PREFACE

Designed for use in the office or courtroom, this pamphlet contains the Florida State Court Rules.

WHAT'S NEW

Florida Rules of Court, Volume I – State, 2015 Revised Edition, includes rules and associated material governing practice before the Florida state courts. It is current with amendments received through August 1, 2015.

CONTACT US

For additional information or research assistance, call the West reference attorneys at 1–800–REF–ATTY (1–800–733–2889). Contact our U.S. legal editorial department directly with your questions and suggestions by e-mail at editors.us-legal@thomsonreuters.com.

Thank you for subscribing to this product. Should you have any questions regarding this product please contact Customer Service at 1–800–328–4880 or by fax at 1–800–340–9378. If you would like to inquire about related publications, or to place an order, please contact us at 1–800–344–5009 or visit us online.

THE PUBLISHER

September, 2015

TABLE OF CONTENTS

TABLE OF CONTENTS

TITLE VII

EVIDENCE

CHAPTER 90

EVIDENCE CODE

Historical and Statutory Notes

Amendment Notes:

Laws 1976, c. 76–237, § 8, provided that the law enacting the Evidence Code take effect July 1, 1977. Laws 1977, c. 77–77, § 1, amended Laws 1976, c. 76–237, § 8, to provide that the Evidence

Code take effect on July 1, 1978. Laws 1978, c. 78–361, § 22, changed the effective date to January 1, 1979; however, Laws 1978, c. 78–379, § 1, amended Laws 1976, c. 76–237, § 8, as amended by Laws 1977, c. 77–77, and Laws 1978, c. 78–361, to provide that the Evidence Code take effect on July 1, 1979.

Although § 90.102 provided that Chapter 90, the Florida Evidence Code, "shall replace and supersede existing statutory or common law in conflict with its provisions", § 90.103(2), as amended by Laws 1978, c. 78–361, § 1, provided that "This act shall apply to civil actions accruing after the effective date of this code, to criminal proceedings related to crimes committed after the effective date of this code, and to other proceedings brought after the effective date of this code."

The sections comprising Fla.St.1975, Chapter 90, Witnesses, were transferred to Fla.St.1976, Supp. Chapter 92, Evidence, Admissibility, or repealed by Laws 1976, c. 76–237, which also enacted the Florida Evidence Code contained in Fla.St.1976, Supp. Chapter 90.

In per curiam opinion of June 28, 1979, (372 So.2d 1369) the Florida Supreme Court transitionally and temporarily approved and adopted the Florida Evidence Code as enacted by Laws 1976, c. 76–237, and as amended by the legislature in 1977 and 1978 to take effect July 1, 1979.

A Florida Supreme Court opinion of Dec. 16, 1993, hearing denied May 19, 1994 (638 So.2d 920), adopted many prior statutory changes to the evidence code as rules of court, to the extent they are procedural. See Historical and Statutory Notes following § 90.101.

90.101. Short title

This chapter shall be known and may be cited as the "Florida Evidence Code."

Laws 1976, c. 76–237, § 1.

Historical and Statutory Notes

Amendment Notes:

The Florida Supreme Court in per curiam opinion dated June 28, 1979 (372 So.2d 1369) provided:

"This Court has jurisdiction to adopt rules of practice and procedure under the provisions of article V, section 2(a), Florida Constitution.

"The Florida Evidence Code was adopted unanimously by the legislature in the 1976 regular session. The act originally was intended to take effect July 1, 1977; the effective date of the code was delayed, however, until July 1, 1979.

"It is generally recognized that the present rules of evidence are derived from multiple sources, specifically, case opinions of this Court, the rules of this Court, and statutes enacted by the legislature. Rules of evidence may in some instances be substantive law and, therefore, the sole responsibility of the legislature. In other instances, evidentiary rules may be procedural and the responsibility of this Court.

"To avoid multiple appeals and confusion in the operation of the courts caused by assertions that portions of the evidence code are procedural and, therefore, unconstitutional because they had not been adopted by this Court under its rule-making authority, the Court hereby adopts temporarily the provisions of the evidence code as enacted by chapter 76-237, Laws of Florida, and subsequently amended by chapters 77–77, 77–174, 78–361, and 78–379, Laws of Florida, to the extent that they are procedural, as rules of this Court effective from and after 12:01 a.m., July 1, 1979. These rules shall govern all proceedings within their scope subsequent to that date, and all present rules of evidence established by case law or express rules of court are hereby superseded to the extent they are in conflict with the code. See In re Clarification of Florida Rules of Practice and Procedure, 281 So.2d 204 (Fla.1973).

"Our approval and adoption of the evidence code is transitional and temporary in nature, and we request The Florida Bar, the Academy of Florida Trial Lawyers, and other interested parties to file any appropriate suggestions or objections on or before October 1, 1979, directed to specific rules of evidence contained in the code and stating (1) the basis why the challenge rule is procedural rather than substantive, and (2) why the rule is inappropriate in its present form."

Section 90.103 of the Florida Evidence Code, which was amended by Laws 1981, c. 81–93, effective October 1, 1981, was acknowledged in a per curiam opinion of the Florida Supreme Court of September 17, 1981, (404 So.2d 743), which provided in regard thereto:

"To the extent that these amendments concern court procedure, we adopt them as part of the Rules of Evidence and hereby modify those rules to incorporate the changes. The amended rules shall become effective October 1, 1981."

Amendments by Laws 1985, c. 85–53, effective July 1, 1985, were adopted as rules of court practice and procedure in a per curiam opinion of the Florida Supreme Court of October 30, 1986 (497 So.2d 239). The decision states that the effective date of the law is not altered by the opinion.

The Florida Supreme Court per curiam opinion of Dec. 16, 1993, rehearing denied May 19, 1994 (638 So.2d 920), provides, in part:

"The Florida Evidence Code [1.] enacted by the Legislature is both substantive and procedural. We previously adopted provisions of the Evidence Code as court rules insofar as they deal with procedural matters. *In re Florida Evidence Code,* 372 So.2d 1369 (Fla.1979), *clarified by In re Florida Evidence Code,* 376 So.2d 1161 (Fla.1979). We also have adopted amendments to the Evidence Code as court rules to the extent that they are procedural. *In re Amendment of Florida Evidence Code,* 497 So.2d 239 (Fla.1986); *In re Amendment of Florida Evidence Code,* 404 So.2d 743 (Fla.1981).

"The Florida Bar has petitioned this Court to amend the Rules of Evidence to conform to statutory changes in the Evidence Code. The changes at issue are: Ch. 81–259, §§ 41, 42, at 1032, 1033, Laws of Florida; ch. 83–284, § 1, at 1468, Laws of Florida; ch. 84–36, § 1, at 80, Laws of Florida; ch. 84–363, § 4, at 2145, Laws of Florida; ch. 87–224, § 11, at 1022, Laws of Florida; ch. 88–33, § 2, at 115, Laws of Florida; ch. 90–40, § 2, at 48, Laws of Florida; ch. 90–123, § 1, at 313, Laws of Florida; ch. 90–139, §§ 2–3, at 492, Laws of Florida; ch. 90–174, §§ 1–4, at 583, 584, Laws of Florida; ch. 90–347, § 40, at 2461, Laws of Florida; ch. 91–255, § 12, at 2043, Laws of Florida; [2.] ch. 92–57, § 1, at 449, Laws of Florida; ch. 92–82, § 57, at 679, Laws of Florida; ch. 92–107, § 1, at 747, Laws of Florida; ch. 92–138, § 16, at 967, Laws of Florida; ch. 93–39, § 19, at 52, Laws of Florida; ch. 93–125, § 2, at 1, Laws of Florida; and ch. 93–156, § 26, at 26, Laws of Florida.

"We adopt the amendments to the Evidence Code to the extent that they concern court procedure. [3.] These amended rules are effective the dates the bills became law."

"1. §§ 90.101–.958, Fla.Stat. (1993).

"2. We note that the adoption of chapter 91–255, § 12, at 2043, Laws of Florida, is *only* for procedural purposes and does not bar a challenge to the statute for any other reason.

"3. We do not adopt the amendments to chapter 85–53, §§ 2–4, at 141, Laws of Florida, as the Bar requested, because we have already adopted the amendments to chapter 85–53 in *In re Amendment of Florida Evidence Code,* 497 So.2d 239 (Fla.1986)."

The Florida Supreme Court, in In re Florida Evidence Code, 675 So.2d 584 (1996), provided, in part:

"The Florida Bar has petitioned this Court to amend the Rules of Evidence to conform to statutory changes in the Evidence Code. The changes at issue are: Ch. 80–155, §§ 1-5, 7-9, Laws of Fla.; Ch. 94–124, § 12, Laws of Fla.; Ch. 95–147, §§ 471-504, 1378, Laws of Fla.; Ch. 95–158, § 1, Laws of Fla.; Ch. 95–179, § 1, Laws of Fla.; Ch. 95–187, § 7, Laws of Fla.; and Ch. 95–286, § 5, Laws of Fla..

"We adopt the amendments to the Evidence Code to the extent that they concern court procedure. These amended rules are effective on the dates the bills became law."

90.102. Construction

This chapter shall replace and supersede existing statutory or common law in conflict with its provisions.

Laws 1976, c. 76–237, § 1.

Historical and Statutory Notes

Uniform Rules of Evidence:

For rule relating to purpose and construction, see Rule 102, Uniform Laws Annotated, Master Edition, vol. 13.

90.103. Scope; applicability

(1) Unless otherwise provided by statute, this code applies to the same proceedings that the general law of evidence applied to before the effective date of this code.

(2) This act shall apply to criminal proceedings related to crimes committed after the effective date of this code and to civil actions and all other proceedings pending on or brought after October 1, 1981.

(3) Nothing in this act shall operate to repeal or modify the parol evidence rule.

Laws 1976, c. 76–237, §§ 1, 5, 7; Laws 1978, c. 78–361, § 1. Amended by Laws 1981, c. 81–93, § 1, eff. Oct. 1, 1981.

Historical and Statutory Notes

Amendment Notes:

Laws 1976, c. 76–237, § 8, provides that this act shall take effect July 1, 1977.

Laws 1977, c. 77–77, § 1, amended Laws 1976, c. 76–237, § 8, to provide that the act take effect July 1, 1978.

Laws 1978, c. 78–361, § 22, amended Laws 1976, c. 76–237, § 8, as amended by Laws 1977, c. 77–77, to provide that the act take effect January 1, 1979; however, Laws 1978, c. 78–379, § 1, amended Laws 1976, c. 76–237, § 8, as amended by Laws 1977, c. 77–77, and Laws 1978, c. 78–361, to provide that the act take effect July 1, 1979.

Laws 1978, c. 78–361, rewrote subsec. (2) which, as it appears in Fla.St.1977 provided:

"(2) This act shall apply to both civil and criminal actions brought after the effective date of this act, unless specifically stated otherwise."

Temporary Florida Supreme Court Approval and Adoption of Evidence Code

The Florida Supreme Court in an opinion dated June 28, 1979 (372 So.2d 1369) provided:

"This Court has jurisdiction to adopt rules of practice and procedure under the provisions of article V, section 2(a), Florida Constitution.

"The Florida Evidence Code was adopted unanimously by the legislature in the 1976 regular session. The act originally was intended to take effect July 1, 1977; the effective date of the code was delayed, however, until July 1, 1979.

"It is generally recognized that the present rules of evidence are derived from multiple sources, specifically, case opinions of this Court, the rules of this Court, and statutes enacted by the legislature. Rules of evidence may in some instances be substantive law and, therefore, the sole responsibility of the legislature. In other instances, evidentiary rules may be procedural and the responsibility of this Court.

"To avoid multiple appeals and confusion in the operation of the courts caused by assertions that portions of the evidence code are procedural and, therefore, unconstitutional because they had not been adopted by this Court under its rule-making authority, the Court hereby adopts temporarily the provisions of the evidence code as enacted by chapter 76-237, Laws of Florida, and subsequently amended by chapters 77–77, 77–174, 78–361, and 78–379, Laws of Florida, to the extent that they are procedural, as rules of this Court effective from and after 12:01 a.m., July 1, 1979. These rules shall govern all proceedings within their scope subsequent to that date, and all present rules of evidence established by case law or express rules of court are hereby superseded to the extent they are in conflict with the code. See In re Clarification of Florida Rules of Practice and Procedure, 281 So.2d 204 (Fla.1973).

"Our approval and adoption of the evidence code is transitional and temporary in nature, and we request The Florida Bar, the Academy of Florida Trial Lawyers, and other interested parties to file any appropriate suggestions or objections on or before October 1, 1979, directed to specific rules of evidence contained in the code and stating (1) the basis why the challenged rule is procedural rather than substantive, and (2) why the rule is inappropriate in its present form."

Effective Date:

The Florida Supreme Court in a per curiam "clarifying opinion" dated November 8, 1979, 376 So.2d 1161, provided in part:

"* * * We affirmatively state that our opinion of June 28, 1979, adopted section 90.103, Florida Statutes, in its entirety. By our prior opinion this Court had no intention to change the effective date and applicability provision contained in section 90.103.

"The Code, as adopted by the legislature, contains section 90.103(2) pertaining to the commencement of its application, which provides:

"This act shall apply to civil actions accruing after the effective date of this code, to criminal proceedings related to crimes committed after the effective date of this code, and to other proceedings brought after the effective date of this code.

Chapter 78–361, Laws of Florida (1978), provides that the act take effect July 1, 1979.

"We read this provision to mean that the Evidence Code, including the procedural portion adopted by this Court, shall apply to (1) criminal proceedings related to crimes committed on or after July 1, 1979; (2) civil actions accruing after July 1, 1979; and (3) other proceedings brought after July 1, 1979.

"The Bar also advocates a change in the applicability of the Code in regard to civil actions. It is recommended that, to avoid potential confusion, the Code should be amended to apply to all civil proceedings pending on or brought after July 1, 1979, rather than to civil actions accruing after July 1, 1979. The Florida Academy of Trial Lawyers endorses the position of the Florida Bar.

"We recognize the merit of the Bar's position. The provision making the Code applicable to civil actions accruing after July 1, 1979, will cause application difficulties in some instances. For example, in a products liability action against both the retailer and the manufacturer, this provision could hold the Code applicable to the retailer of the product but not to the manufacturer We agree that in order to avoid this type of problem, which can cause unnecessary legal disputes and resulting costs and delay to litigants, a concerted effort should be made to have the Code amended to be applicable to all pending proceedings for which the trial has not commenced on the effective date. Unfortunately, we have no authority to change the applicability provision without first finding the entire Code to be procedural. We adopt the Bar recommendation that the legislature act promptly to amend the applicability provision. Should the legislature undertake such action, this Court will act expeditiously concerning the procedural segments of the Code.

"For the reasons expressed, our order in this cause rendered on June 28, 1979, is clarified."

Laws 1981, c. 81–93, § 1, rewrote subsec. (2).

Section 90.103 of the Florida Evidence Code, which was amended by Laws 1981, c. 81–93, effective October 1, 1981, was acknowledged in a per curiam opinion of the Florida Supreme Court of September 17, 1981, (404 So.2d 743), which provides in regard thereto:

"To the extent that these amendments concern court procedure, we adopt them as part of the Rules of Evidence and hereby modify those rules to incorporate the changes. The amended rules shall become effective October 1, 1981."

90.104. Rulings on evidence

(1) A court may predicate error, set aside or reverse a judgment, or grant a new trial on the basis of admitted or excluded evidence when a substantial right of the party is adversely affected and:

(a) When the ruling is one admitting evidence, a timely objection or motion to strike appears on the record, stating the specific ground of objection if the specific ground was not apparent from the context; or

(b) When the ruling is one excluding evidence, the substance of the evidence was made known to the court by offer of proof or was apparent from the context within which the questions were asked.

If the court has made a definitive ruling on the record admitting or excluding evidence, either at or before trial, a party need not renew an objection or offer of proof to preserve a claim of error for appeal.

(2) In cases tried by a jury, a court shall conduct proceedings, to the maximum extent practicable, in such a manner as to prevent inadmissible evidence from being suggested to the jury by any means.

(3) Nothing in this section shall preclude a court from taking notice of fundamental errors affecting substantial rights, even though such errors were not brought to the attention of the trial judge.

Laws 1976, c. 76–237, § 1; Laws 1977, c. 77–174, § 1. Amended by Laws 2003, c. 2003–259, § 1, eff. July 1, 2003.

Historical and Statutory Notes

Amendment Notes:

Laws 1977, c. 77–174, a reviser's bill, amended subsec. (1)(a) of this section by inserting "appears" following "motion to strike" editorially inserted in Fla.St.1976, Supp. in the interest of clarity by the division of statutory revision and indexing.

Laws 2003, c. 2003–259, § 1, added "If the court has made a definitive ruling on the record admitting or excluding evidence, either at or before trial, a party need not renew an objection or offer of proof to preserve a claim of error for appeal" at the end of the subsection.

Federal Evidence Rules:

For rule relating to rulings on evidence, see Rule 103, Fed.Rules Evid., 28 U.S.C.A.

Uniform Rules of Evidence:

For rules relating to rulings on evidence, see Rule 103, Uniform Laws Annotated, Master Edition, vol. 13.

90.105. Preliminary questions

(1) Except as provided in subsection (2), the court shall determine preliminary questions concerning the qualification of a person to be a witness, the existence of a privilege, or the admissibility of evidence.

(2) When the relevancy of evidence depends upon the existence of a preliminary fact, the court shall admit the proffered evidence when there is prima facie evidence sufficient to support a finding of the preliminary fact. If prima facie evidence is not introduced to support a finding of the preliminary fact, the court may admit the proffered evidence subject to the subsequent introduction of prima facie evidence of the preliminary fact.

(3) Hearings on the admissibility of confessions shall be conducted out of the hearing of the jury. Hearings on other preliminary matters shall be similarly conducted when the interests of justice require or when an accused is a witness, if he or she so requests.

Laws 1976, c. 76–237, § 1. Amended by Laws 1995, c. 95–147, § 471, eff. July 10, 1995.

Historical and Statutory Notes

Amendment Notes:

Laws 1995, c. 95–147, a reviser's bill, eliminated gender-specific references without making substantive changes in legal effect.

Uniform Rules of Evidence:

For rule relating to preliminary questions, see Rule 104, Uniform Laws Annotated, Master Edition, vol. 13.

90.106. Summing up and comment by judge

A judge may not sum up the evidence or comment to the jury upon the weight of the evidence, the credibility of the witnesses, or the guilt of the accused.

Laws 1976, c. 76–237, § 1.

90.107. Limited admissibility

When evidence that is admissible as to one party or for one purpose, but inadmissible as to another party or for another purpose, is admitted, the court, upon request, shall restrict such evidence to its proper scope and so inform the jury at the time it is admitted.

Laws 1976, c. 76–237, § 1.

Historical and Statutory Notes

Federal Evidence Rules:

For rule relating to limited admissibility, see Rule 105, Fed.Rules Evid., 28 U.S.C.A.

Uniform Rules of Evidence:

For rule relating to limited admissibility, see Rule 105, Uniform Laws Annotated, Master Edition, vol. 13.

90.108. Introduction of related writings or recorded statements

(1) When a writing or recorded statement or part thereof is introduced by a party, an adverse party may require him or her at that time to introduce any other part or any other writing or recorded statement that in fairness ought to be considered contemporaneously. An adverse party is not bound by evidence introduced under this section.

(2) The report of a court reporter, when certified to by the court reporter as being a correct transcript of the testimony and proceedings in the case, is prima facie a correct statement of such testimony and proceedings.

Laws 1976, c. 76–237, § 1; Laws 1978, c. 78–361, § 2. Amended by Laws 1995, c. 95–147, § 472, eff. July 10, 1995; Laws 1995, c. 95–286, § 5, eff. July 1, 1995.

Historical and Statutory Notes

Amendment Notes:

Laws 1978, c. 78–361, added the second sentence.

Laws 1995, c. 95–147, a reviser's bill, eliminated gender-specific references without making substantive changes in legal effect.

Laws 1995, c. 95–286, § 5, eff. July 1, 1995, designated the former section as subsec. (1); and added subsec. (2), relating to reports of court reporters.

Prior Laws

Fla.St.1993, § 29.06.

Comp.Gen.Laws 1927, § 4877.

Rev.Gen.St.1920, § 3093.

Gen.St.1906, § 1848.

Laws 1903, c. 5122, § 5.

Federal Evidence Rules:

For rule relating to remainder of or related writings or recorded statements, see Rule 106, Fed.Rules Evid., 28 U.S.C.A.

Uniform Rules of Evidence:

For rule relating to remainder of related writings, see Rule 106, Uniform Laws Annotated, Master Edition, vol. 13.

90.201. Matters which must be judicially noticed

A court shall take judicial notice of:

(1) Decisional, constitutional, and public statutory law and resolutions of the Florida Legislature and the Congress of the United States.

(2) Florida rules of court that have statewide application, its own rules, and the rules of United States courts adopted by the United States Supreme Court.

(3) Rules of court of the United States Supreme Court and of the United States Courts of Appeal.

Laws 1976, c. 76–237, § 1; Laws 1978, c. 78–361, § 21.

Historical and Statutory Notes

Amendment Notes:

Laws 1978, c. 78–361, deleted former subsec. (2) which required judicial notice of "ordinances and municipal and county charters, the enforcement of which is within the jurisdiction of the court". Subsections (3) and (4) were redesignated as subsecs. (2) and (3), accordingly.

Prior Laws:

Fla.St.1978, Supp., §§ 92.01 to 92.03.

Comp.Gen.Laws 1927, §§ 4381 to 4383.

Rev.Gen.St.1920, §§ 2714 to 2716.

Gen.St.1906, §§ 1514 to 1516.

Rev.St.1892, §§ 1105 to 1107.

Act March 15, 1843, §§ 27 to 29.

Act Nov. 21, 1828, § 6.

Federal Evidence Rules:

For rule relating to judicial notice of adjudicative facts, see Rule 201, Fed.Rules Evid., 28 U.S.C.A.

Uniform Rules of Evidence:

For rule relating to judicial notice of adjudicative facts, see Rule 201, Uniform Laws Annotated, Master Edition, vol. 13.

90.202. Matters which may be judicially noticed

A court may take judicial notice of the following matters, to the extent that they are not embraced within s. 90.201:

(1) Special, local, and private acts and resolutions of the Congress of the United States and of the Florida Legislature.

(2) Decisional, constitutional, and public statutory law of every other state, territory, and jurisdiction of the United States.

(3) Contents of the Federal Register.

(4) Laws of foreign nations and of an organization of nations.

(5) Official actions of the legislative, executive, and judicial departments of the United States and of any state, territory, or jurisdiction of the United States.

(6) Records of any court of this state or of any court of record of the United States or of any state, territory, or jurisdiction of the United States.

(7) Rules of court of any court of this state or of any court of record of the United States or of any other state, territory, or jurisdiction of the United States.

(8) Provisions of all municipal and county charters and charter amendments of this state, provided they are available in printed copies or as certified copies.

(9) Rules promulgated by governmental agencies of this state which are published in the Florida Administrative Code or in bound written copies.

(10) Duly enacted ordinances and resolutions of municipalities and counties located in Florida, provided such ordinances and resolutions are available in printed copies or as certified copies.

(11) Facts that are not subject to dispute because they are generally known within the territorial jurisdiction of the court.

(12) Facts that are not subject to dispute because they are capable of accurate and ready determination by resort to sources whose accuracy cannot be questioned.

(13) Official seals of governmental agencies and departments of the United States and of any state, territory, or jurisdiction of the United States.

Laws 1976, c. 76–237, § 1; Laws 1977, c. 77–174, § 1; Laws 1978, c. 78–361, § 3.

Historical and Statutory Notes

Amendment Notes:

Laws 1977, c. 77–174, a reviser's bill, amended subsec. (6) of this section to reflect substitution of "or" for "and" preceding "of any state" provided for in Fla.St.1976 Supp. in the interest of clarity by the division of statutory revision and indexing.

Laws 1978, c. 78–361, deleted "reasonable" preceding "dispute" in subsecs. (11) and (12), and "reasonably" preceding "be questioned" in subsec. (12).

Prior Laws:

Fla.St.1978, Supp., §§ 92.01 to 92.04.

Laws 1951, c. 26842, § 1.

Laws 1949, c. 25110, §§ 1 to 8.

Comp.Gen.Laws 1927, §§ 4381 to 4384.

Rev.Gen.St.1920, §§ 2714 to 2717.

Gen.St.1906, §§ 1514 to 1517.

Rev.St.1892, §§ 1105 to 1108.

Act March 15, 1843, §§ 27 to 30.

Act Nov. 21, 1828, § 6.

Federal Evidence Rules:

For rule relating to judicial notice of adjudicative facts, see Rule 201, Fed.Rules Evid., 28 U.S.C.A.

Uniform Rules of Evidence:

For rule relating to judicial notice of adjudicative facts, see Rule 201, Uniform Laws Annotated, Master Edition, vol. 13.

90.203. Compulsory judicial notice upon request

A court shall take judicial notice of any matter in s. 90.202 when a party requests it and:

(1) Gives each adverse party timely written notice of the request, proof of which is filed with the court, to enable the adverse party to prepare to meet the request.

(2) Furnishes the court with sufficient information to enable it to take judicial notice of the matter.

Laws 1976, c. 76–237, § 1.

Historical and Statutory Notes

Federal Evidence Rules:

For rule relating to judicial notice of adjudicative facts, see Rule 201, Fed.Rules Evid., 28 U.S.C.A.

Uniform Rules of Evidence:

For rule relating to judicial notice of adjudicative facts, see Rule 201, Uniform Laws Annotated, Master Edition, vol. 13.

90.204. Determination of propriety of judicial notice and nature of matter noticed

(1) When a court determines upon its own motion that judicial notice of a matter should be taken or when a party requests such notice and shows good cause for not complying with s. 90.203(1), the court shall afford each party reasonable opportunity to present information relevant to the propriety of taking judicial notice and to the nature of the matter noticed.

(2) In determining the propriety of taking judicial notice of a matter or the nature thereof, a court may use any source of pertinent and reliable information, whether or not furnished by a party, without regard to any exclusionary rule except a valid claim of privilege and except for the exclusions provided in s. 90.403.

(3) If a court resorts to any documentary source of information not received in open court, the court shall make the information and its source a part of the record in the action and shall afford each party reasonable opportunity to challenge such information, and to offer additional information, before judicial notice of the matter is taken.

(4) In family cases, the court may take judicial notice of any matter described in s. 90.202(6) when imminent danger to persons or property has been alleged and it is impractical to give prior notice to the parties of the intent to take judicial notice. Opportunity to present evidence relevant to the propriety of taking judicial notice under subsection (1) may be deferred until after judicial action has been taken. If judicial notice is taken under this subsection, the court shall, within 2 business days, file a notice in the pending case of the matters judicially noticed. For purposes of this subsection, the term "family cases" has the same meaning as provided in the Rules of Judicial Administration.

Laws 1976, c. 76–237, § 1. Amended by Laws 2014, c. 2014–35, § 2, eff. May 12, 2014.

Historical and Statutory Notes

Amendment Notes:

Laws 2014, c. 2014–35, § 2, added subsec. (4), relating to family cases.

Federal Evidence Rules:

For rule relating to judicial notice of adjudicative facts, see Rule 201, Fed.Rules Evid., 28 U.S.C.A.

Uniform Rules of Evidence:

For rule relating to judicial notice of adjudicative facts, see Rule 201, Uniform Laws Annotated, Master Edition, vol. 13.

90.205. Denial of a request for judicial notice

Upon request of counsel, when a court denies a request to take judicial notice of any matter, the court shall inform the parties at the earliest practicable time and shall indicate for the record that it has denied the request.

Laws 1976, c. 76–237, § 1.

Historical and Statutory Notes

Federal Evidence Rules:

For rule relating to judicial notice of adjudicative facts, see Rule 201, Fed.Rules Evid., 28 U.S.C.A.

Uniform Rules of Evidence:

For rule relating to judicial notice of adjudicative facts, see Rule 201, Uniform Laws Annotated, Master Edition.

90.206. Instructing jury on judicial notice

The court may instruct the jury during the trial to accept as a fact a matter judicially noticed.

Laws 1976, c. 76–237, § 1; Laws 1978, c. 78–361, § 4.

Historical and Statutory Notes

Amendment Notes:

Laws 1978, c. 78–361, substituted "may" for "shall".

Federal Evidence Rules:

For rule relating to judicial notice of adjudicative facts, see Rule 201, Fed.Rules Evid., 28 U.S.C.A.

Uniform Rules of Evidence:

For rule relating to judicial notice of adjudicative facts, see Rule 201, Uniform Laws Annotated, Master Edition, vol. 13.

90.207. Judicial notice by trial court in subsequent proceedings

The failure or refusal of a court to take judicial notice of a matter does not preclude a court from taking judicial notice of the matter in subsequent proceedings, in accordance with the procedure specified in ss. 90.201–90.206.

Laws 1976, c. 76–237, § 1.

Historical and Statutory Notes

Federal Evidence Rules:

For rule relating to judicial notice of adjudicative facts, see Rule 201, Fed.Rules Evid., 28 U.S.C.A.

Uniform Rules of Evidence:

For rule relating to judicial notice of adjudicative facts, see Rule 201, Uniform Laws Annotated, Master Edition, vol. 13.

90.301. Presumption defined; inferences

(1) For the purposes of this chapter, a presumption is an assumption of fact which the law makes from the existence of another fact or group of facts found or otherwise established.

(2) Except for presumptions that are conclusive under the law from which they arise, a presumption is rebuttable.

(3) Nothing in this chapter shall prevent the drawing of an inference that is appropriate.

(4) Sections 90.301–90.304 are applicable only in civil actions or proceedings.

Laws 1978, c. 78–361, added subsec. (4); Laws 1976, c. 76–237, § 1; Laws 1978, c. 78–361, § 5.

Historical and Statutory Notes

Federal Evidence Rules:

For rules relating to presumptions, see Rules 301, 302, Fed.Rules Evid., 28 U.S.C.A.

Uniform Rules of Evidence:

For rules relating to presumptions, see Rules 301 to 303, Uniform Laws Annotated, Master Edition, vol. 13.

90.302. Classification of rebuttable presumptions

Every rebuttable presumption is either:

(1) A presumption affecting the burden of producing evidence and requiring the trier of fact to assume the existence of the presumed fact, unless credible evidence sufficient to sustain a finding of the nonexistence of the presumed fact is introduced, in which event, the existence or nonexistence of the presumed fact shall be determined from the evidence without regard to the presumption; or

(2) A presumption affecting the burden of proof that imposes upon the party against whom it operates the burden of proof concerning the nonexistence of the presumed fact.

Laws 1976, c. 76–237, § 1.

Historical and Statutory Notes

Federal Evidence Rules:

For rule relating to presumptions in civil actions and proceedings, see Rule 301, Fed.Rules Evid., 28 U.S.C.A.

Uniform Rules of Evidence:

For rule relating to presumptions in civil actions and proceedings, see Rule 301, Uniform Laws Annotated, Master Edition, vol. 13.

90.303. Presumption affecting the burden of producing evidence defined

In a civil action or proceeding, unless otherwise provided by statute, a presumption established primarily to facilitate the determination of the particular action in which the presumption is applied, rather than to implement public policy, is a presumption affecting the burden of producing evidence.

Laws 1976, c. 76–237, § 1.

Historical and Statutory Notes

Federal Evidence Rules:

For rule relating to presumptions in civil actions and proceedings, see Rule 301, Fed.Rules Evid., 28 U.S.C.A.

Uniform Rules of Evidence:

For rule relating to presumptions in civil actions and proceedings, see Rule 301, Uniform Laws Annotated, Master Edition, vol. 13.

90.304. Presumption affecting the burden of proof defined

In civil actions, all rebuttable presumptions which are not defined in s. 90.303 are presumptions affecting the burden of proof.

Laws 1976, c. 76–237, § 1.

Historical and Statutory Notes

Federal Evidence Rules:

For rules relating to presumptions, see Rules 301, 302, Fed.Rules Evid., 28 U.S.C.A.

Uniform Rules of Evidence:

For rules relating to presumptions, see Rules 301 to 303, Uniform Laws Annotated, Master Edition, vol. 13.

90.401. Definition of relevant evidence

Relevant evidence is evidence tending to prove or disprove a material fact.

Laws 1976, c. 76–237, § 1.

Historical and Statutory Notes

Federal Evidence Rules:

For rule relating to the definition of relevant evidence, see Rule 401, Fed.Rules Evid., 28 U.S.C.A.

Uniform Rules of Evidence:

For rule relating to the definition of relevant evidence, see Rule 401, Uniform Laws Annotated, Master Edition, vol. 13.

90.402. Admissibility of relevant evidence

All relevant evidence is admissible, except as provided by law.

Laws 1976, c. 76–237, § 1.

Historical and Statutory Notes

Federal Evidence Rules:

For rule relating to admissibility of relevant evidence, see Rule 402, Fed.Rules Evid., 28 U.S.C.A.

Uniform Rules of Evidence:

For rule relating to admissibility of relevant evidence, see Rule 402, Uniform Laws Annotated, Master Edition, vol. 13.

90.4025. Admissibility of paternity determination in certain criminal prosecutions

If a person less than 18 years of age gives birth to a child and the paternity of that child is established under chapter 742, such evidence of paternity is admissible in a criminal prosecution under ss. 794.011, 794.05, 800.04, and 827.04(3).

Added by Laws 1996, c. 96–215, § 8, eff. Oct. 1, 1996; Laws 1996, c. 96–409, § 2, eff. Oct. 1, 1996; Laws 1999, c. 99–2, § 27, eff. June 29, 1999.

Historical and Statutory Notes

Amendment Notes:

Laws 1999, c. 99–2, § 27, eff. June 29, 1999, amended the section to revise the reference to s. 827.04(4).

90.4026. Statements expressing sympathy; admissibility; definitions

(1) As used in this section:

(a) "Accident" means an occurrence resulting in injury or death to one or more persons which is not the result of willful action by a party.

(b) "Benevolent gestures" means actions that convey a sense of compassion or commiseration emanating from human impulses.

(c) "Family" means the spouse, parent, grandparent, stepmother, stepfather, child, grandchild, brother, sister, half-brother, half-sister, adopted child of parent, or spouse's parent of an injured party.

(2) The portion of statements, writings, or benevolent gestures expressing sympathy or a general sense of benevolence relating to the pain, suffering, or death of a person involved in an accident and made to that person or to the family of that person shall be inadmissible as evidence in a civil action. A statement of fault, however, which is part of, or in addition to, any of the above shall be admissible pursuant to this section.

Added by Laws 2001, c. 2001–132, § 1, eff. June 1, 2001.

Historical and Statutory Notes

Amendment Notes:

The Florida Supreme Court in per curiam opinion dated July 11, 2002 (825 So.2d 339) provided in part:

"Consistent with the committee's recommendations, we adopt chapters 2000–316, sections 1 and 2; and 2001–132, section 1 to the extent they are procedural. However, after hearing oral argument, and carefully considering the committee's recommendation against adopting chapter 2001–221, section 1, as well as the comments that were filed, we decline to follow this recommendation and also adopt the amendments to section 90.404(2) to the extent they are procedural. In the absence of a true 'case and controversy,' we express no opinion on the substance of the amendments or on the challenges to chapter 2001–221, section 1, that were raised in these proceedings. The various amendments are effective on the dates they became law."

90.403. Exclusion on grounds of prejudice or confusion

Relevant evidence is inadmissible if its probative value is substantially outweighed by the danger of unfair prejudice, confusion of issues, misleading the jury, or needless presentation of cumulative evidence. This section shall not be construed to mean that evidence of the existence of available third-party benefits is inadmissible.

Laws 1976, c. 76–237, § 1; Laws 1978, c. 78–361, § 6.

Historical and Statutory Notes

Amendment Notes:

Laws 1978, c. 78–361, deleted "undue waste of time" following "misleading the jury", in the first sentence, and added the second sentence.

Federal Evidence Rules:

For rule relating to exclusion of relevant evidence on grounds of prejudice, confusion, or waste of time, see Rule 403, Fed.Rules Evid., 28 U.S.C.A.

Uniform Rules of Evidence:

For rule relating to exclusion of relevant evidence on grounds of prejudice, confusion, or waste of time, see Rule 403, Uniform Laws Annotated, Master Edition, vol. 13.

90.404. Character evidence; when admissible

(1) Character evidence generally.—Evidence of a person's character or a trait of character is inadmissible to prove action in conformity with it on a particular occasion, except:

(a) *Character of accused.*—Evidence of a pertinent trait of character offered by an accused, or by the prosecution to rebut the trait.

(b) *Character of victim.*—

1. Except as provided in s. 794.022, evidence of a pertinent trait of character of the victim of the crime offered by an accused, or by the prosecution to rebut the trait; or

2. Evidence of a character trait of peacefulness of the victim offered by the prosecution in a homicide case to rebut evidence that the victim was the aggressor.

(c) *Character of witness.*—Evidence of the character of a witness, as provided in ss. 90.608–90.610.

(2) Other crimes, wrongs, or acts.—

(a) Similar fact evidence of other crimes, wrongs, or acts is admissible when relevant to prove a material fact in issue, including, but not limited to, proof of motive, opportunity, intent, preparation, plan, knowledge, identity, or absence of mistake or accident, but it is inadmissible when the evidence is relevant solely to prove bad character or propensity.

(b) 1. In a criminal case in which the defendant is charged with a crime involving child molestation, evidence of the defendant's commission of other crimes, wrongs, or acts of child molestation is admissible and may be considered for its bearing on any matter to which it is relevant.

2. For the purposes of this paragraph, the term "child molestation" means conduct proscribed by s. 787.025(2)(c), s. 787.06(3)(g), former s. 787.06(3)(h), s. 794.011, excluding s. 794.011(10), s. 794.05, former s. 796.03, former s. 796.035, s. 800.04, s. 827.071, s. 847.0135(5), s. 847.0145, or s. 985.701(1) when committed against a person 16 years of age or younger.

(c) 1. In a criminal case in which the defendant is charged with a sexual offense, evidence of the defendant's commission of other crimes, wrongs, or acts involving a sexual offense is admissible and may be considered for its bearing on any matter to which it is relevant.

2. For the purposes of this paragraph, the term "sexual offense" means conduct proscribed by s. 787.025(2)(c), s. 787.06(3)(b), (d), (f), or (g), former s.

787.06(3)(h), s. 794.011, excluding s. 794.011(10), s. 794.05, former s. 796.03, former s. 796.035, s. 825.1025(2)(b), s. 827.071, s. 847.0135(5), s. 847.0145, or s. 985.701(1).

(d) 1. When the state in a criminal action intends to offer evidence of other criminal offenses under paragraph (a), paragraph (b), or paragraph (c), no fewer than 10 days before trial, the state shall furnish to the defendant or to the defendant's counsel a written statement of the acts or offenses it intends to offer, describing them with the particularity required of an indictment or information. No notice is required for evidence of offenses used for impeachment or on rebuttal.

2. When the evidence is admitted, the court shall, if requested, charge the jury on the limited purpose for which the evidence is received and is to be considered. After the close of the evidence, the jury shall be instructed on the limited purpose for which the evidence was received and that the defendant cannot be convicted for a charge not included in the indictment or information.

(3) Nothing in this section affects the admissibility of evidence under s. 90.610.

Laws 1976, c. 76–237, § 1. Amended by Laws 1990, c. 90–40, § 2, eff. June 1, 1990; Laws 1993, c. 93–156, § 26, eff. Oct. 1, 1993; Laws 1995, c. 95–147, § 473, eff. July 10, 1995; Laws 2001, c. 2001–221, § 1, eff. July 1, 2001; Laws 2008, c. 2008–172, § 9, eff. Oct. 1, 2008; Laws 2011, c. 2011–220, § 2, eff. July 1, 2011; Laws 2012, c. 2012–97, § 14, eff. July 1, 2012; Laws 2014, c. 2014–160, § 15, eff. Oct. 1, 2014.

Historical and Statutory Notes

Amendment Notes:

Laws 1990, c. 90–40, § 2, eff. June 1, 1990, reenacted subsec. (1)(b)1. without amendment "for the purpose of incorporating the amendment to section 794.022, Florida Statutes, in a reference thereto".

The 1990 amendment to this section was not adopted as a rule of court at the time of publication. See the Historical and Statutory Notes to § 90.101 for adoption of earlier provisions as a rule of court.

Laws 1993, c. 93–156, § 26, eff. Oct. 1, 1993, reenacted subsec. (1)(b) of this section for the purpose of incorporating the amendment to § 794.022 in a reference thereto.

Laws 1995, c. 95–147, a reviser's bill, eliminated gender-specific references without making substantive changes in legal effect.

Laws 2001, c. 2001–221, § 1, rewrote subsec. (2), which formerly read:

"(2) Other crimes, wrongs, or acts.—

"(a) Similar fact evidence of other crimes, wrongs, or acts is admissible when relevant to prove a material fact in issue, such as proof of motive, opportunity, intent, preparation, plan, knowledge, identity, or absence of mistake or accident, but it is inadmissible when the evidence is relevant solely to prove bad character or propensity.

"(b)1. When the state in a criminal action intends to offer evidence of other criminal offenses under paragraph (a), no fewer than 10 days before trial, the state shall furnish to the accused a written statement of the acts or offenses it intends to offer, describing them with the particularity required of an indictment or information. No notice is required for evidence of offenses used for impeachment or on rebuttal.

"2. When the evidence is admitted, the court shall, if requested, charge the jury on the limited purpose for which the evidence is received and is to be considered. After the close of the evidence, the jury shall be instructed on the limited purpose for which the evidence was received and that the defendant cannot be convicted for a charge not included in the indictment or information."

The Florida Supreme Court in per curiam opinion dated July 11, 2002 (825 So.2d 339) provided in part:

"Consistent with the committee's recommendations, we adopt chapters 2000–316, sections 1 and 2; and 2001–132, section 1 to the extent they are procedural. However, after hearing oral argument, and carefully considering the committee's recommendation against adopting chapter 2001–221, section 1, as well as the comments that were filed, we decline to follow this recommendation and also adopt the amendments to section 90.404(2) to the extent they are procedural. In the absence of a true 'case and controversy,' we express no opinion on the substance of the amendments or on the challenges to chapter 2001–221, section 1, that were raised in these proceedings. The various amendments are effective on the dates they became law."

Laws 2008, c. 2008–172, § 9, in subsec. (2)(b)2., inserted a reference to § 847.0135(5), and made a nonsubstantive language change.

Laws 2011, c. 2011–220, § 2, in subsec. (2), inserted references to §§ 787.025(2)(c), 794.011(10), 794.05, 796.03, 796.035, 796.045, 827.071, 847.0145, and 985.701(1) par. (b)2., inserted a new par. (c), relating to sexual offenses, and redesignated for par. (c) as par. (d) and inserted a reference to par. (c).

Laws 2012, c. 2012–97, § 14, in subsecs. (2)(b)2. and (2)(c)2., inserted references to § 787.06(3)(b), (d), (f), (g), and (h), and deleted references to § 796.045.

Laws 2014, c. 2014–160, § 15, in subsec. (2), substituted references to former §§ 787.06(3)(h), 796.03, and 796.035 for references to §§ 787.06(3)(h), 796.03, and 796.035 in pars. (b)2. and (c)2.

Prior Laws:

Fla.St.1978, Supp. § 90.08.

Laws 1971, c. 71–72, §§ 1, 2.

Fla.St.1969, § 90.07.

Laws 1945, c. 22858, § 7.

Comp.Gen.Laws 1927, §§ 4371, 4373.

Rev.Gen.St.1920, §§ 2704, 2706.

Gen.St.1906, §§ 1504, 1506.

Laws 1901, c. 4966, § 1.

Rev.St.1892, §§ 1096, 1097.

Laws 1861, c. 1096, § 54.

Act March 10, 1845, § 6.

Act March 15, 1843, § 25.

Act Nov. 23, 1828, § 72.

Federal Evidence Rules:

For rule relating to admissibility of character evidence, see Rule 404, Fed.Rules Evid., 28 U.S.C.A.

Uniform Rules of Evidence:

For rule relating to admissibility of character evidence, see Rule 404, Uniform Laws Annotated, Master Edition, vol. 13.

90.405. Methods of proving character

(1) Reputation.—When evidence of the character of a person or of a trait of that person's character is admissible, proof may be made by testimony about that person's reputation.

(2) Specific instances of conduct.—When character or a trait of character of a person is an essential element of a charge, claim, or defense, proof may be made of specific instances of that person's conduct.

Laws 1976, c. 76–237, § 1; Laws 1978, c. 78–361, § 7. Amended by Laws 1995, c. 95–147, § 474, eff. July 10, 1995.

Historical and Statutory Notes

Amendment Notes:

Laws 1978, c. 78–361, deleted from the end of subsec. (1) the words "or by testimony in the form of an opinion. On cross examination, inquiry is allowable into relevant specific instances of conduct."

Laws 1995, c. 95–147, a reviser's bill, eliminated gender-specific references without making substantive changes in legal effect.

Federal Evidence Rules:

For rule relating to Methods of proving character, see Rule 405, Fed.Rules Evid., 28 U.S.C.A.

Uniform Rules of Evidence:

For rule relating to Methods of proving character, see Rule 405, Uniform Laws Annotated, Master Edition, vol. 13.

90.406. Routine practice

Evidence of the routine practice of an organization, whether corroborated or not and regardless of the presence of eyewitnesses, is admissible to prove that the conduct of the organization on a particular occasion was in conformity with the routine practice.

Laws 1976, c. 76–237, § 1.

Historical and Statutory Notes

Federal Evidence Rules:

For rule relating to habit and routine practice, see Rule 406, Fed.Rules Evid., 28 U.S.C.A.

Uniform Rules of Evidence:

For rule relating to habit and routine practice, see Rule 406, Uniform Laws Annotated, Master Edition, vol. 13.

90.407. Subsequent remedial measures

Evidence of measures taken after an injury or harm caused by an event, which measures if taken before the event would have made injury or harm less likely to occur, is not admissible to prove negligence, the existence of a product defect, or culpable conduct in connection with the event. This rule does not require the exclusion of evidence of subsequent remedial measures when offered for another purpose, such as proving ownership, control, or the feasibility of precautionary measures, if controverted, or impeachment.

Laws 1976, c. 76–237, § 1; Laws 1977, c. 77–174, § 1. Amended by Laws 1999, c. 99–225, § 13, eff. Oct. 1, 1999.

Historical and Statutory Notes

Amendment Notes:

Laws 1977, c. 77–174, a reviser's bill, amended this section to reflect inclusion of "it occurred" following "taken before" editorially inserted in Fla.St.1976, Supp. by the division of statutory revision and indexing.

Laws 1999, c. 99–225, § 13, rewrote this section, which formerly read:

"Evidence of measures taken after an event, which measures if taken before it occurred would have made the event less likely to occur, is not admissible to prove negligence or culpable conduct in connection with the event."

Federal Evidence Rules:

For rule relating to subsequent remedial measures, see Rule 407, Fed.Rules Evid., 28 U.S.C.A.

Uniform Rules of Evidence:

For rule relating to subsequent remedial measures, see Rule 407, Uniform Laws Annotated, Master Edition, vol. 13.

90.408. Compromise and offers to compromise

Evidence of an offer to compromise a claim which was disputed as to validity or amount, as well as any relevant conduct or statements made in negotiations concerning a compromise, is inadmissible to prove liability or absence of liability for the claim or its value.

Laws 1976, c. 76–237, § 1.

Historical and Statutory Notes

Federal Evidence Rules:

For rule relating to compromise and offers to compromise, see Rule 408 Fed.Rules Evid., 28 U.S.C.A.

Uniform Rules of Evidence:

For rule relating to compromise and offers to compromise, see Rule 408, Uniform Laws Annotated, Master Edition, vol. 13.

90.409. Payment of medical and similar expenses

Evidence of furnishing, or offering or promising to pay, medical or hospital expenses or other damages occasioned by an injury or accident is inadmissible to prove liability for the injury or accident.

Laws 1976, c. 76–237, § 1.

Historical and Statutory Notes

Federal Evidence Rules:

For rule relating to payment of medical and similar expenses, see Rule 409, Fed.Rules Evid., 28 U.S.C.A.

Uniform Rules of Evidence:

For rule relating to payment of medical and similar expenses, see Rule 409, Uniform Laws Annotated, Master Edition, vol. 13.

90.410. Offer to plead guilty; nolo contendere; withdrawn pleas of guilty

Evidence of a plea of guilty, later withdrawn; a plea of nolo contendere; or an offer to plead guilty or nolo contendere to the crime charged or any other crime is inadmissible in any civil or criminal proceeding. Evidence of statements made in connection with any of the pleas or offers is inadmissible, except when such statements are offered in a prosecution under chapter 837.

Laws 1976, c. 76–237, § 1; Laws 1978, c. 78–361, § 8.

Historical and Statutory Notes

Amendment Notes:

Laws 1978, c. 78–361, deleted "for impeachment or" preceding "in a prosecution under chapter 837."

Federal Evidence Rules:

For rule relating to offer to plead guilty; nolo contendere; withdrawn plea of guilty, see Rule 410, Fed.Rules Evid., 28 U.S.C.A.

Uniform Rules of Evidence:

For rule relating to offer to plead guilty; nolo contendere; withdrawn plea of guilty, see Rule 410, Uniform Laws Annotated, Master Edition, vol. 13.

90.501. Privileges recognized only as provided

Except as otherwise provided by this chapter, any other statute, or the Constitution of the United States or of the State of Florida, no person in a legal proceeding has a privilege to:

(1) Refuse to be a witness.

(2) Refuse to disclose any matter.

(3) Refuse to produce any object or writing.

(4) Prevent another from being a witness, from disclosing any matter, or from producing any object or writing.

Laws 1976, c. 76–237, § 1; Laws 1978, c. 78–361, § 9.

Historical and Statutory Notes

Amendment Notes:

Laws 1978, c. 78–361, inserted in the introductory paragraph "this chapter, any other" preceding "statute".

Federal Evidence Rules:

For rule relating to privileges, see Rule 501, Fed.Rules Evid., 28 U.S.C.A.

Uniform Rules of Evidence:

For rule relating to privileges, see Rule 501, Uniform Laws Annotated, Master Edition, vol. 13.

90.5015. Journalist's privilege

(1) **Definitions.**— For purposes of this section, the term:

(a) "Professional journalist" means a person regularly engaged in collecting, photographing, recording, writing, editing, reporting, or publishing news, for gain or livelihood, who obtained the information sought while working as a salaried employee of, or independent contractor for, a newspaper, news journal, news agency, press association, wire service, radio or television station, network, or news magazine. Book authors and others who are not professional journalists, as defined in this paragraph, are not included in the provisions of this section.

(b) "News" means information of public concern relating to local, statewide, national, or worldwide issues or events.

(2) **Privilege.**— A professional journalist has a qualified privilege not to be a witness concerning, and not to disclose the information, including the identity of any source, that the professional journalist has obtained while actively gathering news. This privilege applies only to information or eyewitness observations obtained within the normal scope of employment and does not apply to physical evidence, eyewitness observations, or visual or audio recording of crimes. A party seeking to overcome this privilege must make a clear and specific showing that:

(a) The information is relevant and material to unresolved issues that have been raised in the proceeding for which the information is sought;

(b) The information cannot be obtained from alternative sources; and

(c) A compelling interest exists for requiring disclosure of the information.

(3) **Disclosure.**— A court shall order disclosure pursuant to subsection (2) only of that portion of the information for which the showing under subsection (2) has been made and shall support such order with clear and specific findings made after a hearing.

(4) **Waiver.**— A professional journalist does not waive the privilege by publishing or broadcasting information.

(5) **Construction.**— This section must not be construed to limit any privilege or right provided to a professional journalist under law.

(6) **Authentication.**— Photographs, diagrams, video recordings, audio recordings, computer records, or other business records maintained, disclosed, provided, or produced by a professional journalist, or by the employer or principal of a professional journalist, may be authenticated for admission in evidence upon a showing, by affidavit of the professional journalist, or other individual with personal knowledge, that the photograph, diagram, video recording, audio recording, computer record, or other business record is a true and accurate copy of the original, and that the copy truly and accurately reflects the observations and facts contained therein.

(7) **Accuracy of evidence.**— If the affidavit of authenticity and accuracy, or other relevant factual circumstance, causes the court to have clear and convincing doubts as to the authenticity or accuracy of the proffered evidence, the court may decline to admit such evidence.

(8) **Severability.**—If any provision of this section or its application to any particular person or circumstance is held invalid, that provision or its application is severable and does not affect the validity of other provisions or applications of this section.

Added by Laws 1998, c. 98–48, § 1, eff. May 12, 1998.

90.502. Lawyer-client privilege

(1) For purposes of this section:

(a) A "lawyer" is a person authorized, or reasonably believed by the client to be authorized, to practice law in any state or nation.

(b) A "client" is any person, public officer, corporation, association, or other organization or entity, either public or private, who consults a lawyer with the purpose of obtaining legal services or who is rendered legal services by a lawyer.

(c) A communication between lawyer and client is "confidential" if it is not intended to be disclosed to third persons other than:

1. Those to whom disclosure is in furtherance of the rendition of legal services to the client.

2. Those reasonably necessary for the transmission of the communication.

(2) A client has a privilege to refuse to disclose, and to prevent any other person from disclosing, the contents of confidential communications when such other

person learned of the communications because they were made in the rendition of legal services to the client.

(3) The privilege may be claimed by:

(a) The client.

(b) A guardian or conservator of the client.

(c) The personal representative of a deceased client.

(d) A successor, assignee, trustee in dissolution, or any similar representative of an organization, corporation, or association or other entity, either public or private, whether or not in existence.

(e) The lawyer, but only on behalf of the client. The lawyer's authority to claim the privilege is presumed in the absence of contrary evidence.

(4) There is no lawyer-client privilege under this section when:

(a) The services of the lawyer were sought or obtained to enable or aid anyone to commit or plan to commit what the client knew was a crime or fraud.

(b) A communication is relevant to an issue between parties who claim through the same deceased client.

(c) A communication is relevant to an issue of breach of duty by the lawyer to the client or by the client to the lawyer, arising from the lawyer-client relationship.

(d) A communication is relevant to an issue concerning the intention or competence of a client executing an attested document to which the lawyer is an attesting witness, or concerning the execution or attestation of the document.

(e) A communication is relevant to a matter of common interest between two or more clients, or their successors in interest, if the communication was made by any of them to a lawyer retained or consulted in common when offered in a civil action between the clients or their successors in interest.

(5) Communications made by a person who seeks or receives services from the Department of Revenue under the child support enforcement program to the attorney representing the department shall be confidential and privileged as provided for in this section. Such communications shall not be disclosed to anyone other than the agency except as provided for in this section. Such disclosures shall be protected as if there were an attorney-client relationship between the attorney for the agency and the person who seeks services from the department.

(6) A discussion or activity that is not a meeting for purposes of s. 286.011 shall not be construed to waive the attorney-client privilege established in this section. This shall not be construed to constitute an exemption to either s. 119.07 or s. 286.011.

Laws 1976, c. 76–237, § 1. Amended by Laws 1992, c. 92–138, § 16, eff. July 1, 1992; Laws 1994, c. 94–124, § 12, eff. July 1, 1994; Laws 1995, c. 95–147, § 1378, eff. July 10, 1995; Laws 2000, c. 2000–316, § 1, eff. July 1, 2000.

Historical and Statutory Notes

Amendment Notes:

Laws 1992, c. 92–138, § 16, eff. July 1, 1992, added subsec. (5).

Laws 1994, c. 94–124, § 12, eff. July 1, 1994, in subsec. (5), substituted "Department of Revenue" for "Department of Health and Rehabilitative Services".

Laws 1995, c. 95–147, a reviser's bill, eliminated gender-specific references without making substantive changes in legal effect.

Laws 2000, c. 2000–316, § 1, added subsec. (6).

The Florida Supreme Court in per curiam opinion dated July 11, 2002 (825 So.2d 339) provided in part:

"Consistent with the committee's recommendations, we adopt chapters 2000–316, sections 1 and 2; and 2001–132, section 1 to the extent they are procedural. However, after hearing oral argument, and carefully considering the committee's recommendation against adopting chapter 2001–221, section 1, as well as the comments that were filed, we decline to follow this recommendation and also adopt the amendments to section 90.404(2) to the extent they are procedural. In the absence of a true 'case and controversy,' we express no opinion on the substance of the amendments or on the challenges to chapter 2001–221, section 1, that were raised in these proceedings. The various amendments are effective on the dates they became law."

Federal Evidence Rules:

For rule relating to privileges, see Rule 501, Fed.Rules Evid., 28 U.S.C.A.

Uniform Rules of Evidence:

For rule relating to lawyer-client privilege, see Rule 501, Uniform Laws Annotated, Master Edition, vol. 13.

90.5021. Fiduciary lawyer-client privilege

(1) For the purpose of this section, a client acts as a fiduciary when serving as a personal representative or a trustee as defined in ss. 731.201 and 736.0103, an administrator ad litem as described in s. 733.308, a curator as described in s. 733.501, a guardian or guardian ad litem as defined in s. 744.102, a conservator as defined in s. 710.102, or an attorney in fact as described in chapter 709.

(2) A communication between a lawyer and a client acting as a fiduciary is privileged and protected from disclosure under s. 90.502 to the same extent as if the client were not acting as a fiduciary. In applying s. 90.502 to a communication under this section, only the person or entity acting as a fiduciary is considered a client of the lawyer.

(3) This section does not affect the crime or fraud exception to the lawyer-client privilege provided in s. 90.502(4)(a).

Added by Laws 2011, c. 2011–183, § 1, eff. June 21, 2011.

Historical and Statutory Notes

Amendment Notes:

Laws 2011, c. 2011–183, § 14, provides:

"Except as otherwise expressly provided in this act, this act shall take effect upon becoming a law [June 21, 2011] and shall apply to all proceedings pending before such date and all cases commenced on or after the effective date."

90.503. Psychotherapist-patient privilege

(1) For purposes of this section:

(a) A "psychotherapist" is:

1. A person authorized to practice medicine in any state or nation, or reasonably believed by the patient

so to be, who is engaged in the diagnosis or treatment of a mental or emotional condition, including alcoholism and other drug addiction;

2. A person licensed or certified as a psychologist under the laws of any state or nation, who is engaged primarily in the diagnosis or treatment of a mental or emotional condition, including alcoholism and other drug addiction;

3. A person licensed or certified as a clinical social worker, marriage and family therapist, or mental health counselor under the laws of this state, who is engaged primarily in the diagnosis or treatment of a mental or emotional condition, including alcoholism and other drug addiction;

4. Treatment personnel of facilities licensed by the state pursuant to chapter 394, chapter 395, or chapter 397, of facilities designated by the Department of Children and Families pursuant to chapter 394 as treatment facilities, or of facilities defined as community mental health centers pursuant to s. 394.907(1), who are engaged primarily in the diagnosis or treatment of a mental or emotional condition, including alcoholism and other drug addiction; or

5. An advanced registered nurse practitioner certified under s. 464.012, whose primary scope of practice is the diagnosis or treatment of mental or emotional conditions, including chemical abuse, and limited only to actions performed in accordance with part I of chapter 464.

(b) A "patient" is a person who consults, or is interviewed by, a psychotherapist for purposes of diagnosis or treatment of a mental or emotional condition, including alcoholism and other drug addiction.

(c) A communication between psychotherapist and patient is "confidential" if it is not intended to be disclosed to third persons other than:

1. Those persons present to further the interest of the patient in the consultation, examination, or interview.

2. Those persons necessary for the transmission of the communication.

3. Those persons who are participating in the diagnosis and treatment under the direction of the psychotherapist.

(2) A patient has a privilege to refuse to disclose, and to prevent any other person from disclosing, confidential communications or records made for the purpose of diagnosis or treatment of the patient's mental or emotional condition, including alcoholism and other drug addiction, between the patient and the psychotherapist, or persons who are participating in the diagnosis or treatment under the direction of the psychotherapist. This privilege includes any diagnosis made, and advice given, by the psychotherapist in the course of that relationship.

(3) The privilege may be claimed by:

(a) The patient or the patient's attorney on the patient's behalf.

(b) A guardian or conservator of the patient.

(c) The personal representative of a deceased patient.

(d) The psychotherapist, but only on behalf of the patient. The authority of a psychotherapist to claim the privilege is presumed in the absence of evidence to the contrary.

(4) There is no privilege under this section:

(a) For communications relevant to an issue in proceedings to compel hospitalization of a patient for mental illness, if the psychotherapist in the course of diagnosis or treatment has reasonable cause to believe the patient is in need of hospitalization.

(b) For communications made in the course of a court-ordered examination of the mental or emotional condition of the patient.

(c) For communications relevant to an issue of the mental or emotional condition of the patient in any proceeding in which the patient relies upon the condition as an element of his or her claim or defense or, after the patient's death, in any proceeding in which any party relies upon the condition as an element of the party's claim or defense.

Laws 1976, c. 76–237, § 1. Amended by Laws 1990, c. 90–347, § 40, eff. Oct. 1, 1990; Laws 1992, c. 92–57, § 1, eff. April 3, 1992; Laws 1993, c. 93–39, § 19, eff. Oct. 1, 1993; Laws 1995, c. 95–147, § 475, eff. July 10, 1995; Laws 1999, c. 99–2, § 28, eff. June 29, 1999; Laws 1999, c. 99–8, § 5, eff. June 29, 1999; Laws 2006, c. 2006–204, § 1, eff. July 1, 2006; Laws 2014, c. 2014–19, § 30, eff. July 1, 2014.

Historical and Statutory Notes

Amendment Notes:

Laws 1990, c. 90–347, § 40, eff. Oct. 1, 1990, in par. (1)(a), added subpar. 3.

See the Historical and Statutory Notes to § 90.101 for adoption of earlier provisions as a rule of court.

Laws 1992, c. 92–57, § 1, eff. April 3, 1992, inserted subpar. 3 of subsec. (1)(a) and redesignated former subpar. 3 as subpar. 4.

Laws 1993, c. 93–39, § 19, eff. Oct. 1, 1993, in subsec. (1), in par. (a), made nonsubstantive changes, and deleted a reference to chapter 396.

Laws 1995, c. 95–147, a reviser's bill, eliminated gender-specific references without making substantive changes in legal effect.

Laws 1999, c. 99–8, § 5, eff. June 29, 1999, amended the section to conform to the name change of the Department of Health and Rehabilitative Services.

Laws 2006, c. 2006–204, § 1, added subsec. (1)(a)5., relating to advanced registered nurse practitioners.

Laws 2014, c. 2014–19, a reviser's bill, deleted obsolete and expired provisions, corrected grammatical and typographical errors, and made other similar changes.

Prior Laws:

Fla.St.1978, Supp., §§ 90.242, 490.32.

Laws 1970, c. 70–294, § 21.

Fla.St.1969, § 490.11.

Laws 1965, c. 65–404, § 1.

Laws 1965, c. 65–386, § 5.

Federal Evidence Rules:

For rule relating to privileges, see Rule 501, Fed.Rules Evid., 28 U.S.C.A.

Uniform Rules of Evidence:

For rule relating to physician and psychotherapist-patient privilege, see Rule 503, Uniform Laws Annotated, Master Edition, vol. 13.

90.5035. Sexual assault counselor-victim privilege

(1) For purposes of this section:

(a) A "rape crisis center" is any public or private agency that offers assistance to victims of sexual assault or sexual battery and their families.

(b) A "sexual assault counselor" is any employee of a rape crisis center whose primary purpose is the rendering of advice, counseling, or assistance to victims of sexual assault or sexual battery.

(c) A "trained volunteer" is a person who volunteers at a rape crisis center, has completed 30 hours of training in assisting victims of sexual violence and related topics provided by the rape crisis center, is supervised by members of the staff of the rape crisis center, and is included on a list of volunteers that is maintained by the rape crisis center.

(d) A "victim" is a person who consults a sexual assault counselor or a trained volunteer for the purpose of securing advice, counseling, or assistance concerning a mental, physical, or emotional condition caused by a sexual assault or sexual battery, an alleged sexual assault or sexual battery, or an attempted sexual assault or sexual battery.

(e) A communication between a sexual assault counselor or trained volunteer and a victim is "confidential" if it is not intended to be disclosed to third persons other than:

1. Those persons present to further the interest of the victim in the consultation, examination, or interview.

2. Those persons necessary for the transmission of the communication.

3. Those persons to whom disclosure is reasonably necessary to accomplish the purposes for which the sexual assault counselor or the trained volunteer is consulted.

(2) A victim has a privilege to refuse to disclose, and to prevent any other person from disclosing, a confidential communication made by the victim to a sexual assault counselor or trained volunteer or any record made in the course of advising, counseling, or assisting the victim. Such confidential communication or record may be disclosed only with the prior written consent of the victim. This privilege includes any advice given by the sexual assault counselor or trained volunteer in the course of that relationship.

(3) The privilege may be claimed by:

(a) The victim or the victim's attorney on his or her behalf.

(b) A guardian or conservator of the victim.

(c) The personal representative of a deceased victim.

(d) The sexual assault counselor or trained volunteer, but only on behalf of the victim. The authority of a sexual assault counselor or trained volunteer to claim the privilege is presumed in the absence of evidence to the contrary.

Added by Laws 1983, c. 83–284, § 1, eff. June 24, 1983. Amended by Laws 1995, c. 95–147, § 476, eff. July 10, 1995; Laws 2002, c. 2002–246, § 1, eff. July 1, 2002.

Historical and Statutory Notes

Amendment Notes:

Laws 1995, c. 95–147, a reviser's bill, eliminated gender-specific references without making substantive changes in legal effect.

Laws 2002, c. 2002–246, § 1, in subsec. (1), inserted the definition of "trained volunteer" and redesignated the subsequent definitions; and, in subsecs. (2) and (3), four times inserted "or trained volunteer".

90.5036. Domestic violence advocate-victim privilege

(1) For purposes of this section:

(a) A "domestic violence center" is any public or private agency that offers assistance to victims of domestic violence, as defined in s. 741.28, and their families.

(b) A "domestic violence advocate" means any employee or volunteer who has 30 hours of training in assisting victims of domestic violence and is an employee of or volunteer for a program for victims of domestic violence whose primary purpose is the rendering of advice, counseling, or assistance to victims of domestic violence.

(c) A "victim" is a person who consults a domestic violence advocate for the purpose of securing advice, counseling, or assistance concerning a mental, physical, or emotional condition caused by an act of domestic violence, an alleged act of domestic violence, or an attempted act of domestic violence.

(d) A communication between a domestic violence advocate and a victim is "confidential" if it relates to the incident of domestic violence for which the victim is seeking assistance and if it is not intended to be disclosed to third persons other than:

1. Those persons present to further the interest of the victim in the consultation, assessment, or interview.

2. Those persons to whom disclosure is reasonably necessary to accomplish the purpose for which the domestic violence advocate is consulted.

(2) A victim has a privilege to refuse to disclose, and to prevent any other person from disclosing, a confidential communication made by the victim to a domestic violence advocate or any record made in the course of advising, counseling, or assisting the victim. The privilege applies to confidential communications made between the victim and the domestic violence advocate and to records of those communications only

if the advocate is registered under s. 39.905 at the time the communication is made. This privilege includes any advice given by the domestic violence advocate in the course of that relationship.

(3) The privilege may be claimed by:

(a) The victim or the victim's attorney on behalf of the victim.

(b) A guardian or conservator of the victim.

(c) The personal representative of a deceased victim.

(d) The domestic violence advocate, but only on behalf of the victim. The authority of a domestic violence advocate to claim the privilege is presumed in the absence of evidence to the contrary.

Added by Laws 1995, c. 95–187, § 7, eff. July 1, 1995. Amended by Laws 1998, c. 98–403, § 127, eff. Oct. 1, 1998.

Historical and Statutory Notes

Amendment Notes:

Laws 1998, c. 98–403, § 127, in subsec. (2), corrected a citation.

90.504. Husband-wife privilege

(1) A spouse has a privilege during and after the marital relationship to refuse to disclose, and to prevent another from disclosing, communications which were intended to be made in confidence between the spouses while they were husband and wife.

(2) The privilege may be claimed by either spouse or by the guardian or conservator of a spouse. The authority of a spouse, or guardian or conservator of a spouse, to claim the privilege is presumed in the absence of contrary evidence.

(3) There is no privilege under this section:

(a) In a proceeding brought by or on behalf of one spouse against the other spouse.

(b) In a criminal proceeding in which one spouse is charged with a crime committed at any time against the person or property of the other spouse, or the person or property of a child of either.

(c) In a criminal proceeding in which the communication is offered in evidence by a defendant-spouse who is one of the spouses between whom the communication was made.

Laws 1976, c. 76–237, § 1; Laws 1978, c. 78–361, § 10.

Historical and Statutory Notes

Amendment Notes:

Laws 1978, c. 78–361, deleted subsec. (3)(b) 2 which provided that there is no privilege under this section in a criminal proceeding in which one spouse is charged with:

"A crime committed at any time against the person or property of a third person, which crime was committed in the course of committing a crime against the person or property of the other spouse."

Prior Laws:

Fla.St.1978, Supp. § 90.04.

Comp.Gen.Laws 1927, § 4369.

Rev.Gen.St.1920, § 2702.

Gen.St.1906, § 1502.

Laws 1891, c. 4029, § 1.

Laws 1879, c. 3124, § 1.

Federal Evidence Rules:

For rule relating to privileges, see Rule 501, Fed.Rules Evid., 28 U.S.C.A.

Uniform Rules of Evidence:

For rule relating to husband and wife privilege, see Rule 504, Uniform Laws Annotated, Master Edition, vol. 13.

90.505. Privilege with respect to communications to clergy

(1) For the purposes of this section:

(a) A "member of the clergy" is a priest, rabbi, practitioner of Christian Science, or minister of any religious organization or denomination usually referred to as a church, or an individual reasonably believed so to be by the person consulting him or her.

(b) A communication between a member of the clergy and a person is "confidential" if made privately for the purpose of seeking spiritual counsel and advice from the member of the clergy in the usual course of his or her practice or discipline and not intended for further disclosure except to other persons present in furtherance of the communication.

(2) A person has a privilege to refuse to disclose, and to prevent another from disclosing, a confidential communication by the person to a member of the clergy in his or her capacity as spiritual adviser.

(3) The privilege may be claimed by:

(a) The person.

(b) The guardian or conservator of a person.

(c) The personal representative of a deceased person.

(d) The member of the clergy, on behalf of the person. The member of the clergy's authority to do so is presumed in the absence of evidence to the contrary.

Laws 1976, c. 76–237, § 1; Laws 1977, c. 77–174, § 1; Laws 1978, c. 78–361, § 11. Amended by Laws 1995, c. 95–147, § 477, eff. July 10, 1995.

Historical and Statutory Notes

Amendment Notes:

Laws 1977, c. 77–174, a reviser's bill, amended subsec. (3)(d) of this section to reflect substitution of "The clergyman's" for "His" at the beginning of the second sentence editorially inserted in Fla.St.1976, Supp. in the interest of clarity by the division of statutory revision and indexing.

Laws 1978, c. 78–361, substituted in the definition of clergyman "priest, rabbi, practitioner of Christian Science, or minister" for "priest, minister, rabbi, or regular minister".

Laws 1995, c. 95–147, a reviser's bill, eliminated gender-specific references without making substantive changes in legal effect.

Prior Laws:

Fla.St.1978, Supp. § 90.241.

Laws 1959, c. 59–144, §§ 1 to 4.

Federal Evidence Rules:

For rule relating to privileges, see Rule 501, Fed.Rules Evid., 28 U.S.C.A.

Uniform Rules of Evidence:

For rule relating to religious privilege, see Rule 505, Uniform Laws Annotated, Master Edition, vol. 13.

90.5055. Accountant-client privilege

(1) For purposes of this section:

(a) An "accountant" is a certified public accountant or a public accountant.

(b) A "client" is any person, public officer, corporation, association, or other organization or entity, either public or private, who consults an accountant with the purpose of obtaining accounting services.

(c) A communication between an accountant and the accountant's client is "confidential" if it is not intended to be disclosed to third persons other than:

1. Those to whom disclosure is in furtherance of the rendition of accounting services to the client.

2. Those reasonably necessary for the transmission of the communication.

(2) A client has a privilege to refuse to disclose, and to prevent any other person from disclosing, the contents of confidential communications with an accountant when such other person learned of the communications because they were made in the rendition of accounting services to the client. This privilege includes other confidential information obtained by the accountant from the client for the purpose of rendering accounting advice.

(3) The privilege may be claimed by:

(a) The client.

(b) A guardian or conservator of the client.

(c) The personal representative of a deceased client.

(d) A successor, assignee, trustee in dissolution, or any similar representative of an organization, corporation, or association or other entity, either public or private, whether or not in existence.

(e) The accountant, but only on behalf of the client. The accountant's authority to claim the privilege is presumed in the absence of contrary evidence.

(4) There is no accountant-client privilege under this section when:

(a) The services of the accountant were sought or obtained to enable or aid anyone to commit or plan to commit what the client knew or should have known was a crime or fraud.

(b) A communication is relevant to an issue of breach of duty by the accountant to the accountant's client or by the client to his or her accountant.

(c) A communication is relevant to a matter of common interest between two or more clients, if the communication was made by any of them to an accountant retained or consulted in common when offered in a civil action between the clients.

Laws 1978, c. 78–361, § 12. Amended by Laws 1995, c. 95–147, § 478, eff. July 10, 1995.

Historical and Statutory Notes

Amendment Notes:

Laws 1979, c. 79–202, § 15, added § 473.316 which is similar to this section with the exception of an additional subsec. (5) contained therein pertaining to disciplinary investigation or proceedings conducted pursuant to the accountancy law.

Laws 1995, c. 95–147, a reviser's bill, eliminated gender-specific references without making substantive changes in legal effect.

Prior Laws:

Fla.St.1978, Supp. § 473.141

Laws 1973, c. 73–117, § 4.

Laws 1969, c. 69–36, § 14.

Fla.St.1967, § 473.15.

Comp.Gen.Laws Supp.1936, § 3935(13).

Laws 1931, Ex.Sess. c. 15637, § 13.

Comp.Gen.Laws 1927, §§ 3917 to 3935, 7874.

Laws 1927, c. 12290, §§ 1 to 21.

Rev.Gen.St.1920, §§ 2507 to 2513, 5670.

Laws 1905, c. 5425, §§ 1 to 9.

90.506. Privilege with respect to trade secrets

A person has a privilege to refuse to disclose, and to prevent other persons from disclosing, a trade secret owned by that person if the allowance of the privilege will not conceal fraud or otherwise work injustice. When the court directs disclosure, it shall take the protective measures that the interests of the holder of the privilege, the interests of the parties, and the furtherance of justice require. The privilege may be claimed by the person or the person's agent or employee.

Laws 1976, c. 76–237, § 1. Amended by Laws 1995, c. 95–147, § 479, eff. July 10, 1995.

Historical and Statutory Notes

Amendment Notes:

Laws 1995, c. 95–147, a reviser's bill, eliminated gender-specific references without making substantive changes in legal effect.

Federal Evidence Rules:

For rule relating to privileges, see Rule 501, Fed.Rules Evid., 28 U.S.C.A.

Uniform Rules of Evidence:

For rule relating to trade secrets, see Rule 507, Uniform Laws Annotated, Master Edition, vol. 13.

90.507. Waiver of privilege by voluntary disclosure

A person who has a privilege against the disclosure of a confidential matter or communication waives the privilege if the person, or the person's predecessor while holder of the privilege, voluntarily discloses or makes the communication when he or she does not have a reasonable expectation of privacy, or consents to disclosure of, any significant part of the matter or communication. This section is not applicable when the disclosure is itself a privileged communication.

Laws 1976, c. 76–237, § 1; Laws 1978, c. 78–361, § 13. Amended by Laws 1995, c. 95–147, § 480, eff. July 10, 1995.

Historical and Statutory Notes

Amendment Notes:

Laws 1978, c. 78–361, inserted in the first sentence "or makes the communication when he does not have a reasonable expectation of privacy".

Laws 1995, c. 95–147, a reviser's bill, eliminated gender-specific references without making substantive changes in legal effect.

Federal Evidence Rules:

For rule relating to privileges, see Rule 501, Fed.Rules Evid., 28 U.S.C.A.

Uniform Rules of Evidence:

For rule relating to waiver of privilege by voluntary disclosure, see Rule 510, Uniform Laws Annotated, Master Edition, vol. 13.

90.508. Privileged matter disclosed under compulsion or without opportunity to claim privilege

Evidence of a statement or other disclosure of privileged matter is inadmissible against the holder of the privilege if the statement or disclosure was compelled erroneously by the court or made without opportunity to claim the privilege.

Laws 1976, c. 76–237, § 1.

Historical and Statutory Notes

Federal Evidence Rules:

For rule relating to privilege, see Rule 501, Fed.Rules Evid., 28 U.S.C.A.

Uniform Rules of Evidence:

For rule relating to privileged matter being disclosed under compulsion or without opportunity to claim privilege, see Rule 511, Uniform Laws Annotated, Master Edition, vol. 13.

90.509. Application of privileged communication

Nothing in this act shall abrogate a privilege for any communication which was made prior to July 1, 1979, if such communication was privileged at the time it was made.

Laws 1976, c. 76–237, § 1. Amended by Laws 1981, c. 81–259, § 41, eff. Aug. 4, 1981.

Historical and Statutory Notes

Amendment Notes:

Laws 1981, c. 81–259, a reviser's correction bill prepared pursuant to § 11.242, substituted "July 1, 1979" for "July 1, 1977".

90.510. Privileged communication necessary to adverse party

In any civil case or proceeding in which a party claims a privilege as to a communication necessary to an adverse party, the court, upon motion, may dismiss the claim for relief or the affirmative defense to which the privileged testimony would relate. In making its determination, the court may engage in an in camera inquiry into the privilege.

Laws 1976, c. 76–237, § 1.

90.601. General rule of competency

Every person is competent to be a witness, except as otherwise provided by statute.

Laws 1976, c. 76–237, § 1.

Historical and Statutory Notes

Federal Evidence Rules:

For rule relating to the general rule of competency, see Rule 601, Fed.Rules Evid., 28 U.S.C.A.

Uniform Rules of Evidence:

For rule relating to the general rule of competency, see Rule 601, Uniform Laws Annotated, Master Edition, vol. 13.

90.603. Disqualification of witness

A person is disqualified to testify as a witness when the court determines that the person is:

(1) Incapable of expressing himself or herself concerning the matter in such a manner as to be understood, either directly or through interpretation by one who can understand him or her.

(2) Incapable of understanding the duty of a witness to tell the truth.

Laws 1976, c. 76–237, § 1. Amended by Laws 1995, c. 95–147, § 482, eff. July 10, 1995.

Historical and Statutory Notes

Amendment Notes:

Laws 1995, c. 95–147, a reviser's bill, eliminated gender-specific references without making substantive changes in legal effect.

90.604. Lack of personal knowledge

Except as otherwise provided in s. 90.702, a witness may not testify to a matter unless evidence is introduced which is sufficient to support a finding that the witness has personal knowledge of the matter. Evidence to prove personal knowledge may be given by the witness's own testimony.

Laws 1976, c. 76–237, § 1. Amended by Laws 1995, c. 95–147, § 483, eff. July 10, 1995.

Historical and Statutory Notes

Amendment Notes:

Laws 1995, c. 95–147, a reviser's bill, eliminated gender-specific references without making substantive changes in legal effect.

Federal Evidence Rules:

For rule relating to lack of personal knowledge, see Rule 602, Fed.Rules Evid., 28 U.S.C.A.

Uniform Rules of Evidence:

For rule relating to lack of personal knowledge, see Rule 602, Uniform Laws Annotated, Master Edition, vol. 13.

90.605. Oath or affirmation of witness

(1) Before testifying, each witness shall declare that he or she will testify truthfully, by taking an oath or affirmation in substantially the following form: "Do you swear or affirm that the evidence you are about to give will be the truth, the whole truth, and nothing but the truth?" The witness's answer shall be noted in the record.

(2) In the court's discretion, a child may testify without taking the oath if the court determines the child understands the duty to tell the truth or the duty not to lie.

Laws 1976, c. 76–237, § 1. Amended by Laws 1985, c. 85–53, § 3, eff. July 1, 1985; Laws 1995, c. 95–147, § 484, eff. July 10, 1995.

Historical and Statutory Notes

Amendment Notes:

Laws 1985, c. 85–53, § 3, eff. July 1, 1985, deleted "young" preceding "child" and inserted language appearing as "or the duty not to lie" at the end of subsec. (2) in Fla.St. 1985.

Laws 1995, c. 95–147, a reviser's bill, eliminated gender-specific references without making substantive changes in legal effect.

Federal Evidence Rules:

For rule relating to oath or affirmation, see Rule 603, Fed.Rules Evid., 28 U.S.C.A.

Uniform Rules of Evidence:

For rule relating to oath or affirmation, see Rule 603, Uniform Laws Annotated, Master Edition, vol. 13.

90.606. Interpreters and translators

(1)(a) When a judge determines that a witness cannot hear or understand the English language, or cannot express himself or herself in English sufficiently to be understood, an interpreter who is duly qualified to interpret for the witness shall be sworn to do so.

(b) This section is not limited to persons who speak a language other than English, but applies also to the language and descriptions of any person, such as a child or a person who is mentally or developmentally disabled, who cannot be reasonably understood, or who cannot understand questioning, without the aid of an interpreter.

(2) A person who serves in the role of interpreter or translator in any action or proceeding is subject to all the provisions of this chapter relating to witnesses.

(3) An interpreter shall take an oath that he or she will make a true interpretation of the questions asked and the answers given and that the interpreter will make a true translation into English of any writing which he or she is required by his or her duties to decipher or translate.

Laws 1976, c. 76–237, § 1. Amended by Laws 1985, c. 85–53, § 2, eff. July 1, 1985; Laws 1995, c. 95–147, § 485, eff. July 10, 1995.

Historical and Statutory Notes

Amendment Notes:

Laws 1985, c. 85–53, § 2, eff. July 1, 1985, added the provisions appearing as subsec. (1)(b) in Fla.St.1985.

Laws 1995, c. 95–147, a reviser's bill, eliminated gender-specific references without making substantive changes in legal effect.

Prior Laws:

Fla.St.1978, Supp. § 90.243.

Laws 1972, c. 72–229, § 1.

Federal Evidence Rules:

For rule relating to interpreters, see Rule 604, Fed.Rules Evid., 28 U.S.C.A.

Uniform Rules of Evidence:

For rule relating to interpreters, see Rule 604, Uniform Laws Annotated, Master Edition, vol. 13.

90.6063. Interpreter services for deaf persons

(1) The Legislature finds that it is an important concern that the rights of deaf citizens be protected. It is the intent of the Legislature to ensure that appropriate and effective interpreter services be made available to Florida's deaf citizens.

(2) In all judicial proceedings and in sessions of a grand jury wherein a deaf person is a complainant, defendant, witness, or otherwise a party, or wherein a deaf person is a juror or grand juror, the court or presiding officer shall appoint a qualified interpreter to interpret the proceedings or deliberations to the deaf person and to interpret the deaf person's testimony, statements, or deliberations to the court, jury, or grand jury. A qualified interpreter shall be appointed, or other auxiliary aid provided as appropriate, for the duration of the trial or other proceeding in which a deaf juror or grand juror is seated.

(3)(a) "Deaf person" means any person whose hearing is so seriously impaired as to prohibit the person from understanding oral communications when spoken in a normal, conversational tone.

(b) For the purposes of this section, the term "qualified interpreter" means an interpreter certified by the National Registry of Interpreters for the Deaf or the Florida Registry of Interpreters for the Deaf or an interpreter whose qualifications are otherwise determined by the appointing authority.

(4) Every deaf person whose appearance before a proceeding entitles him or her to an interpreter shall notify the appointing authority of his or her disability not less than 5 days prior to any appearance and shall request at such time the services of an interpreter. Whenever a deaf person receives notification of the time of an appearance before a proceeding less than 5 days prior to the proceeding, the deaf person shall provide his or her notification and request as soon thereafter as practicable. In any case, nothing in this subsection shall operate to relieve an appointing authority's duty to provide an interpreter for a deaf person so entitled, and failure to strictly comply with the notice requirement will not be deemed a waiver of the right to an interpreter. An appointing authority may require a person requesting the appointment of an interpreter to furnish reasonable proof of the person's disability when the appointing authority has reason to believe that the person is not so disabled.

(5) The appointing authority may channel requests for qualified interpreters through:

(a) The Florida Registry of Interpreters for the Deaf;

(b) The Division of Vocational Rehabilitation of the Department of Education; or

(c) Any other resource wherein the appointing authority knows that qualified interpreters can be found.

(6) No qualified interpreter shall be appointed unless the appointing authority and the deaf person make a preliminary determination that the interpreter is able to communicate readily with the deaf person and is able to repeat and translate statements to and from the deaf person accurately.

(7) Before a qualified interpreter may participate in any proceedings subsequent to an appointment under the provisions of this act, such interpreter shall make an oath or affirmation that he or she will make a true interpretation in an understandable manner to the deaf person for whom the interpreter is appointed and that he or she will repeat the statements of the deaf person in the English language to the best of his or her skill and judgment. Whenever a deaf person communicates through an interpreter to any person under such circumstances that the communication would be privileged, and the recipient of the communication could not be compelled to testify as to the communication, this privilege shall apply to the interpreter.

(8) An interpreter appointed by the court in a criminal matter or in a civil matter shall be entitled to a reasonable fee for such service, in addition to actual expenses for travel, to be paid out of general county funds.

Laws 1980, c. 80–155, §§ 1 to 5, 7 to 9, eff. Oct. 1, 1980. Amended by Laws 1981, c. 81–259, § 42, eff. Aug. 4, 1981; Laws 1990, c. 90–123, § 1, eff. June 21, 1990; Laws 1993, c. 93–125, § 2, eff. Oct. 1, 1993; Laws 1995, c. 95–147, § 486, eff. July 10, 1995; Laws 1999, c. 99–8, § 6, eff. June 29, 1999; Laws 2002, c. 2002–22, § 18, eff. April 11, 2002.

Historical and Statutory Notes

Amendment Notes:

Laws 1981, c. 81–259, a reviser's correction bill prepared pursuant to § 11.242, amended subsec. (7) of this section by substituting "the recipient of the communication" for "such person".

Laws 1990, c. 90–123, § 1, eff. June 21, 1990, in subsec. (8), inserted "or in a civil matter"; and deleted a former second sentence, which read "When the interpreter is appointed in a civil matter, a reasonable fee for such service and actual expenses for travel may be assessed as costs, in the discretion of the court."

The 1990 amendment to this section was not adopted as a rule of court at the time of publication. See the Historical and Statutory Notes to § 90.101 for adoption of earlier provisions as a rule of court.

Laws 1993, c. 93–125, § 2, eff. Oct. 1, 1993, in subsec. (2), in the first sentence, inserted "or wherein a deaf person is a juror or grand juror,"; twice inserted "or deliberations"; inserted ", jury,"; and added the second sentence.

Laws 1995, c. 95–147, a reviser's bill, eliminated gender-specific references without making substantive changes in legal effect.

Laws 1999, c. 99–8, § 6, eff. June 29, 1999, amended the section to conform to the name change of the Department of Health and Rehabilitative Services.

Laws 2002, c. 2002–22, § 18, rewrote subsec. (5)(b), which formerly read:

"(b) The Vocational Rehabilitation Program Office of the Department of Labor and Employment Security; or".

90.607. Competency of certain persons as witnesses

(1)(a) Except as provided in paragraph (b), the judge presiding at the trial of an action is not competent to testify as a witness in that trial. An objection is not necessary to preserve the point.

(b) By agreement of the parties, the trial judge may give evidence on a purely formal matter to facilitate the trial of the action.

(2)(a) A member of the jury is not competent to testify as a witness in a trial when he or she is sitting as a juror. If the juror is called to testify, the opposing party shall be given an opportunity to object out of the presence of the jury.

(b) Upon an inquiry into the validity of a verdict or indictment, a juror is not competent to testify as to any matter which essentially inheres in the verdict or indictment.

Laws 1976, c. 76–237, § 1. Amended by Laws 1995, c. 95–147, § 487, eff. July 10, 1995.

Historical and Statutory Notes

Amendment Notes:

Laws 1995, c. 95–147, a reviser's bill, eliminated gender-specific references without making substantive changes in legal effect.

Federal Evidence Rules:

For rules relating to judge or juror as witness, see Rules 605 and 606, Fed.Rules Evid., 28 U.S.C.A.

Uniform Rules of Evidence:

For rules relating to judge or juror as witness, see Rules 605 and 606, Uniform Laws Annotated, Master Edition, vol. 13.

90.608. Who may impeach

Any party, including the party calling the witness, may attack the credibility of a witness by:

(1) Introducing statements of the witness which are inconsistent with the witness's present testimony.

(2) Showing that the witness is biased.

(3) Attacking the character of the witness in accordance with the provisions of s. 90.609 or s. 90.610.

(4) Showing a defect of capacity, ability, or opportunity in the witness to observe, remember, or recount the matters about which the witness testified.

(5) Proof by other witnesses that material facts are not as testified to by the witness being impeached.

Laws 1976, c. 76–237, § 1; Laws 1978, c. 78–361, § 14. Amended by Laws 1990, c. 90–174, § 1, eff. Oct. 1, 1990; Laws 1995, c. 95–147, § 488, eff. July 10, 1995.

Historical and Statutory Notes

Amendment Notes:

Laws 1978, c. 78–361, inserted ", ability or opportunity" in subsec. (1)(d); and, in subsec. (2), substituted "calling" for "producing" in the first sentence, and added the second sentence.

Laws 1990, c. 90–174, § 1, eff. Oct. 1, 1990, redesignated the paragraphs of the section; in the introductory phrase, substituted "including" for "except"; and deleted former subsec. (2).

Laws 1990, c. 90–174, § 6, provides:

"This act shall apply to cases pending or filed on or after October 1, 1990."

The 1990 amendment to this section was not adopted as a rule of court at the time of publication. See the Historical and Statutory Notes to § 90.101 for adoption of earlier provisions as a rule of court.

Laws 1995, c. 95–147, a reviser's bill, eliminated gender-specific references without making substantive changes in legal effect.

Prior Laws:

Fla.St.1978, Supp. §§ 90.09, 90.10.

Comp.Gen.Laws 1927, §§ 4377, 4378.

Rev.Gen.St.1920, §§ 2710, 2711.

Gen.St.1906, §§ 1510, 1511.

Rev.St.1892, §§ 1101, 1102.

Laws 1891, c. 1096, §§ 52, 53.

Federal Evidence Rules:

For rule relating to who may impeach, see Rule 607, Fed.Rules Evid., 28 U.S.C.A.

Uniform Rules of Evidence:

For rule relating to who may impeach, see Rule 607, Uniform Laws Annotated, Master Edition, vol. 13.

90.609. Character of witness as impeachment

A party may attack or support the credibility of a witness, including an accused, by evidence in the form of reputation, except that:

(1) The evidence may refer only to character relating to truthfulness.

(2) Evidence of a truthful character is admissible only after the character of the witness for truthfulness has been attacked by reputation evidence.

Laws 1976, c. 76–237, § 1; Laws 1978, c. 78–361, § 15.

Historical and Statutory Notes

Amendment Notes:

Laws 1978, c. 78–361, deleted "or opinion" preceding ", except that:" in the introductory paragraph, and deleted "opinion or" preceding "reputation evidence" in subsec. (2).

Prior Laws:

Fla.St.1978, Supp. § 90.10.

Comp.Gen.Laws 1927, § 4378.

Rev.Gen.St.1920, § 2711.

Gen.St.1906, § 1511.

Rev.St.1892, § 1102.

Laws 1891, c. 1096, § 53.

Federal Evidence Rules:

For rule relating to evidence of character and conduct of witness, see Rule 608, Fed.Rules Evid., 28 U.S.C.A.

Uniform Rules of Evidence:

For rule relating to evidence of character and conduct of witness, see Rule 608, Uniform Laws Annotated, Master Edition, vol. 13.

90.610. Conviction of certain crimes as impeachment

(1) A party may attack the credibility of any witness, including an accused, by evidence that the witness has been convicted of a crime if the crime was punishable by death or imprisonment in excess of 1 year under the law under which the witness was convicted, or if the crime involved dishonesty or a false statement regardless of the punishment, with the following exceptions:

(a) Evidence of any such conviction is inadmissible in a civil trial if it is so remote in time as to have no bearing on the present character of the witness.

(b) Evidence of juvenile adjudications are inadmissible under this subsection.

(2) The pendency of an appeal or the granting of a pardon relating to such crime does not render evidence of the conviction from which the appeal was taken or for which the pardon was granted inadmissible. Evidence of the pendency of the appeal is admissible.

(3) Nothing in this section affects the admissibility of evidence under s. 90.404 or s. 90.608.

Laws 1976, c. 76–237, § 1; Laws 1978, c. 78–361, § 16. Amended by Laws 1995, c. 95–147, § 489, eff. July 10, 1995.

Historical and Statutory Notes

Amendment Notes:

Laws 1978, c. 78–361, substantially rewrote subsecs. (1) and (2) which as they appear in Fla.St.1977 provided:

"(1) A party may attack the credibility of any witness, including an accused, by evidence that the witness has been convicted of a crime involving dishonesty or a false statement, with the following exceptions:

"(a) Evidence of any such conviction is inadmissible in a civil trial if it is so remote in time as to have no bearing on the present character of the witness.

"(b) Evidence of a prior conviction, which evidence would be otherwise admissible, is inadmissible if the witness has been the subject of a pardon.

"(c) Evidence of juvenile adjudications are inadmissible under this subsection.

"(2) The pendency of an appeal relating to a crime involving dishonesty or a false statement does not render evidence of the conviction from which the appeal was taken inadmissible. Evidence of the pendency of the appeal is admissible."

Laws 1995, c. 95–147, a reviser's bill, eliminated gender-specific references without making substantive changes in legal effect.

Prior Laws:

Fla.St.1978, Supp. § 90.08.

Laws 1971, c. 71–72, §§ 1, 2.

Fla.St.1969, § 90.07.

Laws 1945, c. 22858, § 7.

Comp.Gen.Laws 1927, §§ 4371, 4373.

Rev.Gen.St.1920, §§ 2704, 2706.

Gen.St.1906, §§ 1504, 1506.

Laws 1901, c. 4966, § 1.

Rev.St.1892, §§ 1096, 1097.

Laws 1861, c. 1096, § 54.

Act March 10, 1845, § 6.

Act March 15, 1843, § 25.

Act Nov. 23, 1828, § 72.

Federal Evidence Rules:

For rule relating to impeachment by evidence of conviction of crime, see Rule 609, Fed.Rules Evid., 28 U.S.C.A.

Uniform Rules of Evidence:

For rule relating to impeachment by evidence of conviction of crime, see Rule 609, Uniform Laws Annotated, Master Edition, vol. 13.

90.611. Religious beliefs or opinions

Evidence of the beliefs or opinions of a witness on matters of religion is inadmissible to show that the witness's credibility is impaired or enhanced thereby.

Laws 1976, c. 76–237, § 1. Amended by Laws 1995, c. 95–147, § 490, eff. July 10, 1995.

Historical and Statutory Notes

Amendment Notes:

Laws 1995, c. 95–147, a reviser's bill, eliminated gender-specific references without making substantive changes in legal effect.

Federal Evidence Rules:

For rule relating to religious beliefs or opinions, see Rule 610, Fed.Rules Evid., 28 U.S.C.A.

Uniform Rules of Evidence:

For rule relating to religious beliefs or opinions, see Rule 610, Uniform Laws Annotated, Master Edition, vol. 13.

90.612. Mode and order of interrogation and presentation

(1) The judge shall exercise reasonable control over the mode and order of the interrogation of witnesses and the presentation of evidence, so as to:

(a) Facilitate, through effective interrogation and presentation, the discovery of the truth.

(b) Avoid needless consumption of time.

(c) Protect witnesses from harassment or undue embarrassment.

(2) Cross–examination of a witness is limited to the subject matter of the direct examination and matters affecting the credibility of the witness. The court may, in its discretion, permit inquiry into additional matters.

(3) Leading questions should not be used on the direct examination of a witness except as may be necessary to develop the witness's testimony. Ordinarily, leading questions should be permitted on cross-examination. When a party calls a hostile witness, an adverse party, or a witness identified with an adverse party, interrogation may be by leading questions. The judge shall take special care to protect a witness under age 14 from questions that are in a form that cannot reasonably be understood by a person of the age and understanding of the witness, and shall take special care to restrict the unnecessary repetition of questions.

Laws 1976, c. 76–237, § 1. Amended by Laws 1995, c. 95–179, § 1, eff. May 10, 1995; Laws 2000, c. 2000–316, § 2, eff. July 1, 2000.

Historical and Statutory Notes

Amendment Notes:

Laws 1995, c. 95–179, § 1, eff. May 10, 1995, rewrote subsec. (3), which formerly read:

"(3) Except as provided by rule of court or when the interests of justice otherwise require:

"(a) A party may not ask a witness a leading question on direct or redirect examination.

"(b) A party may ask a witness a leading question on cross-examination or recross-examination."

Laws 2000, c. 2000–316, § 2, added the last sentence.

The Florida Supreme Court in per curiam opinion dated July 11, 2002 (825 So.2d 339) provided in part:

"Consistent with the committee's recommendations, we adopt chapters 2000–316, sections 1 and 2; and 2001–132, section 1 to the extent they are procedural. However, after hearing oral argument, and carefully considering the committee's recommendation against adopting chapter 2001–221, section 1, as well as the comments that were filed, we decline to follow this recommendation and also adopt the amendments to section 90.404(2) to the extent they are procedural. In the absence of a true 'case and controversy,' we express no opinion on the substance of the amendments or on the challenges to chapter 2001–221, section 1, that were raised in these proceedings. The various amendments are effective on the dates they became law."

Federal Evidence Rules:

For rule relating to mode and order of interrogation and presentation, see Rule 611, Fed.Rules Evid., 28 U.S.C.A.

Uniform Rules of Evidence:

For rule relating to mode and order of interrogation and presentation, see Rule 611, Uniform Laws Annotated, Master Edition, vol. 13.

90.613. Refreshing the memory of a witness

When a witness uses a writing or other item to refresh memory while testifying, an adverse party is entitled to have such writing or other item produced at the hearing, to inspect it, to cross-examine the witness thereon, and to introduce it, or, in the case of a writing, to introduce those portions which relate to the testimony of the witness, in evidence. If it is claimed that the writing contains matters not related to the subject matter of the testimony, the judge shall examine the writing in camera, excise any portions not so related, and order delivery of the remainder to the party entitled thereto. Any portion withheld over objection shall be preserved and made available to the appellate court in the event of an appeal. If a writing or other item is not produced or delivered pursuant to order under this section, the testimony of the witness concerning those matters shall be stricken.

Laws 1976, c. 76–237, § 1. Amended by Laws 1995, c. 95–147, § 491, eff. July 10, 1995.

Historical and Statutory Notes

Amendment Notes:

Laws 1995, c. 95–147, a reviser's bill, eliminated gender-specific references without making substantive changes in legal effect.

Federal Evidence Rules:

For rule relating to writing used to refresh memory, see Rule 612, Fed.Rules Evid., 28 U.S.C.A.

Uniform Rules of Evidence:

For rule relating to writing or object used to refresh memory, see Rule 612, Uniform Laws Annotated, Master Edition, vol. 13.

90.614. Prior statements of witnesses

(1) When a witness is examined concerning the witness's prior written statement or concerning an oral statement that has been reduced to writing, the court, on motion of the adverse party, shall order the statement to be shown to the witness or its contents disclosed to him or her.

(2) Extrinsic evidence of a prior inconsistent statement by a witness is inadmissible unless the witness is first afforded an opportunity to explain or deny the

prior statement and the opposing party is afforded an opportunity to interrogate the witness on it, or the interests of justice otherwise require. If a witness denies making or does not distinctly admit making the prior inconsistent statement, extrinsic evidence of such statement is admissible. This subsection is not applicable to admissions of a party-opponent as defined in s. 90.803(18).

Laws 1976, c. 76–237, § 1; Laws 1978, c. 78–361, § 17. Amended by Laws 1995, c. 95–147, § 492, eff. July 10, 1995.

Historical and Statutory Notes

Amendment Notes:

Laws 1978, c. 78–361, inserted "of the adverse party" in subsec. (1), and inserted "denies making or" preceding "does not distinctly admit" in the second sentence of subsec. (2).

Laws 1995, c. 95–147, a reviser's bill, eliminated gender-specific references without making substantive changes in legal effect.

Prior Laws:

Fla.St.1978, Supp. § 90.10.

Comp.Gen.Laws 1927, § 4378.

Rev.Gen.St.1920, § 2711.

Gen.St.1906, 1511.

Rev.St.1892, 1102.

Laws 1861, c. 1096, § 53.

Federal Evidence Rules:

For rule relating to prior statements of witnesses, see Rule 613, Fed.Rules Evid., 28 U.S.C.A.

Uniform Rules of Evidence:

For rule relating to prior statements of witnesses, see Rule 613, Uniform Laws Annotated, Master Edition, vol. 13.

90.615. Calling witnesses by the court

(1) The court may call witnesses whom all parties may cross-examine.

(2) When required by the interests of justice, the court may interrogate witnesses, whether called by the court or by a party.

Laws 1976, c. 76–237, § 1.

Historical and Statutory Notes

Federal Evidence Rules:

For rule relating to calling and interrogation of witnesses by court, see Rule 614, Fed.Rules Evid., 28 U.S.C.A.

Uniform Rules of Evidence:

For rule relating to calling and interrogation of witnesses by court, see Rule 614, Uniform Laws Annotated, Master Edition, vol. 13.

90.616. Exclusion of witnesses

(1) At the request of a party the court shall order, or upon its own motion the court may order, witnesses excluded from a proceeding so that they cannot hear the testimony of other witnesses except as provided in subsection (2).

(2) A witness may not be excluded if the witness is:

(a) A party who is a natural person.

(b) In a civil case, an officer or employee of a party that is not a natural person. The party's attorney shall designate the officer or employee who shall be the party's representative.

(c) A person whose presence is shown by the party's attorney to be essential to the presentation of the party's cause.

(d) In a criminal case, the victim of the crime, the victim's next of kin, the parent or guardian of a minor child victim, or a lawful representative of such person, unless, upon motion, the court determines such person's presence to be prejudicial.

Added by Laws 1990, c. 90–174, § 2, eff. Oct. 1, 1990. Amended by Laws 1992, c. 92–107, § 1, eff. July 1, 1992; Laws 1995, c. 95–147, § 493, eff. July 10, 1995.

Historical and Statutory Notes

Amendment Notes:

Laws 1990, c. 90–174, § 6, provides:

"This act shall apply to cases pending or filed on or after October 1, 1990."

The 1990 addition of this section was not adopted as a rule of court at the time of publication. See the Historical and Statutory Notes to § 90.101 for adoption of earlier provisions as a rule of court.

Laws 1992, c. 92–107, § 1, eff. July 1, 1992, added subsec. (2)(d) relating to prohibiting exclusion of certain persons, including the crime victim.

Laws 1995, c. 95–147, a reviser's bill, eliminated gender-specific references without making substantive changes in legal effect.

90.701. Opinion testimony of lay witnesses

If a witness is not testifying as an expert, the witness's testimony about what he or she perceived may be in the form of inference and opinion when:

(1) The witness cannot readily, and with equal accuracy and adequacy, communicate what he or she has perceived to the trier of fact without testifying in terms of inferences or opinions and the witness's use of inferences or opinions will not mislead the trier of fact to the prejudice of the objecting party; and

(2) The opinions and inferences do not require a special knowledge, skill, experience, or training.

Laws 1976, c. 76–237, § 1. Amended by Laws 1995, c. 95–147, § 494, eff. July 10, 1995.

Historical and Statutory Notes

Amendment Notes:

Laws 1995, c. 95–147, a reviser's bill, eliminated gender-specific references without making substantive changes in legal effect.

Federal Evidence Rules:

For rule relating to opinion testimony by lay witnesses, see Rule 701, Fed.Rules Evid., 28 U.S.C.A.

Uniform Rules of Evidence:

For rule relating to opinion testimony by lay witnesses, see Rule 701, Uniform Laws Annotated, Master Edition, vol. 13.

90.702. Testimony by experts

If scientific, technical, or other specialized knowledge will assist the trier of fact in understanding the evidence or in determining a fact in issue, a witness qualified as an expert by knowledge, skill, experience, training, or education may testify about it in the form of an opinion or otherwise, if:

(1) The testimony is based upon sufficient facts or data;

(2) The testimony is the product of reliable principles and methods; and

(3) The witness has applied the principles and methods reliably to the facts of the case.

Laws 1976, c. 76–237, § 1. Amended by Laws 2013, c. 2013–107, § 1, eff. July 1, 2013.

Historical and Statutory Notes

Amendment Notes:

Laws 2013, c. 2013–107, § 1, rewrote this section, which formerly read:

"If scientific, technical, or other specialized knowledge will assist the trier of fact in understanding the evidence or in determining a fact in issue, a witness qualified as an expert by knowledge, skill, experience, training, or education may testify about it in the form of an opinion; however, the opinion is admissible only if it can be applied to evidence at trial."

Federal Evidence Rules:

For rule relating to testimony by experts, see Rule 702, Fed.Rules Evid., 28 U.S.C.A.

Uniform Rules of Evidence:

For rule relating to testimony by experts, see Rule 702, Uniform Laws Annotated, Master Edition, vol. 13.

Preamble (Laws 2013, c. 2013– 107):

"WHEREAS, the Supreme Court of the United States in Daubert v. Merrell Dow Pharmaceuticals, Inc., 509 U.S. 579 (1993) replaced the standard for expert testimony in all federal courts that was first articulated in Frye v. United States, 293 F.2d 1013 (D.C. Cir 1923) with a new standard that is known as the Daubert standard, and

"WHEREAS, the United States Supreme Court has subsequently reaffirmed and refined the Daubert standard in the cases of General Electric Co. v. Joiner, 522 U.S. 136 (1997) and Kumho Tire Co. v. Carmichael, 526 U.S. 137 (1999), and

"WHEREAS, Florida's Evidence Code is generally patterned after the Federal Rules of Evidence,

"WHEREAS, Rule 702 of the Federal Rules of Evidence, applicable to all federal courts, was amended in 2000 to reflect the holdings in Daubert v. Merrell Dow Pharmaceuticals, Inc., 509 U.S. 579 (1993), General Electric Co. v. Joiner, 522 U.S. 136 (1997), and Kumho Tire Co. v. Carmichael, 526 U.S. 137 (1999), and

"WHEREAS, as result of the 2000 amendment, Rule 702 of the Federal Rules of Evidence provides that: "A witness who is qualified as an expert by knowledge, skill, experience, training, or education may testify in the form of an opinion or otherwise if:

"(a) The expert's scientific, technical, or other specialized knowledge will help the trier of fact to understand the evidence or to determine a fact in issue;

"(b) The testimony is based on sufficient facts or data;

"(c) The testimony is the product of reliable principles and methods; and

"(d) The expert has reliably applied the principles and methods to the facts of the case, and

"WHEREAS, by amending s. 90.702, Florida Statutes, to pattern it after Rule 702 of the Federal Rules of Evidence as amended in 2000, the Florida Legislature intends to adopt the standards for expert testimony in the courts of this state as provided in Daubert v. Merrell Dow Pharmaceuticals, Inc., 509 U.S. 579 (1993), General Electric Co. v. Joiner, 522 U.S. 136 (1997), and Kumho Tire Co. v. Carmichael, 526 U.S. 137 (1999), and to no longer apply the standard in Frye v. United States, 293 F.2d 1013 (D.C. Cir 1923) in the courts of this state, and

"WHEREAS, by amending s. 90.702, Florida Statutes, the Florida Legislature intends to prohibit in the courts of this state pure opinion testimony as provided in Marsh v. Valyou, 977 So.2d 543 (Fla. 2007), NOW, THEREFORE,"

90.703. Opinion on ultimate issue

Testimony in the form of an opinion or inference otherwise admissible is not objectionable because it includes an ultimate issue to be decided by the trier of fact.

Laws 1976, c. 76–237, § 1.

Historical and Statutory Notes

Federal Evidence Rules:

For rule relating to opinion on ultimate issue, see Rule 704, Fed.Rules Evid., 28 U.S.C.A.

Uniform Rules of Evidence:

For rule relating to opinion on ultimate issue, see Rule 704, Uniform Laws Annotated, Master Edition, vol. 13.

90.704. Basis of opinion testimony by experts

The facts or data upon which an expert bases an opinion or inference may be those perceived by, or made known to, the expert at or before the trial. If the facts or data are of a type reasonably relied upon by experts in the subject to support the opinion expressed, the facts or data need not be admissible in evidence. Facts or data that are otherwise inadmissible may not be disclosed to the jury by the proponent of the opinion or inference unless the court determines that their probative value in assisting the jury to evaluate the expert's opinion substantially outweighs their prejudicial effect.

Laws 1976, c. 76–237, § 1. Amended by Laws 1995, c. 95–147, § 495, eff. July 10, 1995; Laws 2013, c. 2013–107, § 2, eff. July 1, 2013.

Historical and Statutory Notes

Amendment Notes:

Laws 1995, c. 95–147, a reviser's bill, eliminated gender-specific references without making substantive changes in legal effect.

Laws 2013, c. 2013–107, § 2, added the last sentence, relating to disclosure of certain facts and data.

Federal Evidence Rules:

For rule relating to bases of opinion testimony by experts, see Rule 703, Fed.Rules Evid., 28 U.S.C.A.

Uniform Rules of Evidence:

For rule relating to bases of opinion testimony by experts, see Rule 703, Uniform Laws Annotated, Master Edition, vol. 13.

90.705. Disclosure of facts or data underlying expert opinion

(1) Unless otherwise required by the court, an expert may testify in terms of opinion or inferences and give reasons without prior disclosure of the underlying facts or data. On cross-examination the expert shall be required to specify the facts or data.

(2) Prior to the witness giving the opinion, a party against whom the opinion or inference is offered may conduct a voir dire examination of the witness directed to the underlying facts or data for the witness's opinion. If the party establishes prima facie evidence that the expert does not have a sufficient basis for the opinion, the opinions and inferences of the expert are inadmissible unless the party offering the testimony establishes the underlying facts or data.

Laws 1976, c. 76–237, § 1. Amended by Laws 1995, c. 95–147, § 496, eff. July 10, 1995.

Historical and Statutory Notes

Amendment Notes:

Laws 1995, c. 95–147, a reviser's bill, eliminated gender-specific references without making substantive changes in legal effect.

Federal Evidence Rules:

For rule relating to disclosure of facts or data underlying expert opinion, see Rule 705, Fed.Rules Evid., 28 U.S.C.A.

Uniform Rules of Evidence:

For rule relating to disclosure of facts or data underlying expert opinion, see Rule 705, Uniform Laws Annotated, Master Edition, vol. 13.

90.706. Authoritativeness of literature for use in cross-examination

Statements of facts or opinions on a subject of science, art, or specialized knowledge contained in a published treatise, periodical, book, dissertation, pamphlet, or other writing may be used in cross-examination of an expert witness if the expert witness recognizes the author or the treatise, periodical, book, dissertation, pamphlet, or other writing to be authoritative, or, notwithstanding nonrecognition by the expert witness, if the trial court finds the author or the treatise, periodical, book, dissertation, pamphlet, or other writing to be authoritative and relevant to the subject matter.

Laws 1978, c. 78–361, § 18.

90.801. Hearsay; definitions; exceptions

(1) The following definitions apply under this chapter:

(a) A "statement" is:

1. An oral or written assertion; or

2. Nonverbal conduct of a person if it is intended by the person as an assertion.

(b) A "declarant" is a person who makes a statement.

(c) "Hearsay" is a statement, other than one made by the declarant while testifying at the trial or hearing, offered in evidence to prove the truth of the matter asserted.

(2) A statement is not hearsay if the declarant testifies at the trial or hearing and is subject to cross-examination concerning the statement and the statement is:

(a) Inconsistent with the declarant's testimony and was given under oath subject to the penalty of perjury at a trial, hearing, or other proceeding or in a deposition;

(b) Consistent with the declarant's testimony and is offered to rebut an express or implied charge against the declarant of improper influence, motive, or recent fabrication; or

(c) One of identification of a person made after perceiving the person.

Laws 1976, c. 76–237, § 1; Laws 1978, c. 78–361, § 19. Amended by Laws 1981, c. 81–93, § 2, eff. Oct. 1, 1981; Laws 1995, c. 95–147, § 497, eff. July 10, 1995.

Historical and Statutory Notes

Amendment Notes:

Laws 1978, c. 78–361, inserted in subsec. (2)(a) "and was given under oath subject to the penalty of perjury at a trial, hearing, or other proceeding or in a deposition".

Laws 1981, c. 81–93, § 2, redefined "hearsay" in subsec. (1) (c).

Laws 1995, c. 95–147, a reviser's bill, eliminated gender-specific references without making substantive changes in legal effect.

Federal Evidence Rules:

For rule relating to hearsay definitions, see Rule 801, Fed.Rules Evid., 28 U.S.C.A.

Uniform Rules of Evidence:

For rule relating to hearsay definitions, see Rule 801, Uniform Laws Annotated, Master Edition, vol. 13.

90.802. Hearsay rule

Except as provided by statute, hearsay evidence is inadmissible.

Laws 1976, c. 76–237, § 1.

Historical and Statutory Notes

Federal Evidence Rules:

For rule relating to hearsay rule, see Rule 802, Fed.Rules Evid., 28 U.S.C.A.

Uniform Rules of Evidence:

For rule relating to hearsay rule, see Rule 802, Uniform Laws Annotated, Master Edition, vol. 13.

90.803. Hearsay exceptions; availability of declarant immaterial

The provision of s. 90.802 to the contrary notwithstanding, the following are not inadmissible as evidence, even though the declarant is available as a witness:

(1) Spontaneous statement.—A spontaneous statement describing or explaining an event or condition made while the declarant was perceiving the event or condition, or immediately thereafter, except when such statement is made under circumstances that indicate its lack of trustworthiness.

have made the statement unless he or she believed it to be true. A statement tending to expose the declarant to criminal liability and offered to exculpate the accused is inadmissible, unless corroborating circumstances show the trustworthiness of the statement.

(d) *Statement of personal or family history.*—A statement concerning the declarant's own birth, adoption, marriage, divorce, parentage, ancestry, or other similar fact of personal or family history, including relationship by blood, adoption, or marriage, even though the declarant had no means of acquiring personal knowledge of the matter stated.

(e) *Statement by deceased or ill declarant similar to one previously admitted.*—In an action or proceeding brought against the personal representative, heir at law, assignee, legatee, devisee, or survivor of a deceased person, or against a trustee of a trust created by a deceased person, or against the assignee, committee, or guardian of a mentally incompetent person, when a declarant is unavailable as provided in paragraph (1)(d), a written or oral statement made regarding the same subject matter as another statement made by the declarant that has previously been offered by an adverse party and admitted in evidence.

(f) *Statement offered against a party that wrongfully caused the declarant's unavailability.*—A statement offered against a party that wrongfully caused, or acquiesced in wrongfully causing, the declarant's unavailability as a witness, and did so intending that result.

Laws 1976, c. 76-237, § 1. Amended by Laws 1990, c. 90-139, § 3, eff. Oct. 1, 1990; Laws 1990, c. 90–174, § 4, eff. Oct. 1, 1990; Laws 1995, c. 95–147, § 499, eff. July 10, 1995; Laws 2005, c. 2005–46, § 2, eff. July 1, 2005; Laws 2012, c. 2012–152, § 1, eff. April 27, 2012.

Historical and Statutory Notes

Amendment Notes:

Laws 1990, c. 90–139, § 3, eff. Oct. 1, 1990, in subsec. (2)(d), substituted "parentage" for "legitimacy".

Laws 1990, c. 90–174, § 4, eff. Oct. 1, 1990, in subsec. (2)(c), deleted a former last sentence.

Laws 1990, c. 90–174, § 6, provides:

"This act shall apply to cases pending or filed on or after October 1, 1990."

The 1990 amendments to this section were not adopted as a rule of court at the time of publication. See the Historical and Statutory Notes to § 90.101 for adoption of earlier provisions as a rule of court.

Laws 1995, c. 95–147, a reviser's bill, eliminated gender-specific references without making substantive changes in legal effect.

Laws 2005, c. 2005–46, § 2, added subsec. (2)(e), relating to statements by deceased and ill declarants.

Laws 2012, c. 2012–152, § 1, inserted subsec. (2)(f), relating to statements offered against parties that wrongfully caused declarants' unavailability.

Prior Laws:

Fla.St.1978, Supp. § 92.22.

Comp.Gen.Laws 1927, § 4394.

Laws 1921, c. 8572, § 1.

Rev.Gen.St.1920, § 2723.

Laws 1919, c. 7838, § 10, sub. 6.

Laws 1909, c. 5897, § 1.

Gen.St.1906, § 1523.

Laws 1893, c. 4135, § 1.

Federal Evidence Rules:

For rule relating to hearsay exceptions, declarant unavailable, see Rule 804, Fed.Rules Evid., 28 U.S.C.A.

Uniform Rules of Evidence:

For rule relating to hearsay exceptions, declarant unavailable, see Rule 804, Uniform Laws Annotated, Master Edition, vol. 13.

90.805. Hearsay within hearsay

Hearsay within hearsay is not excluded under s. 90.802, provided each part of the combined statements conforms with an exception to the hearsay rule as provided in s. 90.803 or s. 90.804.

Laws 1976, c. 76–237, § 1.

Historical and Statutory Notes

Federal Evidence Rules:

For rule relating to hearsay within hearsay, see Rule 805, Fed. Rules Evid., 28 U.S.C.A.

Uniform Rules of Evidence:

For rule relating to hearsay within hearsay, see Rule 805, Uniform Laws Annotated, Master Edition, vol. 13.

90.806. Attacking and supporting credibility of declarant

(1) When a hearsay statement has been admitted in evidence, credibility of the declarant may be attacked and, if attacked, may be supported by any evidence that would be admissible for those purposes if the declarant had testified as a witness. Evidence of a statement or conduct by the declarant at any time inconsistent with the declarant's hearsay statement is admissible, regardless of whether or not the declarant has been afforded an opportunity to deny or explain it.

(2) If the party against whom a hearsay statement has been admitted calls the declarant as a witness, the party is entitled to examine the declarant on the statement as if under cross-examination.

Amendment Notes:; Laws 1976, c. 76–237, § 1. Amended by Laws 1995, c. 95–147, § 500, eff. July 10, 1995.

Historical and Statutory Notes

Laws 1995, c. 95–147, a reviser's bill, eliminated gender-specific references without making substantive changes in legal effect.

Federal Evidence Rules:

For rule relating to attacking and supporting credibility of declarant, see Rule 806, Fed.Rules Evid., 28 U.S.C.A.

Uniform Rules of Evidence:

For rule relating to attacking and supporting credibility of declarant, see Rule 806, Uniform Laws Annotated, Master Edition, vol. 13.

90.901. Requirement of authentication or identification

Authentication or identification of evidence is required as a condition precedent to its admissibility. The requirements of this section are satisfied by evidence sufficient to support a finding that the matter in question is what its proponent claims.

Laws 1976, c. 76–237, § 1.

Historical and Statutory Notes

Federal Evidence Rules:

For rule relating to requirement of authentication or identification, see Rule 901, Fed.Rules Evid., 28 U.S.C.A.

Uniform Rules of Evidence:

For rule relating to requirement of authentication or identification, see Rule 901, Uniform Laws Annotated, Master Edition, vol. 13.

90.902. Self-authentication

Extrinsic evidence of authenticity as a condition precedent to admissibility is not required for:

(1) A document bearing:

(a) A seal purporting to be that of the United States or any state, district, commonwealth, territory, or insular possession thereof; the Panama Canal Zone; the Trust Territory of the Pacific Islands; or a court, political subdivision, department, officer, or agency of any of them; and

(b) A signature by the custodian of the document attesting to the authenticity of the seal.

(2) A document not bearing a seal but purporting to bear a signature of an officer or employee of any entity listed in subsection (1), affixed in the officer's or employee's official capacity.

(3) An official foreign document, record, or entry that is:

(a) Executed or attested to by a person in the person's official capacity authorized by the laws of a foreign country to make the execution or attestation; and

(b) Accompanied by a final certification, as provided herein, of the genuineness of the signature and official position of:

1. The executing person; or

2. Any foreign official whose certificate of genuineness of signature and official position relates to the execution or attestation or is in a chain of certificates of genuineness of signature and official position relating to the execution or attestation.

The final certification may be made by a secretary of an embassy or legation, consul general, consul, vice consul, or consular agent of the United States or a diplomatic or consular official of the foreign country assigned or accredited to the United States. When the parties receive reasonable opportunity to investigate the authenticity and accuracy of official foreign documents, the court may order that they be treated as presumptively authentic without final certification or permit them in evidence by an attested summary with or without final certification.

(4) A copy of an official public record, report, or entry, or of a document authorized by law to be recorded or filed and actually recorded or filed in a public office, including data compilations in any form, certified as correct by the custodian or other person authorized to make the certification by certificate complying with subsection (1), subsection (2), or subsection (3) or complying with any act of the Legislature or rule adopted by the Supreme Court.

(5) Books, pamphlets, or other publications purporting to be issued by a governmental authority.

(6) Printed materials purporting to be newspapers or periodicals.

(7) Inscriptions, signs, tags, or labels purporting to have been affixed in the course of business and indicating ownership, control, or origin.

(8) Commercial papers and signatures thereon and documents relating to them, to the extent provided in the Uniform Commercial Code.

(9) Any signature, document, or other matter declared by the Legislature to be presumptively or prima facie genuine or authentic.

(10) Any document properly certified under the law of the jurisdiction where the certification is made.

(11) An original or a duplicate of evidence that would be admissible under s. 90.803(6), which is maintained in a foreign country or domestic location and is accompanied by a certification or declaration from the custodian of the records or another qualified person certifying or declaring that the record:

(a) Was made at or near the time of the occurrence of the matters set forth by, or from information transmitted by, a person having knowledge of those matters;

(b) Was kept in the course of the regularly conducted activity; and

(c) Was made as a regular practice in the course of the regularly conducted activity,

provided that falsely making such a certification or declaration would subject the maker to criminal penalty under the laws of the foreign or domestic location in which the certification or declaration was signed.

Laws 1976, c. 76–237, § 1; Laws 1977, c. 77–174, § 1. Amended by Laws 1995, c. 95–147, § 501, eff. July 10, 1995; Laws 2003, c. 2003–259, § 3, eff. July 1, 2003.

Historical and Statutory Notes

Amendment Notes:

Laws 1977, c. 77–174, a reviser's bill, amended subsec. (2) of this section to reflect insertion in Fla.St.1976, Supp. of word "but" preceding "purporting to bear" by the division of statutory revision and indexing.

Laws 1995, c. 95–147, a reviser's bill, eliminated gender-specific references without making substantive changes in legal effect.

Laws 2003, c. 2003–259, § 3, added subsec. (11), relating to an original or duplicate of evidence accompanied by a certification or declaration from the custodian of the records.

Prior Laws:

Fla.St.1978, Supp. §§ 92.032, 92.10, 92.121.

Laws 1951, c. 26842, § 1.

Comp.Gen.Laws 1927, § 4385.

Rev.Gen.St.1920, § 2718.

Gen.St.1906, § 1518.

Rev.St.1892, § 1109.

Const.1885, Art. 16, § 21.

Act March 15, 1843, § 26.

Federal Evidence Rules:

For rule relating to self-authentication, see Rule 902, Fed.Rules Evid., 28 U.S.C.A.

Uniform Rules of Evidence:

For rule relating to self-authentication, see Rule 902, Uniform Laws Annotated, Master Edition, vol. 13.

90.903. Testimony of subscribing witness unnecessary

The testimony of a subscribing witness is not necessary to authenticate a writing unless the statute requiring attestation requires it.

Laws 1976, c. 76–237, § 1.

Historical and Statutory Notes

Federal Evidence Rules:

For rule relating to necessity of subscribing witness' testimony, see Rule 903, Fed.Rules Evid., 28 U.S.C.A.

Uniform Rules of Evidence:

For rule relating to necessity of subscribing witness' testimony, see Rule 903, Uniform Laws Annotated, Master Edition, vol. 13.

90.91. Photographs of property wrongfully taken; use in prosecution, procedure; return of property to owner

In any prosecution for a crime involving the wrongful taking of property, a photograph of the property alleged to have been wrongfully taken may be deemed competent evidence of such property and may be admissible in the prosecution to the same extent as if such property were introduced as evidence. Such photograph shall bear a written description of the property alleged to have been wrongfully taken, the name of the owner of the property, the location where the alleged wrongful taking occurred, the name of the investigating law enforcement officer, the date the photograph was taken, and the name of the photographer. Such writing shall be made under oath by the investigating law enforcement officer, and the photograph shall be identified by the signature of the photographer. Upon the filing of such photograph and writing with the law enforcement authority or court holding such property as evidence, the property may be returned to the owner from whom the property was taken.

Laws 1984, c. 84–363, § 4, eff. Oct. 1, 1984.

90.951. Definitions

For purposes of this chapter:

(1) "Writings" and "recordings" include letters, words, or numbers, or their equivalent, set down by handwriting, typewriting, printing, photostating, photography, magnetic impulse, mechanical or electronic recording, or other form of data compilation, upon paper, wood, stone, recording tape, or other materials.

(2) "Photographs" include still photographs, X-ray films, videotapes, and motion pictures.

(3) An "original" of a writing or recording means the writing or recording itself, or any counterpart intended to have the same effect by a person executing or issuing it. An "original" of a photograph includes the negative or any print made from it. If data are stored in a computer or similar device, any printout or other output readable by sight and shown to reflect the data accurately is an "original."

(4) "Duplicate" includes:

(a) A counterpart produced by the same impression as the original, from the same matrix; by means of photography, including enlargements and miniatures; by mechanical or electronic rerecording; by chemical reproduction; or by other equivalent technique that accurately reproduces the original; or

(b) An executed carbon copy not intended by the parties to be an original.

Laws 1976, c. 76–237, § 1.

Historical and Statutory Notes

Federal Evidence Rules:

For rule relating to definitions pertaining to contents of writings, recordings and photographs, see Rule 1001, Fed.Rules Evid., 28 U.S.C.A.

Uniform Rules of Evidence:

For rule relating to definitions pertaining to contents of writings, recordings and photographs, see Rule 1001, Uniform Laws Annotated, Master Edition, vol. 13.

90.952. Requirement of originals

Except as otherwise provided by statute, an original writing, recording, or photograph is required in order to prove the contents of the writing, recording, or photograph.

Laws 1976, c. 76–237, § 1; Laws 1977, c. 77–174, § 1.

Historical and Statutory Notes

Amendment Notes:

Laws 1977, c. 77–174, a reviser's bill, amended this section by inserting the words "in order" preceding "to prove" as those words were editorially supplied in Fla.St.1976, Supp. by the division of statutory revision and indexing.

Prior Laws:

Fla.St.1978, Supp., § 92.35.

Laws 1951, c. 26901, §§ 1, 3.

Federal Evidence Rules:

For rule relating to requirement of original, see Rule 1002, Fed. Rules Evid., 28 U.S.C.A.

Uniform Rules of Evidence:

For rule relating to requirement of original, see Rule 1002, Uniform Laws Annotated, Master Edition, vol. 13.

90.953. Admissibility of duplicates

A duplicate is admissible to the same extent as an original, unless:

(1) The document or writing is a negotiable instrument as defined in s. 673.1041, a security as defined in s. 678.1021, or any other writing that evidences a right to the payment of money, is not itself a security agreement or lease, and is of a type that is transferred by delivery in the ordinary course of business with any necessary endorsement or assignment.

(2) A genuine question is raised about the authenticity of the original or any other document or writing.

(3) It is unfair, under the circumstance, to admit the duplicate in lieu of the original.

Laws 1976, c. 76–237, § 1. Amended by Laws 1992, c. 92–82, § 57, eff. Jan. 1, 1993; Laws 1999, c. 99–2, § 29, eff. June 29, 1999.

Historical and Statutory Notes

Amendment Notes:

Laws 1992, c. 92–82, § 57, eff. Jan. 1, 1993, correctively substituted "673.1041" for "673.104" in subsec. (1).

Laws 1999, c. 99–2, § 29, eff. June 29, 1999, amended to conform to the repeal of former s. 678.102.

Prior Laws:

Fla.St.1978, Supp. § 92.11.

Comp.Gen.Laws 1927, § 4386.

Rev.Gen.St.1920, § 2719.

Gen.St.1906, § 1519.

Rev.St.1892, § 1110.

Act Nov. 20, 1828, § 20.

Federal Evidence Rules:

For rule relating to admissibility of duplicates, see Rule 1003, Fed.Rules Evid., 28 U.S.C.A.

Uniform Rules of Evidence:

For rule relating to admissibility of duplicates, see Rule 1003, Uniform Laws Annotated, Master Edition, vol. 13.

90.954. Admissibility of other evidence of contents

The original of a writing, recording, or photograph is not required, except as provided in s. 90.953, and other evidence of its contents is admissible when:

(1) All originals are lost or destroyed, unless the proponent lost or destroyed them in bad faith.

(2) An original cannot be obtained in this state by any judicial process or procedure.

(3) An original was under the control of the party against whom offered at a time when that party was put on notice by the pleadings or by written notice from the adverse party that the contents of such original would be subject to proof at the hearing, and such original is not produced at the hearing.

(4) The writing, recording, or photograph is not related to a controlling issue.

Laws 1976, c. 76–237, § 1; Laws 1977, c. 77–174, § 1. Amended by Laws 1995, c. 95–147, § 502, eff. July 10, 1995.

Historical and Statutory Notes

Amendment Notes:

Laws 1977, c. 77–174, a reviser's bill, amended the introductory paragraph of this section by substituting "of" for "or" following "The original" which language was editorially substituted in the interest of clarity in Fla.St.1976, Supp. by the division of statutory revision and indexing.

Laws 1995, c. 95–147, a reviser's bill, eliminated gender-specific references without making substantive changes in legal effect.

Federal Evidence Rules:

For rule relating to admissibility of other evidence of contents, see Rule 1004, Fed.Rules Evid., 28 U.S.C.A.

Uniform Rules of Evidence:

For rule relating to admissibility of other evidence of contents, see Rule 1004, Uniform Laws Annotated, Master Edition, vol. 13.

90.955. Public records

(1) The contents of an official record or of a document authorized to be recorded or filed, and actually recorded or filed, with a governmental agency, either federal, state, county, or municipal, in a place where official records or documents are ordinarily filed, including data compilations in any form, may be proved by a copy authenticated as provided in s. 90.902, if otherwise admissible.

(2) If a party cannot obtain, by the exercise of reasonable diligence, a copy that complies with subsection (1), other evidence of the contents is admissible.

Laws 1976, c. 76–237, § 1.

Historical and Statutory Notes

Prior Laws:

Fla.St.1978, Supp. §§ 92.11, 92.12, 92.121.

Laws 1974, c. 74–39, § 1.

Comp.Gen.Laws 1927, §§ 4386, 4387.

Rev.Gen.St.1920, §§ 2719, 2720.

Gen.St.1906, §§ 1519, 1520.

Rev.St.1892, §§ 1110, 1111.

Const.1885, Art. 16, § 21.

Laws 1846, c. 81, § 1.

Act Nov. 20, 1828, § 12.

Federal Evidence Rules:

For rule relating to public records, see Rule 1005, Fed.Rules Evid., 28 U.S.C.A.

Uniform Rules of Evidence:

For rule relating to public records, see Rule 1005, Uniform Laws Annotated, Master Edition, vol. 13.

90.956. Summaries

When it is not convenient to examine in court the contents of voluminous writings, recordings, or photographs, a party may present them in the form of a chart, summary, or calculation by calling a qualified witness. The party intending to use such a summary must give timely written notice of his or her intention to use the summary, proof of which shall be filed with the court, and shall make the summary and the originals or duplicates of the data from which the summary is compiled available for examination or copying, or both, by other parties at a reasonable time and place. A judge may order that they be produced in court.

Laws 1976, c. 76–237, § 1. Amended by Laws 1995, c. 95–147, § 503, eff. July 10, 1995.

Historical and Statutory Notes

Amendment Notes:

Laws 1995, c. 95–147, a reviser's bill, eliminated gender-specific references without making substantive changes in legal effect.

Federal Evidence Rules:

For rule relating to summaries, see Rule 1006, Fed.Rules Evid., 28 U.S.C.A.

Uniform Rules of Evidence:

For rule relating to summaries, see Rule 1006, Uniform Laws Annotated, Master Edition, vol. 13.

90.957. Testimony or written admissions of a party

A party may prove the contents of writings, recordings, or photographs by the testimony or deposition of the party against whom they are offered or by that party's written admission, without accounting for the nonproduction of the original.

Laws 1976, c. 76–237, § 1. Amended by Laws 1995, c. 95–147, § 504, eff. July 10, 1995.

Historical and Statutory Notes

Amendment Notes:

Laws 1995, c. 95–147, a reviser's bill, eliminated gender-specific references without making substantive changes in legal effect.

Federal Evidence Rules:

For rule relating to testimony or written admission of party, see Rule 1007, Fed.Rules Evid., 28 U.S.C.A.

Uniform Rules of Evidence:

For rule relating to testimony or written admission of party, see Rule 1007, Uniform Laws Annotated, Master Edition, vol. 13.

90.958. Functions of court and jury

(1) Except as provided in subsection (2), when the admissibility under this chapter of other evidence of the contents of writings, recordings, or photographs depends upon the existence of a preliminary fact, the question as to whether the preliminary fact exists is for the court to determine.

(2) The trier of fact shall determine whether:

(a) The asserted writing ever existed.

(b) Another writing, recording, or photograph produced at the trial is the original.

(c) Other evidence of the contents correctly reflects the contents.

Laws 1976, c. 76–237, § 1.

Historical and Statutory Notes

Federal Evidence Rules:

For rule relating to functions of court and jury, see Rule 1008, Fed.Rules Evid., 28 U.S.C.A.

Uniform Rules of Evidence:

For rule relating to functions of court and jury, see Rule 1008, Uniform Laws Annotated, Master Edition, vol. 13.

INDEX TO FLORIDA EVIDENCE CODE

FLORIDA RULES OF CIVIL PROCEDURE

1967 Revision

Effective after Midnight December 31, 1966

Rule 1.010. Scope and Title of Rules

These rules apply to all actions of a civil nature and all special statutory proceedings in the circuit courts and county courts except those to which the Florida Probate Rules, the Florida Family Law Rules of Procedure, or the Small Claims Rules apply. The form, content, procedure, and time for pleading in all special statutory proceedings shall be as prescribed by the statutes governing the proceeding unless these rules specifically provide to the contrary. These rules shall be construed to secure the just, speedy, and inexpensive determination of every action. These rules shall be known as the Florida Rules of Civil Procedure and abbreviated as Fla.R.Civ.P.

Amended June 19, 1968, effective Oct. 1, 1968 (211 So.2d 206); Oct. 9, 1980, effective Jan. 1, 1981 (391 So.2d 165); July 16, 1992, effective Jan. 1, 1993 (604 So.2d 1110); July 7, 1995, effective Jan. 1, 1996 (663 So.2d 1047); Nov. 22, 1995, effective Jan. 1, 1996 (663 So.2d 1049).

Authors' Comment—1967

Rule 1.010 is almost identical to Former Rule A, and now abolishes the distinction between law and equity. The rules supersede all prior rules and are more closely akin to the Federal Rules. Therefore, Barron and Holtzoff, Federal Practice and Procedure (West 1960) should be consulted because of the persuasive influence of the federal interpretations in terms of Florida practice.

Criminal proceedings are the only ones clearly excluded from the coverage of the rules. Rules of Criminal Procedure were adopted by the Supreme Court on March 1, 1967, to be effective January 1, 1968. By being applicable to all suits of a civil nature, the civil rules cover not only law and equity, tort and contract, but also special statutory proceedings and proceedings under the various extraordinary writs which have been classified as civil in nature. (See 4 University of Florida L.Rev. 446 (1951)).

The rules are by their terms clearly applicable to County Judge's courts but, of course, do not control probate proceedings, landlord and tenant proceedings, or other special statutory proceedings in that court. As to whether they can properly apply, see In re McRae's Estate, 1954, 73 So.2d 818.

Small claims courts, justice of the peace courts, and administrative agencies are excluded from the coverage of the rules.

Our rules completely abolish the distinction between law and equity as does Federal Rule 2 which provides that there shall be but one form of action to be known as a "civil action". See Rule 1.040.

The direction that the rules "shall be construed to secure the just, speedy, and inexpensive determination of every action" has two courses. It is, first, a direction that if a rule needs interpretation, the stated objective is the guide. The direction recognizes that procedural law is not an end in itself; it is only the means to an end. And that end is the proper administration of the substantive law. Procedural law fulfills its purpose if the substantive law is thereby administered in a "just, speedy, and inexpensive" manner. This provision does not authorize granting a defendant's motion for involuntary dismissal before the close of the plaintiff's evidence, as recognized in Sapp v. Redding, 178 So.2d 204, (D.C.A.1st 1965).

It is, next, a direction that each rule shall be applied with that objective in mind, especially where the court may exercise a judicial discretion.

The rules, therefore, establish a flexible scheme of civil procedure; but in the last analysis, whether an action is to be determined in the manner contemplated will depend, in great measure, upon the attitudes of judges and lawyers in approaching legal controversies and in employing and applying the rules.

Except where they conflict with statutory provisions, the rules may serve as a useful guide for approved procedure even in courts, agencies, or proceedings to which not expressly applicable.

To the extent that statutes dealing specifically with a particular civil action or proceeding do not set out a specific rule for a particular phase of practice or procedure, such phase would appear to be governed by these rules.

Rule 1.020. Privacy and Court Records

Every pleading or other paper filed with the court shall comply with Florida Rule of Judicial Administration 2.425.

Added Nov. 14, 2013, effective Jan. 1, 2014 (131 So.3d 643).

Rule 1.030. Nonverification of Pleadings

Except when otherwise specifically provided by these rules or an applicable statute, every pleading or other document of a party represented by an attorney need not be verified or accompanied by an affidavit.

Amended Dec. 13, 1976, effective Jan. 1, 1977, (339 So.2d 626); June 14, 1979, effective July 1, 1979 (372 So.2d 449); Oct. 18, 2012, effective Dec. 1, 2012, April 1, 2013, Oct. 1, 2013 (102 So. 3d 451).

Committee Notes

1976 Amendment. Subdivisions (a)–(b) have been amended to require the addition of the filing party's telephone number on all pleadings and papers filed.

Rule 1.040. One Form of Action

There shall be one form of action to be known as "civil action."

Amended July 16, 1992, effective Jan. 1, 1993 (604 So.2d 1110).

Authors' Comment—1967

Rule 1.040 is new to state practice, and perhaps is the most fundamental rule of all. It abolishes the forms of actions as well as eliminating the distinc-

tions between law and equity, in the identical language of Federal Rule 2. Thus, the litigant now may present his claim in an orderly manner to a court empowered to give him whatever relief is appropriate and just.

Rule 1.050. When Action Commenced

Every action of a civil nature shall be deemed commenced when the complaint or petition is filed except that ancillary proceedings shall be deemed commenced when the writ is issued or the pleading setting forth the claim of the party initiating the action is filed.

Authors' Comment—1967

Rule 1.050 is the same as former Rule 1.2(a) and is similar to Federal Rule 3. There is now no difference between law and equity in the commencement of an action, and the keeping of separate dockets as set forth in the prior rule is no longer required.

The first actual step to be taken in the institution of an action is the preparation of a complaint.

Until F.S.A. § 95.01 was repealed, as recommended by the committee, there was a serious question as to whether the statute of limitations was tolled by the filing of a complaint. Section 95.01 provided that for the purposes of that chapter an action was commenced when process was delivered to the proper officer to be served. Section 95.01 was repealed by Laws 1955, c. 29737.

Under the present rule, the time when a suit is commenced determines whether it is prematurely brought, whether it is barred by limitations or laches, or prior or subsequent to another suit. These things are now related by the rule to the time of filing the complaint, not the issuance, delivery for service, or the service of the summons. Under Rule 1.080(e), filing may be with the clerk or the judge. Filing with the clerk is preferable to avoid any question that might arise should there be a failure to transmit to the clerk as required by the rule. Ancillary proceedings are commenced when the pleading is filed or writ issued.

F.S.A. §§ 713.21–713.24 seem to contain no special provision on what constitutes the commencement of an action to enforce a mechanic's lien.

Rule 1.060. Transfers of Actions

(a) Transfers of Courts. If it should appear at any time that an action is pending in the wrong court of any county, it may be transferred to the proper court within said county by the same method as provided in rule 1.170(j).

(b) Wrong Venue. When any action is filed laying venue in the wrong county, the court may transfer the action in the manner provided in rule 1.170(j) to the proper court in any county where it might have been brought in accordance with the venue statutes. When the venue might have been laid in 2 or more counties, the person bringing the action may select the county to which the action is transferred, but if no such selection is made, the matter shall be determined by the court.

(c) Method. The service charge of the clerk of the court to which an action is transferred under this rule shall be paid by the party who commenced the action within 30 days from the date the order of transfer is entered, subject to taxation as provided by law when the action is determined. If the service charge is not paid within the 30 days, the action shall be dismissed without prejudice by the court that entered the order of transfer.

Amended Oct. 9, 1980, effective Jan. 1, 1981 (391 So.2d 165); Sept. 13, 1984, effective Jan. 1, 1985 (458 So.2d 245); July 16, 1992, effective Jan. 1, 1993 (604 So.2d 1110).

Court Commentary

1984 Amendment. Because of confusion in some circuits, subdivision (c) is added:

(a) to specify who is to pay the clerk's service charge on transfer;

(b) to provide for the circumstance in which the service charge is not paid; and

(c) to require the dismissal to be by the court which entered the order of transfer.

Rule 1.061. Choice of Forum

(a) Grounds for Dismissal. An action may be dismissed on the ground that a satisfactory remedy may be more conveniently sought in a jurisdiction other than Florida when:

(1) the trial court finds that an adequate alternate forum exists which possesses jurisdiction over the whole case, including all of the parties;

(2) the trial court finds that all relevant factors of private interest favor the alternate forum, weighing in the balance a strong presumption against disturbing plaintiffs' initial forum choice;

(3) if the balance of private interests is at or near equipoise, the court further finds that factors of public interest tip the balance in favor of trial in the alternate forum; and

(4) the trial judge ensures that plaintiffs can reinstate their suit in the alternate forum without undue inconvenience or prejudice.

The decision to grant or deny the motion for dismissal rests in the sound discretion of the trial court, subject to review for abuse of discretion.

(b) Stipulations in General. The parties to any action for which a satisfactory remedy may be more conveniently sought in a jurisdiction other than Florida may stipulate to conditions upon which a forum-non-conveniens dismissal shall be based, subject to approval by the trial court. The decision to accept or reject the stipulation rests in the sound discretion of the trial court, subject to review for abuse of discretion.

A forum-non-conveniens dismissal shall not be granted unless all defendants agree to the stipulations required by subdivision (c) and any additional stipulations required by the court.

(c) Statutes of Limitation. In moving for forum-non-conveniens dismissal, defendants shall be deemed to automatically stipulate that the action will be treated in the new forum as though it had been filed in that forum on the date it was filed in Florida, with service of process accepted as of that date.

(d) Failure to Refile Promptly. When an action is dismissed in Florida for forum non conveniens, plaintiffs shall automatically be deemed to stipulate that they will lose the benefit of all stipulations made by the defendant, including the stipulation provided in subdivision (c) of this rule, if plaintiffs fail to file the action in the new forum within 120 days after the date the Florida dismissal becomes final.

(e) Waiver of Automatic Stipulations. Upon unanimous agreement, the parties may waive the conditions provided in subdivision (c) or (d), or both, only when they demonstrate and the trial court finds a compelling reason for the waiver. The decision to accept or reject the waiver shall not be disturbed on review if supported by competent, substantial evidence.

(f) Reduction to Writing. The parties shall reduce their stipulation to a writing signed by them, which shall include all stipulations provided by this rule and which shall be deemed incorporated by reference in any subsequent order of dismissal.

(g) Time for Moving for Dismissal. A motion to dismiss based on forum non conveniens shall be served not later than 60 days after service of process on the moving party.

(h) Retention of Jurisdiction. The court shall retain jurisdiction after the dismissal to enforce its order of dismissal and any conditions and stipulations in the order.

Added January 25, 1996 (674 So.2d 86). Amended Oct. 31, 1996, effective Jan. 1, 1997 (682 So.2d 105); Oct. 5, 2000, effective Jan. 1, 2001 (773 So.2d 1098).

Court Commentary

This section was added to elaborate on Florida's adoption of the federal doctrine of forum non conveniens in *Kinney System, Inc. v. Continental Insurance Co.*, 674 So.2d 86 (Fla. 1996), and it should be interpreted in light of that opinion.

Subdivision (a) codifies the federal standard for reviewing motions filed under the forum-non-conveniens doctrine. Orders granting or denying dismissal for forum non conveniens are subject to appellate review under an abuse-of-discretion standard.

As stated in *Kinney*, the phrase "private interests" means adequate access to evidence and relevant sites, adequate access to witnesses, adequate enforcement of judgments, and the practicalities and expenses associated with the litigation. Private interests do not involve consideration of the availability or unavailability of advantageous legal theories, a history of generous or stingy damage awards, or procedural nuances that may affect outcomes but that do not effectively deprive the plaintiff of any remedy.

"Equipoise" means that the advantages and disadvantages of the alternative forum will not significantly undermine or favor the "private interests" of any particular party, as compared with the forum in which suit was filed.

"Public interests" are the ability of courts to protect their dockets from causes that lack significant connection to the jurisdiction; the ability of courts to encourage trial of controversies in the localities in which they arise; and the ability of courts to consider their familiarity with governing law when deciding whether to retain jurisdiction over a case. Even when the private conveniences of the litigants are nearly in balance, a trial court has discretion to grant a forum-non-conveniens dismissal upon finding that retention of jurisdiction would be unduly burdensome to the community, that there is little or no public interest in the dispute, or that foreign law will predominate if jurisdiction is retained.

Subdivision (b) provides that the parties can stipulate to conditions of a forum-non-conveniens dismissal, subject to the trial court's approval. The trial court's acceptance or rejection of the stipulation is subject to appellate review under an abuse-of-discretion standard.

Subdivisions (c) and (d) provide automatic conditions that shall be deemed included in every forum-non-conveniens dismissal. The purpose underlying subdivision (c) is to ensure that any statute of limitation in the new forum is applied as though the action had been filed in that forum on the date it was filed in Florida. The purpose underlying subdivision (d) is to ensure that the action is promptly refiled in the new forum. Both of these stipulations are deemed to be a part of every stipulation that does not expressly state otherwise, subject to the qualification provided in subdivision (e).

Subdivision (e) recognizes that there may be extraordinary conditions associated with the new forum that would require the waiver of the conditions provided in subdivisions (c) and (d). Waivers should be granted sparingly. Thus, the parties by unanimous consent may stipulate to waive those conditions only upon showing a compelling reason to the trial court. The trial court's acceptance or rejection of the waiver may not be reversed on appeal where supported by competent, substantial evidence.

Subdivision (f) requires the parties to reduce their stipulation to written form, which the parties must sign. When and if the trial court accepts the stipulation, the parties' agreement then is treated as though it were incorporated by reference in the trial court's order of dismissal. To avoid confusion, the parties shall include the automatic stipulations provided by subdivisions (c) and (d) of this rule, unless the latter are properly waived under subdivision (e).

However, the failure to include these automatic conditions in the stipulation does not waive them unless the dismissing court has expressly so ruled.

Committee Notes

2000 Amendment. Subdivision (a)(1) is amended to clarify that the alternative forum other than Florida must have jurisdiction over all of the parties for the trial court to grant a dismissal based on forum non conveniens.

Subdivision (b) is amended to clarify that all of the defendants, not just the moving defendant, must agree to the stipulations required by subdivision (c) as well as any additional stipulations required by the trial court before an action may be dismissed based on forum non conveniens.

Subdivision (g) is added to require that a motion to dismiss based on forum non conveniens be served not later than 60 days after service of process on the moving party.

Subdivision (h) is added to require the court to retain jurisdiction over the action after the dismissal for purposes of enforcing its order of dismissal and any conditions and stipulations contained in the order.

Rule 1.070. Process

(a) Summons; Issuance. Upon the commencement of the action, summons or other process authorized by law shall be issued forthwith by the clerk or judge under the clerk's or the judge's signature and the seal of the court and delivered for service without praecipe.

(b) Service; By Whom Made. Service of process may be made by an officer authorized by law to serve process, but the court may appoint any competent person not interested in the action to serve the process. When so appointed, the person serving process shall make proof of service by affidavit promptly and in any event within the time during which the person served must respond to the process. Failure to make proof of service shall not affect the validity of the service. When any process is returned not executed or returned improperly executed for any defendant, the party causing its issuance shall be entitled to such additional process against the unserved party as is required to effect service.

(c) Service; Numerous Defendants. If there is more than 1 defendant, the clerk or judge shall issue as many writs of process against the several defendants as may be directed by the plaintiff or the plaintiff's attorney.

(d) Service by Publication. Service of process by publication may be made as provided by statute.

(e) Copies of Initial Pleading for Persons Served. At the time of personal service of process a copy of the initial pleading shall be delivered to the party upon whom service is made. The date and hour of service shall be endorsed on the original process and all copies of it by the person making the service. The party seeking to effect personal service shall furnish the person making service with the necessary copies. When the service is made by publication, copies of the initial pleadings shall be furnished to the clerk and mailed by the clerk with the notice of action to all parties whose addresses are stated in the initial pleading or sworn statement.

(f) Service of Orders. If personal service of a court order is to be made, the original order shall be filed with the clerk, who shall certify or verify a copy of it without charge. The person making service shall use the certified copy instead of the original order in the same manner as original process in making service.

(g) Fees; Service of Pleadings. The statutory compensation for making service shall not be increased by the simultaneous delivery or mailing of the copy of the initial pleading in conformity with this rule.

(h) Pleading Basis. When service of process is to be made under statutes authorizing service on nonresidents of Florida, it is sufficient to plead the basis for service in the language of the statute without pleading the facts supporting service.

(i) Service of Process by Mail. A defendant may accept service of process by mail.

(1) Acceptance of service of a complaint by mail does not thereby waive any objection to the venue or to the jurisdiction of the court over the person of the defendant.

(2) A plaintiff may notify any defendant of the commencement of the action and request that the defendant waive service of a summons. The notice and request shall:

(A) be in writing and be addressed directly to the defendant, if an individual, or to an officer or managing or general agent of the defendant or other agent authorized by appointment or law to receive service of process;

(B) be dispatched by certified mail, return receipt requested;

(C) be accompanied by a copy of the complaint and shall identify the court in which it has been filed;

(D) inform the defendant of the consequences of compliance and of failure to comply with the request;

(E) state the date on which the request is sent;

(F) allow the defendant 20 days from the date on which the request is received to return the waiver, or, if the address of the defendant is outside of the United States, 30 days from the date on which it is received to return the waiver; and

(G) provide the defendant with an extra copy of the notice and request, including the waiver, as well as a prepaid means of compliance in writing.

(3) If a defendant fails to comply with a request for waiver within the time provided herein, the court shall impose the costs subsequently incurred in effecting service on the defendant unless good cause for the failure is shown.

(4) A defendant who, before being served with process, timely returns a waiver so requested is not required to respond to the complaint until 60 days after the date the defendant received the request for waiver of service. For purposes of computing any time prescribed or allowed by these rules, service of process shall be deemed effected 20 days before the time required to respond to the complaint.

(5) When the plaintiff files a waiver of service with the court, the action shall proceed, except as provided in subdivision (4) above, as if a summons and complaint had been served at the time of filing the waiver, and no further proof of service shall be required.

(j) Summons; Time Limit. If service of the initial process and initial pleading is not made upon a defendant within 120 days after filing of the initial pleading directed to that defendant the court, on its own initiative after notice or on motion, shall direct that service be effected within a specified time or shall dismiss the action without prejudice or drop that defendant as a party; provided that if the plaintiff shows good cause or excusable neglect for the failure, the court shall extend the time for service for an appropriate period. When a motion for leave to amend with the attached proposed amended complaint is filed, the 120–day period for service of amended complaints on the new party or parties shall begin upon the entry of an order granting leave to amend. A dismissal under this subdivision shall not be considered a voluntary dismissal or operate as an adjudication on the merits under rule 1.420(a)(1).

Amended Sept. 29, 1971, effective Dec. 13, 1971 (253 So.2d 404); July 26, 1972, effective Jan. 1, 1973 (265 So.2d 21); Oct. 9, 1980, effective Jan. 1, 1981 (391 So.2d 165); Oct. 6, 1988, effective Jan. 1, 1989 (536 So.2d 974); July 16, 1992, effective Jan. 1, 1993 (604 So.2d 1110); Oct. 31, 1996, effective Jan. 1, 1997 (682 So.2d 105); March 4, 1999 (746 So.2d 1084); Feb. 17, 2000 (754 So.2d 671); Oct. 23, 2003, effective Jan. 1, 2004 (858 So.2d 1013).

Committee Notes

1971 Amendment. Subdivisions (f), (g), and (h) of the existing rule are combined because they deal with the same subject matter. The "notice of suit" is changed to "notice of action" to comply with the statutory change in 1967. Subdivision (g) is new and provides for substitution of a certified or verified copy of a court order that must be served. The original is to be filed with the clerk and not removed. Subdivision (i) is relettered to (h).

1972 Amendment. Subdivision (a) is amended to require the officer issuing the process to sign it and place the court seal on it. This was required by former section 47.04, Florida Statutes, and is essential to the validity of process. When the statute was repealed these procedural requirements were omitted and inadvertently not included in the rule. Subdivision (b) is changed to eliminate the predicate for court appointment of a person to make service of process. This makes the rule more flexible and permits the court to appoint someone to make service at any appropriate time.

1980 Amendment. Subdivision (i) is added to eliminate pleading evidentiary facts for "long arm" service of process. It is based on the long-standing principle in service by publication that pleading the basis for service is sufficient if it is done in the language of the statute. See *McDaniel v. McElvy*, 91 Fla. 770, 108 So. 820 (1926). Confusion has been generated in the decisions under the "long arm" statute. See *Wm. E. Strasser Construction Corp. v. Linn*, 97 So. 2d 458 (Fla. 1957); *Hartman Agency, Inc. v. Indiana Farmers Mutual Insurance Co.*, 353 So. 2d 665 (Fla. 2d DCA 1978); and *Drake v. Scharlau*, 353 So. 2d 961 (Fla. 2d DCA 1978). The amendment is not intended to change the distinction between pleading and proof as enunciated in *Elmex Corp. v. Atlantic Federal Savings & Loan Association of Fort Lauderdale*, 325 So. 2d 58 (Fla. 4th DCA 1976). It is intended to eliminate the necessity of pleading evidentiary facts as well as those of pecuniary benefit that were used in the *Elmex* case. The amendment is limited to pleading. If the statutory allegations are attacked by motion, the pleader must then prove the evidentiary facts to support the statutory requirements. If denied in a pleading, the allegations must be proved at trial. Otherwise, the allegations will be admitted under rule 1.110(e).

1988 Amendment. Subdivision (j) has been added to require plaintiffs to cause service of original summons within 120 days of filing the complaint absent good cause for further delay.

1992 Amendment. Subdivision (d) is repealed because the reason for the rule ceased when process was permitted to run beyond county boundaries. The amendment to subdivision (j) (redesignated as (i)) is intended to clarify that a dismissal under this subdivision is not to be considered as an adjudication on the merits under rule 1.420(a)(1) of these rules.

1996 Amendment. Subdivision (i) is added to provide some formality to the practice of requesting waiver of service of process by a sheriff or person appointed to serve papers or by publication. The committee intends that only the manner of service will be waived by this procedure. By accepting service pursuant to this rule, the defendant will not waive any objection to venue or jurisdiction over the person or admit to the sufficiency of the pleadings or to allegations with regard to long-arm or personal jurisdiction. For example, service of process would be void should a motion to dismiss be granted because the complaint did not allege the basis for long-arm jurisdiction over a nonresident defendant. *City Contract Bus Service, Inc. v. H.E. Woody*, 515 So. 2d 1354 (Fla. 1st DCA 1987). Under such circumstances, the defendant must be served pursuant to law or again waive service pursuant to this rule. Subdivision (i)(2)(F) allows the defendant 20 days from receipt (or 30 days if the defendant is outside of the United States) to return the waiver. Accordingly, the committee intends that the waiver be received by the plaintiff or the plaintiff's attorney by the twentieth day (or the thirtieth day if the defendant is outside of the United States). The former subdivision (i) has been redesignated as subdivision (j). Form 1.902 may be used to give notice of an action and request waiver of process pursuant to this rule.

2003 Amendment. Subdivision (j) is amended in accordance with *Totura & Co., Inc. v. Williams*, 754 So. 2d 671 (Fla. 2000). See the amendment to rule 1.190(a).

Authors' Comment—1967

Rule 1.070 is patterned after former Rule 1.3, 1954 Rules of Civil Procedure as amended. Federal Rule 4 is the federal counterpart to the rule.

A true and correct copy of the complaint must be served. The reason for this is the cutting down of time between pleadings. Placing of time of service on copy is an improvement over the Federal rule which does not have this requirement.

As soon as the complaint is filed, it becomes the duty of the clerk to issue a summons forthwith. The normal practice is for counsel to see that the summons gets into the hands of the proper sheriff or constable with enough copies of the complaint to make effective service and with any instructions for service that may be helpful to the officer. Particularly helpful are instructions or directions as to the likely whereabouts of the parties to be served.

An appropriate certificate of service is all that is required where the service is made by a sheriff or constable. An affidavit of service is required only when the server is specially appointed by the court.

Process and the service thereof are fully covered by F.S.A. Chapters 48 and 49.

Rule 1.071. Constitutional Challenge to State Statute or County or Municipal Charter, Ordinance, or Franchise; Notice by Party

A party that files a pleading, written motion, or other paper drawing into question the constitutionality of a state statute or a county or municipal charter, ordinance, or franchise must promptly

(a) file a notice of constitutional question stating the question and identifying the paper that raises it; and

(b) serve the notice and the pleading, written motion, or other paper drawing into question the constitutionality of a state statute or a county or municipal charter, ordinance, or franchise on the Attorney General or the state attorney of the judicial circuit in which the action is pending, by either certified or registered mail.

Service of the notice and pleading, written motion, or other paper does not require joinder of the Attorney General or the state attorney as a party to the action.

Added Sept. 8, 2010, effective Jan. 1, 2011 (52 So.3d 579).

Committee Notes

2010 Adoption. This rule clarifies that, with respect to challenges to a state statute or municipal charter, ordinance, or franchise, service of the notice does not require joinder of the Attorney General or the state attorney as a party to the action; however, consistent with section 86.091, Florida Statutes, the Florida Attorney General or applicable state attorney has the discretion to participate and be heard on matters affecting the constitutionality of a statute. See, *e.g.*, *Mayo v. National Truck Brokers, Inc.*, 220 So. 2d 11 (Fla. 1969); *State ex rel. Shevin v. Kerwin*, 279 So. 2d 836 (Fla. 1973) (Attorney General may choose to participate in appeal even though he was not required to be a party at the trial court). The rule imposes a new requirement that the party challenging the statute, charter, ordinance, or franchise file verification with the court of compliance with section 86.091, Florida Statutes. See form 1.975.

Rule 1.080. Service and Filing of Pleadings, Orders, and Documents

(a) Service. Every pleading subsequent to the initial pleading, all orders, and every other document filed in the action must be served in conformity with the requirements of Florida Rule of Judicial Administration 2.516.

(b) Filing. All documents shall be filed in conformity with the requirements of Florida Rule of Judicial Administration 2.525.

(c) Writing and written defined. Writing or written means a document containing information, an application, or a stipulation.

Amended Sept. 29, 1971, effective Dec. 13, 1971 (253 So.2d 404); July 26, 1972, effective Jan. 1, 1973 (265 So.2d 21); Dec. 13, 1976, effective Jan. 1, 1977 (339 So.2d 626); Nov. 1, 1979, effective Jan. 1, 1980 (376 So.2d 844); Dec. 13, 1979, effective Jan. 1, 1980 (377 So.2d 971); Sept. 13, 1984, effective Jan. 1, 1985 (458 So.2d 245); July 16, 1992, effective Jan. 1, 1993 (604 So.2d 1110); Oct. 5, 2000, effective Jan. 1, 2001 (773 So.2d 1098); Sept. 8, 2010, effective Jan. 1, 2011 (52 So.3d 579); Oct. 18, 2012, effective, *nunc pro tunc*, Sept. 1, 2012 (102 So.3d 505); Oct. 18, 2012, effective Dec. 1, 2012, April 1, 2013, Oct. 1, 2013 (102 So.3d 451).

Authors' Comment—1967

Rule 1.080 is substantially the same as prior Rule 1.4, 1954 Rules of Civil Procedure, as amended effective January 1, 1966. It is similar to Federal Rule 5, although the latter entitles the rule as Service and Filing of Pleadings and Other Papers, whereas Rule 1.080 labels the contents as Service of Pleadings and Papers. The rule is simple and direct. A change is found in paragraph (e) as amended in 1965, in that the rule no longer states that the clerk shall file papers as of the same date papers were filed with the judge, but returns to its original language of the judge noting the filing date, which eliminates a source of confusion which arose under the 1965 amendment.

Prior to the Common Law and Equity Rules original pleadings were not required to be served on the parties. Usually, however, attorneys forwarded a copy of such pleadings to the opposing attorneys. This practice can no longer be followed because it is necessary to have proof that the pleading has been served.

This Rule provides for three distinct ways of making service, (1) by delivery, (2) by mailing, and (3) by leaving the pleading or other paper with the clerk of court, and then goes on to provide for four distinct methods of delivery.

It should also be noted that service must be made upon the attorney, if the party is represented by an attorney, unless the court orders otherwise. This continues the established practice of serving the attorney in matters arising during the progress of a suit. Where one member of a firm has signed a pleading himself, service should be on him.

Service by Delivery—Handing to Attorney or Party

Service by delivery of a copy to the attorney or party is physical delivery into the hands of the attorney or party personally wherever he may be found.

——Leaving Copy at Office with Clerk or Some Person in Charge

Just who may be deemed "in charge" of the office within the meaning of the provision that service by delivery may be effected by leaving a copy at the office of party or attorney with his clerk or some person in charge thereof, must be determined by the circumstances of the particular office set-up. In some offices the secretary or receptionist may be in charge so as to permit leaving the copy with her, while in other offices she may have so little authority that she cannot be deemed to be in charge. On the other hand, a person may be in charge of an office at one time, as when the employer is out, and not at another.

It should be noted that the copy must be left with the clerk or person in charge of the office when that person is in the office so that giving it to such person in the hall or elevator or giving it to a clerk at the courthouse would not be a valid service within the meaning of the rule, although a similar delivery to the attorney or party personally would be valid.

It should be noted further that there is no requirement that the attorney or party be absent from the office in order to leave a copy with his clerk or other person in charge. It would seem, therefore, that a copy may be left with some person fulfilling the requirements of the Rule even though the party or attorney is in the office at the time.

Where the copy is left with some person, it is advisable to have the certificate of service show the name of the person with whom it is left, as well as his function in the office.

——Leaving Copy at Office in Conspicuous Place

Where no one is in charge of the office, delivery may be made by leaving the copy in a conspicuous place. This provision covers the case where everyone is out of the office but the door is left open and also where the person in the office is deemed not to be in charge of it. What is a conspicuous place must be determined by the physical appearance and arrangement of the office. The copy must be left in the office and cannot be left outside and probably could not be left on the threshold.

——Leaving Copy at Dwelling House

A copy may also be left at the "usual place of abode with some person of his family above fifteen years of age" but this is limited solely to cases where the office is closed or the person to be served has no office and cannot be given a more general application to permit service at the house whenever it is more convenient to make it there.

Service by Mail

The second method of service is by mailing and such service is complete upon mailing. Therefore placing a paper to be served in the mail on the last day is a valid service even though it might not be received for several days after the expiration of the period given for action in the particular case.

But where service is made by mail, three days must be added to the period given to the party served to respond, since by the provisions of a later rule an additional three days is given "whenever a party has the right or is required to do some act or take some proceedings within a prescribed period after the service of a notice or other paper upon him" and service is made by mail (Rule 1.090(e)). So, even though the paper is actually received the same day it is mailed or a day afterward, the party served has an additional three days added to the time given for response.

Filing

Filing is accomplished when the paper is delivered or placed in the hands of the officer entitled to receive it. U.S. v. Missco Homestead Assn. (C.C.A.8th) 185 Fed.2d 283. However, the Florida Courts have strictly construed the filing requirement to mean that that pleading must actually be filed with the court, and mere service is insufficient to present the pleading to the court. Pan American World Airways v. Gregory, 96 So.2d 669 (Fla.App. 1957).

Rule 1.090. Time

(a) Computation. Computation of time shall be governed by Florida Rule of Judicial Administration 2.514.

(b) Enlargement. When an act is required or allowed to be done at or within a specified time by order of court, by these rules, or by notice given thereunder, for cause shown the court at any time in its discretion (1) with or without notice, may order the period enlarged if request therefor is made before the expiration of the period originally prescribed or as extended by a previous order, or (2) upon motion made and notice after the expiration of the specified period, may permit the act to be done when failure to act was the result of excusable neglect, but it may not extend the time for making a motion for new trial, for rehearing, or to alter or amend a judgment; making a motion for relief from a judgment under rule 1.540(b);

taking an appeal or filing a petition for certiorari; or making a motion for a directed verdict.

(c) Unaffected by Expiration of Term. The period of time provided for the doing of any act or the taking of any proceeding shall not be affected or limited by the continued existence or expiration of a term of court. The continued existence or expiration of a term of court in no way affects the power of a court to do any act or take any proceeding in any action which is or has been pending before it.

(d) For Motions. A copy of any written motion which may not be heard ex parte and a copy of the notice of the hearing thereof shall be served a reasonable time before the time specified for the hearing.

Amended Oct. 9, 1980, effective Jan. 1, 1981 (391 So.2d 165); July 16, 1992, effective Jan. 1, 1993 (604 So.2d 1110); July 12, 2012, effective Oct. 1, 2012 (95 So.3d 96).

Authors' Comment—1967

Rule 1.090 is substantially the same as former Rule 1.6, 1954 Rules of Civil Procedure, as amended in 1965, as well as Federal Rule 6.

Rule 1.100. Pleadings and Motions

(a) Pleadings. There shall be a complaint or, when so designated by a statute or rule, a petition, and an answer to it; an answer to a counterclaim denominated as such; an answer to a crossclaim if the answer contains a crossclaim; a third-party complaint if a person who was not an original party is summoned as a third-party defendant; and a third-party answer if a third-party complaint is served. If an answer or third-party answer contains an affirmative defense and the opposing party seeks to avoid it, the opposing party shall file a reply containing the avoidance. No other pleadings shall be allowed.

(b) Motions. An application to the court for an order shall be by motion which shall be made in writing unless made during a hearing or trial, shall state with particularity the grounds therefor, and shall set forth the relief or order sought. The requirement of writing is fulfilled if the motion is stated in a written notice of the hearing of the motion. All notices of hearing shall specify each motion or other matter to be heard.

(c) Caption.

(1) Every pleading, motion, order, judgment, or other paper shall have a caption containing the name of the court, the file number, and except for in rem proceedings, including forfeiture proceedings, the name of the first party on each side with an appropriate indication of other parties, and a designation identifying the party filing it and its nature or the nature of the order, as the case may be. In any in rem proceeding, every pleading, motion, order, judgment, or other paper shall have a caption containing the name of the court, the file number, the style "In re" (followed by the name or general description of the property), and a designation of the person or entity filing it and its nature or the nature of the order, as the case may be. In an in rem forfeiture proceeding, the style shall be "In re forfeiture of" (followed by the name or general description of the property). All papers filed in the action shall be styled in such a manner as to indicate clearly the subject matter of the paper and the party requesting or obtaining relief.

(2) A civil cover sheet (form 1.997) shall be completed and filed with the clerk at the time an initial complaint or petition is filed by the party initiating the action. If the cover sheet is not filed, the clerk shall accept the complaint or petition for filing; but all proceedings in the action shall be abated until a properly executed cover sheet is completed and filed. The clerk shall complete the civil cover sheet for a party appearing pro se.

(3) A final disposition form (form 1.998) shall be filed with the clerk by the prevailing party at the time of the filing of the order or judgment which disposes of the action. If the action is settled without a court order or judgment being entered, or dismissed by the parties, the plaintiff or petitioner immediately shall file a final disposition form (form 1.998) with the clerk. The clerk shall complete the final disposition form for a party appearing pro se, or when the action is dismissed by court order for lack of prosecution pursuant to rule 1.420(e).

(d) Motion in Lieu of Scire Facias. Any relief available by scire facias may be granted on motion after notice without the issuance of a writ of scire facias.

Amended June 19, 1968, effective Oct. 1, 1968 (211 So.2d 206); Sept. 29, 1971, effective Dec. 13, 1971 (253 So.2d 404); July 26, 1972, effective Jan. 1, 1973 (265 So.2d 21); May 1, 1986, effective July 1, 1986 (488 So.2d 57); July 16, 1992, effective Jan. 1, 1993 (604 So.2d 1110); June 3, 2009 (15 So.3d 558); Sept. 8, 2010, effective Jan. 1, 2011 ((52 So.3d 579).

Committee Notes

1971 Amendment. The change requires a more complete designation of the document that is filed so that it may be more rapidly identified. It also specifies the applicability of the subdivision to all of the various documents that can be filed. For example, a motion to dismiss should now be entitled "defendant's motion to dismiss the complaint" rather than merely "motion" or "motion to dismiss."

1972 Amendment. Subdivision (a) is amended to make a reply mandatory when a party seeks to avoid an affirmative defense in an answer or third-party answer. It is intended to eliminate thereby the problems exemplified by *Tuggle v. Maddox*, 60 So.2d 158 (Fla.1952), and *Dickerson v. Orange State Oil Co.*, 123 So.2d 562 (Fla. 2d DCA 1960).

1992 Amendment. Subdivision (b) is amended to require all notices of hearing to specify the motions or other matters to be heard.

2010 Amendment. Subdivision (c) is amended to address separately the caption for in rem proceedings, including in rem forfeiture proceedings.

Authors' Comment—1967

Rule 1.100 is identical to former Rule 1.7, 1954 Rules of Civil Procedure, as amended effective January 1, 1966. It is an adaption of Federal Rules 7(a) and 10(a) and Common Law Rule 8. It reduces the number of pleadings to a minimum. A reply is no longer a part of Florida practice to respond to a counterclaim, but an answer is now required denominated as such. However, a reply may be ordered by the court to an answer, and if there is doubt about affirmative defenses a motion should be filed to require a reply. Under Rule 1.110(e) affirmative defenses are deemed denied if an answer is not filed. An answer setting up matters in avoidance of an affirmative defense may be ordered by the court. The Federal provisions as to a third party complaint are now recognized in the Florida Rules and Rules 1.180, 1.210, 1.170, 1.420, 1.270, 1.110, and 1.510 and should be consulted as to the utilization of this practice. Forms for such practice appear in Forms 1.948 and 1.904.

Section (b) of this rule prohibits the use of a petition with an accompanying order to show cause. The order is obtainable but the application is to be made by motion. For the federal practice see Application of Tracy, 106 F.2d 96 (C.C.A.2, 1939); Walling v. Moore Milling Co., 62 F.Supp. 378 (W.D.Va.1945).

Motions are of many varieties and can be used for many purposes. The common requirements for practically all of them are that they be in writing, state the grounds with particularity and set forth the relief or order sought (1.100(b)). Work can be saved by including the motion in a written notice of hearing but the common practice appears to be to set up the motion and notice of hearing thereon separately.

Only the first party on each side need be stated in the caption, and these are not changed regardless of changes in parties.

A simple motion is to be preferred to a formal order to show cause which the judge may decline to sign and which if entertained at all will be treated as a motion under the rules.

All motions, except those made during a trial or hearing, must be in writing, and the requirements as to form, and signature of pleadings are equally applicable to motions. Care is recommended in complying with these requirements which are few and simple. A motion which is not signed or which is signed with intent to defeat the rule requiring signed pleadings may be stricken as sham and false and the attorney, for wilful violation, may be disciplined.

A motion must specify with particularity the grounds upon which the motion is based and set forth the relief or order sought. These requirements are mandatory.

Rule 1.110. General Rules of Pleading

(a) Forms of Pleadings. Forms of action and technical forms for seeking relief and of pleas, pleadings, or motions are abolished.

(b) Claims for Relief. A pleading which sets forth a claim for relief, whether an original claim, counterclaim, crossclaim, or third-party claim must state a cause of action and shall contain (1) a short and plain statement of the grounds upon which the court's jurisdiction depends, unless the court already has jurisdiction and the claim needs no new grounds of jurisdiction to support it, (2) a short and plain statement of the ultimate facts showing that the pleader is entitled to relief, and (3) a demand for judgment for the relief to which the pleader deems himself or herself entitled. Relief in the alternative or of several different types may be demanded. Every complaint shall be considered to pray for general relief.

(c) The Answer. In the answer a pleader shall state in short and plain terms the pleader's defenses to each claim asserted and shall admit or deny the averments on which the adverse party relies. If the defendant is without knowledge, the defendant shall so state and such statement shall operate as a denial. Denial shall fairly meet the substance of the averments denied. When a pleader intends in good faith to deny only a part of an averment, the pleader shall specify so much of it as is true and shall deny the remainder. Unless the pleader intends in good faith to controvert all of the averments of the preceding pleading, the pleader may make denials as specific denials of designated averments or may generally deny all of the averments except such designated averments as the pleader expressly admits, but when the pleader does so intend to controvert all of its averments, including averments of the grounds upon which the court's jurisdiction depends, the pleader may do so by general denial.

(d) Affirmative Defenses. In pleading to a preceding pleading a party shall set forth affirmatively accord and satisfaction, arbitration and award, assumption of risk, contributory negligence, discharge in bankruptcy, duress, estoppel, failure of consideration, fraud, illegality, injury by fellow servant, laches, license, payment, release, res judicata, statute of frauds, statute of limitations, waiver, and any other matter constituting an avoidance or affirmative defense. When a party has mistakenly designated a defense as a counterclaim or a counterclaim as a defense, the court, on terms if justice so requires, shall treat the pleading as if there had been a proper designation. Affirmative defenses appearing on the face of a prior pleading may be asserted as grounds for a motion or defense under rule 1.140(b); provided this shall not limit amendments under rule 1.190 even if such ground is sustained.

(e) Effect of Failure to Deny. Averments in a pleading to which a responsive pleading is required, other than those as to the amount of damages, are admitted when not denied in the responsive pleading. Averments in a pleading to which no responsive pleading is required or permitted shall be taken as denied or avoided.

(f) Separate Statements. All averments of claim or defense shall be made in consecutively numbered paragraphs, the contents of each of which shall be limited as far as practicable to a statement of a single set of circumstances, and a paragraph may be referred to by number in all subsequent pleadings. Each claim founded upon a separate transaction or occurrence and each defense other than denials shall be stated in a separate count or defense when a separation facilitates the clear presentation of the matter set forth.

(g) Joinder of Causes of Action; Consistency. A pleader may set up in the same action as many claims or causes of action or defenses in the same right as the pleader has, and claims for relief may be stated in the alternative if separate items make up the cause of action, or if 2 or more causes of action are joined. A party may also set forth 2 or more statements of a claim or defense alternatively, either in 1 count or defense or in separate counts or defenses. When 2 or more statements are made in the alternative and 1 of them, if made independently, would be sufficient, the pleading is not made insufficient by the insufficiency of 1 or more of the alternative statements. A party may also state as many separate claims or defenses as that party has, regardless of consistency and whether based on legal or equitable grounds or both. All pleadings shall be construed so as to do substantial justice.

(h) Subsequent Pleadings. When the nature of an action permits pleadings subsequent to final judgment and the jurisdiction of the court over the parties has not terminated, the initial pleading subsequent to final judgment shall be designated a supplemental complaint or petition. The action shall then proceed in the same manner and time as though the supplemental complaint or petition were the initial pleading in the action, including the issuance of any needed process. This subdivision shall not apply to proceedings that may be initiated by motion under these rules.

Amended Sept. 29, 1971, effective Dec. 13, 1971 (253 So.2d 404); July 16, 1992, effective Jan. 1, 1993 (604 So.2d 1110); Oct. 31, 1996, effective Jan. 1, 1997 (682 So.2d 105); Oct. 5, 2000, effective Jan. 1, 2001 (773 So.2d 1098); effective Feb. 11, 2010 (44 So.3d 555); Dec. 11, 2014, effective Dec. 11, 2014 (153 So.3d 258).

Committee Notes

1971 Amendment. Subdivision (h) is added to cover a situation usually arising in divorce judgment modifications, supplemental declaratory relief actions, or trust supervision. When any subsequent proceeding results in a pleading in the strict technical sense under rule 1.100(a), response by opposing parties will follow in the same course as though the new pleading were the initial pleading in the action. The time for answering and authority for defenses under rule 1.140 will apply. The last sentence exempts post judgment motions under rules 1.480(c), 1.530, and 1.540, and similar proceedings from its purview.

2014 Amendment. The last two paragraphs of rule 1.110(b) regarding pleading requirements for certain mortgage foreclosure actions were deleted and incorporated in new rule 1.115.

Authors' Comment—1967

Rule 1.110 is patterned after former Rule 1.8, 1954 Rules of Civil Procedure, as amended effective January 1, 1966. Subsection (b) is in part an adaption of Federal Rule 8(a) with the last sentence being similar to Federal Rule 54(c).

The complete picture in pleadings is to be gathered from Rules 1.030, 1.100, 1.110, 1.120, 1.130, 1.140, 1.150, 1.160, 1.170, 1.180 and 1.190. Pleadings under the Florida Rules are now similar to the Federal Rules.

The permitted types of usual pleading are complaints, petitions, answers and counterclaims, with replies under certain conditions (Rule 1.100). Pleadings are thus limited in number. As to content, brevity, clarity and simplicity are made the goals. Prolixity is forbidden. See Anderson v. Groveland, 113 So.2d 569 (DCA2d 1959).

Each pleading must bear an appropriate caption (1.100(c)) and be properly signed (1.030). The requirement of verification is eliminated even where relief pendente lite is sought (1.030) but constant watch must always be maintained for special verification requirements applicable to the particular subject involved.

The function of the final denial at common law is now performed by Rule 1.110(e) which provides that "averments in a pleading to which no responsive pleading is required or permitted shall be taken as denied or avoided." Accordingly, unless jurisdiction is denied, a general denial of a complaint should not be made, but the factual basis for the denial should be alleged.

The contents of a pleading should not just meet the minimum requirements for that type of pleading. They should clearly and adequately inform the judge, the opposing party and the jury (in cases where the pleadings may be read to the jury) of the position of the pleader. The arrangement should be designed to make an orderly and effective presentation. To guide the pleader along these lines the rules require presentation in separately numbered paragraphs and in counts (1.110(f)).

In dealing with complaints, petitions, counterclaims and cross-claims, the rule requires that they must state a cause of action, set forth a plain statement of the ultimate facts on which the pleader relies, contain allegations of fact sufficient to show the jurisdiction of the court and contain a demand for judgment or decree for the relief to which the pleader deems himself entitled. This is now the same as the Federal Rule and now also requires "a short and plain statement of the claim showing that the pleader is entitled to relief" (F.R. 8(a)). Under the Florida Rule, vague and loose pleading will not be permitted. The complaint must show a legal liability by stating the elements of a cause of action; must plead factual matter sufficient to apprise the adversary of what he is called upon to answer so that the court may determine the legal effect of the complaint. Messana v. Maule Industries, 50 So.2d 874 (Fla.1951); Kislak v. Kreedian, 95 So.2d 510 (Fla.1951).

A complaint or counterclaim need demand no specific amount of damages, although it may do so. The old equity requirement that the complaint show the residence and disability of the parties no longer exists. Residence may, however, in many instances, such as for constructive service, or application of the nonresident motorist statute, be a material factor and where it is, it should be shown.

The common counts are no longer permitted as such but may be used if they satisfy the requirements of Rule 1.110. Moore v. Boyd, 1953, 62 So.2d 427.

The first function of an answer is to admit or deny the allegations of the complaint. It may also include affirmative defenses and a counterclaim. The best practice is to confine the answer first to admissions, then denials in whole or in part, and then lack of knowledge of the allegations of the complaint, paragraph by paragraph, followed by affirmative defenses. Pearson v. Sindelar, 75 So.2d 295 (Fla.1954). Defenses should be set forth separately in numbered paragraphs. If there is to be a counterclaim it should be separated from the answer and defenses and have separately numbered paragraphs, but the numbering should be consecutive throughout the entire pleading for clear reference. A crossclaim should preferably be an entirely separate pleading since it involves persons other than the original plaintiff or plaintiffs.

Affirmative defenses should be timely raised in order to preserve an issue for appellate review, as recognized in Wise v. Quina, 174 So.2d 590. Formerly, they could be raised only by answer rather than by motion to dismiss, but the present rule now authorizes utilization of a motion or defense under Rule 1.140(b). Too often, counsel fail to properly plead valid affirmative defenses, so as to preserve such issues for determination by the court, and thereby waive the issues.

Counsel should be alert to the fact that litigants are bound by the allegations of their pleadings and further, that relief granted cannot be greater than the relief sought.

As provided in official form 1.943 of the rules promulgated by the Supreme Court, it is necessary to allege in a complaint for divorce only the language of the statute for stating the grounds for divorce.

A motion to dismiss may assert an affirmative defense as a ground only within the limitations of Rule 1.110(d); that is, if the affirmative defense appears on the face of a prior pleading.

Rule 1.115. Pleading Mortgage Foreclosures

(a) Claim for Relief. A claim for relief that seeks to foreclose a mortgage or other lien on residential real property, including individual units of condominiums and cooperatives designed principally for occupation by one to four families which secures a promissory note, must: (1) contain affirmative allegations expressly made by the claimant at the time the proceeding is commenced that the claimant is the holder of the original note secured by the mortgage; or (2) allege with specificity the factual basis by which the claimant is a person entitled to enforce the note under section 673.3011, Florida Statutes.

(b) Delegated Claim for Relief. If a claimant has been delegated the authority to institute a mortgage foreclosure action on behalf of the person entitled to enforce the note, the claim for relief shall describe the authority of the claimant and identify with specificity the document that grants the claimant the authority to act on behalf of the person entitled to enforce the note. The term "original note" or "original promissory note" means the signed or executed promissory note rather than a copy of it. The term includes any renewal, replacement, consolidation, or amended and restated note or instrument given in renewal, replacement, or substitution for a previous promissory note. The term also includes a transferrable record, as defined by the Uniform Electronic Transaction Act in section 668.50(16), Florida Statutes.

(c) Possession of Original Promissory Note. If the claimant is in possession of the original promissory note, the claimant must file under penalty of perjury a certification contemporaneously with the filing of the claim for relief for foreclosure that the claimant is in possession of the original promissory note. The certification must set forth the location of the note, the name and title of the individual giving the certification, the name of the person who personally verified such possession, and the time and date on which the possession was verified. Correct copies of the note and all allonges to the note must be attached to the certification. The original note and the allonges must be filed with the court before the entry of any judgment of foreclosure or judgment on the note.

(d) Lost, Destroyed, or Stolen Instrument. If the claimant seeks to enforce a lost, destroyed, or stolen instrument, an affidavit executed under penalty of perjury must be attached to the claim for relief. The affidavit must: (1) detail a clear chain of all endorsements, transfers, or assignments of the promissory note that is the subject of the action; (2) set forth facts showing that the claimant is entitled to enforce a lost, destroyed, or stolen instrument pursuant to section 673.3091, Florida Statutes; and (3) include as exhibits to the affidavit such copies of the note and the allonges to the note, audit reports showing receipt of the original note, or other evidence of the acquisition, ownership, and possession of the note as may be available to the claimant. Adequate protection as required under section 673.3091(2), Florida Statutes, shall be provided before the entry of final judgment.

(e) Verification. When filing an action for foreclosure on a mortgage for residential real property the claim for relief shall be verified by the claimant seeking to foreclose the mortgage. When verification of a document is required, the document filed shall include an oath, affirmation, or the following statement:

"Under penalties of perjury, I declare that I have read the foregoing, and the facts alleged therein are true and correct to the best of my knowledge and belief."

Added Dec. 11, 2014, effective Dec. 11, 2014 (153 So.3d 258).

Rule 1.120. Pleading Special Matters

(a) Capacity. It is not necessary to aver the capacity of a party to sue or be sued, the authority of a party to sue or be sued in a representative capacity, or the legal existence of an organized association of persons that is made a party, except to the extent required to show the jurisdiction of the court. The initial pleading served on behalf of a minor party shall specifically aver the age of the minor party. When a party desires to raise an issue as to the legal existence of any party, the capacity of any party to sue or be sued, or the authority of a party to sue or be sued in a representative capacity, that party shall do so by specific negative averment which shall include such supporting particulars as are peculiarly within the pleader's knowledge.

(b) Fraud, Mistake, Condition of the Mind. In all averments of fraud or mistake, the circumstances constituting fraud or mistake shall be stated with such particularity as the circumstances may permit. Malice, intent, knowledge, mental attitude, and other condition of mind of a person may be averred generally.

(c) Conditions Precedent. In pleading the performance or occurrence of conditions precedent, it is sufficient to aver generally that all conditions precedent have been performed or have occurred. A denial of performance or occurrence shall be made specifically and with particularity.

(d) Official Document or Act. In pleading an official document or official act it is sufficient to aver that the document was issued or the act done in compliance with law.

(e) Judgment or Decree. In pleading a judgment or decree of a domestic or foreign court, a judicial or quasi-judicial tribunal, or a board or officer, it is sufficient to aver the judgment or decree without setting forth matter showing jurisdiction to render it.

(f) Time and Place. For the purpose of testing the sufficiency of a pleading, averments of time and place are material and shall be considered like all other averments of material matter.

(g) Special Damage. When items of special damage are claimed, they shall be specifically stated.

Amended July 16, 1992, effective Jan. 1, 1993 (604 So.2d 1110); Sept. 27, 2007, effective Jan. 1, 2008 (966 So.2d 943).

Authors' Comment—1967

Rule 1.120 is identical to former Rule 1.9, 1954 Rules of Civil Procedure, and almost identical to Federal Rule 9. As such, 1A Barron and Holtzoff, Federal Practice and Procedure, Rules Edition (West 1960) should be consulted as a most helpful guide of construction of the similar federal rule.

Fraud, mistake, breach of trust, wilful default or undue influence cannot be pleaded generally—these defenses must be pleaded specifically as "the circumstances may permit," but malice, intent, knowledge or mental attitude may be averred generally.

As to pleading conditions precedent, this rule alters the common law rule which required the detailed pleading of performance of conditions precedent.

A specific denial of a general allegation of the performance or occurrence of conditions precedent shifts the burden on the plaintiff to prove the allegations.

This rule does not make it mandatory to state acts and contracts according to their legal effect—but if they are so pleaded, the pleading must fairly apprise the adverse party of the facts which it is intended to prove. Time and place are now material allegations under this rule. The circumstances justifying a claim for special damages should be disclosed in the pleadings. Such special damages must be specifically pleaded, if evidence concerning them is to be admissible.

Capacity need not be pleaded. Lack of capacity must be raised by the other party by specific negative averment (not merely by pleading lack of knowledge). Thus it is unnecessary to plead the appointment of a plaintiff or defendant as an executor or administrator. Nevertheless, if a party is involved in a suit in other than his individual capacity, the capacity in which he is a party should be indicated in the caption and the pleadings.

Clear and explicit reference must be made to identify the instruments attached and to be incorporated. Consistency between the allegations of the pleadings and the terms and contents of the exhibits is absolutely essential. In event of inconsistency the exhibits will control. Only documents which give rise to the cause of action or establish the right which has been breached need be attached.

Rule 1.130. Attaching Copy of Cause of Action and Exhibits

(a) Instruments Attached. All bonds, notes, bills of exchange, contracts, accounts, or documents upon which action may be brought or defense made, or a copy thereof or a copy of the portions thereof material to the pleadings, shall be incorporated in or attached to the pleading. No papers shall be unnecessarily annexed as exhibits. The pleadings shall contain no unnecessary recitals of deeds, documents, contracts, or other instruments.

(b) Part for All Purposes. Any exhibit attached to a pleading shall be considered a part thereof for all purposes. Statements in a pleading may be adopted by reference in a different part of the same pleading, in another pleading, or in any motion.

Amended July 16, 1992, effective Jan. 1, 1993 (604 So.2d 1110).

Authors' Comment—1967

This rule is identical to Rule 1.10, 1954 Rules of Civil Procedure, as per amendment effective January 1, 1966. The amendment and the present rule authorize statements in a pleading to be adopted by references in a different part of the same pleading or in another pleading or in any motion, thereby alleviating the necessity of lengthy repetition in the pleadings. This latter authorization made the Rule consistent with Federal Rule 10(c).

Rule 1.140. Defenses

(a) When Presented.

(1) Unless a different time is prescribed in a statute of Florida, a defendant shall serve an answer within 20 days after service of original process and the initial pleading on the defendant, or not later than the date fixed in a notice by publication. A party served with a pleading stating a crossclaim against that party shall serve an answer to it within 20 days after service on that party. The plaintiff shall serve an answer to a counterclaim within 20 days after service of the counterclaim. If a reply is required, the reply shall be served within 20 days after service of the answer.

(2) (A) Except when sued pursuant to section 768.28, Florida Statutes, the state of Florida, an agency of the state, or an officer or employee of the state sued in an official capacity shall serve an answer to the complaint or crossclaim, or a reply to a counterclaim, within 40 days after service.

(B) When sued pursuant to section 768.28, Florida Statutes, the Department of Financial Services or the defendant state agency shall have 30 days from the date of service within which to serve an answer to the complaint or crossclaim or a reply to a counterclaim.

(3) The service of a motion under this rule, except a motion for judgment on the pleadings or a motion to strike under subdivision (f), alters these periods of time so that if the court denies the motion or postpones its disposition until the trial on the merits, the responsive pleadings shall be served within 10 days after notice of the court's action or, if the court grants a motion for a more definite statement, the responsive pleadings shall be served within 10 days after service of the more definite statement unless a different time is fixed by the court in either case.

(4) If the court permits or requires an amended or responsive pleading or a more definite statement, the pleading or statement shall be served within 10 days after notice of the court's action. Responses to the pleadings or statements shall be served within 10 days of service of the pleadings or statements.

(b) How Presented. Every defense in law or fact to a claim for relief in a pleading shall be asserted in the responsive pleading, if one is required, but the following defenses may be made by motion at the option of the pleader: (1) lack of jurisdiction over the subject matter, (2) lack of jurisdiction over the person, (3) improper venue, (4) insufficiency of process, (5) insufficiency of service of process, (6) failure to state a cause of action, and (7) failure to join indispensable parties. A motion making any of these defenses shall be made before pleading if a further pleading is permitted. The grounds on which any of the enumerated defenses are based and the substantial matters of law intended to be argued shall be stated specifically and with particularity in the responsive pleading or motion. Any ground not stated shall be deemed to be waived except any ground showing that the court lacks jurisdiction of the subject matter may be made at any time. No defense or objection is waived by being joined with other defenses or objections in a responsive pleading or motion. If a pleading sets forth a claim for relief to which the adverse party is not required to serve a responsive pleading, the adverse party may assert any defense in law or fact to that claim for relief at the trial, except that the objection of failure to state a legal defense in an answer or reply shall be asserted by motion to strike the defense within 20 days after service of the answer or reply.

(c) Motion for Judgment on the Pleadings. After the pleadings are closed, but within such time as not to delay the trial, any party may move for judgment on the pleadings.

(d) Preliminary Hearings. The defenses 1 to 7 in subdivision (b) of this rule, whether made in a pleading or by motion, and the motion for judgment in subdivision (c) of this rule shall be heard and determined before trial on application of any party unless the court orders that the hearing and determination shall be deferred until the trial.

(e) Motion for More Definite Statement. If a pleading to which a responsive pleading is permitted is so vague or ambiguous that a party cannot reasonably be required to frame a responsive pleading, that party may move for a more definite statement before interposing a responsive pleading. The motion shall point out the defects complained of and the details desired. If the motion is granted and the order of the court is not obeyed within 10 days after notice of the order or such other time as the court may fix, the court may strike the pleading to which the motion was directed or make such order as it deems just.

(f) Motion to Strike. A party may move to strike or the court may strike redundant, immaterial, impertinent, or scandalous matter from any pleading at any time.

(g) Consolidation of Defenses. A party who makes a motion under this rule may join with it the other motions herein provided for and then available to that party. If a party makes a motion under this rule but omits from it any defenses or objections then available to that party that this rule permits to be raised by motion, that party shall not thereafter make a motion based on any of the defenses or objections omitted, except as provided in subdivision (h)(2) of this rule.

(h) Waiver of Defenses.

(1) A party waives all defenses and objections that the party does not present either by motion under subdivisions (b), (e), or (f) of this rule or, if the party has made no motion, in a responsive pleading except as provided in subdivision (h)(2).

(2) The defenses of failure to state a cause of action or a legal defense or to join an indispensable party may be raised by motion for judgment on the pleadings or at the trial on the merits in addition to being raised either in a motion under subdivision (b) or in the answer or reply. The defense of lack of jurisdiction of the subject matter may be raised at any time.

Amended July 26, 1972, effective Jan. 1, 1973 (265 So.2d 21); Oct. 6, 1988, effective Jan. 1, 1989 (536 So.2d 974); July 16, 1992, effective Jan. 1, 1993 (604 So.2d 1110); Oct. 1, 1998 (718 So.2d 795); Oct. 5, 2000, effective Jan. 1, 2001 (773 So.2d 1098); Sept. 27, 2007, effective Jan. 1, 2008 (966 So.2d 943).

Committee Notes

1972 Amendment. Subdivision (a) is amended to eliminate the unnecessary statement of the return date when service is made by publication, and to accommodate the change proposed in rule 1.100(a) making a reply mandatory under certain circumstances. Motions to strike under subdivision (f) are divided into 2 categories, so subdivision (a) is also amended to accommodate this change by eliminating motions to strike under the new subdivision (f) as motions that toll the running of time. A motion to strike an insufficient legal defense will now be available under subdivision (b) and continue to toll the time for responsive pleading. Subdivision (b) is amended to include the defense of failure to state a sufficient legal defense. The proper method of attack for failure to state a legal defense remains a motion to strike. Subdivision (f) is changed to accommodate the 2 types of motions to strike. The motion to strike an insufficient legal defense is now in subdivision (b). The motion to strike under subdivision (f) does not toll the time for responsive pleading and can be made at any time, and the matter can be stricken by the court on its initiative at any time. Subdivision (g) follows the terminology of Federal Rule of Civil Procedure 12(g). Much difficulty has been experienced in the application of this and the succeeding subdivision with the result that the same defenses are being raised several times in an action. The intent of the rule is to permit the defenses to be raised one time, either by motion or by the responsive pleading, and thereafter only by motion for judgment on the pleadings or at the trial. Subdivision (h) also reflects this philosophy. It is based on federal rule 12(h) but more clearly states the purpose of the rule.

1988 Amendment. The amendment to subdivision (a) is to fix a time within which amended pleadings, responsive pleadings, or more definite statements required by the court and responses to those pleadings or statements must be served when no time limit is fixed by the court in its order. The court's authority to alter these time periods is contained in rule 1.090(b).

2007 Amendment. Subdivision (a) is amended to conform rule 1.140 to the statutory requirements of sections 48.111, 48.121, and 768.28, Florida Statutes. The rule is similar to Federal Rule of Civil Procedure 12(a).

Author's Comment—1967

The rule is substantially the same as former Rule No. 1.11, 1954 Rules of Civil Procedure as per amendment effective January 1, 1966. The amendment and present rule added to subsection (b) to restore demurrer practice to the extent of requiring the specific grounds of defensive motions to be stated with particularity. Failure to raise a ground of defense in a proper manner deems the ground waived, except for jurisdictional attacks which are available at any time. The rule is similar to Federal Rule 12 and 1A Barron and Holtzoff, Federal Practice and Procedure, Rules Edition (West 1960) should be consulted for persuasive interpretations by the federal courts.

In view of the construction that all rules of procedure bearing on the method of presenting pleadings to the court should be construed together, as recognized in Pan American World Airways v. Gregory, 96 So.2d 669 (D.C.A.3d 1957), special care should be taken to ensure that the specific requirements of related rules have been complied with.

Affirmative defenses may not be asserted as grounds for a motion to dismiss under this rule, by operation of Rule 1.110(d), unlike the former practice which required such defenses to be presented in an answer.

A motion to dismiss may assert an affirmative defense as a ground only within the limitations of Rule 1.110(d); that is, if the affirmative defense appears on the face of a prior pleading.

In the event a motion to dismiss is granted, the unsuccessful party may seek leave of the court to file an amended pleading in which the defects of the dismissed pleading may be supplied by additional allegations.

It is not necessary to move to strike a complaint, counterclaim, cross-claim or third party claim but certain defenses may be raised by motion.

By motion under paragraph (c) an issue of law is raised and all the facts which are properly pleaded are admitted.

Although paragraph (d) of this rule is in language which is mandatory and which makes it necessary to present the matter on motion, nevertheless the court can hold the matter until trial.

Under paragraph (e) of this rule bills of particulars are superseded. Motions under paragraph (e) now toll the running of the twenty day period.

An insufficient defense or any redundant, immaterial, impertinent or scandalous matter in a pleading may be stricken on the motion of a party or by the court's motion.

Paragraph (g) of this rule is intended to avoid a series of successive motions.

The specified defenses of objections that may be raised by motion need not appear upon the face of the pleading asserting the claim. "Speaking" motions are permissible. If the motion is based upon failure to state a claim, however, and matters outside the pleadings are presented to and not excluded by the court, the motion shall be treated as one for summary judgment.

Rule 1.140 was intended (1) to provide a convenient method for the presentation of defenses and objections and (2) to prevent their use for purposes of delay. All defenses and objections are presented by motion or pleading.

Under prior law, successive motions presenting defenses and objections to pleadings were not only permitted, but, in maintaining the distinction between special and general appearances, were required. The abolition of the special appearance eliminated the need for successive motions, and the rule took the further step of precluding a succession of motions.

A responsive pleading is required, generally, only to a pleading of a claim. In pleading to an answer containing a counterclaim, the plaintiff will present only his defenses to the counterclaim; he should not meet the defenses asserted in the answer to the original claim, for they shall be taken as denied or avoided.

When a responsive pleading is required, the pleader may present "every defense, in law or fact," or objection in the responsive pleading. The objection of lack of jurisdiction over the person, which formerly was required to be made by special appearance, is not waived by joinder with defenses to the merits, or even with the averment of counterclaims or crossclaims.

The pleader may prefer to raise by motion certain defenses or objections which he believes will be sustained and thus obviate the need for pleading to the merits, or the disposition of which will aid in the preparation of his pleading. Rule 1.140 provides seven specific defenses which may be raised by motion before pleading. Although the rules do not refer to any particular type of motion, the usual method of raising the defense of failure to state a cause of action and lack of jurisdiction over the subject matter is by motion to dismiss. Insufficiency of process is attacked by a motion to quash; improper venue by a motion to abate or transfer; failure to join indispensable parties by motion to abate and dismiss. In addition, Rule 1.140(e) provides for a motion for a more definite statement. A motion to strike from any pleading any redundant, immaterial, impertinent or scandalous matter may be made under Rule 1.140(f). If a motion is made on any one of such defenses or objections, all other defenses or objections provided under Rule 1.140 to be raised by motion, and then available, must be joined, and no subsequent motion based on such defenses or objections will be entertained, except as provided in Rule 1.140(h). Grounds for *all* motions must be stated.

Successive motions are therefore allowed only (1) when a defense or objection provided for in Rule 1.140 was not available when the prior motion was made upon one or more of the specified defenses or objections, or (2) when the prior or subsequent motion is based upon a defense or objection provided for by statute or by a rule other than Rule 1.140. For example, since a motion for change of venue upon one of the statutory grounds listed in F.S.A. § 53.03 is not provided for in Rule 1.140, such a motion may be made separately and may then be followed by a motion or by a pleading raising one or more of the defenses or objections enumerated in Rule 1.140.

Motion for more definite statement

In prior practice, the motion for a more definite statement was permissible to aid the responding pleader to prepare his pleading, but also, and more important, to seek information to aid him in his preparation for trial by the formulation of more particular issues, and so prevent surprise at the trial.

The rule, on the other hand, limits the motion for a more definite statement to the needs of a party in framing a responsive pleading. The rules for pretrial discovery are thought to provide more adequate means for supplying detailed information than did the common-law bill of particulars or the motion for more definite statement.

Since the purpose of the motion for a more definite statement is limited to the needs of the party in framing the responsive pleading, the only pleadings subject to the motion are those to which a response is permitted. For all practical purposes, such motion has taken the place of the former motion for compulsory amendment.

Bills of particulars—not available

Neither the Federal Rule nor this rule expressly abolish the bill of particulars, but the historical development and the purposes of the bill indicate that it is no longer available. The historical development of Federal Rule 12(e) makes clear the intention to abolish them. The pre-trial discovery procedures serve the purpose of the old bill of particulars.

General and special appearances

This rule contains no reference to either a general or special appearance. The former practice was to appear specially for the purpose of objecting by motion to the jurisdiction of the court, insufficiency of process or service of process. The fact that the validity of one objection or defense makes unnecessary a determination of others presented by the same motion does not militate against the collective presentation contemplated by the rule in aid of its purpose to avoid successive motions. Motions for a more definite statement or to strike a portion of a pleading might well be excepted from the joinder requirement; but as a practical matter the revision of the pleading required by the granting of such motions would not be likely to afford ground for any defense or objection other than those excepted from the waiver provision of Rule 1.140(h).

There is no longer any necessity for appearing specially, as subdivision (b) provides that every defense may be made either in the responsive pleading or by motion.

The fact that an answer to the merits is an appearance for all purposes, is no longer of much significance. All objections to jurisdiction, venue and process and all defenses in abatement or bar may be set up in a motion or answer to the merits without waiving any of them. Conversely, all objections except jurisdiction of the subject matter and failure to state a cause of action, failure to state a legal defense, or failure to join an indispensable party, are waived by failure to interpose them by motion or answer.

The emphasis is not on the nature of the appearance, whether special or general, but rather upon the precise nature of the objection or defense interposed. This simplification of procedure is a major step forward. It enables counsel to incorporate in one answer all his objections to the proceeding as well as his defenses to the merits and any counterclaims he may have without fear that he may thereby waive any valid objection. Thus the technical niceties of distinction between general and special appearance are abolished and no end is accomplished by retaining the terms.

The elimination of the special appearance encourages a quick presentation of defenses and objections and limits the presentation of successive motions. This is accomplished by the assertion of all defenses and objections in the responsive pleading, and it is partially accomplished even when a motion is used because of the requirement of Rule 1.140 that any motion under Rule 1.140 include all defenses or objections provided in Rule 1.140 and then available. The objection of lack of jurisdiction over the person is not waived by the joinder with other defenses or objections, but it is waived by failure to assert it when any other defense or objection is raised by motion or pleading.

Quaere, whether objection to jurisdiction over the person may be raised in a pleading which asserts a counterclaim. Critics of the Federal Rules state that the pleader may assert in the answer the defense of lack of jurisdiction along with other defenses and objections and counterclaims. The important factor is the sequence of determination of the defenses and objections and counterclaims.

Motion for judgment on the pleadings

The motion for judgment on the pleadings under Rule 1.140(c) falls in a different category. It does not present a "defense" or an "objection"; it is made only after the pleadings are closed, and it calls for a decision on the issues they make. Other defenses and objections are raised by the responding pleading or by motion before pleading. See Miller v. Eatmon, 177 So.2d 523 (DCA 1st 1965), for discussion of applicability of judgment on the pleadings.

Service of defenses

It is failure to "serve" defenses or objections within the required time that places a party in default rather than failure to appear or failure to file. In fact, it has been held that a default cannot be entered if an answer has been served, but not filed. Pan American World Airways v. Gregory, App., 96 So.2d 669. It should be noted that the latter decision sets forth that mere service of a pleading is not enough to present the pleading to the court. The pleading must be filed.

Waiver of defenses

The operation of the waiver provision of Rule 1.140(h) is not limited to the defenses and objections specified in Rule 1.140. All defenses and objections, whether provided for by that rule or by any of the other rules or by statute, are waived unless presented by motion or pleading, except as provided in Rule 1.140(h).

All defenses and objections listed under Rule 1.140 may be made in a single motion. The text indicates that objections made under Rules 1.140(e) and 1.140(f) should be joined with each other, and must likewise be joined with any objection made under Rule 1.140(b) if the objections listed in the latter are then available. The Federal decisions are not in agreement on its interpretation.

It would seem that the objections under Rule 1.140(e) of vagueness and indefiniteness, and under Rule 1.140(f) of redundancy and like defects, would be available from the outset and should therefore be joined in a motion presenting any other defense or objection specified under Rule 1.140.

A motion to strike may be made under this rule, or the court may strike for good reason on its own initiative. See Rule 1.150 for motion to strike sham pleadings.

Rule 1.150. Sham Pleadings

(a) Motion to Strike. If a party deems any pleading or part thereof filed by another party to be a sham, that party may move to strike the pleading or part thereof before the cause is set for trial and the court shall hear the motion, taking evidence of the respective parties, and if the motion is sustained, the pleading to which the motion is directed shall be stricken. Default and summary judgment on the merits may be entered in the discretion of the court or the court may permit additional pleadings to be filed for good cause shown.

(b) Contents of Motion. The motion to strike shall be verified and shall set forth fully the facts on which the movant relies and may be supported by affidavit. No traverse of the motion shall be required.

Amended July 16, 1992, effective Jan. 1, 1993 (604 So.2d 1110).

Authors' Comment—1967

Rule 1.150 is derived from former Rule 1.14, 1954 Rules of Civil Procedure, with the present rule deleting the paragraph pertaining to abolishment of exceptions and the striking of various matters on the court's own initiative or motion. Such striking of matters appears in Rule 1.140(f) and that provision should be studied in connection with any motion to strike. It was redundant to keep the same provision in two rules.

An unsworn motion to strike a pleading and which fails to set forth facts on which the movant relies is insufficient to support striking of an answer. Carapezza v. Pate, 143 So.2d 346 (D.C.A.3d 1962).

In making a determination of the merits of a motion to strike sham pleadings, testimony may be taken by the court from the respective parties.

There is no corresponding provision for the utilization of the motion to strike as sham or false in the Federal practice. There can be no motion to strike parts of a pleading on such ground. It can be used only to attack the pleading as a whole and under the terms of Federal Rule 12, which corresponds to our Rule 1.140(f). The falseness of material determinative matter is probably better determined by motion for summary judgment and in accordance with the rules pertaining to such a motion, in order to obtain a final judgment.

Rule 1.160. Motions

All motions and applications in the clerk's office for the issuance of mesne process and final process to enforce and execute judgments, for entering defaults, and for such other proceedings in the clerk's office as do not require an order of court shall be deemed motions and applications grantable as of course by the clerk. The clerk's action may be suspended or altered or rescinded by the court upon cause shown.

Authors' Comment—1967

Rule 1.160 is substantially the same as former Rule 1.12, 1954 Rules of Civil Procedure, except that the former equity process, procedures and terminology no longer appear in the present rule.

While it was evidently not derived therefrom, this rule is substantially the same as Federal Rule 77(c).

Rule 1.170. Counterclaims and Crossclaims

(a) Compulsory Counterclaims. A pleading shall state as a counterclaim any claim which at the time of serving the pleading the pleader has against any opposing party, provided it arises out of the transaction or occurrence that is the subject matter of the opposing party's claim and does not require for its adjudication the presence of third parties over whom the court cannot acquire jurisdiction. But the pleader need not state a claim if (1) at the time the action was commenced the claim was the subject of another pending action, or (2) the opposing party brought suit upon that party's claim by attachment or other process by which the court did not acquire jurisdiction to render a personal judgment on the claim and the pleader is not stating a counterclaim under this rule.

(b) Permissive Counterclaim. A pleading may state as a counterclaim any claim against an opposing party not arising out of the transaction or occurrence that is the subject matter of the opposing party's claim.

(c) Counterclaim Exceeding Opposing Claim. A counterclaim may or may not diminish or defeat the recovery sought by the opposing party. It may claim relief exceeding in amount or different in kind from that sought in the pleading of the opposing party.

(d) Counterclaim against the State. These rules shall not be construed to enlarge beyond the limits established by law the right to assert counterclaims or to claim credits against the state or any of its subdivisions or other governmental organizations thereof subject to suit or against a municipal corporation or against an officer, agency, or administrative board of the state.

(e) Counterclaim Maturing or Acquired after Pleading. A claim which matured or was acquired by the pleader after serving the pleading may be presented as a counterclaim by supplemental pleading with the permission of the court.

(f) Omitted Counterclaim or Crossclaim. When a pleader fails to set up a counterclaim or crossclaim through oversight, inadvertence, or excusable neglect, or when justice requires, the pleader may set up the counterclaim or crossclaim by amendment with leave of the court.

(g) Crossclaim against Co–Party. A pleading may state as a crossclaim any claim by one party against a co-party arising out of the transaction or occurrence that is the subject matter of either the original action or a counterclaim therein, or relating to any property that is the subject matter of the original action. The crossclaim may include a claim that the party against whom it is asserted is or may be liable to the crossclaimant for all or part of a claim asserted in the action against the crossclaimant. Service of a crossclaim on a party who has appeared in the action shall be made pursuant to rule 1.080. Service of a crossclaim against a party who has not appeared in the action shall be made in the manner provided for service of summons.

(h) Additional Parties May Be Brought In. When the presence of parties other than those to the original action is required to grant complete relief in the determination of a counterclaim or crossclaim, they shall be named in the counterclaim or crossclaim and be served with process and shall be parties to the action thereafter if jurisdiction of them can be obtained and their joinder will not deprive the court of jurisdiction of the action. Rules 1.250(b) and (c) apply to parties brought in under this subdivision.

(i) Separate Trials; Separate Judgment. If the court orders separate trials as provided in rule 1.270(b), judgment on a counterclaim or crossclaim may be rendered when the court has jurisdiction to do so even if a claim of the opposing party has been dismissed or otherwise disposed of.

(j) Demand Exceeding Jurisdiction; Transfer of Action. If the demand of any counterclaim or crossclaim exceeds the jurisdiction of the court in which the action is pending, the action shall be transferred forthwith to the court of the same county having jurisdiction of the demand in the counterclaim or crossclaim with only such alterations in the pleadings as are essential. The court shall order the transfer of the action and the transmittal of all papers in it to the proper court if the party asserting the demand exceeding the jurisdiction deposits with the court having jurisdiction a sum sufficient to pay the clerk's service charge in the court to which the action is transferred at the time of filing the counterclaim or crossclaim. Thereupon the original papers and deposit shall be transmitted and filed with a certified copy of the order. The court to which the action is transferred shall have full power and jurisdiction over the demands of all parties. Failure to make the service charge deposit at the time the counterclaim or crossclaim is filed, or within such further time as the court may allow, shall reduce a claim for damages to an amount within the jurisdiction of the court where the action is pending and waive the claim in other cases.

Amended July 26, 1972, effective Jan. 1, 1973 (265 So.2d 21); Oct. 9, 1980, effective Jan. 1, 1981 (391 So.2d 165); Oct. 6, 1988, effective Jan. 1, 1989 (536 So.2d 974); July 16, 1992, effective Jan. 1, 1993 (604 So.2d 1110); Oct. 18, 2012, effective, *nunc pro tunc*, Sept. 1, 2012 (102 So.3d 505).

Committee Notes

1972 Amendment. Subdivision (h) is amended to conform with the philosophy of the 1968 amendment to rule 1.250(c). No justification exists to require more restrictive joinder provisions for counterclaims and crossclaims than is required for the initial pleading. The only safeguard required is that joinder does not deprive the court of jurisdiction. Subdivision (j) is amended to require deposit of the service charge for transfer when a counterclaim or crossclaim exceeding the jurisdiction of the court in which the action is pending is filed. This cures a practical problem when the defendant files a counterclaim or crossclaim exceeding the jurisdiction but neglects to pay the service charge to the court to which the action is transferred. The matter then remains in limbo and causes procedural difficulties in progressing the action.

1988 Amendment. The last 2 sentences were added to subdivision (g) to counter the construction of these rules and section 48.031(1), Florida Statutes, by an appellate court in *Fundaro v. Canadiana Corp.,* 409 So.2d 1099 (Fla. 4th DCA 1982), to require service of all crossclaims with summons pursuant to rule 1.070. The purpose of this amendment is to make it clear that crossclaims must be served as initial pleadings only against a party who has not previously entered an appearance in the action.

2012 Amendment. Subdivision (g) is amended to reflect the relocation of the service rule from rule 1.080 to Fla. R. Jud. Admin. 2.516.

Authors' Comment—1967

Rule 1.170 is the same as former amended Rule 1.13, 1954 Rules of Civil Procedure which became effective January 1, 1966, and is closely patterned after Federal Rule 13. Therefore, 1A Barron and Holtzoff, Federal Practice and Procedure, Rules Edition (West 1960) should be consulted for an analysis under the similar federal counterpart. The present rule is an adaption of Equity Rule 35, F.S.A. § 52.11 (now repealed) and F.S.A. § 52.12(1) (repealed 1967), as well as former Rule 1.13.

The present rule now permits a counterclaim to be pleaded as a pleading, rather than in just an answer, in conformity with the federal practice.

Because of the mandatory nature of the language requiring transfer of an action if the demand of any counterclaim or cross-claim exceeds the jurisdiction of the original court, careful pleading can effect a transfer to the circuit court, if such be desired for any reason.

The purpose and effect of the rule is to permit any claim that defendant has against the plaintiff to be asserted as a counterclaim, thereby avoiding circuity of action. It is immaterial whether the counterclaim is in contract or in tort, or even whether it has any connection with the plaintiff's claim. If, however, the counterclaim arises out of the transaction or occurrence that forms the basis of the plaintiff's claim, failure to assert it as a counterclaim constitutes a waiver of the right to recover on it. If it is independent of plaintiff's claim, the defendant has the option of asserting it as a counterclaim, but, may, if he prefers, bring a separate action on his claim. A defendant may assert a cross claim against another defendant, provided it arises out of the plaintiff's claim or a counterclaim. Additional parties may be brought in if required for the disposition of a counterclaim or cross-claim.

An interesting case for comparison is the Minnesota case of House v. Hanson, 72 N.W.2d 874. The Minnesota rule makes mandatory the filing of a counterclaim if it arises out of a *"transaction"* that is the subject of the opposing party's claim. The Court held that this did not apply to tort claims arising out of an automobile accident as there was no *"transaction."* The Florida rule, however, refers to an *"occurrence"* as well as a *"transaction."*

On permissive counterclaims, all "subject matter" restrictions are removed. A counterclaim may be pleaded without regard to the subject matter of the claim of the opposing party. See Jones-Mahoney Corp. v. C.A. Fielland, Inc., 114 So.2d 18 (D.C.A.2d 1959) for complete discussion of this area.

The purpose of the rule is to permit the determination in a single proceeding of all controversies between the parties and thus avoid multiplicity of actions.

Cross-Claims

The cross-claim must be distinguished from the counterclaim. The latter is a claim against the opposite party, and the cross-claim is a claim by one party against another party on the same side of the case.

It is normally a claim asserted by a defendant against a codefendant or against a third party who might properly be brought into the cause. See Florida Fuel Oil v. Spring Villas, 95 So.2d 581 (1957) for construction of the rule, prior to the adoption of third party practice in Florida.

Bringing in Additional Parties

Where additional parties should be brought in pursuant to the rule, the counter-claimant or cross-claimant should secure an order from the court that certain named persons be brought in a defendants to the counterclaim or cross-claim, and serve a copy of the summons and the pleading in the manner provided for the service of the summons and complaint.

The pleading of a cross-claim is never compulsory, and is limited to a claim arising out of the transaction or occurrence that is the subject matter either of the original claim or of a counterclaim therein or relating to any property that is the subject matter of the original action.

A cross-claim may apparently be stated in an answer, a reply or a third-party answer.

Rule 1.180. Third-Party Practice

(a) When Available. At any time after commencement of the action a defendant may have a summons and complaint served on a person not a party to the action who is or may be liable to the defendant for all or part of the plaintiff's claim against the defendant, and may also assert any other claim that arises out of the transaction or occurrence that is the subject matter of the plaintiff's claim. The defendant need not obtain leave of court if the defendant files the third-party complaint not later than 20 days after the defendant serves the original answer. Otherwise, the defendant must obtain leave on motion and notice to all parties to the action. The person served with the summons and third-party complaint, herein called the third-party defendant, shall make defenses to the defendant's claim as provided in rules 1.110 and 1.140 and counterclaims against the defendant and cross-claims against other third-party defendants as provided in rule 1.170. The third-party defendant may assert against the plaintiff any defenses that the defendant has to the plaintiff's claim. The third-party defendant may also assert any claim against the plaintiff arising out of the transaction or occurrence that is the subject matter of the plaintiff's claim against the defendant. The plaintiff may assert any claim against the third-party defendant arising out of the transaction or occurrence that is the subject matter of the plaintiff's claim against the defendant, and the third-party defendant thereupon shall assert a defense as provided in rules 1.110 and 1.140 and counterclaims and crossclaims as provided in rule 1.170. Any party may move to strike the third-party claim or for its severance or separate trial. A third-party defendant may proceed under this rule against any person not a party to the action who is or may be liable to the third-party defendant for all or part of the claim made in the action against the third-party defendant.

(b) When Plaintiff May Bring in Third Party. When a counterclaim is asserted against the plaintiff, the plaintiff may bring in a third party under circumstances which would entitle a defendant to do so under this rule.

Amended Sept. 13, 1984, effective Jan. 1, 1985 (458 So.2d 245); July 16, 1992, effective Jan. 1, 1993 (604 So.2d 1110).

Court Commentary

1984 Amendment. Subdivision (a) is amended to permit the defendant to have the same right to assert claims arising out of the transaction or occurrence that all of the other parties to the action have. It overrules the decisions in *Miramar Construction, Inc. v. El Conquistador Condominium,* 303 So.2d 81 (Fla. 3d DCA1974), and *Richard's Paint Mfg. Co. v. Onyx Paints, Inc.,* 363 So.2d 596 (Fla. 4th DCA 1978), to that extent. The term defendant is used throughout instead of third-party plaintiff for clarity and brevity reasons and refers to the defendant serving the summons and third-party complaint on a third-party defendant or, when applicable, to the similar summons and fourth party.

Authors' Comment—1967

Rule 1.180 is derived from former Rule 1.41, 1954 Rules of Civil Procedure which had been added by order of July 28, 1965, effective January 1, 1966. The rule is new to Florida Practice and is almost the same as Federal Rule 14(a) and (b), with minor language changes and the twenty days being substituted for the ten day period within which to file the third party complaint after service of the original answer. In view of the sparsity of Florida cases on the new practice and the similarity to the Federal Rule, 1A Barron and Holtzoff, Federal Practice and Procedure, Rules Edition (West 1960), should be carefully analyzed.

Rule 1.180 does not require leave of court for a defendant, or counter-defendant, as a third party plaintiff, to make the service if he files his third party complaint within 20 days after he serves his original answer. The purpose of the practice is to authorize a defendant to bring in third parties in order to save time and costs of duplicating evidence, to obtain consistent results from identical or similar evidence, and to do away with the serious handicap of a time lag between a judgment against the third party defendant. It permits the disposition of the entire subject matter arising from one set of facts in one action, thereby satisfying the mandate of Rule 1.010 for securing "the just, speedy and inexpensive determination of every action."

The language of the rule is not mandatory, and a party may refrain from impleading a third party defendant and assert his claim in an independent action if he so prefers. The rule furnishes the right to a defendant to implead a person not a party to the action who is or may be liable to him for all or part of the plaintiff's claim against him, but tactical considerations may warrant the utilization of an independent action depending upon the circumstances.

The third party defendant must utilize the rules in the same manner as any other defendant, if he is to protect his interests. He may also implead any person not a party to the action, in the same manner as he was impleaded into the action.

In addition, the provisions of the remainder of the rules which relate to third party practice should be consulted, to-wit: Rules 1.100, 1.210, 1.170, 1.420, 1.270, 1.110 and 1.510. Form 1.948 sets forth the essentials for a third party complaint, and Form 1.904 sets forth the necessary ingredients of a third party summons.

Rule 1.190. Amended and Supplemental Pleadings

(a) Amendments. A party may amend a pleading once as a matter of course at any time before a responsive pleading is served or, if the pleading is one to which no responsive pleading is permitted and the action has not been placed on the trial calendar, may so amend it at any time within 20 days after it is served. Otherwise a party may amend a pleading only by leave of court or by written consent of the adverse party. If a party files a motion to amend a pleading, the party shall attach the proposed amended pleading to the motion. Leave of court shall be given freely when justice so requires. A party shall plead in response to an amended pleading within 10 days after service of the amended pleading unless the court otherwise orders.

(b) Amendments to Conform with the Evidence. When issues not raised by the pleadings are tried by express or implied consent of the parties, they shall be treated in all respects as if they had been raised in the pleadings. Such amendment of the pleadings as may be necessary to cause them to conform to the evidence and to raise these issues may be made upon motion of any party at any time, even after judgment, but failure so to amend shall not affect the result of the trial of these issues. If the evidence is objected to at the trial on the ground that it is not within the issues made by the pleadings, the court may allow the pleadings to be amended to conform with the evidence and shall do so freely when the merits of the cause are more effectually presented thereby and the objecting party fails to satisfy the court that the admission of such evidence will prejudice the objecting party in maintaining an action or defense upon the merits.

(c) Relation Back of Amendments. When the claim or defense asserted in the amended pleading arose out of the conduct, transaction, or occurrence set forth or attempted to be set forth in the original pleading, the amendment shall relate back to the date of the original pleading.

(d) Supplemental Pleadings. Upon motion of a party the court may permit that party, upon reasonable notice and upon such terms as are just, to serve a supplemental pleading setting forth transactions or occurrences or events which have happened since the date of the pleading sought to be supplemented. If the court deems it advisable that the adverse party plead thereto, it shall so order, specifying the time therefor.

(e) Amendments Generally. At any time in furtherance of justice, upon such terms as may be just, the court may permit any process, proceeding, pleading, or record to be amended or material supplemental matter to be set forth in an amended or supplemental pleading. At every stage of the action the court must disregard any error or defect in the proceedings which does not affect the substantial rights of the parties.

(f) Claims for Punitive Damages. A motion for leave to amend a pleading to assert a claim for punitive damages shall make a reasonable showing, by evidence in the record or evidence to be proffered by the claimant, that provides a reasonable basis for recovery of such damages. The motion to amend can be filed separately and before the supporting evidence or proffer, but each shall be served on all parties at least 20 days before the hearing.

Amended Oct. 9, 1980, effective Jan. 1, 1981 (391 So.2d 165); Oct. 6, 1988, effective Jan. 1, 1989 (536 So.2d 974); July 16, 1992, effective Jan. 1, 1993 (604 So.2d 1110); Oct. 23, 2003, effective Jan. 1, 2004 (858 So.2d 1013).

Committee Notes

1980 Amendment. The last clause of subdivision (a) is deleted to restore the decision in *Scarfone v. Denby*, 156 So. 2d 694 (Fla. 2d DCA 1963). The adoption of rule 1.500 requiring notice of an application for default after filing or serving of any paper eliminates the need for the clause. This will permit reinstatement of the procedure in federal practice and earlier Florida practice requiring a response to each amended pleading, thus simplifying the court file under the doctrine of *Dee v. Southern Brewing Co.*, 146 Fla. 588, 1 So. 2d 562 (1941).

2003 Amendment. Subdivision (a) is amended in accordance with *Totura & Co., Inc. v. Williams*, 754 So. 2d 671 (Fla. 2000). See the amendment to rule 1.070(j). Subdivision (f) is added to state the requirements for a party moving for leave of court to amend a pleading to assert a claim for punitive damages. See *Beverly Health & Rehabilitation Services, Inc. v. Meeks*, 778 So. 2d 322 (Fla. 2d DCA 2000).

Authors' Comment—1967

Rule 1.190 is the same as former Rule 1.15, 1954 Rules of Civil Procedure, as per amendment effective January 1, 1966. It is patterned closely after Federal Rule 15, and as such, 1A Barron and Holtzoff, Federal Practice and Procedure, Rules Edition (West 1960) should be carefully studied for a constructive analysis of the similar federal counterpart. The contents of Federal Rule 15(b) authorizing the court to grant a continuance to enable the objecting party to meet evidence which relates to amended pleadings at trial, have been omitted.

The rule now requires a response to an amended pleading to be within 20 days after service of the amended pleading, rather than within the former 10 day requirement or the former remaining time requirement.

Although the rule authorizes an amendment before a responsive pleading is filed, the court in Nenow v. Ceilings and Specialties, Inc., 151 So.2d 28 (D.C.A.2d 1963), ruled that the right to amend before a responsive pleading is filed is not absolute.

In spite of the fact that the policy is liberal to grant amendments freely when justice so requires, the courts have consistently recognized that the trial judge has wide discretion on procedural matters including requests to amend pleadings.

. . .

Amendments can be made by consent or by order of court if they are not made before the responsive pleading is served or within 20 days after service of a pleading if a responsive pleading is not required and the action has not been placed on the trial calendar.

Amendments under paragraph (b) of this rule can be made at any time but they must not prejudice the opposing party. They can be made as late as or after judgment, and this is particularly true if essential to justice or if the presentation of the merits will be more effectively expedited. See Garrett v. Oak Hall Club, 118 So.2d 633 (S.Ct.1960).

The liberal practice giving the right to make one amendment, as of course applies to all types of pleadings, not just complaints. There is no right to file a supplemental pleading as of course.

The rule does not spell out the mechanics of accomplishing an amendment. It can be done by a pleading which merely shows the amendment, addition or change, by interlineation on the original pleading or by a new amended pleading which replaces the original.

The latter method is to be preferred except for minor or formal amendments or changes. Amendment by interlineation is not recommended except on the basis of a court order supporting it to avoid any suspicion that it might be an unauthorized alteration.

Relation Back

The principle of relation back of amended pleadings existed in prior law, but it was limited to an amendment which did not state a new cause of action. The harshness of the rule was modified by a liberal construction of a "cause of action." In accord with this liberal application of the principle, the rule requires only that the amendment arise out of the "conduct, transaction, or occurrence" set forth in the original pleading.

Supplemental Pleadings

Supplemental pleadings are those which set forth new matter which has arisen since the filing of the original pleading. Rule 1.190(d) providing for such pleadings reads: "Upon motion of a party the court may, upon reasonable notice and upon such terms as are just, permit him to serve a supplemental pleading setting forth transactions or occurrences or events which have happened since the date of the pleading sought to be supplemented. If the court deems it advisable that the adverse party plead thereto, it shall so order, specifying the time therefor."

The function of the supplemental pleading is to bring forward new facts or events arising after the filing of the pleading, to cure defects resulting from the occurrence of such events during the progress of the suit. Matters existing at the time of filing the pleading and omitted therefrom because overlooked or unknown should be brought in by amendment.

The necessity for pleading to a supplemental pleading is governed by order of the trial court.

Rule 1.200. Pretrial Procedure

(a) Case Management Conference. At any time after responsive pleadings or motions are due, the court may order, or a party by serving a notice may convene, a case management conference. The matter to be considered shall be specified in the order or notice setting the conference. At such a conference the court may:

(1) schedule or reschedule the service of motions, pleadings, and other papers;

(2) set or reset the time of trials, subject to rule 1.440(c);

(3) coordinate the progress of the action if the complex litigation factors contained in rule 1.201(a)(2)(A)–(a)(2)(H) are present;

(4) limit, schedule, order, or expedite discovery;

(5) consider the possibility of obtaining admissions of fact and voluntary exchange of documents and electronically stored information, and stipulations regarding authenticity of documents and electronically stored information;

(6) consider the need for advance rulings from the court on the admissibility of documents and electronically stored information;

(7) discuss as to electronically stored information, the possibility of agreements from the parties regarding the extent to which such evidence should be preserved, the form in which such evidence should be produced, and whether discovery of such information should be conducted in phases or limited to particular individuals, time periods, or sources;

(8) schedule disclosure of expert witnesses and the discovery of facts known and opinions held by such experts;

(9) schedule or hear motions in limine;

(10) pursue the possibilities of settlement;

(11) require filing of preliminary stipulations if issues can be narrowed;

(12) consider referring issues to a magistrate for findings of fact; and

(13) schedule other conferences or determine other matters that may aid in the disposition of the action.

(b) Pretrial Conference. After the action is at issue the court itself may or shall on the timely motion of any party require the parties to appear for a conference to consider and determine:

(1) the simplification of the issues;

(2) the necessity or desirability of amendments to the pleadings;

(3) the possibility of obtaining admissions of fact and of documents that will avoid unnecessary proof;

(4) the limitation of the number of expert witnesses;

(5) the potential use of juror notebooks; and

(6) any matters permitted under subdivision (a) of this rule.

(c) Notice. Reasonable notice shall be given for a case management conference, and 20 days' notice shall be given for a pretrial conference. On failure of a party to attend a conference, the court may dismiss the action, strike the pleadings, limit proof or witnesses, or take any other appropriate action. Any documents that the court requires for any conference shall be specified in the order. Orders setting pretrial conferences shall be uniform throughout the territorial jurisdiction of the court.

(d) Pretrial Order. The court shall make an order reciting the action taken at a conference and any stipulations made. The order shall control the subsequent course of the action unless modified to prevent injustice.

Amended Sept. 29, 1971, effective Dec. 13, 1971 (253 So.2d 404); July 26, 1972, effective Jan. 1, 1973 (265 So.2d 21); Sept. 13, 1984, effective Jan. 1, 1985 (458 So.2d 245); Oct. 6, 1988, effective Jan. 1, 1989 (536 So.2d 974); July 16, 1992, effective Jan. 1, 1993 (604 So.2d 1110); Oct. 5, 2000, effective Jan. 1, 2001 (773 So.2d 1098); Sept. 30, 2004, effective Oct. 1, 2004 (887 So.2d 1090); Oct. 4, 2007, effective Jan. 1, 2008 (967 So.2d 178); June 3, 2009 (15 So.3d 558); July 5, 2012, effective Sept. 1, 2012 (95 So.3d 76).

Committee Notes

1971 Amendment. The 3 paragraphs of the rule are lettered and given subtitles. The present last paragraph is placed second as subdivision (b) because the proceeding required under it is taken before that in the present second paragraph. The time for implementation is changed from settling the issues because the language is erroneous, the purpose of the conference being to settle some and prepare for the trial of other issues. The last 2 sentences of subdivision (b) are added to require uniformity by all judges of the court and to require specification of the documentary requirements for the conference. The last sentence of subdivision (c) is deleted since it is covered by the local rule provisions of rule 1.020(d). The reference to the parties in substitution for attorneys and counsel is one of style because the rules generally impose obligations on the parties except when the attorneys are specifically intended. It should be understood that those parties represented by attorneys will have the attorneys perform for them in the usual manner.

1972 Amendment. Subdivision (a) is amended to require the motion for a pretrial by a party to be timely. This is done to avoid motions for pretrial conferences made a short time before trial and requests for a continuance of the trial as a result of the pretrial conference order. The subdivision is also amended to require the clerk to send to the judge a copy of the motion by a party for the pretrial conference.

1988 Amendment. The purpose of adding subdivision (a)(5) is to spell out clearly for the bench and bar that case management conferences may be used for scheduling the disclosure of expert witnesses and the discovery of the opinion and factual information held by those experts. Subdivision (5) is not intended to expand discovery.

1992 Amendment. Subdivision (a) is amended to allow a party to set a case management conference in the same manner as a party may set a hearing on a motion. Subdivision (c) is amended to remove the mandatory language and make the notice requirement for a case management conference the same as that for a hearing on a motion; *i.e.*, reasonable notice.

2012 Amendment. Subdivisions (a)(5) to (a)(7) are added to address issues involving electronically stored information.

Court Commentary

1984 Amendment. This is a substantial rewording of rule 1.200. Subdivision (a) is added to authorize case management conferences in an effort to give the court more control over the progress of the action. All of the matters that the court can do under the case management conference can be done at the present time under other rules or because of the court's authority otherwise. The new subdivision merely emphasizes the court's authority and arranges an orderly method for the exercise of that authority. Subdivisions (a), (b), and (c) of the existing rule are relettered accordingly. Subdivision (a) of the existing rule is also amended to delete the reference to requiring the attorneys to appear at a pretrial conference by referring to the parties for that purpose. This is consistent with the language used throughout the rules and does not contemplate a change in present procedure. Subdivisions (a)(5) and (a)(6) of the existing rule are deleted since they are now covered adequately under the new subdivision (a). Subdivisions (b) and (c) of the existing rule are amended to accommodate the 2 types of conferences that are now authorized by the rules.

Authors' Comment—1967

Rule 1.200 is substantially the same as former Rule 1.16, 1954 Rules of Civil Procedure as per amendment effective January 1, 1966, and similar to Federal Rule 16. Thus, 1A Barron & Holtzoff, Federal Practice and Procedure, Rules Edition (West 1960) should be analyzed for construction of the federal counterpart. The most recent change requires the trial court to serve its order setting a pre-trial conference on the attorneys not less than

20 days prior to the conference, and grants the power to dismiss the suit or counterclaim, strike the answer or take other drastic action for failure of counsel to attend.

Pretrial procedure has now been used successfully for several years. Pretrial under the Federal rule is optional. Under Rule 1.200 it is a matter of right if either party moves for it.

This procedure has worked exceptionally well in this as in other jurisdictions. It requires the intelligent cooperation of the attorneys. The attitude of the judge is an important factor. Some types of cases lend themselves to pretrial procedure better than others do.

At a pretrial conference much can be accomplished toward a clarification and simplification of the material issues. Counsel should at the outset make a full opening statement. At such a conference documentary evidence can be identified; certain matters of technical proof can be determined; hospital records can be identified; agency can be established and many other matters can be settled without the necessity of providing technical formal proof at the trial. The proper use of pretrial conferences can do much to keep the calendars up to date, but unless the calendars for such conferences are skillfully handled they can prove a great burden to a lawyer who on short notice is obliged to travel from one county to another to attend such conferences.

The opinion of judges and attorneys experienced with pretrial conferences is that the pretrial conference should be held reasonably soon before the trial, when the parties have utilized the discovery procedures and are fully informed on all aspects of the action and in a position to aid the trial court in its pretrial efforts to simplify and shorten the trial.

Although settlements are only an incident to pretrial conferences and are not to be mentioned in the pretrial order, a skillful judge without forceful tactics can assist in the settlement of a case. It is not the province of the pretrial judge to try to force a settlement and such judicial conduct is subject to censure.

The powers and authority of the trial judge at a pre-trial conference are very broad by the all-embracing language of subsection (6), and he may consider and determine such matters as may aid in the disposition of the action either on his own motion or on motion of either party.

The trial court may on pretrial enter a summary judgment on its own motion. An excellent discussion of this procedure appears in Roberts v. Braynon, 90 So.2d 623 (S.Ct.1956).

Another significant decision on pretrial procedure is Rose v. Yulle, 88 So.2d 318 (S.Ct.1956). This case held that on pretrial the trial court may order a party to disclose the names of all witnesses he expects to question on the trial. This holding of itself is a rather drastic extension of former Rule 1.16 which, as to witnesses, expressly gives only the power to limit the number of *expert* witnesses. But the court went even further and sustained the trial court in its refusal to permit a witness who had not been disclosed on pretrial to testify although notice of disclosure as to this witness was filed and served on the opposing party several days before trial and the opposing party made no objection to the witness testifying. The Supreme Court suggested that the party seeking to have a material witness testify who had not been mentioned at pretrial conference should advise the court and opposing counsel what the witness would testify to, that his testimony was material and essential to prove the party's case and that there could be no lawful objection to its introduction into evidence. The Court noted that its suggestion is substantially the practice followed in moving for a continuance on account of the absence of a material witness and should be followed when a witness is sought to be used, whose name had not been disclosed on pretrial.

Rule 1.201. Complex Litigation

(a) Complex Litigation Defined. At any time after all defendants have been served, and an appearance has been entered in response to the complaint by each party or a default entered, any party, or the court on its own motion, may move to declare an action complex. However, any party may move to designate an action complex before all defendants have been served subject to a showing to the court why service has not been made on all defendants. The court shall convene a hearing to determine whether the action requires the use of complex litigation procedures and enter an order within 10 days of the conclusion of the hearing.

(1) A "complex action" is one that is likely to involve complicated legal or case management issues and that may require extensive judicial management to expedite the action, keep costs reasonable, or promote judicial efficiency.

(2) In deciding whether an action is complex, the court must consider whether the action is likely to involve:

(A) numerous pretrial motions raising difficult or novel legal issues or legal issues that are inextricably intertwined that will be time-consuming to resolve;

(B) management of a large number of separately represented parties;

(C) coordination with related actions pending in one or more courts in other counties, states, or countries, or in a federal court;

(D) pretrial management of a large number of witnesses or a substantial amount of documentary evidence;

(E) substantial time required to complete the trial;

(F) management at trial of a large number of experts, witnesses, attorneys, or exhibits;

(G) substantial post-judgment judicial supervision; and

(H) any other analytical factors identified by the court or a party that tend to complicate comparable actions and which are likely to arise in the context of the instant action.

(3) If all of the parties, pro se or through counsel, sign and file with the clerk of the court a written stipulation to the fact that an action is complex and identifying the factors in (2)(A) through (2)(H) above that apply, the court shall enter an order designating the action as complex without a hearing.

(b) Initial Case Management Report and Conference. The court shall hold an initial case management conference within 60 days from the date of the order declaring the action complex.

(1) At least 20 days prior to the date of the initial case management conference, attorneys for the parties as well as any parties appearing pro se shall confer and prepare a joint statement, which shall be filed with the clerk of the court no later than 14 days before the conference, outlining a discovery plan and stating:

(A) a brief factual statement of the action, which includes the claims and defenses;

(B) a brief statement on the theory of damages by any party seeking affirmative relief;

(C) the likelihood of settlement;

(D) the likelihood of appearance in the action of additional parties and identification of any nonparties to whom any of the parties will seek to allocate fault;

(E) the proposed limits on the time: (i) to join other parties and to amend the pleadings, (ii) to file and hear motions, (iii) to identify any nonparties whose identity is known, or otherwise describe as specifically as practicable any nonparties whose identity is not known, (iv) to disclose expert witnesses, and (v) to complete discovery;

(F) the names of the attorneys responsible for handling the action;

(G) the necessity for a protective order to facilitate discovery;

(H) proposals for the formulation and simplification of issues, including the elimination of frivolous claims or defenses, and the number and timing of motions for summary judgment or partial summary judgment;

(I) the possibility of obtaining admissions of fact and voluntary exchange of documents and electronically stored information, stipulations regarding authenticity of documents, electronically stored information, and the need for advance rulings from the court on admissibility of evidence;

(J) the possibility of obtaining agreements among the parties regarding the extent to which such electronically stored information should be preserved, the form in which such information should be produced, and whether discovery of such information should be conducted in phases or limited to particular individuals, time periods, or sources;

(K) suggestions on the advisability and timing of referring matters to a magistrate, master, other neutral, or mediation;

(L) a preliminary estimate of the time required for trial;

(M) requested date or dates for conferences before trial, a final pretrial conference, and trial;

(N) a description of pertinent documents and a list of fact witnesses the parties believe to be relevant;

(O) number of experts and fields of expertise; and

(P) any other information that might be helpful to the court in setting further conferences and the trial date.

(2) Lead trial counsel and a client representative shall attend the initial case management conference.

(3) Notwithstanding rule 1.440, at the initial case management conference, the court will set the trial date or dates no sooner than 6 months and no later than 24 months from the date of the conference unless good cause is shown for an earlier or later setting. The trial date or dates shall be on a docket having sufficient time within which to try the action and, when feasible, for a date or dates certain. The trial date shall be set after consultation with counsel and in the presence of all clients or authorized client representatives. The court shall, no later than 2 months prior to the date scheduled for jury selection, arrange for a sufficient number of available jurors. Continuance of the trial of a complex action should rarely be granted and then only upon good cause shown.

(c) The Case Management Order. The case management order shall address each matter set forth under rule 1.200(a) and set the action for a pretrial conference and trial. The case management order also shall specify the following:

(1) Dates by which all parties shall name their expert witnesses and provide the expert information required by rule 1.280(b)(5). If a party has named an expert witness in a field in which any other parties have not identified experts, the other parties may name experts in that field within 30 days thereafter. No additional experts may be named unless good cause is shown.

(2) Not more than 10 days after the date set for naming experts, the parties shall meet and schedule dates for deposition of experts and all other witnesses not yet deposed. At the time of the meeting each party is responsible for having secured three confirmed dates for its expert witnesses. In the event the parties cannot agree on a discovery deposition schedule, the court, upon motion, shall set the schedule. Any party may file the completed discovery

deposition schedule agreed upon or entered by the court. Once filed, the deposition dates in the schedule shall not be altered without consent of all parties or upon order of the court. Failure to comply with the discovery schedule may result in sanctions in accordance with rule 1.380.

(3) Dates by which all parties are to complete all other discovery.

(4) The court shall schedule periodic case management conferences and hearings on lengthy motions at reasonable intervals based on the particular needs of the action. The attorneys for the parties as well as any parties appearing pro se shall confer no later than 15 days prior to each case management conference or hearing. They shall notify the court at least 10 days prior to any case management conference or hearing if the parties stipulate that a case management conference or hearing time is unnecessary. Failure to timely notify the court that a case management conference or hearing time is unnecessary may result in sanctions.

(5) The case management order may include a briefing schedule setting forth a time period within which to file briefs or memoranda, responses, and reply briefs or memoranda, prior to the court considering such matters.

(6) A deadline for conducting alternative dispute resolution.

(d) Final Case Management Conference. The court shall schedule a final case management conference not less than 90 days prior to the date the case is set for trial. At least 10 days prior to the final case management conference the parties shall confer to prepare a case status report, which shall be filed with the clerk of the court either prior to or at the time of the final case management conference. The status report shall contain in separately numbered paragraphs:

(1) A list of all pending motions requiring action by the court and the date those motions are set for hearing.

(2) Any change regarding the estimated trial time.

(3) The names of the attorneys who will try the case.

(4) A list of the names and addresses of all non-expert witnesses (including impeachment and rebuttal witnesses) intended to be called at trial. However, impeachment or rebuttal witnesses not identified in the case status report may be allowed to testify if the need for their testimony could not have been reasonably foreseen at the time the case status report was prepared.

(5) A list of all exhibits intended to be offered at trial.

(6) Certification that copies of witness and exhibit lists will be filed with the clerk of the court at least 48 hours prior to the date and time of the final case management conference.

(7) A deadline for the filing of amended lists of witnesses and exhibits, which amendments shall be allowed only upon motion and for good cause shown.

(8) Any other matters which could impact the timely and effective trial of the action.

Added June 3, 2009 (15 So.3d 558). Amended July 5, 2012, effective Sept. 1, 2012 (95 So. 3d 76).

Committee Notes

2012 Amendment. Subdivision (b)(1)(J) is added to address issues involving electronically stored information.

Rule 1.210. Parties

(a) Parties Generally. Every action may be prosecuted in the name of the real party in interest, but a personal representative, administrator, guardian, trustee of an express trust, a party with whom or in whose name a contract has been made for the benefit of another, or a party expressly authorized by statute may sue in that person's own name without joining the party for whose benefit the action is brought. All persons having an interest in the subject of the action and in obtaining the relief demanded may join as plaintiffs and any person may be made a defendant who has or claims an interest adverse to the plaintiff. Any person may at any time be made a party if that person's presence is necessary or proper to a complete determination of the cause. Persons having a united interest may be joined on the same side as plaintiffs or defendants, and anyone who refuses to join may for such reason be made a defendant.

(b) Minors or Incompetent Persons. When a minor or incompetent person has a representative, such as a guardian or other like fiduciary, the representative may sue or defend on behalf of the minor or incompetent person. A minor or incompetent person who does not have a duly appointed representative may sue by next friend or by a guardian ad litem. The court shall appoint a guardian ad litem for a minor or incompetent person not otherwise represented in an action or shall make such other order as it deems proper for the protection of the minor or incompetent person.

Amended Oct. 9, 1980, effective Jan. 1, 1981 (391 So.2d 165); July 16, 1992, effective Jan. 1, 1993 (604 So.2d 1110); Oct. 23, 2003, effective Jan. 1, 2004 (858 So.2d 1013); Sept. 27, 2007, effective Jan. 1, 2008 (966 So.2d 943).

Committee Notes

1980 Amendment. Subdivisions (c) and (d) are deleted. Both are obsolete. They were continued in effect earlier because the committee was uncertain about the need for them at the time. Subdivision (c) has been supplanted by section 737.402(2)(z), Florida Statutes (1979), that gives trustees the power to prosecute and defend actions, regardless of the conditions specified in the subdivision. The adoption of section 733.212, Florida Statutes (1979), eliminates the need for subdivision (d) because it provides an easier and less expensive method of eliminating the interests of an heir at law who is not a beneficiary under the will. To the extent that an heir at law is an indispensable party to a proceeding concerning a testamentary trust, due process requires notice and an opportunity to defend, so the rule would be unconstitutionally applied.

2003 Amendment. In subdivision (a), "an executor" is changed to "a personal representative" to conform to statutory language. See § 731.201(25), Fla. Stat. (2002).

Authors' Comment—1967

Rule 1.210 is a consolidation of former Rules 1.17, 3.3, and 3.5, 1954 Rules of Civil Procedure, thus placing parties with varying statuses within a single rule. Rules 1.100 and 1.180 should be consulted as to pleadings and third party practice respectively, Rule 1.230 as to interventions, and Rule 1.240 as to interpleader, for a more complete picture of parties.

The "real party in interest" identified in subsection (a) is the person in whom rests, by substantive law, the claim sought to be enforced. The real party in interest rule is permissive, not mandatory, unlike Federal Rule 17(a).

The enumerated representatives may sue without joining the person to be benefited.

Subsection (b) is identical to former Rule 1.17(b) and to Federal Rule 17(c). The first sentence expressly permits, but does not require, the enumerated representatives to sue or defend on behalf of the infant or incompetent person. 2 Barron and Holtzoff, Federal Practice and Procedure (West 1961) should be consulted for an analysis of the identical federal counterparts.

Although a subrogee or assignee can sue in his own name, he is not compelled to do so. An insurance company claiming by way of subrogation can sue in the name of its insured and cannot be compelled to sue in its own name. Gould v. Weibel, 62 So.2d 47 (Fla.1952).

* * *

Rule 1.220. Class Actions

(a) Prerequisites to Class Representation. Before any claim or defense may be maintained on behalf of a class by one party or more suing or being sued as the representative of all the members of a class, the court shall first conclude that (1) the members of the class are so numerous that separate joinder of each member is impracticable, (2) the claim or defense of the representative party raises questions of law or fact common to the questions of law or fact raised by the claim or defense of each member of the class, (3) the claim or defense of the representative party is typical of the claim or defense of each member of the class, and (4) the representative party can fairly and adequately protect and represent the interests of each member of the class.

(b) Claims and Defenses Maintainable. A claim or defense may be maintained on behalf of a class if the court concludes that the prerequisites of subdivision (a) are satisfied, and that:

(1) the prosecution of separate claims or defenses by or against individual members of the class would create a risk of either:

(A) inconsistent or varying adjudications concerning individual members of the class which would establish incompatible standards of conduct for the party opposing the class; or

(B) adjudications concerning individual members of the class which would, as a practical matter, be dispositive of the interests of other members of the class who are not parties to the adjudications, or substantially impair or impede the ability of other members of the class who are not parties to the adjudications to protect their interests; or

(2) the party opposing the class has acted or refused to act on grounds generally applicable to all the members of the class, thereby making final injunctive relief or declaratory relief concerning the class as a whole appropriate; or

(3) the claim or defense is not maintainable under either subdivision (b)(1) or (b)(2), but the questions of law or fact common to the claim or defense of the representative party and the claim or defense of each member of the class predominate over any question of law or fact affecting only individual members of the class, and class representation is superior to other available methods for the fair and efficient adjudication of the controversy. The conclusions shall be derived from consideration of all relevant facts and circumstances, including (A) the respective interests of each member of the class in individually controlling the prosecution of separate claims or defenses, (B) the nature and extent of any pending litigation to which any member of the class is a party and in which any question of law or fact controverted in the subject action is to be adjudicated, (C) the desirability or undesirability of concentrating the litigation in the forum where the subject action is instituted, and (D) the difficulties likely to be encountered in the management of the claim or defense on behalf of a class.

(c) Pleading Requirements. Any pleading, counterclaim, or crossclaim alleging the existence of a class shall contain the following:

(1) Next to its caption the designation: "Class Representation."

(2) Under a separate heading, designated as "Class Representation Allegations," specific recitation of:

(A) the particular provision of subdivision (b) under which it is claimed that the claim or defense is maintainable on behalf of a class;

(B) the questions of law or fact that are common to the claim or defense of the representative party and the claim or defense of each member of the class;

(C) the particular facts and circumstances that show the claim or defense advanced by the representative party is typical of the claim or defense of each member of the class;

(D)(i) the approximate number of class members, (ii) a definition of the alleged class, and (iii) the particular facts and circumstances that show the representative party will fairly and adequately protect and represent the interests of each member of the class; and

(E) the particular facts and circumstances that support the conclusions required of the court in determining that the action may be maintained as a class action pursuant to the particular provision of subdivision (b) under which it is claimed that the claim or defense is maintainable on behalf of a class.

(d) Determination of Class Representation; Notice; Judgment: Claim or Defense Maintained Partly on Behalf of a Class.

(1) As soon as practicable after service of any pleading alleging the existence of a class under this rule and before service of an order for pretrial conference or a notice for trial, after hearing the court shall enter an order determining whether the claim or defense is maintainable on behalf of a class on the application of any party or on the court's initiative. Irrespective of whether the court determines that the claim or defense is maintainable on behalf of a class, the order shall separately state the findings of fact and conclusions of law upon which the determination is based. In making the determination the court (A) may allow the claim or defense to be so maintained, and, if so, shall state under which subsection of subdivision (b) the claim or defense is to be maintained, (B) may disallow the class representation and strike the class representation allegations, or (C) may order postponement of the determination pending the completion of discovery concerning whether the claim or defense is maintainable on behalf of a class. If the court rules that the claim or defense shall be maintained on behalf of a class under subdivision (b)(3), the order shall also provide for the notice required by subdivision (d)(2). If the court rules that the claim or defense shall be maintained on behalf of a class under subdivision (b)(1) or subdivision (b)(2), the order shall also provide for the notice required by subdivision (d)(2), except when a showing is made that the notice is not required, the court may provide for another kind of notice to the class as is appropriate. When the court orders postponement of its determination, the court shall also establish a date, if possible, for further consideration and final disposition of the motion. An order under this subsection may be conditional and may be altered or amended before entry of a judgment on the merits of the action.

(2) As soon as is practicable after the court determines that a claim or defense is maintainable on behalf of a class, notice of the pendency of the claim or defense shall be given by the party asserting the existence of the class to all the members of the class. The notice shall be given to each member of the class who can be identified and located through reasonable effort and shall be given to the other members of the class in the manner determined by the court to be most practicable under the circumstances. Unless otherwise ordered by the court, the party asserting the existence of the class shall initially pay for the cost of giving notice. The notice shall inform each member of the class that (A) any member of the class who files a statement with the court by the date specified in the notice asking to be excluded shall be excluded from the class, (B) the judgment, whether favorable or not, will include all members who do not request exclusion, and (C) any member who does not request exclusion may make a separate appearance within the time specified in the notice.

(3) The judgment determining a claim or defense maintained on behalf of a class under subdivision (b)(1) or (b)(2), whether or not favorable to the class, shall include and describe those persons whom the court finds to be members of the class. The judgment determining a claim or defense maintained on behalf of a class under subdivision (b)(3), whether or not favorable to the class, shall include and identify those to whom the notice provided in subdivision (d)(2) was directed, who have not requested exclusion and whom the court finds to be members of the class.

(4) When appropriate, (A) a claim or defense may be brought or maintained on behalf of a class concerning particular issues, or (B) class representation may be divided into subclasses, and each subclass may be treated as a separate and distinct class and the provisions of this rule shall be applied accordingly.

(e) Dismissal or Compromise. After a claim or defense is determined to be maintainable on behalf of a class under subdivision (d), the claim or defense shall not be voluntarily withdrawn, dismissed, or compromised without approval of the court after notice and hearing. Notice of any proposed voluntary withdrawal, dismissal, or compromise shall be given to all members of the class as the court directs.

Amended 347 So.2d 599 at 608; Oct. 9, 1980, effective Jan. 1, 1981 (391 So.2d 165); July 16, 1992, effective Jan. 1, 1993 (604 So.2d 1110).

Committee Notes

1980 Amendment. The class action rule has been completely revised to bring it in line with modern practice. The rule is based on Federal Rule of Civil Procedure 23, but a number of changes have been made to eliminate problems in the federal rule through court decisions. Generally, the rule provides for the prerequisites to class representation, an early determination about whether the claim or defense is maintainable on behalf of a class, notice to all members of the class, provisions for the members of the class to exclude themselves, the form of judgment, and the procedure governing dismissal or compromise of a claim or defense maintained on behalf of a class. The prerequisites of subdivision (a) are changed from those in federal rule 23 only to the extent necessary to incorporate the criteria enunciated in *Port Royal v. Conboy,* 154 So.2d 734 (Fla.2d DCA 1963). The notice requirements have been made more explicit and stringent than those in the federal rule.

Authors' Comment—1967

Rule 1.220 is the same as former Rule 3.6, 1954 Rules of Civil Procedure. The language of the rule sets forth the grounds for its utilization.

Class suits were long a part of Florida and federal equity practice. Florida practice is based upon old federal equity rule 38 which has been carried forward into our present Rule 1.220 without change. The present federal rule (Rule 23) on class actions has made some changes in old federal equity rule 38 and is not limited to suits of equitable character.

It is important that the plaintiff in a class suit should allege facts showing the necessity for bringing the action as a class suit, as well as the plaintiff's right to represent the class. The existence of the class should be alleged as well as described with some degree of certainty, and mention should be made that the members are so numerous as to make it impracticable to bring them all before the court.

In Peters v. Meeks, 163 So.2d 753 (Fla.1964), the Supreme Court of Florida warned that the allegations of a complaint should not be too broad in a class suit, and said decision should be carefully noted. Also refer to 2 Barron & Holtzoff, Federal Practice and Procedure, Rules Edition (West 1961) for a complete analysis of class actions.

Rule 1.221. Homeowners' Associations and Condominium Associations

A homeowners' or condominium association, after control of such association is obtained by homeowners or unit owners other than the developer, may institute, maintain, settle, or appeal actions or hearings in its name on behalf of all association members concerning matters of common interest to the members, including, but not limited to: (1) the common property, area, or elements; (2) the roof or structural components of a building, or other improvements (in the case of homeowners' associations, being specifically limited to those improvements for which the association is responsible); (3) mechanical, electrical, or plumbing elements serving a property or an improvement or building (in the case of homeowners' associations, being specifically limited to those elements for which the association is responsible); (4) representations of the developer pertaining to any existing or proposed commonly used facility; (5) protests of ad valorem taxes on commonly used facilities; and, in the case of homeowners' associations, (6) defense of actions in eminent domain or prosecution of inverse condemnation actions. If an association has the authority to maintain a class action under this rule, the association may be joined in an action as representative of that class with reference to litigation and disputes involving the matters for which the association could bring a class action under this rule. Nothing herein limits any statutory or common law right of any individual homeowner or unit owner, or class of such owners, to bring any action that may otherwise be available. An action under this rule shall not be subject to the requirements of rule 1.220.

Added Oct. 9, 1980, effective Jan. 1, 1981 (391 So.2d 165). Amended July 16, 1992, effective Jan. 1, 1993 (604 So.2d 1110); Sept. 27, 2007, effective Jan. 1, 2008 (966 So.2d 943).

Committee Notes

1980 Adoption. The present rule relating to condominium associations [1.220(b)] is left intact but renumbered as rule 1.221.

2007 Amendment. Consistent with amendments to section 720.303(1), Florida Statutes, homeowners' associations have been added to the rule.

Rule 1.222. Mobile Homeowners' Associations

A mobile homeowners' association may institute, maintain, settle, or appeal actions or hearings in its name on behalf of all homeowners concerning matters of common interest, including, but not limited to: the common property; structural components of a building or other improvements; mechanical, electrical, and plumbing elements serving the park property; and protests of ad valorem taxes on commonly used facilities. If the association has the authority to maintain a class action under this rule, the association may be joined in an action as representative of that class with reference to litigation and disputes involving the matters for which the association could bring a class action under this rule. Nothing herein limits any statutory or common-law right of any individual homeowner or class of homeowners to bring any action which may otherwise be available. An action under this rule shall not be subject to the requirements of rule 1.220.

Added Sept. 22, 1988 (541 So.2d 1121). Amended July 16, 1992, effective Jan. 1, 1993 (604 So.2d 1110).

Rule 1.230. Interventions

Anyone claiming an interest in pending litigation may at any time be permitted to assert a right by intervention, but the intervention shall be in subordination to, and in recognition of, the propriety of the main proceeding, unless otherwise ordered by the court in its discretion.

Amended July 16, 1992, effective Jan. 1, 1993 (604 So.2d 1110).

Authors' Comment—1967

Rule 1.230 is the same as former Rule 3.4, 1954 Rules of Civil Procedure, and may be utilized by the omitted party if the plaintiff has left out a necessary or proper party. It is in accord with the general language of Rule 1.210(a) that: "Any person may at any time be made a party if his presence is necessary or proper to a complete determination of the cause." Previously, the rule was only applicable in equity actions, but now applies to all civil actions.

Under this rule, the court has full control over intervention, including the extent thereof; although intervention under the rule is classified as of right, there must be an application made to the court, and the court in its discretion, considering the time of application as well as other factors, may deny the intervention or allow it upon conditions.

The intervener becomes a party to the action; he has the right to litigate on the merits the claim or defense for which he intervenes. In view of the aim of the rules to allow liberal joinder of parties and claims, the intervener should be permitted to counter-claim, cross-claim, and implead third parties, unless a denial of the right to do so is made a condition of allowing the intervention. In imposing such a condition, the court should consider whether the intervener has an absolute right to intervene or only a permissive one, the stage at which the application for intervention is made, the nature of the intervener's claim, and other factors.

In Federal practice, intervention is covered by Rule 24, Federal Rules of Civil Procedure. This rule was derived from old federal equity rule 37, which formed the basis for our Rule 1.230. Federal Rule 24 omits the requirement that the intervention be in subordination to and in recognition of the propriety of the main proceeding.

Intervention is not to be confused with interpleader. Interpleader is now the subject of Rule 1.240, infra.

Although the general rule is to the effect that it is too late to apply for intervention after final decree has been entered, nevertheless the ends of justice sometimes require that such leave be granted after final decree, as recognized in Wags Transportation System v. City of Miami Beach, 88 So.2d 751 (1956).

The Federal rule spells out the procedure for intervention. Ours fails to do so. The former practice was to apply by petition. Perhaps this should now be called a motion inasmuch as Rule 1.100 does not recognize petitions as a proper form of pleading, except when so designated by statute or rule. Rule 1.100(b) requires an application to the court to be by motion. The Federal rule specifies a motion as the means to intervene. See 2 Barron & Holtzoff, Federal Practice and Procedure, Rules Edition (West 1961) for an excellent discussion of intervention construction.

Notice of the motion is not required but service of a copy would be the better practice in view of Rule 1.080. Former Rule 1.4, 1954 Rules of Civil Procedure, from which Rule 1.080 is adopted, required service of every written motion, whereas the 1965 amendment and the present rule speak of only service of pleadings.

Rule 1.240. Interpleader

Persons having claims against the plaintiff may be joined as defendants and required to interplead when their claims are such that the plaintiff is or may be exposed to double or multiple liability. It is not ground for objection to the joinder that the claim of the several claimants or the titles on which their claims depend do not have common origin or are not identical but are adverse to and independent of one another, or that the plaintiff avers that the plaintiff is not liable in whole or in part to any or all of the claimants. A defendant exposed to similar liability may obtain such interpleader by way of crossclaim or counterclaim. The provisions of this rule supplement and do not in any way limit the joinder of parties otherwise permitted.

Amended July 16, 1992, effective Jan. 1, 1993 (604 So.2d 1110).

Authors' Comment—1967

Rule 1.240 is the same as Rule 3.13, 1954 Rules of Civil Procedure governing interpleader. The original Rule 3.13, 1954 Rules of Civil Procedure relating to time for taking testimony was abolished by order of the Supreme Court of June 30, 1961, effective October 1, 1961 (131 So.2d 475). The subsequent Rule 3.13 adopted in 1962 and the present rule are almost identical with paragraph (1) of Federal Rule 22. Therefore, the annotations under the Federal Rule should be carefully analyzed in view of the absence of abundant precedent in Florida under this rule. The remedy of interpleader, although new to the Florida Rules, has long been recognized as an equitable one. See Jax Ice & Cold Storage Co. v. South Florida Forms Co., 91 Fla. 593, 109 So. 212 (Fla.1926). It is based upon the theory that conflicting claimants should litigate their claims among themselves, without involving the stakeholder in their dispute. In other words, when two or more persons claiming the same thing or fund of a third person, and the latter, laying no claim to it himself, is ignorant as to which of them has a right to it, and fears he may be prejudiced by their proceeding against him to recover it, he may file a complaint against them, the object of which is to make them litigate their title between themselves, instead of litigating it with him.

The rule itself establishes that persons having claims against the plaintiff may be joined as defendants and required to interplead when their claims are such that the plaintiff is or may be exposed to multiple liability. Relief to a defendant is likewise provided for in the rule. Moreover, the rule is supplementary to and does not limit the joinder of parties otherwise permitted by law.

In view of the almost verbatim adherence to Federal Rule 22(1), 2 Barron and Holtzoff, Federal Practice and Procedure, Rules Edition (West 1961) should be carefully analyzed. Interpleader is now also recognized in the Uniform Commercial Code appearing in F.S.A. §§ 676.6–106 and 677.7–603.

The existing law in Florida as to the maintenance of an interpleader action was expanded by the 1962 adoption of a new Rule 3.13, Rules of Civil Procedure. In Ellison v. Riddle, 166 So.2d 840 (Fla. D.C.A.2d 1964), the Court recognized the limitations to obtaining an award of costs and attorneys fees. The Court ruled that in order to obtain such an award, a plaintiff must prove his total disinterest in the stake he holds, other than bringing it into court so that conflicting claims can be judicially determined, and he must also show he did nothing to cause the conflicting claims or give rise to the peril of double vexation.

In Riverside Bank v. Florida Dealers & Growers Bank, 151 So.2d 834 (Fla.D.C.A.1st 1963), four indispensable conditions are outlined which must appear from the pleadings before an action may fall within the category of strict interpleader, to-wit: (1) the claims must be dependent or have a common origin; (2) the same thing, debt (or duty) or stake must be claimed by the defendants; (3) the plaintiff must have no interest in the subject matter—that is, in strict interpleader as distinguished from a suit in the nature of interpleader; and (4) the plaintiff must be in a position of indifference, having incurred no independent liability to either of the claimants, but must stand indifferent between them merely as a stakeholder, and it must appear that no act on his part has caused the embarrassment of conflicting claims and the peril of double vexation.

Rule 1.250. Misjoinder and Nonjoinder of Parties

(a) Misjoinder. Misjoinder of parties is not a ground for dismissal of an action. Any claim against a party may be severed and proceeded with separately.

(b) Dropping Parties. Parties may be dropped by an adverse party in the manner provided for voluntary dismissal in rule 1.420(a)(1) subject to the exception stated in that rule. If notice of lis pendens has been filed in the action against a party so dropped, the notice of dismissal shall be recorded and cancels the notice of lis pendens without the necessity of a court order. Parties may be dropped by order of court on its own initiative or the motion of any party at any stage of the action on such terms as are just.

(c) Adding Parties. Parties may be added once as a matter of course within the same time that pleadings can be so amended under rule 1.190(a). If amendment by leave of court or stipulation of the parties is permitted, parties may be added in the amended pleading without further order of court. Parties may be added by order of court on its own initiative or on motion of any party at any stage of the action and on such terms as are just.

Amended June 19, 1968, effective Oct. 1, 1968 (211 So.2d 206); July 26, 1972, effective Jan. 1, 1973 (265 So.2d 21); July 16, 1992, effective Jan. 1, 1993 (604 So.2d 1110).

Committee Notes

1972 Amendment. Subdivision (c) is amended to permit the addition of parties when the pleadings are amended by stipulation. This conforms the subdivision to all of the permissive types of amendment under rule 1.190(a). It was an inadvertent omission by the committee when the rule in its present form was adopted in 1968 as can be seen by reference to the 1968 committee note.

Authors' Comment—1967

Rule 1.250 is the same as former Rule 1.18, 1954 Rules of Civil Procedure as well as Federal Rule 21. Thus 2 Barron and Holtzoff, Federal Practice and Procedure, Rules Edition (West 1961) should be consulted for an analysis of the identical provision.

A party or the court may add a party at any stage of the action by operation of this rule as well as through Rule 1.210(a) if the added party's presence is necessary or proper to a complete determination of the cause.

Misjoinder of parties is not ground for dismissal of the action. The misjoined party should be dropped on such terms as the court deems just. If there are misjoined claims because of multiple parties, the misjoined claim may be severed and proceeded with separately.

Rule 1.260. Survivor; Substitution of Parties

(a) Death.

(1) If a party dies and the claim is not thereby extinguished, the court may order substitution of the proper parties. The motion for substitution may be made by any party or by the successors or representatives of the deceased party and, together with the notice of hearing, shall be served on all parties as provided in rule 1.080 and upon persons not parties in the manner provided for the service of a summons. Unless the motion for substitution is made within 90 days after the death is suggested upon the record by service of a statement of the fact of the death in the manner provided for the service of the motion, the action shall be dismissed as to the deceased party.

(2) In the event of the death of one or more of the plaintiffs or of one or more of the defendants in an action in which the right sought to be enforced survives only to the surviving plaintiffs or only against the surviving defendants, the action shall not abate. The death shall be suggested upon the record and the action shall proceed in favor of or against the surviving parties.

(b) Incompetency. If a party becomes incompetent, the court, upon motion served as provided in subdivision (a) of this rule, may allow the action to be continued by or against that person's representative.

(c) Transfer of Interest. In case of any transfer of interest, the action may be continued by or against the original party, unless the court upon motion directs the person to whom the interest is transferred to be substituted in the action or joined with the original party. Service of the motion shall be made as provided in subdivision (a) of this rule.

(d) Public Officers; Death or Separation from Office.

(1) When a public officer is a party to an action in an official capacity and during its pendency dies, resigns, or otherwise ceases to hold office, the action does not abate and the officer's successor is automatically substituted as a party. Proceedings following the substitution shall be in the name of the substituted party, but any misnomer not affecting the substantial rights of the parties shall be disregarded. An order of substitution may be entered at any time, but the omission to enter such an order shall not affect the substitution.

(2) When a public officer sues or is sued in an official capacity, the officer may be described as a party by the official title rather than by name but the court may require the officer's name to be added.

Amended July 16, 1992, effective Jan. 1, 1993 (604 So.2d 1110).

Authors' Comment—1967

Rule 1.260 is the same as former Rule 1.19, 1954 Rules of Civil Procedure, as per amendment effective January 1, 1966, except for the numerical reference to a related rule now being in conformity with the new rules. It is almost identical to Federal Rule 25. Thus, 2 Barron and Holtzoff, Federal Practice and Procedure, Rules Edition (West 1961) should be consulted for a persuasive analysis of the construction of the federal counterpart of substitution of parties in civil actions in cases where a party dies, becomes incompetent, transfers his interest, or, if a public officer, is separated from his office.

Rule 1.19, after amendment, differed from the original 1954 Rule in certain important respects. Service of the motion for substitution was authorized on persons *not* parties in the manner provided for the service of a summons. The most vital change was the removal of the two year limit. After amendment, substitution was to be made within 90 days after the death was suggested upon the record, but the time could be extended by the court under Rule 1.090(b) if the request for enlargement of time was made within the 90 days or as extended by previous order, or if beyond the 90 day period, upon motion establishing excusable neglect. However, a danger in relying upon a belated motion alleging excusable neglect is that the mandatory language of the rule requiring dismissal of the action may have already taken effect. In view of the strict Federal construction of the prior two year limitation period, it would always be best to file the motion for substitution within the 90 day period.

Rule 1.260(a) applies to substitution of parties upon the death of a natural party. It has no application to a dissolution of a corporation, since such would be governed by subsection (c).

The rule does not apply to death of a party on appeal since such is governed by Florida Appellate Rule 3.11e.

Serious consideration must be given the effect of F.S.A. § 733.18 as construed in Field v. Newsom, 170 So.2d 50 (D.C.A.3d 1965), and F.S.A. § 733.16 as construed in Davis v. Evans, 132 So.2d 476 (D.C.A. 1st 1961).

It should be noted that the former rule required a substitution order to be made within the two year period whereas the new rule requires an application by motion to be made within the 90 day period.

Since the 1966 amendment, a public officer is automatically substituted as a party, and if he sues or is sued in his official capacity he may be described by his official title only, thereby rendering any later substitution unnecessary.

Rule 1.270. Consolidation; Separate Trials

(a) Consolidation. When actions involving a common question of law or fact are pending before the court, it may order a joint hearing or trial of any or all the matters in issue in the actions; it may order all the actions consolidated; and it may make such orders concerning proceedings therein as may tend to avoid unnecessary costs or delay.

(b) Separate Trials. The court in furtherance of convenience or to avoid prejudice may order a separate trial of any claim, crossclaim, counterclaim, or third–party claim, or of any separate issue or of any number of claims, crossclaims, counterclaims, third–party claims, or issues.

Amended July 16, 1992, effective Jan. 1, 1993 (604 So.2d 1110).

Authors' Comments—1967

Rule 1.270 is the same as former Rule 1.20, 1954 Rules of Civil Procedure as per amendment effective January 1, 1966. It is substantially the same as Federal Rule 42, and thus 2B Barron and Holtzoff, Federal Practice and Procedure, Rules Edition (West 1961) should be consulted for an excellent analysis of the construction of the federal counterpart.

Consistent with the creation of third party practice in Florida by the present rules, the court may order separate trials for third party claims under subsection (b).

Consolidation of cases on appeal may be ordered by Florida Appellate Rules 2.1a(2)(a) and 2.2a(2)(a).

Although the rule does prescribe the manner by which a party may obtain consolidation or a separate trial, such may be accomplished by motion practice pursuant to Rule 1.100(b).

The rule is complementary to the rules dealing with joinder of claims and parties. Liberal provisions have been made for the joinder of claims and parties in the interest of presenting all the controversies between the parties. Where those rules could have been complied with, but were not, and the separate actions present claims or defenses involving a common question of law or fact, the court has authority, upon its own initiative or upon motion, to order consolidated the actions or the trial or hearing of any or all matters in issue in the actions.

The rule is one of trial convenience and the administration of justice. Its use is within the discretion of the trial court. It should not be used to deprive a party of any substantive rights which would be denied unless the actions proceeded separately. The rule is intended to benefit not only the litigants but also the administration of the courts.

Generally, justice requires that an action should not be handled piecemeal when it reasonably can be avoided, and it should be administered with the least expense and vexation to the parties.

The court has authority to order a joint hearing or trial of any matter in issue in the actions, and from that simple consolidation of trials the authority extends through varying degrees of consolidation to the other extreme of the consolidation of actions. The extent of the merger will vary according to what may be necessary to insure the just and expeditious disposition of the controversy.

A common use may be the consolidation for trial of the issue of liability in an automobile accident resulting in personal injuries to several persons with reservation of separate trials of the issues of damages where the latter are extensive and complicated.

The court may exercise its power to consolidate on its own motion, but normally it will be exercised upon the timely motion of a party. Whether consolidation will be ordered lies in the discretion of the court.

Rule 1.280. General Provisions Governing Discovery

(a) Discovery Methods. Parties may obtain discovery by one or more of the following methods: depositions upon oral examination or written questions; written interrogatories; production of documents or things or permission to enter upon land or other property for inspection and other purposes; physical and mental examinations; and requests for admission. Unless the court orders otherwise and under subdivision (c) of this rule, the frequency of use of these methods is not limited, except as provided in rules 1.200, 1.340, and 1.370.

(b) Scope of Discovery. Unless otherwise limited by order of the court in accordance with these rules, the scope of discovery is as follows:

(1) *In General.* Parties may obtain discovery regarding any matter, not privileged, that is relevant to the subject matter of the pending action, whether it relates to the claim or defense of the party seeking discovery or the claim or defense of any other party, including the existence, description, nature, custody, condition, and location of any books, documents, or other tangible things and the identity and location of persons having knowledge of any discoverable matter. It is not ground for objection that the information sought will be inadmissible at the trial if the information sought appears reasonably calculated to lead to the discovery of admissible evidence.

(2) *Indemnity Agreements.* A party may obtain discovery of the existence and contents of any agreement under which any person may be liable to satisfy part or all of a judgment that may be entered in the action or to indemnify or to reimburse a party for payments made to satisfy the judgment. Information concerning the agreement is not admissible in evidence at trial by reason of disclosure.

(3) *Electronically Stored Information.* A party may obtain discovery of electronically stored information in accordance with these rules.

(4) *Trial Preparation: Materials.* Subject to the provisions of subdivision (b)(5) of this rule, a party may obtain discovery of documents and tangible things otherwise discoverable under subdivision (b)(1) of this rule and prepared in anticipation of litigation or for trial by or for another party or by or for that party's representative, including that party's attorney, consultant, surety, indemnitor, insurer, or agent, only upon a showing that the party seeking discovery has need of the materials in the preparation of the case and is unable without undue hardship to obtain the substantial equivalent of the materials by other means. In ordering discovery of the materials when the required showing has been made, the court shall protect against disclosure of the mental impressions, conclusions, opinions, or legal theories of an attorney or other representative of a party concerning the litigation. Without the required showing a party may obtain a copy of a statement concerning the action or its subject matter previously made by that party. Upon request without the required showing a person not a party may obtain a copy of a statement concerning the action or its subject matter previously made by that person. If the request is refused, the person may move for an order to obtain a copy. The provisions of rule 1.380(a)(4) apply to the award of expenses incurred as a result of making the motion. For purposes of this paragraph, a statement previously made is a written statement signed or otherwise adopted or approved by the person making it, or a stenographic, mechanical, electrical, or other recording or transcription of it that is a substantially verbatim recital of an oral statement by the person making it and contemporaneously recorded.

(5) *Trial Preparation: Experts.* Discovery of facts known and opinions held by experts, otherwise discoverable under the provisions of subdivision (b)(1) of this rule and acquired or developed in anticipation of litigation or for trial, may be obtained only as follows:

(A)(i) By interrogatories a party may require any other party to identify each person whom the other party expects to call as an expert witness at trial and to state the subject matter on which the expert is expected to testify, and to state the substance of the facts and opinions to which the expert is expected to testify and a summary of the grounds for each opinion.

(ii) Any person disclosed by interrogatories or otherwise as a person expected to be called as an expert witness at trial may be deposed in accordance with rule 1.390 without motion or order of court.

(iii) A party may obtain the following discovery regarding any person disclosed by interrogatories or otherwise as a person expected to be called as an expert witness at trial:

1. The scope of employment in the pending case and the compensation for such service.

2. The expert's general litigation experience, including the percentage of work performed for plaintiffs and defendants.

3. The identity of other cases, within a reasonable time period, in which the expert has testified by deposition or at trial.

4. An approximation of the portion of the expert's involvement as an expert witness, which may be based on the number of hours, percentage of hours, or percentage of earned income derived from serving as an expert witness; however, the expert shall not be required to disclose his or her earnings as an expert witness or income derived from other services.

An expert may be required to produce financial and business records only under the most unusual or compelling circumstances and may not be compelled to compile or produce nonexistent documents. Upon motion, the court may order further discovery by other means, subject to such restrictions as to scope and other provisions pursuant to subdivision (b)(5)(C) of this rule concerning fees and expenses as the court may deem appropriate.

(B) A party may discover facts known or opinions held by an expert who has been retained or specially employed by another party in anticipation of litigation or preparation for trial and who is not expected to be called as a witness at trial, only as provided in rule 1.360(b) or upon a showing of exceptional circumstances under which it is impracticable for the party seeking discovery to obtain facts or opinions on the same subject by other means.

(C) Unless manifest injustice would result, the court shall require that the party seeking discovery pay the expert a reasonable fee for time spent in responding to discovery under subdivisions (b)(5)(A) and (b)(5)(B) of this rule; and concerning discovery from an expert obtained under subdivision (b)(5)(A) of this rule the court may require, and concerning discovery obtained under subdivision (b)(5)(B) of this rule shall require, the party seeking discovery to pay the other party a fair part of the fees and expenses reasonably incurred by the latter party in obtaining facts and opinions from the expert.

(D) As used in these rules an expert shall be an expert witness as defined in rule 1.390(a).

(6) *Claims of Privilege or Protection of Trial Preparation Materials.* When a party withholds information otherwise discoverable under these rules by claiming that it is privileged or subject to protection as trial preparation material, the party shall make the claim expressly and shall describe the nature of the documents, communications, or things not produced or disclosed in a manner that, without revealing information itself privileged or protected, will enable other parties to assess the applicability of the privilege or protection.

(c) Protective Orders. Upon motion by a party or by the person from whom discovery is sought, and for good cause shown, the court in which the action is pending may make any order to protect a party or person from annoyance, embarrassment, oppression, or undue burden or expense that justice requires, including one or more of the following: (1) that the discovery not be had; (2) that the discovery may be had only on specified terms and conditions, including a designation of the time or place; (3) that the discovery may be had only by a method of discovery other than that selected by the party seeking discovery; (4) that certain matters not be inquired into, or that the scope of the discovery be limited to certain matters; (5) that discovery be conducted with no one present except persons designated by the court; (6) that a deposition after being sealed be opened only by order of the court; (7) that a trade secret or other confidential research, development, or commercial information not be disclosed or be disclosed only in a designated way; and (8) that the parties simultaneously file specified documents or information enclosed in sealed envelopes to be opened as directed by the court. If the motion for a protective order is denied in whole or in part, the court may, on such terms and conditions as are just, order that any party or person provide or permit discovery. The provisions of rule 1.380(a)(4) apply to the award of expenses incurred in relation to the motion.

(d) Limitations on Discovery of Electronically Stored Information.

(1) A person may object to discovery of electronically stored information from sources that the person identifies as not reasonably accessible because of burden or cost. On motion to compel discovery or for a protective order, the person from whom discovery is sought must show that the information sought or the format requested is not reasonably accessible because of undue burden or cost. If that showing is made, the court may nonetheless order the discovery from such sources or in such formats if the requesting party shows good cause. The court may specify conditions of the discovery, including ordering that some or all of the expenses incurred by the person from whom discovery is sought be paid by the party seeking the discovery.

(2) In determining any motion involving discovery of electronically stored information, the court must limit the frequency or extent of discovery otherwise allowed by these rules if it determines that (i) the discovery sought is unreasonably cumulative or duplicative, or can be obtained from another source or in another manner that is more convenient, less burden-

some, or less expensive; or (ii) the burden or expense of the discovery outweighs its likely benefit, considering the needs of the case, the amount in controversy, the parties' resources, the importance of the issues at stake in the action, and the importance of the discovery in resolving the issues.

(e) Sequence and Timing of Discovery. Except as provided in subdivision (b)(5) or unless the court upon motion for the convenience of parties and witnesses and in the interest of justice orders otherwise, methods of discovery may be used in any sequence, and the fact that a party is conducting discovery, whether by deposition or otherwise, shall not delay any other party's discovery.

(f) Supplementing of Responses. A party who has responded to a request for discovery with a response that was complete when made is under no duty to supplement the response to include information thereafter acquired.

(g) Court Filing of Documents and Discovery. Information obtained during discovery shall not be filed with the court until such time as it is filed for good cause. The requirement of good cause is satisfied only where the filing of the information is allowed or required by another applicable rule of procedure or by court order. All filings of discovery documents shall comply with Florida Rule of Judicial Administration 2.425. The court shall have the authority to impose sanctions for violation of this rule.

Amended July 26, 1972, effective Jan. 1, 1973 (265 So.2d 21); Sept. 13, 1984, effective Jan. 1, 1985 (458 So.2d 245); Oct. 6, 1988, effective Jan. 1, 1989 (536 So.2d 974); July 6, 1989 (545 So.2d 866); July 16, 1992, effective Jan. 1, 1993 (604 So.2d 1110); Oct. 31, 1996, effective Jan. 1, 1997 (682 So.2d 105); Oct. 5, 2000, effective Jan. 1, 2001 (773 So.2d 1098); Sept. 27, 2007, effective Jan. 1, 2008 (966 So.2d 943); Nov. 3, 2011, effective, *nunc pro tunc*, Oct. 1, 2011 (78 So.3d 1045); July 5, 2012, effective Sept. 1, 2012 (95 So.3d 76).

Committee Notes

1972 Amendment. The rule is derived from Federal Rule of Civil Procedure 26 as amended in 1970. Subdivisions (a), (b)(2), and (b)(3) are new. Subdivision (c) contains material from former rule 1.310(b). Subdivisions (d) and (e) are new, but the latter is similar to former rule 1. 340(d). Significant changes are made in discovery from experts. The general rearrangement of the discovery rule is more logical and is the result of 35 years of experience under the federal rules.

1988 Amendment. Subdivision (b)(2) has been added to enable discovery of the existence and contents of indemnity agreements and is the result of the enactment of sections 627.7262 and 627.7264, Florida Statutes, proscribing the joinder of insurers but providing for disclosure. This rule is derived from Federal Rule of Civil Procedure 26(b)(2). Subdivisions (b)(2) and (b)(3) have been redesignated as (b)(3) and (b)(4) respectively.

The purpose of the amendment to subdivision (b)(3)(A) (renumbered (b)(4)(A)) is to allow, without leave of court, the depositions of experts who have been disclosed as expected to be used at trial. The purpose of subdivision (b)(4)(D) is to define the term "expert" as used in these rules.

1996 Amendment. The amendments to subdivision (b)(4)(A) are derived from the Supreme Court's decision in *Elkins v. Syken*, 672 So. 2d 517 (Fla. 1996). They are intended to avoid annoyance, embarrassment, and undue expense while still permitting the adverse party to obtain relevant information regarding the potential bias or interest of the expert witness.

Subdivision (b)(5) is added and is derived from Federal Rule of Civil Procedure 26(b)(5) (1993).

2011 Amendment. Subdivision (f) is added to ensure that information obtained during discovery is not filed with the court unless there is good cause for the documents to be filed, and that information obtained during discovery that includes certain private information shall not be filed with the court unless the private information is redacted as required by Florida Rule of Judicial Administration 2.425.

2012 Amendment. Subdivisions (b)(3) and (d) are added to address discovery of electronically stored information.

The parties should consider conferring with one another at the earliest practical opportunity to discuss the reasonable scope of preservation and production of electronically stored information. These issues may also be addressed by means of a rule 1.200 or rule 1.201 case management conference.

Under the good cause test in subdivision (d)(1), the court should balance the costs and burden of the requested discovery, including the potential for disruption of operations or corruption of the electronic devices or systems from which discovery is sought, against the relevance of the information and the requesting party's need for that information. Under the proportionality and reasonableness factors set out in subdivision (d)(2), the court must limit the frequency or extent of discovery if it determines that the discovery sought is excessive in relation to the factors listed.

In evaluating the good cause or proportionality tests, the court may find its task complicated if the parties know little about what information the sources at issue contain, whether the information sought is relevant, or how valuable it may be to the litigation. If appropriate, the court may direct the parties to develop the record further by engaging in focused discovery, including sampling of the sources, to learn more about what electronically stored information may be contained in those sources, what costs and burdens are involved in retrieving, reviewing, and producing the information, and how valuable the information sought may be to the litigation in light of the availability of information from other sources or methods of discovery, and in light of the parties' resources and the issues at stake in the litigation.

Court Commentary

2000 Amendment. *Allstate Insurance Co. v. Boecher*, 733 So.2d 993, 999 (Fla. 1999), clarifies that subdivision (b)(4)(A)(iii) is not intended "to place a blanket bar on discovery from parties about information they have in their possession about an expert, including the party's financial relationship with the expert."

Rule 1.285. Inadvertent Disclosure of Privileged Materials

(a) Assertion of Privilege as to Inadvertently Disclosed Materials. Any party, person, or entity, after inadvertent disclosure of any materials pursuant to these rules, may thereafter assert any privilege recognized by law as to those materials. This right exists without regard to whether the disclosure was made pursuant to formal demand or informal request. In order to assert the privilege, the party, person, or entity shall, within 10 days of actually discovering the inadvertent disclosure, serve written notice of the assertion of privilege on the party to whom the materials were disclosed. The notice shall specify with particularity the materials as to which the privilege is asserted, the nature of the privilege asserted, and the date on which the inadvertent disclosure was actually discovered.

(b) Duty of the Party Receiving Notice of an Assertion of Privilege. A party receiving notice of an assertion of privilege under subdivision (a) shall promptly return, sequester, or destroy the materials specified in the notice, as well as any copies of the material. The party receiving the notice shall also promptly notify any other party, person, or entity to whom it has disclosed the materials of the fact that the notice has been served and of the effect of this rule. That party shall also take reasonable steps to retrieve the materials disclosed. Nothing herein affects any obligation pursuant to R. Regulating Fla. Bar 4–4.4(b).

(c) Right to Challenge Assertion of Privilege. Any party receiving a notice made under subdivision (a) has the right to challenge the assertion of privilege. The grounds for the challenge may include, but are not limited to, the following:

(1) The materials in question are not privileged.

(2) The disclosing party, person, or entity lacks standing to assert the privilege.

(3) The disclosing party, person, or entity has failed to serve timely notice under this rule.

(4) The circumstances surrounding the production or disclosure of the materials warrant a finding that the disclosing party, person, or entity has waived its assertion that the material is protected by a privilege.

Any party seeking to challenge the assertion of privilege shall do so by serving notice of its challenge on the party, person, or entity asserting the privilege. Notice of the challenge shall be served within 20 days of service of the original notice given by the disclosing party, person, or entity. The notice of the recipient's challenge shall specify the grounds for the challenge. Failure to serve timely notice of challenge is a waiver of the right to challenge.

(d) Effect of Determination that Privilege Applies. When an order is entered determining that materials are privileged or that the right to challenge the privilege has been waived, the court shall direct what shall be done with the materials and any copies so as to preserve all rights of appellate review. The recipient of the materials shall also give prompt notice of the court's determination to any other party, person, or entity to whom it had disclosed the materials.

Added Sept. 8, 2010, effective. Jan. 1, 2011 (52 So.3d 579).

Rule 1.290. Depositions Before Action or Pending Appeal

(a) Before Action.

(1) *Petition.* A person who desires to perpetuate that person's own testimony or that of another person regarding any matter that may be cognizable in any court of this state may file a verified petition in the circuit court in the county of the residence of any expected adverse party. The petition shall be entitled in the name of the petitioner and shall show: (1) that the petitioner expects to be a party to an action cognizable in a court of Florida, but is presently unable to bring it or cause it to be brought, (2) the subject matter of the expected action and the petitioner's interest therein, (3) the facts which the petitioner desires to establish by the proposed testimony and the petitioner's reasons for desiring to perpetuate it, (4) the names or a description of the persons the petitioner expects will be adverse parties and their addresses so far as known, and (5) the names and addresses of the persons to be examined and the substance of the testimony which the petitioner expects to elicit from each; and shall ask for an order authorizing the petitioner to take the deposition of the persons to be examined named in the petition for the purpose of perpetuating their testimony.

(2) *Notice and Service.* The petitioner shall thereafter serve a notice upon each person named in the petition as an expected adverse party, together with a copy of the petition, stating that the petitioner will apply to the court at a time and place named therein for an order described in the petition. At least 20 days before the date of hearing the notice shall be served either within or without the county in the manner provided by law for service of summons, but if such service cannot with due diligence be made upon any expected adverse party named in the petition, the court may make an order for service by publication or otherwise, and shall appoint an attorney for persons not served in the manner provided by law for service of summons who shall represent them, and if they are not otherwise represented, shall cross-examine the deponent.

(3) *Order and Examination.* If the court is satisfied that the perpetuation of the testimony may prevent a failure or delay of justice, it shall make an

order designating or describing the persons whose depositions may be taken and specifying the subject matter of the examination and whether the deposition shall be taken upon oral examination or written interrogatories. The deposition may then be taken in accordance with these rules and the court may make orders in accordance with the requirements of these rules. For the purpose of applying these rules to depositions for perpetuating testimony, each reference therein to the court in which the action is pending shall be deemed to refer to the court in which the petition for such deposition was filed.

(4) *Use of Deposition.* A deposition taken under this rule may be used in any action involving the same subject matter subsequently brought in any court in accordance with rule 1.330.

(b) Pending Appeal. If an appeal has been taken from a judgment of any court or before the taking of an appeal if the time therefor has not expired, the court in which the judgment was rendered may allow the taking of the depositions of witnesses to perpetuate their testimony for use in the event of further proceedings in the court. In such case the party who desires to perpetuate the testimony may make a motion for leave to take the deposition upon the same notice and service as if the action was pending in the court. The motion shall show (1) the names and addresses of persons to be examined and the substance of the testimony which the movant expects to elicit from each, and (2) the reason for perpetuating their testimony. If the court finds that the perpetuation of the testimony is proper to avoid a failure or delay in justice, it may make an order allowing the deposition to be taken and may make orders of the character provided for by these rules, and thereupon the deposition may be taken and used in the same manner and under the same conditions as are prescribed in these rules for depositions taken in actions pending in the court.

(c) Perpetuation by Action. This rule does not limit the power of a court to entertain an action to perpetuate testimony.

Amended Oct. 9, 1980, effective Jan. 1, 1981 (391 So.2d 165); Sept. 13, 1984, effective Jan. 1, 1985 (458 So.2d 245); July 16, 1992, effective Jan. 1, 1993 (604 So.2d 1110).

Committee Notes

1980 Amendment. Subdivision (d) is repealed because depositions de bene esse are obsolete. Rules 1.280 and 1.310 with the remainder of this rule cover all needed deposition circumstances and do so better. Subdivision (d) was taken from former chapter 63, Florida Statutes, and is not a complete procedure without reference to the parts of the statute not carried forward in the rule.

Authors' Comment—1967

Rule 1.290 is identical to former Rule 1.22, 1954 Rules of Civil Procedure, as per amendment effective January 1, 1966. The amendment merely deleted the restriction to circuit courts since other trial courts may also utilize the procedure. The rule is patterned closely after Federal Rule 27, and therefore 2A Barron and Holtzoff, Federal Practice and Procedure, Rules Edition (West 1961) should be consulted for a persuasive analysis of the federal rule.

Prior to the order of the Supreme Court of Florida in 131 So.2d 475 (1961), depositions de bene esse were provided for in both Rule 1.22 and Rule 1.32, 1954 Rules of Civil Procedure, but the latter was abolished as redundant.

This is one of the few times a petition is used under the Rules promulgated by the Supreme Court. Prior to adoption of the Rules a bill of complaint or F.S.A. §§ 91.21–91.24, were used to perpetuate testimony.

Rule 1.290 deals with perpetuation of testimony before action. Where a party is unable to bring an action presently, or a defendant knows that an action will be brought against him and he desires to perpetuate testimony he can do so under this rule.

The rule is intended only for the perpetuation of testimony; it is not a discovery procedure. It is not to be used for the purpose of discovery before action is commenced. A party may not "fish" for some ground for bringing suit. The requirement that the petitioner be presently unable to bring his action or cause it to be brought does not encompass the situation of a petitioner who has a matured claim but lacks knowledge of all the facts.

Procedure—Petition

A proceeding to perpetuate testimony is not a separate civil action in the usual sense. Although not based upon a pending action, it is an ancillary or auxiliary proceeding. The proceeding is begun, not by the service of summons and complaint, but by the filing of a "verified petition" in the circuit court of the county of the residence of an expected adverse party.

The petition shall be entitled in the name of the petitioner, such as in other ancillary or auxiliary proceedings, and shall show the requirements enumerated in clause (a) of paragraph (1), concluding with a prayer for an order authorizing the petitioner to take the depositions of the persons named in the petition for the purpose of perpetuating their testimony. The rules applicable to captions, signing, and other matters of form of pleadings apply to the petition. The petitioner may support the petition by affidavits.

Notice and Service

After filing the verified petition with the court, a copy of the petition and a notice of hearing must be served upon each person named in the petition as an expected adverse party. Service shall be made as provided for the service of a summons. Service is not restricted, however, to service "within the state".

Where the service upon named persons cannot with due diligence be made, the court may make such order as is just for service by publication or otherwise. This would include service by registered mail.

Where service must be made upon persons who are described, but not named in the petition, as expected adverse parties, the court may make such order as is just for service by publication or otherwise.

For persons not served in the manner provided for a summons the court shall appoint an attorney to represent them at the hearing on the petition. The rule further directs such attorney, in case any such persons are not otherwise represented, to cross-examine the deponent.

Order and Examination

The rule does not provide for the conduct of the hearing upon the petition. The hearing is intended to be a summary one. The requirement of verification of the petition tends to establish that the averments of the petition have been made in good faith. The expected adverse parties are required to serve and file any responsive papers. It is suggested that the expected adverse parties may serve and file affidavits showing lack of good faith, or that the averments are sham or have no actual basis.

The determination of what is a "delay or failure of justice" upon which is founded the order to perpetuate testimony is aided by the enumerated facts required to appear in the petition.

The court does not itself take the testimony, nor does it necessarily issue a commission or letters rogatory. After the entry of the order, the deposition may be taken in accordance with these rules. If the court has ordered the deposition to be taken orally, Rule 1.310 and related rules apply; and if the order is for deposition by interrogatories, Rule 1.320 and related rules apply. In either case, a notice of the taking of the deposition is required as provided in the rules. Such notice may be served upon the attorney representing the expected adverse party at the hearing upon the petition. If no appearance at the hearing was made by a person personally served, caution would suggest that such a person be served with a notice of the taking of the deposition.

A copy of the order of the court should be served with the notice of the taking of the deposition to avoid dispute over the scope of the examination.

Under subsection (b) this testimony is not for use by the appellate court, but is for use should the case be remitted to the lower court for a new trial. The order required is obtained by motion if court finds that the perpetuation may prevent a failure or delay of justice, and the motion need not be verified as in the case of a petition in subsection (a). See Chaachou v. Chaachou, 102 So.2d 820 (D.C.A.3d 1958).

Rule 1.300. Persons Before Whom Depositions May Be Taken

(a) Persons Authorized. Depositions may be taken before any notary public or judicial officer or before any officer authorized by the statutes of Florida to take acknowledgments or proof of executions of deeds or by any person appointed by the court in which the action is pending.

(b) In Foreign Countries. In a foreign country depositions may be taken (1) on notice before a person authorized to administer oaths in the place in which the examination is held, either by the law thereof or by the law of Florida or of the United States, (2) before a person commissioned by the court, and a person so commissioned shall have the power by virtue of the commission to administer any necessary oath and take testimony, or (3) pursuant to a letter rogatory. A commission or a letter rogatory shall be issued on application and notice and on terms that are just and appropriate. It is not requisite to the issuance of a commission or a letter rogatory that the taking of the deposition in any other manner is impracticable or inconvenient, and both a commission and a letter rogatory may be issued in proper cases. A notice or commission may designate the person before whom the deposition is to be taken either by name or descriptive title. A letter rogatory may be addressed "To the Appropriate Authority in ________ (name of country) ________." Evidence obtained in response to a letter rogatory need not be excluded merely for the reason that it is not a verbatim transcript or that the testimony was not taken under oath or any similar departure from the requirements for depositions taken within Florida under these rules.

(c) Selection by Stipulation. If the parties so stipulate in writing, depositions may be taken before any person at any time or place upon any notice and in any manner and when so taken may be used like other depositions.

(d) Persons Disqualified. Unless so stipulated by the parties, no deposition shall be taken before a person who is a relative, employee, attorney, or counsel of any of the parties, is a relative or employee of any of the parties' attorney or counsel, or is financially interested in the action.

Amended July 16, 1992, effective Jan. 1, 1993 (604 So.2d 1110).

Authors' Comment—1967

Rule 1.300 is the same as former Rule 1.23, 1954 Rules of Civil Procedure, as per amendment effective January 1, 1966. It is quite similar to Federal Rules 28 and 29.

Paragraph (c) requires the cooperation of all the attorneys involved in the litigation. The use of this rule eliminates following the steps prescribed in Rule 1.310(b).

Rule 1.310. Depositions Upon Oral Examination

(a) When Depositions May Be Taken. After commencement of the action any party may take the testimony of any person, including a party, by deposition upon oral examination. Leave of court, granted with or without notice, must be obtained only if the plaintiff seeks to take a deposition within 30 days after service of the process and initial pleading upon any defendant, except that leave is not required (1) if a defendant has served a notice of taking deposition or otherwise sought discovery, or (2) if special notice is given as provided in subdivision (b)(2) of this rule. The attendance of witnesses may be compelled by subpoena as provided in rule 1.410. The deposition of a person confined in prison may be taken only by leave of court on such terms as the court prescribes.

(b) Notice; Method of Taking; Production at Deposition.

(1) A party desiring to take the deposition of any person upon oral examination shall give reasonable notice in writing to every other party to the action. The notice shall state the time and place for taking the deposition and the name and address of each person to be examined, if known, and, if the name is not known, a general description sufficient to identify the person or the particular class or group to which the person belongs. If a subpoena duces tecum is to be served on the person to be examined, the designation of the materials to be produced under the subpoena shall be attached to or included in the notice.

(2) Leave of court is not required for the taking of a deposition by plaintiff if the notice states that the person to be examined is about to go out of the state and will be unavailable for examination unless a deposition is taken before expiration of the 30–day period under subdivision (a). If a party shows that when served with notice under this subdivision that party was unable through the exercise of diligence to obtain counsel to represent the party at the taking of the deposition, the deposition may not be used against that party.

(3) For cause shown the court may enlarge or shorten the time for taking the deposition.

(4) Any deposition may be recorded by videotape without leave of the court or stipulation of the parties, provided the deposition is taken in accordance with this subdivision.

(A) Notice. A party intending to videotape a deposition shall state in the notice that the deposition is to be videotaped and shall give the name and address of the operator. Any subpoena served on the person to be examined shall state the method or methods for recording the testimony.

(B) Stenographer. Videotaped depositions shall also be recorded stenographically, unless all parties agree otherwise.

(C) Procedure. At the beginning of the deposition, the officer before whom it is taken shall, on camera: (i) identify the style of the action, (ii) state the date, and (iii) swear the witness.

(D) Custody of Tape and Copies. The attorney for the party requesting the videotaping of the deposition shall take custody of and be responsible for the safeguarding of the videotape, shall permit the viewing of it by the opposing party, and, if requested, shall provide a copy of the videotape at the expense of the party requesting the copy.

(E) Cost of Videotaped Depositions. The party requesting the videotaping shall bear the initial cost of videotaping.

(5) The notice to a party deponent may be accompanied by a request made in compliance with rule 1.350 for the production of documents and tangible things at the taking of the deposition. The procedure of rule 1.350 shall apply to the request. Rule 1.351 provides the exclusive procedure for obtaining documents or things by subpoena from nonparties without deposing the custodian or other person in possession of the documents.

(6) In the notice a party may name as the deponent a public or private corporation, a partnership or association, or a governmental agency, and designate with reasonable particularity the matters on which examination is requested. The organization so named shall designate one or more officers, directors, or managing agents, or other persons who consent to do so, to testify on its behalf and may state the matters on which each person designated will testify. The persons so designated shall testify about matters known or reasonably available to the organization. This subdivision does not preclude taking a deposition by any other procedure authorized in these rules.

(7) On motion the court may order that the testimony at a deposition be taken by telephone. The order may prescribe the manner in which the deposition will be taken. A party may also arrange for a stenographic transcription at that party's own initial expense.

(8) Any minor subpoenaed for testimony shall have the right to be accompanied by a parent or guardian at all times during the taking of testimony notwithstanding the invocation of the rule of sequestration of section 90.616, Florida Statutes, except upon a showing that the presence of a parent or guardian is likely to have a material, negative impact on the credibility or accuracy of the minor's testimony, or that the interests of the parent or guardian are in actual or potential conflict with the interests of the minor.

(c) Examination and Cross–Examination; Record of Examination; Oath; Objections. Examination and cross-examination of witnesses may proceed as permitted at the trial. The officer before whom the deposition is to be taken shall put the witness on oath and shall personally, or by someone acting under the officer's direction and in the officer's presence, record the testimony of the witness, except that when a deposition is being taken by telephone, the witness shall be sworn by a person present with the witness who is qualified to administer an oath in that location. The testimony shall be taken stenographically or recorded by any other means ordered in accordance with subdivision (b)(4) of this rule. If requested by one of the parties, the testimony shall be transcribed at the initial cost of the requesting party and prompt notice of the request shall be given to all other parties. All objections made at time of the examination to the qualifications of the officer taking the deposition, the manner of taking it, the evidence presented, or the conduct of any party, and any other objection to the proceedings shall be noted by the officer upon the deposition. Any objection during a deposition shall be stated concisely and in a nonargumentative and nonsuggestive manner. A party may instruct a deponent not to answer only when necessary to preserve a privilege, to enforce a limitation on evidence directed by the court, or to present a motion under subdivision (d). Otherwise, evidence objected to shall be taken subject to the objections. Instead of participating in the oral examination, parties may serve written questions in a sealed envelope on the party taking the deposition and that party shall transmit them to the officer, who shall propound them to the witness and record the answers verbatim.

(d) Motion to Terminate or Limit Examination. At any time during the taking of the deposition, on motion of a party or of the deponent and upon a showing that the examination is being conducted in bad faith or in such manner as unreasonably to annoy, embarrass, or oppress the deponent or party, or that objection and instruction to a deponent not to answer are being made in violation of rule 1.310(c), the court in which the action is pending or the circuit court where the deposition is being taken may order the officer conducting the examination to cease forthwith from taking the deposition or may limit the scope and manner of the taking of the deposition under rule 1.280(c). If the order terminates the examination, it shall be resumed thereafter only upon the order of the court in which the action is pending. Upon demand of any party or the deponent, the taking of the deposition shall be suspended for the time necessary to make a motion for an order. The provisions of rule 1.380(a) apply to the award of expenses incurred in relation to the motion.

(e) Witness Review. If the testimony is transcribed, the transcript shall be furnished to the witness for examination and shall be read to or by the witness unless the examination and reading are waived by the witness and by the parties. Any changes in form or substance that the witness wants to make shall be listed in writing by the officer with a statement of the reasons given by the witness for making the changes. The changes shall be attached to the transcript. It shall then be signed by the witness unless the parties waived the signing or the witness is ill, cannot be found, or refuses to sign. If the transcript is not signed by the witness within a reasonable time after it is furnished to the witness, the officer shall sign the transcript and state on the transcript the waiver, illness, absence of the witness, or refusal to sign with any reasons given therefor. The deposition may then be used as fully as though signed unless the court holds that the reasons given for the refusal to sign require rejection of the deposition wholly or partly, on motion under rule 1.330(d)(4).

(f) Filing; Exhibits.

(1) If the deposition is transcribed, the officer shall certify on each copy of the deposition that the witness was duly sworn by the officer and that the deposition is a true record of the testimony given by the witness. Documents and things produced for inspection during the examination of the witness shall be marked for identification and annexed to and returned with the deposition upon the request of a party, and may be inspected and copied by any party, except that the person producing the materials may substitute copies to be marked for identification if that person affords to all parties fair opportunity to verify the copies by comparison with the originals. If the person producing the materials requests their return, the officer shall mark them, give each party an opportunity to inspect and copy them, and return them to the person producing them and the materials may then be used in the same manner as if annexed to and returned with the deposition.

(2) Upon payment of reasonable charges therefor the officer shall furnish a copy of the deposition to any party or to the deponent.

(3) A copy of a deposition may be filed only under the following circumstances:

(A) It may be filed in compliance with Florida Rule of Judicial Administration 2.425 and rule 1.280(f) by a party or the witness when the contents of the deposition must be considered by the court on any matter pending before the court. Prompt notice of the filing of the deposition shall be given to all parties unless notice is waived. A party filing the deposition shall furnish a copy of the deposition or the part being filed to other parties unless the party already has a copy.

(B) If the court determines that a deposition previously taken is necessary for the decision of a matter pending before the court, the court may order that a copy be filed by any party at the initial cost of the party, and the filing party shall comply with rules 2.425 and 1.280(f).

(g) Obtaining Copies. A party or witness who does not have a copy of the deposition may obtain it from the officer taking the deposition unless the court orders otherwise. If the deposition is obtained from a person other than the officer, the reasonable cost of reproducing the copies shall be paid to the person by the requesting party or witness.

(h) Failure to Attend or to Serve Subpoena; Expenses.

(1) If the party giving the notice of the taking of a deposition fails to attend and proceed therewith and another party attends in person or by attorney pursuant to the notice, the court may order the party giving the notice to pay to the other party the reasonable

expenses incurred by the other party and the other party's attorney in attending, including reasonable attorneys' fees.

(2) If the party giving the notice of the taking of a deposition of a witness fails to serve a subpoena upon the witness and the witness because of the failure does not attend and if another party attends in person or by attorney because that other party expects the deposition of that witness to be taken, the court may order the party giving the notice to pay to the other party the reasonable expenses incurred by that other party and that other party's attorney in attending, including reasonable attorneys' fees.

Amended July 26, 1972, effective Jan. 1, 1973 (265 So.2d 21); Dec. 13, 1976, effective Jan. 1, 1977 (339 So.2d 626); June 14, 1979, effective July 1, 1979 (372 So.2d 449); Sept. 10, 1981, effective Jan. 1, 1982 (403 So.2d 926); Sept. 13, 1984, effective Jan. 1, 1985 (458 So.2d 245); Oct. 6, 1988, effective Jan. 1, 1989 (536 So.2d 974); July 16, 1992, effective Jan. 1, 1993 (604 So.2d 1110); Oct. 31, 1996, effective Jan. 1, 1997 (682 So.2d 105); Oct. 5, 2000, effective Jan. 1, 2001 (773 So.2d 1098); Sept. 27, 2007, effective Jan. 1, 2008 (966 So.2d 943); Sept. 8, 2010, effective Jan. 1, 2011 (52 So.3d 579); Nov. 3, 2011, effective, *nunc pro tunc*, Oct. 1, 2011 (78 So.3d 1045).

Committee Notes

1972 Amendment. Derived from Federal Rule of Civil Procedure 30 as amended in 1970. Subdivision (a) is derived from rule 1.280(a); subdivision (b) from rule 1.310(a) with additional matter added; the first sentence of subdivision (c) has been added and clarifying language added throughout the remainder of the rule.

1976 Amendment. Subdivision (b)(4) has been amended to allow the taking of a videotaped deposition as a matter of right. Provisions for the taxation of costs and the entry of a standard order are included as well. This new amendment allows the contemporaneous stenographic transcription of a videotaped deposition.

1988 Amendment. The amendments to subdivision (b)(4) are to provide for depositions by videotape as a matter of right.

The notice provision is to ensure that specific notice is given that the deposition will be videotaped and to disclose the identity of the operator. It was decided not to make special provision for a number of days' notice.

The requirement that a stenographer be present (who is also the person likely to be swearing the deponent) is to ensure the availability of a transcript (although not required). The transcript would be a tool to ensure the accuracy of the videotape and thus eliminate the need to establish other procedures aimed at the same objective (like time clocks in the picture and the like). This does not mean that a transcript must be made. As at ordinary depositions, this would be up to the litigants.

Technical videotaping procedures were not included. It is anticipated that technical problems may be addressed by the court on motions to quash or motions for protective orders.

Subdivision (c) has been amended to accommodate the taking of depositions by telephone. The amendment requires the deponent to be sworn by a person authorized to administer oaths in the deponent's location and who is present with the deponent.

1992 Amendment. Subdivision (b)(4)(D) is amended to clarify an ambiguity in whether the cost of the videotape copy is to be borne by the party requesting the videotaping or by the party requesting the copy. The amendment requires the party requesting the copy to bear the cost of the copy.

1996 Amendment. Subdivision (c) is amended to state the existing law, which authorizes attorneys to instruct deponents not to answer questions only in specific situations. This amendment is derived from Federal Rule of Civil Procedure 30(d) as amended in 1993.

2010 Amendment. Subdivision (b)(5) is amended to clarify that the procedure set forth in rule 1.351 must be followed when requesting or receiving documents or things without testimony, from nonparties pursuant to a subpoena. The amendment is intended to prevent the use of rules 1.310 and 1.410 to request documents from nonparties pursuant to a subpoena without giving the opposing party the opportunity to object to the subpoena before it is served on the nonparty as required by rule 1.351.

2011 Amendment. A reference to Florida Rule of Judicial Administration 2.425 and rule 1.280(f) is added to require persons filing discovery materials with the court to make sure that good cause exists prior to filing discovery materials and that certain specific personal information is redacted.

Court Commentary

1984 Amendment. Subdivision (b)(7) is added to authorize deposition by telephone, with provision for any party to have a stenographic transcription at that party's own initial expense.

Subdivision (d) is changed to permit any party to terminate the deposition, not just the objecting party.

Subdivision (e) is changed to eliminate the confusing requirement that a transcript be submitted to the witness. The term has been construed as requiring the court reporter to travel, if necessary, to the witness, and creates a problem when a witness is deposed in Florida and thereafter leaves the state before signing. The change is intended to permit the parties and the court reporter to handle such situations on an ad hoc basis as is most appropriate.

Subdivision (f) is the committee's action in response to the petition seeking amendment to rule 1.310(f) filed in the Supreme Court Case No. 62,699. Subdivision (f) is changed to clarify the need for furnishing copies when a deposition, or part of it, is properly filed, to authorize the court to require a deposition to be both transcribed and filed, and to specify that a party who does not obtain a copy of the deposition may get it from the court reporter unless ordered otherwise by the court. This eliminates the present requirement of furnishing a copy of the deposition, or material part of it, to a person who already has a copy in subdivision (f)(3)(A).

Subdivision (f)(3)(B) broadens the authority of the court to require the filing of a deposition that has been taken, but not transcribed.

Subdivision (g) requires a party to obtain a copy of the deposition from the court reporter unless the court orders otherwise. Generally, the court should not order a party who has a copy of the deposition to furnish it to someone who has neglected to obtain it when the deposition was transcribed. The person should obtain it from the court reporter unless there is a good reason why it cannot be obtained from the reporter.

Authors' Comment—1967

Rule 1.310 is the same as former Rule 1.24, 1954 Rules of Civil Procedure, as per amendment effective January 1, 1966. It is closely patterned after Federal Rule 30 and thus the excellent analysis found in 2A Barron and Holtzoff, Federal Practice and Procedure, Rules Edition (West 1961) should be carefully analyzed.

Rules 1.310 and 1.320 set out the procedure for taking depositions authorized by Rule 1.280 if they are taken during pendency of an action, and by Rule 1.290 if they are taken before action or pending appeal. Rule 1.310 applies if the depositions are taken upon oral examination, and Rule 1.320 if they are taken upon written interrogatories.

Notice

Under Rule 1.310(a) a party desiring to take the deposition of any person upon oral examination shall give a reasonable notice to every other party.

What is a "reasonable" time will depend upon the facts of each case. Any party upon whom the notice is served may move the court, upon cause shown, to shorten or enlarge the time.

The place for the taking of the deposition of a person other than a party must be selected with Rule 1.410(d)(2)[1] in mind, which limits the place at which a witness may be subpoenaed to attend an examination. The prospective witness may, of course, volunteer to attend an examination at a place where he could not by subpoena be compelled to attend, and such place may be stated in the notice; but the examining party takes all the risk of the witness' nonappearance at the designated place.

It is not necessary to subpoena a party to attend the taking of his deposition; the service of the notice upon his attorney is sufficient to require attendance. If the party does not appear for the taking of his deposition, he is not subject to punishment for contempt of court unless a subpoena was served upon him, but he is subject to the procedural penalties prescribed in Rule 1.380, which should afford sufficient sanctions to compel attendance. Consequently, Rule 1.410(d)(2)[1] does not control the place of the examination of a party, although it controls the effectiveness of a subpoena served upon a party; and a party may be required to attend his examination at any place, subject to timely motion made under Rule 1.310(b) to change the place of examination. Rule 1.310(b) affords means of keeping the examining party within reasonable limits in setting the place of examination of a party.

The notice of the taking of a deposition must state the name and address of each person to be examined, if known. The purpose is to enable the other parties to prepare for cross-examination. But in order to give the discovery aspect of the deposition procedure a wide application, the rule permits, in lieu of the name of the prospective witness, a general description sufficient to identify him or the particular class or group to which he belongs. In view of the penalties provided by Rule 1.310(g), a party should, when the name of the witness is known to another party, obtain it in advance by interrogatories under Rule 1.340.

The notice need not state the name of the person before whom the deposition will be taken, but such statement is the better practice. If the name of the officer is stated, his unavailability may be protected against by adding the phrase, "or before some other officer authorized by law to take depositions".

The notice need not state the subject matter of the examination. Such statement, if made, will limit the examining party accordingly.

Objections

All objections made at the time of the taking of the depositions must be noted by the officer upon or attached to the depositions. All testimony objected to must be taken subject to the objection.

Protection of Parties and Witnesses

Abuse of the almost unlimited scope of examination permitted by Rule 1.280 is safeguarded against by orders made for the protection of parties and witnesses before the examination or production under this rule, and orders made during the examination under Rule 1.310. These rules give the court broad powers to control the use of the discovery procedures, and the exercise of these powers lies in the discretion of the court. Liberality in the exercise of its powers is directed to prevent abuses of the discovery procedures.

A few points may be emphasized:

(a) A party or witness to be examined may not arbitrarily refuse to attend the examination without becoming subject to the penalties prescribed by Rules 1.380 and 1.410. If there exists any objection to the examination, application should be seasonably made under this rule. Either the party or the prospective witness may make such application.

(b) Application for the protective order is made to the court in which the action is pending. The protection authorized by Rule 1.310(d), during the taking of the examination, may be applied for in the court in which the action is pending or the circuit court where the deposition is being taken.

(c) "Seasonably" means as soon as the party or prospective witness learns of the need for a protective order.

(d) The moving party or prospective witness must show "good cause" for the issuance of the order. What is good cause will vary with the nature of the protective order requested. The power of the court, however, is to be exercised with liberality toward the accomplishment of the purpose of the rule to protect parties and witnesses from abuses of the discovery procedures.

(e) The rule lists nine specific types of orders and the general catch-all order "which justice requires to protect the party or witness from annoyance, expense, embarrassment or oppression".

Place of Taking Deposition

Frequently the question arises as to the right of a defendant to take the deposition of a plaintiff who resides outside the jurisdiction of the court where the cause is pending. Under Federal Rule 30, the federal courts have required the plaintiff to appear for deposition on notice of the defendant in the district where the cause is pending, even though the plaintiff may have to travel a long distance unless good cause is shown to the contrary, and a strict view is taken of this. Sometimes the court makes an alternative provision that the plaintiff's deposition may be taken at the place of his residence on condition that the expenses of the defendant's attorney and a reasonable counsel fee in an amount fixed by the court be paid by the plaintiff. Groll v. Stulkin, 12 F.R.D. 262 (1951).

In Montgomery v. Sheldon, 16 F.R.D. 34 (1954), the court said:

"The general rule is that a plaintiff, having chosen the forum, must submit to oral examination within the district that he has chosen." (Plaintiff required to travel from State of Washington to New York.)

And in Slade v. Transatlantic Financing Corporation, 21 F.R.D. 146 (1957), it was stated:

"The rule is well settled that a nonresident plaintiff who chooses this forum makes himself available to examination here in the absence of a showing of unreasonable hardship or in the presence of special circumstances (plaintiff required to travel from London to New York).

The federal courts usually deny the request that plaintiff's deposition be taken by written interrogatories instead of orally, upon the ground that an oral deposition presents greater advantages for discovery. In Solomon v. Teitelbaum, 9 F.R.D. 515 (1949), the court said:

"Nor does it appear where the plaintiffs, having embarked upon this litigation, should not assume all the incidents thereof which the law contemplates."

In Ormond Beach First National Bank v. Montgomery Roofing Company, 189 So.2d 239 (D.C.A.1st 1966), the court held that the officers or managing agents of a corporate plaintiff may ordinarily be required to testify on deposition in the county of the forum. This ruling appears to be sound and there does not appear to be any reason why it should not be applied with equal force to an individual plaintiff. The court recognized that under the rule (now 1.310(b)) for good cause shown the trial court may order that the plaintiff's deposition shall be taken in the county other than that of the forum.

Protection During Course of Examination

The rule provides for protective orders upon motion of any party or witness during the taking of the deposition. There must be a showing that the examination is being conducted in bad faith or in such manner as unreasonably to annoy, embarrass, or oppress the witness or party. The court order may stop the examination or may limit the scope and manner of the taking of the deposition as provided in Rule 1.310(b).

The motion may be made in the court in which the action is pending or the circuit court where the deposition is being taken. When the deposition is being taken out of the state, it would seem that the motion can be made only to the court where the action is pending. The courts might well consider that this situation would warrant a broad application of Rule 1.310(b) as a preventative against the evils condemned by Rule 1.310(d). In any event, the objecting party or witness may demand the suspension of the examination for the time necessary to make a motion for an order.

The last sentence [of Rule 1.310(d)] gives the court power to impose costs or expenses upon either party or upon the witness. In granting the motion, the court may impose costs upon the party taking the deposition for abusing the discovery procedures. In denying the motion, the court may impose costs upon the objecting party or witness if no substantial basis existed for the motion.

If the protective order terminates the taking of the deposition, the examination may be resumed only upon the order of the court in which the action is pending.

Signature and Changes

Changes in the deposition desired by the witness should be made, not be erasure, but by the officer's entering the change on the deposition with the witness' reasons therefor.

The amendments may be of substance as well as of form. The procedure is not applicable to errors made in reporting or transcribing the proceedings. These should be remedied, not by changing, but by correcting the deposition before it is finally certified by the reporter and the officer.

The examination of the transcribed deposition and the reading of it to the witness may be waived only by the witness and the parties jointly. This waiver provision might be convenient when the examination and reading would require another meeting of the parties, the witness, and the officer taking the deposition. Many attorneys oppose the use of the waiver provision as a matter of general policy.

Under paragraph (e) if the reading and signing is to be waived a stipulation to that effect should be incorporated in the stenographic record.

Subpoenas

To avoid being assessed with costs it is recommended that all witnesses be served with subpoenas, then if the witnesses do not appear the party is not liable for costs.

Transcription, Certification and Filing

The rule should be read with Rule 1.330, providing for waiver of errors and irregularities as to the completion and return of the deposition unless a motion to suppress the deposition or some part thereof is made with reasonable promptness after such defect is, or with due diligence might have been, ascertained.

* * * *

While requiring the filing of the deposition with the clerk is essential to its availability for use at the trial, there seems to be no good reason why the filing of a deposition taken solely for discovery purposes cannot be waived. The stipulation of waiver should be signed by all parties, since any party may make use of the deposition at the trial.

* * * *

1 Probably should read Rule 1.410(e)(2).

Rule 1.320. Depositions Upon Written Questions

(a) Serving Questions; Notice. After commencement of the action any party may take the testimony of any person, including a party, by deposition upon written questions. The attendance of witnesses may be compelled by the use of subpoena as provided in rule 1.410. The deposition of a person confined in prison may be taken only by leave of court on such terms as the court prescribes. A party desiring to take a deposition upon written questions shall serve them with a notice stating (1) the name and address of the person who is to answer them, if known, and, if the name is not known, a general description sufficient to identify the person or the particular class or group to which that person belongs, and (2) the name or descriptive title and address of the officer before whom the deposition is to be taken. A deposition upon written questions may be taken of a public or private corporation, a partnership or association, or a governmental agency in accordance with rule 1.310(b)(6). Within 30 days after the notice and written questions are served, a party may serve cross questions upon all other parties. Within 10 days after being served with cross questions, a party may serve redirect questions upon all other parties. Within 10 days after being served with redirect questions, a party may serve recross questions upon all other parties. The court may for cause shown enlarge or shorten the time.

(b) Officer to Take Responses and Prepare Record. A copy of the notice and copies of all questions served shall be delivered by the party taking the depositions to the officer designated in the notice, who shall proceed promptly to take the testimony of the witness in the manner provided by rules 1.310(c), (e), and (f) in response to the questions and to prepare the deposition, attaching the copy of the notice and the questions received by the officer. The questions shall not be filed separately from the deposition unless a party seeks to have the court consider the questions before the questions are submitted to the witness.

Amended July 26, 1972, effective Jan. 1, 1973 (265 So.2d 21); Sept. 10, 1981, effective Jan. 1, 1982 (403 So.2d 926); July 16, 1992, effective Jan. 1, 1993 (604 So.2d 1110).

Committee Notes

1972 Amendment. Derived from Federal Rule of Civil Procedure 31 as amended in 1970. The name of interrogatories has been changed to questions to avoid confusion with interrogatories to parties under rule 1.340. Language changes resulting from the rearrangement of the discovery rules have been inserted and subdivision (d) deleted.

Authors' Comment—1967

The scope of the examination upon written interrogatories is the same as upon oral examination and any matter regarding which a deponent may be examined by oral interrogation may be the subject of written interrogatories.

While the scope of the examination upon written interrogatories is the same as upon oral examination, the procedure for taking depositions on written interrogatories will perhaps be little used for the purpose of discovery because an interrogatory process does not well lend itself to discovery. Its principal use would appear to be to interrogate friendly witnesses at a distance when it is inconvenient to call them and the party taking the deposition knows what their testimony is going to be.

Under the rule, the deposition by interrogatories is taken in the same manner as an oral deposition, i.e., by written notice served upon all other parties stating that the deposition is to be taken before a named or described officer upon the interrogatories served by the parties upon one another. No application need be made to the court except where the plaintiff seeks to take the deposition within 20 days after service of process on the defendant; and the procedure may be utilized whether the witness is within or without the state.

The notice requirements differ from those for the notice of taking a deposition by oral examination. * * * * The name or descriptive title and the address of the officer before whom the deposition is to be taken must be stated in the notice. Time and place for the taking of the deposition need not be stated, but it is proper to state the place if it differs from the address of the officer.

The proposed interrogatories must be served on every party involved in the action. Cross interrogatories and redirect and recross interrogatories are permitted.

Objections to the form of written interrogatories are waived, under Rule 1.330, unless served in writing upon the party propounding them within the time allowed for serving the responsive interrogatories or within three days after service of the last interrogatories authorized.

When objections to the form of the interrogatories are made, the party may reframe the questions to remove the objections or he may leave them unchanged and have the questions presented to the witness subject to the objections. The objections may be renewed at the trial if the deposition is then offered for use.

A copy of the notice and copies of all interrogatories served between the parties are then delivered by the party taking the deposition to the officer designated in the notice. Rule 1.320(b). This should be done as soon as practicable after all interrogatories have been served. The presence of the witness may be required by subpoena.

The testimony of the witness responding to the interrogatories must be read and signed by the witness unless the reading and signing is waived. The notice and the interrogatories must be attached to the deposition. If witness fails or refuses to sign, the deposition must so indicate. See Rule 1.310(e).

The witness is subpoenaed as provided in Rule 1.410(d).

Rule 1.330. Use of Depositions in Court Proceedings

(a) Use of Depositions. At the trial or upon the hearing of a motion or an interlocutory proceeding, any part or all of a deposition may be used against any party who was present or represented at the taking of the deposition or who had reasonable notice of it so far as admissible under the rules of evidence applied as though the witness were then present and testifying in accordance with any of the following provisions:

(1) Any deposition may be used by any party for the purpose of contradicting or impeaching the testimony of the deponent as a witness or for any purpose permitted by the Florida Evidence Code.

(2) The deposition of a party or of anyone who at the time of taking the deposition was an officer, director, or managing agent or a person designated under rule 1.310(b)(6) or 1.320(a) to testify on behalf of a public or private corporation, a partnership or association, or a governmental agency that is a party may be used by an adverse party for any purpose.

(3) The deposition of a witness, whether or not a party, may be used by any party for any purpose if the court finds: (A) that the witness is dead; (B) that the witness is at a greater distance than 100 miles from the place of trial or hearing, or is out of the state, unless it appears that the absence of the witness was procured by the party offering the deposition; (C) that the witness is unable to attend or testify because of age, illness, infirmity, or imprisonment; (D) that the party offering the deposition has been unable to procure the attendance of the witness by subpoena; (E) upon application and notice, that such exceptional circumstances exist as to make it desirable, in the interest of justice and with due regard to the importance of presenting the testimony of witnesses orally in open court, to allow the deposition to be used; or (F) the witness is an expert or skilled witness.

(4) If only part of a deposition is offered in evidence by a party, an adverse party may require the party to introduce any other part that in fairness ought to be considered with the part introduced, and any party may introduce any other parts.

(5) Substitution of parties pursuant to rule 1.260 does not affect the right to use depositions previously taken and, when an action in any court of the United States or of any state has been dismissed and another action involving the same subject matter is afterward brought between the same parties or their representatives or successors in interest, all depositions lawfully taken and duly filed in the former action may be used in the latter as if originally taken for it.

(6) If a civil action is afterward brought, all depositions lawfully taken in a medical liability mediation proceeding may be used in the civil action as if originally taken for it.

(b) Objections to Admissibility. Subject to the provisions of rule 1.300(b) and subdivision (d)(3) of this rule, objection may be made at the trial or hearing to receiving in evidence any deposition or part of it for any reason that would require the exclusion of the evidence if the witness were then present and testifying.

(c) Effect of Taking or Using Depositions. A party does not make a person the party's own witness for any purpose by taking the person's deposition. The introduction in evidence of the deposition or any part of it for any purpose other than that of contradicting or impeaching the deponent makes the deponent the witness of the party introducing the deposition, but this shall not apply to the use by an adverse party of a deposition under subdivision (a)(2) of this rule. At the trial or hearing any party may rebut any relevant evidence contained in a deposition whether introduced by that party or by any other party.

(d) Effect of Errors and Irregularities.

(1) *As to Notice.* All errors and irregularities in the notice for taking a deposition are waived unless written objection is promptly served upon the party giving the notice.

(2) *As to Disqualification of Officer.* Objection to taking a deposition because of disqualification of the officer before whom it is to be taken is waived unless made before the taking of the deposition begins or as soon thereafter as the disqualification becomes known or could be discovered with reasonable diligence.

(3) *As to Taking of Deposition.*

(A) Objections to the competency of a witness or to the competency, relevancy, or materiality of testimony are not waived by failure to make them before or during the taking of the deposition unless the ground of the objection is one that might have been obviated or removed if presented at that time.

(B) Errors and irregularities occurring at the oral examination in the manner of taking the deposition, in the form of the questions or answers, in the oath or affirmation, or in the conduct of parties and errors of any kind that might be obviated, removed, or cured if promptly presented are waived unless timely objection to them is made at the taking of the deposition.

(C) Objections to the form of written questions submitted under rule 1.320 are waived unless served in writing upon the party propounding them within the time allowed for serving the succeeding cross or other questions and within 10 days after service of the last questions authorized.

(4) *As to Completion and Return.* Errors and irregularities in the manner in which the testimony is transcribed or the deposition is prepared, signed, certified, or otherwise dealt with by the officer under rules 1.310 and 1.320 are waived unless a motion to suppress the deposition or some part of it is made with reasonable promptness after the defect is, or with due diligence might have been, discovered.

Amended July 26, 1972, effective Jan. 1, 1973 (265 So.2d 21); July 14, 1977, effective Sept. 1, 1977 (348 So.2d 325); Sept. 10, 1981, effective Jan. 1, 1982 (403 So.2d 926); July 16, 1992, effective Jan. 1, 1993 (604 So.2d 1110); Oct. 1, 1998 (718 So.2d 795).

Committee Notes

1972 Amendment. Derived from Federal Rule of Civil Procedure 32 as amended in 1970. Subdivisions (a), (b), and (c) are former rules 1.280(d), (f), and (g) respectively. Subdivision (d) is derived from the entire former rule 1.330.

1998 Amendment. Subdivision (a)(1) was amended to clarify that, in addition to the uses of depositions prescribed by these rules, depositions may be used for any purpose permitted by the Florida Evidence Code (chapter 90, Fla. Stat.). This amendment is consistent with the 1980 amendment to Rule 32 of the Federal Rules of Civil Procedure.

Authors' Comment—1967

* * * *

Objections to the notice of taking a deposition are waived unless written objection is promptly served upon the party giving the notice. There is no justification for allowing a party served with a notice to permit the deposition to be taken and then move to suppress the deposition because of errors and irregularities in the notice. Objection should be made in time for correction.

In terms of timely objections to testimony at the time of the taking of the deposition, Evans v. Perry, 161 So.2d 27 (D.C.A.2d 1964) specifically held that a party must object at the deposition, and it was too late to interpose objections at trial, since the ground of objection could have been obviated if made at the time of the deposition. Failure to object constituted a waiver.

Rule 1.300(d) specifies grounds which disqualify an officer or a stenographer.

Paragraph (d) deals only with matters after the testimony has been taken stenographically; it has no application to any of the matters covered by (a), (b) and (c) inclusive.

Rule 1.340. Interrogatories to Parties

(a) Procedure for Use. Without leave of court, any party may serve upon any other party written interrogatories to be answered (1) by the party to whom the interrogatories are directed, or (2) if that party is a public or private corporation or partnership or association or governmental agency, by any officer or agent, who shall furnish the information available to that party. Interrogatories may be served on the plaintiff after commencement of the action and on any other party with or after service of the process and initial pleading upon that party. The interrogatories shall not exceed 30, including all subparts, unless the court permits a larger number on motion and notice and for good cause. If the supreme court has approved a form of interrogatories for the type of action, the initial interrogatories on a subject included therein shall be from the form approved by the court. A party may serve fewer than all of the approved interrogatories within a form. Other interrogatories may be added to the approved forms without leave of court, so long as the total of approved and additional interrogatories does not exceed 30. Each interrogatory shall be answered separately and fully in writing under oath unless it is objected to, in which event the grounds for objection shall be stated and signed by the attorney making it. The party to whom the interrogatories are directed shall serve the answers and any objections within 30 days after the service of the interrogatories, except that a defendant may serve answers or objections within 45 days after service of the process and initial pleading upon that defendant. The court may allow a shorter or longer time. The party submitting the interrogatories may move for an order under rule 1.380(a) on any objection to or other failure to answer an interrogatory.

(b) Scope; Use at Trial. Interrogatories may relate to any matters that can be inquired into under rule 1.280(b), and the answers may be used to the extent permitted by the rules of evidence except as otherwise provided in this subdivision. An interrogatory otherwise proper is not objectionable merely because an answer to the interrogatory involves an opinion or contention that relates to fact or calls for a conclusion or asks for information not within the personal knowledge of the party. A party shall respond to such an interrogatory by giving the information the party has and the source on which the information is based. Such a qualified answer may not be used as direct evidence for or impeachment against the party giving the answer unless the court finds it otherwise admissible under the rules of evidence. If a party introduces an answer to an interrogatory, any other party may require that party to introduce any other interrogatory and answer that in fairness ought to be considered with it.

(c) Option to Produce Records. When the answer to an interrogatory may be derived or ascertained from the records (including electronically stored information) of the party to whom the interrogatory is directed or from an examination, audit, or inspection of the records or from a compilation, abstract, or summary based on the records and the burden of deriving or ascertaining the answer is substantially the same for the party serving the interrogatory as for the party to whom it is directed, an answer to the interrogatory specifying the records from which the answer may be derived or ascertained and offering to give the party serving the interrogatory a reasonable opportunity to examine, audit, or inspect the records and to make copies, compilations, abstracts, or summaries is a sufficient answer. An answer shall be in sufficient detail to permit the interrogating party to locate and to identify, as readily as can the party interrogated, the records from which the answer may be derived or ascertained, or shall identify a person or persons representing the interrogated party who will be available to assist the interrogating party in locating and identifying the records at the time they are produced. If the records to be produced consist of electronically stored information, the records shall be produced in a form or forms in which they are ordinarily maintained or in a reasonably usable form or forms.

(d) Effect on Co-Party. Answers made by a party shall not be binding on a co-party.

(e) Service and Filing. Interrogatories shall be arranged so that a blank space is provided after each separately numbered interrogatory. The space shall be reasonably sufficient to enable the answering party to insert the answer within the space. If sufficient space is not provided, the answering party may attach additional papers with answers and refer to them in the space provided in the interrogatories. The interrogatories shall be served on the party to whom the interrogatories are directed and copies shall be served on all other parties. A certificate of service of the interrogatories shall be filed, giving the date of service and the name of the party to whom they were directed. The answers to the interrogatories shall be served upon the party originally propounding the interrogatories and a copy shall be served on all other parties by the answering party. The original or any copy of the answers to interrogatories may be filed in compliance with Florida Rule of Judicial Administration 2.425 and rule 1.280(g) by any party when the court should consider the answers to interrogatories in determining any matter pending before the court. The court may order a copy of the answers to interrogatories filed at any time when the court determines that examination of the answers to interrogatories is necessary to determine any matter pending before the court.

Amended June 19, 1968, effective Oct. 1, 1968 (211 So.2d 206); July 26, 1972, effective Jan. 1, 1973 (265 So.2d 21); Dec. 13, 1976, effective Jan. 1, 1977 (339 So.2d 626); July 14, 1977, effective Sept. 1, 1977 (348 So.2d 325); Oct. 9, 1980, effective Jan. 1, 1981 (391 So.2d 165); Sept. 10, 1981, effective Jan. 1, 1982 (403 So.2d 926); Nov. 12, 1981, effective Jan. 1, 1982 (407 So.2d 197); Sept. 13, 1984, effective Jan. 1, 1985 (458 So.2d 245); Oct. 6, 1988, effective Jan. 1, 1989 (536 So.2d 974); July 16, 1992, effective Jan. 1, 1993 (604 So.2d 1110); Sept. 8, 2010, effective Jan. 1, 2011 (52 So.3d 579); Nov. 3, 2011, effective, *nunc pro tunc*, Oct. 1, 2011 (78 So.3d 1045); July 5, 2012, effective Sept. 1, 2012 (95 So.3d 76).

Committee Notes

1972 Amendment. Subdivisions (a), (b), and (c) are derived from Federal Rule of Civil Procedure 33 as amended in 1970. Changes from the existing rule expand the time for answering, permit interrogatories to be served with the initial pleading or at any time thereafter, and eliminate the requirement of a hearing on objections. If objections are made, the interrogating party has the responsibility of setting a hearing if that party wants an answer. If the interrogatories are not sufficiently important, the interrogating party may let the matter drop. Subdivision (b) covers the same matter as the present rule 1.340(b) except those parts that have been transferred to rule 1.280. It also eliminates the confusion between facts and opinions or contentions by requiring that all be given. Subdivision (c) gives the interrogated party an option to produce business records from which the interrogating party can derive the answers to questions. Subdivision (d) is former subdivision (c) without change. Former subdivision (d) is repealed because it is covered in rule 1.280(e). Subdivision (e) is derived from the New Jersey rules and is intended to place both the interrogatories and the answers to them in a convenient place in the court file so that they can be referred to with less confusion. The requirement for filing a copy before the answers are received is necessary in the event of a dispute concerning what was done or the appropriate times involved.

1988 Amendment. The word "initial" in the 1984 amendment to subdivision (a) resulted in some confusion, so it has been deleted. Also the total number of interrogatories which may be propounded without leave of court is enlarged to 30 from 25. Form interrogatories which have been approved by the supreme court must be used; and those so used, with their subparts, are included in the total number permitted. The amendments are not intended to change any other requirement of the rule.

2011 Amendment. A reference to Florida Rule of Judicial Administration 2.425 and rule 1.280(f) is added to require persons filing discovery materials with the court to make sure that good cause exists prior to filing discovery materials and that certain specific personal information is redacted.

2012 Amendment. Subdivision (c) is amended to provide for the production of electronically stored information in answer to interrogatories and to set out a procedure for determining the form in which to produce electronically stored information.

Court Commentary

1984 Amendment. Subdivision (a) is amended by adding the reference to approved forms of interrogatories. The intent is to eliminate the burden of unnecessary interrogatories.

Subdivision (c) is amended to add the requirement of detail in identifying records when they are produced as an alternative to answering the interrogatory or to designate the persons who will locate the records.

Subdivision (e) is changed to eliminate the requirement of serving an original and a copy of the interrogatories and of the answers in light of the 1981 amendment that no longer permits filing except in special circumstances.

Subdivision (f) is deleted since the Medical Liability Mediation Proceedings have been eliminated.

Authors' Comment—1967

The rule is the same as former Rule 1.27, 1954 Rules of Civil Procedure, as per amendment effective January 1, 1966. This latter amendment lengthened the time for service of answers to interrogatories from 15 days to 20 days, after the service of the interrogatories. The rule is closely patterned after Federal Rule 33, and 2A Barron and Holtzoff, Federal Practice and Procedure, Rules Edition (West 1961) contains an excellent analysis of the interpretations under the similar federal pre-trial discovery method, which should be consulted.

Interrogatories under this rule may be addressed only to a party. Other persons, including a party's attorney, may be examined only by deposition.

Interrogatories to parties under this rule are simpler and less expensive than the taking of a deposition by oral examination or written interrogatories, and are well adapted to actions involving small amounts of money and to obtaining simple facts or information that will be helpful in determining whether other discovery procedures should be used.

The scope of the examination is the same as that afforded by Rule 1.280 for the taking of a deposition. An excellent discussion on the limits of the permissible scope of discovery by interrogatories, as well as as on the limits of the trial court's wide discretion appears in Charles Sales Corp. v. Rovenger, 88 So.2d 551 (Fla.1956).

Interrogatories to parties governed by Rule 1.340 must be carefully distinguished from depositions upon interrogatories under Rule 1.320. Depositions upon interrogatories represent testimony taken out of court before an officer upon notice and under oath, with the right to cross-examine by means of cross-interrogatories. In interrogatories to parties there is no provision for cross-examination, A list of questions is prepared, served upon the adverse party, answers are given and that concludes the examination. Further, the deposition of any person, whether a party or not, may be taken upon interrogatories while interrogatories to parties can be addressed only to parties.

In a landmark case in Florida, Passino v. Sanburn, 190 So.2d 61 (D.C.A.3, 1966), the court held that interrogatories under the Florida Rules of Civil Procedure are continuing in nature, i.e., the answering party is required to furnish appropriate information to the proponent after answers to the interrogatories have been filed.

One of the purposes of interrogatories to parties is to obtain admissions and thus limit subjects of controversy at trial and avoid unnecessary testimony and waste of time in preparation. Another purpose is to provide information which will be useful when taking said party's deposition.

Inasmuch as the interrogatories are submitted directly to the adverse party without the intervention of an officer or the use of cross interrogatories, this method if discovery represents an inexpensive means of securing useful information in preparation for trial or depositions.

The fact that the information needed to answer an interrogatory is within the sole knowledge of the attorney for the party is not a valid objection. The Supreme Court of Florida ruled in Dupree v. Better Way, 86 So.2d 425 (1956), that a party must answer an interrogatory seeking names and addresses of any other persons known by the plaintiff or his attorney to have knowledge of facts pertaining to an accident, against a contention that such information was privileged and the work product of his attorneys. The court held that such inquiry was within the scope of examination permitted by Rule 1.280(b), and thus, the attorney could not have refused to comply.

Under Rule 1.340, an officer or agent of a corporation, partnership or association who answers interrogatories must "furnish such information as is available to the party" on whose behalf he answers. This means that an officer or agent, who has not sufficient familiarity with the facts to answer the interrogatories either as of knowledge or on information, as may be the case in some large corporations, is required to make such inquiry as will enable him to supply the answers, when the information is accessible to the company on whose behalf he answers, as for example, where the information called for in the interrogatories is contained in the company's files.

The Federal courts are split on the question whether copies of documents may be required to be attached to answers to interrogatories. As to documents not exempt, the better reasoning supports the view that copies need not be so supplied. Such a practice would nullify the provisions of Rule 1.350 requiring a motion and order of the court to produce documents upon a showing of good cause. Furthermore, the burden of time and expense in producing the copy would be shifted from the examining party, as under Rule 1.350, to the party interrogated. * * * *

Interrogatories can be served by a defendant before he is required to file an answer. While there does not appear to be a general rule which extends the time within which a pleading must be filed or an action taken when a motion has been made or when interrogatories have been served, it must necessarily follow that there is a suspension of time or a tolling of time within which to file the pleading or to take the action. Rule 1.090(b) would support an application for the extension of time. Interrogatories may be served after a deposition has been taken and a deposition may be taken after interrogatories have been answered.

Frequent attempts have been made under Rule 1.340 to require a party to furnish a "witness list." That is, not only give the names and addresses of persons having knowledge of relevant facts but the names of witnesses which the party or his attorney plans to use on trial. The federal cases are divided on this problem, but under the Federal Rule 33 corresponding to Rule 1.340 most of them have held that a party cannot be compelled to state the names of all witnesses who he would use at trial and thus commit himself in advance. (2A Barron and Holtzoff, Federal Practice and Procedure, Rules Edition, Section 766 (West 1961)).

The Florida Supreme Court has held in Rose v. Yuille, 88 So.2d 318 (1956) that the court has the power to require a "witness list" on pretrial (see comment and notes under Rule 1.200). It has not yet gone so far as to permit witness lists under Rule 1.340. In view of the findings of the Federal Rule Advisory Committee on this problem it is believed that Rule 1.340 should neither be construed nor amended to permit "witness lists" to be demanded. The Circuit Courts are evidently going both ways on the problem. Probably most of them will sustain objections to an interrogatory calling for a "witness list."

Failure to answer interrogatories subjects the defaulting party to severe penalties under Rule 1.380, within the sound judicial discretion of the court, but such discretion is also limited, as noted in State Road Department v. Hufford, 161 So.2d 35 (D.C.A.1st 1964).

Rule 1.350. Production of Documents and Things and Entry Upon Land for Inspection and Other Purposes

(a) Request; Scope. Any party may request any other party (1) to produce and permit the party making the request, or someone acting in the requesting party's behalf, to inspect and copy any designated documents, including electronically stored information, writings, drawings, graphs, charts, photographs, phono-records, and other data compilations from which information can be obtained, translated, if necessary, by the party to whom the request is directed through detection devices into reasonably usable form, that constitute or contain matters within the scope of rule 1.280(b) and that are in the possession, custody, or control of the party to whom the request is directed; (2) to inspect and copy, test, or sample any tangible things that constitute or contain matters within the scope of rule 1.280(b) and that are in the possession, custody, or control of the party to whom the request is directed; or (3) to permit entry upon designated land or other property in the possession or control of the party upon whom the request is served for the purpose of inspection and measuring, surveying, photographing, testing, or sampling the property or any designated object or operation on it within the scope of rule 1.280(b).

(b) Procedure. Without leave of court the request may be served on the plaintiff after commencement of the action and on any other party with or after service of the process and initial pleading on that party. The request shall set forth the items to be inspected, either by individual item or category, and describe each item and category with reasonable particularity. The request shall specify a reasonable time, place, and manner of making the inspection or performing the related acts. The party to whom the request is directed shall serve a written response within 30 days after service of the request, except that a defendant may serve a response within 45 days after service of the process and initial pleading on that defendant. The court may allow a shorter or longer time. For each item or category the response shall state that inspection and related activities will be permitted as requested unless the request is objected to, in which event the reasons for the objection shall be stated. If an objection is made to part of an item or category, the part shall be specified. When producing documents, the producing party shall either produce them as they are kept in the usual course of business or shall identify them to correspond with the categories in the request. A request for electronically stored information may specify the form or forms in which electronically stored information is to be produced. If the responding party objects to a requested form, or if no form is specified in the request, the responding party must state the form or forms it intends to use. If a request for electronically stored information does not specify the form of production, the producing party must produce the information in a form or forms in which it is ordinarily maintained or in a reasonably usable form or forms. The party submitting the request may move for an order under rule 1.380 concerning any objection, failure to respond to the request, or any part of it, or failure to permit the inspection as requested.

(c) Persons Not Parties. This rule does not preclude an independent action against a person not a party for production of documents and things and permission to enter upon land.

(d) Filing of Documents. Unless required by the court, a party shall not file any of the documents or things produced with the response. Documents or things may be filed in compliance with Florida Rule of Judicial Administration 2.425 and rule 1.280(g) when they should be considered by the court in determining a matter pending before the court.

Amended July 26, 1972, effective Jan. 1, 1973 (265 So.2d 21); Oct. 9, 1980, effective Jan. 1, 1981 (391 So.2d 165); Sept. 10, 1981, effective Jan. 1, 1982 (403 So.2d 926); July 16, 1992, effective Jan. 1, 1993 (604 So.2d 1110); Nov. 3, 2011, effective, *nunc pro tunc*, Oct. 1, 2011 (78 So.3d 1045); July 5, 2012, effective Sept. 1, 2012 (95 So.3d 76).

Committee Notes

1972 Amendment. Derived from Federal Rule of Civil Procedure 34 as amended in 1970. The new rule eliminates the good cause requirement of the former rule, changes the time for making the request and responding to it, and changes the procedure for the response. If no objection to the discovery is made, inspection is had without a court order. While the good cause requirement has been eliminated, the change is not intended to overrule cases limiting discovery under this rule to the scope of ordinary discovery, nor is it intended to overrule cases limiting unreasonable requests such as those reviewed in *Van Devere v. Holmes,* 156 So.2d 899 (Fla.3d DCA 1963); *IBM v. Elder,* 187 So.2d 82 (Fla.3d DCA 1966); and *Miami v. Florida Public Service Commission,* 226 So.2d 217 (Fla.1969). It is intended that the court review each objection and weigh the need for discovery and the likely results of it against the right of privacy of the party or witness or custodian.

1980 Amendment. Subdivision (b) is amended to require production of documents as they are kept in the usual course of business or in accordance with the categories in the request.

2011 Amendment. A reference to Florida Rule of Judicial Administration 2.425 and rule 1.280(f) is added to require persons filing discovery materials with the court to make sure that good cause exists prior to filing discovery materials and that certain specific personal information is redacted.

2012 Amendment. Subdivision (a) is amended to address the production of electronically stored information. Subdivision (b) is amended to set out a procedure for determining the form to be used in producing electronically stored information.

Rule 1.351. Production of Documents and Things Without Deposition

(a) Request; Scope. A party may seek inspection and copying of any documents or things within the scope of rule 1.350(a) from a person who is not a party by issuance of a subpoena directing the production of the documents or things when the requesting party does not seek to depose the custodian or other person in possession of the documents or things. This rule provides the exclusive procedure for obtaining documents or things by subpoena from nonparties without deposing the custodian or other person in possession of the documents or things pursuant to rule 1.310.

(b) Procedure. A party desiring production under this rule shall serve notice as provided in rule 1.080 on every other party of the intent to serve a subpoena under this rule at least 10 days before the subpoena is issued if service is by delivery and 15 days before the subpoena is issued if the service is by mail or e-mail. The proposed subpoena shall be attached to the notice and shall state the time, place, and method for production of the documents or things, and the name and address of the person who is to produce the documents or things, if known, and if not known, a general description sufficient to identify the person or the particular class or group to which the person belongs; shall include a designation of the items to be produced; and shall state that the person who will be asked to produce the documents or things has the right to object to the production under this rule and that the person will not be required to surrender the documents or things. A copy of the notice and proposed subpoena shall not be furnished to the person upon whom the subpoena is to be served. If any party serves an objection to production under this rule within 10 days of service of the notice, the documents or things shall not be produced pending resolution of the objection in accordance with subdivision (d).

(c) Subpoena. If no objection is made by a party under subdivision (b), an attorney of record in the action may issue a subpoena or the party desiring production shall deliver to the clerk for issuance a subpoena together with a certificate of counsel or pro se party that no timely objection has been received from any party, and the clerk shall issue the subpoena and deliver it to the party desiring production. Service within the state of Florida of a nonparty subpoena shall be deemed sufficient if it complies with rule 1.410(d) or if (1) service is accomplished by mail or hand delivery by a commercial delivery service, and (2) written confirmation of delivery, with the date of service and the name and signature of the person accepting the subpoena, is obtained and filed by the party seeking production. The subpoena shall be identical to the copy attached to the notice and shall specify that no testimony may be taken and shall require only production of the documents or things specified in it. The subpoena may give the recipient an option to deliver or mail legible copies of the documents or things to the party serving the subpoena. The person upon whom the subpoena is served may condition the preparation of copies on the payment in advance of the reasonable costs of preparing the copies. The subpoena shall require production only in the county of the residence of the custodian or other person in possession of the documents or things or in the county where the documents or things are located or where the custodian or person in possession usually conducts business. If the person upon whom the subpoena is served objects at any time before the production of the documents or things, the documents or things shall not be produced under this rule, and relief may be obtained pursuant to rule 1.310.

(d) Ruling on Objection. If an objection is made by a party under subdivision (b), the party desiring production may file a motion with the court seeking a ruling on the objection or may proceed pursuant to rule 1.310.

(e) Copies Furnished. If the subpoena is complied with by delivery or mailing of copies as provided in subdivision (c), the party receiving the copies shall furnish a legible copy of each item furnished to any other party who requests it upon the payment of the reasonable cost of preparing the copies.

(f) Independent Action. This rule does not affect the right of any party to bring an independent action for production of documents and things or permission to enter upon land.

Added Oct. 9, 1980, effective Jan. 1, 1981 (391 So.2d 165). Amended July 16, 1992, effective Jan. 1, 1993 (604 So.2d 1110); Oct. 31, 1996, effective Jan. 1, 1997 (682 So.2d 105); Sept. 27, 2007, effective Jan. 1, 2008 (966 So.2d 943); Sept. 8, 2010, effective Jan. 1, 2011 (52 So.3d 579); Oct. 18, 2012, effective, *nunc pro tunc*, Sept. 1, 2012 (102 So.3d 505).

Committee Notes

1980 Adoption. This rule is designed to eliminate the need of taking a deposition of a records custodian when the person seeking discovery wants copies of the records only. It authorizes objections by any other party as well as the custodian of the records. If any person objects, recourse must be had to rule 1.310.

1996 Amendment. This rule was amended to avoid premature production of documents by nonparties, to clarify the clerk's role in the process, and to further clarify that any objection to the use of this rule does not contemplate a hearing before the court but directs the party to rule 1.310 to obtain the desired production. This amendment is not intended to preclude all communication between parties and nonparties. It is intended only to prohibit a party from prematurely sending to a nonparty a copy of the required notice or the proposed subpoena. This rule was also amended along with rule 1.410 to allow attorneys to issue subpoenas. See Committee Note for rule 1.410.

2007 Amendment. Subdivisions (b) and (d) were amended to permit a party seeking nonparty discovery to have other parties' objections resolved by the court.

2010 Amendment. Subdivision (a) is amended to clarify that the procedure set forth in rule 1.351, not rule 1.310, shall be followed when requesting or receiving documents or things, without testimony, from nonparties pursuant to a subpoena.

2012 Amendment. Subdivision (b) is amended to include e-mail service as provided in Fla. R. Jud. Admin. 2.516.

Rule 1.360. Examination of Persons

(a) Request; Scope.

(1) A party may request any other party to submit to, or to produce a person in that other party's custody or legal control for, examination by a qualified expert when the condition that is the subject of the requested examination is in controversy.

(A) When the physical condition of a party or other person under subdivision (a)(1) is in controversy, the request may be served on the plaintiff without leave of court after commencement of the action, and on any other person with or after service of the process and initial pleading on that party. The request shall specify a reasonable time, place, manner, conditions, and scope of the examination and the person or persons by whom the examination is to be made. The party to whom the request is directed shall serve a response within 30 days after service of the request, except that a defendant need not serve a response until 45 days after service of the process and initial pleading on that defendant. The court may allow a shorter or longer time. The response shall state that the examination will be permitted as requested unless the request is objected to, in which event the reasons for the objection shall be stated. If the examination is to be recorded or observed by others, the request or response shall also include the number of people attending, their role, and the method or methods of recording.

(B) In cases where the condition in controversy is not physical, a party may move for an examination by a qualified expert as in subdivision (a)(1). The order for examination shall be made only after notice to the person to be examined and to all parties, and shall specify the time, place, manner, conditions, and scope of the examination and the person or persons by whom it is to be made.

(C) Any minor required to submit to examination pursuant to this rule shall have the right to be accompanied by a parent or guardian at all times during the examination, except upon a showing that the presence of a parent or guardian is likely to have a material, negative impact on the minor's examination.

(2) An examination under this rule is authorized only when the party submitting the request has good cause for the examination. At any hearing the party submitting the request shall have the burden of showing good cause.

(3) Upon request of either the party requesting the examination or the party or person to be examined, the court may establish protective rules governing such examination.

(b) Report of Examiner.

(1) If requested by the party to whom a request for examination or against whom an order is made under subdivision (a)(1)(A) or (a)(1)(B) or by the person examined, the party requesting the examination to be made shall deliver to the other party a copy of a detailed written report of the examiner setting out the examiner's findings, including results of all tests made, diagnosis, and conclusions, with similar reports of all earlier examinations of the same condition. After delivery of the detailed written report, the party requesting the examination to be made shall be entitled upon request to receive from the party to whom the request for examination or against whom the order is made a similar report of any examination of the same condition previously or thereafter made, unless in the case of a report of examination of a person not a party the party shows the inability to obtain it. On motion, the court may order delivery of a report on such terms as are just; and if an examiner fails or refuses to make a report, the court may exclude the examiner's testimony if offered at the trial.

(2) By requesting and obtaining a report of the examination so ordered or requested or by taking the deposition of the examiner, the party examined waives any privilege that party may have in that action or any other involving the same controversy regarding the testimony of every other person who has examined or may thereafter examine that party concerning the same condition.

(3) This subdivision applies to examinations made by agreement of the parties unless the agreement provides otherwise. This subdivision does not preclude discovery of a report of an examiner or taking the deposition of the examiner in accordance with any other rule.

(c) Examiner as Witness. The examiner may be called as a witness by any party to the action, but shall not be identified as appointed by the court.

Amended July 26, 1972, effective Jan. 1, 1973 (265 So.2d 21); Oct. 6, 1988, effective Jan. 1, 1989 (536 So.2d 974); July 16, 1992, effective Jan. 1, 1993 (604 So.2d 1110); July 7, 1995, effective Jan. 1, 1996 (663 So.2d 1047); Nov. 22, 1995, effective Jan. 1, 1996 (663 So.2d 1049); Sept. 27, 2007, effective Jan. 1, 2008 (966 So.2d 943); Sept. 8, 2010, effective Jan. 1, 2011 (52 So.3d 579).

Committee Notes

1972 Amendment. Derived from Federal Rule of Civil Procedure 35 as amended in 1970. The good cause requirement under this rule has been retained so that the requirements of *Schlagenhauf v. Holder*, 379 U.S. 104, 85 S.Ct. 234, 13 L.Ed.2d 152 (1964), have not been affected. Subdivision (b) is changed to make it clear that reports can be obtained whether an order for the examination has been entered or not and that all earlier reports of the same condition can also be obtained.

1988 Amendment. This amendment to subdivision (a) is intended to broaden the scope of rule 1.360 to accommodate the examination of a person by experts other than physicians.

Authors' Comment—1967

Rule 1.360 is the same as former Rule 1.29, 1954 Rules of Civil Procedure and quite similar to Federal Rule 35. As such, 2A Barron and Holtzoff, Federal Practice and Procedure, Rules Edition (West 1961) should be consulted.

It should be noted that the order of the court may be made only on good cause shown, and failure to show good cause by the moving party will defeat the issuance of the order. By operation of Rule 1.380(b)(2)(iv), a party is protected from arrest for disobeying an order under this rule, although remaining subject to the other consequences for failure to comply with the order.

Under the practice heretofore in Florida many attorneys have arranged between themselves for examinations without the entry of any order and such practice is not prohibited by this rule. The order provided for under this rule makes it possible to obtain a copy of the physician's report. This rule is not mandatory, the granting of the order is discretionary.

If the examined party takes advantage of this rule, he becomes obligated to furnish all of his medical reports. The plaintiff's physician holds the key to this rule because if he refuses to make the report available the only penalty is that his testimony is barred. Thus the examined person could obtain from the defendant the report of the defendant's physician and then not furnish reports made by his, the plaintiff's physician if that physician fails or refuses to make such report.

Rule 1.370. Requests for Admission

(a) Request for Admission. A party may serve upon any other party a written request for the admission of the truth of any matters within the scope of rule 1.280(b) set forth in the request that relate to statements or opinions of fact or of the application of law to fact, including the genuineness of any documents described in the request. Copies of documents shall be served with the request unless they have been or are otherwise furnished or made available for inspection and copying. Without leave of court the request may be served upon the plaintiff after commencement of the action and upon any other party with or after service of the process and initial pleading upon that party. The request for admission shall not exceed 30 requests, including all subparts, unless the court permits a larger number on motion and notice and for good cause, or the parties propounding and responding to the requests stipulate to a larger number. Each matter of which an admission is requested shall be separately set forth. The matter is admitted unless the party to whom the request is directed serves upon the party requesting the admission a written answer or objection addressed to the matter within 30 days after service of the request or such shorter or longer time as the court may allow but, unless the court shortens the time, a defendant shall not be required to serve answers or objections before the expiration of 45 days after service of the process and initial pleading upon the defendant. If objection is made, the reasons shall be stated. The answer shall specifically deny the matter or set forth in detail the reasons why the answering party cannot truthfully admit or deny the matter. A denial shall fairly meet the substance of the requested admission, and when good faith requires that a party qualify an answer or deny only a part of the matter of which an admission is requested, the party shall specify so much of it as is true and qualify or deny the remainder. An answering party may not give lack of information or knowledge as a reason for failure to admit or deny unless that party states that that party has made reasonable inquiry and that the information known or readily obtainable by that party is insufficient to enable that party to admit or deny. A party who considers that a matter of which an admission has been requested presents a genuine issue for trial may not object to the request on that ground alone; the party may deny the matter or set forth reasons why the party cannot admit or deny it, subject to rule 1.380(c). The party who has requested the admissions may move to determine the sufficiency of the answers or objections. Unless the court determines that an objection is justified, it shall order that an answer be served. If the court determines that an answer does not comply with the requirements of this rule, it may order either that the matter is admitted or that an amended answer be served. Instead of these orders the court may determine that final disposition of the request be made at a pretrial conference or at a designated time before trial. The provisions of rule 1.380(a)(4) apply to the award of expenses incurred in relation to the motion.

(b) Effect of Admission. Any matter admitted under this rule is conclusively established unless the court on motion permits withdrawal or amendment of the admission. Subject to rule 1.200 governing amendment of a pretrial order, the court may permit withdrawal or amendment when the presentation of the merits of the action will be subserved by it and the party who obtained the admission fails to satisfy the court that withdrawal or amendment will prejudice that party in maintaining an action or defense on the merits. Any admission made by a party under this rule is for the purpose of the pending action only and is not an admission for any other purpose nor may it be used against that party in any other proceeding.

Amended June 19, 1968, effective Oct. 1, 1968 (211 So.2d 206); Oct. 1, 1970 (237 So.2d 151); July 26, 1972, effective Jan. 1, 1973 (265 So.2d 21); July 16, 1992, effective Jan. 1, 1993 (604 So.2d 1110); Oct. 23, 2003, effective Jan. 1, 2004 (858 So.2d 1013).

Committee Notes

1972 Amendment. Derived from Federal Rule of Civil Procedure 36 as amended in 1970. The rule is changed to eliminate distinctions between questions of opinion, fact, and mixed questions. The time sequences are changed in accordance with the other discovery rules, and case law is incorporated by providing for amendment and withdrawal of the answers and for judicial scrutiny to determine the sufficiency of the answers.

2003 Amendment. The total number of requests for admission that may be served without leave of court is limited to 30, including all subparts.

Authors' Comment—1967

Rule 1.370 is the same as former Rule 1.30, 1954 Rules of Civil Procedure, as per amendment effective January 1, 1966. The only significant change in said amended rule and present rule from the original 1954 rule is the extension of time to not less than twenty [now thirty] days after service for response to avoid a requested admission from being admitted, in lieu of the former ten day period. The rule is substantially the same as Federal Rule 36, with the exception that the federal rule contains the ten day period after service for response to avoid the admission of requested matters. Therefore, 2A Barron and Holtzoff, Federal Practice and Procedure, Rules Edition (West 1961) should be consulted for a persuasive analysis of the federal counterpart in view of the fact that the Florida courts adhere to the federal constructions. See McKean v. Kloeppel Hotels, Inc., 171 So.2d 552 (D.C.A.1st 1965).

The purpose of the rule is to expedite the trial of the action and to relieve the parties of the time and expense entailed in proving the genuineness of documents or the truth of matters of fact which the adverse party does not intend to litigate or which can be ascertained by reasonable inquiry. One party may not obstinately put the other to his proof. Rule 1.380(c) provides sanctions to compel admissions.

The request for admissions is addressed to the party. It may be served upon the attorney as provided in Rule 1.080 but the party should sign the statement and swear to its truth.

The admission may be made by default, or by serving a written admission upon the party requesting it, as provided in Rule 1.080, and filing the original with the clerk together with proof of service.

Affirmative action is required to avoid the requested admissions. Inadequate reasons for neither admitting nor denying are the equivalent of an admission. At the trial the party requesting the admission should prove the service of the request and the lack of answer. A motion for an order to compel the admission or a statement of reasons for refusal is not contemplated.

Under this rule, an objection may be made to part of a request for admission, but in that event the remainder of the request must be answered and conversely if a denial is made to part of a requested admission, the part denied and the part admitted should be specified. The decisions of the Federal courts are authorities in determining the application of this rule. Wider v. Carraway, 101 So.2d 13 (D.C.A.2d 1958).

As a matter of practice, the date for serving answers to requests for admissions should be designated and this should be not less than 20 [now 30] days; however, the request should designate a definite time for answering. See Campbell v. Blue, 80 So.2d 316 (S.Ct.1955).

The Federal court decisions are in disagreement as to whether a party is required to go beyond his personal knowledge and obtain from third persons the information requested. The better reasoned decisions, and the view entertained by the textwriters, is that the purpose of the rule requires that a party answer, even though he has no personal knowledge, if the means of information are within his reach. An exception to this view is recognized where the fact can be ascertained by the adverse party only from a third person who is hostile or is interested in the outcome of the action.

A plaintiff seeking an admission under this rule may need the information before a responsive pleading is filed and therefore it may be necessary to secure an extension of time to file such pleading under Rule 1.090.

The admissions made are limited to the pending action. Any attempt to use them for any other purpose can be prevented by prompt court application brought on by motion.

Summary judgment can be granted if admissions by failure to deny under this rule remove all material issues of fact from the case, but not if the admissions are uncertain. In Fink v. Powsner, 108 So.2d 324 (D.C.A.3d 1959), the court upheld a summary judgment against a defendant, where defendant's sworn admissions, coupled with an exhibit attached to the plaintiff's motion for summary judgment, resolved all issues of fact under the pleadings in plaintiff's favor.

Rule 1.380(c) provides penalties for refusal to admit if the demanding party thereof proves that which he was seeking and included therein are reasonable attorney fees.

Under certain circumstances, as recognized in Southern Railway Company v. Wood, 171 So.2d 614

(D.C.A.1st 1965) failure to deny admissions in timely fashion can be cured by utilization of Rule 1.540(b).

Rule 1.380. Failure to Make Discovery; Sanctions

(a) Motion for Order Compelling Discovery. Upon reasonable notice to other parties and all persons affected, a party may apply for an order compelling discovery as follows:

(1) *Appropriate Court.* An application for an order to a party may be made to the court in which the action is pending or in accordance with rule 1.310(d). An application for an order to a deponent who is not a party shall be made to the circuit court where the deposition is being taken.

(2) *Motion.* If a deponent fails to answer a question propounded or submitted under rule 1.310 or 1.320, or a corporation or other entity fails to make a designation under rule 1.310(b)(6) or 1.320(a), or a party fails to answer an interrogatory submitted under rule 1.340, or if a party in response to a request for inspection submitted under rule 1.350 fails to respond that inspection will be permitted as requested or fails to permit inspection as requested, or if a party in response to a request for examination of a person submitted under rule 1.360(a) objects to the examination, fails to respond that the examination will be permitted as requested, or fails to submit to or to produce a person in that party's custody or legal control for examination, the discovering party may move for an order compelling an answer, or a designation or an order compelling inspection, or an order compelling an examination in accordance with the request. The motion must include a certification that the movant, in good faith, has conferred or attempted to confer with the person or party failing to make the discovery in an effort to secure the information or material without court action. When taking a deposition on oral examination, the proponent of the question may complete or adjourn the examination before applying for an order. If the court denies the motion in whole or in part, it may make such protective order as it would have been empowered to make on a motion made pursuant to rule 1.280(c).

(3) *Evasive or Incomplete Answer.* For purposes of this subdivision an evasive or incomplete answer shall be treated as a failure to answer.

(4) *Award of Expenses of Motion.* If the motion is granted and after opportunity for hearing, the court shall require the party or deponent whose conduct necessitated the motion or the party or counsel advising the conduct to pay to the moving party the reasonable expenses incurred in obtaining the order that may include attorneys' fees, unless the court finds that the movant failed to certify in the motion that a good faith effort was made to obtain the discovery without court action, that the opposition to the motion was substantially justified, or that other circumstances make an award of expenses unjust. If the motion is denied and after opportunity for hearing, the court shall require the moving party to pay to the party or deponent who opposed the motion the reasonable expenses incurred in opposing the motion that may include attorneys' fees, unless the court finds that the making of the motion was substantially justified or that other circumstances make an award of expenses unjust. If the motion is granted in part and denied in part, the court may apportion the reasonable expenses incurred as a result of making the motion among the parties and persons.

(b) Failure to Comply with Order.

(1) If a deponent fails to be sworn or to answer a question after being directed to do so by the court, the failure may be considered a contempt of the court.

(2) If a party or an officer, director, or managing agent of a party or a person designated under rule 1.310(b)(6) or 1.320(a) to testify on behalf of a party fails to obey an order to provide or permit discovery, including an order made under subdivision (a) of this rule or rule 1.360, the court in which the action is pending may make any of the following orders:

(A) An order that the matters regarding which the questions were asked or any other designated facts shall be taken to be established for the purposes of the action in accordance with the claim of the party obtaining the order.

(B) An order refusing to allow the disobedient party to support or oppose designated claims or defenses, or prohibiting that party from introducing designated matters in evidence.

(C) An order striking out pleadings or parts of them or staying further proceedings until the order is obeyed, or dismissing the action or proceeding or any part of it, or rendering a judgment by default against the disobedient party.

(D) Instead of any of the foregoing orders or in addition to them, an order treating as a contempt of court the failure to obey any orders except an order to submit to an examination made pursuant to rule 1.360(a)(1)(B) or subdivision (a)(2) of this rule.

(E) When a party has failed to comply with an order under rule 1.360(a)(1)(B) requiring that party to produce another for examination, the orders listed in paragraphs (A), (B), and (C) of this subdivision, unless the party failing to comply shows the inability to produce the person for examination.

Instead of any of the foregoing orders or in addition to them, the court shall require the party failing to obey the order to pay the reasonable expenses caused by the failure, which may include attorneys' fees, unless the court finds that the failure was substantially justified or that other circumstances make an award of expenses unjust.

(c) Expenses on Failure to Admit. If a party fails to admit the genuineness of any document or the truth of any matter as requested under rule 1.370 and if the party requesting the admissions thereafter proves the genuineness of the document or the truth of the matter, the requesting party may file a motion for an order requiring the other party to pay the requesting party the reasonable expenses incurred in making that proof, which may include attorneys' fees. The court shall issue such an order at the time a party requesting the admissions proves the genuineness of the document or the truth of the matter, upon motion by the requesting party, unless it finds that (1) the request was held objectionable pursuant to rule 1.370(a), (2) the admission sought was of no substantial importance, or (3) there was other good reason for the failure to admit.

(d) Failure of Party to Attend at Own Deposition or Serve Answers to Interrogatories or Respond to Request for Inspection. If a party or an officer, director, or managing agent of a party or a person designated under rule 1.310(b)(6) or 1.320(a) to testify on behalf of a party fails (1) to appear before the officer who is to take the deposition after being served with a proper notice, (2) to serve answers or objections to interrogatories submitted under rule 1.340 after proper service of the interrogatories, or (3) to serve a written response to a request for inspection submitted under rule 1.350 after proper service of the request, the court in which the action is pending may take any action authorized under paragraphs (A), (B), and (C) of subdivision (b)(2) of this rule. Any motion specifying a failure under clause (2) or (3) of this subdivision shall include a certification that the movant, in good faith, has conferred or attempted to confer with the party failing to answer or respond in an effort to obtain such answer or response without court action. Instead of any order or in addition to it, the court shall require the party failing to act to pay the reasonable expenses caused by the failure, which may include attorneys' fees, unless the court finds that the failure was substantially justified or that other circumstances make an award of expenses unjust. The failure to act described in this subdivision may not be excused on the ground that the discovery sought is objectionable unless the party failing to act has applied for a protective order as provided by rule 1.280(c).

(e) Electronically Stored Information; Sanctions for Failure to Preserve. Absent exceptional circumstances, a court may not impose sanctions under these rules on a party for failing to provide electronically stored information lost as a result of the routine, good faith operation of an electronic information system.

Amended July 26, 1972, effective Jan. 1, 1973 (265 So.2d 21); Sept. 13, 1984, effective Jan. 1, 1985 (458 So.2d 245); Oct. 6, 1988, effective Jan. 1, 1989 (536 So.2d 974); July 16, 1992, effective Jan. 1, 1993 (604 So.2d 1110); Oct. 31, 1996, effective Jan. 1, 1997 (682 So.2d 105); Oct. 5, 2000, effective Jan. 1, 2001 (773 So.2d 1098); Oct. 23, 2003, effective Jan. 1, 2004 (858 So.2d 1013); Dec. 15, 2005, effective Jan. 1, 2006 (917 So.2d 176); July 5, 2012, effective Sept. 1, 2012 (95 So.3d 76); Nov. 14, 2013, effective Jan. 1, 2014 (131 So.3d 643).

Committee Notes

1972 Amendment. Derived from Federal Rule of Civil Procedure 37 as amended in 1970. Subdivision (a)(3) is new and makes it clear that an evasive or incomplete answer is a failure to answer under the rule. Other clarifying changes have been made within the general scope of the rule to ensure that complete coverage of all discovery failures is afforded.

2003 Amendment. Subdivision (c) is amended to require a court to make a ruling on a request for reimbursement at the time of the hearing on the requesting party's motion for entitlement to such relief. The court may, in its discretion, defer ruling on the amount of the costs or fees in order to hold an evidentiary hearing whenever convenient to the court and counsel.

2005 Amendment. Following the example of Federal Rule of Civil Procedure 37 as amended in 1993, language is included in subdivision (a)(2) that requires litigants to seek to resolve discovery disputes by informal means before filing a motion with the court. This requirement is based on successful experience with the federal rule as well as similar local rules of state trial courts. Subdivision (a)(4) is revised to provide that a party should not be awarded its expenses for filing a motion that might have been avoided by conferring with opposing counsel. Subdivision (d) is revised to require that, where a party failed to file any response to a rule 1.340 interrogatory or a rule 1.350 request, the discovering party should attempt to obtain such responses before filing a motion for sanctions.

2012 Amendment. Subdivision (e) is added to make clear that a party should not be sanctioned for the loss of electronic evidence due to the good-faith operation of an electronic information system; the language mirrors that of Federal Rule of Civil Procedure 37(e). Nevertheless, the good-faith requirement contained in subdivision (e) should prevent a party from exploiting the routine operation of an information system to thwart discovery obligations by allowing that operation to destroy information that party is required to preserve or produce. In determining good faith, the court may consider any steps taken by the party to comply with court orders, party agreements, or requests to preserve such information.

2013 Amendment. This rule was amended to add "substantially" before "justified" in subdivisions (a)(4), (b)(2), and (d), to make the rule internally consistent and to make it more consistent with Federal Rule of Civil Procedure 37, from which it was derived.

Authors' Comment—1967

Rule 1.380 is substantially the same as former Rule 1.31, 1954 Rules of Civil Procedure, as per amendment effective January 1, 1966, with only minor language changes. It is similar to Federal Rule 37 [as amended in 1970] and thus 2A Barron and Holtzoff, Federal Practice and Procedure, Rules Edition (West 1961) is of great significance as a guideline to apply in Florida practice.

Rule 1.380 provides the sanctions necessary to make effective the discovery procedures. On the other hand, the person to whom questions are put or upon whom requests are made is afforded substantial protection from abuses and is given opportunity to raise objections by other Rules.

Consequently, the question of the propriety of a particular discovery procedure may be presented to the court by two general routes: (1) the person from whom discovery is sought may seek protective orders or raise objections to particular interrogatories; and (2) the party seeking discovery may invoke the sanctions of Rule 1.380. For this reason, cases under the rules dealing with objections to discovery should be considered in connection with the cases under Rule 1.380 in determining whether a particular discovery may be compelled under Rule 1.380.

The rule contemplates that the officer before whom a deposition is taken may not punish for contempt for failure to answer a question and may not rule upon the admissibility of the information or evidence sought. Rule 1.310(c) provides that "Evidence objected to shall be taken subject to the objections". Objections to the admissibility of evidence are saved for the trial or hearing when the deposition is offered. If a witness refuses to answer a question propounded upon oral examination, the proponent of the question may complete the examination on other matters or may request adjournment; if a witness refuses to answer a question presented by written interrogatories, the officer notes the fact and completes the examination; the proponent of the question may then seek an order that answer be made.

Likewise, when a party has failed to answer an interrogatory submitted under Rule 1.340, the proponent of the question may apply for a similar order.

Upon failure to obey such an order the sanctions provided in Rule 1.380(b) become applicable.

These provisions for payment of expenses, including attorney fees incurred in obtaining the order or opposing the motion, are designed to discourage mere captious refusals to answer and unjustifiable applications for orders where refusals to answer are reasonable.

The rule applies when the witness has appeared for the taking of his deposition and then refuses to answer a question, or when a party refuses to answer an interrogatory submitted under Rule 1.340. If a witness, including a party has been subpoenaed and fails to appear for the taking of the deposition, an order of the court is not a prerequisite to holding him in contempt for such non-appearance. Rule 1.410 provides for contempt. If a party or an officer or managing agent of a party fails to appear for the taking of a deposition after being served with proper notice, or serves no answers to interrogatories submitted under Rule 1.340, the sanctions of Rule 1.380(d) are available.

The failure of a party or an officer or managing agent of a party to appear for the taking of a deposition or to serve answers to interrogatories must be willful to warrant an order under Rule 1.380(d). This order follows the failure to appear after being served with a proper notice or the failure to answer interrogatories properly submitted under Rule 1.340. An anticipatory order is not authorized by this rule.

If the party or an officer or managing agent of a party appears at the taking of the deposition and then refuses to answer a question, or if some interrogatories submitted under Rule 1.340 are answered and others refused or inadequately answered, the proper procedure is to secure an order under Rule 1.380(a) to compel an answer. A refusal to obey such an order, without an affirmative showing of willfulness, will entail the consequences of Rule 1.380(b), among which are the consequences authorized by this rule.

The court may in its discretion grant additional time to answer interrogatories or allow the completion of the deposition, where such action will promote just determination of the action.

It is not necessary to serve a subpoena to require the attendance of a party or an officer or managing agent of a party at the taking of a deposition. This rule provides the sanction for such attendance if proper notice has been given. The party or officer or managing agent is not personally answerable for a contempt unless he has been served with a subpoena; the contempt proceedings are then governed by Rule 1.410.

Although this rule provides for a contempt if a witness refuses to be sworn, an affirmation by a witness who objects to taking an oath should not subject such a witness to a contempt charge on the ground of refusing to be sworn. This rule covers depositions and interrogatories. A refusal to answer thereunder after the court has ordered that the question shall be answered may be held to be a contempt of the court ordering the answer. Subparagraph (b) of this rule only relates to Rules 1.350, 1.360, and subparagraph (a) of this rule; however subparagraph (a) of this rule covers all rules relating to depositions and interrogatories except Rule 1.370 as to admissions. Note that (b)(2) deals only with parties or their officers, or managing or authorized agents and does not deal with witnesses who are not in one of the enumerated categories. Under the four subdivisions of (b)(2) the court is given wide latitude and the penalties are far reaching and may if invoked prevent a proper presentation or a proper defense. Under (c) expenses including attorneys fees may be assessed against a party who denies the genuineness of a document or a fact which denial proves untrue. Therefore care must be exercised in deciding whether to refuse to answer or refuse to admit.

This rule by its language does not include Rule 1.370 as to admissions, except for expenses on a sworn denial where the latter is disproved by the requesting party. These penalties under Rule 1.380(c) do not apply to a failure to serve interrogatories, as carefully explained in State Road Department v. Hufford, 161 So.2d 35 (D.C.A.1st 1964). That decision further outlines the limits of judicial discretion in utilizing the severe sanctions of the rule against a defaulting party.

There is no need to apply to the court to compel answers to requests for admissions served under Rule 1.370. If no affirmative step is taken to deny the requests, or if the responses are inadequate, the facts are deemed admitted by operation of that rule.

The penalty under (d) of this rule is severe because the action can be dismissed or a default judgment can be entered. However, the entry of a default judgment against a party who wilfully fails to serve answers to interrogatories can only be applied against a defendant, quite obviously. See Rashard v. Cappiali, 171 So.2d 581 (D.C.A.3d 1965) [disapproved by Wallraff v. T.G.I. Friday's, Inc., 490 So.2d 50 (Fla., 1986)] for a complete discussion as to the sanctions against a plaintiff and the limitations thereof.

Rule 1.390. Depositions of Expert Witnesses

(a) Definition. The term "expert witness" as used herein applies exclusively to a person duly and regularly engaged in the practice of a profession who holds a professional degree from a university or college and has had special professional training and experience, or one possessed of special knowledge or skill about the subject upon which called to testify.

(b) Procedure. The testimony of an expert or skilled witness may be taken at any time before the trial in accordance with the rules for taking depositions and may be used at trial, regardless of the place of residence of the witness or whether the witness is within the distance prescribed by rule 1.330(a)(3). No special form of notice need be given that the deposition will be used for trial.

(c) Fee. An expert or skilled witness whose deposition is taken shall be allowed a witness fee in such reasonable amount as the court may determine. The court shall also determine a reasonable time within which payment must be made, if the deponent and party cannot agree. All parties and the deponent shall be served with notice of any hearing to determine the fee. Any reasonable fee paid to an expert or skilled witness may be taxed as costs.

(d) Applicability. Nothing in this rule shall prevent the taking of any deposition as otherwise provided by law.

Amended July 26, 1972, effective Jan. 1, 1973 (265 So.2d 21); Oct. 6, 1988, effective Jan. 1, 1989 (536 So.2d 974); July 16, 1992, effective Jan. 1, 1993 (604 So.2d 1110).

Committee Notes

1972 Amendment. This rule has caused more difficulty in recent years than any other discovery rule. It was enacted as a statute originally to make the presentation of expert testimony less expensive and less onerous to the expert and to admit the expert's deposition at trial regardless of the expert's residence. In spite of its intent, courts seem determined to misconstrue the plain language of the rule and cause complications that the committee and the legislature did not envisage. See *Owca v. Zemzicki,* 137 So.2d 876 (Fla.2d DCA 1962); *Cook v. Lichtblau,* 176 So.2d 523 (Fla.2d DCA 1965); and *Bondy v. West,* 219 So.2d 117 (Fla.2d DCA 1969). The committee hopes the amendment to subdivision (b) will show that the intent of the rule is to permit a deposition taken of an expert in conformity with any rule for the taking of a deposition to be admitted, if otherwise admissible under the rules of evidence, regardless of the residence of the expert. In short, the rule eliminates the necessity of any of the requirements of rule 1.330(a)(3) when the deposition offered is that of an expert.

1988 Amendment. Subdivision (c) has been amended to clarify the procedure to be used in paying an expert witness for his or her appearance at a deposition.

Authors' Comment—1967

Rule 1.390 is patterned after former Rule 1.32, 1954 Rules of Civil Procedure, as per amendment effective January 1, 1966. The original Rule 1.32, 1954 Rules of Civil Procedure, relating to depositions de bene esse was abolished by the Supreme Court of Florida in 1961 as appears in 131 So.2d 475 and 132 So.2d 6. The present rule, relating to depositions of expert witnesses altered former amended Rule 1.32 in certain respects and no longer recognizes distinctions between law and equity. A significant change is the last sentence of paragraph (b) which now adds that a deposition taken under this rule and any deposition taken of an expert witness under any other rule may be used in any manner provided for in Rule 1.280(d). This eliminates the confusion about introduction of an expert's deposition resulting from Cook v. Lichtblau, 176 So.2d 523 (D.C.A.2d 1965).

The rule is basically the same as F.S.A. § 90.23 (repealed 1967), with the addition of the last sentence of paragraph (b), as noted above. As commented on in Owca v. Zemzicki, 137 So.2d 876 (D.C.A.2d 1962), the purpose of the statute (and therefore, the present rule) is to supply an expeditious and economical means by which the costs attendant upon the use of expert witnesses might be reduced and the time of such witnesses conserved. If there is no objection to the taking of a deposition, the deposition may be used in evidence, if otherwise admissible.

Reasonable notice that such deposition is to be taken is a mandatory requirement under the rule.

By operation of Rule 1.280(d)(3) opposing counsel is under no obligation to object to the deposition until it is actually proffered, since the party taking it must assume the burden of affirmatively demonstrating that the situation falls within the confines of the circumstances set forth in the rule allowing a deposition of a witness to be used instead of the witness' presence and testimony at trial.

Upon proper objection, the court may disallow the taking of such deposition and require personal appearance at trial, if it finds such is necessary to insure a fair and impartial trial. Such objection must be made prior to the taking of the deposition. From a tactical point, counsel must decide if the deposition is preferable to the testimony of a live witness from the stand. Many subjective value judgments have to be made, depending upon the impression the expert may make by his testimony, the strength of his appearance, and other considerations. However, these factors may not become apparent until the time of the actual taking of the deposition.

See comment to Rule 1.280 regarding notice of taking depositions.

Rule 1.410. Subpoena

(a) Subpoena Generally. Subpoenas for testimony before the court, subpoenas for production of tangible evidence, and subpoenas for taking depositions may be issued by the clerk of court or by any attorney of record in an action.

(b) Subpoena for Testimony before the Court.

(1) Every subpoena for testimony before the court shall be issued by an attorney of record in an action or by the clerk under the seal of the court and shall state the name of the court and the title of the action and shall command each person to whom it is directed to attend and give testimony at a time and place specified in it.

(2) On oral request of an attorney or party and without praecipe, the clerk shall issue a subpoena for testimony before the court or a subpoena for the production of documentary evidence before the court signed and sealed but otherwise in blank, both as to the title of the action and the name of the person to whom it is directed, and the subpoena shall be filled in before service by the attorney or party.

(c) For Production of Documentary Evidence. A subpoena may also command the person to whom it is directed to produce the books, papers, documents (including electronically stored information), or tangible things designated therein, but the court, upon motion made promptly and in any event at or before the time specified in the subpoena for compliance therewith, may (1) quash or modify the subpoena if it is unreasonable and oppressive, or (2) condition denial of the motion upon the advancement by the person in whose behalf the subpoena is issued of the reasonable cost of producing the books, papers, documents, or tangible things. If a subpoena does not specify a form for producing electronically stored information, the person responding must produce it in a form or forms in which it is ordinarily maintained or in a reasonably usable form or forms. A person responding to a subpoena may object to discovery of electronically stored information from sources that the person identifies as not reasonably accessible because of undue costs or burden. On motion to compel discovery or to quash, the person from whom discovery is sought must show that the information sought or the form requested is not reasonably accessible because of undue costs or burden. If that showing is made, the court may nonetheless order discovery from such sources or in such forms if the requesting party shows good cause, considering the limitations set out in rule 1.280(d)(2). The court may specify conditions of the discovery, including ordering that some or all of the expenses of the discovery be paid by the party seeking the discovery. A party seeking a production of evidence at trial which would be subject to a subpoena may compel such production by serving a notice to produce such evidence on an adverse party as provided in rule 1.080. Such notice shall have the same effect and be subject to the same limitations as a subpoena served on the party.

(d) Service. A subpoena may be served by any person authorized by law to serve process or by any other person who is not a party and who is not less than 18 years of age. Service of a subpoena upon a person named therein shall be made as provided by law. Proof of such service shall be made by affidavit of the person making service except as applicable under rule 1.351(c) for the production of documents and things by a nonparty without deposition, if not served by an officer authorized by law to do so.

(e) Subpoena for Taking Depositions.

(1) Filing a notice to take a deposition as provided in rule 1.310(b) or 1.320(a) with a certificate of service on it showing service on all parties to the action constitutes an authorization for the issuance of subpoenas for the persons named or described in the notice by the clerk of the court in which the action is pending or by an attorney of record in the action. The subpoena shall state the method for recording the testimony. The subpoena may command the person to whom it is directed to produce designated books, papers, documents, or tangible things that constitute or contain evidence relating to any of the matters within the scope of the examination permitted by rule 1.280(b), but in that event the subpoena will be subject to the provisions of rule 1.280(c) and subdivision (c) of this rule. Within 10 days after its service, or on or before the time specified in the subpoena for compliance if the time is less than 10 days after service, the person to whom the subpoena is directed may serve written objection to inspection or copying of any of the designated materials. If objection is made, the party serving the subpoena shall not be entitled to inspect and copy the materials except pursuant to an order of the court from which the subpoena was issued. If objection has been made, the party serving the subpoena may move for an order at any time before or during the taking of the deposition upon notice to the deponent.

(2) A person may be required to attend an examination only in the county wherein the person resides or is employed or transacts business in person or at such other convenient place as may be fixed by an order of court.

(f) Contempt. Failure by any person without adequate excuse to obey a subpoena served upon that person may be deemed a contempt of the court from which the subpoena issued.

(g) Depositions before Commissioners Appointed in this State by Courts of Other States; Subpoena Powers; etc. When any person authorized by the laws of Florida to administer oaths is appointed by a court of record of any other state, jurisdiction, or government as commissioner to take the testimony of any named witness within this state, that witness may be compelled to attend and testify before that commissioner by witness subpoena issued by the clerk of any circuit court at the instance of that commissioner or by other process or proceedings in the same manner as if that commissioner had been appointed by a court of this state; provided that no document or paper writing shall be compulsorily annexed as an exhibit to such deposition or otherwise permanently removed from the possession of the witness producing it, but in lieu thereof a photostatic copy may be annexed to and transmitted with such executed commission to the court of issuance.

(h) Subpoena of Minor. Any minor subpoenaed for testimony shall have the right to be accompanied by a parent or guardian at all times during the taking of testimony notwithstanding the invocation of the rule of sequestration of section 90.616, Florida Statutes, except upon a showing that the presence of a parent or guardian is likely to have a material, negative impact on the credibility or accuracy of the minor's testimony, or that the interests of the parent or guardian are in actual or potential conflict with the interests of the minor.

Amended June 19, 1968, effective Oct. 1, 1968 (211 So.2d 206); July 26, 1972, effective Jan. 1, 1973 (265 So.2d 21); Dec. 13, 1976, effective Jan. 1, 1977 (339 So.2d 626); Oct. 9, 1980, effective Jan. 1, 1981 (391 So.2d 165); July 16, 1992, effective Jan. 1, 1993 (604 So.2d 1110); Oct. 31, 1996, effective Jan. 1, 1997 (682 So.2d 105); Sept. 27, 2007, effective Jan. 1, 2008 (966 So.2d 943); Sept. 8, 2010, effective Jan. 1, 2011 (52 So.3d 579); July 5, 2012, effective Sept. 1, 2012 (95 So.3d 76); Oct. 18, 2012, effective, *nunc pro tunc*, Sept. 1, 2012 (102 So.3d 505).

Committee Notes

1972 Amendment. Subdivisions (a) and (d) are amended to show the intent of the rule that subpoenas for deposition may not be issued in blank by the clerk, but only for trial. The reason for the distinction is valid. A subpoena for appearance before the court is not subject to abuse because the court can correct any attempt to abuse the use of blank subpoenas. Since a judge is not present at a deposition, additional protection for the parties and the deponent is required and subpoenas should not be issued in blank. Subdivision (d) is also modified to conform with the revised federal rule on subpoenas for depositions to permit an objection by the deponent to the production of material required by a subpoena to be produced.

1980 Amendment. Subdivision (c) is revised to conform with section 48.031, Florida Statutes (1979).

1996 Amendment. This rule is amended to allow an attorney (as referred to in Fla.R.Jud.Admin. 2.060(a)–(b)), as an officer of the court, and the clerk to issue subpoenas in the name of the court. This amendment is not intended to change any other requirement or precedent for the issuance or use of subpoenas. For example, a notice of taking the deposition must be filed and served before a subpoena for deposition may be issued.

2012 Amendment. Subdivision (c) is amended to reflect the relocation of the service rule from rule 1.080 to Fla. R. Jud. Admin. 2.516.

2012 Amendment. Subdivision (c) is amended to address the production of electronically stored information pursuant to a subpoena. The procedures for dealing with disputes concerning the accessibility of the information sought or the form for its production are intended to correspond to those set out in Rule 1.280(d).

Authors' Comment—1967

Rule 1.410 is similar to former Rule 1.34, 1954 Rules of Civil Procedure, as per amendment effective January 1, 1966. The amendment contained some significant changes from the original rule, with the present rule adding even more procedural clarification. Federal Rule 45 is the same in many respects, and thus 2B Barron and Holtzoff, Federal Practice and Procedure, Rules Edition (West 1961) should be consulted in terms of a comprehensive analysis of the comparable federal counterpart. The Florida courts rely on the federal courts' construction of the rule in the absence of a square holding in Florida. See Franklyn S., Inc. v. Riesenbeck, 166 So.2d 831 (D.C.A.3d 1964), wherein the court ruled that a subpoena duces tecum may run to a party at time of trial, because of the federal interpretation of the rule. However, the problem created in the trial court in that decision is now alleviated by the present rule's addition of the last two sentences to paragraph (b) concerning a notice to produce.

The rule covers subpoenas ad testificandum and duces tecum for appearance or production at a trial or hearing or at the taking of a deposition.

Rule 1.410(b) applies generally to the subpoena duces tecum, whether used for the production of documents and tangible things at the hearing or trial or at the taking of a deposition. If the subpoena calls for production at the taking of a deposition, Rule 1.410(d)(1) governs the scope of the command and affords the additional protection of Rule 1.310(b).

A distinction must be drawn between discovery under Rule 1.350 and the issuance of a subpoena duces tecum under Rule 1.410(b)(d). If it is desired to inspect, copy, or photograph documents or tangible things under the control of a party for purposes of discovery before the trial or hearing, and for the purpose of preparing for trial, good cause must be shown and an order of the court obtained under Rule 1.350. On the other hand, if a party desires the production of documents or tangible things under the control of a party or witness for use at the taking of a deposition or at the hearing or trial, good cause still must be shown but no court order need be obtained; a subpoena duces tecum issued by the clerk under Rule 1.410(b)(d) will be sufficient. As recognized in Brooker v. Smith, 108 So.2d 790 (D.C.A.2d 1959), Rules 1.350 and 1.410 are in pari materia, and a party must make a showing of good cause required by Rule 1.350 in order to utilize Rule 1.410. Such must appear in the notice to produce, as set forth in Metz v. Smith, 141 So.2d 617 (D.C.A.3d 1962).

Upon issuance to a party of a subpoena duces tecum for discovery, said party may not fail to respond, but must promptly object by motion prior to the return date, and thereupon before compliance with the subpoena duces tecum shall be required, the party causing its issuance must show good cause at a hearing on the motion. See Pembroke Park Lakes, Inc. v. High Ridge Water Co., 186 So.2d 85 (D.C.A.3d 1966) for the procedure of obtaining protection by a party from the subpoena duces tecum.

A subpoena duces tecum generally reaches all documents or tangible things under the control of the person or corporation ordered to produce, except for questions of privilege and unreasonableness. It makes no difference that a particular document or tangible thing is at a place outside the state and so without the territorial jurisdiction of the court. The witness being served within the state, the test is one of control, not of location.

Prior to 1955 F.S.A. § 91.27 gave to commissioners appointed by the courts of other states the power to issue subpoenas. This was repealed by Laws 1955, c. 29737, § 1, with the evident thought that the content of F.S.A. Chapter 91 was amply covered by the 1954 Florida Rules of Civil Procedure dealing with the taking of depositions.

The original Rule 1.34 failed to include any provision for compelling the attendance of witnesses before commissioners appointed by other courts. Therefore, effective December 1st, 1956, a new paragraph (f) was added to former Rule 1.34 to cover this problem (Fla.L.J. Nov. 1956, p. 545).

Under F.S.A. § 91.27 commissioners appointed outside the state had the same powers as commissioners appointed by courts of this state. Section 91.25 gave the commissioners themselves the power to issue subpoenas. Now the subpoena is to be issued by the Clerk of the Circuit Court at the instance of the commissioner. This apparently assumes a written request supported by a proper showing of appointment.

Service of a subpoena may now be by any person not a party who is over twenty-one years of age. This is similar to the Federal Rule, except that the latter authorizes service by one over eighteen years of age.

Although a party may move for dismissal of an action or any claim against him for failure to comply with the Rules of Civil Procedure under Rule 1.420(b), failure to obey a subpoena is punishable only by contempt, not dismissal of the complaint. However, if a party makes a motion to produce documents pursuant to Rule 1.350, then upon failure of a plaintiff to comply, the complaint may be dismissed. See Franklin Acceptance Corporation v. Superior Electrical Industries, Inc., 167 So.2d 116 (D.C.A.3d 1964), which decision also required notice.

The provisions in Rule 1.410(b) for a notice to produce at trial on an adverse party in lieu of a subpoena duces tecum being served is intended to make the procedure for obtaining documentary evidence for trial easier. However, the same protection exists for an adverse party to object and require a showing of good cause, since such notice is subject to the limitations of a subpoena.

Rule 1.420. Dismissal of Actions

(a) Voluntary Dismissal.

(1) *By Parties.* Except in actions in which property has been seized or is in the custody of the court, an action, a claim, or any part of an action or claim may be dismissed by plaintiff without order of court (A) before trial by serving, or during trial by stating on the record, a notice of dismissal at any time before a hearing on motion for summary judgment, or if none is served or if the motion is denied, before retirement of the jury in a case tried before a jury or before submission of a nonjury case to the court for decision, or (B) by filing a stipulation of dismissal signed by all current parties to the action. Unless otherwise stated in the notice or stipulation, the dismissal is without prejudice, except that a notice of dismissal operates as an adjudication on the merits when served by a plaintiff who has once dismissed in any court an action based on or including the same claim.

(2) *By Order of Court; If Counterclaim.* Except as provided in subdivision (a)(1) of this rule, an action shall not be dismissed at a party's instance except on order of the court and upon such terms and conditions as the court deems proper. If a counterclaim has been served by a defendant prior to the service upon the defendant of the plaintiff's notice of dismissal, the action shall not be dismissed against defendant's objections unless the counterclaim can remain pending for independent adjudication by the court. Unless otherwise specified in the order, a dismissal under this paragraph is without prejudice.

(b) Involuntary Dismissal. Any party may move for dismissal of an action or of any claim against that party for failure of an adverse party to comply with these rules or any order of court. Notice of hearing on the motion shall be served as required under rule 1.090(d). After a party seeking affirmative relief in an action tried by the court without a jury has completed the presentation of evidence, any other party may move for a dismissal on the ground that on the facts and the law the party seeking affirmative relief has shown no right to relief, without waiving the right to offer evidence if the motion is not granted. The court as trier of the facts may then determine them and render judgment against the party seeking affirmative relief or may decline to render judgment until the close of all the evidence. Unless the court in its order for dismissal otherwise specifies, a dismissal under this subdivision and any dismissal not provided for in this rule, other than a dismissal for lack of jurisdiction or for improper venue or for lack of an indispensable party, operates as an adjudication on the merits.

(c) Dismissal of Counterclaim, Crossclaim, or Third–Party Claim. The provisions of this rule apply to the dismissal of any counterclaim, crossclaim, or third-party claim.

(d) Costs. Costs in any action dismissed under this rule shall be assessed and judgment for costs entered in that action, once the action is concluded as to the party seeking taxation of costs. When one or more other claims remain pending following dismissal of any claim under this rule, taxable costs attributable solely to the dismissed claim may be assessed and judgment for costs in that claim entered in the action, but only when all claims are resolved at the trial court level as to the party seeking taxation of costs. If a party who has once dismissed a claim in any court of this state commences an action based upon or including the same claim against the same adverse party, the court shall make such order for the payment of costs of the claim previously dismissed as it may deem proper and shall stay the proceedings in the action until the party seeking affirmative relief has complied with the order.

(e) Failure to Prosecute. In all actions in which it appears on the face of the record that no activity by filing of pleadings, order of court, or otherwise has occurred for a period of 10 months, and no order staying the action has been issued nor stipulation for stay approved by the court, any interested person, whether a party to the action or not, the court, or the clerk of the court may serve notice to all parties that no such activity has occurred. If no such record activity has occurred within the 10 months immediately preceding the service of such notice, and no record activity occurs within the 60 days immediately following the service of such notice, and if no stay was issued or approved prior to the expiration of such 60–day period, the action shall be dismissed by the court on its own motion or on the motion of any interested person, whether a party to the action or not, after reasonable notice to the parties, unless a party shows good cause in writing at least 5 days before the hearing on the motion why the action should remain pending. Mere inaction for a period of less than 1 year shall not be sufficient cause for dismissal for failure to prosecute.

(f) Effect on Lis Pendens. If a notice of lis pendens has been filed in connection with a claim for affirmative relief that is dismissed under this rule, the notice of lis pendens connected with the dismissed claim is automatically dissolved at the same time. The notice, stipulation, or order shall be recorded.

Amended June 19, 1968, effective Oct. 1, 1968 (211 So.2d 206); Dec. 13, 1976, effective Jan. 1, 1977 (339 So.2d 626); Oct. 9, 1980, effective Jan. 1, 1981 (391 So.2d 165); Sept. 13, 1984, effective Jan. 1, 1985 (458 So.2d 245); July 16, 1992, effective Jan. 1, 1993 (604 So.2d 1110); Dec. 15, 2005, effective Jan. 1, 2006 (917 So.2d 176); Sept. 8, 2010, effective Jan. 1, 2011 (52 So.3d 579).

Committee Notes

1976 Amendment. Subdivision (e) has been amended to prevent the dismissal of an action for inactivity alone unless 1 year has elapsed since the occurrence of activity of record. Nonrecord activity will not toll the 1–year time period.

1980 Amendment. Subdivision (e) has been amended to except from the requirement of record activity a stay that is ordered or approved by the court.

1992 Amendment. Subdivision (f) is amended to provide for automatic dissolution of lis pendens on claims that are settled even though the entire action may not have been dismissed.

2005 Amendment. Subdivision (e) has been amended to provide that an action may not be dismissed for lack of prosecution without prior notice to the claimant and adequate opportunity for the claimant to re-commence prosecution of the action to avert dismissal.

Court Commentary

1984 Amendment. A perennial real property title problem occurs because of the failure to properly dispose of notices of lis pendens in the order of dismissal. Accordingly, the reference in subdivision (a)(1) to disposition of notices of lis pendens has been deleted and a separate subdivision created to automatically dissolve notices of lis pendens whenever an action is dismissed under this rule.

Author's Comment

Rule 1.420 is derived from former Rule 1.35, 1954 Rules of Civil Procedure, as per amendment effective January 1, 1966. It is similar in many respects to Federal Rule 41, and thus, 2B Barron and Holtzoff, Federal Practice and Procedure, Rules Edition (West 1961) should be analyzed for persuasive interpretations under the federal counterpart to the rule.

Paragraph (b) now specifically authorizes dismissal of an action for failure to comply with the *rules* or any order of court. It further provides *in non-jury cases,* that after the party seeking affirmative relief completes his presentation of the evidence, any other party may move to dismiss without waiving his right to offer evidence, if the motion is denied. The original rule contained no such restriction as to non-jury cases. In jury cases, such practice for an involuntary dismissal is treated the same as a motion for directed verdict, as recognized in Gibson v. Gibson, 180 So.2d 388, 392 (D.C.A.1st 1965). The last sentence of this paragraph now provides that dismissal for lack of an indispensable party shall not operate as an adjudication on the merits. This paragraph of the rule is in conformity to the Federal Rule as amended in 1963.

A plaintiff may voluntarily dismiss an action before hearing on a motion for a summary judgment or by filing a dismissal signed by all the appearing parties. An initial dismissal is without prejudice but a subsequent voluntary dismissal operates as an adjudication on the merits if the second action is based on or includes the same claim as the original action. Any other dismissal must be by court order and on terms deemed proper. A dismissal will not defeat a counterclaim previously pleaded.

Under this rule the defendant may move for an involuntary dismissal by motion. He may at conclusion of plaintiff's case except for proof of damages move for a dismissal without waiving the right to offer a defense. The defendant cannot move until the plaintiff has completed his case, however. See Sapp v. Redding, 178 So.2d 204 (D.C.A.1st 1965). The rules as to dismissals should tend to keep the calendar up to date.

Dismissals except a voluntary one constitute an adjudication on the merits unless the court provides otherwise. Nonsuits no longer are recognized in Florida, as stated in Crews v. Dobson, 177 So.2d 202 (S.Ct.1965), since the present rule eliminated such device from Florida practice as no longer necessary. However a failure to object to a voluntary nonsuit, despite the change in the rules, failure to move for dismissal with prejudice, and failure to appeal a voluntary nonsuit constitutes a waiver to a party insisting that a nonsuit order was a dismissal on the merits and thus, res judicata as to a subsequent action. See Florida East Coast Ry. Co. v. Lewis, 167 So.2d 104 (D.C.A.1st 1964), cert. denied 177 So.2d 334.

All of the subdivisions of this rule are applicable to a dismissal of a counterclaim, cross-claim or third party claim. Paragraph (a)(1) deals only with a plaintiff.

Paragraph (d) of this rule applies to any dismissal. It now mandatorily requires staying proceedings of the second action until costs of the original action are paid.

The rule initially differs from the original rule by excluding actions wherein property has been seized or is in the custody of the court. Then it should be carefully noted that a dismissal without order of court can be accomplished voluntarily by *serving* a notice of dismissal, at any time before a summary judgment hearing, in place of *filing* as required by the former rule, prior to service of an answer or of a motion for summary judgment. The present rule also permits stating on the record a notice of dismissal during trial prior to submission to trier of the facts for decision of the cause.

Paragraph (e) is new to the rules and does not appear in the Federal Rule. It is clearly adopted from F.S.A. § 45.19(1) (repealed 1967), and provides for dismissal for lack of prosecution, as well as reinstatement of dismissed actions by motion for good cause. However, such motion for reinstatement must be *served* within one month after the order of dismissal. Service as required by this rule requires compliance with Rule 1.080. Dismissal for lack of prosecution has been construed as not to be an adjudication on the merits so as to bar a subsequent suit on the same subject matter.

Third party claims are also an object of the rule now that third party practice is recognized by the rules.

Voluntary dismissals require a strong showing to be granted after a plaintiff has rested and a defendant has moved for a directed verdict.

Rule 1.430. Demand for Jury Trial; Waiver

(a) Right Preserved. The right of trial by jury as declared by the Constitution or by statute shall be preserved to the parties inviolate.

(b) Demand. Any party may demand a trial by jury of any issue triable of right by a jury by serving upon the other party a demand therefor in writing at any time after commencement of the action and not later than 10 days after the service of the last pleading directed to such issue. The demand may be indorsed upon a pleading of the party.

(c) Specification of Issues. In the demand a party may specify the issues that the party wishes so tried; otherwise, the party is deemed to demand trial by jury for all issues so triable. If a party has demanded trial by jury for only some of the issues, any other party may serve a demand for trial by jury of any other or all of the issues triable by jury 10 days after service of the demand or such lesser time as the court may order.

(d) Waiver. A party who fails to serve a demand as required by this rule waives trial by jury. If waived, a jury trial may not be granted without the consent of the parties, but the court may allow an amendment in the proceedings to demand a trial by jury or order a trial by jury on its own motion. A demand for trial by jury may not be withdrawn without the consent of the parties.

Amended July 26, 1972, effective Jan. 1, 1973 (265 So.2d 21); July 16, 1992, effective Jan. 1, 1993 (604 So.2d 1110).

Committee Notes

1972 Amendment. Subdivision (d) is amended to conform to the decisions construing it. See *Wood v. Warriner,* 62 So.2d 728 (Fla.1953); *Bittner v. Walsh,* 132 So.2d 799 (Fla.1st DCA 1961); and *Shores v. Murphy,* 88 So.2d 294 (Fla.1956). It is not intended to overrule *Wertman v. Tipping,* 166 So.2d 666 (Fla.1st DCA 1964), that requires a moving party to show justice requires a jury.

Authors' Comments—1967

Rule 1.430 is almost identical to former Rule 2.1, 1954 Rules of Civil Procedure, with certain minor language changes appearing in the new rule. This rule is now the same as Federal Rule 38 except that in Rule 1.430(d) the sentence has been inserted: "If waived, a jury trial may not be granted without the consent of the parties."

This is another situation which demonstrates that while under the Federal Rules the procedural differences between law and equity are abolished by the rules, for purposes of determining the right to a jury trial, differences between legal and equitable rights and remedies are preserved just as they are under the Florida Rules.

Whether a jury trial should be demanded will depend upon a counter-balancing of the various factors with which every counsel is familiar.

The right to a jury trial is such a fundamental right that once counsel decides it should be waived he should obtain the client's consent to the waiver.

Rule 1.430 prescribes the procedural step to be taken in order to assure the right of trial by jury. It requires that there be an affirmative demand for jury trial within 10 days after service of the last pleading directed to the issue as to which a jury trial is desired.

No form for the making of the demand is prescribed by the rule other than that it must be in writing. In the absence of any prescribed form, any form adequately expressing the demand, signed by the party or his attorney will suffice. The demand may take the form of an indorsement on a pleading filed in the action.

Of great importance is the fact that Rule 1.430 specifically provides that a party may demand a trial by jury of any issue triable of right by a jury and that the demand be served not later than ten days after the service of the "last pleading directed to such issue." The rule further establishes that the failure of a party to serve a demand as required by it shall constitute a waiver by a party of a trial by jury, and specifically if waived, a jury trial can only be granted with the consent of the parties. However, the decisions under the rule indicate that trial courts are ignoring the mandatory requirements of the rule and exercising broad discretion in subsequently allowing trial by jury, unlike the Federal decisions which consistently deny jury trials when untimely claims are made for same without proper allegation of facts to authorize it. The leading case of Fountain of Youth Broadcasting Company v. Church, 51 So.2d 728 (1951), relying upon earlier authority, indicates that the policy in Florida is to allow a broad discretion in the trial courts in granting jury trials, despite the terminology of the rule. The Supreme Court again in Shores v. Murphy, 88 So.2d 294 (1956), carefully analyzed the provisions of former Rule 2.1 and the fact that it is similar to Federal Rule 38, recognizing that the Florida Rule is even stronger and does not allow the granting of a jury trial under former Rule 2.1 after waiver, without the consent of the parties, but that the Florida courts may exercise an exceedingly broad discretion because of the fundamental nature of the right to trial by jury in ordering a jury trial in the interest of justice, regardless of the failure of a party to properly comply with the rule. The Court recognized that despite the fact that the Florida rules do not include a provision similar to Federal Rule 39 to authorize a trial judge to order a jury trial upon motion, even though neither party is entitled to a jury trial as a matter of right because of waiver that results from a failure to demand trial by jury in accordance with the Federal Rule, Rule 1.15(e) of the Florida Rules of Civil Procedure, now appearing as Rule 1.190(e), grants a trial judge broad discretion in permitting amendments in procedural matters and otherwise disregarding defects which do not affect the substantial rights of the parties, this being construed to include the discretion to order a jury trial if justice required it. Thus, the provisions of the rule requiring the consent of the parties has apparently been ignored by the Florida courts.

An interesting decision is Hightower v. Bigoney, 145 So.2d 505 (D.C.A.2d 1962), wherein the Court ruled that a defendant has no absolute right to a jury trial of the legal issues raised by his compulsory counterclaim to the plaintiff's original complaint in equity. This decision was reversed by the Supreme Court in 156 So.2d 501 (1963) wherein the court held that a compulsory counterclaim presenting a common law action entitled the counterclaimant to demand a jury trial as a matter of right.

The strictness of application of comparable Federal Rule 38, unlike the applications of the Florida Rule, is found in numerous federal decisions. The federal courts have consistently denied jury trials when the applications for same are untimely or not in accordance with the requirements of the rule. In Ward v. Brown, 301 F.2d 445 (1962), the Court of Appeals (C.A.10th) stated that the denial of an oral application for permission to file a written demand for jury trial was not error, in that a timely written demand for jury trial must be served ten days after the service of the last pleading directed to the issues; otherwise the right to a jury trial is waived. Moreover, an amended answer must inject a new issue to authorize a written demand for a jury trial. In Reeves v. Pennsylvania R. Co., 9 F.R.D. 487 (1949), the U.S. District Court refused to allow a jury trial which was demanded after the plaintiff amended her complaint almost a year after the service of an answer to her original complaint. No new issue was raised and the Court refused to exercise its discretion to grant a jury trial in the absence of any allegation of incidents or facts calling for the exercise of such discretion. See also Mack v. 48 Vesey St. Corp., 7 F.R.D. 487 (1947). Waldo Theatre Corp. v. Dondis, 1 F.R.D. 685 (1941); and Telechron, Inc. v. Parissi, 108 F.Supp. 897, 203 F.2d 454, reversed on other grounds, 349 U.S. 46, 99 L.Ed. 867, 75 S.Ct. 577 (1955).

As a practical matter, it appears that in Florida, the final decision rests with the trial judge, and that after final judgment, reversal could be obtained only by establishing that (1) the trial court abused its discretion and (2) there was error in the verdict which injured the defendant.

Rule 1.430(d) provides that "a demand for trial by jury made as herein provided may not be withdrawn without the consent of the parties."

The purpose of the latter provision is to safeguard the existence of the right of jury trial to non-demanding parties where a demand has been made by one of the parties. Without the provision one of the parties might demand a jury and then after the time for making the demand had gone by, withdraw his demand, and leave the non-demanding parties without the right to trial by jury.

Rule 1.431. Trial Jury

(a) Questionnaire.

(1) The circuit court may direct the authority charged by law with the selection of prospective jurors to furnish each prospective juror with a questionnaire

in the form approved by the supreme court from time to time to assist the authority in selecting prospective jurors. The questionnaire shall be used after the names of jurors have been selected as provided by law but before certification and the placing of the names of prospective jurors in the jury box. The questionnaire shall be used to determine those who are not qualified to serve as jurors under any statutory ground of disqualification.

(2) To assist in voir dire examination at trial, any court may direct the clerk to furnish prospective jurors selected for service with a questionnaire in the form approved by the supreme court from time to time. The prospective jurors shall be asked to complete and return the forms. Completed forms may be inspected in the clerk's office and copies shall be available in court during the voir dire examination for use by parties and the court.

(b) Examination by Parties. The parties have the right to examine jurors orally on their voir dire. The order in which the parties may examine each juror shall be determined by the court. The court may ask such questions of the jurors as it deems necessary, but the right of the parties to conduct a reasonable examination of each juror orally shall be preserved.

(c) Challenge for Cause.

(1) On motion of any party, the court shall examine any prospective juror on oath to determine whether that person is related, within the third degree, to (i) any party, (ii) the attorney of any party, or (iii) any other person or entity against whom liability or blame is alleged in the pleadings, or is related to any person alleged to have been wronged or injured by the commission of the wrong for the trial of which the juror is called, or has any interest in the action, or has formed or expressed any opinion, or is sensible of any bias or prejudice concerning it, or is an employee or has been an employee of any party or any other person or entity against whom liability or blame is alleged in the pleadings, within 30 days before the trial. A party objecting to the juror may introduce any other competent evidence to support the objection. If it appears that the juror does not stand indifferent to the action or any of the foregoing grounds of objection exists or that the juror is otherwise incompetent, another shall be called in that juror's place.

(2) The fact that any person selected for jury duty from bystanders or the body of the county and not from a jury list lawfully selected has served as a juror in the court in which that person is called at any other time within 1 year is a ground of challenge for cause.

(3) When the nature of any civil action requires a knowledge of reading, writing, and arithmetic, or any of them, to enable a juror to understand the evidence to be offered, the fact that any prospective juror does not possess the qualifications is a ground of challenge for cause.

(d) Peremptory Challenges. Each party is entitled to 3 peremptory challenges of jurors, but when the number of parties on opposite sides is unequal, the opposing parties are entitled to the same aggregate number of peremptory challenges to be determined on the basis of 3 peremptory challenges to each party on the side with the greater number of parties. The additional peremptory challenges accruing to multiple parties on the opposing side shall be divided equally among them. Any additional peremptory challenges not capable of equal division shall be exercised separately or jointly as determined by the court.

(e) Exercise of Challenges. All challenges shall be addressed to the court outside the hearing of the jury in a manner selected by the court so that the jury panel is not aware of the nature of the challenge, the party making the challenge, or the basis of the court's ruling on the challenge, if for cause.

(f) Swearing of Jurors. No one shall be sworn as a juror until the jury has been accepted by the parties or until all challenges have been exhausted.

(g) Alternate Jurors.

(1) The court may direct that 1 or 2 jurors be impaneled to sit as alternate jurors in addition to the regular panel. Alternate jurors in the order in which they are called shall replace jurors who have become unable or disqualified to perform their duties before the jury retires to consider its verdict. Alternate jurors shall be drawn in the same manner, have the same qualifications, be subject to the same examination, take the same oath, and have the same functions, powers, facilities, and privileges as principal jurors. An alternate juror who does not replace a principal juror shall be discharged when the jury retires to consider the verdict.

(2) If alternate jurors are called, each party shall be entitled to one peremptory challenge in the selection of the alternate juror or jurors, but when the number of parties on opposite sides is unequal, the opposing parties shall be entitled to the same aggregate number of peremptory challenges to be determined on the basis of 1 peremptory challenge to each party on the side with the greater number of parties. The additional peremptory challenges allowed pursuant to this subdivision may be used only against the alternate jurors. The peremptory challenges allowed pursuant to subdivision (d) of this rule shall not be used against the alternate jurors.

(h) Interview of a Juror. A party who believes that grounds for legal challenge to a verdict exist may move for an order permitting an interview of a juror or jurors to determine whether the verdict is subject to the challenge. The motion shall be served within 10 days after rendition of the verdict unless good cause is shown for the failure to make the motion within that time. The motion shall state the name and address of each juror to be interviewed and the grounds for challenge that the party believes may exist. After notice and hearing, the trial judge shall enter an order denying the motion or permitting the interview. If the interview is permitted, the court may prescribe the place, manner, conditions, and scope of the interview.

(i) Communication With the Jury. This rule governs all communication between the judge or courtroom personnel and jurors.

(1) *Communication to be on the Record.* The court shall notify the parties of any communication from the jury pertaining to the action as promptly as practicable and in any event before responding to the communication. Except as set forth below, all communications between the court or courtroom personnel and the jury shall be on the record in open court or shall be in writing and filed in the action. The court or courtroom personnel shall note on any written communication to or from the jury the date and time it was delivered.

(2) *Exception for Certain Routine Communication.* The court shall, by pretrial order or by statement on the record with opportunity for objection, set forth the scope of routine ex parte communication to be permitted and the limits imposed by the court with regard to such communication.

(A) Routine ex parte communication between the bailiff or other courtroom personnel and the jurors, limited to juror comfort and safety, may occur off the record.

(B) In no event shall ex parte communication between courtroom personnel and jurors extend to matters that may affect the outcome of the trial, including statements containing any fact or opinion concerning a party, attorney, or procedural matter or relating to any legal issue or lawsuit.

(3) *Instructions to Jury.* During voir dire, the court shall instruct the jurors and courtroom personnel regarding the limitations on communication between the court or courtroom personnel and jurors. Upon empanelling the jury, the court shall instruct the jurors that their questions are to be submitted in writing to the court, which will review them with the parties and counsel before responding.

(4) *Notification of Jury Communication.* Courtroom personnel shall immediately notify the court of any communication to or from a juror or among jurors in contravention of the court's orders or instructions, including all communication contrary to the requirements of this rule.

Added Sept. 29, 1971, effective Dec. 13, 1971 (253 So.2d 404). Amended July 31, 1973, effective Oct. 1, 1973 (281 So.2d 204); Dec. 13, 1976, effective Jan. 1, 1977 (339 So.2d 626); Oct. 9, 1980, effective Jan. 1, 1981 (391 So.2d 165); Oct. 6, 1988 and Dec. 30, 1988, effective Jan. 1, 1989 (536 So.2d 974); July 16, 1992, effective Jan. 1, 1993 (604 So.2d 1110); Dec. 15, 2005, effective Jan. 1, 2006 (917 So.2d 176); Nov. 14, 2013, effective Jan. 1, 2014 (131 So.3d 643).

Committee Notes

1971 Adoption. Subdivision (a) is new. It is intended to replace section 40.101, Florida Statutes, declared unconstitutional in *Smith v. Portante*, 212 So. 2d 298 (Fla. 1968), after supplying the deficiencies in the statute. It is intended to simplify the task of selecting prospective jurors, both for the venire and for the panel for trial in a particular action. The forms referred to in subdivision (a) are forms 1.983 and 1.984. Subdivisions (b)–(e) are sections 53.031, 53.021, 53.011, and 53.051, Florida Statutes, without substantial change.

1976 Amendment. Subdivision (e) has been added to establish a procedure for challenging jurors without members of the panel knowing the source of the challenge, to avoid prejudice. Subdivision (f) is a renumbering of the previously enacted rule regarding alternate jurors.

Subdivision (g) has been added to establish a procedure for interviewing jurors. See also Canons of Professional Responsibility DR 7–108.

1988 Amendment. Subdivision (f) has been added to ensure the right to "back-strike" prospective jurors until the entire panel has been accepted in civil cases. This right to back-strike until the jurors have been sworn has been long recognized in Florida. *Florida Rock Industries, Inc. v. United Building Systems, Inc.*, 408 So. 2d 630 (Fla. 5th DCA 1982). However, in the recent case of *Valdes v. State*, 443 So. 2d 223 (Fla. 1st DCA 1984), the court held that it was not error for a court to swear jurors one at a time as they were accepted and thereby prevent retrospective peremptory challenges. The purpose of this subdivision is to prevent the use of individual swearing of jurors in civil cases. Former subdivisions (f) and (g) have been redesignated as (g) and (h) respectively.

1992 Amendment. Subdivision (g)(2) is amended to minimize the inequity in numbers of peremptory challenges allowed in selecting alternate jurors in actions with multiple parties.

2005 Amendment. Subdivision (c)(1) is amended to ensure that prospective jurors may be challenged for cause based on bias in favor of or against nonparties against whom liability or blame may be alleged in accordance with the decisions in *Fabre v. Marin*, 623 So. 2d 1182 (Fla. 1993), or *Nash v. Wells Fargo Guard Services, Inc.*, 678 So. 2d 1262 (Fla. 1996).

2013 Amendment. Subdivision (i) governs the responsibility of the court for ensuring that parties and their counsel are aware of all contact with the jury that could affect the outcome of the case. Trial judges may have differing views on what constitutes harmless or routine ex parte communication with jurors. Reasonable variations are therefore permitted, provided the judge adequately advises counsel, before the trial begins, of the specific circumstances under which the court has determined that jury communications will not be reported to the parties. The rule does not prevent the bailiff or other courtroom personnel from discussing such routine matters as juror parking, location of break areas, how and when to assemble for duty, dress, and which items of a juror's personal property may be brought into the courthouse or jury room. However, for example, questions or remarks from a juror about such matters as the length of a witness's testimony, when court will adjourn on a given day, or how long the trial may take to complete should be reported to the judge, as these matters may be of interest to the parties. Any doubt as to whether a communication may or may not be of interest to the parties should be resolved in favor of promptly informing the court, the parties, and counsel, even if it is after the fact. This will best ensure that the parties have the opportunity to object to any improper communication and give the court an opportunity to cure any prejudice, if an objection is made.

Rule 1.440. Setting Action for Trial

(a) When at Issue. An action is at issue after any motions directed to the last pleading served have been disposed of or, if no such motions are served, 20 days after service of the last pleading. The party entitled to serve motions directed to the last pleading may waive the right to do so by filing a notice for trial at any time after the last pleading is served. The existence of crossclaims among the parties shall not prevent the court from setting the action for trial on the issues raised by the complaint, answer, and any answer to a counterclaim.

(b) Notice for Trial. Thereafter any party may file and serve a notice that the action is at issue and ready to be set for trial. The notice shall include an estimate of the time required, whether the trial is to be by a jury or not, and whether the trial is on the original action or a subsequent proceeding. The clerk shall then submit the notice and the case file to the court.

(c) Setting for Trial. If the court finds the action ready to be set for trial, it shall enter an order fixing a date for trial. Trial shall be set not less than 30 days from the service of the notice for trial. By giving the same notice the court may set an action for trial. In actions in which the damages are not liquidated, the order setting an action for trial shall be served on parties who are in default in accordance with rule 1.080.

(d) Applicability. This rule does not apply to actions to which chapter 51, Florida Statutes (1967), applies or to cases designated as complex pursuant to rule 1.201.

Amended June 19, 1968, effective Oct. 1, 1968 (211 So.2d 206); July 26, 1972, effective Jan. 1, 1973 (265 So.2d 21); Dec. 13, 1976, effective Jan. 1, 1977 (339 So.2d 626); Oct. 9, 1980, effective Jan. 1, 1981 (391 So.2d 165); Sept. 13, 1984, effective Jan. 1, 1985 (458 So.2d 245); Oct. 6, 1988, effective Jan. 1, 1989 (536 So.2d 974); July 16, 1992, effective Jan. 1, 1993 (604 So.2d 1110); June 3, 2009 (15 So.3d 558); Oct. 18, 2012, effective, *nunc pro tunc*, Sept. 1, 2012 (102 So.3d 505).

Committee Notes

1972 Amendment. All references to the pretrial conference are deleted because these are covered in rule 1.200.

1980 Amendment. Subdivision (b) is amended to specify whether the trial will be on the original pleadings or subsequent pleadings under rule 1.110(h).

1988 Amendment. Subdivision (c) was amended to clarify a confusion regarding the notice for trial which resulted from a 1968 amendment.

2012 Amendment. Subdivision (c) is amended to reflect the relocation of the service rule from rule 1.080 to Fla. R. Jud. Admin. 2.516.

Court Commentary

1984 Amendment. Subdivision (a) is amended by adding a sentence to emphasize the authority given in rule 1.270(b) for the severing of issues for trial.

Subdivision (c) is amended to delete the reference to law actions so that the rule will apply to all actions in which unliquidated damages are sought.

Authors' Comment—1967

Rule 1.440 is identical to former Rule 2.2, 1954 Rules of Civil Procedure, as amended in 1965, effective January 1, 1966.

Former Rule 2.2 was changed by amendment to eliminate a notice in writing that the case was ready for trial, and substituting in its place that a motion may be filed and served after an action is at issue. An action is deemed at issue twenty (20) days after service of the last pleading, if no motions are served which are directed to the last pleading and the motion that the action be tried eliminates the need for a notice that the case is ready for trial. The time period was substantially changed to provide that no trial date should be less than thirty (30) days from the service of the notice of the trial date by the Court, unless all parties agree to a shorter time. Sub-section (6) of section 28.21, F.S.A., relating to the duty of the Clerk of the Circuit Court to keep a trial docket, should be consulted as to its contents and the annotations thereunder. Any party may file and serve a motion that the action be tried.

Although the new Rule provides that the Court shall set the action for trial, even ex parte, apparently, and notify all parties in writing of the trial date, after the motion that the action be tried is filed, a good practice would be to file along with the motion an Order leaving the trial date blank, along with envelopes addressed to counsel for both parties.

Rule 1.442. Proposals for Settlement

(a) Applicability. This rule applies to all proposals for settlement authorized by Florida law, regardless of the terms used to refer to such offers, demands, or proposals, and supersedes all other provisions of the rules and statutes that may be inconsistent with this rule.

(b) Service of Proposal. A proposal to a defendant shall be served no earlier than 90 days after service of process on that defendant; a proposal to a plaintiff shall be served no earlier than 90 days after the action has been commenced. No proposal shall be served later than 45 days before the date set for trial or the first day of the docket on which the case is set for trial, whichever is earlier.

(c) Form and Content of Proposal for Settlement.

(1) A proposal shall be in writing and shall identify the applicable Florida law under which it is being made.

(2) A proposal shall:

(A) name the party or parties making the proposal and the party or parties to whom the proposal is being made;

(B) state that the proposal resolves all damages that would otherwise be awarded in a final judgment in the action in which the proposal is served, subject to subdivision (F);

(C) state with particularity any relevant conditions;

(D) state the total amount of the proposal and state with particularity all nonmonetary terms of the proposal;

(E) state with particularity the amount proposed to settle a claim for punitive damages, if any;

(F) state whether the proposal includes attorneys' fees and whether attorneys' fees are part of the legal claim; and

(G) include a certificate of service in the form required by rule 1.080.

(3) A proposal may be made by or to any party or parties and by or to any combination of parties properly identified in the proposal. A joint proposal shall state the amount and terms attributable to each party.

(4) Notwithstanding subdivision (c)(3), when a party is alleged to be solely vicariously, constructively, derivatively, or technically liable, whether by operation of law or by contract, a joint proposal made by or served on such a party need not state the apportionment or contribution as to that party. Acceptance by any party shall be without prejudice to rights of contribution or indemnity.

(d) Service and Filing. A proposal shall be served on the party or parties to whom it is made but shall not be filed unless necessary to enforce the provisions of this rule.

(e) Withdrawal. A proposal may be withdrawn in writing provided the written withdrawal is delivered before a written acceptance is delivered. Once withdrawn, a proposal is void.

(f) Acceptance and Rejection.

(1) A proposal shall be deemed rejected unless accepted by delivery of a written notice of acceptance within 30 days after service of the proposal. The provisions of Florida Rule of Judicial Administration 2.514(b) do not apply to this subdivision. No oral communications shall constitute an acceptance, rejection, or counteroffer under the provisions of this rule.

(2) In any case in which the existence of a class is alleged, the time for acceptance of a proposal for settlement is extended to 30 days after the date the order granting or denying certification is filed.

(g) Sanctions. Any party seeking sanctions pursuant to applicable Florida law, based on the failure of the proposal's recipient to accept a proposal, shall do so by serving a motion in accordance with rule 1.525.

(h) Costs and Fees.

(1) If a party is entitled to costs and fees pursuant to applicable Florida law, the court may, in its discretion, determine that a proposal was not made in good faith. In such case, the court may disallow an award of costs and attorneys' fees.

(2) When determining the reasonableness of the amount of an award of attorneys' fees pursuant to this section, the court shall consider, along with all other relevant criteria, the following factors:

(A) The then-apparent merit or lack of merit in the claim.

(B) The number and nature of proposals made by the parties.

(C) The closeness of questions of fact and law at issue.

(D) Whether the party making the proposal had unreasonably refused to furnish information necessary to evaluate the reasonableness of the proposal.

(E) Whether the suit was in the nature of a test case presenting questions of far-reaching importance affecting nonparties.

(F) The amount of the additional delay cost and expense that the party making the proposal reasonably would be expected to incur if the litigation were to be prolonged.

(i) Evidence of Proposal. Evidence of a proposal or acceptance thereof is admissible only in proceedings to enforce an accepted proposal or to determine the imposition of sanctions.

(j) Effect of Mediation. Mediation shall have no effect on the dates during which parties are permitted to make or accept a proposal for settlement under the terms of the rule.

Added July 27, 1989, effective Jan. 1, 1990 (550 So.2d 442). Amended July 16, 1992, effective Jan. 1, 1993 (604 So.2d 1110); Oct. 31, 1996, effective Jan. 1, 1997 (682 So.2d 105); Oct. 5, 2000, effective Jan. 1, 2001 (773 So.2d 1098); Sept. 8, 2010, effective Jan. 1, 2011 (52 So.3d 579); Oct. 18, 2012, effective, *nunc pro tunc*, Sept. 1, 2012 (102 So.3d 505); April 11, 2013 (112 So.3d 1209); Nov. 14, 2013, effective Jan. 1, 2014 (131 So.3d 643).

Committee Notes

1996 Amendment. This rule was amended to reconcile, where possible, sections 44.102(6) (formerly 44.102(5)(b)), 45.061, 73.032, and 768.79, Florida

Statutes, and the decisions of the Florida Supreme Court in *Knealing v. Puleo*, 675 So. 2d 593 (Fla. 1996), *TGI Friday's, Inc. v. Dvorak*, 663 So. 2d 606 (Fla. 1995), and *Timmons v. Combs*, 608 So. 2d 1 (Fla. 1992). This rule replaces former rule 1.442, which was repealed by the *Timmons* decision, and supersedes those sections of the Florida Statutes and the prior decisions of the court, where reconciliation is impossible, in order to provide a workable structure for proposing settlements in civil actions. The provision which requires that a joint proposal state the amount and terms attributable to each party is in order to conform with *Fabre v. Marin*, 623 So. 2d 1182 (Fla. 1993).

2000 Amendment. Subdivision (f)(2) was added to establish the time for acceptance of proposals for settlement in class actions. "Filing" is defined in rule 1.080(e). Subdivision (g) is amended to conform with new rule 1.525.

2012 Amendment. Subdivision (c)(2)(G) is amended to reflect the relocation of the service rule from rule 1.080 to Fla. R. Jud. Admin. 2.516.

2013 Amendment. Subdivision (f)(1) was amended to reflect the relocation of the rule regarding additional time after service by mail or e-mail from rule 1.090(e) to Fla. R. Jud. Admin. 2.514(b).

2013 Amendment. Subdivision (c)(2)(B) is amended to clarify that a proposal for settlement must resolve all claims between the proponent and the party to whom the proposal is made except claims for attorneys' fees, which may or may not be resolved in the proposal.

Rule 1.450. Evidence

(a) Record of Excluded Evidence. In an action tried by a jury if an objection to a question propounded to a witness is sustained by the court, the examining attorney may make a specific offer of what the attorney expects to prove by the answer of the witness. The court may require the offer to be made out of the hearing of the jury. The court may add such other or further statement as clearly shows the character of the evidence, the form in which it was offered, the objection made, and the ruling thereon. In actions tried without a jury the same procedure may be followed except that the court upon request shall take and report the evidence in full unless it clearly appears that the evidence is not admissible on any ground or that the witness is privileged.

(b) Filing. When documentary evidence is introduced in an action, the clerk or the judge shall endorse an identifying number or symbol on it and when proffered or admitted in evidence, it shall be filed by the clerk or judge and considered in the custody of the court and not withdrawn except with written leave of court.

Amended Sept. 29, 1971, effective Dec. 13, 1971 (253 So.2d 404); May 5, 1976 (335 So.2d 802); March 8, 1979 (368 So.2d 1293); Sept. 10, 1981, effective January 1, 1982 (403 So.2d 926); Sept. 13, 1984, effective Jan. 1, 1985 (458 So.2d 245); July 16, 1992, effective Jan. 1, 1993 (604 So.2d 1110); Oct. 31, 1996, effective Jan. 1, 1997 (682 So.2d 105).

Committee Notes

1971 Amendment. Subdivision (d) is amended to eliminate the necessity of a court order for disposal of exhibits. The clerk must retain the exhibits for 1 year unless the court permits removal earlier. If removal is not effected within the year, the clerk may destroy or dispose of the exhibits after giving the specified notice.

1996 Amendment. Former subdivision (a) entitled "Adverse Witness" is deleted because it is no longer needed or appropriate because the matters with which it deals are treated in the Florida Evidence Code.

Court Commentary

1984 Amendment. Subdivision (d) was repealed by the supreme court; see 403 So.2d 926.

Subdivision (e): This rule was originally promulgated by the supreme court in Carter v. Sparkman, 335 So.2d 802, 806 (Fla.1976).

In *The Florida Bar, in re Rules of Civil Procedure*, 391 So.2d 165 (Fla.1980), the court requested the committee to consider the continued appropriateness of rule 1.450(e). In response, the committee recommended its deletion. After oral argument in *The Florida Bar: In re Rules of Civil Procedure*, 429 So.2d 311, the court specifically declined to abolish the rule or to adopt a similar rule for other types of actions.

The committee again considered rule 1.450(e) in depth and at length and again recommends its deletion for the reason that no exception should be made in the rule to a particular type of action.

Subdivision (f): The West's Desk Copy Florida Rules of Court, at page 62, points out:

"The per curiam opinion of the Florida Supreme Court of June 21, 1979 (403 So.2d 926) provides: 'On March 8, 1979, the Court proposed new Rule 1.450 of the Florida Rules of Civil Procedure which would provide for the disposal of exhibits and depositions in civil matters. Absent further action by the Court, the proposed rule was to become effective July 2, 1979. The Court has carefully considered the responses received regarding proposed Rule 1.450(f) and now feels that the July 2, 1979, effective date does not allow sufficient time for full reflection on matters raised in these responses. Therefore, the effective date for Rule 1.450(f) is, by this order, delayed until further order of the Court.'"

The retention of court records is the subject of Florida Rule of Judicial Administration 2.075.

Authors' Comment—1967

Rule 1.450 is identical to former Rule 1.37, 1954 Rules of Civil Procedure, as amended in 1965, effective January 1, 1966. The latter amendment added subsections (c) and (d) to the former rule, and subsection (c) is the same as former Rule 2.5, 1954 Rules of Civil Procedure which was transferred to former Rule 1.37(c) by the 1965 amendment.

Subsections (a) and (b) are the same as Federal Rule 43(b) and (c). The Florida rule omits subsection (a) of Federal Rule 43 which sets forth a general principle of liberality in favor of the admissibility of evidence and the competency of witnesses. It also omits the remaining subsections (d), (e), and (f) of the Federal Rule relating to affirmation in lieu of oath, evidence on motions, and interpreters. Moreover, Federal Rule 44 concerning proof of official records was not incorporated into the Florida Rules.

The rule contains no specific provision concerning the cross-examination, contradiction or impeachment of a witness who is not a party or an officer, director, or managing agent of a party, except that it recognizes the right of a party to interrogate an unwilling or hostile witness by leading questions. However, it would seem to recognize the general principle that a party who calls a witness as his own vouches for his credibility, but that the court may in its own discretion allow a party to cross examine and impeach his own witness if it appears that the witness is hostile.

Excluded evidence in non-jury cases is reported on the request of any party but the reporting of inadmissible evidence is discretionary with the court. Relevant cross-examination and evidence in rebuttal should be allowed and reported. By including the testimony the record will be complete, thus obviating a motion for a new trial and affording the appellate court a basis on which to determine whether harm was done by the exclusion and on which to render a proper judgment without remanding the case for further trial.

Under subsections (c) and (d) (repealed) a document offered, but refused admission in evidence cannot be withdrawn without leave of court.

This rule applies only on trial and not to the taking of depositions.

On depositions, the preferred practice is to allow copies of documents (preferably photostats) to be made to be filed with the deposition and allow the originals to remain with the person having the same.

On trial, each document to be shown to a witness should be marked by the clerk for identification and thereafter referred to by that mark.

As is apparent from a reading of the rule, the field of evidence is left practically untouched by the Florida Rules of Civil Procedure, 1967 Revision. For a full treatment of evidence problems, one should consult McCormick on Evidence (West Publishing Company 1954).

Rule 1.451. Taking Testimony

(a) Testimony at Hearing or Trial. When testifying at a hearing or trial, a witness must be physically present unless otherwise provided by law or rule of procedure.

(b) Communication Equipment. The court may permit a witness to testify at a hearing or trial by contemporaneous audio or video communication equipment (1) by agreement of the parties or (2) for good cause shown upon written request of a party upon reasonable notice to all other parties. The request and notice must contain the substance of the proposed testimony and an estimate of the length of the proposed testimony. In considering sufficient good cause, the court shall weigh and address in its order the reasons stated for testimony by communication equipment against the potential for prejudice to the objecting party.

(c) Required Equipment. Communication equipment as used in this rule means a conference telephone or other electronic device that permits all those appearing or participating to hear and speak to each other simultaneously and permits all conversations of all parties to be audible to all persons present. Contemporaneous video communications equipment must make the witness visible to all participants during the testimony. For testimony by any of the foregoing means, there must be appropriate safeguards for the court to maintain sufficient control over the equipment and the transmission of the testimony so the court may stop the communication to accommodate objection or prevent prejudice.

(d) Oath. Testimony may be taken through communication equipment only if a notary public or other person authorized to administer oaths in the witness's jurisdiction is present with the witness and administers the oath consistent with the laws of the jurisdiction.

(e) Burden of Expense. The cost for the use of the communication equipment is the responsibility of the requesting party unless otherwise ordered by the court.

Added Nov. 14, 2013, effective Jan. 1, 2014 (131 So.3d 643).

Committee Note

2013 Adoption. This rule allows the parties to agree, or one or more parties to request, that the court authorize presentation of witness testimony by contemporaneous video or audio communications equipment. A party seeking to present such testimony over the objection of another party must still satisfy the good-cause standard. In determining whether good cause exists, the trial court may consider such factors as the type and stage of proceeding, the presence or absence of constitutionally protected rights, the importance of the testimony to the resolution of the case, the amount in controversy in the case, the relative cost or inconvenience of requiring the presence of the witness in court, the ability of counsel to use necessary exhibits or demonstrative aids, the limitations (if any) placed on the opportunity for opposing counsel and the finder of fact to observe the witness's demeanor, the potential for unfair surprise, the witness's affiliation with one or more parties, and any other factors the court reasonably deems material to weighing the justification the requesting party has offered in support of the request to allow a witness to testify by communications equipment against the potential for prejudice to the objecting party. With the advance of technology, the cost and availability of contemporaneous video testimony may be considered by the court in determining whether good cause is established for audio testimony.

Rule 1.452. Questions by Jurors

(a) Questions Permitted. The court shall permit jurors to submit to the court written questions directed to witnesses or to the court. Such questions will be submitted after all counsel have concluded their questioning of a witness.

(b) Procedure. Any juror who has a question directed to the witness or the court shall prepare an unsigned, written question and give the question to the bailiff, who will give the question to the judge.

(c) Objections. Out of the presence of the jury, the judge will read the question to all counsel, allow counsel to see the written question, and give counsel an opportunity to object to the question.

Added Oct. 4, 2007, effective Jan. 1, 2008 (967 So.2d 178).

Rule 1.455. Juror Notebooks

In its discretion, the court may authorize documents and exhibits to be included in notebooks for use by the jurors during trial to aid them in performing their duties.

Added Oct. 4, 2007, effective Jan. 1, 2008 (967 So.2d 178).

Rule 1.460. Continuances

A motion for continuance shall be in writing unless made at a trial and, except for good cause shown, shall be signed by the party requesting the continuance. The motion shall state all of the facts that the movant contends entitle the movant to a continuance. If a continuance is sought on the ground of nonavailability of a witness, the motion must show when it is believed the witness will be available.

Amended Oct. 9, 1980, effective Jan. 1, 1981 (391 So.2d 165); Oct. 6, 1988, effective Jan. 1, 1989 (536 So.2d 974); July 16, 1992, effective Jan. 1, 1993 (604 So.2d 1110).

Committee Notes

1980 Amendment. Subdivision (a), deleted by amendment, was initially adopted when trials were set at a docket sounding prescribed by statute. Even then, the rule was honored more in the breach than the observance. Trials are no longer uniformly set in that manner, and continuances are granted generally without reference to the rule. Under the revised rule, motions for continuance can be filed at any time that the need arises and need not be in writing if the parties are before the court.

1988 Amendment. The supreme court, by adopting Florida Rule of Judicial Administration 2.085(c), effective July 1, 1986, required all motions for continuance to be signed by the litigant requesting the continuance. The amendment conforms rule 1.460 to rule 2.085(c); but, by including an exception for good cause, it recognizes that circumstances justifying a continuance may excuse the signature of the party.

Authors' Comment—1967

Rule 1.460 is almost identical to subsections (a), (b), and (d) of former Rule 2.4, 1954 Rules of Civil Procedure. Subsection (c) of the former rule, relating to service of a copy of the motion for continuance was omitted from the present rule inasmuch as Rule 1.080 comprehends service of such motion and other pleadings.

Applications to postpone the trial of a cause are addressed to the sound discretion of the court.

The motion should show that the party applying has used due diligence to prepare for trial and also what diligence has been used; that he cannot safely proceed to trial without certain evidence or witnesses which are not at hand and cannot be at hand if the trial proceeds at once, or showing the materiality of the expected evidence; that due effort constituting due diligence has been used (stating facts) to procure such evidence, or the attendance of such witnesses; the names and residences of such witnesses, and what facts, as distinguished from legal conclusions, they will swear to, and the reasons of the applicant for his belief that they will so swear; also sufficient facts showing reasonable grounds to believe that such testimony or witnesses can be obtained if the action be continued as requested and when, and that there are no other documents or witnesses which can be procured by whom the facts can be proven.

It should be carefully noted that any motion for a continuance must be served upon the attorney of record for the opposing party, together with a notice with the time, place and the judge before whom said motion will be called for hearing. Thus the rule requires the simultaneous service of both the motion and the notice of hearing.

As a matter of practice, although the rule does not require it, many courts require such motions for continuances to be supported by affidavits.

Rule 1.470. Exceptions Unnecessary; Jury Instructions

(a) Adverse Ruling. For appellate purposes no exception shall be necessary to any adverse ruling, order, instruction, or thing whatsoever said or done at the trial or prior thereto or after verdict, which was said or done after objection made and considered by the trial court and which affected the substantial rights of the party complaining and which is assigned as error.

(b) Instructions to Jury. The Florida Standard Jury Instructions appearing on the court's website at www.floridasupremecourt.org/jury_instructions.shtml shall be used by the trial judges of this state in instructing the jury in civil actions to the extent that the Standard Jury Instructions are applicable, unless the trial judge determines that an applicable Standard Jury Instruction is erroneous or inadequate. If the trial judge modifies a Standard Jury Instruction or gives such other instruction as the judge determines necessary to accurately and sufficiently instruct the jury, upon timely objection to the instruction, the trial judge shall state on the record or in a separate order the legal basis for varying from the Standard Jury Instruction. Similarly, in all circumstances in which the notes accompanying the Florida Standard Jury Instructions contain a recommendation that a certain type of instruction not be given, the trial judge shall follow the recommendation unless the judge determines that the giving of such an instruction is necessary to accurately and sufficiently instruct the jury, in which event the judge shall give such instruction as the judge deems appropriate and necessary. If the trial judge does not follow such a recommendation of the Florida Standard Jury Instructions, upon timely objection to the instruction, the trial judge shall state on the record or in a separate order the legal basis of the determination that such instruction is necessary. Not later than at the close of the evidence, the parties shall file written requests that the court instruct the jury on the law set forth in such requests. The court shall then require counsel to appear before it to settle the instructions to be given. At such conference, all objections shall be made and ruled upon and the court shall inform counsel of such instructions as it will give. No party may assign as error the giving of any instruction unless that party objects thereto at such time, or the failure to give any instruction unless that party requested the same. The court shall orally instruct the jury before or after the arguments of counsel and may provide appropriate instructions during the trial. If the instructions are given prior to final argument, the presiding judge shall give the jury final procedural instructions after final arguments are concluded and prior to deliberations. The court shall provide each juror with a written set of the instructions for his or her use in deliberations. The court shall file a copy of such instructions.

(c) Orders on New Trial, Directed Verdicts, etc. It shall not be necessary to object or except to any order granting or denying motions for new trials, directed verdicts, or judgments non obstante veredicto or in arrest of judgment to entitle the party against whom such ruling is made to have the same reviewed by an appellate court.

Amended Oct. 6, effective Jan. 1, 1989 (536 So.2d 974); July 16, 1992, effective Jan. 1, 1993 (604 So.2d 1110); Oct. 4, 2007, effective Jan. 1, 2008 (967 So.2d 178); Sept. 8, 2010, effective Jan. 1, 2011 (52 So.3d 579); Feb. 20, 2014 (133 So.3d 928).

Committee Notes

1988 Amendment. The word "general" in the third sentence of subdivision (b) was deleted to require the court to specifically inform counsel of the charges it intends to give. The last sentence of that subdivision was amended to encourage judges to furnish written copies of their charges to juries.

2010 Amendment. Portions of form 1.985 were modified and moved to subdivision (b) of rule 1.470 to require the court to use published standard instructions where applicable and necessary, to permit the judge to vary from the published standard jury instructions and notes only when necessary to accurately and sufficiently instruct the jury, and to require the parties to object to preserve error in variance from published standard jury instructions and notes.

2014 Amendment. Florida Standard Jury Instructions include the Florida Standard Jury Instructions—Contract and Business Cases.

Authors' Comment—1967

Objections and Exceptions

Rule 1.470 is the same as former Rule 2.6, 1954 Rules of Civil Procedure, as amended in 1965, effective January 1, 1966, with the exception of only certain minor language changes.

Former Rule 2.6(a) abolished exceptions. An objection now serves every purpose of both objection and exception.

For example, if counsel interposes an objection to evidence and his objection is overruled, he need not note an exception. To do so is surplusage and even improper. He must, however, make known his objection at the proper time and not remain silent. Thus, in order to preserve his client's rights, counsel must note objections to a judge's instructions to the jury if he has any. In other words counsel is still under a duty to state objections, but if his objections are overruled, he need not note an exception to the ruling.

An objection must be so definite as to indicate to the trial court the precise ground upon which the evidence is inadmissible or the ruling objectionable. The purpose of an objection is to call the court's attention directly to the matter and thus enable it to avoid error.

Section 59.07, F.S.A. likewise established in appellate procedure relating to civil cases that an exception is not necessary to review an adverse ruling if an objection has been made and considered by the trial court, and Section 924.11(3), F.S.A. established the same rule in criminal appeals. In similar fashion, Florida Appellate Rule 6.7g established that formal exceptions are not necessary to review an issue on appeal, but that an objection or the making known of the action which the party desires the court to take is sufficient.

The most recent amendment to paragraph (c) deleted non-suits from those orders to which an objection would be unnecessary.

The requirements of former subsection Rule 2.6(d)—now deleted, to the effect that the court state grounds for granting a new trial, appear in Rule 1.530(f), infra.

Instructions

The conference on instructions contemplated by Rule 1.470(b) should be held under circumstances calculated to give a reasonable opportunity to take the steps contemplated. In many instances it may be advisable to give advance consideration to the instructions at the pretrial conference under the terms of Rule 1.200(6).

The conference during the course of the trial is usually hurried. Particularly if counsel contemplates an instruction of great difficulty and importance, on which he wishes to give the court ample opportunity for study, he would do well to get it before the court at the pretrial conference. At any rate, requested instructions should be placed in the hands of the court and copies given to opposing counsel at the earliest time possible in the course of the trial.

If there are to be many serious objections to charges proposed by the court, or requested by the parties, the reporter should be present to report the proceedings.

Not only is the court obligated to hold the conference on instructions but it must advise counsel of such general charges as it will give. If counsel is deprived of his opportunity to object because of the failure of the court to perform its duties, the lack of an objection should not be fatal. See Tampa Transit Lines v. Corbin, 62 So.2d 10 (1953). However, if counsel wants a conference he should request it. Luster v. Moore, 78 So.2d 87 (1955).

Rule 1.480. Motion for a Directed Verdict

(a) Effect. A party who moves for a directed verdict at the close of the evidence offered by the adverse party may offer evidence in the event the motion is denied without having reserved the right to do so and to the same extent as if the motion had not been made. The denial of a motion for a directed verdict shall not operate to discharge the jury. A motion for a directed verdict shall state the specific grounds therefor. The order directing a verdict is effective without any assent of the jury.

(b) Reservation of Decision on Motion. When a motion for a directed verdict is denied or for any reason is not granted, the court is deemed to have submitted the action to the jury subject to a later determination of the legal questions raised by the motion. Within 15 days after the return of a verdict, a party who has timely moved for a directed verdict may serve a motion to set aside the verdict and any judgment entered thereon and to enter judgment in accordance with the motion for a directed verdict. If a verdict was not returned, a party who has timely moved for a directed verdict may serve a motion for judgment in accordance with the motion for a directed verdict within 15 days after discharge of the jury.

(c) Joined with Motion for New Trial. A motion for a new trial may be joined with this motion or a new trial may be requested in the alternative. If a verdict was returned, the court may allow the judgment to stand or may reopen the judgment and either order a new trial or direct the entry of judgment as if the requested verdict had been directed. If no verdict was returned, the court may direct the entry of judgment as if the requested verdict had been directed or may order a new trial.

Amended July 16, 1992, effective Jan. 1, 1993 (604 So.2d 1110); Oct. 31, 1996, effective Jan. 1, 1997 (682 So.2d 105); Sept. 8, 2010, effective Jan. 1, 2011 (52 So.3d 579); Nov. 14, 2013, effective Jan. 1, 2014 (131 So.3d 643).

Committee Notes

1996 Amendment. Subdivision (b) is amended to clarify that the time limitations in this rule are based on service.

2010 Amendment. Subdivision (b) is amended to conform to 2006 changes to Federal Rule of Civil Procedure 50(b) eliminating the requirement for renewing at the close of all the evidence a motion for directed verdict already made at the close of an adverse party's evidence.

2013 Amendment. Subdivision (b) is amended to change the time for service of a motion from 10 to 15 days after the specified event.

Authors' Comment—1967

Rule 1.480 is the same as former Rule 2.7, 1954 Rules of Civil Procedure, as amended in 1965, effective January 1, 1966, with the exception of only certain minor language and punctuation changes. Note under this rule alone failure to make a motion for a directed verdict or for a judgment non obstante veredicto prior to or simultaneous with a motion for new trial might prove fatal.

The rule does not require technical precision in stating the grounds of the motion. It does require that they be stated with sufficient certainty to apprise the court of the movant's position with respect thereto. The usual practice, however, is to make such motions orally since ordinarily there is no time or opportunity to formulate them in writing.

It is a well established principle of the common law that although questions of fact must be decided by the jury and may not be reexamined by the court, the question whether there is sufficient evidence to raise a question of fact to be presented to the jury is a question of law to be decided by the court.

Rule 1.480 provides a procedure for the determination of this question of law by the court. Rule 1.480(a) provides for a motion for a directed verdict at the close of the evidence and before the case is submitted to the jury. It enables the court to determine whether there is any question of fact to be submitted to the jury and whether any verdict other than the one directed would be erroneous as a matter of law. Rule 1.480(b) authorizes the court to reserve the decision of this question of law until after the case has been submitted to the jury. If the court decides that a verdict should have been directed, it may set aside the verdict of the jury and enter a judgment notwithstanding the verdict. Rule 1.480(c) also authorizes a motion for a new trial in the alternative.

If after the denial of a motion for a directed verdict, the defendant proceeds to put his case in evidence, it is of paramount importance to renew the motion for directed verdict at the conclusion of all of the testimony, or such motion is deemed to be waived. Likewise, it is incumbent upon a defendant, if his first motion not be denied or granted, to make certain that the legal question presented by his motion for a directed verdict made at the close of the plaintiff's case is reserved for consideration by the trial judge after verdict.

Under Rule 1.480(b) if the jury fails to agree, a party may renew his motion for a directed verdict, but where there is evidence of a substantial character which, if believed by the jury, would require a verdict for his adversary, the court should permit a retrial and deny the motion for a directed verdict.

Under Rule 1.480(c) a motion for a new trial may be joined with a motion for judgment notwithstanding the verdict, or a new trial may be prayed for in the alternative.

In proceeding under this rule, a party should keep in mind the clear distinction between the power of the court, after setting aside a verdict, to enter judgment notwithstanding the verdict in accordance with the prior motion for a directed verdict, and the court's power to grant a new trial. In cases in which a judgment n.o.v. is not proper there may still be grounds to set aside the verdict and grant a new trial. There is no inconsistency in requiring the court to submit the issues to the jury if there is substantial evidence to support a verdict for the adverse party, and at the same time permitting it to set the verdict aside if it is deemed contrary to the weight of evidence. In directing a judgment n.o.v., the court makes a final disposition of the case. On the other hand, in granting a new trial, the court merely makes necessary the submission of issues for determination by another jury.

Rule 1.481. Verdicts

In all actions when punitive damages are sought, the verdict shall state the amount of punitive damages separately from the amounts of other damages awarded.

Added June 19, 1968, effective Oct. 1, 1968 (211 So.2d 206).

Rule 1.490. Magistrates

(a) General Magistrates. Judges of the circuit court may appoint as many general magistrates from among the members of the Bar in the circuit as the judges find necessary, and the general magistrates shall continue in office until removed by the court. The order making an appointment shall be recorded. Every person appointed as a general magistrate shall take the oath required of officers by the Constitution and the oath shall be recorded before the magistrate discharges any duties of that office.

(b) Special Magistrates. The court may appoint members of The Florida Bar as special magistrates for any particular service required by the court, and they shall be governed by all the provisions of law and rules relating to magistrates except they shall not be required to make oath or give bond unless specifically required by the order appointing them. Upon a showing that the appointment is advisable, a person other than a member of the Bar may be appointed.

(c) Reference. No reference shall be to a magistrate, either general or special, without the consent of the parties. When a reference is made to a magistrate, either party may set the action for hearing before the magistrate.

(d) General Powers and Duties. Every magistrate shall perform all of the duties that pertain to the office according to the practice in chancery and under the direction of the court. Process issued by a magistrate shall be directed as provided by law. Hearings before any magistrate, examiner, or commissioner shall be held in the county where the action is pending, but hearings may be held at any place by order of the court within or without the state to meet the convenience of the witnesses or the parties. All grounds of disqualification of a judge shall apply to magistrates. Magistrates shall not practice law of the same case type in the court in any county or circuit the magistrate is appointed to serve.

(e) Bond. When not otherwise provided by law, the court may require magistrates who are appointed to dispose of real or personal property to give bond and surety conditioned for the proper payment of all moneys that may come into their hands and for the due performance of their duties as the court may direct. The bond shall be made payable to the State of Florida and shall be for the benefit of all persons aggrieved by any act of the magistrate.

(f) Notice of Hearings. The magistrate shall assign a time and place for proceedings as soon as reasonably possible after the reference is made and give notice to each of the parties. The notice or order setting a matter for hearing before the magistrate must state if electronic recording or a court reporter will be used to create a record of the proceedings. If electronic recording is to be used, the notice must state that any party may have a court reporter transcribe the record of the proceedings at that party's expense. If any party fails to appear, the magistrate may proceed ex parte or may adjourn the proceeding to a future day, giving notice to the absent party of the adjournment.

(g) Hearings. The magistrate shall proceed with reasonable diligence in every reference and with the least practicable delay. Any party may apply to the court for an order to the magistrate to speed the proceedings and to make the report and to certify to the court the reason for any delay. The evidence shall be taken by the magistrate or by some other person under the magistrate's authority in the magistrate's presence and shall be filed with the magistrate's report. The magistrate shall have authority to examine on oath the parties and all witnesses produced by the parties on all matters contained in the reference and to require production of all books, papers, writings, vouchers, and other documents applicable to the referenced matters. The magistrate shall admit evidence by deposition or that is otherwise admissible in court. The magistrate may take all actions concerning evidence that can be taken by the court and in the same manner. All parties accounting before a magistrate shall bring in their accounts in the form of accounts payable and receivable, and any other parties who are not satisfied with the account may examine the accounting party orally or by interrogatories or deposition as the magistrate directs. All depositions and documents that have been taken or used previously in the action may be used before the magistrate.

(h) Magistrate's Report. The magistrate must file the report on the referenced matters and serve copies on all parties, and include the name and address of any court reporter who transcribed the proceedings. The magistrate's report must contain the following language in bold type:

IF YOU WISH TO SEEK REVIEW OF THE REPORT AND RECOMMENDATIONS MADE BY THE MAGISTRATE, YOU MUST FILE EXCEPTIONS IN ACCORDANCE WITH FLORIDA RULE OF CIVIL PROCEDURE 1.490(i). YOU WILL BE REQUIRED TO PROVIDE THE COURT WITH A RECORD SUFFICIENT TO SUPPORT YOUR EXCEPTIONS OR YOUR EXCEPTIONS WILL BE DENIED. A RECORD ORDINARILY INCLUDES A WRITTEN TRANSCRIPT OF ALL RELEVANT PROCEEDINGS. THE PERSON SEEKING REVIEW MUST HAVE THE TRANSCRIPT PREPARED IF NECESSARY FOR THE COURT'S REVIEW.

(i) Filing Report; Notice; Exceptions. The parties may file exceptions to the report within 10 days after it is served. Any party may file cross-exceptions within 5 days from the service of the exceptions. If no exceptions are timely filed, the court shall take appropriate action on the report. If exceptions are timely filed, the court shall resolve the exceptions at a hearing on reasonable notice. The filing of cross-exceptions shall not delay a hearing on the exceptions and cross-exceptions unless good cause is shown.

(j) Record. A party filing exceptions to the magistrate's report must provide the court in advance of the hearing a record sufficient to support that party's exceptions.

(1) The record shall include the court file, designated portions of the transcript of proceedings before the magistrate, and all depositions and evidence presented to the magistrate. The designated transcript portions must be delivered to the court and all other parties at least 48 hours before the hearing.

(2) If the party filing exceptions has the court reporter prepare less than a full transcript of proceedings before the magistrate, that party must promptly file a notice designating the portions of the transcript that have been ordered. The other parties must be given reasonable time after service of the notice to arrange for the preparation and designation of other portions of the transcript for the court to consider at the hearing.

Amended Sept. 29, 1971, effective Dec. 13, 1971 (253 So.2d 404); Oct. 9, 1980, effective Jan. 1, 1981 (391 So.2d 165); Sept. 13, 1984, effective Jan. 1, 1985 (458 So.2d 245); July 16, 1992, effective Jan. 1, 1993 (604 So.2d 1110); Sept. 30, 2004, effective Oct. 1, 2004 (887 So.2d 1090); May 9, 2013 (113 So.3d 777); Nov. 14, 2013, effective Jan. 1, 2014 (131 So.3d 643); March 13, 2014, effective March 13, 2014 (141 So.3d 179); March 5, 2015, effective March 5, 2015 (159 So.3d 838).

Committee Notes

1971 Amendment. The entire rule has been revised. Obsolete language has been omitted and changes made to meet objections shown by the use of local rules in many circuits. Subdivisions (a) and (b) are not substantially changed. Subdivision (c) is shortened and eliminates the useless priority for setting the matter for hearing to permit either party to go forward. Subdivision (d) eliminates the right of the parties to stipulate to the place of hearing. Subdivision (e) is not substantially changed. Subdivisions (f), (g), (h), and (i) are combined. The right to use affidavits is eliminated because of the unavailability of cross-examination and possible constitutional questions. The vague general authority of the master under subdivision (g) is made specific by limiting it to actions that the court could take. Subdivision (j) is repealed because it is covered in the new subdivision (f). Subdivision (g) is the same as former subdivision (k) after eliminating the reference to affidavits. Subdivision (h) is the same as former subdivision (*l*).

1980 Amendment. Subdivision (d) is amended to delete the specific reference to the direction of process so that process issued by the master will be governed by the law applicable to process generally.

Court Commentary

1984 Amendment. The consent of all parties is required for any reference to a special master. Special masters may be used as provided by statute even with the rule change. See *Slatcoff v. Dezen*, 74 So. 2d 59 (Fla. 1954).

Authors' Comment—1967

This rule is almost the same as former Rule 3.14, 1954 Rules of Civil Procedure, as amended in 1965, effective January 1, 1966. The former rule about masters in chancery had not been amended since 1873; it contained many obsolete provisions and duplications which have been removed and the rule stated in modern language.

The rule is based mainly on the old Chancery Act sections 54 through 65, which were taken in large part from the Federal Equity Rules.

In Federal practice the matter of masters is now covered by Federal Rule 53, which in accordance with previous federal practice makes a reference to a master the exception rather than the rule.

In Florida the former practice in equity was usually to have testimony taken before a master or special examiner.

The practice of furnishing counsel with drafts or notice of proposed reports before filing, to permit as many differences as possible to be ironed out before the final report is filed, appears to be commendable although not expressed in the rule.

The attitude of our Supreme Court giving weight and effect to masters' reports is indicated by the case annotations below.

Rule 1.491. General Magistrates for Residential Mortgage Foreclosure Matters

(a) General Magistrates for Residential Mortgage Foreclosure. The chief judge of each judicial circuit shall appoint such number of general magistrates to handle only residential mortgage foreclosures from among the members of the Bar in the circuit as are necessary to expeditiously preside over all actions and suits for the foreclosure of a mortgage on residential real property; and any other matter concerning the foreclosure of a mortgage on residential real property as allowed by the administrative order of the chief judge. Such general magistrates shall continue in office until removed by the court. The order making an appointment shall be recorded. Every person appointed as a general magistrate shall take the oath required of officers by the Constitution and the oath shall be recorded before the magistrate discharges any duties of that office. General magistrates appointed to handle residential mortgage foreclosure matters only shall not be required to give bond or surety.

(b) Reference.

(1) Consent to a magistrate for residential mortgage foreclosure actions and suits may be express or may be implied in accordance with the requirements of this rule.

(A) A written objection to the referral to a magistrate handling residential mortgage foreclosures must be filed within 10 days of the service of the order of referral or within the time to respond to the initial pleading, whichever is later.

(B) If the time set for the hearing is less than 10 days after service of the order of referral, the objection must be filed before commencement of the hearing.

(C) Failure to file a written objection to a referral to the magistrate handling residential mortgage foreclosures within the applicable time period is deemed to be consent to the order of referral.

(2) The order of referral to a magistrate handling residential mortgage foreclosures shall be in substantial conformity with this rule and shall contain the following language in bold type:

A REFERRAL TO A MAGISTRATE FOR A RESIDENTIAL MORTGAGE FORECLOSURE MATTER REQUIRES THE CONSENT OF ALL PARTIES. YOU ARE ENTITLED TO HAVE THIS MATTER HEARD BEFORE A JUDGE. IF YOU DO NOT WANT TO HAVE THIS MATTER HEARD BEFORE A MAGISTRATE, YOU MUST FILE A WRITTEN OBJECTION TO THE REFERRAL WITHIN 10 DAYS OF THE TIME OF SERVICE OF THIS ORDER OR WITHIN THE TIME TO RESPOND TO THE INITIAL PLEADING, WHICHEVER IS LATER. IF THE TIME SET FOR THE HEARING IS LESS THAN 10 DAYS AFTER THE SERVICE OF THIS ORDER, THE OBJECTION MUST BE MADE BEFORE THE HEARING. FAILURE TO FILE A WRITTEN OBJECTION WITHIN THE APPLICABLE TIME PERIOD IS DEEMED TO BE CONSENT TO THE REFERRAL. REVIEW OF THE REPORT AND RECOMMENDATIONS MADE BY THE MAGISTRATE SHALL BE BY EXCEPTIONS AS PROVIDED IN THIS RULE. A RECORD, WHICH INCLUDES A TRANSCRIPT OF PROCEEDINGS, MAY BE REQUIRED TO SUPPORT THE EXCEPTIONS.

When a reference is made to a magistrate, either party may set the action for hearing before the magistrate.

(c) General Powers and Duties. The provisions for the general powers and duties of a magistrate in rule 1.490(d) shall apply to proceedings under this rule.

(d) Notice of Hearings; Hearings. The provisions for notice of hearings and hearings in rules 1.490(f)-(g) shall apply to proceedings under this rule.

(e) Magistrate's Report. The provisions for the requirement of the magistrate's report in rule 1.490(h) shall apply to proceedings under this rule.

(f) Filing Report; Notice; Exceptions; Record. The provisions for filing the report, notice, exceptions to the report, and requirements for a record in rules 1.490(i)-(j) shall apply to proceedings under this rule.

Added March 13, 2014, effective March 13, 2014 (141 So.3d 179). Amended March 5, 2015, effective March 5, 2015 (159 So.3d 838).

Committee Notes

2014 Adoption. This rule is the result of an emergency petition by the Trial Court Budget Commission and is intended to alleviate the backlog of residential mortgage foreclosure cases that Florida courts are currently facing.

2015 Amendment. The changes are intended to adopt certain procedural changes made to rule 1.490 by *In re Amendments to Florida Rules of Civil Procedure*, 131 So. 3d 643 (Fla. 2013).

Rule 1.500. Defaults and Final Judgments Thereon

(a) By the Clerk. When a party against whom affirmative relief is sought has failed to file or serve any paper in the action, the party seeking relief may have the clerk enter a default against the party failing to serve or file such paper.

(b) By the Court. When a party against whom affirmative relief is sought has failed to plead or otherwise defend as provided by these rules or any applicable statute or any order of court, the court may enter a default against such party; provided that if such party has filed or served any paper in the action, that party shall be served with notice of the application for default.

(c) Right to Plead. A party may plead or otherwise defend at any time before default is entered. If a party in default files any paper after the default is entered, the clerk shall notify the party of the entry of the default. The clerk shall make an entry on the progress docket showing the notification.

(d) Setting aside Default. The court may set aside a default, and if a final judgment consequent thereon has been entered, the court may set it aside in accordance with rule 1.540(b).

(e) Final Judgment. Final judgments after default may be entered by the court at any time, but no judgment may be entered against an infant or incompetent person unless represented in the action by a general guardian, committee, conservator, or other representative who has appeared in it or unless the court has made an order under rule 1.210(b) providing that no representative is necessary for the infant or incompetent. If it is necessary to take an account or to determine the amount of damages or to establish the truth of any averment by evidence or to make an investigation of any other matter to enable the court to enter judgment or to effectuate it, the court may receive affidavits, make references, or conduct hearings as it deems necessary and shall accord a right of trial by jury to the parties when required by the Constitution or any statute.

Amended Sept. 29, 1968, effective Oct. 1, 1968 (211 So.2d 206); July 26, 1972, effective Jan. 1, 1973 (265 So.2d 21); Nov. 29, 1972 (269 So.2d 359); Sept. 13, 1984, effective Jan. 1, 1985 (458 So.2d 245); July 16, 1992, effective Jan. 1, 1993 (604 So.2d 1110).

Court Commentary

1984 Amendment. Subdivision (c) is amended to change the method by which the clerk handles papers filed after a default is entered. Instead of returning the papers to the party in default, the clerk will now be required to file them and merely notify the party that a default has been entered. The party can then take whatever action the party believes is appropriate.

This is to enable the court to judge the effect, if any, of the filing of any paper upon the default and the propriety of entering final judgment without notice to the party against whom the default was entered.

Authors' Comment—1967

Rule 1.500 is a new default rule adopted from Federal Rule 55 in part applying to cases in both law and equity. It replaces former Rules 2.9, 3.9, 3.10 and 3.11, 1954 Rules of Civil Procedure. Subsection (a) is somewhat similar to Federal Rule 55(a). The only substantial difference between the new rule and the Federal rule is one which forbids the clerk to enter a default against a party who has appeared. The court is required to enter such a default *after notice*, and thus the new rule overrules Capers v. Lee, 91 So.2d 337. The rule eliminates entry by clerks of final judgments consequent on default.

The first step to be taken in order to obtain a judgment by default or a former decree pro confesso is the party's filing of an application for entry of default by the clerk or by the court. Unlike the former governing rules, it is the failure to *file or to serve* any paper in the action that places a party in default by the very language of the rule. Rule 1.080 sets forth the requirements of both "filing" and "service" within the meaning of this rule and must be carefully analyzed.

The enactment of the Soldiers' and Sailors' Relief Act of 1940, 50 U.S.C.A.App. § 520, created new requirements relating to the entry of judgments by default. Under that Act, which applies to both federal and state courts, before a judgment based upon a default by the defendant may be entered, the plaintiff must file either: (1) an affidavit setting forth facts showing that the defendant is not in military service, or (2) an affidavit setting forth that the defendant is in military service or that the plaintiff is unable to determine whether or not the defendant is in such service. If the first affidavit, showing that defendant is not in military service, is not filed, a judgment may not be entered without securing an order of court directing its entry. If the defendant is in military service, such an order may not be made until after the court appoints an attorney to represent the defendant and protect his interests. An attorney so appointed has no power to waive any right of the defendant or bind him by his acts. Unless it appears that the defendant is not in military service, the court may require, as a condition before entry of judgment, that the plaintiff file a bond to indemnify the defendant against any loss or damage caused by the judgment if it should thereafter be set aside in whole or in part. The court may make such other orders and enter such judgment as it deems necessary for the protection of the defendant's rights under the Act.

The motion for default should preferably be verified and show: (1) The acquisition of jurisdiction over the defaulting party. (2) The existence of a default by failure to serve or file. (3) That no pleading has been filed containing a certificate of service. (4) The military status of the defendant.

The reason for the third suggested showing is that service by mail is complete on mailing (Rule 1.080(b)) and the certificate is prima facie proof of service (Rule 1.080(b)). If a pleading is on file containing a certificate of service the primary facie proof in the record is that service has been made, although the copy has not been received by the moving party. No default should be entered until this proof is adequately overcome.

Unlike former Rule 2.9 which did not provide for setting aside defaults at law as existed in equity under former Rule 3.10, the new rule specifically authorizes the court to set aside defaults. Moreover, it authorizes setting aside a final judgment entered thereon in accordance with Rule 1.540(b). Thus, the distinction between legal procedure and equity procedure is abolished, and the rule adheres to the policy of liberality alluded to by the Supreme Court of Florida in North Shore Hospital, Inc. v. Barber, 143 So.2d 849 (1962), as well as to the policy of the repealed statute providing for the vacating of defaults in proper cases.

Although the decision of Craver v. Ramagli Realty Co., 109 So.2d 187 (1959), was subsequently considered by the Supreme Court wherein it was determined that the District Court had no jurisdiction to review the initial appeal, the reasoning of the District Court in its initial decision is important to note. Therein, the District Court ruled that where a second amended complaint reworded the claim of a first amended complaint and added another count, an answer to the first amended complaint was sufficient to prevent a default for failure to answer the second amended complaint.

As in the former rules relating to both law and equity, the new rule specifically authorizes a party to plead at any time before a default is entered.

Unlike former Rule 3.10, no ten day period must lapse before a decree becomes final, but the new rule authorizes final judgments after default at any time.

A motion to set aside a default should show proper grounds for vacating said default, as should a motion for setting aside a final judgment in accordance with Rule 1.540(b). Rule 1.540(b) still speaks of decrees, moreover.

In a tort case where a default has been entered against the defendant and no jury demanded in the complaint, there appears to be no reason why evidence of damages should not be received by the court without a jury in determining the amount of the judgment. However, if a jury had been demanded in the complaint, it would seem that the court should empanel a jury to determine the amount of damages; otherwise, the defendant will be denied a procedural right to which he is entitled under the pleadings, even though he is in default.

Rule 1.510. Summary Judgment

(a) For Claimant. A party seeking to recover upon a claim, counterclaim, crossclaim, or third-party claim or to obtain a declaratory judgment may move for a summary judgment in that party's favor upon all or any part thereof with or without supporting affidavits at any time after the expiration of 20 days from the commencement of the action or after service of a motion for summary judgment by the adverse party.

(b) For Defending Party. A party against whom a claim, counterclaim, crossclaim, or third-party claim is asserted or a declaratory judgment is sought may move for a summary judgment in that party's favor as to all or any part thereof at any time with or without supporting affidavits.

(c) Motion and Proceedings Thereon. The motion shall state with particularity the grounds upon which it is based and the substantial matters of law to be argued and shall specifically identify any affidavits, answers to interrogatories, admissions, depositions, and other materials as would be admissible in evidence ("summary judgment evidence") on which the movant relies. The movant shall serve the motion at least 20 days before the time fixed for the hearing, and shall also serve at that time a copy of any summary judgment evidence on which the movant relies that has not already been filed with the court. The adverse party shall identify, by notice served pursuant to rule 1.080 at least 5 days prior to the day of the hearing, or delivered no later than 5:00 p.m. 2 business days prior to the day of the hearing, any summary judgment evidence on which the adverse party relies. To the extent that summary judgment evidence has not already been filed with the court, the adverse party shall serve a copy on the movant pursuant to rule 1.080 at least 5 days prior to the day of the hearing, or by delivery to the movant's attorney no later than 5:00 p.m. 2 business days prior to the day of hearing. The judgment sought shall be rendered forthwith if the pleadings and summary judgment evidence on file show that there is no genuine issue as to any material fact and that the moving party is entitled to a judgment as a matter of law. A summary judgment, interlocutory in character, may be rendered on the issue of liability alone although there is a genuine issue as to the amount of damages.

(d) Case Not Fully Adjudicated on Motion. On motion under this rule if judgment is not rendered upon the whole case or for all the relief asked and a trial or the taking of testimony and a final hearing is necessary, the court at the hearing of the motion, by examining the pleadings and the evidence before it and by interrogating counsel, shall ascertain, if practicable, what material facts exist without substantial controversy and what material facts are actually and in good faith controverted. It shall thereupon make an order specifying the facts that appear without substantial controversy, including the extent to which the amount of damages or other relief is not in controversy, and directing such further proceedings in the action as are just. On the trial or final hearing of the action the facts so specified shall be deemed established, and the trial or final hearing shall be conducted accordingly.

(e) Form of Affidavits; Further Testimony. Supporting and opposing affidavits shall be made on personal knowledge, shall set forth such facts as would be admissible in evidence, and shall show affirmatively that the affiant is competent to testify to the matters stated therein. Sworn or certified copies of all papers or parts thereof referred to in an affidavit shall be attached thereto or served therewith. The court may permit affidavits to be supplemented or opposed by depositions, answers to interrogatories, or by further affidavits.

(f) When Affidavits Are Unavailable. If it appears from the affidavits of a party opposing the motion that the party cannot for reasons stated present by affidavit facts essential to justify opposition, the court may refuse the application for judgment or may order a continuance to permit affidavits to be obtained or depositions to be taken or discovery to be had or may make such other order as is just.

(g) Affidavits Made in Bad Faith. If it appears to the satisfaction of the court at any time that any of the affidavits presented pursuant to this rule are presented in bad faith or solely for the purpose of delay, the court shall forthwith order the party employing them to pay to the other party the amount of the reasonable expenses which the filing of the affidavits caused the other party to incur, including reasonable attorneys' fees, and any offending party or attorney may be adjudged guilty of contempt.

Amended Dec. 13, 1976, effective Jan. 1, 1977 (339 So.2d 626); July 16, 1992, effective Jan. 1, 1993 (604 So.2d 1110); Dec. 15, 2005, effective Jan. 1, 2006 (917 So.2d 176); Sept. 8, 2010, effective Jan. 1, 2011 (52 So.3d 579); Oct. 18, 2012, effective, *nunc pro tunc*, Sept. 1, 2012 (102 So.3d 505).

Committee Notes

1976 Amendment. Subdivision (c) has been amended to require a movant to state with particularity the grounds and legal authority which the movant will rely upon in seeking summary judgment. This amendment will eliminate surprise and bring the summary judgment rule into conformity with the identical provision in rule 1.140(b) with respect to motions to dismiss.

1992 Amendment. The amendment to subdivision (c) will require timely service of opposing affidavits, whether by mail or by delivery, prior to the day of the hearing on a motion for summary judgment.

2005 Amendment. Subdivision (c) has been amended to ensure that the moving party and the adverse party are each given advance notice of and, where appropriate, copies of the evidentiary material on which the other party relies in connection with a summary judgment motion.

2012 Amendment. Subdivision (c) is amended to reflect the relocation of the service rule from rule 1.080 to Fla. R. Jud. Admin. 2.516.

Authors' Comment—1967

The rule is substantially the same as former Rule 1.36 as amended and Federal Rule 56. In terms of former Rule 1.36, there has been much rephrasing of its contents, with *decrees* being deleted from the application of the present rule because of the nonexistence of such an instrument. The present rule now allows answers to interrogatories to be the basis to establish that there is no genuine issue as to any material fact and that the moving party is entitled to judgment as a matter of law, such being in accord with the Federal Rule and the 1965 Florida amendment.

Third party claimants or defendants now have the right to utilize summary judgment practice in order to expedite the administration of justice in the same manner as other parties.

The 20 day time limit allows the defending party to file his answer and defense. The 20 day period may be extended by the court so that in such circumstances the motion for summary judgment by the claimant cannot be made until the extended time has expired. The defending party can move at any time and need not wait 20 days. If the defending party does move for a summary judgment, the claimant is not required to wait the 20 days before moving for a summary judgment.

The function of summary judgment procedure is to supply an efficient procedural device for the prompt disposition of actions, be they legal or equitable, if there be no genuine issue as to any material fact and the moving party is entitled to judgment as a matter of law. Its purposes are those expressed in rule 1.010, i.e. "to secure the just, speedy and inexpensive determination" of the action.

The moving party has the burden of proof in establishing his right to a summary judgment. The procedure utilized for obtaining this relief is not a substitute for a trial of disputed issues of fact. The court is to examine the evidence, not for the purpose of trying the fact issues, but to determine whether there is a genuine issue of fact to be tried; and if there is any issue of fact over which the parties are in disagreement the motion is to be denied. The summary judgment procedure does not include a summary trial of disputed fact issues.

While the rule makes no specific provision for a case in which it develops that the opposing, nonmoving party, is entitled to a summary judgment, the Florida courts now recognize that there are circumstances when such should be done. See Carpineta v. Shields, 70 So.2d 573 (S.Ct.1954), King v. L. & L. Investors, Inc., 133 So.2d 744 (D.C.A.3d 1961), and City of Pinellas Park v. Cross-State Utilities Co., 176 So.2d 384 (D.C.A.2d 1965). These decisions recognize that the advisable procedure is a cross-motion by the successful party, although such is not required. See also John K. Brennan Co. v. Central Bank & Trust Co., 164 So.2d 525 (D.C.A.2d 1964) for a full discussion of the due process elements in entering a summary judgment for a nonmoving party.

The fact that both parties move for summary judgment does not establish that there is no issue of fact. Although a party may on his own motion assert that, accepting his legal theory, the facts are undisputed, he may be able and should be allowed to show that if his opponent's theory is adopted a genuine issue of fact exists.

If the movant sustains his initial burden, the opponent has the burden to come forward with counter-evidence revealing a factual issue. The movant need not exclude every possible inference that the opposing party might have other evidence available to prove his case. Should the opponent not come forward with any affidavit or other proof in opposition to a motion for summary judgment, the movant need only establish a prima facie case, whereupon the court may enter such judgment. See Harvey Building, Inc. v. Haley, 175 So.2d 780 (S.Ct.1965).

Not only is it the duty of the trial judge to exclude facts which would be inadmissible in evidence as recognized in Lake v. Konstantinu, 189 So.2d 171, (D.C.A.2d 1966), the decisions further bear out that the Florida Rule does not permit the taking of any testimony at a hearing on a motion for summary judgment. See Ogden Trucking Company v. Heller Bros. & Co., 130 So.2d 295 (D.C.A.3d 1961).

The question of whether a summary judgment can be entered on a plaintiff's motion prior to the filing of defendant's answer has been settled affirmatively by the Supreme Court of Florida, provided that 20 days had expired from the commencement of the action before the motion for summary judgment was filed. The Supreme Court set for the admonition that such a motion is granted with caution, however, in Coast Cities Coaches, Inc. v. Dade County, 178 So.2d 703 (Fla.1965), and adhered to the federal decisions which uniformly hold that a plaintiff need not wait for a defendant to file answer before moving for a summary decree. Moreover, a motion to dismiss before answer does not prevent a motion for summary judgment since the latter may well be after 20 days have expired.

The new rule requires that a motion for summary judgment be served at least 20 days before the time fixed for hearing, and based upon decisions construing the prior 10 day rule, it would be reversible error to grant relief on shorter notice.

When affirmative defenses are pleaded sufficiently, and such are not contradicted or opposed properly, this will preclude a plaintiff from obtaining a summary judgment.

Under this rule, a summary judgment can be entered as to part of a pleading and the case continues as to the balance. The rule contemplates by its language entertainment of a partial summary judgment and the appellate courts have so held. In Berry v. Pyrofax Gas Corporation, 121 So.2d 447 (D.C.A.1st 1960), the Court upheld the authority to enter partial summary judgment on one of three claims stated in separate paragraphs of a counterclaim. However, such a judgment is interlocutory in character and not appealable, but it may be assigned as error upon an appeal from the final judgment. Moreover, an order denying a motion for summary judgment in its entirety is not a final judgment, but is interlocutory in nature.

Although Florida Appellate Rule 4.2a does not presently permit an interlocutory appeal from an order denying a motion by the plaintiff for a summary judgment on liability in a "law" action, the desirability of such an appeal seems apparent and would in many instances result in the avoidance of a costly and lengthy trial. An excellent commentary construing the similar provisions of Federal Rule 56 is found in 3 Barron and Holtzoff, Federal Practice and Procedure, Rules Edition (West 1958) which should be consulted to determine the federal courts' interpretations of the analogous Federal Rule. In view of the close adherence of the Florida Courts to the federal interpretations, these volumes are of great value to successful utilization of the Florida rule.

Related Motions—Distinguished

It is sometimes difficult to distinguish between a motion for a summary judgment under this rule, a motion to dismiss under Rule 1.140(b), and a motion for judgment on the pleadings under Rule 1.140(c). Technically these three motions have distinct functions. A motion to dismiss for lack of jurisdiction, improper venue, insufficiency of process, insufficiency of service, and failure to join an indispensable party contemplates a dismissal of the claim and not a judgment on the merits for either party. A motion to dismiss for failure to state a cause of action, besides asking for a dismissal, is by its terms a contention that the pleading to which it is addressed does not in itself sufficiently state a case. A motion for judgment on the pleadings is based upon the ground that the moving party is entitled to a judgment on the face of the pleadings themselves. On the other hand a party moving for summary judgment contends that on the basis of the entire record—pleadings, depositions, admissions, answers to interrogatories, and affidavits of both parties—there is no genuine issue as to any material fact and that he is entitled to a judgment as a matter of law. In practice, however, many courts have disregarded these distinctions. In view of the purpose of the rules to secure the just, speedy, and inexpensive determination of every action, the courts have been reluctant to refuse to make the proper disposition of the case merely because of the form of the motion.

Use by Defendant

A defending party is not required to serve his responsive pleading before moving for summary judgment. He may make the motion at any time, setting out his defenses by affidavit, and thus effect a speedy termination of the action if no genuine issue exists as to any fact or facts pertaining to a defense that would defeat the claim.

The defendant party may likewise, before pleading, test the sufficiency of the claim by a motion for dismissal for failure to state a cause of action. If matters outside the pleading are presented to the court on the motion and not excluded, the motion is to be treated as one for summary judgment testing the sufficiency of the claim in fact.

The defending party is not required to wait 20 days. If the defending party moves for a summary judgment and has a hearing on same, Rule 1.420(a)(1) prevents the claimant from voluntarily dismissing his action. Unlike similar Federal Rule 41, Rule 1.420 requires a voluntary dismissal to be taken before a summary judgment hearing, whereas the federal rule and former Florida Rule 1.35(a)(1) allow a voluntary dismissal at any time prior to service of a motion for summary judgment.

Determination of Undisputed Facts

The decisions are not clear whether a motion for summary judgment is available to a party who cannot contend that there is no issue of fact and who makes the motion only to secure an order under Rule 1.510(d) that certain facts appear without substantial controversy and shall be deemed established at the trial. Rules 1.510(a) and 1.510(b) authorize a motion upon any part of a claim, and it is clear by the last sentence of Rule 1.510(c) that the party may seek a summary judgment solely upon the issue of liability, admitting that a controversy exists as to the amount of damages. But it is not clear whether the motion can be made solely for the purpose of obtaining the order provided for in Rule 1.510(d), or whether the order is intended to be only ancillary to a motion seeking a summary judgment as to the whole claim, or at least as to all factual issues bearing on liability.

The court is obliged to make the order provided for by paragraph (d) of this rule. The entire rule is mandatory. Actually an order must be entered—an oral ruling is not sufficient. The order must specify the facts which are not controverted. Upon the trial the order is used to indicate the facts which are established and as to which no proof is necessary. The object is to shorten the trial by eliminating the fact issues shown to be without substantial controversy. The effect of the order is the same as an order under Rule 1.200 for formulation of issues. It is interlocutory in character and therefor non-appealable in a common law claim. To call it a "partial summary judgment" is a misnomer.

Affidavits

Affidavits can be used by any party, be it the claimant, the defending party or a third party claimant or defendant. Such instruments may be in support of or in opposition to a motion for summary judgment. They are the weakest form of evidence and not ordinarily admissible at trial. Their function is to show that there is available competent testimony which can be introduced at the trial.

An affidavit substantially in the form of testimony admissible at a trial should satisfy the requirements that it be made upon personal knowledge and set forth such facts as would be admissible in evidence. The requirement that it show affirmatively that the affiant is competent to testify to the matters stated therein is not satisfied by the statement that he has personal knowledge; there should be stated in detail the facts showing that he has personal knowledge.

If a document is referred to in an affidavit, and the affiant does not have the document or a copy of it, he should so state in the affidavit, describe the document, state when and where he saw it and under what circumstances, who has possession, and what efforts have been made to obtain it or a copy of it.

A movant's affidavits are viewed strictly, whereas counter-affidavits are read more liberally by the courts as a matter of practice. See Holl v. Talcott, 191 So.2d 40 (S.Ct.1966).

If in support of a motion for summary judgment, the affidavit should be filed with the motion so as to allow opposing parties time to controvert it. If the affidavit is in opposition to a motion for summary judgment, it must be filed prior to the day of the hearing.

Under some circumstances, as recognized in Jones v. Stoutenburgh, 91 So.2d 299 (S.Ct.1957), pre-trial discovery procedures can be utilized to reveal that a defending affiant actually has no competent evidentiary support for his affidavit.

A statement in an affidavit which is physically impossible in the light of common knowledge or scientific principles may be disregarded and does not create a genuine issue of fact. Watley v. Florida Power and Light Company, 192 So.2d 27 (D.C.A. 1st 1966).

Affidavits Unavailable

The purpose of Rule 1.510(f) is to protect a party opposing a motion for summary judgment who is unable at the time of the hearing to establish that there is a genuine issue of fact. To be entitled to protection, the party must show by affidavit good grounds why he has been unable to present his proof; the affidavit should show what the proof is and what steps have been taken to obtain it. The court is given wide discretion to deal with the various circumstances, e.g., refuse the application for judgment, order a continuance to permit affidavits to be obtained or depositions to be taken or discovery to be had, or make such other order as is just.

Affidavits In Bad Faith

Under paragraph (g) summary judgment affidavits filed for the purpose of delay will subject the party filing them to costs and counsel fees. The court may adjudge the attorney who files such affidavits in contempt if the court finds that he has acted in bad faith or solely for the purpose of delay.

Answers to Interrogatories

Answers to interrogatories can be the basis to establish that there is no genuine issue as to any material fact and that the moving party is entitled to judgment as a matter of law. This element is new to the Florida Rule by the 1965 amendment to former Rule 1.36, effective January 1, 1966, and became a part of similar Federal Rule 56 in 1963.

Important distinctions exist between answers to interrogatories and affidavits which should be noted. An affidavit is the weakest form of evidence and ordinarily is not admissible at trial, as noted above. Its function on a motion for summary judgment is to show that there is available competent testimony which can be introduced at trial. The answer to an interrogatory, however, similar to an admission, is admissible at trial when offered by the opposing party, since it is an admission of an adverse party.

The rule now authorizes the Court to permit affidavits to be supplemented or opposed by answers to interrogatories. For an excellent discussion of the use of answers to interrogatories, prior to the new rule, as well as function, use and limitations of summary judgments, see Lake v. Konstantinu, *supra*.

Rule 1.520. View

Upon motion of either party the jury may be taken to view the premises or place in question or any property, matter, or thing relating to the controversy between the parties when it appears that view is necessary to a just decision; but the party making the motion shall advance a sum sufficient to defray the expenses of the jury and the officer who attends them in taking the view, which expense shall be taxed as costs if the party who advanced it prevails.

Amended July 16, 1992, effective Jan. 1, 1993 (604 So.2d 1110).

Authors' Comment—1967

Rule 1.520 is identical to former Rule 2.23, 1954 Rules of Civil Procedure which became effective on January 1, 1966.

The rule was new to the Rules of Civil Procedure, beginning Jan. 1, 1966. A similar provision appears in Section 73.071(5), F.S.A., relating to the view of the property by a jury in eminent domain proceedings. It should be noted that the allowance of a view of the premises or place in question, or any property, matter or thing relating to the controversy between the parties, by the very language of the rule, is within the sound discretion of the trial court. See Fontainebleau Hotel Corp. v. Goddard, 177 So.2d 555 (D.C.A.3d 1965).

Rule 1.525. Motions for Costs and Attorneys' Fees

Any party seeking a judgment taxing costs, attorneys' fees, or both shall serve a motion no later than 30 days after filing of the judgment, including a judgment of dismissal, or the service of a notice of voluntary dismissal, which judgment or notice concludes the action as to that party.

Added Oct. 5, 2000, effective Jan. 1, 2001 (773 So.2d 1098). Amended Oct. 23, 2003, effective Jan. 1, 2004 (858 So.2d 1013); Dec. 15, 2005, effective Jan. 1, 2006 (917 So.2d 176); Sept. 8, 2010, effective Jan. 1, 2011 (52 So.3d 579).

Committee Notes

2000 Adoption. This rule is intended to establish a time requirement to serve motions for costs and attorneys' fees.

Court Commentary

2000 Adoption. This rule only establishes time requirements for serving motions for costs, attorneys' fees, or both, and in no way affects or overrules the pleading requirements outlined by this Court in *Stockman v. Downs*, 573 So. 2d 835 (Fla. 1991).

Rule 1.530. Motions for New Trial and Rehearing; Amendments of Judgments

(a) Jury and Non-Jury Actions. A new trial may be granted to all or any of the parties and on all or a part of the issues. On a motion for a rehearing of matters heard without a jury, including summary judgments, the court may open the judgment if one has been entered, take additional testimony, and enter a new judgment.

(b) Time for Motion. A motion for new trial or for rehearing shall be served not later than 15 days after the return of the verdict in a jury action or the date of filing of the judgment in a non-jury action. A timely motion may be amended to state new grounds in the discretion of the court at any time before the motion is determined.

(c) Time for Serving Affidavits. When a motion for a new trial is based on affidavits, the affidavits shall be served with the motion. The opposing party has 10 days after such service within which to serve opposing affidavits, which period may be extended for an additional period not exceeding 20 days either by the court for good cause shown or by the parties by written stipulation. The court may permit reply affidavits.

(d) On Initiative of Court. Not later than 15 days after entry of judgment or within the time of ruling on a timely motion for a rehearing or a new trial made by a party, the court of its own initiative may order a rehearing or a new trial for any reason for which it might have granted a rehearing or a new trial on motion of a party.

(e) When Motion Is Unnecessary; Non-Jury Case. When an action has been tried by the court without a jury, the sufficiency of the evidence to support the judgment may be raised on appeal whether or not the party raising the question has made any objection thereto in the trial court or made a motion for rehearing, for new trial, or to alter or amend the judgment.

(f) Order Granting to Specify Grounds. All orders granting a new trial shall specify the specific grounds therefor. If such an order is appealed and does not state the specific grounds, the appellate court shall relinquish its jurisdiction to the trial court for entry of an order specifying the grounds for granting the new trial.

(g) Motion to Alter or Amend a Judgment. A motion to alter or amend the judgment shall be served not later than 15 days after entry of the judgment, except that this rule does not affect the remedies in rule 1.540(b).

Amended June 19, 1968, effective Oct. 1, 1968 (211 So.2d 206); Sept. 13, 1984, effective Jan. 1, 1985 (458 So.2d 245); July 16, 1992, effective Jan. 1, 1993 (604 So.2d 1110); Nov. 14, 2013, effective Jan. 1, 2014 (131 So.3d 643).

Committee Notes

1992 Amendment. In subdivision (e), the reference to assignments of error is eliminated to conform to amendments to the Florida Rules of Appellate Procedure.

2013 Amendment. Subdivisions (b) and (g) are amended to change the deadlines for service of certain motions from 10 to 15 days after the specified event. Subdivision (d) is amended to change the deadline for a court to act of its own initiative.

Authors' Comment—1967

The present rule is similar to former amended Rule 2.8, 1954 Rules of Civil Procedure which became effective on January 1, 1966, but both Rule 1.530 and amended Rule 2.8 differ in great detail from the various rules which served as their source. The new rule provides for a motion for rehearing of matters heard without a jury wherein the court may open the judgment if one has been entered, take additional testimony and enter a new judgment.

Federal Rules 59 and 52(b) contain similar provisions to the Florida rule. Former amended Rule 3.16, 1954 Rules of Civil Procedure, effective January 1, 1966, included petitions directed to summary decrees within the meaning of rehearings, whereas the new rule includes summary judgments as proper objects for rehearing, and designates a motion for a rehearing as the proper vehicle to obtain such relief. This again is recognition of the abolishing of procedural differences between law and equity.

The rule provides for the service of affidavits with any motion for a new trial based upon affidavits, such to be served with the motion. Paragraph (c) further provides for specified time period in which to serve opposing affidavits.

Paragraph (d) providing for the ordering of a rehearing or new trial within the ten day period after the entry of judgment or within the time of ruling on a timely motion for rehearing or a timely motion for new trial, is much broader than the former paragraph (c) of former Rule 2.8, prior to its amendment, which had referred solely to the rendition of a verdict.

Paragraph (e) is the same as the former rule establishing that in a non-jury case, the sufficiency of the evidence may be raised on appeal by an assignment of error regardless of the fact that the party may not have raised any objection in the trial court in any manner. Paragraph (f) requires every order granting a new trial must specify the particular and specific grounds therefor. Paragraph (g) authorizes a motion to alter or amend a judgment within ten days after the entry of the judgment, without affecting the remedies provided in Rule 1.540(b), the latter providing for relief for specified reasons. The rule refers to such motion to amend judgment as being necessarily filed not later than ten days after the entry of judgment, wherein the former paragraph (d) of Rule 2.8, prior to its amendment, referred to the rendition of a verdict as the focal point within which to move to amend the judgment.

It should be noted that paragraph (f) requires that every order granting a new trial shall specify the particular and specific grounds therefor, whereas such requirement was found prior to the adoption of the new rule, in Rule 2.6(d), the latter having been deleted in the revision, effective July 1, 1962.

It should be noted further that a motion for new trial may be joined with a motion for a directed verdict under Rule 1.480(c). Moreover, it would appear that by operation of Rule 1.470(c), it would not be necessary to object or except to any order granting or denying a motion for new trial to obtain appellate review.

A timely motion under this rule may be amended to state new grounds if allowed by the court prior to ruling on the motion.

Great emphasis should be accorded the timeliness within which a file a proper motion for rehearing, inasmuch as the filing of a motion for rehearing *after* the filing of a notice of appeal destroys the effectiveness of the notice of appeal, and jurisdiction can only be vested in the appellate court by filing another notice of appeal after the disposition of the motion for rehearing or abandonment of same. See State ex rel. Owens v. Pearson, 156 So.2d 4 (1963). The disposition of the motion for rehearing constitutes the rendition point for appellate purposes (Rule 1.3, Fla.App.Rules). However, a notice of appeal filed *after* the motion for rehearing has been filed in the lower court would constitute an abandonment of the motion in all probability. See State ex rel. Faircloth v. District Court of Approval, Third District, 187 So.2d 890 (S.Ct.1966). It is important that the motion for rehearing be timely filed.

Court Commentary

1984 Amendment. Subdivision (b): This clarifies the time in which a motion for rehearing may be served. It specifies that the date of filing as shown on the face of the judgment in a non-jury action is the date from which the time for serving a motion for rehearing is calculated.

There is no change in the time for serving a motion for new trial in a jury action, except the motion may be served before the rendition of the judgment.

Rule 1.540. Relief From Judgment, Decrees, or Orders

(a) Clerical Mistakes. Clerical mistakes in judgments, decrees, or other parts of the record and errors therein arising from oversight or omission may be corrected by the court at any time on its own initiative or on the motion of any party and after such notice, if any, as the court orders. During the pendency of an appeal such mistakes may be so corrected before the record on appeal is docketed in the appellate court, and thereafter while the appeal is pending may be so corrected with leave of the appellate court.

(b) Mistakes; Inadvertence; Excusable Neglect; Newly Discovered Evidence; Fraud; etc. On motion and upon such terms as are just, the court may relieve a party or a party's legal representative from a final judgment, decree, order, or proceeding for the following reasons: (1) mistake, inadvertence, surprise, or excusable neglect; (2) newly discovered evidence which by due diligence could not have been discovered in time to move for a new trial or rehearing; (3) fraud (whether heretofore denominated intrinsic or extrinsic), misrepresentation, or other misconduct of an adverse party; (4) that the judgment or decree is void; or (5) that the judgment or decree has been satisfied, released, or discharged, or a prior judgment or decree upon which it is based has been reversed or otherwise vacated, or it is no longer equitable that the judgment or decree should have prospective application. The motion shall be filed within a reasonable time, and for reasons (1), (2), and (3) not more than 1 year after the judgment, decree, order, or proceeding was entered or taken. A motion under this subdivision does not affect the finality of a judgment or decree or suspend its operation. This rule does not limit the power of a court to entertain an independent action to relieve a party from a judgment, decree, order, or proceeding or to set aside a judgment or decree for fraud upon the court.

Writs of coram nobis, coram vobis, audita querela, and bills of review and bills in the nature of a bill of review are abolished, and the procedure for obtaining any relief from a judgment or decree shall be by motion as prescribed in these rules or by an independent action.

Amended July 16, 1992, effective Jan. 1, 1993 (604 So.2d 1110); July 7, 1995, effective Jan. 1, 1996 (663 So.2d 1047); Nov. 22, 1995, effective Jan. 1, 1996 (663 So.2d 1049); Oct. 23, 2003, effective Jan. 1, 2004 (858 So.2d 1013).

Committee Notes

1992 Amendment. Subdivision (b) is amended to remove the 1–year limitation for a motion under this rule based on fraudulent financial affidavits in marital cases.

2003 Amendment. Subdivision (b) is amended to clarify that motions must be filed.

Authors' Comment—1967

Rule 1.540 is substantially the same as Federal Rule 60, but includes decrees as the object of the relief sought, unlike the Federal Rule. It is identical to former Rule 1.38, 1954 Rules of Civil Procedure, as amended, effective in 1962.

This rule applies to orders, decrees and proceedings as well as to judgments, "decrees" apparently being included because those rendered prior to January 1, 1967, may come within this rule.

Subsection (a) relating to clerical mistakes includes only errors or mistakes arising from accidental slip or omission and not errors or mistakes in the substance of what is decided by the judgment or order. Such may be called to court's attention by motion practiced by any party. Correcting or completing the record-on-appeal is provided for in Florida Appellate Rule 3.6*l*.

Subsection (b) provides for motion practice to relieve a party upon such terms as are just from a final judgment, decree, order, or proceeding on five specified grounds, whereas the comparable Federal Rule provides for an additional reason whenever it justifies relief from operation of the judgment.

The application of the relief provisions is generally within the discretion of the court except when questions of law are involved. For example, if a judgment or decree is void as a matter of law, no discretion would exist but to give proper relief.

The rule requires that the motion for relief be made within a reasonable time, with a one (1) year limitation being applicable to the first three grounds of mistake, et al., newly discovered evidence which could not be discovered by due diligence in time to move for a new trial or rehearing, and fraud or other misconduct of an adverse party.

Since the motion is not in the appellate court, it does not stay proceedings under Florida Appellate Rule 3.9f and will not toll the appeal time. If the motion is granted, the time to appeal will run from the new judgment rendered. Certain former corrective writs for relief are abolished by the rule with relief from a judgment or decree being only by motion as prescribed by the Rules or by an independent action.

When a judgment becomes a judgment of the appellate court, it is necessary to first obtain leave of the appellate court before the lower court has jurisdiction to relieve a party from a judgment. Filing of an appeal, however, does not toll the one year limitation in which a motion to vacate a judgment must be filed.

Subsection (b) is applicable to obtain relief from an unjust prior decree or judgment and has been liberally construed to provide such remedy. While a denial of the motion is appealable as a final judgment or decree, such appeal will not bring up for review the final decree or judgment sought to be vacated; if the motion is granted, the order is interlocutory, which is appealable as such, unless the court's action on granting of motion meets the test of finality, in which event it is appealable as a final judgment. See Odum v. Morningstar, 158 So.2d 776 (Fla.D.C.A.2d 1963).

The power of the court is discretionary and a party has no absolute right to invoke it. It is incumbent upon the moving party to show the existence of adequate grounds to justify the exercise of such power.

Although the rule speaks of abolishing writs of coram nobis and coram vobis, such motions are still available in criminal procedure.

Moreover, as in the Federal Rule, Rule 1.540(b) does not extend to interlocutory judgments.

Finally, it should be carefully noted that there is an express saving clause in Rule 1.540(b) which does not limit the power of the court to set aside a judgment or decree for fraud upon the court. There is no time limit on the exercise of this power, nor on the right to bring an independent action under this rule.

Rule 1.550. Executions and Final Process

(a) Issuance. Executions on judgments shall issue during the life of the judgment on the oral request of the party entitled to it or that party's attorney without praecipe. No execution or other final process shall issue until the judgment on which it is based has been recorded nor within the time for serving a motion for new trial or rehearing, and if a motion for new trial or rehearing is timely served, until it is determined; provided execution or other final process may be issued on special order of the court at any time after judgment.

(b) Stay. The court before which an execution or other process based on a final judgment is returnable may stay such execution or other process and suspend proceedings thereon for good cause on motion and notice to all adverse parties.

Amended June 19, 1968, effective Oct. 1, 1968 (211 So.2d 206); July 16, 1992, effective Jan. 1, 1993 (604 So.2d 1110).

Authors' Comment—1967

Rule 1.550 is almost identical to former Rule 2.13, 1954 Rules of Civil Procedure as amended, effective January 1, 1966. The current rule, however, provides for executions to issue without praecipe. In connection with this rule, consideration should be given to F.S.A. Ch. 55, which deals at length with judgments and executions.

Filing a motion for new trial or rehearing stays the issuance of execution unless the court orders otherwise. This is different from the terminology of former Rule 3.16 which did not permit a petition for rehearing to stay the proceedings unless ordered by the court.

Rule 1.560. Discovery in Aid of Execution

(a) In General. In aid of a judgment, decree, or execution the judgment creditor or the successor in interest, when the interest appears of record, may obtain discovery from any person, including the judgment debtor, in the manner provided in these rules.

(b) Fact Information Sheet. In addition to any other discovery available to a judgment creditor under this rule, the court, at the request of the judgment creditor, shall order the judgment debtor or debtors to complete form 1.977, including all required attachments, within 45 days of the order or such other reasonable time as determined by the court. Failure to obey the order may be considered contempt of court.

(c) Final Judgment Enforcement Paragraph. In any final judgment, the judge shall include the following enforcement paragraph if requested by the prevailing party or attorney:

"It is further ordered and adjudged that the judgment debtor(s) shall complete under oath Florida Rule of Civil Procedure Form 1.977 (Fact Information Sheet), including all required attachments, and serve it on the judgment creditor's attorney, or the judgment creditor if the judgment creditor is not represented by an attorney, within 45 days from the date of this final judgment, unless the final judgment is satisfied or post-judgment discovery is stayed.

Jurisdiction of this case is retained to enter further orders that are proper to compel the judgment debtor(s) to complete form 1.977, including all required attachments, and serve it on the judgment creditor's attorney, or the judgment creditor if the judgment creditor is not represented by an attorney."

(d) Information Regarding Assets of Judgment Debtor's Spouse. In any final judgment, if requested by the judgment creditor, the court shall include the additional Spouse Related Portion of the fact information sheet upon a showing that a proper predicate exists for discovery of separate income and assets of the judgment debtor's spouse.

Amended July 26, 1972, effective Jan. 1, 1973 (265 So.2d 21); July 16, 1992, effective Jan. 1, 1993 (604 So.2d 1110); Oct. 5, 2000, effective Jan. 1, 2001 (773 So.2d 1098); Nov. 14, 2013, effective Jan. 1, 2014 (131 So.3d 643).

Committee Notes

1972 Amendment. The rule is expanded to permit discovery in any manner permitted by the rules and conforms to the 1970 change in Federal Rule of Civil Procedure 69(a).

2000 Amendment. Subdivisions (b)–(e) were added and patterned after Florida Small Claims Rule 7.221(a) and Form 7.343. Although the judgment creditor is entitled to broad discovery into the judgment debtor's finances, Fla. R. Civ. P. 1.280(b); *Jim Appley's Tru–Arc, Inc. v. Liquid Extraction Systems*, 526 So. 2d 177, 179 (Fla. 2d DCA 1988), inquiry into the individual assets of the judgment debtor's spouse may be limited until a proper predicate has been shown. *Tru-Arc, Inc.* 526 So. 2d at 179; *Rose Printing Co. v. D'Amato*, 338 So. 2d 212 (Fla. 3d DCA 1976).

Failure to complete form 1.977 as ordered may be considered contempt of court.

2013 Amendment. Subdivision (e) was deleted because the filing of a notice of compliance is unnecessary for the judgment creditor to seek relief from the court for noncompliance with this rule, and because the Fact Information Sheet itself should not be filed with the clerk of the court.

Authors' Comment—1967

The Rule 1.560 is identical to former Rule 1.40, 1954 Rules of Civil Procedure and to the last sentence of Federal Rule 69(a), except that the latter does not mention decrees. The federal counterpart provides that procedure in aid of judgment or execution may be in the manner provided for taking depositions, as does the Florida Rule, and further allows the manner provided by the practice of the state in which the district court is held.

The Florida procedure provides a flexible and inexpensive method for uncovering assets against which to make a levy.

It does not, however, have the teeth of the supplementary proceedings provided by F.S.A. § 56.36. These proceedings are still available and will often be preferred where third parties or fraudulent transfers are involved or the benefits of Dezen v. Slatcoff, 66 So.2d 483 (Fla.1953) can be obtained.

In some instances it may be found helpful to use discovery as a preliminary aid to supplementary proceedings.

The depositions may be taken at any time after judgment upon notice, without a court order, and before any person authorized to administer an oath. The statutory proceedings supplementary to execution require a return of execution unsatisfied and an application to the court for an order requiring the judgment debtor to appear for examination before the judge or a commissioner appointed in the order. The depositions may supply information in aid of the judgment or execution, while under the statutory proceedings the court may make various orders pertaining to the property discovered. The two procedures are cumulative.

Supplemental proceedings are separate and distinct from the main cause in which judgment is procured and sometimes are said to be collateral to it.

In Olin's Rent-A-Car System, Inc. v. Avis Rental Car System of Florida, Inc., 135 So.2d 434 (D.C.A.3d 1961), the Court ruled that after deposition discovery procedures were utilized by a judgment creditor, there was no legal basis for the issuance of a rule to show cause by the lower court directed to the garnishee judgment debtor to produce its business records prior to the filing of an answer by said garnishee judgment debtor. The Court recognized the possibility of obtaining discovery under Rule 1.350, but stated that the burden would be upon the judgment creditor to show good cause for the order sought.

See 3 Barron and Holtzoff, Federal Practice and Procedure, Rules Edition, Rule 69 (West 1958) for an excellent discussion of the federal counterpart to this rule.

Rule 1.570. Enforcement of Final Judgments

(a) Money Judgments. Final process to enforce a judgment solely for the payment of money shall be by execution, writ of garnishment, or other appropriate process or proceedings.

(b) Property Recovery. Final process to enforce a judgment for the recovery of property shall be by a writ of possession for real property and by a writ of replevin, distress writ, writ of garnishment, or other appropriate process or proceedings for other property.

(c) Performance of an Act. If judgment is for the performance of a specific act or contract:

(1) the judgment shall specify the time within which the act shall be performed. If the act is not performed within the time specified, the party seeking enforcement of the judgment shall make an affidavit that the judgment has not been complied with within the prescribed time and the clerk shall issue a writ of attachment against the delinquent party. The delinquent party shall not be released from the writ of attachment until that party has complied with the judgment and paid all costs accruing because of the failure to perform the act. If the delinquent party cannot be found, the party seeking enforcement of the judgment shall file an affidavit to this effect and the court shall issue a writ of sequestration against the delinquent party's property. The writ of sequestration shall not be dissolved until the delinquent party complies with the judgment;

(2) the court may hold the disobedient party in contempt; or

(3) the court may appoint some person, not a party to the action, to perform the act insofar as practicable. The performance of the act by the person appointed shall have the same effect as if performed by the party against whom the judgment was entered.

(d) Vesting Title. If the judgment is for a conveyance, transfer, release, or acquittance of real or personal property, the judgment shall have the effect of a duly executed conveyance, transfer, release, or acquittance that is recorded in the county where the judgment is recorded. A judgment under this subdivision shall be effective notwithstanding any disability of a party.

Amended Oct. 9, 1980, effective Jan. 1, 1981 (391 So.2d 165); July 16, 1992, effective Jan. 1, 1993 (604 So.2d 1110).

Committee Notes

1980 Amendment. This rule has been subdivided and amended to make it more easily understood. No change in the substance of the rule is intended. Subdivision (d) is partly derived from Federal Rule of Civil Procedure 70.

Authors' Comment—1967

Rule 1.570 rephrases former Rule 3.15, 1954 Rules of Civil Procedure, relating to enforcement of final decrees, with certain modifications and changes. Initially, the term "judgment" is substituted for "decree" throughout the rule.

Old Chancery Act Section 67 from which this rule was taken was based on Federal Equity Rule 8. Federal Rule of Civil Procedure 70 now has somewhat comparable provisions although there are many differences.

By Rule 1.570 provision is made for the enforcement of judgments for the performance of specific acts. Such judgments might become useless, in the absence of convenient and efficient methods for securing their enforcement. The very variety and flexibility of these judgments necessitates greater elasticity and broader scope in the means by which these judgments can be made effective. Such scope and elasticity in these methods are secured by this Rule. If a judgment be for the performance of a specific act, and the act is not performed within the time prescribed by the judgment, the court may direct that the act required to be done be done by some person appointed by the court; or the clerk may issue a writ of attachment or sequestration. A writ of assistance may be obtained for the enforcement of judgments or orders for the delivery of possession.

Rule 1.580. Writ of Possession

(a) Issuance. When a judgment or order is for the delivery of possession of real property, the judgment or order shall direct the clerk to issue a writ of possession. The clerk shall issue the writ forthwith and deliver it to the sheriff for execution.

(b) Third-Party Claims. If a person other than the party against whom the writ of possession is issued is in possession of the property, that person may retain possession of the property by filing with the sheriff an affidavit that the person is entitled to possession of the property, specifying the nature of the claim. Thereupon the sheriff shall desist from enforcing the writ and shall serve a copy of the affidavit on the party causing issuance of the writ of possession. The party causing issuance of the writ may apply to the court for an order directing the sheriff to complete execution of the writ. The court shall determine the right of possession in the property and shall order the sheriff to continue to execute the writ or shall stay execution of the writ, if appropriate.

Amended Oct. 9, 1980, effective Jan. 1, 1981 (391 So.2d 165); July 16, 1992, effective Jan. 1, 1993 (604 So.2d 1110).

Committee Notes

1980 Amendment. There was inadvertently continued the difference between writs of assistance and writs of possession when law and chancery procedure was consolidated. The amendment eliminates the distinction. Writs of assistance are combined with writs of possession. The amendment provides for issuance and the determination of third-party claims. The only change is to shift the burden of the affidavit from the person causing the writ to be executed to the third person who contends that its execution is inappropriate.

Authors' Comment—1967

Rule 1.580 is similar to former Rule 3.17, 1954 Rules of Civil Procedure.

Writs of assistance were long recognized in federal equity practice under Federal Equity 9 which was carried forward in Section 69 of the Chancery Act on which present Rule 1.580 is based. Present Federal Rule 70 recognizes writs of assistance.

Rule 1.590. Process in Behalf of and Against Persons not Parties

Every person who is not a party to the action who has obtained an order, or in whose favor an order has been made, may enforce obedience to such order by the same process as if that person were a party, and every person, not a party, against whom obedience to any order may be enforced shall be liable to the same process for enforcing obedience to such orders as if that person were a party.

Amended July 16, 1992, effective Jan. 1, 1993 (604 So.2d 1110).

Authors' Comment—1967

Rule 1.590 is identical to former Rule 3.18, 1954 Rules of Civil Procedure, as amended in 1965, effective January 1, 1966.

Chancery Act Section 72, on which this rule is based, was taken from Federal Equity Rule 11. Federal Rule 71 now contains similar provisions.

A court may make an order in favor of one not a party. An example of this arises where a foreclosure or other judicial sale is made and the court then orders the property delivered to the purchaser or his assignee. Such purchaser or assignee is entitled to any process to endorse the order to which a party might be entitled. However, the rights of a person not a party to the proceeding cannot be adjudicated.

Under Equity Rule 11, a writ of assistance could be granted in favor of purchasers of land from a party obtaining the decree or order. It could not issue against any but a party to the suit in which it was sought, or his privies or one coming into possession pendente lite. 5 Barron, Darnieder and Keogh, Federal Practice and Procedure, Section 4407.

The rule can have application in class actions, in which rights and obligations may be determined with respect to persons who are not parties to the action except by way of representation.

Rule 1.600. Deposits in Court

In an action in which any part of the relief sought is a judgment for a sum of money or the disposition of a sum of money or the disposition of any other thing capable of delivery, a party may deposit all or any part of such sum or thing with the court upon notice to every other party and by leave of court. Money paid into court under this rule shall be deposited and withdrawn by order of court.

Authors' Comment—1967

Rule 1.600 is almost identical to Federal Rule 67, and the cases thereunder should be consulted. See, also, Phipps v. Watson, 147 So. 234 (Fla.1933). It would appear that the running of interest on a judgment may be stopped by paying the amount of the judgment and costs into the court pending determination of how the proceeds are to be distributed.

See 3 Barron and Holtzoff, Federal Practice and Procedure, Rules Edition, Chapter 12, Rule 67 (West 1958) for a complete discussion of the federal counterpart to the Florida rule.

A deposit of money or thing capable of delivery requires an order of court upon notice. Although the rule provides for withdrawal of money only on order of the court it does not appear to require such an order for withdrawal of any other thing capable of delivery. A deposit with the court may be made prior to any judgment, if a party so desires. The parties to litigation may stipulate as to the disposition of moneys deposited in the court.

Rule 1.610. Injunctions

(a) Temporary Injunction.

(1) A temporary injunction may be granted without written or oral notice to the adverse party only if:

(A) it appears from the specific facts shown by affidavit or verified pleading that immediate and irreparable injury, loss, or damage will result to the movant before the adverse party can be heard in opposition; and

(B) the movant's attorney certifies in writing any efforts that have been made to give notice and the reasons why notice should not be required.

(2) No evidence other than the affidavit or verified pleading shall be used to support the application for a temporary injunction unless the adverse party appears at the hearing or has received reasonable notice of the hearing. Every temporary injunction granted without notice shall be endorsed with the date and hour of entry and shall be filed forthwith in the clerk's office and shall define the injury, state findings by the court why the injury may be irreparable, and give the reasons why the order was granted without notice if notice was not given. The temporary injunction shall remain in effect until the further order of the court.

(b) Bond. No temporary injunction shall be entered unless a bond is given by the movant in an amount the court deems proper, conditioned for the payment of costs and damages sustained by the adverse party if the adverse party is wrongfully enjoined. When any injunction is issued on the pleading of a municipality or the state or any officer, agency, or political subdivision thereof, the court may require or dispense with a bond, with or without surety, and conditioned in the same manner, having due regard for the public interest. No bond shall be required for issuance of a temporary injunction issued solely to prevent physical injury or abuse of a natural person.

(c) Form and Scope. Every injunction shall specify the reasons for entry, shall describe in reasonable detail the act or acts restrained without reference to a pleading or another document, and shall be binding on the parties to the action, their officers, agents, servants, employees, and attorneys and on those persons in active concert or participation with them who receive actual notice of the injunction.

(d) Motion to Dissolve. A party against whom a temporary injunction has been granted may move to dissolve or modify it at any time. If a party moves to dissolve or modify, the motion shall be heard within 5 days after the movant applies for a hearing on the motion.

Amended Oct. 9, 1980, effective Jan. 1, 1981 (391 So.2d 165); Sept. 13, 1984, effective Jan. 1, 1985 (458 So.2d 245); July 16, 1992, effective Jan. 1, 1993 (604 So.2d 1110); Oct. 5, 2000, effective Jan. 1, 2001 (773 So.2d 1098).

Committee Notes

1980 Amendment. This rule has been extensively amended so that it is similar to Federal Rule of Civil Procedure 65. The requirement that an injunction not be issued until a complaint was filed has been deleted as unnecessary. A pleading seeking an injunction or temporary restraining order must still be filed before either can be entered. The rule now provides for a temporary restraining order without notice that will expire automatically unless a hearing on a preliminary injunction is held and a preliminary injunction granted. The contents of an injunctive order are specified. The binding effect of an injunctive order is specified, but does not change existing law. Motions to dissolve may be made and heard at any time. The trial on the merits can be consolidated with a hearing on issuance of a preliminary injunction, and the trial can be advanced to accommodate this.

Court Commentary

1984 Amendment. Considerable dissatisfaction arose on the adoption of the 1980 rule, particularly because of the creation of the temporary restraining order with its inflexible time limits. See *Sun Tech Inc. of South Florida v. Fortune Personnel Agency of Fort Lauderdale*, 412 So. 2d 962 (Fla. 4th DCA 1982). The attempt to balance the rights of the parties in 1980 failed because of court congestion and the inability in the existing circumstances to accommodate the inflexible time limits. These changes will restore injunction procedure to substantially the same as that existing before the 1980 change. The temporary restraining order terminology and procedure is abolished. The former procedure of temporary and permanent injunctions is restored. The requirement of findings and reasons and other details in an injunctive order are retained.

Subdivision (b) eliminates the need for a bond on a temporary injunction issued to prevent physical injury or abuse of a natural person.

Subdivision (e) institutes a requirement that a motion to dissolve an injunction shall be heard within 5 days after the movant applies for it. This provision emphasizes the importance of a prompt determination of the propriety of injunctive relief granted without notice or, if the circumstances have changed since the issuance of the injunctive order, the need for speedy relief as a result of the changes. Former subdivisions (a), (b)(3), and (b)(4) have been repealed because the new procedure makes them superfluous. The right of the court to consolidate the hearing on a temporary injunction with the trial of the action is not affected because that can still be accomplished under rule 1.270(a).

Rule 1.620. Receivers

(a) Notice. The provisions of rule 1.610 as to notice shall apply to applications for the appointment of receivers.

(b) Report. Every receiver shall file in the clerk's office a true and complete inventory under oath of the property coming under the receiver's control or possession under the receiver's appointment within 20 days after appointment. Every 3 months unless the court otherwise orders, the receiver shall file in the same office an inventory and account under oath of any additional property or effects which the receiver has discovered or which shall have come to the receiver's hands since appointment, and of the amount remaining in the hands of or invested by the receiver, and of the manner in which the same is secured or invested, stating the balance due from or to the receiver at the time of rendering the last account and the receipts and expenditures since that time. When a receiver neglects to file the inventory and account, the court shall enter an order requiring the receiver to file such inventory and account and to pay out of the receiver's own funds the expenses of the order and the proceedings thereon within not more than 20 days after being served with a copy of such order.

(c) Bond. The court may grant leave to put the bond of the receiver in suit against the sureties without notice to the sureties of the application for such leave.

Amended July 16, 1992, effective Jan. 1, 1993 (604 So.2d 1110).

Authors' Comment—1967

Rule 1.620 is the same as former Rule 3.20, 1954 Rules of Civil Procedure, as amended in 1965, effective January 1, 1966.

A receiver is a person appointed by the court to take control, custody or management of property involved in litigation and to preserve the property and receive rents, issues and profits. He is an officer of the court, appointed as an incident to other proceedings wherein certain ultimate relief is prayed.

The matter of appointing a receiver rests within the discretion of the court.

Although it may be possible under extreme circumstances to obtain the appointment of a receiver without notice by complying with Rule 1.610, it is better to let the circumstances justify the shortness of the notice rather than no notice.

Former Rule 3.20 was reworded in the most recent amendment and separated into sub-paragraphs. It should be noted that the provisions for attachment against the receiver were eliminated.

Inasmuch as Rule 1.100 restricts pleadings to initiate a cause of action to a complaint, it would appear that a complaint would initially have to be filed for the appointment of a receiver, unless a cause of action has already been filed and thereafter it became necessary to appoint a receiver, in which case a motion, pursuant to Rule 1.100(b), would be appropriate.

Rule 1.625. Proceedings Against Surety on Judicial Bonds

When any rule or statute requires or permits giving of bond by a party in a judicial proceeding, the surety on the bond submits to the jurisdiction of the court when the bond is approved. The surety shall furnish the address for the service of papers affecting the surety's liability on the bond to the officer to whom the bond is given at that time. The liability of the surety may be enforced on motion without the necessity of an independent action. The motion shall be served on the surety at the address furnished to the officer. The surety shall serve a response to the motion within 20 days after service of the motion, asserting any defenses in law or in fact. If the surety fails to serve a response within the time allowed, a default may be taken. If the surety serves a response, the issues raised shall be decided by the court on reasonable notice to the parties. The right to jury trial shall not be abridged in any such proceedings.

Added Oct. 9, 1980, effective Jan. 1, 1981 (391 So.2d 165).

Committee Note

1980 Adoption. This rule is intended to avoid the necessity of an independent action against a surety on judicial bonds. It does not abolish an independent action if the obligee prefers to file one.

Rule 1.630. Extraordinary Remedies

(a) Applicability. This rule applies to actions for the issuance of writs of mandamus, prohibition, quo warranto, and habeas corpus.

(b) Initial Pleading. The initial pleading shall be a complaint. It shall contain:

(1) the facts on which the plaintiff relies for relief;

(2) a request for the relief sought; and

(3) if desired, argument in support of the petition with citations of authority.

The caption shall show the action filed in the name of the plaintiff in all cases and not on the relation of the state. When the complaint seeks a writ directed to a lower court or to a governmental or administrative agency, a copy of as much of the record as is necessary to support the plaintiff's complaint shall be attached.

(c) Time. A complaint shall be filed within the time provided by law.

(d) Process. If the complaint shows a prima facie case for relief, the court shall issue:

(1) an order nisi in prohibition;

(2) an alternative writ in mandamus that may incorporate the complaint by reference only;

(3) a writ of quo warranto; or

(4) a writ of habeas corpus.

The writ shall be served in the manner prescribed by law.

(e) Response. Defendant shall respond to the writ as provided in rule 1.140, but the answer in quo warranto shall show better title to the office when the writ seeks an adjudication of the right to an office held by the defendant.

Added Sept. 13, 1984, effective Jan. 1, 1985 (458 So.2d 245). Amended July 16, 1992, effective Jan. 1, 1993 (604 So.2d 1110); June 16, 1994 (639 So.2d 22); Oct. 18, 2012, effective, *nunc pro tunc*, Sept. 1, 2012 (102 So.3d 505); Nov. 14, 2013, effective Jan. 1, 2014 (131 So.3d 643).

Court Commentary

1984 Amendment. Rule 1.630 replaces rules and statutes used before 1980 when the present Florida Rules of Appellate Procedure were adopted. Experience has shown that rule 9.100 is not designed for use in trial court. The times for proceeding, the methods of proceeding, and the general nature of the procedure is appellate and presumes that the proceeding is basically an appellate proceeding. When the extraordinary remedies are sought in the trial court, these items do not usually exist and thus the rule is difficult to apply. The uniform procedure concept of rule 9.100 has been retained with changes making the procedure fit trial court procedure. The requirement of attaching a copy of the record in subdivision (b) may not be possible within the time allowed for the initial pleading because of the unavailability of the record. In that event the plaintiff should file a motion to extend the time to allow the preparation of the record and supply it when prepared. The filing of a motion to extend the time should be sufficient to extend it until the motion can be decided by the court.

Committee Notes

2012 Amendment. Subdivision (d)(5) is amended to reflect the relocation of the service rule from rule 1.080 to Fla. R. Jud. Admin. 2.516.

2013 Amendment. Rule 1.630 has been amended to remove any reference to certiorari proceedings, which instead are governed by the Florida Rules of Appellate Procedure. The Florida Rules of Appellate Procedure apply when the circuit courts exercise their appellate jurisdiction.

Rule 1.650. Medical Malpractice Presuit Screening Rule

(a) Scope of Rule. This rule applies only to the procedures prescribed by section 766.106, Florida Statutes, for presuit screening of claims for medical malpractice.

(b) Notice.

(1) Notice of intent to initiate litigation sent by certified mail to and received by any prospective defendant shall operate as notice to the person and any other prospective defendant who bears a legal relationship to the prospective defendant receiving the notice. The notice shall make the recipient a party to the proceeding under this rule.

(2) The notice shall include the names and addresses of all other parties and shall be sent to each party.

(3) The court shall decide the issue of receipt of notice when raised in a motion to dismiss or to abate an action for medical malpractice.

(c) Discovery.

(1) *Types.* Upon receipt by a prospective defendant of a notice of intent to initiate litigation, the parties may obtain presuit screening discovery by one or more of the following methods: unsworn statements upon oral examination; production of documents or things; and physical examinations. Unless otherwise provided in this rule, the parties shall make discoverable information available without formal discovery. Evidence of failure to comply with this rule may be grounds for dismissal of claims or defenses ultimately asserted.

(2) *Procedures for Conducting.*

(A) Unsworn Statements. The parties may require other parties to appear for the taking of an unsworn statement. The statements shall only be used for the purpose of presuit screening and are not discoverable or admissible in any civil action for any purpose by any party. A party desiring to take the unsworn statement of any party shall give reasonable notice in writing to all parties. The notice shall state the time and place for taking the statement and the name and address of the party to be examined. Unless otherwise impractical, the examination of any party shall be done at the same time by all other parties. Any party may be represented by an attorney at the taking of an unsworn statement. Statements may be electronically or stenographically recorded, or recorded on video tape. The taking of unsworn statements of minors is subject to the provisions of rule 1.310(b)(8). The taking of unsworn statements is subject to the provisions of rule 1.310(d) and may be terminated for abuses. If abuses occur, the abuses shall be evidence of failure of that party to comply with the good faith requirements of section 766.106, Florida Statutes.

(B) Documents or Things. At any time after receipt by a party of a notice of intent to initiate litigation, a party may request discoverable documents or things. The documents or things shall be produced at the expense of the requesting party within 20 days of the date of receipt of the request. A party is required to produce discoverable documents or things within that party's possession or control. Copies of documents produced in response to the request of any party shall be served on all other parties. The party serving the documents shall list the name and address of the parties upon whom the documents were served, the date of service, the manner of service, and the identity of the document served in the certificate of service. Failure of a party to comply with the above time limits shall not relieve that party of its obligation under the statute but shall be evidence of failure of that party to comply with the good faith requirements of section 766.106, Florida Statutes.

(C) Physical Examinations. Upon receipt by a party of a notice of intent to initiate litigation and within the presuit screening period, a party may require a claimant to submit to a physical examination. The party shall give reasonable notice in writing to all parties of the time and place of the examination. Unless otherwise impractical, a claimant shall be required to submit to only one examination on behalf of all parties. The practicality of a single examination shall be determined by the nature of the claimant's condition as it relates to the potential liability of each party. The report of examination shall be made available to all parties upon payment of the reasonable cost of reproduction. The report shall not be provided to any person not a party at any time. The report shall only be used for the purpose of presuit screening and the examining physician may not testify concerning the examination in any subsequent civil action. All requests for physical examinations or notices of unsworn statements shall be in writing and a copy served upon all parties. The requests or notices shall bear a certificate of service identifying the name and address of the person upon whom the request or notice is served, the date of the request or notice, and the manner of service. Any minor required to submit to examination pursuant to this rule shall have the right to be accompanied by a parent or guardian at all times during the examination, except upon a showing that the presence of a parent or guardian is likely to have a material, negative impact on the minor's examination.

(3) *Work Product.* Work product generated by the presuit screening process that is subject to exclusion in a subsequent proceeding is limited to verbal or written communications that originate pursuant to the presuit screening process.

(d) Time Requirements.

(1) The notice of intent to initiate litigation shall be served by certified mail, return receipt requested, prior to the expiration of any applicable statute of limitations or statute of repose. If an extension has been granted under section 766.104(2), Florida Statutes, or by agreement of the parties, the notice shall be served within the extended period.

(2) The action may not be filed against any defendant until 90 days after the notice of intent to initiate litigation was mailed to that party. The action may be filed against any party at any time after the notice of intent to initiate litigation has been mailed after the claimant has received a written rejection of the claim from that party.

(3) To avoid being barred by the applicable statute of limitations, an action must be filed within 60 days or within the remainder of the time of the statute of limitations after the notice of intent to initiate litigation was received, whichever is longer, after the earliest of the following:

(A) The expiration of 90 days after the date of receipt of the notice of intent to initiate litigation.

(B) The expiration of 180 days after mailing of the notice of intent to initiate litigation if the claim is controlled by section 768.28(6)(a), Florida Statutes.

(C) Receipt by claimant of a written rejection of the claim.

(D) The expiration of any extension of the 90–day presuit screening period stipulated to by the parties in accordance with section 766.106(4), Florida Statutes.

Added Sept. 29, 1988 (536 So.2d 193). Amended Oct. 25, 1990 (568 So.2d 1273); July 16, 1992, effective Jan. 1, 1993 (604 So.2d 1110); Nov. 4, 1993, effective Nov. 19, 1993 So.2d 481); March 11, 1999 (745 So.2d 946); Aug. 19, 1999, Nos. 91,966, 92,382, and 92,451; Oct. 5, 2000, effective Jan. 1, 2001 (773 So.2d 1098); Oct. 23, 2003, effective Jan. 1, 2004 (858 So.2d 1013); Sept. 27, 2007, effective Jan. 1, 2008 (966 So.2d 943).

Committee Notes

2000 Amendment. The reference to the statute of repose was added to subdivision (d)(1) pursuant to *Musculoskeletal Institute Chartered v. Parham*, 745 So.2d 946 (Fla. 1999).

Rule 1.700. Rules Common to Mediation and Arbitration

(a) Referral by Presiding Judge or by Stipulation. Except as hereinafter provided or as otherwise prohibited by law, the presiding judge may enter an order referring all or any part of a contested civil matter to mediation or arbitration. The parties to any contested civil matter may file a written stipulation to mediate or arbitrate any issue between them at any time. Such stipulation shall be incorporated into the order of referral.

(1) *Conference or Hearing Date.* Unless otherwise ordered by the court, the first mediation conference or arbitration hearing shall be held within 60 days of the order of referral.

(2) *Notice.* Within 15 days after the designation of the mediator or the arbitrator, the court or its designee, who may be the mediator or the chief arbitrator, shall notify the parties in writing of the date, time, and place of the conference or hearing unless the order of referral specifies the date, time, and place.

(b) Motion to Dispense with Mediation and Arbitration. A party may move, within 15 days after the order of referral, to dispense with mediation or arbitration, if:

(1) the issue to be considered has been previously mediated or arbitrated between the same parties pursuant to Florida law;

(2) the issue presents a question of law only;

(3) the order violates rule 1.710(b) or rule 1.800; or

(4) other good cause is shown.

(c) Motion to Defer Mediation or Arbitration. Within 15 days of the order of referral, any party may file a motion with the court to defer the proceeding. The movant shall set the motion to defer for hearing prior to the scheduled date for mediation or arbitration. Notice of the hearing shall be provided to all interested parties, including any mediator or arbitrator who has been appointed. The motion shall set forth, in detail, the facts and circumstances supporting the motion. Mediation or arbitration shall be tolled until disposition of the motion.

(d) Disqualification of a Mediator or Arbitrator. Any party may move to enter an order disqualifying a mediator or an arbitrator for good cause. If the court rules that a mediator or arbitrator is disqualified from hearing a case, an order shall be entered setting forth the name of a qualified replacement. Nothing in this provision shall preclude mediators or arbitrators from disqualifying themselves or refusing any assignment. The time for mediation or arbitration shall be tolled during any periods in which a motion to disqualify is pending.

Added Dec. 31, 1987, effective Jan. 1, 1988 (518 So.2d 908). Amended Nov. 23, 1988 (534 So.2d 1150); June 21, 1990, effective July 1, 1990 (563 So.2d 85); July 16, 1992, effective Jan. 1, 1993 (604 So.2d 1110); April 14, 1994, eff. July 1, 1994 (641 So.2d 343).

Rule 1.710. Mediation Rules

(a) Completion of Mediation. Mediation shall be completed within 45 days of the first mediation conference unless extended by order of the court or by stipulation of the parties.

(b) Exclusions from Mediation. A civil action shall be ordered to mediation or mediation in conjunction with arbitration upon stipulation of the parties. A civil action may be ordered to mediation or mediation in conjunction with arbitration upon motion of any party or by the court, if the judge determines the action to be of such a nature that mediation could be of benefit to the litigants or the court. Under no circumstances may the following categories of actions be referred to mediation:

(1) Bond estreatures.

(2) Habeas corpus and extraordinary writs.

(3) Bond validations.

(4) Civil or criminal contempt.

(5) Other matters as may be specified by administrative order of the chief judge in the circuit.

(c) Discovery. Unless stipulated by the parties or ordered by the court, the mediation process shall not suspend discovery.

Added Dec. 31, 1987, effective Jan. 1, 1988 (518 So.2d 908). Amended June 21, 1990, effective July 1, 1990 (563 So.2d 85); July 16, 1992, effective Jan. 1, 1993 (604 So.2d 1110); April 14, 1994, eff. July 1, 1994 (641 So.2d 343); Oct. 31, 1996, effective Jan. 1, 1997 (682 So.2d 105).

Committee Notes

1994 Amendment. The Supreme Court Committee on Mediation and Arbitration Rules encourages crafting a combination of dispute resolution processes without creating an unreasonable barrier to the traditional court system.

Rule 1.720. Mediation Procedures

(a) Interim or Emergency Relief. A party may apply to the court for interim or emergency relief at any time. Mediation shall continue while such a motion is pending absent a contrary order of the court, or a decision of the mediator to adjourn pending disposition of the motion. Time for completing mediation shall be tolled during any periods when mediation is interrupted pending resolution of such a motion.

(b) Appearance at Mediation. Unless otherwise permitted by court order or stipulated by the parties in writing, a party is deemed to appear at a mediation conference if the following persons are physically present:

(1) The party or a party representative having full authority to settle without further consultation; and

(2) The party's counsel of record, if any; and

(3) A representative of the insurance carrier for any insured party who is not such carrier's outside counsel and who has full authority to settle in an amount up to the amount of the plaintiff's last demand or policy limits, whichever is less, without further consultation.

(c) Party Representative Having Full Authority to Settle. A "party representative having full authority to settle" shall mean the final decision maker with respect to all issues presented by the case who has the legal capacity to execute a binding settlement agreement on behalf of the party. Nothing herein shall be deemed to require any party or party representative who appears at a mediation conference in compliance with this rule to enter into a settlement agreement.

(d) Appearance by Public Entity. If a party to mediation is a public entity required to operate in compliance with chapter 286, Florida Statutes, that party shall be deemed to appear at a mediation conference by the physical presence of a representative with full authority to negotiate on behalf of the entity and to recommend settlement to the appropriate decision-making body of the entity.

(e) Certification of Authority. Unless otherwise stipulated by the parties, each party, 10 days prior to appearing at a mediation conference, shall file with the court and serve all parties a written notice identifying the person or persons who will be attending the mediation conference as a party representative or as an insurance carrier representative, and confirming that those persons have the authority required by subdivision (b).

(f) Sanctions for Failure to Appear. If a party fails to appear at a duly noticed mediation conference without good cause, the court, upon motion, shall impose sanctions, including award of mediation fees, attorneys' fees, and costs, against the party failing to appear. The failure to file a confirmation of authority required under subdivision (e) above, or failure of the persons actually identified in the confirmation to appear at the mediation conference, shall create a rebuttable presumption of a failure to appear.

(g) Adjournments. The mediator may adjourn the mediation conference at any time and may set times for reconvening the adjourned conference notwithstanding rule 1.710(a). No further notification is required for parties present at the adjourned conference.

(h) Counsel. The mediator shall at all times be in control of the mediation and the procedures to be followed in the mediation. Counsel shall be permitted to communicate privately with their clients. In the discretion of the mediator and with the agreement of the parties, mediation may proceed in the absence of counsel unless otherwise ordered by the court.

(i) Communication with Parties or Counsel. The mediator may meet and consult privately with any party or parties or their counsel.

(j) Appointment of the Mediator.

(1) Within 10 days of the order of referral, the parties may agree upon a stipulation with the court designating:

(A) a certified mediator, other than a senior judge presiding as a judge in that circuit; or

(B) a mediator, other than a senior judge, who is not certified as a mediator but who, in the opinion of the parties and upon review by the presiding judge, is otherwise qualified by training or experience to mediate all or some of the issues in the particular case.

(2) If the parties cannot agree upon a mediator within 10 days of the order of referral, the plaintiff or petitioner shall so notify the court within 10 days of the expiration of the period to agree on a mediator, and the court shall appoint a certified mediator selected by rotation or by such other procedures as may be adopted by administrative order of the chief judge in the circuit in which the action is pending. At the request of either party, the court shall appoint a certified circuit court mediator who is a member of The Florida Bar.

(3) If a mediator agreed upon by the parties or appointed by a court cannot serve, a substitute mediator can be agreed upon or appointed in the same manner as the original mediator. A mediator shall not mediate a case assigned to another mediator without the agreement of the parties or approval of the court. A substitute mediator shall have the same qualifications as the original mediator.

(k) Compensation of the Mediator. The mediator may be compensated or uncompensated. When the mediator is compensated in whole or part by the parties, the presiding judge may determine the reasonableness of the fees charged by the mediator. In the absence of a written agreement providing for the mediator's compensation, the mediator shall be compensated at the hourly rate set by the presiding judge in the referral order. Where appropriate, each party shall pay a proportionate share of the total charges of the mediator. Parties may object to the rate of the mediator's compensation within 15 days of the order of referral by serving an objection on all other parties and the mediator.

Added Dec. 31, 1987, effective Jan. 1, 1988 (518 So.2d 908). Amended June 21, 1990, effective July 1, 1990 (563 So.2d 85); May 28, 1992 (604 So.2d 764); July 16, 1992, effective Jan. 1, 1993 (604 So.2d 1110); April 14, 1994, eff. July 1, 1994 (641 So.2d 343); Nov. 3, 2005, effective Jan. 1, 2006 (917 So.2d 145); Nov. 15, 2007 (969 So.2d 1003); Nov. 3, 2011, effective Jan. 1, 2012 (75 So.3d 264); June 19, 2014, effective Oct. 1, 2014 (141 So.3d 1172).

Committee Notes

2011 Amendment. Mediated settlement conferences pursuant to this rule are meant to be conducted when the participants actually engaged in the settlement negotiations have full authority to settle the case without further consultation. New language in subdivision (c) now defines "a party representative with full authority to settle" in two parts. First, the party representative must be the final decision maker with respect to all issues presented by the case in question. Second, the party representative must have the legal capacity to execute a binding agreement on behalf of the settling party. These are objective standards. Whether or not these standards have been met can be determined without reference to any confidential mediation communications. A decision by a party representative not to settle does not, in and of itself, signify the absence of full authority to settle. A party may delegate full authority to settle to more than one person, each of whom can serve as the final decision maker. A party may also designate multiple persons to serve together as the final decision maker, all of whom must appear at mediation.

New subdivision (e) provides a process for parties to identify party representative and representatives of insurance carriers who will be attending the mediation conference on behalf of parties and insurance carriers and to confirm their respective settlement authority by means of a direct representation to the court. If necessary, any verification of this representation would be upon motion by a party or inquiry by the court without involvement of the mediator and would not require disclosure of confidential mediation communications. Nothing in this rule shall be deemed to impose any duty or obligation on the mediator selected by the parties or appointed by the court to ensure compliance.

The concept of self determination in mediation also contemplates the parties' free choice in structuring and organizing their mediation sessions, including those who are to participate. Accordingly, elements of this rule are subject to revision or qualification with the mutual consent of the parties.

Rule 1.730. Completion of Mediation

(a) No Agreement. If the parties do not reach an agreement as to any matter as a result of mediation, the mediator shall report the lack of an agreement to the court without comment or recommendation. With the consent of the parties, the mediator's report may also identify any pending motions or outstanding legal issues, discovery process, or other action by any party which, if resolved or completed, would facilitate the possibility of a settlement.

(b) Agreement. If a partial or final agreement is reached, it shall be reduced to writing and signed by the parties and their counsel, if any. The agreement shall be filed when required by law or with the parties' consent. A report of the agreement shall be submitted to the court or a stipulation of dismissal shall be filed. By stipulation of the parties, the agreement may be electronically or stenographically recorded. In such event, the transcript may be filed with the court. The mediator shall report the existence of the signed or transcribed agreement to the court without comment within 10 days thereof. No agreement under this rule shall be reported to the court except as provided herein.

(c) Imposition of Sanctions. In the event of any breach or failure to perform under the agreement, the court upon motion may impose sanctions, including costs, attorneys' fees, or other appropriate remedies including entry of judgment on the agreement.

Added Dec. 31, 1987, effective Jan. 1, 1988 (518 So.2d 908). Amended June 21, 1990, effective July 1, 1990 (563 So.2d 85); July 16, 1992, effective Jan. 1, 1993 (604 So.2d 1110); Oct. 31, 1996, effective Jan. 1, 1997 (682 So.2d 105); Oct. 5, 2000, effective Jan. 1, 2001 (773 So.2d 1098).

Committee Notes

1996 Amendment. Subdivision (b) is amended to provide for partial settlements, to clarify the procedure for concluding mediation by report or stipulation of dismissal, and to specify the procedure for reporting mediated agreements to the court. The reporting requirements are intended to ensure the confidentiality provided for in section 44.102(3), Florida Statutes, and to prevent premature notification to the court.

Rule 1.750. County Court Actions

(a) Applicability. This rule applies to the mediation of county court matters and issues only and controls over conflicting provisions in rules 1.700, 1.710, 1.720, and 1.730.

(b) Limitation on Referral to Mediation. When a mediation program utilizing volunteer mediators is unavailable or otherwise inappropriate, county court matters may be referred to a mediator or mediation program which charges a fee. Such order of referral shall advise the parties that they may object to mediation on grounds of financial hardship or on any ground set forth in rule 1.700(b). If a party objects, mediation shall not be conducted until the court rules on the objection. The court may consider the amount in controversy, the objecting party's ability to pay, and any other pertinent information in determining the propriety of the referral. When appropriate, the court shall apportion mediation fees between the parties.

(c) Scheduling. In small claims actions, the mediator shall be appointed and the mediation conference held during or immediately after the pretrial conference unless otherwise ordered by the court. In no event shall the mediation conference be held more than 14 days after the pretrial conference.

(d) Appointment of the Mediator. In county court actions not subject to the Florida Small Claims Rules, rule 1.720(f) shall apply unless the case is sent to a mediation program provided at no cost to the parties.

(e) Appearance at Mediation. In small claims actions, an attorney may appear on behalf of a party at mediation provided that the attorney has full authority to settle without further consultation. Unless otherwise ordered by the court, a nonlawyer representative may appear on behalf of a party to a small claims mediation if the representative has the party's signed written authority to appear and has full authority to settle without further consultation. In either event, the party need not appear in person. In any other county court action, a party will be deemed to appear if the persons set forth in rule 1.720(b) are physically present.

(f) Agreement. Any agreements reached as a result of small claims mediation shall be written in the form of a stipulation. The stipulation may be entered as an order of the court.

Added Dec. 31, 1987, effective Jan. 1, 1988 (518 So.2d 908). Amended June 21, 1990, effective July 1, 1990 (563 So.2d 85); April 14, 1994, eff. July 1, 1994 (641 So.2d 343); Oct. 31, 1996, effective Jan. 1, 1997 (682 So.2d 105); Oct. 23, 2003, effective Jan. 1, 2004 (858 So.2d 1013).

Rule 1.800. Exclusions From Arbitration

A civil action shall be ordered to arbitration or arbitration in conjunction with mediation upon stipulation of the parties. A civil action may be ordered to arbitration or arbitration in conjunction with mediation upon motion of any party or by the court, if the judge determines the action to be of such a nature that arbitration could be of benefit to the litigants or the court. Under no circumstances may the following categories of actions be referred to arbitration:

(1) Bond estreatures.

(2) Habeas corpus or other extraordinary writs.

(3) Bond validations.

(4) Civil or criminal contempt.

(5) Such other matters as may be specified by order of the chief judge in the circuit.

Added Dec. 31, 1987, effective Jan. 1, 1988 (518 So.2d 908). Amended July 16, 1992, effective Jan. 1, 1993 (604 So.2d 1110); April 14, 1994, eff. July 1, 1994 (641 So.2d 343); Oct. 31, 1996, effective Jan. 1, 1997 (682 So.2d 105).

Committee Notes

1994 Amendment. The Supreme Court Committee on Mediation and Arbitration Rules encourages crafting a combination of dispute resolution processes without creating an unreasonable barrier to the traditional court system.

Rule 1.810. Selection and Compensation of Arbitrators

(a) Selection. The chief judge of the circuit or a designee shall maintain a list of qualified persons who have agreed to serve as arbitrators. Cases assigned to arbitration shall be assigned to an arbitrator or to a panel of 3 arbitrators. The court shall determine the number of arbitrators and designate them within 15 days after service of the order of referral in the absence of an agreement by the parties. In the case of a panel, one of the arbitrators shall be appointed as the chief arbitrator. Where there is only one arbitrator, that person shall be the chief arbitrator.

(b) Compensation. The chief judge of each judicial circuit shall establish the compensation of arbitrators subject to the limitations in section 44.103(3), Florida Statutes.

Added Dec. 31, 1987, effective Jan. 1, 1988 (518 So.2d 908). Amended July 16, 1992, effective Jan. 1, 1993 (604 So.2d 1110); April 14, 1994, eff. July 1, 1994 (641 So.2d 343); Oct. 23, 2003, effective Jan. 1, 2004 (858 So.2d 1013).

Committee Notes

2003 Amendment. The statutory reference in subdivision (b) is changed to reflect changes in the statutory numbering.

Rule 1.820. Hearing Procedures for Non–Binding Arbitration

(a) Authority of the Chief Arbitrator. The chief arbitrator shall have authority to commence and adjourn the arbitration hearing and carry out other such duties as are prescribed by section 44.103, Florida Statutes. The chief arbitrator shall not have authority to hold any person in contempt or to in any way impose sanctions against any person.

(b) Conduct of the Arbitration Hearing.

(1) The chief judge of each judicial circuit shall set procedures for determining the time and place of the arbitration hearing and may establish other procedures for the expeditious and orderly operation of the arbitration hearing to the extent such procedures are not in conflict with any rules of court.

(2) Hearing procedures shall be included in the notice of arbitration hearing sent to the parties and arbitration panel.

(3) Individual parties or authorized representatives of corporate parties shall attend the arbitration hearing unless excused in advance by the chief arbitrator for good cause shown.

(c) Rules of Evidence. The hearing shall be conducted informally. Presentation of testimony shall be kept to a minimum, and matters shall be presented to the arbitrator(s) primarily through the statements and arguments of counsel.

(d) Orders. The chief arbitrator may issue instructions as are necessary for the expeditious and orderly conduct of the hearing. The chief arbitrator's instructions are not appealable. Upon notice to all parties the chief arbitrator may apply to the presiding judge for orders directing compliance with such instructions. Instructions enforced by a court order are appealable as are other orders of the court.

(e) Default of a Party. When a party fails to appear at a hearing, the chief arbitrator may proceed with the hearing and the arbitration panel shall render a decision based upon the facts and circumstances as presented by the parties present.

(f) Record and Transcript. Any party may have a record and transcript made of the arbitration hearing at that party's expense.

(g) Completion of the Arbitration Process.

(1) Arbitration shall be completed within 30 days of the first arbitration hearing unless extended by order of the court on motion of the chief arbitrator or of a party. No extension of time shall be for a period exceeding 60 days from the date of the first arbitration hearing.

(2) Upon the completion of the arbitration process, the arbitrator(s) shall render a decision. In the case of a panel, a decision shall be final upon a majority vote of the panel.

(3) Within 10 days of the final adjournment of the arbitration hearing, the arbitrator(s) shall notify the parties, in writing, of their decision. The arbitration decision may set forth the issues in controversy and the arbitrator('s)(s') conclusions and findings of fact and law. The arbitrator('s)(s') decision and the originals of any transcripts shall be sealed and filed with the clerk at the time the parties are notified of the decision.

(h) Time for Filing Motion for Trial. Any party may file a motion for trial. If a motion for trial is filed by any party, any party having a third-party claim at issue at the time of arbitration may file a motion for trial within 10 days of service of the first motion for trial. If a motion for trial is not made within 20 days of service on the parties of the decision, the decision shall be referred to the presiding judge, who shall enter such orders and judgments as may be required to carry out the terms of the decision as provided by section 44.103(5), Florida Statutes.

Added Dec. 31, 1987, effective Jan. 1, 1988 (518 So.2d 908). Amended July 16, 1992, effective Jan. 1, 1993 (604 So.2d 1110); April 14, 1994, eff. July 1, 1994 (641 So.2d 343); Oct. 23, 2003, effective Jan. 1, 2004 (858 So.2d 1013); Sept. 27, 2007, effective Jan. 1, 2008 (966 So.2d 943).

Committee Notes

1988 Adoption. Arbitration proceedings should be informal and expeditious. The court should take into account the nature of the proceedings when determining whether to award costs and attorneys' fees after a trial de novo. Counsel are free to file exceptions to an arbitration decision or award at the time it is to be considered by the court. The court should consider such exceptions when determining whether to award costs and attorneys' fees. The court should consider rule 1.442 concerning offers of judgment and section 45.061, Florida Statutes (1985), concerning offers of settlement, as statements of public policy in deciding whether fees should be awarded.

1994 Amendment. The Supreme Court Committee on Mediation and Arbitration Rules recommends that a copy of the local arbitration procedures be disseminated to the local bar.

2003 Amendment. The statutory reference in subdivision (h) is changed to reflect changes in the statutory numbering.

2007 Amendment. Subdivision (h) is amended to avoid the unintended consequences for defendants with third-party claims who prevailed at arbitration but could not pursue those claims in a circuit court action because no motion for trial was filed despite a plaintiff or plaintiffs having filed a motion for trial that covered those claims. See *State Dept. of Transportation v. BellSouth Telecommunications, Inc.*, 859 So. 2d 1278 (Fla. 4th DCA 2003).

Rule 1.830. Voluntary Binding Arbitration

(a) Absence of Party Agreement.

(1) *Compensation.* In the absence of an agreement by the parties as to compensation of the arbitrator(s), the court shall determine the amount of compensation subject to the provisions of section 44.104(3), Florida Statutes.

(2) *Hearing Procedures.* Subject to these rules and section 44.104, Florida Statutes, the parties may, by written agreement before the hearing, establish the hearing procedures for voluntary binding arbitration. In the absence of such agreement, the court shall establish the hearing procedures.

(b) Record and Transcript. A record and transcript may be made of the arbitration hearing if requested by any party or at the direction of the chief arbitrator. The record and transcript may be used in subsequent legal proceedings subject to the Florida Rules of Evidence.

(c) Arbitration Decision and Appeal.

(1) The arbitrator(s) shall serve the parties with notice of the decision and file the decision with the court within 10 days of the final adjournment of the arbitration hearing.

(2) A voluntary binding arbitration decision may be appealed within 30 days after service of the decision on the parties. Appeal is limited to the grounds specified in section 44.104(10), Florida Statutes.

(3) If no appeal is filed within the time period set out in subdivision (2) of this rule, the decision shall be referred to the presiding judge who shall enter such orders and judgments as required to carry out the terms of the decision as provided under section 44.104(11), Florida Statutes.

Added Dec. 31, 1987, effective Jan. 1, 1988 (518 So.2d 908). Amended July 16, 1992, effective Jan. 1, 1993 (604 So.2d 1110); April 14, 1994, eff. July 1, 1994 (641 So.2d 343).

Rule 1.900. Forms

(a) Process. The following forms of process, notice of lis pendens, and notice of action are sufficient. Variations from the forms do not void process or notices that are otherwise sufficient.

(b) Other Forms. The other forms are sufficient for the matters that are covered by them. So long as the substance is expressed without prolixity, the forms may be varied to meet the facts of a particular case.

(c) Formal Matters. Captions, except for the designation of the paper, are omitted from the forms. A general form of caption is the first form. Signatures are omitted from pleadings and motions.

Added June 19, 1968, effective Oct. 1, 1968 (211 So.2d 174). Amended July 16, 1992, effective Jan. 1, 1993 (604 So.2d 1110).

FORMS FOR USE WITH RULES OF CIVIL PROCEDURE

Form 1.901. Caption

(a) General Form.

(name of court)

```
A. B.,                 )
        Plaintiff,     )
                       )
        –vs–           ) No. . . . . . . . . . . . . . .
                       )
C. D.,                 )
        Defendant      )
```

(designation of pleading)

(b) Petition.

(name of court)

In re the Petition)
of A. B. for (type of) No. . . . .
relief))

PETITION FOR (type of relief)

(c) In rem proceedings.

(name of court)

In re (name or general)
description of property)) No. . . . .

(designation of pleading)

(d) Forfeiture proceedings.

(name of court)

In re (name or general)
description of property)) No. . . . .

(designation of pleading)

Added June 19, 1968, effective Oct. 1, 1968 (211 So.2d 174). Amended Oct. 9, 1980, effective Jan. 1, 1981 (391 So.2d 165); July 16, 1992, effective Jan. 1, 1993 (604 So.2d 1110); Sept. 8, 2010, effective Jan. 1, 2011 (52 So.3d 579).

Committee Notes

1980 Amendment. Subdivision (b) is added to show the form of caption for a petition.

2010 Amendment. Subdivisions (c) and (d) are added to show the form of caption for in rem proceedings, including in rem forfeiture proceedings.

Form 1.902. Summons

(a) General Form.

SUMMONS

THE STATE OF FLORIDA:

To Each Sheriff of the State:

YOU ARE COMMANDED to serve this summons and a copy of the complaint or petition in this action on defendant . . . .

Each defendant is required to serve written defenses to the complaint or petition on . . . ., plaintiff's attorney, whose address is . . . ., within 20 days [1] after service of this summons on that defendant, exclusive of the day of service, and to file the original of the defenses with the clerk of this court either before service on plaintiff's attorney or immediately thereafter. If a defendant fails to do so, a default will be entered against that defendant for the relief demanded in the complaint or petition.

DATED on . . . .

(Name of Clerk)
As Clerk of the Court
By __________________
As Deputy Clerk

(b) Form for Personal Service on Natural Person.

SUMMONS

THE STATE OF FLORIDA:

To Each Sheriff of the State:

YOU ARE COMMANDED to serve this summons and a copy of the complaint in this lawsuit on defendant . . . .

DATED on . . . .

CLERK OF THE CIRCUIT COURT
(SEAL)
(Name of Clerk)
As Clerk of the Court
By __________________
As Deputy Clerk

IMPORTANT

A lawsuit has been filed against you. You have 20 calendar days after this summons is served on you to file a written response to the attached complaint with the clerk of this court. A phone call will not protect you. Your written response, including the case number given above and the names of the parties, must be filed if you want the court to hear your side of the case. If you do not file your response on time, you may lose the case, and your wages, money, and property may thereafter be taken without further warning from the court. There are other legal requirements. You may want to call an attorney right away. If you do not know an attorney, you may call an attorney referral service or a legal aid office (listed in the phone book).

If you choose to file a written response yourself, at the same time you file your written response to the court you must also mail or take a copy of your written response to the "Plaintiff/Plaintiff's Attorney" named below.

IMPORTANTE

Usted ha sido demandado legalmente. Tiene 20 dias, contados a partir del recibo de esta notificacion, para contestar la demanda adjunta, por escrito, y presentarla ante este tribunal. Una llamada telefonica no lo protegera. Si usted desea que el tribunal considere su defensa, debe presentar su respuesta por escrito, incluyendo el numero del caso y los nombres de las partes interesadas. Si usted no contesta la demanda a tiempo, pudiese perder el caso y podria ser despojado de sus ingresos y propiedades, o privado de sus derechos, sin previo aviso del tribunal. Existen otros requisitos legales. Si lo desea, puede usted consultar a un abogado inmediatamente. Si no conoce a un abogado, puede llamar a una de las oficinas de asistencia legal que aparecen en la guia telefonica.

Si desea responder a la demanda por su cuenta, al mismo tiempo en que presenta su respuesta ante el tribunal, debera usted enviar por correo o entregar una copia de su respuesta a la persona denominada abajo como "Plaintiff/Plaintiff's Attorney" (Demandante o Abogado del Demandante).

IMPORTANT

Des poursuites judiciares ont ete entreprises contre vous. Vous avez 20 jours consecutifs a partir de la date de l'assignation de cette citation pour deposer une reponse ecrite a la plainte ci-jointe aupres de ce tribunal. Un simple coup de telephone est insuffisant pour vous proteger. Vous etes obliges de deposer votre reponse ecrite, avec mention du numero de dossier ci-dessus et du nom des parties nommees ici, si vous souhaitez que le tribunal entende votre cause. Si vous ne deposez pas votre reponse ecrite dans le relai requis, vous risquez de perdre la cause ainsi que votre salaire, votre argent, et vos biens peuvent etre saisis par la suite, sans aucun preavis ulterieur du tribunal. Il y a d'autres obligations juridiques et vous pouvez requerir les services immediats d'un avocat. Si vous ne connaissez pas d'avocat, vous pourriez telephoner a un service de reference d'avocats ou a un bureau d'assistance juridique (figurant a l'annuaire de telephones).

Si vous choisissez de deposer vous-meme une reponse ecrite, il vous faudra egalement, en meme temps que cette formalite, faire parvenir ou expedier une copie de votre reponse ecrite au "Plaintiff/Plaintiff's Attorney" (Plaignant ou a son avocat) nomme ci-dessous.

____

Plaintiff/Plaintiff's Attorney

....

....

Address

Florida Bar No. ....

(c) Forms for Service by Mail.

(1) *Notice of Lawsuit and Request for Waiver of Service of Process.*

NOTICE OF COMMENCEMENT OF ACTION

TO: (Name of defendant or defendant's representative)

A lawsuit has been commenced against you (or the entity on whose behalf you are addressed). A copy of the complaint is attached to this notice. The complaint has been filed in the (Circuit or County) Court for the .... and has been assigned case no.: ....

This is not a formal summons or notification from the court, but is rather my request that you sign the enclosed waiver of service of process form in order to save the cost of serving you with a judicial summons and an additional copy of the complaint. The cost of service will be avoided if I receive a signed copy of the waiver within 20 days (30 days if you do not reside in the United States) after the date you receive this notice and request for waiver. I have enclosed a stamped self-addressed envelope for your use. An extra copy of the notice and request, including the waiver, is also attached for your records.

If you comply with this request and return the signed waiver, it will be filed with the court and no summons will be served on you. The lawsuit will then proceed as if you had been served on the date the waiver is filed, except that you will not be obligated to respond to the complaint until 60 days after the date on which you received the notice and request for waiver.

If I do not receive the signed waiver within 20 days from the date you received the notice and the waiver of service of process form, formal service of process may be initiated in a manner authorized by the Florida Rules of Civil Procedure. You (or the party on whose behalf you are addressed) will be required to pay the full cost of such service unless good cause is shown for the failure to return the waiver of service.

I hereby certify that this notice of lawsuit and request for waiver of service of process has been sent to you on behalf of the plaintiff on .... (date) ....

____

Plaintiff's Attorney or
Unrepresented Plaintiff

(2) *Waiver of Service of Process.*

WAIVER OF SERVICE OF PROCESS

TO: (Name of plaintiff's attorney or unrepresented plaintiff)

I acknowledge receipt of your request that I waive service of process in the lawsuit of .... v. .... in the .... Court in .... I have also received a copy of the complaint, two copies of this waiver, and a means by which I can return the signed waiver to you without cost to me.

I agree to save the cost of service of process and an additional copy of the complaint in this lawsuit by not requiring that I (or the entity on whose behalf I am acting) be served with judicial process in the manner provided by Fla. R. Civ. P. 1.070.

If I am not the defendant to whom the notice of lawsuit and waiver of service of process was sent, I declare that my relationship to the entity or person to whom the notice was sent and my authority to accept service on behalf of such person or entity is as follows:

(describe relationship to person or entity and authority to accept service)

I (or the entity on whose behalf I am acting) will retain all defenses or objections to the lawsuit or to the jurisdiction or venue of the court except for any objections based on a defect in the summons or in the service of the summons.

I understand that a judgment may be entered against me (or the party on whose behalf I am acting) if a written response is not served upon you within 60 days from the date I received the notice of lawsuit and request for waiver of service of process.

DATED on ....

____
Defendant or Defendant's Representative

Added June 19, 1968, effective Oct. 1, 1968 (211 So.2d 174). Amended Oct. 9, 1980, effective Jan. 1, 1981 (391 So.2d 165); Oct. 6, 1988 and Dec. 30, 1988, effective Jan. 1, 1989 (536 So.2d 974); July 16, 1992, effective Jan. 1, 1993 (604 So.2d 1110); Oct. 31, 1996, effective Jan. 1, 1997 (682 So.2d 105); Oct. 5, 2000, effective Jan. 1, 2001 (773 So.2d 1098); Oct. 23, 2003, effective Jan. 1, 2004 (858 So.2d 1013); Sept. 27, 2007, effective Jan. 1, 2008 (966 So.2d 943).

1 Except when suit is brought pursuant to section 768.28, Florida Statutes, if the State of Florida, one of its agencies, or one of its officials or employees sued in his or her official capacity is a defendant, the time to be inserted as to it is 40 days. When suit is brought pursuant to section 768.28, Florida Statutes, the time to be inserted is 30 days.

Committee Notes

1988 Amendment. Two forms are now provided: 1 for personal service on natural persons and 1 for other service by summons. The new form for personal service on natural persons is included to ensure awareness by defendants or respondents of their obligations to respond.

The summons form for personal service on natural persons is to be used for service on natural persons under the following provisions: sections 48.031 (service of process generally), 48.041 (service on minors), 48.042 (service on incompetents), 48.051 (service on state prisoners), 48.183 (service of process in action for possession of residential premises), and 48.194 (personal service outside the state), Florida Statutes.

The former, general summons form is to be used for all other service by summons, including service under sections 48.061 (service on partnership), 48.071 (service on agents of nonresidents doing business in the state), 48.081 (service on corporation), 48.101 (service on dissolved corporations), 48.111 (service on public agencies or officers), 48.121 (service on the state), 48.131 (service on alien property custodian), 48.141 (service on labor unions), 48.151 (service on statutory agents for certain purposes), Florida Statutes, and all statutes providing for substituted service on the secretary of state.

The form for personal service on natural persons contains Spanish and French versions of the English text to ensure effective notice on all Floridians. In the event of space problems in the summons form, the committee recommends that the non–English portions be placed on the reverse side of the summons.

1992 Amendment. (b): The title is amended to eliminate confusion by the sheriffs in effecting service.

1996 Amendment. Form 1.902(c) was added for use with rule 1.070(i).

2007 Amendment. Subdivision (a) is amended to conform form 1.902 to the statutory requirements of sections 48.111, 48.121, and 768.28, Florida Statutes. The form is similar to Federal Rule of Civil Procedure Form 1.

Form 1.903. Crossclaim Summons

CROSSCLAIM SUMMONS

THE STATE OF FLORIDA:
To Each Sheriff of the State:

YOU ARE COMMANDED to serve this summons and a copy of the crossclaim in this action on defendant ....

Each crossclaim defendant is required to serve written defenses to the crossclaim on ...., defendant's attorney, whose address is ...., and on ...., plaintiff's attorney, whose address is ...., within 20 days after service of this summons on that defendant, exclusive of the day of service, and to file the original of the defenses with the clerk of this court either before service on the attorneys or immediately thereafter. If a crossclaim defendant fails to do so, a default will be entered against that defendant for the relief demanded in the crossclaim.

DATED on ....

(Name of Clerk)
As Clerk of the Court
By ______________
As Deputy Clerk

Added June 19, 1968, effective Oct. 1, 1968 (211 So.2d 174). Amended Oct. 9, 1980, effective Jan. 1, 1981 (391 So.2d 165); Oct. 5, 2000, effective Jan. 1, 2001 (773 So.2d 1098).

Form 1.904. Third–Party Summons

THIRD–PARTY SUMMONS

THE STATE OF FLORIDA:
To Each Sheriff of the State:

YOU ARE COMMANDED to serve this summons and a copy of the third-party complaint or petition in this action on third-party defendant, ...

Each third-party defendant is required to serve written defenses to the third-party complaint or petition on ...., plaintiff's attorney, whose address is ...., and on ...., defendant's attorney, whose address is ...., within 20 days after service of this summons on that defendant, exclusive of the date of service, and to file the original of the defenses with the clerk of this court either before service on the attorneys or immediately thereafter. If a third-party defendant fails to do so, a default will be entered against that defendant for the relief demanded in the third-party complaint or petition.

DATED on ....

(Name of Clerk)
As Clerk of the Court
By ____________________
As Deputy Clerk

Added June 19, 1968, effective Oct. 1, 1968 (211 So.2d 174). Amended Oct. 9, 1980, effective Jan. 1, 1981 (391 So.2d 165); Oct. 5, 2000, effective Jan. 1, 2001 (773 So.2d 1098).

Form 1.905. Attachment

WRIT OF ATTACHMENT

THE STATE OF FLORIDA:
To Each Sheriff of the State:

YOU ARE COMMANDED to attach and take into custody so much of the lands, tenements, goods, and chattels of defendant, ..., as is sufficient to satisfy the sum of $ .... and costs.

ORDERED at ...., Florida, on ..... (date) .....

____
Judge

Added June 19, 1968, effective Oct. 1, 1968 (211 So.2d 174). Amended Oct. 9, 1980, effective Jan. 1, 1981 (391 So.2d 165); July 16, 1992, effective Jan. 1, 1993 (604 So.2d 1110); Oct. 5, 2000, effective Jan. 1, 2001 (773 So.2d 1098).

Committee Notes

1980 Amendment. The direction is modernized and the combination with the summons deleted. A writ of attachment must now be issued by a judge under section 76.03, Florida Statutes (1979).

Form 1.906. Attachment—Foreclosure

WRIT OF ATTACHMENT

THE STATE OF FLORIDA:
To Each Sheriff of the State:

YOU ARE COMMANDED to take and hold the following described property:

(describe property)

or so much of it as can be found sufficient to satisfy the debt to be foreclosed.

ORDERED at ...., Florida, on ..... (date) .....

____
Judge

Added June 19, 1968, effective Oct. 1, 1968 (211 So.2d 174). Amended Oct. 9, 1980, effective Jan. 1, 1981 (391 So.2d 165); July 16, 1992, effective Jan. 1, 1993 (604 So.2d 1110); Oct. 5, 2000, effective Jan. 1, 2001 (773 So.2d 1098).

Committee Notes

1980 Amendment. The direction is modernized and the combination with the summons deleted. A writ of attachment must now be issued by a judge under section 76.03, Florida Statutes (1979).

Form 1.907. Garnishment

(a) Writ of Garnishment.

WRIT OF GARNISHMENT

THE STATE OF FLORIDA:
To Each Sheriff of the State:

YOU ARE COMMANDED to summon the garnishee, ..., to serve an answer to this writ on ...., plaintiff's attorney, whose address is ...., within 20 days after service on the garnishee, exclusive of the day of service, and to file the original with the clerk of this court either before service on the attorney or immediately thereafter, stating whether the garnishee is indebted to defendant, ..., at the time of the answer or was indebted at the time of service of the writ, or at any time between such times, and in what sum and what tangible and intangible personal property of the defendant the garnishee is in possession or control of at the time of the answer or had at the time of service of this writ, or at any time between such times, and whether the garnishee knows of any other person indebted to the defendant or who may be in possession or control of any of the property of the defendant. The amount set in plaintiff's motion is $ ....

DATED on ....

(Name of Clerk)
As Clerk of the Court
By ____________________
As Deputy Clerk

(b) Continuing Writ of Garnishment against Salary or Wages.

CONTINUING WRIT OF GARNISHMENT AGAINST SALARY OR WAGES

THE STATE OF FLORIDA:
To Each Sheriff of the State:

YOU ARE COMMANDED to summon the garnishee, ..., whose address is ...., who is required to serve an answer to this writ on ...., plaintiff's attorney, whose address is ...., within 20 days after service of this writ, exclusive of the day of service, and to file the original with the clerk of court either before service on the attorney or immediately thereafter. The answer shall state whether the garnishee is the employer of the defendant .... and whether the garnishee is indebted to the defendant by reason of salary or wages. The garnishee's answer shall specify the periods of payment (for example, weekly, biweekly, or monthly) and amount of salary or wages and be based on the defendant's earnings for the pay period during which this writ is served on the garnishee.

During each pay period, a portion of the defendant's salary or wages as it becomes due shall be held and not disposed of or transferred until further order of this court. The amount of salary or wages to be withheld for each pay period shall be made in accordance with the following paragraph. This writ shall continue until the plaintiff's judgment is paid in full or until otherwise provided by court order.

Federal law (15 U.S.C. §§ 1671–1673) limits the amount to be withheld from salary or wages to no more than 25% of any individual defendant's disposable earnings (the part of earnings remaining after the deduction of any amounts required by law to be deducted) for any pay period or to no more than the amount by which the individual's disposable earnings for the pay period exceed 30 times the federal minimum hourly wage, whichever is less.

For administrative costs, the garnishee may collect $.......... against the salary or wages of the defendant for the first deduction and $.......... for each deduction thereafter.

The total amount of the final judgment outstanding as set out in the plaintiff's motion is $ ....

FAILURE TO FILE AN ANSWER WITHIN THE TIME REQUIRED MAY RESULT IN THE ENTRY OF JUDGMENT AGAINST THE GARNISHEE FOR THE ABOVE TOTAL AMOUNT OF $..........

ORDERED at ...., Florida, on ..... (date) ......

(Name of Clerk)
As Clerk of the Court
By ____________________
As Deputy Clerk

Added June 19, 1968, effective Oct. 1, 1968 (211 So.2d 174). Amended Oct. 9, 1980, effective Jan. 1, 1981 (391 So.2d 165); July 16, 1992, effective Jan. 1, 1993 (604 So.2d 1110); Oct. 31, 1996, effective Jan. 1, 1997 (682 So.2d 105); Oct. 5, 2000, effective Jan. 1, 2001 (773 So.2d 1098).

Committee Notes

1992 Amendment. This form is to be used to effectuate section 77.0305, Florida Statutes.

1996 Amendment. The following was adopted as a committee note, with no changes to the text of the forms: Both forms 1.907(a) and (b) are for use after judgment has been entered against a defendant. If a plaintiff seeks a writ of garnishment before judgment is entered, notice to the defendant of the right to an immediate hearing under sections 73.031 and 77.07, Florida Statutes, must be included in the writ and served on the defendant.

Form 1.908. Writ of Replevin

WRIT OF REPLEVIN

THE STATE OF FLORIDA:
To Each Sheriff of the State:

YOU ARE COMMANDED to replevy the goods and chattels in possession of the defendant, ..., described as follows:

(describe property)

and to dispose of it according to law.

DATED on ....

(Name of Clerk)
As Clerk of the Court
By ____________________
As Deputy Clerk

Added June 19, 1968, effective Oct. 1, 1968 (211 So.2d 174). Amended Oct. 9, 1980, effective Jan. 1, 1981 (391 So.2d 165); July 16, 1992, effective Jan. 1, 1993 (604 So.2d 1110); Oct. 31, 1996, effective Jan. 1, 1997 (682 So.2d 105); Oct. 5, 2000, effective Jan. 1, 2001 (773 So.2d 1098).

Committee Notes

1980 Amendment. The form is amended in accordance with the statutory changes as a result of *Fuentes v. Shevin*, 407 U.S. 67, 92 S. Ct. 1983, 32 L. Ed. 2d 556 (1972). The sheriff is commanded to dispose of the property according to law because of the conflict between sections 78.068(4) and 78.13, Florida Statutes (1979). The former apparently contemplates that the sheriff will hold the property for 5 days within which the bond can be posted, while the latter retains the old 3–day time period.

1996 Amendment. This amendment only changes the name of the form.

Form 1.909. Distress

DISTRESS WRIT

THE STATE OF FLORIDA:
To the Sheriff of .... County, Florida:

YOU ARE COMMANDED to serve this writ and a copy of the complaint on defendant ....

This distress writ subjects all property liable to distress for rent on the following property in .... County, Florida:

(describe property)

Each defendant is enjoined from damaging, disposing of, secreting, or removing any property liable to be distrained from the rented real property after the time of service of this writ until the sheriff levies on the property or this writ is vacated or the court otherwise orders. If a defendant does not move for dissolution of the writ, the court may order the sheriff to levy on the property liable to distress forthwith after 20 days from the time the complaint in this action is served. The amount claimed in the complaint is the sum of $ .... with interest and costs.

DATED on ....

____
Judge

Added June 19, 1968, effective Oct. 1, 1968 (211 So.2d 174). Amended Oct. 9, 1980, effective Jan. 1, 1981 (391 So.2d 165); July 16, 1992, effective Jan. 1, 1993 (604 So.2d 1110); Oct. 5, 2000, effective Jan. 1, 2001 (773 So.2d 1098).

Committee Notes

1980 Amendment. This form is substantially revised to comply with the statutory changes in section 83.12, Florida Statutes, as amended in 1980 to overcome the unconstitutionality of distress proceedings. See *Phillips v. Guin & Hunt, Inc.*, 344 So. 2d 568 (Fla. 1977). Because the revision is substantial, no struck-through or underscored type is indicated.

Form 1.910. Subpoena for Trial

(a) For Issuance by Clerk.

SUBPOENA

THE STATE OF FLORIDA:
TO ....:

YOU ARE COMMANDED to appear before the Honorable ...., Judge of the Court, at the .... County Courthouse in ...., Florida, on ...., at .... m., to testify in this action. If you fail to appear, you may be in contempt of court.

You are subpoenaed to appear by the following attorney, and unless excused from this subpoena by this attorney or the court, you shall respond to this subpoena as directed.

DATED on ....

(Name of Clerk)
As Clerk of the Court
By ____________________
As Deputy Clerk

____
Attorney for ....
....
....
Address
Florida Bar No. ....

Any minor subpoenaed for testimony shall have the right to be accompanied by a parent or guardian at all times during the taking of testimony notwithstanding the invocation of the rule of sequestration of section 90.616, Florida Statutes, except upon a showing that the presence of a parent or guardian is likely to have a material, negative impact on the credibility or accuracy of the minor's testimony, or that the interests of the parent or guardian are in actual or potential conflict with the interests of the minor.

If you are a person with a disability who needs any accommodation in order to participate in this proceeding, you are entitled, at no cost to you, to the provision of certain assistance. Please contact [identify applicable court personnel by name, address, and telephone number] at least 7 days before your scheduled court appearance, or immediately upon receiving this notification if the time before the scheduled appearance is less than 7 days; if you are hearing or voice impaired, call 711.

(b) For Issuance by Attorney of Record.

SUBPOENA

THE STATE OF FLORIDA:
TO ....:

YOU ARE COMMANDED to appear before the Honorable ...., Judge of the Court, at the .... County Courthouse in ...., Florida, on .... (date) ...., at ....

m., to testify in this action. If you fail to appear, you may be in contempt of court.

You are subpoenaed to appear by the following attorney, and unless excused from this subpoena by this attorney or the court, you shall respond to this subpoena as directed.

DATED on ....

(Name of Attorney)
For the Court

____

Attorney for ....

....

....

Address

Florida Bar No. ....

Any minor subpoenaed for testimony shall have the right to be accompanied by a parent or guardian at all times during the taking of testimony notwithstanding the invocation of the rule of sequestration of section 90.616, Florida Statutes, except upon a showing that the presence of a parent or guardian is likely to have a material, negative impact on the credibility or accuracy of the minor's testimony, or that the interests of the parent or guardian are in actual or potential conflict with the interests of the minor.

If you are a person with a disability who needs any accommodation in order to participate in this proceeding, you are entitled, at no cost to you, to the provision of certain assistance. Please contact [identify applicable court personnel by name, address, and telephone number] at least 7 days before your scheduled court appearance, or immediately upon receiving this notification if the time before the scheduled appearance is less than 7 days; if you are hearing or voice impaired, call 711.

Added June 19, 1968, effective Oct. 1, 1968 (211 So.2d 174). Amended Oct. 9, 1980, effective Jan. 1, 1981 (391 So.2d 165); July 16, 1992, effective Jan. 1, 1993 (604 So.2d 1110); Oct. 31, 1996, effective Jan. 1, 1997 (682 So.2d 105); Oct. 5, 2000, effective Jan. 1, 2001 (773 So.2d 1098); Sept. 27, 2007, effective Jan. 1, 2008 (966 So.2d 943); Nov. 14, 2013, effective Jan. 1, 2014 (131 So.3d 643).

Committee Notes

1996 Amendment. Form (b) was added to comply with amendments to rule 1.410.

2013 Amendment. The notice to persons with disabilities was amended to comply with amendments to Fla. R. Jud. Admin. 2.540.

Form 1.911. Subpoena Duces Tecum for Trial

(a) For Issuance by Clerk.

SUBPOENA DUCES TECUM

THE STATE OF FLORIDA:

TO ....:

YOU ARE COMMANDED to appear before the Honorable ...., Judge of the Court, at the .... County Courthouse in ...., Florida, on .... (date) ...., at .... m., to testify in this action and to have with you at that time and place the following: .... If you fail to appear, you may be in contempt of court.

You are subpoenaed to appear by the following attorney, and unless excused from this subpoena by this attorney or the court, you shall respond to this subpoena as directed.

DATED on ....

(Name of Clerk)
As Clerk of the Court
By __________
As Deputy Clerk

____

Attorney for ....

....

....

Address

Florida Bar No. ....

Any minor subpoenaed for testimony shall have the right to be accompanied by a parent or guardian at all times during the taking of testimony notwithstanding the invocation of the rule of sequestration of section 90.616, Florida Statutes, except upon a showing that the presence of a parent or guardian is likely to have a material, negative impact on the credibility or accuracy of the minor's testimony, or that the interests of the parent or guardian are in actual or potential conflict with the interests of the minor.

If you are a person with a disability who needs any accommodation in order to participate in this proceeding, you are entitled, at no cost to you, to the provision of certain assistance. Please contact [identify applicable court personnel by name, address, and telephone number] at least 7 days before your scheduled court appearance, or immediately upon receiving this notification if the time before the scheduled appearance is less than 7 days; if you are hearing or voice impaired, call 711.

(b) For Issuance by Attorney of Record.

SUBPOENA DUCES TECUM

THE STATE OF FLORIDA:

TO ....:

YOU ARE COMMANDED to appear before the Honorable ...., Judge of the Court, at the .... County Courthouse in ...., Florida, on (date), at .... m., to testify in this action and to have with you at that time and place the following: .... If you fail to appear, you may be in contempt of court.

You are subpoenaed to appear by the following attorney, and unless excused from this subpoena by this attorney or the court, you shall respond to this subpoena as directed.

DATED on ....

(Name of Attorney)
For the Court

______

Attorney for ....

....

....

Address

Florida Bar No. ....

Any minor subpoenaed for testimony shall have the right to be accompanied by a parent or guardian at all times during the taking of testimony notwithstanding the invocation of the rule of sequestration of section 90.616, Florida Statutes, except upon a showing that the presence of a parent or guardian is likely to have a material, negative impact on the credibility or accuracy of the minor's testimony, or that the interests of the parent or guardian are in actual or potential conflict with the interests of the minor.

If you are a person with a disability who needs any accommodation in order to participate in this proceeding, you are entitled, at no cost to you, to the provision of certain assistance. Please contact [identify applicable court personnel by name, address, and telephone number] at least 7 days before your scheduled court appearance, or immediately upon receiving this notification if the time before the scheduled appearance is less than 7 days; if you are hearing or voice impaired, call 711.

Added June 19, 1968, effective Oct. 1, 1968 (211 So.2d 174). Amended Oct. 9, 1980, effective Jan. 1, 1981 (391 So.2d 165); July 16, 1992, effective Jan. 1, 1993 (604 So.2d 1110); Oct. 31, 1996, effective Jan. 1, 1997 (682 So.2d 105); Oct. 5, 2000, effective Jan. 1, 2001 (773 So.2d 1098); Sept. 27, 2007, effective Jan. 1, 2008 (966 So.2d 943); Nov. 14, 2013, effective Jan. 1, 2014 (131 So.3d 643).

Committee Notes

1996 Amendment. Form (b) was added to comply with amendments to rule 1.410.

2013 Amendment. The notice to persons with disabilities was amended to comply with amendments to Fla. R. Jud. Admin. 2.540.

Form 1.912. Subpoena for Deposition

(a) For Issuance by Clerk.

SUBPOENA FOR DEPOSITION

THE STATE OF FLORIDA

TO ....:

YOU ARE COMMANDED to appear before a person authorized by law to take depositions at .... in ...., Florida, on ...(date)..., at .... m., for the taking of your deposition in this action. If you fail to appear, you may be in contempt of court.

You are subpoenaed to appear by the following attorney, and unless excused from this subpoena by this attorney or the court, you shall respond to this subpoena as directed.

DATED on ....

(Name of Clerk)
As Clerk of the Court
By ______
As Deputy Clerk

______

Attorney for ....

....

....

Address

Florida Bar No. ....

Any minor subpoenaed for testimony shall have the right to be accompanied by a parent or guardian at all times during the taking of testimony notwithstanding the invocation of the rule of sequestration of section 90.616, Florida Statutes, except upon a showing that the presence of a parent or guardian is likely to have a material, negative impact on the credibility or accuracy of the minor's testimony, or that the interests of the parent or guardian are in actual or potential conflict with the interests of the minor.

If you are a person with a disability who needs any accommodation in order to participate in this deposition, you are entitled, at no cost to you, to the provision of certain assistance. Please contact [identify attorney or party taking deposition by name, address, and telephone number] at least 7 days before your scheduled deposition, or immediately upon receiving this notification if the time before the scheduled appearance is less than 7 days; if you are hearing or voice impaired, call 711.

(b) For Issuance by Attorney of Record.

SUBPOENA FOR DEPOSITION

THE STATE OF FLORIDA:

TO ....:

YOU ARE COMMANDED to appear before a person authorized by law to take depositions at .... in ...., Florida, on .... (date).........., at .... m., for the taking of your deposition in this action. If you fail to appear, you may be in contempt of court.

You are subpoenaed to appear by the following attorney, and unless excused from this subpoena by this attorney or the court, you shall respond to this subpoena as directed.

DATED on ....

(Name of Attorney)
For the Court

Attorney for ....
....
....
Address
Florida Bar No. ....

Any minor subpoenaed for testimony shall have the right to be accompanied by a parent or guardian at all times during the taking of testimony notwithstanding the invocation of the rule of sequestration of section 90.616, Florida Statutes, except upon a showing that the presence of a parent or guardian is likely to have a material, negative impact on the credibility or accuracy of the minor's testimony, or that the interests of the parent or guardian are in actual or potential conflict with the interests of the minor.

If you are a person with a disability who needs any accommodation in order to participate in this deposition, you are entitled, at no cost to you, to the provision of certain assistance. Please contact [identify attorney or party taking the deposition by name, address, and telephone number] at least 7 days before your scheduled deposition, or immediately upon receiving this notification if the time before the scheduled deposition is less than 7 days; if you are hearing or voice impaired, call 711.

Added June 19, 1968, effective Oct. 1, 1968 (211 So.2d 174). Amended Oct. 9, 1980, effective Jan. 1, 1981 (391 So.2d 165); July 16, 1992, effective Jan. 1, 1993 (604 So.2d 1110); Oct. 31, 1996, effective Jan. 1, 1997 (682 So.2d 105); Oct. 5, 2000, effective Jan. 1, 2001 (773 So.2d 1098); Sept. 27, 2007, effective Jan. 1, 2008 (966 So.2d 943); Nov. 14, 2013, effective Jan. 1, 2014 (131 So.3d 643).

Committee Notes

1996 Amendment. Form (b) was added to comply with amendments to rule 1.410.

2013 Amendment. The notice to persons with disabilities was amended to make the procedure for obtaining accommodation consistent with the procedure required in court proceedings.

Form 1.913. Subpoena Duces Tecum for Deposition

(a) For Issuance by Clerk.

SUBPOENA DUCES TECUM FOR

THE STATE OF FLORIDA:
TO ....:

YOU ARE COMMANDED to appear before a person authorized by law to take depositions at .... in ...., Florida, on ...(date)..., at .... m., for the taking of your deposition in this action and to have with you at that time and place the following: .... If you fail to appear, you may be in contempt of court.

You are subpoenaed to appear by the following attorney, and unless excused from this subpoena by this attorney or the court, you shall respond to this subpoena as directed.

DATED on ....

(Name of Clerk)
As Clerk of the Court
By ____________
As Deputy Clerk

Attorney for ....
....
....
Address
Florida Bar No. ....

Any minor subpoenaed for testimony shall have the right to be accompanied by a parent or guardian at all times during the taking of testimony notwithstanding the invocation of the rule of sequestration of section 90.616, Florida Statutes, except upon a showing that the presence of a parent or guardian is likely to have a material, negative impact on the credibility or accuracy of the minor's testimony, or that the interests of the parent or guardian are in actual or potential conflict with the interests of the minor.

If you are a person with a disability who needs any accommodation in order to participate in this deposition you are entitled, at no cost to you, to the provision of certain assistance. Please contact [identify attorney or party taking the deposition by name, address, and telephone number] at least 7 days before your scheduled deposition, or immediately upon receiving this notification if the time before the scheduled deposition is less than 7 days; if you are hearing or voice impaired, call 711.

(b) For Issuance by Attorney of Record.

SUBPOENA DUCES TECUM FOR DEPOSITION

THE STATE OF FLORIDA:
TO ....:

YOU ARE COMMANDED to appear before a person authorized by law to take depositions at .... in ...., Florida, on ...(date)..., at .... m., for the taking of your deposition in this action and to have with you at that time and place the following: .... If you fail to appear, you may be in contempt of court.

You are subpoenaed to appear by the following attorney, and unless excused from this subpoena by this attorney or the court, you shall respond to this subpoena as directed.

DATED on ....

(Name of Attorney)
For the Court

____

Attorney for ....

....

....

Address

Florida Bar No. ....

Any minor subpoenaed for testimony shall have the right to be accompanied by a parent or guardian at all times during the taking of testimony notwithstanding the invocation of the rule of sequestration of section 90.616, Florida Statutes, except upon a showing that the presence of a parent or guardian is likely to have a material, negative impact on the credibility or accuracy of the minor's testimony, or that the interests of the parent or guardian are in actual or potential conflict with the interests of the minor.

If you are a person with a disability who needs any accommodation in order to participate in this deposition, you are entitled, at no cost to you, to the provision of certain assistance. Please contact [identify attorney or party taking the deposition by name, address, and telephone number] at least 7 days before your scheduled deposition, or immediately upon receiving this notification if the time before the scheduled appearance is less than 7 days; if you are hearing or voice impaired, call 711.

Added June 19, 1968, effective Oct. 1, 1968 (211 So.2d 174). Amended Oct. 9, 1980, effective Jan. 1, 1981 (391 So.2d 165); July 16, 1992, effective Jan. 1, 1993 (604 So.2d 1110); Oct. 31, 1996, effective Jan. 1, 1997 (682 So.2d 105); Oct. 5, 2000, effective Jan. 1, 2001 (773 So.2d 1098); Sept. 27, 2007, effective Jan. 1, 2008 (966 So.2d 943); Nov. 14, 2013, effective Jan. 1, 2014 (131 So.3d 643).

Committee Notes

1996 Amendment. Form (b) was added to comply with amendments to rule 1.410.

2013 Amendment. The notice to persons with disabilities was amended to make the procedure for obtaining accommodation consistent with the procedure required in court proceedings.

Form 1.914. Execution

EXECUTION

THE STATE OF FLORIDA:
To Each Sheriff of the State:

YOU ARE COMMANDED to levy on the property subject to execution of .... in the sum of $ .... with interest at ...... % a year from ...... (date) ......, until paid and to have this writ before the court when satisfied.

DATED on ....

(Name of Clerk)
As Clerk of the Court
By ______________
As Deputy Clerk

Added June 19, 1968, effective Oct. 1, 1968 (211 So.2d 174). Amended Oct. 9, 1980, effective Jan. 1, 1981 (391 So.2d 165); Oct. 5, 2000, effective Jan. 1, 2001 (773 So.2d 1098).

Committee Note

1980 Amendment. The description of the property to be levied on has been made general so it encompasses all property subject to execution under section 56.061, Florida Statutes (1979).

Form 1.915. Writ of Possession

WRIT OF POSSESSION

THE STATE OF FLORIDA:
To the Sheriff of .... County, Florida:

YOU ARE COMMANDED to remove all persons from the following described property in .... County, Florida:

(describe property)

and to put .... in possession of it.

DATED on ....

(Name of Clerk)
As Clerk of the Court
By ______________
As Deputy Clerk

Added June 19, 1968, effective Oct. 1, 1968 (211 So.2d 174). Amended July 26, 1972, effective Jan. 1, 1973 (265 So.2d 21); Oct. 9, 1980, effective Jan. 1, 1981 (391 So.2d 165); July 16, 1992, effective Jan. 1, 1993 (604 So.2d 1110); Oct. 5, 2000, effective Jan. 1, 2001 (773 So.2d 1098).

Committee Notes

1973 Amendment. The form is changed to make the direction conform to the statutory requirement in section 48.011, Florida Statutes.

1980 Amendment. The direction on this form is changed to the sheriff of the county where the property is located, and the conclusion is modernized.

Form 1.916. Replevin Order to Show Cause

ORDER TO SHOW CAUSE

THE STATE OF FLORIDA:
To Each Sheriff of the State:

YOU ARE COMMANDED to serve this order on defendant, ..., by personal service as provided by law, if possible, or, if you are unable to personally serve defendant within the time specified, by placing a copy of this order with a copy of the summons on the claimed property located at ...., Florida, at least 5 days before the hearing scheduled below, excluding the day of service and intermediate Saturdays, Sundays, and legal holidays. Nonpersonal service as provided in this order shall be effective to afford notice to defendant of this order, but for no other purpose.

Defendant shall show cause before the Honorable ...., on ..... (date) ....., at ..... m. in the .... County Courthouse in ...., Florida, why the property claimed by plaintiff in the complaint filed in this action should not be taken from the possession of defendant and delivered to plaintiff.

Defendant may file affidavits, appear personally or with an attorney and present testimony at the time of the hearing, or, on a finding by the court pursuant to section 78.067(2), Florida Statutes (1979), that plaintiff is entitled to possession of the property described in the complaint pending final adjudication of the claims of the parties, file with the court a written undertaking executed by a surety approved by the court in an amount equal to the value of the property to stay an order authorizing the delivery of the property to plaintiff.

If defendant fails to appear as ordered, defendant shall be deemed to have waived the right to a hearing. The court may thereupon order the clerk to issue a writ of replevin.

ORDERED at ...., Florida, on ..... (date) ......

____

Judge

Added Oct. 9, 1980, effective Jan. 1, 1981 (391 So.2d 165). Amended July 16, 1992, effective Jan. 1, 1993 (604 So.2d 1110); Oct. 31, 1996, effective Jan. 1, 1997 (682 So.2d 105); Oct. 5, 2000, effective Jan. 1, 2001 (773 So.2d 1098).

Committee Notes

1980 Adoption. Former form 1.916 is repealed because of the consolidation of writs of assistance with writs of possession. The new form is the replevin order to show cause prescribed by section 78.065, Florida Statutes (1979).

1996 Amendment. This form is amended to provide for service at least 5 days before the show cause hearing, rather than by a specified date.

Form 1.917. Ne Exeat

WRIT OF NE EXEAT

THE STATE OF FLORIDA:
To Each Sheriff of the State:

YOU ARE COMMANDED to detain the defendant, ..., and to require the defendant to give bond in the sum of $ .... payable to the Governor of Florida and the Governor's successors in office conditioned that the defendant will answer plaintiff's pleading in this action and will not depart from the state without leave of court and will comply with the lawful orders of this court, with sureties to be approved by the clerk of this court. If the defendant does not give the bond, the defendant shall be taken into custody and be confined in the .... County jail until the defendant gives the bond or until further order of this court. If the defendant does not give the bond, the defendant shall be brought before a judge of this court within 24 hours of confinement.

DATED on ....

(Name of Clerk)
As Clerk of the Court
By ____________________
As Deputy Clerk

Added June 19, 1968, effective Oct. 1, 1968 (211 So.2d 174). Amended Dec. 13, 1976, effective Jan. 1, 1977 (339 So.2d 626); Oct. 9, 1980, effective Jan. 1, 1981 (391 So.2d 165); July 16, 1992, effective Jan. 1, 1993 (604 So.2d 1110); Oct. 5, 2000, effective Jan. 1, 2001 (773 So.2d 1098).

Committee Notes

1976 Amendment. See 1976 Op. Att'y Gen. Fla. 076–13 (Jan. 23, 1976).

Form 1.918. Lis Pendens

NOTICE OF LIS PENDENS

TO DEFENDANT(S) ...., AND ALL OTHERS WHOM IT MAY CONCERN:

YOU ARE NOTIFIED OF THE FOLLOWING:

(a) The plaintiff has instituted this action against you seeking ("to foreclose a mortgage" or "to partition" or "to quiet title" or other type of action) with respect to the property described below.

(b) The plaintiff(s) in this action is/are:

(1) ....

(2) ....

(c) The date of the institution of this action is .... OR: the date on the clerk's electronic receipt for the action's filing is .... OR: the case number of the action is as shown in the caption.

(d) The property that is the subject matter of this action is in .... County, Florida, and is described as follows:

(legal description of property)

DATED on ....

....
Attorney for ....
....
....
Address
Florida Bar No. ....

NOTE: This form is not to be recorded without the clerk's case number.

Added June 19, 1968, effective Oct. 1, 1968 (211 So.2d 174). Amended Oct. 1, 1970; July 16, 1992, effective Jan. 1, 1993 (604 So.2d 1110); July 7, 1995, effective Jan. 1, 1996 (663 So.2d 1047); Nov. 28, 1995, effective Jan. 1, 1996 (663 So.2d 1049) Oct. 5, 2000, effective Jan. 1, 2001 (773 So.2d 1098); Oct. 1, 2009 (20 So.3d 379).

Committee Notes

2009 Amendment. This form was substantially rewritten due to the amendments to section 48.23, Florida Statutes (2009). Section 48.23 provides that the notice must contain the names of all of the parties, the name of the court in which the action is instituted, a description of the property involved or affected, a description of the relief sought as to the property, and one of the following: the date of the institution of the action, the date of the clerk's electronic receipt, or the case number. If the case number is used to satisfy the requirements of section 48.23, it should be inserted in the case caption of the notice.

Form 1.919. Notice of Action; Constructive Service—No Property

NOTICE OF ACTION

TO ....:

YOU ARE NOTIFIED that an action for ("construction of a will" or "re-establishment of a lost deed" or other type of action) has been filed against you and you are required to serve a copy of your written defenses, if any, to it on ...., the plaintiff's attorney, whose address is ...., on or before ..... (date) ....., and file the original with the clerk of this court either before service on the plaintiff's attorney or immediately thereafter; otherwise a default will be entered against you for the relief demanded in the complaint or petition.

DATED on ....

(Name of Clerk)
As Clerk of the Court
By ____________________
As Deputy Clerk

NOTE: This form must be modified to name the other defendants when there are multiple defendants and all are not served under the same notice. See section 49.08(1), Florida Statutes (1979).

Added June 19, 1968, effective Oct. 1, 1968 (211 So.2d 174). Amended Oct. 9, 1980, effective Jan. 1, 1981 (391 So.2d 165); July 16, 1992, effective Jan. 1, 1993 (604 So.2d 1110); July 7, 1995, effective Jan. 1, 1996 (663 So.2d 1047); Nov. 28, 1995, effective Jan. 1, 1996 (663 So.2d 1049); Oct. 5, 2000, effective Jan. 1, 2001 (773 So.2d 1098).

Form 1.920. Notice of Action; Constructive Service—Property

NOTICE OF ACTION

TO ....:

YOU ARE NOTIFIED that an action to ("enforce a lien on" or "foreclose a mortgage on" or "quiet title to" or "partition" or other type of action) the following property in .... County, Florida:

(describe property)

has been filed against you and you are required to serve a copy of your written defenses, if any, to it on ...., the plaintiff's attorney, whose address is ...., on or before ..... (date) ....., and file the original with the clerk of this court either before service on the plaintiff's attorney or immediately thereafter; otherwise a default will be entered against you for the relief demanded in the complaint or petition.

DATED on ....

(Name of Clerk)
As Clerk of the Court
By ____________________
As Deputy Clerk

NOTE: This form must be modified to name the other defendants when there are multiple defendants and all are not served under the same notice. See section 49.08(1), Florida Statutes (1979).

Added June 19, 1968, effective Oct. 1, 1968 (211 So.2d 174). Amended Oct. 9, 1980, effective Jan. 1, 1981 (391 So.2d 165); July 16, 1992, effective Jan. 1, 1993 (604 So.2d 1110); Oct. 5, 2000, effective Jan. 1, 2001 (773 So.2d 1098).

Form 1.921. Notice Of Production From Nonparty

NOTICE OF PRODUCTION

To ....:

YOU ARE NOTIFIED that after 10 days from the date of service of this notice, if service is by delivery, or 15 days from the date of service, if service is by mail, and if no objection is received from any party, the undersigned will issue or apply to the clerk of this court for issuance of the attached subpoena directed to ...., who is not a party and whose address is ...., to produce the items listed at the time and place specified in the subpoena.

DATED on ....

Attorney for ....
....
....
Address
Florida Bar No. ....

NOTE: This form of notice is for use with rule 1.351. A copy of the subpoena must be attached to this form for it to comply with the rule.

Added Oct. 9, 1980, effective Jan. 1, 1981 (391 So.2d 165). Amended July 16, 1992, effective Jan. 1, 1993 (604 So.2d 1110); Oct. 31, 1996, effective Jan. 1, 1997 (682 So.2d 105); Oct. 5, 2000, effective Jan. 1, 2001 (773 So.2d 1098).

Committee Notes

1980 Adoption. This form is new.

1996 Amendment. This form was amended to comply with amendments to rules 1.351 and 1.410.

Form 1.922. Subpoena Duces Tecum Without Deposition

(a) When Witness Has Option to Furnish Records Instead of Attending Deposition; Issuance by Clerk.

SUBPOENA DUCES TECUM

THE STATE OF FLORIDA:

TO ....:

YOU ARE COMMANDED to appear at .... in ...., Florida, on ...(date)..., at .... m., and to have with you at that time and place the following: ....

These items will be inspected and may be copied at that time. You will not be required to surrender the original items. You may comply with this subpoena by providing legible copies of the items to be produced to the attorney whose name appears on this subpoena on or before the scheduled date of production. You may condition the preparation of the copies upon the payment in advance of the reasonable cost of preparation. You may mail or deliver the copies to the attorney whose name appears on this subpoena and thereby eliminate your appearance at the time and place specified above. You have the right to object to the production pursuant to this subpoena at any time before production by giving written notice to the attorney whose name appears on this subpoena. THIS WILL NOT BE A DEPOSITION. NO TESTIMONY WILL BE TAKEN.

If you fail to:

(1) appear as specified; or

(2) furnish the records instead of appearing as provided above; or

(3) object to this subpoena,

you may be in contempt of court. You are subpoenaed to appear by the following attorney, and unless excused from this subpoena by this attorney or the court, you shall respond to this subpoena as directed.

DATED on ....

(Name of Clerk)
As Clerk of the Court
By ____________________
As Deputy Clerk

Attorney for ....
....
....
Address
Florida Bar No. ....

If you are a person with a disability who needs any accommodation in order to respond to this subpoena, you are entitled, at no cost to you, to the provision of certain assistance. Please contact [identify attorney or party taking the deposition by name, address, and telephone number] at least 7 days before your scheduled appearance, or immediately upon receiving this notification if the time before the scheduled appearance is less than 7 days; if you are hearing or voice impaired, call 711.

(b) When Witness Must Appear and Produce the Records; Issuance by Clerk.

SUBPOENA DUCES TECUM

THE STATE OF FLORIDA:

TO: ....:

YOU ARE COMMANDED to appear at .... in ...., Florida, on ...(date)..., at .... m., and to have with you at that time and place the following: ....

These items will be inspected and may be copied at that time. You will not be required to surrender the original items. You have the right to object to the production pursuant to this subpoena at any time before production by giving written notice to the attorney whose name appears on this subpoena. THIS WILL NOT BE A DEPOSITION. NO TESTIMONY WILL BE TAKEN.

If you fail to:

(1) appear or furnish the records at the time and place specified instead of appearing; or

(2) object to this subpoena,

you may be in contempt of court. You are subpoenaed by the attorney whose name appears on this subpoena, and unless excused from this subpoena by the attorney or the court, you shall respond to this subpoena as directed.

DATED on . . . .

(Name of Clerk)
As Clerk of the Court
By ____________________
As Deputy Clerk

____

Attorney for . . . .

. . . .

. . . .

Address

Florida Bar No. . . . .

If you are a person with a disability who needs any accommodation in order respond to this subpoena, you are entitled, at no cost to you, to the provision of certain assistance. Please contact [identify attorney or party taking the deposition by name, address, and telephone number] at least 7 days before your scheduled appearance, or immediately upon receiving this notification if the time before the scheduled appearance is less than 7 days; if you are hearing or voice impaired, call 711.

(c) When Witness Has Option to Furnish Records Instead of Attending Deposition; Issuance by Attorney of Record.

SUBPOENA DUCES TECUM

THE STATE OF FLORIDA:

TO . . . .:

YOU ARE COMMANDED to appear at . . . . in . . . ., Florida, on . . .(date). . ., at . . . . m., and to have with you at that time and place the following: . . . .

These items will be inspected and may be copied at that time. You will not be required to surrender the original items. You may comply with this subpoena by providing legible copies of the items to be produced to the attorney whose name appears on this subpoena on or before the scheduled date of production. You may condition the preparation of the copies upon the payment in advance of the reasonable cost of preparation. You may mail or deliver the copies to the attorney whose name appears on this subpoena and thereby eliminate your appearance at the time and place specified above. You have the right to object to the production pursuant to this subpoena at any time before production by giving written notice to the attorney whose name appears on this subpoena. THIS WILL NOT BE A DEPOSITION. NO TESTIMONY WILL BE TAKEN.

If you fail to:

(1) appear as specified; or

(2) furnish the records instead of appearing as provided above; or

(3) object to this subpoena,

you may be in contempt of court. You are subpoenaed to appear by the following attorney, and unless excused from this subpoena by this attorney or the court, you shall respond to this subpoena as directed.

DATED on . . . .

(Name of Attorney)
For the Court

____

Attorney for . . . .

. . . .

. . . .

Address

Florida Bar No. . . . .

If you are a person with a disability who needs any accommodation in order to respond to this subpoena, you are entitled, at no cost to you, to the provision of certain assistance. Please contact [identify attorney or party taking the deposition by name, address, and telephone number] at least 7 days before your scheduled appearance, or immediately upon receiving this notification if the time before the scheduled appearance is less than 7 days; if you are hearing or voice impaired, call 711.

(d) When Witness Must Appear and Produce the Records; Issuance by Attorney of Record.

THE STATE OF FLORIDA:

TO . . . .:

YOU ARE COMMANDED to appear at . . . . in . . . ., Florida, on . . .(date). . ., at . . . . m., and to have with you at that time and place the following: . . . .

These items will be inspected and may be copied at that time. You will not be required to surrender the original items. You have the right to object to the production pursuant to this subpoena at any time before production by giving written notice to the attorney whose name appears on this subpoena. THIS WILL NOT BE A DEPOSITION. NO TESTIMONY WILL BE TAKEN.

If you fail to:

(1) appear or furnish the records at the time and place specified instead of appearing; or

(2) object to this subpoena,

you may be in contempt of court. You are subpoenaed by the attorney whose name appears on this subpoena, and unless excused from this subpoena by the attorney or the court, you shall respond to this subpoena as directed.

DATED on . . . .

(Name of Attorney)
For the Court

____

Attorney for . . . .

. . . .

. . . .

Address

Florida Bar No. . . . .

If you are a person with a disability who needs any accommodation in order to respond to this subpoena, you are entitled, at no cost to you, to the provision of certain assistance. Please contact [identify attorney or party taking the deposition by name, address, and telephone number] at least 7 days before your scheduled appearance, or immediately upon receiving this notification if the time before the scheduled appearance is less than 7 days; if you are hearing or voice impaired, call 711.

NOTE: These forms are to be used for production of documents under rule 1.351. Form (a) is used when the person having the records may furnish copies to the attorney requesting the subpoena instead of appearing at the time and place specified in the subpoena and the subpoena is to be issued by the clerk. Form (b) is used when the records must be produced at the time and place specified in the subpoena and the subpoena is to be issued by the clerk. Form (c) is used when the person having the records may furnish copies to the attorney requesting the subpoena instead of appearing at the time and place specified in the subpoena and the subpoena is to be issued by an attorney of record. Form (d) is used when the records must be produced at the time and place specified in the subpoena and the subpoena is to be issued by an attorney of record.

Added Oct. 9, 1980, effective Jan. 1, 1981 (391 So.2d 165). Amended by July 16, 1992, effective Jan. 1, 1993 (604 So.2d 1110); Oct. 31, 1996, effective Jan. 1, 1997 (682 So.2d 105); Oct. 5, 2000, effective Jan. 1, 2001 (773 So.2d 1098); Sept. 27, 2007, effective Jan. 1, 2008 (966 So.2d 943); Nov. 14, 2013, effective Jan. 1, 2014 (131 So.3d 643).

Committee Notes

1980 Adoption. This form is new.

1996 Amendment. Forms (a) and (b) were amended and forms (c) and (d) were added to comply with amendments to rules 1.351 and 1.410.

2013 Amendment. The notice to persons with disabilities was amended to make the procedure for obtaining accommodation consistent with the procedure required in court proceedings.

Form 1.923. Eviction Summons/Residential

EVICTION SUMMONS/RESIDENTIAL

TO: . . . .
Defendant(s)

. . . .

. . . .

PLEASE READ CAREFULLY

You are being sued by . . . . to require you to move out of the place where you are living for the reasons given in the attached complaint.

You are entitled to a trial to determine whether you can be required to move, but you MUST do ALL of the things listed below. You must do them within 5 days (not including Saturday, Sunday, or any legal holiday) after the date these papers were given to you or to a person who lives with you or were posted at your home.

THE THINGS YOU MUST DO ARE AS FOLLOWS:

(1) Write down the reason(s) why you think you should not be forced to move. The written reason(s) must be given to the clerk of the court at . . . . County Courthouse

. . . .

. . . ., Florida

(2) Mail or give a copy of your written reason(s) to:

. . . .

Plaintiff/Plaintiff's Attorney

. . . .

. . . .

Address

(3) Pay to the clerk of the court the amount of rent that the attached complaint claims to be due and any rent that becomes due until the lawsuit is over. If you believe that the amount claimed in the complaint is incorrect, you should file with the clerk of the court a motion to have the court determine the amount to be paid. If you file a motion, you must attach to the motion any documents supporting your position and mail or give a copy of the motion to the plaintiff/plaintiff's attorney.

(4) If you file a motion to have the court determine the amount of rent to be paid to the clerk of the court, you must immediately contact the office of the judge to whom the case is assigned to schedule a hearing to decide what amount should be paid to the clerk of the court while the lawsuit is pending.

IF YOU DO NOT DO ALL OF THE THINGS SPECIFIED ABOVE WITHIN 5 WORKING DAYS AFTER THE DATE THAT THESE PAPERS WERE GIVEN TO YOU OR TO A PERSON WHO LIVES WITH YOU OR WERE POSTED AT YOUR HOME, YOU MAY BE EVICTED WITHOUT A HEARING OR FURTHER NOTICE

---

(5) If the attached complaint also contains a claim for money damages (such as unpaid rent), you must

respond to that claim separately. You must write down the reasons why you believe that you do not owe the money claimed. The written reasons must be given to the clerk of the court at the address specified in paragraph (1) above, and you must mail or give a copy of your written reasons to the plaintiff/plaintiff's attorney at the address specified in paragraph (2) above. This must be done within 20 days after the date these papers were given to you or to a person who lives with you. This obligation is separate from the requirement of answering the claim for eviction within 5 working days after these papers were given to you or to a person who lives with you or were posted at your home.

THE STATE OF FLORIDA:

To Each Sheriff of the State: You are commanded to serve this summons and a copy of the complaint in this lawsuit on the above-named defendant.

DATED on ....

Clerk of the County Court
By ____________________
As Deputy Clerk

NOTIFICACION DE DESALOJO/RESIDENCIAL

A: ....
Demandado(s)

....
....

SIRVASE LEER CON CUIDADO

Usted esta siendo demandado por .... para exigirle que desaloje el lugar donde reside por los motivos que se expresan en la demanda adjunta.

Usted tiene derecho a ser sometido a juicio para determinar si se le puede exigir que se mude, pero ES NECESARIO que haga TODO lo que se le pide a continuacion en un plazo de 5 dias (no incluidos los sabados, domingos, ni dias feriados) a partir de la fecha en que estos documentos se le entregaron a usted o a una persona que vive con usted, o se colocaron en su casa.

USTED DEBERA HACER LO SIGUIENTE:

(1) Escribir el (los) motivo(s) por el (los) cual(es) cree que no se le debe obligar a mudarse. El (Los) motivo(s) debera(n) entregarse por escrito al secretario del tribunal en el .... County Courthouse

....
...................., Florida

(2) Enviar por correo o darle su(s) motivo(s) por escrito a:

....
Demandante/Abogado del Demandante

....
....
Direccion

(3) Pagarle al secretario del tribunal el monto del alquiler que la demanda adjunta reclama como adeudado, así como cualquier alquiler pagadero hasta que concluya el litigio. Si usted considera que el monto reclamado en la demanda es incorrecto, debera presentarle al secretario del tribunal una mocion para que el tribunal determine el monto que deba pagarse. Si usted presenta una mocion, debera adjuntarle a esta cualesquiera documentos que respalden su posicion, y enviar por correo o entregar una copia de la misma al demandante/abogado del demandante.

(4) Si usted presenta una mocion para que el tribunal determine el monto del alquiler que deba pagarse al secretario del tribunal, debera comunicarse de inmediato con la oficina del juez al que se le haya asignado el caso para que programe una audiencia con el fin de determinar el monto que deba pagarse al secretario del tribunal mientras el litigio este pendiente.

SI USTED NO LLEVA A CABO LAS ACCIONES QUE SE ESPECIFICAN ANTERIORMENTE EN UN PLAZO DE 5 DIAS LABORABLES A PARTIR DE LA FECHA EN QUE ESTOS DOCUMENTOS SE LE ENTREGARON A USTED O A UNA PERSONA QUE VIVE CON USTED, O SE COLOQUEN EN SU CASA, SE LE PODRA DESALOJAR SIN NECESIDAD DE CELEBRAR UNA AUDIENCIA NI CURSARSELE OTRO AVISO

(5) Si la demanda adjunta tambien incluye una reclamacion por danos y perjuicios pecunarios (tales como el incumplimiento de pago del alquiler), usted debera responder a dicha reclamacion por separado. Debera exponer por escrito los motivos por los cuales considera que usted no debe la suma reclamada, y entregarlos al secretario del tribunal en la direccion que se especifica en el parrafo (1) anterior, asi como enviar por correo o entregar una copia de los mismos al demandante/abogado del demandante en la direccion que se especifica en el parrafo (2) anterior. Esto debera llevarse a cabo en un plazo de 20 dias a partir de la fecha en que estos documentos se le entregaron a usted o a una persona que vive con usted. Esta obligacion es aparte del requisito de responder a la demanda de desalojo en un plazo de 5 dias a partir de la fecha en que estos documentos se le entregaron a usted o a una persona que vive con usted, o se coloquen en su casa.

CITATION D'EVICTION/RESIDENTIELLE

A: ....
Defendeur(s)

. . . .

. . . .

LISEZ ATTENTIVEMENT

Vous etes poursuivi par . . . . pour exiger que vous evacuez les lieux de votre residence pour les raisons enumerees dans la plainte ci-dessous.

Vous avez droit a un proces pour determiner si vous devez demenager, mais vous devez, au prealable, suivre les instructions enumerees ci-dessous, pendant les 5 jours (non compris le samedi, le dimanche, ou un jour ferie) a partir de la date ou ces documents ont ete donnes a vous ou a la personne vivant avec vous, ou ont ete affiches a votre residence.

LISTE DES INSTRUCTIONS A SUIVRE:

(1) Enumerer par ecrit les raisons pour lesquelles vous pensez ne pas avoir a demenager. Elles doivent etre remises au clerc du tribunal a . . . . County Courthouse

. . . .

. . . ., Florida

(2) Envoyer ou donner une copie au:

. . . .

Plaignant/Avocat du Plaignant

. . . .

. . . .

Adresse

(3) Payer au clerc du tribunal le montant des loyers dus comme etabli dans la plainte et le montant des loyers dus jusqu'a la fin du proces. Si vous pensez que le montant etabli dans la plainte est incorrect, vous devez presenter au clerc du tribunal une demande en justice pour determiner la somme a payer. Pour cela vous devez attacher a la demande tous les documents soutenant votre position et faire parvenir une copie de la demande au plaignant/avocat du plaignant.

(4) Si vous faites une demande en justice pour determiner la somme a payer au clerc du tribunal, vous devrez immediatement prevenir le bureau de juge qui presidera au proces pour fixer la date de l'audience qui decidera quelle somme doit etre payee au clerc du tribunal pendant que le proces est en cours.

SI VOUS NE SUIVEZ PAS CES INSTRUCTIONS A LA LETTRE DANS LES 5 JOURS QUE SUIVENT LA DATE OU CES DOCUMENTS ONT ETE REMIS A VOUS OU A LA PERSONNE HABITANT AVEC VOUS, OU ONT ETE AFFICHES A VOTRE RESIDENCE, VOUS POUVEZ ETRE EXPULSES SANS AUDIENCE OU SANS AVIS PREALABLE

---

(5) Si la plainte ci-dessus contient une demande pour dommages pecuniaires, tels des loyers arrieres, vous devez y repondre separement. Vous devez enumerer par ecrit les raisons pour lesquelles vous estimez ne pas devoir le montant demande. Ces raisons ecrites doivent etre donnees au clerc du tribunal a l'adresse specifiee dans le paragraphe (1) et une copie de ces raisons donnee ou envoyee au plaignant/avocat du plaignant a l'adresse specifiee dans le paragraphe (2). Cela doit etre fait dans les 20 jours suivant la date ou ces documents ont ete presentes a vous ou a la personne habitant avec vous. Cette obligation ne fait pas partie des instructions a suivre en reponse au proces d'eviction dans les 5 jours suivant la date ou ces documents ont ete presentes a vous ou a la personne habitant avec vous, ou affiches a votre residence.

Added Oct. 6, 1988, effective Jan. 1, 1989 (536 So.2d 974). Amended July 16, 1992, effective Jan. 1, 1993 (604 So.2d 1110); Oct. 31, 1996, effective Jan. 1, 1997 (682 So.2d 105); Oct. 5, 2000, effective Jan. 1, 2001 (773 So.2d 1098); Sept. 8, 2010, effective Jan. 1, 2011 (52 So.3d 579).

Committee Notes

1988 Adoption. This form was added to inform those sought to be evicted of the procedure they must follow to resist eviction.

1996 Amendment. This is a substantial revision of form 1.923 to comply with the requirements of section 83.60, Florida Statutes, as amended in 1993.

Form 1.924. Affidavit of Diligent Search and Inquiry

I, *(full legal name)* ______________________ (individually or an Employee of ____________________), being sworn, certify that the following information is true:

1. I have made diligent search and inquiry to discover the current residence of ______________________, who is [over 18 years old] [under 18 years old] [age is unknown] (circle one). **Refer to checklist below and identify all actions taken (any additional information included such as the date the action was taken and the person with whom you spoke is helpful) (attach additional sheet if necessary):**

[check **all** that apply]

____ Inquiry of Social Security Information

____ Telephone listings in the last known locations of defendant's residence

____ Statewide directory assistance search

____ Internet people finder search {specify sites searched}

____ Voter Registration in the area where defendant was last known to reside.

____ Nationwide Masterfile Death Search

____ Tax Collector's records in area where defendant was last known to reside.

____ Tax Assessor's records in area where defendant was last known to reside

____ Department of Motor vehicle records in the state of defendant's last known address

____ Driver's License records search in the state of defendant's last known address.

____ Department of Corrections records in the state of defendant's last known address.

____ Federal Prison records search.

____ Regulatory agencies for professional or occupational licensing.

____ Inquiry to determine if defendant is in military service.

____ Last known employment of defendant.

{List all additional efforts made to locate defendant}

____

____

____

Attempts to Serve Process and Results

____

____

____

____ I inquired of the occupant of the premises whether the occupant knows the location of the borrower-defendant, with the following results:

____

____

____

2. ____________________ **current residence**

[check **one** only]

____ a. ____________________'s current residence is unknown to me

____ b. ____________________'s current residence is in some state or country __________ other than Florida and __________'s last known address is:

____

____

____ c. The ____________________, having residence in Florida, has been absent from Florida for more than 60 days prior to the date of this affidavit, or conceals him (her) self so that process cannot be served personally upon him or her, and I believe there is no person in the state upon whom service of process would bind this absent or concealed __________.

I understand that I am swearing or affirming under oath to the truthfulness of the claims made in this affidavit and that the punishment for knowingly making a false statement includes fines and/or imprisonment.

Dated: ____________________

Signature of Affiant
Printed Name: ______
Address: ______
City, State, Zip: ______
Phone: ______
Telefacsimile: ______

STATE OF __________
COUNTY OF __________

Sworn to or affirmed and signed before me on this ____ day of __________, 20____ by __________.

____
NOTARY PUBLIC,
STATE OF ______

____
(Print, Type or Stamp Commissioned Name of Notary Public)

____ Personally known
____ Produced identification
____ Type of identification produced: ______

NOTE: This form is used to obtain constructive service on the defendant.

Added Feb. 11, 2010 (44 So.3d 555).

Form 1.932. Open Account

COMPLAINT

Plaintiff, A. B., sues defendant, C. D., and alleges:

1. This is an action for damages that (insert jurisdictional amount).

2. Defendant owes plaintiff $ .... that is due with interest since ..... (date) ....., according to the attached account.

WHEREFORE plaintiff demands judgment for damages against defendant.

NOTE: A copy of the account showing items, time of accrual of each, and amount of each must be attached.

Added June 19, 1968, effective Oct. 1, 1968 (211 So.2d 174). Amended Oct. 5, 2000, effective Jan. 1, 2001 (773 So.2d 1098).

Form 1.933. Account Stated

COMPLAINT

Plaintiff, A. B., sues defendant, C. D., and alleges:

1. This is an action for damages that (insert jurisdictional amount).

2. Before the institution of this action plaintiff and defendant had business transactions between them and on ..... (date) ....., they agreed to the resulting balance.

3. Plaintiff rendered a statement of it to defendant, a copy being attached, and defendant did not object to the statement.

4. Defendant owes plaintiff $ .... that is due with interest since ..... (date) ....., on the account.

WHEREFORE plaintiff demands judgment for damages against defendant.

NOTE: A copy of the account showing items, time of accrual of each, and amount of each must be attached.

Added June 19, 1968, effective Oct. 1, 1968 (211 So.2d 174). Amended Oct. 5, 2000, effective Jan. 1, 2001 (773 So.2d 1098).

Form 1.934. Promissory Note

COMPLAINT

Plaintiff, A. B., sues defendant, C. D., and alleges:

1. This is an action for damages that (insert jurisdictional amount).

2. On ..... (date) ....., defendant executed and delivered a promissory note, a copy being attached, to plaintiff in .... County, Florida.

3. Plaintiff owns and holds the note.

4. Defendant failed to pay (use a or b)

a. the note when due.

b. the installment payment due on the note on ..... (date) ....., and plaintiff elected to accelerate payment of the balance.

5. Defendant owes plaintiff $ .... that is due with interest since ..... (date) ....., on the note.

6. Plaintiff is obligated to pay his/her attorneys a reasonable fee for their services.

WHEREFORE plaintiff demands judgment for damages against defendant.

NOTE: A copy of the note must be attached. Use paragraph 4a. or b. as applicable and paragraph 6 if appropriate.

Added June 19, 1968, effective Oct. 1, 1968 (211 So.2d 174). Amended Oct. 9, 1980, effective Jan. 1, 1981 (391 So.2d 165); July 16, 1992, effective Jan. 1, 1993 (604 So.2d 1110); Oct. 5, 2000, effective Jan. 1, 2001 (773 So.2d 1098).

Committee Notes

1980 Amendment. Paragraph 3 is added to show ownership of the note, and paragraph 4 is clarified to show that either 4a or 4b is used, but not both.

Form 1.935. Goods Sold

COMPLAINT

Plaintiff, A. B., sues defendant, C. D., and alleges:

1. This is an action for damages that (insert jurisdictional amount).

2. Defendant owes plaintiff $ .... that is due with interest since ..... (date) ....., for the following goods sold and delivered by plaintiff to defendant between ..... (date) ....., and ..... (date) .....:

(list goods and prices)

WHEREFORE plaintiff demands judgment for damages against defendant.

Added June 19, 1968, effective Oct. 1, 1968 (211 So.2d 174). Amended Oct. 5, 2000, effective Jan. 1, 2001 (773 So.2d 1098).

Form 1.936. Money Lent

COMPLAINT

Plaintiff, A. B., sues defendant, C. D., and alleges:

1. This is an action for damages that (insert jurisdictional amount).

2. Defendant owes plaintiff $ .... that is due with interest since ..... (date) ....., for money lent by plaintiff to defendant on ..... (date) .....

WHEREFORE plaintiff demands judgment for damages against defendant.

Added June 19, 1968, effective Oct. 1, 1968 (211 So.2d 174). Amended Oct. 5, 2000, effective Jan. 1, 2001 (773 So.2d 1098).

Form 1.937. Replevin

COMPLAINT

Plaintiff, A. B., sues defendant, C. D., and alleges:

1. This is an action to recover possession of personal property in .... County, Florida.

2. The description of the property is:

(list property)

To the best of plaintiff's knowledge, information, and belief, the value of the property is $ ....

3. Plaintiff is entitled to the possession of the property under a security agreement dated ...., a copy of the agreement being attached.

4. To plaintiff's best knowledge, information, and belief, the property is located at ....

5. The property is wrongfully detained by defendant. Defendant came into possession of the property by (method of possession). To plaintiff's best knowledge, information, and belief, defendant detains the property because (give reasons).

6. The property has not been taken for any tax, assessment, or fine pursuant to law.

7. The property has not been taken under an execution or attachment against plaintiff's property.

WHEREFORE plaintiff demands judgment for possession of the property.

NOTE: Paragraph 3 must be modified if the right to possession arose in another manner. Allegations and a demand for damages, if appropriate, can be added to the form.

Added June 19, 1968, effective Oct. 1, 1968 (211 So.2d 174). Amended Oct. 9, 1980, effective Jan. 1, 1981 (391 So.2d 165); July 16, 1992, effective Jan. 1, 1993 (604 So.2d 1110); Oct. 5, 2000, effective Jan. 1, 2001 (773 So.2d 1098).

Committee Notes

1980 Amendment. The form is amended to comply with the amendments to the replevin statutes pursuant to *Fuentes v. Shevin*, 407 U.S. 67, 92 S. Ct. 1983, 32 L. Ed. 2d 556 (1972).

Form 1.938. Forcible Entry and Detention

COMPLAINT

Plaintiff, A. B., sues defendant, C. D., and alleges:

1. This is an action to recover possession of real property unlawfully (forcibly) detained in ________________ County, Florida.

2. Plaintiff is entitled to possession of the following real property in said county:

(insert description of property)

3. Defendant has unlawfully (forcibly) turned plaintiff out of and withholds possession of the property from plaintiff.

WHEREFORE plaintiff demands judgment for possession of the property and damages against defendant.

NOTE: Substitute "forcibly" for "unlawfully" or add it as an alternative when applicable. This form cannot be used for residential tenancies.

Added June 19, 1968, effective Oct. 1, 1968 (211 So.2d 174). Amended Oct. 9, 1980, effective Jan. 1, 1981 (391 So.2d 165); July 16, 1992, effective Jan. 1, 1993 (604 So.2d 1110).

Form 1.939. Conversion

COMPLAINT

Plaintiff, A. B., sues defendant, C. D., and alleges:

1. This is an action for damages that (insert jurisdictional amount).

2. On or about ..... (date) ....., defendant converted to his/her own use (insert description of property converted) that was then the property of plaintiff of the value of $ ....

WHEREFORE plaintiff demands judgment for damages against defendant.

Added June 19, 1968, effective Oct. 1, 1968 (211 So.2d 174). Amended July 16, 1992, effective Jan. 1, 1993 (604 So.2d 1110); Oct. 5, 2000, effective Jan. 1, 2001 (773 So.2d 1098).

Form 1.940. Ejectment

COMPLAINT

Plaintiff, A.B., sues defendant, C.D., and alleges:

1. This is an action to recover possession of real property in ________________ County, Florida.

2. Defendant is in possession of the following real property in the county:

(describe property)

to which plaintiff claims title as shown by the attached statement of plaintiff's chain of title.

3. Defendant refuses to deliver possession of the property to plaintiff or pay plaintiff the profits from it.

WHEREFORE plaintiff demands judgment for possession of the property and damages against defendant.

NOTE: A statement of plaintiff's chain of title must be attached.

Added June 19, 1968, effective Oct. 1, 1968 (211 So.2d 174). Amended Oct. 9, 1980, effective Jan. 1, 1981 (391 So.2d 165); July 16, 1992, effective Jan. 1, 1993 (604 So.2d 1110).

Committee Notes

1980 Amendment. The words "possession of" are inserted in paragraph 1 for clarification.

Form 1.941. Specific Performance

COMPLAINT

Plaintiff, A. B., sued defendant, C. D., and alleges:

1. This is an action for specific performance of a contract to convey real property in .... County, Florida.

2. On ..... (date) ....., plaintiff and defendant entered into a written contract, a copy being attached.

3. Plaintiff tendered the purchase price to defendant and requested a conveyance of the real property described in the contract.

4. Defendant refused to accept the tender or to make the conveyance.

5. Plaintiff offers to pay the purchase price.

WHEREFORE plaintiff demands judgment that defendant be required to perform the contract for damages.

NOTE: A copy of the sales contract must be attached.

Added June 19, 1968, effective Oct. 1, 1968 (211 So.2d 174). Amended Oct. 9, 1980, effective Jan. 1, 1981 (391 So.2d 165); July 16, 1992, effective Jan. 1, 1993 (604 So.2d 1110); Oct. 5, 2000, effective Jan. 1, 2001 (773 So.2d 1098).

Committee Notes

1980 Amendment. Paragraph 3 is divided into 2 paragraphs to properly accord with rule 1.110(f).

Form 1.942. Check

COMPLAINT

Plaintiff, A. B., sues defendant, C. D., and alleges:

1. This is an action for damages that (insert jurisdictional amount).

2. On ..... (date) ....., defendant executed a written order for the payment of $.........., commonly called a check, a copy being attached, payable to the order of plaintiff and delivered it to plaintiff.

3. The check was presented for payment to the drawee bank but payment was refused.

4. Plaintiff holds the check and it has not been paid.

5. Defendant owes plaintiff $........ that is due with interest from ..... (date) ....., on the check.

WHEREFORE plaintiff demands judgment for damages against defendant.

NOTE: A copy of the check must be attached. Allegations about endorsements are omitted from this form and must be added when proper.

Added June 19, 1968, effective Oct. 1, 1968 (211 So.2d 174). Amended Oct. 9, 1980, effective Jan. 1, 1981 (391 So.2d 165); July 16, 1992, effective Jan. 1, 1993 (604 So.2d 1110); Oct. 5, 2000, effective Jan. 1, 2001 (773 So.2d 1098).

Committee Notes

1980 Amendment. Paragraph 4 is divided into 2 paragraphs to properly accord with rule 1.110(f).

Form 1.944(a). Mortgage Foreclosure

(When location of original note known)

COMPLAINT

Plaintiff, A. B., sues defendant, C. D., and alleges:

1. This is an action to foreclose a mortgage on real property in .... County, Florida.

2. On .....(date)....., defendant executed and delivered a promissory note and a mortgage securing payment of the note to .....(plaintiff or plaintiff's predecessor) .....The mortgage was recorded on .....(date)....., in Official Records Book .... at page .... of the public records of .... County, Florida, and mortgaged the property described in the mortgage then owned by and in possession of the mortgagor, a copy of the mortgage and the note being attached.

3. (Select a, b, or c)

(a) Plaintiff is the holder of the original note secured by the mortgage.

(b) Plaintiff is a person entitled to enforce the note under applicable law because .....(allege specific facts).....

(c) Plaintiff has been delegated the authority to institute a mortgage foreclosure action on behalf of the person entitled to enforce the note. The document(s) that grant(s) plaintiff the authority to act on behalf of the person entitled to enforce the note is/are as follows ....

4. The property is now owned by defendant who holds possession.

5. Defendant has defaulted under the note and mortgage by failing to pay the payment due .....(date)....., and all subsequent payments .....(allege other defaults as applicable).......

6. Plaintiff declares the full amount payable under the note and mortgage to be due.

7. Defendant owes plaintiff $......... that is due on principal on the note and mortgage, interest from .....(date)....., and title search expense for ascertaining necessary parties to this action.

8. Plaintiff is obligated to pay plaintiff's attorneys a reasonable fee for their services. Plaintiff is enti-

tled to recover its attorneys' fees under .....(allege statutory and/or contractual bases, as applicable).....

WHEREFORE, plaintiff demands judgment foreclosing the mortgage, for costs (and, when applicable, for attorneys' fees), and, if the proceeds of the sale are insufficient to pay plaintiff's claim, a deficiency judgment.

NOTE: An action for foreclosure of a mortgage on residential real property must contain an oath, affirmation, or the following statement as required by rule 1.115(e).

VERIFICATION

Under penalty of perjury, I declare that I have read the foregoing, and the facts alleged therein are true and correct to the best of my knowledge and belief.

____

Executed on this .....(date).....

____

[Person Signing Verification]

CERTIFICATION OF POSSESSION OF ORIGINAL NOTE

The undersigned hereby certifies:

1. That plaintiff is in possession of the original promissory note upon which this action is brought.

2. The location of the original promissory note is: .....(location).....

3. The name and title of the person giving the certification is: .....(name and title).....

4. The name of the person who personally verified such possession is: .....(name).....

5. The time and date on which possession was verified were: .....(time and date).....

6. Correct copies of the note (and, if applicable, all endorsements, transfers, allonges, or assignments of the note) are attached to this certification.

7. I give this statement based on my personal knowledge.

Under penalties of perjury, I declare that I have read the foregoing Certification of Possession of Original Note and that the facts stated in it are true.

Executed on .....(date).....

____

[Person Signing Certification]

NOTE: This form is for installment payments with acceleration. It omits allegations about junior encumbrances, unpaid taxes, unpaid insurance premiums, other nonmonetary defaults, and for a receiver. They must be added when appropriate. A copy of the note and mortgage must be attached. This form may require modification. This form is designed to incorporate the pleading requirements of section 702.015, Florida Statutes (2013) and rule 1.115. It is also designed to conform to section 673.3011, Florida Statutes (2013), except that part of section 673.3011, Florida Statutes, which defines a person entitled to enforce an instrument under section 673.3091, Florida Statutes. See form 1.944(b). Pursuant to section 702.015, Florida Statutes (2013), a certification of possession of the original promissory note must be filed contemporaneously with the Complaint (form 1.944(a)) or, in the event that the plaintiff seeks to enforce a lost, destroyed, or stolen instrument, an affidavit setting forth the facts required by law must be attached to the complaint (form 1.944(b)).

Formerly Form 1.944, added June 19, 1968, effective Oct. 1, 1968 (211 So.2d 174). Amended Oct. 9, 1980, effective Jan. 1, 1981 (391 So.2d 165); July 16, 1992, effective Jan. 1, 1993 (604 So.2d 1110); Oct. 5, 2000, effective Jan. 1, 2001 (773 So.2d 1098). Renumbered Form 1.944(a) and amended Dec. 11, 2014, effective Dec. 11, 2014 (153 So.3d 258).

Form 1.944(b). Mortgage Foreclosure

(When location of original note unknown)

COMPLAINT

Plaintiff, ABC, sues defendant, XYZ, and states:

1. This is an action to foreclose a mortgage on real property in .... County, Florida.

2. On .....(date)....., defendant executed and delivered a promissory note and a mortgage securing the payment of said note to .....(plaintiff or plaintiff's predecessor)..... The mortgage was recorded on .....(date)....., in Official Records Book ..... at page ..... of the public records of .... County, Florida, and mortgaged the property described therein which was then owned by and in possession of the mortgagor. A copy of the mortgage and note are attached to the affidavit which is attached hereto as Composite Exhibit "1"; the contents of the affidavit are specifically incorporated by reference.

3. Plaintiff is not in possession of the note but is entitled to enforce it.

4. (select a, b, c, or d) Plaintiff cannot reasonably obtain possession of the note because

(a) the note was destroyed.

(b) the note is lost.

(c) the note is in the wrongful possession of an unknown person.

(d) the note is in the wrongful possession of a person that cannot be found or is not amenable to service of process.

5. (select a, b, c, or d)

(a) At the time the original note was lost, plaintiff was the holder of the original note secured by the mortgage.

(b) At the time the original note was lost, plaintiff was a person entitled to enforce the note under applicable law because .....(allege specific facts).....

(c) Plaintiff has directly or indirectly acquired ownership of the note from a person who was entitled to enforce the note when loss of possession occurred as follows: .....(allege facts as to transfer of ownership).....

(d) Plaintiff has been delegated the authority to institute a mortgage foreclosure action on behalf of the person entitled to enforce the note, and the document(s) that grant(s) plaintiff the authority to act on behalf of the person entitled to enforce the note is/are as follows ....(attach documents if not already attached).

6. Plaintiff did not transfer the note or lose possession of it as the result of a lawful seizure.

7. The property is now owned by defendant who holds possession.

8. Defendant has defaulted under the note and mortgage by failing to pay the payment(s) due .....(date(s))....., and all subsequent payments .....(identify other defaults as applicable).....

9. Plaintiff declares the full amount payable under the note and mortgage to be due.

10. Defendant owes plaintiff $.......... that is due on principal on the note and mortgage, interest from .....(date)....., and title search expense for ascertaining necessary parties to this action.

11. Plaintiff is obligated to pay its attorneys a reasonable fee for their services. Plaintiff is entitled to recover its attorneys' fees for prosecuting this claim pursuant to .....(identify statutory and/or contractual bases, as applicable).....

WHEREFORE, Plaintiff demands judgment foreclosing the mortgage, for costs (and, where applicable, for attorneys' fees), and if the proceeds of the sale are insufficient to pay plaintiff's claim, a deficiency judgment.

NOTE: An action for foreclosure of a mortgage on residential real property must contain an oath, affirmation, or the following statement as required by rule 1.115(e).

VERIFICATION

Under penalty of perjury, I declare that I have read the foregoing, and the facts alleged therein are true and correct to the best of my knowledge and belief.

Executed on .....(date).....

____
(Person Signing Verification)

* * * * *

AFFIDAVIT OF COMPLIANCE

STATE OF FLORIDA
COUNTY OF ....

BEFORE ME, the undersigned authority, personally appeared .....(name)....., who, after being first duly sworn, deposes and states, under penalty of perjury:

1. I am the plaintiff (or plaintiff's ....) (identify relationship to plaintiff).

2. I am executing this affidavit in support of plaintiff's Complaint against defendant and I have personal knowledge of the matters set forth herein.

3. On .....(date)....., the public records reflect that defendant executed and delivered a mortgage securing the payment of the note to .....(plaintiff/plaintiff's predecessor)..... The mortgage was recorded on .....(date)....., in Official Records Book .... at page .... of the public records of .... County, Florida, and mortgaged the property described therein, which was then owned by and in possession of the mortgagor, a copy of the mortgage and the note being attached.

4. (select a, b, c, or d) Plaintiff cannot reasonably obtain possession of the note because

(a) the note was destroyed.

(b) the note is lost.

(c) the note is in the wrongful possession of an unknown person.

(d) the note is in the wrongful possession of a person who cannot be found or is not amenable to service of process.

5. (select a, b, c, or d)

(a) At the time the original note was lost, plaintiff was the holder of the original note secured by the mortgage.

(b) At the time the original note was lost, plaintiff was a person entitled to enforce the note under applicable law because .....(allege specific facts).....

(c) Since the note was lost, plaintiff has directly or indirectly acquired ownership of the note from a person who was entitled to enforce the note when loss of possession occurred as follows: .....(allege facts regarding transfer of ownership).....

(d) Plaintiff has been delegated the authority to institute a mortgage foreclosure action on behalf of the person entitled to enforce the note, and the document(s) that grant(s) plaintiff the authority to act on behalf of the person entitled to enforce the note is/are as follows .... (attach copy of document(s) or relevant portion(s) of the document(s)).

6. Below is the clear chain of the endorsements, transfers, allonges or assignments of the note and all

documents that evidence same as are available to Plaintiff: .....(identify in chronological order all endorsements, transfers, assignments of, allonges to, the note or other evidence of the acquisition, ownership and possession of the note)..... Correct copies of the foregoing documents are attached to this affidavit.

7. Plaintiff did not transfer the note or lose possession of it as the result of a lawful seizure.

FURTHER, AFFIANT SAYETH NAUGHT.

____
[signature]
....
[typed or printed name of affiant]

STATE OF FLORIDA

COUNTY OF ....

BEFORE ME, the undersigned authority appeared .....(name of affiant)....., who .....is personally known to me or ..... produced identification .... and acknowledged that he/she executed the foregoing instrument for the purposes expressed therein and who did take an oath.

WITNESS my hand and seal in the State and County aforesaid, this .....(date).....

____
NOTARY PUBLIC, State of Florida
Print Name: ....
Commission Expires: .....

Added Dec. 11, 2014, effective Dec. 11, 2014 (153 So.3d 258).

Committee Note

2014 Adoption. This form is for installment payments with acceleration. It omits allegations about junior encumbrances, unpaid taxes, unpaid insurance premiums, other nonmonetary defaults, and for a receiver. Allegations must be added when appropriate. This form may require modification. This form is designed to incorporate the pleading requirements of section 702.015, Florida Statutes (2013), and rule 1.115. It is also designed to comply with section 673.3091, Florida Statutes (2013). Adequate protection as required by sections 702.11 (2013) and 673.3091(2), Florida Statutes (2013), must be provided before the entry of final judgment.

Form 1.944(c). Motion for Order to Show Cause

PLAINTIFF'S MOTION FOR ORDER TO SHOW CAUSE FOR ENTRY OF FINAL JUDGMENT OF FORECLOSURE

1. Plaintiff is a lienholder of real property located at .....(address)..... or is a .....Condominium Association/Cooperative Association/Homeowner's Association.....

2. The plaintiff has filed a verified complaint in conformity with applicable law, which is attached.

3. The plaintiff requests this court issue an order requiring defendant(s) to appear before the court to show cause why a final judgment of foreclosure should not be entered against defendant(s).

4. The date of the hearing may not occur sooner than the later of 20 days after service of the order to show cause or 45 days after service of the initial complaint.

OR

COMMENT: Use the following when service is by publication:

4. When service is obtained by publication, the date for the hearing may not be set sooner than 30 days after the first publication.

5. The accompanying proposed order to show cause affords defendant(s) all the rights and obligations as contemplated by applicable law.

6. Upon the entry of the order to show cause, plaintiff shall serve a copy of the executed order to show cause for entry of final judgment as required by law.

7. This is not a residential property for which a homestead exemption for taxation was granted according to the rolls of the latest assessment by the County Property Appraiser.

Plaintiff requests the court review this complaint and grant this motion for order to show cause for entry of final judgment of foreclosure, and grant such further relief as may be awarded at law or in equity.

____
Plaintiff

Certificate of Service

Added Dec. 11, 2014, effective Dec. 11, 2014 (153 So.3d 258).

Committee Note

2014 Adoption. This form is designed to comply with section 702.10, Florida Statutes (2013).

Form 1.944(d). Order to Show Cause

ORDER TO SHOW CAUSE

THIS CAUSE has come before the court on .....plaintiff's/lien holder's..... motion for order to show cause for entry of final judgment of mortgage foreclosure and the court having reviewed the motion and the verified complaint, and being otherwise fully advised in the circumstances, finds and it is

ORDERED AND ADJUDGED that:

1. The defendant(s) shall appear at a hearing on foreclosure on .....(date)..... at .....(time)..... before the undersigned judge, in the .....(county)..... Courthouse at .....(address)....., to show cause why the attached final judgment of foreclosure

should not be entered against the defendant(s) in this cause. This hearing referred to in this order is a "show cause hearing."

2. This ORDER TO SHOW CAUSE shall be served on the defendant(s) in accordance with the Florida Rules of Civil Procedure and applicable law as follows:

a. If the defendant(s) has/have been served under Chapter 48, Florida Statutes, with the verified complaint and original process has already been effectuated, service of this order may be made in the manner provided in the Florida Rules of Civil Procedure; or, if the other party is the plaintiff in the action, service of the order to show cause on that party may be made in the manner provided in the Florida Rules of Civil Procedure.

b. If the defendant(s) has/have not been served under Chapter 48, Florida Statutes, with the verified complaint and original process, the order to show cause, together with the summons and a copy of the verified complaint, shall be served on the party in the same manner as provided by law for original process.

3. The filing of defenses by a motion or verified answer at or before the show cause hearing constitutes cause for which the court may not enter the attached final judgment.

4. Defendant(s) has/have the right to file affidavits or other papers at the time of the show cause hearing and may appear at the hearing personally or by an attorney.

5. If defendant(s) file(s) motions, they may be considered at the time of the show cause hearing.

6. Defendant(s)' failure to appear either in person or by an attorney at the show cause hearing or to file defenses by motion or by a verified or sworn answer, affidavits, or other papers which raise a genuine issue of material fact which would preclude entry of summary judgment or which would otherwise constitute a legal defense to foreclosure, after being served as provided by law with the order to show cause, will be deemed presumptively a waiver of the right to a hearing. In such case, the court may enter a final judgment of foreclosure ordering the clerk of the court to conduct a foreclosure sale. An order requiring defendant(s) to vacate the premises may also be entered.

7. If the mortgage provides for reasonable attorneys' fees and the requested fee does not exceed 3% of the principal amount owed at the time the complaint is filed, the court may not need to hold a hearing to adjudge the requested fee to be reasonable.

8. Any final judgment of foreclosure entered under section 702.10(1) Florida Statutes, shall be only for in rem relief; however, entry of such final judgment of foreclosure shall not preclude entry of an in personam money damages judgment or deficiency judgment where otherwise allowed by law.

9. A copy of the proposed final judgment is attached and will be entered by the court if defendant(s) waive(s) the right to be heard at the show cause hearing.

10. The court finds that this is not a residential property for which a homestead exemption for taxation was granted according to the rolls of the latest assessment by the county property appraiser.

DONE AND ORDERED at ....(county)...., Florida.....(date).....

____

CIRCUIT JUDGE

Copies to:

Added Dec. 11, 2014, effective Dec. 11, 2014 (153 So.3d 258).

Committee Note

2014 Adoption. This form is designed to comply with section 702.10(1), Florida Statutes (2013).

Form 1.945. Motor Vehicle Negligence

COMPLAINT

Plaintiff, A. B., sues defendants, C. D., and E. F., and alleges:

1. This is an action for damages that (insert jurisdictional amount).

2. (Use a or b) a. On or about ..... (date) ....., defendant, C. D., owned a motor vehicle that was operated with his/her consent by defendant, E. F., at .... in ...., Florida.

b. On or about ..... (date)....., defendant owned and operated a motor vehicle at .... in ...., Florida.

3. At that time and place defendants negligently operated or maintained the motor vehicle so that it collided with plaintiff's motor vehicle.

4. As a result plaintiff suffered bodily injury and resulting pain and suffering, disability, disfigurement, mental anguish, loss of capacity for the enjoyment of life, expense of hospitalization, medical and nursing care and treatment, loss of earnings, loss of ability to earn money, and aggravation of a previously existing condition. The losses are either permanent or continuing and plaintiff will suffer the losses in the future. Plaintiff's automobile was damaged and he/she lost the use of it during the period required for its repair or replacement.

WHEREFORE plaintiff demands judgment for damages against defendants.

NOTE: This form, except for paragraph 2b, is for use when owner and driver are different persons. Use paragraph 2b when they are the same. If paragraph 2b is used, "defendants" must be changed to "defendant" wherever it appears.

Added June 19, 1968, effective Oct. 1, 1968 (211 So.2d 174). Amended Oct. 9, 1980, effective Jan. 1, 1981 (391 So.2d 165); July 16, 1992, effective Jan. 1, 1993 (604 So.2d 1110); Oct. 5, 2000, effective Jan. 1, 2001 (773 So.2d 1098).

Committee Notes

1980 Amendment. This form was changed to show that one of the alternatives in paragraph 2 is used, but not both, and paragraph 4 has been changed to paraphrase Standard Jury Instruction 6.2.

Form 1.946. Motor Vehicle Negligence When Plaintiff Is Unable to Determine Who Is Responsible

COMPLAINT

Plaintiff, A. B., sues defendants, C. D., and E. F., and alleges:

1. This is an action for damages that (insert jurisdictional amount).

2. On or about ..... (date) ....., defendant, C. D., or defendant, E. F., or both defendants, owned and operated motor vehicles at .... in ...., Florida.

3. At that time and place defendants, or one of them, negligently operated or maintained their motor vehicles so that one or both of them collided with plaintiff's motor vehicle.

4. As a result plaintiff suffered bodily injury and resulting pain and suffering, disability, disfigurement, mental anguish, loss of capacity for the enjoyment of life, expense of hospitalization, medical and nursing care and treatment, loss of earnings, loss of ability to earn money, and aggravation of a previously existing condition. The losses are either permanent or continuing and plaintiff will suffer the losses in the future. Plaintiff's automobile was damaged and he/she lost the use of it during the period required for its repair or replacement.

WHEREFORE plaintiff demands judgment for damages against defendants.

NOTE: Allegations when owner and driver are different persons are omitted from this form and must be added when proper.

Added June 19, 1968, effective Oct. 1, 1968 (211 So.2d 174). Amended Oct. 9, 1980, effective Jan. 1, 1981 (391 So.2d 165); July 16, 1992, effective Jan. 1, 1993 (604 So.2d 1110); Oct. 5, 2000, effective Jan. 1, 2001 (773 So.2d 1098).

Committee Notes

1980 Amendment. Paragraph 4 is changed to paraphrase Standard Jury Instruction 6.2.

Form 1.947. Tenant Eviction

COMPLAINT

Plaintiff, A. B., sues defendant, C. D., and alleges:

1. This is an action to evict a tenant from real property in .... County, Florida.

2. Plaintiff owns the following described real property in said county:

(describe property)

3. Defendant has possession of the property under (oral, written) agreement to pay rent of $.......... payable ....

4. Defendant failed to pay rent due ..... (date) ......

5. Plaintiff served defendant with a notice on ..... (date) ....., to pay the rent or deliver possession but defendant refuses to do either.

WHEREFORE plaintiff demands judgment for possession of the property against defendant.

NOTE: Paragraph 3 must specify whether the rental agreement is written or oral and if written, a copy must be attached.

Added June 19, 1968, effective Oct. 1, 1968 (211 So.2d 174). Amended Oct. 5, 2000, effective Jan. 1, 2001 (773 So.2d 1098).

Form 1.948. Third–Party Complaint. General Form

THIRD–PARTY COMPLAINT

Defendant, C.D., sues third-party defendant, E.F., and alleges:

1. Plaintiff filed a complaint against defendant, C.D., a copy being attached.

2. (State the cause of action that C.D. has against E.F. for all or part of what A.B. may recover from C.D. as in an original complaint.)

WHEREFORE defendant C.D., demands judgment against the third-party defendant, E.F., for all damages that are adjudged against defendant, C.D., in favor of plaintiff.

NOTE: A copy of the complaint from which the third-party complaint is derived must be attached.

Added June 19, 1968, effective Oct. 1, 1968 (211 So.2d 174). Amended Oct. 9, 1980, effective Jan. 1, 1981 (391 So.2d 165); Oct. 6, 1988, effective Jan. 1, 1989 (536 So.2d 974); July 16, 1992, effective Jan. 1, 1993 (604 So.2d 1110).

Committee Notes

1988 Amendment. The first sentence was changed to eliminate the words "and third party plaintiff."

Form 1.949. Implied Warranty

COMPLAINT

Plaintiff, A. B., sues defendant, C. D., and alleges:

1. This is an action for damages that (insert jurisdictional amount).

2. Defendant manufactured a product known and described as (describe product).

3. Defendant warranted that the product was reasonably fit for its intended use as (describe intended use).

4. On ..... (date) ....., at .... in .... County, Florida, the product (describe the occurrence and defect that resulted in injury) while being used for its intended purpose, causing injuries to plaintiff who was then a user of the product.

5. As a result plaintiff was injured in and about his/her body and extremities, suffered pain therefrom, incurred medical expense in the treatment of the injuries, and suffered physical handicap, and his/her working ability was impaired; the injuries are either permanent or continuing in their nature and plaintiff will suffer the losses and impairment in the future.

WHEREFORE plaintiff demands judgment for damages against defendant.

Added June 19, 1968, effective Oct. 1, 1968 (211 So.2d 174). Amended July 26, 1972, effective Jan. 1, 1973 (265 So.2d 21); July 16, 1992, effective Jan. 1, 1993 (604 So.2d 1110); Oct. 5, 2000, effective Jan. 1, 2001 (773 So.2d 1098).

Committee Notes

1972 Amendment. This form is changed to require an allegation of the defect in paragraph 4. Contentions were made in trial courts that the form as presently authorized eliminated the substantive requirement that the plaintiff prove a defect except under those circumstances when substantive law eliminates the necessity of such proof. Paragraph 4 is amended to show that no substantive law change was intended.

Form 1.951. Fall–Down Negligence Complaint

COMPLAINT

Plaintiff, A. B., sues defendant, C. D., and alleges:

1. This is an action for damages that (insert jurisdictional amount).

2. On ..... (date) ....., defendant was the owner and in possession of a building at .... in ...., Florida, that was used as a (describe use).

3. At that time and place plaintiff went on the property to (state purpose).

4. Defendant negligently maintained (describe item) on the property by (describe negligence or dangerous condition) so that plaintiff fell on the property.

5. The negligent condition was known to defendant or had existed for a sufficient length of time so that defendant should have known of it.

6. As a result plaintiff was injured in and about his/her body and extremities, suffered pain therefrom, incurred medical expense in the treatment of the injuries, and suffered physical handicap, and his/her working ability was impaired; the injuries are either permanent or continuing in nature and plaintiff will suffer the losses and impairment in the future.

WHEREFORE plaintiff demands judgment for damages against defendant.

Added July 26, 1972, effective Jan. 1, 1973 (265 So.2d 21); July 16, 1992, effective Jan. 1, 1993 (604 So.2d 1110); Oct. 5, 2000, effective Jan. 1, 2001 (773 So.2d 1098).

Form 1.960. Bond. General Form

(TYPE OF BOND)

WE, (plaintiff's name), as principal and (surety's name), as Surety, are bound to (defendant's name) in the sum of $ .... for the payment of which we bind ourselves, our heirs, personal representatives, successors, and assigns, jointly and severally.

THE CONDITION OF THIS BOND is that if plaintiff shall (insert condition), then this bond is void; otherwise it remains in force.

SIGNED AND SEALED on ....

____
As Principal

(Surety's name)
By ____________________
As Attorney in Fact
As Surety

Approved on ..... (date) .....
(Name of Clerk)
As Clerk of the Court
By ____________________
As Deputy Clerk

Added June 19, 1968, effective Oct. 1, 1968 (211 So.2d 174). Amended July 16, 1992, effective Jan. 1, 1993 (604 So.2d 1110); Oct. 5, 2000, effective Jan. 1, 2001 (773 So.2d 1098).

Committee Notes

1992 Amendment. The "Approved on [..... (date) .....]" line is moved to a location immediately above the clerk's name.

Form 1.961. Various Bond Conditions

The following conditions are to be inserted in the second paragraph of form 1.960 in the blank provided for the condition of the bond. Other proper conditions must be inserted for other types of bonds.

(a) Attachment, Garnishment, and Distress.

. . . pay all costs and damages that defendant sustains in consequence of plaintiff improperly suing out (type of writ) in this action . . .

NOTE: The condition of an attachment bond in aid of foreclosure when the holder of the property is unknown is different from the foregoing condition. See section 76.12, Florida Statutes.

(b) Costs.

. . . pay all costs and charges that are adjudged against plaintiff in this action . . .

(c) Replevin.

. . . prosecute this action to effect and without delay, and if defendant recovers judgment against plaintiff in this action, plaintiff shall return the property replevied, if return of it is adjudged, and shall pay defendant all money recovered against plaintiff by defendant in this action . . .

Added June 19, 1968, effective Oct. 1, 1968 (211 So.2d 174). Amended July 16, 1992, effective Jan. 1, 1993 (604 So.2d 1110).

Form 1.965. Defense. Statute of Limitations

Each cause of action, claim, and item of damages did not accrue within the time prescribed by law for them before this action was brought.

Added June 19, 1968, effective Oct. 1, 1968 (211 So.2d 174). Amended July 16, 1992, effective Jan. 1, 1993 (604 So.2d 1110).

Form 1.966. Defense. Payment

Before commencement of this action defendant discharged plaintiff's claim and each item of it by payment.

Added June 19, 1968, effective Oct. 1, 1968 (211 So.2d 174).

Form 1.967. Defense. Accord and Satisfaction

On ..... (date) ....., defendant delivered to plaintiff and plaintiff accepted from defendant (specify consideration) in full satisfaction of plaintiff's claim.

Added June 19, 1968, effective Oct. 1, 1968 (211 So.2d 174). Amended Oct. 5, 2000, effective Jan. 1, 2001 (773 So.2d 1098).

Form 1.968. Defense. Failure of Consideration

The sole consideration for the execution and delivery of the promissory note described in paragraph _____ of the complaint was plaintiff's promise to lend defendant $1,000; plaintiff failed to lend the sum to defendant.

NOTE: This form is for failure to complete the loan evidenced by a promissory note. The contract, consideration, and default of the plaintiff must be varied to meet the facts of each case.

Added June 19, 1968, effective Oct. 1, 1968 (211 So.2d 174). Amended July 16, 1992, effective Jan. 1, 1993 (604 So.2d 1110).

Form 1.969. Defense. Statute of Frauds

The agreement alleged in the complaint was not in writing and signed by defendant or by some other person authorized by defendant and was to answer for the debt, default, or miscarriage of another person.

NOTE: This form is for one of the cases covered by the Statute of Frauds. It must be varied to meet the facts of other cases falling within the statute.

Added June 19, 1968, effective Oct. 1, 1968 (211 So.2d 174). Amended July 16, 1992, effective Jan. 1, 1993 (604 So.2d 1110).

Form 1.970. Defense. Release

On ..... (date) ....., and after plaintiff's claim in this action accrued, plaintiff released defendant from it, a copy of the release being attached.

NOTE: This form is for the usual case of a written release. If the release is not in writing, the last clause must be omitted and the word "orally" inserted before "released."

Added June 19, 1968, effective Oct. 1, 1968 (211 So.2d 174). Amended Oct. 5, 2000, effective Jan. 1, 2001 (773 So.2d 1098).

Form 1.971. Defense. Motor Vehicle Contributory Negligence

Plaintiff's negligence contributed to the accident and his/her injury and damages because he/she negligently operated or maintained the motor vehicle in which he/she was riding so that it collided with defendant's motor vehicle.

Added June 19, 1968, effective Oct. 1, 1968 (211 So.2d 174). Amended Oct. 9, 1980, effective Jan. 1, 1981 (391 So.2d 165); July 16, 1992, effective Jan. 1, 1993 (604 So.2d 1110).

Form 1.972. Defense. Assumption of Risk

Plaintiff knew of the existence of the danger complained of in the complaint, realized and appreciated the possibility of injury as a result of the danger, and, having a reasonable opportunity to avoid it, voluntarily exposed himself/herself to the danger.

Added June 19, 1968, effective Oct. 1, 1968 (211 So.2d 174). Amended Oct. 9, 1980, effective Jan. 1, 1981 (391 So.2d 165); July 16, 1992, effective Jan. 1, 1993 (604 So.2d 1110).

Committee Notes

1980 Amendment. This form is amended to show the substantive changes caused by the substitution of the doctrine of comparative negligence for contributory negligence. The form is paraphrased from Standard Jury Instruction 3.8.

Form 1.975. Notice of Compliance When Constitutional Challenge Is Brought

NOTICE OF COMPLIANCE WITH SECTION 86.091, FLORIDA STATUTES

The undersigned hereby gives notice of compliance with Fla. R. Civ. P. 1.071, with respect to the constitutional challenge brought pursuant to .....(Florida statute, charter, ordinance, or franchise challenged)..... The undersigned complied by serving the .....(Attorney General for the state of Florida or State Attorney for the .... Judicial Circuit)..... with a copy of the pleading or motion challenging .....(Florida statute, charter, ordinance, or franchise challenged)....., by .....(certified or registered mail)..... on .....(date).....

____

Attorney for ....

Florida Bar No. ....

Address ....

Telephone No. ....

Added Sept. 8, 2010, effective Jan. 1, 2011 (52 So.3d 579).

Committee Notes

2010 Adoption. This form is to be used to provide notice of a constitutional challenge as required by section 86.091, Florida Statutes. See rule 1.071. This form is to be used when the Attorney General or the State Attorney is not a named party to the action, but must be served solely in order to comply with the notice requirements set forth in section 86.091.

Form 1.976. Standard Interrogatories

The forms of Florida standard interrogatories approved by the supreme court shall be used in the actions to which they apply, subject to the requirements of rule 1.340.

Added Sept. 13, 1984, effective Jan. 1, 1985 (458 So.2d 245). Amended July 16, 1992, effective Jan. 1, 1993 (604 So.2d 1110).

Standard interrogatories promulgated in the order of Sept. 13, 1984, effective Jan. 1, 1985 (458 So.2d 245), are contained in an appendix following text of the Civil Procedure Rules and Forms.

Form 1.977. Fact Information Sheet

(a) For Individuals.

(CAPTION)

FACT INFORMATION SHEET

Full Legal Name: ________________

Nicknames or Aliases: ________________

Residence Address: ________________

Mailing Address (if different): ____________

Telephone Numbers: (Home) __________

(Business) ________________

Name of Employer: ________________

Address of Employer: ________________

Position or Job Description: ____________

Rate of Pay: $ ___ per ___. Average Paycheck: $ ___ per ____________

Average Commissions or Bonuses: $ ___ per ______ Commissions or bonuses are based on ___

Other Personal Income: $ ___ from ______

(Explain details on the back of this sheet or an additional sheet if necessary.)

Social Security Number: ______ Birthdate: ___

Driver's License Number: ____________

Marital Status: ______ Spouse's Name: ____

* * * * * * * *

Spouse Related Portion

Spouse's Address (if different): __________

Spouse's Social Security Number: ______ Birthdate: ________________

Spouse's Employer: ________________

Spouse's Average Paycheck or Income: $ ___ per ___

Other Family Income: $ ___ per ________

(Explain details on back of this sheet or an additional sheet if necessary.) Describe all other accounts or investments you may have, including stocks, mutual funds, savings bonds, or annuities, on the back of this sheet or on an additional sheet if necessary.

* * * * * * * *

Names and Ages of All Your Children (and addresses if not living with you): ____________

Child Support or Alimony Paid: $ ___ per ___

Names of Others You Live With: __________

Who is Head of Your Household? ______ You ___ Spouse ___ Other Person Checking Account at: ______ Account # __________

Savings Account at: ______ Account # ______

For Real Estate (land) You Own or Are Buying:

Address: ________________

All Names on Title: ________________

Mortgage Owed to: ________________

Balance Owed: ________________

Monthly Payment: $ ________________

(Attach a copy of the deed or mortgage, or list the legal description of the property on the back of this sheet or an additional sheet if necessary. Also provide the same information on any other property you own or are buying.)

For All Motor Vehicles You Own or Are Buying:

Year/Make/Model: ______ Color: ______

Vehicle ID No.: ______ Tag No: ______

Mileage: ________________

Names on Title: ______ Present Value: $ ____

Loan Owed to: ____________________

Balance on Loan: $ ____________________

Monthly Payment: $ ____________________

(List all other automobiles, as well as other vehicles, such as boats, motorcycles, bicycles, or aircraft, on the back of this sheet or an additional sheet if necessary.)

Have you given, sold, loaned, or transferred any real or personal property worth more than $100 to any person in the last year? If your answer is "yes," describe the property, market value, and sale price, and give the name and address of the person who received the property.

Does anyone owe you money? Amount Owed: $ ____

Name and Address of Person Owing Money: ______

Reason money is owed: ____________________

Please attach copies of the following:

a. Your last pay stub.

b. Your last 3 statements for each bank, savings, credit union, or other financial account.

c. Your motor vehicle registrations and titles.

d. Any deeds or titles to any real or personal property you own or are buying, or leases to property you are renting.

e. Your financial statements, loan applications, or lists of assets and liabilities submitted to any person or entity within the last 3 years.

f. Your last 2 income tax returns filed.

UNDER PENALTY OF PERJURY, I SWEAR OR AFFIRM THAT THE FOREGOING ANSWERS ARE TRUE AND COMPLETE.

____
Judgment Debtor

STATE OF FLORIDA

COUNTY OF ....

Sworn to (or affirmed) and subscribed before me this ___ day of ___ (year), by (name of person making statement)

____
Notary Public State of Florida
My Commission expires: ....

Personally known ___ OR Produced Identification ___

Type of identification produced ____________________

YOU MUST MAIL OR DELIVER THIS COMPLETED FORM, WITH ALL ATTACHMENTS, TO THE JUDGMENT CREDITOR OR THE JUDGMENT CREDITOR'S ATTORNEY, BUT DO NOT FILE THIS FORM WITH THE CLERK OF THE COURT.

(b) For Corporations and Other Business Entities.

(CAPTION)

FACT INFORMATION SHEET

Name of entity: ____________________

Name and title of person filling out this form: ______

Telephone number: ____________________

Place of business: ____________________

Mailing address (if different): ____________________

Gross/taxable income reported for federal income tax purposes last three years:

$ ___ /$ ___ $ ___ /$ ___ $ ___ /$ ___

Taxpayer identification number: ____________________

Is this entity an S corporation for federal income tax purposes? ________ Yes ________ No

Average number of employees per month ________

Name of each shareholder, member, or partner owning 5% or more of the entity's common stock, preferred stock, or other equity interest:

____

____

____

Names of officers, directors, members, or partners:

____

____

Checking account at: ____________ Account # ______

Savings account at: ____________ Account # ______

Does the entity own any vehicles? ___ Yes ___ No

For each vehicle please state: ____________________

Year/Make/Model: ________ Color: ________

Vehicle ID No: ________ Tag No: ________ Mileage: ________

Names on Title: ________ Present Value: $ ______

Loan Owed to: ____________________

Balance on Loan: $ ____________________

Monthly Payment: $ ____________________

Does the entity own any real property? ___ Yes ___ No

If yes, please state the address(es): ____________

Please check if the entity owns the following: ______

___ Boat

___ Camper

___ Stocks/bonds

___ Other real property

___ Other personal property

Please attach copies of the following:

1. Copies of state and federal income tax returns for the past 3 years.

2. All bank, savings and loan, and other account books and statements for accounts in institutions in

which the entity had any legal or equitable interest for the past 3 years.

3. All canceled checks for the 12 months immediately preceding the service date of this Fact Information Sheet for accounts in which the entity held any legal or equitable interest.

4. All deeds, leases, mortgages, or other written instruments evidencing any interest in or ownership of real property at any time within the 12 months immediately preceding the date this lawsuit was filed.

5. Bills of sale or other written evidence of the gift, sale, purchase, or other transfer of any personal or real property to or from the entity within the 12 months immediately preceding the date this lawsuit was filed.

6. Motor vehicle or vessel documents, including titles and registrations relating to any motor vehicles or vessels owned by the entity alone or with others.

7. Financial statements as to the entity's assets, liabilities, and owner's equity prepared within the 12 months immediately preceding the service date of this Fact Information Sheet.

8. Minutes of all meetings of the entity's members, partners, shareholders, or board of directors held within 2 years of the service date of this Fact Information Sheet.

9. Resolutions of the entity's members, partners, shareholders, or board of directors passed within 2 years of the service date of this Fact Information Sheet.

UNDER PENALTY OF PERJURY, I SWEAR OR AFFIRM THAT THE FOREGOING ANSWERS ARE TRUE AND COMPLETE.

____
Judgment Debtor's Designated Representative/Title

STATE OF FLORIDA

COUNTY OF ....

Sworn to (or affirmed) and subscribed before me this ___ day of _______ (year), by (name of person making statement).

____
Notary Public State of Florida
My Commission expires: ....

Personally known ___ OR Produced identification ___

Type of identification produced ______________

YOU MUST MAIL OR DELIVER THIS COMPLETED FORM, WITH ALL ATTACHMENTS, TO THE PLAINTIFF JUDGMENT CREDITOR OR THE PLAINTIFF'S JUDGMENT CREDITOR'S ATTORNEY, BUT DO NOT FILE THIS FORM WITH THE CLERK OF THE COURT.

Added Oct. 5, 2000, effective Jan. 1, 2001 (773 So.2d 1098). Amended Oct. 3, 2003, effective Jan. 1, 2004 (858 So.2d 1013); Nov. 14, 2013, effective Jan. 1, 2014 (131 So.3d 643).

Committee Notes

2000 Adoption. This form is added to comply with amendments to rule 1.560.

2013 Amendment. This amendment clarifies that the judgment debtor should mail or deliver the Fact Information Sheet only to the judgment creditor or the judgment creditor's attorney, and should not file the Fact Information Sheet with the clerk of the court.

Form 1.980. Default

MOTION FOR DEFAULT

Plaintiff moves for entry of a default by the clerk against defendant .... for failure to serve any paper on the undersigned or file any paper as required by law.

____
Attorney for Plaintiff

DEFAULT

A default is entered in this action against the defendant named in the foregoing motion for failure to serve or file any paper as required by law.

Dated on ....

(Name of Clerk)
As Clerk of the Court
By ______________
As Deputy Clerk

Added June 19, 1968, effective Oct. 1, 1968 (211 So.2d 174). Amended Oct. 9, 1980, effective Jan. 1, 1981 (391 So.2d 165); Oct. 5, 2000, effective Jan. 1, 2001 (773 So.2d 1098).

Form 1.981. Satisfaction of Judgment

SATISFACTION OF JUDGMENT

The undersigned, owner and holder of a final judgment rendered in the above-captioned civil action, dated ...., recorded in .... County, Official Records Book .... beginning at Page ...., acknowledges that all sums due under it have been fully paid and that final judgment is hereby canceled and satisfied of record.

DATED on ....

____
Judgment Owner and Holder (or their attorney)

STATE OF FLORIDA

COUNTY OF ______________

The foregoing instrument was acknowledged before me this ___ day of ___, 20 ___, by (name of person acknowledging).

(NOTARY SEAL) (Signature of Notary Public–State of Florida)
(Name of Notary Typed, Printed, or Stamped)

Personally Known ________ OR Produced Identification ________
Type of Identification Produced ________

Added Oct. 23, 2003, effective Jan. 1, 2004 (858 So.2d 1013). Amended Nov. 14, 2013, effective Jan. 1, 2014 (131 So.3d 643).

Committee Notes

2003 Amendment. This satisfaction of Judgment is a general form. It is a new form. To ensure identity of the signer, notarization is prudent but not required. If a certified copy of the judgment is recorded, it may be prudent to include that recording information.

2013 Amendment. This form has been changed to remove unnecessary language and to include the acknowledgment required by sections 695.03 and 701.04, Florida Statutes.

Form 1.982. Contempt Notice

MOTION AND NOTICE OF HEARING

TO: (name of attorney for party, or party if not represented)

YOU ARE NOTIFIED that plaintiff will apply to the Honorable ...., Circuit Judge, on ... (date) ..., at ... m., in the .... County Courthouse at ...., Florida, for an order adjudging ... (defendant's name) ... in contempt of court for violation of the terms of the order or judgment entered by this court on ... (date) ..., by failing to ...., and I certify that a copy hereof has been furnished to .... by mail on ... (date) ...

If you are a person with a disability who needs any accommodation in order to participate in this proceeding, you are entitled, at no cost to you, to the provision of certain assistance. Please contact [identify applicable court personnel by name, address, and telephone number] at least 7 days before your scheduled court appearance, or immediately upon receiving this notification if the time before your scheduled appearance is less than 7 days; if you are hearing or voice impaired, call 711.

NOTE: The particular violation must be inserted in the motion and notice. A separate motion is unnecessary.

Added June 19, 1968, effective Oct. 1, 1968 (211 So.2d 174). Amended July 16, 1992, effective Jan. 1, 1993 (604 So.2d 1110); July 7, 1995, effective Jan. 1, 1996 (663 So.2d 1047); Nov. 22, 1995, effective Jan. 1, 1996 (663 So.2d 1049); Oct. 5, 2000, effective Jan. 1, 2001 (773 So.2d 1098); Sept. 27, 2007, effective Jan. 1, 2008 (966 So.2d 943); Nov. 14, 2013, effective Jan. 1, 2014 (131 So.3d 643).

Committee Note

2013 Amendment. The notice to persons with disabilities was amended to make the procedure for obtaining accommodation consistent with the procedure required in court proceedings.

Form 1.983. Prospective Juror Questionnaire

QUESTIONNAIRE FOR PROSPECTIVE JURORS

1. Name (print) ....
   (first) (middle) (last)
2. Residence address ....
   (street and number)
   ....
   (city) (zip)
3. Date of birth ....
   Sex .... Occupation ....
4. Do you understand the English language?
   ....
   (yes) (no)
5. Do you read and write the English language?
   ....
   (yes) (no)
6. Have you ever been convicted of a crime and not restored to your civil rights?
   ....
   (yes) (no)
   If "yes," state nature of crime, date of conviction, and name of court in which convicted: ....
7. Are there any criminal charges pending against you of which you are aware?
   ....
   (yes) (no)
   If "yes," state nature of charge and name of court in which the case is pending:
   ....
   ....
8. Are you a bonded deputy sheriff?
   ....
   (yes) (no)
9. List any official executive office you now hold with the federal, state, or county government:
   ....
10. Is your hearing good? ....
    (yes) (no)
    Is your eyesight good? ....
    (yes) (no)
    (The court may require a medical certificate.)
11. Do you have any other physical or mental disability that would interfere with your service as a juror?
    ....
    (yes) (no)
    If "yes," state nature: ....
    (The court may require a medical certificate.)
12. Do you know of any reason why you cannot serve as a juror?
    ....
    (yes) (no)
    If "yes," state reason: ....
13. MOTHERS AND EXPECTANT MOTHERS ONLY: Florida law provides that expectant mothers and mothers with children under 18 years of age residing with them shall be exempt from jury duty upon their request. Do you want to be exempt under this provision?
    ....

(yes) (no)

If "yes," what are the ages of your children?

....

____
Signature

This is not a summons for jury duty. If your name is later drawn for jury service, you will be summoned by the sheriff by registered mail or in person.

NOTE: This form does not use a caption as shown in form 1.901. It may be headed with the designation of the jury-selecting authority such as "Board of County Commissioners of Leon County, Florida," or "Pinellas County Jury Commission."

Added Sept. 29, 1971, effective Dec. 13, 1971 (253 So.2d 404). Amended July 16, 1992, effective Jan. 1, 1993 (604 So.2d 1110).

Form 1.984. Juror Voir Dire Questionnaire

JURY QUESTIONNAIRE

Instructions to Jurors

You have been selected as a prospective juror. It will aid the court and help shorten the trial of cases if you will answer the questions on this form and return it in the enclosed self-addressed stamped envelope within the next 2 days. Please complete the form in blue or black ink and write as dark and legibly as you can.

1. Name (print) ______________________
(first) (middle) (last)
2. Residence address ______________________
3. Years of residence: In Florida ______________
In this county ______________
4. Former residence ______________________
5. Marital status: (married, single, divorced, widow, or widower)______________________
6. Your occupation and employer______________
7. If you are not now employed, give your last occupation and employer______________
8. If married, name and occupation of husband or wife______________________
9. Have you served as a juror before?__________
10. Have you or any member of your immediate family been a party to any lawsuit?________If so, when and in what court?______________________
11. Are you either a close friend of or related to any law enforcement officer?______________
12. Has a claim for personal injuries ever been made against you or any member of your family?________
13. Have you or any member of your family ever made any claim for personal injuries?__________

____
Juror's Signature

NOTE: This form does not have a caption as shown in form 1.901, but should be headed with the name of the court summoning the juror.

Added Sept. 29, 1971, effective Dec. 13, 1971 (253 So.2d 404). Amended July 16, 1992, effective Jan. 1, 1993 (604 So.2d 1110).

Form 1.986. Verdicts

In all civil actions tried to a jury, the parties should refer to the model verdict forms contained in the Florida Standard Jury Instructions in Civil Cases, as applicable.

Added June 19, 1968, effective Oct. 1, 1968 (211 So.2d 174). Amended July 16, 1992, effective Jan. 1, 1993 (604 So.2d 1110); Oct. 5, 2000, effective Jan. 1, 2001 (773 So.2d 1098); Sept. 8, 2010, effective Jan. 1, 2011 (52 So.3d 579).

Form 1.988. Judgment After Default

(a) General Form. This form is the general form for a judgment after default, not including recovery for prejudgment interest and attorneys' fees:

FINAL JUDGMENT

This action was heard after entry of default against defendant and

IT IS ADJUDGED that plaintiff, ... (name and address) ..., recover from defendant, ... (name and address, and last 4 digits of social security number if known) ..., the sum of $ .... with costs in the sum of $ ...., that shall bear interest at the rate of ... % a year, for which let execution issue.

ORDERED at ...., Florida, on ..... (date) .....

____
Judge

(b) Form with Interest and Fees. This form is for judgment after default including prejudgment interest and attorneys' fees recovered:

FINAL JUDGMENT

This action was heard after entry of default against defendant and

IT IS ADJUDGED that plaintiff, ... (name and address) ..., recover from defendant, ... (name and address, and last 4 digits of social security number if known) ..., the sum of $ .... on principal, $ .... for attorneys' fees with costs in the sum of $ ...., and prejudgment interest in the sum of $ ...., making a total of $ .... that shall bear interest at the rate of ... % a year, for which let execution issue.

ORDERED at ...., Florida, on ..... (date) .....

____
Judge

NOTE: The address of the person who claims a lien as a result of the judgment must be included in the judgment in order for the judgment to become a lien on real estate when a certified copy of the judgment is recorded. Alternatively, an affidavit with this information may be simultaneously recorded. For the specific requirements, see section 55.10(1), Florida Statutes; *Hott Interiors, Inc. v. Fostock*, 721 So. 2d 1236 (Fla. 4th DCA 1998). The address and social security number (if known) of each person against whom the judgment is rendered must be included in the judgment, pursuant to section 55.01(2), Florida Statutes. However, for privacy reasons, only the last 4 digits of the social security number should be shown.

Added Oct. 9, 1980, effective Jan. 1, 1981 (391 So.2d 165). Amended Sept. 13, 1984, effective Jan. 1, 1985 (458 So.2d 245); July 16, 1992, effective Jan. 1, 1993 (604 So.2d 1110); Oct. 5, 2000, effective Jan. 1, 2001 (773 So.2d 1098); Oct. 23, 2003, effective Jan. 1, 2004 (858 So.2d 1013); Nov. 3, 2011, effective, *nunc pro tunc*, Oct. 1, 2011 (78 So.3d 1045).

Committee Notes

1980 Adoption. This form is new.

2003 Amendment. Subdivision (b) is amended to include prejudgment interest in the total judgment pursuant to *Quality Engineered Installation, Inc. v. Higley South, Inc.*, 670 So. 2d 929 (Fla. 1996).

Form 1.989. Order of Dismissal for Lack of Prosecution

(a) Notice of Lack of Prosecution.

NOTICE OF LACK OF PROSECUTION

PLEASE TAKE NOTICE that it appears on the face of the record that no activity by filing of pleadings, order of court, or otherwise has occurred for a period of 10 months immediately preceding service of this notice, and no stay has been issued or approved by the court. Pursuant to rule 1.420(e), if no such record activity occurs within 60 days following the service of this notice, and if no stay is issued or approved during such 60–day period, this action may be dismissed by the court on its own motion or on the motion of any interested person, whether a party to the action or not, after reasonable notice to the parties, unless a party shows good cause in writing at least 5 days before the hearing on the motion why the action should remain pending.

(b) Order Dismissing Case for Lack of Prosecution.

ORDER OF DISMISSAL

This action was heard on the ..... respondent's/court's/interested party's ..... motion to dismiss for lack of prosecution served on ..... (date) ...... The court finds that (1) notice prescribed by rule 1.420(e) was served on ..... (date) .....; (2) there was no record activity during the 10 months immediately preceding service of the foregoing notice; (3) there was no record activity during the 60 days immediately following service of the foregoing notice; (4) no stay has been issued or approved by the court; and (5) no party has shown good cause why this action should remain pending. Accordingly,

IT IS ORDERED that this action is dismissed for lack of prosecution.

ORDERED at ...., Florida, on ..... (date) ......

____
Judge

Added Sept. 29, 1971, effective Dec. 13, 1971 (253 So.2d 404). Amended July 16, 1992, effective Jan. 1, 1993 (604 So.2d 1110); Oct. 5, 2000, effective Jan. 1, 2001 (773 So.2d 1098); Dec. 15, 2005, effective Jan. 1, 2006 (917 So.2d 176).

Form 1.990. Final Judgment for Plaintiff. Jury Action for Damages

FINAL JUDGMENT

Pursuant to the verdict rendered in this action

IT IS ADJUDGED that plaintiff, ... (name and address) ..., recover from defendant, ... (name and address, and last 4 digits of social security number if known) ..., the sum of $ .... with costs in the sum of $ ...., making a total of $ ...., that shall bear interest at the rate of ... % a year, for which let execution issue.

ORDERED at ...., Florida, on ..... (date) ....

____
Judge

NOTE: The address of the person who claims a lien as a result of the judgment must be included in the judgment in order for the judgment to become a lien on real estate when a certified copy of the judgment is recorded. Alternatively, an affidavit with this information may be simultaneously recorded. For the specific requirements, see section 55.10(1), Florida Statutes; *Hott Interiors, Inc. v. Fostock*, 721 So. 2d 1236 (Fla. 4th DCA 1998). The address and social security number (if known) of each person against whom the judgment is rendered must be included in the judgment, pursuant to section 55.01(2), Florida Statutes. However, for privacy reasons, only the last 4 digits of the social security number should be shown.

Added June 19, 1968, effective Oct. 1, 1968 (211 So.2d 174). Amended Oct. 9, 1980, effective Jan. 1, 1981 (391 So.2d 165); Sept. 13, 1984, effective Jan. 1, 1985 (458 So.2d 245); July 16, 1992, effective Jan. 1, 1993 (604 So.2d 1110); Oct. 5, 2000, effective Jan. 1, 2001 (773 So.2d 1098); Nov. 3, 2011, effective, *nunc pro tunc*, Oct. 1, 2011 (78 So.3d 1045).

Form 1.991. Final Judgment for Defendant. Jury Action for Damages

FINAL JUDGMENT

Pursuant to the verdict rendered in this action

IT IS ADJUDGED that plaintiff, . . . (name and address, and last 4 digits of social security number if known) . . ., take nothing by this action and that defendant, . . . (name and address) . . ., shall go hence without day and recover costs from plaintiff in the sum of $ . . . . that shall bear interest at the rate of . . . % a year, for which let execution issue.

ORDERED at . . . ., Florida, on . . . . . (date) . . . . .

____

Judge

NOTE: The address of the person who claims a lien as a result of the judgment must be included in the judgment in order for the judgment to become a lien on real estate when a certified copy of the judgment is recorded. Alternatively, an affidavit with this information may be simultaneously recorded. For the specific requirements, see section 55.10(1), Florida Statutes; *Hott Interiors, Inc. v. Fostock*, 721 So. 2d 1236 (Fla. 4th DCA 1998). The address and social security number (if known) of each person against whom the judgment is rendered must be included in the judgment, pursuant to section 55.01(2), Florida Statutes. However, for privacy reasons, only the last 4 digits of the social security number should be shown.

Added June 19, 1968, effective Oct. 1, 1968 (211 So.2d 174). Amended Sept. 13, 1984, effective Jan. 1, 1985 (458 So.2d 245); July 16, 1992, effective Jan. 1, 1993 (604 So.2d 1110); Oct. 5, 2000, effective Jan. 1, 2001 (773 So.2d 1098); Nov. 3, 2011, effective, *nunc pro tunc*, Oct. 1, 2011 (78 So.3d 1045).

Form 1.993. Final Judgment for Plaintiff. General Form. Non–Jury

FINAL JUDGMENT

This action was tried before the court. On the evidence presented

IT IS ADJUDGED that:

1. (list adjudications in numbered paragraphs)
2. . . . .

(See note below on name, address, and social security number requirements.)

ORDERED at . . . ., Florida, on . . . . (date) . . . . .

____

Judge

NOTE: Findings of fact can be inserted after "presented" if desired. The address of the person who claims a lien as a result of the judgment must be included in the judgment in order for the judgment to become a lien on real estate when a certified copy of the judgment is recorded. Alternatively, an affidavit with this information may be simultaneously recorded. For the specific requirements, see section 55.10(1), Florida Statutes; *Hott Interiors, Inc. v. Fostock*, 721 So. 2d 1236 (Fla. 4th DCA 1998). The address and social security number (if known) of each person against whom the judgment is rendered must be included in the judgment, pursuant to section 55.01(2), Florida Statutes. However, for privacy reasons, only the last 4 digits of the social security number should be shown.

Added June 19, 1968, effective Oct. 1, 1968 (211 So.2d 174). Amended Oct. 5, 2000, effective Jan. 1, 2001 (773 So.2d 1098); Nov. 3, 2011, effective, *nunc pro tunc*, Oct. 1, 2011 (78 So.3d 1045).

Form 1.994. Final Judgment for Defendant. General Form. Non–Jury

FINAL JUDGMENT

This action was tried before the court. On the evidence presented

IT IS ADJUDGED that plaintiff, . . . (name and address, and last 4 digits of social security number if known) . . ., take nothing by this action and that defendant, . . . (name and address) . . ., shall go hence without day and recover costs from plaintiff in the sum of $ . . . . that shall bear interest at the rate of . . . % a year, for which let execution issue.

ORDERED at . . . ., Florida, on . . . . . (date) . . . . .

____

Judge

NOTE: Findings of fact can be inserted after "presented" if desired. The address of the person who claims a lien as a result of the judgment must be included in the judgment in order for the judgment to become a lien on real estate when a certified copy of the judgment is recorded. Alternatively, an affidavit with this information may be simultaneously recorded. For the specific requirements, see section 55.10(1), Florida Statutes; *Hott Interiors, Inc. v. Fostock*, 721 So. 2d 1236 (Fla. 4th DCA 1998). The address and social security number (if known) of each person against whom the judgment is rendered must be included in the judgment, pursuant to section 55.01(2), Florida Statutes. However, for privacy reasons, only the last 4 digits of the social security number should be shown.

Added June 19, 1968, effective Oct. 1, 1968 (211 So.2d 174). Amended Sept. 13, 1984, effective Jan. 1, 1985 (458 So.2d 245); July 16, 1992, effective Jan. 1, 1993 (604 So.2d 1110); Oct. 5, 2000, effective Jan. 1, 2001 (773 So.2d 1098); Nov. 3, 2011, effective, *nunc pro tunc*, Oct. 1, 2011 (78 So.3d 1045).

Form 1.995. Final Judgment of Replevin

NOTE APPLICABLE TO FORMS (a)–(d): The address of the person who claims a lien as a result of the judgment must be included in the judgment in order for the judgment to become a lien on real estate when a certified copy of the judgment is recorded. Alternatively, an affidavit with this information may be simultaneously recorded. For the specific requirements, see section 55.10(1), Florida Statutes; *Hott Interiors, Inc. v. Fostock*, 721 So. 2d 1236 (Fla. 4th DCA 1998). The address and social security number (if known) of each person against whom the judgment is rendered must be included in the judgment, pursuant to section 55.01(2), Florida Statutes. However, for privacy reasons, only the last 4 digits of the social security number should be shown.

(a) Judgment in Favor of Plaintiff when Plaintiff Has Possession.

FINAL JUDGMENT OF REPLEVIN

This matter was heard on plaintiff's complaint. On the evidence presented

IT IS ADJUDGED that:

1. Plaintiff, . . . (name and address) . . ., has the right against defendant, . . . (name and address, and last 4 digits of social security if known) . . ., to retain possession of the following described property:

(list the property and include a value for each item)

2. Plaintiff shall recover from defendant the sum of $ .... as damages for the detention of the property and the sum of $ .... as costs, making a total of $ ...., which shall bear interest at the rate of ... % per year, for which let execution issue.

ORDERED at ...., Florida, on ..... (date) .....

____
Judge

NOTE: This form applies when the plaintiff has recovered possession under a writ of replevin and prevailed on the merits. Pursuant to section 78.18, Florida Statutes (1995), paragraph 2 of the form provides that the plaintiff can also recover damages for the wrongful taking and detention of the property, together with costs. Generally these damages are awarded in the form of interest unless loss of use can be proven. *Ocala Foundry & Machine Works v. Lester*, 49 Fla. 199, 38 So. 51 (1905).

If the defendant has possession of part of the property, see form 1.995(b).

(b) Judgment in Favor of Plaintiff when Defendant Has Possession.

FINAL JUDGMENT OF REPLEVIN

This matter was heard on plaintiff's complaint. On the evidence presented

IT IS ADJUDGED that:

1. Plaintiff, . . . (name and address) . . ., has the right against defendant, . . . (name and address, and last 4 digits of social security number if known) . . ., to possession of the following described property:

(list the property and include a value for each item)

for which the clerk of the court shall issue a writ of possession; or

2. Plaintiff shall recover from defendant [if applicable add "and surety on the forthcoming bond"] the sum of $ .... for the value of the property, which shall bear interest at the rate of ... % per year, for which let execution issue.

3. Plaintiff shall recover from defendant the sum of $ .... as damages for the detention of the property and the sum of $ .... as costs, making a total of $ ...., which shall bear interest at the rate of ... % per year, for which let execution issue.

ORDERED at ...., Florida, on ..... (date) .....

____
Judge

NOTE: This form applies when the plaintiff prevails on the merits and the defendant retains possession of the property. Section 78.19, Florida Statutes (1995), allows the plaintiff to recover the property or its value or the value of the plaintiff's lien or special interest. The value for purposes of paragraph 2 is either the value of the property or the value of the plaintiff's lien or special interest.

Paragraph 3 of the form provides for damages for detention only against the defendant because the defendant's surety obligates itself only to ensure forthcoming of the property, not damages for its detention.

Pursuant to section 78.19(2), Florida Statutes, paragraphs 1 and 2 of the form provide the plaintiff the option of obtaining either a writ of possession or execution against the defendant and defendant's surety on a money judgment for property not recovered. *Demetree v. Stramondo*, 621 So. 2d 740 (Fla. 5th DCA 1993). If the plaintiff elects the writ of possession for the property and the sheriff is unable to find it or part of it, the plaintiff may immediately have execution against the defendant for the whole amount recovered or the amount less the value of the property found by the sheriff. If the plaintiff elects execution for the whole amount, the officer shall release all property taken under the writ.

If the plaintiff has possession of part of the property, see form 1.995(a).

(c) Judgment in Favor of Defendant when Defendant Has Possession under Forthcoming Bond.

FINAL JUDGMENT OF REPLEVIN

This matter was heard on plaintiff's complaint. On the evidence presented

IT IS ADJUDGED that:

1. Defendant, . . . (name and address) . . ., has the right against plaintiff, . . . (name and address, and last 4 digits of social security number if known) . . ., to possession of the following described property:

(list the property and include a value for each item)

2. Defendant retook possession of all or part of the property under a forthcoming bond, and defendant's attorney has reasonably expended . . . hours in representing defendant in this action and $ .... is a reasonable hourly rate for the services.

3. Defendant shall recover from plaintiff the sum of $ .... for the wrongful taking of the property, costs in the sum of $ ...., and attorneys' fees in the sum of $ ...., making a total of $ ...., which shall bear interest at the rate of . . . % per year, for which let execution issue.

ORDERED at ...., Florida, on ..... (date) .....

Judge

NOTE: This form applies when the defendant prevails and the property was retained by or redelivered to the defendant. Section 78.20, Florida Statutes (1995), provides for an award of attorneys' fees. The prevailing defendant may be awarded possession, damages, if any, for the taking of the property, costs, and attorneys' fees.

If the plaintiff has possession of part of the property, see form 1.995(d).

(d) Judgment in Favor of Defendant when Plaintiff Has Possession.

FINAL JUDGMENT OF REPLEVIN

This matter was heard on plaintiff's complaint. On the evidence presented

IT IS ADJUDGED that:

1. Defendant, . . . (name and address) . . ., has the right against plaintiff, . . . (name and address, and last four digits of social security number if known) . . ., to recover possession of the following described property:

(list the property and include a value for each item)

for which the clerk of the court shall issue a writ of possession; or

2. Defendant shall recover from plaintiff [if applicable add "and surety on plaintiff's bond"] the sum of $ .... for the value of the property, which shall bear interest at the rate of . . . % per year, for which let execution issue.

3. Defendant shall recover from plaintiff the sum of $ .... as damages for detention of the property and the sum of $ .... as costs, making a total of $ ...., which shall bear interest at the rate of . . . % per year, for which let execution issue.

ORDERED at ...., Florida, on ..... (date) .....

Judge

NOTE: This form should be used when the defendant prevails but the plaintiff has possession of the property. Section 78.21, Florida Statutes (1995), does not provide for an award of attorneys' fees when the defendant prevails and possession had been temporarily retaken by the plaintiff. Sections 78.21 and 78.19 allow the defendant to recover the property or its value or the value of the defendant's special interest.

Paragraphs 1 and 2 of the form provide to the defendant the option of obtaining either a writ of possession or execution against the plaintiff and plaintiff's surety on a money judgment for property not recovered and costs. *Demetree v. Stramondo*, 621 So. 2d 740 (Fla. 5th DCA 1993). If the defendant elects the writ of possession for the property and the sheriff is unable to find it or part of it, the defendant may immediately have execution against the plaintiff and surety for the whole amount recovered or the amount less the value of the property found by the sheriff. If the defendant elects execution for the whole amount, the officer shall release all property taken under the writ.

If the defendant has possession of part of the property, see form 1.995(c).

Added Oct. 15, 1998 (723 So.2d 180). Amended Oct. 5, 2000, effective Jan. 1, 2001 (773 So.2d 1098); Nov. 3, 2011, effective, *nunc pro tunc*, Oct. 1, 2011 (78 So.3d 1045).

Form 1.996(a). Final Judgment of Foreclosure

FINAL JUDGMENT

This action was tried before the court. On the evidence presented

IT IS ADJUDGED that:

1. **Amounts Due.** Plaintiff, ... (name and address) ...., is due

Principal	$.......
Interest to date of this judgment	....
Title search expenses	....
Taxes	....
Attorneys' fees total	....
Court costs, now taxed	....
Other:	....
Subtotal	$........
LESS: Escrow balance	....
LESS: Other	....
TOTAL	$.......

That shall bear interest at a rate of 7% per year.

2. **Lien on Property.** Plaintiff holds a lien for the total sum superior to all claims or estates of defendant(s), on the following described property in .... County, Florida:

(describe property)

3. **Sale of Property.** If the total sum with interest at the rate described in paragraph 1 and all costs accrued subsequent to this judgment are not paid, the clerk of this court shall sell the property at public sale on .... (date) ...., to the highest bidder for cash, except as prescribed in paragraph 4, at the courthouse located at .... (street address of courthouse) .... in .... County in .... (name of city) ...., Florida, in accordance with section 45.031, Florida Statutes (2013), using the following method (CHECK ONE):

.... At .... (location of sale at courthouse; *e.g.*, north door) ...., beginning at .... (time of sale) .... on the prescribed date.

.... By electronic sale beginning at .... (time of sale) .... on the prescribed date at .... (website) ....

4. **Costs.** Plaintiff shall advance all subsequent costs of this action and shall be reimbursed for them by the clerk if plaintiff is not the purchaser of the property for sale, provided, however, that the purchaser of the property for sale shall be responsible for the documentary stamps payable on the certificate of title. If plaintiff is the purchaser, the clerk shall credit plaintiff's bid with the total sum with interest and costs accruing subsequent to this judgment, or such part of it as is necessary to pay the bid in full.

5. **Distribution of Proceeds.** On filing the certificate of title the clerk shall distribute the proceeds of the sale, so far as they are sufficient, by paying: first, all of plaintiff's costs; second, documentary stamps affixed to the certificate; third, plaintiff's attorneys' fees; fourth, the total sum due to plaintiff, less the items paid, plus interest at the rate prescribed in paragraph 1 from this date to the date of the sale; and by retaining any remaining amount pending further order of this court.

6. **Right of Redemption/Right of Possession.** On filing the certificate of sale, defendant(s) and all persons claiming under or against defendant(s) since the filing of the notice of lis pendens shall be foreclosed of all estate or claim in the property and defendant's right of redemption as prescribed by section 45.0315, Florida Statutes (2013) shall be terminated, except as to claims or rights under chapter 718 or chapter 720, Florida Statutes, if any. Upon the filing of the certificate of title, the person named on the certificate of title shall be let into possession of the property.

7. **Attorneys' Fees.**

[If a default judgment has been entered against the mortgagor]

Because a default judgment has been entered against the mortgagor and because the fees requested do not exceed 3% of the principal amount owed at the time the complaint was filed, it is not necessary for the court to hold a hearing or adjudge the requested attorneys' fees to be reasonable.

[If no default judgment has been entered against the mortgagor]

The court finds, based upon the affidavits/testimony presented and upon inquiry of counsel for the plaintiff that ________ hours were reasonably expended by plaintiff's counsel and that an hourly rate of $________ is appropriate. Plaintiff's counsel represents that the attorneys' fees awarded does not exceed its contract fee with the plaintiff. The court finds that there is/are no reduction or enhancement factors for consideration by the court pursuant to *Florida Patients Compensation Fund v. Rowe*, 472 So. 2d 1145 (Fla. 1985). (If the court has found that there are reduction or enhancement factors to be applied, then such factors must be identified and explained herein).

[If the fees to be awarded are a flat fee]

The requested attorneys' fees are a flat rate fee that the firm's client has agreed to pay in this matter. Given the amount of the fee requested and the labor expended, the court finds that a lodestar analysis is not necessary and that the flat fee is reasonable.

8. **Jurisdiction Retained.** Jurisdiction of this action is retained to enter further orders that are proper including, without limitation, a deficiency judgment.

IF THIS PROPERTY IS SOLD AT PUBLIC AUCTION, THERE MAY BE ADDITIONAL MONEY

FROM THE SALE AFTER PAYMENT OF PERSONS WHO ARE ENTITLED TO BE PAID FROM THE SALE PROCEEDS PURSUANT TO THE FINAL JUDGMENT.

IF YOU ARE A SUBORDINATE LIENHOLDER CLAIMING A RIGHT TO FUNDS REMAINING AFTER THE SALE, YOU MUST FILE A CLAIM WITH THE CLERK NO LATER THAN 60 DAYS AFTER THE SALE. IF YOU FAIL TO FILE A CLAIM, YOU WILL NOT BE ENTITLED TO ANY REMAINING FUNDS.

[If the property being foreclosed on has qualified for the homestead tax exemption in the most recent approved tax roll, the final judgment shall additionally contain the following statement in conspicuous type:]

IF YOU ARE THE PROPERTY OWNER, YOU MAY CLAIM THESE FUNDS YOURSELF. YOU ARE NOT REQUIRED TO HAVE A LAWYER OR ANY OTHER REPRESENTATION AND YOU DO NOT HAVE TO ASSIGN YOUR RIGHTS TO ANYONE ELSE IN ORDER FOR YOU TO CLAIM ANY MONEY TO WHICH YOU ARE ENTITLED. PLEASE CONTACT THE CLERK OF THE COURT, (INSERT INFORMATION FOR APPLICABLE COURT) **WITHIN 10 DAYS AFTER THE SALE TO SEE IF THERE IS ADDITIONAL MONEY FROM THE FORECLOSURE SALE THAT THE CLERK HAS IN THE REGISTRY OF THE COURT.**

IF YOU DECIDE TO SELL YOUR HOME OR HIRE SOMEONE TO HELP YOU CLAIM THE ADDITIONAL MONEY, YOU SHOULD READ VERY CAREFULLY ALL PAPERS YOU ARE REQUIRED TO SIGN, ASK SOMEONE ELSE, PREFERABLY AN ATTORNEY WHO IS NOT RELATED TO THE PERSON OFFERING TO HELP YOU, TO MAKE SURE THAT YOU UNDERSTAND WHAT YOU ARE SIGNING AND THAT YOU ARE NOT TRANSFERRING YOUR PROPERTY OR THE EQUITY IN YOUR PROPERTY WITHOUT THE PROPER INFORMATION. IF YOU CANNOT AFFORD TO PAY AN ATTORNEY, YOU MAY CONTACT (INSERT LOCAL OR NEAREST LEGAL AID OFFICE AND TELEPHONE NUMBER) **TO SEE IF YOU QUALIFY FINANCIALLY FOR THEIR SERVICES. IF THEY CANNOT ASSIST YOU, THEY MAY BE ABLE TO REFER YOU TO A LOCAL BAR REFERRAL AGENCY OR SUGGEST OTHER OPTIONS. IF YOU CHOOSE TO CONTACT** (NAME OF LOCAL OR NEAREST LEGAL AID OFFICE AND TELEPHONE NUMBER) **FOR ASSISTANCE, YOU SHOULD DO SO AS SOON AS POSSIBLE AFTER RECEIPT OF THIS NOTICE.**

ORDERED at ...., Florida, on .... (date) ....

____

Judge

NOTE: Paragraph 1 must be varied in accordance with the items unpaid, claimed, and proven. The form does not provide for an adjudication of junior lienors' claims nor for redemption by the United States of America if it is a defendant. The address of the person who claims a lien as a result of the judgment must be included in the judgment in order for the judgment to become a lien on real estate when a certified copy of the judgment is recorded. Alternatively, an affidavit with this information may be simultaneously recorded. For the specific requirements, see section 55.10(1), Florida Statutes; *Hott Interiors, Inc. v. Fostock*, 721 So. 2d 1236 (Fla. 4th DCA 1998).

Added Sept. 29, 1971, effective Dec. 13, 1971 (253 So.2d 404). Amended Oct. 9, 1980 effective Jan. 1, 1981 (391 So.2d 165); Sept. 13, 1984, effective Jan. 1, 1985 (458 So.2d 245); July 16, 1992, effective Jan. 1, 1993 (604 So.2d 1110); Oct. 5, 2000, effective Jan. 1, 2001 (773 So.2d 1098). Renumbered from Form 1.996 and amended effective Feb. 11, 2010 (44 So.3d 555). Amended effective Dec. 9, 2010 (51 So.3d 1140); Dec. 11, 2014, effective Dec. 11, 2014 (153 So.3d 258).

Committee Notes

1980 Amendment. The reference to writs of assistance in paragraph 7 is changed to writs of possession to comply with the consolidation of the 2 writs.

2010 Amendment. Mandatory statements of the mortgagee/property owner's rights are included as required by the 2006 amendment to section 45.031, Florida Statutes. Changes are also made based on 2008 amendments to section 45.031, Florida Statutes, permitting courts to order sale by electronic means.

Additional changes were made to bring the form into compliance with chapters 718 and 720 and section 45.0315, Florida Statutes, and to better align the form with existing practices of clerks and practitioners. The breakdown of the amounts due is now set out in column format to simplify calculations. The requirement that the form include the address and social security number of all defendants was eliminated to protect the privacy interests of those defendants and in recognition of the fact that this form of judgment does not create a personal final money judgment against the defendant borrower, but rather an in rem judgment against the property. The address and social security number of the defendant borrower should be included in any deficiency judgment later obtained against the defendant borrower.

2014 Amendment. These amendments added titles, updated statutory reference to time for right of redemption, and added a paragraph on attorneys' fees.

Form 1.996(b). Final Judgment of Foreclosure for Reestablishment of Lost Note

FINAL JUDGMENT

This action was tried before the court. On the evidence presented

IT IS ADJUDGED that:

1. **Amounts Due.** Plaintiff, . . . (name and address) . . . ., is due

Principal	$ . . . . .
Interest to date of this judgment	. . . .
Title search expenses	. . . .
Taxes	. . . .
Attorneys' fees total	. . . .
Court costs, now taxed	. . . .
Other:	. . . .
Subtotal	$ . . . . . .
LESS: Escrow balance	. . . .
LESS: Other	. . . .
TOTAL	$ . . . . . .

2. **Lien on Property.** Plaintiff holds a lien for the total sum superior to all claims or estates of defendant(s), on the following described property . . . . County, Florida:

(describe property)

3. **Sale of Property.** If the total sum with interest at the rate described in paragraph 1 and all costs accrued subsequent to this judgment are not paid, the clerk of this court shall sell the property at public sale on . . . . (date) . . . ., to the highest bidder for cash, except as prescribed in paragraph 4, at the courthouse located at . . . (street address of courthouse) . . . in . . . . County in . . . . (name of city) . . . ., Florida, in accordance with section 45.031, Florida Statutes (2013), using the following method (CHECK ONE):

At . . . . (location of sale at courthouse; *e.g.*, north door) . . . ., beginning at . . . . (time of sale) . . . . on the prescribed date.

By electronic sale beginning at . . . . (time of sale) . . . . on the prescribed date at . . . . (website) . . . .

4. **Costs.** Plaintiff shall advance all subsequent costs of this action and shall be reimbursed for them by the clerk if plaintiff is not the purchaser of the property for sale, provided, however, that the purchaser of the property for sale shall be responsible for the documentary stamps payable on the certificate of title. If plaintiff is the purchaser, the clerk shall credit plaintiff's bid with the total sum with interest and costs accruing subsequent to this judgment, or such part of it as is necessary to pay the bid in full.

5. **Distribution of Proceeds.** On filing the certificate of title the clerk shall distribute the proceeds of the sale, so far as they are sufficient, by paying: first, all of plaintiff's costs; second, documentary stamps affixed to the certificate; third, plaintiff's attorneys' fees; fourth, the total sum due to plaintiff, less the items paid, plus interest at the rate prescribed in paragraph 1 from this date to the date of the sale; and by retaining any remaining amount pending further order of this court.

6. **Right of Redemption/Right of Possession.** On filing the certificate of sale, defendant(s) and all persons claiming under or against defendant(s) since the filing of the notice of lis pendens shall be foreclosed of all estate or claim in the property and defendant's right of redemption as prescribed by section 45.031, Florida Statutes (2013) shall be terminated, except as to claims or rights under chapter 718 or chapter 720, Florida Statutes, if any. Upon the filing of the certificate of title, the person named on the certificate of title shall be let into possession of the property.

7. **Attorneys' Fees.**

[If a default judgment has been entered against the mortgagor]

Because a default judgment has been entered against the mortgagor and because the fees requested do not exceed 3% of the principal amount owed at the time the complaint was filed, it is not necessary for the court to hold a hearing or adjudge the requested attorneys' fees to be reasonable.

[If no default judgment has been entered against the mortgagor]

The court finds, based upon the affidavits/testimony presented and upon inquiry of counsel for the plaintiff that ______ hours were reasonably expended by plaintiff's counsel and that an hourly rate of $ ________ is appropriate. Plaintiff's counsel represents that the attorney fee awarded does not exceed its contract fee with the plaintiff. The court finds that there are no reduction or enhancement factors for consideration by the court pursuant to *Florida Patients Compensation Fund v. Rowe*, 472 So. 2d 1145 (Fla. 1985). (If the court has found that there are reduction or enhancement factors to be applied, then such factors must be identified and explained herein).

[If the fees to be awarded are a flat fee]

The requested attorneys' fees are a flat rate fee that the firm's client has agreed to pay in this matter. Given the amount of the fee requested and the labor expended, the court finds that a lodestar analysis is not necessary and that the flat fee is reasonable.

8. **Re-establishment of Lost Note.** The court finds that the plaintiff has re-established the terms of the lost note and its right to enforce the instrument as required by applicable law. Plaintiff shall hold the defendant(s) maker of the note harmless and shall

indemnify defendant(s) for any loss defendant(s) may incur by reason of a claim by any other person to enforce the lost note. Adequate protection has been provided as required by law by the following means: .... (identify means of security under applicable law: a written indemnification agreement, a surety bond, include specific detail) ....

Judgment is hereby entered in favor of the plaintiff as to its request to enforce the lost note.

9. **Jurisdiction Retained.** Jurisdiction of this action is retained to enforce the adequate protection ordered and to enter further orders that are proper including, without limitation, a deficiency judgment.

IF THIS PROPERTY IS SOLD AT PUBLIC AUCTION, THERE MAY BE ADDITIONAL MONEY FROM THE SALE AFTER PAYMENT OF PERSONS WHO ARE ENTITLED TO BE PAID FROM THE SALE PROCEEDS PURSUANT TO THE FINAL JUDGMENT.

IF YOU ARE A SUBORDINATE LIENHOLDER CLAIMING A RIGHT TO FUNDS REMAINING AFTER THE SALE, YOU MUST FILE A CLAIM WITH THE CLERK NO LATER THAN 60 DAYS AFTER THE SALE. IF YOU FAIL TO FILE A CLAIM, YOU WILL NOT BE ENTITLED TO ANY REMAINING FUNDS.

[If the property being foreclosed on has qualified for the homestead tax exemption in the most recent approved tax roll, the final judgment shall additionally contain the following statement in conspicuous type:]

IF YOU ARE THE PROPERTY OWNER, YOU MAY CLAIM THESE FUNDS YOURSELF. YOU ARE NOT REQUIRED TO HAVE A LAWYER OR ANY OTHER REPRESENTATION AND YOU DO NOT HAVE TO ASSIGN YOUR RIGHTS TO ANYONE ELSE IN ORDER FOR YOU TO CLAIM ANY MONEY TO WHICH YOU ARE ENTITLED. PLEASE CHECK WITH THE CLERK OF THE COURT, (INSERT INFORMATION FOR APPLICABLE COURT) **WITHIN 10 DAYS AFTER THE SALE TO SEE IF THERE IS ADDITIONAL MONEY FROM THE FORECLOSURE SALE THAT THE CLERK HAS IN THE REGISTRY OF THE COURT.**

IF YOU DECIDE TO SELL YOUR HOME OR HIRE SOMEONE TO HELP YOU CLAIM THE ADDITIONAL MONEY, YOU SHOULD READ VERY CAREFULLY ALL PAPERS YOU ARE REQUIRED TO SIGN, ASK SOMEONE ELSE, PREFERABLY AN ATTORNEY WHO IS NOT RELATED TO THE PERSON OFFERING TO HELP YOU, TO MAKE SURE THAT YOU UNDERSTAND WHAT YOU ARE SIGNING AND THAT YOU ARE NOT TRANSFERRING YOUR PROPERTY OR THE EQUITY IN YOUR PROPERTY WITHOUT THE PROPER INFORMATION. IF YOU CANNOT AFFORD TO PAY AN ATTORNEY, YOU MAY CONTACT (INSERT LOCAL OR NEAREST LEGAL AID OFFICE AND TELEPHONE NUMBER) **TO SEE IF YOU QUALIFY FINANCIALLY FOR THEIR SERVICES. IF THEY CANNOT ASSIST YOU, THEY MAY BE ABLE TO REFER YOU TO A LOCAL BAR REFERRAL AGENCY OR SUGGEST OTHER OPTIONS. IF YOU CHOOSE TO CONTACT** (NAME OF LOCAL OR NEAREST LEGAL AID OFFICE AND TELEPHONE NUMBER) **FOR ASSISTANCE, YOU SHOULD DO SO AS SOON AS POSSIBLE AFTER RECEIPT OF THIS NOTICE.**

ORDERED at ...., Florida, on .... (date) ....

____
Judge

NOTE: Paragraph 1 must be varied in accordance with the items unpaid, claimed, and proven. The form does not provide for an adjudication of junior lienors' claims or for redemption by the United States of America if it is a defendant. The address of the person who claims a lien as a result of the judgment must be included in the judgment in order for the judgment to become a lien on real estate when a certified copy of the judgment is recorded. Alternatively, an affidavit with this information may be simultaneously recorded. For the specific requirements, see section 55.10(1), Florida Statutes; *Hott Interiors, Inc. v. Fostock*, 721 So. 2d 1236 (Fla. 4th DCA 1998).

Added Dec. 11, 2014, effective Dec. 11, 2014 (153 So.3d 258).

Committee Note

2014 Amendment. This new form is to be used when the foreclosure judgment re-establishes a lost note.

Form 1.996(c). Motion to Cancel and Reschedule Foreclosure Sale

Plaintiff moves to cancel and reschedule the mortgage foreclosure sale because:

1. On ..... (date) ..... this court entered a Final Judgment of Foreclosure pursuant to which a foreclosure sale was scheduled for ..... (date) .....

2. The sale needs to be canceled for the following reason(s):

a. ________ Plaintiff and defendant are continuing to be involved in loss mitigation;

b. ________ Defendant is negotiating for the sale of the property that is the subject of this matter and plaintiff wants to allow the defendant an opportunity to sell the property and pay off the debt that is due and owing to plaintiff.

c. ________ Defendant has entered into a contract to sell the property that is the subject of this matter and plaintiff wants to give the defendant an opportunity to consummate the sale and pay off the debt that is due and owing to plaintiff.

d. ________ Defendant has filed a Chapter ________ Petition under the Federal Bankruptcy Code;

e. ________ Plaintiff has ordered but has not received a statement of value/appraisal for the property;

f. ________ Plaintiff and defendant have entered into a Forbearance Agreement;

g. Other

____

____

____

3. If this Court cancels the foreclosure sale, plaintiff moves that it be rescheduled.

I hereby certify that a copy of the foregoing motion has been furnished by ..... (method of service) ..... to ..... (name(s)) ..... on ..... (date) .....

NOTE. This form is used to move the court to cancel and reschedule a foreclosure sale.

Formerly Form 1.996(b), added Feb. 11, 2010 (44 So.3d 555). Renumbered Form 1.996(c) and amended Dec. 11, 2014, effective Dec. 11, 2014 (153 So.3d 258).

Form 1.997. Civil Cover Sheet

The civil cover sheet and the information contained in it neither replace nor supplement the filing and service of pleadings or other papers as required by law. This form shall be filed by the plaintiff or petitioner for the use of the Clerk of Court for the purpose of reporting judicial workload data pursuant to Florida Statutes section 25.075. (See instructions for completion.)

I. CASE STYLE

(Name of Court)

Plaintiff ________________ Case #:

Judge: ________

vs.

Defendant ________________

____

II. TYPE OF CASE (If the case fits more than one type of case, select the most definitive category.) If the most descriptive label is a subcategory (is indented under a broader category), place an x on both the main category and subcategory lines.

___ Condominium
___ Contracts and indebtedness
___ Eminent domain
___ Auto negligence
___ Negligence—other
    ___ Business governance
    ___ Business torts
    ___ Environmental/Toxic tort
    ___ Third party indemnification
    ___ Construction defect
    ___ Mass tort
    ___ Negligent security
    ___ Nursing home negligence
    ___ Premises liability—commercial
    ___ Premises liability—residential
___ Products liability
___ Real property/Mortgage foreclosure
    ___ Commercial foreclosure $0–$50,000
    ___ Commercial foreclosure $50,001–$249,999
    ___ Commercial foreclosure $250,000 or more
    ___ Homestead residential foreclosure $0–$50,000
    ___ Homestead residential foreclosure $50,001–$249,999
    ___ Homestead residential foreclosure $250,000 or more
    ___ Nonhomestead residential foreclosure $0–$50,000
    ___ Nonhomestead residential foreclosure $50,001–$249,999

___ Nonhomestead residential foreclosure $250,000 or more
___ Other real property actions $0–$50,000
___ Other real property actions $50,001–$249,999
___ Other real property actions $250,000 or more
___ Professional malpractice
___ Malpractice—business
___ Malpractice—medical
___ Malpractice—other professional
___ Other
___ Antitrust/Trade regulation
___ Business transactions
___ Constitutional challenge—statute or ordinance
___ Constitutional challenge—proposed amendment
___ Corporate trusts
___ Discrimination—employment or other
___ Insurance claims
___ Intellectual property
___ Libel/Slander
___ Shareholder derivative action
___ Securities litigation
___ Trade secrets
___ Trust litigation

III. REMEDIES SOUGHT (check all that apply):
___ Monetary;
___ Nonmonetary declaratory or injunctive relief;
___ Punitive

IV. NUMBER OF CAUSES OF ACTION: [ ]
(specify) ______________________________
____

V. IS THIS CASE A CLASS ACTION LAWSUIT?
___ yes
___ no

VI. HAS NOTICE OF ANY KNOWN RELATED CASE BEEN FILED?
___ no
___ yes If "yes," list all related cases by name, case number, and court.
____
____

VII. IS JURY TRIAL DEMANDED IN COMPLAINT?
___ yes
___ no

I CERTIFY that the information I have provided in this cover sheet is accurate to the best of my knowledge and belief, and that I have read and will comply with the requirements of Florida Rule of Judicial Administration 2.425.

Signature ______________ Fla. Bar # ______________
Attorney or party (Bar # if attorney)

______________________________ ______________
(type or print name) Date

FORM 1.997. INSTRUCTIONS FOR ATTORNEYS COMPLETING CIVIL COVER SHEET

Plaintiff must file this cover sheet with first paperwork filed in the action or proceeding (except small claims cases or other county court cases, probate, or family cases). Domestic and juvenile cases should be accompanied by a completed Florida Family Law Rules of Procedure Form 12.928, Cover Sheet for Family Court Cases. Failure to file a civil cover sheet in any civil case other than those excepted above may result in sanctions.

I. Case Style. Enter the name of the court, the appropriate case number assigned at the time of filing of the original complaint or petition, the name of the judge assigned (if applicable), and the name (last, first, middle initial) of plaintiff(s) and defendant(s).

II. Type of Case. Place an "X" on the appropriate line. If the cause fits more than one type of case, select the most definitive. If the most definitive label is a subcategory (indented under a broader category label), place an "X" on the category and subcategory lines. Definitions of the cases are provided below in the order they appear on the form.

(A) Condominium—all civil lawsuits pursuant to Chapter 718, Florida Statutes, in which a condominium association is a party.

(B) Contracts and indebtedness—all contract actions relating to promissory notes and other debts, including those arising from the sale of goods, but excluding contract disputes involving condominium associations.

(C) Eminent domain—all matters relating to the taking of private property for public use, including inverse condemnation by state agencies, political subdivisions, or public service corporations.

(D) Auto negligence—all matters arising out of a party's allegedly negligent operation of a motor vehicle.

(E) Negligence—other—all actions sounding in negligence, including statutory claims for relief on account of death or injury, that are not included in other main categories.

(F) Business governance—all matters relating to the management, administration, or control of a company.

(G) Business torts—all matters relating to liability for economic loss allegedly caused by interference with economic or business relationships.

(H) Environmental/Toxic tort—all matters relating to claims that violations of environmental regulatory provisions or exposure to a chemical caused injury or disease.

(I) Third party indemnification—all matters relating to liability transferred to a third party in a financial relationship.

(J) Construction defect—all civil lawsuits in which damage or injury was allegedly caused by defects in the construction of a structure.

(K) Mass tort—all matters relating to a civil action involving numerous plaintiffs against one or more defendants.

(L) Negligent security—all matters involving injury to a person or property allegedly resulting from insufficient security.

(M) Nursing home negligence—all matters involving injury to a nursing home resident resulting from negligence of nursing home staff or facilities.

(N) Premises liability—commercial—all matters involving injury to a person or property allegedly resulting from a defect on the premises of a commercial property.

(O) Premises liability—residential—all matters involving injury to a person or property allegedly resulting from a defect on the premises of a residential property.

(P) Products liability—all matters involving injury to a person or property allegedly resulting from the manufacture or sale of a defective product or from a failure to warn.

(Q) Real property/Mortgage foreclosure—all matters relating to the possession, title, or boundaries of real property. All matters involving foreclosures or sales of real property, including foreclosures associated with condominium associations or condominium units.

(R) Commercial foreclosure—all matters relating to the termination of a business owner's interest in commercial property by a lender to gain title or force a sale to satisfy the unpaid debt secured by the property. Check the category that includes the estimate of the amount in controversy of the claim (section 28.241, Florida Statutes).

(S) Homestead residential foreclosure—all matters relating to the termination of a residential property owner's interest by a lender to gain title or force a sale to satisfy the unpaid debt secured by the property where the property has been granted a homestead exemption.

Check the category that includes the estimate of the amount in controversy of the claim (section 28.241, Florida Statutes).

(T) Nonhomestead residential foreclosure—all matters relating to the termination of a residential property owner's interest by a lender to gain title or force a sale to satisfy the unpaid debt secured by the property where the property has not been granted a homestead exemption. Check the category that includes the estimate of the amount in controversy of the claim (section 28.241, Florida Statutes).

(U) Other real property actions—all matters relating to land, land improvements, or property rights not involving commercial or residential foreclosure. Check the category that includes the estimate of the amount in controversy of the claim (section 28.241, Florida Statutes).

(V) Professional malpractice—all professional malpractice lawsuits.

(W) Malpractice—business—all matters relating to a business's or business person's failure to exercise the degree of care and skill that someone in the same line of work would use under similar circumstances.

(X) Malpractice—medical—all matters relating to a doctor's failure to exercise the degree of care and skill that a physician or surgeon of the same medical specialty would use under similar circumstances.

(Y) Malpractice—other professional—all matters relating to negligence of those other than medical or business professionals.

(Z) Other—all civil matters not included in other categories.

(AA) Antitrust/Trade regulation—all matters relating to unfair methods of competition or unfair or deceptive business acts or practices.

(AB) Business transactions—all matters relating to actions that affect financial or economic interests.

(AC) Constitutional challenge—statute or ordinance—a challenge to a statute or ordinance, citing a violation of the Florida Constitution.

(AD) Constitutional challenge—proposed amendment—a challenge to a legislatively initiated proposed constitutional amendment, but excluding challenges to a citizen-initiated proposed constitutional amendment because the Florida Supreme Court has direct jurisdiction of such challenges.

(AE) Corporate trusts—all matters relating to the business activities of financial services companies or banks acting in a fiduciary capacity for investors.

(AF) Discrimination—employment or other—all matters relating to discrimination, including employment, sex, race, age, handicap, harassment, retaliation, or wages.

(AG) Insurance claims—all matters relating to claims filed with an insurance company.

(AH) Intellectual property—all matters relating to intangible rights protecting commercially valuable products of the human intellect.

(AI) Libel/Slander—all matters relating to written, visual, oral, or aural defamation of character.

(AJ) Shareholder derivative action—all matters relating to actions by a corporation's shareholders to protect and benefit all shareholders against corporate management for improper management.

(AK) Securities litigation—all matters relating to the financial interest or instruments of a company or corporation.

(AL) Trade secrets—all matters relating to a formula, process, device, or other business information that is kept confidential to maintain an advantage over competitors.

(AM) Trust litigation—all civil matters involving guardianships, estates, or trusts and not appropriately filed in probate proceedings.

III. Remedies Sought. Place an "X" on the appropriate line. If more than one remedy is sought in the complaint or petition, check all that apply.

IV. Number of Causes of Action. If the complaint or petition alleges more than one cause of action, note the number and the name of the cause of action.

V. Class Action. Place an "X" on the appropriate line.

VI. Related Cases. Place an "X" on the appropriate line.

VII. Is Jury Trial Demanded In Complaint? Check the appropriate line to indicate whether a jury trial is being demanded in the complaint

ATTORNEY OR PARTY SIGNATURE. Sign the civil cover sheet. Print legibly the name of the person signing the civil cover sheet. Attorneys must include a Florida Bar number. Insert the date the civil cover sheet is signed. Signature is a certification that the filer has provided accurate information on the civil cover sheet**, and has read and complied with the requirements of Florida Rule of Judicial Administration 2.425**.

Added May 1, 1986, effective July 1, 1986 (488 So.2d 57). Amended Oct. 31, 1996, effective Jan. 1, 1997 (682 So.2d 105); Dec. 15, 2005, effective Jan. 1, 2006 (917 So.2d 176); June 3, 2009, effective Jan. 1, 2010 (15 So.3d 558); Oct. 15, 2009, effective Jan. 1, 2010 (30 So.2d 477); Nov. 14, 2013, effective Jan. 1, 2014 (131 So.3d 643).

Form 1.998. Final Disposition Form

This form shall be filed by the prevailing party for the use of the Clerk of Court for the purpose of reporting judicial workload data pursuant to Florida Statutes section 25.075. (See instructions on the reverse of the form.)

I. CASE STYLE

(Name of Court) ______

Plaintiff ______ Case #: ______
______ Judge: ______

vs.

Defendant______
______

II. MEANS OF FINAL DISPOSITION (Place an "x" in one box for major category and one subcategory, if applicable, only)

- ☐ Dismissed Before Hearing
  - ☐ Dismissed Pursuant to Settlement—Before Hearing
  - ☐ Dismissed Pursuant to Mediated Settlement—Before Hearing
  - ☐ Other—Before Hearing
- ☐ Dismissed After Hearing
  - ☐ Dismissed Pursuant to Settlement—After Hearing
  - ☐ Dismissed Pursuant to Mediated Settlement—After Hearing
  - ☐ Other After Hearing—After Hearing
- ☐ Disposed by Default
- ☐ Disposed by Judge
- ☐ Disposed by Non-jury Trial
- ☐ Disposed by Jury Trial
- ☐ Other

DATE ______ ______

SIGNATURE OF ATTORNEY FOR PREVAILING PARTY

INSTRUCTIONS FOR ATTORNEYS COMPLETING FINAL DISPOSITION FORM

I. Case Style. Enter the name of the court, the appropriate case number assigned at the time of filing of the original complaint or petition, the name of the judge assigned to the case and the names (last, first, middle initial) of plaintiff(s) and defendant(s).

II. Means of Final Disposition. Place an "x" in the appropriate major category box and in the appropriate subcategory box, if applicable. The following are the definitions of the disposition categories.

(A) Dismissed Before Hearing—the case is settled, voluntarily dismissed, or otherwise disposed of before a hearing is held;

(B) Dismissal Pursuant to Settlement—Before Hearing—the case is voluntarily dismissed by the plaintiff after a settlement is reached without mediation before a hearing is held;

(C) Dismissal Pursuant to Mediated Settlement—Before Hearing—the case is voluntarily dismissed by the plaintiff after a settlement is reached with mediation before a hearing is held;

(D) Other—Before Hearing—the case is dismissed before hearing in an action that does not fall into one of the other disposition categories listed on this form.

(E) Dismissed After Hearing—the case is dismissed by a judge, voluntarily dismissed, or settled after a hearing is held;

(F) Dismissal Pursuant to Settlement—After Hearing—the case is voluntarily dismissed by the plaintiff after a settlement is reached without mediation after a hearing is held;

(G) Dismissal Pursuant to Mediated Settlement—After Hearing—the case is voluntarily dismissed by the plaintiff after a settlement is reached with mediation after a hearing is held;

(H) Other—After Hearing—the case is dismissed after hearing in an action that does not fall into one of the other disposition categories listed on this form.

(I) Disposed by Default—a defendant chooses not to or fails to contest the plaintiff's allegations and a judgment against the defendant is entered by the court;

(J) Disposed by Judge—a judgment or disposition is reached by the judge in a case that is not dismissed and in which no trial has been held. Includes stipulations by the parties, conditional judgments, summary judgment after hearing, and any matter in which a judgment is entered excluding cases disposed of by default as in category (I) above;

(K) Disposed by Non–Jury Trial—the case is disposed as a result of a contested trial in which there is no jury and in which the judge determines both the issues of fact and law in the case;

(L) Disposed by Jury Trial—the case is disposed as a result of a jury trial (consider the beginning of a jury trial to be when the jurors and alternates are selected and sworn);

(M) Other—the case is consolidated, submitted to arbitration or mediation, transferred, or otherwise disposed of by other means not listed in categories (A) through (L).

DATE AND ATTORNEY SIGNATURE. Date and sign the final disposition form.

Added May 1, 1986, effective July 1, 1986 (488 So.2d 57). Amended June 3, 2009 (15 So.3d 558); Oct. 15, 2009 (30 So.3d 477).

Form 1.999. Order Designating a Case Complex

This form order is for designating a case complex under rule 1.201 and directing the clerk of court to update the court's records and to report the case activity to the Supreme Court.

ORDER DESIGNATING CASE A "COMPLEX CASE" DIRECTIONS TO THE CLERK OF COURT

THIS CAUSE was considered on [the court's own motion] [the motion of a party] to designate this case a "complex case" as defined in rule 1.201, Fla. R. Civ. P. Being fully advised in the circumstances, the court determines that the case meets the criteria for proceeding under the rule and designates it as a "complex case."

The clerk of the court shall designate this case a "complex case," update the court's records accordingly, and report such designation and the case activity to the Supreme Court pursuant to section 25.075, Florida Statutes, and rule 2.245(a), Fla. R. Jud. Admin.

DONE AND ORDERED at ...., County, Florida, on .... (date) ....

____
Judge

Added June 3, 2009 (15 So.3d 558).

APPENDIX I

STANDARD INTERROGATORIES FORMS

Form 1. General Personal Injury Negligence—Interrogatories to Plaintiff

(If answering for another person or entity, answer with respect to that person or entity, unless otherwise stated.)

1. What is the name and address of the person answering these interrogatories, and, if applicable, the person's official position or relationship with the party to whom the interrogatories are directed?

2. List the names, business addresses, dates of employment, and rates of pay regarding all employers, including self-employment, for whom you have worked in the past 10 years.

3. List all former names and when you were known by those names. State all addresses where you have lived for the past 10 years, the dates you lived at each address, your Social Security number, your date of birth, and, if you are or have ever been married, the name of your spouse or spouses.

4. Do you wear glasses, contact lenses, or hearing aids? If so, who prescribed them, when were they prescribed, when were your eyes or ears last examined, and what is the name and address of the examiner?

5. Have you ever been convicted of a crime, other than any juvenile adjudication, which under the law under which you were convicted was punishable by death or imprisonment in excess of 1 year, or that involved dishonesty or a false statement regardless of the punishment? If so, state as to each conviction the specific crime and the date and place of conviction.

6. Were you suffering from physical infirmity, disability, or sickness at the time of the incident described in the complaint? If so, what was the nature of the infirmity, disability, or sickness?

7. Did you consume any alcoholic beverages or take any drugs or medications within 12 hours before the time of the incident described in the complaint? If so, state the type and amount of alcoholic beverages, drugs, or medication which were consumed, and when and where you consumed them.

8. Describe in detail how the incident described in the complaint happened, including all actions taken by you to prevent the incident.

9. Describe in detail each act or omission on the part of any party to this lawsuit that you contend constituted negligence that was a contributing legal cause of the incident in question.

10. Were you charged with any violation of law (including any regulations or ordinances) arising out of the incident described in the complaint? If so, what was the nature of the charge; what plea or answer, if any, did you enter to the charge; what court or agency heard the charge; was any written report prepared by anyone regarding this charge, and, if so, what is the name and address of the person or entity that prepared the report; do you have a copy of the report; and was the testimony at any trial, hearing, or other proceeding on the charge recorded in any manner, and, if so, what is the name and address of the person who recorded the testimony?

11. Describe each injury for which you are claiming damages in this case, specifying the part of your body that was injured, the nature of the injury, and, as to any injuries you contend are permanent, the effects on you that you claim are permanent.

12. List each item of expense or damage, other than loss of income or earning capacity, that you claim to have incurred as a result of the incident described in the complaint, giving for each item the date incurred, the name and business address of the person or entity to whom each was paid or is owed, and the goods or services for which each was incurred.

13. Do you contend that you have lost any income, benefits, or earning capacity in the past or future as a result of the incident described in the complaint? If so, state the nature of the income, benefits, or earning capacity, and the amount and the method that you used in computing the amount.

14. Has anything been paid or is anything payable from any third party for the damages listed in your answers to these interrogatories? If so, state the amounts paid or payable, the name and business address of the person or entity who paid or owes said amounts, and which of those third parties have or claim a right of subrogation.

15. List the names and business addresses of each physician who has treated or examined you, and each medical facility where you have received any treatment or examination for the injuries for which you seek damages in this case; and state as to each the

date of treatment or examination and the injury or condition for which you were examined or treated.

16. List the names and business addresses of all other physicians, medical facilities, or other health care providers by whom or at which you have been examined or treated in the past 10 years; and state as to each the dates of examination or treatment and the condition or injury for which you were examined or treated.

17. List the names and addresses of all persons who are believed or known by you, your agents, or your attorneys to have any knowledge concerning any of the issues in this lawsuit; and specify the subject matter about which the witness has knowledge.

18. Have you heard or do you know about any statement or remark made by or on behalf of any party to this lawsuit, other than yourself, concerning any issue in this lawsuit? If so, state the name and address of each person who made the statement or statements, the name and address of each person who heard it, and the date, time, place, and substance of each statement.

19. State the name and address of every person known to you, your agents, or your attorneys, who has knowledge about, or possession, custody, or control of, any model, plat, map, drawing, motion picture, videotape, or photograph pertaining to any fact or issue involved in this controversy; and describe as to each, what item such person has, the name and address of the person who took or prepared it, and the date it was taken or prepared.

20. Do you intend to call any expert witnesses at the trial of this case? If so, state as to each such witness the name and business address of the witness, the witness's qualifications as an expert, the subject matter upon which the witness is expected to testify, the substance of the facts and opinions to which the witness is expected to testify, and a summary of the grounds for each opinion.

21. Have you made an agreement with anyone that would limit that party's liability to anyone for any of the damages sued upon in this case? If so, state the terms of the agreement and the parties to it.

22. Please state if you have ever been a party, either plaintiff or defendant, in a lawsuit other than the present matter, and, if so, state whether you were plaintiff or defendant, the nature of the action, and the date and court in which such suit was filed.

Added April 4, 1991 (577 So.2d 580). Amended July 16, 1992, effective Jan. 1, 1993 (604 So.2d 1110).

Form 2. General Personal Injury Negligence—Interrogatories to Defendant

(If answering for another person or entity, answer with respect to that person or entity, unless otherwise stated.)

1. What is the name and address of the person answering these interrogatories, and, if applicable, the person's official position or relationship with the party to whom the interrogatories are directed?

2. List all former names and when you were known by those names. State all addresses where you have lived for the past 10 years, the dates you lived at each address, your Social Security number, and your date of birth.

3. Have you ever been convicted of a crime, other than any juvenile adjudication, which under the law under which you were convicted was punishable by death or imprisonment in excess of 1 year, or that involved dishonesty or a false statement regardless of the punishment? If so, state as to each conviction, the specific crime and the date and place of conviction.

4. Describe any and all policies of insurance which you contend cover or may cover you for the allegations set forth in plaintiff's complaint, detailing as to such policies the name of the insurer, the number of the policy, the effective dates of the policy, the available limits of liability, and the name and address of the custodian of the policy.

5. Describe in detail how the incident described in the complaint happened, including all actions taken by you to prevent the incident.

6. Describe in detail each act or omission on the part of any party to this lawsuit that you contend constituted negligence that was a contributing legal cause of the incident in question.

7. State the facts upon which you rely for each affirmative defense in your answer.

8. Do you contend any person or entity other than you is, or may be, liable in whole or part for the claims asserted against you in this lawsuit? If so, state the full name and address of each such person or entity, the legal basis for your contention, the facts or evidence upon which your contention is based, and whether or not you have notified each such person or entity of your contention.

9. Were you charged with any violation of law (including any regulations or ordinances) arising out of the incident described in the complaint? If so, what was the nature of the charge; what plea or answer, if any, did you enter to the charge; what court or agency heard the charge; was any written report prepared by anyone regarding the charge, and, if so, what is the name and address of the person or entity who prepared the report; do you have a copy of the report; and was the testimony at any trial, hearing, or other proceeding on the charge recorded in any manner, and, if so, what is the name and address of the person who recorded the testimony?

10. List the names and addresses of all persons who are believed or known by you, your agents, or your attorneys to have any knowledge concerning any of the issues in this lawsuit; and specify the subject matter about which the witness has knowledge.

11. Have you heard or do you know about any statement or remark made by or on behalf of any party to this lawsuit, other than yourself, concerning any issue in this lawsuit? If so, state the name and address of each person who made the statement or statements, the name and address of each person who heard it, and the date, time, place, and substance of each statement.

12. State the name and address of every person known to you, your agents, or your attorneys who has knowledge about, or possession, custody, or control of, any model, plat, map, drawing, motion picture, videotape, or photograph pertaining to any fact or issue involved in this controversy; and describe as to each, what item such person has, the name and address of the person who took or prepared it, and the date it was taken or prepared.

13. Do you intend to call any expert witnesses at the trial of this case? If so, state as to each such witness the name and business address of the witness, the witness's qualifications as an expert, the subject matter upon which the witness is expected to testify, the substance of the facts and opinions to which the witness is expected to testify, and a summary of the grounds for each opinion.

14. Have you made an agreement with anyone that would limit that party's liability to anyone for any of the damages sued upon in this case? If so, state the terms of the agreement and the parties to it.

15. Please state if you have ever been a party, either plaintiff or defendant, in a lawsuit other than the present matter, and, if so, state whether you were plaintiff or defendant, the nature of the action, and the date and court in which such suit was filed.

Added April 4, 1991 (577 So.2d 580). Amended July 16, 1992, effective Jan. 1, 1993 (604 So.2d 1110).

Form 3. Medical Malpractice—Interrogatories to Plaintiff

(These interrogatories should be used in conjunction with the General Personal Injury Negligence Interrogatories to Plaintiff.)

23. Do you contend that you have experienced any injury or illness as a result of any negligence of this defendant? If so, state the date that each such injury occurred, a description of how the injury was caused, and the exact nature of each such injury.

24. What condition, symptom, or illness caused you to obtain medical care and treatment from this defendant?

25. Do you claim this defendant neglected to inform or instruct or warn you of any risk relating to your condition, care, or treatment? If so, state of what, in your opinion, the defendant failed to inform, instruct, or warn you.

26. If you contend that you were not properly informed by this defendant regarding the risk of the treatment or the procedure performed, state what alternative treatment or procedure, if any, you would have undergone had you been properly informed.

27. State the date and place and a description of each complaint for which you contend the defendant refused to attend or treat you.

28. State the date you became aware of the injuries sued on in this action, and describe in detail the circumstances under which you became aware of each such injury; state the date you became aware that the injuries sued on in this action were caused or may have been caused by medical negligence; and describe in detail the circumstances under which you became aware of the cause of said injuries.

29. State the name and address of every person or organization to whom you have given notice of the occurrence sued on in this case because you, your agents, or your attorneys believe that person or organization may be liable in whole or in part to you.

Added April 4, 1991 (577 So.2d 580). Amended July 16, 1992, effective Jan. 1, 1993 (604 So.2d 1110).

Form 4. Medical Malpractice—Interrogatories to Defendant

(These interrogatories should be used in conjunction with the General Personal Injury Negligence Interrogatories to Defendant.)

NOTE: When the word "Plaintiff" is mentioned, these interrogatories are directed to be answered regarding (name of plaintiff/patient).

16. Please give us your entire educational background, starting with your college education and chronologically indicating by date and place each school, college, course of study, title of seminars, length of study, and honors received by you up to the present time, including internships, residencies, degrees received, licenses earned or revoked, medical specialty training, board memberships, authorship of any books, articles, or texts, including the names of those writings and their location in medical journals, awards or honors received, and continuing medical education.

17. Please give us your entire professional background up to the present time, including dates of employment or association, the names of all physicians with whom you have practiced, the form of employment or business relationship such as whether by partnership, corporation, or sole proprietorship, and the dates of the relationships, including hospital staff privileges and positions, and teaching experience.

18. With respect to your office library or usual place of work, give us the name, author, name of publisher, and date of publication of every medical book or article, journal, or medical text, to which you had access, which deals with the overall subject matter described in paragraph [whatever paragraph number that concerns negligence] of the complaint. (In

lieu of answering this interrogatory you may allow plaintiff's counsel to inspect your library at a reasonable time.)

19. If you believe there was any risk to the treatment you rendered to the plaintiff, state the nature of all risks, including whether the risks were communicated to the plaintiff; when, where, and in what manner they were communicated; and whether any of the risks in fact occurred.

20. Tell us your experience in giving the kind of treatment or examination that you rendered to the plaintiff before it was given to the plaintiff, giving us such information as the approximate number of times you have given similar treatment or examinations, where the prior treatment or examinations took place, and the successful or unsuccessful nature of the outcome of that treatment or those examinations.

21. Please identify, with sufficient particularity to formulate the basis of a request to produce, all medical records of any kind of which you are aware which deal with the medical treatment or examinations furnished to the plaintiff at any time, whether by you or another person or persons.

22. Please state whether any claim for medical malpractice has ever been made against you alleging facts relating to the same or similar subject matter as this lawsuit, and, if so, state as to each such claim the names of the parties, the claim number, the date of the alleged incident, the ultimate disposition of the claim, and the name of your attorney, if any.

Added April 4, 1991 (577 So.2d 580). Amended July 16, 1992, effective Jan. 1, 1993 (604 So.2d 1110).

Form 5. Automobile Negligence—Interrogatories to Plaintiff

(These interrogatories should be used in conjunction with the General Personal Injury Negligence Interrogatories to Plaintiff.)

23. At the time of the incident described in the complaint, were you wearing a seat belt? If not, please state why not; where you were seated in the vehicle; and whether the vehicle was equipped with a seat belt that was operational and available for your use.

24. Did any mechanical defect in the motor vehicle in which you were riding at the time of the incident described in the complaint contribute to the incident? If so, describe the nature of the defect and how it contributed to the incident.

Added April 4, 1991 (577 So.2d 580). Amended July 16, 1992, effective Jan. 1, 1993 (604 So.2d 1110).

Form 6. Automobile Negligence—Interrogatories to Defendant

(These interrogatories should be used in conjunction with the General Personal Injury Negligence Interrogatories to Defendant.)

16. Do you wear glasses, contact lenses, or hearing aids? If so, who prescribed them, when were they prescribed, when were your eyes or ears last examined, and what is the name and address of the examiner?

17. Were you suffering from physical infirmity, disability, or sickness at the time of the incident described in the complaint? If so, what was the nature of the infirmity, disability, or sickness?

18. Did you consume any alcoholic beverages or take any drugs or medications within 12 hours before the time of the incident described in the complaint? If so, state the type and amount of alcoholic beverages, drugs, or medication which were consumed, and when and where you consumed them.

19. Did any mechanical defect in the motor vehicle in which you were riding at the time of the incident described in the complaint contribute to the incident? If so, describe the nature of the defect and how it contributed to the incident.

20. List the name and address of all persons, corporations, or entities who were registered title owners or who had ownership interest in, or right to control, the motor vehicle that the defendant driver was driving at the time of the incident described in the complaint; and describe both the nature of the ownership interest or right to control the vehicle, and the vehicle itself, including the make, model, year, and vehicle identification number.

21. At the time of the incident described in the complaint, did the driver of the vehicle described in your answer to the preceding interrogatory have permission to drive the vehicle? If so, state the names and addresses of all persons who have such permission.

22. At the time of the incident described in the complaint, was the defendant driver engaged in any mission or activity for any other person or entity, including any employer? If so, state the name and address of that person or entity and the nature of the mission or activity.

23. Was the motor vehicle that the defendant driver was driving at the time of the incident described in the complaint damaged in the incident, and, if so, what was the cost to repair the damage?

Added April 4, 1991 (577 So.2d 580). Amended July 16, 1992, effective Jan. 1, 1993 (604 So.2d 1110).

APPENDIX II

STATEWIDE UNIFORM GUIDELINES FOR TAXATION OF COSTS IN CIVIL ACTIONS

Statewide Uniform Guidelines for Taxation of Costs in Civil Actions

Purpose and Application. These guidelines are advisory only. The taxation of costs in any particular proceeding is within the broad discretion of the trial court. The trial court should exercise that discretion in a manner that is consistent with the policy of reducing the overall costs of litigation and of keeping such costs as low as justice will permit. With this goal in mind, the trial court should consider and reward utilization of innovation technologies by a party which subsequently minimizes costs and reduce the award when use of innovation technologies that were not used would have resulted in lowering costs. In addition, these guidelines are not intended to (1) limit the amount of costs recoverable under a contract or statute, or (2) prejudice the rights of any litigant objecting to an assessment of costs on the basis that the assessment is contrary to applicable substantive law.

Burden of Proof. Under these guidelines, it is the burden of the moving party to show that all requested costs were reasonably necessary either to defend or prosecute the case at the time the action precipitating the cost was taken.

I. Litigation Costs That Should Be Taxed.

A. Depositions.

1. The original and one copy of the deposition and court reporter's per diem for all depositions.

2. The original and/or one copy of the electronic deposition and the cost of the services of a technician for electronic depositions used at trial.

3. Telephone toll and electronic conferencing charges for the conduct of telephone and electronic depositions.

B. Documents and Exhibits.

1. The costs of copies of documents filed (in lieu of "actually cited") with the court, which are reasonably necessary to assist the court in reaching a conclusion.

2. The costs of copies obtained in discovery, even if the copies were not used at trial.

C. Expert Witnesses.

1. A reasonable fee for deposition and/or trial testimony, and the costs of preparation of any court ordered report.

D. Witnesses.

1. Costs of subpoena, witness fee, and service of witnesses for deposition and/or trial.

E. Court Reporting Costs Other than for Depositions.

1. Reasonable court reporter's per diem for the reporting of evidentiary hearings, trial and post-trial hearings.

F. Reasonable Charges Incurred for Requiring Special Magistrates, Guardians Ad Litem, and Attorneys Ad Litem.

II. Litigation Costs That May Be Taxed as Costs.

A. Mediation Fees and Expenses.

1. Costs and fees of mediator.

B. Reasonable Travel Expenses.

1. Reasonable travel expenses of expert when traveling in excess of 100 miles from the expert's principal place of business (not to include the expert's time).

2. Reasonable travel expenses of witnesses.

C. Electronic Discovery Expenses.

1. The cost of producing copies of relevant electronic media in response to a discovery request.

2. The cost of converting electronically stored information to a reasonably usable format in response to a discovery request that seeks production in such format.

III. Litigation Costs That Should Not Be Taxed as Costs.

A. The Cost of Long Distance Telephone Calls with Witnesses, both Expert and Non–Expert (including conferences concerning scheduling of depositions or requesting witnesses to attend trial)

B. Any Expenses Relating to Consulting But Non–Testifying Experts

C. Cost Incurred in Connection with Any Matter Which Was Not Reasonably Calculated to Lead to the Discovery of Admissible Evidence

D. Travel Time.

1. Travel time of attorney(s).

2. Travel time of expert(s).

E. Travel Expenses of Attorney(s).

F. The Cost of Privilege Review of Documents, including Electronically Stored Information.

Amended Nov. 17, 2005, effective Jan. 1, 2006 (915 So.2d 612); Nov. 14, 2013, effective Jan. 1, 2014 (131 So.3d 643).

INDEX TO FLORIDA RULES OF CIVIL PROCEDURE

FLORIDA RULES OF JUDICIAL ADMINISTRATION

Adoption

Adopted June 30, 1978, effective July 1, 1978 (360 So.2d 1076)

PART I. GENERAL PROVISIONS

Rule 2.110. Scope and Purpose

These rules, cited as "Florida Rules of Judicial Administration" and abbreviated as "Fla. R. Jud. Admin.," shall take effect at 12:01 a.m. on July 1, 1979. They shall apply to administrative matters in all courts to which the rules are applicable by their terms. The rules shall be construed to secure the speedy and inexpensive determination of every proceeding to which they are applicable. These rules shall supersede all conflicting rules and statutes.

Former Rule 2.010 amended June 14, 1979, effective July 1, 1979 (372 So.2d 449); Oct. 8, 1992, effective Jan. 1, 1993 (609 So.2d 465). Renumbered from Rule 2.010 Sept. 21, 2006 (939 So.2d 966).

Rule 2.120. Definitions

The following terms have the meanings shown as used in these rules:

(a) Court Rule: A rule of practice or procedure adopted to facilitate the uniform conduct of litigation applicable to all proceedings, all parties, and all attorneys.

(b) Local Court Rule:

(1) A rule of practice or procedure for circuit or county application only that, because of local conditions, supplies an omission in or facilitates application of a rule of statewide application and does not conflict therewith.

(2) A rule that addresses other matters that are required by the Florida Constitution, general law, rules of court, or a supreme court opinion to be adopted by or in a local rule.

(c) Administrative Order: A directive necessary to administer properly the court's affairs but not inconsistent with the constitution or with court rules and administrative orders entered by the supreme court.

Former Rule 2.020 amended June 14, 1979, effective July 1, 1979 (372 So.2d 449); Oct. 8, 1992, effective Jan. 1, 1993 (609 So.2d 465); Oct. 5, 2000, effective Jan. 1, 2001 (780 So.2d 819). Renumbered from Rule 2.020 Sept. 21, 2006 (939 So.2d 966).

Rule 2.130. Priority of Florida Rules of Appellate Procedure

The Florida Rules of Appellate Procedure shall control all proceedings in the supreme court and the district courts, and all proceedings in which the circuit courts exercise their appellate jurisdiction, notwithstanding any conflicting rules of procedure.

Former Rule 2.135 added Oct. 24, 1996, effective Jan. 1, 1997 (682 So.2d 89). Renumbered from Rule 2.135 Sept. 21, 2006 (939 So.2d 966). Amended July 10, 2008, effective Jan. 1, 2009 (986 So.2d 560).

Rule 2.140. Amending Rules of Court

(a) Amendments Generally. The following procedure shall be followed for consideration of rule amendments generally other than those adopted under subdivisions (d), (e), (f), and (g):

(1) Proposals for court rules, amendments to them, or abrogation of them may be made by any person.

(2) Proposals shall be submitted to the clerk of the supreme court in writing and shall include a general description of the proposed rule change or a specified proposed change in content. The clerk of the supreme court shall refer proposals to the appropriate committee under subdivision (a)(3).

(3) The Florida Bar shall appoint the following committees to consider rule proposals: Civil Procedure Rules Committee, Criminal Procedure Rules Committee, Small Claims Rules Committee, Traffic Court Rules Committee, Appellate Court Rules Committee, Juvenile Court Rules Committee, Code and Rules of Evidence Committee, Rules of Judicial Administration Committee, Probate Rules Committee, and Family Law Rules Committee.

(4) Each committee shall be composed of attorneys and judges with extensive experience and training in the area of practice of the committee calling for regular, frequent use of the rules. The members of the committee shall serve for 3–year staggered terms. The president of The Florida Bar shall appoint the chair and vice chair of each committee.

(5) The committees shall consider and vote on each proposal. The committees may originate proposals and are charged with the duty of regular review and reevaluation of the rules to advance orderly and inexpensive procedures in the administration of justice. The committees may accept or reject proposed amendments or may amend proposals. The committees shall keep minutes of their activities, which minutes shall reflect the action taken on each proposal. Copies of the minutes shall be furnished to the clerk of the supreme court, to the board of governors of The Florida Bar, and to the proponent of any proposal considered at the meeting.

(6) The Rules of Judicial Administration Committee shall also serve as a rules coordinating committee. Each rules committee shall have at least 1 of its members appointed to the Rules of Judicial Administration Committee to serve as liaison. All committees shall provide a copy of any proposed rules changes to the Rules of Judicial Administration Committee within 30 days of a committee's affirmative vote to recommend the proposed change to the supreme court. The Rules of Judicial Administration Committee shall then refer all proposed rules changes to those rules committees that might be affected by the proposed change.

(7) Whenever the Rules of Judicial Administration Committee receives a request to coordinate the submission of a single comprehensive report of proposed rule amendments on behalf of multiple rules committees, the general procedure shall be as follows:

(A) The subcommittee chairs handling the matter for each committee will constitute an ad hoc committee to discuss the various committees' recommendations and to formulate time frames for the joint response. The chair of the ad hoc committee will be the assigned Rules of Judicial Administration Committee subcommittee chair.

(B) At the conclusion of the work of the ad hoc committee, a proposed joint response will be prepared by the ad hoc committee and distributed to the committee chairs for each committee's review and final comments.

(C) The Rules of Judicial Administration Committee shall be responsible for filing the comprehensive final report.

(b) Schedule for Rules Proposals.

(1) Each committee shall report all proposed rule changes on a staggered basis (with the first cycle starting in 2006). Reports shall be made by the Criminal Procedure Rules Committee, the Traffic Court Rules Committee, and the Juvenile Court Rules Committee in 2006; by the Civil Procedure Rules Committee, the Probate Rules Committee, the Small Claims Rules Committee, and the Code and Rules of Evidence Committee in 2007; and by the Family Law Rules Committee, the Appellate Court Rules Committee, and the Rules of Judicial Administration Committee in 2008. Thereafter, the cycle shall repeat.

(2) No later than June 15 of the year prior to each reporting year or such other date as the board of governors of The Florida Bar may set, each reporting committee shall submit all proposed rule changes to the board of governors with the committee's final numerical voting record on each proposal. Contemporaneously with reporting proposed rule changes to the board of governors, each committee report shall be furnished to the Speaker of the Florida House of Representatives, the President of the Florida Senate, and the chairs of the House and Senate committees as designated by the Speaker and the President, and published on the Internet website of The Florida Bar, and in the Florida Bar Journal or Florida Bar News. Any person desiring to comment upon proposed rule changes shall submit written comments to the appropriate committee chair no later than August 1 of the year prior to each reporting year. Each committee shall consider any comments submitted and thereafter report to the board of governors, no later than October 15 of the year prior to each reporting year, any revisions to the proposed rule changes. Contemporaneously with reporting any revisions to the board of governors, each committee's revised proposed rule changes shall be furnished to the Speaker of the Florida House of Representatives, the President of the Florida Senate, and the chairs of the House and Senate committees as designated by the Speaker and the President, and published on the Internet website of The Florida Bar, and in the Florida Bar Journal or Florida Bar News. Any person desiring to comment thereafter shall submit written comments to the supreme court in accordance with subdivision (b)(6).

(3) No later than December 15 of the year prior to each reporting year, the board of governors shall consider the proposals and shall vote on each proposal to recommend acceptance, rejection, or amendment.

(4) No later than February 1 of each reporting year, each committee shall file a report of its proposed rule changes with the supreme court. Each committee may amend its recommendations to coincide with the recommendations of the board of governors or may decline to do so or may amend its recommendations in another manner. Any such amendments shall also be reported to the supreme court. The report and proposed rule changes must conform to the Guidelines for Rules Submissions approved by administrative order and posted on the Internet websites of the supreme court and The Florida Bar. Consistent with the requirements that are fully set forth in the Guidelines, the report shall include:

(A) a list of the proposed changes, together with a detailed explanation of each proposal that includes a narrative description of how each amendment changes the language of the rule and a thorough discussion of the reason for each change;

(B) the final numerical voting record of the proposals in the committee;

(C) the name and address of the proponent of each change, if other than the rules committee;

(D) a report of the action taken by the committee on comments submitted in accordance with subdivision (b)(2);

(E) a report of the action and voting record of the board of governors;

(F) any dissenting views of the committee and, if available, of the board; and

(G) an appendix containing all comments submitted to the committee, all relevant background documents, and a two-column chart setting forth the proposed changes in legislative format in the first column and a brief explanation of each change in the second column.

The report and the proposed rule changes shall be filed with the supreme court, in legislative format, both on paper and in an electronic format approved by the supreme court.

(5) If oral argument is deemed necessary, the supreme court shall establish a date during the month of May or June of each reporting year for oral argument on the proposals. Notice of the hearing on the proposals and a copy of the proposals shall be furnished to the affected committee chair and vice chair, the executive director of The Florida Bar, all members of the Judicial Management Council, the clerk and chief judge of each district court of appeal, the clerk and chief judge of each judicial circuit, the Speaker of the Florida House of Representatives, the President of the Florida Senate, the chairs of the House and Senate committees as designated by the Speaker and the President, and any person who has asked in writing filed with the clerk of the supreme court for a copy of the notice. The clerk may provide the notice electronically. If the committee modifies its recommendations after considering comments submitted in accordance with subdivision (b)(2), the recommendations or a resume of them shall be published on the Internet websites of the supreme court and The Florida Bar and in the Florida Bar Journal or Florida Bar News before the hearing. Notice of the hearing shall also be published on the Internet websites of the supreme court and The Florida Bar and in the Florida Bar Journal or Florida Bar News.

(6) Before the date of oral argument, any person may file comments concerning the proposals. All comments and other submissions by interested persons shall be filed with the clerk of the supreme court and served on the chair of the appropriate rules committee, and on the proponent of the rule change if other than the rules committee. The chair of the rules committee shall file a response to all comments within the time period set by the court. All comments and other submissions regarding the rule change proposals, in addition to being filed with the supreme court in paper format, shall also be filed in an electronic format approved by the supreme court. Prior to the date of oral argument and as soon as practicable after the date of filing, the clerk of the supreme court shall publish on the Internet websites of the supreme court and The Florida Bar all comments and the responses of the chair of the rules committee that have been filed concerning the rule change proposals. All requests or submissions by a rules committee made in connection with a pending rule change proposal shall be filed with the clerk of the supreme court and thereafter published by the clerk of the supreme court on the Internet websites of the supreme court and The Florida Bar.

(7) Orders of the supreme court on said proposals should be adopted in sufficient time to take effect on January 1 of the year following the reporting year. The supreme court may permit motions for rehearing to be filed on behalf of any person, The Florida Bar, any bar association, and the affected committee.

(c) Rejected Proposals. If a committee rejects a proposal, the proponent may submit the proposed rule to the board of governors and shall notify the chair and vice chair of the affected committee of the submission of the proposed rule to the board of governors. Minority reports of committees are allowed and may be submitted to both the board of governors and the supreme court.

(d) Emergency Amendments by Court. The supreme court, with or without notice, may change court rules at any time if an emergency exists that does not permit reference to the appropriate committee of The Florida Bar for recommendations. If a change is made without reference to the committee, the change may become effective immediately or at a future time. In either event, the court shall fix a date for further consideration of the change. Any person may file comments concerning the change, seeking its abrogation or a delay in the effective date, in accordance with the procedures set forth in subdivision (b)(6) of this rule. The court may allow oral argument in support of such comments by The Florida Bar, by its sections and committees, and by other bar associations. Notice of the hearing on the change and a copy of the change shall be furnished to the affected committee chair and vice chair, the executive director of The Florida Bar, all members of the Judicial Management Council, the clerk and chief judge of each district court of appeal, the clerk and chief judge of each judicial circuit, the Speaker of the Florida House of Representatives, the President of the Florida Senate, the chairs of the House and Senate committees as designated by the Speaker and the President, and any person who has asked in writing filed with the clerk of the supreme court for a copy of the notice. The clerk may provide the notice electronically. The change shall be published on the Internet websites of the supreme court and The Florida Bar, and in the Florida Bar Journal or Florida Bar News before the hearing. Notice of the hearing shall also be published on the Internet websites of the supreme court and The Florida Bar, and in the Florida Bar Journal or Florida Bar News.

(e) Emergency Recommendations by Committee. If, in the opinion of a committee, a proposal is of an emergency nature, and the board of governors concurs, proposals may be made at any time to the supreme court. The report and proposed rule changes must conform to the Guidelines for Rules Submissions approved by administrative order and posted on the Internet websites of the supreme court and The Florida Bar. If the court agrees that an emergency exists, the court may set a time for oral argument and consideration of the proposal. Notice of the hearing on the proposals and a copy of the proposals shall be furnished to the affected committee chair and vice chair, the executive director of The Florida Bar, all members of the Judicial Management Council, the clerk and chief judge of each district court of appeal, the clerk and chief judge of each judicial circuit, the Speaker of the Florida House of Representatives, the President of the Florida Senate, the chairs of the House and Senate committees as designated by the Speaker and the President, and any person who has asked in writing filed with the clerk of the supreme court for a copy of the notice. The clerk may provide the notice electronically. The recommendations or a resume of them shall be published on the Internet websites of the supreme court and The Florida Bar, and in the Florida Bar Journal or Florida Bar News before the hearing. Notice of the hearing shall also be published on the Internet websites of the supreme court and The Florida Bar, and in the Florida Bar Journal or Florida Bar News.

(f) Request by Court. The supreme court may direct special consideration of a proposal at times other than those specified in this rule and may require a committee to report its recommendation with the recommendations of the board of governors. All requests or submissions by a rules committee made in connection with a request under this subdivision shall be filed with the clerk of the supreme court. The report and proposed rule changes must conform to the Guidelines for Rules Submissions approved by administrative order and posted on the Internet websites of the supreme court and The Florida Bar. The supreme court may set oral argument on the report at any time. Notice of the hearing on the proposals and a copy of the proposals shall be furnished to the affected committee chair and vice chair, the executive director of The Florida Bar, all members of the Judicial Management Council, the clerk and chief judge of each district court of appeal, the clerk and chief judge of each judicial circuit, the Speaker of the Florida House of Representatives, the President of the Florida Senate, the chairs of the House and Senate committees as designated by the Speaker and the President, and any person who has asked in writing filed with the clerk of the supreme court for a copy of the notice. The clerk may provide the notice electronically. The recommendations or a resume of them shall be published on the Internet websites of the supreme court and The Florida Bar, and in the Florida Bar Journal or Florida Bar News before the hearing. Notice of the hearing shall also be published on the Internet websites of the supreme court and The Florida Bar, and in the Florida Bar Journal or Florida Bar News.

(g) Amendments to the Rules of Judicial Administration.

(1) *Amendments Without Referral to Rules Committee.* Changes to the Rules of Judicial Administration contained in Part II, State Court Administration, of these rules, and rules 2.310, and 2.320, contained in Part III, Judicial Officers, generally will be considered and adopted by the supreme court without reference to or proposal from the Rules of Judicial Administration Committee. The supreme court may amend rules under this subdivision at any time, with or without notice. If a change is made without notice, the court shall fix a date for future consideration of the change and the change shall be published on the Internet websites of the supreme court and The Florida Bar and in the Florida Bar Journal or Florida Bar News. Any person may file comments concerning the change, in accordance with the procedures set forth in subdivision (b)(6) of this rule. The court may hear oral argument on the change. Notice of the hearing on the change and a copy of the change shall be provided in accordance with subdivision (d) of this rule.

(2) *Other Amendments.* Amendments to all other Rules of Judicial Administration shall be referred to or proposed by the Rules of Judicial Administration Committee and adopted by the supreme court as provided in subdivisions (a), (b), (c), (d), (e), and (f) of this rule.

(h) Local Rules Proposed by Trial Courts. The foregoing procedure shall not apply to local rules proposed by a majority of circuit and county judges in the circuit. The chief justice of the supreme court may appoint a Local Rule Advisory Committee to consider and make recommendations to the court concerning local rules and administrative orders submitted pursuant to rule 2.215(e).

Former Rule 2.130 amended June 14, 1979, effective July 1, 1979 (372 So.2d 449); July 17, 1980, effective Jan. 1, 1981 (389 So.2d 202); Sept. 13, 1984, effective Jan. 1, 1985 (458 So.2d 1110); June 8, 1987, effective July 1, 1987 (509 So.2d 276); Oct. 8, 1992, effective Jan. 1, 1993 (609 So.2d 465); Oct. 22, 1992 (607 So.2d 396); Oct. 5, 2000, effective Jan. 1, 2001 (780 So.2d 819); Sept. 19, 2002 (826 So.2d 233); July 10, 2003 (851 So.2d 698); Nov. 3, 2005 (915 So.2d 157). Renumbered from 2.130 Sept. 21, 2006 (939 So.2d 966). Amended July 10, 2008, effective Jan. 1, 2009 (986 So.2d 560); Feb. 7, 2013, effective Feb. 7, 2013 (124 So.3d 807)

Committee Notes

1980 Amendment. Rule 2.130 is entirely rewritten to codify the procedures for changes to all Florida rules of procedure as set forth by this court in *In re Rules of Court: Procedure for Consideration of Proposals Concerning Practice and Procedure*, 276 So. 2d 467 (Fla. 1972), and to update those procedures based on current practice. The Supreme Court Rules Advisory Committee has been abolished, and the Local Rules Advisory Committee has been established.

PART II. STATE COURT ADMINISTRATION

Rule 2.205. The Supreme Court

(a) Internal Government.

(1) *Exercise of Powers and Jurisdiction.*

(A) The supreme court shall exercise its powers, including establishing policy for the judicial branch, and jurisdiction en banc. Five justices shall constitute a quorum and the concurrence of 4 shall be necessary to a decision. In cases requiring only a panel of 5, if 4 of the 5 justices who consider the case do not concur, it shall be submitted to the other 2 justices.

(B) Consistent with the authority of the supreme court to establish policy, including recommending state budget and compensation priorities for the judicial branch, no judge, supreme court created committee, commission, task force, or similar group, and no conference (Conference of District Court of Appeal Judges, Conference of Circuit Court Judges, Conference of County Court Judges) is permitted to recommend state budget priorities, including compensation and benefits, to the legislative or executive branch that have not been approved by the supreme court. This subdivision is not intended to apply to judges expressing their personal views who affirmatively state that they are not speaking on behalf of the judicial branch.

(C) Newly created judicial branch commissions, committees, task forces, work groups, and similar study or advisory groups must be established by the supreme court, not solely by the chief justice. Such study or advisory groups may be created and charged by rule adopted by the court, or by administrative order issued by the chief justice in accordance with court action. Members of such groups shall be appointed by administrative order of the chief justice, after consultation with the court. When practicable, ad hoc committees and other ad hoc study or advisory groups, which should be used to address specific problems, shall be established under the umbrella of an existing committee or commission, which should be used to address long-term problems.

(2) *Chief Justice.*

(A) The chief justice shall be chosen by majority vote of the justices for a term of 2 years commencing on July 1, 2012. The selection of the chief justice should be based on managerial, administrative, and leadership abilities, without regard to seniority only. A chief justice may serve successive terms limited to a total of 8 years. The chief justice may be removed by a vote of 4 justices. If a vacancy occurs, a successor shall be chosen promptly to serve the balance of the unexpired term.

(B) The chief justice shall be the administrative officer of the judicial branch and of the supreme court and shall be responsible for the dispatch of the business of the branch and of the court and direct the implementation of policies and priorities as determined by the supreme court for the operation of the branch and of the court. The administrative powers and duties of the chief justice shall include, but not be limited to:

(i) the responsibility to serve as the primary spokesperson for the judicial branch regarding policies and practices that have statewide impact including, but not limited to, the judicial branch's management, operation, strategic plan, legislative agenda and budget priorities;

(ii) the power to act on requests for stays during the pendency of proceedings, to order the consolidation of cases, to determine all procedural motions and petitions relating to the time for filing and size of briefs and other papers provided for under the rules of this court, to advance or continue cases, and to rule on other procedural matters relating to any proceeding or process in the court;

(iii) the power to assign active or retired county, circuit, or appellate judges or justices to judicial service in this state, in accordance with subdivisions (a)(3) and (a)(4) of this rule;

(iv) the power, upon request of the chief judge of any circuit or district, or sua sponte, in the event of natural disaster, civil disobedience, or other emergency situation requiring the closure of courts or other circumstances inhibiting the ability of litigants to comply with deadlines imposed by rules of procedure applicable in the courts of this state, to enter such order or orders as may be appropriate to suspend, toll, or otherwise grant relief from time deadlines imposed by otherwise applicable statutes and rules of procedure for such period as may be appropriate, including, without limitation, those affecting speedy trial procedures in criminal and juvenile proceedings, all civil process and proceedings, and all appellate time limitations;

(v) the authority to directly inform all judges on a regular basis by any means, including, but not limited to, email on the state of the judiciary, the state of the budget, issues of importance, priorities and other matters of statewide interest; furthermore, the chief justice shall routinely communicate with the chief judges and leaders of the district courts, circuit and county court conferences by the appropriate means;

(vi) the responsibility to exercise reasonable efforts to promote and encourage diversity in the administration of justice; and

(vii) the power to perform such other administrative duties as may be required and which are not otherwise provided for by law or rule.

(C) The chief justice shall be notified by all justices of any contemplated absences from the court and the reasons therefor. When the chief justice is to be temporarily absent, the chief justice shall select the justice longest in continuous service as acting chief justice.

(D) If the chief justice dies, retires, or is unable to perform the duties of the office, the justice longest in continuous service shall perform the duties during the period of incapacity or until a successor chief justice is elected.

(E) The chief justice shall meet on a regular basis with the chief judges of the district courts and the chief judges of the circuit courts to discuss and provide feedback for implementation of policies and practices that have statewide impact including, but not limited to, the judicial branch's management, operation, strategic plan, legislative agenda and budget priorities. Such meetings shall, if practicable, occur at least quarterly and be conducted in-person. At the discretion of the chief justice, any of these meetings may be combined with other judicial branch and leadership meetings and, where practicable include the justices of the supreme court.

(3) *Administration.*

(A) The chief justice may, either upon request or when otherwise necessary for the prompt dispatch of business in the courts of this state, temporarily assign justices of the supreme court, judges of district courts of appeal, circuit judges, and judges of county courts to any court for which they are qualified to serve. Any consenting retired justice or judge may be assigned to judicial service and receive compensation as provided by law.

(B) For the purpose of judicial administration, a "retired judge" is defined as a judge not engaged in the practice of law who has been a judicial officer of this state. A retired judge shall comply with all requirements that the supreme court deems necessary relating to the recall of retired judges.

(C) When a judge who is eligible to draw retirement compensation has entered the private practice of law, the judge may be eligible for recall to judicial service upon cessation of the private practice of law and approval of the judge's application to the court. The application shall state the period of time the judge has not engaged in the practice of law, and must be approved by the court before the judge shall be eligible for recall to judicial service.

(D) A "senior judge" is a retired judge who is eligible to serve on assignment to temporary judicial duty.

(4) *Assignments of Justices and Judges.*

(A) When a justice of the supreme court is unable to perform the duties of office, or when necessary for the prompt dispatch of the business of the court, the chief justice may assign to the court any judge who is qualified to serve, for such time as the chief justice may direct.

(B) When a judge of any district court of appeal is unable to perform the duties of office, or when necessary for the prompt dispatch of the business of the court, the chief judge shall advise the chief justice and the chief justice may assign to the court any judge who is qualified to serve, for such time or such proceedings as the chief justice may direct.

(C) When any circuit or county judge is unable to perform the duties of office, or when necessary for the prompt dispatch of the business of the court, the chief judge of the circuit may assign any judge in the circuit to temporary service for which the judge is qualified, in accordance with rule 2.215. If the chief judge deems it necessary, the chief judge may request the chief justice to assign a judge to the court for such time or such proceedings as the chief justice may direct.

(b) Clerk.

(1) *Appointment.* The supreme court shall appoint a clerk who shall hold office at the pleasure of the court and perform such duties as the court directs. The clerk's compensation shall be fixed by law. The clerk's office shall be in the supreme court building. The clerk shall devote full time to the duties of the office and shall not engage in the practice of law while in office.

(2) *Custody of Records, Files, and Seal.* All court records and the seal of the court shall be kept in the office and the custody of the clerk. The clerk shall not allow any court record to be taken from the clerk's office or the courtroom, except by a justice of the court or upon the order of the court.

(3) *Records of Proceedings.* The clerk shall keep such records as the court may from time to time order or direct. The clerk shall keep a docket or equivalent electronic record of all cases that are brought for review to, or that originate in, the court. Each case shall be numbered in the order in which the notice, petition, or other initial pleading originating the cause is filed in the court.

(4) *Filing Fee.* In all cases filed in the court, the clerk shall require the payment of a fee as provided by law when the notice, petition, or other initial pleading is filed. The payment shall not be exacted in advance in appeals in which a party has been adjudicated insolvent for the purpose of an appeal or in appeals in which the state is the real party in interest as the moving party. The payment of the fee shall not be required in habeas corpus proceedings, or appeals therefrom, arising out of or in connection with criminal actions.

(5) *Issuance and Recall of Mandate; Recordation and Notification.* The clerk shall issue such mandates or process as may be directed by the court. If, within 120 days after a mandate has been issued, the court directs that a mandate be recalled, then the clerk shall recall the mandate. Upon the issuance or recall of any mandate, the clerk shall record the issuance or recall in a book or equivalent electronic record kept for that purpose, in which the date of issuance or date of recall and the manner of transmittal of the process shall be noted. In proceedings in which no mandate is issued, upon final adjudication of the pending cause the clerk shall transmit to the party affected thereby a copy of the court's order or judgment. The clerk shall notify the attorneys of record of the issuance of any mandate, the recall of any mandate, or the rendition of any final judgment. The clerk shall furnish without charge to all attorneys of record in any cause a copy of any order or written opinion rendered in such action.

(6) *Return of Original Papers.* Upon the conclusion of any proceeding in the supreme court, the clerk shall return to the clerk of the lower court the original papers or files transmitted to the court for use in the cause.

(c) Librarian.

(1) *Appointment.* The supreme court shall appoint a librarian of the supreme court and such assistants as may be necessary. The supreme court library shall be in the custody of the librarian, but under the exclusive control of the court. The library shall be open to members of the bar of the supreme court, to members of the legislature, to law officers of the executive or other departments of the state, and to such other persons as may be allowed to use the library by special permission of the court.

(2) *Library Hours.* The library shall be open during such times as the reasonable needs of the bar require and shall be governed by regulations made by the librarian with the approval of the court.

(3) *Books.* Books shall not be removed from the library except for use by, or upon order of, any justice.

(d) Marshal.

(1) *Appointment.* The supreme court shall appoint a marshal who shall hold office at the pleasure of the court and perform such duties as the court directs. The marshal's compensation shall be fixed by law.

(2) *Duties.* The marshal shall have power to execute process of the court throughout the state and such other powers as may be conferred by law. The marshal may deputize the sheriff or a deputy sheriff in any county to execute process of the court and shall perform such clerical or ministerial duties as the court may direct or as required by law. Subject to the direction of the court, the marshal shall be custodian of the supreme court building and grounds.

(e) State Courts Administrator.

(1) *Appointment.* The supreme court shall appoint a state courts administrator who shall serve at the pleasure of the court and perform such duties as the court directs. The state courts administrator's compensation shall be fixed by law.

(2) *Duties.* The state courts administrator shall supervise the administrative office of the Florida courts, which shall be maintained at such place as directed by the supreme court; shall employ such other personnel as the court deems necessary to aid in the administration of the state courts system; shall represent the state courts system before the legislature and other bodies with respect to matters affecting the state courts system and functions related to and serving the system; shall supervise the preparation and submission to the supreme court, for review and approval, of a tentative budget request for the state courts system and shall appear before the legislature in accordance with the court's directions in support of the final budget request on behalf of the system; shall inform the judiciary of the state courts system's final budget request and any proposed substantive law changes approved by the supreme court; shall assist in the preparation of educational and training materials for the state courts system and related personnel, and shall coordinate or assist in the conduct of educational and training sessions for such personnel; shall assist all courts in the development of improvements in the system, and submit to the chief justice and the court appropriate recommendations to improve the state courts system; and shall collect and compile uniform financial and other statistical data or information reflective of the cost, workloads, business, and other functions related to the state courts system. The state courts administrator is the custodian of all records in the administrator's office.

(f) Open Sessions. All sessions of the court shall be open to the public, except proceedings designated as confidential by the court and conference sessions held for the discussion and consideration of pending cases, for the formulation of opinions by the court, and for the discussion or resolution of other matters related to the administration of the state courts system.

(g) Designation of Assigned Judges. When any judge of another court is assigned for temporary service on the supreme court, that judge shall be designated, as author or participant, by name and initials followed by the words "Associate Justice."

Former Rule 2.030 amended June 14, 1979, effective July 1, 1979 (372 So.2d 449); May 3, 1990, effective June 15, 1990 (560 So.2d 786); Oct. 8, 1992, effective Jan. 1, 1993 (609 So.2d 465); Oct. 24, 1996, effective Jan. 1, 1997 (682 So.2d 89); March 7, 2002 (825 So.2d 889); Nov. 3, 2005, effective Jan. 1, 2006 (915 So.2d 145). Renumbered from Rule 2.030 Sept. 21, 2006 (939 So.2d 966). Amended Feb. 9, 2012 (121 So.3d 1); Dec. 20, 2012 (119 So.3d 1211); Oct. 31, 2013, effective Jan. 1, 2014 (125 So.3d 743).

Rule 2.210. District Courts of Appeal

(a) Internal Government.

(1) *Exercise of Powers and Jurisdiction.* Three judges shall constitute a panel for and shall consider each case, and the concurrence of a majority of the panel shall be necessary to a decision.

(2) *Chief Judge.*

(A) The selection of a chief judge should be based on managerial, administrative, and leadership abilities, without regard to seniority only.

(B) The chief judge shall be the administrative officer of the court, and shall, consistent with branch-wide policies, direct the formation and implementation of policies and priorities for the operation of the court. The chief judge shall exercise administrative supervision over all judges and court personnel. The chief judge shall be responsible to the chief justice of the supreme court. The chief judge may enter and sign administrative orders. The administrative powers and duties of the chief judge include, but are not limited to, the power to order consolidation of cases, and to assign cases to the judges for the preparation of opinions, orders, or judgments. The chief judge shall have the authority to require all judges of the court, court officers and court personnel, to comply with all court and judicial branch policies, administrative orders, procedures, and administrative plans.

(C) The chief judge shall maintain liaison in all judicial administrative matters with the chief justice of the supreme court, and shall, considering available resources, ensure the efficient and proper administration of the court. The chief judge shall develop an administrative plan that shall include an administrative organization capable of effecting the prompt disposition of cases, the assignment of judges, other court officers, and court personnel, and the control of dockets. The administrative plan shall include a consideration of the statistical data developed by the case reporting system.

(D) All judges shall inform the chief judge of any contemplated absences that will affect the progress of the court's business. If a judge is temporarily absent, is disqualified in an action, or is unable to

tion as a public record, and copies shall be provided to any requesting party for the cost of duplication. The chief judge of the circuit may provide for the publication of the rules. The clerk of the supreme court shall furnish copies of each approved local court rule to the executive director of The Florida Bar.

(2) Any judge or member of The Florida Bar who believes that an administrative order promulgated under subdivision (b)(2) of this rule is a court rule or a local rule as defined in rule 2.120, rather than an administrative order, may apply to the Supreme Court Local Rules Advisory Committee for a decision on the question. The decisions of the committee concerning the determination of the question shall be reported to the supreme court, and the court shall follow the procedure set forth in subdivision (D) above in considering the recommendation of the committee.

(3) All administrative orders of a general and continuing nature, and all others designated by the chief judge, shall be indexed and recorded by the clerk of the circuit court in each county where the orders are effective. A set of the recorded copies shall be readily available for inspection as a public record, and copies shall be provided to any requesting party for the cost of duplication. The chief judge shall, on an annual basis, direct a review of all local administrative orders to ensure that the set of copies maintained by the clerk remains current and does not conflict with supreme court or local rules.

(4) All local court rules entered pursuant to this section shall be numbered sequentially for each respective judicial circuit.

(f) Duty to Rule within a Reasonable Time. Every judge has a duty to rule upon and announce an order or judgment on every matter submitted to that judge within a reasonable time. Each judge shall maintain a log of cases under advisement and inform the chief judge of the circuit at the end of each calendar month of each case that has been held under advisement for more than 60 days.

(g) Duty to Expedite Priority Cases. Every judge has a duty to expedite priority cases to the extent reasonably possible. Priority cases are those cases that have been assigned a priority status or assigned an expedited disposition schedule by statute, rule of procedure, case law, or otherwise. Particular attention shall be given to all juvenile dependency and termination of parental rights cases, cases involving families and children in need of services, challenges involving elections and proposed constitutional amendments, and capital postconviction cases. As part of an effort to make capital postconviction cases a priority, the chief judge shall have the discretion to create a postconviction division to handle capital postconviction, as well as non-capital postconviction cases, and may assign one or more judges to that division.

(h) Neglect of Duty. The failure of any judge, clerk, prosecutor, public defender, attorney, court reporter, or other officer of the court to comply with an order or directive of the chief judge shall be considered neglect of duty and shall be reported by the chief judge to the chief justice of the supreme court. The chief justice may report the neglect of duty by a judge to the Judicial Qualifications Commission, and neglect of duty by other officials to the governor of Florida or other appropriate person or body.

(i) Status Conference after Compilation of Record in Death Case. In any proceeding in which a defendant has been sentenced to death, the circuit judge assigned to the case shall take such action as may be necessary to ensure that a complete record on appeal has been properly prepared. To that end, the judge shall convene a status conference with all counsel of record as soon as possible after the record has been prepared pursuant to rule of appellate procedure 9.200(d) but before the record has been transmitted. The purpose of the status conference shall be to ensure that the record is complete.

Former Rule 2.050 amended June 14, 1979, effective July 1, 1979 (372 So.2d 449); July 17, 1980, effective Jan. 1, 1981 (389 So.2d 202); Dec. 4, 1980, effective Jan. 1, 1981 (391 So.2d 214); Jan. 5, 1987, effective Feb. 1, 1987 (500 So.2d 524); May 21, 1987, effective July 1, 1987 (507 So.2d 1390); Sept. 29, 1988, effective Jan. 1, 1989 (536 So.2d 195); Oct. 8, 1992, effective Jan. 1, 1993 (609 So.2d 465); April 11, 1996 (672 So.2d 523); Oct. 24, 1996, effective Jan. 1, 1997 (682 So.2d 89); Feb. 7, 1997 (688 So.2d 320); Nov. 20, 1997 (701 So.2d 864); July 12, 2001, effective Oct. 1, 2001 (797 So.2d 1213); Aug. 29, 2002, effective Oct. 1, 2002 (826 So.2d 233); July 10, 2003 (851 So.2d 698); Nov. 3, 2005, effective Jan. 1, 2006 (915 So.2d 157); Mar. 2, 2006 (923 So.2d 1160). Renumbered from Rule 2.050 Sept. 21, 2006 (939 So.2d 966). Amended Mar. 27, 2008, effective April 1, 2008 (978 So.2d 805); July 10, 2008, effective Jan. 1, 2009 (986 So.2d 560); Sept. 25, 2008, effective Oct. 1, 2008 (992 So.2d 237); Feb. 24, 2011 (75 So.3d 1241); Feb. 9, 2012 (121 So.3d 1); July 3, 2014, effective Jan. 1, 2015 (148 So.3d 1171).

Committee Notes

2008 Amendment. The provisions in subdivision (g) of this rule should be read in conjunction with the provisions of rule 2.545(c) governing priority cases.

Court Commentary

1996 Court Commentary. Rule 2.050(h) should be read in conjunction with Florida Rule of Appellate Procedure 9.140(b)(4)(A).

1997 Court Commentary. [Rule 2.050(b)(10)]. The refresher course may be a six-hour block during any Florida Court Education Council approved course offering sponsored by any approved Florida judicial education provider, including the Florida College of Advanced Judicial Studies or the Florida Conference of Circuit Judges. The block must contain instruction on the following topics: penalty phase, jury selection, and rule 3.850 proceedings.

Failure to complete the refresher course during the three-year judicial education reporting period will necessitate completion of the original "Handling Capital Cases" course.

2002 Court Commentary. Recognizing the inherent differences in trial and appellate court dockets, the last sentence of subdivision (g) is intended to conform to the extent practicable with appellate rule 9.146(g), which requires appellate courts to give priority to appeals in juvenile dependency and termination of parental rights cases, and in cases involving families and children in need of services.

Criminal Court Steering Committee Note

2014 Amendment. Capital postconviction cases were added to the list of priority cases.

Rule 2.220. Conferences of Judges

(a) Conference of County Court Judges.

(1) *Organization.* There shall be a "Conference of County Court Judges of Florida," consisting of the active and senior county court judges of the State of Florida.

(2) *Purpose.* The purpose of the conference shall be:

(A) the betterment of the judicial system of the state;

(B) the improvement of procedure and practice in the several courts;

(C) to conduct conferences and institutes for continuing judicial education and to provide forums in which the county court judges of Florida may meet and discuss mutual problems and solutions; and

(D) to provide input to the Unified Committee on Judicial Compensation on judicial compensation and benefit issues, and to assist the judicial branch in soliciting support and resources on these issues.

(3) *Officers.* Management of the conference shall be vested in the officers of the conference, an executive committee, and a board of directors.

(A) The officers of the conference shall be:

(i) the president, president-elect, immediate past president, secretary, and treasurer, who shall be elected at large; and

(ii) one vice-president elected from each appellate court district.

(B) The executive committee shall consist of the officers of the conference and an executive secretary.

(C) The board of directors shall consist of the executive committee and a member elected from each judicial circuit.

(D) There shall be an annual meeting of the conference.

(E) Between annual meetings of the conference, the affairs of the conference shall be managed by the executive committee.

(4) *Authority.* The conference may adopt governance documents, the provisions of which shall not be inconsistent with this rule.

Subdivision (b) effective upon repeal of F.S.A. § 26.55. See 121 So.3d 1.

(b) Conference of Circuit Court Judges.

(1) *Organization.* There shall be a "Conference of Circuit Court Judges of Florida," consisting of the active and retired circuit judges of the several judicial circuits of the state, excluding retired judges practicing law.

(2) *Purpose.* The purpose of the conference shall be:

(A) the betterment of the judicial system of the state;

(B) the improvement of procedure and practice in the several courts;

(C) to conduct conferences and institutes for continuing judicial education and to provide forums in which the circuit court judges of Florida may meet and discuss mutual problems and solutions;

(D) to provide input to the Unified Committee on Judicial Compensation on judicial compensation and benefit issues, and to assist the judicial branch in soliciting support and resources on these issues;

(E) to report to the Florida Supreme Court recommendations as the conference may have concerning the improvement of procedure and practice in the several courts;

(F) to confer with the Florida Supreme Court regarding concerns the conference may have concerning the laws of this state affecting the administration of justice; and

(G) to provide to the Florida Legislature recommendations as the conference may have concerning laws of this state affecting the administration of justice.

(3) *Officers.* Management of the conference shall be vested in the officers of the conference, an executive committee, and a board of directors.

(A) The officers of the conference shall be the chair, chair-elect, secretary, and treasurer.

(B) The executive committee shall consist of the officers of the conference and such other members as the conference shall determine.

(C) The board of directors shall consist of the executive committee and membership in one shall be identical to membership of the other.

(D) There shall be an annual meeting of the conference.

(E) Between annual meetings of the conference, the affairs of the conference shall be managed by the executive committee.

(4) *Authority.* The conference may adopt governance documents, the provisions of which shall not be inconsistent with this rule.

(c) Conference of District Court of Appeal Judges.

(1) *Organization.* There shall be a "Florida Conference of District Court of Appeal Judges," consisting of the active and senior district court of appeal judges of the State of Florida.

(2) *Purpose.* The purpose of the conference shall be:

(A) the betterment of the judicial system of the state;

(B) the improvement of procedure and practice in the several courts;

(C) to conduct conferences and institutes for continuing judicial education and to provide forums in which the district court of appeal judges of Florida may meet and discuss mutual problems and solutions; and

(D) to provide input to the Unified Committee on Judicial Compensation on judicial compensation and benefit issues, and to assist the judicial branch in soliciting support and resources on these issues.

(3) *Officers.* Management of the conference shall be vested in the officers of the conference and an executive committee.

(A) The officers of the conference shall be the president, president-elect, and secretary-treasurer.

(B) The executive committee shall consist of the president and president-elect of the conference and the chief judge of each district court of appeal.

(C) There shall be an annual meeting of the conference.

(D) Between annual meetings of the conference, the affairs of the conference shall be managed by the executive committee.

(4) *Authority.* The conference may adopt governance documents, the provisions of which shall not be inconsistent with this rule.

Former Rule 2.120 amended June 14, 1979, effective July 1, 1979 (372 So.2d 449); Oct. 8, 1992, effective Jan. 1, 1993 (609 So.2d 465). Renumbered new Rule 2.220 Sept. 21, 2006 (939 So.2d 966). Amended Feb. 9, 2012, effective Feb. 9, 2012 and contingent effective in part (121 So.3d 1); Dec. 20, 2012 (119 So.3d 1211); Oct. 31, 2013 (125 So.3d 754).

Rule 2.225. Judicial Management Council

(a) Creation and Responsibilities. There is hereby created the Judicial Management Council of Florida, which shall meet at least quarterly, and be charged with the following responsibilities:

(1) identifying potential crisis situations affecting the judicial branch and developing strategy to timely and effectively address them;

(2) identifying and evaluating information that would assist in improving the performance and effectiveness of the judicial branch (for example, information including, but not limited to, internal operations for cash flow and budget performance, and statistical information by court and type of cases for (i) number of cases filed, (ii) aged inventory of cases—the number and age of cases pending, (iii) time to disposition—the percentage of cases disposed or otherwise resolved within established time frames, and (iv) clearance rates—the number of outgoing cases as a percentage of the number of incoming cases);

(3) developing and monitoring progress relating to long-range planning for the judicial branch;

(4) reviewing the charges of the various court and Florida Bar commissions and committees, recommending consolidation or revision of the commissions and committees, and recommending a method for the coordination of the work of those bodies based on the proposed revisions; and

(5) addressing issues brought to the council by the supreme court.

(b) Referrals. The chief justice and the supreme court shall consider referring significant new issues or problems with implications for judicial branch policy to the Judicial Management Council prior to the creation of any new committees.

(c) Supreme Court Action on Recommendations by the Judicial Management Council. The supreme court may take any or all of the following actions on recommendations made by the Judicial Management Council:

(1) adopt the recommendation of the council in whole or in part, with or without conditions, including but not limited to:

(A) directing that action be taken to influence or change administrative policy, management practices, rules, or programs that are the subject of the recommendations;

(B) including the recommendation in the judicial branch's legislative agenda or budget requests;

(2) refer specific issues or questions back to the council for further study or alternative recommendations;

(3) reject the recommendation or decision in whole or in part;

(4) refer the recommendation to other entities, such as the Florida Legislature, the governor, the cabinet, executive branch agencies, or The Florida Bar, as the supreme court deems appropriate; or

(5) take alternative action.

(d) Membership.

(1) The council shall consist of 15 voting members, including the chief justice, who shall chair the council, an additional justice of the supreme court, representatives from each level of court, and public members.

(2) All voting members shall be appointed by the supreme court. Each member, other than the chief justice, will initially be appointed for a 2- or 4- year term, with the terms staggered to ensure continuity and experience on the council and for 4–year terms thereafter.

(3) The state courts administrator shall be a non-voting member. The council may request other non-voting persons to participate on an as-needed temporary basis to gain expertise and experience in certain issues on review.

(e) Staff Support and Funding. The Office of the State Courts Administrator shall provide primary staff support to the Judicial Management Council. Adequate staffing and other resources shall be made available to the Office of the State Courts Administrator to ensure the effective and efficient completion of tasks assigned to the Judicial Management Council. Sufficient resources shall also be provided for meetings of the Judicial Management Council and its committees or subcommittees, and other expenses necessary to the satisfactory completion of its work.

Former Rule 2.125 added Feb. 28, 1985, effective March 1, 1985 (465 So.2d 1217). Amended June 1, 1989 (543 So.2d 1244); Nov. 9, 1989 (552 So.2d 194); Jan. 11, 1990 (555 So.2d 848); Oct. 8, 1992, effective Jan. 1, 1993 (609 So.2d 465); March 30, 1995 (652 So.2d 811); June 15, 1995 (656 So.2d 926); Oct. 24, 1996, effective Jan. 1, 1997 (682 So.2d 89). Renumbered from Rule 2.125 Sept. 21, 2006 (939 So.2d 966). Amended Feb. 9, 2012 (121 So.3d 1).

Rule 2.230. Trial Court Budget Commission

(a) Purpose. The purpose of this rule is to establish a Trial Court Budget Commission that will have the responsibility for developing and overseeing the administration of trial court budgets in a manner which ensures equity and fairness in state funding among the 20 judicial circuits.

(b) Responsibilities. The Trial Court Budget Commission is charged with specific responsibility to:

(1) establish budgeting and funding policies and procedures consistent with judicial branch plans and policies, directions from the supreme court, and in consideration of input from the Commission on Trial Court Performance and Accountability and other supreme court committees and from the Florida Conference of Circuit Court Judges and the Florida Conference of County Court Judges;

(2) make recommendations to the supreme court on the trial court component of the annual judicial branch budget request;

(3) advocate for the trial court component of the annual judicial branch budget request and associated statutory changes;

(4) make recommendations to the supreme court on funding allocation formulas and budget implementation and criteria as well as associated accountability mechanisms based on actual legislative appropriations;

(5) monitor trial court expenditure trends and revenue collections to identify unanticipated budget problems and to ensure the efficient use of resources;

(6) recommend statutory and rule changes related to trial court budgets;

(7) develop recommended responses to findings on financial audits and reports from the Supreme Court Inspector General, Auditor General, Office of Program Policy Analysis and Government Accountability, and other governmental entities charged with auditing responsibilities regarding trial court budgeting when appropriate;

(8) recommend to the supreme court trial court budget reductions required by the legislature;

(9) identify potential additional sources of revenue for the trial courts;

(10) recommend to the supreme court legislative pay plan issues for trial court personnel, except the commission shall not make recommendations as to pay or benefits for judges; and

(11) request input from the Commission on Trial Court Performance and Accountability on recommendations from that commission that may impact the trial court budget or require funding.

(c) Operational Procedures. The Trial Court Budget Commission will establish operating procedures necessary to carry out its responsibilities as outlined in subdivision (b), subject to final approval by the supreme court. These procedures shall include:

(1) a method for ensuring input from interested constituencies, including the chief judges and trial court administrators of the trial courts, other members of the trial court judiciary, the Judicial Management Council, the Commission on Trial Court Performance and Accountability, and other judicial branch committees and commissions; and

(2) a method for appeal of the decisions of the Trial Court Budget Commission. Appeals may be made only by a chief judge on behalf of a circuit. Appeals may be heard only by the Trial Court Budget Commission unless the appeal is based on the failure of the commission to adhere to its operating procedures, in which case the appeal may be made to the supreme court.

(d) Action by Supreme Court or Chief Justice on Recommendations of Trial Court Budget Commission. The supreme court or chief justice, as appropriate, may take any or all of the following actions on recommendations made by the Trial Court Budget Commission:

(1) The adoption of the recommendations of the commission made in accordance with the discharge of its responsibilities listed in subdivision (b) in whole.

(2) The adoption of the recommendations in part and referral of specific issues or questions back to the commission for further study or alternative recommendations.

(e) Membership and Organization. The Trial Court Budget Commission will be composed of 21 voting members appointed by the chief justice who will represent the interests of the trial courts generally rather than the individual interests of a particular circuit or division. The respective presidents of the Conference of Circuit Court Judges, and the Conference of County Court Judges, and the chair of the Commission on Trial Court Performance and Accountability shall serve as ex officio nonvoting members of the Commission. The chief justice will make appointments to ensure that the broad interests of the trial courts are represented by including members who have experience in different divisions, who have expertise in court operations or administrative matters, and who offer geographic, racial, ethnic, and gender diversity.

(1) The membership must include 14 trial court judges and 7 trial court administrators.

(2) The chief justice will appoint 1 member to serve as chair and 1 member to serve as vice chair, each for a 2–year term.

(3) A supreme court justice will be appointed by the chief justice to serve as supreme court liaison.

(4) No circuit will have more than 2 members on the commission.

(5) The original members of the commission will be appointed as follows:

(A) 7 members shall be appointed for a 2–year term;

(B) 7 members shall be appointed for a 4–year term; and

(C) 7 members shall be appointed for one 6–year term.

All subsequent members will each be appointed for one 6–year term. In the event of a vacancy, the chief justice will appoint a new member to serve for the remainder of the departing member's term.

(6) The commission may establish subcommittees as necessary to satisfactorily carry out its responsibilities. Subcommittees may make recommendations only to the commission as a whole. The chair of the commission may appoint a non-commission member to serve on a subcommittee.

(f) Staff Support and Funding. The Office of the State Courts Administrator will provide primary staff support to the commission. Adequate staffing and resources will be made available to the Office of the State Courts Administrator to ensure the commission is able to fulfill its responsibilities as outlined in the rule. Sufficient resources will also be provided for the commission and its subcommittees to meet and otherwise complete its work.

Former Rule 2.053 adopted Aug. 31, 2000, effective Dec. 1, 2000 (774 So.2d 625, reissued Nov. 9, 2000). Amended July 10, 2003 (851 So.2d 698). Renumbered from Rule 2.053 Sept. 21, 2006 (939 So.2d 966). Amended Feb. 9, 2012 (121 So.3d 1).

Rule 2.235. District Court of Appeal Budget Commission

(a) Purpose. The purpose of this rule is to establish a District Court of Appeal Budget Commission with responsibility for developing and overseeing the administration of district court budgets in a manner which ensures equity and fairness in state funding among the 5 districts.

(b) Responsibilities. The District Court of Appeal Budget Commission is charged with specific responsibility to:

(1) establish budgeting and funding policies and procedures consistent with judicial branch plans and policies, directions from the supreme court, and in consideration of input from the Commission on District Court of Appeal Performance and Accountability, and other supreme court committees;

(2) make recommendations to the supreme court on a unitary district court component of the annual judicial branch budget request;

(3) advocate for the district court component of the annual judicial branch budget request;

(4) make recommendations to the supreme court on funding allocation formulas and/or criteria as well as associated accountability mechanisms based on actual legislative appropriations;

(5) monitor district court expenditure trends and revenue collections to identify unanticipated budget problems and to ensure the efficient use of resources;

(6) recommend statutory and rule changes related to district court budgets;

(7) develop recommended responses to findings on financial audits and reports from the Supreme Court Inspector General, Auditor General, Office of Program Policy Analysis and Government Accountability, and other governmental entities charged with auditing responsibilities regarding district court budgeting when appropriate;

(8) recommend to the supreme court district court budget reductions required by the legislature;

(9) identify potential additional sources of revenue for the district courts;

(10) recommend to the supreme court legislative pay plan issues for district court personnel, except the commission shall not make recommendations as to pay or benefits for judges; and

(11) request input from the Commission on District Court of Appeal Performance and Accountability on recommendations from that commission that may impact the district court budget or require funding.

(c) Operational Procedures. The District Court of Appeal Budget Commission will establish operating procedures necessary to carry out its responsibilities as outlined in subdivision (b), subject to final approval by the supreme court. These procedures shall include:

(1) a method for ensuring input from interested constituencies, including the chief judges, marshals, and clerks of the district courts, other members of the district court judiciary, the Judicial Management Council, the Commission on District Court of Appeal Performance and Accountability, and other judicial branch committees and commissions; and

(2) a method for appeal of the decisions of the District Court of Appeal Budget Commission. Appeals may be made only by a chief judge on behalf of the district. Appeals may be heard only by the District Court of Appeal Budget Commission unless the appeal is based on the failure of the commission to adhere to its operating procedures, in which case the appeal may be made to the supreme court.

(d) Action by Supreme Court or Chief Justice on Recommendations of District Court of Appeal Budget Commission. The supreme court or chief justice, as appropriate, may take any or all of the following actions on recommendations made by the District Court of Appeal Budget Commission:

(1) The adoption of the recommendations of the commission made in accordance with the discharge of its responsibilities listed in subdivision (b) in whole.

(2) The adoption of the recommendations in part and referral of specific issues or questions back to the commission for further study or alternative recommendations.

(e) Membership and Organization. The District Court of Appeal Budget Commission will be composed of 10 voting members appointed by the chief justice who will represent the interests of the district courts generally rather than the individual interests of a particular district.

(1) The membership shall include the chief judge of each district court of appeal, who shall serve for his or her term as chief judge. The membership shall also include one additional judge from each district court of appeal, appointed by the chief justice, with advice from each chief judge. The marshal of each district court of appeal shall serve as a nonvoting member. Ex officio nonvoting members shall also include the chairs of the District Court of Appeal Performance and Accountability Commission and the Appellate Court Technology Committee, and the president of the District Court of Appeal Judges Conference.

(2) The chief justice will appoint 1 member to serve as chair and 1 member to serve as vice chair, each for a four–year term, or until the member's term on the commission expires.

(3) The commission may establish subcommittees as necessary to satisfactorily carry out its responsibilities. Subcommittees may make recommendations only to the commission as a whole. The chair of the commission may appoint a non-commission member to serve on a subcommittee.

(4) Effective July 1, 2013, the commission shall be reconstituted with staggered terms for voting members, as follows: (A) The chief judge of each district will be appointed for his or her term as chief judge. (B) The additional judge from each odd-numbered district will be appointed for a four-year term. (C) The additional judge from each even-numbered district will be appointed for a two-year term, and thereafter to four-year terms. (D) Each nonvoting member will serve so long as he or she continues to hold the office which entitles him or her to membership on the commission.

(f) Staff Support and Funding. The Office of the State Courts Administrator will provide primary staff support to the commission. Adequate staffing and resources will be made available to the Office of the State Courts Administrator to ensure the commission is able to fulfill its responsibilities as outlined in this rule. Sufficient resources will also be provided for the commission and its subcommittees to meet and otherwise complete its work.

Former Rule 2.054 adopted March 15, 2001, effective July 1, 2001 (796 So.2d 477). Amended Dec. 20, 2001, effective Jan. 1, 2002 (812 So.2d 401). Renumbered from Rule 2.054 Sept. 21, 2006 (939 So.2d 966). Amended Sept. 28, 2006 (939 So.2d 1051); Feb. 9, 2012 (121 So.3d 1).

Rule 2.236. Florida Courts Technology Commission

(a) Purpose. The purpose of this rule is to establish a Florida Courts Technology Commission with responsibility for overseeing, managing, and directing the development and use of technology within the judicial branch under the direction of the supreme court as specified in this rule. For the purpose of this rule, the term "judicial branch" does not include The Florida Bar, the Florida Board of Bar Examiners, or the Judicial Qualifications Commission.

(b) Responsibilities. The Florida Courts Technology Commission is charged with specific responsibility to:

(1) make recommendations to the supreme court on all matters of technology policy impacting the judicial branch to allow the supreme court to establish technology policy in the branch;

(2) make recommendations to the supreme court regarding policies for public access to electronic court records;

(3) make recommendations to the supreme court about the relative priorities of various technology projects within the judicial branch so that the supreme court can establish priorities. The commission should coordinate with the Trial Court Budget Commission and District Court of Appeal Budget Commission to secure funds for allocation of those priorities;

(4) direct and establish priorities for the work of all technology committees in the judicial branch, including the Appellate Court Technology Committee, and

review and approve recommendations made by any court committee concerning technology matters or otherwise implicating court technology policy.

(5) establish, periodically review, and update technical standards for technology used and to be used in the judicial branch to receive, manage, maintain, use, secure, and distribute court records by electronic means, consistent with the technology policies established by the supreme court. These standards shall be coordinated with the strategic plans of the judicial branch, rules of procedure, applicable law, and directions from the supreme court, and shall incorporate input from the public, clerks of court, supreme court committees and commissions, and other groups involved in the application of current technology to the judicial branch;

(6) create procedures whereby courts and clerks and other applicable entities can apply for approval of new systems, or modifications to existing systems, that involve the application of technology to the receipt, management, maintenance, use, securing, and distribution of court records within the judicial branch, and between the public and the judicial branch;

(7) evaluate all such applications to determine whether they comply with the technology policies established by the supreme court and the procedures and standards created pursuant to this rule, and approve those applications deemed to be effective and found to be in compliance;

(8) develop and maintain security policies that must be utilized to ensure the integrity and availability of court technology systems and related data;

(9) ensure principles of accessibility are met for all court technology projects, with consideration and application of the requirements of the Americans with Disabilities Act of 1990 and any other applicable state or federal disability laws;

(10) ensure that the technology utilized in the judicial branch is capable of required integration;

(11) periodically review and evaluate all approved technology in the judicial branch to determine its adherence to current supreme court technology policies and standards;

(12) review annual and periodic reports on the status of court technology systems and proposals for technology improvements and innovation throughout the judicial branch;

(13) recommend statutory and rule changes or additions relating to court technology and the receipt, maintenance, management, use, securing, and distribution of court records by electronic means;

(14) identify technology issues that require attention in the judicial branch upon:

(A) referral from the chief justice;

(B) referral from the supreme court; or

(C) identification by the Florida Courts Technology Commission on its own initiative based on recommendations of the public, commission members, judges, justice system partners, The Florida Bar, clerks of court, the Florida Legislature (either informally or through the passage of legislation), the Governor, the cabinet, or executive branch agencies; and

(15) coordinate proposed amendments to rules of court procedure and judicial administration necessary to effectuate the commission's charge with appropriate Florida Bar rules committees.

If a program, system, or application is found not to comply with the policies established by the supreme court or the standards and procedures established by the commission, the commission may require that it be terminated or modified or subject to such conditions as the commission deems appropriate.

(c) Operational Procedures. The Florida Courts Technology Commission shall establish operating procedures necessary to carry out its responsibilities as outlined in subdivision (b), subject to final approval by the supreme court. These procedures shall include:

(1) a method for ensuring input from all interested constituencies in the state of Florida;

(2) a method for monitoring the development of new court technology projects, reviewing reports on new technology projects, and reviewing the annual reports;

(3) a method whereby courts and clerks and other applicable entities can apply for approval of new technology systems or applications, or modifications to existing systems or applications, that affect the receipt, management, maintenance, use, securing, and distribution of court records;

(4) a system to evaluate all applications for new or modified technology systems to determine whether they comply with the policies and technical standards established by the supreme court and the procedures created pursuant to this rule, and are otherwise appropriate to implement in the judicial branch;

(5) a process for making decisions on all applications for new or modified technology systems and communicating those decisions to interested parties. If an application is found to comply with technology policies and standards, the commission may approve the application and its written approval shall authorize the applicant to proceed. For all applications that are not approved, the commission shall assist the applicant in remedying any deficiencies that the commission identifies;

(6) a method to monitor all technology programs, systems, and applications used in the judicial branch to ensure that such programs, systems, and applications are operating in accordance with the technology policies established by the supreme court and technical standards established by the commission. The

commission may ask any operator of a program, system, or application to appear before it for examination into whether the program, system, or application complies with technology policies and standards;

(7) a process to conduct the limited, short-term work of the commission through work groups that it may constitute from time to time. Work groups may make recommendations to the commission as a whole. The chair of the commission may appoint non-commission members to serve on any work group; and

(8) a process to conduct substantial work of the commission requiring long-term commitment through subcommittees. Subcommittees may make recommendations to the commission as a whole. The chair of the commission may appoint non-commission members to serve on any subcommittee.

(d) Action by Supreme Court or Chief Justice on Recommendations of or Decisions by Florida Courts Technology Commission. The supreme court or chief justice, as appropriate, may take any of the following actions on recommendations or decisions made by the Florida Courts Technology Commission:

(1) Adopt the recommendation or decision of the commission in whole or in part, with or without conditions.

(2) Refer specific issues or questions back to the commission for further study or alternative recommendations.

(3) Reject the recommendation or decision in whole or in part.

(4) Take alternative action.

(e) Membership and Organization.

(1) The Florida Courts Technology Commission shall be composed of 25 voting members appointed by the chief justice after consultation with the court. All members shall represent the interests of the public and of Florida courts generally rather than the separate interests of any particular district, circuit, county, division, or other organization. The membership shall include members who have experience in different divisions of courts, in court operations, and in using technology in court for case processing, management, and administrative purposes, and shall provide geographic, racial, ethnic, gender, and other diversity.

(2) The membership shall include 2 district court judges, 5 circuit court judges (1 of whom must be a chief judge), 2 county court judges, 3 court administrators, 3 court technology officers, 4 clerks of court (1 of whom must be a clerk of an appellate court), 4 members of The Florida Bar (1 of whom must be a member of the Board of Governors of The Florida Bar), and 2 members of the public at large.

(3) The members of the commission who are judicial officers, court technology officers, and court administrators must constitute a majority of the commission and must constitute a majority of any quorum at all meetings of the commission.

(4) A supreme court justice shall be appointed by the chief justice to serve as supreme court liaison to the commission.

(5) Each member will be initially appointed for a 1-, 2-, or 3–year term, with the terms staggered to ensure continuity and experience on the commission and for three year terms thereafter. Retention and reappointment of each member will be at the discretion of the chief justice.

(6) The chief justice shall appoint 1 member to serve as chair for a two-year term.

(f) Schedule of Reports. The Florida Courts Technology Commission shall prepare an annual report of its activities, which shall include its recommendations for changes or additions to the technology policies or standards of Florida courts, its recommendations for setting or changing priorities among the programs within the responsibility of the commission to assist with budget resources available, its recommendations for changes to rules, statutes, or regulations that affect technology in Florida courts and the work of the commission. The report also shall include recommendations of the Appellate Court Technology Committee that implicate court technology policy and the action taken on those recommendations by the commission. This report shall be submitted to the supreme court on April 1 of each year.

(g) Appellate Court Technology Committee.

(1) *Purpose.* The purpose of this subdivision is to establish the Appellate Court Technology Committee as a standing committee of the Florida Courts Technology Commission responsible for providing technical guidance and consultation to the commission regarding information systems development and operational policies and procedures relating to automation in the district courts of appeal.

(2) *Responsibilities.* The Appellate Court Technology Committee is charged with specific responsibility to:

(A) coordinate with and provide advice to the Florida Courts Technology Commission regarding the development of standards and policies for implementing new technologies, system security, public access to district court information, and system support;

(B) develop, recommend, and implement policy and procedures consistent with the overall policy of the supreme court relating to technology issues affecting the district courts of appeal;

(C) recommend and coordinate the purchase and upgrade of hardware and software in relation to the district courts' office automation systems and networks;

(D) oversee and direct expenditures of designated state court system trust funds for technology needs in the district courts;

(E) promote orientation and education programs on technology and its effective utilization in the district court environment;

(F) ensure principles of accessibility are met for all court technology projects, with consideration and application of the requirements of the Americans with Disabilities Act of 1990 and any other applicable state or federal disability laws;

(G) propose amendments to rules of court procedure and judicial administration necessary to effectuate the committee's charge, after coordination with appropriate Florida Bar rules committees; and

(H) identify budget issues and funding sources and coordinate with the District Court of Appeal Budget Commission on recommendations requiring additional funding or resources for implementation in the district courts of appeal.

(3) *Membership and Terms.*

(A) The chief justice will select the chair of the committee from among the judges of the district courts, with input from the chief judges.

(B) The chief judges of the remaining district courts will designate a representative from each of their courts to serve as member of the committee.

(C) The chair and members will serve 3–year terms. Retention and reappointment of the chair will be at the discretion of the chief justice. Retention and reappointment of the representative from each district court will be at the discretion of the district court chief judge.

(4) *Commission Approval and Reporting of Policy Recommendations.* Committee recommendations that implicate court technology policy must be reviewed and approved by the commission. The commission will report the committee's policy recommendations and the action taken on them by the commission to the supreme court. The committee may submit to the court a companion report on its recommendations, supporting or opposing the action taken by the commission.

(h) Staff Support and Funding. The Office of the State Courts Administrator shall provide primary staff support to the Florida Courts Technology Commission and the Appellate Court Technology Committee. Adequate staffing and resources shall be made available by the Office of the State Courts Administrator to ensure that the commission and committee are able to fulfill their responsibilities under this rule.

Added effective July 1, 2010 (41 So.3d 128).

Rule 2.240. Determination of Need for Additional Judges

(a) Purpose. The purpose of this rule is to set forth uniform criteria used by the supreme court in determining the need for additional judges, except supreme court justices, and the necessity for decreasing the number of judges, pursuant to article V, section 9, Florida Constitution. These criteria form the primary basis for the supreme court's determination of need for additional judges. Unforeseen developments, however, may have an impact upon the judiciary resulting in needs which cannot be foreseen or predicted by statistical projections. The supreme court, therefore, may also consider any additional information found by it to be relevant to the process. In establishing criteria for the need for additional appellate court judges, substantial reliance has been placed on the findings and recommendations of the Commission on District Court of Appeal Performance and Accountability. *See In re Report of the Comm'n on Dist. Court of Appeal Performance and Accountability—Rule of Judicial Admin. 2.035*, 933 So. 2d 1136 (Fla. 2006).

(b) Criteria.

(1) *Trial Courts.*

(A) Assessment of judicial need at the trial court level is based primarily upon the application of case weights to circuit and county court caseload statistics supplied to the Office of the State Courts Administrator by the clerks of the circuit courts, pursuant to rule 2.245, Florida Rules of Judicial Administration. Such case weights provide a quantified measure of judicial time spent on case-related activity, translating judicial caseloads into judicial workload by factoring in the relative complexity by case type in the following manner:

(i) The circuit court case weights are applied to forecasted case filings, which include circuit criminal (includes felony, drug court, and worthless check cases), circuit civil (includes matters involving claims of $15,000.01 and above), family (includes domestic relations, juvenile dependency, and juvenile delinquency cases), and probate (includes guardianship, mental health, and trust cases).

(ii) The county court case weights are applied to forecasted filings, which include county criminal (includes misdemeanor, violations of county and municipal ordinance, worthless check, driving under the influence, and other criminal traffic cases), and county civil (includes small claims, matters involving claims ranging from $5,000.01 to $15,000, landlord-tenant, and civil traffic infraction cases).

(B) Other factors may be utilized in the determination of the need for one or more additional judges. These factors include, but are not limited to, the following:

(i) The availability and use of county court judges in circuit court.

(ii) The availability and use of senior judges to serve on a particular court.

(iii) The availability and use of magistrates and hearing officers.

(iv) The extent of use of alternative dispute resolution.

(v) The number of jury trials.

(vi) Foreign language interpretations.

(vii) The geographic size of a circuit, including travel times between courthouses in a particular jurisdiction.

(viii) Law enforcement activities in the court's jurisdiction, including any substantial commitment of additional resources for state attorneys, public defenders, and local law enforcement.

(ix) The availability and use of case-related support staff and case management policies and practices.

(x) Caseload trends.

(C) The Commission on Trial Court Performance and Accountability shall review the trial court workload trends and case weights and consider adjustments no less than every five years.

(2) *District Courts of Appeal.*

(A) The criteria for determining the need to certify the need for increasing or decreasing the number of judges on a district court of appeal shall include the following factors:

(i) workload factors to be considered include: trends in case filings; trends in changes in case mix; trends in the backlog of cases ready for assignment and disposition; trends in the relative weight of cases disposed on the merits per judge; and changes in statutes, rules of court, and case law that directly or indirectly impact judicial workload.

(ii) efficiency factors to be considered include: a court's ability to stay current with its caseload, as indicated by measurements such as trend in clearance rate; trends in a court's percentage of cases disposed within the time standards set forth in the Rules of Judicial Administration and explanation/justification for cases not resolved within the time standards; and a court's utilization of resources, case management techniques and technologies to maximize the efficient adjudication of cases, research of legal issues, and preparation and distribution of decisions.

(iii) effectiveness factors to be considered include the extent to which each judge has adequate time to: thoroughly research legal issues, review briefs and memoranda of law, participate in court conferences on pending cases, hear and dispose of motions, and prepare correspondence, orders, judgments and opinions; expedite appropriate cases; prepare written opinions when warranted; develop, clarify, and maintain consistency in the law within that district; review all decisions rendered by the court; perform administrative duties relating to the court; and participate in the administration of the justice system through work in statewide committees.

(iv) professionalism factors to be considered include: the extent to which judges report that they have time to participate, including teaching, in education programs designed to increase the competency and efficiency of the judiciary and justice system as well as the competency of lawyers; provide guidance and instruction for the professional development of court support staff; and participate in appropriate activities of the legal profession at both the state and local levels to improve the relationship between the bench and bar, to enhance lawyer professionalism, and to improve the administration of justice.

(B) The court will presume that there is a need for an additional appellate court judgeship in any district for which a request is made and where the relative weight of cases disposed on the merits per judge would have exceeded 280 after application of the proposed additional judge(s).

(i) The relative weight of cases disposed on the merits shall be determined based upon case disposition statistics supplied to the state courts administrator by the clerks of the district courts of appeal, multiplied by the relative case weights established pursuant to subdivision (b)(2)(B)(ii), and divided by 100.

(ii) The Commission on District Court of Appeal Performance and Accountability shall review the workload trends of the district courts of appeal and consider adjustments in the relative case weights every four years.

(c) Additional Trial Court Workload Factors. Because summary statistics reflective of the above criteria do not fully measure judicial workload, the supreme court will receive and consider, among other things, information about the time to perform and volume of the following activities, which also comprise the judicial workload of a particular jurisdiction:

(1) review appellate court decisions;

(2) research legal issues;

(3) review briefs and memoranda of law;

(4) participate in court conferences on pending cases;

(5) hear and dispose of motions;

(6) prepare correspondence, orders, judgments, and decisional opinions;

(7) review presentence investigative reports and predispositional reports in delinquency and dependency cases;

(8) review petitions and motions for post-conviction relief;

(9) perform administrative duties relating to the court;

(10) participate in meetings with those involved in the justice system; and

(11) participate in educational programs designed to increase the competency and efficiency of the judiciary.

(d) Certification Process. The process by which certification of the need to increase or decrease the number of judges shall include:

(1) The state courts administrator will distribute a compilation of summary statistics and projections to each chief judge at a time designated by the chief justice.

(2) Each chief judge shall submit to the chief justice a request for any increase or decrease in the number of judges in accordance with the following:

(A) Trial Courts. Each chief judge will then consider these criteria, additional workload factors, and summary statistics, and submit to the chief justice a request for any increases or decreases under article V, section 9, of the Florida Constitution that the chief judge feels are required.

(B) District Courts. Each chief judge will then consider the criteria of this rule and the summary statistics; if a new judge is requested, the chief judge shall prepare a report showing the need for a new judge based upon the application of the criteria in this rule.

(i) Any request for a new district court judge shall be submitted to the District Court of Appeal Budget Commission for review and approval.

(ii) The chief judge of a district court of appeal shall submit the report showing the need together with the approval of the District Court of Appeal Budget Commission to the chief justice.

(3) The chief justice and the state courts administrator may then confer with the chief judge and other representatives of the court submitting the request as well as representatives of The Florida Bar and the public to gather additional information and clarification about the need in the particular jurisdiction.

(4) The chief justice will submit recommendations to the supreme court, which will thereafter certify to the legislature its findings and recommendations concerning such need.

(5) The supreme court, in conjunction with the certification process under this rule, shall also consider the necessity for increasing, decreasing, or redefining appellate districts and judicial circuits as required by article V, section 9, of the Florida Constitution and as set forth in Florida Rule of Judicial Administration 2.241.

Former Rule 2.035 added Nov. 23, 1983, effective Dec. 1, 1983 (442 So.2d 198). Amended Feb. 23, 1984 (446 So.2d 87); Oct. 8, 1992, effective Jan. 1, 1993 (609 So.2d 465); Dec. 21, 1995, effective Jan. 1, 1996 (665 So.2d 218); Oct. 5, 2000, effective Jan. 1, 2001 (780 So.2d 819); Oct. 14, 2004 (888 So.2d 614); July 6, 2006 (933 So.2d 1136). Renumbered from Rule 2.035 Sept. 21, 2006 (939 So.2d 966). Amended Jan. 31, 2008 (974 So.2d 1066); Nov. 14, 2013 (129 So.3d 358).

Court Commentary

1983 Adoption. Article V, section 9, of the Florida Constitution authorizes the establishment, by rule, of uniform criteria for the determination of the need for additional judges, except supreme court justices, the necessity for decreasing the number of judges and for increasing, decreasing, or redefining appellate districts and judicial circuits. Each year since the adoption of article V in 1972, this court, pursuant to section 9, has certified its determination of need to the legislature based upon factors and criteria set forth in our certification decisions. This rule is intended to set forth criteria and workload factors previously developed, adopted, and used in this certification process, as summarized and specifically set forth in *In re Certificate of Judicial Manpower*, 428 So. 2d 229 (Fla. 1983); *In re Certificate of Judicial Manpower*, 396 So. 2d 172 (Fla. 1981); and *In re Certification*, 370 So. 2d 365 (Fla. 1979).

2004 Amendment. Subdivision (b)(2) was amended to provide more specific criteria and workload factors to be used in determining the need for increasing or decreasing the number of judges on the District Courts of Appeal. In addition, the caseload level at which the court will presume that there is a need for an additional appellate judge has been increased from 250 to 350 filings per judge.

2006 Amendment. Subdivision (a) is amended to be consistent with the 2006 adoption of rule 2.036 relating to the criteria for determining the necessity and for increasing, decreasing, or redefining appellate districts and judicial circuits, pursuant to article V, section 9, Florida Constitution. The Court adopts the Commission on District Court of Appeal Performance and Accountability's conclusion that a single case filing threshold is insufficient to capture the intricacies that make up judicial workload in the district courts. The Commission's alternative to the 350–filings–per–judge threshold is a weighted case dispositions per judge, which the Commission determined to be a meaningful measure of judicial workload.

The relative weighted caseload is determined by surveying a representative sample of judges on the relative degree of judicial effort put into each category of cases based upon an agreed typical case having a value of 100. Each category was assigned a relative weight number based upon the statewide average of the weight calculated through the survey. These weights were then applied to each court's dispositions on the merits to determine the weighted caseload value and divided by 100.

This approach accommodates the important distinction between the number of cases filed and the judicial effort required to dispose of those cases. While the number of cases continues to increase, trends in the types of cases filed have dramatically changed the nature of the work that the district court judges handle. The weighted caseload approach not only accommodates the differences in types of cases by measuring their relative workload demands for judges, but it also accommodates the work performed by legal support staff.

Subdivision (b)(2)(B) establishes a presumption that the relative weight of cases disposed on the merits should fall below 280 per judge. Chief judges must consider the impact that the addition of a judge would have on this measure when applied to their courts' dispositions on the merits for the previous year.

Every four years the Commission will measure the relative judicial effort associated with the cases disposed on the merits for the year immediately preceding. This will be accomplished by asking a representative sample of judges to approximate the relative weight of cases in relation to a mid-ranked case. The resulting weights will then be applied to each court's dispositions on the merits to determine the weighted caseload value per judge.

2013 Amendment. Subdivision (d)(5) was added to ensure the certification process under rule 2.240(d) is conducted in conjunction with the related process for determinations regarding increases, decreases, or redefinition of appellate districts and judicial circuits under Florida Rule of Judicial Administration 2.241.

Rule 2.241. Determination of the Necessity to Increase, Decrease, or Redefine Judicial Circuits and Appellate Districts

(a) Purpose. The purpose of this rule is to establish uniform criteria for the supreme court's determination of the necessity for increasing, decreasing, or redefining judicial circuits and appellate districts as required by article V, section 9, of the Florida Constitution. This rule also provides for an assessment committee and a certification process to assist the court in certifying to the legislature its findings and recommendations concerning such need.

(b) Certification Process. A certification process shall be completed in conjunction with the supreme court's annual determination regarding the need for judges under Florida Rule of Judicial Administration 2.240(d) and in accordance with the following:

(1) The supreme court shall certify a necessity to increase, decrease, or redefine judicial circuits and appellate districts when it determines that the judicial process is adversely affected by circumstances that present a compelling need for the certified change.

(2) The supreme court may certify a necessity to increase, decrease, or redefine judicial circuits and appellate districts when it determines that the judicial process would be improved significantly by the certified change.

(3) The state courts administrator will distribute a compilation of summary statistics and projections to each chief judge at a time designated by the chief justice.

(4) Each chief judge shall consider criteria as may apply under rules 2. 241(c) and 2.241(d), as well as any other relevant factors, and shall inform the chief justice of any perceived need to increase, decrease, or redefine the state's judicial circuits or appellate districts.

(5) Having been advised in these matters by the chief justice and taking into consideration other relevant factors, the supreme court, finding cause for further inquiry, may appoint an assessment committee to consider the capacity of the courts to effectively fulfill their constitutional and statutory responsibilities as well as any attendant need to increase, decrease, or redefine appellate districts and judicial circuits.

(6) If an assessment committee is appointed, the committee shall confer with the chief judges and other representatives of appellate districts and judicial circuits, district court of appeal and/or trial court budget commissions, The Florida Bar, and the public for purposes of gathering additional information regarding matters within its charge and shall submit written recommendations to the supreme court.

(7) The supreme court shall consider the assessment committee's recommendations within a timeframe it deems appropriate.

(8) Whether or not an assessment committee is appointed, the supreme court shall balance the potential impact and disruption caused by changes in judicial circuits and appellate districts against the need to address circumstances that limit the quality and efficiency of, and public confidence in, the judicial process. Given the impact and disruption that can arise from any alteration in judicial structure, prior to recommending a change in judicial circuits or appellate districts, the supreme court shall consider less disruptive adjustments including, but not limited to, the addition of judges, the creation of branch locations, geographic or subject-matter divisions within judicial circuits or appellate districts, deployment of new technologies, and increased ratios of support staff per judge.

(c) Criteria for Judicial Circuits. The following criteria shall be considered when determining the necessity for increasing, decreasing, or redefining judicial circuits as required by article V, section 9, of the Florida Constitution:

(1) *Effectiveness.* Factors to be considered for this criterion include the extent to which each court:

(A) expedites appropriate cases;

(B) handles its workload in a manner permitting its judges to prepare written decisions when warranted;

(C) is capable of accommodating changes in statutes or case law impacting workload or court operations; and

(D) handles its workload in a manner permitting its judges to serve on committees for the judicial system.

(2) *Efficiency.* Factors to be considered for this criterion are the extent to which each court:

(A) stays current with its caseload, as indicated by measurements such as the clearance rate;

(B) adjudicates a high percentage of its cases within the time standards set forth in the Rules of Judicial Administration and has adequate procedures to ensure efficient, timely disposition of its cases; and

(C) uses its resources, case management techniques, and technologies to improve the efficient adjudication of cases, research of legal issues, and issuance of decisions.

(3) *Access to Courts.* Factors to be considered for this criterion are the extent to which:

(A) litigants, including self-represented litigants, have meaningful access consistent with due process; and

(B) decisions of a court are available in a timely and efficient manner.

(4) *Professionalism.* Factors to be considered for this criterion are the extent to which each court:

(A) handles workload issues in a manner permitting its judges adequate time and resources to participate in continuing judicial education and to stay abreast of the law in order to maintain a qualified judiciary;

(B) is capable of recruiting and retaining qualified staff; and

(C) affords staff adequate time to participate in continuing education and specialized training.

(5) *Public Trust and Confidence.* Factors to be considered for this criterion are the extent to which each court:

(A) handles workload in a manner permitting its judges adequate time for community involvement;

(B) affords access to open court and other public proceedings for the general public;

(C) fosters public trust and confidence given its geography and demographic composition; and

(D) attracts a diverse group of well-qualified applicants for judicial vacancies, including applicants from all counties within the circuit.

(6) *Additional criteria.* Such other factors as are regularly considered when making a determination with respect to the need for additional judges under Florida Rule of Judicial Administration 2.240(b)(1) and (c).

(d) Criteria for District Courts. The following criteria shall be considered when determining the necessity for increasing, decreasing, or redefining appellate districts as required by article V, section 9, of the Florida Constitution:

(1) *Effectiveness.* Factors to be considered for this criterion are the extent to which each court:

(A) expedites appropriate cases;

(B) handles workload in a manner permitting its judges to prepare written opinions when warranted;

(C) functions in a collegial manner;

(D) handles workload in a manner permitting its judges to develop, clarify, and maintain consistency in the law within that district, including consistency between written opinions and per curiam affirmances without written opinions;

(E) handles its workload in a manner permitting its judges to harmonize decisions of their court with those of other district courts or to certify conflict when appropriate;

(F) handles its workload in a manner permitting its judges to have adequate time to review all decisions rendered by the court;

(G) is capable of accommodating changes in statutes or case law impacting workload or court operations; and

(H) handles its workload in a manner permitting its judges to serve on committees for the judicial system.

(2) *Efficiency.* Factors to be considered for this criterion are the extent to which each court:

(A) stays current with its caseload, as indicated by measurements such as the clearance rate;

(B) adjudicates a high percentage of its cases within the time standards set forth in the Rules of Judicial Administration and has adequate procedures to ensure efficient, timely disposition of its cases; and

(C) uses its resources, case management techniques, and other technologies to improve the efficient adjudication of cases, research of legal issues, and preparation and distribution of decisions.

(3) *Access to Appellate Review.* Factors to be considered for this criterion are the extent to which:

(A) litigants, including self-represented litigants, have meaningful access to a district court for mandatory and discretionary review of cases, consistent with due process;

(B) litigants are afforded efficient access to the court for the filing of pleadings and for oral argument when appropriate; and

(C) orders and opinions of a court are available in a timely and efficient manner.

(4) *Professionalism.* Factors to be considered for this criterion are the extent to which each court:

(A) handles its workload in a manner permitting its judges adequate time and resources to participate in continuing judicial education opportunities and to stay abreast of the law in order to maintain a qualified judiciary;

(B) is capable of recruiting and retaining qualified staff; and

(C) affords staff adequate time to participate in continuing education and specialized training.

(5) *Public Trust and Confidence.* Factors to be considered for this criterion are the extent to which each court:

(A) handles its workload in a manner permitting its judges adequate time for community involvement;

(B) provides adequate access to oral arguments and other public proceedings for the general public within its district;

(C) fosters public trust and confidence given its geography and demographic composition; and

(D) attracts a diverse group of well-qualified applicants for judicial vacancies, including applicants from all circuits within the district.

(e) *Results of determination.* Only upon the supreme court's finding that a need exists for increasing, decreasing, or redefining appellate districts and judicial circuits, shall the court, acting prior to the next regular session of the legislature, certify to the legislature its findings and recommendations concerning such need.

Former Rule 2.036 added Feb. 16, 2006 (921 So.2d 615). Renumbered from Rule 2.036 Sept. 21, 2006 (939 So.2d 966). Amended Nov. 14, 2013 (129 So.3d 358).

District Court of Appeal Workload and Jurisdiction Committee Notes

2006 Adoption. Article V, section 9 of the Florida constitution states that:

The supreme court shall establish by rule uniform criteria for the determination of the need for additional judges except supreme court justices, the *necessity* for decreasing the number of judges and for increasing, decreasing or redefining appellate districts. If the supreme court finds that a *need* exists for . . . increasing, decreasing or redefining appellate districts . . ., it shall, prior to the next regular session of the legislature, certify to the legislature its findings and recommendations concerning such need.

(Emphasis added.) Thus, the constitution uses only "need" when describing the uniform criteria for certifying additional judges, but uses both "necessity" and "need" when describing the uniform criteria for increasing, decreasing, or redefining appellate districts. The supreme court has never determined whether this language compels differing tests for the two certifications. Subdivision (c) of this rule uses the phrase "certify a necessity." The Committee on District Court of Appeal Workload and Jurisdiction determined that the two standards set forth in that subdivision recognize the supreme court's obligation to recommend a change to the structure of the district courts when circumstances reach the level of necessity that compels a change, but also recognize the court's discretion to recommend a change to the structure of the district courts when improvements are needed.

The criteria set forth in this rule are based on studies of the workload, jurisdiction, and performance of the appellate courts, and the work of the Committee on District Court of Appeal Workload and Jurisdiction in 2005. In establishing these criteria, substantial reliance was placed on empirical research conducted by judicial branch committees and on other statistical data concerning cases, caseloads, timeliness of case processing, and manner for disposition of cases, collected by the Office of the State Courts Administrator Office as required by section 25.075, Florida Statutes (2004), and Florida Rule of Judicial Administration 2.030(e)(2).

The workload and jurisdiction committee considered the impact of computer technology on appellate districts. It is clear that, at this time or in the future, technology can be deployed to allow litigants efficient access to a court for filing of pleadings and for participation in oral argument, and that it can expand the general public's access to the courts. It is possible that technology will substantially alter the appellate review process in the future and that appellate courts may find that technology permits or even requires different districting techniques. This rule was designed to allow these issues to be addressed by the assessment committee and the supreme court without mandating any specific approach.

The five basic criteria in subdivision (d) are not listed in any order of priority. Thus, for example, the workload and jurisdiction committee did not intend efficiency to be a more important criterion than engendering public trust and confidence.

Subdivision (d)(2)(A) recognizes that the court currently provides the legislature with an annual measurement of the appellate courts' "clearance rate," which is the ratio between the number of cases that are resolved during a fiscal year and the new cases that are filed during the same period. Thus, a clearance rate of one hundred percent reflects a court that is disposing of pending cases at approximately the same rate that new cases arrive. Given that other measurements may be selected in the future, the rule does not mandate sole reliance on this measurement.

Subdivision (d)(5)(E) recognizes that a district court's geographic territory may be so large that it limits or discourages applicants for judicial vacancies from throughout the district and creates the perception that a court's judges do not reflect the makeup of the territory.

Court Commentary

2013 Amendment. The rule has been amended so the supreme court's annual certification process will include an analysis of the need to increase, decrease, or redefine judicial circuits. The requirement for an assessment committee to analyze, once every eight years, the capacity of the district courts to fulfill their duties has been deleted. Instead, the chief judges of the trial and appellate courts will review annual statistics provided by the state courts administrator, along with the criteria set forth in the rule and any other relevant factors, and inform the chief justice of any perceived need. Taking these and other concerns into consideration, the supreme court may appoint an assessment committee to make further inquiry. If an assessment committee is appointed, the supreme court will consider the committee's recommendations and will certify to the legislature its own findings and recommendations concerning such need.

Rule 2.244. Judicial Compensation

(a) Statement of Purpose. The purpose of this rule is to set forth the official policy of the judicial branch of state government concerning the appropriate salary relationships between justices and judges at the various levels of the state courts system and the mechanism for advancing judicial compensation and benefits issues. Although ultimate discretion in establishing judicial compensation is vested in the Florida Legislature, the salary relationships referenced in this rule reflect the policy of the judicial branch when requesting adjustments to judicial salaries.

(b) Annual Salaries. The annual salary of a district court of appeal judge should be equal to 95 percent of the annual salary of a supreme court justice. The annual salary of a circuit court judge should be equal to 90 percent of the annual salary of a supreme court justice. The annual salary of a county court judge should be equal to 85 percent of the annual salary of a supreme court justice.

(c) Unified Committee on Judicial Compensation.

(1) *Creation.* There shall be created a Unified Committee on Judicial Compensation to address judicial pay and benefits issues.

(2) *Purpose.* The purpose of the Unified Committee on Judicial Compensation shall be to:

(A) develop and recommend to the supreme court judicial pay and benefits priorities; and

(B) advocate for judicial pay and benefits issues approved by the supreme court for inclusion in the annual judicial branch budget request.

(3) *Membership.* The membership shall include the chief justice of the supreme court, the presidents and presidents-elect of the Conference of District Court of Appeal Judges, the Conference of Circuit Court Judges, and the Conference of County Court Judges, and the chairs and vice-chairs of the District Court Budget Commission and the Trial Court Budget Commission.

(4) *Staffing.* The Office of the State Courts Administrator will provide primary staff support to the committee.

Added May 17, 2007 (957 So.2d 1168). Amended Feb. 9, 2012 (121 So.3d 1).

Rule 2.245. Case Reporting System for Trial Courts

(a) Reporting. The clerk of the circuit court shall report the activity of all cases before all courts within the clerk's jurisdiction to the supreme court in the manner and on the forms established by the office of the state courts administrator and approved by order of the court. In those jurisdictions where separate offices of the clerk of the circuit court and clerk of the county court have been established by law, the clerk of the circuit court shall report the activity of all cases before the circuit court, and the clerk of the county court shall report the activity of all cases before the county court.

(b) Uniform Case Numbering System.

(1) The clerk of the circuit court and the clerk of the county court, where that separate office exists, shall use the Uniform Case Numbering System. The uniform case number shall appear upon the case file, the docket and minute books (or their electronic equivalent), and the complaint.

(2) The office of the state courts administrator shall distribute to the respective clerks of the circuit and county courts appropriate instructions regarding the nature and use of the Uniform Case Numbering System.

Former Rule 2.080 amended June 14, 1979, effective July 1, 1979 (372 So.2d 449); Oct. 8, 1992, effective Jan. 1, 1993 (609 So.2d 465). Renumbered from Rule 2.080 Sept. 21, 2006 (939 So.2d 966).

Rule 2.250. Time Standards for Trial and Appellate Courts and Reporting Requirements

(a) Time Standards. The following time standards are hereby established as a presumptively reasonable time period for the completion of cases in the trial and appellate courts of this state. It is recognized that there are cases that, because of their complexity, present problems that cause reasonable delays. However, most cases should be completed within the following time periods:

(1) *Trial Court Time Standards.*

(A) Criminal.

Felony — 180 days (arrest to final disposition)

Misdemeanor — 90 days (arrest to final disposition)

(B) Civil.

Jury cases — 18 months (filing to final disposition)

Non-jury cases — 12 months (filing to final disposition)

Small claims — 95 days (filing to final disposition)

(C) Domestic Relations.

Uncontested — 90 days (filing to final disposition)

Contested — 180 days (filing to final disposition)

(D) Probate.

Uncontested, no federal estate tax return — 12 months (from issuance of letters of administration to final discharge)

Uncontested, with federal estate tax return — 12 months (from the return's due date to final discharge)

Contested — 24 months (from filing to final discharge)

(E) Juvenile Delinquency.

Disposition hearing — 120 days (filing of petition or child being taken into custody to hearing)

Disposition hearing (child detained) — 36 days (date of detention to hearing)

(F) Juvenile Dependency.

Disposition hearing (child sheltered) — 88 days (shelter hearing to disposition)

Disposition hearing (child not sheltered) — 120 days (filing of petition for dependency to hearing)

(G) Permanency Proceedings.

Permanency hearing — 12 months (date child is sheltered to hearing)

(2) *Supreme Court and District Courts of Appeal Time Standards*: Rendering a decision—within 180 days of either oral argument or the submission of the case to the court panel for a decision without oral argument, except in juvenile dependency or termination of parental rights cases, in which a decision should be rendered within 60 days of either oral argument or submission of the case to the court panel for a decision without oral argument.

(3) *Florida Bar Referee Time Standards*: Report of referee — within 180 days of being assigned to hear the case

(4) *Circuit Court Acting as Appellate Court*:

Ninety days from submission of the case to the judge for review

(b) Reporting of Cases. The time standards require that the following monitoring procedures be implemented:

All pending cases in circuit and district courts of appeal exceeding the time standards shall be listed separately on a report submitted quarterly to the chief justice. The report shall include for each case listed the case number, type of case, case status (active or inactive for civil cases and contested or uncontested for domestic relations and probate cases), the date of arrest in criminal cases, and the original filing date in civil cases. The Office of the State Courts Administrator will provide the necessary forms for submission of this data. The report will be due on the 15th day of the month following the last day of the quarter.

Former Rule 2.085 added May 14, 1986, effective July 1, 1986 (493 So.2d 423). Amended Sept. 29, 1988, effective Jan. 1, 1989 (536 So.2d 195); Oct. 8, 1992, effective Jan. 1, 1993 (609 So.2d 465); Aug. 29, 2002, effective Oct. 1, 2002 (826 So.2d 233); July 10, 2003, effective Jan. 1, 2004 (851 So.2d 698); Nov. 18, 2004, effective Jan. 1, 2005 (889 So.2d 68); Nov. 3, 2005, effective Jan. 1, 2006 (915 So.2d 157). Renumbered from Rule 2.085 Sept. 21, 2006 (939 So.2d 966). Amended Nov. 12, 2009 (24 So.3d 47).

Rule 2.255. Statewide Grand Jury

(a) Procedure. The chief judge of each judicial circuit shall cause a list of those persons whose names have been drawn and certified for jury duty in each of the counties within that circuit to be compiled. The lists shall be taken from the male and female population over the age of 18 years and having the other constitutional and statutory qualifications for jury duty in this state not later than the last day of the first week of December of each year. From the lists so compiled, the chief judge shall cause to be selected, by lot and at random, and by any authorized method including mechanical, electronic, or electrical device, a list of prospective grand jurors from each county whose number shall be determined on the basis of 3 jurors for each 3,000 residents or a fraction thereof in each county. The lists from which the names are drawn may be, but are not required to be, the same lists from which petit and grand juries are drawn in each county and circuit. After compilation, the statewide grand jury lists shall be submitted to the state courts administrator not later than February 15 of each year.

(b) Population. For the purposes of this rule, the population of each county shall be in accordance with the latest United States Decennial Census as set forth in the Florida Statutes.

(c) Excuses.

(1) The judge appointed to preside over the statewide grand jury may issue an order appointing the chief judge of the judicial circuit where a prospective grand juror resides to determine whether service on the statewide grand jury will result in an unreasonable personal or financial hardship because of the location or projected length of the grand jury investigation.

(2) The chief judge of the circuit shall determine whether a prospective grand juror fails to meet the qualifications of a juror in the county where the person resides. The determination shall be made only for those prospective grand jurors who contact the chief judge and request disqualification.

(3) The chief judge of the circuit shall excuse any prospective grand juror who requests and is qualified for exemption from grand jury service pursuant to general law, or from service as a juror in the county where the person resides. The chief judge shall inform the judge appointed to preside over the statewide grand jury without delay of any determination.

Former Rule 2.100 amended June 14, 1979, effective July 1, 1979 (372 So.2d 449); Oct. 8, 1992, effective Jan. 1, 1993 (609 So.2d 465). Renumbered from Rule 2.100 Sept. 21, 2006 (939 So.2d 966).

Rule 2.256. Juror Time Management

(a) Optimum Use. The services of prospective jurors should be employed so as to achieve optimum use with a minimum of inconvenience to jurors.

(b) Minimum Number. A minimally sufficient number of jurors needed to accommodate trial activity should be determined. This information and appropriate management techniques should be used to adjust both the number of individuals summoned for jury duty and the number assigned to jury panels, consistent with any administrative orders issued by the Chief Justice.

(c) Courtroom Assignment. Each prospective juror who has reported to the courthouse should be assigned a courtroom for voir dire before any prospective juror is assigned a second time.

(d) Calendar Coordination. Jury management and calendar management should be coordinated to make effective use of jurors.

Added Oct. 4, 2007, effective Jan. 1, 2008 (967 So.2d 178).

Rule 2.260. Change of Venue

(a) Preliminary Procedures. Prior to entering an order to change venue to a particular circuit in a criminal case or in any other case in which change of venue will likely create an unusual burden for the transferee circuit, the chief judge in the circuit in which the case originated shall contact the chief judge in the circuit to which the case is intended to be moved to determine the receiving county's ability to accommodate the change of venue. It is the intent of this rule that the county identified to receive the case shall do so unless the physical facilities or other resources in that county are such that moving the case to that county would either create an unsafe situation or adversely affect the operations of that court. Any conflict between the circuits regarding a potential change of venue shall be referred to the chief justice of the Florida Supreme Court for resolution.

(b) Presiding Judge. The presiding judge from the originating court shall accompany the change of venue case, unless the originating and receiving courts agree otherwise.

(c) Reimbursement of Costs. As a general policy the county in which an action originated shall reimburse the county receiving the change of venue case for any ordinary expenditure and any extraordinary but reasonable and necessary expenditure that would not otherwise have been incurred by the receiving county. For purposes of this section, ordinary expenditure, extraordinary expenditure, and nonreimbursable expenditure are defined as follows:

(1) Ordinary expenditures include:

(A) juror expenses not reimbursed by the State of Florida;

(B) court reporter expenses, including appearances by either official or freelance reporters, transcripts, and other expenses associated with the creation of a court record;

(C) court interpreters;

(D) maintenance of evidence, including the cost of handling, storing, or maintaining the evidence beyond the expenses normally incurred by the receiving county;

(E) services and supplies purchased as a result of the change of venue;

(F) overtime expenditures for regular court and clerk staff attributable to the change of venue; and

(G) trial–related expenses, including conflict attorney fees; all expert, law enforcement, or ordinary witness costs and expenses; and investigator expenses.

(2) Extraordinary but reasonable and necessary expenses include:

(A) security–related expenditures, including overtime for security personnel;

(B) facility remodeling or renovation; and

(C) leasing or renting of space or equipment.

Except in emergencies or unless it is impracticable to do so, a receiving county should give notice to the chief judge and clerk of the county in which the action originated before incurring any extraordinary expenditures.

(3) Nonreimbursable expenses include:

(A) normal operating expenses, including the overhead of the receiving county; and

(B) equipment that is purchased and kept by the receiving county that can be used for other purposes or cases.

(d) Documentation of Costs. No expenses shall be submitted for reimbursement without supporting documentation, such as a claim, invoice, bill, statement, or time sheet. Any required court order or approval of costs shall also be sent to the originating court.

(e) Timing of Reimbursement. Unless both counties agree to other terms, reimbursement of all expenses by the originating county shall be paid or disputed in writing on or before the sixtieth day after the receipt of the claim for reimbursement. Payment of a disputed amount shall be made on or before the sixtieth day after the resolution of this dispute. Any amount subject to dispute shall be expeditiously resolved by authorized representatives of the court administrator's office of the originating and receiving counties.

(f) Media Relations. Procedures to accommodate the media shall be developed by the receiving county immediately upon notice of the change of venue when the change of venue is reasonably expected to generate an unusual amount of publicity. These procedures must be approved by the chief judge of the receiving circuit and implemented pursuant to administrative order by the presiding judge. The presiding judge shall obtain the concurrence of the chief judge before entering any orders that vary from or conflict with existing administrative orders of the receiving circuit.

(g) Case File. The clerk of the circuit court in the originating county shall forward the original case file to the clerk in the receiving county. The receiving clerk shall maintain the file and keep it secure until the trial has been concluded. During the trial, any documents or exhibits that have been added shall be properly marked and added to the file in a manner consistent with the policy and procedures of the receiving county. After the conclusion of the trial, the file shall be returned to the clerk in the county of origin.

Former Rule 2.180 added Oct. 24, 1996, effective Jan. 1, 1997 (682 So.2d 89). Renumbered from Rule 2.180 Sept. 21, 2006 (939 So.2d 966).

Rule 2.265. Municipal Ordinance Violations

(a) References to Abolished Municipal Courts. All references to a municipal court or municipal judge in rules promulgated by the supreme court, in the Florida Statutes, and in any municipal ordinance shall be deemed to refer, respectively, to the county court or county court judge.

(b) Costs in County Courts. The chief judge of a circuit shall by administrative order establish a schedule of costs, in conformity with any provisions of law, to be assessed against a defendant in the county court and paid to the county for violations of municipal ordinances which are prosecuted in county court. The costs shall be assessed as a set dollar amount per conviction, not to exceed $50 excluding any other statutory costs.

(c) Collection of Outstanding Fines. All cases for which outstanding fines, civil penalties, and costs are being collected by a municipality shall be retained by the municipality until collected or until the offender defaults on payment. If a default occurs, the municipality may institute summary claims proceedings to collect the outstanding fines.

(d) Judicial Notice of Municipal Ordinances. The judges of the county courts may take judicial notice of any municipal ordinance if a certified copy of the ordinance has been filed in the office of the clerk of circuit court or, in those counties having a clerk of the county court, filed in that office, and if a certified copy of the ordinance is presented to the court.

(e) Style of Municipal Ordinance Cases. All prosecutions for violations of municipal ordinances in county court shall have the following style: City of . . . . v. . . . .

Former Rule 2.110 amended June 14, 1979, effective July 1, 1979 (372 So.2d 449); Oct. 8, 1992, effective Jan. 1, 1993 (609 So.2d 465); Dec. 23, 1993 (634 So.2d 604). Renumbered from Rule 2.110 Sept. 21, 2006 (939 So.2d 966).

PART III. JUDICIAL OFFICERS

Rule 2.310. Judicial Discipline, Removal, Retirement, and Suspension

(a) Filing. Any recommendations to the supreme court from the Judicial Qualifications Commission pursuant to article V, section 12, of the Florida Constitution shall be in writing. The original and 7 copies shall be filed with the clerk of the court, and a copy shall be served expeditiously on the justice or judge against whom action is sought.

(b) Procedure.

(1) Promptly upon the filing of a recommendation from the commission, the court shall determine whether the commission's recommendation complies with all requirements of the constitution and the commission's rules. Upon determining that the recommendation so complies, and unless the court otherwise directs, an order shall issue directing the justice or judge to show cause in writing why the recommended action should not be taken.

(2) The justice or judge may file a response in writing within the time set by the court in its order to show cause, and the commission may serve a reply within 20 days from service of the response.

(3) If requested by the commission, or by a justice or judge at the time of filing a response, the court may allow oral argument on the commission's recommendation.

(c) Costs. The supreme court may award reasonable and necessary costs, including costs of investigation and prosecution, to the prevailing party. Neither attorneys' fees nor travel expenses of commission personnel shall be included in an award of costs. Taxable costs may include:

(1) court reporters' fees, including per diem fees, deposition costs, and costs associated with the preparation of the transcript and record; and

(2) witness expenses, including travel and out-of-pocket expenses.

Former Rule 2.140 added Sept. 13, 1984, effective Jan. 1, 1985 (458 So.2d 1110). Amended Oct. 8, 1992, effective Jan. 1, 1993 (609 So.2d 465); Oct. 5, 2000, effective Jan. 1, 2001 (780 So.2d 819). Renumbered from Rule 2.140 Sept. 21, 2006 (939 So.2d 966).

Rule 2.320. Continuing Judicial Education

(a) Purpose. This rule sets forth the continuing education requirements for all judges in the state judicial system.

(b) Education Requirements.

(1) *Applicability.* All Florida county, circuit, and appellate judges and Florida supreme court justices shall comply with these judicial education require-

ments. Retired judges who have been approved by the supreme court to be assigned to temporary active duty as authorized by section 25.073, Florida Statutes (1991), shall also comply with the judicial education requirements.

(2) *Minimum Requirements.* Each judge and justice shall complete a minimum of 30 credit hours of approved judicial education programs every 3 years. Beginning January 1, 2012, 4 hours must be in the area of judicial ethics; prior to that date, 2 hours in the area of judicial ethics are required. Approved courses in fairness and diversity also can be used to fulfill the judicial ethics requirement. In addition to the 30–hour requirement, every judge new to a level of trial court must complete the Florida Judicial College program in that judge's first year of judicial service following selection to that level of court; every new appellate court judge or justice must, within 2 years following selection to that level of court, complete an approved appellate-judge program. Every new appellate judge who has never been a trial judge or who has never attended Phase I of the Florida Judicial College as a magistrate must also attend Phase I of the Florida Judicial College in that judge's first year of judicial service following the judge's appointment. Credit for teaching a course for which mandatory judicial education credit is available will be allowed on the basis of 2½ hours' credit for each instructional hour taught, up to a maximum of 5 hours per year.

(3) *Mediation Training.* Prior to conducting any mediation, a senior judge shall have completed a minimum of one judicial education course offered by the Florida Court Education Council. The course shall specifically focus on the areas where the Code of Judicial Conduct or the Florida Rules for Certified and Court–Appointed Mediators could be violated.

(c) Course Approval. The Florida Court Education Council, in consultation with the judicial conferences, shall develop approved courses for each state court jurisdiction. Courses offered by other judicial and legal education entities must be approved by the council before they may be submitted for credit.

(d) Waiver. The Florida Court Education Council is responsible for establishing a procedure for considering and acting upon waiver and extension requests on an individual basis.

(e) Reporting Requirements and Sanctions. The Florida Court Education Council shall establish a procedure for reporting annually to the chief justice on compliance with this rule. Each judge shall submit to the Court Education Division of the Office of the State Courts Administrator an annual report showing the judge's attendance at approved courses. Failure to comply with the requirements of this rule will be reported to the chief justice of the Florida supreme court for such administrative action as deemed necessary. The chief justice may consider a judge's or justice's failure to comply as neglect of duty and report the matter to the Judicial Qualifications Commission.

Former Rule 2.150 added Dec. 31, 1987, effective Jan. 1, 1988 (518 So.2d 258). Amended Oct. 8, 1992, effective Jan. 1, 1993 (609 So.2d 465); Nov. 3, 2005, effective Nov. 3, 2007 (915 So.2d 145). Renumbered from Rule 2.150 Sept. 21, 2006 (939 So.2d 966). Amended effective Dec. 9, 2010 (51 So.3d 1151).

Rule 2.330. Disqualification of Trial Judges

(a) Application. This rule applies only to county and circuit judges in all matters in all divisions of court.

(b) Parties. Any party, including the state, may move to disqualify the trial judge assigned to the case on grounds provided by rule, by statute, or by the Code of Judicial Conduct.

(c) Motion. A motion to disqualify shall:

(1) be in writing;

(2) allege specifically the facts and reasons upon which the movant relies as the grounds for disqualification;

(3) be sworn to by the party by signing the motion under oath or by a separate affidavit; and

(4) include the dates of all previously granted motions to disqualify filed under this rule in the case and the dates of the orders granting those motions.

The attorney for the party shall also separately certify that the motion and the client's statements are made in good faith. In addition to filing with the clerk, the movant shall immediately serve a copy of the motion on the subject judge as set forth in Florida Rule of Civil Procedure 1.080.

(d) Grounds. A motion to disqualify shall show:

(1) that the party fears that he or she will not receive a fair trial or hearing because of specifically described prejudice or bias of the judge; or

(2) that the judge before whom the case is pending, or some person related to said judge by consanguinity or affinity within the third degree, is a party thereto or is interested in the result thereof, or that said judge is related to an attorney or counselor of record in the cause by consanguinity or affinity within the third degree, or that said judge is a material witness for or against one of the parties to the cause.

(e) Time. A motion to disqualify shall be filed within a reasonable time not to exceed 10 days after discovery of the facts constituting the grounds for the motion and shall be promptly presented to the court for an immediate ruling. Any motion for disqualification made during a hearing or trial must be based on facts discovered during the hearing or trial and may be stated on the record, provided that it is also promptly reduced to writing in compliance with subdivision (c) and promptly filed. A motion made during hearing or trial shall be ruled on immediately.

(f) Determination — Initial Motion. The judge against whom an initial motion to disqualify under subdivision (d)(1) is directed shall determine only the legal sufficiency of the motion and shall not pass on the truth of the facts alleged. If the motion is legally sufficient, the judge shall immediately enter an order granting disqualification and proceed no further in the action. If any motion is legally insufficient, an order denying the motion shall immediately be entered. No other reason for denial shall be stated, and an order of denial shall not take issue with the motion.

(g) Determination — Successive Motions. If a judge has been previously disqualified on motion for alleged prejudice or partiality under subdivision (d)(1), a successor judge shall not be disqualified based on a successive motion by the same party unless the successor judge rules that he or she is in fact not fair or impartial in the case. Such a successor judge may rule on the truth of the facts alleged in support of the motion.

(h) Prior Rulings. Prior factual or legal rulings by a disqualified judge may be reconsidered and vacated or amended by a successor judge based upon a motion for reconsideration, which must be filed within 20 days of the order of disqualification, unless good cause is shown for a delay in moving for reconsideration or other grounds for reconsideration exist.

(i) Judge's Initiative. Nothing in this rule limits the judge's authority to enter an order of disqualification on the judge's own initiative.

(j) Time for Determination. The judge shall rule on a motion to disqualify immediately, but no later than 30 days after the service of the motion as set forth in subdivision (c). If not ruled on within 30 days of service, the motion shall be deemed granted and the moving party may seek an order from the court directing the clerk to reassign the case.

Former Rule 2.160 added Oct. 8, 1992, effective Jan. 1, 1993 (609 So.2d 465). Amended July 10, 2003, effective Jan. 1, 2004 (851 So.2d 698); Oct. 7, 2004, effective Jan. 1, 2005 (885 So.2d 870). Renumbered from Rule 2.160 Sept. 21, 2006 (939 So.2d 966). Amended July 10, 2008, effective Jan. 1, 2009 (986 So.2d 560).

PART IV. JUDICIAL PROCEEDINGS AND RECORDS

Rule 2.410. Possession of Court Records

No person other than judges and authorized court employees shall remove court records as defined in rule 2.430 from the clerk's office except by order of the chief judge or chief justice upon a showing of good cause.

Former Rule 2.072 added June 27, 1996 (675 So.2d 1376). Renumbered from Rule 2.072 Sept. 21, 2006 (939 So.2d 966).

Court Commentary

1996 Adoption. This rule was written as a result of the problems being encountered in the removal of files from clerks' offices. While the purpose of the rule is to discourage the removal of court files, it is not intended to prohibit chief judges or the chief justice from issuing for good cause a general order providing that attorneys or authorized individuals may be allowed to check out files on a routine basis to assist in the administrative efficiency of a court. We note that section 28.13, Florida Statutes (1995), similarly prohibits the removal of files from clerks' offices.

Rule 2.420. Public Access to and Protection of Judicial Branch Records

(a) Scope and Purpose. Subject to the rulemaking power of the Florida Supreme Court provided by article V, section 2, Florida Constitution, the following rule shall govern public access to and the protection of the records of the judicial branch of government. The public shall have access to all records of the judicial branch of government, except as provided below. Access to all electronic and other court records shall be governed by the Standards for Access to Electronic Court Records and Access Security Matrix, as adopted by the supreme court in Administrative Order AOSC14–19 or the then-current Standards for Access. Remote access to electronic court records shall be permitted in counties where the supreme court's conditions for release of such records are met.

(b) Definitions.

(1) "Records of the judicial branch" are all records, regardless of physical form, characteristics, or means of transmission, made or received in connection with the transaction of official business by any judicial branch entity and consist of:

(A) "court records," which are the contents of the court file, including the progress docket and other similar records generated to document activity in a case, transcripts filed with the clerk, documentary exhibits in the custody of the clerk, and electronic records, videotapes, or stenographic tapes of depositions or other proceedings filed with the clerk, and electronic records, videotapes, or stenographic tapes of court proceedings; and

(B) "administrative records," which are all other records made or received pursuant to court rule, law, or ordinance, or in connection with the transaction of official business by any judicial branch entity.

(2) "Judicial branch" means the judicial branch of government, which includes the state courts system, the clerk of court when acting as an arm of the court, The Florida Bar, the Florida Board of Bar Examiners, the Judicial Qualifications Commission, and all other

entities established by or operating under the authority of the supreme court or the chief justice.

(3) *"Custodian."* The custodian of all administrative records of any court is the chief justice or chief judge of that court, except that each judge is the custodian of all records that are solely within the possession and control of that judge. As to all other records, the custodian is the official charged with the responsibility for the care, safekeeping, and supervision of such records. All references to "custodian" mean the custodian or the custodian's designee.

(4) "Confidential," as applied to information contained within a record of the judicial branch, means that such information is exempt from the public right of access under article I, section 24(a) of the Florida Constitution and may be released only to the persons or organizations designated by law, statute, or court order. As applied to information contained within a court record, the term "exempt" means that such information is confidential. Confidential information includes information that is confidential under this rule or under a court order entered pursuant to this rule. To the extent reasonably practicable, restriction of access to confidential information shall be implemented in a manner that does not restrict access to any portion of the record that is not confidential.

(5) "Affected non-party" means any non-party identified by name in a court record that contains confidential information pertaining to that non-party.

(6) "Filer" means any person who files a document in court records, except "filer" does not include the clerk of court or designee of the clerk, a judge, magistrate, hearing officer, or designee of a judge, magistrate, or hearing officer.

(c) Confidential and Exempt Records. The following records of the judicial branch shall be confidential:

(1) Trial and appellate court memoranda, drafts of opinions and orders, court conference records, notes, and other written materials of a similar nature prepared by judges or court staff acting on behalf of or at the direction of the court as part of the court's judicial decision-making process utilized in disposing of cases and controversies before Florida courts unless filed as a part of the court record;

(2) Memoranda or advisory opinions that relate to the administration of the court and that require confidentiality to protect a compelling governmental interest, including, but not limited to, maintaining court security, facilitating a criminal investigation, or protecting public safety, which cannot be adequately protected by less restrictive measures. The degree, duration, and manner of confidentiality imposed shall be no broader than necessary to protect the compelling governmental interest involved, and a finding shall be made that no less restrictive measures are available to protect this interest. The decision that confidentiality is required with respect to such administrative memorandum or written advisory opinion shall be made by the chief judge;

(3)(A) Complaints alleging misconduct against judges until probable cause is established;

(B) Complaints alleging misconduct against other entities or individuals licensed or regulated by the courts, until a finding of probable cause or no probable cause is established, unless otherwise provided. Such finding should be made within the time limit set by law or rule. If no time limit is set, the finding should be made within a reasonable period of time;

(4) Periodic evaluations implemented solely to assist judges in improving their performance, all information gathered to form the bases for the evaluations, and the results generated therefrom;

(5) Only the names and qualifications of persons applying to serve or serving as unpaid volunteers to assist the court, at the court's request and direction, shall be accessible to the public. All other information contained in the applications by and evaluations of persons applying to serve or serving as unpaid volunteers shall be confidential unless made public by court order based upon a showing of materiality in a pending court proceeding or upon a showing of good cause;

(6) Copies of arrest and search warrants and supporting affidavits retained by judges, clerks, or other court personnel until execution of said warrants or until a determination is made by law enforcement authorities that execution cannot be made;

(7) All records made confidential under the Florida and United States Constitutions and Florida and federal law;

(8) All records presently deemed to be confidential by court rule, including the Rules for Admission to the Bar, by Florida Statutes, by prior case law of the State of Florida, and by the rules of the Judicial Qualifications Commission;

(9) Any court record determined to be confidential in case decision or court rule on the grounds that

(A) confidentiality is required to

(i) prevent a serious and imminent threat to the fair, impartial, and orderly administration of justice;

(ii) protect trade secrets;

(iii) protect a compelling governmental interest;

(iv) obtain evidence to determine legal issues in a case;

(v) avoid substantial injury to innocent third parties;

(vi) avoid substantial injury to a party by disclosure of matters protected by a common law or privacy right not generally inherent in the specific type of proceeding sought to be closed;

(vii) comply with established public policy set forth in the Florida or United States Constitution or statutes or Florida rules or case law;

(B) the degree, duration, and manner of confidentiality ordered by the court shall be no broader than necessary to protect the interests set forth in subdivision (A); and

(C) no less restrictive measures are available to protect the interests set forth in subdivision (A).

(10) The names and any identifying information of judges mentioned in an advisory opinion of the Judicial Ethics Advisory Committee.

(d) Procedures for Determining Confidentiality of Court Records.

(1) The clerk of the court shall designate and maintain the confidentiality of any information contained within a court record that is described in subdivision (d)(1)(A) or (d)(1)(B) of this rule. The following information shall be maintained as confidential:

(A) information described by any of subdivisions (c)(1) through (c)(6) of this rule; and

(B) except as provided by court order, information subject to subdivision (c)(7) or (c)(8) of this rule that is currently confidential or exempt from section 119.07, Florida Statutes, and article I, section 24(a) of the Florida Constitution as specifically stated in any of the following statutes or as they may be amended or renumbered:

(i) Chapter 39 records relating to dependency matters, termination of parental rights, guardians ad litem, child abuse, neglect, and abandonment. §§ 39.0132(3), 39.0132(4)(a), Fla. Stat.

(ii) Adoption records. § 63.162, Fla. Stat.

(iii) Social Security, bank account, charge, debit, and credit card numbers. § 119.0714(1)(i)–(j), (2)(a)–(e), Fla. Stat. (Unless redaction is requested pursuant to § 119.0714(2), Fla. Stat., this information is exempt only as of January 1, 2012.)

(iv) HIV test results and the identity of any person upon whom an HIV test has been performed. § 381.004(2)(e), Fla. Stat.

(v) Records, including test results, held by the Department of Health or its authorized representatives relating to sexually transmissible diseases. § 384.29, Fla. Stat.

(vi) Birth records and portions of death and fetal death records. §§ 382.008(6), 382.025(1), Fla. Stat.

(vii) Information that can be used to identify a minor petitioning for a waiver of parental notice when seeking to terminate pregnancy. § 390.01116, Fla. Stat.

(viii) Clinical records under the Baker Act. § 394.4615(7), Fla. Stat.

(ix) Records of substance abuse service providers which pertain to the identity, diagnosis, and prognosis of and service provision to individuals. § 397.501(7), Fla. Stat.

(x) Clinical records of criminal defendants found incompetent to proceed or acquitted by reason of insanity. § 916.107(8), Fla. Stat.

(xi) Estate inventories and accountings. § 733.604(1), Fla. Stat.

(xii) The victim's address in a domestic violence action on petitioner's request. § 741.30(3)(b), Fla. Stat.

(xiii) Protected information regarding victims of child abuse or sexual offenses. §§ 119.071(2)(h), 119.0714(1)(h), Fla. Stat.

(xiv) Gestational surrogacy records. § 742.16(9), Fla. Stat.

(xv) Guardianship reports, orders appointing court monitors, and orders relating to findings of no probable cause in guardianship cases. §§ 744.1076, 744.3701, Fla. Stat.

(xvi) Grand jury records. §§ 905.17, 905.28(1), Fla. Stat.

(xvii) Records acquired by courts and law enforcement regarding family services for children. § 984.06(3)–(4), Fla. Stat.

(xviii) Juvenile delinquency records. §§ 985.04(1), 985.045(2), Fla. Stat.

(xix) Records disclosing the identity of persons subject to tuberculosis proceedings and records held by the Department of Health or its authorized representatives relating to known or suspected cases of tuberculosis or exposure to tuberculosis. §§ 392.545, 392.65, Fla. Stat.

(xx) Complete presentence investigation reports. Fla. R. Crim. P. 3.712.

(xxi) Forensic behavioral health evaluations under Chapter 916. § 916.1065, Fla. Stat.

(xxii) Eligibility screening, substance abuse screening, behavioral health evaluations, and treatment status reports for defendants referred to or considered for referral to a drug court program. § 397.334(10)(a), Fla. Stat.

(2) The filer of any document containing confidential information described in subdivision (d)(1)(B) shall, at the time of filing, file with the clerk a "Notice of Confidential Information within Court Filing" in order to indicate that confidential information described in subdivision (d)(1)(B) of this rule is included within the document being filed and also indicate that either the entire document is confidential or identify the precise location of the confidential information within the document being filed. If an entire court file is maintained as confidential, the filer of a document in such a file is not required to file the notice form. A form Notice of Confidential Information within Court Filing accompanies this rule.

(A) If any document in a court file contains confidential information as described in subdivision (d)(1)(B), the filer, a party, or any affected nonparty may file the Notice of Confidential Information within Court Filing if the document was not initially filed with a Notice of Confidential Information within Court Filing and the confidential information is not maintained as confidential by the clerk. The Notice of Confidential Information within Court Filing filed pursuant to this subdivision must also state the title and type of document, date of filing (if known), date of document, docket entry number, indicate that either the entire document is confidential or identify the precise location of the confidential information within the document, and provide any other information the clerk may require to locate the confidential information.

(B) The clerk of court shall review filings identified as containing confidential information to determine whether the purported confidential information is facially subject to confidentiality under subdivision (d)(1)(B). If the clerk determines that filed information is not subject to confidentiality under subdivision (d)(1)(B), the clerk shall notify the filer of the Notice of Confidential Information within Court Filing in writing within 5 days of filing the notice and thereafter shall maintain the information as confidential for 10 days from the date such notification by the clerk is served. The information shall not be held as confidential for more than that 10 day period, unless a motion has been filed pursuant to subdivision (d)(3).

(3) The filer of a document with the court shall ascertain whether any information contained within the document may be confidential under subdivision (c) of this rule notwithstanding that such information is not itemized at subdivision (d)(1) of this rule. If the filer believes in good faith that information is confidential but is not described in subdivision (d)(1) of this rule, the filer shall request that the information be maintained as confidential by filing a "Motion to Determine Confidentiality of Court Records" under the procedures set forth in subdivision (e), (f), or (g), unless

(A) the filer is the only individual whose confidential information is included in the document to be filed or is the attorney representing all such individuals; and

(B) a knowing waiver of the confidential status of that information is intended by the filer. Any interested person may request that information within a court file be maintained as confidential by filing a motion as provided in subdivision (e), (f), or (g).

(4) If a notice of confidential information is filed pursuant to subdivision (d)(2), or a motion is filed pursuant to subdivision (e)(1) or (g)(1) seeking to determine that information contained in court records is confidential, or pursuant to subdivision (e)(5) or (g)(5) seeking to vacate an order that has determined that information in a court record is confidential or seeking to unseal information designated as confidential by the clerk of court, then the person filing the notice or motion shall give notice of such filing to any affected non-party. Notice pursuant to this provision must:

(A) be filed with the court;

(B) identify the case by docket number;

(C) describe the confidential information with as much specificity as possible without revealing the confidential information, including specifying the precise location of the information within the court record; and

(D) include:

(i) in the case of a motion to determine confidentiality of court records, a statement that if the motion is denied then the subject material will not be treated as confidential by the clerk; and

(ii) in the case of a motion to unseal confidential records or a motion to vacate an order deeming records confidential, a statement that if the motion is granted, the subject material will no longer be treated as confidential by the clerk.

Any notice described herein must be served pursuant to subdivision (k), if applicable, together with the motion that gave rise to the notice in accordance with subdivision (e)(5) or (g)(5).

(5) Except when the entire court file is maintained as confidential, if a judge, magistrate, or hearing officer files any document containing confidential information, the confidential information within the document must be identified as "confidential" and the title of the document must include the word "confidential." The clerk must maintain the confidentiality of the identified confidential information. A copy of the document edited to omit the confidential information shall be provided to the clerk for filing and recording purposes.

(e) Request to Determine Confidentiality of Trial Court Records in Noncriminal Cases.

(1) A request to determine the confidentiality of trial court records in noncriminal cases under subdivision (c) must be made in the form of a written motion captioned "Motion to Determine Confidentiality of Court Records." A motion made under this subdivision must:

(A) identify the particular court records or a portion of a record that the movant seeks to have determined as confidential with as much specificity as possible without revealing the information subject to the confidentiality determination;

(B) specify the bases for determining that such court records are confidential without revealing confidential information; and

(C) set forth the specific legal authority and any applicable legal standards for determining such court records to be confidential without revealing confidential information.

Any written motion made under this subdivision must include a signed certification by the party or the attorney for the party making the request that the motion is made in good faith and is supported by a sound factual and legal basis. Information that is subject to such a motion must be treated as confidential by the clerk pending the court's ruling on the motion. A response to a written motion filed under this subdivision may be served within 10 days of service of the motion. Notwithstanding any of the foregoing, the court may not determine that the case number, docket number, or other number used by the clerk's office to identify the case file is confidential.

(2) Except when a motion filed under subdivision (e)(1) represents that all parties agree to all of the relief requested, the court must, as soon as practicable but no later than 30 days after the filing of a motion under this subdivision, hold a hearing before ruling on the motion. Whether or not any motion filed under subdivision (e)(1) is agreed to by the parties, the court may in its discretion hold a hearing on such motion. Any hearing held under this subdivision must be an open proceeding, except that any person may request that the court conduct all or part of the hearing in camera to protect the interests set forth in subdivision (c). Any person may request expedited consideration of and ruling on the motion. The movant shall be responsible for ensuring that a complete record of any hearing held pursuant to this subdivision is created, either by use of a court reporter or by any recording device that is provided as a matter of right by the court. The court may in its discretion require prior public notice of the hearing on such a motion in accordance with the procedure for providing public notice of court orders set forth in subdivision (e)(4) or by providing such other public notice as the court deems appropriate. The court must issue a ruling on the motion within 30 days of the hearing.

(3) Any order granting in whole or in part a motion filed under subdivision (e) must state the following with as much specificity as possible without revealing the confidential information:

(A) The type of case in which the order is being entered;

(B) The particular grounds under subdivision (c) for determining the information is confidential;

(C) Whether any party's name is determined to be confidential and, if so, the particular pseudonym or other term to be substituted for the party's name;

(D) Whether the progress docket or similar records generated to document activity in the case are determined to be confidential;

(E) The particular information that is determined to be confidential;

(F) Identification of persons who are permitted to view the confidential information;

(G) That the court finds that: (i) the degree, duration, and manner of confidentiality ordered by the court are no broader than necessary to protect the interests set forth in subdivision (c); and (ii) no less restrictive measures are available to protect the interests set forth in subdivision (c); and

(H) That the clerk of the court is directed to publish the order in accordance with subdivision (e)(4).

(4) Except as provided by law or court rule, notice must be given of any written order granting in whole or in part a motion made under subdivision (e)(1) as follows:

(A) within 10 days following the entry of the order, the clerk of court must post a copy of the order on the clerk's website and in a prominent public location in the courthouse; and

(B) the order must remain posted in both locations for no less than 30 days. This subdivision shall not apply to orders determining that court records are confidential under subdivision (c)(7) or (c)(8).

(5) If a nonparty requests that the court vacate all or part of an order issued under subdivision (e) or requests that the court order the unsealing of records designated as confidential under subdivision (d), the request must be made by a written motion, filed in that court, that states with as much specificity as possible the bases for the motion. The motion must set forth the specific legal authority and any applicable legal standards supporting the motion. The movant must serve all parties and all affected non-parties with a copy of the motion. Except when a motion filed under this subdivision represents that all parties and affected non-parties agree to all of the relief requested, the court must, as soon as practicable but no later than 30 days after the filing of a motion under this subdivision, hold a hearing on the motion. Regardless of whether any motion filed under this subdivision is agreed to by the parties and affected non-parties, the court may in its discretion hold a hearing on such motion. Any person may request expedited consideration of and ruling on the motion. Any hearing held under this subdivision must be an open proceeding, except that any person may request that the court conduct all or part of the hearing in camera to protect the interests set forth in subdivision (c). The court must issue a ruling on the motion within 30 days of the hearing. The movant shall be responsible for ensuring that a complete record of any hearing held under this subdivision be created, either by use of a court reporter or by any recording device that is provided as a matter of right by the court. This subdivision shall not apply to orders determining that court records are confidential under subdivision (c)(7) or (c)(8).

(f) Request to Determine Confidentiality of Court Records in Criminal Cases.

(1) Subdivisions (e) and (h) shall apply to any motion by the state, a defendant, or an affected non-party to determine the confidentiality of trial court records in criminal cases under subdivision (c), except as provided in subdivision (f)(3). As to any motion filed in the trial court under subdivision (f)(3), the following procedure shall apply:

(A) Unless the motion represents that the State, defendant(s), and all affected non-parties subject to the motion agree to all of the relief requested, the court must hold a hearing on the motion filed under this subdivision within 15 days of the filing of the motion. Any hearing held under this subdivision must be an open proceeding, except that any person may request that the court conduct all or part of the hearing in camera to protect the interests set forth in subdivision (c)(9)(A).

(B) The court shall issue a written ruling on a motion filed under this subdivision within 10 days of the hearing on a contested motion or within 10 days of the filing of an agreed motion.

(2) Subdivision (g) shall apply to any motion to determine the confidentiality of appellate court records under subdivision (c), except as provided in subdivision (f)(3). As to any motion filed in the appellate court under subdivision (f)(3), the following procedure shall apply:

(A) The motion may be made with respect to a record that was presented or presentable to a lower tribunal, but no determination concerning confidentiality was made by the lower tribunal, or a record presented to an appellate court in an original proceeding.

(B) A response to a motion filed under this subdivision may be served within 10 days of service of the motion.

(C) The court shall issue a written ruling on a motion filed under this subdivision within 10 days of the filing of a response on a contested motion or within 10 days of the filing of an uncontested motion.

(3) Any motion to determine whether a court record that pertains to a plea agreement, substantial assistance agreement, or other court record that reveals the identity of a confidential informant or active criminal investigative information is confidential under subdivision (c)(9)(A)(i), (c)(9)(A)(iii), (c)(9)(A)(v), or (c)(9)(A)(vii) of this rule may be made in the form of a written motion captioned "Motion to Determine Confidentiality of Court Records." Any motion made pursuant to this subdivision must be treated as confidential and indicated on the docket by generic title only, pending a ruling on the motion or further order of the court. As to any motion made under this subdivision, the following procedure shall apply:

(A) Information that is the subject of such motion must be treated as confidential by the clerk pending the court's ruling on the motion. Filings containing the information must be indicated on the docket in a manner that does not reveal the confidential nature of the information.

(B) The provisions of subdivisions (e)(3)(A)–(G), (g)(7), (h), and (j), shall apply to motions made under this subdivision. The provisions of subdivisions (e)(1), (e)(2), (e)(3)(H), (e)(4), and (e)(5) shall not apply to motions made under this subdivision.

(C) No order entered under this subdivision may authorize or approve the sealing of court records for any period longer than is necessary to achieve the objective of the motion, and in no event longer than 120 days. Extensions of an order issued hereunder may be granted for 60–day periods, but each such extension may be ordered only upon the filing of another motion in accordance with the procedures set forth under this subdivision. In the event of an appeal or review of a matter in which an order is entered under this subdivision, the lower tribunal shall retain jurisdiction to consider motions to extend orders issued hereunder during the course of the appeal or review proceeding.

(D) The clerk of the court shall not publish any order of the court issued hereunder in accordance with subdivision (e)(4) or (g)(4) unless directed by the court. The docket shall indicate only the entry of the order.

(4) This subdivision does not authorize the falsification of court records or progress dockets.

(g) Request to Determine Confidentiality of Appellate Court Records in Noncriminal Cases.

(1) Subdivision (e)(1) shall apply to any motion filed in the appellate court to determine the confidentiality of appellate court records in noncriminal cases under subdivision (c). Such a motion may be made with respect to a record that was presented or presentable to a lower tribunal, but no determination concerning confidentiality was made by the lower tribunal, or a record presented to an appellate court in an original proceeding.

(2) A response to a motion filed under subdivision (g)(1) may be served within 10 days of service of the motion. The court shall issue a written ruling on a written motion filed under this subdivision within 30 days of the filing of a response on a contested motion or within 30 days of the filing of an uncontested written motion.

(3) Any order granting in whole or in part a motion filed under subdivision (g)(1) must be in compliance with the guidelines set forth in subdivisions (e)(3)(A)–(H). Any order requiring the sealing of an appellate court record operates to also make those same records confidential in the lower tribunal during the pendency of the appellate proceeding.

(4) Except as provided by law, within 10 days following the entry of an order granting a motion under subdivision (g)(1), the clerk of the appellate court

must post a copy of the order on the clerk's website and must provide a copy of the order to the clerk of the lower tribunal, with directions that the clerk of the lower tribunal shall seal the records identified in the order. The order must remain posted by the clerk of the appellate court for no less than 30 days.

(5) If a nonparty requests that the court vacate all or part of an order issued under subdivision (g)(3), or requests that the court order the unsealing of records designated as confidential under subdivision (d), the request must be made by a written motion, filed in that court, that states with as much specificity as possible the bases for the request. The motion must set forth the specific legal authority and any applicable legal standards supporting the motion. The movant must serve all parties and all affected non-parties with a copy of the motion. A response to a motion may be served within 10 days of service of the motion.

(6) The party seeking to have an appellate record sealed under this subdivision has the responsibility to ensure that the clerk of the lower tribunal is alerted to the issuance of the order sealing the records and to ensure that the clerk takes appropriate steps to seal the records in the lower tribunal.

(7) Upon conclusion of the appellate proceeding, the lower tribunal may, upon appropriate motion showing changed circumstances, revisit the appellate court's order directing that the records be sealed.

(8) Records of a lower tribunal determined to be confidential by that tribunal must be treated as confidential during any review proceedings. In any case where information has been determined to be confidential under this rule, the clerk of the lower tribunal shall so indicate in the index transmitted to the appellate court. If the information was determined to be confidential in an order, the clerk's index must identify such order by date or docket number. This subdivision does not preclude review by an appellate court, under Florida Rule of Appellate Procedure 9.100(d), or affect the standard of review by an appellate court, of an order by a lower tribunal determining that a court record is confidential.

(h) Oral Motions to Determine Confidentiality of Trial Court Records.

(1) Notwithstanding the written notice requirements of subdivision (d)(2) and written motion requirements of subdivisions (d)(3), (e)(1), and (f), the movant may make an oral motion to determine the confidentiality of trial court records under subdivision (c), provided:

(A) except for oral motions under subdivision (f)(3), the oral motion otherwise complies with subdivision (e)(1);

(B) all parties and affected non-parties are present or properly noticed or the movant otherwise demonstrates reasonable efforts made to obtain the attendance of any absent party or affected non-party;

(C) the movant shows good cause why the movant was unable to timely comply with the written notice requirements as set forth in subdivision (d)(2) or the written motion requirement as set forth in subdivision (d)(3), (e)(1), or (f), as applicable;

(D) the oral motion is reduced to written form in compliance with subdivision (d), (e)(1), or (f), as applicable, and is filed within 5 days following the date of making the oral motion;

(E) except for oral motions under subdivision (f)(3), the provisions of subdivision (e)(2) shall apply to the oral motion, procedure and hearing;

(F) the provisions of subdivisions (f)(1)(A) and (B) and (f)(3) shall apply to any oral motion under subdivision (f)(3); and

(G) oral motions are not applicable to subdivision (f)(2) or (g) or extensions of orders under subdivision (f)(3)(C).

(2) The court may deny any oral motion made pursuant to subdivision (h)(1) if the court finds that the movant had the ability to timely comply with the written notice requirements in subdivision (d) or the written motion requirements of subdivision (d)(3), (e)(1), or (f), as applicable, or the movant failed to provide adequate notice to the parties and affected non-parties of the confidentiality issues to be presented to the court.

(3) Until the court renders a decision regarding the confidentiality issues raised in any oral motion, all references to purported confidential information as set forth in the oral motion shall occur in a manner that does not allow public access to such information.

(4) If the court grants in whole or in part any oral motion to determine confidentiality, the court shall issue a written order that does not reveal the confidential information and complies with the applicable subdivision of this rule as follows:

(A) For any oral motion under subdivision (e) or (f)(1), except subdivisions (f)(1)(A) and (B), the written order must be issued within 30 days of the hearing and must comply with subdivision (e)(3).

(B) For any oral motion under subdivision (f)(3), the written order must be issued within 10 days of the hearing on a contested motion or filing of an agreed motion and must comply with subdivision (f)(3).

(i) Sanctions. After notice and an opportunity to respond, and upon determining that a motion, filing, or other activity described below was not made in good faith and was not supported by a sound legal or factual basis, the court may impose sanctions against any party or non-party and/or their attorney, if that party or non-party and/or their attorney, in violation of the applicable provisions of this rule:

(1) seeks confidential status for non-confidential information by filing a notice under subdivision (d)(2);

(2) seeks confidential status for non-confidential information by making any oral or written motion under subdivision (d)(3), (e), (f), (g), or (h);

(3) seeks access to confidential information under subdivision (j) or otherwise;

(4) fails to file a Notice of Confidential Information within Court Filing in compliance with subdivision (d)(2);

(5) makes public or attempts to make public by motion or otherwise information that should be maintained as confidential under subdivision (c), (d), (e), (f), (g) or (h); or

(6) otherwise makes or attempts to make confidential information part of a non-confidential court record.

Nothing in this subdivision is intended to limit the authority of a court to enforce any court order entered pursuant to this rule.

(j) Procedure for Obtaining Access to Confidential Court Records.

(1) The clerk of the court must allow access to confidential court records to persons authorized by law, or any person authorized by court order.

(2) A court order allowing access to confidential court records may be obtained by filing a written motion which must:

(A) identify the particular court record(s) or a portion of the court record(s) to which the movant seeks to obtain access with as much specificity as possible without revealing the confidential information;

(B) specify the bases for obtaining access to such court records;

(C) set forth the specific legal authority for obtaining access to such court records; and

(D) contain a certification that the motion is made in good faith and is supported by a sound factual and legal basis.

(3) The movant must serve a copy of the written motion to obtain access to confidential court records on all parties and reasonably ascertainable affected non-parties and the court must hold a hearing on the written motion within a reasonable period of time.

(4) Any order granting access to confidential court records must:

(A) describe the confidential information with as much specificity as possible without revealing the confidential information, including specifying the precise location of the information within the court records;

(B) identify the persons who are permitted to view the confidential information in the court records;

(C) identify any person who is permitted to obtain copies of the confidential court records; and

(D) state the time limits imposed on such access, if any, and any other applicable terms or limitations to such access.

(5) The filer of confidential court records, that filer's attorney of record, or that filer's agent as authorized by that filer in writing may obtain access to such confidential records pursuant to this subdivision.

(6) Unless otherwise provided, an order granting access to confidential court records under this subdivision shall not alter the confidential status of the record.

(k) Procedure for Service on Victims and Affected Non-parties and When Addresses Are Confidential.

(1) In criminal cases, when the defendant is required to serve any notice or motion described in this rule on an alleged victim of a crime, service shall be on the state attorney, who shall send or forward the notice or motion to the alleged victim.

(2) Except as set forth in subdivision (k)(1), when serving any notice or motion described in this rule on any affected non-party whose name or address is not confidential, the filer or movant shall use reasonable efforts to locate the affected non-party and may serve such affected non-party by any method set forth in Florida Rule of Judicial Administration 2.516.

(3) Except as set forth in subdivision (k)(1), when serving any notice or motion described in this rule and the name or address of any party or affected non-party is confidential, the filer or movant must state prominently in the caption of the notice or motion "Confidential Party or Confidential Affected Non–Party—Court Service Requested." When a notice or motion so designated is filed, the court shall be responsible for providing a copy of the notice or motion to the party or affected non-party, by any method permitted in Florida Rule of Judicial Administration 2.516, in such a way as to not reveal the confidential information.

***(l)* Denial of Access Request for Administrative Records.** Expedited review of denials of access to administrative records of the judicial branch shall be provided through an action for mandamus or other appropriate relief, in the following manner:

(1) When a judge who has denied a request for access to records is the custodian, the action shall be filed in the court having appellate jurisdiction to review the decisions of the judge denying access. Upon order issued by the appellate court, the judge denying access to records shall file a sealed copy of the requested records with the appellate court.

(2) All other actions under this rule shall be filed in the circuit court of the circuit in which such denial of access occurs.

(m) Procedure for Public Access to Judicial Branch Records. Requests and responses to requests for access to records under this rule shall be made in a reasonable manner.

(1) Requests for access to judicial branch records shall be in writing and shall be directed to the custodian. The request shall provide sufficient specificity to enable the custodian to identify the requested records. The reason for the request is not required to be disclosed.

(2) The custodian shall be solely responsible for providing access to the records of the custodian's entity. The custodian shall determine whether the requested record is subject to this rule and, if so, whether the record or portions of the record are exempt from disclosure. The custodian shall determine the form in which the record is provided. If the request is denied, the custodian shall state in writing the basis for the denial.

(3) Fees for copies of records in all entities in the judicial branch of government, except for copies of court records, shall be the same as those provided in section 119.07, Florida Statutes.

Former Rule 2.051 added effective Oct. 29, 1992 (608 So.2d 472). Amended March 23, 1995 (651 So.2d 1185); Jan. 28, 1999, effective Feb. 1, 1999 (746 So.2d 1073); March 7, 2002 (825 So.2d 889); Nov. 3, 2005, effective Jan. 1, 2006 (915 So.2d 157). Renumbered from Rule 2.051 Sept. 21, 2006 (939 So.2d 966). Amended April 5, 2007 (954 So.2d 16); March 18, 2010 (31 So.3d 756); Rule 2.420(d) added March 18, 2010, effective Oct. 1, 2010 (31 So.3d 756). Amended July 7, 2011 (68 So.3d 228); March 28, 2013, effective May 1, 2013 (124 So.3d 819); Dec. 18, 2014, effective Dec. 18, 2014 (153 So.3d 896); Jan. 22, 2015, effective Jan. 22, 2015 (156 So.3d 499).

Committee Note

1995 Amendment. This rule was adopted to conform to the 1992 addition of article I, section 24, to the Florida Constitution. Amendments to this rule were adopted in response to the 1994 recommendations of the Study Committee on Confidentiality of Records of the Judicial Branch.

Subdivision (b) has been added by amendment and provides a definition of "judicial records" that is consistent with the definition of "court records" contained in rule 2.075(a)(1) and the definition of "public records" contained in chapter 119, Florida Statutes. The word "exhibits" used in this definition of judicial records is intended to refer only to documentary evidence and does not refer to tangible items of evidence such as firearms, narcotics, etc. Judicial records within this definition include all judicial records and data regardless of the form in which they are kept. Reformatting of information may be necessary to protect copyrighted material. *Seigle v. Barry*, 422 So. 2d 63 (Fla. 4th DCA 1982), *review denied*, 431 So. 2d 988 (Fla. 1983).

The definition of "judicial records" also includes official business information transmitted via an electronic mail (e-mail) system. The judicial branch is presently experimenting with this new technology. For example, e-mail is currently being used by the judicial branch to transmit between judges and staff multiple matters in the courts including direct communications between judges and staff and other judges, proposed drafts of opinions and orders, memoranda concerning pending cases, proposed jury instructions, and even votes on proposed opinions. All of this type of information is exempt from public disclosure under rules 2.051(c)(1) and (c)(2). With few exceptions, these examples of e-mail transmissions are sent and received between judicial officials and employees within a particular court's jurisdiction. This type of e-mail is by its very nature almost always exempt from public record disclosure pursuant to rule 2.051(c). In addition, official business e-mail transmissions sent to or received by judicial officials or employees using dial-in equipment, as well as the use of on-line outside research facilities such as Westlaw, would also be exempt e-mail under rule 2.051(c). On the other hand, we recognize that not all e-mail sent and received within a particular court's jurisdiction will fall into an exception under rule 2.051(c). The fact that a non-exempt e-mail message made or received in connection with official court business is transmitted intra-court does not relieve judicial officials or employees from the obligation of properly having a record made of such messages so they will be available to the public similar to any other written communications. It appears that official business e-mail that is sent or received by persons outside a particular court's jurisdiction is largely non-exempt and is subject to recording in some form as a public record. Each court should develop a means to properly make a record of non-exempt official business e-mail by either electronically storing the mail or by making a hard copy. It is important to note that, although official business communicated by e-mail transmissions is a matter of public record under the rule, the exemptions provided in rule 2.051(c) exempt many of these judge/staff transmissions from the public record. E–mail may also include transmissions that are clearly not official business and are, consequently, not required to be recorded as a public record. Each court should also publish an e-mail address for public access. The individual e-mail addresses of judicial officials and staff are exempt under rule 2.051(c)(2) to protect the compelling interests of maintaining the uninterrupted use of the computer for research, word-processing, preparation of opinions, and communication during trials, and to ensure computer security.

Subdivision (c)(3) was amended by creating subparts (a) and (b) to distinguish between the provisions governing the confidentiality of complaints against judges and complaints against other individuals or entities licensed or regulated by the Supreme Court.

Subdivision (c)(5) was amended to make public the qualifications of persons applying to serve or serving the court as unpaid volunteers such as guardians ad litem, mediators, and arbitrators and to make public the applications and evaluations of such persons upon a showing of materiality in a pending court proceeding or upon a showing of good cause.

Subdivision (c)(9) has also been amended. Subdivision (c)(9) was adopted to incorporate the holdings of judicial decisions establishing that confidentiality may be required to protect the rights of defendants, litigants, or third parties; to further the administration of justice; or to otherwise promote a compelling governmental interest. *Barron v. Florida Freedom Newspapers, Inc.*, 531 So.2d 113 (Fla. 1988); *Miami Herald Publishing Co. v. Lewis*, 426 So.2d 1 (Fla.1982). Such confidentiality may be implemented by court rule, as well as by judicial decision, where necessary for the effective administration of justice. *See, e.g.*, Fla.R.Crim.P. 3.470, (Sealed Verdict); Fla.R.Crim.P. 3.712, (Presentence Investigation Reports); Fla.R.Civ.P. 1.280(c), (Protective Orders).

Subdivision (c)(9)(D) requires that, except where otherwise provided by law or rule of court, reasonable notice shall be given to the public of any order closing a court record. This subdivision is not applicable to court proceedings. Unlike the closure of court proceedings, which has been held to require notice and hearing prior to closure, *see Miami Herald Publishing Co. v. Lewis*, 426 So. 2d 1 (Fla. 1982), the closure of court records has not required prior notice. Requiring prior notice of closure of a court record may be impractical and burdensome in emergency circumstances or when closure of a court record requiring confidentiality is requested during a judicial proceeding. Providing reasonable notice to the public of the entry of a closure order and an opportunity to be heard on the closure issue adequately protects the competing interests of confidentiality and public access to judicial records. *See Florida Freedom Newspapers, Inc. v. Sirmons*, 508 So.2d 462 (Fla. 1st DCA 1987), *approved, Barron v. Florida Freedom Newspapers, Inc.*, 531 So.2d 113 (Fla.1988); *State ex rel. Tallahassee Democrat v. Cooksey*, 371 So.2d 207 (Fla. 1st DCA 1979). Subdivision (c)(9)(D), however, does not preclude the giving of prior notice of closure of a court record, and the court may elect to give prior notice in appropriate cases.

2002 Court Commentary

The custodian is required to provide access to or copies of records but is not required either to provide information from records or to create new records in response to a request. Op. Atty. Gen. Fla. 80–57 (1980); *Wootton v. Cook*, 590 So.2d 1039 (Fla. 1st DCA 1991); *Seigle v. Barry*, 422 So.2d 63 (Fla. 4th DCA 1982).

The writing requirement is not intended to disadvantage any person who may have difficulty writing a request; if any difficulty exists, the custodian should aid the requestor in reducing the request to writing.

It is anticipated that each judicial branch entity will have policies and procedures for responding to public records requests.

The 1995 commentary notes that the definition of "judicial records" added at that time is consistent with the definition of "court records" contained in rule 2.075(a)(1) and the definition of "public records" contained in chapter 119, Florida Statutes. Despite the commentary, these definitions are not the same. The definitions added in 2002 are intended to clarify that records of the judicial branch include court records as defined in rule 2.075(a)(1) and administrative records. The definition of records of the judicial branch is consistent with the definition of "public records" in chapter 119, Florida Statutes.

2005 Court Commentary

Under courts' inherent authority, appellate courts may appoint a special magistrate to serve as commissioner for the court to make findings of fact and oversee discovery in review proceedings under subdivision (d) of this rule. Cf. *State ex rel. Davis v. City of Avon Park*, 158 So. 159 (Fla. 1934) (recognizing appellate courts' inherent authority to do all things reasonably necessary for administration of justice within the scope of courts' jurisdiction, including the appointment of a commissioner to make findings of fact); *Wessells v. State*, 737 So. 2d 1103 (Fla. 1st DCA 1998) (relinquishing jurisdiction to circuit court for appointment of a special master to serve as commissioner for court to make findings of fact).

2007 Court Commentary

New subdivision (d) applies only to motions that seek to make court records in noncriminal cases confidential in accordance with subdivision (c)(9).

2007 Committee Commentary

Subdivision (d)(2) is intended to permit a party to make use of any court-provided recording device or system that is available generally for litigants' use, but is not intended to require the court system to make such devices available where they are not already in use and is not intended to eliminate any cost for use of such system that is generally borne by a party requesting use of such system.

APPENDIX TO RULE 2.420

IN THE .....(NAME OF COURT)....., FLORIDA
CASE NO.: ________

____
Plaintiff/Petitioner,

v.

____
Defendant/Respondent.

________________________/

NOTICE OF CONFIDENTIAL INFORMATION WITHIN COURT FILING

Pursuant to Florida Rule of Judicial Administration 2.420(d)(2), I hereby certify:

( )(1) I am filing herewith a document containing confidential information as described in Rule 2.420(d)(1)(B) and that:

(a) The title/type of document is ________, and:

(b)( ) the entire document is confidential, or

( ) the confidential information within the document is precisely located at: ________.

OR

( )(2) A document was previously filed in this case that contains confidential information as described in Rule 2.420(d)(1)(B), but a Notice of Confidential Information within Court Filing was not filed with the document and the confidential information was not maintained as confidential by the clerk of the court. I hereby notify the clerk that this confidential information is located as follows:

(a) Title/type of document: ________;

(b) Date of filing (if known): ________;

(c) Date of document: ________;

(d) Docket entry number: ________;

(e) ( )Entire document is confidential, or

( ) Precise location of confidential information in document: ________

____

Filer's Signature

CERTIFICATE OF SERVICE

I HEREBY CERTIFY that a copy of the foregoing was furnished by (e–mail) (delivery) (mail) (fax) on: (All parties and Affected Non–Parties. Note: If the name or address of a Party or Affected Non–Party is confidential DO NOT include such information in this Certificate of Service. Instead, serve the State Attorney or request Court Service. See Rule 2.420(k)) ________, on ________, 20___.

Name ....
Address ....
Phone ....
Florida Bar No. (if applicable) ....
E-mail address ....

Note: The clerk of court shall review filings identified as containing confidential information to determine whether the information is facially subject to confidentiality under subdivision (d)(1)(B). The clerk shall notify the filer in writing within 5 days if the clerk determines that the information is NOT subject to confidentiality, and the records shall not be held as confidential for more than 10 days, unless a motion is filed pursuant to subdivision (d)(3) of the Rule. Fla. R. Jud. Admin. 2.420(d)(2).

Rule 2.425. Minimization of the Filing of Sensitive Information

(a) Limitations for Court Filings. Unless authorized by subdivision (b), statute, another rule of court, or the court orders otherwise, designated sensitive information filed with the court must be limited to the following format:

(1) The initials of a person known to be a minor;

(2) The year of birth of a person's birth date;

(3) No portion of any

(A) social security number,

(B) bank account number,

(C) credit card account number,

(D) charge account number, or

(E) debit account number;

(4) The last four digits of any

(A) taxpayer identification number (TIN),

(B) employee identification number,

(C) driver's license number,

(D) passport number,

(E) telephone number,

(F) financial account number, except as set forth in subdivision (a)(3),

(G) brokerage account number,

(H) insurance policy account number,

(I) loan account number,

(J) customer account number, or

(K) patient or health care number;

(5) A truncated version of any

(A) email address,

(B) computer user name,

(C) password, or

(D) personal identification number (PIN); and

(6) A truncated version of any other sensitive information as provided by court order.

(b) Exceptions. Subdivision (a) does not apply to the following:

(1) An account number which identifies the property alleged to be the subject of a proceeding;

(2) The record of an administrative or agency proceeding;

(3) The record in appellate or review proceedings;

(4) The birth date of a minor whenever the birth date is necessary for the court to establish or maintain subject matter jurisdiction;

(5) The name of a minor in any order relating to parental responsibility, time-sharing, or child support;

(6) The name of a minor in any document or order affecting the minor's ownership of real property;

(7) The birth date of a party in a writ of attachment or notice to payor;

(8) In traffic and criminal proceedings

(A) a pro se filing;

(B) a court filing that is related to a criminal matter or investigation and that is prepared before the filing of a criminal charge or is not filed as part of any docketed criminal case;

(C) an arrest or search warrant or any information in support thereof;

(D) a charging document and an affidavit or other documents filed in support of any charging document, including any driving records;

(E) a statement of particulars;

(F) discovery material introduced into evidence or otherwise filed with the court; and

(G) all information necessary for the proper issuance and execution of a subpoena duces tecum;

(9) Information used by the clerk for case maintenance purposes or the courts for case management purposes; and

(10) Information which is relevant and material to an issue before the court.

(c) Remedies. Upon motion by a party or interested person or sua sponte by the court, the court may order remedies, sanctions or both for a violation of subdivision (a). Following notice and an opportunity to respond, the court may impose sanctions if such filing was not made in good faith.

(d) Motions Not Restricted. This rule does not restrict a party's right to move for protective order, to move to file documents under seal, or to request a determination of the confidentiality of records.

(e) Application. This rule does not affect the application of constitutional provisions, statutes, or rules of court regarding confidential information or access to public information.

Added Nov. 3, 2011, effective, *nunc pro tunc*, Oct. 1, 2011 (78 So.3d 1045). Amended July 12, 2012 (95 So.3d 115).

Rule 2.430. Retention of Court Records

(a) Definitions. The following definitions apply to this rule:

(1) "Court records" mean the contents of the court file, including the progress docket and other similar records generated to document activity in a case, transcripts filed with the clerk, documentary exhibits in the custody of the clerk, and electronic records, video tapes, or stenographic tapes of depositions or other proceedings filed with the clerk, and electronic records, videotapes or stenographic tapes of court proceedings.

(2) "After a judgment has become final" means:

(A) when a final order, final judgment, final docket entry, final dismissal, or nolle prosequi has been entered as to all parties, no appeal has been taken, and the time for appeal has expired; or

(B) when a final order, final judgment, or final docket entry has been entered, an appeal has been taken, the appeal has been disposed of, and the time for any further appellate proceedings has expired.

(3) "Permanently recorded" means that a document has been microfilmed, optically imaged, or recorded onto an electronic record keeping system in accordance with standards adopted by the Supreme Court of Florida.

(b) Permanently Recorded Records.

(1) Court records, except exhibits, that have been permanently recorded may be destroyed or otherwise disposed of by the clerk at any time after a judgment has become final.

(2) Any physical media submitted to the clerk for the purpose of filing information contained in the media may be destroyed, retained, or otherwise disposed of by the clerk once the contents of the media have been made a part of the court record.

(c) Records Not Permanently Recorded. No court records under this subdivision shall be destroyed or disposed of until the final order, final docket entry, or final judgment is permanently recorded for, or recorded in, the public records. The time periods shall not apply to any action in which the court orders the court records to be kept until the court orders otherwise. When an order is entered to that effect, the progress docket and the court file shall be marked by the clerk with a legend showing that the court records are not to be destroyed or disposed of without a further order of court. Any person may apply for an order suspending or prohibiting destruction or disposition of court records in any proceeding. Court records, except exhibits, that are not permanently recorded may be destroyed or disposed of by the clerk after a judgment has become final in accordance with the following schedule:

(1) For trial courts

(A) 60 days—Parking tickets and noncriminal traffic infractions after required audits have been completed.

(B) 2 years—Proceedings under the Small Claims Rules, Medical Mediation Proceedings.

(C) 5 years—Noncriminal ordinance violations, civil litigation proceedings in county court other than those under the Small Claims Rules, and civil proceedings in circuit court except marriage dissolutions and adoptions.

(D) 10 years—Probate, guardianship, and mental health proceedings.

(E) 10 years—Felony and misdemeanor cases in which no information or indictment was filed or in which all charges were dismissed, or in which the state announced a nolle prosequi, or in which the defendant was adjudicated not guilty.

(F) 75 years—Juvenile proceedings containing an order permanently depriving a parent of custody of a child, and adoptions, and all felony and misdemeanor cases not previously destroyed.

(G) Juvenile proceedings not otherwise provided for in this subdivision shall be kept for 5 years after the last entry or until the child reaches the age of majority, whichever is later.

(H) Marriage dissolutions—10 years from the last record activity. The court may authorize destruction of court records not involving alimony, support, or custody of children 5 years from the last record activity.

(2) For district courts of appeal

(A) 2 years — noncriminal court records.

(B) 5 years — Criminal court records.

(3) For the Supreme Court

(A) 5 years — All cases disposed of by order not otherwise provided for in this rule.

(B) 10 years — Cases disposed of by order involving individuals licensed or regulated by the court and noncriminal court records involving the unauthorized practice of law.

(d) Records to Be Retained Permanently. The following court records shall be permanently recorded or permanently retained:

(1) progress dockets, and other similar records generated to document activity in a case, and

(2) court records of the supreme court in which the case was disposed of by opinion.

(e) Court Reporters' Notes. Court reporters or persons acting as court reporters for judicial or discovery proceedings shall retain the original notes or electronic records of the proceedings or depositions until the times specified below:

(1) 2 years from the date of preparing the transcript — Judicial proceedings, arbitration hearings, and discovery proceedings when an original transcript has been prepared.

(2) 10 years — Judicial proceedings in felony cases when a transcript has not been prepared.

(3) 5 years — All other judicial proceedings, arbitration hearings, and discovery proceedings when a transcript has not been prepared.

When an agreement has been made between the reporter and any other person and the person has paid the reasonable charges for storage and retention of the notes, the notes or records shall be kept for any longer time agreed on. All reporters' notes shall be retained in a secure place in Florida.

(f) Exhibits.

(1) Exhibits in criminal proceedings shall be disposed of as provided by law.

(2) All other exhibits shall be retained by the clerk until 90 days after a judgment has become final. If an exhibit is not withdrawn pursuant to subdivision (i) within 90 days, the clerk may destroy or dispose of the exhibits after giving the parties or their attorneys of record 30 days' notice of the clerk's intention to do so. Exhibits shall be delivered to any party or attorney of record calling for them during the 30-day time period.

(g) Disposition Other Than Destruction. Before destruction or disposition of court records under this rule, any person may apply to the court for an order requiring the clerk to deliver to the applicant the court records that are to be destroyed or disposed of. All parties shall be given notice of the application. The court shall dispose of that court record as appropriate.

(h) Release of Court Records. This rule does not limit the power of the court to release exhibits or other parts of court records that are the property of the person or party initially placing the items in the court records. The court may require copies to be substituted as a condition to releasing the court records under this subdivision.

(i) Right to Expunge Records. Nothing in this rule shall affect the power of the court to order records expunged.

(j) Sealed Records. No record which has been sealed from public examination by order of court shall be destroyed without hearing after such notice as the court shall require.

(k) Destruction of Jury Notes. At the conclusion of the trial and promptly following discharge of the jury, the court shall collect all juror notes and immediately destroy the juror notes.

Former Rule 2.075 added Sept. 10, 1981, effective Jan. 1, 1982 (403 So.2d 926). Amended Oct. 8, 1992, effective Jan. 1, 1993 (609 So.2d 465); Sept. 26, 1996, effective Jan. 1, 1997 (681 So.2d 698); March 7, 2002 (825 So.2d 889). Renumbered from Rule 2.075 Sept. 21, 2006 (939 So.2d 966). Amended Oct. 4, 2007, effective Jan. 1, 2008 (967 So.2d 178); Jan. 17, 2008, effective Jan. 17, 2008 (973 So.2d 437); Oct. 18, 2012, effective Dec. 1, 2012, April 1, 2013, Oct. 1, 2013 (102 So.3d 451); Oct. 30, 2014, effective Jan. 1, 2015 (150 So.3d 787).

Rule 2.440. Retention of Judicial Branch Administrative Records

(a) Definitions.

(1) "Judicial branch" means the judicial branch of government, which includes the state courts system, the clerk of court when acting as an arm of the court, The Florida Bar, the Florida Board of Bar Examiners, the Judicial Qualifications Commission, and all other entities established by or operating under the authority of the supreme court or the chief justice.

(2) "Records of the judicial branch" means all records, regardless of physical form, characteristics, or means of transmission, made or received in connection with the transaction of official business by any judicial branch entity and consists of:

(A) "court records," which means the contents of the court file, including the progress docket and other similar records generated to document activity in a case, transcripts filed with the clerk, documentary exhibits in the custody of the clerk, and electronic records, videotapes, or stenographic tapes of depositions or other proceedings filed with the clerk, and electronic records, videotapes, or stenographic tapes of court proceedings; and

(B) "administrative records," which means all other records made or received pursuant to court rule, law, or ordinance, or in connection with the transaction of official business by any judicial branch entity.

(b) Retention Requirements. Administrative records in the judicial branch shall be retained in accordance with the Judicial Branch Records Retention Schedule approved by the supreme court.

Former Rule 2.076 added March 7, 2002 (825 So.2d 889). Renumbered from Rule 2.076 Sept. 21, 2006 (939 So.2d 966).

2002 Commentary

This rule does not apply to court records and files that are governed by rule 2.075. This rule applies to administrative records.

To provide a consistent schedule for retention of administrative records in the judicial branch, the Supreme Court Workgroup on Public Records recommended that the Court adopt the Judicial Branch Records Retention Schedule. This schedule uses the legislatively authorized Department of State retention schedules, as appropriate, and includes a schedule for other records that are unique to the judicial branch.

Rule 2.450. Technological Coverage of Judicial Proceedings

(a) Electronic and Still Photography Allowed. Subject at all times to the authority of the presiding judge to: (i) control the conduct of proceedings before the court; (ii) ensure decorum and prevent distractions; and (iii) ensure the fair administration of justice in the pending cause, electronic media and still photography coverage of public judicial proceedings in the appellate and trial courts of this state shall be allowed in accordance with the following standards of conduct and technology promulgated by the Supreme Court of Florida.

(b) Equipment and Personnel.

(1) At least 1 portable television camera, operated by not more than 1 camera person, shall be permitted in any trial or appellate court proceeding. The number of permitted cameras shall be within the sound discretion and authority of the presiding judge.

(2) Not more than 1 still photographer, using not more than 2 still cameras, shall be permitted in any proceeding in a trial or appellate court.

(3) Not more than 1 audio system for radio broadcast purposes shall be permitted in any proceeding in a trial or appellate court. Audio pickup for all media purposes shall be accomplished from existing audio systems present in the court facility. If no technically suitable audio system exists in the court facility, microphones and related wiring essential for media purposes shall be unobtrusive and shall be located in places designated in advance of any proceeding by the chief judge of the judicial circuit or district in which the court facility is located.

(4) Any "pooling" arrangements among the media required by these limitations on equipment and personnel shall be the sole responsibility of the media without calling upon the presiding judge to mediate any dispute as to the appropriate media representative or equipment authorized to cover a particular proceeding. In the absence of advance media agreement on disputed equipment or personnel issues, the presiding judge shall exclude all contesting media personnel from a proceeding.

(c) Sound and Light Criteria.

(1) Only television photographic and audio equipment that does not produce distracting sound or light shall be used to cover judicial proceedings. No artificial lighting device of any kind shall be used in connection with the television camera.

(2) Only still camera equipment that does not produce distracting sound or light shall be used to cover judicial proceedings. No artificial lighting device of any kind shall be used in connection with a still camera.

(3) It shall be the affirmative duty of media personnel to demonstrate to the presiding judge adequately in advance of any proceeding that the equipment sought to be used meets the sound and light criteria enunciated in this rule. A failure to obtain advance judicial approval for equipment shall preclude its use in any proceeding.

(d) Location of Equipment Personnel.

(1) Television camera equipment shall be positioned in such location in the court facility as shall be designated by the chief judge of the judicial circuit or district in which such facility is situated. The area designated shall provide reasonable access to coverage. If and when areas remote from the court facility that permit reasonable access to coverage are provided, all television camera and audio equipment shall be positioned only in such area. Videotape recording equipment that is not a component part of a television camera shall be located in an area remote from the court facility.

(2) A still camera photographer shall position himself or herself in such location in the court facility as shall be designated by the chief judge of the judicial circuit or district in which such facility is situated. The area designated shall provide reasonable access to coverage. Still camera photographers shall assume a fixed position within the designated area and, once established in a shooting position, shall act so as not to call attention to themselves through further movement. Still camera photographers shall not be permitted to move about in order to obtain photographs of court proceedings.

(3) Broadcast media representatives shall not move about the court facility while proceedings are in session, and microphones or taping equipment once positioned as required by subdivision (b)(3) shall not be moved during the pendency of the proceeding.

(e) Movement During Proceedings. News media photographic or audio equipment shall not be placed in or removed from the court facility except before commencement or after adjournment of proceedings each day, or during a recess. Neither television film magazines nor still camera film or lenses shall be changed within a court facility except during a recess in the proceeding.

(f) Courtroom Light Sources. With the concurrence of the chief judge of a judicial circuit or district in which a court facility is situated, modifications and additions may be made in light sources existing in the facility, provided such modifications or additions are installed and maintained without public expense.

(g) Conferences of Counsel. To protect the attorney-client privilege and the effective right to counsel, there shall be no audio pickup or broadcast of conferences that occur in a court facility between attorneys and their clients, between co-counsel of a client, or between counsel and the presiding judge held at the bench.

(h) Impermissible Use of Media Material. None of the film, videotape, still photographs, or audio reproductions developed during or by virtue of coverage of a judicial proceeding shall be admissible as evidence in the proceeding out of which it arose, in any proceeding subsequent or collateral thereto, or upon retrial or appeal of such proceedings.

(i) Appellate Review. Review of an order excluding the electronic media from access to any proceeding, excluding coverage of a particular participant, or upon any other matters arising under these standards shall be pursuant to Florida Rule of Appellate Procedure 9.100(d).

Former Rule 2.170 added Oct. 8, 1992, effective Jan. 1, 1993 (609 So.2d 465). Amended Feb. 9, 1995 (650 So.2d 30); July 10, 2003, effective Jan. 1, 2004 (851 So.2d 698). Renumbered from Rule 2.170 Sept. 21, 2006 (939 So.2d 966).

Court Commentary

1994 Amendment. This rule was copied from Canon 3A(7) of the Code of Judicial Conduct. Canon 3A(7) represented a departure from former Canon 3A(7) [ABA Canon 35]. The former canon generally proscribed electronic media and still photography coverage of judicial proceedings from within and in areas immediately adjacent to the courtroom, with three categories of exceptions — (a) use for judicial administration, (b) coverage of investitive, ceremonial, and naturalization proceedings, and (c) use for instructional purposes in educational institutions. Subject to the limitations and promulgation of standards as mentioned therein, the revised canon constituted a general authorization for electronic media and still photography coverage for all purposes, including the purposes expressed as exceptions in the former canon. Limited only by the authority of the presiding judge in the exercise of sound discretion to prohibit filming or photographing of particular participants, consent of participants to coverage is not required. The text of the rule refers to public judicial proceedings. This is in recognition of the authority reposing in the presiding judge, upon the exercise of sound discretion, to hold certain judicial proceedings or portions thereof in camera, and in recognition of the fact that certain proceedings or portions thereof are made confidential by statute. The term "presiding judge" includes the chief judge of an appellate tribunal.

Rule 2.451. Use of Electronic Devices

(a) Electronic Devices Defined. An electronic device is any device capable of making or transmitting still or moving photographs, video recordings, or images of any kind; any device capable of creating, transmitting, or receiving text or data; and any device capable of receiving, transmitting, or recording sound. Electronic devices include, without limitation, film cameras, digital cameras, video cameras, any other type of camera, cellular telephones, tape recorders, digital voice recorders, any other type of audio recorders, laptop computers, personal digital assistants, or other similar technological devices with the ability to make or transmit video recordings, audio recordings, images, text, or data.

(b) Use of Electronic Devices by Jurors.

(1) Electronic devices, as that term is defined in subdivision (a), may be removed as directed by the presiding judge from all members of a jury panel at any time before deliberations, but such electronic devices must be removed from all members of a jury panel before jury deliberations begin. The electronic devices will be removed and appropriately secured by the bailiff or other person designated by the chief judge.

(2) Any electronic devices removed from members of a jury panel may be returned to the members of the jury panel during recesses in the trial. When jurors are sequestered, the presiding judge may determine whether the electronic devices will be removed from jurors during the entire period of sequestration.

(3) From the time a person reports for jury service until the person is discharged from jury service, that person is prohibited from using electronic devices for any of the following purposes:

(A) making or transmitting still or moving photographs, audio recordings, video recordings, or images of any kind of the court proceedings;

(B) transmitting or accessing text or data during the court proceedings;

(C) transmitting or accessing text or data about the case on which the juror is serving;

(D) researching, transmitting, or accessing information about the case on which the juror is serving;

(E) otherwise communicating about the case on which the juror is serving; or

(F) otherwise communicating about the jury deliberations.

(4) Nothing in this rule is to be construed to limit or impair the authority of a chief judge or presiding judge to grant permission to a juror to retain his or her electronic device during trial proceedings.

(5) The jury summons mailed to prospective jurors should contain a notice that electronic devices will be removed from all members of a jury panel before jury deliberations begin and as directed by the presiding judge, may be removed at other stages of a trial. At the beginning of the trial, the presiding judge should advise the jury panel about the removal of electronic devices.

(c) Use of Electronic Devices by Others.

(1) The use of electronic devices in a courtroom is subject at all times to the authority of the presiding judge or quasi-judicial officer to

(A) control the conduct of proceedings before the court;

(B) ensure decorum and prevent distractions; and

(C) ensure the fair administration of justice in the pending cause.

(2) The use of electronic devices in a courthouse or court facility is subject at all times to the authority of the chief judge to

(A) ensure decorum and prevent distractions;

(B) ensure the fair administration of justice; and

(C) preserve court security.

Adopted July 3, 2013, effective Oct. 1, 2013 (118 So.3d 193).

Committee Note

2013 Adoption. Subdivision (c), Use of Electronic Devices by Others, parallels Florida Rule of Judicial Administration 2.450(a) regarding the use of electronic devices by the media.

PART V. PRACTICE OF LAW

A. ATTORNEYS

Rule 2.505. Attorneys

(a) Scope and Purpose. All persons in good standing as members of The Florida Bar shall be permitted to practice in Florida. Attorneys of other states who are not members of The Florida Bar in good standing shall not engage in the practice of law in Florida except to the extent permitted by rule 2.510.

(b) Persons Employed by the Court. Except as provided in this subdivision, no full-time employee of the court shall practice as an attorney in any court or before any agency of government while continuing in that position. Any attorney designated by the chief justice or chief judge may represent the court, any court employee in the employee's official capacity, or any judge in the judge's official capacity, in any proceeding in which the court, employee, or judge is an interested party. An attorney formerly employed by a court shall not represent anyone in connection with a matter in which the attorney participated personally and substantially while employed by the court, unless all parties to the proceeding consent after disclosure.

(c) Attorney Not to Be Surety. No attorneys or other officers of court shall enter themselves or be taken as bail or surety in any proceeding in court.

(d) Stipulations. No private agreement or consent between parties or their attorneys concerning the practice or procedure in an action shall be of any force unless the evidence of it is in writing, subscribed by the party or the party's attorney against whom it is alleged. Parol agreements may be made before the court if promptly made a part of the record or incorporated in the stenographic notes of the proceedings, and agreements made at depositions that are incorporated in the transcript need not be signed when signing of the deposition is waived. This rule shall not apply to settlements or other substantive agreements.

(e) Appearance of Attorney. An attorney may appear in a proceeding in any of the following ways:

(1) By serving and filing, on behalf of a party, the party's first pleading or paper in the proceeding.

(2) By substitution of counsel, but only by order of court and with written consent of the client, filed with the court. The court may condition substitution upon payment of, or security for, the substituted attorney's fees and expenses, or upon such other terms as may be just.

(3) By filing with the court and serving upon all parties a notice of appearance as counsel for a party that has already appeared in a proceeding pro se or as co-counsel for a party that has already appeared in a proceeding by non-withdrawing counsel.

(f) Termination of Appearance of Attorney. The appearance of an attorney for a party in a proceeding shall terminate only in one of the following ways:

(1) *Withdrawal of Attorney.* By order of court, where the proceeding is continuing, upon motion and hearing, on notice to all parties and the client, such motion setting forth the reasons for withdrawal and the client's last known address, telephone number, including area code, and email address.

(2) *Substitution of Attorney.* By order of court, under the procedure set forth in subdivision (e)(2) of this rule.

(3) *Termination of Proceeding.* Automatically, without order of court, upon the termination of a proceeding, whether by final order of dismissal, by final adjudication, or otherwise, and following the expiration of any applicable time for appeal, where no appeal is taken.

(4) *Filing of Notice of Completion.* For limited representation proceedings under Florida Family Law Rule of Procedure 12.040, automatically, by the filing of a notice of completion titled "Termination of Limited Appearance" pursuant to rule 12.040(c).

(g) Law Student Participation. Eligible law students shall be permitted to participate as provided under the conditions of chapter 11 of the Rules Regulating The Florida Bar as amended from time to time.

(h) Attorney as Agent of Client. In all matters concerning the prosecution or defense of any proceeding in the court, the attorney of record shall be the agent of the client, and any notice by or to the attorney or act by the attorney in the proceeding shall be accepted as the act of or notice to the client.

Former Rule 2.060 amended June 14, 1979, effective July 1, 1979 (372 So.2d 449); Feb. 21, 1980 (380 So.2d 1027); Sept. 29, 1988, effective Jan. 1, 1989 (536 So.2d 195); Oct. 8, 1992, effective Jan. 1, 1993 (609 So.2d 465); Sept. 26, 1996, effective Jan. 1, 1997 (681 So.2d 698); July 17, 1997, effective Jan. 1, 1998 (701 So.2d 1164); Oct. 5, 2000, effective Jan. 1, 2001 (780 So.2d 819); July 10, 2003, effective Jan. 1, 2004 (851 So.2d 698); Nov. 13, 2003, effective Jan. 1, 2004 (860 So.2d 394); Nov. 3, 2005, effective Jan. 1, 2006 (915 So.2d 157). Renumbered from Rule 2.060 Sept. 21, 2006 (939 So.2d 966). Amended Sept. 28, 2011, effective Jan. 1, 2012 (73 So.3d 210).

Court Commentary

1997 Amendment. Originally, the rule provided that the follow-up filing had to occur within ten days. In the 1997 amendment to the rule, that requirement was modified to provide that the follow-up filing must occur "immediately" after a document is electronically filed. The "immediately thereafter" language is consistent with language used in the rules of procedure where, in a somewhat analogous situation, the filing of a document may occur after service. *See, e.g.*, Florida Rule of Civil Procedure 1.080(d) ("All original papers shall be filed with the court either before service or *immediately thereafter.*") (emphasis added). "Immediately thereafter" has been interpreted to mean "filed with reasonable promptness." *Miami Transit Co. v. Ford*, 155 So. 2d 360 (Fla. 1963).

The use of the words "other person" in this rule is not meant to allow a nonlawyer to sign and file pleadings or other papers on behalf of another. Such conduct would constitute the unauthorized practice of law.

2003 Amendment. Rule Regulating the Florida Bar 4–1.12(c), which addresses the imputed disqualification of a law firm, should be looked to in conjunction with the rule 2.060(b) restriction on representation by a former judicial staff attorney or law clerk.

Rule 2.510. Foreign Attorneys

(a) Eligibility. Upon filing a verified motion with the court, an attorney who is an active member in good standing of the bar of another state and currently eligible to practice law in a state other than Florida may be permitted to appear in particular cases in a Florida court upon such conditions as the court may deem appropriate, provided that a member of The Florida Bar in good standing is associated as an attorney of record. The foreign attorney must make application in each court in which a case is filed even if a lower tribunal granted a motion to appear in the same case. In determining whether to permit a foreign attorney to appear pursuant to this rule, the court may consider, among other things, information provided under subdivision (b)(3) concerning discipline in other jurisdictions. No attorney is authorized to appear pursuant to this rule if the attorney (1) is a Florida resident, unless the attorney has an application pending for admission to The Florida Bar and has not previously been denied admission to The Florida Bar; (2) is a member of The Florida Bar but is ineligible to practice law; (3) has previously been disciplined or held in contempt by reason of misconduct committed while engaged in representation permitted pursuant to this rule provided, however, the contempt is final and has not been reversed or abated; (4) has failed to provide notice to The Florida Bar or pay the filing fee as required in subdivision (b)(7); or (5) is engaged in a "general practice" before Florida courts. For purposes of this rule, more than 3 appearances within a 365–day period in separate cases shall be presumed to be a "general practice." Appearances at different levels of the court system in the same case shall be deemed 1 appearance for the purposes of determining whether a foreign attorney has made more than 3 appearances within a 365–day period. In cases involving indigent or pro bono clients, the court may waive the filing fee for good cause shown.

(b) Contents of Verified Motion. A form verified motion accompanies this rule and shall be utilized by the foreign attorney. The verified motion required by subdivision (a) shall include:

(1) a statement identifying all jurisdictions in which the attorney is an active member in good standing and currently eligible to practice law, including all assigned bar numbers and attorney numbers, for which a certificate of good standing is not required;

(2) a statement identifying by date, case name, and case number all other matters in Florida state courts in which pro hac vice admission has been sought in the preceding 5 years, including any lower tribunals for the case in which the motion is filed, and whether such admission was granted or denied;

(3) a statement identifying all jurisdictions in which disciplinary, suspension, disbarment, or contempt proceedings have been initiated against the attorney in the preceding 5 years including the date on which the proceeding was initiated, the nature of the alleged violation, and the result of the proceeding including the sanction, if any, imposed;

(4) a statement identifying the date on which the legal representation at issue commenced, and the party or parties represented;

(5) a statement that all applicable provisions of these rules and the Rules Regulating the Florida Bar have been read, and that the verified motion complies with those rules;

(6) the name, record bar address, and membership status of the Florida Bar member or members associated for purposes of the representation;

(7) a certificate indicating service of the verified motion upon all counsel of record in the matter in which leave to appear pro hac vice is sought and upon The Florida Bar at its Tallahassee office accompanied by a nonrefundable $250.00 filing fee made payable to The Florida Bar or notice that the movant has requested a judicial waiver of said fee; and

(8) a verification by the attorney seeking to appear pursuant to this rule and the signature of the Florida Bar member or members associated for purposes of the representation.

IN THE ______ COURT OF THE ______ JUDICIAL CIRCUIT,
IN AND FOR ______, COUNTY, FLORIDA

____
Plaintiff

vs. Case No. ______________

Division ______________

____
Defendant

VERIFIED MOTION FOR ADMISSION TO APPEAR PRO HAC VICE PURSUANT TO FLORIDA RULE OF JUDICIAL ADMINISTRATION 2.510

Comes now ____,
Movant herein, and respectfully represents the following:

1. [ ] Movant resides in ______________, ______________
(City) (State)

Movant is not a resident of the State of Florida.

[ ] Movant is a resident of the State of Florida and has an application pending for admission to The Florida Bar and has not previously been denied admission to The Florida Bar.

2. Movant is an attorney and a member of the law firm of (or practices law under the name of) ______________________, with offices at

______________, ______________, ______________, ______________,
(Street Address) (City) (County) (State)

______________, ______________
(Zip Code) (Telephone)

3. Movant has been retained personally or as a member of the above named law firm on ______________ by ______________
(Date Representation Commenced) (Name of Party or Parties)
to provide legal representation in connection with the above-styled matter now pending before the above-named court of the State of Florida.

4. Movant is an active member in good standing and currently eligible to practice law in the following jurisdiction(s): Include attorney or bar number(s). (Attach an additional sheet if necessary.)

JURISDICTION ATTORNEY/BAR NUMBER

____

____

____

____

5. There have been no disciplinary, suspension, disbarment, or contempt proceedings initiated against Movant in the preceding 5 years, except as provided below (give jurisdiction of proceeding, date upon which proceeding was initiated, nature of alleged violation, statement of whether the proceeding has concluded or is still pending, and sanction, if any, imposed): (Attach an additional sheet if necessary.)

____

____

____

____

6. Movant, either by resignation, withdrawal, or otherwise, never has terminated or attempted to terminate Movant's office as an attorney in order to avoid administrative, disciplinary, disbarment, or suspension proceedings.

7. Movant is not an inactive member of The Florida Bar.

8. Movant is not now a member of The Florida Bar.

9. Movant is not a suspended member of The Florida Bar.

10. Movant is not a disbarred member of The Florida Bar nor has Movant received a disciplinary resignation from The Florida Bar.

11. Movant has not previously been disciplined or held in contempt by reason of misconduct committed while engaged in representation pursuant to Florida Rule of Judicial Administration 2.510, except as provided below (give date of disciplinary action or contempt, reasons therefor, and court imposing contempt): (Attach an additional sheet if necessary.)

____

____

____

____

____

12. Movant has filed motion(s) to appear as counsel in Florida state courts during the past five (5) years in the following matters: (Attach an additional sheet if necessary.)

Date of Motion	Case Name	Case Number	Court	Date Motion Granted/Denied

13. Local counsel of record associated with Movant in this matter is __________________________who is an active member in good standing of
(Name and Florida Bar Number)
The Florida Bar and has offices at _______________, ___________, ___________,
(Street Address) (City) (County)
___________, ___________, _____________________.
(State) (Zip Code) (Telephone with area code)

(If local counsel is not an active member of The Florida Bar in good standing, please provide information as to local counsel's membership status. ___________)

14. Movant has read the applicable provisions of Florida Rule of Judicial Administration 2.510 and Rule 1–3.10 of the Rules Regulating The Florida Bar and certifies that this verified motion complies with those rules.

15. Movant agrees to comply with the provisions of the Florida Rules of Professional Conduct and consents to the jurisdiction of the courts and the Bar of the State of Florida.

WHEREFORE, Movant respectfully requests permission to appear in this court for this cause only.

DATED this ______________ day of ______________, 20 ______.

____
Movant

____
Address

____
Address

____
City, State, Zip Code

____
Telephone Number

____
E-mail Address

STATE OF ______________
COUNTY OF ______________

I, ______________, do hereby swear or affirm under penalty of perjury that I am the Movant in the above-styled matter; that I have read the foregoing Motion and know the contents thereof, and the contents are true of my own knowledge and belief.

____
Movant

I hereby consent to be associated as local counsel of record in this cause pursuant to Florida Rule of Judicial Administration 2.510.

DATED this ______________ day of ______________, 20 ______.

____
Local Counsel of Record

____
Address

____
Address

____
City, State, Zip Code

____
Telephone Number

____
Florida Bar Number

____
E-mail Address

CERTIFICATE OF SERVICE

I HEREBY CERTIFY that a true and correct copy of the foregoing motion was served by mail to PHV Admissions, The Florida Bar, 651 East Jefferson Street, Tallahassee, Florida 32399–2333 accompanied by payment of the $250.00 filing fee made payable to The Florida Bar, or notice that the movant has requested a judicial waiver of said fee; and by (e-mail) (delivery) (mail) (fax) to (name of attorney or party if not represented)

____

____ this ______________ day of ______________, 20 ______.

____
Movant

Former Rule 2.061 adopted Oct. 5, 2000, effective Jan. 1, 2001 (780 So.2d 819). Amended May 12, 2005 (907 So.2d 1138). Renumbered from Rule 2.061 Sept. 21, 2006 (939 So.2d 966). Amended Sept. 11, 2008, effective Jan. 1, 2009 (991 So.2d 842); Sept. 28, 2011, effective Jan. 1, 2012 (73 So.3d 210); Oct. 18, 2012, effective Dec. 1, 2012, April 1, 2013, Oct. 1, 2013 (102 So.3d 451); Oct. 30, 2014, effective Jan. 1, 2015 (150 So.3d 787).

B. PRACTICE AND LITIGATION PROCEDURES

Rule 2.514. Computing and Extending Time

(a) Computing Time. The following rules apply in computing time periods specified in any rule of procedure, local rule, court order, or statute that does not specify a method of computing time.

(1) *Period Stated in Days or a Longer Unit.* When the period is stated in days or a longer unit of time

(A) exclude the day of the event that triggers the period;

(B) count every day, including intermediate Saturdays, Sundays, and legal holidays; and

(C) include the last day of the period, but if the last day is a Saturday, Sunday, or legal holiday, or falls within any period of time extended through an order of the chief justice under Florida Rule of Judicial Administration 2.205(a)(2)(B)(iv), the period continues to run until the end of the next day that is not a Saturday, Sunday, or legal holiday and does not fall within any period of time extended through an order of the chief justice.

(2) *Period Stated in Hours.* When the period is stated in hours

(A) begin counting immediately on the occurrence of the event that triggers the period;

(B) count every hour, including hours during intermediate Saturdays, Sundays, and legal holidays; and

(C) if the period would end on a Saturday, Sunday, or legal holiday, or during any period of time extended through an order of the chief justice under Florida Rule of Judicial Administration 2.205(a)(2)(B)(iv), the period continues to run until the same time on the next day that is not a Saturday, Sunday, or legal holiday and does not fall within any period of time extended through an order of the chief justice.

(3) *Period Stated in Days Less Than Seven Days.* When the period stated in days is less than 7 days, intermediate Saturdays, Sundays, and legal holidays shall be excluded in the computation.

(4) *"Last Day" Defined.* Unless a different time is set by a statute, local rule, or court order, the last day ends

(A) for electronic filing or for service by any means, at midnight; and

(B) for filing by other means, when the clerk's office is scheduled to close.

(5) *"Next Day" Defined.* The "next day" is determined by continuing to count forward when the period is measured after an event and backward when measured before an event.

(6) *"Legal Holiday" Defined.* "Legal holiday" means

(A) the day set aside by section 110.117, Florida Statutes, for observing New Year's Day, Martin Luther King, Jr.'s Birthday, Memorial Day, Independence Day, Labor Day, Veterans' Day, Thanksgiving Day, the Friday after Thanksgiving Day, or Christmas Day, and

(B) any day observed as a holiday by the clerk's office or as designated by the chief judge.

(b) Additional Time after Service by Mail or E-mail. When a party may or must act within a specified time after service and service is made by mail or e-mail, 5 days are added after the period that would otherwise expire under subdivision (a).

Added July 12, 2012, effective Oct. 1, 2012 (95 So.3d 96).

Rule 2.515. Signature and Certificates of Attorneys and Parties

(a) Attorney's Signature and Certificates. Every document of a party represented by an attorney shall be signed by at least 1 attorney of record in that attorney's individual name whose current record Florida Bar address, telephone number, including area code, primary e-mail address and secondary e-mail addresses, if any, and Florida Bar number shall be stated, and who shall be duly licensed to practice law in Florida or who shall have received permission to appear in the particular case as provided in rule 2.510. The attorney may be required by the court to give the address of, and to vouch for the attorney's authority to represent, the party. Except when otherwise specifically provided by an applicable rule or statute, documents need not be verified or accompanied by affidavit. The signature of an attorney shall constitute a certificate by the attorney that:

(1) the attorney has read the document;

(2) to the best of the attorney's knowledge, information, and belief there is good ground to support the document;

(3) the document is not interposed for delay; and

(4) the document contains no confidential or sensitive information, or that any such confidential or sensitive information has been properly protected by complying with the provisions of rules 2.420 and 2.425. If a document is not signed or is signed with intent to defeat the purpose of this rule, it may be stricken and the action may proceed as though the document had not been served.

(b) Pro Se Litigant Signature. A party who is not represented by an attorney shall sign any document and state the party's address and telephone number, including area code.

(c) Form of Signature.

(1) The signatures required on documents by subdivisions (a) and (b) of this rule may be:

(A) original signatures;

(B) original signatures that have been reproduced by electronic means, such as on electronically transmitted documents or photocopied documents;

(C) an electronic signature indicator using the "/s/", "s/", or "/s" [name] formats authorized by the person signing a document electronically served or filed; or

(D) any other signature format authorized by general law, so long as the clerk where the proceeding is pending has the capability of receiving and has obtained approval from the Supreme Court of Florida to accept pleadings and documents with that signature format.

(2) By serving a document, or by filing a document by electronic transmission using an attorney's assigned electronic filing credentials:

(A) that attorney certifies compliance with subdivision (a)(1) through (a)(4) and accepts responsibility for the document for all purposes under this rule;

(B) that attorney certifies compliance with all rules of procedure regarding service of the document on attorneys and parties;

(C) that attorney certifies that every person identified as a signer in the document as described in subdivision (c)(1)(C) has authorized such signature; and

(D) every signing attorney is as responsible for the document as if that document had been served by such signing attorney or filed using the assigned electronic filing credentials of such signing attorney.

Former Rule 2.060 amended June 14, 1979, effective July 1, 1979 (372 So.2d 449); Feb. 21, 1980 (380 So.2d 1027); Sept. 29, 1988, effective Jan. 1, 1989 (536 So.2d 195); Oct. 8, 1992, effective Jan. 1, 1993 (609 So.2d 465); Sept. 26, 1996, effective Jan. 1, 1997 (681 So.2d 698); July 17, 1997, effective Jan. 1, 1998 (701 So.2d 1164); Oct. 5, 2000, effective Jan. 1, 2001 (780 So.2d 819); July 10, 2003, effective Jan. 1, 2004 (851 So.2d 698); Nov. 13, 2003, effective Jan. 1, 2004 (860 So.2d 394); Nov. 3, 2005, effective Jan. 1, 2006 (915 So.2d 157). Renumbered from Rule 2.060 Sept. 21, 2006 (939 So.2d 966). Amended Oct. 18, 2012, effective, *nunc pro tunc*, Sept. 1, 2012 (102 So.3d 505); Nov. 14, 2013 (126 So.3d 222).

Rule 2.516. Service of Pleadings and Documents

(a) Service; When Required. Unless the court otherwise orders, or a statute or supreme court administrative order specifies a different means of service, every pleading subsequent to the initial pleading and every other document filed in any court proceeding, except applications for witness subpoenas and documents served by formal notice or required to be served in the manner provided for service of formal notice, must be served in accordance with this rule on each party. No service need be made on parties against whom a default has been entered, except that pleadings asserting new or additional claims against them must be served in the manner provided for service of summons.

(b) Service; How Made. When service is required or permitted to be made upon a party represented by an attorney, service must be made upon the attorney unless service upon the party is ordered by the court.

(1) *Service by Electronic Mail ("e-mail").* All documents required or permitted to be served on another party must be served by e-mail, unless the parties otherwise stipulate or this rule otherwise provides. A filer of an electronic document has complied with this subdivision if the Florida Courts e-filing Portal ("Portal") or other authorized electronic filing system with a supreme court approved electronic service system ("e-Service system") served the document by e-mail or provided a link by e-mail to the document on a website maintained by a clerk ("e-Service"). The filer of an electronic document must verify that the Portal or other e-Service system uses the names and e-mail addresses provided by the parties pursuant to subdivision (b)(1)(A).

(A) Service on Attorneys. Upon appearing in a proceeding, an attorney must designate a primary e-mail address and may designate no more than two secondary e-mail addresses and is responsible for the accuracy of and changes to that attorney's own e-mail addresses maintained by the Portal or other e-Service system. Thereafter, service must be directed to all designated e-mail addresses in that proceeding. Every document filed or served by an attorney thereafter must include the primary e-mail address of that attorney and any secondary e-mail addresses. If an attorney does not designate any e-mail address for service, documents may be served on that attorney at the e-mail address on record with The Florida Bar.

(B) Exception to E-mail Service on Attorneys. Upon motion by an attorney demonstrating that the attorney has no e-mail account and lacks access to the Internet at the attorney's office, the court may excuse the attorney from the requirements of e-mail service. Service on and by an attorney excused by the court from e-mail service must be by the means provided in subdivision (b)(2) of this rule.

(C) Service on and by Parties Not Represented by an Attorney. Any party not represented by an attorney may serve a designation of a primary e-mail address and also may designate no more than two secondary e-mail addresses to which service must be directed in that proceeding by the means provided in subdivision (b)(1) of this rule. If a party not represented by an attorney does not designate an e-mail address for service in a proceeding, service on and by that party must be by the means provided in subdivision (b)(2) of this rule.

(D) Time of Service. Service by e-mail is complete on the date it is sent.

(i) If, however, the e-mail is sent by the Portal or other e-Service system, service is complete on the date the served document is electronically filed.

(ii) If the person required to serve a document learns that the e-mail was not received by an intended recipient, the person must immediately resend the document to that intended recipient by e-mail, or by a means authorized by subdivision (b)(2) of this rule.

(iii) E-mail service, including e-Service, is treated as service by mail for the computation of time.

(E) Format of E-mail for Service. Service of a document by e-mail is made by an e-mail sent to all addresses designated by the attorney or party with either (a) a copy of the document in PDF format attached or (b) a link to the document on a website maintained by a clerk.

(i) All documents served by e-mail must be sent by an e-mail message containing a subject line beginning with the words "SERVICE OF COURT DOCUMENT" in all capital letters, followed by the case number of the proceeding in which the documents are being served.

(ii) The body of the e-mail must identify the court in which the proceeding is pending, the case number, the name of the initial party on each side, the title of each document served with that e-mail, and the name and telephone number of the person required to serve the document.

(iii) Any document served by e-mail may be signed by any of the "/s/", "/s", or "s/" formats.

(iv) Any e-mail which, together with its attached documents, exceeds five megabytes (5MB) in size, must be divided and sent as separate e-mails, no one of which may exceed 5MB in size and each of which must be sequentially numbered in the subject line.

(2) *Service by Other Means.* In addition to, and not in lieu of, service by e-mail, service may also be made upon attorneys by any of the means specified in this subdivision. If a document is served by more than one method of service, the computation of time for any response to the served document shall be based on the method of service that provides the shortest response time. Service on and by all parties who are not represented by an attorney and who do not designate an e-mail address, and on and by all attorneys excused from e-mail service, must be made by delivering a copy of the document or by mailing it to the party or attorney at their last known address or, if no address is known, by leaving it with the clerk of the court. Service by mail is complete upon mailing. Delivery of a copy within this rule is complete upon:

(A) handing it to the attorney or to the party,

(B) leaving it at the attorney's or party's office with a clerk or other person in charge thereof,

(C) if there is no one in charge, leaving it in a conspicuous place therein,

(D) if the office is closed or the person to be served has no office, leaving it at the person's usual place of abode with some person of his or her family above 15 years of age and informing such person of the contents, or

(E) transmitting it by facsimile to the attorney's or party's office with a cover sheet containing the sender's name, firm, address, telephone number, and facsimile number, and the number of pages transmitted. When service is made by facsimile, a copy must also be served by any other method permitted by this rule. Facsimile service occurs when transmission is complete.

(F) Service by delivery shall be deemed complete on the date of the delivery.

(c) Service; Numerous Defendants. In actions when the parties are unusually numerous, the court may regulate the service contemplated by these rules on motion or on its own initiative in such manner as may be found to be just and reasonable.

(d) Filing. All documents must be filed with the court either before service or immediately thereafter, unless otherwise provided for by general law or other rules. If the original of any bond or other document required to be an original is not placed in the court file or deposited with the clerk, a certified copy must be so placed by the clerk.

(e) Filing Defined. The filing of documents with the court as required by these rules must be made by filing them with the clerk in accordance with rule 2.525, except that the judge may permit documents to be filed with the judge, in which event the judge must note the filing date before him or her on the documents and transmit them to the clerk. The date of filing is that shown on the face of the document by the judge's notation or the clerk's time stamp, whichever is earlier.

(f) Certificate of Service. When any attorney certifies in substance:

"I certify that the foregoing document has been furnished to (here insert name or names, addresses used for service, and mailing addresses) by (e-mail) (delivery) (mail) (fax) on . . .(date). . .

____

Attorney"

the certificate is taken as prima facie proof of such service in compliance with this rule.

(g) Service by Clerk. When the clerk is required to serve notices and other documents, the clerk may do so by e-mail as provided in subdivision (b)(1) or by any other method permitted under subdivision (b)(2). Service by a clerk is not required to be by e-mail.

(h) Service of Orders.

(1) A copy of all orders or judgments must be transmitted by the court or under its direction to all parties at the time of entry of the order or judgment. No service need be made on parties against whom a default has been entered except orders setting an action for trial and final judgments that must be prepared and served as provided in subdivision (h)(2). The court may require that orders or judgments be prepared by a party, may require the party to furnish the court with stamped, addressed envelopes for service of the order or judgment, and may require that proposed orders and judgments be furnished to all parties before entry by the court of the order or judgment. The court may serve any order or judgment by e-mail to all attorneys who have not been excused from e-mail service and to all parties not represented by an attorney who have designated an e-mail address for service.

(2) When a final judgment is entered against a party in default, the court must mail a conformed copy of it to the party. The party in whose favor the judgment is entered must furnish the court with a copy of the judgment, unless it is prepared by the court, with the address of the party to be served. If the address is unknown, the copy need not be furnished.

(3) This subdivision is directory and a failure to comply with it does not affect the order or judgment, its finality, or any proceedings arising in the action.

Added Oct. 18, 2012, effective, *nunc pro tunc*, Sept. 1, 2012 (102 So.3d 505). Amended Oct. 18, 2012, effective Dec. 1, 2012, April 1, 2013, Oct. 1, 2013 (102 So.3d 451); April 4, 2013 (112 So.3d 1173); Nov. 14, 2013 (126 So.3d 222).

Rule 2.520. Documents

(a) Electronic Filing Mandatory. All documents filed in any court shall be filed by electronic transmission in accordance with rule 2.525. "Documents" means pleadings, motions, petitions, memoranda, briefs, notices, exhibits, declarations, affidavits, orders, judgments, decrees, writs, opinions, and any paper or writing submitted to a court.

(b) Type and Size. Documents subject to the exceptions set forth in rule 2.525(d) shall be legibly typewritten or printed, on only one side of letter sized (8 1/2 by 11 inch) white recycled paper with one inch margins and consecutively numbered pages. For purposes of this rule, paper is recycled if it contains a minimum content of 50 percent waste paper. Reduction of legal-size (8 1/2 by 14 inches) documents to letter size (8 1/2 by 11 inches) is prohibited. All documents filed by electronic transmission shall comply with rule 2.526 and be filed in a format capable of being electronically searched and printed in a format consistent with the provisions of this rule.

(c) Exhibits. Any exhibit or attachment to any document may be filed in its original size.

(d) Recording Space and Space for Date and Time Stamps.

(1) On all documents prepared and filed by the court or by any party to a proceeding which are to be recorded in the public records of any county, including but not limited to final money judgments and notices of lis pendens, a 3–inch by 3–inch space at the top right-hand corner on the first page and a 1–inch by 3–inch space at the top right-hand corner on each subsequent page shall be left blank and reserved for use by the clerk of court.

(2) On all documents filed with the court, a 1–inch margin on all sides must be left blank for date and time stamps.

(A) Format. Date and time stamp formats must include a single line detailing the name of the court or Portal and shall not include clerk seals. Date stamps must be 8 numerical digits separated by slashes with 2 digits for the month, 2 digits for the day, and 4 digits for the year. Time stamps must be formatted in 12 hour time frames with a.m. or p.m. included. The font size and type must meet the Americans with Disabilities Act requirements.

(B) Location. The Portal stamp shall be on the top left of the document. The Florida Supreme Court and district courts of appeal stamps shall be on the left margin horizontally. Any administrative agency stamp shall be on the right margin horizontally. The clerk's stamp for circuit and county courts shall be on the bottom of the document.

(C) Paper Filings. When a document is filed in paper as authorized by rule, the clerk may stamp the paper document in ink with the date and time of filing instead of, or in addition to, placing the electronic stamp as described in subdivision (B). The ink stamp on a paper document must be legible on the electronic version of the document, and must neither obscure the content or other date stamp, nor occupy space otherwise reserved by subdivision (B).

(e) Exceptions to Recording Space. Any documents created by persons or entities over which the filing party has no control, including but not limited to wills, codicils, trusts, or other testamentary documents; documents prepared or executed by any public officer; documents prepared, executed, acknowledged, or proved outside of the State of Florida; or documents created by State or Federal government agencies, may be filed without the space required by this rule.

(f) Noncompliance. No clerk of court shall refuse to file any document because of noncompliance with this rule. However, upon request of the clerk of court, noncomplying documents shall be resubmitted in accordance with this rule.

Former Rule 2.055 added Oct. 19, 1989, effective Jan. 1, 1990 (550 So.2d 457). Amended Oct. 8, 1992, effective Jan. 1, 1993 (609 So.2d 465); Oct. 24, 1996, effective Jan. 1, 1997 (682 So.2d 89); May 21, 1998, effective Jan. 1, 1999 (711 So.2d 29). Renumbered from Rule 2.055 Sept. 21, 2006 (939 So.2d 966). Amended Oct. 18, 2012, effective Dec. 1, 2012, April 1, 2013, Oct. 1, 2013 (102 So.3d 451); April 2, 2015, effective nunc pro tunc Jan. 1, 2015, except subrule (d)(2)(c), effective April 2, 2015 (161 So.3d 1254).

Court Commentary

1989 Adoption. Rule 2.055 is new. This rule aligns Florida's court system with the federal court system and the court systems of the majority of our sister states by requiring in subdivision (a) that all pleadings, motions, petitions, briefs, notices, orders, judgments, decrees, opinions, or other papers filed with any Florida court be submitted on paper measuring 8 1/2 by 11 inches. Subdivision (e) provides a 1–year transition period from the effective date of January 1, 1990, to January 1, 1991, during which time filings that traditionally have been accepted on legal-size paper will be accepted on either legal- or letter-size paper. The 1–year transition period was provided to allow for the depletion of inventories of legal-size paper and forms. The 1–year transition period was not intended to affect compliance with Florida Rule of Appellate Procedure 9. 210(a)(1), which requires that typewritten appellate briefs be filed on paper measuring 8 1/2 by 11 inches. Nor was it intended that the requirement of Florida Rule of Appellate Procedure 9.210(a)(1) that printed briefs measure 6 by 9 inches be affected by the requirements of subdivision (a).

Subdivision (b), which recognizes an exception for exhibits or attachments, is intended to apply to documents such as wills and traffic citations which traditionally have not been generated on letter-size paper.

Subdivision (c) was adopted to ensure that a 1 1/2 inch square at the top right-hand corner of all filings is reserved for use by the clerk of court. Subdivision (d) was adopted to ensure that all papers and documents submitted for filing will be considered filed on the date of submission regardless of paper size. Subdivision (d) also ensures that after the 1–year transition period of subdivision (e), filings that are not in compliance with the rule are resubmitted on paper measuring 8 1/2 by 11 inches.

This rule is not intended to apply to those instruments and documents presented to the clerk of the circuit court for recording in the Official Records under section 28.222, Florida Statutes (1987). It is also not intended to apply to matters submitted to the clerk of the circuit court in the capacity as ex officio clerk of the board of county commissioners pursuant to article VIII, section (1)(d), Florida Constitution.

1996 Amendment. Subdivision (c) was amended to make the blank space requirements for use by the clerk of the court consistent with section 695.26, Florida Statutes (1995). Subdivision (e) was eliminated because the transition period for letter-size and recycled paper was no longer necessary.

Rule 2.525. Electronic Filing

(a) Definition. "Electronic transmission of documents" means the sending of information by electronic signals to, by or from a court or clerk, which when received can be transformed and stored or transmitted on paper, microfilm, magnetic storage device, optical imaging system, CD–ROM, flash drive, other electronic data storage system, server, case maintenance system ("CM"), electronic court filing ("ECF") system, statewide or local electronic portal ("e-portal"), or other electronic record keeping system authorized by the supreme court in a format sufficient to communicate the information on the original document in a readable format. Electronic transmission of documents includes electronic mail ("e-mail") and any internet-based transmission procedure, and may include procedures allowing for documents to be signed or verified by electronic means.

(b) Application. Only the electronic filing credentials of an attorney who has signed a document may be used to file that document by electronic transmission. Any court or clerk may accept the electronic transmission of documents for filing and may send documents by electronic transmission after the clerk, together with input from the chief judge of the circuit, has obtained approval of procedures, programs, and standards for electronic filing from the supreme court ("ECF Procedures"). All ECF Procedures must comply with the then-current e-filing standards, as promulgated by the supreme court in Administrative Order No. AOSC09–30, or subsequent administrative order.

(c) Documents Affected.

(1) All documents that are court records, as defined in rule 2.430(a)(1), must be filed by electronic transmission, provided that:

(A) the clerk has the ability to accept and retain such documents;

(B) the clerk or the chief judge of the circuit has requested permission to accept documents filed by electronic transmission; and

(C) the supreme court has entered an order granting permission to the clerk to accept documents filed by electronic transmission.

(2) The official court file is a set of electronic documents stored in a computer system maintained by the clerk, together with any supplemental nonelectronic

documents and materials authorized by this rule. It consists of:

(A) documents filed by electronic transmission under this rule;

(B) documents filed in paper form under subdivision (d) that have been converted to electronic form by the clerk;

(C) documents filed in paper form before the effective date of this rule that have been converted to electronic form by the clerk;

(D) documents filed in paper form before the effective date of this rule or under subdivision (d), unless such documents are converted into electronic form by the clerk;

(E) electronic documents filed pursuant to subdivision (d)(5); and

(F) materials and documents filed pursuant to any rule, statute or court order that either cannot be converted into electronic form or are required to be maintained in paper form.

(3) The documents in the official court file are deemed originals for all purposes except as otherwise provided by statute or rule.

(4) Any document in paper form submitted under subdivision (d) is filed when it is received by the clerk or court and the clerk shall immediately thereafter convert any filed paper document to an electronic document. "Convert to an electronic document" means optically capturing an image of a paper document and using character recognition software to recover as much of the document's text as practicable and then indexing and storing the document in the official court file.

(5) Any storage medium submitted under subdivision (d)(5) is filed when received by the clerk or court and the clerk shall immediately thereafter transfer the electronic documents from the storage device to the official court file.

(6) If the filer of any paper document authorized under subdivision (d) provides a self-addressed, postage-paid envelope for return of the paper document after it is converted to electronic form by the clerk, the clerk shall place the paper document in the envelope and deposit it in the mail. Except when a paper document is required to be maintained, the clerk may recycle any filed paper document that is not to be returned to the filer.

(7) The clerk may convert any paper document filed before the effective date of this rule to an electronic document. Unless the clerk is required to maintain the paper document, if the paper document has been converted to an electronic document by the clerk, the paper document is no longer part of the official court file and may be removed and recycled.

(d) Exceptions. Paper documents and other submissions may be manually submitted to the clerk or court:

(1) when the clerk does not have the ability to accept and retain documents by electronic filing or has not had ECF Procedures approved by the supreme court;

(2) for filing by any self-represented party or any self-represented nonparty unless specific ECF Procedures provide a means to file documents electronically. However, any self-represented nonparty that is a governmental or public agency and any other agency, partnership, corporation, or business entity acting on behalf of any governmental or public agency may file documents by electronic transmission if such entity has the capability of filing documents electronically;

(3) for filing by attorneys excused from e-mail service in accordance with rule 2.516(b);

(4) when submitting evidentiary exhibits or filing non-documentary materials;

(5) when the filing involves documents in excess of 25 megabytes (25MB) in size. For such filings, documents may be transmitted using an electronic storage medium that the clerk has the ability to accept, which may include a CD–ROM, flash drive, or similar storage medium;

(6) when filed in open court, as permitted by the court;

(7) when paper filing is permitted by any approved statewide or local ECF procedures; and

(8) if any court determines that justice so requires.

(e) Service.

(1) Electronic transmission may be used by a court or clerk for the service of all orders of whatever nature, pursuant to rule 2.516(h), and for the service of any documents pursuant to any ECF Procedures, provided the clerk, together with input from the chief judge of the circuit, has obtained approval from the supreme court of ECF Procedures containing the specific procedures and program to be used in transmitting the orders and documents. All other requirements for the service of such orders must be met.

(2) Any document electronically transmitted to a court or clerk must also be served on all parties and interested persons in accordance with the applicable rules of court.

(f) Administration.

(1) Any clerk who, after obtaining supreme court approval, accepts for filing documents that have been electronically transmitted must:

(A) provide electronic or telephonic access to its equipment, whether through an e-portal or otherwise, during regular business hours, and all other times as practically feasible;

(B) accept electronic transmission of documents up to 25 megabytes (25MB) in size, or until e-filing has been fully implemented, accept facsimile transmissions of documents up to 10 pages in length; and

(C) accept filings in excess of 25 megabytes (25MB) in size by electronic storage device or system, which may include a CD–ROM, flash drive, or similar storage system.

(2) All attorneys, parties, or other persons using this rule to file documents are required to make arrangements with the court or clerk for the payment of any charges authorized by general law or the supreme court before filing any document by electronic transmission.

(3) The filing date for an electronically transmitted document is the date and time that such filing is acknowledged by an electronic stamp or otherwise, pursuant to any procedure set forth in any ECF Procedures approved by the supreme court, or the date the last page of such filing is received by the court or clerk.

(4) Any court or clerk may extend the hours of access or increase the page or size limitations set forth in this subdivision.

(g) Accessibility. All documents transmitted in any electronic form under this rule must comply with the accessibility requirements of Florida Rule of Judicial Administration 2.526.

Former Rule 2.090 amended June 14, 1979, effective July 1, 1979 (372 So.2d 449); Oct. 8, 1992, effective Jan. 1, 1993 (609 So.2d 465); Sept. 26, 1996, effective Jan. 1, 1997 (681 So.2d 698); July 17, 1997, effective Jan. 1, 1998 (701 So.2d 1164). Renumbered from Rule 2.090 Sept. 21, 2006 (939 So.2d 966). Amended Sept. 28, 2011, effective Jan. 1, 2012 (73 So.3d 210); Oct. 18, 2012, effective Dec. 1, 2012, April 1, 2013, Oct. 1, 2013 (102 So.3d 451); Nov. 14, 2013 (126 So.3d 222).

Court Commentary

1997 Amendment. Originally, the rule provided that the follow-up filing had to occur within ten days. In the 1997 amendment to the rule, that requirement was modified to provide that the follow-up filing must occur "immediately" after a document is electronically filed. The "immediately thereafter" language is consistent with language used in the rules of procedure where, in a somewhat analogous situation, the filing of a document may occur after service. *See, e.g.*, Florida Rule of Civil Procedure 1.080(d) ("All original papers shall be filed with the court either before service or *immediately thereafter*.") (emphasis added). "Immediately thereafter" has been interpreted to mean "filed with reasonable promptness." *Miami Transit Co. v. Ford*, 155 So.2d 360 (Fla.1963).

The use of the words "other person" in this rule is not meant to allow a nonlawyer to sign and file pleadings or other papers on behalf of another. Such conduct would constitute the unauthorized practice of law.

Rule 2.526. Accessibility of Information and Technology

Any document that is or will become a judicial branch record, as defined in rule 2.420(b)(1), and that is transmitted in an electronic form, as defined in rule 2.525, must be formatted in a manner that complies with all state and federal laws requiring that electronic judicial records be accessible to persons with disabilities, including without limitation the Americans with Disabilities Act and Section 508 of the federal Rehabilitation Act of 1973 as incorporated into Florida law by section 282.603(1), Florida Statutes (2010), and any related federal or state regulations or administrative rules.

Added Sept. 28, 2011, effective Jan. 1, 2012 (73 So.3d 210).

Rule 2.530. Communication Equipment

(a) Definition. Communication equipment means a conference telephone or other electronic device that permits all those appearing or participating to hear and speak to each other, provided that all conversation of all parties is audible to all persons present.

(b) Use by All Parties. A county or circuit court judge may, upon the court's own motion or upon the written request of a party, direct that communication equipment be used for a motion hearing, pretrial conference, or a status conference. A judge must give notice to the parties and consider any objections they may have to the use of communication equipment before directing that communication equipment be used. The decision to use communication equipment over the objection of parties will be in the sound discretion of the trial court, except as noted below.

(c) Use Only by Requesting Party. A county or circuit court judge may, upon the written request of a party upon reasonable notice to all other parties, permit a requesting party to participate through communication equipment in a scheduled motion hearing; however, any such request (except in criminal, juvenile, and appellate proceedings) must be granted, absent a showing of good cause to deny the same, where the hearing is set for not longer than 15 minutes.

(d) Testimony.

(1) *Generally.* A county or circuit court judge, general magistrate, special magistrate, or hearing officer may allow testimony to be taken through communication equipment if all parties consent or if permitted by another applicable rule of procedure.

(2) *Procedure.* Any party desiring to present testimony through communication equipment shall, prior to the hearing or trial at which the testimony is to be presented, contact all parties to determine whether each party consents to this form of testimony. The party seeking to present the testimony shall move for permission to present testimony through communication equipment, which motion shall set forth good cause as to why the testimony should be allowed in this form.

(3) *Oath.* Testimony may be taken through communication equipment only if a notary public or other person authorized to administer oaths in the witness's jurisdiction is present with the witness and adminis-

ters the oath consistent with the laws of the jurisdiction.

(4) *Confrontation Rights.* In juvenile and criminal proceedings the defendant must make an informed waiver of any confrontation rights that may be abridged by the use of communication equipment.

(5) *Video Testimony.* If the testimony to be presented utilizes video conferencing or comparable two-way visual capabilities, the court in its discretion may modify the procedures set forth in this rule to accommodate the technology utilized.

(e) Burden of Expense. The cost for the use of the communication equipment is the responsibility of the requesting party unless otherwise directed by the court.

(f) Override of Family Violence Indicator. Communications equipment may be used for a hearing on a petition to override a family violence indicator under Florida Family Law Rule of Procedure 12.650.

Former Rule 2.071 added Jan. 2, 1985, effective Jan. 1, 1985 (462 So.2d 444). Amended Oct. 8, 1992, effective Jan. 1, 1993 (609 So.2d 465); May 25, 2000 (766 So.2d 999); Oct. 5, 2000, effective Jan. 1, 2001 (780 So.2d 819); Nov. 3, 2005, effective Jan. 1, 2006 (915 So.2d 157). Renumbered from Rule 2.071 Sept. 21, 2006 (939 So.2d 966). Amended Sept. 28, 2011, effective Jan. 1, 2012 (73 So.3d 210).

Rule 2.535. Court Reporting

(a) Definitions.

(1) "Approved court reporter" means a court employee or contractor who performs court reporting services, including transcription, at public expense and who meets the court's certification, training, and other qualifications for court reporting.

(2) "Approved transcriptionist" means a court employee, contractor, or other individual who performs transcription services at public expense and who meets the court's certification, training, and other qualifications for transcribing proceedings.

(3) "Civil court reporter" means a court reporter who performs court reporting services in civil proceedings not required to be reported at public expense, and who meets the court's certification, training, and other qualifications for court reporting.

(4) "Court reporting" means the act of making a verbatim record of the spoken word, whether by the use of written symbols, stenomask equipment, stenographic equipment, or electronic devices, in any proceedings pending in any of the courts of this state, including all discovery proceedings conducted in connection therewith, any proceedings reported for the court's own use, and all proceedings required by statute to be reported by an approved court reporter or civil court reporter. It does not mean the act of taking witness statements not intended for use in court as substantive evidence.

(5) "Electronic record" means the audio, analog, digital, or video record of a court proceeding.

(6) "Official record" means the transcript, which is the written or electronically stored record of court proceedings and depositions prepared in accordance with the requirements of subdivision (f).

(b) When Court Reporting Required. Any proceeding shall be reported on the request of any party. The party so requesting shall pay the reporting fees, but this requirement shall not preclude the taxation of costs as authorized by law.

(c) Record. When trial proceedings are being reported, no part of the proceedings shall be omitted unless all of the parties agree to do so and the court approves the agreement. When a deposition is being reported, no part of the proceedings shall be omitted unless all of the parties and the witness so agree. When a party or a witness seeks to terminate or suspend the taking of a deposition for the time necessary to seek a court order, the court reporter shall discontinue reporting the testimony of the witness.

(d) Ownership of Records. The chief judge of the circuit in which a proceeding is pending, in his or her official capacity, is the owner of all records and electronic records made by an official court reporter or quasi-judicial officer in proceedings required to be reported at public expense and proceedings reported for the court's own use.

(e) Fees. The chief judge shall have the discretion to adopt an administrative order establishing maximum fees for court reporting services. Any such order must make a specific factual finding that the setting of such maximum fees is necessary to ensure access to the courts. Such finding shall include consideration of the number of court reporters in the county or circuit, any past history of fee schedules, and any other relevant factors.

(f) Transcripts. Transcripts of all judicial proceedings, including depositions, shall be uniform in and for all courts throughout the state and shall be stored in an electronic format sufficient to communicate the information contained in proceedings in a readable format, and capable of being transmitted electronically as set forth in rule 2.525. Any transcripts stored in electronic form must be capable of being printed in accordance with this rule. The form, size, spacing, and method of printing transcripts are as follows:

(1) All proceedings shall be printed on paper 8 1/2 inches by 11 inches in size and bound on the left.

(2) There shall be no fewer than 25 printed lines per page with all lines numbered 1 through 25, respectively, and with no more than a double space between lines.

(3) Font size or print shall be 9 or 10 pica, 12–point courier, or 12–point Times New Roman print with no less than 56 characters per line on questions and answers unless the text of the speaker ends short of marginal requirements.

(4) Colloquy material shall begin on the same line following the identification of the speaker, with no more than 2 spaces between the identification of the speaker and the commencement of the colloquy. The identification of the speaker in colloquy shall begin no more than 10 spaces from the left margin, and carry-over colloquy shall be indented no more than 5 spaces from the left margin.

(5) Each question and answer shall begin on a separate line no more than 5 spaces from the left margin with no more than 5 spaces from the "Q" or "A" to the text. Carry–over question and answer lines shall be brought to the left margin.

(6) Quoted material shall begin no more than 10 spaces from the left margin with carry-over lines beginning no more than 10 spaces from the left margin.

(7) Indentations of no more than 10 spaces may be used for paragraphs, and all spaces on a line as herein provided shall be used unless the text of the speaker ends short of marginal requirements.

(8) One–line parentheticals may begin at any indentation. Parentheticals exceeding 1 line shall begin no more than 10 spaces from the left margin, with carry-over lines being returned to the left margin.

(9) Individual volumes of a transcript, including depositions, shall be no more than 200 pages in length, inclusive of the index.

(10) Deviation from these standards shall not constitute grounds for limiting use of transcripts in the trial or appellate courts.

(g) Officers of the Court. Approved court reporters, civil court reporters, and approved transcriptionists are officers of the court for all purposes while acting as court reporters in judicial proceedings or discovery proceedings or as transcriptionists. Approved court reporters, civil court reporters, and approved transcriptionists shall comply with all rules and statutes governing the proceeding that are applicable to court reporters and approved transcriptionists.

(h) Court Reporting Services at Public Expense.

(1) *When Reporting Is Required.* All proceedings required by law, court rule, or administrative order to be reported shall be reported at public expense.

(2) *When Reporting May Be Required.* Proceedings reported for the court's own use may be reported at public expense.

(3) *Circuit Plan.* The chief judge, after consultation with the circuit court and county court judges in the circuit, shall enter an administrative order developing and implementing a circuit-wide plan for the court reporting of all proceedings required to be reported at public expense using either full or part time court employees or independent contractors. The plan shall ensure that all court reporting services are provided by approved court reporters or approved transcriptionists. This plan may provide for multiple service delivery strategies if they are necessary to ensure the efficient provision of court reporting services. Each circuit's plan for court reporting services shall be developed after consideration of guidelines issued by the Office of the State Courts Administrator.

(4) *Electronic Recording and Transcription of Proceedings Without Court Reporters.* A chief judge may enter a circuit-wide administrative order, which shall be recorded, authorizing the electronic recording and subsequent transcription by approved court reporters or approved transcriptionists, of any judicial proceedings, including depositions, that are otherwise required to be reported by a court reporter. Appropriate procedures shall be prescribed in the order which shall:

(A) set forth responsibilities for the court's support personnel to ensure a reliable record of the proceedings;

(B) provide a means to have the recording transcribed by approved court reporters or approved transcriptionists, either in whole or in part, when necessary for an appeal or for further use in the trial court; and

(C) provide for the safekeeping of such recordings.

(5) *Safeguarding Confidential Communications When Electronic Recording Equipment Is Used in the Courtroom.*

(A) Court personnel shall provide notice to participants in a courtroom proceeding that electronic recording equipment is in use and that they should safeguard information they do not want recorded.

(B) Attorneys shall take all reasonable and available precautions to protect disclosure of confidential communications in the courtroom. Such precautions may include muting microphones or going to a designated location that is inaccessible to the recording equipment.

(C) Participants have a duty to protect confidential information.

(6) *Grand Jury Proceedings.* Testimony in grand jury proceedings shall be reported by an approved court reporter, but shall not be transcribed unless required by order of court. Other parts of grand jury proceedings, including deliberations and voting, shall not be reported. The approved court reporter's work product, including stenographic notes, electronic recordings, and transcripts, shall be filed with the clerk of the court under seal.

(i) Court Reporting Services in Capital Cases. The chief judge, after consultation with the circuit court judges in the circuit, shall enter an administrative order developing and implementing a circuit-wide plan for court reporting in all trials in which the state seeks the death penalty and in capital postconviction proceedings. The plan shall prohibit the use of digital court reporting as the primary court reporting system and shall require the use of all measures necessary to expedite the preparation of the transcript, including but not limited to:

(1) where available, the use of an approved court reporter who has the capacity to provide real-time transcription of the proceedings;

(2) if real-time transcription services are not available, the use of a computer-aided transcription qualified court reporter;

(3) the use of scopists, text editors, alternating court reporters, or other means to expedite the finalization of the certified transcript; and

(4) the imposition of reasonable restrictions on work assignments by employee or contract approved court reporters to ensure that transcript production in capital cases is given a priority.

(j) Juvenile Dependency and Termination of Parental Rights Cases. Transcription of hearings for appeals of orders in juvenile dependency and termination of parental rights cases shall be given priority, consistent with rule 2.215(g), over transcription of all other proceedings, unless otherwise ordered by the court based upon a demonstrated exigency.

Former Rule 2.070 amended Nov. 2, 1978, effective Jan. 1, 1979 (364 So.2d 466); June 14, 1979, effective July 1, 1979 (372 So.2d 449); May 21, 1987, effective July 1, 1987 (507 So.2d 1390); Sept. 29, 1988, effective Jan. 1, 1989 (536 So.2d 195); Oct. 8, 1992, effective Jan. 1, 1993 (609 So.2d 465); Feb. 23, 1995 (650 So.2d 38); May 9, 1995 (654 So.2d 917); Oct. 5, 1995, effective Jan. 1, 1996 (661 So.2d 806); effective July 14, 2000 (772 So.2d 532); Oct. 5, 2000, effective Jan. 1, 2001 (780 So.2d 819); July 10, 2003, effective Jan. 1, 2004 (851 So.2d 698). Renumbered from Rule 2.070 Sept. 21, 2006 (939 So.2d 966). Amended July 16, 2009 (13 So.3d 1044); Nov. 12, 2009 (24 So.3d 47); Oct. 18, 2012, effective Dec. 1, 2012, April 1, 2013, Oct. 1, 2013 (102 So.3d 451); July 3, 2014, effective Jan. 1, 2015 (148 So.3d 1171).

Committee Note

The definitions of "electronic record" in subdivision (a)(5) and of "official record" in subdivision (a)(6) are intended to clarify that when a court proceeding is electronically recorded by means of audio, analog, digital, or video equipment, and is also recorded via a written transcript prepared by a court reporter, the written transcript shall be the "official record" of the proceeding to the exclusion of all electronic records. While the term "record" is used within Rule 2.535 and within Fla. R. App. P. 9.200, it has a different meaning within the unique context of each rule. Accordingly, the meaning of the term "record" as defined for purposes of this rule does not in any way alter, amend, change, or conflict with the meaning of the term "record" as defined for appellate purposes in Fla. R. App. P. 9.200(a).

Rule 2.540. Requests for Accommodations by Persons with Disabilities

(a) Duties of Court. Qualified individuals with a disability will be provided, at the court's expense, with accommodations, reasonable modifications to rules, policies, or practices, or the provision of auxiliary aids and services, in order to participate in programs or activities provided by the courts of this state. The court may deny a request only in accordance with subdivision (e).

(b) Definitions. The definitions encompassed in the Americans with Disabilities Act of 1990, 42 U.S.C. § 12101, et seq., are incorporated into this rule.

(c) Notice Requirement.

(1) All notices of court proceedings to be held in a public facility, and all process compelling appearance at such proceedings, shall include the following statement in bold face, 14–point Times New Roman or Courier font:

"If you are a person with a disability who needs any accommodation in order to participate in this proceeding, you are entitled, at no cost to you, to the provision of certain assistance. Please contact [identify applicable court personnel by name, address, and telephone number] at least 7 days before your scheduled court appearance, or immediately upon receiving this notification if the time before the scheduled appearance is less than 7 days; if you are hearing or voice impaired, call 711."

(2) Each trial and appellate court shall post on its respective website and in each court facility the procedures for obtaining an accommodation as well as the grievance procedure adopted by that court.

(d) Process for Requesting Accommodations. The process for requesting accommodations is as follows:

(1) Requests for accommodations under this rule may be presented on a form approved or substantially similar to one approved by the Office of the State Courts Administrator, in another written format, or orally. Requests must be forwarded to the ADA coordinator, or designee, within the time frame provided in subdivision (d)(3).

(2) Requests for accommodations must include a description of the accommodation sought, along with a statement of the impairment that necessitates the accommodation and the duration that the accommodation is to be provided. The court, in its discretion, may require the individual with a disability to provide additional information about the impairment. Requests for accommodation shall not include any information regarding the merits of the case.

(3) Requests for accommodations must be made at least 7 days before the scheduled court appearance, or immediately upon receiving notification if the time before the scheduled court appearance is less than 7 days. The court may, in its discretion, waive this requirement.

(e) Response to Accommodation Request. The court must respond to a request for accommodation as follows:

(1) The court must consider, but is not limited by, the provisions of the Americans with Disabilities Act of 1990 in determining whether to provide an accommodation or an appropriate alternative accommodation.

(2) The court must inform the individual with a disability of the following:

(A) That the request for accommodation is granted or denied, in whole or in part, and if the request for accommodation is denied, the reason therefor; or that an alternative accommodation is granted;

(B) The nature of the accommodation to be provided, if any; and

(C) The duration of the accommodation to be provided.

If the request for accommodation is granted in its entirety, the court shall respond to the individual with a disability by any appropriate method. If the request is denied or granted only in part, or if an alternative accommodation is granted, the court must respond to the individual with a disability in writing, as may be appropriate, and if applicable, in an alternative format.

(3) If the court determines that a person is a qualified person with a disability and an accommodation is needed, a request for accommodation may be denied only when the court determines that the requested accommodation would create an undue financial or administrative burden on the court or would fundamentally alter the nature of the service, program, or activity.

(f) Grievance Procedure.

(1) Each judicial circuit and appellate court shall establish and publish grievance procedures that allow for the resolution of complaints. Those procedures may be used by anyone who wishes to file a complaint alleging discrimination on the basis of disability in the provision of services, activities, programs, or benefits by the Florida State Courts System.

(2) If such grievance involves a matter that may affect the orderly administration of justice, it is within the discretion of the presiding judge to stay the proceeding and seek expedited resolution of the grievance.

Former Rule 2.065 adopted Oct. 24, 1996, effective Jan. 1, 1997 (682 So.2d 89). Renumbered from Rule 2.065 Sept. 21, 2006 (939 So.2d 966). Amended effective May 20, 2010 (41 So.3d 881).

Rule 2.545. Case Management

(a) Purpose. Judges and lawyers have a professional obligation to conclude litigation as soon as it is reasonably and justly possible to do so. However, parties and counsel shall be afforded a reasonable time to prepare and present their case.

(b) Case Control. The trial judge shall take charge of all cases at an early stage in the litigation and shall control the progress of the case thereafter until the case is determined. The trial judge shall take specific steps to monitor and control the pace of litigation, including the following:

(1) assuming early and continuous control of the court calendar;

(2) identifying priority cases as assigned by statute, rule of procedure, case law, or otherwise;

(3) implementing such docket control policies as may be necessary to advance priority cases to ensure prompt resolution;

(4) identifying cases subject to alternative dispute resolution processes;

(5) developing rational and effective trial setting policies; and

(6) advancing the trial setting of priority cases, older cases, and cases of greater urgency.

(c) Priority Cases.

(1) In all noncriminal cases assigned a priority status by statute, rule of procedure, case law, or otherwise, any party may file a notice of priority status explaining the nature of the case, the source of the priority status, any deadlines imposed by law on any aspect of the case, and any unusual factors that may bear on meeting the imposed deadlines.

(2) If, in any noncriminal case assigned a priority status by statute, rule of procedure, case law, or otherwise, a party is of the good faith opinion that the case has not been appropriately advanced on the docket or has not received priority in scheduling consistent with its priority case status, that party may seek review of such action by motion for review to the chief judge or to the chief judge's designee. The filing of such a motion for review will not toll the time for seeking such other relief as may be afforded by the Florida Rules of Appellate Procedure.

(d) Related Cases.

(1) The petitioner in a family case as defined in this rule shall file with the court a notice of related cases in conformity with family law form 12.900(h), if related cases are known or reasonably ascertainable. A case is related when:

(A) it involves any of the same parties, children, or issues and it is pending at the time the party files a family case; or

(B) it affects the court's jurisdiction to proceed; or

(C) an order in the related case may conflict with an order on the same issues in the new case; or

(D) an order in the new case may conflict with an order in the earlier litigation.

(2) "Family cases" include dissolution of marriage, annulment, support unconnected with dissolution of marriage, paternity, child support, UIFSA, custodial care of and access to children, proceedings for temporary or concurrent custody of minor children by ex-

tended family, adoption, name change, declaratory judgment actions related to premarital, martial, or postmarital agreements, civil domestic, repeat violence, dating violence, stalking, and sexual violence injunctions, juvenile dependency, termination of parental rights, juvenile delinquency, emancipation of a minor, CINS/FINS, truancy, and modification and enforcement of orders entered in these cases.

(3) The notice of related cases shall identify the caption and case number of the related case, contain a brief statement of the relationship of the actions, and contain a statement addressing whether assignment to one judge or another method of coordination will conserve judicial resources and promote an efficient determination of the actions.

(4) The notice of related cases shall be filed with the initial pleading by the filing attorney or self-represented petitioner. The notice shall be filed in each of the related cases that are currently open and pending with the court and served on all other parties in each of the related cases, and as may be directed by the chief judge or designee. Parties may file joint notices. A notice of related cases filed pursuant to this rule is not an appearance. If any related case is confidential and exempt from public access by law, then a Notice of Confidential Information Within Court Filing as required by Florida Rule of Judicial Administration 2.420 shall accompany the notice. Parties shall file supplemental notices as related cases become known or reasonably ascertainable.

(5) Each party has a continuing duty to inform the court of any proceedings in this or any other state that could affect the current proceeding.

(6) Whenever it appears to a party that two or more pending cases present common issues of fact and that assignment to one judge or another method of coordination will significantly promote the efficient administration of justice, conserve judicial resources, avoid inconsistent results, or prevent multiple court appearances by the same parties on the same issues, the party may file a notice of related cases requesting coordination of the litigation.

(e) Continuances. All judges shall apply a firm continuance policy. Continuances should be few, good cause should be required, and all requests should be heard and resolved by a judge. All motions for continuance shall be in writing unless made at a trial and, except for good cause shown, shall be signed by the party requesting the continuance. All motions for continuance in priority cases shall clearly identify such priority status and explain what effect the motion will have on the progress of the case.

Former Rule 2.085, added May 14, 1986, effective July 1, 1986 (493 So.2d 423). Amended Sept. 29, 1988, effective Jan. 1, 1989 (536 So.2d 195); Oct. 8, 1992, effective Jan. 1, 1993 (609 So.2d 465); Aug. 29, 2002, effective Oct. 1, 2002 (826 So.2d 233); July 10, 2003, effective Jan. 1, 2004 (851 So.2d 698); Nov. 18, 2004, effective Jan. 1, 2005 (889 So.2d 68); Nov. 3, 2005, effective Jan. 1, 2006 (915 So.2d 157). Renumbered from Rule 2.085 Sept. 21, 2006 (939 So.2d 966). Amended Oct. 6, 2011 (75 So.3d 203); Jan. 16, 2014, effective April 1, 2014 (132 So.3d 1114).

Committee Notes

The provisions in subdivision (c) of this rule governing priority cases should be read in conjunction with the provisions of rule 2.215(g), governing the duty to expedite priority cases.

Historical Notes

Committee Notes added July 10, 2008, eff. Jan. 1, 2009 (986 So.2d 560).

Rule 2.550. Calendar Conflicts

(a) Guidelines. In resolving calendar conflicts between the state courts of Florida or between a state court and a federal court in Florida, the following guidelines must be considered:

(1) Any case priority status established by statute, rule of procedure, case law, or otherwise shall be evaluated to determine the effect that resolving a calendar conflict might have on the priority case or cases.

(2) Juvenile dependency and termination of parental rights cases are generally to be given preference over other cases, except for speedy trial and capital cases.

(3) Criminal cases are generally to be given preference over civil cases.

(4) Jury trials are generally to be given preference over non-jury trials.

(5) Appellate arguments, hearings, and conferences are generally to be given preference over trial court proceedings.

(6) The case in which the trial date has been first set generally should take precedence.

(b) Additional Circumstances. Factors such as cost, numbers of witnesses and attorneys involved, travel, length of trial, age of case, and other relevant matters may warrant deviation from these case guidelines.

(c) Notice and Agreement; Resolution by Judges. When an attorney is scheduled to appear in 2 courts at the same time and cannot arrange for other counsel to represent the clients' interests, the attorney shall give prompt written notice of the conflict to opposing counsel, the clerk of each court, and the presiding judge of each case, if known. If the presiding judge of the case cannot be identified, written notice of the conflict shall be given to the chief judge of the court having jurisdiction over the case, or to the chief judge's designee. The judges or their designees shall confer and undertake to avoid the conflict by agreement among themselves. Absent agreement, conflicts should be promptly resolved by the judges or their designees in accordance with the above case guidelines.

Former Rule 2.052 adopted Oct. 24, 1996, effective Jan. 1, 1997 (682 So.2d 89). Amended Aug. 29, 2002, effective Oct. 1, 2002 (826 So.2d 233). Renumbered from Rule 2.052 Sept. 21, 2006 (939 So.2d 966).

Committee Notes

1996 Adoption. The adoption of this rule was prompted by the Resolution of the Florida State–Federal Judicial Council Regarding Calendar Conflicts Between State and Federal Courts, which states as follows:

WHEREAS, the great volume of cases filed in the state and federal courts of Florida creates calendar conflicts between the state and federal courts of Florida which should be resolved in a fair, efficient and orderly manner to allow for judicial efficiency and economy; and

WHEREAS, the Florida State–Federal Judicial Council which represents the Bench and Bar of the State of Florida believes that it would be beneficial to formally agree upon and publish recommended procedures and priorities for resolving calendar conflicts between the state and federal courts of Florida;

NOW, THEREFORE, BE IT RESOLVED

In resolving calendar conflicts between the state and federal courts of Florida, the following case priorities should be considered:

1. Criminal cases should prevail over civil cases.

2. Jury trials should prevail over non-jury trials.

3. Appellate arguments, hearings, and conferences should prevail over trials.

4. The case in which the trial date has been first set should take precedence.

5. Circumstances such as cost, numbers of witnesses and attorneys involved, travel, length of trial, age of case and other relevant matters may warrant deviation from this policy. Such matters are encouraged to be resolved through communication between the courts involved.

Where an attorney is scheduled to appear in two courts — trial or appellate, state or federal — at the same time and cannot arrange for other counsel in his or her firm or in the case to represent his or her client's interest, the attorney shall give prompt written notice to opposing counsel, the clerk of each court, and the presiding judge of each case, if known, of the conflict. If the presiding judge of a case cannot be identified, written notice of the conflict shall be given to the chief judge of the court having jurisdiction over the case, or to his or her designee. The judges or their designees shall confer and undertake to avoid the conflict by agreement among themselves. Absent agreement, conflicts should be promptly resolved by the judges or their designees in accordance with the above case priorities.

In jurisdictions where calendar conflicts arise with frequency, it is recommended that each court involved consider appointing a calendar conflict coordinator to assist the judges in resolving calendar conflicts by obtaining information regarding the conflicts and performing such other ministerial duties as directed by the judges.

REVISED AND READOPTED at Miami, Florida, this 13th day of January, 1995.

Court Commentary

2002 Court Commentary. As provided in subdivision (c), when a scheduling conflict involves different courts, the presiding judges should confer and undertake to agree on a resolution, using the guidelines provided in this rule.

Rule 2.555. Initiation of Criminal Proceedings

(a) Major Statutory Offense. Law enforcement officers, at the time of the filing of a complaint with the clerk of court, shall designate whether the most serious charge on the complaint is a felony or a misdemeanor. The state attorney or the state attorney's designee, at the time of the filing of an original information or an original indictment with the clerk of court, shall designate whether the most serious offense on the information or the indictment is a felony or misdemeanor. Complaints, original informations, and original indictments on which the most serious charge is a felony shall be filed with the clerk of the circuit court.

(b) Ordinance Violations. In cases when the state attorney has the responsibility for the prosecution of county or municipal ordinance violations, where such ordinances have state statutory equivalents, the state attorney or the state attorney's designee shall set forth at the top of the face of the accusatory instrument the exact statute number of the single most serious offense charged.

(c) Information or Indictment after County Court Proceedings Begun. When action in a criminal case has been initiated in county court, and subsequently the state attorney files a direct information or the grand jury indicts the defendant, the state attorney or the state attorney's designee shall notify the clerk without delay.

Former Rule 2.080 amended June 14, 1979, effective July 1, 1979 (372 So.2d 449); Oct. 8, 1992, effective Jan. 1, 1993 (609 So.2d 465). Renumbered from Rule 2.080 Sept. 21, 2006 (939 So.2d 966).

Rule 2.560. Appointment of Interpreters for Non–English–Speaking Persons

(a) Criminal or Juvenile Delinquency Proceedings. In any criminal or juvenile delinquency proceeding in which a non–English–speaking person is the accused, an interpreter for the non–English–speaking person shall be appointed. In any criminal or juvenile delinquency proceeding in which a non–English–speaking person is a victim, an interpreter shall be appointed unless the court finds that the victim does not require the services of a court-appointed interpreter.

(b) Other Proceedings. In all other proceedings in which a non–English–speaking person is a litigant, an interpreter for the non–English–speaking litigant shall be appointed if the court determines that the litigant's inability to comprehend English deprives the litigant of an understanding of the court proceedings, that a fundamental interest is at stake (such as in a civil commitment, termination of parental rights, paternity, or dependency proceeding), and that no alternative to the appointment of an interpreter exists.

(c) Witnesses. In any proceeding in which a non–English–speaking person is a witness, the appointment of an interpreter shall be governed by the applicable provisions of the Florida Evidence Code.

(d) Compliance with Title VI of the Civil Rights Act of 1964. In making determinations regarding the appointment of an interpreter, the court should ensure compliance with the requirements of Title VI of the Civil Rights Act of 1964.

(e) Qualifications of Interpreter.

(1) *Appointment of Interpreters when Certified or Duly Qualified Interpreters Are Available.* Whenever possible, a certified or duly qualified interpreter, as defined in the Rules for Certification and Regulation of Court Interpreters, shall be appointed.

(2) *Appointment of Interpreters when Certified or Duly Qualified Interpreters Are Unavailable.* If, after diligent search, a certified or duly qualified interpreter is not available, an interpreter who is neither certified nor duly qualified may be appointed if the judge or hearing officer presiding over the proceeding finds that:

(A) good cause exists for the appointment of an interpreter who is neither certified nor duly qualified, such as the prevention of burdensome delay, the request or consent of the non–English–speaking person, or other unusual circumstance; and

(B) the proposed interpreter is competent to interpret in the proceedings.

(3) *On–the–Record Objections or Waivers in Criminal and Juvenile Delinquency Proceedings.* In any criminal or juvenile delinquency proceeding in which the interpreter is neither certified nor duly qualified, the court shall advise the accused, on the record, that the proposed interpreter is not certified or duly qualified pursuant to the Rules for Certification and Regulation of Court Interpreters. The accused's objection to the appointment of a proposed interpreter, or the accused's waiver of the appointment of a certified or duly qualified interpreter, shall also be on the record.

(4) *Additional on–the–Record Findings, Objections, and Waivers Required at Subsequent Proceedings.* The appointment of an interpreter who is neither certified nor duly qualified shall be limited to a specific proceeding and shall not be extended to subsequent proceedings in a case without additional findings of good cause and qualification as required by subdivision (e)(2) of this rule, and additional compliance with the procedures for on-the-record objections or waivers provided for in subdivision (e)(3) of this rule.

(f) Privileged Communications. Whenever a person communicates through an interpreter to any person under circumstances that would render the communication privileged and such person could not be compelled to testify as to the communication, the privilege shall also apply to the interpreter.

Former Rule 2.073 added June 29, 2006, effective July 1, 2008 (933 So.2d 504). Renumbered from Rule 2.073 Sept. 21, 2006 (939 So.2d 966).

APPENDIX

State of Florida

Judicial Branch Records Retention Schedule for Administrative Records

GENERAL APPLICATION

This record retention schedule does not impose a duty to create records contained in the schedule. The purpose of the schedule is to authorize destruction of records after the retention period has elapsed. The records custodian may retain records longer than required by the schedule. This schedule authorizes destruction of records unless otherwise provided by court rule.

The retention period should be calculated from the time that the record is completed. For purposes of calculating the retention period, fiscal records should be considered completed at the end of a fiscal year. All retention periods are subject to the caveat "provided that applicable audits have been released."

The records custodian of the judicial branch entity that creates a record creates the "record copy" and is responsible for its retention in accordance with this schedule. The records custodian of the judicial branch entity that properly receives a record from outside the judicial branch has the "record copy" and is responsible for its retention in accordance with this schedule. Duplicates are only required to be retained until obsolete, superseded or administrative value is lost.

"Record Series" means a group of related documents arranged under a single filing arrangement or kept together as a unit because they consist of the same form, relate to the same subject, result from the same activity, or have certain common characteristics.

ACQUISITION RECORDS: LIBRARY

This record series consists of information on the acquisition of library materials including: books, periodicals, filmstrips, software, compact discs, video/audio tapes, and other non-print media. This information may include the accession date and method, the publisher and cost, the date entered into the collection, dates removed from collection, and method of final disposal.

RETENTION: Retain for life of material.

ADMINISTRATIVE CONVENIENCE RECORDS

This record series consists of a subject file, generally filed alphabetically, which is located away from the official files, such as in the Director's and other supervisory offices. The file contains DUPLICATES of correspondence, reports, publications, memoranda, etc., and is used as a working file or reference file on subjects which are currently significant or which may become significant in the near future. The material filed in this series is NOT the official file or record copy but is maintained for the convenience of the officials in carrying out their elected or appointed duties.

RETENTION: Retain until obsolete, superseded or administrative value is lost.

ADMINISTRATIVE RECORDS: PUBLIC OFFICIALS/COURT ADMINISTRATORS

This record series consists of office files documenting the substantive actions of elected or appointed officials and the court administrator. These records constitute the official record of a judicial branch entity's performance of its functions and formulation of policy and program initiative. This series will include various types of records such as correspondence; memoranda; statements prepared for delivery at meetings, conventions or other public functions that are designed to advertise and promote programs, activities and policies of the judicial branch entity; interviews; and reports concerning development and implementation of activities of the judicial branch entity. ***"These records may have archival value."***

RETENTION: 10 years.

ADMINISTRATIVE SUPPORT RECORDS

This record series consists of records accumulated relative to internal administrative activities rather than the functions for which the office exists. Normally, these records document procedures; the expenditure of funds, including budget material; day-to-day management of office personnel including training and travel; supplies, office services and equipment requests and receipts and other recorded experiences that do not serve as official documentation of the programs of the office. However, because the content of these records vary so greatly in content and value (containing some duplicates and record copies), a relatively large proportion of them are of continuing value and may be subject to the audit process. Note: Reference a more applicable records series first if one exists. ***"These records may have archival value."***

RETENTION: 2 years.

ADVERTISEMENTS: LEGAL

This record series consists of advertisements which have appeared in newspapers or in the "Administrative Weekly" on matters pertaining to the judicial branch entity and other legal ads which may or may not indirectly affect the judicial branch entity; i.e., bid invitations for construction jobs, public hearings or notices, public sales. See also "BID RECORDS: CAPITAL IMPROVEMENT SUCCESSFUL BID", "BID RECORDS: CAPITAL IMPROVEMENT UNSUCCESSFUL BIDS" and "BID RECORDS: NON–CAPITAL IMPROVEMENT."

RETENTION: 5 years.

AFFIRMATIVE ACTION RECORDS

This record series consists of copies of reports submitted to the Equal Employment Opportunity Commission (EEOC) per their requirements for the judicial branch entity's affirmative action plan. It may also include discrimination complaints, correspondence and investigative papers pertaining to the judicial branch entity's affirmative action plan. See also "EQUAL EMPLOYMENT OPPORTUNITY COMPLIANCE RECORDS."

RETENTION: 2 years.

APPLICATIONS: GUARDIAN AD LITEM, MEDIATION, OTHERS

This record series consists of applications, supporting documents, correspondence and reports relating to the application of a person to be certified as a mediator, a program to be approved to offer training for mediators, a volunteer to be approved by the Guardian ad Litem Program, or other persons or programs regulated in the judicial branch.

RETENTION: 5 years after the person or program is no longer regulated by the judicial branch.

APPLICATIONS: LIBRARY CARDS

This record series consists of library card applications which must be renewed on an annual, bi-annual, or other basis. The application may include the patron's name, address, telephone number, date of birth, as well as a statement of liability for the care and timely return of all materials checked out or utilized by the patron.

RETENTION: Retain for 30 days after expiration.

APPRAISALS: LAND PURCHASES (NOT PURCHASED)

This record series consists of documents pertaining to land not purchased by a judicial branch entity and all supporting documents. See also "APPRAISALS: LAND PURCHASES (PURCHASED)."

RETENTION: 3 years.

APPRAISALS: LAND PURCHASES (PURCHASED)

This record series consists of documents pertaining to land purchased by a judicial branch entity and all supporting documents. See also "APPRAISALS: LAND PURCHASES (NOT PURCHASED)."

RETENTION: Retain as long as judicial branch entity retains property.

ARCHITECTURAL PLANS/SPECIFICATIONS: PRELIMINARY DRAWINGS

This record series consists of those graphic and engineering preliminary drawing records that depict conceptual as well as precise measured information essential for the planning and construction of facilities.

RETENTION: Retain until completion and acceptance.

ATTENDANCE AND LEAVE RECORDS

This record series consists of requests or applications for vacation, sick, family medical leave (FMLA) and other types of leave including leave of absences, timesheets or timecards along with any required documentation (medical statements or excuses from a physician, jury duty summons, or military orders, etc.) submitted by an employee to document authorized absences.

RETENTION: 3 years.

AUDITS: INDEPENDENT

This record series consists of a report issued by an independent auditor to establish the position of the judicial branch entity being audited against its standard of performance. See also, "AUDITS: INTERNAL," "AUDITS: STATE/FEDERAL" and "AUDITS: SUPPORTING DOCUMENTS."

RETENTION: 10 years.

AUDITS: INTERNAL

This record series consists of a report issued by an internal auditor to establish the position of a judicial branch entity being audited against its standard of performance. See also, "AUDITS: INDEPENDENT," "AUDITS: STATE/FEDERAL" and "AUDITS: SUPPORTING DOCUMENTS."

RETENTION: 3 years.

AUDITS: STATE/FEDERAL

This record series consists of a report issued by a federal or state auditor to establish the position of a judicial branch entity being audited against its standard of performance. See also, "AUDITS: INDEPENDENT," "AUDITS: INTERNAL" and "AUDITS: SUPPORTING DOCUMENTS." **"These records may have archival value."**

RETENTION: 10 years.

AUDITS: SUPPORTING DOCUMENTS

This record series consists of the documentation and supporting documents used to develop the audit report with all bills, accounts, records and transactions. See also "AUDITS: INDEPENDENT," "AUDITS: INTERNAL" and "AUDITS: STATE/FEDERAL."

RETENTION: 3 years.

BACKGROUND/Security Checks

This record series consists of background/security checks for potential new hires and promotions. These checks may include a background and driver's license screening, reference check, and verification of academic standing. The files might include notices of not being hired based on the outcome of a security check and a opportunity for rebuttal. Supporting documentation consists of fingerprint cards, copy of the driver's license, copy of the transcript release form, returned form reference letters, and other necessary information.

RETENTION: 4 anniversary years.

BANK ACCOUNT AUTHORIZATION RECORDS

This record series consists of an authorization to maintain a bank account and who is authorized to sign off on the account.

RETENTION: 1 year after superseded by new authorization.

BAR APPLICANTS: ADMITTED

This record series consists of bar applications, supporting documents, all investigative materials, of administrative value, correspondence, reports, and similar materials accumulated during the bar admissions process regarding bar applicants who were subsequently admitted to The Florida Bar.

RETENTION: Bar application and fingerprint card, 5 years; all other materials, 1 year.

BAR APPLICANTS: NOT ADMITTED (WITH NO RECOMMENDATION)

This record series consists of bar applications, supporting documents, all investigative materials of administrative value, correspondence, reports, and similar materials accumulated during the bar admissions process regarding bar applicants who have not been admitted to The Florida Bar and who have not received an unfavorable recommendation by the Florida Board of Bar Examiners.

RETENTION: 20 years or the death of the applicant, whichever is earlier.

BAR APPLICANTS: NOT ADMITTED (WITH UNFAVORABLE RECOMMENDATION)

This record series consists of bar applications, supporting documents, all investigative materials of administrative value, correspondence, reports, and similar materials accumulated during the bar admissions process regarding bar applicants who have not been admitted to The Florida Bar and who have received an unfavorable recommendation by the Florida Board of Bar Examiners by either a negotiated consent judgment or the issuance of findings of fact and conclusions of law.

RETENTION: 40 years or the death of the applicant, whichever is earlier.

BAR EXAMINATION/ANSWERS

This record series consists of answers to essay questions and answer sheets to machine-scored questions submitted by bar applicants during the bar examination administered by the Florida Board of Bar Examiners.

RETENTION: Until the conclusion of the administration of the next successive general bar examination.

BAR EXAMINATION/FLORIDA PREPARED PORTION

This record series consists of the portion of the bar examination prepared by the Florida Board of Bar Examiners.

RETENTION: 10 years from the date of the administration of the examination.

BID RECORDS: CAPITAL IMPROVEMENT SUCCESSFUL BIDS

This record series consists of information relative to the processing and letting of capital improvement successful bids including legal advertisements, "Requests for Proposal," technical specifications, correspondence, "Invitations to Bid," bid tabulations and bid responses. "Capital Improvements" shall mean enhancement to buildings, fixtures and all other improvements to land. See also "BID RECORDS: CAPITAL IMPROVEMENT UNSUCCESSFUL BIDS" and "BID RECORDS: NON–CAPITAL IMPROVEMENT."

RETENTION: 10 years

BID RECORDS: CAPITAL IMPROVEMENT UNSUCCESSFUL BIDS

This record series consists of information relative to the processing and letting of capital improvement unsuccessful bids including legal advertisements, "Requests for Proposal," technical specifications, correspondence, "Invitations to Bid," bid tabulations and bid responses. "Capital Improvements" shall mean enhancement to buildings, fixtures and all other improvements to land. See also "BID RECORDS: CAPITAL IMPROVEMENT SUCCESSFUL BIDS" and "BID RECORDS: NON–CAPITAL IMPROVEMENT."

RETENTION: 5 years.

BID RECORDS: NON–CAPITAL IMPROVEMENT

This record series consists of information relative to the processing and letting of successful and unsuccessful noncapital improvement bids including legal advertisements, "Requests for Proposal," technical specifications, correspondence, "Invitations to Bid," bid tabulations and bid responses. See also "BID RECORDS: CAPITAL IMPROVEMENT SUCCESSFUL BIDS" and "BID RECORDS: CAPITAL IMPROVEMENT UNSUCCESSFUL BIDS."

RETENTION: 5 years.

BIOGRAPHICAL FILES

This record series consists of vitas, biographies, photographs and newspaper clippings of employees.

RETENTION: Retain until obsolete, superseded or administrative value is lost.

BUDGET RECORDS: APPROVED ANNUAL BUDGET

This record series consists of the approved annual budget and its amendments. See also "BUDGET RECORDS: SUPPORTING DOCUMENTS," **"These records may have archival value."**

RETENTION: Permanent.

BUDGET RECORDS: SUPPORTING DOCUMENTS

This record series consists of any supporting documentation supporting budget matters and is filed chronologically. See also "BUDGET RECORDS: APPROVED ANNUAL BUDGET."

RETENTION: 3 years.

BUILDING PLANS

This record series consists of graphic and engineering records that depict conceptual as well as precise measured information essential for the planning and construction of buildings. See also "ARCHITECTURAL PLANS/SPECIFICATIONS: PRELIMINARY DRAWINGS."

RETENTION: Retain for life of structure.

CALENDARS

This record series consists of a calendar showing official daily appointments and meetings.

RETENTION: 1 year.

CASE RELATED RECORDS NOT IN THE CUSTODY OF THE CLERK AND /OR NOT IN CASE FILE

This record series includes records that are related to a trial court records as defined in Rule 2.420, Florida Rules of Judicial Administration, because they are not filed with the clerk of court and are not included in the court file. These records include, but are not limited to, drug court evaluation and progress reports, mediation reports, deferred prosecution and diversion records, and arbitration reports. Case-related trial court documents may be destroyed or disposed of after a judgment has become final in record accordance with the following schedule:

RETENTION:

(A) 60 days—Parking tickets and noncriminal traffic infractions after required audits have been completed.

(B) 2 years—Proceedings under the Small Claims Rules, Medical Mediation Proceedings.

(C) 5 years—Misdemeanor actions, criminal traffic violations, ordinance violations, civil litigation proceedings in county court other than those under the Small Claims Rules, and civil proceedings in circuit court except marriage dissolutions and adoptions.

(D) 10 years—Probate, guardianship, and mental health proceedings.

(E) 10 years—Felony cases in which no information or indictment was filed or in which all charges were dismissed, or in which the state announced a nolle prosequi, or in which the defendant was adjudicated not guilty.

(F) 75 years—juvenile proceedings containing an order permanently depriving a parent of custody of a child, and adoptions and all felony cases not previously destroyed.

(G) Juvenile proceedings not otherwise provided for in this subdivision shall be kept for 5 years after the last entry or until the child reaches the age of majority, whichever is later.

(H) Marriage dissolutions—10 years from the last record activity. The court may authorize destruction of court records not involving alimony, support, or custody of children 5 years from the last record activity.

CERTIFICATION FORWARD DOCUMENTS

This record series consists of lists of encumbrances to be applied against certified forward money which is money brought forward from the previous fiscal year for goods and services which were not received until the current fiscal year. See also "ENCUMBRANCE RECORDS."

RETENTION: 3 years.

CHILD SUPPORT/ALIMONY DISBURSEMENT RECORDS: DETAIL

This series consists of records documenting disbursement of child support or alimony. The series includes, but is not limited to, check registers, check stubs, cancelled checks, cancelled warrants, disbursement ledgers, transaction journals, vendor invoice, refund records and other accounts payable related documentation.

RETENTION: 5 fiscal years

CHILD SUPPORT/ALIMONY DISBURSEMENT RECORDS: SUMMARY

This series consists of records providing summary or aggregate documentation of expenditures or transfers moneys for child support or alimony. The series may include, but is not limited to, trail balance reports, check logs and registers, summary reports, summary journal transactions and other accounts payable summary related documentation.

RETENTION: 10 fiscal years

CHILD SUPPORT/ALIMONY RECEIPT/REVENUE RECORDS: DETAIL

This series consists of records documenting specific receipts/revenues collected for child support or alimony. The series may include, but is not limited to, cash receipts, receipt books, deposit receipts, bank validated deposit slips, depository ledger reports filed with Clerk of Court, transaction journals, refund records, bad check records and other accounts receivable related documentation.

RETENTION: 5 fiscal years

CHILD SUPPORT/ALIMONY RECEIPT/REVENUE RECORDS: SUMMARY

This series consists of records providing summary or aggregate documentation of receipts/revenues collected for child support or alimony. The series may include, but is not limited to, monthly statements of bank accounts, trial balance reports, bank statements, credit and debit card reports, collection balance sheets and other receivable summary related documentation.

RETENTION: 10 fiscal years

COMPLAINTS: CITIZENS/CONSUMERS/EMPLOYEES

This record series consists of individual complaints received from citizens, consumers or employees. This file may include the name, address, date of complaint, telephone number, the complaint to whom referred and date, action taken and signature of person taking the action.

RETENTION: 1 year.

CONTINUING EDUCATION RECORDS

This record series consists of continuing education records, including records of judicial education.

RETENTION: 2 years.

CONTRACTS/LEASES/AGREEMENTS: CAPITAL IMPROVEMENT/REAL PROPERTY

This record series consists of legal documents, correspondence, reports, etc., relating to the negotiation, fulfillment and termination of capital improvement or real property contracts, leases or agreements to which the agency is a party, including contracts, leases or agreements with architects, engineers, builders, and construction companies. "Capital Improvements" shall mean improvements to real property (land, buildings, including appurtenances, fixtures and fixed equipment, structures, etc.), that add to the value and extend the useful life of the property, including construction of new structures, replacement or rehabilitation of existing structures (e.g., major repairs such as roof replacement), or removal of closed structures. "Real Property" means land, buildings, and fixtures. The terms "land," "real estate," "realty" and "real property" may be used interchangeably. See also "CONTRACTS/ LEASES/ AGREEMENTS: NON–CAPITAL IMPROVEMENT."

RETENTION: 10 fiscal years after completion or termination of contract/lease/agreement

CONTRACTS/LEASES/AGREEMENTS: NON–CAPITAL IMPROVEMENT

This record series consists of legal documents, correspondence, reports, etc., relating to the negotiation, fulfillment and termination of non-capital improvement contracts, leases or agreements to which the agency is a party. In addition, it includes the various contracts, leases or agreements entered into for the purchase of goods and services such as the purchase of gas, fuel oil and annual purchases of inventory-maintained items. See also "CONTRACTS/LEASES/AGREEMENTS: CAPITAL IMPROVEMENT/REAL PROPERTY."

RETENTION: 5 fiscal years after completion or termination of contract/lease/agreement

CORRESPONDENCE & MEMORANDA: ADMINISTRATIVE

This record series consists of routine correspondence and memoranda of a general nature that is associated with administrative practices but that does not create policy or procedure, document the business of a particular program, or act as a receipt. See also "INFORMATION REQUEST RECORDS." ***"These records may have archival value."***

RETENTION: 3 years.

CORRESPONDENCE & MEMORANDA: PROGRAM AND POLICY DEVELOPMENT

This record series consists of correspondence and memoranda of any nature that is associated with a specific program or the development of policy and procedure. ***"These records may have archival value."***

RETENTION: 5 years.

COURT REGISTRY

This record series consists of records, ledgers and journals showing amounts paid into the Court Registry, held by the Court, and paid out by the Court.

RETENTION: Permanent.

COURT REPORTS

This record series consists of court reports, including SRS, jury management, witness management, uniform case reporting system records, and other statistical court reports.

RETENTION: 3 years.

DEEDS: PROPERTY

This record series consists of property deeds. Series may include appraisals, surveys, and other supporting documents.

RETENTION: Retain as long as property is retained.

DELAYED BIRTH (APPLICATION/CERTIFICATE/AFFIDAVITS, ETC.)

This record series consists of an application signed by a judge for a birth (other than in a hospital usually). This record is filed with the County Court pursuant to Section 382.0195(4)(a), Florida Statutes. Once signed, the application becomes an order. The record copy is sent to Vital Statistics.

RETENTION: Permanent

DIRECTIVES/POLICIES/PROCEDURES

This record series consists of the official management statements of policy for the organization, supporting documents, and the operating procedures which outline the methods for accomplishing the functions and activities assigned to the judicial branch entity. It includes all memoranda and correspondence generated relating to the policies and procedures which are to be followed by employees. See also "CORRESPONDENCE & MEMORANDA: PROGRAM AND POLICY DEVELOPMENT." **"These records may have archival value."**

RETENTION: 2 years.

DISASTER PREPAREDNESS DRILLS

This record series consists of the results of disaster preparedness exercises and the supporting documents including scenarios, location of safety related drills, time tables, response times, probable outcomes, areas of difficulties, descriptions of how difficulties were resolved, and areas for improvement. Types of drills include: fire, tornado, safety, hurricane and SARA chemical spills. See also "DIRECTIVES/POLICIES/PROCEDURES" and "DISASTER PREPAREDNESS PLANS."

RETENTION: 3 years.

DISASTER PREPAREDNESS PLANS

This record series consists of disaster preparedness and recovery plans adopted by a judicial branch entity. See also "DIRECTIVE/POLICIES/PROCEDURES."

RETENTION: Retain until obsolete, superseded or administrative value is lost.

DISBURSEMENT RECORDS: DETAIL

This series consists of records documenting specific expenditures or transfers of agency moneys for the procurement of commodities and services and other purposes. The series may include, but is not limited to, procurement records such as requisitions, requisition logs, purchase orders, contracts, purchasing card (p-card) receipts, vendor invoices, receiving reports, acceptances of contract deliverables, approvals, and related documentation; and expenditure records for disbursements made through checks, warrants, electronic fund transfers (EFT), purchasing cards, or other methods, such as payment vouchers, approvals, check registers, cancelled checks, check stubs, cancelled warrants, disbursement ledgers, journal transactions, expenditure detail reports, refund records and other accounts payable and related documentation. Retention is based on s. 95.11(2), F.S., Statute of Limitations on contracts, obligations, or liabilities. See also "DISBURSEMENT RECORDS: SUMMARY," "PURCHASING RECORDS," and "TRAVEL RECORDS."

RETENTION: 5 fiscal years

DISBURSEMENT RECORDS: SUMMARY

This series consists of records providing summary or aggregate documentation of expenditures or transfers of agency moneys for the procurement of commodities and services and other purposes. The series may include, but is not limited to, summary records such as trial balance reports, check logs and registers, summary expenditure reports, federal grant final closeout reports, summary journal transactions, and other accounts payable summary and related documentation. See also "DISBURSEMENT RECORDS: DETAIL."

RETENTION: 10 fiscal years

DISCIPLINARY CASE FILES

This record series consists of both sustained formal or informal disciplinary cases investigated that allege employee misconduct or violations of department regulations and orders, and state/federal statutes. It includes statements by the employee, witnesses, and the person filing the complaint. "Formal discipline" is defined as disciplinary action involving demotion, removal from office, suspension, or other similar action. "Informal discipline" is defined as any disciplinary action involving written and verbal reprimands, memoranda, or other similar action. This record series also can consist of formal and informal disciplinary cases that were determined as not sustained, unfounded, or exonerated charges. See also "PERSONNEL RECORDS".

RETENTION: 5 years.

DRAFTS AND WORKING PAPERS

This record series consists of documents, correspondence, reports, memos, and other materials in preliminary or developmental form before their iteration as a final product. Drafts may include copies of materials circulated for review for grammar, spelling, and content. Working papers may include notes and miscellaneous documents and materials used in compiling and assembling the final product. Note that some draft documents and working papers may have long-term value; such documents may even have archival or historical value. Such records might be better placed under the record series "Administrator Records: Public Officials/Court Administrators."

RETENTION: Retain until obsolete, superseded or administrative value is lost.

DRUG TEST RECORDS

This record series consists of the positive or negative results of a drug test under the Drug Free Workplace Act or as required for CDL or other drivers under US DOT regulations as well as records related to canceled tests. This series might include documents generated in decisions to administer reasonable suspicion or post-accident testing, or in verifying the existence of a medical explanation of the inability of the driver to provide adequate breath or to provide a urine specimen for testing. In addition, the case file could include: the employer's copy of an alcohol test form, including the results of the test; a copy of the controlled substances test chain of custody control form; documents sent by the Medical Review Officer (MRO) to the employer; notice to report for testing; affidavit signed by the employee stating any prescription drugs or over the counter medication currently taken; and final clearance to resume working. This record series can also consist of documentation, including memorandum and correspondence, related to an employee's refusal to take or submit samples for an alcohol and/or controlled substances test(s).

RETENTION: 5 years.

ELECTRONIC FUNDS TRANSFER RECORDS

This record series consists of documentation necessary to establish and maintain the electronic transfer of funds from one financial institution to another. The documentation may include, but is not limited to: an agreement between the two parties; a form which lists both institutions' names, their routing numbers, the name of the account holder, and the account's authorizing signature; a canceled deposit slip or check; and the paperwork for the termination of service or transfer of service to a new institution. This series does not include the paperwork on a specific individual deposit or payment.

RETENTION: 5 fiscal years

ELECTRONIC RECORDS SOFTWARE

This record series consists of proprietary and non-proprietary software as well as related documentation that provides information about the content, structure and technical specifications of computer systems necessary for retrieving information retained in machine-readable format. These records may be necessary to an audit process.

RETENTION: Retain as long as there are software dependent records.

EMPLOYEE PRE–COUNSELING RECORDS

This record series consists of material and supporting documentation which provide documentation of initial contact with an employee regarding incidents which may or may not lead to disciplinary action. This series is not considered in and of itself a part of the employee discipline record.

RETENTION: 1 year.

EMPLOYMENT EXAMINATION RECORDS

This record series consists of test plans, announcements, grades, grading scales, keyed exams, test monitor's list of candidates, any research toward the development of the tests, and any other selection or screening criteria. See "PERSONNEL RECORDS" and "RECRUITMENT & SELECTION PACKAGES."

RETENTION: 4 anniversary years

ENCUMBRANCE RECORDS

This record series consists of documents and reports which document funds that have been encumbered. See also "CERTIFICATION FORWARD DOCUMENTS."

RETENTION: 3 years.

ENDOWMENTS, BEQUESTS AND TRUST FUND RECORDS

This record series consists of creating, establishing or contributing to endowments, bequests and trust fund records. **"These records may have archival value."**

RETENTION: Permanent.

ENVIRONMENTAL REGULATION RECORDS

This record series consists of permits, reviews, supporting documents and correspondence resulting from environmental regulation requirements.

RETENTION: 5 years.

EQUAL EMPLOYMENT OPPORTUNITY COMPLIANCE RECORDS

This record series consists of EEO–5 and supporting documents, reviews, background papers and correspondence relating to employment papers and correspondence relating to employment statistics (race, sex, age, etc.). See also "AFFIRMATIVE ACTION RECORDS."

RETENTION: 4 anniversary years after final action

EQUIPMENT/VEHICLE MAINTENANCE RECORDS

This record series documents service, maintenance, and repairs to agency equipment and vehicles, including program changes to electronic equipment. The series may include, but is not limited to, work orders and documentation of dates/history of repairs, locations, cost of parts, hours worked, etc. Records for all agency vehicles, including ground, air, and water vehicles, are covered by this series. See also "VEHICLE RECORDS."

RETENTION: 1 fiscal year after disposition of equipment.

EQUIPMENT/VEHICLE USAGE RECORDS

This record series documents use of agency equipment and vehicles, including, but not limited to, vehicle logs indicating driver, destination, fuel/service stops, and odometer readings and/or total trip mileage; equipment usage logs and/or reports; and other usage documentation. See also "VEHICLE RECORDS."

RETENTION:

a) **Record copy.** 1 calendar year.

b) **Duplicates.** Retain until obsolete, superseded, or administrative value is lost.

EXPENDITURE PLANS: CAPITAL

This record series consists of capital improvement expenditure plans.

RETENTION: Permanent.

FACILITY RESERVATION/Rental records

This record series consists of forms generated in the process of renting or scheduling a public meeting hall or room, conference site, to a citizen or family, private organization, or other public agency. These forms include, but are not limited to, name of renter, renter's address and telephone number, method of payment, acknowledgment of rules, liability, damage waivers, and the date and time of the rental as well as what facility or portion of a facility is to be reserved. These forms may contain a check number, corresponding receipt number, an amount as well as deposit information. There may also be a floor plan denoting the desired arrangement of tables or chairs as requested by the renter.

RETENTION: 5 fiscal years

FEASIBILITY STUDY RECORDS

This record series consists of working papers, correspondence, consulting firm reports and management committee reports investigating various projects of the judicial branch entity.

RETENTION: 3 years.

FEDERAL AND STATE TAX FORMS/REPORTS

This record series consists of W–2 Forms, W–4 Forms, W–9 Forms, 940 Forms, 941–E Forms, 1099 Forms, 1099 Reports and UTC–6 Forms. The retention period mentioned below for the record (master) copy was established pursuant to Section 26 CFR 31.6001–1(2).

RETENTION: 4 calendar years.

GENERAL LEDGERS: ANNUAL SUMMARY

This record series consists of ledgers containing accounts to which debits and credits are posted from supporting documents of original entry. It includes all permanent ledger entries.

RETENTION: Permanent.

GRAND JURY NOTES

This record series consists of stenographic records, notes, and transcriptions made by the court reporter or stenographer during the grand jury session. These records are normally kept in a sealed container and are not subject to public inspection pursuant to Section 905.17(1), Florida Statutes. A Court order must be obtained for disposition.

RETENTION: 10 years from closing of session.

GRAND JURY RECORDS

This record series consists of jury summons, requests for recusal, juror payments, information to jurors' employers, lists of jurors, juror questionnaires, and other records related to a grand jury. This record series includes records related to a grand jury and the statewide grand jury.

RETENTION: 2 years.

GRANT FILES

This record series consists of financial, management and any other related material which is generated subsequent to application for or expenditure of grant funds. These files include all applications, supporting documentation, contracts, agreements, and routine reports. Check with applicable grant agency for any additional requirements. Project completion has not occurred until all reporting requirements are satisfied and final payments have been received. See also "PROJECT FILES: FEDERAL", and "PROJECT FILES: NONCAPITAL IMPROVEMENT". **"These records may have archival value."**

RETENTION: 5 fiscal years after completion of project.

GRIEVANCE FILES (EMPLOYMENT)

This record series consists of records of all proceedings in the settlement of disputes between employer and employee. See also "PERSONNEL RECORDS."

RETENTION: 3 years.

HEALTH RECORDS: BLOOD BORNE PATHOGEN/ASBESTOS/EXPOSURE

This record series consists of medical records of employees who may have or did come into contact with blood or other potentially hazardous materials. These confidential records include the employee's name, social security number, hepatitis B vaccination status including the dates of testing, results of examinations, medical testing, and follow up procedures, a copy of the healthcare professional's written opinion, a list of complaints which may be related to the exposure, and a copy of information provided to the healthcare professional. This record series can also consist of documents which record the exposure or possible exposure of an employee to a blood borne pathogen, contagion, radiation and chemicals above the acceptable limits or dosage. These documents may include statistical analyses, incident reports, material safety data sheets, copies of medical records or reports, risk management assessments, and other necessary data to support the possibility of exposure. *Please refer to 20 CFR 1910.1030.*

RETENTION: 30 years after termination, retirement, or separation from employment.

INCIDENT REPORTS

This record series consists of reports of incidents which occur at a public facility or on publicly owned property. It may include alarm malfunctions, suspicious persons, maintenance problems, or any other circumstance that should be noted for future reference or follow up.

RETENTION: 4 years.

INFORMATION REQUEST RECORDS

This record series consists of correspondence accumulated in answering inquiries from the public. See also "CORRESPONDENCE & MEMORANDA: ADMINISTRATIVE."

RETENTION: 1 year.

INSPECTION RECORDS: FIRE/SECURITY/SAFETY

This record series consists of inspection reports for fire, security, and safety.

RETENTION: 4 years.

INSPECTION REPORTS: FIRE EXTINGUISHER (ANNUAL)

This records series consists of annual fire extinguisher inspection reports.

RETENTION: 1 anniversary year or life of equipment, whichever is sooner.

INSURANCE RECORDS

This record series consists of all policies, claim filing information, correspondence and claims applications made by an agency, premium payment records which includes fire, theft, liability, medical, life, etc. on agency's property or employees. The record series also consists of a list of any insurance carriers and the premium payment amounts paid to them.

RETENTION: 5 years after final disposition of claim or expiration of policy.

INVENTORY RECORDS: PHYSICAL

This record series consists of all information regarding the physical inventory of all Operating Capital Outlay (O.C.O.) items which require an identification number and tag. Included in these reports are items sold through the auctions process as well as the Fixed Inventory Report showing all property owned by the judicial branch entity. See also "SUPPLY RECORDS."

RETENTION: 3 years.

JQC—JUDICIAL FINANCIAL DISCLOSURE FORMS

This record consists of all financial disclosure forms filed by the judiciary with the Judicial Qualifications Commission.

RETENTION: 10 years.

JQC—JUDICIAL COMPLAINTS

This record consists of individual complaints received from citizens, judges, or lawyers against members of the judiciary.

RETENTION: 3 years if complaint summarily dismissed. For the lifetime of the judge against whom the complaint has been filed in all other cases.

JUROR NOTES

Juror notes shall consist of any written notes taken by jurors during civil or criminal trials.

RETENTION: Immediate destruction upon issuance of a verdict or if the trial ends prematurely as a result of a mistrial, plea, or settlement.

JURY RECORDS

This record series consists of jury summons, requests for recusal, juror payments, information to jurors' employers, lists of jurors, juror questionnaires, and other records related to the jury pool. This record series includes records related to petit juries.

RETENTION: 2 years.

KEY AND BADGE ISSUANCE RECORDS

This record series consists of the key control system which includes receipts for keys and security or identification badges issued by employees. See also "VISITOR LOGS."

RETENTION: Retain as long as employee is employed.

LAW OFFICE MANAGEMENT ASSISTANCE SERVICE RECORDS

This record series consists of all materials in connection with consultations or advice given in the course of office management assistance services provided to an attorney, legal office, or law firm.

RETENTION: Retain until obsolete, superseded or administrative value is lost.

LEAVE TRANSACTION REPORTS

This record series consists of the printed record generated through COPES of the total hours used and the accrual earned during a pay period. It also consists of the leave balances of vacation, sick and compensatory leave for all employees in the agency.

RETENTION: 3 years.

LEGISLATION RECORDS

This record series consists of proposed legislation for the Florida Legislature and all supporting documentation, analysis or tracking information. **"These records may have archival value."**

RETENTION: Retain until obsolete, superseded or administrative value is lost.

LIBRARY CIRCULATION RECORDS

This record series consists of the transactions devised to make library materials and equipment available to the entire library clientele. Also, includes delinquent records and charges, copies of incoming and outgoing interlibrary loan requests for books, magazine articles, microfilms, renewals and subject searches.

RETENTION: 3 years.

LITIGATION CASE FILES

This record series consists of legal documents, notes, reports, background material, etc. created in the preparation of handling legal disputes involving a judicial branch entity. See also, "OPINIONS: LEGAL (ATTORNEY)," and "OPINIONS: LEGAL (SUPPORTING DOCUMENTS)."

RETENTION: 5 years after case closed or appeal process expired.

MAIL: UNDELIVERABLE FIRST CLASS

This record series consists of mail from any judicial branch entity, returned due to an incorrect address or postage. See also "MAILING LISTS" and "POSTAGE RECORDS."

RETENTION: 1 year.

MAILING LISTS

This record series consists of mailing lists. See also "MAIL: UNDELIVERABLE FIRST CLASS" and "POSTAGE RECORDS."

RETENTION: Retain until obsolete, superseded or administrative value is lost.

MANAGEMENT SURVEYS/STUDIES: INTERNAL

This record series consists of the raw data and work papers for any survey conducted to study management issues such as client/patron/employee satisfaction and service improvement. This data may include survey response cards, the results of telephone polls, tally sheets, opinion cards for suggestion boxes, and other records related to the study of internal operations. This does not include a consultant report. The final computation of the data is produced as a survey report and may be scheduled either as part of a feasibility study, project case file, or an operational/statistical report—depending on the nature and depth of the survey/study.

RETENTION: 1 year after final data or report released.

MATERIALS SAFETY RECORDS

This record series consists of a list of toxic substances to which an employee is, has been or may be exposed to during the course of their employment with an employer who manufacturers, produces, uses, applies or stores toxic substances in the work place.

RETENTION: 30 years.

MEMORANDA—LEGAL: Court's decision-making

This record series consists of memoranda, drafts or other documents involved in a court's judicial decision-making process.

RETENTION: Retain until obsolete, superseded or administrative value is lost.

MINUTES: OFFICIAL MEETINGS

This record series consists of the minutes of meetings convened to establish policy or precedent and includes meetings of the Board of Governors of The Florida Bar and The Florida Board of Bar Examiners, and court administrative conferences. See also "MINUTES: OTHER MEETINGS" and "MINUTES: OFFICIAL MEETINGS (AUDIO/VISUAL RECORDINGS)." **"These records may have archival value."**

RETENTION: Permanent.

MINUTES: OFFICIAL MEETINGS (AUDIO/VISUAL RECORDINGS)

This record series consists of official audio and video recordings of meetings. See also, "MINUTES: OTHER MEETINGS."

RETENTION: Until minutes are prepared.

MINUTES: OFFICIAL MEETINGS (SUPPORTING DOCUMENTS)

This record series consists of the agenda and supporting documents for official meetings. See also "MIN-

UTES: OTHER MEETINGS" and "MINUTES: OFFICIAL MEETINGS (AUDIO/VISUAL RECORDINGS)."

RETENTION: 3 years.

MINUTES: OTHER MEETINGS

This record series consists of minutes from all meetings which are not included in "MINUTES: OFFICIAL MEETINGS."

RETENTION: 1 year.

MONTHLY DISTRIBUTION OF FINES

This record series consists of monthly reports, prepared by the clerk, of all fines imposed under the penal laws of the state and the proceeds of all forfeited bail bonds or recognizance which are paid into the fine and forfeiture fund. The report contains the amount of fines imposed by the court and of bonds forfeited and judgments rendered on said forfeited bonds, and into whose hands they had been paid or placed for collection, the date of conviction in each case, the term of imprisonment, and the name of the officer to whom commitment was delivered.

RETENTION: 3 fiscal years.

NEWS RELEASES

This record series consists of news releases distributed by the judicial branch entity and news releases received from other offices for informational purposes. See also "PUBLIC INFORMATION CASE FILES" and "PRE–PUBLICATIONS AND MEDIA ITEM RECORDS." **"These records may have archival value."**

RETENTION: 90 days.

OPERATIONAL AND STATISTICAL REPORT RECORDS: OFFICE

This record series consists of daily, weekly, monthly, biannual, and annual narrative and statistical reports of office operations made within and between judicial branch entities. Also included in this series are activity reports demonstrating the productivity of an employee or the work tasks completed for a period of time (hourly/daily/weekly).

RETENTION: Retain until obsolete, superseded or administrative value is lost.

OPINIONS: ETHICS

This record series consists of advisory ethical opinions issued by the appropriate committee in response to an inquiry from a regulated person or entity. **"These records may have archival value."**

RETENTION: Permanent.

OPINIONS: ETHICS (SUPPORTING DOCUMENTS)

This record series consists of supporting documents relating to advisory ethical opinions.

RETENTION: 3 years.

OPINIONS: LEGAL (ATTORNEY)

This record series consists of written opinions of lasting significance establishing policy or precedent answering legal questions involving questions of interpretation of Florida or federal law. This does not include memoranda, drafts or other documents involved in a court's judicial decision-making process. See also "CORRESPONDENCE & MEMORANDA: PROGRAM AND POLICY DEVELOPMENT", "LITIGATION CASE FILES," "MEMORANDA—LEGAL" and "OPINIONS: LEGAL (SUPPORTING DOCUMENTS)." **"These records may have archival value."**

RETENTION: Permanent.

OPINIONS: LEGAL (SUPPORTING DOCUMENTS)

This record series consists of the supporting documentation to the opinions that answer legal questions involving questions of interpretation of Florida or Federal law. See also "LITIGATION CASE FILES" and "OPINIONS: LEGAL (ATTORNEY)."

RETENTION: 3 years.

ORDERS: ADMINISTRATIVE

This record series consists of administrative orders as defined in Rule of Judicial Administration 2.020(c).

RETENTION: Permanent.

ORGANIZATION CHARTS

This record series consists of organizational charts that show lines of authority and responsibility within and between judicial branch entities. See also "DIRECTIVES/POLICIES/PROCEDURES."

RETENTION: Retain until obsolete, superseded or administrative value is lost.

OTHERWISE UNCATEGORIZED RECORDS

This record series consists of all records which are not otherwise specified in this schedule.

RETENTION: Retain until obsolete, superseded or administrative value is lost.

PARKING DECAL/PERMIT RECORDS

This record series consists of parking applications for automobile and motor bike decals for employees. See also "VEHICLE RECORDS."

RETENTION: 2 years.

PAYROLL RECORDS

This record series consists of the following: a form used by staff to rectify errors in payroll processing including: wrong name, incorrect deductions or salary, inaccurate tax information, or other problems; forms authorizing direct deductions for insurance, union dues, credit unions, savings bonds, charitable contributions, deferred compensation, day care, etc.; any payroll record posted to the employee's applicable retirement plan, in any format (plus indices, if applicable), which are used to document payment for retirement or other purposes during an employee's duration of employment and also lists each rate(s) of pay changes.

RETENTION: 4 years.

PAYROLL RECORDS: REGISTERS (POSTED)

This record series consists of records posted to the employee's retirement plan, in any format (plus indexes, if applicable), which are used to document payment for retirement or other purposes during an employee's duration of employment and also lists each rate of pay. Please note that the information in this record series should be posted to an applicable retirement plan. See also other "PAYROLL RECORDS" and "SOCIAL SECURITY CONTROLLED SUMMARY RECORDS."

RETENTION: 4 years.

PERSONNEL RECORDS

This record series consists of an application for employment, resume, personnel action reports, directly related correspondence, oath of loyalty, fingerprints, medical examination reports, performance evaluation reports, worker's compensation reports, and other related materials. See also "EMPLOYMENT EXAMINATION RECORDS," "DISCIPLINARY CASE FILES," and other "PERSONNEL RECORDS."

RETENTION: 25 years after separation or termination of employment.

PERSONNEL RECORDS: LOCATOR

This record series consists of a log or card of where to locate personnel including name of individual, location to be found, date, address, emergency contact and other general information.

RETENTION: Retain until obsolete, superseded or administrative value is lost.

PERSONNEL RECORDS: OPS/TEMPORARY EMPLOYMENT

This record series consists of all information relating to each O.P.S. or temporary employee within each judicial branch entity. Also, records may include an employment application, resume, personnel action forms and any correspondence relating to that individual. Temporary employment may include personnel from a local employment agency. See also "EMPLOYMENT EXAMINATION RECORDS," DISCIPLINARY CASE FILES," and other "PERSONNEL RECORDS."

RETENTION: 3 years.

PETTY CASH DOCUMENTATION RECORDS

This record series consists of receipts, bills and monthly balances indicating amount needed for replenishing this revolving account.

RETENTION: 3 years.

POSITION DESCRIPTION RECORDS

This record series consists of specifically assigned duties and responsibilities for a particular position, including percentage breakdown of duties.

RETENTION: 2 years after superseded.

POSTAGE RECORDS

This record series consists of a detailed listing showing the amount of postage used, date, unused balance and purpose. See also "MAILING LISTS" and "MAIL: UNDELIVERABLE FIRST CLASS."

RETENTION: 3 years.

PRE–PUBLICATIONS AND MEDIA ITEM RECORDS

This record series consists of records used to generate publications such as catalogs, pamphlets and leaflets and other media items including rough, blue lined, and final copies. See also "NEWS RELEASES" and "PUBLIC INFORMATION CASE FILES".

RETENTION: Retain until receipt of final copy.

PROCLAMATIONS/RESOLUTIONS

This record series consists of an expression of a governing body or public official concerning administrative matters, an expression of a temporary character or a provision for the disposition of a particular item of the administrative business of a governing body or judicial branch entity. See also, "DIRECTIVES/POLICIES/PROCEDURES." **"These records may have archival value."**

RETENTION: Permanent.

PROCLAMATIONS/RESOLUTIONS: SUPPORTING DOCUMENTS

This record series consists of documents that were used to prepare a proclamation or resolution. See also "PROCLAMATIONS/RESOLUTIONS" and "DIRECTIVES/POLICIES/PROCEDURES."

RETENTION: 3 years.

PROGRAM/SUBJECT/REFERENCE FILES

This record series may contain correspondence, reports, memoranda, studies, articles, etc. regarding topics of interest to or addressed by a judicial branch entity. See also, "ADMINISTRATIVE RECORDS: PUBLIC OFFICIALS/COURT ADMINISTRATORS".

RETENTION: Retain until obsolete, superseded, or administrative value is lost.

PROJECT FILES: CAPITAL IMPROVEMENT

This record series consists of correspondence or memoranda, drawings, resolutions, narratives, budget revisions, survey information, change orders, computer runs and reports all pertaining to capital improvement projects, construction and contract specifications for various proposed projects sent out for bid. See also "PROJECT FILES: FEDERAL," and "PROJECT FILES: NON–CAPITAL IMPROVEMENT."

RETENTION: 10 years

PROJECT FILES: FEDERAL

This record series consists of original approved project contracts, agreements, awards, and line-item budgets, budget amendments, cash requests, correspondence and audit reports. See also "GRANT FILES" and "PROJECT FILES: CAPITAL IMPROVEMENT."

RETENTION: 5 years.

PROJECT FILES: NON–CAPITAL IMPROVEMENT

This record series consists of correspondence or memoranda, drawings, resolutions, narratives, budget revisions, survey information, change orders, computer runs and reports all pertaining to projects in progress, construction and contract specifications for various proposed projects sent out for bid. See also "GRANT FILES," "PROJECT FILES: CAPITAL IMPROVEMENT," and "PROJECT FILES: FEDERAL."

RETENTION: 5 years.

PROPERTY TRANSFER FORMS

This record series consists of all capital and non-capital property transfer forms to declare surplus or transfer to another unit of local or state government. This series does not include real property transfers.

RETENTION: 1 year.

PUBLIC INFORMATION CASE FILES

This record series consists of speeches and drafts, contact prints, negatives, enlargements from negatives and transparencies created as illustrations in publications or as visual displays of activities of the judicial branch entity. See also "NEWS RELEASES," and "PRE–PUBLICATIONS AND MEDIA ITEM RECORDS." **"These records may have archival value."**

RETENTION: 90 days.

PUBLIC PROGRAM/EVENT RECORDS: CONTRACTED

This record series consists of case files of events or programs which are available to the public or segments of the public. Files may include copies of contracts or agreements, participant or performer information, program details and arrangements, photo or video tapes. See also "PUBLIC PROGRAM/EVENT RECORDS: NON–CONTRACTED."

RETENTION: 5 years.

PUBLIC PROGRAM/EVENT RECORDS: NON–CONTRACTED

This record series consists of case files of events or programs which are available to the public or segments of the public. Files may include copies of contracts or agreements, participant or performer information, program details and arrangements, photo or video tapes. See also "PUBLIC PROGRAM/EVENT RECORDS: CONTRACTED."

RETENTION: 3 years.

PURCHASING RECORDS

This record series consists of a copy of the purchase order which is retained by the originating office while another is sent by the purchasing office to the appropriate vendor for action. The series may include, but is not limited to, copies of requisitions sent by the originating office to supply, purchasing, graphics, duplicating, or other sections for action; copies of receiving reports; and a log of outstanding and paid requisitions and purchase orders used for cross-referencing purposes. See also "DISBURSEMENT RECORDS: DETAIL."

RETENTION: 5 fiscal years

RECEIPT/REVENUE RECORDS: DETAIL

This series consists of records documenting specific receipts/revenues collected by an agency through cash, checks, electronic fund transfers (EFT), credit and debit cards, or other methods. The series may include, but is not limited to, records such as cash collection records and reports, cash receipt books, cash register tapes, deposit/transfer slips, EFT notices, credit and debit card records, receipt ledgers, receipt journal transactions and vouchers, refund records, bad check records, and other accounts receivable and related documentation. Retention is based on s. 95.11(2), F.S., Statute of Limitations on contracts, obligations, or liabilities. See also "RECEIPT/REVENUE RECORDS: SUMMARY."

RETENTION: 5 fiscal years provided applicable audits have been released.

RECEIPT/REVENUE RECORDS: SUMMARY

This series consists of records providing summary or aggregate documentation of receipts/revenues collected by an agency. The series may include, but is not limited to, records such as trial balance reports, bank statements, credit and debit card reports, revenue reconciliations, collection balance sheets, and other accounts receivable summary and related documentation. See also "RECEIPT/REVENUE RECORDS: DETAIL."

RETENTION: 10 fiscal years provided applicable audits have been released.

RECEIPTS: REGISTERED AND CERTIFIED MAIL

This record series consists of receipts for registered and certified mail sent out or received by a particular judicial branch entity. See also "MAIL: UNDELIVERABLE FIRST CLASS," and "POSTAGE RECORDS."

RETENTION: 1 year.

RECRUITMENT & SELECTION PACKAGES

This record series consists of all records which document the selection process and justify the selection process and justify the selection decision including: details of the job analysis and identification of the knowledge, skills and abilities necessary to perform the job; application forms and/or resumes for employment including demographic data of applicants including but not limited to race, sex, age and veteran status; list of all applicants' name and ratings or rankings (if applicable) for each selection technique; description of the selection process; selection techniques used, including samples, supplemental applications, etc.; the current position description; the names and titles of all persons administering the selection process or participating in making selection decisions; the job opportunity announcement and any other recruitment efforts; and other information that affects the selection decisions. See also "EMPLOYMENT EXAMINATION RECORDS".

RETENTION: 4 anniversary years after personnel action and any litigation is resolved.

SALARY COMPARISON REPORTS

This record series consists of a report which is distributed and provided for reference purposes only. This data is compiled from records located in the Personnel Office.

RETENTION: 1 year.

SALARY SCHEDULES

This record series consists of a pay grade comparison chart or log indicating the salary classification for each position.

RETENTION: 10 years.

SEARCH COMMITTEE RECORDS

This record series consists of minutes, reports, vitas, resumes, interview score sheets, interview results, list of priority hires, a personnel requisition, references of applicants and the affirmative action compliance report.

RETENTION: 180 days

SEARCH WARRANTS SERVED: NO ARREST/NO CASE FILED

This record series consists of the original affidavit for search warrant, search warrant and return of the search warrant. Series may also include property inventory and receipt, if any property was obtained. After execution of the warrant it is filed with the Clerk of Court as served with no arrest having been made. Since no court case is generated, these are kept as a separate record series.

RETENTION: 1 year after date of return.

SOCIAL SECURITY CONTROLLED SUMMARY RECORDS

This record series consists of a judicial branch entity's copy of the State's FICA report mailed to the Division of Retirement. Report lists the total taxable wages plus the amount withheld from employee wages plus employer's contribution. See also "PAYROLL RECORDS."

RETENTION: 4 calendar years after due date of tax.

STATE AUTOMATED MANAGEMENT ACCOUNTING SYSTEM (SAMAS) REPORTS

This record series consists of reports of all updated transactions entered into the system and a financial statement for each month for all divisions of judicial branch entities.

RETENTION: 3 years.

STATE AWARDS AND RECOGNITION FILES

This record series consists of data relating to the State Meritorious Service Awards Program. File contains employee suggestion forms (Form DMS/EPE.AWP01), evaluations, adoption forms and payment records. It also contains Superior Accomplishment nomination forms and payment records. Summary information submitted to the Department of Management Services for Annual Workforce Report (Form DMS/EPE.AWP02) is also contained in this record series.

RETENTION: 3 years.

SUPPLY RECORDS

This record series consists of documentation of a perpetual inventory of expendable supplies located in a central supply office for use by judicial branch entity employees. Included in this series is a listing of all available supplies which is distributed periodically or upon request. See also "INVENTORY RECORDS: PHYSICAL."

RETENTION: 3 years.

SURVEILLANCE VIDEO TAPES

This record series consists of surveillance video tapes created to monitor activities occurring both within and outside of public buildings. This tape may play an integral part in prosecution or disciplinary actions.

RETENTION: 30 days, then erase and reuse provided any necessary images are saved.

TELEPHONE CALL RECORDS: LONG DISTANCE

This record series consists of documentation and logs of separately billed long distance telephone service.

RETENTION: 1 year.

TRAINING MATERIAL RECORDS

This record series consists of materials used in training, such as films, slides, commentaries, manuals, workbooks and other related items. This records series does not include individual training records.

RETENTION: Retain until obsolete, superseded or administrative value is lost.

TRAINING RECORDS: EMPLOYEE

This record series consists of a record for each employee which may include all educational and training records of the employee. See also "PERSONNEL RECORDS."

RETENTION: 3 years.

TRANSITORY MESSAGES

This record series consists of those records that are created primarily for the communication of information, as opposed to communications designed for the perpetuation of knowledge. Transitory messages do not set policy, establish guidelines or procedures, certify a transaction, or become a receipt. The informal tone of transitory messages might be compared to the communication that might take place during a telephone conversation or a conversation in an office hallway. Transitory messages would include, but would not be limited to: E-mail messages with short-lived, or no administrative value, voice mail, self-sticking notes, and telephone messages.

RETENTION: Retain until obsolete, superseded or administrative value is lost.

TRAVEL RECORDS

This record series consists of records required to support reimbursement of expenses incurred during official travel.

RETENTION: 5 fiscal years.

UNCLAIMED PROPERTY RECORDS

This record series consists of forms required by the State Comptroller's Office for the registration of abandoned tangible or intangible property. These forms are required under Chapter 717 of the Florida Statutes. The judicial branch entity holding the unclaimed property is to maintain a list of the specific type of property, amount, name, and last known address of the owner.

RETENTION: 5 years after the property becomes reportable.

UNEMPLOYMENT COMPENSATION RECORDS

This record series consists of reports submitted to the State on a quarterly basis stating the name of each employee, employee number, amount of wages paid during quarter subject to unemployment benefits, social security number, number of weeks covered and other pertinent information which is retained by the State for determination of unemployment benefits due to applicants for same. Also includes, receipts and statements of charges.

RETENTION: 5 fiscal years.

VEHICLE ACCIDENT REPORTS

This record series consists of reports of employees that are involved in accidents in a judicial branch entity vehicle or in their own vehicle during the course of official business. See also "VEHICLE RECORDS."

RETENTION: 4 anniversary years.

VEHICLE RECORDS

This record series consists of all pertinent records pertaining to each vehicle owned by the judicial branch entity. The records usually consist of the vehicle registration papers, copy of the title, inspection information, maintenance agreements, credit card information, confidential tag issuance information and any other information relating to the vehicle. See also "VEHICLE ACCIDENT REPORTS."

RETENTION: 1 year after disposition of vehicle.

VENDOR FILES

This record series consists of vendor invoices for items purchased or leased, received and paid for.

RETENTION: 3 years.

VISITOR LOGS

This record series consists of records documenting employees' and visitors' entrance into a judicial branch entity's building during and after office hours. See also "KEY AND BADGE ISSUANCE RECORDS."

RETENTION: 30 days.

WIRE AND ORAL COMMUNICATIONS: APPLICATIONS, ORDERS AND AUDIO RECORDINGS

This record series consists of applications for an order authorizing the interception of a wire or oral communications and orders granted pursuant to Chapter 934, Florida Statutes. Also included are original recordings of the contents of any wire or oral communication made pursuant to Section 934.09, Florida Statutes. They shall not be destroyed except upon an order of the issuing or denying judge, or that judge's successor in office, and in any event shall be kept for ten (10) years.

RETENTION: 10 years (upon permission of the Court).

WITNESS SUBPOENAS/LISTS

This record series consists of subpoena lists that may be used to establish witness payments.

RETENTION: 3 years.

WORK ORDERS

This record series consists of information reflecting the individual history of major or minor maintenance or services requiring a work order request. Work order includes dates, locations, cost of labor, hours worked, equipment cost per hour, material used and cost, and other pertinent details. This item does not include equipment maintenance records. See also "EQUIPMENT/VEHICLE MAINTENANCE RECORDS."

RETENTION: 3 years.

WORK SCHEDULES

This record series consists of any scheduling documentation for shift or part time employees. These records may include hours scheduled to work, the switching of hours with another employee, the location or route of work assignment, and anticipated starting and ending times.

RETENTION: 1 year.

WORKERS' COMPENSATION RECORDS

This record series consists of the first report of injury and the employer's supplemental reports including, if used, OSHA Form No. 200 as well as its predecessor forms No. 100 and 102 and OSHA Form No. 101. These records are created pursuant to Florida Statutes Section 440.09 and OSHA standards 1904.2, 1904.4, and 1904.5.

RETENTION: 5 years.

Added March 7, 2002 (825 So.2d 889). Amended Jan. 6, 2011.

INDEX TO
FLORIDA RULES OF JUDICIAL ADMINISTRATION

FLORIDA RULES OF CRIMINAL PROCEDURE

Adoption

Revision Adopted December 6, 1972, effective February 1, 1973 (272 So.2d 65)

I. SCOPE, PURPOSE, AND CONSTRUCTION

Rule 3.010. Scope

These rules shall govern the procedure in all criminal proceedings in state courts including proceedings involving direct and indirect criminal contempt, proceedings under rule 3.850, and vehicular and pedestrian traffic offenses insofar as these rules are made applicable by the Florida Rules of Practice and Procedure for Traffic Courts. These rules shall not apply to direct or indirect criminal contempt of a court acting in any appellate capacity. These rules shall not apply to rules 3.811 and 3.812. These rules shall be known as the Florida Rules of Criminal Procedure and may be cited as Fla. R. Crim. P.

Amended Sept. 24, 1992, effective Jan. 1, 1993 (606 So.2d 227).

Committee Notes

1968 Adoption. These rules are not intended to apply to municipal courts, but are intended to apply to all state courts where "crimes" are charged.

1972 Amendment. Amended to provide for applicability of rules to vehicular traffic offenses, when made so by the traffic court rules.

1992 Amendment. The rule is amended to refer to "Florida Rules of Criminal Procedure" and "Fla. R.Crim.P." rather than to "Rules of Criminal Procedure" and "R.Crim.P." Although the Florida Bar Rules of Criminal Procedure already contains this language, the West publications, Florida Rules of Court (1991) and Florida Criminal Law and Rules (1991), do not. The published version of rule 3.010, In re Florida Rules of Criminal Procedure, 272 So.2d 65 (Fla.1973), and the single published amendment to the rule, In re Amendments to the Florida Rules of Criminal Procedure, 518 So.2d 256 (Fla.1987), also do not contain these additions. The Florida Bar publication, Florida Criminal Rules and Practice, in a commentary to rule 3.010, indicates that the Florida Supreme Court changed the citation form in an order effective January 1, 1977. The commentary indicates that the order stated in pertinent part:

In order to provide the clarity of citations in briefs filed in this court and other legal writings, the following amendments to the procedural rules adopted by this court pursuant to Article V, Section 2(a), of the Florida Constitution are hereby adopted.

* * *

The last sentence of Rule 3.010 of the Florida Rules of Criminal Procedure is amended as follows: "These Rules shall be known as the Florida Rules of Criminal Procedure and may be cited as Fla. R.Crim.P."

However, these changes were apparently inadvertently omitted when the 1987 amendments were published. The proposed 1992 amendments again incorporate into the rule the language set out in the court's 1977 order.

The amendments would enable clearer identification of the rules and achieve consistency of style with other sets of court rules, in particular, rule 9.800(i), Fla.R.App.P., which provides that the proper citation to the Florida Rules of Criminal Procedure is Fla.R.Crim.P.

Rule 3.020. Purpose and Construction

These rules are intended to provide for the just determination of every criminal proceeding. They shall be construed to secure simplicity in procedure and fairness in administration.

Committee Notes

1968 Adoption. Substantially the same as Federal [Criminal Procedure] Rule 2.

1972 Amendment. Same as prior rule.

Rule 3.025. State and Prosecuting Attorney Defined

Whenever the terms "state," "state attorney," "prosecutor," "prosecution," "prosecuting officer," or "prosecuting attorney" are used in these rules, they shall be construed to mean the prosecuting authority representing the state of Florida.

Added Nov. 2, 2000, effective Jan. 1, 2001 (794 So.2d 457).

Committee Notes

2000 Adoption. This provision is new. Its purpose is to include the Office of Statewide Prosecution as a prosecuting authority under these rules. No substantive changes are intended by the adoption of this rule.

II. GENERAL PROVISIONS

Rule 3.030. Service and Filing of Pleadings, Papers, and Documents

(a) Service. Every pleading subsequent to the initial indictment or information on which a defendant is to be tried unless the court otherwise orders, and every order not entered in open court, every written motion unless it is one about which a hearing ex parte is authorized, and every written notice, demand, and similar document shall be served on each party in conformity with Florida Rule of Judicial Administration 2.516; however, nothing herein shall be construed to require that a plea of not guilty shall be in writing.

(b) Filing. All documents that are "court records" as defined in the Florida Rules of Judicial Administration must be filed with the clerk in accordance with Florida Rules of Judicial Administration 2.520 and 2.525.

(c) Deposit with the Clerk. Any paper document that is a judgment and sentence or required by statute or rule to be sworn to or notarized shall be filed and deposited with the clerk immediately thereafter. The clerk shall maintain deposited original paper documents in accordance with Florida Rule of Judicial Administration 2.430, unless otherwise ordered by the court.

Amended Sept. 24, 1992, effective Jan. 1, 1993 (606 So.2d 227); Nov. 2, 2000, effective Jan. 1, 2001 (794 So.2d 457); Oct. 18, 2012, effective, *nunc pro tunc*, Sept. 1, 2012 (102 So.3d 505); Oct. 18, 2012, effective Dec. 1, 2012, April 1, 2013, Oct. 1, 2013 (102 So.3d 451).

Committee Notes

1968 Adoption. Taken from the Florida Rules of Civil Procedure.

1972 Amendment. Same as prior rule; (a) amended by deleting reference to trial on affidavit.

2000 Amendment. Fraudulent manipulation of electronically transmitted service should be considered contemptuous and dealt with by appropriate sanctions by the court.

[Federal Criminal Procedure Rule 49(a, b, d) contains similar provisions.]

Rule 3.040. Computation of Time

Computation of time shall be governed by Florida Rule of Judicial Administration 2.514(a), except for the periods of time of less than 7 days contained in rules 3.130, 3.132(a) and (c), and 3.133(a).

Amended Sept. 24, 1992, effective Jan. 1, 1993 (606 So.2d 227); July 12, 2012, effective Oct. 1, 2012 (95 So.3d 96).

Committee Notes

1968 Adoption. Taken from the Florida Rules of Civil Procedure.

1972 Amendment. Same as prior rule.

1988 Amendment. The 1983 amendments resulted in the reallocation of the time periods in rule 3.131 to rule 3.133, and also added an important 5-day period in the new rule regarding pretrial detention in rule 3.132.

Court Commentary

1975 Amendment. Underlined portion is the only change. The effect is to remove the 72-hour provision of proposed rule 3.131 from the Saturday, Sunday, and legal holiday exception.

Rule 3.050. Enlargement of Time

When by these rules or by a notice given thereunder or by order of court an act is required or allowed to be done at or within a specified time, the court for good cause shown may, at any time, in its discretion (1) with or without notice, order the period enlarged if a request therefor is made before the expiration of the period originally prescribed or extended by a previous order or (2) upon motion made and notice after the expiration of the specified period, permit the act to be done when the failure to act was the result of excusable neglect; but it may not, except as provided by statute or elsewhere in these rules, extend the time for making a motion for new trial, for taking an appeal, or for making a motion for a judgment of acquittal.

Amended Sept. 24, 1992, effective Jan. 1, 1993 (606 So.2d 227).

Committee Notes

1968 Adoption. Taken from the Florida Rules of Civil Procedure.

1972 Amendment. Same as prior rule.

Rule 3.060. Time for Service of Motions and Notice of Hearing

A copy of any written motion which may not be heard ex parte and a copy of the notice of the hearing thereof, shall be served on the adverse party a reasonable time before the time specified for the hearing.

Committee Notes

1968 Adoption. Taken from rules of civil procedure. [1954 RCP 1.6(d); 1967 RCP 1.090(d).]

[Federal Criminal Procedure Rule 45(d) contains substantially similar provisions. However, the time for service is specified.]

1972 Amendment. Same as prior rule.

Rule 3.070. Additional Time After Service by Mail, When Permitted, or E-Mail

Whenever a party has the right or is required to do some act or take some proceedings within a prescribed period after the service of a notice or other document on the party and the notice or document is served on the party by mail, when permitted, or e-mail, 3 days shall be added to the prescribed period.

Amended Sept. 24, 1992, effective Jan. 1, 1993 (606 So.2d 227); Oct. 18, 2012, effective, *nunc pro tunc*, Sept. 1, 2012 (102 So.3d 505); Oct. 18, 2012, effective Dec. 1, 2012, April 1, 2013, Oct. 1, 2013 (102 So.3d 451).

Committee Notes

1968 Adoption. This is the same as rule 1.6(e), Florida Rules of Civil Procedure, except for the omission of subdivision (c) of the civil rules, which appears to be inapplicable to criminal cases.

1972 Amendment. Same as prior rule.

Rule 3.080. Nonverification of Pleadings

Except when otherwise specifically provided by these rules or an applicable statute, every written pleading or other document of a party represented by an attorney need not be verified or accompanied by an affidavit.

Amended Oct. 18, 2012, effective Dec. 1, 2012, April 1, 2013, Oct. 1, 2013 (102 So.3d 451).

Committee Notes

1968 Adoption. Taken from rules of civil procedure. [1954 RCP 1.5(a); 1967 RCP 1.030(a).]

1972 Amendment. Same as prior rule.

Rule 3.090. Pleading Captions

Every pleading, motion, order, judgment, or other document shall have a caption containing the name of the court, the file number, the name of the first party on each side with an appropriate indication of other parties, and a designation identifying the party filing it and its nature, to include if the pleading or document is sworn or the nature of the order, as the case may be. All documents filed in the action shall be styled in such a manner as to indicate clearly the subject matter of the document and the party requesting or obtaining relief.

Added Nov. 27, 1996, effective Jan. 1, 1997 (685 So.2d 1253). Amended Oct. 18, 2012, effective Dec. 1, 2012, April 1, 2013, Oct. 1, 2013 (102 So.3d 451).

Rule 3.111. Providing Counsel to Indigents

(a) When Counsel Provided. A person entitled to appointment of counsel as provided herein shall have counsel appointed when the person is formally charged with an offense, or as soon as feasible after custodial restraint, or at the first appearance before a committing judge, whichever occurs earliest.

(b) Cases Applicable.

(1) Counsel shall be provided to indigent persons in all prosecutions for offenses punishable by incarceration including appeals from the conviction thereof. In the discretion of the court, counsel does not have to be provided to an indigent person in a prosecution for a misdemeanor or violation of a municipal ordinance if the judge, at least 15 days prior to trial, files in the cause a written order of no incarceration certifying that the defendant will not be incarcerated in the case pending trial or probation violation hearing, or as part of a sentence after trial, guilty or nolo contendere plea, or probation revocation. This 15–day requirement may be waived by the defendant or defense counsel.

(A) If the court issues an order of no incarceration after counsel has been appointed to represent the defendant, the court may discharge appointed counsel unless the defendant is incarcerated or the defendant would be substantially disadvantaged by the discharge of appointed counsel.

(B) If the court determines that the defendant would be substantially disadvantaged by the discharge of appointed counsel, the court shall either:

(i) not discharge appointed counsel; or

(ii) discharge appointed counsel and allow the defendant a reasonable time to obtain private counsel, or if the defendant elects to represent himself or herself, a reasonable time to prepare for trial.

(C) If the court withdraws its order of no incarceration, it shall immediately appoint counsel if the defendant is otherwise eligible for the services of the public defender. The court may not withdraw its order of no incarceration once the defendant has been found guilty or pled nolo contendere.

(2) Counsel may be provided to indigent persons in all proceedings arising from the initiation of a criminal action against a defendant, including postconviction proceedings and appeals therefrom, extradition proceedings, mental competency proceedings, and other proceedings that are adversary in nature, regardless of the designation of the court in which they occur or the classification of the proceedings as civil or criminal.

(3) Counsel may be provided to a partially indigent person on request, provided that the person shall defray that portion of the cost of representation and the reasonable costs of investigation as he or she is able without substantial hardship to the person or the person's family, as directed by the court.

(4) "Indigent" shall mean a person who is unable to pay for the services of an attorney, including costs of investigation, without substantial hardship to the person or the person's family; "partially indigent" shall mean a person unable to pay more than a portion of the fee charged by an attorney, including costs of investigation, without substantial hardship to the person or the person's family.

(5) Before appointing a public defender, the court shall:

(A) inform the accused that, if the public defender or other counsel is appointed, a lien for the services rendered by counsel may be imposed as provided by law;

(B) make inquiry into the financial status of the accused in a manner not inconsistent with the guidelines established by section 27.52, Florida Statutes. The accused shall respond to the inquiry under oath;

(C) require the accused to execute an affidavit of insolvency as required by section 27.52, Florida Statutes.

(c) Duty of Booking Officer. In addition to any other duty, the officer who commits a defendant to custody has the following duties:

(1) The officer shall immediately advise the defendant:

(A) of the right to counsel;

(B) that, if the defendant is unable to pay a lawyer, one will be provided immediately at no charge.

(2) If the defendant requests counsel or advises the officer that he or she cannot afford counsel, the officer shall immediately and effectively place the defendant in communication with the (office of) public defender of the circuit in which the arrest was made.

(3) If the defendant indicates that he or she has an attorney or is able to retain an attorney, the officer shall immediately and effectively place the defendant in communication with the attorney or the Lawyer Referral Service of the local bar association.

(4) The public defender of each judicial circuit may interview a defendant when contacted by, or on behalf of, a defendant who is, or claims to be, indigent as defined by law.

(A) If the defendant is in custody and reasonably appears to be indigent, the public defender shall tender such advice as is indicated by the facts of the case, seek the setting of a reasonable bail, and otherwise represent the defendant pending a formal judicial determination of indigency.

(B) If the defendant is at liberty on bail or otherwise not in custody, the public defender shall elicit from the defendant only the information that may be reasonably relevant to the question of indigency and shall immediately seek a formal judicial determination of indigency. If the court finds the defendant indigent, it shall immediately appoint counsel to represent the defendant.

(d) Waiver of Counsel.

(1) The failure of a defendant to request appointment of counsel or the announced intention of a defendant to plead guilty shall not, in itself, constitute a waiver of counsel at any stage of the proceedings.

(2) A defendant shall not be considered to have waived the assistance of counsel until the entire process of offering counsel has been completed and a thorough inquiry has been made into both the accused's comprehension of that offer and the accused's capacity to make a knowing and intelligent waiver. Before determining whether the waiver is knowing and intelligent, the court shall advise the defendant of the disadvantages and dangers of self-representation.

(3) Regardless of the defendant's legal skills or the complexity of the case, the court shall not deny a defendant's unequivocal request to represent himself or herself, if the court makes a determination of record that the defendant has made a knowing and intelligent waiver of the right to counsel, and does not suffer from severe mental illness to the point where the defendant is not competent to conduct trial proceedings by himself or herself.

(4) A waiver of counsel made in court shall be of record; a waiver made out of court shall be in writing with not less than 2 attesting witnesses. The witnesses shall attest the voluntary execution thereof.

(5) If a waiver is accepted at any stage of the proceedings, the offer of assistance of counsel shall be renewed by the court at each subsequent stage of the proceedings at which the defendant appears without counsel.

(e) Withdrawal of Defense Counsel After Judgment and Sentence. The attorney of record for a defendant in a criminal proceeding shall not be relieved of any duties, nor be permitted to withdraw as counsel of record, except with approval of the lower tribunal on good cause shown on written motion, until after:

(1) the filing of:

(A) a notice of appeal;

(B) a statement of judicial acts to be reviewed, if a transcript will require the expenditure of public funds;

(C) directions to the clerk, if necessary; and

(D) a designation of that portion of the reporter's transcript that supports the statement of judicial acts to be reviewed, if a transcript will require expenditure of public funds; or

(2) substitute counsel has been obtained or appointed, or a statement has been filed with the appellate court that the appellant has exercised the right to self-representation. In publicly funded cases, the public defender for the local circuit court shall be appointed initially until the record is transmitted to the appellate court; or

(3) the time has expired for filing of a notice of appeal, and no notice has been filed.

Orders allowing withdrawal of counsel are conditional, and counsel shall remain of record for the limited purpose of representing the defendant in the lower tribunal regarding any sentencing error that the lower tribunal is authorized to address during the pendency of the direct appeal under rule 3.800(b)(2).

Amended Sept. 24, 1992, effective Jan. 1, 1993 (606 So.2d 227); July 16, 1998 (719 So.2d 873); Nov. 12, 1999 (760 So.2d 67); Jan. 13, 2000 (671 So.2d 1015); Nov. 2, 2000, effective Jan. 1, 2001 (794 So.2d 457); Dec. 5, 2002, effective Jan. 1, 2003 (837 So.2d 924); Sept. 30, 2004, effective Oct. 1, 2004 (887 So.2d 1090); April 7, 2005 (900 So.2d 528); Aug. 27, 2009 (17 So.3d 272); Sept. 23, 2010 (48 So.3d 17); Nov. 8, 2012, effective Jan. 1, 2013 (104 So.3d 304).

Committee Notes

1972 Adoption. Part 1 of the ABA Standard relating to providing defense services deals with the general philosophy for providing criminal defense services and while the committee felt that the philosophy should apply to the Florida Rules of Criminal Procedure, the standards were not in such form to be the subject of that particular rule. Since the standards deal with the national situation, contained in them were alternative methods of providing defense services, i.e., assigned counsel vs. defender system; but, Florida, already having a defender system, need not be concerned with the assigned counsel system.

(a) Taken from the first sentence of ABA Standard 5.1. There was considerable discussion within the committee concerning the time within which counsel should be appointed and who should notify defendant's counsel. The commentary in the ABA Standard under 5.1a, b, convinced the committee to adopt the language here contained.

(b) Standard 4.1 provides that counsel should be provided in all criminal cases punishable by loss of liberty, except those types where such punishment is not likely to be imposed. The committee determined that the philosophy of such standard should be recommended to the Florida Supreme Court. The committee determined that possible deprivation of liberty for any period makes a case serious enough that the accused should have the right to counsel.

(c) Based on the recommendation of ABA Standard 5.1b and the commentary thereunder which provides that implementation of a rule for providing the defendant with counsel should not be limited to providing a means for the accused to contact a lawyer.

(d) From standard 7.2 and the commentaries thereunder.

1980 Amendment. Modification of the existing rule (the addition of (b)(5)(A)–(C)) provides a greater degree of uniformity in appointing counsel to indigent defendants. The defendant is put on notice of the lien for public defender services and must give financial information under oath.

A survey of Florida judicial circuits by the Committee on Representation of Indigents of the Criminal Law Section (1978–79) disclosed the fact that several circuits had no procedure for determining indigency and that there were circuits in which no affidavits of insolvency were executed (and no legal basis for establishing or collecting lien monies).

1992 Amendment. In light of *State v. District Court of Appeal of Florida, First District*, 569 So. 2d 439 (Fla. 1990), in which the supreme court pronounced that motions seeking belated direct appeal based on ineffective assistance of counsel should be filed in the trial court pursuant to rule 3.850, the committee recommends that rule 3.111(e) be amended to detail with specificity defense counsel's duties to perfect an appeal prior to withdrawing after judgment and sentence. The present provision merely notes that such withdrawal is governed by Florida Rule of Appellate Procedure 9.140(b)(3).

1998 Amendment. The amendments to (d)(2)–(3) were adopted to reflect *State v. Bowen*, 698 So. 2d 248 (Fla. 1997), which implicitly overruled *Cappetta v. State*, 204 So. 2d 913 (Fla. 4th DCA 1967), *rev'd on other grounds* 216 So. 2d 749 (Fla. 1968). *See Fitzpatrick v. Wainwright*, 800 F.2d 1057 (11th Cir. 1986), for a list of factors the court may consider. *See also McKaskle v. Wiggins*, 465 U.S. 168, 104 S.Ct. 944, 79 L.Ed.2d 122 (1984), and *Savage v. Estelle*, 924 F.2d 1459 (9th Cir. 1990), *cert. denied* 501 U.S. 1255, 111 S.Ct. 2900, 115 L.Ed.2d 1064 (1992), which suggest that the defendant's right to self-representation is limited when the defendant is not able or willing to abide by the rules of procedure and courtroom protocol.

2000 Amendment. This rule applies only to judicial proceedings and is inapplicable to investigative proceedings and matters. *See* rule 3.010.

2002 Amendment. Indigent defendants are entitled to counsel if they are either currently in custody or might be incarcerated in their case. *See Alabama v. Shelton*, 122 S.Ct. 1764, 1767 (2002) (Sixth Amendment forbids imposition of suspended sentence that may "end up in the actual deprivation of a person's liberty" unless defendant accorded "the guiding hand of counsel"). *See also Tur v. State*, 797 So. 2d 4 (Fla. 3d DCA 2001) (uncounseled plea to criminal charge cannot result in jail sentence based on violation of probationary sentence for that charge); *Harris v. State*, 773 So. 2d 627 (Fla. 4th DCA 2000).

Discharge of the public defender based on an order certifying no incarceration that is entered after the public defender has already spent considerable time and resources investigating the case and preparing a defense may leave the defendant "in a position worse than if no counsel had been appointed in the first place." *State v. Ull*, 642 So. 2d 721, 724 (Fla. 1994).

In determining whether a defendant's due process rights would be violated by the discharge of the public defender, the court should consider all of the relevant circumstances, including, but not limited to:

1. The stage of the proceedings at which the order of no incarceration is entered.

2. The extent of any investigation and pretrial preparation by the public defender.

3. Any prejudice that might result if the public defender is discharged.

4. The nature of the case and the complexity of the issues.

5. The relationship between the defendant and the public defender.

Counsel may be provided to indigent persons in all other proceedings in, or arising from, a criminal case and the court should resolve any doubts in favor of the appointment of counsel for the defendant. *See Graham v. State*, 372 So. 2d 1363, 1365 (Fla. 1979).

See form found at Fla. R. Crim. P. 3.994.

2005 Amendment. *See* Affidavit of Indigent Status as provided by *In re Approval of Form for Use by Clerks of the Circuit Courts Pursuant to Rule*

10–2.1(a) of the Rules Regulating the Florida Bar, 877 So. 2d 720 (Fla. 2004).

Rule 3.112. Minimum Standards for Attorneys in Capital Cases

(a) Statement of Purpose. The purpose of these rules is to set minimum standards for attorneys in capital cases to help ensure that competent representation will be provided to capital defendants in all cases. Minimum standards that have been promulgated concerning representation for defendants in criminal cases generally and the level of adherence to such standards required for noncapital cases should not be adopted as sufficient for death penalty cases. Counsel in death penalty cases should be required to perform at the level of an attorney reasonably skilled in the specialized practice of capital representation, zealously committed to the capital case, who has had adequate time and resources for preparation. These minimum standards for capital cases are not intended to preclude any circuit from adopting or maintaining standards having greater requirements.

(b) Definitions. A capital trial is defined as any first-degree murder case in which the State has not formally waived the death penalty on the record. A capital appeal is any appeal in which the death penalty has been imposed. A capital postconviction proceeding is any postconviction proceeding where the defendant is still under a sentence of death.

(c) Applicability. This rule applies to all defense counsel handling capital trials and capital appeals, who are appointed or retained on or after July 1, 2002. Subdivision (k) of this rule applies to all lead counsel handling capital postconviction cases, who are appointed or retained on or after April 1, 2015.

(d) List of Qualified Conflict Counsel.

(1) Every circuit shall maintain a list of conflict counsel qualified for appointment in capital cases in each of three categories:

(A) lead trial counsel;

(B) trial co-counsel; and

(C) appellate counsel.

(2) The chief judge for each circuit shall maintain a list of qualified counsel pursuant to section 27.40(3)(a), Florida Statutes.

(e) Appointment of Counsel. A court must appoint lead counsel and, upon written application and a showing of need by lead counsel, should appoint co-counsel to handle every capital trial in which the defendant is not represented by retained counsel. Lead counsel shall have the right to select cocounsel from attorneys on the lead counsel or cocounsel list. Both attorneys shall be reasonably compensated for the trial and sentencing phase. Except under extraordinary circumstances, only one attorney may be compensated for other proceedings. In capital cases in which the Public Defender or Criminal Conflict and Civil Regional Counsel is appointed, the Public Defender or Criminal Conflict and Civil Regional Counsel shall designate lead and co-counsel.

(f) Lead Trial Counsel. Lead trial counsel assignments should be given to attorneys who:

(1) are members of the bar admitted to practice in the jurisdiction or admitted to practice *pro hac vice;* and

(2) are experienced and active trial practitioners with at least five years of litigation experience in the field of criminal law; and

(3) have prior experience as lead counsel in no fewer than nine state or federal jury trials of serious and complex cases which were tried to completion, as well as prior experience as lead defense counsel or cocounsel in at least two state or federal cases tried to completion in which the death penalty was sought. In addition, of the nine jury trials which were tried to completion, the attorney should have been lead counsel in at least three cases in which the charge was murder; or alternatively, of the nine jury trials, at least one was a murder trial and an additional five were felony jury trials; and

(4) are familiar with the practice and procedure of the criminal courts of the jurisdiction; and

(5) are familiar with and experienced in the utilization of expert witnesses and evidence, including but not limited to psychiatric and forensic evidence; and

(6) have demonstrated the necessary proficiency and commitment which exemplify the quality of representation appropriate to capital cases, including but not limited to the investigation and presentation of evidence in mitigation of the death penalty; and

(7) have attended within the last two years a continuing legal education program of at least twelve hours' duration devoted specifically to the defense of capital cases.

(g) Co-counsel. Trial co-counsel assignments should be given to attorneys who:

(1) are members of the bar admitted to practice in the jurisdiction or admitted to practice *pro hac vice*; and

(2) qualify as lead counsel under paragraph (f) of these standards or meet the following requirements:

(A) are experienced and active trial practitioners with at least three years of litigation experience in the field of criminal law; and

(B) have prior experience as lead counsel or cocounsel in no fewer than three state or federal jury trials of serious and complex cases which were tried to completion, at least two of which were trials in which the charge was murder; or alternatively, of the three jury trials, at least one was a murder trial and one was a felony jury trial; and

(C) are familiar with the practice and procedure of the criminal courts of the jurisdiction; and

(D) have demonstrated the necessary proficiency and commitment which exemplify the quality of representation appropriate to capital cases, and

(E) have attended within the last two years a continuing legal education program of at least twelve hours' duration devoted specifically to the defense of capital cases.

(h) Appellate Counsel. Appellate counsel assignments should be given to attorneys who:

(1) are members of the bar admitted to practice in the jurisdiction or admitted to practice *pro hac vice*; and

(2) are experienced and active trial or appellate practitioners with at least five years of experience in the field of criminal law; and

(3) have prior experience in the appeal of at least one case where a sentence of death was imposed, as well as prior experience as lead counsel in the appeal of no fewer than three felony convictions in federal or state court, at least one of which was an appeal of a murder conviction; or alternatively, have prior experience as lead counsel in the appeal of no fewer than six felony convictions in federal or state court, at least two of which were appeals of a murder conviction; and

(4) are familiar with the practice and procedure of the appellate courts of the jurisdiction; and

(5) have demonstrated the necessary proficiency and commitment which exemplify the quality of representation appropriate to capital cases; and

(6) have attended within the last two years a continuing legal education program of at least twelve hours' duration devoted specifically to the defense of capital cases.

(i) Notice of Appearance. An attorney who is retained or appointed in place of the Public Defender or Criminal Conflict and Civil Regional Counsel to represent a defendant in a capital case shall immediately file a notice of appearance certifying that he or she meets the qualifications of this rule. If the office of the Public Defender or Criminal Conflict and Civil Regional Counsel is appointed to represent the defendant, the Public Defender or Criminal Conflict and Civil Regional Counsel shall certify that the individuals or assistants assigned as lead and co-counsel meet the requirements of this rule. A notice of appearance filed under this rule shall be served on the defendant.

(j) Limitation on Caseloads.

(1) *Generally.* As soon as practicable, the trial court should conduct an inquiry relating to counsel's availability to provide effective assistance of counsel to the defendant. In assessing the availability of prospective counsel, the court should consider the number of capital or other cases then being handled by the attorney and any other circumstances bearing on the attorney's readiness to provide effective assistance of counsel to the defendant in a timely fashion. No appointment should be made to an attorney who may be unable to provide effective legal representation as a result of an unrealistically high caseload. Likewise, a private attorney should not undertake the representation of a defendant in a capital case if the attorney's caseload is high enough that it might impair the quality of legal representation provided to the defendant.

(2) *Public Defender.* If a Public Defender or Criminal Conflict and Civil Regional Counsel seeks to refuse appointment to a new capital case based on a claim of excessive caseload, the matter should be referred to the Chief Judge of the circuit or to the administrative judge as so designated by the Chief Judge. The Chief Judge or his or her designate should coordinate with the Public Defender or Criminal Conflict and Civil Regional Counsel to assess the number of attorneys involved in capital cases, evaluate the availability of prospective attorneys, and resolve any representation issues.

(k) Qualifications of Lead Counsel in Capital Postconviction Proceedings. In order to serve as lead counsel, as set forth in rule 3.851, for the defendant in a capital postconviction proceeding, an attorney shall have:

(1) been a member of any bar for at least 5 years; and

(2) at least 3 years of experience in the field of postconviction litigation; and

(3) prior participation in a combined total of 5 proceedings in any of the following areas, at least 2 of which shall be from subdivision (k)(3)(C), (k)(3)(D), or (k)(3)(E) below:

(A) capital trials;

(B) capital sentencings;

(C) capital postconviction evidentiary hearings;

(D) capital collateral postconviction appeals;

(E) capital federal habeas proceedings.

***(l)* Exceptional Circumstances.** In the event that the trial court determines that exceptional circumstances require counsel not meeting the requirements of this rule, the trial court shall enter an order specifying, in writing, the exceptional circumstances requiring deviation from the rule and the court's explicit determination that counsel chosen will provide competent representation in accord with the policy concerns of the rule.

Added Oct. 28, 1999, effective July 1, 2000 (759 So.2d 610). Amended July 1, 2002 (820 So.2d 185); Oct. 8, 2008 (993 So.2d 501); Feb. 26, 2009 (3 So.3d 1175); July 3, 2014, corrected Oct. 2, 2014, effective January 1, 2015 and April 1, 2015 (148 So.3d 1171).

Committee Comments

These standards are based on the general premise that the defense of a capital case requires specialized skill and expertise. The Supreme Court has not only the authority, but the constitutional responsibility to ensure that indigent defendants are provided with competent counsel, especially in capital cases where the State seeks to take the life of the indigent defendant. The Supreme Court also has exclusive jurisdiction under Article V section 15 of the Florida Constitution to "[r]egulate the admission of persons to the practice of law and the discipline of persons admitted." Implied in this grant of authority is the power to set the minimum requirements for the admission to practice law, *see In re Florida Board of Bar Examiners*, 353 So. 2d 98 (Fla. 1977), as well as the minimum requirements for certain kinds of specialized legal work. The Supreme Court has adopted minimum educational and experience requirements for board certification in other specialized fields of the law.

The experience and continuing educational requirements in these standards are based on existing local standards in effect throughout the state as well as comparable standards in effect in other states. Specifically, the committee considered the standards for the appointment of counsel in capital cases in the Second, Sixth, Eleventh, Fifteenth, and Seventeenth Circuits, the statewide standards for appointing counsel in capital cases in California, Indiana, Louisiana, Ohio, and New York, and the American Bar Association standards for appointment of counsel in capital cases.

These standards are not intended to establish any independent legal rights. For example, the failure to appoint cocounsel, standing alone, has not been recognized as a ground for relief from a conviction or sentence. *See Ferrell v. State*, 653 So. 2d 367 (Fla. 1995); *Lowe v. State*, 650 So. 2d 969 (Fla. 1994); *Armstrong v. State*, 642 So. 2d 730 (Fla. 1994). Rather, these cases stand for the proposition that a showing of inadequacy of representation in the particular case is required. *See Strickland v. Washington*, 466 U.S. 668, 104 S.Ct. 2052, 80 L.Ed.2d 674 (1984). These rulings are not affected by the adoption of these standards. Any claims of ineffective assistance of counsel will be controlled by *Strickland*.

The American Bar Association Standards and many other state standards require the appointment of two lawyers at the trial level in every prosecution that could result in the imposition of the death penalty. The committee has modified this requirement by allowing the trial court some discretion as to the number of attorneys, and by eliminating certain provisions that may be unnecessary or economically unfeasible. Paragraph (e) minimizes the potential duplication of expenses by limiting the compensable participation of cocounsel. In addition, the standard adopted herein requires an initial showing by lead counsel of the need for cocounsel and, while the standard suggests that cocounsel should ordinarily be appointed, the ultimate decision is left to the discretion of the trial court.

The committee emphasizes that the right to appointed counsel is not enlarged by the application of these standards. The court should appoint conflict counsel only if there is a conflict and the defendant otherwise qualifies for representation by the Public Defender. A defendant who is represented by retained counsel is not entitled to the appointment of a second lawyer at public expense merely because that defendant is unable to bear the cost of retaining two lawyers.

Criminal Court Steering Committee Note

2014 Amendment. The Steering Committee added minimum requirements for lead counsel in capital postconviction proceedings to ensure a requisite level of expertise in capital postconviction cases and to permit the State the opportunity to seek opt-in treatment pursuant to 28 U.S.C. §§ 2261–2266.

Rule 3.113. Minimum Standards for Attorneys in Felony Cases

Text of rule effective May 16, 2016.

Before an attorney may participate as counsel of record in the circuit court for any adult felony case, including postconviction proceedings before the trial court, the attorney must complete a course, approved by The Florida Bar for continuing legal education credits, of at least 100 minutes and covering the legal and ethical obligations of discovery in a criminal case, including the requirements of rule 3.220, and the principles established in *Brady v. Maryland*, 373 U.S. 83 (1963) and *Giglio v. United States*, 405 U.S. 150 (1972).

Added May 15, 2014, effective May 16, 2016 (139 So.3d 292).

Criminal Court Steering Committee Commentary

2014 Adoption. The Supreme Court has exclusive jurisdiction under Article V, section 15 of the Florida Constitution to "regulate the admission of persons to the practice of law and the discipline of persons admitted." Implied in this grant of authority is the power to set minimum requirements for the admission to practice law, *see In re Florida Board of Bar Examiners*, 353 So. 2d 98 (Fla. 1977), as well as minimum requirements for certain kinds of specialized legal work. The Supreme Court has adopted minimum educational and experience requirements for attorneys in capital cases, *see, e.g.*, rule 3.112, and for board certification in other specialized fields of law.

The concept of a two-hour continuing legal education (CLE) requirement was proposed in the 2012 Final Report of the Florida Innocence Commission.

The CLE requirement is not intended to establish any independent legal rights. Any claim of ineffective assistance of counsel will be controlled by *Strickland v. Washington*, 466 U.S. 668 (1984).

It is intended that The Florida Prosecuting Attorneys Association and The Florida Public Defender Association will develop a seminar that will be approved for CLE credit by The Florida Bar. It is also intended that attorneys will be able to electronically access that seminar, at no cost, via The Florida Bar's website, the Florida Prosecuting Attorneys Association's website, and/or the Florida Public Defender Association's website.

The rule is not intended to apply to counsel of record in direct or collateral adult felony appeals.

Rule 3.115. Duties of State Attorney; Criminal Intake

The state attorney shall provide the personnel or procedure for criminal intake in the judicial system. All sworn complaints charging the commission of a criminal offense shall be filed in the office of the clerk of the circuit court and delivered to the state attorney for further proceedings.

Amended Sept. 24, 1992, effective Jan. 1, 1993 (606 So.2d 227).

III. PRELIMINARY PROCEEDINGS

Rule 3.120. Committing Judge

Each state and county judge is a committing judge and may issue a summons to, or a warrant for the arrest of, a person against whom a complaint is made in writing and sworn to before a person authorized to administer oaths, when the complaint states facts that show that such person violated a criminal law of this state within the jurisdiction of the judge to whom the complaint is presented. The judge may take testimony under oath to determine if there is reasonable ground to believe the complaint is true. The judge may commit the offender to jail, may order the defendant to appear before the proper court to answer the charge in the complaint, or may discharge the defendant from custody or from any undertaking to appear. The judge may authorize the clerk to issue a summons.

Amended Sept. 24, 1992, effective Jan. 1, 1993 (606 So.2d 227); Sept. 30, 2004, effective Oct. 1, 2004 (887 So.2d 1090).

Committee Notes

1968 Adoption. This is substantially the same as part of section 901.01, Florida Statutes. (The remaining part should be retained as a statute.) It differs from the statute by requiring the complaint to be in writing and by identifying the initiating instrument as a "complaint," thus adopting the federal terminology which is more meaningful and modern. Some doubt was expressed as to whether the terms of the statute incorporated in the rule are within the rulemaking power of the Supreme Court.

1972 Amendment. Substantially same as former rule. Altered to incorporate the provision for testimony under oath formerly contained in rule 3.121(a), and authorize the execution of the affidavit before a notary or other person authorized to administer oaths.

Rule 3.121. Arrest Warrant

(a) Issuance. An arrest warrant, when issued, shall:

(1) be in writing and in the name of the State of Florida;

(2) set forth substantially the nature of the offense;

(3) command that the person against whom the complaint was made be arrested and brought before a judge;

(4) specify the name of the person to be arrested or, if the name is unknown to the judge, designate the person by any name or description by which the person can be identified with reasonable certainty;

(5) state the date when issued and the county where issued;

(6) be signed by the judge with the title of the office; or, may be electronically signed by the judge if the arrest warrant bears the affiant's signature, or electronic signature, is supported by an oath or affirmation administered by the judge, or other person authorized by law to administer oaths, and, if submitted electronically, is submitted by reliable electronic means; and

(7) in all offenses bailable as of right be endorsed with the amount of bail and the return date.

(b) Amendment. No arrest warrant shall be dismissed nor shall any person in custody be discharged because of any defect as to form in the warrant; but the warrant may be amended by the judge to remedy such defect.

Amended Sept. 24, 1992, effective Jan. 1, 1993 (606 So.2d 227); Sept. 30, 2004, effective Oct. 1, 2004 (887 So.2d 1090); Dec. 12, 2013 (132 So.3d 123).

Committee Notes

1968 Adoption. (a) This is substantially the same as section 901.02, Florida Statutes, except that the rule requires a written complaint. Also, the rule does not incorporate that seldom used part of the statute that permits the magistrate to issue an arrest warrant upon affidavits made before the prosecuting attorney.

(b) This is the same as section 901.03, Florida Statutes.

(c) This is the same as section 901.05, Florida Statutes, except for modernizing the language.

1972 Amendment. (a) of former rule has been deleted, as its substance is now contained in rules 3.120 and 3.130; (b) has been renumbered as (a); (c) has been renumbered as (b).

Rule 3.125. Notice to Appear

(a) Definition. Unless indicated otherwise, notice to appear means a written order issued by a law enforcement officer in lieu of physical arrest requiring a person accused of violating the law to appear in a designated court or governmental office at a specified date and time.

(b) By Arresting Officer. If a person is arrested for an offense declared to be a misdemeanor of the first or second degree or a violation, or is arrested for violation of a municipal or county ordinance triable in the county, and demand to be taken before a judge is not made, notice to appear may be issued by the arresting officer unless:

(1) the accused fails or refuses to sufficiently identify himself or herself or supply the required information;

(2) the accused refuses to sign the notice to appear;

(3) the officer has reason to believe that the continued liberty of the accused constitutes an unreasonable risk of bodily injury to the accused or others;

(4) the accused has no ties with the jurisdiction reasonably sufficient to assure the accused's appearance or there is substantial risk that the accused will refuse to respond to the notice;

(5) the officer has any suspicion that the accused may be wanted in any jurisdiction; or

(6) it appears that the accused previously has failed to respond to a notice or a summons or has violated the conditions of any pretrial release program.

(c) By Booking Officer. If the arresting officer does not issue notice to appear because of one of the exceptions listed in subdivision (b) and takes the accused to police headquarters, the booking officer may issue notice to appear if the officer determines that there is a likelihood that the accused will appear as directed, based on a reasonable investigation of the accused's:

(1) residence and length of residence in the community;

(2) family ties in the community;

(3) employment record;

(4) character and mental condition;

(5) past record of convictions; or

(6) past history of appearance at court proceedings.

(d) How and When Served. If notice to appear is issued, it shall be prepared in quadruplicate. The officer shall deliver 1 copy of the notice to appear to the arrested person and the person, to secure release, shall give a written promise to appear in court by signing the 3 remaining copies: 1 to be retained by the officer and 2 to be filed with the clerk of the court. These 2 copies shall be sworn to by the arresting officer before a notary public or a deputy clerk. If notice to appear is issued under subdivision (b), the notice shall be issued immediately upon arrest. If notice to appear is issued under subdivision (c), the notice shall be issued immediately on completion of the investigation. The arresting officer or other duly authorized official then shall release from custody the person arrested.

(e) Copy to the Clerk of the Court. With the sworn notice to appear, the arresting officer shall file with the clerk a list of witnesses and their addresses and a list of tangible evidence in the cause. One copy shall be retained by the officer and 2 copies shall be filed with the clerk of the court.

(f) Copy to State Attorney. The clerk shall deliver 1 copy of the notice to appear and schedule of witnesses and evidence filed therewith to the state attorney.

(g) Contents. If notice to appear is issued, it shall contain the:

(1) name and address of the accused;

(2) date of offense;

(3) offense(s) charged—by statute and municipal ordinance if applicable;

(4) counts of each offense;

(5) time and place that the accused is to appear in court;

(6) name and address of the trial court having jurisdiction to try the offense(s) charged;

(7) name of the arresting officer;

(8) name(s) of any other person(s) charged at the same time; and

(9) signature of the accused.

(h) Failure to Appear. If a person signs a written notice to appear and fails to respond to the notice to appear, a warrant of arrest shall be issued under rule 3.121.

(i) Traffic Violations Excluded. Nothing contained herein shall prevent the operation of a traffic violations bureau, the issuance of citations for traffic violations, or any procedure under chapter 316, Florida Statutes.

(j) Rules and Regulations. Rules and regulations of procedure governing the exercise of authority to issue notices to appear shall be established by the chief judge of the circuit.

(k) Procedure by Court.

(1) When the accused appears before the court under the requirements of the notice to appear, the court shall advise the defendant as set forth in rule 3.130(b), and the provisions of that rule shall apply. The accused at such appearance may elect to waive the right to counsel and trial and enter a plea of guilty or nolo contendere by executing the waiver form contained on the notice to appear, and the court may enter judgment and sentence in the cause.

(2) In the event the defendant enters a plea of not guilty, the court may set the cause for jury or nonjury trial on the notice to appear under the provisions of rules 3.140 and 3.160. When the court sets a trial date by the court, the clerk shall, without further praecipe, issue witness subpoenas to the law enforcement officer who executed the notice to appear and to the witnesses whose names and addresses appear on the list filed by the officer, requiring their attendance at trial.

(*l*) Form of Notice to Appear and Schedule of Witnesses and Evidence. The notice to appear and schedule of witnesses and evidence shall be in substantially the following form:

IN THE COUNTY COURT, IN AND FOR
__________ COUNTY, FLORIDA
NOTICE TO APPEAR

____
Agency Case #
STATE OF FLORIDA, COUNTY OF __________
In the name of __________ County, Florida: The undersigned certifies that he or she has just and reasonable grounds to believe, and does believe, that:
On . . .(date). . . . ., at ________ ( )a.m. ( )p.m.

________ ________ ________ ________
Last Name First M.I. Aliases

________________ ________________
Street—City and State Date and Place of Birth

____ ____ ____ ____ ____ ____ ____
Phone Race/Sex Height Weight Hair Eyes Scars/Marks

________ ________________ ________
Occupation Place of Employment Employment Phone

________ ________ ____ ________
Complexion Driver's License # Yr./St. Social Security #

at (location) ________________
in ________ County, Florida, committed the following offense(s):
(1) ______________ (2) ______________
in violation of section(s): ____: ____ ( ) State Statute
( ) Municipal Ord.

DID (Narrative): ____________________

____

____

____

____
Name of Officer ID Agency

[ ] Mandatory appearance in court, ____________
Location

on . . .(date). . . . ., at __________ ( )a.m. ( )p.m.

[ ] You need not appear in court, but must comply with instructions on back.

CO–DEFENDANTS:

1. ____ [ ] Cited [ ] Jailed
Name DOB Address

2. ____ [ ] Cited [ ] Jailed
Name DOB Address

If you are a person with a disability who needs any accommodation in order to participate in this proceeding, you are entitled, at no cost to you, to the provision of certain assistance. Please contact [identify applicable court personnel by name, address, and telephone number] at least 7 days before your scheduled court appearance, or immediately upon receiving this notification if the time before the scheduled appearance is less than 7 days; if you are hearing or voice impaired, call 711.

I AGREE TO APPEAR AT THE TIME AND PLACE DESIGNATED ABOVE TO ANSWER THE OFFENSE CHARGED OR TO PAY THE FINE SUBSCRIBED. I UNDERSTAND THAT SHOULD I WILLFULLY FAIL TO APPEAR BEFORE THE COURT AS REQUIRED BY THIS NOTICE TO APPEAR, I MAY BE HELD IN CONTEMPT OF COURT AND A WARRANT FOR MY ARREST SHALL BE ISSUED.

____
Signature of Defendant

I swear the above and reverse and attached statements are true and correct to the best of my knowledge and belief.

____
Complainant

____
Agency or Department

Sworn to and subscribed before me on . . .(date). . . . .

____
Notary Public, State of Florida

WAIVER INFORMATION

If you desire to plead guilty or nolo contendere (no contest) and you need not appear in court as indicated on the face of this notice, you may present this notice at the county court named on the reverse of this page.

From . . .(date). . . . ., __________ to . . .(date). . . . ., __________
Hour Hour

and pay a fine of __________ dollars in cash, money order, or certified check.

The waiver below must be completed and attached. Read carefully.

Your failure to answer this summons in the manner subscribed will result in a warrant being issued on a separate and additional charge.

"In consideration of my not appearing in court, I the undersigned, do hereby enter my appearance on the affidavit for the offense charged on the other side of this notice and waive the reading of the affidavit in the above named cause and the right to be present at the trial of said action. I hereby enter my plea of Guilty [ ] or Nolo Contendere [ ], and waive my right to prosecute appeal or error proceedings.

"I understand the nature of the charge against me; I understand my right to have counsel and waive this right and the right to a continuance. I waive my right to trial before a judge or jury. I plead Guilty [ ] or Nolo Contendere [ ] to the charge, being fully aware that my signature to this plea will have the same effect as a judgment of this court."

Total Fine and Cost ______

Defendant Signature ______

Address ______

______

IN THE COUNTY COURT, IN AND FOR
______ COUNTY, FLORIDA
SCHEDULE OF WITNESSES AND
EVIDENCE FOR NOTICE TO APPEAR

______
Agency Case #

______
Last Name First M.I. Aliases

______
Address

. . .(date of notice to appear). . . . . Offense(s): (1) ______
(2) ______

TANGIBLE EVIDENCE: (If none, write "None")

Item: ______

Obtained from (person and/or place): ______

first received by: ______

given to: ______

WITNESSES: (If none, write "None")

#1 Name: ______

Res. Tel. No. ______ Address: ______

Bus. Tel. No. ______ Business: ______

Testimony: ______

______

#2 Name: ______

Res. Tel. No. ______ Address: ______

Bus. Tel. No. ______ Business: ______

Testimony: ______

______

#3 Name: ______

Res. Tel. No. ______ Address: ______

Bus. Tel. No. ______ Business: ______

Testimony: ______

______

I certify that the foregoing is a complete list of witnesses and evidence known to me.

______

Investigating Officer

____

Agency

Amended Sept. 24, 1992, effective Jan. 1, 1993 (606 So.2d 227); Nov. 2, 2000, effective Jan. 1, 2001 (794 So.2d 457); Sept. 30, 2004, effective Oct. 1, 2004 (887 So.2d 1090); Nov. 8, 2012, effective Jan. 1, 2013 (104 So.3d 304).

Supersedure

This rule supersedes Laws 1973, c. 73–27, enacting §§ 901.27 to 901.32, and repealing §§ 901.06 and 901.23, to the extent that the statutes conflict with this rule. The rule supersedes only that portion of Laws 1973, c. 73–27, as is included in the rule, and the balance of the statute will remain in effect as part of the substantive law.

Committee Notes

1992 Amendment. The amendment deletes subdivision (k) and reletters subdivisions (*l*) and (m). The elimination of subdivision (k) will entitle individuals charged with criminal violations to the same discovery, without regard to the nature of the charging instrument. As amended, persons charged by way of a notice to appear can obtain the same discovery as persons charged by way of either an information or an indictment. In this regard the committee also has proposed amendments to rule 3.220(b)(1), (b)(2), (c)(1), and (h)(1) to change the reference from "indictment or information" to "charging document."

Rule 3.130. First Appearance

(a) Prompt First Appearance. Except when previously released in a lawful manner, every arrested person shall be taken before a judicial officer, either in person or by electronic audiovisual device in the discretion of the court, within 24 hours of arrest. In the case of a child in the custody of juvenile authorities, against whom an information or indictment has been filed, the child shall be taken for a first appearance hearing within 24 hours of the filing of the information or indictment. The chief judge of the circuit for each county within the circuit shall designate 1 or more judicial officers from the circuit court, or county court, to be available for the first appearance and proceedings. The state attorney or an assistant state attorney and public defender or an assistant public defender shall attend the first appearance proceeding either in person or by other electronic means. First appearance hearings shall be held with adequate notice to the public defender and state attorney. An official record of the proceedings shall be maintained. If the defendant has retained counsel or expresses a desire to and is financially able, the attendance of the public defender or assistant public defender is not required at the first appearance, and the judge shall follow the procedure outlined in subdivision (c)(2).

(b) Advice to Defendant. At the defendant's first appearance the judge shall immediately inform the defendant of the charge, including an alleged violation of probation or community control and provide the defendant with a copy of the complaint. The judge shall also adequately advise the defendant that:

(1) the defendant is not required to say anything, and that anything the defendant says may be used against him or her;

(2) if unrepresented, that the defendant has a right to counsel, and, if financially unable to afford counsel, that counsel will be appointed; and

(3) the defendant has a right to communicate with counsel, family, or friends, and if necessary, will be provided reasonable means to do so.

(c) Counsel for Defendant.

(1) *Appointed Counsel.* If practicable, the judge should determine prior to the first appearance whether the defendant is financially able to afford counsel and whether the defendant desires representation. When the judge determines that the defendant is entitled to court-appointed counsel and desires counsel, the judge shall immediately appoint counsel. This determination must be made and, if required, counsel appointed no later than the time of the first appearance and before any other proceedings at the first appearance. If necessary, counsel may be appointed for the limited purpose of representing the defendant only at first appearance or at subsequent proceedings before the judge.

(2) *Retained Counsel.* When the defendant has employed counsel or is financially able and desires to employ counsel to represent him or her at first appearance, the judge shall allow the defendant a reasonable time to send for counsel and shall, if necessary, postpone the first appearance hearing for that purpose. The judge shall also, on request of the defendant, require an officer to communicate a message to such counsel as the defendant may name. The officer shall, with diligence and without cost to the defendant if the counsel is within the county, perform the duty. If the postponement will likely result in the continued incarceration of the defendant beyond a 24–hour period, at the request of the defendant the judge may appoint counsel to represent the defendant for the first appearance hearing.

(3) *Opportunity to Confer.* No further steps in the proceedings should be taken until the defendant and counsel have had an adequate opportunity to confer,

unless the defendant has intelligently waived the right to be represented by counsel.

(4) *Waiver of Counsel.* The defendant may waive the right to counsel at first appearance. The waiver, containing an explanation of the right to counsel, shall be in writing and signed and dated by the defendant. This written waiver of counsel shall, in addition, contain a statement that it is limited to first appearance only and shall in no way be construed to be a waiver of counsel for subsequent proceedings.

(d) Pretrial Release. The judicial officer shall proceed to determine conditions of release pursuant to rule 3.131. For a defendant who has been arrested for violation of his or her probation or community control by committing a new violation of law, the judicial officer:

(1) May order the offender to be taken before the court that granted the probation or community control if the offender admits the violation;

(2) If the offender does not admit the violation at first appearance hearing, the judicial officer may commit and order the offender to be brought before the court that granted probation or community control, or may release the offender with or without bail to await further hearing, notwithstanding section 907.041, Florida Statutes, relating to pretrial detention and release. In determining whether to require or set the amount of bail, the judicial officer may consider whether the offender is more likely than not to receive a prison sanction for the violation.

Amended Dec. 5, 1991, effective Dec. 15, 1991 (591 So.2d 173); Sept. 24, 1992, effective Jan. 1, 1993 (606 So.2d 227); Sept. 30, 2004, effective Oct. 1, 2004 (887 So.2d 1090); June 3, 2009 (11 So.3d 341); March 8, 2012 (84 So.3d 254).

Committee Notes

1972 Amendment. Same as prior rule except (b), which is new.

Rule 3.131. Pretrial Release

(a) Right to Pretrial Release. Unless charged with a capital offense or an offense punishable by life imprisonment and the proof of guilt is evident or the presumption is great, every person charged with a crime or violation of municipal or county ordinance shall be entitled to pretrial release on reasonable conditions. As a condition of pretrial release, whether such release is by surety bail bond or recognizance bond or in some other form, the defendant shall refrain from any contact of any type with the victim, except through pretrial discovery pursuant to the Florida Rules of Criminal Procedure and shall comply with all conditions of pretrial release as ordered by the court. Upon motion by the defendant when bail is set, or upon later motion properly noticed pursuant to law, the court may modify the condition precluding victim contact if good cause is shown and the interests of justice so require. The victim shall be permitted to be heard at any proceeding in which such modification is considered, and the state attorney shall notify the victim of the provisions of this subsection and of the pendency of any such proceeding. If no conditions of release can reasonably protect the community from risk of physical harm to persons, assure the presence of the accused at trial, or assure the integrity of the judicial process, the accused may be detained.

(b) Hearing at First Appearance—Conditions of Release.

(1) Unless the state has filed a motion for pretrial detention pursuant to rule 3.132, the court shall conduct a hearing to determine pretrial release. For the purpose of this rule, bail is defined as any of the forms of release stated below. Except as otherwise provided by this rule, there is a presumption in favor of release on nonmonetary conditions for any person who is granted pretrial release. The judicial officer shall impose the first of the following conditions of release that will reasonably protect the community from risk of physical harm to persons, assure the presence of the accused at trial, or assure the integrity of the judicial process; or, if no single condition gives that assurance, shall impose any combination of the following conditions:

(A) personal recognizance of the defendant;

(B) execution of an unsecured appearance bond in an amount specified by the judge;

(C) placement of restrictions on the travel, association, or place of abode of the defendant during the period of release;

(D) placement of the defendant in the custody of a designated person or organization agreeing to supervise the defendant;

(E) execution of a bail bond with sufficient solvent sureties, or the deposit of cash in lieu thereof; provided, however, that any criminal defendant who is required to meet monetary bail or bail with any monetary component may satisfy the bail by providing an appearance bond; or

(F) any other condition deemed reasonably necessary to assure appearance as required, including a condition requiring that the person return to custody after specified hours.

(2) The judge shall at the defendant's first appearance consider all available relevant factors to determine what form of release is necessary to assure the defendant's appearance. If a monetary bail is required, the judge shall determine the amount. Any judge setting or granting monetary bond shall set a separate and specific bail amount for each charge or offense. When bail is posted each charge or offense requires a separate bond.

(3) In determining whether to release a defendant on bail or other conditions, and what that bail or those conditions may be, the court may consider the nature and circumstances of the offense charged and the penalty provided by law; the weight of the evidence

against the defendant; the defendant's family ties, length of residence in the community, employment history, financial resources, need for substance abuse evaluation and/or treatment, and mental condition; the defendant's past and present conduct, including any record of convictions, previous flight to avoid prosecution, or failure to appear at court proceedings; the nature and probability of danger that the defendant's release poses to the community; the source of funds used to post bail; whether the defendant is already on release pending resolution of another criminal proceeding or is on probation, parole, or other release pending completion of sentence; and any other facts the court considers relevant.

(4) No person charged with a dangerous crime, as defined in section 907. 041(4)(a), Florida Statutes, shall be released on nonmonetary conditions under the supervision of a pretrial release service, unless the service certifies to the court that it has investigated or otherwise verified the conditions set forth in section 907.041(3)(b), Florida Statutes.

(5) All information provided by a defendant in connection with any application for or attempt to secure bail, to any court, court personnel, or individual soliciting or recording such information for the purpose of evaluating eligibility for or securing bail for the defendant, under circumstances such that the defendant knew or should have known that the information was to be used in connection with an application for bail, shall be accurate, truthful, and complete, without omissions, to the best knowledge of the defendant. Failure to comply with the provisions of this subdivision may result in the revocation or modification of bail. However, no defendant shall be compelled to provide information regarding his or her criminal record.

(6) Information stated in, or offered in connection with, any order entered pursuant to this rule need not strictly conform to the rules of evidence.

(c) Consequences of Failure to Appear.

(1) Any defendant who willfully and knowingly fails to appear and breaches a bond as specified in section 903.26, Florida Statutes, and who voluntarily appears or surrenders shall not be eligible for a recognizance bond.

(2) Any defendant who willfully and knowingly fails to appear and breaches a bond as specified in section 903.26, Florida Statutes, and who is arrested at any time following forfeiture shall not be eligible for a recognizance bond or any form of bond that does not require a monetary undertaking or commitment equal to or greater than $2,000 or twice the value of the monetary commitment or undertaking of the original bond, whichever is greater.

(d) Subsequent Application for Setting or Modification of Bail.

(1) When a judicial officer not possessing trial jurisdiction orders a defendant held to answer before a court having jurisdiction to try the defendant, and bail has been denied or sought to be modified, application by motion may be made to the court having jurisdiction to try the defendant or, in the absence of the judge of the trial court, to the circuit court. The motion shall be determined promptly. No judge or a court of equal or inferior jurisdiction may modify or set a condition of release, unless the judge:

(A) imposed the conditions of bail or set the amount of bond required;

(B) is the chief judge of the circuit in which the defendant is to be tried;

(C) has been assigned to preside over the criminal trial of the defendant; or

(D) is the first appearance judge and was authorized by the judge initially setting or denying bail to modify or set conditions of release.

(2) Applications by the defendant for modification of bail on any felony charge must be heard by a court in person at a hearing, with the defendant present and with at least 3 hours' notice to the state attorney and county attorney, if bond forfeiture proceedings are handled by the county attorney. The state may apply for modification of bail by showing good cause and with at least 3 hours' notice to the attorney for the defendant.

(3) If any trial court fixes bail and refuses its reduction before trial, the defendant may institute habeas corpus proceedings seeking reduction of bail. If application is made to the supreme court or district court of appeal, notice and a copy of such application shall be given to the attorney general and the state attorney. Such proceedings shall be determined promptly.

(e) Bail Before Conviction; Condition of Undertaking.

(1) If a person is admitted to bail for appearance for a preliminary hearing or on a charge that a judge is empowered to try, the condition of the undertaking shall be that the person will appear for the hearing or to answer the charge and will submit to the orders and process of the judge trying the same and will not depart without leave.

(2) If a person is admitted to bail after being held to answer by a judge or after an indictment or information on which the person is to be tried has been filed, the condition of the undertaking shall be that the person will appear to answer the charges before the court in which he or she may be prosecuted and submit to the orders and process of the court and will not depart without leave.

(f) Revocation of Bail. The court in its discretion for good cause, any time after a defendant who is at large on bail appears for trial, may commit the defendant to the custody of the proper official to abide by the judgment, sentence, and any further order of the court.

(g) Arrest and Commitment by Court. The court in which the cause is pending may direct the arrest and commitment of the defendant who is at large on bail when:

(1) there has been a breach of the undertaking;

(2) it appears that the defendant's sureties or any of them are dead or cannot be found or are insufficient or have ceased to be residents of the state; or

(3) the court is satisfied that the bail should be increased or new or additional security required.

The order for the commitment of the defendant shall recite generally the facts on which it is based and shall direct that the defendant be arrested by any official authorized to make arrests and that the defendant be committed to the official in whose custody he or she would be if he or she had not been given bail, to be detained by such official until legally discharged. The defendant shall be arrested pursuant to such order on a certified copy thereof, in any county, in the same manner as on a warrant of arrest. If the order provided for is made because of the failure of the defendant to appear for judgment, the defendant shall be committed. If the order is made for any other cause, the court may determine the conditions of release, if any.

(h) Bail after Recommitment. If the defendant applies to be admitted to bail after recommitment, the court that recommitted the defendant shall determine conditions of release, if any, subject to the limitations of (b) above.

(i) Qualifications of Surety after Order of Recommitment. If the defendant offers bail after recommitment, each surety shall possess the qualifications and sufficiency and the bail shall be furnished in all respects in the manner prescribed for admission to bail before recommitment.

(j) Issuance of Capias; Bail Specified. On the filing of either an indictment or information charging the commission of a crime, if the person named therein is not in custody or at large on bail for the offense charged, the judge shall issue or shall direct the clerk to issue, either immediately or when so directed by the prosecuting attorney, a capias for the arrest of the person. If the person named in the indictment or information is a child and the child has been served with a promise to appear under the Florida Rules of Juvenile Procedure, capias need not be issued. Upon the filing of the indictment or information, the judge shall endorse the amount of bail, if any, and may authorize the setting or modification of bail by the judge presiding over the defendant's first appearance hearing. This endorsement shall be made on the capias and signed by the judge.

(k) Summons on Misdemeanor Charge. When a complaint is filed charging the commission of a misdemeanor only and the judge deems that process should issue as a result, or when an indictment or information on which the defendant is to be tried charging the commission of a misdemeanor only, and the person named in it is not in custody or at large on bail for the offense charged, the judge shall direct the clerk to issue a summons instead of a capias unless the judge has reasonable ground to believe that the person will not appear in response to a summons, in which event an arrest warrant or a capias shall be issued with the amount of bail endorsed on it. The summons shall state substantially the nature of the offense and shall command the person against whom the complaint was made to appear before the judge issuing the summons or the judge having jurisdiction of the offense at a time and place stated in it.

(*l*) Summons When Defendant Is Corporation. On the filing of an indictment or information or complaint charging a corporation with the commission of a crime, whether felony or misdemeanor, the judge shall direct the clerk to issue or shall issue a summons to secure its appearance to answer the charge. If, after being summoned, the corporation does not appear, a plea of not guilty shall be entered and trial and judgment shall follow without further process.

Amended Dec. 5, 1991, effective Dec. 15, 1991 (591 So.2d 173); Sept. 24, 1992, effective Jan. 1, 1993 (606 So.2d 227); Sept. 30, 2004, effective Oct. 1, 2004 (887 So.2d 1090); Feb. 1, 2007, effective Apr. 1, 2007 (948 So.2d 731); June 21, 2007 (959 So.2d 250); Nov. 19, 2009, effective Jan. 1, 2010 (26 So.3d 534).

Committee Notes

1968 Adoption. (a) Same as section 903.01, Florida Statutes.

(b) Same as section 903.04, Florida Statutes.

(c) Same as section 903.02, Florida Statutes.

(d) Same as section 903.12, Florida Statutes.

(e) Substantially same as section 903.13, Florida Statutes.

(f) Same as section 903.19, Florida Statutes.

(g) Same as section 918.01, Florida Statutes.

(h) Substantially same as section 903.23, Florida Statutes.

(i) Same as section 903.24, Florida Statutes.

(j) Same as section 903.25, Florida Statutes.

(k) and (*l*) Formerly rule 3.150(c). These proposals contain the essentials of present sections 907.01, 907.02, and 901.09(3), Florida Statutes, a change of some of the terminology being warranted for purpose of clarity.

(m) Formerly rule 3.150(c). This proposal contains all of the essentials of section 907.03, Florida Statutes, and that part of section 901. 14, Florida Statutes, pertaining to postindictment or postinformation procedure. A charge by affidavit is provided.

Although subdivision (g) is the same as section 918.01, Florida Statutes, its constitutionality was questioned by the subcommittee, constitutional right to bail and presumption of innocence.

1972 Amendment. Same as prior rule except (b), which is new. (k), (*l*), and (m) are taken from prior rule 3.150.

1977 Amendment. This proposal amends subdivision (b)(4) of the present rule [formerly rule 3.130(b)(4)] to expand the forms of pretrial release available to the judge. The options are the same as those available under the federal rules without the presumption in favor of release on personal recognizance or unsecured appearance.

This proposal leaves it to the sound discretion of the judge to determine the least onerous form of release which will still insure the defendant's appearance.

It also sets forth the specific factors the judge should take into account in making this determination.

1983 Amendment. Rule 3.131(d) is intended to replace former rule 3.130(f) and therefore contemplates all subsequent modifications of bail including all increases or reductions of monetary bail or any other changes sought by the state or by the defendant.

Court Comment

1977 Amendment. Subdivision (a) was repealed by Chapter 76–138, § 2, Laws of Florida, insofar as it was inconsistent with the provision of that statute. Subdivision (a) has been amended so as to comply with the legislative act.

Rule 3.132. Pretrial Detention

(a) Motion Filed at First Appearance. A person arrested for an offense for which detention may be ordered under section 907.041, Florida Statutes, shall be taken before a judicial officer for a first appearance within 24 hours of arrest. The state may file with the judicial officer at first appearance a motion seeking pretrial detention, signed by the state attorney or an assistant, setting forth with particularity the grounds and the essential facts on which pretrial detention is sought and certifying that the state attorney has received testimony under oath supporting the grounds and the essential facts alleged in the motion. If no such motion is filed, the judicial officer may inquire whether the state intends to file a motion for pretrial detention, and if so, grant the state no more than three days to file a motion under this subdivision. Upon a showing by the state of probable cause that the defendant committed the offense and exigent circumstances, the defendant shall be detained in custody pending the filing of the motion. If, after inquiry, the State indicates it does not intend to file a motion for pretrial detention, or fails to establish exigent circumstances for holding defendant in custody pending the filing of the motion, or files a motion that is facially insufficient, the judicial officer shall proceed to determine the conditions of release pursuant to the provisions of rule 3.131(b). If the motion for pretrial detention is facially sufficient, the judicial officer shall proceed to determine whether there is probable cause that the person committed the offense. If probable cause is found, the person may be detained in custody pending a final hearing on pretrial detention. If probable cause is established after first appearance pursuant to the provisions of rule 3.133 and the person has been released from custody, the person may be recommitted to custody pending a final hearing on pretrial detention.

(b) Motion Filed after First Appearance. A motion for pretrial detention may be filed at any time prior to trial. The motion shall be made to the court with trial jurisdiction. On receipt of a facially sufficient motion and a determination of probable cause, unless otherwise previously established, that an offense eligible for pretrial detention has been committed, the following shall occur:

(1) In the event of exigent circumstances, the court shall issue a warrant for the arrest of the named person, if the person has been released from custody. The person may be detained in custody pending a final hearing on pretrial detention.

(2) In the absence of exigent circumstances, the court shall order a hearing on the motion as provided in (c) below.

(c) Final Order.

(1) *Hearing Required.* A final order of pretrial detention shall be entered only after a hearing in the court of trial jurisdiction. The hearing shall be held within 5 days of the filing of the motion or the date of taking the person in custody pursuant to a motion for pretrial detention, whichever is later. The state attorney has the burden of showing beyond a reasonable doubt the need for pretrial detention pursuant to the criteria in section 907.041, Florida Statutes. The defendant may request a continuance. The state shall be entitled to 1 continuance for good cause. No continuance shall exceed 5 days unless there are extenuating circumstances. The defendant may be detained pending the hearing, but in no case shall the defendant be detained in excess of 10 days, unless the delay is sought by the defendant. The person sought to be detained is entitled to representation by counsel, to present witnesses and evidence, and to cross-examine witnesses. The court may admit relevant evidence and testimony under oath without complying with the rules of evidence, but evidence secured in violation of the United States Constitution or the Constitution of the State of Florida shall not be admissible. A final order of pretrial detention shall not be based exclusively on hearsay evidence. No testimony by the defendant shall be admissible to prove the guilt of the defendant at any other judicial proceeding, but may be admitted in an action for perjury based on the defendant's statements made at the pretrial detention hearing or for impeachment.

(2) *Findings and Conclusions to Be Recorded.* The court's pretrial detention order shall be based solely on evidence produced at the hearing and shall contain findings of fact and conclusions of law to

support it. The order shall be made either in writing or orally on the record. The court shall render its findings within 24 hours of the pretrial detention hearing.

(3) *Dissolution of Order.* The defendant shall be entitled to dissolution of the pretrial detention order whenever the court finds that a subsequent event has eliminated the basis for detention.

(4) *Further Proceedings on Order.* If any trial court enters a final order of pretrial detention, the defendant may obtain review by motion to the appropriate appellate court. If motion for review is taken to the supreme court or the district court of appeal, notice and a copy of the motion shall be served on the attorney general and the state attorney; if review is taken to the circuit court, service shall be on the state attorney.

Amended Sept. 24, 1992, effective Jan. 1, 1993 (606 So.2d 227); Feb. 1, 2007, effective Apr. 1, 2007 (948 So.2d 731); Sept. 17, 2009, effective Jan. 1, 2010 (19 So.3d 306).

Rule 3.133. Pretrial Probable Cause Determinations and Adversary Preliminary Hearings

(a) Nonadversary Probable Cause Determination.

(1) *Defendant in Custody.* In all cases in which the defendant is in custody, a nonadversary probable cause determination shall be held before a judge within 48 hours from the time of the defendant's arrest; provided, however, that this proceeding shall not be required when a probable cause determination has been previously made by a judge and an arrest warrant issued for the specific offense for which the defendant is charged. The judge after a showing of extraordinary circumstance may continue the proceeding for not more than 24 hours beyond the 48-hour period. The judge, after a showing that an extraordinary circumstance still exists, may continue the proceeding for not more than 24 additional hours following the expiration of the initial 24-hour continuance. This determination shall be made if the necessary proof is available at the time of the first appearance as required under rule 3.130, but the holding of this determination at that time shall not affect the fact that it is a nonadversary proceeding.

(2) *Defendant on Pretrial Release.* A defendant who has been released from custody before a probable cause determination is made and who is able to establish that the pretrial release conditions are a significant restraint on his or her liberty may file a written motion for a nonadversary probable cause determination setting forth with specificity the items of significant restraint that a finding of no probable cause would eliminate. The motion shall be filed within 21 days from the date of arrest, and notice shall be given to the state. A judge who finds significant restraints on the defendant's liberty shall make a probable cause determination within 7 days from the filing of the motion.

(3) *Standard of Proof.* Upon presentation of proof, the judge shall determine whether there is probable cause for detaining the arrested person pending further proceedings. The defendant need not be present. In determining probable cause to detain the defendant, the judge shall apply the standard for issuance of an arrest warrant, and the finding may be based on sworn complaint, affidavit, deposition under oath, or, if necessary, on testimony under oath properly recorded.

(4) *Action on Determination.* If probable cause is found, the defendant shall be held to answer the charges. If probable cause is not found or the specified time periods are not complied with, the defendant shall be released from custody unless an information or indictment has been filed, in which event the defendant shall be released on recognizance subject to the condition that he or she appear at all court proceedings or shall be released under a summons to appear before the appropriate court at a time certain. Any release occasioned by a failure to comply with the specified time periods shall be by order of the judge on a written application filed by the defendant with notice sent to the state or by a judge without a written application but with notice to the state. The judge shall order the release of the defendant after it is determined that the defendant is entitled to release and after the state has a reasonable period of time, not to exceed 24 hours, in which to establish probable cause. A release required by this rule does not void further prosecution by information or indictment but does prohibit any restraint on liberty other than appearing for trial. A finding that probable cause does or does not exist shall be made in writing, signed by the judge, and filed, together with the evidence of such probable cause, with the clerk of the court having jurisdiction of the offense for which the defendant is charged.

(b) Adversary Preliminary Hearing.

(1) *When Applicable.* A defendant who is not charged in an information or indictment within 21 days from the date of arrest or service of the capias on him or her shall have a right to an adversary preliminary hearing on any felony charge then pending against the defendant. The subsequent filing of an information or indictment shall not eliminate a defendant's entitlement to this proceeding.

(2) *Process.* The judge shall issue such process as may be necessary to secure attendance of witnesses within the state for the state or the defendant.

(3) *Witnesses.* All witnesses shall be examined in the presence of the defendant and may be cross-examined. Either party may request that the witnesses be sequestered. At the conclusion of the testimony for the prosecution, the defendant who so elects shall be sworn and testify in his or her own behalf, and in such cases the defendant shall be warned in advance of testifying that anything he or she may say can be used against him or her at a subsequent trial.

The defendant may be cross-examined in the same manner as other witnesses, and any witnesses offered by the defendant shall be sworn and examined.

(4) *Record.* At the request of either party, the entire preliminary hearing, including all testimony, shall be recorded verbatim stenographically or by mechanical means and at the request of either party shall be transcribed. If the record of the proceedings, or any part thereof, is transcribed at the request of the prosecuting attorney, a copy of this transcript shall be furnished free of cost to the defendant or the defendant's counsel.

(5) *Action on Hearing.* If from the evidence it appears to the judge that there is probable cause to believe that an offense has been committed and that the defendant has committed it, the judge shall cause the defendant to be held to answer to the circuit court; otherwise, the judge shall release the defendant from custody unless an information or indictment has been filed, in which event the defendant shall be released on recognizance subject to the condition that he or she appear at all court proceedings or shall be released under a summons to appear before the appropriate court at a time certain. Such release does not, however, void further prosecution by information or indictment but does prohibit any restraint on liberty other than appearing for trial. A finding that probable cause does or does not exist shall be made in writing, signed by the judge, and, together with the evidence received in the cause, shall be filed with the clerk of the circuit court.

(c) Additional Nonadversary Probable Cause Determinations and Preliminary Hearings. If there has been a finding of no probable cause at a nonadversary determination or adversary preliminary hearing, or if the specified time periods for holding a nonadversary probable cause determination have not been complied with, a judge may thereafter make a determination of probable cause at a nonadversary probable cause determination, in which event the defendant shall be retained in custody or returned to custody upon appropriate process issued by the judge. A defendant who has been retained in custody or returned to custody by such a determination shall be allowed an adversary preliminary hearing in all instances in which a felony offense is charged.

Amended Jan. 18, 1991, effective April 1, 1991 (573 So.2d 826); Sept. 24, 1992, effective Jan. 1, 1993 (606 So.2d 227); Dec. 23, 1993, effective Jan. 1, 1994 (630 So.2d 552); Sept. 30, 2004 (887 So.2d 1090).

Committee Notes

1968 Adoption. (Notes are to former rule 1.122.)

(a) Substantially the same as section 902.01, Florida Statutes; the word "examination" is changed to "hearing" to conform to modern terminology.

(b) through (j) Substantially the same as sections 902.02 through 902.10, 902.13, and 902.14, Florida Statutes, except for exchange of "hearing" for "examination."

(k) Parts of section 902.11, Florida Statutes, and all of section 902.12, Florida Statutes, were omitted because of conflict with case law: *Escobedo v. Illinois*, 378 U.S. 478, 84 S.Ct. 1758, 12 L.Ed.2d 977 (1964); *White v. Maryland*, 373 U.S. 59, 83 S.Ct. 1050, 10 L.Ed.2d 193 (1963).

(*l*) Taken from Federal Rule of Criminal Procedure 5(c). Previously Florida had no statute or rule defining what the magistrate should do at the conclusion of the preliminary hearing.

(m) Substantially the same as section 902.18, Florida Statutes, except "without delay" changed to "within 7 days." Some specific time limit was felt necessary because of frequent delay by magistrates while defendants remain in jail.

1972 Amendment. The ABA Standards on Pre-Trial Release provide for a person arrested to be taken before a committing magistrate without unreasonable delay for immediate judicial consideration of the release decision. The committee determined that, since a determination of probable cause at this immediate hearing presents difficult logistical problems for the state and defense counsel, the question of probable cause should be decided at a later preliminary hearing. For this reason, subdivisions (c), (d), and (e) of the former rule have been deleted in favor of the hearing provision now contained in rule 3.130.

(a) A revised version of former rule 3.122(a).

(b) New. Establishes the time period in which the preliminary hearing must take place.

(c)(1) Substantially the same as former rule 3.122(b). Amended to provide for advice of counsel relative to waiver and for written waiver.

(c)(2) Amended to delete provisions relating to recording of proceedings as same are now contained in subdivision (h).

(d) Same as prior rule 3.122(g).

(e) Same as prior rule 3.122(h).

(f) Substantially the same as prior rule 3.122(i); language modernized by slight changes.

(g) Same as prior rule 3.122(j).

(h) New rule to provide for record of proceedings.

(i) Same as prior rule 3.122(*l*).

(j) Substantially the same as prior rule 3.122(m). Time period for transmission of papers is reduced. (2) provides for transmission of any transcript of proceedings.

1977 Amendment. The rule corrects several deficiencies in the prior rule:

(1) In the prior rule no specific mechanism was provided to effect the release which is allowed. This revision provides such a mechanism and coordinates the mechanism with the additional procedures created by subdivision (c).

(2) Once a determination of no probable cause was made and the defendant was released, no method was provided for reversing the process in those instances in which the determination is palpably in error or in instances in which it is later possible to establish probable cause.

(3) The prior rule allowed the unconditioned release of a defendant without the possibility of recapture simply because of a technical failure to abide by the rather arbitrary time limits established for the conduct of a nonadversary probable cause determination and regardless of the ability to establish probable cause. The new rule allows a determination or redetermination of probable cause to be made in instances in which to do so is sensible. The defendant is protected by the provision allowing an adversary preliminary hearing as a check against any possible abuse.

Court Comment

1975 Amendment. This is a complete rewrite of the preliminary hearing rule.

Rule 3.134. Time for Filing Formal Charges

The state shall file formal charges on defendants in custody by information, or indictment, or in the case of alleged misdemeanors by whatever documents constitute a formal charge, within 30 days from the date on which the defendants are arrested or from the date of the service of capiases upon them. If the defendants remain uncharged, the court on the 30th day and with notice to the state shall:

(1) Order that the defendants automatically be released on their own recognizance on the 33rd day unless the state files formal charges by that date; or

(2) If good cause is shown by the state, order that the defendants automatically be released on their own recognizance on the 40th day unless the state files formal charges by that date.

In no event shall any defendants remain in custody beyond 40 days unless they have been formally charged with a crime.

Added Jan. 18, 1991, effective April 1, 1991 (573 So.2d 826).

Rule 3.140. Indictments; Informations

(a) Methods of Prosecution.

(1) *Capital Crimes.* An offense that may be punished by death shall be prosecuted by indictment.

(2) *Other Crimes.* The prosecution of all other criminal offenses shall be as follows:

In circuit courts and county courts, prosecution shall be solely by indictment or information, except that prosecution in county courts for violations of municipal ordinances and metropolitan county ordinances may be by affidavit or docket entries and prosecutions for misdemeanors, municipal ordinances, and county ordinances may be by notice to appear issued and served pursuant to rule 3.125. A grand jury may indict for any offense. When a grand jury returns an indictment for an offense not triable in the circuit court, the circuit judge shall either issue a summons returnable in the county court or shall bail the accused for trial in the county court, and the judge, or at the judge's direction, the clerk of the circuit court, shall certify the indictment and file it in the records of the county court.

(b) Nature of Indictment or Information. The indictment or information on which the defendant is to be tried shall be a plain, concise, and definite written statement of the essential facts constituting the offense charged.

(c) Caption, Commencement, Date, and Personal Statistics.

(1) *Caption.* No formal caption is essential to the validity of an indictment or information on which the defendant is to be tried. Upon objection made as to its absence a caption shall be prefixed in substantially the following manner:

In the (name of court)

State of Florida versus (name of defendant)

or, in the case of municipal ordinance cases in county court,

City of ________ / ________ County versus (name of defendant).

Any defect, error, or omission in a caption may be amended as of course,at any stage of the proceeding, whether before or after a plea to the merits, by court order.

(2) *Commencement.* All indictments or informations on which the defendant is to be tried shall expressly state that the prosecution is brought in the name and by the authority of the State of Florida. Indictments shall state that the defendant is charged by the grand jury of the county. Informations shall state that the appropriate prosecuting attorney makes the charge.

(3) *Date.* Every indictment or information on which the defendant is to be tried shall bear the date (day, month, year) that it is filed in each court in which it is so filed.

(4) *Personal Statistics.* Every indictment or information shall include the defendant's race, gender, and date of birth when any of these facts are known. Failure to include these facts shall not invalidate an otherwise sufficient indictment or information.

(d) The Charge.

(1) *Allegation of Facts; Citation of Law Violated.* Each count of an indictment or information on which the defendant is to be tried shall allege the essential facts constituting the offense charged. In addition, each count shall recite the official or customary citation of the statute, rule, regulation, or other provision of law that the defendant is alleged to have violated. Error in or omission of the citation shall not be ground for dismissing the count or for a reversal of a conviction based thereon if the error or omission did not mislead the defendant to the defendant's prejudice.

(2) *Name of Accused.* The name of the accused person shall be stated, if known, and if not known, the

person may be described by any name or description by which the person can be identified with reasonable certainty. If the grand jury, prosecuting attorney, or affiant making the charge does not know either the name of the accused or any name or description by which the accused can be identified with reasonable certainty, the indictment or information, as the case may be, shall so allege and the accused may be charged by a fictitious name.

(3) *Time and Place.* Each count of an indictment or information on which the defendant is to be tried shall contain allegations stating as definitely as possible the time and place of the commission of the offense charged in the act or transaction or on 2 or more acts or transactions connected together, provided the court in which the indictment or information is filed has jurisdiction to try all of the offenses charged.

(4) *Allegation of Intent to Defraud.* If an intent to defraud is required as an element of the offense to be charged, it shall be sufficient to allege an intent to defraud, without naming therein the particular person or body corporate intended to be defrauded.

(e) Incorporation by Reference. Allegations made in 1 count shall not be incorporated by reference in another count.

(f) Endorsement and Signature; Indictment. An indictment shall be signed by the foreperson or the acting foreperson of the grand jury returning it. The state attorney or acting state attorney or an assistant state attorney shall make and sign a statement on the indictment to the effect that he or she has advised the grand jury returning the indictment as authorized and required by law. No objection to the indictment on the ground that the statement has not been made shall be entertained after the defendant pleads to the merits.

(g) Signature, Oath, and Certification; Information. An information charging the commission of a felony shall be signed by the state attorney, or a designated assistant state attorney, under oath stating his or her good faith in instituting the prosecution and certifying that he or she has received testimony under oath from the material witness or witnesses for the offense. An information charging the commission of a misdemeanor shall be signed by the state attorney, or a designated assistant state attorney, under oath stating his or her good faith in instituting the prosecution. No objection to an information on the ground that it was not signed or verified, as herein provided, shall be entertained after the defendant pleads to the merits.

(h) Conclusion. An indictment or information on which the defendant is to be tried need contain no formal conclusion.

(i) Surplusage. An unnecessary allegation may be disregarded as surplusage and, on motion of the defendant, may be stricken from the pleading by the court.

(j) Amendment of Information. An information on which the defendant is to be tried that charges an offense may be amended on the motion of the prosecuting attorney or defendant at any time prior to trial because of formal defects.

(k) Form of Certain Allegations. Allegations concerning the following items may be alleged as indicated below:

(1) *Description of Written Instruments.* Instruments consisting wholly or in part of writing or figures, pictures, or designs may be described by any term by which they are usually known or may be identified, without setting forth a copy or facsimile thereof.

(2) *Words; Pictures.* Necessary averments relative to spoken or written words or pictures may be made by the general purport of such words or pictures without setting forth a copy or facsimile thereof.

(3) *Judgments; Determinations; Proceedings.* A judgment, determination, or proceeding of any court or official, civil or military, may be alleged generally in such a manner as to identify the judgment, determination, or proceeding, without alleging facts conferring jurisdiction on the court or official.

(4) *Exceptions; Excuses; Provisos.* Statutory exceptions, excuses, or provisos relative to offenses created or defined by statute need not be negatived by allegation.

(5) *Alternative or Disjunctive Allegations.* For an offense that may be committed by doing 1 or more of several acts, or by 1 or more of several means, or with 1 or more of several intents or results, it is permissible to allege in the disjunctive or alternative such acts, means, intents, or results.

(6) *Offenses Divided into Degrees.* For an offense divided into degrees it is sufficient to charge the commission of the offense without specifying the degree.

(7) *Felonies.* It shall not be necessary to allege that the offense charged is a felony or was done feloniously.

(*l*) Custody of Indictment or Information. Unless the defendant named therein has been previously released on a citation, order to appear, personal recognizance, or bail, or has been summoned to appear, or unless otherwise ordered by the court having jurisdiction, all indictments or informations and the records thereof shall be in the custody of the clerk of the court to which they are presented and shall not be inspected by any person other than the judge, clerk, attorney general, and prosecuting attorney until the defendant is in custody or until 1 year has elapsed between the return of an indictment or the filing of an information, after which time they shall be opened for public inspection.

(m) Defendant's Right to Copy of Indictment or Information. Each person who has been indicted or informed against for an offense shall, on application to the clerk, be furnished a copy of the indictment or information and the endorsements thereon, at least 24 hours before being required to plead to the indictment or information if a copy has not been so furnished. A failure to furnish a copy shall not affect the validity of any subsequent proceeding against the defendant if he or she pleads to the indictment or information.

(n) Statement of Particulars. The court, on motion, shall order the prosecuting attorney to furnish a statement of particulars when the indictment or information on which the defendant is to be tried fails to inform the defendant of the particulars of the offense sufficiently to enable the defendant to prepare a defense. The statement of particulars shall specify as definitely as possible the place, date, and all other material facts of the crime charged that are specifically requested and are known to the prosecuting attorney, including the names of persons intended to be defrauded. Reasonable doubts concerning the construction of this rule shall be resolved in favor of the defendant.

(*o*) Defects and Variances. No indictment or information, or any count thereof, shall be dismissed or judgment arrested, or new trial granted on account of any defect in the form of the indictment or information or of misjoinder of offenses or for any cause whatsoever, unless the court shall be of the opinion that the indictment or information is so vague, indistinct, and indefinite as to mislead the accused and embarrass him or her in the preparation of a defense or expose the accused after conviction or acquittal to substantial danger of a new prosecution for the same offense.

Amended May 28, 1992 (603 So.2d 1144); Sept. 24, 1992, effective Jan. 1, 1993 (606 So.2d 227); Nov. 3, 2011, effective, *nunc pro tunc*, Oct. 1, 2011 (78 So.3d 1045); Nov. 8, 2012, effective Jan. 1, 2013 (104 So.3d 304).

Committee Notes

1968 Adoption. Introductory Statement: The contention may be made that the authority of the Supreme Court of Florida to govern practice and procedure in all courts by court rule does not include the power to vary in any way from present statutory law governing the work product of the grand jury, viz., the indictment. Such a contention must, of necessity, be based in part, at least, upon the assumption that the grand jury is not an integral part of the judicial system of Florida but is a distinct entity which serves that system. The Supreme Court of Florida, in State v. Clemons, 150 So.2d 231 (Fla.1963), seems to have taken a position contrary to such an assumption.

Regardless of whether such a contention is valid, it seems beyond controversy that the essentials of the indictment, as in the case of an information, are so intimately associated with practice and procedure in the courts that the individual or group having the responsibility of determining its makeup and use is thus empowered to govern a substantial segment of such practice and procedure. The conclusion seems to be inescapable, therefore, that, since the constitution grants to the supreme court authority over this phase of the judicial scheme, the following material is appropriate for consideration as a part of the proposed rules:

(a)(1) *Capital Crimes.* This recommendation is consistent with present Florida law. See § 10 DR, Fla. Const. (1885, as amended) (now Art. I, § 15, Fla. Const. (1968 as amended)); § 904.01, Fla.Stat. (1963). The terminology "which may be punished by death" is deemed preferable to the terminology "capital crime" of the constitution and "capital offenses" of the statute because of its definitive nature. The recommended terminology is utilized in Federal Rule of Criminal Procedure 7(a) and in the American Law Institute's Code of Criminal Procedure, section 115. The terminology used in the 1963 Code of Criminal Procedure of Illinois is "when death is a possible punishment." See § 110–4.

Section 10, DR, Florida Constitution, provides: "No person shall be tried for a capital crime unless on presentment or indictment by a grand jury." No provision is made in the recommendation for prosecution by presentment. This omission is consistent with the apparent legislative construction placed on this section. Section 904.01, Florida Statutes, provides "All capital offenses shall be tried by indictment by a grand jury." Since presentments traditionally have not been used as trial accusatorial writs in Florida, there seems little reason, at this date, to question that the constitution authorizes the implementing authority, be it the legislature or the supreme court, to use one of the specified methods of prosecution to the exclusion of the other.

(a)(2) *Other Crimes.* In criminal courts of record and the Court of Record of Escambia County, the constitution of Florida requires that prosecutions be by information. (§§ 9(5) & 10, Art. V). In county judges' courts having elective prosecuting attorneys, present statutory law permits prosecutions by indictment (§ 904.02) and affidavit (Ch. 937). The additional method of prosecution by information is provided as a step toward attaining uniformity with other courts in the prosecution of noncapital offenses, at least to the extent that a prosecutor desires to use an information. This addition involved consideration of whether a nonelected prosecutor serving in a county judge's court, which often is the case, has the authority to use an information as an accusatorial writ. Since this question has not been definitely resolved under present law, caution dictated the specification that the prosecuting attorney be elected as a prerequisite to the use of an information.

In all courts not hereinabove mentioned that have elective prosecuting attorneys, trial by indictment or information is consistent with present Florida constitutional law and most of the statutory law. (See § 10, DR, Fla. Const., §§ 904.01 & 904.02, Fla.Stat.; cf. § 932.56, where an affidavit may be used in cases appealed from a justice of the peace court and which is tried de novo in a circuit court.) In specially created courts having elective prosecutors and which are not otherwise provided for in foregoing provisions of this rule, it was felt that prosecution by indictment or information should be allowed, even though present statutory authority may limit prosecutions in such courts to the use of an information, e.g., the Court of Record of Alachua County.

In courts not having elective prosecutors, prosecution by information is not recommended because of the aforementioned doubt as to the authority of a nonelected prosecutor to use an information as an accusatorial writ. With reference to the present court structure of Florida this part of the proposal applies only to county judges' courts and justice of the peace courts. The only variation from present procedure contemplated by this part of the proposal is the use of an indictment as a basis for prosecution in a justice of the peace court.

Under this proposal a grand jury may indict for any criminal offense. This recommendation is based on the premise that a grand jury's power to indict should not be limited by virtue of levels in a state court structure. A grand jury should be considered as a guardian of the public peace against all criminal activity and should be in a position to act directly with reference thereto. While practicalities dictate that most non-capital felonies and misdemeanors will be tried by information or affidavit, if appropriate, even if an indictment is permissible as an alternative procedure, it is well to retain the grand jury's check on prosecutors in this area of otherwise practically unrestricted discretion.

The procedure proposed for the circuit judge to follow if a grand jury returns an indictment for an offense not triable in the circuit court applies, with appropriate variations, much of the procedure presently used when a grand jury returns an indictment triable in a criminal court of record. See § 32.18, Fla.Stat.

(b) Nature of Indictment or Information. This provision appears in rule 7(c) of the Rules of Criminal Procedure for the United States District Court (hereafter referred to as the federal rules for purposes of brevity). It may be deemed appropriate for incorporation into the recommendations since it preserves to the defendant expressly the right to a formal written accusation and at the same time permits the simplification of the form of the accusation and the elimination of unnecessary phraseology.

(c) Caption, Commencement, and Date.

(1) *Caption.* Section 906.02, Florida Statutes, contains the essentials of this proposal. It is well settled at common law that the caption is no part of the indictment and that it may be amended. The caption may be considered as serving the purpose of convenience by making more readily identifiable a particular accusatorial writ. The proposal makes it possible for this convenience to be served if either party wishes it, yet does not provide that the caption be a matter of substance. The essentials of this recommendation also appear in section 149 of the American Law Institute's Code of Criminal Procedure.

(2) *Commencement.* This proposal apparently is directly contrary to section 906.02(1), Florida Statutes, which treats the caption and the commencement in the same manner, i.e., that neither is necessary to the validity of the indictment or information but may be present as mere matters of convenience. This legislative assumption may not be a correct one and caution dictates that a meaningful commencement be included. Section 20, article V, of the Constitution of Florida provides that the style of all process shall be: " 'The State of Florida' and all prosecutions shall be conducted in the name and by the authority of the State." As contemplated in the proposal, the commencement expressly states the sovereign authority by which the accusatorial writ is issued and the agent of that authority. Section 906.02(2), Florida Statutes, seems to contemplate that there will be included in the indictment an express provision concerning the agency of the state responsible for its presentation, viz., the grand jury, by stating, "It is unnecessary to allege that the grand jurors were empaneled, sworn or charged, or that they present the indictment upon their oaths or affirmations." The American Law Institute's commentary on the commencement (A.L.I. Code of Criminal Procedure, p. 529 et seq.) indicates that there is much confusion between what information should be in the commencement as distinguished from the caption.

(3) *Date.* Since in many cases the beginning of the prosecution is co-existent with the issuance of the indictment or information, the date the writ bears may be of great significance, particularly with reference to the tolling of a statute of limitations. If the date of a grand jury's vote of a true bill or a prosecutor's making oath to an information differs from the date of filing of the indictment or information with the appropriate clerk, it seems the date of filing is the preferable date for a writ to bear since until the filing transpires there is no absolute certainty that the prosecution actually will leave the province of the grand jury or prosecutor.

(d) The Charge.

(1) *Allegation of Facts; Citation of Law Violated.* This proposal is consistent with various sections of chapter 906, Florida Statutes, in that the charge is adequately alleged when based on the essentials of the offense; surplusage should be guarded against. The citation of the law allegedly violated contributes to defining the charge and conserves time in ascertaining the exact nature of the charge. The 1963 Illinois Criminal Code, section 111–3(a)(2), and Federal Rule of Criminal Procedure 7(c) contain similar provisions.

(2) *Name of Accused.* The provision concerning the method of stating the name of the accused is consistent with the very elaborate section 906.08, Florida Statutes, which seems unnecessarily long. It is deemed desirable that when a fictitious name is used the necessity therefor should be indicated by allegation.

(3) *Time and Place.* This provision is consistent with present Florida law. (See Morgan v. State, 51 Fla. 76, 40 So. 828 (1906), as to "time"; see Rimes v. State, 101 Fla. 1322, 133 So. 550 (1931), as to "place".) The provision is patterned after section 111–3(4) of the 1963 Illinois Code of Criminal Procedure.

(4) *Joinder of Offenses.* The essence of this proposal is presently found in section 906.25, Florida Statutes, federal rule 8(a), and section 111–4(a) of the 1963 Illinois Code of Criminal Procedure.

(5) *Joinder of Defendants.* This proposal is taken from federal rule 8(b). Its substance also appears in section 111–4(b) of the Illinois Code of Criminal Procedure. Although section 906.25, Florida Statutes, does not expressly contain this provision, there is little doubt that its broad language includes it.

(6) *Allegation of Intent to Defraud.* The language of this proposal presently appears in section 906.18, Florida Statutes, except for the provision concerning affidavit. Its continuation seems advisable as an aid to drawing allegations in charging instruments, although such information if known to the prosecutor may be required to be given in a bill of particulars upon motion of the defendant. (See subdivision (n) of this rule.) At times such information may be unknown to the prosecutor. A part of the statute is purposely not included in the proposal. The excluded part states "and on the trial it shall be sufficient, and shall not be deemed a variance, if there appear to be an intent to defraud the United States or any state, county, city, town or parish, or any body corporate, or any public officer in his official capacity, or any copartnership or members thereof, or any particular person." It seems that this part of the statute is stated in terms of the law of evidence rather than practice and procedure and should not be included in the rules, although apparently being a logical conclusion from the part included in the proposal.

(e) Incorporation by Reference. Although provision for incorporation by reference appears in federal rule 7(c), the prohibition of such incorporation is recommended with the thought that even though repetition may be minimized by incorporation, confusion, vagueness, and misunderstanding may be fostered by such procedure.

(f) Endorsement and Signature; Indictment. The requirement that the indictment be endorsed "A true bill" and be signed by the foreman or acting foreman of the grand jury presently appears in section 905.23, Florida Statutes. There apparently is no valid reason for changing this requirement since it serves the useful purpose of lending authenticity to the indictment as a legal product of the grand jury. The requirement of the foreman's signature also appears in federal rule 6(c), 1963, Illinois CCP section 111–3(b), and A.L.I. Model Code of Criminal Procedure section 125.

The provision pertaining to the statement and signature of the prosecuting attorney varies from present Florida law and is offered in alternative form. Florida statutes presently provide that an indictment shall be signed by a state attorney (§§ 27.21 & 27.22). Federal rule 7(c) also provides for the signature of the attorney for the government.

No requirement presently is made in Florida necessitating an express explanatory statement preceding such signature. Presumably the justification for the signature appears in the Florida statutes that require the aforementioned officers to wait upon the grand jury as advisors, as examiners of witnesses, and to draw indictments. (See §§ 905.16, 905.17, 905.19, 905.22, 27.02, 27.16, 27.21, & 27.22, Fla.Stat.)

Vagueness remains concerning the significance of the signature, however. Since the prosecuting attorney cannot be present while the grand jury is deliberating or voting (see section 905.17, Florida Statutes) and has no voice in the decision of whether an indictment is found (see section 905.26, Florida Statutes), a logical question arises concerning the necessity for the prosecuting attorney's signature on the indictment. The provision for the statement is made for the purpose of clarifying the reason for the signature.

(g) Signature, Oath, and Certification; Information. Section 10, DR, Florida Constitution, requires that informations be under oath of the prosecuting attorney of the court in which the information is filed. Article V, section 9(5), Florida Constitution, contains the same requirement concerning informations filed by the prosecuting attorney in a criminal court of record. This proposal also does not deviate from present Florida statutory law as found in section 906.04, Florida Statutes. This statute has received judicial approval. (See Champlin v. State, 122 So.2d 412 (Fla. 2d DCA 1960).) It should be noted here that the prosecutor's statement under oath is defined as to the purpose served by the signature.

(h) Conclusion. A similar provision currently appears in section 906.03, Florida Statutes, and should be included in the rules because of its tendency to minimize unnecessary statements in accusatorial writs. Provision is added for the affidavit as an accusatorial writ.

(i) Surplusage. The first part of the proposal, providing for the disregarding of unnecessary allegations as surplusage, is similar to section 906.24, Florida Statutes. The part concerned with striking such material is patterned after federal rule 7(d). The parts are properly complementary.

(j) Amendment of Information. This proposal contains no provision for an amendment of an indictment since, presumably, a grand jury may not amend an indictment which it has returned and which is pending, although it may return another indictment and the first indictment may be disposed of by a nolle prosequi. (See 17 Fla.Jur. Indictments and Informations, 9 (1958).) A federal indictment cannot be amended without reassembling the grand jury (see Ex parte Bain, 121 U.S. 1 (1887)); consequently the federal rules contain no provision for the amendment of an indictment. (It may be that the Supreme Court of Florida will feel inclined to include in the rules an express statement concerning amendments of an indictment. None is included here, however.)

The proposal is patterned after section 111–5 of the 1963 Illinois Code of Criminal Procedure, with one exception. The exception arises due to the fact that the Illinois Code provision applies to indictments as well as informations, the position in Illinois apparently being assumed that an indictment may be amended, at least with reference to specified items listed in the statute, as well as other formalities.

(k) Form of Certain Allegations. Several statutes in chapter 906, Florida Statutes, are concerned with the manner of making allegations in indictments and informations. Some of these sections are of such general application that it seems advisable to include their substance in the rules; others are so restricted that it may be deemed appropriate to recommend other disposition of them.

The proposals made in (1) through (7) here are based on the substance of the designated Florida statutes:

Proposal (1): section 906.09.

Proposal (2): section 906.10.

Proposal (3): section 906.11.

Proposal (4): section 906.12.

Proposal (5): section 906.13.

Proposal (6): section 906.23.

Proposal (7): section 906.17.

(*l*) Custody and Inspection. The proposal is taken verbatim from section 906.27, Florida Statutes. The necessity for specific provision for the custody and inspection of accusatorial writs seems to be proper to include here.

(m) Defendant's Right to Copy of Indictment or Information. The procedure contained in this proposal is presently required under section 906.28, Florida Statutes, and seems to be unobjectionable.

(n) Statement of Particulars. The phrase, "bill of particulars," has been modernized by changing "bill" to "statement." Historically, a "bill" is a written statement. The first sentence of this proposal is taken from section 906.27, Florida Statutes, the only change being the narrowing of the scope of the judicial discretion now granted by the statute. The latter part of the proposal is recommended in order to clarify the requirements of the rule. Provision for the accusatorial affidavit has been added.

(*o*) Defects and Variances. This proposal presently appears in Florida law in the form of section 906.25, Florida Statutes. The statute has been the object of much judicial construction and it seems inadvisable to divide it into parts merely for convenience in placing these parts under more appropriate titles, such as "Pre–Trial Motions," "Motion for New Trial," etc.

The intimate relation the statute has with indictments and informations justifies its inclusion here. The useful purposes served by the court constructions dictate the use of the statutory language without change.

1972 Amendment. Substantially the same as prior rule. References to trial by affidavit have been deleted throughout this rule and all Florida Rules of Criminal Procedure because of the passage of the 1972 amendment to article V of the Florida Constitution.

(a)(2) Amended to refer only to circuit courts and county courts. Reference to trial of vehicular traffic offenses transferred to rule 3.010 and made applicable to all rules of criminal procedure.

Former rule (d)(4) and (d)(5) transferred to new rule 3.150. Former rule (d)(6) renumbered as (d)(4).

1973 Amendment. The purpose of the amendment is to provide the same method for prosecution of violations of metropolitan county ordinances as for violations of municipal ordinances.

Rule 3.150. Joinder of Offenses and Defendants

(a) Joinder of Offenses. Two or more offenses that are triable in the same court may be charged in the same indictment or information in a separate count for each offense, when the offenses, whether felonies or misdemeanors, or both, are based on the same act or transaction or on 2 or more connected acts or transactions.

(b) Joinder of Defendants. Two or more defendants may be charged in the same indictment or information on which they are to be tried when:

(1) each defendant is charged with accountability for each offense charged;

(2) each defendant is charged with conspiracy and some of the defendants are also charged with 1 or more offenses alleged to have been committed in furtherance of the conspiracy; or

(3) even if conspiracy is not charged and all defendants are not charged in each count, it is alleged that the several offenses charged were part of a common scheme or plan.

Such defendants may be charged in 1 or more counts together or separately, and all of the defendants need not be charged in each count.

(c) Joint Representation. When 2 or more defendants have been jointly charged under rule 3.150(b) or have been joined for trial and are represented by the same attorney or by attorneys who are associated in the practice of law, the court shall, as soon as practicable, inquire into such joint representation and shall personally advise each defendant of the right to effective assistance of counsel, including separate representation. The court shall take such measures as are necessary to protect each defendant's right to counsel.

Amended Sept. 24, 1992, effective Jan. 1, 1993 (606 So.2d 227); Oct. 7, 2004, effective Jan. 1, 2005 (886 So.2d 197).

Committee Notes

1968 Adoption. (Notes are to rule 1.140(d)(4) and (5).)

(4) *Joinder of Offenses.* The essence of this proposal is presently found in section 906.25, Florida Statutes, federal rule 8(a), and section 111–4(a) of the 1963 Illinois Code of Criminal Procedure.

(5) *Joinder of Defendants.* This proposal is taken from federal rule 8(b). Its substance also appears in section 111–4(b) of the Illinois Code of Criminal Procedure. While section 906.25, Florida Statutes, does not expressly contain this provision, there is little doubt that its broad language includes it.

1972 Amendment. Provisions of former rule 3.150 are transferred to and incorporated in rule 3.130, Pretrial Release.

(a) Substantially the same as former rule 3.140(d)(4) except that it omits proviso that the court have jurisdiction to try all offenses charged. The proviso seems redundant.

(b) Substantially the same as ABA Standard 1.2 of ABA Standards Relating to Joinder and Severance but omits subparagraph (c)(2) which would permit joinder of charges "so closely connected in respect to time, place, and occasion that it would be difficult to separate proof of one charge from proof of the others." The ABA commentary on this standard concedes that in such cases the chances are considerable that defendants would have a right to severance. Difficulty of separating proof is a good reason for denying a right to join charges. The committee is of the opinion that defendants not connected in the commission of an act and not connected by conspiracy or by common scheme or plan should not, under any circumstances, be joined. The suggested rule omits the provision of former rule 3.140(d)(4) permitting joinder of 2 or more defendants in a single indictment or information, if they are alleged to have participated in the same series of acts or transactions constituting more than 1 offense. If all defendants participated in a series of connected acts or transactions constituting 2 or more offenses, the offenses can be joined under rule 3.150(a).

The last sentence of the suggested rule is the last sentence of former rule 3.140(d)(5).

2004 Amendment. This rule is intended to provide a uniform procedure for judges to follow when codefendants are represented by the same attorney, by the same law firm, or by attorneys who are associated in the practice of law. This provision is substantially derived from Rule 44, Fed. R. Crim. P. See also *Larzelere v. State*, 676 So. 2d 394 (Fla. 1996).

Court Commentary

2004 Amendment. Like Federal Rule of Criminal Procedure 44(c), new subdivision (c) does not specify the particular measures that the court must take to protect a defendant's right to counsel. Because the measures that will best protect a defendant's right to counsel can vary from case to case, this determination is left within the court's discretion. One possible course of action is to advise the defendant of the possible conflict of interest that could arise from dual representation and to obtain a voluntary, knowing, and intelligent waiver of the right to obtain separate representation. *See Larzelere v. State*, 676 So. 2d 394 (Fla. 1996). Another option is to require separate representation. See Fed. R. Crim. P. 44(c) advisory committee notes 1979 amendment.

Rule 3.151. Consolidation of Related Offenses

(a) Related Offenses. For purposes of these rules, 2 or more offenses are related offenses if they are triable in the same court and are based on the same act or transaction or on 2 or more connected acts or transactions.

(b) Consolidation of Indictments or Informations. Two or more indictments or informations charging related offenses shall be consolidated for trial on a timely motion by a defendant or by the state. The procedure thereafter shall be the same as if the prosecution were under a single indictment or information. Failure to timely move for consolidation constitutes a waiver of the right to consolidation.

(c) Dismissal of Related Offenses after Trial. When a defendant has been tried on a charge of 1 of 2 or more related offenses, the charge of every other related offense shall be dismissed on the defendant's motion unless a motion by the defendant for consolidation of the charges has been previously denied, or unless the defendant has waived the right to consolidation, or unless the prosecution has been unable, by due diligence, to obtain sufficient evidence to warrant charging the other offense or offenses.

(d) Plea. A defendant may plead guilty or nolo contendere to a charge of 1 offense on the condition that other charges of related offenses be dismissed or that no charges of other related offenses be instituted. Should the court find that the condition cannot be fulfilled, the plea shall be considered withdrawn.

Amended Sept. 24, 1992, effective Jan. 1, 1993 (606 So.2d 227).

Committee Notes

1968 Adoption. This rule is almost the same as federal rule 13, with provisions added for trial by affidavit.

1972 Amendment. (a) To same general effect as ABA Standard with changes to conform to rules 3.150(a) and 3.190(k).

(b) Limits motion for consolidation to defendant and provides that defendant waives his or her right to consolidation by failing to file a timely motion. Under standards relating to joinder of offenses and defendants, the prosecution may avoid the necessity for consolidation by charging offenses and defendants in a single indictment or information where consolidation is permissible. Omits provision of ABA Standard authorizing denial of consolidation if prosecuting attorney does not have "sufficient evidence to warrant trying" 1 of the "offenses" or if the court finds that the ends of justice would be defeated by consolidation. The lack of "sufficient evidence to warrant" trial of 1 of several charges of "related offenses" would be quite rare. In the rare case in which there is such a lack of evidence, the appropriate remedy would be a motion for continuance of all pending charges of related offenses, showing that the lack of evidence could probably be cured by a reasonable delay. The committee does not favor separate trials of charges of related offenses over the defendant's objection.

(c) Florida has no similar rule. Omits exception in ABA Standard in case "the prosecuting attorney did not have sufficient evidence to warrant trying (the) offense" or upon a finding that "the ends of justice would be defeated if the motion was granted." See comment on (b). The rule is not intended to restrict defendant's substantive rights.

(d) Florida has no similar rule. The first sentence of ABA Standard is considered by the committee to state a rule of substantive law and is omitted as unnecessary.

1977 Amendment. The changes from the prior rule are intended to provide equal treatment for both the state and the defendant.

Rule 3.152. Severance of Offenses and Defendants

(a) Severance of Offenses.

(1) In case 2 or more offenses are improperly charged in a single indictment or information, the defendant shall have a right to a severance of the charges on timely motion.

(2) In case 2 or more charges of related offenses are joined in a single indictment or information, the court nevertheless shall grant a severance of charges on motion of the state or of a defendant:

(A) before trial on a showing that the severance is appropriate to promote a fair determination of the defendant's guilt or innocence of each offense; or

(B) during trial, only with defendant's consent, on a showing that the severance is necessary to achieve a fair determination of the defendant's guilt or innocence of each offense.

(b) Severance of Defendants.

(1) On motion of the state or a defendant, the court shall order a severance of defendants and separate trials:

(A) before trial, on a showing that the order is necessary to protect a defendant's right to a speedy trial, or is appropriate to promote a fair determination of the guilt or innocence of 1 or more defendants; or

(B) during trial, only with defendant's consent and on a showing that the order is necessary to achieve a fair determination of the guilt or innocence of 1 or more defendants.

(2) If a defendant moves for a severance of defendants on the ground that an oral or written statement of a codefendant makes reference to him or her but is not admissible against him or her, the court shall determine whether the state will offer evidence of the statement at the trial. If the state intends to offer the statement in evidence, the court shall order the state to submit its evidence of the statement for consideration by the court and counsel for defendants and if the court determines that the statement is not admissible against the moving defendant, it shall require the state to elect 1 of the following courses:

(A) a joint trial at which evidence of the statement will not be admitted;

(B) a joint trial at which evidence of the statement will be admitted after all references to the moving defendant have been deleted, provided the court determines that admission of the evidence with deletions will not prejudice the moving defendant; or

(C) severance of the moving defendant.

(3) In cases in which, at the close of the state's case or at the close of all of the evidence, the evidence is not sufficient to support a finding that allegations on which the joinder of a defendant is based have been proved, the court shall, on motion of that defendant, grant a severance unless the court finds that severance is unnecessary to achieve a fair determination of that defendant's guilt or innocence.

Amended Sept. 24, 1992, effective Jan. 1, 1993 (606 So.2d 227).

Committee Notes

1968 Adoption. This subdivision rewords and adds to federal rule 14. It covers subject matter of section 918.02, Florida Statutes.

1972 Amendment. (a)(1) Severance on timely motion by defendant is mandatory if multiple offenses are improperly joined.

(a)(2) Provides for severance of offenses before trial on showing that severance will promote a fair determination of guilt or innocence substantially as provided by former rule 3.190(j)(2) and, unlike any Florida rule, distinguishes motion during trial.

(b)(1) Based on ABA Standard 2.3(b). Expands rule 3.190(j) to include defendant's right to speedy trial as ground for severance and, unlike any Florida rule, distinguishes between motion before and motion during trial.

(b)(2) Based on ABA Standard 2.3, subparagraphs (a) and (c). Requires court to determine whether the statement will be offered as distinguished from asking the state its intention. Requires production of evidence of the statement in the event it will be offered so that the court and counsel can intelligently deal with the problem. Florida has no similar rule.

(b)(3) Substantially the same as ABA Standard, except that the proposed rule requires severance unless the court affirmatively finds that severance is unnecessary. Florida has no similar rule.

Rule 3.153. Timeliness of Defendant's Motion; Waiver

(a) Timeliness; Waiver. A defendant's motion for severance of multiple offenses or defendants charged in a single indictment or information shall be made before trial unless opportunity therefor did not exist or the defendant was not aware of the grounds for such a motion, but the court in its discretion may entertain such a motion at the trial. The right to file such a motion is waived if it is not timely made.

(b) Renewal of Motion. If a defendant's pretrial motion for severance is overruled, the defendant may renew the motion on the same grounds at or before the close of all the evidence at the trial.

Amended Sept. 24, 1992, effective Jan. 1, 1993 (606 So.2d 227).

Committee Notes

1972 Adoption. (a) Relates solely to defendant's motion for severance. Florida has no similar rule.

(b) Florida has no similar rule.

IV. ARRAIGNMENT AND PLEAS

Rule 3.160. Arraignment

(a) Nature of Arraignment. The arraignment shall be conducted in open court or by audiovisual device in the discretion of the court and shall consist of the judge or clerk or prosecuting attorney reading the indictment or information on which the defendant will be tried to the defendant or stating orally to the defendant the substances of the charge or charges and calling on the defendant to plead thereto. The reading or statement as to the charge or charges may be waived by the defendant. If the defendant is represented by counsel, counsel may file a written plea of not guilty at or before arraignment and thereupon arraignment shall be deemed waived.

(b) Effect of Failure to Arraign or Irregularity of Arraignment. Neither a failure to arraign nor an irregularity in the arraignment shall affect the validity of any proceeding in the cause if the defendant pleads to the indictment or information on which the defendant is to be tried or proceeds to trial without objection to such failure or irregularity.

(c) Plea of Guilty after Indictment or Information Filed. If a person who has been indicted or informed against for an offense, but who has not been arraigned, desires to plead guilty thereto, the person may so inform the court having jurisdiction of the offense, and the court shall, as soon as convenient, arraign the defendant and permit the defendant to plead guilty to the indictment or information.

(d) Time to Prepare for Trial. After a plea of not guilty the defendant is entitled to a reasonable time in which to prepare for trial.

(e) Defendant Not Represented by Counsel. Prior to arraignment of any person charged with the commission of a crime, if he or she is not represented by counsel, the court shall advise the person of the right to counsel and, if he or she is financially unable to obtain counsel, of the right to be assigned court-appointed counsel to represent him or her at the arraignment and at all subsequent proceedings. The person shall execute an affidavit that he or she is unable financially or otherwise to obtain counsel, and if the court shall determine the reason to be true, the court shall appoint counsel to represent the person.

If the defendant, however, understandingly waives representation by counsel, he or she shall execute a written waiver of such representation, which shall be filed in the case. If counsel is appointed, a reasonable time shall be accorded to counsel before the defendant shall be required to plead to the indictment or information on which he or she is to be arraigned or tried, or otherwise to proceed further.

Amended Sept. 24, 1992, effective Jan. 1, 1993 (606 So.2d 227).

Committee Notes

1968 Adoption. (a) A combination of section 908.01, Florida Statutes, and Federal Rule of Criminal Procedure 10.

(b) Same as section 908.02, Florida Statutes.

(c) Same as section 909.15, Florida Statutes, except provision is made for trial by affidavit.

(d) Same as section 909.20, Florida Statutes.

(e) Federal rule 44 provides:

"If the defendant appears in court without counsel the court shall advise him of his right to counsel and assign counsel to represent him at every stage of the proceeding unless he elects to proceed without counsel or is able to obtain counsel."

A presently proposed amendment to such rule provides:

"(a) Right to Assigned Counsel. Every defendant who is unable to obtain counsel shall be entitled to have counsel assigned to represent him at every stage of the proceedings from his initial appearance before the commissioner or the court through appeal, unless he waives such appointment.

"(b) Assignment Procedure. The procedures for implementing the right set out in subdivision (a) shall be those provided by law or by local rules of district courts of appeal."

In lieu of such latter, blanket provision, it is suggested that the rule provide, as stated, for inquiry of the defendant and determination by the court as to the defendant's desire for and inability to obtain counsel, after being advised of entitlement thereto. Many defendants, of course, will waive counsel.

In view of Harvey v. Mississippi, 340 F.2d 263 (5th Cir.1965), and White v. Maryland, 373 U.S. 59, 83 S.Ct. 1050, 10 L.Ed.2d 193 (1963), holding that entitlement to counsel does not depend upon whether the offense charged is a felony or misdemeanor, it is suggested that the word "crime" be used instead of "felony" only in the first sentence of the proposed rule.

In Hamilton v. Alabama, 368 U.S. 52, 82 S.Ct. 157, 7 L.Ed.2d 114 (1961), involving breaking and entering with intent to commit rape, the Supreme Court held the defendant was entitled to counsel at the arraignment, if the arraignment be deemed a part of the trial, as apparently it is under Alabama law. In Ex parte Jeffcoat, 109 Fla. 207, 146 So. 827 (1933), the Supreme Court of Florida held the arraignment to be a mere formal preliminary step to an answer or plea. However, in Sardinia v. State, 168 So.2d 674 (Fla.1964), the court recognized the accused's right to counsel upon arraignment. Section 909.21, Florida Statutes, provides for appointment of counsel in capital cases.

1972 Amendment. Substantially the same as prior rule. The committee considered changes recommended by The Florida Bar and incorporated the proposed change relating to written plea of not guilty and waiver of arraignment.

1992 Amendment. The amendment allows the judge to participate in the arraignment process by including the judge as one of the designated individuals who may advise the defendant of the pending charges. Apparently, the 1988 amendment to rule 3.160(a) inadvertently eliminated the judge from the arraignment procedure. In re Rule 3.160(a), Florida Rules of Criminal Procedure, 528 So.2d 1179, 1180 (Fla.1988). The prior amendment did include the judge. The Florida Bar Re: Amendment to Rules—Criminal Procedure, 462 So.2d 386 (Fla. 1984). While the language of rule 3.160(a) as presently set out in the Florida Bar pamphlet, Florida Rules of Criminal Procedure, is identical to the language of this proposed amendment (that is, it includes the judge in the arraignment process), the West publications, Florida Criminal Laws and Rules (1991) and Florida Rules of Court (1991), nevertheless follow the language set out in 528 So.2d at 1180.

Rule 3.170. Pleas

(a) Types of Plea; Court's Discretion. A defendant may plead not guilty, guilty, or, with the consent of the court, nolo contendere. Except as otherwise provided by these rules, all pleas to a charge shall be in open court and shall be entered by the defendant. If the sworn complaint charges the commission of a misdemeanor, the defendant may plead guilty to the charge at the first appearance under rule 3.130, and the judge may thereupon enter judgment and sentence without the necessity of any further formal charges being filed. A plea of not guilty may be entered in writing by counsel. Every plea shall be entered of record, but a failure to enter it shall not affect the validity of any proceeding in the cause.

(b) Pleading to Other Charges. Having entered a plea in accordance with this rule, the defendant may, with the court's permission, enter a plea of guilty or nolo contendere to any and all charges pending against him or her in the State of Florida over which the court would have jurisdiction and, when authorized by law, to charges pending in a court of lesser jurisdiction, if the prosecutor in the other case or cases gives written consent thereto. The court accepting such a plea shall make a disposition of all such charges by judgment, sentence, or otherwise. The record of the plea and its disposition shall be filed in the court of original jurisdiction of the offense. If a defendant secures permission to plead to other pending charges and does so plead, the entry of such a plea shall constitute a waiver by the defendant of venue and all nonjurisdictional defects relating to such charges.

(c) Standing Mute or Pleading Evasively. If a defendant stands mute, or pleads evasively, a plea of not guilty shall be entered.

(d) Failure of Corporation to Appear. If the defendant is a corporation and fails to appear, a plea of not guilty shall be entered of record.

(e) Plea of Not Guilty; Operation in Denial. A plea of not guilty is a denial of every material allegation in the indictment or information on which the defendant is to be tried.

(f) Withdrawal of Plea of Guilty or No Contest. The court may in its discretion, and shall on good cause, at any time before a sentence, permit a plea of guilty or no contest to be withdrawn and, if judgment of conviction has been entered thereon, set aside the judgment and allow a plea of not guilty, or, with the consent of the prosecuting attorney, allow a plea of guilty or no contest of a lesser included offense, or of a lesser degree of the offense charged, to be substituted for the plea of guilty or no contest. The fact that a defendant may have entered a plea of guilty or no contest and later withdrawn the plea may not be used against the defendant in a trial of that cause.

(g) Vacation of Plea and Sentence Due to Defendant's Noncompliance.

(1) Whenever a plea agreement requires the defendant to comply with some specific terms, those terms shall be expressly made a part of the plea entered into in open court.

(2) Unless otherwise stated at the time the plea is entered:

(A) The state may move to vacate a plea and sentence within 60 days of the defendant's noncompliance with the specific terms of a plea agreement.

(B) When a motion is filed pursuant to subdivision (g)(2)(A) of this rule, the court shall hold an evidentiary hearing on the issue unless the defendant admits noncompliance with the specific terms of the plea agreement.

(C) No plea or sentence shall be vacated unless the court finds that there has been substantial noncompliance with the express plea agreement.

(D) When a plea and sentence is vacated pursuant to this rule, the cause shall be set for trial within 90 days of the order vacating the plea and sentence.

(h) Plea of Guilty to Lesser Included Offense or Lesser Degree. The defendant, with the consent of the court and of the prosecuting attorney, may plead guilty to any lesser offense than that charged that is included in the offense charged in the indictment or information or to any lesser degree of the offense charged.

(i) Plea of Guilty to an Offense Divided into Degrees; Determination of the Degree. When an indictment or information charges an offense that is divided into degrees without specifying the degree, if the defendant pleads guilty, generally the court shall, before accepting the plea, examine witnesses to determine the degree of the offense of which the defendant is guilty.

(j) Time and Circumstances of Plea. No defendant, whether represented by counsel or otherwise, shall be called on to plead unless and until he or she has had a reasonable time within which to deliberate thereon.

(k) Responsibility of Court on Pleas. No plea of guilty or nolo contendere shall be accepted by a court without the court first determining, in open court, with means of recording the proceedings stenographically or mechanically, that the circumstances surrounding the plea reflect a full understanding of the significance of the plea and its voluntariness and that there is a factual basis for the plea of guilty. A complete record of the proceedings at which a defendant pleads shall be kept by the court.

(*l*) Motion to Withdraw the Plea after Sentencing. A defendant who pleads guilty or nolo contendere without expressly reserving the right to appeal a legally dispositive issue may file a motion to withdraw the plea within thirty days after rendition of the sentence, but only upon the grounds specified in Florida Rule of Appellate Procedure 9.140(b)(2)(A)(ii)(a)–(e) except as provided by law.

(m) Motion to Withdraw the Plea after Drug Court Transfer. A defendant who pleads guilty or nolo contendere to a charge for the purpose of transferring the case, pursuant to section 910.035, Florida Statutes, may file a motion to withdraw the plea upon successful completion of the drug court treatment program.

Amended Sept. 24, 1992, effective Jan. 1, 1993 (606 So.2d 227); March 10, 1994 (633 So.2d 1056); Nov. 27, 1996, effective Jan. 1, 1997 (685 So.2d 1253); Dec. 5, 2002, effective January 1, 2003 (837 So.2d 924); Sept. 21, 2006 (938 So.2d 978); Nov. 9, 2006, effective January 1, 2007 (942 So.2d 407); March 29, 2007 (953 So.2d 513); June 21, 2007 (959 So.2d 250).

Committee Notes

1968 Adoption.

(a) Patterned after the major portion of Federal Rule of Criminal Procedure 11.

(b) Same as section 909.07, Florida Statutes, except the word "made" is substituted for "pleaded."

(c) Taken from a part of section 908.03, Florida Statutes.

(d) Taken from a part of section 908.03, Florida Statutes.

(e) Same as section 909.16, Florida Statutes, except that provision is added for trial by affidavit.

(f) Essentially the same as section 909.13, Florida Statutes.

(g) Essentially the same as section 909.09, Florida Statutes, except for the addition of the charge by affidavit.

(h) Same as section 909.11, Florida Statutes, except provision is made for a charge by affidavit.

1972 Amendment. This general topic is found in ABA Standard relating to pleas of guilty. The Standards are divided into 3 parts: receiving and acting upon a plea; withdrawal of the plea; and plea discussions and plea agreements. The first and second parts are considered under this rule.

(a) Same as first part of existing rule; substance of second sentence of existing rule transferred to new subdivision (j); new provision permits, with court approval, plea of not guilty to be made in writing.

(b) From ABA Standard 1.2; the purpose of this rule is to permit a defendant to plead guilty or nolo contendere to all cases pending against the defendant, thus avoiding multiple judicial and prosecutorial labors. New concept of permitting this procedure even though the other cases are pending in other counties is taken from Federal Rule of Criminal Procedure 20 which has successfully met the purpose explained above.

(c) Same as prior rule.

(d) Same as prior rule.

(e) Same as prior rule.

(f) Last sentence added from ABA Standard 2.2.

(g) Same as prior rule.

(h) Same as prior rule.

(i) This should be done in accordance with *Boykin v. Alabama*, 395 U.S. 238, 89 S.Ct. 1709, 23 L.Ed.2d 274 (1969), and *Garcia v. State*, 228 So.2d 300 (Fla. 1969). This should also include advising a defendant so pleading of the possibility of an action or charge against him or her as a multiple felon if the circumstances so warrant.

(j) From first sentence of present rule 3.170(a) with addition of requirement of determination of factual basis for a plea of guilty as provided by last sentence of federal rule 11. While requiring the presence of a court reporter, the proposed rule does not require that the reporter transcribe and file a transcript of the proceedings on a plea of guilty or nolo contendere, although the committee considers that such a requirement by the trial judge is desirable.

1973 Amendment. The purpose of this amendment is to provide a method whereby a defendant may plead guilty to a misdemeanor at first appearance without the necessity of the state attorney subsequently filing an information.

Rule 3.171. Plea Discussions and Agreements

(a) In General. Ultimate responsibility for sentence determination rests with the trial judge. However, the prosecuting attorney and the defense attorney, or the defendant when representing himself or herself, are encouraged to discuss and to agree on pleas that may be entered by a defendant. The discussion and agreement must be conducted with the defendant's counsel. If the defendant represents himself or herself, all discussions between the defendant and the prosecuting attorney shall be of record.

(b) Responsibilities of the Prosecuting Attorney.

(1) A prosecuting attorney may:

(A) engage in discussions with defense counsel or a defendant who is without counsel with a view toward reaching an agreement that, upon the defendant's entering a plea of guilty or nolo contendere to a charged offense or to a lesser or related offense, the prosecuting attorney will do any of the following:

(i) abandon other charges; or

(ii) make a recommendation, or agree not to oppose the defendant's request for a particular sentence, with the understanding that such recommendation or request shall not be binding on the trial judge; or

(iii) agree to a specific sentence; and

(B) consult with the victim, investigating officer, or other interested persons and advise the trial judge of their views during the course of plea discussions.

(2) The prosecuting attorney shall:

(A) apprise the trial judge of all material facts known to the attorney regarding the offense and the defendant's background prior to acceptance of a plea by the trial judge; and

(B) maintain the record of direct discussions with a defendant who represents himself or herself and make the record available to the trial judge upon the entry of a plea arising from these discussions.

(c) Responsibilities of Defense Counsel.

(1) Defense counsel shall not conclude any plea agreement on behalf of a defendant-client without the client's full and complete consent thereto, being certain that any decision to plead guilty or nolo contendere is made by the defendant.

(2) Defense counsel shall advise defendant of:

(A) all plea offers; and

(B) all pertinent matters bearing on the choice of which plea to enter and the particulars attendant upon each plea and the likely results thereof, as well as any possible alternatives that may be open to the defendant.

(d) Responsibilities of the Trial Judge. After an agreement on a plea has been reached, the trial judge may have made known to him or her the agreement and reasons therefor prior to the acceptance of the plea. Thereafter, the judge shall advise the parties whether other factors (unknown at the time) may make his or her concurrence impossible.

Amended Sept. 24, 1992, effective Jan. 1, 1993 (606 So.2d 227).

Committee Notes

1972 Amendment. New in Florida. Most criminal cases are disposed of by pleas of guilty arrived at by negotiations between prosecutor and defense counsel, but there was no record of the "plea negotiations," "plea bargaining," or "compromise." The result has been a flood of postconviction claims which require evidentiary hearings and frequently conflicting testimony concerning the plea negotiations. There has also been criticism of the practice of requiring a defendant, upon a negotiated guilty plea, to give a negative reply to the court's inquiry concerning any "promise" made to the defendant. This is designed to avoid the foregoing pitfalls and criticisms by having the negotiations made of record and permitting some control of them. See Commentary to Standard 3.1 ABA Standards relating to pleas of guilty.

(a) From Standard 3.1a.

(b) From Standard 3.2.

(c) From Standard 3.3 except for omission of that part of standard which prohibits trial judge from participating in plea discussions.

(d) From Standard 3.4.

1977 Amendment. This is a rewording of the prior rule in order to set out the responsibilities of the participants. The rule recognizes the ultimate responsibility of the trial judge, but it encourages prosecution and defense counsel to assist the trial judge in this regard. When the circumstances of the case so merit, it is the responsibility of each respective party to discuss a fair disposition in lieu of trial. For protection of the prosecutor and the defendant, plea discussions between the state and a pro se defendant should be recorded, in writing or electronically.

(b) New in Florida.

(1)(i) Restatement of policy followed by extensive revision in the form of Federal Rule of Criminal Procedure 11(e)(1).

(1)(ii) The rule sets out discretionary minimum professional prosecutorial procedure where either victim or law enforcement officers are involved to better guide the trial judge.

(2)(i) Mandatory responsibility of prosecutor contemplates disposition with no presentence investigation.

(2)(ii) Mandatory record protects both the prosecutor and the pro se defendant.

(c)(1) Renumbering subdivision (b) of prior rule.

(2)(i) New in Florida. This proposed language makes it mandatory for defense counsel to advise fully defendant of all plea offers by the state. Defense counsel should also discuss and explain to the defendant those matters which trial judge will inquire about before accepting a plea.

(2)(ii) Same as prior rule 3.171(b), paragraph 2.

(d) Now embraces and renumbers former rule 3.171(c). The content of former rule 3.171(d) now appears as part of new rule 3.172.

Rule 3.172. Acceptance of Guilty or Nolo Contendere Plea

(a) Voluntariness; Factual Basis. Before accepting a plea of guilty or nolo contendere, the trial judge shall determine that the plea is voluntarily entered and that a factual basis for the plea exists. Counsel for the prosecution and the defense shall assist the trial judge in this function.

(b) Open Court. All pleas shall be taken in open court, except that when good cause is shown a plea may be taken in camera.

(c) Determination of Voluntariness. Except when a defendant is not present for a plea, pursuant to the provisions of rule 3.180(d), the trial judge should, when determining voluntariness, place the defendant under oath and shall address the defendant personally and shall determine that he or she understands:

(1) the nature of the charge to which the plea is offered, the maximum possible penalty, and any mandatory minimum penalty provided by law;

(2) if not represented by an attorney, that the defendant has the right to be represented by an attorney at every stage of the proceeding and, if necessary, an attorney will be appointed to represent him or her;

(3) the right to plead not guilty or to persist in that plea if it has already been made, the right to be tried by a jury, and at that trial a defendant has the right to the assistance of counsel, the right to compel attendance of witnesses on his or her behalf, the right to confront and cross-examine witnesses against him or her, and the right not to testify or be compelled to incriminate himself or herself;

(4) that upon a plea of guilty, or nolo contendere without express reservation of the right to appeal, he or she gives up the right to appeal all matters relating to the judgment, including the issue of guilt or innocence, but does not impair the right to review by appropriate collateral attack;

(5) that if the defendant pleads guilty or is adjudged guilty after a plea of nolo contendere there will not be a further trial of any kind, so that by pleading guilty or nolo contendere he or she waives the right to a trial;

(6) that if the defendant pleads guilty or nolo contendere, the trial judge may ask the defendant questions about the offense to which he or she has pleaded, and if the defendant answers these questions under oath, on the record, and in the presence of counsel, the answers may later be used against him or her in a prosecution for perjury;

(7) the complete terms of any plea agreement, including specifically all obligations the defendant will incur as a result;

(8) that if he or she pleads guilty or nolo contendere, if he or she is not a United States citizen, the plea may subject him or her to deportation pursuant to the laws and regulations governing the United States Immigration and Naturalization Service. It shall not be necessary for the trial judge to inquire as to whether the defendant is a United States citizen, as this admonition shall be given to all defendants in all cases; and

(9) that if the defendant pleads guilty or nolo contendere, and the offense to which the defendant is pleading is a sexually violent offense or a sexually motivated offense, or if the defendant has been previously convicted of such an offense, the plea may subject the defendant to involuntary civil commitment as a sexually violent predator upon completion of his or her sentence. It shall not be necessary for the trial judge to determine whether the present or prior offenses were sexually motivated, as this admonition shall be given to all defendants in all cases.

(10) that if the defendant pleads guilty or nolo contendere and the offense to which the defendant is pleading is one for which automatic, mandatory driver's license suspension or revocation is required by law to be imposed (either by the court or by a separate agency), the plea will provide the basis for the suspension or revocation of the defendant's driver's license.

(d) DNA Evidence Inquiry. Before accepting a defendant's plea of guilty or nolo contendere to a felony, the judge must inquire whether counsel for the defense has reviewed the discovery disclosed by the state, whether such discovery included a listing or description of physical items of evidence, and whether counsel has reviewed the nature of the evidence with the defendant. The judge must then inquire of the defendant and counsel for the defendant and the state whether physical evidence containing DNA is known to exist that could exonerate the defendant. If no such physical evidence is known to exist, the court may accept the defendant's plea and impose sentence. If such physical evidence is known to exist, upon defendant's motion specifying the physical evidence to be tested, the court may postpone the proceeding and order DNA testing.

(e) Acknowledgment by Defendant. Before the trial judge accepts a guilty or nolo contendere plea, the judge must determine that the defendant either (1) acknowledges his or her guilt or (2) acknowledges that he or she feels the plea to be in his or her best interest, while maintaining his or her innocence.

(f) Proceedings of Record. The proceedings at which a defendant pleads guilty or nolo contendere shall be of record.

(g) Withdrawal of Plea Offer or Negotiation. No plea offer or negotiation is binding until it is accepted by the trial judge formally after making all the inquiries, advisements, and determinations required by this rule. Until that time, it may be withdrawn by either party without any necessary justification.

(h) Withdrawal of Plea When Judge Does Not Concur. If the trial judge does not concur in a tendered plea of guilty or nolo contendere arising from negotiations, the plea may be withdrawn.

(i) Evidence. Except as otherwise provided in this rule, evidence of an offer or a plea of guilty or nolo contendere, later withdrawn, or of statements made in connection therewith, is not admissible in any civil or criminal proceeding against the person who made the plea or offer.

(j) Prejudice. Failure to follow any of the procedures in this rule shall not render a plea void absent a showing of prejudice.

Amended Sept. 24, 1992, effective Jan. 1, 1993 (606 So.2d 227); Nov. 27, 1996, effective Jan. 1, 1997 (685 So.2d 1253); Sept. 1, 2005, effective Oct. 1, 2005 (911 So.2d 763); Sept. 21, 2006 (938 So.2d 978); March 29, 2007 (953 So.2d 513); Oct. 1, 2009 (20 So.3d 376); Nov. 19, 2009, effective Jan. 1, 2010 (26 So.3d 534).

Committee Notes

1977 Adoption. New in Florida. In view of the supreme court's emphasis on the importance of this procedure as set forth in *Williams v. State*, 316 So. 2d 267 (Fla. 1975), the committee felt it appropriate to expand the language of former rule 3.170(j) (deleted) and establish a separate rule. Incorporates Federal Rule of Criminal Procedure 11(c) and allows for pleas of convenience as provided in *North Carolina v. Alford*, 400 U.S. 25, 91 S. Ct. 160, 27 L.Ed.2d 162 (1970).

(a), (b) Mandatory record of voluntariness and factual predicate is proper responsibility of counsel as well as the court.

(c)(iv) This waiver of right to appeal is a change from the proposed amendments to the rules of criminal procedure now pending. A sentence if lawful is not subject to appellate review; a judgment, however, is. The committee was of the opinion that the proposed rule should be expanded to include a waiver of appeal from the judgment as well as the sentence. Waivers of appeal have been approved. *United States ex rel. Amuso v. LaValle*, 291 F.Supp. 383 (E.D.N.Y. 1968), *aff'd* 427 F.2d 328 (2d Cir. 1970); *State v. Gibson*, 68 N.J. 499, 348 A.2d 769 (1975); *People v. Williams*, 36 N.Y.2d 829, 370 N.Y.S.2d 904, 331 N.E.2d 684 (1975).

(vii) Requires the court to explain the plea agreement to the defendant, including conditions subsequent such as conditions of probation.

(e) Provides a readily available record (either oral or by use of standard forms) in all cases where a felony is charged.

(h) Rewording of federal rule 11(e)(6).

2005 Amendment. Rule 3.172(c)(9) added. See section 394.910, et seq., Fla. Stat.; and *State v. Harris*, 881 So.2d 1079 (Fla. 2004).

Rule 3.180. Presence of Defendant

(a) Presence of Defendant. In all prosecutions for crime the defendant shall be present:

(1) at first appearance;

(2) when a plea is made, unless a written plea of not guilty shall be made in writing under the provisions of rule 3.170(a);

(3) at any pretrial conference, unless waived by the defendant in writing;

(4) at the beginning of the trial during the examination, challenging, impanelling, and swearing of the jury;

(5) at all proceedings before the court when the jury is present;

(6) when evidence is addressed to the court out of the presence of the jury for the purpose of laying the foundation for the introduction of evidence before the jury;

(7) at any view by the jury;

(8) at the rendition of the verdict; and

(9) at the pronouncement of judgment and the imposition of sentence.

(b) Presence; definition. A defendant is present for purposes of this rule if the defendant is physically in attendance for the courtroom proceeding, and has a meaningful opportunity to be heard through counsel on the issues being discussed.

(c) Defendant Absenting Self.

(1) *Trial.* If the defendant is present at the beginning of the trial and thereafter, during the progress of the trial or before the verdict of the jury has been returned into court, voluntarily absents himself or herself from the presence of the court without leave of court, or is removed from the presence of the court because of his or her disruptive conduct during the trial, the trial of the cause or the return of the verdict of the jury in the case shall not thereby be postponed or delayed, but the trial, the submission of the case to the jury for verdict, and the return of the verdict thereon shall proceed in all respects as though the defendant were present in court at all times.

(2) *Sentencing.* If the defendant is present at the beginning of the trial and thereafter absents himself or herself as described in subdivision (1), or if the defendant enters a plea of guilty or no contest and thereafter absents himself or herself from sentencing, the sentencing may proceed in all respects as though the defendant were present at all times.

(d) Defendant May Be Tried in Absentia for Misdemeanors. Persons prosecuted for misdemeanors may, at their own request, by leave of court, be excused from attendance at any or all of the proceedings aforesaid.

(e) Presence of Corporation. A corporation may appear by counsel at all times and for all purposes.

Amended Sept. 24, 1992, effective Jan. 1, 1993 (606 So.2d 227); Nov. 27, 1996, effective Jan. 1, 1997 (685 So.2d 1253); Nov. 9, 2006, effective Jan. 1, 2007 (942 So.2d 407).

Committee Notes

1968 Adoption. (a) The suggested rule is in great part a recopying of section 914.01, Florida Statutes:

In (3) the words "at the beginning of the trial" are recommended for inclusion to avoid questions arising as to the necessity for the defendant's presence at times other than upon trial, such as when the jury venire is ordered, etc.

Subdivision (a)(8) is not in the present statute. However, it is deemed advisable to include it, as the several sections of chapter 921, Florida Statutes, particularly section 921.07, appear to impliedly or expressly require the defendant's presence at such times.

(c) The statute and the suggested rule make no distinction between capital and other cases. In all probability, however, were a person on trial for a capital case to escape during trial, a mistrial should be ordered if such person were not captured within a reasonable time.

(d) It is suggested that this language be used rather than the all-inclusive general language of the present statute as to misdemeanor cases.

(e) This provision does not appear in section 914.01, Florida Statutes, but it is a part of Federal Rule of Criminal Procedure 43. It is deemed useful to include it.

1972 Amendment. Same as prior rule except (3) added to conform to rule 3.220(k); other subdivisions renumbered.

V. PRETRIAL MOTIONS AND DEFENSES

Rule 3.190. Pretrial Motions

(a) In General. Every pretrial motion and pleading in response to a motion shall be in writing and signed by the party making the motion or the attorney for the party. This requirement may be waived by the court for good cause shown. Each motion or other pleading shall state the ground or grounds on which it is based. A copy shall be served on the adverse party. A certificate of service must accompany the filing of any pleading.

(b) Motion to Dismiss; Grounds. All defenses available to a defendant by plea, other than not guilty, shall be made only by motion to dismiss the indictment or information, whether the same shall relate to matters of form, substance, former acquittal, former jeopardy, or any other defense.

(c) Time for Moving to Dismiss. Unless the court grants further time, the defendant shall move to dismiss the indictment or information either before or at arraignment. The court in its discretion may permit the defendant to plead and thereafter to file a motion to dismiss at a time to be set by the court. Except for objections based on fundamental grounds, every ground for a motion to dismiss that is not presented by a motion to dismiss within the time hereinabove provided shall be considered waived. However, the court may at any time entertain a motion to dismiss on any of the following grounds:

(1) The defendant is charged with an offense for which the defendant has been pardoned.

(2) The defendant is charged with an offense for which the defendant previously has been placed in jeopardy.

(3) The defendant is charged with an offense for which the defendant previously has been granted immunity.

(4) There are no material disputed facts and the undisputed facts do not establish a prima facie case of guilt against the defendant.

The facts on which the motion is based should be alleged specifically and the motion sworn to.

(d) Traverse or Demurrer. The state may traverse or demur to a motion to dismiss that alleges factual matters. Factual matters alleged in a motion to dismiss under subdivision (c)(4) of this rule shall be considered admitted unless specifically denied by the state in the traverse. The court may receive evidence on any issue of fact necessary to the decision on the motion. A motion to dismiss under subdivision (c)(4) of this rule shall be denied if the state files a traverse that, with specificity, denies under oath the material fact or facts alleged in the motion to dismiss. The demurrer or traverse shall be filed a reasonable time before the hearing on the motion to dismiss.

(e) Effect of Sustaining a Motion to Dismiss. If the motion to dismiss is sustained, the court may order that the defendant be held in custody or admitted to bail for a reasonable specified time pending the filing of a new indictment or information. If a new indictment or information is not filed within the time specified in the order, or within such additional time as the court may allow for good cause shown, the defendant, if in custody, shall be discharged therefrom, unless some other charge justifies a continuation in custody. If the defendant has been released on bail, the defendant and the sureties shall be exonerated; if money or bonds have been deposited as bail, the money or bonds shall be refunded.

(f) Motion for Continuance.

(1) *Definition.* A continuance within the meaning of this rule is the postponement of a cause for any period of time.

(2) *Cause.* On motion of the state or a defendant or on its own motion, the court may grant a continuance, in its discretion for good cause shown.

(3) *Time for Filing.* A motion for continuance may be made only before or at the time the case is set for trial, unless good cause for failure to so apply is shown or the ground for the motion arose after the cause was set for trial.

(4) *Certificate of Good Faith.* A motion for continuance shall be accompanied by a certificate of the movant's counsel that the motion is made in good faith.

(5) *Affidavits.* The party applying for a continuance may file affidavits in support of the motion, and the adverse party may file counter-affidavits in opposition to the motion.

(g) Motion to Suppress Evidence in Unlawful Search.

(1) *Grounds.* A defendant aggrieved by an unlawful search and seizure may move to suppress anything so obtained for use as evidence because:

(A) the property was illegally seized without a warrant;

(B) the warrant is insufficient on its face;

(C) the property seized is not the property described in the warrant;

(D) there was no probable cause for believing the existence of the grounds on which the warrant was issued; or

(E) the warrant was illegally executed.

(2) *Contents of Motion.* Every motion to suppress evidence shall state clearly the particular evidence sought to be suppressed, the reasons for suppression, and a general statement of the facts on which the motion is based.

(3) *Hearing.* Before hearing evidence, the court shall determine if the motion is legally sufficient. If it is not, the motion shall be denied. If the court hears the motion on its merits, the defendant shall present evidence supporting the defendant's position and the state may offer rebuttal evidence.

(4) *Time for Filing.* The motion to suppress shall be made before trial unless opportunity therefor did not exist or the defendant was not aware of the grounds for the motion, but the court may entertain the motion or an appropriate objection at the trial.

(h) Motion to Suppress a Confession or Admission Illegally Obtained.

(1) *Grounds.* On motion of the defendant or on its own motion, the court shall suppress any confession or admission obtained illegally from the defendant.

(2) *Contents of Motion.* Every motion made by a defendant to suppress a confession or admission shall identify with particularity any statement sought to be suppressed, the reasons for suppression, and a general statement of the facts on which the motion is based.

(3) *Time for Filing.* The motion to suppress shall be made before trial unless opportunity therefor did not exist or the defendant was not aware of the grounds for the motion, but the court in its discretion may entertain the motion or an appropriate objection at the trial.

(4) *Hearing.* The court shall receive evidence on any issue of fact necessary to be decided to rule on the motion.

(i) Motion to Take Deposition to Perpetuate Testimony.

(1) After the filing of an indictment or information on which a defendant is to be tried, the defendant or the state may apply for an order to perpetuate testimony. The application shall be verified or supported by the affidavits of credible persons that a prospective witness resides beyond the territorial jurisdiction of the court or may be unable to attend or be prevented from attending a trial or hearing, that the witness's testimony is material, and that it is necessary to take the deposition to prevent a failure of justice. The court shall order a commission to be issued to take the deposition of the witnesses to be used in the trial and that any nonprivileged designated books, papers, documents, or tangible objects be produced at the same time and place. If the application is made within 10 days before the trial date, the court may deny the application.

(2) If the defendant or the state desires to perpetuate the testimony of a witness living in or out of the state whose testimony is material and necessary to the case, the same proceedings shall be followed as provided in subdivision (i)(1), but the testimony of the witness may be taken before an official court reporter, transcribed by the reporter, and filed in the trial court.

(3) If the deposition is taken on the application of the state, the defendant and the defendant's attorney shall be given reasonable notice of the time and place set for the deposition. The officer having custody of the defendant shall be notified of the time and place and shall produce the defendant at the examination and keep the defendant in the presence of the witness during the examination. A defendant not in custody may be present at the examination, but the failure to appear after notice and tender of expenses shall constitute a waiver of the right to be present. The state shall pay to the defendant's attorney and to a defendant not in custody the expenses of travel and subsistence for attendance at the examination. The state shall make available to the defendant for examination and use at the deposition any statement of the witness being deposed that is in the possession of the state and that the state would be required to make available to the defendant if the witness were testifying at trial.

(4) The application and order to issue the commission may be made either in term time or in vacation. The commission shall be issued at a time to be fixed by the court.

(5) Except as otherwise provided, the rules governing the taking and filing of oral depositions, the objections thereto, the issuing, execution, and return of the commission, and the opening of the depositions in civil actions shall apply in criminal cases.

(6) No deposition shall be used or read into evidence when the attendance of the witness can be procured. If the court determines that any person whose deposition has been taken is absent because of procurement, inducement, or threats of any person on behalf of the state or of the defendant or of any person on the defendant's behalf, the deposition shall not be read in evidence on behalf of the defendant.

(j) Motion to Expedite. On motion by the state, the court, in the exercise of its discretion, shall take into consideration the dictates of sections 825.106 and 918.0155, Florida Statutes (1995).

Amended Sept. 24, 1992, effective Jan. 1, 1993 (606 So.2d 227); Nov. 27, 1996, effective Jan. 1, 1997 (685 So.2d 1253); Nov. 2, 2000, effective Jan. 1, 2001 (794 So.2d 457); Dec. 5, 2002, effective Jan. 1, 2003 (837 So.2d 924); Nov. 19, 2009, effective Jan. 1, 2010 (26 So.3d 534).

Repeal

Laws 1979, c. 79–69, § 3, provided for the repeal of Rule 3.190(j) "insofar as it is inconsistent with the provisions of this act." Section 4 of the law provided: "This act shall take effect upon becoming a law, except that section 3 shall take effect only if passed by a two-thirds vote of the membership of each house of the legislature." The law was passed with the requisite majority vote. The other provisions of the law were designated as F.S.1979 § 918.17 [see, now, § 92.23] which permits video-taping of testimony of certain minors in cases involving sexual battery or child abuse.

Committee Notes

1968 Adoption. (a) New; devised by committee.

(b) Substantially the same as section 909.02, Florida Statutes, except changes name of "motion to quash" to "motion to dismiss." This conforms to the terminology of the Federal Rules of Criminal Procedure. The statute authorizing the state to appeal from certain orders, section 924.07, Florida Statutes, should be amended by substituting the words "motion to dismiss" for "motion to quash."

(c) Combines the substance of sections 909.01 and 909.06, Florida Statutes. Subdivision (4) affords a new remedy to an accused. Although there is now a conclusive presumption of probable cause once an indictment or information is filed (see *Sullivan v. State*, 49 So.2d 794 (Fla. 1951)), it is felt that this rule is necessary. Primarily, this procedure will permit a pretrial determination of the law of the case when the facts are not in dispute. In a sense, this is somewhat similar to summary judgment proceedings in civil cases, but a dismissal under this rule is not a bar to a subsequent prosecution.

(d) New; based on *Marks v. State*, 115 Fla. 497, 155 So. 727 (1934), and what is generally regarded as the better practice. Hearing provision based on federal rule 41(e).

(e) Combines federal rule 12(b)(5) and section 909.05, Florida Statutes. With reference to the maximum time that a defendant will be held in custody or on bail pending the filing of a new indictment or information, the trial court is given discretion in setting such time as to both the indictment and information. This proposal differs from section 909.05, Florida Statutes, with reference to the filing of a new indictment in that the statute requires that the new indictment be found by the same grand jury or the next grand jury having the authority to inquire into the offense. If the supreme court has the authority to deviate from this statutory provision by court rule, it seems that the trial court should be granted the same discretion with reference to the indictment that it is granted concerning the information. The statute is harsh in that under its provisions a person can be in custody or on bail for what may be an unreasonable length of time before a grand jury is required to return an indictment in order that the custody or bail be continued.

(g)(1) This subdivision is almost the same as section 916.02(1), Florida Statutes.

(g)(2) This subdivision is almost the same as section 916.02(2), Florida Statutes.

(g)(3) This subdivision is almost the same as section 916.03, Florida Statutes.

(g)(4) This subdivision rewords a portion of section 916.04, Florida Statutes.

(g)(5) This subdivision rewords section 916.07, Florida Statutes.

(h) Same as federal rule 41(e) as to the points covered.

(i) This rule is based on 38–144–11 of the Illinois Code of Criminal Procedure and federal rule 41(e).

(j) This subdivision rewords and adds to federal rule 14. It covers the subject matter of section 918.02, Florida Statutes.

(k) This rule is almost the same as federal rule 13, with provision added for trial by affidavit.

(*l*) Substantially same as section 916.06, Florida Statutes, with these exceptions: application cannot be made until indictment, information, or trial affidavit is filed; application must be made at least 10 days before trial; oral deposition in addition to written interrogatories is permissible.

1972 Amendment. Subdivision (h) is amended to require the defendant to specify the factual basis behind the grounds for a motion to suppress evidence. Subdivision (*l*) is amended to permit the state to take depositions under the same conditions that the defendant can take them. Former subdivisions (j) and (k) transferred to rules 3.150, 3.151, and 3.152. Subdivisions (*l*) and (m) renumbered (j) and (k) respectively. Otherwise, same as prior rule.

1977 Amendment. This amendment resolves any ambiguity in the rule as to whether the state must file a general or a specific traverse to defeat a motion to dismiss filed under the authority of rule 3.190(c)(4).

See *State v. Kemp*, 305 So.2d 833 (Fla. 3d DCA 1974).

The amendment clearly now requires a specific traverse to specific material fact or facts.

1992 Amendment. The amendments, in addition to gender neutralizing the wording of the rule, make a minor grammatical change by substituting the word "upon" for "on" in several places. The amendments also delete language from subdivision (a) to eliminate from the rule any reference as to when pretrial motions are to be served on the adverse party. Because rule 3.030 addresses the service of pleadings and papers, such language was removed to avoid confusion and reduce redundancy in the rules.

2002 Amendment. If the trial court exercises its discretion to consider the motion to suppress during trial, the court may withhold ruling on the merits of the motion, and motion for a judgment of acquittal, and allow the case to be submitted to the jury. If the defendant is acquitted, no further proceedings regarding the motion to suppress or motion for a judgment of acquittal would be necessary. However, if the jury finds the defendant guilty of the crime charged, the trial court could then consider the motion to suppress post-trial in conjunction with the defendant's renewed motion for a judgment of acquittal or motion for new trial.

Rule 3.191. Speedy Trial

(a) Speedy Trial without Demand. Except as otherwise provided by this rule, and subject to the limitations imposed under subdivisions (e) and (f), every person charged with a crime shall be brought to trial within 90 days of arrest if the crime charged is a misdemeanor, or within 175 days of arrest if the crime charged is a felony. If trial is not commenced within these time periods, the defendant shall be entitled to the appropriate remedy as set forth in subdivision (p). The time periods established by this subdivision shall commence when the person is taken into custody as defined under subdivision (d). A person charged with a crime is entitled to the benefits of this rule whether the person is in custody in a jail or correctional institution of this state or a political subdivision thereof or is at liberty on bail or recognizance or other pretrial release condition. This subdivision shall cease to apply whenever a person files a valid demand for speedy trial under subdivision (b).

(b) Speedy Trial upon Demand. Except as otherwise provided by this rule, and subject to the limitations imposed under subdivisions (e) and (g), every person charged with a crime by indictment or information shall have the right to demand a trial within 60 days, by filing with the court a separate pleading entitled "Demand for Speedy Trial," and serving a copy on the prosecuting authority.

(1) No later than 5 days from the filing of a demand for speedy trial, the court shall hold a calendar call, with notice to all parties, for the express purposes of announcing in open court receipt of the demand and of setting the case for trial.

(2) At the calendar call the court shall set the case for trial to commence at a date no less than 5 days nor more than 45 days from the date of the calendar call.

(3) The failure of the court to hold a calendar call on a demand that has been properly filed and served shall not interrupt the running of any time periods under this subdivision.

(4) If the defendant has not been brought to trial within 50 days of the filing of the demand, the defendant shall have the right to the appropriate remedy as set forth in subdivision (p).

(c) Commencement of Trial. A person shall be considered to have been brought to trial if the trial commences within the time herein provided. The trial is considered to have commenced when the trial jury panel for that specific trial is sworn for voir dire examination or, on waiver of a jury trial, when the trial proceedings begin before the judge.

(d) Custody. For purposes of this rule, a person is taken into custody

(1) when the person is arrested as a result of the conduct or criminal episode that gave rise to the crime charged, or

(2) when the person is served with a notice to appear in lieu of physical arrest.

(e) Prisoners outside Jurisdiction. A person who is in federal custody or incarcerated in a jail or correctional institution outside the jurisdiction of this state or a subdivision thereof, and who is charged with a crime by indictment or information issued or filed under the laws of this state, is not entitled to the benefit of this rule until that person returns or is returned to the jurisdiction of the court within which the Florida charge is pending and until written notice of the person's return is filed with the court and served on the prosecutor. For these persons, the time period under subdivision (a) commences on the date the last act required under this subdivision occurs. For these persons the time period under subdivision (b) commences when the demand is filed so long as the acts required under this subdivision occur before the filing of the demand. If the acts required under this subdivision do not precede the filing of the demand, the demand is invalid and shall be stricken upon motion of the prosecuting attorney. Nothing in this rule shall affect a prisoner's right to speedy trial under law.

(f) Consolidation of Felony and Misdemeanor. When a felony and a misdemeanor are consolidated for disposition in circuit court, the misdemeanor shall be governed by the same time period applicable to the felony.

(g) Demand for Speedy Trial; Accused Is Bound. A demand for speedy trial binds the accused and the state. No demand for speedy trial shall be filed or served unless the accused has a bona fide desire to obtain a trial sooner than otherwise might be provided. A demand for speedy trial shall be considered a pleading that the accused is available for trial, has diligently investigated the case, and is prepared or will be prepared for trial within 5 days. A demand filed by an accused who has not diligently investigated the case or who is not timely prepared for trial shall be stricken as invalid on motion of the prosecuting attorney. A demand may not be withdrawn by the accused except on order of the court, with consent of the state or on good cause shown. Good cause for continuances or delay on behalf of the accused thereafter shall not include nonreadiness for trial, except as to matters that may arise after the demand for trial is filed and that reasonably could not have been anticipated by the accused or counsel for the accused. A person who has demanded speedy trial, who thereafter is not prepared for trial, is not entitled to continuance or delay except as provided in this rule.

(h) Notice of Expiration of Time for Speedy Trial; When Timely. A notice of expiration of speedy trial time shall be timely if filed and served after the expiration of the periods of time for trial provided in this rule. However, a notice of expiration of speedy trial time filed before expiration of the period of time for trial is invalid and shall be stricken on motion of the prosecuting attorney.

(i) When Time May Be Extended. The periods of time established by this rule may be extended, provided the period of time sought to be extended has not expired at the time the extension was procured. An extension may be procured by:

(1) stipulation, announced to the court or signed in proper person or by counsel, by the party against whom the stipulation is sought to be enforced;

(2) written or recorded order of the court on the court's own motion or motion by either party in exceptional circumstances as hereafter defined in subdivision *(l)*;

(3) written or recorded order of the court with good cause shown by the accused;

(4) written or recorded order of the court for a period of reasonable and necessary delay resulting from proceedings including but not limited to an examination and hearing to determine the mental competency or physical ability of the defendant to stand trial, for hearings on pretrial motions, for appeals by the state, for DNA testing ordered on the defendant's behalf upon defendant's motion specifying the physical evidence to be tested pursuant to section 925.12(2), Florida Statutes, and for trial of other pending criminal charges against the accused; or

(5) administrative order issued by the chief justice, under Florida Rule of Judicial Administration 2.205(a)(2)(B)(iv), suspending the speedy trial procedures as stated therein.

(j) Delay and Continuances; Effect on Motion. If trial of the accused does not commence within the periods of time established by this rule, a pending motion for discharge shall be granted by the court unless it is shown that:

(1) a time extension has been ordered under subdivision (i) and that extension has not expired;

(2) the failure to hold trial is attributable to the accused, a codefendant in the same trial, or their counsel;

(3) the accused was unavailable for trial under subdivision (k); or

(4) the demand referred to in subdivision (g) is invalid.

If the court finds that discharge is not appropriate for reasons under subdivisions (j)(2), (3), or (4), the pending motion for discharge shall be denied, provided, however, that trial shall be scheduled and commence within 90 days of a written or recorded order of denial.

(k) Availability for Trial. A person is unavailable for trial if the person or the person's counsel fails to attend a proceeding at which either's presence is required by these rules, or the person or counsel is not ready for trial on the date trial is scheduled. A person who has not been available for trial during the term provided for in this rule is not entitled to be discharged. No presumption of nonavailability attaches, but if the state objects to discharge and presents any evidence tending to show nonavailability, the accused must establish, by competent proof, availability during the term.

(*l*) Exceptional Circumstances. As permitted by subdivision (i) of this rule, the court may order an extension of the time periods provided under this rule when exceptional circumstances are shown to exist. Exceptional circumstances shall not include general congestion of the court's docket, lack of diligent preparation, failure to obtain available witnesses, or other avoidable or foreseeable delays. Exceptional circumstances are those that, as a matter of substantial justice to the accused or the state or both, require an order by the court. These circumstances include:

(1) unexpected illness, unexpected incapacity, or unforeseeable and unavoidable absence of a person whose presence or testimony is uniquely necessary for a full and adequate trial;

(2) a showing by the state that the case is so unusual and so complex, because of the number of defendants or the nature of the prosecution or otherwise, that it is unreasonable to expect adequate investigation or preparation within the periods of time established by this rule;

(3) a showing by the state that specific evidence or testimony is not available despite diligent efforts to secure it, but will become available at a later time;

(4) a showing by the accused or the state of necessity for delay grounded on developments that could not have been anticipated and that materially will affect the trial;

(5) a showing that a delay is necessary to accommodate a codefendant, when there is reason not to sever the cases to proceed promptly with trial of the defendant; and

(6) a showing by the state that the accused has caused major delay or disruption of preparation of proceedings, as by preventing the attendance of witnesses or otherwise.

(m) Effect of Mistrial; Appeal; Order of New Trial. A person who is to be tried again or whose trial has been delayed by an appeal by the state or the defendant shall be brought to trial within 90 days from the date of declaration of a mistrial by the trial court, the date of an order by the trial court granting a new trial, the date of an order by the trial court granting a motion in arrest of judgment, or the date of receipt by the trial court of a mandate, order, or notice of whatever form from a reviewing court that makes possible a new trial for the defendant, whichever is last in time. If a defendant is not brought to trial within the prescribed time periods, the defendant shall be entitled to the appropriate remedy as set forth in subdivision (p).

(n) Discharge from Crime; Effect. Discharge from a crime under this rule shall operate to bar prosecution of the crime charged and of all other crimes on which trial has not commenced nor conviction obtained nor adjudication withheld and that were or might have been charged as a result of the same conduct or criminal episode as a lesser degree or lesser included offense.

(*o*) Nolle Prosequi; Effect. The intent and effect of this rule shall not be avoided by the state by entering a nolle prosequi to a crime charged and by prosecuting a new crime grounded on the same conduct or criminal episode or otherwise by prosecuting new and different charges based on the same conduct or criminal episode, whether or not the pending charge is suspended, continued, or is the subject of entry of a nolle prosequi.

(p) Remedy for Failure to Try Defendant within the Specified Time.

(1) No remedy shall be granted to any defendant under this rule until the court has made the required inquiry under subdivision (j).

(2) At any time after the expiration of the prescribed time period, the defendant may file a separate pleading entitled "Notice of Expiration of Speedy Trial Time," and serve a copy on the prosecuting authority.

(3) No later than 5 days from the date of the filing of a notice of expiration of speedy trial time, the court shall hold a hearing on the notice and, unless the court finds that one of the reasons set forth in subdivision (j) exists, shall order that the defendant be brought to trial within 10 days. A defendant not brought to trial within the 10–day period through no fault of the defendant, on motion of the defendant or the court, shall be forever discharged from the crime.

Amended Sept. 24, 1992, effective Jan. 1, 1993 (606 So.2d 227); April 8, 1993, effective July 1, 1993 (615 So.2d 692); Nov. 2, 2000, effective Jan. 1, 2001 (794 So.2d 457); Oct. 7, 2004, effective Jan. 1, 2005 (886 So.2d 197); Nov. 19, 2009, effective Jan. 1, 2010 (26 So.3d 534); June 9, 2011, effective June 9, 2011 (66 So.3d 851); Nov. 8, 2012, effective Jan. 1, 2013 (104 So.3d 304).

Committee Notes

1972 Amendment. Same as prior rule. The schedule is omitted as being unnecessary.

1977 Amendment. An appeal by the state from an order dismissing the case constitutes an interlocutory appeal and should be treated as such. The additional phrase removes any ambiguities in the existing rule.

1980 Amendment.

(a)(1). Speedy Trial without Demand.

1. Prisoners in Florida institutions are now treated like any other defendant [formerly (b)(1)].

2. Federal prisoners and prisoners outside Florida may claim the benefit of this subdivision once special prerequisites are satisfied under (b)(1).

3. Before a court can discharge a defendant, the court must make complete inquiry to ensure that discharge is appropriate.

(a)(2). Speedy Trial upon Demand.

1. Trial cannot be scheduled within 5 days of the filing of the demand without the consent of both the state and the defendant.

2. Before a court can discharge a defendant, the court must make complete inquiry to ensure that discharge is appropriate.

3. Prisoners in Florida are now treated like any other defendant [formerly (b)(2)].

4. Federal prisoners and prisoners outside Florida may claim the benefit of this subdivision once special prerequisites are satisfied under (b)(1).

(a)(3). Commencement of Trial.

1. Minor change in language to reflect case law.

(a)(4). Custody. [NEW]

1. Custody is defined in terms tantamount to arrest. This definition was formerly contained in (a)(1).

2. Where a notice to appear is served in lieu of arrest, custody results on the date the notice is served.

(b)(1). Prisoners outside Jurisdiction. [NEW]

1. Prisoners outside the jurisdiction of Florida may claim benefit under (a)(1) and (a)(2) after the prisoner returns to the jurisdiction of the court

where the charge is pending and after the prisoner files and serves a notice of this fact.

2. As an alternative, certain prisoners may claim the benefit of sections 941.45–941.50, Florida Statutes (1979).

3. Former (b)(1) is repealed.

(b)(2). [NEW]

1. Where a misdemeanor and felony are consolidated for purposes of trial in circuit court, the misdemeanor is governed by the same time period applicable to the felony. To claim benefit under this provision, the crimes must be consolidated before the normal time period applicable to misdemeanors has expired.

2. Former (b)(2) is repealed.

(b)(3). Repealed and superseded by (b)(1).

(c). Demand for Speedy Trial.

1. The subdivision recognizes that an invalid (spurious) demand must be stricken.

2. The subdivision now puts a 5–day limit on the time when a defendant must be prepared.

(d)(1). Motion for Discharge.

1. Under the amended provision, a prematurely filed motion is invalid and may be stricken.

(d)(2). When Time May Be Extended.

1. The terms "waiver," "tolling," or "suspension" have no meaning within the context of the subdivision as amended. The subdivision addresses extensions for a specified period of time.

2. Except for stipulations, all extensions require an order of the court.

3. The term "recorded order" refers to stenographic recording and not recording of a written order by the clerk.

(d)(3). Delay and Continuances.

1. Even though the normal time limit has expired under (a)(1) or (a)(2), a trial court may not properly discharge a defendant without making a complete inquiry of possible reasons to deny discharge. If the court finds that the time period has been properly extended and the extension has not expired, the court must simply deny the motion. If the court finds that the delay is attributable to the accused, that the accused was unavailable for trial, or that the demand was invalid, the court must deny the motion and schedule trial within 90 days. If the court has before it a valid motion for discharge and none of the above circumstances are present, the court must grant the motion.

(e). Availability for Trial.

1. Availability for trial is now defined solely in terms of required attendance and readiness for trial.

(f). Exceptional Circumstances.

1. The 2 extension limit for unavailable evidence has been discarded.

2. The new trial date paragraph was eliminated because it simply was unnecessary.

(g). Effect of Mistrial; Appeal; Order of New Trial.

1. Makes uniform a 90–day period within which a defendant must be brought to trial after a mistrial, order of new trial, or appeal by the state or defendant.

(h)(1). Discharge from Crime.

1. No change.

(h)(2). Nolle Prosequi.

1. No change.

1984 Amendment.

(a)(1). Repeals the remedy of automatic discharge from the crime and refers instead to the new subdivision on remedies.

(a)(2). Establishes the calendar call for the demand for speedy trial when filed. This provision, especially sought by prosecutors, brings the matter to the attention of both the court and the prosecution. The subdivision again repeals the automatic discharge for failure to meet the mandated time limit, referring to the new subdivision on remedies for the appropriate remedy.

(I). The intent of (I)(4) is to provide the state attorney with 15 days within which to bring a defendant to trial from the date of the filing of the motion for discharge. This time begins with the filing of the motion and continues regardless of whether the judge hears the motion.

This subdivision provides that, upon failure of the prosecution to meet the mandated time periods, the defendant shall file a motion for discharge, which will then be heard by the court within 5 days. The court sets trial of the defendant within 10 additional days. The total 15–day period was chosen carefully by the committee, the consensus being that the period was long enough that the system could, in fact, bring to trial a defendant not yet tried, but short enough that the pressure to try defendants within the prescribed time period would remain. In other words, it gives the system a chance to remedy a mistake; it does not permit the system to forget about the time constraints. It was felt that a period of 10 days was too short, giving the system insufficient time in which to bring a defendant to trial; the period of 30 days was too long, removing incentive to maintain strict docket control in order to remain within the prescribed time periods.

The committee further felt that it was not appropriate to extend the new remedy provisions to misdemeanors, but only to more serious offenses.

1992 Amendment. The purpose of the amendments is to gender neutralize the wording of the rule. In addition, the committee recommends the rule be amended to differentiate between 2 separate and distinct pleadings now referred to as "motion for discharge." The initial "motion for discharge" has been renamed "notice of expiration of speedy trial time."

Rule 3.192. Motions for Rehearing

When an appeal by the state is authorized by Florida Rule of Appellate Procedure 9.140, or sections 924.07 or 924.071, Florida Statutes, the state may file a motion for rehearing within 10 days of an order subject to appellate review. A motion for rehearing shall state with particularity the points of law or fact that, in the opinion of the state, the court has overlooked or misapprehended in its decision, and shall not present issues not previously raised in the proceeding. A response may be filed within 10 days of service of the motion. The trial court's order disposing of the motion for rehearing shall be filed within 15 days of the response but not later than 40 days from the date of the order of which rehearing is sought. A timely filed motion for rehearing shall toll rendition of the order subject to appellate review and the order shall be deemed rendered upon the filing of a signed, written order denying the motion for rehearing. This rule shall not apply to post-conviction proceedings pursuant to rule 3.800(a), 3.850, 3.851, or 3.853. Nothing in this rule precludes the trial court from exercising its inherent authority to reconsider a ruling while the court has jurisdiction of the case.

Added Nov. 19, 2009, effective Jan. 1, 2010 (26 So.3d 534). Amended June 11, 2015, effective June 11, 2015 (167 So.3d 395).

Rule 3.200. Notice of Alibi

On the written demand of the prosecuting attorney, specifying as particularly as is known to the prosecuting attorney the place, date, and time of the commission of the crime charged, a defendant in a criminal case who intends to offer evidence of an alibi in defense shall, not less than 10 days before trial or such other time as the court may direct, file and serve on the prosecuting attorney a notice in writing of an intention to claim an alibi, which notice shall contain specific information as to the place at which the defendant claims to have been at the time of the alleged offense and, as particularly as is known to the defendant or the defendant's attorney, the names and addresses of the witnesses by whom the defendant proposes to establish the alibi. Not more than 5 days after receipt of defendant's witness list, or any other time as the court may direct, the prosecuting attorney shall file and serve on the defendant the names and addresses (as particularly as are known to the prosecuting attorney) of the witnesses the state proposes to offer in rebuttal to discredit the defendant's alibi at the trial of the cause. Both the defendant and the prosecuting attorney shall be under a continuing duty to promptly disclose the names and addresses of additional witnesses who come to the attention of either party subsequent to filing their respective witness lists as provided in this rule. If a defendant fails to file and serve a copy of the notice as herein required, the court may exclude evidence offered by the defendant for the purpose of providing an alibi, except the defendant's own testimony. If the notice is given by a defendant, the court may exclude the testimony of any witness offered by the defendant for the purpose of proving an alibi if the name and address of the witness as particularly as is known to the defendant or the defendant's attorney is not stated in the notice. If the prosecuting attorney fails to file and serve a copy on the defendant of a list of witnesses as herein provided, the court may exclude evidence offered by the state in rebuttal to the defendant's alibi evidence. If notice is given by the prosecuting attorney, the court may exclude the testimony of any witness offered by the prosecuting attorney for the purpose of rebutting the defense of alibi if the name and address of the witness as particularly as is known to the prosecuting attorney is not stated in the notice. For good cause shown the court may waive the requirements of this rule.

Amended Sept. 24, 1992, effective Jan. 1, 1993 (606 So.2d 227).

Committee Notes

1968 Adoption. The rule is completely new in Florida. Fourteen states have adopted notice of alibi statutes or rules: Arizona Supreme Court Rules of Criminal Procedure 192 (enacted in 1940); Ind.Ann.Stat. 9–1631, 9–1632, 9–1633 (1956) (enacted in 1935); Iowa Code Ann. 777 18 (1958) (enacted in 1941); Kan.Gen.Stat.Ann. 62–1341 (1949) (enacted in 1935); Mich.Stat.Ann. 630.14 (1947) (enacted in 1935); N.J. Superior and County Court Criminal Practice Rule 3:5–9 (1948) (enacted in 1934); N.Y.Code of Crim.Proc. 295–L (1935) (enacted in 1935); Ohio Rev.Code Ann. 2945.58 (1953) (enacted in 1929); Okla.Stat.Ann. 22–585 (1937) (enacted in 1935); S.D. Code 34.2801 (1939) (enacted in 1935); Utah Code Ann. 77–22–17 (1953) (enacted in 1935); Vt.Stat.Ann. 13–6561, 6562 (1958) (enacted in 1935); Wis.Stat.Ann. 955.07 (1958) (enacted in 1935).

The rule is modeled after the Ohio, New York, and New Jersey statutes:

(1) The requirement of notice in writing is taken from the Ohio statute.

(2) The requirement of an initial demand by the prosecuting attorney is based on the New York and New Jersey statutes.

(3) The requirement of a mutual exchange of witness lists is based on those statutes which require the defendant to disclose alibi witnesses. In the interest of mutuality, the requirement of a reciprocal exchange of witness lists has been added. The enforcement provision is based on the Ohio and New York statutes. In New York, a defendant who fails to give advance notice of alibi may still give alibi testimony himself. People v. Rakiec, 23 N.Y.S.2d 607, aff'd 45 N.E.2d 812 (1942).

For an excellent article on notice of alibi statutes, court decisions thereunder, and some empirical data on the practical effect of the rules, see David M. Epstein, "Advance Notice of Alibi," 55 J.Crim. Law & Criminology 29 (1964).

1972 Amendment. Same as prior rule.

1992 Amendment. The purpose of the amendments is to gender neutralize the wording of the rule.

Rule 3.201. Battered–Spouse Syndrome Defense

(a) Battered-Spouse Syndrome. When in any criminal case it shall be the intention of the defendant to rely on the defense of battered-spouse syndrome at trial, no evidence offered by the defendant for the purpose of establishing that defense shall be admitted in the case unless advance notice in writing of the defense shall have been given by the defendant as hereinafter provided.

(b) Time for Filing Notice. The defendant shall give notice of intent to rely on the defense of battered-spouse syndrome no later than 30 days prior to trial. The notice shall contain a statement of particulars showing the nature of the defense the defendant expects to prove and the names and addresses of the witnesses by whom the defendant expects to show battered-spouse syndrome, insofar as possible.

Added Oct. 21, 1993 (630 So.2d 172).

Rule 3.202. Expert Testimony of Mental Mitigation During Penalty Phase of Capital Trial: Notice and Examination by State Expert

(a) Notice of Intent to Seek Death Penalty. The provisions of this rule apply only in those capital cases in which the state gives written notice of its intent to seek the death penalty within 45 days from the date of arraignment. Failure to give timely written notice under this subdivision does not preclude the state from seeking the death penalty.

(b) Notice of Intent to Present Expert Testimony of Mental Mitigation. When in any capital case, in which the state has given notice of intent to seek the death penalty under subdivision (a) of this rule, it shall be the intention of the defendant to present, during the penalty phase of the trial, expert testimony of a mental health professional, who has tested, evaluated, or examined the defendant, in order to establish statutory or nonstatutory mental mitigating circumstances, the defendant shall give written notice of intent to present such testimony.

(c) Time for Filing Notice; Contents. The defendant shall give notice of intent to present expert testimony of mental mitigation not less than 20 days before trial. The notice shall contain a statement of particulars listing the statutory and nonstatutory mental mitigating circumstances the defendant expects to establish through expert testimony and the names and addresses of the mental health experts by whom the defendant expects to establish mental mitigation, insofar as is possible.

(d) Appointment of State Expert; Time of Examination. After the filing of such notice and on the motion of the state indicating its desire to seek the death penalty, the court shall order that, within 48 hours after the defendant is convicted of capital murder, the defendant be examined by a mental health expert chosen by the state. Attorneys for the state and defendant may be present at the examination. The examination shall be limited to those mitigating circumstances the defendant expects to establish through expert testimony.

(e) Defendant's Refusal to Cooperate. If the defendant refuses to be examined by or fully cooperate with the state's mental health expert, the court may, in its discretion:

(1) order the defense to allow the state's expert to review all mental health reports, tests, and evaluations by the defendant's mental health expert; or

(2) prohibit defense mental health experts from testifying concerning mental health tests, evaluations, or examinations of the defendant.

Added Nov. 2, 1995, effective Jan. 1, 1996 (674 So.2d 83). Amended on motion for rehearing May 2, 1996 (674 So.2d 83).

Rule 3.203. Defendant's Intellectual Disability as a Bar to Imposition of the Death Penalty

(a) Scope. This rule applies in all first-degree murder cases in which the state attorney has not waived the death penalty on the record and the defendant's intellectual disability becomes an issue.

(b) Definition of Intellectual Disability. As used in this rule, the term "intellectual disability" means significantly subaverage general intellectual functioning existing concurrently with deficits in adaptive behavior and manifested during the period from conception to age 18. The term "significantly subaverage general intellectual functioning," for the purpose of this rule, means performance that is two or more standard deviations from the mean score on a standardized intelligence test authorized by the Department of Children and Family Services in rule 65G–4.011 of the Florida Administrative Code. The term "adaptive behavior," for the purpose of this rule, means the effectiveness or degree with which an individual meets the standards of personal independence and social responsibility expected of his or her age, cultural group, and community.

(c) Motion for Determination of Intellectual Disability as a Bar to Execution: Contents; Procedures.

(1) A defendant who intends to raise intellectual disability as a bar to execution shall file a written motion to establish intellectual disability as a bar to execution with the court.

(2) The motion shall state that the defendant is intellectually disabled and, if the defendant has been tested, evaluated, or examined by one or more experts, the names and addresses of the experts. Copies of reports containing the opinions of any experts named in the motion shall be attached to the motion. The court shall appoint an expert chosen by the state attorney if the state attorney so requests. The expert shall promptly test, evaluate, or examine the defendant and shall submit a written report of any findings to the parties and the court.

(3) If the defendant has not been tested, evaluated, or examined by one or more experts, the motion shall state that fact and the court shall appoint two experts

who shall promptly test, evaluate, or examine the defendant and shall submit a written report of any findings to the parties and the court.

(4) Attorneys for the state and defendant may be present at the examinations conducted by court-appointed experts.

(5) If the defendant refuses to be examined or fully cooperate with the court appointed experts or the state's expert, the court may, in the court's discretion:

(A) order the defense to allow the court-appointed experts to review all mental health reports, tests, and evaluations by the defendant's expert;

(B) prohibit the defense experts from testifying concerning any tests, evaluations, or examinations of the defendant regarding the defendant's intellectual disability; or

(C) order such relief as the court determines to be appropriate.

(d) Time for filing Motion for Determination of Intellectual Disability as a Bar to Execution. The motion for a determination of intellectual disability as a bar to execution shall be filed not later than 90 days prior to trial, or at such time as is ordered by the court.

(e) Hearing on Motion to Determine Intellectual Disability. The circuit court shall conduct an evidentiary hearing on the motion for a determination of intellectual disability. At the hearing, the court shall consider the findings of the experts and all other evidence on the issue of whether the defendant is intellectually disabled. The court shall enter a written order prohibiting the imposition of the death penalty and setting forth the court's specific findings in support of the court's determination if the court finds that the defendant is intellectually disabled as defined in subdivision (b) of this rule. The court shall stay the proceedings for 30 days from the date of rendition of the order prohibiting the death penalty or, if a motion for rehearing is filed, for 30 days following the rendition of the order denying rehearing, to allow the state the opportunity to appeal the order. If the court determines that the defendant has not established intellectual disability, the court shall enter a written order setting forth the court's specific findings in support of the court's determination.

(f) Waiver. A claim authorized under this rule is waived if not filed in accord with the time requirements for filing set out in this rule, unless good cause is shown for the failure to comply with the time requirements.

(g) Finding of Intellectual Disability; Order to Proceed. If, after the evidence presented, the court is of the opinion that the defendant is intellectually disabled, the court shall order the case to proceed without the death penalty as an issue.

(h) Appeal. An appeal may be taken by the state if the court enters an order finding that the defendant is intellectually disabled, which will stay further proceedings in the trial court until a decision on appeal is rendered. Appeals are to proceed according to Florida Rule of Appellate Procedure 9.140(c).

(i) Motion to Establish Intellectual Disability as a Bar to Execution; Stay of Execution. The filing of a motion to establish intellectual disability as a bar to execution shall not stay further proceedings without a separate order staying execution.

Added May 20, 2004, effective Oct. 1, 2004 (875 So.2d 563). Amended Nov. 19, 2009, effective Jan. 1, 2010 (26 So.3d 534); Dec. 12, 2013 (132 So.3d 123).

Rule 3.210. Incompetence to Proceed: Procedure for Raising the Issue

(a) Proceedings Barred during Incompetency. A person accused of an offense or a violation of probation or community control who is mentally incompetent to proceed at any material stage of a criminal proceeding shall not be proceeded against while incompetent.

(1) A "material stage of a criminal proceeding" shall include the trial of the case, pretrial hearings involving questions of fact on which the defendant might be expected to testify, entry of a plea, violation of probation or violation of community control proceedings, sentencing, hearings on issues regarding a defendant's failure to comply with court orders or conditions, or other matters where the mental competence of the defendant is necessary for a just resolution of the issues being considered. The terms "competent," "competence," "incompetent," and "incompetence," as used in rules 3.210–3.219, shall refer to mental competence or incompetence to proceed at a material stage of a criminal proceeding.

(2) The incompetence of the defendant shall not preclude such judicial action, hearings on motions of the parties, discovery proceedings, or other procedures that do not require the personal participation of the defendant.

(b) Motion for Examination. If, at any material stage of a criminal proceeding, the court of its own motion, or on motion of counsel for the defendant or for the state, has reasonable ground to believe that the defendant is not mentally competent to proceed, the court shall immediately enter its order setting a time for a hearing to determine the defendant's mental condition, which shall be held no later than 20 days after the date of the filing of the motion, and may order the defendant to be examined by no more than 3 experts, as needed, prior to the date of the hearing. Attorneys for the state and the defendant may be present at any examination ordered by the court.

(1) A written motion for the examination made by counsel for the defendant shall contain a certificate of counsel that the motion is made in good faith and on reasonable grounds to believe that the defendant is incompetent to proceed. To the extent that it does not invade the lawyer-client privilege, the motion shall

contain a recital of the specific observations of and conversations with the defendant that have formed the basis for the motion.

(2) A written motion for the examination made by counsel for the state shall contain a certificate of counsel that the motion is made in good faith and on reasonable grounds to believe the defendant is incompetent to proceed and shall include a recital of the specific facts that have formed the basis for the motion, including a recitation of the observations of and statements of the defendant that have caused the state to file the motion.

(3) If the defendant has been released on bail or other release provision, the court may order the defendant to appear at a designated place for evaluation at a specific time as a condition of such release. If the court determines that the defendant will not submit to the evaluation or that the defendant is not likely to appear for the scheduled evaluation, the court may order the defendant taken into custody until the determination of the defendant's competency to proceed. A motion made for evaluation under this subdivision shall not otherwise affect the defendant's right to release.

(4) The order appointing experts shall:

(A) identify the purpose or purposes of the evaluation, including the nature of the material proceeding, and specify the area or areas of inquiry that should be addressed by the evaluator;

(B) specify the legal criteria to be applied; and

(C) specify the date by which the report should be submitted and to whom the report should be submitted.

Amended Sept. 24, 1992, effective Jan. 1, 1993 (606 So.2d 227); Nov. 19, 2009, effective Jan. 1, 2010 (26 So.3d 534).

Committee Notes

1968 Adoption. (a) Same as section 917.01, Florida Statutes, except it was felt that court cannot by rule direct institution officials. Thus words, "he shall report this fact to the court which conducted the hearing. If the officer so reports" and concluding sentence, "No defendant committed by a court to an institution, by reason of the examination referred to in this paragraph, shall be released therefrom, without the consent of the court committing him," should be omitted from the rule but retained by statute.

(b) Same as section 909.17, Florida Statutes.

(c) Same as section 917.02, Florida Statutes.

1972 Amendment. Subdivision (a)(3) refers to Jackson v. Indiana, 406 U.S. 715, 730, 92 S.Ct. 1845, 32 L.Ed.2d 435 (1972); also, United States v. Curry, 410 F.2d 1372 (4th Cir.1969). Subdivision (d) is added to give the court authority to confine an insane person who is likely to cause harm to others even if the person is otherwise entitled to bail. The amendment does not apply unless the defendant contends that he or she is insane at the time of trial or at the time the offense was committed. The purpose of the amendment is to prevent admittedly insane persons from being at large when there is a likelihood they may injure themselves or others.

1977 Amendment. This language is taken, almost verbatim, from existing rule 3.210(a). The word "insane" is changed to reflect the new terminology, "competence to stand trial." The definition of competence to stand trial is taken verbatim from the United States Supreme Court formulation of the test in Dusky v. United States, 362 U.S. 402, 80 S.Ct. 788, 4 L.Ed.2d 824 (1960).

(a)(2) The first part of this paragraph is taken, almost verbatim, from the existing rule. The right of counsel for the state to move for such examination has been added.

(b)(1) In order to confine the defendant as incompetent to stand trial, the defendant must be confined under the same standards as those used for civil commitment. These criteria were set forth in the recent U.S. Supreme Court case of Jackson v. Indiana, 406 U.S. 715, 92 S.Ct. 1845, 32 L.Ed.2d 435 (1972), in which it was held to be a denial of equal protection to subject a criminal defendant to a more lenient commitment standard than would be applied to one not charged with a crime. Therefore, the criteria for involuntary civil commitment should be incorporated as the criteria for commitment for incompetence to stand trial.

In this subdivision is found the most difficult of the problems to resolve for the rule. The head-on conflict between the Department of Health and Rehabilitative Services, a part of the executive branch of the government, and the courts occurs when the administrator determines that a defendant no longer should be confined, but the trial judge does not wish the defendant released because the trial judge feels that further commitment is necessary. Under the civil commitment model, the administrator has the power to release a committed patient at such time as the administrator feels the patient no longer meets the standards for commitment. Obviously, since a defendant in a criminal case is under the jurisdiction of the court, such immediate release is unwarranted.

The time period of the initial commitment parallels that of civil commitment.

(b)(2) treats the problem of what the court should do with a defendant who is not competent to stand trial, but who fails to meet the criteria for commitment. If incompetent, but not in need of treatment and not dangerous, then the defendant cannot be committed. The present rule provides for dismissal of the charges immediately. There appears to be no reason why someone in this situation should not be released pending trial on bail, as would other defendants.

The finding of "not guilty by reason of insanity," required under the present rule when a defendant cannot be tried by reason of incompetence, seems inappropriate since such a defense admits the commission of the fact of the crime but denies the defendant's mental state. Since no such finding has been made (and cannot be made), the verdict entered of not guilty by reason of insanity is not appropriate. Further, it would give a defendant, later competent, a res judicata or double jeopardy defense, the verdict being a final determination of guilt or innocence. It would seem far more appropriate to withdraw the charges. A defendant who regains competence within the period of the statute of limitations could still be tried for the offense, if such trial is warranted.

One of the major problems confronting the institution in which an incompetent person is being held is that of obtaining consent for medical procedures and treatment, not necessarily mental treatment. Generally, under the statute, the patient civilly committed is not thereby deemed incompetent to consent. At the commitment hearing in the civil proceedings, the judge may make the general competency determination. It is recommended that the same process apply in the hearing on competency to stand trial, and that, if the trial judge does not find the defendant incompetent for other purposes, the defendant be legally considered competent for such other purposes.

1980 Amendment.

(a) This provision is identical to that which has been contained in all prior rules and statutes relating to competence to stand trial. No change is suggested.

(b) In order to ensure that the proceedings move quickly the court is required to set a hearing within 20 days. This subdivision should be read in conjunction with rule 3.211 which requires the experts to submit their report to the court at such time as the court shall specify. The court therefore determines the time on which the report is to be submitted. The provision requiring at least 2 but no more than 3 experts is meant to coincide with section 394.02, Florida Statutes (1979), in which the legislature provides for the number of experts to be appointed and that at least 1 of such experts be appointed from a group of certain designated state-related professionals. This legislative restriction on appointment will ensure that the Department of Health and Rehabilitative Services will, to some extent, be involved in the hospitalization decision-making process. Other possible procedures were discussed at great length both among members of the committee and with representatives of the legislature, but it was decided that any more specific procedures should be developed on the local level in the individual circuits and that it would be inappropriate to mandate such specific procedures in a statewide court rule. Since it was felt by the committee to be a critical stage in the proceedings and subject to Sixth Amendment provisions, and since no psychiatrist-patient privilege applies to this stage of the proceeding, the committee felt that attorneys for both sides should have the right to be present at such examinations.

(1) and (2) A motion for examination relative to competency to stand trial should not be a "boiler plate" motion filed in every case. The inclusion of specific facts in the motion will give the trial judge a basis on which to determine whether there is sufficient indication of incompetence to stand trial that experts should be appointed to examine the defendant. Provision was made that conversations and observations need not be disclosed if they were felt to violate the lawyer-client privilege. Observations of the defendant were included in this phrase in that these may, in some cases, be considered "verbal acts."

(3) The mere filing of a motion for examination to determine competence to stand trial should not affect in any way the provision for release of a defendant on bail or other pretrial release provision. If a defendant has been released on bail, the judgment already having been made that he or she is so entitled, and as long as the defendant will continue to appear for appropriate evaluations, the mere fact that the motion was filed should not abrogate the right to bail. Obviously, if other factors would affect the defendant's right to release or would affect the right to release on specific release conditions, those conditions could be changed or the release revoked. By making the requirement that the defendant appear for evaluation a condition of release, the court can more easily take back into custody a defendant who has refused to appear for evaluation, and the defendant can then be evaluated in custody.

1988 Amendment. Title. The title is amended to reflect change in subdivision (a)(1), which broadens the issue of competency in criminal proceedings from the narrow issue of competency to stand trial to competency to proceed at any material stage of a criminal proceeding.

(a) This provision is broadened to prohibit proceeding against a defendant accused of a criminal offense or a violation of probation or community control and is broadened from competency to stand trial to competency to proceed at any material stage of a criminal proceeding as defined in subdivision (1).

(1) This new provision defines a material stage of a criminal proceeding when an incompetent defendant may not be proceeded against. This provision includes competence to be sentenced, which was previously addressed in rule 3.740 and is now addressed with more specificity in the new rule 3.214. Under the Florida Supreme Court decision of Jackson v. State, 452 So.2d 533 (Fla. 1984), this definition would not apply to a motion under rule 3.850.

(2) This new provision allows certain matters in a criminal case to proceed, even if a defendant is determined to be incompetent, in areas not requiring the personal participation of the defendant.

(b) This provision is amended to reflect the changes in subdivision (a) above.

(1) Same as above.

(2) Same as above.

(3) Same as above. This provision also changes the phrase "released from custody on a pre-trial release provision" to "released on bail or other release provision" because the term "custody" is subject to several interpretations.

(4) This new provision is designed to specify and clarify in the order appointing experts, the matters the appointed experts are to address, and to specify when and to whom their reports are to be submitted. Court-appointed experts often do not understand the specific purpose of their examination or the specifics of the legal criteria to be applied.

Specifying to whom the experts' reports are to be submitted is designed to avoid confusion.

1992 Amendment. The purpose of the amendment is to gender neutralize the wording of the rule.

Introductory Note Relating to Amendments to Rules 3.210 to 3.219. In 1985, the Florida Legislature enacted amendments to part I of chapter 394, the "Florida Mental Health Act," and substantial amendments to chapter 916 entitled "Mentally Deficient and Mentally Ill Defendants." The effect of the amendments is to avoid tying mentally ill or deficient defendants in the criminal justice system to civil commitment procedures in the "Baker Act." Reference to commitment of a criminal defendant found not guilty by reason of insanity has been removed from section 394.467, Florida Statutes. Chapter 916 now provides for specific commitment criteria of mentally ill or mentally retarded criminal defendants who are either incompetent to proceed or who have been found not guilty by reason of insanity in criminal proceedings.

In part, the following amendments to rules 3.210 to 3.219 are designed to reflect the 1985 amendments to chapters 394 and 916.

Florida judges on the criminal bench are committing and the Department of Health and Rehabilitative Services (HRS) mental health treatment facilities are admitting and treating those mentally ill and mentally retarded defendants in the criminal justice system who have been adjudged incompetent to stand trial and defendants found to be incompetent to proceed with violation of probation and community control proceedings. Judges are also finding such defendants not guilty by reason of insanity and committing them to HRS for treatment, yet there were no provisions for such commitments in the rules.

Some of the amendments to rules 3.210 to 3.219 are designed to provide for determinations of whether a defendant is mentally competent to proceed in any material stage of a criminal proceeding and provide for community treatment or commitment to HRS when a defendant meets commitment criteria under the provisions of chapter 916 as amended in 1985.

Rule 3.211. Competence to Proceed: Scope of Examination and Report

(a) Examination by Experts. Upon appointment by the court, the experts shall examine the defendant with respect to the issue of competence to proceed, as specified by the court in its order appointing the experts to evaluate the defendant, and shall evaluate the defendant as ordered.

(1) The experts shall first consider factors related to the issue of whether the defendant meets the criteria for competence to proceed; that is, whether the defendant has sufficient present ability to consult with counsel with a reasonable degree of rational understanding and whether the defendant has a rational, as well as factual, understanding of the pending proceedings.

(2) In considering the issue of competence to proceed, the examining experts shall consider and include in their report:

(A) the defendant's capacity to:

(i) appreciate the charges or allegations against the defendant;

(ii) appreciate the range and nature of possible penalties, if applicable, that may be imposed in the proceedings against the defendant;

(iii) understand the adversary nature of the legal process;

(iv) disclose to counsel facts pertinent to the proceedings at issue;

(v) manifest appropriate courtroom behavior;

(vi) testify relevantly; and

(B) any other factors deemed relevant by the experts.

(b) Factors to Be Evaluated. If the experts should find that the defendant is incompetent to proceed, the experts shall report on any recommended treatment for the defendant to attain competence to proceed. In considering the issues relating to treatment, the examining experts shall report on:

(1) the mental illness or intellectual disability causing the incompetence;

(2) the treatment or treatments appropriate for the mental illness or intellectual disability of the defendant and an explanation of each of the possible treatment alternatives in order of choices;

(3) the availability of acceptable treatment. If treatment is available in the community, the expert shall so state in the report; and

(4) the likelihood of the defendant attaining competence under the treatment recommended, an assessment of the probable duration of the treatment required to restore competence, and the probability that the defendant will attain competence to proceed in the foreseeable future.

(c) Written Findings of Experts. Any written report submitted by the experts shall:

(1) identify the specific matters referred for evaluation;

(2) describe the evaluative procedures, techniques, and tests used in the examination and the purpose or purposes for each;

(3) state the expert's clinical observations, findings, and opinions on each issue referred for evaluation by the court, and indicate specifically those issues, if any, on which the expert could not give an opinion; and

(4) identify the sources of information used by the expert and present the factual basis for the expert's clinical findings and opinions.

The procedure for determinations of the confidential status of reports is governed by Rule of Judicial Administration 2.420.

(d) Limited Use of Competency Evidence.

(1) The information contained in any motion by the defendant for determination of competency to proceed or in any report of experts filed under this rule insofar as the report relates solely to the issues of competency to proceed and commitment, and any information elicited during a hearing on competency to proceed or commitment held pursuant to this rule, shall be used only in determining the mental competency to proceed or the commitment or other treatment of the defendant.

(2) The defendant waives this provision by using the report, or portions thereof, in any proceeding for any other purpose, in which case disclosure and use of the report, or any portion thereof, shall be governed by applicable rules of evidence and rules of criminal procedure. If a part of the report is used by the defendant, the state may request the production of any other portion of that report that, in fairness, ought to be considered.

Amended Sept. 24, 1992, effective Jan. 1, 1993 (606 So.2d 227); Nov. 19, 2009, effective Jan. 1, 2010 (26 So.3d 534); Nov. 3, 2011, effective, *nunc pro tunc*, Oct. 1, 2011 (78 So.3d 1045); Dec. 12, 2013 (132 So.3d 123).

Committee Notes

1980 Adoption. This rule provides for appointment of experts and for the contents of the report which the experts are to render. Since the issue of competency has been raised, the experts will, of course, report on this issue. If there is reason to believe that involuntary hospitalization is also required, the court should order the experts to make this evaluation as well during their initial examination. It was felt, however, that the experts should not inquire into involuntary hospitalization as a matter of course, but only if sufficient reasonable grounds to do so were alleged in the motion, comparing the procedure to that required by the civil commitment process.

(a) Certain factors relating to competency to stand trial have been determined to be appropriate for analysis by examining experts. Often, with different experts involved, the experts do not use the same criteria in reaching their conclusions. The criteria used by experts who testify at the competency and commitment hearings may not be the same as those used by persons involved in the treatment process or later hearings after treatment. This subdivision, therefore, addresses those factors which, at least, should be considered by experts at both ends of the spectrum. Additional factors may be considered, and these factors listed may be addressed in different ways. At least the requirement that these specific factors be addressed will give a common basis of understanding for the experts at the competency hearing, the trial judge, and the experts who will later receive a defendant who is found to be incompetent to stand trial and in need of involuntary hospitalization. The test for determining competency to stand trial is that which has been contained in both the prior rules and statutes developed from Dusky v. United States, 362 U.S. 402, 80 S.Ct. 788, 4 L.Ed.2d 824 (1960).

(1) The factors set forth in this section have been developed by the Department of Health and Rehabilitative Services (HRS) in its Competency Evaluation Instrument, a refinement of the McGarry Competency Evaluation Procedure.

(b) The issue of involuntary hospitalization is to be considered only if the court has ordered the experts to consider this issue; the court would do so if it found that there existed reasonable grounds to believe that the defendant met the criteria for involuntary hospitalization. The factors set forth in order to determine this issue are those that have been developed through prior statutes relating to involuntary hospitalization, from the case of Jackson v. Indiana, 406 U.S. 715, 92 S.Ct. 1845, 32 L.Ed.2d 435 (1972), and In Re: Beverly, 342 So.2d 481 (Fla.1977).

As to criteria for involuntary hospitalization, see chapter 394, Florida Statutes, or, in the case of mental retardation, see chapter 393, Florida Statutes.

Section 394.467(1), Florida Statutes (1979), prescribes criteria for involuntary hospitalization or placement. In case of mental retardation, section 393.11, Florida Statutes (1979), governs.

(c) In most instances, the issues of incompetency at time of trial and insanity at time of the offense will be raised at the same time or, at least, in the same case. In the event that the 2 are not raised in the same case, there would be no reason for the examining experts to inquire into the mental status of the defendant at the time of the offense itself at the incompetency examination. However, if insanity as a defense is raised, it would be most appropriate for judicial efficiency to have the examining experts inquire into all issues at the same time. This provision permits such inquiry by the experts in the event that notice of intent to rely on the defense of insanity has been filed by the defendant.

(d) This provision is meant to permit local circuits to develop their own forms for such reports if they feel that such forms are appropriate. It does not preclude HRS from suggesting a form that would be of particular assistance to them and requesting its adoption, but adoption is not mandated.

(e) This subdivision provides for the confidentiality of the information obtained by virtue of an examination of the defendant pursuant to this subdivision. Cf. § 90.108, Fla.Stat. (1979); Fla.R.Civ.P. 1.330(6).

Section 916.12, Florida Statutes is a companion statute relating to mental competence to stand trial.

1988 Amendment. Title. The title is amended to reflect changes in rule 3.210.

(a) This subdivision, which was originally an introductory paragraph, is amended to reflect changes in rule 3.210. The deletions related to the extent of the evaluation and when and to whom the experts' reports are to be submitted have been placed in rule 3.210(4) above.

(1) This subdivision, which was formerly subdivision (a), has been amended to reflect changes in rule 3.210 above.

(2) This provision has been amended to reflect the changes to rule 3.210. In addition, the 11 factors previously numbered (i) through (xi) have been reduced to 6 factors. Numbers (v), (vi), (vii), (x), and (xi) have been removed. Those 5 factors were felt to not be directly related to the issue of a defendant having the mental capacity to communicate with his or her attorney or to understand the proceedings against him or her and may have had the effect of confusing the issues the experts are to address in assessing a defendant's competency to proceed. The terms "ability" and "capacity" which were used interchangeably in the prior version of this provision have been changed to the single term "capacity" for continuity. A provision has been added which allows the appointed expert to also include any other factors deemed relevant to take into account different techniques and points of view of the experts.

(b) This subdivision, including its 4 subdivisions, is amended to reflect the changes in rule 3.210. It also expands the determination from the limited area of whether an incompetent defendant should be voluntarily committed to treatment to recommended treatment options designed to restore or maintain competence. Subdivision (v) has been deleted because consideration of less restrictive alternatives is addressed in other amendments. [See rule 3.212(c)(3)(iv).] The amendments further reflect 1985 legislative amendments to chapters 394 and 916, Florida Statutes.

(ii) Appropriate treatment may include maintaining the defendant on psychotropic or other medication. See rule 3.215.

(c) This provision is amended to take into account the defense of insanity both at trial and in violation of probation/community control hearings.

(d) This provision deletes the old language relating to the use of standardized forms. The new provision, with its 4 subdivisions, outlines in detail what the written report of an expert is to include, to ensure the appointed expert understands what issues are to be addressed, and that the report identifies sources of information, tests or evaluation techniques used, and includes the findings and observations upon which the expert's opinion is based. It requires the expert to specify those issues on which the expert could not render an opinion.

(e) This provision is amended to comply with changes in rule 3.210. In addition, the second paragraph has been expanded to clarify under what circumstances the reports of experts in a competency evaluation may be discovered by the prosecution and used as evidence in a hearing other than the hearing on the issue of a defendant's competency to proceed.

1992 Amendment. The purpose of the amendments is to gender neutralize the wording of the rule.

Introductory Note Relating to Amendments to Rules 3.210 to 3.219. See notes following rule 3.210 for the text of this note.

Rule 3.212. Competence to Proceed: Hearing and Disposition

(a) Admissibility of Evidence. The experts preparing the reports may be called by either party or the court, and additional evidence may be introduced by either party. The experts appointed by the court shall be deemed court witnesses whether called by the court or either party and may be examined as such by either party.

(b) Finding of Competence. The court shall first consider the issue of the defendant's competence to proceed. If the court finds the defendant competent to proceed, the court shall enter its order so finding and shall proceed.

(c) Commitment on Finding of Incompetence. If the court finds the defendant is incompetent to proceed, or that the defendant is competent to proceed but that the defendant's competence depends on the continuation of appropriate treatment for a mental illness or intellectual disability, the court shall consider issues relating to treatment necessary to restore or maintain the defendant's competence to proceed.

(1) The court may order the defendant to undergo treatment if the court finds that the defendant is mentally ill or intellectually disabled and is in need of treatment and that treatment appropriate for the defendant's condition is available. If the court finds that the defendant may be treated in the community on bail or other release conditions, the court may make acceptance of reasonable medical treatment a condition of continuing bail or other release conditions.

(2) If the defendant is incarcerated, the court may order treatment to be administered at the custodial facility or may order the defendant transferred to another facility for treatment or may commit the defendant as provided in subdivision (3).

(3) A defendant may be committed for treatment to restore a defendant's competence to proceed if the court finds that:

(A) the defendant meets the criteria for commitment as set forth by statute;

(B) there is a substantial probability that the mental illness or intellectual disability causing the defendant's incompetence will respond to treatment and that the defendant will regain competency to proceed in the reasonably foreseeable future;

(C) treatment appropriate for restoration of the defendant's competence to proceed is available; and

(D) no appropriate treatment alternative less restrictive than that involving commitment is available.

(4) If the court commits the defendant, the order of commitment shall contain:

(A) findings of fact relating to the issues of competency and commitment addressing the factors set forth in rule 3.211 when applicable;

(B) copies of the reports of the experts filed with the court pursuant to the order of examination;

(C) copies of any other psychiatric, psychological, or social work reports submitted to the court relative to the mental state of the defendant; and

(D) copies of the charging instrument and all supporting affidavits or other documents used in the determination of probable cause.

(5) The treatment facility shall admit the defendant for hospitalization and treatment and may retain and treat the defendant. No later than 6 months from the date of admission, the administrator of the facility shall file with the court a report that shall address the issues and consider the factors set forth in rule 3.211, with copies to all parties. If, at any time during the 6–month period or during any period of extended commitment that may be ordered pursuant to this rule, the administrator of the facility determines that the defendant no longer meets the criteria for commitment or has become competent to proceed, the administrator shall notify the court by such a report, with copies to all parties.

(A) If, during the 6–month period of commitment and treatment or during any period of extended commitment that may be ordered pursuant to this rule, counsel for the defendant shall have reasonable grounds to believe that the defendant is competent to proceed or no longer meets the criteria for commitment, counsel may move for a hearing on the issue of the defendant's competence or commitment. The motion shall contain a certificate of counsel that the motion is made in good faith and on reasonable grounds to believe that the defendant is now competent to proceed or no longer meets the criteria for commitment. To the extent that it does not invade the attorney-client privilege, the motion shall contain a recital of the specific observations of and conversations with the defendant that have formed the basis for the motion.

(B) If, upon consideration of a motion filed by counsel for the defendant or the prosecuting attorney and any information offered the court in support thereof, the court has reasonable grounds to believe that the defendant may have regained competence to proceed or no longer meets the criteria for commitment, the court shall order the administrator of the facility to report to the court on such issues, with copies to all parties, and shall order a hearing to be held on those issues.

(6) The court shall hold a hearing within 30 days of the receipt of any such report from the administrator of the facility on the issues raised thereby. If, following the hearing, the court determines that the defendant continues to be incompetent to proceed and that the defendant meets the criteria for continued commitment or treatment, the court shall order continued commitment or treatment for a period not to exceed 1 year. When the defendant is retained by the facility, the same procedure shall be repeated prior to the expiration of each additional 1–year period of extended commitment.

(7) If, at any time after such commitment, the court decides, after hearing, that the defendant is competent to proceed, it shall enter its order so finding and shall proceed.

(8) If, after any such hearing, the court determines that the defendant remains incompetent to proceed but no longer meets the criteria for commitment, the court shall proceed as provided in rule 3.212(d).

(d) Release on Finding of Incompetence. If the court decides that a defendant is not mentally competent to proceed but does not meet the criteria for commitment, the defendant may be released on appropriate release conditions for a period not to exceed 1 year. The court may order that the defendant receive outpatient treatment at an appropriate local facility and that the defendant report for further evaluation at specified times during the release period as conditions of release. A report shall be filed with the court after each evaluation by the persons appointed by the court to make such evaluations, with copies to all parties. The procedure for determinations of the confidential status of reports is governed by Rule of Judicial Administration 2.420.

Amended Sept. 24, 1992, effective Jan. 1, 1993 (606 So.2d 227); Nov. 27, 1996, effective Jan. 1, 1997 (685 So.2d 1253); Nov. 3, 2011, effective, *nunc pro tunc*, Oct. 1, 2011 (78 So.3d 1045); Dec. 12, 2013 (132 So.3d 123).

Committee Notes

1980 Adoption. This rule sets forth the procedure for the hearing itself. If other experts have been involved who were not appointed pursuant to this rule, provision is made that such experts may then be called by either party. Those experts appointed by the court to conduct the examination, if called by the court or by either party to testify at the hearing, will be regarded as court experts. Either party may then examine such experts by leading questions or may impeach such experts. If a party calls an expert witness other than those appointed by the court pursuant to these rules, the usual evidentiary rules of examining such witnesses shall then apply. Following the hearing, the court may come to one of 3 conclusions: (a) the defendant is competent to stand trial, rule 3.212(a); (b) the defendant is incompetent to stand trial and is in need of involuntary hospitalization, rule 3.212(b); or (c) the defendant is incompetent to stand trial but is not in need of involuntary hospitalization, rule 3.212(c).

(a) This provision has been contained in every prior rule or statute relating to the issues of competency to stand trial and provides that if the defendant is competent the trial shall commence. No change is recommended.

(b) This subdivision provides for the second possible finding of the court, namely that the defendant is found incompetent to stand trial and is in need of involuntary hospitalization. It is designed to track the provisions of chapter 394, Florida Statutes, relating to involuntary hospitalization and the provisions of chapter 393 relating to residential services insofar as they may apply to the defendant under criminal charges. In this way, the procedures to be set up by the institution to which a criminal defendant is sent should not vary greatly from procedures common to the institution in the involuntary hospitalization or residential treatment of those not subject to criminal charges.

The criteria for involuntary hospitalization are set forth in section 394.467(1), Florida Statutes (1979). As to involuntary hospitalization for mental retardation, see section 393.11, Florida Statutes (1979); definition of treatment facility, see section 394.455, Florida Statutes (1979); involuntary admission to residential services, see section 393.11, Florida Statutes (1979).

(2) The requirement that there be certain contents to the order of commitment is set forth in order to give greater assistance to the personnel of the treatment facility. The information to be included in the order should give them the benefit of all information that has been before the trial judge and has been considered by that judge in making the decision to involuntarily hospitalize the defendant. This information should then assist the personnel of the receiving institution in making their initial evaluation and in instituting appropriate treatment more quickly. The last requirement, that of supporting affidavits or other documents used in the determination of probable cause, is to give some indication of the nature of the offense to the examining doctors to enable them to determine when the defendant has reached a level of improvement that he or she can discuss the charge with "a reasonable degree of rational understanding."

(3) This subdivision is designed to correspond with a complementary section of the Florida Statutes. It mandates, as does the statute, that the treatment facility must admit the defendant for hospitalization and treatment. The time limitations set forth in this subdivision are designed to coincide with those set forth in chapter 394, Florida Statutes. If, however, the defendant should regain competence or no longer meets hospitalization criteria prior to the expiration of any of the time periods set, the administrator of the facility may report to the court and cause a re-evaluation of the defendant's mental status. At the end of the 6–month period, and every year thereafter, the administrator must report to the court. These time periods are set forth so as to coincide with chapter 394, Florida Statutes.

(i) Permits the defendant's attorney, in an appropriate case, to request a hearing if the attorney believes the defendant to have regained competency. The grounds for such belief are to be contained in the motion, as is a certificate of the good faith of counsel in filing it. If the motion is sufficient to give the court reasonable grounds to believe that the defendant may be competent or no longer meets the criteria for hospitalization, the court can order a report from the administrator and hold a hearing on the issues.

(4) The rule is meant to mandate that the court hold a hearing as quickly as possible, but the hearing must be held at least within 30 days of the receipt of the report from the administrator of the facility.

(c) This rule provides for the disposition of the defendant who falls under the third of the alternatives listed above, that is, one who is incompetent to stand trial but does not meet the provisions for involuntary hospitalization. It is meant to provide as great a flexibility as possible for the trial judge in handling such defendant.

As to criteria for involuntary hospitalization, see section 394.467(1), Florida Statutes (1979).

Section 916.13, Florida Statutes complements this rule and provides for the hospitalization of defendants adjudicated incompetent to stand trial.

1988 Amendment. Title. The title has been amended to reflect changes in rules 3.210 and 3.211.

(a) This provision was formerly the introductory paragraph to this rule. It has been labeled subdivision (a) for consistency in form.

(b) This provision was former subdivision (a). It has been amended to reflect changes in rules 3.210 and 3.211. The former subdivisions (b) and (b)(1) have been deleted because similar language is now found in new subdivision (c).

(c) This new provision, including all its subdivisions, is designed to reflect the commitment criteria in section 916.13(1), Florida Statutes, and to reflect that commitment to the Department of Health and Rehabilitative Services is to be tied to specific commitment criteria when no less restrictive treatment alternative is available.

(1) This provision provides for available community treatment when appropriate.

(2) This provision provides for treatment in a custodial facility or other available community residential program.

(3) This provision, and its subdivisions, outlines when a defendant may be committed and refers to commitment criteria under the provisions of section 916.13(1), Florida Statutes.

(4) This provision, and its subdivisions, was formerly subdivision (b)(2). The language has been amended to reflect changes in chapter 916 relating to the commitment of persons found incompetent to proceed and changes in rules 3.210 and 3.211.

(5) This provision, and its subdivisions, was formerly subdivision (b)(3). The amendments are for the same reasons as (4) above.

(6) This provision was formerly subdivision (b)(4). The amendments are for the same reasons as (4) above.

(7) This provision was formerly subdivision (b)(5). The amendments are for the same reasons as (4) above.

(8) This provision was formerly subdivision (b)(6). The amendments are for the same reasons as (4) above.

(d) The amendments to the provision are for the same reasons as (4) above.

1992 Amendment. The amendments substitute "shall" in place of "may" in subdivision (c)(5)(B) to require the trial court to order the administrator of the facility where an incompetent defendant has been committed to report to the court on the issue of competency when the court has reasonable grounds to believe that the defendant may have regained competence to proceed or no longer meets the criteria for commitment. The amendments also gender neutralize the wording of the rule.

Introductory Note Relating to Amendments to Rules 3.210 to 3.219. See notes following rule 3.210 for the text of this note.

Rule 3.213. Continuing Incompetency to Proceed, Except Incompetency to Proceed With Sentencing: Disposition

(a) Dismissal without Prejudice during Continuing Incompetency.

(1) If at any time after 5 years following a determination that a person is incompetent to stand trial or proceed with a probation or community control violation hearing when charged with a felony, or 1 year when charged with a misdemeanor, the court, after hearing, determines that the defendant remains incompetent to stand trial or proceed with a probation or community control violation hearing, that there is no substantial probability that the defendant will become mentally competent to stand trial or proceed with a probation or community control violation hearing in the foreseeable future, and that the defendant does not meet the criteria for commitment, it shall dismiss the charges against the defendant without prejudice to the state to refile the charges should the defendant be declared competent to proceed in the future.

(2) If the incompetency to stand trial or to proceed is due to intellectual disability or autism, the court shall dismiss the charges within a reasonable time after such determination, not to exceed 2 years for felony charges and 1 year for misdemeanor charges, unless the court specifies in its order the reasons for believing that the defendant will become competent within the foreseeable future and specifies the time within which the defendant is expected to become competent. The dismissal shall be without prejudice to the state to refile should the defendant be declared competent to proceed in the future.

(b) Commitment or Treatment during Continuing Incompetency.

(1) If at any time after 5 years following a determination that a person is incompetent to stand trial or proceed with a probation or community control violation hearing when charged with a felony, or 1 year when charged with a misdemeanor, the court, after hearing, determines that the defendant remains incompetent to stand trial or proceed with a probation or community control violation hearing, that there is no substantial probability that the defendant will become mentally competent to stand trial or proceed with a probation or community control violation hearing in the foreseeable future, and that the defendant does meet the criteria for commitment, the court shall dismiss the charges against the defendant and commit the defendant to the Department of Children and Family Services for involuntary hospitalization or residential services solely under the provisions of law or may order that the defendant receive outpatient treatment at any other facility or service on an outpatient basis subject to the provisions of those statutes. In the order of commitment, the judge shall order that the administrator of the facility notify the state attorney of the committing circuit no less than 30 days prior to the anticipated date of release of the defendant. If charges are dismissed pursuant to this subdivision, the dismissal shall be without prejudice to the state to refile the charges should the defendant be declared competent to proceed in the future.

(2) If the continuing incompetency is due to intellectual disability or autism, and the defendant either lacks the ability to provide for his or her well-being or is likely to physically injure himself or herself, or others, the defendant may be involuntarily admitted to residential services as provided by law.

(c) Applicability. This rule shall not apply to defendants determined to be incompetent to proceed with sentencing, which is addressed in rule 3.214.

Amended Sept. 24, 1992, effective Jan. 1, 1993 (606 So.2d 227); Nov. 2, 2000, effective Jan. 1, 2001 (794 So.2d 457); Nov. 9, 2006, effective Jan. 1, 2007 (942 So.2d 407); Dec. 12, 2013 (132 So.3d 123).

Committee Notes

1980 Adoption. As to involuntary hospitalization, see section 394.467(1), Florida Statutes (1979); as to involuntary admission to residential services, see chapter 393, Florida Statutes (1979).

(b) This provision is meant to deal with the defendant who remains incompetent after 5 years, and who does meet the criteria for involuntary hospitalization. It provides that the criminal charges will be dismissed and the defendant will be involuntarily hospitalized. It further provides that the administrator of the facility must notify the state attorney prior to any release of a defendant committed pursuant to this subdivision.

As to criteria for involuntary hospitalization, see section 394.467(1), Florida Statutes (1979); in case of retardation, see chapter 393, Florida Statutes (1979).

(c) Since commitment criteria for a defendant determined to be incompetent to stand trial are the same as for civil hospitalization, there is no need to continue the difference between felony and misdemeanor procedure.

Section 916.14, Florida Statutes, makes the statute of limitations and defense of former jeopardy inapplicable to criminal charges dismissed because of incompetence of defendant to stand trial.

1988 Amendment. Title. The title has been amended to comply with changes in rule 3.210, but specifically excludes competency to proceed with sentencing, which is addressed in the new rule 3.214.

(a) This provision was amended to reflect changes in rules 3.210 and 3.211. New language is added which specifies that, if charges are dismissed under this rule, it is without prejudice to the state to refile if the defendant is declared competent to proceed in the future. Similar language was previously found in rule 3.214(d), but is more appropriate under this rule.

(b) This provision has been amended for the same reasons as (a) above.

(c) This new provision specifically exempts this rule from being used against a defendant determined to be incompetent to be sentenced, which is now provided in the new rule 3.214. It is replaced by the new rule 3.214.

1992 Amendment. The purpose of the amendment is to gender neutralize the wording of the rule.

Introductory Note Relating to Amendments to Rules 3.210 to 3.219.

See notes following rule 3.210 for the text of this note.

Rule 3.214. Incompetency to Proceed to Sentencing: Disposition

If a defendant is determined to be incompetent to proceed after being found guilty of an offense or violation of probation or community control or after voluntarily entering a plea to an offense or violation of probation or community control, but prior to sentencing, the court shall postpone the pronouncement of sentence and proceed pursuant to rule 3.210 (et seq.) and the following rules.

Amended Sept. 24, 1992, effective Jan. 1, 1993 (606 So.2d 227).

Committee Note

1988 Amendment. Title. This new rule replaces the former rule 3.740. It was felt to be more appropriately addressed in this sequence. The former rule 3.214 is now renumbered 3.215. The former rule 3.740 used the inappropriate phrase "(p)rocedures when insanity is alleged as cause for not pronouncing sentence." Insanity is an affirmative defense to a criminal charge. The more correct term is "incompetence to proceed to sentencing."

(a) This new provision reiterates amendments to rule 3.210 and provides that sentencing shall be postponed for a defendant incompetent to proceed with disposition of a criminal matter—to include a finding of guilt at trial, after entry of a voluntary plea, or after a violation of probation or community control proceeding.

Introductory Note Relating to Amendments to Rules 3.210 to 3.219. See notes following rule 3.210 for the text of this note.

Rule 3.215. Effect of Adjudication of Incompetency to Proceed: Psychotropic Medication

(a) Former Jeopardy. If the defendant is declared incompetent to stand trial during trial and afterwards declared competent to stand trial, the defendant's other uncompleted trial shall not constitute former jeopardy.

(b) Limited Application of Incompetency Adjudication. An adjudication of incompetency to proceed shall not operate as an adjudication of incompetency to consent to medical treatment or for any other purpose unless such other adjudication is specifically set forth in the order.

(c) Psychotropic Medication. A defendant who, because of psychotropic medication, is able to understand the proceedings and to assist in the defense shall not automatically be deemed incompetent to proceed simply because the defendant's satisfactory mental condition is dependent on such medication, nor shall the defendant be prohibited from proceeding solely because the defendant is being administered medication under medical supervision for a mental or emotional condition.

(1) Psychotropic medication is any drug or compound affecting the mind, behavior, intellectual functions, perception, moods, or emotion and includes anti-psychotic, anti-depressant, anti-manic, and anti-anxiety drugs.

(2) If the defendant proceeds to trial with the aid of medication for a mental or emotional condition, on the motion of defense counsel, the jury shall, at the beginning of the trial and in the charge to the jury, be given explanatory instructions regarding such medication.

Amended Sept. 24, 1992, effective Jan. 1, 1993 (606 So.2d 227).

Committee Notes

1980 Adoption. (c) As to psychotropic medications, see section 916.12(2), Florida Statutes (1980).

(d) This subdivision is intended to provide specific exceptions to the speedy trial rule.

1988 Amendment. Title. This rule was formerly rule 3.214.

The amendments to this rule, including the title, are designed to reflect amendments to rules 3.210 and 3.211.

(d) Matters contained in former subsection (d) are covered by the provisions of rule 3.191. That subsection has therefore been deleted.

1992 Amendment. The purpose of the amendment is to gender neutralize the wording of the rule.

Introductory Note Relating to Amendments to Rules 3.210 to 3.219. See notes following rule 3.210 for the text of this note.

Rule 3.216. Insanity at Time of Offense or Probation or Community Control Violation: Notice and Appointment of Experts

(a) Expert to Aid Defense Counsel. When in any criminal case a defendant is adjudged to be indigent or partially indigent, and is not represented by the public defender or regional counsel, and counsel has reason to believe that the defendant may be incompetent to proceed or that the defendant may have been insane at the time of the offense or probation or community control violation, counsel may so inform the court who shall appoint 1 expert to examine the defendant in order to assist counsel in the preparation of the defense. The expert shall report only to the attorney for the defendant and matters related to the expert shall be deemed to fall under the lawyer-client privilege.

(b) Notice of Intent to Rely on Insanity Defense. When in any criminal case it shall be the intention of the defendant to rely on the defense of insanity either at trial or probation or community control violation hearing, no evidence offered by the defendant for the purpose of establishing that defense shall be admitted in the case unless advance notice in writing of the defense shall have been given by the defendant as hereinafter provided.

(c) Time for Filing Notice. The defendant shall give notice of intent to rely on the defense of insanity no later than 15 days after the arraignment or the filing of a written plea of not guilty in the case when the defense of insanity is to be relied on at trial or no later than 15 days after being brought before the appropriate court to answer to the allegations in a violation of probation or community control proceeding. If counsel for the defendant shall have reasonable grounds to believe that the defendant may be incompetent to proceed, the notice shall be given at the same time that the motion for examination into the defendant's competence is filed. The notice shall contain a statement of particulars showing the nature of the insanity the defendant expects to prove and the names and addresses of the witnesses by whom the defendant expects to show insanity, insofar as is possible.

(d) Court –Ordered Evaluations. On the filing of such notice and on motion of the state, the court shall order the defendant to be examined by the state's mental health expert(s) as to the sanity or insanity of the defendant at the time of the commission of the alleged offense or probation or community control violation. Attorneys for the state and defendant may be present at the examination.

(e) Time for Filing Notice of Intent to Rely on a Mental Health Defense Other than Insanity. The defendant shall give notice of intent to rely on any mental health defense other than insanity as soon as a good faith determination has been made to utilize the defense but in no event later than 30 days prior to trial. The notice shall contain a statement of particulars showing the nature of the defense the defendant expects to prove and the names and addresses of the witnesses by whom the defendant expects to prove the defense, insofar as possible. If expert testimony will be presented, the notice shall indicate whether the expert has examined the defendant.

(f) Court–Ordered Experts for Other Mental Health Defenses. If the notice to rely on any mental health defense other than insanity indicates the defendant will rely on the testimony of an expert who has examined the defendant, the court shall upon motion of the state order the defendant be examined by one qualified expert for the state as to the mental health defense raised by the defendant. Upon a showing of good cause, the court may order additional examinations upon motion by the state or the defendant. Attorneys for the state and defendant may be present at the examination. When the defendant relies on the testimony of an expert who has not examined the defendant, the state shall not be entitled to a compulsory examination of the defendant.

(g) Waiver of Time to File. On good cause shown for the omission of the notice of intent to rely on the defense of insanity, or any mental health defense, the court may in its discretion grant the defendant 10 days to comply with the notice requirement. If leave is granted and the defendant files the notice, the defendant is deemed unavailable to proceed. If the trial has already commenced, the court, only on motion of the defendant, may declare a mistrial in order to permit the defendant to raise the defense of insanity pursuant to this rule. Any motion for mistrial shall constitute a waiver of the defendant's right to any claim of former jeopardy arising from the uncompleted trial.

(h) Evaluating Defendant after Pretrial Release. If the defendant has been released on bail or other release conditions, the court may order the defendant to appear at a designated place for evaluation at a specific time as a condition of the release provision. If the court determines that the defendant will not submit to the evaluation provided for herein or that the defendant is not likely to appear for the scheduled evaluation, the court may order the defendant taken into custody until the evaluation is completed. A motion made for evaluation under this subdivision shall not otherwise affect the defendant's right to pretrial release.

(i) Evidence. Any experts appointed by the court may be summoned to testify at the trial, and shall be deemed court witnesses whether called by the court or by either party. Other evidence regarding the defendant's insanity or mental condition may be introduced by either party. At trial, in its instructions to the jury, the court shall include an instruction on the consequences of a verdict of not guilty by reason of insanity.

Amended Sept. 24, 1992, effective Jan. 1, 1993 (606 So.2d 227); Nov. 27, 1996, effective Jan. 1, 1997 (685 So.2d 1253); Nov. 19, 2009, effective Jan. 1, 2010 (26 So.3d 534).

Committee Notes

1980 Adoption.

(a) This subdivision is based on Pouncy v. State, 353 So.2d 640 (Fla. 3d DCA 1977), and provides that an expert may be provided for an indigent defendant. The appointment of the expert will in this way allow the public defender or court-appointed attorney to screen possible incompetency or insanity cases and give a basis for determining whether issues of incompetency or insanity ought to be raised before the court; it will also permit the defense attorney to specify in greater detail in the statement of particulars the nature of the insanity that attorney expects to prove, if any, and the basis for the raising of that defense.

(b) Essentially the same as in prior rules; provides that written notice must be given in advance by the defendant.

(c) Since counsel for indigents often are not appointed until arraignment and since it is sometimes difficult for a defendant to make a determination on whether the defense of insanity should be raised prior to arraignment, a 15-day post-arraignment period is provided for the filing of the notice. The defendant must raise incompetency at the same time as insanity, if at all possible. With the appointment of the expert to assist, the defendant should be able to raise both issues at the same time if grounds for both exist. The remainder of the rule, providing for the statement to be included in the notice, is essentially the same as that in prior rules.

(d) The appointment of experts provision is designed to track, insofar as possible, the provisions for appointment of experts contained in the rules relating to incompetency to stand trial and in the Florida Statutes relating to appointment of expert witnesses. Insofar as possible, the single examination should include incompetency, involuntary commitment issues where there are reasonable grounds for their consideration, and issues of insanity at time of the offense. Judicial economy would mandate such a single examination where possible.

(g) In order to obtain more standardized reports, specific items relating to the examination are required of the examining experts. See note to rule 3.211(a).

(h) Essentially the substance of prior rule 3.210(e)(4) and (5), with some changes. Both prior provisions are combined into a single provision; speedy trial time limits are no longer set forth, but waiver of double jeopardy is mandated.

(i) Same as rule 3.210(b)(3), relating to incompetency to stand trial. See commentary to that rule.

(j) A restatement of former rule 3.210(e)(7). The provision that experts called by the court shall be deemed court witnesses is new. The former provision relating to free access to the defendant is eliminated as unnecessary.

As to appointment of experts, see section 912.11, Florida Statutes.

1988 Amendment. The amendments to this rule, including the title, provide for the affirmative defense of insanity in violation of probation or community control proceedings as well as at trial.

1992 Amendment. The purpose of the amendment is to gender neutralize the wording of the rule.

1996 Amendment. Subdivisions (e) and (f) were added to conform to State v. Hickson, 630 So.2d 172 (Fla. 1993). These amendments are not intended to expand existing case law.

Introductory Note Relating to Amendments to Rules 3.210 to 3.219. See notes following rule 3.210 for the text of this note.

Rule 3.217. Judgment of Not Guilty by Reason of Insanity: Disposition of Defendant

(a) Verdict of Not Guilty by Reason of Insanity. When a person is found by the jury or the court not guilty of the offense or is found not to be in violation of probation or community control by reason of insanity, the jury or judge, in giving the verdict or finding of not guilty judgment, shall state that it was given for that reason.

(b) Treatment, Commitment, or Discharge after Acquittal. When a person is found not guilty of the offense or is found not to be in violation of probation or community control by reason of insanity, if the court then determines that the defendant presently meets the criteria set forth by law, the court shall commit the defendant to the Department of Children and Family Services or shall order outpatient treatment at any other appropriate facility or service, or shall discharge the defendant. Any order committing the defendant or requiring outpatient treatment or other outpatient service shall contain:

(1) findings of fact relating to the issue of commitment or other court-ordered treatment;

(2) copies of any reports of experts filed with the court; and

(3) any other psychiatric, psychological, or social work report submitted to the court relative to the mental state of the defendant.

Amended Sept. 24, 1992, effective Jan. 1, 1993 (606 So.2d 227); Nov. 2, 2000, effective Jan. 1, 2001 (794 So.2d 457).

Committee Notes

1980 Adoption.

(a) Same substance as in prior rule.

(b) The criteria for commitment are set forth in chapter 394, Florida Statutes. This rule incorporates those statutory criteria by reference and then restates the other alternatives available to the judge under former rule 3.210.

See section 912.18, Florida Statutes, for criteria.

(1) This subdivision is equivalent to rule 3.212(b)(2); see commentary to that rule.

1988 Amendment. The amendments to this rule provide for evaluation of a defendant found not guilty by reason of insanity in violation of probation or community control proceedings as well as at trial.

The amendments further reflect 1985 amendments to chapter 916, Florida Statutes.

1992 Amendment. The purpose of the amendment is to gender neutralize the wording of the rule.

Introductory Note Relating to Amendments to Rules 3.210 to 3.219. See notes following rule 3.210 for the text of this note.

Rule 3.218. Commitment of a Defendant Found not Guilty by Reason of Insanity

(a) Commitment; 6–Month Report. The Department of Children and Family Services shall admit to an appropriate facility a defendant found not guilty by reason of insanity under rule 3.217 and found to meet the criteria for commitment for hospitalization and treatment and may retain and treat the defendant. No later than 6 months from the date of admission, the administrator of the facility shall file with the court a report, and provide copies to all parties, which shall address the issues of further commitment of the defendant. If at any time during the 6–month period, or during any period of extended hospitalization that may be ordered under this rule, the administrator of the facility shall determine that the defendant no longer meets the criteria for commitment, the administrator shall notify the court by such a report and provide copies to all parties. The procedure for determinations of the confidential status of reports is governed by Rule of Judicial Administration 2.420.

(b) Right to Hearing if Committed upon Acquittal. The court shall hold a hearing within 30 days of the receipt of any report from the administrator of the facility on the issues raised thereby, and the defendant shall have a right to be present at the hearing. If the court determines that the defendant continues to meet the criteria for continued commitment or treatment, the court shall order further commitment or treatment for a period not to exceed 1 year. The same procedure shall be repeated before the expiration of each additional 1–year period in which the defendant is retained by the facility.

(c) Evidence to Determine Continuing Insanity. Before any hearing held under this rule, the court may, on its own motion, and shall, on motion of counsel for the state or defendant, appoint no fewer than 2 nor more than 3 experts to examine the defendant relative to the criteria for continued commitment or placement of the defendant and shall specify the date by which the experts shall report to the court on these issues and provide copies to all parties.

Amended Sept. 24, 1992, effective Jan. 1, 1993 (606 So.2d 227); Nov. 2, 2000, effective Jan. 1, 2001 (794 So.2d 457); Nov. 3, 2011, effective, *nunc pro tunc*, Oct. 1, 2011 (78 So.3d 1045).

Committee Notes

1980 Adoption. This provision provides for hospitalization of a defendant found not guilty by reason of insanity and is meant to track similar provisions in the rules relating to competency to stand trial and the complementary statutes. It provides for an initial 6–month period of commitment with successive 1–year periods; it provides for reports to the court and for the appointment of experts to examine the defendant when such hearings are necessary. The underlying rationale of this rule is to make standard, insofar as possible, the commitment process, whether it be for incompetency to stand trial or following a judgment of not guilty by reason of insanity.

For complementary statute providing for hospitalization of defendant adjudicated not guilty by reason of insanity, see section 912.15, Florida Statutes.

1988 Amendment. The amendments to this rule, including the title, provide for commitment of defendants found not guilty by reason of insanity in violation of probation or community control proceedings, as well as those so found at trial. The amendments further reflect 1985 amendments to chapter 916, Florida Statutes.

Introductory Note Relating to Amendments to Rules 3.210 to 3.219. See notes following rule 3.210 for the text of this note.

Rule 3.219. Conditional Release

(a) Release Plan. The committing court may order a conditional release of any defendant who has been committed according to a finding of incompetency to proceed or an adjudication of not guilty by reason of insanity based on an approved plan for providing appropriate outpatient care and treatment. When the administrator shall determine outpatient treatment of the defendant to be appropriate, the administrator may file with the court, and provide copies to all parties, a written plan for outpatient treatment, including recommendations from qualified professionals. The plan may be submitted by the defendant. The plan shall include:

(1) special provisions for residential care, adequate supervision of the defendant, or both;

(2) provisions for outpatient mental health services; and

(3) if appropriate, recommendations for auxiliary services such as vocational training, educational services, or special medical care.

In its order of conditional release, the court shall specify the conditions of release based on the release plan and shall direct the appropriate agencies or persons to submit periodic reports to the court regarding the defendant's compliance with the conditions of the release, and progress in treatment, and provide copies to all parties. The procedure for determinations of the confidential status of reports is governed by Rule of Judicial Administration 2.420.

(b) Defendant's Failure to Comply. If it appears at any time that the defendant has failed to comply with the conditions of release, or that the defendant's condition has deteriorated to the point that inpatient care is required, or that the release conditions should be modified, the court, after hearing, may modify the release conditions or, if the court finds the defendant meets the statutory criteria for commitment, may order that the defendant be recommitted to the Department of Children and Family Services for further treatment.

(c) Discharge. If at any time it is determined after hearing that the defendant no longer requires court-supervised follow-up care, the court shall terminate its jurisdiction in the cause and discharge the defendant.

Amended Sept. 24, 1992, effective Jan. 1, 1993 (606 So.2d 227); Nov. 2, 2000, effective Jan. 1, 2001 (794 So.2d 457); Nov. 3, 2011, effective, *nunc pro tunc*, Oct. 1, 2011 (78 So.3d 1045).

Committee Notes

1980 Adoption. This rule implements the prior statutory law permitting conditional release.

For complementary statute providing for conditional release, see section 916.17, Florida Statutes.

1988 Amendment. The amendments to this rule are designed to reflect amendments to rules 3.210, 3.211, and 3.218 as well as 1985 amendments to chapter 916, Florida Statutes.

(b) This provision has been amended to permit the court to recommit a conditionally released defendant to HRS under the provisions of chapter 916 only if the court makes a finding that the defendant currently meets the statutory commitment criteria found in section 916.13(1), Florida Statutes.

1992 Amendment. The purpose of the amendment is to gender neutralize the wording of the rule.

Introductory Note Relating to Amendments to Rules 3.210 to 3.219. See notes following rule 3.210 for the text of this note.

VI. DISCOVERY

Rule 3.220. Discovery

(a) Notice of Discovery. After the filing of the charging document, a defendant may elect to participate in the discovery process provided by these rules, including the taking of discovery depositions, by filing with the court and serving on the prosecuting attorney a "Notice of Discovery" which shall bind both the prosecution and defendant to all discovery procedures contained in these rules. Participation by a defendant in the discovery process, including the taking of any deposition by a defendant or the filing of a public records request under chapter 119, Florida Statutes, for law enforcement records relating to the defendant's pending prosecution, which are nonexempt as a result of a codefendant's participation in discovery, shall be an election to participate in discovery and triggers a reciprocal discovery obligation for the defendant. If any defendant knowingly or purposely shares in discovery obtained by a codefendant, the defendant shall be deemed to have elected to participate in discovery.

(b) Prosecutor's Discovery Obligation.

(1) Within 15 days after service of the Notice of Discovery, the prosecutor shall serve a written Discovery Exhibit which shall disclose to the defendant and permit the defendant to inspect, copy, test, and photograph the following information and material within the state's possession or control, except that any property or material that portrays sexual performance by a child or constitutes child pornography may not be copied, photographed, duplicated, or otherwise reproduced so long as the state attorney makes the property or material reasonably available to the defendant or the defendant's attorney:

(A) a list of the names and addresses of all persons known to the prosecutor to have information that may be relevant to any offense charged or any defense thereto, or to any similar fact evidence to be presented at trial under section 90.404(2), Florida Statutes. The names and addresses of persons listed shall be clearly designated in the following categories:

(i) Category A. These witnesses shall include (1) eye witnesses, (2) alibi witnesses and rebuttal to alibi witnesses, (3) witnesses who were present when a recorded or unrecorded statement was taken from or made by a defendant or codefendant, which shall be separately identified within this category, (4) investigating officers, (5) witnesses known by the prosecutor to have any material information that tends to negate the guilt of the defendant as to any offense charged, (6) child hearsay witnesses, (7) expert witnesses who have not provided a written report and a curriculum vitae or who are going to testify, and (8) informant witnesses, whether in custody, who offer testimony concerning the statements of a defendant about the issues for which the defendant is being tried.

(ii) Category B. All witnesses not listed in either Category A or Category C.

(iii) Category C. All witnesses who performed only ministerial functions or whom the prosecutor does not intend to call at trial and whose involvement with and knowledge of the case is fully set out in a police report or other statement furnished to the defense;

(B) the statement of any person whose name is furnished in compliance with the preceding subdivision. The term "statement" as used herein includes a written statement made by the person and signed or otherwise adopted or approved by the person and also includes any statement of any kind or manner made by the person and written or recorded or summarized in any writing or recording. The term "statement" is specifically intended to include all police and investigative reports of any kind prepared for or in connection with the case, but shall not include the notes from which those reports are compiled;

(C) any written or recorded statements and the substance of any oral statements made by the defendant, including a copy of any statements contained in police reports or report summaries, together with the name and address of each witness to the statements;

(D) any written or recorded statements and the substance of any oral statements made by a codefendant;

(E) those portions of recorded grand jury minutes that contain testimony of the defendant;

(F) any tangible papers or objects that were obtained from or belonged to the defendant;

(G) whether the state has any material or information that has been provided by a confidential informant;

(H) whether there has been any electronic surveillance, including wiretapping, of the premises of the defendant or of conversations to which the defendant was a party and any documents relating thereto;

(I) whether there has been any search or seizure and any documents relating thereto;

(J) reports or statements of experts made in connection with the particular case, including results of physical or mental examinations and of scientific tests, experiments, or comparisons; and

(K) any tangible papers or objects that the prosecuting attorney intends to use in the hearing or trial and that were not obtained from or that did not belong to the defendant.

(L) any tangible paper, objects or substances in the possession of law enforcement that could be tested for DNA.

(M) whether the state has any material or information that has been provided by an informant witness, including:

(i) the substance of any statement allegedly made by the defendant about which the informant witness may testify;

(ii) a summary of the criminal history record of the informant witness;

(iii) the time and place under which the defendant's alleged statement was made;

(iv) whether the informant witness has received, or expects to receive, anything in exchange for his or her testimony;

(v) the informant witness' prior history of cooperation, in return for any benefit, as known to the prosecutor.

(2) If the court determines, in camera, that any police or investigative report contains irrelevant, sensitive information or information interrelated with other crimes or criminal activities and the disclosure of the contents of the police report may seriously impair law enforcement or jeopardize the investigation of those other crimes or activities, the court may prohibit or partially restrict the disclosure.

(3) The court may prohibit the state from introducing into evidence any of the foregoing material not disclosed, so as to secure and maintain fairness in the just determination of the cause.

(4) As soon as practicable after the filing of the charging document the prosecutor shall disclose to the defendant any material information within the state's possession or control that tends to negate the guilt of the defendant as to any offense charged, regardless of whether the defendant has incurred reciprocal discovery obligations.

(c) Disclosure to Prosecution.

(1) After the filing of the charging document and subject to constitutional limitations, the court may require a defendant to:

(A) appear in a lineup;

(B) speak for identification by witnesses to an offense;

(C) be fingerprinted;

(D) pose for photographs not involving re-enactment of a scene;

(E) try on articles of clothing;

(F) permit the taking of specimens of material under the defendant's fingernails;

(G) permit the taking of samples of the defendant's blood, hair, and other materials of the defendant's body that involves no unreasonable intrusion thereof;

(H) provide specimens of the defendant's handwriting; and

(I) submit to a reasonable physical or medical inspection of the defendant's body.

(2) If the personal appearance of a defendant is required for the foregoing purposes, reasonable notice of the time and location of the appearance shall be given by the prosecuting attorney to the defendant and his or her counsel. Provisions may be made for appearances for such purposes in an order admitting a defendant to bail or providing for pretrial release.

(d) Defendant's Obligation.

(1) If a defendant elects to participate in discovery, either through filing the appropriate notice or by participating in any discovery process, including the taking of a discovery deposition, the following disclosures shall be made:

(A) Within 15 days after receipt by the defendant of the Discovery Exhibit furnished by the prosecutor pursuant to subdivision (b)(1)(A) of this rule, the defendant shall furnish to the prosecutor a written list of the names and addresses of all witnesses whom the defendant expects to call as witnesses at the trial or hearing. When the prosecutor subpoenas a witness whose name has been furnished by the defendant, except for trial subpoenas, the rules applicable to the taking of depositions shall apply.

(B) Within 15 days after receipt of the prosecutor's Discovery Exhibit the defendant shall serve a written Discovery Exhibit which shall disclose to and permit the prosecutor to inspect, copy, test, and photograph the following information and material that is in the defendant's possession or control:

(i) the statement of any person listed in subdivision (d)(1)(A), other than that of the defendant;

(ii) reports or statements of experts made in connection with the particular case, including results of physical or mental examinations and of scientific tests, experiments, or comparisons; and

(iii) any tangible papers or objects that the defendant intends to use in the hearing or trial.

(2) The prosecutor and the defendant shall perform their obligations under this rule in a manner mutually agreeable or as ordered by the court.

(3) The filing of a motion for protective order by the prosecutor will automatically stay the times provided for in this subdivision. If a protective order is granted, the defendant may, within 2 days thereafter, or at any time before the prosecutor furnishes the information or material that is the subject of the motion for protective order, withdraw the defendant's notice of discovery and not be required to furnish reciprocal discovery.

(e) Restricting Disclosure. The court on its own initiative or on motion of counsel shall deny or partially restrict disclosures authorized by this rule if it finds there is a substantial risk to any person of physical harm, intimidation, bribery, economic reprisals, or unnecessary annoyance or embarrassment resulting from the disclosure, that outweighs any usefulness of the disclosure to either party.

(f) Additional Discovery. On a showing of materiality, the court may require such other discovery to the parties as justice may require.

(g) Matters Not Subject to Disclosure.

(1) *Work Product.* Disclosure shall not be required of legal research or of records, correspondence, reports, or memoranda to the extent that they contain the opinions, theories, or conclusions of the prosecuting or defense attorney or members of their legal staffs.

(2) *Informants.* Disclosure of a confidential informant shall not be required unless the confidential informant is to be produced at a hearing or trial or a failure to disclose the informant's identity will infringe the constitutional rights of the defendant.

(h) Discovery Depositions.

(1) *Generally.* At any time after the filing of the charging document any party may take the deposition upon oral examination of any person authorized by this rule. A party taking a deposition shall give reasonable written notice to each other party and shall make a good faith effort to coordinate the date, time, and location of the deposition to accommodate the schedules of other parties and the witness to be deposed. The notice shall state the time and the location where the deposition is to be taken, the name of each person to be examined, and a certificate of counsel that a good faith effort was made to coordinate the deposition schedule. After notice to the parties the court may, for good cause shown, extend or shorten the time and may change the location of the deposition. Except as provided herein, the procedure for taking the deposition, including the scope of the examination, and the issuance of a subpoena (except a subpoena duces tecum) for deposition by an attorney of record in the action, shall be the same as that provided in the Florida Rules of Civil Procedure. Any deposition taken pursuant to this rule may be used by any party for the purpose of contradicting or impeaching the testimony of the deponent as a witness. The trial court or the clerk of the court may, upon application by a pro se litigant or the attorney for any party, issue subpoenas for the persons whose depositions are to be taken. In any case, including multiple defendants or consolidated cases, no person shall be deposed more than once except by consent of the parties or by order of the court issued on good cause shown. A witness who refuses to obey a duly served subpoena may be adjudged in contempt of the court from which the subpoena issued.

(A) The defendant may, without leave of court, take the deposition of any witness listed by the prosecutor as a Category A witness or listed by a co-defendant as a witness to be called at a joint trial or hearing. After receipt by the defendant of the Discovery Exhibit, the defendant may, without leave of court, take the deposition of any unlisted witness who may have information relevant to the offense charged. The prosecutor may, without leave of court, take the deposition of any witness listed by the defendant to be called at a trial or hearing.

(B) No party may take the deposition of a witness listed by the prosecutor as a Category B witness except upon leave of court with good cause shown. In determining whether to allow a deposition, the court should consider the consequences to the defendant, the complexities of the issues involved, the complexity of the testimony of the witness (e.g., experts), and the other opportunities available to the defendant to discover the information sought by deposition.

(C) A witness listed by the prosecutor as a Category C witness shall not be subject to deposition unless the court determines that the witness should be listed in another category.

(D) No deposition shall be taken in a case in which the defendant is charged only with a misdemeanor or a criminal traffic offense when all other discovery provided by this rule has been complied with unless good cause can be shown to the trial court. In determining whether to allow a deposition, the court should consider the consequences to the defendant, the complexity of the issues involved, the complexity of the witness' testimony (e.g., experts), and the other opportunities available to the defendant to discover the information sought by deposition. However, this prohibition against the taking of depositions shall not be applicable if following the furnishing of discovery by the defendant the state then takes the statement of a listed defense witness pursuant to section 27.04, Florida Statutes.

(2) *Transcripts.* No transcript of a deposition for which the state may be obligated to expend funds shall be ordered by a party unless it is in compliance with general law.

(3) *Location of Deposition.* Depositions of witnesses residing in the county in which the trial is to take place shall be taken in the building in which the trial shall be held, such other location as is agreed on by the parties, or a location designated by the court. Depositions of witnesses residing outside the county in which the trial is to take place shall be taken in a court reporter's office in the county or state in which the witness resides, such other location as is agreed on by the parties, or a location designated by the court.

(4) *Depositions of Sensitive Witnesses.* Depositions of children under the age of 16 shall be videotaped unless otherwise ordered by the court. The court may order the videotaping of a deposition or the taking of a deposition of a witness with fragile emotional strength to be in the presence of the trial judge or a special magistrate.

(5) *Depositions of Law Enforcement Officers.* Subject to the general provisions of subdivision (h)(1), law enforcement officers shall appear for deposition, without subpoena, upon written notice of taking deposition delivered at the address of the law enforcement agency or department, or an address designated by the law enforcement agency or department, five days prior to the date of the deposition. Law enforcement officers who fail to appear for deposition after being served notice as required by the rule may be adjudged in contempt of court.

(6) *Witness Coordinating Office/Notice of Taking Deposition.* If a witness coordinating office has been established in the jurisdiction pursuant to applicable Florida Statutes, the deposition of any witness should be coordinated through that office. The witness coordinating office should attempt to schedule the depositions of a witness at a time and location convenient for the witness and acceptable to the parties.

(7) *Defendant's Physical Presence.* A defendant shall not be physically present at a deposition except on stipulation of the parties or as provided by this rule. The court may order the physical presence of the defendant on a showing of good cause. The court may consider (A) the need for the physical presence of the defendant to obtain effective discovery, (B) the intimidating effect of the defendant's presence on the witness, if any, (C) any cost or inconvenience which may result, and (D) any alternative electronic or audio/visual means available.

(8) *Telephonic Statements.* On stipulation of the parties and the consent of the witness, the statement of any witness may be taken by telephone in lieu of the deposition of the witness. In such case, the witness need not be under oath. The statement, however, shall be recorded and may be used for impeachment at trial as a prior inconsistent statement pursuant to the Florida Evidence Code.

(i) Investigations Not to Be Impeded. Except as is otherwise provided as to matters not subject to disclosure or restricted by protective orders, neither the counsel for the parties nor other prosecution or defense personnel shall advise persons having relevant material or information (except the defendant) to refrain from discussing the case with opposing counsel or showing opposing counsel any relevant material, nor shall they otherwise impede opposing counsel's investigation of the case.

(j) Continuing Duty to Disclose. If, subsequent to compliance with the rules, a party discovers additional witnesses or material that the party would have been under a duty to disclose or produce at the time of the previous compliance, the party shall promptly disclose or produce the witnesses or material in the same manner as required under these rules for initial discovery.

(k) Court May Alter Times. The court may alter the times for compliance with any discovery under these rules on good cause shown.

***(l)* Protective Orders.**

(1) *Motion to Restrict Disclosure of Matters.* On a showing of good cause, the court shall at any time order that specified disclosures be restricted, deferred, or exempted from discovery, that certain matters not be inquired into, that the scope of the deposition be limited to certain matters, that a deposition be sealed and after being sealed be opened only by order of the court, or make such other order as is appropriate to protect a witness from harassment, unnecessary inconvenience, or invasion of privacy, including prohibiting the taking of a deposition. All material and information to which a party is entitled, however, must be disclosed in time to permit the party to make beneficial use of it.

(2) *Motion to Terminate or Limit Examination.* At any time during the taking of a deposition, on motion of a party or of the deponent, and upon a

showing that the examination is being conducted in bad faith or in such manner as to unreasonably annoy, embarrass, or oppress the deponent or party, the court in which the action is pending or the circuit court where the deposition is being taken may (1) terminate the deposition, (2) limit the scope and manner of the taking of the deposition, (3) limit the time of the deposition, (4) continue the deposition to a later time, (5) order the deposition to be taken in open court, and, in addition, may (6) impose any sanction authorized by this rule. If the order terminates the deposition, it shall be resumed thereafter only upon the order of the court in which the action is pending. Upon demand of any party or deponent, the taking of the deposition shall be suspended for the time necessary to make a motion for an order.

(m) In Camera and Ex Parte Proceedings.

(1) Any person may move for an order denying or regulating disclosure of sensitive matters. The court may consider the matters contained in the motion in camera.

(2) Upon request, the court shall allow the defendant to make an ex parte showing of good cause for taking the deposition of a Category B witness.

(3) A record shall be made of proceedings authorized under this subdivision. If the court enters an order granting relief after an in camera inspection or ex parte showing, the entire record of the proceeding shall be sealed and preserved and be made available to the appellate court in the event of an appeal.

(n) Sanctions.

(1) If, at any time during the course of the proceedings, it is brought to the attention of the court that a party has failed to comply with an applicable discovery rule or with an order issued pursuant to an applicable discovery rule, the court may order the party to comply with the discovery or inspection of materials not previously disclosed or produced, grant a continuance, grant a mistrial, prohibit the party from calling a witness not disclosed or introducing in evidence the material not disclosed, or enter such other order as it deems just under the circumstances.

(2) Willful violation by counsel or a party not represented by counsel of an applicable discovery rule, or an order issued pursuant thereto, shall subject counsel or the unrepresented party to appropriate sanctions by the court. The sanctions may include, but are not limited to, contempt proceedings against the attorney or unrepresented party, as well as the assessment of costs incurred by the opposing party, when appropriate.

(3) Every request for discovery or response or objection, including a notice of deposition made by a party represented by an attorney, shall be signed by at least 1 attorney of record in the attorney's individual name, whose address shall be stated. A party who is not represented by an attorney shall sign the request, response, or objection and list his or her address. The signature of the attorney or party constitutes a certification that the signer has read the request, response, or objection and that to the best of the signer's knowledge, information, or belief formed after a reasonable inquiry it is:

(A) consistent with these rules and warranted by existing law or a good faith argument for the extension, modification, or reversal of existing law;

(B) not interposed for any improper purpose, such as to harass or to cause unnecessary delay or needless increase in the cost of litigation; and

(C) not unreasonable or unduly burdensome or expensive, given the needs of the case and the importance of the issues at stake in the litigation.

If a request, response, or objection is not signed, it shall be stricken unless it is signed promptly after the omission is called to the attention of the party making the request, response, or objection, and a party shall not be obligated to take any action with respect to it until it is signed.

If a certification is made in violation of this rule, the court, on motion or on its own initiative, shall impose on the person who made the certification, the firm or agency with which the person is affiliated, the party on whose behalf the request, response, or objection is made, or any or all of the above an appropriate sanction, which may include an order to pay the amount of the reasonable expenses incurred because of the violation, including a reasonable attorney's fee.

(*o*) Pretrial Conference.

(1) The trial court may hold 1 or more pretrial conferences, with trial counsel present, to consider such matters as will promote a fair and expeditious trial. The defendant shall be present unless the defendant waives this in writing.

(2) The court may set, and upon the request of any party shall set, a discovery schedule, including a discovery cut-off date, at the pretrial conference.

Amended Sept. 24, 1992, effective Jan. 1, 1993 (606 So.2d 227); Sept. 12, 1996, effective Oct. 1, 1996 (681 So.2d 666); April 2, 1998 (710 So.2d 961); Dec. 3, 1998 (721 So.2d 1162); Feb. 18, 1999 (745 So.2d 319); Feb. 10, 2000 (763 So.2d 274); Sept. 30, 2004, effective Oct. 1, 2004 (887 So.2d 1090); April 7, 2005 (900 So.2d 528); Nov. 19, 2009, effective Jan. 1, 2010 (26 So.3d 534); Dec. 20, 2012 (105 So.3d 1275); Nov. 8, 2012, effective Jan. 1, 2013 (104 So.3d 304); May 23, 2013 (115 So.3d 207); May 29, 2014, effective July 1, 2014 (140 So.3d 538).

Committee Notes

1968 Adoption.

(a)(1) This is substantially the same as section 925.05, Florida Statutes.

(a)(2) This is new and allows a defendant rights which he did not have, but must be considered in light of subdivision (c).

(a)(3) This is a slight enlargement upon the present practice; however, from a practical standpoint, it is not an enlargement, but merely a codification of section 925.05, Florida Statutes, with respect to the defendant's testimony before a grand jury.

(b) This is a restatement of section 925.04, Florida Statutes, except for the change of the word "may" to "shall."

(c) This is new and affords discovery to the state within the trial judge's discretion by allowing the trial judge to make discovery under (a)(2) and (b) conditioned upon the defendant giving the state some information if the defendant has it. This affords the state some area of discovery which it did not previously have with respect to (b). A question was raised concerning the effect of (a)(2) on FBI reports and other reports which are submitted to a prosecutor as "confidential" but it was agreed that the interests of justice would be better served by allowing this rule and that, after the appropriate governmental authorities are made aware of the fact that their reports may be subject to compulsory disclosure, no harm to the state will be done.

(d) and (e) This gives the defendant optional procedures. (d) is simply a codification of section 906.29, Florida Statutes, except for the addition of "addresses." The defendant is allowed this procedure in any event. (e) affords the defendant the additional practice of obtaining all of the state's witnesses, as distinguished from merely those on whose evidence the information, or indictment, is based, but only if the defendant is willing to give the state a list of all defense witnesses, which must be done to take advantage of this rule. The confidential informant who is to be used as a witness must be disclosed; but it was expressly viewed that this should not otherwise overrule present case law on the subject of disclosure of confidential informants, either where disclosure is required or not required.

(f) This is new and is a compromise between the philosophy that the defendant should be allowed unlimited discovery depositions and the philosophy that the defendant should not be allowed any discovery depositions at all. The purpose of the rule is to afford the defendant relief from situations when witnesses refuse to "cooperate" by making pretrial disclosures to the defense. It was determined to be necessary that the written signed statement be a criterion because this is the only way witnesses can be impeached by prior contradictory statements. The word "cooperate" was intentionally left in the rule, although the word is a loose one, so that it can be given a liberal interpretation, i.e., a witness may claim to be available and yet never actually submit to an interview. Some express the view that the defendant is not being afforded adequate protection because the cooperating witness will not have been under oath, but the subcommittee felt that the only alternative would be to make unlimited discovery depositions available to the defendant which was a view not approved by a majority of the subcommittee. Each minority is expressed by the following alternative proposals:

Alternative Proposal (1): When a person is charged with an offense, at any time after the filing of the indictment, information, or affidavit upon which the defendant is to be tried, such person may take the deposition of any person by deposition upon oral examination for the purpose of discovery. The attendance of witnesses may be compelled by the use of subpoenas as provided by law. The deposition of a person confined in prison may be taken only by leave of court on such terms as the court prescribes. The scope of examination and the manner and method of taking such deposition shall be as provided in the Florida Rules of Civil Procedure and the deposition may be used for the purpose of contradicting or impeaching the testimony of a deponent as a witness.

Alternative Proposal (2): If a defendant signs and files a written waiver of his or her privilege against self-incrimination and submits to interrogation under oath by the prosecuting attorney, then the defendant shall be entitled to compulsory process for any or all witnesses to enable the defendant to interrogate them under oath, before trial, for discovery purposes.

A view was expressed that some limitation should be placed on the state's rights under sections 27.04 and 32.20, Florida Statutes, which allow the prosecutor to take all depositions unilaterally at any time. It was agreed by all members of the subcommittee that this right should not be curtailed until some specific time after the filing of an indictment, information, or affidavit, because circumstances sometimes require the filing of the charge and a studied marshalling of evidence thereafter. Criticism of the present practice lies in the fact that any time up to and during the course of the trial the prosecutor can subpoena any person to the privacy of the prosecutor's office without notice to the defense and there take a statement of such person under oath. The subcommittee was divided, however, on the method of altering this situation and the end result was that this subcommittee itself should not undertake to change the existing practice, but should make the Supreme Court aware of this apparent imbalance.

(g) This is new and is required in order to make effective the preceding rules.

(h) This is new and, although it encompasses relief for both the state and the defense, its primary purpose is to afford relief in situations when witnesses may be intimidated and a prosecuting attorney's heavy docket might not allow compliance with discovery within the time limitations set forth in the rules. The words, "sufficient showing" were intentionally included in order to permit the trial judge to have discretion in granting the protective relief. It would be impossible to specify all possible grounds which can be the basis of a protective order. This verbiage also permits a possible abuse by a prosecution-minded trial judge, but the subcommittee felt that the appellate court would remedy any such abuse in the course of making appellate decisions.

(i) This is new and, although it will entail additional expense to counties, it was determined that it was necessary in order to comply with the recent trend of federal decisions which hold that due process is violated when a person who has the money with which to resist criminal prosecution gains an advantage over the person who is not so endowed. Actually, there is serious doubt that the intent of this subdivision can be accomplished by a rule of procedure; a statute is needed. It is recognized that such a statute may be unpopular with the legislature and not enacted. But, if this subdivision has not given effect there is a likelihood that a constitutional infirmity (equal protection of the law) will be found and either the entire rule with all subdivisions will be held void or confusion in application will result.

(j) This provision is necessary since the prosecutor is required to assume many responsibilities under the various subdivisions under the rule. There are no prosecuting attorneys, either elected or regularly assigned, in justice of the peace courts. County judge's courts, as distinguished from county courts, do not have elected prosecutors. Prosecuting attorneys in such courts are employed by county commissions and may be handicapped in meeting the requirements of the rule due to the irregularity and uncertainty of such employment. This subdivision is inserted as a method of achieving as much uniformity as possible in all of the courts of Florida having jurisdictions to try criminal cases.

1972 Amendment. The committee studied the ABA Standards for Criminal Justice relating to discovery and procedure before trial. Some of the standards are incorporated in the committee's proposal, others are not. Generally, the standards are divided into 5 parts:

Part I deals with policy and philosophy and, while the committee approves the substance of Part I, it was determined that specific rules setting out this policy and philosophy should not be proposed.

Part II provides for automatic disclosures (avoiding judicial labor) by the prosecutor to the defense of almost everything within the prosecutor's knowledge, except for work product and the identity of confidential informants. The committee adopted much of Part II, but felt that the disclosure should not be automatic in every case; the disclosure should be made only after request or demand and within certain time limitations. The ABA Standards do not recommend reciprocity of discovery, but the committee deemed that a large degree of reciprocity is in order and made appropriate recommendations.

Part III of the ABA Standards recommends some disclosure by the defense (not reciprocal) to which the state was not previously entitled. The committee adopted Part III and enlarged upon it.

Part IV of the Standards sets forth methods of regulation of discovery by the court. Under the Standards the discovery mentioned in Parts II and III would have been automatic and without the necessity of court orders or court intervention. Part III provides for procedures of protection of the parties and was generally incorporated in the recommendations of the committee.

Part V of the ABA Standards deals with omnibus hearings and pretrial conferences. The committee rejected part of the Standards dealing with omnibus hearings because it felt that it was superfluous under Florida procedure. The Florida committee determined that a trial court may, at its discretion, schedule a hearing for the purposes enumerated in the ABA Omnibus Hearing and that a rule authorizing it is not necessary. Some of the provisions of the ABA Omnibus Hearing were rejected by the Florida committee, i.e., stipulations as to issues, waivers by defendant, etc. A modified form of pretrial conference was provided in the proposals by the Florida committee.

(a)(1)(i) Same as ABA Standard 2.1(a)(i) and substance of Standard 2.1(e). Formerly Florida Rule of Criminal Procedure 3.220(e) authorized exchange of witness lists. When considered with proposal 3.220(a)(3), it is seen that the proposal represents no significant change.

(ii) This rule is a modification of Standard 2.1(a)(ii) and is new in Florida, although some such statements might have been discoverable under rule 3.220(f). Definition of "statement" is derived from 18 U.S.C. § 3500.

Requiring law enforcement officers to include irrelevant or sensitive material in their disclosures to the defense would not serve justice. Many investigations overlap and information developed as a by-product of one investigation may form the basis and starting point for a new and entirely separate one. Also, the disclosure of any information obtained from computerized records of the Florida Crime Information Center and the National Crime Information Center should be subject to the regulations prescribing the confidentiality of such information so as to safeguard the right of the innocent to privacy.

(iii) Same as Standard 2.1(a)(ii) relating to statements of accused; words "known to the prosecutor, together with the name and address of each witness to the statement" added and is new in Florida.

(iv) From Standard 2.1(a)(ii). New in Florida.

(v) From Standard 2.1(a)(iii) except for addition of words, "that have been recorded" which were inserted to avoid any inference that the proposed rule makes recording of grand jury testimony mandatory. This discovery was formerly available under rule 3.220(a)(3).

(vi) From Standard 2.1(a)(v). Words, "books, papers, documents, photographs" were condensed to "papers or objects" without intending to change their meaning. This was previously available under rule 3.220(b).

(vii) From Standard 2.1(b)(i) except word "confidential" was added to clarify meaning. This is new in this form.

(viii) From Standard 2.1(b)(iii) and is new in Florida in this form. Previously this was disclosed upon motion and order.

(ix) From Standard 2.3(a), but also requiring production of "documents relating thereto" such as search warrants and affidavits. Previously this was disclosed upon motion and order.

(x) From Standard 2.1(a)(iv). Previously available under rule 3.220(a)(2). Defendant must reciprocate under proposed rule 3.220(b)(4).

(xi) Same committee note as (b) under this subdivision.

(2) From Standard 2.1(c) except omission of words "or would tend to reduce his punishment therefore" which should be included in sentencing.

(3) Based upon Standard 2.2(a) and (b) except Standards required prosecutor to furnish voluntarily and without demand while this proposal requires defendant to make demand and permits prosecutor 15 days in which to respond.

(4) From Standards 2.5(b) and 4.4. Substance of this proposal previously available under rule 3.220(h).

(5) From Standard 2.5. New in Florida.

(b)(1) From Standard 3.1(a). New in Florida.

(2) From Standard 3.1(b). New in Florida.

(3) Standards did not recommend that defendant furnish prosecution with reciprocal witness list; however, formerly, rule 3.220(e) did make such provision. The committee recommended continuation of reciprocity.

(4) Standards did not recommend reciprocity of discovery. Previously, Florida rules required some reciprocity. The committee recommended continuation of former reciprocity and addition of exchanging witness' statement other than defendants'.

(c) From Standard 2.6. New in Florida, but generally recognized in decisions.

(d) Not recommended by Standards. Previously permitted under rule 3.220(f) except for change limiting the place of taking the deposition and eliminating requirement that witness refuse to give voluntary signed statement.

(e) From Standard 4.1. New in Florida.

(f) Same as rule 3.220(g).

(g) From Standard 4.4 and rule 3.220(h).

(h) From Standard 4.4 and rule 3.220(h).

(i) From Standard 4.6. Not previously covered by rule in Florida, but permitted by decisions.

(j)(1) From Standard 4.7(a). New in Florida except court discretion permitted by rule 3.220(g).

(2) From Standard 4.7(b). New in Florida.

(k) Same as prior rule.

(*l*) Modified Standard 5.4. New in Florida.

1977 Amendment. The proposed change only removes the comma which currently appears after (a)(1).

1980 Amendment. The intent of the rule change is to guarantee that the accused will receive those portions of police reports or report summaries which contain any written, recorded, or oral statements made by the accused.

1986 Amendment. The showing of good cause under (d)(2) of this rule may be presented ex parte or in camera to the court.

1989 Amendment. 3.220(a). The purpose of this change is to ensure reciprocity of discovery. Under the previous rule, the defendant could tailor discovery, demanding only certain items of discovery with no requirement to reciprocate items other than those demanded. A defendant could avoid reciprocal discovery by taking depositions, thereby learning of witnesses through the deposition process, and then deposing those witnesses without filing a demand for discovery. With this change, once a defendant opts to use any discovery device, the defendant is required to produce all items designated under the discovery rule, whether or not the defendant has specifically requested production of those items.

Former subdivision (c) is relettered (b). Under (b)(1) the prosecutor's obligation to furnish a witness list is conditioned upon the defendant filing a "Notice of Discovery."

Former subdivision (a)(1)(i) is renumbered (b)(1)(i) and, as amended, limits the ability of the defense to take depositions of those persons designated by the prosecutor as witnesses who should not be deposed because of their tangential relationship to the case. This does not preclude the defense attorney or a defense investigator from interviewing any witness, including a police witness, about the witness's knowledge of the case.

This change is intended to meet a primary complaint of law enforcement agencies that depositions are frequently taken of persons who have no knowledge of the events leading to the charge, but whose names are disclosed on the witness list. Examples of these persons are transport officers, evidence technicians, etc.

In order to permit the defense to evaluate the potential testimony of those individuals designated by the prosecutor, their testimony must be fully set forth in some document, generally a police report.

(a)(1)(ii) is renumbered (b)(1)(ii). This subdivision is amended to require full production of all police incident and investigative reports, of any kind, that are discoverable, provided there is no independent reason for restricting their disclosure. The term "statement" is intended to include summaries of statements of witnesses made by investigating officers as well as statements adopted by the witnesses themselves.

The protection against disclosure of sensitive information, or information that otherwise should not be disclosed, formerly set forth in (a)(1)(i), is retained, but transferred to subdivision (b)(1)(xii).

The prohibition sanction is not eliminated, but is transferred to subdivision (b)(1)(xiii). "Shall" has been changed to "may" in order to reflect the procedure for imposition of sanctions specified in *Richardson v. State,* 246 So. 2d 771 (Fla. 1971).

The last phrase of renumbered subdivision (b)(2) is added to emphasize that constitutionally required Brady material must be produced regardless of the defendant's election to participate in the discovery process.

Former subdivision (b) is relettered (c).

Former subdivisions (b)(3) and (4) are now included in new subdivision (d). An introductory phrase has been added to subdivision (d). Subdivision (d) reflects the change in nomenclature from a "Demand for Discovery" to the filing of a "Notice of Discovery."

As used in subdivision (d), the word "defendant" is intended to refer to the party rather than to the person. Any obligations incurred by the "defendant" are incurred by the defendant's attorney if the defendant is represented by counsel and by the defendant personally if the defendant is not represented.

The right of the defendant to be present and to examine witnesses, set forth in renumbered subdivision (d)(1), refers to the right of the defense, as party to the action. The term refers to the attorney for the defendant if the defendant is represented by counsel. The right of the defendant to be physically present at the deposition is controlled by new subdivision (h)(6).

Renumbered subdivision (d)(2), as amended, reflects the new notice of discovery procedure. If the defendant elects to participate in discovery, the defendant is obligated to furnish full reciprocal disclosure.

Subdivision (e) was previously numbered (a)(4). This subdivision has been modified to permit the remedy to be sought by either prosecution or defense.

Subdivision (f) was previously numbered (a)(5) and has been modified to permit the prosecutor, as well as the defense attorney, to seek additional discovery.

Former subdivision (c) is relettered (g).

Former subdivision (d) is relettered (h). Renumbered subdivision (h)(1) has been amended to reflect the restrictions on deposing a witness designated by the prosecution under (b)(1)(i) (designation of a witness performing ministerial duties only or one who will not be called at trial).

(h)(1)(i) is added to provide that a deposition of a witness designated by the prosecutor under (b)(1)(i) may be taken only upon good cause shown by the defendant to the court.

(h)(1)(ii) is added to provide that abuses by attorneys of the provisions of (b)(1)(i) are subject to stringent sanctions.

New subdivision (h)(1)(iii) abolishes depositions in misdemeanor cases except when good cause is shown.

A portion of former subdivision (d)(1) is renumbered (h)(3). This subdivision now permits the administrative judge or chief judge, in addition to the trial judge, to designate the place for taking the deposition.

New subdivision (h)(4) recognizes that children and some adults are especially vulnerable to intimidation tactics. Although it has been shown that such tactics are infrequent, they should not be tolerated because of the traumatic effect on the witness. The videotaping of the deposition will enable the trial judge to control such tactics. Provision is also made to protect witnesses of fragile emotional strength because of their vulnerability to intimidation tactics.

New subdivision (h)(5) emphasizes the necessity for the establishment, in each jurisdiction, of an effective witness coordinating office. The Florida Legislature has authorized the establishment of such office through section 43.35, Florida Statutes. This subdivision is intended to make depositions of witnesses and law enforcement officers as convenient as possible for the witnesses and with minimal disruption of law enforcement officers' official duties.

New subdivision (h)(6) recognizes that one of the most frequent complaints from child protection workers and from rape victim counselors is that the presence of the defendant intimidates the witnesses. The trauma to the victim surpasses the benefit to the defense of having the defendant present at the deposition. Since there is no right, other than that given by the rules of procedure, for a defendant to attend a deposition, the Florida Supreme Court Commission on Criminal Discovery believes that no such right should exist in those cases. The "defense," of course, as a party to the action, has a right to be present through counsel at the deposition. In this subdivision, the word "defendant" is meant to refer to the person of the defendant, not to the defense as a party. *See* comments to rules 3.220(d) and 3.220(d)(1).

Although defendants have no right to be present at depositions and generally there is no legitimate reason for their presence, their presence is appropriate in certain cases. An example is a complex white collar fraud prosecution in which the defendant must explain the meaning of technical documents or terms. Cases requiring the defendant's presence are the exception rather than the rule. Accordingly, (h)(6)(i)–(ii) preclude the presence of defendants at depositions unless agreed to by the parties or ordered by the court. These subdivisions set forth factors that a court should take into account in considering motions to allow a defendant's presence.

New subdivision (h)(7) permits the defense to obtain needed factual information from law enforcement officers by informal telephone deposition. Recognizing that the formal deposition of a law enforcement officer is often unnecessary, this procedure will permit such discovery at a significant reduction of costs.

Former subdivisions (e), (f), and (g) are relettered (i), (j), and (k), respectively.

Former subdivision (h) is relettered (*l*) and is modified to emphasize the use of protective orders to protect witnesses from harassment or intimidation and to provide for limiting the scope of the deposition as to certain matters.

Former subdivision (i) is relettered (m).

Former subdivision (j) is relettered (n).

Renumbered (n)(2) is amended to provide that sanctions are mandatory if the court finds willful abuse of discovery. Although the amount of sanction is discretionary, some sanction must be imposed.

(n)(3) is new and tracks the certification provisions of federal procedure. The very fact of signing such a certification will make counsel cognizant of the effect of that action.

Subdivision (k) is relettered (*o*).

Subdivision (*l*) is relettered (p).

1992 Amendment. The proposed amendments change the references to "indictment or information" in subdivisions (b)(1), (b)(2), (c)(1), and (h)(1) to "charging document." This amendment is proposed in conjunction with amendments to rule 3.125 to provide that all individuals charged with a criminal violation would be entitled to the same discovery regardless of the nature of the charging document (i.e., indictment, information, or notice to appear).

1996 Amendment. This is a substantial rewording of the rule as it pertains to depositions and pretrial case management. The amendment was in response to allegations of discovery abuse and a call for a more cost conscious approach to discovery by the Florida Supreme Court. In felony cases, the rule requires prosecutors to list witnesses in categories A, B, and C. Category A witnesses are subject to deposition as under the former rule. Category B witnesses are subject to deposition only upon leave of court. Category B witnesses include, but are not limited to, witnesses whose only connection to the case is the fact that they are the owners of property; transporting officers; booking officers; records and evidence custodians; and experts who have filed a report and curriculum vitae and who will not offer opinions subject to the *Frye* test. Category C witnesses may not be deposed. The trial courts are given more responsibility to regulate discovery by pretrial conference and by determining which category B witnesses should be deposed in a given case.

The rule was not amended for the purpose of prohibiting discovery. Instead, the rule recognized that many circuits now have "early resolution" or "rocket dockets" in which "open file discovery" is used to resolve a substantial percentage of cases at or before arraignment. The committee encourages that procedure. If a case cannot be resolved early, the committee believes that resolution of typical cases will occur after the depositions of the most essential witnesses (category A) are taken. Cases which do not resolve after the depositions of category A, may resolve if one or more category B witnesses are deposed. If the case is still unresolved, it is probably going to be a case that needs to be tried. In that event, judges may determine which additional depositions, if any, are necessary for pretrial preparation. A method for making that determination is provided in the rule.

Additionally, trial judges may regulate the taking of depositions in a number of ways to both facilitate resolution of a case and protect a witness from unnecessary inconvenience or harassment. There is a provision for setting a discovery schedule, including a discovery cut-off date as is common in civil practice. Also, a specific method is provided for application for protective orders.

One feature of the new rule relates to the deposition of law enforcement officers. Subpoenas are no longer required.

The rule has standardized the time for serving papers relating to discovery at fifteen days.

Discovery in misdemeanor cases has not been changed.

(b)(1)(A)(i) An investigating officer is an officer who has directed the collection of evidence, interviewed material witnesses, or who was assigned as the case investigator.

(h)(1) The prosecutor and defense counsel are encouraged to be present for the depositions of essential witnesses, and judges are encouraged to provide calendar time for the taking of depositions so that counsel for all parties can attend. This will 1) diminish the potential for the abuse of witnesses, 2) place the parties in a position to timely and effectively avail themselves of the remedies and sanctions established in this rule, 3) promote an expeditious and timely resolution of the cause, and 4) diminish the need to order transcripts of the deposition, thereby reducing costs.

1998 Amendment. This rule governs only the location of depositions. The procedure for procuring out-of-state witnesses for depositions is governed by statute.

Court Commentary

1996 Amendment. The designation of a witness who will present similar fact evidence will be dependent upon the witness's relationship to the similar crime, wrong, or act about which testimony will be given rather than the witness's relationship to the crime with which the defendant is currently charged.

1999/2000 Amendment. This rule does not affect requests for nonexempt law enforcement records as provided in chapter 119, Florida Statutes, other than those that are nonexempt as a result of a codefendant's participation in discovery. *See Henderson v. State*, 745 So. 2d 319 (Fla. Feb. 18, 1999).

2014 Amendment. The amendment to subdivision (b)(1)(A)(i)(8) is not intended to limit in any manner whatsoever the discovery obligations under the other provisions of the rule. With respect to subdivision (b)(1)(M)(iv), the Florida Innocence Commission recognized the impossibility of listing in the body of the rule every possible permutation expressing a benefit by the state to the informant witness. Although the term "anything" is not defined in the rule, the following are examples of benefits that may be considered by the trial court in determining whether the state has complied with its discovery obligations. The term "anything" includes, but is not limited to, any deal, promise, inducement, pay, leniency, immunity, personal advantage, vindication, or other benefit that the prosecution, or any person acting on behalf of the prosecution, has knowingly made or may make in the future.

VII. SUBSTITUTION OF JUDGE

Rule 3.231. Substitution of Judge

If by reason of death or disability the judge before whom a trial has commenced is unable to proceed with the trial, or posttrial proceedings, another judge, certifying that he or she has become familiar with the case, may proceed with the disposition of the case, except in death penalty sentencing proceedings. In death penalty sentencing proceedings, a successor judge who did not hear the evidence during the penalty phase of the trial shall conduct a new sentencing proceeding before a new jury.

Amended Sept. 24, 1992, effective Jan. 1, 1993 (606 So.2d 227); Nov. 19, 2009, effective Jan. 1, 2010 (26 So.3d 534).

Committee Notes

1972 Adoption. New. Follows ABA Standard 4.3, Trial by Jury. Inserted to provide for substitution of trial judge in specified instances.

VIII. CHANGE OF VENUE

Rule 3.240. Change of Venue

(a) Grounds for Motion. The state or the defendant may move for a change of venue on the ground that a fair and impartial trial cannot be had in the county where the case is pending for any reason other than the interest and prejudice of the trial judge.

(b) Contents of Motion. Every motion for change of venue shall be in writing and be accompanied by:

(1) affidavits of the movant and 2 or more other persons setting forth facts on which the motion is based; and

(2) a certificate by the movant's counsel that the motion is made in good faith.

(c) Time for Filing. A motion for change of venue shall be filed no less than 10 days before the time the case is called for trial unless good cause is shown for failure to file within such time.

(d) Action on Motion. The court shall consider the affidavits filed by all parties and receive evidence on every issue of fact necessary to its decision. If the court grants the motion it shall make an order removing the cause to the court having jurisdiction to try such offense in some other convenient county where a fair and impartial trial can be had.

(e) Defendant in Custody. If the defendant is in custody, the order shall direct that the defendant be forthwith delivered to the custody of the sheriff of the county to which the cause is removed.

(f) Transmittal of Documents. The clerk shall enter on the minutes the order of removal and transmit to the court to which the cause is removed a certified copy of the order of removal and of the record and proceedings and of the undertakings of the witnesses and the accused.

(g) Attendance by Witnesses. When the cause is removed to another court, witnesses who have been lawfully subpoenaed or ordered to appear at the trial shall, on notice of such removal, attend the court to which the cause is removed at the time specified in the order of removal. A witness who refuses to obey a duly served subpoena may be adjudged in contempt of court.

(h) Multiple Defendants. If there are several defendants and an order is made removing the cause on the application of one or more but not all of them, the other defendants shall be tried and all proceedings had against them in the county in which the cause is pending in all respects as if no order of removal had been made as to any defendant.

(i) Action of Receiving Court. The court to which the cause is removed shall proceed to trial and judgment therein as if the cause had originated in that court. If it is necessary to have any of the original pleadings or other documents before that court, the court from which the cause is removed shall at any time on application of the prosecuting attorney or the defendant order such documents or pleadings to be transmitted by the clerk, a certified copy thereof being retained.

(j) Prosecuting Attorney's Obligation. The prosecuting attorney of the court to which the cause is removed may amend the information, or file a new information, and such new information shall be entitled in the county in which the trial is had, but the allegations as to the place of commission of the crime shall refer to the county in which the crime was actually committed.

Amended Sept. 24, 1992, effective Jan. 1, 1993 (606 So.2d 227); Nov. 19, 2009, effective Jan. 1, 2010 (26 So.3d 534); Oct. 18, 2012, effective Dec. 1, 2012, April 1, 2013, Oct. 1, 2013 (102 So.3d 451).

Committee Notes

1968 Adoption. (a) through (d) substantially same as sections 911.02 through 911.05, Florida Statutes. Language is simplified and requirement pertaining to cases in criminal courts of record that removal be to adjoining county is omitted. Modern communications and distribution of television and press makes old requirements impractical. Designation of county left to discretion of the trial judge.

(e) through (i) same as corresponding sections 911.06 through 911.10, Florida Statutes.

1972 Amendment. Same as prior rule.

IX. THE TRIAL

Rule 3.250. Accused as Witness

In all criminal prosecutions the accused may choose to be sworn as a witness in the accused's own behalf and shall in that case be subject to examination as other witnesses, but no accused person shall be compelled to give testimony against himself or herself, nor shall any prosecuting attorney be permitted before the jury or court to comment on the failure of the accused to testify in his or her own behalf.

Amended Sept. 24, 1992, effective Jan. 1, 1993 (606 So.2d 227); May 3, 2007 (957 So.2d 1164).

Repeal

Laws 2006, c. 2006–96, § 2 provides:
"Rule 3.250, Florida Rules of Criminal Procedure, is repealed to the extent that it is inconsistent with this act."

Committee Notes

1968 Adoption. Same as section 918.09, Florida Statutes.

1972 Amendment. Same as prior rule. The committee considered The Florida Bar proposed amendment to this rule, but makes no recommendation with respect thereto.

Rule 3.251. Right to Trial by Jury

In all criminal prosecutions the accused shall have the right to a speedy and public trial by an impartial jury in the county where the crime was committed.

Committee Notes

1972 Adoption. Substance of Art. I, § 16, Florida Constitution.

Rule 3.260. Waiver of Jury Trial

A defendant may in writing waive a jury trial with the consent of the state.

Amended Sept. 24, 1992, effective Jan. 1, 1993 (606 So.2d 227).

Committee Notes

1968 Adoption. This is the same as Federal Rule of Criminal Procedure 23(a). This changes existing law by providing for consent of state.

1972 Amendment. Changes former rule by deleting "the approval of the Court," thus making trial by judge mandatory where both parties agree. The committee felt that the matter of withdrawal of a waiver was a matter within the inherent discretion of the trial judge and that no rule is required.

Rule 3.270. Number of Jurors

Twelve persons shall constitute a jury to try all capital cases, and 6 persons shall constitute a jury to try all other criminal cases.

Amended Sept. 24, 1992, effective Jan. 1, 1993 (606 So.2d 227).

Committee Notes

1968 Adoption. Except for substituting the word "persons" for "men," the suggested rule is a transcription of section 913.10, Florida Statutes. The standing committee on Florida court rules raised the question as to whether this rule is procedural or substantive and directed the subcommittee to call this fact to the attention of the Supreme Court.

1972 Amendment. Same as prior rule.

Rule 3.280. Alternate Jurors

(a) Selection. The court may direct that jurors, in addition to the regular panel, be called and impanelled to sit as alternate jurors. Alternate jurors, in the order in which they are impanelled, shall replace jurors who, prior to the time the jury retires to consider its verdict, become unable or disqualified to perform their duties. Alternate jurors shall be drawn in the same manner, have the same qualifications, be subject to the same examination, take the same oath, and have the same functions, powers, facilities, and privileges as the principal jurors. Except as hereinafter provided regarding capital cases, an alternate juror who does not replace a principal juror shall be discharged at the same time the jury retires to consider its verdict.

(b) Responsibilities. At the conclusion of the guilt or innocence phase of the trial, each alternate juror will be excused with instructions to remain in the courtroom. The jury will then retire to consider its verdict, and each alternate will be excused with appropriate instructions that the alternate juror may have to return for an additional hearing should the defendant be convicted of a capital offense.

Amended Sept. 24, 1992, effective Jan. 1, 1993 (606 So.2d 227).

Committee Notes

1968 Adoption. Save for certain rewording, the suggested rule is a transcription of section 913.10(2), Florida Statutes, except that the provisions for the challenging of the alternate jurors has been included more appropriately in the rule relating to challenges.

1972 Amendment. Same as prior rule.

1977 Amendment. This rule clarifies any ambiguities as to what should be done with alternate jurors at the conclusion of a capital case and whether they should be available for the penalty phase of the trial. The change specifies that they will not be instructed as to any further participation until the other jurors who are deliberating on guilt or innocence are out of the courtroom, in order not to influence the deliberating jurors or in any way convey that the trial judge feels that a capital conviction is imminent.

Rule 3.281. List of Prospective Jurors

Upon request, any party shall be furnished by the clerk of the court with a list containing names and addresses of prospective jurors summoned to try the case together with copies of all jury questionnaires returned by the prospective jurors.

Amended Sept. 24, 1992, effective Jan. 1, 1993 (606 So.2d 227).

Committee Note

1972 Adoption. ABA Standard 2.2. The furnishing of such a list should result in considerable time being saved at voir dire. Also includes those questionnaires authorized by section 40.101, Florida Statutes, although the statute itself provides for such disclosure.

Rule 3.290. Challenge to Panel

The state or defendant may challenge the panel. A challenge to the panel may be made only on the ground that the prospective jurors were not selected or drawn according to law. Challenges to the panel shall be made and decided before any individual juror is examined, unless otherwise ordered by the court. A challenge to the panel shall be in writing and shall specify the facts constituting the ground of the challenge. Challenges to the panel shall be tried by the court. Upon the trial of a challenge to the panel the witnesses may be examined on oath by the court and may be so examined by either party. If the challenge to the panel is sustained, the court shall discharge the panel. If the challenge is not sustained, the individual jurors shall be called.

Amended Sept. 24, 1992, effective Jan. 1, 1993 (606 So.2d 227).

Committee Notes

1968 Adoption. This is a transcription of section 913.01, Florida Statutes.

1972 Amendment. Same as prior rule 3.300; order of rule changed to improve chronology.

Rule 3.300. Voir Dire Examination, Oath, and Excusing of Member

(a) Oath. The prospective jurors shall be sworn collectively or individually, as the court may decide. The form of oath shall be as follows:

"Do your solemnly swear (or affirm) that you will answer truthfully all questions asked of you as prospective jurors, so help you God?"

If any prospective juror affirms, the clause "so help you God" shall be omitted.

(b) Examination. The court may then examine each prospective juror individually or may examine the prospective jurors collectively. Counsel for both the state and defendant shall have the right to examine jurors orally on their voir dire. The order in which the parties may examine each juror shall be determined by the court. The right of the parties to conduct an examination of each juror orally shall be preserved.

(c) Prospective Jurors Excused. If, after the examination of any prospective juror, the court is of the opinion that the juror is not qualified to serve as a trial juror, the court shall excuse the juror from the trial of the cause. If, however, the court does not excuse the juror, either party may then challenge the juror, as provided by law or by these rules.

Amended Sept. 24, 1992, effective Jan. 1, 1993 (606 So.2d 227).

Committee Notes

1968 Adoption.

(a) Save for the inclusion of the form of oath, the suggested rule is a transcription of a part of section 913.02(1), Florida Statutes. The form of oath paraphrases in pertinent part the oath set out in section 913.11, Florida Statutes.

(b) The suggested rule is a transcription of the remainder of section 913.02(1), Florida Statutes.

(c) Substantially same as section 913.02(2), Florida Statutes.

1972 Amendment. (a) The language relating to competence to serve as jurors deleted as superfluous, (c) amended for clarification by inserting the clause "the such juror is not qualified to serve as a trial juror" for the clause "that such juror is incompetent."

1980 Amendment. As to examination by parties, this brings rule 3.300(b) into conformity with Florida Rule of Civil Procedure 1.431(b). This rule also allows the court to examine each prospective juror individually or collectively.

Rule 3.310. Time for Challenge

The state or defendant may challenge an individual prospective juror before the juror is sworn to try the cause; except that the court may, for good cause, permit a challenge to be made after the juror is sworn, but before any evidence is presented.

Amended Sept. 24, 1992, effective Jan. 1, 1993 (606 So.2d 227).

Committee Notes

1968 Adoption. Save for the heading and for the inclusion of the phrase, "for cause or peremptorily," the suggested rule is a transcription of the provisions of section 913.04, Florida Statutes.

1972 Amendment. Prior rule amended only by deleting some language felt by the committee to be superfluous.

Rule 3.315. Exercise of Challenges

On the motion of any party, all challenges shall be addressed to the court outside the hearing of the jury panel in a manner selected by the court so that the jury panel is not aware of the nature of the challenge, the party making the challenge, or the basis of the court's ruling on the challenge, if for cause.

Amended Sept. 24, 1992, effective Jan. 1, 1993 (606 So.2d 227).

Committee Note

1980 Adoption. With the exception of "Upon the motion of any party," the language is taken directly from Florida Rule of Civil Procedure 1.431(c)(3). This rule had no counterpart in the criminal rules.

Rule 3.320. Manner of Challenge

A challenge to an individual juror may be oral. When a juror is challenged for cause the ground of the challenge shall be stated.

Committee Notes

1968 Adoption. Save for the heading and the insertion of the word "the," the suggested rule is a transcription of the provisions of section 913.05, Florida Statutes. The phrase "for cause or peremptorily" has been added.

1972 Amendment. Same as prior rule [but some terminology has been changed].

Same as prior rule.

Rule 3.330. Determination of Challenge for Cause

The court shall determine the validity of a challenge of an individual juror for cause. In making such determination the juror challenged and any other material witnesses, produced by the parties, may be examined on oath by either party. The court may consider also any other evidence material to such challenge.

Committee Notes

1968 Adoption. The suggested rule is essentially a transcription of sections 913.06 and 913.07, Florida Statutes, except for the first and last sentences.

1972 Amendment. Same as prior rule [but some terminology has been changed].

Rule 3.340. Effect of Sustaining Challenge

If a challenge for cause of an individual juror is sustained, the juror shall be discharged from the trial of the cause. If a peremptory challenge to an individual juror is made, the juror shall be discharged likewise from the trial of the cause.

Amended Sept. 24, 1992, effective Jan. 1, 1993 (606 So.2d 227).

Committee Notes

1968 Adoption. The first sentence of the suggested rule except for the inclusion of the words "for cause" is a transcription of section 913.09, Florida Statutes. The last sentence has been added.

1972 Amendment. Same as prior rule.

Rule 3.350. Peremptory Challenges

(a) Number. Each party shall be allowed the following number of peremptory challenges:

(1) *Felonies Punishable by Death or Imprisonment for Life.* Ten, if the offense charged is punishable by death or imprisonment for life.

(2) *All Other Felonies.* Six, if the offense charged is a felony not punishable by death or imprisonment for life.

(3) *Misdemeanors.* Three, if the offense charged is a misdemeanor.

(b) Codefendants. If 2 or more defendants are jointly tried, each defendant shall be allowed the number of peremptory challenges specified above, and in such case the state shall be allowed as many challenges as are allowed to all of the defendants.

(c) Multiple Counts and Multiple Charging Documents. If an indictment or information contains 2 or more counts or if 2 or more indictments or informations are consolidated for trial, the defendant shall be allowed the number of peremptory challenges that would be permissible in a single case, but in the interest of justice the judge may use judicial discretion in extenuating circumstances to grant additional challenges to the accumulated maximum based on the number of charges or cases included when it appears that there is a possibility that the state or the defendant may be prejudiced. The state and the defendant shall be allowed an equal number of challenges.

(d) Alternate Jurors. If 1 or 2 alternate jurors are called, each party is entitled to 1 peremptory challenge, in addition to those otherwise allowed by law, for each alternate juror so called. The additional peremptory challenge may be used only against the alternate juror and the other peremptory challenges allowed by law shall not be used against the alternate juror.

(e) Additional Challenges. The trial judge may exercise discretion to allow additional peremptory challenges when appropriate.

Amended Sept. 24, 1992, effective Jan. 1, 1993 (606 So.2d 227).

Committee Notes

1968 Adoption. The suggested rule is a transcription of section 913.08, Florida Statutes, excluding subdivision (5), which is lifted from section 913.10(2), Florida Statutes, and included since the several provisions relate to peremptory challenges. The question was raised regarding multiple counts or consolidation in their relation to the number of challenges. It was decided not to imply approval of multiple counts or consolidation. The standing committee on Florida court rules raised the question as to whether or not this rule is procedural or substantive and directed the subcommittee to call this fact to the attention of the supreme court.

1972 Amendment. Substantially same as prior rule; introductory language modernized.

1977 Amendment. This proposed rule amends rule 3.350(e) to allow the defendant and the state an equal number of peremptory challenges and to permit the court to grant additional challenges to both parties where it appears that the state would otherwise be prejudiced.

1992 Amendment. The amendment adds (e) that specifically sets out the trial court's discretion to allow peremptory challenges in addition to those provided for in the rule. This amendment was one of several proposed by the jury management committee that provided for a reduction in the number of peremptory challenges allowed by the rule. The majority of the criminal procedure rules committee, while recommending against adoption of the remaining proposals of the jury management committee, nevertheless felt it would be appropriate to add (e) to clarify that the trial court's discretion is not limited to those situations set out in (c) of the rule (i.e., multiple counts or informations or indictments consolidated for trial).

Rule 3.360. Oath of Trial Jurors

The following oath shall be administered to the jurors: "Do you solemnly swear (or affirm) that you will well and truly try the issues between the State of Florida and the defendant and render a true verdict according to the law and the evidence, so help you God?" If any juror affirms, the clause "so help you God" shall be omitted.

Committee Notes

1967 Adoption. The suggested rule is a transcription of FS 913.11.

1972 Adoption. Language of prior rule amended slightly to modernize.

Rule 3.361. Witness Attendance and Subpoenas

(a) Subpoenas generally. Subpoenas for testimony before the court and subpoenas for production of tangible evidence before the court may be issued by the clerk of the court or by any attorney of record in an action.

(b) Subpoena for testimony or production of tangible evidence.

(1) A subpoena for testimony or production of tangible evidence before the court shall state the name of the court and the title of the action and shall command each person to whom it is directed to attend and give testimony or produce the evidence at a time and place specified in the subpoena.

(2) On oral request of an attorney, the clerk shall issue a subpoena for testimony before the court or a subpoena for the production of tangible evidence before the court, signed and sealed but otherwise in blank, and the subpoena shall be filled in by the attorney before service.

(c) For production of tangible evidence.

(1) If a subpoena commands a person or entity to produce books, papers, documents, or tangible things,the person or entity may move the court to quash or modify the subpoena before the time specified in the subpoena for compliance.

(2) The court may (A) quash or modify the subpoena if it is unreasonable and oppressive, or (B) require the person in whose behalf the subpoena is issued to advance the reasonable cost of producing the books, papers, documents, or tangible things.

(d) Attendance and enforcement. A witness subpoenaed for testimony before the court or for production of tangible evidence before the court shall appear and remain in attendance until excused by the court or by all parties. A witness who refuses to obey a subpoena or who departs without being excused properly may be held in contempt.

Added Nov. 27, 1996, effective Jan. 1, 1997 (685 So.2d 1253). Amended Dec. 3, 1998 (724 So.2d 1162); Dec. 5, 2002, effective Jan. 1, 2003 (837 So.2d 924).

X. CONDUCT OF TRIAL; JURY INSTRUCTIONS

Rule 3.370. Regulation and Separation of Jurors

(a) During Trial. After the jurors have been sworn they shall hear the case as a body and, within the discretion of the trial judge, may be sequestered. In capital cases, absent a showing of prejudice, the trial court may order that between the guilt and penalty phases of the trial the jurors may separate for a definite time to be fixed by the court and then reconvene before the beginning of the penalty phase.

(b) After Submission of Cause. Unless the jurors have been kept together during the trial the court may, after the final submission of the cause, order that the jurors may separate for a definite time to be fixed by the court and then reconvene in the courtroom before retiring for consideration of their verdict.

(c) During Deliberations. Absent exceptional circumstances of emergency, accident, or other special necessity or unless sequestration is waived by the state and the defendant, in all capital cases in which the death penalty is sought by the state, once the jurors have retired for consideration of their verdict, they must be sequestered until such time as they have reached a verdict or have otherwise been discharged by the court. In all other cases, the court, in its discretion, either on the motion of counsel or on the court's initiative, may order that the jurors be permitted to separate. If jurors are allowed to separate, the trial judge shall give appropriate cautionary instructions.

Amended March 26, 1992 (596 So.2d 1036).

Committee Notes

1968 Adoption—Rule 1.380 [3.380].

(a) Taken from [F.S.A. §] 919.01.

(b) Taken from [F.S.A. §] 919.02.

1972 Amendment. (a) and (b) substantially the same as former rule 3.380, except that some language has been modernized. New provision permits nonsequestered jury to separate after receiving case for consideration.

Former Rule 3.370 has been deleted as its substance is now contained in new Rules 3.150 through 3.153 on Joinder and Severance.

Rule 3.371. Juror Questions of Witnesses

(a) Judicial Discretion. At the discretion of the presiding trial judge, jurors may be allowed to submit questions of witnesses during the trial.

(b) Procedure. The trial judge shall utilize the following procedure if a juror indicates that the juror wishes to ask a question:

(1) the questions must be submitted in writing;

(2) the trial judge shall review the question outside the presence of the jury;

(3) counsel shall have an opportunity to object to the question outside the presence of the jury;

(4) counsel shall be allowed to ask follow up questions; and

(5) the jury must be advised that if a question submitted by a juror is not allowed for any reason, the juror must not discuss it with the other jurors and must not hold it against either party.

Added Oct. 4, 2007, effective Jan. 1, 2008 (967 So.2d 178).

Rule 3.372. Juror Notebooks

In its discretion, the court may authorize documents and exhibits to be included in notebooks for use by the jurors during trial to aid them in performing their duties.

Added Oct. 4, 2007, effective Jan. 1, 2008 (967 So.2d 178).

Rule 3.380. Motion for Judgment of Acquittal

(a) Timing. If, at the close of the evidence for the state or at the close of all the evidence in the cause, the court is of the opinion that the evidence is insufficient to warrant a conviction, it may, and on the motion of the prosecuting attorney or the defendant shall, enter a judgment of acquittal.

(b) Waiver. A motion for judgment of acquittal is not waived by subsequent introduction of evidence on behalf of the defendant. The motion must fully set forth the grounds on which it is based.

(c) Renewal. If the jury returns a verdict of guilty or is discharged without having returned a verdict, the defendant's motion may be made or renewed within 10 days after the reception of a verdict and the jury is discharged or such further time as the court may allow.

Amended Sept. 24, 1992, effective Jan. 1, 1993 (606 So.2d 227); Dec. 10, 1998 (721 So.2d 725).

Committee Notes

1968 Adoption. Substantially same as section 918.08, Florida Statutes, except as follows:

(a) The existing statutory practice of granting directed verdicts is abolished in favor of the federal practice of having the judge enter a judgment of acquittal.

(b) The wording was changed to comply with the judgment of acquittal theory. A majority of the committee felt that the substance of the existing statute was all right, but a minority felt that the language should be changed so that a defendant would waive an erroneous denial of his motion for judgment of acquittal by introducing evidence. This point was raised in Wiggins v. State, 101 So.2d 833 (Fla.1st DCA 1958), wherein the court said that this statute is "ineptly worded."

1972 Amendment. (a) and (b) same as prior rule 3.660, transferred to better follow trial chronology. (c) provides time period for renewal of motion and is new.

1980 Amendment. This brings rule 3.380(c) into conformity with Florida Rule of Civil Procedure 1.480(b) as it relates to the number of days (10) within which a party, either in a civil or criminal case, may make or renew a motion for judgment of acquittal. There appears to be no sound reason for the distinction between the criminal rule (4 days or such greater time as the court may allow, not to exceed 15 days) and the civil rule (10 days).

Rule 3.381. Final Arguments

In all criminal trials, excluding the sentencing phase of a capital case, at the close of all the evidence, the prosecuting attorney shall be entitled to an initial closing argument and a rebuttal closing argument before the jury or the court sitting without a jury. Failure of the prosecuting attorney to make a closing argument shall not deprive the defense of its right to make a closing argument or the prosecuting attorney's right to then make a rebuttal argument. If the defendant does not present a closing argument, the prosecuting attorney will not be permitted a rebuttal argument.

Added May 3, 2007 (957 So.2d 1164).

Rule 3.390. Jury Instructions

(a) Subject of Instructions. The presiding judge shall instruct the jury only on the law of the case before or after the argument of counsel and may provide appropriate instructions during the trial. If the instructions are given prior to final argument, the presiding judge shall give the jury final procedural instructions after final arguments are concluded and prior to deliberations. Except in capital cases, the judge shall not instruct the jury on the sentence that may be imposed for the offense for which the accused is on trial.

(b) Form of Instructions. The instruction to a jury shall be orally delivered and shall also be in writing. All written instructions shall also be filed in the cause.

(c) Written Request. At the close of the evidence, or at such earlier time during the trial as the court reasonably directs, any party may file written requests that the court instruct the jury on the law as set forth in the requests. The court shall inform counsel of its proposed action on the request and of the instructions that will be given prior to their argument to the jury.

(d) Objections. No party may raise on appeal the giving or failure to give an instruction unless the party objects thereto before the jury retires to consider its verdict, stating distinctly the matter to which the party objects and the grounds of the objection. Opportunity shall be given to make the objection out of the presence of the jury.

(e) Transcript and Review. When an objection is made to the giving of or failure to give an instruction, no exception need be made to the court's ruling thereon in order to have the ruling reviewed, and the grounds of objection and ruling thereon shall be taken by the court reporter and, if the jury returns a verdict of guilty, transcribed by the court reporter and filed in the cause.

Amended Sept. 24, 1992, effective Jan. 1, 1993 (606 So.2d 227); Oct. 4, 2007, effective Jan. 1, 2008 (967 So.2d 178).

Committee Notes

1972 Adoption. The committee adopted section 918.10, Florida Statutes, with only minor modification as to terminology.

1988 Amendment. To assist the jury in understanding the jury instructions.

1992 Amendment: Suggested change in wording to make (d) clearer and easier to understand and also so it more closely follows its federal counterpart, Federal Rule of Criminal Procedure 30.

Rule 3.391. Selection of Foreperson of Jury

The court shall instruct the jurors to select one of their number foreperson.

Amended Sept. 24, 1992, effective Jan. 1, 1993 (606 So.2d 227).

Committee Notes

1968 Adoption. This rule was inserted in order to clarify the system of selecting jury foreman.

1972 Amendment. Same as former rule 3.390.

Rule 3.400. Materials to the Jury Room

(a) Discretionary Materials. The court may permit the jury, upon retiring for deliberation, to take to the jury room:

(1) a copy of the charges against the defendant;

(2) forms of verdict approved by the court, after being first submitted to counsel;

(3) all things received in evidence other than depositions. If the thing received in evidence is a public record or a private document which, in the opinion of the court, ought not to be taken from the person having it in custody, a copy shall be taken or sent instead of the original.

(b) Mandatory Materials. The court must provide the jury, upon retiring for deliberation, with a written copy of the instructions given to take to the jury room.

Amended March 2, 1995, effective May 31, 1995 (657 So.2d 1134); Oct. 4, 2007, effective Jan. 1, 2008 (967 So.2d 178).

Committee Notes

1968 Adoption. (1) and (2) same as [F.S.A. §] 919.04(1) and (2).

[It was proposed that written or recorded statements or confessions be included among the items not to be taken with or sent to the jury. "It was felt by the committee that the present practice of allowing such things to be taken with the jury is unfair and emphasizes such statements or confessions to the jury. Since they are always read to the jury they should receive no additional emphasis than the testimony of any witness from the stand." However, the proposal was not adopted, and F.S.A. § 919.04(3) was transferred unchanged to Rule 1.400(c).]

1972 Amendment. (a) permits a copy of the indictment or information to be taken to the jury room. The Committee deliberated at length about this provision but finally approved same. (b), (c), and (d) are same as former rule 3.400(a), (b), and (c) [but some terminology has been changed].

Rule 3.410. Jury Request to Review Evidence or for Additional Instructions

After the jurors have retired to consider their verdict, if they request additional instructions or to have any testimony read or played back to them they may be conducted into the courtroom by the officer who has them in charge and the court may give them the additional instructions or may order the testimony read or played back to them. The instructions shall be given and the testimony presented only after notice to the prosecuting attorney and to counsel for the defendant. All testimony read or played back must be done in open court in the presence of all parties. In its discretion, the court may respond in writing to the inquiry without having the jury brought before the court, provided the parties have received the opportunity to place objections on the record and both the inquiry and response are made part of the record.

Amended Sept. 24, 1992, effective Jan. 1, 1993 (606 So.2d 227); Nov. 8, 2012, effective Jan. 1, 2013 (104 So.3d 304).

Committee Notes

1968 Adoption. Same as section 919.05, Florida Statutes.

1972 Amendment. This is the same as former rule 3.410, except that the former rule made it mandatory for the trial judge to give additional instructions upon request. The committee feels that this should be discretionary.

Rule 3.420. Recall of Jury for Additional Instructions

The court may recall the jurors after they have retired to consider their verdict to give them additional instructions or to correct any erroneous instructions given them. The additional or corrective instructions may be given only after notice to the prosecuting attorney and to counsel for the defendant.

Amended Sept. 24, 1992, effective Jan. 1, 1993 (606 So.2d 227).

Committee Notes

1968 Adoption. Same as section 919.06, Florida Statutes.

1972 Amendment. Same as former rule.

Rule 3.430. Jury Not Recallable to Hear Additional Evidence

After the jurors have retired to consider their verdict the court shall not recall the jurors to hear additional evidence.

Committee Notes

1967 Adoption. Same as [F.S.A. §] 919.07.

1972 Revision. Same as prior rule.

XI. THE VERDICT

Rule 3.440. Rendition of Verdict; Reception and Recording

When the jurors have agreed upon a verdict they shall be conducted into the courtroom by the officer having them in charge. The court shall ask the foreperson if an agreement has been reached on a verdict. If the foreperson answers in the affirmative, the judge shall call on the foreperson to deliver the verdict in writing to the clerk. The court may then examine the verdict and correct it as to matters of form with the unanimous consent of the jurors. The clerk shall then read the verdict to the jurors and, unless disagreement is expressed by one or more of them or the jury is polled, the verdict shall be entered of record, and the jurors discharged from the cause. No verdict may be rendered unless all of the trial jurors concur in it.

Amended Sept. 24, 1992, effective Jan. 1, 1993 (606 So.2d 227).

Committee Notes

1968 Adoption. Same as section 919.09, Florida Statutes.

1972 Amendment. Same as prior rule.

Rule 3.450. Polling the Jury

On the motion of either the state or the defendant or on its own motion, the court shall cause the jurors to be asked severally if the verdict rendered is their verdict. If a juror dissents, the court must direct that the jury be sent back for further consideration. If there is no dissent the verdict shall be entered of record and the jurors discharged. However, no motion to poll the jury shall be entertained after the jury is discharged or the verdict recorded.

Amended Sept. 24, 1992, effective Jan. 1, 1993 (606 So.2d 227).

Committee Notes

1968 Adoption. Same as section 919.10, Florida Statutes, except elimination of polling jury after directed verdict in view of innovation of "judgment of acquittal."

1972 Amendment. Same as prior rule.

Rule 3.451. Judicial Comment on Verdict

While it is appropriate for the court to thank jurors at the conclusion of a trial for their public service, the court shall not praise or criticize their verdict.

Committee Notes

1972 Adoption. From ABA Standard 5.6, Trial by Jury.

Rule 3.470. Proceedings on Sealed Verdict

The court may, with the consent of the prosecuting attorney and the defendant, direct the jurors that if they should agree upon a verdict during a temporary adjournment of the court, the foreperson and each juror shall sign the same, and the verdict shall be sealed in an envelope and delivered to the officer having charge of the jury, after which the jury may separate until the next convening of the court. When the court authorizes the rendition of a sealed verdict, it shall admonish the jurors not to make any disclosure concerning it or to speak with other persons concerning the cause, until their verdict shall have been rendered in open court. The officer shall, forthwith, deliver the sealed verdict to the clerk. When the jurors have reassembled in open court, the envelope shall be opened by the court or clerk and the same proceedings shall be had as in the receiving of other verdicts.

Amended Sept. 24, 1992, effective Jan. 1, 1993 (606 So.2d 227).

Committee Notes

1968 Adoption of Rule 3.470. Same as section 919.12, Florida Statutes.

1968 Adoption of Rule 3.480. Same as section 919.13, Florida Statutes.

1972 Amendment. Former rule 3.480 has been deleted, its substance now contained in rule 3.470. Substantially same as former rules 3.470 and 3.480.

Rule 3.490. Determination of Degree of Offense

If the indictment or information charges an offense divided into degrees, the jury may find the defendant guilty of the offense charged or any lesser degree supported by the evidence. The judge shall not instruct on any degree as to which there is no evidence.

Committee Notes

1968 Adoption. Same as [F.S.A.] § 919.14.

1972 Amendment. Same as prior rule except references to affidavit have been deleted.

Rule 3.500. Verdict of Guilty Where More Than One Count

If different offenses are charged in the indictment or information on which the defendant is tried, the jurors shall, if they convict the defendant, make it appear by their verdict on which counts or of which offenses they find the defendant guilty.

Amended Sept. 24, 1992, effective Jan. 1, 1993 (606 So.2d 227).

Committee Notes

1968 Adoption. Same as section 919.15, Florida Statutes.

1972 Amendment. Amended to modernize the language of the rule. Substantially the same as prior rule.

Rule 3.505. Inconsistent Verdicts

The state need not elect between inconsistent counts, but the trial court shall submit to the jury verdict forms as to each count with instructions applicable to returning its verdicts from the inconsistent counts.

Amended Sept. 24, 1992, effective Jan. 1, 1993 (606 So.2d 227).

Committee Note

1977 Adoption. Although there appears to be no rule or statute relating to "election," many Florida cases refer to the fact that the trial court is required to make the state elect, before or during trial, between inconsistent counts. Many times the circumstances show conclusively that the accused is guilty of one or the other of inconsistent offenses. Since the evidence is then inconsistent with any reasonable hypothesis of innocence, the circumstantial rule is satisfied and the evidence should support a verdict of guilty as to either offense. In such a case the state should not be required to elect. This new rule is intended to lead to uniformity throughout the state on this issue and is more consonant with rule 3.140(k)(5).

Rule 3.510. Determination of Attempts and Lesser Included Offenses

On an indictment or information on which the defendant is to be tried for any offense the jury may convict the defendant of:

(a) an attempt to commit the offense if such attempt is an offense and is supported by the evidence. The judge shall not instruct the jury if there is no evidence to support the attempt and the only evidence proves a completed offense; or

(b) any offense that as a matter of law is a necessarily included offense or a lesser included offense of the offense charged in the indictment or information and is supported by the evidence. The judge shall not instruct on any lesser included offense as to which there is no evidence.

Amended Sept. 24, 1992, effective Jan. 1, 1993 (606 So.2d 227).

Committee Notes

1968 Adoption. Same as section 919.16, Florida Statutes. The standing committee on Florida court rules raised the question as to whether this rule is procedural or substantive and directed the subcommittee to call this fact to the attention of the supreme court.

1972 Amendment. Same as prior rule except that references to affidavit have been deleted.

Rule 3.520. Verdict in Case of Joint Defendants

On the trial of 2 or more defendants jointly the jurors may render a verdict as to any defendant in regard to whom the jurors agree.

Amended Sept. 24, 1992, effective Jan. 1, 1993 (606 So.2d 227).

Committee Notes

1968 Adoption. Same as section 919.17, Florida Statutes.

1972 Amendment. Same as prior rule.

Rule 3.530. Reconsideration of Ambiguous or Defective Verdict

If a verdict is so defective that the court cannot determine from it whether the jurors intended to acquit the defendant or to convict the defendant of an offense for which judgment could be entered under the indictment or information on which the defendant is tried, or cannot determine from it on what count or counts the jurors intended to acquit or convict the defendant, the court shall, with proper instructions, direct the jurors to reconsider the verdict, and the verdict shall not be received until it shall clearly appear therefrom whether the jurors intended to convict or acquit the defendant and on what count or counts they intended to acquit or convict the defendant. If the jury persists in rendering a defective verdict, the court shall declare a mistrial.

Amended Sept. 24, 1992, effective Jan. 1, 1993 (606 So.2d 227).

Committee Notes

1968 Adoption. Same as section 919.18, Florida Statutes.

1972 Amendment. Same as prior rule.

Rule 3.540. When Verdict May Be Rendered

A verdict may be rendered and additional or corrective instructions given on any day, including Sunday or any legal holiday.

Committee Notes

1968 Adoption. Same as [F.S.A. §] 919.19.

1972 Amendment. Same as prior rule.

Rule 3.550. Disposition of Defendant

If a verdict of guilty is rendered the defendant shall, if in custody, be remanded. If the defendant is at large on bail, the defendant may be taken into custody and committed to the proper official or remain at liberty on the same or additional bail as the court may direct.

Amended Sept. 24, 1992, effective Jan. 1, 1993 (606 So.2d 227).

Committee Notes

1968 Adoption. Same as section 919.20, Florida Statutes.

Rule 3.560. Discharge of Jurors

After the jurors have retired to consider their verdict, the court shall discharge them from the cause when:

(a) their verdict has been received;

(b) on the expiration of such time as the court deems proper, if the court finds there is no reasonable probability that the jurors can agree on a verdict; or

(c) a necessity exists for their discharge.

The court may in any event discharge the jurors from the cause if the prosecuting attorney and the defendant consent to the discharge.

Amended Sept. 24, 1992, effective Jan. 1, 1993 (606 So.2d 227).

Committee Notes

1968 Adoption. Same as section 919.21, Florida Statutes, except (4) omitted.

1972 Amendment. Same as prior rule.

Rule 3.570. Irregularity in Rendition, Reception, and Recording of Verdict

No irregularity in the rendition or reception of a verdict may be raised unless it is raised before the jury is discharged. No irregularity in the recording of a verdict shall affect its validity unless the defendant was in fact prejudiced by the irregularity.

Amended Sept. 24, 1992, effective Jan. 1, 1993 (606 So.2d 227).

Committee Notes

1968 Adoption. Rule 3.570 is same as section 919.22, Florida Statutes.

Section 919.23, Florida Statutes, was not included in the rules. This deals with the recommendation of mercy and it was felt that this was not procedural but substantive and not within the scope of the rulemaking power of the supreme court.

1972 Amendment. Same as prior rule.

Rule 3.575. Motion to Interview Juror

A party who has reason to believe that the verdict may be subject to legal challenge may move the court for an order permitting an interview of a juror or jurors to so determine. The motion shall be filed within 10 days after the rendition of the verdict, unless good cause is shown for the failure to make the motion within that time. The motion shall state the name of any juror to be interviewed and the reasons that the party has to believe that the verdict may be subject to challenge. After notice and hearing, the trial judge, upon a finding that the verdict may be subject to challenge, shall enter an order permitting the interview, and setting therein a time and a place for the interview of the juror or jurors, which shall be conducted in the presence of the court and the parties. If no reason is found to believe that the verdict may be subject to challenge, the court shall enter its order denying permission to interview.

Added Oct. 7, 2004, effective Jan. 1, 2005 (886 So.2d 197).

Court Commentary

2004 Amendment. This rule does not abrogate Rule Regulating The Florida Bar 4–3.5(d)(4), which allows an attorney to interview a juror to determine whether the verdict may be subject to legal challenge after filing a notice of intention to interview.

XII. POSTTRIAL MOTIONS

Rule 3.580. Court May Grant New Trial

When a verdict has been rendered against the defendant or the defendant has been found guilty by the court, the court on motion of the defendant, or on its own motion, may grant a new trial or arrest judgment.

Committee Notes

1968 Adoption. Same as [F.S.A.] Section 920.01 except arrest of judgment is added.

1972 Amendment. Same as prior rule.

Rule 3.590. Time for and Method of Making Motions; Procedure; Custody Pending Hearing

(a) Time for Filing in Noncapital Cases. A motion for new trial or in arrest of judgment, or both, in cases in which the state does not seek the death penalty, may be made within 10 days after the rendition of the verdict or the finding of the court. A timely motion may be amended to state new grounds without leave of court prior to expiration of the 10–day period and in the discretion of the court at any other time before the motion is determined.

(b) Time for Filing in Capital Cases Where the Death Penalty Is an Issue. A motion for new trial or arrest of judgment, or both, or for a new penalty phase hearing may be made within 10 days after written final judgment of conviction and sentence of life imprisonment or death is filed. The motion may address grounds which arose in the guilt phase and the penalty phase of the trial. Separate motions for the guilt phase and the penalty phase may be filed. The motion or motions may be amended without leave of court prior to the expiration of the 10 day period, and in the discretion of the court, at any other time before the motion is determined.

(c) Oral Motions. When the defendant has been found guilty by a jury or by the court, the motion may be dictated into the record, if a court reporter is present, and may be argued immediately after the return of the verdict or the finding of the court. The court may immediately rule on the motion.

(d) Written Motions. The motion may be in writing, filed with the clerk; it shall state the grounds on which it is based. A copy of a written motion shall be served on the prosecuting attorney. When the court sets a time for the hearing thereon, the clerk may notify counsel for the respective parties or the attorney for the defendant may serve notice of hearing on the prosecuting officer.

(e) Custody Pending Motion. Until the motion is disposed of, a defendant who is not already at liberty on bail shall remain in custody and not be allowed liberty on bail unless the court on good cause shown (if the offense for which the defendant is convicted is bailable) permits the defendant to be released on bail until the motion is disposed of. If the defendant is already at liberty on bail that is deemed by the court to be good and sufficient, it may permit the defendant to continue at large on such bail until the motion for new trial is heard and disposed of.

Amended Sept. 24, 1992, effective Jan. 1, 1993 (606 So.2d 227); Dec. 7, 2006, effective Jan. 1, 2007 (945 So.2d 1124); Nov. 8, 2012, effective Jan. 1, 2013 (104 So.3d 304).

Committee Notes

1968 Adoption. (a) The same as the first part of section 920.02(3), Florida Statutes, except that the statutory word "further" is changed to "greater" in the rule and provision for motion in arrest of judgment is added.

(b) Substantially the same as first part of section 920.02(2), Florida Statutes. The rule omits the requirement that the defendant be sentenced immediately on the denial of a motion for new trial (the court might wish to place the defendant on probation or might desire to call for a presentence investigation). The rule also omits the statute's requirement that an order of denial be dictated to the court reporter, because the clerk is supposed to be taking minutes at this stage.

NOTE: The provisions of the last part of section 920.02(2), Florida Statutes, as to supersedeas and appeal are not incorporated into this rule; such provisions are not germane to motions for new trial or arrest of judgment.

(c) Substantially same as section 920.03, Florida Statutes.

(d) Substantially same as last part of section 920.02(3), Florida Statutes, except that the last sentence of the rule is new.

NOTE: The provisions of section 920.02(4), Florida Statutes, relating to supersedeas on appeal and the steps that are necessary to obtain one, are not incorporated into a rule. The provisions of section 920.02(4) do not belong in a group of rules dealing with motions for new trial.

1972 Amendment. Substantially the same as prior rule.

1980 Amendment. This brings rule 3.590(a) into conformity with Florida Rule of Civil Procedure 1.530(b) as it relates to the time within which a motion for new trial or in arrest of judgment may be filed. It also allows the defendant in a criminal case the opportunity to amend the motion. The opportunity to amend already exists in a civil case. No sound reason exists to justify the disparities in the rules.

2006 Amendment. This amendment provides the time limitations and procedures for moving for new trial, arrest of judgment or a new penalty phase in capital cases in which the death penalty is an issue. The motion may be made within ten days after written final judgment of conviction and sentence of life imprisonment or death is filed.

Rule 3.600. Grounds for New Trial

(a) Grounds for Granting. The court shall grant a new trial if any of the following grounds is established.

(1) The jurors decided the verdict by lot.

(2) The verdict is contrary to law or the weight of the evidence.

(3) New and material evidence, which, if introduced at the trial would probably have changed the verdict or finding of the court, and which the defendant could

not with reasonable diligence have discovered and produced at the trial, has been discovered.

(b) Grounds for Granting if Prejudice Established. The court shall grant a new trial if any of the following grounds is established, providing substantial rights of the defendant were prejudiced thereby.

(1) The defendant was not present at any proceeding at which the defendant's presence is required by these rules.

(2) The jury received any evidence out of court, other than that resulting from an authorized view of the premises.

(3) The jurors, after retiring to deliberate upon the verdict, separated without leave of court.

(4) Any juror was guilty of misconduct.

(5) The prosecuting attorney was guilty of misconduct.

(6) The court erred in the decision of any matter of law arising during the course of the trial.

(7) The court erroneously instructed the jury on a matter of law or refused to give a proper instruction requested by the defendant.

(8) For any other cause not due to the defendant's own fault, the defendant did not receive a fair and impartial trial.

(c) Evidence. When a motion for new trial calls for a decision on any question of fact, the court may consider evidence on the motion by affidavit or otherwise.

Amended Sept. 24, 1992, effective Jan. 1, 1993 (606 So.2d 227).

Committee Notes

1968 Adoption. Same as sections 920.04 and 920.05, Florida Statutes, except that the last paragraph of section 920.05 is omitted from the rule. The provision of the omitted paragraph that a new trial shall be granted to a defendant who has not received a fair and impartial trial through no personal fault is inserted in the rule as subdivision (b)(8). The provision of the omitted paragraph of the statute which requires a new trial when the sentence exceeds the penalty provided by law is omitted from the rule because no defendant is entitled to a new trial merely because an excessive sentence has been pronounced. The standing committee on Florida court rules questioned whether this rule is procedural or substantive and directed the subcommittee to call this fact to the attention of the supreme court.

(c) Same as second paragraph of section 920.07, Florida Statutes.

1972 Amendment. Same as prior rule.

Rule 3.610. Motion for Arrest of Judgment; Grounds

The court shall grant a motion in arrest of judgment only on 1 or more of the following grounds:

(a) The indictment or information on which the defendant was tried is so defective that it will not support a judgment of conviction.

(b) The court is without jurisdiction of the cause.

(c) The verdict is so uncertain that it does not appear therefrom that the jurors intended to convict the defendant of an offense of which the defendant could be convicted under the indictment or information under which the defendant was tried.

(d) The defendant was convicted of an offense for which the defendant could not be convicted under the indictment or information under which the defendant was tried.

Amended Sept. 24, 1992, effective Jan. 1, 1993 (606 So.2d 227).

Committee Notes

1968 Adoption. Note that (a)(1) of the rule revamps section 920.05(2)(a) through (d), Florida Statutes, in an effort to better take into account the fact that an accusatorial writ that would not withstand a motion to quash (dismiss) might well support a judgment of conviction if no such motion is filed. See Sinclair v. State, 46 So.2d 453 (1950).

Note also that, where appropriate, the rule mentions "affidavit" in addition to "indictment" and "information." The standing committee on Florida court rules questioned whether this rule is procedural or substantive and directed the subcommittee to call this fact to the attention of the supreme court.

1972 Amendment. Same as prior rule. References to trial affidavit deleted.

Rule 3.620. When Evidence Sustains Only Conviction of Lesser Offense

When the offense is divided into degrees or necessarily includes lesser offenses and the court, on a motion for new trial, is of the opinion that the evidence does not sustain the verdict but is sufficient to sustain a finding of guilt of a lesser degree or of a lesser offense necessarily included in the one charged, the court shall not grant a new trial but shall find or adjudge the defendant guilty of the lesser degree or lesser offense necessarily included in the charge, unless a new trial is granted by reason of some other prejudicial error.

Amended Sept. 24, 1992, effective Jan. 1, 1993 (606 So.2d 227).

Committee Notes

1968 Adoption. Substantially the same as section 920.06, Florida Statutes.

1972 Amendment. Same as prior rule.

Rule 3.630. Sentence Before or After Motion Filed

The court in its discretion may sentence the defendant either before or after the filing of a motion for new trial or arrest of judgment.

Amended Sept. 24, 1992, effective Jan. 1, 1993 (606 So.2d 227).

Committee Notes

1968 Adoption. Same as first paragraph of section 920.07, Florida Statutes. Provision for arrest of judgment is added.

1972 Amendment. Same as prior rule.

Rule 3.640. Effect of Granting New Trial

When a new trial is granted, the new trial shall proceed in all respects as if no former trial had occurred except that when an offense is divided into degrees or the charge includes a lesser offense, and the defendant has been found guilty of a lesser degree or lesser included offense, the defendant cannot thereafter be prosecuted for a higher degree of the same offense or for a higher offense than that of which the defendant was convicted.

Amended Sept. 24, 1992, effective Jan. 1, 1993 (606 So.2d 227); Nov. 1, 2006, effective Jan. 1, 2007 (945 So.2d 407).

Committee Notes

1968 Adoption. Based on section 920.09, Florida Statutes. The second paragraph of the existing statute allows the testimony of an absent witness, given at a former trial, to be used only if the witness is absent from the state or dead. This has been enlarged to include absent witnesses who are physically incapacitated to attend court or who have become mentally incapacitated to testify since the former trial.

1972 Committee Note. Same as prior rule.

XIII. JUDGMENT

Rule 3.650. Judgment Defined

The term "judgment" means the adjudication by the court that the defendant is guilty or not guilty.

Committee Notes

1968 Adoption. Substantially the same as [F.S.A.] Section 921.01.

1972 Amendment. Same as prior rule.

Rule 3.670. Rendition of Judgment

If the defendant is found guilty, a judgment of guilty and, if the defendant has been acquitted, a judgment of not guilty shall be rendered in open court and in writing, signed by the judge, filed, and recorded. However, where allowed by law, the judge may withhold an adjudication of guilt if the judge places the defendant on probation.

When a judge renders a final judgment of conviction, withholds adjudication of guilt after a verdict of guilty, imposes a sentence, grants probation, or revokes probation, the judge shall forthwith inform the defendant concerning the rights of appeal therefrom, including the time allowed by law for taking an appeal. Within 15 days after the signed written judgment and sentence is filed with the clerk of court, the clerk of the court shall serve on counsel for the defendant and counsel for the state a copy of the judgment of conviction and sentence entered, noting thereon the date of service by a certificate of service. If it is the practice of the trial court or the clerk of court to hand deliver copies of the judgment and sentence at the time of sentencing and copies are in fact hand delivered at that time, hand delivery shall be noted in the court file, but no further service shall be required and the certificate of service need not be included on the hand-delivered copy.

Amended Sept. 24, 1992, effective Jan. 1, 1993 (606 So.2d 227); Nov. 12, 1999, effective Jan. 1, 2000 (760 So.2d 67); April 7, 2005 (900 So.2d 528).

Committee Notes

1968 Adoption. To the same effect as section 921.02, Florida Statutes, except the portion reading "in writing, signed by the judge" which was added. Last sentence was added to permit the judge to operate under section 948.01(3), Florida Statutes.

The Florida law forming the basis of this proposal is found in article V, sections 4 and 5, Constitution of Florida, concerning the right of appeal from a judgment of conviction; section 924.06, Florida Statutes, specifying when a defendant may take an appeal; section 924.09, Florida Statutes, and Florida Criminal Appellate Rule 6.2 concerning the time for taking appeals by a defendant in criminal cases; and section 948.011, Florida Statutes, providing for a sentence of a fine and probation as to imprisonment.

The purpose of the proposed rule is to provide assurance that a defendant, represented or unrepresented by counsel, will have authoritative and timely notice of the right to appeal.

1972 Amendment. Same as prior rule [but some terminology has been changed].

2005 Amendment. Amended to conform with section 775.08435, Florida Statutes (2004), effective July 1, 2004 (ch. 2004–60, Laws of Fla.).

Rule 3.680. Judgment on Informal Verdict

If a verdict is rendered from which it can be clearly understood that the jurors intended to acquit the defendant, a judgment of not guilty shall be rendered thereon even though the verdict is defective. No judgment of guilty shall be rendered on a verdict unless the jurors clearly express in it a finding of guilt of the defendant.

Amended Sept. 24, 1992, effective Jan. 1, 1993 (606 So.2d 227).

Committee Notes

1968 Adoption. Same as section 921.02, Florida Statutes.

1972 Amendment. Same as prior rule.

Rule 3.690. Judgment of Not Guilty; Defendant Discharged and Sureties Exonerated

When a judgment of not guilty is entered, the defendant, if in custody, shall be immediately discharged unless the defendant is in custody on some other charge. If the defendant is at large on bail, the defendant's sureties shall be exonerated and, if money or bonds have been deposited as bail, the money or bonds shall be refunded.

Amended Sept. 24, 1992, effective Jan. 1, 1993 (606 So.2d 227).

Committee Notes

1968 Adoption. Same as section 921.04, Florida Statutes.

1972 Amendment. Same as prior rule.

Rule 3.691. Post–Trial Release

(a) When Authorized. All persons who have been adjudicated guilty of the commission of any offense, not capital, may be released, pending review of the conviction, at the discretion of either the trial or appellate court, applying the principles enunciated in Younghans v. State, 90 So.2d 308 (Fla.1956), provided that no person may be admitted to bail on appeal from a conviction of a felony unless the defendant establishes that the appeal is taken in good faith, on grounds fairly debatable, and not frivolous. However, in no case shall bail be granted if such person has previously been convicted of a felony, the commission of which occurred prior to the commission of the subsequent felony, and the person's civil rights have not been restored or if other felony charges are pending against the person and probable cause has been found that the person has committed the felony or felonies at the time the request for bail is made.

(b) Written Findings. In any case in which the court has the discretion to release the defendant pending review of the conviction and, after the defendant's conviction, denies release, it shall state in writing its reasons for the denial.

(c) Review of Denial. An order by a trial court denying bail to a person pursuant to the provisions of subdivision (a) may be reviewed by motion to the appellate court and the motion shall be advanced on the calendar of the appellate court for expeditious review.

(d) Conditions of Release. If the defendant is released after conviction and on appeal, the condition shall be: (1) the defendant will duly prosecute the appeal; (2) the defendant will surrender himself or herself in execution of the judgment or sentence on its being affirmed or modified or on the appeal being dismissed; or in case the judgment is reversed and the cause remanded for a new trial, the defendant will appear in the court to which the cause may be remanded for a new trial, that the defendant will appear in the court to which the cause may be remanded and submit to the orders and process thereof and will not depart the jurisdiction of the court without leave.

(e) Approval of Bond. The court shall approve the sufficiency and adequacy of the bond, its security, and sureties, prior to the release of the defendant.

Amended Sept. 24, 1992, effective Jan. 1, 1993 (606 So.2d 227); Nov. 8, 2012, effective Jan. 1, 2013 (104 So.3d 304).

Committee Notes

1977 Amendment. Chapter 76–138, section 2, Laws of Florida, by appropriate vote, repealed the provisions of rule 3.691, insofar as they were inconsistent with the legislative act. This rule has been amended to include the provisions of Chapter 76–138, Laws of Florida.

Rule 3.692. Petition to Seal or Expunge

(a) Requirements of Petition.

(1) All relief sought by reason of sections 943.0585–943.059, Florida Statutes, shall be by written petition, filed with the clerk. The petition shall state the grounds on which it is based and the official records to which it is directed and shall be supported by an affidavit of the party seeking relief, which affidavit shall state with particularity the statutory grounds and the facts in support of the motion. A petition seeking to seal or expunge nonjudicial criminal history records must be accompanied by a certificate of eligibility issued to the petitioner by the Florida Department of Law Enforcement. A copy of the completed petition and affidavit shall be served on the prosecuting attorney and the arresting authority. Notice and hearing shall be as provided in rule 3.590(c).

(2) All relief sought by reason of section 943.0583, Florida Statutes, shall be by written petition, filed with the clerk. The petition shall state the grounds on which it is based and the official records to which it is directed; shall be supported by the petitioner's sworn statement attesting that the petitioner is eligible for such an expunction; and to the best of his or her knowledge or belief that the petitioner does not have any other petition to expunge or any petition to seal pending before any court; and shall be accompanied by official documentation of the petitioner's status as a victim of human trafficking, if any exists. A petition to expunge, filed under section 943.0583, Florida Statutes, is not required to be accompanied by a certificate of eligibility from the Florida Department of Law Enforcement. A copy of the completed petition, sworn statement, and any other official documentation of the petitioner's status as a victim of human trafficking, shall be served on the prosecuting attorney and the arresting authority. Notice and hearing shall be as provided in rule 3.590(c).

(b) State's Response; Evidence. The state may traverse or demur to the petition and affidavit. The court may receive evidence on any issue of fact necessary to the decision of the petition.

(c) Written Order. If the petition is granted, the court shall enter its written order so stating and further setting forth the records and agencies or departments to which it is directed.

(d) Copies of Order. On the receipt of an order sealing or expunging nonjudicial criminal history records, the clerk shall furnish a certified copy thereof to each agency or department named therein except the court.

(e) Clerk's Duties. In regard to the official records of the court, including the court file of the cause, the clerk shall:

(1) remove from the official records of the court, excepting the court file, all entries and records subject to the order, provided that, if it is not practical to remove the entries and records, the clerk shall make certified copies thereof and then expunge by appropriate means the original entries and records;

(2) seal the entries and records, or certified copies thereof, together with the court file and retain the same in a nonpublic index, subject to further order of the court (see *Johnson v. State*, 336 So. 2d 93 (Fla. 1976));

(3) in multi-defendant cases, make a certified copy of the contents of the court file that shall be sealed under subdivision (2). Thereafter, all references to the petitioner shall be expunged from the original court file.

(f) Costs. All costs of certified copies involved herein shall be borne by the movant, unless the movant is indigent.

Amended Dec. 23, 1993 (630 So.2d 552); June 16, 1994 (639 So.2d 15); Nov. 2, 2000, effective Jan. 1, 2001 (794 So.2d 457); Dec. 12, 2013, effective Jan. 1, 2014 (132 So.3d 123); April 24, 2014, effective April 24, 2014 (137 So.3d 1015).

Committee Notes

1984 Amendment. Substantially the same as the former rule. The statutory reference in (1) was changed to cite the current statute and terminology was changed accordingly. Subdivision (f) of the former rule was deleted because it dealt with substantive matters covered by section 943.058, Florida Statutes (1981).

2000 Amendment. Substantially the same as the former rule, but references to certificate of eligibility for obtaining nonjudicial criminal history records were added pursuant to *State v. D.H.W.*, 686 So. 2d 1331 (Fla. 1996).

XIV. SENTENCE

Orders Imposing Death Sentence

Grossman v. State, 525 So.2d 833, filed February 18, 1988, ordered establishment of a procedural rule that all written orders imposing a death sentence be prepared prior to the oral pronouncement of sentence for filing concurrent with the pronouncement, such order to be effective thirty days after the decision becomes final.

Rule 3.700. Sentence Defined; Pronouncement and Entry; Sentencing Judge

(a) Sentence Defined. The term sentence means the pronouncement by the court of the penalty imposed on a defendant for the offense of which the defendant has been adjudged guilty.

(b) Pronouncement and Entry. Every sentence or other final disposition of the case shall be pronounced in open court, including, if available at the time of sentencing, the amount of jail time credit the defendant is to receive. The final disposition of every case shall be entered in the minutes in courts in which minutes are kept and shall be docketed in courts that do not maintain minutes.

(c) Sentencing Judge.

(1) *Noncapital Cases.* In any case, other than a capital case, in which it is necessary that sentence be pronounced by a judge other than the judge who presided at trial or accepted the plea, the sentencing judge shall not pass sentence until the judge becomes acquainted with what transpired at the trial, or the facts, including any plea discussions, concerning the plea and the offense.

(2) *Capital Cases.* In any capital case in which it is necessary that sentence be pronounced by a judge other than the judge who presided at the capital trial, the sentencing judge shall conduct a new sentencing proceeding before a jury prior to passing sentence.

Amended Sept. 24, 1992, effective Jan. 1, 1993 (606 So.2d 227); March 10, 1994 (633 So.2d 1056); Nov. 12, 1999 (760 So.2d 67).

Committee Notes

1968 Adoption. This rule is a revamped version of section 921.05, Florida Statutes.

1972 Amendment. Subdivisions (a) and (b) are substantially the same as in former rule. Subdivision (c) was added to emphasize that the sentencing procedure should be conducted by the trial judge or the judge taking the plea. The rule makes provision for emergency situations when such judge is unavailable.

Rule 3.701. Sentencing Guidelines

(a) Use with Forms. This rule is to be used in conjunction with forms 3.988(a)–(i).

(b) Statement of Purpose. The purpose of sentencing guidelines is to establish a uniform set of standards to guide the sentencing judge in the sentence decision-making process. The guidelines represent a synthesis of current sentencing theory and historic sentencing practices throughout the state. Sentencing guidelines are intended to eliminate unwarranted variation in the sentencing process by reducing the subjectivity in interpreting specific offense-related and offender-related criteria and in defining their relative importance in the sentencing decision. The sentencing guidelines embody the following principles:

(1) Sentencing should be neutral with respect to race, gender, and social and economic status.

(2) The primary purpose of sentencing is to punish the offender. Rehabilitation and other traditional considerations continue to be desired goals of the criminal justice system but must assume a subordinate role.

(3) The penalty imposed should be commensurate with the severity of the convicted offense and the circumstances surrounding the offense.

(4) The severity of the sanction should increase with the length and nature of the offender's criminal history.

(5) The sentence imposed by the sentencing judge should reflect the length of time to be served, shortened only by the application of gain time.

(6) While the sentencing guidelines are designed to aid the judge in the sentencing decision and are not intended to usurp judicial discretion, departures from the presumptive sentences established in the guidelines shall be articulated in writing and made when circumstances or factors reasonably justify the aggravation or mitigation of the sentence. The level of proof necessary to establish facts supporting a departure from a sentence under the guidelines is a preponderance of the evidence.

(7) Because the capacities of state and local correctional facilities are finite, use of incarcerative sanctions should be limited to those persons convicted of more serious offenses or those who have longer criminal histories. To ensure such usage of finite resources, sanctions used in sentencing convicted felons should be the least restrictive necessary to achieve the purposes of the sentence.

(c) Offense Categories. Offenses have been grouped into 9 offense categories encompassing the following statutes:

Category 1: Murder, manslaughter: Chapter 782 (except subsection 782.04(1)(a)), subsection 316.193(3)(c)3, and subsection 327.351(2).

Category 2: Sexual offenses: Section 775.22, chapters 794 and 800, section 826.04, and section 491.0112.

Category 3: Robbery: Section 812.13, and sections 812.133 and 812.135.

Category 4: Violent personal crimes: Section 231.06, chapters 784 and 836, section 843.01, and subsection 381.411(4).

Category 5: Burglary: Chapter 810, section 817.025, and subsection 806.13(3).

Category 6: Thefts, forgery, fraud: Sections 192.037 and 206.56, chapters 322 and 409, section 370.142, section 415.111, chapter 443, section 493.3175, sections 494.0018, 496.413, and 496.417, chapter 509, subsection 517.301(1)(a), subsections 585.145(3) and 585.85(2), section 687.146, and chapters 812 (except section 812.13), 815, 817, 831, and 832.

Category 7: Drugs: Section 499.005 and chapter 893.

Category 8: Weapons: Chapter 790 and section 944.40.

Category 9: All other felony offenses.

(d) General Rules and Definitions.

(1) One guideline scoresheet shall be utilized for each defendant covering all offenses pending before the court for sentencing. The state attorney's office will prepare the scoresheets and present them to defense counsel for review as to accuracy in all cases unless the judge directs otherwise. The sentencing judge shall approve all scoresheets.

(2) "Conviction" means a determination of guilt resulting from plea or trial, regardless of whether adjudication was withheld or whether imposition of sentence was suspended.

(3) "Primary offense" is defined as the offense at conviction that, when scored on the guidelines scoresheet, recommends the most severe sanction. In the case of multiple offenses, the primary offense is determined in the following manner:

(A) A separate guidelines scoresheet shall be prepared scoring each offense at conviction as the "primary offense at conviction" with the other offenses at conviction scored as "additional offenses at conviction."

(B) The guidelines scoresheet that recommends the most severe sentence range shall be the scoresheet to be utilized by the sentencing judge pursuant to these guidelines.

(4) All other offenses for which the offender is convicted and that are pending before the court for sentencing at the same time shall be scored as additional offenses based on their degree and the number of counts of each.

(5) "Prior record" refers to any past criminal conduct on the part of the offender, resulting in conviction, prior to the commission of the primary offense. Prior record includes all prior Florida, federal, out-of-state, military, and foreign convictions, as well as convictions for violation of municipal or county ordinances that bring within the municipal or county code

the violation of a state statute or statutes. Provided, however, that:

(A) Entries in criminal histories that show no disposition, disposition unknown, arrest only, or other nonconviction disposition shall not be scored.

(B) When scoring federal, foreign, military, or out-of-state convictions, assign the score for the analogous or parallel Florida statute.

(C) When unable to determine whether an offense at conviction is a felony or a misdemeanor, the offense should be scored as a misdemeanor. When the degree of the felony is ambiguous or impossible to determine, score the offense as a third-degree felony.

(D) Prior record shall include criminal traffic offenses, which shall be scored as misdemeanors.

(E) Convictions that do not constitute violations of a parallel or analogous state criminal statute shall not be scored.

(F) An offender's prior record shall not be scored if the offender has maintained a conviction-free record for a period of 10 consecutive years from the most recent date of release from confinement, supervision, or sanction, whichever is later, to the date of the primary offense.

(G) All prior juvenile dispositions that are the equivalent of convictions as defined in subdivision (d)(2), occurring within 3 years of the commission of the primary offense and that would have been criminal if committed by an adult, shall be included in prior record.

(6) "Legal status at time of offense" is defined as follows: Offenders on parole, probation, or community control; offenders in custody serving a sentence; escapees; fugitives who have fled to avoid prosecution or who have failed to appear for a criminal judicial proceeding or who have violated conditions of a supersedeas bond; and offenders in pretrial intervention or diversion programs. Legal status points are to be assessed where these forms of legal constraint existed at the time of the commission of offenses scored as primary or additional offenses at conviction. Legal status points are to be assessed only once whether there are one or more offenses at conviction.

(7) Victim injury shall be scored for each victim physically injured during a criminal episode or transaction, and for each count resulting in such injury whether there are one or more victims.

(8) The recommended sentences provided in the guideline grids are assumed to be appropriate for the composite score of the offender. A range is provided to permit some discretion. The permitted ranges allow the sentencing judge additional discretion when the particular circumstances of a crime or defendant make it appropriate to increase or decrease the recommended sentence without the requirement of finding reasonable justification to do so and without the requirement of a written explanation.

(9) For those offenses having a mandatory penalty, a scoresheet should be completed and the guideline sentence calculated. If the recommended sentence is less than the mandatory penalty, the mandatory sentence takes precedence. If the guideline sentence exceeds the mandatory sentence, the guideline sentence should be imposed.

(10) If the composite score for a defendant charged with a single offense indicates a guideline sentence that exceeds the maximum sentence provided by statute for that offense, the statutory maximum sentence should be imposed.

(11) Departures from the recommended or permitted guideline sentence should be avoided unless there are circumstances or factors that reasonably justify aggravating or mitigating the sentence. Any sentence outside the permitted guideline range must be accompanied by a written statement delineating the reasons for the departure. Reasons for deviating from the guidelines shall not include factors relating to prior arrests without conviction or the instant offenses for which convictions have not been obtained.

(12) A sentence must be imposed for each offense. However, the total sentence cannot exceed the total guideline sentence unless a written reason is given. Where the offender is being sentenced for a capital felony and other noncapital felonies that arose out of the same criminal episode or transaction, the sentencing court may impose any sentence authorized by law for the noncapital felonies.

(13) Community control is a form of intensive supervised custody in the community involving restriction of the freedom of the offender. When community control is imposed, it shall not exceed the term provided by general law.

(14) Sentences imposed after revocation of probation or community control must be in accordance with the guidelines. The sentence imposed after revocation of probation or community control may be included within the original cell (guidelines range) or may be increased to the next higher cell (guidelines range) without requiring a reason for departure.

(15) Categories 3, 5, and 6 contain an additional factor to be scored under the heading of Prior Record: Prior convictions for similar offenses. Prior convictions scored under this factor should be calculated in addition to the general prior record score. Scoring is limited to prior felony convictions included within the category.

Amended April 12, 1990, and Sept. 6, 1990 (566 So.2d 770); March 7, 1991 (576 So.2d 1307); Nov. 7, 1991 (589 So.2d 271); Sept. 24, 1992, effective Jan. 1, 1993 (606 So.2d 227); Feb. 11, 1993 (613 So.2d 1307); Nov. 30, 1993 (628 So.2d 1084).

Sentencing Guidelines Commission Notes

1988 Amendments. (a) The operation of this rule is not intended to change the law or requirements of proof as regards sentencing.

(b) These principles are binding on the sentencing court.

(c) Only 1 category is proper in any particular case. Category 9, "All Other Felony Offenses," should be used only when the primary offense at conviction is not included in another, more specific category. The guidelines do not apply to capital felonies.

Inchoate offenses are included within the category of the offense attempted, solicited, or conspired to, as modified by chapter 777.

The form appearing at Florida Rule of Criminal Procedure 3.988(a) has been revised to incorporate a point value for inclusion in the prior record factor utilized in the determination of recommended sentence by scoring each prior conviction under section 316.193, Florida Statutes (Supp.1984), or section 316.1931, Florida Statutes (Supp.1984), or section 327.351, Florida Statutes (Supp.1984), at a value of 32 points. This point value will be applied only if the offender is convicted for a violation of section 316.193(3)(c)3, Florida Statutes (Supp.1986), or section 327.351, Florida Statutes (Supp.1984), if the operation of a motor vehicle or vessel by the offender while intoxicated as defined in section 316.193(1), Florida Statutes (Supp.1986), or section 327.351(1), Florida Statutes (Supp.1984), results in the death of any human being and the scoresheet utilized in sentencing is the form appearing at Florida Rule of Criminal Procedure 3.988(a). For purposes of determining a prior conviction for a violation of the above enumerated statute, a prior conviction for violation of section 316.1931 or section 316.193 or former section 860.01 or former section 316.028, or a previous conviction for any substantially similar alcohol-related or drug-related traffic offense outside this state shall also be considered a prior conviction.

(d)(1) Ultimate responsibility for ensuring that scoresheets are accurately prepared rests with the sentencing court. Due to ethical considerations, defense counsel may not be compelled to submit a scoresheet. Probation and parole officers may be directed to compile guidelines scoresheets only when a presentence investigation has been ordered. The forms for calculating the guidelines are forms 3.988(a)–(i).

(d)(2) This definition applies to both instant offense and prior record scoring.

(d)(3) The proper offense category is identified on determination of the primary offense. When the defendant is convicted of violations of more than 1 unique statute, the offenses are to be sorted by statutory degree.

(d)(4) No points shall be scored for lesser and included offenses. In the event of multiple counts of the same distinct offense and degree of felony being scored as primary offense, it shall be scored as additional counts of the primary offense. All other offenses for which the defendant is convicted that are pending before the court for sentencing shall be scored as additional offenses.

(d)(5) Each separate prior felony and misdemeanor conviction in an offender's prior record that amounts to a violation of Florida law shall be scored, unless discharged by the passage of time. Any uncertainty in the scoring of the defendant's prior record shall be resolved in favor of the defendant, and disagreement as to the propriety of scoring specific entries in the prior record should be resolved by the trial judge.

Prior record includes all offenses for which the defendant has been found guilty, regardless of whether adjudication was withheld or the record has been expunged.

Juvenile dispositions, with the exclusion of status offenses, are included and considered along with adult convictions by operation of this provision. However, each separate adjudication is discharged from consideration if 3 years have passed between the date of disposition and the commission of the instant offense.

For any offense where sentence was previously suspended pursuant to the imposition of probation and such offense is now before the court for sentencing, upon a revocation of that probation based upon a subsequent criminal offense (which subsequent offense is also before the court for sentencing at the same time), the earlier offense shall be scored as "prior record" and not as "additional offense."

(d)(7) This provision implements the intention of the commission that points for victim injury be added for each victim injured during a criminal transaction or episode. The injury need not be an element of the crime for which the defendant is convicted, but is limited to physical trauma. However, if the victim injury is the result of a crime for which the defendant has been acquitted, it shall not be scored.

(d)(8) The first guideline cell in each category (any nonstate prison sanction) allows the court the flexibility to impose any lawful term of probation with or without a period of incarceration as a condition of probation, a county jail term alone, or any nonincarcerative disposition. Any sentence may include the requirement that a fine be paid. The sentences are found in forms 3.988(a)–(i).

(d)(10) If an offender is convicted under an enhancement statute, the reclassified degree should be used as the basis for scoring the primary offense in the appropriate category. If the offender is sentenced under section 775.084 (habitual offender), the maximum allowable sentence is increased as provided by the operation of that statute. If the sentence imposed departs from the recommended sentence, the provisions of (d)(11) shall apply.

(d)(11) A sentencing judge may depart from the recommended sentence and impose a sentence within the permitted range without giving reasons therefor. If a sentencing judge departs from the permitted range, reasons for departure shall be articulated at the time sentence is imposed. The written statement shall be made a part of the record, with sufficient specificity to inform all parties, as well as the public, of the reasons for departure. The court is prohibited from considering offenses for which the defendant has not been convicted. Other factors, consistent and not in conflict with the statement of purpose, may be considered and utilized by the sentencing judge.

(d)(12) The sentencing court shall impose or suspend sentence for each separate count, as convicted. The total sentence shall not exceed the guideline sentence, unless the provisions of subdivision (d)(11) are complied with.

If a split sentence is imposed (i.e., a combination of state prison and probation supervision), the incarcerative portion imposed shall not be less than the minimum of the guideline range nor exceed the maximum of the range. The total sanction (incarceration and probation) shall not exceed the term provided by general law.

(d)(13) Community control is a viable alternative for any state prison sentence less than 24 months without requiring a reason for departure. It is appropriate to impose a sentence of community control to be followed by a term of probation. The total sanction (community control and probation) shall not exceed the term provided by general law.

Community control is not an alternative sanction from the recommended range of any nonstate prison sanction unless the provisions of rule 3.701(d)(11) are applied.

1991 Amendment. The purpose of the 1991 revision to rule 3.701(d)(6) is to clarify the original intent that legal constraint is a status consideration and is not to be considered a function of the number of offenses at conviction.

1991 Amendment. The purpose of the 1991 revision to rule 3.701(d)(7) is to provide consistency in the scoring of victim injury by scoring each offense at conviction for which victim injury can appropriately be scored, whether committed against a single or multiple victims.

1993 Amendments. Inchoate offenses are included within the category of the offense attempted, solicited, or conspired to, as modified by chapter 777. An attempt, solicitation, or conspiracy to commit first-degree murder as defined in subsection 782.04(1)(a) shall be scored in category 1. An attempt, solicitation, or conspiracy to commit capital sexual battery as defined in subsection 794.011(2) shall be scored in category 2.

Rule 3.702. Sentencing Guidelines (1994)

(a) Use. This rule is to be used in conjunction with the forms located at rule 3.990. This rule is intended to implement the 1994 revised sentencing guidelines in strict accordance with chapter 921, Florida Statutes, as revised by chapter 93–406, Laws of Florida.

(b) Purpose and Construction. The purpose of the 1994 revised sentencing guidelines and the principles they embody are set out in subsection 921.001(4). Existing caselaw construing the application of sentencing guidelines that is in conflict with the provisions of this rule or the statement of purpose or the principles embodied by the 1994 sentencing guidelines set out in subsection 921.001(4) is superseded by the operation of this rule.

(c) Offense Severity Ranking. Felony offenses subject to the 1994 revised sentencing guidelines are listed in a single offense severity ranking chart located at section 921.0012. The offense severity ranking chart employs 10 offense levels, ranked from least severe to most severe. Each felony offense is assigned to a level according to the severity of the offense, commensurate with the harm or potential for harm to the community that is caused by the offense. Felony offenses not listed in section 921.0012 are to be assigned a severity level as described in section 921.0013.

(d) General Rules and Definitions.

(1) A comprehensive guidelines scoresheet shall be prepared for each defendant covering all offenses pending before the court for sentencing, including offenses for which the defendant has been adjudicated an habitual felony offender or an habitual violent felony offender. The office of the state attorney or the probation services office, or both where appropriate, will prepare the scoresheets and present them to defense counsel for review as to accuracy. Where the defendant is alleged to have violated probation or community control and probation services will recommend revocation, probation services shall prepare a comprehensive guidelines scoresheet for use at sentencing after revocation of probation or community control. The sentencing judge shall review the scoresheet for accuracy.

(2) "Conviction" means a determination of guilt resulting from plea or trial, regardless of whether adjudication was withheld or whether imposition of sentence was suspended.

(3) "Primary offense" is the offense pending for sentencing that results in the highest number of total sentence points. Only one offense may be scored as the primary offense.

(4) "Additional offense" is any offense, other than the primary offense, pending before the court for sentencing. Sentence points for additional offenses are determined by the severity level and the number of offenses at a particular severity level. Misdemeanors are scored at level "M" regardless of degree.

(5) "Victim injury" is scored for physical injury or death suffered by a person as a direct result of any offense pending before the court for sentencing. If an offense pending before the court for sentencing involves sexual penetration, victim injury is to be scored. If an offense pending before the court for sentencing involves sexual contact, but no penetration, victim injury shall be scored. If the victim of an offense involving sexual penetration or sexual contact without penetration suffers any physical injury as a direct result of an offense pending before the court for sentencing, that physical injury is to be scored separately and in addition to any points scored for the sexual contact or sexual penetration.

Victim injury shall be scored for each victim physically injured and for each offense resulting in physical injury whether there are one or more victims. However, if the victim injury is the result of a crime of which the defendant has been acquitted, it shall not be scored.

(6) Attempts, conspiracies, and solicitations charged under chapter 777 are scored at severity levels below the level at which the completed offense is located. Attempts and solicitations are scored 2 severity levels below the completed offense. Criminal conspiracies are scored 1 severity level below the completed offense.

(7) "Total offense score" results from adding the sentence points for primary offense, additional offense, and victim injury.

(8) "Prior record" refers to any conviction for an offense committed by the defendant prior to the commission of the primary offense. Prior record shall include convictions for offenses committed by the defendant as an adult or as a juvenile, convictions by federal, out-of-state, military, or foreign courts, and convictions for violations of county or municipal ordinances that incorporate by reference a penalty under state law. Federal, out-of-state, military, or foreign convictions are scored at the severity level at which the analogous or parallel Florida crime is located.

(A) Convictions for offenses committed more than 10 years prior to the date of the commission of the primary offense are not scored as prior record if the defendant has not been convicted of any other crime for a period of 10 consecutive years from the most recent date of release from confinement, supervision, or other sanction, whichever is later, to the date of the commission of the primary offense.

(B) Juvenile dispositions of offenses committed by the defendant within 3 years prior to the date of the commission of the primary offense are scored as prior record if the offense would have been a crime if committed by an adult. Juvenile dispositions of sexual offenses committed by the defendant more than 3 years prior to the date of the primary offense are to be scored as prior record if the defendant has not maintained a conviction-free record, either as an adult or as a juvenile, for a period of 3 consecutive years from the most recent date of release from confinement, supervision, or sanction, whichever is later, to the date of commission of the primary offense.

(C) Entries in criminal histories that show no disposition, disposition unknown, arrest only, or a disposition other than conviction shall not be scored. Criminal history records expunged or sealed under section 943.058 or other provisions of law, including former sections 893.14 and 901.33, shall be scored as prior record where the defendant whose record has been expunged or sealed is before the court for sentencing.

(D) Any uncertainty in the scoring of the defendant's prior record shall be resolved in favor of the defendant, and disagreement as to the propriety of scoring specific entries in the prior record shall be resolved by the sentencing judge.

(E) When unable to determine whether the conviction to be scored as prior record is a felony or a misdemeanor, the conviction should be scored as a misdemeanor. When the degree of felony is ambiguous or the severity level cannot be determined, the conviction should be scored at severity level 1.

(9) "Legal status violations" occur when a defendant, while under any of the forms of legal status listed in subsection 921.0011(3), commits an offense that results in conviction. Legal status violations receive a score of 4 sentence points and are scored when the offense committed while under legal status is before the court for sentencing. Points for a legal status violation are to be assessed only once regardless of the existence of more than one form of legal status at the time an offense is committed or the number of offenses committed while under any form of legal status.

(10) "Release program violations" occur when the defendant is found to have violated a condition of a release program designated in subsection 921.0011(6). Six points shall be assessed for each violation up to a maximum of 18 points in the case of multiple violations. Where there are multiple violations, points in excess of 6 may be assessed only for each successive violation that follows the reinstatement or modification of the release program and are not to be assessed for violation of several conditions of a single release program order.

(11) "Total prior record score" results from adding sentence points for prior record, legal status violations, and release program violations.

(12) Possession of a firearm, destructive device, semiautomatic weapon, or a machine gun during the commission or attempt to commit a crime will result in additional sentence points. Eighteen sentence points shall be assessed where the defendant is convicted of committing or attempting to commit any felony other than those enumerated in subsection 775.087(2) while having in his or her possession a firearm as defined in subsection 790.001(6) or a destructive device as defined in subsection 790.001(4). Twenty-five sentence points shall be assessed where the offender is convicted of committing or attempting to commit any felony other than those enumerated in subsection 775.087(2) while having in his or her possession a semiautomatic weapon as defined in subsection 775.087(2) or a machine gun as defined in subsection 790.001(9).

(13) "Subtotal sentence points" result from adding the total offense score, the total prior record score, and any additional points for possession of a firearm, destructive device, semiautomatic weapon, or machine gun.

(14) If the primary offense is drug trafficking under section 893.135, the subtotal sentence points may be multiplied, at the discretion of the sentencing court, by a factor of 1.5. If the primary offense is a violation of the Law Enforcement Protection Act under subsections 775.0823(2), (3), (4), or (5), the subtotal sentence points shall be multiplied by a factor of 2. If the primary offense is a violation of subsection 775.087(2)(a)(2) or subsections 775.0823(6) or (7), the subtotal sentence points shall be multiplied by a factor of 1.5. If both enhancements are applicable, only the enhancement with the higher multiplier is to be used.

(15) "Total sentence points" result from the enhancement, if applicable, of the subtotal sentence points. If no enhancement is applicable, the subtotal sentence points are the total sentence points.

(16) "Presumptive sentence" is determined by the total sentence points. If the total sentence points are less than or equal to 40, the recommended sentence, absent a departure, shall not be state prison. However, the sentencing court may increase sentence points less than or equal to 40 by up to and including 15 percent to arrive at total sentence points in excess of 40. If the total sentence points are greater than 40 but less than or equal to 52, the decision to sentence the defendant to state prison or a nonstate prison sanction is left to the discretion of the sentencing court. If the total sentence points are greater than 52, the sentence, absent a departure, must be to state prison.

A state prison sentence is calculated by deducting 28 points from the total sentence points where total sentence points exceed 40. The resulting number represents state prison months. State prison months may be increased or decreased by up to and including 25 percent at the discretion of the sentencing court. State prison months may not be increased where the sentencing court has exercised discretion to increase total sentence points under 40 points to achieve a state prison sentence. The sentence imposed must be entered on the scoresheet.

(17) For those offenses having a mandatory penalty, a scoresheet should be completed and the guidelines presumptive sentence calculated. If the presumptive sentence is less than the mandatory penalty, the mandatory sentence takes precedence. If the presumptive sentence exceeds the mandatory sentence, the presumptive sentence should be imposed.

(18) Departure from the recommended guidelines sentence provided by the total sentence points should be avoided unless there are circumstances or factors that reasonably justify aggravating or mitigating the sentence. A state prison sentence that deviates from the recommended prison sentence by more than 25 percent, a state prison sentence where the total sentence points are equal to or less than 40, or a sentence other than state prison where the total sentence points are greater than 52 must be accompanied by a written statement delineating the reasons for departure. Circumstances or factors that can be considered include, but are not limited to, those listed in subsections 921.0016(3) and (4). Reasons for departing from the recommended guidelines sentence shall not include circumstances or factors relating to prior arrests without conviction or charged offenses for which convictions have not been obtained.

(A) If a sentencing judge imposes a sentence that departs from the recommended guidelines sentence, the reasons for departure shall be orally articulated at the time sentence is imposed. Any departure sentence must be accompanied by a written statement, signed by the sentencing judge, delineating the reasons for departure. The written statement shall be filed in the court file within 15 days of the date of sentencing. A written transcription of orally stated reasons for departure articulated at the time sentence was imposed is sufficient if it is signed by the sentencing judge and filed in the court file within 15 days of the date of sentencing. The sentencing judge may also list the written reasons for departure in the space provided on the guidelines scoresheet and shall sign the scoresheet.

(B) The written statement delineating the reasons for departure shall be made a part of the record. The written statement, if it is a separate document, must accompany the guidelines scoresheet required to be provided to the Department of Corrections pursuant to subsection 921.0014(5).

(19) The sentencing court shall impose or suspend sentence for each separate count, as convicted. The total sentence shall be within the guidelines sentence unless a departure is ordered.

If a split sentence is imposed, the incarcerative portion of the sentence must not deviate more than 25 percent from the recommended guidelines prison sentence. The total sanction (incarceration and community control or probation) shall not exceed the term provided by general law or the guidelines recommended sentence where the provisions of subsection 921.001(5) apply.

(20) Sentences imposed after revocation of probation or community control must be in accordance with the guidelines. Cumulative incarceration imposed after revocation of probation or community control is subject to limitations imposed by the guidelines. A violation of probation or community control may not be the basis for a departure sentence.

Added Nov. 30, 1993, effective Jan. 1, 1994 (628 So.2d 1084). Amended April 2, 1998 (711 So.2d 27).

Committee Notes

1993 Adoption. (d)(1) If sentences are imposed under section 775.084 and the sentencing guidelines, a scoresheet listing only those offenses sentenced under the sentencing guidelines must be prepared and utilized in lieu of the comprehensive scoresheet.

Due to ethical considerations, defense counsel may not be compelled to submit or sign a scoresheet.

(d)(3) The primary offense need not be the highest ranked offense pending for sentencing where scoring the less severe offense as the primary offense will result in higher total sentence points. This can occur where the multipliers for drug trafficking or violations of the Law Enforcement Protection Act are applied or where past convictions can be included as prior record that could not be scored if the offense ranked at a higher severity level was the primary offense.

(d)(16) The presumptive sentence is assumed to be appropriate for the composite score of the defendant. Where the total sentence points do not exceed 40, the court has the flexibility to impose any lawful term of probation with or without a period of incarceration as a condition of probation, a county jail term alone, or any nonincarcerative disposition. Any sentence may include a requirement that a fine be paid.

Rule 3.703. Sentencing Guidelines (1994 as amended)

(a) Use. This rule is to be used in conjunction with the forms located at rule 3.991. This rule implements the 1994 sentencing guidelines, as amended, in strict accordance with chapter 921, Florida Statutes. This rule applies to offenses committed on or after October 1, 1995, or as otherwise indicated.

(b) Purpose and Construction. The purpose of the 1994 sentencing guidelines and the principles they embody are set out in subsection 921.001(4). Existing caselaw construing the application of sentencing guidelines that is in conflict with the provisions of this rule or the statement of purpose or the principles embodied by the 1994 sentencing guidelines set out in subsection 921.001(4) is superseded by the operation of this rule.

(c) Offense Severity Ranking.

(1) Felony offenses subject to the 1994 sentencing guidelines, as amended, are listed in a single offense severity ranking chart located at section 921.0012. The offense severity ranking chart employs 10 offense levels, ranked from least severe to most severe. Each felony offense is assigned to a level according to the severity of the offense, commensurate with the harm or potential for harm to the community that is caused by the offense. The numerical statutory reference in the left column of the chart and the felony degree designations in the middle column of the chart determine whether felony offenses are specifically listed in the offense severity ranking chart and the appropriate severity level. The language in the right column is merely descriptive.

(2) Felony offenses not listed in section 921.0012 are to be assigned a severity level in accordance with section 921.0013, as follows:

(A) A felony of the third degree within offense level 1.

(B) A felony of the second degree within offense level 4.

(C) A felony of the first degree within offense level 7.

(D) A felony of the first degree punishable by life within offense level 9.

(E) A life felony within offense level 10.

An offense does not become unlisted and subject to the provisions of section 921.0013, because of a reclassification of the degree of felony pursuant to section 775.0845, section 775.087, section 775.0875 or section 794.023.

(d) General Rules and Definitions.

(1) One or more sentencing guidelines scoresheets shall be prepared for each offender covering all offenses pending before the court for sentencing, including offenses for which the offender has been adjudicated an habitual felony offender, an habitual violent felony offender or violent career criminal. The office of the state attorney or the Department of Corrections, or both where appropriate, will prepare the scoresheets and present them to defense counsel for review as to accuracy. The Department of Corrections shall prepare sentencing guidelines scoresheets if the offender is alleged to have violated probation or community control and revocation is recommended.

(2) One scoresheet shall be prepared for all offenses committed under any single version or revision of the guidelines, pending before the court for sentencing.

(3) If an offender is before the court for sentencing for more than one felony and the felonies were committed under more than one version or revision of the guidelines, separate scoresheets must be prepared and used at sentencing. The sentencing court may impose such sentence concurrently or consecutively.

(4) The sentencing judge shall review the scoresheet for accuracy and sign it.

(5) Felonies, except capital felonies, with continuing dates of enterprise are to be sentenced under the guidelines in effect on the beginning date of the criminal activity.

(6) "Conviction" means a determination of guilt resulting from plea or trial, regardless of whether adjudication was withheld or whether imposition of sentence was suspended.

(7) "Primary offense" is the offense pending for sentencing that results in the highest number of total sentence points. Only one offense may be scored as the primary offense.

(8) "Additional offense" is any offense, other than the primary offense, pending before the court for sentencing. Sentence points for additional offenses are determined by the severity level and the number

of offenses at a particular severity level. Misdemeanors are scored at level "M" regardless of degree.

(9) "Victim injury" is scored for physical injury or death suffered by a person as a direct result of any offense pending before the court for sentencing. Except as otherwise provided by law, the sexual penetration and sexual contact points will be scored as follows. Sexual penetration points are scored if an offense pending before the court for sentencing involves sexual penetration. Sexual contact points are scored if an offense pending before the court for sentencing involves sexual contact, but no penetration. If the victim of an offense involving sexual penetration or sexual contact without penetration suffers any physical injury as a direct result of an offense pending before the court for sentencing, that physical injury is to be scored in addition to any points scored for the sexual contact or sexual penetration.

Victim injury shall be scored for each victim physically injured and for each offense resulting in physical injury whether there are one or more victims. However, victim injury shall not be scored for an offense for which the offender has not been convicted.

Victim injury resultant from one or more capital felonies before the court for sentencing is not to be included upon any scoresheet prepared for non-capital felonies also pending before the court for sentencing. This in no way prohibits the scoring of victim injury as a result from the non-capital felonies before the court for sentencing.

(10) Unless specifically provided otherwise by statute, attempts, conspiracies, and solicitations are indicated in the space provided on the guidelines scoresheet and are scored at one severity level below the completed offense.

Attempts, solicitations, and conspiracies of third-degree felonies located in offense severity levels 1 and 2 are to be scored as misdemeanors. Attempts, solicitations, and conspiracies of third-degree felonies located in offense severity levels 3, 4, 5, 6, 7, 8, 9, and 10 are to be scored as felonies one offense level beneath the incomplete or inchoate offense.

(11) An increase in offense severity level may result from a reclassification of felony degrees pursuant to sections 775.0845, 775.087, 775.0875, or 794.023. Any such increase should be indicated in the space provided on the sentencing guidelines scoresheet.

(12) A single assessment of thirty prior serious felony points is added if the offender has a primary offense or any additional offense ranked in level 8, 9, or 10 and one or more prior serious felonies. A "prior serious felony" is an offense in the offender's prior record ranked in level 8, 9, or 10 and for which the offender is serving a sentence of confinement, supervision or other sanction or for which the offender's date of release from confinement, supervision or other sanction, whichever is later is within 3 years before the date the primary offense or any additional offenses were committed. Out of state convictions wherein the analogous or parallel Florida offenses are located in offense severity level 8, 9, or 10 are to be considered prior serious felonies.

(13) If the offender has one or more prior capital felonies, points shall be added to the subtotal sentence points of the offender equal to twice the number of points the offender receives for the primary offense and any additional offense. Out-of-state convictions wherein the analogous or parallel Florida offenses are capital offenses are to be considered capital offenses for purposes of operation of this section.

(14) "Total offense score" is the sum of the sentence points for primary offense, any additional offenses and victim injury.

(15) "Prior record" refers to any conviction for an offense committed by the offender prior to the commission of the primary offense, excluding any additional offenses pending before the court for sentencing. Prior record shall include convictions for offenses committed by the offender as an adult or as a juvenile, convictions by federal, out of state, military, or foreign courts and convictions for violations of county or municipal ordinances that incorporate by reference a penalty under state law. Federal, out of state, military, or foreign convictions are scored at the severity level at which the analogous or parallel Florida crime is located.

(A) Convictions for offenses committed more than 10 years prior to the date of the commission of the primary offense are not scored as prior record if the offender has not been convicted of any other crime for a period of 10 consecutive years from the most recent date of release from confinement, supervision, or other sanction, whichever is later, to the date of the commission of the primary offense.

(B) Juvenile dispositions of offenses committed by the offender within 3 years prior to the date of the commission of the primary offense are scored as prior record if the offense would have been a crime if committed by an adult. Juvenile dispositions of sexual offenses committed by the offender more than 3 years prior to the date of the primary offense are to be scored as prior record if the offender has not maintained a conviction-free record, either as an adult or as a juvenile, for a period of 3 consecutive years from the most recent date of release from confinement, supervision, or sanction, whichever is later, to the date of commission of the primary offense.

(C) Entries in criminal histories that show no disposition, disposition unknown, arrest only, or a disposition other than conviction are not scored. Criminal history records expunged or sealed under section 943.058 or other provisions of law, including former sections 893.14 and 901.33, are scored as prior record where the offender whose record has been expunged or sealed is before the court for sentencing.

(D) Any uncertainty in the scoring of the offender's prior record shall be resolved in favor of the offender and disagreement as to the propriety of scoring specific entries in the prior record shall be resolved by the sentencing judge.

(E) When unable to determine whether the conviction to be scored as prior record is a felony or a misdemeanor, the conviction should be scored as a misdemeanor. When the degree of felony is ambiguous or the severity level cannot be determined, the conviction should be scored at severity level 1.

(16) "Legal status points" are assessed when an offender:

(A) Escapes from incarceration;

(B) Flees to avoid prosecution;

(C) Fails to appear for a criminal proceeding;

(D) Violates any condition of a supersedeas bond;

(E) Is incarcerated;

(F) Is under any form of a pretrial intervention or diversion program; or

(G) Is under any form of court-imposed or post-prison release community supervision and commits an offense that results in conviction. Legal status violations receive a score of 4 sentence points and are scored when the offense committed while under legal status is before the court for sentencing. Points for a legal status violation are to be assessed only once regardless of the existence of more than one form of legal status at the time an offense is committed or the number of offenses committed while under any form of legal status.

(17) Community sanction violation points occur when the offender is found to have violated a condition of:

(A) Probation;

(B) Community Control; or

(C) Pretrial Intervention or diversion.

Community sanction violation points are assessed when a community sanction violation is before the court for sentencing. Six community sanction violation points shall be assessed for each violation or if the violation results from a new felony conviction, 12 community sanction violation points shall be assessed. Where there are multiple violations, points may be assessed only for each successive violation that follows a continuation of supervision, or modification or revocation of the community sanction before the court for sentencing and are not to be assessed for violation of several conditions of a single community sanction. Multiple counts of community sanction violations before the sentencing court shall not be the basis for multiplying the assessment of community sanction violation points.

(18) "Total prior record score" is the sum of all sentence points for prior record.

(19) Possession of a firearm, semiautomatic firearm, or a machine gun during the commission or attempt to commit a crime will result in additional sentence points. Eighteen sentence points are assessed if the offender is convicted of committing or attempting to commit any felony other than those enumerated in subsection 775.087(2) while having in his or her possession a firearm as defined in subsection 790.001(6). Twenty-five sentence points are assessed if the offender is convicted of committing or attempting to commit any felony other than those enumerated in subsection 775.087(3) while having in his or her possession a semiautomatic firearm as defined in subsection 775.087(3) or a machine gun as defined in subsection 790.001(9). Only one assessment of either 18 or 25 points shall apply.

(20) "Subtotal sentence points" are the sum of the total offense score, the total prior record score, any legal status points, community sanction points, prior serious felony points, prior capital felony points or points for possession of a firearm or semiautomatic weapon.

(21) If the primary offense is drug trafficking under section 893.135 ranked in offense severity level 7 or 8, the subtotal sentence points may be multiplied, at the discretion of the sentencing court, by a factor of 1.5.

(22) If the primary offense is a violation of the Law Enforcement Protection Act under subsection 775.0823(2), the subtotal sentence points are multiplied by a factor of 2.5. If the primary offense is a violation of subsection 775.0823(3), (4), (5), (6), (7), or (8) the subtotal sentence points are multiplied by a factor of 2.0. If the primary offense is a violation of the Law Enforcement Protection Act under subsection 775.0823(9) or (10) or section 784.07(3) or section 775.0875(1), the subtotal sentence points are multiplied by a factor of 1.5.

(23) If the primary offense is grand theft of the third degree of a motor vehicle and the offender's prior record includes three or more grand thefts of the third degree of a motor vehicle, the subtotal sentence points are multiplied by 1.5.

(24) If the offender is found to be a member of a criminal street gang pursuant to section 874.04, at the time of the commission of the primary offense, the subtotal sentence points are multiplied by 1.5.

(25) If the primary offense is determined to be a crime of domestic violence as defined in section 741.28 and to have been committed in the presence of a child who is related by blood or marriage to the victim or perpetrator and who is under the age of 16, the subtotal sentence points are multiplied, at the discretion of the court, by 1.5.

(26) "Total sentence points" are the subtotal sentence points or the enhanced subtotal sentence points.

(27) "Presumptive sentence" is determined by the total sentence points. A person sentenced for a felony committed on or after July 1, 1997, who has at least one prior felony conviction and whose recommended sentence is any nonstate prison sanction may be sentenced to community control or a term of incarceration not to exceed 22 months. A person sentenced for a felony committed on or after July 1, 1997, who has at least one prior felony conviction and whose minimum recommended sentence is less than 22 months in state prison may be sentenced to a term of incarceration not to exceed 22 months.

In all other cases, if the total sentence points are less than or equal to 40, the recommended sentence, absent a departure, shall not be state prison. The court may impose any nonstate prison sanction authorized by law, including community control. However, the sentencing court may increase sentence points less than or equal to 40 by up to and including 15% to arrive at total sentence points in excess of 40. If the total sentence points are greater than 40 but less than or equal to 52, the decision to sentence the defendant to state prison or a nonstate prison sanction is left to the discretion of the sentencing court. If the total sentence points are greater than 52, the sentence, absent a departure, must be to state prison.

A state prison sentence is calculated by deducting 28 points from the total sentence points where total sentence points exceed 40. The resulting number represents state prison months. State prison months may be increased or decreased by up to and including 25% at the discretion of the sentencing court. State prison months may not be increased where the sentencing court has exercised discretion to increase total sentence points under 40 points to achieve a state prison sentence. The sentence imposed must be entered on the scoresheet.

If the total sentence points are equal to or greater than 363, the court may sentence the offender to life imprisonment.

(28) If the recommended sentence under the sentencing guidelines exceeds the maximum sentence authorized for the pending felony offenses, the guidelines sentence must be imposed, absent a departure. Such downward departure must be equal to or less than the maximum sentence authorized by section 775.082.

(29) For those offenses having a mandatory penalty, a scoresheet should be completed and the guidelines presumptive sentence calculated. If the presumptive sentence is less than the mandatory penalty, the mandatory sentence takes precedence. If the presumptive sentence exceeds the mandatory sentence, the presumptive sentence should be imposed.

(30) Departure from the recommended guidelines sentence provided by the total sentence points should be avoided unless there are circumstances or factors that reasonably justify aggravating or mitigating the sentence. A state prison sentence that deviates from the recommended prison sentence by more than 25%, a state prison sentence where the total sentence points are equal to or less than 40, or a sentence other than state prison where the total sentence points are greater than 52 must be accompanied by a written statement delineating the reasons for departure. Circumstances or factors that can be considered include, but are not limited to, those listed in subsections 921.0016(3) and (4). Reasons for departing from the recommended guidelines sentence shall not include circumstances or factors relating to prior arrests without conviction or charged offenses for which convictions have not been obtained.

(A) If a sentencing judge imposes a sentence that departs from the recommended guidelines sentence, the reasons for departure shall be orally articulated at the time sentence is imposed. Any departure sentence must be accompanied by a written statement, signed by the sentencing judge, delineating the reasons for departure. The written statement shall be filed in the court file within 7 days after the date of sentencing. A written transcription of orally stated reasons for departure articulated at the time sentence was imposed is sufficient if it is signed by the sentencing judge and filed in the court file within 7 days after the date of sentencing. The sentencing judge may also list the written reasons for departure in the space provided on the guidelines scoresheet and shall sign the scoresheet.

(B) The written statement delineating the reasons for departure shall be made a part of the record. The written statement, if it is a separate document, must accompany the guidelines scoresheet required to be provided to the Department of Corrections pursuant to subsection 921.0014(5).

(31) The sentencing court shall impose or suspend sentence for each separate count, as convicted. The total sentence shall be within the guidelines sentence unless a departure is ordered.

If a split sentence is imposed, the incarcerative portion of the sentence must not deviate more than 25 percent from the recommended guidelines prison sentence. The total sanction (incarceration and community control or probation) shall not exceed the term provided by general law or the guidelines recommended sentence where the provisions of subsection 921.001(5) apply.

(32) Sentences imposed after revocation of probation or community control must be in accordance with the guidelines. Cumulative incarceration imposed after revocation of probation or community control is subject to limitations imposed by the guidelines. A violation of probation or community control may not be the basis for a departure sentence.

Added Sept. 21, 1995, effective Oct. 1, 1995 (660 So.2d 1374). Amended Sept. 26, 1996, effective Oct. 1, 1996 (685 So.2d 1213); June 26, 1997, eff. July 1, 1997 and Oct. 1, 1997 (696 So.2d 1171).

Committee Notes

1996 Amendments.

(a) This portion was amended to show that the earliest offense date to which this rule applies is October 1, 1995 and that all subsequent changes are incorporated. It is intended that Committee Notes will be used to indicate effective dates of changes.

(c) This amendment applies to offenses committed on or after October 1, 1996.

(d)(9) The 1996 Legislature created two crimes for which sexual penetration or sexual contact points are not scored. That exception applies to offenses committed on or after October 1, 1996 pursuant to section 872.06, Florida Statutes or section 944.35(3)(b)2, Florida Statutes.

(d)(12) The amendment applies to offenses committed on or after October 1, 1996.

(d)(13) The amendment applies on or after October 1, 1996.

(d)(17) This amendment, which applies on or after October 1, 1996, clarifies when points may be assessed for multiple violations. It also incorporates legislative changes that indicate that multiple assessments may not be made for multiple counts of community sanction violations.

(d)(24) The amendment applies to crimes committed on or after October 1, 1996.

1997 Amendments.

(d)(25) The amendment applies to crimes committed on or after October 1, 1997.

Rule 3.704. The Criminal Punishment Code

(a) Use. This rule is to be used in conjunction with the forms located at rule 3.992. This rule implements the 1998 Criminal Punishment Code, in compliance with chapter 921, Florida Statutes. This rule applies to offenses committed on or after October 1, 1998, or as otherwise required by law.

(b) Purpose and Construction. The purpose of the 1998 Criminal Punishment Code and the principles it embodies are set out in subsection 921.002(1), Florida Statutes. Existing case law construing the application of sentencing guidelines will continue as precedent unless in conflict with the provisions of this rule or the 1998 Criminal Punishment Code.

(c) Offense Severity Ranking.

(1) Felony offenses subject to the 1998 Criminal Punishment Code are listed in a single offense severity ranking chart located at section 921.0022, Florida Statutes. The offense severity ranking chart employs 10 offense levels, ranked from least severe to most severe. Each felony offense is assigned to a level according to the severity of the offense, commensurate with the harm or potential for harm to the community that is caused by the offense, as determined by statute. The numerical statutory reference in the left column of the chart and the felony degree designations in the middle column of the chart determine whether felony offenses are specifically listed in the offense severity ranking chart and the appropriate severity level. The language in the right column is merely descriptive.

(2) Felony offenses not listed in section 921.0022 are assigned a severity level in accordance with section 921.0023, Florida Statutes, as follows:

(A) A felony of the third degree within offense level 1.

(B) A felony of the second degree within offense level 4.

(C) A felony of the first degree within offense level 7.

(D) A felony of the first degree punishable by life within offense level 9.

(E) A life felony within offense level 10.

An offense does not become unlisted and subject to the provisions of section 921.0023 because of a reclassification of the degree of felony under section 775.0845, section 775.087, section 775.0875 or section 794.023, Florida Statutes, or any other law that provides an enhanced penalty for a felony offense.

(d) General Rules and Definitions.

(1) One or more Criminal Punishment Code scoresheets must be prepared for each offender covering all offenses pending before the court for sentencing, including offenses for which the offender may qualify as an habitual felony offender, an habitual violent felony offender, a violent career criminal, or a prison releasee reoffender. The office of the state attorney must prepare the scoresheets and present them to defense counsel for review as to accuracy. If sentences are imposed under section 775.084, or section 775.082(9), Florida Statutes, and the Criminal Punishment Code, a scoresheet listing only those offenses sentenced under the Criminal Punishment Code must be filed in addition to any sentencing documents filed under section 775.084 or section 775.082(9).

(2) One scoresheet must be prepared for all offenses committed under any single version or revision of the guidelines or Criminal Punishment Code pending before the court for sentencing.

(3) If an offender is before the court for sentencing for more than one felony and the felonies were committed under more than one version or revision of the guidelines or Criminal Punishment Code, separate scoresheets must be prepared and used at sentencing. The sentencing court may impose such sentence concurrently or consecutively.

(4) The sentencing judge must review the scoresheet for accuracy and sign it.

(5) Felonies, except capital felonies, with continuing dates of enterprise are to be sentenced under the guidelines or Criminal Punishment Code in effect on the beginning date of the criminal activity.

(6) "Conviction" means a determination of guilt that is the result of a plea or trial, regardless of whether adjudication is withheld.

(7) "Primary offense" means the offense at conviction pending before the court for sentencing for which the total sentence points recommend a sanction that is as severe as, or more severe than, the sanction recommended for any other offense committed by the offender and pending before the court at sentencing. Only one count of one offense before the court for sentencing shall be classified as the primary offense.

(8) "Additional offense" means any offense other than the primary offense for which an offender is convicted and which is pending before the court for sentencing at the time of the primary offense.

(9) "Victim injury" is scored for physical injury or death suffered by a person as a direct result of any offense pending before the court for sentencing. Except as otherwise provided by law, the sexual penetration and sexual contact points will be scored as follows. Sexual penetration points are scored if an offense pending before the court for sentencing involves sexual penetration. Sexual contact points are scored if an offense pending before the court for sentencing involves sexual contact, but no penetration. If the victim of an offense involving sexual penetration or sexual contact without penetration suffers any physical injury as a direct result of an offense pending before the court for sentencing, that physical injury must be scored in addition to any points scored for the sexual contact or sexual penetration.

Victim injury must be scored for each victim physically injured and for each offense resulting in physical injury whether there are one or more victims. However, victim injury must not be scored for an offense for which the offender has not been convicted.

Victim injury resulting from one or more capital offenses before the court for sentencing must not be included upon any scoresheet prepared for non-capital offenses also pending before the court for sentencing. This does not prohibit the scoring of victim injury as a result of the non-capital offense or offenses before the court for sentencing.

(10) Unless specifically provided otherwise by statute, attempts, conspiracies, and solicitations must be indicated in the space provided on the Criminal Punishment Code scoresheet and must be scored at one severity level below the completed offense.

Attempts, solicitations, and conspiracies of third-degree felonies located in offense severity levels 1 and 2 must be scored as misdemeanors. Attempts, solicitations, and conspiracies of third-degree felonies located in offense severity levels 3, 4, 5, 6, 7, 8, 9, and 10 must be scored as felonies one offense level beneath the incomplete or inchoate offense.

(11) An increase in offense severity level may result from a reclassification of felony degrees under sections 775.0845, 775.087, 775.0875, or 794.023. Any such increase must be indicated in the space provided on the Criminal Punishment Code scoresheet.

(12) A single assessment of thirty prior serious felony points is added if the offender has a primary offense or any additional offense ranked in level 8, 9, or 10 and one or more prior serious felonies. A 'prior serious felony' is an offense in the offender's prior record ranked in level 8, 9, or 10 and for which the offender is serving a sentence of confinement, supervision or other sanction or for which the offender's date of release from confinement, supervision, or other sanction, whichever is later, is within 3 years before the date the primary offense or any additional offenses were committed. Out of state convictions wherein the analogous or parallel Florida offenses are located in offense severity level 8, 9, or 10 must be considered prior serious felonies.

(13) If the offender has one or more prior capital felonies, points must be added to the subtotal sentence points of the offender equal to twice the number of points the offender receives for the primary offense and any additional offense. Out-of-state convictions wherein the analogous or parallel Florida offenses are capital offenses must be considered capital offenses for purposes of operation of this section.

(14) "Prior record" refers to any conviction for an offense committed by the offender prior to the commission of the primary offense. Prior record includes convictions for offenses committed by the offender as an adult or as a juvenile, convictions by federal, out of state, military, or foreign courts and convictions for violations of county or municipal ordinances that incorporate by reference a penalty under state law. Federal, out of state, military or foreign convictions are scored at the severity level at which the analogous or parallel Florida crime is located.

(A) Convictions for offenses committed more than 10 years before the date of the commission of the primary offense must not be scored as prior record if the offender has not been convicted of any other crime for a period of 10 consecutive years from the most recent date of release from confinement, supervision, or other sanction, whichever is later, to the date of the commission of the primary offense.

(B) Juvenile dispositions of offenses committed by the offender within 5 years before the date of the commission of the primary offense must be scored as prior record if the offense would have been a crime if committed by an adult. Juvenile dispositions of sexual offenses committed by the offender more than 5 years before the date of the primary offense must be scored as prior record if the offender has not maintained a conviction-free record, either as an adult or as a juvenile, for a period of 5 consecutive years from the most recent date of release from confinement, supervision, or sanction, whichever is later, to the date of commission of the primary offense.

(C) Entries in criminal histories that show no disposition, disposition unknown, arrest only, or a disposition other than conviction must not be scored. Criminal history records expunged or sealed under section 943.058, Florida Statutes, or other provisions of law, including former sections 893.14 and 901.33, Florida Statutes, must be scored as prior record where the offender whose record has been expunged or sealed is before the court for sentencing.

(D) Any uncertainty in the scoring of the offender's prior record must be resolved in favor of the offender and disagreement as to the propriety of scoring specific entries in the prior record must be resolved by the sentencing judge.

(E) When unable to determine whether the conviction to be scored as prior record is a felony or a misdemeanor, the conviction must be scored as a misdemeanor. When the degree of felony is ambiguous or the severity level cannot be determined, the conviction must be scored at severity level 1.

(15) "Legal status points" are assessed when an offender:

(A) Escapes from incarceration;

(B) Flees to avoid prosecution;

(C) Fails to appear for a criminal proceeding;

(D) Violates any condition of a supersedeas bond;

(E) Is incarcerated;

(F) Is under any form of a pretrial intervention or diversion program; or

(G) Is under any form of court-imposed or post-prison release community supervision and commits an offense that results in conviction. Legal status violations receive a score of 4 sentence points and are scored when the offense committed while under legal status is before the court for sentencing. Points for a legal status violation must only be assessed once regardless of the existence of more than one form of legal status at the time an offense is committed or the number of offenses committed while under any form of legal status.

(16) Community sanction violation points occur when the offender is found to have violated a condition of:

(A) Probation;

(B) Community Control; or

(C) Pretrial intervention or diversion.

Community sanction violation points are assessed when a community sanction violation is before the court for sentencing. Six community sanction violation points must be assessed for each violation or if the violation results from a new felony conviction, 12 community sanction violation points must be assessed. For violations occurring on or after March 12, 2007, if the community sanction violation that is not based upon a failure to pay fines, costs, or restitution is committed by a violent felony offender of special concern as defined in s. 948.06, twelve community sanction violation points must be assessed or if the violation results from a new felony conviction, 24 community sanction points must be assessed. Where there are multiple violations, points may be assessed only for each successive violation that follows a continuation of supervision, or modification or revocation of the community sanction before the court for sentencing and are not to be assessed for violation of several conditions of a single community sanction. Multiple counts of community sanction violations before the sentencing court may not be the basis for multiplying the assessment of community sanction violation points.

(17) Possession of a firearm, semiautomatic firearm, or a machine gun during the commission or attempt to commit a crime will result in additional sentence points. Eighteen sentence points are assessed if the offender is convicted of committing or attempting to commit any felony other than those enumerated in subsection 775.087(2) while having in his or her possession a firearm as defined in subsection 790.001(6), Florida Statutes. Twenty-five sentence points are assessed if the offender is convicted of committing or attempting to commit any felony other than those enumerated in subsection 775.087(3) while having in his or her possession a semiautomatic firearm as defined in subsection 775.087(3) or a machine gun as defined in subsection 790.001(9). Only one assessment of either 18 or 25 points can be made.

(18) "Subtotal sentence points" are the sum of the primary offense points, the total additional offense points, the total victim injury points, the total prior record points, any legal status points, community sanction points, prior serious felony points, prior capital felony points and points for possession of a firearm or semiautomatic weapon.

(19) If the primary offense is drug trafficking under section 893.135, Florida Statutes, ranked in offense severity level 7 or 8, the subtotal sentence points may be multiplied, at the discretion of the sentencing court, by a factor of 1.5.

(20) If the primary offense is a violation of the Law Enforcement Protection Act under subsection 775.0823(2), (3), or (4), Florida Statutes, the subtotal sentence points are multiplied by 2.5. If the primary offense is a violation of subsection 775.0823(5), (6), (7), (8), or (9), the subtotal sentence points are multiplied by 2.0. If the primary offense is a violation of section 784.07(3) or 775.0875(1) or the Law Enforcement Protection Act under subsection 775.0823(10) or (11), the subtotal sentence points are multiplied by 1.5.

(21) If the primary offense is grand theft of the third degree of a motor vehicle and the offender's prior record includes three or more grand thefts of the third degree of a motor vehicle, the subtotal sentence points are multiplied by 1.5.

(22) If the offender is found to have committed the offense for the purpose of benefiting, promoting, or furthering the interests of a criminal gang under

section 874.04, Florida Statutes, at the time of the commission of the primary offense, the subtotal sentence points are multiplied by 1.5.

(23) If the primary offense is a crime of domestic violence as defined in section 741.28, Florida Statutes, which was committed in the presence of a child under 16 years of age who is a family household member as defined in section 741.28(2) with the victim or perpetrator, the subtotal sentence points are multiplied by 1.5.

(24) "Total sentence points" are the subtotal sentence points or the enhanced subtotal sentence points.

(25) The lowest permissible sentence is the minimum sentence that may be imposed by the trial court, absent a valid reason for departure. The lowest permissible sentence is any nonstate prison sanction in which the total sentence points equals or is less than 44 points, unless the court determines within its discretion that a prison sentence, which may be up to the statutory maximums for the offenses committed, is appropriate. When the total sentence points exceeds 44 points, the lowest permissible sentence in prison months must be calculated by subtracting 28 points from the total sentence points and decreasing the remaining total by 25 percent. The total sentence points must be calculated only as a means of determining the lowest permissible sentence. The permissible range for sentencing must be the lowest permissible sentence up to and including the statutory maximum, as defined in section 775.082, for the primary offense and any additional offenses before the court for sentencing. The sentencing court may impose such sentences concurrently or consecutively. However, any sentence to state prison must exceed 1 year. If the lowest permissible sentence under the Code exceeds the statutory maximum sentence as provided in section 775.082, the sentence required by the Code must be imposed. If the total sentence points are greater than or equal to 363, the court may sentence the offender to life imprisonment. The sentence imposed must be entered on the scoresheet.

(26) For those offenses having a mandatory minimum sentence, a scoresheet must be completed and the lowest permissible sentence under the Code calculated. If the lowest permissible sentence is less than the mandatory minimum sentence, the mandatory minimum sentence takes precedence. If the lowest permissible sentence exceeds the mandatory sentence, the requirements of the Criminal Punishment Code and any mandatory minimum penalties apply. Mandatory minimum sentences must be recorded on the scoresheet.

(27) Any downward departure from the lowest permissible sentence, as calculated according to the total sentence points under section 921.0024, Florida Statutes, is prohibited unless there are circumstances or factors that reasonably justify the downward departure. Circumstances or factors that can be considered include, but are not limited to, those listed in subsection 921.0026(2), Florida Statutes.

(A) If a sentencing judge imposes a sentence that is below the lowest permissible sentence, it is a departure sentence and must be accompanied by a written statement by the sentencing court delineating the reasons for the departure, filed within 7 days after the date of sentencing. A written transcription of orally stated reasons for departure articulated at the time sentence was imposed is sufficient if it is filed by the court within 7 days after the date of sentencing. The sentencing judge may also list the written reasons for departure in the space provided on the Criminal Punishment Code scoresheet.

(B) The written statement delineating the reasons for departure must be made a part of the record. The written statement, if it is a separate document, must accompany the scoresheet required to be provided to the Department of Corrections under subsection 921.0024(6).

If a split sentence is imposed, the total sanction (incarceration and community control or probation) must not exceed the term provided by general law or the maximum sentence under the Criminal Punishment Code.

(28) If the lowest permissible sentence under the criminal punishment code is a state prison sanction but the total sentencing points do not exceed 48 points (or 54 points if six of those points are for a violation of probation, community control, or other community supervision that does not involve a new crime), the court may sentence the defendant to probation, community control, or community supervision with mandatory participation in a prison diversion program, as provided for in s. 921.00241, Florida Statutes, if the defendant meets the requirements for that program as set forth in section 921.00241.

(29) If the total sentence points equal 22 or less, the court must sentence the offender to a nonstate prison sanction unless it makes written findings that a nonstate prison sanction could present a danger to the public.

(30) Sentences imposed after revocation of probation or community control must be imposed according to the sentencing law applicable at the time of the commission of the original offense.

Added Sept. 24, 1998, effective Oct. 1, 1998 (721 So.2d 265). Amended December 9, 1999 (763 So.2d 997); Sept. 26, 2001 (810 So.2d 826); April 19, 2007 (957 So.2d 1160); Nov. 20, 2008 (998 So.2d 1128); Sept. 10, 2009 (22 So.3d 1); Sept. 23, 2010 (46 So.3d 17).

Committee Note

The terms must and shall, as used in this rule, are mandatory and not permissive.

2001 Amendment. 3.704(d)(14)(B). The definition of "prior record" was amended to include juvenile dispositions of offenses committed within 5 years prior to the date of the commission of the primary offense. "Prior record" was previously defined to include juvenile disposition of offenses committed within 3 years prior to the date of the commission of the primary offense. This amendment reflects the legislative change to section 921.0021, Florida Statutes, effective July 1, 2001. This new definition of prior record applies to primary offenses committed on or after July 1, 2001.

Rule 3.710. Presentence Report

(a) Cases In Which Court Has Discretion. In all cases in which the court has discretion as to what sentence may be imposed, the court may refer the case to the Department of Corrections for investigation and recommendation. No sentence or sentences other than probation shall be imposed on any defendant found guilty of a first felony offense or found guilty of a felony while under the age of 18 years, until after such investigation has first been made and the recommendations of the Department of Corrections received and considered by the sentencing judge.

(b) Capital Defendant Who Refuses To Present Mitigation Evidence. Should a defendant in a capital case choose not to challenge the death penalty and refuse to present mitigation evidence, the court shall refer the case to the Department of Corrections for the preparation of a presentence report. The report shall be comprehensive and should include information such as previous mental health problems (including hospitalizations), school records, and relevant family background.

Amended Oct. 7, 2004, effective Jan. 1, 2005 (886 So.2d 197).

Committee Notes

1972 Adoption. The rule provides for the utilization of a pre-sentence report as part of the sentencing process. While use of the report is discretionary in all cases, it is mandatory in two instances, the sentencing of a first felony offender and of a defendant under 18 years of age. Of course, no report is necessary where the specific sentence is mandatory, e.g., the sentence of death or life imprisonment in a verdict of first degree murder.

1988 Amendment. This amendment changes wording to conform with current responsibility of the Department of Corrections to prepare the presentence investigation and report.

2004 Amendment. The amendment adds subdivision (b). Section 948. 015, Florida Statutes, is by its own terms inapplicable to those cases described in this new subdivision. Nonetheless, subdivision (b) requires a report that is "comprehensive." Accordingly, the report should include, if reasonably available, in addition to those matters specifically listed in *Muhammad v. State*, 782 So.2d 343, 363 (Fla. 2000), a description of the status of all of the charges in the indictment as well as any other pending offenses; the defendant's medical history; and those matters listed in sections 948.015 (3)–(8) and (13), Florida Statutes. The Department of Corrections should not recommend a sentence.

Rule 3.711. Presentence Report: When Prepared

(a) Except as provided in subdivision (b), the sentencing court shall not authorize the commencement of the presentence investigation until there has been a finding of guilt.

(b) The sentencing court may authorize the commencement of the presentence investigation prior to finding of guilt if:

(1) the defendant has consented to such action; and

(2) nothing disclosed by the presentence investigation comes to the attention of the prosecution, the court, or the jury prior to an adjudication of guilt. Upon motion of the defense and prosecution, the court may examine the presentence investigation prior to the entry of a plea.

Amended Sept. 24, 1992, effective Jan. 1, 1993 (606 So.2d 227).

Committee Notes

1972 Adoption. The rule permits presentence investigations to be initiated prior to finding of guilt. Its purpose is to reduce unwarranted jail time by a defendant who expects to plead guilty and who may well merit probation or commitment to facilities other than prison.

Rule 3.712. Presentence Report: Disclosure

The presentence investigation shall not be a public record and shall be available only to the following persons under the following stated conditions:

(a) To the sentencing court to assist it in determining an appropriate sentence.

(b) To persons or agencies having a legitimate professional interest in the information that it would contain.

(c) To reviewing courts if relevant to an issue on which an appeal has been taken.

(d) To the parties as rule 3.713 provides.

Amended Sept. 24, 1992, effective Jan. 1, 1993 (606 So.2d 227).

Committee Notes

1972 Amendment. Provides for disclosure of the report to the trial court, appropriate agencies of the state, and appellate courts, if needed.

Rule 3.713. Presentence Investigation Disclosure: Parties

(a) The trial judge may disclose any of the contents of the presentence investigation to the parties prior to sentencing. Any information so disclosed to one party shall be disclosed to the opposing party.

(b) The trial judge shall disclose all factual material, including but not limited to the defendant's education, prior occupation, prior arrests, prior convictions, military service, and the like, to the defendant and the state a reasonable time prior to sentencing.

If any physical or mental evaluations of the defendant have been made and are to be considered for the purposes of sentencing or release, such reports shall be disclosed to counsel for both parties.

(c) On motion of the defendant or the prosecutor or on its own motion, the sentencing court may order the defendant to submit to a mental or physical examination that would be relevant to the sentencing decision. Copies of the examination or any other examination to be considered for the purpose of sentencing shall be disclosed to counsel for the parties subject to the limitation of rule 3.713(b).

Amended Sept. 24, 1992, effective Jan. 1, 1993 (606 So.2d 227).

Committee Notes

1972 Adoption. This rule represents a compromise between the philosophy that presentence investigations should be fully disclosed to a defendant and the objection that such disclosure would dry up sources of confidential information and render such report virtually useless. (a) gives the trial judge discretion to disclose any or all of the report to the parties. (b) makes mandatory the disclosure of factual and physical and mental evaluation material only. In this way, it is left to the discretion of the trial judge to disclose to a defendant or defendant's counsel any other evaluative material. The judicial discretion should amply protect the confidentiality of those sources who do not wish to be disclosed, while the availability of all factual material will permit the defendant to discover and make known to the sentencing court any errors that may appear in the report.

Rule 3.720. Sentencing Hearing

As soon as practicable after the determination of guilt and after the examination of any presentence reports, the sentencing court shall order a sentencing hearing. At the hearing:

(a) The court shall inform the defendant of the finding of guilt against the defendant and of the judgment and ask the defendant whether there is any legal cause to show why sentence should not be pronounced. The defendant may allege and show as legal cause why sentence should not be pronounced only:

(1) that the defendant is insane;

(2) that the defendant has been pardoned of the offense for which he or she is about to be sentenced;

(3) that the defendant is not the same person against whom the verdict or finding of the court or judgment was rendered; or

(4) if the defendant is a woman and sentence of death is to be pronounced, that she is pregnant.

(b) The court shall entertain submissions and evidence by the parties that are relevant to the sentence.

(c) In cases where guilt was determined by plea, the court shall inform itself, if not previously informed, of the existence of plea discussions or agreements and the extent to which they involve recommendations as to the appropriate sentence.

(d)(1) If the accused was represented by a public defender or other court appointed counsel, the court shall notify the accused of the imposition of a lien pursuant to section 938.29, Florida Statutes. The amount of the lien shall be given and a judgment entered in that amount against the accused. Notice of the accused's right to a hearing to contest the amount of the lien shall be given at the time of sentence.

(2) If the accused requests a hearing to contest the amount of the lien, the court shall set a hearing date within 30 days of the date of sentencing.

Amended Sept. 24, 1992, effective Jan. 1, 1993 (606 So.2d 227); Sept. 23, 2010 (48 So.3d 17).

Committee Notes

1968 Adoption (of Rule 3.730). A revamped version of section 921.08, Florida Statutes.

1972 Amendment. 3.720(a): Substantially the same as former rule 3.730. 3.720(b): The defendant is to be permitted to challenge factual bases for the sentence that the defendant believes to be incorrect. When possible, submissions should be done informally, but the rule does not preclude an evidentiary hearing if it should be necessary. 3.720(c): Provides for plea discussions to be made a part of the record.

1980 Amendment. Modification of the rule by the addition of (d)(1) and (d)(2) requires a trial judge to adequately inform a defendant of the imposition of a lien for public defender services. A uniform procedure for scheduling hearings to contest liens would reduce the number of postsentence petitions from incarcerated defendants at times remote from sentencing. The procedure is designed to complete all lien requirements established by section 27.56, Florida Statutes, before defendants are removed from the jurisdiction of the trial court.

Rule 3.721. Record of the Proceedings

The sentencing court shall ensure that a record of the entire sentencing proceeding is made and preserved in such a manner that it can be transcribed as needed.

Committee Notes

1972 Adoption. New, providing for a record of the sentencing proceeding.

Rule 3.730. Issuance of Capias When Necessary to Bring Defendant Before Court

Whenever the court deems it necessary to do so in order to procure the presence of the defendant before it for the adjudication of guilt or the pronouncement of sentence, or both, when the defendant is not in custody, it shall direct the clerk to issue immediately or when directed by the prosecuting attorney a capias for the arrest of the defendant. Subsequent capiases may be issued from time to time by direction of the court or the prosecuting attorney.

Amended Sept. 24, 1992, effective Jan. 1, 1993 (606 So.2d 227).

Committee Notes

1968 Adoption (of Rule 3.710). A revamped version of section 921.06, Florida Statutes, adding provision that defendant be required to be present at the adjudication of guilt.

1972 Amendment. Same as prior rule 3.710.

Rule 3.750. Procedure When Pardon Is Alleged as Cause for Not Pronouncing Sentence

When the cause alleged for not pronouncing sentence is that the defendant has been pardoned for the offense for which the defendant is about to be sentenced, the court, if necessary, shall postpone the pronouncement of sentence for the purpose of hearing evidence on the allegation. If the court decides that the allegation is true, it shall discharge the defendant from custody unless the defendant is in custody on some other charge. If, however, it decides that the allegation is not true, it shall proceed to pronounce sentence.

Amended Sept. 24, 1992, effective Jan. 1, 1993 (606 So.2d 227).

Committee Notes

1968 Adoption. A revamped version of section 921.10, Florida Statutes.

1972 Amendment. Same as prior rule.

Rule 3.760. Procedure When Nonidentity Is Alleged as Cause for Not Pronouncing Sentence

When the cause alleged for not pronouncing sentence is that the person brought before the court to be sentenced is not the same person against whom the verdict, finding of the court, or judgment was rendered, the court, if necessary, shall postpone the pronouncement of sentence for the purpose of hearing evidence on the allegation. If the court decides that the allegation is true, it shall discharge the person from custody unless the person is in custody on some other charge. If, however, it decides that the allegation is not true, it shall proceed to pronounce sentence.

Amended Sept. 24, 1992, effective Jan. 1, 1993 (606 So.2d 227).

Committee Notes

1968 Adoption. A revamped version of section 921.11, Florida Statutes.

1972 Amendment. Same as prior rule.

Rule 3.770. Procedure When Pregnancy Is Alleged as Cause for Not Pronouncing Death Sentence

When pregnancy of a female defendant is alleged as the cause for not pronouncing the death sentence, the court shall postpone the pronouncement of sentence until after it has decided the truth of that allegation. If necessary in order to arrive at such a decision, it shall immediately fix a time for a hearing to determine whether the defendant is pregnant and shall appoint not exceeding 3 competent disinterested physicians to examine the defendant as to her alleged pregnancy and to testify at the hearing as to whether she is pregnant. Other evidence regarding whether the defendant is pregnant may be introduced at the hearing by either party. If the court decides that the defendant is not pregnant, it shall proceed to pronounce sentence. If it decides that she is pregnant, it shall commit her to prison until it appears that she is not pregnant and shall then pronounce sentence upon her.

Amended Sept. 24, 1992, effective Jan. 1, 1993 (606 So.2d 227).

Committee Notes

1968 Adoption. A revamped version of section 921.12, Florida Statutes.

Note that the rule omits the statutory provisions for the payment of fees to the examining physicians. The supreme court probably does not have the power to make rules governing such matters.

1972 Amendment. Same as prior rule.

Rule 3.780. Sentencing Hearing for Capital Cases

(a) Evidence. In all proceedings based on section 921.141, Florida Statutes, the state and defendant will be permitted to present evidence of an aggravating or mitigating nature, consistent with the requirements of the statute. Each side will be permitted to cross-examine the witnesses presented by the other side. The state will present evidence first.

(b) Rebuttal. The trial judge shall permit rebuttal testimony.

(c) Opening Statement and Closing Argument. Both the state and the defendant will be given an equal opportunity for one opening statement and one closing argument. The state will proceed first.

Amended Sept. 24, 1992, effective Jan. 1, 1993 (606 So.2d 227); Nov. 27, 1996, effective Jan. 1, 1997 (685 So.2d 1253).

Committee Notes

1977 Adoption. This is a new rule designed to create a uniform procedure that will be consistent with both section 921.141, Florida Statutes, and State v. Dixon, 283 So.2d 1 (Fla. 1973).

Rule 3.790. Probation and Community Control

(a) Suspension of the Pronouncement and Imposition of Sentence; Probation or Community Control. Pronouncement and imposition of sentence of imprisonment shall not be made on a defendant who is to be placed on probation, regardless of whether the defendant has been adjudicated guilty. An order of the court placing a person on probation or community control shall place the probationer under the authority of the Department of Corrections to be supervised as provided by law. The court shall specify the length of time during which the defendant is to be supervised.

(b) Revocation of Probation or Community Control; Judgment; Sentence.

(1) *Generally.* Except as otherwise provided in subdivisions (b)(2) and (b)(3) below, when a probationer or a community controllee is brought before a court of competent jurisdiction charged with a violation of probation or community control, the court shall advise the person of the charge and, if the charge is admitted to be true, may immediately enter an order revoking, modifying, or continuing the probation or community control. If the violation of probation or community control is not admitted by the probationer or community controllee, the court may commit the person or release the person with or without bail to await further hearing or it may dismiss the charge of violation of probation or community control. If the charge is not admitted by the probationer or community controllee and if it is not dismissed, the court, as soon as practicable, shall give the probationer or community controllee an opportunity to be fully heard in person, by counsel, or both. After the hearing, the court may enter an order revoking, modifying, or continuing the probation or community control. Following a revocation of probation or community control, the trial court shall adjudicate the defendant guilty of the crime forming the basis of the probation or community control if no such adjudication has been made previously. Pronouncement and imposition of sentence then shall be made on the defendant.

(2) *Lunsford Act Proceedings.* When a probationer or community controllee is arrested for violating his or her probation or community control in a material respect and is under supervision for any criminal offense proscribed in chapter 794, Florida Statutes, section 800.04(4), Florida Statutes, section 800.04(5), Florida Statutes, section 800.04(6), Florida Statutes, section 827.071, Florida Statutes, or section 847.0145, Florida Statutes, or is a registered sexual predator or a registered sexual offender, or is under supervision for a criminal offense for which, but for the effective date, he or she would meet the registration criteria of section 775.21, Florida Statutes, section 943.0435, Florida Statutes, or section 944.607, Florida Statutes, the court must make a finding that the probationer or community controllee is not a danger to the public prior to release with or without bail.

(A) The hearing to determine whether the defendant is a danger to the public shall be conducted by a court of competent jurisdiction no sooner than 24 hours after arrest. The time for conducting the hearing may be extended at the request of the accused, or at the request of the state upon a showing of good cause.

(B) At the hearing, the defendant shall have the right to be heard in person or through counsel, to present witnesses and evidence, and to cross-examine witnesses.

(C) In determining the danger posed by the defendant's release, the court may consider:

(i) the nature and circumstances of the violation and any new offenses charged;

(ii) the defendant's past and present conduct, including convictions of crimes;

(iii) any record of arrests without conviction for crimes involving violence or sexual crimes;

(iv) any other evidence of allegations of unlawful sexual conduct or the use of violence by the defendant;

(v) the defendant's family ties, length of residence in the community, employment history, and mental condition;

(vi) the defendant's history and conduct during the probation or community control supervision from which the violation arises and any other previous supervisions, including disciplinary records of previous incarcerations;

(vii) the likelihood that the defendant will engage again in a criminal course of conduct;

(viii) the weight of the evidence against the defendant; and

(ix) any other facts the court considers relevant.

(3) *Anti–Murder Act Proceedings.* The provisions of this subdivision shall control over any conflicting provisions in subdivision (b)(2). When a probationer or community controllee is arrested for violating his or her probation or community control in a material respect and meets the criteria for a violent felony offender of special concern, or for certain other related categories of offender, as set forth in section 948.06(8), Florida Statutes, the defendant shall be brought before the court that granted the probation or community control and, except when the alleged violation is based solely on the defendant's failure to pay costs, fines, or restitution, shall not be granted bail or any other form of pretrial release prior to the resolution of the probation or community control violation hearing.

(A) The court shall not dismiss the probation or community control violation warrant pending against the defendant without holding a recorded violation hearing at which both the state and the accused are represented.

(B) If, after conducting the hearing, the court determines that the defendant has committed a violation of probation or community control other than a failure to pay costs, fines, or restitution, the court shall make written findings as to whether the defendant poses a danger to the community. In determining the danger to the community posed by the defendant's release, the court shall base its findings on one or more of the following:

(i) The nature and circumstances of the violation and any new offenses charged;

(ii) The defendant's present conduct, including criminal convictions;

(iii) The defendant's amenability to nonincarcerative sanctions based on his or her history and conduct during the probation or community control supervision from which the violation hearing arises and any other previous supervisions, including disciplinary records of previous incarcerations;

(iv) The weight of the evidence against the defendant; and

(v) Any other facts the court considers relevant.

(C) If the court finds that the defendant poses a danger to the community, the court shall revoke probation or community control and sentence the defendant up to the statutory maximum, or longer if permitted by law.

(D) If the court finds that the defendant does not pose a danger to the community, the court may revoke, modify, or continue the probation or community control or may place the probationer into community control as provided in section 948.06, Florida Statutes.

Amended Sept. 24, 1992, effective Jan. 1, 1993 (606 So.2d 227); July 5, 2007 (959 So.2d 1187).

Committee Notes

1968 Adoption. Subdivisions (a) and (b) contain the procedural aspects of section 948.01(1), (2), and (3), Florida Statutes. It should be noted that in (b) provision is made for no pronouncements in addition to no imposition of sentence prior to the granting of probation. The terminology in section 948.01(3), Florida Statutes, is that the trial court shall "withhold the imposition of sentence." The selected terminology is deemed preferable to the present statutory language since the latter is apparently subject to misconstruction whereby a sentence may be pronounced and merely the execution of the sentence is suspended.

The Third District Court of Appeal has indicated that the proper procedure to be followed is that probation be granted prior to sentencing. A sentence, therefore, is not a prerequisite of probation. See Yates v. Buchanan, 170 So.2d 72 (Fla.3d DCA 1964); also see Bateh v. State, 101 So.2d 869 (Fla.1st DCA 1958), decided by the First District Court of Appeal to the same effect.

While a trial court initially can set a probationary period at less than the maximum allowed by law, this period may be extended to the maximum prior to the expiration of the initially-set probationary period. Pickman v. State, 155 So.2d 646 (Fla.1st DCA 1963). This means, therefore, that any specific time set by the court as to the probationary period is not binding if the court acts timely in modifying it. It is clear, in view of the foregoing, that if a trial judge pronounces a definite sentence and then purports to suspend its execution and place the defendant on probation for the period of time specified in the sentence, matters may become unduly complicated.

If such procedure is considered to be nothing more than an informal manner of suspending the imposition of sentence and thus adhering to present statutory requirements, it should be noted that the time specified in the "sentence" is not binding on the court with reference to subsequent modification, if timely action follows. On the other hand, if the action of the trial court is considered strictly, it would be held to be void as not in conformity with statutory requirements.

A probationary period is not a sentence, and any procedure that tends to mix them is undesirable, even if this mixture is accomplished by nothing more than the terminology used by the trial court in its desire to place a person on probation. See sections 948.04 and 948.06(1), Florida Statutes, in which clear distinctions are drawn between the period of a sentence and the period of probation.

(c) Contains the procedural aspects of section 948.06(1), Florida Statutes.

1972 Amendment. (a) of former rule deleted, as its substance is now contained in rules 3.710, 3.711, and 3.713. Former subdivisions (b) and (c) are now renumbered (a) and (b) respectively.

1988 Amendment. This amendment changes wording to conform with current responsibilities of the Department of Corrections to supervise a person placed on either probation or community control and brings community control within the scope of the rule.

Rule 3.800. Correction, Reduction, and Modification of Sentences

(a) Correction. A court may at any time correct an illegal sentence imposed by it, or an incorrect calculation made by it in a sentencing scoresheet, when it is affirmatively alleged that the court records demonstrate on their face an entitlement to that relief, provided that a party may not file a motion to correct an illegal sentence under this subdivision during the time allowed for the filing of a motion under subdivision (b)(1) or during the pendency of a direct appeal. A defendant may seek correction of an allegedly erroneous sexual predator designation under this subdivision, but only when it is apparent from the face of the record that the defendant did not meet the criteria for designation as a sexual predator. All orders denying motions under this subdivision shall include a statement that the movant has the right to appeal within 30 days of rendition of the order.

(b) Motion to Correct Sentencing Error. A motion to correct any sentencing error, including an illegal sentence, may be filed as allowed by this subdivision. This subdivision shall not be applicable to those cases in which the death sentence has been imposed and direct appeal jurisdiction is in the Supreme Court under article V, section 3(b)(1) of the Florida Constitution. The motion must identify the error with specificity and provide a proposed correction. A response to the motion may be filed within 15 days, either admitting or contesting the alleged error. Motions may be filed by the state under this subdivision only if the correction of the sentencing error would benefit the defendant or to correct a scrivener's error.

(1) *Motion Before Appeal.* During the time allowed for the filing of a notice of appeal of a sentence, a defendant or the state may file a motion to correct a sentencing error.

(A) This motion shall stay rendition under Florida Rule of Appellate Procedure 9.020(i).

(B) Unless the trial court determines that the motion can be resolved as a matter of law without a hearing, it shall hold a calendar call no later than 20 days from the filing of the motion, with notice to all parties, for the express purpose of either ruling on the motion or determining the need for an evidentiary hearing. If an evidentiary hearing is needed, it shall be set no more than 20 days from the date of the calendar call. Within 60 days from the filing of the motion, the trial court shall file an order ruling on the motion. A party may file a motion for rehearing of any signed, written order entered under subdivisions (a) and (b) of this rule within 15 days of the date of service of the order or within 15 days of the expiration of the time period for filing an order if no order is filed. A response may be filed within 10 days of service of the motion. The trial court's order disposing of the motion for rehearing shall be filed within 15 days of the response but not later than 40 days from the date of the order of which rehearing is sought. A timely filed motion for rehearing shall toll rendition of the order subject to appellate review and the order shall be deemed rendered upon the filing of a signed, written order denying the motion for rehearing.

(2) *Motion Pending Appeal.* If an appeal is pending, a defendant or the state may file in the trial court a motion to correct a sentencing error. The motion may be filed by appellate counsel and must be served before the party's first brief is served. A notice of pending motion to correct sentencing error shall be filed in the appellate court, which notice automatically shall extend the time for the filing of the brief until 10 days after the clerk of circuit court transmits the supplemental record under Florida Rule of Appellate Procedure 9.140(f)(6).

(A) The motion shall be served on the trial court and on all trial and appellate counsel of record. Unless the motion expressly states that appellate counsel will represent the movant in the trial court, trial counsel will represent the movant on the motion under Florida Rule of Appellate Procedure 9.140(d). If the state is the movant, trial counsel will represent the defendant unless appellate counsel for the defendant notifies trial counsel and the trial court that he or she will represent the defendant on the state's motion.

(B) The trial court shall resolve this motion in accordance with the procedures in subdivision (b)(1)(B), except that if the trial court does not file an order ruling on the motion within 60 days, the motion shall be deemed denied. Similarly, if the trial court does not file an order ruling on a timely motion for rehearing within 40 days from the date of the order of which rehearing is sought, the motion for rehearing shall be deemed denied.

(C) In accordance with Florida Rule of Appellate Procedure 9.140(f)(6), the clerk of circuit court shall supplement the appellate record with the motion, the order, any amended sentence, and, if designated, a transcript of any additional portion of the proceedings.

(c) Reduction and Modification. A court may reduce or modify to include any of the provisions of chapter 948, Florida Statutes, a legal sentence imposed by it, sua sponte, or upon motion filed, within 60 days after the imposition, or within 60 days after receipt by the court of a mandate issued by the appellate court on affirmance of the judgment and/or sentence on an original appeal, or within 60 days after receipt by the court of a certified copy of an order of the appellate court dismissing an original appeal from the judgment and/or sentence, or, if further appellate review is sought in a higher court or in successively higher courts, within 60 days after the highest state or federal court to which a timely appeal has been taken under authority of law, or in which a petition for certiorari has been timely filed under authority of law, has entered an order of affirmance or an order dismissing the appeal and/or denying certiorari. If review is upon motion, the trial court shall have 90 days from the date the motion is filed or such time as agreed by the parties or as extended by the trial court to enter an order ruling on the motion. This subdivision shall not be applicable to those cases in which the death sentence is imposed or those cases in which the trial judge has imposed the minimum mandatory sentence or has no sentencing discretion.

Amended Sept. 24, 1992, effective Jan. 1, 1993 (606 So.2d 227); June 27, 1996, effective July 1, 1996 (675 So.2d 1374); Nov. 27, 1996, effective Jan. 1, 1997 (685 So.2d 1253); Nov. 12, 1999 (760 So.2d 67); Jan. 13, 2000 (761 So.2d 1015); Nov. 2, 2000, effective Jan. 1, 2001 (794 So.2d 457); Oct. 7, 2004, effective Jan. 1, 2005 (886 So.2d 197); Feb. 8, 2007 (949 So.2d 196); Nov. 19, 2009, effective Jan. 1, 2010 (26 So.3d 534); Dec. 8, 2011 (76 So.3d 913); Nov. 8, 2012, effective Jan. 1, 2013 (104 So.3d 304); April 18, 2013, revised Dec. 5, 2013, effective, *nunc pro tunc*, July 1, 2013 (132 So.3d 734); June 11, 2015, effective June 11, 2015 (167 So.3d 395).

Committee Notes

1968 Adoption. Same as sections 921.24 and 921.25, Florida Statutes. Similar to Federal Rule of Criminal Procedure 35.

1972 Amendment. Same as prior rule.

1977 Amendment. This amendment provides a uniform time within which a defendant may seek a reduction in sentence and excludes death and minimum mandatory sentences from its operation.

1980 Amendment. Permits the sentencing judge, within the 60–day time period, to modify as well as to reduce the sentence originally imposed. Such modification would permit the judge to impose, in the modification, any sentence which could have been imposed initially, including split sentence or probation. The trial judge may not, in such modification, increase the original sentence.

1996 Amendments. Subdivision (b) was added and existing subdivision (b) was renumbered as subdivision (c) in order to authorize the filing of a motion to correct a sentence or order of probation, thereby providing a vehicle to correct sentencing errors in the trial court and to preserve the issue should the motion be denied. A motion filed under subdivision (b) is an authorized motion which tolls the time for filing the notice of appeal. The presence of a defendant who is represented by counsel would not be required at the hearing on the disposition of such a motion if it only involved a question of law.

2000 Amendment. The amendment to subdivision (a) is intended to conform the rule with *State v. Mancino*, 714 So.2d 429 (Fla. 1998).

Court Commentary

1999 Amendments. Rule 3.800(b) was substantially rewritten to accomplish the goals of the Criminal Appeal Reform Act of 1996 (Ch. 96–248, Laws of Fla.). As revised, this rule permits the filing of a motion during the initial stages of an appeal. A motion pursuant to this rule is needed only if the sentencing error has not been adequately preserved for review at an earlier time in the trial court.

The State may file a motion to correct a sentencing error pursuant to rule 3.800(b) only if the correction of that error will benefit the defendant or correct a scrivener's error. This amendment is not intended to alter the substantive law of the State concerning whether a change to the defendant's sentence violates the constitutional prohibition against double jeopardy. *See, e.g., Cheshire v. State*, 568 So.2d 908 (Fla. 1990); *Goene v. State*, 577 So.2d 1306, 1309 (Fla.1991); Troupe v. Rowe, 283 So.2d 857, 859 (Fla. 1973).

A scrivener's error in this context describes clerical or ministerial errors in a criminal case that occur in the written sentence, judgment, or order of probation or restitution. The term scrivener's error refers to a mistake in the written sentence that is at variance with the oral pronouncement of sentence or the record but not those errors that are the result of a judicial determination or error. *See, e.g., Allen v. State*, 739 So.2d 166 (Fla. 3rd DCA 1999) (correcting a "scrivener's error" in the written order that adjudicated the appellant in contempt for "jailing polygraph exam"); *Pressley v. State*, 726 So.2d 403 (Fla. 2d DCA 1999) (correcting scrivener's error in the sentencing documents that identified the defendant as a habitual offender when he was not sentenced as a habitual offender); *Ricks v. State*, 725 So.2d 1205 (Fla. 2d DCA 1999) (correcting scrivener's error that resulted from the written sentence not identifying the defendant as a habitual offender although the court had orally pronounced a habitual offender sentence), *review denied*, 732 So.2d 328 (Fla. 1999); *McKee v. State*, 712 So.2d 837 (Fla. 2d DCA 1998) (remanding for the trial court to determine whether a scrivener's error occurred where the written order of probation imposed six years' probation, which conflicted with the written sentence and the trial court minutes that reflected only five years' probation had been imposed); *Florczak v. State*, 712 So.2d 467, 467 (Fla. 4th DCA 1998) (correcting a scrivener's error in the judgment of conviction where the defendant was acquitted of grand theft but the written judgment stated otherwise); *Stombaugh v. State*, 704 So.2d 723, 725–26 (Fla. 5th DCA 1998) (finding a scrivener's error occurred where the State had nol prossed a count of the information as part of plea bargain but the written sentence reflected that the defendant was sentenced under that count). But see *Carridine v. State*, 721 So.2d 818, 819 (Fla. 4th DCA 1998) (trial court's failure to sign written reasons for imposing an upward departure sentence did not constitute a scrivener's error that could be corrected nunc pro tunc by the trial court), and cases cited therein.

When a trial court determines that an evidentiary hearing is necessary to resolve a factual issue, it is possible that the court will need to utilize the entire 60–day period authorized by this rule. However, trial courts and counsel are strongly encouraged to cooperate to resolve these motions as expeditiously as possible because they delay the appellate process. For purposes of this rule, sentencing errors include harmful errors in orders entered as a result of the sentencing process. This includes errors in orders of probation, orders of community control, cost and restitution orders, as well as errors within the sentence itself.

Rule 3.801. Correction of Jail Credit

(a) Correction of Jail Credit. A court may correct a sentence that fails to allow a defendant credit for all of the time he or she spent in the county jail before sentencing as provided in section 921.161, Florida Statutes.

(b) Time Limitations. No motion shall be filed or considered pursuant to this rule if filed more than 1 year after the sentence becomes final. For sentences imposed prior to July 1, 2013, a motion under this rule may be filed on or before July 1, 2014.

(c) Contents of Motion. The motion shall be under oath and include:

(1) a brief statement of the facts relied on in support of the motion;

(2) the dates, location of incarceration and total time for credit already provided;

(3) the dates, location of incarceration and total time for credit the defendant contends was not properly awarded;

(4) whether any other criminal charges were pending at the time of the incarceration noted in subdivi-

sion (c)(3), and if so, the location, case number and resolution of the charges; and

(5) whether the defendant waived any county jail credit at the time of sentencing, and if so, the number of days waived.

(d) Successive Motions. No successive motions for jail credit will be considered.

(e) Incorporation of Portions of Florida Rule of Criminal Procedure 3. 850. The following subdivisions of Florida Rule of Criminal Procedure 3.850 apply to proceedings under this rule: 3.850(e), (f), (j), (k), and (n).

Adopted April 18, 2013, revised Dec. 5, 2013, effective, *nunc pro tunc*, July 1, 2013 (132 So.3d 734).

Court Commentary

2013 Adoption. All jail credit issues must be handled pursuant to this rule. The rule is intended to require that jail credit issues be dealt with promptly, within 1 year of the sentence becoming final. No successive motions for jail credit will be allowed.

XV. EXECUTION OF SENTENCE

Rule 3.810. Commitment of Defendant; Duty of Sheriff

On pronouncement of a sentence imposing a penalty other than a fine only or death, the court shall, unless the execution of the sentence is suspended or stayed, and, in such case, on termination of the suspension or stay, forthwith commit the defendant to the custody of the sheriff under a commitment to which shall be attached a certified copy of the sentence and, unless both are contained in the same instrument if the sentence is imprisonment in the state prison, a certified copy of the judgment of conviction and a certified copy of the indictment or information, and the sheriff shall thereupon, within a reasonable time, if the sheriff is not the proper official to execute the sentence, transfer the defendant, together with the commitment and attached certified copies, to the custody of the official whose duty it is to execute the sentence and shall take from that person a receipt for the defendant and make a return thereof to the court.

Amended Sept. 24, 1992, effective Jan. 1, 1993 (606 So.2d 227).

Committee Notes

1968 Adoption. Substantially the same as section 922.01, Florida Statutes. There has been added to the rule the requirement that, if the commitment is to the state prison, it shall be accompanied by a certified copy of the judgment of conviction and a certified copy of the indictment or information. (Section 944.18, Florida Statutes, requires a certified copy of the indictment or information to be transmitted to the Division of Corrections; the Division of Corrections should also have a certified copy of the judgment.)

1972 Amendment. Same as prior rule.

Rule 3.811. Insanity at Time of Execution: Capital Cases

(a) Insanity to Be Executed. A person under sentence of death shall not be executed while insane to be executed.

(b) Insanity Defined. A person under sentence of death is insane for purposes of execution if the person lacks the mental capacity to understand the fact of the impending execution and the reason for it.

(c) Stay of Execution. No motion for a stay of execution pending hearing, based on grounds of the prisoner's insanity to be executed, shall be entertained by any court until such time as the Governor of Florida shall have held appropriate proceedings for determining the issue pursuant to the appropriate Florida Statutes.

(d) Motion for Stay after Governor's Determination of Sanity to Be Executed. On determination of the Governor of Florida, subsequent to the signing of a death warrant for a prisoner under sentence of death and pursuant to the applicable Florida Statutes relating to insanity at time of execution, that the prisoner is sane to be executed, counsel for the prisoner may move for a stay of execution and a hearing based on the prisoner's insanity to be executed.

(1) The motion shall be filed in the circuit court of the circuit in which the execution is to take place and shall be heard by one of the judges of that circuit or such other judge as shall be assigned by the chief justice of the supreme court to hear the motion. The state attorney of the circuit shall represent the State of Florida in any proceedings held on the motion.

(2) The motion shall be in writing and shall contain a certificate of counsel that the motion is made in good faith and on reasonable grounds to believe that the prisoner is insane to be executed.

(3) Counsel for the prisoner shall file, along with the motion, all reports of experts that were submitted to the governor pursuant to the statutory procedure for executive determination of sanity to be executed. If any of the evidence is not available to counsel for the prisoner, counsel shall attach to the motion an affidavit so stating, with an explanation of why the evidence is unavailable.

(4) Counsel for the prisoner and the state may submit such other evidentiary material and written submissions including reports of experts on behalf of the prisoner as shall be relevant to determination of the issue.

(5) A copy of the motion and all supporting documents shall be served on the Florida Department of Legal Affairs and the state attorney of the circuit in which the motion has been filed.

(e) Order Granting. If the circuit judge, upon review of the motion and submissions, has reasonable grounds to believe that the prisoner is insane to be executed, the judge shall grant a stay of execution and may order further proceedings which may include a hearing pursuant to rule 3.812.

Amended Sept. 24, 1992, effective Jan. 1, 1993 (606 So.2d 227).

Committee Notes

1988 Adoption. This rule is not intended to preclude the Office of the Attorney General or the state attorney of the circuit in which the trial was held from appearing on behalf of the State of Florida under circumstances when permitted by law.

Rule 3.812. Hearing on Insanity at Time of Execution: Capital Cases

(a) Hearing on Insanity to Be Executed. The hearing on the prisoner's insanity to be executed shall not be a review of the governor's determination, but shall be a hearing de novo.

(b) Issue at Hearing. At the hearing the issue shall be whether the prisoner presently meets the criteria for insanity at time of execution, that is, whether the prisoner lacks the mental capacity to understand the fact of the pending execution and the reason for it.

(c) Procedure. The court may do any of the following as may be appropriate and adequate for a just resolution of the issues raised:

(1) require the presence of the prisoner at the hearing;

(2) appoint no more than 3 disinterested mental health experts to examine the prisoner with respect to the criteria for insanity to be executed and to report their findings and conclusions to the court; or

(3) enter such other orders as may be appropriate to effectuate a speedy and just resolution of the issues raised.

(d) Evidence. At hearings held pursuant to this rule, the court may admit such evidence as the court deems relevant to the issues, including but not limited to the reports of expert witnesses, and the court shall not be strictly bound by the rules of evidence.

(e) Order. If, at the conclusion of the hearing, the court shall find, by clear and convincing evidence, that the prisoner is insane to be executed, the court shall enter its order continuing the stay of the death warrant; otherwise, the court shall deny the motion and enter its order dissolving the stay of execution.

Amended Sept. 24, 1992, effective Jan. 1, 1993 (606 So.2d 227).

Rule 3.820. Habeas Corpus

(a) Custody Pending Appeal of Order of Denial. When a defendant has been sentenced, and is actually serving the sentence, and has not appealed from the judgment or sentence, but seeks a release from imprisonment by habeas corpus proceedings, and the writ has been discharged after it has been issued, the custody of the prisoner shall not be disturbed, pending review by the appellate court.

(b) Custody Pending Appeal of Order Granting. Pending review of a decision discharging a prisoner on habeas corpus, the prisoner shall be discharged on bail, with sureties to be approved as other bail bonds are approved for the prisoner's appearance to answer and abide by the judgment of the appellate court.

Amended Sept. 24, 1992, effective Jan. 1, 1993 (606 So.2d 227).

Committee Notes

1968 Adoption. Same as section 922.03, Florida Statutes.

1972 Amendment. Same as prior rule, but some terminology has been changed.

XVI. CRIMINAL CONTEMPT

Rule 3.830. Direct Criminal Contempt

A criminal contempt may be punished summarily if the court saw or heard the conduct constituting the contempt committed in the actual presence of the court. The judgment of guilt of contempt shall include a recital of those facts on which the adjudication of guilt is based. Prior to the adjudication of guilt the judge shall inform the defendant of the accusation against the defendant and inquire as to whether the defendant has any cause to show why he or she should not be adjudged guilty of contempt by the court and sentenced therefor. The defendant shall be given the opportunity to present evidence of excusing or mitigating circumstances. The judgment shall be signed by the judge and entered of record. Sentence shall be pronounced in open court.

Amended Sept. 24, 1992, effective Jan. 1, 1993 (606 So.2d 227).

Committee Notes

1968 Adoption. This proposal is consistent with present Florida practice in authorizing summary proceedings in direct criminal contempt cases. See Ballengee v. State, 144 So.2d 68 (Fla.2d DCA 1962); Baumgartner v. Joughin, 105 Fla. 334, 141 So. 185 (1932); also see State v. Lehman, 100 Fla. 481, 129 So. 818 (1930), holding that the defendant is not entitled to notice of the accusation or a motion for attachment. Fairness dictates that the defendant be allowed to present excusing or mitigating evidence even in direct criminal contempt cases.

Much of the terminology of the proposal is patterned after Federal Rule of Criminal Procedure 42(a) with variations for purposes of clarity. What may be considered a significant change from the terminology of the federal rule is that the proposal provides for a "judgment" of contempt, whereas the term "order" of contempt is used in the federal rule. Both terms have been used in Florida appellate cases. The term "judgment" is preferred here since it is consistent with the procedure of adjudicating guilt and is more easily reconciled with a "conviction" of contempt, common terminology on the trial and appellate levels in Florida. It also is consistent with appeals in contempt cases. See, e.g., State ex rel. Shotkin v. Buchanan, 149 So.2d 574, 98 A.L.R.2d 683 (Fla.3d DCA 1963), for the use of the term "judgment".

1972 Amendment. Same as prior rule.

Rule 3.840. Indirect Criminal Contempt

A criminal contempt, except as provided in rule 3.830 concerning direct contempts, shall be prosecuted in the following manner:

(a) Order to Show Cause. The judge, on the judge's own motion or on affidavit of any person having knowledge of the facts, may issue and sign an order directed to the defendant, stating the essential facts constituting the criminal contempt charged and requiring the defendant to appear before the court to show cause why the defendant should not be held in contempt of court. The order shall specify the time and place of the hearing, with a reasonable time allowed for preparation of the defense after service of the order on the defendant.

(b) Motions; Answer. The defendant, personally or by counsel, may move to dismiss the order to show cause, move for a statement of particulars, or answer the order by way of explanation or defense. All motions and the answer shall be in writing unless specified otherwise by the judge. A defendant's omission to file motions or answer shall not be deemed as an admission of guilt of the contempt charged.

(c) Order of Arrest; Bail. The judge may issue an order of arrest of the defendant if the judge has reason to believe the defendant will not appear in response to the order to show cause. The defendant shall be admitted to bail in the manner provided by law in criminal cases.

(d) Arraignment; Hearing. The defendant may be arraigned at the time of the hearing, or prior thereto at the defendant's request. A hearing to determine the guilt or innocence of the defendant shall follow a plea of not guilty. The judge may conduct a hearing without assistance of counsel or may be assisted by the prosecuting attorney or by an attorney appointed for that purpose. The defendant is entitled to be represented by counsel, have compulsory process for the attendance of witnesses, and testify in his or her own defense. All issues of law and fact shall be heard and determined by the judge.

(e) Disqualification of Judge. If the contempt charged involves disrespect to or criticism of a judge, the judge shall disqualify himself or herself from presiding at the hearing. Another judge shall be designated by the chief justice of the supreme court.

(f) Verdict; Judgment. At the conclusion of the hearing the judge shall sign and enter of record a judgment of guilty or not guilty. There should be included in a judgment of guilty a recital of the facts constituting the contempt of which the defendant has been found and adjudicated guilty.

(g) Sentence; Indirect Contempt. Prior to the pronouncement of sentence, the judge shall inform the defendant of the accusation and judgment against the defendant and inquire as to whether the defendant has any cause to show why sentence should not be pronounced. The defendant shall be afforded the opportunity to present evidence of mitigating circumstances. The sentence shall be pronounced in open court and in the presence of the defendant.

Amended Sept. 24, 1992, effective Jan. 1, 1993 (606 So.2d 227).

Committee Notes

1968 Adoption.

(a)(1) Order to Show Cause. The courts have used various and, at times, misleading terminology with reference to this phase of the procedure, viz. "citation," "rule nisi," "rule," "rule to show cause," "information," "indicted," and "order to show cause." Although all apparently have been used with the same connotation the terminology chosen probably is more readily understandable than the others. This term is used in Federal Rule of Criminal Procedure 42(b) dealing with indirect criminal contempts.

In proceedings for indirect contempt, due process of law requires that the accused be given notice of the charge and a reasonable opportunity to meet it by way of defense or explanation. State ex rel. Giblin v. Sullivan, 157 Fla. 496, 26 So.2d 509 (1946); State ex rel. Geary v. Kelly, 137 So.2d 262, 263 (Fla. 3d DCA 1962).

The petition (affidavit is used here) must be filed by someone having actual knowledge of the facts and must be under oath. Phillips v. State, 147 So.2d 163 (Fla. 3d DCA 1962); see also Croft v. Culbreath, 150 Fla. 60, 6 So.2d 638 (1942); Ex parte Biggers, 85 Fla. 322, 95 So. 763 (1923).

(2) Motions; Answer. The appellate courts of Florida, while apparently refraining from making motions and answers indispensable parts of the procedure, seem to regard them with favor in appropriate situations. Regarding motions to quash and motion for bill of particulars, see Geary v. State, 139 So.2d 891 (Fla. 3d DCA 1962); regarding the answer, see State ex. rel. Huie v. Lewis, 80 So.2d 685 (Fla.1955).

Elsewhere in these rules is a recommended proposal that a motion to dismiss replace the present motion to quash; hence, the motion to dismiss is recommended here.

The proposal contains no requirement that the motions or answer be under oath. Until section 38.22, Florida Statutes, was amended in 1945 there prevailed in Florida the common law rule that denial under oath is conclusive and requires discharge of the defendant in indirect contempt cases; the discharge was considered as justified because the defendant could be convicted of perjury if the defendant had sworn falsely in the answer or in a motion denying the charge. The amendment of section 38.22, Florida Statutes, however, has been construed to no longer justify the discharge of the defendant merely because the defendant denies the charge under oath. See Ex parte Earman, 85 Fla. 297, 95 So. 755 (1923), re the common law; see Dodd v. State, 110 So.2d 22 (Fla. 3d DCA 1959) re the construction of section 38.22, Florida Statutes, as amended. There appears, therefore, no necessity of requiring that a pleading directed to the order to show cause be under oath, except as a matter of policy of holding potential perjury prosecutions over the heads of defendants. It is recommended, therefore, that no oath be required at this stage of the proceeding.

Due process of law in the prosecution for indirect contempt requires that the defendant have the right to assistance by counsel. Baumgartner v. Joughin, 105 Fla. 335, 141 So. 185 (1932), adhered to, 107 Fla. 858, 143 So. 436 (1932).

(3) Order of Arrest; Bail. Arrest and bail, although apparently used only rarely, were permissible at common law and, accordingly, are unobjectionable under present Florida law. At times each should serve a useful purpose in contempt proceedings and should be included in the rule. As to the common law, see Ex parte Biggers, supra.

(4) Arraignment; Hearing. Provision is made for a prehearing arraignment in case the defendant wishes to plead guilty to the charge prior to the date set for the hearing. The defendant has a constitutional right to a hearing under the due process clauses of the state and federal constitutions. State ex rel. Pipia v. Buchanan, 168 So.2d 783 (Fla. 3d DCA 1964). This right includes the right to assistance of counsel and the right to call witnesses. Baumgartner v. Joughin, supra. The defendant cannot be compelled to testify against himself. Demetree v. State ex rel. Marsh, 89 So.2d 498 (Fla.1956).

Section 38.22, Florida Statutes, as amended in 1945, provides that all issues of law or fact shall be heard and determined by the judge. Apparently under this statute the defendant is not only precluded from considering a jury trial as a right but also the judge has no discretion to allow the defendant a jury trial. See State ex rel. Huie v. Lewis, supra, and Dodd v. State, supra, in which the court seems to assume this, such assumption seemingly being warranted by the terminology of the statute.

There is no reason to believe that the statute is unconstitutional as being in violation of section 11 of the Declaration of Rights of the Florida Constitution which provides, in part, that the accused in all criminal prosecutions shall have the right to a public trial by an impartial jury. Criminal contempt is not a crime; consequently, no criminal prosecution is involved. Neering v. State, 155 So.2d 874 (Fla. 1963); State ex rel. Saunders v. Boyer, 166 So.2d 694 (Fla. 2d DCA 1964); Ballengee v. State, 144 So.2d 68 (Fla. 2d DCA 1962).

Section 3 of the Declaration of Rights, providing that the right of trial by jury shall be secured to all and remain inviolate forever, also apparently is not violated. This provision has been construed many times as guaranteeing a jury trial in proceedings at common law, as practiced at the time of the adoption of the constitution (see, e.g., Hawkins v. Rellim Inv. Co., 92 Fla. 784, 110 So. 350 (1926)), i.e., it is applicable only to cases in which the right existed before the adoption of the constitution (see, e.g., State ex rel. Sellers v. Parker, 87 Fla. 181, 100 So. 260 (1924)). Section 3 was never intended to extend the right of a trial by jury beyond this point. Boyd v. Dade County, 123 So.2d 323 (Fla.1960).

There is some authority that trial by jury in indirect criminal contempt existed in the early common law, but this practice was eliminated by the Star Chamber with the result that for centuries the common law courts have punished indirect contempts without a jury trial. See 36 Mississippi Law Journal 106. The practice in Florida to date apparently has been consistent with this position. No case has been found in this state in which a person was tried by a jury for criminal contempt. See Justice Terrell's comment adverse to such jury trials in State ex rel. Huie v. Lewis, supra.

The United States Supreme Court has assumed the same position with reference to the dictates of the common law. Quoting from Eilenbecker v. District Court, 134 U.S. 31, 36, 10 S.Ct. 424, 33 L.Ed. 801 (1890), the Court stated, "If it has ever been understood that proceedings according to the common law for contempt of court have been subject to the right of trial by jury, we have been unable to find any instance of it." United States v. Barnett, 376 U.S. 681, 696, 84 S.Ct. 984, 12 L.Ed.2d 23 (1964). In answer to the contention that contempt proceedings without a jury were limited to trivial offenses, the Court stated, "[W]e find no basis for a determination that, at the time the Constitution was adopted, contempt was generally regarded as not extending to cases of serious misconduct." 376 U.S. at 701. There is little doubt, therefore, that a defendant in a criminal contempt case in Florida has no constitutional right to a trial by jury.

Proponents for such trials seemingly must depend on authorization by the legislature or Supreme Court of Florida to attain their objective. By enacting section 38.22, Florida Statutes, which impliedly prohibits trial by jury the legislature exhibited a legislative intent to remain consistent with the common law rule. A possible alternative is for the Supreme Court of Florida to promulgate a rule providing for such trials and assume the position that under its constitutional right to govern practice and procedure in the courts of Florida such rule would supersede section 38.22, Florida Statutes. It is believed that the supreme court has such authority. Accordingly, alternate proposals are offered for the court's consideration; the first provides for a jury trial unless waived by the defendant and the alternate is consistent with present practice.

(5) Disqualification of Judge. Provision for the disqualification of the judge is made in federal rule 42(b). The proposal is patterned after this rule.

Favorable comments concerning disqualification of judges in appropriate cases may be found in opinions of the Supreme Court of Florida. See Pennekamp v. State, 156 Fla. 227, 22 So.2d 875 (1945), and concurring opinion in State ex rel. Huie v. Lewis, supra.

(6) Verdict; Judgment. "Judgment" is deemed preferable to the term "order," since the proper procedure involves an adjudication of guilty. The use of "judgment" is consistent with present Florida practice. E.g., Dinnen v. State, 168 So.2d 703 (Fla. 2d DCA 1964); State ex rel. Byrd v. Anderson, 168 So.2d 554 (Fla. 1st DCA 1964).

The recital in the judgment of facts constituting the contempt serves to preserve for postconviction purposes a composite record of the offense by the person best qualified to make such recital: the judge. See Ryals v. United States, 69 F.2d 946 (5th Cir.1934), in which such procedure is referred to as "good practice."

(7) Sentence; Indirect Contempt. The substance of this subdivision is found in present sections 921.05(2), 921.07 and 921.13, Florida Statutes. While these sections are concerned with sentences in criminal cases, the First District Court of Appeal in 1964 held that unless a defendant convicted of criminal contempt is paid the same deference the defendant is not being accorded due process of law as provided in section 12 of the Declaration of Rights of the Florida Constitution and the Fourteenth Amendment of the Constitution of the United States. Neering v. State, 164 So.2d 29 (Fla. 1st DCA 1964).

Statement concerning the effect the adoption of this proposed rule will have on contempt statutes:

This rule is not concerned with the source of the power of courts to punish for contempt. It is concerned with desirable procedure to be employed in the implementation of such power. Consequently, its adoption will in no way affect the Florida statutes purporting to be legislative grants of authority to the courts to punish for contempt, viz., sections 38.22 (dealing with "all" courts), 932.03 (dealing with courts having original jurisdiction in criminal cases), and 39.13 (dealing with juvenile courts). This is true regardless of whether the source of power is considered to lie exclusively with the courts as an inherent power or is subject, at least in part, to legislative grant.

The adoption of the rule also will leave unaffected the numerous Florida statutes concerned with various situations considered by the legislature to be punishable as contempt (e.g., section 38.23, Florida Statutes), since these statutes deal with substantive rather than procedural law.

Section 38.22, Florida Statutes, as discussed in the preceding notes, is concerned with procedure in that it requires the court to hear and determine all questions of law or fact. Insofar, therefore, as criminal contempts are concerned the adoption of the alternate proposal providing for a jury trial will mean that the rule supersedes this aspect of the statute and the statute should be amended accordingly.

1972 Amendment. Same as prior rule.

XVII. POSTCONVICTION RELIEF

Rule 3.850. Motion to Vacate, Set Aside, or Correct Sentence

(a) Grounds for Motion. The following grounds may be claims for relief from judgment or release from custody by a person who has been tried and found guilty or has entered a plea of guilty or nolo contendere before a court established by the laws of Florida:

(1) The judgment was entered or sentence was imposed in violation of the Constitution or laws of the United States or the State of Florida.

(2) The court did not have jurisdiction to enter the judgment.

(3) The court did not have jurisdiction to impose the sentence.

(4) The sentence exceeded the maximum authorized by law.

(5) The plea was involuntary.

(6) The judgment or sentence is otherwise subject to collateral attack.

(b) Time Limitations. A motion to vacate a sentence that exceeds the limits provided by law may be filed at any time. No other motion shall be filed or considered pursuant to this rule if filed more than 2 years after the judgment and sentence become final unless it alleges that

(1) the facts on which the claim is predicated were unknown to the movant or the movant's attorney and could not have been ascertained by the exercise of due diligence, and the claim is made within 2 years of the time the new facts were or could have been discovered with the exercise of due diligence, or

(2) the fundamental constitutional right asserted was not established within the period provided for herein and has been held to apply retroactively, and the claim is made within 2 years of the date of the mandate of the decision announcing the retroactivity, or

(3) the defendant retained counsel to timely file a 3.850 motion and counsel, through neglect, failed to file the motion. A claim based on this exception shall

not be filed more than 2 years after the expiration of the time for filing a motion for postconviction relief.

(c) Contents of Motion. The motion must be under oath stating that the defendant has read the motion or that it has been read to him or her, that the defendant understands its content, and that all of the facts stated therein are true and correct. The motion must also include an explanation of:

(1) the judgment or sentence under attack and the court that rendered the same;

(2) whether the judgment resulted from a plea or a trial;

(3) whether there was an appeal from the judgment or sentence and the disposition thereof;

(4) whether a previous postconviction motion has been filed, and if so, how many;

(5) if a previous motion or motions have been filed, the reason or reasons the claim or claims in the present motion were not raised in the former motion or motions;

(6) the nature of the relief sought; and

(7) a brief statement of the facts and other conditions relied on in support of the motion.

This rule does not authorize relief based on grounds that could have or should have been raised at trial and, if properly preserved, on direct appeal of the judgment and sentence. If the defendant is filing a newly discovered evidence claim based on recanted trial testimony or on a newly discovered witness, the defendant shall include an affidavit from that person as an attachment to his or her motion. For all other newly discovered evidence claims, the defendant shall attach an affidavit from any person whose testimony is necessary to factually support the defendant's claim for relief. If the affidavit is not attached to the motion, the defendant shall provide an explanation why the required affidavit could not be obtained.

(d) Form of Motion. Motions shall be typewritten or hand-written in legible printed lettering, in blue or black ink, double-spaced, with margins no less than 1 inch on white 8 1/2–by–11 inch paper. No motion, including any memorandum of law, shall exceed 50 pages without leave of the court upon a showing of good cause.

(e) Amendments to Motion. When the court has entered an order under subdivision (f)(2) or (f)(3), granting the defendant an opportunity to amend the motion, any amendment to the motion must be served within 60 days. A motion may otherwise be amended at any time prior to either the entry of an order disposing of the motion or the entry of an order pursuant to subdivision (f)(5) or directing that an answer to the motion be filed pursuant to (f)(6), whichever occurs first. Leave of court is required for the filing of an amendment after the entry of an order pursuant to subdivision (f)(5) or (f)(6). Notwithstanding the timeliness of an amendment, the court need not consider new factual assertions contained in an amendment unless the amendment is under oath. New claims for relief contained in an amendment need not be considered by the court unless the amendment is filed within the time frame specified in subdivision (b).

(f) Procedure; Evidentiary Hearing; Disposition. On filing of a motion under this rule, the clerk shall forward the motion and file to the court. Disposition of the motion shall be in accordance with the following procedures, which are intended to result in a single, final, appealable order that disposes of all claims raised in the motion.

(1) *Untimely and Insufficient Motions.* If the motion is insufficient on its face, and the time to file a motion under this rule has expired prior to the filing of the motion, the court shall enter a final appealable order summarily denying the motion with prejudice.

(2) *Timely but Insufficient Motions.* If the motion is insufficient on its face, and the motion is timely filed under this rule, the court shall enter a nonfinal, nonappealable order allowing the defendant 60 days to amend the motion. If the amended motion is still insufficient or if the defendant fails to file an amended motion within the time allowed for such amendment, the court, in its discretion, may permit the defendant an additional opportunity to amend the motion or may enter a final, appealable order summarily denying the motion with prejudice.

(3) *Timely Motions Containing Some Insufficient Claims.* If the motion sufficiently states one or more claims for relief and it also attempts but fails to state additional claims, and the motion is timely filed under this rule, the court shall enter a nonappealable order granting the defendant 60 days to amend the motion to sufficiently state additional claims for relief. Any claim for which the insufficiency has not been cured within the time allowed for such amendment shall be summarily denied in an order that is a nonfinal, nonappealable order, which may be reviewed when a final, appealable order is entered.

(4) *Motions Partially Disposed of by the Court Record.* If the motion sufficiently states one or more claims for relief but the files and records in the case conclusively show that the defendant is not entitled to relief as to one or more claims, the claims that are conclusively refuted shall be summarily denied on the merits without a hearing. A copy of that portion of the files and records in the case that conclusively shows that the defendant is not entitled to relief as to one or more claims shall be attached to the order summarily denying these claims. The files and records in the case are the documents and exhibits previously filed in the case and those portions of the other proceedings in the case that can be transcribed. An order that does not resolve all the claims is a nonfinal, nonappealable order, which may be reviewed when a final, appealable order is entered.

(5) *Motions Conclusively Resolved by the Court Record.* If the motion is legally sufficient but all grounds in the motion can be conclusively resolved either as a matter of law or by reliance upon the records in the case, the motion shall be denied without a hearing by the entry of a final order. If the denial is based on the records in the case, a copy of that portion of the files and records that conclusively shows that the defendant is entitled to no relief shall be attached to the final order.

(6) *Motions Requiring a Response from the State Attorney.* Unless the motion, files, and records in the case conclusively show that the defendant is entitled to no relief, the court shall order the state attorney to file, within the time fixed by the court, an answer to the motion. The answer shall respond to the allegations contained in the defendant's sufficiently pleaded claims, describe any matters in avoidance of the sufficiently pleaded claims, state whether the defendant has used any other available state postconviction remedies including any other motion under this rule, and state whether the defendant has previously been afforded an evidentiary hearing.

(7) *Appointment of Counsel.* The court may appoint counsel to represent the defendant under this rule. The factors to be considered by the court in making this determination include: the adversary nature of the proceeding, the complexity of the proceeding, the complexity of the claims presented, the defendant's apparent level of intelligence and education, the need for an evidentiary hearing, and the need for substantial legal research.

(8) *Disposition by Evidentiary Hearing.*

(A) If an evidentiary hearing is required, the court shall grant a prompt hearing and shall cause notice to be served on the state attorney and the defendant or defendant's counsel, and shall determine the issues, and make findings of fact and conclusions of law with respect thereto.

(B) At an evidentiary hearing, the defendant shall have the burden of presenting evidence and the burden of proof in support of his or her motion, unless otherwise provided by law.

(C) The order issued after the evidentiary hearing shall resolve all the claims raised in the motion and shall be considered the final order for purposes of appeal.

(g) Defendant's Presence Not Required. The defendant's presence shall not be required at any hearing or conference held under this rule except at the evidentiary hearing on the merits of any claim.

(h) Successive Motions.

(1) A second or successive motion must be titled: "Second or Successive Motion for Postconviction Relief."

(2) A second or successive motion is an extraordinary pleading. Accordingly, a court may dismiss a second or successive motion if the court finds that it fails to allege new or different grounds for relief and the prior determination was on the merits or, if new and different grounds are alleged, the judge finds that the failure of the defendant or the attorney to assert those grounds in a prior motion constituted an abuse of the procedure or there was no good cause for the failure of the defendant or defendant's counsel to have asserted those grounds in a prior motion. When a motion is dismissed under this subdivision, a copy of that portion of the files and records necessary to support the court's ruling shall accompany the order denying the motion.

(i) Service on Parties. The clerk of the court shall promptly serve on the parties a copy of any order entered under this rule, noting thereon the date of service by an appropriate certificate of service.

(j) Rehearing. Any party may file a motion for rehearing of any order addressing a motion under this rule within 15 days of the date of service of the order. A motion for rehearing is not required to preserve any issue for review in the appellate court. A motion for rehearing must be based on a good faith belief that the court has overlooked a previously argued issue of fact or law or an argument based on a legal precedent or statute not available prior to the court's ruling. A response may be filed within 10 days of service of the motion. The trial court's order disposing of the motion for rehearing shall be filed within 15 days of the response but not later than 40 days from the date of the order of which rehearing is sought.

(k) Appeals. An appeal may be taken to the appropriate appellate court only from the final order disposing of the motion. All final orders denying motions for postconviction relief shall include a statement that the defendant has the right to appeal within 30 days of the rendition of the order. All nonfinal, nonappealable orders entered pursuant to subdivision (f) should include a statement that the defendant has no right to appeal the order until entry of the final order.

(*l*) Belated Appeals and Discretionary Review. Pursuant to the procedures outlined in Florida Rule of Appellate Procedure 9.141, a defendant may seek a belated appeal or discretionary review.

(m) Habeas Corpus. An application for writ of habeas corpus on behalf of a prisoner who is authorized to apply for relief by motion pursuant to this rule shall not be entertained if it appears that the applicant has failed to apply for relief, by motion, to the court that sentenced the applicant or that the court has denied the applicant relief, unless it also appears that the remedy by motion is inadequate or ineffective to test the legality of the applicant's detention.

(n) Certification of Defendant; Sanctions. No motion may be filed pursuant to this rule unless it is filed in good faith and with a reasonable belief that it is timely, has potential merit, and does not duplicate previous motions that have been disposed of by the court.

(1) By signing a motion pursuant to this rule, the defendant certifies that: the defendant has read the motion or that it has been read to the defendant and that the defendant understands its content; the motion is filed in good faith and with a reasonable belief that it is timely filed, has potential merit, and does not duplicate previous motions that have been disposed of by the court; and, the facts contained in the motion are true and correct.

(2) The defendant shall either certify that the defendant can understand English or, if the defendant cannot understand English, that the defendant has had the motion translated completely into a language that the defendant understands. The motion shall contain the name and address of the person who translated the motion and that person shall certify that he or she provided an accurate and complete translation to the defendant. Failure to include this information and certification in a motion shall be grounds for the entry of an order dismissing the motion pursuant to subdivision (f)(1), (f)(2), or (f)(3).

(3) Conduct prohibited under this rule includes, but is not limited to, the following: the filing of frivolous or malicious claims; the filing of any motion in bad faith or with reckless disregard for the truth; the filing of an application for habeas corpus subject to dismissal pursuant to subdivision (m); the willful violation of any provision of this rule; and the abuse of the legal process or procedures governed by this rule.

The court, upon its own motion or on the motion of a party, may determine whether a motion has been filed in violation of this rule. The court shall issue an order setting forth the facts indicating that the defendant has or may have engaged in prohibited conduct. The order shall direct the defendant to show cause, within a reasonable time limit set by the court, why the court should not find that the defendant has engaged in prohibited conduct under this rule and impose an appropriate sanction. Following the issuance of the order to show cause and the filing of any response by the defendant, and after such further hearing as the court may deem appropriate, the court shall make a final determination of whether the defendant engaged in prohibited conduct under this subsection.

(4) If the court finds by the greater weight of the evidence that the defendant has engaged in prohibited conduct under this rule, the court may impose one or more sanctions, including:

(A) contempt as otherwise provided by law;

(B) assessing the costs of the proceeding against the defendant;

(C) dismissal with prejudice of the defendant's motion;

(D) prohibiting the filing of further pro se motions under this rule and directing the clerk of court to summarily reject any further pro se motion under this rule;

(E) requiring that any further motions under this rule be signed by a member in good standing of The Florida Bar, who shall certify that there is a good faith basis for each claim asserted in the motion; and/or

(F) if the defendant is a prisoner, a certified copy of the order be forwarded to the appropriate institution or facility for consideration of disciplinary action against the defendant, including forfeiture of gain time pursuant to Chapter 944, Florida Statutes.

(5) If the court determines there is probable cause to believe that a sworn motion contains a false statement of fact constituting perjury, the court may refer the matter to the state attorney.

Amended Sept. 24, 1992, effective Jan. 1, 1993 (606 So.2d 227); Oct. 21, 1993, effective Jan. 1, 1994 (626 So.2d 198); May 27, 1999 (747 So.2d 931); May 27, 1999 (750 So.2d 592); Oct. 19, 2000 (779 So.2d 1290); Nov. 22, 2000 (789 So.2d 262); June 23, 2011, eff. July 1, 2011 (72 So.3d 735); April 18, 2013, revised Dec. 5, 2013, effective, *nunc pro tunc*, July 1, 2013 (132 So.3d 734); June 11, 2015, effective June 11, 2015 (167 So.3d 395).

Repeal

Rule 3.850 was repealed effective January 14, 2000, under the provisions of Laws 2000, c. 2000–3, § 10, to the extent that it was inconsistent with that act.

Readoption

Rule 3.850 was readopted as it existed prior to the effective date of Laws 2000, c. 2000–3, under the provisions of the Florida Supreme Court Order of February 7, 2000, 763 So.2d 273. See, also, Allen v. Butterworth, 756 So.2d 52.

Committee Notes

1972 Amendment. Same as prior rule. Former rule 3.860, previously deleted, now found in article 18, The Florida Bar Integration Rules.

1977 Amendment. Nothing has been taken from proposed rule 3.850. Additions have been made. The committee proceeded on the theory that generally the motions coming under the purview of the rule were filed by prisoners and will be considered ex parte.

The proposed amendment contemplates that in those cases where the trial court found the movant entitled to some relief, the state attorney would be noticed and given an opportunity to be heard. The rule further contemplates that if the appellate court reverses, it would do so with directions to conduct a hearing with notice to all parties.

(a), (b), (c), (d), (e)

The committee was of the opinion that the motion should contain the minimum prerequisites indicated in the lettered portions to permit the trial court to quickly ascertain whether or not the motion was entitled to consideration and, if not, provide for its return to the movant as unacceptable. This procedure is similar to federal rules dealing with postconviction motions.

The committee perceives that denial of a motion will either be based on the insufficiency of the motion itself or on the basis of the file or record which the trial court will have before it. The proposal provides for a simplified expeditious disposition of appeals in such cases. It is to be noted, however, that in those cases where the record is relied on as a basis for denial of the motion, it may in exceptional cases involve a substantial record, but the advantages of this procedure seem to justify coping with the unusual or exceptional case. It is the opinion of the committee that, in any order of denial based on the insufficiency of the motion or on the face of the record, trial courts will set forth specifically the basis of the court's ruling with sufficient specificity to delineate the issue for the benefit of appellate courts.

The committee thought that the provision permitting ex parte denial of a motion based on the face of the record was appropriate inasmuch as the movant was granted an opportunity for rehearing in which to point out any errors the court may have made, thus providing sufficient safeguards to ensure consideration of the prisoner's contentions.

The prisoner or movant's motion for rehearing will be a part of the record on appeal, thereby alerting the appellate court to the movant's dissatisfaction with the trial court's ruling.

1984 Amendment. The committee felt that provisions should be added to allow the court to consider why a subsequent motion was being filed and whether it was properly filed, similar to Federal Rule of Criminal Procedure 9(b) or 35.

The committee also felt that the court should have the authority to order the state to respond to a 3.850 motion by answer or other pleading as the court may direct.

The committee felt that even if a motion filed under rule 3.850 does not substantially comply with the requirements of the rule, the motion should still be filed and ruled on by the court. Hence the former provision authorizing the court to refuse to receive such a nonconforming motion has been removed and words allowing the presiding judge to summarily deny a noncomplying motion have been satisfied.

1992 Amendment. Pursuant to State v. District Court of Appeal of Florida, First District, 569 So.2d 439 (Fla.1990), motions seeking a belated direct appeal based on the ineffective assistance of counsel should be filed in the trial court under rule 3.850. Also, see rule 3.111(e) regarding trial counsel's duties before withdrawal after judgment and sentence.

1993 Amendment. This amendment is necessary to make this rule consistent with rule 3.851.

Court Commentary

1996 Court Commentary. Florida Rule of Judicial Administration 2.071(b) allows for telephonic and teleconferencing communication equipment to be utilized "for a motion hearing, pretrial conference, or a status conference." Teleconferencing sites have been established by the Department of Management Services, Division of Communications at various metropolitan locations in the state. The "Shevin Study" [1] examined, at this Court's request, the issue of delays in capital postconviction relief proceedings and noted that travel problems of counsel cause part of those delays. The Court strongly encourages the use of the new telephonic and teleconferencing technology for postconviction relief proceedings that do not require evidentiary hearings.

1. Letter from Robert L. Shevin "Re: Study of the Capital Collateral Representative" to Chief Justice Stephen H. Grimes (Feb. 26, 1996) (on file with the Supreme Court of Florida in No. 87,688).

2013 Amendment.

Rule 3.850 has been revised to address several issues identified by the Postconviction Rules Workgroup in 2006 and by the Criminal Court Steering Committee and the Subcommittee on Postconviction Relief in 2011.

Rule 3.850(d). New subdivision (d) is derived from the final two sentences formerly contained in subdivision (c).

Rule 3.850(e). Subdivision (e) was added to codify existing case law on amendments to postconviction motions and to comport with subdivision (f).

Rule 3.850(f). Subdivision (f) attempts to set out each of the different options that a trial judge has when considering a motion under this rule. It reflects the timeframe requirement of subdivision (b) and codifies existing case law regarding timely but facially insufficient motions, partial orders of denial, and the appointment of counsel. *See, e. g., Spera v. State*, 971 So. 2d 754 (Fla. 2007).

Rule 3.850(g). Subdivision (g) was previously contained in subdivision (e), but the language is largely derived from rule 3.851(c)(3).

Rule 3.850(h). Subdivision (h), formerly rule 3.850(f), was substantially rewritten.

Rule 3.850(i). Subdivision (i) is substantially the same as former subdivision (g).

Rule 3.850(j). Subdivision (j) allows both the state and the defendant the right to rehearing and is intended to allow the court to correct an obvious error without the expense and delay of a state appeal. *See King v. State*, 870 So. 2d 69 (Fla. 2d DCA 2003). The statement regarding finality is consistent with Florida Rule of Appellate Procedure 9.020(i) and is intended to clarify the date of rendition of the final order disposing of any motion under this rule.

Rule 3.850(k). Subdivision (k), formerly rule 3.850(i), was substantially rewritten to simplify the review process in both the trial and appellate courts and to provide for the efficient disposition of all claims in both courts. The requirement of a statement indicating whether the order is a nonfinal or final order subject to appeal is intended to ensure that all claims will be disposed of by the trial court and addressed in a single appeal.

Rule 3.850(*l*). Subdivision (*l*), formerly rule 3.850(j), reflects the consolidation of the subdivision with former rule 3.850(k).

Rule 3.850(n). Subdivision (n) is a substantial rewrite of former subdivision (m).

Rule 3.851. Collateral Relief After Death Sentence has Been Imposed and Affirmed on Direct Appeal

(a) Scope. This rule shall apply to all postconviction proceedings that commence upon issuance of the appellate mandate affirming the death sentence to include all motions and petitions for any type of postconviction or collateral relief brought by a defendant in state custody who has been sentenced to death and whose conviction and death sentence have been affirmed on direct appeal. It shall apply to all postconviction motions filed on or after January 1, 2015, by defendants who are under sentence of death. Motions pending on that date are governed by the version of this rule in effect immediately prior to that date.

(b) Appointment of Postconviction Counsel.

(1) Upon the issuance of the mandate affirming a judgment and sentence of death on direct appeal, the Supreme Court of Florida shall at the same time issue an order appointing the appropriate office of the Capital Collateral Regional Counsel or directing the trial court to immediately appoint counsel from the Registry of Attorneys maintained by the Justice Administrative Commission. The name of Registry Counsel shall be filed with the Supreme Court of Florida.

(2) Within 30 days of the issuance of the mandate, the Capital Collateral Regional Counsel or Registry Counsel shall file either a notice of appearance or a motion to withdraw in the trial court. Motions to withdraw filed more than 30 days after the issuance of the mandate shall not be entertained unless based on a specific conflict of interest as set forth in section 27.703, Florida Statutes.

(3) Within 15 days after Capital Collateral Regional Counsel or Registry Counsel files a motion to withdraw, the chief judge or assigned judge shall rule on the motion and appoint new postconviction counsel if necessary. The appointment of new collateral counsel shall be from the Registry of attorneys maintained by the Justice Administrative Commission unless the case is administratively transferred to another Capital Collateral Regional Counsel.

(4) In every capital postconviction case, one lawyer shall be designated as lead counsel for the defendant. The lead counsel shall be the defendant's primary lawyer in all state court litigation. No lead counsel shall be permitted to appear for a limited purpose on behalf of a defendant in a capital postconviction proceeding.

(5) After the filing of a notice of appearance, Capital Collateral Regional Counsel, Registry Counsel, or a private attorney shall represent the defendant in the state courts until a judge allows withdrawal or until the sentence is reversed, reduced, or carried out, regardless of whether another attorney represents the defendant in a federal court.

(6) A defendant who has been sentenced to death may not represent himself or herself in a capital postconviction proceeding in state court. The only bases for a defendant to seek to dismiss postconviction counsel in state court shall be pursuant to statute due to actual conflict or subdivision (i) of this rule.

(c) Preliminary Procedures.

(1) *Judicial Assignment and Responsibilities.* Within 30 days of the issuance of mandate affirming a judgment and sentence of death on direct appeal, the chief judge shall assign the case to a judge qualified under the Rules of Judicial Administration to conduct capital proceedings. The assigned judge is responsible for case management to ensure compliance with statutes, rules, and administrative orders that impose processing steps, time deadlines, and reporting requirements for capital postconviction litigation. From the time of assignment, the judge must issue case management orders for every step of the capital postconviction process, including at the conclusion of all hearings and conferences.

(2) *Status Conferences.* The assigned judge shall conduct a status conference not later than 90 days after the judicial assignment, and shall hold status conferences at least every 90 days thereafter until the evidentiary hearing has been completed or the motion has been ruled on without a hearing. The attorneys, with leave of the trial court, may appear electronically at the status conferences. Requests to appear electronically shall be liberally granted. Pending motions, disputes involving public records, or any other matters ordered by the court shall be heard at the status conferences.

(3) *Defendant's Presence Not Required.* The defendant's presence shall not be required at any hearing or conference held under this rule, except at the evidentiary hearing on the merits of any claim and at any hearing involving conflict with or removal of collateral counsel.

(4) *Duties of Defense Counsel.* Within 45 days of appointment of postconviction counsel, the defendant's trial counsel shall provide to postconviction counsel a copy of the original file including all work product not otherwise subject to a protective order and information pertaining to the defendant's capital case which was created and obtained during the representation of the defendant. Postconviction counsel shall maintain the confidentiality of all confidential information received. Postconviction counsel shall bear the costs of

any copying. The defendant's trial counsel must retain the defendant's original file.

(5) *Record on Direct Appeal.* The Clerk of the Circuit Court shall retain a copy of the record for the direct appeal when the record is transmitted to the Supreme Court of Florida. The Clerk of the Supreme Court of Florida shall deliver the record on appeal to the records repository within 30 days after the appointment of postconviction counsel.

(d) Time Limitation.

(1) Any motion to vacate judgment of conviction and sentence of death shall be filed by the defendant within 1 year after the judgment and sentence become final. For the purposes of this rule, a judgment is final:

(A) on the expiration of the time permitted to file in the United States Supreme Court a petition for writ of certiorari seeking review of the Supreme Court of Florida decision affirming a judgment and sentence of death (90 days after the opinion becomes final); or

(B) on the disposition of the petition for writ of certiorari by the United States Supreme Court, if filed.

(2) No motion shall be filed or considered pursuant to this rule if filed beyond the time limitation provided in subdivision (d)(1) unless it alleges:

(A) the facts on which the claim is predicated were unknown to the movant or the movant's attorney and could not have been ascertained by the exercise of due diligence, or

(B) the fundamental constitutional right asserted was not established within the period provided for in subdivision (d)(1) and has been held to apply retroactively, or

(C) postconviction counsel, through neglect, failed to file the motion.

(3) All petitions for extraordinary relief in which the Supreme Court of Florida has original jurisdiction, including petitions for writs of habeas corpus, shall be filed simultaneously with the initial brief filed on behalf of the death-sentenced defendant in the appeal of the circuit court's order on the initial motion for postconviction relief filed under this rule.

(4) If the governor signs a death warrant before the expiration of the time limitation in subdivision (d)(1), the Supreme Court of Florida, on a defendant's request, will grant a stay of execution to allow any postconviction relief motions to proceed in a timely and orderly manner.

(5) An extension of time may be granted by the Supreme Court of Florida for the filing of postconviction pleadings if the defendant's counsel makes a showing that due to exceptional circumstances, counsel was unable to file the postconviction pleadings within the 1–year period established by this rule.

(e) Contents of Motion.

(1) *Initial Motion.* A motion filed under this rule is an initial postconviction motion if no state court has previously ruled on a postconviction motion challenging the same judgment and sentence. An initial motion and memorandum of law filed under this rule shall not exceed 75 pages exclusive of the attachments. Each claim or subclaim shall be separately pled and shall be sequentially numbered beginning with claim number 1. If upon motion or upon the court's own motion, a judge determines that this portion of the rule has not been followed, the judge shall give the movant 30 days to amend. If no amended motion is filed, the judge shall deem the noncompliant claim, subclaim, and/or argument waived. Attachments shall include, but are not limited to, the judgment and sentence. The memorandum of law shall set forth the applicable case law supporting the granting of relief as to each separately pled claim. This rule does not authorize relief based upon claims that could have or should have been raised at trial and, if properly preserved, on direct appeal of the judgment and sentence. If claims that were raised on appeal or should have or could have been raised on appeal are contained in the motion, the memorandum of law shall contain a brief statement explaining why these claims are being raised on postconviction relief. The motion need not be under oath or signed by the defendant but shall include:

(A) a description of the judgment and sentence under attack and the court that rendered the same;

(B) a statement of each issue raised on appeal and the disposition thereof;

(C) the nature of the relief sought;

(D) a detailed allegation of the factual basis for any claim for which an evidentiary hearing is sought;

(E) a detailed allegation as to the basis for any purely legal or constitutional claim for which an evidentiary hearing is not required and the reason that this claim could not have been or was not raised on direct appeal; and

(F) a certification from the attorney that he or she has discussed the contents of the motion fully with the defendant, that he or she has complied with Rule 4–1.4 of the Rules of Professional Conduct, and that the motion is filed in good faith.

(2) *Successive Motion.* A motion filed under this rule is successive if a state court has previously ruled on a postconviction motion challenging the same judgment and sentence. A claim raised in a successive motion shall be dismissed if the trial court finds that it fails to allege new or different grounds for relief and the prior determination was on the merits; or, if new and different grounds are alleged, the trial court finds that the failure to assert those grounds in a prior motion constituted an abuse of the procedure; or, if the trial court finds there was no good cause for

failing to assert those grounds in a prior motion; or, if the trial court finds the claim fails to meet the time limitation exceptions set forth in subdivision (d)(2)(A), (d)(2)(B), or (d)(2)(C).

A successive motion shall not exceed 25 pages, exclusive of attachments, and shall include:

(A) all of the pleading requirements of an initial motion under subdivision (e)(1);

(B) the disposition of all previous claims raised in postconviction proceedings and the reason or reasons the claim or claims raised in the present motion were not raised in the former motion or motions;

(C) if based upon newly discovered evidence, *Brady v. Maryland*, 373 U.S. 83 (1963), or *Giglio v. United States*, 405 U.S. 150 (1972), the following:

(i) the names, addresses, and telephone numbers of all witnesses supporting the claim;

(ii) a statement that the witness will be available, should an evidentiary hearing be scheduled, to testify under oath to the facts alleged in the motion or affidavit;

(iii) if evidentiary support is in the form of documents, copies of all documents shall be attached, including any affidavits obtained; and

(iv) as to any witness or document listed in the motion or attachment to the motion, a statement of the reason why the witness or document was not previously available.

(f) Procedure; Evidentiary Hearing; Disposition.

(1) *Filing and Service.* All pleadings in the postconviction proceeding shall be filed with the clerk of the trial court and served on the assigned judge, opposing party, and the attorney general. Upon the filing of any original court document in the postconviction proceeding, the clerk of the trial court shall determine that the assigned judge has received a copy. All motions other than the postconviction motion itself shall be accompanied by a notice of hearing.

(2) *Duty of Clerk.* A motion filed under this rule shall be immediately delivered to the chief judge or the assigned judge along with the court file.

(3) *Answer.*

(A) Answer to the Initial Motion. Within 60 days of the filing of an initial motion, the state shall file its answer. The answer and accompanying memorandum of law shall not exceed 75 pages, exclusive of attachments and exhibits. The answer shall address the legal insufficiency of any claim in the motion, respond to the allegations of the motion, and address any procedural bars. The answer shall use the same claim numbering system contained in the defendant's initial motion. As to any claims of legal insufficiency or procedural bar, the state shall include a short statement of any applicable case law.

(B) Answer to a Successive Motion. Within 20 days of the filing of a successive motion, the state shall file its answer. The answer shall not exceed 25 pages, exclusive of attachments and exhibits. The answer shall use the same claim numbering system contained in the defendant's motion. The answer shall specifically respond to each claim in the motion and state the reason(s) that an evidentiary hearing is or is not required.

(4) *Amendments.* A motion filed under this rule may not be amended unless good cause is shown. A copy of the claim sought to be added must be attached to the motion to amend. The trial court may in its discretion grant a motion to amend provided that the motion to amend was filed at least 45 days before the scheduled evidentiary hearing. Granting a motion under this subdivision shall not be a basis for granting a continuance of the evidentiary hearing unless a manifest injustice would occur if a continuance was not granted. If amendment is allowed, the state shall file an amended answer within 20 days after the judge allows the motion to be amended.

(5) *Case Management Conference; Evidentiary Hearing.*

(A) Initial Postconviction Motion. No later than 90 days after the state files its answer to an initial motion, the trial court shall hold a case management conference. At the case management conference, the defendant shall disclose all documentary exhibits that he or she intends to offer at the evidentiary hearing and shall file and serve an exhibit list of all such exhibits and a witness list with the names and addresses of any potential witnesses. All expert witnesses shall be specifically designated on the witness list and copies of all expert reports shall be attached. Within 60 days after the case management conference, the state shall disclose all documentary exhibits that it intends to offer at the evidentiary hearing and shall file and serve an exhibit list of all such exhibits and a witness list with the names and addresses of any potential witnesses. All expert witnesses shall be specifically designated on the witness list and copies of all expert reports shall be attached. At the case management conference, the trial court shall:

(i) schedule an evidentiary hearing, to be held within 150 days, on claims listed by the defendant as requiring a factual determination;

(ii) hear argument on any purely legal claims not based on disputed facts; and

(iii) resolve disputes arising from the exchange of information under this subdivision.

(B) Successive Postconviction Motion. Within 30 days after the state files its answer to a successive motion for postconviction relief, the trial court shall hold a case management conference. At the case management conference, the trial court also shall determine whether an evidentiary hearing should be held and hear argument on any purely legal claims not based on disputed facts. If the motion, files, and records in the case conclusively show that the movant is entitled to no relief, the motion may be denied without an evidentiary hearing. If the trial court determines that an evidentiary hearing should be held, the court shall schedule the hearing to be held within 90 days. If a death warrant has been signed, the trial court shall expedite these time periods in accordance with subdivision (h) of this rule.

(C) Extension of Time to Hold Evidentiary Hearing. The trial court also may for good cause extend the time for holding an evidentiary hearing for up to 90 days.

(D) Taking Testimony. Upon motion, or upon its own motion and without the consent of any party, the court may permit a witness to testify at the evidentiary hearing by contemporaneous video communication equipment that makes the witness visible to all parties during the testimony. There must be appropriate safeguards for the court to maintain sufficient control over the equipment and the transmission of the testimony so the court may stop the communication to accommodate objections or prevent prejudice. If testimony is taken through video communication equipment, there must be a notary public or other person authorized to administer oaths in the witness's jurisdiction who is present with the witness and who administers the oath consistent with the laws of the jurisdiction where the witness is located. The cost for the use of video communication equipment is the responsibility of either the requesting party or, if upon its own motion, the court.

(E) Procedures After Evidentiary Hearing. Immediately following an evidentiary hearing, the trial court shall order a transcript of the hearing, which shall be filed within 10 days if real-time transcription was utilized, or within 45 days if real-time transcription was not utilized. The trial judge may permit written closing arguments instead of oral closing arguments. If the trial court permits the parties to submit written closing arguments, the arguments shall be filed by both parties within 30 days of the filing of the transcript of the hearing. No answer or reply arguments shall be allowed. Written arguments shall be in compliance with the requirements for briefs in rule 9.210(a)(1) and (a)(2), shall not exceed 60 pages without leave of court, and shall include proposed findings of facts and conclusions of law, with citations to authority and to appropriate portions of the transcript of the hearing.

(F) Rendition of the Order. If the court does not permit written closing arguments, the court shall render its order within 30 days of the filing of the transcript of the hearing. If the court permits written closing arguments, the court shall render its order within 30 days of the filing of the last written closing argument and no later than 60 days from the filing of the transcript of the hearing. The court shall rule on each claim considered at the evidentiary hearing and all other claims raised in the motion, making detailed findings of fact and conclusions of law with respect to each claim, and attaching or referencing such portions of the record as are necessary to allow for meaningful appellate review. The order issued after the evidentiary hearing shall resolve all the claims raised in the motion and shall be considered the final order for purposes of appeal. The clerk of the trial court shall promptly serve upon the parties and the attorney general a copy of the final order, with a certificate of service.

(6) *Experts and Other Witnesses.* All expert witnesses who will testify at the evidentiary hearing must submit written reports, which shall be disclosed to opposing counsel as provided in subdivision (f)(5)(A). If the defendant intends to offer expert testimony of his or her mental status, the state shall be entitled to have the defendant examined by its own mental health expert. If the defendant fails to cooperate with the state's expert, the trial court may, in its discretion, proceed as provided in rule 3.202(e).

(7) *Rehearing.* Motions for rehearing shall be filed within 15 days of the rendition of the trial court's order and a response thereto filed within 10 days thereafter. A motion for rehearing shall be based on a good faith belief that the court has overlooked a previously argued issue of fact or law or an argument based on a legal precedent or statute not available prior to the court's ruling. The trial court's order disposing of the motion for rehearing shall be rendered not later than 30 days from the filing of the motion for rehearing. If no order is filed within 30 days from the filing of the motion for rehearing, the motion is deemed denied. A motion for rehearing is not required to preserve any issue for review.

(8) *Appeals.* Any party may appeal a final order entered on a defendant's motion for rule 3.851 relief by filing a notice of appeal with the clerk of the lower tribunal within 30 days of the rendition of the order to be reviewed. Pursuant to the procedures outlined in Florida Rule of Appellate Procedure 9.142, a defendant under sentence of death may petition for a belated appeal.

(g) Incompetence to Proceed in Capital Collateral Proceedings.

(1) A death-sentenced defendant pursuing collateral relief under this rule who is found by the court to be mentally incompetent shall not be proceeded against if there are factual matters at issue, the development or resolution of which require the defendant's input. However, all collateral relief issues that involve only matters of record and claims that do not require the defendant's input shall proceed in collateral proceedings notwithstanding the defendant's incompetency.

(2) Collateral counsel may file a motion for competency determination and an accompanying certificate of counsel that the motion is made in good faith and on reasonable grounds to believe that the death-sentenced defendant is incompetent to proceed.

(3) If, at any stage of a postconviction proceeding, the court determines that there are reasonable grounds to believe that a death-sentenced defendant is incompetent to proceed and that factual matters are at issue, the development or resolution of which require the defendant's input, a judicial determination of incompetency is required.

(4) The motion for competency examination shall be in writing and shall allege with specificity the factual matters at issue and the reason that competent consultation with the defendant is necessary with respect to each factual matter specified. To the extent that it does not invade the lawyer-client privilege with collateral counsel, the motion shall contain a recital of the specific observations of, and conversations with, the death-sentenced defendant that have formed the basis of the motion.

(5) If the court finds that there are reasonable grounds to believe that a death-sentenced defendant is incompetent to proceed in a postconviction proceeding in which factual matters are at issue, the development or resolution of which require the defendant's input, the court shall order the defendant examined by no more than 3, nor fewer than 2, experts before setting the matter for a hearing. The court may seek input from the death-sentenced defendant's counsel and the state attorney before appointment of the experts.

(6) The order appointing experts shall:

(A) identify the purpose of the evaluation and specify the area of inquiry that should be addressed;

(B) specify the legal criteria to be applied; and

(C) specify the date by which the report shall be submitted and to whom it shall be submitted.

(7) Counsel for both the death-sentenced defendant and the state may be present at the examination, which shall be conducted at a date and time convenient for all parties and the Department of Corrections.

(8) On appointment by the court, the experts shall examine the death-sentenced defendant with respect to the issue of competence to proceed, as specified by the court in its order appointing the experts to evaluate the defendant, and shall evaluate the defendant as ordered.

(A) The experts first shall consider factors related to the issue of whether the death-sentenced defendant meets the criteria for competence to proceed, that is, whether the defendant has sufficient present ability to consult with counsel with a reasonable degree of rational understanding and whether the defendant has a rational as well as factual understanding of the pending collateral proceedings.

(B) In considering the issue of competence to proceed, the experts shall consider and include in their report:

(i) the defendant's capacity to understand the adversary nature of the legal process and the collateral proceedings;

(ii) the defendant's ability to disclose to collateral counsel facts pertinent to the postconviction proceeding at issue; and

(iii) any other factors considered relevant by the experts and the court as specified in the order appointing the experts.

(C) Any written report submitted by an expert shall:

(i) identify the specific matters referred for evaluation;

(ii) describe the evaluative procedures, techniques, and tests used in the examination and the purpose or purposes for each;

(iii) state the expert's clinical observations, findings, and opinions on each issue referred by the court for evaluation, and indicate specifically those issues, if any, on which the expert could not give an opinion; and

(iv) identify the sources of information used by the expert and present the factual basis for the expert's clinical findings and opinions.

(9) If the experts find that the death-sentenced defendant is incompetent to proceed, the experts shall report on any recommended treatment for the defendant to attain competence to proceed. In considering the issues relating to treatment, the experts shall report on:

(A) the mental illness or intellectual disability causing the incompetence;

(B) the treatment or treatments appropriate for the mental illness or intellectual disability of the defendant and an explanation of each of the possible treatment alternatives in order of choices; and

(C) the likelihood of the defendant attaining competence under the treatment recommended, an assessment of the probable duration of the treatment required to restore competence, and the probability that the defendant will attain competence to proceed in the foreseeable future.

(10) Within 30 days after the experts have completed their examinations of the death-sentenced defendant, the court shall schedule a hearing on the issue of the defendant's competence to proceed.

(11) If, after a hearing, the court finds the defendant competent to proceed, or, after having found the defendant incompetent, finds that competency has been restored, the court shall enter its order so finding and shall proceed with a postconviction motion. The defendant shall have 60 days to amend his or her

rule 3.851 motion only as to those issues that the court found required factual consultation with counsel.

(12) If the court does not find the defendant incompetent, the order shall contain:

(A) findings of fact relating to the issues of competency;

(B) copies of the reports of the examining experts; and

(C) copies of any other psychiatric, psychological, or social work reports submitted to the court relative to the mental state of the death-sentenced defendant.

(13) If the court finds the defendant incompetent or finds the defendant competent subject to the continuation of appropriate treatment, the court shall follow the procedures set forth in rule 3.212(c), except that, to the extent practicable, any treatment shall take place at a custodial facility under the direct supervision of the Department of Corrections.

(h) After Death Warrant Signed.

(1) *Judicial Assignment.* The chief judge of the circuit shall assign the case to a judge qualified under the Rules of Judicial Administration to conduct capital cases as soon as notification of the death warrant is received.

(2) *Calendar Advancement.* Proceedings after a death warrant has been issued shall take precedence over all other cases. The assigned judge shall make every effort to resolve scheduling conflicts with other cases including cancellation or rescheduling of hearings or trials and requesting senior judge assistance.

(3) *Schedule of Proceedings.* The time limitations in this rule shall not apply after a death warrant has been signed. All motions shall be heard expeditiously considering the time limitations set by the date of execution and the time required for appellate review.

(4) *Location of Hearings.* The location of hearings after a death warrant is signed shall be determined by the trial judge considering the availability of witnesses or evidence, the security problems involved in the case, and any other factor determined by the trial court.

(5) *Postconviction Motions.* All motions filed after a death warrant is issued shall be considered successive motions and subject to the content requirement of subdivision (e)(2) of this rule.

(6) *Case Management Conference.* The assigned judge shall schedule a case management conference as soon as reasonably possible after receiving notification that a death warrant has been signed. During the case management conference the court shall set a time for filing a postconviction motion and shall schedule a hearing to determine whether an evidentiary hearing should be held and hear argument on any purely legal claims not based on disputed facts. If the motion, files, and records in the case conclusively show that the movant is entitled to no relief, the motion may be denied without an evidentiary hearing. If the trial court determines that an evidentiary hearing should be held, the court shall schedule the hearing to be held as soon as reasonably possible considering the time limitations set by the date of execution and the time required for appellate review.

(7) *Reporting.* The assigned judge shall require the proceedings conducted under death warrant to be reported using the most advanced and accurate technology available in general use at the location of the hearing. The proceedings shall be transcribed expeditiously considering the time limitations set by the execution date.

(8) *Procedures After Hearing.* The court shall obtain a transcript of all proceedings and shall render its order as soon as possible after the hearing is concluded. A copy of the final order shall be electronically transmitted to the Supreme Court of Florida and to the attorneys of record.

(9) *Transmittal of Record.* The record shall be immediately delivered to the clerk of the Supreme Court of Florida by the clerk of the trial court or as ordered by the assigned judge. The record shall also be electronically transmitted if the technology is available. A notice of appeal shall not be required to transmit the record.

(i) Dismissal of Postconviction Proceedings.

(1) This subdivision applies only when a defendant seeks both to dismiss pending postconviction proceedings and to discharge collateral counsel.

(2) If the defendant files the motion pro se, the Clerk of the Court shall serve copies of the motion on counsel of record for both the defendant and the state. Counsel of record may file responses within 10 days.

(3) The trial judge shall review the motion and the responses and schedule a hearing. The defendant, collateral counsel, and the state shall be present at the hearing.

(4) The judge shall examine the defendant at the hearing and shall hear argument of the defendant, collateral counsel, and the state. No fewer than 2 or more than 3 qualified experts shall be appointed to examine the defendant if the judge concludes that there are reasonable grounds to believe the defendant is not mentally competent for purposes of this rule. The experts shall file reports with the court setting forth their findings. Thereafter, the court shall conduct an evidentiary hearing and enter an order setting forth findings of competency or incompetency.

(5) If the defendant is found to be incompetent for purposes of this rule, the court shall deny the motion without prejudice.

(6) If the defendant is found to be competent for purposes of this rule, the court shall conduct a complete (*Durocher/Faretta*) inquiry to determine whether the defendant knowingly, freely and voluntarily

wants to dismiss pending postconviction proceedings and discharge collateral counsel.

(7) If the court determines that the defendant has made the decision to dismiss pending postconviction proceedings and discharge collateral counsel knowingly, freely, and voluntarily, the court shall enter an order dismissing all pending postconviction proceedings and discharging collateral counsel. But if the court determines that the defendant has not made the decision to dismiss pending postconviction proceedings and discharge collateral counsel knowingly, freely, and voluntarily, the court shall enter an order denying the motion without prejudice.

(8) If the court grants the motion:

(A) a copy of the motion, the order, and the transcript of the hearing or hearings conducted on the motion shall be forwarded to the Clerk of the Supreme Court of Florida within 30 days; and

(B) discharged counsel shall, within 10 days after issuance of the order, file with the clerk of the circuit court 2 copies of a notice seeking review in the Supreme Court of Florida, and shall, within 20 days after the filing of the transcript, serve an initial brief. Both the defendant and the state may serve responsive briefs. Briefs shall be served as prescribed by rule 9.210.

(9) If the court denies the motion, the defendant may seek review as prescribed by Florida Rule of Appellate Procedure 9.142(b).

(j) Attorney General Notification to Clerk. The Office of the Attorney General shall notify the clerk of the supreme court when it believes the defendant has completed his or her direct appeal, initial postconviction proceeding in state court, and habeas corpus proceeding and appeal therefrom in federal court. The Office of the Attorney General shall serve a copy of the notification on defendant's counsel of record.

Amended July 12, 2001, effective Oct. 1, 2001; Oct. 1, 2001 (802 So.2d 298); Sept. 19, 2002 (828 So.2d 999); Dec. 7, 2006, effective Jan. 1, 2007 (945 So.2d 1124); Dec. 30, 2008 (1 So.3d 163); Nov. 19, 2009, effective Jan. 1, 2010 (26 So.3d 534); June 23, 2011, eff. July 1, 2011 (72 So.3d 735); Oct. 18, 2012, effective Dec. 1, 2012, April 1, 2013, Oct. 1, 2013 (102 So.3d 451); Nov. 8, 2012, effective Jan. 1, 2013 (104 So.3d 304); April 18, 2013, revised Dec. 5, 2013, effective, *nunc pro tunc*, July 1, 2013 (132 So.3d 734); Dec. 12, 2013 (132 So.3d 123); July 3, 2014, effective Jan. 1, 2015 (148 So.3d 1171); Jan. 29, 2015, effective Jan. 29, 2015 (156 So.3d 1036).

Repeal

Rule 3.851 was repealed effective January 14, 2000, under the provisions of Laws 2000, c. 2000–3, § 10.

Readoption

Rule 3.851 was readopted as it existed prior to the effective date of Laws 2000, c. 2000–3, under the provisions of the Florida Supreme Court Order of February 7, 2000, 763 So.2d 273. See, also, Allen v. Butterworth, 756 So.2d 52.

Court Commentary

1993 Adoption. This rule is consistent with the recommendation of the Supreme Court Committee on Postconviction Relief in Capital Cases, which was created because of the substantial delays in the death penalty postconviction relief process. The committee was created because of the inability of the capital collateral representative to properly represent all death penalty inmates in postconviction relief cases and because of the resulting substantial delays in those cases. That committee recognized that, to make the process work properly, each death row prisoner should have counsel available to represent him or her in postconviction relief proceedings. The committee found that one of the major problems with the process was that the triggering mechanism to start or assure movement of the postconviction relief proceedings was the signing of a death warrant. In a number of instances, the courts were not aware of the problems concerning representation of a defendant until a death warrant was signed. In other instances, the committee found that, when postconviction relief motions had been filed, they clearly had not moved at an orderly pace and the signing of a death warrant was being used as a means to expedite the process. The committee recommended that specific named counsel should be designated to represent each prisoner not later than 30 days after the defendant's judgment and sentence of death becomes final. To assure that representation, the committee's report noted that it was essential that there be adequate funding of the capital collateral representative and sought temporary assistance from The Florida Bar in providing pro bono representation for some inmates.

There is a justification for the reduction of the time period for a capital prisoner as distinguished from a noncapital prisoner, who has two years to file a postconviction relief proceeding. A capital prisoner will have counsel immediately available to represent him or her in a postconviction relief proceeding, while counsel is not provided or constitutionally required for noncapital defendants to whom the two-year period applies.

In the event the capital collateral representative is not fully funded and available to provide proper representation for all death penalty defendants, the reduction in the time period would not be justified and would necessarily have to be repealed, and this Court will forthwith entertain a petition for the repeal of the rule. In this context, it is important to emphasize that the governor agrees that absent the circumstance where a competent death-sentenced individual voluntarily requests that a death warrant be signed, no death warrants will be issued during the initial round of federal and state review, provided that counsel for death penalty defendants is proceeding in a timely and diligent manner. This Court agrees that the initial round of postconviction proceedings should proceed in a deliberate but timely manner without the pressure of a pending death warrant. Subdivision 3.851(b)(4) above addresses concerns of The Florida Bar and The Florida Bar Foundation.

The provisions of the present rule 3.851 providing for time periods where a 60–day warrant is signed by the governor are abolished because they are unnecessary if the guidelines are followed. The proceedings and grounds for postconviction relief remain as provided under Florida Rule of Criminal Procedure 3.850, which include, as one of the grounds, the opportunity for a defendant to present newly discovered evidence in accordance with Scott v. Dugger, 604 So. 2d 465 (Fla. 1992), Jones v. State, 591 So. 2d 911 (Fla. 1991), and Richardson v. State, 546 So. 2d 1037 (Fla. 1989).

1996 Amendment. Subdivision (c) is added to make the Court's decision in Huff v. State, 622 So. 2d 982 (Fla. 1993), applicable to all rule 3.850 motions filed by a prisoner who has been sentenced to death. Florida Rule of Judicial Administration 2.071(b) allows for telephonic and teleconferencing communication equipment to be utilized "for a motion hearing, pretrial conference, or a status conference." Teleconferencing sites have been established by the Department of Management Services, Division of Communications at various metropolitan locations in the state. The "Shevin Study" examined, at this Court's request, the issue of delays in capital postconviction relief proceedings and noted that travel problems of counsel cause part of those delays. The Court strongly encourages the use of the new telephonic and teleconferencing technology for postconviction relief proceedings that do not require evidentiary hearings, such as the hearing required under subdivision (c) of this rule. Only the attorneys need be involved in a hearing held under subdivision (c) of this rule; attendance of the postconviction defendant is not required.

2001 Amendment. Several new procedures are added to rule 3.851. New subdivision (b), Appointment of Postconviction Counsel, is added to ensure appointment of postconviction counsel upon the Supreme Court of Florida's issuance of mandate on direct appeal. New subdivision (c), Preliminary Procedures, provides for, among other things, the assignment of a qualified judge within 30 days after mandate issues on direct appeal and status conferences every 90 days after the assignment until the evidentiary hearing has been completed or the motion has been ruled on without a hearing. These status conferences are intended to provide a forum for the timely resolution of public records issues and other preliminary matters. New subdivision (f), Procedure; Evidentiary Hearing; Disposition, sets forth general procedures. Most significantly, that subdivision requires an evidentiary hearing on claims listed in an initial motion as requiring a factual determination. The Court has identified the failure to hold evidentiary hearings on initial motions as a major cause of delay in the capital postconviction process and has determined that, in most cases, requiring an evidentiary hearing on initial motions presenting factually based claims will avoid this cause of delay. See Amendments to Florida Rules of Criminal Procedure 3.851, 3.852 and 3.993, 772 So. 2d 488, 491 (Fla. 2000).

2006 Amendment. The amendments provide for the appointment of Registry Counsel in areas of the state that are not served by a Capital Collateral Regional Counsel. Counsel are allowed to appear at status conferences electronically to authorize both telephonic and video appearances.

2013 Amendment. Only minor amendments are made to rule 3.851.

Criminal Court Steering Committee Note

2014 Amendment. The rule was amended to comply with the "Timely Justice Act of 2013," chapter 2013–216, Laws of Florida, and to preclude extended postconviction litigation. Because the Sixth Amendment does not apply to postconviction proceedings, the Steering Committee concluded that a defendant has no constitutional right to self-representation in postconviction matters. The Steering Committee also concluded that the capital postconviction process would function more effectively if a defendant were represented by an attorney, unless the defendant seeks to dismiss postconviction proceedings and discharge counsel pursuant to subdivision (i). The Steering Committee concluded that the lead attorney should not be allowed to participate in capital postconviction litigation on a limited basis and that the lead attorney should remain in the case until the litigation is concluded or until the court allows withdrawal. The Steering Committee also determined that the postconviction process would not work efficiently unless the trial judge was responsible for case management. Case management orders are required throughout the postconviction process in order to maintain a capital postconviction computer database.

Under the amended rule, the clerk of the trial court is required to retain a copy of the record so that it will be available for postconviction litigation, especially following issuance of the death warrant. Additionally, the Steering Committee added provisions to the pleading requirements for motions and created a provision that allows for written closing argument memoranda, formalizing by rule a practice that is already utilized throughout the state in capital postconviction proceedings. In an effort to prevent delay, the amended rule requires written reports from experts who will testify at the evidentiary hearing, and allows for witnesses to testify via videoconferencing, even over the objections of the parties. Finally, the amended rule requires the Attorney General to inform the Clerk of the Florida Supreme Court and the defendant's counsel of record when a defendant has completed his or her litigation in order for the Clerk to report to the Governor pursuant to Florida Statute 922.052.

Rule 3.852. Capital Postconviction Public Records Production

(a) Applicability and Scope.

(1) This rule is applicable only to the production of public records for capital postconviction defendants and does not change or alter the time periods specified in Florida Rule of Criminal Procedure 3.851. Furthermore, this rule does not affect, expand, or

limit the production of public records for any purposes other than use in a proceeding held pursuant to rule 3.850 or rule 3.851.

(2) This rule shall not be a basis for renewing requests that have been initiated previously or for relitigating issues pertaining to production of public records upon which a court has ruled prior to October 1, 1998.

(3) This rule is to be used in conjunction with the forms found at Florida Rule of Criminal Procedure 3.993.

(b) Definitions.

(1) "Public records" has the meaning set forth in section 119.011, Florida Statutes.

(2) "Trial court" means:

(A) the judge who entered the judgment and imposed the sentence of death; or

(B) the judge assigned by the chief judge.

(3) "Records repository" means the location designated by the secretary of state pursuant to section 27.7081, Florida Statutes, for archiving capital postconviction public records.

(4) "Collateral counsel" means a capital collateral regional counsel from one of the three regions in Florida; a private attorney who has been appointed to represent a capital defendant for postconviction litigation; or a private attorney who has been hired by the capital defendant or who has agreed to work pro bono for a capital defendant for postconviction litigation.

(5) "Agency" means an entity or individual as defined in section 119.011, Florida Statutes, that is subject to the requirements of producing public records for inspection under section 119.07, Florida Statutes.

(6) "Index" means a list of the public records included in each container of public records sent to the records repository.

(c) Filing and Service.

(1) The original of all notices, requests, or objections filed under this rule must be filed with the clerk of the trial court. Copies must be served on the trial court, the attorney general, the state attorney, collateral counsel, and any affected person or agency, unless otherwise required by this rule.

(2) Service shall be made pursuant to Florida Rule of Criminal Procedure 3.030.

(3) In all instances requiring written notification or request, the party who has the obligation of providing a notification or request shall provide proof of receipt.

(4) Persons and agencies receiving postconviction public records notifications or requests pursuant to this rule are not required to furnish records filed in a trial court prior to the receipt of the notice.

(d) Action Upon Issuance of Mandate.

(1) Within 15 days after receiving written notification of the Supreme Court of Florida's mandate affirming the sentence of death, the attorney general shall file with the trial court a written notice of the mandate and serve a copy of it upon the state attorney who prosecuted the case, the Department of Corrections, and the defendant's trial counsel. The notice to the state attorney shall direct the state attorney to submit public records to the records repository within 90 days after receipt of written notification and to notify each law enforcement agency involved in the investigation of the capital offense, with a copy to the trial court, to submit public records to the records repository within 90 days after receipt of written notification. The notice to the Department of Corrections shall direct the department to submit public records to the records repository within 90 days after receipt of written notification. The attorney general shall make a good faith effort to assist in the timely production of public records and written notices of compliance by the state attorney and the Department of Corrections with copies to the trial court.

(2) Within 90 days after receiving written notification of issuance of the Supreme Court of Florida's mandate affirming a death sentence, the state attorney shall provide written notification to the attorney general and to the trial court of the name and address of any additional person or agency that has public records pertinent to the case.

(3) Within 90 days after receiving written notification of issuance of the Supreme Court of Florida's mandate affirming a death sentence, the defendant's trial counsel shall provide written notification to the attorney general and to the trial court of the name and address of any person or agency with information pertinent to the case which has not previously been provided to collateral counsel.

(4) Within 15 days after receiving written notification of any additional person or agency pursuant to subdivision (d)(2) or (d)(3) of this rule, the attorney general shall notify all persons or agencies identified pursuant to subdivisions (d)(2) or (d)(3), with a copy to the trial court, that these persons or agencies are required by law to copy, index, and deliver to the records repository all public records pertaining to the case that are in their possession. The person or agency shall bear the costs related to copying, indexing, and delivering the records. The attorney general shall make a good faith effort to assist in the timely production of public records and a written notice of compliance by each additional person or agency with a copy to the trial court.

(e) Action Upon Receipt of Notice of Mandate.

(1) Within 15 days after receipt of a written notice of the mandate from the attorney general, the state attorney shall provide written notification to each law enforcement agency involved in the specific case to submit public records to the records repository within 90 days after receipt of written notification. A copy of the notice shall be served upon the defendant's trial counsel and the trial court. The state attorney shall

make a good faith effort to assist in the timely production of public records and a written notice of compliance by each law enforcement agency with a copy to the trial court.

(2) Within 90 days after receipt of a written notice of the mandate from the attorney general, the state attorney shall copy, index, and deliver to the records repository all public records, in a current, nonproprietary technology format, that were produced in the state attorney's investigation or prosecution of the case. The state attorney shall bear the costs. The state attorney shall also provide written notification to the attorney general and the trial court of compliance with this section, including certifying that, to the best of the state attorney's knowledge or belief, all public records in the state attorney's possession have been copied, indexed, and delivered to the records repository as required by this rule.

(3) Within 90 days after receipt of written notification of the mandate from the attorney general, the Department of Corrections shall copy, index, and deliver to the records repository all public records, in a current, nonproprietary technology format, determined by the department to be relevant to the subject matter of a proceeding under rule 3.851, unless such copying, indexing, and delivering would be unduly burdensome. To the extent that the records determined by the department to be relevant to the subject matter of a proceeding under rule 3.851 are the defendant's medical, psychological, substance abuse, or psychiatric records, upon receipt of express consent by the defendant or pursuant to the authority of a court of competent jurisdiction, the department shall provide a copy of the defendant's medical, psychological, substance abuse, and psychiatric records to the defendant's counsel of record. The department shall bear the costs. The secretary of the department shall provide written notification to the attorney general and the trial court of compliance with this section certifying that, to the best of the secretary of the department's knowledge or belief, all such public records in the possession of the secretary of the department have been copied, indexed, and delivered to the records repository.

(4) Within 90 days after receipt of written notification of the mandate from the state attorney, a law enforcement agency shall copy, index, and deliver to the records repository all public records, in a current, nonproprietary technology format, which were produced in the investigation or prosecution of the case. Each agency shall bear the costs. The chief law enforcement officer of each law enforcement agency shall provide written notification to the attorney general and the trial court of compliance with this section including certifying that, to the best of the chief law enforcement officer's knowledge or belief, all such public records in possession of the agency or in possession of any employee of the agency, have been copied, indexed, and delivered to the records repository.

(5) Within 90 days after receipt of written notification of the mandate from the attorney general, each additional person or agency identified pursuant to subdivision (d)(2) or (d)(3) of this rule shall copy, index, and deliver to the records repository all public records, in a current, nonproprietary technology format, which were produced during the prosecution of the case. The person or agency shall bear the costs. The person or agency shall provide written notification to the attorney general and the trial court of compliance with this subdivision and shall certify, to the best of the person or agency's knowledge and belief, all such public records in the possession of the person or agency have been copied, indexed, and delivered to the records repository.

(f) Exempt or Confidential Public Records.

(1) Any public records delivered to the records repository pursuant to these rules that are confidential or exempt from the requirements of section 119.07, Florida Statutes, or article I, section 24(a), Florida Constitution, must be separately contained, without being redacted, and sealed. The outside of the container must clearly identify that the public record is confidential or exempt and that the seal may not be broken without an order of the trial court. The outside of the container must identify the nature of the public records and the legal basis for the exemption.

(2) Upon the entry of an appropriate court order, sealed containers subject to an inspection by the trial court shall be shipped to the clerk of court. The containers may be opened only for inspection by the trial court in camera. The moving party shall bear all costs associated with the transportation and inspection of such records by the trial court. The trial court shall perform the unsealing and inspection without ex parte communications and in accord with procedures for reviewing sealed documents.

(3) Collateral counsel must file a motion for in camera inspection within 30 days of receipt of the notice of delivery of the sealed records to the central records repository, or the in camera inspection will be deemed waived.

(g) Demand for Additional Public Records.

(1) Within 240 days after collateral counsel is appointed, retained, or appears pro bono, such counsel shall send a written demand for additional public records to each person or agency submitting public records or identified as having information pertinent to the case under subdivision (d) of this rule, with a copy to the trial court. However, if collateral counsel was appointed prior to October 1, 2001, then within 90 days after collateral counsel is appointed, retained, or appears pro bono, such counsel shall send a written demand for additional public records to each person or agency submitting public records or identified as hav-

ing information pertinent to the case under subdivision (d) of this rule.

(2) Within 90 days of receipt of the written demand, each person or agency notified under this subdivision shall deliver to the records repository any additional public records in the possession of the person or agency that pertain to the case and shall certify to the best of the person or agency's knowledge and belief that all additional public records have been delivered to the records repository or, if no additional public records are found, shall recertify that the public records previously delivered are complete. To the extent that the additional public records are the defendant's Department of Corrections' medical, psychological, substance abuse, or psychiatric records, upon receipt of express consent by the defendant or pursuant to the authority of a court of competent jurisdiction, the department shall provide a copy of the defendant's medical, psychological, substance abuse, and psychiatric records to the defendant's counsel of record. A copy of each person's or agency's certification shall be provided to the trial court.

(3) Within 60 days of receipt of the written demand, any person or agency may file with the trial court an objection to the written demand described in subdivision (g)(1). The trial court shall hear and rule on any objection no later than the next 90–day status conference after the filing of the objection, ordering a person or agency to produce additional public records if the court determines each of the following exists:

(A) Collateral counsel has made a timely and diligent search as provided in this rule.

(B) Collateral counsel's written demand identifies, with specificity, those additional public records that are not at the records repository.

(C) The additional public records sought are relevant to the subject matter of a proceeding under rule 3.851, or appear reasonably calculated to lead to the discovery of admissible evidence.

(D) The additional public records request is not overly broad or unduly burdensome.

(h) Cases in Which Mandate was Issued Prior to Effective Date of Rule.

(1) If the mandate affirming a defendant's conviction and sentence of death was issued prior to October 1, 1998, and no initial public records requests have been made by collateral counsel by that date, the attorney general and the state attorney shall file notifications with the trial court as required by subdivisions (d) and (e) of this rule.

(2) If on October 1, 1998, a defendant is represented by collateral counsel and has initiated the public records process, collateral counsel shall, within 90 days after October 1, 1998, or within 90 days after the production of records which were requested prior to October 1, 1998, whichever is later, file with the trial court and serve a written demand for any additional public records that have not previously been the subject of a request for public records. The request for these records shall be treated the same as a request pursuant to subdivisions (d)(3) and (d)(4) of this rule, and the records shall be copied, indexed, and delivered to the repository as required in subdivision (e)(5) of this rule.

(3) Within 10 days of the signing of a defendant's death warrant, collateral counsel may request in writing the production of public records from a person or agency from which collateral counsel has previously requested public records. A person or agency shall copy, index, and deliver to the repository any public record:

(A) that was not previously the subject of an objection;

(B) that was received or produced since the previous request; or

(C) that was, for any reason, not produced previously.

The person or agency providing the records shall bear the costs of copying, indexing, and delivering such records. If none of these circumstances exist, the person or agency shall file with the trial court and the parties an affidavit stating that no other records exist and that all public records have been produced previously. A person or agency shall comply with this subdivision within 10 days from the date of the written request or such shorter time period as is ordered by the court.

(4) In all instances in subdivision (h) which require written notification the receiving party shall provide proof of receipt by return mail or other carrier.

(i) Limitation on Postproduction Request for Additional Records.

(1) In order to obtain public records in addition to those provided under subdivisions (e), (f), (g), and (h) of this rule, collateral counsel shall file an affidavit in the trial court which:

(A) attests that collateral counsel has made a timely and diligent search of the records repository; and

(B) identifies with specificity those public records not at the records repository; and

(C) establishes that the additional public records are either relevant to the subject matter of the postconviction proceeding or are reasonably calculated to lead to the discovery of admissible evidence; and

(D) shall be served in accord with subdivision (c)(1) of this rule.

(2) Within 30 days after the affidavit of collateral counsel is filed, the trial court may order a person or agency to produce additional public records only upon finding each of the following:

(A) collateral counsel has made a timely and diligent search of the records repository;

(B) collateral counsel's affidavit identifies with specificity those additional public records that are not at the records repository;

(C) the additional public records sought are either relevant to the subject matter of a proceeding under rule 3.851 or appear reasonably calculated to lead to the discovery of admissible evidence; and

(D) the additional records request is not overly broad or unduly burdensome.

(j) Authority of the Court. In proceedings under this rule the trial court may:

(1) compel or deny disclosure of records;

(2) conduct an in-camera inspection;

(3) extend the times in this rule upon a showing of good cause;

(4) require representatives from government agencies to appear at status conferences to address public records issues;

(5) impose sanctions upon any party, person, or agency affected by this rule including initiating contempt proceedings, taxing expenses, extending time, ordering facts to be established, and granting other relief; and

(6) resolve any dispute arising under this rule unless jurisdiction is in an appellate court.

(k) Scope of Production and Resolution of Production Issues.

(1) Unless otherwise limited, the scope of production under any part of this rule shall be that the public records sought are not privileged or immune from production and are either relevant to the subject matter of the proceeding under rule 3.851 or are reasonably calculated to lead to the discovery of admissible evidence.

(2) Any objections or motions to compel production of public records pursuant to this rule shall be filed within 30 days after the end of the production time period provided by this rule. Counsel for the party objecting or moving to compel shall file a copy of the objection or motion directly with the trial court. The trial court shall hold a hearing on the objection or motion on an expedited basis.

***(l)* Destruction of Records Repository Records.** Sixty days after a capital sentence is carried out, after a defendant is released from incarceration following the granting of a pardon or reversal of the sentence, or after a defendant has been resentenced to a term of years, the attorney general shall provide written notification of this occurrence to the secretary of state with service in accord with subdivision (c)(1). After the expiration of the 60 days, the secretary of state may then destroy the copies of the records held by the records repository that pertain to that case, unless an objection to the destruction is filed in the trial court and served upon the secretary of state and in accord with subdivision (c)(1). If no objection has been served within the 60–day period, the records may then be destroyed. If an objection is served, the records shall not be destroyed until a final disposition of the objection.

Added September 18, 1998, effective Oct. 1, 1998 (723 So.2d 163). Amended July 1, 1999 (754 So.2d 640); July 1, 1999 (754 So.2d 640); Oct. 1, 2001 (802 So.2d 298); Sept. 30, 2004, effective Oct. 1, 2004 (887 So.2d 1090); Nov. 19, 2009, effective Jan. 1, 2010 (26 So.3d 534); Oct. 18, 2012, effective, *nunc pro tunc*, Sept. 1, 2012 (102 So.3d 505); Dec. 12, 2013 (132 So.3d 123); April 24, 2014, corrected June 19, 2014, effective July 1, 2014 (140 So.3d 507); July 3, 2014, effective January 1, 2015 (148 So.3d 1171); April 30, 2015, effective April 30, 2015 (140 So.3d 507).

Repeal

Rule 3.852 was repealed effective January 14, 2000, under the provisions of Laws 2000, c. 2000–3, § 10.

Readoption

Rule 3.852 was readopted as it existed prior to the effective date of Laws 2000, c. 2000–3, under the provisions of the Florida Supreme Court Order of February 7, 2000, 763 So.2d 273. See, also, Allen v. Butterworth, 756 So.2d 52.

Criminal Court Steering Committee Note

2014 Amendment. The rule is amended to require the state attorney and attorney general to manage compliance with the public records process.

Rule 3.853. Motion for Postconviction DNA Testing

(a) Purpose. This rule provides procedures for obtaining DNA (deoxyribonucleic acid) testing under sections 925.11 and 925.12, Florida Statutes.

(b) Contents of Motion. The motion for postconviction DNA testing must be under oath and must include the following:

(1) a statement of the facts relied upon in support of the motion, including a description of the physical evidence containing DNA to be tested and, if known, the present location or last known location of the evidence and how it originally was obtained;

(2) a statement that the evidence was not previously tested for DNA, or a statement that the results of previous DNA testing were inconclusive and that subsequent scientific developments in DNA testing techniques likely would produce a definitive result establishing that the movant is not the person who committed the crime;

(3) a statement that the movant is innocent and how the DNA testing requested by the motion will exonerate the movant of the crime for which the movant was sentenced, or a statement how the DNA testing will mitigate the sentence received by the movant for that crime;

(4) a statement that identification of the movant is a genuinely disputed issue in the case and why it is an issue or an explanation of how the DNA evidence would either exonerate the defendant or mitigate the sentence that the movant received;

(5) a statement of any other facts relevant to the motion; and

(6) a certificate that a copy of the motion has been served on the prosecuting authority.

(c) Procedure.

(1) Upon receipt of the motion, the clerk of the court shall file it and deliver the court file to the assigned judge.

(2) The court shall review the motion and deny it if it is facially insufficient. If the motion is facially sufficient, the prosecuting authority shall be ordered to respond to the motion within 30 days or such other time as may be ordered by the court.

(3) Upon receipt of the response of the prosecuting authority, the court shall review the response and enter an order on the merits of the motion or set the motion for hearing.

(4) In the event that the motion shall proceed to a hearing, the court may appoint counsel to assist the movant if the court determines that assistance of counsel is necessary and upon a determination of indigency pursuant to section 27.52, Florida Statutes.

(5) The court shall make the following findings when ruling on the motion:

(A) Whether it has been shown that physical evidence that may contain DNA still exists.

(B) Whether the results of DNA testing of that physical evidence likely would be admissible at trial and whether there exists reliable proof to establish that the evidence containing the tested DNA is authentic and would be admissible at a future hearing.

(C) Whether there is a reasonable probability that the movant would have been acquitted or would have received a lesser sentence if the DNA evidence had been admitted at trial.

(6) If the court orders DNA testing of the physical evidence, the cost of the testing may be assessed against the movant, unless the movant is indigent. If the movant is indigent, the state shall bear the cost of the DNA testing ordered by the court.

(7) The court-ordered DNA testing shall be ordered to be conducted by the Department of Law Enforcement or its designee, as provided by statute. However, the court, upon a showing of good cause, may order testing by another laboratory or agency certified by the American Society of Crime Laboratory Directors/Laboratory Accreditation Board (ASCLD/LAB) or Forensic Quality Services, Inc. (FQS) if requested by a movant who can bear the cost of such testing.

(8) The results of the DNA testing ordered by the court shall be provided in writing to the court, the movant, and the prosecuting authority.

(d) Time Limitations. The motion for postconviction DNA testing may be filed or considered at any time following the date that the judgment and sentence in the case becomes final.

(e) Rehearing. The movant may file a motion for rehearing of any order denying relief within 15 days after service of the order denying relief. The time for filing an appeal shall be tolled until an order on the motion for rehearing has been entered.

(f) Appeal. An appeal may be taken by any adversely affected party within 30 days from the date the order on the motion is rendered. All orders denying relief must include a statement that the movant has the right to appeal within 30 days after the order denying relief is rendered.

Added October 18, 2001 (807 So.2d 633). Amended September 15, 2004 (884 So.2d 934); September 29, 2005 (935 So.2d 1218); September 21, 2006 (938 So.2d 977); March 29, 2007 (953 So.2d 513); Nov. 19, 2009, effective Jan. 1, 2010 (26 So.3d 534); September 2, 2010 (43 So.3d 688).

Repeal

Laws 2006, c. 2006–292, § 3, provides:

"Rule 3.853, Florida Rules of Criminal Procedure, is repealed to the extent it is inconsistent with this act."

Retroactivity

Laws 2006, c. 2006–292, § 4, provides:

"This act shall take effect upon becoming a law [June 23, 2006] and shall apply retroactively to October 1, 2005; but section 3 shall take effect only if this act is passed by the affirmative vote of two-thirds of the membership of each house of the Legislature [this act passed the House of Representatives by a vote of 113 yeas to 1 nay and the Senate by a vote of 40 yeas to 0 nays]".

XVIII. FORMS

Rule 3.984. Application for Criminal Indigent Status

IN THE CIRCUIT/COUNTY COURT OF THE ______ JUDICIAL CIRCUIT IN AND FOR ______ COUNTY, FLORIDA

STATE OF FLORIDA vs. CASE NO.______

______
Defendant/Minor Child

APPLICATION FOR CRIMINAL INDIGENT STATUS

______ I AM SEEKING THE APPOINTMENT OF THE PUBLIC DEFENDER
OR
______ I HAVE A PRIVATE ATTORNEY OR AM SELF–REPRESENTED AND SEEK DETERMINATION OF INDIGENCE STATUS FOR COSTS

Notice to Applicant: The provision of a public defender/court appointed lawyer and costs/due process services are not free. A judgment and lien may be imposed against all real or personal property you own to pay for legal and other services provided on your behalf or on behalf of the person for whom you are making this application. There is a $50.00 fee for each application filed.
If the application fee is not paid to the Clerk of the Court within 7 days, it will be added to any costs that may be assessed against you at the conclusion of this case. If you are a parent/guardian making this affidavit on behalf of a minor or tax-dependent adult, the information contained in this application must include your income and assets.

1. **I have ___ dependents.** *(Do not include children not living at home and do not include a working spouse or yourself.)*

2. **I have a take home income of $** ______ paid ( ) weekly ( ) bi-weekly ( ) semi-monthly ( ) monthly ( ) yearly
(Take home income equals salary, wages, bonuses, commissions, allowances, overtime, tips and similar payments, ***minus*** *deductions required by law and other court ordered support payments)*

3. **I have other income** paid ( ) weekly ( ) bi-weekly ( ) semi- monthly ( ) monthly ( ) yearly: *(Circle "Yes" and fill in the amount if you have this kind of income, otherwise circle "No".)*
Social Security benefit .... Yes $ ____ No
Unemployment compensation ..... Yes $ ____ No
Union Funds .... Yes $ ____ No
Workers compensation .... Yes $ ____ No
Retirement/pensions .... Yes $ ____ No
Trusts or gifts .... Yes $ ____ No
Veterans' benefit .... Yes $ ____ No
Child support or other regular support from family members/spouse .... Yes $ ____ No
Rental income .... Yes $ ____ No
Dividends or interest .... Yes $ ____ No
Other kinds of income not on the list .... Yes $ ____ No

4. **I have other assets:** *(Circle "yes" and fill in the value of the property, otherwise circle "No.")*
Cash .... Yes $ ____ No
Bank account(s) .... Yes $ ____ No
Certificates of deposit or money market accounts .... Yes $ ____ No
* Equity in Motor vehicles/Boats/Other tangible property .... Yes $ ____ No
Savings .... Yes $ ____ No
Stocks/bonds .... Yes $ ____ No
* Equity in Real estate (excluding homestead) .... Yes $ ____ No
* include expectancy of an interest in such property

5. **I have a total amount of liabilities and debts in the amount of $ ______.**

6. **I receive:** *(Circle "Yes" or "No.")*
Temporary Assistance for Needy Families–Cash Assistance .... Yes No
Poverty-related veterans' benefits.... Yes No
Supplemental Security Income (SSI) .. Yes No

7. **I have been released on bail in the amount of $ ______. Cash ___ Surety ___ Posted by:** Self ___ Family ___ Other___

A person who knowingly provides false information to the clerk or the court in seeking a determination of indigent status under s. 27.52, F.S. commits a misdemeanor of the first degree, punishable as provided in s. 775.082, F.S. or s. 775.083, F.S. **I attest that the information I have provided on this Application is true and accurate to the best of my knowledge.**

Signed this ___ day of ________, 20 ___.

Date of Birth ________ Signature of applicant for indigent status

Driver's license or ID number ____ Print full legal name ______
Address ______
City, State, Zip ______
Phone number ______

CLERK'S DETERMINATION

___Based on the information in this Application, I have determined the applicant to be ( ) Indigent ( ) Not Indigent

___The Public Defender is hereby appointed to the case listed above until relieved by the Court.

Dated this ___ day of ________, 20 ___.

____
Clerk of the Circuit Court

This form was completed with the assistance of __________
Clerk/Deputy Clerk/Other authorized person

APPLICANTS FOUND NOT INDIGENT MAY SEEK REVIEW BY ASKING FOR A HEARING TIME. Sign here if you want the judge to review the clerk's decision of not indigent. ________

Added April 7, 2005 (900 So.2d 528). Amended June 30, 2005, eff. July 1, 2005 (910 So.2d 194); March 19, 2009 (5 So.3d 662).

Rule 3.985. Standard Jury Instructions

The forms of Florida Standard Jury Instructions in Criminal Cases appearing on the court's website at www.floridasupremecourt.org/jury_instructions/instructions.shtml may be used by the trial judges of this state in charging the jury in every criminal case to the extent that the forms are applicable, unless the trial judge shall determine that an applicable form of instruction is erroneous or inadequate, in which event the judge shall modify or amend the form or give such other instruction as the trial judge shall determine to be necessary to instruct the jury accurately and sufficiently on the circumstances of the case; and, in such event, the trial judge shall state on the record or in a separate order the respect in which the judge finds the standard form erroneous or inadequate and the legal basis of the judge's finding. Similarly, in all circumstances in which the notes accompanying the Florida Standard Jury Instructions in Criminal Cases contain a recommendation that a certain type of instruction not be given, the trial judge may follow the recommendation unless the judge shall determine that the giving of such an instruction is necessary to instruct the jury accurately and sufficiently, in which event the judge shall give such instruction as the judge shall deem appropriate and necessary; and, in such event, the trial judge shall state on the record or in a separate order the legal basis of the determination that the instruction is necessary.

Amended Sept. 24, 1992, effective Jan. 1, 1993 (606 So.2d 227); Oct. 1, 2009 (20 So.3d 376).

Committee Notes

1972 Amendment. Same as prior rule.

Rule 3.9855. Juror Voir Dire Questionnaire

JUROR VOIR DIRE QUESTIONNAIRE

1. Name and date of birth ________
2. What city, town or area of the county do you live in? ________
Zip code ________
3. Years of residence: In Florida ________
In this county ________
4. Former residence ________
5. Marital status (married, single, divorced, widow, or widower) ________
6. Your occupation and employer ________

____
7. If you are not now employed, give your last occupation and employer

____

____
8. If married, name and occupation of spouse

____

____
9. Have you ever served as a juror before? yes ___ no ________
If yes, civil ___ criminal
Did the jury reach a verdict? yes ___ no ___
Were you the foreperson? yes ___ no
10. If you have children, give the age, sex and occupation of those children

____

____
11. Are you either a close friend or relative of any law enforcement officer? ________
12. Have you, a close friend, or family member been the victim of a crime? ________
13. Have you, a close friend, or family member been arrested or accused of a crime? ________

Added Oct. 4, 2007, effective Jan. 1, 2008 (967 So.2d 178).

Rule 3.986. Forms Related to Judgment and Sentence

(a) Sufficiency of Forms. The forms as set forth below, or computer generated formats that duplicate these forms, shall be used by all courts. Variations from these forms do not void a judgment, sentence, order, or fingerprints that are otherwise sufficient.

(b) Form for Judgment.

___ Probation Violator
___ Community Control Violator
___ Retrial
___ Resentence

In the Circuit Court,
_____ Judicial Circuit, in and for
_____ County, Florida
Division
Case Number ________

State of Florida

v.

____
Defendant

JUDGMENT

The defendant, ________, being personally before this court represented by ______, the attorney of record, and the state represented by ________, and having

___ been tried and found guilty by jury/by court of the following crime(s)

___ entered a plea of guilty to the following crime(s)

___ entered a plea of nolo contendere to the following crime(s)

Count	Crime	Offense Statute Number(s)	Degree Of Crime	Case Number	OBTS Number
____	____	____	____	____	____
____	____	____	____	____	____
____	____	____	____	____	____
____	____	____	____	____	____
____	____	____	____	____	____

___ and no cause being shown why the defendant should not be adjudicated guilty, IT IS ORDERED THAT the defendant is hereby ADJUDICATED GUILTY of the above crime(s).

___ and being a qualified offender pursuant to s. 943.325, the defendant shall be required to submit DNA samples as required by law.

___ and good cause being shown; IT IS ORDERED THAT ADJUDICATION OF GUILT BE WITHHELD.

DONE AND ORDERED in open court in ________ County, Florida, on .... (date)..........

____
Judge

State of Florida

v.

____
Defendant Case Number_____

FINGERPRINTS OF DEFENDANT

R. Thumb	R. Index	R. Middle	R. Ring	R. Little
L. Thumb	L. Index	L. Middle	L. Ring	L. Little

Fingerprints taken by: ______________________
(Name) (Title)

I HEREBY CERTIFY that the above and foregoing fingerprints on this judgment are the fingerprints of the defendant, ________, and that they were placed thereon by the defendant in my presence in open court this date.

____
Judge

(c) Form for Charges, Costs, and Fees.

In the Circuit Court,
___ Judicial Circuit, in and for
___ County, Florida
Division
Case Number ___

State of Florida

v.

____
Defendant

CHARGES/COSTS/FEES

The defendant is hereby ordered to pay the following sums if checked:

___ $50.00 pursuant to section 938.03, Florida Statutes (Crimes Compensation Trust Fund).

___ $3.00 as a court cost pursuant to section 938.01, Florida Statutes (Criminal Justice Trust Fund).

___ $2.00 as a court cost pursuant to section 938.15, Florida Statutes (Criminal Justice Education by Municipalities and Counties).

___ A fine in the sum of $ ________ pursuant to section 775.0835, Florida Statutes. (This provision refers to the optional fine for the Crimes Compensation Trust Fund and is not applicable unless checked and completed. Fines imposed as part of a sentence to section 775.083, Florida Statutes, are to be recorded on the sentence page(s).)

___ A sum of $ ________ pursuant to section 938.27, Florida Statutes (Prosecution/Investigative Costs).

___ A sum of $ ________ pursuant to section 938.29, Florida Statutes (Public Defender/Appointed Counsel Fees).

___ Restitution in accordance with attached order.

___ $201 pursuant to section 938.08, Florida Statutes (Funding Programs in Domestic Violence).

___ A sum of $ _________ for the cost of collecting the DNA sample required by s. 943.325, Florida Statutes.

___ Other ______________________________
____

DONE AND ORDERED in open court in _________ County, Florida, on (date)

____
Judge

(d) Form for Sentencing.

Defendant ______ Case Number ______ OBTS Number______

SENTENCE

(As to Count ___)

The defendant, being personally before this court, accompanied by the defendant's attorney of record, ___, and having been adjudicated guilty herein, and the court having given the defendant an opportunity to be heard and to offer matters in mitigation of sentence, and to show cause why the defendant should not be sentenced as provided by law, and no cause being shown,

(Check one if applicable)

___ and the court having on ..... (date) ..... deferred imposition of sentence until this date

___ and the court having previously entered a judgment in this case on ..... (date) ..... now resentences the defendant

___ and the court having placed the defendant on probation/community control and having subsequently revoked the defendant's probation/community control

It Is The Sentence Of The Court That:

___ The defendant pay a fine of $ ___, pursuant to section 775.083, Florida Statutes, plus $ ___ as the 5% surcharge required by section 938.04, Florida Statutes.

___ The defendant is hereby committed to the custody of the Department of Corrections.

___ The defendant is hereby committed to the custody of the Sheriff of ___ County, Florida.

___ The defendant is sentenced as a youthful offender in accordance with section 958.04, Florida Statutes.

To Be Imprisoned (check one; unmarked sections are inapplicable):

___ For a term of natural life.

___ For a term of ___.

___ Said SENTENCE SUSPENDED for a period of ___ subject to conditions set forth in this order.

If "split" sentence complete the appropriate paragraph

___ Followed by a period of ___ on probation/community control under the supervision of the Department of Corrections according to the terms and conditions of supervision set forth in a separate order entered herein.

___ However, after serving a period of ___ imprisonment in ___ the balance of the sentence shall be suspended and the defendant shall be placed on probation/community control for a period of ___ under supervision of the Department of Corrections according to the terms and conditions of probation/community control set forth in a separate order entered herein.

In the event the defendant is ordered to serve additional split sentences, all incarceration portions shall be satisfied before the defendant begins service of the supervision terms.

SPECIAL PROVISIONS

(As to Count ___)

By appropriate notation, the following provisions apply to the sentence imposed:

Mandatory/Minimum Provisions:

Firearm

___ It is further ordered that the 3–year minimum imprisonment provision of section 775.087(2), Florida Statutes, is hereby imposed for the sentence specified in this count.

Drug Trafficking

___ It is further ordered that the ___ mandatory minimum imprisonment provision of section 893.135(1), Florida Statutes, is hereby imposed for the sentence specified in this count.

Controlled Substance Within 1,000 Feet of School

___ It is further ordered that the 3–year minimum imprisonment provision of section

893.13(1)(c)1, Florida Statutes, is hereby imposed for the sentence specified in this count.

Habitual Felony Offender

___ The defendant is adjudicated a habitual felony offender and has been sentenced to an extended term in accordance with the provisions of section 775.084(4)(a), Florida Statutes. The requisite findings by the court are set forth in a separate order or stated on the record in open court.

Habitual Violent Felony Offender

___ The defendant is adjudicated a habitual violent felony offender and has been sentenced to an extended term in accordance with the provisions of section 775.084(4)(b), Florida Statutes. A minimum term of ___ year(s) must be served prior to release. The requisite findings of the court are set forth in a separate order or stated on the record in open court.

Law Enforcement Protection Act

___ It is further ordered that the defendant shall serve a minimum of ___ years before release in accordance with section 775.0823, Florida Statutes. (Offenses committed before January 1, 1994).

Capital Offense

___ It is further ordered that the defendant shall serve no less than 25 years in accordance with the provisions of section 775.082(1), Florida Statutes. (Offenses committed before October 1, 1995).

Short–Barreled Rifle, Shotgun, Machine Gun

___ It is further ordered that the 5–year minimum provisions of section 790.221(2), Florida Statutes, are hereby imposed for the sentence specified in this count. (Offenses committed before January 1, 1994).

Continuing Criminal Enterprise

___ It is further ordered that the 25–year minimum sentence provisions of section 893.20, Florida Statutes, are hereby imposed for the sentence specified in this count. (Offenses committed before January 1, 1994).

Taking a Law Enforcement Officer's Firearm

___ It is further ordered that the 3–year mandatory minimum imprisonment provision of section 775.0875(1), Florida Statutes, is hereby imposed for the sentence specified in this count. (Offenses committed before January 1, 1994).

Sexual Offender/Sexual Predator Determinations:

Sexual Predator

The defendant is adjudicated a sexual predator as set forth in section 775.21, Florida Statutes.

Sexual Offender

The defendant meets the criteria for a sexual offender as set forth in section 943.0435(1)(a)1a., b., c., or d.

Age of Victim

The victim was ___ years of age at the time of the offense.

Age of Defendant

The defendant was ___ years of age at the time of the offense.

Relationship to Victim

The defendant is not the victim's parent or guardian.

Sexual Activity [F.S. 800.04(4)]

The offense ___ did ___ did not involve sexual activity.

Use of Force or Coercion [F.S. 800.04(4)]

The sexual activity described herein ___ did ___ did not involve the use of force or coercion.

Use of Force or Coercion/unclothed Genitals [F.S. 800.04(5)]

The molestation ___ did ___ did not involve unclothed genitals or genital area.

The molestation ___ did ___ did not involve the use of force or coercion.

Other Provisions:

Criminal Gang Activity

___ The felony conviction is for an offense that was found, pursuant to section 874.04, Florida Statutes, to have been committed for the purpose of benefiting, promoting, or furthering the interests of a criminal gang.

Retention of Jurisdiction

___ The court retains jurisdiction over the defendant pursuant to section 947.16(4), Florida Statutes (1983).

Jail Credit

___ It is further ordered that the defendant shall be allowed a total of ___ days as credit for time incarcerated before imposition of this sentence.

CREDIT FOR TIME SERVED IN RESENTENCING AFTER VIOLATION OF PROBATION OR COMMUNITY CONTROL

___ It is further ordered that the defendant be allowed ___ days time served between date of arrest as a violator following release from prison to the date of resentencing. The Department of Corrections shall apply original jail time credit and shall compute and apply credit for time served and unforfeited gain time previously awarded on case/count ________. (Offenses committed before October 1, 1989)

___ It is further ordered that the defendant be allowed ___ days time served between date of arrest as a violator following release from prison to the date of resentencing. The Department of Corrections shall apply original jail time credit and shall compute and apply credit for time served on case/count ________. (Offenses committed between October 1, 1989, and December 31, 1993)

___ The Court deems the unforfeited gain time previously awarded on the above case/count forfeited under section 948.06(7).

___ The Court allows unforfeited gain time previously awarded on the above case/count. (Gain time may be subject to forfeiture by the Department of Corrections under section 944.28(1)).

___ It is further ordered that the defendant be allowed ___ days time served between date of arrest as a violator following release from prison to the date of resentencing. The Department of Corrections shall apply original jail time credit and shall compute and apply credit for time served only pursuant to section 921.0017, Florida Statutes, on case/count ________. (Offenses committed on or after January 1, 1994)

Consecutive/Concurrent as to Other Counts

It is further ordered that the sentence imposed for this count shall run (check one) ___ consecutive to ___ concurrent with the sentence set forth in count ___ of this case.

Consecutive/Concurrent as to Other Convictions

It is further ordered that the composite term of all sentences imposed for the counts specified in this order shall run (check one) ___ consecutive to ___ concurrent with (check one) the following:

___ any active sentence being served.

___ specific sentences: ________________

____

In the event the above sentence is to the Department of Corrections, the Sheriff of ___ County, Florida, is hereby ordered and directed to deliver the defendant to the Department of Corrections at the facility designated by the department together with a copy of this judgment and sentence and any other documents specified by Florida Statute.

The defendant in open court was advised of the right to appeal from this sentence by filing notice of appeal within 30 days from this date with the clerk of this court and the defendant's right to the assistance of counsel in taking the appeal at the expense of the state on showing of indigency.

In imposing the above sentence, the court further recommends ________.

____

____

DONE AND ORDERED in open court at ________ County, Florida, on .... (date)......

____
Judge

(e) Form for Order of Probation.

In the ___ Court
of ______ County, Florida
Case Number ________

State of Florida

v.

____
Defendant

ORDER OF PROBATION

This cause coming on this day to be heard before me, and you, the defendant, ________, being now present before me, and you having

(check one)

___ entered a plea of guilty to

___ entered a plea of nolo contendere to

___ been found guilty by jury verdict of

___ been found guilty by the court trying the case without a jury of the offense(s) of ________

____

____

SECTION 1: Judgment Of Guilt

___ The Court hereby adjudges you to be guilty of the above offense(s).

Now, therefore, it is ordered and adjudged that the imposition of sentence is hereby withheld and that you be placed on probation for a period of ________ under the supervision of the Department of Corrections, subject to Florida law.

SECTION 2: Order Withholding Adjudication

___ Now, therefore, it is ordered and adjudged that the adjudication of guilt is hereby withheld and that you be placed on probation for a period of ________ under the supervision of the Department of Corrections, subject to Florida law.

SECTION 3: Probation During Portion Of Sentence

It is hereby ordered and adjudged that you be

___ committed to the Department of Corrections

___ confined in the County Jail

for a term of ___ with credit for ___ jail time. After you have served ___ of the term you shall be placed on probation for a period of ___ under the supervision of the Department of Corrections, subject to Florida law.

___ confined in the County Jail

for a term of ___ with credit for ___ jail time, as a special condition of probation.

It is further ordered that you shall comply with the following conditions of probation during the probationary period.

(1) Not later than the fifth day of each month, you will make a full and truthful report to your officer on the form provided for that purpose.

(2) You will pay the State of Florida the amount of $ ________ per month toward the cost of your supervision, unless otherwise waived in compliance with Florida Statutes.

(3) You will not change your residence or employment or leave the county of your residence without first procuring the consent of your officer.

(4) You will not possess, carry, or own any firearm. You will not possess, carry, or own any weapons without first procuring the consent of your officer.

(5) You will live without violating the law. A conviction in a court of law shall not be necessary for such a violation to constitute a violation of your probation.

(6) You will not associate with any person engaged in any criminal activity.

(7) You will not use intoxicants to excess or possess any drugs or narcotics unless prescribed by a physician. Nor will you visit places where intoxicants, drugs, or other dangerous substances are unlawfully sold, dispensed, or used.

(8) You will work diligently at a lawful occupation, advise your employer of your probation status, and support any dependents to the best of your ability, as directed by your officer.

(9) You will promptly and truthfully answer all inquiries directed to you by the court or the officer, and allow your officer to visit in your home, at your employment site, or elsewhere, and you will comply with all instructions your officer may give you.

(10) You will pay restitution, costs, and/or fees in accordance with the attached orders.

(11) You will report in person within 72 hours of your release from confinement to the probation office in ______ County, Florida, unless otherwise instructed by your officer. (This condition applies only if section 3 on the previous page is checked.) Otherwise, you must report immediately to the probation office located at ________.

(12) You shall submit to the drawing of blood or other biological specimens as required by s. 943.325, Florida Statutes.

(13) You shall submit to the taking of a digitized photograph as required by s. 948.03, Florida Statutes.

SPECIAL CONDITIONS

___ You must undergo a (drug/alcohol) evaluation and, if treatment is deemed necessary, you must successfully complete the treatment.

___ You will submit to urinalysis, breathalyzer, or blood tests at any time requested by your officer, or the professional staff of any treatment center where you are receiving treatment, to determine possible use of alcohol, drugs, or controlled substances. You shall be required to pay for the tests unless payment is waived by your officer.

___ You must undergo a mental health evaluation, and if treatment is deemed necessary, you must successfully complete the treatment.

___ You will not associate with ___ during the period of probation.

___ You will not associate with other criminal gang members or associates, except as authorized by law enforcement officials, prosecutorial authorities, or the court, for the purpose of aiding in the investigation of criminal activity.

___ You will not contact ___ during the period of probation.

___ You will attend and successfully complete an approved batterers' intervention program.

___ Other ______________________________

____

(Use the space below for additional conditions as necessary.)

You are hereby placed on notice that the court may at any time rescind or modify any of the conditions of your probation, or may extend the period of probation as authorized by law, or may discharge you from further supervision. If you violate any of the conditions of your probation, you may be arrested and the court may revoke your probation, adjudicate you guilty if adjudication of guilt was withheld, and impose any sentence that it might have imposed before placing you on probation or require you to serve the balance of the sentence.

It is further ordered that when you have been instructed as to the conditions of probation, you shall be released from custody if you are in custody, and if you are at liberty on bond, the sureties thereon shall stand discharged from liability. (This paragraph applies only if section 1 or section 2 is checked.)

It is further ordered that the clerk of this court file this order in the clerk's office and provide certified copies of same to the officer for use in compliance with the requirements of law.

DONE AND ORDERED, on ...... (date)......

____

Judge

I acknowledge receipt of a certified copy of this order. The conditions have been explained to me and I agree to abide by them.

.....(date)..... Probationer ______

Instructed by ______

Original:	Clerk of the Court
Certified Copies:	Probationer
	Florida Department of Corrections, Probation and Parole Services

(f) Form for Community Control.

In the ___ Court
of ______ County, Florida
Case Number ______

State of Florida

v.

____
Defendant

ORDER OF COMMUNITY CONTROL

This cause coming on this day to be heard before me, and you, the defendant, __________, being now present before me, and you having

(check one)

___ entered a plea of guilty to

___ entered a plea of nolo contendere to

___ been found guilty by jury verdict of

___ been found guilty by the court trying the case without a jury of the offense(s) of ______________

____

____

SECTION 1: Judgment of Guilt

___ The court hereby adjudges you to be guilty of the above offense(s).

Now, therefore, it is ordered and adjudged that you be placed on community control for a period of ___ under the supervision of the Department of Corrections, subject to Florida law.

SECTION 2: Order Withholding Adjudication

___ Now, therefore, it is ordered and adjudged that the adjudication of guilt is hereby withheld and that you be placed on Community Control for a period of ___ under the supervision of the Department of Corrections, subject to Florida law.

SECTION 3: Community Control During Portion Of Sentence

It is hereby ordered and adjudged that you be

___ committed to the Department of Corrections

___ confined in the County Jail

for a term of ___ with credit for ___ jail time. After you have served ___ of the term, you shall be placed on community control for a period of ___ under the supervision of the Department of Corrections, subject to Florida law.

___ confined in the County Jail

for a term of ___ with credit for ___ jail time, as a special condition of community control.

It is further ordered that you shall comply with the following conditions of community control during the community control period.

(1) Not later than the fifth day of each month, you will make a full and truthful report to your officer on the form provided for that purpose.

(2) You will pay the State of Florida the amount of $___ per month toward the cost of your supervision, unless otherwise waived in compliance with Florida Statutes.

(3) You will not change your residence or employment or leave the county of your residence without first procuring the consent of your officer.

(4) You will not possess, carry, or own any firearm. You will not possess, carry, or own other weapons without first procuring the consent of your officer.

(5) You will live without violating the law. A conviction in a court of law shall not be necessary for such a violation to constitute a violation of your community control.

(6) You will not associate with any person engaged in any criminal activity.

(7) You will not use intoxicants to excess or possess any drugs or narcotics unless prescribed by a physician. Nor will you visit places where intoxicants, drugs, or other dangerous substances are unlawfully sold, dispensed, or used.

(8) You will work diligently at a lawful occupation, advise your employer of your community control status, and support any dependents to the best of your ability as directed by your officer.

(9) You will promptly and truthfully answer all inquiries directed to you by the court or your officer and allow your officer to visit in your home, at your employment site or elsewhere, and you will comply with all instructions your officer may give you.

(10) You will report to your officer at least 4 times a week, or, if unemployed full time, daily.

(11) You will perform ___ hours of public service work as directed by your officer.

(12) You will remain confined to your approved residence except for one half hour before and after your approved employment, public service work, or any other special activities approved by your officer.

(13) You will pay restitution, costs, and/or fees in accordance with the attached orders.

(14) You will report in person within 72 hours of your release from confinement to the probation office in ___ County, Florida, unless otherwise instructed by your officer. (This condition applies only if section 3 on the previous page is checked.) Otherwise, you must report immediately to the probation office located at ___.

(15) You shall submit to the drawing of blood or other biological specimens as required by s. 943.325, Florida Statutes.

(16) You shall submit to the taking of a digitized photograph as required by s. 948.101, Florida Statutes.

SPECIAL CONDITIONS

___ You must undergo a (drug/alcohol) evaluation, and if treatment is deemed necessary, you must successfully complete the treatment.

___ You must undergo a mental health evaluation, and if treatment is deemed necessary, you must successfully complete the treatment.

___ You will submit to urinalysis, breathalyzer, or blood tests at any time requested by your officer, or the professional staff of any treatment center where you are receiving treatment, to determine possible use of alcohol, drugs, or controlled substances. You shall be required to pay for the tests unless payment is waived by your officer.

___ You will not associate with ___ during the period of community control.

___ You will not associate with other criminal gang members or associates, except as authorized by law enforcement officials, prosecutorial authorities, or the court, for the purpose of aiding in the investigation of criminal activity.

___ You will not contact ___ during the period of community control.

___ You will maintain an hourly accounting of all your activities on a daily log which you will submit to your officer on request.

___ You will participate in self-improvement programs as determined by the court or your officer.

___ You will submit to electronic monitoring of your whereabouts as required by the Florida Department of Corrections.

___ You will attend and successfully complete an approved batterers' intervention program.

___ Other ________________________________

____

(Use the space below for additional conditions as necessary.)

You are hereby placed on notice that the court may at any time rescind or modify any of the conditions of your community control, or may extend the period of community control as authorized by law, or may discharge you from further supervision or return you to a program of regular probation supervision. If you violate any of the conditions and sanctions of your community control, you may be arrested, and the court may adjudicate you guilty if adjudication of guilt was withheld, revoke your community control, and impose any sentence that it might have imposed before placing you on community control.

It is further ordered that when you have reported to your officer and have been instructed as to the conditions of community control, you shall be released from custody if you are in custody, and if you are at liberty on bond, the sureties thereon shall stand discharged from liability. (This paragraph applies only if section 1 or section 2 is checked.)

It is further ordered that the clerk of this court file this order in the clerk's office, and forthwith provide certified copies of same to the officer for use in compliance with the requirements of law.

DONE AND ORDERED, on ......(date)......

____

Judge

I acknowledge receipt of a certified copy of this order. The conditions have been explained to me and I agree to abide by them.

. . . . (date) . . . . Community controller ______

Instructed by ______

Original: Clerk of the Court
Certified Copies: Community Controlee
Florida Department of Corrections, Probation and Parole Services

(g) Form for Restitution Order.

In the Circuit Court,
______ Judicial Circuit, in and for
______ County, Florida
Division ______
Case Number ______

State of Florida

v.

______
Defendant

RESTITUTION ORDER

By appropriate notation, the following provisions apply to the sentence imposed in this section:

___ Restitution is not ordered as it is not applicable.

___ Restitution is not ordered due to the financial resources of the defendant.

___ Restitution is not ordered due to ______.

___ Due to the financial resources of the defendant, restitution of a portion of the damages is ordered as prescribed below.

___ Restitution is ordered as prescribed below.

___ Restitution is ordered for the following victim. (Victim refers to the aggrieved party, aggrieved party's estate, or aggrieved party's next of kin if the aggrieved party is deceased as a result of the offense. In lieu of the victim's address and phone number, the address and phone number of the prosecuting attorney, victim's attorney, or victim advocate may be used.)

______ ______
Name of victim — Name of attorney or advocate if applicable

Address ______
City, State, and Zip Code ______
Phone Number ______

___ The sum of $ ____ for medical and related services and devices relating to physical, psychiatric, and psychological care, including non- medical care and treatment rendered in accordance with a recognized method of healing.

___ The sum of $ ____ for necessary physical and occupational therapy and rehabilitation.

___ The sum of $ ____ to reimburse the victim for income lost as a result of the offense.

___ The sum of $ ____ for necessary funeral and related services if the offense resulted in bodily injury resulting in the death of the victim.

___ The sum of $ ____ for damages resulting from the offense.

___ The sum of $ ____ for ______
______

It is further ordered that the defendant fulfill restitution obligations in the following manner:

___ Total monetary restitution is determined to be $ ____ to be paid at a rate of $ ____ per (check one) ____ month ____ week ____ other (specify) ____ and is to be paid (check one) ____ through the clerk of the circuit court, ____ to the victim's designee, or ____ through the Department of Corrections, with an additional 4% fee of $ ____ for handling, processing, and forwarding the restitution to the victim(s).

___ For which sum let execution issue.

DONE AND ORDERED at ____ County, Florida, on ___ (date) ___

______
Judge
Original: Clerk of the Court
Certified Copy: Victim

Amended May 28, 1992 (603 So.2d 1144); Sept. 24, 1992, effective Jan. 1, 1993 (603 So.2d 1144); Dec. 23, 1993, effective Jan. 1, 1994 (630 So.2d 552); Oct. 31, 1996, effective Nov. 15, 1996 (684 So.2d 173); Nov. 27, 1996, effective Jan. 1, 1997 (685 So.2d 1253); Nov. 2, 2000, effective Jan. 1, 2001 (794 So.2d 457); Oct. 7, 2004, effective Jan. 1, 2005 (886 So.2d 197); Nov. 20, 2008 (998 So.2d 1128); Sept. 10, 2009 (22 So.3d 1); Nov. 19, 2009, effective Jan. 1, 2010 (26 So.3d 534); Sept. 23, 2010 (48 So.3d 17).

Committee Note

1980 Amendment. The proposed changes to rule 3.986 are housekeeping in nature. References to the Department of Offender Rehabilitation have been changed to Department of Corrections to reflect a legislative change. See section 20.315, Florida Statutes (Supp. 1978). The reference to "hard labor" has been stricken as the courts have consistently held such a condition of sentence is not authorized by statute. See, *e.g., McDonald v. State*, 321 So.2d 453, 458 (Fla. 4th DCA 1975).

Rule 3.987. Motion for Postconviction Relief

MODEL FORM FOR USE IN MOTIONS FOR POSTCONVICTION RELIEF PURSUANT TO FLORIDA RULE OF CRIMINAL PROCEDURE 3.850

In the Circuit Court of the ________ Judicial Circuit, in and for ________ County, Florida

State of Florida	)	
	)	
v.	)	Criminal Division
	)	
________________	)	Case No.: ________
(your name)	)	(the original case number)
	)	
________________	)	

MOTION FOR POSTCONVICTION RELIEF

Instructions—Read Carefully

(1) This motion must be legibly handwritten or typewritten, signed by the defendant, and contain either the first or second oath set out at the end of this rule. Any false statement of a material fact may serve as the basis for prosecution and conviction for perjury. All questions must be answered concisely in the proper space on the form.

(2) Additional pages are not permitted except with respect to the facts that you rely upon to support your grounds for relief. No citation of authorities need be furnished. If briefs or arguments are submitted in support of your legal claims (as opposed to your factual claims), they should be submitted in the form of a separate memorandum of law. This memorandum should have the same caption as this motion.

(3) No filing fee is required when submitting a motion for postconviction relief.

(4) Only the judgment of one case may be challenged in a single motion for postconviction relief. If you seek to challenge judgments entered in different cases, or different courts, you must file separate motions as to each such case. The single exception to this is if you are challenging the judgments in the different cases that were consolidated for trial. In this event, show each case number involved in the caption.

(5) Your attention is directed to the fact that you must include all grounds for relief, and all facts that support such grounds, in the motion you file seeking relief from any judgment of conviction.

(6) When the motion is fully completed, the original must be mailed to the clerk of the court whose address is ____________ (county where sentence was imposed) County Courthouse, ____________ (address of clerk), Florida.

MOTION

1. Name and location of the court that entered the judgment of conviction under attack: ____________
____

2. Date of judgment of conviction: ____________

3. Length of sentence: ____________

4. Nature of offense(s) involved (all counts): ____________
____
____

5. What was your plea? (check only one)

(a) Not guilty ____

(b) Guilty ____

(c) Nolo contendere ____

(d) Not guilty by reason of insanity ____

If you entered one plea to one count and a different plea to another count, give details: ____________
____
____

6. Kind of trial: (check only one)

(a) Jury ____

(b) Judge only without jury ____

7. Did you testify at the trial or at any pretrial hearing?

Yes ____ No ____

If yes, list each such occasion: ____________
____

8. Did you appeal from the judgment of conviction?

Yes ____ No ____

9. If you did appeal, answer the following:

(a) Name of court: ____________

(b) Result: ____________

(c) Date of result: ____________

(d) Citation (if known): ____________

10. Other than a direct appeal from the judgment of conviction and sentence, have you previously filed any petitions, applications, motions, etc., with respect to this judgment in this court?

Yes ____ No ____

11. If your answer to number 10 was "yes," give the following information (applies only to proceedings in this court):

(a)(1) Nature of the proceeding: ______

______

(2) Grounds raised: ______

______

______

(3) Did you receive an evidentiary hearing on your petition, application, motion, etc.?

Yes ____ No ____

(4) Result: ______

(5) Date of result: ______

(b) As to any second petition, application, motion, etc., give the same information:

(1) Nature of the proceeding: ______

______

(2) Grounds raised: ______

______

______

(3) Did you receive an evidentiary hearing on your petition, application, motion, etc.?

Yes ____ No ____

(4) Result: ______

(5) Date of result: ______

12. Other than a direct appeal from the judgment of conviction and sentence, have you previously filed any petitions, applications, motions, etc., with respect to this judgment in any other court?

Yes ____ No ____

13. If your answer to number 12 was "yes," give the following information:

(a)(1) Name of court: ______

(2) Nature of the proceeding: ______

______

______

(3) Grounds raised: ______

______

______

(4) Did you receive an evidentiary hearing on your petition, application, motion, etc.?

Yes ____ No ____

(5) Result: ______

(6) Date of result: ______

(b) As to any second petition, application, motion, etc., give the same information:

(1) Name of court: ______

(2) Nature of the proceeding: ______

______

______

(3) Grounds raised: ______

______

______

(4) Did you receive an evidentiary hearing on your petition, application, motion, etc.?

Yes ____ No ____

(5) Result: ______

(6) Date of result: ______

(c) As to any third petition, application, motion, etc., give the same information:

(1) Name of court: ______

(2) Nature of the proceeding: ______

______

______

(3) Grounds raised: ______

______

______

(4) Did you receive an evidentiary hearing on your petition, application, motion, etc.?

Yes ____ No ____

(5) Result: ______

(6) Date of result: ______

14. State concisely every ground on which you claim that the judgment or sentence is unlawful. Summarize briefly the facts supporting each ground. If necessary, you may attach pages stating additional grounds and the facts supporting them.

For your information, the following is a list of the most frequently raised grounds for postconviction relief. Each statement preceded by a letter constitutes a separate ground for possible relief. You may raise any grounds that you may have other than those listed. However, you should raise in this motion all available grounds (relating to this conviction) on which you base your allegations that your conviction or sentence is unlawful.

DO NOT CHECK ANY OF THESE LISTED GROUNDS. If you select one or more of these grounds for relief, you must allege facts. The motion will not be accepted by the court if you merely check (a) through (i).

(a) Conviction obtained by plea of guilty or nolo contendere that was unlawfully induced or not made voluntarily with understanding of the nature of the charge and the consequences of the plea.

(b) Conviction obtained by the unconstitutional failure of the prosecution to disclose to the defendant evidence favorable to the defendant.

(c) Conviction obtained by a violation of the protection against double jeopardy.

(d) Denial of effective assistance of counsel.

(e) Denial of right of appeal.

(f) Lack of jurisdiction of the court to enter the judgment or impose sentence (such as an unconstitutional statute).

(g) Sentence in excess of the maximum authorized by law.

(h) Newly discovered evidence.

(i) Changes in the law that would be retroactive.

A. Ground 1: ______________________________

____

Supporting FACTS (tell your story briefly without citing cases or law):

____

____

____

____

____

B. Ground 2: ______________________________

____

Supporting FACTS (tell your story briefly without citing cases or law):

____

____

____

____

____

____

C. Ground 3: ______________________________

____

Supporting FACTS (tell your story briefly without citing cases or law):

____

____

____

____

____

____

D. Ground 4: ______________________________

____

Supporting FACTS (tell your story briefly without citing cases or law):

____

____

____

____

____

____

15. If any of the grounds listed in 14 A, B, C, and D were not previously presented on your direct appeal, state briefly what grounds were not so presented and give your reasons they were not so presented:

____

____

____

____

____

____

16. Do you have any petition, application, appeal, motion, etc., now pending in any court, either state or federal, as to the judgment under attack?

Yes _____ No _____

17. If your answer to number 16 was "yes," give the following information:

(a) Name of court: ______________________________

(b) Nature of the proceeding: ______________________________

(c) Grounds raised: ______________________________

____

____

(d) Status of the proceedings: ______________________________

____

18. Give the name and address, if known, of each attorney who represented you in the following stages of the judgment attacked herein.

(a) At preliminary hearing: ______________________________

____

(b) At arraignment and plea: ______________________________

____

(c) At trial: ______________________________

____

(d) At sentencing: ______________________________

____

(e) On appeal: ______________________________

____

(f) In any postconviction proceeding: ______________________________

____

(g) On appeal from any adverse ruling in a postconviction proceeding: ______________________________

____

WHEREFORE, movant requests that the court grant all relief to which the movant may be entitled in this proceeding, including but not limited to (here list the nature of the relief sought):

1. ______________________________

____

____

____

____

____

____

2. Such other and further relief as the court deems just and proper.

OATH

(Complete 1 or 2)

1. Notarized Oath.

STATE OF FLORIDA)
)
COUNTY OF ________)

Before me, the undersigned authority, this day personally appeared ________________, who first being duly sworn, says that he or she is the defendant in the above-styled cause, that he or she has read the foregoing motion for postconviction relief and has personal knowledge of the facts and matters therein set forth and alleged and that each and all of these facts and matters are true and correct.

____
(your signature)

SWORN AND SUBSCRIBED TO before me on _____ (date) _____.

____
NOTARY PUBLIC or other person authorized to administer an oath (print, type, or stamp commissioned name of notary public)

Personally known _____ or produced identification _____

Type of Identification produced _____

2. Unnotarized Oath.

Under penalties of perjury, I declare that I have read the foregoing motion and that the facts stated in it are true.

____
(your signature)

Amended Sept. 24, 1992, effective Jan. 1, 1993 (606 So.2d 227); Dec. 2, 1993 (628 So.2d 1102); Dec. 23, 1993, effective Jan. 1, 1994 (630 So.2d 552); Nov. 2, 2000, effective Jan. 1, 2001 (794 So.2d 457).

Rule 3.988. Sentencing Guidelines

Rule 3.988(a)

Category 1: Murder, Manslaughter

I. Primary Offense at Conviction

Degree	Counts 1	2	3	4	Points
Life	165	226	286	346	_____
1st pbl	150	195	276	336	_____
1st	136	165	226	286	_____
2nd	77	93	106	121	_____
3rd	45	55	65	75	_____

Primary offense counts in excess of four:

Add 60 for each additional life _____
Add 60 for each additional 1st pbl _____
Add 60 for each additional 1st _____
Add 15 for each additional 2nd _____
Add 10 for each additional 3rd _____
Total _____

II. Additional Offenses at Conviction

Degree	Counts 1	2	3	4	Points
Life	61	73	79	85	_____
1st pbl	45	54	58	63	_____
1st	29	35	38	41	_____
2nd	16	19	21	22	_____
3rd	10	12	13	14	_____
MM	2	3	4	5	_____

Additional offense counts in excess of four:

Add 6 for each additional life _____
Add 5 for each additional 1st pbl _____
Add 3 for each additional 1st _____
Add 1 for each additional 2nd _____
Add 1 for each additional 3rd _____
Add 1 for each additional MM _____
Total _____

III. A. Prior Record

Degree	Counts 1	2	3	4	Points
Life	50	110	180	270	_____
1st pbl	40	88	138	216	_____
1st	30	66	96	162	_____
2nd	15	33	48	81	_____
3rd	5	11	18	27	_____
MM	1	2	4	6	_____

Prior convictions in excess of four:

Add 90 for each additional life _____
Add 78 for each additional 1st pbl _____
Add 66 for each additional 1st _____
Add 33 for each additional 2nd _____
Add 9 for each additional 3rd _____
Add 2 for each additional MM _____
Total _____

III. B. Prior DUI Convictions

Add 32 for each prior DUI conviction only where primary offense is DUI manslaughter.

_____ Priors × 32 = _____ Total Points

IV. Legal Status at Time of Offense

Status	Points
No restrictions	0
Legal constraint	21

Total _____

V. Victim Injury (physical)

Degree of Injury		× Number	= Points
None	0	_____	_____
Slight	7	_____	_____
Moderate	14	_____	_____
Death or severe	21	_____	_____

Total _____

[G7567]

Chapter 782—Homicide (except subsection 782.04(1)(a)—capital murder)

Subsection 316.193(3)(c)(3)—DUI Manslaughter (automobile)

Subsection 327.351(2)—DUI Manslaughter (vessel)

GUIDELINE SENTENCE

Points	Recommended Range	Permitted Range
66	any nonstate prison sanction	any nonstate prison sanction

Points	Recommended Range	Permitted Range
67– 92	community control or 12–30 months incarceration	any nonstate prison sanction or community control or 1–7 years incarceration
93–135	5 (3–7)	community control or 1–12 years incarceration
136–164	10 (7–12)	3–17
165–225	15 (12–17)	7–22
226–285	20 (17–22)	12–27
286–345	25 (22–27)	17–40
346–381	30 (27–40)	22–Life
382 +	Life	27–Life

Note—Any person sentenced for a felony offense committed after October 1, 1988, whose presumptive sentence is any nonstate prison sanction may be sentenced to community control or to a term of incarceration not to exceed 22 months. Such sentence is not subject to appeal. However, before imposing such sentence, the court shall give due consideration to the criteria in s. 921.005(1). § 921.001(5), Fla. Stat. (Supp. 1988).

Rule 3.988(b)

Category 2: Sexual Offenses

I. Primary Offense at Conviction

	Counts				Points
Degree	1	2	3	4	
Life	262	314	340	366	____
1st	216	259	281	302	____
2nd	158	190	206	222	____
3rd	149	179	193	209	____

Primary offense counts in excess of four:

Add 26 for each additional life ____
Add 21 for each additional 1st ____
Add 16 for each additional 2nd ____
Add 16 for each additional 3rd ____
Total ____

II. Additional Offenses at Conviction

	Counts				Points
Degree	1	2	3	4	
Life	44	53	69	97	____
1st pbl	40	48	62	88	____
1st	36	43	56	78	____
2nd	26	31	40	56	____
3rd	25	30	39	55	____
MM	5	6	8	11	____

Additional offense counts in excess of four:

Add 28 for each additional life ____
Add 26 for each additional 1st pbl ____
Add 22 for each additional 1st ____
Add 16 for each additional 2nd ____
Add 16 for each additional 3rd ____
Add 3 for each additional MM ____
Total ____

III. Prior Record

	Counts				Points
Degree	1	2	3	4	
Life	264	530	810	1100	____
1st pbl	211	424	648	880	____
1st	158	318	486	660	____
2nd	80	159	243	330	____
3rd	26	53	81	110	____
MM	5	10	15	20	____

Prior convictions in excess of four:

Add 290 for each additional life	____
Add 232 for each additional 1st pbl	____
Add 174 for each additional 1st	____
Add 87 for each additional 2nd	____
Add 29 for each additional 3rd	____
Add 5 for each additional MM	____
Total	____

IV. Legal Status at Time of Offense

Status	Points
No restrictions	0
Legal constraint	30

Total ____

V. Victim Injury (physical)

Degree of Injury		× Number	= Points
No Contact	0		
Contact but no penetration	20		
Penetration or slight injury	40		
Death or serious injury	85		
		Total	

Chapter 794—Sexual Battery

Chapter 800—Lewdness; Indecent Exposure

Section 826.04—Incest

Section 491.0112—Sexual Misconduct by a Psychotherapist

Section 775.22—Sexual Predator Registration

GUIDELINE SENTENCE

Points	Recommended Range	Permitted Range
149–169	any nonstate prison sanction	any nonstate prison sanction
170–185	community control or 12–30 months incarceration	any nonstate prison sanction or community control or 1–3 1/2 years incarceration
186–207	3 (2 1/2–3 1/2)	community control or 1–4 1/2 years incarceration
208–229	4 (3 1/2–4 1/2)	2 1/2–5 1/2
230–250	5 (4 1/2–5 1/2)	3 1/2–7
251–278	6 (5 1/2–7)	4 1/2–9
279–312	8 (7–9)	5 1/2–12
313–354	10 (9–12)	7–17
355–422	15 (12–17)	9–22
423–486	20 (17 –22)	12–27
487–546	25 (22–27)	17–40
547–582	30 (27–40)	22–Life

Points	Recommended Range	Permitted Range
583 +	Life	27–Life

Note—Any person sentenced for a felony offense committed after October 1, 1988, whose presumptive sentence is any nonstate prison sanction may be sentenced to community control or to a term of incarceration not to exceed 22 months. Such sentence is not subject to appeal. However, before imposing such sentence, the court shall give due consideration to the criteria in s. 921.005(1). § 921.001(5), Fla. Stat. (Supp. 1988).

Rule 3.988(c)

Category 3: Robbery

I. Primary Offense at Conviction

	Counts				Points
Degree	1	2	3	4	
Life	102	122	133	148	____
1st pbl	82	98	107	119	____
1st	70	84	91	101	____
2nd	50	60	65	75	____
3rd	34	41	44	54	____

Primary offense counts in excess of four:

Add 15 for each additional life ____
Add 12 for each additional 1st pbl ____
Add 10 for each additional 1st ____
Add 10 for each additional 2nd ____
Add 10 for each additional 3rd ____
Total ____

II. Additional Offenses at Conviction

	Counts				Points
Degree	1	2	3	4	
Life	20	24	20	28	____
1st pbl	17	20	22	24	____
1st	14	17	18	19	____
2nd	10	12	13	14	____
3rd	7	8	9	10	____
MM	1	2	3	4	____

Additional offense counts in excess of four:

Add 2 for each additional life ____
Add 2 for each additional 1st pbl ____
Add 1 for each additional 1st ____
Add 1 for each additional 2nd ____
Add 1 for each additional 3rd ____
Add 1 for each additional MM ____
Total ____

III. A. Prior Record

	Counts				Points
Degree	1	2	3	4	
Life	100	210	330	460	____
1st pbl	80	168	264	368	____
1st	60	126	198	276	____
2nd	30	63	99	138	____
3rd	10	21	33	46	____
MM	2	5	8	12	____

Prior convictions in excess of four:

Add 130 for each additional life ____
Add 104 for each additional 1st pbl ____
Add 78 for each additional 1st ____
Add 39 for each additional 2nd ____
Add 13 for each additional 3rd ____
Add 4 for each additional MM ____
Total ____

III. B. Same Category Priors

Add 25 for each prior category 3 offense

____ Priors × 25 = ____ Total Points

IV. Legal Status at Time of Offense

Status	Points
No restrictions	0
Legal constraint	17

Total ____

V. Victim injury (physical)

Degree of Injury		× Number	= Points
None	0	____	____
Slight	7	____	____
Moderate	14	____	____
Death or severe	21	____	____

Total ____

Section 812.13—Robbery

Section 812.131—Carjacking

Section 812.135—Home Invasion Robbery

GUIDELINE SENTENCE

Points	Recommended Range	Permitted Range
34– 53	any nonstate prison sanction	any nonstate prison sanction
54– 65	community control or 12–30 months incarceration	any nonstate prison sanction or community control or 1–3 1/2 years incarceration
66– 81	3 (2 1/2–3 1/2)	community control or 1–4 1/2 years incarceration
82–101	4 (3 1/2–4 1/2)	2 1/2–5 1/2
102–121	5 (4 1/2–5 1/2)	3 1/2–7
122–151	6 (5 1/2–7)	4 1/2–9
152–183	8 (7–9)	5 1/2–12
184–229	10 (9–12)	7–17
230–295	15 (12–17)	9–22
296–357	20 (17–22)	12–27
358–417	25 (22–27)	17–40
418–453	30 (27–40)	22–Life
454 +	Life	27–Life

Note—Any person sentenced for a felony offense committed after October 1, 1988, whose presumptive sentence is any nonstate prison sanction may be sentenced to community control or to a term of incarceration not to exceed 22 months. Such sentence is not subject to appeal. However, before imposing such sentence, the court shall give due consideration to the criteria in s. 921.005(1). § 921.001(5), Fla. Stat. (Supp. 1988).

Rule 3.988(d)

Category 4: Violent Personal Crimes

I. Primary Offense at Conviction

Degree	Counts 1	2	3	4	Points
1st	147	176	191	206	____
2nd	105	126	136	146	____
3rd	73	88	95	102	____

Primary offense counts in excess of four:

Add 15 for each additional 1st ____
Add 10 for each additional 2nd ____
Add 7 for each additional 3rd ____
Total ____

II. Additional Offenses at Conviction

Degree	Counts 1	2	3	4	Points
1st	29	35	38	41	____
2nd	21	25	27	29	____
3rd	15	18	20	21	____
MM	3	4	5	6	____

Additional offense counts in excess of four:

Add 3 for each additional 1st ____
Add 2 for each additional 2nd ____
Add 1 for each additional 3rd ____
Add 1 for each additional MM ____
Total ____

III. Prior Record

Degree	Counts 1	2	3	4	Points
Life	50	110	160	270	____
1st pbl	40	88	128	216	____
1st	30	66	96	162	____
2nd	15	33	48	81	____
3rd	5	11	18	27	____
MM	1	2	4	6	____

Prior convictions in excess of four:

Add 90 for each additional life ____
Add 88 for each additional 1st pbl ____
Add 66 for each additional 1st ____
Add 33 for each additional 2nd ____
Add 9 for each additional 3rd ____
Add 2 for each additional MM ____
Total ____

IV. Legal Status at Time of Offense

Status	Points
No restrictions	0
Legal constraint	36

Total ____

V. Victim Injury (physical)

Degree of Injury		× Number	= Points
None	0	____	____
Slight	12	____	____
Moderate	24	____	____
Death or severe	36	____	____

Total ____

Section 231.06—Assault or Battery Upon District School Board Employee

Chapter 784—Assault, Battery

Section 836.05—Threats, Extortion

Section 836.10—Written Threats to Kill or Do Bodily Injury

Section 843.01—Resisting Officer with Violence

Subsection 381.411(4)(b)—Battery on HRS Employee

GUIDELINE SENTENCE

Points	Recommended Range	Permitted Range
73–112	any nonstate prison sanction	any nonstate prison sanction
113–154	community control or 12–30 months incarceration	any nonstate prison sanction or community control or 1–3 1/2 years incarceration
155–176	3 (2 1/2–3 1/2)	community control or 1–4 1/2 years incarceration
177–192	4 (3 1/2–4 1/2)	2 1/2–5 1/2

Points	Recommended Range	Permitted Range
193–206	5 (4 1/2–5 1/2)	3 1/2–7
207–228	6 (5 1/2–7)	4 1/2–9
229–254	8 (7–9)	5 1/2–12
255–292	10 (9–12)	7–17
293–352	15 (12–17)	9–22
353–412	20 (17–22)	12–27
413–472	25 (22–27)	17–40
473 +	30 (27–40)	22–40

Note—Any person sentenced for a felony offense committed after October 1, 1988, whose presumptive sentence is any nonstate prison sanction may be sentenced to community control or to a term of incarceration not to exceed 22 months. Such sentence is not subject to appeal. However, before imposing such sentence, the court shall give due consideration to the criteria in s. 921.005(1). § 921.001(5), Fla. Stat. (Supp. 1988).

Rule 3.988(e)

Category 5: Burglary

I. Primary Offense at Conviction

	Counts				Points
Degree	1	2	3	4	
Life	80	96	104	112	_____
1st pbl	70	84	91	98	_____
1st	60	72	78	84	_____
2nd	30	36	39	42	_____
3rd	20	24	26	28	_____

Primary offense counts in excess of four:

Add 8 for each additional life _____
Add 7 for each additional 1st pbl _____
Add 6 for each additional 1st _____
Add 3 for each additional 2nd _____
Add 2 for each additional 3rd _____
Total _____

II. Additional Offenses at Conviction

	Counts				Points
Degree	1	2	3	4	
Life	16	19	21	23	_____
1st pbl	14	16	18	20	_____
1st	12	14	16	17	_____
2nd	6	7	8	9	_____
3rd	4	5	6	7	_____
MM	1	2	3	4	_____

Additional offense counts in excess of four:

Add 2 for each additional life _____
Add 2 for each additional 1st pbl _____
Add 1 for each additional 1st _____
Add 1 for each additional 2nd _____
Add 1 for each additional 3rd _____
Add 1 for each additional MM _____
Total _____

III. A. Prior Record

	Counts				Points
Degree	1	2	3	4	
Life	60	130	210	307	_____
1st pbl	48	104	168	246	_____
1st	36	78	126	184	_____
2nd	18	39	63	90	_____
3rd	6	13	21	30	_____
MM	1	2	3	4	_____

Primary convictions in excess of four:

Add 97 for each additional life	____
Add 78 for each additional 1st pbl	____
Add 58 for each additional 1st	____
Add 27 for each additional 2nd	____
Add 9 for each additional 3rd	____
Add 1 for each additional MM	____
Total	____

III. B. Same Category Priors

Add 5 for each prior category 5 offense

____ Priors × 5 = ____ Total Points

IV. Legal Status at Time of Offense

Status	Points
No restrictions	0
Legal constraint	10
Total	____

V. Victim Injury (physical)

Degree of Injury		× Number =	Points
None	0		
Slight	5	____	____
Moderate	10	____	____
Death or severe	15	____	____
		Total	____

[G7572]

GUIDELINE SENTENCE

Points	Recommended Range	Permitted Range
20–46	any nonstate prison sanction	any nonstate prison sanction
47–71	community control or 12–30 months incarceration	any nonstate prison sanction or community control or 1–3 1/2 years incarceration
72–90	3 (2 1/2–3 1/2)	community control or 1–4 1/2 years incarceration
91–106	4 (3 1/2–4 1/2)	2 1/2–5 1/2
107–120	5 (4 1/2–5 1/2)	3 1/2–7
121–143	6 (5 1/2–7)	4 1/2–9
144–164	8 (7–9)	5 1/2–12
165–205	10 (9–12)	7–17
206–265	15 (12–17)	9–22
266–325	20 (17–22)	12–27
326–385	25 (22–27)	17–40

Chapter 810—Burglary

Subsection 806.13(3)—Criminal Mischief

Section 817.025—Obtaining Access to a Home or Private Business by False Personation or Representation

Points	Recommended Range	Permitted Range
386–445	30 (27–40)	22–Life
446 +	Life	27–Life

Note—Any person sentenced for a felony offense committed after October 1, 1988, whose presumptive sentence is any nonstate prison sanction may be sentenced to community control or to a term of incarceration not to exceed 22 months. Such sentence is not subject to appeal. However, before imposing such sentence, the court shall give due consideration to the criteria in s. 921.005(1). § 921.001(5), Fla. Stat. (Supp. 1988).

Rule 3.988(f)

Category 6: Thefts, Forgery, Fraud

I. Primary Offense at Conviction

Degree	Counts 1	2	3	4	Points
Life	86	103	112	120	____
1st	70	84	91	98	____
2nd	35	42	46	49	____
3rd	13	16	17	18	____

Primary offense counts in excess of four:

Add 8 for each additional life ____
Add 7 for each additional 1st ____
Add 3 for each additional 2nd ____
Add 1 for each additional 3rd ____
Total ____

II. Additional Offenses at Conviction

Degree	Counts 1	2	3	4	Points
Life	17	20	22	24	____
1st pbl	16	18	20	22	____
1st	14	17	18	19	____
2nd	7	8	9	10	____
3rd	3	4	5	6	____
MM	1	2	3	4	____

Additional offense counts in excess of four:

Add 2 for each additional life ____
Add 2 for each additional 1st pbl ____
Add 1 for each additional 1st ____
Add 1 for each additional 2nd ____
Add 1 for each additional 3rd ____
Add 1 for each additional MM ____
Total ____

III. A. Prior Record

Degree	Counts 1	2	3	4	Points
Life	50	110	180	270	____
1st pbl	40	88	138	216	____
1st	30	66	96	162	____
2nd	15	33	48	81	____
3rd	5	11	18	27	____
MM	1	2	4	6	____

Prior convictions in excess of four:

Add 90 for each additional life ____
Add 78 for each additional 1st pbl ____
Add 66 for each additional 1st ____
Add 33 for each additional 2nd ____
Add 9 for each additional 3rd ____
Add 2 for each additional MM ____
Total ____

III. B. Same Category Priors

Add 5 for each prior category 6 offense

____ Priors × 5 = ____ Total Points

IV. Legal Status at Time of Offense

Status	Points
No restrictions	0
Legal constraint	6
Total	____

V. Victim Injury (physical)

Degree of Injury		× Number =	Points
None	0	____	____
Slight	3	____	____
Moderate	6	____	____
Death or severe	9	____	____
		Total	____

Chapter 322—Drivers' Licenses

Chapter 409—Social and Economic Assistance

Chapter 443—Unemployment Compensation

Chapter 509—Public Lodging and Public Food Service Establishments

Chapter 812—Theft (except section 812.13—Robbery)

Chapter 815—Computer-Related Crimes

Chapter 817—Fraudulent Practices

Chapter 831—Forgery and Counterfeiting

Chapter 832—Worthless Checks

Section 192.037—Escrow Accounts

Section 206.56—Theft of State Funds

Section 370.142—Lobster Trap Tags

Section 415.11—Abuse, Neglect or Exploitation of Aged Person or Disabled Adult

Section 493.3175—Sale of Property by a Licensee

Section 494.0018—Mortgage Brokers

Section 496.413, 496.417—Solicitation of Contributions

Section 517.301(1)(a)—Fraudulent Securities Transactions

Subsections 585.145(3), 585.85(2)—Veterinary Inspection

Section 687.146—Loan Brokers

GUIDELINE SENTENCE

Points	Recommended Range	Permitted Range
13–36	any nonstate prison sanction	any nonstate prison sanction
37–56	community control or 12–30 months incarceration	any nonstate prison sanction or community control or 1–3 1/2 years incarceration
57–74	3 (2 1/2–3 1/2)	community control or 1–4 1/2 years incarceration
75–90	4 (3 1/2–4 1/2)	2 1/2–5 1/2
91–104	5 (4 1/2–5 1/2)	3 1/2–7
105–122	6 (5 1/2–7)	4 1/2–9
123–146	8 (7–9)	5 1/2–12
147–180	10 (9–12)	7–17
181–240	15 (12–17)	9–22
241–300	20 (17–22)	12–27
301–360	25 (22–27)	17–40
361–420	30 (27–40)	22–Life
421 +	Life	27–Life

Note—Any person sentenced for a felony offense committed after October 1, 1988, whose presumptive sentence is any nonstate prison sanction may be sentenced to community control or to a term of incarceration not to exceed 22 months. Such sentence is not subject to appeal. However, before imposing such sentence, the court shall give due consideration to the criteria in s. 921.005(1). § 921.001(5), Fla. Stat. (Supp. 1988).

Rule 3.988(g)

Category 7: Drugs

I. Primary Offense at Conviction

Degree	Counts 1	2	3	4	Points
Life	151	181	196	211	______
1st	137	164	178	192	______
2nd	65	78	84	91	______
3rd	42	50	55	59	______

Primary offense counts in excess of four:

Add 15 for each additional life ______
Add 14 for each additional 1st ______
Add 7 for each additional 2nd ______
Add 4 for each additional 3rd ______
Total ______

II. Additional Offenses at Conviction

Degree	Counts 1	2	3	4	Points
Life	30	36	39	42	______
1st pbl	28	34	37	40	______
1st	27	32	35	38	______
2nd	13	16	17	18	______
3rd	8	10	11	12	______
MM	2	3	4	5	______

Additional offense counts in excess of four:

Add 3 for each additional life ______
Add 3 for each additional 1st pbl ______
Add 3 for each additional 1st ______
Add 1 for each additional 2nd ______
Add 1 for each additional 3rd ______
Add 1 for each additional MM ______
Total ______

III. Prior Record

Degree	Counts 1	2	3	4	Points
Life	60	130	210	300	______
1st pbl	48	104	168	240	______
1st	36	78	126	180	______
2nd	18	39	63	90	______
3rd	6	13	21	30	______
MM	1	2	3	4	______

Prior convictions in excess of four:

Add 90 for each additional life ______
Add 72 for each additional 1st pbl ______
Add 54 for each additional 1st ______
Add 27 for each additional 2nd ______
Add 9 for each additional 3rd ______
Add 1 for each additional MM ______
Total ______

IV. Legal Status at Time of Offense

Status	Points
No restrictions	0
Legal constraint	14

Total ______

V. Victim Injury (physical)

Degree of Injury		× Number	= Points
None	0	______	______
Slight	5	______	______
Moderate	10	______	______
Death or severe	15	______	______

Total ______

Section 499.005—Regulation of Drugs and Cosmetics

Chapter 893—Drugs

GUIDELINE SENTENCE

Points	Recommended Range	Permitted Range
42–75	any nonstate prison sanction	any nonstate prison sanction
76–113	community control or 12–30 months incarceration	any nonstate prison sanction or community control or 1–3 1/2 years incarceration
114–133	3 (2 1/2–3 1/2)	community control or 1–4 1/2 years incarceration
134–147	4 (3 1/2–4 1/2)	2 1/2–5 1/2

Points	Recommended Range	Permitted Range
148–162	5 (4 1/2–5 1/2)	3 1/2–7
163–184	6 (5 1/2–7)	4 1/2–9
185–208	8 (7–9)	5 1/2–12
209–244	10 (9–12)	7–17
245–304	15 (12–17)	9–22
305–364	20 (17–22)	12–27
365–424	25 (22–27)	17–40
425–483	30 (27–40)	22–Life
484 +	Life	27–Life

Note—Any person sentenced for a felony offense committed after October 1, 1988, whose presumptive sentence is any nonstate prison sanction may be sentenced to community control or to a term of incarceration not to exceed 22 months. Such sentence is not subject to appeal. However, before imposing such sentence, the court shall give due consideration to the criteria in s. 921.005(1). § 921.001(5), Fla. Stat. (Supp. 1988).

Rule 3.988(h)

Category 8: Weapons and Escape

I. Primary Offense at Conviction

Degree	Counts 1	2	3	4	Points
1st	70	84	91	98	____
2nd	45	54	58	63	____
3rd	15	18	20	21	____

Primary offense counts in excess of four:

Add 7 for each additional 1st ____
Add 5 for each additional 2nd ____
Add 1 for each additional 3rd ____
Total ____

II. Additional Offenses at Conviction

Degree	Counts 1	2	3	4	Points
1st	14	17	18	19	____
2nd	9	11	12	13	____
3rd	3	4	5	6	____
MM	1	2	3	4	____

Additional offense counts in excess of four:

Add 1 for each additional 1st ____
Add 1 for each additional 2nd ____
Add 1 for each additional 3rd ____
Add 1 for each additional MM ____
Total ____

III. Prior Record

Degree	Counts 1	2	3	4	Points
Life	10	20	40	60	____
1st pbl	8	16	32	48	____
1st	6	12	24	36	____
2nd	3	6	12	18	____
3rd	1	2	4	6	____
MM	1	2	3	4	____

Primary convictions in excess of four:

Add 20 for each additional life	____
Add 16 for each additional 1st pbl	____
Add 12 for each additional 1st	____
Add 6 for each additional 2nd	____
Add 2 for each additional 3rd	____
Add 1 for each additional MM	____
Total	____

IV. Legal Status at Time of Offense

Status	Points
No restrictions	0
Legal constraint	12
Total	____

V. Victim Injury (physical)

Degree of Injury		× Number =	Points
None	0	____	____
Slight	4	____	____
Moderate	8	____	____
Death or severe	12	____	____
		Total	____

Chapter 790—Weapons and Firearms
Section 944.40—Escape

GUIDELINE SENTENCE

Points	Recommended Range	Permitted Range
15–49	any nonstate prison sanction	any nonstate prison sanction
50–75	community control or 12–30 months incarceration	any nonstate prison sanction or community control or 1–3 1/2 years incarceration
76–91	3 (2 1/2–3 1/2)	community control or 1–4 1/2 years incarceration
92–105	4 (3 1/2–4 1/2)	2 1/2–5 1/2
106–115	5 (4 1/2–5 1/2)	3 1/2–7
116–133	6 (5 1/2–7)	4 1/2–9
134–157	8 (7–9)	5 1/2–12
158–193	10 (9–12)	7–17
194–253	15 (12–17)	9–22
254–313	20 (17–22)	12–27
314–373	25 (22–27)	17–40
374 +	30 (27–40)	22–40

Note—Any person sentenced for a felony offense committed after October 1, 1988, whose presumptive sentence is any nonstate prison sanction may be sentenced to community control or to a term of incarceration not to exceed 22 months. Such sentence is not subject to appeal.

However, before imposing such sentence, the court shall give due consideration to the criteria in s. 921.005(1). § 921.001(5), Fla. Stat. (Supp. 1988).

Rule 3.988(i)

Category 9: All Other Felony Offenses

I. Primary Offense at Conviction

Degree	Counts 1	2	3	4	Points
Life	241	289	376	526	_____
1st pbl	181	217	282	395	_____
1st	133	160	207	290	_____
2nd	108	130	140	150	_____
3rd	52	62	68	72	_____

Primary offense counts in excess of four:

Add 150 for each additional life	_____
Add 213 for each additional 1st	_____
Add 83 for each additional 1st	_____
Add 10 for each additional 2nd	_____
Add 4 for each additional 3rd	_____
Total	_____

II. Additional Offenses at Conviction

Degree	Counts 1	2	3	4	Points
Life	48	58	75	105	_____
1st pbl	38	45	58	82	_____
1st	27	32	42	59	_____
2nd	22	26	34	48	_____
3rd	10	12	16	22	_____
MM	2	3	4	5	_____

Additional offense counts in excess of four:

Add 30 for each additional life	_____
Add 24 for each additional 1st pbl	_____
Add 17 for each additional 1st	_____
Add 14 for each additional 2nd	_____
Add 6 for each additional 3rd	_____
Add 1 for each additional MM	_____
Total	_____

III. Prior Record

Degree	Counts 1	2	3	4	Points
Life	100	210	330	460	_____
1st pbl	80	168	264	368	_____
1st	60	126	198	276	_____
2nd	30	63	99	138	_____
3rd	10	21	33	46	_____
MM	2	5	8	12	_____

Primary convictions in excess of four:

Add 130 for each additional life	_____
Add 104 for each additional 1st pbl	_____
Add 78 for each additional 1st	_____
Add 39 for each additional 2nd	_____
Add 13 for each additional 3rd	_____
Add 4 for each additional MM	_____
Total	_____

IV. Legal Status at Time of Offense

Status	Points
No restrictions	0
Legal constraint	24
Total	_____

V. Victim Injury (physical)

Degree of Injury		× Number	= Points
None	0	_____	_____
Slight	8	_____	_____
Moderate	16	_____	_____
Death or severe	24	_____	_____
		Total	_____

All felonies not included in categories one through eight.

GUIDELINE SENTENCE

Points	Recommended Range	Permitted Range
52–108	any nonstate prison sanction	any nonstate prison sanction
109–132	community control or 12–30 months incarceration	any nonstate prison sanction or community control or 1–3 1/2 years incarceration

Points	Recommended Range	Permitted Range
133–148	3 (2 1/2–3 1/2)	community control or 1–4 1/2 years incarceration
149–162	4 (3 1/2–4 1/2)	2 1/2–5 1/2
163–180	5 (4 1/2–5 1/2)	3 1/2–7
181–208	6 (5 1/2–7)	4 1/2–9
209–240	8 (7–9)	5 1/2–12
241–282	10 (9–12)	7–17
283–348	15 (12–17)	9–22
349–410	20 (17–22)	12–27
411–470	25 (22–27)	17–40
471–506	30 (27–40)	22–Life
507 +	Life	27–Life

Note—Any person sentenced for a felony offense committed after October 1, 1988, whose presumptive sentence is any nonstate prison sanction may be sentenced to community control or to a term of incarceration not to exceed 22 months. Such sentence is not subject to appeal. However, before imposing such sentence, the court shall give due consideration to the criteria in s. 921.005(1). § 921.001(5), Fla. Stat. (Supp. 1988).

Rule 3.988(j)

SENTENCING GUIDELINES SCORESHEET

1. Primary Docket Number 2. Additional Docket Numbers 3. OBTS Number 4. Category: ☐1 ☐2 ☐3 ☐4 ☐5 ☐6 ☐7 ☐8 ☐9

5. Name (Last Name First) 6. Date of Birth 7. Sex: ☐M ☐F 8. Race: ☐B ☐W ☐Other 9. Violation ☐Prob ☐CC 10. County

11. Judge at Sentencing 12. Date of Offense 13. Date of Sentence 14. ☐Plea ☐Trial 15. DOC Number

OFFICE USE ONLY POINTS

I. PRIMARY OFFENSE AT CONVICTION

Counts Degree Statute Description ______ I. ______

II. ADDITIONAL OFFENSES AT CONVICTION

Counts Fel/Misd Degree Statute Description

______

______

______

______

______ II. ______

(Continue on Separate Page)

III. A. PRIOR RECORD

Counts Fel/Misd Degree Statute Description

______

______

______

______

______

OFFICE USE ONLY POINTS

______ ______ ______ ______ ______ III. A. ______

(Continue on Separate Page)

______ III. B. SAME CATEGORY PRIORS (categories 3, 5 and 6 only) III. B. ______

______ III. C. PRIOR DUI CONVICTIONS (category 1 only) III. C. ______

______ IV. LEGAL STATUS AT TIME OF OFFENSE

____ (1) no restrictions ____ (2) legal constraint IV. ______

V. VICTIM INJURY

Number of Scoreable Victim Injuries	Degree of Injury
______	none or no contact
______	slight or contact but no penetration
______	moderate or penetration
______	severe or death

V. ______

TOTAL POINTS ______

RECOMMENDED SENTENCE ______ PERMITTED SENTENCE ______

TOTAL SENTENCE IMPOSED ______

______ REASONS FOR DEPARTURE ______

JUDGE ______ PREPARER ______

OFFICE USE ONLY T.S. ______ C.C. ______ Prob. ______ S.P. ______ C.J. ______ E.F. ______

Effective Date: Jan. 1, 1991

Distributions	Court File	Sentencing Guidelines Commission	Department of Corrections	Defendant
	Original	First Copy	Second Copy	Third Copy

[G7556]

Sentencing Guidelines Scoresheet, continued

Primary Document Number ______ OBTS Number ______

Name (Last Name First) ______ County ______

OFFICE USE ONLY

II. CONTINUATION OF ADDITIONAL OFFENSES AT CONVICTION

	Counts	Fel/Misd	Degree	Statute	Description
______	______	______	______	______	______
______	______	______	______	______	______
______	______	______	______	______	______
______	______	______	______	______	______
______	______	______	______	______	______
______	______	______	______	______	______
______	______	______	______	______	______
______	______	______	______	______	______
______	______	______	______	______	______
______	______	______	______	______	______

III. A. CONTINUATION OF PRIOR RECORD

	Counts	Fel/Misd	Degree	Statute	Description
______	______	______	______	______	______
______	______	______	______	______	______
______	______	______	______	______	______
______	______	______	______	______	______
______	______	______	______	______	______
______	______	______	______	______	______
______	______	______	______	______	______
______	______	______	______	______	______
______	______	______	______	______	______
______	______	______	______	______	______

REASONS FOR DEPARTURE ______

____
Judge

[G7576]

Amended Sept. 6, 1990, effective Jan. 1, 1991 (566 So.2d 770); March 7, 1991 (576 So.2d 1307); Nov. 7, 1991 (589 So.2d 271); Feb. 11, 1993 (613 So.2d 1307); Nov. 30, 1993 (628 So.2d 1084).

Rule 3.989. Affidavit, Petition, and Order to Expunge or Seal Forms

(a) Affidavit in Support of Petition.

In the Circuit Court of the
__________ Judicial Circuit,
in and for __________
County, Florida

Case No.: __________
Division __________

State of Florida,)
Plaintiff,)
v.)
__________________)
Defendant/Petitioner)
__________________)

AFFIDAVIT

State of Florida

County of __________

I, _____ (name of defendant/petitioner) _____, am the defendant/petitioner in the above-styled cause and I do hereby swear or affirm that:

1. I fully understand the meaning of all of the terms of this affidavit.

2. I have never been adjudicated guilty of a criminal offense or a comparable ordinance violation nor adjudicated delinquent for committing a felony or a misdemeanor specified in section 943.051(3)(b), Florida Statutes.

3. I was arrested on _____ (date) _____, by _____ (arresting agency) _____, and I have not been adjudicated guilty of, nor adjudicated delinquent for committing, any of the acts stemming from that arrest or the alleged criminal activity surrounding my arrest.

4. I am eligible for the relief requested, to the best of my knowledge and belief, and do not have any other petition to expunge or seal pending before any court.

5. I have never secured a prior records expunction or sealing under any law.

6. (For use in expunction petitions only.) My record of arrest for this date has been sealed for at least 10 years; or an indictment, information, or other charging document was not filed against me for the above criminal transaction; or an indictment, information, or other charging document filed against me was dismissed by the prosecutor or the court.

____
Petitioner

Sworn to and subscribed before me on _____ (date)

____
NOTARY PUBLIC, or other person authorized to administer an oath

Printed, typed, or stamped commissioned name of Notary Public

Personally known _____ or produced identification _____

Type of identification produced __________

My commission expires:

(b) Order to Expunge.

In the Circuit Court of the
__________ Judicial Circuit,
in and for __________
County, Florida

Case No.: __________
Division __________

State of Florida,)
Plaintiff,)
v.)
__________________,)
Defendant/Petitioner)
__________________)

ORDER TO EXPUNGE UNDER SECTION 943.0585, FLORIDA STATUTES, AND FLORIDA RULE OF CRIMINAL PROCEDURE 3.692

THIS CAUSE having come on to be heard before me this date on a petition to expunge certain records of the petitioner's arrest on _____ (date) _____, by _____ (arresting agency) _____, for _____ (charges)

_____, and the court having heard argument of counsel and being otherwise fully advised in the premises, the court hereby finds the following:

1. The petitioner has never previously been adjudicated guilty of a criminal offense or a comparable ordinance violation nor adjudicated delinquent for committing a felony or a misdemeanor specified in section 943.051(3)(b), Florida Statutes.

2. The petitioner was not adjudicated guilty of nor adjudicated delinquent for committing any of the acts stemming from the arrest or criminal activity to which this expunction petition pertains.

3. The petitioner has not secured a prior records expunction or sealing.

4. This record has either been sealed for at least 10 years; or no indictment, information, or other charging document was ever filed in this case against the petitioner; or an indictment, information, or other charging document filed against the defendant was dismissed by the prosecutor or the court.

5. A Certificate of Eligibility issued by the Florida Department of Law Enforcement accompanied the petition for expunction of nonjudicial criminal history records. Whereupon it is

ORDERED AND ADJUDGED that the petition to expunge is granted. All court records pertaining to the above-styled case shall be sealed in accordance with the procedures set forth in Florida Rule of Criminal Procedure 3.692; and it is further

ORDERED AND ADJUDGED that the clerk of this court shall forward a certified copy of this order to the (check one) _____ state attorney, _____ special prosecutor, _____ statewide prosecutor, _____ (arresting agency) _____, and the Sheriff of ____________ County, who will comply with the procedures set forth in section 943.0585, Florida Statutes, and appropriate regulations of the Florida Department of Law Enforcement, and who will further forward a copy of this order to any agency that their records reflect has received the instant criminal history record information; and it is further

ORDERED AND ADJUDGED that _____ (arresting agency) _____ shall expunge all information concerning indicia of arrest or criminal history record information regarding the arrest or alleged criminal activity to which this petition pertains in accordance with the procedures set forth in section 943.0585, Florida Statutes, and Florida Rule of Criminal Procedure 3.692.

All costs of certified copies involved herein are to be borne by the ____________.

DONE AND ORDERED in Chambers at ________ County, Florida, on _____ (date) ______

____
Circuit Court Judge

(c) Order to Seal.

In the Circuit Court of the
________ Judicial Circuit,
in and for ________
County, Florida

Case No.: ________
Division ________

State of Florida,)
)
Plaintiff,)
)
v.)
)
____________,)
Defendant/Petitioner)
____________)

ORDER TO SEAL RECORDS UNDER SECTION 943.059, FLORIDA STATUTES, AND FLORIDA RULE OF CRIMINAL PROCEDURE 3.692

THIS CAUSE having come on to be heard before me this date on petitioner's petition to seal records concerning the petitioner's arrest on _____ (date) _____, by the _____ (arresting agency) _____, and the court having heard argument of counsel and being otherwise advised in the premises, the court hereby finds:

1. The petitioner has never been previously adjudicated guilty of a criminal offense or comparable ordinance violation nor adjudicated delinquent for committing a felony or a misdemeanor specified in section 943.051(3)(b), Florida Statutes.

2. The petitioner was not adjudicated guilty of nor adjudicated delinquent for committing any of the acts stemming from the arrest or criminal activity to which the instant petition pertains.

3. The petitioner has not secured a prior records expunction or sealing.

4. A Certificate of Eligibility issued by the Florida Department of Law Enforcement accompanied the instant petition for sealing nonjudicial criminal history records. Whereupon it is

ORDERED AND ADJUDGED that the petition to seal records is granted. All court records pertaining to the above-styled case shall be sealed in accordance with the procedures set forth in Florida Rule of Criminal Procedure 3.692; and it is further

ORDERED AND ADJUDGED that the clerk of this court shall forward a certified copy of this order to the (check one) _____ state attorney, _____ special prosecutor, _____ statewide prosecutor, _____ (arresting agency) _____, and the Sheriff of ____________ County, who will comply with the procedures set forth in section 943.059, Florida Statutes, and appropriate regulations of the Florida Department of Law Enforcement, and who will further forward a copy of this order to any agency that their records reflect has received the instant criminal history record information; and it is further

ORDERED AND ADJUDGED that ____ (arresting agency) ____ shall seal all information concerning indicia of arrest or criminal history record information regarding the arrest or alleged criminal activity to which this petition pertains in accordance with the procedures set forth in section 943.059, Florida Statutes, and Florida Rule of Criminal Procedure 3.692.

All costs of certified copies involved herein are to be borne by the ____________

DONE AND ORDERED in Chambers at ____________ County, Florida, on ____ (date) ____

____
Circuit Court Judge

(d) Petition to Expunge or Seal.

In the Circuit Court of the
________ Judicial Circuit,
in and for ________
County, Florida

Case No.: ________
Division ________

State of Florida,)
Plaintiff,)
v.)
______________,)
Defendant/Petitioner)
______________)

PETITION TO EXPUNGE OR SEAL

The petitioner, ____________, by and through the undersigned attorney, petitions this honorable court, under Florida Rule of Criminal Procedure 3.692 and section ____ 943.0585, or ____ section 943.059 Florida Statutes, to ____ expunge/seal ____ all criminal history record information in the custody of any criminal justice agency and the official records of the court concerning the petitioner's arrest on ____ (date) ____, by ____ (arresting agency) ____, for ____ (charges) ____, and as grounds therefor shows:

1. On ____ (date) ____, the petitioner, ____________, a ____ (race/sex) ____, whose date of birth is ____ (date of birth) ____, was arrested by ____ (arresting agency) ____, and charged with ____ (charges) ____

2. The petitioner has not been adjudicated guilty of nor adjudicated guilty of committing any of the acts stemming from this arrest or alleged criminal activity.

3. The petitioner has not been previously adjudicated guilty of a criminal offense or a comparable ordinance violation nor adjudicated delinquent for committing a felony or a misdemeanor specified in section 943.051(3)(b), Florida Statutes.

4. The petitioner has not secured a prior records expunction or sealing under section 943.0585, or 943.059, Florida Statutes, former section 943.058, Florida Statutes, former section 893.14, Florida Statutes, or former section 901.33, Florida Statutes, or any other law, rule, or authority.

5. (To be used only when requesting expunction.) The petitioner's record has been sealed under section 943.059, Florida Statutes, former section 943.058, Florida Statutes, former section 893.14, Florida Statutes, or former section 901.33, Florida Statutes, for at least 10 years; or there has not been an indictment, information, or other charging document filed against the petitioner who is the subject of this criminal history record information; or an indictment, information, or other charging document filed against the petitioner who is the subject of this criminal history information was dismissed by the prosecutor or the court.

6. A Certificate of Eligibility for ____ expunction/sealing ____ of nonjudicial criminal history records issued by the Florida Department of Law Enforcement accompanies this petition.

WHEREFORE, the petitioner moves to ____ expunge/seal ____ any criminal history record information and any official court records regarding his/her arrest by ____ (arresting agency) ____, for ____ (charges) ____, on ____ (date) ____.

I HEREBY CERTIFY that a true and correct copy of the foregoing pleading has been served on ____ (name of prosecuting authority) ____, (check one) ____ State Attorney for the ________ Judicial Circuit, in and for ________ County, ____ Special Prosecutor, ____ Statewide Prosecutor); ____ (arresting agency) ____; ________ (Sheriff of county in which defendant was arrested, if different); and the Florida Department of Law Enforcement, on ____ (date) ____.

____
Name:
Address:
City/State:
Telephone Number:
Fla. Bar No.:

(e) Petition to Expunge; Human Trafficking Victim.

In the Circuit Court of the
____________ Judicial Circuit,

in and for ____________
County, Florida

Case No.: ____________
Division ____________

State of Florida,)
)
Plaintiff,)
)
v.)
)
____________,)
)
Defendant/Petitioner.)

PETITION TO EXPUNGE/HUMAN TRAFFICKING VICTIM

The petitioner, ..., by and through the undersigned attorney, petitions this honorable court, under Florida Rule of Criminal Procedure 3.692 and section .... 943.0583, Florida Statutes, to expunge all criminal history record information in the custody of any criminal justice agency and the official records of the court concerning the petitioner's arrest and/or conviction on .... (date(s)) ...., by .... (arresting agency and/or prosecuting authority) ...., for .... (charges and/or offenses) ...., and as grounds therefor shows:

1. On .... (date(s)) ...., the petitioner, ..., a .... (race/sex) ...., whose date of birth is .... (date of birth) ...., was arrested by .... (arresting agency) ...., and charged with .... (charges) .... or was convicted by .... (name of prosecuting authority) .... of .... (offenses) ....

2. The petitioner has been the victim of human trafficking, as discussed in section 787.06, Florida Statutes, and has committed an offense, other than those offenses listed in 775.084(1)(b)1, which was committed as a part of a human trafficking scheme of which he/she was the victim or at the direction of an operator of the scheme as evidenced by the attached official documentation of his/her status, or may be shown by clear and convincing evidence presented to the Court.

WHEREFORE, the petitioner moves to .... expunge any criminal history record information and any official court records regarding his/her arrest and/or conviction by .... (arresting agency and/or name of prosecuting authority) ...., for .... (charges and/or offenses) ...., on .... (date(s)) ....

I HEREBY CERTIFY that a true and correct copy of the foregoing pleading has been served on .... (name of prosecuting authority) ...., (check one) .... State Attorney for the .... Judicial Circuit, in and for .... County, ... Special Prosecutor, ... Statewide Prosecutor; .... (arresting agency) .... ; .... (Sheriff of county in which defendant was arrested, if different); and the Florida Department of Law Enforcement, on .... (date) ....

____
Name:
Address:
City/State:
Telephone Number:
E-mail Address:
Fla. Bar No.:

.... or produced identification ....

Type of identification produced

(f) Affidavit in Support of Petition; Human Trafficking Victim.

In the Circuit Court of the
____________ Judicial Circuit,
in and for ____________
County, Florida

Case No.: ____________
Division ____________

State of Florida,)
)
Plaintiff,)
)
v.)
)
____________,)
)
Defendant/Petitioner.)
____________)

AFFIDAVIT/HUMAN TRAFFICKING VICTIM

State of Florida

County of ____________

I, ...(name of defendant/petitioner)..., am the defendant/petitioner in the above-styled cause and I do hereby swear or affirm that:

1. I fully understand the meaning of all of the terms of this affidavit.

2. I have been the victim of human trafficking, as discussed in section 787.06, Florida Statutes, and have committed an offense, other than those offenses listed in 775.084(1)(b)1, which was committed as a part of a human trafficking scheme of which I was the victim or at the direction of an operator of the scheme.

3. I was arrested and/or convicted on ...(date(s))..., by ...(arresting agency and/or name of prosecuting authority)...

4. I am eligible for the relief requested, to the best of my knowledge and belief, and . . .(do or do not). . . have any other petition to expunge or seal pending before any court.

____
Petitioner

Sworn to and subscribed before me on . . .(date). . .

____
NOTARY PUBLIC, or other person authorized to administer an oath
Printed, typed, or stamped commissioned name of Notary Public

Personally known . . . . or produced identification . . . .

Type of identification produced . . . .

My commission expires:

(g) Order to Expunge; Human Trafficking Victim.

In the Circuit Court of the
____
Judicial Circuit, in and for
____
County, Florida

Case No.: ______________
Division _______________

State of Florida,)
)
Plaintiff,)
)
v.)
)
________________________,)
)
Defendant/Petitioner.)
)

ORDER TO EXPUNGE, HUMAN TRAFFICKING VICTIM,
UNDER SECTION 943.0585, FLORIDA STATUTES,
AND FLORIDA RULE OF CRIMINAL PROCEDURE 3.692

THIS CAUSE, having come on to be heard before me this date upon a petition to expunge certain records of the petitioner's arrest and/or conviction on . . . . (date(s)) . . . ., by . . . . (arresting agency and/or name of prosecuting authority) . . . ., for . . . . (charges and/or offenses) . . . ., and the court having heard argument of counsel and being otherwise fully advised in the premises, the court hereby finds the following:

The petitioner has been the victim of human trafficking, as discussed in section 787.06, Florida Statutes, and has committed an offense, other than those offenses listed in 775.084(1)(b)1, which was committed as a part of a human trafficking scheme of which he/she was the victim, or at the direction of an operator of the scheme. A conviction expunged under this section is deemed to have been vacated due to a substantive defect in the underlying criminal proceedings.

Whereupon it is

ORDERED AND ADJUDGED that the petition to expunge is granted. All court records pertaining to the above-styled case shall be sealed in accordance with the procedures set forth in Florida Rule of Criminal Procedure 3.692; and it is further

ORDERED AND ADJUDGED that the clerk of this court shall forward a certified copy of this order to the (check one) . . . . state attorney, ... special prosecutor, ... statewide prosecutor, ... (arresting agency) . . . ., and the Sheriff of . . . . County, who will comply with the procedures set forth in section 943.0583, Florida Statutes, and appropriate regulations of the Florida Department of Law Enforcement, and who will further forward a copy of this order to any agency that their records reflect has received the instant criminal history record information; and it is further

ORDERED AND ADJUDGED that . . . . (arresting agency) . . . . shall expunge all information concerning indicia of arrest, conviction, or criminal history record information regarding the arrest, conviction, or alleged criminal activity to which this petition pertains in accordance with the procedures set forth in section 943.0583, Florida Statutes, and Florida Rule of Criminal Procedure 3.692.

All costs of certified copies involved herein are to be borne by the . . . .

DONE AND ORDERED in Chambers at . . . . County, Florida, on . . . . (date) . . . .

____
Circuit Court Judge

Amended Dec. 23, 1993 (630 So.2d 552); June 16, 1994 (639 So.2d 15); Nov. 2, 2000, effective Jan. 1, 2001 (794 So.2d 457); Dec. 12, 2013, effective Jan. 1, 2014 (132 So.3d 123); April 24, 2014, effective April 24, 2014 (137 So.3d 1015).

Committee Notes

1984 Adoption. In order to have uniformity throughout the state, the committee proposes these forms for petition to expunge or seal, order to seal, and order to expunge and affidavit. These also should be a great asset to counsel and an invaluable asset to the clerks and FDLE, etc., who will be receiving orders in the future. The subcommittee working on these proposed forms has contacted law enforcement agencies, clerks, etc., for their input as to these proposed forms.

Rule 3.990. Sentencing Guidelines Scoresheet

RULE 3.990(a) SENTENCING GUIDELINES SCORESHEET

1. DATE OF SENTENCE ☐☐ ☐☐ ☐☐ MO DY YR
2. PREPARED BY ☐ DC ☐ SAO
3. COUNTY
4. SENTENCING JUDGE

5. NAME (LAST,FIRST,M.I.)
6. DOB ☐☐ ☐☐ ☐☐ MO DY YR
7. DC ☐☐☐☐☐☐
8. OBTS # ☐☐☐☐☐☐☐☐☐☐
9. RACE ☐B ☐W ☐OTH HISP. ☐YES ☐NO
10. GENDER ☐M ☐F
11. ☐PLEA ☐TRIAL

☐ Check here if that sentencing is for only a revocation of probation or community control

I. PRIMARY OFFENSE: If Qualifier, please check___A___S___C (A=Attempt, S=Solicitation, C=Conspiracy) POINTS

CODES DC USE ONLY	DOCKET#	FELONY DEGREE	F.S.#	OFFENSE LEVEL	OFF. DATE
☐☐☐☐	____ /	____ /	____	☐☐	☐☐ ☐☐ ☐☐ MO DY YR

Description __________

(Level = Pts: 1=4, 2=10, 3=16, 4=22, 5=28, 6=36, 7=56, 8=74, 9=92, 10=116)

I. ____

II. ADDITIONAL OFFENSE(S): Supplemental page attached ☐

	DOCKET#	FEL/MM	F.S.#	OFFENSE LEVEL	QUALIFY A S C	CNTS		POINTS	
☐☐☐☐	____ /	____ /	____ /	____	☐☐☐	____	×	____	= ____
Description:									
☐☐☐☐	____ /	____ /	____ /	____	☐☐☐	____	×	____	= ____
Description:									
☐☐☐☐	____ /	____ /	____ /	____	☐☐☐	____	×	____	= ____
Description									

(Level = Pts: M=0.2, 1=0.7, 2=1.2, 3=2.4, 4=3.6, 5=5.4, 6=7.2, 7=8.4, 8=9.6, 9=10.8, 10=12.0)

Supplemental page points ____

II. ____

III. VICTIM INJURY:

			Number		Total				Number		Total
2ND Degree Murder	120	×	____	=	____	Slight	4	×	____	=	____
Death	60	×	____	=	____	Sex Penetration	40	×	____	=	____
Severe	40	×	____	=	____	Sex Contact	18	×	____	=	____
Moderate	18	×	____	=	____						

III. ____

IV. PRIOR RECORD: Supplemental page attached ☐

	FEL/MM DEGREE	F.S.#	OFFENSE LEVEL	QUALIFY: A S C	DESCRIPTION	NUM		POINTS	
☐☐☐☐	____	____	____	☐☐☐	____	____	×	____	= ____
☐☐☐☐	____	____	____	☐☐☐	____	____	×	____	= ____
☐☐☐☐	____	____	____	☐☐☐	____	____	×	____	= ____
☐☐☐☐	____	____	____	☐☐☐	____	____	×	____	= ____
☐☐☐☐	____	____	____	☐☐☐	____	____	×	____	= ____

(Level = Pts: M=0.2, 1=0.5, 2=0.8, 3=1.6, 4=2.4, 5=3.6, 6=4.8 7=5.6, 8=6.4, 9=7.2, 10=8.0)

Supplemental page point ____

IV. ____

Page Subtotal ____

Effective Date: January 1, 1994

Page 1 Subtotal ____

V. Legal Status Violation = 4 Points V. ____

VI. Release Program Violation—6 Points X Number of Violations (Max 18 Pts) = VI. ____

VII. Firearm or Destructive Device = 18 Points VII. ____

VIII. Semi–Automatic Weapon or Machine Gun = 25 Points VIII. ____

Subtotal Sentence Points. ______

IX. Enhancements (only one multiplier may be used)

Law Enforcement Protection	Drug Trafficking
☐ 1.5 Multiplier ☐ 2.0 Multiplier	☐ 1.5 Multiplier

Enhanced Subtotal Sentence Points IX. ______

TOTAL SENTENCE POINTS ______

SENTENCE COMPUTATION

- If total sentence points are less than, or equal to 40, the sentencing court may not impose a state prison sentence. The sentencing court may increase total sentence points that are less than or equal to 40 by up to 15 percent and may impose a state prison sentence if the increased total exceeds 40 points.

______ × 1.15 = ______

Total Sentence Points Increased Sentence Points

- If total sentence points are greater than 40 and less than or equal to 52 the decision to incarcerate in a state prison is left to the discretion of the court. If total sentence points are greater than 5% the sentence must be a state prison sentence. A state prison sentence is calculated by deducting 28 from total or increased sentence points.

______ minus 28 = ______

Total Or Increased Sentence Pts. State Prison Months

- The sentencing court may increase or decrease state prison months by up to 25 percent except where the total sentence points were less than or equal to 40 but have been increased by up to 15 percent to exceed 40 points. Any state prison sentence must exceed 12 months.

× .75 ______
Minimum State Prison Months

______ / \
State Prison Months

× 1.25 ______
Maximum State Prison Months

TOTAL SENTENCE IMPOSED

	Years	Months	Days
☐ State Prison	______	______	______
☐ County Jail	______	______	______
☐ Community Control	______	______	______
☐ Probation	______	______	______

- Please designate the particular type of sentence where an enhanced or mandatory sentence imposed.

☐ Habitual Felony Offender ☐ Guidelines Aggravated Departure
☐ Habitual Violent Felony Offender ☐ Guidelines Mitigated Departure
Mandatory pursuant to: ☐ s.775.087 ☐ s.893.13 ☐ s.893.135

RULE 3.990(b) SUPPLEMENTAL SENTENCING GUIDELINES SCORESHEET

NAME (LAST,FIRST,M.I.) DOCKET # DATE OF SENTENCE
M O D Y Y R
☐☐ ☐☐ ☐☐

CODES DC USE ONLY	II. ADDITIONAL OFFENSE(S) DOCKET#	FEL/MM	F.S. #	LEVEL	QUALIFY A S C	CNTS		POINTS	
□□□□	______	/	______ / ______	/	□□□		× ______	=	______
	Description: ______								
□□□□	______	/	______ / ______	/	□□□		× ______	=	______
	Description: ______								
□□□□	______	/	______ / ______	/	□□□		× ______	=	______
	Description: ______								
□□□□	______	/	______ / ______	/	□□□		× ______	=	______
	Description: ______								
□□□□	______	/	______ / ______	/	□□□		× ______	=	______
	Description: ______								

(Level = Pts: M=0.2, 1=0.7, 2=1.2, 3=2.4, 4=3.6, 5=5.4, 6=7.2, 7=8.4, 8=9.6, 9=10.8, 10=12.0)

II. ______

IV. **PRIOR RECORD:** Supplemental page attached

	FEL/MM DEGREE	F.S. #	LEVEL	QUALIFY: A S C	DESCRIPTION	NUM		POINTS(s)	
□□□□	______	______ /	______	□□□	______	______	× ______	=	______
□□□□	______	______ /	______	□□□	______	______	× ______	=	______
□□□□	______	______ /	______	□□□	______	______	× ______	=	______
□□□□	______	______ /	______	□□□	______	______	× ______	=	______
□□□□	______	______ /	______	□□□	______	______	× ______	=	______
□□□□	______	______ /	______	□□□	______	______	× ______	=	______

(Level = Pts: M=0.2, 1=0.5, 2=0.8, 3=1.6, 4=2.4, 5=3.6, 6=4.8, 7=5.6, 8=6.4, 9=7.2, 10=8.0)

IV. ______

REASONS FOR DEPARTURE ______

______

______

______

______

______

______

______

JUDGE'S SIGNATURE

Effective Date: January 1, 1994

If reasons cited for departure are not listed below, please write reasons on the reverse side in the area specified "Reasons for Departure"

Reasons for Departure—Aggravating Circumstances

- ☐ Legitimate, uncoerced, plea bargain.
- ☐ Offense was one of violence and was committed in a manner that was especially heinous, atrocious or cruel.
- ☐ Offenses arose from separate episodes. Primary offense is at level 4 or higher and the defendant has committed 5 or more offenses within a 180 day period that have resulted in convictions.
- ☐ Primary offense is scored at level 3 and the defendant has committed 8 or more offenses within a 180 day period that have resulted in convictions.
- ☐ Offense was committed within 6 months of defendant's discharge from a release program or state prison.
- ☐ Defendant occupied a leadership role in a criminal organization.
- ☐ Offense committed by a public official under color of office.
- ☐ Defendant knew victim to be a law enforcement officer at the time of the offense, the offense was a violent offense; and that status is not an element of the primary offense.

- ☐ Offense created substantial risk of death or great bodily harm to many persons or to one or more small children.
- ☐ Victim especially vulnerable due to age or physical or mental disability.
- ☐ Offense was motivated by prejudice based on race, color, ancestry, ethnicity, religion, sexual orientation or national origin of the victim.
- ☐ Victim suffered extraordinary physical or emotional trauma or permanent physical injury, or was treated with particular cruelty.
- ☐ Victim was physically attacked by the defendant in the presence of one or more members of the victim's family.
- ☐ Offense resulted in substantial economic hardship to a victim and consisted of an illegal act or acts committed by means of concealment, guile or fraud to obtain money or property, to avoid payment or loss of money or property or to obtain business or professional advantage when two or more of the following circumstances were present:
  - ☐ Offense involved multiple victims or multiple incidents per victim.
  - ☐ Offense involved a high degree of sophistication or planning or occurred over a lengthy period of time;
  - ☐ The defendant used position or status to facilitate the commission of the offense, including positions of trust, confidence, or fiduciary relationship; or
  - ☐ The defendant was in the past involved in other conduct similar to that involved in the current offense.
- ☐ Offense committed in order to prevent or avoid arrest, to impede or prevent prosecution for the conduct underlying the arrest, or to effect an escape from custody.
- ☐ Defendant is not amenable to rehabilitation or supervision, as evidenced by an escalating pattern of criminal conduct as described in s. 921.001(8).
- ☐ Defendant induced a minor to participate in any of the offenses pending before the court for disposition.
- ☐ Primary offense is scored at level 7 or higher and the defendant has been convicted of one or more offense that scored, or would have scored, at an offense level 8 or higher.
- ☐ Defendant has an extensive unscoreable juvenile record.

Reasons for Departure—Mitigating Circumstances

- ☐ Legitimate, uncoerced plea bargain.
- ☐ Defendant was an accomplice to the offense and was a relatively minor participant in the criminal conduct.
- ☐ The capacity of the defendant to appreciate the criminal nature of the conduct or to conform that conduct to the requirements of law was substantially impaired.
- ☐ Defendant requires specialized treatment for addiction, mental disorder, or physical disability and the defendant is amenable to treatment.
- ☐ The need for payment of restitution to the victim outweighs the need for a prison sentence.
- ☐ The victim was an initiator, willing participant, aggressor, or provoker of the incident.
- ☐ The defendant acted under extreme duress or under the domination of another person.
- ☐ Before the identity of the defendant was determined, the victim was substantially compensated.
- ☐ Defendant cooperated with the State to resolve the current offense or any other offense.
- ☐ The offense was committed in an unsophisticated manner and was an isolated incident for which the defendant has shown remorse.
- ☐ At the time of the offense the defendant was too young to appreciate the consequences of the offense.
- ☐ Defendant to be sentenced as a youthful offender.

Added Nov. 30, 1993, effective Jan. 1, 1994 (628 So.2d 1084).

Rule 3.991. Sentencing Guidelines Scoresheets [1]

(a) Sentencing Guidelines Scoresheet

1. DATE OF SENTENCE ☐☐ ☐☐ ☐☐ MO DY YR 2. PREPARED BY ☐ DC ☐ SAO 3. COUNTY 4. SENTENCING JUDGE

5. NAME (LAST,FIRST,M.I.) 6. DOB MO DY YR ☐☐ ☐☐ ☐☐ 7. DC # ☐☐☐☐☐☐ 8. OBTS # ☐☐☐☐☐☐☐☐☐☐ 9. RACE ☐ B ☐ W ☐ OTH 10. GENDER ☐ M ☐ F 11. ☐ PLEA ☐ TRIAL

I. **PRIMARY OFFENSE:** If Qualifier, please check ___ A ___ S ___ C ___ R (A=Attempt, S=Solicitation, C=Conspiracy, R=Reclassification)

CODES DC USE ONLY	DOCKET#	FELONY DEGREE	F.S. #	OFFENSE LEVEL	OFFENSE DATE	POINTS
☐☐☐☐	____/	____/	____	☐☐	☐☐ ☐☐ ☐☐ MO DY YR	

Description: ____

(Level = Pts: 1=4, 2=10, 3=16, 4=22, 5=28, 6=36, 7=56, 8=74, 9=92, 10=116)

Prior capital felony triples primary offense points ☐   I. ____

II. **ADDITIONAL OFFENSE(S):** Supplemental page attached ☐

	DOCKET#	FEL/MM	F.S. #	OFFENSE LEVEL	QUALIFY A S C R	CNTS				POINTS
☐☐☐☐	____/	____/	____/	____	☐☐☐☐	____	×	____	=	____
	Description: ____									
☐☐☐☐	____/	____/	____/	____	☐☐☐☐	____	×	____	=	____
	Description: ____									
☐☐☐☐	____/	____/	____/	____	☐☐☐☐	____	×	____	=	____
	Description: ____									

(Level = Pts: M=0.2, 1=0.7, 2=1.2, 3=2.4, 4=3.6, 5=5.4, 6=18, 7=28, 8=37, 9=45, 10=58)

Prior capital felony triples additional offense points ☐   Supplemental page points ____

II. ____

III. **VICTIM INJURY:**

			Number		Total				Number		Total
2nd Degree Murder	240	×	____	=	____	Slight	4	×	____	=	____
Death	120	×	____	=	____	Sex Penetration	80	×	____	=	____
Severe	40	×	____	=	____	Sex Contact	40	×	____	=	____
Moderate	18	×	____	=	____						

III. ____

IV. **PRIOR RECORD:** Supplemental page attached ☐

	FEL/MM DEGREE	F.S. #	DEFENSE LEVEL	QUALIFY: A S C R	DESCRIPTION	NUM		POINTS		
☐☐☐☐	____	____/	____	☐☐☐☐	____	____	×	____	=	____
☐☐☐☐	____	____/	____	☐☐☐☐	____	____	×	____	=	____
☐☐☐☐	____	____/	____	☐☐☐☐	____	____	×	____	=	____
☐☐☐☐	____	____/	____	☐☐☐☐	____	____	×	____	=	____
☐☐☐☐	____	____/	____	☐☐☐☐	____	____	×	____	=	____

(Level = Pts: M=0.2, 1=0.5, 2=0.8, 3=1.6, 4=2.4, 5=3.6, 6=9, 7=14, 8=19, 9=23, 10=29)

Supplemental page points ____

IV. ____

Effective Date: For offenses committed on or after October 1, 1995   Page Subtotal ____

Page 1 Subtotal ______

V. Legal Status Violation = 4 Points V. ______

VI. Community Sanction Violation before the court for sentencing
A) 6 Pts × each such successive violation OR VI. A. ______
B) New Felony Conviction = 12 Pts × each such successive violation B. ______

VII. Firearm/Semi–Automatic or Machine Gun = 18 or 25 Points VII. ______

VIII. Prior Serious Felony = 30 Pts VIII. ______

Subtotal Sentence Points. ______

IX. Enhancements (only if the primary offense qualifies for enhancement)

Law Enforcement Protection	Drug Trafficking	Grand Theft Motor Vehicle
☐ × 1.5 ☐ × 2.0 ☐ × 2.5	☐ × 1.5	☐ × 1.5

Enhanced Subtotal Sentence Points IX. ______

TOTAL SENTENCE POINTS ______

SENTENCE COMPUTATION

- 40 or less total sentence points mandates a non state prison sanction. Sentence points less than or equal to 40 may be increased by 15 percent.

______ × 1.15 = ______
Total Sentence Points — Increased Sentence Points

- If total or increased sentence points are greater than 40 or equal to 52, state incarceration is discretionary. A total of more than 52 total or increased sentence points must be a state prison sentence. A life sentence may be imposed at the discretion of the court if total sentence points are 363 or greater.

______ minus 28 = ______
Total/Increased Points — State Prison Months

- The sentencing court may increase or decrease prison months by up to 25 percent except where total sentence points were originally increased by 15 percent to exceed 40 points. Any state prison sentence must exceed 12 months.

______ / × .75 = ______ Min. Prison Months
State Prison Months
\\ × 1.25 = ______ Max. Prison Months

TOTAL SENTENCE IMPOSED

	Years	Months	Days
☐ State Prison ☐ Life			
☐ County Jail ☐ Time Served			
☐ Community Control			
☐ Probation			

Has more than one scoresheet been used at sentencing?
____ Yes ____ No

- Please designate the particular type of sentence where an enhanced or mandatory sentence imposed.

☐ Habitual Felony/Habitual Violent Offender ☐ Guideline Aggravated Departure
☐ Violent Career Criminal ☐ Guideline Mitigated Departure
☐ Mandatory pursuant to: ☐ § 775.087 ☐ § 893.13 ☐ § 893.135

JUDGE'S SIGNATURE

____

(b) Supplemental Sentencing Guidelines Scoresheet

NAME (LAST,FIRST,M.I.) DOCKET # DATE OF SENTENCE
M O D Y Y R
☐☐ ☐☐ ☐☐

CODES DC USE ONLY	II. ADDITIONAL OFFENSE(S) DOCKET#	FEL/MM	F.S. #	LEVEL	QUALIFY A S C R	CNTS		POINTS
□□□□	____/	____/	____/	____	□□□□	___ × ___	=	____
	Description: ____							
□□□□	____/	____/	____/	____	□□□□	___ × ___	=	____
	Description: ____							
□□□□	____/	____/	____/	____	□□□□	___ × ___	=	____
	Description: ____							
□□□□	____/	____/	____/	____	□□□□	___ × ___	=	____
	Description: ____							
□□□□	____/	____/	____/	____	□□□□	___ × ___	=	____
	Description: ____							

(Level = Pts: M=0.2, 1=0.7, 2=1.2, 3=2.4, 4=3.6, 5=5.4, 6=18, 7=28, 8=37, 9=46, 10=58)

II.____

IV. **PRIOR RECORD**: Supplemental page attached

	FEL/MM DEGREE	F.S.#	LEVEL	QUALIFY: A S C R	DESCRIPTION	NUM		POINTS(s)
□□□□	____	____/	____	□□□□	____	____ ×	=	____
□□□□	____	____/	____	□□□□	____	____ ×	=	____
□□□□	____	____/	____	□□□□	____	____ ×	=	____
□□□□	____	____/	____	□□□□	____	____ ×	=	____
□□□□	____	____/	____	□□□□	____	____ ×	=	____
□□□□	____	____/	____	□□□□	____	____ ×	=	____

(Level = Pts: M=0.2, 1=0.5, 2=0.8, 3=1.6, 4=2.4, 5=3.6, 6=9, 7=14, 8=19, 9=23, 10=29)

IV.____

REASONS FOR DEPARTURE ____________________

____

____

____

____

____

____

JUDGE'S SIGNATURE

Effective Date: For offenses committed an or after October 1, 1995

If reasons cited for departure are not listed below, please write reasons on the reverse side.

Reasons for Departure—Aggravating Circumstances

[ ] Legitimate, uncoerced, plea bargain.

[ ] Offense was one of violence and was committed in a manner that was especially heinous, atrocious or cruel.

[ ] Offenses arose from separate episodes. Primary offense is at level 4 or higher and the defendant has committed 5 or more offenses within a 180 day period that have resulted in convictions.

[ ] Primary offense is scored at level 3 and the defendant has committed 8 or more offenses within a 180 day period that have resulted in convictions.

[ ] Offense was committed within 6 months of defendant's discharge from a release program or state prison.

[ ] Defendant occupied leadership role in a criminal organization.

[ ] Offense committed by a public official under color of office.

[ ] Defendant knew victim was a law enforcement officer at the time of the offense; the offense was a violent offense; and that status is not an element of the primary offense.

[ ] Offense created substantial risk of death or great bodily harm to many persons or to one or more small children.

[ ] Victim especially vulnerable due to age or physical or mental disability.

[ ] Offense was motivated by prejudice based on race, color, ancestry, ethnicity, religion, sexual orientation, or national origin of the victim.

[ ] Victim suffered extraordinary physical or emotional trauma or permanent physical injury, or was treated with particular cruelty.

[ ] Victim was physically attacked by the defendant in the presence of one or more members of the victim's family.

[ ] Offense resulted in substantial economic hardship to a victim and consisted of an illegal act or acts committed by means of concealment, guile, or fraud to obtain money or property, to avoid payment or loss of money or property, or to obtain business or professional advantage, when two or more of the following circumstances were present:

[ ] Offense involved multiple victims or multiple incidents per victim;

[ ] Offense involved a high degree of sophistication or planning or occurred over a lengthy period of time;

[ ] The defendant used position or status to facilitate the commission of the offense, including positions of trust, confidence, or fiduciary relationship; or

[ ] The defendant was in the past involved in other conduct similar to that involved in the current offense.

[ ] Offense committed in order to prevent or avoid arrest, to impede or prevent prosecution for the conduct underlying the arrest, or to effect an escape from custody.

[ ] Defendant is not amenable to rehabilitation or supervision, as evidenced by an escalating pattern of criminal conduct as described in s. 921.001(8).

[ ] Defendant induced a minor to participate in any of the offenses pending before the court for disposition.

[ ] Primary offense is scored at level 7 or higher and the defendant has been convicted of one or more offense that scored, or would have scored, at an offense 8 or higher.

[ ] Defendant has an extensive unscoreable juvenile record.

[ ] Effective for offenses committed on or after January 1, 1997—Defendant committed an offense involving sexual contact or sexual penetration and as a direct result of the offense, the victim contracted a sexually transmissible disease.

Reasons for Departure—Mitigating Circumstances

[ ] Legitimate, uncoerced plea bargain.

[ ] Defendant was an accomplice to the offense and was a relatively minor participant in the criminal conduct.

[ ] The capacity of the defendant to appreciate the criminal nature of the conduct or to conform that conduct to the requirement of law was substantially impaired.

[ ] Defendant requires specialized treatment for a mental disorder that is unrelated to substance abuse or addiction, or for a physical disability, and the defendant is amenable to treatment.

[ ] Effective only for offenses committed prior to July 1, 1997—Defendant requires specialized treatment for addiction and is amenable to treatment.

[ ] The need for payment of restitution to the victim outweighs the need for a prison sentence.

[ ] The victim was an initiator, willing participant, aggressor, or provoker of the incident.

[ ] The defendant acted under extreme duress or under the domination of another person.

[ ] Before the identity of the defendant was determined, the victim was substantially compensated.

[ ] Defendant cooperated with the State to resolve the current offense or any other offense.

[ ] The offense was committed in an unsophisticated manner and was an isolated incident for which the defendant has shown remorse.

[ ] At the time of the offense the defendant was too young to appreciate the consequences of the offense.

[ ] Defendant to be sentenced as a youthful offender.

Added Sept. 21, 1995, effective Oct. 1, 1995 (660 So.2d 1374). Amended Sept. 26, 1996, effective Jan. 1, 1997 (685 So.2d 1213); June 26, 1997, eff. July 1, 1997 and Oct. 1, 1997 (696 So.2d 1171); April 2, 1998 (711 So.2d 27).

1 Name line supplied by Publisher.

Rule 3.992. Criminal Punishment Code Scoresheets

(a) Criminal Punishment Code Scoresheet. The Criminal Punishment Code Scoresheet Preparation Manual is available at: *http://www.dc.state.fl.us/pub/sen_cpcm/index.html*

The Criminal Punishment Code Scoresheet Preparation Manual is available at: *http://www.dc.state.fl.us/pub/sen_cpcm/index.html*

1. DATE OF SENTENCE	2. PREPARER'S NAME	3. COUNTY	4. SENTENCING JUDGE	
5. NAME (LAST, FIRST, M.I.)	6. DOB	8. RACE ☐B ☐W ☐OTHER	10. PRIMARY OFF. DATE	12. PLEA ☐
	7. DC #	9. GENDER ☐M ☐F	11. PRIMARY DOCKET #	TRIAL ☐

I. **PRIMARY OFFENSE:** If Qualifier, please check ___A ___S ___C ___R (A=Attempt, S=Solicitation, C=Conspiracy, R=Reclassification)

FELONY DEGREE	F.S.#	DESCRIPTION	OFFENSE LEVEL	POINTS
______/	______/	______/	______/	

(Level - Points: 1=4, 2=10, 3=16, 4=22, 5=28, 6=36, 7=56, 8=74, 9=92, 10=116)

Prior capital felony triples Primary Offense points ☐ I. ______

II. **ADDITIONAL OFFENSE(S):** Supplemental page attached ☐

DOCKET#	FEL/MM DEGREE	F.S.#	OFFENSE LEVEL	QUALIFY A S C R	COUNTS		POINTS		TOTAL
______/	______/	______/	______	☐☐☐☐	______	x	______	=	______
DESCRIPTION ______									
______/	______/	______/	______	☐☐☐☐	______	x	______	=	______
DESCRIPTION ______									
______/	______/	______/	______	☐☐☐☐	______	x	______	=	______
DESCRIPTION ______									
______/	______/	______/	______	☐☐☐☐	______	x	______	=	______
DESCRIPTION ______									

(Level - Points: M=0.2, 1=0.7, 2=1.2, 3=2.4, 4=3.6, 5=5.4, 6=18, 7=28, 8=37, 9=46, 10=58)

Prior capital felony triples Additional Offense points ☐

Supplemental page points ______

II. ______

III. **VICTIM INJURY:**

		Number		Total			Number		Total
2nd Degree Murder	240 x	______	=	______	Slight	4 x	______	=	______
Death	120 x	______	=	______	Sex Penetration	80 x	______	=	______
Severe	40 x	______	=	______	Sex Contact	40 x	______	=	______
Moderate	18 x	______	=	______					

III. ______

IV. **PRIOR RECORD:** Supplemental page attached ☐

FEL/MM DEGREE	F.S.#	OFFENSE LEVEL	QUALIFY: A S C R	DESCRIPTION	NUMBER		POINTS		TOTAL
______	______/	______	☐☐☐☐	______	______	X	______	=	______
______	______/	______	☐☐☐☐	______	______	X	______	=	______
______	______/	______	☐☐☐☐	______	______	X	______	=	______
______	______/	______	☐☐☐☐	______	______	X	______	=	______
______	______/	______	☐☐☐☐	______	______	X	______	=	______
______	______/	______	☐☐☐☐	______	______	X	______	=	______
______	______/	______	☐☐☐☐	______	______	X	______	=	______
______	______/	______	☐☐☐☐	______	______	X	______	=	______
______	______/	______	☐☐☐☐	______	______	X	______	=	______

(Level = Points: M=0.2, 1=0.5, 2=0.8, 3=1.6, 4=2.4, 5=3.6, 6=9, 7=14, 8=19, 9=23, 10=29)

Supplemental page points ______

IV. ______

Page 1 Subtotal: ______

Effective Date: For offenses committed under the Criminal Punishment Code effective for offenses committed on or after October 1, 1998 and subsequent revisions.

NAME (LAST, FIRST, M.I.)	DOCKET #

Page 1 Subtotal: ______

V. Legal Status violation = 4 Points

☐ Escape ☐ Fleeing ☐ Failure to appear ☐ Supersedeas bond ☐ Incarceration ☐ Pretrial intervention or diversion program

☐ Court imposed or post prison release community supervision resulting in a conviction V. ______

VI. Community Sanction violation before the court for sentencing

☐ Probation ☐ Community Control ☐ Pretrial Intervention or diversion VI. ______

☐ 6 points for any violation other than new felony conviction x ______ each successive violation OR

☐ New felony conviction = 12 points x ______ each successive violation if new offense results in conviction before or at same time as sentence for violation of probation OR

☐ 12 points x ______ each successive violation for a violent felony offender of special concern when the violation is not based solely on failure to pay costs, fines, or restitution OR

☐ New felony conviction = 24 points x ______ each successive violation for a violent felony offender of special concern if new offense results in a conviction before or at the same time for violation of probation

VII. Firearm/Semi-Automatic or Machine Gun = 18 or 25 Points VII. ______

VIII. Prior Serious Felony - 30 Points VIII. ______

Subtotal Sentence Points ______

IX. Enhancements (only if the primary offense qualifies for enhancement)

Law Enf. Protect.	Drug Trafficker	Motor Vehicle Theft	Criminal Gang Offense	Domestic Violence in the Presence of Related Child (offenses committed on or after 3/12/07)	Adult-on-Minor Sex Offense (offenses committed on or after 10/1/14)
___x 1.5 ___x 2.0 ___x 2.5	____x 1.5	___x 1.5	___x 1.5	___x 1.5	___x 2.0

Enhanced Subtotal Sentence Points IX. ______

TOTAL SENTENCE POINTS ______

SENTENCE COMPUTATION

If total sentence points are less than or equal to 44, the lowest permissible sentence is any non-state prison sanction. If the total sentence points are 22 points or less, see Section 775.082(10), Florida Statutes, to determine if the court must sentence the offender to a non-state prison sanction.

If total sentence points are greater than 44:

______ minus 28 = ______ x .75 = ______

total sentence points — lowest permissible prison sentence in months

If total sentence points are 60 points or less and court makes findings pursuant to both Florida Statute 948.20 and 397.334(3), the court may place the defendant into a treatment-based drug court program.

The maximum sentence is up to the statutory maximum for the primary and any additional offenses as provided in s. 775.082, F.S., unless the lowest permissible sentence under the Code exceeds the statutory maximum. Such sentences may be imposed concurrently or consecutively. If total sentence points are greater than or equal to 363, a life sentence may be imposed.

______
maximum sentence in years

TOTAL SENTENCE IMPOSED

	Years	Months	Days
☐ State Prison ☐ Life	____	____	____
☐ County Jail ☐ Time Served	____	____	____
☐ Community Control			
☐ Probation ☐ Modified	____	____	____

Please check if sentenced as ☐ habitual offender, ☐habitual violent offender, ☐ violent career criminal, ☐ prison releasee reoffender, or a ☐ mandatory minimum applies.

☐ Mitigated Departure ☐ Plea Bargain ☐ Prison Diversion Program

Other Reason ______

JUDGE'S SIGNATURE

Effective Date: For offenses committed under the Criminal Punishment Code effective for offenses committed on or after October 1, 1998, and subsequent revisions.

(b) Supplemental Criminal Punishment Code Scoresheet

NAME (LAST, FIRST, M.I.) DOCKET # DATE OF SENTENCE

II. ADDITIONAL OFFENSES(S):

DOCKET#	FEL/MM DEGREE	F.S.#	OFFENSE LEVEL	QUALIFY A S C R	COUNTS		POINTS		TOTAL
______/	______/	______/	______	☐☐☐☐	______	×	______	=	______
DESCRIPTION ______									
______/	______/	______/	______	☐☐☐☐	______	×	______	=	______
DESCRIPTION ______									
______/	______/	______/	______	☐☐☐☐	______	×	______	=	______
DESCRIPTION ______									
______/	______/	______/	______	☐☐☐☐	______	×	______	=	______
DESCRIPTION ______									
______/	______/	______/	______	☐☐☐☐	______	×	______	=	______
DESCRIPTION ______									

(Level—Points: M=0.2, 1=0.7, 2=1.2, 3=2.4, 4=3.6, 5=5.4, 6=18, 7=28, 8=37, 9=46, 10=58)

II. ______

IV. PRIOR RECORD

FEL/MM DEGREE	F.S.#	OFFENSE LEVEL	QUALIFY: A S C R	DESCRIPTION	NUMBER		POINTS		TOTAL
______	______/	______	☐☐☐☐	______	______	×	______	=	______
______	______/	______	☐☐☐☐	______	______	×	______	=	______
______	______/	______	☐☐☐☐	______	______	×	______	=	______
______	______/	______	☐☐☐☐	______	______	×	______	=	______
______	______/	______	☐☐☐☐	______	______	×	______	=	______
______	______/	______	☐☐☐☐	______	______	×	______	=	______

(Level = Points: M=0.2, 1=0.5, 2=0.8, 3=1.6, 4=2.4, 5=3.6, 6=9, 7 =14, 8=19, 9=23, 10=29)

IV. ______

REASONS FOR DEPARTURE—MITIGATING CIRCUMSTANCES

(reasons may be checked here or written on the scoresheet)

☐ Legitimate, uncoerced plea bargain.

☐ The defendant was an accomplice to the offense and was a relatively minor participant in the criminal conduct.

☐ The capacity of the defendant to appreciate the criminal nature of the conduct or to conform that conduct to the requirements of law was substantially impaired.

☐ The defendant requires specialized treatment for a mental disorder that is unrelated to substance abuse or addiction, or for a physical disability, and the defendant is amenable to treatment.

☐ The need for payment of restitution to the victim outweighs the need for a prison sentence.

☐ The victim was an initiator, willing participant, aggressor, or provoker of the incident.

☐ The defendant acted under extreme duress or under the domination of another person.

☐ Before the identity of the defendant was determined, the victim was substantially compensated.

☐ The defendant cooperated with the State to resolve the current offense or any other offense.

☐ The offense was committed in an unsophisticated manner and was an isolated incident for which the defendant has shown remorse.

☐ At the time of the offense the defendant was too young to appreciate the consequences of the offense.

☐ The defendant is to be sentenced as a youthful offender.

☐ The defendant is amenable to the services of a postadjudicatory treatment-based drug court program and is otherwise qualified to participate in the program.

☐ The defendant was making a good faith effort to obtain or provide medical assistance for an individual experiencing a drug-related overdose.

Pursuant to 921.0026(3) the defendant's substance abuse or addiction does not justify a downward departure from the lowest permissible sentence, except for the provisions of s. 921.0026(2)(m).

Effective Date: For offenses committed under the Criminal Punishment Code effective for offenses committed on or after October 1, 1998 and subsequent revisions.

Added Sept. 24, 1998, effective Oct. 1, 1998 (721 So.2d 265). Amended Sept. 26, 2001 (810 So.2d 826); April 19, 2007 (957 So.2d 1160); Jan. 10, 2008 (972 So.2d 862); Sept. 25, 2008, eff. Oct. 1, 2008 (992 So.2d 239); Dec. 3, 2009 (30 So.3d 491); Sept. 28, 2011 (73 So.3d 202); Oct. 11, 2012 (101 So.3d 1263); Sept. 4, 2014, effective Oct. 1, 2014 (147 So.3d 515).

Rule 3.993. Forms Related to Capital Postconviction Records Production

(a) Notice to State Attorney of Affirmance of Death Penalty.

In the Circuit Court of the ____
Judicial Circuit, in and for ____
County, Florida
Case No. ____________
Division ____________

State of Florida,

Plaintiff,

v.

________________,

Defendant.

NOTICE TO STATE ATTORNEY OF AFFIRMANCE OF DEATH PENALTY

TO: ____________________________
[name of state attorney and circuit]

The Attorney General of the State of Florida, under Florida Rule of Criminal Procedure 3.852(d)(1), gives notice that on .....(date)....., the Florida Supreme Court issued its mandate affirming the death sentence in this case.

Within 15 days after receipt of this notice, you should provide written notice to each law enforcement agency involved in this case.

Within 90 days after receipt of this notice, you and each law enforcement agency involved in this case, should copy, index, and deliver to the records repository of the Secretary of State all public records that were produced in the investigation or prosecution of this case, except those previously filed in the trial court.

I HEREBY CERTIFY that a true and correct copy of the foregoing has been served on _________ [name of trial court], _________ [name of state attorney], and _________ [name of trial counsel for defendant] on .....(date).,

____
[name and address of attorney general]

(b) Notice to Secretary of Department of Corrections of Affirmance of Death Penalty.

In the Circuit Court of the ____
Judicial Circuit, in and for ____
County, Florida
Case No. ____________
Division ____________

State of Florida,

Plaintiff,

v.

________________,

Defendant.

NOTICE TO SECRETARY OF DEPARTMENT OF CORRECTIONS OF AFFIRMANCE OF DEATH PENALTY

TO: ____________________________
[name of Secretary of Department of Corrections]

The Attorney General of the State of Florida, under Florida Rule of Criminal Procedure 3.852(d)(1), gives notice that on _____ (date) _____, the Florida Supreme Court issued its mandate affirming the death sentence in this case.

Within 90 days after receipt of this notice, you should copy, index, and deliver to the records repository of the Secretary of State all public records determined by your department to be relevant to the subject matter of a proceeding under Florida Rule of Criminal Procedure 3.850 or 3.851 unless the production of these records would be unduly burdensome.

I HEREBY CERTIFY that a true and correct copy of the foregoing has been served on _________ [name of trial court], _________ [name of Secretary of Department of Corrections], and _________ [name of trial counsel for defendant] on _____ (date) _____.

____
[name and address of attorney general]

(c) Notice by State Attorney to Law Enforcement Agency.

In the Circuit Court of the ____
Judicial Circuit, in and for ____
County, Florida
Case No. ____________
Division ____________

State of Florida,

Plaintiff,

v.

________________,

Defendant.

NOTICE OF AFFIRMANCE OF DEATH PENALTY AND TO PRODUCE PUBLIC RECORDS

TO: ______________________________
[name of chief law enforcement officer]

The State Attorney of the ________ Judicial Circuit of the State of Florida, under Florida Rule of Criminal Procedure 3.852(e)(1), hereby gives notice to ______________ [name of chief law enforcement officer and agency], that was involved in this case by investigation, arrest, prosecution or incarceration, that on ____ (date) ____, the Florida Supreme Court issued its mandate affirming the death sentence in this case.

Within 90 days after receipt of this notice, you and each law enforcement agency involved in this case should copy, index, and deliver to the records repository of the Secretary of State all public records that were produced in the investigation, arrest, prosecution, or incarceration of this case, except those filed in the trial court.

I HEREBY CERTIFY that a true and correct copy of the foregoing has been served on ________ [name of trial court], ________ [name of chief law enforcement officer], ________ [name of attorney general], and ________ [name of collateral counsel], on ____ (date) ____.

____
[name and address of state attorney]

(d) Notice of Compliance by State Attorney.

In the Circuit Court of the ____
Judicial Circuit, in and for ____
County, Florida
Case No. ____________
Division ____________

State of Florida,

Plaintiff,

v.

______________,

Defendant.

NOTICE OF COMPLIANCE BY STATE ATTORNEY

TO: ______________________________
[name and address of attorney general]

The State Attorney for the ______________ Judicial Circuit gives notice to the Attorney General of compliance by delivery of public records involving this case to the records repository of the Secretary of State. To the best of my knowledge and belief, all public records in my possession that were produced in the investigation or prosecution of the case, except those previously filed in the trial court, have been copied, indexed, and delivered to the records repository of the Secretary of State as required by Florida Rule of Criminal Procedure 3.852(e)(2).

I HEREBY CERTIFY that a true and correct copy of the foregoing has been served on ________ [name of trial court], ________ [name of attorney general], and ________ [name of collateral counsel] on ____ (date) ____.

____
[name and address of state attorney]

(e) Notice of Compliance by the Secretary of the Department of Corrections.

In the Circuit Court of the ____
Judicial Circuit, in and for ____
County, Florida
Case No. ____________
Division ____________

State of Florida,

Plaintiff,

v.

______________,

Defendant.

NOTICE OF COMPLIANCE BY THE SECRETARY OF THE DEPARTMENT OF CORRECTIONS

TO: ______________________________
[name and address of attorney general]

The Secretary of the Department of Corrections, having received notice of the affirmance of the death penalty in this case from the Attorney General on ____ (date) ____, hereby gives notice and certifies that, to the best of my knowledge and belief, all public records determined by the Department to be relevant to the subject matter of a proceeding under Florida Rule of Criminal Procedure 3.850 or 3.851, except those previously filed in the trial court, have been copied, indexed, and delivered to the records repository of the Secretary of State.

I HEREBY CERTIFY that a true and correct copy of the foregoing has been served on ________ [name of trial court], ________ [name of attorney general], ________ [name of state attorney], and ________ [name of collateral counsel], on ____ (date) ____.

____
[name and address of Secretary of Department of Corrections]

(f) Notice of Compliance by Law Enforcement Agency.

In the Circuit Court of the ____ Judicial Circuit, in and for ____ County, Florida
Case No. ____________
Division ____________

State of Florida,

Plaintiff,

v.

______________,

Defendant.

NOTICE OF COMPLIANCE BY LAW ENFORCEMENT AGENCY

TO: ______________________________
[name and address of attorney general]

______[name of chief law enforcement officer and agency] that was involved in this case by an investigation, arrest, prosecution, or incarceration, hereby gives notice to the Attorney General of compliance by delivery of public records involving this case to the records repository of the Secretary of State. I further certify that, to the best of my knowledge and belief, all public records in possession of this agency or in the possession of any employee of this agency that were produced in the investigation or prosecution of the case, except those previously filed in the trial court, have been copied, indexed, and delivered to the records repository of the Secretary of State.

I HEREBY CERTIFY that a true and correct copy of the foregoing has been served on ________ [name of trial court], _________ [name of attorney general], _________ [name of state attorney], and ______ [name of collateral counsel], on ____ (date) ____.

____
[name and address of chief law enforcement officer]

(g) Notice to Attorney General of Pertinent Information.

In the Circuit Court of the ____ Judicial Circuit, in and for ____ County, Florida
Case No. ____________
Division ____________

State of Florida,

Plaintiff,

v.

______________,

Defendant.

STATE ATTORNEY'S NOTICE TO ATTORNEY GENERAL OF PERTINENT INFORMATION

TO: ______________________________
[name and address of attorney general]

The undersigned ______[name of state attorney] hereby gives notice to the Attorney General of the following name(s) and address(es) of any person or agency having information pertinent to this case in addition to those persons and agencies who previously furnished public records to the records repository of the Secretary of State:

[list names and addresses of persons or agencies]

Please provide prompt written notification to each identified person or agency of the duty to deliver to the records respository of the Secretary of State all public records pertaining to this case, except those previously filed in the trial court.

I HEREBY CERTIFY that a true and correct copy of the foregoing has been served on ________ [name of trial court], ________ [name of attorney general], and ________ [name of public defender or defense counsel], on _____ (date) _____

____
[name and address of state attorney]

(h) Notice to Attorney General of Pertinent Information.

In the Circuit Court of the ____ Judicial Circuit, in and for ____ County, Florida
Case No. ____________
Division ____________

State of Florida,

Plaintiff,

v.

______________,

Defendant.

TRIAL COUNSEL'S NOTICE TO ATTORNEY GENERAL OF PERTINENT INFORMATION

TO: ______________________________
[name and address of attorney general]

The undersigned ________ [name of public defender or other counsel], for ________ [name of defendant], hereby gives notice to the Attorney General of the following name(s) and address(es) of persons or agencies that may have information pertinent to this case, in addition to those previously furnished to collateral counsel.

[list names and addresses of persons or agencies]

Please provide prompt written notification to each identified person or agency of the duty to deliver to the records repository of the Secretary of State all public records pertaining to this case, except those previously filed in the trial court.

I HEREBY CERTIFY that a true and correct copy of the foregoing has been served on ________ [name of trial court], ________ [name of attorney general], and ________ [name of state attorney], on ____ (date) ____.

____
[name and address of trial counsel]

(i) Notice by Attorney General to Person or Agency Having Pertinent Information.

In the Circuit Court of the ____
Judicial Circuit, in and for ____
County, Florida
Case No. ________
Division ________

State of Florida,

Plaintiff,

v.

__________,

Defendant.

NOTICE BY ATTORNEY GENERAL TO PERSON OR AGENCY HAVING PERTINENT INFORMATION

TO: ____________________
[name and address of person or agency]

Pursuant to Florida Rule of Criminal Procedure 3.852(d)(2), the undersigned has been notified by ________ [name of trial counsel or state attorney], that you have public records pertinent to this case.

Under the provisions of rule 3.852(e)(5), you must:

1. Within 90 days of receipt of this notice, copy, index, and deliver to the records repository of the Secretary of State all public records in your possession pertinent to this case, except those previously filed in the trial court; and

2. Provide written notice to me that you have complied with these provisions.

I HEREBY CERTIFY that a true and correct copy of the pleading has been served on ________ [name of person or agency]and ________ [name of trial court], on ____ (date) ____.

____
[name and address of attorney general]

(j) Notice of Compliance by Person or Agency.

In the Circuit Court of the ____
Judicial Circuit, in and for ____
County, Florida
Case No. ________
Division ________

State of Florida,

Plaintiff,

v.

__________,

Defendant.

NOTICE OF COMPLIANCE BY PERSON OR AGENCY

TO: ____________________
[name and address of attorney general]

The undersigned having received notice under Florida Rule of Criminal Procedure 3.852(e)(5) from the Attorney General on ____ (date) ____, to copy, index, and deliver all public records in my possession or in the possession of the undersigned agency to the records repository of the Secretary of State, hereby gives notice to the Attorney General and further certifies that, to the best of my knowledge and belief, all of these public records in my possession or in the possession of the undersigned agency pertaining to this case, except those previously filed in the trial court, have been copied, indexed, and delivered to the records repository of the Secretary of State.

I HEREBY CERTIFY that a true and correct copy of the foregoing has been served on ________ [name of trial court], ________ [name of attorney general], ________ [name of state attorney], and ________ [name of collateral counsel], on ____ (date) ____.

____
[name and address of person or agency]

(k) Defendant's Demand for Production of Additional Public Records Pertaining to Defendant's Case.

In the Circuit Court of the ____
Judicial Circuit, in and for ____
County, Florida
Case No. ________
Division ________

State of Florida,

Plaintiff,

v.

__________,

Defendant.

DEFENDANT'S DEMAND FOR ADDITIONAL PUBLIC RECORDS PERTAINING TO DEFENDANT'S CASE

TO: ______________________

[name and address of person or agency]

The defendant, by and through undersigned counsel, hereby makes demand of __________[name of person or agency submitting public records], under Florida Rule of Criminal Procedure 3.852(i), for additional public records pertinent to this case.

1. Undersigned counsel represents that, after a timely and diligent search, the records specifically described below:

(a) are relevant to a pending proceeding under rule 3. 850; or

(b) appear reasonably calculated to lead to the discovery of admissible evidence; and

(c) have not been obtained previously in discovery or from a prior public records request from either the above-named person or agency or any other; and

(d) presently are not available from the public records repository.

2. The public records requested are as follows:

[list public records requested]

3. Under rule 3.852, any objection to production, including any claim of exemption, must be filed with the trial court and served on all counsel of record within 60 days of receipt of this demand, or that objection will be considered waived.

4. Under rule 3.852, you shall, within 90 days after receipt of this demand:

(a) copy, index, and deliver to the records repository of the Secretary of State any additional public records in the possession of your agency that pertain to this case; and

(b) certify that, to the best of your knowledge and belief, all additional public records have been delivered to the records repository of the Secretary of State; and

(c) recertify that the public records previously delivered are complete if no additional public records are found.

____

[name of attorney for defendant]

I HEREBY CERTIFY that a true and correct copy of the foregoing has been served on __________ [name of trial court], __________ [name of person or agency], __________ [name of attorney general], and __________ [name of state attorney], on _____ (date) _____.

____

[name and address of attorney for defendant]

(*l*) Objection to Defendant's Request for Production of Additional Public Records Pertaining to Defendant's Case and Motion for Hearing.

In the Circuit Court of the ____ Judicial Circuit, in and for ____ County, Florida
Case No. __________
Division __________

State of Florida,

Plaintiff,

v.

______________,

Defendant.

OBJECTION TO DEFENDANT'S REQUEST FOR PRODUCTION OF ADDITIONAL PUBLIC RECORDS PERTAINING TO DEFENDANT'S CASE AND MOTION FOR HEARING

The undersigned person or agency, having received on _____ (date) _____ defendant's demand for production of additional public records pertaining to defendant's case hereby files this objection and respectfully moves the court to hold a hearing to determine if the requirements of Florida Rule of Criminal Procedure 3.852 have been met. The grounds for this objection are:

[specify grounds and identify records]

Respectfully submitted,

____

[name of attorney]

Attorney for __________

[name of person or agency]

I HEREBY CERTIFY that a true and correct copy of the foregoing has been served on __________ [name of trial court], __________ [name of attorney for defendant], and __________ [name of attorney general], on _____ (date) _____.

____

[name of attorney]

(m) Notice of Delivery of Exempt Public Records to Records Repository.

In the Circuit Court of the ____ Judicial Circuit, in and for ____ County, Florida
Case No. __________
Division __________

State of Florida,

Plaintiff,

v.

_______________,

Defendant.

NOTICE OF DELIVERY OF EXEMPT PUBLIC RECORDS TO RECORDS REPOSITORY

TO: Records Repository

____
[address of records repository]

The undersigned, ________[name of person or agency], hereby gives notice to the records repository of the Secretary of State that certain delivered records are confidential or exempt from the requirements of section 119.07(1), Florida Statutes. These public records have been separately contained without being redacted, sealed, and the nature of the public records and the legal basis under which the public records are exempt has been identified.

I HEREBY CERTIFY that a true and correct copy of the foregoing has been served on ________[name of trial court], ________[name of records repository], ________[name of attorney general], [name of state attorney], and ________[name of collateral counsel] on _____ (date) _____.

____
[name and address of person or agency]

(n) Order to Deliver Exempt Public Records to the Clerk of Circuit Court.

In the Circuit Court of the ____
Judicial Circuit, in and for ____
County, Florida
Case No. ________
Division ________

State of Florida,

Plaintiff,

v.

_______________,

Defendant.

ORDER TO DELIVER EXEMPT PUBLIC RECORDS

TO: Records Repository

____
[address of records repository]

This court having received notice on _____ (date) _____, that certain records for which a claim of confidentiality or exemption from disclosure has been made have been copied, indexed, separately contained without being redacted, sealed, identified as to their nature and the legal basis for their confidentiality or exemption, and delivered to the records repository of the Secretary of State, it is ordered that said records be delivered to ________[name of clerk of circuit court] for further proceedings consistent with Florida Rule of Criminal Procedure 3.852(f). ________[name of moving party] shall bear all costs associated with the transportation and inspection of these records by the trial court.

DONE AND ORDERED in ________ County, Florida, on _____ (date) _____.

____
Judge

(*o*) Notice of Delivery of Exempt Public Records to the Clerk of Circuit Court.

In the Circuit Court of the ____
Judicial Circuit, in and for ____
County, Florida
Case No. ________
Division ________

State of Florida,

Plaintiff,

v.

_______________,

Defendant.

NOTICE OF DELIVERY OF EXEMPT PUBLIC RECORDS TO CLERK OF CIRCUIT COURT

TO: _______________________________
[name and address of clerk of circuit court]

The Secretary of State, by and through the undersigned, having received an appropriate court order under Florida Rule of Criminal Procedure 3.852, hereby gives notice that the sealed container(s) of exempt public records has/have been shipped to the above-listed clerk of circuit court. Under the provisions of rule 3.852(f)(2), these public records may be opened only for an inspection by the trial court in camera.

I HEREBY CERTIFY that a true and correct copy of the foregoing has been served on ________ [name of trial court], ________ [name of clerk of circuit court], ________ [name of attorney general], and ________ [name of collateral counsel], on _____ (date) _____.

____
[name of secretary of state]
By: ________________

[name of representative of secretary of state]

Added Sept. 18, 1998, eff. Oct. 1, 1998 (723 So.2d 163). Amended July 1, 1999 (754 So.2d 640); Nov. 2, 2000, effective Jan. 1, 2001 (794 So.2d 457).

Rule 3.994. Order Certifying No Incarceration

In the ________ Court of the
________ Judicial Circuit,
in and for ________
County, Florida
Case No.: ________
Division: ________

State of Florida,
Plaintiff,
v.
________ (name) ___,
Defendant.

ORDER CERTIFYING NO INCARCERATION

1. The court hereby certifies that it will not impose any period of incarceration upon the defendant if there is a finding of guilt, a plea of guilty or nolo contendere on the substantive charge(s), or any probation revocation in this case.

2. The court hereby finds that the defendant is not incarcerated in this case.

3. Accordingly,

☐ The court declines to appoint counsel in this case.

☐ The court having found that the defendant will not be substantially prejudiced by the discharge of appointed counsel, counsel is discharged in this case.

☐ The court finds that the defendant would be substantially prejudiced by the discharge of appointed counsel and, therefore, the Court will not discharge counsel in this case.

4. This certification of no incarceration may be withdrawn by the court after notice to the defendant unless the court has made a finding of guilt or the defendant has pled guilty or nolo contendere.

5. If this order certifying no incarceration is withdrawn after appointed counsel has been discharged pursuant to this order, there shall be an immediate redetermination of indigency and appointment of counsel.

DONE AND ORDERED at ________, Florida, on ________ (date) ________.

____
Judge

Added Dec. 5, 2002, effective Jan. 1, 2003 (837 So.2d 924).

Rule 3.995. Order of Revocation of Probation / Community Control

Officer ________
Office Location ________
Judge/Division ________

In the Circuit/County Court,
________ County, Florida
Case Number ________

State of Florida

v.

____
Defendant

ORDER OF REVOCATION OF PROBATION/COMMUNITY CONTROL

THIS CAUSE, having been brought upon an affidavit of violation of probation/community control, and it appearing that the defendant was placed on probation /community control in accordance with the provisions of Chapter 948, Florida Statutes and, it further appearing that the defendant,

___ entered an admission to a material violation(s), or

___ after hearing has been found by the Court to be in material violation of the following conditions(s):

IT IS THEREFORE ORDERED AND ADJUDGED that the probation/community control of the defendant be revoked in accordance with Section 948.06, Florida Statutes.

DONE AND ORDERED IN OPEN COURT, this ___ day of ________.

____
Judge

Added Oct. 7, 2004, effective Jan. 1, 2005 (886 So.2d 197).

INDEX TO
FLORIDA RULES OF CRIMINAL PROCEDURE

FLORIDA RULES OF CIVIL PROCEDURE FOR INVOLUNTARY COMMITMENT OF SEXUALLY VIOLENT PREDATORS

Rule 4.010. Scope and Title of Rules

These rules shall apply to all civil actions filed in the circuit courts of the State of Florida pursuant to part V, chapter 394, Florida Statutes. These rules shall be known as the Florida Rules of Civil Procedure for Involuntary Commitment of Sexually Violent Predators and abbreviated as Fla. R. Civ. P.—S.V.P.

Added July 9, 2009 (13 So.3d 1025).

Rule 4.030. Nonverification of Pleadings

Every pleading or other document of a party represented by an attorney need not be verified or accompanied by an affidavit except when otherwise specifically provided by these rules or an applicable statute.

Added July 9, 2009 (13 So.3d 1025). Amended July 11, 2013, effective Oct. 1, 2013 (118 So.3d 196).

Rule 4.040. Parties

The State of Florida shall be the petitioner in actions brought under these rules. Any person who is alleged to be a sexually violent predator shall be designated as the respondent.

Added July 9, 2009 (13 So.3d 1025).

Rule 4.060. Venue and Transfers of Actions

Venue for bringing a petition under Part V, chapter 394, Florida Statutes, shall be (1) in the county where the respondent was last charged and convicted of a qualifying offense; (2) if the person has never been convicted of a qualifying offense in this state but has been convicted of such an offense in another state or in federal court, in the county where the person was last convicted of any offense in this state; or (3) if the person is being confined in this state pursuant to interstate compact and has a prior or current conviction for a sexually violent offense, in the county where the person plans to reside upon release or, if no residence in this state is planned, in the county where the facility from which the person to be released is located. If it should appear at any time that the action is pending in the wrong county it may be transferred by motion of any party or on motion by the court.

Added July 9, 2009 (13 So.3d 1025).

Rule 4.070. Process

(a) Issuance. The clerk of the court shall issue a summons, a copy of the petition, any accompanying affidavits, and a copy of the order finding probable cause to the respondent upon receipt of an order finding probable cause signed by a circuit judge. The summons shall direct the respondent to file an answer to the petition within ten days after the date of service. The state attorney shall serve a copy of the petition and related documents upon the attorney appointed to represent the respondent pursuant to rule 4.080. The finding of probable cause shall not become effective until the summons is returned served and filed with the clerk of the court.

(b) Service; By Whom Made. The state attorney shall electronically transmit a copy of the summons, petition, any accompanying affidavits, and the order finding probable cause to the person in charge of the facility in which the respondent is confined. The person in charge of the facility shall serve a printed copy of the summons, the petition, any accompanying affidavits, and order finding probable cause on the respondent within 24 hours after receiving it and before the respondent is transferred to a secure facility. The person in charge of the facility in which the respondent is confined shall make a return on the summons within 24 hours after making service, by electronically confirming to the state attorney that service has been made. The state attorney shall file a printed copy of the return with the clerk, along with the summons, on the first business day after receiving it. Additional process may be issued as in other civil actions.

Added July 9, 2009 (13 So.3d 1025).

Rule 4.080. Service and Filing of Pleadings, Papers, and Documents

(a) Service; When Required. Unless the court otherwise orders, every pleading subsequent to the initial pleading and every other document filed in the action, except applications for a witness subpoena, shall be served on the opposing party.

(b) Service of Subsequent Pleadings Other Than Original Petition; How Made. When service is required or permitted to be made upon a party represented by an attorney, service shall be made upon the attorney unless service upon the party is ordered by the court. Service on the attorney or party shall be as required by Fla. R. Jud. Admin. 2.516.

(c) Filing. All documents that are "court records" as defined in the Florida Rules of Judicial Administration must be filed with the clerk in accordance with Fla. R. Jud. Admin. 2.520 and 2.525.

(d) Deposit with the Clerk. Any paper document that is a judgment or required by statute or rule to be sworn to or notarized shall be filed and deposited with the clerk immediately thereafter. The clerk shall maintain deposited original paper documents in accordance with Fla. R. Jud. Admin. 2.430, unless otherwise ordered by the court.

Added July 9, 2009 (13 So.3d 1025). Amended July 11, 2013, effective Oct. 1, 2013 (118 So.3d 196).

Rule 4.090. Time

(a) Computation. Computation of time shall be governed by Florida Rule of Judicial Administration 2.514.

(b) Enlargement. When an act is required or allowed to be done at or within a specified time by order of court, by these rules, or by notice given thereunder, for cause shown, the court at any time in its discretion (1) with or without notice, may order the period enlarged if request therefor is made before the expiration of the period originally prescribed or as extended by a previous order, or (2) upon motion made and notice after the expiration of the specified period, may permit the act to be done when failure to act was the result of excusable neglect, but it may not extend the time for making a motion for new trial, for rehearing, or to alter or amend a judgment.

Added July 9, 2009 (13 So.3d 1025). Amended July 12, 2012, effective Oct. 1, 2012 (95 So.3d 96).

Rule 4.100. Pleadings and Motions

(a) Pleadings. There shall be a petition and an answer to it. The answer shall set forth any affirmative defense to the petition, including the failure of the petition to state a cause of action. No other pleadings shall be allowed. All pleadings shall comply with the rules governing pleadings in other civil actions. (Rules 1.100 and 1.110, Fla. R. Civ. P.)

(b) Motions. An application to the court for an order shall be by motion which shall be made in writing unless made during a hearing or trial, shall state with particularity the grounds therefor, and shall set forth the relief or order sought. The requirement of writing is fulfilled if the motion is stated in a written notice of the hearing of the motion. All notices of hearing shall specify each motion or other matter to be heard.

(c) Caption. Every pleading, motion, order, judgment, or other document shall have a caption containing the name of the court, the uniform case number, the name of the party on each side, and a designation identifying the party filing it and its nature or the nature of the order, as the case may be. All documents filed in the action shall be styled in such a manner as to indicate clearly the subject matter of the paper and the party requesting or obtaining relief.

Added July 9, 2009 (13 So.3d 1025). Amended July 11, 2013, effective Oct. 1, 2013 (118 So.3d 196).

Rule 4.110. Motions

(a) Motion for Summary Judgment. After the pleadings and discovery are closed, but within such time as not to delay the trial, any party may move for summary judgment. Summary judgment practice shall be governed by Fla. R. Civ. P. 1.510.

(b) Motions to Dismiss. Motions directed to the sufficiency of the petition shall be contained in the answer as an affirmative defense.

(c) Motion for More Definite Statement. A respondent may file a motion for a more definite statement which shall be considered a motion for a statement of particulars in response to the original petition. The motion shall disclose the defects in the petition.

Added July 9, 2009 (13 So.3d 1025).

Rule 4.200. Appointment of Counsel

(a) Appointment of Attorney. The presiding judge shall appoint an attorney to represent the respondent at the time an order finding probable cause is entered. The appointment shall continue until the court determines whether the respondent is not entitled to court appointed counsel, private counsel represents the respondent, or the respondent waives the right to counsel. Stand-by counsel may be appointed if the respondent waives the right to counsel.

(b) Waiver of Counsel. The court shall conduct a thorough inquiry as set forth in *Faretta v. California*, 422 U.S. 406 (1975), in the event the respondent requests self representation, and shall consider appointment of stand-by counsel if the respondent proceeds unrepresented.

Added July 9, 2009 (13 So.3d 1025).

Rule 4.220. Adversarial Probable Cause Hearing

(a) An adversarial probable cause hearing shall be held, within 5 days after service of a demand upon the petitioner, if the court determines that the failure to begin a trial in accordance with the time provided in rule 4.240(a) is not the result of any delay caused by the respondent and the time limitation to begin the hearing has not been waived. The respondent may waive the adversarial probable cause hearing in writing or on the record in open court.

(b) An adversarial probable cause hearing shall be held, within 5 days after service of a demand upon the petitioner, if the respondent's incarcerative sentence has expired and the respondent has been transferred to the custody of the Department of Children and Family Services.

(c) The court shall receive evidence, hear argument of the attorneys, and determine whether probable cause exists to believe that the person is a sexually violent predator at the adversarial probable cause hearing.

(d) At the adversarial probable cause hearing, the respondent has the right to:

(1) be represented by counsel;

(2) present testimony and other evidence;

(3) cross–examine any witnesses who testify against the respondent; and

(4) view and copy all petitions and reports in the court file.

(e) The court shall issue an Order of No Probable Cause and release the respondent from custody if the evidence does not establish probable cause to believe the respondent is a sexually violent predator.

Added July 9, 2009 (13 So.3d 1025).

Rule 4.240. Trial Proceedings After Finding of Probable Cause; 5 Day Status Hearing; Determination of Counsel for the Respondent; Waiver of Time Limitations

(a) The court shall conduct a status hearing within 5 days after the summons is served. At the hearing, the court shall determine if the respondent is entitled to court appointed counsel, and appoint counsel if the respondent requests it. The respondent shall be given a reasonable time to obtain private counsel if time is requested for that purpose. A *Faretta* inquiry shall be conducted if the respondent elects self representation. The trial to determine if the respondent is a sexually violent predator shall be commenced within 30 days after the summons has been returned served and filed with the clerk of the court, unless the respondent waives the 30 day time period in writing, with a copy to the assigned judge, or on the record in open court. The court shall set a trial date not less than 90 days after the date of the waiver of the 30 day period. Further continuances shall be allowed only on good cause shown. A future trial date shall be set if a further continuance is allowed.

(b) The trial shall be to the court without a jury unless the state attorney or the respondent files a demand for jury trial in accordance with rule 4.430.

(c) The burden of proof for the judge or jury to determine if the respondent is a sexually violent predator is clear and convincing evidence.

(d) The court shall enter final judgment for the petitioner if the jury unanimously finds the respondent to be a sexually violent predator.

(e) The court shall declare a mistrial if the jury cannot reach a unanimous verdict. The court shall poll the jury before it is discharged to determine if at least four jurors would have found the respondent to be a sexually violent predator.

(1) A re-trial shall be scheduled if at least four jurors would have found the respondent to be a sexually violent predator. The re-trial on the petition must commence within 90 days after the date of the mistrial, unless the case is continued at the request of the respondent for good cause. The court shall enter final judgment for the respondent if the re-trial is not commenced within 90 days from the date of the mistrial unless the respondent has waived the time limit by receiving a continuance.

(2) If three or more jurors do not find that the respondent is a sexually violent predator, the court shall enter a final judgment in favor of the respondent.

Added July 9, 2009 (13 So.3d 1025).

Rule 4.260. Continuance of Trial

A motion for continuance by either party shall be in writing unless made in a hearing in open court and shall be signed by the party or attorney requesting the continuance. The motion shall state all of the facts that the movant contends entitles the movant to a continuance. If a continuance is sought on the ground of non-availability of a witness, the motion must show when the witness will be available. The trial may be continued once upon the request of either party for not more than 120 days upon a showing of good cause, or by the court on its own motion in the interests of justice, when the person will not be substantially prejudiced. No additional continuances may be granted unless the court finds that a manifest injustice would otherwise occur. Continuances should only be ordered upon a showing of good cause. A motion for continuance on behalf of the respondent shall state that the respondent has been advised of all consequences of the request and of any rights waived by the motion.

Added July 9, 2009 (13 So.3d 1025).

Rule 4.280. General Provisions Governing Discovery

(a) Discovery methods. Parties may obtain discovery by one or more of the following methods: depositions upon oral examination; production of documents or things for inspection and other purposes; and physical and mental examinations.

(b) Scope of Discovery. Unless otherwise limited by order of the court in accordance with these rules, the scope of discovery is as follows:

(1) *In General.* Parties may obtain discovery regarding any matter, not privileged, that is relevant to the subject matter of the pending action, whether it relates to the claim or defense of the party seeking discovery, including the existence, description, nature, custody, condition, and location of any books, documents, or other tangible things and the identity and location of persons having knowledge of any discoverable matter. It is not ground for objection that the information sought will be inadmissible at the trial if the information sought appears reasonably calculated to lead to the discovery of admissible evidence.

(2) *Trial Preparation: Materials.* Subject to the provisions of subdivision (b)(1) of this rule, a party may obtain discovery of documents and tangible things otherwise discoverable under subdivision (b)(1) of this rule and prepared in anticipation of litigation for trial only upon a showing that the party seeking discovery has need of the materials in the preparation of the case and is unable without undue hardship to obtain the substantial equivalent of the materials by other means. In ordering discovery of the materials when the required showing has been made, the court shall protect against disclosure of the mental impressions, conclusions, opinions, or legal theories of an attorney or other representative of a party concerning the litigation.

(3) *Trial Preparation.*

(A)(i) The state attorney bringing the action shall disclose the names and addresses of all witnesses to be called by the petitioner to testify at trial at the time of the filing of the petition. The respondent shall disclose the names and addresses of all witnesses to be called by the respondent at trial at the time of filing the answer to the petition. The list of witnesses may be amended without leave of court until ten days prior to trial. Thereafter, the witness lists may be amended by leave of court.

(ii) The witness list shall include the names and addresses of expert witnesses. A copy of all reports made by experts shall be disclosed as soon as they are received. An expert may be required to produce financial and business records only under the most unusual or compelling circumstances and may not be compelled to compile or produce nonexistent documents. Upon motion, the court may order further discovery by other means, subject to such restrictions as to scope and other provisions pursuant to subdivision (b)(1) of this rule concerning fees and expenses as the court may deem appropriate.

(iii) The state attorney shall provide the respondent with copies of case reports, depositions, witness statements and other records regarding the respondent's prior criminal history and confinement, and any other document or material reviewed and relied upon by the multidisciplinary team in evaluating the respondent, within ten days after the summons has been returned served and filed with the clerk of the court.

(B) A party may discover facts known or opinions held by an expert who has been retained or specially employed by another party in anticipation of litigation or preparation for trial, and who is not expected to be called as a witness at trial, only upon a showing of exceptional circumstances under which it is impracticable for the party seeking discovery to obtain facts or opinions on the same subject by other means.

(C) Expert witnesses shall be paid a reasonable fee for time spent responding to discovery under subdivision (b)(3)(A) and (b)(3)(B) of this rule unless a manifest injustice would result. Respondents who are not indigent may be required to pay for discovery obtained under (b)(3)(A) and shall be responsible for discovery obtained under (b)(3)(B). The state attorney and indigent respondents shall apply for compensation for experts in the manner prescribed by law.

(4) *Claims of Privilege or Protection of Trial Preparation Materials.* When a party withholds information otherwise discoverable under these rules by claiming that it is privileged or subject to protection as trial preparation material, the party shall make the claim expressly and shall describe the nature of the documents, communications, or things not produced or disclosed in a manner that, without revealing information itself privileged or protected, will enable other parties to assess the applicability of the privilege or protection. Attorney work product claims and preparation for trial privilege claims shall be allowed.

(c) Protective Orders. Upon motion by a party, or by the person from whom discovery is sought, and for good cause shown, the court may make any order to protect a party or person from annoyance, embarrassment, oppression, or undue burden or expense that justice requires, including one or more of the following:

(1) the discovery not be had;

(2) the discovery may be had only on specified terms and conditions, including a designation of the time or place;

(3) the discovery may be had only by a method of discovery other than that selected by the party seeking discovery;

(4) certain matters not be inquired into, or that the scope of the discovery be limited to certain matters;

(5) the discovery be conducted with no one present except persons designated by the court;

(6) a deposition after being sealed be opened only by order of the court; and

(7) the parties simultaneously file specified documents or information enclosed in sealed envelopes to be opened as directed by the court. If the motion for a protective order is denied in whole or in part, the court may, on such terms and conditions as are just, order that any party or person provide or permit discovery.

(d) Sequence and Timing of Discovery. Except as provided in subdivision (b)(1) or unless the court upon motion for the convenience of parties and witnesses and in the interest of justice orders otherwise, methods of discovery may be used in any sequence, and the fact that a party is conducting discovery, whether by deposition or otherwise, shall not delay any other party's discovery.

(e) Supplementing of Responses. A party who has responded to a request for discovery with a response that was complete when made is under a continuing duty to supplement the response to include information thereafter acquired. This provision shall apply to the reciprocal discovery obligation of the petitioner and the respondent to reveal witnesses' names and addresses on a continuing basis. The court shall inquire into all claims of failure to disclose and rule appropriately as to duties to disclose and as to sanctions.

Added July 9, 2009 (13 So.3d 1025).

Rule 4.310. Depositions Upon Oral Examination

(a) When Depositions May Be Taken. Any party may take the testimony of any person, including the respondent, by deposition upon oral examination after the action is commenced. The attendance of witnesses may be compelled by subpoena as provided in Fla. R. Civ. P. 1.410. The deposition of a person in custody, except the respondent, may be taken only by leave of court on such terms as the court prescribes.

(b) Notice; Method of Taking; Production at Deposition.

(1) A party desiring to take the deposition of any person upon oral examination shall give reasonable notice in writing to every party to the action. The notice shall state the time and place for taking the deposition and the name and address of each person to be examined. If a subpoena duces tecum is to be served on the person to be examined, the designation of the materials to be produced under the subpoena shall be attached to or included in the notice.

(2) For cause shown, the court may enlarge or shorten the time for taking the deposition.

(3) Any deposition may be recorded by videotape without leave of the court or stipulation of the parties, provided the deposition is taken in accordance with this subdivision.

(4) On motion the court may order that the testimony at a deposition be taken by telephone. The order may prescribe the manner in which the deposition will be taken. A party may also arrange for a stenographic transcription at that party's own initial expense.

(A) Notice. A party intending to videotape a deposition shall state in the notice that the deposition is to be videotaped and shall give the name and address of the operator.

(B) Stenographer. Videotaped depositions shall also be recorded stenographically, unless all parties agree otherwise.

(C) Procedure. At the beginning of the deposition, the officer before whom it is taken shall, on camera: (i) identify the style of the action, (ii) state the date, and (iii) swear the witness.

(D) Custody of Tape and Copies. The attorney for the party requesting the videotaping of the deposition shall take custody of and be responsible for the safeguarding of the videotape, shall permit the viewing of it by the opposing party, and, if requested, shall provide a copy of the videotape at the expense of the party requesting the copy.

(E) Cost of Videotaped Depositions. The party requesting the videotaping shall bear the initial cost of videotaping.

(c) Examination and Cross–Examination; Record of Examination; Oath; Objections. Examination and cross-examination of witnesses may proceed as permitted at trial. The officer before whom the deposition is to be taken shall put the witness on oath and shall personally, or by someone acting under the officer's direction, and in the officer's presence, record the testimony of the witness, except that when a deposition is taken by telephone, the witness shall be sworn by a person present with the witness who is qualified to administer the oath in that location. The testimony shall be taken stenographically or recorded by any means ordered in accordance with subdivision (b). If requested by one of the parties, the testimony shall be transcribed at the initial cost of the requesting party and prompt notice of the request shall be given to all other parties. All objections made at the time of the examination to the qualifications of the officer taking the deposition, the manner of taking it, the evidence presented, or the conduct of any party, and any other objection to the proceedings shall be noted by the officer upon the deposition. Any objection during a deposition shall be stated concisely and in a non-argumentative and non-suggestive manner. A party may instruct a deponent not to answer only when necessary to preserve a privilege, to enforce a limitation on evidence directed by the court, or to present a motion under subdivision (d). Otherwise, evidence objected to shall be taken subject to the objections.

(d) Motion to Terminate or Limit Examination. At any time during the taking of the deposition, on motion of a party or of the deponent and upon a showing that the examination is being conducted in bad faith or in such manner as unreasonably to annoy, embarrass, or oppress the deponent or party, or that objection and instruction to a deponent not to answer are being made in violation of rule 4.310(c), the court in which the action is pending or the circuit court where the deposition is being taken may order the officer conducting the examination to cease forthwith from taking the deposition or may limit the scope and manner of the taking of the deposition under rule 4.280(c). If the order terminates the examination, it shall be resumed thereafter only upon the order of the court in which the action is pending. Upon demand of any party or the deponent, the taking of the deposition shall be suspended for the time necessary to make a motion for an order.

(e) Witness Review. A transcript of the testimony shall be furnished to the witness for examination and shall be read to or by the witness unless the witness cannot be found or the examination and reading are waived by the witness and the parties. Any changes in form or substance that the witness wants to make shall be listed in writing by the officer with a statement of the reasons given by the witness for making the changes. The changes shall be attached to the transcript. It shall then be signed by the witness unless the parties waived the signing or the witness refuses to sign. Transcripts that are not signed by the witness after being made available for a reasonable time shall be signed by the officer, who shall state on the transcript the reason why the witness did not sign it, such as waiver, illness, absence, or refusal to sign. The deposition may then be used as fully as though signed unless a motion to suppress the deposition, or part of it, is made with reasonable promptness after the defect is, or with due diligence might have been, discovered and the court holds that the reasons given for the refusal to sign require rejection of the deposition wholly or partly.

(f) Filing; Exhibits.

(1) If the deposition is transcribed, the officer shall certify on each copy of the deposition that the witness was duly sworn by the officer and that the deposition is a true record of the testimony given by the witness. Documents and things produced for inspection during the deposition shall be marked for identification and annexed to and returned with the deposition upon the request of a party, and may be inspected and copied by any party except that the person producing the materials may substitute copies to be marked for identification if that person affords to all parties fair opportunity to verify the copies by comparison with the originals. If the person producing the materials requests their return, the officer shall mark them, give each party an opportunity to inspect and copy them, and return them to the person producing them and the materials may then be used in the same manner as if annexed to and returned with the deposition.

(2) The officer shall furnish a copy of the deposition to any party, or to the deponent, upon payment of reasonable charges. The cost of transcripts ordered by the state attorney or an indigent respondent shall be paid in the manner prescribed by law.

(3) A copy of a deposition may be filed only under the following circumstances:

(A) It may be filed by a party or the witness when the contents of the deposition must be considered by the court on any matter pending before the court. Prompt notice of the filing on the deposition shall be given to all parties unless notice is waived. A party filing the deposition shall furnish a copy of the deposition or the part being filed to other parties unless the party already has a copy.

(B) The court may order a copy of the deposition be filed by any party if the deposition is necessary to decide a matter pending before the court.

(g) Obtaining Copies. A party or witness who does not have a copy of the deposition may obtain it from the officer taking the deposition unless the court orders otherwise. If the deposition is obtained from a person other than the officer, the reasonable cost of reproducing the copies shall be paid to the person by the requesting party or witness.

Added July 9, 2009 (13 So.3d 1025).

Rule 4.330. Use of Deposition in Court Proceedings

(a) Use of Depositions. At the trial or upon the hearing of a motion or an interlocutory proceeding, any part or all of a deposition may be used against any party who was present or represented at the taking of the deposition or who had reasonable notice of it so far as admissible under the rules of evidence applied as though the witness were then present and testifying in accordance with any of the following provisions:

(1) Any deposition may be used by any party for the purpose of contradicting or impeaching the testimony of the deponent as a witness or for any purpose permitted by the Florida Evidence Code.

(2) The deposition of a witness, whether or not a party, may be used by any party for any purpose if the court finds:

(A) the witness is dead;

(B) the witness is at a greater distance than 100 miles from the place of trial or hearing, or is out of the state, unless it appears that the absence of the witness was procured by the party offering the deposition;

(C) the witness is unable to attend or testify because of age, illness, infirmity, or imprisonment;

(D) the party offering the deposition has been unable to procure the attendance of the witness by subpoena;

(E) upon application and notice, that such exceptional circumstances exist as to make it desirable, in the interest of justice and with due regard to the importance of presenting the testimony of witnesses orally in open court, to allow the deposition to be used; or

(F) the witness is an expert or skilled witness.

(3) If only part of a deposition is offered in evidence by a party, an adverse party may require the party to introduce any other part that in fairness ought to be considered with the part introduced, and any party may introduce any other parts.

(b) Objections to Admissibility. Subject to the provisions of rule 4. 310(c), objection may be made at the trial or hearing to receiving in evidence any deposition or part of it for any reason that would require the exclusion of the evidence if the witness were then present and testifying.

(c) Effect of Taking or Using Depositions. A party does not make a person the party's own witness for any purpose by taking the person's deposition. The introduction in evidence of the deposition or any part of it for any purpose other than that of contradicting or impeaching the deponent makes the deponent the witness of the party introducing the deposition, but this shall not apply to the use by an adverse party of a deposition under subdivision (a) of this rule. At the trial or hearing any party may rebut any relevant evidence contained in a deposition whether introduced by that party or by any other party.

(d) Effect of Errors and Irregularities.

(1) *As to Notice.* All errors and irregularities in the notice for taking deposition are waived unless a written objection is promptly served upon the party giving the notice.

(2) *As to Disqualification of Officer.* Objection to taking a deposition because of disqualification of the officer before whom it is to be taken is waived unless the objection is made before the taking of the deposition begins or as soon thereafter as the disqualification becomes known or could be discovered with reasonable diligence.

Added July 9, 2009 (13 So.3d 1025).

Rule 4.380. Failure to Make Discovery; Sanctions

(a) Motion for Order Compelling Discovery. A party may apply for an order compelling discovery upon reasonable notice to the other party and all persons affected, as follows:

(1) *Motion.* If a deponent fails to answer a question propounded or submitted under rule 4.310, fails to respond that the examination will be permitted as requested, or fails to submit to or to produce a person in that party's custody or legal control for examination, the discovering party may move for an order compelling an answer, or a designation or an order compelling inspection, or an order compelling an examination in accordance with the request. The motion must include a certification that the movant, in good faith, has conferred or attempted to confer with the person or party failing to make the discovery in an effort to secure the information or material without court action. When taking a deposition on oral examination, the proponent of the question may complete or adjourn the examination before applying for an order. If the court denies the motion in whole or in part, it may make such protective order as it would have been empowered to make on a motion made pursuant to rule 4.280(c).

(2) *Evasive or Incomplete Answer.* For purposes of this subdivision an evasive or incomplete answer shall be treated as a failure to answer.

(b) Failure to Comply with Order.

If a deponent fails to be sworn or to answer a question after being directed to do so by the court, the failure may be considered a contempt of the court, or, if the deponent is a party, the court may enter any of the following orders:

(1) an order that the matters regarding which the questions were asked or any other designated facts shall be taken to be established for the purposes of the action in accordance with the claim of the party obtaining the order;

(2) an order refusing to allow the disobedient party to support or oppose designated claims or defenses, or prohibiting that party from introducing designated matters in evidence;

(3) an order striking out pleadings or parts of them or staying further proceedings until the order is obeyed, or dismissing the action or proceeding or any part of it, or rendering a judgment by default against the disobedient party;

(4) instead of any of the foregoing orders or in addition to them, an order treating as a contempt of court the failure to obey any orders except an order to submit to an examination made pursuant to rule 4.360(b)(2); or

(5) an order imposing the sanctions listed in paragraph (1), (2), or (3) of this subdivision if the respondent fails to submit to an examination as ordered.

Added July 9, 2009 (13 So.3d 1025).

Rule 4.390. Depositions of Expert Witnesses

(a) Definition. The term "expert witness" as used herein applies exclusively to a person duly and regularly engaged in the practice of a profession who holds a professional degree from a university or college and has had special professional training and experience, or one possessed of special knowledge or skill about the subject upon which called to testify.

(b) Procedure. The testimony of an expert or skilled witness may be taken at any time before the trial in accordance with the rules for taking depositions and may be used at trial, regardless of the place of residence of the witness or whether the witness is within the distance prescribed by rule 4.330(a)(2)(B). No special form of notice need be given that the deposition will be used for trial.

(c) Fee. An expert or skilled witness whose deposition is taken shall be allowed a witness fee in such reasonable amount as the court may determine. The court shall also determine a reasonable time within which payment must be made, if the deponent and party cannot agree. All parties and the deponent shall be served with notice of any hearing to determine the fee.

(d) Applicability. Nothing in this rule shall prevent the taking of any deposition as otherwise provided by law.

Added July 9, 2009 (13 So.3d 1025).

Rule 4.410. Subpoena

(a) Subpoena Generally. Subpoenas for testimony before the court, subpoenas for production of tangible evidence, and subpoenas for taking depositions may be issued by the clerk of court or by any attorney of record in an action.

(b) Subpoena for Testimony before the Court. Every subpoena for testimony before the court shall be issued by an attorney of record in an action or by the clerk under the seal of the court and shall state the name of the court and the title of the action and shall command each person to whom it is directed to attend and give testimony at a time and place specified in it. On oral request of an attorney or party and without praecipe, the clerk shall issue a subpoena for testimony before the court or a subpoena for the production of documentary evidence before the court signed and sealed but otherwise in blank, both as to the title of the action and the name of the person to whom it is directed, and the subpoena shall be filled in before service by the attorney or party.

(c) For Production of Documentary Evidence. A subpoena may also command the person to whom it is directed to produce the books, papers, documents, or tangible things designated therein, but the court, upon motion made promptly and in any event at or before the time specified in the subpoena for compliance therewith, may:

(1) quash or modify the subpoena if it is unreasonable and oppressive, or

(2) condition denial of the motion upon the advancement by the person in whose behalf the subpoena is issued of the reasonable cost of producing the books, papers, documents, or tangible things. A party seeking production of evidence at trial which would be subject to a subpoena may compel such production by serving a notice to produce such evidence on an adverse party as provided in rule 4.070(b). Such notice shall have the same effect and be subject to the same limitations as a subpoena served on the party.

(d) Service. A subpoena may be served by any person authorized by law to serve process or by any other person who is not a party and who is not less than 18 years of age. Service of a subpoena upon a person named therein shall be made as provided by law. Proof of such service shall be made by affidavit of the person making service if not served by an officer authorized by law to do so.

(e) Subpoena for Taking Depositions.

(1) Filing a notice to take a deposition as provided in rule 4.310(b) with a certificate of service on it showing service on all parties to the action constitutes an authorization for the issuance of subpoenas for the persons named or described in the notice by the clerk of the court in which the action is pending or by an attorney of record in the action. The subpoena may command the person to whom it is directed to produce designated books, papers, documents, or tangible things that constitute or contain evidence relating to any of the matters within the scope of the examination permitted by rule 4.280(b), but in that event the subpoena will be subject to the provisions of rule 4.280(c) and subdivision (c) of this rule. Within 10 days after its service, or on or before the time specified in the subpoena for compliance if the time is less than 10 days after service, the person to whom the subpoena is directed may serve written objection to inspection or copying of any of the designated materials. If objection is made, the party serving the subpoena shall not be entitled to inspect and copy the materials except pursuant to an order of the court from which the subpoena was issued. If objection has been made, the party serving the subpoena may move for an order at any time before or during the taking of the deposition upon notice to the deponent.

(2) A person may be required to attend an examination only in the county wherein the person resides or is employed or transacts business in person or at such other convenient place as may be fixed by an order of court.

(f) Contempt. Failure by any person without adequate excuse to obey a subpoena served upon that person may be deemed contempt of the court from which the subpoena issued.

(g) Subpoena of Minor. Any minor subpoenaed for testimony shall have the right to be accompanied by a parent or guardian at all times during the taking of testimony notwithstanding the invocation of the rule of sequestration of section 90.616, Florida Statutes, except upon a showing that the presence of a parent or guardian is likely to have a material, negative impact on the credibility or accuracy of the minor's testimony, or that the interests of the parent or guardian are in actual or potential conflict with the interests of the minor.

Added July 9, 2009 (13 So.3d 1025).

Rule 4.430. Demand for Jury Trial; Waiver

(a) Right Preserved. The right of trial by jury as declared by the constitution or by statute shall be preserved to the parties inviolate.

(b) Waiver of Jury Trial; Demand. The trial shall be before the court without a jury unless the petitioner files a demand for jury trial with the petition or the respondent files such a demand with the answer.

(c) Late Demand for Jury Trial. If waived, a jury trial may not be granted without the consent of the parties, but the court may allow an amendment in the proceedings to demand a trial by jury or order a trial by jury on its own motion.

Added July 9, 2009 (13 So.3d 1025).

Rule 4.431. Trial by Jury

(a) Number of Jurors.

(1) The jury shall be composed of six persons.

(2) The court may direct that 1 or more jurors be impaneled to sit as alternate jurors in addition to the regular panel. Alternate jurors shall replace jurors who have become unable or disqualified to perform their duties, in the order in which they are called, before the jury retires to consider its verdict. Alternate jurors shall be drawn in the same manner, have the same qualifications, be subject to the same examination, take the same oath, and have the same functions, powers, facilities, and privileges as principal jurors. An alternate juror who does not replace a principal juror shall be discharged when the jury retires to consider the verdict.

(3) If alternate jurors are called, each party shall be entitled to one peremptory challenge in the selection of each alternate juror. Additional peremptory challenges allowed pursuant to this subdivision may be used only against the alternate jurors. The peremptory challenges allowed pursuant to subdivision (d) of this rule shall not be used against the alternate jurors.

(b) Questionnaire. The circuit court may require prospective jurors to complete a questionnaire in the form approved by the Supreme Court of Florida to assist in selecting prospective jurors. The questionnaire shall be used after the names of jurors have been selected as provided by law but before certification and the placing of the names of prospective jurors in the jury box.

(c) Examination by Parties. The parties have the right to examine jurors orally on their voir dire. The order in which the parties may examine each juror shall be determined by the court. The court may ask such questions of the jurors as it deems necessary, but the right of the parties to conduct a reasonable examination of each juror orally shall be preserved.

(d) Juror List. Upon request, any party shall be furnished by the clerk of the court with a list containing names and addresses of prospective jurors summoned to try the case together with copies of all jury questionnaires returned by the prospective jurors.

(e) Challenge to the Panel. The state or defendant may challenge the panel. A challenge to the panel may be made only on the ground that the prospective jurors were not selected or drawn according to law. Challenges to the panel shall be made and decided before any individual juror is examined, unless otherwise ordered by the court. A challenge to the panel shall be in writing and shall specify the facts constituting the ground of the challenge. Challenges to the panel shall be tried by the court. Upon the trial of a challenge to the panel the witnesses may be examined on oath by the court and may be so examined by either party. If the challenge to the panel is sustained, the court shall discharge the panel. If the challenge is not sustained, the individual jurors shall be called.

(f) Oath for Voir Dire. The prospective jurors shall be sworn collectively or individually, as the court may decide. The form of oath shall be as follows:

"Do your solemnly swear (or affirm) that you will answer truthfully all questions asked of you as prospective jurors, so help you God?"

If any prospective juror affirms, the clause "so help you God" shall be omitted.

(g) Examination. The court may then examine each prospective juror individually or may examine the prospective jurors collectively. Counsel for both the state and defendant shall have the right to examine jurors orally on their voir dire. The order in which the parties may examine each juror shall be determined by the court. The right of the parties to conduct an examination of each juror orally shall be preserved.

(h) Prospective Jurors Excused. If, after the examination of any prospective juror, the court is of the opinion that the juror is not qualified to serve as a trial juror, the court shall excuse the juror from the trial of the cause. If, however, the court does not excuse the juror, either party may then challenge the juror, as provided by law or by these rules.

(i) Time for Challenge. The state or defendant may challenge an individual prospective juror before the juror is sworn to try the cause; except that the court may, for good cause, permit a challenge to be made after the juror is sworn, but before any evidence is presented.

(j) Exercise of Challenge. On the motion of any party, all challenges shall be addressed to the court outside the hearing of the jury panel in a manner selected by the court so that the jury panel is not aware of the nature of the challenge, the party making the challenge, or the basis of the court's ruling on the challenge, if for cause.

(k) Manner of Challenge. A challenge to an individual juror may be oral. When a juror is challenged for cause the ground of the challenge shall be stated.

(*l*) Determination of Challenge for Cause. The court shall determine the validity of a challenge of an individual juror for cause. In making such determination the juror challenged and any other material witnesses, produced by the parties, may be examined on oath by either party. The court may consider also any other evidence material to such challenge

(m) Number of Challenges. Each party shall be allowed three peremptory challenges.

(n) Alternate Jurors. If 1 or 2 alternate jurors are called, each party is entitled to 1 peremptory challenge, in addition to those otherwise allowed by law, for each alternate juror so called. The additional peremptory challenge may be used only against the alternate juror and the other peremptory challenges allowed by law shall not be used against the alternate juror.

(*o*) Additional Challenges. The trial judge may exercise discretion to allow additional peremptory challenges when appropriate.

(p) Oath of Trial Jurors. The following oath shall be administered to the jurors:

"Do you solemnly swear (or affirm) that you will well and truly try the issues between the State of Florida and the respondent and render a true verdict according to the law and the evidence, so help you God?"

If any juror affirms, the clause "so help you God" shall be omitted.

(q) Interview of a Juror. A party who believes that grounds for legal challenge to a verdict exist may move for an order permitting an interview of a juror or jurors to determine whether the verdict is subject to the challenge. The motion shall be served within 10 days after rendition of the verdict unless good cause is shown for the failure to make the motion within that time. The motion shall state the name and address of each juror to be interviewed and the grounds for challenge that the party believes may exist. After notice and hearing, the trial judge shall enter an order denying the motion or permitting the interview. If the interview is permitted, the court may prescribe the place, manner, conditions, and scope of the interview.

Added July 9, 2009 (13 So.3d 1025).

Rule 4.440. Rules of Procedure and Evidence

(a) In all commitment proceedings initiated under part V, chapter 394, Florida Statutes and this rule, the following applies:

(1) The Florida Rules of Civil Procedure and Florida Rules of Judicial Administration apply unless otherwise superseded by these rules.

(2) The Florida Rules of Evidence apply unless superseded by these rules.

(3) The psychotherapist-patient privilege under section 90.503, Florida Statutes, does not apply to any communication relevant to an issue pertaining to an involuntary civil commitment proceeding.

(4) Evidence of prior behavior by the person subject to the proceedings, if relevant to prove the person is a sexually violent predator, may be considered by the judge or jury.

(5) Hearsay evidence, including reports of the multidisciplinary team or reports prepared on behalf of the multidisciplinary team, is admissible unless the trial judge finds that the evidence is not reliable. However, hearsay evidence may not serve as the sole basis for the involuntary civil commitment of a person subject to the proceedings.

(b) No rule adopted by the Department of Children and Family Services pursuant to section 394.930, Florida Statutes, as amended, shall constitute (1) an evidentiary predicate for the admission of any testimony of physical evidence; (2) a basis for excluding or limiting the presentation of any testimony or physical evidence; or (3) elements of the cause of action the state must allege or prove, in any proceeding initiated under part V, chapter 394 Florida Statutes, and these rules.

(c) The failure of either party to comply with these rules does not constitute a defense in any proceedings initiated under part V, chapter 394, Florida Statutes.

Added July 9, 2009 (13 So.3d 1025). Amended July 11, 2013, effective Oct. 1, 2013 (118 So.3d 196).

Rule 4.450. Appeal

(a) An appeal to review a final judgment shall be pursuant Rule 9.110, Florida Rules of Appellate Procedure, as amended.

(b) An indigent respondent who requests the appointment of counsel for appeal must file an affidavit to establish entitlement to the appointment. The public defender of the circuit in which the respondent was determined to be a sexually violent predator shall be appointed to represent an indigent respondent on appeal. The public defender may request the public defender who handles criminal appeals to represent a respondent as provided in section 27.51(4), Florida Statutes.

Added July 9, 2009 (13 So.3d 1025).

Rule 4.460. Post Judgment Habeas Corpus

The respondent may file a petition for habeas corpus alleging ineffective assistance of counsel in the county in which the judgment was rendered within two years after the judgment becomes final. All other habeas corpus petitions, including petitions filed pursuant to section 394.9215(1)(a), Florida Statutes, must be filed in the county where the facility in which the petitioner is confined is located. Habeas corpus proceedings brought under this rule shall be governed by Fla. R. Crim. P. 3.850.

Added July 9, 2009 (13 So.3d 1025).

Rule 4.470. Post Commitment Proceedings

(a) A respondent committed after a trial shall be entitled to examination of his or her mental condition at least one time each year. Examinations may be ordered more frequently at the discretion of the court.

(b) The respondent may retain, or if indigent, the court may appoint, a qualified professional to conduct the examination. The examiner shall be given access to all records concerning the respondent.

(c) The report stating the result of any examination conducted pursuant to paragraph (a) or (b) shall be provided to the court for review.

(d) A respondent who receives written notice of the examination, and waives his or her rights to confidentiality of the result, and who petitions the court over the objection of the director of the facility where the respondent is housed, has the right to a hearing limited to determining whether probable cause exists to believe the respondent's condition has so changed, that it is safe for the respondent to be at large, and that the respondent will not engage in acts of sexual violence if discharged. Both the state attorney and the respondent may present evidence. The respondent has the right to be represented by counsel and the right to be present at the hearing.

(e) If it is determined that there is sufficient probable cause to believe it is safe to release the person, the court shall set the petition for a non-jury trial.

(f) The state attorney shall have the right to have the person examined by professionals chosen by the state prior to the trial.

(g) The burden is on the state to prove, by clear and convincing evidence, that it is not safe for the person to be at large and that, if released, the person is likely to engage in acts of sexual violence.

(h) At the conclusion of any trial conducted under this rule, the judge shall enter an appropriate final judgment which shall be appealable pursuant to the applicable Rules of Appellate Procedure.

Added July 9, 2009 (13 So.3d 1025). Amended June 5, 2014, effective July 1, 2014 (140 So.3d 996).

INDEX TO

FLORIDA RULES OF CIVIL PROCEDURE FOR INVOLUNTARY COMMITMENT OF SEXUALLY VIOLENT PREDATORS

PROBATE RULES

PART I. GENERAL

PART II. PROBATE

PART III. GUARDIANSHIP

Effective Date

Rules of Probate and Guardianship promulgated by order of the Florida Supreme Court on July 26, 1967, to take effect on January 1, 1968, (201 So.2d 409), as amended, were superseded by the following rules adopted December 17, 1975, to take effect January 1, 1976 (324 So.2d 38).

Revision

The rules were revised March 31, 1977, effective July 1, 1977 (344 So.2d 828); September 29, 1988, effective January 1, 1989 (531 So.2d 1261); August 22, 1991, effective October 1, 1991 (584 So.2d 964); September 24, 1992, effective January 1, 1993 (607 So.2d 1306); September 28, 2000, effective January 1, 2001 (778 So.2d 272); October 11, 2001, effective October 11, 2001 (807 So.2d 622); May 2, 2002 (824 So.2d 849); revised June 19, 2003 (848 So.2d 1069); September 30, 2004, effective October 1, 2004 (887 So.2d 1090); September 29, 2005, effective January 1, 2006 (912 So.2d 1178); February 1, 2007 (948 So.2d 735); July 5, 2007, eff. January 1, 2008 (959 So.2d 1170); July 12, 2007 (964 So.2d 140); July 10, 2008 (986 So.2d 576); September 2, 2010 (50 So.3d 578); July 7, 2011 (67 So.3d 1035); September 28, 2011 (73 So.3d 205); September 28, 2011 (73 So.3d 205); October 1, 2011 (78 So.3d 1045); September 2, 2010, effective January 1, 2011 (50 So.3d 578); July 12, 2012, effective October 1, 2012 (95 So.3d 96); October 18, 2012, effective nunc pro tunc September 1, 2012 (102 So.3d 505); October 18, 2012, effective December 1, 2012, April 1, 2013, October 1, 2013 (102 So.3d 451); September 26, 2013, effective January 1, 2014 (123 So.3d 31); November 27, 2013, effective November 27, 2013 (131 So. 3d 717); May 22, 2014, effective May 22, 2014 (139 So.3d 875).

PART I. GENERAL

Rule 5.010. Scope

These rules govern the procedure in all probate and guardianship proceedings and shall be known as the Florida Probate Rules and may be cited as Fla. Prob. R. Part I applies to all proceedings. Part II applies to probate alone, Part III applies to guardianship alone, and Part IV applies to expedited judicial intervention concerning medical treatment procedures. The Florida Rules of Civil Procedure apply only as provided herein.

Amended March 31, 1977, effective July 1, 1977 (344 So.2d 828); Sept. 29, 1988, effective Jan. 1. 1989 (531 So.2d 1261); Aug. 22, 1991, effective Oct. 1, 1991 (584 So.2d 964); Sept. 24, 1992, effective Jan. 1, 1993 (607 So.2d 1306).

Committee Notes

Rule History

1975 Revision: These rules shall govern the procedures to be followed in all matters pending on or commenced after January 1, 1976, including procedures for the enforcement of substantive rights that have vested before that date. See section 731.011, Florida Statutes.

1977 Revision: The changes in these rules shall take effect on July 1, 1977.

1988 Revision: In the opinion reported at 460 So. 2d 906, the Florida Supreme Court directed the Probate and Guardianship Rules Committee to study the statutes and attempt to identify those portions of the Florida Probate Code, the Florida Guardianship Law, and other statutes that contained procedural provisions. When those procedural provisions were identified, the committee was charged to promulgate rules incorporating those procedures.

The committee has reviewed the statutes and has found a substantial measure of procedure that was contained only in the statutes for which there were no corresponding rules. The committee also determined that much of the procedure in the statutes already had a rule counterpart.

New rules added, or prior rules amended, in 1988 to add procedural matters previously found only in the statutes are rules 5.050, 5.122, 5.171, 5.180, 5.201, 5.235, 5.270, 5.275, 5.355, 5.360, 5.385, 5.386, 5.400, 5.440, 5.475, 5.490, and 5.510. With only one exception (see rule 5.050), the only portion of the statutes that has been reviewed in detail, and for which rules have been created, is the Florida Probate Code. Other portions of the statutes mentioned in the opinion cited above remain for the next cycle of this committee to review.

As the committee wrote rules to transfer the statutory procedure into these rules, an attempt was made to write the rule without changing the meaning of the statute. It was not possible or advisable to use the exact wording of the statute in some instances, and in those instances the committee rewrote the statutory language in the format used in the rules generally. Even under those circumstances, the committee attempted to transfer the entire procedural portion of the statute without changing its meaning. Where it was specifically intended in a few instances to add to existing statutory procedure, that fact is noted in the relevant committee note. The committee felt strongly that it would be detrimental to the orderly process of estate probate and related procedures if a rule specified a different procedure than was specified in the related statute, even though the statute must, under the Florida Constitution, yield to the rule when there is a conflict.

The committee, through the proper channels in The Florida Bar (initially, the Probate Law Committee of the Real Property, Probate and Trust Law Section), intends to ask the legislature to repeal those portions of the statutes that are procedural when there are similar rules already in place, or when similar new rules are added by this opinion. It is the opinion of the committee that continuing to maintain procedure in the statutes when there is a rule specifying that procedure is detrimental to the orderly process of the court and the public that it serves, especially when, over time, the statute and the rule may diverge.

Although the supreme court has adopted these recommended rules, it has not specifically determined that all of the provisions of the statutes that were procedural have now been adopted as a rule. This is a continuing project for the committee and although these new rules and changes represent a substantial transition of procedure into the rules, the committee does not suggest that the transition is complete. The court is not precluded from examining any particular statute or rule in the context of a particular actual dispute.

1991 Revision: Rule revised to reflect addition of new Part IV dealing with expedited judicial intervention concerning medical treatment procedures.

1992 Revision: In 1989, the Florida Legislature enacted a comprehensive revision to Florida's guardianship law. In response, the Florida Supreme Court appointed an ad hoc committee to recommend temporary rules of procedure for the new law. In an opinion at 551 So. 2d 452 (Fla. 1989), the court adopted the temporary rules recommended by the ad hoc committee, to replace Part III of the then-existing Florida Probate Rules, effective October 1, 1989. In its opinion, the court also directed the Florida Probate Rules Committee to review the new laws and, on a priority basis, to recommend permanent rules of procedure.

The committee reviewed the Florida Guardianship Law enacted in 1989, as well as revisions to the law enacted in 1990, and presented its rule recommendations to the court in 1991. The court, in an opinion at 584 So. 2d 964, adopted the recommendations with minor exceptions, to be effective October 1, 1991.

In 1990, the court also rendered its opinion in In re Guardianship of Browning, 568 So. 2d 4 (Fla. 1990), regarding a person's right to refuse life-prolonging medical procedures. In that decision, the court directed the committee to recommend a rule to provide for expedited judicial intervention. In response, the committee created a new Part IV of these rules and recommended rule 5.900, which was adopted by the court, with minor changes, in its opinion at 584 So. 2d 964, effective October 1, 1991.

The committee continued its efforts to review the Florida Probate Code and to promulgate or amend rules regarding any procedural portions of those statutes. As a result of those efforts, as well as the efforts described above, the committee recommended amendments to rules 5.010, 5.025, 5.040, 5.050, 5.200, 5.240, 5.310, 5.346, 5.400, 5.470, 5.550, 5.560, 5.590, 5.600, 5.610, 5.620, 5.630, 5.640, 5.650, 5.660, 5.670, 5.680, 5.695, 5.700, 5.710, and 5.800; creation of new rules 5.496, 5.540, 5.541, 5.555, 5.635, 5.636, 5.690, 5.696, 5.697, 5.705, and 5.900; and deletion of rule 5.495. In addition, the committee recommended editorial changes in virtually all the rules so that they would conform stylistically to one another and to all other rules promulgated by the supreme court.

2003 Revision: The committee has promulgated numerous changes in the rules and in the committee notes to many of the rules, in response to legislative amendments that deleted procedural aspects of a number of statutes in the Florida Probate Code, including deletion and re-titling of some statutes. See Ch. 2001–226, Laws of Fla.

Rule References

Fla. Prob. R. 5.025 Adversary proceedings.

Fla. Prob. R. 5.040(a)(3)(B) Notice.

Fla. Prob. R. 5.050 Transfer of proceedings.

Fla. Prob. R. 5.080 Discovery and subpoena.

Fla. Prob. R. 5.230(e) Commission to prove will.

Fla. R. App. P. 9.800 Uniform citation system.

Rule 5.015. General Definitions

(a) General. The definitions and rules of construction stated or referred to in sections 1.01 and 393.12, Florida Statutes, and chapters 731, 732, 733, 734, 735, 736, 738, 739, and 744, Florida Statutes, as amended from time to time, shall apply to these rules, unless otherwise defined in these rules.

(b) Specific Definitions. When used in these rules

(1) "Certified copy" means a copy of a document signed and verified as a true copy by the officer to whose custody the original is entrusted;

(2) "formal notice" means notice under rule 5.040(a);

(3) "informal notice" means notice under rule 5.040(b);

(4) "judge" means a judge of the circuit court, including any judge elected, appointed, substituted, or assigned to serve as judge of the court;

(5) "guardian advocate" means a person appointed for a person with a developmental disability pursuant to section 393.12, Florida Statutes;

(6) "guardian" means a person appointed pursuant to chapter 744, Florida Statutes, or a guardian advocate unless a rule indicates otherwise;

(7) "ward" means an individual for whom a guardian is appointed.

Amended March 31, 1977, effective July 1, 1977 (344 So.2d 828); Sept. 29, 1988, effective Jan. 1, 1989 (537 So.2d 500); Sept. 29, 1989, effective Oct. 1, 1989 (549 So.2d 665); Nov. 17, 1989 (551 So.2d 452); Sept. 24, 1992, effective Jan. 1, 1993 (607 So.2d 1306); Sept. 28, 2000, effective Jan. 1, 2001 (778 So.2d 272); July 12, 2007 (964 So.2d 140); July 10, 2008 (986 So.2d 576).

Committee Notes

Rule History

1977 Revision: No change in rule. Correction of typographical error in committee note.

This is intended to simplify drafting of these rules and should be liberally construed. See Fla. Prob. R. 5.190 and 5.540 and also §§ 731.201 and 744.102, Fla. Stat.

1988 Revision: Rule was expanded due to deletion of rule 5.190. Committee notes expanded. Citation form changes in rule and committee notes.

1992 Revision: Citation form changes in rule and committee notes.

2000 Revision: Subdivision (b)(2) amended to delete outdated reference to rule 5.550(c).

2007 Revision: Subdivision (a) amended to add reference to chapter 736, Florida Statutes, which was added to the statutes effective July 1, 2007 and which replaces deleted chapter 737, and to add reference to chapter 739, Florida Statutes, which was added effective July 1, 2005. Committee notes revised.

2008 Revision: Subdivision (a) amended to add reference to section 393.12, Florida Statutes, which governs guardian advocates for persons with developmental disabilities. As provided by section 744.102(11), the term "guardian advocate" as used in the Florida Guardianship Law and these rules does not include a guardian advocate appointed for a person determined to lack capacity to consent to treatment under section 394.4598, Florida Statutes. Subdivisions (b)(5) through (b)(7) added to reflect 2008 amendments to section 393.12, Florida Statutes. Committee notes revised.

Statutory References

§ 1.01, Fla. Stat. Definitions.

§ 393.063, Fla. Stat. Definitions.

§ 393.12, Fla. Stat. Capacity; appointment of guardian advocate.

§ 731.201, Fla. Stat. General definitions.

§ 736.0103, Fla. Stat. Definitions.

§ 738.102, Fla. Stat. Definitions.

§ 739.102, Fla. Stat. Definitions.

§ 744.102, Fla. Stat. Definitions.

Rule 5.020. Pleadings; Verification; Motions

(a) Forms of Pleading. Pleadings shall be signed by the attorney of record, and by the pleader when required by these rules. All technical forms of pleadings are abolished. No defect of form impairs substantial rights, and no defect in the statement of jurisdictional facts actually existing renders any proceeding void.

(b) Petition. A petition shall contain a short and plain statement of the relief sought, the grounds therefor, and the jurisdiction of the court where the jurisdiction has not already been shown.

(c) Motions. Any other application to the court for an order shall be by written motion, unless made orally during a hearing or trial. The motion shall state with particularity the grounds therefor and shall set forth the relief or order sought.

(d) Rehearing. A motion for rehearing of any order or judgment shall be served not later than 10 days after the date of filing the order or judgment with the clerk as shown on the face of the order or judgment.

(e) Verification. When verification of a document is required, the document filed shall include an oath, affirmation, or the following statement:

"Under penalties of perjury, I declare that I have read the foregoing, and the facts alleged are true, to the best of my knowledge and belief."

Amended March 31, 1977, effective July 1, 1977 (344 So.2d 828); Sept. 4, 1980, effective Jan. 1, 1981 (387 So.2d 949); Sept. 13, 1984, effective Jan. 1, 1985 (458 So.2d 1079); Sept. 29, 1988, effective Jan. 1, 1989 (537 So.2d 500); Sept. 24, 1992, effective Jan. 1, 1993 (986 So.2d 576).

Committee Notes

The time for determining when a motion for rehearing must be served has been clarified in view of Casto v. Casto, 404 So. 2d 1046 (Fla. 1981).

Rule History

1977 Revision: Editorial change (rule) and expansion of committee note. Subdivisions (a), (b), and (d) substantially the same as subdivisions (a), (b), and (f) of prior rule 5.030. Subdivision (c) taken from section 731.104, Florida Statutes. For adversary proceedings see new rule 5.025. Notice of administration is not a pleading within the meaning of this rule.

1980 Revision: Subdivisions (c) and (d) have been redesignated as (e) and (f). New subdivisions (c) and (d) are added to provide for the use of motions in probate proceedings other than adversary proceedings and to specifically authorize a procedure for rehearing.

1984 Revision: Minor editorial changes. Subdivision (f) of prior rule has been deleted as it is now covered under the adversary rules.

1988 Revision: Editorial change in caption of (a). Committee notes revised. Citation form change in committee notes.

1992 Revision: Editorial changes. Committee notes revised. Citation form changes in rule and committee notes.

2003 Revision: Committee notes revised.

2008 Revision: Committee notes revised.

2010 Revision: Committee notes revised.

Statutory References

§ 393.12, Fla. Stat. Capacity; appointment of guardian advocate.

§ 731.104, Fla. Stat. Verification of documents.

§ 731.201, Fla. Stat. General definitions.

§ 733.202, Fla. Stat. Petition.

§ 733.604(1), Fla. Stat. Inventories and accountings; public records exemptions.

§ 733.901, Fla. Stat. Final discharge.

§ 735.203, Fla. Stat. Petition for summary administration.

§ 744.104, Fla. Stat. Verification of documents.

§ 744.3085, Fla. Stat. Guardian advocates.

§ 744.3201, Fla. Stat. Petition to determine incapacity.

§ 744.331, Fla. Stat. Procedures to determine incapacity.

§ 744.334, Fla. Stat. Petition for appointment of guardian or professional guardian; contents.

Rule References

Fla. Prob. R. 5.025 Adversary proceedings.

Fla. Prob. R. 5.200 Petition for administration.

Fla. Prob. R. 5.205(b) Filing evidence of death.

Fla. Prob. R. 5.320 Oath of personal representative.

Fla. Prob. R. 5.330 Execution by personal representative.

Fla. Prob. R. 5.350 Continuance of unincorporated business or venture.

Fla. Prob. R. 5.370(a) Sales of real property where no power conferred.

Fla. Prob. R. 5.405(b) Proceedings to determine homestead real property.

Fla. Prob. R. 5.530 Summary administration.

Fla. Prob. R. 5.550 Petition to determine incapacity.

Fla. Prob. R. 5.560 Petition for appointment of guardian of an incapacitated person.

Fla. Prob. R. 5.600 Oath.

Fla. Prob. R. 5.649 Guardian advocate.

Rule 5.025. Adversary Proceedings

(a) Specific Adversary Proceedings. The following are adversary proceedings unless otherwise ordered by the court: proceedings to remove a personal representative, surcharge a personal representative, remove a guardian, surcharge a guardian, probate a lost or destroyed will or later-discovered will, determine beneficiaries, construe a will, reform a will, modify a will, cancel a devise, partition property for the purposes of distribution, determine pretermitted status, determine pretermitted share, determine amount of elective share and contribution, and for revocation of probate of a will.

(b) Declared Adversary Proceedings. Other proceedings may be declared adversary by service on interested persons of a separate declaration that the proceeding is adversary.

(1) If served by the petitioner, the declaration must be served with the petition to which it relates.

(2) If served by the respondent, the declaration and a written response to the petition must be served at the earlier of:

(A) within 20 days after service of the petition, or

(B) prior to the hearing date on the petition.

(3) When the declaration is served by a respondent, the petitioner must promptly serve formal notice on all other interested persons.

(c) Adversary Status by Order. The court may determine any proceeding to be an adversary proceeding at any time.

(d) Notice and Procedure in Adversary Proceedings.

(1) Petitioner must serve formal notice.

(2) After service of formal notice, the proceedings, as nearly as practicable, must be conducted similar to suits of a civil nature, including entry of defaults. The Florida Rules of Civil Procedure govern, except for rule 1.525.

(3) The court on its motion or on motion of any interested person may enter orders to avoid undue delay in the main administration.

(4) If a proceeding is already commenced when an order is entered determining the proceeding to be adversary, it must thereafter be conducted as an adversary proceeding. The order must require interested persons to serve written defenses, if any, within 20 days from the date of the order. It is not necessary to re-serve the petition except as ordered by the court.

(5) When the proceedings are adversary, the caption of subsequent pleadings, as an extension of the

probate caption, must include the name of the first petitioner and the name of the first respondent.

Amended March 31, 1977, effective July 1, 1977 (344 So.2d 828); Sept. 13, 1984, effective Jan. 1, 1985 (458 So.2d 1079); Sept. 29, 1988, effective Jan. 1, 1989 (537 So.2d 500); Sept. 24, 1992, effective Jan. 1, 1993 (607 So.2d 1306); Oct. 11, 2001 (807 So.2d 622); Jan. 10, 2002 (816 So.2d 1095); Sept. 28, 2011 (73 So.3d 205).

Committee Notes

The court on its initiative or on motion of any party may order any proceeding to be adversary or nonadversary or enter any order that will avoid undue delay. The personal representative would be an interested person in all adversary proceedings. A prescribed form for the caption is provided that will facilitate the clerk's and the court's ability to segregate such adversary proceeding from other adversary proceedings and from the main probate file:

	Court Case #
In Re Estate of John B. Jones	)
Julia Jones,	)
Petitioner,	)
v.	)
Harold Jones, as Personal Representative, et al.,	)
Respondents.	)

Rule History

1975 Revision: New rule. 324 So. 2d 38.

1977 Revision: Editorial changes to (a)(1).

1984 Revision: Extensive changes, Committee notes revised and expanded.

1988 Revision: Changes in (a) add proceedings to remove a guardian and to surcharge a guardian to the list of specific adversary proceedings and delete proceedings to determine and award the elective share from the list. Change in (b)(4) clarifies on whom the petitioner must serve formal notice. Editorial change in (d)(2) and (d)(5). Committee notes revised. Citation form changes in committee notes.

1992 Revision: Deletion of (b)(3) as unnecessary. Former (b)(4) renumbered as new (b)(3). Committee notes revised. Citation form changes in committee notes.

2001 Revision: Change in (a) to add determination of amount of elective share and contribution as specific adversary proceedings. Committee notes revised.

2003 Revision: Committee notes revised.

2008 Revision: Committee notes revised.

2011 Revision: Subdivision (a) revised to add "reform a will, modify a will" and "determine pretermitted status." Subdivision (d)(2) modified to insure that an award of attorneys' fees in a probate or guardianship proceeding follows the law and procedures established for such proceedings, rather than the law and procedures for civil proceedings. *See Amendments to the Florida Family Law Rules of Procedure (Rule 12.525)*, 897 So. 2d 467 (Fla. 2005). Editorial changes to conform to the court's guidelines for rules submissions as set forth in Administrative Order AOSC06-14. Committee Notes revised.

Statutory References

§ 393.12, Fla. Stat. Capacity; appointment of guardian advocate.

§§ 732.201–732.2155, Fla. Stat. Elective share of surviving spouse.

§ 732.301, Fla. Stat. Pretermitted spouse.

§ 732.302, Fla. Stat. Pretermitted children.

§ 732.507, Fla. Stat. Effect of subsequent marriage, birth, adoption, or dissolution of marriage.

§§ 732.6005–732.611, Fla. Stat. Rules of construction.

§ 732.615, Fla. Stat. Reformation to correct mistakes.

§ 732.616, Fla. Stat. Modification to achieve testator's tax objectives.

§ 733.105, Fla. Stat. Determination of beneficiaries.

§ 733.107, Fla. Stat. Burden of proof in contests; presumption of undue influence.

§ 733.109, Fla. Stat. Revocation of probate.

§ 733.207, Fla. Stat. Establishment and probate of lost or destroyed will.

§ 733.208, Fla. Stat. Discovery of later will.

§ 733.504, Fla. Stat. Removal of personal representative; causes for removal.

§ 733.505, Fla. Stat. Jurisdiction in removal proceedings.

§ 733.506, Fla. Stat. Proceedings for removal.

§ 733.5061, Fla. Stat. Appointment of successor upon removal.

§ 733.603, Fla. Stat. Personal representative to proceed without court order.

§ 733.609, Fla. Stat. Improper exercise of power; breach of fiduciary duty.

§ 733.619(2), (4), Fla. Stat. Individual liability of personal representative.

§ 733.814, Fla. Stat. Partition for purpose of distribution.

§ 744.3085, Fla. Stat. Guardian advocates.

§ 744.474, Fla. Stat. Reasons for removal of guardian.

§ 744.477, Fla. Stat. Proceedings for removal of a guardian.

Rule References

Fla. Prob. R. 5.040 Notice.

Fla. Prob. R. 5.270 Revocation of probate.

Fla. Prob. R. 5.360 Elective share.

Fla. Prob. R. 5.365 Petition for dower.

Fla. Prob. R. 5.440 Proceedings for removal.

Fla. Prob. R. 5.649 Guardian advocate.

Fla. Prob. R. 5.660 Proceedings for removal of guardian.

Fla. Prob. R. 5.681 Restoration of rights of person with developmental disability.

Fla. R. Civ. P. 1.140 Defenses.

Fla. R. Civ. P. 1.160 Motions.

Fla. R. Civ. P. 1.200 Pretrial procedure.

Fla. R. Civ. P. 1.280 General provisions governing discovery.

Fla. R. Civ. P. 1.290 Depositions before action or pending appeal.

Fla. R. Civ. P. 1.310 Depositions upon oral examination.

Fla. R. Civ. P. 1.340 Interrogatories to parties.

Fla. R. Civ. P. 1.380 Failure to make discovery; sanctions.

Rule 5.030. Attorneys

(a) Required; Exception. Every guardian and every personal representative, unless the personal representative remains the sole interested person, shall be represented by an attorney admitted to practice in Florida. A guardian or personal representative who is an attorney admitted to practice in Florida may represent himself or herself as guardian or personal representative. A guardian advocate is not required to be represented by an attorney unless otherwise required by law or the court.

(b) Limited Appearance Without Court Order. An attorney of record for an interested person in a proceeding governed by these rules shall be the attorney of record in all other proceedings in the administration of the same estate or guardianship, except service of process in an independent action on a claim, unless at the time of appearance the attorney files a notice specifically limiting the attorney's appearance only to the particular proceeding or matter in which the attorney appears. At the conclusion of that proceeding or matter, the attorney's role terminates upon the attorney filing notice of completion of limited appearance and serving a copy on the client and other interested persons.

(c) Withdrawal or Limited Appearance With Court Order. An attorney of record may withdraw or limit the attorney's appearance with approval of the court, after filing a motion setting forth the reasons and serving a copy on the client and other interested persons.

Amended March 31, 1977, effective July 1, 1977 (344 So.2d 828); June 14, 1979, effective July 1, 1979 (372 So.2d 449); Sept. 13, 1984, effective Jan. 1, 1985 (458 So.2d 1079); Sept. 29, 1988, effective Jan. 1, 1989 (537 So.2d 500); Sept. 24, 1992, effective Jan. 1, 1993 (607 So.2d 1306); Sept. 29, 2005, effective Jan. 1, 2006 (912 So.2d 1178); Feb. 1, 2007 (948 So.2d 735); July 10, 2008 (986 So.2d 576); Sept. 2, 2010, effective Jan. 1, 2011 (50 So.3d 578).

Committee Notes

The appearance of an attorney in an estate is a general appearance unless (i) specifically limited at the time of such appearance or (ii) the court orders otherwise. This rule does not affect the right of a party to employ additional attorneys who, if members of The Florida Bar, may appear at any time.

Rule History

1975 Revision: Subdivision (a) is same as prior rule 5.040 with added provision for withdrawal of attorney similar to Florida Rule of Appellate Procedure 2.3(d)(2). Subdivision (b) reflects ruling in case of State ex rel. Falkner v. Blanton, 297 So. 2d 825 (Fla. 1974).

1977 Revision: Editorial change requiring filing of petition for withdrawal and service of copy upon interested persons. Editorial change in citation forms in rule and committee note.

1984 Revision: Minor editorial changes and addition of subdivision (c). Committee notes expanded.

1988 Revision: Editorial changes and order of subdivisions rearranged. Committee notes expanded. Citation form changes in committee notes.

1992 Revision: Editorial changes. Committee notes revised. Citation form changes in committee notes.

2003 Revision: Committee notes revised.

2005 Revision: Committee notes revised.

2006 Revision: Committee notes revised.

2008 Revision: Subdivision (a) amended to reflect that a guardian advocate may not be required to be represented by an attorney in some instances. Committee notes revised.

2010 Revision: Subdivisions (b) and (c) amended to clarify the procedure for termination of an attorney's representation of an interested person either with or without court order.

2012 Revision: Committee notes revised.

Statutory References

§ 393.12, Fla. Stat. Capacity; appointment of guardian advocate.

§ 731.301, Fla. Stat. Notice.

§ 733.106, Fla. Stat. Costs and attorney's fees.

§ 733.212, Fla. Stat. Notice of administration; filing of objections.

§ 733.6175, Fla. Stat. Proceedings for review of employment of agents and compensation of personal representatives and employees of estate.

§ 744.108, Fla. Stat. Guardian's and attorney's fees and expenses.

§ 744.3085, Fla. Stat. Guardian advocates.

Rule References

Fla. Prob. R. 5.041 Service of pleadings and documents.

Fla. Prob. R. 5.110(b), (c) Resident agent.

Fla. R. Jud. Admin. 2.505 Attorneys.

Fla. R. Jud. Admin. 2.516 Service of pleadings and documents.

Fla. R. App. P. 9.440 Attorneys.

Rule 5.040. Notice

(a) Formal Notice.

(1) When formal notice is given, a copy of the pleading or motion shall be served on interested persons, together with a notice requiring the person served to serve written defenses on the person giving notice within 20 days after service of the notice, exclusive of the day of service, and to file the original of the written defenses with the clerk of the court either before service or immediately thereafter, and notifying the person served that failure to serve written defenses as required may result in a judgment or order for the relief demanded in the pleading or motion, without further notice.

(2) After service of formal notice, informal notice of any hearing on the pleading or motion shall be served on interested persons, provided that if no written defense is served within 20 days after service of formal notice on an interested person, the pleading or motion may be considered ex parte as to that person, unless the court orders otherwise.

(3) Formal notice shall be served:

(A) by sending a copy by any commercial delivery service requiring a signed receipt or by any form of mail requiring a signed receipt as follows:

(i) to the attorney representing an interested person; or

(ii) to an interested person who has filed a request for notice at the address given in the request for notice; or

(iii) to an incapacitated person or a person with a developmental disability to the person's usual place of abode and to the person's legal guardian, if any, at the guardian's usual place of abode or regular place of business; or, if there is no legal guardian, to the incapacitated person or person with a developmental disability at the person's usual place of abode and on the person, if any, having care or custody of the incapacitated person or person with a developmental disability at the usual place of abode or regular place of business of such custodian; or

(iv) to a minor whose disabilities of nonage are not removed, by serving the persons designated to accept service of process on a minor under chapter 48, Florida Statutes; or

(v) on any other individual to the individual's usual place of abode or to the place where the individual regularly conducts business; or

(vi) on a corporation or other business entity to its registered office in Florida or its principal business office in Florida or, if neither is known after reasonable inquiry, to its last known address; or

(B) as provided in the Florida Rules of Civil Procedure for service of process; or

(C) as otherwise provided by Florida law for service of process.

(4) Service of formal notice pursuant to subdivision (3)(A) shall be complete on receipt of the notice. Proof of service shall be by verified statement of the person giving the notice; and there shall be attached to the verified statement the signed receipt or other evidence satisfactory to the court that delivery was made to the addressee or the addressee's agent.

(5) If service of process is made pursuant to Florida law, proof of service shall be made as provided therein.

(b) Informal Notice. When informal notice of a petition or other proceeding is required or permitted, it shall be served as provided in rule 5.041.

(c) "Notice" Defined. In these rules, the Florida Probate Code, and the Florida Guardianship Law "notice" shall mean informal notice unless formal notice is specified.

(d) Formal Notice Optional. Formal notice may be given in lieu of informal notice at the option of the person giving notice unless the court orders otherwise. When formal notice is given in lieu of informal notice, formal notice shall be given to all interested persons entitled to notice. When formal notice is given in lieu of informal notice, that notice does not modify any time period otherwise specified by statute or these rules.

Amended March 31, 1977, effective July 1, 1977 (344 So.2d 828); Sept. 4, 1980, effective Jan. 1, 1981 (387 So.2d 949); Sept. 13, 1984, effective Jan. 1, 1985 (458 So.2d 1079); Sept. 29, 1988, effective Jan. 1, 1989 (537 So.2d 500); Aug. 22, 1991, effective Oct. 1, 1991 (584 So.2d 964); Sept. 24, 1992, effective Jan. 1, 1993 (607 So.2d 1306); Oct. 3, 1996, effective Jan. 1, 1997 (683 So.2d 78); Sept. 28, 2000, effective Jan. 1, 2001 (778 So.2d 272); Sept. 29, 2005, effective Jan. 1, 2006 (912 So.2d 1178); Feb. 1, 2007 (948 So.2d 735); July 5, 2007, effective Jan. 1, 2008 (959 So.2d 1170); July 12, 2007 (964 So.2d 140); July 10, 2008 (986 So.2d 576); Sept. 2, 2010, effective Jan. 1, 2011 (50 So.3d 578); Oct. 18, 2012, effective, *nunc pro tunc*, Sept. 1, 2012 (102 So.3d 505).

Committee Notes

Formal notice is the method of service used in probate proceedings and the method of service of process for obtaining jurisdiction over the person receiving the notice. "The manner provided for service of formal notice" is as provided in rule 5.040(a)(3).

Informal notice is the method of service of notice given to interested persons entitled to notice when formal notice is not given or required.

Reference in this rule to the terms "mail" or "mailing" refers to use of the United States Postal Service.

Rule History

1975 Revision: Implements section 731.301, Florida Statutes.

1977 Revision: Reference to elisor.

1980 Revision: Editorial changes. Clarification of time for filing defenses after formal notice. Authorizes court to give relief to delinquent respondent from ex parte status; relief from service on numerous persons; allows optional use of formal notice.

1984 Revision: Editorial changes. Eliminates deadline for filing as opposed to serving defenses after formal notice; defines procedure subsequent to service of defenses after formal notice; new requirements for service of formal notice on incompetents and corporations; defines when service of formal notice is deemed complete; provisions relating to method of service of informal notice transferred to new rules 5.041 and 5.042; eliminates waiver of notice by will.

1988 Revision: Editorial changes. Committee notes revised. Citation form changes in committee notes.

1991 Revision: Subdivision (b) amended to define informal notice more clearly.

1992 Revision: Editorial changes. Committee notes revised. Citation form changes in committee notes.

1996 Revision: Subdivision (a) amended to permit service of formal notice by commercial delivery service to conform to 1993 amendment to section 731.301(1), Florida Statutes. Editorial changes.

2001 Revision: Editorial changes in subdivision (a)(3)(A) to clarify requirements for service of formal notice.

2003 Revision: Committee notes revised.

2005 Revision: Subdivision (a)(3)(A) amended to delete requirement of court approval of commercial delivery service.

2006 Revision: Committee notes revised.

2007 Revision: Committee notes revised.

2007 Revision: New subdivision (a)(3)(A)(iv) inserted in response to Cason ex rel. Saferight v. Hammock, 908 So.2d 512 (Fla. 5th DCA 2005), and subsequent subdivisions renumbered accordingly. Committee notes revised.

2008 Revision: Subdivision (a)(3)(A)(iii) revised to include "person with a developmental disability." Committee notes revised.

2010 Revision: Subdivision (d) amended to clarify that the optional use of formal notice when only informal notice is required does not modify any time period otherwise specified by statute or rule. Committee notes revised.

2012 Revision: Subdivision (b) revised to reflect amendment to rule 5.041.

Statutory References

§ 1.01(3), Fla. Stat. Definitions.

ch. 48, Fla. Stat. Process and service of process.

ch. 49, Fla. Stat. Constructive service of process.

§ 393.12, Fla. Stat. Capacity; appointment of guardian advocate.

§ 731.105, Fla. Stat. In rem proceeding.

§ 731.201(18), (22), Fla. Stat. General definitions.

§ 731.301, Fla. Stat. Notice.

§ 731.302, Fla. Stat. Waiver and consent by interested person.

§ 733.212, Fla. Stat. Notice of administration; filing of objections.

§ 733.2123, Fla. Stat. Adjudication before issuance of letters.

§ 733.502, Fla. Stat. Resignation of personal representative.

§ 733.613, Fla. Stat. Personal representative's right to sell real property.

§ 733.6175, Fla. Stat. Proceedings for review of employment of agents and compensation of personal representatives and employees of estate.

§ 733.901, Fla. Stat. Final discharge.

ch. 743, Fla. Stat. Disability of nonage of minors removed.

§ 744.106, Fla. Stat. Notice.

§ 744.301, Fla. Stat. Natural guardians.

§ 744.3085, Fla. Stat. Guardian advocates.

§ 744.3201, Fla. Stat. Petition to determine incapacity.

§ 744.331, Fla. Stat. Procedures to determine incapacity.

§ 744.3371, Fla. Stat. Notice of petition for appointment of guardian and hearing.

§ 744.441, Fla. Stat. Powers of guardian upon court approval.

§ 744.447, Fla. Stat. Petition for authorization to act.

§ 744.477, Fla. Stat. Proceedings for removal of a guardian.

Rule References

Fla. Prob. R. 5.025 Adversary proceedings.

Fla. Prob. R. 5.030 Attorneys.

Fla. Prob. R. 5.041 Service of pleadings and documents.

Fla. Prob. R. 5.042 Time.

Fla. Prob. R. 5.060 Request for notices and copies of pleadings.

Fla. Prob. R. 5.180 Waiver and consent.

Fla. Prob. R. 5.560 Petition for appointment of guardian of an incapacitated person.

Fla. Prob. R. 5.649 Guardian advocate.

Fla. Prob. R. 5.681 Restoration of rights of person with developmental disability.

Fla. R. Jud. Admin. 2.505 Attorneys.

Fla. R. Jud. Admin. 2.516 Service of pleadings and documents.

Fla. R. Civ. P. 1.070 Process.

Fla. R. Civ. P. Form 1.902 Summons.

Rule 5.041. Service of Pleadings and Documents

Unless the court orders otherwise, every petition or motion for an order determining rights of an interested person, and every other pleading or document filed in the particular proceeding which is the subject matter of such petition or motion, except applications for witness subpoenas, shall be served on interested persons as set forth in Florida Rule of Judicial Administration 2.516 unless these rules, the Florida Probate Code, or the Florida Guardianship Law provides otherwise. No service need be made on interested persons against whom a default has been entered, or against whom the matter may otherwise proceed ex parte, unless a new or additional right or demand is asserted. For purposes of this rule an interested person shall be deemed a party under rule 2.516.

If the interested person is a minor whose disabilities of nonage are not removed, and who is not represented by an attorney, then service shall be on the persons designated to accept service of process on a minor under chapter 48, Florida Statutes.

Added Sept. 13, 1984, effective Jan. 1, 1985 (458 So.2d 1079). Amended Sept. 24, 1992, effective Jan. 1, 1993 (607 So.2d 1306); Oct. 3, 1996, effective Jan. 1, 1997 (683 So.2d 78); Sept. 28, 2000, effective Jan. 1, 2001 (778 So.2d 272); Sept. 29, 2005, effective Jan. 1, 2006 (912 So.2d 1178); Feb. 1, 2007 (948 So.2d 735); July 5, 2007, effective Jan. 1, 2008 (959 So.2d 1170); Oct. 18, 2012, effective, *nunc pro tunc*, Sept. 1, 2012 (102 So.3d 505).

Committee Notes

Derived from Florida Rule of Civil Procedure 1.080. Regulates the service of pleadings and papers in proceedings on petitions or motions for determination of rights. It is not applicable to every pleading and paper served or filed in the administration of a guardianship or decedent's estate.

Rule History

1984 Revision: New rule. Subdivision (c) is same as former rule 5.040(d).

1988 Revision: Committee notes revised. Citation form changes in committee notes.

1992 Revision: Editorial changes. Committee notes revised. Citation form changes in committee notes.

1996 Revision: Subdivision (b) amended to allow service to be made by facsimile. Committee notes revised.

2000 Revision: Subdivision (b) amended to clarify requirements for service of pleadings and papers. Subdivision (e) amended to clarify date of filing. Editorial changes in subdivision (f).

2003 Revision: Committee notes revised.

2005 Revision: Changes in subdivisions (b) and (f) to clarify service requirements, and editorial changes in (e).

2006 Revision: Committee notes revised.

2007 Revision: Provisions regarding service on a minor added in subdivision (b) in response to *Cason ex rel. Saferight v. Hammock*, 908 So.2d 512 (Fla. 5th DCA 2005). Committee notes revised.

2008 Revision: Committee notes revised.

2010 Revision: Committee notes revised.

2012 Revision: Portions of subdivision (b) and all of subdivisions (d), (e), (f), and (g) deleted in response to creation of Rule 2.516 of the Rules of Judicial Administration. Committee notes revised.

Statutory References

ch. 39, Fla. Stat. Proceedings relating to children.

ch. 48, Fla. Stat. Process and service of process.

ch. 61, Fla. Stat. Dissolution of marriage; support; time-sharing.

ch. 63, Fla. Stat. Adoption.

§ 393.12, Fla. Stat. Capacity; appointment of guardian advocate.

§ 731.201, Fla. Stat. General definitions.

§ 731.301, Fla. Stat. Notice.

§ 733.212, Fla. Stat. Notice of administration; filing of objections.

§ 733.2123, Fla. Stat. Adjudication before issuance of letters.

§ 733.705(2), (4), Fla. Stat. Payment of and objection to claims.

ch. 743, Fla. Stat. Disability of nonage of minors removed.

§ 744.3085, Fla. Stat. Guardian advocates.

§ 744.3201, Fla. Stat. Petition to determine incapacity.

§ 744.331, Fla. Stat. Procedures to determine incapacity.

§ 744.3371, Fla. Stat. Notice of petition for appointment of guardian and hearing.

§ 744.447, Fla. Stat. Petition for authorization to act.

ch. 751, Fla. Stat. Temporary custody of minor children by extended family.

Rule References

Fla. Prob. R. 5.020 Pleadings; verification; motions.

Fla. Prob. R. 5.025 Adversary proceedings.

Fla. Prob. R. 5.030 Attorneys.

Fla. Prob. R. 5.040 Notice.

Fla. Prob. R. 5.042 Time.

Fla. Prob. R. 5.150(c) Order requiring accounting.

Fla. Prob. R. 5.180 Waiver and consent.

Fla. Prob. R. 5.240(a) Notice of administration.

Fla. Prob. R. 5.340(d) Inventory.

Fla. Prob. R. 5.550 Petition to determine incapacity.

Fla. Prob. R. 5.560 Petition for appointment of guardian of an incapacitated person.

Fla. Prob. R. 5.649 Guardian advocate.

Fla. Prob. R. 5.681 Restoration of rights of person with developmental disability.

Fla. R. Civ. P. 1.080 Service of pleadings and papers.

Fla. R. Jud. Admin. 2.505 Attorneys.

Fla. R. Jud. Admin. 2.516 Service of pleadings and documents.

Rule 5.042. Time

(a) Computation. Computation of time shall be governed by Florida Rule of Judicial Administration 2.514.

(b) Enlargement. When an act is required or allowed to be done at or within a specified time by these rules, by order of court, or by notice given thereunder, for cause shown the court at any time in its discretion

(1) with or without notice may order the period enlarged if request therefor is made before the expiration of the period originally prescribed or as extended by a previous order, or

(2) on motion made and notice after the expiration of the specified period may permit the act to be done when failure to act was the result of excusable neglect. The court under this rule may not extend the time for serving a motion for rehearing or to enlarge any period of time governed by the Florida Rules of Appellate Procedure.

(c) Service for Hearings. A copy of any written petition or motion which may not be heard ex parte and a copy of the notice of the hearing thereon shall be served a reasonable time before the time specified for the hearing.

(d) Additional Time after Service by Mail or E-mail. Except when serving formal notice, or when serving a motion, pleading, or other document in the manner provided for service of formal notice, Florida Rule of Judicial Administration 2.514 shall apply to the computation of time following service.

Added Sept. 13, 1984, effective Jan. 1, 1985 (458 So.2d 1079). Amended Sept. 29, 1988, effective Jan. 1, 1989 (537 So.2d 500); Sept. 24, 1992, effective Jan. 1, 1993 (607 So.2d 1306); Sept. 29, 2005, effective Jan. 1, 2006 (912 So.2d 1178); July 12, 2012, effective Oct. 1, 2012 (95 So.3d 96).

Committee Notes

This rule is derived from Florida Rule of Civil Procedure 1.090.

Rule History

1984 Revision: New rule.

1988 Revision: Editorial changes in (a) and (b). Subdivision (a) enlarged to include closing of the clerk's office as a legal holiday. In *Clara P. Diamond, Inc. v. Tam–Bay Realty, Inc.*, 462 So. 2d 1168 (Fla. 2d DCA 1984), the Second District Court of Appeal suggested that Florida Rule of Civil Procedure 1.090(b) be clarified to leave no question that the court may not extend the time for rehearing, appeal, or petition for certiorari regardless of whether a request to enlarge the time therefor was made before the expiration of the time allowed. Because the format of rule 5.042(b) was substantially the same as the format of rule 1.090(b), subdivision (b) is amended to conform for the sake of clarity. Committee notes revised.

1992 Revision: Editorial changes. Committee notes revised. Citation form changes in committee notes.

2003 Revision: Committee notes revised.

2005 Revision: Subdivision (d) amended to clarify exception to mailing rule for service of formal notice and service in the manner provided for service of formal notice. Committee notes revised.

2008 Revision: Committee notes revised.

2012 Revision: Subdivision (a) revised to refer to Rule 2.514 and delete duplicative provisions. Subdivision (d) revised to incorporate service by e-mail and the filing and service of documents, rather than papers. Committee notes revised.

Statutory References

§ 393.12, Fla. Stat. Capacity; appointment of guardian advocate.

§ 683.01, Fla. Stat. Legal holidays.

§ 731.301, Fla. Stat. Notice.

§ 732.107, Fla. Stat. Escheat.

§ 732.2135, Fla. Stat. Time of election; extensions; withdrawal.

§ 732.402, Fla. Stat. Exempt property.

§ 732.901, Fla. Stat. Production of wills.

§ 733.104, Fla. Stat. Suspension of statutes of limitation in favor of the personal representative.

§ 733.212, Fla. Stat. Notice of administration; filing of objections.

§ 733.2121, Fla. Stat. Notice to creditors; filing of claims.

§ 733.701, Fla. Stat. Notifying creditors.

§ 733.702, Fla. Stat. Limitations on presentation of claims.

§ 733.705, Fla. Stat. Payment of and objection to claims.

§ 733.710, Fla. Stat. Limitations on claims against estates.

§ 733.816, Fla. Stat. Disposition of unclaimed property held by personal representatives.

§ 744.3085, Fla. Stat. Guardian advocates.

Rule References

Fla. Prob. R. 5.040(a)(1) Notice.

Fla. Prob. R. 5.150 Order requiring accounting.

Fla. Prob. R. 5.240 Notice of administration.

Fla. Prob. R. 5.241 Notice to creditors.

Fla. Prob. R. 5.340(a)–(b) Inventory.

Fla. Prob. R. 5.345 Accountings other than personal representatives' final accountings.

Fla. Prob. R. 5.395 Notice of federal estate tax return.

Fla. Prob. R. 5.400 Distribution and discharge.

Fla. Prob. R. 5.649 Guardian advocate.

Fla. Prob. R. 5.681 Restoration of rights of person with developmental disability.

Fla. Prob. R. 5.700 Objection to guardianship reports.

Fla. R. Civ. P. 1.090 Time.

Fla. R. Jud. Admin. 2.514 Computing and extending time.

Rule 5.043. Deposit of Wills and Codicils

Notwithstanding any rule to the contrary, and unless the court orders otherwise, any original executed will or codicil deposited with the court must be retained by the clerk in its original form and must not be destroyed or disposed of by the clerk for 20 years after submission regardless of whether the will or codicil has been permanently recorded as defined by Florida Rule of Judicial Administration 2.430.

Added Oct. 18, 2012, effective Dec. 1, 2012, April 1, 2013, Oct. 1, 2013 (102 So.3d 451).

Committee Notes

2012 Adoption. Florida Rule of Judicial Administration 2.525 requires that all documents be filed with the court electronically. Although the Florida Statutes direct the deposit of a will, rather than the filing of the will, the committee believes that original wills and codicils should be retained in their original form longer than other documents filed with the court due to the unique evidentiary aspects of the actual document. These unique aspects could be lost forever if the original document were converted to electronic form and the original destroyed.

Rule History

2012 Revision: New Rule.

Statutory References

§ 731.201(16), Fla. Stat. General definitions.

§ 732.901, Fla. Stat. Production of wills.

Rule References

Fla. R. Jud. Admin. 2.430 Retention of court records.

Fla. R. Jud. Admin. 2.525 Electronic filing.

Rule 5.050. Transfer of Proceedings

(a) Incorrect Venue. When any proceeding is filed laying venue in the wrong county, the court may transfer the proceeding in the same manner as provided in the Florida Rules of Civil Procedure. Any action taken by the court or the parties before the transfer is not affected because of the improper venue.

(b) Change of Residence of Ward. When the residence of a ward is changed to another county, the guardian of the person or the guardian advocate shall have the venue of the guardianship changed to the county of the acquired residence.

Amended Sept. 29, 1988, effective Jan. 1, 1989 (537 So.2d 500); Aug. 22, 1991, effective Oct. 1, 1991 (584 So.2d 964); July 10, 2008 (986 So.2d 576).

Committee Notes

Subdivision (b) of this rule represents a rule implementation of the procedure found in section 744.202(3), Florida Statutes.

Rule History

1975 Revision: Same as section 733.101(3), Florida Statutes.

1977 Revision: Title changed to indicate that the rule is one dealing with transfer.

1988 Revision: Prior rule renumbered as (a). New (b) is rule implementation of procedure in section 744.202(2), Florida Statutes. Editorial changes. Committee notes expanded. Citation form changes in rule and committee notes.

1991 Revision: Editorial changes.

1992 Revision: Committee notes revised. Citation form changes in committee notes.

2003 Revision: Committee notes revised.

2008 Revision: Change in (b) to add reference to guardian advocate. Committee notes revised.

Statutory References

ch. 47, Fla. Stat. Venue.

§ 393.12, Fla. Stat. Capacity; appointment of guardian advocate.

§ 733.101, Fla. Stat. Venue of probate proceedings.

§ 744.106, Fla. Stat. Notice.

§ 744.201, Fla. Stat. Domicile of ward.

§ 744.202, Fla. Stat. Venue.

§ 744.2025, Fla. Stat. Change of ward's residence.

§ 744.306, Fla. Stat. Foreign guardians.

§ 744.3085, Fla. Stat. Guardian advocates.

§ 744.3201, Fla. Stat. Petition to determine incapacity.

Rule References

Fla. Prob. R. 5.200(d) Petition for administration.

Fla. Prob. R. 5.240(b)(3), (d) Notice of administration.

Fla. Prob. R. 5.649 Guardian advocate.

Fla. R. Civ. P. 1.060 Transfers of actions.

Rule 5.060. Request for Notices and Copies of Pleadings

(a) Request. Any interested person who desires notice of proceedings in the estate of a decedent or ward may file a separate written request for notice of further proceedings, designating therein such person's residence and post office address. When such person's residence or post office address changes, a new designation of such change shall be filed in the proceedings. A person filing such request, or address change, must serve a copy on the attorney for the personal representative or guardian, and include a certificate of service.

(b) Notice and Copies. A party filing a request shall be served thereafter by the moving party with notice of further proceedings and with copies of subsequent pleadings and documents as long as the party is an interested person.

Amended Sept. 4, 1980, effective Jan. 1, 1981 (387 So.2d 949); Sept. 29, 1988, effective Jan. 1, 1989 (537 So.2d 500); Sept. 24, 1992, effective Jan. 1, 1993 (607 So.2d 1306); Sept. 26, 2013, effective Jan. 1, 2014 (123 So.3d 31).

Committee Notes

Rule History

1975 Revision: This rule substantially incorporates the provisions of prior rule 5.060 except that now a copy of the request shall be mailed by the clerk only to the attorney for the personal representative or guardian. Even though a request under this rule has not been made, informal notice as provided in rule 5.040(b)(3) may still be required.

1977 Revision: Editorial and citation form change in committee note.

1980 Revision: Caveat, the personal representative may want to give notice to parties even though not required, for example, where an independent action has been filed on an objected claim.

1988 Revision: Captions added to subdivisions. Committee notes expanded. Citation form changes in committee notes.

1992 Revision: Editorial changes. Committee notes revised. Citation form changes in committee notes.

2003 Revision: Committee notes revised.

2010 Revision: Committee notes revised.

2012 Revision: Committee notes revised.

2013 Revision: Subdivisions (a) and (b) revised to reflect service of documents, rather than papers. Subdivision (a) revised to shift responsibility for service of the request from the clerk to the interested person making the request for notice and copies. Editorial changes to conform to the court's guidelines for rule submissions as set forth in AOSC06–14.

Statutory References

§ 731.201, Fla. Stat. General definitions.

§ 733.604, Fla. Stat. Inventories and accountings; public records exemptions.

Rule References

Fla. Prob. R. 5.040 Notice.

Fla. Prob. R. 5.041 Service of pleadings and documents.

Fla. Prob. R. 5.340 Inventory.

Fla. Prob. R. 5.341 Estate information.

Fla. R. Jud. Admin. 2.516 Service of pleadings and documents.

Rule 5.065. Notice of Civil Action or Ancillary Administration

(a) Civil Action. A personal representative and a guardian shall file a notice when a civil action has been instituted by or against the personal representative or the guardian. The notice shall contain:

(1) the names of the parties;

(2) the style of the court and the case number;

(3) the county and state where the proceeding is pending;

(4) the date of commencement of the proceeding; and

(5) a brief statement of the nature of the proceeding.

(b) Ancillary Administration. The domiciliary personal representative shall file a notice when an ancillary administration has commenced, which notice shall contain:

(1) the name and residence address of the ancillary personal representative; and

(2) the information required in subdivisions (a)(2), (3), and (4) above.

(c) Copies Exhibited. A copy of the initial pleading may be attached to the notice. To the extent an attached initial pleading states the required information, the notice need not restate it.

Added Sept. 13, 1984, effective Jan. 1, 1985 (458 So.2d 1079). Amended Sept. 24, 1992, effective Jan. 1, 1993 (607 So.2d 1306); Sept. 28, 2000, effective Jan. 1, 2001 (778 So.2d 272).

Committee Notes

This rule reflects a procedural requirement not founded on a statute or rule.

Rule History

1984 Revision: New rule.

1988 Revision: Committee notes expanded.

1992 Revision: Editorial change. Citation form changes in committee notes.

2000 Revision: Subdivision (b) amended to eliminate requirement to set forth nature and value of ancillary assets.

Statutory References

§ 733.612(20), Fla.Stat. Transactions authorized for the personal representative; exceptions.

§ 744.441(11), Fla.Stat. Powers of guardian upon court approval.

Rule 5.080. Discovery and Subpoena

(a) Adoption of Civil Rules. The following Florida Rules of Civil Procedure shall apply in all probate and guardianship proceedings:

(1) Rule 1.280, general provisions governing discovery.

(2) Rule 1.290, depositions before action or pending appeal.

(3) Rule 1.300, persons before whom depositions may be taken.

(4) Rule 1.310, depositions upon oral examination.

(5) Rule 1.320, depositions upon written questions.

(6) Rule 1.330, use of depositions in court proceedings.

(7) Rule 1.340, interrogatories to parties.

(8) Rule 1.350, production of documents and things and entry upon land for inspection and other purposes.

(9) Rule 1.351, production of documents and things without deposition.

(10) Rule 1.360, examination of persons.

(11) Rule 1.370, requests for admission.

(12) Rule 1.380, failure to make discovery; sanctions.

(13) Rule 1.390, depositions of expert witnesses.

(14) Rule 1.410, subpoena.

(b) Limitations and Costs. In order to conserve the assets of the estate, the court has broad discretion to limit the scope and the place and manner of the discovery and to assess the costs, including attorneys' fees, of the discovery against the party making it or against 1 or more of the beneficiaries of the estate or against the ward in such proportions as the court determines, considering, among other factors, the benefit derived therefrom.

(c) Application. It is not necessary to have an adversary proceeding under rule 5.025 to utilize the rules adopted in subdivision (a) above. Any interested person may utilize the rules adopted in subdivision (a).

Amended March 31, 1977, effective July 1, 1977 (344 So.2d 828); Sept. 13, 1984, effective Jan. 1, 1985 (458 So.2d 1079); Sept. 29, 1988, effective Jan. 1, 1989 (537 So.2d 500); Sept. 24, 1992, effective Jan. 1, 1993 (607 So.2d 1306); Oct. 3, 1996, effective Jan. 1, 1997 (683 So.2d 78); May 2, 2002 (824 So.2d 849); Feb. 1, 2007 (948 So.2d 735); July 12, 2007 (964 So.2d 140).

Committee Notes

Subdivision (b) is not intended to result in the assessment of costs, including attorney's fees, in every instance in which discovery is sought. Subdivision (c) is not intended to overrule the holdings in *In re Estate of Shaw*, 340 So. 2d 491 (Fla. 3d DCA 1976), and *In re Estate of Posner*, 492 So. 2d 1093 (Fla. 3d DCA 1986).

Rule History

1975 Revision: This rule is the same as prior rule 5.080, broadened to include guardianships and intended to clearly permit the use of discovery practices in nonadversary probate and guardianship matters.

1977 Revision: Editorial change in citation form in committee note.

1984 Revision: Florida Rules of Civil Procedure 1.290, 1.300, 1.351, and 1.410 have been added.

1988 Revision: Subdivision (a)(15) deleted as duplicative of rule 5.070 Subpoena. Editorial change in (b). Citation form change in committee notes.

1992 Revision: Editorial changes. Committee notes revised. Citation form changes in committee notes.

1996 Revision: Reference to rule 1.400 eliminated because of deletion of that rule from the Florida Rules of Civil Procedure. Editorial change.

2002 Revision: Reference to rule 1.410 transferred to subdivision (a) from former rule 5.070. Subdivision (b) amended to give court discretion to assess attorneys' fees. Subdivision (c) added. Committee notes revised.

2006 Revision: Committee notes revised.

2007 Revision: Committee notes revised.

Statutory References

§ 731.201(23), Fla. Stat. General definitions.

§ 733.106, Fla. Stat. Costs and attorney's fees.

§ 744.105, Fla. Stat. Costs.

§ 744.108, Fla. Stat. Guardian's and attorney's fees and expenses.

Rule References

Fla. Prob. R. 5.025 Adversary proceedings.

Fla. R. Jud. Admin. 2.535 Court reporting.

Rule 5.095. General and Special Magistrates

(a) General Magistrates. The court may appoint general magistrates as the court finds necessary. General magistrates shall be members of The Florida Bar and shall continue in office until removed by the court. The order making an appointment shall be recorded. Each general magistrate shall take the oath required of officers by the Florida Constitution. The oath shall be recorded before the magistrate begins to act.

(b) Special Magistrates. The court may appoint members of The Florida Bar as special magistrates for any particular service required by the court. Special magistrates shall be governed by all laws and rules relating to general magistrates, except special magistrates shall not be required to make oath unless specifically required by the court. For good cause shown, the court may appoint a person other than a member of The Florida Bar as a special magistrate.

(c) Reference. No referral shall be made to a magistrate without the consent of the parties. When a referral is made to a magistrate, either party may set the action for hearing before the magistrate.

(d) General Powers and Duties. Every magistrate shall act under the direction of the court. Process issued by a magistrate shall be directed as provided by law. All grounds for disqualification of a judge shall apply to magistrates.

(e) Bond. When not otherwise provided by law, the court may require magistrates who are appointed to dispose of real or personal property to give bond and surety conditioned for the proper payment of all money that may come into their hands and for the due performance of their duties. The bond shall be made payable to the State of Florida and shall be for the benefit of all persons aggrieved by any act of the magistrate.

(f) Hearings. Hearings before any magistrate may be held in the county where the action is pending or at any other place by order of the court for the convenience of the witnesses or the parties. The magistrate shall assign a time and place for proceedings as soon as reasonably possible after a referral is made and give notice to all parties. If any party fails to appear, the magistrate may proceed ex parte or may continue the hearing to a future day, with notice to the absent party. The magistrate shall proceed with reasonable diligence and the least practicable delay. Any party may apply to the court for an order directing the magistrate to accelerate the proceedings and to make a report promptly. Evidence shall be taken in writing or by electronic recording by the magistrate or by some other person under the magistrate's authority in the magistrate's presence and shall be filed with the magistrate's report. The magistrate may examine and take testimony from the parties and their witnesses under oath on all matters contained in the referral and may require production of all books, papers, writings, vouchers, and other documents applicable to those matters. The magistrate shall admit only evidence that would be admissible in court. The magistrate may take all actions concerning evidence that may be taken by the court. All parties accounting before a magistrate shall bring in their accounts in the form of accounts payable and receivable, and any other parties who are not satisfied with the account may examine the accounting party orally or by interrogatories or deposition as the magistrate directs. All depositions and documents that have been taken or used previously in the action may be used before the magistrate.

(g) Magistrate's Report. The magistrate's report shall contain a description of the matters considered and the magistrate's conclusion and any recommendations. No part of any statement of facts, account, charge, deposition, examination, or answer used before the magistrate shall be recited.

(h) Filing Report; Notice; Exceptions. The magistrate shall file the report and serve copies on the parties. The parties may serve exceptions to the report within 10 days from the time it is served on them. If no exceptions are filed within that period, the court shall take appropriate action on the report. All timely filed exceptions shall be heard on reasonable notice by either party.

(i) Application of Rule. This rule shall not apply to the appointment of magistrates for the specific purpose of reviewing guardianship inventories, accountings, and plans as otherwise governed by law and these rules.

Added July 5, 2007, effective Jan. 1, 2008 (959 So.2d 1170).

Committee Notes

Rule History

2007 Revision: This rule, patterned after Florida Rule of Civil Procedure 1.490, is created to implement the use of magistrates in probate and guardianship proceedings other than those specifically addressed in rule 5.697.

Rule References

Fla. Prob. R. 5.697 Magistrates' review of guardianship inventories, accountings, and plans.

Fla. R. Civ. P. 1.490 Magistrates.

Rule 5.100. Right of Appeal

Appeal of final orders and discretionary appellate review of non-final orders are governed by the Florida Rules of Appellate Procedure.

Amended Sept. 29, 1988, effective Jan. 1, 1989 (537 So.2d 500); Sept. 24, 1992, effective Jan. 1, 1993 (607 So.2d 1306); Oct. 3, 1996, effective Jan. 1, 1997 (683 So.2d 78); Sept. 28, 2000, effective Jan. 1, 2001 (778 So.2d 272).

Committee Notes

For purposes of appellate review, the service of a motion for rehearing postpones rendition of final orders only. A motion for rehearing of a non-final order does not toll the running of the time to seek review of that order.

Rule History

1975 Revision: Same as prior rule 5.100 with editorial changes.

1977 Revision: Citation form change in committee note.

1988 Revision: Committee notes expanded. Citation form changes in rule and committee notes.

1992 Revision: Editorial changes. Citation form changes in committee notes.

1996 Revision: Superseded by Florida Rule of Appellate Procedure 9. 110(a)(2).

2000 Revision: Rewritten because former rule was superseded. Revisions to committee notes to amend text and to include cross-references to other rules.

2003 Revision: Committee notes revised.

Rule References

Fla. Prob. R. 5.020(d) Pleadings; verification; motions.

Fla. R. App. P. 9.020(h) Definitions.

Fla. R. App. P. 9.110(a)(2), (b) Appeal proceedings to review final orders of lower tribunals and orders granting new trial in jury and non-jury cases.

Fla. R. App. P. 9.130(b) Proceedings to review non-final orders and specified final orders.

Rule 5.110. Address Designation for Personal Representative or Guardian; Designation of Resident Agent and Acceptance

(a) Address Designation of Personal Representative or Guardian. Before letters are issued, the personal representative or guardian must file a designation of street address, and mailing address. If the personal representative or guardian is an individual, the designation must also include the individual's residence address. The personal representative or guardian must notify the court of any change in its residence address, street address, or mailing address within 20 days of the change.

(b) Designation of Resident Agent. Before letters are issued, a personal representative or guardian must file a designation of resident agent for service of process or notice, and the acceptance by the resident agent. A designation of resident agent is not required if a personal representative or guardian is (1) a corporate fiduciary having an office in Florida, or (2) a Florida Bar member who is a resident of and has an office in Florida. The designation must contain the name, street address, and mailing address of the resident agent. If the resident agent is an individual who is not an attorney, the designation must also include the individual's residence address.

(c) Residency Requirement. A resident agent, other than a member of The Florida Bar who is a resident of Florida, must be a resident of the county where the proceedings are pending.

(d) Acceptance by Resident Agent. The resident agent must sign a written acceptance of designation.

(e) Incorporation in Other Pleadings. The designation of the address of the personal representative or guardian, the designation of resident agent, or acceptance may be incorporated in the petition for administration, the petition for appointment of guardian, or the personal representative's or guardian's oath.

(f) Effect of Designation and Acceptance. The designation of and acceptance by the resident agent shall constitute consent to service of process or notice on the agent and shall be sufficient to bind the personal representative or guardian:

(1) in its representative capacity in any action; and

(2) in its personal capacity only in those actions in which the personal representative or guardian is sued personally for claims arising from the administration of the estate or guardianship.

(g) Successor Agent. If the resident agent dies, resigns, or is unable to act for any other reason, the personal representative or guardian must appoint a successor agent within 10 days after receiving notice that such event has occurred.

Amended Sept. 13, 1984, effective Jan. 1, 1985 (458 So.2d 1079); Sept. 29, 1988, effective Jan. 1, 1989 (537 So.2d 500); Sept. 24, 1992, effective Jan. 1, 1993 (607 So.2d 1306); September 28, 2000, effective Jan. 1, 2001 (778 So.2d 272); Sept. 2, 2010, effective Jan. 1, 2011 (50 So.3d 578); Sept. 26, 2013, effective Jan. 1, 2014 (123 So.3d 31).

Committee Notes

Rule History

1977 Revision: Change in committee note to conform to statutory renumbering.

Substantially the same as prior rule 5.210, except that under prior rule, designation was required to be filed within 10 days after letters issued.

1984 Revision: Captions added to subdivisions. New subdivision (b) added. Requires filing acceptance at the same time as filing designation. Committee notes revised.

1988 Revision: Change in (c) to clarify that the personal representative, if a member of The Florida Bar, may not also serve as resident agent for service of process or notice. Citation form change in committee notes.

1992 Revision: Editorial changes. Committee notes revised. Citation form changes in committee notes.

2000 Revision: Extensive editorial changes to rule. Rule reformatted for clarity and revised to permit an attorney serving as resident agent to designate a business address in lieu of a residence address.

2003 Revision: Committee notes revised.

2008 Revision: Committee notes revised.

2010 Revision: Subdivision (a) amended to require the personal representative or guardian to notify the court of any change of address to facilitate timely communication with the personal representative or guardian.

2013 Revision: Subdivision (b) amended to limit to individuals the requirement that the guardian or personal representative provide a designation of residence address, excluding corporate fiduciaries. Editorial changes to conform to the court's guidelines for rules submissions as set forth in AOSC06–14.

Rule References

Fla. Prob. R. 5.200 Petition for administration.

Fla. Prob. R. 5.320 Oath of personal representative.

Fla. Prob. R. 5.560 Petition for appointment of guardian of an incapacitated person.

Fla. Prob. R. 5.649 Guardian advocate.

Rule 5.120. Administrator Ad Litem and Guardian Ad Litem

(a) Appointment. When it is necessary that the estate of a decedent or a ward be represented in any probate or guardianship proceeding and there is no personal representative of the estate or guardian of the ward, or the personal representative or guardian is or may be interested adversely to the estate or ward, or is enforcing the personal representative's or guardian's own debt or claim against the estate or ward, or the necessity arises otherwise, the court may appoint an administrator ad litem or a guardian ad litem, as the case may be, without bond or notice for that particular proceeding. At any point in a proceeding, a court may appoint a guardian ad litem to represent the interests of an incapacitated person, an unborn or unascertained person, a minor or any other person otherwise under a legal disability, a person with a developmental disability, or a person whose identity or address is unknown, if the court determines that representation of the interest otherwise would be inadequate. If not precluded by conflict of interest, a guardian ad litem may be appointed to represent several persons or interests. The administrator ad litem or guardian ad litem shall file an oath to discharge all duties faithfully and upon the filing shall be qualified to act. No process need be served upon the administrator ad litem or guardian ad litem, but such person shall appear and defend as directed by the court.

(b) Petition. The petition for appointment of a guardian ad litem shall state to the best of petitioner's information and belief:

(1) the initials and residence address of each minor, person with a developmental disability, or incapacitated person and year of birth of each minor who has an interest in the proceedings;

(2) the name and address of any guardian appointed for each minor, person with a developmental disability, or incapacitated person;

(3) the name and residence address of any living natural guardians or living natural guardian having

legal custody of each minor, person with a developmental disability, or incapacitated person;

(4) a description of the interest in the proceedings of each minor, person with a developmental disability, or incapacitated person; and

(5) the facts showing the necessity for the appointment of a guardian ad litem.

(c) Notice. Within 10 days after appointment, the petitioner shall serve conformed copies of the petition for appointment of a guardian ad litem and order to any guardian, or if there is no guardian, to the living natural guardians or the living natural guardian having legal custody of the minor, person with a developmental disability, or incapacitated person.

(d) Report. The guardian ad litem shall serve conformed copies of any written report or finding of the guardian ad litem's investigation and answer filed in the proceedings, petition for compensation and discharge, and the notice of hearing on the petition to any guardian, or in the event that there is no guardian, to the living natural guardians or the living natural guardian having legal custody of the minor, person with a developmental disability, or incapacitated person.

(e) Service of Petition and Order. Within 10 days after appointment, the petitioner for an administrator ad litem shall serve conformed copies of the petition for appointment and order to the attorney of record of each beneficiary and to each known beneficiary not represented by an attorney of record.

(f) Enforcement of Judgments. When an administrator ad litem or guardian ad litem recovers any judgment or other relief, it shall be enforced as other judgments. Execution shall issue in favor of the administrator ad litem or guardian ad litem for the use of the estate or ward and the money collected shall be paid to the personal representative or guardian, or as otherwise ordered by the court.

(g) Claim of Personal Representative. The fact that the personal representative is seeking reimbursement for claims against the decedent paid by the personal representative does not require appointment of an administrator ad litem.

Amended March 31, 1977, effective July 1, 1977 (344 So.2d 828); Sept. 29, 1988, effective Jan. 1, 1989 (537 So.2d 500); Sept. 24, 1992, effective Jan. 1, 1993 (607 So.2d 1306); Feb. 1, 2007 (948 So.2d 735); July 10, 2008 (986 So.2d 576); Oct. 18, 2012, effective, *nunc pro tunc*, Sept. 1, 2012 (102 So.3d 505); May 22, 2014, effective May 22, 2014 (139 So.3d 875).

Committee Notes

Rule History

1977 Revision: Editorial change in (a) limiting application of rule to probate and guardianship proceedings. In (b) the petition for appointment of a guardian need not be verified. Deletion of (g) as being substantive rather than procedural and changing former (h) to new (g). Change in committee note to conform to statutory renumbering.

This rule implements sections 731.303(5), 733.308, and 744.391, Florida Statutes, and includes some of the provisions of prior rule 5.230.

1988 Revision: Editorial changes; captions added to paragraphs. Citation form changes in committee notes.

1992 Revision: Addition of phrase in subdivision (a) to conform to 1992 amendment to section 731.303(5), Florida Statutes. Editorial changes. Committee notes revised. Citation form changes in committee notes.

2003 Revision: Committee notes revised.

2006 Revision: Committee notes revised.

2008 Revision: Subdivisions (a), (b), (c), and (d) amended to include persons with a developmental disability. Committee notes revised.

2012 Revision: The phrase "deliver or mail" in subdivisions (c), (d), and (e) has been replaced with the word "serve" to comply with other rules relating to service of pleadings and documents. Committee notes revised.

2014 Revision: Amends subdivision (b)(1) to conform to Fla. R. Jud. Admin. 2.425. Committee notes revised.

Statutory References

§ 393.12, Fla. Stat. Capacity; appointment of guardian advocate.

§ 731.303, Fla. Stat. Representation.

§ 733.308, Fla. Stat. Administrator ad litem.

§ 733.708, Fla. Stat. Compromise.

§ 744.3025, Fla. Stat. Claims of minors.

§ 744.3085, Fla. Stat. Guardian advocates.

§ 744.387, Fla. Stat. Settlement of claims.

§ 744.391, Fla. Stat. Actions by and against guardian or ward.

§ 744.446, Fla. Stat. Conflicts of interest; prohibited activities; court approval; breach of fiduciary duty.

Rule References

Fla. Prob. R. 5.041 Service of pleadings and documents.

Fla. R. Jud. Admin. 2.516 Service of pleadings and documents.

Fla. R. Jud. Admin. 2.425 Minimization of the Filing of Sensitive Information.

Rule 5.122. Curators

(a) Petition for Appointment. The petition for appointment of a curator shall be verified and shall contain:

(1) the petitioner's name, address, and interest, if any, in the estate;

(2) the decedent's name, address, date and place of death, and state and county of domicile;

(3) the names and addresses of the persons apparently entitled to letters of administration and any known beneficiaries;

(4) the nature and approximate value of the assets;

(5) a statement showing venue;

(6) a statement as to why a curator should be appointed; and

(7) the name and address of any proposed curator.

The court may appoint a curator sua sponte.

(b) Appointment. Before letters of curatorship are issued, the curator shall file a designation of resident agent and acceptance, and an oath, as is required for personal representatives under these rules. The court shall issue letters of curatorship that shall entitle the curator to possess or control the decedent's property, which the court may enforce through contempt proceedings.

(c) Notice. Formal notice shall be given to the person apparently entitled to letters, if any. If it is likely that the decedent's property will be wasted, destroyed, or removed beyond the jurisdiction of the court and if the appointment of a curator would be delayed by giving notice, the court may appoint a curator without notice.

(d) Powers. By order, the court may authorize the curator to perform any duty or function of a personal representative, including publication and service of notice to creditors, or if a will has been admitted, service of notice of administration.

(e) Inventory and Accounting. The curator shall file an inventory within 30 days after issuance of letters of curatorship. When the personal representative is appointed, the curator shall account for and deliver all estate assets in the curator's possession to the personal representative within 30 days after issuance of letters of administration.

(f) Petition to Reconsider. If a curator has been appointed without notice, any interested party who did not receive notice may, at any time, petition to reconsider the appointment.

(g) Subject to Other Provisions. Curators shall be subject to the provisions of these rules and other applicable law concerning personal representatives.

Added Sept. 29, 1988, effective Jan. 1, 1989 (537 So.2d 500). Amended Sept. 24, 1992, effective Jan. 1, 1993 (607 So.2d 1306); June 19, 2003 (848 So.2d 1069).

Committee Notes

This rule implements the procedure found in section 733.501, Florida Statutes, as amended in 1997 and 2001. The rule has been modified, in part, to reflect the addition of new rule 5.241 regarding notice to creditors. Because the fundamental concern of curatorship is protection of estate property, the procedure facilitates speed and flexibility while recognizing due process concerns. It is not intended that this rule change the effect of the statute from which it has been derived, but the rule has been reformatted to conform to the structure of these rules. Furthermore, the Committee does not intend to create a new procedure, except that subdivision (d) specifies certain acts that the court may authorize the curator to perform. This specificity of example, while not included in the statute, is not intended to limit the authorized acts to those specified in the rule. The appointment of a curator without notice is tantamount to a temporary injunction. Thus, due process considerations suggest an expedited hearing to reconsider the appointment of a curator by any interested party who did not receive notice.

Rule History

1988 Revision: New rule.

1992 Revision: Editorial changes. Citation form changes in committee notes.

2003 Revision: Extensive changes to rule to clarify procedure for appointment of curator. Committee notes revised.

Statutory References

§ 733.402, Fla. Stat. Bond of fiduciary; when required; form.

§ 733.501, Fla. Stat. Curators.

Rule Reference

Fla. Prob. R. 5.020 Pleadings; verification; motions.

Rule 5.150. Order Requiring Accounting

(a) Accountings Required by Statute. When any personal representative or guardian fails to file an accounting or return required by statute or rule, the court on its own motion or on the petition of an interested person shall order the personal representative or guardian to file the accounting or return within 15 days from the service on the personal representative or guardian of the order, or show cause why he or she should not be compelled to do so.

(b) Accountings Not Required by Statute. On the petition of an interested person, or on its own motion, the court may require the personal representative or guardian to file an accounting or return not otherwise required by statute or rule. The order requiring an accounting or return shall order the personal representative or guardian to file the accounting or return within a specified time from service on the personal representative or guardian of the order, or show cause why he or she should not be compelled to do so.

(c) Service. A copy of the order shall be served on the personal representative or guardian and the personal representative's or guardian's attorney.

Amended Sept. 13, 1984, effective Jan. 1, 1985 (458 So.2d 1079); Sept. 24, 1992, effective Jan. 1, 1993 (607 So.2d 1306); Sept. 30, 2004, effective Oct. 1, 2004 (887 So.2d 1090).

Committee Notes

The court on its motion or on petition of an interested person may require a personal representative or guardian to file an accounting or return not otherwise required by statute.

Rule History

1977 Revision: Change in committee notes.

1984 Revision: Extensive editorial changes. Committee notes revised and expanded.

1992 Revision: Editorial changes. Committee notes revised. Citation form changes in committee notes.

2003 Revision: Committee notes revised.

2008 Revision: Committee notes revised.

Statutory References

§ 38.22, Fla. Stat. Power to punish contempts.

§ 38.23, Fla. Stat. Contempts defined.

§ 393.12(2)(h), Fla. Stat. Capacity; appointment of guardian advocate.

§ 733.5036, Fla. Stat. Accounting and discharge following resignation.

§ 733.508, Fla. Stat. Accounting and discharge of removed personal representatives upon removal.

§ 733.901, Fla. Stat. Final discharge.

ch. 738, Fla. Stat. Principal and income.

§ 744.3085, Fla. Stat. Guardian advocates.

§ 744.367, Fla. Stat. Duty to file annual guardianship report.

§ 744.3678, Fla. Stat. Annual accounting.

§ 744.3685, Fla. Stat. Order requiring guardianship report; contempt.

§ 744.369, Fla. Stat. Judicial review of guardianship reports.

§ 744.467, Fla. Stat. Resignation of guardian.

§ 744.511, Fla. Stat. Accounting upon removal.

§ 744.517, Fla. Stat. Proceedings for contempt.

§ 744.521, Fla. Stat. Termination of guardianship.

§ 744.524, Fla. Stat. Termination of guardianship on change of domicile of resident ward.

§ 744.527, Fla. Stat. Final reports and applications for discharge; hearing.

Rule References

Fla. Prob. R. 5.649 Guardian advocate.

Fla. Prob. R. 5.650 Resignation or disqualification of guardian; appointment of successor.

Fla. Prob. R. 5.660 Proceedings for removal of guardian.

Fla. Prob. R. 5.670 Termination of guardianship on change of domicile of resident ward.

Fla. Prob. R. 5.680 Termination of guardianship.

Fla. Prob. R. 5.681 Restoration of rights of person with developmental disability.

Fla. Prob. R. 5.695 Annual guardianship report.

Fla. Prob. R. 5.696 Annual accounting.

Fla. Prob. R. 5.697 Magistrates' review of guardianship accountings and plans.

Rule 5.160. Production of Assets

On the petition of an interested person, or on its own motion, the court may require any personal representative or guardian to produce satisfactory evidence that the assets of the estate are in the possession or under the control of the personal representative or guardian and may order production of the assets in the manner and for the purposes directed by the court.

Amended Sept. 13, 1984, effective Jan. 1, 1985 (458 So.2d 1079); Sept. 29, 1988, effective Jan. 1, 1989 (537 So.2d 500); Sept. 24, 1992, effective Jan. 1, 1993 (607 So.2d 1306).

Committee Notes

Rule History

1977 Revision: Change in committee notes.

1984 Revision: Minor editorial changes. Committee notes revised.

1988 Revision: Editorial changes.

1992 Revision: Editorial changes. Committee notes revised.

Statutory Reference

§ 744.373, Fla.Stat. Production of property.

Rule 5.170. Evidence

In proceedings under the Florida Probate Code and the Florida Guardianship Law the rules of evidence in civil actions are applicable unless specifically changed by the Florida Probate Code, the Florida Guardianship Law, or these rules.

Amended March 31, 1977, effective July 1, 1977 (344 So.2d 828); Sept. 13, 1984, effective Jan. 1, 1985 (458 So.2d 1079).

Committee Notes

Rule History

1977 Revision: New rule.

1984 Revision: To further clarify the intent of the rule to incorporate the provisions of the Florida Evidence Code (chapter 90, Florida Statutes) when not in conflict with the Florida Probate Code or Florida Guardianship Law, or rules applicable to these particular proceedings.

1992 Revision: Citation form changes in committee notes.

2003 Revision: Committee notes revised.

Statutory References

ch. 90, Fla. Stat. Florida Evidence Code.

§ 733.107, Fla. Stat. Burden of proof in contests; presumption of undue influence.

Rule 5.171. Evidence of Death

In a proceeding under these rules, the following shall apply:

(a) Death Certificate. An authenticated copy of a death certificate issued by an official or agency of the place where the death purportedly occurred or by an official or agency of the United States is prima facie proof of the fact, place, date, and time of death and the identity of the decedent.

(b) Other Records. A copy of any record or report of a governmental agency, domestic or foreign, that a person is dead, alive, missing, detained, or, from the facts related, presumed dead is prima facie evidence of the status, dates, circumstances, and places disclosed by the record or report.

(c) Extended Absence. A person who is absent from the place of that person's last known domicile for a continuous period of 5 years and whose absence is not satisfactorily explained after diligent search and inquiry is presumed dead. The person's death is presumed to have occurred at the end of the period unless there is evidence establishing that death occurred earlier.

Added Sept. 29, 1988, effective Jan. 1, 1989 (537 So.2d 500). Amended Sept. 24, 1992, effective Jan. 1, 1993 (607 So.2d 1306).

Committee Notes

This rule represents a rule implementation of the procedure found in section 731.103, Florida Statutes. It is not intended to change the effect of the statute from which it was derived but has been reformatted to conform with the structure of these rules. It is not intended to create a new procedure or modify an existing procedure, except that additional language has been added which was not in the statute, to permit issuance of a death certificate by an official or agency of the United States. An example would be such a certificate issued by the Department of State or the Department of Defense.

Rule History

1988 Revision: New rule.

1992 Revision: Editorial changes. Committee notes revised. Citation form changes in committee notes.

Statutory References

§ 731.103, Fla.Stat. Evidence as to death or status.

§ 744.521, Fla.Stat. Termination of guardianship.

Rule References

Fla.Prob.R. 5.205 Filing evidence of death.

Fla.Prob.R. 5.680 Termination of guardianship.

Rule 5.180. Waiver and Consent

(a) Manner of Execution. A waiver or consent as authorized by law shall be in writing and signed by the person executing the waiver or consent.

(b) Contents. The waiver or consent shall state:

(1) the person's interest in the subject of the waiver or consent;

(2) if the person is signing in a fiduciary or representative capacity, the nature of the capacity;

(3) expressly what is being waived or consented to; and

(4) if the waiver pertains to compensation, language declaring that the waiving party has actual knowledge of the amount and manner of determining the compensation and, in addition, either:

(A) that the party has agreed to the amount and manner of determining that compensation and waives any objection to payment; or

(B) that the party has the right to petition the court to determine the compensation and waives that right.

(c) Filing. The waiver or consent shall be filed.

Amended March 31, 1977, effective July 1, 1977 (344 So.2d 828); Sept. 13, 1984, effective Jan. 1, 1985 (458 So.2d 1079); Sept. 29, 1988, effective Jan. 1, 1989 (537 So.2d 500); Sept. 24, 1992, effective Jan. 1, 1993 (607 So.2d 1306); Oct. 3, 1996, effective Jan. 1, 1997 (683 So.2d 78); Feb. 1, 2007 (948 So.2d 735).

Committee Notes

One person who serves in two fiduciary capacities may not waive or consent to the person's acts without the approval of those whom the person represents. This rule represents a rule implementation of the procedure found in section 731.302, Florida Statutes.

Rule History

1977 Revision: Extends right of waiver to natural guardian; clarifies right to waive service of notice of administration.

1984 Revision: Extends waiver to disclosure of compensation and distribution of assets. Committee notes revised.

1988 Revision: Procedure from section 731.302, Florida Statutes, inserted as new (1)(f), and a new requirement that the waiver be in writing has been added. Editorial changes. Committee notes expanded. Citation form changes in committee notes.

1992 Revision: Editorial changes. Committee notes revised. Citation form changes in committee notes.

1996 Revision: Addition of specific fee waiver disclosure requirements found in § 733.6171(9), Florida Statutes, and expanded to cover all fees. Committee notes revised.

2003 Revision: Committee notes revised.

2006 Revision: Rule extensively amended to remove references to interested persons' right to waive or consent, which is governed by section 731.302, Florida Statutes, and to address manner of execution and contents of waiver. Committee notes revised.

Statutory References

§ 731.302, Fla. Stat. Waiver and consent by interested person.

§ 731.303, Fla. Stat. Representation.

§ 733.6171, Fla. Stat. Compensation of attorney for the personal representative.

PART II. PROBATE

Rule 5.200. Petition for Administration

The petition for administration shall be verified by the petitioner and shall contain:

(a) a statement of the interest of the petitioner, the petitioner's name and address, and the name and office address of the petitioner's attorney;

(b) the name and last known address of the decedent, last 4 digits of the decedent's social security number, date and place of death of the decedent, and state and county of the decedent's domicile;

(c) so far as is known, the names and addresses of the surviving spouse, if any, the beneficiaries and their relationship to the decedent and the year of birth of any beneficiaries who are minors;

(d) a statement showing venue;

(e) the priority, under the Florida Probate Code, of the person whose appointment as the personal representative is sought and a statement that the person is qualified to serve under the laws of Florida;

(f) a statement whether domiciliary or principal proceedings are pending in another state or country, if known, and the name and address of the foreign personal representative and the court issuing letters;

(g) a statement of the approximate value and nature of the assets;

(h) in an intestate estate, a statement that after the exercise of reasonable diligence the petitioner is unaware of any unrevoked wills or codicils, or if the petitioner is aware of any unrevoked wills or codicils, a statement why the wills or codicils are not being probated;

(i) in a testate estate, a statement identifying all unrevoked wills and codicils being presented for probate, and a statement that the petitioner is unaware of any other unrevoked wills or codicils or, if the petitioner is aware of any other unrevoked wills or codicils, a statement why the other wills or codicils are not being probated; and

(j) in a testate estate, a statement that the original of the decedent's last will is in the possession of the court or accompanies the petition, or that an authenticated copy of a will deposited with or probated in another jurisdiction or that an authenticated copy of a notarial will, the original of which is in the possession of a foreign notary, accompanies the petition.

Amended March 31, 1977, effective July 1, 1977 (344 So.2d 828); Sept. 29, 1988, effective Jan. 1, 1989 (537 So.2d 500); Sept. 24, 1992, effective Jan. 1, 1993 (607 So.2d 1306); May 2, 2002 (824 So.2d 849); July 5, 2007, effective Jan. 1, 2008 (959 So.2d 1170); July 12, 2007 (964 So.2d 140); Sept. 2, 2010, effective Jan. 1, 2011 (50 So.3d 578); Nov. 3, 2011, effective, *nunc pro tunc*, Oct. 1, 2011 (78 So.3d 1045); May 22, 2014, effective May 22, 2014 (139 So.3d 875).

Committee Notes

Rule History

1977 Revision: Addition to (b)(5) to require an affirmative statement that the person sought to be appointed as personal representative is qualified to serve. Committee note expanded to include additional statutory references.

Substantially the same as section 733.202, Florida Statutes, and implementing sections 733.301 through 733.305, Florida Statutes.

1988 Revision: Editorial changes. Committee notes revised.

1992 Revision: Addition of phrase in subdivision (b) to conform to 1992 amendment to section 733.202(2)(b), Florida Statutes. Reference to clerk ascertaining the amount of the filing fee deleted in subdivision (g) because of repeal of sliding scale of filing fees. The remaining language was deemed unnecessary. Editorial changes. Committee notes revised. Citation form changes in committee notes.

2002 Revision: Addition of phrases in subdivision (j) to add references to wills probated in Florida where the original is in the possession of a foreign official. Editorial changes. Committee notes revised.

2003 Revision: Committee notes revised.

2007 Revision: Committee notes revised.

2007 Revision: Editorial changes in (h) and (i).

2010 Revision: Editorial change in (e) to clarify reference to Florida Probate Code.

2011 Revision: Subdivision (b) amended to limit listing of decedent's social security number to last four digits.

2012 Revision: Committee notes revised.

2014 Revision: Subdivision (c) amended to conform to Fla. R. Jud. Admin. 2.425. Committee notes revised.

Statutory References

§ 731.201(23), Fla. Stat. General definitions.

§ 731.301, Fla. Stat. Notice.

§ 733.202, Fla. Stat. Petition.

§ 733.301, Fla. Stat. Preference in appointment of personal representative.

§ 733.302, Fla. Stat. Who may be appointed personal representative.

§ 733.303, Fla. Stat. Persons not qualified.

§ 733.304, Fla. Stat. Nonresidents.

§ 733.305, Fla. Stat. Trust companies and other corporations and associations.

Rule References

Fla. Prob. R. 5.020 Pleadings; verification; motions.

Fla. Prob. R. 5.040 Notice.

Fla. Prob. R. 5.041 Service of pleadings and documents.

Fla. Prob. R. 5.180 Waiver and consent.

Fla. Prob. R. 5.201 Notice of petition for administration.

Fla. R. Jud. Admin. 2.516 Service of pleadings and documents.

Fla. R. Jud. Admin. 2.425 Minimization of the Filing of Sensitive Information.

Rule 5.201. Notice of Petition for Administration

(a) Petitioner Entitled to Preference of Appointment. Except as may otherwise be required by these rules or the Florida Probate Code, no notice need be given of the petition for administration or the issuance of letters when it appears that the petitioner is entitled to preference of appointment as personal representative.

(b) Petitioner Not Entitled to Preference. Before letters shall be issued to any person who is not entitled to preference, formal notice must be served on all known persons qualified to act as personal representative and entitled to preference equal to or greater than the applicant, unless those entitled to preference waive it in writing.

(c) Service of Petition by Formal Notice. If the petitioner elects or is required to serve formal notice of the petition for administration prior to the issuance of letters, a copy of the will offered for probate must be attached to the notice.

Added Sept. 29, 1988, effective Jan. 1, 1989 (537 So.2d 500). Amended effective Dec. 9, 2010 (51 So.3d 1146).

Committee Notes

This rule represents a rule implementation of the procedure formerly found in section 733.203(2), Florida Statutes, which was repealed as procedural in 2001.

Rule History

1988 Revision: New rule.

1992 Revision: Committee notes revised. Citation form changes in committee notes.

2003 Revision: Committee notes revised.

2010 Revision: Subdivision (c) added to require service of a copy of the will offered for probate. This requirement was included in section 733.2123, Florida Statutes, but was removed in 2010 because it was deemed to be a procedural requirement. Committee notes revised. Editorial changes.

Statutory References

§ 731.301, Fla. Stat. Notice.

§ 733.212, Fla. Stat. Notice of administration; filing of objections.

§ 733.2123 Fla. Stat. Adjudication before issuance of letters.

Rule References

Fla. Prob. R. 5.040 Notice.

Fla. Prob. R. 5.060 Request for notices and copies of pleadings.

Fla. Prob. R. 5.200 Petition for administration.

Rule 5.205. Filing Evidence of Death

(a) Requirements for Filing. A copy of an official record of the death of a decedent shall be filed by the personal representative, if any, or the petitioner in each of the following proceedings and at the times specified:

(1) *Administration of decedent's estate*: not later than 3 months following the date of the first publication of the notice to creditors.

(2) *Ancillary proceedings*: not later than 3 months following the date of first publication of notice to creditors.

(3) *Summary administration*: at any time prior to entry of the order of summary administration.

(4) *Disposition without administration*: at the time of filing the application for disposition without administration.

(5) *Determination of beneficiaries*: at any time prior to entry of the final judgment determining beneficiaries.

(6) *Determination of protected homestead*: at any time prior to entry of the final judgment determining protected homestead status of real property.

(7) *Probate of will without administration*: at any time prior to entry of the order admitting will to probate.

(b) Waiver. On verified petition by the personal representative, if any, or the petitioner the court may enter an order dispensing with this rule, without notice or hearing.

(c) Authority to Require Filing. The court may, without notice or hearing, enter an order requiring the personal representative, if any, or the petitioner to file a copy of an official record of death at any time during the proceedings.

Added Sept. 4, 1980, effective Jan. 1, 1981 (387 So.2d 949). Amended Sept. 13, 1984, effective Jan. 1, 1985 (458 So.2d 1079); Sept. 29, 1988, effective Jan. 1, 1989 (537 So.2d 500); Sept. 24, 1992, effective Jan. 1, 1993 (607 So.2d 1306); May 2, 2002 (824 So.2d 849); June 19, 2003 (848 So.2d 1069).

Committee Notes

A short form certificate of death, which does not disclose the cause of death, should be filed.

Rule History

1980 Revision: This rule is intended to provide a uniform procedure for filing an official record of death in any judicial or statutory proceeding upon the death of a decedent. The court may, upon ex parte application, waive compliance with this rule or require filing at any stage in the proceedings.

1984 Revision: Captions and minor editorial changes. Committee notes revised.

1988 Revision: Editorial and substantive changes. Adds (a)(8) to require filing when will is admitted to probate without administration of the estate or an order disposing of property. Committee notes revised.

1992 Revision: Editorial changes. Committee notes revised. Citation form changes in committee notes.

2002 Revision: Replaces "homestead" with "protected homestead" in (a)(7) to conform to addition of term in section 731.201(29), Florida Statutes. Committee notes revised.

2003 Revision: Revises subdivision (a)(1) to change notice of administration to notice to creditors. Deletes subdivision (a)(3) referring to family administration, and renumbers subsequent subdivisions. Committee notes revised.

2010 Revision: Committee notes revised.

Statutory References

§ 28.222(3)(g), Fla. Stat. Clerk to be county recorder.

§ 382.008(6), Fla. Stat. Death and fetal death registration.

§ 731.103, Fla. Stat. Evidence as to death or status.

§ 733.2121, Fla. Stat. Notice to creditors; filing of claims.

Rule References

Fla. Prob. R. 5.042(a) Time.

Fla. Prob. R. 5.171 Evidence of death.

Fla. Prob. R. 5.241 Notice to creditors.

Rule 5.210. Probate of Wills Without Administration

(a) Petition and Contents. A petition to admit a decedent's will to probate without administration shall be verified by the petitioner and shall contain:

(1) a statement of the interest of the petitioner, the petitioner's name and address, and the name and office address of the petitioner's attorney;

(2) the name and last known address of the decedent, last 4 digits of the decedent's social security number, date and place of death of the decedent, and state and county of the decedent's domicile;

(3) so far as is known, the names and addresses of the surviving spouse, if any, the beneficiaries and their relationships to the decedent, and the name and year of birth of any who are minors;

(4) a statement showing venue;

(5) a statement whether domiciliary or principal proceedings are pending in another state or country, if known, and the name and address of the foreign personal representative and the court issuing letters;

(6) a statement that there are no assets subject to administration in Florida;

(7) a statement identifying all unrevoked wills and codicils being presented for probate and a statement that the petitioner is unaware of any other unrevoked wills or codicils or, if the petitioner is aware of any other unrevoked wills or codicils, a statement why the other wills or codicils are not being probated; and

(8) a statement that the original of the decedent's last will is in the possession of the court or accompanies the petition, or that an authenticated copy of a will deposited with or probated in another jurisdiction or that an authenticated copy of a notarial will, the original of which is in the possession of a foreign notary, accompanies the petition.

(b) Service. The petitioner shall serve a copy of the petition on those persons who would be entitled to service under rule 5.240.

(c) Objections. Objections to the validity of the will shall follow the form and procedure set forth in these rules pertaining to revocation of probate. Objections to the venue or jurisdiction of the court shall follow the form and procedure set forth in the Florida Rules of Civil Procedure.

(d) Order. An order admitting the will to probate shall include a finding that the will has been executed as required by law.

Amended Sept. 13, 1984, effective Jan. 1, 1985 (458 So.2d 1079); Sept. 29, 1988, effective Jan. 1, 1989 (537 So.2d 500); Sept. 24, 1992, effective Jan. 1, 1993 (607 So.2d 1306); Oct. 3, 1996, effective Jan. 1, 1997 (683 So.2d 78); May 2, 2002 (824 So.2d 849); July 5, 2007, effective Jan. 1, 2008 (959 So.2d 1170); Sept. 2, 2010, effective Jan. 1, 2011 (50 So.3d 578); Nov. 3, 2011, effective, *nunc pro tunc*, Oct. 1, 2011 (78 So.3d 1045); May 22, 2014, effective May 22, 2014 (139 So.3d 875).

Committee Notes

Examples illustrating when a will might be admitted to probate are when an instrument (such as a will or trust agreement) gives the decedent a power exercisable by will, such as the power to appoint a successor trustee or a testamentary power of appointment. In each instance, the will of the person holding the power has no legal significance until admitted to probate. There may be no assets, creditors' issues, or other need for a probate beyond admitting the will to establish the exercise or nonexercise of such powers.

Rule History

1975 Revision: Proof of will may be taken by any Florida circuit judge or clerk without issuance of commission.

1984 Revision: This rule has been completely revised to set forth the procedure for proving all wills except lost or destroyed wills and the title changed. The rule requires an oath attesting to the statutory requirements for execution of wills and the will must be proved before an order can be entered admitting it to probate. Former rules 5.280, 5.290, and 5.500 are included in this rule. Committee notes revised.

1988 Revision: Editorial and substantive changes. Change in (a)(3) to clarify which law determines validity of a notarial will; change in (a)(4) to clarify requirement that will of a Florida resident must comply with Florida law; adds new subdivision (b) to set forth required contents of petition for probate of will; moves former (b) to (c). Committee notes expanded; citation form change in committee notes.

1992 Revision: Editorial changes. Committee notes revised. Citation form changes in committee notes.

1996 Revision: Subdivision (a)(4) changed to allow authenticated copies of wills to be admitted to probate if the original is filed or deposited in another jurisdiction.

2002 Revision: Substantial revision to the rule setting forth the requirements of a petition to admit a will to probate when administration is not required. Self proof of wills is governed by the Florida Statutes. Former subdivision (a)(4) amended and transferred to new rule 5.215. Former subdivision (a)(5) amended and transferred to new rule 5.216.

2003 Revision: Committee notes revised.

2007 Revision: Existing text redesignated as subdivision (a) and editorial change made in (a)(7). New subdivisions (b) and (c) added to provide for service of the petition and the procedure for objections consistent with the procedures for probate of a will with administration. Committee notes revised.

2010 Revision: Subdivision (b) amended to reflect that service of the petition to admit a decedent's will to probate without administration shall be served on the persons who would be entitled to service of the notice of administration in a formal administration as set forth in rule 5.240. New subdivision (d) added to provide that any order admitting the decedent's will to probate without administration contain a finding that the will was executed as required by law. Committee notes revised.

2011 Revision: Subdivision (a)(2) amended to limit listing of decedent's social security number to last four digits.

2014 Revision: Subdivision (a)(3) amended to conform to Fla. R. Jud. Admin. 2.425. Committee notes revised.

Statutory References

§ 731.201, Fla. Stat. General definitions.

§ 731.301, Fla. Stat. Notice.

§ 732.502, Fla. Stat. Execution of wills.

§ 732.503, Fla. Stat. Self–proof of will.

§ 733.103, Fla. Stat. Effect of probate.

§ 733.201, Fla. Stat. Proof of wills.

§ 733.202, Fla. Stat. Petition.

§ 733.204, Fla. Stat. Probate of a will written in a foreign language.

§ 733.205, Fla. Stat. Probate of notarial will.

§ 733.206, Fla. Stat. Probate of will of resident after foreign probate.

§ 733.207, Fla. Stat. Establishment and probate of lost or destroyed will.

§ 734.104, Fla. Stat. Foreign wills; admission to record; effect on title.

Rule References

Fla. Prob. R. 5.015 General definitions.

Fla. Prob. R. 5.020 Pleadings, verification; motions.

Fla. Prob. R. 5.205(a)(7) Filing evidence of death.

Fla. Prob. R. 5.215 Authenticated copy of will.

Fla. Prob. R. 5.216 Will written in foreign language.

Fla. Prob. R. 5.230 Commission to prove will.

Fla. Prob. R. 5.240 Notice of administration.

Fla. Prob. R. 5.270 Revocation of probate.

Fla. R. Jud. Admin. 2.425 Minimization of the Filing of Sensitive Information.

Rule 5.215. Authenticated Copy of Will

An authenticated copy of a will may be admitted to probate if the original could be admitted to probate in Florida.

Added May 2, 2002 (824 So.2d 849).

Committee Notes

Rule History

2002 Revision: New rule, derived from former rule 5.210(a)(4).

2003 Revision: Committee notes revised.

Statutory References

§ 733.205, Fla. Stat. Probate of notarial will.

§ 733.206, Fla. Stat. Probate of will of resident after foreign probate.

§ 734.102, Fla. Stat. Ancillary administration.

§ 734.1025, Fla. Stat. Nonresident decedent's testate estate with property not exceeding $50,000 in this state; determination of claims.

§ 734.104, Fla. Stat. Foreign wills; admission to record; effect on title.

Rule References

Fla. Prob. R. 5.200 Petition for administration.

Fla. Prob. R. 5.210 Probate of wills without administration.

Fla. Prob. R. 5.470 Ancillary administration.

Fla. Prob. R. 5.475 Ancillary administration, short form.

Rule 5.216. Will Written in Foreign Language

A will written in a foreign language being offered for probate shall be accompanied by a true and complete English translation. In the order admitting the foreign language will to probate, the court shall establish the correct English translation. At any time during administration, any interested person may have the correctness of the translation redetermined after formal notice to all other interested persons.

Added May 2, 2002 (824 So.2d 849).

Committee Notes

Rule History

2002 Revision: New rule, derived from former rule 5.210(a)(5) and section 733.204(2), Florida Statutes.

Statutory Reference

§ 733.204, Fla. Stat. Probate of a will written in a foreign language.

Rule 5.230. Commission to Prove Will

(a) Petition. On petition the court may appoint a commissioner to take the oath of any person qualified to prove the will under Florida law. The petition must set forth the date of the will and the place where it was executed, if known; the names of the witnesses and address of the witness whose oath is to be taken; and the name, title, and address of the proposed commissioner.

(b) Commission. The commission must be directed to a person who is authorized to administer an oath by the laws of Florida, the United States of America, or the state or country where the witness may be found, and it shall empower the commissioner to take the oath of the witness to prove the will and shall direct the commissioner to certify the oath and file the executed commission, copy of the will, oath of the witness, and certificate of commissioner. An oath of the commissioner is not required.

(c) Mailing or Delivery. The petitioner or the petitioner's attorney must cause the commission, together with a copy of the will, the oath, and the certificate of commissioner, to be mailed or delivered to the commissioner.

(d) Filing. The executed commission, copy of the will, oath of the witness, and certificate of commissioner must be filed.

Amended Sept. 13, 1984, effective Jan. 1, 1985 (458 So.2d 1079); Sept. 29, 1988, effective Jan. 1, 1989 (537 So.2d 500); Sept. 24, 1992, effective Jan. 1, 1993 (607 So.2d 1306); Sept. 26, 2013, effective Jan. 1, 2014 (123 So.3d 31).

Committee Notes

Rule History

1975 Revision: Substantially the same as prior rule 5.130(a) and (b) and carries forward prior procedures as to a matter upon which Florida Probate Code is silent.

1984 Revision: This rule has been completely changed to set forth the procedure for the issuance and return of a commission. The rule has been broadened to allow anyone authorized by Florida Statutes or by the U.S. Code to be a commissioner as well as those authorized by the state or country where the witness resides.

The rule now provides that the petitioner or his attorney shall forward the commission to the commissioner. The rule also contemplates that a Florida notary may be appointed as commissioner to take the proof of a witness outside the State of Florida. Committee notes revised and expanded.

1988 Revision: Editorial and substantive changes. Change in (a) to provide that the commissioner may take the oath of not only the attesting witness to the will but also the oath of any other person qualified to prove the will; change in (c) to permit copies other than photographic copies to be furnished to the commissioner, and to permit delivery of documents in a manner other than by mailing; change in (d) to require the filing of documents with the court. Committee notes revised. Citation form changes in rule and committee notes.

1992 Revision: Editorial change. Committee notes revised. Citation form changes in committee notes.

2003 Revision: Committee notes revised.

2013 Revision: Subdivision (e) deleted because it duplicates subdivision (d) in Rule 5.240. Committee notes revised. Editorial changes to conform to the court's guidelines for rules submissions as set forth in AOSC06–14.

Statutory References

§ 92.50, Fla. Stat. Oaths, affidavits, and acknowledgments; who may take or administer; requirements.

§ 733.101, Fla. Stat. Venue of probate proceedings.

§ 733.201, Fla. Stat. Proof of wills.

§ 22 U.S.C. 4215 Notarial acts, oaths, affirmations, affidavits, and depositions; fees.

Rule References

Fla. Prob. R. 5.050 Transfer of proceedings.

Fla. R. Civ. P. 1.060 Transfers of actions.

Rule 5.235. Issuance of Letters, Bond

(a) Appointment of Personal Representative. After the petition for administration is filed and the will, if any, is admitted to probate:

(1) the court shall appoint the person entitled and qualified to be personal representative;

(2) the court shall determine the amount of any bond required. The clerk may approve the bond in the amount determined by the court; and

(3) any required oath or designation of, and acceptance by, a resident agent shall be filed.

(b) Issuance of Letters. Upon compliance with all of the foregoing, letters shall be issued to the personal representative.

(c) Bond. On petition by any interested person or on the court's own motion, the court may waive the requirement of filing a bond, require a personal representative or curator to give bond, increase or decrease the bond, or require additional surety.

Added Sept. 29, 1988, effective Jan. 1, 1989 (537 So.2d 500). Amended Sept. 24, 1992, effective Jan. 1, 1993 (607 So.2d 1306); Oct. 3, 1996, effective Jan. 1, 1997 (683 So.2d 78).

Committee Notes

This rule represents a rule implementation of the procedure formerly found in sections 733.401 and 733.403(2), Florida Statutes, both of which were repealed in 2001. It is not intended to change the effect of the statutes from which it was derived but has been reformatted to conform with the structure of these rules. It is not intended to create a new procedure or modify an existing procedure.

Rule History

1988 Revision: New rule.

1992 Revision: Editorial changes. Committee notes revised. Citation form changes in committee notes.

1996 Revision: Mandate in subdivision (a)(2) prohibiting charge of service fee by clerk deleted. Statutory references added.

2003 Revision: Committee notes revised.

2010 Revision: Committee notes revised.

Statutory References

§ 28.24(19), Fla. Stat. Service charges by clerk of the circuit court.

§ 28.2401, Fla. Stat. Service charges in probate matters.

§ 733.402, Fla. Stat. Bond of fiduciary; when required; form.

§ 733.403, Fla. Stat. Amount of bond.

§ 733.405, Fla. Stat. Release of surety.

§ 733.501, Fla. Stat. Curators.

Rule References

Fla. Prob. R. 5.110 Address designation for personal representative or guardian; designation of resident agent and acceptance.

Fla. Prob. R. 5.122 Curators.

Fla. Prob. R. 5.320 Oath of personal representative.

Rule 5.240. Notice of Administration

(a) Service. The personal representative shall promptly serve a copy of the notice of administration on the following persons who are known to the personal representative and who were not previously served under section 733.2123, Florida Statutes:

(1) the decedent's surviving spouse;

(2) all beneficiaries;

(3) a trustee of any trust described in section 733.707(3), Florida Statutes and each qualified beneficiary of the trust as defined in section 736.0103(16), if each trustee is also a personal representative of the estate; and

(4) persons who may be entitled to exempt property in the manner provided for service of formal notice. The personal representative may similarly serve a copy of the notice on any devisee under another will or heirs or others who claim or may claim an interest in the estate.

(b) Contents. The notice shall state:

(1) the name of the decedent, the file number of the estate, the designation and address of the court in which the proceedings are pending, whether the estate is testate or intestate, and, if testate, the date of the will and any codicils;

(2) the name and address of the personal representative and of the personal representative's attorney, and that the fiduciary lawyer-client privilege in section 90.5021, Florida Statutes, applies with respect to the personal representative and any attorney employed by the personal representative;

(3) that any interested person on whom the notice is served who challenges the validity of the will, the qualifications of the personal representative, venue, or jurisdiction of the court must file any objections with the court in the manner provided in the Florida Probate Rules within the time required by law or those objections are forever barred;

(4) that any person entitled to exempt property must file a petition for determination of exempt property within the time provided by law or the right to exempt property is deemed waived; and

(5) that an election to take an elective share must be filed within the time provided by law.

(c) Copy of Will. Unless the court directs otherwise, the personal representative of a testate estate must, upon written request, furnish a copy of the will and all codicils admitted to probate to any person on whom the notice of administration was served.

(d) Objections. Objections to the validity of the will shall follow the form and procedure set forth in these rules pertaining to revocation of probate. Objections to the qualifications of the personal representative shall follow the form and procedure set forth in these rules pertaining to removal of a personal representative. Objections to the venue or jurisdiction of the court shall follow the form and procedure set forth in the Florida Rules of Civil Procedure.

(e) Waiver of Service. For the purpose of determining deadlines established by reference to the date of service of a copy of the notice of administration in cases in which service has been waived, service on a person who has waived notice is deemed to occur on the date the waiver is filed.

Amended March 31, 1977, effective July 1, 1977 (344 So.2d 828); Sept. 13, 1984, effective Jan. 1, 1985 (458 So.2d 1079); Sept. 29, 1988, effective Jan. 1, 1989 (537 So.2d 500); Aug. 22, 1991, effective Oct. 1, 1991 (584 So.2d 964); Sept. 24, 1992, effective Jan. 1, 1993 (607 So.2d 1306); Oct. 3, 1996, effective Jan. 1, 1997 (683 So.2d 78); May 2, 2002 (824 So.2d 849); June 19, 2003, (848 So.2d 1069); Sept. 29, 2005, effective Jan.1, 2006 (912 So.2d 1178); July 12, 2007 (964 So.2d 140); Sept. 28, 2011 (73 So.3d 205); Nov. 27, 2013 (131 So.3d 717).

Committee Notes

Rule History

1977 Revision: Former subdivision (c) is deleted as being substantive rather than procedural.

1984 Revision: Editorial changes; new requirement to file proof of publication; new requirements as to form of objections to will and qualifications of personal representative. Committee notes revised.

1988 Revision: The obligation to mail notice of administration to all known or reasonably ascertainable creditors has been added to comply with the dictates of *Tulsa Professional Collection Services, Inc. v. Pope*, 485 U.S. 478, 108 S. Ct. 1340, 99 L. Ed. 2d 565 (1988).

This rule does not require sending notice of administration to creditors in estates where the time for filing claims has expired before the effective date of this rule. However, no opinion is offered whether such claims are barred by the provisions of section 733.702, Florida Statutes.

Committee notes revised. Citation form changes in committee notes.

1991 Revision: Subdivision (a) modified to make it consistent with recent changes to sections 733.212 and 733.702, Florida Statutes. Those statutes were amended to comply with the dictates of *Tulsa Professional Collection Services, Inc. v. Pope*, 485 U.S. 478, 108 S. Ct. 1340, 99 L. Ed. 2d 565 (1988). For the same reason, subdivision (e) was eliminated.

1992 Revision: Former subdivision (e) revised and reinstated to emphasize need for personal representative to determine all known or reasonably ascertainable creditors. Editorial changes; committee notes revised; citation form changes in committee notes.

1996 Revision: Subdivision (a) amended to require service of notice of administration on trustees of certain revocable trusts as defined by Florida statute. Editorial changes.

2002 Revision: Procedures for notifying creditors are now governed by new rule 5.241. Committee notes revised.

2003 Revision: Change in title of (a) to reflect elimination of publication of notice. Committee notes revised.

2005 Revision: Subdivision (a)(3) amended to make it consistent with 2003 change to section 733.212(1)(c), Florida Statutes, regarding when service on trust beneficiaries is required, and clarifying editorial change made in (a). New subdivision (b)(5) added regarding notice to file election to take elective share. Committee notes revised.

2007 Revision: Subdivision (a)(3) amended to replace reference to "beneficiary" with "qualified beneficiary" and to change reference from former section 737.303(4)(b) to new section 736.0103(14), which defines that term. Subdivision (b)(5) amended to delete the reference to the surviving spouse filing the election as another person can file the election on behalf of the surviving spouse. New subdivision (e) added to provide a deadline for objection by a person who waives service. Committee notes revised.

2011 Revision: Subdivision (b)(2) amended to conform to amendment to section 732.212, Florida Statutes, relating to attorney-client privilege for fiduciaries and their attorneys. Editorial changes to conform to the court's guidelines for rules submissions as set forth in Administrative Order AOSC06–14. Statutory reference to section 732.402, Florida Statutes, added. Committee Notes revised.

2013 Revision: Updated statutory reference in subdivision (a)(3). Committee notes revised.

Statutory References

§ 731.201(23), Fla. Stat. General definitions.

§ 731.301, Fla. Stat. Notice.

§ 731.302, Fla. Stat. Waiver and consent by interested person.

§ 732.2135, Fla. Stat. Time of election; extensions; withdrawal.

§ 732.402, Fla. Stat. Exempt property.

§ 732.5165, Fla. Stat. Effect of fraud, duress, mistake, and undue influence.

§ 733.101, Fla. Stat. Venue of probate proceedings.

§ 733.109, Fla. Stat. Revocation of probate.

§ 733.212, Fla. Stat. Notice of administration; filing of objections.

§ 733.2123, Fla. Stat. Adjudication before issuance of letters.

§ 733.302, Fla. Stat. Who may be appointed personal representative.

§ 733.303, Fla. Stat. Persons not qualified.

§ 733.305, Fla. Stat. Trust companies and other corporations and associations.

§ 733.504, Fla. Stat. Removal of personal representative; causes for removal.

§ 733.506, Fla. Stat. Proceedings for removal.

Rule References

Fla. Prob. R. 5.025 Adversary proceedings.

Fla. Prob. R. 5.040 Notice.

Fla. Prob. R. 5.050 Transfer of proceedings.

Fla. Prob. R. 5.180 Waiver and consent.

Fla. Prob. R. 5.270 Revocation of probate.

Fla. Prob. R. 5.440 Proceedings for removal.

Fla. R. Civ. P. 1.060 Transfers of actions.

Rule 5.2405. Service of Notice of Administration on Personal Representative

(a) Date Notice of Administration is Considered Served on Person who is Personal Representative. Unless service of the notice of administration is waived pursuant to Rule 5.240(e), when a person who is entitled to service of the notice of administration pursuant to Rule 5.240(a) is also a personal representative, the notice of administration shall be deemed served upon the person on the earliest of the following dates:

(1) the date on which the person acknowledges in writing receipt of the notice of administration;

(2) the date on which the notice of administration is first served on any other person entitled to service of the notice of administration (or the first among multiple persons entitled to service); or

(3) the date that is 30 days after the date letters of administration are issued.

(b) Date Other Notices are Considered Served on Person who is Personal Representative. When a person who is entitled to service of notice under these rules or the Florida Probate Code (other than the notice of administration) is also a personal representative, any notice shall be deemed as having been served on the personal representative on the earliest of the following dates:

(1) the date on which the person acknowledges in writing receipt of the notice;

(2) the date on which the notice is required to be served by the personal representative under these rules or the Florida Probate Code; or,

(3) the date on which the notice is first served by the personal representative on any other person entitled to service of the same notice.

Added Sept. 26, 2013, effective Jan. 1, 2014 (123 So.3d 31).

Committee Notes

This rule is intended to address situations in which the personal representative is also an interested person in an estate, but claims that he or she has not received the notice of administration, despite the personal representative being required to serve the notice. The receipt of the notice of administration can trigger time limits for the person receiving the notice with regard to certain rights, such as the right to claim an elective share.

Rule History

2013 Revision: New rule.

Statutory References

§ 731.201(23), Fla. Stat. General definitions.

§ 731.301, Fla. Stat. Notice.

§ 731.302, Fla. Stat. Waiver and consent by interested person.

§ 732.2135, Fla. Stat. Time of election; extensions; withdrawal.

§ 732.5165, Fla. Stat. Effect of fraud, duress, mistake, and undue influence.

§ 733.101, Fla. Stat. Venue of probate proceedings.

§ 733.109, Fla. Stat. Revocation of probate.

§ 733.212, Fla. Stat. Notice of administration; filing of objections.

§ 733.2123, Fla. Stat. Adjudication before issuance of letters.

§ 733.302, Fla. Stat. Who may be appointed personal representative.

§ 733.303, Fla. Stat. Persons not qualified.

§ 733.305, Fla. Stat. Trust companies and other corporations and associations.

§ 733.504, Fla. Stat. Removal of personal representative; causes for removal.

§ 733.506, Fla. Stat. Proceedings for removal.

Rule References

Fla. Prob. R. 5.025 Adversary proceedings.

Fla. Prob. R. 5.040 Notice.

Fla. Prob. R. 5.050 Transfer of proceedings.

Fla. Prob. R. 5.180 Waiver and consent.

Fla. Prob. R. 5.270 Revocation of probate.

Fla. Prob. R. 5.440 Proceedings for removal of personal representative.

Fla. R. Civ. P. 1.060 Transfers of actions.

Rule 5.241. Notice to Creditors

(a) Publication and Service. Unless creditors' claims are otherwise barred by law, the personal representative shall promptly publish a notice to creditors and serve a copy of the notice on all creditors of the decedent who are reasonably ascertainable and, if required by law, on the Agency for Health Care Administration. Service of the notice shall be either by informal notice, or in the manner provided for service of formal notice at the option of the personal representative. Service on one creditor by a chosen method shall not preclude service on another creditor by another method.

(b) Contents. The notice to creditors shall contain the name of the decedent, the file number of the estate, the designation and address of the court, the name and address of the personal representative and of the personal representative's attorney, and the date of first publication of the notice to creditors. The notice shall require all creditors to file all claims against the estate with the court, within the time provided by law.

(c) Method of Publication and Proof. Publication shall be made as required by law. The personal representative shall file proof of publication with the court within 45 days after the date of first publication of the notice to creditors.

(d) Statement Regarding Creditors. Within 4 months after the date of the first publication of notice to creditors, the personal representative shall file a verified statement that diligent search has been made to ascertain the name and address of each person having a claim against the estate. The statement shall indicate the name and address of each person at that time known to the personal representative who has or may have a claim against the estate and whether such person was served with the notice to creditors or otherwise received actual notice of the information contained in the notice to creditors; provided that the statement need not include persons who have filed a timely claim or who were included in the personal representative's proof of claim.

(e) Service of Death Certificate. If service of the notice on the Agency for Health Care Administration is required, it shall be accompanied by a death certificate.

Added May 2, 2002 (824 So.2d 849). Amended Sept. 29, 2005, effective Jan. 1, 2006 (912 So.2d 1178); July 5, 2007, effective Jan. 1, 2008 (959 So.2d 1170); July 12, 2007 (964 So.2d 140).

Committee Notes

It is the committee's opinion that the failure to timely file the proof of publication of the notice to creditors shall not affect time limitations for filing claims or objections.

On April 19, 1988, the United States Supreme Court decided *Tulsa Professional Collection Services, Inc. v. Pope*, 485 U.S. 478, 108 S. Ct. 1340, 99

L. Ed. 2d 565. This case substantially impacted the method for handling (and barring) creditors' claims. This case stands for the proposition that a creditor may not be barred by the usual publication if that creditor was actually known to or reasonably ascertainable by the personal representative, and the personal representative failed to give notice to the creditor by mail or other means as certain to ensure actual notice. Less than actual notice in these circumstances would deprive the creditor of due process rights under the 14th Amendment to the U.S. Constitution. Probably actual notice of the death (as in the case of a hospital where the decedent died as a patient) without notice of the institution of probate proceedings is not sufficient.

An elementary and fundamental requirement of due process in any proceeding which is to be accorded finality is notice reasonably calculated, under all the circumstances, to apprise interested persons of the pendency of the proceeding and afford them an opportunity to present their claims.

The steps to be taken by a personal representative in conducting a diligent search for creditors depends, in large measure, on how familiar the personal representative is with the decedent's affairs. Therefore, the committee believes it is inappropriate to list particular steps to be taken in each estate, since the circumstances will vary from case to case.

The statement required by this rule is not intended to be jurisdictional but rather to provide evidence of satisfaction (or lack thereof) of the due process requirements.

Rule History

2002 Revision: New rule to implement procedures consistent with new section 733.2121, Florida Statutes.

2003 Revision: Committee notes revised.

2005 Revision: Subdivision (a) amended to clarify approved methods of service on creditors. Committee notes revised.

2007 Revision: New subdivision (e) added to require service of a copy of the decedent's death certificate on the Agency for Health Care Administration, as is now required by section 733.2121(3)(d), Florida Statutes.

Statutory References

ch. 50, Fla. Stat. Legal and official advertisements.

§ 731.301, Fla. Stat. Notice.

§ 733.2121, Fla. Stat. Notice to creditors; filing of claims.

§ 733.702, Fla. Stat. Limitations on presentation of claims.

§ 733.703, Fla. Stat. Form and manner of presenting claim.

§ 733.704, Fla. Stat. Amendment of claims.

§ 733.705, Fla. Stat. Payment of and objection to claims.

§ 733.708, Fla. Stat. Compromise.

Rule Reference

Fla. Prob. R. 5.490 Form and manner of presenting claim.

Rule 5.260. Caveat; Proceedings

(a) Filing. Any creditor or interested person other than a creditor may file a caveat with the court. The caveat of an interested person, other than a creditor, may be filed before or after the death of the person for whom the estate will be, or is being, administered. The caveat of a creditor may be filed only after the person's death.

(b) Contents. The caveat shall contain the name of the person for whom the estate will be, or is being, administered, the last 4 digits of the person's social security number or year of birth, if known, a statement of the interest of the caveator in the estate, and the name and specific mailing address of the caveator.

(c) Resident Agent of Caveator; Service. If the caveator is not a resident of Florida, the caveator must file a designation of the name and specific mailing address and residence address of a resident in the county where the caveat is filed as the caveator's agent for service of notice. The written acceptance by the person appointed as resident agent must be filed with the designation or included in the caveat. The designation and acceptance shall constitute the consent of the caveator that service of notice upon the designated resident agent shall bind the caveator. If the caveator is represented by an attorney admitted to practice in Florida who signs the caveat, it shall not be necessary to designate a resident agent under this rule.

(d) Filing after Commencement. If at the time of the filing of any caveat the decedent's will has been admitted to probate or letters of administration have been issued, the clerk must promptly notify the caveator in writing of the date of issuance of letters and the names and addresses of the personal representative and the personal representative's attorney.

(e) Creditor. When letters of administration issue after the filing of a caveat by a creditor, the clerk must promptly notify the caveator, in writing, advising the caveator of the date of issuance of letters and the names and addresses of the personal representative and the personal representative's attorney, unless notice has previously been served on the caveator. A copy of any notice given by the clerk, together with a certificate of the mailing of the original notice, must be filed in the estate proceedings.

(f) Other Interested Persons; Before Commencement. After the filing of a caveat by an interested person other than a creditor, the court must not admit a will of the decedent to probate or appoint a personal representative without service of formal notice on the caveator or the caveator's designated agent. A caveator is not required to be served with formal notice of its own petition for administration.

Amended March 31, 1977, effective July 1, 1977 (344 So.2d 828); Sept. 13, 1984, effective Jan. 1, 1985 (458 So.2d 1079); Sept. 24, 1992, effective Jan. 1, 1993 (607 So.2d 1306); Sept. 2, 2010, effective Jan. 1, 2011 (50 So.3d 578); Subsecs. (a), (b), (d), (e), and (f) amended effective Dec. 9, 2010; Subsec. (c) amended effective Jan. 1, 2011 (51 So.3d 1146); Subsec. (b) amended effective July 7, 2011 (67 So.3d 1035); Nov. 27, 2013 (131 So.3d 717).

Committee Notes

Caveat proceedings permit a decedent's creditor or other interested person to be notified when letters of administration are issued. Thereafter, the caveator must take appropriate action to protect the caveator's interests.

This rule treats the creditor caveator differently from other caveators.

An attorney admitted to practice in Florida who represents the caveator may sign the caveat on behalf of the client.

Rule History

1977 Revision: Carried forward prior rule 5.150.

1984 Revision: Changes in (a), (b), and (d) are editorial. Change in (c) eliminates resident agent requirement for Florida residents and for nonresidents represented by a Florida attorney. Service on the attorney binds caveator. Former (e) is now subdivisions (e) and (f) and treats creditor caveator differently from other interested persons. Change in (f) requires formal notice. Committee notes revised.

1988 Revision: Committee notes revised. Citation form changes in committee notes.

1992 Revision: Addition of language in subdivision (b) to implement 1992 amendment to section 731.110(2), Florida Statutes. Editorial changes. Citation form changes in committee notes.

2003 Revision: Committee notes revised.

2010 Cycle Report Revision: Subdivision (c) amended to clarify that a state agency filing a caveat need not designate an agent for service of process, and to provide that a caveator who is not a resident of the county where the caveat is filed must designate either a resident of that county or an attorney licensed and residing in Florida as the caveator's agent. Editorial changes in (d) and (e). Committee notes revised.

2010 Out-of-Cycle Report Revision: Subdivisions (a) and (b) amended to conform with statutory changes. Subdivision (c) amended to read as it existed prior to SC10–171 (35 FLW S482) due to a subsequent legislative amendment (Chapter 2010–132, § 3, Laws of Fla.). Editorial changes in (d), (e), and (f). Committee notes revised.

2011 Revision: Subdivision (b) amended to replace language removed in 2010 out-of-cycle revision, to replace term "decedent" with "person for whom the estate will be, or is being, administered," and to limit listing of a social security number to the last four digits and a date of birth to the year of birth.

2013 Revision: Subdivision (f) is updated to provide that a caveator is not required to be served with formal notice of its own petition for administration. Committee notes revised.

Statutory Reference

§ 731.110, Fla. Stat. Caveat; proceedings.

Rule Reference

Fla. Prob. R. 5.040(a) Notice.

Rule 5.270. Revocation of Probate

(a) Petition and Contents. A petition for revocation of probate shall state the interest of the petitioner in the estate and the facts constituting the grounds on which revocation is demanded.

(b) Continued Administration. Pending the determination of any issue for revocation of probate, the personal representative shall proceed with the administration of the estate as if no revocation proceeding had been commenced, except that no distribution may be made to beneficiaries in contravention of the rights of those who, but for the will, would be entitled to the property disposed of.

Amended Sept. 13, 1984, effective Jan. 1, 1985 (458 So.2d 1079); Sept. 29, 1988, effective Jan. 1, 1989 (537 So.2d 500); Sept. 29, 2005, effective Jan. 1, 2006 (912 So.2d 1178); July 12, 2007 (964 So.2d 140).

Committee Notes

This rule represents a rule implementation of the procedure found in section 733.109(2), Florida Statutes. It is not intended to change the effect of the statute from which it was derived but has been reformatted to conform with the structure of these rules. It is not intended to create a new procedure or modify an existing procedure. The committee believes that subsections (1) and (3) of the statute are substantive, and have therefore not been included. Further, this rule revises subdivision (b) of the prior similar rule to track the language in the statute from which it was derived.

Rule History

1984 Revision: Extensive changes. Committee notes revised.

1988 Revision: Language of subdivision (b) of the rule rewritten to track the statute more closely. Committee notes expanded. Citation form change in committee notes.

1992 Revision: Committee notes revised. Citation form changes in committee notes.

2003 Revision: Committee notes revised.

2005 Revision: "Beneficiaries" substituted for "devisees" in subdivision (b) to conform language to section 733.109(2), Florida Statutes.

2007 Revision: Committee notes revised.

Statutory References

§ 731.201(23), Fla. Stat. General definitions.

§ 732.5165, Fla. Stat. Effect of fraud, duress, mistake, and undue influence.

§ 733.109, Fla. Stat. Revocation of probate.

§ 733.212, Fla. Stat. Notice of administration; filing of objections.

§ 733.2123, Fla. Stat. Adjudication before issuance of letters.

Rule References

Fla. Prob. R. 5.025 Adversary proceedings.

Fla. Prob. R. 5.040 Notice.

Fla. Prob. R. 5.240 Notice of administration.

Rule 5.275. Burden of Proof in Will Contests

In all proceedings contesting the validity of a will, the burden shall be upon the proponent of the will to establish prima facie its formal execution and attestation. Thereafter, the contestant shall have the burden of establishing the grounds on which the probate of the will is opposed or revocation sought.

Added Sept. 29, 1988, effective Jan. 1, 1989 (537 So.2d 500).

Committee Notes

This rule represents a rule implementation of the procedure found in section 733.107, Florida Statutes. The presumption of undue influence implements public policy against abuse of fiduciary or confidential relationships and is therefore a presumption shifting the burden of proof under sections 90.301–90.304, Florida Statutes.

Rule History

1988 Revision: New rule.

1992 Revision: Citation form changes in committee notes.

2003 Revision: Committee notes revised.

Statutory References

§ 90.301, Fla. Stat. Presumption defined; inferences.

§ 90.302, Fla. Stat. Classification of rebuttable presumptions.

§ 90.303, Fla. Stat. Presumption affecting the burden of producing evidence defined.

§ 90.304, Fla. Stat. Presumption affecting the burden of proof defined.

§ 733.107, Fla. Stat. Burden of proof in contests; presumption of undue influence.

Rule 5.310. Disqualification of Personal Representative; Notification

Any personal representative who was not qualified to act at the time of appointment or who would not be qualified for appointment if application for appointment were then made shall immediately file and serve on all interested persons a notice describing:

(a) the reason the personal representative was not qualified at the time of appointment; or

(b) the reason the personal representative would not be qualified for appointment if application for appointment were then made and the date on which the disqualifying event occurred.

The personal representative's notice shall state that any interested person may petition to remove the personal representative.

Amended Sept. 24, 1992, effective Jan. 1, 1993 (607 So.2d 1306); May 2, 2002 (824 So.2d 849).

Committee Notes

Notification under this rule or section 733.3101, Florida Statutes, does not automatically affect the authority of the personal representative to act. The personal representative may resign or interested persons or the court must act to remove the personal representative.

Rule History

1975 Revision: This is same as old rule 5.220 and old section 732.47(3), Florida Statutes. The rule sets forth the imperative need for timely action and the inherent responsibility of a fiduciary to effect orderly succession. It further implies the inherent jurisdiction of the court to control by judicial overview the succession.

1977 Revision: Citation form change in committee note.

1988 Revision: Committee notes revised. Citation form changes in committee notes.

1992 Revision: Editorial changes to clarify rule. Committee notes revised. Citation form changes in committee notes.

2002 Revision: Rule amended to implement procedures found in section 733.3101, Florida Statutes. Committee notes revised.

Statutory References

§ 731.301, Fla. Stat. Notice.

§ 733.302, Fla. Stat. Who may be appointed personal representative.

§ 733.303, Fla. Stat. Persons not qualified.

§ 733.3101, Fla. Stat. Personal representative not qualified.

§ 733.502, Fla. Stat. Resignation of personal representative.

§ 733.504, Fla. Stat. Removal of personal representative; causes for removal.

§ 733.505, Fla. Stat. Jurisdiction in removal proceedings.

§ 733.506, Fla. Stat. Proceedings for removal.

Rule References

Fla. Prob. R. 5.040 Notice.

Fla. Prob. R. 5.430 Resignation of personal representative.

Fla. Prob. R. 5.440 Proceedings for removal.

Rule 5.320. Oath of Personal Representative

Before the granting of letters of administration, the personal representative shall file an oath to faithfully administer the estate of the decedent. If the petition is verified by the prospective personal representative individually, the oath may be incorporated in the petition or in the designation of resident agent.

Amended Sept. 24, 1992, effective Jan. 1, 1993 (607 So.2d 1306).

Committee Notes

It is contemplated the oath may be signed concurrently with the petition for administration and will be valid even if it predates the order appointing the personal representative.

Rule History

1977 Revision: No change in rule. Change in committee note to conform to statutory renumbering.

This rule establishes the uniform requirement for an oath of faithful performance of fiduciary duties within the permissiveness of section 733.401(1)(d), Florida Statutes. Should be taken together with new rule 5.110, Resident Agent.

1988 Revision: Committee notes expanded. Citation form changes in committee notes.

1992 Revision: Editorial change. Committee notes revised. Citation form changes in committee notes.

2003 Revision: Committee notes revised.

Rule References

Fla. Prob. R. 5.110 Address designation for personal representative or guardian; designation of resident agent and acceptance.

Fla. Prob. R. 5.235 Issuance of letters, bond.

Rule 5.330. Execution by Personal Representative

Notwithstanding any other provisions of these rules, the personal representative shall sign the:

(a) inventory;

(b) accountings;

(c) petition for sale or confirmation of sale or encumbrance of real or personal property;

(d) petition to continue business of decedent;

(e) petition to compromise or settle claim;

(f) petition to purchase on credit;

(g) petition for distribution and discharge; and

(h) resignation of personal representative.

Amended Sept. 29, 1988, effective Jan. 1, 1989 (537 So.2d 500); Sept. 24, 1992, effective Jan. 1, 1993 (607 So.2d 1306).

Committee Notes

Rule History

1975 Revision: Where the jurisdiction of the court is invoked voluntarily pursuant to section 733.603, Florida Statutes, or otherwise, the rule requires that the personal representative have actual knowledge of the more important steps and acts of administration.

1977 Revision: Citation form change in committee note.

1988 Revision: Editorial changes. Citation form changes in committee notes.

1992 Revision: Editorial changes. Committee notes revised. Citation form changes in committee notes.

2003 Revision: Committee notes revised.

2010 Revision: Committee notes revised.

Statutory References

§ 733.502, Fla. Stat. Resignation of personal representative.

§ 733.604, Fla. Stat. Inventories and accountings; public records exemptions.

§ 733.612(5), (22), (24), Fla. Stat. Transactions authorized for the personal representative; exceptions.

§ 733.613, Fla. Stat. Personal representative's right to sell real property.

§ 733.708, Fla. Stat. Compromise.

§ 733.901, Fla. Stat. Final discharge.

Rule References

Fla. Prob. R. 5.340 Inventory.

Fla. Prob. R. 5.345 Accountings other than personal representatives' final accountings.

Fla. Prob. R. 5.346 Fiduciary accounting.

Fla. Prob. R. 5.350 Continuance of unincorporated business or venture.

Fla. Prob. R. 5.370 Sales of real property where no power conferred.

Fla. Prob. R. 5.400 Distribution and discharge.

Fla. Prob. R. 5.430 Resignation of personal representative.

Rule 5.340. Inventory

(a) Contents and Filing. Unless an inventory has been previously filed, the personal representative shall file an inventory of the estate within 60 days after issuance of letters. The inventory shall contain notice of the beneficiaries' rights under subdivision (e), list the estate with reasonable detail, and include for each listed item (excluding real property appearing to be protected homestead property) its estimated fair market value at the date of the decedent's death. Real property appearing to be protected homestead property shall be listed and so designated.

(b) Extension. On petition the time for filing the inventory may be extended by the court for cause shown without notice, except that the personal representative shall serve copies of the petition and order on the persons described in subdivision (d).

(c) Amendments. A supplementary or amended inventory containing the information required by subdivision (a) as to each affected item shall be filed and served by the personal representative if:

(1) the personal representative learns of property not included in the original inventory; or

(2) the personal representative learns that the estimated value or description indicated in the original inventory for any item is erroneous or misleading; or

(3) the personal representative determines the estimated fair market value of an item whose value was described as unknown in the original inventory.

(d) Service. The personal representative shall serve a copy of the inventory and all supplemental and amended inventories on the surviving spouse, each heir at law in an intestate estate, each residuary beneficiary in a testate estate, and any other interested person who may request it in writing.

(e) Information. On request in writing, the personal representative shall provide the following:

(1) To the requesting residuary beneficiary or heir in an intestate estate, a written explanation of how the

inventory value for an asset was determined or, if an appraisal was obtained, a copy of the appraisal.

(2) To any other requesting beneficiary, a written explanation of how the inventory value for each asset distributed or proposed to be distributed to that beneficiary was determined or, if an appraisal of that asset was obtained, a copy of the appraisal.

(f) Notice to Nonresiduary Beneficiaries. The personal representative shall provide to each nonresiduary beneficiary written notice of that beneficiary's right to receive a written explanation of how the inventory value for each asset distributed or proposed to be distributed to that beneficiary was determined or a copy of an appraisal, if any, of the asset.

(g) Elective Share Proceedings. Upon entry of an order determining the surviving spouse's entitlement to the elective share, the personal representative shall file an inventory of the property entering into the elective estate which shall identify the direct recipient, if any, of that property. The personal representative shall serve the inventory of the elective estate as provided in rule 5.360. On request in writing, the personal representative shall provide an interested person with a written explanation of how the inventory value for an asset was determined and shall permit an interested person to examine appraisals on which the inventory values are based.

(h) Verification. All inventories shall be verified by the personal representative.

Amended Sept. 4, 1980, effective Jan. 1, 1981 (387 So.2d 949); Sept. 13, 1984, effective Jan. 1, 1985 (458 So.2d 1079); Nov. 30, 1984, effective Jan. 1, 1985 (460 So.2d 906); Sept. 29, 1988, effective Jan. 1, 1989 (537 So.2d 500); Sept. 24, 1992, effective Jan. 1, 1993 (607 So.2d 1306); Oct. 11, 2001 (807 So.2d 622); Jan. 10, 2002 (816 So.2d 1095); May 2, 2002 (824 So.2d 849); Sept. 2, 2010, effective Jan. 1, 2011 (50 So.3d 578); Oct. 18, 2012, effective, *nunc pro tunc*, Sept. 1, 2012 (102 So.3d 505).

Committee Notes

Inventories of the elective estate under subdivision (f) shall be afforded the same confidentiality as probate inventories. § 733.604(1) and (2), Fla. Stat.

Inventories are still required to be filed. Once filed, however, they are subject to the confidentiality provisions found in sections 733.604(1) and (2), Florida Statutes.

Constitutional protected homestead real property is not necessarily a probatable asset. Disclosure on the inventory of real property appearing to be constitutional protected homestead property informs interested persons of the homestead issue.

Interested persons are entitled to reasonable information about estate proceedings on proper request, including a copy of the inventory, an opportunity to examine appraisals, and other information pertinent to their interests in the estate. The rights of beneficiaries to information contained in estate inventories is limited by section 733.604(3), Florida Statutes. Inventories of the elective estate under subdivision (f) affects a broader class of interested persons who may obtain information regarding the assets disclosed therein subject to control by the court and the confidentiality afforded such inventories under section 733.604(1) and (2).

Rule History

1980 Revision: Eliminated the time limit in requesting a copy of the inventory by an interested person or in furnishing it by the personal representative.

1984 (First) Revision: Extensive changes. Committee notes revised.

1984 (Second) Revision: Subdivision (a) modified to clarify or re-insert continued filing requirement for inventory.

1988 Revision: Editorial changes in (b) and (d). Committee notes revised. Citation form changes in committee notes.

1992 Revision: Editorial changes. Committee notes revised. Citation form changes in committee notes.

2001 Revision: Subdivision (a) amended to conform to statutory changes. Subdivision (d) amended to add requirement of filing of proof of service. Subdivision (e) amended to clarify personal representative's duty to furnish explanation of how inventory values were determined. Subdivision (f) added to require personal representative to file inventory of property entering into elective share. Subdivision (g) added to require verification of inventories. Committee notes revised.

2002 Revision: Subdivision (e) amended to conform to section 733.604(3), Florida Statutes. Subdivision (f) amended to establish procedures for interested persons to obtain information about assets and values listed in the inventory of the elective estate. Committee notes revised.

2003 Revision: Committee notes revised.

2010 Revision: Subdivisions (d) and (g) (former (f)) amended to delete the requirement to serve a copy of the inventory on the Department of Revenue. Subdivision (e) amended, and new (f) created, to limit the kind of information available to nonresiduary beneficiaries, and subsequent subdivisions relettered. Editorial changes in (a), (e), and (g). Committee notes revised.

2012 Revision: The last sentence of subdivision (d) is deleted to remove duplicative requirement of filing a proof of service for a document which includes a certificate of service as provided in Fla. R Jud. Admin. 2. 516. If service of the inventory is b service in the manner provided for service of form notice, then proof of service should be filed provided in rule 5.040(a)(5). Committee note vised.

Constitutional Reference

Art. X, § 4, Fla. Const.

Statutory References

§ 732.401, Fla. Stat. Descent of homest

§ 732.4015, Fla. Stat. Devise of homes

§ 733.604, Fla. Stat. Inventories and public records exemptions.

Rule References

Fla. Prob. R. 5.041 Service of pleadings and documents.

Fla. Prob. R. 5.060 Request for notices and copies of pleadings.

Fla. Prob. R. 5.330 Execution by personal representative.

Fla. Prob. R. 5.360 Elective share.

Fla. Prob. R. 5.405 Proceedings to determine homestead real property.

Fla. R. Jud. Admin. 2.516 Service of pleadings and documents.

Rule 5.341. Estate Information

On reasonable request in writing, the personal representative shall provide an interested person with information about the estate and its administration.

Added May 2, 2002 (824 So.2d 849).

Committee Notes

This rule is not intended to overrule the holdings in *In re Estate of Shaw*, 340 So. 2d 491 (Fla. 3d DCA 1976), and *In re Estate of Posner*, 492 So. 2d 1093 (Fla. 3d DCA 1986).

Rule History

2002 Revision: New rule.

Rule 5.342. Inventory of Safe–Deposit Box

(a) Filing. The personal representative shall file an inventory of the contents of the decedent's safe-deposit box within 10 days of the initial opening of the box by the personal representative or the personal representative's attorney of record. The inventory shall include a copy of the financial institution's entry record for the box from a date that is six months prior to the decedent's date of death to the date of the initial opening by the personal representative or the personal representative's attorney of record.

(b) Verification. Each person who was present at initial opening must verify the contents of the box ...ning a copy of the inventory under penalties of

...**ice.** The personal representative shall ...f the inventory on the surviving spouse, ... in an intestate estate, each residuary ...state estate, and any other interest- ...request it in writing.

...8 So.2d 1069). Amended Oct. 18, ...*nc*, Sept. 1, 2012 (102 So.3d 505).

...tee Notes

...cords, once filed, shall be ...iality as probate inven-

...d pursuant to section ...o written inventory ...ed.

2012 Revision: The last sentence of subdivision (c) is deleted to remove duplicative requirement of filing a proof of service for a document which includes a certificate of service as provided in Fla. R. Jud. Admin. 2. 516. If service of the inventory is by service in the manner provided for service of formal notice, then proof of service should be filed as provided in rule 5.040(a)(5). Committee notes revised.

Statutory References

§ 655.935, Fla. Stat. Search procedure on death of lessee.

§ 655.936, Fla. Stat. Delivery of safe-deposit box contents or property held in safekeeping to personal representative.

§ 733.6065, Fla. Stat. Opening safe-deposit box.

Rule References

Fla. Prob. R. 5.041 Service of pleadings and documents.

Fla. Prob. R. 5.340 Inventory.

Fla. R. Jud. Admin. 2.516 Service of pleadings and documents.

Rule 5.3425. Search of Safe Deposit Box

(a) Petition for Order Authorizing Search. The petition for an order authorizing the search of a safe deposit box leased or co-leased by a decedent must be verified and must contain:

(1) The petitioner's name, address, and interest, if any, in the estate;

(2) The decedent's name, address, date and place of death, and state and county of domicile;

(3) A description of the safe deposit box leased by the decedent and, if known, the name of any co-lessee;

(4) The name and address of the institution where the safe deposit box is located; and

(5) A statement that the petitioner believes that the decedent may have left in the safe deposit box one or more of the following:

(A) A will or codicil of the decedent, or a writing described in section 732.515 of the Code;

(B) A deed to a burial plot;

(C) A writing giving burial instructions; or

(D) Insurance policies on the life of the decedent.

(b) Order. If the Court determines that the petitioner is entitled to an order authorizing a search of the decedent's safe deposit box, it must enter an order

(1) authorizing the petitioner to open the safe deposit box in the presence of an officer of the lessor and, if requested by the petitioner, to remove and deliver

(A) to the court having probate jurisdiction in the county where the lessor is located any writing purporting to be a will or codicil of the decedent and any writing purporting to identify devises of tangible property;

(B) to the petitioner, any writing purporting to be a deed to a burial plot to give burial instructions; and

(C) to the beneficiary named therein, any document purporting to be an insurance policy on the life of the decedent.

(2) directing the officer of the lessor to make a complete copy of any document removed and delivered pursuant to the court order, together with a memorandum of delivery identifying the name of the officer, the person to whom the document was delivered, and the date of delivery, to be placed in the safe deposit box leased or co-leased by the decedent.

Added effective Dec. 9, 2010 (51 So.3d 1146).

Committee Notes

The search of the safe deposit box is not considered an initial opening and is not subject to the inventory requirements of rule 5.342.

Rule History

2010 Revision: New rule.

Statutory References

§ 655.935, Fla. Stat. Search procedure on death of lessee.

Rule 5.345. Accountings Other Than Personal Representatives' Final Accountings

(a) Applicability and Accounting Periods. This rule applies to the interim accounting of any fiduciary of a probate estate, the accounting of a personal representative who has resigned or been removed, and the accounting of a curator upon the appointment of a successor fiduciary. The fiduciary may elect to file an interim accounting at any time, or the court may require an interim or supplemental accounting. The ending date of the accounting period for any accounting to which this rule applies shall be as follows:

(1) For an interim accounting, any date selected by the fiduciary, including a fiscal or calendar year, or as may be determined by the court.

(2) For the accounting of a personal representative who has resigned or has been removed, the date the personal representative's letters are revoked.

(3) For a curator who has been replaced by a successor fiduciary, the date of appointment of the successor fiduciary.

(b) Notice of Filing. Notice of filing and a copy of any accounting to which this rule applies shall be served on all interested persons. The notice shall state that objections to the accounting must be filed within 30 days from the date of service of notice.

(c) Objection. Any interested person may file an objection to any accounting to which this rule applies within 30 days from the date of service of notice on that person. Any objection not filed within 30 days from the date of service shall be deemed abandoned. An objection shall be in writing and shall state with particularity the item or items to which the objection is directed and the grounds upon which the objection is based.

(d) Service of Objections. The objecting party shall serve a copy of the objection on the fiduciary filing the accounting and other interested persons.

(e) Disposition of Objections and Approval of Accountings. The court shall sustain or overrule any objection filed as provided in this rule. If no objection is filed, any accounting to which this rule applies shall be deemed approved 30 days from the date of service of the accounting on interested persons.

(f) Substantiating Papers. On reasonable written request, the fiduciary shall permit an interested person to examine papers substantiating items in any accounting to which this rule applies.

(g) Supplemental Accountings. The court, on its own motion or on that of any interested person, may require a fiduciary who has been replaced by a successor fiduciary to file a supplemental accounting, the beginning date of which shall be the ending date of the accounting as specified in subdivision (a) of this rule and the ending date of which is the date of delivery of all of the estate's property to the successor fiduciary, or such other date as the court may order.

(h) Verification. All accountings shall be verified by the fiduciary filing the accounting.

Amended March 31, 1977, effective July 1, 1977 (344 So.2d 828); Sept. 4, 1980, effective Jan. 1, 1981 (387 So.2d 949); Sept. 13, 1984, effective Jan. 1, 1985 (458 So.2d 1079); Sept. 24, 1992, effective Jan. 1, 1993 (607 So.2d 1306); May 2, 2002 (824 So.2d 849); Sept. 29, 2005, effective Jan. 1, 2006 (912 So.2d 1178).

Committee Notes

The personal representative is required to file a final accounting when administration is complete, unless filing is waived by interested persons. Additionally, a fiduciary of a probate estate may elect, but is not required, to file interim accountings at any time. An accounting is required for resigning or removed fiduciaries. The filing, notice, objection, and approval procedure is similar to that for final accounts.

Rule History

1977 Revision: Change in (a) to authorize selection of fiscal year.

1980 Revision: Change in (d) of prior rule to require the notice to state that the basis for an objection is necessary. Change in (e) of prior rule to require any person filing an objection to set forth the basis of such objection.

1984 Revision: Extensive changes. Committee notes revised.

1988 Revision: Citation form change in committee notes.

1992 Revision: Editorial change. Committee notes revised. Citation form changes in committee notes.

2002 Revision: Implements procedures for interim accountings and accountings by resigning or removed fiduciaries. Committee notes revised.

2003 Revision: Committee notes revised.

2005 Revision: Verification requirement added as new (h). Committee notes revised.

Statutory References

§ 733.3101, Fla. Stat. Personal representative not qualified.

§ 733.501, Fla. Stat. Curators.

§ 733.5035, Fla. Stat. Surrender of assets after resignation.

§ 733.5036, Fla. Stat. Accounting and discharge following resignation.

§ 733.508, Fla. Stat. Accounting and discharge of removed personal representatives upon removal.

§ 733.509, Fla. Stat. Surrender of assets upon removal.

ch. 738, Fla. Stat. Principal and income.

Rule References

Fla. Prob. R. 5.020 Pleadings; verification; motions.

Fla. Prob. R. 5.122 Curators.

Fla. Prob. R. 5.150 Order requiring accounting.

Fla. Prob. R. 5.330 Execution by personal representative.

Fla. Prob. R. 5.346 Fiduciary accounting.

Fla. Prob. R. 5.430 Resignation of personal representative.

Fla. Prob. R. 5.440 Proceedings for removal.

Rule 5.346. Fiduciary Accounting

(a) Contents. A fiduciary accounting shall include:

(1) all cash and property transactions since the date of the last accounting or, if none, from the commencement of administration, and

(2) a schedule of assets at the end of the accounting period.

(b) Accounting Standards. The following standards are required for the accounting of all transactions occurring on or after January 1, 1994:

(1) Accountings shall be stated in a manner that is understandable to persons who are not familiar with practices and terminology peculiar to the administration of estates and trusts.

(2) The accounting shall begin with a concise summary of its purpose and content.

(3) The accounting shall contain sufficient information to put interested persons on notice as to all significant transactions affecting administration during the accounting period.

(4) The accounting shall contain 2 values in the schedule of assets at the end of the accounting period, the asset acquisition value or carrying value, and estimated current value.

(5) Gains and losses incurred during the accounting period shall be shown separately in the same schedule.

(6) The accounting shall show significant transactions that do not affect the amount for which the fiduciary is accountable.

(c) Accounting Format. A model format for an accounting is attached to this rule as Appendix A.

(d) Verification. All accountings shall be verified by the fiduciary filing the accounting.

Added Sept. 29, 1988, effective Jan. 1, 1989 (537 So.2d 500). Amended Sept. 24, 1992, effective Jan. 1, 1993 (607 So.2d 1306); Oct. 3, 1996, effective Jan. 1, 1997 (683 So.2d 78); May 2, 2002 (824 So.2d 849); Sept. 29, 2005, effective Jan. 1, 2006 (912 So.2d 1178); July 12, 2007 (964 So.2d 140).

Committee Notes

This rule substantially adopts the Uniform Fiduciary Accounting Principles and Model Formats adopted by the Committee on National Fiduciary Accounting Standards of the American Bar Association: Section of Real Property, Probate and Trust Law, the American College of Probate Counsel, the American Bankers Association: Trust Division, and other organizations.

Accountings shall also comply with the Florida principal and income law, chapter 738, Florida Statutes.

Attached as Appendix B to this rule are an explanation and commentary for each of the foregoing standards, which shall be considered as a Committee Note to this rule.

Accountings that substantially conform to the model formats are acceptable. The model accounting format included in Appendix A is only a suggested form.

Rule History

1988 Revision: New rule.

1992 Revision: Editorial changes throughout. Rule changed to require compliance with the Uniform Fiduciary Accounting Principles and Model Formats for accounting of all transactions occurring on or after January 1, 1994. Committee notes revised. Citation form changes in committee notes.

1996 Revision: Committee notes revised.

1999 Revision: Committee notes revised to correct rule reference and to reflect formatting changes in accounting formats.

2002 Revision: Subdivisions (a) and (b) amended to clarify contents of accounting. Committee notes revised.

2003 Revision: Committee notes revised.

2005 Revision: Verification requirement added as new (d). Committee notes revised.

2007 Revision: Committee notes revised.

2010 Revision: Committee notes revised.

Statutory References

§ 733.501, Fla. Stat. Curators.

§ 733.5036, Fla. Stat. Accounting and discharge following resignation.

§ 733.508, Fla. Stat. Accounting and discharge of removed personal representatives upon removal.

§ 733.602(1), Fla. Stat. General duties.

§ 733.612(18), Fla. Stat. Transactions authorized for the personal representative; exceptions.

ch. 738, Fla. Stat. Principal and income.

Rule References

Fla. Prob. R. 5.020 Pleadings; verification; motions.

Fla. Prob. R. 5.040 Notice.

Fla. Prob. R. 5.122 Curators.

Fla. Prob. R. 5.180 Waiver and consent.

Fla. Prob. R. 5.330 Execution by personal representative.

Fla. Prob. R. 5.345 Accountings other than personal representatives' final accountings.

Fla. Prob. R. 5.400 Distribution and discharge.

Fla. Prob. R. 5.430 Resignation of personal representative.

Fla. Prob. R. 5.440 Proceedings for removal.

APPENDIX A

IN THE CIRCUIT COURT FOR ________ COUNTY, FLORIDA

IN RE: ESTATE OF PROBATE DIVISION

File Number

Deceased. Division

__________ACCOUNTING OF PERSONAL REPRESENTATIVE(S)

From: __________, ___, Through: __________, ______________

The purpose of this accounting is to acquaint all interested persons with the transactions that have occurred during the period covered by the accounting and the assets that remain on hand. It consists of a SUMMARY sheet and Schedule A showing all Receipts, Schedule B showing all Disbursements, Schedule C showing all Distributions, Schedule D showing all Capital Transactions and Adjustments (the effect of which are also reflected in other schedules, if appropriate), and Schedule E showing assets on hand at the end of the accounting period.

It is important that this accounting be carefully examined. Requests for additional information and any questions should be addressed to the personal representative(s) or the attorneys for the personal representative(s), the names and addresses of whom are set forth below.

Under penalties of perjury, the undersigned personal representative(s) declare(s) that I (we) have read and examined this accounting and that the facts and figures set forth in the Summary and the attached Schedules are true, to the best of my (our) knowledge and belief, and that it is a complete report of all cash and property transactions and of all receipts and disbursements by me (us) as personal representative(s) of the estate of ________ deceased, from __________, ___ through __________, ___.

Signed on __________, ___.

Attorney for Personal Representative: Personal Representative:

______________________________ ______________________________

Attorney ______________________________

Name

Florida Bar No. ______________________________

______________________________ ______________________________

______________________________ ______________________________

______________________________ ______________________________

(address) (address)

Telephone: ______________________________ [Print or Type Names Under All Signature Lines]

IN THE CIRCUIT COURT FOR ________ COUNTY, FLORIDA

IN RE: ESTATE OF PROBATE DIVISION

File Number

Deceased. Division

__________ACCOUNTING OF PERSONAL REPRESENTATIVE

From: __________________, ___, Through: ________, ______________

SUMMARY

		Income	Principal	Totals
I.	**Starting Balance** Assets per Inventory or on Hand at Close of Last Accounting Period			
II.	**Receipts** Schedule A:	______	______	______
III.	**Disbursements** Schedule B:	______	______	______
IV.	**Distributions** Schedule C:	______	______	______
V.	**Capital Transactions and Adjustments** Schedule D: Net Gain or (Loss)		$______	______
VI.	**Assets on Hand at Close of Accounting Period** Schedule E: Cash and Other Assets	______	______	______

NOTE: Refer to Fla. Prob. R. 5.330(b), 5.345, 5.346, and 5.400.

Also see Accountings, Chapter 12 of Practice Under Florida Probate Code (Fla. Bar CLE).

Entries on Summary are to be taken from totals on Schedules A, B, C, D and E.

The Summary and Schedules A, B, C, D and E are to constitute the full accounting. Every transaction occurring during the accounting period should be reflected on the Schedules.

All purchases and sales, all adjustments to the inventory or carrying value of any asset, and any other changes in the assets (such as stock splits) should be described on Schedule D.

The amount in the "Total" column for Item VI must agree with the total inventory or adjusted carrying value of all assets on hand at the close of the accounting period on Schedule E.

______ACCOUNTING OF PERSONAL REPRESENTATIVE,

ESTATE OF ______________________________

From:____________________, ___, Through:______________________,

SCHEDULE A Receipts

Date	Brief Description of Items	Income	Principal

NOTE: Schedule A should reflect only those items received during administration that are not shown on the inventory. Classification of items as income or principal is to be in accordance with the provisions of the Florida Principal and Income Act, Chapter 738, Florida Statutes.

Entries involving the sale of assets or other adjustments to the carrying values of assets are to be shown on Schedule D, and not on Schedule A.

__________ACCOUNTING OF PERSONAL REPRESENTATIVE,

ESTATE OF ____

From:____________________, ___, Through:____________________________,

SCHEDULE B Disbursements

Date	Brief Description of Items	Income	Principal

NOTE: Schedule B should reflect only those items paid out during the accounting period. Classification of disbursements as income or principal is to be in accordance with the provisions of the Florida Principal and Income Act, Chapter 738, Florida Statutes.

Entries involving the purchase of assets or adjustments to the carrying values of assets are to be shown on Schedule D, and not on Schedule B.

__________ACCOUNTING OF PERSONAL REPRESENTATIVE,

ESTATE OF ____

From:____________________, ___, Through:____________________________,

SCHEDULE C Distributions

Date	Brief Description of Items	Income	Principal

NOTE: Schedule C should reflect only those items or amounts distributed to beneficiaries during the accounting period. Assets distributed should be shown at their inventory or adjusted carrying values. Classification of distributions as income or principal is to be in accordance with the provisions of the Florida Principal and Income Act, Chapter 738, Florida Statutes.

Entries involving adjustments to the carrying values of assets are to be shown on Schedule D, and not on Schedule C.

__________ACCOUNTING OF PERSONAL REPRESENTATIVE,

ESTATE OF ____________________________________

From:________________, ___, Through:____________________,

SCHEDULE D Capital Transactions and Adjustments

(Does not include distributions. Distributions are shown on Schedule C.)

Date	Brief Description of Transactions	Net Gain	Net Loss
	TOTAL NET GAINS AND LOSSES		
	NET GAIN OR (LOSS)		

NOTE: Schedule D should reflect all purchases and sales of assets and any adjustments to the carrying values of any assets.

Entries reflecting sales should show the inventory or adjusted carrying values, the costs and expenses of the sale, and the net proceeds received. The net gain or loss should be extended in the appropriate column on the right side of Schedule D.

Entries reflecting purchases should reflect the purchase price, any expenses of purchase or other adjustments to the purchase price, and the total amount paid. Presumably no gain or loss would be shown for purchases.

Entries reflecting adjustments in capital assets should explain the change (such as a stock split) and the net gain or loss should be shown in the appropriate column on the right side of Schedule D.

The NET gain or loss should be entered in the Principal column of the Summary.

__________ACCOUNTING OF PERSONAL REPRESENTATIVE,

ESTATE OF ________________________________

From:_______________, ___, Through:____________________,

SCHEDULE E Assets on Hand at Close of Accounting Period

(Indicate where held and legal description, certificate numbers or other identification.)

	Estimated Current Value	Carrying Value
ASSETS OTHER THAN CASH:		
OTHER ASSETS TOTAL		
CASH:		
CASH TOTAL		
TOTAL ASSETS (must agree with the Total for Item VI on Summary)		

NOTE: Schedule E should be a complete list of all assets on hand reflecting inventory values for each item, adjusted in accordance with any appropriate entries on Schedule D.

Current market values for any assets that are known to be different from the inventory or carrying values as of the close of the accounting period should be shown in the column marked "Current Value." The total inventory or adjusted carrying value (not Current Value) must agree with the Total for Item VI on Summary.

APPENDIX B

UNIFORM FIDUCIARY ACCOUNTING PRINCIPLES

I. ACCOUNTS SHOULD BE STATED IN A MANNER THAT IS UNDERSTANDABLE BY PERSONS WHO ARE NOT FAMILIAR WITH PRACTICES AND TERMINOLOGY PECULIAR TO THE ADMINISTRATION OF ESTATES AND TRUSTS.

Commentary: In order for an account to fulfill its basic function of communication, it is essential that it be stated in a manner that recognizes that the interested parties are not usually familiar with fiduciary accounts. It is neither practical nor desirable to require that accounts be tailored to meet individual disabilities of particular parties but any account should be capable of being understood by a person of average intelligence, literate in English, and familiar with basic financial terms who has read it with care and attention.

Problems arising from terminology or style are usually a reflection of the fact that people who become versed in a particular form of practice tend to forget that terms which are familiar and useful to them may convey nothing to someone else or may even be affirmatively misleading. For example, the terms "debit" and "credit" are generally incomprehensible to people with no knowledge of bookkeeping and many people who are familiar with them in other contexts would assume that in the context of fiduciary accounting, the receipt of an item is a "credit" to the fund rather than a "debit" to the fiduciary.

While the need for concise presentation makes a certain amount of abbreviation both acceptable and necessary, uncommon abbreviation of matters essential to an understanding of the account should be avoided or explained.

No position is taken for or against the use of direct print-outs from machine accounting systems. The quality of the accounts produced by these systems varies widely in the extent to which they can be understood by persons who are not familiar with them. To endorse or object to a direct print-out because it is produced by machine from previously stored data would miss the essential point by focusing attention upon the manner of preparation rather than the product.

II. A FIDUCIARY ACCOUNT SHALL BEGIN WITH A CONCISE SUMMARY OF ITS PURPOSE AND CONTENT.

Commentary: Very few people can be expected to pay much attention to a document unless they have some understanding of its general purpose and its significance to them. Even with such an understanding, impressions derived from the first page or two will often determine whether the rest is read. The use that is made of these pages is therefore of particular significance.

The cover page should disclose the nature and function of the account. While a complete explanation of the significance of the account and the effect of its presentation upon the rights of the parties is obviously impractical for inclusion at this point, there should be at least a brief statement identifying the fiduciary and the subject matter, noting the importance of examining the account and giving an address where more information can be obtained.

It is assumed that the parties would also have enough information from other sources to understand the nature of their relationship to the fund (e.g., residuary legatee, life tenant, remainderman), the function of the account, and the obligation of the fiduciary to supply further relevant information upon request. It is also assumed that notice will be given of any significant procedural considerations such as limitation on the time within which objections must be presented. This would normally be provided by prior or contemporaneous memoranda, correspondence, or discussions.

A summary of the account shall also be presented at the outset. This summary, organized as a table of contents, shall indicate the order of the details presented in the account and shall show separate totals for the aggregate of the assets on hand at the beginning of the accounting period; transactions during the period; and the assets remaining on hand at the end of the period. Each entry in the summary shall be supported by a schedule in the account that provides the details on which the summary is based.

III. A FIDUCIARY ACCOUNT SHALL CONTAIN SUFFICIENT INFORMATION TO PUT THE INTERESTED PARTIES ON NOTICE AS TO ALL SIGNIFICANT TRANSACTIONS AFFECTING ADMINISTRATION DURING THE ACCOUNTING PERIOD.

Commentary: The presentation of the information account shall allow an interested party to follow the progress of the fiduciary's administration of assets during the accounting period.

An account is not complete if it does not itemize, or make reference to, assets on hand at the beginning of the accounting period.

Illustration:

3.1 The first account for a decedent's estate or a trust may detail the items received by the fiduciary and for which the fiduciary is responsible. It may refer to the total amount of an inventory filed elsewhere or assets described in a schedule attached to a trust agreement.

Instead of retyping the complete list of assets in the opening balance, the preparer may prefer to attach as an exhibit a copy of the inventory, closing balance from the last account, etc., as appropriate, or may refer to them if previously provided to the interested parties who will receive it.

Transactions shall be described in sufficient detail to give interested parties notice of their purpose and effect. It should be recognized that too much detail may be counterproductive to making the account understandable. In accounts covering long periods or dealing with extensive assets, it is usually desirable to consolidate information. For instance, where income from a number of securities is being accounted for over a long period of time, a statement of the total dividends received on each security with appropriate indication of changes in the number of shares held will be more readily understandable and easier to check for completeness than a chronological listing of all dividends received.

Although detail should generally be avoided for routine transactions, it will often be necessary to proper understanding of an event that is somewhat out of the ordinary.

Illustrations:

3.2 Extraordinary appraisal costs should be shown separately and explained.

3.3 Interest and penalties in connection with late filing of tax returns should be shown separately and explained.

3.4 An extraordinary allocation between principal and income such as apportionment of proceeds of property acquired on foreclosure should be separately stated and explained.

3.5 Computation of a formula marital deduction gift involving non-probate assets should be explained.

IV. A FIDUCIARY ACCOUNT SHALL CONTAIN TWO VALUES, THE ASSET ACQUISITION VALUE OR CARRYING VALUE, AND CURRENT VALUE.

Commentary: In order for transactions to be reported on a consistent basis, an appropriate carrying value for assets must be chosen and employed consistently.

The carrying value of an asset should reflect its value at the time it is acquired by the fiduciary (or a predecessor fiduciary). When such a value is not precisely determinable, the figure used should reflect a thoughtful decision by the fiduciary. For assets owned by a decedent, inventory values or estate tax values – generally reflective of date of death – would be appropriate. Assets received in kind by a trustee from a settlor of an inter vivos trust should be carried at their value at the time of receipt. For assets purchased during the administration of the fund, cost would normally be used. Use of Federal income tax basis for carrying value is acceptable when basis is reasonably representative of real values at the time of acquisition. Use of tax basis as a carrying value under other circumstances could be affirmatively misleading to beneficiaries and therefore is not appropriate.

In the Model Account, carrying value is referred to as "fiduciary acquisition value." The Model Account establishes the initial carrying value of assets as their value at date of death for inventoried assets, date of receipt for subsequent receipts, and cost for investments.

Carrying value would not normally be adjusted for depreciation.

Except for adjustments that occur normally under the accounting system in use, carrying values should generally be continued unchanged through successive accounts and assets should not be arbitrarily "written up" or "written down." In some circumstances, however, with proper disclosure and explanation, carrying value may be adjusted.

Illustrations:

4.1 Carrying values based on date of death may be adjusted to reflect changes on audit of estate or inheritance tax returns.

4.2 Where appropriate under applicable local law, a successor fiduciary may adjust the carrying value of assets to reflect values at the start of that fiduciary's administration.

4.3 Assets received in kind in satisfaction of a pecuniary legacy should be carried at the value used for purposes of distribution.

Though essential for accounting purposes, carrying values are commonly misunderstood by laypersons as being a representation of actual values. To avoid this, the account should include both current values and carrying values.

The value of assets at the beginning and ending of each accounting period is necessary information for the evaluation of investment performance. Therefore, the account should show, or make reference to, current values at the start of the period for all assets whose carrying values were established in a prior accounting period.

Illustrations:

4.4 The opening balance of the first account of a testamentary trustee will usually contain assets received in kind from the executor. Unless the carrying value was written up at the time of distribution (e.g., 4.2 or 4.3 supra) these assets will be carried at a value established during the executor's administration. The current value at the beginning of the accounting period should also be shown.

4.5 An executor's first account will normally carry assets at inventory (date of death) values or costs. No separate listing of current values at the beginning of the accounting period is necessary.

Current values should also be shown for all assets on hand at the close of the accounting period. The date on which current values are determined shall be stated and shall be the last day of the accounting period, or a date as close thereto as reasonably possible.

Current values should be shown in a column parallel to the column of carrying values. Both columns should be totalled.

In determining current values for assets for which there is no readily ascertainable current value, the source of the value stated in the account shall be explained. The fiduciary shall make a good faith effort to determine realistic values but should not be expected to incur expenses for appraisals or similar costs when there is no reason to expect that the resulting information will be of practical consequence to the administration of the estate or the protection of the interests of the parties.

Illustrations:

4.6 When an asset is held under circumstances that make it clear that it will not be sold (e.g., a residence held for use of a beneficiary) the fiduciary's estimate of value would be acceptable in lieu of an appraisal.

4.7 Considerations such as a pending tax audit or offer of the property for sale may indicate the advisability of not publishing the fiduciary's best estimate of value. In such circumstances, a statement that value was fixed by some method such as "per company books," "formula under buy-sell agreement," or "300% of assessed value" would be acceptable, but the fiduciary would be expected to provide further information to interested parties upon request.

V. GAINS AND LOSSES INCURRED DURING THE ACCOUNTING PERIOD SHALL BE SHOWN SEPARATELY IN THE SAME SCHEDULE.

Commentary: Each transaction involving the sale or other disposition of securities during the accounting period shall be shown as a separate item in one combined schedule of the account indicating the transaction, date, explanation, and any gain or loss.

Although gains and losses from the sale of securities can be shown separately in accounts, the preferred method of presentation is to present this information in a single schedule. Such a presentation provides the most meaningful description of investment performance and will tend to clarify relationships between gains and losses that are deliberately realized at the same time.

VI. THE ACCOUNT SHALL SHOW SIGNIFICANT TRANSACTIONS THAT DO NOT AFFECT THE AMOUNT FOR WHICH THE FIDUCIARY IS ACCOUNTABLE.

Commentary: Transactions such as the purchase of an investment, receipt of a stock split, or change of a corporate name do not alter the total fund for which a fiduciary is accountable but must be shown in order to permit analysis and an understanding of the administration of the fund. These can be best shown in information schedules.

One schedule should list all investments made during the accounting period. It should include those subsequently sold as well as those still on hand. Frequently the same money will be used for a series of investments. Therefore, the schedule should not be totalled in order to avoid giving an exaggerated idea of the size of the fund.

A second schedule (entitled "Changes in Investment Holdings" in the Model Account) should show all transactions affecting a particular security holding, such as purchase of additional shares, partial sales, stock splits, change of corporate name, divestment distributions, etc. This schedule, similar to a ledger account for each holding, will reconcile opening and closing entries for particular holdings, explain changes in carrying value, and avoid extensive searches through the account for information scattered among other schedules.

Rule 5.350. Continuance of Unincorporated Business or Venture

(a) Separate Accounts and Reports. In the conduct of an unincorporated business or venture, the personal representative shall keep separate, full, and accurate accounts of all receipts and expenditures and make reports as the court may require.

(b) Petition. If the personal representative determines it to be in the best interest of the estate to continue an unincorporated business or venture beyond the time authorized by statute or will, the personal representative shall file a verified petition which shall include:

(1) a statement of the nature of that business or venture;

(2) a schedule of specific assets and liabilities;

(3) the reasons for continuation;

(4) the proposed form and times of accounting for that business or venture;

(5) the period for which the continuation is requested; and

(6) any other information pertinent to the petition.

(c) Order. If the continuation is authorized, the order shall state:

(1) the period for which that business or venture is to continue;

(2) the particular powers of the personal representative in the continuation of that business or venture; and

(3) the form and frequency of accounting by that business or venture.

(d) Petition by Interested Person. Any interested person, at any time, may petition the court for an order regarding the operation of, accounting for, or termination of an unincorporated business or venture, and the court shall enter an order thereon.

Amended Sept. 13, 1984, effective Jan. 1, 1985 (458 So.2d 1079); Sept. 29, 1988, effective Jan. 1, 1989 (537 So.2d 500).

Committee Notes

Rule History

1975 Revision: New rule, § 733.612, Fla.Stat.

1984 Revision: Extensive changes in rule and title. Clarifies procedural steps to be taken by a personal representative who determines it to be in the best interest of an estate to continue any unincorporated business beyond the time authorized by statute. Information required to be filed in a verified petition is specified, and normal information to be included in a court order is listed. Other pertinent information under (b)(6) may include provisions for insurance of business or venture, proposed professionals to be used in connection with such activities, how the business or venture shall be managed, the person or persons proposed for managerial positions, a list of all other employees, agents, or independent contractors employed by or affiliated with the business or venture, and proposed compensation for all such management personnel, agents, employees, and independent contractors. Committee notes revised and expanded.

1988 Revision: Editorial change in caption of (b). Committee notes revised. Citation form changes in committee notes.

1992 Revision: Committee notes revised. Citation form changes in committee notes.

2012 Revision: Committee notes revised.

Statutory References

§ 733.612(22), Fla.Stat. Transactions authorized for the personal representative; exceptions.

Rule References

Fla. Prob. R. 5.020 Pleadings; verification; motions.

Fla. Prob. R. 5.040 Notice.

Fla. Prob. R. 5.041 Service of pleadings and documents.

Fla. Prob. R. 5.330 Execution by personal representative.

Fla. R. Jud. Admin. 2.516 Service of pleadings and documents.

Rule 5.355. Proceedings for Review of Employment of Agents and Compensation of Personal Representatives and Estate Employees

After notice to all interested persons and upon petition of an interested person bearing all or a part of the impact of the payment of compensation to the personal representative or any person employed by the personal representative, the propriety of the employment and the reasonableness of the compensation or payment may be reviewed by the court. The petition shall state the grounds on which it is based. The burden of proving the propriety of the employment and the reasonableness of the compensation shall be upon the personal representative and the person employed by the personal representative. Any person who is determined to have received excessive compensation from an estate may be ordered to make appropriate refunds.

Added Sept. 29, 1988, effective Jan. 1, 1989 (537 So.2d 500). Amended Sept. 24, 1992, effective Jan. 1, 1993 (607 So.2d 1306); Oct. 3, 1996, effective Jan. 1, 1997 (683 So.2d 78); July 12, 2007 (964 So.2d 140).

Committee Notes

This rule represents a rule implementation of the procedure formerly found in section 733.6175, Florida Statutes. It is not intended to change the effect of the statute from which it was derived but has been reformatted to conform with the structure of these rules. It is not intended to create a new procedure or modify an existing procedure.

Rule History

1988 Revision: New rule.

1992 Revision: Editorial changes. Committee notes revised. Citation form changes in committee notes.

1996 Revision: Committee notes revised.

2003 Revision: Committee notes revised.

2007 Revision: Committee notes revised.

2012 Revision: Committee notes revised.

Statutory References

§ 731.201(23), Fla. Stat. General definitions.

§ 731.301, Fla. Stat. Notice.

§ 733.612(19), Fla. Stat. Transactions authorized for the personal representative; exceptions.

§ 733.617, Fla. Stat. Compensation of personal representative.

§ 733.6171, Fla. Stat. Compensation of attorney for the personal representative.

§ 733.6175, Fla. Stat. Proceedings for review of employment of agents and compensation of personal representatives and employees of estate.

Rule References

Fla. Prob. R. 5.040 Notice.

Fla. Prob. R. 5.041 Service of pleadings and documents.

Fla. R. Jud. Admin. 2.516 Service of pleadings and documents.

Rule 5.360. Elective Share

(a) Election. An election to take the elective share may be filed by the surviving spouse, or on behalf of the surviving spouse by an attorney-in-fact or guardian of the property of the surviving spouse.

(1) *Election by Surviving Spouse.* An electing surviving spouse must file the election within the time required by law and promptly serve a copy of the election on the personal representative in the manner provided for service of formal notice.

(2) *Election by Attorney-in-Fact or Guardian of the Property of Surviving Spouse.*

(A) Petition for Approval. Before filing the election, the attorney-in-fact or guardian of the property of the surviving spouse must petition the court having jurisdiction of the probate proceeding for approval to make the election. The petition for approval must allege the authority to act on behalf of the surviving spouse and facts supporting the election.

(B) Notice of Petition. Upon receipt of the petition, the personal representative must promptly serve a copy of the petition by formal notice on all interested persons.

(C) Order Authorizing Election. If the election is approved, the order must include a finding that the election is in the best interests of the surviving spouse during the spouse's probable lifetime.

(D) Filing the Election. Upon entry of an order authorizing the filing of an election, the attorney-in-fact or guardian of the property must file the election within the later of the time provided by law or 30 days from service of the order and promptly serve a copy of the election on the personal representative in the manner provided for service of formal notice.

(b) Procedure for Election.

(1) *Extension.* Within the period provided by law to make the election, the surviving spouse or an attorney-in-fact or guardian of the property of the surviving spouse may petition the court for an extension of time for making an election or for approval to make the election. After notice and hearing the court

for good cause shown may extend the time for election. If the court grants the petition for an extension, the election must be filed within the time allowed by the extension.

(2) *Withdrawal of Election.* The surviving spouse, an attorney-in-fact, a guardian of the property of the surviving spouse, or the personal representative of the surviving spouse's estate may withdraw the election within the time provided by law.

(3) *Service of Notice.* Upon receipt of an election the personal representative must serve a notice of election within 20 days following service of the election, together with a copy of the election, on all interested persons in the manner provided for service of formal notice. The notice of election must indicate the names and addresses of the attorneys for the surviving spouse and the personal representative and must state that:

(A) persons receiving a notice of election may be required to contribute toward the satisfaction of the elective share;

(B) objections to the election must be served within 20 days after service of the copy of the notice of election; and

(C) if no objection to the election is timely served, an order determining the surviving spouse's entitlement to the elective share may be granted without further notice.

(4) *Objection to Election.* Within 20 days after service of the notice of election, an interested person may serve an objection to the election which must state with particularity the grounds on which the objection is based. The objecting party must serve copies of the objection on the surviving spouse and the personal representative. If an objection is served, the personal representative must promptly serve a copy of the objection on all other interested persons who have not previously been served with a copy of the objection.

(c) Determination of Entitlement.

(1) *No Objection Served.* If no objection to the election is timely served, the court must enter an order determining the spouse's entitlement to the elective share.

(2) *Objection Served.* If an objection to the election is timely served, the court must determine the surviving spouse's entitlement to the elective share after notice and hearing.

(d) Procedure to Determine Amount of Elective Share and Contribution.

(1) *Petition by Personal Representative.* After entry of the order determining the surviving spouse's entitlement to the elective share, the personal representative must file and serve a petition to determine the amount of the elective share. The petition must

(A) give the name and address of each direct recipient known to the personal representative;

(B) describe the proposed distribution of assets to satisfy the elective share, and the time and manner of distribution; and

(C) identify those direct recipients, if any, from whom a specified contribution will be required and state the amount of contribution sought from each.

(2) *Service of Inventory.* The inventory of the elective estate required by rule 5.340, together with the petition, must be served within 60 days after entry of the order determining entitlement to the elective share on all interested persons in the manner provided for service of formal notice.

(3) *Petition by Spouse.* If the personal representative does not file the petition to determine the amount of the elective share within 90 days from rendition of the order of entitlement, the electing spouse or the attorney-in-fact or the guardian of the property or personal representative of the electing spouse may file the petition specifying as particularly as is known the value of the elective share.

(4) *Objection to Amount of Elective Share.* Within 20 days after service of the petition to determine the amount of the elective share, an interested person may serve an objection to the amount of or distribution of assets to satisfy the elective share. The objection must state with particularity the grounds on which the objection is based. The objecting party must serve copies of the objection on the surviving spouse and the personal representative. If an objection is served, the personal representative must promptly serve a copy of the objection on all interested persons who have not previously been served.

(5) *Determination of Amount of Elective Share and Contribution.*

(A) No Objection Served. If no objection is timely served to the petition to determine the amount of the elective share, the court must enter an order on the petition.

(B) Objection Served. If an objection is timely served to the petition to determine the amount of the elective share, the court must determine the amount of the elective share and contribution after notice and hearing.

(6) *Order Determining Amount of Elective Share and Contribution.* The order must:

(A) set forth the amount of the elective share;

(B) identify the assets to be distributed to the surviving spouse in satisfaction of the elective share; and

(C) if contribution is necessary, specify the amount of contribution for which each direct recipient is liable.

(e) Relief From Duty to Enforce Contribution. A petition to relieve the personal representative from the duty to enforce contribution must state the grounds on which it is based and notice must be served on interested persons.

Amended Sept. 13, 1984, effective Jan. 1, 1985 (458 So.2d 1079); Sept. 29, 1988, effective Jan. 1, 1989 (537 So.2d 500); Sept. 24, 1992, effective Jan. 1, 1993 (607 So.2d 1306); Oct. 11, 2001 (807 So.2d 622); Sept. 29, 2005, effective Jan. 1, 2006 (912 So.2d 1178); Dec. 9, 2010 (51 So.3d 1146).

Committee Notes

The extensive rewrite of this rule in 2001 is intended to conform it with and provide procedures to accommodate amendments to Florida's elective share statutes, §§ 732.201 *et seq.*, Fla. Stat. Proceedings to determine entitlement to elective share are not specific adversary proceedings under rule 5.025(a), but may be declared adversary at the option of the party. Proceedings to determine the amount of elective share and contribution are specific adversary proceedings under rule 5.025(a). Requirements for service are intended to be consistent with the requirements for formal notice. Rule 5.040. Service of process may be required to obtain personal jurisdiction over direct recipients who are not otherwise interested persons and who have not voluntarily submitted themselves to the jurisdiction of the court. Rule 5.040(a)(3)(C); ch. 48, Fla. Stat. Process and Service of Process; ch. 49, Fla. Stat., Constructive Service of Process. An inventory of the elective estate should be afforded the same confidentiality as other estate inventories. § 733.604(1) and (2), Fla. Stat. In fulfilling his or her obligations under this rule, a personal representative is not required to make impractical or extended searches for property entering into the elective estate and the identities of direct recipients. Preexisting rights to dower and curtesy formerly addressed in subdivision (e) of this rule are now governed by new rule 5.365.

Counsel's attention is directed to Fla. Ethics Opinion 76–16, dated April 4, 1977, for guidance regarding the duties of an attorney with respect to spousal rights.

Rule History

1984 Revision: Extensive changes. Clarifies information to be included in a petition for elective share filed by a personal representative and specifies information to be included in an order determining elective share. Committee notes revised and expanded.

1988 Revision: Extensive changes. A new procedure has been added providing for optional service of a notice of election together with a copy of the election and a procedure to expose objections to and determine right to entitlement, separate from the pre-existing procedure of determination of amount and setting aside. Subdivisions (c) and (d) represent rule implementation of procedure in statute. Committee notes revised and expanded. Citation form changes in committee notes.

1992 Revision: Editorial change. Committee notes revised. Citation form changes in committee notes.

2001 Revision: Entire rule rewritten. Committee notes revised.

2003 Revision: Committee notes revised.

2005 Revision: Subdivision (a) amended to require service in the manner of formal notice of the notice of election. Subdivision (b)(3) amended to provide time period for personal representative to service notice of election on interested persons, and title revised. Subdivision (d)(2) amended to provide time limit and service requirement for elective estate inventory and petition for determination of amount of elective share. Committee notes revised.

2010 Cycle Report Revision: Committee notes revised.

2010 Out-of-Cycle Report Revision: Subdivision (a)(2) amended to conform to an amendment to § 732.2125, Florida Statutes.

2012 Revision: Committee notes revised.

Statutory References

§ 732.201, Fla. Stat. Right to elective share.

§ 732.2025, Fla. Stat. Definitions.

§ 732.2035, Fla. Stat. Property entering into elective estate.

§ 732.2045, Fla. Stat. Exclusions and overlapping application.

§ 732.2055, Fla. Stat. Valuation of the elective estate.

§ 732.2065, Fla. Stat. Amount of the elective share.

§ 732.2075, Fla. Stat. Sources from which elective share payable; abatement.

§ 732.2085, Fla. Stat. Liability of direct recipients and beneficiaries.

§ 732.2095, Fla. Stat. Valuation of property used to satisfy elective share.

§ 732.2125, Fla. Stat. Right of election; by whom exercisable.

§ 732.2135, Fla. Stat. Time of election; extensions; withdrawal.

§ 732.2145, Fla. Stat. Order of contribution; personal representative's duty to collect contribution.

§ 733.604, Fla. Stat. Inventories and accountings; public records exemptions.

Rule References

Fla. Prob. R. 5.025 Adversary proceedings.

Fla. Prob. R. 5.040 Notice.

Fla. Prob. R. 5.041 Service of pleadings and documents.

Fla. Prob. R. 5.340 Inventory.

Fla. R. Jud. Admin. 2.516 Service of pleadings and documents.

Fla. R. App. P. 9.020(h) Definitions.

Rule 5.365. Petition for Dower

A widow may file an extraordinary petition for assignment of dower. The petition shall be filed in the court of each county where the widow's husband had conveyed land in which the widow had not relinquished her right of dower before October 1, 1973. Formal notice shall be served on persons adversely affected. The proceedings shall be as similar as possible to those formerly existing for the ordinary assignment of dower.

Added Oct. 11, 2001 (807 So.2d 622). Amended Jan. 10, 2002 (816 So.2d 1095).

Committee Notes

Rule History

2001 Revision: Derived from former rule 5.360(e).

Statutory Reference

§ 732.111, Fla.Stat. Dower and curtesy abolished.

Rule 5.370. Sales of Real Property Where No Power Conferred

(a) Petition. When authorization or confirmation of the sale of real property is required, the personal representative shall file a verified petition setting forth the reasons for the sale, a description of the real property sold or proposed to be sold, and the price and terms of the sale.

(b) Order. If the sale is authorized or confirmed, the order shall describe the real property. An order authorizing a sale may provide for the public or private sale of the real property described therein, in parcels or as a whole. An order authorizing a private sale shall specify the price and terms of the sale. An order authorizing a public sale shall specify the type of notice of sale to be given by the personal representative.

Amended Sept. 13, 1984, effective Jan. 1, 1985 (458 So.2d 1079); Oct. 3, 1996, effective Jan. 1, 1997 (683 So.2d 78).

Committee Notes

Petitions under the rule are governed by section 733.610, Florida Statutes, under which sales are voidable by interested persons if there was a conflict of interest without full disclosure and consent, unless the will or contract entered into by the decedent authorized the transaction or it was approved by the court after notice to all interested persons, and by section 733.609, Florida Statutes, involving bad faith actions by the personal representative. Note provision for attorneys' fees.

Rule History

1984 Revision: Extensive changes. Notice of hearing on any petition concerning sale of real property is required by statute unless waived. The requirement to record a certified copy of the order approving sale of real estate in each county where the real property or any part thereof is situated has been deleted. Committee notes revised and expanded.

1988 Revision: Committee notes expanded. Citation form changes in committee notes.

1992 Revision: Committee notes revised. Citation form changes in committee notes.

1996 Revision: Editorial changes.

2012 Revision: Committee notes revised.

Statutory References

§ 733.609, Fla.Stat. Improper exercise of power; breach of fiduciary duty.

§ 733.610, Fla.Stat. Sale, encumbrance or transaction involving conflict of interest.

§ 733.613(1), Fla.Stat. Personal representative's right to sell real property.

§ 733.810, Fla.Stat. Distribution in kind; valuation.

Rule References

Fla. Prob. R. 5.020 Pleadings; verification; motions.

Fla. Prob. R. 5.040 Notice.

Fla. Prob. R. 5.041 Service of pleadings and documents.

Fla. Prob. R. 5.180 Waiver and consent.

Fla. R. Jud. Admin. 2.516 Service of pleadings and documents.

Rule 5.380. Compulsory Payment of Devises or Distributive Interests

(a) Petition. A beneficiary may file a petition setting forth the facts that entitle the beneficiary to compel payment of devises or distributive interests stating that the property will not be required for the payment of debts, family allowance, spouse's elective share, estate and inheritance taxes, claims, charges, and expenses of administration, or for providing funds for contribution or enforcing equalization in case of advancements.

(b) Order. If the court finds that the property will not be required for the purposes set forth in subdivision (a), it may enter an order describing the property to be surrendered or delivered and compelling the personal representative, prior to the final settlement of the personal representative's accounts, to do one or more of the following:

(1) Pay all or any part of a devise in money.

(2) Deliver specific personal property within the personal representative's custody and control.

(3) Pay all or any part of a distributive interest in the personal estate of a decedent.

(4) Surrender real property.

(c) Bond. Before the entry of an order of partial distribution, the court may require the person entitled to distribution to give a bond with sureties as prescribed by law.

Amended Sept. 13, 1984, effective Jan. 1, 1985 (458 So.2d 1079); Sept. 29, 1988, effective Jan. 1, 1989 (537 So.2d 500); Sept. 24, 1992, effective Jan. 1, 1993 (607 So.2d 1306).

Committee Notes

Rule History

1984 Revision: Extensive changes. Committee notes revised.

1988 Revision: Editorial change in caption of (a). Citation form change in committee notes.

1992 Revision: Editorial changes. Committee notes revised. Citation form changes in committee notes.

2003 Revision: Committee notes revised.

2012 Revision: Committee notes revised.

Statutory References

§ 731.301, Fla. Stat. Notice.

§ 733.802, Fla. Stat. Proceedings for compulsory payment of devises or distributive interest.

Rule References

Fla. Prob. R. 5.020 Pleadings; verification; motions.

Fla. Prob. R. 5.040 Notice.

Fla. Prob. R. 5.041 Service of pleadings and documents.

Fla. R. Jud. Admin. 2.516 Service of pleadings and documents.

Rule 5.385. Determination of Beneficiaries and Shares

(a) Beneficiaries and Shares. If a personal representative or other interested person is in doubt or is unable to determine with certainty beneficiaries entitled to an estate or the shares of any beneficiary of an estate, or a beneficiary entitled to any asset or interest in an estate, the personal representative or other interested person may petition the court to determine beneficiaries.

(b) Petition. The petition shall include:

(1) the names, residences, and post office addresses of all persons who may have an interest, except creditors of the decedent, known to the petitioner or ascertainable by diligent search and inquiry;

(2) a statement of the nature of the interest of each person;

(3) designation of any person believed to be a minor or incapacitated, and whether any person so designated is under legal guardianship in this state;

(4) a statement as to whether petitioner believes that there are, or may be, persons whose names are not known to petitioner who have claims against, or interest in, the estate as beneficiaries.

(c) Order. After formal notice and hearing, the court shall enter an order determining the beneficiaries or the shares and amounts they are entitled to receive, or both.

Added Sept. 29, 1988, effective Jan. 1, 1989 (537 So.2d 500). Amended Sept. 24, 1992, effective Jan. 1, 1993 (607 So.2d 1306); May 2, 2002 (824 So.2d 849); June 19, 2003 (848 So.2d 1069); July 12, 2007 (964 So.2d 140).

Committee Notes

This rule represents a rule implementation of the procedure formerly found in section 733.105, Florida Statutes. It is not intended to change the effect of the statute from which it was derived but has been reformatted to conform with the structure of these rules. It is not intended to create a new procedure or modify an existing procedure.

Rule History

1988 Revision: New rule.

1992 Revision: Editorial changes. Committee notes revised. Citation form changes in committee notes.

2002 Revision: Subdivision (c) added to implement procedure formerly found in section 733.105(2), Florida Statutes. Committee notes revised.

2003 Revision: Change in subdivision (c) to replace "heirs or devisees" with "beneficiaries" to incorporate term used in section 733.105, Florida Statutes. Committee notes revised.

2007 Revision: Committee notes revised.

2012 Revision: Committee notes revised.

2014 Revision: Fla. R. Jud. Admin. 2.425(b)(6) provides an exception for the full name of any minor "in any document or order affecting minor's ownership of real property." Committee notes revised.

Statutory References

ch. 49, Fla. Stat. Constructive service of process.

§ 731.201(2), (23), Fla. Stat. General definitions.

§ 731.301, Fla. Stat. Notice.

§ 733.105, Fla. Stat. Determination of beneficiaries.

Rule References

Fla. Prob. R. 5.025 Adversary proceedings.

Fla. Prob. R. 5.040 Notice.

Fla. Prob. Rule 5.041 Service of pleadings and documents.

Fla. Prob. R. 5.120 Administrator ad litem and guardian ad litem.

Fla. Prob. R. 5.205(a)(5) Filing evidence of death.

Fla. R. Jud. Admin. 2.516 Service of pleadings and documents.

Fla. R. Jud. Admin. 2.425 Minimization of the Filing of Sensitive Information.

Rule 5.386. Escheat

(a) Escheat Proceeding. If it appears to the personal representative that an estate may escheat or there is doubt about the existence of any person entitled to the estate, the personal representative shall institute a proceeding to determine beneficiaries within 1 year after letters have been issued to the personal representative, and notice shall be served on the Department of Legal Affairs. If the personal representative fails to institute the proceeding within the time fixed, it may be instituted by the Department of Legal Affairs.

(b) Court's Report. On or before January 15 of each year, each court shall furnish to the Department of Legal Affairs a list of all estates being administered in which no person appears to be entitled to the property and the personal representative has not instituted a proceeding for the determination of beneficiaries.

(c) Administration. Except as herein provided, escheated estates shall be administered as other estates.

Added Sept. 29, 1988, effective Jan. 1, 1989 (537 So.2d 500). Amended Sept. 24, 1992, effective Jan. 1, 1993 (607 So.2d 1306).

Committee Notes

This rule represents a rule implementation of the procedure formerly found in section 732.107, Florida Statutes. It is not intended to change the effect of the statute from which it was derived but has been reformatted to conform with the structure of these rules. It is not intended to create a new procedure or modify an existing procedure.

Rule History

1988 Revision: New rule.

1992 Revision: Editorial change. Committee notes revised. Citation form changes in committee notes.

2003 Revision: Committee notes revised.

2012 Revision: Committee notes revised.

Statutory References

§ 732.107, Fla. Stat. Escheat.

§ 733.105, Fla. Stat. Determination of beneficiaries.

§ 733.816, Fla. Stat. Disposition of unclaimed property held by personal representatives.

Rule References

Fla. Prob. R. 5.020 Pleadings; verification; motions.

Fla. Prob. R. 5.040 Notice.

Fla. Prob. R. 5.041 Service of pleadings and documents.

Fla. Prob. R. 5.042 Time.

Fla. Prob. R. 5.385 Determination of beneficiaries and shares.

Fla. R. Jud. Admin. 2.516 Service of pleadings and documents.

Rule 5.395. Notice of Federal Estate Tax Return

When a federal estate tax return is filed, required to be filed, or will be filed, the personal representative shall file a notice stating the due date of the return. The notice shall be filed within 12 months from the date letters are issued and copies of the notice shall be served on interested persons. Whenever the due date is subsequently extended, similar notice shall be filed and served.

Added Sept. 13, 1984, effective Jan. 1, 1985 (458 So.2d 1079). Amended Sept. 26, 2013, effective Jan. 1, 2014 (123 So.3d 31).

Committee Notes

The purpose of the rule is to require notification to the court and all interested persons that the time for closing the estate is extended when a federal estate tax return is required.

Rule History

1984 Revision: New rule.

1988 Revision: Citation form change in committee notes.

1992 Revision: Committee notes revised. Citation form changes in committee notes.

2003 Revision: Committee notes revised.

2013 Revision: Clarifies the available option to file a federal tax return even if one is not required by state or federal rule or law.

Rule Reference

Fla. Prob. R. 5.400 Distribution and discharge.

Rule 5.400. Distribution and Discharge

(a) Petition for Discharge; Final Accounting. A personal representative who has completed administration except for distribution shall file a final accounting and a petition for discharge including a plan of distribution.

(b) Contents.

The petition for discharge shall contain a statement:

(1) that the personal representative has fully administered the estate;

(2) that all claims which were presented have been paid, settled, or otherwise disposed of;

(3) that the personal representative has paid or made provision for taxes and expenses of administration;

(4) showing the amount of compensation paid or to be paid to the personal representative, attorneys, accountants, appraisers, or other agents employed by the personal representative and the manner of determining that compensation;

(5) showing a plan of distribution which shall include:

(A) a schedule of all prior distributions;

(B) the property remaining in the hands of the personal representative for distribution;

(C) a schedule describing the proposed distribution of the remaining assets; and

(D) the amount of funds retained by the personal representative to pay expenses that are incurred in the distribution of the remaining assets and termination of the estate administration;

(6) that any objections to the accounting, the compensation paid or proposed to be paid, or the proposed distribution of assets must be filed within 30 days from the date of service of the last of the petition for discharge or final accounting; and also that within 90 days after filing of the objection, a notice of hearing thereon must be served or the objection is abandoned; and

(7) that objections, if any, shall be in writing and shall state with particularity the item or items to which the objection is directed and the grounds on which the objection is based.

(c) Closing Estate; Extension. The final accounting and petition for discharge shall be filed and served on interested persons within 12 months after issuance of letters for an estate not filing a federal estate tax return, otherwise within 12 months from the date the return is due, unless the time is extended by the court for cause shown after notice to interested persons. The petition to extend time shall state the status of the estate and the reason for the extension.

(d) Distribution. The personal representative shall promptly distribute the estate property in accordance with the plan of distribution, unless objections are filed as provided in these rules.

(e) Discharge. On receipt of evidence that the estate has been fully administered and properly distributed, the court shall enter an order discharging the personal representative and releasing the surety on any bond.

Amended March 31, 1977, effective July 1, 1977 (344 So.2d 828); Sept. 4, 1980, effective Jan. 1, 1981 (387 So.2d 949); Sept. 13, 1984, effective Jan. 1, 1985 (458 So.2d 1079); Sept. 29, 1988, effective Jan. 1, 1989 (537 So.2d 500); Sept. 24, 1992, effective Jan. 1, 1993 (607 So.2d 1306); Oct. 3, 1996, effective Jan. 1, 1997 (683 So.2d 78); Sept. 29, 2005, effective Jan. 1, 2006 (912 So.2d 1178); Feb. 1, 2007 (948 So.2d 735); July 12, 2007 (964 So.2d 140); Sept. 26, 2013, effective Jan. 1, 2014 (123 So.3d 31).

Committee Notes

The rule establishes a procedure for giving notice and serving the final accounting, petition for discharge, and plan of distribution to all interested persons prior to distribution and discharge. No distinction is made in plans of distribution which distribute estate property in kind among multiple residual beneficiaries proportionate to their respective interests and those which include equalizing adjustments in cash or property and which do not make prorated distribution. If disclosure of the compensation or disclosure of the manner of determining the compensation in the petition for discharge is to be waived, the form of waiver must conform to rule 5.180(b).

Rule History

1980 Revision: Change in prior (a)(6) to require that an objection set forth the basis on which it is being made.

1984 Revision: This rule has been substantially revised. Portions of the prior rule are now incorporated in rules 5.400 and 5.401. The committee has included the procedure for filing and serving of objections to the final accounting, petition for discharge, plan of distribution, or compensation in rule 5.401.

1988 Revision: Subdivision (b)(1) is deleted to avoid duplication with rule 5.346. Subdivision (c) is amended to add the 12–month time specification of section 733.901(1), Florida Statutes. Committee notes revised. Citation form changes in committee notes.

1992 Revision: Subdivision (b)(5)(D) is added. Editorial changes. Committee notes revised. Citation form changes in committee notes.

1996 Revision: Addition in (a)(4) of specific attorney fee compensation disclosure requirements found in § 733.6171(9), Florida Statutes, and expanded to cover all compensation. Committee notes revised.

2003 Revision: Committee notes revised.

2005 Revision: Subdivision (f) deleted to avoid duplication with rule 5.180.

2006 Revision: Committee notes revised.

2007 Revision: Committee notes revised.

2012 Revision: Committee notes revised.

2013 Revision: Clarifies the available option to file a federal tax return even if one is not required by state or federal rule or law.

Statutory References

§ 731.201(12), (23), Fla. Stat. General definitions.

§ 731.302, Fla. Stat. Waiver and consent by interested person.

§ 733.809, Fla. Stat. Right of retainer.

§ 733.810, Fla. Stat. Distribution in kind; valuation.

§ 733.811, Fla. Stat. Distribution; right or title of distributee.

§ 733.812, Fla. Stat. Improper distribution or payment; liability of distributee or payee.

§ 733.901, Fla. Stat. Final discharge.

Rule References

Fla. Prob. R. 5.020 Pleadings; verification; motions.

Fla. Prob. R. 5.040 Notice.

Fla. Prob. R. 5.041 Service of pleadings and documents.

Fla. Prob. R. 5.042 Time.

Fla. Prob. R. 5.180 Waiver and consent.

Fla. Prob. R. 5.330 Execution by personal representative.

Fla. Prob. R. 5.346 Fiduciary accounting.

Fla. Prob. R. 5.401 Objections to petition for discharge or final accounting.

Fla. R. Jud. Admin. 2.250(a)(1)(D) Time standards for trial and appellate courts and reporting requirements.

Fla. R. Jud. Admin. 2.516 Service of pleadings and documents.

Rule 5.401. Objections to Petition for Discharge or Final Accounting

(a) Objections. An interested person may object to the petition for discharge or final accounting within 30 days after the service of the later of the petition or final accounting on that interested person.

(b) Contents. Written objections to the petition for discharge or final accounting must state with particularity the items to which the objections are directed and must state the grounds on which the objections are based.

(c) Service. Copies of the objections shall be served by the objector on the personal representative and interested persons not later than 30 days after the last date on which the petition for discharge or final accounting was served on the objector.

(d) Hearing on Objections. Any interested person may set a hearing on the objections. Notice of the hearing shall be given to all interested persons. If a notice of hearing on the objections is not served within 90 days of filing of the objections, the objections shall be deemed abandoned and the personal representative may make distribution as set forth in the plan of distribution.

(e) Order on Objections. The court shall sustain or overrule any objections to the petition for discharge and final accounting and shall determine a plan of distribution.

(f) Discharge. On receipt of evidence that the estate has been distributed according to the plan determined by the court and the claims of creditors have been paid or otherwise disposed of, the court shall enter an order discharging the personal representative and releasing the surety on any bond.

Added Sept. 13, 1984, effective Jan. 1, 1985 (458 So.2d 1079). Amended Sept. 29, 1988, effective Jan. 1, 1989 (537 So.2d 500); Oct. 3, 1996, effective Jan. 1, 1997 (683 So.2d 78); July 12, 2007 (964 So.2d 140).

Committee Notes

Rule History

1984 Revision: New rule. Objections to the petition for discharge or final accounting were formerly under prior rule 5.400. Clarifies procedure for objections.

1988 Revision: Editorial changes in (a). Committee notes revised. Citation form changes in committee notes.

1992 Revision: Committee notes revised. Citation form changes in committee notes.

1996 Revision: Subdivision (d) amended to clarify that 90–day period pertains to service of hearing notice, not the actual hearing date.

2003 Revision: Committee notes revised.

2007 Revision: Committee notes revised.

2012 Revision: Committee notes revised.

Statutory References

§ 731.201(12), (23), Fla. Stat. General definitions.

§ 733.6175, Fla. Stat. Proceedings for review of employment of agents and compensation of personal representatives and employees of estate.

§ 733.901, Fla. Stat. Final discharge.

Rule References

Fla. Prob. R. 5.020 Pleadings; verification; motions.

Fla. Prob. R. 5.040 Notice.

Fla. Prob. R. 5.041 Service of pleadings and documents.

Fla. Prob. R. 5.042 Time.

Fla. Prob. R. 5.180 Waiver and consent.

Fla. Prob. R. 5.400 Distribution and discharge.

Fla. R. Jud. Admin. 2.516 Service of pleadings and documents.

Rule 5.402. Notice of Lien on Protected Homestead

(a) Filing. If the personal representative has recorded a notice of lien on protected homestead, the personal representative shall file a copy of the recorded notice in the probate proceeding.

(b) Contents. The notice of lien shall contain:

(1) the name and address of the personal representative and the personal representative's attorney;

(2) the legal description of the real property;

(3) to the extent known, the name and address of each person appearing to have an interest in the property; and

(4) a statement that the personal representative has expended or is obligated to expend funds to preserve, maintain, insure, or protect the property and that the lien stands as security for recovery of those expenditures and obligations incurred, including fees and costs.

(c) Service. A copy of the recorded notice of lien shall be served on interested persons in the manner provided for service of formal notice.

Added Sept. 29, 2005, effective Jan. 1, 2006 (912 So.2d 1178).

Committee Notes

Rule History

2005 Revision: New rule.

2012 Revision: Committee notes revised.

Statutory References

§ 733.608, Fla. Stat. General power of the personal representative.

Rule References

Fla. Prob. R. 5.040 Notice.

Fla. Prob. R. 5.041 Service of pleadings and documents.

Fla. Prob. R. 5.403 Proceedings to determine amount of lien on protected homestead.

Fla. Prob. R. 5.404 Notice of taking possession of protected homestead.

Fla. Prob. R. 5.405 Proceedings to determine protected homestead real property.

Fla. R. Jud. Admin. 2.516 Service of pleadings and documents.

Rule 5.403. Proceedings to Determine Amount of Lien on Protected Homestead

(a) Petition. A personal representative or interested person may file a petition to determine the amount of any lien on protected homestead.

(b) Contents. The petition shall be verified by the petitioner and shall state:

(1) the name and address of the personal representative and the personal representative's attorney;

(2) the interest of the petitioner;

(3) the legal description of the real property;

(4) to the extent known, the name and address of each person appearing to have an interest in the property; and

(5) to the extent known, the amounts paid or obligated to be paid by the personal representative to preserve, maintain, insure, or protect the protected homestead, including fees and costs.

(c) Service. The petition shall be served on interested persons by formal notice.

Added Sept. 29, 2005, effective January 1, 2006 (912 So.2d 1178).

Committee Notes

Rule History

2005 Revision: New rule.

2012 Revision: Committee notes revised.

Statutory References

§ 733.608, Fla. Stat. General power of the personal representative.

Rule References

Fla. Prob. R. 5.040 Notice.

Fla. Prob. R. 5.041 Service of pleadings and documents.

Fla. Prob. R. 5.402 Notice of lien on protected homestead.

Fla. Prob. R. 5.404 Notice of taking possession of protected homestead.

Fla. Prob. R. 5.405 Proceedings to determine protected homestead real property.

Fla. R. Jud. Admin. 2.516 Service of pleadings and documents.

Rule 5.404. Notice of Taking Possession of Protected Homestead

(a) Filing of Notice. If a personal representative takes possession of what appears reasonably to be protected homestead pending a determination of its homestead status, the personal representative shall file a notice of that act.

(b) Contents of Notice. The notice shall contain:

(1) a legal description of the property;

(2) a statement of the limited purpose for preserving, insuring, and protecting it for the heirs or devisees pending a determination of the homestead status;

(3) the name and address of the personal representative and the personal representative's attorney;

(4) if the personal representative is in possession when the notice is filed, the date the personal representative took possession.

(c) Service of Notice. The notice shall be served in the manner provided for service of formal notice on interested persons and on any person in actual possession of the property.

Added May 2, 2002 (824 So.2d 849). Amended Sept. 29, 2005, effective Jan. 1, 2006 (912 So.2d 1178); Sept. 26, 2013, effective Jan. 1, 2014 (123 So.3d 31).

Committee Notes

Rule History

2002 Revision: New rule.

2005 Revision: Term "devisees" substituted for "beneficiaries" in subdivision (b)(2) to clarify the status of persons interested in protected homestead. Committee notes revised.

2013 Revision: Deletes subdivision (b)(4) because the required information is not appropriate for a Notice of Taking possession, nor does it comply with the Americans with Disabilities Act requirements.

Statutory References

§ 732.401, Fla. Stat. Descent of homestead.

§ 732.4015, Fla. Stat. Devise of homestead.

§ 733.608(2), Fla. Stat. General power of the personal representative.

Rule References

Fla. Prob. R. 5.402 Notice of lien on protected homestead.

Fla. Prob. R. 5.403 Proceedings to determine amount of lien on protected homestead.

Fla. Prob. R. 5.405 Proceedings to determine protected homestead real property.

Rule 5.405. Proceedings to Determine Protected Homestead Real Property

(a) Petition. An interested person may file a petition to determine protected homestead real property owned by the decedent.

(b) Contents. The petition shall be verified by the petitioner and shall state:

(1) the date of the decedent's death;

(2) the county of the decedent's domicile at the time of death;

(3) the name of the decedent's surviving spouse and the names of surviving descendants, and a statement as to whether the decedent had any minor children as of the date of death. If so, they should be identified with name and year of birth;

(4) a legal description of the property owned by the decedent on which the decedent resided; and

(5) any other facts in support of the petition.

(c) Order. The court's order on the petition shall describe the real property and determine whether any of the real property constituted the protected homestead of the decedent. If the court determines that any of the real property was the protected homestead of the decedent, the order shall identify by name the person or persons entitled to the protected homestead real property and define the interest of each.

Added Sept. 13, 1984, effective Jan. 1, 1985 (458 So.2d 1079). Amended Sept. 29, 1988, effective Jan. 1, 1989 (537 So.2d 500); Sept. 24, 1992, effective Jan. 1, 1993 (607 So.2d 1306); Oct. 3, 1996, effective Jan. 1, 1997 (683 So.2d 78); May 2, 2002 (824 So.2d 849); July 12, 2007 (964 So.2d 140); May 22, 2014, effective May 22, 2014 (139 So.3d 875).

Committee Notes

This rule establishes the procedure by which the personal representative or any interested person may petition the court for a determination that certain real property constituted the decedent's protected homestead property, in accordance with article X, section 4 of the Florida Constitution. The jurisdiction of the court to determine constitutional protected homestead property was established by *In re Noble's Estate*, 73 So. 2d 873 (Fla. 1954).

Rule History

1984 Revision: New rule.

1988 Revision: Editorial change in (a). Subdivision (b)(4) amended to conform to constitutional change. Committee notes revised. Citation form change in committee notes.

1992 Revision: Editorial change. Committee notes revised. Citation form changes in committee notes.

1996 Revision: Subdivision (c) amended to require description of real property that is the subject of the petition, description of any homestead property, and definition of specific interests of persons entitled to homestead real property.

2002 Revision: Replaces "homestead" with "protected homestead" throughout to conform to addition of term in section 731.201(29), Florida Statutes. Committee notes revised.

2003 Revision: Committee notes revised.

2007 Revision: Committee notes revised.

2010 Revision: Committee notes revised.

2012 Revision: Committee notes revised.

2014 Revision: Amends subdivisions (b)(3) and (c) to conform to Fla. R. Jud. Admin. 2.425. Committee notes revised.

Constitutional Reference

Art. X, § 4, Fla. Const.

Statutory References

§ 731.104, Fla. Stat. Verification of documents.

§ 731.201(33), Fla. Stat. General definitions.

§ 732.401, Fla. Stat. Descent of homestead.

§ 732.4015, Fla. Stat. Devise of homestead.

§ 733.607, Fla. Stat. Possession of estate.

§ 733.608, Fla. Stat. General power of the personal representative.

Rule References

Fla. Prob. R. 5.020 Pleadings; verification; motions.

Fla. Prob. R. 5.040 Notice.

Fla. Prob. R. 5.041 Service of pleadings and documents.

Fla. Prob. R. 5.205(a)(6) Filing evidence of death.

Fla. Prob. R. 5.340 Inventory.

Fla. Prob. R. 5.404 Notice of taking possession of protected homestead.

Fla. R. Jud. Admin. 2.516 Service of pleadings and documents.

Fla. R. Jud. Admin. 2.425 Minimization of the Filing of Sensitive Information.

Rule 5.406. Proceedings to Determine Exempt Property

(a) Petition. An interested person may file a petition to determine exempt property within the time allowed by law.

(b) Contents. The petition shall be verified by the petitioner and shall:

(1) describe the property and the basis on which it is claimed as exempt property; and

(2) state the name and address of the decedent's surviving spouse or, if none, the names and addresses of decedent's children entitled by law to the exempt property and the year of birth of those who are minors.

(c) Order. The court shall determine each item of exempt property and its value, if necessary to determine its exempt status, and order the surrender of that property to the persons entitled to it.

Added Sept. 13, 1984, effective Jan. 1, 1985 (458 So.2d 1079). Amended Sept. 29, 1988, effective Jan. 1, 1989 (537 So.2d 500); Oct. 3, 1996, effective Jan. 1, 1997 (683 So.2d 78); Sept. 2, 2010, effective Jan. 1, 2011 (50 So.3d 578); May 22, 2014, effective May 22, 2014 (139 So.3d 875).

Committee Notes

This rule establishes the procedure by which the personal representative or any interested person may petition the court for determination of exempt property in accordance with article X, section 4 of the Florida Constitution and section 732.402, Florida Statutes.

Section 732.402, Florida Statutes, specifies the time within which the petition to determine exempt property must be filed, within 4 months after the date of service of the notice of administration, unless extended as provided in the statute.

Rule History

1984 Revision: New rule.

1988 Revision: Subdivision (a) revised to reflect editorial changes and to require verification. Subdivision (b)(1) revised to require the basis for asserting exempt property status. Subdivision (b)(2) added the requirement of stating addresses of those entitled to exempt property. Subdivision (c) revised to reflect editorial changes and to require determination of the value of each item of exempt property. Committee notes revised.

1992 Revision: Committee notes revised. Citation form changes in committee notes.

1996 Revision: Editorial changes in rule to conform to similar language in rule 5.405. Committee notes revised.

2003 Revision: Committee notes revised.

2010 Revision: Subdivision (c) amended to limit the instances in which the value of the property claimed as exempt needs to be stated in the order.

2012 Revision: Committee notes revised.

2014 Revision: Subdivision (b)(2) amended to conform to Fla. R. Jud. Admin. 2.425 and provide the year of birth of a minor. Committee notes revised.

Statutory References

§ 731.104, Fla. Stat. Verification of documents.

§ 732.402, Fla. Stat. Exempt property.

Rule References

Fla. Prob. R. 5.020 Pleadings; verification; motions.

Fla. Prob. R. 5.040 Notice.

Fla. Prob. R. 5.041 Service of pleadings and documents.

Fla. Prob. R. 5.042 Time.

Fla. Prob. R. 5.420 Disposition of personal property without administration.

Fla. R. Jud. Admin. 2.516 Service of pleadings and documents.

Fla. R. Jud. Admin. 2.425 Minimization of the Filing of Sensitive Information.

Rule 5.407. Proceedings to Determine Family Allowance

(a) Petition. An interested person may file a petition to determine family allowance.

(b) Contents. The petition shall be verified by the petitioner and shall:

(1) state the names and addresses of the decedent's surviving spouse and the decedent's adult lineal heirs and the initials, address, and year of birth of the decedents' lineal heirs who are minors and who were being supported by the decedent or who were entitled to be supported by the decedent at the time of the decedent's death; and

(2) for each person for whom an allowance is sought, state the adult person's name, or minor child's initials, and relationship to the decedent, the basis on which the allowance is claimed, and the amount sought.

(c) Order. The order shall identify the persons entitled to the allowance, the amount to which each is entitled, the method of payment, and to whom payment should be made.

Added June 19, 2003, effective Jan. 1, 2004 (848 So.2d 1069). Amended Oct. 18, 2012, effective, *nunc pro tunc*, Sept. 1, 2012 (102 So.3d 505); May 22, 2014, effective May 22, 2014 (139 So.3d 875).

Committee Notes

Rule History

2003 Revision: New rule.

2012 Revision: Editorial change in (b)(1) for gender neutrality. Committee notes revised.

2014 Revision: Subdivisions (b)(1) and (b)(2) are amended to conform to Fla. R. Jud. Admin. 2.425. Committee notes revised.

Statutory References

§ 731.104, Fla. Stat. Verification of documents.

§ 732.403, Fla. Stat. Family allowance.

Rule References

Fla. Prob. R. 5.020 Pleadings; verification; motions.

Fla. Prob. R. 5.040 Notice.

Fla. Prob. R. 5.041 Service of pleadings and documents.

Fla. R. Jud. Admin. 2.516 Service of pleadings and documents.

Fla. R. Jud. Admin. 2.425 Minimization of the Filing of Sensitive Information.

Rule 5.420. Disposition of Personal Property Without Administration

(a) Application. An interested person may request a disposition of the decedent's personal property without administration. An application signed by the applicant shall set forth:

(1) the description and value of the exempt property;

(2) the description and value of the other assets of the decedent;

(3) the amount of preferred funeral expenses and reasonable and necessary medical and hospital expenses for the last 60 days of the last illness together with accompanying statements or payment receipts; and

(4) each requested payment or distribution of personal property.

(b) Exempt Property. If the decedent's personal property includes exempt property, or property that can be determined to be exempt property, the application must also be signed by all persons entitled to the exempt property or by their representative.

(c) Preparation. On request, the clerk shall assist the applicant in the preparation of the required writing.

(d) Disposition. If the court is satisfied that disposition without administration is appropriate, the court may, without hearing, by letter or other writing authorize the payment, transfer, or disposition of the decedent's personal property to those persons entitled to it.

Amended March 31, 1977, effective July 1, 1977 (344 So.2d 828); Sept. 13, 1984, effective Jan. 1, 1985 (458 So.2d 1079); Sept. 29, 1988, effective Jan. 1, 1989 (531 So.2d 1261); Sept. 24, 1992, effective Jan. 1, 1993 (607 So.2d 1306).

Committee Notes

Section 732.402, Florida Statutes, requires persons entitled to exempt property, which excludes property specifically or demonstratively devised, to file timely a petition to determine exempt property. Accordingly, disposition of personal property under this rule should not be granted if decedent's personal property includes exempt property without all persons entitled thereto agreeing to such disposition.

Rule History

1977 Revision: Permits the clerk to perform limited ministerial acts in the completion of the application.

1984 Revision: Editorial changes. Delineates the required contents of the application. Committee notes revised.

1988 Revision: Subdivision (a)(3) changed to require applicant to attach accompanying statements or payment receipts regarding priority expenses. Subdivision (b) added to require persons entitled to exempt property to agree to the proposed disposition. Committee notes expanded.

1992 Revision: Editorial change. Committee notes revised. Citation form changes in committee notes.

2003 Revision: Committee notes revised.

Statutory References

§ 732.402, Fla. Stat. Exempt property.

§ 735.301, Fla. Stat. Disposition without administration.

Rule Reference

Fla. Prob. R. 5.205(a)(4) Filing evidence of death.

Rule 5.430. Resignation of Personal Representative

(a) Resignation. A personal representative may resign with court approval.

(b) Petition for Resignation. The personal representative seeking to resign shall file a petition for resignation. The petition shall be verified and shall state:

(1) the personal representative desires to resign and be relieved of all powers, duties, and obligations as personal representative;

(2) the status of the estate administration and that the interests of the estate will not be jeopardized if the resignation is accepted;

(3) whether a proceeding for accounting, surcharge, or indemnification or other proceeding against the resigning personal representative is pending; and

(4) whether the appointment of a successor fiduciary is necessary. If the petition nominates a successor fiduciary, it shall state the nominee's priority under the Florida Probate Code, if any, and that the nominee is qualified to serve under the laws of Florida.

(c) Service. The petition shall be served by formal notice on all interested persons and the personal representative's surety, if any.

(d) Appointment of Successor. Before accepting the resignation, the court shall determine the necessity for appointment of a successor fiduciary. If there is no joint personal representative serving, the court shall appoint a successor fiduciary.

(e) Acceptance of Resignation. The court may accept the resignation and revoke the letters of the resigning personal representative if the interests of the estate are not jeopardized. Acceptance of the resignation shall not exonerate the resigning personal representative or the resigning personal representative's surety from liability.

(f) Delivery of Records and Property. The resigning personal representative shall immediately upon acceptance of the resignation by the court deliver to the remaining personal representative or the successor fiduciary all of the records of the estate and all property of the estate, unless otherwise directed by the court.

(g) Petition for Discharge; Accounting. The resigning personal representative shall file an accounting and a petition for discharge within 30 days after the date that the letters of the resigning personal representative are revoked by the court. The petition for discharge shall be verified and shall state:

(1) that the letters of the resigning personal representative have been revoked;

(2) that the resigning personal representative has surrendered all undistributed estate assets, records, documents, papers, and other property of or concerning the estate to the remaining personal representative or the successor fiduciary; and

(3) the amount of compensation paid or to be paid the resigning personal representative and the attorney and other persons employed by the resigning personal representative.

(h) Notice, Filing, and Objections to Accounting. Notice of, filing of, and objections to the accounting of the resigning personal representative shall be as provided in rule 5.345.

(i) Notice of Filing and Objections to Petition for Discharge.

(1) Notice of filing and a copy of the petition for discharge shall be served on all interested persons. The notice shall state that objections to the petition for discharge must be filed within 30 days after the later of service of the petition or service of the accounting on that interested person.

(2) Any interested person may file an objection to the petition for discharge within 30 days after the later of service of the petition or service of the accounting on that interested person. Any objection not filed within such time shall be deemed abandoned. An objection shall be in writing and shall state with particularity the item or items to which the objection is directed and the grounds on which the objection is based.

(3) The objecting party shall serve a copy of the objection on the resigning personal representative and other interested persons.

(4) Any interested person may set a hearing on the objections. Notice of the hearing shall be given to the resigning personal representative and other interested persons.

(j) Failure to File Accounting or Deliver Records or Property. The resigning personal representative shall be subject to contempt proceedings if the resigning personal representative fails to file an accounting or fails to deliver all property of the estate and all estate records under the control of the resigning personal representative to the remaining personal representative or the successor fiduciary within the time prescribed by this rule or by court order.

(k) Discharge. The court shall enter an order discharging the resigning personal representative and releasing the surety on any bond after the court is satisfied that the resigning personal representative has delivered all records and property of the estate to the remaining personal representative or the successor fiduciary; that all objections, if any, to the accounting of the resigning personal representative have been withdrawn, abandoned, or judicially resolved; and that the liability of the resigning personal representative has been determined and satisfied.

Amended Sept. 29, 1988, effective Jan. 1, 1989 (537 So.2d 500); Sept. 24, 1992, effective Jan. 1, 1993 (607 So.2d 1306); June 19, 2003 (848 So.2d 1069); July 12, 2007 (964 So.2d 140).

Committee Notes

In the event of resignation of a personal representative, if a joint personal representative is not serving, the successor fiduciary must file an oath and designation of a successor resident agent.

This rule was revised to implement the revisions to the probate code that govern resignation of personal representative. The committee intended to separate the procedure with respect to resignation from removal because these proceedings may differ in practice.

Rule History

1975 Revision: The rule provides for the orderly succession of personal representatives in the event a personal representative resigns or is removed.

1977 Revision: Editorial change in committee note.

1988 Revision: Editorial changes; captions added to subdivisions. Committee notes revised. Citation form changes in committee notes.

1992 Revision: Editorial changes. Committee notes revised. Citation form changes in committee notes.

2003 Revision: Rule completely revised to comply with statutory changes. Committee notes revised.

2007 Revision: Committee notes revised.

2012 Revision: Committee notes revised.

Statutory References

§ 731.104, Fla. Stat. Verification of documents.

§ 731.201(23), Fla. Stat. General definitions.

§ 733.101, Fla. Stat. Venue of probate proceedings.

§ 733.502, Fla. Stat. Resignation of personal representative.

§ 733.503, Fla. Stat. Appointment of successor upon resignation.

§ 733.5035, Fla. Stat. Surrender of assets after resignation.

§ 733.5036, Fla. Stat. Accounting and discharge following resignation.

Rule References

Fla. Prob. R. 5.020 Pleadings; verification; motions.

Fla. Prob. R. 5.040 Notice.

Fla. Prob. R. 5.041 Service of pleadings and documents.

Fla. Prob. R. 5.180 Waiver and consent.

Fla. Prob. R. 5.310 Disqualification of personal representative; notification.

Fla. Prob. R. 5.330 Execution by personal representative.

Fla. Prob. R. 5.345 Accountings other than personal representatives' final accountings.

Fla. Prob. R. 5.346 Fiduciary accounting.

Fla. Prob. R. 5.401 Objections to petition for discharge or final accounting.

Fla. R. Jud. Admin. 2.516 Service of pleadings and documents.

Rule 5.440. Proceedings for Removal of Personal Representative

(a) Commencement of Proceeding. The court on its own motion may remove, or any interested person by petition may commence a proceeding to remove, a personal representative. A petition for removal shall state the facts constituting the grounds upon which removal is sought, and shall be filed in the court having jurisdiction over the administration of the estate.

(b) Accounting. A removed personal representative shall file an accounting within 30 days after removal.

(c) Delivery of Records and Property. A removed personal representative shall, immediately after removal or within such time prescribed by court order, deliver to the remaining personal representative or to the successor fiduciary all of the records of the estate and all of the property of the estate.

(d) Failure to File Accounting or Deliver Records and Property. If a removed personal representative fails to file an accounting or fails to deliver all property of the estate and all estate records under the control of the removed personal representative to the remaining personal representative or to the successor fiduciary within the time prescribed by this rule or by court order, the removed personal representative shall be subject to contempt proceedings.

Amended Sept. 4, 1980, effective Jan. 1, 1981 (387 So.2d 949); Sept. 13, 1984, effective Jan. 1, 1985 (458 So.2d 1079); Sept. 29, 1988, effective Jan. 1, 1989 (537 So.2d 500); Sept. 24, 1992, effective Jan. 1, 1993 (607 So.2d 1306); May 2, 2002 (824 So.2d 849); July 12, 2007 (964 So.2d 140); Dec. 9, 2010 (51 So.3d 1146).

Committee Notes

The revision of subdivision (a) of this rule by the addition of its final phrase represents a rule implementation of the procedure found in section 733.505, Florida Statutes. It is not intended to change the effect of the statute from which it was derived but has been reformatted to conform with the structure of these rules. It is not intended to create a new procedure or modify an existing procedure.

Rule History

1980 Revision: Subdivision (a) amended to require formal notice to interested persons and to delete requirement that court give directions as to mode of notice. Surety authorized to petition for removal.

1984 Revision: Editorial changes. Provisions in prior rule for contempt have been deleted since the court has the inherent power to punish for contempt. Committee notes revised.

1988 Revision: Last phrase of (a) added to implement the procedure found in section 733.505, Florida Statutes. Subdivision (b) amended to parallel interim accounting rules. Deletes ability to extend time to file and adds reference to court power to punish for contempt. Committee notes expanded. Editorial changes. Citation form changes in committee notes.

1992 Revision: Editorial changes. Committee notes revised. Citation form changes in committee notes.

2002 Revision: Entire rule amended. Contents of accountings by removed fiduciaries are now governed by rule 5.346. Editorial changes in (a), (c), and (d). Committee notes revised.

2003 Revision: Committee notes revised.

2007 Revision: Committee notes revised.

2010 Revision: Editorial change in title to clarify scope of rule.

2012 Revision: Committee notes revised.

Statutory References

§ 731.201(23), Fla. Stat. General definitions.

§ 733.504, Fla. Stat. Removal of personal representative; causes of removal.

§ 733.505, Fla. Stat. Jurisdiction in removal proceedings.

§ 733.506, Fla. Stat. Proceedings for removal.

§ 733.5061, Fla. Stat. Appointment of successor upon removal.

§ 733.508, Fla. Stat. Accounting and discharge of removed personal representatives upon removal.

§ 733.509, Fla. Stat. Surrender of assets upon removal.

Rule References

Fla. Prob. R. 5.020 Pleadings; verification; motions.

Fla. Prob. R. 5.025 Adversary proceedings.

Fla. Prob. R. 5.040 Notice.

Fla. Prob. R. 5.041 Service of pleadings and documents.

Fla. Prob. R. 5.042 Time.

Fla. Prob. R. 5.150 Order requiring accounting.

Fla. Prob. R. 5.310 Disqualification of personal representative; notification.

Fla. Prob. R. 5.345 Accountings other than personal representatives' final accountings.

Fla. Prob. R. 5.346 Fiduciary accounting.

Fla. R. Jud. Admin. 2.516 Service of pleadings and documents.

Rule 5.460. Subsequent Administration

(a) Petition. If, after an estate is closed, additional property of the decedent is discovered or if further administration of the estate is required for any other reason, any interested person may file a petition for further administration of the estate. The petition shall be filed in the same probate file as the original administration.

(b) Contents. The petition shall state:

(1) the name, address, and interest of the petitioner in the estate;

(2) the reason for further administration of the estate;

(3) the description, approximate value, and location of any asset not included among the assets of the prior administration; and

(4) a statement of the relief sought.

(c) Order. The court shall enter such orders as appropriate. Unless required, the court need not revoke the order of discharge, reissue letters, or require bond.

Amended Sept. 13, 1984, effective Jan. 1, 1985 (458 So.2d 1079).

Committee Notes

This rule establishes a procedure for further administration after estate is closed, which may be summary in nature.

Rule History

1984 Revision: Extensive changes. Committee notes revised.

1992 Revision: Citation form change in committee notes.

2003 Revision: Committee notes revised.

2012 Revision: Committee notes revised.

Statutory Reference

§ 733.903, Fla. Stat. Subsequent administration.

Rule References

Fla. Prob. R. 5.020 Pleadings; verification; motions.

Fla. Prob. R. 5.040 Notice.

Fla. Prob. R. 5.041 Service of pleadings and documents.

Fla. R. Jud. Admin. 2.516 Service of pleadings and documents.

Rule 5.470. Ancillary Administration

(a) Petition. The petition for ancillary letters shall include an authenticated copy of so much of the domiciliary proceedings as will show:

(1) for a testate estate the will, petition for probate, order admitting the will to probate, and authority of the personal representative; or

(2) for an intestate estate the petition for administration and authority of the personal representative to act.

(b) Notice. Before ancillary letters shall be issued to any person, formal notice shall be given to:

(1) all known persons qualified to act as ancillary personal representative and whose entitlement to preference of appointment is equal to or greater than petitioner's and who have not waived notice or joined in the petition; and

(2) all domiciliary personal representatives who have not waived notice or joined in the petition.

(c) Probate of Will. On filing the authenticated copy of a will, the court shall determine whether the will complies with Florida law to entitle it to probate. If it does comply, the court shall admit the will to probate.

Amended Sept. 13, 1984, effective Jan. 1, 1985 (458 So.2d 1079); Sept. 24, 1992, effective Jan. 1, 1993 (607 So.2d 1306); Oct. 3, 1996, effective Jan. 1, 1997 (683 So.2d 78); Sept. 29, 2005, effective Jan. 1, 2006 (912 So.2d 1178).

Committee Notes

Rule History

1975 Revision: The rule sets out the procedural requirements for issuance of ancillary letters.

1984 Revision: Editorial changes with addition of notice requirement in (b). Committee notes revised.

1988 Revision: Committee notes revised.

1992 Revision: Changed rule to require that notice be given to persons qualified to act as ancillary personal representative whose entitlement to preference of appointment is equal to or greater than petitioner's and to all domiciliary personal representatives prior to entry of an order admitting the will to probate. Committee notes revised. Citation form changes in committee notes.

1996 Revision: The requirement that a filing of an authenticated copy of a will be a "probated" will is removed from subdivision (c). There may be circumstances in which a will is on deposit or file in a foreign jurisdiction but is not being offered for probate. That should not preclude an ancillary administration in Florida of that estate. This change is not intended to allow an authenticated copy of any document other than an original instrument to be filed under this rule and considered for probate.

2003 Revision: Committee notes revised.

2005 Revision: Committee notes revised.

2010 Revision: Committee notes revised.

2012 Revision: Committee notes revised.

Statutory References

§ 731.201(1), Fla. Stat. General definitions.

§ 733.212, Fla. Stat. Notice of administration; filing of objections.

§ 733.2121, Fla. Stat. Notice to creditors; filing of claims.

§ 734.102, Fla. Stat. Ancillary administration.

§ 734.1025, Fla. Stat. Nonresident decedent's testate estate with property not exceeding $50,000 in this state; determination of claims.

Rule References

Fla. Prob. R. 5.020 Pleadings; verification; motions.

Fla. Prob. R. 5.040 Notice.

Fla. Prob. R. 5.041 Service of pleadings and documents.

Fla. Prob. R. 5.042 Time.

Fla. Prob. R. 5.065(b) Notice of civil action or ancillary administration.

Fla. Prob. R. 5.205(a)(2) Filing evidence of death.

Fla. Prob. R. 5.215 Authenticated copy of will.

Fla. Prob. R. 5.240 Notice of administration.

Fla. Prob. R. 5.241 Notice to creditors.

Fla. Prob. R. 5.475 Ancillary administration, short form.

Fed. R. Civ. P. 44(a) Proving an official record.

Fla. R. Jud. Admin. 2.516 Service of pleadings and documents.

Rule 5.475. Ancillary Administration, Short Form

(a) Filing Requirements. The foreign personal representative of a testate estate that meets the requirements of section 734.1025, Florida Statutes, may file with the clerk in the county where any property is located an authenticated copy of so much of the transcript of the foreign proceedings as will show:

(1) the probated will and all probated codicils of the decedent;

(2) the order admitting them to probate;

(3) the letters or their equivalent; and

(4) the part of the record showing the names of the beneficiaries of the estate or an affidavit of the foreign personal representative reciting that the names are not shown or not fully disclosed by the foreign record and specifying the names.

On presentation of the foregoing, the court shall admit the will and any codicils to probate if they comply with section 732.502(1) or section 732.502(2), Florida Statutes.

(b) Notice to Creditors. After complying with the foregoing requirements, the foreign personal representative may cause a notice to creditors to be published as required by these rules.

(c) Claims Procedure. The procedure for filing or barring claims and objecting to them and for suing on them shall be the same as for other estates, except as provided in this rule.

(d) Order. If no claims are filed against the estate within the time allowed, the court shall enter an order adjudging that notice to creditors has been duly published and proof thereof filed and that no claims have been filed against the estate or that all claims have been satisfied.

(e) Notification of Claims Filed. If any claim is filed against the estate within the time allowed, the clerk shall send to the foreign personal representative a copy of the claim and a notice setting a date for a hearing to appoint an ancillary personal representative. At the hearing, the court shall appoint an ancillary personal representative according to the preferences as provided by law.

(f) Objections to Claims. If an ancillary personal representative is appointed pursuant to this rule, the procedure for filing, objecting to, and suing on claims shall be the same as for other estates, except that the ancillary personal representative appointed shall have not less than 30 days from the date of appointment within which to object to any claim filed.

Added Sept. 29, 1988, effective Jan. 1, 1989 (537 So.2d 500). Amended Sept. 24, 1992, effective Jan. 1, 1993 (607 So.2d 1306); Sept. 29, 2005, effective Jan. 1, 2006 (912 So.2d 1178).

Committee Notes

This rule represents a rule implementation of the procedure found in section 734.1025, Florida Statutes. It is not intended to change the effect of the statute from which it was derived but has been reformatted to conform with the structure of these rules. It is not intended to create a new procedure or modify an existing procedure.

Rule History

1988 Revision: New rule.

1992 Revision: Editorial changes. Committee notes revised. Citation form changes in committee notes.

2003 Revision: Committee notes revised.

2005 Revision: Deletion of reference to intestate estates in subdivision (a) to conform to 2001 amendments to section 734.1025, Florida Statutes. Editorial changes throughout.

2012 Revision: Committee notes revised.

Statutory References

§ 733.2121, Fla. Stat. Notice to creditors; filing of claims.

§ 734.102, Fla. Stat. Ancillary administration.

§ 734.1025, Fla. Stat. Nonresident decedent's testate estate with property not exceeding $50,000 in this state; determination of claims.

Rule References

Fla. Prob. R. 5.020 Pleadings; verification; motions.

Fla. Prob. R. 5.040 Notice.

Fla. Prob. R. 5.041 Service of pleadings and documents.

Fla. Prob. R. 5.042 Time.

Fla. Prob. R. 5.065(b) Notice of civil action or ancillary administration.

Fla. Prob. R. 5.205(a)(2) Filing evidence of death.

Fla. Prob. R. 5.215 Authenticated copy of will.

Fla. Prob. R. 5.240 Notice of administration.

Fla. Prob. R. 5.241 Notice to creditors.

Fla. Prob. R. 5.470 Ancillary administration.

Fla. R. Jud. Admin. 2.516 Service of pleadings and documents.

Rule 5.490. Form and Manner of Presenting Claim

(a) Form. A creditor's statement of claim shall be verified and filed with the clerk and shall state:

(1) the basis for the claim;

(2) the amount claimed;

(3) the name and address of the creditor;

(4) the security for the claim, if any; and

(5) whether the claim is currently due or involves an uncertainty and, if not due, then the due date and, if contingent or unliquidated, the nature of the uncertainty.

(b) Copy. At the time of filing the claim, the creditor shall also furnish the clerk with a copy thereof.

(c) Mailing. The clerk shall mail a copy of claims, noting the fact and date of mailing on the original, to the attorney for the personal representative unless all personal representatives file a notice directing that copies of claims be mailed to a designated personal representative or attorney of record. Absent designation, a copy of claims shall be mailed to the attorney for the personal representative named first in the letters of administration.

(d) Validity of Claim. Failure to deliver or receive a copy of the claim shall not affect the validity of the claim.

(e) Amending Claims. If a claim as filed is sufficient to notify interested persons of its substance but is otherwise defective as to form, the court may permit the claim to be amended at any time.

(f) Service by Personal Representative. If the personal representative files a claim individually, or in any other capacity creating a conflict of interest between the personal representative and any interested person, then at the time the claim is filed, the personal representative shall serve all interested persons with a copy of the claim and notice of the right to object to the claim. The notice shall state that an interested person may object to a claim as provided by law and rule 5.496. Service shall be either by informal notice or in the manner provided for service of formal notice. Service on one interested person by a chosen method shall not preclude service on another interested person by another method.

Amended Sept. 13, 1984, effective Jan. 1, 1985 (458 So.2d 1079); Sept. 29, 1988, effective Jan. 1, 1989 (537 So.2d 500); July 5, 2007, effective Jan. 1, 2008 (959 So.2d 1170).

Committee Notes

Subdivision (e) of this rule represents a rule implementation of the procedure found in section 733.704, Florida Statutes. It is not intended to change the effect of the statute from which it was derived but has been reformatted to conform with the structure of these rules. It is not intended to create a new procedure or modify an existing procedure.

Rule History

1975 Revision: Sets forth the claims procedure to be followed and clarifies the matter of delivery of copies where there are multiple personal representatives or where the attorney of record desires to accept such delivery.

1984 Revision: Extensive editorial changes and requires furnishing of copy of claim to the attorney for the personal representative. Committee notes revised.

1988 Revision: Clarifies the matter of delivery of copies and directs the clerk to mail the same to the attorney for the personal representative unless designations are filed by all personal representatives to the contrary. Subdivision (e) added to implement the procedure found in section 733.704, Florida Statutes. Editorial changes. Committee notes expanded. Citation form change in committee notes.

1992 Revision: Committee notes revised. Citation form changes in committee notes.

1999 Revision: Reference to repealed rule deleted from committee notes.

2003 Revision: Committee notes revised.

2007 Revision: Editorial change in (a). New (f) added, providing procedure for notice when personal representative files a claim individually or otherwise has a conflict of interest with any interested person regarding a claim.

Statutory References

§ 731.104, Fla. Stat. Verification of documents.

§ 733.2121, Fla. Stat. Notice to creditors; filing of claims.

§ 733.702, Fla. Stat. Limitations on presentation of claims.

§ 733.703, Fla. Stat. Form and manner of presenting claim.

§ 733.704, Fla. Stat. Amendment of claims.

§ 733.708, Fla. Stat. Compromise.

§ 733.710, Fla. Stat. Limitations on claims against estates.

§ 734.102, Fla. Stat. Ancillary administration.

Rule References

Fla. Prob. R. 5.020 Pleadings; verification; motions.

Fla. Prob. R. 5.241 Notice to creditors.

Fla. Prob. R. 5.470 Ancillary administration.

Fla. Prob. R. 5.475 Ancillary administration, short form.

Fla. Prob. R. 5.530 Summary administration.

Rule 5.496. Form and Manner of Objecting to Claim

(a) Filing. An objection to a claim, other than a personal representative's proof of claim, shall be in writing and filed on or before the expiration of 4 months from the first publication of notice to creditors or within 30 days from the timely filing or amendment of the claim, whichever occurs later.

(b) Service. A personal representative or other interested person who files an objection to the claim shall serve a copy of the objection on the claimant. If the objection is filed by an interested person other than the personal representative, a copy of the objection shall also be served on the personal representative. Any objection shall include a certificate of service.

(c) Notice to Claimant. An objection shall contain a statement that the claimant is limited to a period of 30 days from the date of service of an objection within which to bring an action as provided by law.

Added Sept. 24, 1992, effective Jan. 1, 1993 (607 So.2d 1306). Amended June 19, 2003 (848 So.2d 1069); Sept. 29, 2005, effective Jan. 1, 2006 (912 So.2d 1178); July 5, 2007, effective Jan. 1, 2008 (959 So.2d 1170); Sept. 2, 2010, effective Jan. 1, 2011 (50 So.3d 578).

Committee Notes

This rule represents an implementation of the procedure found in section 733.705, Florida Statutes, and adds a requirement to furnish notice of the time limitation in which an independent action or declaratory action must be filed after objection to a claim.

Rule History

1992 Revision: New rule.

2003 Revision: Reference in (a) to notice of administration changed to notice to creditors. Committee notes revised.

2005 Revision: Removed provision for objections to personal representative's proof of claim, now addressed in rule 5.498, and subsequent subdivisions relettered. Reference to service on the claimant's attorney removed because service on the attorney is required by rule 5.041(b). Committee notes revised.

2007 Revision: Editorial change in (a). Second sentence of (b) added to specify that the objection must include a certificate of service.

2010 Revision: Subdivision (b) amended to delete the requirement to serve a copy of an objection to a claim within 10 days, and to clarify the requirement to include a certificate of service.

2012 Revision: Committee notes revised.

Statutory References

§ 731.201(4), Fla. Stat. General definitions.

§ 733.705, Fla. Stat. Payment of and objection to claims.

Rule References

Fla. Prob. R. 5.040 Notice.

Fla. Prob. R. 5.041 Service of pleadings and documents.

Fla. Prob. R. 5.498 Personal representative's proof of claim.

Fla. Prob. R. 5.499 Form and manner of objecting to personal representative's proof of claim.

Fla. R. Jud. Admin. 2.516 Service of pleadings and documents.

Rule 5.498. Personal Representative's Proof of Claim

(a) Contents. A personal representative's proof of claim shall state:

(1) the basis for each claim;

(2) the amount claimed;

(3) the name and address of the claimant;

(4) the security for the claim, if any;

(5) whether the claim is matured, unmatured, contingent, or unliquidated;

(6) whether the claim has been paid or is to be paid; and

(7) that any objection to a claim listed as to be paid shall be filed no later than 4 months from first publication of the notice to creditors or 30 days from the date of the filing of the proof of claim, whichever occurs later.

(b) Service. The proof of claim shall be served at the time of filing or promptly thereafter on all interested persons.

Added Sept. 29, 2005, effective Jan. 1, 2006 (912 So.2d 1178). Amended July 5, 2007, effective Jan. 1, 2008 (959 So.2d 1170).

Committee Notes

This rule represents an implementation of the procedure found in section 733.703(2), Florida Statutes, with respect to a proof of claim filed by the personal representative.

Rule History

2005 Revision: New rule.

2007 Revision: Subdivision (b) amended to eliminate the need to serve claimants listed as paid on the proof of claim, and clarifying editorial change.

2012 Revision: Committee notes revised.

Statutory References

§ 733.703(2), Fla. Stat. Form and manner of presenting claim.

§ 733.705, Fla. Stat. Payment of and objection to claims.

Rule References

Fla. Prob. R. 5.041 Service of pleadings and documents.

Fla. Prob. R. 5.499 Form and manner of objecting to personal representative's proof of claim.

Fla. R. Jud. Admin. 2.516 Service of pleadings and documents.

Rule 5.499. Form and Manner of Objecting to Personal Representative's Proof of Claim

(a) Filing. An objection to a personal representative's proof of claim shall be in writing and filed on or before the expiration of 4 months from the first publication of notice to creditors or within 30 days from the timely filing of the proof of claim, whichever occurs later.

(b) Contents. The objection shall identify the particular item or items to which objection is made. An objection to an item listed on the proof of claim as to be paid shall also contain a statement that the claimant is limited to a period of 30 days from the date of service of an objection within which to bring an independent action as provided by law.

(c) Items Listed as Paid. If an objection is filed to an item listed on the proof of claim as paid, it shall not be necessary for the claimant to file an independent action as to that item. Liability as between estate and the personal representative individually for claims listed on the proof of claim as paid, or for claims treated as if they were listed on the proof of claim as paid, shall be determined in the estate administration, in a proceeding for accounting or surcharge, or in another appropriate proceeding, whether or not an objection has been filed.

(d) Items Paid Before Objection. If an item listed as to be paid is paid by the personal representative prior to the filing of an objection as to that item, the item shall be treated as if it were listed on the proof of claim as paid.

(e) Service. The objector shall serve a copy of the objection on the personal representative and, in the case of any objection to an item listed as to be paid, shall also serve a copy on that claimant within 10 days after the filing of the objection. In the case of an objection to an item listed as to be paid, the objection shall include a certificate of service.

Added Sept. 29, 2005, effective Jan. 1, 2006 (912 So.2d 1178). Amended July 5, 2007, effective Jan. 1, 2008 (959 So.2d 1170).

Committee Notes

This rule represents an implementation of the procedure found in section 733.705, Florida Statutes, with respect to a proof of claim filed by the personal representative. The rule recognizes the different treatment between items listed on a proof of claim as having been paid versus items listed as to be paid. An objection to an item listed as to be paid is treated in the same manner as a creditor's claim and there is a requirement to furnish notice of the time limitation in which an independent action or declaratory action must be filed after objection to a claim.

Rule History

2005 Revision: New rule.

2007 Revision: Editorial change in (a). Extensive revisions to rest of rule to clarify the differences in procedure between items listed as paid and items listed as to be paid. Committee notes revised.

2012 Revision: Committee notes revised.

Statutory Reference

§ 733.705, Fla. Stat. Payment of and objection to claims.

Rule References

Fla. Prob. R. 5.040 Notice.

Fla. Prob. R. 5.041 Service of pleadings and documents.

Fla. Prob. R. 5.496 Form and manner of objecting to claim.

Fla. Prob. R. 5.498 Personal representative's proof of claim.

Fla. R. Jud. Admin. 2.516 Service of pleadings and documents.

Rule 5.510. Establishment and Probate of Lost or Destroyed Will

(a) Proceeding. The establishment and probate of a lost or destroyed will shall be in one proceeding.

(b) Petition. The petition, in addition to reciting information required under these rules for petition for administration, shall include a statement of the facts constituting grounds on which relief is sought, and a statement of the contents of the will or, if available, a copy of the will.

(c) Testimony. The testimony of each witness in the proceeding shall be reduced to writing and filed and may be used as evidence in any contest of the will if the witness has died or moved from the state.

(d) Notice. No lost or destroyed will shall be admitted to probate unless formal notice has been given to those who, but for the will, would be entitled to the property thereby devised.

(e) Order. The order admitting the will to probate shall state in full its terms and provisions.

Amended March 31, 1977, effective July 1, 1977 (344 So.2d 828); Sept. 13, 1984, effective Jan. 1, 1985 (458 So.2d 1079); Sept. 29, 1988, effective Jan. 1, 1989 (537 So.2d 500); May 2, 2002 (824 So.2d 849).

Committee Notes

This rule represents a rule implementation of the procedure formerly found in section 733.207, Florida Statutes. It is not intended to change the effect of the statute from which it was derived but has been reformatted to conform with the structure of these rules. It is not intended to create a new procedure or modify an existing procedure.

Rule History

1977 Revision: Editorial change in subdivision (c) of prior rule.

1984 Revision: Extensive changes. Committee notes revised.

1988 Revision: Rule rewritten to conform to statute. Committee notes expanded. Citation form change in committee notes.

1992 Revision: Committee notes revised. Citation form changes in committee notes.

2002 Revision: Subdivision (d) added to implement procedure formerly found in section 733.207(3), Florida Statutes. Committee notes revised.

2003 Revision: Committee notes revised.

2012 Revision: Committee notes revised.

Statutory Reference

§ 733.207, Fla. Stat. Establishment and probate of lost or destroyed will.

Rule References

Fla. Prob. R. 5.020 Pleadings; verification; motions.

Fla. Prob. R. 5.025 Adversary proceedings.

Fla. Prob. R. 5.040 Notice.

Fla. Prob. R. 5.041 Service of pleadings and documents.

Fla. Prob. R. 5.042 Time.

Fla. Prob. R. 5.200 Petition for administration.

Fla. R. Jud. Admin. 2.516 Service of pleadings and documents.

Rule 5.530. Summary Administration

(a) Petition. The petition must be verified as required by law and must contain:

(1) a statement of the interest of each petitioner, each petitioner's name and address, and the name and office address of each petitioner's attorney;

(2) the name and last known address of the decedent, last 4 digits of the decedent's social security number, date and place of death of the decedent, and state and county of the decedent's domicile;

(3) so far as is known, the names and addresses of the surviving spouse, if any, and the beneficiaries and their relationship to the decedent and the year of birth of any who are minors;

(4) a statement showing venue;

(5) a statement whether domiciliary or principal proceedings are pending in another state or country, if known, and the name and address of the foreign personal representative and the court issuing letters;

(6) a statement that the decedent's will, if any, does not direct administration as required by chapter 733, Florida Statutes;

(7) a statement that the value of the entire estate subject to administration in this state, less the value of property exempt from the claims of creditors, does not exceed $75,000 or that the decedent has been dead for more than 2 years;

(8) a description of all assets in the estate and the estimated value of each, and a separate description of any protected homestead and exempt property;

(9) a statement either;

(A) that all creditors' claims are barred or

(B) that a diligent search and reasonable inquiry for any known or reasonably ascertainable creditors has been made and one of the following:

(i) A statement that the estate is not indebted.

(ii) The name and address of each creditor, the nature of the debt, the amount of the debt and whether the amount is estimated or exact, and when the debt is due. If provision for payment of the debt has been made other than for full payment in the proposed order of distribution, the following information must be shown:

(a) The name of the person who will pay the debt.

(b) The creditor's written consent for substitution or assumption of the debt by another person.

(c) The amount to be paid if the debt has been compromised.

(d) The terms for payment and any limitations on the liability of the person paying the debt.

(10) in an intestate estate, a statement that after the exercise of reasonable diligence each petitioner is unaware of any unrevoked wills or codicils;

(11) in a testate estate, a statement identifying all unrevoked wills and codicils being presented for probate, and a statement that each petitioner is unaware of any other unrevoked will or codicil; and

(12) a schedule of proposed distribution of all probate assets and the person to whom each asset is to be distributed.

(b) Service. The joinder in, or consent to, a petition for summary administration is not required of a beneficiary who will receive full distributive share under the proposed distribution. Any beneficiary and any known or reasonably ascertainable creditor not joining or consenting must receive formal notice of the petition.

(c) Testate Estate. In a testate estate, on the filing of the petition for summary administration, the decedent's will must be proved and admitted to probate.

(d) Order. If the court determines that the decedent's estate qualifies for summary administration, it must enter an order distributing the probate assets and specifically designating the person to whom each asset is to be distributed.

Amended March 31, 1977, effective July 1, 1977 (344 So.2d 828); Sept. 13, 1984, effective Jan. 1, 1985 (458 So.2d 1079); Sept. 29, 1988, effective Jan. 1, 1989 (537 So.2d 500); Sept. 24, 1992, effective Jan. 1, 1993 (607 So.2d 1306); May 2, 2002 (824 So.2d 849); Sept. 29, 2005, effective Jan. 1, 2006 (912 So.2d 1178); July 5, 2007, effective Jan. 1, 2008 (959 So.2d 1170); Nov. 3, 2011, effective, *nunc pro tunc*, Oct. 1, 2011 (78 So.3d 1045); Sept. 26, 2013, effective Jan. 1, 2014 (123 So.3d 31); May 22, 2014, effective May 22, 2014 (139 So.3d 875).

Committee Notes

Verification and service of a petition for summary administration are governed by rules 5.020, 5.040, and 5.041. Section 735.206(2), Florida Statutes, relating to diligent search for, and service of the petition for summary administration on, reasonably ascertainable creditors is substantive. Nothing in this rule is intended to change the effect of the statutory amendments.

Rule History

1977 Revision: Changes to conform to 1975 statutory revision. Established the requirements of a petition for summary administration and provided for the hearing thereon and the entry of the order of distribution of the assets.

1984 Revision: Extensive revisions and editorial changes. Committee notes revised.

1988 Revision: Editorial change in caption of (a). Committee notes revised.

1992 Revision: Editorial changes. Committee notes revised. Citation form changes in committee notes.

2002 Revision: Replaces "homestead" with "protected homestead" in (a)(2) to conform to addition of term in section 731.201(29), Florida Statutes. Committee notes revised.

2003 Revision: Committee notes revised.

2005 Revision: Subdivision (a)(3) amended to include requirements of section 735.206(2), Florida Statutes.

2007 Revision: Rule substantially rewritten to require petition to include essentially the same information required to be stated in a petition for administration and to require the petitioners to specify facts showing they are entitled to summary administration. New subdivision (b) added to provide for formal notice of the petition, and subsequent subdivisions relettered.

2011 Revision: Subdivision (a)(2) amended to limit listing of decedent's social security number to last four digits.

2012 Revision: Committee notes revised.

2013 Revision: Subdivision (a)(9) reorganized to avoid the misconception that a diligent search and reasonable inquiry for known or reasonably ascertainable creditors is required when creditor claims are barred. Committee notes revised. Editorial changes to conform to the court's guidelines for rules submissions as set forth in AOSC06-14.

2014 Revision: Subdivision (a)(3) amended to provide only the year of birth of a minor to conform to Fla. R. Jud. Admin. 2.425. Committee notes revised.

Statutory References

§ 731.104, Fla. Stat. Verification of documents.

§§ 735.201–735.2063, Fla. Stat. Summary administration.

Rule References

Fla. Prob. R. 5.020 Pleadings; verification; motions.

Fla. Prob. R. 5.040 Notice.

Fla. Prob. R. 5.041 Service of pleadings and documents.

Fla. Prob. R. 5.205(a)(3) Filing evidence of death.

Fla. R. Jud. Admin. 2.420 Public access to judicial branch records.

Fla. R. Jud. Admin. 2.425 Minimization of the filing of sensitive information.

Fla. R. Jud. Admin. 2.516 Service of pleadings and documents.

PART III. GUARDIANSHIP

Rule 5.540. Hearings

(a) Application. All hearings under chapter 744 and under section 393.12, Florida Statutes, shall be open unless the alleged incapacitated person, adjudicated ward, or person alleged to have a developmental disability elects to have the hearing closed.

(b) Election. An election to close a hearing may be made before the hearing by filing a written notice. Subject to the court's approval, an election to close or reopen a hearing may be made at any time during the hearing by oral or written motion.

Added Aug. 22, 1991, effective Oct. 1, 1991 (584 So.2d 964). Amended July 10, 2008 (986 So.2d 576).

Committee Notes

This rule permits an alleged incapacitated person, adjudicated ward, or person alleged to have a developmental disability to elect to have all hearings open or closed at any time by oral or written election.

Rule History

1991 Revision: New rule.

1992 Revision: Committee notes revised.

2008 Revision: Subdivision (a) amended to include persons with a developmental disability. Committee notes revised.

Statutory References

§ 393.12, Fla. Stat. Capacity; appointment of guardian advocate.

§ 744.1095, Fla. Stat. Hearings.

§ 744.3085, Fla. Stat. Guardian advocates.

Rule References

Fla. Prob. R. 5.541 Recording of hearings.

Rule 5.541. Recording of Hearings

Electronic or stenographic recordings shall be made of all hearings on the:

(a) adjudication of incapacity;

(b) appointment of a guardian;

(c) modification, termination, or revocation of the adjudication of incapacity;

(d) restoration of capacity; or

(e) restoration of rights.

Added Aug. 22, 1991, effective Oct. 1, 1991 (584 So.2d 964). Amended Sept. 24, 1992, effective Jan. 1, 1993 (607 So.2d 1306); July 10, 2008 (986 So.2d 576).

Committee Notes

This rule represents a rule implementation of the procedure found in sections 744.109 and 744.3031, Florida Statutes. It is not intended to change the effect of the statutes from which it is derived, or to create a new procedure or modify an existing procedure.

Rule History

1991 Revision: New rule.

1992 Revision: Editorial changes. Committee notes revised. Citation form change in committee notes.

2003 Revision: Committee notes revised.

2008 Revision: New subdivision (e) added for proceedings involving guardian advocates. Committee notes revised.

Statutory References

§ 393.12, Fla. Stat. Capacity; appointment of guardian advocate.

§ 744.109, Fla. Stat. Records.

§ 744.3031, Fla. Stat. Emergency temporary guardianship.

§ 744.3085, Fla. Stat. Guardian advocates.

§ 744.3371, Fla. Stat. Notice of petition for appointment of guardian and hearing.

Rule 5.550. Petition to Determine Incapacity

(a) Contents. The petition to determine incapacity shall be verified by the petitioner and shall state:

(1) the name, age, and present address of the petitioner and the petitioner's relationship to the alleged incapacitated person;

(2) the name, age, county of residence, and present address of the alleged incapacitated person, and specify the primary language spoken by the alleged incapacitated person, if known;

(3) that the petitioner believes the alleged incapacitated person to be incapacitated, the facts on which such belief is based, and the names and addresses of all persons known to the petitioner who have knowledge of such facts through personal observation;

(4) the name and address of the alleged incapacitated person's attending or family physician, if known;

(5) which rights the alleged incapacitated person is incapable of exercising to the best of the petitioner's knowledge; and, if the petitioner has insufficient experience to make that judgment, the petitioner shall so indicate;

(6) whether plenary or limited guardianship is sought for the alleged incapacitated person; and

(7) the names, relationships, and addresses of the next of kin of the alleged incapacitated person, specifying the year of birth of any who are minors, to the extent known to the petitioner.

(b) Notice.

(1) *Contents.* The notice of filing the petition to determine incapacity shall state:

(A) the time and place of the hearing to inquire into the capacity of the alleged incapacitated person;

(B) that an attorney has been appointed to represent such person; and

(C) that if the court determines that such person is incapable of exercising any of the rights enumerated in the petition a guardian may be appointed.

(2) *Service on Alleged Incapacitated Person.* The notice and a copy of the petition to determine incapacity shall be personally served by an elisor appointed by the court, who may be the court appointed counsel for the alleged incapacitated person. The elisor shall read the notice to the alleged incapacitated person, but need not read the petition. A return of service shall be filed by the elisor certifying that the notice and petition have been served on and the notice read to the alleged incapacitated person. No responsive pleading is required and no default may be entered for failure to file a responsive pleading. The allegations of the petition are deemed denied.

(3) *Service on Others.* A copy of the petition and the notice shall also be served on counsel for the alleged incapacitated person, and on all next of kin.

(c) Verified Statement. An interested person may file a verified statement that shall state:

(1) that he or she has a good faith belief that the alleged incapacitated person's trust, trust amendment, or durable power of attorney is invalid; and

(2) facts constituting a reasonable basis for that belief.

(d) Order. When an order determines that a person is incapable of exercising delegable rights, it shall specify whether there is an alternative to guardianship that will sufficiently address the problems of the incapacitated person.

Amended Sept. 4, 1980, effective Jan. 1, 1981 (387 So.2d 949); Sept. 13, 1984, effective Jan. 1, 1985 (458 So.2d 1079); Sept. 29, 1989, effective Oct. 1, 1989 (549 So.2d 665); Nov. 17, 1989 (551 So.2d 452); Aug. 22, 1991, effective Oct. 1, 1991 (584 So.2d 964); Feb. 1, 2007 (948 So.2d 735); May 22, 2014, effective May 22, 2014 (139 So.3d 875).

Committee Notes

Rule History

1980 Revision: Implements 1979 amendments to section 744.331, Florida Statutes.

1984 Revision: Change in title of rule. Editorial changes and adds a provision for service of petition. Committee notes revised.

1988 Revision: Committee notes revised. Citation form changes in committee notes.

1989 Revision by Ad Hoc Committee: The committee realized that formal notice as defined in rule 5.040(a)(1) requires the recipient of notice to file a responsive pleading within 20 days after the service of the notice. The committee believed that to impose such a requirement on the alleged incapacitated person would contravene the legislative intent of the 1989 revisions to chapter 744, Florida Statutes. The committee observed that the time required for appointment of mandatory appointed counsel might render a responsive pleading within 20 days impossible for the alleged incapacitated person. The committee concluded that, procedurally, notice upon the alleged incapacitated person should occur in the same manner as formal notice in rule 5.040, but the required response under that rule should not be imposed upon the alleged incapacitated person.

1991 Revision: Implements 1989 amendments to sections 744.3201 and 744. 331, Florida Statutes, and 1990 technical amendments.

1992 Revision: Citation form changes in committee notes.

2006 Revision: Subdivisions (c) and (d) added to incorporate 2006 amendment to section 744.441 and creation of section 744.462, Florida Statutes. Committee notes revised.

2014 Revision: Amends subdivision (a)(7) to conform with Fla. R. Jud. Admin. 2.425. Committee notes revised.

Statutory References

§ 744.3201, Fla. Stat. Petition to determine incapacity.

§ 744.331, Fla. Stat. Procedures to determine incapacity.

§ 744.3371, Fla. Stat. Notice of petition for appointment of guardian and hearing.

§ 744.441(11), Fla. Stat. Powers of guardian upon court approval.

§ 744.462, Fla. Stat. Determination regarding alternatives to guardianship.

Rule References

Fla. Prob. R. 5.020 Pleadings; verification; motions.

Fla. Prob. R. 5.040(a)(3) Notice.

Fla. Prob. R. 5.800(a) Application of revised chapter 744 to existing guardianships.

Fla. R. Jud. Admin. 2.425 Minimization of the Filing of Sensitive Information.

Rule 5.552. Voluntary Guardianship of Property

(a) Petition for Appointment of Guardian. The petition for voluntary guardianship shall be verified by the petitioner and shall state:

(1) the facts to establish venue;

(2) the petitioner's residence and post office address;

(3) that the petitioner although mentally competent is incapable of the care, custody, and management of the petitioner's estate by reason of age or physical infirmity, and is voluntarily petitioning to have a guardian of the petitioner's property appointed;

(4) whether the guardianship shall apply to all of the petitioner's property or less than all of the petitioner's property; and if less than all of the petitioner's property, the specific property to which the guardianship is to apply;

(5) the name and residence and post office address of any proposed guardian;

(6) that the proposed guardian is qualified to serve or that a willing and qualified proposed guardian has not been located; and

(7) the names and post office addresses of persons to whom the petitioner requests that notice of the hearing for the appointment of the guardian, and any petition for authority to act, be given.

(b) Certificate of Licensed Physician. The petition shall be accompanied by a certificate of a licensed physician as required by law.

(c) Notice of Hearing. Notice of hearing on the petition for appointment, and any petition for authority to act, shall be given to the ward and any person to whom the ward requests notice be given, which request can be made in the petition for appointment or a subsequent written request for notice signed by the ward.

(d) Annual Report. The annual report shall be accompanied by a certificate from a licensed physician as required by law.

(e) Termination. The ward may terminate a voluntary guardianship by filing a notice of termination. Copies of the notice shall be served on all interested persons. The guardian shall file a petition for discharge in accordance with these rules.

Added June 19, 2003, effective Jan. 1, 2004 (848 So.2d 1069); Feb. 1, 2007 (948 So.2d 735).

Committee Notes

Rule History

2003 Revision: New rule.

2006 Revision: New (d) added to incorporate 2006 amendment to section 744.341, Florida Statutes, requiring inclusion of physician's certificate in annual report, and subsequent subdivision relettered. Committee notes revised.

Statutory References

§ 744.341, Fla. Stat. Voluntary guardianship.

Rule References

Fla. Prob. R. 5.680 Termination of guardianship.

Fla. Prob. R. 5.695 Annual guardianship report.

Rule 5.555. Guardianships of Minors

(a) Application. This rule shall apply to any guardianship for a minor.

(b) Petition to Determine Incapacity. No petition to determine incapacity need be filed.

(c) Petition for Appointment of Guardian. The petition shall be verified by the petitioner and shall state:

(1) the facts to establish venue;

(2) the petitioner's residence and post office address;

(3) the name, age, and residence and post office address of the minor;

(4) the names and addresses of the parents of the minor and if none, the next of kin known to the petitioner;

(5) the name and residence and post office address of the proposed guardian, and that the proposed guardian is qualified to serve; or, that a willing and qualified guardian has not been located;

(6) the proposed guardian's relationship to and any previous association with the minor;

(7) the reasons why the proposed guardian should be appointed; and

(8) the nature and value of the property subject to the guardianship.

(d) Notice. Formal notice of the petition for appointment of guardian shall be served on any parent who is not a petitioner or, if there is no parent, on the persons with whom the minor resides and on such other persons as the court may direct.

(e) Initial and Annual Guardianship Reports.

(1) The initial guardianship report shall consist only of the verified inventory. The annual guardianship report shall consist only of the annual accounting.

(2) The guardian shall file an initial and annual guardianship plan as required by law.

(3) Unless otherwise ordered by the court or required by law, the guardian need not serve a copy of the initial guardianship report and the annual guardianship reports on the ward.

(f) Inspection of Inventory or Accounting. Unless otherwise ordered by the court for good cause shown, any inventory, amended or supplementary inventory, or accounting is subject to inspection only by the clerk, the ward or the ward's attorney, and the guardian or the guardian's attorney.

Added Aug. 22, 1991, effective Oct. 1, 1991 (584 So.2d 964). Amended Oct. 3, 1996, effective Jan. 1, 1997 (683 So.2d 78); Sept. 28, 2000, effective Jan. 1, 2001 (778 So.2d 272); June 19, 2003, effective Jan. 1, 2004 (848 So.2d 1069); Feb. 1, 2007 (948 So.2d 735).

Committee Notes

The provisions of chapter 744, Florida Statutes, and the guardianship rules enacted in 1989 leave some uncertainty with respect to the procedural requirements in guardianships for minors who are not incapacitated persons. This rule is intended to address only certain procedures with respect to the establishment and administration of guardianships over minors. The committee believes that certain provisions of the guardianship law and rules apply to both guardianships of minors as well as guardianships of incapacitated persons and no change has been suggested with respect to such rules. Because no adjudication of a minor is required by statute, it is contemplated that appointment of a guardian for a minor may be accomplished without a hearing. Initial and annual guardianship reports for minors have been simplified where all assets are on deposit with a designated financial institution under applicable Florida law.

Rule History

1991 Revision: New rule adopted to apply to guardianships over minors who are not incapacitated persons.

1992 Revision: Committee notes revised. Citation form changes in committee notes.

1996 Revision: Committee notes revised.

2000 Revision: Deletes requirement in subdivision (c) to report social security number of proposed guardian.

2003 Revision: Deletes requirement in subdivision (c) to report social security number of minor. Committee notes revised.

2006 Revision: Subdivision (e)(2) amended to conform to requirement in sections 744.362(1) and 744.3675, Florida Statutes, to file initial and annual guardianship plans. Subdivision (e)(3) amended to eliminate requirement of service on ward unless ordered by court or required by statute.

2014 Revision: Fla. R. Jud. Admin. 2.425(b)(4)—(5) provides exceptions for using the birth date of any minor "whenever the birth date is necessary for the court to establish or maintain subject matter jurisdiction," as well as using the full name in situations in which the "name of the minor in any order relating to parental responsibility, time-sharing, or child support." Committee notes revised.

Statutory References

§ 69.031, Fla. Stat. Designated financial institutions for assets in hands of guardians, curators, administrators, trustees, receivers, or other officers.

§ 744.3021, Fla. Stat. Guardians of minors.

§ 744.334, Fla. Stat. Petition for appointment of guardian or professional guardian; contents.

§ 744.3371(2), Fla. Stat. Notice of petition for appointment of guardian and hearing.

§ 744.342, Fla. Stat. Minors; guardianship.

§ 744.362, Fla. Stat. Initial guardianship report.

§ 744.363, Fla. Stat. Initial guardianship plan.

§ 744.365, Fla. Stat. Verified inventory.

§ 744.367, Fla. Stat. Duty to file annual guardianship report.

§ 744.3675, Fla. Stat. Annual guardianship plan.

§ 744.3678, Fla. Stat. Annual accounting.

§ 744.3679, Fla. Stat. Simplified accounting procedures in certain cases.

Rule References

Fla. Prob. R. 5.040 Notice.

Fla. Prob. R. 5.541 Recording of hearings.

Fla. Prob. R. 5.560 Petition for appointment of guardian of an incapacitated person.

Fla. Prob. R. 5.620 Inventory.

Fla. Prob. R. 5.636 Settlement of minors' claims.

Fla. Prob. R. 5.690 Initial guardianship report.

Fla. R. Jud. Admin. 2.425 Minimization of the Filing of Sensitive Information.

Rule 5.560. Petition for Appointment of Guardian of an Incapacitated Person

(a) Contents. The petition shall be verified by the petitioner and shall state:

(1) the facts to establish venue;

(2) the petitioner's residence and post office address;

(3) the name, age, and residence and post office address of the alleged incapacitated person;

(4) the nature of the incapacity, the extent of guardianship, either limited or plenary, requested for the alleged incapacitated person, and the nature and value of property subject to the guardianship;

(5) the names and addresses of the next of kin of the alleged incapacitated person known to the petitioner;

(6) the name and residence and post office address of the proposed guardian, and that the proposed guardian is qualified to serve, or that a willing and qualified guardian has not been located;

(7) the proposed guardian's relationship to and any previous association with the alleged incapacitated person;

(8) the reasons why the proposed guardian should be appointed;

(9) whether there are alternatives to guardianship known to the petitioner that may sufficiently address the problems of the alleged incapacitated person in whole or in part; and

(10) if the proposed guardian is a professional guardian, a statement that the proposed guardian has complied with the registration requirements of section 744.1083, Florida Statutes.

(b) Notice. Notice of filing the petition for appointment of guardian may be served as a part of the notice of filing the petition to determine incapacity, but shall be served a reasonable time before the hearing on the petition or other pleading seeking appointment of a guardian.

(c) Service on Public Guardian. If the petitioner requests appointment of the public guardian, a copy of the petition and the notice shall be served on the public guardian.

Amended Sept. 4, 1980, effective Jan. 1, 1981 (387 So.2d 949); Sept. 13, 1984, effective Jan. 1, 1985 (458 So.2d 1079); Dec. 23, 1987 (517 So.2d 675); Sept. 29, 1988, effective Jan. 1, 1989 (537 So.2d 500); Sept. 29, 1989, effective Oct. 1, 1989 (549 So.2d 665); Nov. 17, 1989 (551 So.2d 452); Aug. 22, 1991, effective Oct. 1, 1991 (584 So.2d 964); Oct. 3, 1996, effective Jan. 1, 1997 (683 So.2d 78); Sept. 28, 2000, effective Jan. 1, 2001 (778 So.2d 272); Feb. 1, 2007 (948 So.2d 140).

Committee Notes

Rule History

1975 Revision: Substantially the same as section 744.334, Florida Statutes, expanded to include provisions of section 744.302, Florida Statutes, and section 744.312, Florida Statutes, by reference.

1977 Revision: Change in committee notes to conform to statutory renumbering.

1980 Revision: Implements 1979 amendment to section 744.334, Florida Statutes.

1984 Revision: Combines rule 5.560 and part of prior rule 5.570. Editorial changes and committee notes revised.

1988 Revision: Editorial changes. Committee notes revised. Citation form changes in committee notes.

1989 Revision by Ad Hoc Committee: Subdivision (a)(4) of the former rule has been deleted altogether because the date and court of adjudication will probably not be known at the time of filing the petition for the appointment since petition for appointment will henceforth be filed contemporaneously with the petition to determine incapacity.

1991 Revision: Implements 1989 amendments to sections 744.334 and 744.331(1), Florida Statutes, and 1990 technical amendments. Subdivision (c)(1) deleted because rule 5.555(d) addresses service on parents.

1992 Revision: Citation form changes in committee notes.

1996 Revision: Deletes requirement in subdivision (a) to report social security number of alleged incapacitated person. Adds provision to subdivision (b) for notice before hearing when petition is not served simultaneously with petition to determine incapacity.

2000 Revision: Deletes requirement in subdivision (a) to report social security number of proposed guardian.

2003 Revision: Committee notes revised.

2006 Revision: New (a)(9) added to incorporate 2006 passage of section 744.462, Florida Statutes. Subdivision (a)(10) added to implement section 744.1083, Florida Statutes. Committee notes revised.

2014 Revision: Fla. R. Jud. Admin. 2.425(b)(4)—(5) provides exceptions for using the birth date of any minor "whenever the birth date is necessary for the court to establish or maintain subject matter jurisdiction," as well as using the full name in situations in which the "name of the minor in any order relating to parental responsibility, time-sharing, or child support." Committee notes revised.

Statutory References

§ 744.1083, Fla. Stat. Professional guardian registration.

§ 744.309, Fla. Stat. Who may be appointed guardian of a resident ward.

§ 744.312, Fla. Stat. Considerations in appointment of guardian.

§ 744.331, Fla. Stat. Procedures to determine incapacity.

§ 744.334, Fla. Stat. Petition for appointment of guardian or professional guardian; contents.

§ 744.3371(1), Fla. Stat. Notice of petition for appointment of guardian and hearing.

§ 744.341, Fla. Stat. Voluntary guardianship.

§ 744.344, Fla. Stat. Order of appointment.

§ 744.462, Fla. Stat. Determination regarding alternatives to guardianship.

§ 744.703, Fla. Stat. Office of public guardian; appointment, notification.

Rule References

Fla. Prob. R. 5.020 Pleadings; verification; motions.

Fla. Prob. R. 5.040 Notice.

Fla. Prob. R. 5.550 Petition to determine incapacity.

Fla. R. Jud. Admin. 2.425 Minimization of the Filing of Sensitive Information.

Rule 5.590. Application For Appointment as Guardian; Disclosure Statement; Filing

(a) Individual Applicants.

(1) The application for appointment shall contain:

(A) the applicant's qualifications to serve as a guardian, including a statement indicating whether the applicant has ever been (i) arrested or (ii) convicted of a felony, even if the record of such arrest or conviction has been expunged, unless the expunction was ordered pursuant to section 943.0583, Florida Statutes; and

(B) the names of all wards who are adults and the initials of any ward who is a minor for whom the applicant is then acting as guardian, the court file number and circuit court in which each case is pending, and a statement as to whether the applicant is acting as a limited or plenary guardian of the person or property, or both, of each ward.

(2) The application for appointment shall be filed and served a reasonable time before the hearing on the appointment of a guardian.

(b) Nonprofit Corporate Guardians.

(1) No application for appointment shall be required of a nonprofit corporate guardian.

(2) A disclosure statement shall contain:

(A) the corporation's qualifications to serve as a guardian; and

(B) the names of all wards who are adults and the initials of any ward who is a minor for whom the corporation is then acting as guardian, the court file number and circuit court in which each case is pending, and a statement as to whether the corporation is acting as a limited or plenary guardian of the person or property, or both, of each ward.

(3) The disclosure statement of a nonprofit corporate guardian shall be filed quarterly with the clerk of the court for each circuit in which the corporation has been appointed, or is seeking appointment, as guardian.

(c) For Profit Corporations and Associations. No application for appointment or disclosure statement shall be required of any for profit corporation or association authorized to exercise fiduciary powers under Florida law.

(d) Public Guardians. No application for appointment or disclosure statement shall be required of a public guardian.

Added Sept. 29, 1989, effective Oct. 1, 1989 (551 So.2d 452). Amended Aug. 22, 1991, effective Oct. 1, 1991 (584 So.2d 964); Oct. 3, 1996, effective Jan. 1, 1997 (683 So.2d 78); Feb. 1, 2007 (948 So.2d 140); May 22, 2014, effective May 22, 2014 (139 So.3d 875); Nov. 6, 2014, effective Nov. 6, 2014 (150 So.3d 1100).

Committee Notes

Rule History

1988 Revision: Prior rule deleted; text of rule moved to rule 5.650.

1989 Revision: Rule reactivated with different title and text.

1991 Revision: Implements 1989 and 1990 amendments to section 744.3125, Florida Statutes.

1992 Revision: Citation form change in committee notes.

1996 Revision: Adds filing and service provisions consistent with rule 5.560. Corrects reference to corporations qualified to exercise fiduciary powers. Editorial changes. Adds statutory references.

2003 Revision: Committee notes revised.

2006 Revision: Committee notes revised.

2008 Revision: Committee notes revised.

2014 Revision: Amends subdivisions (a)(1)(B) and (b)(1)(B) to conform to Fla. R. Jud. Admin. 2.425. Creates a rule reference. Committee notes revised.

2014 Revision: Amends subdivision (a)(1)(A) to conform to sections 744.309(3), 943.0583, and 943.0585, Florida Statutes. Committee notes revised.

Statutory References

§ 393.063(17), Fla. Stat. Definitions.

§ 393.12, Fla. Stat. Capacity; appointment of guardian advocate.

§ 744.102(4), (9), (11), (14), (22) Fla. Stat. Definitions.

§ 744.3085, Fla. Stat. Guardian advocates.

§ 744.309, Fla. Stat. Who may be appointed guardian of a resident ward.

§ 744.3125, Fla. Stat. Application for appointment.

§ 744.331(1), Fla. Stat. Procedures to determine incapacity.

§ 744.3371, Fla. Stat. Notice of petition for appointment of guardian and hearing.

§ 943.0583, Fla. Stat. Human trafficking victim expunction.

§ 943.0585, Fla. Stat. Court-ordered expunction of criminal history records.

Rule References

Fla. R. Jud. Admin. 2.425 Minimization of the Filing of Sensitive Information.

Rule 5.600. Oath

Every guardian or emergency temporary guardian shall take an oath to perform faithfully the duties of guardian or emergency temporary guardian before exercising such authority. The oath may be incorporated in the petition for appointment of guardian, or petition for appointment of emergency temporary guardian, if verified by the prospective guardian.

Amended Sept. 13, 1984, effective Jan. 1, 1985 (458 So.2d 1079); Sept. 29, 1989, effective Oct. 1, 1989 (549 So.2d 665); Nov. 17, 1989 (551 So.2d 452); Aug. 22, 1991, effective Oct. 1, 1991 (584 So.2d 964); Sept. 24, 1992, effective Jan. 1, 1993 (607 So.2d 1306).

Committee Notes

Rule History

1977 Revision: Change in committee notes to conform to statutory renumbering. Rule permits oath of guardian to be incorporated in petition for appointment and in designation of resident agent.

1984 Revision: Editorial change and deletes genders.

1989 Revision: Prior rule adopted as temporary emergency rule.

1991 Revision: Permits oath to be incorporated in application for appointment of guardian, adds reference to temporary emergency guardian, and makes editorial change.

1992 Revision: Editorial changes.

2008 Revision: Committee notes revised.

Statutory References

§ 393.12, Fla. Stat. Capacity; appointment of guardian advocate.

§ 744.347, Fla. Stat. Oath of guardian.

Rule 5.610. Execution by Guardian

The guardian shall sign the:

(a) initial guardianship plan;

(b) inventory, amended inventory, or supplemental inventory;

(c) annual guardianship plan;

(d) annual accounting;

(e) guardian's petition for court approval required by law;

(f) petition for discharge;

(g) final report; and

(h) resignation of guardian.

Amended March 31, 1977, effective July 1, 1977 (344 So.2d 828); Sept. 29, 1988, effective Jan. 1, 1989 (537 So.2d 500); Sept. 29, 1989, effective Oct. 1, 1989 (549 So.2d 665); Nov. 17, 1989 (551 So.2d 452); Aug. 22, 1991, effective Oct. 1, 1991 (584 So.2d 964).

Committee Notes

Rule History

1975 Revision: Rule lists what guardian shall sign and includes any petition for court approval required by section 744.441, Florida Statutes. The rule requires that the guardian have actual knowledge of the more important steps and acts of administration.

1977 Revision: Change in statutory reference in rule and in committee note to conform to statutory renumbering.

1988 Revision: Editorial changes. Committee notes revised. Citation form changes in rule and committee notes.

1989 Revision: Prior rule deleted and replaced by temporary emergency rule.

1991 Revision: Changes to conform to 1989 and 1990 revisions to guardianship law. Adds additional documents to be signed by the guardian. Statutory references added.

2003 Revision: Committee notes revised.

2008 Revision: Committee notes revised.

Statutory References

§ 393.12, Fla. Stat. Capacity; appointment of guardian advocate.

§ 744.362, Fla. Stat. Initial guardianship report.

§ 744.363, Fla. Stat. Initial guardianship plan.

§ 744.365, Fla. Stat. Verified inventory.

§ 744.367, Fla. Stat. Duty to file annual guardianship report.

§ 744.3675, Fla. Stat. Annual guardianship plan.

§ 744.3678, Fla. Stat. Annual accounting.

§ 744.387, Fla. Stat. Settlement of claims.

§ 744.441, Fla. Stat. Powers of guardian upon court approval.

§ 744.446, Fla. Stat. Conflicts of interest; prohibited activities; court approval; breach of fiduciary duty.

§ 744.447, Fla. Stat. Petition for authorization to act.

§ 744.451, Fla. Stat. Order.

§ 744.467, Fla. Stat. Resignation of guardian.

§ 744.511, Fla. Stat. Accounting upon removal.

§ 744.521, Fla. Stat. Termination of guardianship.

§ 744.524, Fla. Stat. Termination of guardianship on change of domicile of resident ward.

§ 744.527(1), Fla. Stat. Final reports and application for discharge; hearing.

§ 744.534, Fla. Stat. Disposition of unclaimed funds held by guardian.

Rule 5.620. Inventory

(a) Inventory. Within 60 days after issuance of letters, the guardian of the property shall file a verified inventory as required by law. All property not in the guardian's possession as of the date the inventory is filed shall be so identified.

(b) Amended or Supplemental Inventory. If the guardian of the property learns of any property not included in the inventory, or learns that the description in the inventory is inaccurate, the guardian shall, within 30 days of this discovery, file a verified amended or supplemental inventory showing the change.

(c) Substantiating Papers. Unless ordered by the court, the guardian need not file the papers substantiating the inventory. Upon reasonable written request, the guardian of the property shall make the substantiating papers available for examination to those persons entitled to receive or inspect the inventory.

(d) Safe–Deposit Box Inventory. If the ward has a safe-deposit box, a copy of the safe-deposit box inventory shall be filed as part of the verified inventory.

(e) Guardian Advocates. This rule shall apply to a guardian advocate to the extent that the guardian advocate was granted authority over the property of the person with a developmental disability.

Amended Sept. 13, 1984, effective Jan. 1, 1985 (458 So.2d 1079); Sept. 29, 1988, effective Jan. 1, 1989 (537 So.2d 500); Sept. 29, 1989, effective Oct. 1, 1989 (549 So.2d 665); Nov. 17, 1989 (551 So.2d 452); Aug. 22, 1991, effective Oct. 1, 1991 (584 So.2d 964); Sept. 29, 2005, effective Jan. 1, 2006 (912 So.2d 1178); July 12, 2007 (964 So.2d 140); July 10, 2008 (986 So.2d 576).

Committee Notes

Rule History

1977 Revision: Change in committee notes to conform to statutory renumbering.

1984 Revision: Change to require inventory to be filed within 60 days after issuance of letters, rather than after appointment. Committee notes revised.

1988 Revision: Editorial changes. Committee notes revised. Citation form change in committee notes.

1989 Revision: Prior rule deleted and replaced by temporary emergency rule.

1991 Revision: Former rule 5.620(b) has been deleted as partly substantive and addressed in section 744.381, Florida Statutes, and the procedural part is unnecessary.

The committee recognizes the conflict between this rule and section 744. 362, Florida Statutes, which requires the filing of the initial guardianship report (which includes the inventory) within 60 days after appointment. The committee believes this provision, which attempts to regulate when a paper must be filed with the court, is procedural and that a guardian may not receive letters of guardianship empowering the guardian to act contemporaneously with the appointment. Therefore, the issuance of letters is a more practical time from which to measure the beginning of the time period for the accomplishment of this act.

1992 Revision: Citation form changes in committee notes.

2005 Revision: Editorial changes in (d).

2007 Revision: Committee notes revised.

2008 Revision: Adds reference to guardian advocate in new (e). Committee notes revised.

2012 Revision: Committee notes revised.

Statutory References

§ 393.12, Fla. Stat. Capacity; appointment of guardian advocate.

§ 744.362, Fla. Stat. Initial guardianship report.

§ 744.365, Fla. Stat. Verified inventory.

§ 744.3701, Fla. Stat. Inspection of report.

§ 744.381, Fla. Stat. Appraisals.

§ 744.384, Fla. Stat. Subsequently discovered or acquired property.

Rule References

Fla. Prob. R. 5.020 Pleadings; verification; motions.

Fla. Prob. R. 5.041 Service of pleadings and documents.

Fla. Prob. R. 5.060 Request for notices and copies of pleadings.

Fla. Prob. R. 5.610 Execution by guardian.

Fla. Prob. R. 5.649 Guardian advocate.

Fla. Prob. R. 5.690 Initial guardianship report.

Fla. Prob. R. 5.700 Objection to guardianship reports.

Fla. R. Jud. Admin. 2.516 Service of pleadings and documents.

Rule 5.625. Notice of Completion of Guardian Education Requirements

(a) Filing. Unless the guardian education requirement is waived by the court, each guardian, other than a professional guardian, shall file with the court within 4 months after the issuance of letters of guardianship or letters of guardian advocacy a notice of completion of guardian education requirements.

(b) Content. The notice shall state:

(1) that the guardian has completed the required number of hours of course instruction and training covering the legal duties and responsibilities of a guardian, the rights of a ward, the availability of local resources to aid a ward, and the preparation of habilitation plans and annual guardianship reports, including accountings;

(2) the date the course was completed;

(3) the name of the course completed; and

(4) the name of the entity or instructor that taught the course.

(c) Verification. The notice shall be verified by the guardian.

Added Sept. 29, 2005, effective Jan. 1, 2006 (912 So.2d 1178). Amended Feb. 1, 2007 (948 So.2d 735); July 10, 2008 (986 So.2d 576).

Committee Notes

Rule History

2005 Revision: New rule.

2006 Revision: Subdivision (a) amended to conform to 2006 amendment to section 744.3145(4), Florida Statutes.

2008 Revision: Adds reference in (a) to guardian advocacy. Committee notes revised.

Statutory References

§ 393.12, Fla. Stat. Capacity; appointment of guardian advocate.

§ 744.3145, Fla. Stat. Guardian education requirements.

Rule 5.630. Petition for Approval of Acts

(a) Contents. When authorization or confirmation of any act of the guardian is required, application shall be made by verified petition stating the facts showing:

(1) the expediency or necessity for the action;

(2) a description of any property involved;

(3) the price and terms of any sale, mortgage, or other contract;

(4) whether the ward has been adjudicated incapacitated to act with respect to the rights to be exercised;

(5) whether the action requested conforms to the guardianship plan; and

(6) the basis for the relief sought.

(b) Notice. No notice of a petition to authorize sale of perishable personal property or of property rapidly deteriorating shall be required. Notice of a petition to perform any other act requiring a court order shall be given to the ward, to the next of kin, if any, and to those persons who have filed requests for notices and copies of pleadings.

(c) Order.

(1) If the act is authorized or confirmed, the order shall describe the permitted act and authorize the guardian to perform it or confirm its performance.

(2) If a sale or mortgage is authorized or confirmed, the order shall describe the property. If a sale is to be private, the order shall specify the price and the terms of the sale. If a sale is to be public, the order shall state that the sale shall be made to the highest bidder and that the court reserves the right to reject all bids.

(3) If the guardian is authorized to bring an action to contest the validity of all or part of a revocable trust, the order shall contain a finding that the action appears to be in the ward's best interests during the

ward's probable lifetime. If the guardian is not authorized to bring such an action, the order shall contain a finding concerning the continued need for a guardian and the extent of the need for delegation of the ward's rights.

Amended March 31, 1977, effective July 1, 1977 (344 So.2d 828); Sept. 4, 1980, effective Jan. 1, 1981 (387 So.2d 949); Sept. 29, 1988, effective Jan. 1, 1989 (537 So.2d 500); Sept. 29, 1989, effective Oct. 1, 1989 (549 So.2d 665); Nov. 17, 1989 (551 So.2d 452); Aug. 22, 1991, effective Oct. 1, 1991 (584 So.2d 964); Feb. 1, 2007 (948 So.2d 735); July 12, 2007 (964 So.2d 140).

Committee Notes

Rule History

1975 Revision: Substantially the same as sections 744.503, 744.447, and 744.451, Florida Statutes, with editorial changes.

1977 Revision: Change in statutory reference in rule and in committee note to conform to statutory renumbering.

1980 Revision: Implements 1979 amendment to section 744.447(2), Florida Statutes.

1988 Revision: Editorial changes; captions added to subdivisions. Committee notes revised. Citation form changes in rule and committee notes.

1989 Revision: Prior rule deleted and replaced by temporary emergency rule.

1991 Revision: Changes to conform to 1989 revised guardianship law.

1992 Revision: Committee notes revised. Citation form changes in committee notes.

2006 Revision: New (a)(6) added to incorporate 2006 amendment to section 744.441, Florida Statutes. New (c)(3) added to reflect passage of 2006 amendment to section 737.2065, Florida Statutes. Committee notes revised.

2007 Revision: Committee notes revised.

2008 Revision: Committee notes revised.

2012 Revision: Committee notes revised.

Statutory References

§ 393.12, Fla. Stat. Capacity; appointment of guardian advocate.

§ 736.0207, Fla. Stat. Trust contests.

§ 744.3215, Fla. Stat. Rights of persons determined incapacitated.

§ 744.441, Fla. Stat. Powers of guardian upon court approval.

§ 744.447, Fla. Stat. Petition for authorization to act.

§ 744.451, Fla. Stat. Order.

Rule References

Fla. Prob. R. 5.020 Pleadings; verification; motions.

Fla. Prob. R. 5.025 Adversary proceedings.

Fla. Prob. R. 5.040 Notice.

Fla. Prob. R. 5.041 Service of pleadings and documents.

Fla. Prob. R. 5.060 Request for notices and copies of pleadings.

Fla. Prob. R. 5.610 Execution by guardian.

Fla. Prob. R. 5.636 Settlement of minors' claims.

Fla. Prob. R. 5.649 Guardian advocate.

Fla. R. Jud. Admin. 2.516 Service of pleadings and documents.

Rule 5.635. Petition for Extraordinary Authority

(a) Contents. When authorization for extraordinary authority is sought as permitted by law, application shall be made by verified petition stating:

(1) the petitioner's interest in the proceeding;

(2) the specific authority requested; and

(3) the facts constituting the basis for the relief sought and that the authority being requested is in the best interest of the ward.

(b) Notice.

(1) The petition shall be served by formal notice. For good cause shown, the court may shorten the time for response to the formal notice and may set an expedited hearing.

(2) The petition shall be served on the guardian of the person, if the guardian is not the petitioner, the ward, the next of kin, if any, those interested persons who have filed requests for notices and copies of pleadings, and such other persons as the court may direct.

(c) Hearing. The hearing shall be at a time and place that will enable the ward to express the ward's views to the court.

Added Aug. 22, 1991, effective Oct. 1, 1991 (584 So.2d 964).

Committee Notes

Rule History

1991 Revision: New rule.

1992 Revision: Committee notes revised.

2008 Revision: Committee notes revised.

Statutory References

§ 393.12, Fla. Stat. Capacity; appointment of guardian advocate.

§ 744.3215(4), Fla. Stat. Rights of persons determined incapacitated.

§ 744.3725, Fla. Stat. Procedure for extraordinary authority.

Rule 5.636. Settlement of Minors' Claims

(a) Time of Settlement. Claims on behalf of minors may be settled either before or after an action is filed.

(b) Petition. The petition for approval of a settlement shall contain:

(1) the initials, residence address, and the year of birth of the minor;

(2) the name and address of any guardian appointed for the minor;

(3) the name and residence address of the natural guardians or other persons having legal custody of the minor;

(4) a statement disclosing the interests of any natural or court-appointed guardian whose interest may be in conflict with that of the minor;

(5) a description of the cause of action in which the minor's interest arises;

(6) a summary of the terms of the proposed settlement; and

(7) copies of all agreements, releases, or other documents to be executed on behalf of the minor.

(c) Notice. Notice of the petition shall be given to the court-appointed guardians for the minor, to the natural guardians or other persons with legal custody of the minor, to the minor if age 14 or older, and to the minor's next of kin if required by the court.

(d) Guardian Ad Litem. The court shall appoint a guardian ad litem on behalf of a minor, without bond or notice, with respect to any proposed settlement that exceeds $50,000 and affects the interests of the minor, if:

(1) there is no court-appointed guardian of the minor;

(2) the court-appointed guardian may have an interest adverse to the minor; or

(3) the court determines that representation of the minor's interest is otherwise inadequate.

(e) Valuation of Proposed Settlement. A proposed settlement is deemed to exceed $50,000 if the gross amount payable exceeds $50,000, without reduction to reflect present value or fees and costs.

(f) Report. A guardian ad litem appointed with respect to a proposed settlement affecting the interests of a minor shall, not later than 5 days prior to the hearing on a petition for order authorizing settlement, file and serve a report indicating the guardian ad litem's determination regarding whether the proposed settlement will be in the best interest of the minor. The report shall include:

(1) a statement of the facts of the minor's claim and the terms of the proposed settlement, including any benefits to any persons or parties with related claims;

(2) a list of the persons interviewed and documents reviewed by the guardian ad litem in evaluating the minor's claim and proposed settlement; and

(3) the guardian ad litem's analysis of whether the proposed settlement will be in the best interest of the minor.

A copy of the report shall be served on those persons on whom service is required in subdivision (c) of this rule.

Added Sept. 24, 1992, effective Jan. 1, 1993 (607 So.2d 1306). Amended Feb. 1, 2007 (948 So.2d 735); May 22, 2014, effective May 22, 2014 (139 So.3d 875).

Committee Notes

When a civil action is pending, the petition for approval of settlement should be filed in that civil action. In all other circumstances, the petition for approval of settlement should be filed in the same court and assigned to a judge who would preside over a petition for appointment of guardian of a minor.

The total settlement to be considered under subdivisions (d) and (e) is not limited to the amounts received only by the minor, but includes all settlement payments or proceeds received by all parties to the claim or action. For example, the proposed settlement may have a gross value of $60,000, with $30,000 payable to the minor and $30,000 payable to another party. In that instance the total proposed settlement exceeds $50,000. Further, the "gross amount payable" under subdivision (e) is the total sum payable, without reducing the settlement amount by fees and costs that might be paid from the proceeds of the settlement. For example, if the proposed settlement is $60,000 but $20,000 of that sum will be paid to the attorneys representing the minor's interest in the action, the "gross amount payable" still exceeds $50,000. Likewise, the "gross amount payable" cannot be reduced to reflect the present value of the proposed settlement on behalf of the minor.

Rule History

1992 Revision: New rule.

2003 Revision: Committee notes revised.

2006 Revision: Amended to reflect 2006 passage of new section 744.3025, Claims of Minors, increasing dollar figure from $25,000 to $50,000 as threshold amount requiring appointment of guardian ad litem if interests of minor are not otherwise adequately represented. Committee notes revised.

2014 Revision: Amends subdivision (b)(1) to conform to Fla. R. Jud. Admin. 2.425. Committee notes revised.

Statutory References

§ 744.3025, Fla. Stat. Claims of minors.

§ 744.387, Fla. Stat. Settlement of claims.

§ 744.391, Fla. Stat. Actions by and against guardian or ward.

§ 744.441, Fla. Stat. Powers of guardian upon court approval.

§ 744.446, Fla. Stat. Conflicts of interest; prohibited activities; court approval; breach of fiduciary duty.

§ 744.447, Fla. Stat. Petition for authorization to act.

§ 768.23, Fla. Stat. Protection of minors and incompetents.

§ 768.25, Fla. Stat. Court approval of settlements.

Rule References

Fla. Prob. R. 5.040 Notice.

Fla. Prob. R. 5.042 Time.

Fla. Prob. R. 5.120 Administrator ad litem and guardian ad litem.

Fla. Prob. R. 5.610 Execution by guardian.

Fla. Prob. R. 5.630 Petition for approval of acts.

Fla. R. Jud. Admin. 2.425 Minimization of the Filing of Sensitive Information.

Rule 5.640. Continuance of Unincorporated Business or Venture of Ward

(a) Continuance of Business. When the ward is adjudicated incapacitated while engaged in any unincorporated business or venture, or the court finds that a person with a developmental disability lacks capacity to manage an unincorporated business or venture, the court may authorize the guardian to continue the business or venture for a reasonable time under the supervision of the court.

(b) Petition. Before an order is made under subdivision (a), the guardian shall file a verified petition, alleging sufficient facts to make it appear that it is in the best interest of the ward's estate to continue the business or venture.

(c) Order. The order authorizing the continuance of the business or venture may empower the guardian to make contracts necessary to conduct the business or venture and to incur debts and pay out money in the proper conduct of the business or venture. The net profits only of the business or venture are to be added to the assets of the ward's estate.

(d) Accounts and Reports. In the conduct of the business or venture, the guardian shall keep full and accurate accounts of all receipts and expenditures and make reports as the court requires.

(e) Discontinuance of Business. Any person interested in the ward's estate may at any time petition the court for an order requiring the guardian to discontinue and to wind up the business or venture, and the court, after notice to the guardian, shall enter such order thereon as is in the best interest of the ward's estate.

Amended Sept. 29, 1988, effective Jan. 1, 1989 (537 So.2d 500); Sept. 29, 1989, effective Oct. 1, 1989 (549 So.2d 665); Nov. 17, 1989 (551 So.2d 452); Aug. 22, 1991, effective Oct. 1, 1991 (584 So.2d 964); July 10, 2008 (986 So.2d 576).

Committee Notes

Rule History

1975 Revision: Implements section 744.441(16), Florida Statutes. The rule is patterned after rule 5.350 pertaining to the continuation of a business of a decedent by a personal representative.

1977 Revision: No change in rule. Change in committee note to conform to statutory renumbering.

1988 Revision: Change in title of rule; captions added to subdivisions. Committee notes revised. Citation form changes in committee notes.

1989 Revision: Prior rule deleted and replaced by temporary emergency rule.

1991 Revision: Editorial changes in (a), (b), and (e).

1992 Revision: Citation form changes in committee notes.

2008 Revision: Subdivision (a) amended to include persons with a developmental disability. Committee notes revised.

Statutory References

§ 393.12, Fla. Stat. Capacity; appointment of guardian advocate.

§ 744.3085, Fla. Stat. Guardian advocates.

§ 744.441(13), Fla. Stat. Powers of guardian upon court approval.

§ 744.447, Fla. Stat. Petition for authorization to act.

Rule Reference

Fla. Prob. R. 5.350 Continuance of unincorporated business or venture.

Rule 5.645. Management of Property of Nonresident Ward by Foreign Guardian

(a) Petition. A guardian of the property of a nonresident ward, duly appointed by a court of another state, territory, or country, who desires to manage any part or all of the property of the ward located in this state, may file a verified petition for authority to manage the property. The petition shall state:

(1) the circumstances of the guardian's appointment;

(2) a description of the property and its estimated value; and

(3) the indebtedness, if any, existing against the ward in this state.

(b) Designation of Resident Agent. The guardian shall designate a resident agent as required by these rules.

(c) Oath. The guardian shall file an oath as required by these rules.

(d) Filing of Authenticated Copies. The guardian shall file authenticated copies of:

(1) letters of guardianship or other authority to act as guardian; and

(2) bond or other security, if any.

(e) Order. The court shall determine if the foreign bond or other security is sufficient to guarantee the faithful management of the ward's property in this state. The court may require a new guardian's bond in this state in an amount it deems necessary. The order shall authorize the guardian to manage the property and shall specifically describe the property.

Added July 5, 2007, effective Jan. 1, 2008 (959 So.2d 1170).

Committee Notes

Rule History

2007 Revision: New rule.

Statutory References

§ 744.306, Fla. Stat. Foreign guardians.

§ 744.307, Fla. Stat. Foreign guardian may manage the property of nonresident ward.

Rule References

Fla. Prob. R. 5.110 Address designation for personal representative or guardian; designation of resident agent and acceptance.

Fla. Prob. R. 5.600 Oath.

Rule 5.646. Standby Guardians

(a) Petition for Appointment of Standby Guardian for Minor.

(1) *Contents.* A minor's guardian or the natural guardians of a minor may petition for the appointment of a standby guardian of the person or property of the minor. The petition shall be verified by the petitioner and shall state:

(A) the facts to establish venue;

(B) the petitioner's residence and post office address;

(C) the name, age, and residence and post office address of the minor;

(D) the names and addresses of the parents of the minor and, if none, the next of kin known to the petitioner;

(E) the name and residence and post office address of the proposed standby guardian, and that the proposed standby guardian is qualified to serve;

(F) the proposed standby guardian's relationship to and any previous association with the minor;

(G) the reasons why the proposed standby guardian should be appointed; and

(H) the nature and value of the property subject to the guardianship.

(2) *Notice and Waiver of Notice.* Notice of the hearing on the petition must be served on the parents, natural or adoptive, of the minor and on any guardian for the minor. Notice may be waived by those required to receive notice or by the court for good cause.

(b) Petition for Appointment of Standby Guardian for Incapacitated Person.

(1) *Contents.* A currently serving guardian may petition for the appointment of a standby guardian of the person or property of an incapacitated person. The petition shall be verified by the petitioner and shall state:

(A) the petitioner's residence and post office address;

(B) the name, age, and residence and post office address of the incapacitated person;

(C) the nature of the incapacity, the extent of guardianship, either limited or plenary, and the nature and value of property subject to the guardianship;

(D) the names and addresses of the next of kin of the incapacitated person known to the petitioner;

(E) the name and residence and post office address of the proposed standby guardian, and that the proposed standby guardian is qualified to serve;

(F) the proposed standby guardian's relationship to and any previous association with the incapacitated person; and

(G) the reasons why the proposed standby guardian should be appointed.

(2) *Notice.* Notice of the hearing on the petition must be served on the incapacitated person's next of kin.

(c) Petition for Confirmation.

(1) *Contents.* A standby guardian, not later than 20 days after the assumption of duties as guardian, shall petition for confirmation of appointment. The petition shall be verified by the petitioner and shall state:

(A) the petitioners's residence and post office address;

(B) the name, age, and residence and post office address of the adult incapacitated person or initials, year of birth, and residence address of minor;

(C) the nature of the incapacity, the extent of guardianship, either limited or plenary, and the nature and value of property subject to the guardianship;

(D) the names and addresses of the next of kin of the incapacitated person or minor known to the petitioner;

(E) the name and residence and post office address of the proposed guardian, and that the proposed guardian is qualified to serve;

(F) the proposed guardian's relationship to and any previous association with the incapacitated person or minor;

(G) the reasons why appointment of the proposed guardian should be confirmed; and

(H) if the proposed guardian is a professional guardian, a statement that the proposed guardian has complied with the educational requirements of section 744.1083, Florida Statutes.

(2) *Service.* The petition for confirmation and notice of hearing shall be served on the incapacitated person's next of kin a reasonable time before the hearing on the petition or other pleading seeking confirmation of the guardian.

Added Feb. 1, 2007 (948 So.2d 735). Amended May 22, 2014 (139 So.3d 875).

Committee Notes

The standby guardian must file an oath pursuant to rule 5.600 before commencing the exercise of authority as guardian. Prior to appointment, the standby guardian must file an application pursuant to rule 5.590.

Section 393.12(10), Florida Statutes, provides that a guardian advocate shall have all of the duties, responsibilities, and powers of a guardian under Chapter 744, Florida Statutes. However, section 744.304 authorizes the appointment of a standby guardian only for a minor or incapacitated person.

Rule History

2006 Revision: New rule.

2008 Revision: Committee notes revised.

2014 Revision: Subdivision (c)(1)(B) amended to conform to Fla. R. Jud. Admin. 2.425. Committee notes revised.

Statutory Reference

§ 744.304, Fla. Stat. Standby guardianship.

Rule References

Fla. Prob. R. 5.590 Application for appointment as guardian; disclosure statement; filing.

Fla. Prob. R. 5.600 Oath.

Fla. R. Jud. Admin. 2.425 Minimization of the Filing of Sensitive Information.

Rule 5.647. Surrogate Guardian

(a) Petition for Designation of Surrogate Guardian. A guardian may file a petition to designate a surrogate guardian to exercise the powers of the guardian if the guardian is unavailable to act. The surrogate must be a professional guardian. The petition shall state:

(1) the name and business address of the surrogate guardian;

(2) the requested duration of the appointment; and

(3) the powers to be exercised by the surrogate guardian.

(b) Service. The petition for appointment of a surrogate guardian shall be served on all interested persons and the ward, unless the ward is a minor.

(c) Oath. The surrogate guardian must file with the court an oath swearing or affirming that the surrogate guardian will faithfully perform the duties delegated.

(d) Termination. Prior to the expiration of the period granted by court order, the guardian may terminate the authority of the surrogate guardian by filing a written notice of the termination with the court and serving it on the surrogate guardian.

Added Feb. 1, 2007 (948 So.2d 735).

Committee Notes

Rule History

2006 Revision: New rule.

2008 Revision. Committee notes revised.

Statutory References

§ 393.12, Fla. Stat. Capacity; appointment of guardian advocate.

§ 744.442, Fla. Stat. Delegation of authority.

Rule 5.648. Emergency Temporary Guardian

(a) Petition for Appointment of Emergency Temporary Guardian. Prior to appointment of a guardian but after a petition for determination of incapacity has been filed, the alleged incapacitated person or any adult interested in the welfare of that person may petition for the appointment of an emergency temporary guardian of the person or property. The petition shall be verified and shall state:

(1) the petitioner's residence and post office address;

(2) the name, age, and residence and post office address of the alleged incapacitated person;

(3) that there appears to be imminent danger that the physical or mental health or safety of the alleged incapacitated person will be seriously impaired or that the alleged incapacitated person's property is in danger of being wasted, misappropriated, or lost unless immediate action is taken;

(4) the nature of the emergency and the reason immediate action must be taken;

(5) the extent of the emergency temporary guardianship, either limited or plenary, requested for the alleged incapacitated person, and, if known, the nature and value of the property to be subject to the emergency temporary guardianship;

(6) the names and addresses of the next of kin of the alleged incapacitated person known to the petitioner;

(7) the name and residence and post office address of the proposed emergency temporary guardian, and that the proposed emergency temporary guardian is qualified to serve, or that a willing and qualified emergency temporary guardian has not been located; and

(8) the proposed emergency temporary guardian's relationship to or any previous association with the alleged incapacitated person.

(b) Notice. Unless the court orders otherwise, notice of filing of the petition for appointment of an emergency temporary guardian and any hearing on the petition shall be served before the hearing on the petition on the alleged incapacitated person and on the alleged incapacitated person's attorney.

(c) Service on Public Guardian. If the petitioner requests appointment of the public guardian as emergency temporary guardian, a copy of the petition and notice shall be served on the public guardian.

(d) Order. The order appointing the emergency temporary guardian shall specify the powers and duties of the emergency temporary guardian.

(e) Extension of Authority. Prior to the expiration of the authority of the emergency temporary guardian, any interested person may file a verified petition for extension of authority of the emergency temporary guardian. The petition must show that the conditions that warranted the initial appointment of the emergency temporary guardian still exist. The petition shall be served on the ward's attorney and on the emergency temporary guardian.

(f) Final Report. An emergency temporary guardian shall file a final report no later than 30 days after the expiration of the emergency temporary guardianship. A copy of the final report shall be served on the successor guardian, if any, the ward, and the ward's attorney. With approval of the court, service on the ward may be accomplished by serving the attorney for the ward.

(1) If the emergency temporary guardian is a guardian of the property, the final report shall consist of a verified inventory of the ward's property as of the date letters of emergency temporary guardianship were issued, a final accounting that gives a full and correct account of the receipts and disbursements of all the ward's property over which the guardian had control, and a statement of the property on hand at the end of the emergency temporary guardianship.

(2) If the emergency temporary guardian is a guardian of the person, the final report shall summarize the activities of the guardian with regard to residential placement, medical condition, mental health and rehabilitative services, and the social condition of the ward to the extent of the authority granted to the emergency temporary guardian.

(3) If the emergency temporary guardian becomes the successor guardian of the property or person of the ward, the final report must satisfy the requirements of, and shall serve as, the initial report of the guardian of the property or person of the ward, as the case may be, as set forth in rule 5.690.

Added July 12, 2007 (964 So.2d 140).

Committee Notes

Rule History

2007 Revision: New rule.

Statutory References

§ 744.3031, Fla. Stat. Emergency temporary guardianship.

§ 744.344(4), Fla. Stat. Order of appointment.

Rule References

Fla. Prob. R. 5.600 Oath.

Fla. Prob. R. 5.690 Initial Guardianship Report.

Rule 5.649. Guardian Advocate

(a) Petition for Appointment of Guardian Advocate. A petition to appoint a guardian advocate for a person with a developmental disability may be executed by an adult person who is a resident of this state. The petition must be verified by the petitioner and must state:

(1) the name, age, and present address of the petitioner and the petitioner's relationship to the person with a developmental disability;

(2) the name, age, county of residence, and present address of the person with a developmental disability;

(3) that the petitioner believes that the person needs a guardian advocate and the factual information on which such belief is based;

(4) the exact areas in which the person lacks the ability to make informed decisions about the person's care and treatment services or to meet the essential requirements for the person's physical health or safety;

(5) the legal disabilities to which the person is subject;

(6) if authority is sought over any property of the person, a description of that property and the reason why management or control of that property should be placed with a guardian advocate;

(7) the name of the proposed guardian advocate, the relationship of the proposed guardian advocate to the person with a developmental disability, the relationship of the proposed guardian advocate with the providers of health care services, residential services, or other services to the person with developmental disabilities, and the reason why the proposed guardian advocate should be appointed. If a willing and qualified guardian advocate cannot be located, the petition must so state; and

(8) whether the petitioner has knowledge, information, or belief that the person with a developmental disability has executed an advance directive under chapter 765, Florida Statutes, or a durable power of attorney under chapter 709, Florida Statutes.

(b) Notice.

(1) Notice of the filing of the petition must be given to the person with a developmental disability, both verbally and in writing, in the language of the person and in English. Notice must also be given to the person with a developmental disability's next of kin, any designated health care surrogate, an attorney-in-fact designated in a durable power of attorney, and such other persons as the court may direct. A copy of the petition to appoint a guardian advocate must be served with the notice.

(2) The notice must state that a hearing will be held to inquire into the capacity of the person with a developmental disability to exercise the rights enumerated in the petition. The notice must also state the date of the hearing on the petition.

(3) The notice must state that the person with a developmental disability has the right to be represented by counsel of the person's own choice and the court must initially appoint counsel.

(c) Counsel. Within 3 days after a petition has been filed, the court must appoint an attorney to represent a person with a developmental disability who is the subject of a petition to appoint a guardian advocate. The person with a developmental disability may substitute his or her own attorney for the attorney appointed by the court.

(d) Order. If the court finds the person with a developmental disability requires the appointment of a guardian advocate, the order appointing the guardian advocate must contain findings of facts and conclusions of law, including:

(1) the nature and scope of the person's inability to make decisions;

(2) the exact areas in which the person lacks ability to make informed decisions about care and treatment services or to meet the essential requirements for the individual's physical health and safety;

(3) if any property of the person is to be placed under the management or control of the guardian advocate, a description of that property, any limitations as to the extent of such management or control, and the reason why management or control by the guardian advocate of that property is in the best interest of the person;

(4) if the person has executed an advance directive or durable power of attorney, a determination as to whether the documents sufficiently address the needs of the person and a finding that the advance directive or durable power of attorney does not provide an alternative to the appointment of a guardian advocate that sufficiently addresses the needs of the person with a developmental disability;

(5) if a durable power of attorney exists, the powers of the attorney-in-fact, if any, that are suspended and granted to the guardian advocate;

(6) if an advance directive exists and the court determines that the appointment of a guardian advocate is necessary, the authority, if any, the guardian advocate exercises over the health care surrogate;

(7) the specific legal disabilities to which the person with a developmental disability is subject;

(8) the name of the person selected as guardian advocate; and

(9) the powers, duties, and responsibilities of the guardian advocate, including bonding of the guardian advocate as provided by law.

(e) Issuance of Letters. Upon compliance with all of the foregoing, letters of guardian advocacy must be issued to the guardian advocate.

Added July 10, 2008 (986 So.2d 576). Amended Sept. 26, 2013, effective Jan. 1, 2014 (123 So.3d 31).

Committee Notes

Rule History

2008 Revision: New rule.

2013 Revision: New subdivisions (a)(6) and (d)(3) added to address situations in which the guardian advocate will have authority over the property of the person with a developmental disability. New subdivision (e) added to provide for the issuance of letters of guardian advocacy. Editorial changes to subdivisions (a)(7) and (b)(3). Editorial changes to conform to the court's guidelines for rules submissions as set forth in AOSC06–14.

Statutory References

§ 393.063(9), Fla. Stat. Definitions.

§ 393.12, Fla. Stat. Capacity; appointment of guardian advocate.

§ 709.08, Fla. Stat. Durable power of attorney.

§ 765.101, Fla. Stat. Definitions.

§ 765.104, Fla. Stat. Amendment or revocation.

§ 765.202, Fla. Stat. Designation of a health care surrogate.

§ 765.204, Fla. Stat. Capacity of principal; procedure.

§ 765.205(3), Fla. Stat. Responsibility of the surrogate.

§ 765.302, Fla. Stat. Procedure for making a living will; notice to physician.

§ 765.401, Fla. Stat. The proxy.

Rule References

Fla. Prob. R. 5.020 Pleadings; verification; motions.

Fla. Prob. R. 5.540 Hearings.

Fla. Prob. R. 5.681 Restoration of rights of person with developmental disability.

Rule 5.650. Resignation or Disqualification of Guardian; Appointment of Successor

(a) Resignation and Petition for Discharge. A guardian seeking to resign shall file a resignation and petition for discharge.

(b) Contents. The resignation and petition for discharge shall state:

(1) that the guardian wishes to resign and be relieved of all duties as guardian;

(2) the amount of compensation to be paid to the guardian and to the attorneys, accountants, or other agents employed by the guardian; and

(3) the names and addresses of the successor guardian and the successor guardian's attorney, or that a successor guardian has not yet been appointed or duly qualified.

(c) Final Report. A resigning guardian of the property shall file a final report showing receipts, disbursements, amounts reserved for unpaid and anticipated costs and fees, and other relevant financial information from the date of the previous annual accounting, and a list of assets to be turned over to the successor guardian.

(d) Notice. A notice shall be served stating that:

(1) any objection shall be in writing and shall state with particularity each item to which the objection is directed and the grounds on which the objection is based;

(2) any objection to the resignation, petition for discharge, or final report shall be filed within 30 days

from the date of service of the petition for discharge; and

(3) within 90 days after filing of the objection, a notice of hearing thereon shall be served or the objection is abandoned.

(e) Service. A copy of the resignation, petition for discharge, final report, and notice of resignation and petition for discharge shall be served on the ward, any surety on the guardian's bond, any successor guardian, and such other persons as the court may direct.

(f) Objections. Objections shall be in the form and be filed within the time set forth in the notice of resignation and petition for discharge. A copy of the objections shall be served by the objector on the ward, all guardians, any surety on the guardian's bond, and any successor guardian.

(g) Disposition of Objections. Any interested person may set a hearing on the objections. Notice of the hearing shall be served on the guardian, the successor guardian, if any, and any other interested persons. If a notice of hearing on the objections is not served within 90 days of filing of the objections, the objections will be deemed abandoned.

(h) Discharge. The guardian's resignation shall not be accepted and the guardian shall not be discharged until all objections have been withdrawn, abandoned, or judicially resolved and a successor guardian has been appointed and duly qualified. After all objections have been withdrawn, abandoned, or judicially resolved, if the court is satisfied that the resigning guardian has faithfully discharged the duties of the guardianship and the interests of the ward are protected, and the resigning guardian of the property has delivered the assets of the ward, all guardianship records, and all money due to the ward from the guardian to the remaining or successor guardian, the court shall enter an order accepting resignation of guardian and granting discharge.

(i) Disqualification. Any guardian who is improperly appointed, or who becomes disqualified to act after appointment, shall immediately file a resignation and petition for discharge and proceed in accordance with this rule.

(j) Nonresident Guardians. Nonresident guardians appointed before October 1, 1989, shall not be automatically disqualified to serve and shall not be required to resign and initiate their own removal.

(k) Guardian Advocates. This rule shall apply to guardian advocates, except that a final report shall be required of a guardian advocate only if the guardian advocate's authority included the management of the property of the person with a developmental disability.

Amended Sept. 29, 1988, effective Jan. 1, 1989 (537 So.2d 500); Sept. 29, 1989, effective Oct. 1, 1989 (549 So.2d 665); Nov. 17, 1989 (551 So.2d 452); Aug. 22, 1991, effective Oct. 1, 1991 (584 So.2d 964); July 5, 2007, effective Jan. 1, 2008 (959 So.2d 1170); July 10, 2008 (986 So.2d 576).

Committee Notes

Rule History

1975 Revision: Substantially the same as sections 744.467 and 744.471, Florida Statutes, with editorial changes.

1977 Revision: No change in rule. Change in committee note to conform to statutory renumbering.

1988 Revision: Editorial changes in (a). Text of rule 5.590 inserted in (b). Editorial change in (c). Captions added to subdivisions. Committee notes revised. Citation form changes in committee notes.

1989 Revision: Prior rule deleted and replaced by temporary emergency rule.

1991 Revision: Substantial revision of entire rule to harmonize with procedure for termination of guardianship under rules 5.670 and 5.680. Subdivision (k) transferred from temporary emergency rule 5.800.

1992 Revision: Committee notes revised. Citation form changes in committee notes.

2007 Revision: Subdivision (i) deleted because right of waiver is substantive. Subsequent subdivisions relettered.

2008 Revision: Subdivision (k) added to include guardian advocates. Committee notes revised.

2012 Revision: Committee notes revised.

Statutory References

§ 393.12, Fla. Stat. Capacity; appointment of guardian advocate.

§ 744.102(11), Fla. Stat. Definitions.

§ 744.3085, Fla. Stat. Guardian advocates.

§ 744.467, Fla. Stat. Resignation of guardian.

§ 744.471, Fla. Stat. Appointment of successor.

Rule References

Fla. Prob. R. 5.040 Notice.

Fla. Prob. R. 5.041 Service of pleadings and documents.

Fla. Prob. R. 5.180 Waiver and consent.

Fla. Prob. R. 5.610 Execution by guardian.

Fla. Prob. R. 5.649 Guardian advocate.

Fla. Prob. R. 5.681 Restoration of rights of person with developmental disability.

Fla. R. Jud. Admin. 2.516 Service of pleadings and documents.

Rule 5.660. Proceedings for Removal of Guardian

(a) Notice. Proceedings for removal of a guardian may be instituted by a court, by any surety or other interested person, or by the ward, and formal notice of the petition for removal of a guardian must be served on all guardians, other interested persons, next of kin, and the ward. The pleading must state with particularity the reasons why the guardian should be removed.

(b) Accounting. A removed guardian must file with the court an accounting for the guardianship within 20 days after the guardian's removal. A copy of the accounting must be served on the successor guardian and the ward, unless the ward is a minor or has been determined to be totally incapacitated.

(c) Transfer of Property and Records. The removed guardian (or the guardian's heirs, personal representative, or surety) must turn over all the property of the ward in the removed guardian's control and all guardianship records to the duly qualified successor. The successor guardian must, or the ward may, demand of the removed guardian (or the guardian's heirs, personal representative, or surety) all of those items.

(d) Failure to Comply. If a removed guardian fails to file a true, complete, and final accounting for the guardianship or to turn over to the successor all property of the ward in the removed guardian's control and all guardianship records, the court must issue a show-cause order.

(e) Guardian Advocates. Subdivisions (b) through (d) of this rule apply to guardian advocates only to the extent that the guardian advocate was granted authority over the property of the person with a developmental disability.

Amended Sept. 4, 1980, effective Jan. 1, 1981 (387 So.2d 949); Sept. 13, 1984, effective Jan. 1, 1985 (458 So.2d 1079); Sept. 29, 1988, effective Jan. 1, 1989 (537 So.2d 500); Sept. 29, 1989, effective Oct. 1, 1989 (549 So.2d 665); Nov. 17, 1989 (551 So.2d 452); Aug. 22, 1991, effective Oct. 1, 1991 (584 So.2d 964); Feb. 1, 2007 (948 So.2d 735); July 10, 2008 (986 So.2d 576); Sept. 26, 2013, effective Jan. 1, 2014 (123 So.3d 31).

Committee Notes

Rule History

1977 Revision: No change in rule. Change in committee notes to conform to statutory renumbering.

1980 Revision: Subdivision (a) amended to specifically authorize any guardian or next of kin to file the petition and to require formal notice in conformity with rule 5.630(b).

1984 Revision: Subdivision (b) amended to conform to statute. Editorial changes and Committee notes revised.

1988 Revision: Subdivision (a) rewritten for clarity. Language in (b) deleted as surplusage. Editorial change in caption of (c). Committee notes revised. Citation form change in committee notes.

1989 Revision: Prior rule deleted and replaced by temporary emergency rule.

1991 Revision: Subdivision (a) amended to require that the petition allege specific reasons why the guardian should be removed and to require service of the petition on the ward. Otherwise, editorial changes in all subdivisions.

1992 Revision: Citation form changes in committee notes.

2006 Revision: Requirement in (b) to serve minors deleted to conform to 2006 amendment to section 744.511, Florida Statutes.

2008 Revision: Subdivision (e) added to include guardian advocates. Committee notes revised.

2012 Revision: Committee notes revised.

2013 Revision: Subdivision (b) revised to conform to section 744.511, Florida Statutes. Committee notes revised. Editorial changes to conform to the court's guidelines for rules submissions as set forth in AOSC06–14.

Statutory References

§ 393.12, Fla. Stat. Capacity; appointment of guardian advocate.

§ 744.3085, Fla. Stat. Guardian advocates.

§ 744.474, Fla. Stat. Reasons for removal of guardian.

§ 744.477, Fla. Stat. Proceedings for removal of a guardian.

§ 744.511, Fla. Stat. Accounting upon removal.

§ 744.514, Fla. Stat. Surrender of property upon removal.

§ 744.517, Fla. Stat. Proceedings for contempt.

Rule References

Fla. Prob. R. 5.025 Adversary proceedings.

Fla. Prob. R. 5.040 Notice.

Fla. Prob. R. 5.041 Service of pleadings and documents.

Fla. Prob. R. 5.649 Guardian advocate.

Fla. R. Jud. Admin. 2.420 Public access to judicial branch records.

Fla. R. Jud. Admin. 2.516 Service of pleadings and documents.

Rule 5.670. Termination of Guardianship on Change of Domicile of Resident Ward

(a) Petition for Discharge. The Florida guardian may file a petition for discharge when the domicile of a resident ward has changed to a foreign jurisdiction, the foreign court having jurisdiction over the ward at the ward's new domicile has appointed a foreign guardian, and the foreign guardian has qualified and posted a bond in the amount required by the foreign court.

(b) Contents of Petition. The petition for discharge shall state:

(1) that the grounds set forth in subdivision (a) have occurred;

(2) that the guardian has fully administered the Florida guardianship; and

(3) the amount of compensation to be paid to the guardian and to the attorneys, accountants, or other agents employed by the guardian.

(c) Final Report. The Florida guardian of the property shall file a final report showing receipts, disbursements, amounts reserved for unpaid and anticipated costs and fees, and other relevant financial information from the date of the previous annual accounting, and a list of the assets to be turned over to the foreign guardian.

(d) Notice. The Florida guardian of the property shall publish a notice as required by law, which shall state:

(1) the name of the ward;

(2) the file number of the guardianship;

(3) the designation and address of the court;

(4) the name and address of the guardian and the guardian's attorney;

(5) the name and address of the foreign guardian and the foreign guardian's attorney, if any;

(6) the date of first publication;

(7) that a petition for discharge has been filed upon the grounds of change of domicile of the ward;

(8) the date the guardian will apply for discharge;

(9) that the jurisdiction of the ward will be transferred to the foreign jurisdiction;

(10) that any objection shall be in writing and shall state with particularity each item to which the objection is directed and the grounds on which the objection is based;

(11) that any objection to the final report or the petition for discharge shall be filed within the later of 30 days from the date of service of the petition for discharge or the date of first publication of the notice; and

(12) that within 90 days after filing of the objection, a notice of hearing thereon shall be served or the objection is abandoned.

(e) Service. A copy of the petition for discharge and of the notice of petition for discharge shall be served on the foreign guardian and such other persons as the court may direct.

(f) Objections. Objections shall be in the form and be filed within the time set forth in the notice of petition for discharge. A copy of the objections shall be served by the objector on the Florida guardian and the foreign guardian.

(g) Disposition of Objections. Any interested person may set a hearing on the objections. Notice of the hearing shall be served on the Florida guardian, the foreign guardian, and any other interested persons. If a notice of hearing on the objections is not served within 90 days of filing of the objections, the objections will be deemed abandoned.

(h) Discharge. The Florida guardian may not be discharged until all objections have been withdrawn, abandoned, or judicially resolved. After all objections have been withdrawn, abandoned, or judicially resolved, if the court is satisfied that the Florida guardian has faithfully discharged the duties of the guardianship and the interests of the ward are protected, and the Florida guardian of the property has delivered the assets of the ward to the foreign guardian, the court shall enter an order of discharge.

Amended Sept. 13, 1984, effective Jan. 1, 1985 (458 So.2d 1079); Sept. 29, 1988, effective Jan. 1, 1989 (537 So.2d 500); Sept. 29, 1989, effective Oct. 1, 1989 (549 So. 2d 665); Nov. 17, 1989 (551 So.2d 452); Aug. 22, 1991, effective Oct. 1, 1991 (584 So.2d 964); July 5, 2007, effective Jan. 1, 2008 (959 So.2d 1170).

Committee Notes

Rule History

1977 Revision: Change in committee notes to conform to statutory renumbering.

1984 Revision: Adds 30–day requirement for filing objections. Editorial changes and Committee notes revised.

1988 Revision: Editorial change in (c). First and last sentences of (d) deleted and clarifying word added.

1989 Revision: Prior rule adopted as temporary emergency rule.

1991 Revision: Substantial revision of entire rule to harmonize with procedure for discharge of guardian under rule 5.680 and to conform to section 744.524, Florida Statutes.

1992 Revision: Committee notes revised. Citation form changes in committee notes.

2007 Revision: Subdivision (i) deleted because right of waiver is substantive. Committee notes revised.

2008 Revision: Committee notes revised.

2012 Revision: Committee notes revised.

Statutory References

§ 393.12, Fla. Stat. Capacity; appointment of guardian advocate.

§ 744.102(8), (9), Fla. Stat. Definitions.

§ 744.201, Fla. Stat. Domicile of ward.

§ 744.202, Fla. Stat. Venue.

§ 744.2025, Fla. Stat. Change of ward's residence.

§ 744.524, Fla. Stat. Termination of guardianship on change of domicile of resident ward.

§ 744.531, Fla. Stat. Order of discharge.

Rule References

Fla. Prob. R. 5.041 Service of pleadings and documents.

Fla. Prob. R. 5.180 Waiver and consent.

Fla. Prob. R. 5.610 Execution by guardian.

Fla. Prob. R. 5.680 Termination of guardianship.

Fla. R. Jud. Admin. 2.516 Service of pleadings and documents.

Rule 5.680. Termination of Guardianship

(a) Petition for Discharge. When the ward has become sui juris, has terminated a voluntary guardianship, has been restored to capacity, has had all rights restored, or has died, or when the guardian has been unable to locate the ward after diligent search, or, for a guardian of the property, when the property subject to the guardianship has been exhausted, the guardian shall file a petition for discharge. A guardian of the person is discharged without further proceeding upon filing a certified copy of the ward's death certificate.

(b) Contents of Petition. The petition for discharge shall state:

(1) the reason for termination of the guardianship;

(2) that the guardian has fully administered the guardianship; and

(3) the amount of unpaid and anticipated costs and fees to be paid to the guardian and to the attorneys, accountants, or other agents employed by the guardian.

(c) Final Report. The guardian of the property shall promptly file a final report. If the ward has died, the guardian must file the report no later than 45 days after he or she has been served with letters of administration, letters of curatorship, or an order of summary administration. The report shall show receipts, disbursements, amounts reserved for unpaid and anticipated disbursements, costs, and fees, including the amounts set forth in subdivision (b)(3), and other relevant financial information from the date of the previous annual accounting, and a list of the assets to be turned over to the person entitled to them.

(d) Notice. A notice shall be served stating:

(1) that any objection shall be in writing and shall state with particularity each item to which the objection is directed and the grounds on which the objection is based;

(2) that any objection to the final report or the petition for discharge shall be filed within 30 days from the date of service of the petition for discharge; and

(3) that within 90 days after filing of the objection, a notice of hearing thereon shall be served or the objection is abandoned.

(e) Service. The guardian applying for discharge shall serve a copy of the petition for discharge and final report on the ward, on the personal representative of a deceased ward, or if there are no assets justifying qualification of a personal representative for the estate of a deceased ward, on the known next of kin of the deceased ward, or such other persons as the court may direct; provided however, that a guardian of the property who is subsequently appointed personal representative shall serve a copy of the petition for discharge and final report on all beneficiaries of the ward's estate.

(f) Objections. All persons served shall have 30 days to file objections to the petition for discharge and final report. The objections shall state with particularity the items to which the objections are directed and shall state the grounds on which the objections are based. Copies of the objections shall be served by the objector on the guardian. Any interested person may set a hearing on the objections. Notice of the hearing shall be served on the guardian and any other interested persons. If a notice of hearing on the objections is not served within 90 days of filing of the objections, the objections will be deemed abandoned. The guardian may not be discharged until all objections have been withdrawn, abandoned, or judicially resolved, and the petition for discharge of the guardian is granted by the court.

(g) Discharge. The guardian may not be discharged until all objections are withdrawn, abandoned, or judicially resolved. After all objections are withdrawn, abandoned, or judicially resolved, and if it appears that the guardian has paid all amounts reserved to the persons entitled to them and has made full and complete distribution of the ward's assets to the persons entitled to them and has otherwise faithfully discharged the duties of the guardian, the court shall grant the petition for discharge and enter an order of discharge. If objections are filed and are not withdrawn, abandoned, or judicially resolved, the court shall conduct a hearing in the same manner as for a hearing on objections to annual guardianship plans. After hearing, if the court is satisfied that the guardian has faithfully discharged the duties of the guardianship and the interests of the ward are protected, and the guardian has rendered a complete and accurate final report and has delivered the assets of the ward to the person entitled to them, the court shall enter an order of discharge.

Amended Sept. 29, 1988, effective Jan. 1, 1989 (537 So.2d 500); Sept. 29, 1989, effective Oct. 1, 1989 (549 So.2d 665); Nov. 17, 1989 (551 So.2d 452); Aug. 22, 1991, effective Oct. 1, 1991 (584 So.2d 964); Sept. 24, 1992, effective Jan. 1, 1993 (607 So.2d 1306); Oct. 3, 1996, effective Jan. 1, 1997 (683 So.2d 78); June 19, 2003, effective Jan. 1, 2004 (848 So.2d 1069); Feb. 1, 2007 (948 So.2d 735); July 10, 2008 (986 So.2d 576).

Committee Notes

Rule History

1975 Revision: Implements sections 744.527 and 744.531, Florida Statutes, and also requires the guardian applying for discharge to do so by filing a petition for discharge and provides the procedure pertaining thereto.

1977 Revision: No change in rule. Change in committee note to conform to statutory renumbering.

1988 Revision: Captions added to subdivisions. Committee notes revised. Citation form changes in committee notes.

1989 Revision: Prior rule deleted and replaced by temporary emergency rule.

1991 Revision: Substantial revision of entire rule to harmonize with procedure for discharge of personal representatives under rules 5.400 and 5.401.

1992 Revision: Committee notes revised. Citation form changes in committee notes.

1996 Revision: Editorial changes to clarify that all anticipated costs and fees should be shown on final report and thereafter paid prior to transfer of assets and discharge of guardian.

2003 Revision: Subdivision (a) amended to reflect addition of rule 5.552 dealing with voluntary guardianship of property. Committee notes revised.

2006 Revision: Subdivision (c) amended to conform to 2006 amendments to section 744.527, Florida Statutes. Subdivision (h) deleted as unnecessary because substantive right of waiver is provided by section 731.302, Florida Statutes.

2008 Revision: Reference to restoration of rights added in subdivision (a). Committee notes revised.

2012 Revision: Committee notes revised.

Statutory References

§ 393.12, Fla. Stat. Capacity; appointment of guardian advocate.

§ 744.521, Fla. Stat. Termination of guardianship.

§ 744.527, Fla. Stat. Final reports and application for discharge; hearing.

§ 744.528, Fla. Stat. Discharge of guardian named as personal representative.

§ 744.531, Fla. Stat. Order of discharge.

§ 744.534, Fla. Stat. Disposition of unclaimed funds held by guardian.

Rule References

Fla. Prob. R. 5.040 Notice.

Fla. Prob. R. 5.041 Service of pleadings and documents.

Fla. Prob. R. 5.180 Waiver and consent.

Fla. Prob. R. 5.552 Voluntary guardianship of property.

Fla. Prob. R. 5.610 Execution by guardian.

Fla. Prob. R. 5.681 Restoration of rights of person with developmental disability.

Fla. R. Jud. Admin. 2.516 Service of pleadings and documents.

Rule 5.681. Restoration of Rights of Person With Developmental Disability

(a) Suggestion of Restoration of Rights. A suggestion of restoration of rights of a person with a developmental disability may be executed by any interested person, including the person with a developmental disability. The suggestion must contain:

(1) a statement that the person with a developmental disability is capable of exercising some or all of the rights that were granted to the guardian advocate;

(2) evidentiary support for the filing as provided by law; and

(3) the name and address of the attorney representing the person with a developmental disability, if any, known to the petitioner.

(b) Counsel. Within 3 days after the suggestion has been filed, the court must appoint an attorney to represent a person with a developmental disability who is not then represented by counsel as stated in the suggestion.

(c) Notice. Upon filing of the suggestion, if the name and address of the attorney representing the person with a developmental disability is listed in the suggestion, or upon the appointment of counsel, if no name and address of an attorney are listed in the suggestion, the clerk must immediately send notice of the filing of the suggestion, together with a copy of the suggestion, to the person with a developmental disability, the person's guardian advocate, the person's attorney, the attorney for the guardian advocate, if any, and any other interested person as directed by the court. The notice must contain a statement that all objections to the suggestion must be filed within 20 days after service of the notice. Formal notice must be served on the guardian advocate. Informal notice may be served on the other persons. Notice need not be served on the petitioner. The clerk must file proof of service.

(d) Objections. Any objection must be in writing and must state with particularity each item to which the objection is directed and the grounds on which the objection is based. The objector must serve notice of hearing on the objection and a copy of the objection on the person with the developmental disability, the person's attorney, the person's guardian advocate, the attorney for the guardian advocate, if any, the next of kin of the person with a developmental disability, and any other interested persons as directed by the court.

(e) Order.

The court must enter an order denying the suggestion or restoring all or some of the rights that were granted to the guardian advocate. If only some rights are restored to the person with a developmental disability, the order must state which rights are restored and amend the letters of guardian advocacy accordingly. The court need not hold a hearing prior to entering an order restoring rights if no objections are filed and the court is satisfied with the evidentiary support for restoration supplied by the petitioner.

(f) Additional Requirements. If personal rights are restored, the guardian advocate must file an amended plan within 60 days after the order restoring rights. If all property rights are restored, a guardian advocate previously granted management or control over property must file a final accounting within 60 days after the order restoring rights. A copy of any amended plan and accounting must be promptly served on the person with a developmental disability and the person's attorney.

Added July 10, 2008 (986 So.2d 576). Amended Sept. 26, 2013, effective Jan. 1, 2014 (123 So.3d 31).

Committee Notes

Rule History

2008 Revision: New rule.

2013 Revision: Substantial revisions to reflect the designation of the pleading as a Suggestion of Restoration of Rights; the requirement for a statement of evidentiary support, the identification and address of the attorney for the person with a developmental disability; procedures for service of objections; clarification of requirements following a restoration of rights; and editorial changes. Editorial changes to conform to the court's guidelines for rule submissions as set forth in AOSC06–14.

Statutory References

§ 393.063(9), Fla. Stat. Definitions.

§ 393.12, Fla. Stat. Capacity; appointment of guardian advocate.

§ 709.08, Fla. Stat. Durable power of attorney.

§ 765.101, Fla. Stat. Definitions.

§ 765.104, Fla. Stat. Amendment or revocation.

§ 765.202, Fla. Stat. Designation of a health care surrogate.

§ 765.204, Fla. Stat. Capacity of principal; procedure.

§ 765.205(3), Fla. Stat. Responsibility of the surrogate.

§ 765.302, Fla. Stat. Procedure for making a living will; notice to physician.

§ 765.401, Fla. Stat. The proxy.

Rule References

Fla. Prob. R. 5.020 Pleadings; verification; motions.

Fla. Prob. R. 5.540 Hearings.

Fla. Prob. R. 5.541 Recording of hearings.

Fla. Prob. R. 5.680 Termination of guardianship.

Rule 5.685. Determination Regarding Alternatives to Guardianship

(a) Reporting by Guardian. The guardian shall promptly file a report attaching a copy of a final order or judgment that determines the validity of a ward's durable power of attorney, trust, or trust amendment.

(b) Petition. At any time after the appointment of a guardian, the guardian, the ward, the ward's attorney, if any, or any other interested person may file a verified petition stating that there is an alternative to guardianship that will sufficiently address the problems of the ward.

(c) Contents of Petition. The petition to determine alternatives to guardianship shall state:

(1) the petitioner's interest in the proceeding; and

(2) the facts constituting the basis for the relief sought and that the proposed alternative to guardianship will sufficiently address the problems of the ward and is in the ward's best interest.

(d) Service. The petition shall be served on the guardian, the ward, the ward's attorney, if any, those interested persons who have filed requests for notices and copies of pleadings, and such other persons as the court may direct.

(e) Order. The order shall specify whether there is an alternative to guardianship that will sufficiently address the problems of the ward, the continued need for a guardian, and the extent of the need for delegation of the ward's rights.

Added Feb. 1, 2007 (948 So.2d 735).

Committee Notes

Rule History

2006 Revision: New rule.

Statutory References

§ 744.331, Fla. Stat. Procedures to determine incapacity.

§ 744.462, Fla. Stat. Determination regarding alternatives to guardianship.

Rule 5.690. Initial Guardianship Report

(a) Contents and Filing. An initial guardianship report shall be filed within 60 days after the issuance of letters of guardianship. The guardian of the property shall file the initial guardianship report consisting of the verified inventory. The guardian of the person shall file the initial guardianship report consisting of the guardianship plan.

(b) Service. Copies of the initial guardianship report shall be served on the ward, unless the ward is a minor under the age of 14 years or is totally incapacitated, and the attorney for the ward, if any. With approval of the court, service on the ward may be accomplished by serving the attorney for the ward.

Added Aug. 22, 1991, effective Oct. 1, 1991 (584 So.2d 964). Amended Sept. 24, 1992, effective Jan. 1, 1993 (607 So.2d 1306).

Committee Notes

The committee recognizes the conflict between this rule and section 744.362, Florida Statutes, which requires the filing of the initial guardianship report (which includes the inventory) within 60 days after appointment. The committee believes this provision, which attempts to regulate when a paper must be filed with the court, is procedural and that a guardian may not receive letters of guardianship empowering the guardian to act contemporaneously with the appointment. Therefore, the issuance of letters is a more practical time from which to measure the beginning of the time period for the accomplishment of this act.

In the event the guardian of the property and the guardian of the person are not the same entity or person, they shall make a good faith effort to jointly file the initial guardianship report.

Rule History

1991 Revision: New rule.

1992 Revision: Addition of phrase in subdivision (b) to conform to 1992 amendment to section 744.362(1), Florida Statutes. Citation form changes in committee notes.

2012 Revision: Committee notes revised.

Statutory References

§ 744.362, Fla.Stat. Initial guardianship report.

§ 744.363, Fla.Stat. Initial guardianship plan.

§ 744.365, Fla.Stat. Verified inventory.

§ 744.3701, Fla.Stat. Inspection of report.

§ 744.384, Fla.Stat. Subsequently discovered or acquired property.

Rule References

Fla. Prob. R. 5.020 Pleadings; verification; motions.

Fla. Prob. R. 5.041 Service of pleadings and documents.

Fla. Prob. R. 5.060 Request for notices and copies of pleadings.

Fla. Prob. R. 5.180 Waiver and consent.

Fla. Prob. R. 5.610 Execution by guardian.

Fla. Prob. R. 5.620 Inventory.

Fla. Prob. R. 5.700 Objection to guardianship reports.

Fla. R. Jud. Admin. 2.516 Service of pleadings and documents.

Rule 5.695. Annual Guardianship Reports

(a) Contents and Filing.

(1) *Guardian of the Person.* Unless the court requires reporting on a calendar year basis, the guardian of the person shall file an annual guardianship plan within 90 days after the last day of the anniversary month in which the letters of guardianship were issued. The plan shall be for the year ending on the last day of such anniversary month. If the court requires reporting on a calendar year basis, the guardianship plan shall be filed on or before April 1 of each year.

(2) *Guardian of the Property.* Unless the court requires or authorizes reporting on a fiscal year basis, the guardian of the property shall file an annual accounting on or before April 1 of each year. The annual accounting shall cover the preceding annual accounting period. If the court requires or authorizes reporting on a fiscal year basis, the annual accounting shall be filed on or before the first day of the fourth month after the end of the fiscal year.

(b) Service. Copies of the annual plan and accounting shall be served on the ward, unless the ward is a minor or is totally incapacitated, and the attorney for the ward, if any. With the approval of the court, service on the ward may be accomplished by serving the attorney for the ward. The guardian shall serve copies on such other persons as the court may direct.

Former Rule 5.690. Amended Sept. 4, 1980, effective Jan. 1, 1981 (387 So.2d 949); Sept. 29, 1988, effective Jan. 1, 1989 (537 So.2d 500); Sept. 29, 1989, effective Oct. 1, 1989 (549 So.2d 665); Nov. 17, 1989 (551 So.2d 452). Renumbered as Rule 5.695 and amended Aug. 22, 1991, effective Oct. 1, 1991 (584 So.2d 964). Amended Sept. 24, 1992, effective Jan. 1, 1993 (607 So.2d 1306); Feb. 1, 2007 (948 So.2d 735).

Committee Notes

The annual guardianship report consists of the annual plan for the guardian of the person and the annual accounting for the guardian of the property.

For annual guardianship reports regarding minors, see rule 5.555.

With approval of the court, service on the ward may be accomplished by service on the attorney for the ward, if any. The committee was concerned that actual service on a ward of the accounting or guardianship plan may give uninterested persons access to financial or personal information to the detriment of the ward. The committee believes that under such circumstances, the guardian of the property could seek an order under section 744.371(5), Florida Statutes, even if the ward's circumstances were set out in detail in a pleading other than the annual guardianship report. Such court order may be sought in appropriate circumstances at the time of the initial hearing to determine incapacity.

Rule History

1975 Revision: Substantially the same as section 744.427(1), (2), and (4), Florida Statutes, and section 744.437, Florida Statutes, with editorial changes and providing for the waiving, by a ward who has become sui juris or by the personal representative of a deceased ward, of the filing of an annual accounting. The rule requires the guardian of the property of a ward to appear before the court at the time he files his annual accounting or at such time the court shall determine in order that the court may inquire as to any matter relating to the physical and financial well-being of the ward. This appears to be in conflict with section 744.437, Florida Statutes, which refers to "every guardian" but in the same sentence it refers to "at the time the guardian files his annual return" and only the guardian of the property is required to file an annual accounting.

1977 Revision: No change in rule. Change in committee note to conform to statutory renumbering.

1980 Revision: Subdivision (e) amended to avoid conflict with statutory changes in section 744.437, Florida Statutes (1979).

1988 Revision: Matter in (b) deleted; covered in sections 744.427(2) and 744.434, Florida Statutes. Subdivision (c) deleted; covered in section 744.427(4), Florida Statutes. Captions added to subdivisions. Committee notes revised. Citation form changes in committee notes.

1989 Revision: Prior rule deleted and replaced by temporary emergency rule.

1991 Revision: Substantial changes and rule renumbered.

1992 Revision: Addition of language in subdivisions (a)(1) and (a)(2) to implement 1992 amendments to sections 744.367(1) and (2), Florida Statutes. Committee notes revised. Citation form changes in committee notes.

2006 Revision: Requirement in (b) to serve minors age 14 and above deleted to conform to amendment to section 744.367(3), Florida Statutes. Committee notes revised.

2012 Revision: Committee notes revised.

Statutory References

§ 744.367, Fla. Stat. Duty to file annual guardianship report.

§ 744.3675, Fla. Stat. Annual guardianship plan.

§ 744.3678, Fla. Stat. Annual accounting.

§ 744.3685, Fla. Stat. Order requiring guardianship report; contempt.

§ 744.3701, Fla. Stat. Inspection of report.

§ 744.371, Fla. Stat. Relief to be granted.

§ 744.3735, Fla. Stat. Annual appearance of the guardian.

Rule References

Fla. Prob. R. 5.020 Pleadings; verification; motions.

Fla. Prob. R. 5.041 Service of pleadings and documents.

Fla. Prob. R. 5.060 Request for notices and copies of pleadings.

Fla. Prob. R. 5.180 Waiver and consent.

Fla. Prob. R. 5.552 Voluntary guardianship of property.

Fla. Prob. R. 5.555 Guardianships of minors.

Fla. Prob. R. 5.610 Execution by guardian.

Fla. Prob. R. 5.700 Objection to guardianship reports.

Fla. Prob. R. 5.800(b) Application of revised chapter 744 to existing guardianships.

Fla. R. Jud. Admin. 2.516 Service of pleadings and documents.

Rule 5.696. Annual Accounting

(a) Contents and Filing. The guardian of the property must file an annual accounting as required by law. The annual accounting must include:

(1) a full and correct account of the receipts and disbursements of all of the ward's property over which the guardian has control and a statement of the ward's property on hand at the end of the accounting period; and

(2) a copy of the statements of all of the ward's cash accounts as of the end of the accounting period from each institution where the cash is deposited.

(b) Substantiating Documents. Unless otherwise ordered by the court, the guardian need not file the documents substantiating the annual accounting. Upon reasonable written request, the guardian of the property shall make the substantiating documents available for examination to persons entitled to receive or inspect the annual accounting.

(c) Interim Inspection of Records. Upon reasonable written request and notice, the guardian of the property shall make all material financial records pertaining to the guardianship available for inspections to those persons entitled to receive or inspect the annual accounting.

Added Aug. 22, 1991, effective Oct. 1, 1991 (584 So.2d 964). Amended Sept. 2, 2010, effective Jan. 1, 2011 (50 So.3d 578); Sept. 26, 2013, effective Jan. 1, 2014 (123 So.3d 31).

Committee Notes

Rule History

1991 Revision: New rule.

1992 Revision: Citation form changes in committee notes.

2010 Revision: Editorial change in (b) to delete redundant language.

2012 Revision: Committee notes revised.

2013 Revision: Subdivision (b) revised to substitute "documents" for "papers." Committee notes revised. Editorial changes to conform to the court's guidelines for rule submissions as set forth in AOSC06–14.

Statutory References

§ 744.367, Fla.Stat. Duty to file annual guardianship report.

§ 744.3678, Fla.Stat. Annual accounting.

§ 744.3701, Fla.Stat. Inspection of report.

§ 744.3735, Fla.Stat. Annual appearance of the guardian.

Rule References

Fla. Prob. R. 5.020 Pleadings; verification; motions.

Fla. Prob. R. 5.041 Service of pleadings and documents.

Fla. Prob. R. 5.060 Request for notices and copies of pleadings.

Fla. Prob. R. 5.610 Execution by guardian.

Fla. Prob. R. 5.695 Annual guardianship report.

Fla. Prob. R. 5.700 Objection to guardianship reports.

Fla. R. Jud. Admin. 2.516 Service of pleadings and documents.

Rule 5.697. Magistrates' Review of Guardianship Inventories, Accountings, and Plans

(a) General Magistrates. The court may appoint general magistrates to review guardianship inventories, accountings, and plans. General magistrates shall be members of The Florida Bar and shall continue in office until removed by the court. The order appointing a general magistrate shall be recorded. Each general magistrate shall take the oath required of officers of the court by the Florida Constitution. The oath shall be recorded before the magistrate begins to act.

(b) Special Magistrates. In connection with the court's review of guardianship inventories, accountings, and plans, the court may appoint members of The Florida Bar as special magistrates for any particular service required by the court. Special magistrates shall be governed by all laws and rules relating to general magistrates except special magistrates shall not be required to take an oath unless specifically required by the court. For good cause shown, the court may appoint a person other than a member of The Florida Bar as a special magistrate.

(c) General Powers and Duties. Every magistrate shall act under the direction of the court. Process issued by a magistrate shall be directed as provided by law. All grounds for disqualification of a judge shall apply to magistrates.

(d) Hearings. Hearings before any magistrate may be held in the county where the action is pending, or at any other place by order of the court for the convenience of the witnesses or the parties. A magistrate shall give notice of hearings to all parties. If any party fails to appear, the magistrate may proceed ex parte or may continue the hearing to a future day, with notice to the absent party. The magistrate shall proceed with reasonable diligence and the least practicable delay. Any party may apply to the court for an order directing the magistrate to accelerate the proceedings and to make a report promptly. Evidence shall be taken in writing or by electronic recording by the magistrate or by some other person under the magistrate's authority in the magistrate's presence and shall be filed with the magistrate's report. The magistrate may examine and take testimony from the parties and their witnesses under oath, on all matters authorized by the court for review by the magistrate and may require production of all books, papers, writings, vouchers, and other documents applicable to those matters. The magistrate shall admit only evidence that would be admissible in court. The magistrate may take all actions concerning evidence that may be taken by the court.

(e) Magistrate's Report. The magistrate's report shall contain a description of the matters considered and the magistrate's conclusions and any recommendations. No part of any statement of facts, account, charge, deposition, examination, or answer used before the magistrate shall be recited. The magistrate shall be required to file a report only if a hearing is held pursuant to subdivision (d) of this rule or if specifically directed to do so by the court.

(f) Filing Report; Service; Exceptions. The magistrate shall file a report with the court and serve copies on the parties. The parties may serve exceptions to the report within 10 days from the date the report is served on them. If no exceptions are timely filed, the court shall take appropriate action on the report. All timely filed exceptions shall be heard by the court on reasonable notice by any party.

Added Aug. 22, 1991, effective Oct. 1, 1991 (584 So.2d 964). Amended Sept. 24, 1992, effective Jan. 1, 1993 (607 So.2d 1306); Sept. 30, 2004, effective Oct. 1, 2004 (887 So.2d 1090); July 5, 2007, effective Jan. 1, 2008 (959 So.2d 1170).

Committee Notes

Rule History

1991 Revision: This is a new rule, patterned after Florida Rule of Civil Procedure 1.490.

1992 Revision: Editorial change. Citation form change in committee notes.

2004 Revision: Change in nomenclature from "master" to "magistrate" to track similar change in the Florida Statutes.

2007 Revision: Title of rule and subdivisions (a) and (b) amended to include inventories. "Shall" substituted for "may" in last sentence of subdivision (f). Committee notes revised.

Statutory Reference

§ 744.369(2), Fla. Stat. Judicial review of guardianship reports.

Rule References

Fla. Prob. R. 5.095 General and special magistrates.

Fla. R. Civ. P. 1.490 Magistrates.

Rule 5.700. Objection to Guardianship Reports

(a) Objections. The ward, or any other interested person, may file an objection to any part of a guardianship report within the time provided by law.

(b) Contents. Any objection shall be in writing and shall state with particularity each item to which the objection is directed and the grounds on which the objection is based.

(c) Service. The objector shall serve a copy of the objection on each guardian and on any other person as directed by the court.

Amended Sept. 29, 1988, effective Jan. 1, 1989 (537 So.2d 500); Sept. 29, 1989, effective Oct. 1, 1989 (549 So.2d 665); Nov. 17, 1989 (551 So.2d 452); Aug. 22, 1991, effective Oct. 1, 1991 (584 So.2d 964).

Committee Notes

Rule History

1975 Revision: Substantially the same as section 744.427(3), (5), and (6), Florida Statutes, with editorial changes.

1977 Revision: No change in rule. Change in committee note to conform to statutory renumbering.

1988 Revision: Captions added to subdivisions. Committee notes revised. Citation form change in committee notes.

1989 Revision: Prior rule deleted and replaced by temporary emergency rule.

1991 Revision: Revised to conform with new statutory requirements.

1992 Revision: Citation form changes in committee notes.

2008 Revision: Committee notes revised.

2012 Revision: Committee notes revised.

Statutory References

§ 393.12, Fla. Stat. Capacity; appointment of guardian advocate.

§ 744.362, Fla. Stat. Initial guardianship report.

§ 744.363, Fla. Stat. Initial guardianship plan.

§ 744.365, Fla. Stat. Verified inventory.

§ 744.367, Fla. Stat. Duty to file annual guardianship report.

§ 744.3675, Fla. Stat. Annual guardianship plan.

§ 744.3678, Fla. Stat. Annual accounting.

Rule References

Fla. Prob. R. 5.020 Pleadings; verification; motions.

Fla. Prob. R. 5.041 Service of pleadings and documents.

Fla. Prob. R. 5.060 Request for notices and copies of pleadings.

Fla. Prob. R. 5.180 Waiver and consent.

Fla. Prob. R. 5.610 Execution by guardian.

Fla. R. Jud. Admin. 2.516 Service of pleadings and documents.

Rule 5.705. Petition for Interim Judicial Review

(a) Contents. A petition for interim judicial review shall be verified, state the petitioner's interest in the proceeding, state with particularity the manner in which the guardian's action or proposed action does not comply with or exceeds the guardian's authority under the guardian plan, and state why the action or proposed action of the guardian is not in the best interest of the ward.

(b) Service. The petition shall be served by formal notice.

(c) Hearing. The petitioner or any interested person may set the matter for hearing.

(d) Expedited Proceedings. For good cause shown, the court may shorten the time for response to the formal notice and may set an expedited hearing.

Added Aug. 22, 1991, effective Oct. 1, 1991 (584 So.2d 964). Amended September 28, 2000, effective Jan. 1, 2001 (778 So.2d 272).

Committee Notes

Rule History

1991 Revision: New rule.

2000 Revision: Subdivision (d) added to permit expedited proceedings.

2008 Revision: Committee notes revised.

Statutory References

§ 393.12, Fla. Stat. Capacity; appointment of guardian advocate.

§ 744.3715, Fla. Stat. Petition for interim judicial review.

Rule 5.710. Reports of Public Guardian

The public guardian, as the guardian of a ward, shall file:

(a) an initial report as required by law;

(b) annual guardianship reports, which shall include the dates of quarterly visits to the ward, as required by law;

(c) a report within 6 months of his or her appointment as guardian of a ward, which shall also be filed with the executive director of the Statewide Public Guardianship Office, stating:

(1) the public guardian's efforts to locate a family member or friend, other person, bank, or corporation to act as guardian of the ward; and

(2) the ward's potential to be restored to capacity;

(d) an annual report, filed with the Statewide Public Guardianship Office, by September 1 for the preceding fiscal year, on the operations of the office of public guardian; and

(e) a report of an independent audit by a qualified certified public accountant, to be filed with the Statewide Public Guardianship Office every 2 years.

Added effective Dec. 23, 1987 (517 So.2d 675). Amended Sept. 29, 1989, effective Oct. 1, 1989 (549 So.2d 665); Nov. 17, 1989 (551 So.2d 452); Aug. 22, 1991, effective Oct. 1, 1991 (584 So.2d 964); July 5, 2007, effective Jan. 1, 2007 (959 So.2d 1170); Sept. 2, 2010, effective Jan. 1, 2011 (50 So.3d 578).

Committee Notes

Rule History

1987 Revision: This is a new rule and was promulgated to establish procedures to accommodate the Public Guardian Act. See § 744.701, et seq., Fla. Stat. See also Fla. Prob. R. 5.560.

1989 Revision: Prior rule adopted as temporary emergency rule.

1991 Revision: Editorial changes.

1992 Revision: Citation form changes in committee notes.

2007 Revision: Rule extensively amended to specify reports a public guardian is required to file.

2010 Revision: Editorial change in (e).

Statutory Reference

§§ 744.701–744.709, Fla.Stat. Public Guardianship Act.

Rule Reference

Fla.Prob.R. 5.560 Petition for appointment of guardian of an incapacitated person.

Rule 5.720. Court Monitor

(a) Appointment. Upon motion or inquiry by any interested person or upon its own motion, the court may appoint a court monitor in any proceeding over which it has jurisdiction.

(b) Order of Appointment. The order of appointment shall state the name, address, and phone number of the monitor and shall set forth the matters to be investigated. The order may authorize the monitor to investigate, seek information, examine documents, or interview the ward. The order of appointment shall be served upon the guardian, the ward, and such other persons as the court may determine.

(c) Report. The monitor shall file a verified written report with the court setting forth the monitor's findings. The report shall be served on the guardian, the ward, and such other persons as the court may determine.

(d) Protection of Ward. If it appears from the monitor's report that further action by the court to protect the interests of the ward is necessary, the court shall, after a hearing with notice, enter any order necessary to protect the ward or the ward's property, including amending the plan, requiring an accounting, ordering production of assets, or initiating proceedings to remove a guardian. Notice of the hearing shall be served on the guardian, the ward, and such other persons as the court may determine.

Added Feb. 1, 2007 (948 So.2d 735). Amended July 10, 2008 (986 So.2d 576).

Committee Notes

This rule applies to the non-emergency appointment of court monitors.

Rule History

2006 Revision: New rule.

2008 Revision: Editorial change in (d). Committee notes revised.

Statutory References

§ 393.12, Fla. Stat. Capacity; appointment of guardian advocate.

§ 744.107, Fla. Stat. Court monitors.

§ 744.3701, Fla. Stat. Inspection of report.

Rule 5.725. Emergency Court Monitor

(a) Appointment. Upon motion or inquiry by any interested person or upon its own motion, the court may appoint a court monitor on an emergency basis without notice in any proceeding over which it has jurisdiction.

(b) Order of Appointment. The order of appointment shall specifically find that there appears to be imminent danger that the physical or mental health or safety of the ward will be seriously impaired or that the ward's property is in danger of being wasted, misappropriated, or lost unless immediate action is taken. The scope of the matters to be investigated and the powers and duties of the monitor must be specifically enumerated in the order.

(c) Duration of Authority. The authority of a monitor expires 60 days after the date of appointment or upon a finding of no probable cause, whichever occurs first. The court may enter an order extending the authority of the monitor for an additional 30 days upon a showing that an emergency condition still exists.

(d) Report. Within 15 days after the entry of an order of appointment, the monitor shall file a verified written report setting forth the monitor's findings and recommendations. The report may be supported by documents or other evidence. The time for filing the report may be extended by the court for good cause.

(e) Review. Upon review of the report, the court shall enter an order determining whether there is probable cause to take further action to protect the person or property of the ward.

(1) If the court finds no probable cause, the court shall enter an order finding no probable cause and discharging the monitor.

(2) If the court finds probable cause, the court shall enter an order directed to the respondent stating the essential facts constituting the conduct charged and requiring the respondent to appear before the court to show cause why the court should not take further action. The order shall specify the time and place of the hearing with a reasonable time to allow for the preparation of a defense after service of the order. A copy of the order to show cause together with the order of appointment and report of the monitor shall be served upon the guardian, the ward, the ward's attorney, if any, and the respondent.

(f) Protecting Ward. If at any time prior to the hearing on the order to show cause the court enters a temporary injunction, a restraining order, an order freezing assets, an order suspending the guardian or appointing a guardian ad litem, or any other order to protect the physical or mental health, safety, or property of the ward, the order or injunction shall be served on the guardian, the ward, the ward's attorney, if any, and such other persons as the court may determine.

Added Feb. 1, 2007 (948 so.2d 735). Amended Sept. 2, 2010, effective Jan. 1, 2011 (50 So.3d 578).

Committee Notes

Rule History

2006 Revision: New rule.

2008 Revision: Committee notes revised.

2010 Revision: Editorial change in (c).

Statutory references

§ 393.12, Fla. Stat. Capacity; appointment of guardian advocate.

§ 744.1075, Fla. Stat. Emergency court monitor.

Rule 5.800. Application of Revised Chapter 744 to Existing Guardianships

(a) Prior Adjudication of Incompetency. When an adjudication of incompetency has taken place under chapter 744, Florida Statutes, before October 1, 1989, no readjudication of incapacity shall be required.

(b) Annual Guardianship Reports. Guardians appointed before October 1, 1989, shall file annual guardianship reports as required by law.

Added Sept. 29, 1989, effective Oct. 1, 1989 (549 So.2d 665); Nov. 17, 1989 (551 So.2d 452). Amended Aug. 22, 1991, effective Oct. 1, 1991 (584 So.2d 964).

Committee Notes

Rule History

1989 Revision by Ad Hoc Committee: The committee adopted a position that guardians appointed before the effective date of the 1989 revisions to chapter 744, Florida Statutes, should comply with all sections of the law that apply to future acts of the guardian. For example, all guardians will in the future file annual reports and will be responsible for the continuing well-being of their wards. The committee recognized a distinction between those actions that will necessarily occur on a continuing basis throughout the guardianship and those actions that happen at a particular moment in time but are not necessarily ongoing duties. There are two and only two specific examples to which the statutory reforms would not apply retrospectively if the above distinction is adopted. First, the initial adjudication of incapacity occurs only once in any guardianship. Although guardianships are reevaluated annually, the statute does not contemplate a complete readjudication procedure every year. Therefore, the committee concluded that the initial adjudicatory hearing need not be repeated for wards adjudicated incompetent before October 1, 1989. Second, as concerns nonresident guardians appointed before October 1, 1989, normally, a guardian is appointed only once at the beginning of the guardianship. While these nonresident guardians would be expected to obey all provisions of the law prospectively, they would not be required to initiate their own removal.

1991 Revision: Editorial changes in first sentence of (a), and rest of subdivision deleted as unnecessary. Subdivision (b) has been transferred to rule 5.650. Date reference no longer required in (c), and modified to make filing requirement of preexisting guardianships consistent with the current statutory provisions.

1992 Revision: Citation form changes in committee notes.

Statutory References

§ 744.367, Fla.Stat. Duty to file annual guardianship report.

§ 744.3675, Fla.Stat. Annual guardianship plan.

§ 744.3678, Fla.Stat. Annual accounting.

Rule References

Fla.Prob.R. 5.695 Annual guardianship report.

Fla.Prob.R. 5.696 Annual accounting.

PART IV. EXPEDITED JUDICIAL INTERVENTION CONCERNING MEDICAL TREATMENT PROCEDURES

Rule 5.900. Expedited Judicial Intervention Concerning Medical Treatment Procedures

(a) Petition. Any proceeding for expedited judicial intervention concerning medical treatment procedures may be brought by any interested adult person and shall be commenced by the filing of a verified petition which states:

(1) the name and address of the petitioner;

(2) the name and location of the person who is the subject of the petition (hereinafter referred to as the "patient");

(3) the relationship of the petitioner to the patient;

(4) the names, relationship to the patient, and addresses if known to the petitioner, of:

(A) the patient's spouse and adult children;

(B) the patient's parents (if the patient is a minor);

(C) if none of the above, the patient's next of kin;

(D) any guardian and any court-appointed health care decision-maker;

(E) any person designated by the patient in a living will or other document to exercise the patient's health care decision in the event of the patient's incapacity;

(F) the administrator of the hospital, nursing home, or other facility where the patient is located;

(G) the patient's principal treating physician and other physicians known to have provided any medical opinion or advice about any condition of the patient relevant to this petition; and

(H) all other persons the petitioner believes may have information concerning the expressed wishes of the patient; and

(5) facts sufficient to establish the need for the relief requested, including, but not limited to, facts to support the allegation that the patient lacks the capacity to make the requisite medical treatment decision.

(b) Supporting Documentation. Any affidavits and supporting documentation, including any living will or designation of health care decision-maker, shall be attached to the petition.

(c) Notice. Unless waived by the court, notice of the petition and the preliminary hearing shall be served on the following persons who have not joined in the petition or otherwise consented to the proceedings:

(1) the patient;

(2) the patient's spouse and the patient's parents, if the patient is a minor;

(3) the patient's adult children;

(4) any guardian and any court-appointed health care decision-maker;

(5) any person designated by the patient in a living will or other document to exercise the patient's health care decision in the event of the patient's incapacity;

(6) the administrator of the hospital, nursing home, or other facility where the patient is located;

(7) the patient's principal treating physician and other physicians believed to have provided any medical opinion or advice about any condition of the patient relevant to this petition;

(8) all other persons the petitioner believes may have information concerning the expressed wishes of the patient; and

(9) such other persons as the court may direct.

(d) Hearing. A preliminary hearing on the petition shall be held within 72 hours after the filing of the petition. At that time the court shall review the petition and supporting documentation. In its discretion the court shall either:

(1) rule on the relief requested immediately after the preliminary hearing; or

(2) conduct an evidentiary hearing not later than 4 days after the preliminary hearing and rule on the relief requested immediately after the evidentiary hearing.

Added Aug. 22, 1991, effective Oct. 1, 1991 (584 So.2d 964). Amended Sept. 24, 1992, effective Jan. 1, 1993 (607 So.2d 1306).

Committee Notes

This rule was submitted by the committee in response to the request contained in footnote 17 of *In re Guardianship of Browning*, 568 So.2d 4 (Fla. 1990). See also *Cruzan by Cruzan v. Director*, Missouri Department of Health, 497 U.S. 261, 110 S.Ct. 2841, 111 L. Ed.2d 224 (1990).

The promulgation of this rule is not intended to imply that judicial intervention is required to terminate life-prolonging procedures.

Practitioners should note that the criteria and standards of proof contained in Browning differ from the criteria and standards of proof presently existing in chapter 765, Florida Statutes.

Rule History

1991 Revision: New rule.

1992 Revision: This rule was created on an emergency basis and on further review, the committee decided it needed to clarify that the petition should include an allegation that the patient lacks capacity to make the requisite medical treatment decision, and that the patient should receive notice of the petition and hearing. Committee notes revised. Citation form changes in committee notes.

2008 Revision: Committee notes revised.

Constitutional Reference

Art. I, § 23, Fla. Const.

Statutory References

§ 393.12, Fla. Stat. Capacity; appointment of guardian advocate.

§ 709.08, Fla. Stat. Durable power of attorney.

§ 731.302, Fla. Stat. Waiver and consent by interested person.

§ 744.102, Fla. Stat. Definitions.

§ 744.104, Fla. Stat. Verification of documents.

§ 744.3115, Fla. Stat. Advance directives for health care.

ch. 765, Fla. Stat. Health care advance directives.

Rule References

Fla. Prob. R. 5.020 Pleadings; verification; motions.

Fla. Prob. R. 5.040 Notice.

INDEX TO FLORIDA PROBATE RULES

FLORIDA RULES OF TRAFFIC COURT

Adoption

Adopted December 9, 1974, effective January 1, 1975 (306 So.2d 489)

I. SCOPE, PURPOSE, AND CONSTRUCTION

II. GENERAL PROVISIONS

III. CRIMINAL OFFENSES

IV. TRAFFIC INFRACTIONS

I. SCOPE, PURPOSE, AND CONSTRUCTION

Rule 6.010. Scope

(a) Application. These rules govern practice and procedure in any traffic case and specifically apply to practice and procedure in county courts and before civil traffic infraction hearing officers.

(b) Part III. The rules under Part III of these rules apply to all criminal traffic offenses, whether prosecuted in the name of the state or any subdivision of it.

(c) Part IV. The rules under Part IV of these rules apply only to traffic infractions adjudicated in a court of the state, whether by a county court judge or civil traffic infraction hearing officer.

Amended April 25, 1975, effective May 1, 1975 (311 So.2d 665); Dec. 14, 1978 (366 So.2d 400); Feb. 11, 1982 (410 So.2d 1337); March 29, 1990 (559 So.2d 1101); Oct. 22, 1992, effective Jan. 1, 1993 (608 So.2d 451); Oct. 17, 1996, effective Jan. 1, 1997 (685 So.2d 1242).

Committee Notes

1990 Amendment. The statutory authorization of civil traffic infraction hearing officers by chapter 89–337, Laws of Florida, necessitates reference to such hearing officers (statutorily referred to interchangeably as magistrates) in the traffic court rules. Reference in the proposed rule to traffic magistrate rather than merely magistrate is designed to distinguish the former from other magistrates, especially in relation to the applicability of the Code of Judicial Conduct (see section of code entitled "Compliance with the Code of Judicial Conduct"), thereby avoiding the possibility of conflict with authorizing statute.

1992 Amendment. Because traffic violations are contained in several chapters of Florida Statutes, references to chapter 318 have been deleted to eliminate latent inconsistencies.

1996 Amendment. Enactment of chapter 94–202, Laws of Florida, necessitated the deletion of all references in the rules to traffic "magistrates" in favor of the term traffic "hearing officers."

Rule 6.020. Purpose and Construction

These rules shall be construed to secure simplicity and uniformity in procedure, fairness in administration and the elimination of unnecessary expense and delay.

II. GENERAL PROVISIONS

Rule 6.040. Definitions

The following definitions apply:

(a) "Court" means any county court to which these rules apply and the judge thereof or any civil traffic hearing officer program and the traffic hearing officer thereof.

(b) "Charging document" means any information, uniform traffic citation, complaint affidavit, or any other manner of charging a criminal traffic offense under law.

(c) "Judge" means any judicial officer elected or appointed by the governor authorized by law to preside over a court to which these rules apply.

(d) "Law" includes the constitutions of the United States and the State of Florida, statutes, ordinances, judicial decisions, and these rules.

(e) "Oath" includes affirmations.

(f) "Clerk" means clerk of the initiating court or trial court.

(g) "Open court" means in a courtroom as provided or judge's or traffic hearing officer's chambers of suitable judicial decorum.

(h) "Prosecutor" means any attorney who represents a state, county, city, town, or village in the prosecution of a defendant for the violation of a statute or ordinance.

(i) "Criminal traffic offense" means a violation that may subject a defendant upon conviction to incarceration, within the jurisdiction of a court to which these rules apply.

(j) "Warrant" includes capias.

(k) "Infraction" means a noncriminal traffic violation that is not punishable by incarceration and for which there is no right to a trial by jury or a right to court-appointed counsel.

(*l*) "Official" means any state judge or traffic hearing officer authorized by law to preside over a court or at a hearing adjudicating traffic infractions.

(m) "Department" means the Department of Highway Safety and Motor Vehicles, defined in section 20.24, Florida Statutes, or the appropriate division thereof.

(n) "Officer" means any enforcement officer charged with and acting under authority to arrest or cite persons suspected or known to be violating the statutes or ordinances regulating the operation of equipment or vehicles or the regulation of traffic.

(*o*) "Infraction requiring a mandatory hearing" refers to an infraction listed in section 318.19, Florida Statutes, which requires an appearance before a designated official at the time and location of the scheduled hearing.

(p) "Traffic hearing officer" means an official appointed under the civil traffic infraction hearing officer program who shall have the power to adjudicate civil traffic infractions subject to certain exceptions.

(q) "Counsel" means any attorney who represents a defendant.

Amended Dec. 14, 1978 (366 So.2d 400); Feb. 11, 1982 (410 So.2d 1337); Sept. 13, 1984, effective Jan. 1, 1985 (458 So.2d 1112); March 29, 1990 (559 So.2d 1101); Oct. 22, 1992, effective Jan. 1, 1993 (608 So.2d 451); July 1, 1993 (621 So.2d 1063); Oct. 17, 1996, effective Jan. 1, 1997 (685 So.2d 1242); Sept. 21, 2006, eff. Jan. 1, 2007 (938 So.2d 983).

Committee Notes

1990 Amendment. In order to accommodate both the court and hearing officer program as alternative sources for the adjudication of civil infractions, the definition of court has been expanded. The term judge has been redefined to limit its reference to only county court judges and the reference to official has been expanded to include the traffic magistrate. In addition, a separate definition for traffic magistrate has been added.

1992 Amendment. Defines charging document and more precisely defines criminal traffic offense.

1996 Amendment. Enactment of chapter 94–202, Laws of Florida, necessitated the deletion of all references in the rules to traffic "magistrates" in favor of the term traffic "hearing officers."

Rule 6.080. Improper Disposition of Traffic Ticket

Any person who solicits or aids in the disposition of a traffic complaint or summons in any manner other than that authorized by the court or who willfully violates any provision of these rules shall be proceeded against for criminal contempt (in the manner provided in these rules). However, a traffic hearing officer shall not have the power to hold any person in contempt of court, but shall be permitted to file a verified motion for order of contempt before any state trial court judge of the same county in which the alleged contempt occurred. Such matter shall be handled as an indirect contempt of court pursuant to the provisions of Florida Rule of Criminal Procedure 3.840.

Amended March 29, 1990 (559 So.2d 1101); Oct. 17, 1996, effective Jan. 1, 1997 (685 So.2d 1242).

Committee Notes

1990 Amendment. This rule expands the statutory mandate of Chapter 89–337, section 3(1) which deprives magistrates of the power of contempt with respect to defendants only. The rule extends the prohibition of a magistrate's direct contempt powers to cover any person. The Committee expressed concern that if the contempt prohibition were limited to only the defendant, it might be assumed that such powers existed with respect to others such as attorneys, court personnel and witnesses. This rule also incorporates reference to the provisions of Florida Rule of Criminal Procedure 3.840 by specifying that magistrates may initiate indirect contempt proceedings by filing a verified motion for order of contempt pursuant to the Rule of Criminal Procedure.

1996 Amendment. Enactment of chapter 94–202, Laws of Florida, necessitated the deletion of all references in the rules to traffic "magistrates" in favor of the term traffic "hearing officers."

Rule 6.090. Direct and Indirect Criminal Contempt

Direct and indirect criminal contempt shall be proceeded upon in the same manner as in the Criminal Rules of Procedure.

Amended April 25, 1975, effective May 1, 1975 (311 So.2d 665); Feb. 11, 1982 (410 So.2d 1337; Aug. 25, 1988, effective Jan. 1, 1989 (536 So.2d 181).

Committee Comments

1988 Amendment: The change from the word "punished" to the words "proceeded upon" were needed to make clear that the Committee intended to follow the procedure as outlined in Rule 3.830 and Rule 3.840, Criminal Procedure Rules. Those rules are procedural and contain no penalties.

Rule 6.100. Traffic Violations Bureau

(a) **Establishment and Function.** A traffic violations bureau shall be established in each county court by administrative order of the chief judge of the circuit in which the county court is located. The function of the bureau shall be to accept appearances, waivers of non- criminal hearings, admissions, payment of civil penalties for traffic infractions not requiring a mandatory hearing, and nolo contendere pleas under the authority of section 318.14(9) and (10), Florida Statutes. If any person's sentence for a criminal traffic offense or penalty for a traffic infraction requiring a mandatory hearing or a traffic infraction in which the person elects to appear before an official includes the payment of a fine or civil penalty, payment may be made before the bureau. The bureau may also accept appearances, waivers of hearings, admissions, and payment of civil penalties as provided in section 318.18, Florida Statutes, in traffic infraction cases in which the driver originally elected, but was not required, to appear before an official prior to the date of the hearing. The bureau shall act under the direction and control of the judges of the court.

(b) **Civil Penalty Schedule; Payment and Accounting.** The court shall post in the place where civil penalties are to be paid in the violations bureau the schedule of the amount of the civil penalty as provided in section 318.18, Florida Statutes. All fines, civil penalties, and costs shall be paid to, receipted by, and accounted for by the violations bureau or proper authority in accordance with these rules.

(c) **Statistical Reports.** All cases processed in the violations bureau shall be numbered, tabulated, and reported for identification and statistical purposes. In any statistical reports required by law, the number of cases disposed of by the violations bureau shall be listed separately from those disposed of in open court.

Amended Feb. 11, 1982 (410 So.2d 1337); Sept. 30, 1985, effective Oct. 1, 1985 (477 So.2d 542); March 29, 1990 (559 So.2d 1101); Oct. 7, 2004, effective Jan. 1, 2005 (890 So.2d 1111).

Committee Comments

1990 Amendment: This amendment was proposed to avoid possible confusion as to any authority traffic magistrates could have in relation to the operation of traffic violations bureaus.

Rule 6.110. Driver Improvement, Student Traffic Safety Council, and Substance Abuse Education Courses

(a) Designation of School. In those areas where defendants are ordered or are allowed to elect to attend a driver improvement school or student traffic safety council school, or are sentenced to a substance abuse education course, the chief judge of the circuit shall issue an administrative order designating the schools at which attendance is required. No substance abuse education course shall be approved by the chief judges until approval is first granted by the DUI Programs Director. For persons ordered to attend driver improvement schools, those schools approved by the department shall be considered approved for purposes of this rule.

(b) Inspection and Supervision. Any programs designated to serve an area of the state are subject to the inspection and supervision of the DUI Programs Director.

(c) Out-of-State Residents. Out-of-state residents sentenced to a driver improvement school course or substance abuse program may elect to complete a substantially similar program or school in their home state, province, or country.

Amended April 25, 1975, effective May 1, 1975 (311 So.2d 665); March 31, 1976 (330 So.2d 129); June 2, 1977 (347 So.2d 413); Nov. 1, 1979 (376 So.2d 1157); Feb. 11, 1982 (410 So.2d 1337); Sept. 30, 1985, effective Oct. 1, 1985 (477 So.2d 542); Aug. 25, 1988, effective Jan. 1, 1989 (536 So.2d 181); Oct. 11, 1990 (567 So.2d 1380); Oct. 22, 1992, effective Jan. 1, 1993 (608 So.2d 451); July 1, 1993 (621 So.2d 1063).

Committee Notes

1988 Amendment. The reason for the change was to bring subdivision (a) into conformity with the statutory language in section 322.282, Florida Statutes, which states "substance abuse education course" rather than a "DWI Counter Attack School."

Subdivision (d) [now (c)] is new and was designed to allow compliance with section 316.193(5), Florida Statutes, when the person did not reside in Florida, was in Florida for only a short, temporary stay, and attendance at a substance abuse course in Florida would constitute a hardship. Section 316.193(5) requires only that the substance abuse course be "specified by the court."

1990 Amendment. The offense of Driving While Intoxicated was abolished by statute, thereby making reference to DWI inappropriate. The title of the person coordinating Substance Abuse Education Courses has been changed from that of Schools Coordinator to that of Programs Director.

Rule 6.130. Case Consolidation

When a defendant is cited for the commission of both a criminal and a civil traffic violation, or both a civil traffic infraction requiring a mandatory hearing and a civil traffic infraction not requiring a hearing, the cases may be heard simultaneously if they arose out of the same set of facts.

However, in no case shall a traffic hearing officer hear a criminal traffic case or a case involving a civil traffic infraction issued in conjunction with a criminal traffic offense.

Under any of these circumstances the civil traffic infraction shall be treated as continued for the purpose of reporting to the department. Prior to the date of the scheduled hearing or trial, a defendant may dispose of any nonmandatory civil traffic infraction in the manner provided by these rules and section 318.14, Florida Statutes.

Amended April 25, 1975, effective May 1, 1975 (311 So.2d 665); Dec. 14, 1978 (366 So.2d 400); Sept. 13, 1984, effective Jan. 1, 1985 (458 So.2d 1112); March 29, 1990 (559 So.2d 1101); Oct. 22, 1992, effective Jan. 1, 1993 (608 So.2d 451); Oct. 17, 1996, effective Jan. 1, 1997 (685 So.2d 1242).

Committee Notes

1990 Amendment. The rule on case consolidation was amended to include language from chapter 89–337, Laws of Florida, which prohibits traffic magistrates from hearing civil infractions arising out of same facts as criminal traffic offenses.

1996 Amendment. Enactment of chapter 94–202, Laws of Florida, necessitated the deletion of all references in the rules to traffic "magistrates" in favor of the term traffic "hearing officers."

Rule 6.140. Conduct of Trial

All trials and hearings shall be held in open court and shall be conducted in an orderly manner according to law and applicable rules. All proceedings for the trial of traffic cases shall be held in a place suitable for the purpose.

Amended Feb. 11, 1982 (410 So.2d 1337); Aug. 25, 1988, effective Jan. 1, 1989 (536 So.2d 181); July 1, 1993 (621 So.2d 1063).

Committee Comments

1988 Amendment: There was a major elimination in this particular rule, as the Committee felt that all questions pertaining to the conduct of any trial or hearing were covered by case decision, law, and the rules and that an official should not be permitted to decide on any other basis. It was also felt that the word *place*, should be substituted for the word *room* as in some emergency situations hearings had been held outside, etc.

Rule 6.150. Witnesses

(a) Procedure. The procedure prescribed by law in civil and criminal cases concerning the attendance and testimony of witnesses, the administration of oaths and affirmations, and proceedings to enforce the remedies and protect the rights of the parties shall govern traffic cases as far as they are applicable unless provided otherwise by these rules or by the law. Payment of witness fees and costs of serving witnesses in civil traffic cases shall be made in the same manner as in a criminal traffic case.

(b) Use of Affidavits. A defendant in a civil infraction case may offer evidence of other witnesses through use of one or more affidavits. The affidavits shall be considered by the court only as to the facts therein that are based on the personal knowledge and observation of the affiant as to relevant material facts. However, the affidavits shall not be admissible for the purpose of establishing character or reputation.

Amended April 25, 1975, effective May 1, 1975 (311 So.2d 665); Sept. 13, 1984, effective Jan. 1, 1985 (458 So.2d 1112); Oct. 22, 1992, effective Jan. 1, 1993 (608 So.2d 451).

III. CRIMINAL OFFENSES

Rule 6.160. Practice as in Criminal Rules

Except as provided, the Florida Rules of Criminal Procedure shall govern this part. A defendant shall be considered "taken into custody" for the purpose of rule 3.191 when the defendant is arrested, or when a traffic citation, notice to appear, summons, information, or indictment is served on the defendant in lieu of arrest.

Amended Feb. 11, 1982 (410 So.2d 1337); Sept. 13, 1984, effective Jan. 1, 1985 (458 So.2d 1112); Aug. 25, 1988, effective Jan. 1, 1989 (536 So.2d 181); Oct. 22, 1992, effective Jan. 1, 1993 (608 So.2d 451).

Committee Notes

1988 Amendments. The purpose of the change was to make clear that both pretrial and trial procedures, under this part, are governed by the Florida Rules of Criminal Procedure, unless there is a conflict. The previous rule had only applied to "trial"—and the committee felt that pretrial and post-trial procedures should also apply.

Rule 6.165. Complaint; Summons; Form; Use

(a) Uniform Traffic Citation. All prosecutions for criminal traffic offenses by law enforcement officers shall be by uniform traffic citation as provided for in section 316.650, Florida Statutes, or other applicable statutes, or by affidavit, information, or indictment as provided for in the Florida Rules of Criminal Procedure. If prosecution is by affidavit, information, or indictment, a uniform traffic citation shall be prepared by the arresting officer at the direction of the prosecutor or, in the absence of the arresting officer, by the prosecutor and submitted to the department.

(b) Amendment of Citation. The court may allow the prosecutor to amend in open court a traffic citation alleging a criminal traffic offense to state a different traffic offense. No new traffic citation need be issued by the arresting officer. The court shall grant additional time to the defendant for the purpose of preparing a defense if the amendment has prejudiced the defendant.

Added Feb. 11, 1982 (410 So.2d 1337). Amended Sept. 13, 1984, effective Jan. 1, 1985 (458 So.2d 1112); Aug. 25, 1988, effective Jan. 1, 1989 (536 So.2d 181); Oct. 22, 1992, effective Jan. 1, 1993 (608 So.2d 451).

Committee Notes

1988 Amendment. It was felt that due process required the court to grant a continuance to the defendant as a matter of right, if the amendment prejudiced the defendant. The committee felt that this should be mandatory and not discretionary.

Rule 6.180. Sentencing Repeat Offenders

(a) Defendant's Rights. A defendant alleged to have a prior conviction for a criminal traffic offense shall have a right to remain silent concerning any prior conviction at the time of plea or sentence.

(b) Proof of Prior Convictions. If the right to remain silent is invoked by the defendant, the state shall have a reasonable time, if requested, to determine if any prior convictions exist. If the state is unable to prove any prior convictions, the defendant shall be treated as if no prior convictions exist.

(c) Suspension by Department. This provision shall not prevent the department from suspending a defendant's driving privilege for a longer period than the court has entered if a prior record is discovered by the department.

Added Aug. 25, 1988, effective Jan. 1, 1989 (536 So.2d 181). Amended Oct. 22, 1992, effective Jan. 1, 1993 (608 So.2d 451).

Committee Notes

1988 Adoption. Rule 6.180 is new and is designed to codify existing procedures in DUI cases. The rule sets forth what has become known as a "Meehan plea." Meehan v. State, 397 So.2d 1214 (Fla.2d DCA 1981).

1992 Amendment. Makes a "Meehan plea" applicable to all criminal traffic offenses.

Rule 6.183. Peremptory Challenges

In every jury trial in which a defendant is charged with a violation of section 316.193, Florida Statutes, each party shall have 3 peremptory challenges, but the trial court, in the interest of justice, in its discretion may permit additional challenges.

Added Aug. 25, 1988, effective Jan. 1, 1989 (536 So.2d 181). Amended Oct. 22, 1992, effective Jan. 1, 1993 (608 So.2d 451).

Committee Notes

1988 Adoption. This rule was initially drafted to allow 6 peremptory challenges per side in all DUI trials on the basis that the penalties in a DUI were normally more severe than most third-degree felonies, that the trial was as complicated as any second-degree felony, and that it was also subject to extreme jury prejudice due to "media blitz" publicity and the pressures from citizen action groups, as well as the numbers of prospective jurors who were nondrinkers or had religious reasons against drinking. The proposed rule met with strong opposition from the committee as drafted, with an almost even split vote. An amendment was proposed, which is the above rule as written, which satisfied all members of the committee, as it was recognized that the outlined problems existed, and the committee felt that a rule was needed to affirmatively show that additional peremptories should be freely granted by the court when the need arises.

Rule 6.190. Procedure on Failure to Appear; Warrant; Notice

Text of rule effective until January 1, 2016. See, also, rule effective January 1, 2016.

(a) Issuance of Warrants. The court may direct the issuance of a warrant for the arrest of any resident of this state, or any non-resident on whom process may be served in this state, who fails to appear and answer a criminal traffic complaint or summons lawfully served on such person and against whom a complaint or information has been filed. The warrant shall be directed to all law enforcement officers, state, county, and municipal, in the state and may be executed in any county in this state.

(b) Warrant Not Issued or Served; Disposition of Case. If a warrant is not issued or is not served within 30 days after issuance, the court may place the case in an inactive file or file of cases disposed of and shall report only bond forfeiture cases and cases finally adjudicated to the driver license issuing authority of the department. For all other purposes, including final disposition reports, the cases shall be reported as disposed of, subject to being reopened if thereafter the defendant appears or is apprehended.

(c) Nonresident of State; Failure to Appear or Answer Summons. If a defendant is not a resident of this state and fails to appear or answer a traffic complaint, the clerk of the court or the court shall mail notice to the defendant at the address stated in the complaint and to the department. The department shall send notice to the license issuing agency in the defendant's home state. If the defendant fails to appear or answer within 30 days after the mailing of notice, the court shall place the case in an inactive file or file of cases disposed of, subject to being reopened if thereafter the defendant appears or answers or a warrant is issued and served.

(d) Forfeiture of Bail. The waiting period imposed herein shall not affect any proceedings for forfeiture of bail.

Amended April 25, 1975, effective May 1, 1975 (311 So.2d 665); Oct. 7, 2004, effective Jan. 1, 2005 (890 So.2d 1111).

Rule 6.190. Procedure on Failure to Appear; Warrant; Notice

Text of rule effective January 1, 2016. See, also, rule effective until January 1, 2016.

(a) Issuance of Warrants. The court may direct the issuance of a warrant for the arrest of any resident of this state, or any non-resident on whom process may be served in this state, who fails to appear and answer a criminal traffic complaint or summons lawfully served on such person and against whom a complaint or information has been filed. The warrant shall be directed to all law enforcement officers, state, county, and municipal, in the state and may be executed in any county in this state.

(b) Warrant Not Issued or Served; Disposition of Case. If a warrant is not issued or is not served within 30 days after issuance, the court may place the case in an inactive file or file of cases disposed of and shall report only bond forfeiture cases and cases finally adjudicated to the driver license issuing authority of the department. For all other purposes, including final disposition reports, the cases shall be reported as disposed of, subject to being reopened if thereafter the defendant appears or is apprehended.

(c) Nonresident of State; Failure to Appear or Answer Summons. If a defendant is not a resident of this state and fails to appear or answer a traffic complaint, the clerk of the court or the court shall send notice to the defendant at the address stated in the complaint and to the department. The department shall send notice to the license issuing agency in the defendant's home state. If the defendant fails to appear or answer within 30 days after notice is sent, the court shall place the case in an inactive file or file of cases disposed of, subject to being reopened if thereafter the defendant appears or answers or a warrant is issued and served.

(d) Forfeiture of Bail. The waiting period imposed herein shall not affect any proceedings for forfeiture of bail.

Amended April 25, 1975, effective May 1, 1975 (311 So.2d 665); Oct. 7, 2004, effective Jan. 1, 2005 (890 So.2d 1111); June 4, 2015, effective Jan. 1, 2016 (166 So.3d 179).

Rule 6.200. Pleas and Affidavits of Defense

(a) Record of Pleas. All pleas entered in open court shall be recorded by an official court reporter or electronic means, unless the defendant signs a written waiver of this right.

(b) Written Pleas of Guilty or Nolo Contendere. Subject to the approval of the court, written pleas of guilty or nolo contendere may be entered in criminal traffic offenses not designated felonies under the laws of the state, and sentence imposed thereon.

(c) Nonresident of County; Affidavit of Defense. Any person charged with the commission of a criminal traffic offense who is not a resident of or domiciled in a county where the alleged offense took place may, at the discretion of the court, file a written statement setting forth facts justifying the filing of an affidavit of defense or file an affidavit of defense directly, if practicable, upon posting a reasonable bond set by the court.

Amended July 18, 1979 (372 So.2d 1377); Feb. 11, 1982 (410 So.2d 1337); Oct. 7, 2004, effective Jan. 1, 2005 (890 So.2d 1111).

Rule 6.290. Withholding Adjudication Prohibited

Pursuant to section 316.656, Florida Statutes, no court shall suspend, defer, or withhold adjudication of guilt or the imposition of sentence for the offense of driving or being in actual physical control of a motor vehicle while having an unlawful blood alcohol level or while under the influence of alcoholic beverages, any chemical substance set forth in section 877.111, Florida Statutes, or any substance controlled by chapter 893, Florida Statutes.

Amended May 11, 1978 (358 So.2d 1360); Dec. 14, 1978 (366 So.2d 400); Feb. 11, 1982 (410 So.2d 1337); Sept. 13, 1984, effective Jan. 1, 1985 (458 So.2d 1112); Aug. 25, 1988, effective Jan. 1, 1989 (536 So.2d 181); Oct. 22, 1992, effective Jan. 1, 1993 (608 So.2d 451).

Committee Notes

1988 Amendment. Subdivision (b) was eliminated by the committee as there is no "lesser offense" for a DUI. Moreover, the enhanced penalty under section 316.193(4), Florida Statutes, for a blood alcohol level of .20 or above has inherently changed the entire previous meaning of the eliminated subdivision. The new enhanced penalty portion of the statute creates a "lesser offense" to the "enhancement"—but not to the DUI.

Rule 6.291. Procedures on Withheld Adjudication in Driving While License Suspended; Costs and Enlargement of Time to Comply; Record of Convictions

(a) Costs. When a defendant charged with a criminal offense elects to exercise the option of receiving a withheld adjudication under section 318.14(10), Florida Statutes, law enforcement education assessments under section 943.25, Florida Statutes, and victims-of-crimes compensation costs and surcharges under sections 938.03 and 938.04, Florida Statutes, must be assessed, in addition to the court costs assessed by section 318.14(10), Florida Statutes.

(b) Additional Costs. In addition to any other allowable costs, additional court costs of up to $5 may be assessed, if authorized by administrative order of the chief judge of the circuit.

(c) Time to Comply. When a defendant elects to exercise the option of receiving a withheld adjudication pursuant to section 318.14(10), Florida Statutes, the clerk shall allow the defendant such additional time as may be reasonably necessary, not exceeding 60 days, to fulfill statutory requirements. If the defendant has not been able to comply with the statutory requirements within 60 days, the court, for good cause shown, may extend the time necessary for the defendant to comply.

(d) Convictions. Elections under section 318.14(10), Florida Statutes, when adjudication is withheld, shall not constitute convictions as that term is used in chapter 322, Florida Statutes.

Added Sept. 30, 1985, effective Oct. 1, 1985 (477 So.2d 542). Amended Sept. 18, 1986, effective Oct. 1, 1986 (494 So.2d 1129); Oct. 11, 1990 (567 So.2d 1380); Oct. 22, 1992, effective Jan. 1, 1993 (608 So.2d 451); Dec. 3, 2009, effective Jan. 1, 2010 (24 So.3d 176).

Committee Notes

1990 Amendment. Section 27.3455(1), Florida Statutes, was amended to provide that any person who pleads nolo contendere to a misdemeanor or criminal traffic offense under section 318.14(10)(a) shall be assessed costs of $50 for the local government criminal justice trust fund. This enactment requires the deletion of the previously existing rule provision that prohibited an assessment of costs for the local government criminal justice trust fund.

1992 Amendment. This rule consolidates rules 6.291, 6.292, and 6.293. It also sets a limit on the amount of time a clerk can allow a defendant to process an administrative withheld adjudication through the clerk, without leave of court.

Rule 6.300. Driver License Revocation; Maintaining List

In order to comply with the provisions of section 322.282(1), Florida Statutes, the clerk need not maintain a separate list of driver license revocations or suspensions from his or her existing records.

Amended Feb. 11, 1982 (410 So.2d 1337); Sept. 18, 1986, effective Oct. 1, 1986 (494 So.2d 1129).

Rule 6.310. Lesser Included Offenses

No civil traffic infraction shall be considered a lesser included offense of any criminal traffic offense.

Amended April 25, 1975, effective May 1, 1975 (311 So.2d 665); Dec. 14, 1978 (366 So.2d 400); Feb. 11, 1982 (410 So.2d 1337).

IV. TRAFFIC INFRACTIONS

Rule 6.320. Complaint; Summons; Forms; Use

All citations for traffic infractions shall be by uniform traffic citation as provided in section 316.650, Florida Statutes, or other applicable statutes or by affidavit. If the complaint is made by affidavit a uniform traffic citation shall be prepared by the clerk and submitted to the department.

Amended April 25, 1975, effective May 1, 1975 (311 So.2d 665); Dec. 14, 1978 (366 So.2d 400); Feb. 11, 1982 (410 So.2d 1337).

Rule 6.325. Speedy Trial: Infractions Only

(a) General Rule. Except as otherwise provided in this rule, every defendant charged with a noncriminal traffic infraction shall be brought to trial within 180 days of the date the defendant is served with the uniform traffic citation or other charging document. If trial is not commenced within 180 days, the defendant shall be entitled to dismissal of the infraction charge.

(b) Effect of Delay or Continuances. If the trial of the defendant is not commenced within the 180–day requirement established by this rule, a motion for dismissal shall be granted by the court unless it is shown that

(1) failure to hold trial was attributable to the defendant or the defendant's counsel, or

(2) the defendant was unavailable for trial.

If the court finds that dismissal is not appropriate for the reasons listed in this subdivision, the motion for dismissal shall be denied.

(c) Application of Rule. This rule shall not apply to any infraction that is a part of a single episode or occurrence, which is attached to, consolidated with, or associated with a criminal traffic offense.

Added Oct. 22, 1992, effective Jan. 1, 1994 (608 So.2d 451). Amended Jan. 11, 1996 (667 So.2d 188).

Committee Notes

1992 Adoption. This rule establishes a speedy trial rule for traffic infractions and provides for automatic dismissal upon motion after the expiration of 180 days.

1995 Amendment. Subdivision (a) was amended to make it clear that the speedy trial rule was not meant to be a "statute of limitations." Under the existing statute of limitations (section 775.15(2)(d), Florida Statutes) infractions must be filed within one year of the date of the event that is the reason for the charge. This amendment makes it clear that the state can bring the charge within one year from the date of the infraction, but the charge must be tried within 180 days from the date of service of the infraction upon the accused. Subdivision (d) was entirely eliminated as unnecessary.

Rule 6.330. Election to Attend Traffic School

(a) Attendance at School. Unless a mandatory hearing is required, or the defendant appears at a hearing before an official, a defendant may elect to attend a driver improvement school pursuant to section 318.14(9), Florida Statutes, within 30 days of receiving a citation or, if a hearing was requested, at any time before trial. Attendance at a driver improvement school shall not operate to waive the law enforcement education assessments under section 943.25, Florida Statutes. Any defendant electing to attend driver improvement school under section 318.14(9), Florida Statutes, will receive a withheld adjudication and not be assessed points.

(b) Location of School. A defendant who is sentenced to or elects to attend a driver improvement school shall have the right to attend an approved school in the location of the defendant's choice.

Amended April 25, 1975, effective May 1, 1975 (311 So.2d 665); Jan. 27, 1977 (342 So.2d 80); Feb. 11, 1982 (410 So.2d 1337); Sept. 13, 1984, effective Jan. 1, 1985 (458 So.2d 1112); Sept. 30, 1985, effective Oct. 1, 1985 (477 So.2d 542); Sept. 18, 1986, effective Oct. 1, 1986 (494 So.2d 1129); Oct. 22, 1992, effective Jan. 1, 1993 (608 So.2d 451); Dec. 3, 2009, effective Jan. 1, 2010 (24 So.3d 176).

Committee Notes

2009 Amendment. The rule change in subdivision (a) was necessary to create a uniform time period throughout the state by which a clerk must allow a defendant to elect to attend a driver improvement school.

Rule 6.340. Affidavit of Defense or Admission and Waiver of Appearance

(a) Appearance in Court. Any defendant charged with an infraction may, in lieu of a personal appearance at trial, file an affidavit of defense or an admission that the infraction was committed as provided in this rule.

(b) Posting of Bond. The trial court may require a bond to be posted before the court will accept an affidavit in lieu of appearance at trial. The defendant shall be given reasonable notice if required to post a bond.

(c) Attorney Representation. If a defendant is represented by an attorney in an infraction case, said attorney may represent the defendant in the absence of the defendant at a hearing or trial without the defendant being required to file an affidavit of defense. The attorney shall file a written notice of appearance. The attorney may enter any plea, proceed to trial, present evidence other than the defendant's statements, and examine and cross examine witnesses without the defendant being required to file an affidavit of defense. Nonetheless, a defendant represented by an attorney may file an affidavit of defense. If a represented defendant files such an affidavit, the affidavit must be signed and properly notarized, subjecting the affiant to perjury prosecution for false statements.

(d) Sample Affidavit of Defense or Admission and Waiver of Appearance.

	*	IN THE COUNTY COURT,
STATE OF FLORIDA,	*	COUNTY, FLORIDA
Plaintiff,	*	
	*	CASE NO.
vs.	*	
	*	CITATION NO.
________,	*	
Defendant.	*	DRIVER'S LICENSE NO.
________	*	________

AFFIDAVIT OF DEFENSE OR ADMISSION AND WAIVER OF APPEARANCE

Before me personally appeared ________________, who after first being placed under oath, swears or affirms as follows:

1. My name, address, and telephone number are:
Name: ________
Address: ________
____
Telephone No.: ________

2. I am the defendant in the above-referenced case and am charged with the following violation(s): (List the charges as you understand them to be.)
____
____
____
[Note: This is not an admission that you violated any law.]

3. Check **only one** as your plea:

I hereby plead NOT GUILTY and file this affidavit of defense as my sworn statement herein. I understand that when I plead not guilty, I do not have to supply any further statement. I understand that by my filing this affidavit, the hearing officer or judge will have to make a decision as to whether I committed the alleged violation by the sworn testimony of the witnesses, other evidence, and my statement. I understand that I am waiving my personal appearance at the final hearing of this matter.

I hereby plead GUILTY and file this affidavit as an explanation of what happened and as a statement that the hearing officer or judge can consider before pronouncing a sentence. I understand that I am not required to make any statement. I understand that the hearing officer or judge will determine the appropriate sentence and decide whether to adjudicate me guilty.

I hereby plead NO CONTEST and file this affidavit as an explanation of what happened and as a statement that the hearing officer or judge can consider before pronouncing a sentence. By pleading no contest, I understand that I am not admitting or denying that the infraction was committed but do not contest the charges, and I understand that I may be sentenced and found guilty even though I entered a plea of no contest. I understand that I am not required to make any statement. I understand that the hearing officer or judge will determine any appropriate sentence and decide whether to adjudicate me guilty.

4. Defendant's Statement: (additional papers, documents, photos, etc. can be attached but should be mentioned herein).

____

____

____

____

____

____

I understand that any material misrepresentation could cause me to be prosecuted for a separate criminal law violation.

/s/______________________

Affiant/Defendant

Sworn to (or affirmed) and subscribed before me, the undersigned authority, on ______________

Personally known ____

Produced identification ____ Type of ID produced ____

/s/______________________________

Notary Public, Deputy Clerk, or other authority

NAME:

Commission No.

My Commission Expires:

NOTE: It is your responsibility to make sure this affidavit is in the court file before the hearing date. If Affiant/Defendant is under the age of 18, a parent or guardian must sign this affidavit:

____

Parent or Guardian

Amended April 25, 1975, effective May 1, 1975 (311 So.2d 665); June 30, 1976 (335 So.2d 2); Feb. 11, 1982 (410 So.2d 1337); Aug. 25, 1988, effective Jan. 1, 1989 (536 So.2d 181); Oct. 22, 1992, effective Jan. 1, 1993 (608 So.2d 451); Oct. 17, 1996, effective Jan. 1, 1997 (685 So.2d 1242).

Committee Notes

1996 Amendment. The committee completely revised this rule to conform to the common practice of attorneys practicing in the traffic courts of Florida.

Rule 6.350. Computation of Time

Computation of time shall be governed by Florida Rule of Judicial Administration 2.514.

Amended Oct. 22, 1992, effective Jan. 1, 1993 (608 So.2d 451); July 12, 2012, effective Oct. 1, 2012 (95 So.3d 96).

Rule 6.360. Enlargement of Time

(a) Procedure. When by these rules or by a notice given thereunder or by order of an official an act is required, or allowed to be done at or within a specified time, the official for good cause shown, at any time, in the official's discretion may

(1) order the period enlarged if request therefor is made before the expiration of the period originally prescribed or as extended by a previous order; or

(2) on motion made after the expiration of the specified period, permit the act to be done when the failure to act was the result of excusable neglect. However, except as provided by statute or elsewhere in these rules, the official may not extend the time for making a motion for a new hearing, or for taking an appeal.

(b) Withheld Adjudications. When a defendant elects to exercise the option of receiving a withheld adjudication pursuant to section 318.14(9) or (10), Florida Statutes, the clerk shall allow the defendant such additional time, not exceeding 60 days, as may be reasonably necessary to fulfill the statutory requirements. If the defendant has not been able to comply with the statutory requirements within 60 days, the court, for good cause shown, may extend the time necessary for the defendant to comply.

Amended Sept. 30, 1985, effective Oct. 1, 1985 (477 So.2d 542); Sept. 18, 1986, effective Oct. 1, 1986 (494 So.2d 1129); Oct. 22, 1992, effective Jan. 1, 1993 (608 So.2d 451).

Rule 6.380. Nonverification of Pleadings

Text of rule effective until January 1, 2016. See, also, rule effective January 1, 2016.

Except when otherwise specifically provided by these rules or an applicable statute, every written pleading or other paper of a defendant represented by an attorney need not be verified or accompanied by an affidavit.

Amended June 14, 1979, effective July 1, 1979 (372 So.2d 449); Oct. 22, 1992, effective Jan. 1, 1993 (608 So.2d 451).

Rule 6.380. Nonverification of Pleadings

Text of rule effective January 1, 2016. See, also, rule effective until January 1, 2016.

Except when otherwise specifically provided by these rules or an applicable statute, every written pleading or other document of a defendant represented by an attorney need not be verified or accompanied by an affidavit.

Amended June 14, 1979, effective July 1, 1979 (372 So.2d 449); Oct. 22, 1992, effective Jan. 1, 1993 (608 So.2d 451); June 4, 2015, effective Jan. 1, 2016 (166 So.3d 179).

Rule 6.400. Clerk to Prepare and Send Reports

When reports or forms are to be sent to the department, the clerk or traffic violations bureau shall prepare and send the reports or forms.

Amended Oct. 22, 1992, effective Jan. 1, 1993 (608 So.2d 451).

Rule 6.445. Discovery: Infractions Only

If an electronic or mechanical speed measuring device is used by the citing officer, the type of device and the manufacturer's serial number must be included in the body of the citation. If any relevant supporting documentation regarding such device is in the officer's possession at the time of trial, the defendant or defendant's attorney shall be entitled to review that documentation immediately before that trial.

Added Oct. 17, 1996, effective Jan. 1, 1997 (685 So.2d 1242). Amended Dec. 3, 2009, effective Jan. 1, 2010 (24 So.3d 176).

Committee Notes

2009 Amendment. This amendment is based on the fact that currently to the committee's knowledge there are 5 different measuring devices or types: Radar, Laser, Pace Car, Vascar, and airplane with stopwatch. It is believed that identifying the type of measuring device is not unduly burdensome to the state and it is necessary in the preparation of a defense. Withholding this information until the time of trial unduly prejudices the defense. This amendment is also forward-looking in that as new measuring devices appear, they can be effectively used as long as they are disclosed.

Rule 6.450. Order of Hearing

(a) When Traffic Infraction Admitted. If a defendant admits that the traffic infraction was committed, the official shall permit the defendant to offer a statement concerning the commission of the infraction. The official may examine the defendant and issuing officer concerning the infraction prior to making a determination as to the civil penalty to be imposed.

(b) Description of Procedure. Before the commencement of a hearing the official shall briefly describe and explain the purposes and procedure of the hearing and the rights of the defendant.

(c) Defense. The defendant may offer sworn testimony and evidence and, after such testimony is offered, shall answer any questions asked by the official.

(d) Additional Witnesses. If the testimony of additional witnesses is to be offered, the order in which the witnesses shall testify shall be determined by the official conducting the hearing. Any such witness shall be sworn and shall testify, and may then be questioned by the official, and thereafter may be questioned by the defendant or counsel.

(e) Further Examination. Upon the conclusion of such testimony and examination, the official may further examine or allow such examination as the official deems appropriate.

(f) Closing Statement. At the conclusion of all testimony and examination, the defendant or counsel shall be permitted to make a statement in the nature of a closing argument.

(g) Failure to Appear at Contested Hearing. In any case in which a contested infraction hearing is held, and the defendant, who either has asked for the contested hearing or otherwise received proper notice of the hearing, fails to appear for the hearing, the official can proceed with the hearing, take testimony, and, if it is determined that the infraction was committed, impose a penalty as if the defendant had attended the hearing. In the interests of justice, the court may vacate the judgment upon a showing of good cause by the defendant.

Amended Sept. 13, 1984, effective Jan. 1, 1985 (458 So.2d 1112); Oct. 22, 1992, effective Jan. 1, 1993 (608 So.2d 451).

Rule 6.455. Amendments

The charging document may be amended by the issuing officer in open court at the time of a scheduled hearing before it commences, subject to the approval of the official. The official shall grant a continuance if the amendment requires one in the interests of justice. No case shall be dismissed by reason of any informality or irregularity in the charging instrument.

Added Sept. 13, 1984, effective Jan. 1, 1985 (458 So.2d 1112). Amended Aug. 25, 1988, effective Jan. 1, 1989 (536 So.2d 181); Oct. 22, 1992, effective Jan. 1, 1993 (608 So.2d 451); Sept. 21, 2006, effective Jan. 1, 2007 (938 So.2d 983).

Committee Notes

1988 Amendment. The revision deletes the word "may" and substitutes the word "shall." This brings the rule in accord with due process.

Rule 6.460. Evidence

Text of rule effective until January 1, 2016. See, also, rule effective January 1, 2016.

(a) Applicable Rules. The rules of evidence applicable in all hearings for traffic infractions shall be the same as in civil cases, except to the extent inconsistent with these rules, and shall be liberally construed by the official hearing the case.

(b) Tape Recording of Hearing. Any party to a noncriminal traffic infraction may make a tape recording of the hearing. The provision and operation of the recording equipment shall be the responsibility of the defendant unless otherwise provided by the court. The original recording shall be delivered immediately after the hearing to the clerk, who shall seal and file it. Such tape shall be transcribed for an appeal if ordered by the defendant. Transcription shall only be by an official court reporter at the defendant's expense.

Amended Sept. 13, 1984, effective Jan. 1, 1985 (458 So.2d 1112); Oct. 22, 1992, effective Jan. 1, 1993 (608 So.2d 451).

Rule 6.460. Evidence

Text of rule effective January 1, 2016. See, also, rule effective until January 1, 2016.

(a) Applicable Rules. The rules of evidence applicable in all hearings for traffic infractions shall be the same as in civil cases, except to the extent inconsistent with these rules, and shall be liberally construed by the official hearing the case.

(b) Recording of Hearing. Any party to a noncriminal traffic infraction may make a recording of the hearing. The provision and operation of the recording equipment shall be the responsibility of that party unless otherwise provided by the court, and shall be in a recording format acceptable to the clerk. A recording of the proceeding that is made by a party shall be delivered immediately after the hearing to the clerk, who shall secure and file it. A certified copy of such recording shall be furnished by the clerk and transcribed for an appeal if ordered by a party at that party's expense. Transcription shall only be by an official court reporter at the requesting party's expense.

Amended Sept. 13, 1984, effective Jan. 1, 1985 (458 So.2d 1112); Oct. 22, 1992, effective Jan. 1, 1993 (608 So.2d 451); June 4, 2015, effective Jan. 1, 2016 (166 So.3d 179).

Committee Notes

2015 Amendment. In light of continuing technological advances, this rule was amended to accommodate continuing changes in technology and the ability to use various types of equipment when recording a traffic infraction hearing. Parties are encouraged to contact the clerk of court prior to their hearing to confirm that the recording equipment they intend to use will produce a recording in a format that is acceptable to the clerk.

Rule 6.470. Costs

(a) Hearing Required. In those cases in which a hearing is held to determine whether a traffic infraction was committed, court costs and surcharges as authorized by law may be assessed by the official against the defendant in addition to the penalty imposed.

(b) No Hearing Required. When no hearing is required or held and the defendant admits the commission of the offense by paying the penalty or receiving a withheld adjudication pursuant to section 318.14(9) or (10), Florida Statutes, costs and surcharges as provided by law or administrative order may be imposed.

(c) Election to Attend School. If a defendant elects to attend a driver improvement school as provided in rule 6.330, the law enforcement education assessments shall be collected at the time the defendant appears before the traffic violations bureau to make the election.

Amended Jan. 13, 1975, effective Jan. 20, 1975 (306 So.2d 505); Dec. 14, 1978 (366 So.2d 400); July 18, 1979 (372 So.2d 1377); Feb. 11, 1982 (410 So.2d 1337); Sept. 13, 1984, effective Jan. 1, 1985 (458 So.2d 1112); Oct. 18, 1984, effective Jan. 1, 1985 (458 So.2d 1115); Sept. 30, 1985, effective Oct. 1, 1985 (477 So.2d 542); Sept. 18, 1986, effective Oct. 1, 1986 (494 So.2d 1129); Oct. 22, 1992, effective Jan. 1, 1993 (608 So.2d 451).

Committee Notes

1992 Amendment. The proposed amendment deletes reference to specific costs to avoid annual revision.

Rule 6.480. Deferred Payment of Penalty Imposed

(a) Procedure. On motion of the defendant or on the official's own motion, an official must allow a reasonable amount of time, no less than 30 days, before requiring the payment of any penalty imposed. If payment is not made after such extension or further extensions, such action will be considered a failure to comply for purposes of section 318.15, Florida Statutes.

(b) Administrative Order to Clerk. In relation to elections under section 318.14(9) or (10), Florida Statutes, the clerk, under the authority of an administrative order, may allow a reasonable amount of time before requiring the payment of civil penalties or costs.

Amended Sept.13, 1984, effective Jan. 1, 1985 (458 So.2d 1112); Sept. 30, 1985, effective Oct. 1, 1985 (477 So.2d 542); Sept. 18, 1986, effective Oct. 1, 1986 (494 So.2d 1129); Oct. 22, 1992, effective Jan. 1, 1993 (608 So.2d 451); Dec. 3, 2009, effective Jan. 1, 2010 (24 So.3d 176).

Committee Notes

2009 Amendment. Too often, defendants, represented by counsel and exercising use of Traffic Court Rule 6.340 (Waiver of Appearance), will resolve a case and be forced to make payment immediately, within 5 or 10 days. This type of sanction does not allow for the defendant to be notified by counsel in a reasonable amount of time. The amendment relieves the defendant from this undue hardship.

Rule 6.490. Correction and Reduction of Penalty

(a) Correction of Penalty. An official may at any time correct an illegal penalty.

(b) Reduction of Penalty. An official may reduce a legal penalty

(1) within 60 days after its imposition;

(2) within 60 days after receipt by the official of a mandate issued by the appellate court upon affirmance of the judgment and/or penalty on an original appeal;

(3) within 60 days after receipt by the official of a certified copy of an order of the appellate court dismissing an original appeal from the judgment and/or penalty; or

(4) if further appellate review is sought in a higher court or in successively higher courts, then within 60 days after the highest state or federal court to which a timely appeal has been taken under authority of law, or in which a petition for certiorari has been timely filed under authority of law, has entered an order of affirmance or an order dismissing the appeal and/or denying certiorari.

Amended Oct. 22, 1992, effective Jan. 1, 1993 (608 So.2d 451).

Rule 6.500. Pronouncement and Entry of Penalty; Penalizing Official

(a) Entry of Penalty. The final disposition of every case shall be entered in the minutes in courts in which minutes are kept, and shall be docketed in courts which do not maintain minutes.

(b) Pronouncement of Penalty; Obligations of Penalizing Official. In those cases in which it is necessary that the penalty be pronounced by an official other than the official who presided at the hearing, or accepted an admission, the penalizing official shall not impose a penalty without first becoming acquainted with what transpired at the hearing or the facts concerning the admission and the infraction.

Amended April 25, 1975, effective May 1, 1975 (311 So.2d 665); Feb. 11, 1982 (410 So.2d 1337); Oct. 7, 2004, effective Jan. 1, 2005 (890 So.2d 1111).

Rule 6.510. Determination That Infraction Was Not Committed; Bond Refunded

When it is determined that a defendant did not commit an alleged traffic infraction and a bond has been posted, the money or bond shall be refunded.

Amended Oct. 22, 1992, effective Jan. 1, 1993 (608 So.2d 451).

Rule 6.520. Effect of Granting New Hearing

When a new hearing is granted, the new hearing shall proceed in all respects as if no former trial had been had.

Rule 6.530. Imposition of Penalty Before or After Motion Filed

The official has the discretion to impose the civil penalty either before or after the filing of a motion for new hearing or arrest of judgment.

Amended Oct. 22, 1992, effective Jan. 1, 1993 (608 So.2d 451).

Rule 6.540. Time for and Method of Making Motions; Procedure

(a) Time. A motion for new hearing or in arrest of judgment, or both, may be made within 10 days, or such greater time as the official may allow, not to exceed 30 days, after the finding of the official.

(b) Method. When the defendant has been found to have committed the infraction, the motion may be dictated into the record, if a court reporter is present, and may be argued immediately after the finding of the official. The official may immediately rule on the motion.

(c) Procedure. The motion may be in writing, filed with the clerk or violations bureau and shall state the grounds on which it is based. When the official sets a time for the hearing, the clerk or bureau shall notify the counsel, if any, for the defendant or, if no attorney has been retained, the defendant.

Amended Sept. 13, 1984, effective Jan. 1, 1985 (458 So.2d 1112); Aug. 25, 1988, effective Jan. 1, 1989 (536 So.2d 181); Oct. 22, 1992, effective Jan. 1, 1993 (608 So.2d 451).

Committee Notes

1988 Amendment. The committee changed the time period to become uniform with Florida Rule of Criminal Procedure 3.590.

Rule 6.550. Official May Grant New Hearing

When, following a hearing, a determination has been made that the traffic infraction was committed, the official on motion of the defendant, or on the official's own motion, may grant a new hearing.

Amended Oct. 22, 1992, effective Jan. 1, 1993 (608 So.2d 451).

Rule 6.560. Conviction of Traffic Infraction

An admission or determination that a defendant has committed a traffic infraction shall constitute a conviction as that term is used in chapter 322, Florida Statutes, and section 943.25, Florida Statutes, unless adjudication is withheld by an official in those cases in which withholding of adjudication is not otherwise prohibited by statute or rule of procedure. Elections under section 318.14(9) or (10), Florida Statutes, when adjudication is withheld, shall not constitute convictions, but shall involve the collections of assessments pursuant to section 943.25, Florida Statutes.

Amended Jan. 13, 1975, effective Jan. 20, 1975 (306 So.2d 505); Dec. 14, 1978 (366 So.2d 400); Feb. 11, 1982 (410 So.2d 1337); Sept. 13, 1984, effective Jan. 1, 1985 (458 So.2d 1112); Sept. 30, 1985, effective Oct. 1, 1985 (477 So.2d 542); Sept. 18, 1986, effective Oct. 1, 1986 (494 So.2d 1129); Oct. 22, 1992, effective Jan. 1, 1993 (608 So.2d 451).

Rule 6.570. Reporting Action Requiring Suspension of Driver License

Any noncompliance with the provisions of chapter 318, Florida Statutes, resulting in the suspension of a driver license shall be reported to the department within 5 days after an offender's failure to comply on a form to be supplied by the department. Any noncompliance may be determined without the necessity of holding a hearing.

Amended Feb. 11, 1982 (410 So.2d 1337); Sept. 13, 1984, effective Jan. 1, 1985 (458 So.2d 1112); Sept. 18, 1986, effective Oct. 1, 1986 (494 So.2d 1129); Oct. 22, 1992, effective Jan. 1, 1993 (608 So.2d 451).

Rule 6.575. Retention of Case Files

For the purpose of record retention pursuant to the General Records Schedule D–T 1, case files with an outstanding or unsatisfied D–6 shall be considered disposed of 7 years after the submission of the D–6 by the clerk to the department. If the clerk disposes of a file, the department shall be notified.

Added May 11, 1978 (358 So.2d 1360). Amended Feb. 11, 1982 (410 So.2d 1337); Aug. 25, 1988, effective Jan. 1, 1989 (536 So.2d 181); Oct. 22, 1992, effective Jan. 1, 1993 (608 So.2d 451).

Committee Notes

1988 Amendment. In light of a recent statutory change providing for the 6 year (rather than 4) renewal of driver licenses, a corresponding change in records retention was deemed appropriate.

Rule 6.580. Completion of Driver School; Conditions

(a) **Approval by Chief Judge.** All driver schools selected by the chief judge of the circuit shall establish the conditions for the successful completion of the driver course. The conditions shall be submitted in writing for approval of the chief judge.

(b) **Failure to Meet Conditions; Reporting.** Any failure to meet the conditions for successful completion of the course shall be reported to the official having jurisdiction of the case or the clerk or traffic violations bureau if designated by the official of the school.

Amended Oct. 7, 2004, effective Jan. 1, 2005 (890 So.2d 1111).

Rule 6.590. Failure to Complete Driver School; Reinstatement of Driver License

(a) Notice of Failure to Complete Course. In any case in which a defendant elects to attend driver school but fails to appear for or complete the course, a notice of failure to complete the course shall be sent to the department within 5 days after the failure to comply, in order to comply with the requirements of section 318.15(1), Florida Statutes.

(b) Appearance After Notice Sent. If the defendant appears after notice has been sent but before the department has suspended the driver license, the department shall be notified on a form to be supplied by the department immediately after the civil penalty as provided in section 318.18, Florida Statutes, has been fulfilled.

(c) Reinstatement of License. If the defendant appears after the driver license has been suspended, the defendant must fulfill the civil penalty as provided in section 318.18, Florida Statutes, and may be required to agree again to attend a driver school. The defendant shall be given a form supplied by the department, certified by the official, to be taken to the nearest driver license examining station to have the driving privilege reinstated.

Amended Feb. 11, 1982 (410 So.2d 1337); Sept. 18, 1986, effective Oct. 1, 1986 (494 So.2d 1129); Oct. 22, 1992, effective Jan. 1, 1993 (608 So.2d 451).

Rule 6.600. Failure to Appear or Pay Civil Penalty; Reinstatement of Driver License

(a) Notice of Failure to Comply. In any case in which no mandatory hearing is required and the defendant has signed and accepted a citation but fails to pay the civil penalty or appear, notice of such failure shall be sent to the department within 5 days after the failure to comply, in order to comply with the requirements of section 318.15(1), Florida Statutes.

(b) Appearance After Notice Sent. If the defendant appears after the notice has been sent but before the department has suspended the driver license, the civil penalty may be paid without a hearing or the defendant may request a hearing. If the defendant requests a hearing, the clerk must set the case for hearing upon payment of the costs specified in section 318.18(8)(a), Florida Statutes. The department must be notified immediately on a form to be supplied by the department.

(c) Reinstatement of License. If the defendant appears after the driver license has been suspended, the defendant may pay the civil penalty, elect to attend a driver improvement school, or request a hearing. Any request for a hearing shall be made within a reasonable period of time after the commission of the alleged offense. If an election to attend a hearing is granted and it is determined that the infraction was committed, the defendant shall be subject to the penalty provisions of section 318.14(5), Florida Statutes. The defendant shall be given a form supplied by the department, certified by the official, to be taken to the nearest driver license examining station to have the driving privilege reinstated.

Amended Feb. 11, 1982 (410 So.2d 1337); Sept. 18, 1986, effective Oct. 1, 1986 (494 So.2d 1129); Aug. 25, 1988, effective Jan. 1, 1989 (536 So.2d 181); Oct. 22, 1992, effective Jan. 1, 1993 (608 So.2d 451); Dec. 20, 2012, effective Jan. 1, 2013 (105 So.3d 1267).

Committee Notes

1988 Amendment. It was thought that a defendant who fails to appear until after his or her driver license has been suspended (which could be years later) should not be allowed to elect a hearing in those cases where the state has been prejudiced by the passage of time.

Rule 6.610. Failure to Fulfill Penalty Imposed After a Hearing; Reinstatement of Driver License

(a) Notice of Failure to Comply. In any case in which a hearing is held, if it is determined that the infraction was committed and a penalty is imposed but the penalty is not fulfilled, notice of such failure shall be sent to the department within 5 days after the failure to comply, in order to comply with the requirements of section 318.15(1), Florida Statutes.

(b) Appearance After Notice Sent. If the defendant appears after notice has been sent but before the department has suspended the driver license, the department shall be notified on a form to be supplied by the department after the penalty imposed has been fulfilled.

(c) Reinstatement of License. If the defendant appears after the driver license has been suspended, the defendant must fulfill the penalty and, if it is not a part of the penalty originally imposed, may be required to agree to attend a driver school if available. The defendant shall be given a form supplied by the department, certified by the official, to be taken to the nearest driver license examining station to have the driving privilege reinstated.

Amended Feb. 11, 1982 (410 So.2d 1337); Sept. 18, 1986, effective Oct. 1, 1986 (494 So.2d 1129); Oct. 22, 1992, effective Jan. 1, 1993 (608 So.2d 451).

Rule 6.620. Failure to Appear for Mandatory Hearing; Reinstatement of Driver License

(a) Notice of Failure to Appear. In any case in which a mandatory hearing is required and the defendant fails to appear, notice of such failure to appear shall be sent to the department within 5 days after the failure to comply, in order to comply with the requirements of section 318.15(1), Florida Statutes.

(b) Appearance After Notice Sent. If the defendant appears after notice has been sent, the department shall be notified immediately on a form to be supplied by the department and a hearing shall be held to determine whether the infraction was committed.

(c) Reinstatement of License. If the defendant's driver license has been suspended by the department and, after a hearing, it is found that the infraction was committed, the official may require that driver school, if available, be attended as part of the penalty. The defendant shall be given a form supplied by the department, certified by the official, to be taken to the nearest driver license examining station to have the driving privilege reinstated.

Amended Feb. 11, 1982 (410 So.2d 1337); Sept. 18, 1986, effective Oct. 1, 1986 (494 So.2d 1129); Oct. 22, 1992, effective Jan. 1, 1993 (608 So.2d 451).

Rule 6.630. Civil Traffic Infraction Hearing Officer Program; Traffic Hearing Officers

Text of rule effective until January 1, 2016. See, also, rule effective January 1, 2016.

Under the authority of sections 318.30–318.38, Florida Statutes, and article V, section 2, Florida Constitution, this court adopts the following rules and procedure for the Civil Traffic Infraction Hearing Officer Program:

(a) Eligibility of County. Pursuant to section 318.30, Florida Statutes, any county shall be eligible to participate in the Civil Traffic Infraction Hearing Officer Program.

(b) Participation. Any county electing to participate in the program shall be subject to the supervision of the Florida Supreme Court. The decision on whether to participate shall be made by the chief judge.

(c) Appointment of Traffic Hearing Officers. The appointment of such hearing officers shall be made by the chief judge, after consultation with the county judges in the county affected, and shall be approved by the chief justice. Once approval has been granted by the chief justice, the traffic hearing officers shall serve at the will of the chief judge.

(d) Jurisdiction. Traffic hearing officers shall have the power to accept pleas from defendants, hear and rule upon motions, decide whether a defendant has committed an infraction, and adjudicate or withhold adjudication in the same manner as a county court judge. However, a traffic hearing officer shall not:

(1) have the power to hold any person in contempt of court, but shall be permitted to file a verified motion for order of contempt with an appropriate state trial court judge pursuant to Florida Rule of Criminal Procedure 3.840;

(2) hear a case involving an accident resulting in injury or death; or

(3) hear a criminal traffic offense case or a case involving a civil traffic infraction issued in conjunction with a criminal traffic offense.

(e) Appeals. Appeals from decisions of a traffic hearing officer shall be to circuit court pursuant to the relevant provisions of the Florida Rules of Appellate Procedure in the same manner as appeals from the county court, except that traffic hearing officers shall not have the power to certify questions to district courts of appeal. The appellant shall be responsible for producing the record for such appeal.

(f) Membership in The Florida Bar. A traffic hearing officer shall be a member in good standing of The Florida Bar.

(g) Training. Traffic hearing officers must complete 40 hours of standardized training that has been approved by the supreme court. Instructors must be county court judges, hearing officers, and persons with expertise or knowledge with regard to specific traffic violations or traffic court. Curriculum and materials must be submitted to the Office of the State Courts Administrator. The standardized training must contain, at a minimum, all of the following:

(1) 28 hours of lecture sessions including 2.5 hours of ethics, 5 hours of courtroom procedure and control (which must include handling of situations in which a defendant's constitutional right against self-incrimination may be implicated), 11 hours of basic traffic court law and evidence, 3 hours of clerk's office/DMV training, 2 hours of participant perspective sessions/demonstrations, 3 hours of dispositions/penalties, and 1.5 hours of civil infractions/jurisdiction;

(2) 4 hours of role playing including mock opening statements, pretrial and trial sessions, and direct observation;

(3) 4 hours of observation including 2 hours of on-road observation of traffic enforcement;

(4) 4 hours of mentored participation in traffic court proceedings in the hiring county. Mentors must be county court judges or traffic hearing officers; and

(5) written training manuals for reference.

(h) Continuing Legal Education. Traffic hearing officers must complete 4 hours of continuing legal education per year. The continuing legal education program must be approved by the supreme court and must contain a minimum of 2 hours of ethics or professionalism. Curriculum materials must be submitted to the Office of the State Courts Administrator.

(i) Hours. Traffic hearing officers may serve either full time or part time at the discretion of the chief judge.

(j) Code of Judicial Conduct. All traffic hearing officers shall be subject to the Code of Judicial Conduct as provided in the application section of the code.

(k) Implementation of Program. In any county electing to establish a program, the chief judge shall develop a plan for its implementation and shall submit the plan to the Office of the State Courts Administrator. Funds for the program shall be used for traffic hearing officer program salaries and other necessary expenses, such as training, office rental, furniture, and administrative staff salaries. Any county electing to establish a traffic hearing officer program shall provide the funds necessary to operate the program.

(*l*) Robes. Traffic hearing officers shall not wear robes.

(m) Concurrent Jurisdiction. A county judge may exercise concurrent jurisdiction with a traffic hearing officer.

(n) Assignment to County Judge. On written request of the defendant, within 30 days of the issuance of the uniform traffic citation, the case shall be assigned to a county judge.

Amended June 6, 2002, effective January 1, 2003 (822 So.2d 1239); Sept. 21, 2006, effective Jan. 1, 2007 (938 So.2d 983); Nov. 27, 2013, effective Jan. 1, 2014 (131 So.3d 714).

Committee Notes

1990 Adoption. The rule attempts to incorporate relevant provisions of chapter 89–337, Laws of Florida, with minor modifications.

The provision in subdivision (c) that the traffic magistrate shall serve at the will of the chief judge is implicit in chapter 89–337, and is believed to be a good policy since it makes irrelevant consideration of the necessity of any involvement by the Judicial Qualifications Commission.

(d)(1) See 1990 Committee Note concerning rule 6.080.

In relation to subdivision (e) on appeals, the subcommittee believes that the addition of the language on the certifications to district courts, while making an obvious point, would avoid any possible confusion. It was also the consensus that there would be no need to recommend amendments to the Florida Rules of Appellate Procedure since rules 9.030(b)(4)(A) and 9.030(c)(1)(A) would appear to cover the matter adequately without further amendment.

Subdivision (g) goes into less detail concerning the actual length of training (40 hours preservice/10 hours continuing) required by chapter 89–337. A special plan for such training will be provided separately, including a recommendation for the waiver of such training for recently retired county court judges.

This rule expands the statutory prohibition of chapter 89–337, section 7, which prohibits traffic magistrates from practicing before other civil traffic magistrates and handling traffic appeals. The committee expressed concern that a limited prohibition extending only to practice before other magistrates might be read as condoning magistrate practice in traffic cases in front of county court judges. Given the contemplated relationship between county court judges and magistrates in education, training, and professional duties, such practice would give the appearance of conflict and should be prohibited.

In relation to subdivision (k), it was the opinion of the subcommittee that the wearing of robes might lead to confusion and interfere with the informal setting of the hearings.

1990 Amendment. Amendment of section 318.30, Florida Statutes (1990), reduced the case load requirement from 20,000 to 15,000 for purposes of allowing a county's participation in the Civil Traffic Infraction Hearing Officer Program. This amendment is necessary to conform the rule to the provisions of the amended statute.

1995 Amendment. Language was added to subdivision (d) to make it clear that hearing officers/magistrates can hear and rule upon motions, such as continuance motions, and otherwise handle normal motion practice in infraction cases.

1996 Amendment. Enactment of chapter 94–202, Laws of Florida, necessitated the deletion of all references in the rules to traffic "magistrates" in favor of the term traffic "hearing officers."

Subsection (a) reflects the legislative intent of section 318.30, Florida Statutes (1994). No longer is a minimum number of cases required before a county can establish a traffic infraction hearing officer program.

Changes to subsection (m) are intended to make uniform the procedure for assignment to a county judge for hearing.

2001 Amendment. Subdivision (g) provides detailed requirements for standardized initial training of traffic hearing officers. A statewide survey of judges and traffic hearing officers was taken and the rule then amended to incorporate the current statewide practice.

Subdivision (h) was added to resolve a conflict that existed between the rules and section 318.34, Florida Statutes.

Subdivision (i) was amended to conform the rule to the current practice prohibitions for hearing officers contained in the Code of Judicial Conduct. The code reflects the consensus of the committee as to appropriate prohibitions.

Rule 6.630. Civil Traffic Infraction Hearing Officer Program; Traffic Hearing Officers

Text of rule effective January 1, 2016. See, also, rule effective until January 1, 2016.

Under the authority of sections 318.30–318.38, Florida Statutes, and article V, section 2, Florida Constitution, this court adopts the following rules and procedure for the Civil Traffic Infraction Hearing Officer Program:

(a) Eligibility of County. Pursuant to section 318.30, Florida Statutes, any county shall be eligible to participate in the Civil Traffic Infraction Hearing Officer Program.

(b) Participation. Any county electing to participate in the program shall be subject to the supervision of the Florida Supreme Court. The decision on whether to participate shall be made by the chief judge.

(c) Appointment of Traffic Hearing Officers. The appointment of such hearing officers shall be made by the chief judge, after consultation with the county judges in the county affected, and shall be approved by the chief justice. Once approval has been granted by the chief justice, the traffic hearing officers shall serve at the will of the chief judge.

(d) Jurisdiction. Traffic hearing officers shall have the power to accept pleas from defendants, hear and rule upon motions, decide whether a defendant has committed an infraction, and adjudicate or withhold adjudication in the same manner as a county court judge. However, a traffic hearing officer shall not:

(1) have the power to hold any person in contempt of court, but shall be permitted to file a verified motion for order of contempt with an appropriate state trial court judge pursuant to Florida Rule of Criminal Procedure 3.840;

(2) hear a case involving an accident resulting in injury or death; or

(3) hear a criminal traffic offense case or a case involving a civil traffic infraction issued in conjunction with a criminal traffic offense.

(e) Appeals. Appeals from decisions of a traffic hearing officer shall be to circuit court pursuant to the relevant provisions of the Florida Rules of Appellate Procedure in the same manner as appeals from the county court, except that traffic hearing officers shall not have the power to certify questions to district courts of appeal. The appellant shall be responsible for producing the record for such appeal.

(f) Membership in The Florida Bar. A traffic hearing officer shall be a member in good standing of The Florida Bar.

(g) Training. Traffic hearing officers must complete 40 hours of standardized training that has been approved by the supreme court. Instructors must be judges, hearing officers, and persons with expertise or knowledge with regard to specific traffic violations or traffic court. Curriculum and materials must be submitted to the Office of the State Courts Administrator. The standardized training must contain, at a minimum, all of the following:

(1) 28 hours of lecture sessions including 2.5 hours of ethics, 5 hours of courtroom control management, 11 hours of basic traffic court law and evidence (which must include handling of situations in which a defendant's constitutional right against self-incrimination may be implicated), 3 hours of clerk's office/DMV training, 2 hours of participant perspective sessions/demonstrations, 3 hours of dispositions/penalties, and 1.5 hours of civil infractions/jurisdiction;

(2) 4 hours of role playing including mock opening statements, pretrial and trial sessions, and direct observation;

(3) 4 hours of observation including 2 hours of on-road observation of traffic enforcement;

(4) 4 hours of mentored participation in traffic court proceedings in the hiring county. Mentors must be county court judges or traffic hearing officers; and

(5) written training manuals for reference.

(h) Continuing Legal Education. Traffic hearing officers must complete 4 hours of continuing legal education per year. The continuing legal education program must be approved by the supreme court and must contain a minimum of 2 hours of ethics or professionalism, and 2 hours of civil traffic infraction related education. Curriculum materials must be submitted to the Office of the State Courts Administrator.

(i) Hours. Traffic hearing officers may serve either full time or part time at the discretion of the chief judge.

(j) Code of Judicial Conduct. All traffic hearing officers shall be subject to the Code of Judicial Conduct as provided in the application section of the code.

(k) Implementation of Program. In any county electing to establish a program, the chief judge shall develop a plan for its implementation and shall submit the plan to the Office of the State Courts Administrator. Funds for the program shall be used for traffic hearing officer program salaries and other necessary expenses, such as training, office rental, furniture, and administrative staff salaries. Any county electing to establish a traffic hearing officer program shall provide the funds necessary to operate the program.

(*l*) Robes. Traffic hearing officers shall not wear robes.

(m) Concurrent Jurisdiction. A county judge may exercise concurrent jurisdiction with a traffic hearing officer.

(n) Assignment to County Judge. On written request of the defendant, within 30 days of the issuance of the uniform traffic citation, the case shall be assigned to a county judge.

Amended June 6, 2002, effective January 1, 2003 (822 So.2d 1239); Sept. 21, 2006, effective Jan. 1, 2007 (938 So.2d 983); Nov. 27, 2013, effective Jan. 1, 2014 (131 So.3d 714); June 4, 2015, effective Jan. 1, 2016 (166 So.3d 179).

Committee Notes

1990 Adoption. The rule attempts to incorporate relevant provisions of chapter 89–337, Laws of Florida, with minor modifications.

The provision in subdivision (c) that the traffic magistrate shall serve at the will of the chief judge is implicit in chapter 89–337, and is believed to be a good policy since it makes irrelevant consideration of the necessity of any involvement by the Judicial Qualifications Commission.

(d)(1) See 1990 Committee Note concerning rule 6.080.

In relation to subdivision (e) on appeals, the subcommittee believes that the addition of the language on the certifications to district courts, while making an obvious point, would avoid any possible confusion. It was also the consensus that there would be no need to recommend amendments to the Florida Rules of Appellate Procedure since rules 9.030(b)(4)(A) and 9.030(c)(1)(A) would appear to cover the matter adequately without further amendment.

Subdivision (g) goes into less detail concerning the actual length of training (40 hours preservice/10 hours continuing) required by chapter 89–337. A special plan for such training will be provided separately, including a recommendation for the waiver of such training for recently retired county court judges.

This rule expands the statutory prohibition of chapter 89–337, section 7, which prohibits traffic magistrates from practicing before other civil traffic magistrates and handling traffic appeals. The committee expressed concern that a limited prohibition extending only to practice before other magistrates might be read as condoning magistrate practice in traffic cases in front of county court judges. Given the contemplated relationship between county court judges and magistrates in education, training, and professional duties, such practice would give the appearance of conflict and should be prohibited.

In relation to subdivision (k), it was the opinion of the subcommittee that the wearing of robes might lead to confusion and interfere with the informal setting of the hearings.

1990 Amendment. Amendment of section 318.30, Florida Statutes (1990), reduced the case load requirement from 20,000 to 15,000 for purposes of allowing a county's participation in the Civil Traffic Infraction Hearing Officer Program. This amendment is necessary to conform the rule to the provisions of the amended statute.

1995 Amendment. Language was added to subdivision (d) to make it clear that hearing officers/magistrates can hear and rule upon motions, such as continuance motions, and otherwise handle normal motion practice in infraction cases.

1996 Amendment. Enactment of chapter 94–202, Laws of Florida, necessitated the deletion of all references in the rules to traffic "magistrates" in favor of the term traffic "hearing officers."

Subsection (a) reflects the legislative intent of section 318.30, Florida Statutes (1994). No longer is a minimum number of cases required before a county can establish a traffic infraction hearing officer program.

Changes to subsection (m) are intended to make uniform the procedure for assignment to a county judge for hearing.

2001 Amendment. Subdivision (g) provides detailed requirements for standardized initial training of traffic hearing officers. A statewide survey of judges and traffic hearing officers was taken and the rule then amended to incorporate the current statewide practice.

Subdivision (h) was added to resolve a conflict that existed between the rules and section 318.34, Florida Statutes.

Subdivision (i) was amended to conform the rule to the current practice prohibitions for hearing officers contained in the Code of Judicial Conduct. The code reflects the consensus of the committee as to appropriate prohibitions.

INDEX TO FLORIDA RULES OF TRAFFIC COURT

FLORIDA SMALL CLAIMS RULES

1967 Compilation

The Supreme Court of Florida, on October 4, 1967 (203 So.2d 616), in response to petition of the Florida Bar, adopted an order to which was appended a complete compilation of the Summary Claims Procedure Rules. The court declared that the compilation should supersede all conflicting rules and statutes and should govern all proceedings within the scope of the rules after midnight, December 31, 1967. The order further declared that all statutes not superseded by, nor in conflict with the rules, should remain in effect as rules promulgated by the Supreme Court of Florida.

1972 Revision

The Florida Supreme Court on December 13, 1972 (270 So.2d 729) adopted a revision of the rules effective February 1, 1973. The court provided: "This revision shall govern all proceedings within the scope of these rules after 12:01 a.m., February 1, 1973. This revision shall supersede all conflicting rules and statutes. All statutes not superseded hereby or in conflict herewith shall remain in effect as rules promulgated by the Supreme Court of Florida."

Rule 7.010. Title and Scope

(a) Title. These rules shall be cited as Florida Small Claims Rules and may be abbreviated "Fla. Sm. Cl. R." These rules shall be construed to implement the simple, speedy, and inexpensive trial of actions at law in county courts.

(b) Scope. These rules are applicable to all actions of a civil nature in the county courts which contain a demand for money or property, the value of which does not exceed $5,000 exclusive of costs, interest, and attorneys' fees. If there is a difference between the time period prescribed by these rules and section 51.011, Florida Statutes, the statutory provision shall govern.

Amended Dec. 14, 1978, effective Jan. 1, 1979 (366 So.2d 398); Sept. 13, 1984, effective Jan. 1, 1985 and Jan. 10, 1985 (461 So.2d 1344, 1347); July 16, 1992, effective Jan. 1, 1993 (601 So.2d 1201); Oct. 10, 1996, effective Jan. 1, 1997 (682 So.2d 1075); Oct. 12, 2000, effective Jan. 1, 2001 (785 So.2d 401); Sept. 26, 2013, effective Jan. 1, 2014 (123 So.3d 41).

Committee Notes

1978 Amendment. The addition to (b) is designed to eliminate confusion caused by denomination of section 51.011, Florida Statutes, as "Summary Procedure."

2013 Amendment. Subdivision (b) is amended to clarify that the Florida Small Claims Rules apply to a claim for money or property even when expressed as, or coupled with, a claim for equitable relief. *State Farm Mutual Automobile Insurance Company v. Green*, 579 So. 2d 402 (Fla. 5th DCA 1991).

Rule 7.020. Applicability of Rules of Civil Procedure

(a) Generally. Florida Rules of Civil Procedure 1.090(a), (b), and (c); 1.190(e); 1.210(b); 1.260; 1.410; and 1.560 are applicable in all actions covered by these rules.

(b) Discovery. Any party represented by an attorney is subject to discovery pursuant to Florida Rules of Civil Procedure 1.280-1.380 directed at said party, without order of court. If a party proceeding without an attorney directs discovery to a party represented by an attorney, the represented party may also use discovery pursuant to the above-mentioned rules without leave of court. When a party is unrepresented and has not initiated discovery pursuant to Florida Rules of Civil Procedure 1.280–1.380, the opposing party shall not be entitled to initiate such discovery without leave of court. However, the time for such discovery procedures may be prescribed by the court.

(c) Additional Rules. In any particular action, the court may order that action to proceed under 1 or more additional Florida Rules of Civil Procedure on application of any party or the stipulation of all parties or on the court's own motion.

Amended Dec. 14, 1978, effective Jan. 1, 1979 (366 So.2d 398); July 16, 1992, effective Jan. 1, 1993 (601 So.2d 1201); Oct. 10, 1996, effective Jan. 1, 1997 (682 So.2d 1075); Oct. 12, 2000, effective Jan. 1, 2001 (785 So.2d 401).

Committee Notes

1972 Amendment. Subdivision (a) is amended by giving the court authority to apply additional rules of civil procedure in any particular case on the application of a party, stipulation of all parties, or order on the court's own motion.

1978 Amendment. These proposed amendments would help prevent overreaching and the ability of one party to obtain judgment without giving the court the full opportunity to consider the merits of the case. When attorneys are involved, the rule would preserve the ability of the parties to fully develop their cases.

1996 Amendment. The addition of Fla. R. Civ. P. 1.380 enables the court to issue and impose sanctions for failure to comply with discovery requests.

Rule 7.040. Clerical and Administrative Duties of Clerk

(a) Generally. The clerk of the circuit court or the clerk of the county court in those counties where such a clerk is provided (hereinafter referred to as the clerk) shall:

(1) maintain a trial calendar. The placing of any action thereon with the date and time of trial is notice to all concerned of the order in which they may expect such action to be called;

(2) maintain a docket book and a judgment book (which may be the same book) in which accurate entries of all actions brought before the court and notations of the proceedings shall comply with Florida Rule of Judicial Administration 2.425 and shall be made including the date of filing; the date of issuance, service, and return of process; the appearance of such parties as may appear; the fact of trial, whether by court or jury; the issuance of execution and to whom issued and the date thereof and return thereon and, when satisfied, a marginal entry of the date thereof; the issuance of a certified copy; a memorandum of the items of costs including witness fees; and the record of the verdict of the jury or finding of the judge, and the judgment, including damages and costs, which judgments may be kept in a separate judgment book; and

(3) maintain an alphabetical index by parties' names with reference to action and case number.

(b) Minute Book. It shall not be necessary for the clerk to maintain a minute book for small claims.

Amended July 16, 1992, effective Jan. 1, 1993 (601 So.2d 1201); Oct. 12, 2000, effective Jan. 1, 2001 (785 So.2d 401); Dec. 15, 2011 (78 So.3d 1303).

Court Commentary

1972 Amendment. See also rule 7.050(c).

Rule 7.050. Commencement of Action; Statement of Claim

(a) Commencement.

(1) *Statement of Claim.* Actions are commenced by the filing of a statement of claim in concise form, which shall inform the defendant of the basis and the amount of the claim. If the claim is based on a written document, a copy or the material part thereof shall be attached to the statement of claim. All documents served upon the defendant with initial process shall be filed with the court.

(2) *Party Not Represented by Attorney to Sign.* A party, individual, or business entity recognized under Florida law who or which has no attorney handling such cause shall sign that party's statement of claim or other paper and state that party's address and telephone number, including area code, and may include an e-mail address. However, if the trial court in its discretion determines that the plaintiff is engaged in the business of collecting claims and holds such claim being sued upon by purchase, assignment, or management arrangement in the operation of such business, the court may require that business entity to provide counsel in the prosecution of the cause. Any business entity recognized under Florida law may be represented at any stage of the trial court proceedings

by any principal of the business entity who has legal authority to bind the business entity or any employee authorized in writing by a principal of the business entity. A principal is defined as being an officer, member, managing member, or partner of the business entity.

(b) Parties. The names, addresses, and, if known, telephone numbers, including area code, of all parties or their attorneys, if any, must be stated on the statement of claim. A party not represented by an attorney may include an e-mail address. Additionally, attorneys must include their Florida Bar number on all papers filed with the court, as well as an e-mail address, in compliance with the Florida Rules of Judicial Administration. A statement of claim shall not be subject to dismissal for the failure to include a telephone number.

(c) Clerk's Duties. The clerk shall assist in the preparation of a statement of claim and other papers to be filed in the action at the request of any litigant. The clerk shall not be required to prepare papers on constructive service, substituted service, proceedings supplementary to execution, or discovery procedures.

(d) Memorandum on Hearing Date. The court shall furnish all parties with a memorandum of the day and hour set for the hearing.

(e) Replevin. In those replevin cases to which these rules are applicable, the clerk of the county court shall set the hearing required by section 78.065(2)(a), Florida Statutes (prejudgment replevin order to show cause hearings) and rule 7.050(d) (pretrial conferences) at the same time.

Amended June 14, 1979, effective July 1, 1979 (372 So.2d 449); Sept. 8, 1988, effective Jan. 1, 1989 (537 So.2d 81); July 16, 1992, effective Jan. 1, 1993 (601 So.2d 1201); Oct. 12, 2000, effective Jan. 1, 2001 (785 So.2d 401); June 20, 2003, effective Jan. 1, 2004 (849 So.2d 293); Jan. 1, 2011 (44 So.3d 573); Oct. 18, 2012, effective, *nunc pro tunc*, Sept. 1, 2012 (102 So.3d 505); Sept. 26, 2013, effective Jan. 1, 2014 (123 So.3d 41).

Committee Notes

1988 Amendment. Subdivision (a)(2): To clarify who may appear and represent a corporation in a small claims case.

Subdivision (b): First sentence is to conform Florida Small Claims Rules with Florida Rules of Judicial Administration 2.060(d) and 2.060(e). Second sentence is to conform to proposed amendment to rules of judicial administration.

Subdivision (e): Require that the order to show cause hearing required in small claims replevin cases and the pretrial conference required by the small claims rules be held at the same time to save time and avoid confusion.

2010 Amendment. A sentence is added to subdivision (a)(1) to ensure that the courts have access to all documents served with initial process.

2013 Amendment. Subdivision (b) is amended to clarify that a party is required to list an opposing party's telephone number only if that telephone number is known. Additionally, the rule is amended to clarify that the requirement of including a telephone number is not grounds for dismissal.

Court Commentary

1972 Amendment. The statement of claim need not be verified.

Subdivision (c) is amended so as to provide that the clerk shall not be required to prepare papers on substituted service.

Rule 7.060. Process and Venue

(a) Summons Required. A summons entitled Notice to Appear stating the time and place of hearing shall be served on the defendant. The summons or notice to appear shall inform the defendant, in a separate paragraph containing bold type, of the defendant's right of venue. This paragraph on venue shall read:

Right to Venue. The law gives the person or company who has sued you the right to file suit in any one of several places as listed below. However, if you have been sued in any place other than one of these places, you, as the defendant, have the right to request that the case be moved to a proper location or venue. A proper location or venue may be one of the following:

1. Where the contract was entered into.

2. If the suit is on an unsecured promissory note, where the note is signed or where the maker resides.

3. If the suit is to recover property or to foreclose a lien, where the property is located.

4. Where the event giving rise to the suit occurred.

5. Where any one or more of the defendants sued reside.

6. Any location agreed to in a contract.

7. In an action for money due, if there is no agreement as to where suit may be filed, where payment is to be made.

If you, as a defendant, believe the plaintiff has not sued in one of these correct places, you must appear on your court date and orally request a transfer or you must file a written request for transfer in affidavit form (sworn to under oath) with the court 7 days prior to your first court date and send a copy to the plaintiff or plaintiff's attorney, if any.

(b) Copy of Claim to Be Served. A copy of the statement of claim shall be served with the summons/notice to appear.

Amended Dec. 14, 1978, effective Jan. 1, 1979 (366 So.2d 398); July 3, 1980, effective Jan. 1, 1981 (385 So.2d 1367); Sept. 8, 1988, effective Jan. 1, 1989 (537 So.2d 81); July 16, 1992, effective Jan. 1, 1993 (601 So.2d 1201); Oct. 12, 2000, effective Jan. 1, 2001 (785 So.2d 401).

Committee Notes

1988 Amendment. A statement is added to the "right to venue notice" on the summons/notice to appear that proper venue also lies in the county where payment is to be made. This conforms with Florida law.

Clarification has been made that the notice is now known as the summons/notice to appear.

Court Commentary

1980 Amendment. If the statutory venue, chapter 47, Florida Statutes, is changed by the legislature, this change should be reflected in the required notice.

Rule 7.070. Method of Service of Process

Service of process shall be effected as provided by law or as provided by Florida Rules of Civil Procedure 1.070(a)-(h). Constructive service or substituted service of process may be effected as provided by law. Service of process on Florida residents only may also be effected by certified mail, return receipt signed by the defendant, or someone authorized to receive mail at the residence or principal place of business of the defendant. Either the clerk or an attorney of record may mail the certified mail, the cost of which is in addition to the filing fee.

Amended Dec. 14, 1978, effective Jan. 1, 1979 (366 So.2d 398); Sept. 13, 1984, effective Jan. 1, 1985 (461 So.2d 1344); July 16, 1992, effective Jan. 1, 1993 (601 So.2d 1201); Oct. 10, 1996, effective Jan. 1, 1997 (682 So.2d 1075); Oct. 12, 2000, effective Jan. 1, 2001 (785 So.2d 401).

Committee Notes

1978 Amendment. Present rule provides for certified or registered mail. Certified mail has not been satisfactory since the Postal Service does not deliver to the defendant in all cases.

1984 Amendment. Mail service is allowed on persons authorized to receive mail for the defendant similar to substituted service by the sheriff on a resident of the defendant's abode. The proposal clarifies the rule that service by mail is not available for out-of-state defendants.

1992 Amendment. The committee has found that most jurisdictions forward the summons and complaint for service by certified mail rather than registered mail. Therefore, the rule is changed to conform to the custom and to be more in keeping with the other service requirements that are required by certified mail as opposed to registered mail.

1996 Amendment. The rule is being modified to exclude Fla. R. Civ. P. 1.070(i) because Small Claims Rule 7.110(e) provides for dismissal of a claim for failure to prosecute after 6 months of inactivity.

Court Commentary

1972 Amendment. The payment of costs of service by certified or registered mail from the filing fee is authorized by section 34.041(1), Florida Statutes; chapter 72–404, Laws of Florida.

Rule 7.080. Service and Filing of Pleadings and Documents Other than Statement of Claim

(a) When Required. Copies of all pleadings and papers subsequent to the notice to appear, except applications for witness subpoenas and orders and judgments entered in open court, shall be served on each party. One against whom a default has been entered is entitled to be served only with pleadings asserting new or additional claims.

(b) How Made. When a party is represented by an attorney, service of papers other than the statement of claim and notice to appear shall be made on the attorney unless the court orders service to be made on the party. When an attorney is serving another attorney, service must be made in compliance with the Florida Rules of Judicial Administration. In all other instances, service must be made by delivering the paper to the party or the party's attorney, as the case may be, or by mailing it to the party's last known address.

(c) Filing. All original pleadings and papers shall be filed with the court either before service or immediately thereafter. The court may allow a copy to be substituted for the original of any document.

(d) Filing with the Court Defined. The filing of documents with the court as required by these rules is made by filing them with the clerk, except that the judge may permit the documents to be filed with the judge, in which event the judge shall note thereon the filing date and transmit them to the clerk, and the clerk shall file them as of the same date they were filed with the judge. Parties represented by an attorney must file documents in compliance with the electronic filing (e-filing) requirements set forth in the Florida Rules of Judicial Administration. Parties not represented by an attorney may file documents in compliance with the e-filing requirement if permitted by the Florida Rules of Judicial Administration.

(e) Certificate of Service.

(1) When any party or attorney in substance certifies:

"I certify that a copy hereof has been furnished to (here insert name or names and address or addresses) by (delivery) (mail) (e-mail if an attorney) on ..... (date) .....

____

Party or party's attorney"

the certificate is prima facie proof of such service in compliance with all rules of court and law.

(2) When any paper is served by the clerk, a docket entry shall be made showing the mode and date of service. Such entry is sufficient proof of service without a separate certificate of service.

(f) When Unrepresented Party Fails to Show Service. If a party who is not represented by an attorney files a paper that does not show service of a copy on all other parties, the clerk shall serve a copy of it on all other parties.

Amended July 16, 1992, effective Jan. 1, 1993 (601 So.2d 1201); Oct. 12, 2000, effective Jan. 1, 2001 (785 So.2d 401); Oct. 18, 2012, effective, *nunc pro tunc*, Sept. 1, 2012 (102 So.3d 505); Oct. 18, 2012, effective Dec. 1, 2012, April 1, 2013, Oct. 1, 2013 (102 So.3d 451).

Court Commentary

1972 Amendment. Subdivisions (a), (b), (c), (d), and (e) are substantially the same as Florida Rule of Civil Procedure 1.080(a), (b), (d), (e), and (f).

Rule 7.090. Appearance; Defensive Pleadings; Trial Date

(a) Appearance. On the date and time appointed in the notice to appear, the plaintiff and defendant shall appear personally or by counsel.

(b) Notice to Appear; Pretrial Conference. The summons/notice to appear shall specify that the initial appearance shall be for a pretrial conference. The initial pretrial conference shall be set by the clerk not more than 50 days from the date of the filing of the action. The pretrial conference may be managed by nonjudicial personnel employed by or under contract with the court. Nonjudicial personnel must be subject to direct oversight by the court. A judge must be available to hear any motions or resolve any legal issues. At the pretrial conference, all of the following matters shall be considered:

(1) The simplification of issues.

(2) The necessity or desirability of amendments to the pleadings.

(3) The possibility of obtaining admissions of fact and of documents that avoid unnecessary proof.

(4) The limitations on the number of witnesses.

(5) The possibilities of settlement.

(6) Such other matters as the court in its discretion deems necessary.

Form 7.322 shall and form 7.323 may be used in conjunction with this rule.

(c) Defensive Pleadings. Unless required by order of court, written pretrial motions and defensive pleadings are not necessary. If filed, copies of such pleadings shall be served on all other parties to the action at or prior to the pretrial conference or within such time as the court may designate. The filing of a motion or a defensive pleading shall not excuse the personal appearance of a party or attorney on the initial appearance date (pretrial conference).

(d) Trial Date. The court shall set the case for trial not more than 60 days from the date of the pretrial conference. At least 10 days' notice of the time of trial shall be given. The parties may stipulate to a shorter or longer time for setting trial with the approval of the court. This rule does not apply to actions to which chapter 51, Florida Statutes, applies.

(e) Waiver of Appearance at Pretrial Conference. Where all parties are represented by an attorney, counsel may agree to waive personal appearance at the initial pretrial conference, if a written agreement of waiver signed by all attorneys is presented to the court prior to or at the pretrial conference. The agreement shall contain a short statement of the disputed issues of fact and law, the number of witnesses expected to testify, an estimate of the time needed to try the case, and any stipulations of fact. The court shall forthwith set the case for trial within the time prescribed by these rules.

(f) Appearance at Mediation; Sanctions. In small claims actions, an attorney may appear on behalf of a party at mediation if the attorney has full authority to settle without further consultation. Unless otherwise ordered by the court, a nonlawyer representative may appear on behalf of a party to a small claims mediation if the representative has the party's signed written authority to appear and has full authority to settle without further consultation. In either event, the party need not appear in person. Mediation may take place at the pretrial conference. Whoever appears for a party must have full authority to settle. Failure to comply with this subdivision may result in the imposition costs and attorney fees incurred by the opposing party.

(g) Agreement. Any agreements reached as a result of small claims mediation shall be written in the form of a stipulation. The stipulation may be entered as an order of the court.

Amended Sept. 13, 1984, effective Jan. 1, 1985 (461 So.2d 1344); Sept. 8, 1988, effective Jan. 1, 1989 (537 So.2d 81); July 16, 1992, effective Jan. 1, 1993 (601 So.2d 1201); Oct. 12, 2000, effective Jan. 1, 2001 (785 So.2d 401); June 20, 2003, effective Jan. 1, 2004 (849 So.2d 293); June 19, 2008, effective Oct. 1, 2008 (985 So.2d 1033); May 12, 2011, effective July 1, 2011 (64 So.3d 1196).

Committee Notes

1972 Amendment. Rule 7.120 is incorporated in subdivision (c). It is slightly expanded to provide for a computation period from service by mail and to give the parties the right to stipulate to a shorter time for the trial.

1984 Amendment. This change requires the use of a pretrial procedure and requires both parties to attend the pretrial conference which can be used to resolve pretrial motions. The use of a pretrial previously varied from county to county.

1988 Amendment. (b) 1st sentence – Chair's clarification.

2nd sentence – Require the clerk to set the initial pretrial conference within a reasonable time after filing of the action taking into consideration the fact that the time standards guideline for small claims cases is 95 days.

3rd sentence – State within the small claims rules what matters shall be considered at the pretrial conference rather than by reference to Florida Rule of Civil Procedure 1.220(a), which has been amended several times and is generally not applicable to small claims cases.

4th sentence – Direct that new form 7.322 shall and that new• form 7.323 may be used statewide.

(c) Clarifies that a personal appearance is required at the pretrial conference when a defense motion is filed.

(e) Adds a provision for waiving counsel's appearance at the pretrial conference where all parties are represented by counsel.

Court Commentary

2008 Amendment. The requirement that an attorney attending mediation on behalf of the client have full authority to settle should not be equated to a requirement to settle where one or more parties wants to proceed to trial.

Rule 7.100. Counterclaims, Setoffs, Third–Party Complaints, Transfer When Jurisdiction Exceeded

(a) Compulsory Counterclaim. Any claim of the defendant against the plaintiff, arising out of the same transaction or occurrence which is the subject matter of the plaintiff's claim, shall be filed not less than 5 days prior to the initial appearance date (pretrial conference) or within such time as the court designates or it is deemed to be abandoned.

(b) Permissive Counterclaim. Any claim or setoff of the defendant against the plaintiff, not arising out of the transaction or occurrence which is the subject matter of the plaintiff's claim, may be filed not less than 5 days before the initial appearance date (pretrial conference) or within such time as the court designates, and tried, providing that such permissive claim is within the jurisdiction of the court.

(c) How Filed. Counterclaims and setoffs shall be filed in writing. If additional time is needed to prepare a defense, the court may continue the action.

(d) Transfer When Beyond Jurisdiction. When a counterclaim or setoff exceeds the jurisdiction of the court, it shall be filed in writing before or at the hearing, and the action shall then be transferred to the court having jurisdiction thereof. As evidence of good faith, the counterclaimant shall deposit a sum sufficient to pay the filing fee in the court to which the case is to be transferred with the counterclaim, which shall be sent with the record to the court to which transferred. Failure to make the deposit waives the right to transfer.

(e) Third-Party Complaints. A defendant may cause a statement of claim to be served on a person not a party to the action who is or may be liable to the defendant for all or part of the plaintiff's claim against the defendant. A defendant must obtain leave of court on motion made at the initial appearance date (pretrial conference) and must file the third-party complaint within such time as the court may allow. The clerk shall schedule a supplemental pretrial conference, and on the date and time appointed in the notice to appear the third-party plaintiff and the third-party defendant shall appear personally or by counsel. If additional time is needed for the third-party defendant to prepare a defense, the court may continue the action. Any party may move to strike the third-party claim or for its severance or separate trial. When a counterclaim is asserted against the plaintiff, the plaintiff may bring in a third-party defendant under circumstances that would entitle a defendant to do so under this rule.

Amended Sept. 8, 1988, effective Jan. 1, 1989 (537 So.2d 81); July 16, 1992, effective Jan. 1, 1993 (601 So.2d 1201); Oct. 12, 2000, effective Jan. 1, 2001 (785 So.2d 401).

Committee Notes

1988 Amendment. Provides for and authorizes third-party claims so that all issues may be addressed and resolved. Also provides for a title change.

Rule 7.110. Dismissal of Actions

(a) Voluntary Dismissal; Effect Thereof.

(1) *By Parties.* Except in actions where property has been seized or is in the custody of the court, an action may be dismissed by the plaintiff without order of court (A) by the plaintiff informing the defendant and clerk of the dismissal before the trial date fixed in the notice to appear, or before retirement of the jury in a case tried before a jury or before submission of a nonjury case to the court for decision, or (B) by filing a stipulation of dismissal signed by all parties who have appeared in the action. Unless otherwise stated, the dismissal is without prejudice, except that a dismissal operates as an adjudication on the merits when a plaintiff has once dismissed in any court an action based on or including the same claim.

(2) *By Order of the Court; If Counterclaim.* Except as provided in subdivision (a)(1) of this rule, an action shall not be dismissed at a party's instance except upon order of the court and on such terms and conditions as the court deems proper. If a counterclaim has been made by the defendant before the plaintiff dismisses voluntarily, the action shall not be dismissed against the defendant's objections unless the counterclaim can remain pending for independent adjudication. Unless otherwise specified in the order, a dismissal under this subdivision is without prejudice.

(b) Involuntary Dismissal. Any party may move for dismissal of an action or of any claim against that party for failure of an adverse party to comply with these rules or any order of court. After a party seeking affirmative relief in an action has completed the presentation of evidence, any other party may move for a dismissal on the ground that upon the facts and the law the party seeking affirmative relief has shown no right to relief without waiving the right to offer evidence in the event the motion is not granted. The court may then determine them and render judgment against the party seeking affirmative relief or may decline to render any judgment until the close of all the evidence. Unless the court in its order for dismissal otherwise specifies, a dismissal under this subdivision and any dismissal not provided for in this rule, other than a dismissal for lack of jurisdiction or for improper venue or for lack of an indispensable party, operates as an adjudication on the merits.

(c) Dismissal of Counterclaim. The provisions of this rule apply to the dismissal of any counterclaim.

(d) Costs. Costs in any action dismissed under this rule shall be assessed and judgment for costs entered in that action. If a party who has once dismissed a claim in any court of this state commences an action based on or including the same claim against the same adverse party, the court shall make such order for the payment of costs of the claim previously dismissed as it may deem proper and shall stay the proceedings in the action until the party seeking affirmative relief has complied with the order.

(e) Failure to Prosecute. All actions in which it affirmatively appears that no action has been taken by filing of pleadings, order of court, or otherwise for a period of 6 months shall be dismissed by the court on its own motion or on motion of any interested person, whether a party to the action or not, after 30 days' notice to the parties, unless a stipulation staying the action has been filed with the court, or a stay order has been filed, or a party shows good cause in writing at least 5 days before the hearing on the motion why the action should remain pending.

Amended Dec. 14, 1978, effective Jan. 1, 1979 (366 So.2d 398); Sept. 13, 1984, effective Jan. 1, 1985 (461 So.2d 1344); July 16, 1992, effective Jan. 1, 1993 (601 So.2d 1201); Oct. 10, 1996, effective Jan. 1, 1997 (682 So.2d 1075); Oct. 12, 2000, effective Jan. 1, 2001 (785 So.2d 401).

Committee Notes

1978 Amendment. Former subdivision (e) provided for 1 year rather than 6 months.

1984 Amendment. Subdivision (e) is changed to allow more time for an attorney to inquire about the status of a claim. Many actions are disposed of by a stipulation to pay, and it may take longer than 10 days to determine the amount due, if any.

1996 Amendment. Subdivision (e) is amended to be consistent with Fla. R. Civ. P. 1.420(e), which includes specific language concerning a stipulation staying the action approved by the court or a stay order as a condition when an action would not automatically be up for dismissal based on lack of prosecution.

Court Commentary

1972 Amendment. Substantially the same as Florida Rule of Civil Procedure 1.420.

Rule 7.130. Continuances and Settlements

(a) Continuances. A continuance may be granted only upon good cause shown. The motion for continuance may be oral, but the court may require that it be reduced to writing. The action shall be set again for trial as soon as practicable and the parties shall be given timely notice.

(b) Settlements. Settlements in full or by installment payments made by the parties out of the presence of the court are encouraged. The plaintiff shall notify the clerk of settlement, and the case may be dismissed or continued pending payments. Upon failure of a party to perform the terms of any stipulation or agreement for settlement of the claim before judgment, the court may enter appropriate judgment without notice upon the creditor's filing of an affidavit of the amount due.

Amended Sept. 13, 1984, effective Jan. 1, 1985 (461 So.2d 1344); July 16, 1992, effective Jan. 1, 1993 (601 So.2d 1201).

Committee Notes

1984 Amendment. Subdivision (b) is altered to conform with rule 7.210(c), which provides for an affidavit but no notice.

Rule 7.135. Summary Disposition

At pretrial conference or at any subsequent hearing, if there is no triable issue, the court shall summarily enter an appropriate order or judgment.

Amended July 16, 1992, effective Jan. 1, 1993 (601 So.2d 1201); Oct. 12, 2000, effective Jan. 1, 2001 (785 So.2d 401).

Rule 7.140. Trial

(a) Time. The trial date shall be set by the court at the pretrial conference.

(b) Determination. Issues shall be settled and motions determined summarily.

(c) Pretrial. The pretrial conference should narrow contested factual issues. The case may proceed to trial with the consent of both parties.

(d) Settlement. At any time before judgment, the judge shall make an effort to assist the parties in settling the controversy by conciliation or compromise.

(e) Unrepresented Parties. In an effort to further the proceedings and in the interest of securing substantial justice, the court shall assist any party not represented by an attorney on:

(1) courtroom decorum;

(2) order of presentation of material evidence; and

(3) handling private information.

The court may not instruct any party not represented by an attorney on accepted rules of law. The court shall not act as an advocate for a party.

(f) How Conducted. The trial may be conducted informally but with decorum befitting a court of justice. The rules of evidence applicable to trial of civil actions apply but are to be liberally construed. At the discretion of the court, testimony of any party or witness may be presented over the telephone.

Additionally, at the discretion of the court an attorney may represent a party or witness over the telephone without being physically present before the court. Any witness utilizing the privilege of testimony by telephone as permitted in this rule shall be treated for all purposes as a live witness, and shall not receive any relaxation of evidentiary rules or other special allowance. A witness may not testify over the telephone in order to avoid either the application of Florida's perjury laws or the rules of evidence.

Amended Sept. 13, 1984, effective Jan. 1, 1985 (461 So.2d 1344); Sept. 8, 1988, effective Jan. 1, 1989 (537 So.2d 81); July 16, 1992, effective Jan. 1, 1993 (601 So.2d 1201); Oct. 10, 1996, effective Jan. 1, 1997 (682 So.2d 1075); Oct. 12, 2000, effective Jan. 1, 2001 (785 So.2d 401); Nov. 3, 2011, effective, *nunc pro tunc*, Oct. 1, 2011 (78 So.3d 1045); Sept. 26, 2013, effective Jan. 1, 2014 (123 So.3d 41).

Committee Notes

1984 Amendment. (a) Changed to conform this rule with the requirement for pretrials.

(c) Allows the cases to proceed to trial with consent of the parties.

(f) This is similar to the proposed amendment to the Florida Rules of Civil Procedure to allow depositions by telephone. Since the court has discretion to allow this testimony, all procedural safeguards could be maintained by the court. Since the court is also the trier of fact, the testimony could be rejected if unreliable.

1988 Amendment. Extends the taking of testimony over the telephone to include parties, deletes the agreement of the parties provision, and adds authorization for an attorney to represent a party or witness over the telephone without being physically present before the court.

1996 Amendment. The revised version of subdivision (e) addresses the need to expressly provide that the judge, while able to assist an unrepresented party, should not act as an advocate for that party.

2011 Amendment. Subdivision (e)(3) was added so that a judge can assist an unrepresented party in the handling of private information that might otherwise inadvertently become public by placement in the court file.

Rule 7.150. Jury Trials

Jury trials may be had upon written demand of the plaintiff at the time of the commencement of the suit, or by the defendant within 5 days after service of notice of suit or at the pretrial conference, if any. Otherwise jury trial shall be deemed waived.

Amended Dec. 14, 1978, effective Jan. 1, 1979 (366 So.2d 398); Sept. 13, 1984, effective Jan. 1, 1985 (461 So.2d 1344); July 16, 1992, effective Jan. 1, 1993 (601 So.2d 1201); Oct. 12, 2000, effective Jan. 1, 2001 (785 So.2d 401).

Committee Notes

1984 Amendment. The purpose of the cost deposit formerly required was to discourage frivolous demands for jury trials. The committee feels that there should be no distinction between the taxation of costs in a $300 claim and a $3,000 claim.

Rule 7.160. Failure of Plaintiff or Both Parties to Appear

(a) Plaintiff. If plaintiff fails to appear on the initial appearance date (pretrial conference), or fails to appear at trial, the action may be dismissed for want of prosecution, defendant may proceed to trial on the merits, or the action may be continued as the judge may direct.

(b) Both Parties. If both parties fail to appear, the judge may continue the action or dismiss it for want of prosecution at that time or later as justice requires.

Amended Oct. 12, 2000, effective Jan. 1, 2001 (785 So.2d 401).

Rule 7.170. Default; Judgment

(a) Default. If the defendant does not appear at the scheduled time, the plaintiff is entitled to a default to be entered by either the judge or clerk.

(b) Final Judgment. After default is entered, the judge shall receive evidence establishing the damages and enter judgment in accordance with the evidence and the law. The judge may inquire into and prevent abuses of venue prior to entering judgment.

Amended Dec. 14, 1978, effective Jan. 1, 1979 (366 So.2d 398); July 3, 1980, effective Jan. 1, 1981 (385 So.2d 1367); Sept. 13, 1984, effective Jan. 1, 1985 and Jan. 10, 1985 (461 So.2d 1344, 1347); July 16, 1992, effective Jan. 1, 1993 (601 So.2d 1201); Oct. 12, 2000, effective Jan. 1, 2001 (785 So.2d 401).

Court Commentary

1972 Amendment. Evidence may be by testimony, affidavit, or other competent means.

1980 Amendment. By the amendment to this rule, the judge is permitted to ensure by any means which the judge deems appropriate that venue is not being abused.

Rule 7.175. Motions for Costs and Attorneys' Fees

Any party seeking a judgment taxing costs or attorneys' fees, or both, shall serve a motion no later than 30 days after filing of the judgment, including a judgment of dismissal, or the service of a notice of voluntary dismissal. In the event of a default judgment, no further motions are needed if costs or attorneys' fees, or both, were sought in the statement of claim.

Added Dec. 15, 2005, effective Jan. 1, 2006 (931 So.2d 78).

Rule 7.180. Motions for New Trial; Time for; Contents

(a) Time. A motion for new trial shall be filed not later than 10 days after return of verdict in a jury action or the date of filing of the judgment in a nonjury action. A timely motion may be amended to state new grounds at any time before it is disposed of in the discretion of the court.

(b) Determination. The motion shall set forth the basis with particularity. Upon examination of the motion, the court may find it without merit and deny it summarily, or may grant a hearing on it with notice.

(c) Grounds. All orders granting a new trial shall specify the specific grounds therefor. If such an order is appealed and does not state the specific grounds, the appellate court shall relinquish its jurisdiction to the trial court for entry of an order specifying the grounds for granting the new trial.

Amended Sept. 13, 1984, effective Jan. 1, 1985 (461 So.2d 1344); July 16, 1992, effective Jan. 1, 1993 (601 So.2d 1201).

Committee Notes

1972 Amendment. Subdivisions (a) and (c) are substantially the same as Florida Rule of Civil Procedure 1.530(b) and (f).

1984 Amendment. This change will be in conformity with the proposed amendment to Florida Rule of Civil Procedure 1.530.

Rule 7.190. Relief From Judgment or Order; Clerical Mistakes

(a) Clerical Mistakes. Clerical mistakes in judgments, orders, or other parts of the record and errors therein arising from oversight or omission may be corrected by the court at any time on its own initiative or on the motion of any party and after such notice, if any, as the court orders. During the pendency of an appeal, such mistakes may be so corrected before the record on appeal is docketed in the appellate court, and thereafter while the appeal is pending may be so corrected with leave of the appellate court.

(b) Mistakes; Inadvertence; Excusable Neglect; Newly Discovered Evidence; Fraud; etc. On motion and on such terms as are just, the court may relieve a party or a party's legal representative from a final judgment, order, or proceeding for the following reasons: (1) mistake, inadvertence, surprise, or excusable neglect; (2) newly discovered evidence which by due diligence could not have been discovered in time to move for a new trial or rehearing; (3) fraud (whether heretofore denominated intrinsic or extrinsic), misrepresentation, or other misconduct of an adverse party; (4) the judgment is void; or (5) the judgment has been satisfied, released, or discharged or a prior judgment on which it is based has been reversed or otherwise vacated or it is no longer equitable that the judgment should have prospective application. The motion shall be made within a reasonable time, and for reasons (1), (2), and (3) not more than 1 year after the judgment, order, or proceeding was entered or taken. A motion under this subdivision does not affect the finality of a judgment or suspend its operation.

Amended July 16, 1992, effective Jan. 1, 1993 (601 So.2d 1201).

Rule 7.200. Executions

Executions on judgments shall issue during the life of the judgment on the oral request of the party entitled to it or that party's attorney without praecipe. No execution or other final process shall issue until the judgment on which it is based has been rendered or within the time for serving a motion for new trial and, if a motion for new trial is timely served, until it is determined; provided execution or other final process may be issued on special order of the court at any time after judgment.

Amended July 16, 1992, effective Jan. 1, 1993 (601 So.2d 1201).

Rule 7.210. Stay of Judgment and Execution

(a) Judgment or Execution or Levy Stayed. When judgment is to be entered against a party, the judge may inquire and permit inquiry about the earnings and financial status of the party and has discretionary power to stay an entry of judgment or, if entered, to stay execution or levy on such terms as are just and in consideration of a stipulation on the part of the judgment debtor to make such payments as will ensure a periodic reduction of the judgment until it is satisfied.

(b) Stipulation. The judge shall note the terms of such stipulation in the file; the stipulation may be set out in the judgment or made a part of the judgment by reference to "the stipulation made in open court."

(c) Execution. When judgment is entered and execution stayed pending payments, if the judgment debtor fails to pay the installment payments, the judgment creditor may have execution without further notice for the unpaid amount of the judgment upon filing an affidavit of the amount due.

(d) Oral Stipulations. Oral stipulations may be made in the presence of the court that upon failure of the judgment debtor to comply with any agreement, judgment may be entered or execution issued, or both, without further notice.

Amended Dec. 14, 1978, effective Jan. 1, 1979 (366 So.2d 398); Sept. 8, 1988, effective Jan. 1, 1989 (537 So.2d 81); July 16, 1992, effective Jan. 1, 1993 (601 So.2d 1201).

Committee Notes

1988 Amendment. Adds the staying of levy as an alternative for the court when arranging payment. Provides lien rights priority protection for judgment creditors.

Rule 7.220. Supplementary Proceedings

Proceedings supplementary to execution may be had in accordance with proceedings provided by law or by the Florida Rules of Civil Procedure.

Amended July 16, 1992, effective Jan. 1, 1993 (601 So.2d 1201).

Rule 7.221. Hearing in Aid of Execution

(a) Use of Form 7.343. In any final judgment, the judge shall include the Enforcement Paragraph of form 7.340 if requested by the prevailing party or attorney. In addition to the forms of discovery available to the judgment creditor under Fla. R. Civ. P. 1.560, the judge, at the request of the judgment creditor or the judgment creditor's attorney, shall order a judgment debtor to complete form 7.343 within 30 days of the order or other such reasonable time determined by the court. If the judgment debtor fails to obey the order, Fla. R. Civ. P. Form 1.982 may be used in conjunction with this subdivision of this rule.

(b) Purpose of Hearing. The judge, at the request of the judgment creditor, shall order a judgment debtor to appear at a hearing in aid of execution at a time certain 30 or more days from the date of entry of a judgment for the purpose of inquiring of the judgment debtor under oath as to earnings, financial status, and any assets available in excess of exemptions to be applied towards satisfaction of judgment. The provisions of this subdivision of this rule shall only apply to a judgment creditor who is a natural person and was not represented by an attorney prior to judgment. Forms 7.342, 7.343, and 7.344 shall be used in connection with this subdivision of this rule.

Added Sept. 8, 1988, effective Jan. 1, 1989 (537 So.2d 81). Amended July 16, 1992, effective Jan. 1, 1993 (601 So.2d 1201); Oct. 10, 1996, effective Jan. 1, 1997 (682 So.2d 1075); Oct. 12, 2000, effective Jan. 1, 2001 (785 So.2d 401).

Committee Notes

1988 Amendment. Provides a procedure for post-judgment, court-assisted discovery for natural person judgment creditors, unrepresented by counsel prior to judgment.

1996 Amendment. The purpose of the change is to make form 7.343 (Fact Information Sheet) available for use by both a party and the party's attorney, even though the hearing in aid of execution is not available to the attorney. The rule will allow the court to include the order as part of the final judgment or to issue the order after the judgment. The court may adjust the time allowed for the response to the Fact Information Sheet to fit the circumstances.

Rule 7.230. Appellate Review

Review of orders and judgments of the courts governed by these rules shall be prosecuted in accordance with the Florida Rules of Appellate Procedure.

Amended July 16, 1992, effective Jan. 1, 1993 (601 So.2d 1201).

Committee Notes

1972 Amendment. Attention is directed to Florida Appellate Rule 4.7, which authorizes the circuit court to modify or dispense with any of the steps to be taken after filing of the notice of appeal.

Rule 7.300. Forms

The following forms of process are sufficient in all actions.

The following forms of statements of claim and other papers are sufficient for the types of actions which they respectively cover. They are intended for illustration only. They and like forms may be used with such modifications as may be necessary to meet the facts of each particular action so long as the substance thereof is expressed without prolixity. The common counts are not sufficient. The complaint forms appended to the Florida Rules of Civil Procedure may be utilized if appropriate.

The following forms are approved:

Form 7.310. Caption

(name of court)

A. B.,)
)
Plaintiff,)
)
-vs-) No. ______
)
C. D.,)
)
Defendant.)

(designation of pleading)

Amended July 16, 1992, effective Jan. 1, 1993 (601 So.2d 1201).

Form 7.322. Summons/Notice to Appear for Pretrial Conference

(CAPTION)

STATE OF FLORIDA—NOTICE TO PLAINTIFF(S) AND DEFENDANT(S)

....

....

....

....

....

YOU ARE HEREBY NOTIFIED that you are required to appear in person or by attorney at the .... in Courtroom # ...., located at ...., on (date), at .... m, for a PRETRIAL CONFERENCE before a judge of this court.

IMPORTANT—READ CAREFULLY THE CASE WILL NOT BE TRIED AT THAT TIME. DO NOT BRING WITNESSES—APPEAR IN PERSON OR BY ATTORNEY

The defendant(s) must appear in court on the date specified in order to avoid a default judgment. The plaintiff(s) must appear to avoid having the case dismissed for lack of prosecution. A written MOTION or ANSWER to the court by the plaintiff(s) or the defendant(s) shall not excuse the personal appearance of a party or its attorney in the PRETRIAL CONFERENCE. The date and time of the pretrial conference CANNOT be rescheduled without good cause and prior court approval.

Any business entity recognized under Florida law may be represented at any stage of the trial court proceedings by any principal of the business entity who has legal authority to bind the business entity or any employee authorized in writing by a principal of the business entity. A principal is defined as being an officer, member, managing member, or partner of the business entity. Written authorization must be brought to the Pretrial Conference.

The purpose of the pretrial conference is to record your appearance, to determine if you admit all or part of the claim, to enable the court to determine the nature of the case, and to set the case for trial if the case cannot be resolved at the pretrial conference. You or your attorney should be prepared to confer with the court and to explain briefly the nature of your dispute, state what efforts have been made to settle the dispute, exhibit any documents necessary to prove the case, state the names and addresses of your witnesses, stipulate to the facts that will require no proof and will expedite the trial, and estimate how long it will take to try the case.

Mediation may take place at the pretrial conference. Whoever appears for a party must have full authority to settle. Failure to have full authority to settle at this pretrial conference may result in the imposition of costs and attorney fees incurred by the opposing party.

If you admit the claim, but desire additional time to pay, you must come and state the circumstances to the court. The court may or may not approve a payment plan and withhold judgment or execution or levy.

RIGHT TO VENUE. The law gives the person or company who has sued you the right to file in any one of several places as listed below. However, if you have been sued in any place other than one of these places, you, as the defendant(s), have the right to request that the case be moved to a proper location or venue. A proper location or venue may be one of the following: (1) where the contract was entered into; (2) if the suit is on an unsecured promissory note, where the note is signed or where the maker resides; (3) if the suit is to recover property or to foreclose a lien, where the property is located; (4) where the event giving rise to the suit occurred; (5) where any one or more of the defendants sued reside; (6) any location agreed to in a contract; (7) in an action for money due, if there is no agreement as to where suit may be filed, where payment is to be made.

If you, as the defendant(s), believe the plaintiff(s) has/have not sued in one of these correct places, you must appear on your court date and orally request a transfer, or you must file a WRITTEN request for transfer in affidavit form (sworn to under oath) with the court 7 days prior to your first court date and send a copy to the plaintiff(s) or plaintiff's(s') attorney, if any.

A copy of the statement of claim shall be served with this summons.

DATED at ...., Florida, on ...(date)...

____

As Clerk of the County Court

Added Sept. 8, 1988, effective Jan. 1, 1989 (537 So.2d 81). Amended July 16, 1992, effective Jan. 1, 1993 (601 So.2d 1201); Oct. 12, 2000, effective Jan. 1, 2001 (785 So.2d 401); June 20, 2003, effective Jan. 1, 2004 (849 So.2d 1069); June 19, 2008, effective Oct. 1, 2008 (985 So.2d 1033); Sept. 26, 2013, effective Jan. 1, 2014 (123 So.3d 41).

Form 7.323. Pretrial Conference Order and Notice of Trial

IN THE COUNTY COURT FOR _____ COUNTY, FLORIDA CIVIL DIVISION

CASE NO _____

__________ ___ by self
__________ ___ by agent
Plaintiff Telephone _____ ___ by attorney

vs.

__________ ___ by self
__________ ___ by agent
Defendant Telephone _____ ___ by attorney

PRETRIAL CONFERENCE ORDER AND NOTICE OF TRIAL

1. DEFENDANT: ISSUES:
___ denies liability and damages ___ Liability and damages
___ admits liability—denies damages ___ Liability only
___ granted ___ days to file a counterclaim and/or third-party complaint ___ Damages only
___ advised of probable need for expert testimony from _____

2. WITNESSES (total)
___ Plaintiff ___ Defendant ___ Parties advised of availability of subpoena power

3. EXHIBITS, DOCUMENTS, AND TANGIBLE EVIDENCE
Plaintiff __________ Parties instructed that they must permit inspection after notice or furnish copies to opposite party within ___ days:
____
Defendant __________ ___ Witnesses' names and addresses
__________ ___ Documents and things to be used at trial

4. DISCOVERY MAY BE HAD IN ACCORDANCE WITH SMALL CLAIMS RULE 7.020.

5. STIPULATION OR OTHER:
TRIAL DATE: (date) , at ___m., for ___ hour(s)
PLACE: ______ County Courthouse, ______, Courtroom No. ______, ______, FL
JUDGE: ______, Telephone No.: ______
ORDERED ON (date)

IMPORTANT—TURN OVER AND READ TRIAL INSTRUCTIONS ON REVERSE SIDE.

RECEIVED FOR: ______________ ______________
For Plaintiff For Defendant

[The following instructions are to be placed on the reverse side of the order and notice of trial.]

IMPORTANT—READ CAREFULLY!

YOU HAVE NOW ATTENDED A PRETRIAL CONFERENCE ON A SMALL CLAIMS ACTION. THIS WILL BE THE ONLY NOTICE YOU WILL RECEIVE CONCERNING YOUR TRIAL DATE AND WHAT YOU NEED TO DO TO PREPARE FOR YOUR TRIAL. DO NOT LOSE THIS ORDER AND NOTICE OF TRIAL. YOU ARE NOW SCHEDULED FOR A TRIAL AS LISTED ON THE REVERSE SIDE OF THIS PAPER. MAKE SURE YOU ARE AWARE OF ALL OF THE FOLLOWING:

1. NONJURY TRIAL—You are now scheduled for a nonjury trial before a county court judge.

2. TRIAL DATE—Do not forget your trial date. Failure to come to court on the given date at the right time may result in your losing the case and the other party winning.

3. EXCHANGE OF DOCUMENTS AND INFORMATION—If the judge told you to submit any documents or give any information to the other party (such as a list of your witnesses' names and addresses), DO IT. Failure to do this as directed by the judge may cause court sanctions against you such as extra court costs, contempt of court, or delays.

4. COUNTERCLAIMS—If you are the plaintiff and you have been given a written notice that a counterclaim has been filed against you in this lawsuit, this means that you are now being sued by the defendant. Also, if at the pretrial conference the judge allowed the defendant a certain number of days to file a counterclaim, the defendant must file that counterclaim within that number of days from the date of this pretrial conference order. If the defendant does that, the defendant has a claim now pending against you. If, at the time of the trial, the counterclaim has been properly filed, there are 2 lawsuits being considered by the judge at the same time: the plaintiff's suit against the defendant and the defendant's suit against the plaintiff. In the event that both claims are settled by the parties, both parties should notify the Clerk of the County Court, Civil Division, ______, IN WRITING, of the settlement. Only after both the plaintiff and the defendant have notified the clerk in writing of the settlement is it not necessary for the parties to appear in court. Settlement of one claim, either the plaintiff's claim against the defendant or the defendant's claim against the plaintiff, has no effect as to the other claim, and that remaining claim will proceed to trial on the trial date listed on the pretrial conference order.

5. THIRD-PARTY COMPLAINTS—If you are the defendant and you believe that the plaintiff may win the suit against you, but, if the plaintiff does, someone else should pay you so you can pay the plaintiff, then you must file a third-party complaint against that person and serve that person with notice of your claim. Once served, that person must appear in court as you have to answer your complaint against that person. This must be done prior to trial within the time allowed you by the judge.

6. TRIAL PREPARATION—Bring all witnesses and all documents and all other evidence you plan to use at the trial. There is only one trial! Have everything ready and be on time. If the judge advised you at the pretrial conference hearing that you needed something for the trial, such as an expert witness (an automobile mechanic, an automobile body worker, a carpenter, a painter, etc.) or a particular document (a note, a lease, receipts, statements, etc.), make sure that you have that necessary person or evidence at the trial. Written estimates of repairs are usually not acceptable as evidence in court unless both parties agree that the written estimates are proper for the judge to consider or unless the person who wrote the estimates is present to testify as to how that person arrived at the amounts on the estimates and that those amounts are reasonable in that particular line of business.

7. COURT REPORTER AND APPEALS—Your nonjury trial will not be recorded. If you wish a record of the proceedings, a court reporter is necessary. To obtain a court reporter to record your final hearing, you must immediately contact the official court reporter, ______, Florida ______, Phone (___) ______. The cost to secure the presence of a court reporter is a minimum of $______ for the first one-half hour or any portion thereof and $______ per each additional half hour or portion thereof. To have the record of the proceeding transcribed, the cost is $______ per page for the original and ______ per page for each copy. Payment for the court reporter's appearance must be made in advance to ______, the official court reporter. Appeals to a higher court because you are not satisfied with the outcome of the trial are governed by special rules. One of these rules requires that the appellate court have a complete record of the trial to review for errors. If you do not have a court reporter at your trial, your chances for success on appeal will be severely limited.

8. SETTLEMENT—If all parties agree on settlement of all claims before trial, each party must notify the judge by telephone so that the allotted trial time may be reassigned to someone else. Immediately thereafter, the parties must, in writing, notify the clerk of the settlement, and the court will thereafter dismiss the case. The mailing address is: Clerk of the County Court, Civil Division, ______.

9. ADDRESS CHANGES—All changes in mailing addresses must be furnished in writing to the clerk and to the opposing party.

10. ADDITIONAL PROBLEMS—For anything you do not understand about the above information and for any additional questions you may have concerning the preparation of your case for trial, please contact the Clerk of the County Court, Civil Division, in person or by telephone (___) ______. The clerk is not authorized to practice law and therefore cannot give you legal advice on how to prove your case. However, the clerk can be of assistance to you in questions of procedure. If you need legal advice, please contact an attorney of your choice. If you know of none, call the ______ County Bar Association, Lawyer Referral Service, for assistance, (___) ______.

Added Sept. 8, 1988, effective Jan. 1, 1989 (537 So.2d 81). Amended July 16, 1992, effective Jan. 1, 1993 (601 So.2d 1201); Oct. 12, 2000, effective Jan. 1, 2001 (785 So.2d 401).

Form 7.330. Statement of Claim (Auto Negligence)

(CAPTION)

STATEMENT OF CLAIM

The plaintiff sues the defendant and says: On or about ______________, in the vicinity of ______________, on a public highway in ______________ County, Florida, plaintiff's motor vehicle, being operated by ______________, collided with defendant's motor vehicle, being operated by ______________; and the collision with plaintiff's vehicle was caused by the negligent and careless operation of defendant's vehicle, whereby plaintiff's vehicle was damaged and depreciated in value.

WHEREFORE, plaintiff demands judgment in the sum of $______.

Amended July 16, 1992, effective Jan. 1, 1993 (601 So.2d 1201).

Form 7.331. Statement of Claim (for Goods Sold)

(CAPTION)

STATEMENT OF CLAIM

Plaintiff, A.B., sues defendant, C.D., and alleges: There is now due, owing, and unpaid from defendant to plaintiff $ ______ with interest since ____ (date) ____, for the following goods sold and delivered by plaintiff to defendant between ____ (date) ____, and ____ (date) ____:

(list goods and prices and any credits)

WHEREFORE, plaintiff demands judgment for damages against defendant.

Amended July 16, 1992, effective Jan. 1, 1993 (601 So.2d 1201); Oct. 12, 2000, effective Jan. 1, 2001 (785 So.2d 401).

Form 7.332. Statement of Claim (for Work Done and Materials Furnished)

(CAPTION)

STATEMENT OF CLAIM

Plaintiff, A.B., sues defendant, C.D., and alleges: There is now due, owing, and unpaid from defendant to plaintiff $ ______ with interest since ____ (date) ____, for the following items of labor and materials furnished to defendant at his/her request between ____ (date) ____, and ____ (date) ____:

(list time and materials, showing charges therefor and any credits)

WHEREFORE, plaintiff demands judgment for damages against defendant.

Amended July 16, 1992, effective Jan. 1, 1993 (601 So.2d 1201); Oct. 12, 2000, effective Jan. 1, 2001 (785 So.2d 401).

Form 7.333. Statement of Claim (for Money Lent)

(CAPTION)

STATEMENT OF CLAIM

Plaintiff, A.B., sues defendant, C.D., and alleges: There is now due, owing, and unpaid from defendant to plaintiff $ ______ for money lent by plaintiff to defendant on ____ (date) ____, with interest thereon since ____ (date) ____

WHEREFORE, plaintiff demands judgment for damages against defendant.

Amended July 16, 1992, effective Jan. 1, 1993 (601 So.2d 1201); Oct. 12, 2000, effective Jan. 1, 2001 (785 So.2d 401).

Form 7.334. Statement of Claim (Promissory Note)

(CAPTION)

STATEMENT OF CLAIM

Plaintiff, A.B., sues defendant, C.D., and alleges:

1. This is an action for damages that do not exceed the sum of $______ (insert jurisdictional amount of court).

2. On ____ (date) ____, defendant executed and delivered to plaintiff a promissory note, a copy being attached, in ______ County, Florida.

3. Defendant failed to pay

(a) said note when due; or

(b) the installment payment due on said note on _____ (date) _____, and plaintiff elected to accelerate payment of the balance.

4. There is now due, owing, and unpaid from defendant to plaintiff $ .... on said note with interest since _____ (date) _____.

5. Plaintiff has obligated himself/herself to pay his/her attorneys a reasonable fee for their services in bringing this action.

WHEREFORE, plaintiff demands judgment for damages against defendant.

Amended July 16, 1992, effective Jan. 1, 1993 (601 So.2d 1201); Oct. 12, 2000, effective Jan. 1, 2001 (785 So.2d 401).

Committee Notes

1972 Amendment. Attach copy of note to each copy of the statement of claim. Use 3(a) or (b) and 5 as applicable.

Form 7.335. Statement of Claim (for Return of Stolen Property From Pawnbroker)

IN THE COUNTY COURT, IN AND
FOR _____ COUNTY, FLORIDA
CASE NO.: _____

_____
Plaintiff,

vs.

_____
Defendant/Pawnbroker.

STATEMENT OF CLAIM FOR
RETURN OF PROPERTY FROM PAWNBROKER

Plaintiff, ..., sues defendant/pawnbroker, ..., and says:

1. This is an action for the return of stolen or misappropriated property pursuant to section 539.001, Florida Statutes.

2. Plaintiff is the owner of the following described property:

_____
_____
_____
_____.

3. The above-described property was stolen or otherwise misappropriated from plaintiff on or about the .... day of ...., 20 .... A copy of the law enforcement report outlining the theft/misappropriation is attached hereto and incorporated into this statement of claim.

4. The above-described property is currently in the possession of defendant and is located at a pawnshop as defined in section 539.001, Florida Statutes, the address of which is _____.

5. Plaintiff has complied with the procedural requirements of section 539. 001, Florida Statutes. Specifically, plaintiff notified the pawnbroker of plaintiff's claim to the property:

___by certified mail, return receipt requested, OR

___in person evidenced by a signed receipt.

The notice contains a complete and accurate description of the purchased or pledged goods and was accompanied by a legible copy of the aforementioned police report regarding the theft or misappropriation of the property. No resolution between plaintiff and defendant pawnbroker could be reached within 10 days after the delivery of the notice.

WHEREFORE, the plaintiff demands judgment for the return of the property. Plaintiff further asks this court to award plaintiff the costs of this action, including reasonable attorneys' fees.

_____
Plaintiff (signature)

_____
Name

_____
Address

_____
City, State, Zip code

_____
Day telephone number

State of Florida
County of _____

The foregoing instrument was acknowledged before me on ....(date).........., by ...., who is personally known to me or has produced .... as identification and who ... did/did not ... take an oath.

WITNESS my hand and official seal, on ....(date)..........

_____
Notary Public
State of Florida

Note to Clerk of Court and to Sheriff: Pursuant to Section 539.001(15), filing fees and service fees shall be waived. Waiver does not require the filing of an affidavit of insolvency.

Added Dec. 15, 2005, effective Jan. 1, 2006 (931 So.2d 78); Jan. 1, 2011 (44 So.3d 573).

Form 7.336. Statement of Claim for Replevin (for Return of Personal Property/Weapon from Government Entity)

(CAPTION)

STATEMENT OF CLAIMS FOR REPLEVIN

Plaintiff(s) .... sues Defendant(s) .... and alleges:

1. This is an action to recover possession of personal property.

2. The description of the property is: ....

....

....

3. To Plaintiff's best knowledge, information, and belief the value of the property is $ .... and its location is ....

4. Plaintiff is the owner of the claimed property or is entitled to possession of it by virtue of the following source of title, or right of possession: ....

....

....

....

(If interest is based on a written instrument a copy is attached.)

5. The property cannot be released by the defendant without a court order, or the property is wrongfully detained by the defendant who obtained possession by:

....

....

6. To Plaintiff's best knowledge, information, and belief, defendant detains property because:

....

....

7. The property has not been taken for any tax, assessment, or fine pursuant to law, nor has it been taken under an execution or attachment against plaintiff's property, or if so taken, it is by law exempt from such taking by the following reference to the exemption law relied upon: ....

8. Written demand for return of the property was provided to Defendant and [if Defendant is not a municipality] also to the Department of Financial Services at least 90 days prior to the filing of this Complaint. Section 768.28(6)(a), Florida Statutes. A copy of the demand is attached hereto.

9. The property is not contraband, was not the fruit of criminal activity, and is not being held for some evidentiary purposes.

10. The property came into possession of Defendant on or about (date)

11. Plaintiff has the legal right to possess the property and is not subject to any legal prohibition against such possession.

Pursuant to section 92.525, Florida Statutes, under penalties of perjury, I declare that I have read the foregoing Statement of Claim and the facts stated in it are true.

____

Plaintiff

NOTE: This form is to be used by those seeking return of personal property (including weapons) taken by a government entity for purposes other than for a criminal investigation, as an incident to arrest, pursuant to a search warrant, or any other seizure for which the Florida Statutes provide a specific procedure for return. Rather, this form is for use by those who seek return of personal property taken for other purposes, such as "safekeeping," and for which the Florida Statutes provide no procedures.

Added Sept. 26, 2013, effective Jan. 1, 2014 (123 So.3d 41).

Form 7.340. Final Judgment

(CAPTION)

FINAL JUDGMENT AGAINST (DEFENDANT(S)'S NAME)

It is adjudged that the plaintiff(s), ..., recover from the defendant(s), ..., the sum of $ .... on principal, $ .... as prejudgment interest, $ .... for attorneys' fees, with costs of $ ...., all of which shall bear interest at the rate of ... % per year as provided for by Florida Statute, for all of which let execution issue.

ORDERED at ...., Florida, on .... (date) ....

____

County Court Judge

Copies furnished to:

PLAINTIFF(S)

DEFENDANT(S)

Plaintiff(s)'s address:

....

....

Defendant(s)'s last known address and last four digits of defendant(s)'s Social Security Number (if known):

....

....

....

(OPTIONAL ENFORCEMENT PARAGRAPH—TO BE INCLUDED UPON REQUEST PURSUANT TO RULE 7.221)

It is further ordered and adjudged that the defendant(s) shall complete Florida Small Claims Rules Form 7.343 (Fact Information Sheet) and return it to the plaintiff's attorney, or to the plaintiff if the plaintiff is not represented by an attorney, within 45 days from the date of this final judgment, unless the final judgment is satisfied or a motion for new trial or notice of appeal is filed. **The defendant should NOT file the completed form 7.343 with the court.**

Jurisdiction of this case is retained to enter further orders that are proper to compel the defendant(s) to complete form 7.343 and return it to the plaintiff's attorney, or the plaintiff if the plaintiff is not represented by an attorney.

Amended Sept. 8, 1988, effective Jan. 1, 1989 (537 So.2d 81); July 16, 1992, effective Jan. 1, 1993 (601 So.2d 1201); Oct. 10, 1996, effective Jan. 1, 1997 (682 So.2d 1075); Oct. 12, 2000, effective Jan. 1, 2001 (785 So.2d 401); Dec. 15, 2005, effective Jan. 1, 2006 (931 So.2d 78); Nov. 3, 2011, effective, *nunc pro tunc*, Oct. 1, 2011 (78 So.3d 1045).

Committee Notes

1992 Amendment. The optional enforcement paragraph was added to facilitate discovery.

Form 7.341. Execution

(CAPTION)

EXECUTION

THE STATE OF FLORIDA:

To Each Sheriff of the State:

YOU ARE HEREBY COMMANDED to levy on the goods and chattels, lands, and tenements of ______ in the sum of $______ with legal interest thereon from _____ (date) _____, until paid and that you have this writ before the court when satisfied.

WITNESS my hand and the seal of the court on ____ (date) ______

(SEAL)

____
Clerk of the Court

Amended July 16, 1992, effective Jan. 1, 1993 (601 So.2d 1201); Oct. 12, 2000, effective Jan. 1, 2001 (785 So.2d 401).

Form 7.342. Ex Parte Motion and Order for Hearing in Aid of Execution

(CAPTION)

EX PARTE MOTION FOR HEARING IN AID OF EXECUTION

The judgment creditor, ..., pursuant to Florida Small Claims Rule 7.221, moves for an order requiring the judgment debtor(s), ..., to appear at a hearing in aid of execution for the purpose of examining the judgment debtor(s) regarding his/her/their ability to satisfy the final judgment entered in this cause and requiring the judgment debtor(s) to complete a FACT INFORMATION SHEET and bring it to the hearing in aid of execution.

____
Judgment Creditor

ORDER FOR HEARING IN AID OF EXECUTION

IT IS ORDERED AND ADJUDGED that the judgment debtor(s), ..., Address: ...., shall:

1. appear before Judge .... on ...(date)..., at .... o'clock ...m., in Courtroom ...., located at: ...., ..., Florida, to be examined as to the judgment debtor('s)(s') ability to satisfy the final judgment entered in this cause; and

2. bring to the hearing all documents and papers that relate to the judgment debtor('s)(s') financial condition and the completed, notarized fact information sheet attached hereto.

Judgment debtor('s)(s') failure to comply with this order shall be grounds for contempt.

ORDERED at ...., Florida, on ...(date)...

____
County Court Judge

Added Sept. 8, 1988, effective Jan. 1, 1989 (537 So.2d 81). Amended July 16, 1992, effective Jan. 1, 1993 (601 So.2d 1201); Oct. 12, 2000, effective Jan. 1, 2001 (785 So.2d 401); Jan. 1, 2011 (44 So.3d 573).

Form 7.343. Fact Information Sheet

(a) For Individuals

(CAPTION)

FACT INFORMATION SHEET—INDIVIDUAL

Full Legal Name: ______________________
Nicknames or Aliases: ______________________
Residence Address: ______________________
Mailing Address (if different): ______________________
Telephone Numbers: (Home) __________ (Business) __________
Name of Employer: ______________________
Address of Employer: ______________________

Position or Job Description: ______________________________
Rate of Pay: $ _____ per ________. Average Paycheck: $ _____ per _______
Average Commissions or Bonuses: $ _____ per _____. Commissions or bonuses are based on ______________________________
Other Personal Income: $ _______ from ______________________________
(Explain details on the back of this sheet or an additional sheet if necessary.)
Social Security Number: ____________ Birthdate: ____________
Driver's License Number: ______________________________
Marital Status: ____________ Spouse's Name: ______________________________
Spouse's Address (if different): ______________________________
Spouse's Social Security Number: ____________ Birthdate: ____________
Spouse's Employer: ______________________________
Spouse's Average Paycheck or Income: $ _____ per ____________
Other Family Income: $ ___ per _____ (Explain details on back of this sheet or an additional sheet if necessary.)
Names and Ages of All Your Children (and addresses if not living with you): ______________________________
Child Support or Alimony Paid: $ _____ per ____________
Names of Others You Live With: ______________________________
Who is Head of Your Household? _____ You _____ Spouse _____ Other Person
Checking Account at: ____________ Account # ____________
Savings Account at: ____________ Account # ____________
(Describe all other accounts or investments you may have, including stocks, mutual funds, savings bonds, or annuities, on the back of this sheet or an additional sheet if necessary.)

For Real Estate (land) You Own or Are Buying:
Address: ______________________________
All Names on Title: ______________________________
Mortgage Owed to: ______________________________
Balance Owed: ______________________________
Monthly Payment: $ ______________________________
(Attach a copy of the deed or mortgage, or list the legal description of the property on the back of this sheet or an additional sheet if necessary. Also provide the same information on any other property you own or are buying.)

For All Motor Vehicles You Own or Are Buying:
Year/Make/Model: ____________ Color: ____________
Vehicle ID #: ________ Tag No: ________ Mileage: ________
Names on Title: ____________ Present Value: $ ____________
Loan Owed to: ______________________________
Balance on Loan: $______________________________
Monthly Payment: $ ________ (List all other automobiles, as well as other vehicles, such as boats, motorcycles, bicycles, or aircraft, on the back of this sheet or an additional sheet if necessary.)
Have you given, sold, loaned, or transferred any real or personal property worth more than $100 to any person in the last year? If your answer is "yes," describe the property and sale price, and give the name and address of the person who received the property.

Does anyone owe you money? Amount Owed: $______________
Name and Address of Person Owing Money: ______________________________
Reason money is owed: ______________________________

Please attach copies of the following:

1. Your last pay stub.
2. Your last 3 statements for each bank, savings, credit union, or other financial account.
3. Your motor vehicle registrations and titles.

4. Any deeds or titles to any real or personal property you own or are buying, or leases to property you are renting.

UNDER PENALTY OF PERJURY, I SWEAR OR AFFIRM THAT THE FOREGOING ANSWERS ARE TRUE AND COMPLETE.

____
Judgment Debtor

STATE OF FLORIDA

COUNTY OF ....

The foregoing instrument was acknowledged before me on ... (date) ..., by ..., who is personally known to me or has produced ... as identification and who did/did not ... take an oath.

WITNESS my hand and official seal, on ..... (date) .....

____
Notary Public
State of Florida

My Commission expires:

MAIL OR DELIVER THE COMPLETED FORM TO THE JUDGMENT CREDITOR OR THE JUDGMENT CREDITOR'S ATTORNEY. DO NOT FILE THIS FORM WITH THE COURT.

(b) For Corporate Entities

(CAPTION)

FACT INFORMATION SHEET—BUSINESS ENTITY

Name/Title of person filling out this form: ______________________
Address: ______________________
Telephone Number: Home: __________ Business: __________
Address of Business Entity: ______________________
Type of Entity: (Check One) ☐ Corporation ☐ Partnership ☐ Limited Partnership ☐ Sole Proprietorship ☐ Limited Liability Corporation (LLC) ☐ Professional Association (PA) ☐ Other: (Please Explain)
Does Business Entity own/have interest in any other business entity? If so please explain. Gross/Taxable income reported for Federal Income Tax purposes last three years:
$ ______________ $ ______________ $ ______________
Taxpayer Identification Number: ______________________
List Partners (General or Limited and Designate Percentage of Ownership): ______
Average No. of Employees/Month: ______________________
Names of Officers and Directors: ______________________
Checking Account at: ______________ Account No: __________
Savings Account At: ______________ Account No: __________
Does the Business Entity own any vehicles:
Years/Makes/Models: ______________________
Vehicle I.D. Nos.: ______________________
Tag Nos.: ______________________
Loans Outstanding: ______________________
Does the Business Entity own any real property: YES __________ NO __________
If Yes: Address: ______________________
Please check if the business entity owns the following:

_____ Boat
_____ Stocks/Bonds
_____ Other Personal Property
_____ Camper
_____ Other Real Property
_____ Intangible Property

Please attach copies of the following:

1. All tax returns for the past 3 years, including but not limited to state and federal income tax returns and tangible personal property tax returns.

2. All bank, savings and loan, and other account books or statements for accounts in institutions in which the defendant had any legal or equitable interest for the past 3 years.

3. All canceled checks for the 12 months immediately preceding the date of this judgment for accounts in which the defendant held any legal or equitable interest.

4. All deeds, leases, mortgages, or other written instruments evidencing any interest in or ownership of real property at any time within the 12 months immediately preceding the date of this judgment.

5. Bills of sale or other written evidence of the gift, sale, purchase, or other transfer of any personal or real property to or from the defendant within the 12 months immediately preceding the date of filing this lawsuit. Any transfer of property within the last year other than ordinary course of business transactions.

6. Motor vehicle documents, including titles and registrations relating to any motor vehicles owned by the defendant alone or with others.

7. Financial statements and any other business records, including but not limited to accounts payable and accounts receivable ledgers, as to the defendant's assets and liabilities prepared within the 12 months immediately preceding the date of this judgment.

8. Copies of articles, by-laws, partnership agreement, operating agreement, and any other governing documents, and minutes of all meetings of the defendant's shareholders, board of directors, or members held within 2 years of the date of this judgment.

9. Resolutions of the shareholders, board of directors, or members passed within 2 years of the date of this judgment.

10. A list or schedule of all inventory and equipment.

UNDER PENALTY OF PERJURY, I SWEAR OR AFFIRM THAT THE FOREGOING ANSWERS ARE TRUE AND COMPLETE.

____
Defendant's Designated Representative
Title: ....

STATE OF FLORIDA
COUNTY OF ....

The foregoing instrument was acknowledged before me on ... (date) ..., by ..., as the defendant's duly authorized representative, who is personally known to me or has produced ... as identification and who ... did/did not ... take an oath.

WITNESS my hand and official seal, on ... (date) ...

____
Notary Public
State of Florida

My Commission expires: ....

MAIL OR DELIVER THE COMPLETED FORM TO THE JUDGMENT CREDITOR OR THE JUDGMENT CREDITOR'S ATTORNEY. DO NOT FILE THIS FORM WITH THE COURT.

Added Sept. 8, 1988, effective Jan. 1, 1989 (537 So.2d 81). Amended July 16, 1992, effective Jan. 1, 1993 (601 So.2d 1201); Oct. 10, 1996, effective Jan. 1, 1997 (682 So.2d 1075); Oct. 12, 2000, effective Jan. 1, 2001 (785 So.2d 401); Dec. 15, 2005, effective Jan. 1, 2006 (931 So.2d 78); Jan. 1, 2011 (44 So.3d 573); Nov. 3, 2011, effective, *nunc pro tunc*, Oct. 1, 2011 (78 So.3d 1045).

Form 7.344. Order to Show Cause

(CAPTION)

ORDER TO SHOW CAUSE

IN THE NAME OF THE STATE OF FLORIDA:
TO:

YOU ARE HEREBY COMMANDED TO APPEAR before this court on _____ (date) _____, at _____ m., in Courtroom _____ at the ________ County Courthouse, Address: ________ , ________, Florida, to show cause, if any, why you should not be adjudged in contempt of court for your failure to appear in court on ____ (date) ____, at ____ m., as required by the court's order issued on ____(date) ____, for a hearing in aid of execution.

ORDERED at ________, Florida, on ____ (date) ____

____
County Court Judge

Added Sept. 8, 1988, effective Jan. 1, 1989 (537 So.2d 81). Amended July 16, 1992, effective Jan. 1, 1993 (601 So.2d 1201); Oct. 12, 2000, effective Jan. 1, 2001 (785 So.2d 401).

Form 7.345. Stipulation for Installment Settlement, Order Approving Stipulation, and Dismissal

(CAPTION)

STIPULATION FOR INSTALLMENT SETTLEMENT, ORDER APPROVING STIPULATION, AND DISMISSAL

Plaintiff and defendant(s), by the signatures below, stipulate that defendant(s) is/are indebted to plaintiff in the sum of $ ________, plus court costs of $ ________, interest of $ ________, and attorneys' fees of $ ________, which defendant(s) agree(s) to pay in installments of $ ...., the first of such payments to be due on ____ (date) ____, and continuing each ________ until paid in full. If the total sum is paid timely and in full, plaintiff agrees that no judgment shall be entered against the defendant(s), and that additional costs, interest, and attorneys' fees, if any, shall be waived. If the defendant(s) shall default in payment hereunder, plaintiff shall be entitled to judgment, execution, costs, interest at the rate provided by law, and attorneys' fees, after written application to the court, without notice. Defendant(s) acknowledge(s) delivery of a true copy hereof at ________, ________ County, Florida. ALL PAYMENTS ARE TO BE MADE PAYABLE TO: ________, and mailed or delivered to: ________

TIME IS OF THE ESSENCE IN THIS AGREEMENT.

________________________	________________________
Plaintiff/Attorney for Plaintiff	Defendant (signature)
Telephone: ____________	________________________
	________________________
BY: ____________________	Address
	Telephone: ____________
	________________________
	Defendant (signature)
	________________________
	________________________
	Address
	Telephone: ____________

ORDER DISMISSING CAUSE AND APPROVING STIPULATION

On the foregoing stipulation signed, delivered, and confirmed at ________ County, Florida, the cause is dismissed. This court retains jurisdiction to enforce the terms of this stipulation.

ORDERED at ________, Florida, on ____ (date) ____

____
County Court Judge

Conformed copies furnished by hand delivery to:
Plaintiff/Attorney for Plaintiff
Defendant(s)

Added July 16, 1992, effective Jan. 1, 1993 (601 So.2d 1201). Amended Oct. 10, 1996, effective Jan. 1, 1997 (682 So.2d 1075); Oct. 12, 2000, effective Jan. 1, 2001 (785 So.2d 401).

Committee Notes

1992 Adoption. Many parties and attorneys litigate in various jurisdictions in the state, and the committee felt that a standard form for settlement would be much more convenient for the litigants and the court system.

1996 Amendment. This form has been modified to reflect recent changes in the statutory rate of interest calculated on final judgment amounts.

Form 7.347. Satisfaction of Judgment

SATISFACTION OF JUDGMENT

The undersigned, the owner and holder of that certain final judgment rendered in the above-captioned civil action, dated ...., recorded in .... County, Official Records Book ... beginning at Page ..., does hereby acknowledge that all sums due under it have been fully paid and that final judgment is hereby satisfied and is canceled and satisfied of record.

DATED on ....

____
Judgment Owner and Holder (or their attorney)

Added July 5, 2007, effective Jan. 1, 2008 (959 So.2d 1169).

Committee Notes

2008 Note. This form is suggested for use by the parties. To avoid possible confusion, when disbursing funds from the court registry in satisfaction of a judgment, the clerk of the court should instead use the form required by the 2005 amendment to section 55.141, Florida Statutes.

2007 Amendment. This satisfaction of judgment is a general form. It is a new form. To ensure identity of the signer, notarization is prudent but not required. If a certified copy of the judgment is recorded, it may be prudent to include that recording information.

Historical Notes

The 2008 Committee Note was added April 17, 2007 (980 So.2d 1054).

Form 7.350. Authorization to Allow Employee to Represent Business Entity at any Stage of Lawsuit

(CAPTION)

AUTHORIZATION OF PRINCIPAL

. . .(name). . . is an employee of . . .(name of business entity under Florida law that is a party to this action). . . This individual has authority to represent the business entity at any stage of the trial court proceedings, including mediation.

The undersigned giving the authority is a principal of the business entity.

Pursuant to section 92.525, Florida Statutes, under penalties of perjury, I declare that I have read the foregoing Authorization and that the facts stated in it are true.

Dated: . . . .

SIGNING AUTHORITY: ____________________

Print name and title: . . . .

Address: . . . .

. . . .

Phone number: . . . .

I certify that a copy of this form has been furnished to [list all parties to this action] by . . .(hand delivery/mail/fax). . . on . . .(date). . .

____

Name and title: . . . .

Added Dec. 15, 2005, effective Jan. 1, 2006 (931 So.2d 78). Amended Sept. 26, 2013, effective Jan. 1, 2014 (123 So.3d 41).

INDEX TO FLORIDA SMALL CLAIMS RULES

FLORIDA RULES OF JUVENILE PROCEDURE

1972 Adoption

The Florida Supreme Court adopted on December 20, 1972, effective January 1, 1973 (270 So.2d 715), temporary rules of juvenile procedure as an emergency matter to govern the procedure in the juvenile division of the circuit court, in order to effect an orderly transition of the courts under revised Article 5 of the Florida Constitution.

1977 and 1980 Revisions

The Florida Supreme Court on March 17, 1977 adopted a revision of the rules to take effect on July 1, 1977 (345 So.2d 655) and adopted a further revision on December 24, 1980 to take effect January 1, 1981 (393 So.2d 1077).

1991 Revision

The Florida Rules of Juvenile Procedure were substantially revised by the Florida Supreme Court in the opinion of May 9, 1991, effective July 1, 1991. The Juvenile Court Rules Committee's Motion for Clarification was granted and a corrected opinion, also dated May 9, 1991, was substituted in lieu of the first opinion (589 So.2d 818).

PART I. RULES OF GENERAL APPLICATION

2012 Revision

Part I, "Rules of General Application", consisting of Rules 8.000 to 8.004, was added by Florida Supreme Court Opinion No. SC11-399 (102 So.3d 451).

Former Part I, "Delinquency Proceedings", consisting of Rules 8.003 to 8.185, was renumbered as Part II, consisting of Rules 8.005 to 8.185, by Florida Supreme Court Opinion No. SC11-399 (102 So.3d 451).

Rule 8.000. Scope and Purpose

These rules shall govern the procedures in the juvenile division of the circuit court in the exercise of its jurisdiction under Florida law.

Part II of these rules governs the procedures for delinquency cases in the juvenile court. Part IV governs the procedures for families and children in need of services cases in the juvenile court. The Department of Juvenile Justice shall be referred to as the "department" in these parts.

Part III of these rules governs the procedures for dependency cases in the juvenile court. The Department of Children and Family Services shall be referred to as the "department" in that part.

These rules are intended to provide a just, speedy, and efficient determination of the procedures covered by them and shall be construed to secure simplicity in procedure and fairness in administration.

They shall be known as the Florida Rules of Juvenile Procedure and may be cited as Fla. R. Juv. P.

When appropriate the use of singular nouns and pronouns shall be construed to include the plural and the use of plural nouns and pronouns shall be construed to include the singular.

Former Rule 8.010 amended Dec. 28, 1984, effective Jan. 1, 1985 (462 So.2d 399). Renumbered as new Rule 8.000 and amended May 9, 1991, effective July 1, 1991 (589 So.2d 818). Amended Nov. 5, 1992, effective Jan. 1, 1993 (608 So.2d 478); Sept. 18, 1998, effective Oct. 1, 1998 (725 So.2d 296); Oct. 18, 2012, effective Dec. 1, 2012, April 1, 2013, Oct. 1, 2013 (102 So.3d 451).

Committee Notes

1991 Amendment. All rules have been edited for style and to remove gender bias. The rules have been reorganized and renumbered to correspond to the types and stages of juvenile proceedings. Cross-references have been changed accordingly.

1992 Amendment. Scope and Purpose, previously found in rules 8.000, 8.200, 8.600, and 8.700, has been consolidated into one rule. Designations of subparts within the delinquency part of the rules have been changed accordingly. Reference to the civil rules, previously found in rule 8.200, has been removed because the rules governing dependency and termination of parental rights proceedings are self-contained and no longer need to reference the Florida Rules of Civil Procedure.

Rule 8.003. Family Law Cover Sheet

The party opening or reopening a case under Part II, III, IV, or V of these rules shall file with the clerk of the circuit court Florida Family Law Rules of Procedure Form 12.928, Cover Sheet for Family Law Cases.

Added effective June 24, 2010 (41 So.3d 888). Amended Oct. 18, 2012, effective Dec. 1, 2012, April 1, 2013, Oct. 1, 2013 (102 So.3d 451).

Rule 8.004. Electronic Filing

(a) All documents that are court records, as defined in Florida Rule of Judicial Administration 2.430(a)(1), are to be filed by electronic transmission, consistent with the requirements of Florida Rule of Judicial Administration 2.525, provided that:

(1) the clerk has the ability to accept and retain such documents;

(2) the clerk or the chief judge of the circuit has requested permission to accept documents filed by electronic transmission; and

(3) the supreme court has entered an order granting permission to the clerk to accept documents filed by electronic transmission.

(b) All documents filed by electronic transmission under this rule satisfy any requirement for the filing of an original, except where the court, law, or these rules otherwise provide for the submittal of an original.

(c) The following paper documents or other submissions may be manually submitted to the clerk for filing under the following circumstances:

(1) when the clerk does not have the ability to accept and retain documents by electronic filing or has not had electronic court filing procedures (ECF Procedures) approved by the supreme court;

(2) by any self-represented party or any self-represented nonparty unless specific ECF Procedures provide a means to file documents electronically. However, any self-represented nonparty that is a governmental or public agency and any other agency, partnership, corporation, or business entity acting on behalf of any governmental or public agency may file documents by electronic transmission if such entity has the capability of filing documents electronically;

(3) by attorneys excused from e-mail service pursuant to these rules or Florida Rule of Judicial Administration 2.516;

(4) when submitting evidentiary exhibits or filing non-documentary materials;

(5) when the filing involves documents in excess of 25 megabytes (25 MB) in size. For such filings, documents may be transmitted using an electronic storage medium that the clerk has the ability to accept, which may include a CD–ROM, flash drive, or similar storage medium;

(6) when filed in open court, as permitted by the court;

(7) when paper filing is permitted by any approved statewide or local ECF procedures; and

(8) if any court determines that justice so requires.

(d) The filing date for an electronically transmitted document is the date and time that such filing is acknowledged by an electronic stamp, or otherwise, pursuant to any procedure set forth in any electronic court filing procedures (ECF Procedures) approved by the supreme court, or the date the last page of such filing is received by the court or clerk.

(e) Where these rules are silent, Florida Rule of Judicial Administration 2.525 controls.

(f) Electronic transmission may be used by a court for the service of all orders, pursuant to Florida Rule of Judicial Administration 2.516, and for the service of filings pursuant to any ECF Procedures, provided the clerk, together with input from the chief judge of the circuit, has obtained approval from the supreme court of ECF Procedures containing the specific procedures and program to be used in transmitting the orders and filings.

Added Oct. 18, 2012, effective Dec. 1, 2012, April 1, 2013, Oct. 1, 2013 (102 So.3d 451).

PART II. DELINQUENCY PROCEEDINGS

2012 Revision

Part II, "Delinquency Proceedings", added as Part I, was renumbered as Part II by Florida Supreme Court Opinion No. SC11-399 (102 So.3d 451).

Former Part II, "Dependency and Termination of Parental Rights Proceedings", was renumbered as Part III, consisting of Rules 8.201 to 8.535, by Florida Supreme Court Opinion No. SC11-399 (102 So.3d 451).

A. PRELIMINARY PROCEEDINGS

2012 Revision

Part II.A, "Preliminary Proceedings", added as Part I.A, consisting of Rules 8.003 to 8.015, was redesignated as Part II.A, consisting of Rules 8.005 to 8.015, by Florida Supreme Court Opinion No. SC11-399.

Rule 8.005. Ordering Children Into Custody

If a verified petition has been filed, or if, prior to the filing of a petition, an affidavit or sworn testimony is presented to the court, either of which alleges facts which under existing law are sufficient to authorize that a child be taken into custody, the court may issue an order to a person, authorized to do so, directing that the child be taken into custody. The order shall:

(a) be in writing;

(b) specify the name and address of the child or, if unknown, designate the child by any name or description by which the child can be identified with reasonable certainty;

(c) specify the age and sex of the child or, if the child's age is unknown, that he or she is believed to be of an age subject to the jurisdiction of the circuit court as a juvenile case;

(d) state the reasons why the child is being taken into custody;

(e) order that the child be brought immediately before the court or be taken to a place of detention designated by the court to be detained pending a detention hearing;

(f) state the date when issued and the county and court where issued; and

(g) be signed by the court with the title of office.

Former Rule 8.030 amended Dec. 28, 1984, effective Jan. 1, 1985 (462 So.2d 399). Renumbered as new Rule 8.005 and amended May 9, 1991, effective July 1, 1991 (589 So.2d 818).

Rule 8.010. Detention Hearing

(a) When Required. No detention order provided for in rule 8.013 shall be entered without a hearing at which all parties shall have an opportunity to be heard on the necessity for the child's being held in detention, unless the court finds that the parent or custodian cannot be located or that the child's mental or physical condition is such that a court appearance is not in the child's best interest.

(b) Time. The detention hearing shall be held within the time limits as provided by law. A child who is detained shall be given a hearing within 24 hours after being taken into custody.

(c) Place. The detention hearing may be held in the county where the incident occurred, where the child is taken into custody, or where the child is detained.

(d) Notice. The intake officer shall make a diligent effort to notify the parent or custodian of the child of the time and place of the hearing. The notice may be by the most expeditious method available. Failure of notice to parents or custodians or their nonattendance at the hearing shall not invalidate the proceeding or the order of detention.

(e) Appointment of Counsel. At the detention hearing, the child shall be advised of the right to be represented by counsel. Counsel shall be appointed if the child qualifies, unless the child waives counsel in writing subject to the requirements of rule 8.165.

(f) Advice of Rights. At the detention hearing the persons present shall be advised of the purpose of the hearing and the child shall be advised of:

(1) the nature of the charge for which he or she was taken into custody;

(2) that the child is not required to say anything and that anything said may be used against him or her;

(3) if the child's parent, custodian, or counsel is not present, that he or she has a right to communicate

with them and that, if necessary, reasonable means will be provided to do so; and

(4) the reason continued detention is requested.

(g) Issues. At this hearing the court shall determine the following:

(1) The existence of probable cause to believe the child has committed a delinquent act. This issue shall be determined in a nonadversary proceeding. The court shall apply the standard of proof necessary for an arrest warrant and its finding may be based upon a sworn complaint, affidavit, deposition under oath, or, if necessary, upon testimony under oath properly recorded.

(2) The need for detention according to the criteria provided by law. In making this determination in addition to the sworn testimony of available witnesses all relevant and material evidence helpful in determining the specific issue, including oral and written reports, may be relied upon to the extent of its probative value, even though it would not be competent at an adjudicatory hearing.

(3) The need to release the juvenile from detention and return the child to the child's nonresidential commitment program.

(h) Probable Cause. If the court finds that such probable cause exists, it shall enter an order making such a finding and may, if other statutory needs of detention exist, retain the child in detention. If the court finds that such probable cause does not exist, it shall forthwith release the child from detention. If the court finds that one or more of the statutory needs of detention exists, but is unable to make a finding on the existence of probable cause, it may retain the child in detention and continue the hearing for the purpose of determining the existence of probable cause to a time within 72 hours of the time the child was taken into custody. The court may, on a showing of good cause, continue the hearing a second time for not more than 24 hours beyond the 72–hour period. Release of the child based on no probable cause existing shall not prohibit the filing of a petition and further proceedings thereunder, but shall prohibit holding the child in detention prior to an adjudicatory hearing.

(i) Presence of Counsel. The state attorney or assistant state attorney and public defender or assistant public defender shall attend the detention hearing. Detention hearings shall be held with adequate notice to the public defender and state attorney. An official record of the proceedings shall be maintained. If the child has retained counsel or expresses a desire to retain counsel and is financially able, the attendance of the public defender or assistant public defender is not required at the detention hearing.

Former Rule 8.050 amended Dec. 28, 1984, effective Jan. 1, 1985 (462 So.2d 399); Aug. 25, 1988, effective Jan. 1, 1989 (536 So.2d 178). Renumbered as new Rule 8.010 and amended May 9, 1991, effective July 1, 1991 (589 So.2d 818). Amended Nov. 17, 2005 (915 So.2d 592); Dec. 17, 2009, effective Jan. 1, 2010 (26 So.3d 552); Nov. 10, 2010, effective Jan. 1, 2011 (48 So.3d 809).

Rule 8.013. Detention Petition and Order

(a) Time Limitation. No child taken into custody shall be detained, as a result of the incident for which taken into custody, longer than as provided by law unless a detention order so directing is made by the court following a detention hearing.

(b) Petition. The detention petition shall:

(1) be in writing and be filed with the court;

(2) state the name and address of the child or, if unknown, designate the child by any name or description by which he or she can be identified with reasonable certainty;

(3) state the age and sex of the child or, if the age is unknown, that the child is believed to be of an age which will make him or her subject to the procedures covered by these rules;

(4) state the reasons why the child is in custody and needs to be detained;

(5) recommend the place where the child is to be detained or the agency to be responsible for the detention; and

(6) be signed by an authorized agent of the Department of Juvenile Justice or by the state attorney or assistant state attorney.

(c) Order. The detention order shall:

(1) be in writing;

(2) state the name and address of the child or, if unknown, designate the child by any name or description by which he or she can be identified with reasonable certainty;

(3) state the age and sex of the child or, if the age is unknown, that the child is believed to be of an age which will make him or her subject to the procedures covered by these rules;

(4) order that the child shall be held in detention and state the reasons therefore, or, if appropriate, order that the child be released from detention and returned to his or her nonresidential commitment program;

(5) make a finding that probable cause exists that the child is delinquent or that such a finding cannot be made at this time and that the case is continued for such a determination to a time certain within 72 hours from the time the child is taken into custody unless this time is extended by the court for good cause shown for not longer than an additional 24 hours;

(6) designate the place where the child is to be detained or the person or agency that will be responsible for the detention and state any special conditions found to be necessary;

(7) state the date and time when issued and the county and court where issued, together with the date and time the child was taken into custody;

(8) direct that the child be released no later than 5:00 p.m. on the last day of the specified statutory

detention period, unless a continuance has been granted to the state or the child for cause; and

(9) be signed by the court with the title of office.

Former Rule 8.040 amended Dec. 28, 1984, effective Jan. 1, 1985 (462 So.2d 399); amended and effective Sept. 19, 1985 (475 So.2d 1240). Renumbered as new Rule 8.013 and amended May 9, 1991, effective July 1, 1991 (589 So.2d 818). Amended Oct. 31, 1996, effective Jan. 1, 1997 (684 So.2d 756); Oct. 26, 2000, effective Jan. 1, 2001 (783 So.2d 138); Nov. 17, 2005 (915 So.2d 592).

Rule 8.015. Arraignment of Detained Child

(a) When Required. If a petition for delinquency is filed and the child is being detained, whether in secure, nonsecure, or home detention, the child shall be given a copy of the petition and shall be arraigned within 48 hours of the filing of the petition, excluding Saturdays, Sundays, or legal holidays.

(b) Notice.

(1) Personal appearance of any person in a hearing before the court shall obviate the necessity of serving process on that person.

(2) The clerk of the court shall give notice of the time and place of the arraignment to the parent or guardian of the child and the superintendent of the detention center by:

(A) summons;

(B) written notice; or

(C) telephone notice.

(3) The superintendent of the detention center, or designee, also shall verify that a diligent effort has been made to notify the parent or guardian of the child of the time and place of the arraignment.

(4) Failure of notice to the parent or guardian, or nonattendance of the parent or guardian at the hearing, shall not invalidate the proceeding.

Amended Oct. 26, 2000, effective Jan. 1, 2001 (783 So.2d 138).

Committee Notes

This rule corresponds to section 985.215(7), Florida Statutes, which requires detained children to be arraigned within 48 hours of the filing of the delinquency petition. This statutory requirement does not allow the normal summons process to take place. The rule, therefore, creates an option for the clerk of the court to notice the parent by phone or in writing.

Rule 8.020. [Reserved]

B. PLEADINGS, PROCESS, AND ORDERS

Rule 8.025. Style of Pleadings and Orders

All pleadings and orders shall be styled: "In the interest of ______, a child," or: "In the interest of ______, children."

Former Rule 8.090 amended Dec. 28, 1984, effective Jan. 1, 1985 (462 So.2d 399). Renumbered as new Rule 8.025 May 9, 1991, effective July 1, 1991 (589 So.2d 818).

Rule 8.030. Commencement of Formal Proceedings

(a) Allegations as to Child. All proceedings shall be initiated by the filing of a petition by a person authorized by law to do so. A uniform traffic complaint may be considered a petition, but shall not be subject to the requirements of rule 8.035.

(b) Allegations as to Parents or Legal Guardians. In any delinquency proceeding in which the state is seeking payment of restitution or the performance of community service work by the child's parents or legal guardians, a separate petition alleging the parents' or legal guardians' responsibility shall be filed and served on the parents or legal guardians of the child.

Former Rule 8.100 amended Dec. 28, 1984, effective Jan. 1, 1985 (462 So.2d 399). Renumbered as new Rule 8.030 and amended May 9, 1991, effective July 1, 1991 (589 So.2d 818). Amended Oct. 26, 2000, effective Jan. 1, 2001 (783 So.2d 138); Sept. 5, 2002, effective Jan. 1, 2003 (827 So.2d 219).

Rule 8.031. Petition for Parental Sanctions

(a) Contents. Each petition directed to the child's parents or legal guardians shall be entitled a petition for parental sanctions and shall allege all facts showing the appropriateness of the requested sanction against the child's parents or legal guardians.

(b) Verification. The petition shall be signed by the state attorney or assistant state attorney, stating under oath the petitioner's good faith in filing the petition.

(c) Amendments. At any time before the hearing, an amended petition for parental sanctions may be filed or the petition may be amended on motion. Amendments shall be freely permitted in the interest of justice and the welfare of the child. A continuance may be granted on motion and a showing that the amendment prejudices or materially affects any party.

Added Oct. 26, 2000, effective Jan. 1, 2001 (783 So.2d 138). Amended Sept. 5, 2002, effective Jan. 1, 2003 (827 So.2d 219).

Rule 8.035. Petitions for Delinquency

(a) Contents of Petition.

(1) Each petition shall be entitled a petition for delinquency and shall allege facts showing the child to have committed a delinquent act. The petition must be a plain, concise, and definite written statement of the essential facts constituting the offense charged.

(2) The petition shall contain allegations as to the identity and residence of the parents or custodians, if known.

(3) In petitions alleging delinquency, each count shall recite the official or customary citations of the

statute, ordinance, rule, regulation, or other provision of the law which the child is alleged to have violated, including the degree of each offense.

(4) Two or more allegations of the commission of delinquent acts may appear in the same petition, in separate counts.

(5) Two or more children may be the subject of the same petition if they are alleged to have participated in the same act or transaction or in the same series of acts or transactions constituting an offense or offenses. The children may be named in one or more counts together or separately and all of them need not be named in each count.

(6) Allegations made in one count shall not be incorporated by reference in another count.

(b) Verification. The petition shall be signed by the state attorney or assistant state attorney, stating under oath the petitioner's good faith in filing the petition. No objection to a petition on the grounds that it was not signed or verified, as herein provided, shall be entertained after a plea to the merits.

(c) Child's Right to Copy of Petition. Upon application to the clerk, a child must be furnished a copy of the petition and the endorsements on it at least 24 hours before being required to plead to the petition.

(d) Amendments. At any time prior to the adjudicatory hearing an amended petition may be filed or the petition may be amended on motion. Amendments shall be freely permitted in the interest of justice and the welfare of the child. A continuance may be granted upon motion and a showing that the amendment prejudices or materially affects any party.

(e) Statement of Particulars. The court, on motion, must order the prosecuting attorney to furnish a statement of particulars when the petition on which the child is to be tried fails to inform the child of the particulars of the offense sufficiently to enable the child to prepare a defense. The statement of particulars must specify as definitely as possible the place, date, and all other material facts of the crime charged that are specifically requested and are known to the prosecuting attorney. Reasonable doubts concerning the construction of this rule shall be resolved in favor of the child.

(f) Defects and Variances. No petition or any count thereof shall be dismissed, or any judgment vacated, on account of any defect in the form of the petition or of misjoinder of offenses or for any cause whatsoever.

Former Rule 8.110 amended Dec. 28, 1984, effective Jan. 1, 1985 (462 So.2d 399). Renumbered as new Rule 8.035 and amended May 9, 1991, effective July 1, 1991 (589 So.2d 818). Amended Nov. 5, 1992, effective Jan. 1, 1993 (608 So.2d 478); Oct. 31, 1996, effective Jan. 1, 1997 (684 So.2d 756); May 23, 2013, effective July 1, 2013 (115 So.3d 286).

Rule 8.040. Process

(a) Summons.

(1) Upon the filing of a petition upon a child who is not detained by order of the court, the clerk shall issue a summons. The summons shall require the person on whom it is served to appear for a hearing at a time and place specified. The time of the hearing shall not be less than 24 hours after service of the summons. The summons shall require the custodian to produce the child at the said time and place. A copy of the delinquency petition shall be attached to the summons.

(2) If the child is being detained by order of the court, process shall be in accordance with the rule pertaining to the arraignment of a detained child.

(b) Service.

(1) *Generally.* The summons and other process shall be served upon such persons and in such manner as required by law. If the parents or custodian are out of the state and their address is known the clerk shall give them notice of the proceedings by mail. Service of process may be waived.

(2) *Petition for Parental Sanctions.* A petition for parental sanctions may be served on the child's parents or legal guardians in open court at any hearing concerning the child, but must be served at least 72 hours before the hearing at which parental sanctions are being sought. The petition for parental sanctions also may be served in accordance with chapter 48, Florida Statutes.

Amended Oct. 26, 2000, effective Jan. 1, 2001, (783 So.2d 138).

Committee Notes

1991 Amendment. This rule clearly defines the difference in procedures for summons for detained and nondetained children.

2000 Amendment. Subsection (b)(2) was added to provide requisite notice to the parents or legal guardians of a child when the state is seeking restitution or wishes to impose other sanctions against the parent or legal guardian. See *S.B.L., Natural Mother of J.J. v. State*, 737 So. 2d 1131 (Fla. 1st DCA 1999); *A.G., Natural Mother of S.B. v. State*, 736 So. 2d 151 (Fla. 1st DCA 1999).

Rule 8.041. Witness Attendance and Subpoenas

(a) Attendance. A witness summoned by a subpoena in an adjudicatory hearing shall remain in attendance at the adjudicatory hearing until excused by the court or by both parties. A witness who departs without being excused properly may be held in criminal contempt of court.

(b) Subpoenas Generally.

(1) Subpoenas for testimony before the court and subpoenas for production of tangible evidence before the court may be issued by the clerk of the court, by any attorney of record in an action, or by the court on its own motion.

(2) Except as otherwise required by this rule, the procedure for issuance of a subpoena (except for a subpoena duces tecum) by an attorney of record in a proceeding shall be as provided in the Florida Rules of Civil Procedure.

(c) Subpoenas for Testimony or Production of Tangible Evidence.

(1) Every subpoena for testimony or production of tangible evidence before the court shall be issued by an attorney of record in an action or by the clerk under the seal of the court. The subpoena shall state the name of the court and the title of the action and shall command each person to whom it is directed to attend and give testimony or produce evidence at a time and place specified.

(2) On oral request of an attorney of record, and without a witness praecipe, the clerk shall issue a subpoena for testimony before the court or a subpoena for tangible evidence before the court. The subpoena shall be signed and sealed but otherwise blank, both as to the title of the action and the name of the person to whom it is directed. The subpoena shall be filled in before service by the attorney.

(d) Subpoenas for Production of Tangible Evidence. If a subpoena commands the person to whom it is directed to produce the books, papers, documents, or tangible things designated in it, the court, on motion made promptly and in any event at or before the time specified in the subpoena for compliance with it, may

(1) quash or modify the subpoena if it is unreasonable and oppressive, or

(2) condition denial of the motion on the advancement by the person in whose behalf the subpoena is issued of the reasonable cost of producing the books, papers, documents, or tangible things.

Added Oct. 26, 2000, effective Jan. 1, 2001 (783 So.2d 138). Amended Mar. 3, 2005 (898 So.2d 47).

Rule 8.045. Notice to Appear

(a) Definition. A notice to appear, unless indicated otherwise, means a written order issued by a law enforcement officer or authorized agent of the department, in lieu of taking a child into custody or detaining a child, which requires a child accused of violating the law to appear in a designated court or governmental office at a specified date and time.

(b) By Arresting Officer. If a child is taken into custody for a violation of law and the officer elects to release the child as provided by law to a parent, responsible adult relative, or legal guardian, a notice to appear may be issued to the child by the officer unless:

(1) the child fails or refuses to sufficiently identify himself or herself or supply the required information;

(2) the child refuses to sign the notice to appear;

(3) the officer has reason to believe that the continued liberty of the child constitutes an unreasonable risk of bodily injury to the child or others;

(4) the child has no ties with the jurisdiction reasonably sufficient to ensure an appearance or there is substantial risk that the child will refuse to respond to the notice;

(5) the officer has any suspicion that the child may be wanted in any jurisdiction; or

(6) it appears that the child has previously failed to respond to a notice or a summons or has violated the conditions of any pretrial release program.

(c) By Departmental Agent. If a child is taken into custody by an authorized agent of the department as provided by law, or if an authorized agent of the department takes custody of a child from a law enforcement officer and the child is not detained, the agent shall issue a notice to appear to the child upon the child's release to a parent, responsible adult relative, or legal guardian.

(d) How and When Served. If a notice to appear is issued, 6 copies shall be prepared. One copy of the notice shall be delivered to the child and 1 copy shall be delivered to the person to whom the child is released. In order to secure the child's release, the child and the person to whom the child is released shall give their written promise that the child will appear as directed in the notice by signing the remaining copies. One copy is to be retained by the issuer and 3 copies are to be filed with the clerk of the court.

(e) Distribution of Copies. The clerk shall deliver 1 copy of the notice to appear to the state attorney and 1 copy to the department and shall retain 1 copy in the court's file.

(f) Contents. A notice to appear shall contain the following information:

(1) The name and address of the child and the person to whom the child was released.

(2) The date of the offense(s).

(3) The offense(s) charged by statute and municipal ordinance, if applicable.

(4) The counts of each offense.

(5) The time and place where the child is to appear.

(6) The name and address of the trial court having jurisdiction to try the offense(s) charged.

(7) The name of the arresting officer or authorized agent of the department.

(8) The signatures of the child and the person to whom the child was released.

(g) Failure to Appear. When a child signs a written notice to appear and fails to respond to the notice, an order to take into custody shall be issued.

(h) Form of Notice. The notice to appear shall be substantially as found in form 8.930.

Added May 9, 1991, effective July 1, 1991 (589 So.2d 818). Amended Nov. 5, 1992, effective Jan. 1, 1993 (608 So.2d 478); amended Sept. 21, 2006, effective Jan. 1, 2007 (939 So.2d 74).

Committee Notes

1991 Adoption. This rule allows juveniles to be released with definite notice as to when they must return to court. This should help decrease the number of juveniles held in detention centers awaiting a court date. It also should provide a mechanism to divert juveniles to programs more efficiently. The change also should decrease the number of summons issued by the clerk.

1992 Amendment. A summons is not sworn but the arrest affidavit that is filed with the notice to appear is sworn. The notice to appear, which is more like a summons, does not need to be sworn.

Rule 8.055. Orders

All orders of the court shall be reduced to writing as soon after they are entered as is consistent with orderly procedure and shall contain findings of fact as required by law.

Former Rule 8.140 amended Dec. 28, 1984, effective Jan. 1, 1985 (462 So.2d 399). Renumbered as new Rule 8.055 May 9, 1991, effective July 1, 1991 (589 So.2d 818).

C. DISCOVERY

Rule 8.060. Discovery

(a) Notice of Discovery.

(1) After the filing of the petition, a child may elect to utilize the discovery process provided by these rules, including the taking of discovery depositions, by filing with the court and serving upon the petitioner a "notice of discovery" which shall bind both the petitioner and the child to all discovery procedures contained in these rules. Participation by a child in the discovery process, including the taking of any deposition by a child, shall be an election to participate in discovery. If any child knowingly or purposely shares in discovery obtained by a codefendant, the child shall be deemed to have elected to participate in discovery.

(2) Within 5 days of service of the child's notice of discovery, the petitioner shall serve a written discovery exhibit which shall disclose to the child or the child's counsel and permit the child or the child's counsel to inspect, copy, test, and photograph the following information and material within the petitioner's possession or control:

(A) A list of the names and addresses of all persons known to the petitioner to have information which may be relevant to the allegations, to any defense with respect thereto, or to any similar fact evidence to be presented at trial under section 90.402(2), Florida Statutes. The names and addresses of persons listed shall be clearly designated in the following categories:

(i) Category A. These witnesses shall include

(a) eye witnesses;

(b) alibi witnesses and rebuttal to alibi witnesses;

(c) witnesses who were present when a recorded or unrecorded statement was taken from or made by the child or codefendant, which shall be separately identified within this category;

(d) investigating officers;

(e) witnesses known by the petitioner to have any material information that tends to negate the guilt of the child as to the petition's allegations;

(f) child hearsay witnesses; and

(g) expert witnesses who have not provided a written report and a curriculum vitae or who are going to testify.

(ii) Category B. All witnesses not listed in either Category A or Category C.

(iii) Category C. All witnesses who performed only ministerial functions or whom the petitioner does not intend to call at the hearing and whose involvement with and knowledge of the case is fully set out in a police report or other statement furnished to the defense.

(B) The statement of any person whose name is furnished in compliance with the preceding paragraph. The term "statement" as used herein means a written statement made by said person and signed or otherwise adopted by him or her and also includes any statement of any kind or manner made by such person and written or recorded or summarized in any writing or recording. The term "statement" is specifically intended to include all police and investigative reports of any kind prepared for or in connection with the case, but shall not include the notes from which such reports are compiled.

(C) Any written or recorded statements and the substance of any oral statements made by the child and known to the petitioner, including a copy of any statements contained in police reports or summaries, together with the name and address of each witness to the statements.

(D) Any written or recorded statements, and the substance of any oral statements, made by a codefendant if the hearing is to be a joint one.

(E) Those portions of recorded grand jury minutes that contain testimony of the child.

(F) Any tangible papers or objects which were obtained from or belonged to the child.

(G) Whether the petitioner has any material or information which has been provided by a confidential informant.

(H) Whether there has been any electronic surveillance, including wiretapping, of the premises of the child, or of conversations to which the child was a party, and any documents relating thereto.

(I) Whether there has been any search or seizure and any document relating thereto.

(J) Reports or statements of experts made in connection with the particular case, including results of physical or mental examinations and of scientific tests, experiments, or comparisons.

(K) Any tangible papers or objects which the petitioner intends to use in the hearing and which were not obtained from or belonged to the child.

(3) As soon as practicable after the filing of the petition, the petitioner shall disclose to the child any material information within the state's possession or control which tends to negate the guilt of the child as to the petition's allegations.

(4) The petitioner shall perform the foregoing obligations in any manner mutually agreeable to the petitioner and the child or as ordered by the court.

(5) Upon a showing of materiality to the preparation of the defense, the court may require such other discovery to the child as justice may require.

(b) Required Disclosure to Petitioner.

(1) If a child elects to participate in discovery, within 5 days after receipt by the child of the discovery exhibit furnished by the petitioner under this rule, the following disclosures shall be made:

(A) The child shall furnish to the petitioner a written list of all persons whom the child expects to call as witnesses at the hearing. When the petitioner subpoenas a witness whose name has been furnished by the child, except for hearing subpoenas, reasonable notice shall be given to the child as to the time and location of examination pursuant to the subpoena. At such examination, the child through counsel shall have the right to be present and to examine the witness. The physical presence of the child shall be governed by rule 8.060(d)(6).

(B) The child shall serve a written discovery exhibit which shall disclose to the petitioner and permit the petitioner to inspect, copy, test, and photograph the following information and material which is in the child's possession or control:

(i) The statement of any person whom the child expects to call as a trial witness other than that of the child.

(ii) Reports or statements of experts made in connection with the particular case, including results of physical or mental examinations and of scientific tests, experiments, or comparisons.

(iii) Any tangible papers or objects which the child intends to use in the hearing.

(2) The child shall perform the foregoing obligations in any manner mutually agreeable to the child and the petitioner or as ordered by the court.

(3) The filing of a motion for protective order by the petitioner will automatically stay the times provided for in this subdivision. If a protective order is granted, the child may, within 2 days thereafter, or at any time before the petitioner furnishes the information or material which is the subject of the motion for protective order, withdraw the demand and not be required to furnish reciprocal discovery.

(c) Limitations on Disclosure.

(1) Upon application, the court may deny or partially restrict disclosure authorized by this rule if it finds there is a substantial risk to any person of physical harm, intimidation, bribery, economic reprisals, or unnecessary annoyance or embarrassment resulting from such disclosure, which outweighs any usefulness of the disclosure to the party requesting it.

(2) The following matters shall not be subject to disclosure:

(A) Disclosure shall not be required of legal research or of records, correspondence, or memoranda, to the extent that they contain the opinion, theories, or conclusions of the prosecuting or defense attorney or members of their legal staff.

(B) Disclosure of a confidential informant shall not be required unless the confidential informant is to be produced at a hearing or a failure to disclose the informant's identity will infringe upon the constitutional rights of the child.

(d) Depositions.

(1) *Time and Location.*

(A) At any time after the filing of the petition alleging a child to be delinquent, any party may take the deposition upon oral examination of any person authorized by this rule.

(B) Depositions of witnesses residing in the county in which the adjudicatory hearing is to take place shall be taken in the building in which the adjudicatory hearing is to be held, another location agreed on by the parties, or a location designated by the court. Depositions of witnesses residing outside the county in which the adjudicatory hearing is to take place shall take place in a court reporter's office in the county and state in which the witness resides, another location agreed to by the parties, or a location designated by the court.

(2) *Procedure.*

(A) The party taking the deposition shall give reasonable written notice to each other party and shall make a good faith effort to coordinate the date, time, and location of the deposition to accommodate the schedules of other parties and the witness to be deposed. The notice shall state the time and the location of the deposition and the name of each person to be examined, and include a certificate of counsel that a good faith effort was made to coordinate the deposition schedule.

(B) Upon application, the court or the clerk of the court may issue subpoenas for the persons whose depositions are to be taken.

(C) After notice to the parties the court, for good cause shown, may change the time or location of the deposition.

(D) In any case, no person shall be deposed more than once except by consent of the parties or by order of the court issued on good cause shown.

(E) Except as otherwise provided by this rule, the procedure for taking the deposition, including the scope of the examination and the issuance of a subpoena (except for a subpoena duces tecum) for deposition by an attorney of record in the action shall be the same as that provided in the Florida Rules of Civil Procedure.

(F) The child, without leave of court, may take the deposition of any witness listed by the petitioner as a Category A witness or listed by a codefendant as a witness to be called at a joint hearing. After receipt by the child of the discovery exhibit, the child, without leave of court, may take the deposition of any unlisted witness who may have information relevant to the petition's allegations. The petitioner, without leave of court, may take the deposition of any witness listed by the child to be called at a hearing.

(G) No party may take the deposition of a witness listed by the petitioner as a Category B witness except upon leave of court with good cause shown. In determining whether to allow a deposition, the court should consider the consequences to the child, the complexities of the issues involved, the complexity of the testimony of the witness (e.g., experts), and the other opportunities available to the child to discover the information sought by deposition.

(H) A witness listed by the petitioner as a Category C witness shall not be subject to deposition unless the court determines that the witness should be listed in another category.

(I) No deposition shall be taken in a case in which a petition has been filed alleging that the child committed only a misdemeanor or a criminal traffic offense when all other discovery provided by this rule has been complied with unless good cause can be shown to the trial court. In determining whether to allow a deposition, the court should consider the consequences to the child, the complexity of the issues involved, the complexity of the witness's testimony (e.g., experts), and the other opportunities available to the child to discover the information sought by deposition. However, this prohibition against the taking of depositions shall not be applicable if following the furnishing of discovery by the child the petitioner then takes the statement of a listed defense witness pursuant to section 27.04, Florida Statutes.

(3) *Use of Deposition.* Any deposition taken pursuant to this rule may be used at any hearing covered by these rules by any party for the purpose of impeaching the testimony of the deponent as a witness.

(4) *Introduction of Part of Deposition.* If only part of a deposition is offered in evidence by a party, an adverse party may require the introduction of any other part that in fairness ought to be considered with the part introduced, and any party may introduce any other parts.

(5) *Sanctions.* A witness who refuses to obey a duly served subpoena for the taking of a deposition may be adjudged in contempt of the court from which the subpoena issued.

(6) *Physical Presence of Child.* The child shall not be physically present at a deposition except upon stipulation of the parties or as provided by this rule.

The court may order the physical presence of the child upon a showing of good cause. In ruling, the court may consider

(A) the need for the physical presence of the child to obtain effective discovery;

(B) the intimidating effect of the child's presence on the witness, if any;

(C) any cost or inconvenience which may result; and

(D) any alternative electronic or audio-visual means available to protect the child's ability to participate in discovery without the child's physical presence.

(7) *Statements of Law Enforcement Officers.* Upon stipulation of the parties and the consent of the witness, the statement of a law enforcement officer may be taken by telephone in lieu of deposition of the officer. In such case, the officer need not be under oath. The statement, however, shall be recorded and may be used for impeachment at trial as a prior inconsistent statement pursuant to the Florida Evidence Code.

(8) *Depositions of Law Enforcement Officers.* Subject to the general provisions of this rule, law enforcement officers shall appear for deposition, without subpoena, upon written notice of taking deposition delivered at the address designated by the law enforcement agency or department or, if no address has been designated, to the address of the law enforcement agency or department, 5 days prior to the date of the deposition. Law enforcement officers who fail to appear for deposition after being served notice are subject to contempt proceedings.

(9) *Videotaped Depositions.* Depositions of children under the age of 16 shall be videotaped upon

demand of any party unless otherwise ordered by the court. The court may order videotaping of a deposition or taking of a deposition of a witness with fragile emotional strength to be in the presence of the trial judge or a special magistrate.

(e) Perpetuating Testimony.

(1) After the filing of the petition and upon reasonable notice, any party may apply for an order to perpetuate testimony of a witness. The application shall be verified or supported by the affidavits of credible persons, and shall state that the prospective witness resides beyond the territorial jurisdiction of the court or may be unable to attend or be prevented from attending the subsequent court proceedings, or that grounds exist to believe that the witness will absent himself or herself from the jurisdiction of the court, that the testimony is material, and that it is necessary to take the deposition to prevent a failure of justice.

(2) If the application is well founded and timely made, the court shall order a commission to be issued to take the deposition of the witness to be used in subsequent court proceedings and that any designated books, papers, documents, or tangible objects, not privileged, be produced at the same time and place. The commission may be issued to any official court reporter, whether the witness be within or without the state, transcribed by the reporter, and filed in the court. The commission shall state the time and place of the deposition and be served on all parties.

(3) No deposition shall be used or read in evidence when the attendance of the witness can be procured. If it shall appear to the court that any person whose deposition has been taken has absented himself or herself by procurement, inducements, or threats by or on behalf of any party, the deposition shall not be read in evidence on behalf of that party.

(f) Nontestimonial Discovery. After the filing of the petition, upon application, and subject to constitutional limitations, the court may with directions as to time, place, and method, and upon conditions which are just, require:

(1) the child in all proceedings to:

(A) appear in a lineup;

(B) speak for identification by a witness to an offense;

(C) be fingerprinted;

(D) pose for photographs not involving reenactment of a scene;

(E) try on articles of clothing;

(F) permit the taking of specimens of material under the fingernails;

(G) permit the taking of samples of blood, hair, and other materials of the body which involve no unreasonable intrusion thereof;

(H) provide specimens of handwriting; or

(I) submit to a reasonable physical or medical inspection of his or her body; and

(2) such other discovery as justice may require upon a showing that such would be relevant or material.

(g) Court May Alter Times. The court may alter the times for compliance with any discovery under these rules on good cause shown.

(h) Supplemental Discovery. If, subsequent to compliance with these rules, a party discovers additional witnesses, evidence, or material which the party would have been under a duty to disclose or produce at the time of such previous compliance, the party shall promptly disclose or produce such witnesses, evidence, or material in the same manner as required under these rules for initial discovery.

(i) Investigations Not to Be Impeded. Except as otherwise provided for matters not subject to disclosure or restricted by protective orders, neither the counsel for the parties nor other prosecution or defense personnel shall advise persons having relevant material or information, except for the child, to refrain from discussing the case with opposing counsel or showing opposing counsel any relevant material, nor shall they otherwise impede opposing counsel's investigation of the case.

(j) Protective Orders. Upon a showing of good cause, the court shall at any time order that specified disclosures be restricted, deferred, or exempted from discovery, that certain matters are not to be inquired into or that the scope of the deposition be limited to certain matters, that a deposition be sealed and after being sealed be opened only by order of the court, or make such other order as is appropriate to protect a witness from harassment, unnecessary inconvenience, or invasion of privacy, including prohibiting the taking of a deposition. All material and information to which a party is entitled, however, must be disclosed in time to permit such party to make beneficial use of it.

(k) Motion to Terminate or Limit Examination. At any time during the taking of a deposition, on motion of a party or of the deponent, and upon a showing that the examination is being conducted in bad faith or in such manner as to unreasonably annoy, embarrass, or oppress the deponent or party, the court in which the action is pending or the circuit court where the deposition is being taken may (1) terminate the deposition, (2) limit the scope and manner of the taking of the deposition, (3) limit the time of the deposition, (4) continue the deposition to a later time, (5) order the deposition to be taken in open court and, in addition, (6) may impose any sanction authorized by this rule. If the order terminates the deposition, it shall be resumed thereafter only upon the order of the court in which the action is pending. Upon demand of any party or deponent, the taking of the deposition shall be suspended for the time necessary to make a motion for an order.

(*l*) In Camera and Ex Parte Proceedings.

(1) Any person may move for an order denying or regulating disclosure of sensitive matters. The court may consider the matters contained in the motion in camera.

(2) Upon request, the court shall allow the child to make an ex parte showing of good cause for taking the deposition of a Category B witness.

(3) A record shall be made of proceedings authorized under this subdivision. If the court enters an order granting relief after an in camera inspection or ex parte showing, the entire record of the proceeding shall be sealed and preserved in the records of the court, to be made available to the appellate court in the event of an appeal.

(m) Sanctions.

(1) If at any time during the course of the proceedings it is brought to the attention of the court that a party has failed to comply with an applicable discovery rule or with an order issued pursuant to an applicable discovery rule, the court may:

(A) order such party to comply with the discovery or inspection of materials not previously disclosed or produced;

(B) grant a continuance;

(C) grant a mistrial;

(D) prohibit the party from calling a witness not disclosed or introducing in evidence the material not disclosed; or

(E) enter such order as it deems just under the circumstances.

(2) Willful violation by counsel or a party not represented by counsel of an applicable discovery rule or an order issued pursuant thereto may subject counsel or a party not represented by counsel to appropriate sanction by the court. The sanctions may include, but are not limited to, contempt proceedings against the attorney or party not represented by counsel, as well as the assessment of costs incurred by the opposing party, when appropriate.

Former Rule 8.070 amended Dec. 28, 1984, effective Jan. 1, 1985 (462 So.2d 399). Renumbered as new Rule 8.060 and amended May 9, 1991, effective July 1, 1991 (589 So.2d 818). Amended Nov. 5, 1992, effective Jan. 1, 1993 (608 So.2d 478); Sept. 12, 1996, effective Oct. 1, 1996 (681 So.2d 666); Dec. 3, 1998 (724 So.2d 1153); Oct. 26, 2000, effective Jan. 1, 2001 (783 So.2d 138); Sept. 30, 2004, effective Oct. 1, 2004 (887 So.2d 1090); Oct. 3, 2013 (123 So.3d 1128).

Committee Notes

[Deleted by 1996 amendment.]

Court Commentary

1996 Amendment. This amendment generally conforms the rule to the 1996 amendment to Florida Rule of Criminal Procedure 3.220.

Rule 8.065. Notice of Defense of Alibi

(a) Notice to State Attorney. After a petition has been served the state attorney may demand in writing that the child, who intends to offer an alibi defense, shall provide the state attorney with the details of the alibi as to the time and place where the child claims to have been at the time of the alleged offense and the names and addresses of such witnesses as may appear to testify thereon. The child shall comply as above not less than 10 days before the trial date.

(b) Rebuttal Witness List. The state attorney shall, within 5 days of the receipt thereof, provide the child with a list of such witnesses to be called to rebut the alibi testimony.

(c) Sanctions. Should the child fail or refuse to comply with the provisions hereof, the court may in its discretion exclude testimony of alibi witnesses other than the child or, should the state attorney fail to comply herewith, the court may in its discretion exclude rebuttal testimony offered by the state.

(d) Waiver of Rule. For good cause shown, the court may waive the requirements of this rule.

Former Rule 8.080 amended Dec. 28, 1984, effective Jan. 1, 1985 (462 So.2d 399). Renumbered as new Rule 8.065 and amended May 9, 1991, effective July 1, 1991 (589 So.2d 818).

D. ARRAIGNMENTS AND PLEAS

Rule 8.070. Arraignments

(a) Appointment of Counsel. Prior to the adjudicatory hearing, the court may conduct a hearing to determine whether a guilty, nolo contendere, or not guilty plea to the petition shall be entered and whether the child is represented by counsel or entitled to appointed counsel as provided by law. Counsel shall be appointed if the child qualifies for such appointment and does not waive counsel in writing subject to the requirements of rule 8.165.

(b) Plea. The reading or statement as to the charge or charges may be waived by the child. No child, whether represented by counsel or otherwise, shall be called on to plead unless and until he or she has had a reasonable time within which to deliberate thereon. If the child is represented by counsel, counsel may file a written plea of not guilty at or before arraignment and arraignment shall then be deemed waived. If a plea of guilty or nolo contendere is entered, the court shall proceed as set forth under rule 8.115, disposition hearings. If a plea of not guilty is entered, the court shall set an adjudicatory hearing within the period of time provided by law. The child is entitled to a reasonable time in which to prepare for trial.

Added May 9, 1991, effective July 1, 1991 (589 So.2d 818). Amended Dec. 17, 2009, effective Jan. 1, 2010 (26 So.3d 552); May 23, 2013, effective July 1, 2013 (115 So.3d 286).

Committee Notes

1991 Adoption. This rule creates an arraignment proceeding that is referred to in section 985.215(7), Florida Statutes.

Rule 8.075. Pleas

No written answer to the petition nor any other pleading need be filed. No child, whether represented by counsel or otherwise, shall be called upon to plead until he or she has had a reasonable time within which to deliberate thereon.

(a) Acceptance of Plea. In delinquency cases the child may plead guilty, nolo contendere, or not guilty. The court may refuse to accept a plea of guilty or nolo contendere, and shall not accept either plea without first determining that the plea is made voluntarily and with a full understanding of the nature of the allegations and the possible consequences of such plea and that there is a factual basis for such plea.

(b) Plan of Proposed Treatment, Training, or Conduct. After the filing of a petition and prior to the adjudicatory hearing, a plan of proposed treatment, training, or conduct may be submitted on behalf of the child in lieu of a plea. The appropriate agencies of the Department of Juvenile Justice or other agency as designated by the court shall be the supervising agencies for said plan and the terms and conditions of all such plans shall be formulated in conjunction with the supervising agency involved. The submission of a plan is not an admission of the allegations of the petition of delinquency.

If such a plan is submitted the procedure shall be as follows:

(1) The plan must be in writing, agreed to and signed in all cases by the state attorney, the child, and, when represented, by the child's counsel, and, unless excused by the court, by the parents or custodian. An authorized agent of the supervising agency involved shall indicate whether the agency recommends the acceptance of the plan.

(2) The plan shall contain a stipulation that the speedy trial rule is waived and shall include the state attorney's consent to defer the prosecution of the petition.

(3) After hearing, which may be waived by stipulation of the parties and the supervising agency, the court may accept the plan and order compliance therewith, or may reject it. If the plan is rejected by the court, the court shall state on the record the reasons for rejection.

(4) Violations of the conditions of the plan shall be presented to the court by motion by the supervising agency or by any party. If the court, after hearing, finds a violation has occurred, it may take such action as is appropriate to enforce the plan, modify the plan by supplemental agreement, or set the case for hearing on the original petition.

(5) The plan shall be effective for an indeterminate period, for such period as is stated therein, or until the petition is dismissed.

(6) Unless otherwise dismissed, the petition may be dismissed on the motion of the person submitting the plan or the supervising agency, after notice of hearing and a finding of substantial compliance with the provisions and intent of the plan.

(c) Written Answer. A written answer admitting or denying the allegations of the petition may be filed by the child joined by a parent, custodian, or the child's counsel. If the answer admits the allegations of the petition it must acknowledge that the child has been advised of the right to counsel, the right to remain silent, and the possible dispositions available to the court and shall include a consent to a predispositional study. Upon the filing of such an answer, a hearing for adjudication or adjudication and disposition shall be set at the earliest practicable time.

(d) Entry of Plea by Court. If a child stands mute or pleads evasively, a plea of not guilty shall be entered by the court.

(e) Withdrawal of Plea. The court may for good cause shown at any time prior to the beginning of a disposition hearing permit a plea of guilty or nolo contendere to be withdrawn, and if a finding that the child committed a delinquent act has been entered thereon, set aside such finding and allow another plea to be substituted for the plea of guilty or nolo contendere. In the subsequent adjudicatory hearing, the court shall not consider the plea which was withdrawn as an admission.

(f) Withdrawal of Plea After Drug Court Transfer. A child who pleads guilty or nolo contendere to a charge for the purpose of transferring the case, under section 910.035, Florida Statutes, may file a motion to withdraw the plea upon successful completion of the juvenile drug court treatment program.

Former Rule 8.130(a) amended Dec. 28, 1984, effective Jan. 1, 1985 (462 So.2d 399). Renumbered as new Rule 8.075 and amended May 9, 1991, effective July 1, 1991 (589 So.2d 818). Amended Oct. 31, 1996, effective Jan. 1, 1997 (684 So.2d 756); June 21, 2007 (959 So.2d 250); May 23, 2013, effective July 1, 2013 (115 So.3d 286).

Rule 8.080. Acceptance of Guilty or Nolo Contendere Plea

(a) Voluntariness. Before accepting a plea of guilty or nolo contendere, the court shall determine that the plea is knowingly and voluntarily entered and that there is a factual basis for it. Counsel for the prosecution and the defense shall assist the court in this determination.

(b) Open Court. All pleas shall be taken in open court, except the hearing may be closed as provided by law.

(c) Determination by Court. The court, when making this determination, should place the child under oath and shall address the child personally. The court shall determine that the child understands each of the following rights and consequences of entering a guilty or nolo contendere plea:

(1) The nature of the charge to which the plea is offered and the possible dispositions available to the court.

(2) If the child is not represented by an attorney, that the child has the right to be represented by an attorney at every stage of the proceedings and, if necessary, one will be appointed. Counsel shall be appointed if the child qualifies for such appointment and does not waive counsel in writing subject to the requirements of rule 8.165.

(3) That the child has the right to plead not guilty, or to persist in that plea if it had already been made, and that the child has the right to an adjudicatory hearing and at that hearing has the right to the assistance of counsel, the right to compel the attendance of witnesses on his or her behalf, the right to confront and cross-examine witnesses against him or her, and the right not to be compelled to incriminate himself or herself.

(4) That, if the child pleads guilty or nolo contendere, without express reservation of the right to appeal, the right to appeal all matters relating to the judgment, including the issue of guilt or innocence, is relinquished, but the right to review by appropriate collateral attack is not impaired.

(5) That, if the child pleads guilty or nolo contendere, there will not be a further adjudicatory hearing of any kind, so that by pleading so the right to an adjudicatory hearing is waived.

(6) That, if the child pleads guilty or nolo contendere, the court may ask the child questions about the offense to which the child has pleaded, and, if those questions are answered under oath, on the record, the answers may later be used against the child in a prosecution for perjury.

(7) The complete terms of any plea agreement including specifically all obligations the child will incur as a result.

(8) That, if the child pleads guilty or nolo contendere to certain sexual offenses, the child may be required to register as a sexual offender.

(9) That, if the child pleads guilty or nolo contendere, and the offense to which the child is pleading is a sexually violent offense or a sexually motivated offense, or if the child has been previously adjudicated for such an offense, the plea may subject the child to involuntary civil commitment as a sexually violent predator on completion of his or her sentence. It shall not be necessary for the trial judge to determine whether the present or prior offenses were sexually motivated, as this admonition shall be given to all children in all cases.

(10) That, if the child pleads guilty or nolo contendere, and the child is not a United States citizen, the facts underlying the plea may subject the child to deportation pursuant to the laws and regulations governing the United States Citizenship and Immigration Services. It shall not be necessary for the trial judge to inquire as to whether the child is a United States citizen, as this admonition shall be given to all children in all cases.

(d) Acknowledgment by Child. Before the court accepts a guilty or nolo contendere plea, the court must determine that the child either:

(1) acknowledges guilt; or

(2) acknowledges that the plea is in the child's best interest, while maintaining innocence.

(e) Of Record. These proceedings shall be of record.

(f) When Binding. Prior to the court's acceptance of a plea, the parties must notify the court of any plea agreement and may notify the court of the reasons for the plea agreement. Thereafter, the court must advise the parties whether the court accepts or rejects the plea agreement and may state its reasons for a rejection of the plea agreement. No plea offer or negotiation is binding until it is accepted by the court after making all the inquiries, advisements, and determinations required by this rule. Until that time, it may be withdrawn by either party without any necessary justification.

(g) Withdrawal of Plea When Judge Does Not Concur. If the trial judge does not concur in a tendered plea of guilty or nolo contendere arising from negotiations, the plea may be withdrawn.

(h) Failure to Follow Procedures. Failure to follow any of the procedures in this rule shall not render a plea void, absent a showing of prejudice.

Added May 9, 1991, effective July 1, 1991 (589 So.2d 818). Amended Dec. 17, 2009, effective Jan. 1, 2010 (26 So.3d 552); May 23, 2013, effective July 1, 2013 (115 So.3d 286).

E. MOTIONS AND SERVICE OF PLEADINGS

Rule 8.085. Prehearing Motions and Service

(a) Prehearing Motions.

(1) *Motions in General.* Every motion made before a hearing and any pleading in response to the motion shall be in writing and shall be signed by the party making the motion and the party's attorney. This requirement may be waived by the court for good cause shown.

(2) *Motion to Dismiss.* All defenses not raised by a plea of not guilty or denial of the allegations of the

petition shall be made by a motion to dismiss the petition. If a motion to dismiss is granted, the child who is detained under an order entered under rule 8.013 may be continued in detention under the said order upon the representation that a new or amended petition will be filed.

(3) *Motion to Suppress.* Any confession or admission obtained illegally or any evidence obtained by an unlawful search and seizure may be suppressed on motion by the child.

(A) Every motion to suppress shall clearly state the particular evidence sought to be suppressed, the reason for the suppression, and a general statement of the facts on which the motion is based.

(B) Before hearing evidence, the court shall determine if the motion is legally sufficient. If it is not, the motion shall be denied. If the court hears the motion on its merits, the moving party shall present evidence in support thereof and the state may offer rebuttal evidence.

(4) *Motion to Sever.* A motion may be made for the severance of 2 or more counts in a multi-count petition, or for the severance of the cases of 2 or more children to be adjudicated in the same hearing. The court may grant motions for severance of counts and severance of jointly brought cases for good cause shown.

(5) *Time for Filing.* Any motion to suppress, sever, or dismiss shall be made prior to the date of the adjudicatory hearing unless an opportunity to make such motion previously did not exist or the party making the motion was not aware of the grounds for the motion.

(6) *Sworn Motions to Dismiss.* Before the adjudicatory hearing the court may entertain a motion to dismiss on the ground that there are no material disputed facts and the undisputed facts do not establish a prima facie case of guilt against the child. The facts on which such motion is based shall be specifically alleged and the motion sworn to by the child. The motion shall be filed a reasonable time before the date of the adjudicatory hearing. The state may traverse or demur to this motion. Factual matters alleged in it shall be deemed admitted unless specifically denied by the state in a traverse. The court, in its discretion, may receive evidence on any issue of fact necessary to decide the motion. The motion shall be dismissed if the state files a written traverse that with specificity denies under oath the material fact or facts alleged in the motion to dismiss. Any demurrer or traverse shall be filed a reasonable time before the hearing on the motion to dismiss.

(b) Service of Pleadings and Papers.

(1) *When Required.* Unless the court orders otherwise, every pleading subsequent to the initial petition, every order, every written motion, unless it is one as to which hearing ex parte is authorized, and every written notice filed in the case shall be served on each party; however, nothing herein shall be construed to require that a plea be in writing or that an application for witness subpoena be served.

(2) *How Made.* When service is required or permitted to be made upon a party represented by an attorney, service shall be made upon the attorney unless service upon the party is ordered by the court. Service upon the attorney or party shall be made by electronic mail (e-mail) consistent with the requirements of Florida Rule of Judicial Administration 2.516, unless the parties stipulate otherwise. Service on and by all parties who are not represented by an attorney and who do not designate an e-mail address, and on and by all attorneys excused from e-mail service, must be made by delivering a copy or by mailing it to the attorney or party's last known address or, if no address is known, by leaving it with the clerk of the court. Service by mail shall be complete upon mailing. Delivery of a copy within this rule shall mean:

(A) handing it to the attorney or the party;

(B) leaving it at the attorney's office, with the person in charge thereof;

(C) if there is no one in charge of the office, leaving it in a conspicuous place therein;

(D) if the office is closed or the person to serve has no office, leaving it at his or her usual place of abode with some person of the family above 15 years of age and informing such person of the contents thereof; or

(E) transmitting it by facsimile to the attorney's or party's office with a cover sheet containing the sender's name, firm, address, telephone number, and facsimile number, the number of pages transmitted, and the recipient's facsimile number. When service is made by facsimile, a copy shall also be served by any other method permitted by this rule. Facsimile service occurs when the transmission is complete.

(3) *Filing.* All documents must be filed with the court either before service or immediately thereafter. If the document required to be filed is to be an original and is not placed in the court file or deposited with the clerk, a certified copy must be so placed by the clerk.

(4) *Filing with Court Defined.* The filing of documents with the court as required by these rules shall be made by filing them with the clerk of the court in accordance with rule 8.004, except that the judge may permit documents to be filed with the judge, in which event the judge must note the filing date before him or her on the documents and transmit them to the clerk. The date of filing is that shown on the face of the document by the notation of the judge or the time stamp of the clerk, whichever is earlier.

(5) *Certificate of Service.* When any authorized person shall in substance certify:

"I certify that a copy/copies has/have been furnished to (insert name or names) by (e-mail) (delivery) (mail) (fax) on (date).

____

Title"

the certificate shall be taken as prima facie proof of such service in compliance with all rules of court and law.

(6) *People Who May Certify Service.* Service of pleadings and orders required to be served as provided by subdivision (2) may be certified by an attorney of record, clerk or deputy clerk, court, or authorized agent of the Department of Juvenile Justice in the form provided in subdivision (b)(5).

(c) Format for E-mail Service. All documents served by e-mail must be sent by an e-mail message containing a subject line beginning with the words "SERVICE OF COURT DOCUMENT" in all capital letters, followed by the case number of the proceeding in which the documents are being served. The body of the e-mail must identify the court in which the proceeding is pending, the case number, the name of the parties on each side, the style of the proceeding, the title of each document served with that e-mail, and the sender's name and telephone number. Any e-mail which, together with its attachments, exceeds five megabytes (5MB) in size, must be divided and sent as separate e-mails, numbered in the subject line, no one of which may exceed 5 MB in size.

(d) Time for Service of Motions and Notice of Hearing. Service by e-mail is complete on the date it is sent and must be treated as service by mail for the computation of time. If the sender learns that the e-mail did not reach the address of the person to be served, the sender must immediately send another copy by e-mail, or by means authorized by subdivision (b)(2). If e-mail service is excused, a copy of any written motion which may not be heard ex parte and a copy of the notice of the hearing thereof shall be served a reasonable time before the time specified for the hearing. If a document is served by more than one method of service, the computation of time for any response to the served document shall be based on the method of service that provides the shortest response time.

(e) Pleading to Be Signed by Attorney. Every written paper or pleading of a party represented by an attorney shall be signed in the attorney's individual name by such attorney, whose mailing address, primary e-mail address and telephone number, including area code, and Florida Bar number shall be stated, and who shall be duly licensed to practice law in Florida. Any document served by e-mail may be signed by any of the "/s/," "/s," or "s/" formats. The attorney may be required by an order of court to vouch for the authority to represent such party and to give the address of such party. Except when otherwise specifically provided by these rules or applicable statute, pleadings as such need not be verified or accompanied by affidavit.

(f) Pleading to Be Signed by Unrepresented Party. A party who has no attorney but represents himself or herself shall sign the written pleading or other paper to be filed and state his or her primary e-mail address, mailing address, and telephone number, including area code.

(g) Effect of Signing Pleading. The signature of a person shall constitute a certificate that the paper or pleading has been read; that to the best of the person's knowledge, information, and belief there is good ground to support it; and that it is not interposed for delay. If a pleading or paper is not signed, or is signed with intent to defeat the purpose of this rule, it may be stricken and the action may proceed as though the pleading or paper had not been served.

(h) Service of Orders. A copy of all orders must be transmitted by the court or under its direction to all parties at the time of the entry of the order. The court may require that orders be prepared by a party, may require the party to furnish the court with stamped addressed envelopes for service of the order or judgment, and may require that proposed orders be furnished to all parties before entry by the court of the order. The court may serve any order by e-mail to all attorneys who were not excused from e-mail service and to all parties not represented by an attorney who have designated an e-mail address for service. This subdivision is directory, and a failure to comply with it does not affect the order or its finality or any proceedings arising in the matter.

Former Rule 8.130(b)–(g) amended Dec. 28, 1984, effective Jan. 1, 1985 (462 So.2d 399). Renumbered as new Rule 8.085 and amended May 9, 1991, effective July 1, 1991 (589 So.2d 818). Amended Nov. 5, 1992, effective Jan. 1, 1993 (608 So.2d 478); Oct. 31, 1996, effective Jan. 1, 1997 (684 So.2d 756); Oct. 26, 2000, effective Jan. 1, 2001 (783 So.2d 138); Sept. 5, 2002, effective Jan. 1, 2003 (827 So.2d 219); Oct. 18, 2012, effective, *nunc pro tunc*, Sept. 1, 2012 (102 So.3d 505); July 1, 2012, effective Oct. 1, 2012 (95 So.3d 96); Oct. 3, 2013, effective Oct. 3, 2013 (123 So.3d 1139).

Committee Notes

1991 Amendment. (a)(6) This creates a procedure for dismissal similar to Florida Rule of Criminal Procedure 3.190(c)(4).

1992 Amendments. (d) Rules 8.240(c)(2) and 8.630(c)(2) allow 5 days for service by mail. This change conforms this rule.

(f) The current rule implies that a written pleading must be filed. No written pleadings are required.

(e) and (g) The language from (e) was moved to create this new subdivision. The current rule applies only to attorneys. These requirements also should apply to nonattorneys who sign and file papers. This rule conforms with proposed revisions to rules 8.230 and 8.640.

Rule 8.090. Speedy Trial

(a) Time. If a petition has been filed alleging a child to have committed a delinquent act, the child shall be brought to an adjudicatory hearing without demand within 90 days of the earlier of the following:

(1) The date the child was taken into custody.

(2) The date of service of the summons that is issued when the petition is filed.

(b) Dismissal. If an adjudicatory hearing has not commenced within 90 days, upon motion timely filed with the court and served upon the prosecuting attorney, the respondent shall be entitled to the appropriate remedy as set forth in subdivision (m). The court before granting such motion shall make the required inquiry under subdivision (d).

(c) Commencement. A child shall be deemed to have been brought to trial if the adjudicatory hearing begins before the court within the time provided.

(d) Motion to Dismiss. If the adjudicatory hearing is not commenced within the periods of time established, the respondent shall be entitled to the appropriate remedy as set forth in subdivision (m) unless any of the following situations exist:

(1) The child has voluntarily waived the right to speedy trial.

(2) An extension of time has been ordered under subdivision (f).

(3) The failure to hold an adjudicatory hearing is attributable to the child, a co-respondent in the same adjudicatory hearing, or their counsel.

(4) The child was unavailable for the adjudicatory hearing. A child is unavailable if:

(A) the child or the child's counsel fails to attend a proceeding when their presence is required; or

(B) the child or the child's counsel is not ready for the adjudicatory hearing on the date it is scheduled.

No presumption of nonavailability attaches, but if the state objects to dismissal and presents any evidence tending to show nonavailability, the child must, by competent proof, establish availability during the term.

(5) The demand referred to in subdivision (g) is invalid.

(6) If the court finds dismissal is not appropriate, the pending motion to dismiss shall be denied, and an adjudicatory hearing shall commence within 90 days of a written or recorded order of denial.

(e) Incompetency of Child. Upon the filing of a motion to declare the child incompetent, the speedy trial period shall be tolled until a subsequent finding of the court that the child is competent to proceed.

(f) Extension of Time. The period of time established by subdivision (a) may be extended as follows:

(1) Upon stipulation, announced to the court or signed by the child or the child's counsel and the state.

(2) By written or recorded order of the court on the court's own motion or motion by either party in exceptional circumstances. The order extending the period shall recite the reasons for the extension and the length of the extension. Exceptional circumstances are those which require an extension as a matter of substantial justice to the child or the state or both. Such circumstances include:

(A) unexpected illness or unexpected incapacity or unforeseeable and unavoidable absence of a person whose presence or testimony is uniquely necessary for a full and adequate trial;

(B) a showing by the state that the case is so unusual and so complex, due to the number of respondents or the nature of the prosecution or otherwise, that it is unreasonable to expect adequate investigation or preparation within the periods of time established by this rule;

(C) a showing by the state that specific evidence or testimony is not available, despite diligent efforts to secure it, but will become available at a later time;

(D) a showing by the child or the state of necessity for delay grounded on developments which could not have been anticipated and which will materially affect the trial;

(E) a showing that a delay is necessary to accommodate a co-respondent, where there is a reason not to sever the cases in order to proceed promptly with trial of the respondent; or

(F) a showing by the state that the child has caused major delay or disruption of preparation or proceedings, such as by preventing the attendance of witnesses or otherwise.

Exceptional circumstances shall not include general congestion of the court's docket, lack of diligent preparation or failure to obtain available witnesses, or other avoidable or foreseeable delays.

(3) By written or recorded order of the court for a period of reasonable and necessary delay resulting from proceedings including, but not limited to, an examination and hearing to determine the mental competency or physical ability of the respondent to stand trial for hearings or pretrial motions, for appeals by the state, and for adjudicatory hearings of other pending charges against the child.

(g) Speedy Trial Upon Demand. Except as otherwise provided by this rule and subject to the limitations imposed by subdivision (h), the child shall have the right to demand a trial within 60 days, by filing a written pleading entitled "Demand for Speedy Trial" with the court and serving it upon the prosecuting attorney.

(1) No later than 5 days from the filing of a demand for speedy trial, the court shall set the matter for report, with notice to all parties, for the express purposes of announcing in open court receipt of the demand and of setting the case for trial.

(2) At the report the court shall set the case for trial to commence at a date no less than 5 days nor more than 45 days from the date of the report.

(3) The failure of the court to hold such a report date on a demand which has been properly filed shall not interrupt the running of any time periods under this subdivision (g).

(4) In the event that the child shall not have been brought to trial within 50 days of the filing of the demand, the child shall have the right to the appropriate remedy as set forth in subdivision (m).

(h) Demand for Speedy Trial; Effect. A demand for speedy trial shall be deemed a pleading by the respondent that he or she is available for the adjudicatory hearing, has diligently investigated the case, and is prepared or will be prepared for the adjudicatory hearing within 5 days. A demand may not be withdrawn by the child except on order of the court, with consent of the state, or on good cause shown. Good cause for continuance or delay on behalf of the accused shall not thereafter include nonreadiness for the adjudicatory hearing, except as to matters which may arise after the demand for the adjudicatory hearing is filed and which could not reasonably have been anticipated by the accused or defense counsel.

(i) Dismissal After Demand. If an adjudicatory hearing has not commenced within 50 days after a demand for speedy trial, upon motion timely filed with the court having jurisdiction and served upon the prosecuting attorney, the child shall have the right to the appropriate remedy as set forth in subdivision (m), provided the court has made the required inquiry under subdivision (d).

(j) Effect of Mistrial, Appeal, or Order of New Trial. A child who is to be tried again or whose adjudicatory hearing has been delayed by an appeal by the state or the respondent shall be brought to trial within 90 days from the date of declaration of a mistrial by the trial court, the date of an order by the trial court granting a new trial, or the date of receipt by the trial court of a mandate, order, or notice of whatever form from an appellate or other reviewing court which makes possible a new trial for the respondent, whichever is last. If the child is not brought to trial within the prescribed time periods, the child shall be entitled to the appropriate remedy as set forth in subdivision (m).

(k) Discharge from Delinquent Act or Violation of Law; Effect. Discharge from a delinquent act or violation of law under this rule shall operate to bar prosecution of the delinquent act or violation of law charged and all other offenses on which an adjudicatory hearing has not begun or adjudication obtained or withheld and that were, or might have been, charged as a lesser degree or lesser included offense.

(*l*) Nolle Prosequi; Effect. The intent and effect of this rule shall not be avoided by the state entering a nolle prosequi to a delinquent act or violation of law charged and by prosecuting a new delinquent act or violation of law grounded on the same conduct or episode or otherwise by prosecuting new and different charges based on the same delinquent conduct or episode, whether or not the pending charge is suspended, continued, or the subject of the entry of a nolle prosequi.

(m) Remedy for Failure to Try Respondent Within the Specified Time.

(1) No remedy shall be granted to any respondent under this rule until the court shall have made the required inquiry under subdivision (d).

(2) The respondent may, at any time after the expiration of the prescribed time period, file a motion for discharge. Upon filing the motion the respondent shall simultaneously file a notice of hearing. The motion for discharge and its notice of hearing shall be served upon the prosecuting attorney.

(3) No later than 5 days from the date of the filing of a motion for discharge, the court shall hold a hearing on the motion and, unless the court finds that one of the reasons set forth in subdivision (d) exists, shall order that the respondent be brought to trial within 10 days. If the respondent is not brought to trial within the 10–day period through no fault of the respondent, the respondent shall be forever discharged from the crime.

Former Rule 8.180 amended Dec. 28, 1984, effective Jan. 1, 1985 (462 So.2d 399); Oct. 27, 1988, effective Jan. 1, 1989 (536 So.2d 199). Renumbered as new Rule 8.090 and amended May 9, 1991, effective July 1, 1991 (589 So.2d 818). Amended Nov. 5, 1992, effective Jan. 1, 1993 (608 So.2d 478); Dec. 22, 1994 (648 So.2d 115); Jan. 26, 1995 (649 So.2d 1370); Sept. 21, 2006, effective Jan. 1, 2007 (939 So.2d 74).

Committee Notes

1991 Amendment. (m)(2) This rule requires a notice of hearing at the time of filing the motion for discharge to ensure that the child's motion is heard in a timely manner. A dissenting opinion in the committee was that this change does not protect the child's rights but merely ensures that the case is not dismissed because of clerical error.

Rule 8.095. Procedure When Child Believed to Be Incompetent or Insane

(a) Incompetency At Time of Adjudicatory Hearing or Hearing on Petition Alleging Violation of Juvenile Probation in Delinquency Cases.

(1) *Motion.*

(A) A written motion for examination of the child made by counsel for the child shall contain a certificate of counsel that the motion is made in good faith and on reasonable grounds to believe that the child is incompetent to proceed. To the extent that it does not invade the lawyer-client privilege, the motion shall contain a recital of the specific observations of and conversations with the child that have formed the basis for the motion.

(B) A written motion for examination of the child made by counsel for the state shall contain a certificate of counsel that the motion is made in good faith and on reasonable grounds to believe the child is incompetent to proceed and shall include a recital of the specific facts that have formed the basis for the motion, including a recitation of the observations of and statements of the child that have caused the state to file the motion.

(2) *Setting Hearing.* If at any time prior to or during the adjudicatory hearing or hearing on a violation of juvenile probation the court has reasonable grounds to believe the child named in the petition may be incompetent to proceed with an adjudicatory hearing, the court on its own motion or motion of counsel for the child or the state shall immediately stay the proceedings and fix a time for a hearing for the determination of the child's mental condition.

(3) *Child Found Competent to Proceed.* If at the hearing provided for in subdivision (a)(2) the child is found to be competent to proceed with an adjudicatory hearing, the court shall enter an order so finding and proceed accordingly.

(4) *Child Found Incompetent to Proceed.* If at the hearing provided for in subdivision (a)(2) the child is found to be incompetent to proceed, the child must be adjudicated incompetent to proceed and may be involuntarily committed as provided by law to the Department of Children and Families for treatment upon a finding of clear and convincing evidence that:

(A) The child is mentally ill or intellectually disabled and because of the mental illness or intellectual disability of the child:

(i) the child is manifestly incapable of surviving with the help of willing and responsible family or friends, including available alternative services, and without treatment the child is likely to either suffer from neglect or refuse to care for himself or herself, and such neglect or refusal poses a real and present threat of substantial harm to the child's well-being; or

(ii) there is a substantial likelihood that in the near future the child will inflict serious bodily harm on himself or herself or others, as evidenced by recent behavior causing, attempting, or threatening such harm; and

(B) All available less restrictive treatment alternatives, including treatment in community residential facilities or community inpatient settings which would offer an opportunity for improvement of the child's condition are inappropriate.

(5) *Hearing on Competency.* Not later than 6 months after the date of commitment, or at the end of any period of extended treatment or training, or at any time the service provider determines the child has attained competency or no longer meets the criteria for commitment, the service provider must file a report with the court and all parties. Upon receipt of this report, the court shall set a hearing to determine the child's competency.

(A) If the court determines that the child continues to remain incompetent, the court shall order appropriate nondelinquent hospitalization or treatment in conformity with this rule and the applicable provisions of chapter 985, Florida Statutes.

(B) If the court determines the child to be competent, it shall enter an order so finding and proceed accordingly.

(6) *Commitment.* Each child who has been adjudicated incompetent to proceed and who meets the criteria for commitment in subdivision (a)(4) must be committed to the Department of Children and Families. The department must train or treat the child in the least restrictive alternative consistent with public safety. Any commitment of a child to a secure residential program must be to a program separate from adult forensic programs. If the child attains competency, case management and supervision of the child will be transferred to the Department of Juvenile Justice to continue delinquency proceedings. The court retains authority, however, to order the Department of Children and Families to provide continued treatment to maintain competency.

(A) A child adjudicated incompetent because of intellectual disability may be ordered into a program designated by the Department of Children and Families for intellectually disabled children.

(B) A child adjudicated incompetent because of mental illness may be ordered into a program designated by the Department of Children and Families for mentally ill children.

(7) *Continuing Jurisdiction and Dismissal of Jurisdiction.*

(A) If a child is determined to be incompetent to proceed, the court shall retain jurisdiction of the child for up to 2 years after the date of the order of incompetency, with reviews at least every 6 months to determine competency. If the court determines at any time that the child will never become competent to proceed, the court may dismiss the delinquency petition or petition alleging violation of juvenile probation.

(B) If, at the end of the 2–year period following the date of the order of incompetency, the child has not attained competency and there is no evidence that the child will attain competency within a year, the court must dismiss the delinquency petition.

(C) If necessary, the court may order that proceedings under chapter 393 or 394, Florida Statutes, be instituted. Such proceedings must be instituted no less than 60 days before the dismissal of the delinquency petition. The juvenile court may conduct all proceedings and make all determinations under chapter 393 or 394, Florida Statutes.

(8) *Treatment Alternatives to Commitment.* If a child who is found to be incompetent does not meet the commitment criteria of subdivision (a)(4), the court shall order the Department of Children and Families to provide appropriate treatment and training in the community. All court-ordered treatment must be in the least restrictive setting consistent with public safety. Any residential program must be separate from an adult forensic program. If a child is ordered to receive such services, the services shall be provided by the Department of Children and Families. The competency determination must be reviewed at least every 6 months, or at the end of any extended period of treatment or training, and any time the child appears to have attained competency or will never attain competency, by the service provider. A copy of a written report evaluating the child's competency must be filed by the provider with the court, the Department of Children and Families, the Department of Juvenile Justice, the state, and counsel for the child.

(9) *Speedy Trial Tolled.* Upon the filing of a motion by the child's counsel alleging the child to be incompetent to proceed or upon an order of the court finding a child incompetent to proceed, speedy trial shall be tolled until a subsequent finding of the court that the child is competent to proceed. Proceedings under this subdivision initiated by the court on its own motion or the state's motion may toll the speedy trial period pursuant to rule 8.090(e).

(b) Insanity at Time of Delinquent Act or Violation of Juvenile Probation.

(1) If the child named in the petition intends to plead insanity as a defense, the child shall advise the court in writing not less than 10 days before the adjudicatory hearing and shall provide the court with a statement of particulars showing as nearly as possible the nature of the insanity expected to be proved and the names and addresses of witnesses expected to prove it. Upon the filing of this statement, on motion of the state, or on its own motion, the court may cause the child to be examined in accordance with the procedures in this rule.

(2) The court, upon good cause shown and in its discretion, may waive these requirements and permit the introduction of the defense, or may continue the hearing for the purpose of an examination in accordance with the procedures in this rule. A continuance granted for this purpose will toll the speedy trial rule and the limitation on detention pending adjudication.

(c) Appointment of Expert Witnesses; Detention of Child for Examination.

(1) When a question has been raised concerning the sanity or competency of the child named in the petition and the court has set the matter for an adjudicatory hearing, hearing on violation of juvenile probation, or a hearing to determine the mental condition of the child, the court may on its own motion, and shall on motion of the state or the child, appoint no more than 3, nor fewer than 2, disinterested qualified experts to examine the child as to competency or sanity of the child at the time of the commission of the alleged delinquent act or violation of juvenile probation. Attorneys for the state and the child may be present at the examination. An examination regarding sanity should take place at the same time as the examination into the competence of the child to proceed, if the issue of competency has been raised. Other competent evidence may be introduced at the hearing. The appointment of experts by the court shall not preclude the state or the child from calling other expert witnesses to testify at the adjudicatory hearing, hearing on violation of juvenile probation, or at the hearing to determine the mental condition of the child.

(2) The court only as provided by general law may order the child held in detention pending examination. This rule shall in no way be construed to add any detention powers not provided by statute or case law.

(3) When counsel for a child adjudged to be indigent or partially indigent, whether public defender or court appointed, shall have reason to believe that the child may be incompetent to proceed or may have been insane at the time of the alleged delinquent act or juvenile probation violation, counsel may so inform the court. The court shall appoint 1 expert to examine the child to assist in the preparation of the defense. The expert shall report only to counsel for the child, and all matters related to the expert shall be deemed to fall under the lawyer-client privilege.

(4) For competency evaluations related to intellectual disability, the court shall order the Developmental Services Program Office of the Department of Children and Families to examine the child to determine if the child meets the definition of intellectual disability in section 393.063, Florida Statutes, and, if so, whether the child is competent to proceed or amenable to treatment through the Department of Children and Families' intellectual disability services or programs.

(d) Competence to Proceed; Scope of Examination and Report.

(1) *Examination by Experts.* On appointment by the court, the experts shall examine the child with respect to the issue of competence to proceed as specified by the court in its order appointing the experts.

(A) The experts first shall consider factors related to whether the child meets the criteria for competence to proceed; that is, whether the child has sufficient present ability to consult with counsel with a reasonable degree of rational understanding and whether the child has a rational and factual understanding of the present proceedings.

(B) In considering the competence of the child to proceed, the examining experts shall consider and include in their reports the child's capacity to:

(i) appreciate the charges or allegations against the child;

(ii) appreciate the range and nature of possible penalties that may be imposed in the proceedings against the child, if applicable;

(iii) understand the adversary nature of the legal process;

(iv) disclose to counsel facts pertinent to the proceedings at issue;

(v) display appropriate courtroom behavior; and

(vi) testify relevantly.

The experts also may consider any other factors they deem to be relevant.

(C) Any report concluding that a child is not competent must include the basis for the competency determination.

(2) *Treatment Recommendations.* If the experts find that the child is incompetent to proceed, they shall report on any recommended treatment for the child to attain competence to proceed. A recommendation as to whether residential or nonresidential treatment or training is required must be included. In considering issues related to treatment, the experts shall report on the following:

(A) The mental illness, intellectual disability, or mental age causing incompetence.

(B) The treatment or education appropriate for the mental illness or intellectual disability of the child and an explanation of each of the possible treatment or education alternatives, in order of recommendation.

(C) The availability of acceptable treatment or education. If treatment or education is available in the community, the experts shall so state in the report.

(D) The likelihood of the child attaining competence under the treatment or education recommended, an assessment of the probable duration of the treatment required to restore competence, and the probability that the child will attain competence to proceed in the foreseeable future.

(E) Whether the child meets the criteria for involuntary hospitalization or involuntary admissions to residential services under chapter 985, Florida Statutes.

(3) *Insanity.* If a notice of intent to rely on an insanity defense has been filed before an adjudicatory hearing or a hearing on an alleged violation of juvenile probation, when ordered by the court the experts shall report on the issue of the child's sanity at the time of the delinquent act or violation of juvenile probation.

(4) *Written Findings of Experts.* Any written report submitted by the experts shall:

(A) identify the specific matters referred for evaluation;

(B) describe the procedures, techniques, and tests used in the examination and the purposes of each;

(C) state the expert's clinical observations, findings, and opinions on each issue referred for evaluation by the court and indicate specifically those issues, if any, on which the expert could not give an opinion; and

(D) identify the sources of information used by the expert and present the factual basis for the expert's clinical findings and opinions.

(5) *Limited Use of Competency Evidence.*

(A) The information contained in any motion by the child for determination of competency to proceed or in any report filed under this rule as it relates solely to the issues of competency to proceed and commitment, and any information elicited during a hearing on competency to proceed or commitment held under this rule, shall be used only in determining the mental competency to proceed, the commitment of the child, or other treatment of the child.

(B) The child waives this provision by using the report, or any parts of it, in any proceeding for any other purpose. If so waived, the disclosure or use of the report, or any portion of it, shall be governed by the applicable rules of evidence and juvenile procedure. If a part of a report is used by the child, the state may request the production of any other portion that, in fairness, ought to be considered.

(e) Procedures After Judgment of Not Guilty by Reason of Insanity.

(1) When the child is found not guilty of the delinquent act or violation of juvenile probation because of insanity, the court shall enter such a finding and judgment.

(2) After finding the child not guilty by reason of insanity, the court shall conduct a hearing to determine if the child presently meets the statutory criteria for involuntary commitment to a residential psychiatric facility.

(A) If the court determines that the required criteria have been met, the child shall be committed by the juvenile court to the Department of Children and Families for immediate placement in a residential psychiatric facility.

(B) If the court determines that such commitment criteria have not been established, the court, after hearing, shall order that the child receive recommended and appropriate treatment at an outpatient facility or service.

(C) If the court determines that treatment is not needed, it shall discharge the child.

(D) Commitment to a residential psychiatric facility of a child adjudged not guilty by reason of insanity shall be governed by the provisions of chapters 985 or 394, Florida Statutes, except that requests for discharge or continued involuntary hospitalization of the child shall be directed to the court that committed the child.

(E) If a child is not committed to a residential psychiatric facility and has been ordered to receive appropriate treatment at an outpatient facility or service and it appears during the course of the ordered treatment

(i) that treatment is not being provided or that the child now meets the criteria for hospitalization, the court shall conduct a hearing pursuant to subdivision (e)(2) of this rule.

(ii) that the child no longer requires treatment at an outpatient facility or service, the court shall enter an order discharging the child.

(F) During the time the child is receiving treatment, either by hospitalization or through an outpatient facility or service, any party may request the court to conduct a hearing to determine the nature, quality, and need for continued treatment. The hearing shall be conducted in conformity with subdivision (e)(2) of this rule.

(G) No later than 30 days before reaching age 19, a child still under supervision of the court under this rule shall be afforded a hearing. At the hearing, a determination shall be made as to the need for continued hospitalization or treatment. If the court determines that continued care is appropriate, proceedings shall be initiated under chapter 394, Florida Statutes. If the court determines further care to be unnecessary, the court shall discharge the child.

Former Rule 8.170 amended Aug. 31, 1982, effective Sept. 1, 1982 (418 So.2d 1004); Dec. 28, 1984, effective Jan. 1, 1985 (462 So.2d 399). Renumbered as new Rule 8.095 and amended May 9, 1991, effective July 1, 1991 (589 So.2d 818). Amended Jan. 26, 1995 (649 So.2d 1370); Oct. 31, 1996, effective Jan. 1, 1997 (684 So.2d 756); Oct. 26, 2000, effective Jan. 1, 2001 (783 So.2d 138); Oct. 3, 2013 (123 So.3d 1128).

F. HEARINGS

Rule 8.100. General Provisions for Hearings

Unless otherwise provided, the following provisions apply to all hearings:

(a) Presence of the Child. The child shall be present unless the court finds that the child's mental or physical condition is such that a court appearance is not in the child's best interests.

(b) Use of Restraints on the Child. Instruments of restraint, such as handcuffs, chains, irons, or straitjackets, may not be used on a child during a court proceeding and must be removed prior to the child's appearance before the court unless the court finds both that:

(1) The use of restraints is necessary due to one of the following factors:

(A) Instruments of restraint are necessary to prevent physical harm to the child or another person;

(B) The child has a history of disruptive courtroom behavior that has placed others in potentially harmful situations or presents a substantial risk of inflicting physical harm on himself or herself or others as evidenced by recent behavior; or

(C) There is a founded belief that the child presents a substantial risk of flight from the courtroom; and

(2) There are no less restrictive alternatives to restraints that will prevent flight or physical harm to the child or another person, including, but not limited to, the presence of court personnel, law enforcement officers, or bailiffs.

(c) Absence of the Child. If the child is present at the beginning of a hearing and during the progress of the hearing voluntarily absents himself or herself from the presence of the court without leave of the court, or is removed from the presence of the court because of disruptive conduct during the hearing, the hearing shall not be postponed or delayed, but shall proceed in all respects as if the child were present in court at all times.

(d) Invoking the Rule. Prior to the examination of any witness the court may, and on the request of any party in an adjudicatory hearing shall, exclude all other witnesses. The court may cause witnesses to be kept separate and to be prevented from communicating with each other until all are examined.

(e) Continuances. The court may grant a continuance before or during a hearing for good cause shown by any party.

(f) Record of Testimony. A record of the testimony in all hearings shall be made by an official court reporter, a court approved stenographer, or a recording device. The records shall be preserved for 5 years from the date of the hearing. Official records of testimony shall be provided only on request of a party or a party's attorney or on a court order.

(g) Notice. When these rules do not require a specific notice, all parties will be given reasonable notice of any hearing.

Former Rule 8.220 amended Dec. 28, 1984, effective Jan. 1, 1985 (462 So.2d 399). Renumbered as new Rule 8.100 and amended May 9, 1991, effective July 1, 1991 (589 So.2d 818). Amended Nov. 5, 1992, effective Jan. 1, 1993 (608 So.2d 478); Jan. 26, 1995 (649 So.2d 1370); April 29, 1999 (753 So.2d 541); July 6, 2000 (opinion withdrawn on denial of rehearing March 15, 2001); March 15, 2001 (796 So.2d 470); June 26, 2008 (985 So.2d 534); Dec. 17, 2009, effective Jan. 1, 2010 (26 So.3d 552).

Rule 8.104. Testimony by Closed–Circuit Television

(a) Requirements for Use. In any case the trial court may order the testimony of a victim or witness under the age of 16 to be taken outside the courtroom and shown by means of closed-circuit television if on motion and hearing in camera, the trial court determines that the victim or witness would suffer at least moderate emotional or mental harm due to the presence of the defendant child if the witness is required to testify in open court.

(b) Persons Who May File Motion. The motion may be filed by:

(1) the victim or witness or his or her attorney, parent, legal guardian, or guardian ad litem;

(2) the trial judge on his or her own motion;

(3) the prosecuting attorney; or

(4) the defendant child or his or her counsel.

(c) Person Who May Be Present During Testimony. Only the judge, prosecutor, witness or victim, attorney for the witness or victim, defendant child's attorney, operator of the equipment, an interpreter, and some other person who in the opinion of the court contributes to the well-being of the victim or witness and who will not be a witness in the case may be in the room during the recording of the testimony.

(d) Presence of Defendant Child. During the testimony of the victim or witness by closed-circuit television, the court may require the defendant child to view the testimony from the courtroom. In such case, the court shall permit the defendant child to observe and hear the testimony, but shall ensure that the victim or witness cannot hear or see the defendant child. The defendant child's right to assistance of counsel, which includes the right to immediate and direct communication with counsel conducting cross examination, shall be protected and, on the defendant child's request, such communication shall be provided by any appropriate electronic method.

(e) Findings of Fact. The court shall make specific findings of fact on the record as to the basis for its ruling under this rule.

(f) Time for Motion. The motion referred to in subdivision (a) may be made at any time with reasonable notice to each party.

Added Nov. 5, 1992, effective Jan. 1, 1993 (608 So.2d 478). Amended Jan. 26, 1995 (649 So.2d 1370).

Committee Notes

1992 Adoption. Addition of this rule is mandated by section 92.55, Florida Statutes (1989).

Rule 8.105. Waiver of Jurisdiction

(a) On Demand. On demand for waiver of jurisdiction, the court shall enter a written order setting forth the demand, waiving jurisdiction, and certifying the case for trial as if the child were an adult. The demand shall be made in the form provided by law prior to the commencement of an adjudicatory hearing. A certified copy of the order shall be furnished to the clerk of the court having jurisdiction to try the child as an adult and to the prosecuting officer of the said child within 5 days of the demand being made. The court may order that the child be delivered to the sheriff of the county in which the court that is to try the child is located.

(b) Involuntary Waiver; Hearing.

(1) As provided by law, the state attorney may or, if required, shall, file a motion requesting the court to waive its jurisdiction and certify the case to the appropriate court for trial as if the child were an adult.

(2) Following the filing of the motion of the state attorney, summons shall be issued and served in conformity with the provision of rule 8.040. A copy of the motion and a copy of the delinquency petition, if not already served, shall be attached to each summons.

(3) No plea to a petition shall be accepted by the court prior to the disposition of the motion to waive jurisdiction.

(4) After the filing of the report required by law, the court shall conduct a hearing on the motion to determine the existence of the criteria established by law for waiver of jurisdiction.

(5) After hearing as provided in this rule:

(A) The court may enter an order waiving jurisdiction and certifying the case for trial as if the child were an adult as provided by law. The order shall set forth the basis for waiver of jurisdiction and certification to the appropriate court, with copies provided to all parties and the department. A certified copy of the order shall be furnished to the clerk of the court having jurisdiction to try the child as an adult and to the prosecuting officer of the said court within 5 days of the date of the order. The child shall be delivered immediately to the sheriff of the county in which the court that is to try the child as an adult is located.

(B) The court may enter an order denying waiver of jurisdiction, and give reasons for this denial, as provided by law. If the waiver is denied, the same judge, with the consent of the child and the state, may proceed immediately with the adjudicatory hearing.

(c) Bail. If the child is delivered to the sheriff under subdivision (a) or (b) the court shall fix bail. A certified copy of the order shall be furnished to the sheriff.

Former Rule 8.150 amended Dec. 28, 1984, effective Jan. 1, 1985 (462 So.2d 399). Renumbered as new Rule 8.105 and amended May 9, 1991, effective July 1, 1991 (589 So.2d 818). Amended Oct. 31, 1996, effective Jan. 1, 1997 (684 So.2d 756).

Rule 8.110. Adjudicatory Hearings

(a) Appearances; Pleas. The child shall appear before the court at the time set and, unless a written plea has been filed, enter a plea of guilty, not guilty, or, with the consent of the court, nolo contendere.

(b) Preparation of Case. If the child pleads not guilty the court may proceed at once to an adjudicatory hearing, or may continue the case to allow sufficient time on the court calendar for a hearing or to give the state or the child a reasonable time for the preparation of the case.

(c) Trial by Judge. The adjudicatory hearing shall be conducted by the judge without a jury. At this hearing the court determines whether the allegations of the petition have been sustained.

(d) Testimony. The child may be sworn and testify in his or her own behalf. The child may be cross-examined as other witnesses. No child shall be compelled to give testimony against himself or herself, nor shall any prosecuting attorney be permitted to comment on the failure of the child to testify in his or her own behalf. A child offering no testimony in his or her own behalf except his or her own shall be entitled to the concluding argument.

(e) Joint and Separate Trials. When 2 or more children are alleged to have committed a delinquent act or violation of law, they shall be tried jointly unless the court in its discretion orders separate trials.

(f) Dismissal. If the court finds that the allegations in the petition have not been sustained, it shall enter an order so finding and dismissing the case.

(g) Dispositional Alternatives. If the court finds that the evidence supports the allegations of the petition, it may enter an order of adjudication or withhold adjudication as provided by law. If the pre-disposition report required by law is available, the court may proceed immediately to disposition or continue the case for a disposition hearing. If the report is not available, the court will continue the case for a disposition hearing and refer it to the appropriate agency or agencies for a study and recommendation. If the case is continued the court may order the child detained.

(h) Degree of Offense. If in a petition there is alleged an offense which is divided into degrees, the court may find the child committed an offense of the degree alleged or of any lesser degree.

(i) Specifying Offense Committed. If in a petition more than one offense is alleged the court shall state in its order which offense or offenses it finds the child committed.

(j) Lesser Included Offenses. On a petition on which the child is to be tried for any offense, the court may find the child committed:

(1) an attempt to commit the offense, if the attempt is an offense and is supported by the evidence; or

(2) any offense that as a matter of law is a necessarily included offense or a lesser included offense of the offense charged in the petition and is supported by the evidence.

(k) Motion for Judgment of Dismissal. If at the close of the evidence for the petitioner, the court is of the opinion that the evidence is insufficient to establish a prima facie case of guilt against the child, it may, or on the motion of the state attorney or the child shall, enter an order dismissing the petition for insufficiency of the evidence.

Former Rule 8.190 amended Dec. 28, 1984, effective Jan. 1, 1985 (462 So.2d 399); Aug. 25, 1988, effective Jan. 1, 1989 (536 So.2d 178). Renumbered as new Rule 8.110 and amended May 9, 1991, effective July 1, 1991 (589 So.2d 818). Amended Sept. 5, 2002, effective Jan. 1, 2003 (827 So.2d 219).

Rule 8.115. Disposition Hearing

(a) Information Available to Court. At the disposition hearing the court, after establishing compliance with the dispositional considerations, determinations, and discussions required by law, may receive any relevant and material evidence helpful in determining the proper disposition to be made. It shall include written reports required by law, and may include, but shall not be limited to, the child's need for substance abuse evaluation and/or treatment, and any psychiatric or psychological evaluations of the child that may be obtained and that are relevant and material. Such evidence may be received by the court and may be relied upon to the extent of its probative value, even though not competent in an adjudicatory hearing. In any case in which it is necessary or consented to by the parties that disposition be pronounced by a judge other than the judge who presided at the adjudicatory hearing or accepted a plea of guilty or nolo contendere, the sentencing judge shall not pronounce disposition until the judge becomes acquainted with what transpired at the adjudicatory hearing, or the facts concerning the plea and the offense, including any plea discussions if a plea of guilty or nolo contendere was entered.

(b) Appointment of Counsel. Counsel shall be appointed at all disposition hearings, including cases transferred from other counties and restitution hearings, if the child qualifies for such appointment and does not waive counsel in writing as required by rule 8.165.

(c) Disclosure. The child, the child's attorney, the child's parent or custodian, and the state attorney shall be entitled to disclosure of all information in the predisposition report and all reports and evaluations used by the department in the preparation of the report.

(d) Disposition Order. The disposition order shall be prepared and distributed by the clerk of the court. Copies shall be provided to the child, defense attorney, state attorney, and department representative.

Each case requires a separate disposition order. The order shall:

(1) state the name and age of the child;

(2) state the disposition of each count, specifying the charge title, degree of offense, and maximum penalty defined by statute and specifying the amount of time served in secure detention before disposition;

(3) state general and specific conditions or sanctions;

(4) make all findings of fact required by law;

(5) state the date and time when issued and the county and court where issued; and

(6) be signed by the court with the title of office.

(e) Fingerprints. The child's fingerprints shall be affixed to the order of disposition.

Former Rule 8.200 amended Dec. 28, 1984, effective Jan. 1, 1985 (462 So.2d 399). Renumbered as new Rule 8.115 and amended May 9, 1991, effective July 1, 1991 (589 So.2d 818). Amended Oct. 31, 1996, effective Jan. 1, 1997 (684 So.2d 756); Oct. 26, 2000, effective Jan. 1, 2001 (783 So.2d 138); June 21, 2007 (959 So.2d 250); Dec. 17, 2009, effective Jan. 1, 2010 (26 So.3d 552); May 23, 2013, effective July 1, 2013 (115 So.3d 286).

Committee Notes

1991 Amendment. (c) Section 985.23(3)(e), Florida Statutes, requires the court to fingerprint any child who is adjudicated or has adjudication withheld for a felony. This rule extends this requirement to all dispositions. Sentencing guidelines include scorable points for misdemeanor offenses as well as for felonies. This procedure also should assist in identifying juveniles who use false names and birthdates, which can result in the arrest of an innocent child whose name was used by the offender.

Rule 8.120. Post–Disposition Hearing

(a) Revocation of Juvenile Probation.

(1) A child who has been placed on juvenile probation may be brought before the court upon allegations of violation(s).

(2) Any proceeding alleging a violation shall be initiated by the filing of a sworn affidavit of the material facts supporting the allegation(s). The affidavit shall be executed by the child's juvenile probation officer or other person having actual knowledge of the facts. Copies of the affidavit shall be provided to the court, the state attorney, and the Department of Juvenile Justice.

(3) When revocation proceedings are sought by the state attorney or the Department of Juvenile Justice, the proceedings shall be initiated by the filing of a petition alleging violation of juvenile probation. The petition shall incorporate and reference the affidavit described in subdivision (a)(2). All such petitions must be signed and filed by legal counsel.

(4) The court may initiate revocation proceedings by the entry of an order initiating revocation proceedings. The order must incorporate and reference the affidavit described in subdivision (a)(2).

(5) All interested persons, including the child, shall have an opportunity to be heard. After such hearing, the court shall enter an order revoking, modifying, terminating, or continuing juvenile probation. Upon the revocation of juvenile probation, the court shall, when the child has been placed on juvenile probation and adjudication has been withheld, adjudicate the child delinquent. In all cases after a revocation of juvenile probation, the court shall enter a new disposition order.

(b) Retention of Authority over Discharge. When the court has retained authority over discharge of a delinquent child from placement or commitment as provided by law, prior to any discharge from placement or commitment, the Department of Juvenile Justice shall notify the court, the state attorney, the victim of the offense or offenses for which the child was placed under supervision of the department, and the child of its intention to discharge the child. Thereafter, any interested party may request a hearing, within the time prescribed by law, to address the discharge.

Former Rule 8.210 amended Dec. 28, 1984, effective Jan. 1, 1985 (462 So.2d 399). Renumbered as new Rule 8.120 and amended May 9, 1991, effective July 1, 1991 (589 So.2d 818). Amended Nov. 5, 1992, effective Jan. 1, 1993 (608 So.2d 478); Jan. 26, 1995 (649 So.2d 1370); Oct. 31, 1996, effective Jan. 1, 1997 (684 So.2d 756); Oct. 26, 2000, effective Jan. 1, 2001 (783 So.2d 138).

G. RELIEF FROM ORDERS AND JUDGMENTS

Rule 8.130. Motion for Rehearing

(a) Basis. After the court has entered an order ruling on a pretrial motion, an order of adjudication, or an order withholding adjudication, any party may move for rehearing upon one or more of the following grounds:

(1) That the court erred in the decision of any matter of law arising during the hearing.

(2) That a party did not receive a fair and impartial hearing.

(3) That any party required to be present at the hearing was not present.

(4) That there exists new and material evidence which, if introduced at the hearing, would probably have changed the court's decision and could not with reasonable diligence have been discovered before and produced at the hearing.

(5) That the court is without jurisdiction of the proceeding.

(6) That the judgment is contrary to the law and evidence.

(b) Time and Method.

(1) A motion for rehearing may be made and ruled upon immediately after the court announces its judgment but must be made within 10 days of the entry of the order being challenged.

(2) If the motion is made in writing, it shall be served as provided in these rules for service of other pleadings.

(3) A motion for rehearing shall toll the time for the taking of an appeal.

(c) Court Action.

(1) If the motion for rehearing is granted, the court may vacate or modify the order or any part thereof and allow additional proceedings as it deems just. It may enter a new judgment, and may order or continue the child in detention pending further proceedings.

(2) The court on its own initiative may vacate or modify any order within the time limitation provided in subdivision (b).

Former Rule 8.230 amended Dec. 28, 1984, effective Jan. 1, 1985 (462 So.2d 399); Aug. 25, 1988, effective Jan. 1, 1989 (536 So.2d 178). Renumbered as new Rule 8.130 and amended May 9, 1991, effective July 1, 1991 (589 So.2d 818). Amended Dec. 17, 2009, effective Jan. 1, 2010 (26 So.3d 552).

Rule 8.135. Correction of Disposition or Commitment Orders

(a) Correction. A court at any time may correct an illegal disposition or commitment order imposed by it. However, a party may not file a motion to correct under this subdivision during the time allowed for the filing of a motion under subdivision (b)(1) or during the pendency of a direct appeal.

(b) Motion to Correct Disposition or Commitment Error. A motion to correct any disposition or commitment order error, including an illegal disposition or commitment, may be filed as allowed by this subdivision. The motion must identify the error with specificity and provide a proposed correction. A response to the motion may be filed within 15 days either admitting or contesting the alleged error. Motions may be filed by the state under this subdivision only if the correction of the error would benefit the child or to correct a scrivener's error.

(1) *Motion Before Appeal.* During the time allowed for the filing of a notice of appeal, a child, the state, or the department may file a motion to correct a disposition or commitment order error.

(A) This motion stays rendition under Florida Rule of Appellate Procedure 9.020(i).

(B) Unless the trial court determines that the motion can be resolved as a matter of law without a hearing, it shall hold an initial hearing no later than 10 days from the filing of the motion, with notice to all parties, for the express purpose of either ruling on the motion or determining the need for an evidentiary hearing. If an evidentiary hearing is needed, it shall be set no more than 10 days from the date of the initial hearing. Within 30 days from the filing of the motion, the trial court shall file an order ruling on the motion. If no order is filed within 30 days, the motion shall be deemed denied.

(2) *Motion Pending Appeal.* If an appeal is pending, a child or the state may file in the trial court a motion to correct a disposition or commitment order error. The motion may be filed by appellate counsel and must be served before the party's first brief is served. A notice of pending motion to correct disposition or commitment error shall be filed in the appellate court, which notice shall automatically extend the time for the filing of the brief, until 10 days after the clerk of the circuit court transmits the supplemental record under Florida Rule of Appellate Procedure 9.140(f)(6).

(A) The motion shall be served on the trial court and on all trial and appellate counsel of record. Unless the motion expressly states that appellate counsel will represent the movant in the trial court, trial counsel will represent the movant on the motion under Florida Rule of Appellate Procedure 9.140(d). If the state is the movant, trial counsel will represent the child unless appellate counsel for the child notifies trial counsel and the trial court that appellate counsel will represent the child on the state's motion.

(B) The trial court shall resolve this motion in accordance with subdivision (b)(1)(B) of this rule.

(C) Under Florida Rule of Appellate Procedure 9.140(f)(6), the clerk of the circuit court shall supplement the appellate record with the motion, the order, any amended disposition, and, if designated, a transcript of any additional portion of the proceedings.

Former Rule 8.240 amended Dec. 28, 1984, effective Jan. 1, 1985 (462 So.2d 399). Renumbered as new Rule 8.135 May 9, 1991, effective July 1, 1991 (589 So.2d 818). Amended Jan. 3, 2002, effective Jan. 15, 2002 (816 So.2d 536); Sept. 21, 2006, effective Jan. 1, 2007 (939 So.2d 74); Oct. 3, 2013 (123 So.3d 1128).

Rule 8.140. Extraordinary Relief

(a) Basis. On motion and upon such terms as are just, the court may relieve a party or the party's legal representative from an order, judgment, or proceeding for the following reasons:

(1) Mistake, inadvertence, surprise, or excusable neglect.

(2) Newly discovered evidence which by due diligence could not have been discovered in time to move for rehearing.

(3) Fraud (intrinsic or extrinsic), misrepresentation, or other misconduct of any other party.

(4) That the order or judgment is void.

(b) Time. The motion shall be made within a reasonable time and, for reasons (1), (2), and (3), not more than 1 year after the judgment, order, or proceeding was taken.

Former Rule 8.240(b) renumbered as Rule 8.250 and amended Dec. 28, 1984, effective Jan. 1, 1985 (462 So.2d 399). Renumbered as new Rule 8.140 and amended May 9, 1991, effective July 1, 1991 (589 So.2d 818).

Rule 8.145. Supersedeas on Appeal

(a) Granting of Supersedeas. The court in considering the welfare and best interest of the child and the interest of the public may grant a supersedeas in its discretion on such conditions as it may determine are appropriate.

(b) Preeminence of Rule. This rule shall be to the exclusion of any other court rule providing for supersedeas on appeal.

Former Rule 8.250 renumbered as Rule 8.260 and amended Dec. 28, 1984, effective Jan. 1, 1985 (462 So.2d 399). Renumbered as new Rule 8.145 May 9, 1991, effective July 1, 1991 (589 So.2d 818).

H. CONTEMPT

Rule 8.150. Contempt

(a) Direct Contempt. A contempt may be punished summarily if the court saw or heard the conduct constituting the contempt committed in the actual presence of the court. The judgment of guilt of contempt shall include a recital of those facts upon which the adjudication of guilt is based. Prior to the adjudication of guilt the court shall inform the person accused of the accusation and inquire as to whether there is any cause to show why he or she should not be adjudged guilty of contempt by the court and sentenced therefor. The accused shall be given the opportunity to present evidence of excusing or mitigating circumstances. The judgment shall be signed by the court and entered of record. Sentence shall be pronounced in open court.

(b) Indirect Contempt. An indirect contempt may be prosecuted in the following manner:

(1) *Order to Show Cause.* The court on its own motion or upon affidavit of any person having knowledge of the facts, may issue and sign an order directed to the one accused of contempt, stating the essential facts constituting the contempt charged and requiring the accused to appear before the court to show cause why he or she should not be held in contempt of court. The order shall specify the time and place of the hearing, with a reasonable time allowed for the preparation of a defense after service of the order on the one accused. It shall be served in the same manner as a summons. Nothing herein shall be construed to prevent the one accused of contempt from waiving the service of process.

(2) *Motions; Answer.* The accused, personally or by counsel, may move to dismiss the order to show cause, move for a statement of particulars, or answer such order by way of explanation or defense. All motions and the answers shall be in writing unless specified otherwise by the court. The accused's omission to file a motion or answer shall not be deemed an admission of guilt of the contempt charged.

(3) *Order of Arrest; Bail.* The court may issue an order of arrest of the one accused of contempt if the court has reason to believe the accused will not appear in response to the order to show cause. The accused shall be admitted to bail in the manner provided by law in criminal cases.

(4) *Arraignment; Hearing.* The accused may be arraigned at the hearing, or prior thereto upon request. A hearing to determine the guilt or innocence of the accused shall follow a plea of not guilty. The court may conduct a hearing without assistance of counsel or may be assisted by the state attorney or by an attorney appointed for that purpose. The accused is entitled to be represented by counsel, have compulsory process for the attendance of witnesses, and may testify in his or her own defense. All issues of law and fact shall be determined by the court.

(5) *Disqualification of the Judge.* If the contempt charged involves disrespect to or criticism of a judge, the judge shall be disqualified by the chief judge of the circuit.

(6) *Verdict; Judgment.* At the conclusion of the hearing the court shall sign and enter of record a judgment of guilty or not guilty. There should be included in a judgment of guilty a recital of the facts constituting the contempt of which the accused has been found and adjudicated guilty.

(7) *Sentence.* Prior to the pronouncement of sentence the court shall inform the accused of the accusation and judgment against him or her and inquire as to whether there is any cause to show why sentence should not be pronounced. The accused shall be afforded the opportunity to present evidence of mitigating circumstances. The sentence shall be pronounced in open court and in the presence of the one found guilty of contempt.

Former Rules 8.270 and 8.280 amended Dec. 28, 1984, effective Jan. 1, 1985 (462 So.2d 399). Renumbered as new Rule 8.150 and amended May 9, 1991, effective July 1, 1991 (589 So.2d 818).

I. GENERAL PROVISIONS

Rule 8.160. Transfer of Cases

The court may transfer any case, after adjudication or when adjudication is withheld, to the circuit court for the county of the circuit in which is located the domicile or usual residence of the child or such other circuit court as the court may determine to be for the best interest of the child. No case shall be transferred to another county under this rule unless a plea of nolo contendere or guilty has been entered by the child on the charge being transferred, or until the transferring court has found the child committed the offense in question after an adjudicatory hearing in the county where the offense occurred. Any action challenging the entry of a plea or the adjudicatory hearing result must be brought in the transferring court's county. The transferring court shall enter an order transferring its jurisdiction and certifying the case to the proper court. The transferring court shall furnish the following to the state attorney, the public defender, if counsel was previously appointed, and the clerk of the receiving court within 5 days:

(a) A certified copy of the order of transfer, which shall include, but not be limited to:

(1) specific offense that the child was found to have committed;

(2) degree of the offense;

(3) name of parent/custodian to be summoned;

(4) address at which the child should be summoned for disposition;

(5) name and address of victim;

(6) whether the child was represented by counsel; and

(7) findings of fact, after hearing or stipulation, regarding the amount of damages or loss caused directly or indirectly by the child's offense, for purposes of restitution.

(b) A certified copy of the delinquency petition.

(c) A copy of the juvenile referral or complaint.

(d) Any reports and all previous orders including orders appointing counsel entered by the court in the interest of that child.

Former Rule 8.060 renumbered as new Rule 8.160 Dec. 28, 1984, effective Jan. 1, 1985 (462 So.2d 399). Amended Aug. 25, 1988, effective Jan. 1, 1989 (536 So.2d 178); May 9, 1991, effective July 1, 1991 (589 So.2d 818); Nov. 5, 1992, effective Jan. 1, 1993 (608 So.2d 478).

Committee Notes

1991 Amendment. This rule requires the transferring court to provide sufficient information to the receiving court when transferring the case to another jurisdiction to comply with the requirements of chapter 39, Florida Statutes.

1992 Amendment. The purpose of this amendment is to require the court hearing the substantive charge to determine the value of the victim's damage or loss caused by the child's offense. The victim and witnesses necessary to testify as to damage and loss are more often residents of the transferring court's county, rather than the receiving court's.

Rule 8.165. Providing Counsel to Parties

(a) Duty of the Court. The court shall advise the child of the child's right to counsel. The court shall appoint counsel as provided by law unless waived by the child at each stage of the proceeding. Waiver of counsel can occur only after the child has had a meaningful opportunity to confer with counsel regarding the child's right to counsel, the consequences of waiving counsel, and any other factors that would assist the child in making the decision to waive counsel. This waiver shall be in writing.

(b) Waiver of Counsel.

(1) The failure of a child to request appointment of counsel at a particular stage in the proceedings or the child's announced intention to plead guilty shall not, in itself, constitute a waiver of counsel at any subsequent stage of the proceedings.

(2) A child shall not be deemed to have waived the assistance of counsel until the entire process of offering counsel has been completed and a thorough inquiry into the child's comprehension of that offer and the capacity to make that choice intelligently and understandingly has been made.

(3) If the child is entering a plea to or being tried on an allegation of committing a delinquent act, the written waiver shall also be submitted to the court in the presence of a parent, legal custodian, responsible adult relative, or attorney assigned by the court to assist the child, who shall verify on the written waiver that the child's decision to waive counsel has been discussed with the child and appears to be knowing and voluntary.

(4) No waiver shall be accepted if it appears that the party is unable to make an intelligent and understanding choice because of mental condition, age, education, experience, the nature or complexity of the case, or other factors.

(5) If a waiver is accepted at any stage of the proceedings, the offer of assistance of counsel shall be renewed by the court at each subsequent stage of the proceedings at which the party appears without counsel.

Former Rule 8.290 amended Dec. 28, 1984, effective Jan. 1, 1985 (462 So.2d 399); Aug. 25, 1988, effective Jan. 1, 1989 (536 So.2d 178). Renumbered as new Rule 8.165 and amended May 9, 1991, effective July 1, 1991 (589 So.2d 818). Amended Jan. 27, 2005 (894 So.2d 875); May 1, 2008, effective July 1, 2008 (981 So.2d 463).

Rule 8.170. Guardian Ad Litem

At any stage of the proceedings, the court may appoint a guardian ad litem for the child.

A guardian ad litem shall not be required to post bond but shall file an acceptance of the office.

Former Rule 8.300 amended Aug. 31, 1982, effective Sept. 1, 1982 (418 So.2d 1004); Dec. 28, 1984, effective Jan. 1, 1985 (462 So.2d 399). Renumbered as new Rule 8.170 May 9, 1991, effective July 1, 1991 (589 So.2d 818).

Rule 8.180. Computation and Enlargement of Time

(a) Computation. Computation of time shall be governed by Florida Rule of Judicial Administration 2.514, except for rules 8.013 and 8.010, to which rule 2.514(a)(2)(C) shall not apply and the statutory time period shall govern.

(b) Enlargement of Time. When by these rules or by a notice given thereunder or by order of court an act is required or allowed to be done at or within a specified time, the court for good cause shown may, at any time, in its discretion:

(1) with or without notice, order the period enlarged if request therefor is made before the expiration of the period originally prescribed or as extended by a previous order; or

(2) upon motion made and notice after the expiration of the specified period, permit the act to be done where the failure to act was the result of excusable neglect.

But it may not, except as provided by law or elsewhere in these rules, extend the time for making a motion for a new trial, a motion for rehearing, judgment of acquittal, vacation of judgment, or for taking an appeal. This rule shall not be construed to apply to detention hearings.

Former Rule 8.330 amended Dec. 28, 1984, effective Jan. 1, 1985 (462 So.2d 399). Renumbered as new Rule 8.180 and amended May 9, 1991, effective July 1, 1991 (589 So.2d 818). Amended July 12, 2012, effective Oct. 1, 2012 (95 So.3d 96).

Rule 8.185. Community Arbitration

(a) Referral. A case may be referred to community arbitration as provided by law. The chief judge of each judicial circuit shall maintain a list of qualified persons who have agreed to serve as community arbitrators for the purpose of carrying out the provisions of chapter 985, Florida Statutes.

(b) Arbitrator Qualifications. Each community arbitrator or member of a community arbitration panel shall be selected pursuant to law and shall meet the following minimum qualification and training requirements:

(1) Be at least 18 years of age.

(2) Be a person of the temperament necessary to deal properly with cases involving children and with the family crises likely to be presented.

(3) Pass a law enforcement records check and a Department of Children and Family Services abuse registry background check, as determined by the written guidelines developed by the chief judge of the circuit, the senior circuit court judge assigned to juvenile cases in the circuit, and the state attorney.

(4) Observe a minimum of 3 community arbitration hearings conducted by an approved arbitrator in a juvenile case.

(5) Conduct at least 1 juvenile community arbitration hearing under the personal observation of an approved community arbitrator.

(6) Successfully complete a training program consisting of not less than 8 hours of instruction including, but not limited to, instruction in:

(A) conflict resolution;

(B) juvenile delinquency law;

(C) child psychology; and

(D) availability of community resources.

The chief judge of the circuit, the senior circuit judge assigned to juvenile cases in the circuit, and the state attorney shall develop specific written guidelines for the training program and may specify additional qualifications as necessary.

Added Nov. 5, 1992, effective Jan. 1, 1993 (608 So.2d 478). Amended Oct. 26, 2000, effective Jan. 1, 2001 (783 So.2d 138); Sept. 5, 2002, effective Jan. 1, 2003 (827 So.2d 219).

Committee Notes

1992 Adoption. This rule provides qualification and training requirements for arbitrators as required by section 985.304(3), Florida Statutes. It was the committee's intention to set minimal qualifications and to allow local programs to determine additional requirements.

PART III. DEPENDENCY AND TERMINATION OF PARENTAL RIGHTS PROCEEDINGS

2012 Revision

Part III, "Dependency and Termination of Parental Rights Proceedings", added as Part II, was renumbered as Part III by Florida Supreme Court Opinion No. SC11-399 (102 So.3d 451).

Former Part III, "Proceedings for Families and Children in Need of Services", was renumbered as Part IV by Florida Supreme Court Opinion No. SC11-399 (102 So.3d 451).

A. GENERAL PROVISIONS

Rule 8.201. Commencement of Proceedings

(a) Commencement of Proceedings. Proceedings are commenced when:

(1) an initial shelter petition is filed;

(2) a petition alleging dependency is filed;

(3) a petition for termination of parental rights is filed;

(4) a petition for an injunction to prevent child abuse under chapter 39, Florida Statutes, is filed;

(5) a petition or affidavit for an order to take into custody is filed; or

(6) any other petition authorized by chapter 39, Florida Statutes, is filed.

(b) File to Be Opened. Upon commencement of any proceeding, the clerk shall open a file and assign a case number.

Former Rule 8.510 added Dec. 28, 1984, effective Jan. 1, 1985 (462 So.2d 399). Renumbered as new Rule 8.201 and amended May 9, 1991, effective July 1, 1991 (589 So.2d 818). Amended Sept. 18, 1998, effective Oct. 1, 1998 (724 So.2d 1153); Sept. 5, 2002, effective Jan. 1, 2003 (827 So.2d 219); Oct. 11, 2012 (101 So.3d 368); May 23, 2013, effective July 1, 2013 (115 So.3d 286).

Rule 8.203. Application of Uniform Child Custody Jurisdiction and Enforcement Act

Any pleading filed commencing proceedings as set forth in rule 8.201 shall be accompanied by an affidavit, to the extent of affiant's personal knowledge, under the Uniform Child Custody Jurisdiction and Enforcement Act. Each party has a continuing duty to inform the court of any custody proceeding in this or any other state of which information is obtained during the proceeding.

Former Rule 8.520 added Dec. 28, 1984, effective Jan. 1, 1985 (462 So.2d 399). Renumbered as new Rule 8.203 and amended May 9, 1991, effective July 1, 1991 (589 So.2d 818). Amended Jan. 27, 2005 (894 So.2d 875).

Rule 8.205. Transfer of Cases

(a) Transfer of Cases Within Circuit Court. If it should appear at any time in a proceeding initiated in a division other than the division of the circuit court assigned to handle dependency matters that facts are alleged that essentially constitute a dependency or the termination of parental rights, the court may upon consultation with the administrative judge assigned to dependency cases order the transfer of action and the transmittal of all relevant documents to the division assigned to handle dependency matters. The division assigned to handle dependency matters shall then assume jurisdiction only over matters pertaining to dependency, custody, visitation, and child support.

(b) Transfer of Cases Within the State of Florida. The court may transfer any case after adjudication, when adjudication is withheld, or before adjudication where witnesses are available in another jurisdiction, to the circuit court for the county in which is located the domicile or usual residence of the child or such other circuit as the court may determine to be for the best interest of the child and to promote the efficient administration of justice. The transferring court shall enter an order transferring its jurisdiction and certifying the case to the proper court, furnishing all parties, the clerk, and the attorney's office handling dependency matters for the state in the receiving court a copy of the order of transfer within 5 days. The clerk shall also transmit a certified copy of the file to the receiving court within 5 days.

(c) Transfer of Cases Among States. If it should appear at any time that an action is pending in another state, the court may transfer jurisdiction over the action to a more convenient forum state, may stay the proceedings, or may dismiss the action.

Former Rule 8.530 added Dec. 28, 1984, effective Jan. 1, 1985 (462 So.2d 399). Amended Aug. 25, 1988, effective Jan. 1, 1989 (536 So.2d 178). Renumbered as new Rule 8.205 and amended May 9, 1991, effective July 1, 1991 (589 So.2d 818). Amended Nov. 5, 1992, effective Jan. 1, 1993 (608 So.2d 478); Sept. 18, 1998, effective Oct. 1, 1998 (725 So.2d 296); Oct. 26, 2000, effective Jan. 1, 2001, (783 So.2d 138); Oct. 18, 2012, effective Dec. 1, 2012, April 1, 2013, Oct. 1, 2013 (102 So.3d 451).

Committee Notes

1992 Amendment. Plans under rule 8.327 were deleted in the 1991 revision to the rules, but are being reinstated as "stipulations" in the 1992 revisions. This change corrects the cross-reference.

Rule 8.210. Parties and Participants

(a) Parties. For the purpose of these rules the terms "party" and "parties" shall include the petitioner, the child, the parent(s) of the child, the department, and the guardian ad litem or the representative of the guardian ad litem program, when the program has been appointed.

(b) Participants. "Participant" means any person who is not a party but who should receive notice of hearings involving the child. Participants include foster parents or the legal custodian of the child, identified prospective parents, actual custodians of the child, grandparents entitled to notice of an adoption proceeding as provided by law, the state attorney, and any other person whose participation may be in the best interest of the child. The court may add additional participants. Participants may be granted leave by the court to be heard without the necessity of filing a motion to intervene and shall have no other rights of a party except as provided by law.

(c) Parent or Legal Custodian. For the purposes of these rules, when the phrase "parent(s) or legal custodian(s)" is used, it refers to the rights or responsibilities of the parent and, only if there is no living parent with intact parental rights, to the rights or responsibilities of the legal custodian who has assumed the role of the parent.

Former Rule 8.540 added Dec. 28, 1984, effective Jan. 1, 1985 (462 So.2d 399). Renumbered as new Rule 8.210 and amended May 9, 1991, effective July 1, 1991 (589 So.2d 818). Amended Nov. 5, 1992, effective Jan. 1, 1993 (608 So.2d 478); Sept. 28, 1995 (661 So.2d 800); Sept. 18, 1998, effective Oct. 1, 1998 (725 So.2d 296); June 10, 1999, effective July 1, 1999 (753 So.2d 1214); Oct. 26, 2000, effective Jan. 1, 2001 (783 So.2d 138); Sept. 5, 2002, effective Jan. 1, 2003 (827 So.2d 219); Sept. 21, 2006, effective Jan. 1, 2007 (939 So.2d 74).

Rule 8.215. Guardian Ad Litem

(a) Request. At any stage of the proceedings, any party may request or the court may appoint a guardian ad litem to represent any child alleged to be dependent.

(b) Appointment. The court shall appoint a guardian ad litem to represent the child in any proceeding as required by law and shall ascertain at each stage of the proceeding whether a guardian ad litem should be appointed if one has not yet been appointed.

(c) Duties and Responsibilities. The guardian ad litem shall be a responsible adult, who may or may not be an attorney, or a certified guardian ad litem program, and shall have the following responsibilities:

(1) To gather information concerning the allegations of the petition and any subsequent matters arising in the case and, unless excused by the court, to file a written report. This report shall include a summary of the guardian ad litem's findings, a statement of the wishes of the child, and the recommendations of the guardian ad litem and shall be provided to all parties and the court at least 72 hours before the hearing for which the report is prepared.

(2) To be present at all court hearings unless excused by the court.

(3) To represent the interests of the child until the jurisdiction of the court over the child terminates, or until excused by the court.

(4) To perform such other duties as are consistent with the scope of the appointment.

(d) Bond. A guardian ad litem shall not be required to post bond but shall file an acceptance of the office.

(e) Service. A guardian ad litem shall be entitled to receive service of pleadings and papers as provided by rule 8.225.

(f) Practice of Law by Lay Guardians. The duties of lay guardians shall not include the practice of law.

(g) Substitution or Discharge. The court, on its own motion or that of any party, including the child, may substitute or discharge the guardian ad litem for reasonable cause.

Former Rule 8.590 added Dec. 28, 1984, effective Jan. 1, 1985 (462 So.2d 399). Renumbered as new Rule 8.215 and amended May 9, 1991, effective July 1, 1991 (589 So.2d 818). Amended Oct. 31, 1996, effective Jan. 1, 1997 (684 So.2d 756); Sept. 18, 1998, effective Oct. 1, 1998 (725 So.2d 296); Oct. 26, 2000, effective Jan. 1, 2001 (783 So.2d 138).

Committee Notes

1991 Amendment. (c)(1) This section allows a report to be submitted before any hearing, not only the disposition hearing.

Rule 8.217. Attorney Ad Litem

(a) Request. At any stage of the proceedings, any party may request or the court may consider whether an attorney ad litem is necessary to represent any child alleged, or found, to be dependent, if one has not already been appointed.

(b) Appointment. The court may appoint an attorney ad litem to represent the child in any proceeding as allowed by law.

(c) Duties and Responsibilities. The attorney ad litem shall be an attorney who has completed any additional requirements as provided by law. The attorney ad litem shall have the responsibilities provided by law.

(d) Service. An attorney ad litem shall be entitled to receive and must provide service of pleadings and documents as provided by rule 8.225.

Added March 1, 2001 (796 So.2d 468). Amended Oct. 18, 2012, effective Dec. 1, 2012, April 1, 2013, Oct. 1, 2013 (102 So.3d 451).

Rule 8.220. Style of Pleading and Orders

All pleadings and orders shall be styled: "In the interest of ______, a child," or: "In the interest of ______, children."

Former Rule 8.600 added Dec. 28, 1984, effective Jan. 1, 1985 (462 So.2d 399). Renumbered as new Rule 8.220 May 9, 1991, effective July 1, 1991 (589 So.2d 818).

Rule 8.224. Permanent Mailing Address

(a) Designation. On the first appearance before the court, each party shall provide a permanent mailing address to the court. The court shall advise each party that this address will be used by the court, the petitioner, and other parties for notice unless and until the party notifies the court and the petitioner, in writing, of a new address.

(b) Effect of Filing. On the filing of a permanent address designation with the court, the party then has an affirmative duty to keep the court and the petitioner informed of any address change. Any address change must be filed with the court as an amendment to the permanent address designation.

(c) Service to Permanent Mailing Address. Service of any summons, notice, pleadings, subpoenas, or other papers to the permanent mailing address on file with the court will be presumed to be appropriate service.

Added Oct. 26, 2000, effective Jan. 1, 2001 (783 So.2d 183).

Rule 8.225. Process, Diligent Searches, and Service of Pleadings and Papers

(a) Summons and Subpoenas.

(1) *Summons.* Upon the filing of a dependency petition, the clerk shall issue a summons. The summons shall require the person on whom it is served to appear for a hearing at a time and place specified not less than 72 hours after service of the summons. A copy of the petition shall be attached to the summons.

(2) *Subpoenas.* Subpoenas for testimony before the court, for production of tangible evidence, and for taking depositions shall be issued by the clerk of the court, the court on its own motion, or any attorney of record for a party. Subpoenas may be served within the state by any person over 18 years of age who is not a party to the proceeding. In dependency and termination of parental rights proceedings, subpoenas may also be served by authorized agents of the department or the guardian ad litem. Except as otherwise required by this rule, the procedure for issuance of a subpoena by an attorney of record in a proceeding shall be as provided in the Florida Rules of Civil Procedure.

(3) *Service of Summons and Other Process to Persons Residing in the State.* The summons and other process shall be served upon all parties other than the petitioner as required by law. The summons and other process may be served by authorized agents of the department or the guardian ad litem.

(A) Service by publication shall not be required for dependency hearings and shall be required only for service of summons in a termination of parental rights proceeding for parents whose identities are known but whose whereabouts cannot be determined despite a diligent search. Service by publication in these circumstances shall be considered valid service.

(B) The failure to serve a party or give notice to a participant in a dependency hearing shall not affect the validity of an order of adjudication or disposition if the court finds that the petitioner has completed a diligent search that failed to ascertain the identity or location of that party.

(C) Personal appearance of any person in a hearing before the court eliminates the requirement for serving process upon that person.

(4) *Service of Summons and Other Process to Persons Residing Outside of the State in Dependency Proceedings.*

(A) Service of the summons and other process on parents, parties, participants, petitioners, or persons outside this state shall be in a manner reasonably calculated to give actual notice, and may be made:

(i) by personal delivery outside this state in a manner prescribed for service of process within this state;

(ii) in a manner prescribed by the law of the place in which service is made for service of process in that place in an action in any of its courts of general jurisdiction;

(iii) by any form of mail addressed to the person to be served and requesting a receipt; or

(iv) as directed by the court. Service by publication shall not be required for dependency hearings.

(B) Notice under this rule shall be served, mailed, delivered, or last published at least 20 days before any hearing in this state.

(C) Proof of service outside this state may be made by affidavit of the person who made the service or in the manner prescribed by the law of this state, the order pursuant to which the service is made, or the law of the place in which the service is made. If service is made by mail, proof may be in a receipt signed by the addressee or other evidence of delivery to the addressee.

(D) Personal appearance of any person in a hearing before the court eliminates the requirement for serving process upon that person.

(b) Diligent Search.

(1) *Location Unknown.* If the location of a parent is unknown and that parent has not filed a permanent address designation with the court, the petitioner shall complete a diligent search as required by law.

(2) *Affidavit of Diligent Search.* If the location of a parent is unknown after the diligent search has been completed, the petitioner shall file with the court an affidavit of diligent search executed by the person who made the search and inquiry.

(3) *Court Review of Affidavit.* The court must review the affidavit of diligent search and enter an order determining whether the petitioner has completed a diligent search as required by law. In termination of parental rights proceedings, the clerk must not certify a notice of action until the court enters an order finding that the petitioner has conducted a diligent search as required by law. In a dependency proceeding, if the court finds that the petitioner has conducted a diligent search, the court may proceed to grant the requested relief of the petitioner as to the parent whose location is unknown without further notice.

(4) *Continuing Duty.* After filing an affidavit of diligent search in a dependency or termination of parental rights proceeding, the petitioner, and, if the court requires, the department, are under a continuing duty to search for and attempt to serve the parent whose location is unknown until excused from further diligent search by the court. The department shall report on the results of the continuing search at each court hearing until the person is located or until further search is excused by the court.

(c) Identity of Parent Unknown.

(1) If the identity of a parent is unknown, and a petition for dependency, shelter care, or termination of parental rights is filed, the court shall conduct the inquiry required by law. The information required by law may be submitted to the court in the form of a sworn affidavit executed by a person having personal knowledge of the facts.

(2) If the court inquiry fails to identify any person as a parent or prospective parent, the court shall so find and may proceed to grant the requested relief of the petitioner as to the unknown parent without further notice.

(d) Identity and Location Determined. If an inquiry or diligent search identifies and locates any person who may be a parent or prospective parent, the court must require that notice of the hearing be provided to that person.

(e) Effect of Failure to Serve. Failure to serve parents whose identity or residence is unknown shall not affect the validity of an order of adjudication or disposition if the court finds the petitioner has completed a diligent search.

(f) Notice and Service of Pleadings and Papers.

(1) *Notice of Arraignment Hearings in Dependency Cases.* Notice of the arraignment hearing must be served on all parties with the summons and petition. The document containing the notice to appear in a dependency arraignment hearing must contain, in type at least as large as the balance of the document, the following or substantially similar language: "FAILURE TO PERSONALLY APPEAR AT THE ARRAIGNMENT HEARING CONSTITUTES CONSENT TO THE ADJUDICATION OF THIS CHILD (OR THESE CHILDREN) AS A DEPENDENT CHILD (OR CHILDREN) AND MAY ULTIMATELY RESULT IN LOSS OF CUSTODY OF THIS CHILD (OR THESE CHILDREN)." Any preadoptive parents of the children and all participants, including the child's foster parents and relative caregivers, must be notified of the arraignment hearing.

(2) *Notice of Assessment of Child Support.* Other than as part of a disposition order, if the court, on its own motion or at the request of any party, seeks to impose or enforce a child support obligation on any parent, all parties and participants are entitled to reasonable notice that child support will be addressed at a future hearing.

(3) *Notice of Hearings to Participants and Parties Whose Identity or Address are Known.* Any preadoptive parents, all participants, including foster parents and relative caregivers, and parties whose identity and address are known must be notified of all proceedings and hearings, unless otherwise provided by law. Notice involving emergency hearings must be that which is most likely to result in actual notice. It is the duty of the petitioner or moving party to notify any preadoptive parents, all participants, including foster parents and relative caregivers, and parties known to the petitioner or moving party of all hearings, except hearings which must be noticed by the court. Additional notice is not required if notice was provided to the parties in writing by the court or is contained in prior court orders and those orders were provided to the participant or party. All foster or preadoptive parents must be provided at least 72 hours notice, verbally or in writing, of all proceedings or hearings relating to children in their care or children they are seeking to adopt to ensure the ability to provide input to the court. This subdivision shall not be construed to require that any foster parent, preadoptive parent, or relative caregiver be made a party to the proceedings solely on the basis of notice and a right to be heard.

(4) *Service of Pleadings, Orders, and Papers.* Unless the court orders otherwise, every pleading, order, and paper filed in the action after the initial petition, shall be served on each party or the party's attorney. Nothing herein shall be construed to require that a

plea be in writing or that an application for witness subpoena be served.

(5) *Method of Service.* When service is required or permitted to be made upon a party or participant represented by an attorney, service shall be made upon the attorney unless service upon the party or participant is ordered by the court.

(A) Excusing of Service. Service is excused if the identity or residence of the party or participant is unknown and a diligent search for that person has been completed in accordance with law.

(B) Service by Electronic Mail ("e-mail"). Service of a document by e-mail is made by an e-mail sent to all addresses designated by the attorney or party with either (a) a copy of the document in PDF format attached or (b) a link to the document on a website maintained by a clerk.

(i) Service on Attorneys. Upon appearing in a proceeding, an attorney must designate a primary e-mail address and may designate no more than two secondary e-mail addresses to which service must be directed in that proceeding. Every document filed by an attorney thereafter must include the primary e-mail address of that attorney and any secondary e-mail addresses. If an attorney does not designate any e-mail address for service, documents may be served on that attorney at the e-mail address on record with The Florida Bar.

(ii) Exception to E-mail Service on Attorneys. Service by an attorney on another attorney must be made by e-mail unless the parties stipulate otherwise. Upon motion by an attorney demonstrating that the attorney has no e-mail account and lacks access to the Internet at the attorney's office, the court may excuse the attorney from the requirements of e-mail service. Service on and by an attorney excused by the court from e-mail service must be by the means provided in subdivision (c)(6) of this rule.

(iii) Service on and by Parties Not Represented by an Attorney. Any party not represented by an attorney may serve a designation of a primary e-mail address and also may designate no more than two secondary e-mail addresses to which service must be directed in that proceeding. If a party not represented by an attorney does not designate an e-mail address for service in a proceeding, service on and by that party must be by the means provided in subdivision (c)(6) of this rule.

(iv) Format of E–mail for Service. All documents served by e-mail must be sent by an e-mail message containing a subject line beginning with the words "SERVICE OF COURT DOCUMENT" in all capital letters, followed by the case number of the proceeding in which the documents are being served. The body of the e-mail must identify the court in which the proceeding is pending, the case number, the name of the initial party on each side, the title of each document served with that e-mail, and the sender's name and telephone number. Any e-mail which, together with its attachments, exceeds five megabytes (5MB) in size, must be divided and sent as separate e-mails, numbered in the subject line, no one of which may exceed 5MB in size.

(v) Time of Service. Service by e-mail is complete on the date sent and must be treated as service by mail for the computation of time. If the sender learns that the e-mail did not reach the address of the person to be served, the sender must immediately send another copy by e-mail or by a means authorized by subdivision (f)(6).

(6) *Service by Other Means.* In addition to, and not in lieu of, service by e-mail, service may also be made upon attorneys by any of the means specified in this subdivision. If a document is served by more than one method of service, the computation of time for any response to the served document shall be based on the method of service that provides the shortest response time. Service on and by all parties and participants who are not represented by an attorney and who do not designate an e-mail address, and on and by all attorneys excused from e-mail service, must be made by delivering a copy of the document or by mailing it to the party or participant at their permanent mailing address if one has been provided to the court or to the party, participant, or attorney at their last known address or, if no address is known, by leaving it with the clerk of the court. Service by mail is complete upon mailing. Delivery of a copy within this rule is complete upon:

(A) handing it to the attorney or to the party or participant,

(B) leaving it at the attorney's, party's or participant's office with a clerk or other person in charge thereof,

(C) if there is no one in charge, leaving it in a conspicuous place therein,

(D) if the office is closed or the person to be served has no office, leaving it at the person's usual place of abode with some person of his or her family above 15 years of age and informing such person of the contents, or

(E) transmitting it by facsimile to the attorney's, party's, or participant's office with a cover sheet containing the sender's name, firm, address, telephone number, and facsimile number, and the number of pages transmitted. When service is made by facsimile, a copy must also be served by any other method permitted by this rule. Facsimile service occurs when transmission is complete.

(F) Service by delivery shall be deemed complete on the date of the delivery.

(7) *Filing.* All documents must be filed with the court either before service or immediately thereafter.

If the original of any bond or other document is required to be an original and is not placed in the court file or deposited with the clerk, a certified copy must be so placed by the clerk.

(8) *Filing Defined.* The filing of documents with the court as required by these rules must be made by filing them with the clerk, except that the judge may permit documents to be filed with the judge, in which event the judge must note the filing date before him or her on the documents and transmit them to the clerk. The date of filing is that shown on the face of the document by the judge's notation or the clerk's time stamp, whichever is earlier.

(9) *Certificate of Service.* When any attorney certifies in substance:

"I certify that a copy hereof has been furnished to (here insert name or names and addresses used for service) by (e-mail) (delivery) (mail) (fax) on (date) ....

____
Attorney"

the certificate must be taken as prima facie proof of such service in compliance with this rule.

(10) *Service by Clerk.* When the clerk is required to serve notices and other documents, the clerk may do so by e-mail or by another method permitted under subdivision (c). Service by a clerk is not required to be by e-mail.

(11) *Service of Orders.*

(A) A copy of all orders or judgments must be transmitted by the court or under its direction to all parties at the time of entry of the order or judgment. No service need be made on parties against whom a default has been entered except orders setting an action for trial and final judgments that must be prepared and served as provided in subdivision (c)(11)(B). The court may require that orders or judgments be prepared by a party, may require the party to furnish the court with stamped addressed envelopes for service of the order or judgment, and may require that proposed orders and judgments be furnished to all parties before entry by the court of the order or judgment. The court may serve any order or judgment by e-mail to all attorneys who have not been excused from e-mail service and to all parties not represented by an attorney who have designated an email address for service.

(B) When a final judgment is entered against a party in default, the court must mail a conformed copy of it to the party. The party in whose favor the judgment is entered must furnish the court with a copy of the judgment, unless it is prepared by the court and with the address of the party to be served. If the address is unknown, the copy need not be furnished.

(C) This subdivision is directory and a failure to comply with it does not affect the order or judgment or its finality or any proceedings arising in the action.

Former Rule 8.630 added Dec. 28, 1984, effective Jan. 1, 1985 (462 So.2d 399). Amended March 1, 1990 (557 So.2d 1360). Renumbered as new Rule 8.225 and amended May 9, 1991, effective July 1, 1991 (589 So.2d 818). Amended Nov. 5, 1992, effective Jan. 1, 1993 (608 So.2d 478); Oct. 31, 1996, effective Jan. 1, 1997 (684 So.2d 756); Sept. 18, 1998, effective Oct. 1, 1998 (725 So.2d 296); June 10, 1999, effective July 1, 1999 (753 So.2d 214); Oct. 26, 2000, effective Jan. 1, 2001 (783 So.2d 138); Sept. 5, 2002, effective Jan. 1, 2003 (827 So.2d 219); Mar. 3, 2005 (898 So.2d 47); Sept. 25, 2008 (992 So.2d 242); Mar. 19, 2009 (5 So.3d 665); Oct. 18, 2012, effective, *nunc pro tunc*, Sept. 1, 2012 (102 So.3d 505); May 23, 2013, effective July 1, 2013 (115 So.3d 286); Oct. 3, 2013, effective Oct. 2, 2013 (123 So.3d 1139).

Rule 8.226. Determination of Parenthood

(a) In General. The court must determine the identity of all parents and prospective parents at the initial hearing in proceedings under chapter 39, Florida Statutes, as provided by law. Nothing in this rule prevents a parent or prospective parent from pursuing remedies under chapter 742, Florida Statutes. The court having jurisdiction over the dependency matter may conduct proceedings under chapter 742, Florida Statutes, either as part of the chapter 39, Florida Statutes, proceeding or in a separate action under chapter 742, Florida Statutes.

(b) Appearance of Prospective Parent.

(1) If a prospective parent appears in the chapter 39, Florida Statutes, proceeding, the court shall advise the prospective parent of the right to become a parent in the proceeding by completing a sworn affidavit of parenthood and filing the affidavit with the court or the department. This subdivision shall not apply if the court has identified both parents of the child as defined by law.

(2) If the prospective parent seeks to become a parent in the chapter 39, Florida Statutes, proceeding, the prospective parent shall complete a sworn affidavit of parenthood and file the affidavit with the court or the department. If a party objects to the entry of the finding that the prospective parent is a parent in the proceeding, or if the court on its own motion requires further proceedings to determine parenthood, the court shall not enter an order finding parenthood until proceedings under chapter 742, Florida Statutes, have been concluded. The prospective parent shall continue to receive notice of hearings as a participant pending the proceedings under chapter 742, Florida Statutes. If no other party objects and the court does not require further proceedings to determine parenthood, the court shall enter an order finding that the prospective parent is a parent in the proceeding.

(3) If the prospective parent is uncertain about parenthood and requests further proof of parenthood, or if there is more than one prospective parent for the

same child, the juvenile court may conduct proceedings under chapter 742, Florida Statutes, to determine parenthood. At the conclusion of the chapter 742, Florida Statutes, proceedings, the court shall enter an order determining parenthood.

(4) Provided that paternity has not otherwise been established by operation of law or court order, at any time prior to the court entering a finding that the prospective parent is the parent in the proceeding, the prospective parent may complete and file with the court or the department a sworn affidavit of nonpaternity declaring that the prospective parent is not the parent of the child and waiving all potential rights to the child and rights to further notices of hearing and court filings in the proceeding.

(5) If the court has identified both parents of a child as defined by law, the court shall not recognize an alleged biological parent as a parent in the proceeding until a court enters an order pursuant to law establishing the alleged biological parent as a parent in the proceeding.

Adopted May 23, 2013, effective July 1, 2013 (115 So.3d 286).

Rule 8.230. Pleadings to be Signed

(a) Pleading to Be Signed by Attorney. Every written document or pleading of a party represented by an attorney shall be signed in the attorney's individual name by such attorney, whose Florida Bar number, address, and telephone number, including area code, shall be stated and who shall be duly licensed to practice law in Florida. The attorney may be required by an order of court to vouch for the authority to represent such party and to give the address of such party. Except when otherwise specifically provided by these rules or applicable statute, pleadings as such need not be verified or accompanied by affidavit.

(b) Pleading to Be Signed by Unrepresented Party. A party who has no attorney but who represents himself or herself shall sign a written pleading or other document to be filed and state his or her address and telephone number, including area code.

(c) Effect of Signing Pleading. The signature of a person shall constitute a certificate that the document or pleading has been read; that to the best of the person's knowledge, information, and belief there is good ground to support it; and that it is not interposed for delay. If a pleading or document is not signed, or is signed with intent to defeat the purpose of this rule, it may be stricken and the action may proceed as though the pleading or document had not been filed.

Former Rule 8.640 added Dec. 28, 1984, effective Jan. 1, 1985 (462 So.2d 399). Renumbered as new Rule 8.230 and amended May 9, 1991, effective July 1, 1991 (589 So.2d 818). Amended Nov. 5, 1992, effective Jan. 1, 1993 (608 So.2d 478); Oct. 26, 2000, effective Jan. 1, 2001 (783 So.2d 138); Oct. 18, 2012, effective Dec. 1, 2012, April 1, 2013, Oct. 1, 2013 (102 So.3d 451).

Committee Notes

1991 Amendment. The current rule implies that a written pleading must be filed. No written pleadings are required.

1992 Amendments. (a) and (c) The language from (a) was moved to create this new subdivision. The current rule only applies to attorneys. These requirements also should apply to nonattorneys who sign and file papers. This change conforms to proposed changes for rules 8.085 and 8.640.

Rule 8.231. Providing Counsel to Dependent Children With Special Needs

(a) Duty of Court.

(1) The court shall appoint an attorney to represent any child who is determined to be a child of special needs and who is subject to any proceeding under chapter 39, Florida Statutes.

(A) The court must first request a recommendation from the Statewide Guardian Ad Litem Office for an attorney who is willing to represent a child without additional compensation. If such an attorney is available within 15 days after the court's request, the court must appoint that attorney.

(B) If no attorney is available to represent a child without compensation, the court must appoint a compensated attorney. A compensated attorney may be appointed within the 15–day period if the Statewide Guardian Ad Litem Office informs the court it will not be able to recommend an attorney within that time period.

(C) The appointment continues until the attorney is allowed to withdraw, is discharged by the court, or until the case is dismissed.

(D) The court order appointing an attorney must be in writing.

(b) Determination of Dependent Child of Special Needs.

(1) A dependent child of special needs is a child who:

(A) resides in a skilled nursing facility or is being considered for placement in a skilled nursing home;

(B) is prescribed psychotropic medication but declines assent to the psychotropic medication;

(C) has a diagnosis of a developmental disability as defined in section 393.063, Florida Statutes;

(D) is being placed in a residential treatment center or being considered for placement in a residential treatment center; or

(E) is a victim of human trafficking as defined in section 787.06(2)(d), Florida Statutes.

(c) Duties of Attorney. The attorney shall provide the child the complete range of legal services, from the removal from the home or from the initial appointment through all available appellate proceedings. With permission of the court, the attorney may arrange for supplemental or separate counsel to represent the child in appellate proceedings.

Added Feb. 19, 2015, effective Feb. 19, 2015 (158 So.3d 523).

Rule 8.235. Motions

(a) Motions in General. An application to the court for an order shall be made by motion which shall be in writing unless made during a hearing; shall be signed by the party making the motion or by the party's attorney; shall state with particularity the grounds therefor; and shall set forth the relief or order sought. The requirement of writing is fulfilled if the motion is stated in a written notice of the hearing of the motion or in a written report to the court for a scheduled hearing provided the notice or report are served on the parties as required by law.

(b) Motion to Dismiss. Any party may file a motion to dismiss any petition, allegations in the petition, or other pleading, setting forth the grounds on which the motion is based. If a motion to dismiss the petition is granted when a child is being sheltered under an order, the child may be continued in shelter under previous order of the court upon the representation that a new or amended petition will be filed.

(c) Sworn Motion to Dismiss. Before the adjudicatory hearing the court may entertain a motion to dismiss the petition or allegations in the petition on the ground that there are no material disputed facts and the undisputed facts do not establish a prima facie case of dependency. The facts on which such motion is based shall be specifically alleged and the motion sworn to by the party. The motion shall be filed a reasonable time before the date of the adjudicatory hearing. The opposing parties may traverse or demur to this motion. Factual matters alleged in it shall be deemed admitted unless specifically denied by the party. The motion shall be denied if the party files a written traverse that with specificity denies under oath the material fact or facts alleged in the motion to dismiss.

(d) Motion to Sever. A motion may be made for a severance of 2 or more counts of a multi-count petition, or for the severance of the cases of 2 or more children alleged to be dependent in the same petition. The court may grant motions for severance of jointly-brought cases for good cause shown.

Former Rule 8.740 added Dec. 28, 1984, effective Jan. 1, 1985 (462 So.2d 399). Renumbered as new Rule 8.235 and amended May 9, 1991, effective July 1, 1991 (589 So.2d 818). Amended Nov. 5, 1992, effective Jan. 1, 1993 (608 So.2d 478); June 10, 1999, effective July 1, 1999 (753 So.2d 1214); Oct. 26, 2000, effective Jan. 1, 2001 (783 So.2d 138); Dec. 17, 2009, effective Jan. 1, 2010 (26 So.3d 552).

Committee Notes

1992 Amendment. This rule allows any party to move for dismissal based on the grounds that there are no material facts in dispute and that these facts are not legally sufficient to prove dependency.

Rule 8.240. Computation, Continuance, Extension, and Enlargement of Time

(a) Computation. Computation of time shall be governed by Florida Rule of Judicial Administration 2.514, except for rules 8.300 and 8.305, to which rule 2.514(a)(2)(C) shall not apply and the statutory time period shall govern.

(b) Enlargement of Time. When by these rules, by a notice given under them, or by order of court an act is required or allowed to be done at or within a specified time, the court for good cause shown, within the limits established by law, and subject to the provisions of subdivision (d) of this rule, may, at any time, in its discretion (1) with or without notice, order the period enlarged if a request is made before the expiration of the period originally prescribed or as extended by a previous order, or (2) on motion made and notice after the expiration of the specified period permit the act to be done when the failure to act was the result of excusable neglect. The court may not, except as provided by law or elsewhere in these rules, extend the time for making a motion for new trial, for rehearing, or vacation of judgment, or for taking an appeal. This rule shall not be construed to apply to shelter hearings.

(c) Time for Service of Motions and Notice of Hearing. A copy of any written motion that may not be heard ex parte and a copy of the notice of hearing shall be served a reasonable time before the time specified for the hearing.

(d) Continuances and Extensions of Time.

(1) A motion for continuance, extension, or waiver of the time standards provided by law and found in this rule shall be in writing and signed by the requesting party. On a showing of good cause, the court shall allow a motion for continuance or extension to be made ore tenus at any time during the proceedings.

(2) A motion for continuance, extension, or waiver of the time standards provided by law shall not be made in advance of the particular circumstance or need that would warrant delay of the proceedings.

(3) A motion for continuance, extension, or waiver of the time standards provided by law shall state all of the facts that the movant contends entitle the movant to a continuance, extension, or waiver of time including:

(A) the task that must be completed by the movant to preserve the rights of a party or the best interests of the child who is the subject of the proceedings;

(B) the minimum number of days absolutely necessary to complete this task; and

(C) the total number of days the proceedings have been continued at the request of any party within any 12–month period.

(4) These time limitations do not include the following:

(A) Periods of delay resulting from a continuance granted at the request of the child's counsel or the child's guardian ad litem or, if the child is of sufficient capacity to express reasonable consent, at the request of or with the consent of the child.

(B) Periods of delay because of unavailability of evidence that is material to the case if the requesting party has exercised due diligence to obtain the evidence and there are substantial grounds to believe that the evidence will be available within 30 days. However, if the requesting party is not prepared to proceed within 30 days, any other party may move for issuance of an order to show cause or the court on its own motion may impose appropriate sanctions, which may include dismissal of the petition.

(C) Periods of delay to allow the requesting party additional time to prepare the case and additional time is justified because of an exceptional circumstance.

(D) Reasonable periods of delay necessary to accomplish notice of the hearing to the parent or legal custodian.

(5) Notwithstanding subdivision (4), proceedings may not be continued or extended for more than a total of 60 days for all parties within any 12–month period. A continuance or extension of time standards beyond 60 days in any 12–month period may be granted only on a finding by the court of extraordinary circumstances and that the continuance or extension of time standards is necessary to preserve the constitutional rights of a party or that there is substantial evidence demonstrating that the child's best interests will be affirmatively harmed without the granting of a continuance or extension of time.

Former Rule 8.620 added Dec. 28, 1984, effective Jan. 1, 1985 (462 So.2d 399). Renumbered as new Rule 8.240 and amended May 9, 1991, effective July 1, 1991 (589 So.2d 818). Amended Sept. 18, 1998, effective Oct. 1, 1998 (725 So.2d 296); Oct. 26, 2000, effective Jan. 1, 2001 (783 So.2d 138); Jan. 27, 2005 (894 So.2d 875); Feb. 8, 2007 (951 So.2d 804); July 12, 2012, effective Oct. 1, 2012 (95 So.3d 96).

Rule 8.245. Discovery

(a) Scope of Discovery. Unless otherwise limited by the court in accordance with these rules, the scope of discovery is as follows:

(1) *In General.* Parties may obtain discovery regarding any matter, not privileged, that is relevant to the subject matter of the pending action, whether it relates to the claim or defense of the party seeking discovery or the claim or defense of any other party, including the existence, description, nature, custody, condition, and location of any books, documents, or other tangible things and the identity and location of persons having knowledge of any discoverable matter. It is not ground for objection that the information sought will be inadmissible at the hearing if the information sought appears reasonably calculated to lead to the discovery of admissible evidence.

(2) *Claims of Privilege or Protection of Trial Preparation Materials.* When a party withholds information otherwise discoverable under these rules by claiming that it is privileged or subject to protection as trial preparation material, the party shall make the claim expressly and describe the nature of the document, communications, or things not produced or disclosed in a manner that, without revealing information itself privileged or protected, will allow other parties to assess the applicability of the privilege or protection.

(b) Required Disclosure.

(1) At any time after the filing of a shelter petition, a petition alleging a child to be a dependent child, or a petition for termination of parental rights, on written demand of any party, the party to whom the demand is directed shall disclose and permit inspecting, copying, testing, or photographing matters material to the cause. If the child had no living parent with intact parental rights at the time the dependency allegations arose, then the person who was serving as the legal custodian of the child at that time is entitled to obtain discovery during the pendency of a shelter or dependency petition.

(2) The following information shall be disclosed by any party on demand:

(A) The names and addresses of all persons known to have information relevant to the proof or defense of the petition's allegations.

(B) The statement of any person furnished in compliance with the preceding paragraph. The term "statement" means a written statement made by this person and signed or otherwise adopted or approved by the person, or a stenographic, mechanical, electronic, or other recording, or a transcript of it, or that is a substantially verbatim recital of an oral statement made by this person to an officer or agent of the state and recorded contemporaneously with the making of the oral statement. The court may prohibit any party from introducing in evidence the material not disclosed, to secure and maintain fairness in the just determination of the cause.

(C) Any written or recorded statement and the substance of any oral statement made by the demanding party or a person alleged to be involved in the same transaction. If the number of oral statements made to any person are so numerous that, as a practical matter, it would be impossible to list the substance of all the oral statements, then the party to whom the demand is directed will disclose that person's identity and the fact that this person has knowledge of numerous statements. This disclosure will allow the demanding party to depose that person.

(D) Tangible papers or objects belonging to the demanding party that are to be used at the adjudicatory hearing.

(E) Reports or statements of experts, including results of physical or mental examinations and of scientific tests, experiments, or comparisons.

(3) The disclosures required by subdivision (a)[1] of this rule shall be made within 10 days from the receipt of the demand for them. Disclosure may be made by allowing the requesting party to review the files of the party from whom discovery is requested after redaction of nondiscoverable information.

(c) Limitations on Disclosure.

(1) On application, the court may deny or partially restrict disclosure authorized by this rule if it finds there is a substantial risk to any person of physical harm, intimidation, bribery, economic reprisals, or unnecessary annoyance or embarrassment resulting from the disclosure, that outweighs any usefulness of the disclosure to the party requesting it.

(2) Disclosure shall not be required of legal research or of records, correspondence, or memoranda, to the extent that they contain the opinion, theories, or conclusions of the parties' attorneys or members of their legal staff.

(d) Production of Documents and Things for Inspection and Other Purposes.

(1) *Request; Scope.* Any party may request any other party

(A) to produce and permit the party making the request, or someone acting on the requesting party's behalf, to inspect and copy any designated documents, including writings, drawings, graphs, charts, photographs, phono-records, and other data compilations from which information can be obtained, translated, if necessary, by the party to whom the request is directed through detection devices into reasonably usable form, that constitute or contain matters within the scope of subdivision (a) and that are in the possession, custody, or control of the party to whom the request is directed; and

(B) to inspect and copy, test, or sample any tangible things that constitute or contain matters within the scope of subdivision (a) and that are in the possession, custody, or control of the party to whom the request is directed.

(2) *Procedure.* Without leave of court the request may be served on the petitioner after commencement of proceedings and on any other party with or after service of the summons and initial petition on that party. The request shall set forth the items to be inspected, either by individual item or category, and describe each item and category with reasonable particularity. The request shall specify a reasonable time, place, and manner of making the inspection or performing the related acts. The party to whom the request is directed shall serve a written response within 15 days after service of the request, except that a respondent may serve a response within 30 days after service of the process and initial pleading on that respondent. The court may allow a shorter or longer time. For each item or category the response shall state that inspection and related activities will be permitted as requested unless the request is objected to, in which event the reasons for the objection shall be stated. If an objection is made to part of an item or category, the part shall be specified. When producing documents, the producing party shall either produce them as they are kept in the usual course of business or shall identify them to correspond with the categories in the request. The party submitting the request may move for an order under subdivision (k) concerning any objection, failure to respond to the request, or any part of it, or failure to permit inspection as requested.

(3) *Persons Not Parties.* This rule does not preclude an independent action against a person not a party for production of documents and things.

(4) *Filing of Documents.* Unless required by the court, a party shall not file any of the documents or things produced with the response. Documents or things may be filed when they should be considered by the court in determining a matter pending before the court.

(e) Production of Documents and Things Without Deposition.

(1) *Request; Scope.* A party may seek inspection and copying of any documents or things within the scope of subdivision (d)(1) from a person who is not a party by issuance of a subpoena directing the production of the documents or things when the requesting party does not seek to depose the custodian or other person in possession of the documents or things.

(2) *Procedure.* A party desiring production under this rule shall serve notice on every other party of the intent to serve a subpoena under this rule at least 5 days before the subpoena is issued if service is by delivery and 10 days before the subpoena is issued if service is by mail. The proposed subpoena shall be attached to the notice and shall state the time, place, and method for production of the documents or things, and the name and address of the person who is to produce the documents or things, if known, and if not known, a general description sufficient to identify the person or the particular class or group to which the person belongs; shall include a designation of the items to be produced; and shall state that the person who will be asked to produce the documents or things has the right to object to the production under this rule and that the person will not be required to surrender the documents or things. A copy of the notice and proposed subpoena shall not be furnished to the person on whom the subpoena is to be served. If any party serves an objection to production under this rule within 10 days of service of the notice, the

documents or things shall not be produced under this rule and relief may be obtained under subdivision (g).

(3) *Subpoena.* If no objection is made by a party under subdivision (e)(2), an attorney of record in the action may issue a subpoena or the party desiring production shall deliver to the clerk for issuance a subpoena and a certificate of counsel or pro se party that no timely objection has been received from any party. The clerk shall issue the subpoena and deliver it to the party desiring production. The subpoena shall be identical to the copy attached to the notice, shall specify that no testimony may be taken, and shall require only production of the documents or things specified in it. The subpoena may give the recipient an option to deliver or mail legible copies of the documents or things to the party serving the subpoena. The person on whom the subpoena is served may condition the preparation of copies on the payment in advance of the reasonable costs of preparing the copies. The subpoena shall require production only in the county of the residence of the custodian or other person in possession of the documents or things or in the county where the documents or things are located or where the custodian or person in possession usually conducts business. If the person on whom the subpoena is served objects at any time before the production of the documents or things, the documents or things shall not be produced under this rule, and relief may be obtained under subdivision (g).

(4) *Copies Furnished.* If the subpoena is complied with by delivery or mailing of copies as provided in subdivision (e)(3), the party receiving the copies shall furnish a legible copy of each item furnished to any other party who requests it on the payment of the reasonable cost of preparing the copies.

(5) *Independent Action.* This rule does not affect the right of any party to bring an independent action for production of documents and things.

(f) Protective Orders. On motion by a party or by the person from whom discovery is sought, and for good cause shown, the court in which the action is pending may make any order to protect a party or person from annoyance, embarrassment, oppression, or undue burden or expense that justice requires, including one or more of the following:

(1) that the discovery not be had;

(2) that the discovery may be had only on specified terms and conditions, including a designation of the time or place;

(3) that the discovery may be had only by a method of discovery other than that selected by the party seeking discovery;

(4) that certain matters not be inquired into, or that the scope of the discovery be limited to certain matters;

(5) that discovery be conducted with no one present except persons designated by the court;

(6) that a deposition after being sealed be opened only by order of the court;

(7) that confidential research or information not be disclosed or be disclosed only in a designated way; and

(8) that the parties simultaneously file specified documents or information enclosed in sealed envelopes to be opened as directed by the court.

If the motion for a protective order is denied in whole or in part, the court may, on such terms and conditions as are just, order that any party or person provide or permit discovery.

(g) Depositions.

(1) *Time and Place.*

(A) At any time after the filing of the petition alleging a child to be dependent or a petition for termination of parental rights, any party may take the deposition on oral examination of any person who may have information relevant to the allegations of the petition.

(B) The deposition shall be taken in a building in which the adjudicatory hearing may be held, in another place agreed on by the parties, or where the trial court may designate by special or general order. A resident of the state may be required to attend an examination only in the county in which he or she resides, is employed, or regularly transacts business in person.

(2) *Procedure.*

(A) The party taking the deposition shall give written notice to each other party. The notice shall state the time and place the deposition is to be taken and the name of each person to be examined.

(B) Subpoenas for taking depositions shall be issued by the clerk of the court, the court, or any attorney of record for a party.

(C) After notice to the parties the court, for good cause shown, may extend or shorten the time and may change the place of taking.

(D) Except as otherwise provided by this rule, the procedure for taking the deposition, including the scope of the examination and obtaining protective orders, shall be the same as that provided by the Florida Rules of Civil Procedure.

(3) *Use of Deposition.* Any deposition taken under this rule may be used at any hearing covered by these rules by any party for the following purposes:

(A) For the purpose of impeaching the testimony of the deponent as a witness.

(B) For testimonial evidence, when the deponent, whether or not a party, is unavailable to testify because of one or more of the following reasons:

(i) He or she is dead.

(ii) He or she is at a greater distance than 100 miles from the place of hearing or is out of the state, unless it appears that the absence of the witness was procured by the party offering the deposition.

(iii) The party offering the deposition has been unable to procure the attendance of the witness by subpoena.

(iv) He or she is unable to attend or testify because of age, illness, infirmity, or imprisonment.

(v) It has been shown on application and notice that such exceptional circumstances exist as to make it desirable, in the interest of justice and with due regard to the importance of presenting the testimony of witnesses orally in open court, to allow the deposition to be used.

(vi) The witness is an expert or skilled witness.

(4) *Use of Part of Deposition.* If only part of a deposition is offered in evidence by a party, an adverse party may require the party to introduce any other part that in fairness ought to be considered with the part introduced, and any party may introduce any other parts.

(5) *Refusal to Obey Subpoena.* A person who refuses to obey a subpoena served on the person for the taking of a deposition may be adjudged in contempt of the court from which the subpoena issued.

(6) *Limitations on Use.* Except as provided in subdivision (3), no deposition shall be used or read in evidence when the attendance of the witness can be procured. If it appears to the court that any person whose deposition has been taken has absented himself or herself by procurement, inducements, or threats by or on behalf of any party, the deposition shall not be read in evidence on behalf of that party.

(h) Perpetuating Testimony Before Action or Pending Appeal.

(1) *Before Action.*

(A) Petition. A person who desires to perpetuate the person's own testimony or that of another person regarding any matter that may be cognizable in any court of this state may file a verified petition in the circuit court in the county of the residence of any expected adverse party. The petition shall be titled in the name of the petitioner and shall show:

(i) that the petitioner expects to be a party to an action cognizable in a court of Florida, but is presently unable to bring it or cause it to be brought;

(ii) the subject matter of the expected action and the person's interest in it;

(iii) the facts that the person desires to establish by the proposed testimony and the reasons for desiring to perpetuate it;

(iv) the names or a description of the persons expected to be adverse parties and their names and addresses so far as known; and

(v) the names and addresses of the persons to be examined and the substance of the testimony expected to be elicited from each and asking for an order authorizing the petitioner to take the deposition of the persons to be examined named in the petition for the purpose of perpetuating their testimony.

(B) Notice and Service. The petitioner shall serve a notice on each person named in the petition as an expected adverse party, with a copy of the petition, stating that the petitioner will apply to the court at a time and place in the notice for an order described in the petition. At least 20 days before the date of the hearing, the notice shall be served either within or without the county in the manner provided by law for serving of summons. However, if service cannot with due diligence be made on any expected adverse party named in the petition, the court may order service by publication or otherwise and shall appoint an attorney for persons not served in the manner provided by law for service of summons. The attorney shall represent the adverse party and, if he or she is not otherwise represented, shall cross-examine the deponent.

(C) Order and Examination. If the court is satisfied that the perpetuation of the testimony may prevent a failure or delay of justice, it shall make an order designating or describing the persons whose depositions may be taken and specifying the subject matter of the examination and whether the deposition shall be taken on oral examination or written interrogatories. The deposition may then be taken in accordance with these rules and the court may make orders in accordance with the requirements of these rules. For the purpose of applying these rules to depositions for perpetuating testimony, each reference in them to the court in which the action is pending shall be deemed to refer to the court in which the petition for the deposition was filed.

(D) Use of Deposition. If a deposition to perpetuate testimony is taken under these rules, it may be used in any action involving the same subject matter subsequently brought in any court of Florida in accordance with the provisions of subdivision (g)(3).

(2) *Pending Appeal.* If an appeal has been taken from a judgment of any court or before the taking of an appeal if the time for it has not expired, the court in which the judgment was rendered may allow the taking of the depositions of witnesses to perpetuate their testimony for use in further proceedings in the court. In such case, the party who desires to perpetuate the testimony may move for leave to take the deposition on the same notice and service as if the action were pending in the court. The motion shall show the names and addresses of persons to be examined, the substance of the testimony expected to be elicited from each, and the reasons for perpetuating the testimony. If the court finds that the perpetua-

tion is proper to avoid a failure or delay in justice, it may make orders as provided for by this rule and the deposition may then be taken and used in the same manner and under the same conditions as are prescribed in these rules for depositions taken in actions pending in the court.

(3) *Perpetuation Action.* This rule does not limit the power of a court to entertain an action to perpetuate testimony.

(i) Rules Governing Depositions of Children Under 16.

(1) The taking of a deposition of a child witness or victim under the age of 16 may be limited or precluded by the court for good cause shown.

(2) The court, after proper notice to all parties and an evidentiary hearing, based on good cause shown, may set conditions for the deposition of a child under the age of 16 including:

(A) designating the place of the deposition;

(B) designating the length of time of the deposition;

(C) permitting or prohibiting the attendance of any person at the deposition;

(D) requiring the submission of questions before the examination;

(E) choosing a skilled interviewer to pose the questions;

(F) limiting the number or scope of the questions to be asked; or

(G) imposing any other conditions the court feels are necessary for the protection of the child.

(3) Good cause is shown based on, but not limited to, one or more of the following considerations:

(A) The age of the child.

(B) The nature of the allegations.

(C) The relationship between the child victim and the alleged abuser.

(D) The child has undergone previous interviews for the purposes of criminal or civil proceedings that were recorded either by videotape or some other manner of recording and the requesting party has access to the recording.

(E) The examination would adversely affect the child.

(F) The manifest best interests of the child require the limitations or restrictions.

(4) The court, in its discretion, may order the consolidation of the taking of depositions of a child under the age of 16 when the child is the victim or witness in a pending proceeding arising from similar facts or circumstances.

(j) Supplemental Discovery. If, subsequent to compliance with these rules, a party discovers additional witnesses, evidence, or material that the party would have been under a duty to disclose or produce at the time of the previous compliance, the party shall promptly disclose or produce such witnesses, evidence, or material in the same manner as required under these rules for initial discovery.

(k) Sanctions.

(1) If at any time during the course of the proceedings, it is brought to the attention of the court that a party has failed to comply with an applicable discovery rule or with an order issued under an applicable discovery rule, the court may:

(A) order the party to comply with the discovery or inspection of materials not previously disclosed or produced;

(B) grant a continuance;

(C) order a new hearing;

(D) prohibit the party from calling a witness not disclosed or introducing in evidence the material not disclosed; or

(E) enter an order that it deems just under the circumstances.

(2) Willful violation by counsel of an applicable discovery rule or an order issued under it may subject counsel to appropriate sanction by the court.

Former Rule 8.770 added Dec. 28, 1984, effective Jan. 1, 1985 (462 So.2d 399). Renumbered as new Rule 8.245 and amended May 9, 1991, effective July 1, 1991 (589 So.2d 818). Amended Jan. 26, 1995 (649 So.2d 1370); Sept. 18, 1998, effective Oct. 1, 1998 (725 So.2d 296); Oct. 26, 2000, effective Jan. 1, 2001 (783 So.2d 138); Sept. 5, 2002, effective Jan. 1, 2003 (827 So.2d 219); Jan. 27, 2005 (894 So.2d 875).

1 So in original, probably should read "subdivision (b)".

Committee Notes

1991 Amendment. (a)(1) Termination of parental rights proceedings have been added to discovery procedures.

Rule 8.250. Examinations, Evaluation, and Treatment

(a) Child. Mental or physical examination of a child may be obtained as provided by law.

(b) Parent, Legal Custodian, or Other Person who has Custody or is Requesting Custody. At any time after the filing of a shelter, dependency, or termination of parental rights petition, or after an adjudication of dependency or a finding of dependency when adjudication is withheld, when the mental or physical condition, including the blood group, of a parent, legal custodian, or other person who has custody or is requesting custody of a child is in controversy, any party may request the court to order the person to submit to a physical or mental examination or a substance abuse evaluation or assessment by a qualified professional. The order may be made only on good cause shown and after notice to the person to be examined and to all parties and shall specify the time, place, manner, conditions, and scope of the examination and the person or persons by whom it is to be made. The person whose examination is sought may, after receiving notice of the request for an examination, request a hearing seeking to quash the request. The court may, on its own motion, order a parent, legal custodian, or other person who has custody or is requesting custody to undergo such evaluation, treatment, or counseling activities as authorized by law.

Former Rule 8.750 added Dec. 28, 1984, effective Jan. 1, 1985 (462 So.2d 399). Renumbered as new Rule 8.250 and amended May 9, 1991, effective July 1, 1991 (589 So.2d 818). Amended Sept. 18, 1998, effective Oct. 1, 1998 (725 So.2d 296); Oct. 26, 2000, effective Jan. 1, 2001 (783 So.2d 138); Feb. 8, 2007 (951 So.2d 804).

Committee Notes

1991 Amendment. This rule allows any party to request an evaluation but provides a mechanism for a hearing to quash the request.

Rule 8.255. General Provisions for Hearings

(a) Presence of Counsel. The department must be represented by an attorney at every stage of these proceedings.

(b) Presence of Child.

(1) The child has a right to be present at all hearings.

(2) If the child is present at the hearing, the court may excuse the child from any portion of the hearing when the court determines that it would not be in the child's best interest to remain.

(3) If a child is not present at a hearing, the court shall inquire and determine the reason for the absence of the child. The court shall determine whether it is in the best interest of the child to conduct the hearing without the presence of the child or to continue the hearing to provide the child an opportunity to be present at the hearing.

(4) Any party may file a motion to require or excuse the presence of the child.

(c) Separate Examinations. The child and the parents, caregivers, or legal custodians of the child may be examined separately and apart from each other.

(d) Examination of Child; Special Protections.

(1) *Testimony by Child.* A child may be called to testify in open court by any party to the proceeding or the court, and may be examined or cross-examined.

(2) *In–Camera Examination.*

(A) On motion and hearing, the child may be examined by the court outside the presence of other parties as provided by law. The court shall assure that proceedings are recorded, unless otherwise stipulated by the parties.

(B) The motion may be filed by any party or the trial court on its own motion.

(C) The court shall make specific written findings of fact, on the record, as to the basis for its ruling. These findings may include but are not limited to:

(i) the age of the child;

(ii) the nature of the allegation;

(iii) the relationship between the child and the alleged abuser;

(iv) the likelihood that the child would suffer emotional or mental harm if required to testify in open court;

(v) whether the child's testimony is more likely to be truthful if given outside the presence of other parties;

(vi) whether cross-examination would adversely affect the child; and

(vii) the manifest best interest of the child.

(D) The child may be called to testify by means of closed-circuit television or by videotaping as provided by law.

(e) Invoking the Rule. Before the examination of any witness the court may, and on the request of any party shall, exclude all other witnesses. The court may cause witnesses to be kept separate and to be prevented from communicating with each other until all are examined.

(f) Continuances. As permitted by law, the court may grant a continuance before or during a hearing for good cause shown by any party.

(g) Record. A record of the testimony in all hearings shall be made by an official court reporter, a court-approved stenographer, or a recording device. The records of testimony shall be preserved as required by law. Official records of testimony shall be transcribed only on order of the court.

(h) Notice. When these rules do not require a specific notice, all parties will be given reasonable notice of any hearing.

(i) Advising Parents. At any hearing when it has been determined that reunification is not a viable alternative, and prior to the filing of the petition for termination of parental rights, the court shall advise the parent of the availability of private placement of the child with an adoption entity as defined in Chapter 63, Florida Statutes.

Former Rule 8.610 added Dec. 28, 1984, effective Jan. 1, 1985 (462 So.2d 399). Amended March 1, 1990 (557 So.2d 1360). Renumbered as new Rule 8.255 and amended May 9, 1991, effective July 1, 1991 (589 So.2d 818). Amended Nov. 5, 1992, effective Jan. 1, 1993 (608 So.2d 478); Sept. 18, 1998, effective Oct. 1, 1998 (725 So.2d 296); Oct. 26, 2000, effective Jan. 1, 2001 (783 So.2d 138); Sept. 5, 2002, effective Jan. 1, 2003 (827 So.2d 219); Jan. 27, 2005 (894 So.2d 875); April 26, 2012, effective June 1, 2012 (88 So.3d 142); Oct. 3, 2013, effective Oct. 3, 2013 (123 So.3d 1128).

Committee Notes

1991 Amendment. (b) This change allows a child to be present instead of mandating the child's presence when the child's presence would not be in his or her best interest. The court is given the discretion to determine the need for the child to be present.

1992 Amendment. This change was made to reflect a moderated standard for in-camera examination of a child less rigid than the criminal law standard adopted by the committee in the 1991 rule revisions.

2005 Amendment. Subdivision (i) was deleted because provisions for general masters were transferred to rule 8.257.

Rule 8.257. General Magistrates

(a) Appointment. Judges of the circuit court may appoint as many general magistrates from among the members of The Florida Bar in the circuit as the judges find necessary, and the general magistrates shall continue in office until removed by the court. The order of appointment shall be recorded. Every person appointed as a general magistrate shall take the oath required of officers by the Constitution and the oath shall be recorded before the magistrate discharges any duties of that office.

(b) Referral.

(1) *Consent.* No matter shall be heard by a general magistrate without an appropriate order of referral and the consent to the referral of all parties. Consent, as defined in this rule, to a specific referral, once given, cannot be withdrawn without good cause shown before the hearing on the merits of the matter referred. Consent may be express or implied in accordance with the requirements of this rule.

(2) *Objection.* A written objection to the referral to a general magistrate must be filed within 10 days of the service of the order of referral. If the time set for the hearing is less than 10 days after service of the order of referral, the objection must be filed before commencement of the hearing. Failure to file a written objection within the applicable time period is deemed to be consent to the order of referral.

(3) *Order.*

(A) The order of referral shall contain the following language in bold type:

A REFERRAL TO A GENERAL MAGISTRATE REQUIRES THE CONSENT OF ALL PARTIES. YOU ARE ENTITLED TO HAVE THIS MATTER HEARD BEFORE A JUDGE. IF YOU DO NOT WANT TO HAVE THIS MATTER HEARD BEFORE THE GENERAL MAGISTRATE, YOU MUST FILE A WRITTEN OBJECTION TO THE REFERRAL WITHIN 10 DAYS OF THE TIME OF SERVICE OF THIS ORDER. IF THE TIME SET FOR THE HEARING IS LESS THAN 10 DAYS AFTER THE SERVICE OF THIS ORDER, THE OBJECTION MUST BE MADE BEFORE THE HEARING. FAILURE TO FILE A WRITTEN OBJECTION WITHIN THE APPLICABLE TIME PERIOD IS DEEMED TO BE A CONSENT TO THE REFERRAL. REVIEW OF THE REPORT AND RECOMMENDATIONS MADE BY THE GENERAL MAGISTRATE SHALL BE BY EXCEPTIONS AS PROVIDED IN FLORIDA RULE OF JUVENILE PROCEDURE 8.257(f). A RECORD, WHICH INCLUDES A TRANSCRIPT OF PROCEEDINGS, ELECTRONIC RECORDING OF PROCEEDINGS, OR STIPULATION BY THE PARTIES OF THE EVIDENCE CONSIDERED BY THE GENERAL MAGISTRATE AT THE PROCEEDINGS, WILL BE REQUIRED TO SUPPORT THE EXCEPTIONS.

(B) The order of referral shall state with specificity the matter or matters being referred. The order of referral shall also state whether electronic recording or a court reporter is provided by the court.

(4) *Setting Hearing.* When a referral is made to a general magistrate, any party or the general magistrate may set the action for hearing.

(c) General Powers and Duties. Every general magistrate shall perform all of the duties that pertain to the office according to the practice in chancery and rules of court and under the direction of the court. A general magistrate shall be empowered to administer oaths and conduct hearings, which may include the taking of evidence. All grounds for disqualification of a judge shall apply to general magistrates.

(d) Hearings.

(1) The general magistrate shall assign a time and place for proceedings as soon as reasonably possible after the referral is made and give notice to each of the parties either directly or by directing counsel to file and serve a notice of hearing. If any party fails to appear, the general magistrate may proceed ex parte or may adjourn the proceeding to a future day, giving notice of the adjournment to the absent party. The general magistrate shall proceed with reasonable diligence in every referral and with the least delay practicable. Any party may apply to the court for an order to the general magistrate to speed the proceedings and to make the report and to certify to the court the reason for any delay.

(2) The general magistrate shall take testimony and establish a record which may be by electronic means as provided by Florida Rule of Judicial Administration 2.535(g)(3) or by a court reporter. The parties may not waive this requirement.

(3) The general magistrate shall have authority to examine under oath the parties and all witnesses on all matters contained in the referral, to require production of all books, papers, writings, vouchers, and other documents applicable to it, and to examine on oath orally all witnesses produced by the parties. The general magistrate may take all actions concerning evidence that can be taken by the circuit court and in

the same manner. The general magistrate shall have the same powers as a circuit judge to use communications equipment as defined and regulated by Florida Rule of Judicial Administration 2.530.

(4) The notice or order setting a matter for hearing shall state whether electronic recording or a court reporter is provided by the court. If the court provides electronic recording, the notice shall also state that any party may provide a court reporter at that party's expense, subject to the court's approval.

(e) Report.

(1) The general magistrate shall file a report that includes findings of fact, conclusions of law, and recommendations and serve copies on all parties. If a court reporter was present, the report shall contain the name and address of the reporter.

(2) The report and recommendations shall contain the following language in bold type:

SHOULD YOU WISH TO SEEK REVIEW OF THE REPORT AND RECOMMENDATIONS MADE BY THE GENERAL MAGISTRATE, YOU MUST FILE EXCEPTIONS WITHIN 10 DAYS OF SERVICE OF THE REPORT AND RECOMMENDATIONS IN ACCORDANCE WITH FLORIDA RULE OF JUVENILE PROCEDURE 8.257(f). YOU WILL BE REQUIRED TO PROVIDE THE COURT WITH A RECORD SUFFICIENT TO SUPPORT YOUR EXCEPTIONS WITHIN 10 DAYS OF SERVICE OF THE REPORT AND RECOMMENDATIONS OR YOUR EXCEPTIONS WILL BE DENIED. A RECORD ORDINARILY INCLUDES A TRANSCRIPT OF PROCEEDINGS, ELECTRONIC RECORDING OF PROCEEDINGS, OR STIPULATION BY THE PARTIES OF THE EVIDENCE CONSIDERED BY THE GENERAL MAGISTRATE AT THE PROCEEDINGS. THE PERSON SEEKING REVIEW MUST HAVE THE TRANSCRIPT PREPARED FOR THE COURT'S REVIEW.

(f) Exceptions. The parties may file exceptions to the report within 10 days from the time it is served on them. Any party may file cross-exceptions within 5 days from the service of the exceptions. However, the filing of cross-exceptions shall not delay the hearing on the exceptions unless good cause is shown. If no exceptions are filed within that period, the court shall take appropriate action on the report. If exceptions are filed, they shall be heard on reasonable notice by either party or the court.

(g) Record.

(1) For the purpose of the hearing on exceptions, a record, substantially in conformity with this rule, shall be provided to the court by the party seeking review. The record shall consist of

(A) the court file;

(B) all depositions and evidence presented to the general magistrate; and

(C) the transcript of the proceedings, electronic recording of the proceedings, or stipulation by the parties of the evidence considered by the general magistrate at the proceedings.

(2) The transcript of the proceedings, electronic recording of the proceedings, or stipulation by the parties of the evidence considered by the general magistrate at the proceedings, if any, shall be delivered to the judge and provided to all other parties not less than 48 hours before the hearing on exceptions.

(3) If less than a full transcript or electronic recording of the proceedings taken before the general magistrate is ordered prepared by the excepting party, that party shall promptly file a notice setting forth the portions of the transcript or electronic recording that have been ordered. The responding party shall be permitted to designate any additional portions of the transcript or electronic recording necessary to the adjudication of the issues raised in the exceptions or cross-exceptions.

(4) The cost of the original and all copies of the transcript or electronic recording of the proceedings shall be borne initially by the party seeking review. Should any portion of the transcript or electronic recording be required as a result of a designation filed by the responding party, the party making the designation shall bear the initial cost of the additional transcript or electronic recording.

(h) Prohibition on Magistrate Presiding over Certain Hearings. Notwithstanding the provisions of this rule, a general magistrate shall not preside over a shelter hearing under section 39.402, Florida Statutes, an adjudicatory hearing under section 39.507, Florida Statutes, or an adjudicatory hearing under section 39.809, Florida Statutes.

Added Jan. 27, 2005 (894 So.2d 875). Amended Sept. 21, 2006, effective. Jan. 1, 2007 (939 So.2d 74); Feb. 8, 2007 (951 So.2d 804); Dec. 17, 2009, effective Jan. 1, 2010 (26 So.3d 552).

Rule 8.260. Orders

(a) General Requirements. All orders of the court must be reduced to writing as soon after they are entered as is consistent with orderly procedure, and must contain specific findings of fact and conclusions of law, and must be signed by the judge as provided by law.

(b) Transmittal to Parties. A copy of all orders must be transmitted by the court or under its direction to all parties at the time of entry of the order.

(c) Other Options. The court may require

(1) that orders be prepared by a party;

(2) that the party serve the order; and

(3) on a case-by-case basis, that proposed orders be furnished to all parties before entry of the order by the court.

(d) Precedence of Orders. Orders of the circuit court hearing dependency matters must be filed in any dissolution or other custody action or proceeding involving the same child. These orders must take precedence over other orders affecting the placement of, access to, parental time with, adoption of, or parental rights and responsibilities for the same minor child, unless jurisdiction has been terminated. These orders may be filed under seal and need not be open to inspection by the public.

Former Rule 8.650 added Dec. 28, 1984, effective Jan. 1, 1985 (462 So.2d 399). Renumbered as new Rule 8.260 and amended May 9, 1991, effective July 1, 1991 (589 So.2d 818). Amended Oct. 26, 2000, effective Jan. 1, 2001 (783 So.2d 138); May 23, 2013, effective July 1, 2013 (115 So.3d 286).

Rule 8.265. Motion for Rehearing

(a) Basis. After the court has entered an order, any party may move for rehearing upon one or more of the following grounds:

(1) That the court erred in the decision of any matter of law arising during the hearing.

(2) That a party did not receive a fair and impartial hearing.

(3) That any party required to be present at the hearing was not present.

(4) That there exists new and material evidence, which, if introduced at the hearing would probably have changed the court's decision and could not with reasonable diligence have been discovered before and produced at the hearing.

(5) That the court is without jurisdiction of the proceeding.

(6) That the judgment is contrary to the law and evidence.

(b) Time and Method.

(1) A motion for rehearing may be made and ruled upon immediately after the court announces its judgment but must be made within 10 days of the entry of the order.

(2) If the motion is made in writing, it shall be served as provided in these rules for service of other pleadings.

(3) A motion for rehearing shall not toll the time for the taking of an appeal. The court shall rule on the motion for rehearing within 10 days of filing or it is deemed denied.

(c) Court Action.

(1) A rehearing may be granted to all or any of the parties on all or any part of the issues. All orders granting a rehearing shall state the specific issues to be reheard.

(2) If the motion for rehearing is granted the court may vacate or modify the order or any part of it and allow additional proceedings as it deems just. It may enter a new judgment, and may order or continue the child in a shelter or out-of-home placement pending further proceedings.

(3) The court on its own initiative may vacate or modify any order within the time limitation provided in subdivision (b).

Former Rule 8.820 added Dec. 28, 1984, effective Jan. 1, 1985 (462 So.2d 399). Renumbered as new Rule 8.265 and amended May 9, 1991, effective July 1, 1991 (589 So.2d 818). Amended Oct. 31, 1996, effective Jan. 1, 1997 (684 So.2d 756); Sept. 5, 2002, effective Jan. 1, 2003 (827 So.2d 219); Dec. 17, 2009, effective Jan. 1, 2010 (26 So.3d 552).

Rule 8.270. Relief From Judgments or Orders

(a) Clerical Mistakes. Clerical mistakes in judgments, orders, or other parts of the record and errors therein arising from oversight or omission may be corrected by the court at any time on its own initiative or on motion of any party, after such notice, if any, as the court orders. During the pendency of an appeal such mistakes may be so corrected before the record on appeal is docketed in the appellate court and thereafter while the appeal is pending may be so corrected with leave of the appellate court.

(b) Extraordinary Relief. On motion and upon such terms as are just, the court may relieve a party or the party's legal representative from an order, judgment, or proceeding for the following reasons:

(1) Mistake, inadvertence, surprise, or excusable neglect.

(2) Newly discovered evidence which by due diligence could not have been discovered in time to move for rehearing.

(3) Fraud (intrinsic or extrinsic), misrepresentation, or other misconduct of any other party.

(4) That the order or judgment or any part thereof is void.

The motion shall be made within a reasonable time and for reasons (1), (2), and (3) not more than 1 year after the judgment, order, or proceeding was taken.

(c) Limitation. After the court loses jurisdiction of the cause, as provided by law, a motion for relief of judgment or order under subdivision (b) shall not be heard.

Former Rule 8.830 added Dec. 28, 1984, effective Jan. 1, 1985 (462 So.2d 399). Renumbered as new Rule 8.270 and amended May 9, 1991, effective July 1, 1991 (589 So.2d 818).

Rule 8.276. Appeal Procedures

Florida Rule of Appellate Procedure 9.146 generally governs appeals in juvenile dependency and termination of parental rights cases.

Added Nov. 12, 2009 (24 So.3d 47).

Rule 8.285. Criminal Contempt

(a) Direct Contempt. A contempt may be punished summarily if the court saw or heard the conduct constituting the contempt committed in the actual presence of the court. The judgment of guilt of contempt shall include a recital of those facts upon which the adjudication of guilt is based. Prior to the adjudication of guilt the court shall inform the person accused of the accusation and inquire as to whether there is any cause to show why he or she should not be adjudged guilty of contempt by the court and sentenced. The accused shall be given the opportunity to present evidence of excusing or mitigating circumstances. The judgment shall be signed by the court and entered of record. Sentence shall be pronounced in open court.

(b) Indirect Contempt. An indirect contempt shall be prosecuted in the following manner:

(1) *Order to Show Cause.* The court on its own motion or upon affidavit of any person having knowledge of the facts may issue and sign an order directed to the one accused of contempt, stating the essential facts constituting the contempt charged and requiring the accused to appear before the court to show cause why he or she should not be held in contempt of court. The order shall specify the time and place of the hearing, with a reasonable time allowed for the preparation of a defense after service of the order on the one accused. It shall be served in the same manner as a summons. Nothing herein shall be construed to prevent the one accused of contempt from waiving the service of process.

(2) *Motions; Answer.* The accused, personally or by counsel, may move to dismiss the order to show cause, move for a statement of particulars, or answer such order by way of explanation or defense. All motions and the answer shall be in writing unless specified otherwise by the court. The accused's omission to file a motion or answer shall not be deemed an admission of guilt of the contempt charged.

(3) *Order of Arrest; Bail.* The court may issue an order of arrest of the one accused of contempt if the court has reason to believe the accused will not appear in response to the order to show cause. The accused shall be entitled to bail in the manner provided by law in criminal cases.

(4) *Arraignment; Hearing.* The accused may be arraigned at the hearing, or prior thereto upon request. A hearing to determine the guilt or innocence of the accused shall follow a plea of not guilty. The court may conduct a hearing without assistance of counsel or may be assisted by the state attorney or by an attorney appointed for the purpose. The accused is entitled to be represented by counsel, have compulsory process for the attendance of witnesses, and may testify in his or her own defense. All issues of law and fact shall be determined by the court.

(5) *Disqualification of the Judge.* If the contempt charged involves disrespect to or criticism of a judge, the judge shall be disqualified by the chief judge of the circuit.

(6) *Verdict; Judgment.* At the conclusion of the hearing the court shall sign and enter of record a judgment of guilty or not guilty. There should be included in a judgment of guilty a recital of the facts constituting the contempt of which the accused has been found and adjudicated guilty.

(7) *Sentence.* Prior to the pronouncement of sentence the court shall inform the accused of the accusation and judgment against him or her and inquire as to whether there is any cause to show why sentence should not be pronounced. The accused shall be afforded the opportunity to present evidence of mitigating circumstances. The sentence shall be pronounced in open court and in the presence of the one found guilty of contempt.

Former Rules 8.860 and 8.870 added Dec. 28, 1984, effective Jan. 1, 1985 (462 So.2d 399). Renumbered as new Rule 8.285 and amended May 9, 1991, effective July 1, 1991 (589 So.2d 818). Amended May 23, 2013, effective July 1, 2013 (115 So.3d 286).

Rule 8.286. Civil Contempt

(a) Applicability. This rule governs indirect civil contempt proceedings in matters related to juvenile dependency. The use of civil contempt sanctions under this rule must be limited to those used to compel compliance with a court order or to compensate a movant for losses sustained as a result of a contemnor's willful failure to comply with a court order. Contempt sanctions intended to punish an offender or to vindicate the authority of the court are criminal in nature and are governed by rule 8.285.

(b) Motion and Notice. Civil contempt may be initiated by motion. The motion must recite the essential facts constituting the acts alleged to be contemptuous. No civil contempt may be imposed without notice to the alleged contemnor and without providing the alleged contemnor with an opportunity to be heard. The civil contempt motion and notice of hearing may be served by mail provided notice by mail is reasonably calculated to apprise the alleged contemnor of the pendency of the proceedings. The notice must specify the time and place of the hearing and must contain the following language: "FAILURE TO APPEAR AT THE HEARING MAY RESULT IN THE COURT ISSUING A WRIT OF BODILY ATTACHMENT FOR YOUR ARREST. IF YOU ARE ARRESTED, YOU MAY BE HELD IN JAIL UP TO 48 HOURS BEFORE A HEARING IS HELD."

(c) Hearing. In any civil contempt hearing, after the court makes an express finding that the alleged contemnor had notice of the motion and hearing:

(1) The court shall determine whether the movant has established that a prior order was entered and

that the alleged contemnor has failed to comply with all or part of the prior order.

(2) If the court finds the movant has established all of the requirements in subdivision (c)(1) of this rule, the court must,

(A) if the alleged contemnor is present, determine whether the alleged contemnor had the present ability to comply with the prior court order; or

(B) if the alleged contemnor fails to appear, set a reasonable purge based on the circumstances of the parties.

The court may issue a writ of bodily attachment and direct that, upon execution of the writ of bodily attachment, the alleged contemnor be brought before the court within 48 hours for a hearing on whether the alleged contemnor has the present ability to comply with the prior court order and, if so, whether the failure to comply is willful.

(d) Order and Sanctions. After hearing the testimony and evidence presented, the court must enter a written order granting or denying the motion for contempt.

(1) An order finding the alleged contemnor to be in contempt must contain a finding that a prior order was entered, that the alleged contemnor has failed to comply with the prior court order, that the alleged contemnor had the present ability to comply, and that the alleged contemnor willfully failed to comply with the prior court order. The order must contain a recital of the facts on which these findings are based.

(2) If the court grants the motion for contempt, the court may impose appropriate sanctions to obtain compliance with the order including incarceration, attorneys' fees and costs, compensatory or coercive fines, and any other coercive sanction or relief permitted by law provided the order includes a purge provision as set forth in subdivision (e) of this rule.

(e) Purge. If the court orders incarceration, a coercive fine, or any other coercive sanction for failure to comply with a prior order, the court must set conditions for purge of the contempt, based on the contemnor's present ability to comply. The court must include in its order a separate affirmative finding that the contemnor has the present ability to comply with the purge and the factual basis for that finding. The court may grant the contemnor a reasonable time to comply with the purge conditions. If the court orders incarceration but defers incarceration for more than 48 hours to allow the contemnor a reasonable time to comply with the purge conditions, and the contemnor fails to comply within the time provided, the movant must file an affidavit of noncompliance with the court. The court then may issue a writ of bodily attachment. Upon incarceration, the contemnor must be brought before the court within 48 hours for a determination of whether the contemnor continues to have the present ability to comply with the purge.

(f) Review after Incarceration. Notwithstanding the provisions of this rule, at any time after a contemnor is incarcerated, the court on its own motion or motion of any party may review the contemnor's present ability to comply with the purge and the duration of incarceration and modify any prior orders.

(g) Other Relief. When there is a failure to comply with a court order but the failure is not willful, nothing in this rule shall be construed as precluding the court from granting such relief as may be appropriate under the circumstances.

Adopted May 23, 2013, effective July 1, 2013 (115 So.3d 286).

Rule 8.290. Dependency Mediation

(a) Definitions. The following definitions apply to this rule:

(1) "Dependency matters" means proceedings arising under Chapter 39, Florida Statutes.

(2) "Dependency mediation" means mediation of dependency matters.

(3) "Mediation" means a process whereby a neutral third person called a mediator acts to encourage and facilitate the resolution of a dispute between two or more parties. It is an informal and nonadversarial process with the objective of helping the disputing parties reach a mutually acceptable and voluntary agreement. In mediation, decision-making authority rests with the parties. The role of the mediator includes, but is not limited to, assisting the parties in identifying issues, fostering joint problem-solving, and exploring settlement alternatives.

(b) Applicability. This rule applies only to mediation of dependency matters.

(c) Compliance with Statutory Time Requirements. Dependency mediation shall be conducted in compliance with the statutory time requirements for dependency matters.

(d) Referral. Except as provided by this rule, all matters and issues described in subdivision (a)(1) may be referred to mediation. All referrals to mediation shall be in written form, shall advise the parties of their right to counsel, and shall set a date for hearing before the court to review the progress of the mediation. The mediator or mediation program shall be appointed by the court or stipulated to by the parties. If the court refers the matter to mediation, the mediation order shall address all applicable provisions of this rule. The mediation order shall be served on all parties and on counsel under the provisions of the Florida Rules of Juvenile Procedure.

(e) Appointment of the Mediator.

(1) *Court Appointment.* The court, in the order of referral to mediation, shall appoint a certified dependency mediator selected by rotation or by such other procedures as may be adopted by administrative order of the chief judge in the circuit in which the action is pending.

(2) *Party Stipulation.* Within 10 days of the filing of the order of referral to mediation, the parties may agree upon a stipulation with the court designating:

(A) another certified dependency mediator, other than a senior judge presiding as a judge in that circuit, to replace the one selected by the judge; or

(B) a mediator, other than a senior judge, who is not certified as a mediator but who, in the opinion of the parties and upon review by the presiding judge, is otherwise qualified by training or experience to mediate all or some of the issues in the particular case.

(f) Fees. Dependency mediation referrals may be made to a mediator or mediation program that charges a fee. Any order of referral to a mediator or mediation program charging a fee shall advise the parties that they may timely object to mediation on grounds of financial hardship.On the objection of a party or the court's own motion, the court may, after considering the objecting party's ability to pay and any other pertinent information, reduce or eliminate the fee.

(g) Objection to Mediation. Within 10 days of the filing of the order of referral to mediation, any party or participant ordered to mediation may make a written objection to the court about the order of referral if good cause for such objection exists. If a party objects, mediation shall not be conducted until the court rules on the objection.

(h) Scheduling. The mediation conference may be held at any stage of the proceedings. Unless otherwise scheduled by the court, the mediator or the mediation program shall schedule the mediation conference.

(i) Disqualification of the Mediator. Any party may move to enter an order disqualifying a mediator for good cause. If the court rules that a mediator is disqualified from mediating a case, an order shall be entered with the name of a qualified replacement. Nothing in this provision shall preclude mediators from disqualifying themselves or refusing any assignment.

(j) Substitute Mediator. If a mediator agreed upon by the parties or appointed by a court cannot serve, a substitute mediator can be agreed upon or appointed in the same manner as the original mediator. A mediator shall not mediate a case assigned to another mediator without the agreement of the parties or approval of the court. A substitute mediator shall have the same qualifications as the original mediator.

(k) Discovery. Unless stipulated by the parties or ordered by the court, the mediation process shall not suspend discovery.

(*l*) Appearances.

(1) *Order Naming or Prohibiting Attendance of Parties.* The court shall enter an order naming the parties and the participants who must appear at the mediation and any parties or participants who are prohibited from attending the mediation. Additional participants may be included by court order or by mutual agreement of all parties.

(2) *Physical Presence of Adult Parties and Participants.* Unless otherwise agreed to by the parties or ordered by the court, any party or participant ordered to mediation shall be physically present at the mediation conference. Persons representing an agency, department, or program must have full authority to enter into an agreement that shall be binding on that agency, department, or program. In the discretion of the mediator, and with the agreement of the attending parties, dependency mediation may proceed in the absence of any party or participant ordered to mediation.

(3) *Appearance of Counsel.* In the discretion of the mediator, and with the agreement of the attending parties, dependency mediation may proceed in the absence of counsel unless otherwise ordered by the court.

(4) *Appearance of Child.* The court may prohibit the child from appearing at mediation upon determining that such appearance is not in the best interest of the child. No minor child shall be required to appear at mediation unless the court has previously determined by written order that it is in the child's best interest to be physically present. The court shall specify in the written order of referral to mediation any special protections necessary for the child's appearance.

(5) *Sanctions for Failure to Appear.* If a party or participant ordered to mediation fails to appear at a duly-noticed mediation conference without good cause, the court, on motion of any party or on its own motion, may impose sanctions. Sanctions against the party or participant failing to appear may include one or more of the following: contempt of court, an award of mediator fees, an award of attorney fees, an award of costs, or other remedies as deemed appropriate by the court.

(m) Caucus with Parties and Participants. During the mediation session, the mediator may meet and consult privately with any party, participant, or counsel.

(n) Continuances. The mediator may end the mediation session at any time and may set new times for reconvening the mediation. No further notification shall be required for parties or participants present at the mediation session.

(*o*) Report on Mediation.

(1) If agreement is reached on all or part of any matter or issue, including legal or factual issues to be determined by the court, the agreement shall be immediately reduced to writing, signed by the attending parties, and promptly submitted to the court by the mediator with copies to all parties and counsel.

(2) If the parties do not reach an agreement as to any matter as a result of mediation, the mediator shall report the lack of an agreement to the court without comment or recommendation.

(p) Court Hearing and Order On Mediated Agreement. On receipt of a full or partial mediation agreement, the court shall hold a hearing and enter an order accepting or rejecting the agreement consistent with the best interest of the child. The court may modify the terms of the agreement with the consent of all parties to the agreement.

(q) Imposition of Sanctions On Breach of Agreement. In the event of any breach or failure to perform under the court-approved agreement, the court, on a motion of any party or on its own motion, may impose sanctions. The sanctions may include contempt of court, vacating the agreement, imposition of costs and attorney fees, or any other remedy deemed appropriate by the court.

Added July 10, 1997 (696 So.2d 763). Amended Sept. 18, 1998, effective Oct. 1, 1998 (725 So.2d 296); Oct. 26, 2000, effective Jan. 1, 2001 (783 So.2d 138); Jan. 27, 2005 (894 So.2d 875); Nov. 3, 2005, effective Jan. 1, 2006 (915 So.2d 145); June 19, 2014, effective Oct. 1, 2014 (141 So.3d 1172).

Committee Notes

1997 Adoption. In considering the provision regarding the appearance of the child found in subsection (*l*)(4), the Supreme Court Mediation and Arbitration Rules Committee considered issues concerning the child's right to participate and be heard in mediation and the need to protect the child from participating in proceedings when such participation would not be in the best interest of the child. The Committee has addressed only the issue of mandating participation of the child in mediation. In circumstances where the court has not mandated that the child appear in mediation, the Committee believes that, in the absence of an order prohibiting the child from mediation, the participation of the child in mediation will be determined by the parties.

Whenever the court, pursuant to subdivision (p) determines whether to accept, reject, or modify the mediation agreement, the Committee believes that the court shall act in accordance with the confidentiality requirements of chapter 44, Florida Statutes.

Rule 8.292. Appointment and Discharge of Surrogate Parent

(a) Appointment. Unless appointed by the district school superintendent, the court must appoint a surrogate parent for a child known to the department who has or is suspected of having a disability when

(1) after reasonable efforts, no parent can be located; or

(2) a court of competent jurisdiction over a child under Chapter 39, Florida Statutes, has determined that no person has the authority under the Individuals with Disabilities Education Act, including the parent or parents subject to the dependency action, or no person has the authority, willingness, or ability to serve as the educational decision maker for the child without judicial action.

(b) Who May Be Appointed. The surrogate parent must meet the minimum criteria established by law.

(c) Recognition of Surrogate Parent. The dependency court and school district must recognize the initial individual appointed as surrogate parent.

(d) Duties and Responsibilities. The surrogate parent must be acquainted with the child and become knowledgeable about the child's disability and educational needs and

(1) must represent the child in all matters relating to identification, evaluation, and educational placement and the provision of a free and appropriate education to the child;

(2) must represent the interests and safeguard the rights of the child in educational decisions that affect the child, and enjoy all the procedural safeguards afforded a parent regarding the identification, evaluation, and educational placement of a student with a disability or a student who is suspected of having a disability; and

(3) does not have the authority to represent the interests of the child regarding the child's care, maintenance, custody, residential placement, or any other area not specifically related to the education of the child, unless the same person is appointed by the court for these other purposes.

(e) Notice of Appointment. When the court appoints a surrogate parent, notice must be provided as soon as practicable to the child's school.

(f) Substitution or Discharge. The court may, through a determination of the best interest of the child or as otherwise established by law, find that it is appropriate to substitute or discharge the surrogate parent. The surrogate parent must continue in the appointed role until discharged.

Added Oct. 1, 2009 (22 So.3d 9).

B. TAKING CHILDREN INTO CUSTODY AND SHELTER HEARINGS

Rule 8.300. Taking Into Custody

(a) Affidavit. An affidavit or verified petition may be filed alleging facts under existing law sufficient to establish grounds to take a child into custody. The affidavit or verified petition shall:

(1) be in writing and signed;

(2) specify the name, address, date of birth, and sex of the child, or, if unknown, designate the child by any name or description by which he or she can be identified with reasonable certainty;

(3) specify that the child is of an age subject to the jurisdiction of the court; and

(4) state the reasons the child should be taken into custody.

(b) Criteria for Order. The court may issue an order to take a child into custody based on sworn testimony meeting the criteria in subdivision (a).

(c) Order. The order to take into custody shall:

(1) be in writing and signed;

(2) specify the name, address, and sex of the child or, if unknown, designate the child by any name or description by which he or she can be identified with reasonable certainty;

(3) specify that the child is of an age subject to the jurisdiction of the court;

(4) state the reasons the child should be taken into custody;

(5) order that the child be held in a suitable place pending transfer of physical custody to an authorized agent of the department; and

(6) state the date when issued, and the county and court where issued.

Former Rule 8.700 added Dec. 28, 1984, effective Jan. 1, 1985 (462 So.2d 399). Renumbered as new Rule 8.300 and amended May 9, 1991, effective July 1, 1991 (589 So.2d 818). Amended Oct. 26, 2000, effective Jan. 1, 2001 (783 So.2d 138); Jan. 27, 2005 (894 So.2d 875).

Rule 8.305. Shelter Petition, Hearing, and Order

(a) Shelter Petition. If a child has been or is to be removed from the home and maintained in an out-of-home placement for more than 24 hours, the person requesting placement shall file a written petition that shall:

(1) specify the name, address, date of birth, and sex of the child or, if unknown, designate the child by any name or description by which he or she can be identified with reasonable certainty;

(2) specify the name and address, if known, of the child's parents or legal custodian and how each was notified of the shelter hearing;

(3) if the child has been removed from the home, state the date and time of the removal;

(4) specify that the child is of an age subject to the jurisdiction of the court;

(5) state the reasons the child needs to be placed in a shelter;

(6) list the reasonable efforts, if any, that were made by the department to prevent or eliminate the need for the removal or continued removal of the child from the home or, if no such efforts were made, a description of the emergency that prevented these efforts;

(7) recommend where the child is to be placed or the agency to be responsible for placement;

(8) if the children are currently not placed together, specify the reasonable efforts of the department to keep the siblings together after the removal from the home, why a foster home is not available to place the siblings, or why it is not in the best interest of the child that all the siblings be placed together in out-of-home care;

(9) specify ongoing visitation or interaction between the siblings or if sibling visitation or interaction is not recommended, specify why visitation or interaction would be contrary to the safety or well-being of the child; and

(10) be signed by the petitioner and, if represented by counsel, by the petitioner's attorney.

(b) Shelter Hearing.

(1) The parents or legal custodians of the child shall be given actual notice of the date, time, and location of the shelter hearing. If the parents are outside the jurisdiction of the court, are not known, cannot be located, or refuse or evade service, they shall be given such notice as best ensures their actual knowledge of the date, time, and location of the shelter hearing. If the parents or legal custodians are not present at the hearing, the person providing, or attempting to provide, notice to the parents or legal custodians shall advise the court in person or by sworn affidavit of the attempts made to provide notice and the results of those attempts.

(2) The court shall conduct an informal hearing on the petition within the time limits provided by law. The court shall determine at the hearing the existence of probable cause to believe the child is dependent and whether the other criteria provided by law for placement in a shelter have been met. The shelter hearing may be continued for up to 72 hours with the child remaining in shelter care if either:

(A) the parents or legal custodians appear for the shelter hearing without legal counsel and request a continuance to consult with legal counsel; or

(B) the court determines that additional time is necessary to obtain and review documents pertaining to the family to appropriately determine the risk to the child.

(3) The issue of probable cause shall be determined in a nonadversarial manner, applying the standard of proof necessary for an arrest warrant.

(4) At the hearing, all interested persons present shall have an opportunity to be heard and present evidence on the criteria for placement provided by law.

(5) The court may base its determination on a sworn complaint, testimony, or an affidavit and may hear all relevant and material evidence, including oral

and written reports, to the extent of its probative value even though it would not be competent at an adjudicatory hearing.

(6) The court shall advise the parent or legal custodian of:

(A) the right to be represented by counsel as provided by law;

(B) the reason the child is in custody and why continued placement is requested;

(C) the right to present placement alternatives; and

(D) the time, date, and location of the next hearing and of the importance of the parents' or legal custodians' active participation in subsequent proceedings and hearings.

(7) The court shall appoint:

(A) a guardian ad litem to represent the child unless the court finds representation unnecessary;

(B) an attorney ad litem to represent the child if the court finds the appointment necessary and authorized by law; and

(C) an attorney for indigent parents unless waived by the parent.

(8) The court shall determine visitation rights absent a clear and convincing showing that visitation is not in the best interest of the child.

(9) The court shall inquire of the parents whether the parents have relatives who might be considered for placement of the child. The parents shall provide to the court and all parties identification and location information regarding the relatives. The court shall advise the parents that the parents have a continuing duty to inform the department of any relative who should be considered for placement of the child.

(10) The court shall advise the parents that if the parents fail to substantially comply with the case plan their parental rights may be terminated and the child's out-of-home placement may become permanent.

(11) The court must request that the parents consent to provide access to the child's medical and educational records and provide information to the court, the department, or its contract agencies, and any guardian ad litem or attorney for the child. If a parent is unavailable, is unable to consent, or withholds consent and the court determines access to the records and information is necessary to provide services for the child, the court shall issue an order granting access.

(12) The court may order the parents to provide all known medical information to the department and to any others granted access.

(13) If the child has or is suspected of having a disability and the parent is unavailable pursuant to law, the court must appoint a surrogate parent or refer the child to the district school superintendent for appointment of a surrogate parent.

(14) If the shelter hearing is conducted by a judge other than a judge assigned to hear dependency cases, a judge assigned to hear dependency cases shall hold a shelter review on the status of the child within 2 working days after the shelter hearing.

(c) Shelter Order. An order granting shelter care must identify the parties present at the hearing and contain written findings that:

(1) placement in shelter care is necessary based on the criteria provided by law;

(2) placement in shelter care is in the best interest of the child;

(3) the department made reasonable efforts to keep the siblings together after the removal from the home and specifies if the children are currently not placed together, why a foster home is not available or why it is not in the best interest of the child that all the siblings be placed together in out-of-home care;

(4) specifies on-going visitation or interaction between the siblings or if sibling visitation or interaction is not recommended, specifies why visitation or interaction would be contrary to the safety or well-being of the child;

(5) continuation of the child in the home is contrary to the welfare of the child because the home situation presents a substantial and immediate danger to the child's physical, mental, or emotional health or safety that cannot be mitigated by the provision of preventive services;

(6) there is probable cause to believe the child is dependent;

(7) the department has made reasonable efforts to prevent or eliminate the need for removal of the child from the home, including a description of which specific services, if available, could prevent or eliminate the need for removal or continued removal from the home, the date by which the services are expected to become available, and, if services are not available to prevent or eliminate the need for removal or continued removal of the child from the home, an explanation of why the services are not available for the child;

(8) the court notified the parents or legal custodians of the time, date, and location of the next dependency hearing, and of the importance of their active participation in all subsequent proceedings and hearings; and

(9) the court notified the parents or legal custodians of their right to counsel as provided by law.

(d) Release from Shelter Care. No child shall be released from shelter care after a shelter order has been entered except on order of the court unless the shelter order authorized release by the department.

Former Rule 8.710 added Dec. 28, 1984, effective Jan. 1, 1985 (462 So.2d 399). Amended Aug. 25, 1988, effective Jan. 1, 1989 (536 So.2d 178); March 1, 1990 (557 So.2d 1360). Renumbered as new Rule 8.305 and amended May 9, 1991, effective July 1, 1991 (589 So.2d 818). Amended Oct. 31, 1996, effective Jan. 1, 1997 (684 So.2d 756); Sept. 18, 1998, effective Oct. 1, 1998 (725 So.2d 296); June 10, 1999, effective July 1, 1999 (753 So.2d 1214); Oct. 26, 2000, effective Jan. 1, 2001 (783 So.2d 138); March 1, 2001 (796 So.2d 468); Jan. 27, 2005 (894 So.2d 875); Feb. 8, 2007 (951 So.2d 804); Oct. 1, 2009 (22 So.3d 9); Feb. 19, 2015, effective Feb. 19, 2015 (158 So.3d 523).

C. PETITION, ARRAIGNMENT, ADJUDICATION, AND DISPOSITION

Rule 8.310. Dependency Petitions

(a) Contents.

(1) A dependency petition may be filed as provided by law. Each petition shall be entitled a petition for dependency and shall allege sufficient facts showing the child to be dependent based upon applicable law.

(2) The petition shall contain allegations as to the identity and residence of the parents or legal custodians, if known.

(3) The petition shall identify the age, sex, and name of the child. Two or more children may be the subject of the same petition.

(4) Two or more allegations of dependency may appear in the same petition, in separate counts. The petition need not contain allegations of acts or omissions by both parents.

(5) The petition must describe what voluntary services, safety planning and/or dependency mediation the parents or legal custodians were offered and the outcome of each.

(b) Verification. The petition shall be signed stating under oath the signer's good faith in filing the petition. No objection to a petition on the grounds that it was not signed or verified, as herein provided, shall be entertained after a plea to the merits.

(c) Amendments. At any time prior to the conclusion of an adjudicatory hearing, an amended petition may be filed or the petition may be amended by motion; however, after a written answer or plan has been filed, amendments shall be permitted only with the permission of the court, unless all parties consent. Amendments shall be freely permitted in the interest of justice and the welfare of the child. A continuance may be granted on motion and a showing that the amendment prejudices or materially affects any party.

(d) Defects and Variances. No petition or any count thereof shall be dismissed, or any judgment vacated, on account of any defect in the form of the petition or of misjoinder of counts. If the court is of the opinion that the petition is so vague, indistinct, and indefinite as to mislead the child, parent, or legal custodian and prejudice any of them in the preparation of a defense, the petitioner may be required to furnish a more definite statement.

(e) Voluntary Dismissal. The petitioner without leave of the court, at any time prior to entry of an order of adjudication, may request a voluntary dismissal of the petition or any allegations of the petition by serving a notice requesting dismissal on all parties, or, if during a hearing, by so stating on the record. The petition or any allegations in the petition shall be dismissed. If the petition is dismissed, the court loses jurisdiction unless another party adopts the petition within 72 hours.

Former Rule 8.720 added Dec. 28, 1984, effective Jan. 1, 1985 (462 So.2d 399). Amended Aug. 25, 1988, effective Jan. 1, 1989 (536 So.2d 178). Renumbered as new Rule 8.310 and amended May 9, 1991, effective July 1, 1991 (589 So.2d 818). Amended Sept. 18, 1998, effective Oct. 1, 1998 (725 So.2d 296); June 10, 1999, effective July 1, 1999 (753 So.2d 1214); Oct. 26, 2000, effective Jan. 1 2001 (783 So.2d 138); Dec. 17, 2009, effective Jan. 1, 2010 (26 So.3d 552); Feb. 19, 2015, effective Feb. 19, 2015 (158 So.3d 523).

Committee Notes

1991 Amendment. (c) The time limit for amending a petition has been extended to be consistent with civil pleading procedures. The best interest of the child requires liberal amendments. The procedures for determining if a party has been prejudiced have not been changed.

(e) This section has been reworded to provide a procedure for notice to all parties before dismissal and to allow adoption of a petition by another party.

Rule 8.315. Arraignments and Prehearing Conferences

(a) Arraignment. Before the adjudicatory hearing, the court shall conduct a hearing to determine whether an admission, consent, or denial to the petition shall be entered, and whether the parties are represented by counsel or are entitled to appointed counsel as provided by law. If an admission or consent is entered and no denial is entered by any other parent or legal custodian, the court shall schedule a disposition hearing to be conducted within 15 days. If a denial is entered, the court shall set an adjudicatory hearing within the period of time provided by law and appoint counsel when required.

(b) Withdrawal of Plea. The court may for good cause, at any time before the beginning of a disposition hearing, permit an admission of the allegations of the petition or a consent to dependency to be withdrawn and, if an adjudication has been entered, set aside the adjudication. In a subsequent adjudicatory hearing the court shall disregard an admission or consent that has been withdrawn.

(c) Prehearing Conference. Before any adjudicatory hearing, the court may set or the parties may request that a prehearing conference be held to determine the order in which each party may present witnesses or evidence and the order in which cross-examination and argument shall occur. The court may also enter findings on the record of any stipulations entered into by the parties and consider any other matters that may aid in the conduct of the adjudicatory hearing.

(d) Status Hearing. Within 60 days of the filing of the petition, a status hearing shall be held with all parties present unless an adjudicatory or disposition hearing has begun. Subsequent status hearings shall be held every 30 days unless an adjudicatory or disposition hearing has begun.

Former Rule 8.730 added Dec. 28, 1984, effective Jan. 1, 1985 (462 So.2d 399). Renumbered as new Rule 8.315 and amended May 9, 1991, effective July 1, 1991 (589 So.2d 818). Amended Oct. 31, 1996, effective Jan. 1, 1997 (684 So.2d 756); Sept. 18, 1998, effective Oct. 1, 1998 (725 So.2d 296); Oct. 26, 2000, effective Jan. 1, 2001 (783 So.2d 138); Jan. 27, 2005 (894 So.2d 875).

Committee Notes

1991 Amendment. (d) This section requires a status hearing every 30 days to ensure prompt resolution of the case while preserving the rights of all parties.

Rule 8.320. Providing Counsel to Parties

(a) Duty of the Court.

(1) At each stage of the dependency proceeding the court shall advise the parent of the right to have counsel present.

(2) The court shall appoint counsel to indigent parents or others who are so entitled as provided by law, unless appointment of counsel is waived by that person.

(3) The court shall ascertain whether the right to counsel is understood.

(b) Waiver of Counsel.

(1) No waiver of counsel shall be accepted where it appears that the parent is unable to make an intelligent and understanding choice because of age, education, experience, the nature or complexity of the case, or other factors.

(2) A waiver of counsel made in court shall be of record. The court shall question the party in sufficient detail to ascertain that the waiver is made knowingly, intelligently, and voluntarily.

(3) If a waiver is accepted at any stage of the proceedings, the offer of assistance of counsel shall be renewed by the court at each subsequent stage of the proceedings at which the party appears without counsel.

Former Rule 8.560 added Dec. 28, 1984, effective Jan. 1, 1985 (462 So.2d 399). Renumbered as new Rule 8.320 and amended May 9, 1991, effective July 1, 1991 (589 So.2d 818). Amended Sept. 18, 1998, effective Oct. 1, 1998 (725 So.2d 296); June 10, 1999, effective July 1, 1999 (753 So.2d 1214); Oct. 26, 2000, effective Jan. 1, 2001 (783 So.2d 138).

Rule 8.325. Answers and Pleadings

(a) No Answer Required. No written answer to the petition need be filed by the parent or legal custodian. The parent or legal custodian of the child may enter an oral or written answer to the petition or remain silent.

(b) Denial of Allegations. If the parent or legal custodian denies the allegations of the petition, remains silent, or pleads evasively, the court shall enter a denial of dependency and set the case for an adjudicatory hearing.

(c) Admission of or Consent to Dependency. The parent or legal custodian may admit or consent to a finding of dependency. The court shall determine that any admission or consent to a finding of dependency is made voluntarily and with a full understanding of the nature of the allegations and the possible consequences of the admission or consent, and that the parent has been advised of the right to be represented by counsel. The court shall incorporate these findings into its order in addition to findings of fact specifying the act or acts causing dependency, by whom committed, and facts on which the findings are based. If the answer admits the allegations of the petition it shall constitute consent to a predisposition study.

Added May 9, 1991, effective July 1, 1991 (589 So.2d 818). Amended Nov. 5, 1992, effective Jan. 1, 1993 (608 So.2d 478); Sept. 18, 1998, effective Oct. 1, 1998 (725 So.2d 296); June 10, 1999, effective July 1, 1999 (753 So.2d 1214); Jan. 27, 2005 (894 So.2d 875).

Rule 8.330. Adjudicatory Hearings

(a) Hearing by Judge. The adjudicatory hearing shall be conducted by the judge, without a jury, utilizing the rules of evidence in use in civil cases. At this hearing the court shall determine whether the allegations of the dependency petition have been sustained by a preponderance of the evidence. If the court is of the opinion that the allegations are sustained by clear and convincing evidence, it may enter an order so stating.

(b) Examination of Witnesses. A party may call any person as a witness. A party shall have the right to examine or cross-examine all witnesses. However, the child and the parents, caregivers, or legal custodians of the child may be examined separately and apart from each other.

(c) Presence of Parties. All parties have the right to be present at all hearings. A party may appear in person or, at the discretion of the court for good cause shown, by an audio or audiovisual device. No party shall be excluded from any hearing unless so ordered by the court for disruptive behavior or as provided by law. If a person appears for the arraignment hearing and the court orders that person to personally appear at the adjudicatory hearing for dependency, stating the date, time, and place of the adjudicatory hearing, then that person's failure to appear for the scheduled adjudicatory hearing constitutes consent to a dependency adjudication.

(d) Joint and Separate Hearings. When 2 or more children are alleged to be dependent children, the hearing may be held simultaneously when the several children involved are related to each other or involved in the same case, unless the court orders separate hearings.

(e) Motion for Judgment of Dismissal. In all proceedings, if at the close of the evidence for the petitioner the court is of the opinion that the evidence is insufficient to warrant a finding of dependency, it may, and on the motion of any party shall, enter an order dismissing the petition for insufficiency of the evidence or find that allegations in the petition have not been sustained. If the court finds that allegations in the petition have not been sustained but does not dismiss the petition, the parties, including all parents, shall continue to receive pleadings, notices, and documents and to have the right to be heard.

(f) Dismissal. If the court shall find that the allegations in the petition have not been sustained, it shall enter an order dismissing the case for insufficiency of the evidence or find that allegations in the petition have not been sustained. If the court finds that allegations in the petition have not been sustained but does not dismiss the petition, the parties, including all parents, shall continue to receive pleadings, notices, and documents and to have the right to be heard.

Former Rule 8.780(a)–(g), (i) added Dec. 28, 1984, effective Jan. 1, 1985 (462 So.2d 399). Renumbered as new Rule 8.330 and amended May 9, 1991, effective July 1, 1991 (589 So.2d 818). Amended Sept. 18, 1998, effective Oct. 1, 1998 (725 So.2d 296); June 10, 1999, effective July 1, 1999 (753 So.2d 1214); Oct. 26, 2000, effective Jan. 1, 2001 (783 So.2d 138); Nov. 22, 2000, effective Jan. 1, 2001 (789 So.2d 951); Feb. 8, 2007 (951 So.2d 804); Nov. 12, 2009 (24 So.3d 47).

Committee Notes

1991 Amendment. (a) This change gives the court the option of making a finding based on a higher burden of proof to eliminate the need for a repetitive hearing on the same evidence if a termination of parental rights petition is filed.

Rule 8.332. Order Finding Dependency

(a) Finding of Dependency. In all cases in which dependency is established, the court shall enter a written order stating the legal basis for a finding of dependency, specifying the facts upon which the finding of dependency is based, and stating whether the court made the finding by a preponderance of the evidence or by clear and convincing evidence. The court shall include the dates of the adjudicatory hearing, if any, in the order.

(b) Adjudication of Dependency. If the court finds that the child named in the petition is dependent, the court shall enter an order adjudicating the child dependent if the child is placed or will continue to be placed in an out-of-home placement. The court may enter an order adjudicating the child dependent if the child remains in or is returned to the home. The court shall conduct a disposition hearing.

(c) Withhold of Adjudication of Dependency.

(1) If the court finds that the child named in the petition is dependent, but finds that no action other than supervision in the child's home is required, it may enter an order briefly stating the facts on which its finding is based, but withholding an order of adjudication and placing the child in the child's home under the supervision of the department. The department shall file a case plan and the court shall review the case plan pursuant to these rules.

(2) If the court later finds that the parents of the child have not complied with the conditions of supervision imposed, including the case plan, the court may, after a hearing to establish the noncompliance, but without further evidence of the state of dependency, enter an order of adjudication and shall thereafter have full authority under this chapter to provide for the child as adjudicated. If the child is to remain in an out-of-home placement by order of the court, the court must adjudicate the child dependent. If the court adjudicates the child dependent, the court shall then conduct a disposition hearing.

(d) Failure to Substantially Comply. The court shall advise the parents that if the parents fail to substantially comply with the case plan, their parental rights may be terminated.

(e) Inquiry Regarding Relatives for Placement. If the child is in out-of-home placement, the court shall inquire of the parents whether the parents have relatives who might be considered as placement for the child. The parents shall provide to the court and all parties identification and location information for the relatives.

Added Nov. 12, 2009 (24 So.3d 47).

Rule 8.335. Alternatives Pending Disposition

If the court finds that the evidence supports the allegations of the petition, it may make a finding of dependency as provided by law. If the predisposition and other reports required by law are available, the court may proceed to disposition or continue the case for a disposition hearing. If the case is continued, the court may refer the case to appropriate agencies for additional study and recommendation. The court may order the child continued in placement, designate the placement or the agency that will be responsible for the child's placement, and enter such other orders deemed necessary to protect the health, safety, and well-being of the child, including diagnosis, evaluation, treatment, and visitation.

Former Rule 8.780(h) added Dec. 28, 1984, effective Jan. 1, 1985 (462 So.2d 399). Renumbered as new Rule 8.335 and amended May 9, 1991, effective July 1, 1991 (589 So.2d 818).

Rule 8.340. Disposition Hearings

(a) Information Available to Court. At the disposition hearing, the court, after establishing compliance with the dispositional considerations, determinations, and discussions required by law, may receive any relevant and material evidence helpful in determining the proper disposition to be made. It must include written reports required by law, and may include, but is not limited to, any psychiatric or psychological evaluations of the child or his or her parent, caregiver, or legal custodian that may be obtained and that are relevant and material. Such evidence may be received by the court and may be relied upon to the extent of its probative value, even though not competent in an adjudicatory hearing.

(b) Disclosure to Parties. All parties are entitled to disclosure of all information in all reports submitted to the court.

(c) Orders of Disposition. The court shall in its written order of disposition include:

(1) the placement or custody of the child;

(2) special conditions of placement and visitation;

(3) evaluation, counseling, treatment activities, and other actions to be taken by the parties, if ordered;

(4) persons or entities responsible for supervising or monitoring services to the child and parent;

(5) continuation or discharge of the guardian ad litem, as appropriate;

(6) date, time, and location of next scheduled review hearing, as required by law;

(7) child support payments, if the child is in an out-of-home placement;

(8) if the child is placed in foster care, the reasons why the child was not placed in the legal custody of an adult relative, legal custodian, or other adult approved by the court and a further determination as to whether diligent efforts were made by the department to locate an adult relative, legal custodian, or other adult willing to care for the child instead of placement with the department;

(9) such other requirements to protect the health, safety, and well-being of the child, to preserve the stability of the child's educational placement, and to promote family preservation or reunification whenever possible; and

(10) approval of the case plan as filed with the court. If the court does not approve the case plan at the disposition hearing, the court must set a hearing within 30 days after the disposition hearing to review and approve the case plan.

Former Rule 8.790 added Dec. 28, 1984, effective Jan. 1, 1985 (462 So.2d 399). Renumbered as new Rule 8.340 and amended May 9, 1991, effective July 1, 1991 (589 So.2d 818). Amended Nov. 5, 1992, effective Jan. 1, 1993 (609 So.2d 478); Sept. 18, 1998, effective Oct. 1, 1998 (725 So.2d 296); Oct. 26, 2000, effective Jan. 1, 2001 (783 So.2d 138); May 23, 2013, effective July 1, 2013 (115 So.3d 286).

Committee Notes

1992 Amendment. Dismissal of a petition is not appropriate after adjudication.

Rule 8.345. Post-Disposition Relief

(a) Motion for Modification of Placement. A child who has been placed in his or her own home, in the home of a relative, or in some other place, under the supervision or legal custody of the department, may be brought before the court by the department or any interested person on a motion for modification of placement. If neither the parents, the legal custodian, nor any appointed guardian ad litem or attorney ad litem object to the change, then the court may enter an order making the change in placement without a hearing. If the parents, the legal custodian, or any appointed guardian ad litem or attorney ad litem object to the change of placement, the court shall conduct a hearing and thereafter enter an order changing the placement, modifying the conditions of placement, continuing placement as previously ordered, or placing the child with the department or a licensed child-caring agency.

(1) In cases in which the issue before the court is whether a child should be reunited with a parent, and the child is currently placed with someone other than a parent, the court must determine whether the parent has substantially complied with the terms of the case plan to the extent that the safety, well-being, and physical, mental, and emotional health of the child is not endangered by the return of the child to the home.

(2) In cases in which the issue before the court is whether a child who is placed in the custody of a parent should be reunited with the other parent upon a finding of substantial compliance with the terms of the case plan, the court must determine that the safety, well-being, and physical, mental, and emotional health of the child would not be endangered by reunification and that reunification would be in the best interest of the child.

(b) Motion for Termination of Supervision or Jurisdiction. Any party requesting termination of agency supervision or the jurisdiction of the court or both shall do so by written motion or in a written report to the court. The court must hear all parties present and enter an order terminating supervision or terminating jurisdiction and supervision or continuing them as previously ordered. The court shall not terminate jurisdiction unless the child is returned to the parent and has been in the placement for at least 6 months, the child is adopted, or the child attains the age of 18, unless the court has extended jurisdiction.

Former Rule 8.800(a) and (b) added Dec. 28, 1984, effective Jan. 1, 1985 (462 So.2d 399). Renumbered as new Rule 8.345 and amended May 9, 1991, effective July 1, 1991 (589 So.2d 818). Amended Sept. 18, 1998, effective Oct. 1, 1998 (725 So.2d 296); June 10, 1999, effective July 1, 1999 (753 So.2d 1214); Oct. 26, 2000, effective Jan. 1, 2001 (783 So.2d 138); Sept. 5, 2002, effective Jan. 1, 2003 (827 So.2d 219); May 23, 2013, effective July 1, 2013 (115 So.3d 286); Oct. 3, 2013, effective Oct. 3, 2013 (123 So.3d 1128).

Rule 8.347. Motion to Supplement Order of Adjudication, Disposition Order, and Case Plan

(a) Motion. After the court has entered an order of adjudication of dependency, any party may file a motion for the court to supplement the order of adjudication with findings that a parent or legal custodian contributed to the dependency status of the child pursuant to the statutory definition of a dependent child. The motion may also request that the court supplement the disposition order and the case plan.

(b) Contents.

(1) The motion must identify the age, sex, and name of the children whose parent or legal custodian is the subject of the motion.

(2) The motion must specifically identify the parent or legal custodian who is the subject of the motion.

(3) The motion must allege sufficient facts showing that a parent or legal custodian contributed to the dependency status of the child pursuant to the statutory definition of a dependent child.

(c) Verification. The motion must be signed under oath, stating that the signer is filing the motion in good faith.

(d) Amendments. At any time prior to the conclusion of an evidentiary hearing on the motion, an amended motion may be filed or the motion may be amended by oral motion. A continuance may be granted on motion and a showing that the amendment prejudices or materially affects any party.

(e) Notice.

(1) *In General.* Parents or legal custodians who have previously been properly served with the dependency petition or who have previously appeared in the dependency proceeding shall be served with a notice of hearing and copies of the motion and the initial order of adjudication of dependency in the same manner as the service of documents that are filed after the service of the initial dependency petition as provided in these rules.

(2) *Summons.*

(A) Parents or legal custodians who have not been properly served with the dependency petition or who have not previously appeared in the dependency proceeding must be properly served with a summons and copies of the motion and the initial order of adjudication of dependency. The summons must require the person on whom it is served to appear for a preliminary hearing on the motion at a time and place specified, not less than 72 hours after service of the summons.

(B) Upon the filing of the motion and upon request, the clerk shall issue a summons.

(C) The movant shall not be required to serve a summons on a parent or legal custodian who has previously been properly served with the dependency petition or who has appeared in the dependency proceeding.

(D) The summons shall be served in the same manner as service of a dependency petition as required by law.

(E) Service by publication of the motion shall not be required.

(F) If the location of the party to be served is unknown, the court may enter an order granting the motion only if the movant has properly served the person subject to the motion, the person subject to the motion has appeared in the proceeding, or the movant has conducted a diligent search and filed with the court an affidavit of diligent search.

(G) Personal appearance of any person in a hearing before the court on the motion eliminates the requirement for serving process upon that person.

(f) Preliminary Hearing on Motion.

(1) The court must conduct a preliminary hearing and determine whether the parent or legal custodian who is the subject of the motion:

(A) has been properly served with the summons or notice, and with copies of the motion and initial order of adjudication of dependency;

(B) is represented by counsel or is entitled to appointed counsel as provided by law; and

(C) wishes to challenge the motion or consent to the court granting the motion.

(2) If the parent or legal custodian who is the subject of the motion wishes to challenge the motion or if the parent or legal custodian was properly served and fails to appear at the preliminary hearing, the court must schedule an evidentiary hearing on the motion within 30 days.

(3) If the parent or legal custodian who is the subject of the motion wishes to consent to the motion without admitting or denying the allegations of the motion, the court shall enter an order supplementing the initial order of adjudication of dependency based on the sworn allegations of the motion.

(g) Evidentiary Hearing.

(1) *Hearing Procedures.* The hearing shall be conducted in the same manner and with the same procedures as the adjudicatory hearing on the dependency petition as provided in these rules.

(2) *Motion for Judgment Denying Motion.* In all proceedings, if at the close of the evidence for the movant, the court is of the opinion that the evidence is insufficient to warrant findings that a parent or legal custodian contributed to the dependency status of the child pursuant to the statutory definition of a dependent child, it may, and on the motion of any party must, enter an order denying the motion for insufficiency of the evidence.

(3) *Denial of Motion.* If the court, at the conclusion of the evidence, finds that the allegations in the

motion have not been sustained, the court shall enter an order denying the motion.

(4) *Granting of the Motion.* If the court finds that the movant has proven the allegations of the motion, the court shall enter an order granting the motion as provided in these rules.

(h) Supplemental Order of Adjudication.

(1) If the parent or legal custodian consents to the motion and its allegations or if the court finds that the movant has proven the allegations of the motion at an evidentiary hearing, the court shall enter a written order granting the motion and specifying facts that support findings that a parent or legal custodian contributed to the dependency status of the child pursuant to the statutory definition of a dependent child and stating whether the court made the finding by a preponderance of the evidence or by clear and convincing evidence.

(2) If necessary, the court shall schedule a supplemental disposition hearing within 15 days.

(3) The court shall advise the parent who is the subject of the motion that if the parent fails to substantially comply with the case plan, parental rights may be terminated.

(4) If the child is in out-of-home placement, the court shall inquire of the parents whether the parents have relatives who might be considered as placement for the child. The parents shall provide to the court and to all parties the identity and location of the relatives.

(i) Supplemental Disposition Hearing.

(1) *Hearing.* If necessary, the court shall conduct a supplemental disposition hearing pursuant to the same procedures for a disposition hearing and case plan review hearing as provided by law.

(2) *Supplemental Predisposition Study and Case Plan.*

(A) A written case plan and a predisposition study prepared by an authorized agent of the department must be filed with the court, served upon the parents of the child, provided to the representative of the guardian ad litem program, if the program has been appointed, and provided to all other parties not less than 72 hours before the supplemental disposition hearing.

(B) The court may grant an exception to the requirement for a predisposition study by separate order or within the judge's order of disposition upon a finding that all the family and child information required by law is available in other documents filed with the court.

(3) *Supplemental Order of Disposition.* The court shall in its written supplemental order of disposition include:

(A) the placement or custody of the child;

(B) special conditions of placement and visitation;

(C) evaluation, counseling, treatment activities, and other actions to be taken by the parties, when ordered;

(D) the names of the supervising or monitoring agencies, and the continuation or discharge of the guardian ad litem, when appropriate;

(E) the date, time, and location for the next case review as required by law;

(F) child support payments, if the child is in an out-of-home placement;

(G) if the child is placed in foster care, the reasons why the child was not placed in the legal custody of an adult relative, legal custodian, or other adult approved by the court;

(H) approval of the case plan or direction to amend the case plan within 30 days; and

(I) such other requirements as are deemed necessary to protect the health, safety, and well-being of the child.

Adopted May 23, 2013, effective July 1, 2013 (115 So.3d 286).

Rule 8.350. Placement of Child Into Residential Treatment Center After Adjudication of Dependency

(a) Placement.

(1) *Treatment Center Defined.* Any reference in this rule to a residential treatment center is to a residential treatment center or facility licensed under section 394.875, Florida Statutes, for residential mental health treatment. Any reference to hospital is to a hospital licensed under chapter 395, Florida Statutes, for residential mental health treatment. This rule does not apply to placement under sections 394.463 or 394.467, Florida Statutes.

(2) *Basis for Placement.* The placement of any child who has been adjudicated dependent for residential mental health treatment shall be as provided by law.

(3) *Assessment by Qualified Evaluator.* Whenever the department believes that a child in its legal custody may require placement in a residential treatment center or hospital, the department shall arrange to have the child assessed by a qualified evaluator as provided by law and shall file notice of this with the court and all parties. Upon the filing of this notice by the department, the court shall appoint a guardian ad litem for the child, if one has not already been appointed, and shall also appoint an attorney for the child. All appointments pursuant to this rule shall conform to the provisions of rule 8.231. Both the guardian ad litem and attorney shall meet the child and shall have the opportunity to discuss the child's suitability for residential treatment with the qualified evaluator conducting the assessment. Upon the completion of the evaluator's written assessment, the department shall provide a copy to the court and to all parties. The guardian ad litem shall also provide a

written report to the court and to all parties indicating the guardian ad litem's recommendation as to the child's placement in residential treatment and the child's wishes.

(4) *Motion for Placement.* If the department seeks to place the child in a residential treatment center or hospital, the department shall immediately file a motion for placement of the child with the court. This motion shall include a statement as to why the child is suitable for this placement and why less restrictive alternatives are not appropriate and also shall include the written findings of the qualified evaluator. The motion shall state whether all parties, including the child, are in agreement. Copies of the motion must be served on the child's attorney and all parties and participants.

(5) *Immediate Placement.* If the evaluator's written assessment indicates that the child requires immediate placement in a residential treatment center or hospital and that such placement cannot wait for a hearing, then the department may place the child pending a hearing, unless the court orders otherwise.

(6) *Guardian ad Litem.* The guardian ad litem must be represented by an attorney at all proceedings under this rule, unless the guardian ad litem is acting as an attorney.

(7) *Status Hearing.* Upon the filing of a motion for placement, the court shall set the matter for a status hearing within 48 hours, excluding weekends and holidays. The department shall timely provide notice of the date, time, and place of the hearing to all parties and participants.

(8) *Notice of Hearing.* The child's attorney or guardian ad litem shall notify the child of the date, time, and place of the hearing. No hearing shall proceed without the presence of the child's attorney. The guardian ad litem may be excused by the court for good cause shown.

(9) *Disagreement with Placement.* If no party disagrees with the department's motion at the status hearing, then the motion for placement may be approved by the court. However, if any party, including the child, disagrees, then the court shall set the matter for hearing within 10 working days.

(10) *Presence of Child.* The child shall be present at the hearing unless the court determines pursuant to subdivision (c) that a court appearance is not in the child's best interest. In such circumstances, the child shall be provided the opportunity to express his or her views to the court by a method deemed appropriate by the court.

(11) *Hearing on Placement.*

(A) At the hearing, the court shall consider, at a minimum, all of the following:

(i) based on an independent assessment of the child, the recommendation of a department representative or authorized agent that the residential treatment or hospitalization is in the child's best interest and a showing that the placement is the least restrictive available alternative;

(ii) the recommendation of the guardian ad litem;

(iii) the written findings of the evaluation and suitability assessment prepared by a qualified evaluator; and

(iv) the views regarding placement in residential treatment that the child expresses to the court.

(B) All parties shall be permitted to present evidence and witnesses concerning the suitability of the placement.

(C) If the court determines that the child is not suitable for residential treatment, the court shall order the department to place the child in the least restrictive setting that is best suited to meet the child's needs.

(b) Continuing Residential Placement Review.

(1) The court shall conduct a hearing to review the status of the child's residential treatment plan no later than 3 months after the child's admission to the residential treatment program. An independent review of the child's progress toward achieving the goals and objectives of the treatment plan must be completed by a qualified evaluator and submitted to the court, the child's attorney, and all parties in writing at least 72 hours before the 3–month review hearing.

(2) Review hearings shall be conducted every 3 months thereafter, until the child is placed in a less restrictive setting. At each 3–month review hearing, if the child is not represented by an attorney, the court shall appoint counsel. At the 3–month review hearing the court shall determine whether the child disagrees with continued placement.

(3) If the court determines at any hearing that the child is not suitable for continued residential treatment, the court shall order the department to place the child in the least restrictive setting that is best suited to meet the child's needs.

(c) Presence of Child. The child shall be present at all court hearings unless the court finds that the child's mental or physical condition is such that a court appearance is not in the child's best interest. In such circumstances, the child shall be provided the opportunity to express his or her views to the court by a method deemed appropriate by the court.

(d) Standard of Proof. At the hearing, the court shall determine whether the evidence supporting involuntary commitment of a dependent child to a residential mental health treatment facility is clear and convincing.

Added March 6, 2003 (842 So.2d 763). Amended Sept. 21, 2006, effective. Jan. 1, 2007 (939 So.2d 74); May 23, 2013, effective July 1, 2013 (115 So.3d 286); Feb. 19, 2015, effective Feb. 19, 2015 (158 So.3d 523).

Rule 8.355. Administration of Psychotropic Medication to a Child in Shelter Care or in Foster Care When Parental Consent Has Not Been Obtained

(a) Motion for Court Authorization for Administration of Psychotropic Medications.

(1) Whenever the department believes that a child in its physical or legal custody requires the administration of a psychotropic medication, and the child's parents or legal guardians have not provided express and informed consent as provided by law, the department or its agent shall file a motion with the court to authorize the administration of the psychotropic medication before the administration of the medication, except as provided in subdivision (c) of this rule. In all cases in which a motion is required, the motion shall include the following information:

(A) The written report of the department describing the efforts made to enable the prescribing physician to obtain express and informed consent for providing the medication to the child and describing other treatments considered or recommended for the child;

(B) The prescribing physician's signed medical report, as required by law; and

(C) Whether the child assents to the medication.

(2) If the child declines to assent to the proposed administration of psychotropic medication the court shall appoint an attorney to represent the child and a hearing shall be held on the department's motion. The appointment shall conform to the provisions of rule 8.231.

(3) The department must serve a copy of the motion, and notify all parties of its proposed administration of psychotropic medication to the child in writing, or by whatever other method best ensures that all parties receive notification of the proposed action, within 48 hours after filing the motion for court authorization. When an attorney is appointed to represent the child a copy of the motion must be served on the attorney.

(4) If any party other than the child objects to the proposed administration of the psychotropic medication to the child, that party must file its objection within 2 working days after being notified of the department's motion.

(b) Court Action on Department's Motion for Administration of Psychotropic Medication.

(1) If the child assents and no party timely files an objection to the department's motion, the court may enter its order authorizing the proposed administration of the psychotropic medication without a hearing. Based on its determination of the best interests of the child, the court may order additional medical consultation or require the department to obtain a second opinion within a reasonable time, not more than 21 calendar days. When the court orders an additional medical consultation or second medical opinion, the department shall file a written report including the results of this additional consultation or a copy of the second medical opinion with the court within the time required by the court, and shall serve a copy of the report as required by subdivision (a)(2) of this rule.

(2) If the child does not assent to the medication or any party timely files its objection to the proposed administration of the psychotropic medication to the child, the court shall hold a hearing as soon as possible on the department's motion.

(A) At such hearing, the medical report of the prescribing physician is admissible in evidence.

(B) At such hearing, the court shall ask the department whether additional medical, mental health, behavioral, counseling, or other services are being provided to the child that the prescribing physician considers to be necessary or beneficial in treating the child's medical condition, and which the physician recommends or expects to be provided to the child with the medication.

(C) The court may order additional medical consultation or a second medical opinion, as provided in subdivision (b)(1) of this rule.

(D) After considering the department's motion and any testimony received, the court may order that the department provide or continue to provide the proposed psychotropic medication to the child, on a determination that it is in the child's best interest to do so.

(c) Emergency Situations.

(1) *Shelter Care.* When a child is initially removed from the home and taken into custody under section 39.401, Florida Statutes, and the department continues to administer a current prescription of psychotropic medication to the child, the department shall request court authorization for the continued administration of the medication at the shelter hearing. This request shall be included in the shelter petition.

(A) The department shall provide all information in its possession to the court in support of its request at the shelter hearing. The court may authorize the continued administration of the psychotropic medication only until the arraignment hearing on the petition for adjudication, or for 28 days following the date of the child's removal, whichever occurs first.

(B) When the department believes, based on the required physician's evaluation, that it is appropriate to continue the psychotropic medication beyond the time authorized by the court at the shelter hearing, the department shall file a motion seeking continued court authorization at the same time as it files the dependency petition, within 21 days after the shelter hearing.

(2) *When Delay Would Cause Significant Harm.* Whenever the department believes, based on the cer-

tification of the prescribing physician, that delay in providing the prescribed psychotropic medication to the child would, more likely than not, cause significant harm to the child, the department must submit a motion to the court seeking continuation of the medication within 3 working days after the department begins providing the medication to the child.

(A) The motion seeking authorization for the continued administration of the psychotropic medication to the child shall include all information required in subdivision (a)(1) of this rule. The required medical report must also include the specific reasons why the child may experience significant harm, and the nature and the extent of the potential harm, resulting from a delay in authorizing the prescribed medication.

(B) The department shall serve the motion on all parties within 3 working days after the department begins providing the medication to the child.

(C) The court shall hear the department's motion at the next regularly scheduled court hearing required by law, or within 30 days after the date of the prescription, whichever occurs sooner. However, if any party files an objection to the motion, the court shall hold a hearing within 7 days.

(3) *In Emergency Psychiatric Placements.* The department may authorize the administration of psychotropic medications to a child in its custody in advance of a court order in hospitals, crisis stabilization units, and in statewide inpatient psychiatric programs. Should the department do so, it must seek court authorization for the continued administration of the medication as required in subdivision (a) of this rule.

Added Nov. 17, 2005 (915 So.2d 592). Amended Feb. 19, 2015, effective Feb. 19, 2015 (158 So.3d 523).

D. CASE PLANS

Rule 8.400. Case Plan Development

(a) Case Planning Conference. The case plan must be developed in a face-to-face conference with the parents, the guardian ad litem, attorney ad litem and, if appropriate, the child and the temporary custodian of the child.

(b) Contents. The case plan must be written simply and clearly in English and the principal language of the parents, if possible. Each case plan must contain

(1) a description of the problem being addressed, including the parent's behavior or acts resulting in risk to the child and the reason for the intervention by the department;

(2) a permanency goal;

(3) if it is a concurrent plan, a description of the permanency goal of reunification with the parent or legal custodian and one of the remaining permanency goals;

(4) the date the compliance period expires; and

(5) a written notice to the parent that failure of the parent to substantially comply with the case plan may result in the termination of parental rights, and that a material breach of the case plan may result in the filing of a petition for termination of parental rights sooner than the expiration of the compliance period.

(c) Expiration of Case Plan. The case plan compliance period expires no later than 12 months after the date the child was initially removed from the home or the date the case plan was accepted by the court, whichever occurs first.

(d) Department Responsibility.

(1) The department shall prepare a draft of a case plan for each child receiving services under Chapter 39, Florida Statutes.

(2) The department shall document, in writing, a parent's unwillingness or inability to participate in the development of the case plan, provide the written documentation to the parent when available for the court record, and prepare a case plan.

(3) After the case plan has been developed, and before acceptance by the court, the department shall make the appropriate referrals for services that will allow the parents to begin the agreed-upon tasks and services immediately if the parents agree to begin compliance.

(4) The department must immediately give the parties, including the child if appropriate, a signed copy of the agreed-upon case plan.

(5) The department must prepare, but need not submit to the court, a case plan for a child who will be in care no longer than 30 days unless that child is placed in out of home care a second time within a 12–month period.

(6) The department must prepare a case plan for a child in out of home care within 60 days after the department removes the child from the home and shall submit the plan to the court before the disposition hearing for the court to review and approve.

(7) Not less than 3 business days before the disposition or case plan review hearing, the department must file a case plan with the court.

(8) After jurisdiction attaches, the department shall file with the court all case plans, including all case plans prepared before jurisdiction of the court attached. The department shall provide a copy of the case plans filed to all the parties whose whereabouts are known, not less than 3 business days before the disposition or case plan review hearing.

(e) Signature. The case plan must be signed by all parties except the child, if the child is not of an age or capacity to participate in the case planning process.

(f) Service. Each party, including the child, if appropriate, must be provided with a copy of the case plan not less than 3 business days before the disposition or case plan review hearing. If the location of a parent is unknown, this fact must be documented in writing and included in the plan.

Former Rule 8.800(c) added Dec. 28, 1984, effective Jan. 1, 1985 (462 So.2d 399). Amended March 1, 1990 (557 So.2d 1360). Renumbered as new Rule 8.400 and amended May 9, 1991, effective July 1, 1991 (589 So.2d 818). Amended Sept. 28, 1995 (661 So.2d 800); Sept. 18, 1998, effective Oct. 1, 1998 (725 So.2d 296); June 10, 1999, effective July 1, 1999 (753 So.2d 1214); Oct. 26, 2000, effective Jan. 1, 2001 (783 So.2d 138); March 1, 2001 (796 So.2d 468); Jan. 27, 2005 (894 So.2d 875); Feb. 8, 2007 (951 So.2d 804); Dec. 17, 2009, effective Jan. 1, 2010 (26 So.3d 552).

Rule 8.401. Case Plan Development for Young Adults

(a) Case Planning Conference. The case plan must be developed in a face-to-face conference with the young adult, the guardian ad litem, attorney ad litem and, when appropriate, the legal guardian of the young adult, if the young adult is not of the capacity to participate in the case planning process.

(b) Contents. The case plan must be written simply and clearly in English and the principal language of the young adult. Each case plan must contain

(1) A description of the services, including independent living services, to be provided to the young adult;

(2) A copy of the young adult's transition plan;

(3) The permanency goal of transition from licensed care to independent living; and

(4) The date the compliance period expires.

(c) Department Responsibility.

(1) After the case plan has been developed, the department must prepare the written case plan for each young adult receiving services under Chapter 39, Florida Statutes.

(2) After the case plan has been developed, and before acceptance by the court, the department must make the appropriate referrals for services that will allow the young adult to begin receiving the agreed-upon services immediately.

(3) The department must immediately provide the young adult a signed copy of the agreed-upon case plan.

(4) Not less than 3 business days before a judicial review or permanency hearing, the department must file the case plan with the court.

(d) Signature. The case plan must be signed by the young adult, all parties and, when appropriate, the legal guardian if the young adult is not of the capacity to participate in the case planning process.

(e) Service. Each party must be served with a copy of the case plan not less than 3 business days before the judicial review hearing. If the location of the young adult is unknown, this fact must be documented in writing and filed with the court.

(f) Re-admitted to Care. If the department petitions the court for reinstatement of jurisdiction after a young adult has been re-admitted to care under Chapter 39, Florida Statutes, the department must file an updated case plan.

Added March 20, 2014, effective March 20, 2014 (136 So.3d 508).

Rule 8.410. Approval of Case Plans

(a) Hearing. The court shall review the contents of the case plan at the disposition or case plan review hearing unless a continuance for the filing of the case plan has been granted by the court.

(b) Determinations by Court. At the hearing, the court shall determine if:

(1) The plan is consistent with the previous orders of the court placing the child in care.

(2) The plan is consistent with the requirements for the content of a case plan as provided by law.

(3) The parents were advised of their right to have counsel present at all prior hearings and the parents were advised of their right to participate in the preparation of the case plan and to have counsel or any other person assist in the preparation of the case plan.

(4) The case plan is meaningful and designed to address the facts, circumstances, and problems on which the court based its order of dependency for the child.

(5) The plan adequately addresses the goals and needs of the child.

(c) Amendment of Initial Case Plan. During the hearing, if the court determines that the case plan does not meet statutory requirements and include previous court orders, it shall order the parties to make amendments to the plan. The amended plan must be submitted to the court within 30 days for another hearing and approval. A copy of the amended plan must be provided to each party, if the location of the party is known, at least 3 business days before filing with the court. If the parties do not agree on the final terms, the court shall order those conditions and tasks it believes must be accomplished to obtain permanency for the child. In addition, the court may order the department to provide those services necessary to assist in achieving the goal of the case plan.

(d) Entry of Findings. The court shall enter its findings with respect to the review of the case plan in writing and make specific findings on each element required by law to be included in a case plan.

(e) Review Hearing. The court will set a hearing to review the performance of the parties to the case plan no later than 90 days after the disposition hearing or the hearing at which the case plan was approved,6 months from the date on which the child was removed from the home, or 6 months from the date of the last judicial review, whichever comes first.

Added May 9, 1991, effective July 1, 1991 (589 So.2d 818). Amended Sept. 28, 1995 (661 So.2d 800); Oct. 31, 1996, effective Jan. 1, 1997 (684 So.2d 756); Sept. 18, 1998, effective Oct. 1, 1998 (725 So.2d 296); June 10, 1999, effective July 1, 1999 (753 So.2d 1214); Oct. 26, 2000, effective Jan. 1, 2001 (783 So.2d 138); Jan. 27, 2005 (894 So.2d 875); Feb. 8, 2007 (851 So.2d 804); Dec. 17, 2009, effective Jan. 1, 2010 (26 So.3d 552).

Rule 8.415. Judicial Review of Dependency Cases

(a) Required Review. All dependent children must have their status reviewed as provided by law. Any party may petition the court for a judicial review as provided by law.

(b) Scheduling Hearings.

(1) *Initial Review Hearing.* The court must determine when the first review hearing must be held and the clerk of the court must immediately schedule the review hearing. In no case may the hearing be scheduled for later than 6 months from the date of removal from the home or 90 days from the disposition or case plan approval hearing, whichever comes first. In every case, the court must conduct a judicial review at least every 6 months.

(2) *Subsequent Review Hearings.* At each judicial review hearing, the court must schedule the next judicial review hearing which must be conducted within 6 months. The clerk of the court, at the judicial review hearing, must provide the parties, the social service agency charged with the supervision of care, custody, or guardianship of the child, the foster parent or legal custodian in whose home the child resides, any preadoptive parent, and such other persons as the court may direct with written notice of the date, time, and location of the next judicial review hearing.

(3) *Review Hearings for Children 17 Years of Age.* The court must hold a judicial review hearing within 90 days after a child's 17th birthday. The court must also issue an order, separate from the order on judicial review, that the specific disabilities of nonage of the child have been removed pursuant to sections 743.044, 743.045, 743.046, and 743.047, Florida Statutes, as well as any other disabilities of nonage that the court finds to be in the child's best interest to remove. The court must continue to hold timely judicial review hearings. If necessary, the court may review the status of the child more frequently during the year before the child's 18th birthday. At the last review hearing before the child reaches 18 years of age, the court must also address whether the child plans to remain in foster care, and, if so, ensure that the child's transition plan complies with the law.

(4) *Review Hearings for Young Adults in Foster Care.* The court must review the status of a young adult at least every six months and must hold a permanency review hearing at least annually while the young adult remains in foster care. The young adult or any other party to the dependency case may request an additional hearing or judicial review.

(c) Report. In all cases, the department or its agent must prepare a report to the court. The report must contain facts showing the court to have jurisdiction of the cause as a dependency case. It must contain information as to the identity and residence of the parent, if known, and the legal custodian, the dates of the original dependency adjudication and any subsequent judicial review proceedings, the results of any safe-harbor placement assessment including the status of the child's placement, and a request for one or more of the following forms of relief:

(1) that the child's placement be changed;

(2) that the case plan be continued to permit the parents or social service agency to complete the tasks assigned to them in the agreement; or

(3) that proceedings be instituted to terminate parental rights and legally free the child for adoption.

(d) Service. A copy of the report containing recommendations and, if not previously provided by the court, a notice of review hearing must be served on all persons who are required by law to be served at least 72 hours before the judicial review hearing.

(e) Information Available to Court. At the judicial review hearing the court may receive any relevant and material evidence pertinent to the cause. This must include written reports required by law and may include, but must not be limited to, any psychiatric or psychological evaluations of the child or parent, caregiver, or legal custodian that may be obtained and that are material and relevant. This evidence may be received by the court and relied on to the extent of its probative value, even though it may not be competent in an adjudicatory hearing.

(f) Court Action.

(1) The court must hold a hearing to review the compliance of the parties with the case plan and to determine what assigned tasks were and were not accomplished and the reasons for any noncompliance. The court must also determine the frequency, kind, and duration of contacts among siblings who have been separated during placement, as well as any efforts undertaken to reunite separated siblings, if doing so is in the best interest of each child.

(2) If the court finds that the parents have substantially complied with the case plan, the court must return the child to the custody of the parents if the court is satisfied that reunification will not be detrimental to the child's safety, well-being, or physical, mental, or emotional health.

(3) If the court finds that the social service agency has not complied with its obligations, the court may find the social service agency to be in contempt, must order the social service agency to submit its plan for

compliance with the case plan, and must require the social service agency to show why the child could not be safely returned to the home of the parents. If the court finds that the child could not be safely returned to the parents, it must extend the case plan for a period of not more than 6 months to allow the social service agency to comply with its obligations under the case plan.

(4) At any judicial review held under section 39.701(3), Florida Statutes, if, in the opinion of the court, the department has not met its obligations to the child as stated in the written case plan or in the provision of independent living services, the court may issue an order directing the department to show cause as to why it has not done so. If the department cannot justify its noncompliance, the court may give the department 30 days within which to comply and, on failure to comply, the court may hold the department in contempt.

(5) The court must enter a written order on the conclusion of the review hearing including a statement of the facts, those findings it was directed to determine by law, a determination of the future course of the proceedings, and the date, time, and place of the next hearing.

(g) Jurisdiction.

(1) When a child is returned to the parents, the court must not terminate its jurisdiction over the child until 6 months after the return. Based on a report of the department and any other relevant factors, the court must then determine whether jurisdiction should be continued or terminated. If its jurisdiction is to be terminated, it must enter an order to that effect.

(2) When a child has not been returned to the parent, but has been permanently committed to the department for subsequent adoption, the court must continue to hold judicial review hearings on the status of the child at least every 6 months until the adoption is finalized. These hearings must be held in accordance with these rules.

(3) If a young adult petitions the court at any time before his or her 19th birthday requesting the court's continued jurisdiction, the court may retain or reinstate jurisdiction for a period of time not to continue beyond the date of the young adult's 19th birthday for the purpose of determining whether appropriate services that were required to be provided to the young adult before reaching 18 years of age have been provided.

(4) If a young adult has chosen to remain in extended foster care after he or she has reached 18 years of age, the department may not close a case and the court may not terminate jurisdiction until the court finds, following a hearing, that the appropriate statutory criteria have been met.

(5) If a petition for special immigrant juvenile status and an application for adjustment of status have been filed on behalf of a foster child and the petition and application have not been granted by the time the child reaches 18 years of age, the court may retain jurisdiction solely for the purpose of allowing the continued consideration of the petition and application by federal authorities. Review hearings must be set solely for the purpose of determining the status of the petition and application. The court's jurisdiction must terminate on the final decision of the federal authorities, or on the immigrant child's 22nd birthday, whichever occurs first.

(h) Administrative Review. The department, under a formal agreement with the court in particular cases, may conduct administrative reviews instead of judicial reviews for children in out-of-home placement. Notice must be provided to all parties. An administrative review may not be substituted for the first judicial review or any subsequent 6–month review. Any party may petition the court for a judicial review as provided by law.

(i) Concurrent Planning.

(1) At the initial judicial review hearing, the court must make findings regarding the likelihood of the child's reunification with the parent or legal custodian within 12 months after the removal of the child from the home.

(2) If the court makes a written finding that it is not likely that the child will be reunified with the parent or legal custodian within 12 months after the child was removed from the home, the department must file a motion to amend the case plan and declare that it will use concurrent planning for the case plan.

(3) The department must file the motion to amend the case plan no later than 10 business days after receiving the written finding of the court and attach the proposed amended case plan to the motion.

(4) If concurrent planning is already being used, the case plan must document the efforts the department is making to complete the concurrent goal.

Former Rule 8.800(d) added Dec. 28, 1984, effective Jan. 1, 1985 (462 So.2d 399). Amended March 1, 1990 (557 So.2d 1360). Renumbered as new Rule 8.415 and amended May 9, 1991, effective July 1, 1991 (589 So.2d 818). Amended Nov. 5, 1992, effective Jan. 1, 1993 (608 So.2d 478); Dec. 22, 1994 (648 So.2d 115); Sept. 18, 1998, effective Oct. 1, 1998 (725 So.2d 296); June 10, 1999, effective July 1, 1999 (753 So.2d 1214); Oct. 26, 2000, effective Jan. 1, 2001 (783 So.2d 138); Jan. 27, 2005 (894 So.2d 875); Mar. 3, 2005 (898 So.2d 47); Nov. 17, 2005 (915 So.2d 592); Feb. 8, 2007 (951 So.2d 804); Oct. 11, 2012, effective Jan. 1, 2013 (101 So.3d 368); March 20, 2014, effective March 20, 2014 (136 So.3d 508); Feb. 19, 2015, effective Feb. 19, 2015 (158 So.3d 523).

Committee Notes

1991 Adoption. The rule allows for certain forms of relief pertinent to foster care review. It allows the court to order commencement of a termination of parental rights proceeding if the parents are not in compliance. The court is also permitted to extend or modify the plan.

Rule 8.420. Case Plan Amendments

(a) Modifications. After the case plan has been developed, the tasks and services agreed upon in the plan may not be changed or altered except as follows.

(1) The case plan may be amended at any time to change the goal of the plan, employ the use of concurrent planning, add or remove tasks the parent must complete to substantially comply with the plan, provide appropriate services for the child, and update the child's health, mental health, and education records.

(2) The case plan may be amended on approval of the court if all parties are in agreement regarding the amendments to the plan and the amended plan is signed by all parties and submitted to the court with a memorandum of explanation.

(3) The case plan may be amended by the court or on motion of any party at any hearing to change the goal of the plan, employ the use of concurrent planning, or add or remove the tasks the parent must complete in order to substantially comply with the plan, if there is a preponderance of evidence demonstrating the need for the amendment.

(4) The case plan may be amended by the court or on motion of any party at any hearing to provide appropriate services to the child if there is competent evidence demonstrating the need for the amendment.

(5) The case plan is deemed amended as to the child's health, mental health, and education records when the child's updated health and education records are filed by the department.

(b) Basis to Amend the Case Plan. The need to amend the case plan may be based on information discovered or circumstances arising after the approval of the case plan for:

(1) a previously unaddressed condition that, without services, may prevent the child from safely returning to or remaining in the home;

(2) the child's need for permanency;

(3) the failure of a party to substantially comply with a task in the original case plan, including the ineffectiveness of a previously offered service;

(4) an error or oversight in the case plan; or

(5) information discovered or circumstances arising after the approval of the plan regarding the provision of safe and proper care for the child.

(c) Service. A copy of the amended plan must be immediately given to all parties.

Added Feb. 8, 2007 (951 So.2d 804).

Rule 8.425. Permanency Hearings

(a) Required Review. A permanency hearing must be held no later than 12 months after the date the child was removed from the home or within 30 days after a court determines that reasonable efforts to return a child to either parent are not required, whichever occurs first. A permanency hearing must be held at least every 12 months for any child who continues to be supervised by the department or awaits adoption.

(b) Determinations at Hearing.

(1) The court shall determine

(A) whether the current permanency goal for the child is appropriate or should be changed;

(B) when the child will achieve one of the permanency goals; and

(C) whether the department has made reasonable efforts to finalize the permanency plan currently in effect.

(2) The court shall approve a permanency goal for the child as provided by law choosing from the following options, listed in order of preference:

(A) reunification;

(B) adoption, if a petition for termination of parental rights has been or will be filed;

(C) permanent guardianship of a dependent child under section 39.6221, Florida Statutes;

(D) permanent placement with a fit and willing relative under section 39.6231, Florida Statutes; or

(E) placement in another planned permanent living arrangement under section 39.6241, Florida Statutes.

(3) The best interest of the child is the primary consideration in determining the permanency goal. The court must also consider the reasonable preference of the child if the court has found the child to be of sufficient intelligence, understanding, and experience to express a preference and any recommendation of the guardian ad litem.

(4) If the court approves a permanency goal of adoption, the court shall advise the parents of the availability of private placement of the child with an adoption entity, as defined in chapter 63, Florida Statutes.

(c) Case Plan. The case plan must list the tasks necessary to finalize the permanency placement and shall be amended at the permanency hearing if necessary. If a concurrent case plan is in place, the court shall approve a single goal that is in the child's best interest.

(d) Permanency Order.

(1) The findings of the court regarding reasonable efforts to finalize the permanency plan must be explicitly documented, made on a case-by-case basis, and stated in the court order.

(2) The court shall enter an order approving the permanency goal for the child.

(3) If the court approves a permanency goal of adoption, the order approving this goal shall include a provision stating that the court advised the parents of the availability of private placement of the child with

an adoption entity as defined in chapter 63, Florida Statutes, during the permanency hearing.

(4) If the court approves a permanency goal of permanent guardianship of a dependent child, placement with a fit and willing relative, or another planned permanent living arrangement, the court shall make findings as to why this permanent placement is established without adoption of the child to follow. The department and the guardian ad litem must provide the court with a recommended list and description of services needed by the child, such as independent living services and medical, dental, educational, or psychological referrals, and a recommended list and description of services needed by his or her caregiver.

(5) If the court establishes a permanent guardianship for the child, the court's written order shall

(A) transfer parental rights with respect to the child relating to protection, education, care and control of the person, custody of the person, and decision-making on behalf of the child to the permanent guardian;

(B) list the circumstances or reasons why the child's parents are not fit to care for the child and why reunification is not possible by referring to specific findings of fact made in its order adjudicating the child dependent or by making separate findings of fact;

(C) state the reasons why a permanent guardianship is being established instead of adoption;

(D) specify the frequency and nature of visitation or contact between the child and his or her parents, siblings, and grandparents; and

(E) require that the permanent guardian not return the child to the physical care and custody of the person from whom the child was removed without the approval of the court.

(6) The court shall retain jurisdiction over the case and the child shall remain in the custody of the permanent guardian unless the order creating the permanent guardianship is modified by the court. The court shall discontinue regular review hearings and relieve the department of the responsibility for supervising the placement of the child. Notwithstanding the retention of jurisdiction, the placement shall be considered permanency for the child.

(7) If the court permanently places a child with a fit and willing relative, the court's written order shall

(A) list the circumstances or reasons why reunification is not possible by referring to specific findings of fact made in its order adjudicating the child dependent or by making separate findings of fact;

(B) state the reasons why permanent placement with a fit and willing relative is being established instead of adoption;

(C) specify the frequency and nature of visitation or contact between the child and his or her parents, siblings, and grandparents; and

(D) require that the relative not return the child to the physical care and custody of the person from whom the child was removed without the approval of the court.

(8) If the court establishes another planned permanent living arrangement as the child's permanency option:

(A) The court must find that a more permanent placement, such as adoption, permanent guardianship, or placement with a fit and willing relative, is not in the best interests of the child.

(B) The department shall document reasons why the placement will endure and how the proposed arrangement will be more stable and secure than ordinary foster care.

(C) The court must find that the health, safety, and well-being of the child will not be jeopardized by such an arrangement.

(D) The court must find that compelling reasons exist to show that placement in another planned permanent living arrangement is the most appropriate permanency goal.

(e) Entry of Separate Order Establishing Permanency. If the court permanently places a child in a permanent guardianship or with a fit and willing relative, the court shall enter a separate order establishing the authority of the permanent guardian or relative to care for the child, reciting that individual's powers and authority with respect to the child and providing any other information the court deems proper which can be provided to persons who are not parties to the proceeding as necessary, notwithstanding the confidentiality provisions of Chapter 39, Florida Statutes.

(f) Recommendations for Sustaining Permanency. If the court approves a goal of placement with a fit and willing relative or another planned permanent living arrangement, the department and the guardian ad litem must provide the court with a recommended list and description of services needed by the child, and a recommended list and description of services needed by his or her caregiver.

Added Feb. 8, 2007 (951 So.2d 804). Amended Oct. 11, 2012 (101 So.3d 368); Oct. 3, 2013 (123 So.3d 1128).

Rule 8.430. Modification of Permanency Order

(a) Best Interests of Child. The permanency placement is intended to continue until the child reaches the age of majority and may not be disturbed absent a finding by the court that the circumstances of the permanency placement are no longer in the best interest of the child.

(b) Request for Modification by a Parent.

(1) If a parent who has not had his or her parental rights terminated makes a motion for reunification or increased contact with the child, the court shall first hold a hearing to determine whether the dependency

case should be reopened and whether there should be a modification of the order. At the hearing, the parent must demonstrate that the safety, well-being, and physical, mental, and emotional health of the child is not endangered by the modification.

(2) The court shall base its decision concerning any motion by a parent for reunification or increased contact with a child on the effect of the decision on the safety, well-being, and physical and emotional health of the child. Factors that must be considered and addressed in the findings of fact of the order on the motion must include

(A) the compliance or noncompliance of the parent with the case plan;

(B) the circumstances which caused the child's dependency and whether those circumstances have been resolved;

(C) the stability and length of the child's placement;

(D) the preference of the child, if the child is of sufficient age and understanding to express a preference;

(E) the recommendation of the current custodian; and

(F) the recommendation of the guardian ad litem, if one has been appointed.

Added Feb. 8, 2007 (951 So.2d 804).

Rule 8.435. Reinstatement of Jurisdiction for Young Adult

(a) Petition for Reinstatement of Jurisdiction.

(1) If a young adult who is between the ages of 18 and 21 is re-admitted to foster care, the department shall petition the court to reinstate jurisdiction over the young adult.

(2) The petition for reinstatement of jurisdiction must be in writing and specify that the young adult meets the eligibility requirements for readmission to foster care as provided by law. The petition is not required to be sworn and notarized.

(3) The department shall serve the young adult and any party a copy of the petition for reinstatement of jurisdiction.

(b) Hearing on Petition for Reinstatement of Jurisdiction.

(1) Upon filing of the petition for reinstatement of jurisdiction, the court shall schedule and conduct a hearing on the petition for reinstatement of jurisdiction.

(2) The department shall serve the young adult and any party a notice of the hearing on the petition for reinstatement of jurisdiction.

(c) Order on Petition for Reinstatement of Jurisdiction.

(1) If the department establishes that the young adult meets the eligibility requirements for readmission to foster care as provided by law, the court shall enter an order reinstating jurisdiction over the young adult.

(2) In the order reinstating jurisdiction, the court shall schedule a judicial review hearing to take place within 6 months.

Added March 20, 2014, effective March 20, 2014 (136 So.3d 508).

E. TERMINATION OF PARENTAL RIGHTS

Rule 8.500. Petition

(a) Initiation of Proceedings.

(1) All proceedings seeking the termination of parental rights to a child shall be initiated by the filing of an original petition in the pending dependency action, if any.

(2) A petition for termination of parental rights may be filed at any time by the department, the guardian ad litem, or any person having knowledge of the facts. Each petition shall be titled a petition for termination of parental rights.

(3) When provided by law, a separate petition for dependency need not be filed.

(b) Contents.

(1) The petition shall contain allegations as to the identity and residence of the parents, if known.

(2) The petition shall identify the age, sex, and name of the child. Two or more children may be the subject of the same petition.

(3) The petition shall include facts supporting allegations that each of the applicable statutory elements for termination of parental rights has been met.

(4) When required by law, the petition shall contain a showing that the parents were offered a case plan and did not substantially comply with it.

(5) The petition shall contain an allegation that the parents will be informed of the availability of private placement of the child with an adoption entity, as defined in chapter 63, Florida Statutes.

(6) The petition shall have a certified copy of the birth certificate of each child named in it attached unless the petitioner, after diligent search and inquiry, is unable to produce it, in which case the petition shall state the date and place of birth of each child, unless these matters cannot be ascertained after diligent search and inquiry or for other good cause.

(c) Verification. The petition shall be signed under oath stating the good faith of the petitioner in filing it. No objection to a petition on the grounds that it was not signed or verified as required shall be entertained after a plea to the merits.

(d) Amendments. At any time before the conclusion of an adjudicatory hearing, an amended petition may be filed or the petition may be amended by motion. However, after a written answer has been filed or the adjudicatory hearing has commenced, amendments shall be permitted only with the permission of the court unless all parties consent. Amendments shall be freely permitted in the interest of justice and the welfare of the child. A continuance shall be granted on motion and a showing that the amendment prejudices or materially affects any party.

(e) Defects and Variances. No petition or any count of it shall be dismissed, or any judgment vacated, because of any defect in the form of the petition or of misjoinder of counts. If the court is of the opinion that the petition is so vague, indistinct, and indefinite as to mislead the parent and prejudice him or her in the preparation of a defense, the petitioner will be required to furnish a more definite statement.

(f) Voluntary Dismissal. The petitioner, without leave of the court, at any time before entry of an order of adjudication, may request a voluntary dismissal of the petition by serving a notice of request of dismissal on all parties or, if during a hearing, by so stating on the record. The petition shall be dismissed and the court loses jurisdiction unless another party adopts the petition within 72 hours. Unless otherwise stated, the dismissal shall be without prejudice.

(g) Parental Consent.

(1) The parents of the child may consent to the petition for termination of parental rights at any time, in writing or orally, on the record.

(2) If, before the filing of the petition for termination of parental rights, the parents have consented to the termination of parental rights and executed surrenders and waivers of notice of hearing as provided by law, this shall be alleged in the petition and copies shall be attached to the petition and presented to the court.

(3) If the parents appear and enter an oral consent on the record to the termination of parental rights, the court shall determine the basis on which a factual finding may be made and shall incorporate these findings into its order of disposition.

Added May 9, 1991, effective July 1, 1991 (589 So.2d 818). Amended Sept. 28, 1995 (661 So.2d 800); Sept. 18, 1998, effective Oct. 1, 1998 (725 So.2d 296); June 10, 1999, effective July 1, 1999 (753 So.2d 1214); Oct. 26, 2000, effective Jan. 1, 2001 (783 So.2d 138); Jan. 27, 2005 (894 So.2d 875); Oct. 11, 2012 (101 So.3d 368).

Rule 8.505. Process and Service

(a) Personal Service. On the filing of a petition requesting the termination of parental rights, a copy of the petition and notice of the date, time, and place of the advisory hearing must be personally served on

(1) the parents;

(2) the legal custodians or caregivers of the child;

(3) if the natural parents are dead or unknown, a living relative of the child, unless on diligent search and inquiry no relative can be found;

(4) any person who has physical custody of the child;

(5) any grandparents entitled by law to notice of the adoption proceeding;

(6) any prospective parent identified by law;

(7) the guardian ad litem for the child or the representative of the guardian ad litem program, if the program has been appointed;

(8) the attorney ad litem for the child if one has been appointed; and

(9) any other person as provided by law.

(b) Contents. The document containing the notice to appear shall notify the required persons of the filing of the petition and must contain in type at least as large as the balance of the document the following or substantially similar language:

"FAILURE TO PERSONALLY APPEAR AT THE ADVISORY HEARING CONSTITUTES CONSENT TO THE TERMINATION OF PARENTAL RIGHTS OF THIS CHILD (THESE CHILDREN). IF YOU FAIL TO APPEAR ON THE DATE AND TIME SPECIFIED, YOU MAY LOSE ALL LEGAL RIGHTS AS A PARENT TO THE CHILD OR CHILDREN NAMED IN THE PETITION ATTACHED TO THIS NOTICE."

(c) Constructive Service. Parties whose identities are known and on whom personal service of process cannot be effected shall be served by publication as provided by law. The notice of action shall contain the initials of the child and the child's date of birth. There shall be no other identifying information of the child in the notice of action. The notice of action shall include the full name and last known address of the person subject to the notice. The notice of action shall not contain the name or any other identifying information of the other parents or prospective parents who are not subject to the notice.

(d) Waiver of Service. Service of process may be waived, as provided by law, for persons who have executed a written surrender of the child to the department.

Added May 9, 1991, effective July 1, 1991 (589 So.2d 818). Amended Sept. 28, 1995 (661 So.2d 800); Sept. 18, 1998, effective Oct. 1, 1998 (725 So.2d 296); June 10, 1999, effective July 1, 1999 (753 So.2d 1214); Oct. 26, 2000, effective Jan. 1, 2001 (783 So.2d 138); March 1, 2001 (796 So.2d 468); Jan. 27, 2005 (894 So.2d 875); Dec. 17, 2009, effective Jan. 1, 2010 (26 So.3d 552).

Rule 8.510. Advisory Hearing and Pretrial Status Conferences

(a) Advisory Hearing.

(1) An advisory hearing on the petition to terminate parental rights must be held as soon as possible after service of process can be effected, but no less than 72 hours following service of process. Personal appearance of any person at the advisory hearing eliminates the time requirement for serving process on that person.

(2) The court must:

(A) advise the parents of their right to counsel and appoint counsel in accordance with legal requirements;

(B) advise the parents of the availability of private placement of the child with an adoption entity, as defined in chapter 63, Florida Statutes;

(C) determine whether an admission, consent, or denial to the petition shall be entered; and

(D) appoint a guardian ad litem if one has not already been appointed.

(3) If a parent served with notice fails to personally appear at the advisory hearing, the court shall enter a consent to the termination of parental rights petition for the parent who failed to personally appear.

(4) If an admission or consent is entered by all parents for a named child included in the petition for termination of parental rights and the court finds that termination of parental rights is in the best interest of the child, the court shall proceed to disposition alternatives as provided by law.

(5) If a denial is entered, the court shall set an adjudicatory hearing within the period of time provided by law or grant a continuance until the parties have sufficient time to proceed to an adjudicatory hearing.

(b) Pretrial Status Conference. Not less than 10 days before the adjudicatory hearing on a petition for involuntary termination of parental rights, the court shall conduct a pretrial status conference to determine the order in which each party may present witnesses or evidence, the order in which cross-examination and argument shall occur, and any other matters that may aid in the conduct of the adjudicatory hearing.

(c) Voluntary Terminations. An advisory hearing may not be held if a petition is filed seeking an adjudication to voluntarily terminate parental rights. Adjudicatory hearings for petitions for voluntary termination must be set within 21 days of the filing of the petition. Notice of intent to rely on this subdivision must be filed with the court as required by law.

Added May 9, 1991, effective July 1, 1991 (589 So.2d 818). Amended Oct. 31, 1996, effective Jan. 1, 1997 (684 So.2d 756); Sept. 18, 1998, effective Oct. 1, 1998 (725 So.2d 296); June 10, 1999, effective July 1, 1999 (753 So.2d 1214); Oct. 26, 2000, effective Jan. 1, 2001 (783 So.2d 138); Jan. 3, 2002, effective Jan. 15, 2002 (816 So.2d 536); Jan. 27, 2005 (894 So.2d 875); Oct. 11, 2012 (101 So.3d 368).

Rule 8.515. Providing Counsel to Parties

(a) Duty of the Court.

(1) At each hearing, the court shall advise unrepresented parents of their right to have counsel present, unless the parents have voluntarily executed a written surrender of the child and consent to the entry of a court order terminating parental rights.

(2) The court shall appoint counsel for indigent parents as provided by law. The court may appoint counsel for other parties as provided by law.

(3) The court shall ascertain whether the right to counsel is understood. If the right to counsel is waived by any parent the court shall ascertain if the right to counsel is knowingly and intelligently waived.

(4) The court shall enter its findings with respect to the appointment or waiver of counsel of indigent parents or the waiver of the right to have counsel present.

(5) Once counsel has been retained or appointed to represent a parent, the attorney shall continue to represent the parent throughout the proceedings or until the court has approved discontinuing the attorney-client relationship. If the attorney-client relationship is discontinued, the court shall advise the parent of the right to have new counsel retained or appointed for the remainder of the proceedings.

(b) Waiver of Counsel.

(1) No waiver shall be accepted if it appears that the parent is unable to make an intelligent and understanding choice because of mental condition, age, education, experience, the nature or complexity of the case, or other factors.

(2) A waiver of counsel shall be made in court and be of record. The court shall question the parent in sufficient detail to ascertain that the waiver is made knowingly and intelligently.

(3) If a waiver is accepted at any hearing, the offer of assistance of counsel shall be renewed by the court at each subsequent hearing at which the parent appears without counsel.

Added May 9, 1991, effective July 1, 1991 (589 So.2d 818). Amended Nov. 5, 1992, effective Jan. 1, 1993 (608 So.2d 478); Sept. 18, 1998, effective Oct. 1, 1998 (725 So.2d 296); Jan. 27, 2005 (894 So.2d 875); Sept. 21, 2006, effective Jan. 1, 2007 (939 So.2d 74).

Rule 8.517. Withdrawal and Appointment of Counsel

(a) Order Adjudicating Child Dependent or Terminating Parental Rights. After an order of adjudication of dependency, an order of disposition, or an order terminating parental rights has been entered, the counsel of record for a parent or legal custodian in a dependency proceeding or a parent in a termination of parental rights proceeding shall not be permitted to withdraw as counsel of record until the following have occurred:

(1) The attorney certifies that the attorney has discussed appellate remedies with the parent or legal custodian.

(A) The attorney certifies that after discussing appellate remedies with the parent or legal custodian, the parent or legal custodian does not want to appeal the order; or

(B) The attorney certifies that after discussing appellate remedies with the parent or legal custodian, the parent or legal custodian wants to appeal the order, and

(i) a notice of appeal containing the signatures of counsel and the parent or legal custodian has been filed;

(ii) directions to clerk, if necessary, have been filed;

(iii) a motion to transcribe the requisite proceedings has been filed;

(iv) a designation to the court reporter specifying the proceedings that must be transcribed in order to obtain review of the issues on appeal and designating the parties to receive a copy of the transcripts has been filed; and

(v) an order appointing appellate counsel, if any, has been entered.

Conformed copies of each of these documents shall be attached to the motion to withdraw.

(2) If the attorney has been unable to contact the parent or legal custodian regarding appellate remedies, the attorney certifies the efforts made to contact the parent or legal custodian.

(b) Service of Order Appointing Counsel. Following rendition of an order appointing appellate counsel, the court shall serve a copy of the order on the appointed appellate counsel and the clerk of the appellate court.

Adopted May 23, 2013, effective July 1, 2013 (115 So.3d 286).

Rule 8.520. Answers and Responsive Pleadings

(a) No Written Answer Required. No answer to the petition need be filed by the parent. The parent of the child may enter an oral or written answer to the petition or appear and remain silent.

(b) Plea of Denial. If the parent denies the allegations of the petition, appears and remains silent, or pleads evasively, the court shall enter a denial and shall set the case for an adjudicatory hearing.

(c) Plea of Admission or Consent. If the parent appears and enters a plea of admission or consent to the termination of parental rights, the court shall determine that the admission or consent is made voluntarily and with a full understanding of the nature of the allegations and the possible consequences of the plea and that the parent has been advised of the right to be represented by counsel. The court shall incorporate these findings into its order of disposition, in addition to findings of fact specifying the act or acts causing the termination of parental rights.

Added May 9, 1991, effective July 1, 1991 (589 So.2d 818). Amended Sept. 28, 1995 (661 So.2d 800); Sept. 18, 1998, effective Oct. 1, 1998 (725 So.2d 296); Oct. 26, 2000, effective Jan. 1, 2001 (783 So.2d 138).

Rule 8.525. Adjudicatory Hearings

(a) Hearing by Judge. The adjudicatory hearing shall be conducted by the judge without a jury using the rules of evidence for civil cases. At this hearing the court shall determine whether the elements required by law for termination of parental rights have been established by clear and convincing evidence.

(b) Time of Hearing. The adjudicatory hearing shall be held within 45 days after the advisory hearing, unless all necessary parties stipulate to some other hearing date. Reasonable continuances may be granted for purposes of investigation, discovery, procuring counsel or witnesses, or for other good cause shown.

(c) Examination of Witnesses. A party may call any person, including a child, as a witness. A party shall have the right to examine or cross-examine all witnesses.

(d) Presence of Parties. All parties have the right to be present at all termination hearings. A party may appear in person or, at the discretion of the court for good cause shown, by an audio or audiovisual device. No party shall be excluded from any hearing unless so ordered by the court for disruptive behavior or as provided by law. If a parent appears for the advisory hearing and the court orders that parent to personally appear at the adjudicatory hearing for the petition for termination of parental rights, stating the date, time, and location of this hearing, then failure of that parent to personally appear at the adjudicatory hearing shall constitute consent for termination of parental rights.

(e) Examination of Child. The court may hear the testimony of the child outside the physical presence of the parties as provided by rule 8.255. Counsel for the parties shall be present during all examinations. The court may limit the manner in which counsel examine the child.

(f) Previous Testimony Admissible. To avoid unnecessary duplication of expenses, in-court testimony previously given at any properly noticed hearing may be admitted, without regard to the availability of the witnesses, if the recorded testimony itself is made available. Consideration of previous testimony does not preclude the parties from calling the witness to answer supplemental questions.

(g) Joint and Separate Hearings. When 2 or more children are the subject of a petition for termination of parental rights, the hearings may be held simultaneously if the children are related to each other or involved in the same case, unless the court orders separate hearings.

(h) Motion for Judgment of Dismissal. In all termination of parental rights proceedings, if at the close of the evidence for the petitioner the parents move for a judgment of dismissal and the court is of the opinion that the evidence is insufficient to sustain the grounds for termination alleged in the petition, it shall enter an order denying the termination and proceed with dispositional alternatives as provided by law.

(i) Final Judgment.

(1) *Terminating Parental Rights.* If the court finds after all of the evidence has been presented that the elements and one of the grounds for termination of parental rights have been established by clear and convincing evidence, the court shall enter a final judgment terminating parental rights and proceed with dispositional alternatives as provided by law. The order must contain the findings of fact and conclusions of law on which the decision was based. The court shall include the dates of the adjudicatory hearing in the order. The parties may stipulate, or the court may order, that parents or relatives of the parent whose rights are terminated be allowed to maintain some contact with the child. If the court orders continued contact, the nature and frequency of this contact must be stated in a written order. The visitation order may be reviewed on motion of any party, including a prospective adoptive parent, and must be reviewed by the court at the time the child is placed for adoption.

(2) *Denying Termination of Parental Rights.* If the court finds after all of the evidence has been presented that the grounds for termination of parental rights have not been established by clear and convincing evidence, but that the grounds for dependency have been established by a preponderance of the evidence, the court shall adjudicate or readjudicate the child dependent and proceed with dispositional alternatives as provided by law.

(3) *Dismissing Petition.* If the court finds after all of the evidence has been presented that the allegations in the petition do not establish grounds for dependency or termination of parental rights, it shall enter an order dismissing the petition.

Added May 9, 1991, effective July 1, 1991 (589 So.2d 818). Amended Oct. 31, 1996, effective Jan. 1, 1997 (684 So.2d 756); Sept. 18, 1998, effective Oct. 1, 1998 (725 So.2d 296); June 10, 1999, effective July 1, 1999 (753 So.2d 1214); Nov. 22, 2000, effective Jan. 1, 2001 (789 So.2d 951); Sept. 5, 2002, effective Jan. 1, 2003 (827 So.2d 219); Jan. 27, 2005 (894 So.2d 875); Nov. 12, 2009 (24 So.3d 47).

Rule 8.535. Postdisposition Hearings

(a) Initial Hearing. If the court terminates parental rights, a postdisposition hearing must be set within 30 days after the date of disposition. At the hearing, the department or licensed child-placing agency shall provide to the court a plan for permanency for the child.

(b) Subsequent Hearings. Following the initial postdisposition hearing, the court shall hold hearings every 6 months to review progress being made toward permanency for the child until the child is adopted or reaches the age of 18, whichever occurs first. Review hearings for alternative forms of permanent placement shall be held as provided by law.

(c) Continuing Jurisdiction. The court that terminates the parental rights to a child under chapter 39, Florida Statutes, shall retain exclusive jurisdiction in all matters pertaining to the child's adoption under chapter 63, Florida Statutes. The petition for adoption must be filed in the division of the circuit court that entered the judgment terminating parental rights, unless a motion for change of venue is granted as provided by law.

(d) Withholding Consent to Adopt.

(1) When a petition for adoption and a favorable home study under section 39.812(5), Florida Statutes, have been filed and the department's consent has not been filed, the court shall conduct a hearing to determine if the department has unreasonably withheld consent.

(2) In reviewing whether the department unreasonably withheld its consent to adopt, the court shall determine whether the department abused its discretion by withholding consent to the adoption by the petitioner. In making this determination, the court shall consider all relevant information, including information obtained or otherwise used by the department in selecting the adoptive family, pursuant to Florida Administrative Code Chapter 65C.

(3) If the court determines that the department unreasonably withheld consent to adopt, and the petitioner has filed with the court a favorable home study as required by law, the court shall incorporate its findings into a written order with specific findings of fact as to how the department abused its discretion in withholding its consent to adopt, and the consent of the department shall be waived.

Added Oct. 31, 1996, effective Jan. 1, 1997 (684 So.2d 756). Amended Sept. 18, 1998, effective Oct. 1, 1998 (725 So.2d 296); Jan. 27, 2005 (894 So.2d 875); Sept. 21, 2006, effective Jan. 1, 2007 (939 So.2d 74).

PART IV. PROCEEDINGS FOR FAMILIES AND CHILDREN IN NEED OF SERVICES

2012 Revision

Part IV, "Proceedings for Families and Children in Need of Services", added as Part III, was renumbered as Part IV by Florida Supreme Court Opinion No. SC11-399 (102 So.3d 451).

Former Part IV, "Other Proceedings", was renumbered as Part V by Florida Supreme Court Opinion No. SC11-399 (102 So.3d 451).

Rule 8.601. Commencement of Proceedings

(a) Pleadings. All proceedings shall be initiated by the filing of:

(1) a request to take into custody;

(2) a petition for children in need of services; or

(3) a shelter petition.

(b) File to Be Opened. Upon commencement of any proceeding, the clerk shall open a file and assign a case number.

Added May 9, 1991, effective July 1, 1991 (589 So.2d 818).

Rule 8.603. Application of Uniform Child Custody Jurisdiction and Enforcement Act

Any pleading filed commencing proceedings as set forth in rule 8.601 shall be accompanied by an affidavit, to the extent of affiant's personal knowledge, under the Uniform Child Custody Jurisdiction and Enforcement Act. Each party has a continuing duty to inform the court of any custody, dependency, or children in need of services proceeding in this or any other state of which the party obtains information during the proceeding.

Added May 9, 1991, effective July 1, 1991 (589 So.2d 818). Amended Jan. 27, 2005 (894 So.2d 875).

Rule 8.605. Transfer of Cases

(a) Transfer of Cases Within the State of Florida. After the commencement of a proceeding pursuant to rule 8.601, the court may transfer any case after adjudication, when adjudication is withheld, or before adjudication where witnesses are available in another jurisdiction, to the circuit court for the county in which is located the domicile or usual residence of the child or such other circuit as the court may determine to be for the best interest of the child and to promote the efficient administration of justice. The transferring court shall enter an order transferring its jurisdiction and certifying the case to the proper court, furnishing all parties, the clerk, and the state attorney of the receiving court a copy of the order of transfer within 5 days. The clerk shall also transmit a certified copy of the file to the receiving court within 5 days.

(b) Transfer of Cases Among States. If it should appear at any time that an action involving the child is pending in another state, the court may transfer jurisdiction, stay the proceedings, or dismiss the action as provided by law.

Added May 9, 1991, effective July 1, 1991 (589 So.2d 818).

Rule 8.610. Parties

(a) Definitions. For the purposes of these rules the terms "party" and "parties" shall include the petitioner, the child, the parent, the guardian ad litem where appointed, the custodian, and every person upon whom service of summons is required by law.

(b) Other Parties. The state attorney's office, the Department of Children and Family Services, or the Department of Juvenile Justice may become a party upon notice to all other parties and the court. The court may add additional parties.

Added May 9, 1991, effective July 1, 1991 (589 So.2d 818). Amended Oct. 31, 1996, effective Jan. 1, 1997 (684 So.2d 756); Oct. 26, 2000, effective Jan. 1, 2001 (783 So.2d 138).

Rule 8.615. Providing Counsel to Parties

(a) Duty of the Court.

(1) At each stage of the proceeding the court shall advise all parties of their right to have counsel present. The court shall appoint counsel to insolvent persons who are so entitled as provided by law. The court shall ascertain whether the right to counsel is understood and, where appropriate, knowingly and intelligently waived. The court shall enter its findings in writing with respect to the appointment or waiver of counsel for insolvent parties.

(2) The court may appoint an attorney for the child or parent, guardian, or custodian of the child as provided by law.

(b) Waiver of Counsel.

(1) No waiver shall be accepted where it appears that the party is unable to make an intelligent and understanding choice because of mental condition, age, education, experience, the nature or complexity of the case, or other factors.

(2) A waiver of counsel shall be made in court and be of record.

(3) If a waiver is accepted at any stage of the proceedings, the offer of assistance of counsel shall be renewed by the court at each subsequent stage of the

proceedings at which the party appears without counsel.

Added May 9, 1991, effective July 1, 1991 (589 So.2d 818).

Rule 8.617. Guardian Ad Litem

(a) Appointment. At any stage of the proceedings any party may request, or the court may appoint, a guardian ad litem to represent any child alleged to be in need of services or from a family in need of services.

(b) Qualifications; Responsibilities. The guardian ad litem shall be an attorney or other responsible adult and shall have the following responsibilities:

(1) To investigate the allegations of the petition and any subsequent matters arising in the case and, unless excused by the court, to file a written report. This report shall include a statement of the wishes of the child and the recommendations of the guardian ad litem and shall be provided to all parties and the court at least 48 hours before the disposition hearing.

(2) To be present at all court hearings unless excused by the court.

(3) To represent the interest of the child until the jurisdiction of the court over the child terminates or until excused by the court.

(4) To perform such other duties and undertake such other responsibilities as the court may direct.

(c) Bond Not Required. A guardian ad litem shall not be required to post bond but shall file an acceptance of the office.

(d) Receiving Service. A guardian ad litem shall be entitled to receive service of pleadings and papers as provided by rule 8.635.

(e) Lay Guardians' Duties. The duties of lay guardians shall not include the practice of law.

(f) Substitution or Discharge. The court, on its own motion or that of any party, including the child, may substitute or discharge the guardian ad litem for reasonable cause.

Added May 9, 1991, effective July 1, 1991 (589 So.2d 818). Amended Oct. 31, 1996, effective Jan. 1, 1997 (684 So.2d 756).

Rule 8.620. Style of Pleadings and Orders

All pleadings and orders shall be styled: "In the interest of ______, a child", or "In the interest of ______, children."

Added May 9, 1991, effective July 1, 1991 (589 So.2d 818).

Rule 8.625. General Provisions for Hearings

(a) Presence of Counsel. The Department of Children and Family Services or the Department of Juvenile Justice must be represented by an attorney at every stage of these proceedings when such department is a party.

(b) Presence of Child. The child shall be present unless the child's presence is waived. If the child is present at the beginning of a hearing and during the progress of the hearing voluntarily absents himself or herself from the presence of the court without leave of the court, or is removed from the presence of the court because of disruptive conduct during the hearing, the hearing shall not be postponed or delayed, but shall proceed in all respects as if the child were present in court at all times.

(c) In Camera Proceedings. The child may be examined by the court outside the presence of other parties under circumstances as provided by law. The court shall assure that the proceedings are recorded unless otherwise stipulated by the parties.

(d) Invoking the Rule. Before the examination of any witness the court may, and on the request of any party shall, exclude all other witnesses. The court may cause witnesses to be kept separate and to be prevented from communicating with each other until all are examined.

(e) Continuances. The court may grant a continuance before or during a hearing for good cause shown by any party.

(f) Record. A record of the testimony in all hearings shall be made by an official court reporter, a court-approved stenographer, or a recording device. The records of testimony shall be preserved as required by law. Official records of testimony shall be transcribed only on order of the court.

(g) Notice. Where these rules do not require a specific notice, all parties will be given reasonable notice of any hearing.

(h) Magistrates. Pursuant to the Florida Rules of Civil Procedure, both general and special magistrates may be appointed to hear issues involved in proceedings under this part.

Added May 9, 1991, effective July 1, 1991 (589 So.2d 818). Amended Oct. 31, 1996, effective Jan. 1, 1997 (684 So.2d 756); Oct. 26, 2000, effective Jan. 1, 2001 (783 So.2d 138); Sept. 30, 2004, effective Oct. 1, 2004 (887 So.2d 1090).

Rule 8.630. Computation and Enlargement of Time

(a) Computation. Computation of time shall be governed by Florida Rule of Judicial Administration, except for rule 8.655, to which rule 2.514(a)(2)(C) shall not apply and the statutory time period shall govern.

(b) Enlargement of Time. When by these rules, by a notice given thereunder, or by order of court an act is required or allowed to be done at or within a specified time, the court for good cause shown may, at any time in its discretion, (1) with or without notice order the period enlarged if the request is made before the expiration of the period originally prescribed or as extended by a previous order, or (2) upon motion made and notice after the expiration of the specified period permit the act to be done where the failure to act was the result of excusable neglect; but it may not, except as provided by law or elsewhere in these rules, extend the time for making motion for new trial, for rehearing, or for vacation of judgment or for taking an appeal. This rule shall not be construed to apply to detention or shelter hearings.

(c) Time for Service of Motions and Notice of Hearing. A copy of any written motion which may not be heard ex parte and a copy of the notice of the hearing thereof shall be served a reasonable time before the time specified for the hearing.

Added May 9, 1991, effective July 1, 1991 (589 So.2d 818). Amended July 12, 2012, effective Oct. 1, 2012 (95 So.3d 96).

Rule 8.635. Process

(a) Summons and Subpoenas.

(1) *Summons.* Upon the filing of a petition, the clerk shall issue a summons. The summons shall require the person on whom it is served to appear for a hearing at a time and place specified. Except in cases of medical emergency, the time of hearing shall not be less than 24 hours after service of the summons. If the child is not detained by an order of the court, the summons shall require the custodian to produce the child at the said time and place. A copy of the petition shall be attached to the summons.

(2) *Subpoenas.* Upon the application of a party, the clerk shall issue, and the court on its own motion may issue, subpoenas requiring attendance and testimony of witnesses and production of records, documents, or other tangible objects at any hearing. This subdivision shall not in any way limit the state attorney's power to issue subpoenas.

(3) *Service.* The summons and other process shall be served upon such persons and in such manner as required by law. If the parents or custodian are out of the state and their address is known, the clerk shall give them notice of the proceedings by mail. Service of process may be waived. Authorized agents of the Department of Juvenile Justice may also serve summons and other process upon such persons and in such manner as required by law.

(b) Service of Pleadings and Papers.

(1) *When Required.* Unless the court orders otherwise, or a statute or supreme court administrative order specifies a different means of service, every pleading subsequent to the initial petition, every order, every written motion, unless it is one as to which hearing ex parte is authorized, and every written notice filed in the case shall be served on each party; however, nothing herein shall be construed to require that a plea be in writing or that an application for witness subpoenas be served.

(2) *How Made.* When service is required or permitted to be made upon a party represented by an attorney, service shall be made upon the attorney unless service upon the party is ordered by the court. All documents required or permitted to be served on another party must be served by e-mail, unless the parties otherwise stipulate or this rule otherwise provides.

(A) Service by Electronic Mail ("e-mail"). Service of a document by e-mail is made by an e-mail sent to all addresses designated by the attorney or party with either (a) a copy of the document in PDF format attached or (b) a link to the document on a website maintained by a clerk. Any document served by e-mail may be signed by any of the "/s/," "/s," or "s/" formats, so long as the filed document is signed in accordance with the applicable rules of court.

(i) Service on Attorneys. Upon appearing in any proceeding, an attorney must designate a principal e-mail address and may designate no more than two secondary e-mail addresses to which service must be directed in that proceeding. Every document filed by an attorney thereafter must include in the signature block the principal e-mail address of that attorney and any secondary e-mail addresses. If an attorney does not designate any e-mail address for service, documents may be served on that attorney at the e-mail address on record with The Florida Bar.

(ii) Exception to E-mail Service on Attorneys. Upon motion by an attorney demonstrating that the attorney has no e-mail account and lacks access to the Internet at the attorney's office, the court may excuse the attorney from the requirements of e-mail service. Service on and by an attorney excused by the court from e-mail service must be by the means provided in subdivision (b)(2)(B) of this rule.

(iii) Service on and by Parties not Represented by an Attorney. Any party not represented by an attorney may serve a designation of a principal e-mail address and also may designate no more than two secondary e-mail addresses to which service must be directed in that proceeding by the means provided in subdivision (b)(2)(A) of this rule. If a party not represented by an attorney does not designate an e-mail address for service in a proceeding, service on and by that party must be by the means provided in subdivision (b)(2)(B) of this rule.

(iv) Format of E–mail for Service. All documents served by e-mail must be sent by an e-mail message containing a subject line beginning with the words "SERVICE OF COURT DOCUMENT" in all capital letters, followed by the case number of the proceeding in which the documents are being served. The body of the e-mail must identify the court in which the proceeding is pending, the case number, the name of the initial party on each side, the title of each document served with that e-mail, and the sender's name and telephone number. Any e-mail which, together with its attachments, exceeds five megabytes (5MB) in size, must be divided and sent as separate e-mails, numbered in the subject line, no one of which may exceed 5MB in size.

(v) Time of Service. Service by e-mail is complete on the day it is sent and must be treated as service by mail for the computation of time. If the sender learns that the e-mail did not reach the address of the person to be served, the sender must immediately serve another copy by e-mail, or by a means authorized by subdivision (b)(2)(B) of this rule.

(B) Service by Other Means. In addition to, and not in lieu of, service by e-mail, service may also be made upon attorneys by the means specified in this subdivision. Service on and by all parties who are not represented by an attorney and who do not designate an e-mail address, and on and by all attorneys excused from e-mail service, must be made by delivering a copy of the document or by mailing it to the party or attorney at their last known address or, if no address is known, by leaving it with the clerk of the court. Service by mail is complete upon mailing. Delivery of a copy within this rule is complete upon:

(i) handing it to the attorney or to the party;

(ii) leaving it at the attorney's or party's office with a clerk or other person in charge thereof;

(iii) if there is no one in charge, leaving it in a conspicuous place therein;

(iv) if the office is closed or the person to be served has no office, leaving it at the person's usual place of abode with some person of his or her family above 15 years of age and informing such person of the contents; or

(v) transmitting it by facsimile to the attorney's or party's office with a cover sheet containing the sender's name, firm, address, telephone number, and facsimile number, and the number of pages transmitted. When service is made by facsimile, a copy must also be served by any other method permitted by this rule. Facsimile service occurs when transmission is complete.

(vi) Service by delivery shall be deemed complete on the date of the delivery.

(C) Numerous Parties. In an action where the parties are unusually numerous, the court may regulate the service contemplated by these rules on motion or on its own initiative in such manner as may be found to be just and reasonable.

(3) *Filing.* All documents must be filed with the court either before service or immediately thereafter, unless otherwise provided for by general law or other rules. If the original of any bond or document required to be an original is not placed in the court file or deposited with the clerk, a certified copy may be so placed by the clerk.

(4) *Filing with Court Defined.* The filing of documents with the court as required by these rules shall be made by filing them with the clerk in accordance with rule 8.004 except that the judge may permit documents to be filed with the judge, in which event the judge must note the filing date before him or her on the documents and transmit them to the clerk. The date of filing is the date shown on the face of the document by the judge's notation or the clerk's time stamp, whichever is earlier.

(5) *Certificate of Service.* When any attorney shall in substance certify:

"I certify that a copy/copies has/have been furnished to (insert name or names) by (e-mail) (delivery) (mail) (fax) on (date).

____

Title"

this certificate shall be taken as prima facie proof of such service in compliance with this rule.

(6) *Service by Clerk.* When the clerk is required to serve notices and other documents, the clerk may do so by e-mail or by any other method permitted in subdivision (b)(2). Service by a clerk is not required to be by e-mail.

(c) Service of Orders. A copy of all orders or judgments must be transmitted by the court or under its direction to all parties at the time of entry of the order or judgment. The court may require that orders or judgments be prepared by a party, may require the party to furnish the court with stamped addressed envelopes for service of the order or judgment, and may require that proposed orders and judgments be furnished to all parties before entry by the court of the order or judgment. The court may serve any order or judgment by e-mail to all attorneys who have designated an e-mail address for service and to all parties not represented by an attorney who have designated an e-mail address for service. This subdivision is directory and a failure to comply with it does not affect the order or its finality or any proceedings arising in the action.

Added May 9, 1991, effective July 1, 1991 (589 So.2d 818). Amended Nov. 5, 1992, effective Jan. 1, 1993 (608 So.2d 478); Oct. 31, 1996, effective Jan. 1, 1997 (684 So.2d 756); Oct. 26, 2000, effective Jan. 1, 2001 (783 So.2d 138); Sept. 5, 2002, effective Jan. 1, 2003 (827 So.2d 219); Oct. 18, 2012, effective, *nunc pro tunc*, Sept. 1, 2012 (102 So.3d 505); Oct. 3, 2013 (123 So.3d 1139).

Rule 8.640. Pleadings to Be Signed

(a) Pleadings to Be Signed by Attorney. Every written paper or pleading of a party represented by an attorney shall be signed in the attorney's individual name by the attorney, whose Florida Bar number, address, and telephone number, including area code, shall be stated, and who shall be duly licensed to practice law in Florida. The attorney may be required by an order of court to vouch for the authority to represent such party and to give the address of such party. Except when otherwise specifically provided by these rules or applicable statute, pleadings need not be verified or accompanied by affidavit.

(b) Pleadings to Be Signed by Unrepresented Party. A party who is unrepresented shall sign a written pleading or other paper to be filed and state the party's address and telephone number, including area code.

(c) Effect of Signing Pleading. The signature of a person shall constitute a certificate that the paper or pleading has been read; that to the best of the person's knowledge, information, and belief there is good ground to support it; and that it is not interposed for delay. If a pleading or paper is not signed, or is signed with intent to defeat the purpose of this rule, it may be stricken and the action may proceed as though the pleading or paper had not been served.

Added May 9, 1991, effective July 1, 1991 (589 So.2d 818). Amended Nov. 5, 1992, effective Jan. 1, 1993 (608 So.2d 478).

Committee Notes

1992 Amendment. (a) and (c) The language from (a) was moved to create this new subdivision. The current rule applies only to attorneys. These requirements also should apply to nonattorneys who sign and file papers. This rule conforms to proposed revisions to rules 8.085 and 8.230.

(b) The current rule implies that a written pleading must be filed. No written pleadings are required.

Rule 8.645. Orders

Upon the conclusion of all hearings, the court shall enter its decisions in a written order. All orders of the court shall be reduced to writing as soon after they are entered as is consistent with orderly procedure and shall contain findings of fact and conclusions of law.

Added May 9, 1991, effective July 1, 1991 (589 So.2d 818).

Rule 8.650. Taking into Custody

(a) Affidavit. An affidavit may be filed by any person alleging facts under existing law sufficient to establish grounds to take a child into custody. The affidavit shall:

(1) be in writing and signed;

(2) specify the name, address, and sex of the child or, if unknown, designate the child by any name or description by which the child can be identified with reasonable certainty;

(3) specify that the child is of an age subject to the jurisdiction of the court; and

(4) state the reasons why the child is being taken into custody.

(b) Criteria for Order. The court may issue an order to take a child into custody based on sworn testimony meeting the criteria set forth in subdivision (a).

(c) Order. The order to take into custody shall:

(1) be in writing and signed;

(2) specify the name, address, and sex of the child or, if unknown, designate the child by any name or description by which the child can be identified with reasonable certainty;

(3) specify that the child is of an age subject to the jurisdiction of the court;

(4) state the reasons why the child is being taken into custody;

(5) order that the child be placed in a suitable place pending a shelter hearing as provided by law; and

(6) state the date when issued and the county and court where issued.

Added May 9, 1991, effective July 1, 1991 (589 So.2d 818).

Rule 8.655. Shelter Petition, Hearing, and Order

(a) Shelter Petition. If a child is to be placed in a shelter after being taken into custody for a period longer than 24 hours, the person requesting placement shall file a written petition which shall:

(1) specify the name, address, and sex of the child or, if unknown, designate the child by any name or description by which the child can be identified with reasonable certainty;

(2) specify that the child is of an age subject to the jurisdiction of the court;

(3) state the reasons why the child needs to be placed in a shelter;

(4) recommend where the child is to be placed or the agency to be responsible for placement;

(5) be signed by the attorney for the petitioner; and

(6) include a certificate of service to all parties and their attorneys of record.

(b) Shelter Hearing.

(1) The petitioner shall make a diligent effort to notify the parent or custodian of the child and shall notify his or her attorney of record of the date, time, and place of the hearing. The petitioner shall list all parties notified of the hearing on the certificate of service on the shelter petition.

(2) The court shall conduct an informal hearing on the petition within the time period provided by law. The court shall determine at the hearing whether the criteria provided by law for placement in a shelter have been met.

(3) At the hearing all interested persons present shall have an opportunity to be heard on the criteria for placement as provided by law.

(4) The court may base its determination on a sworn complaint, testimony, or affidavit and may hear all relevant and material evidence, including oral and written reports, to the extent of its probative value even though it would not be competent at an adjudicatory hearing.

(5) The court shall advise the parties of:

(A) their right to be represented by counsel as provided by law;

(B) the reason for the child being in custody and why continued placement is requested; and

(C) their right to present placement alternatives.

(c) Shelter Order.

The order shall be in writing and shall:

(1) state the name, age, and sex of the child and, if the child's age is unknown, that the child is believed to be of an age which makes him or her subject to the jurisdiction of the court;

(2) include findings as provided by law;

(3) designate the place where the child is to be placed or the person or agency that will be responsible for this placement along with any special conditions found to be necessary;

(4) state the date and time where issued;

(5) indicate when the child shall be released from the shelter or set a review of shelter hearing within the time limits provided by law; and

(6) include a certificate of service to all parties and their attorneys of record.

(d) Release From Shelter Care. No child shall be released from shelter after a shelter order has been entered except on order of the court unless the shelter order authorizes release by the department.

Added May 9, 1991, effective July 1, 1991 (589 So.2d 818). Amended Oct. 26, 2000, effective Jan. 1, 2001 (783 So.2d 138).

Rule 8.660. Petitions

(a) Contents of Petition.

(1) Only those authorized by law may file a petition alleging that a child is in need of services. Each petition shall be entitled a petition for child(ren) in need of services and shall allege sufficient facts showing the child to be in need of services based upon applicable law.

(2) The petition shall contain allegations as to the identity and residence of the parents or custodians, if known.

(3) The petition shall identify the age, sex, and name of the child. Two or more children may be the subject of the same petition.

(4) More than one allegation of children in need of services may appear in the same petition, in separate counts.

(b) Verification. The petition shall be signed by the petitioner, stating under oath the petitioner's good faith. No objection to the petition on the grounds that it was not signed or verified, as herein provided, shall be entertained after a plea to the merits.

(c) Amendments. At any time before or during an adjudicatory hearing, an amended petition may be filed or the petition may be amended by motion. Amendments shall be freely permitted in the interest of justice and the welfare of the child. A continuance may be granted upon motion and a showing that the amendment prejudices or materially affects any party.

(d) Defects and Variances. No petition or any count thereof shall be dismissed, or any judgment vacated, on account of any defect in the form of the petition or of misjoinder of counts. If the court is of the opinion that the petition is so vague, indistinct, and indefinite as to mislead the child, parent, or custodian and prejudice any of them in the preparation of a defense, the petitioner may be required to furnish a more definite statement.

(e) Voluntary Dismissal. At any time before entry of an order of adjudication, the child(ren) in need of services petition may be voluntarily dismissed by petitioner without leave of the court by serving a notice of dismissal on all parties or, if during a hearing, by so stating on the record. Unless otherwise stated, the dismissal shall be without prejudice.

Added May 9, 1991, effective July 1, 1991 (589 So.2d 818).

Rule 8.665. Answers, Arraignments, and Prehearing Conferences

(a) Answers. The child, parent, or custodian of the child may enter an oral or written answer to the petition or remain silent. If the child remains silent or pleads evasively, or the parent, guardian, or legal custodian denies it, the court shall enter a denial of the petition. The court shall determine that any admission or consent to the petition is made voluntarily and with a full understanding of the nature of the allegations and the possible consequences of such admission or consent and that the parties have been advised of the right to be represented by counsel. The court shall incorporate these findings into its order in addition to findings of fact specifying the act or acts, by whom committed, and facts upon which the findings are based. If the answer admits the allegations of the petition it shall constitute consent to a predisposition study.

(b) Arraignment. If a written answer has not been filed by the child, parent, guardian, or legal custodian before the adjudicatory hearing, the court shall conduct a hearing to determine whether an admission, consent, or denial of the petition shall be entered and whether the parties are represented by counsel or are entitled to appointed counsel as provided by law. If an admission or consent is entered, the court shall proceed as set forth in rule 8.690. If a denial is entered, the court shall set an adjudicatory hearing within the period of time provided by law and appoint counsel when required.

(c) Withdrawal of Plea. The court may at any time before the beginning of a disposition hearing permit an admission of the allegations of the petition to be withdrawn and, if an adjudication has been entered thereon, set aside such adjudication. In the subsequent adjudicatory hearing the court shall disregard an admission that has been withdrawn.

(d) Prehearing Conference. Before the conduct of any adjudicatory hearing the court may set or the parties may request that a prehearing conference be held to determine the order in which each party may present witnesses or evidence and the order in which cross-examination and argument shall occur. The court also may enter findings on the record of any stipulations entered into by the parties and consider any other matters which may aid in the conduct of the adjudicatory hearing.

Added May 9, 1991, effective July 1, 1991 (589 So.2d 818).

Rule 8.670. Motions

(a) Motions in General. An application to the court for an order shall be made by a motion which shall be in writing, unless made during a hearing; be signed by the party making the motion or by the party's attorney; state with particularity the grounds therefor; and set forth the relief or order sought. The requirement of writing is fulfilled if the motion is stated in the written notice of the hearing of the motion.

(b) Motion to Dismiss. Any party may file a motion to dismiss any petition or other pleading, setting forth the grounds on which the motion is based. If a motion to dismiss is granted where a child is being detained under an order, the child may be continued in shelter under previous order of the court upon the representation that a new or amended petition will be filed.

(c) Motion to Sever. A motion may be made to sever 2 or more counts of a multicount petition or to sever the cases of 2 or more children alleged to be in need of services in the same petition. The court may grant motions for severance of jointly brought cases for good cause shown.

Added May 9, 1991, effective July 1, 1991 (589 So.2d 818).

Rule 8.675. Examinations, Evaluation, and Treatment

(a) Child. Mental or physical examination of a child may be obtained as provided by law.

(b) Parent, Guardian, or Other Person Requesting Custody. At any time after the filing of a petition, when the mental or physical condition, including the blood group, of a parent, guardian, or other person requesting custody of a child is in controversy, the court may order the person to submit to a physical or mental examination by a qualified professional. The order may be made only on good cause shown and on notice to the person as to the time, place, manner, conditions, and scope of the examination and the person or persons by whom it is to be made. The court may, on its own motion or the motion of any party, order a parent, guardian, or other person requesting custody of the child to undergo such evaluation, treatment, or counseling activities as authorized by law.

Added May 9, 1991, effective July 1, 1991 (589 So.2d 818).

Rule 8.680. Discovery

Discovery will be allowed only upon order of the court and then as provided by rule 8.245.

Added May 9, 1991, effective July 1, 1991 (589 So.2d 818). Amended Nov. 5, 1992, effective Jan. 1, 1993 (608 So.2d 478).

Committee Notes

1992 Amendment. The present wording is somewhat ambiguous in the use of the word "and." The change clarifies the committee's intent.

Rule 8.685. Adjudicatory Hearings

(a) Hearing by Judge. The adjudicatory hearing shall be conducted by the judge without a jury utilizing the rules of evidence. At this hearing the court shall determine whether the allegations of the petition have been sustained.

(b) Examination of Witnesses. Any party shall have the right to examine or cross-examine the witnesses.

(c) Presence of Parties. All parties have the right to be present at all adjudicatory hearings. No party shall be excluded from the hearing unless so ordered by the court for disruptive behavior.

(d) Joint and Separate Hearings. When 2 or more children are alleged to be children in need of services, the hearing may be held simultaneously when the several children involved are related to each other or involved in the same case, unless the court orders separate hearings.

(e) Motion for Judgment of Dismissal. In all proceedings if at the close of the evidence for the petitioner the court is of the opinion that the evidence is insufficient as a matter of law to warrant a finding of child(ren) in need of services, it may, and on the motion of any party shall, enter an order dismissing the petition for insufficiency of evidence.

(f) Findings and Orders. If the court finds that the evidence supports the allegations of the petition, it may make a finding that the child is in need of services as provided by law. In all cases the court shall enter a written order specifying the facts upon which the findings are based. If the predisposition and other reports required by law are unavailable, or by order of the court, any portion of the disposition hearing may be reset within a reasonable time. If the case is continued the court may refer the case to appropriate agencies for additional study and recommendation. The court may order the child into a suitable placement under such reasonable conditions as the court may direct.

Added May 9, 1991, effective July 1, 1991 (589 So.2d 818).

Rule 8.690. Disposition Hearings

(a) Information Available to Court. At the disposition hearing the court, after establishing compliance with the dispositional considerations, determinations, and discussions required by law, may receive any relevant and material evidence helpful in determining the proper disposition to be made. It shall include written reports required by law and may include evaluations of the child or the parent or custodian that may be obtained and that are relevant and material. Such evidence may be received by the court and may be relied upon to the extent of its probative value even though not competent in an adjudicatory hearing.

(b) Disclosure to Parties. All parties shall be entitled to disclosure of all information in all reports submitted to the court.

(c) Orders of Disposition. The court shall in its written order of disposition include:

(1) the placement or custody of the child;

(2) special conditions of placement and visitation;

(3) evaluation, counseling, treatment activities, and other actions to be taken by the parties where ordered;

(4) supervising or monitoring agencies and continuation or discharge of the guardian ad litem, when appropriate;

(5) the period of time or date for subsequent case review when required by law; and

(6) such other requirements deemed necessary to protect the health, safety, and well-being of the child.

(d) Out-of-Home Placement. If the court places the child in out-of-home placement, subsequent proceedings shall be governed by part IIID of these rules.

Added May 9, 1991, effective July 1, 1991 (589 So.2d 818). Amended Oct. 26, 2000, effective Jan. 1, 2001 (783 So.2d 138); Oct. 18, 2012, effective Dec. 1, 2012, April 1, 2013, Oct. 1, 2013 (102 So.3d 451).

Rule 8.695. Postdisposition Relief

(a) Modification of Placement. A child who has been placed in the child's own home, in the home of a relative, or in some other place under the supervision of the department may be brought before the court by the parent, guardian, or any interested person on a motion for modification of placement. Upon notice to all parties, the court shall conduct a hearing and enter an order changing the placement, modifying the conditions of placement, continuing placement as previously ordered, or placing the child with the department or a licensed child-caring agency.

(b) Motion for Termination of Supervision or Jurisdiction. Any party requesting termination of agency supervision or the jurisdiction of the court, or both, shall do so by motion. The court shall hear all parties present and enter an order terminating supervision or terminating jurisdiction and supervision or continuing them as previously ordered. The court shall not terminate jurisdiction unless the child is returned to the parent or placed with a legal guardian.

Added May 9, 1991, effective July 1, 1991 (589 So.2d 818). Amended Oct. 26, 2000, effective Jan. 1, 2001 (783 So.2d 138).

PART V. OTHER PROCEEDINGS

2012 Revision

Part V, "Other Proceedings", added as Part IV, was renumbered as Part V by Florida Supreme Court Opinion No. SC11-399 (102 So.3d 451).

Former Part V, "Forms for Use with the Rules of Juvenile Procedure", was renumbered as Part VI by Florida Supreme Court Opinion No. SC11-399 (102 So.3d 451).

A. GUARDIAN ADVOCATES FOR DRUG–DEPENDENT NEWBORNS

Rule 8.705. Commencement of Proceedings

(a) Petition to Be Filed. All proceedings under this part shall be initiated by the filing of a petition for the appointment of a guardian advocate.

(b) File to Be Opened. Upon commencement of any proceeding, the clerk shall open a file and assign a case number.

Former Rule 8.881 added Sept. 29, 1989, effective Oct. 1, 1989 (549 So.2d 663). Renumbered as new Rule 8.705 and amended May 9, 1991, effective July 1, 1991 (589 So.2d 818).

Rule 8.710. Parties

(a) Definitions. For the purpose of these rules the terms "party" and "parties" shall include the petitioner, the child, the parent, the guardian ad litem where appointed, the custodian, and every person upon whom service of summons is required by law.

(b) Other Parties. The state attorney's office or the Department of Children and Family Services may become a party upon notice to all other parties and notice to the court. The court may add additional parties.

Former Rule 8.882 added Sept. 29, 1989, effective Oct. 1, 1989 (549 So.2d 663). Renumbered as new Rule 8.710 and amended May 9, 1991, effective July 1, 1991 (589 So.2d 818). Amended Oct. 26, 2000, effective Jan. 1, 2001 (783 So.2d 138).

Rule 8.715. Guardian Ad Litem

The court may appoint a guardian ad litem to represent the interests of the child.

Former Rule 8.883 added Sept. 29, 1989, effective Oct. 1, 1989 (549 So.2d 663). Renumbered as new Rule 8.715 May 9, 1991, effective July 1, 1991 (589 So.2d 818).

Rule 8.720. Process and Service

(a) Summons.

(1) Personal appearance of a person in a hearing before the court shall obviate the necessity of serving process upon that person.

(2) Upon the filing of the petition, and upon request of the petitioner, the clerk or deputy clerk shall issue a summons.

(3) The summons shall require the person on whom it is served to appear for a hearing at a time and place specified. Except in cases of medical emergency, the time of hearing shall not be less than 24 hours after service of the summons. The summons shall be directed to and shall be served upon the parents. It shall not be necessary to the validity of the proceedings that the parents be present if their identity or presence is unknown after a diligent search and inquiry have been made; if they have become residents of a state other than this state; or if they evade service or ignore summons, but in this event the person who made the search and inquiry shall file a certificate of those facts.

(b) Subpoenas. Upon the application of a party, the clerk or deputy clerk shall issue, and the court on its own motion may issue, subpoenas requiring attendance and testimony of witnesses and production of records, documents, or other tangible objects at any hearing.

Former Rule 8.884 added Sept. 29, 1989, effective Oct. 1, 1989 (549 So.2d 663). Renumbered as new Rule 8.720 and amended May 9, 1991, effective July 1, 1991 (589 So.2d 818).

Rule 8.725. Petition

(a) Contents of Petition.

(1) The petition shall allege sufficient facts showing grounds for appointment of a guardian advocate based upon applicable law.

(2) The petition shall contain allegations as to the identity and residence of the parents or custodians, if known.

(3) The petition shall identify the age, sex, and name of the child. Two or more children may be the subject of the same petition.

(b) Voluntary Dismissal. The petitioner without leave of the court, at any time prior to the entry of the order, may request a voluntary dismissal of the petition by serving a notice of request for dismissal on all parties or, if during a hearing, by so stating on the record. The petition shall be dismissed and the court loses jurisdiction unless another party adopts the petition within 48 hours. Unless otherwise stated, the dismissal shall be without prejudice.

Former Rule 8.885 added Sept. 29, 1989, effective Oct. 1, 1989 (549 So.2d 663). Renumbered as new Rule 8.725 and amended May 9, 1991, effective July 1, 1991 (589 So.2d 818).

Rule 8.730. Hearing

(a) Time Limit. All hearings shall be carried out as provided by law within the time limits proscribed therein.

(b) Orders.

(1) In all cases at the conclusion of the hearing the court shall enter a written order granting or denying the petition.

(2) An order granting the appointment of a guardian advocate shall specify the term of appointment and not exceed that provided by law.

Former Rule 8.886 added Sept. 29, 1989, effective Oct. 1, 1989 (549 So.2d 663). Renumbered as new Rule 8.730 May 9, 1991, effective July 1, 1991 (589 So.2d 818).

Rule 8.735. Review and Removal

(a) Review by Court. The court may review the appointment of a guardian advocate at any time but shall review the appointment within the time limits as provided by law.

(b) Reauthorization or Removal. The reauthorization or removal of the guardian advocate shall be governed as provided by law.

Former Rule 8.887 added Sept. 29, 1989, effective Oct. 1, 1989 (549 So.2d 663). Renumbered as new Rule 8.735 and amended May 9, 1991, effective July 1, 1991 (589 So.2d 818).

B. JUDICIAL WAIVER OF PARENTAL NOTICE OF TERMINATION OF PREGNANCY

Rule 8.800. Applicability

These rules apply to proceedings instituted pursuant to section 390.01114, Florida Statutes.

Added June 30, 2005 (907 So.2d 1161).

Rule 8.805. Commencement of Proceedings

(a) Petition to Be Filed. Proceedings for a judicial waiver of parental notice of termination of pregnancy shall be commenced by the filing of a petition in circuit court.

(b) Pseudonymous Petitions. Petitions filed under a pseudonym or initials shall be filed simultaneously with a sworn statement containing the minor's true name, date of birth, address and the case number. A certified copy of this Sworn Statement of True Name and Pseudonym shall be given to the minor at the time it is filed. The original sworn statement shall be kept under seal at all times and may only be opened at the minor's request or by court order.

(c) Notice Under Pseudonymous Petitions. So that the minor may receive notice in a safe and secure manner, the minor shall elect to receive notice through the address and phone number of a trusted third person or by personally contacting the clerk's office. If the minor elects to personally contact the clerk's office, she must still provide an address and phone number of a third person through which to receive notice in the event that the court needs to provide notice at a time other than when the minor personally contacts the clerk's office.

(d) Procedures Upon Filing Petition. Upon the filing of a petition, the clerk of the circuit court shall immediately:

(1) open a new file and assign a new case number;

(2) provide the minor with a certified copy of Form 8.988 Sworn Statement of True Name and Pseudonym;

(3) provide the minor with Form 8.989 Advisory Notice to Minor;

(4) present the petition to the court for scheduling of the hearing and appointment of counsel, if requested; and

(5) provide notice of the hearing to the minor. If it is not possible for the clerk to immediately provide notice at the time the minor files the petition, the clerk shall provide notice through the method elected by the minor in the petition.

(e) Fees and Costs. No filing fees or court costs shall be assessed against any pregnant minor who petitions a court for a waiver of parental notice.

Added June 30, 2005 (907 So.2d 1161). Amended July 6, 2006 (934 So.2d 438).

Rule 8.810. Petition

The petition shall include:

(a) the pseudonym or initials of the minor;

(b) the age of the minor;

(c) a statement that the minor is pregnant and notice has not been waived;

(d) a statement that the minor desires to terminate her pregnancy without notice to a parent or legal guardian; and

(e) a short and plain statement of facts to establish any of the following:

(1) The minor is sufficiently mature to decide whether to terminate her pregnancy.

(2) The minor is a victim of child abuse or sexual abuse by one or both of her parents or a guardian.

(3) Notification of a parent or guardian is not in the best interest of the minor.

Added June 30, 2005 (907 So.2d 1161).

Rule 8.815. Counsel

As provided by section 390.01114(4)(a), Florida Statutes, the circuit court shall advise the minor that she has a right to court-appointed counsel and shall provide her with counsel upon her request at no cost.

Added June 30, 2005 (907 So.2d 1161).

Rule 8.820. Hearing

(a) Hearing by Judge. A judge shall conduct an informal hearing on the petition within the time limits provided by law and these rules. General magistrates and special magistrates shall not hear a petition for a judicial waiver of parental notice of termination of pregnancy.

(b) Evidence. The judge shall hear evidence relating to the emotional development, maturity, intellect, and understanding of the minor, and all other relevant evidence.

(c) Burdens of Proof.

(1) A finding that the minor is sufficiently mature to decide whether to terminate her pregnancy requires proof by clear and convincing evidence.

(2) A finding that the minor is a victim of child abuse or sexual abuse inflicted by one or both of her parents or a guardian requires proof by a preponderance of the evidence.

(3) A finding that notification of a parent or guardian is not in the best interest of the minor requires proof by clear and convincing evidence.

(d) Time Limits. As provided by section 390.01114(4)(b), Florida Statutes:

(1) Cases commenced under this rule take precedence over other pending matters as necessary to ensure that the court can make its ruling and issue written findings of fact and conclusions of law within 3 business days of the filing of the petition.

(2) The 3–business-day time limit may be extended at the request of the minor; however, the court remains under an obligation to rule on the petition as soon as practically possible.

(3) If the court fails to rule within the 3–business-day period and an extension has not been requested by the minor, the minor may immediately thereafter petition the chief judge of the circuit for a hearing. The chief judge must ensure that a hearing is held within 48 hours after receipt of the minor's petition, and an order is entered within 24 hours after the hearing.

(e) Confidentiality of Hearings. Hearings under this part shall be closed to the public and all records thereof shall remain confidential as provided by sections 390.01114(4)(e) and 390.01116, Florida Statutes. Persons other than the petitioner may be permitted to attend the hearing at the request of the petitioner. The court shall advise all persons in attendance that the hearing is confidential.

Added June 30, 2005 (907 So.2d 1161). Amended July 6, 2006 (934 So.2d 438); Oct. 20, 2011 (75 So.3d 216).

Rule 8.825. Order and Judgment

At the conclusion of the hearing, the court shall issue written and specific findings of fact and conclusions of law in support of its decision, including findings of fact and conclusions of law relating to the maturity of the minor, and order that a confidential record be maintained.

Added June 30, 2005 (907 So.2d 1161). Amended Oct. 20, 2011 (75 So.3d 216).

Rule 8.830. Transcripts

A court that conducts proceedings pursuant to these rules shall provide for a written transcript of all testimony and proceedings as provided by section 390.01114(4)(e), Florida Statutes.

Added June 30, 2005 (907 So.2d 1161).

Rule 8.835. Confidentiality of Records

(a) As provided by section 390.01116, Florida Statutes, any information including the petition, documents, transcripts, recordings of cases, and any other information that could be used to identify a minor who has petitioned the court for a judicial waiver of parental notice of termination of pregnancy is confidential and exempt from section 119.07(1), Florida Statutes, and section 24(a), Article I of the State Constitution.

(b) So that the minor shall remain anonymous, the court file shall be sealed unless otherwise ordered by the court.

Added June 30, 2005 (907 So.2d 1161).

Rule 8.840. Remand of Proceedings

In the event the minor appeals a determination by the circuit court under these rules and the appellate court remands the matter to the trial court, the trial court must enter its ruling within 3 business days after the remand.

Added Oct. 20, 2011 (75 So.3d 216).

PART VI. FORMS FOR USE WITH THE RULES OF JUVENILE PROCEDURE

2012 Revision

Part VI, "Forms for Use with the Rules of Juvenile Procedure", added as Part V, was renumbered as Part VI by Florida Supreme Court Opinion No. SC11-399 (102 So.3d 451).

Part VI. Forms for Use With the Rules of Juvenile Procedure

The following forms are sufficient for the matters that are covered by them. So long as the substance is expressed without prolixity, the forms may be varied to meet the facts of a particular case. Captions, verifications, and certificates of service, except for the designation of the paper, are omitted from most forms. General forms for these are provided at the beginning of the forms.

Former Part V, amended May 9, 1991, effective July 1, 1991 (589 So.2d 818). Renumbered as Part VI Oct. 18, 2012, effective Dec. 1, 2012, April 1, 2013, Oct. 1, 2013 (102 So.3d 451).

Committee Comments

1991 Amendment. These forms have been updated to conform to revisions to chapter 39, Florida Statutes, and the Florida Rules of Juvenile Procedure. As the court has stated before, the forms are not intended to be part of the rules and are provided for convenience only.

A. GENERAL FORMS

Form 8.901. Caption of Pleadings and Orders

NAME OF COURT

In the Interest of

_____, _____ a child/children _____

___ (Designation of Pleading or Order)

Amended Nov. 5, 1992, effective Jan. 1, 1993 (608 So.2d 478).

Form 8.902. Verification

STATE OF FLORIDA

COUNTY OF ....

Before me, the undersigned authority, personally appeared ..... (name) ....., who, being sworn, says the ..... (document) ..... is filed in good faith and on information, knowledge, and belief is true.

Sworn to and subscribed before me on ..... (date) ......

(Title)

Added May 9, 1991, effective July 1, 1991 (589 So.2d 818). Amended Oct. 26, 2000, effective Jan. 1, 2001 (783 So.2d 138).

Committee Notes

1991 Adoption. The above verification should be added to petitions and motions as required by law.

Form 8.903. Certificate of Service

I certify that a copy of .... (document) .... has been furnished to .... (name(s)) .... by e-mail/U.S.mail/hand delivery/fax on .... (date) ....

____

(Title)

Added May 9, 1991, effective July 1, 1991 (589 So.2d 818). Amended Oct. 26, 2000, effective Jan. 1, 2001 (783 So.2d 138); Oct. 18, 2012, effective, *nunc pro tunc*, Sept. 1, 2012 (102 So.3d 451).

Committee Notes

1991 Adoption. The above may be added to petitions, orders, and other forms as required.

Form 8.904. Affidavit for Order to Take Into Custody

AFFIDAVIT

STATE OF FLORIDA

COUNTY OF ______

Before me, the undersigned authority, personally appeared affiant, who, being sworn, made the following allegations of facts: ______ and requested that the court issue an order to take into custody the below-________________ child(ren)
named/described

Name(s) ____________________

Age(s) ______ Sex ______

Date(s) of birth ________________

Race ____________________

Address ____________________

Identifying description ____________

Parent/Custodian ________________

Address ____________________

____

Affiant

Address ____________

Former Form 8.902 renumbered as new Form 8.904 and amended May 9, 1991, effective July 1, 1991 (589 So.2d 818).

Form 8.905. Order to Take Into Custody

ORDER TO TAKE INTO CUSTODY

TO: ....

A ..... verified petition/affidavit ..... having been filed in this case, alleging facts which under existing law are determined to be sufficient to authorize taking into custody the ..... below-named/identified .... child/children ..... , believed to be of an age subject to the juvenile jurisdiction of the circuit court; therefore

You are commanded to take the following ..... child/children ..... into custody:

Name(s) ....

Age(s) .... Sex ....

Date(s) of Birth ....

Race ....

Address ....

Identifying Description ....

Parent/Custodian ....

Address ....

For the following reasons: ....

Upon taking the ..... child/children ..... into custody, you will deliver ..... him/her/them ..... to .... to be held pending a ..... detention/shelter ..... hearing or upon further order of this court.

ORDERED in the circuit court in and for .... County, Florida, on ..... (date) ......

Circuit Judge

RETURN

This order to take into custody was executed at ..... m., on ..... (date) ....., by the undersigned.

____

(Title)

RETURN TO ISSUING COURT UPON THE CHILD'S 19TH BIRTHDAY

Former Form 8.903 renumbered as new Form 8.905 and amended May 9, 1991, effective July 1, 1991 (589 So.2d 818). Amended Oct. 26, 2000, effective Jan.1, 2001 (783 So.2d 138).

Form 8.906. Release Order

RELEASE ORDER

The court now finding that the above-named ..... child/children ....., previously .... placed in shelter care/detained ....., should be released.

It is ADJUDGED:

1. That .... shall be released immediately to ....

2. It is FURTHER ADJUDGED that ....

ORDERED in the circuit court in and for .... County, Florida, on (date) ......

____

Circuit Judge

Former Form 8.905 renumbered as new Form 8.906 and amended May 9, 1991, effective July 1, 1991 (589 So.2d 818). Amended Oct. 26, 2000, effective Jan. 1, 2001 (783 So.2d 138).

Form 8.907. Transfer Order

TRANSFER ORDER

This case being before this court for consideration of transfer to a court having juvenile jurisdiction in another county, the court finds:

1. That on ..... (date) ....., following a hearing on the petition of ...., the court ..... entered an order of adjudication/withheld adjudication/accepted a plan of proposed treatment, training, or conduct ....

2. That it would be in the best interest of the above-named ..... child/children ..... that this case be transferred to the circuit court of another county because: ....

3. That a dispositional order ..... was/was not ..... made in this case.

It is recommended to the receiving court that: ....

It is ADJUDGED:

1. That the jurisdiction of this court in this case and of the ..... child/children ..... involved is transferred to the circuit court in and for .... County, Florida, of the ..... Judicial Circuit, for any and all proceedings deemed necessary.

2. That within 5 days from the date of this order the clerk of this court shall forward a certified copy of:

(a) The order of transfer, which shall include but not be limited to:

(i) Specific offense that the child was found to have committed;

(ii) Degree of offense;

(iii) Name of parent/custodian to be summoned;

(iv) Address at which the child should be summoned for disposition;

(v) Name and address of the victim; and

(vi) Whether the child was represented by counsel.

(b) A certified copy of the delinquency petition;

(c) A copy of the juvenile referral or complaint; and

(d) Any reports and all previous orders including orders appointing counsel entered by the court in the interest of that child.

These documents shall be forwarded to the clerk of the receiving court; state attorney of the receiving court; public defender of the receiving court, if counsel previously has been appointed; and ....

ORDERED in the circuit court in and for .... County, Florida, on ..... (date) ......

____

Circuit Judge

Amended May 9, 1991, effective July 1, 1991 (589 So.2d 818); Oct. 26, 2000, effective Jan. 1, 2001 (783 So.2d 138).

Form 8.908. Summons

SUMMONS

STATE OF FLORIDA

TO ...., ... a child/children .... and ...., ... parent(s)/custodian ....:

A petition under oath has been filed in this court alleging the above-named .... child/children .... to be .... under the laws of the State of Florida, a copy of which was attached hereto;

You are to appear before the Honorable ...., Circuit Judge, at .... m., on .... (date) ...., at the county courthouse of .... County, at ...., Florida for the hearing of this petition. The ....

parent(s)/custodian .... is/are .... required to produce the .... child/children .... at that time and place unless the .... child/children .... is/are .... in detention or shelter care at that time.

COMMENT: The following paragraph must be in bold, 14 pt. Times New Roman or Courier font.

If you are a person with a disability who needs any accommodation to participate in this proceeding, you are entitled, at no cost to you, to the provision of certain assistance. Please contact .... (name, address, telephone number) .... at least 7 days before your scheduled court appearance, or immediately upon receiving this notification if the time before the scheduled appearance is less than 7 days. If you are hearing or voice impaired, call 711.

You may be held in contempt of court if you fail to appear.

WITNESS my hand and seal of this court at .... County, Florida, on .... (date) ..

.........., Clerk of Circuit Court
.... County, Florida
By: __________, D.C.

Former Form 8.910 renumbered as new Form 8.908 and amended May 9, 1991, effective July 1, 1991 (589 So.2d 818). Amended Oct. 26, 2000, effective Jan. 1, 2001 (783 So.2d 138); Jan. 27, 2005 (894 So.2d 875); May 23, 2013, effective July 1, 2013 (115 So.3d 286).

Form 8.909. Plan For Treatment, Training, or Conduct

PLAN FOR TREATMENT, TRAINING, OR CONDUCT

TO: ...., Circuit Judge

Instead of a plea to the petition filed on ..... (date) ....., alleging the above-named ..... child/children ..... to be ...., the following proposed plan for treatment, training, or conduct, formulated in conjunction with the supervising agency, is now submitted, with the request that it be accepted by the court and that prosecution of the said petition be deferred.

This agreement is entered into with full knowledge and disclosure of all the facts and circumstances of this case, and in consideration thereof, and the promise of fulfillment of its terms and conditions, each of the undersigned agrees as follows: ....

It is further agreed:

1. That the speedy trial rule is waived,
2. That a hearing for the acceptance of this plan ..... is/is not ..... waived,
3. That this plan, as agreed to here, shall be in effect until ....

In witness whereof the undersigned have affixed their hands on ..... (date) .....

____
Child

____
Parent(s) or Custodian(s)

____
Attorney for Child/Parent(s)/Custodian(s) ...

......., Department of Juvenile Justice, Supervising Agency, Recommends: ..... Acceptance/ Rejection .....

____
Authorized Agent

CONSENT IN DELINQUENCY CASES

The undersigned, being familiar with the contents of this plan for treatment, training, or conduct and the delinquency petition on which it is based, consents to defer prosecution of the petition.

Dated: ....

....
State Attorney
By ______________________
Assistant State Attorney

ORDER

The foregoing plan for treatment, training, or conduct having been properly submitted and having been given consideration by the court,

It is ADJUDGED:

___ 1. That the plan is approved and the parties thereto shall comply with its terms and conditions.

___ 2. That the plan is disapproved and an adjudicatory hearing on the petition shall be scheduled.

ORDERED at .... County, Florida, on ..... (date) .....

____
Circuit Judge

Former Form 8.911 renumbered as new Form 8.909 and amended May 9, 1991, effective July 1, 1991 (589 So.2d 818). Amended Nov. 5, 1992, effective Jan. 1, 1993 (608 So.2d 478); Oct. 31, 1996, effective Jan. 1, 1997 (684 So.2d 756); Oct. 26, 2000, effective Jan. 1, 2001 (783 So.2d 138).

Form 8.911. Uniform Child Custody Jurisdiction and Enforcement Act Affidavit

See Fla. Sup. Ct. App. Fam. L. Form 12.902(d).

Added May 9, 1991, effective July 1, 1991 (589 So.2d 818). Amended Jan. 27, 2005 (894 So.2d 875); Sept. 21, 2006, effective Jan. 1, 2007 (939 So.2d 74).

Form 8.912. Petition to Show Cause

PETITION BY AFFIDAVIT FOR ORDER TO SHOW CAUSE

1. This is a proceeding for an order to show why the below-named witness, ______, should not be held in contempt of court.

2. Petitioner is ______________ (title)

3. A subpoena was duly served on ________ (name), at ________ (time) by ________ (name) who was then and there authorized to serve said subpoena. A copy of the receipt evidencing service is attached and incorporated by reference. Said ________ (name) did not appear on ________ (date), at ________ (time) in response to that subpoena and to this date has not appeared.

WHEREFORE, the undersigned does respectfully request the court to issue an order to direct ____________ (name) to appear before the court to show cause why ____________ (name) should not be held in contempt of court.

____
Petitioner

Added May 9, 1991, effective July 1, 1991 (589 So.2d 818).

Form 8.913. Order to Show Cause

ORDER TO SHOW CAUSE

This cause came on to be heard on the petition for order to show cause directed to ..... (name) ..... for failure ..... (specify) ..... on ..... (date) ..... (See attached affidavit.)

NOW, THEREFORE, you, ... (name) ....., are hereby ORDERED to appear before this court located at ...., on ..... (date) ....., at ..... (time) ....., to show cause why you should not be held in contempt of this court, for your failure to ..... (specify) .....

DONE AND ORDERED on ..... (date) ....., at ...., ... County, Florida.

____
Circuit Judge

Added May 9, 1991, effective July 1, 1991 (589 So.2d 818). Amended Oct. 26, 2000, effective Jan. 1, 2001 (783 So.2d 138).

B. DELINQUENCY FORMS

Form 8.929. Detention Order

DETENTION HEARING ORDER

Pick up order for absconding from:

..... home detention
..... probation
..... commitment
..... other: ....

Present before the court:

..... the child;
....(name)....., Assistant State Attorney;
....(name)....., Assistant Public Defender/defense attorney;
....(name)....., parent/legal guardian;
....(name)....., DJJ juvenile probation officer;
....(name)....., Department of Children and Family Services
....(name)....., guardian ad litem

DJJ Supervision status:

..... None
..... Home detention
..... Probation
..... Committed to ..... level
..... CINS/FINS
..... Conditional release

Other court involvement:

Dependency:	..... Yes	..... No	..... Unknown
Domestic relations:	..... Yes	..... No	..... Unknown
Domestic violence:	..... Yes	..... No	..... Unknown

The court finds that the child was taken into custody at ..... a.m./p.m., on ..... (date)

Probable cause that the child committed delinquent acts was:

..... found.
..... not found.
..... reset within 48 hours of custody.

Risk assessment instrument (RAI) score: ....
Score amended to: ....
..... Meets detention criteria.

IT IS ORDERED that the above-named child be:

..... released to the custody of ..... (name) .....
..... held in secure detention for domestic violence charge under section 985.245, Florida Statutes.

The court finds:

..... respite care is not available for the child; and

..... it is necessary to place the child in secure detention to protect the victim from injury.

..... detained by the Department of Juvenile Justice in

..... home detention.

..... home detention with electronic monitoring.

..... secure detention.

with the following special conditions:

..... attend school regularly.

..... attend evaluation as follows:

..... physical.

..... psychological.

..... ADM.

..... other

....

..... no (..... harmful) contact with ..... (name) .....

..... drug testing.

..... no drug and alcohol use.

..... other: ....

..... released from detention and returned to the child's nonresidential commitment program.

Reasons for court ordering more restrictive placement than RAI score: ....

It is FURTHER ORDERED that unless an adjudicatory hearing has begun or a subsequent modification order is entered, the child shall be released no later than 5:00 p.m. on ..... (date) ..... to ..... (name(s)) ....., who is/are ..... the parent(s) ..... a relative .... foster care .... program .... him/her ..... self ..... other ....

IT IS FURTHER ORDERED under section 985.039, Florida Statutes

..... The parent/guardian of the child, ... (name) ...., shall pay to the Department of Juvenile Justice, 2737 Centerview Drive, Tallahassee, FL 32399–3100, $5 per day for each day the juvenile is in secure detention.

..... The parent/guardian of the child, ... (name) ...., shall pay to the Department of Juvenile Justice, 2737 Centerview Drive, Tallahassee, FL 32399–3100, $1 per day for each day the child is in home detention.

..... The parent/guardian of the child, ... (name) ...., shall pay to the Department of Juvenile Justice, 2737 Centerview Drive, Tallahassee, FL 32399–3100, a REDUCED rate of $ .... per day for each day the child is in detention status. This 8.965 reduced fee is based on the court's finding

..... that the parent/guardian was the victim of the delinquent act or violation of law for which the child is currently detained and is cooperating in the investigation of the offense; or

..... of indigency or significant financial hardship. The facts supporting this finding are: ....

..... The parent/guardian of the child, ... (name) ...., ... (address) ...., shall be liable for .... % of the payment. The parent/guardian of the child, ... (name) ...., ... (address) ...., shall be liable for .... % of the payment.

..... The ..... supervision fee/cost of care .... is WAIVED based on the court's finding

..... that the parent/guardian was the victim of the delinquent act or violation of law for which the child is currently detained and is cooperating in the investigation of the offense; or

..... of indigency or significant financial hardship. The facts supporting this finding are: ....

If the child's case is dismissed or if the child is found not guilty of the charges or court order, then the parent/guardian shall not be liable for fees under this order.

Unless modified by subsequent notice, the NEXT COURT APPEARANCE:

..... will be at ..... (time) ..... on ..... (date) .... at ..... (location) ....

..... is to be set.

COMMENT: The following paragraph must be in bold, 14 pt. Times New Roman or Courier font. **If you are a person with a disability who needs any accommodation in order to participate in this proceeding, you are entitled, at no cost to you, to the provision of certain assistance. Please contact ..... (name, address, telephone number) ..... at least 7 days before your scheduled court appearance, or immediately upon receiving this notification if the time before the scheduled appearance is less than 7 days. If you are hearing or voice impaired, call 711.**

Note: The child's parent/legal guardian shall advise Clerk's Office and DJJ of any address change.

..... Department of Juvenile Justice shall transfer the child to .... Detention Center.

.... Other: ....

DONE AND ORDERED in .... County, Florida at .... a.m./p.m. on ..... (date) .....

Circuit Judge

Copies to:

....

Added Sept. 5, 2002, effective Jan. 1, 2003 (827 So.2d 219). Amended Mar. 3, 2005 (898 So.2d 47); Nov. 17, 2005 (915 So.2d 592); Feb. 8, 2007 (951 So.2d 804); May 23, 2013, effective July 1, 2013 (115 So.3d 286).

Form 8.930. Juvenile Notice to Appear

JUVENILE NOTICE TO APPEAR

DATE .... AGENCY ....
CASE NO. ....

PARENT, ADULT RELATIVE, LEGAL GUARDIAN .... (name) ....

I am the .... (relationship to child) .... of .... (child's name) .... and promise to ensure that the child appears on .... (date) .... at .... (time) .... at .... (location) .... I also promise immediately to notify the office of the state attorney at .... (telephone number) .... and the clerk of the court at .... (telephone number) .... of any change in the child's address.

Signature of Parent/Adult Relative/Legal Guardian
..... (address) .....
..... (telephone number) .....
..... (date) .....
..... (address and telephone number of child, if different)

I, ... (child's name) ...., understand that I have been charged with a law violation, ... (offense(s)) ...., and that I am being released at this time to the custody of .... (parent, adult relative, or legal guardian's name) ....

I promise to appear on .... (date) .... at .... (time) .... at .... (location) ...., and to appear as required for any additional conferences or appearances scheduled by DJJ or the court. I understand that my failure to appear shall result in a custody order being issued and that I will be picked up and taken to detention.

Child's Signature

Date ....

Arresting Officer ....

Releasing officer or DJJ counselor authorizing release

DJJ Intake Telephone Number ....

ATTACH TO ARREST AFFIDAVIT

Former Form 8.930 deleted May 9, 1991, effective July 1, 1991. New Form 8.930 added May 9, 1991, effective July 1, 1991 (589 So.2d 818). Amended Oct. 26, 2000, effective Jan. 1, 2001 (783 So.2d 138); Sept. 21, 2006, effective Jan. 1, 2007 (939 So.2d 74).

Form 8.931. Delinquency Petition

PETITION

Your petitioner respectfully represents that ______ whose date(s) of birth ______ is/are and who reside(s) at ______ ______ is/are delinquent and that this court has jurisdiction of this cause because of the following allegations of facts: ______

That the parents or custodians are:

Mother	Residence
Father	Residence
Custodian	Residence

WHEREFORE, your petitioner requests process may issue to bring the above-named parties before the court on a day and time designated to be dealt with according to law.

Dated: ______

Petitioner

Former Form 8.908 renumbered as new Form 8.931 and amended May 9, 1991, effective July 1, 1991 (589 So.2d 818).

Form 8.932. Application for Counsel and Order

APPLICATION FOR COUNSEL AND ORDER

STATE OF FLORIDA
COUNTY OF ....

Before me, the undersigned authority, personally appeared affiant, who, being duly sworn, says:

1. That I understand a delinquency complaint has been made against me and, being advised of my right to an attorney, now request appointment of counsel.

2. Being without sufficient funds, property or assets of any kind, I will be deprived of my right to representation unless I am adjudged insolvent and counsel appointed to represent me.

3. That I have been informed that a lien for the value of the legal services rendered to me by the public defender may be imposed by law on any property I now or may hereafter have in this state.

Dated: ....

____

Affiant Child

STATEMENT OF PARENT(S)

The undersigned are informed and understand that liability for cost of representation of this child by the public defender can be assessed against the parent(s) by court order in an amount not to exceed the amount provided by law.

____

Parent

____

Parent

ORDER

The court finds that this child is indigent, as defined by law, and is desirous of counsel; it is, therefore,

ORDERED

1. That this child is declared to be insolvent.

2. That ...., Public Defender for the ..... Judicial Circuit, State of Florida, is hereby appointed as counsel to represent this child in all matters in defense of the delinquency complaint herein made.

DONE AND ORDERED in the circuit court in and for .... County, Florida, on ..... (date) .....

____

Circuit Judge

Former Form 8.928 renumbered as new Form 8.932 and amended May 9, 1991, effective July 1, 1991 (589 So.2d 818). Amended Oct. 26, 2000, effective Jan. 1, 2001 (783 So.2d 138).

Form 8.933. Waiver of Counsel

WAIVER OF COUNSEL

I, the undersigned child, ... years of age, understand:

(1) That a complaint of delinquency alleging that I did: .... has been made against me;

(2) That I have a right to a lawyer and that if I am unable to pay a lawyer and wish to have one appointed, a lawyer will be provided immediately.

I understand this right to and offer of a lawyer and, being aware of the effect of this waiver, I knowingly, intelligently, understandingly and of my own free will now choose to and, by the signing of this waiver, do hereby waive my right to a lawyer and elect to proceed in this case without benefit of a lawyer.

DATE: __________ ____________________

CHILD

This waiver of counsel was signed in the presence of the undersigned witnesses who, by their signature, attest to its voluntary execution by this child.

WITNESS: ____________________

WITNESS: ____________________

STATEMENT OF PARENT OR RESPONSIBLE ADULT

This waiver of counsel was read by me and explained fully to this child in my presence. I understand the right of this child to an attorney and as the .... of this child I consent to a waiver of this right.

Date: ....

....

ORDER ASSESSING ATTORNEY'S FEE

The child herein, having been represented by the Public Defender in this cause pursuant to Section 27.52, Florida Statutes, it is

ORDERED AND ADJUDGED that a reasonable attorney's fee for services rendered by the Public Defender to the child in this cause is $ .... and that said fee is hereby assessed against ...., the father, and ...., the mother, in favor of the State of Florida.

DONE AND ORDERED at ...., Florida, on ..... (date) .....

____

Circuit Judge

Former Form 8.929 renumbered as new Form 8.933 May 9, 1991, effective July 1, 1991 (589 So.2d 818). Amended Oct. 26, 2000, effective Jan. 1, 2001 (783 So.2d 138).

Form 8.934. Order to Determine Mental Condition

ORDER TO DETERMINE MENTAL CONDITION

It having been made known to the court and the court finding that reasonable grounds exist to believe that this child may be incompetent to proceed with an adjudicatory hearing, and that a hearing should be scheduled to examine this child and determine ..... his/her ..... mental condition, it is

ADJUDGED:

1. That all proceedings in this case are now stayed, pending further order of this court.

2. That a hearing to determine the mental condition of this child is scheduled before me at ... M., on ..... (date) .....

3. That the following named persons are hereby appointed as disinterested qualified experts to examine this child as to competency and to testify as to the child's mental condition at the hearing above scheduled:

(1) ....
Name Address

(2) ....
Name Address

(3) ....
Name Address

4. That this child shall be held temporarily in the custody of ...., who shall produce the child for examination by the above-named at a time and place to be arranged.

ORDERED at ...., ... County, Florida, on ..... (date) .....

____
Circuit Judge

Former Form 8.917 renumbered as new Form 8.934 May 9, 1991, effective July 1, 1991 (589 So.2d 818). Amended Nov. 5, 1992, effective Jan. 1, 1993 (608 So.2d 478); Oct. 26, 2000, effective Jan. 1, 2001 (783 So.2d 138).

Form 8.935. Order of Incompetency

ORDER OF INCOMPETENCY

The above-named child being before the court for inquiry into ..... his/her ..... mental condition and a determination of ..... his/her ..... competency to proceed with an adjudicatory hearing, from the evidence the court finds:

That the said child is mentally incompetent to proceed with the adjudicatory hearing.

It is, therefore, ADJUDGED that proceedings shall be commenced immediately for the involuntary hospitalization of this child by ...., as provided by law, and the said child shall .... pending disposition of those proceedings.

All proceedings in this case are stayed pending such action.

ORDERED at ...., Florida, on ..... (date) .....

____
Circuit Judge

Former Form 8.918 renumbered as new Form 8.935 May 9, 1991, effective July 1, 1991 (589 So.2d 818). Amended Nov. 5, 1992, effective Jan. 1, 1993 (608 So.2d 478); Oct. 26, 2000, effective Jan. 1, 2001 (783 So.2d 138).

Form 8.936. Order of Competency

ORDER OF COMPETENCY

The above-named child being before the court for inquiry into ..... his/her ..... mental condition and a determination of ..... his/her ..... competency to proceed with an adjudicatory hearing, from the evidence the court finds:

That the child is mentally competent to proceed with the adjudicatory hearing.

It is, therefore, ADJUDGED that the adjudicatory hearing in this case shall ..... commence/resume ..... at ... M., on ..... (date) .....

ORDERED at ...., Florida, on ..... (date) .....

____
Circuit Judge

Former Form 8.919 renumbered as new Form 8.936 May 9, 1991, effective July 1, 1991 (589 So.2d 818). Amended Nov. 5, 1992, effective Jan. 1, 1993 (608 So.2d 478); Oct. 26, 2000, effective Jan. 1, 2001 (783 So.2d 138).

Form 8.937. Demand for Voluntary Waiver

DEMAND FOR VOLUNTARY WAIVER OF JURISDICTION

The child files this demand for voluntary waiver of jurisdiction pursuant to rule 8.105, Florida Rules of Juvenile Procedure, and shows that the child desires the court to waive jurisdiction and certify the case for trial in adult court as if the child were an adult to face adult punishments or penalties.

Date ______

____
Child

____
Parent/Legal Guardian

Added May 9, 1991, effective July 1, 1991 (589 So.2d 818).

Form 8.938. Order of Voluntary Waiver

VOLUNTARY WAIVER ORDER

Upon the demand for voluntary waiver filed by the child, it is hereby ORDERED AND ADJUDGED as follows:

1. A demand for voluntary waiver of jurisdiction was filed by the child and parent/legal guardian on ..... (date) .....

2. The court waives jurisdiction to try the child pursuant to chapter 985, Florida Statutes.

3. The above cause is certified for trial as if the child were an adult.

4. A certified copy of this order shall be furnished to the clerk of the court having jurisdiction to try the child as an adult and to the prosecuting officer of said child.

5. The child shall be forthwith delivered to the sheriff of the county in which the court that is to try the child is located. Bond is set at $ ....

DONE AND ORDERED in chambers at ...., ... (date) .....

____
Circuit Judge

Added May 9, 1991, effective July 1, 1991 (589 So.2d 818). Amended Oct. 26, 2000, effective Jan. 1, 2001 (783 So.2d 138).

Form 8.939. Motion for Involuntary Waiver

MOTION FOR INVOLUNTARY WAIVER

The State of Florida, having considered the recommendation of the intake officer, petitions the court to waive jurisdiction pursuant to rule 8.105, Florida Rules of Juvenile Procedure, and shows:

The child was 14 or more years of age at the alleged time of commission of the violation of law for which the child is charged.

[Add the following paragraph, if applicable]

The child has been previously adjudicated delinquent for a violent crime against a person, to wit __________, and is currently charged with a second or
(offense)
subsequent offense.

Wherefore, the State of Florida requests the court to conduct a hearing on this motion for the purpose of determining whether the court should waive its jurisdiction and certify the case to the appropriate court for trial as if the child were an adult.

____
Petitioner

Added May 9, 1991, effective July 1, 1991 (589 So.2d 818).

Form 8.940. Motion to Compile Report

MOTION TO COMPILE REPORT

The State of Florida, having filed a petition for involuntary waiver, moves the court for an order requiring the department to prepare a study and report to the court, in writing, considering the following relevant factors:

1. The seriousness of the alleged offense to the community and whether the protection of the community is best served by transferring the child for adult sanctions.

2. Whether the alleged offense was committed in an aggressive, violent, premeditated, or willful manner.

3. Whether the alleged offense was against persons or against property.

4. The probable cause as found in the report, affidavit, or complaint.

5. The desirability of trial and disposition of the entire offense in one court when the child's associates in the alleged crime are adults or children who are to be tried as adults who will be or have been charged with a crime.

6. The sophistication and maturity of the child.

7. The record and previous history of the child including:

a. Previous contact with the department, other law enforcement agencies, and the courts;

b. Prior periods of juvenile probation;

c. Prior adjudications that the child committed a delinquent act or violation of law, greater weight being given if the child previously had been found by a court to have committed a delinquent act involving an offense classified as a felony or had twice previously been found to have committed a delinquent act involving an offense classified as a misdemeanor; and

d. Prior commitments to institutions.

8. The prospects for adequate protection of the public and the likelihood of reasonable rehabilitation of the child, if found to have committed the alleged offense, by the use of procedures, services, and facilities currently available to the court.

WHEREFORE, the State of Florida requests an order directing the department to prepare a study and report in writing prior to the waiver hearing.

____
Petitioner

Added May 9, 1991, effective July 1, 1991 (589 So.2d 818). Amended Oct. 31, 1996, effective Jan. 1, 1997 (684 So.2d 756); Oct. 26, 2000, effective Jan. 1, 2001 (783 So.2d 138).

Form 8.941. Order to Compile Report

ORDER TO COMPILE REPORT

Upon the motion of the State of Florida, the department shall prepare a study and report to the court, in writing, considering the following relevant factors:

1. The seriousness of the alleged offense to the community and whether the protection of the community is best served by transferring the child for adult sanctions.

2. Whether the alleged offense was committed in an aggressive, violent, premeditated, or willful manner.

3. Whether the alleged offense was against persons or against property.

4. The probable cause as found in the report, affidavit, or complaint.

5. The desirability of trial and disposition of the entire offense in one court when the child's associates in the alleged crime are adults or children who are to be tried as adults who will be or have been charged with a crime.

6. The sophistication and maturity of the child.

7. The record and previous history of the child including:

a. Previous contact with the department, other law enforcement agencies, and the courts;

b. Prior periods of juvenile probation;

c. Prior adjudications that the child committed a delinquent act or violation of law, greater weight being given if the child had previously been found by a court to have committed a delinquent act involving an offense classified as a felony or had twice previously been found to have committed a delinquent act involving an offense classified as a misdemeanor; and

d. Prior commitments to institutions.

8. The prospects for adequate protection of the public and the likelihood of reasonable rehabilitation of the child, if found to have committed the alleged offense, by the use of procedures, services, and facilities currently available to the court.

DONE AND ORDERED in chambers at ...., Florida, ... (date) .....

____

Circuit Judge

Added May 9, 1991, effective July 1, 1991 (589 So.2d 818). Amended Oct. 31, 1996, effective Jan. 1, 1997 (684 So.2d 756); Oct. 26, 2000, effective Jan. 1, 2001 (783 So.2d 138).

Form 8.942. Order of Involuntary Waiver

ORDER OF INVOLUNTARY WAIVER

A petition was filed in this cause on ..... (date) ..... Prior to the adjudicatory hearing on the petition, the State of Florida filed a motion requesting that the court waive its jurisdiction and certify the case to the appropriate court for trial as if the child were an adult. This cause came before the court on the motion.

The following were present ..... (names) ..... with ..... (name) ....., representing the State of Florida and ..... (name) ....., representing the Department of Juvenile Justice.

The court heard the evidence presented by the State of Florida and the child to determine whether the jurisdiction of this court should be waived and the case certified to the appropriate court for trial as if the child were an adult. The court finds that it is in the public interest that the jurisdiction of this court be waived and that the case be certified to the appropriate court having jurisdiction to try an adult who is charged with a like offense based on the following findings of fact:

1. Age of child ....

2. Seriousness of alleged offense ....

3. Manner of commission of offense ....

4. Nature of offense (person or property) ....

5. Probable cause as found in the report, affidavit, or complaint ....

6. Desirability of trial and disposition of entire offense in one court ....

7. Sophistication and maturity of the child ....

8. Record and previous history of the child ....

9. Prospects for adequate protection of the public and rehabilitation of child ....

IT IS ADJUDGED that the jurisdiction of this court is waived and that this case is transferred to the ..... (court) ..... for trial as if the child were an adult.

The child shall be held by the sheriff of this county unless a bond in the amount of $ .... is posted. The child shall appear before ..... (court) ..... on ..... (date) ..... to answer the State of Florida on the foregoing charges.

DONE AND ORDERED in chambers at ...., Florida, on .... (date) ......

____

Circuit Judge

Added May 9, 1991, effective July 1, 1991 (589 So.2d 818). Amended Oct. 31, 1996, effective Jan. 1, 1997 (684 So.2d 756); Oct. 26, 2000, effective Jan. 1, 2001 (783 So.2d 138).

Form 8.947. Disposition Order—Delinquency

DISPOSITION ORDER

A petition was filed on ...(date)..., alleging ...(name)..., ... age, to be a delinquent child. The court finds that it has jurisdiction of the proceedings.

Present before the court were:

.... the child;

.............(name)..., Assistant State Attorney;

.............(name)..., Assistant Public Defender/defense attorney;

. . . .(name). . ., guardian;

. . . .(name). . ., DJJ juvenile probation officer.

At the hearing on . . .(date). . ., after . . . entry of a plea/an adjudicatory hearing. . ., the child was found to have committed the delinquent acts listed below:

	Count	Count	Count	Count
Charge	. . . . .	. . . . .	. . . . .	. . . . .
Lesser	. . . . .	. . . . .	. . . . .	. . . . .
Maximum	. . . . .	. . . . .	. . . . .	. . . . .
Degree	. . . . .	. . . . .	. . . . .	. . . . .
Guilty	. . . . .	. . . . .	. . . . .	. . . . .
Nolo contendere	. . . . .	. . . . .	. . . . .	. . . . .
Nolle prosse	. . . . .	. . . . .	. . . . .	. . . . .
Adjudicated	. . . . .	. . . . .	. . . . .	. . . . .
Adj. withheld	. . . . .	. . . . .	. . . . .	. . . . .

The predisposition report was . . . received and considered/waived by the child . . .

The court, having considered the evidence and comments offered by those present, having inquired, and being otherwise fully advised in the premises ORDERS THAT:

. . . Adjudication of delinquency is withheld.

. . . The child is adjudicated delinquent,

. . . The child is committed to a . . . licensed child caring agency . . . the Department of Juvenile Justice for placement in:

. . . a minimum-risk nonresidential commitment program, for an indeterminate period, but no longer than the child's 21st birthday or the maximum term of imprisonment an adult may serve for each count listed above, whichever comes first.

. . . a . . . low- or . . . moderate-risk commitment program, for an indeterminate period, but no longer than the child's 21st birthday or the maximum term of imprisonment an adult may serve for each count listed above, whichever comes first, because:

. . . the child is before the court for disposition of a felony;

. . . the child has previously been adjudicated for a felony offense;

. . . the child previously has been adjudicated or had adjudication withheld for three or more misdemeanor offenses;

. . . the child is before the court for disposition for a violation of sections 800.03, 806.031, or 828.12, Florida Statutes; or

. . . the court finds by a preponderance of the evidence that the protection of the public requires such placement or that the particular needs of the child would be best served by such placement. The facts supporting this finding are: . . . .

. . . a high-risk commitment program for an indeterminate period, but no longer than the child's 21st birthday or the maximum term of imprisonment an adult may serve for each count listed above, whichever comes first, because the child is before the court for disposition of a felony.

. . . a maximum-risk commitment program, for an indeterminate period, but no longer than the child's 21st birthday or the maximum term of imprisonment an adult may serve for each count listed above, whichever comes first, because the child meets the criteria in section 985.465 or 985.494, Florida Statutes.

. . . The child is allowed . . . . days credit for time spent in secure detention or incarceration before this date.

The child shall be placed on

. . . home detention . . . with/without . . . electronic monitoring until placement.

. . . secure detention until placement.

. . . The court has orally pronounced its reasons for adjudicating and committing this child.

. . . The court retains jurisdiction to accept or reject the discharge of this child from commitment, as provided by law.

. . . The child is placed on post-commitment juvenile probation for an indefinite period not to exceed the child's 19th birthday or the maximum term of imprisonment an adult could receive for each count listed above, whichever comes first.

. . . JUVENILE PROBATION: The child is . . . placed on/continued in . . . juvenile probation under supervision of . . . the Department of Juvenile Justice/ . . . (name) . . . . and

. . . the court having withheld adjudication of delinquency, for an indefinite period not to exceed the child's 19th birthday.

. . . the court having adjudicated the child delinquent, for an indefinite period not to exceed the child's 19th birthday or the maximum term of imprisonment an adult could receive for each count listed above, except for a second degree misdemeanor, six months, whichever comes first.

. . . DISMISS: The case is dismissed.

. . . Disposition on each count is . . . concurrent/consecutive . . .

. . . This case disposition is . . . concurrent/consecutive . . . with case number . . . .

GENERAL CONDITIONS OF JUVENILE PROBATION. The child shall abide by all of the following conditions:

1. The child shall obey all laws.

2. The child shall be employed full-time or attend school with no unexcused absences, suspensions, or disciplinary referrals.

3. The child shall not change or leave . . . his/her . . . residence, school, or place of employment without the consent of . . . his/her . . . parents and juvenile probation officer.

4. The child shall answer truthfully all questions of ... his/her ... juvenile probation officer and carry out all instructions of the court and juvenile probation officer.

5. The child shall keep in contact with the juvenile probation officer in the manner prescribed by the juvenile probation officer.

6. The child shall not use or possess alcoholic beverages or controlled substances.

SPECIAL CONDITIONS OF JUVENILE PROBATION. The child shall abide by all of the conditions marked below:

... Restitution is ordered. Parent and child are responsible, ... jointly and severally.

... Amount is reserved.

... $ .... to be paid to ... (name) ... Payments shall begin ... (date) ... and continue at the rate of $ .... each month.

... The court retains jurisdiction under Chapter 985, Florida Statutes, to enforce its restitution order, regardless of the age of the child.

... Community Service. ... hours are to be performed by the child at the rate of ... hours per month. Written proof is to be provided to the juvenile probation officer.

... A letter of apology to be written by the child to ... (name) ... within ... days. The letter must be a minimum of ... words.

... A ... word essay to be written by the child on ... (subject) ... and provided to the juvenile probation officer within 30 days.

... The child may have no .... contact with victim(s), ... (name(s)) ...

... A ... mental health/substance abuse ... evaluation to be completed by the child within ... days. The child will attend and participate in every scheduled appointment and successfully attend and complete any and all recommended evaluations and treatment.

... The parent(s) ... is/are ... to complete counseling in ....

... A curfew is set for the child at ... p.m. Sunday through Thursday and ... p.m. Friday and Saturday.

... The child's driver's license is ... suspended/revoked/withheld ... for ... (time period) ...

... The child is to complete a ... detention/jail/prison ... tour within .... days.

... The child will be subject to random urinalysis.

... The child will be electronically monitored.

... The child will successfully complete all sanctions of the original juvenile probation order.

... Other: ....

... The child must pay court costs of $ ...., as specified below.

GUN CHARGES

... The court finds that one of the above charges involves the use or possession of a firearm and further ORDERS the following:

... The child's driver's license is ... suspended/revoked ... for ... 1/2 ... years.

... The child is to serve ... 15/21 ... days in the Juvenile Detention Center, and shall not receive credit for time served prior to adjudication.

THE COURT FURTHER FINDS AND ORDERS:

... The child must:

... pay $ .... (no less than $50 per case when a misdemeanor offense is charged) or $ .... (no less than $100 per case when a felony offense is charged), the costs of prosecution and investigation, under sections 938.27 and 985.032, Florida Statutes.

... pay $ ...., the Victim's Crime Compensation Trust Fund fee, under section 938.03, Florida Statutes;

... pay $ ...., the Teen Court cost, under section 938.19, Florida Statutes (if authorized by county ordinance);

... pay $ ...., the Public Defender application fee, under section 27.52, Florida Statutes;

... pay $ ...., the Public Defender attorney fee, under section 938.29, Florida Statutes;

... pay $ ...., other costs, under section(s) ...., Florida Statutes.

... The child has been adjudicated delinquent and the child is required to pay $ ... an Additional cost, under section 939.185, Florida Statutes, if authorized by county ordinance.

... The child has been adjudicated delinquent and assessed a fine and the child is required to pay $ .... to the Crime Prevention Trust Fund, under section 775.083(2), Florida Statutes.

... The child has committed an enumerated crime against a minor and the child is required to pay $ ...., under section 938.10, Florida Statutes.

... The child has violated chapter 794, Florida Statutes (sexual battery) or chapter 800 (lewd or lascivious) and is ordered to make restitution to the Crimes Compensation Trust Fund under section 960.28(5), Florida Statutes, for the cost of the forensic physical examination.

... The child has the inability to pay all court costs, including costs of prosecution, public defender application fees and costs of representation, and shall perform ... hours of community service in lieu of these costs and fees.

... The child ... has been adjudicated delinquent/has entered a plea of no contest/has entered a plea of guilty ... to a felony or an enumerated misdemeanor, and the child is required to submit specimens under section 943.325, Florida Statutes.

. . . Under section 985.039, Florida Statutes:

. . . the parent/legal guardian, . . . (name) . . ., shall pay to the Department of Juvenile Justice, 2737 Centerview Drive, Tallahassee, FL 32399–3100, $5 per day for each day the child is in residential commitment.

. . . the parent/legal guardian, . . . (name) . . ., shall pay to the Department of Juvenile Justice, 2737 Centerview Drive, Tallahassee, FL 32399–3100, $1 per day for each day the child is on probation, nonresidential commitment, or conditional release.

. . . the parent/legal guardian, . . . (name) . . ., shall pay to the Department of Juvenile Justice, 2737 Centerview Drive, Tallahassee, FL 32399–3100, a REDUCED fee of $ . . . per day for each day the child is in the custody of or supervised by the department. This reduced fee is based on the court's finding:

. . . that the parent/legal guardian was the victim of the delinquent act or violation of law for which the child is currently before the court and is cooperating in the investigation of the offense.

. . . of indigency or significant financial hardship. The facts supporting this finding are: . . . .

. . . The cost of care/supervision fee is WAIVED based on the court's finding:

. . . that the parent/legal guardian was the victim of the delinquent act or violation of law for which the child is currently before the court and is cooperating in the investigation of the offense.

. . . of indigency or significant financial hardship. The facts supporting this finding are: . . . .

. . . The parent/guardian, . . . (name) . . ., . . . (address) . . ., shall be liable for . . . % of the payment. The parent/guardian, . . . (name) . . ., . . . (address) . . ., shall be liable for . . . % of the payment.

The child is placed on notice that the court may modify the conditions of . . . his/her . . . juvenile probation at any time and may revoke the juvenile probation if there is a violation of the conditions imposed.

The parties are advised that an appeal is allowed within 30 days of the date of this order.

DONE AND ORDERED in . . . (city) . . ., ... County, Florida on . . . (date) . . ., at . . . a.m./p.m.

____

Circuit Judge

Copies to: . . . .

Added May 9, 1991, effective July 1, 1991 (589 So.2d 818). Amended Jan. 26, 1995 (649 So.2d 1370); Oct. 31, 1996, effective Jan. 1, 1997 (684 So.2d 756); Oct. 26, 2000, effective Jan. 1, 2001 (783 So.2d 138); Mar. 3, 2005 (898 So.2d 47); Nov. 17, 2005 (915 So.2d 592); Feb. 8, 2007 (851 So.2d 804); Oct. 20, 2011 (75 So.3d 216); May 23, 2013, effective July 1, 2013 (115 So.3d 286); Oct. 3, 2013 (123 So.3d 1128).

Form 8.948. Petition For Revocation of Juvenile Probation

PETITION FOR REVOCATION OF JUVENILE PROBATION

The petitioner represents to the court that . . . ., whose residence and address is . . . . was adjudicated a . . . . child and placed on juvenile probation by order of this court dated . . . ., and that the child has violated the conditions of juvenile probation in a material respect by: . . . .

The petitioner represents further that the parent(s) or custodian(s) . . . . . is/are . . . . .:

. . . .	. . . .
Mother	Residence
. . . .	. . . .
Father	Residence
. . . .	. . . .
Custodian	Residence

WHEREFORE, your petitioner requests that process may issue to bring the above-named child before this court to be dealt with according to law.

Date: . . . .

____

Petitioner

Former Form 8.920 renumbered as new Form 8.948 and amended May 9, 1991, effective July 1, 1991 (589 So.2d 818). Amended Oct. 26, 2000, effective Jan. 1, 2001 (783 So.2d 138).

Form 8.949. Order For HIV Testing

ORDER FOR HUMAN IMMUNODEFICIENCY VIRUS (HIV) TESTING

The court having been requested by the . . . . . victim/victim's legal guardian/minor victim's parent . . . . . for disclosure of the child's HIV test results FINDS that:

The child, ... (name) . . . . . , ... is alleged by petition for delinquency to have committed/has been adjudicated delinquent for . . . . a sexual offense proscribed in chapter 794 or section 800.04, Florida Statutes, involving the transmission of body fluids from one person to another.

It is ORDERED AND ADJUDGED that:

1. The child, ... (name) ....., shall immediately undergo Human Immunodeficiency Virus testing.

2. The testing shall be performed under the direction of the Department of Health in accordance with section 381.004, Florida Statutes.

3. The results of the test performed on the child pursuant to this order shall not be admissible in any juvenile proceeding arising out of the ..... alleged sexual offense/sexual offense .....

4. The results of the test shall be disclosed, under the direction of the department, to the child and to the ..... victim/victim's legal guardian/minor victim's parent ..... The department shall ensure that the provisions of section 381.004, Florida Statutes, for personal counseling are available to the party requesting the test results.

DONE AND ORDERED at ...., Florida, ... (date) .....

Circuit Judge

Added Jan. 26, 1995 (649 So.2d 1370). Amended Oct. 26, 2000, effective Jan. 1, 2001 (783 So.2d 138).

Form 8.950. Restitution Order

JUDGMENT AND RESTITUTION ORDER

THIS CAUSE was heard on .... (date) ...., on the state's motion for an order requiring the child, born .... (date) ...., or .... his/her .... parent(s), to pay restitution costs for the benefit of the victim pursuant to sections 985.0301(5)(i), 985.437, and 775.089, Florida Statutes.

Name of victim: ....

Attorney or Advocate: ....

Address: ....

The court being fully advised in the premises, it is ORDERED AND ADJUDGED:

The state's motion is granted and the .... child/child's parent(s), ... (name(s)) ...., shall pay restitution for the benefit of the victim named above as follows:

..... $..... for medical and related services and devices relating to physical, psychiatric, and psychological care, including nonmedical care rendered in accordance with a recognized method of healing.

..... $..... for necessary physical and occupational therapy and rehabilitation.

..... $..... to reimburse the victim for income lost as a result of the offense.

..... $..... for necessary funeral and related services, if the offense caused bodily injury resulting in the death of the victim.

..... $..... for damages resulting from the offense.

..... $..... for ....

The total amount of restitution due is $ ....

Payment shall be made to the clerk of the circuit court.

Payment schedule:

..... Installment payments of $..... payable on a ..... weekly/monthly ..... basis.

..... Payment is due in full.

.... The court finds that the .... child/child's parent(s) .... is/are .... unable to pay and orders the child to perform .... hours of community service in lieu of .... partial/total .... restitution.

The court retains jurisdiction over this child beyond .... his/her .... nineteenth birthday in order to enforce the provisions of this order and retains jurisdiction to modify the restitution in this case.

Other, specified conditions: ....

IT IS FURTHER ORDERED AND ADJUDGED that the clerk of the court shall provide the victim named above a certified copy of this order for the victim to record this judgment as a lien, pursuant to section 55.10, Florida Statutes.

IT IS FURTHER ORDERED AND ADJUDGED that this judgment may be enforced by the state or the victim in order to receive restitution in the same manner as a judgment in a civil action. Execution shall issue for all payments required under this order.

DONE AND ORDERED AT .... (city) ...., ... (county) ...., Florida, on .... (date) ....

Circuit Judge

Copies to:

State Attorney

Counsel for Child

Victim

Department of Juvenile Justice

Parent(s)

Added Jan. 26, 1995 (649 So.2d 1370). Amended Oct. 31, 1996, effective Jan. 1, 1997 (684 So.2d 756); Oct. 26, 2000, effective Jan. 1, 2001 (783 So.2d 138); Feb. 8, 2007 (951 So.2d 804).

Form 8.951. Motion For Juvenile Sexual Offender Placement

MOTION FOR JUVENILE SEXUAL OFFENDER PLACEMENT

Comes now the .... State of Florida, by and through the undersigned assistant state attorney/Department of Juvenile Justice, by and through its undersigned counsel ...., and moves the court for Juvenile Sexual Offender placement. In support thereof, movant would show:

..... that the juvenile has been found by the court, under section 985.35, Florida Statutes, to have committed a violation of chapter 794, chapter 796, chapter 800, section 827.071, or section 847.0133, Florida Statutes; or

..... that the juvenile has been found to have committed any violation of law or delinquent act involving juvenile sexual abuse as defined in section 985.475(1), Florida Statutes.

Placement in a juvenile sexual offender program is required for the protection of the public and would best serve the needs of this juvenile.

WHEREFORE, as this child meets the juvenile sexual offender placement criteria, the .... state/ department .... respectfully requests this court to enter an order placing the child as a juvenile sexual offender under section 985.48, Florida Statutes.

Date: ....

____

Assistant State Attorney/DJJ Attorney

.... (address & phone no.) ....

Florida Bar No.: ....

Added Oct. 31, 1996, effective Jan. 1, 1997 (684 So.2d 756). Amended Oct. 26, 2000, effective Jan. 1, 2001 (783 So.2d 138); Feb. 8, 2007 (951 So.2d 804).

Form 8.952. Findings for Juvenile Sexual Offender Registration

REQUIRED FINDINGS FOR JUVENILE SEXUAL OFFENDER REGISTRATION

The following findings are to be made for adjudications of delinquency made on or after July 1,2007, for committing, or attempting, soliciting, or conspiring to commit any of the following offenses, when the offender is 14 years of age or older at the time of the offense. Check the appropriate charge and make the corresponding findings:

Date of the offense: ....

Offender's age at date of offense: ....

Victim's age at date of offense: ....

..... **F.S. 794.011: Sexual Battery:** Oral, anal, or vaginal penetration by, or union with, the sexual organ of another, or the anal or vaginal penetration of another by any other object.

(Sexual offender registration is required if the offender is 14 years of age or older at the time of the offense.)

..... **F.S. 800.40(4)(b): Lewd or Lascivious Battery:** Encouraging, forcing, or enticing any person less than 16 years of age to engage in sadomasochistic abuse, sexual bestiality, prostitution, or any other act involving sexual activity.

(Sexual offender registration is required if the offender is 14 years of age or older at the time of the offense and at least one of the lines below is checked "Yes.")

Was the victim under the age of 12 at the time of the offense? Yes ..... No .....

Did the sexual activity involve force or coercion? Yes ..... No ....

..... **F.S. 800.04(5)(d): Lewd or Lascivious Molestation—Victim 12–15:** Intentionally touching the breasts, genitals, genital area, buttocks, or the clothing covering them, of a person 12 years of age or older but less than 16 years of age, or forcing or enticing a person less than 16 years of age to so touch the perpetrator.

(Sexual offender registration is required if the offender is 14 years of age or older at the time of the offense and **both** boxes below are checked "Yes.")

Did the sexual activity involve unclothed genitals? Yes ..... No .....

Did the sexual activity involve force or coercion? Yes ..... No ....

..... **F.S. 800.04(5)(c): Lewd or Lascivious Molestation—Victim under 12:** Intentionally touching the breasts, genitals, genital area, buttocks, or the clothing covering them, of a person less than 12 years of age, or forcing or enticing a person less than 12 years of age to so touch the perpetrator.

(Sexual offender registration is required if the offender is 14 years of age or older at the time of the offense and the box below is checked "Yes.")

Did the sexual activity involve unclothed genitals? Yes ..... No .....

(Check one only)

SEXUAL OFFENDER REGISTRATION IS REQUIRED .....

SEXUAL OFFENDER REGISTRATION IS NOT REQUIRED .....

DONE AND ORDERED ON ..... (date) .....

____

Circuit Judge

Added May 23, 2013, effective July 1, 2013 (115 So.3d 286).

C. DEPENDENCY FORMS

Form 8.958. Order Appointing Surrogate Parent

ORDER APPOINTING SURROGATE PARENT FOR DEPENDENT CHILD WHO HAS OR IS SUSPECTED OF HAVING A DISABILITY

The court finds that:

1. The child has, or is suspected of having, a disability as defined in the Individuals with Disabilities in Education Act ("IDEA") and F.S. 1003.01(3).

2. A surrogate parent is needed to act in the place of a parent in educational decision-making and in safeguarding the child's rights under the IDEA.

3. The child is entitled, under the Individuals with Disabilities in Education Act ("IDEA"), 20 U.S.C. § 1415(b)(2); 34 C.F.R. §§ 300.515 and 303.406; F.S. 39.0016(3)–(4), 39.4085(17); and Fla. Admin. Code 6A–6.0333, to the assistance of a surrogate parent because (check all that apply):

.... Parental rights have been terminated

.... Parents cannot be located

.... No parent is available to make education decisions related to the child's disability

.... Foster parent is unwilling or unable to make educational decisions related to the child's disability

.... Relative or non-relative caregiver is unwilling or unable to make educational decisions related to the child's disability

.... Child resides in a group home or therapeutic foster home

.... Other: ....

ACCORDINGLY, it is **ORDERED** that:

1. .... (Name) .... is appointed as a surrogate parent for .... (child's name) ...

2. The surrogate parent named above has the following rights, duties, and responsibilities:

a. to request or respond to requests for evaluations of the child;

b. to review and keep confidential the child's educational records;

c. to request and participate in school meetings including Individual Education Plan (IEP) meetings;

d. to express approval or disapproval of a child's educational placement or IEP;

e. to monitor the child's educational development;

f. to help the child access available and needed educational services;

g. to aid the child in securing all rights provided the child under the IDEA;

h. to meet the child face-to-face

i. to be afforded all of the due process rights parents hold under the IDEA

3. The surrogate parent may also do the following: (check all that apply)

.... attend appropriate court hearings to address the educational needs of the child. The surrogate parent will be provided notice of all dependency court hearings.

.... attend dependency staffings. The community-based care provider will invite the surrogate parent to all permanency staffings and any other staffings when the child's educational needs will be addressed. See F.A.C. 65C–28.006.

....

....

4. As to issues affecting the provision of a Free Appropriate Public Education, principals, teachers, administrators, and other employees of the .... County Public Schools shall communicate with the surrogate parent and accept the requests or decisions of the surrogate parent in the same manner as if he or she were the child's parent.

5. Unless the court explicitly orders otherwise, the surrogate parent does not have the right and responsibility to register the child in school, and grant or withhold consent for ordinary school decisions not related to IDEA (such as field trips, sports and club activities, medical care, etc.).

6. The surrogate parent must have access to and keep confidential the child's records including, but not limited to, records from the school system, community-based care provider or agency, and any mental health or medical evaluations or assessments.

7. By law, the surrogate parent has no liability for actions taken in good faith on behalf of the child in protecting the special education rights of the child.

ORDERED on .... (date) ...., in ...., ... County, Florida.

____
Circuit Judge

Copies to:

County Public Schools c/o Director, Exceptional Student Education, Surrogate parent named above

(Check all that apply)

.... Attorney for DCF: .... (name) ....

.... DCF caseworker: .... (name) ....

.... Guardian ad Litem: ... (name) ....

.... Attorney for mother: .... (name) ....

.... Attorney for father: .... (name) ....

.... Attorney for child: .... (name) ....

.... Child named above .... (name) ....

.... Foster parent: .... (name) ....

.... Relative caregiver: .... (name) ....

.... Child's principal: .... (name) .... at .... School

.... Other: ....

.... Other: ....

Added Oct. 1, 2009 (22 So.3d 9).

Form 8.959. Summons for Dependency Arraignment

SUMMONS AND NOTICE OF HEARING

STATE OF FLORIDA

TO: ..... (name and address of person being summoned) .....

..... (Petitioner's name) .... has filed in this court a petition, alleging under oath that the above-named child(ren) is/are dependent under the laws of the State of Florida and requesting that a summons issue in due course requiring that you appear before this court to be dealt with according to law. A copy of the petition is attached to this summons.

You are to appear before this Court at .... (location of hearing) ...., at .... (time and date of hearing) ....

FAILURE TO PERSONALLY APPEAR AT THE ARRAIGNMENT HEARING CONSTITUTES CONSENT TO THE ADJUDICATION OF THIS CHILD (OR CHILDREN) AS A DEPENDENT CHILD (OR CHILDREN) AND MAY ULTIMATELY RESULT IN LOSS OF CUSTODY OF THIS CHILD (OR CHILDREN).

IF YOU FAIL TO APPEAR YOU MAY BE HELD IN CONTEMPT OF COURT.

COMMENT: The following paragraph must be in bold, 14 pt. Times New Roman or Courier font.

If you are a person with a disability who needs any accommodation to participate in this proceeding, you are entitled, at no cost to you, to the provision of certain assistance. Please contact .... (name, address, telephone number) .... at least 7 days before your scheduled court appearance, or immediately upon receiving this notification if the time before the scheduled appearance is less than 7 days. If you are hearing or voice impaired, call 711.

Witness my hand and seal of this court at .... (city, county, and state) ...., on .... (date) ....

CLERK OF COURT
BY: ____________________
DEPUTY CLERK

NOTIFICACIÓN Y CITACIÓN
PARA LA AUDIENCIA

ESTADO DE LA FLORIDA

PARA: ____________________

(Nombre y dirección de la persona a ser citada)

CONSIDERANDO, que ____________________

(Nombre del(a) demandante)

ha interpuesto en este Juzgado una petición en la cual alega bajo juramente la dependencia del(los) niño(s) según las leyes del Estado de la Florida, adjuntándose copia de la misma, y está solicitando la emisión oportuna de una citación para exigir su comparecencia ante este juzgado para tratar el asunto conforme a la ley.

POR LO TANTO, se le ordena comparecer ante este Juzgado en ____________________ a las ____________________

(lugar de la audiencia) (hora y fecha de la audiencia)

SI USTED NO COMPARECE PERSONALMENTE A LA AUDIENCIA INCOATORIA, ESTO SIGNIFICARÁ QUE USTED ACCEDE A LA ADJUDICACIÓN DE DEPENDENCIA DE ESTE(OS) NIÑO(S) Y FINALMENTE, PODRÁ RESULTAR EN LA PERDIDA DE LA TUTELA DEL(OS) NIÑO(S).

SI USTED NO COMPARECE, SE LO PODRÁ JUZGAR EN DESACATO DEL TRIBUNAL.

Si usted es una persona con una discapacidad que necesita cualquier tipo de trato especial para participar en este procedimiento, usted tiene derecho, sin costa alguno para usted, para la presetación de asistencia determinadas. Póngase en contacto con .... (nombre, dirección, número de teléfono) .... por lo menos 7 dias antes la aparición en la corte programado, o immediatamente después de reciber esta notification, si el tiempo antes de la comparecencia prevista es inferiof a 7 dias. Si usted está oyendo o voz alterada, llame al 711.

Firmado y sigilado en este Juzgado en ____________________

(ciudad, condado y estado)

el ____________

(fecha)

ESCRIBANO DEL TRIBUNAL
POR: ____________________
ESCRIBANO DELEGADO

MANDA AK AVÈTISMAN POU
YON CHITA TANDE

Leta Florid

Pou: ..... (non ak adrès pou moun yo voye manda-a) .....

kÒm, tantiske, ... (non pati ki fé demann–nan) .... fé yon demann devan tribinal-la, epi li sèmante timounnan (yo), swa dizan bezwen pwoteksyon leta dapre règ lalwa nan Leta Florid, yon kopi enfòmasyon sou akizasyon-an kwoke nan lèt sa-a. Yo mande pou yo sèvi–w ak yon manda touswit, ki pou fose-w prezante devan tribinal la pou yo ka koresponn avèk ou, dapre lalwa.

Alò, pou sa yo kòmande–w pou prezante devan tribinal sa-a, ki nan ...., (adrès tribinal-la) ...., a .... (nan dat ak lè, chita tande-a) ....

SI OU PA PREZANTE PESONÈLMAN NAN CHITA TANDE–A, POU YO KA AVÈTI–W AK AKIZASYON OFISYÈL–LA, SA KA LAKÒZ YO DESIDE OU KONSANTI TIMOUN-NAN(YO), BEZWEN PWOTEKSYON LETA, EPI LI KA LAKÒZ OU PÈDI DWA–OU KÒM PARAN TIMOUN SA–A(YO).

SI OU PA PREZANTE, YO GEN DWA CHAJE–W, KÒMKWA OU MANKE TRIBINAL LA DEGA.

Si ou se yon moun infirm, ki beswen 'ed ou ki bewsen ke o akomode w pou ou patispe nan pwosedi sa yo, ou genyen dwa, san ke ou pa peye, a setin 'ed. Silvouple kontake .... (non, address, telephone) .... o moin 7 jou avan dat ou genyen rendevou pou ale nan tribunal, ou si le ou resevwa avi a, genyen mouins ke 7 jou avan date endevou tribunal la. Ou si ou pa tande pale, rele nan nimerro sa 711.

Mwen siyen non mwen, epi mete so mwen, nan dokiman tribinal-la sa-a, kòm temwen, nan (vil, distrik, eta) ...., nan .... (dat) ....

GREFYE TRIBINAL–LA

PA: ______________________

Asistan Grefye Tribinal-la

Added Sept. 18, 1998, effective Oct. 1, 1998 (724 So.2d 1153). Amended Oct. 26, 2000, effective Jan. 1, 2001 (783 So.2d 138); Sept. 5, 2002, effective Jan. 1, 2003 (827 So.2d 219); Jan. 27, 2005 (894 So.2d 875); May 23, 2013, effective July 1, 2013 (115 So.3d 286).

Form 8.960. Shelter Petition

AFFIDAVIT AND PETITION FOR PLACEMENT IN SHELTER

COMES NOW, the undersigned, who being first duly sworn says:

1. On... (date) ... at .... a.m./p.m. the above named minor child(ren) was/were found within the jurisdiction of this court.

..... The child(ren) was/were taken into custody by ....

..... The child(ren) need(s) to be taken into protective custody.

2. The name, age, and residence of this/these child(ren) is/are:

Name	Birth date	Sex	Address
....	....	....	....
....	....	....	....
....	....	....	....

3. The name, relationship to the child(ren), and address of the child(ren)'s parents or other legal custodian(s) is/are:

Name	Relationship	Address
....	....	....
....	....	....

4. The following individuals who were listed in #3 above have been notified in the following manner of the date, time, and location of this hearing:

Name	Manner Notified
....	....
....	....
....	....

5. There is probable cause that the child(ren)

... a. has/have been abused, abandoned, or neglected ort[1] is/are in imminent danger of illness or injury as a result of abuse, abandonment, or neglect;

... b. was/were with a parent or legal custodian who has materially violated a condition of placement imposed by the court;

... c. has/have no legal custodian, or responsible adult relative immediately known and available to provide supervision and care; because ....

6. The provision of appropriate and available services will not eliminate the need for placement of the child(ren) in shelter care because:

... a. an emergency existed in which the child(ren) could not safely remain in the home;

... b. the home situation presents a substantial and immediate danger to the child(ren) which cannot be mitigated by the provision of preventive services;

... c. the child(ren) could not be protected in the home despite the provision of the following services and efforts made by the Department of Children and Families to prevent or eliminate the need for placement in shelter care;

... d. the child(ren) cannot safely remain at home because there are no preventive services that can ensure the safety of the children.

7. The department has made reasonable efforts to keep the siblings together after the removal from the home. The reasonable efforts of the department were ....

... a. The children are currently placed together ....

... b. A foster home is not available to place the siblings together because ....

... c. It is not in the best interest of each child that all the siblings be placed together in out-of-home care because ....

8. On-going visitation or interaction between the siblings ... (list) ... is

... a. recommended as follows ....

... b. not recommended because visitation or interaction would be contrary to the safety or well-being of ... (name(s)) ... because ....

9. The child(ren) is/are in need of and the petitioner requests the appointment of a guardian ad litem.

10. The petitioner requests that the parents, if able, be ordered to pay fees for the care, support, and maintenance of the child(ren) as established by the department under chapter 39, Florida Statutes.

11. The petitioner requests that the parents be ordered to provide to the Department of Children and Families and the Department of Revenue financial information necessary to accurately calculate child support under section 61.30, Florida Statutes, within 28 days of this order.

12. This affidavit and petition is filed in good faith and under oath.

WHEREFORE, the affiant requests that this court order that this/these child(ren) be placed in the custody of the department until this/these child(ren) be placed in the custody of the department until further order of this court and that the place of such custody shall be:

... at the discretion of the Department of Children and Families;

... at the home of a responsible adult relative, ... (name) ..., whose address is ....;

... other.

____

Moving Party

____

... (attorney's name) ...

... (address and telephone number) ...

E-mail address: ....

Florida Bar number: ....

[1] So in original.

Verification

NOTICE TO PARENTS/GUARDIANS/LEGAL CUSTODIANS

A date and time for an arraignment hearing is normally set at this shelter hearing. If one is not set or if there are questions, you should contact the Juvenile Court Clerk's Office at .... A copy of the Petition for Dependency will be given to you or to your attorney, if you have one. A copy will also be available in the clerk's office. You have a right to have an attorney represent you at this hearing and during the dependency proceedings and an attorney will be appointed for you if you request an attorney and the court finds that you are unable to afford an attorney.

COMMENT: The following paragraph must be in bold, 14 pt. Times New Roman or Courier font.

If you are a person with a disability who needs any accommodation to participate in this proceeding, you are entitled, at no cost to you, to the provision of certain assistance. Please contact ... (name, address, telephone number) ... at least 7 days before your scheduled court appearance, or immediately upon receiving this notification if the time before the scheduled appearance is less than 7 days. If you are hearing or voice impaired, call 711.

Added May 9, 1991, effective July 1, 1991 (589 So.2d 818). Amended Sept. 18, 1998, effective Oct. 1, 1998 (725 So.2d 296); Oct. 26, 2000, effective Jan. 1, 2001 (783 So.2d 138); Sept. 5, 2002, effective Jan. 1, 2003 (827 So.2d 219); Jan. 27, 2005 (894 So.2d 875); May 23, 2013, effective July 1, 2013 (115 So.3d 286); Feb. 19, 2015, effective Feb. 19, 2015 (158 So.3d 523).

Form 8.961. Shelter Order

ORDER FOR PLACEMENT IN SHELTER

THIS CAUSE came on to be heard under chapter 39, Florida Statutes, on the sworn AFFIDAVIT AND PETITION FOR PLACEMENT IN SHELTER CARE filed by ...(petitioner's name)..., on ...(date)... The following persons appeared before the court:

... Petitioner ....

... Petitioner's attorney ....

... Mother ....

... Father(s) ....

... Legal custodian(s) ....

... Guardian ad litem ....

... GAL attorney. ....

... Attorney for the Child ....

... Other: ....

and the Court having reviewed its file and having been otherwise duly advised in the premises finds as follows:

1. The minor child(ren), ..., was/were found within the jurisdiction of this court and is/are of an age subject to the jurisdiction of this court.

2. PLACEMENT IN SHELTER.

... The minor child(ren) was/were placed in shelter on ...(date)... at ... a.m./p.m. by ...(name)..., a duly authorized agent of the department.

... The minor child(ren) need(s) to be placed in shelter at the request of the petitioner for the reasons stated in this order.

3. PARENTS/CUSTODIANS. The parents/custodians of the minor child(ren) are:

	Name	Address
Mother:	....	....
Father of .....(child's name) ......:		
	....	....
Other: .....(relationship and to which child)......		
	....	....

4. INABILITY TO NOTIFY AND/OR LOCATE PARENTS/CUSTODIANS. The petitioner has made a good faith effort to notify and/or locate, but was unable to notify and/or locate ...(name(s))..., a parent or legal custodian of the minor child(ren).

5. NOTIFICATION. Each parent/legal custodian not listed in #4 above was:

... duly notified that the child(ren) was/were taken into custody;

... duly notified to be present at this hearing;

... served with a statement setting forth a summary of procedures involved in dependency cases;

... advised of their right to counsel; and

... was represented by counsel, ...(name)...

... knowingly, voluntarily, and intelligently waived the right; or

... the court declined to accept the waiver because ....

... requested appointment of counsel, but the court declined appointment because he/she did not qualify as indigent.

... requested appointment of counsel and counsel was appointed.

6. PROBABLE CAUSE.

... Based on the allegations in the Affidavit and Petition for Placement in Shelter, there is probable cause to believe that the child(ren) is/are dependent based on allegations of abuse, abandonment, or neglect or substantial risk of same.

... A finding of probable cause cannot be made at this time and the court requires additional information to determine the risk to the child(ren). The following information must be provided to the court during the continuation of this hearing: ...(information to be provided)... This hearing is continued for 72 hours, until ...(date and time)... The children will remain in shelter care.

7. NEED FOR PLACEMENT. Placement of the child(ren) in shelter care is in the best interest of the child(ren). Continuation in the home is contrary to the welfare of the child(ren) because the home situation presents a substantial and immediate danger which cannot be mitigated by the provision of preventive services and placement is necessary to protect the child(ren) as shown by the following facts:

... the child(ren) was/were abused, abandoned, or neglected, or is/are suffering from or in imminent danger of injury or illness as a result of abuse, abandonment, or neglect, specifically: ....

... the custodian has materially violated a condition of placement imposed by the court, specifically: ....

... the child(ren) has/have no parent, legal custodian, or responsible adult relative immediately known and available to provide supervision and care, specifically: ....

....

8. REASONABLE EFFORTS.

... Reasonable efforts to prevent or eliminate the need for removing the child(ren) from the home have been made by the department, which provided the following services to the family: ....

... The following specific services, if available, could prevent or eliminate the need for removal or continued removal of the child from the home . . . .

. . . The date these services are expected to be available is . . . .

The department is deemed to have made reasonable efforts to prevent or eliminate the need for removal from the home because:

. . . The first contact with the department occurred during an emergency.

. . . The appraisal of the home situation by the department indicates a substantial and immediate danger to the child(ren) which cannot be mitigated by the provision of preventive services.

. . . The child(ren) cannot safely remain at home because no services exist that can ensure the safety of the child(ren). Services are not available because . . . .

. . . Even with appropriate services, the child(ren)'s safety cannot be ensured.

. . . The department has made reasonable efforts to keep siblings together after the removal from the home. The reasonable efforts of the department were . . . .

. . . It is not in the best interest of each child that all the siblings be placed together in out-of-home care because . . . .

9. RELATIVE PLACEMENT

. . . The court asked any parents present whether the parents have relatives that might be considered as a placement for the child(ren).

. . . The court advised any parents present that the parents have a continuing duty to inform The department of any relative who should be considered for placement of the child.

. . . By this order, the court notifies the relatives who are providing out-of-home care for the child(ren) of the right to attend all subsequent hearings, to submit reports to the court, and to speak to the court regarding the child(ren), if they so desire.

It is, therefore, ORDERED AND ADJUDGED, as follows:

. . . 1. The child(ren) shall remain/be placed in the shelter custody of:

. . . the department, with the department having the discretion to shelter the child(ren) with a relative or other responsible adult on completion of a positive homestudy, abuse registry, and criminal background checks.

. . . all the children shall be placed together in a foster home if available.

. . . a foster home is not available for all the children because . . . .

. . . placement of all the children in the same foster home is not in the best interest of the child(ren) . . . (identify the child(ren)) . . . because . . . .

. . . Other: . . . .

2. The child(ren) . . . may . . . may not be returned to the parent/custodian without further order of this court.

3. The Guardian Ad Litem Program is appointed.

4. The parents, within 28 days of the date of this order, shall provide to the department the information necessary to accurately calculate child support under section 61.30, Florida Statutes. The parents shall pay child support in accordance with Florida Statutes.

5. The legal custodian, or in the absence of the legal custodian, the department and its agents, are hereby authorized to provide consent for and to obtain ordinary and necessary medical and dental treatment and examination for the above child(ren) including blood testing deemed medically appropriate, and necessary preventive care, including ordinary immunizations and tuberculin testing.

6. Visitation with the child(ren) shall be as follows:

By the parents . . . .

Between the sibling children . . . .

Visitation or interaction between the children . . . (identify child(ren)) . . . is not ordered as it will be contrary to the safety or well-being of . . . (identify child(ren)) . . . because . . . .

7. The parents shall provide to the court and all parties identification and location information regarding potential relative placements.

8. The relatives who are providing out-of-home care for the child(ren) have the right to attend all subsequent hearings, to submit reports to the court, and to speak to the court regarding the child(ren), if they so desire.

9. **IF THE PARENTS FAIL TO SUBSTANTIALLY COMPLY WITH THE CASE PLAN, THEIR PARENTAL RIGHTS MAY BE TERMINATED AND THE CHILD(REN)'S OUT–OF–HOME PLACEMENT MAY BECOME PERMANENT.**

10. Special conditions: . . . .

11. This court retains jurisdiction over this matter to enter any other and further orders as may be deemed to be in the best interest and welfare of this/these child(ren).

12. If a Petition for Dependency is subsequently filed in this cause, **the Arraignment Hearing is scheduled for . . . (date) . . . , at . . . a.m./p.m. At . . . (location of arraignment) . . . The parents have a right to be represented by an attorney at the arraignment hearing and during the dependency proceedings.**

COMMENT: The following paragraph must be in bold, 14 pt. Times New Roman or Courier font.

If you are a person with a disability who needs any accommodation in order to participate in this proceeding, you are entitled, at no cost to you, to the provision of certain assistance. Please contact . . . (name, address, telephone number) . . . at least

7 days before your scheduled court appearance, or immediately upon receiving this notification if the time before the scheduled appearance is less than 7 days. If you are hearing or voice impaired, call 711.

ORDERED in .... County, Florida on ...(date)..., at ... a.m./p.m.

____
Circuit Judge

Added May 9, 1991, effective July 1, 1991 (589 So.2d 818). Amended Jan. 26, 1995 (649 So.2d 1370); Oct. 31, 1996, effective Jan. 1, 1997 (684 So.2d 756); Sept. 18, 1998, effective Oct. 1, 1998 (725 So.2d 296); Oct. 26, 2000, effective Jan. 1, 2001 (783 So.2d 138); Feb. 8, 2007 (951 So.2d 804); Oct. 1, 2009 (220 So.3d 9); May 23, 2013, effective July 1, 2013 (115 So.3d 286); Feb. 19, 2015, effective Feb. 19, 2015 (158 So.3d 523).

Form 8.961(a). Order Authorizing Access to Child's Medical and Educational Records

ORDER AUTHORIZING ACCESS TO CHILD'S MEDICAL AND EDUCATIONAL RECORDS

THIS CAUSE came on to be heard under sec. 39.402, Florida Statutes, concerning access to the medical and educational records of ...., a child.

The Court finds:

A. As to medical records and information:

.............................., mother/father of ...., the child, consents to the entry of this order, and to the court's providing access to the child's medical records to the department, its contract agencies, and any guardian ad litem and attorney for the child, and to provide the child's medical information to the court.

.... No parent or legal guardian of the child is available or able to consent to the entry of this order, or the parents withhold consent to providing access to the child's medical records and/or to providing the requested medical information.

.... Access to the child's medical records and information is necessary to provide services to the child.

B. As to educational records and information:

...., mother/father of ...., the child, consents to the entry of this order, and to the court's providing access to the child's educational records to the department, its contract agencies, and any guardian ad litem and attorney for the child, and to provide the child's educational information to the court.

.... No parent or legal guardian of the child is available or able to consent to the entry of this order, or the parents withhold consent to providing access to the child's educational records and/or to providing the requested educational information.

.... Access to the child's educational records and information is necessary to provide services to the child.

Therefore, it is ORDERED:

The department, ... (name of CBC) ...., its contract agencies, ... (name) ...., guardian ad litem, and .... (name) ...., attorney for child, are authorized to access .... (child's name) ....'s medical and educational records and information, until further order of this court.

.... This order does not address the child's privacy rights to any of these records or information that may exist under Florida law. The child may assert to this court any objection under privacy rights to the release of this information.

ORDERED on .... (date) ...., in .... County, Florida.

____
Circuit Judge

Copies to:
(Check all that apply)

.... Attorney for DCF: .... (name) ....

.... Caseworker: .... (name) ....

.... Guardian ad litem: ... (name) ....

.... Attorney for mother: .... (name) ....

.... Attorney for father: .... (name) ....

.... Attorney ad litem for child: ... (name) ....

.... Child named above .... (name) ....

.... Other: ....

.... Other: ....

Added Oct. 1, 2009 (22 So.3d 9).

Form 8.962. Motion for Injunction

VERIFIED MOTION FOR CHAPTER 39 INJUNCTION FOR PROTECTION AGAINST ANY ACT OF CHILD ABUSE OR DOMESTIC VIOLENCE

Movant ( ) Department of Children and Family Services ( ) law enforcement officer ( ) state attorney ( ) responsible person ( ) the court on its own motion, ...(name)......., ...(address)......., requests this court under section 39.504, Florida Statutes, to issue an injunction against Respondent, ...(name)......, ...(address)......

1. The minor child(ren) subject to this request is/are:

Name	Birth date
....	....
....	....
....	....
....	....

2. Reasonable cause for the issuance of an injunction exists based on the following ......(evidence of child abuse or domestic violence and/or recent overt act(s) or failure(s) to act that provide a basis that there is a reasonable likelihood that such abuse or offense will occur)......

3. ..... Respondent, ...(name)..... was noticed of the hearing on this motion on .....(date).....

..... Movant requests that an injunction be issued without notice t o Respondent because the children are in imminent danger in that (5) 27(explain why there would be immediate danger and irreparable harm if Respondent is given notice).....

4. Respondent, ... (name and address) .... can be identified by the following:

Race .... Gender: .... Male .... Female

Birth date .... Ht. .... Wt. ....

Eye color .... Hair color ....

Distinguishing marks or scars ....

Vehicle: make, model, and year .... color ....

Tag number ....

Wherefore, Movant requests that the court enter an injunction under Chapter 39, Florida Statutes, to protect the minor child(ren) against any act of abuse or domestic violence and order Respondent to do the following:

.....a. Refrain from further child abuse of the minor child(ren) or exposure of the minor child(ren) to acts of domestic violence.

.....b. Participate in a specialized treatment program including ....

.....c. Have limited contact with the child(ren) as follows:

..... Supervised visitation with the child(ren). The visitation shall be supervised at all times by the department or an adult approved by the department or the court. The visitation shall occur on a schedule agreed by the parties and at the department's office, a supervised visitation center, or another place agreed by the parties. The frequency of the visitation shall be ....

..... No contact with the child(ren) at home, school, work, or wherever the child(ren may be found except as otherwise provided by this motion.

.....d. Pay $ ..... ( ) weekly ( ) bi-weekly ( ) monthly temporary support for the ( ) child(ren) ( ) family members.

.....e. Pay the costs of medical, psychiatric, and psychological treatment for ( ) the child(ren) ( ) family members incurred as a result of the offenses described in this motion.

.....f. Vacate the home in which ..... (child(ren)'s name(s)) ..... reside(s) and not return until further order of the court.

.....g. Due to any domestic violence described in this motion, Movant also request the court to:

..... Award exclusive use and possession of the dwelling to the caregiver, ...(name) .....

..... Exclude Respondent from the residence, ... (address) ..... of the caregiver, ... (name) .....

..... Award temporary custody of the child(ren) to the caregiver, ... (name) .....

..... Other requests ....

I certify that a copy of this document was ...... mailed ...... faxed and mailed ...... hand delivered to the person(s) listed below on ......(date)...... or ...... was not delivered to the person(s) listed below because ....

Other party or his/her attorney:

Name: ....

Address: ....

Fax Number: ....

I understand that I am swearing or affirming under oath to the truthfulness of the claims made in this verified motion and that punishment for knowingly making a false statement includes fines and/or imprisonment.

. . . . . Moving Party . . . . .

STATE OF FLORIDA
COUNTY OF . . . .

Sworn to or affirmed and signed before me on . . . . . .(date). . . . . by . . . . . .(name). . . . . .

NOTARY PUBLIC OR DEPUTY CLERK

Print, type, or stamp name of notary or clerk

. . . . . .Personally known
. . . . . .Produced identification

Type of identification produced . . . . . .

If the party filing this motion is represented by an attorney, the attorney must complete the following:

I, the undersigned attorney for Movant hereby certify that the following efforts have been made to give notice: . . . . . .(efforts made or if none made, state why). . . . . .

. . . . . .(attorney's name). . . . . .
. . . . . .(address and phone number). . . . . .
. . . . . .(Florida Bar number). . . . . .

Added May 9, 1991, effective July 1, 1991 (589 So.2d 818). Amended Sept. 18, 1998, effective Oct. 1, 1998 (725 So.2d 296); Sept. 25, 2008 (992 So.2d 242).

Form 8.963. Injunction Order

ORDER ON VERIFIED MOTION FOR CHAPTER 39 INJUNCTION

THIS CAUSE came before this court on . . . . (date). . . . ., pursuant to section 39.504, Florida Statutes. Present before the court were . . . . (name(s)) . . . .; and the court having reviewed the verified motion, heard testimony and argument, and being otherwise fully advised in the premises finds:

1. That this court has jurisdiction to issue an injunction in this cause.

2. The minor children subject to this request are:

Name	Birth date
. . . .	. . . .
. . . .	. . . .
. . . .	. . . .
. . . .	. . . .

3. . . . .(Name and address of person(s) against whom injunction is requested) . . . . was noticed of the hearing on this motion on . . . . date . . . .

. . . . . This injunction is being issued without notice because . . . . (child(ren)'s name(s)) . . . . is/are in imminent danger, in that . . . . (explain why there would be immediate and irreparable harm if the other party is given notice) . . . .

4. Reasonable cause for the issuance of an injunction . . . . does . . . . does not exist based on the following: . . . .

5. . . . . .(Name and address of person against whom injunction is requested) . . . . . can be identified by the following:

Race: . . . . Gender: Male . . . . Female . . . .
Date of Birth: . . . .
Height: . . . . Weight: . . . . Eye Color: . . . .
Hair Color:
Distinguishing marks and/or scars: . . . .
Vehicle (make/model/year): . . . .
Color: . . . .
Tag Number: . . . .

THEREFORE, based upon the foregoing findings, it is hereby ORDERED AND ADJUDGED that:

1. This court . . . . grants . . . . denies the motion for injunction.

2. Until . . . . ( ) . . . . (date) . . . ./( ) modified or dissolved by this court . . . ., Respondent, ... (name) and address) . . . . shall:

. . . . . Refrain from further child abuse of the minor child(ren) or exposure of the child(ren) to acts of domestic violence.

. . . . . Participate in a specialized treatment program including . . . .

. . . . . Have limited contact with the children as follows:

. . . . . Supervised visitation with the child(ren). The visitation shall be supervised at all times by the Department or an adult approved by the Department or the court. The visitation shall occur on a schedule agreed by the parties and at the Department's office, a supervised visitation center, or another place agreed by the parties.

The frequency of the visitation shall be . . . .

. . . . . No contact with the child(ren) at home, school, work, or wherever the child(ren) may be found except as otherwise provided by this order.

. . . . . Other conditions . . . .

. . . . . Pay $ . . . . ( ) weekly ( ) biweekly ( ) monthly temporary support for the ( ) child(ren) ( ) family members.

. . . . . Pay the costs of medical, psychiatric and psychological treatment for ( ) the child(ren) ( ) family members incurred as a result of the offenses described in the verified motion.

..... Vacate the home in which .... (child(ren)'s name(s)) .... resides(s) and not return until further order of the court.

..... OTHER CONDITIONS: ....

3. Due to any domestic violence, the court hereby

..... Awards the exclusive use and possession of the dwelling, ... (address) .... to the caregiver .... (name) .... or excludes Respondent from the residence of the caregiver.

..... Awards temporary custody of the child(ren) to the caregiver, ... (name) ....

4. This court retains jurisdiction over this cause to enter any further orders that may be deemed necessary for the best interest and welfare of the minor child(ren).

5. All prior orders not inconsistent with the present Order shall remain in full force and effect.

DONE AND ORDERED on ..... (date) .....

Circuit Judge

Copies furnished to:

COMMENT: If injunction is issued ex parte, include the following:

NOTICE OF HEARING

The Juvenile Court hereby gives notice of hearing in the above styled cause on .... (date) .... at .... a.m./p.m., before .... (judge) ...., at .... (location) .... or as soon thereafter as counsel can be heard.

COMMENT: The following paragraph must be in bold, 14 pt. Times New Roman or Courier font.

If you are a person with a disability who needs any accommodation in order to participate in this proceeding, you are entitled, at no cost to you, to the provision of certain assistance. Please contact .... (name, address, and telephone number) .... at least 7 days before your scheduled court appearance, or immediately upon receiving this notification if the time before the scheduled appearance is less than 7 days. If you are hearing or voice impaired, call 711.

PLEASE BE GOVERNED ACCORDINGLY.

Added May 9, 1991, effective July 1, 1991 (589 So.2d 818). Amended Sept. 18, 1998, effective Oct. 1, 1998 (725 So.2d 296); Sept. 25, 2008 (992 So.2d 242); May 23, 2013, effective July 1, 2013 (115 So.3d 286).

Form 8.964. Dependency Petition

PETITION FOR DEPENDENCY

COMES NOW, Petitioner, ... (name) ...., by and through undersigned counsel, and petitions this court to adjudicate the above- named minor child(ren) to be dependent within the meaning and intent of chapter 39, Florida Statutes. As grounds, petitioner alleges the following:

1. This court has jurisdiction over the minor child(ren), ... (name(s)) ...., a .... (gender) .... child, whose date(s) of birth is/are ...., and who, at the time the dependency arose, was/were in the custody of .... (name(s)) ....

2. The natural mother of the minor child(ren) is .... (name) ...., a resident of .... (state) ...., whose address is ....

3. The father of the minor child(ren), ... (name(s)) .... is .... (name) ...., whose address is .... The father .... is .... is not married to the mother, and .... is .... is not listed on the child(ren)'s birth certificate(s). The mother filed a Sworn Statement About Identity or Location of Father with this court on .... (date) ...., which named .... as the father.

4. The UCCJEA Affidavit .... is attached .... was filed with the Court on .... (date) .... and is incorporated by reference.

5. The child(ren) is/are dependent within the meaning and intent of chapter 39, Florida Statutes, in that the mother/father/parents/legal custodian/caregiver(s) abused, abandoned, or neglected the minor child(ren) on or about .... (date) ...., by: .... and that these activities and environments cause the child(ren)'s physical, mental, or emotional health to be in danger of being significantly impaired.

OR

5. The above named child(ren) is/are presently under substantial risk or imminent threat of harm or abuse or neglect, within the meaning and intent of chapter 39, Florida Statutes, which is likely to cause the child(ren)'s physical health to be significantly impaired because ....

6. The department is unable to ensure the protection of the minor child(ren) without judicial intervention.

7. The mother/father/parents has/have received the following services: ....

8. A shelter hearing was held on .... (date) ...., and the child(ren) was/were placed in the custody of ....

9. An arraignment hearing

..... needs to be scheduled.

..... is scheduled for .... (date and time) ....

10. A guardian ad litem

..... needs to be appointed.

..... was appointed at the shelter hearing to represent the child(ren).

11. Under chapter 39, Florida Statutes, the clerk of the court is required to issue a summons to the following parents or custodians:

The natural mother, ... (name) ...., whose address is ....

The natural father, ... (name) ...., whose address is ....

..... (Additional fathers and their addresses) .....

WHEREFORE, the petitioner asks that process may issue in due course to bring the above-named parties before the court to be dealt with according to the law, to adjudicate the named minor child(ren) named to be dependent.

..... (Petitioner's name) .....

..... (Attorney's name) .....
..... (address and telephone number) .....
..... Florida Bar number .....

Verification
Certificate of service

NOTICE OF RIGHTS

PLEASE READ THIS PETITION BEFORE ENTERING THE COURTROOM.

YOU HAVE A RIGHT TO HAVE COUNSEL PRESENT AT THIS HEARING.

BY COPY OF THIS PETITION, THE PARENTS, CAREGIVERS, AND/OR LEGAL CUSTODIANS ARE NOTIFIED OF THEIR RIGHT TO HAVE LEGAL COUNSEL PRESENT FOR ANY PROCEEDING RESULTING FROM THIS

PETITION OR TO REQUEST THE COURT TO HAVE COUNSEL APPOINTED, IF INDIGENT.

Further, these persons are informed of the following:

An arraignment is set on this matter for .... (date) ...., at .... a.m./p.m., at .... (location) .... The purpose of the arraignment is to advise as to the allegations contained in the Petition For Dependency. When your case is called, the Judge will ask you to enter a plea to this petition. The plea entered may be one of the following:

1. Admit: This means you admit that the petition states the truth and you do not want a trial.

2. Consent: This means you neither admit nor deny the petition, but do not want a trial.

(If you enter either of the above two pleas, the court will set a disposition date for the matter. At disposition, the court will decide where the child will stay and under what conditions).

3. Deny: This means you deny the allegations of the petition and wish the state to attempt to prove them at a trial.

4. Continue: This means you wish time to confer with an attorney, before entering a plea. If you enter this plea, the court will schedule another hearing in approximately 2 weeks. At that time, another arraignment hearing will be held, and you (or your attorney) must enter one of the above three pleas.

COMMENT: The following paragraph must be in bold, 14 pt. Times New Roman or Courier font.

If you are a person with a disability who needs any accommodation in order to participate in this proceeding, you are entitled, at no cost to you, to the provision of certain assistance. Please contact .... (name, address, and telephone number) .... at least 7 days before your scheduled court appearance, or immediately upon receiving this notification if the time before the scheduled appearance is less than 7 days. If you are hearing or voice impaired, call 711.

Added May 9, 1991, effective July 1, 1991 (589 So.2d 818). Amended Oct. 31, 1996, effective Jan. 1, 1997 (684 So.2d 756); Sept. 18, 1998, effective Oct. 1, 1998 (725 So.2d 296); Oct. 26, 2000, effective Jan. 1, 2001 (783 So.2d 138); Sept. 21, 2006, effective Jan. 1, 2007 (939 So.2d 74); May 23, 2013, effective July 1, 2013 (115 So.3d 286).

Form 8.965. Arraignment Order

NOTICE OF NEXT HEARING

THIS CAUSE came to be heard on .... (date) ...., under chapter 39, Florida Statutes, on the Petition For Dependency filed by .... (name) ...., for arraignment of .... (name(s)) .... The following persons appeared before the Court:

.... (Name) ....., Petitioner
.... (Name) ....., Attorney for the petitioner
.... (Name) ....., Attorney for the department
.... (Name) ....., Department caseworker
.... (Name) ....., Mother
.... (Name) ....., Attorney for mother
.... (Name) ....., Father of .... (child) ....
.... (Name) ....., Attorney for father
.... (Name) ....., Guardian ad litem
.... (Name) ....., Attorney for guardian ad litem
.... (Name) ....., Legal custodian
.... (Name) ....., Attorney for legal custodian
.... (Name) ....., Other ....

The court having considered the Petition for Dependency and having heard testimony and argument, and having been otherwise duly advised in the premises finds:

1. This court has jurisdiction over the subject matter of this action; and

2. The mother, ... (name) ....:

..... was .... was not noticed of this hearing;

..... did not appear, and the court:

..... entered a consent by default

..... did not enter a consent by default;

..... appeared with counsel .... appeared without counsel and:

..... was .... was not advised of her right to legal counsel; knowingly, intelligently, and voluntarily, ... waived .... did not waive her right to legal counsel; and

..... was .... was not determined to qualify as indigent and .... was .... was not appointed an attorney.

..... was served with a petition for dependency and entered a plea of: .... Admit, ... Deny, ... Consent, ... No Plea, ... Continuance

..... The Petitioner

.... will continue a diligent search and will attempt service.

..... has conducted an adequate diligent search and is excused from further diligent search and further attempts at service.

3. The father, ... (name) ....:

..... was .... was not noticed of this hearing;

..... did not appear, and the court:

..... entered a consent by default
..... did not enter a consent by default;

..... appeared with counsel .... appeared without counsel and:

..... was .... was not advised of his right to legal counsel;
..... knowingly, intelligently, and voluntarily .... waived .... did not waive his right to legal counsel; and

..... was .... was not determined qualify as indigent and .... was .... was not appointed an attorney.

..... was served with a petition for dependency, and entered a plea of: .... Admit, ... Deny, ... Consent, ... No Plea, ... Continuance

..... The Petitioner

..... will continue a diligent search and will attempt service.

..... has conducted an adequate diligent search and is excused from further diligent search and further attempts at service.

4. That the child(ren)'s current placement in shelter care:

..... is no longer appropriate, and the child(ren) shall be returned to ....

..... is appropriate, in that the child(ren) is/are in a setting which is as family-like as possible, consistent with the child(ren)'s best interest and special needs and, that returning the child(ren) to the home would be contrary to the best interest of the minor child(ren); and, that every reasonable effort has been made to eliminate the need for placement of the child(ren) in shelter care, but present circumstances of the child(ren) and the family are such that shelter care is the only way to ensure the child(ren)'s health, safety, and well-being.

5. Additional findings: ....

THEREFORE, based on the foregoing findings of fact, it is hereby ORDERED and ADJUDGED that:

1. The minor child(ren) shall

..... be .... returned to .... remain in the care and custody of .... (name) ....

..... remain in the care and custody of the department in shelter care pending adjudication and disposition or until further order of this court.

2. The child(ren): .... is/are .... is/are not adjudicated dependent at this hearing.

3. .... Mediation .... A case planning conference is/ are ordered at this time and shall be conducted on .... (date) ...., at .... a.m./p.m., at .... (location) .... All parties, unless otherwise specified, shall attend.

4. As to the mother, ... (name) ...., the court:

Accepts the plea of: .... Admit, ... Deny, ... Consent, ... Continuance.

..... Appoints ..... Does not appoint an attorney.

Sets a hearing for .... re-arraignment .... adjudicatory trial .... disposition and case plan hearing .... trial status on .... (date) .... at .... a.m./p.m.

5. As to the father, ... (name) ...., the court:

Accepts the plea of: ..... Admit, ... Deny, ... Consent, ... Continuance.

..... Appoints ..... Does not appoint an attorney.

Sets a hearing for .... re-arraignment .... adjudicatory trial .... disposition and case plan hearing .... trial status on .... (date) .... at .... a.m./p.m.

6. All prior orders not inconsistent with the present order shall remain in full force and effect.

DONE AND ORDERED on ..... (date) .....

____
Circuit Judge

NOTICE OF HEARING

The Juvenile Court hereby gives notice of hearing in the above-styled cause on .... (date) .... at .... a.m./p.m., before .... (judge) ...., at .... (location) .... or as soon thereafter as counsel can be heard.

COMMENT: The following paragraph must be in bold, 14 pt. Times New Roman or Courier font.

If you are a person with a disability who needs any accommodation in order to participate in this proceeding, you are entitled, at no cost to you, to the provision of certain assistance. Please contact .... (name, address, and telephone number) .... at least 7 days before your scheduled court appearance, or immediately upon receiving this notification if the time before the scheduled appearance is less than 7 days. If you are hearing or voice impaired, call 711.

PLEASE BE GOVERNED ACCORDINGLY.

Copies furnished to:

Added Sept. 18, 1998, effective Oct. 1, 1998 (725 So.2d 296). Amended Oct. 26, 2000, effective Jan. 1, 2001 (783 So.2d 138); May 23, 2013, effective July 1, 2013 (115 So.3d 286).

Form 8.966. Adjudication Order—Dependency

ORDER OF ADJUDICATION

THIS CAUSE came before this court on .... (date).........................., under chapter 39, Florida Statutes, for adjudication of the Petition for Dependency filed by .... (petitioner's name) .... Present before the court were

.... (Name) ....., Petitioner
.... (Name) ....., Attorney for the petitioner
.... (Name) ....., Attorney for the department
.... (Name) ....., Department caseworker
.... (Name) ....., Mother
.... (Name) ....., Attorney for mother
.... (Name) ....., Father of .... (child) ....
.... (Name) ....., Attorney for father
.... (Name) ....., Guardian ad litem
.... (Name) ....., Attorney for guardian ad litem
.... (Name) ....., Legal custodian
.... (Name) ....., Attorney for legal custodian
.... (Name(s)) ....., Minor child(ren)
.... (Name) ....., Attorney ad litem for minor child(ren)
.... (Name) ....., Other ....

The court having heard testimony and argument and being otherwise fully advised in the premises finds:

1. That the minor child(ren) who is/are the subject matter of these proceedings, is/are dependent within the meaning and intent of chapter 39, Florida Statutes, and is/are (a) resident(s) of the State of Florida.

2. The mother, ... (name) ....:

..... was ..... was not noticed of this hearing;

..... did not appear, and the court:

..... entered a Consent for failure to appear after proper notice.

..... did not enter a Consent for failure to appear after proper notice.

..... appeared with counsel;

..... appeared without counsel and:

..... was ..... was not advised of her right to legal counsel,

..... knowingly, intelligently, and voluntarily waived .... did not waive her right to legal counsel and

..... was ..... was not determined to qualify as indigent and .... was .... was not appointed an attorney.

3. The father, ... (name) ....:
..... was ..... was not noticed of this hearing;

..... did not appear, and the court:

..... entered a Consent for failure to appear after proper notice.

..... did not enter a Consent for failure to appear after proper notice.

..... appeared with counsel;

..... appeared without counsel and:

..... was ..... was not advised of his right to legal counsel,

..... knowingly, intelligently, and voluntarily waived .... did not waive his right to legal counsel and

..... was .... was not determined to qualify as indigent and .... was .... was not appointed an attorney.

4. That the child(ren) is/are dependent within the meaning and intent of chapter 39, Florida Statutes, in that the mother, ... (name) ...., abused, neglected, or abandoned the minor child(ren) by .... These facts were proven by .... preponderance of the evidence .... clear and convincing evidence.

5. That the child(ren) is/are dependent within the meaning and intent of chapter 39, Florida Statutes, in that the father, ... (name) ...., abused, neglected, or abandoned the minor child(ren) by .... These facts were proven by .... preponderance of the evidence .... clear and convincing evidence.

COMMENT: Use 6, 7, and 8 only if the child is in out-of-home placement.

6. That the Court finds that it is in the best interest of the child(ren) to remain in out-of-home care.

7. That every reasonable effort was made to eliminate the need for placement of the child(ren) in out-of-home care but the present circumstances of the child(ren) and the .... mother .... father are such that out-of-home care is the only way to ensure the health, safety, and well being of the child(ren), in that ....

8. That the child(ren)'s placement in .... (type of placement) .... is in a setting which is as family like and as close to the home as possible, consistent with the child(ren)'s best interests and special needs.

9. That returning the minor child(ren) to the custody of .... (person who had previous legal custody) .... would be contrary to the best interest and welfare of the minor child(ren).

10. The Court inquired of any parents present whether they have relatives who might be considered for placement of the child(ren).

THEREFORE, based upon the foregoing findings, it is ORDERED AND ADJUDGED that:

1. The minor child(ren), ... (name(s)) ...., is/are adjudicated dependent.

2. The child(ren) shall remain in the care and custody of
..... the department in shelter care

..... other ..... (name) ..... pending disposition.

3. The parents shall provide to the Court and all parties identification and location information regarding potential relative placements.

4. **THE COURT ADVISED THE PARENTS THAT IF THE PARENTS FAIL TO SUBSTANTIALLY COMPLY WITH THE CASE PLAN THEIR PARENTAL RIGHTS MAY BE TERMINATED AND THE CHILD(REN)'S OUT–OF–HOME PLACEMENT MAY BECOME PERMANENT.**

5. This court shall retain jurisdiction over this cause to enter any such further orders that may be deemed necessary for the best interest and welfare of the minor child(ren).

6. All prior orders not inconsistent with the present order shall remain in full force and effect.

7. Disposition is scheduled for .... (date) ...., at .... a.m./p.m.

DONE AND ORDERED on .... date .... at .... (city) ...., Florida.

____
Circuit Judge

NOTICE OF HEARING

The Juvenile Court hereby gives notice of hearing in the above styled cause on .... (date) .... at .... a.m./p.m., before .... (judge) ...., at .... (location) ...., or as soon thereafter as counsel can be heard.

COMMENT: The following paragraph must be in bold, 14 pt. Times New Roman or Courier font.

If you are a person with a disability who needs any accommodation in order to participate in this proceeding, you are entitled, at no cost to you, to the provision of certain assistance. Please contact .... (name, address, and telephone number) .... at least 7 days before your scheduled court appearance, or immediately upon receiving this notification if the time before the scheduled appearance is less than 7 days. If you are hearing or voice impaired, call 711.

PLEASE BE GOVERNED ACCORDINGLY.

Copies furnished to:

Former Form 8.913 renumbered as new Form 8.965 and amended May 9, 1991, effective July 1, 1991 (589 So.2d 818). Amended Nov. 5, 1992, effective Jan. 1, 1993 (608 So.2d 478); Oct. 31, 1996, effective Jan. 1, 1997 (684 So.2d 756). Renumbered as Form 8.966 and amended Sept. 18, 1998, effective Oct. 1, 1998 (725 So.2d 296). Amended Oct. 26, 2000, effective Jan. 1, 2001 (783 So.2d 138); Sept. 21, 2006, effective Jan. 1, 2007 (939 So.2d 74); Feb. 8, 2007 (951 So.2d 804); May 23, 2013, effective July 1, 2013 (115 So.3d 286).

Form 8.967. Order of Disposition, Acceptance of Case Plan, and Notice of Hearing

ORDER OF DISPOSITION, ACCEPTANCE OF CASE PLAN, AND NOTICE OF HEARING

THIS CAUSE came before this court on .... (date) ...., under chapter 39, Florida Statutes, for disposition of the Petition for Dependency and acceptance of the Case Plan filed by the Department of Children and Family Services.

The following persons appeared before the court:
.... (Name) ....., Petitioner
.... (Name) ....., Attorney for the petitioner
.... (Name) ....., Attorney for the department
.... (Name) ....., Department caseworker

.... (Name) ....., Mother
.... (Name) ....., Attorney for mother
.... (Name) ....., Father of .... (child) .....
.... (Name) ....., Attorney for father
.... (Name) ....., Guardian ad litem
.... (Name) ....., Attorney for guardian ad litem
.... (Name) ....., Legal custodian
.... (Name) ....., Attorney for legal custodian
.... (Name) ....., Other: ....

The court having considered the Predisposition Study and Case Plan filed by the department and having heard testimony and argument and being otherwise fully advised in the premises finds that:

1. The minor child(ren) who is/are the subject matter of these proceedings, was/were adjudicated dependent within the meaning and intent of chapter 39, Florida Statutes, continue to be dependent, and is/are residents of the State of Florida.

2. The minor child(ren) is/are of an age subject to the jurisdiction of this Court.

3. The following parties were notified of this hearing and provided a copy of the Case Plan and Predisposition Report filed in this cause:

.... (Name) ....., Petitioner
.... (Name) ....., Attorney for the petitioner
.... (Name) ....., Attorney for the department
.... (Name) ....., Department caseworker
.... (Name) ....., Mother
.... (Name) ....., Attorney for mother
.... (Name) ....., Father of .... (child) .....
.... (Name) ....., Attorney for father
.... (Name) ....., Guardian ad litem
.... (Name) ....., Attorney for guardian ad litem
.... (Name) ....., Other: ....

4. The mother, ... (name) .... :

..... did not appear and .... was .... was not represented by legal counsel;

..... appeared .... with .... without legal counsel and .... was .... was not advised of her right to legal counsel;

..... knowingly, intelligently, and voluntarily waived .... did not waive her right to legal counsel; and

..... was .... was not determined to qualify as indigent and .... was .... was not appointed an attorney.

5. The father, ... (name) .... :

..... did not appear and .... was .... was not represented by legal counsel;

..... appeared .... with .... without legal counsel and .... was .... was not advised of his right to legal counsel;

..... knowingly, intelligently, and voluntarily waived .... did not waive his right to legal counsel; and

..... was .... was not determined to qualify as indigent and .... was .... was not appointed an attorney.

6. The following parents/legal custodians were notified of their right to participate in the preparation of the case plan and to receive assistance from any other person in the preparation of the case plan: .... (names of persons notified) ....

7. The department filed a predisposition study with the court on .... (date) .... This predisposition study .... is .... is not in compliance with the statutory requirements.

8. The department filed a case plan with the court on .... (date) ....

a. The terms of the case plan .... are .... are not consistent with the requirements of the law and previous orders of this court.

b. The case plan .... is .... is not meaningful and designed to address the facts and circumstances on which the court based the finding of dependency.

c. The case plan .... is .... is not in the best interest of the minor child(ren).

d. The case plan's stated goal of .... is .... is not a reasonable goal.

e. The parents .... have .... do not have the ability to comply with the terms of the case plan.

9. There is a need for temporary child support from .... (noncustodial parent(s)) .... and that he/she/they .... has/have .... do/does not have the ability to pay child support.

COMMENT: Use 10, 11 & 12 if child(ren) is/are not placed in the home of a parent.

10. It is in the best interest of the minor child(ren) to be placed in the care and custody of .... (placement ordered) ....

11. Placement of the minor child(ren) in the care and custody of .... (placement ordered) .... is in a setting which is as family like and as close to the home as possible, consistent with the child(ren)'s best interests and special needs.

12. Return of the minor child(ren) to the custody of .... (person from whom child(ren) was/were originally removed) .... would be contrary to the best interest and welfare of the minor child(ren). The child(ren) cannot safely .... remain .... return home with services and removal of the child(ren) is necessary to protect the child(ren), in that ....

13. Prevention or reunification services .... were not .... were indicated and are as listed: .... (services indicated) .... Further efforts could not have shortened separation of this family because: ....

COMMENT: Use 14 if the goal of the case plan is reunification.

14. Reasonable efforts to prevent or eliminate the need for removal of the child(ren) have been made by the department, which provided the following services:

....

COMMENT: Use 15 if child(ren) remain(s) or is/are returned to the parent(s).

15. The child(ren) can safely .... remain with .... be returned to .... (parent(s)'s name(s)) .... as long as he/she/they comply(ies) with the following:

....

THEREFORE, based upon the foregoing findings, it is hereby ORDERED AND ADJUDGED that:

1. The minor child(ren), ... (name(s)) .... be placed in the custody of .... (name) ...., under supervision of the department.

2. The predisposition study report filed by the department is:

..... not accepted and a continuance was requested.

..... accepted by the court.

..... accepted by the court with the following amendments: ..

3. The case plan filed by the department is:

..... not accepted and a continuance is granted for 30 days or less.

..... accepted by the court.

..... accepted by the court with the following amendments: ..

4. All parties are ordered to comply with the provisions of the case plan and any amendments made to it.

COMMENT: Use 5, 6 & 7 if child(ren) is/are placed outside the home.

5. The mother, ... (name) ...., shall pay child support in the amount of $ .... by the .... (day) .... of each month to .... (where money is to be paid) ...., beginning on .... (date) .... and continuing until such time as payments begin to be deducted by income deduction order. All child support payments shall be paid to the

Clerk of the Circuit Court designated to receive child support payments.

6. The father, ... (name) ...., shall pay child support in the amount of $ .... by the .... (day) .... of each month to .... (where money is to be paid) ...., beginning on .... (date) .... and continuing until such time as payments begin to be deducted by income deduction order. All child support payments shall be paid to the Clerk of the Circuit Court designated to receive child support payments.

7. The legal custodian shall have the right to authorize for the child(ren) any emergency medical treatment and any ordinary and necessary medical and dental examinations and treatment, including blood testing, preventive care including ordinary immunizations, tuberculin testing, and well-child care, but not including nonemergency surgery, general anesthesia, provision of psychotropic medications, or other extraordinary procedures for which a separate order or informed consent as provided by law is required.

8. Other: ....

9. All prior orders not inconsistent with the present order shall remain in full force and effect.

10. This court shall retain jurisdiction over this cause to enter any such further orders that may be deemed necessary for the best interest and welfare of the minor child(ren).

11. This matter is scheduled for Judicial Review on .... (date) .... at .... (time) ....

DONE AND ORDERED in ...., Florida, on ..... (date) .....

____
Circuit Judge

NOTICE OF HEARING

The Juvenile Court hereby gives notice of hearing in the above-styled cause on .... (date) .... at .... a.m./p.m., before .... (judge) ...., at .... (location) ...., or as soon thereafter as counsel can be heard.

COMMENT: The following paragraph must be in bold, 14 pt. Times New Roman or Courier font.

If you are a person with a disability who needs any accommodation in order to participate in this proceeding, you are entitled, at no cost to you, to the provision of certain assistance. Please contact .... (name, address, and telephone number) .... at least 7 days before your scheduled court appearance, or immediately upon receiving this notification if the time before the scheduled appearance is less than 7 days. If you are hearing or voice impaired, call 711.

PLEASE BE GOVERNED ACCORDINGLY.

Copies furnished to:

Form 8.966 added May 9, 1991, effective July 1, 1991 (589 So.2d 818). Amended Oct. 31, 1996, effective Jan. 1, 1997 (684 So.2d 756). Renumbered as Form 8.967 and amended Sept. 18, 1998, effective Oct. 1, 1998 (725 So.2d 296). Amended Sept. 5, 2002, effective Jan. 1, 2003 (827 So.2d 219); May 23, 2013, effective July 1, 2013 (115 So.3d 286).

Form 8.968. Affidavit of Diligent Search

AFFIDAVIT OF DILIGENT SEARCH

STATE OF FLORIDA

COUNTY OF ....

BEFORE ME, the undersigned authority, personally appeared ......(name)......, affiant, who, being first duly sworn, deposes and says that ......he/she...... made a diligent search and inquiry to determine the residence of ......(name)......, the ......parent/prospective parent...... of ......(name(s) of child(ren))......, and the results are as follows:

1. Affiant has received the name of the ......(parent/prospective parent)...... from ......(name)......

2. Affiant has had no face-to-face contact with ......(name of parent/prospective parent)......

3. On ......(date)...... affiant telephoned information at ......(name)...... and was informed that there was no listing for ......(name of parent/prospective parent)......

4. On ......(date)...... affiant searched the ......(city)...... telephone directory and was unable to locate a listing for ......(name of parent/prospective parent)......

5. On ......(date)...... affiant sent a certified letter, return receipt requested, to ......(address)......, a last known address of ......(name of parent/prospective parent)...... On ......(date)...... affiant received the unclaimed receipt by return mail.

6. On ......(date)...... affiant visited ......(address)......, the last known address of ......(name of parent/prospective parent)......, and was informed by ......(name)...... that ......(name of parent/prospective parent)...... no longer resides there.

7. Affiant has made inquiries of all relatives of ......(name of parent/prospective parent)...... of the child, including the other parent, made known to me by the petitioner and ......(name)...... The names, addresses, and telephone numbers of those relatives contacted are: .... None of the relatives contacted know the current residence or whereabouts of ......(name of parent/prospective parent)......

8. Affiant has made inquiries of all offices of program areas, including but not limited to mental health, of the Department of Children and Family Services likely to have information about ......(name of parent/prospective parent)...... The names, addresses, and/or telephone numbers of those offices are: .... No one in any of these offices knows the current residence or address of ......(name of parent/prospective parent)......

9. Affiant has made inquiries of other state and federal agencies likely to have information about ......(name of parent/prospective parent)...... The names, addresses, and/or telephone numbers of those agencies: .... No one in any of these agencies

knows the current residence or whereabouts of ......(name of parent/prospective parent)......

10. Affiant has made inquiries of appropriate utility and postal providers. The names, addresses, and/or telephone numbers of those providers are: .... None of those providers know the current residence or whereabouts of ......(name of parent/prospective parent)......

11. Affiant has made inquiries of appropriate law enforcement agencies. The names, addresses, and/or telephone numbers of those agencies are: ....(Name of parent/prospective parent)...... is not known to any of these agencies.

12. Affiant has made inquiries of the federal armed services, including the United States Army, Navy, Air Force, Marine Corps, and National Guard. ......(Name of parent/prospective parent)...... is not currently a member of these services.

13. Affiant has made inquiries of all the hospitals in the .... area. The names, addresses, and/or telephone numbers of those hospitals are: ....(Name of parent/prospective parent)...... is not currently a patient at, nor has ...... he/she ...... recently been admitted to, these hospitals.

14. Affiant has conducted a thorough search of at least one electronic database specifically designed for locating persons including ......(name of database)...... No information regarding ......(name of parent/prospective parent)...... was found in this electronic database.

15. ......(Name of parent/prospective parent).............is/is not...... over 18 years of age.

16. Affiant is unable to determine the residence or whereabouts of ......(name of parent/prospective parent)...... and thus cannot personally serve process upon ......him/her......

Affiant

Before me, the undersigned authority, personally appeared ......(name)......, the petitioner in this action, who ......is personally known to me/produced ......(document)...... as identification......, and who affirms that the allegations are filed in good faith and are true and correct to the best of petitioner's knowledge.

SWORN TO AND SUBSCRIBED before me ......(date)......

NOTARY PUBLIC
Name: ....
Commission No.: ....
My commission expires: ....

OR

Verification (see Form 8.902)

Added Oct. 31, 1996, effective Jan. 1, 1997 (684 So.2d 756). Amended Oct. 26, 2000, effective Jan. 1, 2001 (783 So.2d 138); Sept. 25, 2008 (992 So.2d 242).

Form 8.969. Sworn Statement Regarding Identity or Location of Father

SWORN STATEMENT REGARDING IDENTITY OR LOCATION OF FATHER

1. My name is: ....
My address is: ....

2. I am related to .....(child's name)..... because I am his/her ....

3. I understand that I am answering these questio [1]n under oath and from my own personal knowledge and I swear to tell the truth. I understand that this sworn statement will be filed with the court.

4. The mother of the child WAS married to .....(name)..... at the probable time of conception of the child.

OR

The mother of the child WAS NOT married at the probable time of conception of the child.

OR

I do not know whether or not the mother was married at the probable time of conception of the child.

5. The mother of this child WAS married to .....(name)..... at the time of this child's birth.

OR

The mother of this child WAS NOT married at the time of this child's birth.

OR

I do not know whether the mother of this child was married at the time of this child's birth.

6. The mother of this child WAS living with/cohabiting with .....(name)..... at the time of the probable conception of this child.

OR

The mother of this child WAS NOT living with/cohabiting with any man at the to me [2] of the probable conception of this child.

OR

I do not know whether the mother of this child was living with/cohabiting with any man at the probable time of conception of this child.

7. The mother of this child HAS received payments or promises of child support with respect to this child or because of her pregnancy from .....(name) ......

OR

The mother of this child HAS NOT received payments or promises of child support with respect to this child or because of her pregnancy from anyone.

OR

I do not know whether the mother has received any payments.

8. The mother named .... as the father on the child's birth certificate.

OR

The mother DID NOT name a father on the child's birth certificate.

OR

I do not know whether the mother named a father on the child's birth certificate.

9. The mother named .... as the father of this child in connection with applying for public assistance.

OR

The mother HAS NOT named anyone as the father of this child in connection with applying for public assistance.

OR

I do not know whether the mother has named anyone as the father of this child in connection with applying for public assistance benefits.

10. .....(Name) ..... has been named in a paternity case or acknowledged paternity in a jurisdiction where the mother lived at the time of or since the conception of this child or where this child resides or has resided.

OR

No man has been named in a paternity case or acknowledged paternity of this child in a jurisdiction where the mother lived at the time of or since the conception of this child or where this child resides or has resided.

OR

I do not know if any man has been named in a paternity suit regarding this child.

11. List the name, date of birth, social security number, and last-known address of any man listed in this sworn statement:

Name: ....

Date of birth: .... Social Security No.: ..

Last-known address: ....

12. Do you know any other information about the identity or location of any man listed in this sworn statement? ..... Yes ..... No. If so, please give that information: ....

....

I UNDERSTAND THAT THIS DOCUMENT WILL BE FILED WITH THE COURT. UNDER PENALTY OF PERJURY, I DECLARE THAT I HAVE READ IT AND THAT THE FACTS STATED ARE TRUE.

Date: ....

____
Signature

Witnessed by .....(name) ....., who is an authorized agent of the Department of Children and Family Services and who attests that the person who signed this statement provided proof of identify as indicated:

..... Driver's license, number: ....

..... Passport, number and country: ....

..... Resident Alien (Green Card), number: .....

..... Armed Forces Identification, number: ....

..... Other: ....

Added Oct. 31, 1996, effective Jan. 1, 1997 (684 So.2d 756). Amended Sept. 18, 1998, effective Oct. 1, 1998 (725 So.2d 296).

[1] So in original, should probably read "questions".

[2] So in original, should probably read "at the time".

Form 8.970. Order on Judicial Review

ORDER ON JUDICIAL REVIEW AND NOTICE OF NEXT HEARING

THIS CAUSE came on to be heard on ... (date) ... for Judicial Review on the report filed by the Department of Children and Families in this cause under chapter 39, Florida Statutes.

The following persons appeared before the court:

.... (name) ..., Child
.... (name) ..., Attorney/Attorney ad litem for the child
.... (name) ..., Petitioner
.... (name) ..., Attorney for the petitioner
.... (name) ..., Attorney for the department
.... (name) ..., Department caseworker
.... (name) ..., Mother
.... (name) ..., Attorney for mother
.... (name) ..., Father of ... (child) ...
.... (name) ..., Attorney for father
.... (name) ..., Guardian ad litem
.... (name) ..., Attorney for guardian ad litem
.... (name) ..., Legal custodian
.... (name) ..., Attorney for legal custodian
.... (name) ..., Other ....

And the court having considered

..... Judicial Review and Social Study Report filed by the Department
..... Statement/home study filed by the Department
..... Report of the Guardian Ad Litem
..... Case plan filed by the Department
..... Statement by the Child's Caretaker
..... Whether or not the child is a citizen and, if the child is not a citizen, the steps that have been taken to address the citizenship or residency status of the child
..... Other ....

AND THE COURT having heard testimony and argument, and having been otherwise duly advised in the premises finds:

1. That the minor child(ren) who is/are the subject matter of these proceedings was/were adjudicated dependent, continue to be dependent, is/are of an age subject to the jurisdiction of the court, and is/are resident(s) of the state of Florida.

2. The following parties were notified of this hearing and provided a copy of the documents filed for this hearing:

.... (name) ..., Petitioner
.... (name) ..., Attorney for the petitioner
.... (name) ..., Attorney for the department
.... (name) ..., Department caseworker
.... (name) ..., Mother
.... (name) ..., Attorney for mother
.... (name) ..., Father of ... (child) ...
.... (name) ..., Attorney for father
.... (name) ..., Guardian ad litem
.... (name) ..., Attorney for guardian ad litem
.... (name) ..., Legal custodian
.... (name) ..., Attorney for legal custodian
.... (name) ..., Attorney ad litem for the child
.... (name) ..., Other ....

3. The mother, ... (name) ...:

..... did not appear and ... was ... was not represented by legal counsel;
..... appeared ... with ... without legal counsel and ... was ... was not advised of her right to legal counsel; knowingly, intelligently, and voluntarily ... waived ... did not waive her right to legal counsel; and
... was ... was not determined to qualify as indigent and
... was ... was not appointed an attorney.

4. The father, ... (name) ...:

..... did not appear and ... was ... was not represented by legal counsel;
..... appeared ... with ... without legal counsel and ... was ... was not advised of his right to legal counsel; knowingly, intelligently, and voluntarily ... waived ... did not waive her right to legal counsel; and
... was ... was not determined to qualify as indigent and
... was ... was not appointed an attorney.

COMMENT: Repeat above for each father.

5. The department filed a judicial review report with the court on ... (date) ... This judicial review report ... is ... is not in compliance with the statutory requirements.

6. The following parents/legal custodians were notified of their right to participate in the preparation of the case plan and to receive assistance from any other person in the preparation of the case plan: ... (names of those notified) ...

7. The mother has complied with the following tasks in the case plan: ... (list tasks complied with) ...

8. The mother has not complied with the following tasks in the case plan: ... (list tasks not complied with) ...

9. The father, ... (father's name) ..., has complied with the following tasks in the case plan: ... (list tasks complied with) ...

10. The father, ... (father's name) ..., has not complied with the following tasks in the case plan: ... (list tasks not complied with) ...

11. The mother ... has ... has not complied with court ordered visitation as follows: ... (explanation of visitation compliance) ...

12. The father, ... (father's name) ..., ... has ... has not complied with court ordered visitation as follows: ... (explanation of visitation compliance) ...

13. The department ... has ... has not complied with court ordered visitation as follows: ... (explanation of visitation compliance) ...

14. The mother . . . has . . . has not complied with court ordered financial support for the child as follows: . . . (explanation of financial compliance) . . .

15. The father, . . . (father's name) . . ., . . . has . . . has not complied with court ordered financial support for the child as follows: . . . (explanation of financial compliance) . . .

16. The mother . . . has . . . has not complied with court ordered meetings with the department as follows: . . . (explanation of meetings compliance) . . .

17. The father, . . . (father's name) . . ., . . . has . . . has not complied with court ordered meetings with the department as follows: . . . (explanation of meetings compliance) . . .

18. The department . . . has . . . has not complied with court ordered meetings with the parents as follows: . . . (explanation of meetings compliance) . . .

COMMENT: Use 19, 20, 21, 22, 23, & 24 if child(ren) is/are not placed in the home of a parent.

. . . 19. It is in the best interest of the minor child(ren) to be placed in the care and custody of . . . (placement ordered) . . .

. . . 20. Placement of the minor child(ren) in the care and custody of . . . (placement ordered) . . . is in a setting which is as family like and as close to the home as possible, consistent with the child(ren)'s best interests and special needs.

. . . 21. The children . . . are . . . are not separated in their placements. The following efforts have been made to reunite separated siblings:

. . . .

. . . .

. . . .

. . . It is not in the best interest of each sibling to be reunited in their placement because:

. . . .

. . . .

. . . Each sibling has the following frequency, kind and duration of contacts:

. . . .

. . . .

. . . .

. . . 22. Return of the minor child(ren) to the custody of . . . (person(s) from whom child(ren) was/were originally removed) . . . . would be contrary to the best interest and welfare of the minor child(ren). The child(ren) cannot safely . . . remain . . . return home with services and removal of the child(ren) is necessary to protect the child(ren).

. . . 23. Prevention or reunification services . . . were not . . . were indicated and are as follows: . . . (services indicated) . . . Further efforts could not have shortened separation of this family because . . . .

. . . 24. The likelihood of the children's reunification with the parent or legal custodian within 12 months is . . . .

COMMENT: Use 25 if child(ren) remain(s) or is/are returned to the parent(s).

. . . 25. The child(ren) can safely . . . remain with . . . be returned to . . . (parent('s)(s') name(s)) . . . as long as he/she/they comply(ies) with the following: . . . .

The safety, well-being, and physical, mental, and emotional health of the child(ren) are not endangered by allowing the child(ren) to . . . remain . . . return home.

THEREFORE, based upon the foregoing findings, it is hereby ORDERED AND ADJUDGED that:

1. The minor child(ren), . . . (name(s)) . . ., be placed in the custody of . . . (name) . . ., under supervision of the department.

2. The judicial review report filed by the department is:

. . . not accepted and a continuance was requested.

. . . accepted by the court.

. . . 3. The court finds that it is not likely that the child(ren) will be reunified with the parent or legal custodian within 12 months after the child was removed from the home. The department shall file a motion within 10 days of receipt of this written order to amend the case plan to incorporate concurrent planning into the case plan.

4. The court inquired of any parents present whether they have relatives who might be considered for placement of the children.

5. Other: . . . .

6. All prior orders not inconsistent with the present order shall remain in full force and effect.

7. This court shall retain jurisdiction over this cause to enter any such further orders as may be deemed necessary for the best interest and welfare of the minor child(ren).

8. This matter is scheduled for Judicial Review on . . . (date) . . . at . . . (time) . . .

DONE AND ORDERED in . . . ., Florida on . . . (date) . . . at . . . (time) . . .

____

Circuit Judge

NOTICE OF HEARING

The Juvenile Court hereby gives notice of hearing in the above-styled cause on . . . (date) . . . at . . . . a.m./p.m., before . . . (judge) . . ., at . . . (location) . . ., or as soon thereafter as counsel can be heard.

COMMENT: The following paragraph must be in bold, 14 pt. Times New Roman or Courier font.

If you are a person with a disability who needs any accommodation in order to participate in this proceeding, you are entitled, at no cost to you, to the provision of certain assistance. Please contact . . . (name, address, and telephone number) . . . at least 7 days before your scheduled court appearance, or immediately upon receiving this notification if the time before the scheduled appearance is less than 7 days. If you are hearing or voice impaired, call 711.

PLEASE BE GOVERNED ACCORDINGLY.

Copies furnished to:

Added Sept. 18, 1998, effective Oct. 1, 1998 (725 So.2d 296). Amended Nov. 17, 2005 (915 So.2d 592); Feb. 8, 2007 (851 So.2d 804); May 23, 2013, effective July 1, 2013 (115 So.3d 286); Feb. 19, 2015, effective Feb. 19, 2015, effective Feb. 19, 2015 (158 So.3d 523).

Form 8.973A. Order on Judicial Review for Child Age 17 or Older

ORDER ON JUDICIAL REVIEW FOR CHILD OVER AGE 17 AND NOTICE OF NEXT HEARING

THIS CAUSE came on to be heard on . . . (date) . . . for Judicial Review on the report filed by the Department of Children and Families in this cause under chapter 39, Florida Statutes.

The following persons appeared before the court:

The following persons appeared before the court:

. . . . . . (name) . . ., Child

. . . . . . (name) . . ., Attorney/Attorney ad litem for the Child

. . . . . . (name) . . ., Petitioner

. . . . . . (name) . . ., Attorney for the petitioner

. . . . . . (name) . . ., Attorney for the department

. . . . . . (name) . . ., Department caseworker

. . . . . . (name) . . ., Mother

. . . . . . (name) . . ., Attorney for mother

. . . . . . (name) . . ., Father of . . . (child) . .

. . . . . . (name) . . ., Attorney for father

. . . . . . (name) . . ., Guardian ad litem

. . . . . . (name) . . ., Attorney for guardian ad litem

. . . . . . (name) . . ., Legal custodian

. . . . . . (name) . . ., Attorney for legal custodian

. . . . . . (name) . . ., Other . . . .

and the court having considered:

. . . Judicial Review Social Study Report filed by the Department;

. . . Because the child reached the age of 17 within the past 90 days, written verification that the child:

. . . . . Has been provided with a current Medicaid card and has been provided all necessary information concerning the Medicaid program;

. . . . . Has been provided with a certified copy of his or her birth certificate and has a valid Florida driver's license or has been provided with a Florida identification card;

. . . . . Has a social security card and has been provided information relating to Social Security Insurance benefits, if the child is believed to be eligible;

. . . . . Has received a full accounting if there is a Master Trust for the child and has been informed as to how to access those funds;

. . . . . Has been provided with information related to the Road-to-Independence Program, including eligibility requirements, information on participation, and assistance in gaining admission to the program. If the child is eligible for the Road-to-Independence Program, has been informed that he or she may reside with the licensed foster family or group care provider with whom the child was residing at the time of attaining his or her 18th birthday or may reside in another licensed foster home or with a group care provider arranged by the department;

. . . . . Has an open bank account or the identification necessary to open a bank account and the information necessary to acquire essential banking and budgeting skills;

. . . . . Has been provided with information on public assistance and how to apply;

. . . . . Has been provided a clear understanding of where he or she will be living on his or her 18th birthday, how living expenses will be paid, and what educational program the child will be enrolled in.

. . . . . Has been provided with information as to the child's ability to remain in care until he/she reaches 21 years of age;

. . . . . Has been provided with a letter stating the dates that the child is under the jurisdiction of the court;

. . . . . Has been provided with a letter stating that the child is in compliance with financial aid documentation requirements;

. . . . . Has been provided his or her educational records;

. . . . . Has been provided his or her entire health and mental health records;

..... Has been provided with information concerning the process for accessing his or her case file; and

..... Has been provided with a statement encouraging the child to attend all judicial review hearings occurring after his or her 17th birthday.

..... Statement/homestudy filed by the Department;

..... Report of the Guardian Ad Litem;

..... A case plan, dated ...., filed by the Department that includes information related to independent living services that have been provided since the child's 13th birthday or since the date the child came into foster care, whichever came later;

..... Statement by the child's caretaker on the progress the child has made in acquiring independent living skills;

..... Whether or not the child is a citizen and, if the child is not a citizen, the steps that have been taken to address the citizenship or residency status of the child;

..... Other ....

AND THE COURT having heard testimony and argument, and having been otherwise duly advised in the premises finds:

1. That the minor child(ren) who is/are the subject matter of these proceedings was/were adjudicated dependent, continue to be dependent, is/are of an age subject to the jurisdiction of the court, and is/are resident(s) of the state of Florida.

2. The following parties were notified of this hearing and provided a copy of the documents filed for this hearing:

...... (Name) ..., Child

...... (Name) ..., Attorney/Attorney ad Litem for the Child

...... (Name) ..., Petitioner

...... (Name) ..., Attorney for the petitioner

...... (Name) ..., Attorney for the department

...... (Name) ..., Department caseworker

...... (Name) ..., Mother

...... (Name) ..., Attorney for mother

...... (Name) ..., Father of ... (child) ...

...... (Name) ..., Attorney for father

...... (Name) ..., Guardian ad litem

...... (Name) ..., Attorney for guardian ad litem

...... (Name) ..., Legal custodian

...... (Name) ..., Attorney for legal custodian

...... (Name) ..., Other: ....

3. The child has been given the opportunity to address the court with any information relevant to the child's best interests.

4. The mother, ... (name) ...:

... did not appear and ... was ... was not represented by legal counsel;

... appeared ... with ... without legal counsel and ... was ... was not advised of her right to legal counsel;

knowingly, intelligently, and voluntarily ... waived ... did not waive her right to legal counsel; and ... was ... was not determined to qualify as indigent and

... was ... was not appointed an attorney.

5. The father, ... (name) ...:

... did not appear and ... was ... was not represented by legal counsel;

... appeared ... with ... without legal counsel and ... was ... was not advised of his right to legal counsel;

knowingly, intelligently, and voluntarily ... waived ... did not waive his right to legal counsel; and ... was ... was not determined to qualify as indigent and

... was ... was not appointed an attorney.

COMMENT: Repeat above for each father.

6. The department filed a judicial review report with the court on ... (date) ... This judicial review report ... is ... is not in compliance with the statutory requirements.

7. The following parents/legal custodians were notified of their right to participate in the preparation of the case plan and to receive assistance from any other person in the preparation of the case plan: (names of those notified) ...

8. The mother has complied with the following tasks in the case plan: ... (list tasks complied with) ...

9. The mother has not complied with the following tasks in the case plan: ... (list tasks not complied with) ...

10. The father, ... (father's name) ..., has complied with the following tasks in the case plan: ... (list tasks complied with) ...

11. The father, ... (father's name) ..., has not complied with the following tasks in the case plan: ... (list tasks not complied with) ...

12. The mother ... has ... has not complied with court ordered visitation as follows: ... (explanation of visitation compliance) ...

13. The father, ... (father's name) ..., ... has ... has not complied with court ordered visitation as follows: ... (explanation of visitation compliance) ...

14. The department ... has ... has not complied with court ordered visitation as follows: ... (explanation of visitation compliance) ...

15. The mother . . . has . . . has not complied with court ordered financial support for the child as follows: . . . (explanation of financial compliance) . . .

16. The father, . . . (father's name) . . ., . . . has . . . has not complied with court ordered financial support for the child as follows: . . . (explanation of financial compliance) . . .

17. The mother . . . has . . . has not complied with court ordered meetings with the department as follows: . . . (explanation of meetings compliance) . . .

18. The father, . . . (father's name) . . ., . . . has . . . has not complied with court ordered meetings with the department as follows: . . . (explanation of meetings compliance) . . .

19. The department . . . has . . . has not complied with court ordered meetings with the parents as follows: . . . (explanation of meetings compliance) . . .

COMMENT: Use 20, 21, 22, 23, & 24 if child(ren) is/are not placed in the home of a parent.

. . . 20. It is in the best interest of the minor child(ren) to be placed in the care and custody of . . . (placement ordered) . . .

. . . 21. Placement of the minor child(ren) in the care and custody of . . . (placement ordered) . . . is in a setting which is as family like and as close to the home as possible, consistent with the child(ren)'s best interests and special needs.

. . . 22. The children . . . are . . . are not separated in their placements. The following efforts have been made to reunite the siblings: . . . .

. . . It is not in the siblings' best interest to be reunited in their placement because: . . . .

. . . The separate siblings have the following frequency, kind and duration of contacts: . . . .

. . . 23. Return of the minor child(ren) to the custody of . . . (person(s) from whom child(ren) was/were originally removed) . . . would be contrary to the best interest and welfare of the minor child(ren). The child(ren) cannot safely . . . remain . . . return home with services and removal of the child(ren) is necessary to protect the child(ren).

. . . 24. Prevention or reunification services . . . were not . . . were indicated and are as follows: . . . (services indicated) . . . Further efforts could not have shortened separation of this family because . . . .

COMMENT: Use 25 if child(ren) remain(s) or is/are returned to the parent(s).

. . . 25. The child(ren) can safely . . . remain with . . . be returned to . . . (parent('s)(s') name(s)) . . . as long as he/she/they comply(ies) with the following: . . . . The safety, well-being, and physical, mental, and emotional health of the child(ren) are not endangered by allowing the child(ren) to . . . remain . . . return home.

. . . 26. The child's petition and application for special immigrant juvenile status or other immigration decision remains pending.

. . . 27. The department . . . has . . . has not complied with its obligation as specified in the written case plan or in the provision of independent living services as required by Florida Statutes.

THEREFORE, based upon the foregoing findings, it is hereby ORDERED AND ADJUDGED that:

1. The minor child(ren), . . . name(s)) . . ., be placed in the custody of . . . (name) . . ., under supervision of the department.

2. The judicial review report filed by the department is:

. . . not accepted and a continuance was requested.

. . . accepted by the court.

3. Other: . . . .

4. All prior orders not inconsistent with the present order shall remain in full force and effect.

5. This court shall retain jurisdiction over this cause to enter any such further orders as may be deemed necessary for the best interest and welfare of the minor child(ren).

6. This court shall retain jurisdiction until the final decision is rendered by the federal immigration authorities, or upon the immigrant child's 22nd birthday, whichever shall occur first.

7. This court shall retain jurisdiction until the child's 19th birthday for the purpose of determining whether appropriate services that were required to be provided to the young adult before reaching 18 years of age have been provided to the youth.

8. This court shall retain jurisdiction until the child's 21st birthday, unless the young adult chooses to leave foster care upon reaching 18 years of age, or if the young adult does not meet the eligibility requirements to remain in foster care or chooses to leave care at any time prior to the 21st birthday.

9. This matter is scheduled for Judicial Review on . . . (date) . . . at . . . (time) . . .

DONE AND ORDERED in . . . ., Florida, on . . . (date) . . .

____

Circuit Judge

NOTICE OF HEARING

The Juvenile Court hereby gives notice of hearing in the above-styled cause on . . . (date) . . . at . . . a.m./p.m . . ., before . . . (judge) . . ., at . . . (loca-

tion) . . ., or as soon thereafter as counsel can be heard.

COMMENT: The following paragraph must be in bold, 14 pt. Times New Roman or Courier font.

If you are a person with a disability who needs any accommodation in order to participate in this proceeding, you are entitled, at no cost to you, to the provision of certain assistance. Please contact . . . (name, address, and telephone number) . . . at least 7 days before your scheduled court appearance, or immediately upon receiving this notification if the time before the scheduled appearance is less than 7 days. If you are hearing or voice impaired, call 711.

PLEASE BE GOVERNED ACCORDINGLY.

Copies furnished to . . . .

Formerly Form 8.973, added Nov. 17, 2005 (915 So.2d 592). Amended May 23, 2013, effective July 1, 2013 (115 So.3d 286). Renumbered Form 8.937A and amended March 20, 2014 (136 So.3d 508). Amended Feb. 19, 2015, effective Feb. 19, 2015 (158 So.3d 523).

Form 8.973B. Order on Judicial Review

ORDER ON LAST JUDICIAL REVIEW BEFORE CHILD REACHES AGE 18 AND NOTICE OF NEXT HEARING

THIS CAUSE came on to be heard on . . . (date) . . . for Judicial Review on the report filed by the Department of Children and Families in this cause under chapter 39, Florida Statutes.

The following persons appeared before the court:

. . . . (Name) . . ., Child
. . . . (Name) . . ., Attorney/Attorney ad Litem for the Child
. . . . (Name) . . ., Petitioner
. . . . (Name) . . ., Attorney for the petitioner
. . . . (Name) . . ., Attorney for the department
. . . . (Name) . . ., Department caseworker
. . . . (Name) . . ., Mother
. . . . (Name) . . ., Attorney for mother
. . . . (Name) . . ., Father of . . . (child) . . .
. . . . (Name) . . ., Attorney for father
. . . . (Name) . . ., Guardian ad litem
. . . . (Name) . . ., Attorney for guardian ad litem
. . . . (Name) . . ., Legal custodian
. . . . (Name) . . ., Attorney for legal custodian
. . . . (Name) . . ., Other: . . . .

and the court having considered:

. . . . . Judicial Review Social Study Report filed by the Department;
. . . . . Statement/homestudy filed by the Department;
. . . . . Report of the Guardian Ad Litem;
. . . . . A case plan, dated . . . ., filed by the Department that includes information related to independent living services that have been provided since the child's 13th birthday or since the date the child came into foster care, whichever came later;
. . . . . Statement by the child's caretaker on the progress the child has made in acquiring independent living skills;
. . . . . Whether or not the child is a citizen and, if the child is not a citizen, the steps that have been taken to address the citizenship or residency status of the child;
. . . . . Other: . . . .

AND THE COURT having heard testimony and argument, and having been otherwise duly advised in the premises finds:

1. That the minor child(ren) who . . . is/are . . . the subject matter of these proceedings . . . was/were . . . adjudicated dependent, continue to be dependent, is/are of an age subject to the jurisdiction of the court, and . . . is/are . . . resident(s) of the state of Florida.

2. The following parties were notified of this hearing and provided a copy of the documents filed for this hearing:

. . . . (Name) . . ., Child
. . . . (Name) . . ., Attorney/Attorney ad Litem for the Child
. . . . (Name) . . ., Petitioner
. . . . (Name) . . ., Attorney for the petitioner
. . . . (Name) . . ., Attorney for the department
. . . . (Name) . . ., Department caseworker
. . . . (Name) . . ., Mother
. . . . (Name) . . ., Attorney for mother
. . . . (Name) . . ., Father of . . . (child) . . .
. . . . (Name) . . ., Attorney for father
. . . . (Name) . . ., Guardian ad litem
. . . . (Name) . . ., Attorney for guardian ad litem
. . . . (Name) . . ., Legal custodian
. . . . (Name) . . ., Attorney for legal custodian
. . . . (Name) . . ., Other: . . . .

3. The child has been given the opportunity to address the court with any information relevant to the child's best interests.

4. The mother, . . . (name) . . .:

. . . . . did not appear and . . . was . . . was not represented by legal counsel;
. . . . . appeared . . . with . . . without legal counsel and . . . was . . . was not advised of her right to legal counsel; knowingly, intelligently, and voluntarily . . . waived . . . did not waive her right to legal counsel; and

. . . was . . . was not determined to qualify as indigent and

. . . was . . . was not appointed an attorney.

5. The father, . . . (name) . . . :

. . . . . . did not appear and . . . . was

. . . . was not represented by legal counsel;

. . . . . . appeared with

. . . . without legal counsel and

. . . . was . . . . was not advised of his right to legal counsel;

knowingly, intelligently, and voluntarily

. . . . waived . . . . did not waive his right to legal counsel; and

. . . . was . . . . was not determined to qualify as indigent and

. . . . was . . . . was not appointed an attorney.

COMMENT: Repeat above for each father.

6. The department filed a judicial review report with the court on . . . (date) . . . The judicial review report . . . is . . . is not in compliance with statutory requirements.

7. The following parents/legal custodians were notified of their right to participate in the preparation of the case plan and to receive assistance from any other person in the preparation of the case plan: . . . (names of those notified) . . .

8. The mother has complied with the following tasks in the case plan: . . . (list tasks complied with) . . .

9. The mother has not complied with the following tasks in the case plan: . . . (list tasks not complied with) . . .

10. The father, . . . (father's name) . . ., has complied with the following tasks in the case plan: . . . (list tasks complied with) . . .

11. The father, . . . (father's name) . . ., has not complied with the following tasks in the case plan: . . . (list tasks not complied with) . . .

12. The mother . . . has . . . has not complied with court ordered visitation as follows: . . . (explanation of visitation compliance) . . .

13. The father, . . . (father's name) . . ., . . . has . . . has not complied with court ordered visitation as follows: . . . (explanation of visitation compliance) . . .

14. The department . . . has . . . has not complied with court ordered visitation as follows: . . . (explanation of visitation compliance) . . . .

15. The mother . . . has . . . has not complied with court ordered financial support for the child as follows: . . . (explanation of financial compliance) . . .

16. The father, . . . (father's name) . . ., . . . has . . . has not complied with court ordered financial support for the child as follows: . . . (explanation of financial compliance) . . .

17. The mother . . . has . . . has not complied with court ordered meetings with the department as follows: . . . (explanation of meetings compliance) . . .

18. The father, . . . (father's name) . . ., . . . has . . . has not complied with court ordered meetings with the department as follows: . . . (explanation of meetings compliance) . . .

19. The department . . . has . . . has not complied with court ordered meetings with the parents as follows: . . . (explanation of meetings compliance) . . .

COMMENT: Use 20, 21, 22, 23, & 24 if child(ren) is/are not placed in the home of a parent.

20. It is in the best interest of the minor child(ren) to be placed in the care and custody of . . . (placement ordered) . . .

21. Placement of the minor child(ren) in the care and custody of . . . (placement ordered) . . . is in a setting which is as family like and as close to the home as possible, consistent with the child(ren)'s best interests and special needs.

. . . 22. The children . . . are . . . are not separated in their placements. The following efforts have been made to reunite separated siblings:

. . . .

. . . It is not in the best interest of each sibling to be reunited in their placement because:

. . . .

. . . Each sibling has the following frequency, kind and duration of contacts:

. . . .

23. Return of the minor child(ren) to the custody of . . . (person(s) from whom child(ren) was/were originally removed) . . . would be contrary to the best interest and welfare of the minor child(ren). The child(ren) cannot safely . . . remain . . . return home with services and removal of the child(ren) is necessary to protect the child(ren).

24. Prevention or reunification services . . . were not . . . were indicated and are as follows: . . . (services indicated) . . . Further efforts could not have shortened separation of this family because . . . .

COMMENT: Use 25 if child(ren) remain(s) or is/are returned to the parent(s).

25. The child(ren) can safely . . . remain with . . . be returned to . . . (parent('s)(s') name(s)) . . . as long as he/she/they comply(ies) with the following: . . . . The safety, well-being, and physical, mental, and emotional health of the child(ren) are not endangered by allowing the child(ren) to . . . remain . . . return home.

26. The child's petition and application for special immigrant juvenile status or other immigration decision remains pending.

27. The department . . . has . . . has not complied with its obligation as specified in the written case plan or in the provision of independent living services as required by Florida Statutes.

. . . 28. The child does plan on remaining in foster care.

a. the child will meet the requirements by ....

b. the supervised living arrangement will be ....

c. the child has been informed of

. . . (1) the right to continued support and services;

. . . (2) the right to request termination of this court's jurisdiction and to be discharged from foster care;

. . . (3) the opportunity to reenter foster care pursuant to Florida law.

. . . 29. The child does not plan on remaining in foster care. The child has been informed of:

. . . a. services or benefits for which the child may be eligible based upon the child's placement and length of time spent in licensed foster care;

. . . b. services or benefits that may be lost through a termination of the court's jurisdiction; and

. . . c. other federal, state, local, or community-based services or supports available to the child.

THEREFORE, based upon the foregoing findings, it is hereby ORDERED AND ADJUDGED that:

1. The minor child(ren), . . . (name(s)) . . ., be placed in the custody of . . . (name) . . ., under supervision of the department.

2. The judicial review report filed by the department is: . . . not accepted and a continuance was requested . . . accepted by the court.

3. Other: ....

4. All prior orders not inconsistent with the present order shall remain in full force and effect.

5. This court shall retain jurisdiction over this cause to enter any such further orders as may be deemed necessary for the best interest and welfare of the minor child(ren).

6. This court shall retain jurisdiction until the final decision is rendered by the federal immigration authorities, or upon the immigrant child's 22nd birthday, whichever shall occur first.

7. This court shall retain jurisdiction until the child's 19th birthday for the purpose of determining whether appropriate services that were required to be provided to the young adult before reaching 18 years of age have been provided to the youth.

8. This court shall retain jurisdiction until the child's 21st birthday, unless the young adult chooses to leave foster care upon reaching 18 years of age, or if the young adult does not meet the eligibility requirements to remain in foster care or chooses to leave care at any time prior to the 21st birthday.

9. This matter is scheduled for Judicial Review on . . . (date) . . . at . . . (time) . . .

DONE AND ORDERED in ...., Florida, on . . . (date) . . .

Circuit Judge

NOTICE OF HEARING

The Juvenile Court hereby gives notice of hearing in the above-styled cause on . . . (date) . . . at .... a.m./p.m., before . . . (judge) . . ., at . . . (location) . . ., or as soon thereafter as counsel can be heard.

COMMENT: The following paragraph must be in bold, 14 pt. Times New Roman or Courier font.

If you are a person with a disability who needs any accommodation in order to participate in this proceeding, you are entitled, at no cost to you, to the provision of certain assistance. Please contact . . . (name, address, and telephone number) . . . at least 7 days before your scheduled court appearance, or immediately upon receiving this notification if the time before the scheduled appearance is less than 7 days. If you are hearing or voice impaired, call 711.

PLEASE BE GOVERNED ACCORDINGLY.

Copies furnished to: ....

Added March 20, 2014, effective March 20, 2014 (136 So.3d 508). Amended Feb. 19, 2015, effective Feb. 19, 2015 (158 So.3d 523).

Form 8.973C. Order on Judicial Review for Young Adults in Extended Foster Care

ORDER ON JUDICIAL REVIEW FOR YOUNG ADULTS IN EXTENDED FOSTER CARE AND NOTICE OF NEXT HEARING

THIS CAUSE came on to be heard on . . . (date) . . . for Judicial Review on the report filed by the Department of Children and Families in this cause under chapter 39, Florida Statutes.

The following persons appeared before the court:

. . . . (Name) . . ., Young Adult

. . . . (Name) . . ., Attorney for the Young Adult

. . . . (Name) . . ., Petitioner

. . . . (Name) . . ., Attorney for the petitioner

. . . . (Name) . . ., Attorney for the department

. . . . (Name) . . ., Department caseworker

.... (Name) ..., Guardian ad litem
.... (Name) ..., Attorney for the guardian ad litem
.... (Name) ..., Other: ....
and the court having considered:
..... Judicial Review Social Study Report filed by the Department;
..... Case Plan filed by the Department
..... Report of the Guardian Ad Litem;
..... Other: ....

AND THE COURT having heard testimony and argument, and having been otherwise duly advised in the premises finds:

1. The young adult ... is ... is not making progress in meeting the case plan goals, as follows: ....

2. The case plan and/or the young adult's transition plan shall be amended as follows: ....

3. The Department and all services providers ... have ... have not provided the appropriate services listed in the case plan. The Department must take the following action to ensure the young adult receives identified services that have not been provided:

... 4. The young adult ... is ... is not separated from siblings in out-of-home care. The following efforts have been made to reunite separated siblings:

....

....

....

... It is not in the best interest of each sibling to be reunited in their placement because:

....

....

... Each sibling has the following frequency, kind and duration of contacts:

....

....

....

5. Jurisdiction in this case should be terminated based on the following facts:

... a. The young adult has requested termination of jurisdiction; or

... b. The young adult has been informed by the department of his or her right to attend this hearing and has provided written consent to waive this right, and

... c. The young adult has been informed of the potential negative effects of early termination of care, the option to reenter care before reaching 21 years of age, the procedure for and the limitations on reentering care, and the availability of alternative services, and has signed a document attesting that he or she has been so informed and understands these provisions; or

... d. The young adult has voluntarily left the program, has not signed the document indicated above, and is unwilling to participate in any further court proceeding; or

... e. The young adult has been involuntarily discharged from the program by written notification dated ...., and the young adult has not appealed the discharge decision.

THEREFORE, based upon the foregoing findings, it is hereby ORDERED AND ADJUDGED that:

1. The judicial review report filed by the department is:

... not accepted and a continuance was requested.

... accepted by the court.

2. All prior orders not inconsistent with the present order shall remain in full force and effect.

... 3. This court shall retain jurisdiction until the young adult's 19th birthday for the purpose of determining whether appropriate services that were required to be provided to the young adult before reaching 18 years of age have been provided to the youth; or

... 4. This court shall retain jurisdiction until the young adult's 21st birthday, unless the young adult chooses to leave foster care upon reaching 18 years of age, or if the young adult does not meet the eligibility requirements to remain in foster care or chooses to leave care at any time prior to the 21st birthday; or

... 5. Jurisdiction over this cause is hereby terminated.

... 6. Other: ....

... 7. This matter is scheduled for Judicial Review on ... (date) ... at ... (time) ...

DONE AND ORDERED in ...., Florida, on (date)

____
Circuit Judge

NOTICE OF HEARING

The Juvenile Court hereby gives notice of hearing in the above-styled cause on ... (date) ... at .... a.m./p.m., before ... (judge) ..., at ... (location) ..., or as soon thereafter as counsel can be heard.

COMMENT: The following paragraph must be in bold, 14 pt. Times New Roman or Courier font.

If you are a person with a disability who needs any accommodation in order to participate in this proceeding, you are entitled, at no cost to you, to the provision of certain assistance. Please contact ... (name, address, and telephone number) ... at least 7 days before your scheduled court appearance, or immediately upon receiving this notification if the time before the scheduled appearance is

less than 7 days. If you are hearing or voice impaired, call 711.

PLEASE BE GOVERNED ACCORDINGLY.

Copies furnished to: ....

Added March 20, 2014 (136 So.3d 508). Amended Feb. 19, 2015, effective Feb. 19, 2015 (158 So.3d 523).

Form 8.974. Petition to Extend or Reinstate Court's Jurisdiction

PETITION TO EXTEND JURISDICTION OR TO REINSTATE JURISDICTION AND TO SCHEDULE HEARING

I, ... (name, address, and date of birth) ..... request the court, under section 39.013(2), Florida Statutes to

..... extend jurisdiction, or

..... reinstate jurisdiction,

and to schedule a hearing in this matter.

1. I am currently or was on my 18th birthday in the legal custody of the Department of Children and Family Services.

2. ..... a. I am requesting that the court review the aftercare support, Road-to-Independence scholarship, transitional support, mental health services, and/or developmental disability services to the extent authorized by law.

..... b. A petition for special immigrant juvenile status has been filed on my behalf and the application will not be granted by the time I reach 18 years of age.

WHEREFORE, I request this court extend or reinstate jurisdiction in this case and schedule a hearing as soon as possible.

____
..... (name) .....
..... (address) .....
..... (phone number) .....

Added Nov. 17, 2005 (915 So.2d 952).

Form 8.975. Dependency Order Withholding Adjudication

ORDER OF ADJUDICATION

THIS CAUSE came before this court on .... (date)........................, under chapter 39, Florida Statutes, for adjudication of the Petition for Dependency filed by .... (petitioner's name) .... Present before the court were

.... (Name) ....., Petitioner
.... (Name) ....., Attorney for the petitioner
.... (Name) ....., Attorney for the department
.... (Name) ....., Department caseworker
.... (Name) ....., Mother
.... (Name) ....., Attorney for mother
.... (Name) ....., Father of ..... (child) .....
.... (Name) ....., Attorney for father
.... (Name) ....., Guardian ad litem
.... (Name) ....., Attorney for guardian ad litem
.... (Name) ....., Legal custodian
.... (Name) ....., Attorney for legal custodian
.... (Name) ....., Other ....

The court having heard testimony and argument and being otherwise fully advised in the premises finds:

1. That the minor child(ren) who is/are the subject matter of these proceedings, is/are dependent within the meaning and intent of chapter 39, Florida Statutes, and is/are (a) resident(s) of the State of Florida.

2. The mother, ... (name) ....:

..... was ..... was not noticed of this hearing;

..... did not appear, and the court:

..... entered a Consent for failure to appear after proper notice.

..... did not enter a Consent for failure to appear after proper notice.

..... appeared with counsel;

..... appeared without counsel and:

..... was ..... was not advised of her right to legal counsel,

..... knowingly, intelligently, and voluntarily waived ..... did not waive her right to legal counsel and

..... was ..... was not determined to qualify as indigent and

..... was ..... was not appointed an attorney.

3. The father, ... (name) .....:

..... was ..... was not noticed of this hearing;

..... did not appear, and the court:

..... entered a Consent for failure to appear after proper notice.

..... did not enter a Consent for failure to appear after proper notice.

..... appeared with counsel;

..... appeared without counsel and:

..... was ..... was not advised of his right to legal counsel,

..... knowingly, intelligently, and voluntarily waived ..... did not waive his right to legal counsel and

..... was ..... was not determined to qualify as indigent and

..... was ..... was not appointed an attorney.

4. That the child(ren) is/are dependent within the meaning and intent of chapter 39, Florida Statutes, in that the mother, ... (name) ....., abused, neglected or abandoned the minor child(ren) by .... These facts were proven by ..... preponderance of the evidence ..... clear and convincing evidence.

5. That the child(ren) is/are dependent within the meaning and intent of chapter 39, Florida Statutes, in that the father, ... (name) ....., abused, neglected or abandoned the minor child(ren) by .... These facts were proven by ..... preponderance of the evidence ..... clear and convincing evidence.

6. That the parties have filed a mediation agreement in which the parent(s) consent(s) to the adjudication of dependency of the child(ren) in conjunction with a withhold of adjudication, which the court accepts.

7. Under section 39.507(5), Florida Statutes, the Court finds that the child(ren) named in the petition are dependent, but finds that no action other than supervision in the child(ren)'s home is required.

THEREFORE, based upon the foregoing findings, it is ORDERED AND ADJUDGED that:

1. Under section 39.507(5), Florida Statutes, the Court hereby withholds adjudication of dependency of the minor child(ren). The child(ren) shall be ..... returned/continued ..... in (child(ren)'s home) under the supervision of the department. If this court later finds that the parents have not complied with the conditions of supervision imposed, the court may, after a hearing to establish the noncompliance, but without further evidence of the state of dependency, enter an order of adjudication.

2. This court shall retain jurisdiction over this cause to enter any such further orders that may be deemed necessary for the best interest and welfare of the minor child(ren).

3. All prior orders not inconsistent with the present order shall remain in full force and effect.

4. Disposition is scheduled for ..... (date) ....., at .... a.m./p.m.

DONE AND ORDERED on .... date ....

____
Circuit Judge

NOTICE OF HEARING

The Juvenile Court hereby gives notice of hearing in the above styled cause on .... (date) .... at .... a.m./p.m., before .... (judge) ...., at .... (location) ...., or as soon thereafter as counsel can be heard.

COMMENT: The following paragraph must be in bold, 14 pt. Times New Roman or Courier font.

If you are a person with a disability who needs any accommodation in order to participate in this proceeding, you are entitled, at no cost to you, to the provision of certain assistance. Please contact .... (name, address, and telephone number) .... at least 7 days before your scheduled court appearance, or immediately upon receiving this notification if the time before the scheduled appearance is less than 7 days. If you are hearing or voice impaired, call 711.

PLEASE BE GOVERNED ACCORDINGLY.

Copies furnished to:

Added Sept. 21, 2006, effective Jan. 1, 2007 (951 So.2d 804). Amended May 23, 2013, effective July 1, 2013 (115 So.3d 286).

Form 8.976. Proposed Relative Placement

PROPOSED RELATIVES FOR PLACEMENT

Pursuant to Chapter 39, Florida Statutes, the .... mother/father .... hereby provides the court and the parties with the names and location of relatives who might be considered for placement of the child(ren). The .... mother/father .... will continue to inform the court and the parties of any relative who should be considered for placement of the child(ren) with the filing of subsequent forms.

MATERNAL	PATERNAL
Name:	Name: ....
Address:	Address: ....
Phone number:	Phone number: ....
Relationship to child:	Relationship to child: ....
Name:	Name: ....
Address:	Address: ....
Phone number:	Phone number: ....
Relationship to child:	Relationship to child: ....
Name:	Name: ....
Address:	Address: ....
Phone number:	Phone number: ....
Relationship to child:	Relationship to child: ....
Name:	Name: ....
Address:	Address: ....
Phone number:	Phone number:

. . . .

Relationship to child: Relationship to child:

. . . .

Name: Name:

. . . .

Address: Address:

. . . .

Phone number: Phone number:

. . . .

Relationship to child: Relationship to child:

. . . .

The above information is true and correct to the best of my knowledge.

Dated ________________

(Mother's Signature) (Father's Signature)
Printed name: . . . . Printed name:

Added Feb. 8, 2007 (951 So.2d 804).

Form 8.977. Order Authorizing Child to Enter Into Residential Leasehold and Secure Utility Services Before The Child's 18th Birthday

ORDER AUTHORIZING CHILD TO ENTER INTO RESIDENTIAL LEASEHOLD AND TO SECURE RESIDENTIAL UTILITY SERVICES BEFORE THE CHILD'S 18TH BIRTHDAY

THIS CAUSE came before the court to remove the disabilities of nonage of . . . . . .(name) . . . . . ., for the purposes of entering into a residential leasehold and to secure residential utility services. The court being fully advised in the premises FINDS as follows:

. . . . . .(Name) . . . . . . is 17 years of age, meets the requirements of sections 743.045 and 743.046, Florida Statutes, and is entitled to the benefits of those statutes.

THEREFORE, based on these findings of fact, it is ORDERED AND ADJUDGED that the disabilities of nonage of . . . . . .(name) . . . . . . are hereby removed for the purposes of entering a residential leasehold and securing residential utility services. . . . . . .(Name) . . . . . . is hereby authorized to make and execute contracts, releases, and all other instruments necessary for the purposes of entering into a residential leasehold and securing residential utility services. The contracts or other instruments made by . . . . . .(name) . . . . . . for the purposes of entering into a residential leasehold and securing residential utility services shall have the same effect as though they were the obligations of a person who is not a minor.

ORDERED at . . . ., Florida, on . . . . . .(date) . . . . . .

____
Circuit Judge

Copies to:

Added Feb. 8, 2007 (951 So.2d 804). Amended Sept. 25, 2008 (992 So.2d 242)

Form 8.978. Order Authorizing Child to Secure Depository Financial Services Before the Child's 18th Birthday

ORDER AUTHORIZING CHILD TO SECURE DEPOSITORY FINANCIAL SERVICES BEFORE THE CHILD'S 18TH BIRTHDAY

THIS CAUSE came before the court to remove the disabilities of nonage of . . . . (name) . . . ., for the purpose of securing depository financial services, and the court being fully advised in the premises FINDS as follows:

. . . . (Name) . . . . is at least 16 years of age, meets the requirements of section 743.044, Florida Statutes, and is entitled to the benefits of that statute.

THEREFORE, based on these findings of fact, it is ORDERED AND ADJUDGED that the disabilities of nonage of . . . . (name) . . . . are hereby removed for the purpose of securing depository financial services. . . . . (Name) . . . . is hereby authorized to make and execute contracts, releases, and all other instruments necessary for the purpose of securing depository financial services. The contracts or other instruments made by . . . . (name) . . . . for the purpose of securing depository financial services have the same effect as though they were the obligations of a person who is not a minor.

ORDERED at . . . . Florida, on . . . . (date) . . . .

____
Circuit Judge

Copies to:

Added July 12, 2007 (960 So.2d 764).

Form 8.978(a). Order Concerning Youth's Eligibility for Florida's Tuition and Fee Exemption

ORDER CONCERNING ELIGIBILITY FOR FLORIDA'S TUITION AND FEE EXEMPTION

THIS CAUSE comes before the court to determine . . . . (name) . . . .'s eligibility for the tuition and fee exemption under Chapter 1009, Florida Statutes, and the court being fully advised in the premises, it is

ORDERED AND ADJUDGED that . . . . (name) . . . . is eligible, under Chapter 1009, Florida Statutes, and therefore exempt from the payment of tuition and fees, including lab fees, at a school district that provides postsecondary career programs, community college, or state university.

ORDERED at .... Florida, on .... (date) ....

____
Circuit Judge

Copies to:

Added Dec. 17, 2009, effective Jan. 1, 2010 (26 So.3d 552).

D. TERMINATION OF PARENTAL RIGHTS FORMS

Form 8.979. Summons for Advisory Hearing

SUMMONS AND NOTICE OF ADVISORY HEARING FOR TERMINATION OF PARENTAL RIGHTS AND GUARDIANSHIP

STATE OF FLORIDA

TO: .... (name and address of person being summoned) ....

A Petition for Termination of Parental Rights under oath has been filed in this court regarding the above-referenced child(ren), a copy of which is attached. You are to appear before .... (judge) ...., at .... (time and location of hearing) ...., for a TERMINATION OF PARENTAL RIGHTS ADVISORY HEARING. You must appear on the date and at the time specified.

FAILURE TO PERSONALLY APPEAR AT THIS ADVISORY HEARING CONSTITUTES CONSENT TO THE TERMINATION OF PARENTAL RIGHTS TO THIS CHILD (THESE CHILDREN). IF YOU FAIL TO APPEAR ON THE DATE AND TIME SPECIFIED YOU MAY LOSE ALL LEGAL RIGHTS TO THE CHILD (OR CHILDREN) NAMED IN THE PETITION ATTACHED TO THIS NOTICE.

COMMENT: The following paragraph must be in bold, 14 pt. Times New Roman or Courier font.

If you are a person with a disability who needs any accommodation to participate in this proceeding, you are entitled, at no cost to you, to the provision of certain assistance. Please contact .... (name, address, telephone number) at least 7 days before your scheduled court appearance, or immediately upon receiving this notification if the time before the scheduled appearance is less than 7 days. If you are hearing or voice impaired, call 711.

Witness my hand and seal of this court at .... (city, county, state) .... on .... (date) ....

CLERK OF COURT
BY: ______________
DEPUTY CLERK

AVISO Y CITACIÓN PARA LA AUDIENCIA INFORMATIVA SOBRE LA TERMINACIÓN DE LOS DERECHOS PATERNALES Y DE LA TUTELA

ESTADO DE LA FLORIDA

PARA: ______________________
(Nombre y dirección de la persona a ser citada)

CONSIDERANDO que se ha interpuesto en este Juzgado una solicitud bajo juramento para la terminación de los derechos paternales con respecto al(os) niño(s) en referencia, adjuntándose copia de la misma. Mediante la presente se le ordena comparecer ante el ________ a las ________________ para una AUDIENCIA
(Juez) (hora y lugar de la audiencia)

INFORMATIVA SOBRE LA TERMINACIÓN DE LOS DERECHOS PATERNALES. Usted deberá comparecer en le fecha y hora indicadas.

SI USTED NO COMPARECE PERSONALMENTE A LA AUDIENCIA INFORMATIVA, ESTO SIGNIFICARÁ QUE USTED ACCEDE A LA TERMINACIÓN DE SUS DERECHOS PATERNALES CON RESPECTO A ESTE(OS) NIÑO(S). SI USTED NO COMPARECE EN LA FECHA Y HORA INDICADAS, USTED PODRÁ PERDER TODOS SUS DERECHOS LEGALES CON RESPECTO AL/LOS NIÑO(S) MENCIONADO(S) EN LA PETICIÓN ADJUNTA A ESTE AVISO.

Si usted es una persona con una discapacidad que necesita cualquier tipo de trato especial para participar en este procedimiento, usted tiene derecho, sin costa alguno para usted, para la presetación de asistencia determinadas. Póngase en contacto con .... (nombre, dirección, número de teléfono) .... por lo menos 7 dias antes la aparición en la corte programado, o immediatamente después de recibir esta notification, si el tiempo antes de la comparecencia prevista es inferiof a 7 dias. Si usted está oyendo o voz alterada, llame al 711.

Firmado y sigilado en este Juzgado ____________

______________el ____________
(ciudad, condado, estado) (fecha)

ESCRIBANO DEL TRIBUNAL
POR: ____________
ESCRIBANO DELEGADO

MANDA AK AVÈTISMAN POU ENFOME–W SOU YON CHITA TANDE, POU YO ANILE DWA–W KÒM PARAN AK KÒM GADYEN

Leta Florid

POU: .... (non ak adrès moun yo voye manda-a) ....

KÒM, tandiske, gen yon demann sèmante pou anile dwa paran-yo, ki prezante devan tribinal-la, konsènan timoun ki nonmen nan lèt sa-a, piwo-a, yon kopi dokiman-an kwoke nan dosye-a., yo bay lòd pou prezante devan .... (Jij–la) ...., a .... (nan.lè ak adrès chita tande–a) ...., NAN YON CHITA TANDE POU YO ENFÒME–W, YO GEN LENTANSYON POU ANILE DWA–OU KÒM PARAN. Ou fèt pou prezante nan dat ak lè ki endike-a.

SI OU PA PREZANTE PÈSONÈLMAN NAN CHITA TANDE–A, POU YO ENFÒME–W, YO GEN LENTANSYON POU ANILE DWA–OU KÒM PARAN, SA KA LAKÒZ YO DESIDE OU KONSANTI TIMOUN SA–A (YO), BEZWEN PWOTEKSYON LETA EPI SA KA LAKÒZ OU PÈDI DWA–OU KÒM PARAN TIMOUN SAA(YO), KI GEN NON YO MAKE NAN KOPI DEMANN–NAN, KI KWOKE NAN AVÈTISMAN–AN

Si ou se yon moun infirm, ki beswen 'ed ou ki bewsen ke o akomode w pou ou patispe nan pwosedi sa yo, ou genyen dwa, san ke ou pa peye, a setin 'ed. Silvouple kontake .... (non, address, telephone) .... o moin 7 jou avan dat ou genyen rendevou pou ale nan tribunal, ou si le ou resevwa avi a, genyen mouins ke 7 jou avan date endevou tribunal la. Ou si ou pa tande pale, rele nan nimerro sa 711.

Mwen siyen non mwen e mete so mwen nan dokiman tribinal-la kòm temwen nan (vil, distrik, eta) ...., nan .... (dat) ....

GREFYE TRIBINAL–LA
PA: ____________________
ASISTAN GREFYE TRIBINAL–LA

Added Sept. 18, 1998, effective Oct. 1, 1998 (725 So.2d 296). Amended Sept. 5, 2002, effective Jan. 1, 2003 (827 So.2d 219); Jan. 27, 2005 (894 So.2d 875); May 23, 2013, effective July 1, 2013 (115 So.3d 286).

Form 8.980. Petition for Termination of Parental Rights Based on Voluntary Relinquishment

PETITION FOR TERMINATION
OF PARENTAL RIGHTS

Petitioner, ...(name)..., respectfully petitions this Court for termination of parental rights and permanent commitment of the minor child(ren), ...(name(s))..., to ...(agency name)... for the purpose of subsequent adoption, and as grounds states the following:

A. PARTIES

1. The child, ...(name)..., is a male/female child born on ...(date)..., at ...(city, county, state).... At the time of the filing of this petition, the child is ...(age).... A copy of the child's birth certificate is attached to this Petition and incorporated as Petitioner's Exhibit ....

COMMENT: Repeat above for each child on petition.

2. The child(ren) is/are presently in the care and custody of ...(name)..., and is/are residing in .... County, Florida.

3. An affidavit under the Uniform Child Custody Jurisdiction and Enforcement Act is attached to this as Petitioner's Exhibit ....

4. The natural mother of the child(ren) is ...(name)..., who resides at ....

5. The natural/alleged/putative father of the child(ren) ...(name(s))... is ...(name)..., who resides at ....

COMMENT: Repeat #5 as necessary.

6. A guardian ad litem ... has ... has not been appointed to represent the interests of the child(ren) in this cause.

B. GROUNDS FOR TERMINATION

1. The parent(s) have been advised of their right to legal counsel at all hearings that they attended.

2. The parents will be informed of the availability of private placement of the child with an adoption entity as defined in chapter 63, Florida Statutes.

3. The mother, ...(name)..., freely, knowingly, voluntarily, and .... with .... without advice of legal counsel executed an Affidavit and Acknowledgment of Surrender, Consent, and Waiver of Notice on ...(date)..., for termination of her parental rights to the minor child, ...(name)..., under section 39.806(1)(a), Florida Statutes.

COMMENT: Repeat above as necessary.

4. The father, ...(name)..., freely, knowingly, and voluntarily, and .... with .... without advice of legal counsel executed an Affidavit and Acknowledgment of Surrender, Consent, and Waiver of Notice on ...(date)..., for termination of his parental rights to the minor child, ...(name)..., under section 39.806(1)(a), Florida Statutes.

COMMENT: Repeat above as necessary.

5. Under the provisions of chapter 39, Florida Statutes, it is in the manifest best interest of the child(ren) for parental rights to be terminated for the following reasons:

.... allegations which correspond to sections 39.810(1)–(11), Florida Statutes.

6. A copy of this petition shall be served on the natural mother, ...(name)...; the father(s), ...(name(s))...; the custodian, ...(name)...; and the guardian ad litem, ...(name)...

7. This petition is filed in good faith and under oath.

WHEREFORE, the petitioner respectfully requests that this court grant this petition; find that the parents have voluntarily surrendered their parental rights to the minor child(ren); find that termination of parental rights is in the manifest best interests of this/these child(ren); and that this court enter an order permanently committing this/these child(ren) to the ...(name)... for subsequent adoption.

____
...(petitioner's name and identifying information)...

Verification

____

. . .(attorney's name). . .
. . .(address and telephone number). . .
. . .(email address(es). . .
. . .(Florida Bar number). . .

Certificate of Service

Former Form 8.922 renumbered as new Form 8.980 and amended May 9, 1991, effective July 1, 1991 (589 So.2d 818). Amended Sept. 18, 1998, effective Oct. 1, 1998 (725 So.2d 296); Sept. 21, 2006, effective Jan. 1, 2007 (939 So.2d 74); Oct. 11, 2012 (101 So.3d 368).

Form 8.981. Petition for Involuntary Termination of Parental Rights

PETITION FOR TERMINATION OF PARENTAL RIGHTS

Petitioner, ... (petitioner's name) ...., respectfully petitions this court for termination of parental rights and permanent commitment of the minor child(ren), ... (name(s)) ...., to .... (agency name) .... for the purpose of subsequent adoption, and as grounds states the following:

A. PARTIES

1. The child, ... (name) ...., is a male/female child born on .... (date) ...., at .... (city, county, state) .... At the time of the filing of this petition, the child is .... (age) .... A copy of the child's birth certificate is attached to this Petition and incorporated as Petitioner's Exhibit ....

COMMENT: Repeat above for each child on petition.

2. The child(ren) is/are presently in the care and custody of .... (name) ...., and is/are residing in .... County, Florida.

3. An affidavit under the Uniform Child Custody Jurisdiction and Enforcement Act is attached to this as Petitioner's Exhibit ....

4. The natural mother of the child(ren) is .... (name) ...., who resides at ....

5. The natural/alleged/putative father of the child(ren) .... (name(s)) .... is .... (name) ...., who resides at ....

COMMENT: Repeat #5 as necessary.

6. A guardian ad litem .... has .... has not been appointed to represent the interests of the child(ren) in this cause.

B. GROUNDS FOR TERMINATION

1. The parents have been advised of their right to legal counsel at all hearings that they attended.

2. On or about .... (date(s)) ...., the following occurred: .... (acts which were basis for dependency or TPR, if filed directly) ....

3. The mother has .... (grounds for TPR) .... the minor child(ren) within the meaning and intent of section 39.806, Florida Statutes, in that: .... (allegations which form the statutory basis for grounds) ....

4. The father has .... (grounds for TPR) .... the minor child(ren) within the meaning and intent of section 39.806, Florida Statutes, in that: .... (allegations which form the statutory basis for grounds) ....

5. Under the provisions of sections 39.810(1)–(11), Florida Statutes, it is in the manifest best interests of the child(ren) for parental rights of .... (name(s)) .... to be terminated for the following reasons: .... (allegations for each statutory factor in the manifest best interest test) ....

6. A copy of this petition shall be served on the natural mother, ... (name) ...., father(s), ... (name(s)) ...., the custodian, ... (name) ....; and the guardian ad litem, ... (name) ....

7. This petition is filed by the petitioner in good faith and under oath.

WHEREFORE, the petitioner respectfully requests that this court grant this petition; find that the parents have abused, neglected, or abandoned the minor child(ren); find that termination of parental rights is in the manifest best interests of this/these child(ren); and that this court enter an order permanently committing this/these child(ren) to .... (agency) .... for subsequent adoption.

____
. . . . (petitioner's name and identifying information) . . . .

Verification

____
. . . . (attorney's name) . . . .
. . . . (address and telephone number) . . . .
. . . . (Florida Bar number) . . . .

Certificate of Service

Added May 9, 1991, effective July 1, 1991 (589 So.2d 818). Amended Sept. 18, 1998, effective Oct. 1, 1998 (725 So.2d 296); Sept. 21, 2006, effective Jan. 1, 2007 (939 So.2d 74).

Form 8.982. Notice of Action for Advisory Hearing

.... (Child(ren)'s initials and date(s) of birth) ....

NOTICE OF ACTION AND OF ADVISORY HEARING FOR TERMINATION OF PARENTAL RIGHTS AND GUARDIANSHIP

STATE OF FLORIDA

TO: ....(name and address of person being summoned) ....

A Petition for Termination of Parental Rights under oath has been filed in this court regarding the above-referenced child(ren). You are to appear before .... (judge) ...., at .... (time and address of hearing) ...., for a TERMINATION OF PARENTAL RIGHTS ADVISORY HEARING. You must appear on the date and at the time specified.

FAILURE TO PERSONALLY APPEAR AT THIS ADVISORY HEARING CONSTITUTES CONSENT TO THE TERMINATION OF PARENTAL RIGHTS TO THIS CHILD (THESE CHILDREN). IF YOU FAIL TO APPEAR ON THE DATE AND TIME SPECIFIED YOU MAY LOSE ALL LEGAL RIGHTS TO THE CHILD (OR CHILDREN) WHOSE INITIALS APPEAR ABOVE.

COMMENT: The following paragraph must be in bold, 14 pt. Times New Roman or Courier font.

If you are a person with a disability who needs any accomodation [1] to particiapte [1] in this proceeding, you are entitled, at no cost to you, to the provision of certain assistance. Please contact .... (name, address, telephone number) .... at least 7 days before your scheduled court appearance, or immediately upon receiving this notification if the time before the scheduled appearance is less than 7 days. If you are hearing or voice impaired, call 711.

Witness my hand and seal of this court at .... (city, county, state) .... on .... (date) ....

CLERK OF COURT
BY: ____________
DEPUTY CLERK

AVISO Y CITACION PARA LA AUDIENCIA INFORMATIVA SOBRE LA TERMINACION DE LOS DERECHOS PATERNALES Y DE LA TUTELA

ESTADO DE LA FLORIDA

PARA: (Nombre y direccion de la persona a ser citada)

CONSIDERANDO que se ha interpuesto en este Juzgado una solicitud bajo juramento para la terminacion de los derechos paternales con respecto al(os) nino(s) en referencia, adjuntandose copia de la misma. Mediante la presente se le ordena comparecer ante el ________ a las ____________________ para una AUDIENCIA
(Juez) (hora y lugar de la audiencia)
INFORMATIVA SOBRE LA TERMINACION DE LOS DERECHOS PATERNALES. Usted debera comparecer en le fecha y hora indicadas.

SI USTED NO COMPARECE PERSONALMENTE A LA AUDIENCIA INFORMATIVA, ESTO SIGNIFICARA QUE USTED ACCEDE A LA TERMINACION DE SUS DERECHOS PATERNALES CON RESPECTO A ESTE(OS) NINO(S). SI USTED NO COMPARECE EN LA FECHA Y HORA INDICADAS, USTED PODRA PERDER TODOS SUS DERECHOS LEGALES CON RESPECTO AL/LOS NINO(S) MENCIONADO(S) EN LA PETICION ADJUNTA A ESTE AVISO.

Si usted es una persona con una discapacidad que necesita cualquier tipo de trato especial para participar en este procedimiento, usted tiene derecho, sin costa alguno para usted, para la presetación de asistencia determinadas. Póngase en contacto con .... (nombre, dirección, número de teléfono) .... por lo menos 7 dias antes la aparición en la corte programado, o immediatamente después de reciber esta notification, si el tiempo antes de la comparecencia prevista es inferiof a 7 dias. Si usted está oyendo o voz alterada, llame al 711.

Firmado y sigilado en este Juzgado ____________
____________________ el ________
(ciudad, condado, estado) (fecha)

ESCRIBANO DEL TRIBUNAL
POR: ____________
ESCRIBANO DELEGADO

MANDA AK AVTISMAN POU ENFOME–W SOU YON CHITA TANDE, POU YO ANILE DWA–W KM PARAN AK KM GADYEN.

LETA FLORID

POU: ....(non ak adrs moun yo voye manda-a) ....

KOM, tandiske, gen yon demann smante pou anile dwa paran-yo, ki prezante devan tribinal-la, konsnan timoun ki nonmen nan lt sa-a, piwo-a, yon kopi dokiman-an kwoke nan dosye-a., yo bay ld pou prezante devan .... (Jij-la) ...., a .... (nan.l ak adrs chita tande-a) ...., NAN YON CHITA TANDE POU YO ENFME–W, YO GEN LENTANSYON POU ANILE DWA–OU KM PARAN. Ou ft pou prezante nan dat ak l ki endike-a.

SI OU PA PREZANTE PSONLMAN NAN CHITA TANDE–A, POU YO ENFME–W, YO GEN LENTANSYON POU ANILE DWA–OU KM PARAN, SA KA LAKZ YO DESIDE OU KONSANTI TIMOUN SA–A (YO), BEZWEN PWOTEKSYON LETA EPI SA KA LAKZ OU PDI DWA–OU KM PARAN TIMOUN SA–A(YO), KI GEN NON YO MAKE NAN KOPI DEMANN–NAN, KI KWOKE NAN AVTISMAN–AN

Si ou se yon moun infirm, ki beswen 'ed ou ki bewsen ke o akomode w pou ou patispe nan pwosedi sa yo, ou genyen dwa, san ke ou pa peye, a setin 'ed. Silvouple kontake .... (non, address, telephone) .... o moin 7 jou avan dat ou genyen rendevou pou ale nan tribunal, ou si le ou resevwa avi a, genyen mouins ke 7 jou avan date endevou tribunal la. Ou si ou pa tande pale, rele nan nimerro sa 711.

Mwen siyen non mwen e mete so mwen nan dokiman tribinal-la km temwen nan .... (vil, distrik, eta) ...., nan .... (dat) ....

GREFYE TRIBINAL–LA
PA: ____________________

ASISTAN GREFYE TRIBINALA–L

Added Dec. 17, 2009, effective Jan. 1, 2010 (26 So.3d 552). Amended May 23, 2013, effective July 1, 2013 (115 So.3d 286).

[1] So in original.

Form 8.983. Adjudication Order and Judgment of Involuntary Termination of Parental Rights

ORDER OF ADJUDICATION AND JUDGMENT OF INVOLUNTARY TERMINATION OF PARENTAL RIGHTS

THIS CAUSE came before this court on .... (all dates of the adjudicatory hearing) .... for an adjudicatory hearing on the Petition for Termination of Parental Rights filed by .... (name) .... Present before the court were:

..........(Name) ...., Petitioner

..........(Name) ...., Attorney for the petitioner

..........(Name) ...., Attorney for the department

..........(Name) ...., Department caseworker

..........(Name) ...., Child

..........(Name) ...., Attorney for Child

..........(Name) ...., Mother

..........(Name) ...., Attorney for mother

..........(Name) ...., Father of .... (child)..........

..........(Name) ...., Attorney for father

..........(Name) ...., Guardian ad litem

..........(Name) ...., Attorney for guardian ad litem

..........(Name) ...., Legal custodian

..........(Name) ...., Attorney for legal custodian

..........(Name) ...., Other..........

The court has carefully considered and weighed the testimony of all witnesses. The court has received and reviewed all exhibits.

COMMENT: Add the following only if necessary.

The petitioner has sought termination of the parental rights of .... (parent(s)) who is/are subject of petition)..........

The court finds that the parent(s), ... (name(s)) ...., has/have .... (list grounds proved) ...., under chapter 39, Florida Statutes. The grounds were proved by clear and convincing evidence. Further, the court finds that termination of parental rights of the parent(s), ... name(s) ...., is clearly in the manifest best interests of the child(ren). The findings of fact and conclusions of law supporting this decision are as follows:

1. At all stages of these proceedings the parent(s) was/were advised of his/her/their right to legal counsel, or was/were in fact represented by counsel.

2. On or about .... (date(s)) ...., the following occurred: .... (acts which were basis for dependency or TPR, if filed directly)..........

3. The mother has .... (grounds for TPR) .... the minor child(ren) within the meaning and intent of section 39.806, Florida Statutes, in that: .... (findings that form the statutory basis for grounds)..........

4. The father has .... (grounds for TPR) .... the minor child(ren) within the meaning and intent of section 39.806, Florida Statutes, in that: .... (findings that form the statutory basis for grounds)..........

5. The minor child(ren) to whom .... (parent's(s') name(s)) .... parental rights are being terminated are at substantial risk of significant harm. Termination of parental rights is the least restrictive means to protect the child(ren) from harm.

6. Under the provisions of sections 39.810(1)–(11), Florida Statutes, it is in the manifest best interests of the child(ren) for parental rights of .... (name(s)) .... to be terminated for the reasons below. The court has considered all relevant factors and finds as follows:

(a) Regarding any suitable permanent custody arrangement with a relative of the child, the court finds..........

(b) Regarding the ability and disposition of the parent or parents to provide the child with food, clothing, medical care, or other remedial care recognized and permitted under state law instead of medical care, and other material needs of the child, the court finds..........

(c) Regarding the capacity of the parent or parents to care for the child to the extent that the child's safety, well-being, and physical, mental, and emotional health will not be endangered upon the child's return home, the court finds..........

(d) Regarding the present mental and physical health needs of the child and such future needs of the child to the extent that such future needs can be ascertained based on the present condition of the child, the court finds..........

(e) Regarding the love, affection, and other emotional ties existing between the child and the child's parent or parents, siblings, and other relatives, and the degree of harm to the child that would arise from the termination of parental rights and duties, the court finds..........

(f) Regarding the likelihood of an older child remaining in long-term foster care upon termination of parental rights, due to emotional or behavioral problems or any special needs of the child, the court finds..........

(g) Regarding the child's ability to form a significant relationship with a parental substitute and the likelihood that the child will enter into a more stable and permanent family relationship as a result of permanent termination of parental rights and duties, the court finds..........

(h) Regarding the length of time that the child has lived in a stable, satisfactory environment and the desirability of maintaining continuity, the court finds..........

(i) Regarding the depth of the relationship existing between the child and present custodian, the court finds..........

(j) Regarding the reasonable preferences and wishes of the child, if the court deems the child to be of sufficient intelligence, understanding, and experience to express a preference, the court finds..........

(k) Regarding the recommendations for the child provided by the child's guardian ad litem or the legal representative, the court finds..........

(*l*) Regarding other relevant factors including ...., the court finds..........

COMMENT: Add items 7, 8, and 9 as applicable.

7. Under section 39.811(6)(..........), Florida Statutes, the court terminates the parental rights of only .... (parent whose rights are being terminated) .... as to the minor child(ren), ... (child(ren)'s name(s)) .... Specifically, the court finds that .... (specific findings of fact under section 39.811(6), Florida Statutes)..........

8. Under sections 39.509(5) and 39.811(7)(a), Florida Statutes, the court finds that continued grandparental visitation is not in the best interests of the child(ren) or that such visitation would interfere with the permanency goals for the child(ren) for the following reasons..........

9. Under section 39.811(7)(b), Florida Statutes, the court finds that although parental rights are being terminated, the best interests of .... (names of child(ren) to which this provision applies) .... support continued communication or contact by .... (names of parents, siblings, or relatives of the parent whose rights are terminated and to which this provision applies) .... except as provided above. The nature and frequency of the communication or contact shall be as follows .... It may be reviewed on motion of any party or an identified prospective adoptive parent.

THEREFORE, after weighing the credibility of the witnesses, weighing all statutory factors, and based on the findings of fact and conclusions of law above, the court hereby ORDERS AND ADJUDGES THAT:

1. The petition filed by .... (name) .... is granted as to the parent(s), ... (name(s))..........

2. The parental rights of the father, ... (name) ...., and of the mother, ... (name) ...., to the child, ... (name) ...., are hereby terminated under section 39.806(..........), Florida Statutes.

COMMENT: Repeat the above for each child and parent, as necessary.

3. Under sections 39.811(2) and (5), Florida Statutes, the child(ren), ... (name(s)) ...., are placed in the custody of .... (agency) .... for the purpose of subsequent adoption.

4. The 30–day permanency plan required by section 39.811(8), Florida Statutes, shall be filed and heard at .... (time) .... on .... (date) .... in .... (location)..........

DONE AND ORDERED on .... (date) ...., in .... (city and county) ...., Florida.

____
Circuit Judge

NOTICE

Under section 39.815, Florida Statutes, any child, any parent, guardian ad litem, or legal custodian of any child, any other party to the proceeding who is affected by an order of the court, or the department may appeal to the appropriate District Court of Appeal within the time and in the manner prescribed by the Florida Rules of Appellate Procedure, which is 30 days from the date this order is rendered (filed).

Copies to:

Added May 9, 1991, effective July 1, 1991 (589 So.2d 818). Amended Sept. 18, 1998, effective Oct. 1, 1998 (725 So.2d 296); Sept. 21, 2006, effective Jan. 1, 2007 (939 So.2d 74); Nov. 12, 2009 (24 So.3d 47).

Form 8.984. Judgment of Voluntary Termination of Parental Rights

ADJUDICATORY ORDER AND FINAL JUDGMENT OF TERMINATION OF PARENTAL RIGHTS AND GUARDIANSHIP

THIS CAUSE came before this court on .... (all dates of the adjudicatory hearing) .... for an adjudicatory hearing on the petition for termination of parental rights filed by .... (name) .... Present before the court were:

.... (Name) ...., Petitioner

.... (Name) ...., Attorney for the petitioner

.... (Name) ...., Attorney for the department

.... (Name) ...., Department/agency caseworker

.... (Name) ...., Child

.... (Name) ...., Attorney/Attorney ad litem for Child

.... (Name) ...., Mother

.... (Name) ...., Attorney for mother

.... (Name) ...., Father of .... (child) ....

.... (Name) ...., Attorney for father

.... (Name) ...., Guardian ad litem

.... (Name) ...., Attorney for guardian ad litem

.... (Name) ...., Legal custodian

.... (Name) ...., Attorney for legal custodian

.... (Name) ...., Other ....

___ The mother, ... (name) ...., executed a voluntary surrender of her parental rights for the minor child(ren), ... (name(s)) ...., which is accepted by the court without objection.

COMMENT: Repeat the following as necessary.

___ The father, ... (name) ...., executed a voluntary surrender of his parental rights for the minor child(ren), ... (name(s)) ...., which is accepted by the court without objection.

The court has carefully considered the testimony of witnesses, reviewed the exhibits, reviewed the file, heard argument of counsel, and considered recommendations and arguments of all parties. The court finds by clear and convincing evidence that the parents, ... (names) ...., have surrendered their parental rights to the minor child(ren) under section 39.806(1)(a), Florida Statutes, and that termination of parental rights is in the manifest best interest of the child(ren). The specific facts and findings supporting this decision are as follows:

1. That the mother, ... (name) ...., ... was .... was not personally served with the summons and the petition.

COMMENT: Service is not required if surrender was signed before filing of petition.

2. That the father, ... (name) ...., ... was .... was not personally served with the summons and the petition.

COMMENT: Service is not required if surrender was signed before filing of petition.

3. That the parents were advised of their right to counsel in all prior dependency court proceedings which they attended. The mother has been represented by legal counsel, ... (name) ...., starting on or about .... (date) .... The father has been represented by legal counsel, ... (name) ...., starting on or about .... (date)..........

4. The mother, ... (name) ...., freely, knowingly, voluntarily, and .... with .... without advice of legal counsel executed an affidavit and acknowledgment of surrender, consent, and waiver of notice on .... (date) ...., for termination of her parental rights to the minor child(ren), under section 39.806(1)(a), Florida Statutes.

5. The father, ... (name) ...., freely, knowingly, voluntarily, and .... with .... without advice of legal counsel executed an affidavit and acknowledgment of surrender, consent, and waiver of notice on .... (date) ...., for termination of his parental rights to the minor child(ren), under section 39.806(1)(a), Florida Statutes.

6. That at all times relevant to this action the interests of this/these child(ren) has/have been represented by a guardian ad litem. The guardian ad litem, ... (name) ...., ... agrees .... does not agree that it is in the best interest of the child(ren) for parental rights to be terminated in this cause.

COMMENT: Guardian ad litem not required in voluntary surrender.

7. Under the provisions of sections 39.810(1)–(11), Florida Statutes, it is in the manifest best interest of the child(ren) for parental rights to be terminated for the following reasons:

(a) Regarding any suitable permanency custody arrangement with a relative of the child, the court finds ....

(b) Regarding the ability and disposition of the parent or parents to provide the child with food, clothing, medical care or other remedial care recognized and permitted under state law instead of medical care, and other materials needs of the child, the court finds ....

(c) Regarding the capacity of the parent or parents to care for the child to the extent that the child's safety, well-being, and physical, mental, and emotional health will not be endangered upon the child's return home, the court finds ....

(d) Regarding the present mental and physical health needs of the child and such future needs of the child to the extent that such future needs can be ascertained based on the present condition of the child, the court finds . . . .

(e) Regarding the love, affection, and other emotional ties existing between the child and the child's parent or parents, siblings, and other relatives, and the degree of harm to the child that would arise from the termination of parental rights and duties, the court finds . . . .

(f) Regarding the likelihood of an older child remaining in long-term foster care upon termination of parental rights, due to emotional or behavioral problems or any special needs of the child, the court finds . . . .

(g) Regarding the child's ability to form a significant relationship with a parental substitute and the likelihood that the child will enter into a more stable and permanent family relationship as a result of permanent termination of parental rights and duties, the court finds . . . .

(h) Regarding the length of time that the child has lived in a stable, satisfactory environment and the desirability of maintaining continuity, the court finds . . . .

(i) Regarding the depth of the relationship existing between the child and present custodian, the court finds . . . .

(j) Regarding the reasonable preferences and wishes of the child, if the court deems the child to be of sufficient intelligence, understanding, and experience to express a preference, the court finds . . . .

(k) Regarding the recommendations for the child provided by the child's guardian ad litem or the legal representative, the court finds . . . .

(*l*) Regarding other relevant factors including . . . ., the court finds . . . .

THEREFORE, it is ORDERED AND ADJUDGED that:

1. The petition for termination of parental rights is GRANTED.

2. The parental rights of the father, ... (name) . . . ., and of the mother, ... (name) . . . ., to the child, ... (name) . . . ., are hereby terminated under section 39.806(. . . . .), Florida Statutes.

COMMENT: Repeat the above for each child and parent on petition.

3. The child(ren), ... (name(s)) . . . ., is/are hereby placed in the permanent care and custody of . . . . (agency name) . . . . for subsequent adoption.

4. A hearing for the department to provide a plan for permanency for the child(ren) shall be held on . . . . (date) . . . ., within 30 days of rendering of order, at . . . . (time) . . . .

DONE AND ORDERED on . . . . (date) . . . ., in . . . . County, Florida.

____

Circuit Judge

Copies furnished to: ____________________

NOTICE

Under section 39.815, Florida Statutes, any child, any parent, guardian ad litem, or legal custodian of any child, any other party to the proceeding who is affected by an order of the court, or the department may appeal to the appropriate District Court of Appeal within the time and in the manner prescribed by the Florida Rules of Appellate Procedure, which is 30 days from the date this order is rendered (filed).

Added May 9, 1991, effective July 1, 1991 (589 So.2d 818). Amended Sept. 18, 1998, effective Oct. 1, 1998 (725 So.2d 296); Nov. 12, 2009 (24 So.3d 47).

Form 8.985. Motion to Terminate Supervision and Jurisdiction

MOTION TO TERMINATE SUPERVISION AND JURISDICTION

The Department of Children and Family Services, by and through its undersigned counsel, moves this court for an order terminating the department's supervision and the court's jurisdiction and closing the file in the above-styled cause, and as grounds states:

1. The parental rights previously were terminated and the child(ren) was/were permanently committed to the care and custody of the department for adoption by order of this court.

2. The adoption was finalized on . . . . .(date) . . . . .

WHEREFORE, the Department of Children and Family Services requests that this court terminate jurisdiction and the department's supervision and that the file be closed.

____

. . . . .(attorney's name) . . . . .

. . . . .(address and telephone number) . . . . .

. . . . .(Florida Bar number) . . . . .

Certificate of Service

Added Sept. 18, 1998, effective Oct. 1, 1998 (725 So.2d 296).

Form 8.986. Order Terminating Supervision and Jurisdiction

ORDER TERMINATING SUPERVISION AND JURISDICTION

THIS CAUSE having come before the court on motion to terminate supervision and jurisdiction filed by the Department of Children and Family Services, and the court being otherwise advised in the premises, find the following:

1. The parental rights previously were terminated and the child(ren) was/were permanently committed to the care and custody of the department for subsequent adoption by order of this court.

2. The adoption was finalized on .....(date) ......

THEREFORE, based on these findings of fact, it is ORDERED AND ADJUDGED:

That the supervision of the Department of Children and Family Services and this court's jurisdiction are terminated.

DONE AND ORDERED on .....(date) ......

____
Circuit Judge

Copies furnished to: ____________________

Added Sept. 18, 1998, effective Oct. 1, 1998 (725 So.2d 296).

E. JUDICIAL WAIVER OF PARENTAL NOTICE OF TERMINATION OF PREGNANCY FORMS

2012 Revision

Part VI.E, "Judicial Waiver of Parental Notice of Termination of Pregnancy Forms", was added by Florida Supreme Court Opinion No. SC11-399 (102 So.3d 451).

Form 8.987. Petition for Judicial Waiver of Parental Notification of Termination of Pregnancy

IN THE CIRCUIT COURT OF THE .... JUDICIAL CIRCUIT
IN AND FOR .... COUNTY, FLORIDA

In the Interest of ....(pseudonym or initials of minor)

Case No.: ....
Division: ....

PETITION FOR JUDICIAL WAIVER OF PARENTAL NOTICE OF TERMINATION OF PREGNANCY

I certify that the following information is true and correct:

(1) The pseudonym or initials of the minor (is/are) ...., and the minor has filed a Sworn Statement of True Name and Pseudonym with the clerk.

(2) The minor is .... years old.

(3) The minor is pregnant and notice has not been waived.

(4) The minor desires to terminate her pregnancy without notice to a parent or legal guardian for one or more of the following reasons:

[check all that apply]

.... a. The minor is sufficiently mature to decide whether to terminate her pregnancy, for the following reason(s): ....
....

.... b. The minor is a victim of child abuse or sexual abuse inflicted by one or both of her parents or a guardian.

.... c. Notification of a parent or guardian is not in the best interest of the minor, for the following reason(s): ....
....

(5) The minor requests that the court enter an order authorizing her to consent to the performance or inducement of a termination of pregnancy without notification of a parent or guardian.

(6) The minor requests the appointment of an attorney to represent her in this matter: [check one]

.... yes

.... no

(7) The minor elects the following method or methods for receiving notices of hearings or other court actions in this case:

.... Through a third party whose name is .... and whose address and phone number for purposes of notice are ...., ...

.... The minor will contact the office of the clerk of court at the following phone number ......

I understand that by signing this form I am swearing to or affirming the truthfulness of the claims made in this petition and that the punishment for knowingly making a false statement includes fines, imprisonment, or both.

Signature: ____________________

Date: ....

(You may sign a name other than your true name, such as Jane Doe or other pseudonym under which your petition is being filed.)

Added June 30, 2005 (907 So.2d 1161). Amended July 6, 2006 (934 So.2d 438); Oct. 20, 2011 (75 So.3d 216).

Form 8.988. Sworn Statement of True Name and Pseudonym

SWORN STATEMENT OF TRUE NAME AND PSEUDONYM

NOTICE TO THE CLERK OF COURT: A CERTIFIED COPY OF THIS DECLARATION WITH

THE CASE NUMBER NOTED ON IT SHALL BE GIVEN TO THE MINOR AFTER SHE SIGNS IT.

THE ORIGINAL SHALL IMMEDIATELY BE PLACED IN A SEALED ENVELOPE WHICH SHALL BE FILED UNDER SEAL AND KEPT UNDER SEAL AT ALL TIMES.

(1) My true name is ______, and my address is
(print your name)

______.
(print your address)

(2) My date of birth is ______.

(3) I have filed a Petition for Judicial Waiver of Parental Notice of Termination of Pregnancy under the name or initials ______ on ______.
(date)

I understand that by signing this form I am swearing to or affirming the truthfulness of the information herein and that the punishment for knowingly making a false statement includes fines, imprisonment or both.

Dated:____ Signature: ______
(You must sign your true name.)

Added June 30, 2005 (907 So.2d 1161).

Form 8.989. Advisory Notice to Minor

ADVISORY NOTICE TO MINOR

YOU ARE NOTIFIED as follows:

YOUR CASE NUMBER APPEARS AT THE TOP OF THIS FORM. KEEP IT IN A SAFE PLACE. YOU CAN NOT GET INFORMATION FROM THE CLERK WITHOUT YOUR CASE NUMBER.

YOU HAVE BEEN GIVEN A COPY OF THE SWORN STATEMENT YOU SIGNED WITH YOUR TRUE NAME. KEEP IT IN A SAFE PLACE. YOU MAY NEED TO SHOW IT AND THE FINAL JUDGMENT IN YOUR CASE TO YOUR DOCTOR BEFORE TERMINATING YOUR PREGNANCY.

All information in your case is confidential. No papers will be sent to your home, and you will be contacted by this court only through the method you elected in the petition. Your name will not be on your court papers.

If you would like an attorney to help you with your case, the court will appoint one for you at no cost to you. Your attorney will receive notices about your case so he or she can prepare for and attend hearings with you. You may also name someone else you trust to receive notices for you. You can also contact the clerk of court yourself to check on your case.

You have a right to a hearing and a decision on your case within 48 hours of filing your petition unless you or your attorney waives this right or asks for an extension of time. If this time limit is not met you have the right to ask the clerk for a form that will allow your doctor to perform a termination of pregnancy without notifying a parent.

If the court dismisses your petition, you have the right to appeal. You will be given information regarding how to proceed with an appeal, and if you would like an attorney to help you with an appeal, you may request that the court appoint one.

I certify that I have given a copy of this advisory form to the minor.

Dated: ______ ______ Clerk of the Court
______ County Courthouse
______, Florida.

Added June 30, 2005 (907 So.2d 1161).

Form 8.990. Final Order Granting Petition for Judicial Waiver of Parental Notice of Termination of Pregnancy

FINAL ORDER GRANTING PETITION FOR JUDICIAL WAIVER OF PARENTAL NOTICE OF TERMINATION OF PREGNANCY

THIS CAUSE having come before the court on a petition for judicial waiver of parental notice of termination of pregnancy and the court being otherwise advised in the premises, finds the following:

.... The minor has proven by clear and convincing evidence that she is sufficiently mature to decide whether to terminate her pregnancy, for the following reason(s): ....
....
....
....

The court has considered the following factors in reaching this decision that the minor is sufficiently mature to decide whether to terminate her pregnancy and makes the following findings:

The minor's age is ....

The minor's overall intelligence indicates ......

The minor's emotional development and stability indicates ....

The minor's credibility and demeanor as a witness indicates ....

The minor's ability to accept responsibility is demonstrated by ....

The minor's ability to assess both the immediate and long-range consequences of the minor's choices is demonstrated by ....

The minor's ability to understand and explain the medical risks of terminating her pregnancy and to apply that understanding to her decision is indicated by ....
....

Whether there may be any undue influence by another on the minor's decision to have an abortion .....

.... The minor has proven by a preponderance of the evidence that she is a victim of child abuse or sexual abuse inflicted by one or both of her parents or a guardian, for the following reason(s):

....

....

....

....

The court, having made a finding under this section, will report the abuse as is required by section 39.201, Florida Statutes.

.... The minor has proven by clear and convincing evidence that notification of a parent or guardian is not in the best interest of the minor, for the following reason(s): ....

....

....

....

....

THEREFORE, it is ORDERED AND ADJUDGED that:

1. The petition for judicial waiver of parental notice of termination of pregnancy is GRANTED.

2. The minor may consent to the performance or inducement of a termination of pregnancy without notice to a parent or guardian.

3. The clerk shall keep and maintain a confidential record of these proceedings as provided by section 390.01116, Florida Statutes, and shall seal the record.

DONE AND ORDERED in the .... court in and for .... County, Florida, on ....(date)..........

____

.... Judge

Added June 30, 2005 (907 So.2d 1161). Amended Oct. 20, 2011 (75 So.3d 216).

Form 8.991. Final Order Dismissing Petition for Judicial Waiver of Parental Notice of Termination Of Pregnancy

IN THE CIRCUIT COURT OF THE ______ JUDICIAL CIRCUIT, IN AND FOR ______ COUNTY, FLORIDA

In the interest of ______________ Case No:______
(pseudonym or initials of minor) Division:______

FINAL ORDER DISMISSING PETITION FOR JUDICIAL WAIVER OF PARENTAL NOTICE OF TERMINATION OF PREGNANCY

THIS CAUSE having come before the court on a petition for judicial waiver of parental notice of termination of pregnancy and the court being otherwise advised in the premises, finds the following:

The minor has not proven by sufficient evidence any of the criteria that would permit a judicial waiver of the parental notification requirements of section 390.01114(3), Florida Statutes, for the following reasons:

____

THEREFORE, it is ORDERED AND ADJUDGED that:

1. The petition for judicial waiver of parental notice of termination of pregnancy is DISMISSED.

2. The clerk shall keep and maintain a confidential record of these proceedings as provided by section 390.01116, Florida Statutes, and shall seal the record.

3. The clerk shall immediately provide Form 9.900(f) Notice of Appeal of an Order Dismissing a Petition for Judicial Waiver of Parental Notice of Termination of Pregnancy and Advisory Notice to Minor to the minor or petitioner if other than the minor.

DONE AND ORDERED in the .... court in and for .... County, Florida, on .... (date) ....

____

.... Judge

Added June 30, 2005 (907 So.2d 1161). Amended July 6, 2006 (934 So.2d 438).

Form 8.992. Minor's Petition to Chief Judge to Require a Hearing on her Petition for Judicial Waiver of Notice

MINOR'S PETITION TO CHIEF JUDGE TO REQUIRE A HEARING ON HER PETITION FOR JUDICIAL WAIVER OF NOTICE

I, ...(name)........, hereby petition the chief judge of this judicial circuit for an order directing the judge to whom this case is assigned to hold a hearing within 48 hours after receipt of this petition by the chief judge, and requiring the court to enter an order on my petition for judicial waiver of notice within 24 hours after the hearing.

In support of this petition, I say:

My petition for judicial waiver of notice was filed with the Clerk on ....(date)..........

The third business day from the date of filing my petition was ....(date)..........

I have not requested an extension of time for the hearing required to be conducted.

No hearing has been conducted by the court within the time required by statute.

WHEREFORE, I ask the chief judge to enter an order requiring the hearing on the petition for judicial waiver to be conducted within the next 48 hours, and requiring the court to enter its order within 24 hours after that hearing.

Signature: ______________
Date: __________________
Time: __________________
[to be stamped by Clerk]

Added July 6, 2006 (934 So.2d 438). Amended Oct. 20, 2011 (75 So.3d 216).

INDEX TO
FLORIDA RULES OF JUVENILE PROCEDURE

FLORIDA RULES OF APPELLATE PROCEDURE

Adoption

Adopted October 27, 1977, reconsidered December 22, 1977, effective March 1, 1978 (351 So.2d 981)

Rule 9.010. Effective Date and Scope

These rules, cited as "Florida Rules of Appellate Procedure," and abbreviated "Fla. R. App. P.," shall take effect at 12:01 a.m. on March 1, 1978. They shall govern all proceedings commenced on or after that date in the supreme court, the district courts of appeal, and the circuit courts in the exercise of the jurisdiction described by rule 9.030(c); provided that any appellate proceeding commenced before March 1, 1978, shall continue to its conclusion in the court in which it is then pending in accordance with the Florida Appellate Rules, 1962 Amendment. These rules shall supersede all conflicting statutes and, as provided in Florida Rule of Judicial Administration 2.130, all conflicting rules of procedure.

Amended Oct. 22, 1992, effective Jan. 1, 1993 (609 So.2d 516); Nov. 22, 1996, effective Jan. 1, 1997 (685 So.2d 773); Nov.13, 2008, effective Jan. 1, 2009 (2 So.3d 89).

Committee Notes

1977 Amendment. The rules have been re-numbered to conform with the numbering system adopted by the Florida Supreme Court for all of its rules of practice and procedure, and to avoid confusion with the former rules, which have been extensively revised. The abbreviated citation form to be used for these rules appears in this rule and in rule 9.800.

This rule sets an effective date and retains the substance of former rules 1.1, 1.2, and 1.4. A transition provision has been incorporated to make clear that proceedings already in the appellate stage before the effective date will continue to be governed by the former rules until the completion of appellate review in the court in which it is pending on the effective date. If review is sought after March 1, 1978, of an appellate determination made in a proceeding filed in the appellate court before that date, the higher court may allow review to proceed under the former rules if an injustice would result from required adherence to the new rules. Unnecessary language has been deleted and the wording has been simplified. Specific reference has been made to rule 9.030(c) to clarify those aspects of the jurisdiction of the circuit courts governed by these rules.

1992 Amendment. This rule was amended to eliminate the statement that the Florida Rules of Appellate Procedure supersede all conflicting rules. Other sets of Florida rules contain provisions applicable to certain appellate proceedings, and, in certain instances, those rules conflict with the procedures set forth for other appeals under these rules. In the absence of a clear mandate from the supreme court that only the Florida Rules of Appellate Procedure are to address appellate concerns, the committee felt that these rules should not automatically supersede other rules. See, e.g., *In the Interest of E.P. v. Department of Health and Rehabilitative Services,* 544 So.2d 1000 (Fla. 1989).

1996 Amendment. Rule of Judicial Administration 2.135 now mandates that the Rules of Appellate Procedure control in all appellate proceedings.

Rule 9.020. Definitions

The following terms have the meanings shown as used in these rules:

(a) Administrative Action. Administrative action shall include:

(1) final agency action as defined in the Administrative Procedure Act, chapter 120, Florida Statutes;

(2) non–final action by an agency or administrative law judge reviewable under the Administrative Procedure Act;

(3) quasi–judicial decisions by any administrative body, agency, board or commission not subject to the Administrative Procedure Act; and

(4) administrative action for which judicial review is provided by general law.

(b) Clerk. The person or official specifically designated as such for the court or lower tribunal; if no person or official has been specifically so designated, the official or agent who most closely resembles a clerk in the functions performed.

(c) Court. The supreme court; the district courts of appeal; and the circuit courts in the exercise of the jurisdiction described by rule 9.030(c), including the chief justice of the supreme court and the chief judge of a district court of appeal in the exercise of constitutional, administrative, or supervisory powers on behalf of such courts.

(d) Family Law Matter. A matter governed by the Florida Family Law Rules of Procedure.

(e) Lower Tribunal. The court, agency, officer, board, commission, judge of compensation claims, or body whose order is to be reviewed.

(f) Order. A decision, order, judgment, decree, or rule of a lower tribunal, excluding minutes and minute book entries.

(g) Parties.

(1) *Appellant.* A party who seeks to invoke the appeal jurisdiction of a court.

(2) *Appellee.* Every party in the proceeding in the lower tribunal other than an appellant.

(3) *Petitioner.* A party who seeks an order under rule 9.100 or rule 9.120.

(4) *Respondent.* Every other party in a proceeding brought by a petitioner.

(h) Applicability of Florida Rules of Judicial Administration. The Florida Rules of Judicial Administration are applicable in all proceedings governed by these rules, except as otherwise provided in these rules. These rules shall govern where in conflict with the Florida Rules of Judicial Administration.

(i) Rendition (of an Order). An order is rendered when a signed, written order is filed with the clerk of the lower tribunal. However, unless another applicable rule of procedure specifically provides to the contrary, if a final order has been entered and there has been filed in the lower tribunal an authorized and timely motion for new trial, for rehearing, for certification, to alter or amend, for judgment in accordance with prior motion for directed verdict, for arrest of judgment, to challenge the verdict, to correct a sentence or order of probation pursuant to Florida Rule of Criminal Procedure 3.800(b)(1), to withdraw a plea after sentencing pursuant to Florida Rule of Criminal Procedure 3.170(*l*), or to vacate an order based upon the recommendations of a hearing officer in accordance with Florida Family Law Rule of Procedure 12.491, the following exceptions apply:

(1) If such a motion or motions have been filed, the final order shall not be deemed rendered as to any existing party until the filing of a signed, written order disposing of the last of such motions.

(2) If such a motion or motions have been filed, a signed, written order granting a new trial shall be deemed rendered when filed with the clerk, notwithstanding that other such motions may remain pending at the time.

(3) If such a motion or motions have been filed and a notice of appeal is filed before the filing of a signed, written order disposing of all such motions, the appeal shall be held in abeyance until the filing of a signed, written order disposing of the last such motion.

(j) Rendition of an Appellate Order. If any timely and authorized motion under rule 9.330 or 9.331 is filed, the order shall not be deemed rendered as to any party until all of the motions are either withdrawn or resolved by the filing of a written order.

(k) Signed. A signed document is one containing a signature as provided by Florida Rule of Judicial Administration 2.515(c).

Amended July 14, 1988, effective Jan. 1, 1989 (529 So.2d 687); Dec. 30, 1988, effective Jan. 1, 1989 (536 So.2d 240); March 23, 1989 (541 So.2d 1142); Oct. 22, 1992, effective Jan. 1, 1993 (609 So.2d 516); June 27, 1996, effective July 1, 1996 (675 So.2d 1374); Sept. 27, 1996, effective Oct. 1, 1996 (681 So.2d 1132); Nov. 22, 1996, effective Jan. 1, 1997 (685 So.2d 773); Nov. 12, 1999 (760 So.2d 67); Jan. 13, 2000 (761 So.2d 1015); Oct. 12, 2000, effective Jan. 1, 2001 (780 So.2d 834); Aug. 29, 2002, effective Jan. 1, 2003 (827 So.2d 888); Feb. 3, 2005 (894 So.2d 202); Oct. 18, 2012, effective Dec. 1, 2012, April 1, 2013, Oct. 1, 2013 (102 So.3d 451); Nov. 6, 2014, effective Jan. 1, 2015 (2014 WL 5714099).

Committee Notes

1977 Amendment. This rule supersedes former rule 1.3. Throughout these rules the defined terms have been used in their technical sense only, and are not intended to alter substantive law. Instances may arise in which the context of the rule requires a different meaning for a defined term, but these should be rare.

The term "administrative action" is new and has been defined to make clear the application of these rules to judicial review of administrative agency action. This definition was not intended to conflict with the Administrative Procedure Act, chapter 120, Florida Statutes (1975), but was intended to include all administrative agency action as defined in the Administrative Procedure Act. The reference to municipalities is not intended to conflict with article VIII, section 1(a), Florida Constitution, which makes counties the only political subdivisions of the state.

The term "clerk" retains the substance of the term "clerk" defined in the former rules. This term includes the person who in fact maintains records of proceedings in the lower tribunal if no person is specifically and officially given that duty.

The term "court" retains the substance of the term "court" defined in the former rules, but has been modified to recognize the authority delegated to the chief justice of the supreme court and the chief judges of the district courts of appeal. This definition was not intended to broaden the scope of these rules in regard to the administrative responsibilities of the mentioned judicial officers. The term is used in these rules to designate the court to which a proceeding governed by these rules is taken. If supreme court review of a district court of appeal decision is involved, the district court of appeal is the "lower tribunal."

The term "lower tribunal" includes courts and administrative agencies. It replaces the terms "commission," "board," and "lower court" defined in the former rules.

The term "order" has been broadly defined to include all final and interlocutory rulings of a lower tribunal and rules adopted by an administrative agency. Minute book entries are excluded from the definition in recognition of the decision in *Employers' Fire Ins. Co. v. Continental Ins. Co.*, 326 So.2d 177 (Fla. 1976). It was intended that this rule encourage the entry of written orders in every case.

The terms "appellant," "appellee," "petitioner," and "respondent" have been defined according to the rule applicable to a particular proceeding and generally not according to the legal nature of the proceeding before the court. The term "appellee" has been defined to include the parties against whom relief is sought and all others necessary to the cause. This rule supersedes all statutes concerning the same subject matter, such as section 924.03, Florida Statutes (1975). It should be noted that if a certiorari proceeding is specifically governed by a rule that only refers to "appellant" and "appellee," a "petitioner" and "respondent" should proceed as if they were "appellant" and "appellee," respectively. For example, certiorari proceedings in the supreme court involving the Public Service Commission and Industrial Relations Commission are specifically governed by rule 9.110 even though that rule only refers to "appellant" and "appellee." The parties in such a certiorari proceeding remain designated as "petitioner" and "respondent," because as a matter of substantive law the party invoking the court's jurisdiction is seeking a writ of certiorari. The same is true of rule 9.200 governing the record in such certiorari proceedings.

The term "rendition" has been simplified and unnecessary language deleted. The filing requirement of the definition was not intended to conflict with the substantive right of review guaranteed by the Administrative Procedure Act, section 120.68(1), Florida Statutes (Supp. 1976), but to set a point from which certain procedural times could be measured. Motions that postpone the date of rendition have been narrowly limited to prevent deliberate delaying tactics. To postpone rendition the motion must be timely, authorized, and one of those listed. However, if the lower tribunal is an administrative agency whose rules of practice denominate motions identical to those listed by a different label, the substance of the motion controls and rendition is postponed accordingly.

The definition of "legal holiday" has been eliminated but its substance has been retained in rule 9.420(e).

The term "bond" is defined in rule 9.310(c)(1).

Terms defined in the former rules and not defined here are intended to have their ordinary meanings in accordance with the context of these rules.

1992 Amendment. Subdivision (a) has been amended to reflect properly that deputy commissioners presently are designated as judges of compensation claims.

Subdivision (g) has been rewritten extensively. The first change in this rule was to ensure that an authorized motion for clarification (such as under rule 9.330) was included in those types of motions that delay rendition.

Subdivision (g) also has been revised in several respects to clarify some problems presented by the generality of the prior definition of "rendition." Although rendition is postponed in most types of cases by the filing of timely and authorized post-judgment motions, some rules of procedure explicitly provide to the contrary. The subdivision therefore has been qualified to provide that conflicting rules shall control over the general rule stated in the subdivision. See In Re Interest of E. P., 544 So. 2d 1000 (Fla. 1989). The subdivision also has been revised to make explicit a qualification of long standing in the decisional law, that rendition of non-final orders cannot be postponed by motions directed to them. Not all final orders are subject to postponement of rendition, however. Rendition of a final order can be postponed only by an "authorized" motion, and whether any of the listed motions is an "authorized" motion depends on the rules of procedure governing the proceeding in which the final order is entered. *See Francisco v. Victoria Marine Shipping, Inc.*, 486 So.2d 1386 (Fla. 3d DCA 1986), *review denied* 494 So.2d 1153.

Subdivision (g)(1) has been added to clarify the date of rendition when post-judgment motions have been filed. If there is only 1 plaintiff and 1 defendant in the case, the filing of a post-judgment motion or motions by either party (or both parties) will postpone rendition of the entire final order as to all claims between the parties. If there are multiple parties on either or both sides of the case and less than all parties file post-judgment motions, rendition of the final order will be postponed as to all claims between moving parties and parties moved against, but rendition will not be postponed with respect to claims disposed of in the final order between parties who have no post-judgment motions pending between them with respect to any of those claims. See, e.g., *Phillips v. Ostrer*, 442 So.2d 1084 (Fla. 3d DCA 1983).

Ideally, all post-judgment motions should be disposed of at the same time. See *Winn–Dixie Stores, Inc. v. Robinson*, 472 So. 2d 722 (Fla. 1985). If that occurs, the final order is deemed rendered as to all claims when the order disposing of the motions is filed with the clerk. If all motions are not disposed of at the same time, the final order is deemed rendered as to all claims between a moving party and a party moved against when the written order disposing of the last remaining motion addressed to those claims is filed with the clerk, notwithstanding that other motions filed by co-parties may remain pending. If such motions remain, the date of rendition with respect to the claims between the parties involved in those motions shall be determined in the same way.

Subdivision (g)(2) has been added to govern the special circumstance that arises when rendition of a final order has been postponed initially by post-judgment motions, and a motion for new trial then is granted. If the new trial has been granted simply as an alternative to a new final order, the appeal will be from the new final order. However, if a new trial alone has been ordered, the appeal will be from the new trial order. See rule 9.110. According to the decisional law, rendition of such an order is not postponed by the pendency of any additional, previously filed post-judgment motions, nor can rendition of such an order be postponed by the filing of any further motion. See *Frazier v. Seaboard System Railroad, Inc.*, 508 So.2d 345 (Fla. 1987). To ensure that subdivision (g)(1) is not read as a modification of this special rule, subdivision (g)(2) has been added to make it clear that a separately appealable new trial order is deemed rendered when filed, notwithstanding that other post-judgment motions directed to the initial final order may remain pending at the time.

Subdivision (g)(3) has been added to clarify the confusion generated by a dictum in *Williams v. State*, 324 So.2d 74 (Fla. 1975), which appeared contrary to the settled rule that post-judgment motions were considered abandoned by a party who filed a notice of appeal before their disposition. See *In Re: Forfeiture of $104,591 in U.S. Currency*, 578 So.2d 727 (Fla. 3d DCA 1991). The new subdivision confirms that rule, and provides that the final order is rendered as to the appealing party when the notice of appeal is filed. Although the final order is rendered as to the appealing party, it is not rendered as to any other party whose post-judgment motions are pending when the notice of appeal is filed.

1996 Amendment. Subdivision (a) was amended to reflect the current state of the law. When the term "administrative action" is used in the Florida Rules of Appellate Procedure, it encompasses proceedings under the Administrative Procedure Act, quasi-judicial proceedings before local government agencies, boards, and commissions, and administrative action for which judicial review is provided by general law.

Addition of language in subdivision (i) is intended to toll the time for the filing of a notice of appeal until the resolution of a timely filed motion to vacate when an order has been entered based on the recommendation of a hearing officer in a family law matter. Under the prior rules, a motion to vacate was not an authorized motion to toll the time for the filing of an appeal, and too often the motion to vacate could not be heard within 30 days of the rendition of the order. This rule change permits the lower tribunal to complete its review prior to the time an appeal must be filed.

2000 Amendment. The text of subdivision (i) was moved into the main body of subdivision (h) to retain consistency in the definitional portions of the rule.

Court Commentary

1996 Amendment. Subdivision (h) was amended to ensure that a motion to correct sentence or order of probation and a motion to withdraw the plea after sentencing would postpone rendition. Subdivision (h)(3) was amended to explain that such a motion is not waived by an appeal from a judgment of guilt.

Rule 9.030. Jurisdiction of Courts

(a) Jurisdiction of Supreme Court.

(1) *Appeal Jurisdiction.*

(A) The supreme court shall review, by appeal

(i) final orders of courts imposing sentences of death;[1]

(ii) decisions of district courts of appeal declaring invalid a state statute or a provision of the state constitution.[2]

(B) If provided by general law, the supreme court shall review

(i) by appeal final orders entered in proceedings for the validation of bonds or certificates of indebtedness;[3]

(ii) action of statewide agencies relating to rates or service of utilities providing electric, gas, or telephone service.[4]

(2) *Discretionary Jurisdiction.* The discretionary jurisdiction of the supreme court may be sought to review

(A) decisions of district courts of appeal that [5]

(i) expressly declare valid a state statute;

(ii) expressly construe a provision of the state or federal constitution;

(iii) expressly affect a class of constitutional or state officers;

(iv) expressly and directly conflict with a decision of another district court of appeal or of the supreme court on the same question of law;

(v) pass upon a question certified to be of great public importance;

(vi) are certified to be in direct conflict with decisions of other district courts of appeal;

(B) orders and judgments of trial courts certified by the district court of appeal in which the appeal is pending to require immediate resolution by the supreme court, and [6]

(i) to be of great public importance, or

(ii) to have a great effect on the proper administration of justice;

(C) questions of law certified by the Supreme Court of the United States or a United States court of appeals that are determinative of the cause of action and for which there is no controlling precedent of the Supreme Court of Florida.[7]

(3) *Original Jurisdiction.* The supreme court may issue writs of prohibition to courts and all writs necessary to the complete exercise of its jurisdiction, and may issue writs of mandamus and quo warranto to state officers and state agencies. The supreme court or any justice may issue writs of habeas corpus returnable before the supreme court or any justice, a district court of appeal or any judge thereof, or any circuit judge.[8]

(b) Jurisdiction of District Courts of Appeal.

(1) *Appeal Jurisdiction.* District courts of appeal shall review, by appeal

(A) final orders of trial courts,[1 2] not directly reviewable by the supreme court or a circuit court, including county court final orders declaring invalid a state statute or provision of the state constitution;

(B) non–final orders of circuit courts as prescribed by rule 9.130;[9]

(C) administrative action if provided by general law.[2]

(2) *Certiorari Jurisdiction.*[8] The certiorari jurisdiction of district courts of appeal may be sought to review

(A) non–final orders of lower tribunals other than as prescribed by rule 9.130;

(B) final orders of circuit courts acting in their review capacity.

(3) *Original Jurisdiction.*[8] District courts of appeal may issue writs of mandamus, prohibition, quo warranto, and common law certiorari, and all writs necessary to the complete exercise of the courts' jurisdiction; or any judge thereof may issue writs of habeas corpus returnable before the court or any judge thereof, or before any circuit judge within the territorial jurisdiction of the court.

(4) *Discretionary Review.*[10] District courts of appeal, in their discretion, may review by appeal

(A) final orders of the county court, otherwise appealable to the circuit court under these rules, that the county court has certified to be of great public importance;

(B) non–final orders, otherwise appealable to the circuit court under rule 9.140(c), that the county court has certified to be of great public importance.

(c) Jurisdiction of Circuit Courts.

(1) *Appeal Jurisdiction.* The circuit courts shall review, by appeal

(A) final orders of lower tribunals as provided by general law;[1 2]

(B) non–final orders of lower tribunals as provided by general law;

(C) administrative action if provided by general law.

(2) *Certiorari Jurisdiction.*[8] The certiorari jurisdiction of circuit courts may be sought to review non-final orders of lower tribunals other than as prescribed by rule 9.130.

(3) *Original Jurisdiction.*[8] Circuit courts may issue writs of mandamus, prohibition, quo warranto, common law certiorari, and habeas corpus, and all writs necessary to the complete exercise of the courts' jurisdiction.

Amended March 27, 1980, effective April 1, 1980 (381 So.2d 1370); Nov. 26, 1980, effective Jan. 1, 1981 (391 So.2d 203); Sept. 13, 1984, effective Oct. 1, 1984 (463 So.2d 1114); Feb. 14, 1985, effective March 1, 1985 (463 So.2d 1124); July 14, 1988, effective Jan. 1, 1989 (529 So.2d 687); Dec. 30, 1988, effective Jan. 1, 1989 (536 So.2d 240); Oct. 22, 1992, effective Jan. 1, 1993 (609 So.2d 516); Oct. 12, 2000, effective Jan. 1, 2001 (780 So.2d 834); Feb. 3, 2005 (894 So.2d 202).

1 9.140: Appeal Proceedings in Criminal Cases.
2 9.110: Appeal Proceedings: Final Orders.
3 9.110(i): Validation of Bonds.
4 9.110: Appeal Proceedings: Final Orders; 9.100: Original Proceedings.
5 9.120: Discretionary Review of District Court Decisions.
6 9.125: Discretionary Review of Trial Court Orders and Judgments Certified by the District Court.
7 9.150: Certified Questions from Federal Courts.
8 9.100: Original Proceedings.
9 9.130: Appeal Proceedings: Non–Final Orders.
10 9.160: Discretionary Review of County Court Decisions.

Committee Notes

1977 Amendment. This rule replaces former rules 2.1(a)(5) and 2.2(a)(4). It sets forth the jurisdiction of the supreme court, district courts of appeal, and that portion of the jurisdiction of the circuit courts to which these rules apply. It paraphrases sections 3(b), 4(b), and, in relevant part, 5(b) of article V of the Florida Constitution. The items stating the certiorari jurisdiction of the supreme court and district courts of appeal refer to the constitutional jurisdiction popularly known as the "constitutional certiorari" jurisdiction of the supreme court and "common law certiorari" jurisdiction of the district courts of appeal. This rule is not intended to affect the substantive law governing the jurisdiction of any court and should not be considered as authority for the resolution of disputes concerning any court's jurisdiction. Its purpose is to provide a tool of reference to the practitioner so that ready reference may be made to the specific procedural rule or rules governing a particular proceeding. Footnote references have been made to the rule or rules governing proceedings invoking the listed areas of jurisdiction.

This rule does not set forth the basis for the issuance of advisory opinions by the supreme court to the governor because the power to advise rests with the justices under article IV, section 1(c), Florida Constitution, and not the supreme court as a body. The procedure governing requests from the governor for advice are set forth in rule 9.500.

The advisory committee considered and rejected as unwise a proposal to permit the chief judge of each judicial circuit to modify the applicability of these rules to that particular circuit. These rules may be modified in a particular case, of course, by an agreed joint motion of the parties granted by the court so long as the change does not affect jurisdiction.

1980 Amendment. Subdivision (a) of this rule has been extensively revised to reflect the constitutional modifications in the supreme court's jurisdiction as approved by the electorate on March 11, 1980. See art. V, § 3(b), Fla. Const. (1980). The impetus for these modifications was a burgeoning caseload and the attendant need to make more efficient use of limited appellate resources. Consistent with this purpose, revised subdivision (a) limits the supreme court's appellate, discretionary, and original jurisdiction to cases that substantially affect the law of the state. The district courts of appeal will constitute the courts of last resort for the vast majority of litigants under amended article V.

Subdivision (a)(1)(A)(i) retains the mandatory appellate jurisdiction of the supreme court to review final orders of trial courts imposing death sentences.

Subdivision (a)(1)(A)(ii) has been substantively changed in accordance with amended article V, section 3(b)(1), Florida Constitution (1980), to eliminate the court's mandatory appellate review of final orders of trial courts and decisions of district courts of appeal initially and directly passing on the validity of a state statute or a federal statute or treaty, or construing a provision of the state or federal constitution. Mandatory supreme court review under this subdivision is now limited to district court decisions "declaring invalid" a state statute or a provision of the state constitution. Jurisdiction to review final orders of trial courts in all instances enumerated in former subdivision (a)(1)(A)(ii) now reposes in the appropriate district court of appeal.

Revised subdivision (a)(1)(B) enumerates the 2 classes of cases that the supreme court may review if provided by general law. See art. V, § 3(b) (2), Fla. Const. (1980). Eliminated from the amended article V and rule is the legislative authority, never exercised, to require supreme court review of trial court orders imposing sentences of life imprisonment.

Subdivision (a)(1)(B)(i), pertaining to bond validation proceedings, replaces former subdivision (a)(1)(B)(ii). Its phraseology remains unchanged. Enabling legislation already exists for supreme court review of bond validation proceedings. See § 75.08, Fla. Stat. (1979).

Subdivision (a)(1)(B)(ii) is new. See art. V, § 3(b)(2), Fla. Const. (1980). Under the earlier constitutional scheme, the supreme court was vested with certiorari jurisdiction (which in practice was always exercised) to review orders of "commissions established by general law having statewide jurisdiction," including orders of the Florida Public Service Commission. See art. V, § 3(b)(3), Fla. Const. (1968); § 350.641, Fla. Stat. (1979). This jurisdiction has been abolished. In its stead, amended article V limits the supreme court's review of Public Service Commission orders to those "relating to rates or services of utilities providing electric, gas, or telephone service." Enabling legislation will be required to effectuate this jurisdiction. Review of Public Service Commission orders other than those relating to electric, gas, or utility cases now reposes in the appropriate district court of appeal. See art. V, § 4(b)(2), Fla. Const. (1968); Fla. R. App. P. 9.030(b)(1)(C); and § 120.68(2), Fla. Stat. (1979).

Subdivision (a)(2) has been substantially revised in accordance with amended article V, section 3(b)(3), Florida Constitution (1980), to restrict the scope of review under the supreme court's discretionary jurisdiction. Under the earlier constitution, this jurisdiction was exercised by writ of certiorari. Constitutional certiorari is abolished under amended article V. Reflecting this change, revised subdivision (a)(2) of this rule substitutes the phrase "discretionary jurisdiction" for "certiorari jurisdiction" in the predecessor rule. This discretionary jurisdiction is restricted, moreover, to 6 designated categories of district court decisions, discussed below.

Amended article V eliminates the supreme court's discretionary power to review "any interlocutory order passing upon a matter which upon final judgment would be directly appealable to the Supreme Court" as reflected in subdivision (a)(2)(B) of the predecessor rule. It also eliminates the supreme court's certiorari review of "commissions established by general law having statewide jurisdiction" as reflected in subdivision (a)(2)(C) of the predecessor rule.

Subdivision (a)(2)(A) specifies the 6 categories of district court decisions reviewable by the supreme court under its discretionary jurisdiction.

Subdivisions (a)(2)(A)(i) and (a)(2)(A)(ii) are new and pertain to matters formerly reviewable under the court's mandatory appellate jurisdiction. Under former rule 9.030(a)(1)(A)(ii), the supreme court's mandatory appellate jurisdiction could be invoked if a lower tribunal "inherently" declared a statute valid. See *Harrell's Candy Kitchen, Inc. v. Sarasota–Manatee Airport Auth.*, 111 So. 2d 439 (Fla. 1959). The 1980 amendments to article V and this subdivision require a district court to "expressly declare" a state statute valid before the supreme court's discretionary jurisdiction may be invoked.

Subdivision (a)(2)(A)(iii), pertaining to supreme court review of district court decisions affecting a class of constitutional or state officers, has been renumbered. It tracks the language of the predecessor constitution and rule, with the addition of the restrictive word "expressly" found in amended article V.

Subdivision (a)(2)(A)(iv) represents the most radical change in the supreme court's discretionary jurisdiction. The predecessor article V vested the supreme court with power to review district court decisions "in direct conflict with a decision of any district court of appeal or of the Supreme Court on the same point of law." These cases comprised the overwhelming bulk of the court's caseload and gave rise to an intricate body of case law interpreting the requirements for discretionary conflict review. With the enunciation of the "record proper rule" in *Foley v. Weaver Drugs, Inc.*, 177 So. 2d 221 (Fla. 1965), the supreme court extended its discretionary review in instances of discernible conflict to district court decisions affirming without opinion the orders of trial courts. Amended article V abolishes the Foley doctrine by requiring an "express" as well as a "direct" conflict of district court decisions as a prerequisite to supreme court review. The new article also terminates supreme court jurisdiction over purely intradistrict conflicts, the resolution of which is addressed in rule 9.331.

Subdivision (a)(2)(A)(v) substitutes the phrase "great public importance" for "great public interest" in the predecessor constitution and rule. The change was to recognize the fact that some legal issues may have "great public importance," but may not be sufficiently known by the public to have "great public interest."

Subdivision (a)(2)(A)(vi) is new and tracks the language of article V, section 3(b)(4), Florida Constitution (1980).

Subdivisions (a)(2)(B) and (a)(2)(C) are new. See art. V, §§ 3(b)(5), (3)(b)(6), Fla. Const. (1980). Certification procedures under these subdivisions are addressed in rule 9.125 and rule 9.150, respectively.

Subdivision (a)(3) is identical to the predecessor article V and rule, except it limits the issuance of writs of prohibition to "courts" rather than "courts and commissions" and limits the issuance of writs of mandamus and quo warranto to "state agencies" rather than "agencies."

1984 Amendment. Subdivision (b)(4) was added to implement legislation authorizing district courts of appeal discretion to review by appeal orders and judgments of county courts certified to be of great public importance.

1992 Amendment. Subdivision (c)(1)(B) was amended to reflect correctly that the appellate jurisdiction of circuit courts extended to all non-final orders of lower tribunals as prescribed by rule 9.130, and not only those defined in subdivision (a)(3) of that rule.

Subdivision (c)(1)(C) was amended to reflect the jurisdiction conferred on circuit courts by article V, section 5, Florida Constitution, which provides that "[t]hey shall have the power of direct review of administrative action prescribed by general law."

2000 Amendment. Subdivision (c)(1)(B) was amended to reflect that the appellate jurisdiction of circuit courts is prescribed by general law and not by rule 9.130, as clarified in *Blore v. Fierro*, 636 So. 2d 1329 (Fla. 1994).

Rule 9.040. General Provisions

(a) Complete Determination. In all proceedings a court shall have such jurisdiction as may be necessary for a complete determination of the cause.

(b) Forum.

(1) If a proceeding is commenced in an inappropriate court, that court shall transfer the cause to an appropriate court.

(2) After a lower tribunal renders an order transferring venue, the appropriate court to review otherwise reviewable non-final orders is as follows:

(A) After rendition of an order transferring venue, the appropriate court to review the non-final venue order, all other reviewable non-final orders rendered prior to or simultaneously with the venue order, any order staying, vacating, or modifying the transfer of venue order, or an order dismissing a cause for failure to pay venue transfer fees, is the court that would review non-final orders in the cause, had venue not been transferred.

(B) After rendition of an order transferring venue, the appropriate court to review any subsequently rendered reviewable non-final order, except for those orders listed in subdivision (b)(2)(A), is the court which would review the order, if the cause had been filed in the lower tribunal to which venue was transferred.

(C) The clerk of the lower tribunal whose order is being reviewed shall perform the procedures required by these provisions regarding transfer of venue, including accepting and filing a notice of appeal. If necessary to facilitate non-final review, after an order transferring venue has been rendered, the clerk of the lower tribunal shall copy and retain such portions of the record as are necessary for review of the non-final order. If the file of the cause has been transferred to the transferee tribunal before the notice of appeal is filed in the transferring tribunal, the clerk of the transferee tribunal shall copy and transmit to the transferring tribunal such portions of the record as are necessary for review of the non-final order.

(c) Remedy. If a party seeks an improper remedy, the cause shall be treated as if the proper remedy had been sought; provided that it shall not be the responsibility of the court to seek the proper remedy.

(d) Amendment. At any time in the interest of justice, the court may permit any part of the proceeding to be amended so that it may be disposed of on the merits. In the absence of amendment, the court may disregard any procedural error or defect that does not adversely affect the substantial rights of the parties.

(e) Assignments of Error. Assignments of error are neither required nor permitted.

(f) Filing Fees. Filing fees may be paid by check or money order.

(g) Clerks' Duties. On filing of a notice prescribed by these rules, the clerk shall forthwith transmit the fee and a certified copy of the notice, showing the date of filing, to the court. If jurisdiction has been invoked under rule 9.030(a)(2)(A)(v) or (a)(2)(A)(vi), or if a certificate has been issued by a district court under rule 9.030(a)(2)(B), the clerk of the district court of appeal shall transmit copies of the certificate and decision or order and any suggestion, replies, or appendices with the certified copy of the notice. Notices to review final orders of county and circuit courts in civil cases shall be recorded.

(h) Non–Jurisdictional Matters. Failure of a clerk or a party timely to file fees or additional copies of notices or petitions or the conformed copy of the order or orders designated in the notice of appeal shall not be jurisdictional; provided that such failure may be the subject of appropriate sanction.

(i) Requests to Determine Confidentiality of Appellate Court Records. Requests to determine the confidentiality of appellate records are governed by Florida Rule of Judicial Administration 2.420.

Amended March 27, 1980, effective April 1, 1980 (381 So.2d 1370); Oct. 22, 1992, effective Jan. 1, 1993 (609 So.2d 516); Nov. 22, 1996, effective Jan. 1, 1997 (685 So.2d 773); Oct. 12, 2000, effective Jan. 1, 2001 (780 So.2d 834); Aug. 29, 2002, effective Jan. 1, 2003 (827 So.2d 888); March 18, 2010 (31 So.3d 756).

Committee Notes

1977 Amendment. This rule sets forth several miscellaneous matters of general applicability.

Subdivision (a) is derived from the last sentence of former rule 2.1(a)(5)(a), which concerned direct appeals to the supreme court. This provision is intended to guarantee that once the jurisdiction of any court is properly invoked, the court may determine the entire case to the extent permitted by substantive law. This rule does not extend or limit the constitutional or statutory jurisdiction of any court.

Subdivisions (b) and (c) implement article V, section 2(a), Florida Constitution. Former rule 2.1(a)(5)(d) authorized transfer if an improper forum was chosen, but the former rules did not address the problem of improper remedies being sought. The advisory committee does not consider it to be the responsibility of the court to seek the proper remedy for any party, but a court may not deny relief because a different remedy is proper. Under these provisions a case will not be dismissed automatically because a party seeks an improper remedy or invokes the jurisdiction of the wrong court. The court must instead treat the case as if the proper remedy had been sought and transfer it to the court having jurisdiction. All filings in the case have the same legal effect as though originally filed in the court to which transfer is made. This rule is intended to supersede *Nellen v. State*, 226 So.2d 354 (Fla. 1st DCA 1969), in which a petition for a common law writ of certiorari was dismissed by the district court of appeal because review was properly by appeal to the appropriate circuit court, and *Engel v. City of North Miami*, 115 So.2d 1 (Fla. 1959), in which a petition for a writ of certiorari was dismissed because review should have been by appeal. Under this rule, a petition for a writ of certiorari should be treated as a notice of appeal, if timely.

Subdivision (d) is the appellate procedure counterpart of the harmless error statute, section 59.041, Florida Statutes (1975). It incorporates the concept contained in former rule 3.2(c), which provided that deficiencies in the form or substance of a notice of appeal were not grounds for dismissal, absent a clear showing that the adversary had been misled or prejudiced. Amendments should be liberally allowed under this rule, including pleadings in the lower tribunal, if it would not result in irremediable prejudice.

Subdivision (e) is intended to make clear that assignments of error have been abolished by these rules. It is not intended to extend the scope of review to matters other than judicial acts. If less than the entire record as defined in rule 9.200(a)(1) is to be filed, rule 9.200(a)(2) requires service of a statement of the judicial acts for which review is sought. This requirement also applies under rule 9.140(d). As explained in the commentary accompanying those provisions, such a statement does not have the same legal effect as an assignment of error under the former rules.

Subdivision (f) permits payment of filing fees by check or money order and carries forward the substance of former rule 3.2(a), which allowed payments in cash.

Subdivision (g) is derived from former rules 3.2(a) and 3.2(e). Under these rules, notices and fees are filed in the lower tribunal unless specifically stated otherwise. The clerk must transmit the notice and fees immediately. This requirement replaces the provision of the former rules that the notice be transmitted within 5 days. The advisory committee was of the view that no reason existed for any delays. The term "forthwith" should not be construed to prevent the clerk from delaying transmittal of a notice of criminal appeal for which no fee has been filed for the period of time necessary to obtain an order regarding solvency for appellate purposes and the appointment of the public defender for an insolvent defendant. This provision requires recording of the notice if review of a final trial court order in a civil case is sought. When supreme court jurisdiction is invoked on the basis of the certification of a question of great public interest, the clerk of the district court of appeal is required to transmit a copy of the certificate and the decision to the court along with the notice and fees.

Subdivision (h) is intended to implement the decision in *Williams v. State*, 324 So.2d 74 (Fla. 1975), in which it was held that only the timely filing of the notice of appeal is jurisdictional. The proviso permits the court to impose sanctions if there is a failure to timely file fees or copies of the notice or petition.

The advisory committee considered and rejected as too difficult to implement a proposal of the bar committee that the style of a cause should remain the same as in the lower tribunal.

It should be noted that these rules abolish the practice of permitting Florida trial courts to certify questions to an appellate court. The former rules relating to the internal government of the courts and the creation of the advisory committee have been eliminated as irrelevant to appellate procedure. At its conference of June 27, however, the court unanimously voted to establish a committee to, among other things, prepare a set of administrative rules to incorporate matters of internal governance formerly contained in the appellate rules. The advisory committee has recommended that its existence be continued by the supreme court.

1980 Amendment. Subdivision (g) was amended to direct the clerk of the district court to transmit copies of the district court decision, the certificate, the order of the trial court, and the suggestion, replies, and appendices in all cases certified to the supreme court under rule 9.030(a)(2)(B) or otherwise certified under rule 9.030(a)(2)(A)(v) or (a)(2)(A)(vi).

1992 Amendment. Subdivision (h) was amended to provide that the failure to attach conformed copies of the order or orders designated in a notice of appeal as is now required by rules 9.110(d), 9.130(c), and 9.160(c) would not be a jurisdictional defect, but could be the basis of appropriate sanction by the court if the conformed copies were not included with the notice of appeal.

2000 Amendment. In the event non-final or interlocutory review of a reviewable, non-final order is sought, new subdivision 9.040(b)(2) specifies which court should review such order, after rendition of an order transferring venue to another lower tribunal outside the appellate district of the transferor lower tribunal. It is intended to change and clarify the rules announced in *Vasilinda v. Lozano*, 631 So.2d 1082 (Fla. 1994), and *Cottingham v. State*, 672 So.2d 28 (Fla. 1996). The subdivision makes the time a venue order is rendered the critical factor in determining which court should review such non-final orders, rather than the time fees are paid, or the time the file is received by the transferee lower tribunal, and it applies equally to civil as well as criminal cases. If review is sought of the order transferring venue, as well as other reviewable non-final orders rendered before the change of venue order is rendered, or ones rendered simultaneously with it, review should be by the court that reviews such orders from the transferring lower tribunal. If review is sought of reviewable, non-final orders rendered after the time the venue order is rendered, review should be by the court that reviews such orders from the transferee lower tribunal. The only exceptions are for review of orders staying or vacating the transfer of venue order, or an order dismissing the cause for failure to pay fees, which should be reviewed by the court that reviews orders from the transferring lower tribunal. This paragraph is not intended to apply to review of reviewable non-final orders, for which non-final or interlocutory review is not timely sought or perfected.

Rule 9.050. Maintaining Privacy of Personal Data

(a) Application. Unless otherwise required by another rule of court or permitted by leave of court, all briefs, petitions, replies, appendices, motions, notices, stipulations, and responses and any attachment thereto filed with the court shall comply with the requirements of Florida Rule of Judicial Administration 2.425.

(b) Limitation. This rule does not require redaction of personal data from the record.

(c) Motions Not Restricted. This rule does not restrict a party's right to move to file documents under seal.

Added Nov. 3, 2011, effective, *nunc pro tunc*, Oct. 1, 2011 (78 So.3d 1045).

Rule 9.100. Original Proceedings

(a) Applicability. This rule applies to those proceedings that invoke the jurisdiction of the courts described in rules 9.030(a)(3), (b)(2), (b)(3), (c)(2), and (c)(3) for the issuance of writs of mandamus, prohibition, quo warranto, certiorari, and habeas corpus, and all writs necessary to the complete exercise of the courts' jurisdiction; and for review of non-final administrative action.

(b) Commencement; Parties. The original jurisdiction of the court shall be invoked by filing a petition, accompanied by any filing fees prescribed by law, with the clerk of the court having jurisdiction. The parties to the proceeding shall be as follows:

(1) If the petition seeks review of an order entered by a lower tribunal, all parties to the proceeding in the lower tribunal who are not named as petitioners shall be named as respondents.

(2) If the original jurisdiction of the court is invoked to enforce a private right, the proceedings shall not be brought on the relation of the state.

(3) The following officials shall not be named as respondents to a petition, but a copy of the petition shall be served on the official who issued the order that is the subject of the petition:

(A) Judges of lower tribunals shall not be named as respondents to petitions for certiorari;

(B) Individual members of agencies, boards, and commissions of local governments shall not be named as respondents to petitions for review of quasi-judicial action; and

(C) Officers presiding over administrative proceedings, such as hearing officers and administrative law judges, shall not be named as respondents to petitions for review of non-final agency action.

(c) Petitions for Certiorari; Review of Non–Final Agency Action; Review of Prisoner Disciplinary Action. The following shall be filed within 30 days of rendition of the order to be reviewed:

(1) A petition for certiorari.

(2) A petition to review quasi-judicial action of agencies, boards, and commissions of local government, which action is not directly appealable under any other provision of general law but may be subject to review by certiorari.

(3) A petition to review non-final agency action under the Administrative Procedure Act.

(4) A petition challenging an order of the Department of Corrections entered in prisoner disciplinary proceedings.

(d) Orders Excluding or Granting Access to Press or Public.

(1) A petition to review an order excluding the press or public from, or granting the press or public access to, any proceeding, any part of a proceeding, or any records of the judicial branch, shall be filed in the court as soon as practicable following rendition of the order to be reviewed, if written, or announcement of the order to be reviewed, if oral, but no later than 30 days after rendition of the order. A copy of the petition shall be furnished to the person (or chairperson of the collegial administrative agency) issuing the order, the parties to the proceeding, and any affected non-parties, as defined in Florida Rule of Judicial Administration 2.420.

(2) The court shall immediately consider the petition to determine whether a stay of proceedings in the lower tribunal or the order under review is appropriate and, on its own motion or that of any party, the court may order a stay on such conditions as may be appropriate. Any motion to stay an order granting access to a proceeding, any part of a proceeding, or any records of the judicial branch made under this subdivision must include a signed certification by the movant that the motion is made in good faith and is supported by a sound factual and legal basis. Pending the court's ruling on the motion to stay, the clerk of the court and the lower tribunal shall treat as confidential those proceedings or those records of the judicial branch that are the subject of the motion to stay.

(3) Review of orders under this subdivision shall be expedited.

(e) Petitions for Writs of Mandamus and Prohibition Directed to a Judge or Lower Tribunal. When a petition for a writ of mandamus or prohibition seeks a writ directed to a judge or lower tribunal, the following procedures apply:

(1) *Caption.* The name of the judge or lower tribunal shall be omitted from the caption. The caption shall bear the name of the petitioner and other parties to the proceeding in the lower tribunal who are not petitioners shall be named in the caption as respondents.

(2) *Parties.* The judge or the lower tribunal is a formal party to the petition for mandamus or prohibition and must be named as such in the body of the petition (but not in the caption). The petition must be served on all parties, including any judge or lower tribunal who is a formal party to the petition.

(3) *Response.* Following the issuance of an order pursuant to subdivision (h), the responsibility for responding to a petition is that of the litigant opposing the relief requested in the petition. Unless otherwise specifically ordered, the judge or lower tribunal has no obligation to file a response. The judge or lower tribunal retains the discretion to file a separate response should the judge or lower tribunal choose to do so. The absence of a separate response by the judge or lower tribunal shall not be deemed to admit the allegations of the petition.

(f) Review Proceedings in Circuit Court.

(1) *Applicability.* The following additional requirements apply to those proceedings that invoke the jurisdiction of the circuit court described in rules 9.030(c)(2) and (c)(3) to the extent that the petition involves review of judicial or quasi-judicial action.

(2) *Caption.* The caption shall contain a statement that the petition is filed pursuant to this subdivision.

(3) *Duties of the Circuit Court Clerk.* When a petition prescribed by this subdivision is filed, the circuit court clerk shall forthwith transmit the petition to the administrative judge of the appellate division, or other appellate judge or judges as prescribed by

administrative order, for a determination as to whether an order to show cause should be issued.

(4) *Default*. The clerk of the circuit court shall not enter a default in a proceeding where a petition has been filed pursuant to this subdivision.

(g) Petition. The caption shall contain the name of the court and the name and designation of all parties on each side. The petition shall not exceed 50 pages in length and shall contain

(1) the basis for invoking the jurisdiction of the court;

(2) the facts on which the petitioner relies;

(3) the nature of the relief sought; and

(4) argument in support of the petition and appropriate citations of authority.

If the petition seeks an order directed to a lower tribunal, the petition shall be accompanied by an appendix as prescribed by rule 9.220, and the petition shall contain references to the appropriate pages of the supporting appendix.

(h) Order to Show Cause. If the petition demonstrates a preliminary basis for relief, a departure from the essential requirements of law that will cause material injury for which there is no adequate remedy by appeal, or that review of final administrative action would not provide an adequate remedy, the court may issue an order either directing the respondent to show cause, within the time set by the court, why relief should not be granted or directing the respondent to otherwise file, within the time set by the court, a response to the petition. In prohibition proceedings, the issuance of an order directing the respondent to show cause shall stay further proceedings in the lower tribunal.

(i) Record. A record shall not be transmitted to the court unless ordered.

(j) Response. Within the time set by the court, the respondent may serve a response, which shall not exceed 50 pages in length and which shall include argument in support of the response, appropriate citations of authority, and references to the appropriate pages of the supporting appendices.

(k) Reply. Within 20 days thereafter or such other time set by the court, the petitioner may serve a reply, which shall not exceed 15 pages in length, and supplemental appendix.

(*l*) General Requirements; Fonts. The lettering in all petitions, responses, and replies filed under this rule shall be black and in distinct type, double-spaced, with margins no less than 1 inch. Lettering in script or type made in imitation of handwriting shall not be permitted. Footnotes and quotations may be single spaced and shall be in the same size type, with the same spacing between characters, as the text. Computer-generated petitions, responses, and replies shall be submitted in either Times New Roman 14–point font or Courier New 12–point font. All computer-generated petitions, responses, and replies shall contain a certificate of compliance signed by counsel, or the party if unrepresented, certifying that the petition, response, or reply complies with the font requirements of this rule. The certificate of compliance shall be contained in the petition, response, or reply immediately following the certificate of service.

Amended March 27, 1980, effective April 1, 1980 (381 So.2d 1370); July 3, 1980, effective Jan. 1, 1981 (387 So.2d 920); Nov. 26, 1980, effective Jan. 1, 1981 (391 So.2d 203); July 14, 1988, effective Jan. 1, 1989 (529 So.2d 687); Dec. 30, 1988, effective Jan. 1, 1989 (536 So.2d 240); Oct. 22, 1992, effective Jan. 1, 1993 (609 So.2d 516); Nov. 22, 1996, effective Jan. 1, 1997 (685 So.2d 773); Nov. 24, 1999, effective Jan. 1, 2000 (760 So.2d 74); Oct. 12, 2000, effective Jan. 1, 2001 (780 So.2d 834); March 18, 2010 (31 So.3d 756); Nov. 3, 2011, effective Jan. 1, 2012 (75 So.3d 239); Nov. 6, 2014, effective Jan. 1, 2015 (2014 WL 5714099).

Committee Notes

1977 Amendment. This rule replaces former rule 4.5, except that the procedures applicable to supreme court review of decisions of the district courts of appeal on writs of constitutional certiorari are set forth in rule 9.120; and supreme court direct review of administrative action on writs of certiorari is governed by rule 9.100. This rule governs proceedings invoking the supreme court's jurisdiction to review an interlocutory order passing on a matter where, on final judgment, a direct appeal would lie in the supreme court. The procedures set forth in this rule implement the supreme court's decision in *Burnsed v. Seaboard Coastline R.R.*, 290 So.2d 13 (Fla. 1974), that such interlocutory review rests solely within its discretionary certiorari jurisdiction under article V, section 3(b)(3), Florida Constitution, and that its jurisdiction would be exercised only when, on the peculiar circumstances of a particular case, the public interest required it. This rule abolishes the wasteful current practice in such cases of following the procedures governing appeals, with the supreme court treating such appeals as petitions for the writ of certiorari. This rule requires that these cases be prosecuted as petitions for the writ of certiorari.

This rule also provides the procedures necessary to implement the Administrative Procedure Act, section 120.68(1), Florida Statutes (Supp. 1976), which provides for judicial review of non-final agency action "if review of the final agency decision would not provide an adequate remedy." It was the opinion of the advisory committee that such a right of review is guaranteed by the statute and is not dependent on a court rule, because article V, section 4(b)(2), Florida Constitution provides for legislative grants of jurisdiction to the district courts to review administrative action without regard to the finality of that action. The advisory committee was also of the view that the right of review guaranteed by the statute is no broader than the generally available common law writ of certiorari, although the statutory remedy would prevent resort to an extraordinary writ.

Subdivisions (b) and (c) set forth the procedure for commencing an extraordinary writ proceeding.

The time for filing a petition for common law certiorari is jurisdictional. If common law certiorari is sought to review an order issued by a lower tribunal consisting of more than 1 person, a copy of the petition should be furnished to the chairperson of that tribunal.

Subdivision (d) sets forth the procedure for appellate review of orders excluding the press or public from access to proceedings or records in the lower tribunal. It establishes an entirely new and independent means of review in the district courts, in recognition of the decision in *English v. McCrary*, 348 So.2d 293 (Fla. 1977), to the effect that a writ of prohibition is not available as a means to obtain review of such orders. Copies of the notice must be served on all parties to the proceeding in the lower tribunal, as well as the person who, or the chairperson of the agency that, issued the order.

No provision has been made for an automatic stay of proceedings, but the district court is directed to consider the appropriateness of a stay immediately on the notice being filed. Ordinarily an order excluding the press and public will be entered well in advance of the closed proceedings in the lower tribunal, so that there will be no interruption of the proceeding by reason of the appellate review. In the event a challenged order is entered immediately before or during the course of a proceeding and it appears that a disruption of the proceeding will be prejudicial to 1 or more parties, the reviewing court on its own motion or at the request of any party shall determine whether to enter a stay or to allow the lower tribunal to proceed pending review of the challenged order. *See State ex rel. Miami Herald Publishing Co. v. McIntosh*, 340 So.2d 904, 911 (Fla. 1977).

This new provision implements the "strict procedural safeguards" requirement laid down by the United States Supreme Court in *National Socialist Party of America v. Village of Skokie*, 432 U.S. 43, 97 S.Ct. 2205, 53 L.Ed.2d 96 (1977). In that case the Court held that state restraints imposed on activities protected by the First Amendment must be either immediately reviewable or subject to a stay pending review.

Subdivision (e) sets forth the contents of the initial pleading. The party seeking relief must file a petition stating the authority by which the court has jurisdiction of the case, the relevant facts, the relief sought, and argument supported by citations of authority. This rule does not allow the petitioner to file a brief. Any argument or citations of authority that the petitioner desires to present to the court must be contained in the petition. This change in procedure is intended to eliminate the wasteful current practice of filing repetitive petitions and briefs. Under subdivision (g) no record is required to be filed unless the court so orders, but under subdivision (e) the petitioner must file an appendix to the petition containing conformed copies of the order to be reviewed and other relevant material, including portions of the record, if a record exists. The appendix should also contain any documents that support the allegations of fact contained in the petition. A lack of supporting documents may, of course, be considered by the court in exercising its discretion not to issue an order to show cause.

Under subdivisions (f), (h), and (i), if the allegations of the petition, if true, would constitute grounds for relief, the court may exercise its discretion to issue an order requiring the respondent to show cause why the requested relief should not be granted. A single responsive pleading (without a brief) may then be served, accompanied by a supplemental appendix, within the time period set by the court in its order to show cause. The petitioner is then allowed 20 days to serve a reply and supplemental appendix, unless the court sets another time. It should be noted that the times for response and reply are computed by reference to service rather than filing. This practice is consistent throughout these rules except for initial, jurisdictional filings. The emphasis on service, of course, does not relieve counsel of the responsibility for filing original documents with the court as required by rule 9.420(b); it merely affects the time measurements.

Except as provided automatically under subdivision (f), a stay pending resolution of the original proceeding may be obtained under rule 9.310.

Transmittal of the record under order of the court under subdivision (g) shall be in accordance with the instructions and times set forth in the order.

1980 Amendment. The rule was amended by deleting its reference to former rule 9.030(a)(2)(B) to reflect the 1980 revisions to article V, section 3(b), Florida Constitution that eliminated supreme court review by certiorari of non-final orders that would have been appealable if they had been final orders. The procedures applicable to discretionary supreme court review of district court decisions under rule 9.030(a)(2)(A) are governed by rule 9.120. The procedures applicable to supreme court discretionary review of trial court orders and judgments certified by the district courts under rule 9.030(a)(2)(B) are set forth in rule 9.125.

Subdivision (d) was amended to delete references to the district courts of appeal as the proper court for review of orders excluding the press and public, because the appropriate court could also be a circuit court or the supreme court.

1992 Amendment. Subdivision (b) was amended to add 2 provisions clarifying designation of parties to original proceedings. The first change eliminates the practice of bringing original proceedings on the relation of the state and instead requires that if a private right is being enforced, an action must be brought in the names of the parties. Second, this subdivision now requires that all parties not named as petitioners be included in the style as respondents, consistent with rules 9.020(f)(3) and (f)(4).

Subdivision (c) was amended to eliminate the practice of naming lower court judges, members of administrative bodies, and hearing officers as respondents in petitions for certiorari and for review of non-final agency action. Such individuals still are to be served a copy of the petition, but the amendment is to eliminate any suggestion that they are parties or adverse to the petitioner.

Subdivision (c) also was amended to reflect that review of final administrative action, taken by local government agencies, boards, and commissions acting in a quasi-judicial capacity, is subject to the requirement that the petition for writ of certiorari be filed within 30 days of rendition of the order to be reviewed.

Subdivision (e) was amended to require that the petition, the jurisdictional document, identify all parties on each side to assist the court in identifying any potential conflicts and to identify all parties to the proceeding as required by subdivision (b) of this rule. Additionally, this subdivision was amended to require, consistent with rule 9.210(b)(3), that the petition make references to the appropriate pages of the appendix that is required to accompany the petition.

Subdivision (f) was amended to add the existing requirement in the law that a petition must demonstrate not only that there has been a departure from the essential requirements of law, but also that that departure will cause material injury for which there is no adequate remedy by appeal. This subdivision, without amendment, suggested that it established a standard other than that recognized by Florida decisional law.

Subdivision (h) was amended to require that any response, like the petition, contain references to the appropriate pages of appendices, consistent with subdivision (f) of this rule and rules 9.210(b)(3) and 9.210(c).

1996 Amendment. The reference to "common law" certiorari in subdivision (c)(1) was removed so as to make clear that the 30–day filing limit applies to all petitions for writ of certiorari.

Subdivision (c)(4) is new and pertains to review formerly available under rule 1.630. It provides that a prisoner's petition for extraordinary relief, within the original jurisdiction of the circuit court under rule 9.030(c)(3) must be filed within 30 days after final disposition of the prisoner disciplinary proceedings conducted through the administrative grievance process under chapter 33, Florida Administrative Code. *See Jones v. Florida Department of Corrections*, 615 So. 2d 798 (Fla. 1st DCA 1993).

Subdivision (e) was added, and subsequent subdivisions re-lettered, in order to alter the procedural requirements placed or apparently placed on lower court judges in prohibition and mandamus proceedings. The duty to respond to an Order to Show Cause is expressly placed on the party opposing the relief requested in the petition, and any suggestion of a duty to respond on the part of the lower court judge is removed. The lower court judge retains the option to file a response. In those circumstances in which a response from the lower tribunal is desirable, the court may so order.

Subdivision (f) was added to clarify that in extraordinary proceedings to review lower tribunal action this rule, and not Florida Rule of Civil Procedure 1.630, applies and to specify the duties of the clerk in such proceedings, and to provide a mechanism for alerting the clerk to the necessity of following these procedures. If the proceeding before the circuit court is or may be evidentiary in nature, then the procedures of the Florida Rules of Civil Procedure should be followed.

1999 Amendment. Page limits were added to impose text limitations on petitions, responses and replies consistent with the text limitations applicable to briefs under Rule 9.210.

2010 Amendment. Subdivision (d) is revised to allow review not only of orders that deny access to records of the judicial branch or judicial proceedings, but also those orders that deny motions to seal or otherwise grant access to such records or proceedings claimed to be confidential. This revision is intended to recognize and balance the equal importance of the constitutional right of privacy, which includes confidentiality, and the constitutional right of access to judicial records and proceedings. The previous rule allowed review of orders denying access only "if the proceedings or records are not required by law to be confidential." This provision is eliminated because it is unworkable in that such a determination of what is required by law to be confidential usually concerns the merits of whether the proceedings or records should be confidential in the first instance. Outer time limits for seeking review are added. Subdivision (d)(2) is revised to provide continued confidentiality of judicial proceedings and records to which the order under review has granted access upon the filing of a motion to stay that order until the court rules on the motion to stay. The former subdivision (d)(3) concerning oral argument is deleted as unnecessary in light of Rule 9.320. New subdivision (d)(3) is a recognition of the public policy that favors expedited review of orders denying access and the provision for expedited review in Florida Rule of Judicial Administration 2.420.

2010 Note. As provided in Rule 9.040, request to determine the confidentiality of appellate court records are governed by Florida Rule of Judicial Administration 2.420.

Court Commentary

2000. As to computer-generated petitions, responses, and replies, strict font requirements were imposed in subdivision (*l*) for at least three reasons:

First and foremost, appellate petitions, responses, and replies are public records that the people have a right to inspect. The clear policy of the Florida Supreme Court is that advances in technology should benefit the people whenever possible by lowering financial and physical barriers to public record inspection. The Court's eventual goal is to make all public records widely and readily available, especially via the Internet. Unlike paper documents, electronic documents on the Internet will not display properly on all computers if they are set in fonts that are unusual. In some instances, such electronic documents may even be unreadable. Thus, the Court adopted the policy that all computer-generated appellate petitions, responses, and replies be filed in one of two fonts—either Times New Roman 14–point or Courier New 12–point—that are commonplace on computers with Internet connections. This step will help ensure that the right to inspect public records on the Internet will be genuinely available to the largest number of people.

Second, Florida's court system as a whole is working toward the day when electronic filing of all court documents will be an everyday reality. Though the technology involved in electronic filing is changing rapidly, it is clear that the Internet is the single most significant factor influencing the development of this technology. Electronic filing must be compatible with Internet standards as they evolve over time. It is imperative for the legal profession to become accustomed to using electronic document formats that are most consistent with the Internet.

Third, the proliferation of vast new varieties of fonts in recent years poses a real threat that page-limitation rules can be circumvented through computerized typesetting. The only way to prevent this is to establish an enforceable rule on standards for font use. The subject font requirements are most consistent with this purpose and the other two purposes noted above.

Subdivision (*l*) was also amended to require that immediately after the certificate of service in computer-generated petitions, responses, and replies, counsel (or the party if unrepresented) shall sign a certificate of compliance with the font standards set forth in this rule for computer-generated petitions, responses, and replies.

Rule 9.110. Appeal Proceedings to Review Final Orders of Lower Tribunals and Orders Granting New Trial in Jury and Non–jury Cases

(a) Applicability. This rule applies to those proceedings that

(1) invoke the appeal jurisdiction of the courts described in rules 9.030(a)(1), (b)(1)(A), and (c)(1)(A);

(2) seek review of administrative action described in rules 9.030(b)(1)(C) and (c)(1)(C); and

(3) seek review of orders granting a new trial in jury and non-jury civil and criminal cases described in rules 9.130(a)(4) and 9.140(c)(1)(C).

(b) Commencement. Jurisdiction of the court under this rule shall be invoked by filing a notice, accompanied by any filing fees prescribed by law, with the clerk of the lower tribunal within 30 days of rendition of the order to be reviewed, except as provided in rule 9.140(c)(3).

(c) Exception; Administrative Action. In an appeal to review final orders of lower administrative tribunals, the appellant shall file the notice with the clerk of the lower administrative tribunal within 30 days of rendition of the order to be reviewed, and shall also file a copy of the notice, accompanied by any filing fees prescribed by law, with the clerk of the court.

(d) Notice of Appeal. The notice of appeal shall be substantially in the form prescribed by rule 9.900(a). The caption shall contain the name of the lower tribunal, the name and designation of at least 1 party on each side, and the case number in the lower tribunal. The notice shall contain the name of the court to which the appeal is taken, the date of rendition, and the nature of the order to be reviewed. Except in criminal cases, a conformed copy of the order or orders designated in the notice of appeal shall be attached to the notice together with any order entered on a timely motion postponing rendition of the order or orders appealed.

(e) Record. Within 50 days of filing the notice, the clerk shall prepare the record prescribed by rule 9.200 and serve copies of the index on all parties. Within 110 days of filing the notice, the clerk shall electronically transmit the record to the court.

(f) Briefs. Appellant's initial brief shall be served within 70 days of filing the notice. Additional briefs shall be served as prescribed by rule 9.210.

(g) Cross–Appeal. An appellee may cross-appeal by serving a notice within 10 days of service of the appellant's timely filed notice of appeal or within the time prescribed for filing a notice of appeal, whichever is later. The notice of cross-appeal, accompanied by any filing fees prescribed by law, shall be filed either before service or immediately thereafter in the same manner as the notice of appeal.

(h) Scope of Review. The court may review any ruling or matter occurring before filing of the notice. Multiple final orders may be reviewed by a single notice, if the notice is timely filed as to each such order.

(i) Exception; Bond Validation Proceedings. If the appeal is from an order in a proceeding to validate bonds or certificates of indebtedness, the record shall not be transmitted unless ordered by the supreme court. Appellant's initial brief, accompanied by an appendix as prescribed by rule 9.220, shall be served within 20 days of filing the notice. Additional briefs shall be served as prescribed by rule 9.210.

(j) Exception; Appeal Proceedings from District Courts of Appeal. If the appeal is from an order of a district court of appeal, the clerk shall electronically transmit the record to the court within 60 days of filing the notice. Appellant's initial brief shall be served within 20 days of filing the notice. Additional briefs shall be served as prescribed by rule 9.210.

(k) Review of Partial Final Judgments. Except as otherwise provided herein, partial final judgments are reviewable either on appeal from the partial final judgment or on appeal from the final judgment in the entire case. A partial final judgment, other than one that disposes of an entire case as to any party, is one that disposes of a separate and distinct cause of action that is not interdependent with other pleaded claims. If a partial final judgment totally disposes of an entire case as to any party, it must be appealed within 30 days of rendition.

(*l*) Premature Appeals. Except as provided in rule 9.020(i), if a notice of appeal is filed before rendition of a final order, the appeal shall be subject to dismissal as premature. However, the lower tribunal retains jurisdiction to render a final order, and if a final order is rendered before dismissal of the premature appeal, the premature notice of appeal shall be considered effective to vest jurisdiction in the court to review the final order. Before dismissal, the court in its discretion may grant the parties additional time to obtain a final order from the lower tribunal.

(m) Exception; Insurance Coverage Appeals. Judgments that determine the existence or nonexistence of insurance coverage in cases in which a claim has been made against an insured and coverage thereof is disputed by the insurer may be reviewed either by the method prescribed in this rule or that in rule 9.130.

Amended March 27, 1980, effective April 1, 1980 (381 So.2d 1370); Nov. 26, 1980, effective Jan. 1, 1981 (391 So.2d 203); Sept. 13, 1984, effective Jan. 1, 1985 (463 So.2d 1114); Oct. 17, 1988 (536 So.2d 198); Oct. 22, 1992, effective Jan. 1, 1993 (609 So.2d 516); Nov. 22, 1996, effective Jan. 1, 1997 (685 So.2d 773); June 24, 1999, effective July 1, 1999 (756 So.2d 27); Oct. 23, 2003 (858 So.2d 1013); June 30, 2005 (907 So.2d 1161); July 6, 2006 (934 So.2d 438); Jan. 29, 2009 (1 So.3d 166); Nov. 3, 2011, effective Jan. 1, 2012 (75 So.3d 239); March 1, 2012 (84 So.3d 224); Oct. 18, 2012, effective Dec. 1, 2012, April 1, 2013, Oct. 1, 2013 (102 So.3d 451); Feb. 20, 2014, effective *nunc pro tunc* March 1, 2012 (133 So.3d 927); Nov. 6, 2014, effective Jan. 1, 2015 (2014 WL 5714099).

Committee Notes

1977 Amendment. This rule replaces former rules 3.1, 3.5, 4.1, 4.3, 4.4, and 4.7. It applies when (1) a final order has been entered by a court or administrative agency; (2) a motion for a new trial in a jury case is granted; or (3) a motion for rehearing in a non-jury case is granted and the lower tribunal orders new testimony. It should be noted that certain other non-final orders entered after the final order are reviewable under the procedure set forth in rule 9.130. This rule does not apply to review proceedings in such cases.

Except to the extent of conflict with rule 9.140 governing appeals in criminal cases, this rule governs: (1) appeals as of right to the supreme court; (2) certiorari proceedings before the supreme court seeking direct review of administrative action (for example, Industrial Relations Commission and Public Service Commission); (3) appeals as of right to a district court of appeal, including petitions for review of administrative action under the Administrative Procedure Act, section 120.68, Florida Statutes (Supp. 1976); (4) appeals as of right to a circuit court, including review of administrative action if provided by law.

This rule is intended to clarify the procedure for review of orders granting a new trial. Rules 9.130(a)(4) and 9.140(c)(1)(C) authorize the appeal of orders granting a motion for new trial. Those rules supersede *Clement v. Aztec Sales, Inc.*, 297 So. 2d 1 (Fla. 1974), and are consistent with the decision there. Under subdivision (h) of this rule the scope of review of the court is not necessarily limited to the order granting a new trial. The supreme court has held that "appeals taken from new trial orders shall be treated as appeals from final judgments to the extent possible." *Bowen v. Willard*, 340 So. 2d 110, 112 (Fla. 1976). This rule implements that decision.

Subdivisions (b) and (c) establish the procedure for commencing an appeal proceeding. Within 30 days of the rendition of the final order the appellant must file 2 copies of the notice of appeal, accompanied by the appropriate fees, with the clerk of the lower tribunal; except that if review of administrative action is sought, 1 copy of the notice and the applicable fees must be filed in the court. Failure to file any notice within the 30–day period constitutes an irremediable jurisdictional defect, but the second copy and fees may be filed after the 30–day period, subject to sanctions imposed by the court. See *Williams v. State*, 324 So. 2d 74 (Fla. 1975); Fla. R. App. P. 9.040(h).

Subdivision (d) sets forth the contents of the notice and eliminates the requirement of the former rule that the notice show the place of recordation of the order to be reviewed. The rule requires substantial compliance with the form approved by the supreme court. The date of rendition of the order for which review is sought must appear on the face of the notice. See the definition of "rendition" in Florida Rule of Appellate Procedure 9.020, and see the judicial construction of "rendition" for an administrative rule in *Florida Admin. Comm'n v. Judges of the District Court*, 351 So. 2d 712 (Fla. 1977), on review of *Riley–Field Co. v. Askew*, 336 So. 2d 383 (Fla. 1st DCA 1976). This requirement is intended to allow the clerk of the court to determine the timeliness of the notice from its face. The advisory committee intended that defects in the notice would not be jurisdictional or grounds for disposition unless the complaining party was substantially prejudiced.

This rule works significant changes in the review of final administrative action. The former rules required that a traditional petition for the writ of certiorari be filed if supreme court review was appropriate, and the practice under the Administrative Procedure Act, section 120.68, Florida Statutes (Supp. 1976), has been for the "petition for review" to be substantially similar to a petition for the writ of certiorari. See *Yamaha Int'l Corp. v. Ehrman*, 318 So. 2d 196 (Fla. 1st DCA 1975). This rule eliminates the need for true petitions in such cases. Instead, a simple notice is filed, to be followed later by briefs. It is intended that the notice constitute the petition required in section 120.68(2), Florida Statutes (Supp. 1976). There is no conflict with the statute because the substance of the review proceeding remains controlled by the statute, and the legislature directed that review be under the procedures set forth in these rules. Because it is a requirement of rendition that an order be written and filed, this rule supersedes *Shevin ex rel. State v. Public Service Comm'n*, 333 So. 2d 9 (Fla. 1976), and *School Bd. v. Malbon*, 341 So. 2d 523 (Fla. 2d DCA 1977), to the extent that those decisions assume that reduction of an order to writing is unnecessary for judicial review.

This rule is not intended to affect the discretionary nature of direct supreme court review of administrative action taken under the certiorari jurisdiction of that court set forth in article V, section 3(b)(3), Florida Constitution. Such proceedings remain in certiorari with the only change being to replace wasteful, repetitive petitions for the writ of certiorari with concise notices followed at a later date by briefs. The parties to such actions should be designated as "petitioner" and "respondent" despite the use of the terms "appellant" and "appellee" in this rule. See commentary, Fla. R. App. P. 9.020.

Subdivisions (e), (f), and (g) set the times for preparation of the record, serving copies of the index on the parties, serving briefs, and serving notices of cross-appeal. Provision for cross-appeal notices has been made to replace the cross-assignments of error eliminated by these rules. In certiorari proceedings governed by this rule the term "cross- appeal" should be read as equivalent to "cross-petition." It should be noted that if time is measured by service, rule 9.420(b) requires filing to be made before service or immediately thereafter.

Subdivision (h) permits a party to file a single notice of appeal if a single proceeding in the lower tribunal, whether criminal or civil, results in more than 1 final judgment and an appeal of more than 1 is sought. This rule is intended to further the policies underlying the decisions of the supreme court in *Scheel v. Advance Marketing Consultants, Inc.*, 277 So. 2d 773 (Fla. 1973), and *Hollimon v. State*, 232 So. 2d 394 (Fla. 1970). This rule does not authorize the appeal of multiple final judgments unless otherwise proper as to each. If a prematurely filed notice is held in abeyance in accordance with *Williams v. State*, 324 So. 2d 74 (Fla. 1975), the date of filing is intended to be the date the notice becomes effective.

Subdivision (i) provides an expedited procedure in appeals as of right to the supreme court in bond validation proceedings. An appendix is mandatory.

Subdivision (j) provides for an expedited procedure in appeals as of right to the supreme court from an order of a district court of appeal.

1980 Amendment. The rule has been amended to incorporate changes in rule 9.030 and to reflect the abolition of supreme court jurisdiction to review, if provided by general law, final orders of trial courts imposing sentences of life imprisonment.

The reference indicated (2) in the second paragraph of this committee note for 1977 amendment should be disregarded. See amended rule 9.030(a)(1)(B)(ii) and accompanying committee note.

1984 Amendment. Subdivision (k) was added to remedy a pitfall in the application of case law under *Mendez v. West Flagler Family Association*, 303 So. 2d 1 (Fla. 1974). Appeals may now be taken immediately or delayed until the end of the entire case, under the rationale of *Mendez*.

1992 Amendment. Subdivision (d) was amended to require that the appellant, except in criminal cases, attach to its notice of appeal a conformed copy of any orders designated in the notice of appeal, along with any orders on motions that postponed the rendition of orders appealed. This amendment is designed to assist the clerk in determining the nature and type of order being appealed and the timeliness of any such appeal.

Subdivision (m) was added to clarify the effect of a notice of appeal filed by a party before the lower court renders a final appealable order. Under this subdivision, such a notice of appeal is subject to dismissal as premature, but a final order rendered before the dismissal of the appeal will vest the appellate court with jurisdiction to review that final order. It further provides that the appellate court may relinquish jurisdiction or otherwise allow the lower court to render such a final order before dismissal of the appeal. If the only motion that is delaying rendition has been filed by the party filing the notice of appeal, under rule 9.020(g)(3), such motion is deemed abandoned and the final order is deemed rendered by the filing of a notice of appeal.

1996 Amendment. The addition of new subdivision (a)(2) is a restatement of former Florida Rule of Probate Procedure 5.100, and is not intended to change the definition of final order for appellate purposes. It recognizes that in probate and guardianship proceedings it is not unusual to have several final orders entered during the course of the proceeding that address many different issues and involve many different persons. An order of the circuit court that determines a right, an obligation, or the standing of an interested person as defined in the Florida Probate Code may be appealed before the administration of the probate or guardianship is complete and the fiduciary is discharged.

Subdivision (c) was amended to reflect that in appeals of administrative orders, the appellate court filing fees should be filed in the appellate court, not the administrative tribunal.

Subdivision (n) was added by the committee in response to the opinion in *Canal Insurance Co. v. Reed*, 666 So. 2d 888 (Fla. 1996), suggesting that the Appellate Court Rules Committee consider an appropriate method for providing expedited review of these cases to avoid unnecessary delays in the final resolution of the underlying actions. Expedited review in the manner provided in rule 9.130 is available for such judgments in cases where a claim against the insured is pending and early resolution of the coverage issue is in the best interest of the parties. The notice of appeal should identify whether a party is seeking review pursuant to the procedure provided in this rule or in rule 9.130.

2006 Amendment. Rule 9.110(n) has been amended to clarify that the word "clerk" in the first sentence of the rule refers to the clerk of the lower tribunal. The amendment also permits the minor to ask for leave to file a brief or to request oral argument. The amendment clarifies that the district court does not grant the minor's petition, but rather may reverse the circuit court's dismissal of the petition.

2010 Note. As provided in Rule 9.040, requests to determine the confidentiality of appellate court records are governed by Florida Rule of Judicial Administration 2.420.

2014 Amendments. The amendment to subdivision (*l*) is intended to clarify that it is neither necessary nor appropriate to request a relinquishment of jurisdiction from the court to enable the lower tribunal to render a final order. Subdivision (n) has been moved to rule 9.147.

Court Commentary

2003 Amendment. Subdivision (*l*) was deleted to reflect the holding in *North Florida Women's Health & Counseling Services, Inc. v. State*, 28 Fla. L. Weekly S549 (Fla. July 10, 2003).

Rule 9.120. Discretionary Proceedings to Review Decisions of District Courts of Appeal

(a) Applicability. This rule applies to those proceedings that invoke the discretionary jurisdiction of the supreme court described in rule 9.030(a)(2)(A).

(b) Commencement. The jurisdiction of the supreme court described in rule 9.030(a)(2)(A) shall be invoked by filing a notice, accompanied by any filing fees prescribed by law, with the clerk of the district court of appeal within 30 days of rendition of the order to be reviewed.

(c) Notice. The notice shall be substantially in the form prescribed by rule 9.900. The caption shall contain the name of the lower tribunal, the name and designation of at least 1 party on each side, and the case number in the lower tribunal. The notice shall contain the date of rendition of the order to be reviewed and the basis for invoking the jurisdiction of the court.

(d) Briefs on Jurisdiction. Petitioner's brief, limited solely to the issue of the supreme court's jurisdiction and accompanied by an appendix containing only a conformed copy of the decision of the district court of appeal, shall be served within 10 days of filing the notice. Respondent's brief on jurisdiction shall be served within 20 days after service of petitioner's brief. Formal requirements for both briefs are specified in rule 9.210. No reply brief shall be permitted. If jurisdiction is invoked under rule 9.030(a)(2)(A)(v) (certifications of questions of great public importance by the district courts to the supreme court), no briefs on jurisdiction shall be filed.

(e) Accepting or Postponing Decision on Jurisdiction; Record. If the supreme court accepts or postpones decision on jurisdiction, the court shall so order and advise the parties and the clerk of the district court of appeal. Within 60 days thereafter or such other time set by the court, the clerk shall electronically transmit the record.

(f) Briefs on Merits. Within 20 days of rendition of the order accepting or postponing decision on jurisdiction, the petitioner shall serve the initial brief on the merits, accompanied by an appendix that must include a conformed copy of the decision of the district court of appeal. Additional briefs shall be served as prescribed by rule 9.210.

Amended March 27, 1980, effective April 1, 1980 (381 So.2d 1370); Nov. 26, 1980, effective Jan. 1, 1981 (391 So.2d 203); Oct. 22, 1992, effective Jan. 1, 1993 (609 So.2d 516); Oct. 12, 2000, effective Jan. 1, 2001 (780 So.2d 834); Aug. 29, 2002, effective Jan. 1, 2003 (827 So.2d 888); Oct. 26, 2006, effective Jan. 1, 2007 (941 So.2d 352); Nov. 3, 2011, effective Jan. 1, 2012 (75 So.3d 239); Oct. 18, 2012, effective Dec. 1, 2012, April 1, 2013, Oct. 1, 2013 (102 So.3d 451).

Committee Notes

1977 Amendment. This rule replaces former rule 4.5(c) and governs all certiorari proceedings to review final decisions of the district courts. Certiorari proceedings to review interlocutory orders of the district courts if supreme court jurisdiction exists under article V, section 3(b)(3), Florida Constitution are governed by rule 9.100.

Subdivision (b) sets forth the manner in which certiorari proceedings in the supreme court are to be commenced. Petitions for the writ are abolished and replaced by a simple notice to be followed by briefs. Two copies of the notice, which must substantially comply with the form approved by the supreme court, are to be filed with the clerk of the district court within 30 days of rendition along with the requisite fees. Failure to timely file the fees is not jurisdictional.

Subdivision (c) sets forth the contents of the notice. The requirement that the notice state the date of rendition, as defined in rule 9.020, is intended to permit the clerk of the court to determine timeliness from the face of the notice. The statement of the basis for jurisdiction should be a concise reference to whether the order sought to be reviewed (1) conflicts with other Florida appellate decisions; (2) affects a class of constitutional or state officers; or (3) involves a question of great public interest certified by the district court.

Subdivision (d) establishes the time for filing jurisdictional briefs and prescribes their content. If supreme court jurisdiction is based on certification of a question of great public interest, no jurisdictional briefs are permitted. Briefs on the merits in such cases are to be prepared in the same manner as in other cases. Briefs on the merits are to be served within the time provided after the court has ruled that it will accept jurisdiction or has ruled that it will postpone decision on jurisdiction.

The jurisdictional brief should be a short, concise statement of the grounds for invoking jurisdiction and the necessary facts. It is not appropriate to argue the merits of the substantive issues involved in the case or discuss any matters not relevant to the threshold jurisdictional issue. The petitioner may wish to include a very short statement of why the supreme court should exercise its discretion and entertain the case on the merits if it finds it does have certiorari jurisdiction. An appendix must be filed containing a conformed copy of the decision of the district court. If the decision of the district court was without opinion, or otherwise does not set forth the basis of decision with sufficient clarity to enable the supreme court to determine whether grounds for jurisdiction exist, a conformed copy of the order of the trial court should also be included in the appendix.

Subdivisions (e) and (f) provide that within 60 days of the date of the order accepting jurisdiction, or postponing decision on jurisdiction, the clerk of the district court must transmit the record to the court. The petitioner has 20 days from the date of the order to serve the initial brief on the merits. Other briefs may then be served in accordance with rule 9.210. Briefs that are served must be filed in accordance with rule 9.420.

It should be noted that the automatic stay provided by former rule 4.5(c)(6) has been abolished because it encouraged the filing of frivolous petitions and was regularly abused. A stay pending review may be obtained under rule 9.310. If a stay has been ordered pending appeal to a district court, it remains effective under rule 9.310(e) unless the mandate issues or the district court vacates it. The advisory committee was of the view that the district courts should permit such stays only when essential. Factors to be considered are the likelihood that jurisdiction will be accepted by the supreme court, the likelihood of ultimate success on the merits, the likelihood of harm if no stay is granted, and the remediable quality of any such harm.

1980 Amendment. The rule has been amended to reflect the 1980 revisions to article V, section 3, Florida Constitution creating the additional categories of certifications by the district courts to the supreme court enumerated in rule 9.030(a)(2)(A).

District court decisions that (a) expressly declare valid a state statute, (b) expressly construe a provision of the state or federal constitution, (c) expressly affect a class of constitutional or state officers, (d) expressly and directly conflict with a decision of another district court or the supreme court on the same point of law, (e) pass upon a question certified to be of great public importance, or (f) are certified to be in direct conflict with decisions of other district courts, are reviewed according to the procedures set forth in this rule. No jurisdictional briefs are permitted if jurisdiction is based on certification of a question of great public importance or certification that the decision is in direct conflict with a decision of another district court.

The mandatory appendix must contain a copy of the district court decision sought to be reviewed and should be prepared in accordance with rule 9.220.

Supreme court review of trial court orders and judgments certified by the district court under rule 9.030(a)(2)(B) is governed by the procedures set forth in rule 9.125.

Reply briefs from petitioners are prohibited, and the court will decide whether to accept the case for review solely on the basis of petitioner's initial and respondent's responsive jurisdictional briefs.

1992 Amendment. Subdivision (d) was amended to provide that jurisdictional briefs must conform to the same requirements set forth in rule 9.210.

Rule 9.125. Review of Trial Court Orders and Judgments Certified by the District Courts of Appeal as Requiring Immediate Resolution by the Supreme Court

(a) Applicability. This rule applies to any order or judgment of a trial court that has been certified by the district court of appeal to require immediate resolution by the supreme court because the issues pending in the district court are of great public importance or have a great effect on the proper administration of justice throughout the state. The district court of appeal may make such certification on its own motion or on suggestion by a party.

(b) Commencement. The jurisdiction of the supreme court is invoked on rendition of the certificate by the district court of appeal.

(c) Suggestion. Any party may file with the district court and serve on the parties a suggestion that the order to be reviewed should be certified by the district court to the supreme court. The suggestion shall be substantially in the form prescribed by this rule and shall be filed within 10 days from the filing of the notice of appeal.

(d) Response. Any party may file a response within 5 days of the service of the suggestion.

(e) Form. The suggestion shall be limited to 5 pages and shall contain all of the following elements:

(1) A statement of why the appeal requires immediate resolution by the supreme court.

(2) A statement of why the appeal

(A) is of great public importance, or

(B) will have a great effect on the proper administration of justice throughout the state.

(3) A certificate signed by the attorney stating:

I express a belief, based on a reasoned and studied professional judgment, that this appeal requires immediate resolution by the supreme court and (a) is of great public importance, or (b) will have a great effect on the administration of justice throughout the state.

/s/ ____________
Attorney for . . . (name of party). . .
. . . (address and phone number)
Florida Bar No. . . . .
E-mail Address: . . . .

(4) An appendix containing a conformed copy of the order to be reviewed.

(f) Effect of Suggestion. The district court shall not be required to rule on the suggestion and neither the filing of a suggestion nor the rendition by the district court of its certificate shall alter the applicable time limitations or place of filing. If an order is rendered granting or denying certification, no rehearing shall be permitted.

(g) Procedure When Supreme Court Accepts Jurisdiction. The jurisdiction of the supreme court attaches on rendition of the order accepting jurisdiction. If the supreme court accepts jurisdiction, it shall so order and advise the parties, the clerk of the district court, and the clerk of the lower tribunal. The clerk of the court in possession of the record shall electronically transmit the record in the case to the supreme court within 10 days thereafter. The supreme court shall issue a briefing schedule and all papers formerly required to be filed in the district court shall be filed in the supreme court. If the supreme court denies jurisdiction, it shall so order and advise the parties and the clerk of the district court.

Added March 27, 1980, effective April 1, 1980 (381 So.2d 1370). Amended Nov. 26, 1980, effective Jan. 1, 1981 (391 So.2d 203); Oct. 22, 1992, effective Jan. 1, 1993 (609 So.2d 516); Oct. 12, 2000, effective Jan. 1, 2001 (780 So.2d 834); Nov. 3, 2011, effective Jan. 1, 2012 (75 So.3d 239); Oct. 18, 2012, effective Dec. 1, 2012, April 1, 2013, Oct. 1, 2013 (102 So.3d 451).

Committee Notes

1980 Amendment. This rule is entirely new and governs all discretionary proceedings to review trial court orders or judgments that have been certified by the district court under rule 9.030(a)(2)(B) to require immediate resolution by the supreme court and to be of great public importance or to have a great effect on the proper administration of justice throughout the state. Final and non-final orders are covered by this rule. Discretionary review of other district court decisions if supreme court jurisdiction exists under rule 9.030(a)(2)(A) is governed by rule 9.120.

Subdivision (b) makes clear that certification by the district court is self-executing.

Subdivision (c) sets forth the manner in which a party may file a suggestion that the order to be reviewed should be certified by the district court to the supreme court and requires the suggestion be filed within 10 days from the filing of the notice of appeal. It is contemplated that suggestions under this rule will be rare. A suggestion should be filed only if, under the peculiar circumstances of a case, all the elements contained in subdivision (e) of the rule are present.

Subdivision (d) provides that any other party may file a response to a suggestion within 5 days of the service of the suggestion.

Subdivision (e) provides for the form of the suggestion. All suggestions must be substantially in this form. The suggestion is limited to 5 pages and must contain (1) a statement of why the appeal requires immediate resolution by the supreme court, and (2) a statement of why the appeal either is of great public importance or will have a great effect on the proper administration of justice throughout the state. The suggestion must be accompanied by an appendix containing a copy of the order to be reviewed. The suggestion also must include a certificate signed by the attorney in the form appearing in the rule.

To ensure that no proceeding is delayed because of this rule, subdivisions (f) and (g) provide that the filing of a suggestion will not alter the applicable time limitations or the place of filing. The district court shall not be required to rule on a suggestion. The parties should follow the time limitations contained in the rule through which jurisdiction of the district court was invoked. See rules 9.100, 9.110, 9.130, and 9.140.

Rule 9.130. Proceedings to Review Non–Final Orders and Specified Final Orders

(a) Applicability.

(1) This rule applies to appeals to the district courts of appeal of the non-final orders authorized herein and to appeals to the circuit court of non-final orders when provided by general law. Review of other non-final orders in such courts and non-final administrative action shall be by the method prescribed by rule 9.100.

(2) Appeals of non-final orders in criminal cases shall be as prescribed by rule 9.140.

(3) Appeals to the district courts of appeal of non-final orders are limited to those that

(A) concern venue;

(B) grant, continue, modify, deny, or dissolve injunctions, or refuse to modify or dissolve injunctions;

(C) determine

(i) the jurisdiction of the person;

(ii) the right to immediate possession of property, including but not limited to orders that grant, modify, dissolve or refuse to grant, modify, or dissolve writs of replevin, garnishment, or attachment;

(iii) in family law matters:

a. the right to immediate monetary relief;

b. the rights or obligations of a party regarding child custody or time-sharing under a parenting plan; or

c. that a marital agreement is invalid in its entirety;

(iv) the entitlement of a party to arbitration, or to an appraisal under an insurance policy;

(v) that, as a matter of law, a party is not entitled to workers' compensation immunity;

(vi) whether to certify a class;

(vii) that, as a matter of law, a party is not entitled to absolute or qualified immunity in a civil rights claim arising under federal law;

(viii) that a governmental entity has taken action that has inordinately burdened real property within the meaning of section 70.001(6)(a), Florida Statutes;

(ix) the issue of forum non conveniens;

(x) that, as a matter of law, a party is not entitled to immunity under section 768.28(9), Florida Statutes; or

(xi) that, as a matter of law, a party is not entitled to sovereign immunity.

(D) grant or deny the appointment of a receiver, and terminate or refuse to terminate a receivership.

(4) Orders disposing of motions that suspend rendition are not reviewable separately from a review of the final order; provided that orders granting motions for new trial in jury and non-jury cases are reviewable by the method prescribed in rule 9.110.

(5) Orders entered on an authorized and timely motion for relief from judgment are reviewable by the method prescribed by this rule. Motions for rehearing

directed to these orders will not toll the time for filing a notice of appeal.

(b) Commencement. Jurisdiction of the court under subdivisions (a)(3)–(a)(5) of this rule shall be invoked by filing a notice, accompanied by any filing fees prescribed by law, with the clerk of the lower tribunal within 30 days of rendition of the order to be reviewed.

(c) Notice. The notice, designated as a notice of appeal of non-final order, shall be substantially in the form prescribed by rule 9.900(c). Except in criminal cases, a conformed copy of the order or orders designated in the notice of appeal shall be attached to the notice.

(d) Record. A record shall not be transmitted to the court unless ordered.

(e) Briefs. Appellant's initial brief, accompanied by an appendix as prescribed by rule 9.220, shall be served within 15 days of filing the notice. Additional briefs shall be served as prescribed by rule 9.210.

(f) Stay of Proceedings. In the absence of a stay, during the pendency of a review of a non-final order, the lower tribunal may proceed with all matters, including trial or final hearing, except that the lower tribunal may not render a final order disposing of the cause pending such review absent leave of the court.

(g) Cross–Appeal. An appellee may cross-appeal the order or orders designated by the appellant, to review any ruling described in subdivisions (a)(3)–(a)(5), by serving a notice within 10 days of service of the appellant's timely filed notice of appeal or within the time prescribed for filing a notice of appeal, whichever is later. A notice of cross-appeal, accompanied by any filing fees prescribed by law, shall be filed either before service or immediately thereafter in the same manner as the notice of appeal.

(h) Review on Full Appeal. This rule shall not preclude initial review of a non-final order on appeal from the final order in the cause.

(i) Scope of Review. Multiple non-final orders that are listed in rule 9.130(a)(3) may be reviewed by a single notice if the notice is timely filed as to each such order.

Amended March 27, 1980, effective April 1, 1980 (381 So.2d 1370); Nov. 26, 1980, effective Jan. 1, 1981 (391 So.2d 203); Sept. 13, 1984, effective Jan. 1, 1985 (463 So.2d 1114); July 9, 1992 (605 So.2d 850); Oct. 22, 1992, effective Jan. 1, 1993 (609 So.2d 516); Nov. 22, 1995, effective Jan. 1, 1996 (663 So.2d 1314); Nov. 22, 1996, effective Jan. 1, 1997 (685 So.2d 773); Oct. 12, 2000, effective Jan. 1, 2001 (780 So.2d 834); Feb. 3, 2005 (894 So.2d 202); Nov. 13, 2008, effective Jan. 1, 2009 (2 So.3d 89); Nov. 3, 2011, effective Jan. 1, 2012 (75 So.3d 239); Oct. 18, 2012, effective Dec. 1, 2012, April 1, 2013, Oct. 1, 2013 (102 So.3d 451); Nov. 6, 2014, effective Jan. 1, 2015 (2014 WL 5714099); Nov. 13, 2014, effective Jan. 1, 2015 (151 So.3d 1217).

Committee Notes

1977 Amendment. This rule replaces former rule 4.2 and substantially alters current practice. This rule applies to review of all non-final orders, except those entered in criminal cases, and those specifically governed by rules 9.100 and 9.110.

The advisory committee was aware that the common law writ of certiorari is available at any time and did not intend to abolish that writ. However, because that writ provides a remedy only if the petitioner meets the heavy burden of showing that a clear departure from the essential requirements of law has resulted in otherwise irreparable harm, it is extremely rare that erroneous interlocutory rulings can be corrected by resort to common law certiorari. It is anticipated that because the most urgent interlocutory orders are appealable under this rule, there will be very few cases in which common law certiorari will provide relief. See *Taylor v. Board of Pub. Instruction*, 131 So. 2d 504 (Fla. 1st DCA 1961).

Subdivision (a)(3) designates certain instances in which interlocutory appeals may be prosecuted under the procedures set forth in this rule. Under these rules there are no mandatory interlocutory appeals. This rule eliminates interlocutory appeals as a matter of right from all orders "formerly cognizable in equity," and provides for review of certain interlocutory orders based on the necessity or desirability of expeditious review. Allowable interlocutory appeals from orders in actions formerly cognizable as civil actions are specified, and are essentially the same as under former rule 4.2. Item (A) permits review of orders concerning venue. Item (C)(i) has been limited to jurisdiction over the person because the writ of prohibition provides an adequate remedy in cases involving jurisdiction of the subject matter. Because the purpose of these items is to eliminate useless labor, the advisory committee is of the view that stays of proceedings in lower tribunals should be liberally granted if the interlocutory appeal involves venue or jurisdiction over the person. Because this rule only applies to civil cases, item (C)(ii) does not include within its ambit rulings on motions to suppress seized evidence in criminal cases. Item (C)(ii) is intended to apply whether the property involved is real or personal. It applies to such cases as condemnation suits in which a condemnor is permitted to take possession and title to real property in advance of final judgment. See ch. 74, Fla. Stat. (1975). Item (C)(iii) is intended to apply to such matters as temporary child custody or support, alimony, suit money, and attorneys' fees. Item (C)(iv) allows appeals from interlocutory orders that determine liability in favor of a claimant.

Subdivision (a)(4) grants a right of review if the lower tribunal grants a motion for new trial whether in a jury or non-jury case. The procedures set forth in rule 9.110, and not those set forth in this rule, apply in such cases. This rule has been phrased so that the granting of rehearing in a non-jury case under Florida Rule of Civil Procedure 1.530 may not be the subject of an interlocutory appeal unless the trial judge orders the taking of evidence. Other non-final orders that postpone rendition are not reviewable in an independent proceeding. Other non-final orders entered by a lower tribunal after final order are reviewable and are to be governed by this rule. Such orders include, for example, an order granting a motion to vacate default.

Subdivision (a)(5) grants a right of review of orders on motions seeking relief from a previous court order on the grounds of mistake, fraud, satisfaction of judgment, or other grounds listed in Florida Rule of Civil Procedure 1.540.

Subdivision (a)(6) provides that interlocutory review is to be in the court that would have jurisdiction to review the final order in the cause as of the time of the interlocutory appeal.

Subdivisions (b) and (c) state the manner for commencing an interlocutory appeal governed by this rule. Two copies of the notice must be filed with the clerk of the lower tribunal within 30 days of rendition of the order. Under rule 9.040(g) the notice and fee must be transmitted immediately to the court by the clerk of the lower tribunal.

Subdivision (d) provides for transmittal of the record only on order of the court. Transmittal should be in accordance with instructions contained in the order.

Subdivision (e) replaces former rule 4.2(e) and governs the service of briefs on interlocutory appeals. The time to serve the appellant's brief has been reduced to 15 days so as to minimize interruption of lower tribunal proceedings. The brief must be accompanied by an appendix containing a conformed copy of the order to be reviewed and should also contain all relevant portions of the record.

Subdivision (f) makes clear that unless a stay is granted under rule 9.310, the lower tribunal is only divested of jurisdiction to enter a final order disposing of the case. This follows the historical rule that trial courts are divested of jurisdiction only to the extent that their actions are under review by an appellate court. Thus, the lower tribunal has jurisdiction to proceed with matters not before the court. This rule is intended to resolve the confusion spawned by *De la Portilla v. De la Portilla*, 304 So. 2d 116 (Fla. 1974), and its progeny.

Subdivision (g) was embodied in former rule 4.2(a) and is intended to make clear that the failure to take an interlocutory appeal does not constitute a waiver of any sort on appeal of a final judgment, although an improper ruling might not then constitute prejudicial error warranting reversal.

1992 Amendment. Subdivisions (a)(3)(C)(vii) and (a)(6) were added to permit appeals from non-final orders that either granted or denied a party's request that a class be certified. The committee was of the opinion that orders determining the nature of an action and the extent of the parties before the court were analogous to other orders reviewable under rule 9.130. Therefore, these 2 subdivisions were added to the other limited enumeration of orders appealable by the procedures established in this rule.

Subdivision (a)(3)(D) was added by the committee in response to the decision in *Twin Jay Chambers Partnership v. Suarez*, 556 So. 2d 781 (Fla. 2d DCA 1990). It was the opinion of the committee that orders that deny the appointment of receivers or terminate or refuse to terminate receiverships are of the same quality as those that grant the appointment of a receiver. Rather than base the appealability of such orders on subdivision (a)(3)(C)(ii), the committee felt it preferable to specifically identify those orders with respect to a receivership that were non-final orders subject to appeal by this rule.

Subdivision (c) was amended to require the attachment of a conformed copy of the order or orders designated in the notice of appeal consistent with the amendment to rule 9.110(d).

1996 Amendment. The amendment to subdivision (a)(3)(C)(vi) moves the phrase "as a matter of law" from the end of the subdivision to its beginning. This is to resolve the confusion evidenced in *Breakers Palm Beach v. Gloger*, 646 So. 2d 237 (Fla. 4th DCA 1994), *City of Lake Mary v. Franklin*, 668 So. 2d 712 (Fla. 5th DCA 1996), and their progeny by clarifying that this subdivision was not intended to grant a right of nonfinal review if the lower tribunal denies a motion for summary judgment based on the existence of a material fact dispute.

Subdivision (a)(3)(C)(viii) was added in response to the supreme court's request in *Tucker v. Resha*, 648 So. 2d 1187 (Fla. 1994). The court directed the committee to propose a new rule regarding procedures for appeal of orders denying immunity in federal civil rights cases consistent with federal procedure. Compare *Johnson v. Jones*, 115 S. Ct. 2151, 132 L. Ed. 2d 238 (1995), with *Mitchell v. Forsyth*, 472 U.S. 511, 105 S. Ct. 2806, 86 L. Ed. 2d 411 (1985). The Florida Supreme Court held that such orders are "subject to interlocutory review to the extent that the order turns on an issue of law."

2000 Amendment. The title to this rule was amended to reflect that some of the review proceedings specified in this rule may involve review of final orders.

Subdivision (a)(1) was amended to reflect that the appellate jurisdiction of circuit courts is prescribed by general law and not by this rule, as clarified in *Blore v. Fierro*, 636 So. 2d 1329 (Fla. 1994).

Subdivision (a)(3)(C)(iv) allowing review of orders determining "the issue of liability in favor of a party seeking affirmative relief" was deleted so that such orders are not appealable until the conclusion of the case.

Subdivision (a)(7) was deleted because it is superseded by proposed rule 9.040(b)(2), which determines the appropriate court to review non-final orders after a change of venue.

2008 Amendment. Subdivision 9.130(a)(3)(C)(ii) was amended to address a conflict in the case law concerning whether orders granting, modifying, dissolving, or refusing to grant, modify, or dissolve garnishments are appealable under this subdivision. Compare *Ramseyer v. Williamson*, 639 So. 2d 205 (Fla. 5th DCA 1994) (garnishment order not appealable), with *5361 N. Dixie Highway v. Capital Bank*, 658 So. 2d 1037 (Fla. 4th DCA 1995) (permitting appeal from garnishment order and acknowledging conflict). The amendment is not intended to limit or expand the scope of matters covered under this rule. In that vein, replevin and attachment were included as examples of similar writs covered by this rule.

Subdivision (a)(3)(C)(iv) has been amended to clarify that nonfinal orders determining a party's entitlement to an appraisal under an insurance policy are added to the category of nonfinal orders appealable to the district courts of appeal.

Subdivision 9.130(a)(5) is intended to authorize appeals from orders entered on motions for relief from judgment that are specifically contemplated by a specific rule of procedure (e.g., the current versions of Florida Rule of Civil Procedure 1.540, Small Claims Rule 7.190, Florida Family Law Rule of Procedure 12.540, and Florida Rule of Juvenile Procedure 8.150 and 8.270).

Subdivision (a)(5) has been amended to recognize the unique nature of the orders listed in this subdivision and to codify the holdings of all of Florida's district courts of appeal on this subject. The amendment also clarifies that motions for rehearing directed to these particular types of orders are unauthorized and will not toll the time for filing a notice of appeal.

2014 Amendment. Subdivision (a)(4) has been amended to clarify that an order disposing of a motion that suspends rendition is reviewable, but only in conjunction with, and as a part of, the review of the final order. Additionally, the following sentence has been deleted from subdivision (a)(4): "Other non-final orders entered after final order on authorized motions are reviewable by the method prescribed by this rule." Its deletion clarifies that non-final orders entered after a final order are no more or less reviewable than the same type of order would be if issued before a final order. Non–final orders entered after a final order remain reviewable as part of a subsequent final order or as otherwise provided by statute or court rule. This amendment resolves conflict over the language being stricken and the different approaches to review during post-decretal proceedings that have resulted. *See, e.g., Tubero v. Ellis*, 469 So. 2d 206 (Fla. 4th DCA 1985) (Hurley, J., dissenting). This amendment also cures the mistaken reference in the original 1977 committee note to "orders granting motions to vacate default" as examples of nonfinal orders intended for review under the stricken sentence. An order vacating a default is generally not reviewable absent a final default judgment. *See, e.g., Howard v. McAuley*, 436 So. 2d 392 (Fla. 2d DCA 1983). Orders vacating final default judgments remain reviewable under rule 9.130(a)(5). Essentially, this amendment will delay some courts' review of some non-final orders entered after a final order until rendition of another, subsequent final order. But the amendment is not intended to alter the Court's ultimate authority to review any order.

Rule 9.140. Appeal Proceedings in Criminal Cases

(a) Applicability. Appeal proceedings in criminal cases shall be as in civil cases except as modified by this rule.

(b) Appeals by Defendant.

(1) *Appeals Permitted.* A defendant may appeal

(A) a final judgment adjudicating guilt;

(B) a final order withholding adjudication after a finding of guilt;

(C) an order granting probation or community control, or both, whether or not guilt has been adjudicated;

(D) orders entered after final judgment or finding of guilt, including orders revoking or modifying probation or community control, or both, or orders denying relief under Florida Rule of Criminal Procedure 3.800(a), 3.801, 3.850, 3.851, or 3.853;

(E) an unlawful or illegal sentence;

(F) a sentence, if the appeal is required or permitted by general law; or

(G) as otherwise provided by general law.

(2) *Guilty or Nolo Contendere Pleas.*

(A) Pleas. A defendant may not appeal from a guilty or nolo contendere plea except as follows:

(i) Reservation of Right to Appeal. A defendant who pleads guilty or nolo contendere may expressly reserve the right to appeal a prior dispositive order of the lower tribunal, identifying with particularity the point of law being reserved.

(ii) Appeals Otherwise Allowed. A defendant who pleads guilty or nolo contendere may otherwise directly appeal only

a. the lower tribunal's lack of subject matter jurisdiction;

b. a violation of the plea agreement, if preserved by a motion to withdraw plea;

c. an involuntary plea, if preserved by a motion to withdraw plea;

d. a sentencing error, if preserved; or

e. as otherwise provided by law.

(B) Record.

(i) Except for appeals under subdivision (b)(2)(A)(i) of this rule, the record for appeals involving a plea of guilty or nolo contendere shall be limited to:

a. all indictments, informations, affidavits of violation of probation or community control, and other charging documents;

b. the plea and sentencing hearing transcripts;

c. any written plea agreements;

d. any judgments, sentences, scoresheets, motions, and orders to correct or modify sentences, orders imposing, modifying, or revoking probation or community control, orders assessing costs, fees, fines, or restitution against the defendant, and any other documents relating to sentencing;

e. any motion to withdraw plea and order thereon;

f. notice of appeal, statement of judicial acts to be reviewed, directions to the clerk, and designation to the approved court reporter or approved transcriptionist.

(ii) Upon good cause shown, the court, or the lower tribunal before the record is electronically transmitted, may expand the record.

(3) *Commencement.* The defendant shall file the notice prescribed by rule 9.110(d) with the clerk of the lower tribunal at any time between rendition of a final judgment and 30 days following rendition of a written order imposing sentence. Copies shall be served on the state attorney and attorney general.

(4) *Cross–Appeal.* A defendant may cross-appeal by serving a notice within 10 days of service of the state's notice or service of an order on a motion pursuant to Florida Rule of Criminal Procedure 3.800(b)(2). Review of cross-appeals before trial is limited to related issues resolved in the same order being appealed.

(c) Appeals by the State.

(1) *Appeals Permitted.* The state may appeal an order

(A) dismissing an indictment or information or any count thereof or dismissing an affidavit charging the commission of a criminal offense, the violation of probation, the violation of community control, or the violation of any supervised correctional release;

(B) suppressing before trial confessions, admissions, or evidence obtained by search and seizure;

(C) granting a new trial;

(D) arresting judgment;

(E) granting a motion for judgment of acquittal after a jury verdict;

(F) discharging a defendant under Florida Rule of Criminal Procedure 3.191;

(G) discharging a prisoner on habeas corpus;

(H) finding a defendant incompetent or insane;

(I) finding a defendant intellectually disabled under Florida Rule of Criminal Procedure 3.203;

(J) granting relief under Florida Rule of Criminal Procedure 3.801, 3.850, 3.851, or 3.853;

(K) ruling on a question of law if a convicted defendant appeals the judgment of conviction;

(L) withholding adjudication of guilt in violation of general law;

(M) imposing an unlawful or illegal sentence or imposing a sentence outside the range permitted by the sentencing guidelines;

(N) imposing a sentence outside the range recommended by the sentencing guidelines;

(O) denying restitution; or

(P) as otherwise provided by general law for final orders.

(2) *Non–Final Orders.* The state as provided by general law may appeal to the circuit court non-final orders rendered in the county court.

(3) *Commencement.* The state shall file the notice prescribed by rule 9.110(d) with the clerk of the lower tribunal within 15 days of rendition of the order to be reviewed; provided that in an appeal by the state under rule 9.140(c)(1)(K), the state's notice of cross-appeal shall be filed within 10 days of service of defendant's notice or service of an order on a motion pursuant to Florida Rule of Criminal Procedure 3.800(b)(2). Copies shall be served on the defendant and the attorney of record. An appeal by the state shall stay further proceedings in the lower tribunal only by order of the lower tribunal.

(d) Withdrawal of Defense Counsel after Judgment and Sentence or after Appeal by State.

(1) The attorney of record for a defendant in a criminal proceeding shall not be relieved of any professional duties, or be permitted to withdraw as defense counsel of record, except with approval of the lower tribunal on good cause shown on written motion, until either the time has expired for filing an authorized notice of appeal and no such notice has been filed by the defendant or the state, or after the following have been completed:

(A) a notice of appeal or cross-appeal has been filed on behalf of the defendant or the state;

(B) a statement of judicial acts to be reviewed has been filed if a transcript will require the expenditure of public funds;

(C) the defendant's directions to the clerk have been filed, if necessary;

(D) designations to the approved court reporter or approved transcriptionist have been filed for transcripts of those portions of the proceedings necessary to support the issues on appeal or, if transcripts will require the expenditure of public funds for the defendant, of those portions of the proceedings necessary to support the statement of judicial acts to be reviewed; and

(E) in publicly funded defense and state appeals, when the lower tribunal has entered an order appointing the office of the public defender for the local circuit, the district office of criminal conflict and civil regional counsel, or private counsel as provided by chapter 27, Florida Statutes, that office, or attorney shall remain counsel for the appeal until the record is electronically transmitted to the court. In publicly funded state appeals, defense counsel shall additionally file with the court a copy of the lower tribunal's order appointing the local public defender, the office of criminal conflict and civil regional counsel, or private counsel. In non-publicly funded defense and state appeals, retained appellate counsel shall file a notice of appearance in the court, or defense counsel of record shall file a motion to withdraw in the court, with service on the defendant, that states what the defendant's legal representation on appeal, if any, is expected to be. Documents filed in the court shall be served on the attorney general (or state attorney in appeals to the circuit court).

(2) Orders allowing withdrawal of counsel are conditional and counsel shall remain of record for the limited purpose of representing the defendant in the lower tribunal regarding any sentencing error the lower tribunal is authorized to address during the pendency of the direct appeal pursuant to Florida Rule of Criminal Procedure 3.800(b)(2).

(e) Sentencing Errors. A sentencing error may not be raised on appeal unless the alleged error has first been brought to the attention of the lower tribunal:

(1) at the time of sentencing; or

(2) by motion pursuant to Florida Rule of Criminal Procedure 3.800(b).

(f) Record.

(1) *Service.* The clerk of the lower tribunal shall prepare and serve the record prescribed by rule 9.200 within 50 days of the filing of the notice of appeal. However, the clerk shall not serve the record until all proceedings designated for transcription have been transcribed by the court reporter(s) and filed with the clerk. If the designated transcripts have not been filed by the date required for service of the record, the clerk shall file with the court, and serve on all parties and any court reporter whose transcript has not been filed, a notice of inability to complete the record, listing the transcripts not yet received. In cases where the transcripts are filed after a notice from the clerk, the clerk shall prepare and file the record within 20 days of receipt of the transcripts. An order granting an extension to the court reporter to transcribe designated proceedings shall toll the time for the clerk to serve this notice or the record on appeal.

(2) *Transcripts.*

(A) If a defendant's designation of a transcript of proceedings requires expenditure of public funds, trial counsel for the defendant (in conjunction with appellate counsel, if possible) shall serve, within 10 days of filing the notice, a statement of judicial acts to be reviewed, and a designation to the approved court reporter or approved transcriptionist requiring preparation of only so much of the proceedings as fairly supports the issue raised.

(B) Either party may file motions in the lower tribunal to reduce or expand the transcripts.

(C) Except as permitted in subdivision (f)(2)(D) of this rule, the parties shall designate the approved court reporter or approved transcriptionist to file with the clerk of the lower tribunal the transcripts for the court and sufficient paper copies for all parties exempt from service by e-mail as set forth in the Florida Rules of Judicial Administration.

(D) Non-indigent defendants represented by counsel may designate the approved court reporter or approved transcriptionist to prepare the transcripts. Counsel adopting this procedure shall, within 5 days of receipt of the transcripts from the approved court reporter or approved transcriptionist, file the transcripts. Counsel shall serve notice of the use of this procedure on the attorney general (or the state attorney in appeals to circuit court) and the clerk of the lower tribunal. Counsel shall attach a certificate to each transcript certifying that it is accurate and complete. When this procedure is used, the clerk of the lower tribunal upon conclusion of the appeal shall retain the transcript(s) for use as needed by the state in any collateral proceedings and shall not dispose of the transcripts without the consent of the Office of the Attorney General.

(E) In state appeals, the state shall designate the approved court reporter or approved transcriptionist to prepare and file with the clerk of the lower tribunal the transcripts and sufficient copies for all parties exempt from service by e-mail as set forth in the Florida Rules of Judicial Administration. Alternatively, the state may elect to use the procedure specified in subdivision (f)(2)(D) of this rule.

(F) The lower tribunal may by administrative order in publicly-funded cases direct the clerk of the lower tribunal rather than the approved court reporter or approved transcriptionist to prepare the necessary transcripts.

(3) *Retention of Documents.* Unless otherwise ordered by the court, the clerk of the lower tribunal shall retain any original documents.

(4) *Service of Copies.* The clerk of the lower tribunal shall serve copies of the record to the court, attorney general (or state attorney in appeals to circuit court), and all counsel appointed to represent indigent defendants on appeal. The clerk of the lower tribunal shall simultaneously serve copies of the index to all non-indigent defendants and, upon their request, copies of the record or portions thereof at the cost prescribed by law.

(5) *Return of Record.* Except in death penalty cases, the court shall return the record to the lower tribunal after final disposition of the appeal.

(6) *Supplemental Record for Motion to Correct Sentencing Error Pursuant to Florida Rule of Criminal Procedure 3.800(b)(2).*

(A) The clerk of circuit court shall automatically supplement the appellate record with any motion pursuant to Florida Rule of Criminal Procedure 3.800(b)(2), any response, any resulting order, and any amended sentence. The clerk shall electronically transmit the supplement to the court within 5 days of the filing of the order ruling on the motion. If an order is not filed within 60 days from the filing of the motion, this time shall run from the expiration of the 60 day period, and the clerk shall supplement the record with the motion and a statement that no order was timely filed.

(B) If any appellate counsel determines that a transcript of a proceeding relating to such a motion is required to review the sentencing issue, appellate counsel shall, within 5 days from the transmittal of the supplement described in subdivision (A), designate those portions of the proceedings not on file deemed necessary for transcription and inclusion in the record. A copy of the designation shall be filed with the court. The procedure for this supplementation shall be in accordance with this subdivision, except that counsel is not required to file a revised statement of judicial acts to be reviewed, the approved court reporter or approved transcriptionist shall deliver the transcript within 15 days, and the clerk shall supplement the record with the transcript within 5 days of its receipt.

(g) Briefs. Initial briefs shall be served within 30 days of service of the record or designation of appointed counsel, whichever is later. Additional briefs shall be served as prescribed by rule 9.210.

(h) Post–Trial Release.

(1) *Appeal by Defendant.* The lower tribunal may hear a motion for post-trial release pending appeal before or after a notice is filed; provided that the defendant may not be released from custody until the notice is filed.

(2) *Appeal by State.* An incarcerated defendant charged with a bailable offense shall on motion be released on the defendant's own recognizance pending an appeal by the state, unless the lower tribunal for good cause stated in an order determines otherwise.

(3) *Denial of Post–Trial Release.* All orders denying post-trial release shall set forth the factual basis on which the decision was made and the reasons therefor.

(4) *Review.* Review of an order relating to post-trial release shall be by the court on motion.

(i) Scope of Review. The court shall review all rulings and orders appearing in the record necessary to pass upon the grounds of an appeal. In the interest of justice, the court may grant any relief to which any party is entitled.

Amended Nov. 1, 1979, effective Jan. 1, 1980 (376 So.2d 844); March 27, 1980, effective April 1, 1980 (381 So.2d 1370); Dec. 15, 1983 (443 So.2d 972); Sept. 13, 1984, effective Jan. 1, 1985 (463 So.2d 1114); June 8, 1987, effective July 1, 1987 (509 So.2d 276); Oct. 22, 1992, effective Jan. 1, 1993 (609 So.2d 516); Nov. 22, 1996, effective Jan. 1, 1997 (685 So.2d 773); Nov. 12, 1999 (760 So.2d 67); Jan. 13, 2000 (761 So.2d 1015); Oct. 12, 2000, effective Jan. 1, 2001 (780 So.2d 834); Oct. 18, 2001, (807 So.2d 633); Aug. 29, 2002, effective Jan. 1, 2003 (827 So.2d 888); Oct. 31, 2002, effective Jan. 1, 2003 (837 So.2d 911); May 20, 2004, effective Oct. 1, 2004 (875 So.2d 563); April 7, 2005 (901 So.2d 109); Oct. 26, 2006, effective Jan. 1, 2007 (941 So.2d 352); Nov. 13, 2008, effective Jan. 1, 2009 (2 So.3d 89); July 16, 2009 (13 So.3d 1044); Nov. 3, 2011, effective Jan. 1, 2012 (75 So.3d 239); Oct. 18, 2012, effective Dec. 1, 2012, April 1, 2013, Oct. 1, 2013 (102 So.3d 451); April 18, 2013, revised Dec. 5, 2013, effective, *nunc pro tunc*, July 1, 2013 (132 So.3d 734); Nov. 6, 2014, effective Jan. 1, 2015 (2014 WL 5714099).

Committee Notes

1977 Amendment. This rule represents a substantial revision of the procedure in criminal appeals.

Subdivision (a) makes clear the policy of these rules that procedures be standardized to the maximum extent possible. Criminal appeals are to be governed by the same rules as other cases, except for those matters unique to criminal law that are identified and controlled by this rule.

Subdivision (b)(1) lists the only matters that may be appealed by a criminal defendant, and it is intended to supersede all other rules of practice and procedure. This rule has no effect on either the availability of extraordinary writs otherwise within the jurisdiction of the court to grant, or the supreme court's jurisdiction to entertain petitions for the constitutional writ of certiorari to review interlocutory orders. This rule also incorporates the holding in *State v. Ashby*, 245 So. 2d 225 (Fla. 1971), and is intended to make clear that the reservation of the right to appeal a judgment based on the plea of no contest must be express and must identify the particular point of law being reserved; any issues not expressly reserved are waived. No direct appeal of a judgment based on a guilty plea is allowed. It was not intended that this rule affect the substantive law governing collateral review.

Subdivision (b)(2) replaces former rule 6.2. Specific reference is made to rule 9.110(d) to emphasize that criminal appeals are to be prosecuted in substantially the same manner as other cases. Copies of the notice, however, must be served on both the state attorney and the attorney general. The time for taking an appeal has been made to run from the date judgment is rendered to 30 days after an order imposing sentence is rendered or otherwise reduced to writing. The former rule provided for appeal within 30 days of rendition of judgment or within 30 days of entry of sentence. The advisory committee debated the intent of the literal language of the former rule. Arguably, under the former rule an appeal could not be taken by a defendant during the "gap period" that occurs when sentencing is postponed more than 30 days after entry of judgment. The advisory committee concluded that no purpose was served by such an interpretation because the full case would be reviewable when the "gap" closed. This modification of the former rule promotes the policies underlying *Williams v. State*, 324 So. 2d 74 (Fla. 1975), in which it was held that a notice of appeal prematurely filed should not be dismissed, but held in abeyance until it becomes effective. This rule does not specifically address the issue of whether full review is available if re-sentencing occurs on order of a court in a collateral proceeding. Such cases should be resolved in accordance with the underlying policies of these rules. Compare *Wade v. State*, 222 So. 2d 434 (Fla. 2d DCA 1969), with *Neary v. State*, 285 So. 2d 47 (Fla. 4th DCA 1973). If a defendant appeals a judgment of conviction of a capital offense before sentencing and sentencing is anticipated, the district court of appeal (as the court then with jurisdiction) should hold the case in abeyance until the sentence has been imposed. If the death penalty is imposed, the district court of appeal should transfer the case to the supreme court for review. See § 921.141(4), Fla. Stat. (1975); Fla. R. App. P. 9.040(b).

Subdivision (b)(3) governs the service of briefs. Filing should be made in accordance with rule 9.420.

Subdivision (c)(1) lists the only matters that may be appealed by the state, but it is not intended to affect the jurisdiction of the supreme court to entertain by certiorari interlocutory appeals governed by rule 9.100, or the jurisdiction of circuit courts to entertain interlocutory appeals of pretrial orders from the county courts. See *State v. Smith*, 260 So. 2d 489 (Fla. 1972). No provision of this rule is intended to conflict with a defendant's constitutional right not to be placed twice in jeopardy, and it should be interpreted accordingly. If there is an appeal under item (A), a motion for a stay of the lower tribunal proceeding should be liberally granted in cases in which there appears to be a substantial possibility that trial of any non-dismissed charges would bar prosecution of the dismissed charges if the dismissal were reversed, such as in cases involving the so-called "single transaction rule." Item (E) refers to the popularly known "speedy trial rule," and items (F), (G), and (H) track the balance of state appellate rights in section 924.07, Florida Statutes (1975).

Subdivision (c)(2) parallels subdivision (b)(2) regarding appeals by defendants except that a maximum of 15 days is allowed for filing the notice. An appeal by the state stays further proceedings in the lower tribunal only if an order has been entered by the trial court.

Subdivision (c)(3) governs the service of briefs.

Subdivision (d) applies rule 9.200 to criminal appeals and sets forth the time for preparation and service of the record, and additional matters peculiar to criminal cases. It has been made mandatory that the original record be held by the lower tribunal to avoid loss and destruction of original papers while in transit. To meet the needs of appellate counsel for indigents, provision has been made for automatic transmittal of a copy of the record to the public defender appointed to represent an indigent defendant on appeal, which in any particular case may be the public defender either in the judicial circuit where the trial took place or in the judicial circuit wherein the appellate court is located. See § 27.51(4), Fla. Stat. (1975). Counsel for a non-indigent defendant may obtain a copy of the record at the cost prescribed by law. At the present time, section 28.24(13), Florida Statutes (1975), as amended by chapter 77–284, § 1, Laws of Florida, prescribes a cost of $1 per page.

To conserve the public treasury, appeals by indigent defendants and other criminal defendants in cases in which a free transcript is provided, have been specially treated. Only the essential portions of the transcript are to be prepared. The appellant must file a statement of the judicial acts to be reviewed on appeal and the parties are to file and serve designations of the relevant portions of the record. (This procedure emphasizes the obligation of trial counsel to cooperate with appellate counsel, if the two are different, in identifying alleged trial errors.) The statement is necessary to afford the appellee an opportunity to make a reasonable determination of the portions of the record required. The statement should be sufficiently definite to enable the opposing party to make that determination, but greater specificity is unnecessary. The statement of judicial acts contemplated by this rule is not intended to be the equivalent of assignments of error under former rule 3.5. Therefore, an error or inadequacy in the statement should not be relevant to the disposition of any case. In such circumstances, the appropriate procedure would be to supplement the record under rule 9.200(f) to cure any potential or actual prejudice. Either party may move in the lower tribunal to strike unnecessary portions before they are prepared or to expand the transcript. The ruling of the lower tribunal on such motion is reviewable by motion to the court under rule 9.200(f) if a party asserts additional portions are required.

Subdivision (e) replaces former rule 6.15. Subdivision (e)(1) governs if an appeal is taken by a defendant and permits a motion to grant post-trial release pending appeal to be heard although a notice of appeal has not yet been filed. The lower tribunal may then grant the motion effective on the notice being filed. This rule is intended to eliminate practical difficulties that on occasion have frustrated the cause of justice, as in cases in which a defendant's attorney has not prepared a notice of appeal in advance of judgment. Consideration of such motions shall be in accordance with section 903.132, Florida Statutes (Supp. 1976), and Florida Rule of Criminal Procedure 3.691. This rule does not apply if the judgment is based on a guilty plea because no right to appeal such a conviction is recognized by these rules.

Subdivision (e)(2) governs if the state takes an appeal and authorizes release of the defendant without bond, if charged with a bailable offense, unless the lower tribunal for good cause orders otherwise. The "good cause" standard was adopted to ensure that bond be required only in rare circumstances. The advisory committee was of the view that because the state generally will not be able to gain a conviction unless it prevails, the presumed innocent defendant should not be required to undergo incarceration without strong reasons, especially if a pretrial appeal is involved. "Good cause" therefore includes such factors as the likelihood of success on appeal and the likelihood the defendant will leave the jurisdiction in light of the current status of the charges against the defendant.

Subdivision (e)(3) retains the substance of former rules 6.15(b) and (c). The lower tribunal's order must contain a statement of facts as well as the reasons for the action taken, in accordance with *Younghans v. State*, 90 So. 2d 308 (Fla. 1956).

Subdivision (e)(4) allows review only by motion so that no order regarding post-trial relief is reviewable unless jurisdiction has been vested in the court by the filing of a notice of appeal. It is intended that the amount of bail be reviewable for excessiveness.

Subdivision (f) interacts with rule 9.110(h) to allow review of multiple judgments and sentences in 1 proceeding.

Subdivision (g) sets forth the procedure to be followed if there is a summary denial without hearing of a motion for post-conviction relief under Florida Rule of Criminal Procedure 3.850. This rule does not limit the right to appeal a denial of such a motion after hearing under rule 9.140(b)(1)(C).

1980 Amendment. Although the substance of this rule has not been changed, the practitioner should note that references in the 1977 committee notes to supreme court jurisdiction to review non-final orders that would have been appealable if they had been final orders are obsolete because jurisdiction to review those orders no longer reposes in the supreme court.

1984 Amendment. Subdivision (b)(4) was added to give effect to the administrative order entered by the supreme court on May 6, 1981 (6 Fla. L. Weekly 336), which recognized that the procedures set forth in the rules for criminal appeals were inappropriate for capital cases.

1992 Amendment. Subdivision (b)(3) was amended to provide that, in cases in which public funds would be used to prepare the record on appeal, the attorney of record would not be allowed to withdraw until substitute counsel has been obtained or appointed.

Subdivision (g) was amended to provide a specific procedure to be followed by the courts in considering appeals from summary denial of Florida Rule of Criminal Procedure 3.800(a) motions. Because such motions are in many respects comparable to Florida Rule of Criminal Procedure 3.850 motions, it was decided to use the available format already created by existing subdivision (g) of this rule. Because a Florida Rule of Criminal Procedure 3.800(a) motion does not have the same detailed requirements as does a Florida Rule of Criminal Procedure 3.850 motion, this subdivision also was amended to require the transmittal of any attachments to the motions in the lower court.

1996 Amendment. The 1996 amendments are intended to consolidate and clarify the rules to reflect current law unless otherwise specified.

Rule 9.140(b)(2)(B) was added to accurately reflect the limited right of direct appeal after a plea of guilty or nolo contendere. See *Robinson v. State*, 373 So. 2d 898 (Fla. 1979), and *Counts v. State*, 376 So. 2d 59 (Fla. 2d DCA 1979).

New subdivision (b)(4) reflects *Lopez v. State*, 638 So. 2d 931 (Fla. 1994). A defendant may cross-appeal as provided, but if the defendant chooses not to do so, the defendant retains the right to raise any properly preserved issue on plenary appeal. It is the committee's intention that the 10–day period for filing notice of the cross-appeal should be interpreted in the same manner as in civil cases under rule 9.110(g).

Rule 9.140(b)(6)(E) adopts Florida Rule of Criminal Procedure 3.851(b)(2) and is intended to supersede that rule. See Fla. R. Jud. Admin. 2.135. The rule also makes clear that the time periods in rule 9.140(j) do not apply to death penalty cases.

The revised rules 9.140(e)(2)(D) and 9.140(e)(2)(E) are intended to supersede *Brown v. State*, 639 So. 2d 634 (Fla. 5th DCA 1994), and allow non-indigent defendants represented by counsel, and the state, to order just the original transcript from the court reporter and to make copies. However, the original and copies for all other parties must then be served on the clerk of the lower tribunal for inclusion in the record. The revised rule 9.140(e)(2)(F) also allows chief judges for each circuit to promulgate an administrative order requiring the lower tribunal clerk's office to make copies of the transcript when the defendant is indigent. In the absence of such an administrative order, the court reporter will furnish an original and copies for all parties in indigent appeals.

Rule 9.140(j)(3) imposes a two-year time limit on proceedings to obtain delayed appellate review based on either the ineffectiveness of counsel on a prior appeal or the failure to timely initiate an appeal by appointed counsel. The former was previously applied for by a petition for writ of habeas corpus in the appellate court and the latter by motion pursuant to Florida Rule of Criminal Procedure 3.850 in the trial court. Because both of these remedies did not require a filing fee, it is contemplated that no fee will be required for the filing of petitions under this rule. Subdivision (j)(3)(B) allows two years "after the conviction becomes final. " For purposes of the subdivision a conviction becomes final after issuance of the mandate or other final process of the highest court to which direct review is taken, including review in the Florida Supreme Court and United States Supreme Court. Any collateral review shall not stay the time period under this subdivision. Subdivision (j)(3)(C) under this rule makes clear that defendants who were convicted before the effective date of the rule will not have their rights retroactively extinguished but will be subject to the time limits as calculated from the effective date of the rule unless the time has already commenced to run under rule 3.850.

Rule 9.140(j)(5) was added to provide a uniform procedure for requesting belated appeal and to supersede *State v. District Court of Appeal of Florida, First District*, 569 So. 2d 439 (Fla. 1990). This decision resulted in there being two procedures for requesting belated appeal: Florida Rule of Criminal Procedure 3.850 when the criminal appeal was frustrated by ineffective assistance of trial counsel, *id.*; and habeas corpus for everything else. See *Scalf v. Singletary*, 589 So. 2d 986 (Fla. 2d DCA 1991). Experience showed that filing in the appellate court was more efficient. This rule is intended to reinstate the procedure as it existed prior to *State v. District Court of Appeal, First District*. See *Baggett v. Wainwright*, 229 So. 2d 239 (Fla. 1969); *State v. Meyer*, 430 So. 2d 440 (Fla. 1983).

In the rare case where entitlement to belated appeal depends on a determination of disputed facts, the appellate court may appoint a commissioner to make a report and recommendation.

2000 Amendment. Subdivision (b)(1)(B) was added to reflect the holding of *State v. Schultz*, 720

So. 2d 247 (Fla. 1998). The amendment to renumber subdivision (b)(1)(D), regarding appeals from orders denying relief under Florida Rules of Criminal Procedure 3.800(a) or 3.850, reflects current practice.

The committee added language to subdivision (b)(6)(B) to require court reporters to file transcripts on computer disks in death penalty cases. Death penalty transcripts typically are lengthy, and many persons review and use them over the years. In these cases, filing lengthy transcripts on computer disks makes them easier to use for all parties and increases their longevity.

The committee deleted the last sentence of subdivision (b)(6)(E) because its substance is now included in rule 9.141(a). The committee also amended and transferred subdivisions (i) and (j) to rule 9.141 for the reasons specified in the committee note for that rule.

2005 Amendment. New subdivision (L) was added to (c)(1) in response to the Florida legislature's enactment of section 775.08435(3), Florida Statutes (2004), which provides that "[t]he withholding of adjudication in violation of this section is subject to appellate review under chapter 924."

Court Commentary

1996. Rule 9.140 was substantially rewritten so as to harmonize with the Criminal Appeal Reform Act of 1996 (CS/HB 211). The reference to unlawful sentences in rule 9.140(b)(1)(D) and (c)(1)(J) means those sentences not meeting the definition of illegal under *Davis v. State*, 661 So. 2d 1193 (Fla. 1995), but, nevertheless, subject to correction on direct appeal.

Rule 9.141. Review Proceedings in Collateral or Post-Conviction Criminal Cases

(a) Death Penalty Cases. This rule does not apply to death penalty cases.

(b) Appeals from Post-Conviction Proceedings Under Florida Rule of Criminal Procedure 3.800(a), 3.801, 3.850, or 3.853.

(1) *Applicability of Civil Appellate Procedures.* Appeal proceedings under this subdivision shall be as in civil cases, except as modified by this rule.

(2) *Summary Grant or Denial of All Claims Raised in a Motion Without Evidentiary Hearing.*

(A) Record. When a motion for post-conviction relief under rule 3.800(a), 3.801, 3.850, or 3.853 is granted or denied without an evidentiary hearing, the clerk of the lower tribunal shall electronically transmit to the court, as the record, the motion, response, reply, order on the motion, motion for rehearing, response, reply, order on the motion for rehearing, and attachments to any of the foregoing, together with the certified copy of the notice of appeal.

(B) Index. Unless directed otherwise by the court, the clerk of the lower tribunal shall not index or paginate the record or send copies of the index or record to the parties.

(C) Briefs or Responses.

(i) Briefs are not required, but the appellant may serve an initial brief within 30 days of filing the notice of appeal. The appellee need not file an answer brief unless directed by the court. The appellant may serve a reply brief as prescribed by rule 9.210.

(ii) The court may request a response from the appellee before ruling, regardless of whether the appellant filed an initial brief. The appellant may serve a reply within 20 days after service of the response. The response and reply shall not exceed the page limits set forth in rule 9.210 for answer briefs and reply briefs.

(D) Disposition. On appeal from the denial of relief, unless the record shows conclusively that the appellant is entitled to no relief, the order shall be reversed and the cause remanded for an evidentiary hearing or other appropriate relief.

(3) *Grant or Denial of Motion after an Evidentiary Hearing was Held on One or More Claims.*

(A) Transcription. In the absence of designations to the court reporter, the notice of appeal filed by an indigent pro se litigant in a rule 3.801, 3.850, or 3.853 appeal after an evidentiary hearing shall serve as the designation to the court reporter for the transcript of the evidentiary hearing. Within 5 days of receipt of the notice of appeal, the clerk of the lower tribunal shall request the appropriate court reporter to transcribe the evidentiary hearing and shall send the court reporter a copy of the notice, the date of the hearing to be transcribed, the name of the judge, and a copy of this rule.

(B) Record.

(i) When a motion for post-conviction relief under rule 3.801, 3.850, or 3.853 is granted or denied after an evidentiary hearing, the clerk of the lower tribunal shall index, paginate, and electronically transmit to the court as the record, within 50 days of the filing of the notice of appeal, the notice of appeal, motion, response, reply, order on the motion, motion for rehearing, response, reply, order on the motion for rehearing, and attachments to any of the foregoing, as well as the transcript of the evidentiary hearing.

(ii) Appellant may direct the clerk to include in the record any other documents that were before the lower tribunal at the hearing. If the clerk is directed to include in the record a previously prepared appellate record involving the appellant, the clerk need not reindex or repaginate it.

(iii) The clerk of the lower tribunal shall serve copies of the record on the attorney general (or state attorney in appeals to the circuit court), all counsel appointed to represent indigent defendants on appeal, and any pro se indigent defendant. The clerk of the lower tribunal shall simultaneously serve copies of the index on all nonindigent defendants and, at their request, copies of the record or portions of it at the cost prescribed by law.

(C) Briefs. Initial briefs shall be served within 30 days of service of the record or its index. Additional briefs shall be served as prescribed by rule 9.210.

(c) Petitions Seeking Belated Appeal or Belated Discretionary Review.

(1) *Applicability.* This subdivision governs petitions seeking belated appeals or belated discretionary review.

(2) *Treatment as Original Proceedings.* Review proceedings under this subdivision shall be treated as original proceedings under rule 9.100, except as modified by this rule.

(3) *Forum.* Petitions seeking belated review shall be filed in the court to which the appeal or discretionary review should have been taken.

(4) *Contents.* The petition shall be in the form prescribed by rule 9.100, may include supporting documents, and shall recite in the statement of facts

(A) the date and nature of the lower tribunal's order sought to be reviewed;

(B) the name of the lower tribunal rendering the order;

(C) the nature, disposition, and dates of all previous court proceedings;

(D) if a previous petition was filed, the reason the claim in the present petition was not raised previously;

(E) the nature of the relief sought; and

(F) the specific acts sworn to by the petitioner or petitioner's counsel that constitute the basis for entitlement to belated appeal or belated discretionary review, as outlined below:

(i) A petition seeking belated appeal must state whether the petitioner requested counsel to proceed with the appeal and the date of any such request, or if the petitioner was misadvised as to the availability of appellate review or the status of filing a notice of appeal. A petition seeking belated discretionary review must state whether counsel advised the petitioner of the results of the appeal and the date of any such notification, or if counsel misadvised the petitioner as to the opportunity for seeking discretionary review, or

(ii) A petition seeking belated appeal or belated discretionary review must identify the circumstances unrelated to counsel's action or inaction, including names of individuals involved and date(s) of the occurrence(s), that were beyond the petitioner's control and otherwise interfered with the petitioner's ability to file a timely appeal or notice to invoke, as applicable.

(5) *Time Limits.*

(A) A petition for belated appeal shall not be filed more than 2 years after the expiration of time for filing the notice of appeal from a final order, unless it alleges under oath with a specific factual basis that the petitioner was unaware a notice of appeal had not been timely filed or was not advised of the right to an appeal or was otherwise prevented from timely filing the notice of appeal due to circumstances beyond the petitioner's control, and could not have ascertained such facts by the exercise of reasonable diligence. In no case shall a petition for belated appeal be filed more than 4 years after the expiration of time for filing the notice of appeal.

(B) A petition for belated discretionary review shall not be filed more than 2 years after the expiration of time for filing the notice to invoke discretionary review from a final order, unless it alleges under oath with a specific factual basis that the petitioner was unaware such notice had not been timely filed or was not advised of the results of the appeal, or was otherwise prevented from timely filing the notice due to circumstances beyond the petitioner's control, and that the petitioner could not have ascertained such facts by the exercise of reasonable diligence. In no case shall a petition for belated discretionary review be filed more than 4 years after the expiration of time for filing the notice to invoke discretionary review from a final order.

(6) *Procedure.*

(A) The petitioner shall serve a copy of a petition for belated appeal on the attorney general and state attorney. The petitioner shall serve a copy of a petition for belated discretionary review on the attorney general.

(B) The court may by order identify any provision of this rule that the petition fails to satisfy and, pursuant to rule 9.040(d), allow the petitioner a specified time to serve an amended petition.

(C) The court may dismiss a second or successive petition if it does not allege new grounds and the prior determination was on the merits, or if a failure to assert the grounds was an abuse of procedure.

(D) An order granting a petition for belated appeal shall be filed with the lower tribunal and treated as the notice of appeal, if no previous notice has been filed. An order granting a petition for belated discretionary review or belated appeal of a decision of a district court of appeal shall be filed with the district court and treated as a notice to invoke discretionary jurisdiction or notice of appeal, if no previous notice has been filed.

(d) Petitions Alleging Ineffective Assistance of Appellate Counsel.

(1) *Applicability.* This subdivision governs petitions alleging ineffective assistance of appellate counsel.

(2) *Treatment as Original Proceedings.* Review proceedings under this subdivision shall be treated as original proceedings under rule 9.100, except as modified by this rule.

(3) *Forum.* Petitions alleging ineffective assistance of appellate counsel shall be filed in the court to which the appeal was taken.

(4) *Contents.* The petition shall be in the form prescribed by rule 9.100, may include supporting documents, and shall recite in the statement of facts:

(A) the date and nature of the lower tribunal's order subject to the disputed appeal;

(B) the name of the lower tribunal rendering the order;

(C) the nature, disposition, and dates of all previous court proceedings;

(D) if a previous petition was filed, the reason the claim in the present petition was not raised previously;

(E) the nature of the relief sought; and

(F) the specific acts sworn to by the petitioner or petitioner's counsel that constitute the alleged ineffective assistance of counsel.

(5) *Time Limits.* A petition alleging ineffective assistance of appellate counsel on direct review shall not be filed more than 2 years after the judgment and sentence become final on direct review unless it alleges under oath with a specific factual basis that the petitioner was affirmatively misled about the results of the appeal by counsel. In no case shall a petition alleging ineffective assistance of appellate counsel on direct review be filed more than 4 years after the judgment and sentence become final on direct review.

(6) *Procedure.*

(A) The petitioner shall serve a copy of the petition on the attorney general.

(B) The court may by order identify any provision of this rule that the petition fails to satisfy and, pursuant to rule 9.040(d), allow the petitioner a specified time to serve an amended petition.

(C) The court may dismiss a second or successive petition if it does not allege new grounds and the prior determination was on the merits, or if a failure to assert the grounds was an abuse of procedure.

Adopted Oct. 12, 2000, effective Jan. 1, 2001 (780 So.2d 834). Amended Oct. 18, 2001 (807 So.2d 633); Nov. 15, 2007 (969 So.2d 357); Sept. 25, 2008 (992 So.2d 233); Jan. 29, 2009 (1 So.3d 168); June 23, 2011, eff. July 1, 2011 (72 So.3d 735); Oct. 18, 2012, effective Dec. 1, 2012, April 1, 2013, Oct. 1, 2013 (102 So.3d 451); April 18, 2013, revised Dec. 5, 2013, effective *nunc pro tunc* July 1, 2013 (132 So.3d 734); Nov. 6, 2014, effective Jan. 1, 2015 (2014 WL 5714099).

Committee Notes

2000 Amendment. Rule 9.141 is a new rule governing review of collateral or post-conviction criminal cases. It covers topics formerly included in rules 9.140(i) and (j). The committee opted to transfer these subjects to a new rule, in part because rule 9.140 was becoming lengthy. In addition, review proceedings for collateral criminal cases are in some respects treated as civil appeals or as extraordinary writs, rather than criminal appeals under rule 9.140.

Subdivision (a) clarifies that this rule does not apply to death penalty cases. The Supreme Court has its own procedures for these cases, and the committee did not attempt to codify them.

Subdivision (b)(2) amends former rule 9.140(i) and addresses review of summary grants or denials of post-conviction motions under Florida Rules of Criminal Procedure 3.800(a) or 3.850. Amended language in subdivision (b)(2)(A) makes minor changes to the contents of the record in such cases. Subdivision (b)(2)(B) addresses a conflict between *Summers v. State*, 570 So.2d 990 (Fla. 1st DCA 1990), and *Fleming v. State*, 709 So.2d 135 (Fla. 2d DCA 1998), regarding indexing and pagination of records. The First District requires clerks to index and paginate the records, while the other district courts do not. The committee determined not to require indexing and pagination unless the court directs otherwise, thereby allowing individual courts to require indexing and pagination if they so desire. Subdivision (b)(2)(B) also provides that neither the state nor the defendant should get a copy of the record in these cases, because they should already have all of the relevant documents. Subdivision (b)(2)(D) reflects current case law that the court can reverse not only for an evidentiary hearing but also for other appropriate relief.

Subdivision (b)(3) addresses review of grants or denials of post-conviction motions under rule 3.850 after an evidentiary hearing. Subdivision (b)(3)(A) provides for the preparation of a transcript if an indigent pro se litigant fails to request the court reporter to prepare it. The court cannot effectively carry out its duties without a transcript to review, and an indigent litigant will usually be entitled to preparation of the transcript and a copy of the record at no charge. *See Colonel v. State*, 723 So.2d 853 (Fla. 3d DCA 1998). The procedures in subdivisions (b)(3)(B) and (C) for preparation of the record and service of briefs are intended to be similar to those provided in rule 9.140 for direct appeals from judgments and sentences.

Subdivision (c) is a slightly reorganized and clarified version of former rule 9.140(j). No substantive changes are intended.

Rule 9.142. Procedures for Review in Death Penalty Cases

(a) Procedure in Death Penalty Appeals.

(1) *Record.*

(A) When the notice of appeal is filed in the supreme court, the chief justice will direct the appropriate chief judge of the circuit court to monitor the preparation of the complete record for timely filing in the supreme court. Transcripts of all proceedings conducted in the lower tribunal shall be included in the record under these rules.

(B) The complete record in a death penalty appeal shall include all items required by rule 9.200 and by any order issued by the supreme court. In any appeal following the initial direct appeal, the record that is electronically transmitted shall begin with the most recent mandate issued by the supreme court, or the most recent filing not already electronically transmitted in a prior record in the event the preceding appeal was disposed of without a mandate, and shall exclude any materials already transmitted to the supreme court as the record in any prior appeal. The clerk of the lower tribunal shall retain a copy of the complete record when it transmits the record to the Supreme Court.

(C) The supreme court shall take judicial notice of the appellate records in all prior appeals and writ proceedings involving a challenge to the same judgment of conviction and sentence of death. Appellate records subject to judicial notice under this subdivision shall not be duplicated in the record transmitted for the appeal under review.

(2) *Briefs; Transcripts.* After the record is filed, the clerk will promptly establish a briefing schedule allowing the defendant 60 days from the date the record is filed, the state 45 days from the date the defendant's brief is served, and the defendant 30 days from the date the state's brief is served to serve their respective briefs. On appeals from orders ruling on applications for relief under Florida Rule of Criminal Procedure 3.851 or 3.853, and on resentencing matters, the schedules set forth in rule 9.140(g) will control.

(3) *Sanctions.* If any brief is delinquent, an order to show cause may issue under Florida Rule of Criminal Procedure 3.840, and sanctions may be imposed.

(4) *Oral Argument.* Oral argument will be scheduled after the filing of the defendant's reply brief.

(5) *Scope of Review.* On direct appeal in death penalty cases, whether or not insufficiency of the evidence or proportionality is an issue presented for review, the court shall review these issues and, if necessary, remand for the appropriate relief.

(b) Petitions for Extraordinary Relief.

(1) *Treatment as Original Proceedings.* Review proceedings under this subdivision shall be treated as original proceedings under rule 9.100, except as modified by this rule.

(2) *Contents.* Any petition filed pursuant to this subdivision shall be in the form prescribed by rule 9.100, may include supporting documents, and shall recite in the statement of facts

(A) the date and nature of the lower tribunal's order sought to be reviewed;

(B) the name of the lower tribunal rendering the order;

(C) the nature, disposition, and dates of all previous court proceedings;

(D) if a previous petition was filed, the reason the claim in the present petition was not raised previously;

(E) the nature of the relief sought.

(3) *Petitions Seeking Belated Appeal.*

(A) **Contents.** A petition for belated appeal shall include a detailed allegation of the specific acts sworn to by the petitioner or petitioner's counsel that constitute the basis for entitlement to belated appeal, including whether petitioner requested counsel to proceed with the appeal and the date of any such request, whether counsel misadvised the petitioner as to the availability of appellate review or the filing of the notice of appeal, or whether there were circumstances unrelated to counsel's action or inaction, including names of individuals involved and date(s) of the occurrence(s), that were beyond the petitioner's control and otherwise interfered with the petitioner's ability to file a timely appeal.

(B) **Time limits.** A petition for belated appeal shall not be filed more than 1 year after the expiration of time for filing the notice of appeal from a final order denying rule 3.851 relief, unless it alleges under oath with a specific factual basis that the petitioner

(i) was unaware an appeal had not been timely filed, was not advised of the right to an appeal, was misadvised as to the right to an appeal, or was prevented from timely filing a notice of appeal due to circumstances beyond the petitioner's control; and

(ii) could not have ascertained such facts by the exercise of due diligence.

In no case shall a petition for belated appeal be filed more than 2 years after the expiration of time for filing the notice of appeal.

(4) *Petitions Alleging Ineffective Assistance of Appellate Counsel.*

(A) **Contents.** A petition alleging ineffective assistance of appellate counsel shall include detailed allegations of the specific acts that constitute the alleged ineffective assistance of counsel on direct appeal.

(B) **Time limits.** A petition alleging ineffective assistance of appellate counsel shall be filed simultaneously with the initial brief in the appeal from the lower tribunal's order on the defendant's application for relief under Florida Rule of Criminal Procedure 3.851.

(c) Petition Seeking Review of Nonfinal Orders in Death Penalty Postconviction Proceedings.

(1) *Applicability.* This rule applies to proceedings that invoke the jurisdiction of the supreme court for review of nonfinal orders issued in postconviction proceedings following the imposition of the death penalty.

(2) *Treatment as Original Proceedings.* Review proceedings under this subdivision shall be treated as original proceedings under rule 9.100 unless modified by this subdivision.

(3) *Commencement; Parties.*

(A) Jurisdiction of the supreme court shall be invoked by filing a petition with the clerk of the supreme court within 30 days of rendition of the nonfinal order to be reviewed. A copy of the petition shall be served on the opposing party and furnished to the judge who issued the order to be reviewed.

(B) Either party to the death penalty postconviction proceedings may seek review under this rule.

(4) *Contents.* The petition shall be in the form prescribed by rule 9.100, and shall contain

(A) the basis for invoking the jurisdiction of the court;

(B) the date and nature of the order sought to be reviewed;

(C) the name of the lower tribunal rendering the order;

(D) the name, disposition, and dates of all previous trial, appellate, and postconviction proceedings relating to the conviction and death sentence that are the subject of the proceedings in which the order sought to be reviewed was entered;

(E) the facts on which the petitioner relies, with references to the appropriate pages of the supporting appendix;

(F) argument in support of the petition, including an explanation of why the order departs from the essential requirements of law and how the order may cause material injury for which there is no adequate remedy on appeal, and appropriate citations of authority; and

(G) the nature of the relief sought.

(5) *Appendix.* The petition shall be accompanied by an appendix, as prescribed by rule 9.220, which shall contain the portions of the record necessary for a determination of the issues presented.

(6) *Order to Show Cause.* If the petition demonstrates a preliminary basis for relief or a departure from the essential requirements of law that may cause material injury for which there is no adequate remedy by appeal, the court may issue an order directing the respondent to show cause, within the time set by the court, why relief should not be granted.

(7) *Response.* No response shall be permitted unless ordered by the court.

(8) *Reply.* Within 20 days after service of the response or such other time set by the court, the petitioner may serve a reply, which shall not exceed 15 pages in length, and supplemental appendix.

(9) *Stay.*

(A) A stay of proceedings under this rule is not automatic; the party seeking a stay must petition the supreme court for a stay of proceedings.

(B) During the pendency of a review of a nonfinal order, unless a stay is granted by the supreme court, the lower tribunal may proceed with all matters, except that the lower tribunal may not render a final order disposing of the cause pending review of the nonfinal order.

(10) *Other Pleadings.* The parties shall not file any other pleadings, motions, replies, or miscellaneous documents without leave of court.

(11) *Time Limitations.* Seeking review under this rule shall not extend the time limitations in rule 3.851 or 3.852.

(d) Review of Dismissal of Post–Conviction Proceedings and Discharge of Counsel in Florida Rule of Criminal Procedure 3. 851(i) Cases.

(1) *Applicability.* This rule applies when the circuit court enters an order dismissing postconviction proceedings and discharging counsel under Florida Rule of Criminal Procedure 3.851(i).

(2) *Procedure Following Rendition of Order of Dismissal and Discharge.*

(A) **Notice to Lower Tribunal.** Within 10 days of the rendition of an order granting a prisoner's motion to discharge counsel and dismiss the motion for post-conviction relief, discharged counsel shall file with the clerk of the circuit court a notice seeking review in the supreme court.

(B) **Transcription.** The circuit judge presiding over any hearing on a motion to dismiss and discharge counsel shall order a transcript of the hearing to be prepared and filed with the clerk of the circuit court no later than 25 days from rendition of the final order.

(C) **Record.** Within 30 days of the granting of a motion to dismiss and discharge counsel, the clerk of the circuit court shall electronically transmit a copy of the motion, order, and transcripts of all hearings held on the motion to the clerk of the supreme court.

(D) **Proceedings in Supreme Court.** Within 20 days of the filing of the record in the supreme court, discharged counsel shall serve an initial brief. Both the state and the prisoner may serve responsive briefs. All briefs must be served and filed as prescribed by rule 9.210.

Added Oct. 31, 2002, effective Jan. 1, 2003 (837 So.2d 911). Amended Feb. 3, 2005 (894 So.2d 202); Nov. 15, 2007 (969 So.2d 357); Dec. 30, 2008 (1 So.3d 163); Oct. 15, 2009 (20 So.3d 380); June 23, 2011, eff. July 1, 2011 (72 So.3d 735); Oct. 18, 2012, effective Dec. 1, 2012, April 1, 2013, Oct. 1, 2013 (102 So.3d 451); July 3, 2014, effective January 1, 2015 (151 So.3d 1217); Nov. 6, 2014, effective Jan. 1, 2015 (2014 WL 5714099).

Committee Notes

2009 Amendment. Subdivision (a)(1) has been amended to clarify what is meant by the phrase "complete record" in any death penalty appeal. A complete record in a death penalty appeal includes all items required by rule 9.200 and by any order issued by the supreme court, including any administrative orders such as In Re: Record in Capital Cases (Fla. July 6, 1995). It is necessary for transcripts of all hearings to be prepared and designated for inclusion in the record in all death penalty cases under rules 9.200(b), 9.140(f)(2), and 9.142(a)(2), to ensure completeness for both present and future review. The supreme court permanently retains the records in all death penalty appeals and writ proceedings arising from a death penalty case. See rule 9.140(f)(5); Florida Rule of Judicial Administration 2.430(e)(2). These records are available to the supreme court when reviewing any subsequent proceeding involving the same defendant without the need for inclusion of copies of these records in the record for the appeal under review. Subdivision (a)(1) does not limit the ability of the parties to rely on prior appellate records involving the same defendant and the same judgment of conviction and sentence of death. Subdivision (a)(1)(B) is intended to ensure, among other things, that all documents filed in the lower tribunal under Florida Rule of Criminal Procedure 3.852 are included in the records for all appeals from final orders disposing of motions for postconviction relief filed under rule 3.851. This rule does not limit the authority to file directions under rule 9.200(a)(3), or to correct or supplement the record under rule 9.200(f).

Criminal Court Steering Committee Note

2014 Amendment. Rule 9.142(a)(1)(B) was amended for the clerk of the lower court to retain a copy of the complete record for use in a subsequent postconviction proceeding.

Rule 9.145. Appeal Proceedings in Juvenile Delinquency Cases

(a) Applicability. Appeal proceedings in juvenile delinquency cases shall be as in rule 9.140 except as modified by this rule.

(b) Appeals by Child. To the extent adversely affected, a child or any parent, legal guardian, or custodian of a child may appeal

(1) an order of adjudication of delinquency or withholding adjudication of delinquency, or any disposition order entered thereon;

(2) orders entered after adjudication or withholding of adjudication of delinquency, including orders revoking or modifying the community control;

(3) an illegal disposition; or

(4) any other final order as provided by law.

(c) Appeals by the State.

(1) *Appeals Permitted.* The state may appeal an order

(A) dismissing a petition for delinquency or any part of it, if the order is entered before the commencement of an adjudicatory hearing;

(B) suppressing confessions, admissions, or evidence obtained by search or seizure before the adjudicatory hearing;

(C) granting a new adjudicatory hearing;

(D) arresting judgment;

(E) discharging a child under Florida Rule of Juvenile Procedure 8.090;

(F) ruling on a question of law if a child appeals an order of disposition;

(G) constituting an illegal disposition;

(H) discharging a child on habeas corpus; or

(I) finding a child incompetent pursuant to the Florida Rules of Juvenile Procedure.

(2) *Non–Final State Appeals.* If the state appeals a pre-adjudicatory hearing order of the trial court, the notice of appeal must be filed within 15 days of rendition of the order to be reviewed and before commencement of the adjudicatory hearing.

(A) A child in detention whose case is stayed pending state appeal shall be released from detention pending the appeal if the child is charged with an offense that would be bailable if the child were charged as an adult, unless the lower tribunal for good cause stated in an order determines otherwise. The lower tribunal retains discretion to release from detention any child who is not otherwise entitled to release under the provisions of this rule.

(B) If a child has been found incompetent to proceed, any order staying the proceedings on a state appeal shall have no effect on any order entered for the purpose of treatment.

(d) References to Child. The appeal shall be entitled and docketed with the initials, but not the name, of the child and the court case number. All references to the child in briefs, other papers, and the decision of the court shall be by initials.

(e) Confidentiality. All documents that are filed in paper format under seal shall remain sealed in the office of the clerk of court when not in use by the court, and shall not be open to inspection except by the parties and their counsel, or as otherwise ordered.

Added Nov. 22, 1996, effective Jan. 1, 1997 (685 So.2d 773). Amended Feb. 3, 2005 (894 So.2d 202); Oct. 18, 2012, effective Dec. 1, 2012, April 1, 2013, Oct. 1, 2013 (102 So.3d 451); Nov. 6, 2014, effective Jan. 1, 2015 (2014 WL 5714099).

Committee Notes

1996 Adoption. Subdivision (c)(2) is intended to make clear that in non-final state appeals, the notice of appeal must be filed before commencement of the adjudicatory hearing. However, the notice of appeal must still be filed within 15 days of rendition of the order to be reviewed as provided by rule 9.140(c)(3). These two rules together provide that when an adjudicatory hearing occurs within 15 days or less of rendition of an order to be reviewed, the notice of appeal must be filed before commencement of the adjudicatory hearing. This rule is not intended to extend the 15 days allowed for filing the notice of appeal as provided by rule 9.140(c)(3).

Subdivision (d) requires the parties to use initials in all references to the child in all briefs and other papers filed in the court in furtherance of the appeal. It does not require the deletion of the name of the child from pleadings or other papers transmitted to the court from the lower tribunal.

Rule 9.146. Appeal Proceedings in Juvenile Dependency and Termination of Parental Rights Cases and Cases Involving Families and Children in Need of Services

(a) Applicability. Appeals proceedings in juvenile dependency and termination of parental rights cases and cases involving families and children in need of services shall be as in civil cases except to the extent those rules are modified by this rule.

(b) Who May Appeal. Any child, any parent, guardian ad litem, or any other party to the proceeding affected by an order of the lower tribunal, or the appropriate state agency as provided by law may appeal to the appropriate court within the time and in the manner prescribed by these rules.

(c) Stay of Proceedings.

(1) *Application.* Except as provided by general law and in subdivision (c)(2) of this rule, a party seeking to stay a final or non-final order pending review shall file a motion in the lower tribunal, which shall have continuing jurisdiction, in its discretion, to grant, modify, or deny such relief, after considering the welfare and best interest of the child.

(2) *Termination of Parental Rights.* The taking of an appeal shall not operate as a stay in any case unless pursuant to an order of the court or the lower tribunal, except that a termination of parental rights order with placement of the child with a licensed child-placing agency or the Department of Children and Families for subsequent adoption shall be suspended while the appeal is pending, but the child shall continue in custody under the order until the appeal is decided.

(d) Retention of Jurisdiction. Transmittal of the record to the court does not remove the jurisdiction of the lower tribunal to conduct judicial reviews or other proceedings related to the health and welfare of the child pending appeal.

(e) References to Child or Parents. When the parent or child is a party to the appeal, the appeal shall be docketed and any documents filed in the court shall be titled with the initials, but not the name, of the child or parent and the court case number. All references to the child or parent in briefs, other documents, and the decision of the court shall be by initials.

(f) Confidentiality. All documents that are filed in paper format under seal shall remain sealed in the office of the clerk of the court when not in use by the court, and shall not be open to inspection except by the parties and their counsel, or as otherwise ordered.

(g) Special Procedures and Time Limitations Applicable to Appeals of Final Orders in Dependency or Termination of Parental Rights Proceedings.

(1) *Applicability.* This subdivision applies only to appeals of final orders to the district courts of appeal.

(2) *The Record.*

(A) Contents. The record shall be prepared in accordance with rule 9.200, except as modified by this subdivision.

(B) Transcripts of Proceedings. The appellant shall file a designation to the court reporter, including the name(s) of the individual court reporter(s), if applicable, with the notice of appeal. The designation shall be served on the court reporter on the date of filing and shall state that the appeal is from a final order of termination of parental rights or of dependency, and that the court reporter shall provide the transcript(s) designated within 20 days of the date of service. Within 20 days of the date of service of the designation, the court reporter shall transcribe and file with the clerk of the lower tribunal the transcripts and sufficient copies for all parties exempt from service by e-mail as set forth in the Florida Rules of Judicial Administration. If extraordinary reasons prevent the reporter from preparing the transcript(s) within the 20 days, the reporter shall request an extension of time, shall state the number of additional days requested, and shall state the extraordinary reasons that would justify the extension.

(C) Directions to the Clerk, Duties of the Clerk, Preparation and Transmittal of the Record. The appellant shall file directions to the clerk with the notice of appeal. The clerk shall electronically transmit the record to the court within 5 days of the date the court reporter files the transcript(s) or, if a designation to the court reporter has not been filed, within 5 days of the filing of the notice of appeal. When the record is electronically transmitted to the court, the clerk shall simultaneously electronically transmit the record to the Department of Children and Families, the guardian ad litem, counsel appointed to represent any indigent parties, and shall simultaneously serve copies of the index to all non-indigent parties, and, upon their request, copies of the record or portions thereof. The clerk shall provide the record in paper form to all parties exempt from service by e-mail as set forth in the Florida Rules of Judicial Administration.

(3) *Briefs.*

(A) In General. Briefs shall be prepared and filed in accordance with rule 9.210(a)–(e), (g), and (h).

(B) Times for Service. The initial brief shall be served within 20 days of service of the record on appeal or the index to the record on appeal. The answer brief shall be served within 20 days of service of the initial brief. The reply brief, if any, shall be served within 10 days of the service of the answer brief.

(4) *Motions.*

(A) Motions for Appointment of Appellate Counsel; Authorization of Payment of Transcription Costs. A motion for the appointment of appellate counsel, when authorized by general law, and a motion for authorization of payment of transcription costs, when appropriate, shall be filed with the notice of appeal. The motion and a copy of the notice of appeal shall be served on the presiding judge in the lower tribunal. The presiding judge shall promptly enter an order on the motion.

(B) Motions to Withdraw as Counsel. If appellate counsel seeks leave to withdraw from representation of an indigent parent, the motion to withdraw shall be served on the parent and shall contain a certification that, after a conscientious review of the record, the attorney has determined in good faith that there are no meritorious grounds on which to base an appeal. The parent shall be permitted to file a brief pro se, or through subsequently retained counsel, within 20 days of the issuance of an order granting the motion to withdraw.

(C) Motions for Extensions of Time. An extension of time will be granted only for extraordinary circumstances in which the extension is necessary to preserve the constitutional rights of a party, or in which substantial evidence exists to demonstrate that without the extension the child's best interests will be harmed. The extension will be limited to the number of days necessary to preserve the rights of the party or the best interests of the child. The motion shall state that the appeal is from a final order of termination of parental rights or of dependency, and shall set out the extraordinary circumstances that necessitate an extension, the amount of time requested, and the effect an extension will have on the progress of the case.

(5) *Oral Argument.* A request for oral argument shall be in a separate document served by a party not later than the time when the first brief of that party is due.

(6) *Rehearing; Rehearing En Banc; Clarification; Certification; Issuance of Written Opinion.* Motions for rehearing, rehearing en banc, clarification, certification, and issuance of a written opinion shall be in accordance with rules 9.330 and 9.331, except that no response to these motions is permitted unless ordered by the court.

(7) *The Mandate.* The clerk shall issue such mandate or process as may be directed by the court as soon as practicable.

(h) Expedited Review. The court shall give priority to appeals under this rule.

Added Nov. 22, 1996, effective Jan. 1, 1997 (685 So.2d 773). Amended Oct. 12, 2000, effective Jan. 1, 2001 (780 So.2d 834); Oct. 26, 2006, effective Jan. 1, 2007 (941 So.2d 352); Nov. 12, 2009 (24 So.3d 47); Oct. 18, 2012, effective Dec. 1, 2012, April 1, 2013, Oct. 1, 2013 (102 So.3d 451); Nov. 6, 2014, effective Jan. 1, 2015 (2014 WL 5714099).

Supersedure

Paragraph (b) of Rule 9.146 was found to be superseded by F.S.A. § 39.510(1) by the Florida Second District Court of Appeal in In Re K.M., Fla.App. 2 Dist., 978 So.2d 211 (2008).

Committee Notes

1996 Adoption. The reference in subdivision (a) to cases involving families and children in need of services encompasses only those cases in which an order has been entered adjudicating a child or family in need of services under chapter 39, Florida Statutes.

Subdivision (c) requires the parties to use initials in all references to the child and parents in all briefs and other papers filed in the court in furtherance of the appeal. It does not require the deletion of the names of the child and parents from pleadings and other papers transmitted to the court from the lower tribunal.

2006 Amendment. The title to subdivision (b) was changed from "Appeals Permitted" to clarify that this rule addresses who may take an appeal in matters covered by this rule. The amendment is intended to approve the holding in *D.K.B. v. Department of Children & Families*, 890 So. 2d 1288 (Fla. 2d DCA 2005), that non-final orders in these matters may be appealed only if listed in rule 9.130.

2009 Amendment. The rule was substantially amended following the release of the Study of Delay in Dependency/Parental Termination Appeals Supplemental Report and Recommendations (June 2007) by the Commission on District Court of Appeal Performance and Accountability. The amendments are generally intended to facilitate expedited filing and resolution of appellate cases arising from dependency and termination of parental rights proceedings in the lower tribunal. Subdivision (g)(4)(A) authorizes motions requesting appointment of appellate counsel only when a substantive provision of general law provides for appointment of appellate counsel. Section 27.5304(6), Florida Statutes (2008), limits appointment of appellate counsel for indigent parents to appeals from final orders adjudicating or denying dependency or termination of parental rights. In all other instances, section 27.5304(6), Florida Statutes, requires appointed trial counsel to prosecute or defend appellate cases arising from a dependency or parental termination proceeding in the lower tribunal.

Rule 9.147. Appeal Proceedings to Review Final Orders Dismissing Petitions for Judicial Waiver of Parental Notice of Termination of Pregnancy

(a) Applicability. Appeal proceedings to review final orders dismissing a petition for judicial waiver of parental notice of the termination of a pregnancy shall be as in civil cases, except as modified by this rule.

(b) Fees. No filing fee shall be required for any part of an appeal of the dismissal of a petition for a judicial waiver of parental notice of the termination of a pregnancy.

(c) Record. If an unmarried minor or another person on her behalf appeals an order dismissing a petition for judicial waiver of parental notice of the termination of a pregnancy, the clerk of the lower tribunal shall prepare and electronically transmit the record as described in rule 9.200(d) within 2 days from the filing of the notice of appeal.

(d) Disposition of Appeal. The court shall render its decision on the appeal as expeditiously as possible and no later than 7 days from the transmittal of the record. If no decision is rendered within that time period, the order shall be deemed reversed, the petition shall be deemed granted, and the clerk shall place a certificate to that effect in the file and provide the appellant, without charge, with a certified copy of the certificate.

(e) Briefs and Oral Argument. Briefs, oral argument, or both may be ordered at the discretion of the court. The appellant may move for leave to file a brief and may request oral argument.

(f) Confidentiality of Proceedings. The appeal and all proceedings therein shall be confidential so that the minor shall remain anonymous. The file shall remain sealed unless otherwise ordered by the court.

(g) Procedure Following Reversal. If the dismissal of the petition is reversed on appeal, the clerk shall furnish the appellant, without charge, with either a certified copy of the decision or the clerk's certificate for delivery to the minor's physician.

Added Nov. 6, 2014, effective Jan. 1, 2015 (2014 WL 5714099).

Committee Notes

2014 Amendment. The previous version of this rule was found at rule 9.110(n).

Rule 9.150. Discretionary Proceedings to Review Certified Questions from Federal Courts

(a) Applicability. On either its own motion or that of a party, the Supreme Court of the United States or a United States court of appeals may certify one or more questions of law to the Supreme Court of Florida if the answer is determinative of the cause and there is no controlling precedent of the Supreme Court of Florida.

(b) Certificate. The question(s) may be certified in an opinion by the federal court or by a separate certificate, but the federal court should provide the style of the case, a statement of the facts showing the nature of the cause and the circumstances out of which the questions of law arise, and the questions of law to be answered. The certificate shall be certified to the Supreme Court of Florida by the clerk of the federal court.

(c) Record. The Supreme Court of Florida, in its discretion, may require copies of all or any portion of the record before the federal court to be filed if the record may be necessary to the determination of the cause.

(d) Briefs. If the Supreme Court of Florida, in its discretion, requires briefing, it will issue an order establishing the order and schedule of briefs.

(e) Costs. The taxation of costs for these proceedings is a matter for the federal court and is not governed by these rules.

Added March 27, 1980, effective April 1, 1980 (381 So.2d 1370). Amended Oct. 22, 1992, effective Jan. 1, 1993 (609 So.2d 516); Nov. 3, 2011, effective Jan. 1, 2012 (75 So.3d 239).

Committee Notes

1977 Amendment. This rule retains the substance of former rule 4.61. Except for simplification of language, the only change from the former rule is that answer and reply briefs are governed by the same time schedule as other cases. It is contemplated that the federal courts will continue the current practice of directing the parties to present a stipulated statement of the facts.

1980 Amendment. This rule is identical to former rule 9.510. It has been renumbered to reflect the addition to the Florida Constitution of article V, section 3(b)(6), which permits discretionary supreme court review of certified questions from the federal courts. Answer briefs and reply briefs will continue to be governed by the same time schedule as in other cases.

Rule 9.160. Discretionary Proceedings to Review Decisions of County Courts

(a) Applicability. This rule applies to those proceedings that invoke the discretionary jurisdiction of the district courts of appeal to review county court orders described in rule 9.030(b)(4).

(b) Commencement. Any appeal of an order certified by the county court to be of great public importance must be taken to the district court of appeal. Jurisdiction of the district court of appeal under this rule shall be invoked by filing a notice and the order containing certification, accompanied by any filing fees prescribed by law, with the clerk of the lower tribunal. The time for filing the appeal shall be the same as if the appeal were being taken to the circuit court.

(c) **Notice.** The notice shall be in substantially the form prescribed by rule 9.900(a) or rule 9.900(c), depending on whether the order sought to be appealed is a final or a non-final order, except that such notice should refer to the fact of certification. Except in criminal cases, a conformed copy of the order or orders designated in the notice of appeal shall be attached to the notice together with any order entered on a timely motion postponing rendition of the order or orders appealed.

(d) **Method of Certification.** The certification may be made in the order subject to appeal or in any order disposing of a motion that has postponed rendition as defined in rule 9.020(h). The certification shall include (1) findings of fact and conclusions of law and (2) a concise statement of the issue or issues of great public importance.

(e) **Discretion.**

(1) Any party may suggest that an order be certified to be of great public importance. However, the decision to certify shall be within the absolute discretion of the county court and may be made by the county court on its own motion.

(2) The district court of appeal, in its absolute discretion, shall by order accept or reject jurisdiction. Until the entry of such order, temporary jurisdiction shall be in the district court of appeal.

(f) **Scope of Review.**

(1) If the district court of appeal accepts the appeal, it will decide all issues that would have been subject to appeal if the appeal had been taken to the circuit court.

(2) If the district court declines to accept the appeal, it shall transfer the case together with the filing fee to the circuit court that has appellate jurisdiction.

(g) **Record.** The record shall be prepared and filed in accord with rule 9.110(e) or 9.140(f), depending on the nature of the appeal.

(h) **Briefs.** The form of the briefs and the briefing schedule shall be in accord with rules 9.110(f), 9.140, 9.210, and 9.220, depending on the nature of the appeal.

(i) **Cross–Appeal.** Cross-appeals shall be permitted according to the applicable rules only in those cases in which a cross-appeal would have been authorized if the appeal had been taken to circuit court.

(j) **Applicability of Other Rules.** All other matters pertaining to the appeal shall be governed by the rules that would be applicable if the appeal had been taken to circuit court.

Added Sept. 13, 1984, effective Oct. 1, 1984 (463 So.2d 1114). Amended Feb. 14, 1985, effective March 1, 1985 (463 So.2d 1124); Oct. 22, 1992, effective Jan. 1, 1993 (609 So.2d 516); Nov. 22, 1996, effective Jan. 1, 1997 (685 So.2d 773); Jan. 19, 2006 (919 So.2d 431); Nov. 3, 2011, effective Jan. 1, 2012 (75 So.3d 239); Oct. 18, 2012, effective Dec. 1, 2012, April 1, 2013, Oct. 1, 2013 (102 So.3d 451); Nov. 6, 2014, effective Jan. 1, 2015 (2014 WL 5714099).

Committee Notes

1984 Amendment. This rule was added to implement the amendments to sections 26.012 and 924.08 and the adoption of section 34.195 by the 1984 Legislature. Section 34.195 authorizes only the certification of final judgments, but section 924.08 authorizes the certification of non-final orders in criminal cases. Therefore, this rule does not provide for appeals from non-final orders in civil cases. Under the rationale of *State v. Smith,* 260 So. 2d 489 (Fla. 1972), the authority to provide for appeals from non-final orders may rest in the supreme court rather than in the legislature. However, in keeping with the spirit of the legislation, the rule was drafted to permit certification of those non-final orders in criminal cases that would otherwise be appealable to the circuit court.

Sections 26.012 and 924.08 authorize only the certification of orders deemed to be of great public importance. However, section 34.195 refers to the certification of questions in final judgments if the question may have statewide application and is of great public importance or affects the uniform administration of justice. The committee concluded that any order certified to be of great public importance might have statewide application and that any order that would affect the uniform administration of justice would also be of great public importance. Therefore, the additional statutory language was deemed to be surplusage, and the rule refers only to the requirement of certifying the order to be of great public importance.

The district court of appeal may, in its discretion, decline to accept the appeal, in which event it shall be transferred to the appropriate circuit court for disposition in the ordinary manner. Except as stated in the rule, the procedure shall be the same as would be followed if the appeal were being taken to circuit court. The rule does not authorize review of certified orders by common law certiorari.

It is recommended that in those cases involving issues of great public importance, parties should file suggestions for certification before the entry of the order from which the appeal may be taken. However, parties are not precluded from suggesting certification following the entry of the order except that such suggestion, by itself, will not postpone rendition as defined in rule 9.020(h).

1992 Amendment. Subdivision (c) was amended to require that the appellant, except in criminal cases, attach to its notice of appeal a conformed copy of any orders designated in the notice of appeal, along with any orders on motions that postponed the rendition of orders appealed.

Rule 9.170. Appeal Proceedings in Probate and Guardianship Cases

(a) Applicability. Appeal proceedings in probate and guardianship cases shall be as in civil cases, except as modified by this rule.

(b) Appealable Orders. Except for proceedings under rule 9.100 and rule 9.130(a), appeals of orders rendered in probate and guardianship cases shall be limited to orders that finally determine a right or obligation of an interested person as defined in the Florida Probate Code. Orders that finally determine a right or obligation include, but are not limited to, orders that:

(1) determine a petition or motion to revoke letters of administration or letters of guardianship;

(2) determine a petition or motion to revoke probate of a will;

(3) determine a petition for probate of a lost or destroyed will;

(4) grant or deny a petition for administration pursuant to section 733. 2123, Florida Statutes;

(5) grant heirship, succession, entitlement, or determine the persons to whom distribution should be made;

(6) remove or refuse to remove a fiduciary;

(7) refuse to appoint a personal representative or guardian;

(8) determine a petition or motion to determine incapacity or to remove rights of an alleged incapacitated person or ward;

(9) determine a motion or petition to restore capacity or rights of a ward;

(10) determine a petition to approve the settlement of minors' claims;

(11) determine apportionment or contribution of estate taxes;

(12) determine an estate's interest in any property;

(13) determine exempt property, family allowance, or the homestead status of real property;

(14) authorize or confirm a sale of real or personal property by a personal representative;

(15) make distributions to any beneficiary;

(16) determine amount and order contribution in satisfaction of elective share;

(17) determine a motion or petition for enlargement of time to file a claim against an estate;

(18) determine a motion or petition to strike an objection to a claim against an estate;

(19) determine a motion or petition to extend the time to file an objection to a claim against an estate;

(20) determine a motion or petition to enlarge the time to file an independent action on a claim filed against an estate;

(21) settle an account of a personal representative, guardian, or other fiduciary;

(22) discharge a fiduciary or the fiduciary's surety;

(23) award attorneys' fees or costs; or

(24) approve a settlement agreement on any of the matters listed above in (1)–(23) or authorizing a compromise pursuant to section 733.708, Florida Statutes.

(c) Record; Alternative Appendix. An appeal under this rule may proceed on a record prepared by the clerk of the lower tribunal or on appendices to the briefs, as elected by the parties within the time frames set forth in rule 9.200(a)(3) for designating the record. The clerk of the lower tribunal shall prepare a record on appeal in accordance with rule 9.200 unless the appellant directs that no record shall be prepared. However, any other party may direct the clerk to prepare a record in accordance with rule 9.200. If no record is prepared under this rule, the appeal shall proceed using appendices pursuant to rule 9.220.

(d) Briefs. The appellant's initial brief, accompanied by an appendix as prescribed by rule 9.220 (if applicable), shall be served within 70 days of filing the notice of appeal. Additional briefs shall be served as prescribed by rule 9.210.

(e) Scope of Review. The court may review any ruling or matter related to the order on appeal occurring before the filing of the notice of appeal, except any order that was appealable under this rule. Multiple orders that are separately appealable under rule 9.170(b) may be reviewed by a single notice if the notice is timely filed as to each such order.

Added Nov. 3, 2011, effective Jan. 1, 2012 (75 So.3d 239).

Rule 9.180. Appeal Proceedings to Review Workers' Compensation Cases

(a) Applicability. Appellate review of proceedings in workers' compensation cases shall be as in civil cases except as specifically modified in this rule.

(b) Jurisdiction.

(1) *Appeal.* The First District Court of Appeal (the court) shall review by appeal any final order, as well as any nonfinal order of a lower tribunal that adjudicates

(A) jurisdiction;

(B) venue; or

(C) compensability, provided that the order expressly finds an injury occurred within the scope and course of employment and that claimant is entitled to receive causally related benefits in some amount, and provided further that the lower tribunal certifies in the order that determination of the exact nature and amount of benefits due to claimant will require substantial expense and time.

(2) *Waiver of Review: Abbreviated Final Orders.* Unless a request for findings of fact and conclusions of law is timely filed, review by appeal of an abbreviated

final order shall be deemed waived. The filing of a timely request tolls the time within which an abbreviated final order becomes final or an appeal may be filed.

(3) *Commencement.* Jurisdiction of the court shall be invoked by filing a notice of appeal with the lower tribunal within 30 days of the date the lower tribunal sends to the parties the order to be reviewed either by mail or by electronic means approved by the deputy chief judge, which date shall be the date of rendition. The filing fee prescribed by law must be provided to the clerk or a verified petition for relief of payment of the fee must be filed with the notice of appeal.

(4) *Notice of Appeal.* The notice shall be substantially in the form prescribed by rule 9.900(a) or (c), and shall contain a brief summary of the type of benefits affected, including a statement setting forth the time periods involved which shall be substantially in the following form:

I hereby certify that this appeal affects only the following periods and classifications of benefits and medical treatment:

1. Compensation for ..... (TTD, TPD, wage loss, impairment benefits, PTD, funeral benefits, or death benefits) ..... from ..... (date) ..... to ..... (date) .....
2. Medical benefits.
3. Rehabilitation.
4. Reimbursement from the SDTF for benefits paid from ..... (date) ..... to ..... (date) .....
5. Contribution for benefits paid from ..... (date) ..... to ..... (date) .....

(c) Jurisdiction of Lower Tribunal.

(1) *Substantive Issues.* The lower tribunal retains jurisdiction to decide the issues that have not been adjudicated and are not the subject of pending appellate review.

(2) *Settlement.* At any time before the record on appeal is filed with the court, the lower tribunal shall have the authority to approve settlements or correct clerical errors in the order appealed.

(3) *Relinquishment of Jurisdiction by Court to Consider Settlement.* If, after the record on appeal is filed, settlement is reached, the parties shall file a joint motion stating that a settlement has been reached and requesting relinquishment of jurisdiction to the lower tribunal for any necessary approval of the settlement. The court may relinquish jurisdiction for a specified period for entry of an appropriate order. In the event the Division of Workers' Compensation has advanced the costs of preparing the record on appeal or the filing fee, a copy of the joint motion shall be furnished to the division by the appellant.

(A) Notice. On or before the date specified in the order relinquishing jurisdiction, the parties shall file a joint notice of disposition of the settlement with a conformed copy of any order entered on the settlement.

(B) Costs. Any order approving a settlement shall provide where appropriate for the assessment and recovery of appellate costs, including any costs incurred by the division for insolvent appellants.

(d) Benefits Affected. Benefits specifically referenced in the notice of appeal may be withheld as provided by law pending the outcome of the appeal. Otherwise, benefits awarded shall be paid as required by law.

(1) *Abandonment.* If the appellant or cross-appellant fails to argue entitlement to benefits set forth in the notice of appeal in the appellant's or cross-appellant's initial brief, the challenge to such benefits shall be deemed abandoned. If there is a dispute as to whether a challenge to certain benefits has been abandoned, the court upon motion shall make that determination.

(2) *Payments of Benefits When Challenged Benefits Are Abandoned.* When benefits challenged on appeal have been abandoned under subdivision (d)(1) above, benefits no longer affected by the appeal are payable within 30 days of the service of the brief together with interest as required under section 440.20, Florida Statutes, from the date of the order of the lower tribunal making the award.

(3) *Payment of Benefits After Appeal.* If benefits are ordered paid by the court on completion of the appeal, they shall be paid, together with interest as required under section 440.20, Florida Statutes, within 30 days after the court's mandate. If the order of the court is appealed to the supreme court, benefits determined due by the court may be stayed in accordance with rule 9.310. Benefits ordered paid by the supreme court shall be paid within 30 days of the court's mandate.

(e) Intervention by Division of Workers' Compensation.

(1) *District Court.* Within 30 days of the date of filing a notice or petition invoking the jurisdiction of the court the Division of Workers' Compensation may intervene by filing a notice of intervention as a party appellant/petitioner or appellee/respondent with the court and take positions on any relevant matters.

(2) *Supreme Court.* If review of an order of the court is sought in the supreme court, the division may intervene in accordance with these rules. The clerk of the supreme court shall provide a copy of the pertinent documents to the division.

(3) *Division Not a Party Until Notice to Intervene Is Filed.* Until the notice of intervention is filed, the division shall not be considered a party.

(f) Record Contents: Final Orders.

(1) *Transcript, Order, and Other Documents.* The record shall contain the claim(s) or petition(s) for benefits, notice(s) of denial, pretrial stipulation, pre-

trial order, trial memoranda, depositions or exhibits admitted into evidence, any motion for rehearing and response, order on motion for rehearing, transcripts of any hearings before the lower tribunal and the order appealed. The parties may designate other items for inclusion in or omission from the record in accordance with rule 9.200.

(2) *Proffered Evidence.* Evidence proffered but not introduced into evidence at the hearing shall not be considered unless its admissibility is an issue on appeal and the question is properly designated for inclusion in the record by a party.

(3) *Certification and Transmittal.* The lower tribunal shall certify and transmit the record to the court as prescribed by these rules.

(4) *Stipulated Record.* The parties may stipulate to the contents of the record. In such a case the record shall consist of the stipulated statement and the order appealed which the lower tribunal shall certify as the record on appeal.

(5) *Costs.*

(A) Notice of Estimated Costs. Within 5 days after the contents of the record have been determined under these rules, the lower tribunal shall notify the appellant of the estimated cost of preparing the record. The lower tribunal also shall notify the Division of Workers' Compensation of the estimated record costs if the appellant files a verified petition to be relieved of costs and a sworn financial affidavit.

(B) Deposit of Estimated Costs. Within 15 days after the notice of estimated costs is served, the appellant shall deposit a sum of money equal to the estimated costs with the lower tribunal.

(C) Failure to Deposit Costs. If the appellant fails to deposit the estimated costs within the time prescribed, the lower tribunal shall notify the court, which may dismiss the appeal.

(D) State Agencies: Waiver of Costs. Any self-insured state agency or branch of state government, including the Division of Workers' Compensation and the Special Disability Trust Fund, need not deposit the estimated costs.

(E) Costs. If additional costs are incurred in correcting, amending, or supplementing the record, the lower tribunal shall assess such costs against the appropriate party. If the Division of Workers' Compensation is obligated to pay the costs of the appeal due to appellant's indigency, it must be given notice of any proceeding to assess additional costs. Within 15 days after the entry of the order assessing costs, the assessed party must deposit the sums so ordered with the lower tribunal. The lower tribunal shall promptly notify the court if costs are not deposited as required.

(6) *Transcript(s) of Proceedings.*

(A) Selection of Reporter by Lower Tribunal. The deputy chief judge of compensation claims shall select the reporter or transcriber to transcribe any hearing(s). The deputy chief judge who makes the selection shall give the parties notice of the selection.

(B) Objection to Reporter or Transcriber Selected. Any party may object to the reporter or transcriber selected by filing written objections with the judge who made the selection within 15 days after service of notice of the selection. Within 5 days after filing the objection, the judge shall hold a hearing on the issue. In such a case, the time limits mandated by these rules shall be appropriately extended.

(C) Certification of Transcript by Court Reporter or Transcriber. The reporter or transcriber designated by the deputy chief judge of compensation claims shall certify and deliver an electronic version of the transcript(s) to the clerk of the office of the judges of compensation claims. The transcript(s) shall be delivered in sufficient time for the clerk of the office of the judges of compensation claims to incorporate transcript(s) in the record. The reporter or transcriber shall promptly notify all parties in writing when the transcript(s) is delivered to the clerk of the office of the judges of compensation claims.

(7) *Preparation, Certification, and Transmittal of the Record.* The deputy chief judge of compensation claims shall designate the person to prepare the record. The clerk of the office of the judges of compensation claims shall supervise the preparation of the record. The record shall be delivered to the lower tribunal in sufficient time for the lower tribunal to review the record and send it to the court. The lower tribunal shall review the original record, certify that it was prepared in accordance with these rules, and within 60 days of the notice of appeal being filed transmit the record to the court. The lower tribunal shall provide an electronic image copy of the record to all counsel of record and all unrepresented parties.

(8) *Extensions.* For good cause, the lower tribunal may extend by no more than 30 days the time for filing the record with the court. Any further extension of time may be granted by the court.

(9) *Applicability of Rule 9.200.* Rules 9.200(a)(3), (c), and (f) shall apply to preparation of the record in appeals under this rule.

(g) Relief From Filing Fee and Costs: Indigency.

(1) *Indigency Defined.* Indigency for the purpose of this rule is synonymous with insolvency as defined by section 440.02, Florida Statutes.

(2) *Filing Fee.*

(A) Authority. An appellant may be relieved of paying filing fees by filing a verified petition or motion of indigency under section 57.081(1), Florida Statutes, with the lower tribunal.

(B) Time. The verified petition or motion of indigency must be filed with the lower tribunal together with the notice of appeal.

(C) Verified Petition: Contents. The verified petition or motion shall contain a statement by the appellant to be relieved of paying filing fees due to indigency and appellant's inability to pay the charges. The petition shall request that the lower tribunal enter an order or certificate of indigency. One of the following shall also be filed in support of the verified petition or motion:

(i) If the appellant is unrepresented by counsel, a financial affidavit; or

(ii) If the appellant is represented by counsel, counsel shall certify that counsel has investigated (a) the appellant's financial condition and finds appellant indigent; and (b) the nature of appellant's position and believes it to be meritorious as a matter of law. Counsel shall also certify that counsel has not been paid or promised payment of a fee or other remuneration for such legal services except for the amount, if any, ultimately approved by the lower tribunal to be paid by the employer/carrier if such entitlement is determined by the court.

(D) Service. Appellant shall serve a copy of the verified petition or motion of indigency, including appellant's financial affidavit or counsel's certificate, whichever is applicable, on all interested parties and the clerk of the court.

(E) Order or Certificate of Indigency. The lower tribunal shall review the verified petition or motion for indigency and supporting documents without a hearing, and if the lower tribunal finds compliance with section 57.081(1), Florida Statutes, may issue a certificate of indigency or enter an order granting said relief, at which time appellant may proceed without further application to the court and without payment of any filing fees. If the lower tribunal enters an order denying relief, appellant shall deposit the filing fee with the lower tribunal within 15 days from the date of the order unless timely review is sought by motion filed with the court.

(3) *Costs of Preparation of Record.*

(A) Authority. An appellant may be relieved in whole or in part from the costs of the preparation of the record on appeal by filing with the lower tribunal a verified petition to be relieved of costs and a copy of the designation of the record on appeal. The verified petition to be relieved of costs shall contain a sworn financial affidavit as described in subdivision (D).

(B) Time. The verified petition to be relieved of costs must be filed within 15 days after service of the notice of estimated costs. A verified petition filed prior to the date of service of the notice of estimated costs shall be deemed not timely.

(C) Verified Petition: Contents. The verified petition shall contain a request by appellant to be relieved of costs due to insolvency. The petition also shall include a statement by the appellant's attorney or the appellant, if not represented by an attorney, that the appeal was filed in good faith and the court reasonably could find reversible error in the record and shall state with particularity the specific legal and factual grounds for that opinion.

(D) Sworn Financial Affidavit: Contents. With the verified petition to be relieved of costs, the appellant shall file a sworn financial affidavit listing income and assets, including marital income and assets, and expenses and liabilities.

(E) Verified Petition and Sworn Financial Affidavit: Service. The appellant shall serve a copy of the verified petition to be relieved of costs, including the sworn financial affidavit, on all interested parties, including the Division of Workers' Compensation, the office of general counsel of the Department of Financial Services, and the clerk of the court.

(F) Hearing on Petition to Be Relieved of Costs. After giving 15 days' notice to the Division of Workers' Compensation and all parties, the lower tribunal shall promptly hold a hearing and rule on the merits of the petition to be relieved of costs. However, if no objection to the petition is filed by the division or a party within 20 days after the petition is served, the lower tribunal may enter an order on the merits of the petition without a hearing.

(G) Extension of Appeal Deadlines. If the petition to be relieved of the entire cost of the preparation of the record on appeal is granted, the 60–day period allowed under these rules for the preparation of the record shall begin to run from the date of the order granting the petition. If the petition to be relieved of the cost of the record is denied or only granted in part, the petitioner shall deposit the estimated costs with the lower tribunal within 15 days from the date the order denying the petition is entered. The 60–day period allowed under these rules for the preparation of the record shall begin from the date the estimated cost is deposited with the lower tribunal. If the petition to be relieved of the cost of the record is withdrawn before ruling, then the petitioner shall deposit the estimated costs with the lower tribunal at the time the petition is withdrawn and the 60–day period for preparation of the record shall begin to run from the date the petition is withdrawn.

(H) Payment of Cost for Preparation of Record by Administration Trust Fund. If the petition to be relieved of costs is granted, the lower tribunal may order the Workers' Compensation Administration Trust Fund to pay the cost of the preparation of the record on appeal pending the final disposition of the appeal. The lower tribunal shall provide a copy of such order to all interested parties, including the division, general counsel of the Department of Financial Services, and the clerk of the court.

(I) Reimbursement of Administration Trust Fund If Appeal Is Successful. If the Administration Trust Fund has paid the costs of the preparation of the record and the appellant prevails at the conclusion of the appeal, the appellee shall reimburse the fund the costs paid within 30 days of the mandate issued by the court or supreme court under these rules.

(h) Briefs and Motions Directed to Briefs.

(1) *Briefs: Final Order Appeals.* Within 30 days after the lower tribunal certifies the record to the court, the appellant shall serve the initial brief. Additional briefs shall be served as prescribed by rule 9.210.

(2) *Briefs: Non–Final Appeals.* Appellant's initial brief, accompanied by an appendix as prescribed by rule 9.220, shall be served within 15 days of filing the notice. Additional briefs shall be served as prescribed by rule 9.210.

(3) *Motions to Strike.* Motions to strike a brief or portions of a brief will not be entertained by the court. However, a party, in its own brief, may call to the court's attention a breach of these rules. If no further responsive brief is authorized, noncompliance may be brought to the court's attention by filing a suggestion of noncompliance. Statements in briefs not supported by the record shall be disregarded and may constitute cause for imposition of sanctions.

(i) Attorneys' Fees and Appellate Costs.

(1) *Costs.* Appellate costs shall be taxed as provided by law. Taxable costs shall include those items listed in rule 9.400 and costs for a transcript included in an appendix as part of an appeal of a nonfinal order.

(2) *Attorneys' Fees.* A motion for attorneys' fees shall be served in accordance with rule 9.400(b).

(3) *Entitlement and Amount of Fees and Costs.* If the court determines that an appellate fee is due, the lower tribunal shall have jurisdiction to conduct hearings and consider evidence regarding the amount of the attorney fee and costs due at any time after the mandate is issued.

(4) *Review.* Review shall be in accordance with rule 9.400(c).

Added Nov. 22, 1996, effective Jan. 1, 1997 (685 So.2d 773). Amended Oct. 12, 2000, effective Jan. 1, 2001 (780 So.2d 834); Aug. 29, 2002, effective Jan. 1, 2003 (827 So.2d 888); Feb. 3, 2005 (894 So.2d 202); Oct. 26, 2006, effective Jan. 1, 2007 (941 So.2d 352); Nov. 3, 2011, effective Jan. 1, 2012 (75 So.3d 239); Oct. 18, 2012, effective Dec. 1, 2012, April 1, 2013, Oct. 1, 2013 (102 So.3d 451); Nov. 6, 2014, effective Jan. 1, 2015 (2014 WL 5714099).

Committee Notes

1996 Adoption. Rule 9.180 is intended to supersede rules 4.160, 4.161, 4. 165, 4.166, 4.170, 4.180, 4.190, 4.220, 4.225, 4.230, 4.240, 4.250, 4.260, 4. 265, 4.270, and 4.280 of the Rules of Workers' Compensation Procedure. In consolidating those rules into one rule and incorporating them into the Rules of Appellate Procedure, duplicative rules have been eliminated. The change was not intended to change the general nature of workers' compensation appeals. It is contemplated there still may be multiple "final orders." See 1980 Committee Note, Fla. R. Work. Comp. P. 4.160.

The orders listed in rules 9.180(b)(1)(A), (B), and (C) are the only nonfinal orders appealable before entry of a final order in workers' compensation cases.

Rule 9.180(b)(2) now limits the place for filing the notice of appeal to the lower tribunal that entered the order and not any judge of compensation claims as the former rule provided.

Rule 9.180(f)(6)(E) provides that the lower tribunal shall provide a copy of the record to all counsel of record and all unrepresented parties. It is contemplated that the lower tribunal can accomplish that in whatever manner the lower tribunal deems most convenient for itself, such as, having copies available that counsel or the parties may pick up.

2011 Amendments. Subdivision (b)(4) was amended to provide for the use of form 9.900(c) in appeal of non-final orders.

Subdivisions (f)(6) and (f)(7) were amended to conform to section 440. 29(2), Florida Statutes, providing that the deputy chief judge, not the lower tribunal, is authorized to designate the manner in which hearings are recorded and arrange for the preparation of records on appeal. Moreover, it provides statewide uniformity and consistency in the preparation of records on appeal by incorporating electronic and other technological means to promote efficiency and cost reduction. Currently the electronic version of the transcript is the Portable Document Format (PDF).

Rule 9.190. Judicial Review of Administrative Action

(a) Applicability. Judicial review of administrative action shall be as in civil cases except as specifically modified by this rule.

(b) Commencement.

(1) An appeal from final agency action as defined in the Administrative Procedure Act, chapter 120, Florida Statutes, including immediate final orders entered pursuant to section 120.569(2)(n), Florida Statutes, or other administrative action for which judicial review is provided by general law shall be commenced in accordance with rule 9.110(c).

(2) Review of non-final agency action under the Administrative Procedure Act, including non-final action by an administrative law judge, and agency orders entered pursuant to section 120.60(6), Florida

Statutes, shall be commenced by filing a petition for review in accordance with rules 9.100(b) and (c).

(3) Review of quasi-judicial decisions of any administrative body, agency, board, or commission not subject to the Administrative Procedure Act shall be commenced by filing a petition for certiorari in accordance with rules 9.100(b) and (c), unless judicial review by appeal is provided by general law.

(c) The Record.

(1) *Generally.* As further described in this rule, the record shall include only materials furnished to and reviewed by the lower tribunal in advance of the administrative action to be reviewed by the court.

(2) *Review of Final Action Pursuant to the Administrative Procedure Act.*

(A) In an appeal from any proceeding conducted pursuant to section 120.56 (rule challenges) or sections 120.569 (decisions which affect substantial interests) and 120.57(1), Florida Statutes (decisions which affect substantial interests involving disputed material facts), the record shall consist of all notices, pleadings, motions, and intermediate rulings; evidence admitted; those matters officially recognized; proffers of proof and objections and rulings thereon; proposed findings and exceptions; any decision, opinion, order, or report by the presiding officer; all staff memoranda or data submitted to the presiding officer during the hearing or prior to its disposition, after notice of submission to all parties, except communications by advisory staff as permitted under section 120.66(1), Florida Statutes, if such communications are public records; all matters placed on the record after an ex parte communication; and the official transcript.

(B) In an appeal from any proceeding pursuant to sections 120.569 (decisions which affect substantial interests) and 120.57(2), Florida Statutes (decisions which affect substantial interests involving no disputed issue of material fact), the record shall consist of the notice and summary of grounds; evidence received; all written statements submitted; any decisions overruling objections; all matters placed on the record after an ex parte communication; the official transcript; and any decision, opinion, order, or report by the presiding officer.

(C) In an appeal from any proceeding pursuant to section 120.565, Florida Statutes (declaratory statements), the record shall consist of the petition seeking a declaratory statement and any pleadings filed with the agency; all notices relating to the petition published in the Florida Administrative Weekly; the declaratory statement issued by the agency or the agency's denial of the petition; and all matters listed in subdivision (c)(2)(A) or (c)(2)(B) of this rule, whichever is appropriate, if a hearing is held on the declaratory statement petition.

(D) In an appeal from any proceeding pursuant to section 120.574, Florida Statutes (summary proceeding), the record shall consist of all notices, pleadings, motions, and intermediate rulings; evidence received; a statement of matters officially recognized; proffers of proof and objections and rulings thereon; matters placed on the record after an ex parte communication; the written decision of the administrative law judge presiding at the final hearing; and the official transcript of the final hearing.

(E) In an appeal from a rule adoption pursuant to sections 120.54 (rule adoption) and 120.68(9), Florida Statutes, in which the sole issue presented by the petition is the constitutionality of a rule and there are no disputed issues of fact, the record shall consist only of those documents from the rulemaking record compiled by the agency that materially address the constitutional issue. The agency's rulemaking record consists of all notices given for the proposed rule; any statement of estimated regulatory costs for the rule; a written summary of hearings on the proposed rule; the written comments and responses to written comments as required by sections 120.54 (rule adoption) and 120.541, Florida Statutes (statement of estimated regulatory costs); all notices and findings made pursuant to section 120.54(4), Florida Statutes (adoption of emergency rules); all materials filed by the agency with the Administrative Procedures Committee pursuant to section 120.54(3), Florida Statutes (rule adoption procedure); all materials filed with the Department of State pursuant to section 120.54(3), Florida Statutes (rule adoption procedure); and all written inquiries from standing committees of the legislature concerning the rule.

(F) In an appeal from an immediate final order entered pursuant to section 120.569(2)(n), Florida Statutes, the record shall be compiled in an appendix pursuant to rule 9.220 and served with the briefs.

(3) *Review of Non–Final Action Pursuant to the Administrative Procedure Act.* The provisions of rules 9.100 and 9.220 govern the record in proceedings seeking review of non-final administrative action.

(4) *Review of Administrative Action Not Subject to the Administrative Procedure Act.* In proceedings seeking review of administrative action not governed by the Administrative Procedure Act, the clerk of the lower tribunal shall not be required to prepare a record or record index. The petitioner or appellant shall submit an appendix in accordance with rule 9.220. Supplemental appendices may be submitted by any party. Appendices may not contain any matter not made part of the record in the lower tribunal.

(5) *Videotaped Testimony.* In any circumstance in which hearing testimony is preserved through the use of videotape rather than through an official transcript, the testimony from the videotape shall be transcribed and the transcript shall be made a part of the record before the record is transmitted to the court.

(6) *Modified Record.* The contents of the record may be modified as provided in rule 9.200(a)(3).

(d) Attorneys' Fees.

(1) *Attorneys' Fees.* A motion for attorneys' fees may be served not later than the time for service of the reply brief and shall state the grounds on which the recovery is sought, citing all pertinent statutes.

(2) *Disputes As To Amount.* If the court decides to award attorneys' fees, the court may either remand the matter to the lower tribunal or to the administrative law judge for determination of the amount, or refer the matter to a special magistrate.

(3) *Review.* Review of orders entered by the lower tribunal or the administrative law judge under this rule shall be by motion filed in the court within 30 days of rendition of the order. Objections to reports of special magistrates shall be filed with the court within 30 days after the special magistrate's report is filed with the court.

(e) Stays Pending Review.

(1) *Effect of Initiating Review.* The filing of a notice of administrative appeal or a petition seeking review of administrative action shall not operate as a stay, except that such filing shall give rise to an automatic stay as provided in rule 9.310(b)(2) or chapter 120, Florida Statutes, or when timely review is sought of an award by an administrative law judge on a claim for birth-related neurological injuries.

(2) *Application for Stay Under the Administrative Procedure Act.*

(A) A party seeking to stay administrative action may file a motion either with the lower tribunal or, for good cause shown, with the court in which the notice or petition has been filed. The filing of the motion shall not operate as a stay. The lower tribunal or court may grant a stay upon appropriate terms. Review of orders entered by lower tribunals shall be by the court on motion.

(B) When an agency has ordered emergency suspension, restriction, or limitations of a license under section 120.60(6), Florida Statutes, or issued an immediate final order under section 120.569(2)(n), Florida Statutes, the affected party may file with the reviewing court a motion for stay on an expedited basis. The court may issue an order to show cause and, after considering the agency's response, if timely filed, grant a stay on appropriate terms.

(C) When an agency has suspended or revoked a license other than on an emergency basis, a licensee may file with the court a motion for stay on an expedited basis.. The agency may file a response within 10 days of the filing of the motion, or within a shorter time period set by the court. Unless the agency files a timely response demonstrating that a stay would constitute a probable danger to the health, safety, or welfare of the state, the court shall grant the motion and issue a stay.

(D) When an order suspending or revoking a license has been stayed pursuant to subdivision (2)(C), an agency may apply to the court for dissolution or modification of the stay on grounds that subsequently acquired information demonstrates that failure to dissolve or modify the stay would constitute a probable danger to the public health, safety, or welfare of the state.

(3) *Application for Stay or Supersedeas of Other Administrative Action.* A party seeking to stay administrative action, not governed by the Administrative Procedure Act, shall file a motion in the lower tribunal, which shall have continuing jurisdiction, in its discretion, to grant, modify, or deny such relief. A stay pending review may be conditioned on the posting of a good and sufficient bond, other conditions, or both. Review of orders entered by lower tribunals shall be by the court on motion.

(4) *Duration.* A stay entered by a lower tribunal or a court shall remain in effect during the pendency of all review proceedings in Florida courts until a mandate issues, unless otherwise modified or vacated.

Added Sept. 27, 1996, effective Oct. 1, 1996 (681 So.2d 1132). Amended Oct. 12, 2000, effective Jan. 1, 2001 (780 So.2d 834); Aug. 29, 2002, effective Jan. 1, 2003 (827 So.2d 888); Sept. 30, 2004, effective Oct. 1, 2004 (887 So.2d 1090); Feb. 3, 2005 (894 So.2d 202); Nov. 13, 2008, effective Jan. 1, 2009 (2 So.3d 89); Nov. 3, 2011, effective Jan. 1, 2012 (75 So.3d 239); Nov. 6, 2014, effective Jan. 1, 2015 (2014 WL 5714099).

Committee Notes

1996 Amendment. Appeals which fall within the exception included in subdivision (b)(3) are commenced in accordance with subdivision (b)(1). Therefore, administrative action by appeal in a circuit court, if prescribed by general law, is commenced pursuant to subdivision (b)(1). Unless review of administrative action in circuit court is prescribed by general law to be by appeal, review in circuit court is by petition for an extraordinary writ commenced pursuant to subdivision (b)(3). See *Board of County Commissioners v. Snyder*, 627 So.2d 469 (Fla. 1993); *Grace v. Town of Palm Beach*, 656 So.2d 945 (Fla. 4th DCA 1995). Subdivision (b)(3) supersedes all local government charters, ordinances, rules and regulations which purport to provide a method of review in conflict herewith.

Subdivision (c) was adopted to identify more clearly what constitutes the record in appeals from administrative proceedings. Several sections of the Florida Administrative Procedure Act, as revised in 1996, specifically state what shall constitute the record in certain types of proceedings, and this rule incorporates that statutory language. The rule makes clear that the record shall include only materials that were furnished to and reviewed by the lower tribunal in advance of the administrative action to be reviewed. The intent of this statement is to avoid the inclusion of extraneous materials in the record that were never reviewed by the lower tribunal.

Subdivision (c)(2)(A) is based on provisions of section 120.57(1)(f), Florida Statutes. This subdivision of the rule governs the record from proceedings conducted pursuant to section 120.56 and sections 120.569 and 120.57(1), Florida Statutes. This is because section 120.56(1)(e), Florida Statutes, states that hearings under section 120.56, Florida Statutes, shall be conducted in the same manner as provided by sections 120.569 and 120.57, Florida Statutes.

Subdivision (c)(2)(B) lists the provisions of section 120.57(2)(b), Florida Statutes. Subdivision (c)(2)(B)(vii), which refers to "any decision, opinion, order, or report by the presiding officer," was added by the committee to the list of statutory requirements.

Subdivision (c)(2)(C) addresses the record on appeal from declaratory statement requests pursuant to section 120.565, while subdivision (c)(2)(D) lists the provisions of section 120.574(2)(d), Florida Statutes. Subdivision (c)(2)(E) of the rule addresses proceedings governed by sections 120.54 and 120.68(9), Florida Statutes. The definition of the rulemaking record tracks language in section 120.54(8), Florida Statutes.

Subdivision (c)(3) makes clear that rules 9.100 and 9.220 govern the record in proceedings seeking review of non-final administrative action, while subdivision (c)(4) governs the record in administrative proceedings not subject to the Administrative Procedure Act.

Subdivision (c)(5) states that if videotape is used to preserve hearing testimony, the videotape shall be transcribed before the record is transmitted to the court.

Subdivision (d) was adopted to conform to the 1996 revisions to the Administrative Procedure Act. Recoupment of costs is still governed by rule 9.400.

2000 Amendment. Subdivision (e) was added to address stays pending judicial review of administrative action. Ordinarily, application for a stay must first be made to the lower tribunal, but some agencies have collegial heads who meet only occasionally. If a party can show good cause for applying initially to the court for a stay, it may do so. When an appeal has been taken from a license suspension or revocation under the Administrative Procedure Act, good cause for not applying first to the lower tribunal is presumed.

Subdivision (e)(2)(B) deals with stays of orders which suspend licenses on an emergency basis. Before entering an emergency suspension order, the agency must make a finding that immediate suspension is necessary to protect the public health, safety, or welfare. § 120.60(6), Fla. Stat. (1999). In effect, the agency makes a finding that would be sufficient to defeat issuance of the " stay as a matter of right" contemplated by section 120.68(3), Florida Statutes. The agency's finding is subject to judicial review, however, on application for a stay under subdivision (e)(2)(B).

Absent an emergency suspension order, the court grants a stay as of right in Administrative Procedure Act license suspension and revocation cases unless the licensing agency makes a timely showing that a stay "would constitute a probable danger to the health, safety, or welfare of the state." § 120.68(3), Fla. Stat. (1999). The court can shorten the 10 day period specified in subdivision (e)(2)(c). If the court stays a nonemergency suspension or revocation, the licensing agency can move to modify or dissolve the stay on the basis of material information that comes to light after the stay is issued.

Nothing in subdivision (e) precludes licensing agencies from making suspension or revocation orders effective 30 days after entry, granting stays pending judicial review, or taking other steps to implement section 120.68(3), Florida Statutes.

2004 Amendment. Subdivision (e)(2)(C) was amended to clarify that the ten days (or shorter period set by the court) within which the agency has to respond runs from the filing of the motion for stay. See *Ludwig v. Dept. of Health*, 778 So. 2d 531 (Fla. 1st DCA 2001).

2011 Amendment. Subdivisions (b)(1) and (b)(2) were amended to clarify the procedures for seeking judicial review of immediate final orders and emergency orders suspending, restricting, or limiting a license. Subdivision (c)(2)(F) was added and subdivision (c)(2) was amended to clarify the record for purposes of judicial review of immediate final orders.

Rule 9.200. The Record

Text of rule effective until October 1, 2015. See, also, rule effective October 1, 2015.

(a) Contents.

(1) Except as otherwise designated by the parties, the record shall consist of the original documents, all exhibits that are not physical evidence, and any transcript(s) of proceedings filed in the lower tribunal, except summonses, praecipes, subpoenas, returns, notices of hearing or of taking deposition, depositions, and other discovery. In criminal cases, when any exhibit, including physical evidence, is to be included in the record, the clerk of the lower tribunal shall not, unless ordered by the court, transmit the original and, if capable of reproduction, shall transmit a copy, including but not limited to copies of any tapes, CDs, DVDs, or similar electronically recorded evidence. The record shall also include a progress docket.

(2) In family law, juvenile dependency, and termination of parental rights cases, and cases involving families and children in need of services, the record shall include those items designated in subdivision (a)(1) except that the clerk of the lower tribunal shall retain the original orders, reports and recommendations of magistrates or hearing officers, and judgments within the file of the lower tribunal and shall include copies thereof within the record.

(3) Within 10 days of filing the notice of appeal, an appellant may direct the clerk to include or exclude other documents or exhibits filed in the lower tribunal. The directions shall be substantially in the form prescribed by rule 9.900(g). If the clerk is directed to transmit less than the entire record or a transcript of

trial with less than all of the testimony, the appellant shall serve with such direction a statement of the judicial acts to be reviewed. Within 20 days of filing the notice, an appellee may direct the clerk to include additional documents and exhibits.

(4) The parties may prepare a stipulated statement showing how the issues to be presented arose and were decided in the lower tribunal, attaching a copy of the order to be reviewed and as much of the record in the lower tribunal as is necessary to a determination of the issues to be presented. The parties shall advise the clerk of the lower tribunal of their intention to rely on a stipulated statement in lieu of the record as early in advance of filing as possible. The stipulated statement shall be filed by the parties and transmitted to the court by the clerk of the lower tribunal within the time prescribed for transmittal of the record.

(5) Where any court record, as defined in Florida Rule of Judicial Administration 2.420(b)(1)(A), of proceedings in the lower tribunal has been made or maintained in one of the following electronic formats: fully searchable indexed PDF; fully searchable non-indexed PDF; or, non-searchable PDF

(A) the record, as defined in subdivision (a)(1) through (a)(3), shall be comprised of the electronic form of those items described in subdivision (a)(1) that were created or maintained in the aforementioned electronic formats; or

(B) where the parties elect to prepare a stipulated statement in accordance with subdivision (a)(4), the stipulated statement and its attachments shall be filed electronically in one of the aforementioned electronic formats.

(b) Transcript(s) of Proceedings.

(1) Within 10 days of filing the notice, the appellant shall designate those portions of the proceedings not on file deemed necessary for transcription and inclusion in the record. Within 20 days of filing the notice, an appellee may designate additional portions of the proceedings. Copies of designations shall be served on the approved court reporter, civil court reporter, or approved transcriptionist. Costs of the transcript(s) so designated shall be borne initially by the designating party, subject to appropriate taxation of costs as prescribed by rule 9.400. At the time of the designation, unless other satisfactory arrangements have been made, the designating party must make a deposit of 1/2 of the estimated transcript costs, and must pay the full balance of the fee on delivery of the completed transcript(s).

(2) Within 30 days of service of a designation, or within the additional time provided for under subdivision (b)(3) of this rule, the approved court reporter, civil court reporter, or approved transcriptionist shall transcribe and file with the clerk of the lower tribunal the designated proceedings and shall serve copies as requested in the designation. If a designating party directs the approved court reporter, civil court reporter, or approved transcriptionist to furnish the transcript(s) to fewer than all parties, that designating party shall serve a copy of the designated transcript(s) on the parties within 5 days of receipt from the approved court reporter, civil court reporter, or approved transcriptionist. The transcript of the trial shall be organized in consecutively numbered volumes not to exceed 200 pages each, and each page shall be numbered consecutively. Each volume shall be prefaced by an index containing the names of the witnesses, a list of all exhibits offered and introduced in evidence, and the pages where each may be found.

(3) On service of a designation, the approved court reporter, civil court reporter, or approved transcriptionist shall acknowledge at the foot of the designation the fact that it has been received and the date on which the approved court reporter, civil court reporter, or approved transcriptionist expects to have the transcript(s) completed and shall serve the so-endorsed designation on the parties and file it with the clerk of the court within 5 days of service. If the transcript(s) cannot be completed within 30 days of service of the designation, the approved court reporter, civil court reporter, or approved transcriptionist shall request such additional time as is reasonably necessary and shall state the reasons therefor. If the approved court reporter, civil court reporter, or approved transcriptionist requests an extension of time, the court shall allow the parties 5 days in which to object or agree. The court shall approve the request or take other appropriate action and shall notify the reporter and the parties of the due date of the transcript(s).

(4) If no report of the proceedings was made, or if the transcript is unavailable, a party may prepare a statement of the evidence or proceedings from the best available means, including the party's recollection. The statement shall be served on all other parties, who may serve objections or proposed amendments to it within 10 days of service. Thereafter, the statement and any objections or proposed amendments shall be filed with the lower tribunal for settlement and approval. As settled and approved, the statement shall be included by the clerk of the lower tribunal in the record.

(c) Cross–Appeals. Within 20 days of filing the notice, a cross-appellant may direct that additional documents, exhibits, or transcript(s) be included in the record. If less than the entire record is designated, the cross-appellant shall serve, with the directions, a statement of the judicial acts to be reviewed. The cross-appellee shall have 10 days after such service to direct further additions. The time for preparation and transmittal of the record shall be extended by 10 days.

(d) Duties of Clerk; Preparation and Transmittal of Record.

(1) The clerk of the lower tribunal shall prepare the record as follows:

(A) The clerk of the lower tribunal shall not be required to verify and shall not charge for the incorporation of any transcript(s) into the record. The transcript of the trial shall be incorporated at the end of the record, and shall not be renumbered by the clerk. The progress docket shall be incorporated into the record immediately after the index.

(B) The remainder of the record, including all supplements and any transcripts other than the transcript of the trial, shall be consecutively numbered. The record shall be organized in consecutively numbered volumes not to exceed 200 pages each. The cover sheet of each volume shall contain the name of the lower tribunal and the style and number of the case. Any volume of the record that is prepared in paper format shall be securely bound.

(C) The record, or portions of the record, prepared in accordance with subdivision (a)(5) shall be organized, numbered, and formatted in accordance with subdivision (d)(1)(A)–(d)(1)(B), except that each such volume shall be prepared in electronic format as a PDF file having the indexing and searching characteristics of the electronic items comprising that volume of the record. The index and progress docket shall also be included as a separate indexed, fully searchable PDF file.

(2) The clerk of the lower tribunal shall prepare a complete index to the record and shall attach a copy of the progress docket to the index.

(3) The clerk of the lower tribunal shall certify and transmit the record to the court as prescribed by these rules.

(e) Duties of Appellant or Petitioner. The burden to ensure that the record is prepared and transmitted in accordance with these rules shall be on the petitioner or appellant. Any party may enforce the provisions of this rule by motion.

(f) Correcting and Supplementing Record.

(1) If there is an error or omission in the record, the parties by stipulation, the lower tribunal before the record is transmitted, or the court may correct the record.

(2) If the court finds the record is incomplete, it shall direct a party to supply the omitted parts of the record. No proceeding shall be determined, because of an incomplete record, until an opportunity to supplement the record has been given.

(g) Return of Record. In civil cases, the record shall be returned to the lower tribunal after final disposition by the court.

Amended July 3, 1980, effective Jan. 1, 1981 (387 So.2d 920); Nov. 26, 1980, effective Jan. 1, 1981 (391 So.2d 203); June 8, 1987, effective July 1, 1987 (509 So.2d 276); July 14, 1988, effective Jan. 1, 1989 (529 So.2d 687); Dec. 30, 1988, effective Jan. 1, 1989 (536 So.2d 240); Oct. 22, 1992, effective Jan. 1, 1993 (609 So.2d 516); Nov. 22, 1996, effective Jan. 1, 1997 (685 So.2d 773); Oct. 12, 2000, effective Jan. 1, 2001 (780 So.2d 834); Sept. 30, 2004 (887 So.2d 1090); Oct. 26, 2006, effective Jan. 1, 2007 (941 So.2d 352); Nov. 13, 2008, effective Jan. 1, 2009 (2 So.3d 89); July 16, 2009 (13 So.3d 1044); Oct. 15, 2009 (20 So.3d 380); Nov. 3, 2011, effective Jan. 1, 2012 (75 So.3d 239); June 14, 2012, (93 So.3d 325); Oct. 18, 2012, effective Dec. 1, 2012, April 1, 2013, Oct. 1, 2013 (102 So.3d 451); Nov. 6, 2014, effective Jan. 1, 2015 (2014 WL 5714099).

Committee Notes

1977 Amendment. This rule replaces former rule 3.6 and represents a complete revision of the matters pertaining to the record for an appellate proceeding. References in this rule to "appellant" and "appellee" should be treated as equivalent to "petitioner" and "respondent," respectively. See Commentary, Fla. R. App. P. 9.020. This rule is based in part on Federal Rule of Appellate Procedure 10(b).

Subdivision (a)(1) establishes the content of the record unless an appellant within 10 days of filing the notice directs the clerk to exclude portions of the record or to include additional portions, or the appellee within 20 days of the notice being filed directs inclusion of additional portions. In lieu of a record, the parties may prepare a stipulated statement, attaching a copy of the order that is sought to be reviewed and essential portions of the record. If a stipulated statement is prepared, the parties must advise the clerk not to prepare the record. The stipulated statement is to be filed and transmitted within the time prescribed for transmittal of the record. If less than a full record is to be used, the initiating party must serve a statement of the judicial acts to be reviewed so that the opposing party may determine whether additional portions of the record are required. Such a statement is not intended to be the equivalent of assignments of error under former rule 3.5. Any inadequacy in the statement may be cured by motion to supplement the record under subdivision (f) of this rule.

Subdivision (a) interacts with subdivision (b) so that as soon as the notice is filed the clerk of the lower tribunal will prepare and transmit the complete record of the case as described by the rule. To include in the record any of the items automatically omitted, a party must designate the items desired. A transcript of the proceedings in the lower tribunal will not be prepared or transmitted unless already filed, or the parties designate the portions of the transcript desired to be transmitted. Subdivision (b)(2) imposes on the reporter an affirmative duty to prepare the transcript of the proceedings as soon as designated. It is intended that to complete the preparation of all official papers to be filed with the court, the appellant need only file the notice, designate omitted portions of the record that are desired, and designate the desired portions of the transcript. It therefore will be unnecessary to file directions with the clerk of the lower tribunal in most cases.

Subdivision (b)(1) replaces former rule 3.6(d)(2), and specifically requires service of the designation on the court reporter. This is intended to avoid delays that sometimes occur when a party files the designation, but fails to notify the court reporter that a transcript is needed. The rule also establishes the responsibility of the designating party to initially bear the cost of the transcript.

Subdivision (b)(2) replaces former rule 3.6(e). This rule provides for the form of the transcript, and imposes on the reporter the affirmative duty of delivering copies of the transcript to the ordering parties on request. Such a request may be included in the designation. Under subdivision (e), however, the responsibility for ensuring performance remains with the parties. The requirement that pages be consecutively numbered is new and is deemed necessary to assure continuity and ease of reference for the convenience of the court. This requirement applies even if 2 or more parties designate portions of the proceedings for transcription. It is intended that the transcript portions transmitted to the court constitute a single consecutively numbered document in 1 or more volumes not exceeding 200 pages each. If there is more than 1 court reporter, the clerk will renumber the pages of the transcript copies so that they are sequential. The requirement of a complete index at the beginning of each volume is new, and is necessary to standardize the format and to guide those preparing transcripts.

Subdivision (b)(3) provides the procedures to be followed if no transcript is available.

Subdivision (c) provides the procedures to be followed if there is a cross-appeal or cross-petition.

Subdivision (d) sets forth the manner in which the clerk of the lower tribunal is to prepare the record. The original record is to be transmitted unless the parties stipulate or the lower court orders the original be retained, except that under rule 9.140(d) (governing criminal cases), the original is to be retained unless the court orders otherwise.

Subdivision (e) places the burden of enforcement of this rule on the appellant or petitioner, but any party may move for an order requiring adherence to the rule.

Subdivision (f) replaces former rule 3.6(*l*). The new rule is intended to ensure that appellate proceedings will be decided on their merits and that no showing of good cause, negligence, or accident is required before the lower tribunal or the court orders the completion of the record. This rule is intended to ensure that any portion of the record in the lower tribunal that is material to a decision by the court will be available to the court. It is specifically intended to avoid those situations that have occurred in the past when an order has been affirmed because appellate counsel failed to bring up the portions of the record necessary to determine whether there was an error. See *Pan American Metal Prods. Co. v. Healy*, 138 So.2d 96 (Fla. 3d DCA 1962). The rule is not intended to cure inadequacies in the record that result from the failure of a party to make a proper record during the proceedings in the lower tribunal. The purpose of the rule is to give the parties an opportunity to have the appellate proceedings decided on the record developed in the lower tribunal. This rule does not impose on the lower tribunal or the court a duty to review on their own the adequacy of the preparation of the record. A failure to supplement the record after notice by the court may be held against the party at fault.

Subdivision (g) requires that the record in civil cases be returned to the lower tribunal after final disposition by the court regardless of whether the original record or a copy was used. The court may retain or return the record in criminal cases according to its internal administration policies.

1980 Amendment. Subdivisions (b)(1) and (b)(2) were amended to specify that the party designating portions of the transcript for inclusion in the record on appeal shall pay for the cost of transcription and shall pay for and furnish a copy of the portions designated for all opposing parties. See rule 9.420(b) and 1980 committee note thereto relating to limitations of number of copies.

1987 Amendment. Subdivision (b)(3) above is patterned after Federal Rule of Appellate Procedure 11(b).

1992 Amendment. Subdivisions (b)(2), (d)(1)(A), and (d)(1)(B) were amended to standardize the lower court clerk's procedure with respect to the placement and pagination of the transcript in the record on appeal. This amendment places the duty of paginating the transcript on the court reporter and requires the clerk to include the transcript at the end of the record, without repagination.

1996 Amendment. Subdivision (a)(2) was added because family law cases frequently have continuing activity at the lower tribunal level during the pendency of appellate proceedings and that continued activity may be hampered by the absence of orders being enforced during the pendency of the appeal.

Subdivision (b)(2) was amended to change the wording in the third sentence from "transcript of proceedings" to "transcript of the trial" to be consistent with and to clarify the requirement in subdivision (d)(1)(B) that it is only the transcript of trial that is not to be renumbered by the clerk. Pursuant to subdivision (d)(1)(B), it remains the duty of the clerk to consecutively number transcripts other than the transcript of the trial. Subdivision (b)(2) retains the requirement that the court reporter is to number each page of the transcript of the trial consecutively, but it is the committee's view that if the consecutive pagination requirement is impracticable or becomes a hardship for the court reporting entity, relief may be sought from the court.

2006 Amendment. Subdivision (a)(2) is amended to apply to juvenile dependency and termination of parental rights cases and cases involving families and children in need of services. The justification for retaining the original orders, reports, and recommendations of magistrate or hearing officers, and judgments within the file of the lower tribunal in family law cases applies with equal force in juvenile dependency and termination of parental rights cases, and cases involving families and children in need of services.

2014 Amendment. The phrase "all exhibits that are not physical evidence" in subdivision (a)(1) is intended to encompass all exhibits that are capable of reproduction, including, but not limited to, documents, photographs, tapes, CDs, DVDs, and similar reproducible material. Exhibits that are physical evidence include items that are not capable of reproduction, such as weapons, clothes, biological material, or any physical item that cannot be reproduced as a copy by the clerk's office.

Rule 9.200. The Record

Text of rule effective October 1, 2015. See, also, rule effective until October 1, 2015.

(a) Contents.

(1) Except as otherwise designated by the parties, the record shall consist of all documents filed in the lower tribunal, all exhibits that are not physical evidence, and any transcript(s) of proceedings filed in the lower tribunal, except summonses, praecipes, subpoenas, returns, notices of hearing or of taking deposition, depositions, and other discovery. In criminal cases, when any exhibit, including physical evidence, is to be included in the record, the clerk of the lower tribunal shall not, unless ordered by the court, transmit the original and, if capable of reproduction, shall transmit a copy, including but not limited to copies of any tapes, CDs, DVDs, or similar electronically recorded evidence. The record shall also include a progress docket.

(2) Within 10 days of filing the notice of appeal, an appellant may direct the clerk to include or exclude other documents or exhibits filed in the lower tribunal. The directions shall be substantially in the form prescribed by rule 9.900(g). If the clerk is directed to transmit less than the entire record or a transcript of trial with less than all of the testimony, the appellant shall serve with such direction a statement of the judicial acts to be reviewed. Within 20 days of filing the notice, an appellee may direct the clerk to include additional documents and exhibits.

(3) The parties may prepare a stipulated statement showing how the issues to be presented arose and were decided in the lower tribunal, attaching a copy of the order to be reviewed and as much of the record in the lower tribunal as is necessary to a determination of the issues to be presented. The parties shall advise the clerk of the lower tribunal of their intention to rely on a stipulated statement in lieu of the record as early in advance of filing as possible. The stipulated statement shall be filed by the parties and transmitted to the court by the clerk of the lower tribunal within the time prescribed for transmittal of the record.

(b) Transcript(s) of Proceedings.

(1) Within 10 days of filing the notice, the appellant shall designate those portions of the proceedings not on file deemed necessary for transcription and inclusion in the record. Within 20 days of filing the notice, an appellee may designate additional portions of the proceedings. Copies of designations shall be served on the approved court reporter, civil court reporter, or approved transcriptionist. Costs of the transcript(s) so designated shall be borne initially by the designating party, subject to appropriate taxation of costs as prescribed by rule 9.400. At the time of the designation, unless other satisfactory arrangements have been made, the designating party must make a deposit of 1/2 of the estimated transcript costs, and must pay the full balance of the fee on delivery of the completed transcript(s).

(2) Within 30 days of service of a designation, or within the additional time provided for under subdivision (b)(3) of this rule, the approved court reporter, civil court reporter, or approved transcriptionist shall transcribe and file with the clerk of the lower tribunal the designated proceedings and shall serve copies as requested in the designation. If a designating party directs the approved court reporter, civil court reporter, or approved transcriptionist to furnish the transcript(s) to fewer than all parties, that designating party shall serve a copy of the designated transcript(s) on the parties within 5 days of receipt from the approved court reporter, civil court reporter, or approved transcriptionist. The transcript of the trial shall be filed with the clerk separately from the transcript(s) of any other designated proceedings. The transcript of the trial shall be prefaced by an index containing the names of the witnesses, a list of all exhibits offered and introduced in evidence, and the pages where each may be found. The pages, including the index pages, shall be consecutively numbered, beginning with page 1.

(3) On service of a designation, the approved court reporter, civil court reporter, or approved transcriptionist shall acknowledge at the foot of the designation the fact that it has been received and the date on which the approved court reporter, civil court reporter, or approved transcriptionist expects to have the transcript(s) completed and shall serve the so-endorsed designation on the parties and file it with the clerk of the court within 5 days of service. If the transcript(s) cannot be completed within 30 days of service of the designation, the approved court reporter, civil court reporter, or approved transcriptionist shall request such additional time as is reasonably necessary and shall state the reasons therefor. If the approved court reporter, civil court reporter, or approved transcriptionist requests an extension of time, the court shall allow the parties 5 days in which to object or agree. The court shall approve the request or take other appropriate action and shall notify the reporter and the parties of the due date of the transcript(s).

(4) If no report of the proceedings was made, or if the transcript is unavailable, a party may prepare a statement of the evidence or proceedings from the best available means, including the party's recollection. The statement shall be served on all other parties, who may serve objections or proposed amendments to it within 10 days of service. Thereafter, the statement and any objections or proposed amendments shall be filed with the lower tribunal for settlement and approval. As settled and approved, the statement shall be included by the clerk of the lower tribunal in the record.

(c) Cross–Appeals. Within 20 days of filing the notice, a cross-appellant may direct that additional documents, exhibits, or transcript(s) be included in the record. If less than the entire record is designated, the cross-appellant shall serve, with the directions, a statement of the judicial acts to be reviewed. The cross-appellee shall have 10 days after such service to direct further additions. The time for preparation and transmittal of the record shall be extended by 10 days.

(d) Duties of Clerk; Preparation and Transmittal of Electronic Record.

(1) The clerk of the lower tribunal shall prepare the record as follows:

(A) The clerk of the lower tribunal shall assemble the record on appeal and prepare a cover page and a complete index to the record. Consistent with Florida Rule of Judicial Administration 2.420(g)(8), the index shall indicate any confidential information in the record and if the information was determined to be confidential in an order, identify such order by date or docket number and record page number. The clerk of the lower tribunal shall not be required to verify and shall not charge for the incorporation of any transcript(s) into the record. The transcript of the trial shall be kept separate from the remainder of the record on appeal and shall not be renumbered by the clerk. The progress docket shall be incorporated into the record immediately after the index.

(B) All pages of the remainder of the record, including the cover page, the index, and the progress docket, shall be consecutively numbered. The first page shall be the cover page that includes the name of the lower tribunal, the style and number of the case, and the caption RECORD ON APPEAL in 48 point bold font. All remaining pages, including all supplements and any transcripts other than the transcript of the trial, shall continue the pagination of the cover page, the index, and the progress docket.

(C) The entire record, except for the transcript of the trial, shall be compiled into a single PDF file. The PDF file shall include all filings in their unredacted form. The PDF file shall be:

(i) text searchable;

(ii) paginated to exactly match the pagination of the index; and

(iii) bookmarked, consistently with the index, such that each bookmark states the date, name, and record page of the filing and the bookmarks are viewable in a separate (and/or side) window.

(2) The transcript of the trial shall be converted into a second PDF file. The PDF file shall be:

(i) text searchable; and

(ii) paginated to exactly match the pagination of the index of the transcript of the trial filed under subdivision (b)(2).

(3) The clerk of the lower tribunal shall certify the record and transmit the record and the transcript of the trial to the court by uploading the PDF files:

(A) via the Florida Courts E–Filing Portal; or

(B) in accordance with the procedures established by the appellate court's administrative order governing transmission of the record.

(e) Duties of Appellant or Petitioner. The burden to ensure that the record is prepared and transmitted in accordance with these rules shall be on the petitioner or appellant. Any party may enforce the provisions of this rule by motion.

(f) Correcting and Supplementing Record.

(1) If there is an error or omission in the record, the parties by stipulation, the lower tribunal before the record is transmitted, or the court may correct the record.

(2) If the court finds the record is incomplete, it shall direct a party to supply the omitted parts of the record. No proceeding shall be determined, because of an incomplete record, until an opportunity to supplement the record has been given.

Amended July 3, 1980, effective Jan. 1, 1981 (387 So.2d 920); Nov. 26, 1980, effective Jan. 1, 1981 (391 So.2d 203); June 8, 1987, effective July 1, 1987 (509 So.2d 276); July 14, 1988, effective Jan. 1, 1989 (529 So.2d 687); Dec. 30, 1988, effective Jan. 1, 1989 (536 So.2d 240); Oct. 22, 1992, effective Jan. 1, 1993 (609 So.2d 516); Nov. 22, 1996, effective Jan. 1, 1997 (685 So.2d 773); Oct. 12, 2000, effective Jan. 1, 2001 (780 So.2d 834); Sept. 30, 2004 (887 So.2d 1090); Oct. 26, 2006, effective Jan. 1, 2007 (941 So.2d 352); Nov. 13, 2008, effective Jan. 1, 2009 (2 So.3d 89); July 16, 2009 (13 So.3d 1044); Oct. 15, 2009 (20 So.3d 380); Nov. 3, 2011, effective Jan. 1, 2012 (75 So.3d 239); June 14, 2012, (93 So.3d 325); Oct. 18, 2012, effective Dec. 1, 2012, April 1, 2013, Oct. 1, 2013 (102 So.3d 451); Nov. 6, 2014, effective Jan. 1, 2015 (2014 WL 5714099); May 14, 2015, effective Oct. 1, 2015, (164 So.3d 668).

Committee Notes

1977 Amendment. This rule replaces former rule 3.6 and represents a complete revision of the matters pertaining to the record for an appellate proceeding. References in this rule to "appellant" and "appellee" should be treated as equivalent to "petitioner" and "respondent," respectively. See Commentary, Fla. R. App. P. 9.020. This rule is based in part on Federal Rule of Appellate Procedure 10(b).

Subdivision (a)(1) establishes the content of the record unless an appellant within 10 days of filing the notice directs the clerk to exclude portions of the record or to include additional portions, or the appellee within 20 days of the notice being filed directs inclusion of additional portions. In lieu of a record, the parties may prepare a stipulated statement, attaching a copy of the order that is sought to be reviewed and essential portions of the record. If a stipulated statement is prepared, the parties must advise the clerk not to prepare the record. The stipulated statement is to be filed and transmitted within the time prescribed for transmittal of the record. If less than a full record is to be used, the initiating party must serve a statement of the judicial acts to be reviewed so that the opposing party may determine whether additional portions of the record are required. Such a statement is not intended to be the equivalent of assignments of error under former rule 3.5. Any inadequacy in the statement may be cured by motion to supplement the record under subdivision (f) of this rule.

Subdivision (a) interacts with subdivision (b) so that as soon as the notice is filed the clerk of the lower tribunal will prepare and transmit the complete record of the case as described by the rule. To include in the record any of the items automatically omitted, a party must designate the items desired. A transcript of the proceedings in the lower tribunal will not be prepared or transmitted unless already filed, or the parties designate the portions of the transcript desired to be transmitted. Subdivision (b)(2) imposes on the reporter an affirmative duty to prepare the transcript of the proceedings as soon as designated. It is intended that to complete the preparation of all official papers to be filed with the court, the appellant need only file the notice, designate omitted portions of the record that are desired, and designate the desired portions of the transcript. It therefore will be unnecessary to file directions with the clerk of the lower tribunal in most cases.

Subdivision (b)(1) replaces former rule 3.6(d)(2), and specifically requires service of the designation on the court reporter. This is intended to avoid delays that sometimes occur when a party files the designation, but fails to notify the court reporter that a transcript is needed. The rule also establishes the responsibility of the designating party to initially bear the cost of the transcript.

Subdivision (b)(2) replaces former rule 3.6(e). This rule provides for the form of the transcript, and imposes on the reporter the affirmative duty of delivering copies of the transcript to the ordering parties on request. Such a request may be included in the designation. Under subdivision (e), however, the responsibility for ensuring performance remains with the parties. The requirement that pages be consecutively numbered is new and is deemed necessary to assure continuity and ease of reference for the convenience of the court. This requirement applies even if 2 or more parties designate portions of the proceedings for transcription. It is intended that the transcript portions transmitted to the court constitute a single consecutively numbered document in 1 or more volumes not exceeding 200 pages each. If there is more than 1 court reporter, the clerk will renumber the pages of the transcript copies so that they are sequential. The requirement of a complete index at the beginning of each volume is new, and is necessary to standardize the format and to guide those preparing transcripts.

Subdivision (b)(3) provides the procedures to be followed if no transcript is available.

Subdivision (c) provides the procedures to be followed if there is a cross-appeal or cross-petition.

Subdivision (d) sets forth the manner in which the clerk of the lower tribunal is to prepare the record. The original record is to be transmitted unless the parties stipulate or the lower court orders the original be retained, except that under rule 9.140(d) (governing criminal cases), the original is to be retained unless the court orders otherwise.

Subdivision (e) places the burden of enforcement of this rule on the appellant or petitioner, but any party may move for an order requiring adherence to the rule.

Subdivision (f) replaces former rule 3.6(*l*). The new rule is intended to ensure that appellate proceedings will be decided on their merits and that no showing of good cause, negligence, or accident is required before the lower tribunal or the court orders the completion of the record. This rule is intended to ensure that any portion of the record in the lower tribunal that is material to a decision by the court will be available to the court. It is specifically intended to avoid those situations that have occurred in the past when an order has been affirmed because appellate counsel failed to bring up the portions of the record necessary to determine whether there was an error. See *Pan American Metal Prods. Co. v. Healy*, 138 So.2d 96 (Fla. 3d DCA 1962). The rule is not intended to cure inadequacies in the record that result from the failure of a party to make a proper record during the proceedings in the lower tribunal. The purpose of the rule is to give the parties an opportunity to have the appellate proceedings decided on the record developed in the lower tribunal. This rule does not impose on the lower tribunal or the court a duty to review on their own the adequacy of the preparation of the record. A failure to supplement the record after notice by the court may be held against the party at fault.

Subdivision (g) requires that the record in civil cases be returned to the lower tribunal after final disposition by the court regardless of whether the original record or a copy was used. The court may retain or return the record in criminal cases according to its internal administration policies.

1980 Amendment. Subdivisions (b)(1) and (b)(2) were amended to specify that the party designating portions of the transcript for inclusion in the record on appeal shall pay for the cost of transcription and shall pay for and furnish a copy of the portions designated for all opposing parties. See rule 9.420(b) and 1980 committee note thereto relating to limitations of number of copies.

1987 Amendment. Subdivision (b)(3) above is patterned after Federal Rule of Appellate Procedure 11(b).

1992 Amendment. Subdivisions (b)(2), (d)(1)(A), and (d)(1)(B) were amended to standardize the lower court clerk's procedure with respect to the placement and pagination of the transcript in the record on appeal. This amendment places the duty of paginating the transcript on the court reporter and requires the clerk to include the transcript at the end of the record, without repagination.

1996 Amendment. Subdivision (a)(2) was added because family law cases frequently have continuing activity at the lower tribunal level during the pendency of appellate proceedings and that continued activity may be hampered by the absence of orders being enforced during the pendency of the appeal.

Subdivision (b)(2) was amended to change the wording in the third sentence from "transcript of proceedings" to "transcript of the trial" to be consistent with and to clarify the requirement in subdivision (d)(1)(B) that it is only the transcript of trial that is not to be renumbered by the clerk. Pursuant to subdivision (d)(1)(B), it remains the duty of the clerk to consecutively number transcripts other than the transcript of the trial. Subdivision (b)(2) retains the requirement that the court reporter is to number each page of the transcript of the trial consecutively, but it is the committee's view that if the consecutive pagination requirement is impracticable or becomes a hardship for the court reporting entity, relief may be sought from the court.

2006 Amendment. Subdivision (a)(2) is amended to apply to juvenile dependency and termination of parental rights cases and cases involving families and children in need of services. The justification for retaining the original orders, reports, and recommendations of magistrate or hearing officers, and judgments within the file of the lower tribunal in family law cases applies with equal force in juvenile dependency and termination of parental rights cases, and cases involving families and children in need of services.

2014 Amendment. The phrase "all exhibits that are not physical evidence" in subdivision (a)(1) is intended to encompass all exhibits that are capable of reproduction, including, but not limited to, documents, photographs, tapes, CDs, DVDs, and similar reproducible material. Exhibits that are physical evidence include items that are not capable of reproduction, such as weapons, clothes, biological material, or any physical item that cannot be reproduced as a copy by the clerk's office.

Rule 9.210. Briefs

(a) Generally. In addition to briefs on jurisdiction under rule 9.120(d), the only briefs permitted to be filed by the parties in any one proceeding are the initial brief, the answer brief, a reply brief, and a cross-reply brief. All briefs required by these rules shall be prepared as follows:

(1) When not filed in electronic format, briefs shall be printed, typewritten, or duplicated on opaque, white, unglossed paper. The dimensions of each page of a brief, regardless of format, shall be 8 ½ by 11 inches.

(2) The lettering in briefs shall be black and in distinct type, double-spaced, with margins no less than 1 inch. Lettering in script or type made in imitation of handwriting shall not be permitted. Footnotes and quotations may be single spaced and shall be in the same size type, with the same spacing between characters, as the text in the body of the brief. Headings and subheadings shall be at least as large as the brief's text and may be single-spaced. Computer-generated briefs shall be filed in either Times New Roman 14–point font or Courier New 12–point font. All computer-generated briefs shall contain a certificate of compliance signed by counsel, or the party if unrepresented, certifying that the brief complies with the font requirements of this rule. The certificate of compliance shall be contained in the brief immediately following the certificate of service.

(3) Paper copies of briefs shall be securely bound in book form and fastened along the left side in a manner that will allow them to lie flat when opened or be securely stapled in the upper left corner.

(4) The cover sheet of each brief shall state the name of the court, the style of the cause, including the case number if assigned, the lower tribunal, the party on whose behalf the brief is filed, the type of brief, and the name and address of the attorney filing the brief.

(5) Except as provided in subdivision (a)(6) of this rule, the initial and answer briefs shall not exceed 50 pages in length, provided that if a cross-appeal has been filed, the answer brief/initial brief on cross-appeal shall not exceed 85 pages. Reply briefs shall not exceed 15 pages in length; provided that if a cross-appeal has been filed, the reply brief shall not exceed 50 pages, not more than 15 of which shall be devoted to argument replying to the answer portion of the appellee/cross–appellant's brief. Cross–reply briefs shall not exceed 15 pages. Briefs on jurisdiction shall not exceed 10 pages. The tables of contents and citations, the certificates of service and compliance, and the signature block for the brief's author, shall be excluded from the computation. Longer briefs may be permitted by the court.

(6) In an appeal from a judgment of conviction imposing a sentence of death or in an appeal from an order ruling on, after an evidentiary hearing, an initial postconviction motion filed under Florida Rule of Criminal Procedure 3.851, the initial and answer briefs shall not exceed 100 pages in length, provided that if a cross-appeal has been filed, the answer brief/initial brief on cross-appeal shall not exceed 150 pages. Reply briefs shall not exceed 35 pages in length, provided that if a cross-appeal has been filed, the reply brief shall not exceed 100 pages, not more than 35 of which shall be devoted to argument replying to the answer portion of the appellee/cross–appellant's brief. Cross–reply briefs shall not exceed 35 pages. In an appeal from an order summarily denying an initial postconviction motion filed under Florida Rule of Criminal Procedure 3.851, ruling on a successive postconviction motion filed under Florida Rule of Criminal Procedure 3.851, finding that a defendant is intellectually disabled as a bar to execution under Florida Rule of Criminal Procedure 3.203, or ruling on a motion for postconviction DNA testing filed under Florida Rule of Criminal Procedure 3.853, the initial and answer briefs shall not exceed 75 pages in length. Reply briefs shall not exceed 25 pages in length. The tables of contents and citations, the certificates of service and compliance, and the signature block for

the brief's author, shall be excluded from the computation. Longer briefs may be permitted by the court.

(b) Contents of Initial Brief. The initial brief shall contain the following, in order:

(1) A table of contents listing the sections of the brief, including headings and subheadings that identify the issues presented for review, with references to the pages on which each appears.

(2) A table of citations with cases listed alphabetically, statutes and other authorities, and the pages of the brief on which each citation appears. See rule 9.800 for a uniform citation system.

(3) A statement of the case and of the facts, which shall include the nature of the case, the course of the proceedings, and the disposition in the lower tribunal. References to the appropriate volume and pages of the record or transcript shall be made.

(4) A summary of argument, suitably paragraphed, condensing succinctly, accurately, and clearly the argument actually made in the body of the brief. It should not be a mere repetition of the headings under which the argument is arranged. It should seldom exceed 2 and never 5 pages.

(5) Argument with regard to each issue, with citation to appropriate authorities, and including the applicable appellate standard of review.

(6) A conclusion, of not more than 1 page, setting forth the precise relief sought.

(7) A certificate of service.

(8) A certificate of compliance for computer-generated briefs.

(c) Contents of Answer Brief. The answer brief shall be prepared in the same manner as the initial brief, provided that the statement of the case and of the facts may be omitted, if the corresponding section of the initial brief is deemed satisfactory. If a cross-appeal has been filed, the answer brief shall include the issues in the cross-appeal that are presented for review, and argument in support of those issues.

(d) Contents of Reply Brief. The reply brief shall contain argument in response and rebuttal to argument presented in the answer brief. A table of contents, a table of citations, a certificate of service, and, for computer-generated briefs, a certificate of compliance shall be included in the same manner as in the initial brief.

(e) Contents of Cross–Reply Brief. The cross-reply brief is limited to rebuttal of argument of the cross-appellee. A table of contents, a table of citations, a certificate of service, and, for computer-generated briefs, a certificate of compliance shall be included in the same manner as in the initial brief.

(f) Times for Service of Briefs. The times for serving jurisdiction and initial briefs are prescribed by rules 9.110, 9.120, 9.130, and 9.140. Unless otherwise required, the answer brief shall be served within 20 days after service of the initial brief; the reply brief, if any, shall be served within 20 days after service of the answer brief; and the cross-reply brief, if any, shall be served within 20 days thereafter.

(g) Citations. Counsel are requested to use the uniform citation system prescribed by rule 9.800.

Amended Nov. 26, 1980, effective Jan. 1, 1981 (391 So.2d 203); Sept. 13, 1984, effective Jan. 1, 1985 (463 So.2d 1114); Oct. 22, 1992, effective Jan. 1, 1993 (609 So.2d 516); Nov. 22, 1996, effective Jan. 1, 1997 (685 So.2d 773); Oct. 12, 2000, effective Jan. 1, 2001 (780 So.2d 834); Oct. 26, 2006, effective Jan. 1, 2007 (941 So.2d 352); Nov. 13, 2008, effective Jan. 1, 2009 (2 So.3d 89); Oct. 18, 2012, effective Dec. 1, 2012, April 1, 2013, Oct. 1, 2013 (102 So.3d 451); Nov. 6, 2014, effective Jan. 1, 2015 (2014 WL 5714099); March 12, 2015, effective March 12, 2015 (160 So.3d 62).

Committee Notes

1977 Amendment. This rule essentially retains the substance of former rule 3.7. Under subdivision (a) only 4 briefs on the merits are permitted to be filed in any 1 proceeding: an initial brief by the appellant or petitioner, an answer brief by the appellee or respondent, a reply brief by the appellant or petitioner, and a cross-reply brief by the appellee or respondent (if a cross-appeal or petition has been filed). A limit of 50 pages has been placed on the length of the initial and answer briefs, 15 pages for reply and cross-reply briefs (unless a cross-appeal or petition has been filed), and 20 pages for jurisdictional briefs, exclusive of the table of contents and citations of authorities. Although the court may by order permit briefs longer than allowed by this rule, the advisory committee contemplates that extensions in length will not be readily granted by the courts under these rules. General experience has been that even briefs within the limits of the rule are usually excessively long.

Subdivisions (b), (c), (d), and (e) set forth the format for briefs and retain the substance of former rules 3.7(f), (g), and (h). Particular note must be taken of the requirement that the statement of the case and facts include reference to the record. The abolition of assignments of error requires that counsel be vigilant in specifying for the court the errors committed; that greater attention be given the formulation of questions presented; and that counsel comply with subdivision (b)(5) by setting forth the precise relief sought. The table of contents will contain the statement of issues presented. The pages of the brief on which argument on each issue begins must be given. It is optional to have a second, separate listing of the issues. Subdivision (c) affirmatively requires that no statement of the facts of the case be made by an appellee or respondent unless there is disagreement with the initial brief, and then only to the extent of disagreement. It is unacceptable in an answer brief to make a general statement that the facts in the initial brief are accepted, except as rejected in the argument section of the answer brief. Parties are encouraged to place every fact utilized in the argument section of the brief in the statement of facts.

Subdivision (f) sets forth the times for service of briefs after service of the initial brief. Times for service of the initial brief are governed by the relevant rule.

Subdivision (g) authorizes the filing of notices of supplemental authority at any time between the submission of briefs and rendition of a decision. Argument in such a notice is absolutely prohibited.

Subdivision (h) states the number of copies of each brief that must be filed with the clerk of the court involved 1 copy for each judge or justice in addition to the original for the permanent court file. This rule is not intended to limit the power of the court to require additional briefs at any time.

The style and form for the citation of authorities should conform to the uniform citation system adopted by the Supreme Court of Florida, which is reproduced in rule 9.800.

The advisory committee urges counsel to minimize references in their briefs to the parties by such designations as "appellant," "appellee," "petitioner," and "respondent." It promotes clarity to use actual names or descriptive terms such as "the employee," "the taxpayer," "the agency," etc. See Fed. R. App. P. 28(d).

1980 Amendment. Jurisdictional briefs, now limited to 10 pages by subdivision (a), are to be filed only in the 4 situations presented in rules 9.030(a)(2)(A)(i), (ii), (iii), and (iv).

A district court decision without opinion is not reviewable on discretionary conflict jurisdiction. See *Jenkins v. State*, 385 So. 2d 1356 (Fla. 1980); *Dodi Publishing Co. v. Editorial Am., S.A.*, 385 So. 2d 1369 (Fla. 1980). The discussion of jurisdictional brief requirements in such cases that is contained in the 1977 revision of the committee notes to rule 9.120 should be disregarded.

1984 Amendment. Subdivision (b)(4) is new; subdivision (b)(5) has been renumbered from former (b)(4); subdivision (b)(6) has been renumbered from former (b)(5). Subdivision (g) has been amended.

The summary of argument required by (b)(4) is designed to assist the court in studying briefs and preparing for argument; the rule is similar to rules of the various United States courts of appeals.

1992 Amendment. Subdivision (a)(2) was amended to bring into uniformity the type size and spacing on all briefs filed under these rules. Practice under the previous rule allowed briefs to be filed with footnotes and quotations in different, usually smaller, type sizes and spacing. Use of such smaller type allowed some overly long briefs to circumvent the reasonable length requirements established by subdivision (a)(5) of this rule. The small type size and spacing of briefs allowed under the old rule also resulted in briefs that were difficult to read. The amended rule requires that all textual material wherever found in the brief will be printed in the same size type with the same spacing.

Subdivision (g) was amended to provide that notices of supplemental authority may call the court's attention, not only to decisions, rules, or statutes, but also to other authorities that have been discovered since the last brief was served. The amendment further provides that the notice may identify briefly the points on appeal to which the supplemental authorities are pertinent. This amendment continues to prohibit argument in such notices, but should allow the court and opposing counsel to identify more quickly those issues on appeal to which these notices are relevant.

1996 Amendment. Former subdivision (g) concerning notices of supplemental authority was transferred to new rule 9.225.

Court Commentary

1987. The commission expressed the view that the existing page limits for briefs, in cases other than those in the Supreme Court of Florida, are tailored to the "extraordinary" case rather than the "ordinary" case. In accordance with this view, the commission proposed that the page limits of briefs in appellate courts other than the supreme court be reduced. The appellate courts would, however, be given discretion to expand the reduced page limits in the "extraordinary" case.

2000. As to computer-generated briefs, strict font requirements were imposed in subdivision (a)(2) for at least three reasons:

First and foremost, appellate briefs are public records that the people have a right to inspect. The clear policy of the Florida Supreme Court is that advances in technology should benefit the people whenever possible by lowering financial and physical barriers to public record inspection. The Court's eventual goal is to make all public records widely and readily available, especially via the Internet. Unlike paper documents, electronic documents on the Internet will not display properly on all computers if they are set in fonts that are unusual. In some instances, such electronic documents may even be unreadable. Thus, the Court adopted the policy that all computer-generated appellate briefs be filed in one of two fonts—either Times New Roman 14-point or Courier New 12-point—that are commonplace on computers with Internet connections. This step will help ensure that the right to inspect public records on the Internet will be genuinely available to the largest number of people.

Second, Florida's court system as a whole is working toward the day when electronic filing of all court documents will be an everyday reality. Though the technology involved in electronic filing is changing rapidly, it is clear that the Internet is the single most significant factor influencing the development of this technology. Electronic filing must be compatible with Internet standards as they evolve over time. It is imperative for the legal profession to become accustomed to using electronic document formats that are most consistent with the Internet.

Third, the proliferation of vast new varieties of fonts in recent years poses a real threat that page-limitation rules can be circumvented through computerized typesetting. The only way to prevent this is to establish an enforceable rule on standards for font use. The subject font requirements are most consistent with this purpose and the other two purposes noted above.

Subdivision (a)(2) was also amended to require that immediately after the certificate of service in computer-generated briefs, counsel (or the party if unrepresented) shall sign a certificate of compliance with the font standards set forth in this rule for computer-generated briefs.

Rule 9.220. Appendix

(a) Purpose. The purpose of an appendix is to permit the parties to prepare and transmit copies of those portions of the record deemed necessary to an understanding of the issues presented. It may be served with any petition, brief, motion, response, or reply but shall be served as otherwise required by these rules. In any proceeding in which an appendix is required, if the court finds that the appendix is incomplete, it shall direct a party to supply the omitted parts of the appendix. No proceeding shall be determined until an opportunity to supplement the appendix has been given.

(b) Contents. The appendix shall contain an index and a conformed copy of the opinion or order to be reviewed and may contain any other portions of the record and other authorities. Asterisks should be used to indicate omissions in documents or testimony of witnesses.

(c) Format. Unless otherwise authorized by court order or court rule, the appendix shall be prepared and filed electronically with the clerk as an independent PDF file or series of independent PDF files. When a paper appendix is authorized, it shall be separately bound or separated from the petition, brief, motion, response, or reply by a divider and appropriate tab, and the following requirements shall apply: (1) if the appendix includes documents filed before January 1991 on paper measuring 8 ½ by 14 inches, the documents should be reduced in copying to 8 ½ by 11 inches, if practicable; and (2) if reduction is impracticable, the appendix may measure 8 ½ by 14 inches, but it should be bound separately from the document that it accompanies.

Amended March 27, 1980, effective April 1, 1980 (381 So.2d 1370); Oct. 22, 1992, effective Jan. 1, 1993 (609 So.2d 516); Feb. 3, 2005 (894 So.2d 202); Oct. 18, 2012, effective Dec. 1, 2012, April 1, 2013, Oct. 1, 2013 (102 So.3d 451).

Committee Notes

1977 Adoption. This rule is new and has been adopted to encourage the use of an appendix either as a separate document or as a part of another matter. An appendix is optional, except under rules 9.100, 9.110(i), 9.120, and 9.130. If a legal size (8 ½ by 14 inches) appendix is used, counsel should make it a separate document. The term "conformed copy" is used throughout these rules to mean a true and accurate copy. In an appendix the formal parts of a document may be omitted if not relevant.

1980 Amendment. The rule has been amended to reflect the requirement that an appendix accompany a suggestion filed under rule 9.125.

1992 Amendment. This amendment addresses the transitional problem that arises if legal documents filed before January 1991 must be included in an appendix filed after that date. It encourages the reduction of 8 ½ by 14 inch papers to 8 ½ by 11 inches if practicable, and requires such documents to be bound separately if reduction is impracticable.

Rule 9.225. Notice of Supplemental Authority

Notices of supplemental authority may be filed with the court before a decision has been rendered to call attention to decisions, rules, statutes, or other authorities that are significant to the issues raised and that have been discovered after the last brief served in the cause. The notice shall not contain argument, but may identify briefly the issues argued on appeal to which the supplemental authorities are pertinent if the notice is substantially in the form prescribed by rule 9.900(j). Copies of the supplemental authorities shall be attached to the notice.

Added Nov. 22, 1996, effective Jan. 1, 1997 (685 So.2d 773). Amended Nov. 3, 2011, effective Jan. 1, 2012 (75 So.3d 239).

Committee Notes

1996 Adoption. Formerly rule 9.210(g) with the addition of language that requires that supplemental authorities be significant to the issues raised.

2011 Amendment. When filing a notice of supplemental authority, attorneys and parties are encouraged to use pinpoint citations to direct the court to specific pages or sections of any cited supplemental authority.

Rule 9.300. Motions

(a) Contents of Motion; Response. Unless otherwise prescribed by these rules, an application for an order or other relief available under these rules shall be made by filing a motion therefor. The motion shall state the grounds on which it is based, the relief sought, argument in support thereof, and appropriate citations of authority. A motion for an extension of time shall, and other motions if appropriate may, contain a certificate that the movant's counsel has consulted opposing counsel and that the movant's counsel is authorized to represent that opposing counsel either has no objection or will promptly file an objection. A motion may be accompanied by an appendix, which may include affidavits and other appropriate supporting documents not contained in the record. With the exception of motions filed pursuant to rule 9.410(b), a party may serve 1 response to a motion within 10 days of service of the motion. The court may shorten or extend the time for response to a motion.

(b) Effect on Proceedings. Except as prescribed by subdivision (d) of this rule, service of a motion shall toll the time schedule of any proceeding in the court until disposition of the motion. An order granting an extension of time for any act shall automatically extend the time for all other acts that bear a time relation to it. An order granting an extension of time for preparation of the record, or the index to the record, or for filing of the transcript of proceedings, shall extend automatically, for a like period, the time for service of the next brief due in the proceedings. A conformed copy of an order extending time shall be transmitted forthwith to the clerk of the lower tribunal until the record has been transmitted to the court.

(c) Emergency Relief; Notice. A party seeking emergency relief shall, if practicable, give reasonable notice to all parties.

(d) Motions Not Tolling Time.

(1) Motions for post-trial release, rule 9.140(g).

(2) Motions for stay pending appeal, rule 9.310.

(3) Motions relating to oral argument, rule 9.320.

(4) Motions relating to joinder and substitution of parties, rule 9.360.

(5) Motions relating to amicus curiae, rule 9.370.

(6) Motions relating to attorneys' fees on appeal, rule 9.400.

(7) Motions relating to service, rule 9.420.

(8) Motions relating to admission or withdrawal of attorneys, rule 9.440.

(9) Motions relating to sanctions, rule 9.410.

(10) Motions relating to expediting the appeal.

(11) Motions relating to appeal proceedings to review a final order dismissing a petition for judicial waiver of parental notice of termination of pregnancy, rule 9.147.

(12) Motions for mediation filed more than 30 days after the notice of appeal, rule 9.700(d).

(13) All motions filed in the supreme court, unless accompanied by a separate request to toll time.

Amended July 3, 1980, effective Jan. 1, 1981 (387 So.2d 920); Oct. 22, 1992, effective Jan. 1, 1993 (609 So.2d 516); Nov. 22, 1996, effective Jan. 1, 1997 (685 So.2d 773); Oct. 26, 2006, effective Jan. 1, 2007 (941 So.2d 352); Oct. 18, 2007, effective Jan. 1, 2008 (967 So.2d 194); June 24, 2010, effective Dec. 1, 2010 (41 So.3d 885); Nov. 6, 2014, effective Jan. 1, 2015 (2014 WL 5714099).

Committee Notes

1977 Amendment. This rule replaces former rule 3.9.

Subdivision (a) is new, except to the extent it replaces former rule 3.9(g), and is intended to outline matters required to be included in motions. These provisions are necessary because it is anticipated that oral argument will only rarely be permitted. Any matters that formerly would have been included in a brief on a motion should be included in the motion. Although affidavits and other documents not appearing in the record may be included in the appendix, it is to be emphasized that such materials are limited to matter germane to the motion, and are not to include matters related to the merits of the case. The advisory committee was of the view that briefs on motions are cumbersome and unnecessary. The advisory committee anticipates that the motion document will become simple and unified, with unnecessary technical language eliminated. Routine motions usually require only limited argument. Provision is made for a response by the opposing party. No further responses by either party are permitted, however, without an order of the court entered on the court's own motion or the motion of a party. To ensure cooperation and communication between opposing counsel, and conservation of judicial resources, a party moving for an extension of time is required to certify that opposing counsel has been consulted, and either has no objection or intends to serve an objection promptly. The certificate may also be used for other motions if appropriate. Only the motions listed in subdivision (d) do not toll the time for performance of the next act. Subdivision (d)(9) codifies current practice in the supreme court, where motions do not toll time unless the court approves a specific request, for good cause shown, to toll time for the performance of the next act. Very few motions filed in that court warrant a delay in further procedural steps to be taken in a case.

The advisory committee considered and rejected as unwise a proposal to allow at least 15 days to perform the next act after a motion tolling time was disposed.

Subdivision (b) replaces former rule 3.9(f).

Subdivision (c) is new and has been included at the request of members of the judiciary. It is intended to require that counsel make a reasonable effort to give actual notice to opposing counsel when emergency relief is sought from a court.

Specific reference to motions to quash or dismiss appeals contained in former rules 3.9(b) and (c) has been eliminated as unnecessary. It is not intended that such motions be abolished. Courts have the inherent power to quash frivolous appeals, and subdivision (a) guarantees to any party the right to file a motion. Although no special time limitations are placed on such motions, delay in presenting any motion may influence the relief granted or sanctions imposed under rule 9.410.

As was the case under former rule 3.8, a motion may be filed in either the lower tribunal or the court, in accordance with rule 9.600.

1980 Amendment. Subdivision (b) was amended to require the clerk of either court to notify the other clerk when an extension of time has been granted, up to the time that the record on appeal has been transmitted to the court, so that the clerk of the lower tribunal will be able to properly compute the time for transmitting the record on appeal, and that both courts may properly compute the time for performing subsequent acts.

1992 Amendment. Subdivision (b) was amended to clarify an uncertainty over time deadlines. The existing rule provided that an extension of time for performing an act automatically extended for a comparable period any other act that had a time relation thereto. The briefing schedule, however, is related by time only to the filing of the notice of appeal. Accordingly, this amendment provides that orders extending the time for preparation of the record, the index to the record, or a transcript, automatically extends for the same period the time for service of the initial brief. Subdivision (b) also was amended to correlate with rule 9.600(a), which provides that only an appellate court may grant an extension of time.

Rule 9.310. Stay Pending Review

(a) Application. Except as provided by general law and in subdivision (b) of this rule, a party seeking to stay a final or non-final order pending review shall file a motion in the lower tribunal, which shall have continuing jurisdiction, in its discretion, to grant, modify, or deny such relief. A stay pending review may be conditioned on the posting of a good and sufficient bond, other conditions, or both.

(b) Exceptions.

(1) *Money Judgments.* If the order is a judgment solely for the payment of money, a party may obtain an automatic stay of execution pending review, without the necessity of a motion or order, by posting a good and sufficient bond equal to the principal amount of the judgment plus twice the statutory rate of interest on judgments on the total amount on which the party has an obligation to pay interest. Multiple parties having common liability may file a single bond satisfying the above criteria.

(2) *Public Bodies; Public Officers.* The timely filing of a notice shall automatically operate as a stay pending review, except in criminal cases, in administrative actions under the Administrative Procedure Act, or as otherwise provided by chapter 120, Florida Statutes, when the state, any public officer in an official capacity, board, commission, or other public body seeks review; provided that an automatic stay shall exist for 48 hours after the filing of the notice of appeal for public records and public meeting cases. On motion, the lower tribunal or the court may extend a stay, impose any lawful conditions, or vacate the stay.

(c) Bond.

(1) *Defined.* A good and sufficient bond is a bond with a principal and a surety company authorized to do business in the State of Florida, or cash deposited in the circuit court clerk's office. The lower tribunal shall have continuing jurisdiction to determine the actual sufficiency of any such bond.

(2) *Conditions.* The conditions of a bond shall include a condition to pay or comply with the order in full, including costs; interest; fees; and damages for delay, use, detention, and depreciation of property, if the review is dismissed or order affirmed; and may include such other conditions as may be required by the lower tribunal.

(d) Judgment Against a Surety. A surety on a bond conditioning a stay submits to the jurisdiction of the lower tribunal and the court. The liability of the surety on such bond may be enforced by the lower tribunal or the court, after motion and notice, without the necessity of an independent action.

(e) Duration. A stay entered by a lower tribunal shall remain in effect during the pendency of all review proceedings in Florida courts until a mandate issues, or unless otherwise modified or vacated.

(f) Review. Review of orders entered by lower tribunals under this rule shall be by the court on motion.

Amended Sept. 13, 1984, effective Jan. 1, 1985 (463 So.2d 1114); July 14, 1988, effective Jan. 1, 1989 (529 So.2d 687); Dec. 30, 1988, effective Jan. 1, 1989 (536 So.2d 240); March 23, 1989 (541 So.2d 1142); Oct. 22, 1992, effective Jan. 1, 1993 (609 So.2d 516); Nov. 22, 1996, effective Jan. 1, 1997 (685 So.2d 773); Nov. 13, 2008, effective Jan. 1, 2009 (2 So.3d 89).

Committee Notes

1977 Amendment. This rule replaces former rules 5.1 through 5.12. It implements the Administrative Procedure Act, section 120.68(3), Florida Statutes (Supp.1976).

Subdivision (a) provides for obtaining a stay pending review by filing a motion in the lower tribunal, and clarifies the authority of the lower tribunal to increase or decrease the bond or deal with other conditions of the stay, even though the case is pending before the court. Exceptions are provided in subdivision (b). The rule preserves any statutory right to a stay. The court has plenary power to alter any requirements imposed by the lower tribunal. A party desiring exercise of the court's power may seek review by motion under subdivision (f) of this rule.

Subdivision (b)(1) replaces former rule 5.7. It establishes a fixed formula for determining the amount of the bond if there is a judgment solely for money. This formula shall be automatically accepted by the clerk. If an insurance company is a party to an action with its insured, and the judgment exceeds the insurance company's limits of liability, the rule permits the insurance company to supersede by posting a bond in the amount of its limits of liability, plus 15 percent. For the insured co-defendant to obtain a stay, bond must be posted for the portion of the judgment entered against the insured co-defendant plus 15 percent. The 15 percent figure was chosen as a reasonable estimate of 2 years' interest and costs, it being very likely that the stay would remain in effect for over 1 year.

Subdivision (b)(2) replaces former rule 5.12. It provides for an automatic stay without bond as soon as a notice invoking jurisdiction is filed by the state or any other public body, other than in criminal cases, which are covered by rule 9.140(c)(3), but the lower tribunal may vacate the stay or require a bond. This rule supersedes *Lewis v. Career Service Commission*, 332 So. 2d 371 (Fla. 1st DCA 1976).

Subdivision (c) retains the substance of former rule 5.6, and states the mandatory conditions of the bond.

Subdivision (d) retains the substance of former rule 5.11, with an additional provision for entry of judgment by the court so that if the lower tribunal is an agency, resort to an independent action is unnecessary.

Subdivision (e) is new and is intended to permit a stay for which a single bond premium has been paid to remain effective during all review proceedings. The stay is vacated by issuance of mandate or an order vacating it. There are no automatic stays of mandate under these rules, except for the state or a public body under subdivision (b)(2) of this rule, or if a stay as of right is guaranteed by statute. See, e.g., § 120.68(3), Fla. Stat. (Supp. 1976). This rule interacts with rule 9.340, however, so that a party has 15 days between rendition of the court's decision and issuance of mandate (unless issuance of mandate is expedited) to move for a stay of mandate pending review. If such motion is granted, any stay and bond previously in effect continues, except to the extent of any modifications, by operation of this rule. If circumstances arise requiring alteration of the terms of the stay, the party asserting the need for such change should apply by motion for the appropriate order.

Subdivision (f) provides for review of orders regarding stays pending appeal by motion in the court.

Although the normal and preferred procedure is for the parties to seek the stay in the lower court, this rule is not intended to limit the constitutional power of the court to issue stay orders after its jurisdiction has been invoked. It is intended that if review of the decision of a Florida court is sought in the United States Supreme Court, a party may move for a stay of mandate, but subdivision (e) does not apply in such cases.

1984 Amendment. Because of recent increases in the statutory rate of interest on judgments, subdivision (b)(1) was amended to provide that 2 years' interest on the judgment, rather than 15 percent of the judgment, be posted in addition to the principal amount of the judgment. In addition, the subdivision was amended to cure a deficiency in the prior rule revealed by *Proprietors Insurance Co. v. Valsecchi*, 385 So. 2d 749 (Fla. 3d DCA 1980). As under the former rule, if a party has an obligation to pay interest only on the judgment, the bond required for that party shall be equal to the principal amount of the judgment plus 2 years' interest on it. In some cases, however, an insurer may be liable under its policy to pay interest on the entire amount of the judgment against its insured, notwithstanding that the judgment against it may be limited to a lesser amount by its policy limits. See *Highway Casualty Co. v. Johnston*, 104 So. 2d 734 (Fla. 1958). In that situation, the amended rule requires the insurance company to supersede the limited judgment against it by posting a bond in the amount of the judgment plus 2 years' interest on the judgment against its insured, so that the bond will more closely approximate the insurer's actual liability to the plaintiff at the end of the duration of the stay. If such a bond is posted by an insurer, the insured may obtain a stay by posting a bond in the amount of the judgment against it in excess of that superseded by the insurer. The extent of coverage and obligation to pay interest may, in certain cases, require an evidentiary determination by the court.

1992 Amendment. Subdivision (c)(1) was amended to eliminate the ability of a party posting a bond to do so through the use of 2 personal sureties. The committee was of the opinion that a meaningful supersedeas could be obtained only through the use of either a surety company or the posting of cash. The committee also felt, however, that it was appropriate to note that the lower tribunal retained continuing jurisdiction over the actual sufficiency of any such bond.

Rule 9.315. Summary Disposition

(a) Summary Affirmance. After service of the initial brief in appeals under rule 9.110, 9.130, or 9.140, or after service of the answer brief if a cross-appeal has been filed, the court may summarily affirm the order to be reviewed if the court finds that no preliminary basis for reversal has been demonstrated.

(b) Summary Reversal. After service of the answer brief in appeals under rule 9.110, 9.130, or 9.140, or after service of the reply brief if a cross-appeal has been filed, the court may summarily reverse the order to be reviewed if the court finds that no meritorious basis exists for affirmance and the order otherwise is subject to reversal.

(c) Motions Not Permitted. This rule may be invoked only on the court's own motion. A party may not request summary disposition.

Added June 8, 1987, effective July 1, 1987 (509 So.2d 276). Amended Oct. 22, 1992, effective Jan. 1, 1993 (609 So.2d 516); Nov. 22, 1996, effective Jan. 1, 1997 (685 So.2d 773).

Court Commentary

1987. This rule contemplates a screening process by the appellate courts. More time will be spent early in the case to save more time later. The rule is fair in that appellant has an opportunity to file a full brief. The thought behind this proposal is to allow expeditious disposition of nonmeritorious appeals or obviously meritorious appeals.

Rule 9.320. Oral Argument

Oral argument may be permitted in any proceeding. A request for oral argument shall be in a separate document served by a party:

(a) in appeals, not later than 10 days after the last brief is due to be served;

(b) in proceedings commenced by the filing of a petition, not later than 10 days after the reply is due to be served; and

(c) in proceedings governed by rule 9.146, in accordance with rule 9.146(g)(5).

Each side will be allowed 20 minutes for oral argument, except in capital cases in which each side will be allowed 30 minutes. On its own motion or that of a party, the court may require, limit, expand, or dispense with oral argument.

Amended Sept. 13, 1984, effective Jan. 1, 1985 (463 So.2d 1114); Oct. 22, 1992, effective Jan. 1, 1993 (609 So.2d 516); Nov. 6, 2014, effective Jan. 1, 2015 (2014 WL 5714099).

Committee Notes

1977 Amendment. This rule replaces former rule 3.10. As under the former rules, there is no right to oral argument. It is contemplated that oral argument will be granted only if the court believes its consideration of the issues raised will be enhanced. The time ordinarily allowable to each party has been reduced from 30 minutes to 20 minutes to conform with the prevailing practice in the courts. If oral argument is permitted, the order of the court will state the time and place.

Rule 9.330. Rehearing; Clarification; Certification

(a) Time for Filing; Contents; Response. A motion for rehearing, clarification, certification, or issuance of a written opinion may be filed within 15 days of an order or within such other time set by the court. A motion for rehearing shall state with particularity the points of law or fact that, in the opinion of the movant, the court has overlooked or misapprehended in its decision, and shall not present issues not previously raised in the proceeding. A motion for clarification shall state with particularity the points of law or fact in the court's decision that, in the opinion of the movant, are in need of clarification. A response may be served within 10 days of service of the motion. When a decision is entered without opinion, and a party believes that a written opinion would provide a legitimate basis for supreme court review, the party may request that the court issue a written opinion. If such a request is made by an attorney, it shall include the following statement:

> I express a belief, based upon a reasoned and studied professional judgment, that a written opinion will provide a legitimate basis for supreme court review because (state with specificity the reasons why the supreme court would be likely to grant review if an opinion were written).
>
> s/ ____________
> Attorney for ____________
> (Name of Party)
> ____________
> ____________
> ____________
> (address, e-mail address, and phone number)
> ____________
> (Florida Bar number)

(b) Limitation. A party shall not file more than 1 motion for rehearing or for clarification of decision and 1 motion for certification with respect to a particular decision.

(c) Exception; Bond Validation Proceedings. A motion for rehearing or for clarification of a decision in proceedings for the validation of bonds or certificates of indebtedness as provided by rule 9.030(a)(1)(B)(ii) may be filed within 10 days of an order or within such other time set by the court. A reply may be served within 5 days of service of the motion. The mandate shall issue forthwith if a timely motion has not been filed. A timely motion shall receive immediate consideration by the court and, if denied, the mandate shall issue forthwith.

(d) Exception; Review of District Court Decisions. No motion for rehearing or clarification may be filed in the supreme court addressing:

(1) the dismissal of an appeal that attempts to invoke the court's mandatory jurisdiction under rule 9.030(a)(1)(A)(ii) when the appeal seeks to review a decision of a district court of appeal without opinion, or

(2) the grant or denial of a request for the court to exercise its discretion to review a decision described in rule 9.030(a)(2)(A), or

(3) the dismissal of a petition for an extraordinary writ described in rule 9.030(a)(3) when such writ is used to seek review of a district court decision without opinion.

Amended July 14, 1988, effective Jan. 1, 1989 (529 So.2d 687); Dec. 30, 1988, effective Jan. 1, 1989 (536 So.2d 240); Oct. 22, 1992, effective Jan. 1, 1993 (609 So.2d 516); Oct. 12, 2000, effective Jan. 1, 2001 (780 So.2d 834); Aug. 29, 2002, effective Jan. 1, 2003 (827 So.2d 888); Nov. 13, 2008, effective Jan. 1, 2008 (2 So.3d 89); Nov. 6, 2014, effective Jan. 1, 2015 (2014 WL 5714099).

Committee Notes

1977 Amendment. This rule replaces former rule 3.14. Rehearing now must be sought by motion, not by petition. The motion must be filed within 15 days of rendition and a response may be served within 10 days of service of the motion. Only 1 motion will be accepted by the clerk. Reargument of the issues involved in the case is prohibited.

Subdivision (c) provides expedited procedures for issuing a mandate in bond validation cases, in lieu of those prescribed by rule 9.340.

Subdivision (d) makes clear that motions for rehearing or for clarification are not permitted as to any decision of the supreme court granting or denying discretionary review under rule 9.120.

2000 Amendment. The amendment has a dual purpose. By omitting the sentence "The motion shall not re-argue the merits of the court's order," the amendment is intended to clarify the permissible scope of motions for rehearing and clarification. Nevertheless, the essential purpose of a motion for rehearing remains the same. It should be utilized to bring to the attention of the court points of law or fact that it has overlooked or misapprehended in its decision, not to express mere disagreement with its resolution of the issues on appeal. The amendment also codifies the decisional law's prohibition against issues in post-decision motions that have not previously been raised in the proceeding.

2002 Amendment. The addition of the language at the end of subdivision (a) allows a party to request the court to issue a written opinion that would allow review to the supreme court, if the initial decision is issued without opinion. This language is not intended to restrict the ability of parties to seek rehearing or clarification of such decisions on other grounds.

2008 Amendment. Subdivision (d) has been amended to reflect the holding in *Jackson v. State*, 926 So. 2d 1262 (Fla. 2006).

Rule 9.331. Determination of Causes in a District Court of Appeal En Banc

(a) En Banc Proceedings: Generally. A majority of the judges of a district court of appeal participating may order that a proceeding pending before the court be determined en banc. A district court of appeal en banc shall consist of the judges in regular active service on the court. En banc hearings and rehearing shall not be ordered unless the case is of exceptional importance or unless necessary to maintain uniformity in the court's decisions. The en banc decision shall be by a majority of the active judges actually participating and voting on the case. In the event of a tie vote, the panel decision of the district court shall stand as the decision of the court. If there is no panel decision, a tie vote will affirm the trial court decision.

(b) En Banc Proceedings by Divisions. If a district court of appeal chooses to sit in subject-matter divisions as approved by the Supreme Court, en banc determinations shall be limited to those regular active judges within the division to which the case is assigned, unless the chief judge determines that the case involves matters of general application and that en banc determination should be made by all regular active judges. However, in the absence of such determination by the chief judge, the full court may determine by an affirmative vote of three-fifths of the active judges that the case involves matters that should be heard and decided by the full court, in which event en banc determination on the merits of the case shall be made by an affirmative vote of a majority of the regular active judges participating.

(c) Hearings En Banc. A hearing en banc may be ordered only by a district court of appeal on its own motion. A party may not request an en banc hearing. A motion seeking the hearing shall be stricken.

(d) Rehearings En Banc.

(1) *Generally.* A rehearing en banc may be ordered by a district court of appeal on its own motion or on motion of a party. Within the time prescribed by rule 9.330, a party may move for an en banc rehearing solely on the grounds that the case or issue is of exceptional importance or that such consideration is necessary to maintain uniformity in the court's decisions. A motion based on any other ground shall be stricken. A response may be served within 10 days of service of the motion. A vote will not be taken on the motion unless requested by a judge on the panel that heard the proceeding, or by any judge in regular active service on the court. Judges who did not sit on the panel are under no obligation to consider the motion unless a vote is requested.

(2) *Required Statement for Rehearing En Banc.* A rehearing en banc is an extraordinary proceeding. In every case the duty of counsel is discharged without filing a motion for rehearing en banc unless one of the grounds set forth in (1) is clearly met. If filed by an attorney, the motion shall contain either or both of the following statements:

> I express a belief, based on a reasoned and studied professional judgment, that the case or issue is of exceptional importance.
>
> Or
>
> I express a belief, based on a reasoned and studied professional judgment, that the panel decision is contrary to the following decision(s) of this court and that a consideration by the full court is necessary to maintain uniformity of decisions in this court (citing specifically the case or cases).

/s/ ________________

Attorney for ________
(name of party)

____

(address, e-mail address, and phone number)
Florida Bar No. ________

(3) *Disposition of Motion for Rehearing En Banc.* A motion for rehearing en banc shall be disposed of by order. If rehearing en banc is granted, the court may limit the issues to be reheard, require the filing of additional briefs, and may require additional argument.

Added Sept. 20, 1979, effective Jan. 1, 1980 (374 So.2d 992). Amended Dec. 6, 1979, effective Jan. 1, 1980 (377 So.2d 700); June 24, 1982, effective Oct. 1, 1982 (416 So.2d 1127); Sept. 13, 1984, effective Jan. 1, 1985 (463 So.2d 1114); Oct. 22, 1992, effective Jan. 1, 1993 (609 So.2d 516); Dec. 15, 1994 (646 So.2d 730); Feb. 3, 2005 (894 So.2d 202); Nov. 6, 2014, effective Jan. 1, 2015 (2014 WL 5714099).

Committee Notes

1982 Amendment. This rule is patterned in part after the en banc rule of the United States Court of Appeals for the Fifth and Eleventh Circuits. The rule is an essential part of the philosophy of our present appellate structure because the supreme court no longer has jurisdiction to review intra-district conflict. The new appellate structural scheme requires the district courts of appeal to resolve conflict within their respective districts through the en banc process. By so doing, this should result in a clear statement of the law applicable to that particular district.

Subdivision (a) provides that a majority vote of the active and participating members of the district court is necessary to set a case for hearing en banc or rehearing en banc. The issues on the merits will be decided by a simple majority of the judges actually participating in the en banc process, without regard to recusals or a judge's absence for illness. All judges in regular active service, not excluded for cause, will constitute the en banc panel. Counsel are reminded that en banc proceedings are extraordinary and will be ordered only in the enumerated circumstances. The ground, maintenance of uniformity in the court's decisions, is the equivalent of decisional conflict as developed by supreme court precedent in the exercise of its conflict jurisdiction. The district courts are free, however, to develop their own concept of decisional uniformity. The effect of an en banc tie vote is self-explanatory, but such a vote does suggest that the matter is one that should be certified to the supreme court for resolution.

Subdivision (b) provides that hearings en banc may not be sought by the litigants; such hearings may be ordered only by the district court sua sponte.

Subdivision (c)(1) governs rehearings en banc. A litigant may apply for an en banc rehearing only on the ground that intra-district conflict of decisions exists, and then only in conjunction with a timely filed motion for rehearing under rule 9.330. The en banc rule does not allow for a separate motion for an en banc rehearing nor does it require the district court to enter a separate order on such request. Once a timely motion for rehearing en banc is filed in conjunction with a traditional petition for rehearing, the 3 judges on the initial panel must consider the motion. A vote of the entire court may be initiated by any single judge on the panel. Any other judge on the court may also trigger a vote by the entire court. Nonpanel judges are not required to review petitions for rehearing en banc until a vote is requested by another judge, although all petitions for rehearing en banc should be circulated to nonpanel judges. The court may on its own motion order a rehearing en banc.

Subdivision (c)(2) requires a signed statement of counsel certifying a bona fide belief that an en banc hearing is necessary to ensure decisional harmony within the district.

Subdivision (c)(3) is intended to prevent baseless motions for en banc rehearings from absorbing excessive judicial time and labor. The district courts will not enter orders denying motions for en banc rehearings. If a rehearing en banc is granted, the court may order briefs from the parties and set the case for oral argument.

1992 Amendment. Subdivision (c)(3) was amended to correct a linguistic error found in the original subdivision.

Court Commentary

1994 Amendment. The intent of this amendment is to authorize courts sitting in subject-matter divisions to have cases that are assigned to a division decided en banc by that division without participation by the regular active judges assigned to another division. The presumption is that en banc consideration will usually be limited to the division in which the case is pending. However, recognizing that in exceptional instances it may be preferable for the matter under review to be considered by the whole court, the case can be brought before all regular active judges by the chief judge or by an affirmative vote of three-fifths of the regular active judges on the whole court. Once the matter is before the whole court en banc, a vote on the merits will be by a majority of the regular active judges as now provided in rule 9.331.

Rule 9.340. Mandate

(a) Issuance and Recall of Mandate. Unless otherwise ordered by the court or provided by these rules, the clerk shall issue such mandate or process as may be directed by the court after expiration of 15 days from the date of an order or decision. A copy thereof, or notice of its issuance, shall be served on all parties. The court may direct the clerk to recall the mandate, but not more than 120 days after its issuance.

(b) Extension of Time for Issuance of Mandate. Unless otherwise provided by these rules, if a timely motion for rehearing, clarification, certification, or issuance of a written opinion has been filed, the time for issuance of the mandate or other process shall be extended until 15 days after rendition of the order denying the motion, or, if granted, until 15 days after the cause has been fully determined.

(c) Entry of Money Judgment. If a judgment of reversal is entered that requires the entry of a money judgment on a verdict, the mandate shall be deemed to require such money judgment to be entered as of the date of the verdict.

Amended Sept. 13, 1984, effective Jan. 1, 1985 (463 So.2d 1114); July 14, 1988, effective Jan. 1, 1989 (529 So.2d 687); Dec. 30, 1988, effective Jan. 1, 1989 (536 So.2d 240); Oct. 22, 1992, effective Jan. 1, 1993 (609 So.2d 516); Nov. 12, 2009 (24 So.3d 47); Oct. 31, 2013, effective Jan. 1, 2014 (125 So.3d 743); Nov. 6, 2014, effective Jan. 1, 2015 (2014 WL 5714099).

Committee Notes

1977 Amendment. This rule replaces former rule 3.15. The power of the court to expedite as well as delay issuance of the mandate, with or without motion, has been made express. That part of former rule 3.15(a) regarding money judgments has been eliminated as unnecessary. It is not intended to change the substantive law there stated. The 15-day delay in issuance of mandate is necessary to allow a stay to remain in effect for purposes of rule 9.310(e). This automatic delay is inapplicable to bond validation proceedings, which are governed by rule 9.330(c).

1984 Amendment. Subdivision (c) was added. It is a repromulgation of former rule 3.15(a), which was deleted in 1977 as being unnecessary. Experience proved it to be necessary.

Rule 9.350. Dismissal of Causes

(a) Dismissal of Causes When Settled. When any cause pending in the court is settled before a decision on the merits, the parties shall immediately notify the court by filing a signed stipulation for dismissal.

(b) Voluntary Dismissal. A proceeding of an appellant or petitioner may be dismissed before a decision on the merits by filing a notice of dismissal with the clerk of the court without affecting the proceedings filed by joinder or cross-appeal; provided that dismissal shall not be effective until 10 days after filing the notice of appeal or until 10 days after the time prescribed by rule 9.110(b), whichever is later.

(c) Clerk's Duty. When a proceeding is dismissed under this rule, the clerk of the court shall notify the clerk of the lower tribunal.

(d) Automatic Stay. The filing of a stipulation for dismissal or notice of dismissal automatically stays that portion of the proceedings for which a dismissal is being sought, pending further order of the court.

Amended Sept. 13, 1984, effective Jan. 1, 1985 (463 So.2d 1114); Oct. 22, 1992, effective Jan. 1, 1993 (609 So.2d 516); Oct. 12, 2000, effective Jan. 1, 2001 (780 So.2d 834); Nov. 6, 2014, effective Jan. 1, 2015 (2014 WL 5714099).

Committee Notes

1977 Amendment. Subdivision (a) retains the substance of former rule 3.13(a). On the filing of a stipulation of dismissal, the clerk of the court will dismiss the case as to the parties signing the stipulation.

Subdivision (b) is intended to allow an appellant to dismiss the appeal but a timely perfected cross-appeal would continue. A voluntary dismissal would not be effective until after the time for joinder in appeal or cross-appeal. This limitation was created so that an opposing party desiring to have adverse rulings reviewed by a cross-appeal cannot be trapped by a voluntary dismissal by the appellant after the appeal time has run, but before an appellee has filed the notice of joinder or cross-appeal.

Subdivision (c) retains the substance of former rule 3.13(c).

2014 Amendment. The addition of subdivision (d) clarifies that the filing of a stipulation or notice of dismissal does not itself dismiss the cause, while now providing for an automatic stay once a stipulation or notice is filed. The amendment is intended to limit any further litigation regarding matters that are settled or may be voluntarily dismissed, until the court determines whether to recognize the dismissal.

Rule 9.360. Parties

(a) Joinder. A party to the cause in the lower tribunal who desires to join in a proceeding as a petitioner or appellant shall serve a notice to that effect no later than the latest of the following: (i) within 10 days of service of a timely filed petition or notice of appeal; (ii) within the time prescribed for filing a notice of appeal; or (iii) within the time prescribed in rule 9.100(c). The notice of joinder, accompanied by any filing fees prescribed by law, shall be filed either before service or immediately thereafter in the same manner as the petition or notice of appeal.

(b) Attorneys, Representatives, and Guardians Ad Litem. Attorneys, representatives, and guardians ad litem in the lower tribunal shall retain their status in the court unless others are duly appointed or substituted; however, for limited representation proceedings under Florida Family Law Rule of Procedure 12.040, representation terminates upon the filing of a notice of completion titled "Termination of Limited Appearance" pursuant to rule 12.040(c).

(c) Substitution of Parties.

(1) If substitution of a party is necessary for any reason, the court may so order on its own motion or that of a party.

(2) Public officers as parties in their official capacities may be described by their official titles rather than by name. Their successors in office shall be automatically substituted as parties.

(3) If a party dies while a proceeding is pending and that party's rights survive, the court may order the substitution of the proper party on its own motion or that of any interested person.

(4) If a person entitled to file a notice dies before filing and that person's rights survive, the notice may be filed by the personal representative, attorney of record, or, if none, by any interested person. Following filing, the proper party shall be substituted.

Amended Oct. 22, 1992, effective Jan. 1, 1993 (609 So.2d 516); Nov. 13, 2003, effective Jan. 1, 2004 (860 So.2d 394); Jan. 29, 2009 (1 So.3d 166); Oct. 18, 2012, effective Dec. 1, 2012, April 1, 2013, Oct. 1, 2013 (102 So.3d 451).

Committee Notes

1977 Amendment. This rule is intended as a simplification of the former rules with no substantial change in practice.

Subdivision (a) is a simplification of the provisions of former rule 3.11(b), with modifications recognizing the elimination of assignments of error.

Subdivision (b) retains the substance of former rule 3.11(d).

Subdivision (c)(1) substantially simplifies the procedure for substituting parties. This change is in keeping with the overall concept of this revision that these rules should identify material events that may or should occur in appellate proceedings and specify in general terms how that event should be brought to the attention of the court and how the parties should proceed. The manner in which these events shall be resolved is left to the courts, the parties, the substantive law, and the circumstances of the particular case.

Subdivision (c)(2) is new and is intended to avoid the necessity of motions for substitution if the person holding a public office is changed during the course of proceedings. It should be noted that the style of the case does not necessarily change.

Subdivision (c)(4) is new, and is intended to simplify the procedure and avoid confusion if a party dies before an appellate proceeding is instituted. Substitutions in such cases are to be made according to subdivision (c)(1).

Rule 9.370. Amicus Curiae

(a) When Permitted. An amicus curiae may file a brief only by leave of court. A motion for leave to file must state the movant's interest, the particular issue to be addressed, how the movant can assist the court in the disposition of the case, and whether all parties consent to the filing of the brief.

(b) Contents and Form. An amicus brief must comply with Rule 9.210(b) but shall omit a statement of the case and facts and may not exceed 20 pages. The cover must identify the party or parties supported. An amicus brief must include a concise statement of the identity of the amicus curiae and its interest in the case.

(c) Time for Service. An amicus curiae must serve its brief no later than 10 days after the first brief, petition, or response of the party being supported is filed. An amicus curiae that does not support either party must serve its brief no later than 10 days after the initial brief or petition is filed. A court may grant leave for later service, specifying the time within which an opposing party may respond. The service of an amicus curiae brief does not alter or extend the briefing deadlines for the parties. An amicus curiae may not file a reply brief.

(d) Notice of Intent to File Amicus Brief in Supreme Court. When a party has invoked the discretionary jurisdiction of the supreme court, an amicus curiae may file a notice with the court indicating its intent to seek leave to file an amicus brief on the merits should the court accept jurisdiction. The notice shall state briefly why the case is of interest to the amicus curiae, but shall not contain argument. The body of the notice shall not exceed one page.

Amended Oct. 22, 1992, effective Jan. 1, 1993 (609 So.2d 516); Aug. 29, 2002, effective Jan. 1, 2003 (827 So.2d 888); Feb. 3, 2005 (894 So.2d 202); Oct. 26, 2006, effective Jan. 1, 2007 (941 So.2d 352); Nov. 13, 2008, effective Jan. 1, 2009 (2 So.3d 89); Nov. 3, 2011, effective Jan. 1, 2012 (75 So.3d 239).

Committee Note

1977 Amendment. This rule replaces former rule 3.7(k) and expands the circumstances in which amicus curiae briefs may be filed to recognize the power of the court to request amicus curiae briefs.

2008 Amendment. Subdivision (d) was added to establish a procedure for an amicus curiae to expeditiously inform the supreme court of its intent to seek leave to file an amicus brief on the merits should the court accept jurisdiction. This rule imposes no obligation on the supreme court to delay its determination of jurisdiction. Thus, an amicus curiae should file its notice as soon as possible after the filing of the notice to invoke the discretionary jurisdiction of the supreme court. The filing of a notice under subdivision (d) is optional and shall not relieve an amicus curiae from compliance with the provisions of subdivision (a) of this rule if the court accepts jurisdiction.

Rule 9.400. Costs and Attorneys' Fees

(a) Costs. Costs shall be taxed in favor of the prevailing party unless the court orders otherwise. Taxable costs shall include

(1) fees for filing and service of process;

(2) charges for preparation of the record and any hearing or trial transcripts necessary to determine the proceeding;

(3) bond premiums; and

(4) other costs permitted by law.

Costs shall be taxed by the lower tribunal on a motion served no later than 45 days after rendition of the court's order. If an order is entered either staying the issuance of or recalling a mandate, the lower tribunal is prohibited from taking any further action on costs pending the issuance of a mandate or further order of the court.

(b) Attorneys' Fees. With the exception of motions filed pursuant to rule 9.410(b), a motion for attorneys' fees shall state the grounds on which recovery is sought and shall be served not later than:

(1) in appeals, the time for service of the reply brief; or

(2) in original proceedings, the time for service of the petitioner's reply to the response to the petition.

The assessment of attorneys' fees may be remanded to the lower tribunal. If attorneys' fees are assessed by the court, the lower tribunal may enforce payment.

(c) Review. Review of orders rendered by the lower tribunal under this rule shall be by motion filed in the court within 30 days of rendition.

Amended Oct. 22, 1992, effective Jan. 1, 1993 (609 So.2d 516); Nov. 22, 1996, effective Jan. 1, 1997 (685 So.2d 773); June 24, 2010, effective Dec. 1, 2010 (41 So.3d 885); Nov. 6, 2014, effective Jan. 1, 2015 (2014 WL 5714099).

Committee Notes

1977 Amendment. Subdivision (a) replaces former rules 3.16(a) and (b). It specifies allowable cost items according to the current practice. Item (3) is not intended to apply to bail bond premiums. Item

(4) is intended to permit future flexibility. This rule provides that the prevailing party must move for costs in the lower tribunal within 30 days after issuance of the mandate.

Subdivision (b) retains the substance of former rule 3.16(e). The motion for attorneys' fees must contain a statement of the legal basis for recovery. The elimination of the reference in the former rule to attorneys' fees "allowable by law" is not intended to give a right to assessment of attorneys' fees unless otherwise permitted by substantive law.

Subdivision (c) replaces former rules 3.16(c) and (d). It changes from 20 days to 30 days the time for filing a motion to review an assessment of costs or attorneys' fees by a lower tribunal acting under order of the court.

Rule 9.410. Sanctions

(a) Court's Motion. After 10 days' notice, on its own motion, the court may impose sanctions for any violation of these rules, or for the filing of any proceeding, motion, brief, or other paper that is frivolous or in bad faith. Such sanctions may include reprimand, contempt, striking of briefs or pleadings, dismissal of proceedings, costs, attorneys' fees, or other sanctions.

(b) Motion by a Party.

(1) *Applicability.* Any contrary requirements in these rules notwithstanding, the following procedures apply to a party seeking an award of attorneys' fees as a sanction against another party or its counsel pursuant to general law.

(2) *Proof of Service.* A motion seeking attorneys' fees as a sanction shall include an initial certificate of service, pursuant to rule 9.420(d) and subdivision (3) of this rule, and a certificate of filing, pursuant to subdivision (4) of this rule.

(3) *Initial Service.* A copy of a motion for attorneys' fees as a sanction must initially be served only on the party against whom sanctions are sought. That motion shall be served no later than the time for serving any permitted response to a challenged paper or, if no response is permitted as of right, within 15 days after a challenged paper is served or a challenged claim, defense, contention, allegation, or denial is made at oral argument. A certificate of service that complies with rule 9.420(d) and that reflects service pursuant to this subdivision shall accompany the motion and shall be taken as prima facie proof of the date of service pursuant to this subdivision. A certificate of filing pursuant to subdivision (4) of this rule shall also accompany the motion, but should remain undated and unsigned at the time of the initial service pursuant to this subdivision.

(4) *Filing and Final Service.* If the challenged paper, claim, defense, contention, allegation, or denial is not withdrawn or appropriately corrected within 21 days after initial service of the motion under subdivision (3), the movant may file the motion for attorneys' fees as a sanction with the court (a) no later than the time for service of the reply brief, if applicable, or (b) no later than 45 days after initial service of the motion, whichever is later.

The movant shall serve upon all parties the motion filed with the court. A certificate of filing which complies in substance with the form below, and which shall be dated and signed at the time of final service pursuant to this subdivision, shall be taken as prima facie proof of such final service.

I certify that on .....(date) ....., a copy of this previously served motion has been furnished to .....(court) .....by .....hand delivery/mail/other delivery source .....and has been furnished to .....(name or names) .....by .....hand delivery/mail/other delivery source ......

/s/ ____________________
Attorney for ...(name of party)...
...(address, e-mail address, and phone number)...
Florida Bar No. ....

(5) *Response.* A party against whom sanctions are sought may serve 1 response to the motion within 10 days of the final service of the motion. The court may shorten or extend the time for response to the motion.

Amended July 14, 1988, effective Jan. 1, 1989 (529 So.2d 687); Dec. 30, 1988, effective Jan. 1, 1989 (536 So.2d 240); Oct. 22, 1992, effective Jan. 1, 1993 (609 So.2d 516); June 24, 2010, effective Dec. 1, 2010 (41 So.3d 885); Nov. 6, 2014, effective Jan. 1, 2015 (2014 WL 5714099).

Committee Notes

1977 Amendment. This rule replaces former rule 3.17. This rule specifies the penalties or sanctions that generally are imposed, but does not limit the sanctions available to the court. The only change in substance is that this rule provides for 10 days notice to the offending party before imposition of sanctions.

2010 Amendment. Subdivision (b) is adopted to make rule 9.410 consistent with section 57.105, Florida Statutes (2009).

Rule 9.420. Filing; Service of Copies; Computation of Time

(a) Filing.

(1) *Generally.* Filing may be accomplished in a manner in conformity with the requirements of Florida Rule of Judicial Administration 2.525.

(2) *Inmate Filing.* The filing date of a document filed by a pro se inmate confined in an institution shall be presumed to be the date it is stamped for filing by the clerk of the court, except as follows:

(A) The document shall be presumed to be filed on the date the inmate places it in the hands of an institutional official for mailing if the institution has a system designed for legal mail, the inmate uses that system, and the institution's system records that date, or

(B) The document shall be presumed to be filed on the date reflected on a certificate of service contained in the document if the certificate is in substantially the form prescribed by subdivision (d)(1) of this rule and either:

(i) the institution does not have a system designed for legal mail; or

(ii) the inmate used the institution's system designed for legal mail, if any, but the institution's system does not provide for a way to record the date the inmate places the document in the hands of an institutional official for mailing.

(b) Service.

(1) *By a Party or Amicus Curiae.* All documents shall be filed either before service or immediately thereafter. A copy of all documents filed under these rules shall, before filing or immediately thereafter, be served on each of the parties. The lower tribunal, before the record is transmitted, or the court, on motion, may limit the number of copies to be served.

(2) *By the Clerk of Court.* A copy of all orders and decisions shall be transmitted, in the manner set forth for service in rule 9.420(c), by the clerk of the court to all parties at the time of entry of the order or decision, without first requiring payment of any costs for the copies of those orders and decisions. Prior to the court's entry of an order or decision, the court may require that the parties furnish the court with stamped, addressed envelopes for transmittal of the order or decision.

(c) Method of Service. Service of every document filed in a proceeding governed by these rules (including any briefs, motions, notices, responses, petitions, and appendices) shall be made in conformity with the requirements of Florida Rule of Judicial Administration 2.516, except that the initial document filed in a proceeding governed by these rules (including any notice to invoke jurisdiction, notice of appeal, or petition for an original writ) shall be served both by e-mail pursuant to rule 2.516(b)(1) and in paper form pursuant to rule 2.516(b)(2).

(d) Proof of Service. A certificate of service by an attorney that complies in substance with the requirements of Florida Rule of Judicial Administration 2.516(f) and a certificate of service by a pro se party that complies in substance with the appropriate form below shall be taken as prima facie proof of service in compliance with these rules. The certificate shall specify the party each attorney represents.

(1) *By Pro Se Inmate*:

I certify that I placed this document in the hands of .... (here insert name of institution official) .... for mailing to .... (here insert name or names and addresses used for service) .... on .... (date) ....

____
.... (name)
....
.... (address)
....
.... (prison identification number) ....

(2) *By Other Pro Se Litigants*:

I certify that a copy hereof has been furnished to .... (here insert name or names and addresses used for service) .... by .... (e-mail) (delivery) (mail) .... on .... (date) ....

____
.... (name)
....
.... (address)
....
.... (phone number)

(e) Computation. Computation of time shall be governed by Florida Rule of Judicial Administration 2.514.

Amended July 3, 1980, effective Jan. 1, 1981 (387 So.2d 920); March 19, 1987 (505 So.2d 1087); June 8, 1987, effective July 1, 1987 (509 So.2d 276); Oct. 22, 1992, effective Jan. 1, 1993 (609 So.2d 516); Nov. 22, 1996, effective Jan. 1, 1997 (685 So.2d 773); Oct. 12, 2000, effective Jan. 1, 2001 (780 So.2d 834); Feb. 3, 2005 (894 So.2d 202); Jan. 19, 2006 (919 So.2d 431); Nov. 3, 2011, effective Jan. 1, 2012 (75 So.3d 239); July 12, 2012, effective Oct. 1, 2012 (95 So.3d 96); Oct. 18, 2012, effective, *nunc pro tunc*, Sept. 1, 2012 (102 So.3d 505); Nov. 6, 2014, effective Jan. 1, 2015 (2014 WL 5714099).

Committee Notes

1977 Amendment. Subdivision (a) replaces former rule 3.4(a). The last sentence of former rule 3.4(a) was eliminated as superfluous. The filing of papers with a judge or justice is permitted at the discretion of the judge or justice. The advisory committee recommends that the ability to file with a judge or justice be exercised only if necessary, and that care be taken not to discuss in any manner the merits of the document being filed. See Fla. Code Prof. Resp., DR 7–110(B) (now R. Regulating Fla. Bar 4–3.5(b)); Fla. Code Jud. Conduct, Canon 3(A)(4).

Subdivision (b) replaces and simplifies former rules 3.4(b)(5) and 3.6(i)(3). The substance of the last sentence of former rule 3.4(b)(5) is preserved. It should be noted that except for the notices or petitions that invoke jurisdiction, these rules generally provide for service by a certain time rather than filing. Under this provision filing must be done before service or immediately thereafter. Emphasis has been placed on service so as to eliminate the hardship on parties caused by tardy service under the former rules and to eliminate the burden placed on the courts by motions for extension of time resulting from such tardy service. It is anticipated that tardy filing will occur less frequently under these rules than tardy service under the former rules because the parties are unlikely to act in a manner that would irritate the court. The manner for service and proof thereof is provided in subdivision (c).

Subdivision (d) replaces former rule 3.4(b)(3) and provides that if a party or clerk is required or permitted to do an act within a prescribed time after service, 5 days (instead of 3 days under the former rule) shall be added to the time if service is by mail.

Subdivision (e) replaces former rule 3.18 with no substantial change. "Holiday" is defined to include any day the clerk's office is closed whether or not done by order of the court. The holidays specifically listed have been included, even though many courts do not recognize them as holidays, to not place a burden on practitioners to check whether an individual court plans to observe a particular holiday.

1980 Amendment. Subdivision (b) was amended to provide that either the lower tribunal or the court may limit the number of copies to be served. The rule contemplates that the number of copies may be limited on any showing of good cause, for example, that the number of copies involved is onerous or that the appeal involves questions with which some parties have no interest in the outcome or are so remotely involved as not to justify furnishing a complete record to them at appellant's initial cost. The availability of the original record at the clerk's office of the lower tribunal until due at the appellate court is a factor to be considered.

2014 Amendment. Subdivision (a)(2) has been completely rewritten to conform this rule to *Thompson v. State*, 761 So. 2d 324 (Fla. 2000), and the federal mailbox rule adopted in *Haag v. State*, 591 So. 2d 614 (Fla. 1992). The amendment clarifies that an inmate is required to use the institutional system designed for legal mail, if there is one, in order to receive the benefits of the mailbox rule embodied in this subdivision. If the institution's legal mail system records the date the document is provided to institutional officials for mailing (e.g. Rule 33-210.102(8), Florida Administrative Code (2010)), that date is presumed to be the date of filing. If the institution's legal mail system does not record the date the document is provided to institutional officials—or if the institution does not have a system for legal mail at all—the date of filing is presumed to be the date reflected on the certificate of service contained in the document, if the certificate of service is in substantial conformity with subdivision (d)(1) of this rule. If the inmate does not use the institution's legal mail system when one exists—or if the inmate does not include in the document a certificate of service when the institution does not have a legal mail system—the date the document is filed is presumed to be the date it is stamped for filing by the clerk of the court.

Court Commentary

2000. Subdivision (a)(2) codifies the Florida Supreme Court's holding in *Thompson v. State*, 761 So. 2d 324 (Fla. 2000).

Rule 9.430. Proceedings by Indigents

(a) Appeals. A party who has the right to seek review by appeal without payment of costs shall, unless the court directs otherwise, file a signed application for determination of indigent status with the clerk of the lower tribunal, using an application form approved by the Supreme Court for use by circuit court clerks. The clerk of the lower tribunal's reasons for denying the application shall be stated in writing and are reviewable by the lower tribunal. Review of decisions by the lower tribunal shall be by motion filed in the court.

(b) Original Proceedings. A party who seeks review by an original proceeding under rule 9.100 without the payment of costs shall, unless the court directs otherwise, file with the court a motion to proceed in forma pauperis. If the motion is granted, the party may proceed without further application to the court.

(c) Incarcerated Parties.

(1) *Presumptions.* In the absence of evidence to the contrary, court may, in its discretion, presume that

(A) assertions in an application for determination of indigent status filed by an incarcerated party under this rule are true, and

(B) in cases involving criminal or collateral criminal proceedings, an incarcerated party who has been declared indigent for purposes of proceedings in the lower tribunal remains indigent.

(2) *Non–Criminal Proceedings.* Except in cases involving criminal or collateral proceedings, an application for determination of indigent status filed under this rule by a person who has been convicted of a crime and is incarcerated for that crime or who is being held in custody pending extradition or sentencing shall contain substantially the same information as required by an application form approved by the Supreme Court for use by circuit court clerks. The determination of whether the case involves an appeal from an original criminal or collateral proceeding depends on the substance of the issues raised and not on the form or title of the petition or complaint. In these non-criminal cases, the clerk of the lower tribunal shall require the party to make a partial prepayment of court costs or fees and to make continued partial payments until the full amount is paid.

(d) Parties in Juvenile Dependency and Termination of Parental Rights Cases; Presumption. In cases involving dependency or termination of parental rights, court may, in its discretion, presume that any party who has been declared indigent for purposes of proceedings by the lower tribunal remains indigent, in the absence of evidence to the contrary.

Amended Oct. 22, 1992, effective Jan. 1, 1993 (609 So.2d 516); April 25, 1996, with amendment stayed May 2, 1996, *nunc pro tunc* to April 25, 1996 (682 So.2d 1068); Nov. 22, 1996, effective Jan. 1, 1997 (685 So.2d 773) Feb. 3, 2005 (894 So.2d 202); Nov. 13, 2008, effective Jan. 1, 2009 (2 So.3d 89); Nov. 12, 2009 (24 So.3d 47); Nov. 6, 2014, effective Jan. 1, 2015 (2014 WL 5714099).

Committee Notes

1977 Adoption. This rule governs the manner in which an indigent may proceed with an appeal without payment of fees or costs and without bond. Adverse rulings by the lower tribunal must state in writing the reasons for denial. Provision is made for review by motion. Such motion may be made without the filing of fees as long as a notice has been filed, the filing of fees not being jurisdictional. This rule is not intended to expand the rights of indigents to proceed with an appeal without payment of fees or costs. The existence of such rights is a matter governed by substantive law.

2008 Amendment. Subdivision (b) was created to differentiate the treatment of original proceedings from appeals under this rule. Each subdivision was further amended to comply with statutory amendments to section 27.52, Florida Statutes, the legislature's enactment of section 57.082, Florida Statutes, and the Florida Supreme Court's opinion in *In re Approval of Application for Determination of Indigent Status Forms for Use by Clerks*, 910 So. 2d 194 (Fla. 2005).

Rule 9.440. Attorneys

(a) Foreign Attorneys. An attorney who is an active member in good standing of the bar of another state may be permitted to appear in a proceeding upon compliance with Florida Rule of Judicial Administration 2.510.

(b) Withdrawal of Attorneys. An attorney shall not be permitted to withdraw unless the withdrawal is approved by the court. The attorney shall file a motion for that purpose stating the reasons for withdrawal and the client's address. A copy of the motion shall be served on the client and adverse parties.

Amended Oct. 22, 1992, effective Jan. 1, 1993 (609 So.2d 516); Aug. 29 2002, effective Jan. 1, 2003 (827 So.2d 888).

Committee Notes

1977 Amendment. This rule replaces former rule 2.3 with unnecessary subdivisions deleted. The deletion of former rule 2.3(c) was not intended to authorize the practice of law by research aides or secretaries to any justice or judge or otherwise approve actions inconsistent with the high standards of ethical conduct expected of such persons.

Subdivision (a) permits foreign attorneys to appear on motion filed and granted at any time. See Fla. Bar Integr. Rule By–Laws, art. II, § 2. There is no requirement that the foreign attorney be from a jurisdiction giving a reciprocal right to members of The Florida Bar. This rule leaves disposition of motions to appear to the discretion of the court.

Subdivision (b) is intended to protect the rights of parties and attorneys, and the needs of the judicial system.

This rule does not affect the right of a party to employ additional attorneys who, if members of The Florida Bar, may appear at any time.

2002 Amendment. The amendments to subdivision (a) are intended to make that subdivision consistent with Florida Rule of Judicial Administration 2.061, which was adopted in 2001, and the amendments to subdivision (b) are intended to make that subdivision consistent with Florida Rule of Judicial Administration 2.060(i).

Rule 9.500. Advisory Opinions to Governor

(a) Filing. A request by the governor for an advisory opinion from the justices of the supreme court on a question affecting gubernatorial powers and duties shall be in writing. The request shall be filed with the clerk of the supreme court.

(b) Procedure. As soon as practicable after the filing of the request, the justices shall determine whether the request is within the purview of article IV, section 1(c), Florida Constitution, and proceed as follows:

(1) If 4 justices concur that the question is not within that purview, the governor shall be advised forthwith in writing and a copy shall be filed in the clerk's office.

(2) If the request is within that purview, the court may permit persons whose substantial interests may be affected to be heard on the questions presented through briefs, oral argument, or both. If the court determines to receive briefs or hear oral argument, it shall set the time for filing briefs, the date of argument, and the time allotted. The court may appoint amicus curiae and prescribe their duties.

(3) The justices shall file their opinions in the clerk's office. Copies shall be delivered to the governor.

Amended Oct. 22, 1992, effective Jan. 1, 1993 (609 So.2d 516); Oct. 18, 2012, effective Dec. 1, 2012, April 1, 2013, Oct. 1, 2013 (102 So.3d 451).

Committee Notes

1977 Amendment. This rule simplifies former rule 2.1(h) without material change.

Rule 9.510. Advisory Opinions to Attorney General

(a) Filing. A request by the attorney general for an advisory opinion from the justices of the supreme court concerning the validity of an initiative petition for the amendment of the Florida Constitution shall be in writing. The request shall be filed with the clerk of the supreme court.

(b) Contents of Request. In addition to the language of the proposed amendment, the request referenced in subdivision (a) must contain the following information:

(1) the name and address of the sponsor of the initiative petition;

(2) the name and address of the sponsor's attorney, if the sponsor is represented;

(3) a statement as to whether the sponsor has obtained the requisite number of signatures on the initiative petition to have the proposed amendment put on the ballot;

(4) if the sponsor has not obtained the requisite number of signatures on the initiative petition to have the proposed amendment put on the ballot, the current status of the signature-collection process;

(5) the date of the election during which the sponsor is planning to submit the proposed amendment to the voters;

(6) the last possible date that the ballot for the target election can be printed in order to be ready for the election;

(7) a statement identifying the date by which the Financial Impact Statement will be filed, if the Financial Impact Statement is not filed concurrently with the request; and

(8) the names and complete mailing addresses of all of the parties who are to be served.

(c) Procedure. The justices must initially determine whether the request is within the purview of article V, section 3(b)(10), Florida Constitution, and proceed as follows:

(1) If 4 justices concur that the request is not within that purview, the attorney general will be advised immediately in writing and a copy will be filed in the clerk's office.

(2) If the request is within the purview, the court may permit the attorney general and other interested persons to be heard on the questions presented through briefs, oral argument, or both. If the court decides to receive briefs or hear oral argument, it will establish the time for filing briefs, the date of argument, and the time allotted.

Added Nov. 9, 2006 (942 So.2d 406). Amended Oct. 18, 2012, effective Dec. 1, 2012, April 1, 2013, Oct. 1, 2013 (102 So.3d 451).

Committee Notes

1980 Amendment. This rule has been replaced in its entirety by new Rule 9.150.

Rule 9.600. Jurisdiction of Lower Tribunal Pending Review

(a) Concurrent Jurisdiction. Only the court may grant an extension of time for any act required by these rules. Before the record is docketed, the lower tribunal shall have concurrent jurisdiction with the court to render orders on any other procedural matter relating to the cause, subject to the control of the court, provided that clerical mistakes in judgments, decrees, or other parts of the record arising from oversight or omission may be corrected by the lower tribunal on its own initiative after notice or on motion of any party before the record is docketed in the court, and, thereafter with leave of the court.

(b) Further Proceedings. If the jurisdiction of the lower tribunal has been divested by an appeal from a final order, the court by order may permit the lower tribunal to proceed with specifically stated matters during the pendency of the appeal.

(c) Family Law Matters. In family law matters:

(1) The lower tribunal shall retain jurisdiction to enter and enforce orders awarding separate maintenance, child support, alimony, attorneys' fees and costs for services rendered in the lower tribunal, temporary attorneys' fees and costs reasonably necessary to prosecute or defend an appeal, or other awards necessary to protect the welfare and rights of any party pending appeal.

(2) The receipt, payment, or transfer of funds or property under an order in a family law matter shall not prejudice the rights of appeal of any party. The lower tribunal shall have the jurisdiction to impose, modify, or dissolve conditions upon the receipt or payment of such awards in order to protect the interests of the parties during the appeal.

(3) Review of orders entered pursuant to this subdivision shall be by motion filed in the court within 30 days of rendition.

(d) Criminal Cases. The lower tribunal shall retain jurisdiction to consider motions pursuant to Florida Rules of Criminal Procedure 3.800(b)(2) and in conjunction with post-trial release pursuant to rule 9.140(h).

Amended July 3, 1980, effective Jan. 1, 1981 (387 So.2d 920); June 8, 1987, effective July 1, 1987 (509 So.2d 276); Oct. 22, 1992, effective Jan. 1, 1993 (609 So.2d 516); June 15, 1995 (657 So.2d 897); Nov. 22, 1996, effective Jan. 1, 1997 (685 So.2d 773); Nov. 12, 1999 (760 So.2d 67); Jan. 13, 2000 (761 So.2d 1015); Nov. 13, 2008, effective Jan. 1, 2009 (2 So.3d 89); Nov. 6, 2014, effective Jan. 1, 2015 (2014 WL 5714099).

Committee Notes

1977 Amendment. This rule governs the jurisdiction of the lower tribunal during the pendency of review proceedings, except for interlocutory appeals. If an interlocutory appeal is taken, the lower tribunal's jurisdiction is governed by rule 9.130(f).

Subdivision (b) replaces former rule 3.8(a). It allows for continuation of various aspects of the proceeding in the lower tribunal, as may be allowed by the court, without a formal remand of the cause. This rule is intended to prevent unnecessary delays in the resolution of disputes.

Subdivision (c) is derived from former rule 3.8(b). It provides for jurisdiction in the lower tribunal to enter and enforce orders awarding separate maintenance, child support, alimony, temporary suit money, and attorneys' fees. Such orders may be reviewed by motion.

1980 Amendment. Subdivision (a) was amended to clarify the appellate court's paramount control over the lower tribunal in the exercise of its concurrent jurisdiction over procedural matters. This amendment would allow the appellate court to limit the number of extensions of time granted by a lower tribunal, for example.

1994 Amendment. Subdivision (c) was amended to conform to and implement section 61.16(1), Florida Statutes (1994 Supp.), authorizing the lower tribunal to award temporary appellate attorneys' fees, suit money, and costs.

1996 Amendment. New rule 9.600(d) recognizes the jurisdiction of the trial courts, while an appeal is pending, to rule on motions for post-trial release, as authorized by rule 9.140(g), and to decide motions pursuant to Florida Rule of Criminal Procedure 3.800(a), as authorized by case law such as *Barber v. State,* 590 So. 2d 527 (Fla. 2d DCA 1991).

Rule 9.700. Mediation Rules

(a) Applicability. Rules 9.700—9.740 apply to all appellate courts, including circuit courts exercising jurisdiction under rule 9.030(c), district courts of appeal, and the Supreme Court of Florida.

(b) Referral. The court, upon its own motion or upon motion of a party, may refer a case to mediation at any time. Such motion from a party shall contain a certificate that the movant has consulted opposing counsel or unrepresented party and that the movant is authorized to represent that opposing counsel or unrepresented party:

(1) has no objection;

(2) objects and cites the specific reasons for objection; or

(3) will promptly file an objection.

(c) Time Frames for Mediation. The first mediation conference shall be commenced within 45 days of referral by the court, unless the parties agree to postpone mediation until after the period for filing briefs has expired. The mediation shall be completed within 30 days of the first mediation conference. These times may be modified by order of the court.

(d) Tolling of Times. Unless otherwise ordered, or upon agreement of the parties to postpone mediation until after the expiration of time for filing the appellate briefs, all times under these rules for the processing of cases shall be tolled for the period of time from the referral of a case to mediation until mediation ends pursuant to section 44.404, Florida Statutes. The court, by administrative order, may provide for additional tolling of deadlines. A motion for mediation filed by a party within 30 days of the notice of appeal shall toll all deadlines under these rules until the motion is ruled upon by the court.

(e) Motion to Dispense with Mediation. A motion to dispense with mediation may be served not later than 10 days after the discovery of the facts which constitute the grounds for the motion, if:

(1) the order violates rule 9.710; or

(2) other good cause is shown.

Added July 1, 2010 (41 So.3d 161).

Rule 9.710. Eligibility for Mediation

Any case filed may be referred to mediation at the discretion of the court, but under no circumstances may the following categories of actions be referred:

(a) Criminal and post-conviction cases.

(b) Habeas corpus and extraordinary writs.

(c) Civil or criminal contempt.

(d) Involuntary civil commitments of sexually violent predators.

(e) Collateral criminal cases.

(f) Other matters as may be specified by administrative order.

Added effective July 1, 2010 (41 So.3d 161).

Rule 9.720. Mediation Procedures

(a) Appearance. If a party to mediation is a public entity required to conduct its business pursuant to chapter 286, Florida Statutes, that party shall be deemed to appear at a mediation conference by the physical presence of a representative with full authority to negotiate on behalf of the entity and to recommend settlement to the appropriate decision-making body of the entity. Otherwise, unless changed by order of the court, a party is deemed to appear at a mediation conference if the following persons are physically present or appear electronically upon agreement of the parties:

(1) The party or its representative having full authority to settle without further consultation.

(2) The party's trial or appellate counsel of record, if any. If a party has more than one counsel, the appearance of only one counsel is required.

(3) A representative of the insurance carrier for any insured party who is not such carrier's outside counsel and who has full authority to settle without further consultation.

(b) Sanctions. If a party fails to appear at a duly noticed mediation conference without good cause, the court, upon motion of a party or upon its own motion, may impose sanctions, including, but not limited to, any or all of the following, against the party failing to appear:

(1) An award of mediator and attorney fees and other costs or monetary sanctions.

(2) The striking of briefs.

(3) Elimination of oral argument.

(4) Dismissal or summary affirmance.

(c) Scheduling and Adjournments. Consistent with the time frames established in rule 9.700(c) and after consulting with the parties, the mediator shall set the initial conference date. The mediator may adjourn the mediation conference at any time and may set times for reconvening the adjourned conference. The mediator shall notify the parties in writing of the date, time, and place of any mediation conference, except no further notification is required for parties present at an adjourned mediation conference.

(d) Control of Procedures. The mediator shall at all times be in control of the procedures to be followed in the mediation.

(e) Communication with Parties. The mediator may meet and consult privately with any party or parties or their counsel. Counsel shall be permitted to communicate privately with their clients.

(f) Party Representative Having Full Authority to Settle. Except as provided in subdivision (a) as to public entities, a "party or its representative having full authority to settle" shall mean the final decision maker with respect to all issues presented by the case who has the legal capacity to execute a binding settlement agreement on behalf of the party. Nothing herein shall be deemed to require any party or party representative who appears at a mediation conference in compliance with this rule to enter into a settlement agreement.

(g) Certificate of Authority. Unless otherwise stipulated by the parties, each party, 10 days prior to appearing at a mediation conference, shall file with the court and serve upon all parties a written notice identifying the person or persons who will be attending the mediation conference as a party representative or as an insurance carrier representative, and confirming that those persons have the authority required by this rule.

Added effective July 1, 2010 (41 So.3d 161). Amended Nov. 6, 2014, effective Jan. 1, 2015 (2014 WL 5714099).

Committee Note

2014 Amendment. The amendment adding subdivisions (f) and (g) is intended to make this rule consistent with the November 2011 amendments to Florida Rule of Civil Procedure 1.720.

Rule 9.730. Appointment and Compensation of the Mediator

(a) Appointment by Agreement. Within 10 days of the court order of referral, the parties may file a stipulation with the court designating a mediator certified as an appellate mediator pursuant to rule 10.100(f), Florida Rules for Certified and Court–Appointed Mediators. Unless otherwise agreed to by the parties, the mediator shall be licensed to practice law in any United States jurisdiction.

(b) Appointment by Court. If the parties cannot agree upon a mediator within 10 days of the order of referral, the appellant shall notify the court immediately and the court shall appoint a certified appellate mediator selected by such procedure as is designated by administrative order. The court shall appoint a certified appellate mediator who is licensed to practice law in any United States jurisdiction, unless otherwise requested upon agreement of the parties.

(c) Disqualification of Mediator. Any party may move to enter an order disqualifying a mediator for good cause. Such a motion to disqualify shall be filed within a reasonable time, not to exceed 10 days after discovery of the facts constituting the grounds for the motion, and shall be promptly presented to the court for an immediate ruling. If the court rules that a mediator is disqualified from a case, an order shall be entered setting forth the name of a qualified replacement. The time for mediation shall be tolled during any periods in which a motion to disqualify is pending.

(d) Substitute Mediator. If a mediator agreed upon by the parties or appointed by the court cannot serve, a substitute mediator may be agreed upon or appointed in the same manner as the original mediator.

(e) Compensation of a Court–Selected Mediator. If the court selects the mediator pursuant to subdivision (b), the mediator shall be compensated at the hourly rate set by the court in the referral order or applicable administrative order. Unless otherwise agreed, the compensation of the mediator should be prorated among the named parties.

Added effective July 1, 2010 (41 So.3d 161).

Committee Notes

This rule is not intended to limit the parties from exercising self-determination in the selection of any appropriate form of alternative dispute resolution or to deny the right of the parties to select a neutral. The rule does not prohibit parties from selecting an otherwise qualified non-certified appellate mediator prior to the court's order of referral. Parties may pursue settlement with a non-certified appellate mediator even within the ten-day period following the referral. However, once parties agree on a certified appellate mediator, or notify the court of their inability to do so, the parties can satisfy the court's referral to mediation pursuant to these rules only by appearing at a mediation conducted by a supreme court certified appellate mediator.

Rule 9.740. Completion of Mediation

(a) No Agreement. If the parties do not reach an agreement as a result of mediation, the mediator shall report, within 10 days, the lack of an agreement to the court without comment or recommendation.

(b) Agreement. If a partial or final agreement is reached, it shall be reduced to writing and signed by the parties and their counsel, if any. Within 10 days thereafter, the mediator shall file a report with the court on a form approved by the court.

Added effective July 1, 2010 (41 So.3d 161).

Rule 9.800. Uniform Citation System

This rule applies to all legal documents, including court opinions. Except for citations to case reporters, all citation forms should be spelled out in full if used as an integral part of a sentence either in the text or in footnotes. Abbreviated forms as shown in this rule should be used if the citation is intended to stand alone either in the text or in footnotes.

(a) Florida Supreme Court.

(1) 1846–1886: *Livingston v. L'Engle*, 22 Fla. 427 (1886).

(2) *Fenelon v. State*, 594 So. 2d 292 (Fla. 1992).

(3) For recent opinions not yet published in the Southern Reporter, cite to Florida Law Weekly: *Traylor v. State*, 17 Fla. L. Weekly S42 (Fla. Jan. 16, 1992). If not therein, cite to the slip opinion: *Medina v. State*, No. SC00–280 (Fla. Mar. 14, 2002).

(b) Florida District Courts of Appeal.

(1) *Sotolongo v. State*, 530 So. 2d 514 (Fla. 2d DCA 1988); *Buncayo v. Dribin*, 533 So. 2d 935 (Fla. 3d DCA 1988).

(2) For recent opinions not yet published in Southern Reporter, cite to Florida Law Weekly: *Myers v. State*, 16 Fla. L. Weekly D1507 (Fla. 4th DCA June 5, 1991). If not therein, cite to the slip opinion: *Fleming v. State*, No. 1D01–2734 (Fla. 1st DCA Mar. 6, 2002).

(c) Florida Circuit Courts and County Courts.

(1) *Whidden v. Francis*, 27 Fla. Supp. 80 (Fla. 11th Cir. Ct. 1966).

(2) *State v. Alvarez*, 42 Fla. Supp. 83 (Fla. Dade Cty. Ct. 1975).

(3) For opinions not published in Florida Supplement, cite to Florida Law Weekly Supplement: *State* v. *Ruoff*, 17 Fla. L. Weekly Supp. 619 (Fla. 17th Cir. Ct. Feb. 13, 2010). If not therein, cite to Florida Law Weekly: *State* v. *Cahill*, 16 Fla. L. Weekly C41 (Fla. 19th Cir. Ct. Mar. 5, 1991). If not therein, cite to the slip opinion: *Jones* v. *City of Ocoee*, No. CVAI–93–18 (Fla. 9th Cir. Ct. Dec. 9, 1996).

(d) Florida Administrative Agencies. (Cite if not in Southern Reporter.)

(1) For decisions of the Public Employees Relations Commission: *Indian River Educ. Ass'n v. School Bd.*, 4 F.P.E.R. 4262 (1978).

(2) For decisions of the Florida Public Service Commission: *In re Application of Tampa Elec. Co.*, 81 F.P.S.C. 2:120 (1981).

(3) For decisions posted on the Division of Administrative Hearings' website: *Big Bend Hospice, Inc. v. Agency for Health Care Administration*, Case No. 01–4415 CON (Fla. DOAH Nov. 7, 2002; Fla. AHCA Apr. 8, 2003).

(4) For decisions that are not posted on the Division of Administrative Hearings' website but are reported in the Florida Administrative Law Reports: *Insurance Co. v. Dep't of Ins.*, 2 F.A.L.R. 648–A (Fla. Dep't of Ins. 1980).

(5) For orders that are not posted on the Division of Administrative Hearings' website or reported in one of the above reporters: *In re Town of Inglis Petition for Waiver*, Final Order No. 07–0590 (Fla. DEP Apr. 12, 2007) (available from the agency clerk).

(e) Florida Constitution. (Year of adoption should be given if necessary to avoid confusion.)

Art. V, § 3(b)(3), Fla. Const.

(f) Florida Statutes (Official).

§ 350.34, Fla. Stat. (1973).

§ 120.53, Fla. Stat. (Supp. 1974).

(g) Florida Statutes Annotated. (To be used only for court-adopted rules, or references to other nonstatutory materials that do not appear in an official publication.)

32 Fla. Stat. Ann. 116 (Supp. 1975).

(h) Florida Laws. (Cite if not in Fla. Stat. or if desired for clarity or adoption reference.)

(1) After 1956: Ch. 74–177, § 5, at 473, Laws of Fla.

(2) Before 1957: Ch. 22000, Laws of Fla. (1943).

(i) Florida Rules.

Fla. R. Civ. P. 1.180.

Fla. R. Civ. P.—S.V.P. 4.010.

Fla. R. Jud. Admin. 2.110.

Fla. R. Crim. P. 3.850.

Fla. Prob. R. 5.120.

Fla. R. Traf. Ct. 6.165.

Fla. Sm. Cl. R. 7.070.

Fla. R. Juv. P. 8.070.

Fla. R. App. P. 9.100.

Fla. R. Med. 10.100.

Fla. R. Arb. 11.010.

Fla. Fam. L. R. P. 12.010.

Fla. Admin. Code R. 62D–2.014.

R. Regulating Fla. Bar 4–1.10.

Fla. Bar Found. By–Laws, art. 2.19(b).

Fla. Bar Found. Charter, art. III, § 3.4.

Fla. Bar Integr. R., art. XI, § 11.09.

Fla. Jud. Qual. Comm'n R. 9.

Fla. Std. Jury Instr. (Civ.) 601.4.

Fla. Std. Jury Instr. (Crim.) 3.7.

Fla. Stds. Imposing Law. Sancs. 9.32(a).

Fla. Bar Admiss. R. 3–23.1.

(j) Florida Attorney General Opinions.

Op. Att'y Gen. Fla. 73–178 (1973).

(k) United States Supreme Court.

Sansone v. United States, 380 U.S. 343 (1965).

(Cite to United States Reports, if published therein; otherwise cite to Supreme Court Reporter, Lawyer's Edition, or United States Law Week, in that order of preference. For opinions not published in these reporters, cite to Florida Law Weekly Federal: *California v. Hodari D.*, 13 Fla. L. Weekly Fed. S249 (U.S. Apr. 23, 1991).

(*l*) Federal Courts of Appeals.

Gulf Oil Corp. v. Bivins, 276 F.2d 753 (5th Cir. 1960).

For opinions not published in the Federal Reporter, cite to Florida Law Weekly Federal: *Cunningham v. Zant*, 13 Fla. L. Weekly Fed. C591 (11th Cir. March 27, 1991).

(m) Federal District Courts.

Pugh v. Rainwater, 332 F. Supp. 1107 (S.D. Fla. 1971).

For opinions not published in the Federal Supplement, cite to Florida Law Weekly Federal: *Wasko v. Dugger*, 13 Fla. L. Weekly Fed. D183 (S.D. Fla. Apr. 2, 1991).

(n) United States Constitution. Art. IV, § 2, cl. 2, U.S. Const. Amend. V, U.S. Const.

(*o*) Other Citations. When referring to specific material within a Florida court's opinion, pinpoint citation to the page of the Southern Reporter where that material occurs is optional, although preferred. All other citations shall be in the form prescribed by the latest edition of The Bluebook: A Uniform System of Citation, The Harvard Law Review Association, Gannett House, Cambridge, MA 02138. Citations not covered in this rule or in The Bluebook shall be in the form prescribed by the Florida Style Manual published by the Florida State University Law Review, Tallahassee, FL 32306.

(p) Case Names. Case names shall be underscored (or italicized) in text and in footnotes.

Amended Sept. 13, 1984, effective Jan. 1, 1985 (463 So.2d 1114); Oct. 22, 1992, effective Jan. 1, 1993 (609 So.2d 516); October 12, 1995 (661 So.2d 815); Nov. 22, 1996, effective Jan. 1, 1997 (685 So.2d 773); Oct. 12, 2000, effective Jan. 1, 2001 (780 So.2d 834); Aug. 29, 2002, effective Jan. 1, 2003 (827 So.2d 888); Feb. 3, 2005 (894 So.2d 202); Nov. 13, 2008, effective Jan. 1, 2009 (2 So.3d 89); Nov. 3, 2011, effective Jan. 1, 2012 (75 So.3d 239); Nov. 6, 2014, effective Jan. 1, 2015 (2014 WL 5714099).

Committee Notes

1977 Adoption. This rule is new and is included to standardize appellate practice and ease the burdens on the courts. It is the duty of each litigant and counsel to assist the judicial system by use of these standard forms of citation. Use of these citation forms, however, has not been made mandatory.

1992 Amendment. Rule 9.800 was updated to reflect changes in the available reporters. Additionally, the citations to new rules have been added and citations to rules no longer in use have been deleted.

2011 Amendment. Subdivision (d)(3) was revised and subdivisions (d)(4) and (d)(5) were added to reflect changes in how agencies are publishing their decisions. Section 120.53(2)(a), Florida Statutes, was revised in 2008 to allow agencies to electronically transmit their decisions to the Division of Administrative Hearings for posting on the Division's website in lieu of publishing them in an official reporter. Additionally, recommended and final orders in cases heard by the Division are available on the Division's website, www.doah.state.fl.us. See § 120.57(1)(m), Fla. Stat. Final orders in cases not heard by the Division or electronically submitted to the Division by an agency for posting on the Division's website or published in a reporter should be available from the agency that issues the order.

Rule 9.900. Forms

(a) Notice of Appeal.

IN THE .....(NAME OF THE LOWER TRIBUNAL WHOSE ORDER IS TO BE REVIEWED).....

Case No. ______

______________________,	)	
Defendant/Appellant,	)	
	)	NOTICE OF APPEAL
v.	)	
	)	
______________________,	)	
Plaintiff/Appellee.	)	
	)	
______________________	)	

NOTICE IS GIVEN that ...., Defendant/Appellant, appeals to the ...(name of court that has appellate jurisdiction)..., the order of this court rendered [see rule 9.020(i)] ...(date)... [Conformed copies of orders designated in the notice of appeal shall be attached in accordance with rules 9.110(d), and 9.160(c).] The nature of the order is a final order ...(state nature of the order)....

____

Attorney for ...(name of party)...
...(address, e-mail address, and phone number)...
Florida Bar No. ....

(b) Notice of Cross–Appeal.

IN THE .....(NAME OF THE LOWER TRIBUNAL WHOSE ORDER IS TO BE REVIEWED).....
Case No. ______

______________________,	)	
Defendant/Appellant,	)	
Cross–Appellee,	)	
	)	NOTICE OF CROSS–APPEAL
v.	)	
	)	
______________________,	)	
Plaintiff/Appellee,	)	
Cross–Appellant.	)	
______________________	)	

NOTICE IS GIVEN that ______, Plaintiff/Cross–Appellant, appeals to the . . .(name of court that has appellate jurisdiction). . ., the order of this court rendered [see rule 9.020(i)] . . .(date). . . The nature of the order is a final order . . .(state nature of the order). . . .

____

Attorney for . . .(name of party). . .
. . .(address, e-mail address, and phone number). . .
Florida Bar No. . . . .

(c) Notice of Appeal of Non–Final Order.

(1) *Notice of Appeal of Non–Final Order*

IN THE . . . . .(NAME OF THE LOWER TRIBUNAL WHOSE ORDER IS TO BE REVIEWED) . . . . .
Case No. ______

______________________,)
Defendant/Appellant,)
v.)
______________________,)
Plaintiff/Appellee.)

NOTICE OF APPEAL OF A NON–F INAL ORDER

NOTICE IS GIVEN that ______, Defendant/Appellant, appeals to the . . .(name of court that has appellate jurisdiction). . ., the order of this court rendered [see rule 9.020(i)] . . .(date). . . [Conformed copies of orders designated in the notice of appeal shall be attached in accordance with rules 9.110(d), 9.130(c), and 9.160(c).] The nature of the order is a non-final order . . .(state nature of the order). . . .

____

Attorney for . . .(name of party). . .
. . .(address, e-mail address, and phone number). . .
Florida Bar No. . . . .

(2) *Notice of Cross–Appeal of Non–Final Order.*

IN THE . . . . .(NAME OF THE LOWER TRIBUNAL WHOSE ORDER IS TO BE REVIEWED) . . . . .
Case No. ______

______________________,)
Defendant/Appellant Cross–Appellee,)
v.)
______________________,)
Plaintiff/Appellee/ Cross–Appellant.)

NOTICE OF CROSS–APPEAL OF A NON–FINAL ORDER

NOTICE IS GIVEN that ______, Plaintiff/Cross–Appellant, appeals to the . . .(name of court that has appellate jurisdiction). . ., the order of this court rendered [see rule 9.020(i)] . . .(date). . . The nature of the order is a non-final order . . .(state nature of the order). . . .

____

Attorney for . . .(name of party). . .
. . .(address, e-mail address, and phone number). . .
Florida Bar No. . . . .

(d) Notice to Invoke Discretionary Jurisdiction of Supreme Court.

IN THE DISTRICT COURT OF APPEAL OF FLORIDA, ______ DISTRICT
Case No. ______

______________________,)
Defendant/Petitioner,)
v.)
______________________,)
Plaintiff/Respondent.)

NOTICE TO INVOKE DISCRETIONARY JURISDICTION

NOTICE IS GIVEN that ______, Defendant/Petitioner, invokes the discretionary jurisdiction of the supreme court to review the decision of this court rendered [see rule 9.020(j)] . . .(date). . . The decision . . .(state why the decision is within the supreme court's jurisdiction). . . .[1]

____

Attorney for . . .(name of party). . .
. . .(address, e-mail address, and phone number). . .
Florida Bar No. . . . .

(e) Notice of Administrative Appeal.

IN THE . . . . .(NAME OF AGENCY, OFFICER, BOARD, COMMISSION, OR BODY WHOSE ORDER IS TO BE REVIEWED) . . . . .
Case No. ______

______________________,)
Defendant */Appellant,)
v.)
______________________,)
Plaintiff */Appellee.)

NOTICE OF ADMINISTRATIVE APPEAL

NOTICE IS GIVEN that ______, Appellant, appeals to the . . .(name of court that has appellate jurisdiction). . ., the order of this . . .(name of agency, officer, board, commission, or body whose order is to be reviewed). . . rendered [see rule 9.020(i)] . . .(date). . . [Conformed copies of orders designated in the notice of appeal shall be attached in accordance with rules 9.110(d) and 9.130(c).] The nature of the order is . . .(state nature of the order). . . .

____
Attorney for . . .(name of party). . .
. . .(address, e-mail address, and phone number). . .
Florida Bar No. . . . .

(f) Notice of Appeal of an Order Dismissing a Petition for a Judicial Waiver of Parental Notice of Termination of Pregnancy and Advisory Notice to Minor.

IN THE CIRCUIT COURT FOR THE ________ JUDICIAL CIRCUIT (NUMERICAL DESIGNATION OF THE CIRCUIT) IN AND FOR ________ COUNTY, FLORIDA

Case No. ________

In re: Petition for a Judicial Waiver of Parental Notice of Termination of Pregnancy.

____
(Your pseudonym or initials)

Appellant.

NOTICE IS GIVEN that ________ (your pseudonym or initials), appeals to the ___(District Court with appellate jurisdiction), the order of this court rendered ________ (enter the date that the order was filed on the clerk's docket) [See rule 9.020(i)]. The nature of the order is a final order dismissing a petition for a judicial waiver of parental notice of termination of pregnancy.

Signature: ____________
(As signed on your petition for judicial waiver if you are representing yourself)
Date: ____________
OR
Attorney for ____________
(pseudonym or initials of appellant)
(address, e-mail address, and phone number of attorney)
Florida Bar No. ________

ADVISORY NOTICE TO THE MINOR YOU ARE NOTIFIED AS FOLLOWS:

1. You are entitled to appeal the order dismissing your petition for a judicial waiver of parental notice of termination of pregnancy. You do not have to pay a filing fee for the appeal.

2. If you wish to appeal, you must file a notice of appeal. A form for the notice of appeal (Fla. R. App. P. 9.900(f)) will be provided to you with the order dismissing your petition. You must fill in every blank on the form with the information requested. If you need assistance with the form, the clerk of the circuit court will help you complete it.

3. You must file the notice of appeal with the clerk of the circuit court where your case was heard. The notice of appeal must be filed within thirty (30) days of the date when the judge's written order dismissing your petition was filed with the clerk of the circuit court. If you do not file your notice of appeal within this time period your appeal will not be heard.

4. The notice of appeal is the only document you need to file in connection with your appeal. You may file a motion to seek permission to file a brief in your case, or to request oral argument of your case. These motions or any other motions or documents you file concerning your appeal, except the notice of appeal, must be mailed or delivered to the appellate court for filing. The appellate court that will be reviewing your case is:

The ________ District Court of Appeal

____

____

(address of the District Court)

Telephone number: ________

(Note: The clerk of the circuit court will fill in the blanks above with the appropriate court information).

5. You may request a lawyer to represent you in your appeal. You must tell the judge who heard your petition for a judicial waiver of parental notification of termination of pregnancy that you wish to have a lawyer appointed.

(g) Directions to Clerk.

IN THE . . . (NAME OF LOWER TRIBUNAL WHOSE ORDER IS TO BE REVIEWED) . . .

Case No. ________

________________,
Plaintiff/Appellant,

v.

DIRECTIONS TO CLERK

________________,
Defendant/Appellee.

Plaintiff/Appellant, ____________, directs the clerk to . . . (include/exclude) . . . the following items . . . (in/from) . . . the record described in rule 9.200(a)(1):

ITEM	DATE FILED
1.	

[List of Desired Items]

2.

Note: This form is necessary only if a party does not wish to rely on the record that will be automatically prepared by the clerk under rule 9.200(a)(1).

(h) Designation to Approved Court Reporter, Civil Court Reporter, or Approved Transcriptionist.

IN THE . . . (NAME OF LOWER TRIBUNAL WHOSE ORDER IS TO BE REVIEWED) . . .

Case No. ____________

____________,)
Plaintiff/Appellant,) DESIGNATION TO APPROVED
) COURT REPORTER, CIVIL COURT
v.) REPORTER, OR APPROVED
) TRANSCRIPTIONIST, AND
____________,) REPORTER'S OR APPROVED
Defendant/Appellee.) TRANSCRIPTIONIST'S
____________) ACKNOWLEDGEMENT

I. DESIGNATION

Plaintiff/Appellant, ________, files this Designation to Approved Court Reporter, Civil Court Reporter, or Approved Transcriptionist and directs . . . (name of approved court reporter, civil court reporter, or approved transcriptionist) . . . to transcribe the following portions of the trial proceedings to be used in this appeal [for cases where a party is exempt from service by electronic mail as set forth in the Florida Rules of Judicial Administration, state the following and provide paper copies of the transcript(s)]:

1. The entire trial proceedings recorded by the reporter on . . . (date) . . . before the Honorable . . . (judge) . . ., except ____________.

2. [Indicate all other portions of reported proceedings.]

3. The approved court reporter, civil court reporter, or approved transcriptionist is directed to file the original with the clerk of the lower tribunal and to serve one copy on each of the following:

1.
2.
3.

I, counsel for Appellant, certify that satisfactory financial arrangements have been made with the approved court reporter, civil court reporter, or approved transcriptionist for preparation of the transcript.

____
Attorney for . . . (name of party) . . .
. . . (address, e-mail address, and phone number) . . .
Florida Bar No. . . . .

II. APPROVED COURT REPORTER'S, CIVIL COURT REPORTER'S, OR APPROVED TRANSCRIPTIONIST'S ACKNOWLEDGMENT

1. The foregoing designation was served on . . . (date) . . ., and received on . . . (date) . . .

2. Satisfactory arrangements have ( ) have not ( ) been made for payment of the transcript cost. These financial arrangements were completed on . . . (date) . . .

3. Number of trial or hearing days ___.

4. Estimated number of transcript pages ___.

5a. The transcript will be available within 30 days of service of the foregoing designation and will be filed on or before . . . (date) . . . .

OR

5b. For the following reason(s) the approved court reporter, civil court reporter, or approved transcriptionist requests an extension of time of ___ days for preparation of the transcript that will be filed on or before . . . (date) . . . .

6. Completion and filing of this acknowledgment by the approved court reporter, civil court reporter, or approved transcriptionist constitutes submission to the jurisdiction of the court for all purposes in connection with these appellate proceedings.

7. The undersigned approved court reporter, civil court reporter, or approved transcriptionist certifies that the foregoing is true and correct and that a copy has been furnished by mail ( ) hand delivery ( ) on . . . (date) . . ., to each of the parties or their counsel.

____
Approved Court Reporter, Civil Court Reporter, or Approved Transcriptionist
. . . (address) . . .

Note: The foregoing approved court reporter's, civil court reporter's, or approved transcriptionist's acknowledgment to be placed "at the foot of" or attached to a copy of the designation, shall be properly completed, signed by the approved court reporter, and filed with the clerk of the appellate court within 5 days of service of the designation on the approved court reporter, civil court reporter, or approved transcriptionist. A copy shall be served on all parties or their counsel, who shall have 5 days to object to any requested extension of time. See Fla. R. App. P. 9.200(b)(1), (2), & (3).

(i) Civil Supersedeas Bond.

. . . .(Title of Court). . . .
Case No. ____________

____________,)
Plaintiff,)
)
v.) CIVIL SUPERSEDEAS
) BOND

__________,)
Defendant.)
__________)

We, ______ as Principal, and ______ as Surety, are held and firmly bound unto ______ in the principal sum of $ ___, for the payment of which we bind ourselves, our heirs, personal representatives, successors, and assigns, jointly and severally.

The condition of this obligation is: the above-named Principal has entered an appeal to the .... (court) .... to review the .... (judgment or order) .... entered in the above case on .... (date) ...., and filed in the records of said court in book ______ at page ___.

NOW THEREFORE, if the Principal shall satisfy any money judgment contained in the judgment in full, including, if allowed by law, costs, interest, and attorneys' fees, and damages for delay in the event said appeal is dismissed or said judgment is affirmed, then this obligation shall be null and void; otherwise to remain in full force and effect.

Signed on .... (date) ...., at .... (place) ....

/s/ ______
Principal

Signed on .... (date) ...., at .... (place) ....

/s/ ______
Surety

(j) Notice of Supplemental Authority.

. . . (Title of Court) . . .

Case No.: ______

__________,)
Appellant/Petitioner,)
)
v.) NOTICE OF SUPPLEMENTAL
) AUTHORITY
__________,)
Appellee/Respondent.)
__________)

[Appellant/Petitioner] [Appellee/Respondent], ______, submits as supplemental authority the [decision/rule/statute/other authority] of ______, a copy of which is attached to this notice. The supplemental authority is pertinent to the issue on appeal identified as ______ and [discussed on pages ______ of the ______ brief] [raised at oral argument].

______
Attorney for . . . (name of party) . . .
. . . (address, e-mail address, and phone number); . . .
Florida Bar No. ....

Amended Nov. 26, 1980, effective Jan. 1, 1981 (391 So.2d 203); Sept. 13, 1984, effective Jan. 1, 1985 (463 So.2d 1114); June 8, 1987, effective July 1, 1987 (509 So.2d 276); July 14, 1988, effective Jan. 1, 1989 (529 So.2d 687); Dec. 30, 1988, effective Jan. 1, 1989 (536 So.2d 240); Oct. 22, 1992, effective Jan. 1, 1993 (609 So.2d 516); Nov. 22, 1996, effective Jan. 1, 1997 (685 So.2d 773); Oct. 12, 2000, effective Jan. 1, 2001 (780 So.2d 834); Feb. 3, 2005 (894 So.2d 202); July 6, 2006 (934 So.2d 438); Nov. 13, 2008, effective Jan. 1, 2009 (2 So.3d 89); July 16, 2009 (13 So.3d 1044); Nov. 3, 2011, effective Jan. 1, 2012 (75 So.3d 239); Oct. 18, 2012, effective Dec. 1, 2012, April 1, 2013, Oct. 1, 2013 (102 So.3d 451); Nov. 6, 2014, effective Jan. 1, 2015 (2014 WL 5714099).

[1]The choices are:

a. expressly declares valid a state statute.

b. expressly construes a provision of the state or federal constitution.

c. expressly affects a class of constitutional or state officers.

d. expressly and directly conflicts with a decision of another district court of appeal or of the supreme court on the same question of law.

e. passes on a question certified to be of great public importance.

f. is certified to be in direct conflict with decisions of other district courts of appeal.

See rule 9.030(a)(2)(A).

* or other appropriate designation

Committee Notes

1980 Amendment. Forms 9.900(a) and (b) under the 1977 rules are modified, and additional forms are provided.

1992 Amendment. Forms 9.900(a), (c), and (e) were revised to remind the practitioner that conformed copies of the order or orders designated in the notice of appeal should be attached to the notice of appeal as provided in rules 9.110(d), 9.130(c), and 9.160(c).

INDEX TO
FLORIDA RULES OF APPELLATE PROCEDURE

FLORIDA RULES FOR CERTIFIED AND COURT–APPOINTED MEDIATORS

PART I. MEDIATOR QUALIFICATIONS

PART II. STANDARDS OF PROFESSIONAL CONDUCT

PART III. DISCIPLINE

Date Effective

Added effective May 28, 1992 (604 So.2d 764)

PART I. MEDIATOR QUALIFICATIONS

Rule 10.100. Certification Requirements

(a) General. For certification as a county court, family, circuit court, dependency, or appellate mediator, a mediator must be at least 21 years of age and be of good moral character. For certification as a county court, family, circuit court, or dependency mediator, one must have the required number of points for the type of certification sought as specifically required in rule 10.105.

(b) County Court Mediators. For initial certification as a mediator of county court matters, an applicant must have at least a high school diploma or a General Equivalency Diploma (GED) and 100 points, which shall include:

(1) 30 points for successful completion of a Florida Supreme Court certified county court mediation training program;

(2) 10 points for education; and

(3) 60 points for mentorship.

(c) Family Mediators. For initial certification as a mediator of family and dissolution of marriage issues, an applicant must have at least a bachelor's degree and 100 points, which shall include, at a minimum:

(1) 30 points for successful completion of a Florida Supreme Court certified family mediation training program;

(2) 25 points for education/mediation experience; and

(3) 30 points for mentorship.

Additional points above the minimum requirements may be awarded for completion of additional education/mediation experience, mentorship, and miscellaneous activities.

(d) Circuit Court Mediators. For initial certification as a mediator of circuit court matters, other than family matters, an applicant must have at least a bachelor's degree and 100 points, which shall include, at a minimum:

(1) 30 points for successful completion of a Florida Supreme Court certified circuit mediation training program;

(2) 25 points for education/mediation experience; and

(3) 30 points for mentorship.

Additional points above the minimum requirements may be awarded for completion of additional education/mediation experience, mentorship, and miscellaneous activities.

(e) Dependency Mediators. For initial certification as a mediator of dependency matters, as defined in Florida Rule of Juvenile Procedure 8.290, an applicant must have at least a bachelor's degree and 100 points, which shall include, at a minimum:

(1) 30 points for successful completion of a Florida Supreme Court certified dependency mediation training program;

(2) 25 points for education/mediation experience; and

(3) 40 points for mentorship.

Additional points above the minimum requirements may be awarded for completion of additional education/mediation experience, mentorship, and miscellaneous activities.

(f) Appellate Mediators. For initial certification as a mediator of appellate matters, an applicant must be a Florida Supreme Court certified circuit, family or dependency mediator and successfully complete a Florida Supreme Court certified appellate mediation training program.

(g) Senior Judges Serving As Mediators. A senior judge may serve as a mediator in a court-ordered mediation in a circuit in which the senior judge is not presiding as a judge only if certified by the Florida Supreme Court as a mediator for that type of mediation.

(h) Referral for Discipline. If the certification or licensure necessary for any person to be certified as a family or circuit mediator is suspended or revoked, or if the mediator holding such certification or licensure is in any other manner disciplined, such matter shall be referred to the Mediator Qualifications Board for appropriate action pursuant to rule 10.800.

(i) Special Conditions. Mediators who are certified prior to August 1, 2006, shall not be subject to the point requirements for any category of certification in relation to which continuing certification is maintained.

Former Rule 10.010 added effective May 28, 1992 (604 So.2d 764). Amended April 14, 1994, eff. July 1, 1994 (641 So.2d 343); July 10, 1997 (696 So.2d 763). Renumbered as new Rule 10.100 and amended Feb. 3, 2000, effective April 1, 2000 (762 So.2d 441); Nov. 3, 2005, effective Jan. 1, 2006 (915 So.2d 145); May 11, 2006, effective Aug. 1, 2006 (931 So.2d 877); Nov. 15, 2007 (969 So.2d 1003); July 1, 2010 (41 So.3d 161); June 19, 2014, effective Oct. 1, 2014 (141 So.3d 1172).

Rule 10.105. Point System Categories

(a) Education. Points shall be awarded in accordance with the following schedule (points are only awarded for the highest level of education completed and honorary degrees are not included):

High School Diploma/GED	10 points
Associate's Degree	15 points
Bachelor's Degree	20 points
Master's Degree	25 points
Master's Degree in Conflict Resolution	30 points
Doctorate (e.g., Ph.D., J.D., M.D., Ed. D., LL.M.)	30 points
Ph.D. from Accredited Conflict Resolution Program	40 points

An additional five points will be awarded for completion of a graduate level conflict resolution certificate program in an institution which has been accredited by Middle States Association of Colleges and Schools, the New England Association of Schools and Colleges, the North Central Association of Colleges and Schools, the Northwest Association of Schools and Colleges, the Southern Association of Colleges and Schools, the Western Association of Schools and Colleges, the American Bar Association, or an entity of equal status.

(b) Mediation Experience. One point per year will be awarded to a Florida Supreme Court certified mediator for each year that mediator has mediated at least 15 cases of any type. In the alternative, a maximum of five points will be awarded to any mediator, regardless of Florida Supreme Court certification, who has conducted a minimum of 100 mediations over a consecutive five-year period.

(c) Mentorship. Ten points will be awarded for each supervised mediation completed of the type for which certification is sought and five points will be awarded for each mediation session of the type for which certification is sought which is observed.

(d) Miscellaneous Points.

1. Five points shall be awarded to applicants currently licensed or certified in any United States jurisdiction in psychology, accounting, social work, mental health, health care, education or the practice of law or mediation. Such award shall not exceed a total of five points regardless of the number of licenses or certifications obtained.

2. Five points shall be awarded for possessing conversational ability in a foreign language as demonstrated by certification by the American Council on the Teaching of Foreign Languages (ACTFL) Oral Proficiency Test, qualification as a court interpreter, accreditation by the American Translators Association, or approval as a sign language interpreter by the Registry of Interpreters for the Deaf. Such award shall not exceed a total of five points regardless of the number of languages in which the applicant is proficient.

3. Five points shall be awarded for the successful completion of a mediation training program (minimum 30 hours in length) which is certified or approved by a jurisdiction other than Florida and which may not be the required Florida Supreme Court certified mediation training program. Such award shall not exceed five points regardless of the number of training programs completed.

4. Five points shall be awarded for certification as a mediator by the Florida Supreme Court. Such award shall not exceed five points per category regardless of the number of training programs completed or certifications obtained.

Added Nov. 15, 2007 (969 So.2d 1003).

Committee Notes

The following table is intended to illustrate the point system established in this rule. Any discrepancy between the table and the written certification requirements shall be resolved in favor of the latter.

Points Needed Per Area of Certification		**Minimum Points Required in Each Area**
County	100	30 certified county mediation training; 10 education (minimum HS Diploma/GED); 60 mentorship
Family	100	30 certified family mediation training; 25 education/ mediation experience (minimum Bachelor's Degree); 30 mentorship [and requires 15 additional points]
Dependency	100	30 certified dependency mediation training; 25 education/mediation experience (minimum Bachelor's Degree); 40 mentorship [and requires 5 additional points]
Circuit	100	30 certified circuit mediation training, 25 education/mediation experience (minimum Bachelor's Degree); 30 mentorship; [and requires 15 additional points]

Education/Mediation Experience (points awarded for highest level of education received)

HS Diploma/GED	10 points	Master's Degree in Conflict Resolution	30
Associate's Degree	15 points	Doctorate (e.g., J.D., M.D., Ph.D., Ed.D., LL.M.)	30
Bachelor's Degree	20 points	Ph.D. from accredited CR Program	40
Master's Degree	25 points	Graduate Certificate CR Program	+5
Florida certified mediator: 1 point per year in which mediated at least 15 mediations (any type) OR any mediator: - 5 points for minimum of 100 mediations (any type) over a 5 year period			

Mentorship- must work with at least 2 different certified mediators and must be completed for the type of certification sought

Observation	5 points each session
Supervised Mediation	10 points each complete mediation

Miscellaneous Points

Licensed to practice law, psychology, accounting, social work, mental health, health care, education or mediation in any US jurisdiction	5 points (total)
Florida Certified Mediator	5 points (total)
Foreign Language Conversational Ability as demonstrated by certification by ACTFL Oral Proficiency Test; qualified as a court	5 points (total)

Miscellaneous Points	
interpreter; or accredited by the American Translators Association; Sign Language Interpreter as demonstrated by approval by the Registry of Interpreters for the Deaf	
Completion of additional mediation training program (minimum 30 hours in length) certified/approved by a state or court other than Florida	5 points (total)

Rule 10.110. Good Moral Character

(a) General Requirement. No person shall be certified by this Court as a mediator unless such person first produces satisfactory evidence of good moral character as required by rule 10.100.

(b) Purpose. The primary purpose of the requirement of good moral character is to ensure protection of the participants in mediation and the public, as well as to safeguard the justice system. A mediator shall have, as a prerequisite to certification and as a requirement for continuing certification, the good moral character sufficient to meet all of the Mediator Standards of Professional Conduct set out in rules 10.200–10.690.

(c) Certification. The following shall apply in relation to determining the good moral character required for initial and continuing mediator certification:

(1) The applicant's or mediator's good moral character may be subject to inquiry when the applicant's or mediator's conduct is relevant to the qualifications of a mediator.

(2) An applicant for initial certification who has been convicted of a felony shall not be eligible for certification until such person has received a restoration of civil rights.

(3) An applicant for initial certification who is serving a sentence of felony probation shall not be eligible for certification until termination of the period of probation.

(4) In assessing whether the applicant's or mediator's conduct demonstrates a present lack of good moral character the following factors shall be relevant:

(A) the extent to which the conduct would interfere with a mediator's duties and responsibilities;

(B) the area of mediation in which certification is sought or held;

(C) the factors underlying the conduct;

(D) the applicant's or mediator's age at the time of the conduct;

(E) the recency of the conduct;

(F) the reliability of the information concerning the conduct;

(G) the seriousness of the conduct as it relates to mediator qualifications;

(H) the cumulative effect of the conduct or information;

(I) any evidence of rehabilitation;

(J) the applicant's or mediator's candor; and

(K) denial of application, disbarment, or suspension from any profession.

(d) Decertification. A certified mediator shall be subject to decertification for any knowing and willful incorrect material information contained in any mediator application. There is a presumption of knowing and willful violation if the application is completed, signed, and notarized.

Added effective April 1, 2000 (762 So.2d 441). Amended May 11, 2006, effective August 1, 2006 (931 So.2d 877).

Rule 10.120. Notice of Change of Address or Name.

(a) Address Change. Whenever any certified mediator changes residence or mailing address, that person must within 30 days thereafter notify the center of such change.

(b) Name Change. Whenever any certified mediator changes legal name, that person must within 30 days thereafter notify the center of such change.

Added May 11, 2006, effective August 1, 2006 (931 So.2d 877).

Rule 10.130. Notification of Conviction

(a) Definition. "Conviction" means a determination of guilt which is the result of a trial, or entry of a plea of guilty or no contest, regardless of whether adjudication of guilt or imposition of sentence was suspended, deferred, or withheld, and applies in relation to any of the following:

(1) a felony, misdemeanor of the first degree, or misdemeanor of the second degree involving dishonesty or false statement;

(2) a conviction of a similar offense described in subdivision (1) that includes a conviction by a federal, military, or tribal tribunal, including courts-martial conducted by the Armed Forces of the United States;

(3) a conviction of a similar offense described in subdivision (1) that includes a conviction or entry of a plea of guilty or no contest resulting in a sanction in any jurisdiction of the United States or any foreign jurisdiction. A sanction includes, but is not limited to, a fine, incarceration in a state prison, federal prison, private correctional facility, or local detention facility; or

(4) a conviction of a similar offense described in subdivision (1) of a municipal or county ordinance in this or any other state.

(b) Report of Conviction. A conviction shall be reported in writing to the center within 30 days of such conviction. A report of conviction shall include a copy of the order or orders pursuant to which the conviction was entered.

(c) Suspension. Upon receipt of a report of felony conviction, the center shall immediately suspend all certifications and refer the matter to the qualifications complaint committee.

(d) Referral. Upon receipt of a report of a misdemeanor conviction, the center shall refer the matter to the qualifications complaint committee for appropriate action. If the center becomes aware of a conviction prior to the required notification, it shall refer the matter to the qualifications complaint committee for appropriate action.

Added May 11, 2006, effective August 1, 2006 (931 So.2d 877). Amended effective May 19, 2011 (64 So.3d 1200).

PART II. STANDARDS OF PROFESSIONAL CONDUCT

Rule 10.200. Scope and Purpose

These Rules provide ethical standards of conduct for certified and court-appointed mediators. They are intended to both guide mediators in the performance of their services and instill public confidence in the mediation process. The public's use, understanding, and satisfaction with mediation can only be achieved if mediators embrace the highest ethical principles. Whether the parties involved in a mediation choose to resolve their dispute is secondary in importance to whether the mediator conducts the mediation in accordance with these ethical standards.

Added effective April 1, 2000 (762 So.2d 441).

Committee Notes

2000 Revision. In early 1991, the Florida Supreme Court Standing Committee on Mediation and Arbitration Rules was commissioned by the Chief Justice to research, draft and present for adoption both a comprehensive set of ethical standards for Florida mediators and procedural rules for their enforcement. To accomplish this task, the Committee divided itself into two sub-committees and, over the remainder of the year, launched parallel programs to research and develop the requested ethical standards and grievance procedures.

The Subcommittee on Ethical Standards began its task by searching the nation for other states or private dispute resolution organizations who had completed any significant work in defining the ethical responsibilities of professional mediators. After searching for guidance outside the state, the subcommittee turned to Florida's own core group of certified mediators for more direct and firsthand data. Through a series of statewide public hearings and meetings, the subcommittee gathered current information on ethical concerns based upon the expanding experiences of practicing Florida certified mediators. In May of 1992, The "Florida Rules for Certified and Court Appointed Mediators" became effective.

In the years following the adoption of those ethical rules, the Committee observed their impact on the mediation profession. By 1998, several other states and dispute resolution organizations initiated research into ethical standards for mediation which also became instructive to the Committee. In addition, Florida's Mediator Qualifications Advisory Panel, created to field ethical questions from practicing mediators, gained a wealth of pragmatic experience in the application of ethical concepts to actual practice that became available to the Committee. Finally, The Florida Mediator Qualifications Board, the disciplinary body for mediators, developed specific data from actual grievances filed against mediators over the past several years, which also added to the available body of knowledge.

Using this new body of information and experience, the Committee undertook a year long study program to determine if Florida's ethical rules for mediators would benefit from review and revision.

Upon reviewing the 1992 ethical Rules, it immediately became apparent to the Committee that reorganization, renumbering, and more descriptive titles would make the Rules more useful. For that reason, the Rules were reorganized into four substantive groups which recognized a mediator's ethical responsibilities to the "parties," the "process," the "profession" and the "courts." The intent of the Committee here was to simply make the Rules easier to locate. There is no official significance in the order in which the Rules appear; any one area is equally important as all other areas. The Committee recognizes many rules overlap and define specific ethical responsibilities which impact more than one area. Clearly, a violation of a rule in one section may very well injure relationships protected in another section.

Titles to the Rules were changed to more accurately reflect their content. Additionally, redundancies were eliminated, phrasing tightened, and grammatical changes made to more clearly state their scope and purpose.

Finally, the Committee sought to apply what had been learned. The 2000 revisions are the result of that effort.

Rule 10.210. Mediation Defined

Mediation is a process whereby a neutral and impartial third person acts to encourage and facilitate the resolution of a dispute without prescribing what it should be. It is an informal and non-adversarial process intended to help disputing parties reach a mutually acceptable agreement.

Added effective April 1, 2000 (762 So.2d 441).

Rule 10.220. Mediator's Role

The role of the mediator is to reduce obstacles to communication, assist in the identification of issues and exploration of alternatives, and otherwise facilitate voluntary agreements resolving the dispute. The ultimate decision-making authority, however, rests solely with the parties.

Added effective April 1, 2000 (762 So.2d 441).

Rule 10.230. Mediation Concepts

Mediation is based on concepts of communication, negotiation, facilitation, and problem-solving that emphasize:

(a) self determination;

(b) the needs and interests of the parties;

(c) fairness;

(d) procedural flexibility;

(e) confidentiality; and

(f) full disclosure.

Added effective April 1, 2000 (762 So.2d 441).

Rule 10.300. Mediator's Responsibility to the Parties

The purpose of mediation is to provide a forum for consensual dispute resolution by the parties. It is not an adjudicatory procedure. Accordingly, a mediator's responsibility to the parties includes honoring their right of self-determination; acting with impartiality; and avoiding coercion, improper influence, and conflicts of interest. A mediator is also responsible for maintaining an appropriate demeanor, preserving confidentiality, and promoting the awareness by the parties of the interests of non-participating persons. A mediator's business practices should reflect fairness, integrity and impartiality.

Added effective April 1, 2000 (762 So.2d 441).

Committee Notes

2000 Revision. Rules 10.300–10.380 include a collection of specific ethical concerns involving a mediator's responsibility to the parties to a dispute. Incorporated in this new section are the concepts formerly found in Rule 10.060 (Self Determination); Rule 10.070 (Impartiality/Conflict of Interest); Rule 10.080 (Confidentiality); Rule 10.090 (Professional Advice); and Rule 10.100 (Fees and Expenses). In addition, the Committee grouped under this heading ethical concerns dealing with the mediator's demeanor and courtesy, contractual relationships, and responsibility to non-participating persons.

Rule 10.310. Self–Determination

(a) Decision-Making. Decisions made during a mediation are to be made by the parties. A mediator shall not make substantive decisions for any party. A mediator is responsible for assisting the parties in reaching informed and voluntary decisions while protecting their right of self-determination.

(b) Coercion Prohibited. A mediator shall not coerce or improperly influence any party to make a decision or unwillingly participate in a mediation.

(c) Misrepresentation Prohibited. A mediator shall not intentionally or knowingly misrepresent any material fact or circumstance in the course of conducting a mediation.

(d) Postponement or Cancellation. If, for any reason, a party is unable to freely exercise self-determination, a mediator shall cancel or postpone a mediation.

Added effective April 1, 2000 (762 So.2d 441).

Committee Notes

2000 Revision. Mediation is a process to facilitate consensual agreement between parties in conflict and to assist them in voluntarily resolving their dispute. It is critical that the parties' right to self-determination (a free and informed choice to agree or not to agree) is preserved during all phases of mediation. A mediator must not substitute the judgment of the mediator for the judgment of the parties, coerce or compel a party to make a decision, knowingly allow a participant to make a decision based on misrepresented facts or circumstances, or in any other way impair or interfere with the parties' right of self-determination.

While mediation techniques and practice styles may vary from mediator to mediator and mediation to mediation, a line is crossed and ethical standards are violated when any conduct of the mediator serves to compromise the parties' basic right to agree or not to agree. Special care should be taken to preserve the party's right to self-determination if the mediator provides input to the mediation process. See rule 10.370.

On occasion, a mediator may be requested by the parties to serve as a decision-maker. If the mediator decides to serve in such a capacity, compliance with this request results in a change in the dispute resolution process impacting self-determination, impartiality, confidentiality, and other ethical standards. Before providing decision-making services, therefore, the mediator shall ensure that all parties understand and consent to those changes. See rules 10.330 and 10.340.

Under subdivision (d), postponement or cancellation of a mediation is necessary if the mediator reasonably believes the threat of domestic violence, existence of substance abuse, physical threat or undue psychological dominance are present and existing factors which would impair any party's ability to freely and willingly enter into an informed agreement.

Rule 10.320. Nonparticipating Persons

A mediator shall promote awareness by the parties of the interests of persons affected by actual or potential agreements who are not represented at mediation.

Added effective April 1, 2000 (762 So.2d 441).

Committee Notes

2000 Revision. Mediated agreements will often impact persons or entities not participating in the process. Examples include lienholders, governmental agencies, shareholders, and related commercial entities. In family and dependency mediations, the interests of children, grandparents or other related persons are also often affected. A mediator is responsible for making the parties aware of the potential interests of such non-participating persons.

In raising awareness of the interests of non-participating persons, however, the mediator should still respect the rights of the parties to make their own decisions. Further, raising awareness of possible interests of related entities should not involve advocacy or judgments as to the merits of those interests. In family mediations, for example, a mediator should make the parents aware of the children's interests without interfering with self-determination or advocating a particular position.

Rule 10.330. Impartiality

(a) Generally. A mediator shall maintain impartiality throughout the mediation process. Impartiality means freedom from favoritism or bias in word, action, or appearance, and includes a commitment to assist all parties, as opposed to any one individual.

(b) Withdrawal for Partiality. A mediator shall withdraw from mediation if the mediator is no longer impartial.

(c) Gifts and Solicitation. A mediator shall neither give nor accept a gift, favor, loan, or other item of value in any mediation process. During the mediation process, a mediator shall not solicit or otherwise attempt to procure future professional services.

Added effective April 1, 2000 (762 So.2d 441).

Committee Notes

2000 Revision. A mediator has an affirmative obligation to maintain impartiality throughout the entire mediation process. The duty to maintain impartiality arises immediately upon learning of a potential engagement for providing mediation services. A mediator shall not accept or continue any engagement for mediation services in which the ability to maintain impartiality is reasonably impaired or compromised. As soon as practical, a mediator shall make reasonable inquiry as to the identity of the parties or other circumstances which could compromise the mediator's impartiality.

During the mediation, a mediator shall maintain impartiality even while raising questions regarding the reality, fairness, equity, durability and feasibility of proposed options for settlement. In the event circumstances arise during a mediation that would reasonably be construed to impair or compromise a mediator's impartiality, the mediator is obligated to withdraw.

Subdivision (c) does not preclude a mediator from giving or accepting de minimis gifts or incidental items provided to facilitate the mediation.

Rule 10.340. Conflicts of Interest

(a) Generally. A mediator shall not mediate a matter that presents a clear or undisclosed conflict of interest. A conflict of interest arises when any relationship between the mediator and the mediation participants or the subject matter of the dispute compromises or appears to compromise the mediator's impartiality.

(b) Burden of Disclosure. The burden of disclosure of any potential conflict of interest rests on the mediator. Disclosure shall be made as soon as practical after the mediator becomes aware of the interest or relationship giving rise to the potential conflict of interest.

(c) Effect of Disclosure. After appropriate disclosure, the mediator may serve if all parties agree. However, if a conflict of interest clearly impairs a mediator's impartiality, the mediator shall withdraw regardless of the express agreement of the parties.

(d) Conflict During Mediation. A mediator shall not create a conflict of interest during the mediation. During a mediation, a mediator shall not provide any services that are not directly related to the mediation process.

(e) Senior and Retired Judges. If a mediator who is a senior judge or retired judge not eligible for assignment to temporary judicial duty has presided over a case involving any party, attorney, or law firm in the mediation, the mediator shall disclose such fact prior to mediation. A mediator shall not serve as a mediator in any case in a circuit in which the mediator is currently presiding as a senior judge. Absent express consent of the parties, a mediator shall not serve as a senior judge over any case involving any party, attorney, or law firm that is utilizing or has utilized the judge as a mediator within the previous three years. A senior judge who provides mediation services shall not preside over any case in the circuit where the mediation services are provided; however, a senior judge may preside over cases in circuits in which the judge does not provide mediation services.

Added effective April 1, 2000 (762 So.2d 441). Amended Nov. 3, 2005, effective Jan. 1, 2006 (915 So.2d 145); June 19, 2014, effective Oct. 1, 2014 (141 So.3d 1172).

Committee Notes

2000 Revision. Potential conflicts of interests which require disclosure include the fact of a mediator's membership on a related board of directors, full or part time service by the mediator as a representative, advocate, or consultant to a mediation participant, present stock or bond ownership by the mediator in a corporate mediation participant, or any other form of managerial, financial, or family interest by the mediator in any mediation participant involved in a mediation. A mediator who is a member of a law firm or other professional organization is obliged to disclose any past or present client relationship that firm or organization may have with any party involved in a mediation.

The duty to disclose thus includes information relating to a mediator's ongoing financial or professional relationship with any of the parties, counsel, or related entities. Disclosure is required with respect to any significant past, present, or promised future relationship with any party involved in a proposed mediation. While impartiality is not necessarily compromised, full disclosure and a reasonable opportunity for the parties to react are essential.

Disclosure of relationships or circumstances which would create the potential for a conflict of interest should be made at the earliest possible opportunity and under circumstances which will allow the parties to freely exercise their right of self determination as to both the selection of the mediator and participation in the mediation process.

A conflict of interest which clearly impairs a mediator's impartiality is not resolved by mere disclosure to, or waiver by, the parties. Such conflicts occur when circumstances or relationships involving the mediator cannot be reasonably regarded as allowing the mediator to maintain impartiality.

To maintain an appropriate level of impartiality and to avoid creating conflicts of interest, a mediator's professional input to a mediation proceeding must be confined to the services necessary to provide the parties a process to reach a self-determined agreement. Under subsection (d), a mediator is accordingly prohibited from utilizing a mediation to supply any other services which do not directly relate to the conduct of the mediation itself. By way of example, a mediator would therefore be prohibited from providing accounting, psychiatric or legal services, psychological or social counseling, therapy, or business consultations of any sort during the mediation process.

Mediators establish personal relationships with many representatives, attorneys, mediators, and other members of various professional associations. There should be no attempt to be secretive about such friendships or acquaintances, but disclosure is not necessary unless some feature of a particular relationship might reasonably appear to impair impartiality.

Rule 10.350. Demeanor

A mediator shall be patient, dignified, and courteous during the mediation process.

Added effective April 1, 2000 (762 So.2d 441).

Rule 10.360. Confidentiality

(a) Scope. A mediator shall maintain confidentiality of all information revealed during mediation except where disclosure is required or permitted by law or is agreed to by all parties.

(b) Caucus. Information obtained during caucus may not be revealed by the mediator to any other mediation participant without the consent of the disclosing party.

(c) Record Keeping. A mediator shall maintain confidentiality in the storage and disposal of records and shall not disclose any identifying information when materials are used for research, training, or statistical compilations.

Added effective April 1, 2000 (762 So.2d 441). Amended May 11, 2006, effective August 1, 2006 (931 So.2d 877).

Rule 10.370. Advice, Opinions, or Information

(a) Providing Information. Consistent with standards of impartiality and preserving party self-determination, a mediator may provide information that the mediator is qualified by training or experience to provide.

(b) Independent Legal Advice. When a mediator believes a party does not understand or appreciate how an agreement may adversely affect legal rights or obligations, the mediator shall advise the party of the right to seek independent legal counsel.

(c) Personal or Professional Opinion. A mediator shall not offer a personal or professional opinion intended to coerce the parties, unduly influence the parties, decide the dispute, or direct a resolution of any issue. Consistent with standards of impartiality and preserving party self-determination however, a mediator may point out possible outcomes of the case and discuss the merits of a claim or defense. A mediator shall not offer a personal or professional opinion as to how the court in which the case has been filed will resolve the dispute.

Added effective April 1, 2000 (762 So.2d 441). Amended May 11, 2006, effective August 1, 2006 (931 So.2d 877).

Committee Notes

2000 Revision. (previously Committee Note to 1992 adoption of former rule 10.090). Mediators who are attorneys should note Florida Bar Committee on Professional Ethics, formal opinion 86–8 at 1239, which states that the lawyer-mediator should "explain the risks of proceeding without independent counsel and advise the parties to consult counsel during the course of the mediation and before signing any settlement agreement that he might prepare for them."

2000 Revision. The primary role of the mediator is to facilitate a process which will provide the parties an opportunity to resolve all or part of a dispute by agreement if they choose to do so. A mediator may assist in that endeavor by providing relevant information or helping the parties obtain such information from other sources. A mediator may also raise issues and discuss strengths and weaknesses of positions underlying the dispute. Finally, a mediator may help the parties evaluate resolution options and draft settlement proposals. In providing these services however, it is imperative that the mediator maintain impartiality and avoid any activity which would have the effect of overriding the parties' rights of self-determination. While mediators may call upon their own qualifications and experience to supply information and options, the parties must be given the opportunity to freely decide upon any agreement. Mediators shall not utilize their opinions to decide any aspect of the dispute or to coerce the parties or their representatives to accept any resolution option.

While a mediator has no duty to specifically advise a party as to the legal ramifications or consequences of a proposed agreement, there is a duty for the mediator to advise the parties of the importance of understanding such matters and giving them the opportunity to seek such advice if they desire.

Rule 10.380. Fees and Expenses

(a) Generally. A mediator holds a position of trust. Fees charged for mediation services shall be reasonable and consistent with the nature of the case.

(b) Guiding Principles in Determining Fees. A mediator shall be guided by the following general principles in determining fees:

(1) Any charges for mediation services based on time shall not exceed actual time spent or allocated.

(2) Charges for costs shall be for those actually incurred.

(3) All fees and costs shall be appropriately divided between the parties.

(4) When time or expenses involve two or more mediations on the same day or trip, the time and expense charges shall be prorated appropriately.

(c) Written Explanation of Fees. A mediator shall give the parties or their counsel a written explanation of any fees and costs prior to mediation. The explanation shall include:

(1) the basis for and amount of any charges for services to be rendered, including minimum fees and travel time;

(2) the amount charged for the postponement or cancellation of mediation sessions and the circumstances under which such charges will be assessed or waived;

(3) the basis and amount of charges for any other items; and

(4) the parties' pro rata share of mediation fees and costs if previously determined by the court or agreed to by the parties.

(d) Maintenance of Records. A mediator shall maintain records necessary to support charges for services and expenses and upon request shall make an accounting to the parties, their counsel, or the court.

(e) Remuneration for Referrals. No commissions, rebates, or similar remuneration shall be given or received by a mediator for a mediation referral.

(f) Contingency Fees Prohibited. A mediator shall not charge a contingent fee or base a fee on the outcome of the process.

Added effective April 1, 2000 (762 So.2d 441).

Rule 10.400. Mediator's Responsibility to the Mediation Process

A mediator is responsible for safeguarding the mediation process. The benefits of the process are best achieved if the mediation is conducted in an informed, balanced and timely fashion. A mediator is responsible for confirming that mediation is an appropriate dispute resolution process under the circumstances of each case.

Added effective April 1, 2000 (762 So.2d 441).

Committee Notes

2000 Revision. Rules 10.400–10.430 include a collection of specific ethical concerns involved in a mediator's responsibility to the mediation process. Incorporated in this new section are the concepts formerly found in rule 10.060 (Self–Determination), rule 10.090 (Professional Advice); and rule 10.110 (Concluding Mediation). In addition, the Committee grouped under this heading ethical concerns dealing with the mediator's duty to determine the existence of potential conflicts, a mandate for adequate time for mediation sessions, and the process for adjournment.

Rule 10.410. Balanced Process

A mediator shall conduct mediation sessions in an even-handed, balanced manner. A mediator shall promote mutual respect among the mediation participants throughout the mediation process and encourage the participants to conduct themselves in a collaborative, non-coercive, and non-adversarial manner.

Added effective April 1, 2000 (762 So.2d 441).

Committee Notes

2000 Revision. A mediator should be aware that the presence or threat of domestic violence or abuse among the parties can endanger the parties, the mediator, and others. Domestic violence and abuse can undermine the exercise of self-determination and the ability to reach a voluntary and mutually acceptable agreement.

Rule 10.420. Conduct of Mediation

(a) Orientation Session. Upon commencement of the mediation session, a mediator shall describe the mediation process and the role of the mediator, and shall inform the mediation participants that:

(1) mediation is a consensual process;

(2) the mediator is an impartial facilitator without authority to impose a resolution or adjudicate any aspect of the dispute; and

(3) communications made during the process are confidential, except where disclosure is required or permitted by law.

(b) Adjournment or Termination. A mediator shall:

(1) adjourn the mediation upon agreement of the parties;

(2) adjourn or terminate any mediation which, if continued, would result in unreasonable emotional or monetary costs to the parties;

(3) adjourn or terminate the mediation if the mediator believes the case is unsuitable for mediation or any party is unable or unwilling to participate meaningfully in the process;

(4) terminate a mediation entailing fraud, duress, the absence of bargaining ability, or unconscionability; and

(5) terminate any mediation if the physical safety of any person is endangered by the continuation of mediation.

(c) Closure. The mediator shall cause the terms of any agreement reached to be memorialized appropriately and discuss with the parties and counsel the process for formalization and implementation of the agreement.

Added effective April 1, 2000 (762 So.2d 441). Amended May 11, 2006, effective August 1, 2006 (931 So.2d 877).

Committee Notes

2000 Revision. In defining the role of the mediator during the course of an opening session, a mediator should ensure that the participants fully understand the nature of the process and the limits on the mediator's authority. See rule 10.370(c). It is also appropriate for the mediator to inform the parties that mediators are ethically precluded from providing non-mediation services to any party. See rule 10.340(d).

Florida Rule of Civil Procedure 1.730(b), Florida Rule of Juvenile Procedure 8.290(*o*), and Florida Family Law Rule of Procedure 12.740(f) require that any mediated agreement be reduced to writing. Mediators have an obligation to ensure these rules are complied with, but are not required to write the agreement themselves.

Rule 10.430. Scheduling Mediation

A mediator shall schedule a mediation in a manner that provides adequate time for the parties to fully exercise their right of self-determination. A mediator shall perform mediation services in a timely fashion, avoiding delays whenever possible.

Added effective April 1, 2000 (762 So.2d 441).

Rule 10.500. Mediator's Responsibility to the Courts

A mediator is accountable to the referring court with ultimate authority over the case. Any interaction discharging this responsibility, however, shall be conducted in a manner consistent with these ethical rules.

Added effective April 1, 2000 (762 So.2d 441).

Committee Notes

2000 Revision. Rules 10.500–10.540 include a collection of specific ethical concerns involved in a mediator's responsibility to the courts. Incorporated in this new section are the concepts formerly found in rule 10.040 (Responsibilities to Courts).

Rule 10.510. Information to the Court

A mediator shall be candid, accurate, and fully responsive to the court concerning the mediator's qualifications, availability, and other administrative matters.

Added effective April 1, 2000 (762 So.2d 441).

Rule 10.520. Compliance with Authority

A mediator shall comply with all statutes, court rules, local court rules, and administrative orders relevant to the practice of mediation.

Added effective April 1, 2000 (762 So.2d 441).

Rule 10.530. Improper Influence

A mediator shall refrain from any activity that has the appearance of improperly influencing a court to secure an appointment to a case.

Added effective April 1, 2000 (762 So.2d 441).

Committee Notes

2000 Revision. Giving gifts to court personnel in exchange for case assignments is improper. De minimis gifts generally distributed as part of an overall business development plan are excepted. See also rule 10.330.

Rule 10.600. Mediator's Responsibility to The Mediation Profession

A mediator shall preserve the quality of the profession. A mediator is responsible for maintaining professional competence and forthright business practices, fostering good relationships, assisting new mediators, and generally supporting the advancement of mediation.

Added effective April 1, 2000 (762 So.2d 441).

Committee Notes

2000 Revision. Rules 10.600–10.690 include a collection of specific ethical concerns involving a mediator's responsibility to the mediation profession. Incorporated in this new section are the concepts formerly found in rule 10.030 (General Standards and Qualifications), rule 10.120 (Training and Education), rule 10.130 (Advertising), rule 10.140 (Relationships with Other Professionals), and rule 10.150 (Advancement of Mediation).

Rule 10.610. Marketing Practices

(a) False or Misleading Marketing Practices. A mediator shall not engage in any marketing practice, including advertising, which contains false or misleading information. A mediator shall ensure that any marketing of the mediator's qualifications, services to be rendered, or the mediation process is accurate and honest.

(b) Supreme Court Certification. Any marketing practice in which a mediator indicates that such mediator is "Florida Supreme Court certified" is misleading unless it also identifies at least one area of certification in which the mediator is certified.

(c) Other Certifications. Any marketing publication that generally refers to a mediator being "certified" is misleading unless the advertising mediator has successfully completed an established process for certifying mediators that involves actual instruction rather than the mere payment of a fee. Use of the term "certified" in advertising is also misleading unless the mediator identifies the entity issuing the referenced certification and the area or field of certification earned, if applicable.

(d) Prior Adjudicative Experience. Any marketing practice is misleading if the mediator states or implies that prior adjudicative experience, including, but not limited to, service as a judge, magistrate, or administrative hearing officer, makes one a better or more qualified mediator.

(e) Prohibited Claims or Promises. A mediator shall not make claims of achieving specific outcomes or promises implying favoritism for the purpose of obtaining business.

(f) Additional Prohibited Marketing Practices. A mediator shall not engage in any marketing practice that diminishes the importance of a party's right to self-determination or the impartiality of the mediator, or that demeans the dignity of the mediation process or the judicial system.

Added effective April 1, 2000 (762 So.2d 441). Amended effective April 1, 2010 (32 So.3d 611).

Commentary

2010 Revision. Areas of certification in subdivision (b) include county, family, circuit, dependency and other Supreme Court certifications.

The roles of a mediator and an adjudicator are fundamentally distinct. The integrity of the judicial system may be impugned when the prestige of the judicial office is used for commercial purposes. When engaging in any mediation marketing practice, a former adjudicative officer should not lend the prestige of the judicial office to advance private interests in a manner inconsistent with this rule. For example, the depiction of a mediator in judicial robes or use of the word "judge" with or without modifiers to the mediator's name would be inappropriate. However, an accurate representation of the mediator's judicial experience would not be inappropriate.

Rule 10.620. Integrity and Impartiality

A mediator shall not accept any engagement, provide any service, or perform any act that would compromise the mediator's integrity or impartiality.

Added effective April 1, 2000 (762 So.2d 441).

Rule 10.630. Professional Competence

A mediator shall acquire and maintain professional competence in mediation. A mediator shall regularly participate in educational activities promoting professional growth.

Added effective April 1, 2000 (762 So.2d 441).

Rule 10.640. Skill and Experience

A mediator shall decline an appointment, withdraw, or request appropriate assistance when the facts and circumstances of the case are beyond the mediator's skill or experience.

Added effective April 1, 2000 (762 So.2d 441).

Rule 10.650. Concurrent Standards

Other ethical standards to which a mediator may be professionally bound are not abrogated by these rules. In the course of performing mediation services, however, these rules prevail over any conflicting ethical standards to which a mediator may otherwise be bound.

Added effective April 1, 2000 (762 So.2d 441).

Rule 10.660. Relationships with Other Mediators

A mediator shall respect the professional relationships of another mediator.

Added effective April 1, 2000 (762 So.2d 441).

Rule 10.670. Relationship with Other Professionals

A mediator shall respect the roles of other professional disciplines in the mediation process and shall promote cooperation between mediators and other professionals.

Added effective April 1, 2000 (762 So.2d 441).

Rule 10.680. Prohibited Agreements

With the exception of an agreement conferring benefits upon retirement, a mediator shall not restrict or limit another mediator's practice following termination of a professional relationship.

Added effective April 1, 2000 (762 So.2d 441).

Committee Notes

2000 Revision. Rule 10.680 is intended to discourage covenants not to compete or other practice restrictions arising upon the termination of a relationship with another mediator or mediation firm. In situations where a retirement program is being contractually funded or supported by a surviving mediator or mediation firm, however, reasonable restraints on competition are acceptable.

Rule 10.690. Advancement of Mediation

(a) Pro Bono Service. Mediators have a responsibility to provide competent services to persons seeking their assistance, including those unable to pay for services. A mediator should provide mediation services pro bono or at a reduced rate of compensation whenever appropriate.

(b) New Mediator Training. An experienced mediator should cooperate in training new mediators, including serving as a mentor.

(c) Support of Mediation. A mediator should support the advancement of mediation by encouraging and participating in research, evaluation, or other forms of professional development and public education.

Added effective April 1, 2000 (762 So.2d 441).

PART III. DISCIPLINE

Rule 10.700. Scope and Purpose

These rules apply to all proceedings before all panels and committees of the mediator qualifications board involving the discipline or suspension of certified mediators or noncertified mediators appointed to mediate a case pursuant to court rules. The purpose of these rules of discipline is to provide a means for enforcing the Florida Rules for Certified and Court–Appointed Mediators.

Former Rule 10.160 added effective May 28, 1992 (604 So.2d 764). Amended April 14, 1994, eff. July 1, 1994 (641 So.2d 343). Renumbered as new Rule 10.700 and amended Feb. 3, 2000, effective April 1, 2000 (762 So.2d 441).

Rule 10.710. Privilege to Mediate

Certification to mediate confers no vested right to the holder thereof, but is a conditional privilege that is revocable for cause.

Former Rule 10.170 added effective May 28, 1992 (604 So.2d 764). Renumbered as new Rule 10.710 and amended Feb. 3, 2000, effective April 1, 2000 (762 So.2d 441).

Rule 10.720. Definitions

(a) Board. The mediator qualifications board.

(b) Center. The Florida Dispute Resolution Center of the Office of the State Courts Administrator.

(c) Complaint. Formal submission of an alleged violation of the Rules for Certified and Court–Appointed Mediators, including allegations of a lack of good moral character. A complaint may originate from any person or from the center.

(d) Complaint Committee. Three members of the board from the division in which a complaint against a mediator originates.

(e) Counsel. Counsel appointed by the center, at the direction of the complaint committee, responsible for presenting the complaint to the panel.

(f) Division. One of 3 standing divisions of the mediator qualifications board, established on a regional basis.

(g) Investigator. A certified mediator, attorney, or other qualified individual appointed by the center at the direction of a complaint committee.

(h) Mediator. A person certified by the Florida Supreme Court or an individual mediating pursuant to court order.

(i) Panel. Five members of the board from the division in which a complaint against a mediator originates.

(j) Qualifications Complaint Committee. Three members of the board selected for the purpose of considering referrals pursuant to rule 10.800.

Former Rule 10.180 added effective May 28, 1992 (604 So.2d 764). Amended Oct. 5, 1995 (661 So.2d 807). Renumbered as new Rule 10.720 and amended Feb. 3, 2000, effective April 1, 2000 (762 So.2d 441). Amended May 11, 2006, effective August 1, 2006 (931 So.2d 877).

Rule 10.730. Mediator Qualifications Board

(a) Generally. The mediator qualifications board shall be composed of 3 standing divisions that shall be located in the following regions:

(1) One division in north Florida, encompassing the First, Second, Third, Fourth, Eighth, and Fourteenth judicial circuits;

(2) One division in central Florida, encompassing the Fifth, Sixth, Seventh, Ninth, Tenth, Twelfth, Thirteenth, and Eighteenth judicial circuits;

(3) One division in south Florida, encompassing the Eleventh, Fifteenth, Sixteenth, Seventeenth, Nineteenth, and Twentieth judicial circuits.

Other divisions may be formed by the supreme court based on need.

(b) Composition of Divisions. Each division of the board shall be composed of:

(1) three circuit or county judges;

(2) three certified county mediators;

(3) three certified circuit mediators;

(4) three certified family mediators, at least 2 of whom shall be nonlawyers;

(5) not less than 1 nor more than 3 certified dependency mediators;

(6) not less than 1 nor more than 3 certified appellate mediators; and

(7) three attorneys licensed to practice law in Florida who have a substantial trial practice and are neither certified as mediators nor judicial officers during their terms of service on the board, at least 1 of whom shall have a substantial dissolution of marriage law practice.

(c) Appointment; Terms. Eligible persons shall be appointed to the board by the chief justice of the Supreme Court of Florida for a period of 4 years. The terms of the board members shall be staggered.

(d) Complaint Committee. Each complaint committee of the board shall be composed of 3 members. A complaint committee shall cease to exist after disposing of all assigned cases. Each complaint committee shall be composed of:

(1) one judge or attorney, who shall act as the chair of the committee;

(2) one mediator, who is certified in the area to which the complaint refers; and

(3) one other certified mediator.

(e) Qualifications Complaint Committee. One member of each division shall serve as a member of the qualifications complaint committee for a period of 1 year. The qualifications complaint committee shall be composed of:

(1) one judge or attorney, who shall act as the chair of the committee; and

(2) two certified mediators.

(f) Panels. Each panel of the board shall be composed of 5 members. A panel shall cease to exist after disposing of all assigned cases. Each panel shall be composed of:

(1) one circuit or county judge, who shall serve as the chair;

(2) three certified mediators, at least 1 of whom shall be certified in the area to which the complaint refers; and

(3) one attorney.

(g) Panel Vice-Chair. Each panel once appointed shall elect a vice-chair. The vice-chair shall act as the chair of the panel in the absence of the chair.

Former Rule 10.190 added effective May 28, 1992, (604 So.2d 764). Amended April 14, 1994, eff. July 1, 1994 (641 So.2d 343); Amended Oct. 5, 1995 (661 So.2d 807). Renumbered as new Rule 10.730 and amended Feb. 3, 2000, effective April 1, 2000 (762 So.2d 441). Amended effective July 1, 2010 (41 So.3d 161).

Committee Notes

2000 Revision. In relation to (b)(5), the Committee believes that the Chief Justice should have discretion in the number of dependency mediators appointed to the Board depending on the number of certified dependency mediators available for appointment. It is the intention of the Committee that when dependency mediation reaches a comparable level of activity to the other three areas of certification, the full complement of three representatives per division should be realized.

Rule 10.740. Jurisdiction

(a) Complaint Committee. Each complaint committee shall have such jurisdiction and powers as are necessary to conduct the proper and speedy investigation and disposition of any complaint. The judge or attorney presiding over the complaint committee shall have the power to compel the attendance of witnesses, to take or to cause to be taken the depositions of witnesses, and to order the production of records or other documentary evidence, and the power of contempt. The complaint committee shall perform its investigatory function and have concomitant power to resolve cases prior to panel referral.

(b) Qualifications Complaint Committee. The qualifications complaint committee shall have jurisdiction over all matters referred pursuant to rule 10.800. The qualifications complaint committee shall have such jurisdiction and powers as are necessary to conduct the proper and speedy investigation and disposition of any good moral character complaint or other matter referred by the center. The judge or attorney presiding over the qualifications complaint committee shall have the power to compel the attendance of witnesses, to take or to cause to be taken the depositions of witnesses, and to order the production of records or other documentary evidence, and the power of contempt. The qualifications complaint committee shall perform its investigatory function and have concomitant power to resolve cases prior to panel referral.

(c) Panel. Each panel shall have such jurisdiction and powers as are necessary to conduct the proper and speedy adjudication and disposition of any proceeding. The judge presiding over each panel shall have the power to compel the attendance of witnesses, to take or to cause to be taken the depositions of witnesses, to order the production of records or other documentary evidence, and the power of contempt. The panel shall perform the adjudicatory function, but shall not have any investigatory functions.

(d) Contempt. Should any witness fail, without justification, to respond to the lawful subpoena of the complaint committee, the qualifications complaint committee, or the panel or, having responded, fail or refuse to answer all inquiries or to turn over evidence that has been lawfully subpoenaed, or should any person be guilty of disorderly or contemptuous conduct before any proceeding of the complaint committee, the qualifications complaint committee, or the panel, a motion may be filed by the complaint committee, the qualifications complaint committee, or the panel before the circuit court of the county in which the contemptuous act was committed. The motion shall allege the specific failure on the part of the witness or the specific disorderly or contemptuous act of the person which forms the basis of the alleged contempt of the complaint committee, the qualifications complaint committee, or the panel. Such motion shall pray for the issuance of an order to show cause before the circuit court why the circuit court should not find the person in contempt of the complaint committee, the qualifications complaint committee, or the panel and the person should not be punished by the court therefor. The circuit court shall issue such orders and judgments therein as the court deems appropriate.

Former Rule 10.200 added effective May 28, 1992 (604 So.2d 764). Amended April 14, 1994, eff. July 1, 1994 (641 So.2d 343); amended Oct. 5, 1995 (661 So.2d 807). Renumbered as new Rule 10.740 and amended Feb. 3, 2000, effective April 1, 2000 (762 So.2d 441). Amended May 11, 2006, effective August 1, 2006 (931 So.2d 877).

Rule 10.750. Staff

The center shall provide all staff support to the board necessary to fulfill its duties and responsibilities under these rules and perform all other functions specified in these rules.

Former Rule 10.210 added effective May 28, 1992 (604 So.2d 764). Renumbered as new Rule 10.750 and amended Feb. 3, 2000, effective April 1, 2000 (762 So.2d 441).

Rule 10.800. Good Moral Character; Professional Discipline

(a) Good Moral Character.

(1) Prior to approving an applicant for certification or renewal as a mediator the center shall review the application to determine whether the applicant appears to meet the standards for good moral character. If the center's review of an application for certification or renewal raises any questions regarding the applicant's good moral character, the center shall request the applicant to supply additional information as necessary. Upon completing this extended review, the center shall forward the application and supporting material as a complaint to the qualifications complaint committee.

(2) If the center becomes aware of any information concerning a certified mediator which could constitute credible evidence of a lack of good moral character, the center shall refer such information as a complaint to the qualifications complaint committee.

(3) The qualifications complaint committee shall review all documentation relating to the good moral character of any applicant or certified mediator in a manner consistent, insofar as applicable, with rule 10.810. In relation to an applicant, the qualifications complaint committee shall either recommend approval or, if it finds there is probable cause to believe that the applicant lacks good moral character, it shall refer the matter to a hearing panel for further action. In relation to a certified mediator, the qualifications complaint committee shall dismiss or, if there is probable cause to believe that the mediator lacks good moral character, refer the matter to a hearing panel for further action.

(4) The panel shall take appropriate action on the issue of good moral character by dismissing the charges, denying the application in relation to an applicant, or imposing sanctions against a certified mediator pursuant to rule 10.830.

(5) All such hearings shall be held in a manner consistent, insofar as applicable, with rule 10.820.

(b) Professional Licenses and Certifications.

(1) A certified mediator shall inform the center, in writing, of the change in status of any professional license held by the mediator within 30 days of such change.

(2) Upon becoming aware that a certified mediator has been disciplined by a professional organization of which that mediator is a member, the center shall refer the matter to the qualifications complaint committee.

Added effective April 1, 2000 (762 So.2d 441). Amended May 11, 2006, effective August 1, 2006 (931 So.2d 877).

Rule 10.810. Committee Process

(a) Initiation of Complaint. Any individual wishing to make a complaint alleging that a mediator has violated one or more provisions of these rules shall do so in writing under oath. The complaint shall state with particularity the specific facts that form the basis of the complaint.

(b) Filing. The complaint shall be filed with the center, or, in the alternative, the complaint may be filed in the office of the court administrator in the circuit in which the case originated or, if not case specific, in the circuit where the alleged misconduct occurred.

(c) Referral. The complaint, if filed in the office of the court administrator, shall be referred to the center within 5 days of filing.

(d) Assignment to Committee. Upon receipt of a complaint in proper form, the center shall assign the complaint to a complaint committee or the qualifications complaint committee within 10 days.

(e) Facial Sufficiency Determination. The complaint committee or the qualifications complaint committee shall convene, either in person or by conference call, to determine whether the allegation(s), if true, would constitute a violation of these rules. If the committee finds a complaint against a certified mediator to be facially insufficient, the complaint shall be dismissed without prejudice and the complainant and the mediator shall be so notified. If the qualifications complaint committee finds a complaint against an applicant to be facially insufficient, the complaint shall be dismissed and the application approved if all other requirements are met. If the complaint is found to be facially sufficient, the committee shall prepare a list of any rule or rules which may have been violated and shall submit such to the center.

(f) Service. The center shall serve a copy of the list of alleged rule violations prepared by the committee, a copy of the complaint, and a copy of these rules to the mediator or applicant in question. Service on the mediator or applicant shall be made by certified mail addressed to the mediator or applicant at the mediator's or applicant's place of business or residence on file with the center. Mailing to such an address shall constitute service.

(g) Response. Within 20 days of the receipt of the list of violations prepared by the committee and the complaint, the mediator or applicant shall send a written, sworn response to the center by registered or certified mail. If the mediator or applicant does not respond, the allegations shall be deemed admitted.

(h) Preliminary Review. Upon review of the complaint and the mediator's or applicant's response, the committee may find that no violation has occurred and dismiss the complaint. The committee may also resolve the issue pursuant to subdivision (j) of this rule.

(i) Appointment of Investigator. The committee, after review of the complaint and response, may direct the center to appoint an investigator to assist the committee in any of its functions. Such person shall investigate the complaint and advise the committee when it meets to determine the existence of probable cause. In the alternative to appointing an investigator, the committee or any member or members thereof may investigate the allegations, if so directed by the committee chair. Such investigation may include meeting with the mediator, the applicant and the complainant.

(j) Committee Meeting with the Mediator or Applicant. Notwithstanding any other provision in this rule, at any time while the committee has jurisdiction, it may meet with the complainant and the mediator or applicant, jointly or separately, in an effort to resolve the matter. This resolution may include sanctions if agreed to by the mediator or applicant. If sanctions are accepted, all relevant documentation shall be forwarded to the center. Such conferences shall be in person, by video-conference or teleconference at the discretion of the committee.

(k) Review. If no other disposition has occurred, the committee shall review the complaint, the response, and any investigative report, including any underlying documentation, to determine whether there is probable cause to believe that the alleged misconduct occurred and would constitute a violation of the rules.

(*l*) No Probable Cause. If the committee finds no probable cause, it shall dismiss the complaint and so advise the complainant and the mediator or applicant in writing.

(m) Probable Cause Found. If probable cause exists, the committee may draft formal charges and forward such charges to the center for assignment to a panel. In the alternative, the committee may decide not to pursue the case by filing a short and plain statement of the reason or reasons for non-referral and so advise the complainant and the mediator or applicant in writing.

(n) Formal Charges and Counsel. If the committee refers a complaint to the center, the committee shall submit to the center formal charges which shall include a short and plain statement of the matters asserted in the complaint and references to the particular sections of the rules involved. After considering the circumstances of the complaint and the complexity of the issues to be heard, the committee may direct the center to appoint a member of The Florida Bar to investigate and prosecute the complaint. Such counsel may be the investigator appointed pursuant to this rule if such person is otherwise qualified.

(*o*) Dismissal. Upon the filing of a stipulation of dismissal signed by the complainant and the mediator with the concurrence of the complaint committee, the action shall be dismissed. If an application is withdrawn by the applicant, the complaint shall be dismissed with or without prejudice depending on the circumstances.

Former Rule 10.220 added effective May 28, 1992 (604 So.2d 764). Amended Oct. 5, 1995 (661 So.2d 807). Renumbered as new Rule 10.810 and amended Feb. 3, 2000, effective April 1, 2000 (762 So.2d 441). Amended May 11, 2006, effective August 1, 2006 (931 So.2d 877).

Rule 10.820. Hearing Procedures

(a) Assignment to Panel. Upon referral of a complaint and formal charges from a committee, the center shall assign the complaint and formal charges or other matter to a panel for hearing, with notice of assignment to the complainant and the mediator or applicant. No member of the committee shall serve as a member of the panel.

(b) Hearing. The center shall schedule a hearing not more than 90 days nor less than 30 days from the date of notice of assignment of the matter to the panel. At any time prior to the hearing, the panel may accept an admission to any or all charges and impose sanctions upon the mediator. The panel shall not be required to physically meet in person to accept such admission.

(c) Dismissal. Upon the filing of a stipulation of dismissal signed by the complainant and the mediator, and with the concurrence of the panel, a complaint shall be dismissed.

(d) Procedures for Hearing. The procedures for hearing shall be as follows:

(1) No hearing shall be conducted without 5 panel members being physically present.

(2) The hearing may be conducted informally but with decorum.

(3) The rules of evidence applicable to trial of civil actions apply but are to be liberally construed.

(4) Upon a showing of good cause to the panel, testimony of any party or witness may be presented over the telephone.

(e) Right to Defend. A mediator or applicant shall have the right to defend against all charges and shall have the right to be represented by an attorney, to examine and cross-examine witnesses, to compel the attendance of witnesses to testify, and to compel the production of documents and other evidentiary matter through the subpoena power of the panel.

(f) Mediator or Applicant Discovery. The center shall, upon written demand of a mediator, applicant, or counsel of record, promptly furnish the following: the names and addresses of all witnesses whose testimony is expected to be offered at the hearing, together with copies of all written statements and transcripts of the testimony of such witnesses in the possession of the counsel or the center which are relevant to the subject matter of the hearing and which have not previously been furnished.

(g) Panel Discovery. The mediator, applicant, or counsel of record shall, upon written demand of the counsel or the center, promptly furnish the following: the names and addresses of all witnesses whose testimony is expected to be offered at the hearing, together with copies of all written statements and transcripts of the testimony of such witnesses in the possession of the mediator, applicant, or counsel of record which are relevant to the subject matter of the hearing and which have not previously been furnished.

(h) Failure to Appear. Absent a showing of good cause, if the complainant fails to appear at the hearing, the panel may dismiss a complaint for want of prosecution.

(i) Mediator's or Applicant's Absence. If the mediator or applicant fails to appear, absent a showing of good cause, the hearing shall proceed.

(j) Rehearing. If the matter is heard in the mediator's or applicant's absence, the mediator or applicant may petition for rehearing, for good cause, within 10 days of the date of the hearing.

(k) Recording. Any party shall have the right, without any order or approval, to have all or any portion of the testimony in the proceedings reported and transcribed by a court reporter at the party's expense.

(*l*) Dismissal. Upon dismissal, the panel shall promptly file a copy of the dismissal order with the center.

(m) Sanctions. If, after the hearing, a majority of the panel finds that there is clear and convincing evidence to support a violation of the rules, the panel shall impose such sanctions included in rule 10.830 as it deems appropriate and report such action to the center.

(n) Denial of Application for Certification. If, after a hearing, a majority of the panel finds by the preponderance of the evidence that an applicant should not be certified as a mediator, the panel shall deny the application and report such action to the center.

Former Rule 10.230 added effective May 28, 1992 (604 So.2d 764). Amended Oct. 5, 1995 (661 So.2d 807). Renumbered as new Rule 10.820 and amended Feb. 3, 2000, effective April 1, 2000 (762 So.2d 441). Amended May 11, 2006, effective August 1, 2006 (931 So.2d 877).

Rule 10.830. Sanctions

(a) Generally. The panel may impose one or more of the following sanctions:

(1) Imposition of costs of the proceeding.

(2) Oral admonishment.

(3) Written reprimand.

(4) Additional training, which may include the observation of mediations.

(5) Restriction on types of cases which can be mediated in the future.

(6) Suspension for a period of up to 1 year.

(7) Decertification or, if the mediator is not certified, bar from service as a mediator under Florida Rules of Civil Procedure.

(8) Such other sanctions as are agreed to by the mediator and the panel.

(b) Conviction of Felony. If the panel finds that a certified mediator has a felony conviction, it shall decertify the mediator for a period of not less than two years or until restoration of civil rights, whichever comes later. In order to become reinstated, such decertified mediator must comply with the requirements of subdivision (h).

(c) Failure to Comply. If there is reason to believe that the mediator failed to timely comply with any imposed sanction, a hearing shall be held before a panel convened for that purpose within 60 days of the date when the center learned of the alleged failure to comply. The hearing shall also include any additional alleged failures to comply of which the center becomes aware prior to the date of the hearing. The holding of a hearing shall not preclude a subsequent hearing on an alleged failure occurring after the first alleged failure. Any suspension in effect at the time of the discovery of the violation by the center shall continue in effect until a decision is reached at the hearing. A finding of the panel that there was a willful failure to substantially comply with any imposed sanction shall result in the decertification of the mediator.

(d) Decertified Mediators. If a mediator has been decertified or barred from service pursuant to these rules, the mediator shall not thereafter be certified or assigned to mediate a case pursuant to court rule or be designated as mediator pursuant to court rule unless reinstated.

(e) Decision to be Filed. Upon making a determination that discipline is appropriate, the panel shall promptly file with the center a copy of the decision including findings and conclusions certified by the chair of the panel. The center shall promptly mail to all parties notice of such filing, together with a copy of the decision.

(f) Notice to Circuits. The center shall notify all circuits of any mediator who has been decertified or suspended unless otherwise ordered by the Supreme Court of Florida.

(g) Publication. Upon the imposition of sanctions, the center shall publish the name of the mediator, a short summary of the rule or rules which were violated, the circumstances surrounding the violation, and any sanctions imposed.

(h) Reinstatement After Suspension. Except if inconsistent with rule 10.110, a mediator who has been suspended shall be reinstated as a certified mediator upon the expiration of the imposed or accepted suspension period and satisfaction of any additional renewal obligations.

(i) Reinstatement After Decertification. Except if inconsistent with rule 10.110, a mediator who has been decertified may be reinstated as a certified mediator. Except as otherwise provided in the decision of the panel, no application for reinstatement may be tendered within 2 years after the date of decertification. The reinstatement procedures shall be as follows:

(1) A petition for reinstatement, together with 6 copies, shall be made in writing, verified by the petitioner, and filed with the center.

(2) The petition for reinstatement shall contain:

(A) the name, age, residence, and address of the petitioner;

(B) the offense or misconduct upon which the decertification was based, together with the date of such decertification; and

(C) a concise statement of facts claimed to justify reinstatement as a certified mediator.

(3) The center shall refer the petition for reinstatement to a hearing panel in the appropriate division for review.

(4) The panel shall review the petition and, if the petitioner is found to be unfit to mediate, the petition shall be dismissed. If the petitioner is found fit to mediate, the panel shall notify the center and the center shall reinstate the petitioner as a certified mediator contingent on the petitioner's completion of a certified mediation training program of the type for which the petitioner seeks to be reinstated. Successive petitions for reinstatement based upon the same grounds may be reviewed without a hearing.

Former Rule 10.240 added effective May 28, 1992 (604 So.2d 764). Amended April 14, 1994, eff. July 1, 1994 (641 So.2d 343); amended Oct. 5, 1995 (661 So.2d 807). Renumbered as new Rule 10.830 and amended Feb. 3, 2000, effective April 1, 2000 (762 So.2d 441). Amended May 11, 2006, effective August 1, 2006 (931 So.2d 877); May 19, 2011 (64 So.3d 1200).

Rule 10.840. Subpoenas

(a) Issuance. Subpoenas for the attendance of witnesses and the production of documentary evidence for discovery and for the appearance of any person before a complaint committee, a panel, or any member thereof, may be issued by the chair of the complaint committee or panel or, if the chair of the panel is absent, by the vice-chair. Such subpoenas may be served in any manner provided by law for the service of witness subpoenas in a civil action.

(b) Failure to Obey. Any person who, without adequate excuse, fails to obey a duly served subpoena may be cited for contempt of the committee or panel in accordance with rule 10.740.

Former Rule 10.250 added effective May 28, 1992 (604 So.2d 764). Amended Oct. 5, 1995 (661 So.2d 807). Renumbered as new Rule 10.840 and amended Feb. 3, 2000, effective April 1, 2000 (762 So.2d 441).

Rule 10.850. Confidentiality

(a) Generally. Until sanctions are imposed, whether by the panel or upon agreement of the mediator, all proceedings shall be confidential. After sanctions are imposed by a panel or an application is denied, all documentation including and subsequent to the filing of formal charges shall be public with the exception of those matters which are otherwise confidential under law or rule of the supreme court, regardless of the outcome of any appeal. If a consensual agreement is reached between a mediator and a complaint committee, only the basis of the complaint and the agreement shall be released to the public.

(b) Witnesses. Each witness in every proceeding under these disciplinary rules shall be sworn to tell the truth and not disclose the existence of the proceeding, the subject matter thereof, or the identity of the mediator until the proceeding is no longer confidential under these disciplinary rules. Violation of this oath shall be considered an act of contempt of the complaint committee or the panel.

(c) Papers to be Marked. All notices, papers, and pleadings mailed prior to formal charges being filed shall be enclosed in a cover marked "confidential."

(d) Breach of Confidentiality. Violation of confidentiality by a member of the board shall subject the member to removal by the chief justice of the Supreme Court of Florida.

Former Rule 10.260 added effective May 28, 1992 (604 So.2d 764). Amended Oct. 5, 1995 (661 So.2d 807). Renumbered as new Rule 10.850 and amended Feb. 3, 2000, effective April 1, 2000 (762 So.2d 441); Oct. 16, 2008 (993 So.2d 505).

Committee Notes

1995 Revision: The Committee believed the rule regarding confidentiality should be amended in deference to the 1993 amendment to section 44.102, Florida Statutes, that engrafted an exception to the general confidentiality requirement for all mediation sessions for the purpose of investigating complaints filed against mediators. Section 44.102(4) specifically provides that "the disclosure of an otherwise privileged communication shall be used only for the internal use of the body conducting the investigation" and that "[Prior] to the release of any disciplinary files to the public, all references to otherwise privileged communications shall be deleted from the record."

These provisions created a substantial potential problem when read in conjunction with the previous rule on confidentiality, which made public all proceedings after formal charges were filed. In addition to the possibly substantial burden of redacting the files for public release, there was the potentially greater problem of conducting panel hearings in such a manner as to preclude the possibility that confidential communications would be revealed during testimony, specifically the possibility that any public observers would have to be removed prior to the elicitation of any such communication only to be allowed to return until the next potentially confidential revelation. The Committee believes that under the amended rule the integrity of the disciplinary system can be maintained by releasing the results of any disciplinary action together with a redacted transcript of panel proceedings, while still maintaining the integrity of the mediation process.

2008 Revision: The recent adoption of the Florida Mediation Confidentiality and Privilege Act, sections 44.401—44.406, Florida Statutes, renders the first paragraph of the 1995 Revision Committee Notes inoperative. The second paragraph explains the initial rationale for the rule, which is useful now from a historical standpoint.

Rule 10.860. Interested Party

A mediator is disqualified from serving on a committee or panel proceeding involving the mediator's own discipline or decertification.

Former Rule 10.270 added effective May 28, 1992 (604 So.2d 764). Renumbered as new Rule 10.860 and amended Feb.3, 2000, effective April 1, 2000 (762 So.2d 441).

Rule 10.870. Disqualification of Members of a Panel or Committee

(a) Procedure. In any case, any party may at any time before final disciplinary action show by a suggestion filed in the case that a member of the board before which the case is pending, or some person related to that member, is a party to the case or is interested in the result of the case or that the member is related to an attorney or counselor of record in the case or that the member is a material witness for or against one of the parties to the case.

(b) Facts to be Alleged. A motion to disqualify shall allege the facts relied on to show the grounds for disqualification and shall be verified by the party.

(c) Time for Motion. A motion to disqualify shall be made within a reasonable time after discovery of the facts constituting grounds for disqualification.

(d) Action by Chair. The chair of the appropriate committee or panel shall determine only the legal sufficiency of the motion. The chair shall not pass on the truth of the facts alleged. If the motion is legally sufficient, the chair shall enter an order of disqualification and the disqualified committee or panel member shall proceed no further in the action. In the event that the chair is the challenged member, the vice-chair shall perform the acts required under this subdivision.

(e) Recusals. Nothing in this rule limits a board member's authority to enter an order of recusal on the board member's own initiative.

(f) Replacement. The center shall assign a board member to take the place of any disqualified or recused member.

(g) Qualifications. Each assignee shall have the same qualifications as the disqualified or recused member.

Former Rule 10.280 added effective May 28, 1992 (604 So.2d 764). Amended Oct. 5, 1995 (661 So.2d 807). Renumbered as new Rule 10.870 and amended Feb. 3, 2000, effective April 1, 2000 (762 So.2d 441).

Rule 10.880. Supreme Court Chief Justice Review

(a) Right of Review. Any mediator or applicant found to have committed a violation of these rules or otherwise sanctioned by a hearing panel shall have a right of review of that action. Review of this type shall be by the chief justice of the Supreme Court of Florida or by the chief justice's designee. A mediator shall have no right of review of any resolution reached under rule 10.810(j).

(b) Rules of Procedure. The Florida Rules of Appellate Procedure, to the extent applicable and except as otherwise provided in this rule, shall control all appeals of mediator disciplinary matters.

(1) The jurisdiction to seek review of disciplinary action shall be invoked by submitting an original and one copy of a Notice of Review of Mediator Disciplinary Action to the chief justice within 30 days of the panel's decision. A copy shall also be provided to the Center.

(2) The notice of review shall be substantially in the form prescribed by rule 9.900(a), Florida Rules of Appellate Procedure. A copy of the panel decision shall be attached to the notice.

(3) Appellant's initial brief, accompanied by an appendix as prescribed by rule 9.220, Florida Rules of Appellate Procedure, shall be served within 30 days of submitting the notice of review. Additional briefs shall be served as prescribed by rule 9.210, Florida Rules of Appellate Procedure.

(c) Standard of Review. The review shall be conducted in accordance with the following standard of review:

(1) The chief justice or designee shall review the findings and conclusions of the panel using a competent substantial evidence standard, neither reweighing the evidence in the record nor substituting the reviewer's judgment for that of the panel.

(2) Decisions of the chief justice or designee shall be final upon issuance of a mandate under rule 9.340, Florida Rules of Appellate Procedure.

Former Rule 10.290 added effective May 28, 1992 (604 So.2d 764). Amended April 14, 1994, eff. July 1, 1994 (641 So.2d 343); Oct. 5, 1995 (661 So.2d 807). Renumbered as new Rule 10.880 and amended Feb. 3, 2000, effective April 1, 2000 (762 So.2d 441). Amended May 11, 2006, effective August 1, 2006 (931 So.2d 877); Oct. 16, 2008 (993 So.2d 505).

Rule 10.900. Mediator Ethics Advisory Committee

(a) Scope and Purpose. The Mediator Ethics Advisory Committee shall provide written advisory opinions to mediators subject to these rules in response to ethical questions arising from the Standards of Professional Conduct. Such opinions shall be consistent with supreme court decisions on mediator discipline.

(b) Appointment. The Mediator Ethics Advisory Committee shall be composed of 9 members, 3 from each geographic division served by the Mediator Qualifications Board. No member of the Mediator Qualifications Board shall serve on the committee.

(c) Membership and Terms. The membership of the committee shall be composed of 1 county mediator, 1 family mediator, and 1 circuit mediator from each division and shall be appointed by the chief justice. At least one of the 9 members shall also be a certified dependency mediator, and at least one of the 9 members shall also be a certified appellate mediator. All appointments shall be for 4 years. No member shall serve more than 2 consecutive terms. The committee shall select 1 member as chair and 1 member as vice-chair.

(d) Meetings. The committee shall meet in person or by telephone conference as necessary at the direction of the chair to consider requests for advisory opinions. A quorum shall consist of a majority of the members appointed to the committee. All requests for advisory opinions shall be in writing. The committee may vote by any means as directed by the chair.

(e) Opinions.. Upon due deliberation, and upon the concurrence of a majority of the committee, the committee shall render opinions. A majority of all members shall be required to concur in any advisory opinion issued by the committee. The opinions shall be signed by the chair, or vice-chair in the absence of the chair, filed with the Dispute Resolution Center, published in the Dispute Resolution Center newsletter, and be made available upon request.

(f) Effect of Opinions. While reliance by a mediator on an opinion of the committee shall not constitute a defense in any disciplinary proceeding, it shall be evidence of good faith and may be considered by the board in relation to any determination of guilt or in mitigation of punishment.

(g) Confidentiality. Prior to publication, all references to the requesting mediator or any other real person, firm, organization, or corporation shall be deleted from any request for an opinion, any document associated with the preparation of an opinion, and any opinion issued by the committee. This rule shall apply to all opinions, past and future.

(h) Support. The Dispute Resolution Center shall provide all support necessary for the committee to fulfil its duties under these rules.

Former Rule 10.300 added April 14, 1994, eff. July 1, 1994 (641 So.2d 343). Amended Oct. 5, 1995 (661 So.2d 807). Renumbered as new Rule 10.900 and amended Feb. 3, 2000, effective April 1, 2000 (762 So.2d 441). Amended July 1, 2010 (41 So.3d 161).

Committee Notes

2000 Revision. The Mediator Ethics Advisory Committee was formerly the Mediator Qualifications Advisory Panel.

INDEX TO
FLORIDA RULES FOR CERTIFIED AND COURT—APPOINTED MEDIATORS

FLORIDA RULES FOR COURT-APPOINTED ARBITRATORS

PART I. ARBITRATOR QUALIFICATIONS

Rule 11.010. Qualification

Arbitrators shall be members of The Florida Bar, except where otherwise agreed by the parties. The chief arbitrator shall have been a member of The Florida Bar for at least 5 years. Individuals who are not members of The Florida Bar may serve as arbitrators only on an arbitration panel and then only upon the written agreement of all parties.

Added April 14, 1994, eff. July 1, 1994 (641 So.2d 343).

Rule 11.020. Training

All arbitrators, except as noted below, shall attend 4 hours of training in a program approved by the Supreme Court of Florida. This rule shall not preclude the parties from agreeing to use the services of an arbitrator who has not completed the required training. Any former Florida trial judge who has not completed the training shall be exempt from the training requirements upon submission of documentation of such experience to the chief judge. The supreme court or chief justice may grant a waiver of the training requirement to any group possessing special qualifications which obviate the necessity of such training.

Added April 14, 1994, eff. July 1, 1994 (641 So.2d 343).

PART II. STANDARDS OF PROFESSIONAL CONDUCT

Rule 11.030. Preamble

(a) Scope; Purpose. These rules are intended to instill and promote public confidence in arbitration conducted pursuant to chapter 44, Florida Statutes, and to be a guide to arbitrator conduct. As with other forms of dispute resolution, arbitration must be built on public understanding and confidence. Persons serving as arbitrators are responsible to the parties, the public, and the courts to conduct themselves in a manner which will merit that confidence. These rules apply to all arbitrators who participate in arbitration conducted pursuant to chapter 44 and are a guide to arbitrator conduct in discharging their professional responsibilities in the arbitration of cases in the State of Florida.

(b) Arbitration Defined. Pursuant to chapter 44, Florida Statutes, arbitration is a process whereby a neutral third person or panel considers the facts and arguments presented by the parties and renders a decision which may be binding or nonbinding.

Added April 14, 1994, eff. July 1, 1994 (641 So.2d 343).

Rule 11.040. General Standards and Qualifications

(a) Integrity, Impartiality, and Competence. Integrity, impartiality, and professional competence are essential qualifications of any arbitrator. An arbitrator is in a relation of trust to the parties and shall adhere to the highest standards of integrity, impartiality, and professional competence in rendering professional service.

(1) An arbitrator shall not accept any engagement, perform any service, or undertake any act which would compromise the arbitrator's integrity.

(2) An arbitrator shall maintain professional competence in arbitration skills including, but not limited to:

(A) staying informed of and abiding by all statutes, rules, and administrative orders relevant to the practice of arbitration conducted pursuant to chapter 44, Florida Statutes; and

(B) regularly engaging in educational activities promoting professional growth.

(3) An arbitrator shall decline appointment, withdraw, or request technical assistance when the arbitrator decides that a case is beyond the arbitrator's competence.

(b) Concurrent Standards. Nothing herein shall replace, eliminate, or render inapplicable relevant ethical standards, not in conflict with these rules, which may be imposed upon any arbitrator by virtue of the arbitrator's professional calling.

(c) Continuing Obligations. The ethical obligations begin upon acceptance of the appointment and continue throughout all stages of the proceeding. In addition, whenever specifically set forth in these rules, certain ethical obligations begin as soon as a person is requested to serve as an arbitrator, and certain ethical obligations continue even after the decision in the case has been given to the parties.

Added April 14, 1994, eff. July 1, 1994 (641 So.2d 343).

Rule 11.050. Responsibilities to the Courts

An arbitrator shall be candid, accurate, and fully responsive to a court concerning the arbitrator's qualifications, availability, and all other pertinent matters. An arbitrator shall observe all administrative policies, local rules of court, applicable procedural rules, and statutes. An arbitrator is responsible to the judiciary for the propriety of the arbitrator's activities and must observe judicial standards of fidelity and diligence. An arbitrator shall refrain from any activity which has the appearance of improperly influencing a court to secure placement on a roster or appointment to a case, including gifts or other inducements to court personnel.

Added April 14, 1994, eff. July 1, 1994 (641 So.2d 343).

Rule 11.060. The Arbitration Process

(a) Avoidance of Delays. An arbitrator shall plan a work schedule so that present and future commitments will be fulfilled in a timely manner. An arbitrator shall refrain from accepting appointments when it becomes apparent that completion of the arbitration assignments accepted cannot be completed in a timely fashion. An arbitrator shall perform the arbitrator's services in a timely and expeditious fashion, avoiding delays whenever possible.

(b) Conduct of Proceedings.

(1) An arbitrator shall conduct the proceedings evenhandedly and treat all parties with equality and fairness at all stages of the proceedings.

(2) An arbitrator must afford a hearing which provides both parties the opportunity to present their respective positions pursuant to the arbitration rules.

(3) An arbitrator should be patient and courteous to the parties, to their lawyers, and to the witnesses and should encourage similar conduct by all participants in the proceedings.

(c) Decision–Making.

(1) An arbitrator should, after careful deliberation, decide all issues submitted for determination. An arbitrator should decide no other issues.

(2) An arbitrator should not delegate the duty to decide to any other person.

(3) If all parties agree upon a settlement of the issues in dispute and request an arbitrator to embody that agreement in an award, an arbitrator may do so, but is not required to do so unless satisfied with the propriety of the terms of the settlement. Whenever an arbitrator embodies a settlement by the parties in an award, the arbitrator should state in the award that it is based on an agreement of the parties.

(d) The Award. The award should be definite, certain, and as concise as possible.

Added April 14, 1994, eff. July 1, 1994 (641 So.2d 343).

Rule 11.070. Ex Parte Communication

(a) General. Arbitrators communicating with the parties should avoid impropriety or the appearance of impropriety.

(b) When Permissible. Arbitrators should not discuss a case with any party in the absence of each other party, except in the following circumstances:

(1) Discussions may be held with a party concerning such matters as setting the time and place of hearings or making other arrangements for the conduct of the proceedings. However, the arbitrator should promptly inform each other party of the discussion and should not make any final determination concerning the matter discussed before giving each absent party an opportunity to express its views.

(2) If a party fails to be present at a hearing after having been given due notice, the arbitrator may discuss the case with any party who is present.

(3) If all parties request or consent, such discussion may take place.

(c) Written Communications. Whenever an arbitrator communicates in writing with one party, the arbitrator should at the same time send a copy of the communication to each other party. Whenever an arbitrator receives any written communication concerning the case from one party which has not already been sent to each other party, the arbitrator should do so.

Added April 14, 1994, eff. July 1, 1994 (641 So.2d 343).

Rule 11.080. Impartiality

(a) Impartiality. An arbitrator shall be impartial and advise all parties of any circumstances bearing on possible bias, prejudice, or impartiality. Impartiality means freedom from favoritism or bias in word, action, and appearance.

(1) Arbitrators should conduct themselves in a way that is fair to all parties and should not be swayed by outside pressure, public clamor, fear of criticism, or self-interest.

(2) An arbitrator shall withdraw from an arbitration if the arbitrator believes the arbitrator can no longer be impartial.

(3) An arbitrator shall not give or accept a gift, request, favor, loan, or other item of value to or from a party, attorney, or any other person involved in and arising from any arbitration process.

(4) After accepting appointment, and for a reasonable period of time after the decision of the case, an arbitrator should avoid entering into family, business, or personal relationships which could affect impartiality or give the appearance of partiality, bias, or influence.

(b) Conflicts of Interest and Relationships; Required Disclosures; Prohibitions

(1) An arbitrator must disclose any current, past, or possible future representation or consulting relationship with any party or attorney involved in the arbitration. Disclosure must also be made of any pertinent pecuniary interest. All such disclosures shall be made as soon as practical after the arbitrator becomes aware of the interest or relationship.

(2) An arbitrator must disclose to the parties or to the court involved any close personal relationship or other circumstance, in addition to those specifically mentioned earlier in this rule, which might reasonably raise a question as to the arbitrator's impartiality. All such disclosures shall be made as soon as practical after the arbitrator becomes aware of the interest or relationship.

(3) The burden of disclosure rests on the arbitrator. After disclosure, the arbitrator may serve if both parties so desire. If the arbitrator believes or perceives that there is a clear conflict of interest, the arbitrator should withdraw, irrespective of the expressed desire of the parties.

(4) An arbitrator shall not use the arbitration process to solicit, encourage, or otherwise incur future professional services with either party.

Added April 14, 1994, eff. July 1, 1994 (641 So.2d 343).

Committee Notes

1994 Adoption. The duty to disclose potential conflicts includes the fact of membership on a board of directors, full-time or part-time service as a representative or advocate, consultation work for a fee, current stock or bond ownership (other than mutual fund shares or appropriate trust arrangements), or any other pertinent form of managerial, financial, or immediate family interest of the party involved. An arbitrator who is a member of a law firm is obliged to disclose any representational relationship the member firm may have had with the parties.

Arbitrators establish personal relationships with many representatives, attorneys, arbitrators, and other members of various professional associations. There should be no attempt to be secretive about such friendships or acquaintances, but disclosure is not necessary unless some feature of a particular relationship might reasonably appear to impair impartiality.

Rule 11.090. Relationship With Other Professionals

When there is more than one arbitrator, the arbitrators should afford each other the full opportunity to participate in all aspects of the proceedings.

Added April 14, 1994, eff. July 1, 1994 (641 So.2d 343).

Rule 11.100. Fees and Expenses

An arbitrator occupies a position of trust with respect to the parties and the courts. In charging for services and expenses, the arbitrator must be governed by the same high standard of honor and integrity which applies to all other phases of the arbitrator's work. An arbitrator must keep total charges for services and expenses reasonable and consistent with the nature of the case or within statutory payment limitations.

Added April 14, 1994, eff. July 1, 1994 (641 So.2d 343).

Rule 11.110. Training and Education

(a) Training. An arbitrator is obligated to acquire knowledge and training in the arbitration process, including an understanding of appropriate professional ethics, standards, and responsibilities. Upon request, an arbitrator is required to disclose the extent and nature of the arbitrator's training and experience.

(b) Continuing Education. It is important that arbitrators continue their professional education throughout the period of their active service. An arbitrator shall be personally responsible for ongoing professional growth, including participation in such continuing education as may be required by law.

(c) New Arbitrator Training. An experienced arbitrator should cooperate in the training of new arbitrators.

Added April 14, 1994, eff. July 1, 1994 (641 So.2d 343).

Rule 11.120. Advertising

All advertising by an arbitrator must represent honestly the services to be rendered. No claims of specific results or promises which imply favoritism to one side should be made for the purpose of obtaining business. An arbitrator shall make only accurate statements about the arbitration process, its costs and benefits, and the arbitrator's qualifications.

Added April 14, 1994, eff. July 1, 1994 (641 So.2d 343).

PART III. DISCIPLINE

Rule 11.130. Chief Judge's Responsibility

Arbitrators shall serve at the pleasure of the chief judge, who shall be responsible for enforcing the rules of conduct for arbitrators appointed pursuant to chapter 44, Florida Statutes.

Added April 14, 1994, eff. July 1, 1994 (641 So.2d 343).

Committee Notes

1994 Adoption. The Florida Supreme Court Standing Committee on Mediator and Arbitrator Rules believes that arbitrator discipline, unlike mediator discipline, should be administered by the chief judge rather than by a board appointed for that purpose. The primary reason for this distinction is that there is presently no statewide arbitrator certification process. Rather, arbitrators are made eligible by placement on a list by the chief judge. See Florida Rule of Civil Procedure 1.810(a). It was the feeling of the committee that a method of removal consistent with that of appointment, that is, discretion of the chief judge, would also be appropriate. The rules make the chief judge responsible for enforcing the rules of conduct for arbitrators appointed pursuant to chapter 44, Florida Statutes.

The committee reserves the right to reconsider the effectiveness of this method of discipline after observing operation for a period of time. If this method of removal proves to be ineffective, a board to conduct discipline may need to be appointed. It should, however, be noted that a similar system for the removal of quasi-judicial officers exists in relation to masters, Florida Rule of Civil Procedure 1.490(a), child support enforcement officers, Florida Rule of Civil Procedure 1.491(c), and traffic magistrates, Florida Rule of Traffic Court 6.630(c).

Appeals from decisions of the chief judge shall be taken in the same manner as any other matter appealed from the chief judge.

INDEX TO
FLORIDA RULES FOR COURT—APPOINTED ARBITRATORS

FLORIDA FAMILY LAW RULES OF PROCEDURE

Date Effective

Adopted July 7, 1995, effective January 1, 1996 (663 So.2d 1047); November 22, 1995, effective January 1, 1996 (663 So.2d 1049).

Rule 12.000. Preface

These rules consist of two separate sections. Section I contains the procedural rules governing family law matters and their commentary. Section II contains forms.

Amended Sept. 21, 2000 (810 So.2d 1).

Commentary

1995 Adoption. These rules were adopted after the Florida Supreme Court determined that separate rules for family court procedure were necessary. See *In re Florida R. Fam. Ct. P.*, 607 So.2d 396 (Fla. 1992). The court recognized that family law cases are different from other civil matters, emphasizing that the 1993 creation of family divisions in the circuit courts underscored the differences between family law matters and other civil matters. In adopting the family law rules, the Court stressed the need for simplicity due to the large number of pro se litigants (parties without counsel) in family law matters. In an effort to assist the many pro se litigants in this field, the Court has included simplified forms and instructional commentary in these rules. *See* Section II. The instructional commentary to the forms refers to these rules or the Florida Rules of Civil Procedure, where applicable.

The forms originally were adopted by the Court pursuant to *Family Law Rules of Procedure*, No. 84,337 (Fla. July 7, 1995); *In re Petition for Approval of Forms Pursuant to Rule 10–1.1(b) of the Rules Regulating the Florida Bar-Stepparent Adoption Forms*, 613 So.2d 900 (Fla. 1992); *Rules Regulating the Florida Bar-Approval of Forms*, 581 So.2d 902 (Fla. 1991).

SECTION I. FAMILY LAW RULES OF PROCEDURE

Rule 12.003. Coordination Of Related Family Cases and Hearings

(a) Assignment to One Judge.

(1) All related family cases must be handled before one judge unless impractical.

(2) If it is impractical for one judge to handle all related family cases, the judges assigned to hear the related cases involving the same family and/or children may confer for the purpose of case management and coordination of the cases. Notice and communication shall comply with Canon 3.B.(7) of the Code of Judicial Conduct. The party who filed the notice of related cases or the court may coordinate a case management conference under rule 12.200 between the parties and the judges hearing the related cases. In addition to the issues that may be considered, the court shall:

(A) consolidate as many issues as is practical to be heard by one judge;

(B) coordinate the progress of the remaining issues to facilitate the resolution of the pending actions and to avoid inconsistent rulings;

(C) determine the attendance or participation of any minor child in the proceedings if the related cases include a juvenile action; and

(D) determine the access of the parties to court records if a related case is confidential pursuant to Florida Rule of Judicial Administration 2.420.

(b) Joint Hearings or Trials.

(1) The court may order joint hearings or trials of any issues in related family cases.

(2) For joint or coordinated hearings, notice to all parties and to all attorneys of record in each related case shall be provided by the court, the moving party, or other party as ordered by the court, regardless of whether or not the party providing notice is a party in every case number that will be called for hearing.

Added Jan. 16, 2014, effective April 1, 2014 (132 So.3d 1114).

Rule 12.004. Judicial Access and Review of Related Family Files

(a) In General. A judge hearing a family case may access and review the files of any related case either pending or closed, to aid in carrying out his or her adjudicative responsibilities. Authorized court staff and personnel may also access and review the file of any related case.

(b) Family Case Defined. For purposes of this rule, a related family case is another pending or closed case separate from the pending case, as defined in Rule of Judicial Administration 2.545(d).

(c) Nondisclosure of Confidential Information. Judges or authorized court personnel shall not disclose confidential information and documents contained in related case files except in accordance with applicable state and federal confidentiality laws.

(d) Notice by Court Staff. Authorized court staff may advise the court about the existence of related legal proceedings, the legal issues involved, and administrative information about such cases.

Added Jan. 16, 2014, effective April 1, 2014 (132 So.3d 1114).

Rule 12.005. Transition Rule

These rules shall apply to all family law cases effective January 1, 1996. Any action taken in a family law case before January 1, 1996, that conformed to the then-effective rules or statutes governing family law cases, will be regarded as valid during the pendency of the litigation.

Commentary

1995 Adoption. This rule provides for an effective date of January 1, 1996, for these Florida Family Law Rules of Procedure. Under this rule, any action taken in a family law matter before January 1, 1996, will be regarded as valid during the pendency of the litigation so long as that action was taken in accordance with the then-effective rules or statutes governing family law cases. Any action taken after January 1, 1996, in new or pending family law cases will be governed by these rules.

Rule 12.006. Filing Copies Of Orders in Related Family Cases

The court may file copies of court orders in related family cases involving the same parties. All relevant case numbers should be placed on the order and a separate copy placed in each related case file.

Added Jan. 16, 2014, effective April 1, 2014 (132 So.3d 1114).

Rule 12.007. Access and Review of Related Family Files by Parties

(a) In General. Access to confidential files in related cases shall not be granted except as authorized by Florida Rule of Judicial Administration 2.420.

(b) Confidentiality of Address. When a petitioner for domestic violence injunction requests that his or her address be kept confidential pursuant to section 741.30, Florida Statutes, this information is exempt from the public records provisions of section 119.07(1), Florida Statutes and article I, section 24(a), Florida Constitution, and is a confidential court record under Rule of Judicial Administration 2.420(d). Persons with authorized access to confidential information shall develop methods to ensure that the address remains confidential as provided by law.

(c) Disclosure Prohibited. Disclosure by parties of confidential information and documents contained in court files for related family cases, except in accordance with applicable state and federal confidentiality statutes, is prohibited.

Added Jan. 16, 2014, effective April 1, 2014 (132 So.3d 1114).

Rule 12.010. Scope, Purpose, and Title

(a) Scope.

(1) These rules apply to all actions concerning family matters, including injunctions for protection against domestic, repeat, dating, and sexual violence, and stalking, except as otherwise provided by the Florida Rules of Juvenile Procedure or the Florida Probate Rules. "Family matters," "family law matters," or "family law cases" as used within these rules include, but are not limited to, matters arising from dissolution of marriage, annulment, support unconnected with dissolution of marriage, paternity, child support, an action involving a parenting plan for a minor child or children (except as otherwise provided by the Florida Rules of Juvenile Procedure), proceedings for temporary or concurrent custody of minor children by extended family, adoption, proceedings for emancipation of a minor, declaratory judgment actions related to premarital, marital, or postmarital agreements (except as otherwise provided, when applicable, by the Florida Probate Rules), injunctions for protection against domestic, repeat, dating, and sexual violence, and stalking, and all proceedings for modification, enforcement, and civil contempt of these actions.

(2) The form, content, procedure, and time for pleading in all special statutory proceedings shall be as prescribed by the statutes governing the proceeding unless these rules or the Florida Rules of Civil Procedure, where applicable, specifically provide to the contrary. All actions governed by these rules shall also be governed by the Florida Evidence Code, which shall govern in cases where a conflict with these rules may occur.

(b) Purpose.

(1) These rules are intended to facilitate access to the court and to provide procedural fairness to all parties, to save time and expense through active case management, setting timetables, and the use of alternatives to litigation, and to enable the court to coordinate related cases and proceedings to avoid multiple appearances by the same parties on the same or similar issues and to avoid inconsistent court orders.

(2) Nothing shall prohibit any intake personnel in family law divisions from assisting in the preparation of documents or forms to be filed in any action under these rules.

(c) Title. These rules shall be known as the Florida Family Law Rules of Procedure and abbreviated as Fla. Fam. L. R. P.

Amended June 2, 2005 (905 So.2d 865); Oct. 16, 2008 (995 So.2d 445); Dec. 11, 2008 (997 So.2d 401); Oct. 6, 2011 (75 So.3d 203); July 12, 2012, effective Oct. 1, 2012 (95 So.3d 126); Oct. 18, 2012, effective Dec. 1, 2012, April 1, 2013, Oct. 1, 2013 (102 So.3d 451).

Rule 12.012. Minimization of Sensitive Information

Every pleading or other document filed with the court shall comply with Florida Rule of Judicial Administration 2.425, Minimization of the Filing of Sensitive Information.

Added Dec. 18, 2014, effective Jan. 1, 2015 (154 So.3d 301).

Rule 12.015. Family Law Forms

(a) Forms Adopted as Rules. The forms listed in this rule shall be adopted by the rulemaking process in Fla. R. Jud. Admin. 2.140. The Family Law Rules Committee of The Florida Bar shall propose amendments to these forms and any associated instructions. These forms shall be designated "Florida Family Law

Rules of Procedure Forms." Forms coming under this provision are:

(1) 12.900(a), Disclosure From Nonlawyer;

(2) 12.900(b), Notice of Limited Appearance;

(3) 12.900(c), Consent to Limited Appearance by Attorney;

(4) 12.900(d), Termination of Limited Appearance;

(5) 12.900(e), Acknowledgment of Assistance by Attorney;

(6) 12.900(f), Signature Block for Attorney Making Limited Appearance;

(7) 12.900(g), Agreement Limiting Representation;

(8) 12.900(h), Notice of Related Cases;

(9) 12.901(a), Petition for Simplified Dissolution of Marriage;

(10) 12.902(b), Family Law Financial Affidavit (Short Form);

(11) 12.902(c), Family Law Financial Affidavit;

(12) 12.902(e), Child Support Guidelines Worksheet;

(13) 12.902(f)(3), Marital Settlement Agreement for Simplified Dissolution of Marriage;

(14) 12.910(a), Summons: Personal Service on an Individual;

(15) 12.913(b), Affidavit of Diligent Search and Inquiry;

(16) 12.913(c), Affidavit of Diligent Search;

(17) 12.920(a), Motion for Referral to General Magistrate;

(18) 12.920(b), Order of Referral to General Magistrate;

(19) 12.920(c), Notice of Hearing Before General Magistrate;

(20) 12.928, Cover Sheet for Family Court Cases;

(21) 12.930(a), Notice of Service of Standard Family Law Interrogatories;

(22) 12.930(b), Standard Family Law Interrogatories for Original or Enforcement Proceedings;

(23) 12.930(c), Standard Family Law Interrogatories for Modification Proceedings;

(24) 12.932, Certificate of Compliance with Mandatory Disclosure;

(25) 12.984, Response by Parenting Coordinator;

(26) 12.990(a), Final Judgment of Simplified Dissolution of Marriage;

(27) 12.996(a), Income Deduction Order;

(28) 12.996(b), Notice to Payor;

(29) 12.996(c), Notice of Filing Return Receipt; and

(30) 12.996(d), Florida Addendum to Income Withholding Order; and

(31) 12.998, Order of Referral to Parenting Coordinator.

(b) Other Family Law Forms. All additional Supreme Court approved forms shall be adopted by opinion of the Supreme Court of Florida and outside of the rulemaking procedures required by rule 2.140. These forms shall be designated "Florida Supreme Court Approved Family Law Forms."

Added Sept. 21, 2000 (810 So.2d 1). Amended Sept. 15, 2004 (883 So.2d 1285); Sept. 30, 2004, effective Oct. 1, 2004 (887 So.2d 1090); Oct. 16, 2008, effective Jan. 1, 2009 (995 So.2d 407); Oct. 15, 2009 (30 So.3d 477); Jan. 28, 2010 (27 So.3d 650); March 4, 2010 (39 So.3d 227); June 28, 2012, (94 So.3d 558).

Commentary

2000 Adoption. To help the many people in family law court cases who do not have attorneys to represent them (pro se litigants), the Florida Supreme Court added simplified forms and directions to the Florida Family Law Rules of Procedure when adopting the rules in 1995. These forms initially had been adopted by the Court in *In re Family Law Rules of Procedure*, 663 So. 2d 1049 (Fla. 1995); *In re Petition for Approval of Forms Pursuant to Rule 10–1.1(b) of the Rules Regulating the Florida Bar—Stepparent Adoption Forms*, 613 So. 2d 900 (Fla. 1992), and *Rules Regulating The Florida Bar—Approval of Forms*, 581 So. 2d 902 (Fla. 1991).

In 1997, in an effort to fulfill the spirit of the Court's directives to simplify the process of litigation in family law matters, the Family Court Steering Committee completely revised the existing forms and added new forms and instructions. The rules and forms then constituted more than 500 pages.

Subdivision (b) of this rule was adopted in recognition that the forms would require continuous updating and that the rulemaking process was too cumbersome for such an undertaking.

2009 Amendment. In 2009, Subdivision (a)(20) was adopted to require the filing of a Cover Sheet for Family Court Cases, Form 12.928, in every proceeding to which the Florida Family Law Rules of Procedure apply and to require the Family Law Rules Committee to be responsible for proposing amendments as necessary.

Rule 12.020. Applicability of Florida Rules of Civil Procedure

The Florida Rules of Civil Procedure are applicable in all family law matters except as otherwise provided in these rules. These rules shall govern in cases where a conflict with the Florida Rules of Civil Procedure may occur. Whenever the Florida Rules of Civil Procedure apply to family matters, the use of the words plaintiff, defendant, and complaint within the context of the civil rules shall be interchangeable, where appropriate, with the words, petitioner, respondent, and petition, respectively.

Commentary

1995 Adoption. To avoid confusion among members of the Bar who practice in both family law and civil law areas, it is intended that as much uniformity as possible be maintained between the Florida Family Law Rules of Procedure and the Florida Rules of Civil Procedure. To assist in this effort, the Florida Supreme Court determined that the Florida Rules of Civil Procedure were to apply except as set forth herein. Exceptions and additions to the Florida Rules of Civil Procedure are contained in Florida Family Law Rules of Procedure that are numbered to correspond to their civil rule counterparts. For example, exceptions to Florida Rule of Civil Procedure 1.080 are contained in Florida Family Law Rule of Procedure 12.080.

Rule 12.025. Applicability of Rules of Judicial Administration

(a) Electronic Filing. Florida Rules of Judicial Administration 2.520 and 2.525 are applicable in all family law matters except as otherwise provided in these rules.

(b) Exceptions. Any document filed pursuant to any proceeding under Chapter 63, Florida Statutes, which may be relied upon by the court to terminate parental rights, including consent for adoption or affidavit of nonpaternity, shall be exempt from the requirements of Rule of Judicial Administration 2.525(c).

Added Oct. 18, 2012, effective Dec. 1, 2012, April 1, 2013, Oct. 1, 2013 (102 So.3d 451).

Rule 12.030. Nonverification of Pleadings

Verification of pleadings shall be governed by Florida Rule of Civil Procedure 1.030.

Rule 12.040. Attorneys

(a) Limited Appearance. An attorney of record for a party, in a family law matter governed by these rules, shall be the attorney of record throughout the same family law matter, unless at the time of appearance the attorney files a notice, signed by the party, specifically limiting the attorney's appearance only to the particular proceeding or matter in which the attorney appears.

(b) Withdrawal or Limiting Appearance.

(1) Prior to the completion of a family law matter or prior to the completion of a limited appearance, an attorney of record, with approval of the court, may withdraw or partially withdraw, thereby limiting the scope of the attorney's original appearance to a particular proceeding or matter. A motion setting forth the reasons must be filed with the court and served upon the client and interested persons.

(2) The attorney shall remain attorney of record until such time as the court enters an order, except as set forth in subdivision (c) below.

(c) Scope of Representation.

(1) If an attorney appears of record for a particular limited proceeding or matter, as provided by this rule, that attorney shall be deemed "of record" for only that particular proceeding or matter. Any notice of limited appearance filed shall include the name, address, e-mail address(es), and telephone number of the attorney and the name, address, and telephone number of the party. If the party designates e-mail address(es) for service on and by that party, the party's e-mail address(es) shall also be included. At the conclusion of such proceeding or matter, the attorney's role terminates without the necessity of leave of court, upon the attorney filing a notice of completion of limited appearance. The notice, which shall be titled "Termination of Limited Appearance," shall include the names and last known addresses of the person(s) represented by the withdrawing attorney.

(2) An attorney for the State's Title IV–D child support enforcement agency who appears in a family law matter governed by these rules shall file a notice informing the recipient of Title IV–D services and other parties to the case that the IV–D attorney represents only the Title IV–D agency and not the recipient of IV–D services. The notice must state that the IV–D attorney may only address issues concerning determination of paternity, and establishment, modification, and enforcement of support obligations. The notice may be incorporated into a pleading, motion, or other document filed with the court when the attorney first appears.

(d) Preparation of Pleadings or Other Documents. A party who files a pleading or other document of record pro se with the assistance of an attorney shall certify that the party has received assistance from an attorney in the preparation of the pleading or other document. The name, address, and telephone number of the party shall appear on all pleadings or other documents filed with the court. If the party designates e-mail address(es) for service on and by that party, the party's e-mail address(es) shall also be included.

(e) Notice of Limited Appearance. Any pleading or other document filed by a limited appearance attorney shall state in bold type on the signature page of that pleading or other document: "Attorney for [Petitioner] [Respondent] [attorney's address, e-mail address(es), and telephone number] for the limited purpose of [matter or proceeding]" to be followed by the name of the petitioner or respondent represented and the current address and telephone number of that party. If the party designates e-mail address(es) for service on and by that party, the party's e-mail address(es) shall also be included.

(f) Service. During the attorney's limited appearance, all pleadings or other documents and all notices of hearing shall be served upon both the attorney and the party. If the attorney receives notice of a hearing that is not within the scope of the limited representation, the attorney shall notify the court and the opposing party that the attorney will not attend the court proceeding or hearing because it is outside the scope of the representation.

Added Nov. 13, 2003, effective Jan. 1, 2004 (860 So.2d 394). Amended Oct. 16, 2008, effective Jan. 1, 2009 (995 So.2d 407); Oct. 18, 2012, effective, *nunc pro tunc*, Sept. 1, 2012 (102 So.3d 505); Oct. 18, 2012, effective Dec. 1, 2012, April 1, 2013, Oct. 1, 2013 (102 So.3d 451).

Committee Notes

2012 Amendment. Subdivisions (c), (d), and (e) are amended to provide e-mail addresses in accordance with Florida Rule of Judicial Administration 2.516.

Rule 12.050. When Action Commenced

Commencement of actions shall be governed by Florida Rule of Civil Procedure 1.050.

Rule 12.060. Transfers of Actions

Transfers of actions shall be governed by Florida Rule of Civil Procedure 1.060.

Rule 12.070. Process

(a) Service of Initial Process. Upon the commencement of all family law actions, including proceedings to modify a final judgment, service of process shall be as set forth in Florida Rule of Civil Procedure 1.070.

(b) Summons. The summons, cross-claim summons, and third-party summons in family law matters shall be patterned after Florida Family Law Rules of Procedure Form 12.910(a) and shall specifically contain the following language:

WARNING: Rule 12.285, Florida Family Law Rules of Procedure, requires certain automatic disclosure of documents and information. Failure to comply can result in sanctions, including dismissal or striking of pleadings.

(c) Constructive Service.

(1) For constructive service of process on the legal father in any case or proceeding to establish paternity which would result in termination of the legal father's parental rights, the petitioner shall file an affidavit of diligent search and inquiry that conforms with Florida Family Law Rules of Procedure Form 12.913(c). If the legal father cannot be located, he shall be served with process by publication in the manner provided by chapter 49, Florida Statutes. The notice shall be published in the county where the legal father was last known to have resided. The clerk of the circuit court shall mail a copy of the notice to the legal father at his last known address.

(2) For constructive service of process in any case or proceeding involving parental responsibility, custody, or time-sharing with a minor child, the petitioner shall file an affidavit of diligent search and inquiry that conforms with Florida Family Law Rules of Procedure Form 12.913(c). If the responding party cannot be located, the party shall be served with process by publication in the manner provided by chapter 49, Florida Statutes. The clerk of the circuit court shall mail a copy of the notice to the party's last known address.

(3) For constructive service of process in all other cases, an affidavit of diligent search and inquiry in substantial conformity with Florida Family Law Rules of Procedure Form 12.913(b), must be filed.

(d) Domestic, Repeat, Dating, and Sexual Violence, and Stalking Proceedings. This rule does not govern service of process in proceedings for injunctions for protection against domestic, repeat, dating, and sexual violence, and stalking.

Amended Feb. 26, 1998, eff. March 16, 1998 (713 So.2d 1); Sept. 21, 2000 (810 So.2d 1); June 2, 2005 (905 So.2d 865); July 12, 2007 (962 So.2d 302); July 12, 2012, effective Oct. 1, 2012 (95 So.3d 126); Dec. 18, 2014, effective Jan. 1, 2015 (154 So.3d 301).

Rule 12.071. Constitutional Challenge to State Statute or County or Municipal Charter, Ordinance, or Franchise; Notice by Party

Constitutional challenges to a state statute or county or municipal charter, ordinance, or franchise, and the notice requirements of such challenges shall be governed by Florida Rule of Civil Procedure 1.071.

Adopted Oct. 4, 2012, effective Oct. 4, 2012 (101 So.3d 360).

Rule 12.080. Service of Pleadings and Filing of Documents

(a) Service.

(1) *Family Law Actions Generally.* Service of pleadings and documents after commencement of all family law actions except proceedings for injunctions for protection against domestic, repeat, dating, and sexual violence, and stalking shall be as set forth in Florida Rule of Judicial Administration 2.516, except that rule 2.516 shall also apply to service on the party during the attorney's limited appearance as provided in rule 12.040(f) and be expanded as set forth in subdivisions (b) and (c) to include additional requirements for service of recommended orders and for service on defaulted parties.

(2) *Domestic, Repeat, Dating, and Sexual Violence, and Stalking Actions.* Service of pleadings and documents regarding proceedings for injunctions against domestic, repeat, dating, and sexual violence, and stalking shall be governed by Florida Family Law Rule of Procedure 12.610, where it is in conflict with this rule.

(b) Service and Preparation of Orders and Judgments. A copy of all orders or judgments involving family law matters except proceedings for injunctions for protection against domestic, repeat, dating, and sexual violence, and stalking shall be transmitted by the court or under its direction to all parties at the time of entry of the order or judgment. The court may require that recommended orders, orders, or judgments be prepared by a party. If the court requires that a party prepare the recommended order, order, or judgment, the party shall furnish the court with stamped, addressed envelopes to all parties for service of the recommended order, order, or judgment. The court may also require that any proposed recommended order, order, or judgment that is prepared by a party be furnished to all parties no less than 24 hours before submission to the court of the recommended order, order, or judgment.

(c) Defaulted Parties. No service need be made on parties against whom a default has been entered, except that:

(1) Pleadings asserting new or additional claims against defaulted parties shall be served in the manner provided for service of summons contained in Florida Rule of Civil Procedure 1.070.

(2) Notice of final hearings or trials and court orders shall be served on defaulted parties in the manner provided for service of pleadings and documents contained in Florida Rule of Judicial Administration 2.516.

(3) Final judgments shall be served on defaulted parties as set forth in Florida Rule of Judicial Administration 2.516(h).

Amended Feb. 26, 1998, effective March 16, 1998 (713 So.2d 1); Oct. 29, 1998, effective Feb. 1, 1999 (723 So.2d 208); June 2, 2005 (905 So.2d 865); Oct. 18, 2012, effective, *nunc pro tunc,* Sept. 1, 2012 (102 So.3d 505); July 12, 2012, effective Oct. 1, 2012 (95 So.3d 126); Oct. 18, 2012, effective Dec. 1, 2012, April 1, 2013, Oct. 1, 2013 (102 So.3d 451).

Commentary

1995 Adoption. This rule provides that the procedure for service shall be as set forth in Florida Rule of Civil Procedure 1.080 with the following exceptions or additions to that rule. First, subdivision (b) corresponds to and replaces subdivision (h)(1) of rule 1.080 and expands the rule to include recommended orders. Second, this rule expands items that must be served on defaulted parties to ensure that defaulted parties are at least minimally advised of the progress of the proceedings. This rule is not intended to require the furnishing of a proposed recommended order, proposed order, or proposed final judgment to a defaulted party.

Committee Notes

2012 Amendment. Subdivision (a)(1) is amended to provide for service on the party during the attorney's limited appearance. Subdivision (a)(1), (c)(2), and (c)(3) are amended to provide for service in accordance with Florida Rule of Judicial Administration 2.516.

Rule 12.090. Time

Computation of time shall be governed by Florida Rule of Judicial Administration 2.514. Other aspects of time shall be governed by Florida Rules of Civil Procedure 1.090(b)–(d).

Amended July 12, 2012, effective Oct. 1, 2012 (95 So.3d 96); Oct. 18, 2012, effective, *nunc pro tunc,* Sept. 1, 2012 (102 So.3d 505).

Committee Notes

2012 Amendment. The rule is amended to treat e-mail service as service by mail for the computation of time in accordance with Florida Rule of Judicial Administration 2.516(b)(1)(D)(iii).

Rule 12.100. Pleadings and Motions

Pleadings and motions shall be governed by Florida Rule of Civil Procedure 1.100, except that

(a) the party opening or reopening a case under these rules shall file with the clerk of the circuit court Florida Family Law Rules of Procedure Form 12.928, Cover Sheet for Family Court Cases; and

(b) the requirement in rule 1.100(c)(3) that parties file a final disposition form with the clerk if the action is settled without a court order or judgment being entered or if the action is dismissed by the parties, shall not apply to proceedings governed by these rules.

Amended June 3, 2009 (15 So.3d 558); Oct. 15, 2009 (30 So.3d 477).

Commentary

1995 Adoption. This rule provides that pleadings and motions are to be governed by Florida Rule of Civil Procedure 1.100. The cover sheets and disposition forms described in that rule shall be the same cover sheets and disposition forms used in family law proceedings.

Rule 12.105. Simplified Dissolution Procedure

(a) Requirements for Use. The parties to the dissolution may file a petition for simplified dissolution if they certify under oath that

(1) the parties do not have any minor or dependent children together, the wife does not have any minor or dependent children who were born during the marriage, and the wife is not now pregnant;

(2) the parties have made a satisfactory division of their property and have agreed as to payment of their joint obligations; and

(3) the other facts set forth in Florida Family Law Rules of Procedure Form 12.901(a) (Petition for Simplified Dissolution of Marriage) are true.

(b) Consideration by Court. The clerk shall submit the petition to the court. The court shall consider the cause expeditiously. The parties shall appear before the court in every case and, if the court so directs, testify. The court, after examination of the petition and personal appearance of the parties, shall enter a judgment granting the dissolution (Florida Family Law Rules of Procedure Form 12.990(a)) if the requirements of this rule have been established and there has been compliance with the waiting period required by statute.

(c) Final Judgment. Upon the entry of the judgment, the clerk shall furnish to each party a certified copy of the final judgment of dissolution, which shall be in substantially the form provided in Florida Family Law Rules of Procedure Form 12.990(a).

(d) Forms. The clerk or family law intake personnel shall provide forms for the parties whose circumstances meet the requirements of this rule and shall assist in the preparation of the petition for dissolution and other papers to be filed in the action.

Amended Sept. 21, 2000 (810 So.2d 1); Nov. 3, 2011, effective, *nunc pro tunc*, Oct. 1, 2011 (78 So.3d 1045).

Commentary

1995 Adoption. This rule was previously contained in Florida Rule of Civil Procedure 1.611, which included several unrelated issues. Those issues are now governed by separate family law rules for automatic disclosure, central governmental depository, and this rule for simplified dissolution procedure. Under this rule, the parties must file a financial affidavit (Florida Family Law Rules of Procedure Form 12.902(b) or 12.902(c)), depending on their income and expenses) and a marital settlement agreement (Florida Family Law Rules of Procedure Form 12.902(f)(3)).

Rule 12.110. General Rules of Pleading

The general rules of pleading in Florida Rule of Civil Procedure 1.110 shall apply to these proceedings except that proceedings to modify a final judgment in a family law matter shall be initiated only pursuant to rule 1.110(h) and not by motion.

Commentary

1995 Adoption. This rule clarifies that final judgment modifications must be initiated pursuant to a supplemental petition as set forth in rule 1.110(h), rather than through a motion. Rule 1.110(h) is to be interpreted to require service of process on a supplemental petition as set forth in Florida Family Law Rule of Procedure 12.070.

Rule 12.120. Pleading Special Matters

Pleading of special matters shall be governed by Florida Rule of Civil Procedure 1.120.

Rule 12.130. Documents Supporting Action or Defense

(a) Documents Attached. If it is essential to state a cause of action, a copy of the bonds, notes, bills of exchange, contracts, accounts, or other documents or the relevant portions of the documents shall be incorporated in or attached to the pleadings.

(b) Part for All Purposes. Any exhibit attached to a pleading shall be considered part of the pleading. Statements in a pleading may be adopted by reference in a different part of the same pleading, in another pleading, or in any motion.

(c) Protection of Account and Personal Identifying Numbers. Any reference in any pleading or exhibit filed with the court to account numbers, social security numbers, employee identification numbers, driver's license numbers, passport numbers, or other personal identifying information shall be presented as provided in Florida Rule of Judicial Administration 2.425.

Amended Nov. 3, 2011, effective, *nunc pro tunc*, Oct. 1, 2011 (78 So.3d 1045).

Rule 12.140. Defenses

Defenses shall be governed by Florida Rule of Civil Procedure 1.140.

Rule 12.150. Sham Pleadings

Sham Pleadings shall be governed by Florida Rule of Civil Procedure 1.150.

Rule 12.160. Motions

Motions shall be governed by Florida Rule of Civil Procedure 1.160.

Rule 12.170. Counterclaims and Crossclaims

Counterclaims and crossclaims shall be governed by Florida Rule of Civil Procedure 1.170, except that service of a crossclaim on a party who has appeared in the action, as provided in rule 1.170(g), shall be made pursuant to Florida Rule of Judicial Administration 2.516(b).

Amended Oct. 29, 1998, effective Feb. 1, 1999 (723 So.2d 208); Oct. 18, 2012, effective, *nunc pro tunc*, Sept. 1, 2012 (102 So.3d 505).

Committee Notes

2012 Amendment. This rule is amended to provide for service in accordance with Florida Rule of Judicial Administration 2.516.

Rule 12.180. Third–Party Practice

Third-party practice shall be governed by Florida Rule of Civil Procedure 1.180.

Rule 12.190. Amended and Supplemental Pleadings

Amended and supplemental pleadings shall be governed by Florida Rule of Civil Procedure 1.190.

Rule 12.200. Case Management and Pretrial Conferences

(a) Case Management Conference.

(1) *Family Law Proceedings, Generally.* A case management conference may be ordered by the court at any time on the court's initiative. A party may

request a case management conference 30 days after service of a petition or complaint. At such a conference the court may:

(A) schedule or reschedule the service of motions, pleadings, and other documents;

(B) set or reset the time of trials, subject to rule 12.440;

(C) coordinate the progress of the action if complex litigation factors are present;

(D) limit, schedule, order, or expedite discovery;

(E) schedule disclosure of expert witnesses and the discovery of facts known and opinions held by such experts;

(F) schedule or hear motions related to admission or exclusion of evidence;

(G) pursue the possibilities of settlement;

(H) require filing of preliminary stipulations if issues can be narrowed;

(I) refer issues to a magistrate for findings of fact, if consent is obtained as provided in rules 12.490 and 12.492 and if no significant history of domestic, repeat, dating, or sexual violence, or stalking that would compromise the process is involved in the case;

(J) refer the parties to mediation if no significant history of domestic, repeat, dating, or sexual violence, or stalking that would compromise the mediation process is involved in the case and consider allocation of expenses related to the referral; or refer the parties to counseling if no significant history of domestic, repeat, dating, or sexual violence or stalking that would compromise the process is involved in the case and consider allocation of expenses related to the referral;

(K) coordinate voluntary binding arbitration consistent with Florida law if no significant history of domestic, repeat, dating, or sexual violence or stalking that would compromise the process is involved in the case;

(L) appoint court experts and allocate the expenses for the appointments;

(M) refer the cause for a parenting plan recommendation, social investigation and study, home study, or psychological evaluation and allocate the initial expense for that study;

(N) appoint an attorney or guardian ad litem for a minor child or children if required and allocate the expense of the appointment;

(O) schedule other conferences or determine other matters that may aid in the disposition of the action; and

(P) consider any agreements, objections, or form of production of electronically stored information.

(2) *Adoption Proceedings.* A case management conference shall be ordered by the court within 60 days of the filing of a petition when

(A) there is a request for a waiver of consent to a termination of parental rights of any person required to consent by section 63.062, Florida Statutes;

(B) notice of the hearing on the petition to terminate parental rights pending adoption is not being afforded a person whose consent is required but who has not consented;

(C) there is an objection to venue, which was made after the waiver of venue was signed;

(D) an intermediary, attorney, or agency is seeking fees, costs, or other expenses in excess of those provided under section 63.097 or 63.212(5), Florida Statutes;

(E) an affidavit of diligent search and inquiry is filed in lieu of personal service under section 63.088(4), Florida Statutes; or

(F) the court is otherwise aware that any person having standing objects to the termination of parental rights pending adoption.

(b) Pretrial Conference. After the action is at issue the court itself may or shall on the timely motion of any party require the parties to appear for a conference to consider and determine:

(1) proposed stipulations and the simplification of the issues;

(2) the necessity or desirability of amendments to the pleadings;

(3) the possibility of obtaining admissions of fact and of documents that will avoid unnecessary proof;

(4) the limitation of the number of expert witnesses; and

(5) any matters permitted under subdivision (a) of this rule.

(c) Notice. Reasonable notice shall be given for a case management conference, and 20 days' notice shall be given for a pretrial conference. On failure of a party to attend a conference, the court may dismiss the action, strike the pleadings, limit proof or witnesses, or take any other appropriate action. Any documents that the court requires for any conference shall be specified in the order. Orders setting pretrial conferences shall be uniform throughout the territorial jurisdiction of the court.

(d) Case Management and Pretrial Order. The court shall make an order reciting the action taken at a conference and any stipulations made. The order shall control the subsequent course of the action unless modified to prevent injustice.

Amended Feb. 26, 1998, effective March 16, 1998 (713 So.2d 1); May 30, 2002 (824 So.2d 95); Oct. 3, 2002 (833 So.2d 682); July 10, 2003 (853 So.2d 303); Sept. 30, 2004, effective Oct. 1, 2004 (887 So.2d 1090); June 2, 2005 (905 So.2d 865); Oct. 16, 2008 (995 So.2d 445); July 12, 2012, effective Oct. 1, 2012 (95 So.3d 126); Oct. 18, 2012, effective Dec. 1, 2012, April 1, 2013, Oct. 1, 2013 (102 So.3d 451); Dec. 18, 2014, effective Jan. 1, 2015 (154 So.3d 301).

Commentary

1995 Adoption. This rule addresses issues raised by decisions such as *Dralus v. Dralus*, 627 So. 2d 505 (Fla. 2d DCA 1993); *Wrona v. Wrona*, 592 So. 2d 694 (Fla. 2d DCA 1991); and *Katz v. Katz*, 505 So. 2d 25 (Fla. 4th DCA 1987), regarding the cost of marital litigation. This rule provides an orderly method for the just, speedy, and inexpensive determination of issues and promotes amicable resolution of disputes.

This rule replaces and substantially expands Florida Rule of Civil Procedure 1.200 as it pertained to family law matters. Under this rule, a court may convene a case management conference at any time and a party may request a case management conference 30 days after service of a petition or complaint. The court may consider the following additional items at the conference: motions related to admission or exclusion of evidence, referral of issues to a master if consent is obtained pursuant to the rules, referral of the parties to mediation, referral of the parties to counseling, coordination of voluntary binding arbitration, appointment of court experts, referral of the cause for a home study psychological evaluation, and appointment of an attorney or guardian ad litem for a minor child.

Committee Note

1997 Amendment. In *In re Adoption of Baby E.A.W.*, 658 So. 2d 961 (Fla. 1995), and other cases involving protracted adoption litigation, it becomes clear that the earlier the issue of notice is decided by the court, the earlier the balance of the issues can be litigated. Because both parents' constitutional standing and guarantees of due process require notice and an opportunity to be heard, this rule amendment will help solve the problems of adoption litigation lasting until a child's third, fourth, or even fifth birthday. Furthermore, this rule will encourage both parents to be more candid with intermediaries and attorneys involved in the adoption process.

In *E.A.W.*, 658 So. 2d at 979, Justice Kogan, concurring in part and dissenting in part, stated: "I personally urge the Family Law Rules Committee . . . to study possible methods of expediting review of disputes between biological and adoptive parents." This rule expedites resolution of preliminary matters concerning due process in difficult adoption disputes. This rule also mandates early consideration of the child's rights to due process at early stages of adoption litigation.

Noncompliance with subdivision (a)(2) of this rule shall not invalidate an otherwise valid adoption.

Rule 12.201. Complex Litigation

Florida Rule of Civil Procedure 1.201 shall not apply in proceedings governed by these rules.

Added June 3, 2009 (15 So.3d 558).

Rule 12.210. Parties

Parties to an action filed under the Florida Family Law Rules of Procedure shall be governed by Florida Rule of Civil Procedure 1.210, except that rule 1.210 shall not be read to require that a child is an indispensable party for a dissolution of marriage or action involving a parenting plan for a minor child or children.

Amended Oct. 16, 2008 (995 So.2d 445).

Rule 12.230. Interventions

Interventions shall be governed by Florida Rule of Civil Procedure 1.230.

Rule 12.240. Interpleader

Interpleaders shall be governed by Florida Rule of Civil Procedure 1.240.

Rule 12.250. Misjoinder and Nonjoinder of Parties

Misjoinder and nonjoinder of parties shall be governed by Florida Rule of Civil Procedure 1.250.

Rule 12.260. Survivor; Substitution of Parties

Survivors and the substitution of parties shall be governed by Florida Rule of Civil Procedure 1.260.

Rule 12.270. Consolidation; Separate Trials

Consolidation or separation of trials shall be governed by Florida Rule of Civil Procedure 1.270.

Rule 12.271. Confidentiality of Related Family Hearings

(a) Confidentiality of Coordinated or Joint Hearings. When related family cases are coordinated or joint hearings ordered, any hearings or proceedings involving more than one related family case are subject to the applicable state and federal confidentiality statutes pertaining to each case as if heard separately.

(b) No Waiver. The confidentiality of a case or issue is not waived by coordination or a joint hearing.

Added Jan. 16, 2014, effective April 1, 2014 (132 So.3d 1114).

Rule 12.280. General Provisions Governing Discovery

Florida Rule of Civil Procedure 1.280 shall govern general provisions concerning discovery in family law matters with the following exceptions:

(a) Redaction of Personal Information. All filings of discovery information shall comply with Florida Rule of Judicial Administration 2.425. The court shall have authority to impose sanctions for violation of this rule.

(b) Supplementing of Responses. A party is under a duty to amend a prior response or disclosure if the party:

(1) obtains information or otherwise determines that the prior response or disclosure was incorrect when made; or

(2) obtains information or otherwise determines that the prior response or disclosure, although correct when made, is no longer materially true or complete.

(c) Time for Serving Supplemental Responses. Any supplemental response served pursuant to this rule shall be served as soon as possible after discovery of the incorrect information or change, but in no case shall the supplemental response be served later than 24 hours before any applicable hearing absent a showing of good cause.

(d) Documents Considered Confidential. A determination as to the confidentiality of a court record shall be made in accordance with Florida Rule of Judicial Administration 2.420.

(e) Sealing of Records. Records found to be confidential under Florida Rule of Judicial Administration 2.420 shall be sealed on request of a party.

Amended Dec. 21, 1995, effective Jan. 1, 1996 (663 So.2d 1315); July 10, 2003, effective Jan. 1, 2004 (853 So.2d 303); Sept. 30, 2010 (55 So.3d 381); Nov. 3, 2011, effective, *nunc pro tunc*, Oct. 1, 2011 (78 So.3d 1045).

Commentary

1995 Adoption. Florida Rule of Civil Procedure 1.280 is to govern the general discovery provisions in family law matters with the exceptions set forth above. Subdivision (a) of this rule alters rule 1.280(e) by placing a duty on parties in family law matters to supplement responses. Under rule 1.280(e), no supplemental response is required. Subdivisions (b), (c), and (d) of this rule are in addition to the general requirements of rule 1.280 and have no counterparts in the Rules of Civil Procedure. Subdivisions (c) and (d) have been implemented in recognition of the fact that family law cases often involve sensitive information that should be deemed confidential under Florida Rule of Judicial Administration 2.051. For instance, financial records filed may contain information regarding a family business, which, if public, could provide competitors with an advantage and adversely affect the family business.

Rule 12.281. Inadvertent Disclosure of Privileged Materials

Inadvertent disclosure of privileged materials shall be governed by Florida Rule of Civil Procedure 1.285.

Adopted Oct. 4, 2012, effective Oct. 4, 2012 (101 So.3d 360).

Rule 12.285. Mandatory Disclosure

(a) Application.

(1) *Scope.* This rule shall apply to all proceedings within the scope of these rules except proceedings involving adoption, simplified dissolution, enforcement, contempt, injunctions for protection against domestic, repeat, dating, or sexual violence, or stalking, and uncontested dissolutions when the respondent is served by publication and does not file an answer. Additionally, no financial affidavit or other documents shall be required under this rule from a party seeking attorneys' fees, suit money, or costs, if the basis for the request is solely under section 57.105, Florida Statutes, or any successor statute. Except for the provisions as to financial affidavits and child support guidelines worksheets, any portion of this rule may be modified by order of the court or agreement of the parties.

(2) *Original and Duplicate Copies.* Unless otherwise agreed by the parties or ordered by the court, copies of documents required under this rule may be produced in lieu of originals. Originals, when available, shall be produced for inspection upon request. Parties shall not be required to serve duplicates of documents previously served.

(3) *Documents Not to be Filed with Court; Sanctions.*

(A) Except for the financial affidavit and child support guidelines worksheet, no documents produced under this rule shall be filed in the court file without first obtaining a court order.

(B) References to account numbers and personal identifying information to be filed in the court file shall be governed by Florida Rule of Judicial Administration 2.425.

(C) Sanctions shall be governed by Florida Rule of Civil Procedure 1.280(f).

(b) Time for Production of Documents.

(1) *Temporary Financial Hearings.* Any document required under this rule in any temporary financial relief proceeding shall be served on the other party for inspection and copying as follows.

(A) The party seeking relief shall serve the required documents on the other party with the notice of temporary financial hearing, unless the documents have been served under subdivision (b)(2) of this rule.

(B) The responding party shall serve the required documents on the party seeking relief on or before 5:00 p.m., 2 business days before the day of the temporary financial hearing if served by delivery or 7 days before the day of the temporary financial hearing if served by mail or e-mail, unless the documents have been received previously by the party seeking relief under subdivision (b)(2) of this rule. A responding party shall be given no less than 12 days to serve the documents required under this rule, unless otherwise ordered by the court. If the 45–day period for exchange of documents provided for in subdivision (b)(2) of this rule will occur before the expiration of the 12 days, the provisions of subdivision (b)(2) control.

(2) *Initial and Supplemental Proceedings.* Any document required under this rule for any initial or supplemental proceeding shall be served on the other party for inspection and copying within 45 days of service of the initial pleading on the respondent.

(c) Exemption from Requirement to File and Serve Financial Affidavit. The parties shall not be required to file and serve a financial affidavit under subdivisions (d) and (e) if they are seeking a simplified dissolution of marriage under rule 12.105, they have no minor children, have no support issues, and have filed a written settlement agreement disposing of all financial issues, or if the court lacks jurisdiction to determine any financial issues.

(d) Disclosure Requirements for Temporary Financial Relief. In any proceeding for temporary financial relief heard within 45 days of the service of the initial pleading or within any extension of the time for complying with mandatory disclosure granted by the court or agreed to by the parties, the following documents shall be served on the other party:

(1) A financial affidavit in substantial conformity with Florida Family Law Rules of Procedure Form 12.902(b) if the party's gross annual income is less than $50,000, or Florida Family Law Rules of Procedure Form 12.902(c) if the party's gross annual income is equal to or more than $50,000. This requirement cannot be waived by the parties. The affidavit must also be filed with the court.

(2) All federal and state income tax returns, gift tax returns, and intangible personal property tax returns filed by the party or on the party's behalf for the past year. A party may file a transcript of the tax return as provided by Internal Revenue Service Form 4506 T in lieu of his or her individual federal income tax return for purposes of a temporary hearing.

(3) IRS forms W–2, 1099, and K–1 for the past year, if the income tax return for that year has not been prepared.

(4) Pay stubs or other evidence of earned income for the 3 months prior to service of the financial affidavit.

(e) Parties' Disclosure Requirements for Initial or Supplemental Proceedings. A party shall serve the following documents in any proceeding for an initial or supplemental request for permanent financial relief, including, but not limited to, a request for child support, alimony, equitable distribution of assets or debts, or attorneys' fees, suit money, or costs:

(1) A financial affidavit in substantial conformity with Florida Family Law Rules of Procedure Form 12.902(b) if the party's gross annual income is less than $50,000, or Florida Family Law Rules of Procedure Form 12.902(c) if the party's gross annual income is equal to or more than $50,000, which requirement cannot be waived by the parties. The financial affidavits must also be filed with the court. A party may request, by using the Standard Family Law Interrogatories, or the court on its own motion may order, a party whose gross annual income is less than $50,000 to complete Florida Family Law Rules of Procedure Form 12.902(c).

(2) All federal and state income tax returns, gift tax returns, and intangible personal property tax returns filed by the party or on the party's behalf for the past 3 years.

(3) IRS forms W–2, 1099, and K–1 for the past year, if the income tax return for that year has not been prepared.

(4) Pay stubs or other evidence of earned income for the 3 months prior to service of the financial affidavit.

(5) A statement by the producing party identifying the amount and source of all income received from any source during the 3 months preceding the service of the financial affidavit required by this rule if not reflected on the pay stubs produced.

(6) All loan applications and financial statements prepared or used within the 12 months preceding service of that party's financial affidavit required by this rule, whether for the purpose of obtaining or attempting to obtain credit or for any other purpose.

(7) All deeds within the last 3 years, all promissory notes within the last 12 months, and all present leases, in which the party owns or owned an interest, whether held in the party's name individually, in the party's name jointly with any other person or entity, in the party's name as trustee or guardian for any other person, or in someone else's name on the party's behalf.

(8) All periodic statements from the last 3 months for all checking accounts, and from the last 12 months for all other accounts (for example, savings accounts, money market funds, certificates of deposit, etc.), regardless of whether or not the account has been closed, including those held in the party's name individually, in the party's name jointly with any other person or entity, in the party's name as trustee or guardian for any other person, or in someone else's name on the party's behalf.

(9) All brokerage account statements in which either party to this action held within the last 12 months or holds an interest including those held in the party's name individually, in the party's name jointly with any person or entity, in the party's name as trustee or guardian for any other person, or in someone else's name on the party's behalf.

(10) The most recent statement for any profit sharing, retirement, deferred compensation, or pension plan (for example, IRA, 401(k), 403(b), SEP, KEOGH, or other similar account) in which the party is a participant or alternate payee and the summary plan description for any retirement, profit sharing, or pension plan in which the party is a participant or an alternate payee. (The summary plan description must be furnished to the party on request by the plan administrator as required by 29 U.S.C. § 1024(b)(4).)

(11) The declarations page, the last periodic statement, and the certificate for all life insurance policies

insuring the party's life or the life of the party's spouse, whether group insurance or otherwise, and all current health and dental insurance cards covering either of the parties and/or their dependent children.

(12) Corporate, partnership, and trust tax returns for the last 3 tax years if the party has an ownership or interest in a corporation, partnership, or trust greater than or equal to 30%.

(13) All promissory notes for the last 12 months, all credit card and charge account statements and other records showing the party's indebtedness as of the date of the filing of this action and for the last 3 months, and all present lease agreements, whether owed in the party's name individually, in the party's name jointly with any other person or entity, in the party's name as trustee or guardian for any other person, or in someone else's name on the party's behalf.

(14) All written premarital or marital agreements entered into at any time between the parties to this marriage, whether before or during the marriage. Additionally, in any modification proceeding, each party shall serve on the opposing party all written agreements entered into between them at any time since the order to be modified was entered.

(15) All documents and tangible evidence supporting the producing party's claim that an asset or liability is nonmarital, for enhancement or appreciation of nonmarital property, or for an unequal distribution of marital property. The documents and tangible evidence produced shall be for the time period from the date of acquisition of the asset or debt to the date of production or from the date of the marriage, if based on premarital acquisition.

(16) Any court orders directing a party to pay or receive spousal or child support.

(f) Duty to Supplement Disclosure; Amended Financial Affidavit.

(1) Parties have a continuing duty to supplement documents described in this rule, including financial affidavits, whenever a material change in their financial status occurs.

(2) If an amended financial affidavit or an amendment to a financial affidavit is filed, the amending party shall also serve any subsequently discovered or acquired documents supporting the amendments to the financial affidavit.

(g) Sanctions. Any document to be produced under this rule that is served on the opposing party fewer than 24 hours before a nonfinal hearing or in violation of the court's pretrial order shall not be admissible in evidence at that hearing unless the court finds good cause for the delay. In addition, the court may impose other sanctions authorized by rule 12.380 as may be equitable under the circumstances. The court may also impose sanctions upon the offending lawyer in lieu of imposing sanctions on a party.

(h) Extensions of Time for Complying with Mandatory Disclosure. By agreement of the parties, the time for complying with mandatory disclosure may be extended. Either party may also file, at least 5 days before the due date, a motion to enlarge the time for complying with mandatory disclosure. The court shall grant the request for good cause shown.

(i) Objections to Mandatory Automatic Disclosure. Objections to the mandatory automatic disclosure required by this rule shall be served in writing at least 5 days prior to the due date for the disclosure or the objections shall be deemed waived. The filing of a timely objection, with a notice of hearing on the objection, automatically stays mandatory disclosure for those matters within the scope of the objection. For good cause shown, the court may extend the time for the filing of an objection or permit the filing of an otherwise untimely objection. The court shall impose sanctions for the filing of meritless or frivolous objections.

(j) Certificate of Compliance. All parties subject to automatic mandatory disclosure shall file with the court a certificate of compliance, Florida Family Law Rules of Procedure Form 12.932, identifying with particularity the documents which have been delivered and certifying the date of service of the financial affidavit and documents by that party. The party shall swear or affirm under oath that the disclosure is complete, accurate, and in compliance with this rule, unless the party indicates otherwise, with specificity, in the certificate of compliance.

(k) Child Support Guidelines Worksheet. If the case involves child support, the parties shall file with the court at or prior to a hearing to establish or modify child support a Child Support Guidelines Worksheet in substantial conformity with Florida Family Law Rules of Procedure Form 12.902(e). This requirement cannot be waived by the parties.

(*l*) Place of Production.

(1) Unless otherwise agreed by the parties or ordered by the court, all production required by this rule shall take place in the county where the action is pending and in the office of the attorney for the party receiving production. Unless otherwise agreed by the parties or ordered by the court, if a party does not have an attorney or if the attorney does not have an office in the county where the action is pending, production shall take place in the county where the action is pending at a place designated in writing by the party receiving production, served at least 5 days before the due date for production.

(2) If venue is contested, on motion by a party the court shall designate the place where production will occur pending determination of the venue issue.

(m) Failure of Defaulted Party to Comply. Nothing in this rule shall be deemed to preclude the entry of a final judgment when a party in default has failed to comply with this rule.

Amended Dec. 21, 1995, effective Jan. 1, 1996 (663 So.2d 1315); Feb. 26, 1998, effective March 16, 1998 (713 So.2d 1); Oct. 29, 1998, effective Feb. 1, 1999 (723 So.2d 208); Sept. 21, 2000 (810 So.2d 1); July 10, 2003 (853 So.2d 303); June 2, 2005 (905 So.2d 865); Oct. 6, 2005, effective Jan. 1, 2006 (913 So.2d 545); July 10, 2008 (987 So.2d 65); Nov. 3, 2011, effective, *nunc pro tunc*, Oct. 1, 2011 (78 So.3d 1045); July 12, 2012, effective Oct. 1, 2012 (95 So.3d 126); Oct. 18, 2012, effective, *nunc pro tunc*, Sept. 1, 2012 (102 So.3d 505).

Commentary

1995 Adoption. This rule creates a procedure for automatic financial disclosure in family law cases. By requiring production at an early stage in the proceedings, it is hoped that the expense of litigation will be minimized. *See Dralus v. Dralus*, 627 So. 2d 505 (Fla. 2d DCA 1993); *Wrona v. Wrona*, 592 So. 2d 694 (Fla. 2d DCA 1991); and *Katz v. Katz*, 505 So. 2d 25 (Fla. 4th DCA 1987). A limited number of requirements have been placed upon parties making and spending less than $50,000 annually unless otherwise ordered by the court. In cases where the income or expenses of a party are equal to or exceed $50,000 annually, the requirements are much greater. Except for the provisions as to financial affidavits, other than as set forth in subdivision (k), any portion of this rule may be modified by agreement of the parties or by order of the court. For instance, upon the request of any party or on the court's own motion, the court may order that the parties to the proceeding comply with some or all of the automatic mandatory disclosure provisions of this rule even though the parties do not meet the income requirements set forth in subdivision (d). Additionally, the court may, on the motion of a party or on its own motion, limit the disclosure requirements in this rule should it find good cause for doing so.

Committee Notes

1997 Amendment. Except for the form of financial affidavit used, mandatory disclosure is made the same for all parties subject to the rule, regardless of income. The amount of information required to be disclosed is increased for parties in the under–$50,000 category and decreased for parties in the $50,000–or–over category. The standard family law interrogatories are no longer mandatory, and their answers are designed to be supplemental and not duplicative of information contained in the financial affidavits.

1998 Amendment. If one party has not provided necessary financial information for the other party to complete a child support guidelines worksheet, a good faith estimate should be made.

2005 Amendment. The requirement that a party certify compliance with mandatory disclosure is intended to facilitate full disclosure and prevent a party from alleging that he or she did not know he or she had to provide documents required by this rule. This certification does not relieve the party of the duty to supplement disclosure.

2012 Amendment. Subdivision (b)(1)(B) is amended to provide for e-mail service in accordance with Florida Rule of Judicial Administration 2.516.

Rule 12.287. Financial Affidavits in Enforcement and Contempt Proceedings

Any party in an enforcement or contempt proceeding may serve upon any other party a written request to serve a financial affidavit if the other party's financial circumstances are relevant in the proceeding. The party to whom the request is made shall serve the requested financial affidavit and file a notice of compliance within 10 days after the service of the written request. The court may allow a shorter or longer time. The financial affidavit shall be in substantial conformity with Florida Family Law Rules of Procedure Form 12.902(b) (Short Form), all sections of which shall be completed.

Added Feb. 26, 1998, effective March 16, 1998 (713 So.2d 1). Amended Sept. 21, 2000 (810 So.2d 1); Nov. 3, 2011, effective, *nunc pro tunc*, Oct. 1, 2011 (78 So.3d 1045).

Rule 12.290. Depositions Before Action or Pending Appeal

Depositions before an action or pending an appeal shall be governed by Florida Rule of Civil Procedure 1.290.

Rule 12.300. Persons Before Whom Depositions May Be Taken

Provisions regarding who may take depositions shall be governed by Florida Rule of Civil Procedure 1.300.

Rule 12.310. Depositions Upon Oral Examination

Depositions upon oral examination shall be governed by Florida Rule of Civil Procedure 1.310.

Amended Oct. 16, 2008, effective Jan. 1, 2009 (995 So.2d 407).

Committee Note

2008 Amendment. The provisions of *Fla. R. Civ. P.* 1.310(b)(8) do not alter the requirements of *Rule* 12.407 that a court order must be obtained before deposing a minor child.

Rule 12.320. Depositions Upon Written Questions

Depositions upon written questions shall be governed by Florida Rule of Civil Procedure 1.320.

Rule 12.330. Use of Depositions in Court Proceedings

Use of depositions in court proceedings shall be governed by Florida Rule of Civil Procedure 1.330.

Rule 12.340. Interrogatories to Parties

Interrogatories to parties shall be governed generally by Florida Rule of Civil Procedure 1.340, with the following exceptions.

(a) Service of Interrogatories.

(1) *Initial Interrogatories.* Initial interrogatories to parties in original and enforcement actions shall be those set forth in Florida Family Law Rules of Procedure Form 12.930(b). Parties governed by the mandatory disclosure requirements of rule 12.285 may serve the interrogatories set forth in Florida Family Law Rules of Procedure Form 12.930(b) as set forth in rule 1.340. A party may serve fewer than the interrogatories set forth in Florida Family Law Rules of Procedure Form 12.930(b).

(2) *Modification Interrogatories.* Interrogatories to parties in cases involving modification of a final judgment shall be those set forth in Florida Family Law Rules of Procedure Form 12.930(c). Parties governed by the mandatory disclosure requirements of rule 12.285 may serve the interrogatories set forth in Florida Family Law Rules of Procedure Form 12.930(c) as set forth in rule 1.340. A party may serve fewer than the interrogatories set forth in Florida Family Law Rules of Procedure Form 12.930(c).

(b) Additional Interrogatories. Ten interrogatories, including subparts, may be sent to a party, in addition to the standard interrogatories contained in Florida Family Law Rules of Procedure Form 12.930(b) or Florida Family Law Rules of Procedure Form 12.930(c). A party must obtain permission of the court to send more than 10 additional interrogatories.

(c) Serving of Responses. Parties shall serve responses to interrogatories on the requesting party. Responses shall not be filed with the court unless they are admitted into evidence by the court and are in compliance with Florida Rule of Judicial Administration 2.425. The responding party shall file with the court Florida Family Law Rules of Procedure Form 12.930(d), Notice of Service of Answers to Standard Family Law Interrogatories.

Amended Feb. 26, 1998, effective March 16, 1998 (713 So.2d 1); Sept. 21, 2000 (810 So.2d 1); July 10, 2003, effective Jan. 1, 2004 (853 So.2d 303); Nov. 3, 2011, effective, *nunc pro tunc*, Oct. 1, 2011 (78 So.3d 1045); Oct. 4, 2012 (101 So.3d 360).

Commentary

1995 Adoption. For parties governed under the disclosure requirements of rule 12.285(d) (income or expenses of $50,000 or more), the answers to the interrogatories contained in Form 12.930(b) must be automatically served on the other party. For parties governed under the disclosure requirements of rule 12.285(c) (income and expenses under $50,000), the service of the interrogatories contained in Form 12.930(b) is optional as provided in Florida Rule of Civil Procedure 1.340. Additionally, under this rule, 10 additional interrogatories, including subparts, may be submitted beyond those contained in Florida Family Law Rules of Procedure Form 12.930(b). Leave of court is required to exceed 10 additional interrogatories. The provisions of Florida Rule of Civil Procedure 1.340 are to govern the procedures and scope of the additional interrogatories.

Committee Note

1997 Amendment. The rule was amended to conform to the changes made to rule 12.285, Mandatory Disclosure.

Rule 12.350. Production of Documents and Things and Entry Upon Land for Inspection and Other Purposes

Production of documents and things and entry upon land for inspection and other purposes shall be governed by Florida Rule of Civil Procedure 1.350.

Rule 12.351. Production of Documents and Things Without Deposition

Production of documents and things without deposition shall be governed by Florida Rule of Civil Procedure 1.351, except that a party desiring production under this rule, as provided in rule 1.351(b), shall serve notice as provided in Florida Rule of Judicial Administration 2.516 on every other party of the intent to serve a subpoena under this rule at least 10 days before the subpoena is issued if service is by delivery and 15 days before the subpoena is issued if the service is by mail or e-mail.

Amended Oct. 18, 2012, effective, *nunc pro tunc*, Sept. 1, 2012 (102 So.3d 505).

Committee Notes

2012 Amendment. This rule is amended to provide for service in accordance with Florida Rule of Judicial Administration 2.516.

Rule 12.360. Examination of Persons

Florida Rule of Civil Procedure 1.360 shall govern general provisions concerning the examination of persons in family law matters, except that examinations permitted under rule 1.360(a)(1) may include, but are not limited to, examinations involving physical or mental condition, employability or vocational testing, genetic testing, or any other type of examination related to a matter in controversy.

Commentary

1995 Adoption. This rule expands Florida Rule of Civil Procedure 1.360 to specify common examinations in family law matters, but this rule is not intended to be an exclusive list of allowable examinations. Rule 1.360 should be interpreted to discourage subjecting children to multiple interviews, testing, and evaluations.

Rule 12.363. Evaluation of Minor Child

(a) Appointment of Expert.

(1) The court, on motion of any party or the court's own motion, may appoint an expert for an examination, evaluation, testing, or interview of any minor

child. The parties may agree on the particular expert to be appointed, subject to approval by the court. If the parties have agreed, they shall submit an order including the name, address, telephone number, area of expertise, and professional qualifications of the expert. If there has been a determination of the need for the appointment of an expert and the parties cannot agree on the selection of the expert, the court shall appoint an expert.

(2) After the examination, evaluation, or investigation, any party may file a motion for an additional expert examination, evaluation, interview, testing, or investigation by another expert. The court upon hearing may permit the additional examination, evaluation, testing, or interview only on a showing of good cause and only upon a finding that further examinations, testing, interviews, or evaluations would be in the best interests of the minor child.

(3) Any order entered under this rule shall specify the issues to be addressed by the expert.

(4) Any order entered under this rule may require that all interviews of the child be recorded and the tapes be maintained as part of the expert's file.

(5) The order appointing the expert shall include an initial allocation of responsibility for payment.

(6) A copy of the order of appointment shall be provided immediately to the expert by the court unless otherwise directed by the court. The order shall direct the parties to contact the expert appointed by the court to establish an appointment schedule to facilitate timely completion of the evaluation.

(b) Providing of Reports.

(1) Unless otherwise ordered, the expert shall prepare and provide a written report to each party and the guardian ad litem, if appointed, a reasonable time before any evidentiary hearing on the matter at issue. The expert also shall send written notice to the court that the report has been completed and that a copy of the written report has been provided to each party and the guardian ad litem, if appointed. In any event, the written report shall be prepared and provided no later than 30 days before trial or 75 days from the order of appointment, unless the time is extended by order of the court. The expert shall not send a copy of the report to the court unless the parties and their attorneys have agreed in writing that the report will be considered by the court and filed in the court files as provided in subdivision (e).

(2) On motion of any party, the court may order the expert to produce the expert's complete file to another expert at the initial cost of the requesting party, for review by such expert, who may testify.

(c) Testimony of Other Experts. Any other expert who has treated, tested, interviewed, examined, or evaluated a child may testify only if the court determines that good cause exists to permit the testimony. The fact that no notice of such treatment, testing, interview, examination, or evaluation of a child was given to both parents shall be considered by the court as a basis for preventing such testimony.

(d) Communications with Court by Expert. No expert may communicate with the court without prior notice to the parties, who shall be afforded the opportunity to be present and heard during any such communication between the expert and the court. A request for communication with the court may be informally conveyed by letter or telephone. Further communication with the court, which may be conducted informally, shall be done only with notice to the parties.

(e) Use of Evidence. An expert appointed by the court shall be subject to the same examination as a privately retained expert and the court shall not entertain any presumption in favor of the appointed expert's findings. Any finding or report by an expert appointed by the court may be entered into evidence on the court's own motion or the motion of any party in a manner consistent with the rules of evidence, subject to cross-examination by the parties. Any report filed with the court shall be in compliance with Florida Rule of Judicial Administration 2.425. The report shall not be filed in the court file unless or until it is properly admitted into evidence and considered by the court. The court shall consider whether the report should be sealed as provided by Florida Rule of Judicial Administration 2.420.

(f) Limitation of Scope. This rule shall not apply to parenting coordinators or social investigators.

Added Feb. 26, 1998, effective March 16, 1998 (713 So.2d 1). Amended Oct. 16, 2008 (995 So.2d 445); Sept. 3, 2009 (19 So.3d 950); Nov. 3, 2011, effective, *nunc pro tunc*, Oct. 1, 2011 (78 So.3d 1045); Dec. 18, 2014, effective Jan. 1, 2015 (154 So.3d 301).

Committee Note

1997 Adoption. This rule should be interpreted to discourage subjecting children to multiple interviews, testing, and evaluations, without good cause shown. The court should consider the best interests of the child in permitting evaluations, testing, or interviews of the child. The parties should cooperate in choosing a mental health professional or individual to perform this function to lessen the need for multiple evaluations.

This rule is not intended to prevent additional mental health professionals who have not treated, interviewed, or evaluated the child from testifying concerning review of the data produced pursuant to this rule.

This rule is not intended to prevent a mental health professional who has engaged in long-term treatment of the child from testifying about the minor child.

Rule 12.364. Social Investigations

(a) Applicable to Social Investigations. This rule shall apply to the appointment of an investigator to conduct a social investigation and study under section 61.20, Florida Statutes.

(b) Appointment of Social Investigator. When the issue of time-sharing, parental responsibility, ultimate decision-making, or a parenting plan for a minor child is in controversy, the court, on motion of any party or the court's own motion, may appoint an investigator under section 61.20, Florida Statutes. The parties may agree on the particular investigator to be appointed, subject to approval by the court. If the parties have agreed on the need for a social investigation or the court has determined there is such need, and the parties cannot agree on the selection, the court shall select and appoint an investigator. The social investigator must be qualified as an expert under section 90.702, Florida Statutes, to testify regarding the written study.

(c) Order for Social Investigation. The order for a social investigation shall state whether this is an initial establishment of a parenting plan or a modification of an existing parenting plan. The investigator shall be required to consider the best interests of the child based upon all of factors affecting the welfare and interest of the particular minor child and the circumstances of that family, including, but not limited to the statutory factors set forth in section 61.13, Florida Statutes.

(d) Order Appointing Social Investigator. An order appointing a social investigator shall state that the investigator is being appointed under section 61.20, Florida Statutes, and shall state:

(1) The name, address, and telephone number for each parent.

(2) The name, address, and telephone number of the investigator being appointed.

(3) Any specific issues to be addressed.

(4) An initial allocation of responsibility for payment of the costs for the social investigation. The court may consider taxing the costs at a final hearing.

(5) The order shall direct the parties to contact the investigator appointed by the court to establish an appointment schedule to facilitate timely completion of the investigation. A copy of the order of appointment shall be provided immediately to the investigator by the court, unless otherwise directed by the court.

(e) Written Study with Recommendations. The investigator shall prepare a written study with recommendations regarding a parenting plan, including a written statement of facts found in the social investigation on which the recommendations are based. The written study with recommendations shall be furnished to the court and a copy provided to all parties of record by the investigator at least 30 days before any hearing at which the court is to consider the written study and recommendations, unless otherwise ordered by the court.

(f) Additional Investigation. After the written study is furnished to the court, any party may file a motion for an additional expert examination, evaluation, interview, testing, or investigation. The court upon hearing may order the additional examination, evaluation, testing, or interview of the minor child based on the court finding that the investigation is insufficient and that further examinations, testing, interviews, or evaluations of the minor child would be in the best interests of the minor child.

(g) Production of File. On motion of any party, the court may order the investigator to produce the investigator's complete file to another qualified investigator for review by such investigator, who may render an opinion and testify.

Added Dec. 18, 2014, effective Jan. 1, 2015 (154 So.3d 301).

Rule 12.365. Expert Witnesses

(a) Application. The procedural requirements in this rule shall apply whenever an expert is appointed by the court or retained by a party. This rule applies to all experts including, but not limited to, medical, psychological, social, financial, vocational, and economic experts. Where in conflict, this rule shall supersede Florida Rule of Civil Procedure 1.360.

(b) Communication with Court by Expert. No expert may communicate with the court without prior notice to the parties and their attorneys, who shall be afforded the opportunity to be present and heard during the communication between the expert and the court. A request for communication with the court may be conveyed informally by letter or telephone. Further communication with the court, which may be conducted informally, shall be done only with notice to all parties.

(c) Use of Evidence. The court shall not entertain any presumption in favor of a court-appointed expert's opinion. Any opinion by an expert may be entered into evidence on the court's own motion or the motion of any party in a manner consistent with the rules of evidence, subject to cross-examination by the parties.

(d) Evaluation of Minor Child. This rule shall not apply to any evaluation of a minor child under rule 12.363.

Added Oct. 29, 1998, effective Feb. 1, 1999 (723 So.2d 208). Amended Jan. 28, 1999, effective Feb. 1, 1999 (746 So.2d 1073).

Committee Note

1998 Adoption. This rule establishes the procedure to be followed for the use of experts. The District Court of Appeal, Fourth District, has encouraged the use of court-appointed experts to review financial information and reduce the cost of divorce litigation. *Tomaino v. Tomaino*, 629 So. 2d 874 (Fla. 4th DCA 1993). Additionally, section 90.615(1), Florida Statutes, allows the court to call witnesses whom all parties may cross-examine. *See also* Fed. R. Evid. 706 (trial courts have authority to appoint expert witnesses).

Rule 12.370. Requests for Admission

Requests for admission shall be governed by Florida Rule of Civil Procedure 1.370, except that

(a) the request and any response to it must comply with Florida Rule of Judicial Administration 2.425; and

(b) documents attached to the request for admission shall not be filed with the court and shall only be attached to the copy served on the party to whom the request for admissions is directed.

Amended Nov. 3, 2011, effective, *nunc pro tunc*, Oct. 1, 2011 (78 So.3d 1045).

Rule 12.380. Failure to Make Discovery; Sanctions

Florida Rule of Civil Procedure 1.380 shall govern the failure to make discovery in family law matters and related sanctions, with the following additions.

(a) A party may apply for an order compelling discovery in the manner set forth in rule 1.380 for the failure of any person to comply with any discovery request or requirement under the family law rules, including, but not limited to, the failure to comply with rule 12.285.

(b) In the case of rule 1.380(c), the court may defer ruling on the party's motion for sanctions until the conclusion of the matter in controversy.

Amended July 10, 2003, effective Jan. 1, 2004 (853 So.2d 303).

Rule 12.390. Depositions of Expert Witnesses

Depositions of expert witnesses shall be governed by Florida Rule of Civil Procedure 1.390.

Rule 12.400. Confidentiality of Records and Proceedings

(a) Closure of Proceedings or Records. Closure of court proceedings or sealing of records may be ordered by the court only as provided by Florida Rule of Judicial Administration 2.420.

(b) In Camera Inspections. The court shall conduct an in camera inspection of any records sought to be sealed and consider the contents of the records in determining whether they should be sealed.

(c) Conditional Sealing of Financial Information.

(1) The court has the authority to conditionally seal the financial information required by rule 12.285 if it is likely that access to the information would subject a party to abuse, such as the use of the information by third parties for purposes unrelated to government or judicial accountability or to first amendment rights. Any such order sealing the financial information is conditional in that the information shall be disclosed to any person who establishes that disclosure of the information is necessary for government or judicial accountability or has a proper first amendment right to the information.

(2) Notice of conditional sealing shall be as required by Florida Rule of Judicial Administration 2.420(d).

(3) Upon receipt of a motion to reopen conditionally sealed financial information, the court shall schedule a hearing on the motion with notice provided to the movant and parties.

Amended July 10, 2003, effective Jan. 1, 2004 (853 So.2d 303); Oct. 16, 2008, effective Jan. 1, 2009 (995 So.2d 407).

Commentary

1995 Adoption. Judicial proceedings and records should be public except when substantial compelling circumstances, especially the protection of children or of business trade secrets, require otherwise. Family law matters frequently present such circumstances. It is intended that this rule be applied to protect the interests of minor children from offensive testimony and to protect children in a divorce proceeding.

2003 Amendment. The adoption of a procedure for conditional sealing of the financial information does not change the burden of proof for closure of filed records of court proceedings set forth in Barron v. Florida Freedom Newspapers, Inc., 531 So. 2d 113, 118 (Fla. 1988).

Rule 12.407. Testimony and Attendance of Minor Child

No minor child shall be deposed or brought to a deposition, brought to court to appear as a witness or to attend a hearing, or subpoenaed to appear at a hearing without prior order of the court based on good cause shown unless in an emergency situation. This provision shall not apply to uncontested adoption proceedings.

Commentary

1995 Adoption. This rule is intended to afford additional protection to minor children by avoiding any unnecessary involvement of children in family law litigation. While due process considerations prohibit an absolute ban on child testimony, this rule requires that a judge determine whether a child's testimony is necessary and relevant to issues before the court prior to a child being required to testify.

Rule 12.410. Subpoena

Subpoenas shall be governed by Florida Rule of Civil Procedure 1.410, except as follows:

(a) Subpoenas. No subpoena issued under Florida Rule of Civil Procedure 1.410, even if for the purpose of proof of service or nonservice of the subpoena, shall be filed with the court unless in compliance with Florida Rule of Judicial Administration 2.425.

(b) Notice of Issuance of Subpoena. A party issuing a subpoena through an attorney of record or clerk of the court under Florida Rule of Civil Procedure 1.410 shall, on the same day as the subpoena is issued, serve each party to the proceeding with a notice of issuance of subpoena and file this notice with the court. The notice of issuance of subpoena shall identify the person or entity subject to the subpoena, the date the subpoena was issued, and the date and time for appearance or production, and shall recite that all references to account numbers or personal identifying numbers are in compliance with Florida Rule of Judicial Administration 2.425.

(c) Notice to Produce. Any notice to produce issued under Florida Rule of Civil Procedure 1.410 shall comply with Florida Rule of Judicial Administration 2.425.

(d) Production of Evidence at Trial. A party seeking production of evidence at trial, as provided in rule 1.410(c), which would be subject to a subpoena, as provided in rule 1.410(c), may compel such production by serving a notice to produce such evidence on an adverse party as provided in Florida Rule of Judicial Administration 2.516.

Amended Nov. 3, 2011, effective, *nunc pro tunc*, Oct. 1, 2011 (78 So.3d 1045)); Oct. 18, 2012, effective, *nunc pro tunc*, Sept. 1, 2012 (102 So.3d 505).

Committee Note

2008 Amendment. The provisions of Fla. R. Civ. P. 1.410(h) do not alter the requirements of rule 12.407 that a court order must be obtained before a minor child may be subpoenaed to appear at a hearing.

2012 Amendment. This rule is amended to provide for service in accordance with Florida Rule of Judicial Administration 2.516.

Rule 12.420. Dismissal of Actions

Dismissal of actions shall be governed by Florida Rule of Civil Procedure 1.420, with the following two exceptions.

(a) Voluntary Dismissal. Unless otherwise specified in a notice or stipulation, a voluntary dismissal shall be without prejudice and shall not operate as an adjudication on the merits.

(b) Costs. Costs shall be assessed as provided in rule 1.420(d), except that the court shall not require the payment of costs of a previously dismissed claim, which was based upon or included the same claim against the same adverse party as the current action.

Commentary

1995 Adoption. Subdivision (a), which amends Florida Rule of Civil Procedure 1.420(a)(1), was added to eliminate the language of that subdivision which reads “except that a notice of dismissal operates as an adjudication on the merits when served by a plaintiff who has once dismissed in any court an action based on or including the same claim” and to specifically provide to the contrary. Subdivision (b), which amends rule 1.420(d), was added to prevent the discouragement of reconciliation.

Rule 12.430. Demand for Jury Trial; Waiver

Demands for and waivers of jury trial shall be governed by Florida Rule of Civil Procedure 1.430.

Rule 12.431. Trial Jury

Trials by jury shall be governed by Florida Rule of Civil Procedure 1.431.

Rule 12.440. Setting Action for Trial

Florida Rule of Civil Procedure 1.440 shall govern general provisions concerning setting an action for trial in family law matters, with the following exceptions and additions.

(a) Setting for Trial. If the court finds the action ready to be set for trial, it shall enter an order setting the action for trial, fixing a date for trial, and setting a pretrial conference, if necessary. In the event a default has been entered, reasonable notice of not less than 10 days shall be given unless otherwise required by law. In actions in which the damages are not liquidated, the order setting an action for trial shall be served on parties who are in default in accordance with Florida Rule of Judicial Administration 2.516. Trial shall be set within a reasonable time from the service of the notice for trial. At the pretrial conference, the parties should be prepared, consistent with Florida Family Law Rule of Procedure 12.200, to present any matter that will prepare the parties for trial and that can expedite the resolution of the case. The trial court may also direct the parties to reciprocally exchange and file with the court all documents relative to the outcome of the case; a list of all witnesses, all issues to be tried, and all undisposed motions; an estimate of the time needed to try the case; and any other information the court deems appropriate. Any court filings shall be in conformity with Florida Rule of Judicial Administration 2.425. This information should be served and filed no later than 72 hours before the pretrial conference or 30 days before the trial.

(b) Sanctions. The failure to comply with the requirements of the order setting the action for trial shall subject the party or attorney to appropriate court sanctions.

Amended Nov. 3, 2011, effective, *nunc pro tunc*, Oct. 1, 2011 (78 So.3d 1045); Oct. 18, 2012, effective, *nunc pro tunc*, Sept. 1, 2012 (102 So.3d 505).

Commentary

1995 Adoption. This rule amends Florida Rule of Civil Procedure 1.440(c), Setting for Trial, and creates a procedure to facilitate setting an action for trial. Proper pretrial compliance will foster knowledgeable settlement discussion and expedite an orderly trial. The rule also adds a provision for sanctions.

Rule 12.442. Proposals for Settlement

Florida Rule of Civil Procedure 1.442 shall not apply in proceedings governed by these rules.

Adopted Oct. 4, 2012, effective Oct. 4, 2012 (101 So.3d 360).

Rule 12.450. Evidence

Adverse witnesses, the record of excluded evidence, and the filing of evidence shall be governed by Florida Rule of Civil Procedure 1.450.

Rule 12.451. Taking Testimony

(a) Testimony at Hearing or Trial. When testifying at a hearing or trial, a witness must be physically present unless otherwise provided by law or rule of procedure.

(b) Communication Equipment. The court may permit a witness to testify at a hearing or trial by contemporaneous audio or video communication equipment (1) by agreement of the parties or (2) for good cause shown upon written request of a party upon reasonable notice to all other parties. The request and notice must contain the substance of the proposed testimony and an estimate of the length of the proposed testimony. In considering sufficient good cause, the court shall weigh and address in its order the reasons stated for testimony by communication equipment against the potential for prejudice to the objecting party.

(c) Required Equipment. Communication equipment as used in this rule means a conference telephone or other electronic device that permits all those appearing or participating to hear and speak to each other simultaneously and permits all conversations of all parties to be audible to all persons present. Contemporaneous video communication equipment must make the witness visible to all participants during the testimony. For testimony by any of the foregoing means, there must be appropriate safeguards for the court to maintain sufficient control over the equipment and the transmission of the testimony, so that the court may stop the communication to accommodate objection or prevent prejudice.

(d) Oath. Testimony may be taken through communication equipment only if a notary public or other person authorized to administer oaths in the witness's jurisdiction is present with the witness and administers the oath consistent with the laws of that jurisdiction.

(e) Burden of Expense. The cost for the use of the communication equipment is the responsibility of the requesting party unless otherwise ordered by the court.

Added Jan. 22, 2015, effective Jan. 22, 2015 (156 So.3d 493).

Committee Note

2015 Adoption. This rule allows the parties to agree, or one or more parties to request, that the court authorize presentation of witness testimony by contemporaneous video or audio communications equipment. A party seeking to present such testimony over the objection of another party must still satisfy the good-cause standard. In determining whether good cause exists, the trial court may consider such factors as the type and stage of proceeding, the presence or absence of constitutionally protected rights, the importance of the testimony to the resolution of the case, the amount in controversy in the case, the relative cost or inconvenience of requiring the presence of the witness in court, the ability of counsel to use necessary exhibits or demonstrative aids, the limitation (if any) placed on the opportunity for opposing counsel and the finder of fact to observe the witness's demeanor, the potential for unfair surprise, the witness's affiliation with one or more parties, any other factors the court reasonably deems material to weighing the justification the requesting party has offered in support of the request to allow a witness to testify by communications equipment against the potential prejudice to the objecting party. With the advance of technology, the cost and availability of contemporaneous video testimony may be considered by the court in determining whether good cause is established for audio testimony.

Rule 12.460. Continuances

Continuances shall be governed by Florida Rule of Civil Procedure 1.460.

Rule 12.470. Exceptions Unnecessary

Exceptions shall be governed by Florida Rule of Civil Procedure 1.470 except that no exception shall be necessary to an adverse ruling other than as provided in rules 12.490 and 12.492.

Commentary

1995 Adoption. This rule amends subdivision (a) of rule 1.470 as it applies to family law matters to eliminate possible confusion between common law exceptions and exceptions to recommendations of a general master under rule 12.490 or a special master under rule 12.492.

Rule 12.480. Motion for a Directed Verdict

Motions for directed verdict shall be governed by Florida Rule of Civil Procedure 1.480.

Rule 12.481. Verdicts

Verdicts shall be governed by Florida Rule of Civil Procedure 1.481.

Rule 12.490. General Magistrates

(a) General Magistrates. Judges of the circuit court may appoint as many general magistrates from among the members of The Florida Bar in the circuit as the judges find necessary, and the general magistrates shall continue in office until removed by the court. The order making an appointment shall be recorded. Every person appointed as a general magistrate shall take the oath required of officers by the constitution and the oath shall be recorded before the magistrate discharges any duties of that office.

(b) Reference.

(1) No matter shall be heard by a general magistrate without an appropriate order of reference and the consent to the referral of all parties. Consent, as defined in this rule, to a specific referral, once given, cannot be withdrawn without good cause shown before the hearing on the merits of the matter referred. Consent may be express or may be implied in accordance with the requirements of this rule.

(A) A written objection to the referral to a general magistrate must be filed within 10 days of the service of the order of referral.

(B) If the time set for the hearing is less than 10 days after service of the order of referral, the objection must be filed before commencement of the hearing.

(C) If the order of referral is served within the first 20 days after the service of the initial process, the time to file an objection is extended to the time within which to file a responsive pleading.

(D) Failure to file a written objection within the applicable time period is deemed to be consent to the order of referral.

(2) The order of referral shall be in substantial conformity with Florida Family Law Rules of Procedure Form 12.920(b), and shall contain the following language in bold type:

A REFERRAL TO A GENERAL MAGISTRATE REQUIRES THE CONSENT OF ALL PARTIES. YOU ARE ENTITLED TO HAVE THIS MATTER HEARD BEFORE A JUDGE. IF YOU DO NOT WANT TO HAVE THIS MATTER HEARD BEFORE THE GENERAL MAGISTRATE, YOU MUST FILE A WRITTEN OBJECTION TO THE REFERRAL WITHIN 10 DAYS OF THE TIME OF SERVICE OF THIS ORDER. IF THE TIME SET FOR THE HEARING IS LESS THAN 10 DAYS AFTER THE SERVICE OF THIS ORDER, THE OBJECTION MUST BE MADE BEFORE THE HEARING. IF THIS ORDER IS SERVED WITHIN THE FIRST 20 DAYS AFTER SERVICE OF PROCESS, THE TIME TO FILE AN OBJECTION IS EXTENDED TO THE TIME WITHIN WHICH A RESPONSIVE PLEADING IS DUE. FAILURE TO FILE A WRITTEN OBJECTION WITHIN THE APPLICABLE TIME PERIOD IS DEEMED TO BE A CONSENT TO THE REFERRAL.

REVIEW OF THE REPORT AND RECOMMENDATIONS MADE BY THE GENERAL MAGISTRATE SHALL BE BY EXCEPTIONS AS PROVIDED IN RULE 12.490(f), FLA. FAM. L. R. P. A RECORD, WHICH INCLUDES A TRANSCRIPT OF PROCEEDINGS, MAY BE REQUIRED TO SUPPORT THE EXCEPTIONS.

(3) The order of referral shall state with specificity the matter or matters being referred and the name of the specific general magistrate to whom the matter is referred. The order of referral shall also state whether electronic recording or a court reporter is provided by the court, or whether a court reporter, if desired, must be provided by the litigants.

(4) When a reference is made to a general magistrate, any party or the general magistrate may set the action for hearing.

(c) General Powers and Duties. Every general magistrate shall perform all of the duties that pertain to the office according to the practice in chancery and rules of court and under the direction of the court except those duties related to injunctions for protection against domestic, repeat, dating, and sexual violence, and stalking. A general magistrate shall be empowered to administer oaths and conduct hearings, which may include the taking of evidence. All grounds for disqualification of a judge shall apply to general magistrates.

(d) Hearings.

(1) The general magistrate shall assign a time and place for proceedings as soon as reasonably possible after the reference is made and give notice to each of the parties either directly or by directing counsel to file and serve a notice of hearing. If any party fails to appear, the general magistrate may proceed ex parte or may adjourn the proceeding to a future day, giving notice to the absent party of the adjournment. The general magistrate shall proceed with reasonable diligence in every reference and with the least delay practicable. Any party may apply to the court for an order to the general magistrate to speed the proceedings and to make the report and to certify to the court the reason for any delay.

(2) The general magistrate shall take testimony and establish a record which may be by electronic means as provided by Florida Rule of Judicial Administration 2.535(g)(3) or by a court reporter. The parties may not waive this requirement.

(3) The general magistrate shall have authority to examine under oath the parties and all witnesses upon all matters contained in the reference, to require production of all books, documents, writings, vouchers, and other documents applicable to it, and to examine on oath orally all witnesses produced by the parties. The general magistrate may take all actions concerning evidence that can be taken by the circuit court and in the same manner. The general magistrate shall have the same powers as a circuit judge to utilize communications equipment as defined and regulated by Florida Rule of Judicial Administration 2.530.

(4) The notice or order setting the cause for hearing shall be in substantial conformity with Florida

Family Law Rules of Procedure Form 12.920(c) and shall contain the following language in bold type:

SHOULD YOU WISH TO SEEK REVIEW OF THE REPORT AND RECOMMENDATION MADE BY THE GENERAL MAGISTRATE, YOU MUST FILE EXCEPTIONS IN ACCORDANCE WITH RULE 12.490(f), FLA. FAM. L. R. P. YOU WILL BE REQUIRED TO PROVIDE THE COURT WITH A RECORD SUFFICIENT TO SUPPORT YOUR EXCEPTIONS OR YOUR EXCEPTIONS WILL BE DENIED. A RECORD ORDINARILY INCLUDES A WRITTEN TRANSCRIPT OF ALL RELEVANT PROCEEDINGS. THE PERSON SEEKING REVIEW MUST HAVE THE TRANSCRIPT PREPARED IF NECESSARY FOR THE COURT'S REVIEW.

(5) The notice or order setting a matter for hearing shall state whether electronic recording or a court reporter is provided by the court. If the court provides electronic recording, the notice shall also state that any party may provide a court reporter at that party's expense.

(e) General Magistrate's Report. The general magistrate shall file a report that includes findings of fact and conclusions of law, together with recommendations. If a court reporter was present, the report shall contain the name and address of the reporter.

(f) Filing Report; Notice; Exceptions. The general magistrate shall file the report and recommendations and serve copies on all parties. The parties may file exceptions to the report within 10 days from the time it is served on them. Any party may file cross-exceptions within 5 days from the service of the exceptions, provided, however, that the filing of cross-exceptions shall not delay the hearing on the exceptions unless good cause is shown. If no exceptions are filed within that period, the court shall take appropriate action on the report. If exceptions are filed, they shall be heard on reasonable notice by either party or the court.

(g) Record. For the purpose of the hearing on exceptions, a record, substantially in conformity with this rule, shall be provided to the court by the party seeking review if necessary for the court's review.

(1) The record shall consist of the court file, including the transcript of the relevant proceedings before the general magistrate and all depositions and evidence presented to the general magistrate.

(2) The transcript of all relevant proceedings, if any, shall be delivered to the judge and provided to all other parties not less than 48 hours before the hearing on exceptions. If less than a full transcript of the proceedings taken before the general magistrate is ordered prepared by the excepting party, that party shall promptly file a notice setting forth the portions of the transcript that have been ordered. The responding parties shall be permitted to designate any additional portions of the transcript necessary to the adjudication of the issues raised in the exceptions or cross-exceptions.

(3) The cost of the original and all copies of the transcript of the proceedings shall be borne initially by the party seeking review, subject to appropriate assessment of suit monies. Should any portion of the transcript be required as a result of a designation filed by the responding party, the party making the designation shall bear the initial cost of the additional transcript.

Amended Sept. 21, 2000 (810 So.2d 1); July 10, 2003 (853 So.2d 303); Sept. 30, 2004, effective Oct. 1, 2004 (887 So.2d 1090); June 2, 2005 (905 So.2d 865); Oct. 16, 2008, effective Jan. 1, 2009 (995 So.2d 407); July 12, 2012, effective Oct. 1, 2012 (95 So.3d 126); Dec. 18, 2014, effective Jan. 1, 2015 (154 So.3d 301).

Commentary

1995 Adoption. This rule is a modification of Florida Rule of Civil Procedure 1.490. That rule governed the appointment of both general and special masters. The appointment of special masters is now governed by Florida Family Law Rule of Procedure 12.492. This rule is intended to clarify procedures that were required under rule 1.490, and it creates additional procedures. The use of general masters should be implemented only when such use will reduce costs and expedite cases in accordance with *Dralus v. Dralus*, 627 So. 2d 505 (Fla. 2d DCA 1993), *Wrona v. Wrona*, 592 So. 2d 694 (Fla. 2d DCA 1991), and *Katz v. Katz*, 505 So. 2d 25 (Fla. 4th DCA 1987).

Committee Notes

2004 Amendment. In accordance with Chapter 2004–11, Laws of Florida, all references to general master were changed to general magistrate.

2015 Amendment. Subdivision (b)(3) has been amended to clarify that the order of referral must include the name of the specific general magistrate to whom the matter is being referred and who will conduct the hearing and that concurrent referrals to multiple general magistrates is inappropriate.

Rule 12.491. Child Support Enforcement

(a) Limited Application. This rule shall be effective only when specifically invoked by administrative order of the chief justice for use in a particular county or circuit.

(b) Scope. This rule shall apply to proceedings for

(1) the establishment, enforcement, or modification of child support, or

(2) the enforcement of any support order for the parent or other person entitled to receive child support in conjunction with an ongoing child support or child support arrearage order,

when a party seeking support is receiving services pursuant to Title IV–D of the Social Security Act (42

U.S.C. §§ 651 et seq.) and to non-Title IV–D proceedings upon administrative order of the chief justice.

(c) Support Enforcement Hearing Officers. The chief judge of each judicial circuit shall appoint such number of support enforcement hearing officers for the circuit or any county within the circuit as are necessary to expeditiously perform the duties prescribed by this rule. A hearing officer shall be a member of The Florida Bar unless waived by the chief justice and shall serve at the pleasure of the chief judge and a majority of the circuit judges in the circuit.

(d) Referral. Upon the filing of a cause of action or other proceeding for the establishment, enforcement, or modification of support to which this rule applies, the court or clerk of the circuit court shall refer such proceedings to a support enforcement hearing officer, pursuant to procedures to be established by administrative order of the chief judge.

(e) General Powers and Duties. The support enforcement hearing officer shall be empowered to issue process, administer oaths, require the production of documents, and conduct hearings for the purpose of taking evidence. A support enforcement hearing officer does not have the authority to hear contested paternity cases. Upon the receipt of a support proceeding, the support enforcement hearing officer shall:

(1) assign a time and place for an appropriate hearing and give notice to each of the parties as may be required by law;

(2) take testimony and establish a record, which record may be by electronic means as provided by Florida Rule of Judicial Administration 2.535(h);

(3) accept voluntary acknowledgment of paternity and support liability and stipulated agreements setting the amount of support to be paid; and

(4) evaluate the evidence and promptly make a recommended order to the court. Such order shall set forth findings of fact.

(f) Entry of Order and Relief from Order. Upon receipt of a recommended order, the court shall review the recommended order and shall enter an order promptly unless good cause appears to amend the order, conduct further proceedings, or refer the matter back to the hearing officer to conduct further proceedings. Any party affected by the order may move to vacate the order by filing a motion to vacate within 10 days from the date of entry. Any party may file a cross-motion to vacate within 5 days of service of a motion to vacate, provided, however, that the filing of a cross-motion to vacate shall not delay the hearing on the motion to vacate unless good cause is shown. A motion to vacate the order shall be heard within 10 days after the movant applies for hearing on the motion.

(g) Modification of Order. Any party affected by the order may move to modify the order at any time.

(h) Record. For the purpose of hearing on a motion to vacate, a record, substantially in conformity with this rule, shall be provided to the court by the party seeking review.

(1) The record shall consist of the court file, including the transcript of the proceedings before the hearing officer, if filed, and all depositions and evidence presented to the hearing officer.

(2) The transcript of all relevant proceedings shall be delivered to the judge and provided to opposing counsel not less than 48 hours before the hearing on the motion to vacate. If less than a full transcript of the proceedings taken before the hearing officer is ordered prepared by the moving party, that party shall promptly file a notice setting forth the portions of the transcript that have been ordered. The responding party shall be permitted to designate any additional portions of the transcript necessary to the adjudication of the issues raised in the motion to vacate or cross-motion to vacate.

(3) The cost of the original and all copies of the transcript of the proceedings shall be borne initially by the party seeking review, subject to appropriate assessment of suit monies. Should any portion of the transcript be required as a result of a designation filed by the responding party, the party making the designation shall bear the initial cost of the additional transcript.

Amended Feb. 26, 1998, effective March 16, 1998 (713 So.2d 1); Oct. 29, 1998, effective Feb. 1, 1999 (723 So.2d 208); July 10, 2003, effective Jan. 1, 2004 (853 So.2d 303); Oct. 16, 2008, effective Jan. 1, 2009 (995 So.2d 407); Oct. 16, 2008 (995 So.2d 445); Dec. 18, 2014, effective Jan. 1, 2015 (154 So.3d 301).

Commentary

1995 Adoption. Previously, this rule was contained in Florida Rule of Civil Procedure 1.491. The new rule is substantially the same as previous rule 1.491, with the following additions.

It is intended that any administrative order issued by the chief justice of the Florida Supreme Court under rule 1.491(a) shall remain in full force and effect as though such order was rendered under this rule until changed by order of that same court.

Subdivision (e) now makes clear that contested paternity cases are *not* to be heard by support enforcement hearing officers.

Subdivision (h) has been added to provide requirements for a record.

The following notes and commentary have been carried forward from rule 1.491.

1988 Adoption. Title: The terminology "hearing officer" is used rather than "master" to avoid confusion or conflict with rule 1.490.

Subdivision (a): The rule is intended as a fall back mechanism to be used by the chief justice as the need may arise.

Subdivision (b): The expedited process provisions of the applicable federal regulations apply only to matters which fall within the purview of Title IV–D. The committee recognizes, however, that the use of hearing officers could provide a useful case flow management tool in non-Title IV–D support proceedings.

It is contemplated that a circuit could make application to the chief justice for expansion of the scope of the rule upon a showing of necessity and good cause. It is the position of the representative of the Family Law Section of The Florida Bar that reference of non-Title IV–D proceedings should require the consent of the parties as is required by rule 1.490(c).

Subdivision (c): It is the position of the committee that hearing officers should be members of the Bar in that jurisdictional and other legal issues are likely to arise in proceedings of this nature. The waiver provision is directed to small counties in which it may be difficult or impossible to find a lawyer willing to serve and to such other special circumstances as may be determined by the chief justice.

Subdivision (d): This paragraph recognizes that the mechanics of reference and operation of a program are best determined at the local level.

Subdivision (e): This paragraph is intended to empower the hearing officer to fully carry out his or her responsibilities without becoming overly complicated. The authority to enter defaults which is referred to in the federal regulations is omitted, the committee feeling that the subject matter is fully and adequately covered by rule 1.500.

The authority to accept voluntary acknowledgments of paternity is included at the request of the Department of Health and Rehabilitative Services. Findings of fact are included in the recommended order to provide the judge to whom the order is referred basic information relating to the subject matter.

Subdivision (f): Expedited process is intended to eliminate or minimize delays which are perceived to exist in the normal processing of cases. This paragraph is intended to require the prompt entry of an order and to guarantee due process to the obligee.

General Note: This proposed rule, in substantially the same form, was circulated to each of the chief judges for comment. Five responses were received. Two responding endorsed the procedure, and 3 responding felt that any rule of this kind would be inappropriate. The committee did not address the question of funding, which included not only salaries of hearing officers and support personnel, but also capital outlay for furniture, fixtures, equipment and space, and normal operating costs. The committee recognizes that the operational costs of such programs may be substantial and recommends that this matter be addressed by an appropriate body.

Committee Note

1998 Amendment. This rule shall not apply to proceedings to establish or modify alimony.

Rule 12.492. Special Magistrates

(a) Special Magistrates. The court may appoint members of The Florida Bar as special magistrates for any particular service required by the court in a family law matter other than those involving injunctions for protection against domestic, repeat, dating, and sexual violence, and stalking. The special magistrates shall be governed by all the provisions of law and rules relating to general magistrates except as otherwise provided by this rule. Additionally, they shall not be required to make oath or give bond unless specifically required by the order appointing them. Upon a showing that the appointment is advisable, a person other than a member of The Florida Bar may be appointed.

(b) Reference. No reference shall be to a special magistrate without the express prior consent of the parties, except that the court upon good cause shown and without consent of the parties may appoint an attorney as a special magistrate to preside over depositions and rule upon objections.

(c) General Powers and Duties. Every special magistrate shall perform all of the duties that pertain to the office according to the practice in chancery and rules of court and under the direction of the court. Hearings before any special magistrate shall be held in the county where the action is pending, but hearings may be held at any place by order of the court within or without the state to meet the convenience of the witnesses or the parties. All grounds for disqualification of a judge shall apply to special magistrates.

(d) Bond. When not otherwise provided by law, the court may require special magistrates who are appointed to dispose of real or personal property to give bond and surety conditioned for the proper payment of all moneys that may come into their hands and for the due performance of their duties as the court may direct. The bond shall be made payable to the State of Florida and shall be for the benefit of all persons aggrieved by any act of the special magistrate.

(e) Hearings. When a reference is made to a special magistrate, any party or the special magistrate may set the action for hearing. The special magistrate shall assign a time and place for proceedings as soon as reasonably possible after the reference is made and give notice to each of the parties either directly or by requiring counsel to file and serve a notice of hearing. If any party fails to appear, the special magistrate may proceed ex parte or may adjourn the proceeding to a future day, giving notice to the absent party of the adjournment. The special magistrate shall proceed with reasonable diligence in every reference and with the least delay practicable. Any party may apply to the court for an order to the special magistrate to speed the proceedings and to make the report and to certify to the court the reason for any delay. Unless otherwise ordered by the court, or agreed to by all parties, all parties shall equally share the cost of the presence of a court reporter at a special magistrate's proceedings. If all parties waive the presence of a court reporter, they must do so in writing. The special magistrate shall have authority to examine the parties and all witnesses under oath upon all matters contained in the reference and to require production of all books, papers, writings, vouchers, and other documents applicable to it. The special magistrate shall admit evidence by deposition or that is otherwise admissible in court. The special magistrate may take all actions concerning evidence that can be taken by the court and in the same manner. All parties accounting before a special magistrate shall bring in their accounts in the form of accounts payable and receivable, and any other parties who are not satisfied with the account may examine the accounting party orally or by interrogatories or deposition as the special magistrate directs. All depositions and documents that have been taken or used previously in the action may be used before the special magistrate.

(f) Special Magistrate's Report. The special magistrate shall file a report that includes findings of fact and conclusions of law, together with recommendations. In the report made by the special magistrate no part of any statement of facts, account, charge, deposition, examination, or answer used before the special magistrate need be recited. The matters shall be identified to inform the court what items were used. The report shall include the name and address of the court reporter present, if any.

(g) Filing Report; Notice; Exceptions. The special magistrate shall file the report and recommendations and serve copies on the parties. The parties may file exceptions to the report within 10 days from the time it is served on them. If no exceptions are filed within that period, the court shall take appropriate action on the report. Any party may file cross-exceptions within 5 days from the filing of the exceptions, provided, however, that the filing of cross-exceptions shall not delay the hearing on the exceptions unless good cause is shown. If exceptions are filed, they shall be heard on reasonable notice by either party. The party seeking to have exceptions heard shall be responsible for the preparation of the transcript of proceedings before the special magistrate.

(h) Expenses of Special Magistrate. The costs of a special magistrate may be assessed as any other suit money in family proceedings and all or part of it may be ordered prepaid by order of the court.

Amended Sept. 30, 2004, effective Oct. 1, 2004 (887 So.2d 1090); June 2, 2005 (905 So.2d 865); Oct. 16, 2008, effective Jan. 1, 2009 (995 So.2d 407); July 12, 2012, effective Oct. 1, 2012 (95 So.3d 126).

Commentary

1995 Adoption. Originally, both general and special masters were governed under Florida Rule of Civil Procedure 1.490. General and special masters are now governed under Florida Family Law Rules of Procedure 12.490 and 12.492, respectively. The requirements for appointing special masters are essentially the same as under the previous rule; but this rule eliminates the need for consent for the court to appoint an attorney/special master to preside over depositions and rule on objections. It also provides for the assessment of suit monies and allows for the filing of cross-exceptions.

Committee Note

2004 Amendment. In accordance with Chapter 2004–11, Laws of Florida, all references to special master were changed to special magistrate.

Rule 12.500. Defaults and Final Judgments Thereon

Defaults and final judgments thereon shall be governed by Florida Rule of Civil Procedure 1.500.

Rule 12.510. Summary Judgment

Summary judgment shall be governed by Florida Rule of Civil Procedure 1.510, except that service by the adverse party, as set forth in for rule 1.510(c), shall be on the movant in accordance with Florida Rule of Judicial Administration 2.516.

Amended Oct. 18, 2012, effective, *nunc pro tunc*, Sept. 1, 2012 (102 So.3d 505).

Committee Notes

2012 Amendment. This rule is amended to state who the adverse party serves and provide for service in accordance with Florida Rule of Judicial Administration 2.516.

Rule 12.520. View

Upon motion of either party or on the court's own motion, the trier of fact may view the premises or place in question or any property, matter, or thing relating to the controversy between the parties when it appears that view is necessary to a just decision.

Commentary

1995 Adoption. This rule replaces Florida Rule of Civil Procedure 1.520 and eliminates the advancement of costs imposed by rule 1.520.

Rule 12.525. Motions for Costs and Attorneys' Fees

Florida Rule of Civil Procedure 1.525 shall not apply in proceedings governed by these rules.

Added Mar. 3, 2005 (897 So.2d 467).

Rule 12.530. Motions for New Trial and Rehearing; Amendments of Judgments

Motions for new trial and rehearing and amendments of judgments shall be governed by Florida Rule of Civil Procedure 1.530.

Rule 12.540. Relief From Judgment, Decrees, or Orders

Florida Rule of Civil Procedure 1.540 shall govern general provision concerning relief from judgment, decrees, or orders, except:

(a) there shall be no time limit for motions based on fraudulent financial affidavits in marital or paternity cases; and

(b) the motion and any attachment or exhibit to it shall be in compliance with Florida Rule of Judicial Administration 2.425.

Amended Nov. 3, 2011, effective, *nunc pro tunc*, Oct. 1, 2011 (78 So.3d 1045).

Commentary

1995 Adoption. Under this provision, Florida Rule of Civil Procedure 1.540 applies to all family law issues involving relief from judgment, decrees, or orders, except that there shall be no time limit for motions filed under rule 1.540(b) based on fraudulent financial affidavits in marital or paternity cases. Rule 1.540 was expanded to include marital cases through the rule making procedure subsequent to the Florida Supreme Court's decision in *DeClaire v. Yohanan*, 453 So. 2d 375 (Fla.1984).

Rule 12.550. Executions and Final Process

Executions and final process shall be governed by Florida Rule of Civil Procedure 1.550.

Rule 12.560. Discovery in Aid of Execution

(a) In General. In aid of a judgment, decree, or execution the judgment creditor or the successor in interest, when the interest appears of record, may obtain discovery from any person, including the judgment debtor, in the manner provided in these rules.

(b) Fact Information Sheet. In addition to any other discovery available to a judgment creditor under this rule, the court, at the request of the judgment creditor, shall order the judgment debtor or debtors to complete Florida Rules of Civil Procedure Form 1.977 (Fact Information Sheet), including all required attachments, within 45 days of the order or such other reasonable time as determined by the court.

(c) Final Judgment Enforcement Paragraph. In any final judgment which awards money damages, the judge shall include the following enforcement paragraph if requested at the final hearing or a subsequently noticed hearing by the prevailing party or attorney:

"It is further ordered and adjudged that the judgment debtor(s) shall complete under oath Florida Rule of Civil Procedure Form 1.977 (Fact Information Sheet), including all required attachments, and serve it on the judgment creditor's attorney, or the judgment creditor if the judgment creditor is not represented by an attorney, within 45 days from the date of this final judgment, unless the final judgment is satisfied or post-judgment discovery is stayed.

"Jurisdiction of this case is retained to enter further orders that are proper to compel the judgment debtor(s) to complete form 1.977, including all required attachments, and serve it on the judgment creditor's attorney, or the judgment creditor if the judgment creditor is not represented by an attorney."

(d) Information Regarding Assets of Judgment Debtor's Spouse. In any final judgment which awards money damages, if requested by the judgment creditor at a duly noticed hearing, the court shall require all or part of the additional Spouse Related Portion of the fact information sheet to be filled out by the judgment debtor only upon a showing that a proper predicate exists for discovery of separate income and assets of the judgment debtor's spouse.

Amended Oct. 19, 2000 (783 So.2d 937); Nov. 3, 2011, effective, *nunc pro tunc*, Oct. 1, 2011 (78 So.3d 1045); Dec. 18, 2014, effective Jan. 1, 2015 (154 So.3d 301).

Committee Notes

2000 Amendment. Subdivisions (b)—(e) were added to the Florida Rules of Civil Procedure and adopted with amendments into the Family Law Rules of Procedure. The amendments to the Civil Rules were patterned after Florida Small Claims Rule 7.221(a) and Form 7.343. Although the judgment creditor is entitled to broad discovery into the judgment debtor's finances (Fla. R. Civ. P. 1.280(b); *Jim Appley's Tru–Arc, Inc. v. Liquid Extraction Systems*, 526 So. 2d 177, 179 (Fla. 2d DCA 1988)), in family law cases inquiry into the individual assets of the judgment debtor's spouse must be precluded until a proper predicate has been shown. *Tru–Arc, Inc.*, 526 So. 2d at 179; *Rose Printing Co. v. D'Amato*, 338 So. 2d 212 (Fla. 3d DCA 1976).

2015 Amendment. Subdivision (e) was deleted because the filing of a notice of compliance is unnecessary for the judgment creditor to seek relief from the court for noncompliance with this rule and because the Fact Information Sheet should not be filed with the clerk of the court.

Rule 12.570. Enforcement of Judgments

Enforcement of judgments shall be governed by Florida Rule of Civil Procedure 1.570. Money judgments, as governed by rule 1.570(a) shall include, but not be limited to, judgments for alimony, child support, attorneys' fees, suit money, and costs, and equitable distribution.

Commentary

1995 Adoption. Nothing in this rule or Florida Rule of Civil Procedure 1.570 should be read to preclude the use of other remedies to enforce judgments.

Rule 12.580. Writ of Possession

Writs of possession shall be governed by Florida Rule of Civil Procedure 1.580.

Rule 12.590. Process in Behalf of and Against Persons Not Parties

Process in behalf of and against persons not parties shall be governed by Florida Rule of Civil Procedure 1.590.

Rule 12.600. Deposits in Court

Deposits in court shall be governed by Florida Rule of Civil Procedure 1.600, with the following addition. The party depositing money or depositing the thing capable of delivery shall pay any fee imposed by the clerk of the court, unless the court orders otherwise.

Commentary

1995 Adoption. The addition to Florida Rule of Civil Procedure 1.600 included in this rule is intended to clarify responsibility for the payment of clerk's fees.

Rule 12.610. Injunctions for Protection Against Domestic, Repeat, Dating, and Sexual Violence, and Stalking

(a) Application. This rule shall apply only to temporary and permanent injunctions for protection against domestic violence and temporary and permanent injunctions for protection against repeat violence, dating violence, or sexual violence, and stalking. All other injunctive relief sought in cases to which the Family Law Rules apply shall be governed by Florida Rule of Civil Procedure 1.610.

(b) Petitions.

(1) *Requirements for Use.*

(A) Domestic Violence. Any person may file a petition for an injunction for protection against domestic violence as provided by law.

(B) Repeat Violence. Any person may file a petition for an injunction for protection against repeat violence as provided by law.

(C) Dating Violence. Any person may file a petition for an injunction for protection against dating violence as provided by law.

(D) Sexual Violence. Any person may file a petition for an injunction for protection against sexual violence as provided by law.

(E) Stalking. Any person may file a petition for an injunction for protection against stalking as provided by law.

(2) *Service of Petitions.*

(A) Domestic Violence. Personal service by a law enforcement agency is required. The clerk of the court shall furnish a copy of the petition for an injunction for protection against domestic violence, financial affidavit (if support is sought), Uniform Child Custody Jurisdiction and Enforcement Act affidavit (if custody is sought), temporary injunction (if one has been entered), and notice of hearing to the appropriate sheriff or law enforcement agency of the county where the respondent resides or can be found for expeditious service of process.

(B) Repeat Violence, Dating Violence, Sexual Violence, and Stalking. Personal service by a law enforcement agency is required. The clerk of the court shall furnish a copy of the petition for an injunction for protection against repeat violence, dating violence, sexual violence, or stalking, temporary injunction (if one has been entered), and notice of hearing to the appropriate sheriff or law enforcement agency of the county where the respondent resides or can be found for expeditious service of process.

(C) Additional Documents. Service of pleadings in cases of domestic, repeat, dating, or sexual violence, or stalking other than petitions, supplemental petitions, and orders granting injunctions shall be governed by rule 12.080, except that service of a motion to modify or vacate an injunction should be by notice that is reasonably calculated to apprise the nonmoving party of the pendency of the proceedings.

(3) *Consideration by Court.*

(A) Domestic Violence and Stalking Injunctions. Upon the filing of a petition, the court shall set a hearing to be held at the earliest possible time. A denial of a petition for an ex parte injunction shall be by written order noting the legal grounds for denial. When the only ground for denial is no appearance of an immediate and present danger of domestic violence or stalking, the court shall set a full hearing on the petition for injunction with notice at the earliest possible time. Nothing herein affects a petitioner's right to promptly amend any petition, or otherwise be heard in person on any petition consistent with these rules.

(B) Repeat, Dating, or Sexual Violence Injunctions. Upon the filing of a petition, the court shall set a hearing to be held at the earliest possible time. Nothing herein affects a petitioner's right to promptly amend any petition or otherwise be heard in person on any petition consistent with these rules.

(4) *Forms.*

(A) Provision of Forms. The clerk of the court or family or injunctions for protection intake personnel shall provide simplified forms, including instructions for completion, for any person whose circumstances meet the requirements of this rule and shall assist the petitioner in obtaining an injunction for protection against domestic, repeat, dating, or sexual violence, or stalking as provided by law.

(B) Confidential Filing of Address. A petitioner's address may be furnished to the court in a confidential filing separate from a petition or other form if, for safety reasons, a petitioner believes that the address should be concealed. The ultimate determination of a need for confidentiality must be made by the court as provided in Florida Rule of Judicial Administration 2.420.

(c) Orders of Injunction.

(1) *Consideration by Court.*

(A) Temporary Injunction.

(i) Domestic, Repeat, Dating, or Sexual Violence. For the injunction for protection to be issued ex parte, it must appear to the court that an immediate and present danger of domestic, repeat, dating, or sexual violence exists. In an ex parte hearing for the purpose of obtaining an ex parte temporary injunction, the court may limit the evidence to the verified pleadings or affidavits for a determination of whether there is an imminent danger that the petitioner will become a victim of domestic, repeat, dating, or sexual violence. If the respondent appears at the hearing or has received reasonable notice of the hearing, the court may hold a hearing on the petition. If a verified petition and affidavit are amended, the court shall consider the amendments as if originally filed.

(ii) Stalking. For the injunction for protection to be issued ex parte, it must appear to the court that stalking exists. In an ex parte hearing for the purpose of obtaining an ex parte temporary injunction, the court may limit the evidence to the verified pleadings or affidavits for a determination of whether stalking exists. If the respondent appears at the hearing or has received reasonable notice of the hearing, the court may hold the hearing on the petition. If a verified petition and affidavit are amended, the court shall consider the amendments as if originally filed.

(B) Final Judgment of Injunction for Protection Against Repeat, Dating, or Sexual Violence or Stalking. A hearing shall be conducted.

(C) Final Judgment of Injunction for Protection Against Domestic Violence. The court shall conduct a hearing and make a finding of whether domestic violence occurred or whether imminent danger of domestic violence exists. If the court determines that an injunction will be issued, the court shall also rule on the following:

(i) whether the respondent may have any contact with the petitioner, and if so, under what conditions;

(ii) exclusive use of the parties' shared residence;

(iii) petitioner's temporary time-sharing with the minor child or children;

(iv) whether respondent will have temporary time-sharing with the minor child or children and whether it will be supervised;

(v) whether temporary child support will be ordered;

(vi) whether temporary spousal support will be ordered; and

(vii) such other relief as the court deems necessary for the protection of the petitioner.

The court, with the consent of the parties, may refer the parties to mediation by a certified family mediator to attempt to resolve the details as to the above rulings. This mediation shall be the only alternative dispute resolution process offered by the court. Any agreement reached by the parties through mediation shall be reviewed by the court and, if approved, incorporated into the final judgment. If no agreement is reached the matters referred shall be returned to the court for appropriate rulings. Regardless of whether all issues are resolved in mediation, an injunction for protection against domestic violence shall be entered or extended the same day as the hearing on the petition commences.

(2) *Issuing of Injunction.*

(A) Standardized Forms. The temporary and permanent injunction forms approved by the Florida Supreme Court for domestic, repeat, dating, and sexual violence, and stalking injunctions shall be the forms used in the issuance of injunctions under chapters 741 and 784, Florida Statutes. Additional standard provisions, not inconsistent with the standardized portions of those forms, may be added to the special provisions section of the temporary and permanent injunction forms, or at the end of each section to which they apply, on the written approval of the chief judge of the circuit, and upon final review and written approval by the chief justice. Copies of such additional standard provisions, once approved by the chief justice, shall be sent to the chair of the Family Law Rules Committee of The Florida Bar, the chair of the Steering Committee on Families and Children in the Court, and the chair of The Governor's Task Force on Domestic and Sexual Violence.

(B) Bond. No bond shall be required by the court for the entry of an injunction for protection against domestic, repeat, dating, or sexual violence, or stalking. The clerk of the court shall provide the parties with sufficient certified copies of the order of injunction for service.

(3) *Service of Injunctions.*

(A) Temporary Injunction. A temporary injunction for protection against domestic, repeat, dating, or sexual violence, or stalking must be personally served. When the respondent has been served previously with the temporary injunction and has failed to appear at the initial hearing on the temporary injunction, any subsequent pleadings seeking an extension of time may be served on the respondent by the clerk of the court by certified mail in lieu of personal service by a law enforcement officer. If the temporary injunction was issued after a hearing because the respondent was present at the hearing or had reasonable notice of the hearing, the injunction may be served in the manner provided for a permanent injunction.

(B) Permanent Injunction.

(i) Party Present at Hearing. The parties may acknowledge receipt of the permanent injunction for protection against domestic, repeat, dating, or sexual violence, or stalking in writing on the face of the original order. If a party is present at the hearing and that party fails or refuses to acknowledge the receipt of a certified copy of the injunction, the clerk shall cause the order to be served by mailing certified copies of the injunction to the parties who were present at the hearing at the last known address of each party. Service by mail is complete upon mailing. When an order is served pursuant to this subdivision, the clerk shall prepare a written certification to be placed in the court file specifying the time, date, and method of service and within 24 hours shall forward a copy of the injunction and the clerk's affidavit of service to the sheriff with jurisdiction over the residence of the petitioner. This procedure applies to service of orders to modify or vacate injunctions for protection against domestic, repeat, dating, or sexual violence, or stalking.

(ii) Party not Present at Hearing. Within 24 hours after the court issues, continues, modifies, or vacates an injunction for protection against domestic, repeat, dating, or sexual violence, or stalking the clerk shall forward a copy of the injunction to the sheriff with jurisdiction over the residence of the petitioner for service.

(4) *Duration.*

(A) Temporary Injunction. Any temporary injunction shall be effective for a fixed period not to exceed 15 days. A full hearing shall be set for a date no later than the date when the temporary injunction ceases to be effective. The court may grant a continuance of the temporary injunction and of the full hearing for good cause shown by any party, or upon its own motion for good cause, including failure to obtain service.

(B) Permanent Injunction. Any relief granted by an injunction for protection against domestic, repeat, dating, or sexual violence, or stalking shall be granted for a fixed period or until further order of court. Such relief may be granted in addition to other civil and criminal remedies. Upon petition of the victim, the court may extend the injunction for successive periods or until further order of court. Broad discretion resides with the court to grant an extension after considering the circumstances. No specific allegations are required.

(5) *Enforcement.* The court may enforce violations of an injunction for protection against domestic, repeat, dating, or sexual violence, or stalking in civil contempt proceedings, which are governed by rule 12.570, or in criminal contempt proceedings, which are governed by Florida Rule of Criminal Procedure 3.840, or, if the violation meets the statutory criteria, it may be prosecuted as a crime under Florida Statutes.

(6) *Motion to Modify or Vacate Injunction.* The petitioner or respondent may move the court to modify or vacate an injunction at any time. Service of a motion to modify or vacate injunctions shall be governed by subdivision (b)(2) of this rule. However, for service of a motion to modify to be sufficient if a party is not represented by an attorney, service must be in accordance with rule 12.070, or in the alternative, there must be filed in the record proof of receipt of this motion by the nonmoving party personally.

(7) *Forms.* The clerk of the court or family or injunction for protection intake personnel shall provide simplified forms including instructions for completion, for the persons whose circumstances meet the requirements of this rule and shall assist in the preparation of the affidavit in support of the violation of an order of injunction for protection against domestic, repeat, dating, or sexual violence, or stalking.

Amended Feb. 26, 1998, effective March 16, 1998 (713 So.2d 1); Oct. 29, 1998, effective Feb. 1, 1999 (723 So.2d 208); Jan. 28, 1999, effective Feb. 1, 1999 (746 So.2d 1073); Sept. 21, 2000 (810 So.2d 1); Oct. 19, 2000 (783 So.2d 937); May 1, 2003 (845 So.2d 174); July 10, 2003 (853 So.2d 303); June 2, 2005 (905 So.2d 865); Oct. 16, 2008, effective Jan. 1, 2009 (995 So.2d 407); Oct. 16, 2008 (995 So.2d 445); July 12, 2012, effective Oct. 1, 2012 (95 So.3d 126); Nov. 14, 2013 (126 So.3d 228).

Commentary

2003 Amendment. This rule was amended to emphasize the importance of judicial involvement in resolving injunction for protection against domestic violence cases and to establish protections if mediation is used. In performing case management, court staff may interview the parties separately to identify and clarify their positions. Court staff may present this information to the court along with a proposed order for the court's consideration in the hearing required by subdivision (b). The first sentence of (c)(1)(C) contemplates that an injunction will not be entered unless there is a finding that domestic violence occurred or that there is imminent danger of domestic violence. Subdivision (c)(1)(C) also enumerates certain rulings that a judge must make after deciding to issue an injunction and before referring parties to mediation. This is intended to ensure that issues involving safety are decided by the judge and not left to the parties to resolve. The list is not meant to be exhaustive, as indicated by subdivision (c)(1)(C)(vii), which provides for "other relief," such as retrieval of personal property and referrals to batterers' intervention programs. The prohibition against use of any "alternative dispute resolution" other than mediation is intended to preclude any court-based process that encourages or facilitates, through mediation or negotiation, agreement as to one or more issues, but does not preclude the parties through their attorneys from presenting agreements to the court. All agreements must be consistent with this rule regarding findings. Prior to ordering the parties to mediate, the court should consider risk factors in the case and the suitability of the case for mediation. The court should not refer the case to mediation if there has been a high degree of past violence, a potential for future lethality exists, or there are other factors which would compromise the mediation process.

1995 Adoption. A cause of action for an injunction for protection against domestic violence and repeat violence has been created by section 741.30, Florida Statutes (Supp.1994) (modified by chapter 95–195, Laws of Florida), and section 784.046, Florida Statutes (Supp. 1994), respectively. This rule implements those provisions and is intended to be consistent with the procedures set out in those provisions except as indicated in this commentary. To the extent a domestic or repeat violence matter becomes criminal or is to be enforced by direct or indirect criminal contempt, the appropriate Florida Rules of Criminal Procedure will apply.

The facts and circumstances to be alleged under subdivision 12.610(b)(1)(A) include those set forth in Florida Supreme Court Approved Family Law Form 12.980(b). An injunction for protection against domestic or repeat violence may be sought whether or not any other cause of action is currently pending between the parties. However, the pendency of any such cause of action must be alleged in the petition. The relief the court may grant in a temporary or permanent injunction against domestic violence is set forth in sections 741.30(5)–(6).

The facts and circumstances to be alleged under subdivision (b)(1)(B) include those set forth in Florida Supreme Court Approved Family Law Form 12.980(g). The relief the court may grant in a temporary or permanent injunction against repeat violence is set forth in section 784.046(7), Florida Statutes.

Subdivision (b)(4) expands sections 741.30(2)(c)1 and (2)(c)2, Florida Statutes, to provide that the responsibility to assist the petitioner may be assigned not only to the clerk of court but also to the appropriate intake unit of the court. Florida Supreme Court Approved Family Law Form 12.980(b) provides the form for a petition for injunction against domestic violence. If the custody of a child is at issue, a Uniform Child Custody Jurisdiction and Enforcement Act affidavit must be provided and completed in conformity with Florida Supreme Court Approved Family Law Form 12.902(d). If alimony or child support is sought a Financial Affidavit must be provided and completed in conformity with Florida Family Law Rules of Procedure Form 12.902(b) or 12.902(c).

Subdivision (c)(1)(A) expands chapter 95–195, Laws of Florida, and section 784.046(6)(b), Florida Statutes, to make the limitation of evidence presented at an ex parte hearing permissive rather than mandatory given the due process concerns raised by the statutory restrictions on the taking of evidence.

Unlike traditional injunctions, under subdivision (c)(2), no bond will be required for the issuance of injunctions for protection against domestic or repeat violence. This provision is consistent with the statutes except that, unlike the statutes, it does not set a precise number of copies to be provided for service.

Subdivision (c)(3)(A) makes the procedure for service of a temporary order of injunction for protection against domestic violence and repeat violence consistent. This is intended to replace the differing requirements contained in sections 741.30(8)(a)1 and (8)(c)1 and 784.046(8)(a)1, Florida Statutes.

Subdivision (c)(3)(B) makes the procedure for service of a permanent order of injunction for protection against domestic violence and repeat violence consistent. This is intended to replace the differing requirements contained in sections 741.30(8)(a)3 and (8)(c)1 and 784.046(8)(c)1, Florida Statutes, and to specifically clarify that service of the permanent injunction by mail is only effective upon a party who is present at the hearing which resulted in the issuance of the injunction.

Subdivision (c)(4)(A) restates sections 741.30(5)(c) and 784.046(6)(c), Florida Statutes, with some expansion. This subdivision allows the court upon its own motion to extend the protection of the temporary injunction for protection against domestic or repeat violence for good cause shown, which shall include, but not be limited to, failure to obtain service. This subdivision also makes the procedures in cases of domestic and repeat violence identical, resolving the inconsistencies in the statutes.

Subdivision (c)(4)(B) makes the procedures in cases of domestic and repeat violence identical, resolving inconsistencies in the statutes. As stated in section 741.30(1)(c), Florida Statutes, in the event a subsequent cause of action is filed under chapter 61, Florida Statutes, any orders entered therein shall take precedence over any inconsistent provisions of an injunction for protection against domestic violence which addresses matters governed by chapter 61, Florida Statutes.

Subdivision (c)(5) implements a number of statutes governing enforcement of injunctions against domestic or repeat violence. It is intended by these rules that procedures in cases of domestic and repeat violence be identical to resolve inconsistencies in the statutes. As such, the procedures set out in section 741.31(1), Florida Statutes, are to be followed for violations of injunctions for protection of both domestic and repeat violence. Pursuant to that statute, the petitioner may contact the clerk of the circuit court of the county in which the violation is alleged to have occurred to obtain information regarding enforcement.

Subdivision (c)(7) expands sections 741.30(2)(c)1 and (2)(c)2, Florida Statutes, to provide that the responsibility to assist a petitioner may not only be assigned to the clerk of court but also to the appropriate intake unit of the court. This subdivision makes the procedures in cases of domestic and cases of repeat violence identical to resolve inconsistencies in the statutes.

Committee Note

1997 Amendment. This change mandates use of the injunction forms provided with these rules to give law enforcement a standardized form to assist in enforcement of injunctions. In order to address local concerns, circuits may add special provisions not inconsistent with the mandatory portions.

Rule 12.611. Central Governmental Depository

(a) Administrative Order. If the chief judge of the circuit by administrative order authorizes the creation of a central governmental depository for the circuit or county within the circuit to receive, record, and disburse all support alimony or maintenance payments, as provided in section 61.181, Florida Statutes (1983), the court may direct that payment be made to the officer designated in the administrative order.

(b) Payments to Public Officer.

(1) If the court so directs, the payments shall be made to the officer designated.

(2) The officer shall keep complete and accurate accounts of all payments received. Payments shall be made by cash, money order, cashier's check, or certified check. The officer shall promptly disburse the proceeds to the party entitled to receive them under the judgment or order.

(3) Payment may be enforced by the party entitled to it or the court may establish a system under which the officer issues a motion for enforcement and a notice of hearing in the form approved by the supreme court. The motion and notice shall be served on the defaulting party in accordance with Florida Rule of Judicial Administration 2.516. At the hearing the court shall enter an appropriate order based on the testimony presented to it.

Amended Oct. 18, 2012, effective, *nunc pro tunc*, Sept. 1, 2012 (102 So.3d 505).

Commentary

1995 Adoption. This rule is a remnant of Florida Rule of Civil Procedure 1.611, which contained several unrelated issues. Those issues are now governed by separate rules for automatic disclosure, simplified dissolution procedure, and this rule for central governmental depository.

Committee Notes

2012 Amendment. Subdivision (b)(3) is amended to provide for service in accordance with Florida Rule of Judicial Administration 2.516.

Rule 12.615. Civil Contempt in Support Matters

(a) Applicability. This rule governs civil contempt proceedings in support matters related to family law cases. The use of civil contempt sanctions under this rule shall be limited to those used to compel compliance with a court order or to compensate a movant for losses sustained as a result of a contemnor's willful failure to comply with a court order. Contempt sanctions intended to punish an offender or to vindicate the authority of the court are criminal in nature and are governed by Florida Rules of Criminal Procedure 3.830 and 3.840.

(b) Motion and Notice. Civil contempt may be initiated by motion. The motion must recite the essential facts constituting the acts alleged to be contemptuous. No civil contempt may be imposed without notice to the alleged contemnor and without providing the alleged contemnor with an opportunity to be heard. The civil contempt motion and notice of hearing may be served in accordance with Florida Rule of Judicial Administration 2.516 provided notice is reasonably calculated to apprise the alleged contemnor of the pendency of the proceedings. The notice must specify the time and place of the hearing and must contain the following language: "FAILURE TO APPEAR AT THE HEARING MAY RESULT IN THE COURT ISSUING A WRIT OF BODILY ATTACHMENT FOR YOUR ARREST. IF YOU ARE ARRESTED, YOU MAY BE HELD IN JAIL UP TO 48 HOURS BEFORE A HEARING IS HELD." This notice must also state whether electronic recording or a court reporter is provided by the court or whether a court reporter, if desired, must be provided by the party.

(c) Hearing. In any civil contempt hearing, after the court makes an express finding that the alleged contemnor had notice of the motion and hearing:

(1) the court shall determine whether the movant has established that a prior order directing payment of support was entered and that the alleged contemnor has failed to pay all or part of the support set forth in the prior order; and

(2) if the court finds the movant has established all of the requirements in subdivision (c)(1) of this rule, the court shall,

(A) if the alleged contemnor is present, determine whether the alleged contemnor had the present ability to pay support and willfully failed to pay such support.

(B) if the alleged contemnor fails to appear, set a reasonable purge amount based on the individual circumstances of the parties. The court may issue a writ of bodily attachment and direct that, upon execution of the writ of bodily attachment, the alleged contemnor be brought before the court within 48 hours for a hearing on whether the alleged contemnor has the present ability to pay support and, if so, whether the failure to pay such support is willful.

(d) Order and Sanctions. After hearing the testimony and evidence presented, the court shall enter a written order granting or denying the motion for contempt.

(1) An order finding the alleged contemnor to be in contempt shall contain a finding that a prior order of support was entered, that the alleged contemnor has failed to pay part or all of the support ordered, that the alleged contemnor had the present ability to pay support, and that the alleged contemnor willfully failed to comply with the prior court order. The order shall contain a recital of the facts on which these findings are based.

(2) If the court grants the motion for contempt, the court may impose appropriate sanctions to obtain compliance with the order including incarceration, attorneys' fees, suit money and costs, compensatory or coercive fines, and any other coercive sanction or relief permitted by law provided the order includes a purge provision as set forth in subdivision (e) of this rule.

(e) Purge. If the court orders incarceration, a coercive fine, or any other coercive sanction for failure to comply with a prior support order, the court shall set conditions for purge of the contempt, based on the contemnor's present ability to comply. The court shall include in its order a separate affirmative finding that the contemnor has the present ability to comply with the purge and the factual basis for that finding. The court may grant the contemnor a reasonable time to comply with the purge conditions. If the court orders incarceration but defers incarceration for more than 48 hours to allow the contemnor a reasonable time to comply with the purge conditions, and the contemnor fails to comply within the time provided, the movant shall file an affidavit of noncompliance with the court. If payment is being made through the Central Governmental Depository, a certificate from the depository shall be attached to the affidavit. The court then may issue a writ of bodily attachment. Upon incarceration, the contemnor must be brought before the court within 48 hours for a determination of whether the contemnor continues to have the present ability to pay the purge.

(f) Review after Incarceration. Notwithstanding the provisions of this rule, at any time after a contemnor is incarcerated, the court on its own motion or motion of any party may review the contemnor's present ability to comply with the purge condition and the duration of incarceration and modify any prior orders.

(g) Other Relief. Where there is a failure to pay support or to pay support on a timely basis but the failure is not willful, nothing in this rule shall be construed as precluding the court from granting such relief as may be appropriate under the circumstances.

Added Oct. 29, 1998, effective Feb. 1, 1999 (723 So.2d 208). Amended Jan. 28, 1999, effective Feb. 1, 1999 (746 So.2d 1073); July 10, 2003, effective Jan. 1, 2004 (853 So.2d 303); Oct. 18, 2012, effective, *nunc pro tunc*, Sept. 1, 2012 (102 So.3d 505).

Commentary

1998 Adoption. This rule is limited to civil contempt proceedings. Should a court wish to impose sanctions for criminal contempt, the court must refer to Florida Rules of Criminal Procedure 3.830 and 3.840 and must provide the alleged contemnor with all of the constitutional due process protections afforded to criminal defendants. This rule is created to assist the trial courts in ensuring that the due process rights of alleged contemnors are protected. A court that adjudges an individual to be in civil contempt must always afford the contemnor the opportunity to purge the contempt.

Committee Notes

2012 Amendment. Subdivision (b) is amended to provide for service in accordance with Florida Rule of Judicial Administration 2.516.

Rule 12.620. Receivers

Receivers shall be governed by Florida Rule of Civil Procedure 1.620, except that any inventory filed with the court shall be in compliance with Florida Rule of Judicial Administration 2.425.

Amended Nov. 3, 2011, effective, *nunc pro tunc*, Oct. 1, 2011 (78 So.3d 1045).

Rule 12.625. Proceedings Against Surety on Judicial Bonds

Proceedings against sureties on judicial bonds shall be governed by Florida Rule of Civil Procedure 1.625.

Rule 12.630. Extraordinary Remedies

Extraordinary remedies shall be governed by Florida Rule of Civil Procedure 1.630, except summons in certiorari, as set forth in rule 1.630(d)(5), shall be served as provided in Florida Rule of Judicial Administration 2.516.

Amended Oct. 18, 2012, effective, *nunc pro tunc*, Sept. 1, 2012 (102 So.3d 505).

Committee Notes

2012 Amendment. This rule is amended to provide for service in accordance with Florida Rule of Judicial Administration 2.516.

Rule 12.650. Override of Family Violence Indicator

(a) Application. This rule shall apply only to proceedings instituted pursuant to 42 U.S.C. § 653, which authorizes a state court to override a family violence indicator and release information from the Federal Parent Locator Service notwithstanding the family violence indicator.

(b) Definitions.

(1) "Authorized person" means a person as defined in 42 U.S.C. § 653(c) and § 663(d)(2). It includes any agent or attorney of the Title IV–D agency of this or any other state, the court that has authority to issue

an order or to serve as the initiating court in an action to seek an order against a parent or other person obligated to pay child support, or any agent of such court, the parent or other person entitled to receive child support, legal guardian, attorney, or agent of a child (other than a child receiving assistance under 42 U.S.C. §§ 601 et seq.), and any state agency that administers a child welfare, family preservation, or foster care program. It also includes any agent or attorney of this or any other state who has the duty or authority under the law of such state to enforce a child custody or visitation determination or order establishing a parenting plan; the court that has jurisdiction to make or enforce such a child custody or visitation determination or order establishing a parenting plan, or any agent of such court; and any agent or attorney of the United States, or of a state, who has the duty or authority to investigate, enforce, or bring a prosecution with respect to the unlawful taking or restraint of a child.

(2) "Authorized purpose" means a purpose as defined in 42 U.S.C. § 653(a)(2) and § 663(b). It includes establishing parentage, establishing, setting the amount of, modifying, or enforcing child support obligations, or making or enforcing child custody or visitation orders or orders establishing parenting plans. It also includes enforcing any state or federal law with respect to the unlawful taking or restraint of a child.

(3) "Department" means the Florida Department of Revenue as the state's Title IV–D agency.

(4) "Family violence indicator" means a notation in the Federal Parent Locator Service that has been placed on a record when a state has reasonable evidence of domestic violence or child abuse as defined by that state.

(5) "Federal Parent Locator Service" means the information service established by 42 U.S.C. § 653.

(6) "Petitioner" means an authorized person or an individual on whose behalf an authorized person has requested a Federal Parent Locator Service search and who has been notified that the information from the Federal Parent Locator Service cannot be released because of a family violence indicator.

(7) "Respondent" means the individual whose record at the Federal Parent Locator Service includes a family violence indicator and ordinarily does not want his or her location information disclosed. The department, the Florida Department of Law Enforcement, or the state entity that placed the family violence indicator on the record may be required to respond to an order to show cause; however, they are not considered respondents in these proceedings.

(c) Initiating Proceedings. When an authorized person has attempted to obtain information from the Federal Parent Locator Service and has been notified by the Federal Parent Locator Service that it has location information but cannot disclose the information because a family violence indicator has been placed on the record, a petitioner may institute an action to override the family violence indicator. An action is instituted by filing a sworn complaint in the circuit court. The complaint must:

(1) allege that the petitioner is an authorized person or an authorized person has requested information on his or her behalf from the Federal Parent Locator Service and must include the factual basis for the allegation;

(2) allege that the petitioner is requesting the information for an authorized purpose and state the purpose for which the information is sought;

(3) include the social security number, sex, race, current address, and date of birth of the petitioner and any alias or prior name used by the petitioner;

(4) include the social security number and date of birth of the respondent and any children in common between the petitioner and the respondent, if known;

(5) disclose any prior litigation between the petitioner and the respondent, if known;

(6) disclose whether the petitioner has been arrested for any felony or misdemeanor in this or any other state and the disposition of the arrest; and

(7) include notice from the Federal Parent Locator Service that location information on the respondent cannot be released because of a family violence indicator.

(d) Initial Court Review. When a complaint is filed, the court shall review the complaint ex parte for legal sufficiency to determine that it is from an authorized person or an individual on whose behalf an authorized person requested information from the Federal Parent Locator Service, is for an authorized purpose, and includes the information required in subdivision (c). If the complaint is legally sufficient, the court shall order the department to request the information from the Federal Parent Locator Service and order the department to keep any information received from the Federal Parent Locator Service in its original sealed envelope and provide it to the court within 45 days in the manner described in subdivision (e).

(e) Receipt of information. When sealed information from the Federal Parent Locator Service is obtained, the department shall file the information with the court. The information from the Federal Parent Locator Service shall remain in its original sealed envelope and the outside of the envelope shall be clearly labeled with the case number and the words "sealed information from Federal Parent Locator Service." The clerk of the court shall ensure that the sealed information from the Federal Parent Locator Service is not disclosed to any person other than those specifically authorized by the court. Court files in these proceedings shall be separately secured in the Clerk's office in accordance with the requirements of subdivision (i).

(f) Review of Information by the Court. The court shall conduct an in-camera examination of the contents of the sealed envelope from the Federal Parent Locator Service.

(1) If the information from the sealed envelope does not include an address for the respondent or an address for the respondent's employer, the petitioner and the department will be notified that no information is available and no further action will be taken. The name of the state that placed the family violence indicator on the record will not be released.

(2) If the information from the sealed envelope includes an address for the respondent or the respondent's employer, the court shall issue an order to show cause to the respondent, the department, the Florida Department of Law Enforcement (FDLE), and the state entity that placed the family violence indicator on the record. The order to show cause shall

(A) give the respondent at least 45 days to show cause why the location information should not be released to the petitioner;

(B) clearly state that the failure to respond may result in disclosure of the respondent's location information;

(C) direct the parties to file with the court all documentary evidence which supports their respective positions, including any prior court orders;

(D) direct the department to search its child support enforcement statewide automated system and case file for the presence of a Florida family violence indicator, for any other information in that system or file that is relevant to the issue of whether release of the respondent's location information to the petitioner could be harmful to the respondent or the child, and whether an application for good cause under section 414.32, Florida Statutes, is pending or has been granted and if so, file documentation with the court within 30 days;

(E) unless the FDLE is the petitioner, direct the FDLE to conduct a search of its Florida criminal history records on the petitioner, including information from the Domestic and Repeat Violence Injunction Statewide Verification system, and file it with the court within 30 days; and

(F) set a hearing date within 60 days.

(3) The order to show cause shall be served as follows:

(A) By regular mail and by certified mail, return receipt requested, to the respondent. If a receipt is not returned or a responsive pleading is not filed, the court may extend the time for response and provide for personal service on the respondent. The petitioner also may request that the respondent be initially served by personal service, and if so, the petitioner shall pay into the registry of the court the cost of effecting personal service.

(B) By certified mail, return receipt requested, to the department, the FDLE, and the state entity that placed the family violence indicator on the record.

(C) A copy of the order to show cause shall be provided to the petitioner. However, the copy shall not include any information that may identify the respondent's location, including but not limited to the name or address of the state entity that placed the family violence indicator on the record.

(g) Providing Information to Court.

(1) *Information from Department.* The department shall submit the information it obtains in response to the order to show cause by filing the information with the court in a sealed envelope. The outside of the envelope shall be clearly labeled with the case number and the words "sealed information from the Department of Revenue." Any information that may reveal the location of the respondent should be distinctly noted so that this information is not inadvertently disclosed.

(2) *Information from FDLE.* When it has searched its records in response to the order to show cause, the FDLE shall file a report with the court. The report shall include the case number and results of the search of its records.

(h) Hearing on Order to Show Cause.

(1) At the hearing on the order to show cause, the court shall determine whether release of the respondent's location information to the petitioner could be harmful to the parent or the child. The petitioner has the burden of proof to show that release of information to the petitioner would not be harmful to the parent or the child.

(A) If the court finds that release of the location information could be harmful, the information shall not be released and the petition shall be denied.

(B) If the court finds that release of the location information would not be harmful, the court shall disclose the location information to the petitioner. The disclosure of the location information shall be made only to the petitioner, and the court shall require that the petitioner not disclose the information to other persons. The disclosure of location information to the petitioner in these proceedings does not entitle the petitioner to future disclosure of the respondent's location information.

(C) The court may deny the request for location information if the respondent agrees to designate a third party for service of process for proceedings between the parties.

(2) Notwithstanding the provisions of Florida Rule of Judicial Administration 2.530, the court may conduct a hearing on the order to show cause by means of communications equipment without consent of the parties and without a limitation on the time of the hearing. The communications equipment shall be config-

ured to ensure that the location of the respondent is not disclosed.

(i) Confidentiality. The clerk of the court shall ensure that all court records in these proceedings are protected according to the requirements of this rule. Court records in these proceedings shall be segregated and secured so that information is not disclosed inadvertently from the court file. All court records in these proceedings are confidential and are not available for public inspection until the court issues a final judgment in the case. After the court issues a final judgment in the case, the location information from the Federal Parent Locator Service and any other information that may lead to disclosure of the respondent's location, including but not limited to the respondent's address, employment information, the name or address of the state that placed the family violence indicator on the record, and the telephone number of the respondent, shall remain confidential and not available for public inspection unless otherwise ordered by the court. After the court issues a final judgment in the case, the court shall release nonconfidential information upon motion.

Added May 17, 2000, effective May 25, 2000 (766 So.2d 999). Amended Oct. 16, 2008, effective Jan. 1, 2009 (995 So.2d 407); Oct. 16, 2008 (995 So.2d 445).

Commentary

This rule implements the requirements of 42 U.S.C. § 653, providing for a state court to override a family violence indicator on a record at the Federal Parent Locator Service. It does not apply to any other proceeding involving family violence or any other court records. The limitations on access to the Federal Parent Locator Service and this override process are governed by federal law.

Proceedings under this rule would arise when an authorized person has attempted to obtain information from the Federal Parent Locator Service but has been notified that the information cannot be released because of a family violence indicator. For example, a petitioner may be a noncustodial parent who has attempted to serve the custodial parent in an action to enforce visitation but was unable to effect service of process on the custodial parent. The court may have authorized access to the Federal Parent Locator Service in order to locate the custodial parent for purposes of service of process. If the report from the Federal Parent Locator Service indicates that the information cannot be released because of a family violence indicator, the noncustodial parent would be authorized to petition the court pursuant to this rule to override the family violence indicator.

The purpose of these proceedings is to determine whether to release location information from the Federal Parent Locator Service notwithstanding the family violence indicator. The court must determine whether release of the location information to the petitioner would be harmful to the respondent. If the court determines that release of the location information would not be harmful, the information may be released to the petitioner. If the respondent agrees to designate a third party for service of process, the court may deny the request for location information. In these circumstances, the designation of a third party for service of process is procedural only and does not provide a separate basis for jurisdiction over the respondent.

The court must use care to ensure that information from the Federal Parent Locator Service or other location information in the court record is not inadvertently released to the petitioner, thus defeating any interest of the respondent in maintaining nondisclosure.

The name of the state that placed the family violence indicator on the record may assist the petitioner in obtaining access to the respondent. If the name of the state that placed the family violence indicator on the record is supplied from the Federal Parent Locator Service, but an address for the respondent is not provided, the court should not release the name of the state to the petitioner. Disclosure of this information could assist the petitioner in locating the respondent, may place the respondent in danger, and does not give the respondent an opportunity to be heard by the court prior to release of the information.

Because the interest of the respondent is to keep location information from the petitioner, having both the petitioner and respondent appear at a hearing at the same time may also result in the petitioner obtaining location information about the respondent. If a hearing must be held where both the petitioner and respondent are present, the court should use whatever security measures are available to prevent inadvertent disclosure of the respondent's location information.

Each state establishes its own criteria, consistent with federal law, for placing a family violence indicator on a record. Some states require a judicial determination of domestic violence or child abuse before a family violence indicator is placed on a record. The criteria for a family violence indicator in Florida are in section 61.1825, Florida Statutes.

The records in these proceedings are confidential under 42 U.S.C. §§ 653 and 654. Florida Rule of Judicial Administration 2.051 [renumbered as 2.420 in 2006] also exempts from public disclosure any records made confidential by federal law.

Committee Note

2008 Amendment. Chapter 2008–61, Laws of Florida, effective October 1, 2008, eliminated such terms as "custodial parent," "noncustodial parent," and "visitation" from Chapter 61, Florida Statutes. Instead, the court adopts or establishes a parenting plan that includes, among other things, a time-sharing schedule for the minor children. These statutory changes are reflected in the amendments to the definitions in this rule. However, because 42 *U.S.C.* § 653 includes the terms "custody" and "visitation," these terms have not been excised from the remainder of the rule.

Rule 12.740. Family Mediation

(a) Applicability. This rule governs mediation of family matters and related issues.

(b) Referral. Except as provided by law and this rule, all contested family matters and issues may be referred to mediation. Every effort shall be made to expedite mediation of family issues.

(c) Limitation on Referral to Mediation. Unless otherwise agreed by the parties, family matters and issues may be referred to a mediator or mediation program which charges a fee only after the court has determined that the parties have the financial ability to pay such a fee. This determination may be based upon the parties' financial affidavits or other financial information available to the court. When the mediator's fee is not established under section 44.108, Florida Statutes, or when there is no written agreement providing for the mediator's compensation, the mediator shall be compensated at an hourly rate set by the presiding judge in the referral order. The presiding judge may also determine the reasonableness of the fees charged by the mediator. When appropriate, the court shall apportion mediation fees between the parties and shall state each party's share in the order of referral. Parties may object to the rate of the mediator's compensation within 15 days of the order of referral by serving an objection on all other parties and the mediator.

(d) Appearances. Unless otherwise stipulated by the parties, a party is deemed to appear at a family mediation convened pursuant to this rule if the named party is physically present at the mediation conference. In the discretion of the mediator and with the agreement of the parties, family mediation may proceed in the absence of counsel unless otherwise ordered by the court.

(e) Completion of Mediation. Mediation shall be completed within 75 days of the first mediation conference unless otherwise ordered by the court.

(f) Report on Mediation.

(1) If agreement is reached as to any matter or issue, including legal or factual issues to be determined by the court, the agreement shall be reduced to writing, signed by the parties and their counsel, if any and if present, and submitted to the court unless the parties agree otherwise. By stipulation of the parties, the agreement may be electronically or stenographically recorded and made under oath or affirmed. In such event, an appropriately signed transcript may be filed with the court.

(2) After the agreement is filed, the court shall take action as required by law. When court approval is not necessary, the agreement shall become binding upon filing. When court approval is necessary, the agreement shall become binding upon approval. In either event, the agreement shall be made part of the final judgment or order in the case.

(3) If the parties do not reach an agreement as to any matter as a result of mediation, the mediator shall report the lack of an agreement to the court without comment or recommendation. With the consent of the parties, the mediator's report may also identify any pending motions or outstanding legal issues, discovery process, or other action by any party which, if resolved or completed, would facilitate the possibility of a settlement.

Amended June 2, 2005 (905 So.2d 865); Dec. 6, 2012, effective Jan. 1, 2013 (104 So.3d 1043).

Commentary

1995 Adoption. This rule is similar to former Florida Rule of Civil Procedure 1.740. All provisions concerning the compensation of the mediator have been incorporated into this rule so that all mediator compensation provisions are contained in one rule. Additionally, this rule clarifies language regarding the filing of transcripts, the mediator's responsibility for mailing a copy of the agreement to counsel, and counsel's filing of written objections to mediation agreements.

Rule 12.741. Mediation Rules

(a) Discovery. Unless stipulated by the parties or ordered by the court, the mediation process shall not suspend discovery.

(b) General Procedures.

(1) *Interim or Emergency Relief.* A party may apply to the court for interim or emergency relief at any time. Mediation shall continue while such a motion is pending absent a contrary order of the court, or a decision of the mediator to adjourn pending disposition of the motion. Time for completing mediation shall be tolled during any periods when mediation is interrupted pending resolution of such a motion.

(2) *Sanctions.* If a party fails to appear at a duly noticed mediation conference without good cause, or knowingly and willfully violates any confidentiality provision under section 44.405, Florida Statutes, the court upon motion shall impose sanctions, including an award of mediator and attorneys' fees and other costs, against the party.

(3) *Adjournments.* The mediator may adjourn the mediation conference at any time and may set times for reconvening the adjourned conference. No further notification is required for parties present at the adjourned conference.

(4) *Counsel.* Counsel shall be permitted to communicate privately with their clients. The mediator shall at all times be in control of the mediation and the procedures to be followed in the mediation.

(5) *Communication with Parties.* The mediator may meet and consult privately with any party or parties or their counsel.

(6) *Appointment of the Mediator.*

(A) Within 10 days of the order of referral, the parties may agree upon a stipulation with the court designating:

(i) a certified mediator, other than a senior judge presiding as a judge in that circuit; or

(ii) a mediator, other than a senior judge, who is not certified as a mediator but who, in the opinion of the parties and upon review by the presiding judge, is otherwise qualified by training or experience to mediate all or some of the issues in the particular case.

(B) If the parties cannot agree upon a mediator within 10 days of the order of referral, the plaintiff or petitioner shall so notify the court within 10 days of the expiration of the period to agree on a mediator, and the court shall appoint a certified mediator selected by rotation or by such other procedures as may be adopted by administrative order of the chief judge in the circuit in which the action is pending.

(C) If a mediator agreed upon by the parties or appointed by a court cannot serve, a substitute mediator can be agreed upon or appointed in the same manner as the original mediator. A mediator shall not mediate a case assigned to another mediator without the agreement of the parties or approval of the court. A substitute mediator shall have the same qualifications as the original mediator.

Amended June 2, 2005 (905 So.2d 865); Nov. 3, 2005, effective Jan. 1, 2006 (915 So.2d 145); June 19, 2014, effective Oct. 1, 2014 (141 So.3d 1172).

Commentary

1995 Adoption. This rule combines and replaces Florida Rules of Civil Procedure 1.710, 1.720, and 1.730. The rule, as combined, is substantially similar to those three previous rules, with the following exceptions. This rule deletes subdivisions (a) and (b) of rule 1.710 and subdivisions (b) and (c) of rule 1.730. This rule compliments Florida Family Law Rule of Procedure 12.740 by providing direction regarding various procedures to be followed in family law mediation proceedings.

Rule 12.742. Parenting Coordination

(a) Applicability. This rule applies to parenting coordination.

(b) Qualification Process. Each judicial circuit shall establish a process for determining that a parenting coordinator is qualified in accordance with the requirements established in the parenting coordination section of Chapter 61, Florida Statutes.

(c) Order Referring Parties to Parenting Coordinator. An order referring the parties to a parenting coordinator must be in substantial compliance with Florida Family Law Rules of Procedure Form 12.984(a). The order must specify the role, responsibility, and authority of the parenting coordinator.

(d) Appointment of Parenting Coordinator. The parties may agree in writing on a parenting coordinator subject to the court's approval. If the parties cannot agree on a parenting coordinator, the court shall appoint a parenting coordinator qualified by law.

(e) Response by Parenting Coordinator. The parenting coordinator must file a response accepting or declining the appointment in substantial compliance with Florida Family Law Rules of Procedure Form 12.984(b).

(f) Term of Service. The term of the parenting coordinator shall be as specified in the order of appointment or as extended by the court. The initial term of service shall not exceed two years. The court shall terminate the service on:

(1) The parenting coordinator's resignation or disqualification; or

(2) A finding of good cause shown based on the court's own motion or a party's written motion. Good cause includes, but is not limited to the occurrence of domestic violence; circumstances that compromise the safety of any person or the integrity of the process; or a finding that there is no longer a need for the service of the parenting coordinator. The motion and notice of hearing shall also be served on the parenting coordinator.

(g) Removal of Parenting Coordinator. The court shall remove the parenting coordinator if the parenting coordinator becomes disqualified under the parenting coordination section of Chapter 61, Florida Statutes, or if good cause is shown.

(h) Appointment of Substitute Parenting Coordinator. If a parenting coordinator cannot serve or continue to serve, a substitute parenting coordinator may be chosen in the same manner as the original.

(i) Authority with Consent. The parenting coordinator may have additional authority with express written consent. If there has been a history of domestic violence the court must find that consent has been freely and voluntarily given.

(1) With the express written consent of both parties, the parenting coordinator may

(A) have temporary decision-making authority to resolve specific non-substantive disputes between the parties until such time as a court order is entered modifying the decision; or

(B) make recommendations to the court concerning modifications to the parenting plan or time-sharing.

(2) With the express written consent of a party, a parenting coordinator may

(A) have access to confidential and privileged records and information of that party; or

(B) provide confidential and privileged information for that party to health care providers and to any other third parties.

(3) With the express approval of the court, the parenting coordinator may

(A) have access to a child's confidential and privileged records and information; or

(B) provide confidential and privileged information for that child to health care providers and to any other third parties.

(j) Limitation of Authority.

(1) A parenting coordinator shall not have decision making authority to resolve substantive disputes between the parties. A dispute is substantive if it would

(A) significantly change the quantity or decrease the quality of time a child spends with either parent; or

(B) modify parental responsibility.

(2) A parenting coordinator shall not make a substantive recommendation concerning parental responsibility or timesharing to the court unless the court on its own motion or a joint motion of the parties determines that:

(A) there is an emergency as defined by the parenting coordination section of Chapter 61, Florida Statutes,

(B) the recommendation would be in the best interest of the child, and

(C) the parties agree that any parenting coordination communications that may be raised to support or challenge the recommendation of the parenting coordinator will be permitted.

(k) Emergency Order.

(1) *Consideration by the Court.* Upon the filing of an affidavit or verified report of an emergency by the parenting coordinator, the court shall determine whether the facts and circumstances contained in the report constitute an emergency and whether an emergency order needs to be entered with or without notice to the parties to prevent or stop furtherance of the emergency. Except for the entry of an ex parte order in accordance with (k)(2), the court shall set a hearing with notice to the parties to be held at the earliest possible time.

(2) *Ex Parte Order.* An emergency order may be entered without notice to the parties if it appears from the facts shown by the affidavit or verified report that there is an immediate and present danger that the emergency situation will occur before the parties can be heard. No evidence other than the affidavit or verified report shall be used to support the emergency being reported unless the parties appear at the hearing or have received notice of a hearing. Every temporary order entered without notice in accordance with this rule shall be endorsed with the date and hour of entry, be filed forthwith in the clerk's office, and define the injury or potential injury, state findings by the court why the injury or potential injury may be irreparable, and give the reasons why the order was granted without notice. The court shall provide the parties and attorney ad litem, if one is appointed, with a copy of the parenting coordinator's affidavit or verified report giving rise to the ex parte order. A return hearing shall be scheduled if the court issues an emergency ex parte order.

(3) *Duration.* The emergency order shall remain in effect until further order.

(4) *Motion to Dissolve or Modify Ex Parte Order.* A motion to modify or dissolve an ex parte emergency order must be heard within 5 days after the movant applies for a hearing.

(*l*) Written Communication with Court. The parenting coordinator may submit a written report or other written communication regarding any nonconfidential matter to the court. Parenting coordinators are required, pursuant to the parenting coordination section of Chapter 61, Florida Statutes, to report certain emergencies to the court without giving notice to the parties. The parenting coordinator shall use a form in substantial compliance with Florida Family Law Rules of Procedure Form 12.984(c) when reporting any emergency to the court, whether or not notice to the parties is required by law. If the parenting coordinator is unable to adequately perform the duties in accordance with the court's direction, the parenting coordinator shall file a written request for a status conference and the court shall set a timely status hearing. The parenting coordinator shall use a form in substantial compliance with Florida Family Law Rules of Procedure Form 12.984(d) to request a status conference. When notice to the parties is required, the parenting coordinator must contemporaneously serve each party with a copy of the written communication.

(m) Testimony and Discovery. A parenting coordinator shall not be called to testify or be subject to the discovery rules of the Florida Family Law Rules of Procedure unless the court makes a prior finding of good cause. A party must file a motion, alleging good cause why the court should allow the parenting coordinator to testify or be subject to discovery. The requesting party shall serve the motion and notice of hearing on the parenting coordinator. The requesting party shall initially be responsible for the parenting coordinator's fees and costs incurred as a result of the motion.

(n) Parenting Coordination Session. A parenting coordination session occurs when a party and the parenting coordinator communicate with one another. A parenting coordination session may occur in the presence or with the participation of persons in addition to a party and the parenting coordinator. Unless otherwise directed by the court, the parenting coordinator shall determine who may be present during each parenting coordination session including, without limitation, attorneys, parties, and other persons.

Added Jan. 28, 2010 (27 So.3d 650). Amended July 3, 2014, effective July 3, 2014 (142 So.3d 831).

Committee Notes

2010 Adoption. The provisions of subdivision (k) do not abrogate the confidentiality provisions of section 61.125, Florida Statutes. An exception to confidentiality must apply before invoking this subdivision of the rule.

2014 Revision. Parties are more likely to comply with a parenting plan which has been voluntarily and mutually self-determined by the parties without undue outside influence. Courts therefore should consider referring parties to mediation prior to parenting coordination when a parenting plan has not been agreed to by the parties or adopted by the court. Courts are also encouraged to review what additional forms of alternative dispute resolution as well as social, psychological and educational interventions may best assist the parties in a timely manner. In cases where parties are referred to a parenting coordinator to adopt or create a parenting plan, the court should consider whether the parties would be better served by the court determining certain aspects of the parenting plan (such as parental responsibility, time sharing schedule, etc.) prior to referral to a parenting coordinator. New subdivisions (b), (g), (j)(2), (*l*), and (n) were added and others were renumbered accordingly.

Rule 12.750. Family Self–Help Programs

(a) Establishment of Programs. A chief judge, by administrative order, may establish a self-help program to facilitate access to family courts. The purpose of a self-help program is to assist self-represented litigants, within the bounds of this rule, to achieve fair and efficient resolution of their family law case. The purpose of a self-help program is not to provide legal advice to self-represented litigants. This rule applies only to programs established and operating under the auspices of the court pursuant to this rule.

(b) Definitions.

(1) "Family law case" means any case in the circuit that is assigned to the family law division.

(2) "Self-represented litigant" means any individual who seeks information to file, pursue, or respond to a family law case without the assistance of a lawyer authorized to practice before the court.

(3) "Self-help personnel" means lawyer and nonlawyer personnel in a self-help program.

(4) "Self-help program" means a program established and operating under the authority of this rule.

(5) "Approved form" means (A) Florida Family Law Rules of Procedure Forms or Florida Supreme Court Approved Family Law Forms or (B) forms that have been approved in writing by the chief judge of a circuit and that are not inconsistent with the Supreme Court approved forms, copies of which are to be sent to the chief justice, the chair of the Family Law Rules Committee of The Florida Bar, the chair of the Family Law Section of The Florida Bar, and the chair of the Family Court Steering Committee. Forms approved by a chief judge may be used unless specifically rejected by the Supreme Court.

(c) Services Provided. Self-help personnel may:

(1) encourage self-represented litigants to obtain legal advice;

(2) provide information about available pro bono legal services, low cost legal services, legal aid programs, and lawyer referral services;

(3) provide information about available approved forms, without providing advice or recommendation as to any specific course of action;

(4) provide approved forms and approved instructions on how to complete the forms;

(5) engage in limited oral communications to assist a person in the completion of blanks on approved forms;

(6) record information provided by a self-represented litigant on approved forms;

(7) provide, either orally or in writing, definitions of legal terminology from widely accepted legal dictionaries or other dictionaries without advising whether or not a particular definition is applicable to the self-represented litigant's situation;

(8) provide, either orally or in writing, citations of statutes and rules, without advising whether or not a particular statute or rule is applicable to the self-represented litigant's situation;

(9) provide docketed case information;

(10) provide general information about court process, practice, and procedure;

(11) provide information about mediation, required parenting courses, and courses for children of divorcing parents;

(12) provide, either orally or in writing, information from local rules or administrative orders;

(13) provide general information about local court operations;

(14) provide information about community services; and

(15) facilitate the setting of hearings.

(d) Limitations on Services. Self-help personnel shall not:

(1) provide legal advice or recommend a specific course of action for a self-represented litigant;

(2) provide interpretation of legal terminology, statutes, rules, orders, cases, or the constitution;

(3) provide information that must be kept confidential by statute, rule, or case law;

(4) deny a litigant's access to the court;

(5) encourage or discourage litigation;

(6) record information on forms for a self-represented litigant, except as otherwise provided by this rule;

(7) engage in oral communications other than those reasonably necessary to elicit factual information to complete the blanks on forms except as otherwise authorized by this rule;

(8) perform legal research for litigants;

(9) represent litigants in court; and

(10) lead litigants to believe that they are representing them as lawyers in any capacity or induce the public to rely upon them for legal advice.

(e) Unauthorized Practice of Law. The services listed in subdivision (c), when performed by nonlawyer personnel in a self-help program, shall not be the unauthorized practice of law.

(f) No Confidentiality. Notwithstanding ethics rules that govern attorneys, certified legal interns, and other persons working under the supervision of an attorney, information given by a self-represented litigant to self-help personnel is not confidential or privileged.

(g) No Conflict. Notwithstanding ethics rules that govern attorneys, certified legal interns, and other persons working under the supervision of an attorney, there is no conflict of interest in providing services to both parties.

(h) Notice of Limitation of Services Provided. Before receiving the services of a self-help program, self-help personnel shall thoroughly explain the "Notice of Limitation of Services Provided" disclaimer below. Each self-represented litigant, after receiving an explanation of the disclaimer, shall sign an acknowledgment that the disclaimer has been explained to the self-represented litigant and that the self-represented litigant understands the limitation of the services provided. The self-help personnel shall sign the acknowledgment certifying compliance with this requirement. The original shall be filed by the self-help personnel in the court file and a copy shall be provided to the self-represented litigant.

NOTICE OF LIMITATION OF SERVICES PROVIDED

THE PERSONNEL IN THIS SELF–HELP PROGRAM ARE NOT ACTING AS YOUR LAWYER OR PROVIDING LEGAL ADVICE TO YOU.

SELF–HELP PERSONNEL ARE NOT ACTING ON BEHALF OF THE COURT OR ANY JUDGE. THE PRESIDING JUDGE IN YOUR CASE MAY REQUIRE AMENDMENT OF A FORM OR SUBSTITUTION OF A DIFFERENT FORM. THE JUDGE IS NOT REQUIRED TO GRANT THE RELIEF REQUESTED IN A FORM.

THE PERSONNEL IN THIS SELF–HELP PROGRAM CANNOT TELL YOU WHAT YOUR LEGAL RIGHTS OR REMEDIES ARE, REPRESENT YOU IN COURT, OR TELL YOU HOW TO TESTIFY IN COURT.

SELF–HELP SERVICES ARE AVAILABLE TO ALL PERSONS WHO ARE OR WILL BE PARTIES TO A FAMILY CASE.

THE INFORMATION THAT YOU GIVE TO AND RECEIVE FROM SELF–HELP PERSONNEL IS NOT CONFIDENTIAL AND MAY BE SUBJECT TO DISCLOSURE AT A LATER DATE. IF ANOTHER PERSON INVOLVED IN YOUR CASE SEEKS ASSISTANCE FROM THIS SELF–HELP PROGRAM, THAT PERSON WILL BE GIVEN THE SAME TYPE OF ASSISTANCE THAT YOU RECEIVE.

IN ALL CASES, IT IS BEST TO CONSULT WITH YOUR OWN ATTORNEY, ESPECIALLY IF YOUR CASE PRESENTS SIGNIFICANT ISSUES REGARDING CHILDREN, CHILD SUPPORT, ALIMONY, RETIREMENT OR PENSION BENEFITS, ASSETS, OR LIABILITIES.

___ I CAN READ ENGLISH.

___ I CANNOT READ ENGLISH. THIS NOTICE WAS READ TO ME BY {*NAME*} _________ IN {*LANGUAGE*} _________.

____

SIGNATURE

AVISO DE LIMITACION DE SERVICIOS OFRECIDOS

EL PERSONAL DE ESTE PROGRAMA DE AYUDA PROPIA NO ESTA ACTUANDO COMO SU ABOGADO NI LE ESTA DANDO CONSEJOS LEGALES.

ESTE PERSONAL NO REPRESENTA NI LA CORTE NI NINGUN JUEZ. EL JUEZ ASIGNADO A SU CASO PUEDE REQUERIR UN CAMBIO DE ESTA FORMA O UNA FORMA DIFERENTE. EL JUEZ NO ESTA OBLIGADO A CONCEDER LA REPARACION QUE USTED PIDE EN ESTA FORMA.

EL PERSONAL DE ESTE PROGRAMA DE AYUDA PROPIA NO LE PUEDE DECIR CUALES SON SUS DERECHOS NI SOLUCIONES LEGALES, NO PUEDE REPRESENTARLO EN CORTE, NI DECIRLE COMO TESTIFICAR EN CORTE.

SERVICIOS DE AYUDA PROPIA ESTAN DISPONIBLES A TODAS LAS PERSONAS QUE SON O SERAN PARTES DE UN CASO FAMILIAR.

LA INFORMACION QUE USTED DA Y RECIBE DE ESTE PERSONAL NO ES CONFIDENCIAL Y PUEDE SER DESCUBIERTA MAS ADELANTE. SI OTRA PERSONA ENVUELTA EN SU CASO PIDE AYUDA DE ESTE PRO-

GRAMA, ELLOS RECIBIRAN EL MISMO TIPO DE ASISTENCIA QUE USTED RECIBE.

EN TODOS LOS CASOS, ES MEJOR CONSULTAR CON SU PROPIO ABOGADO, ESPECIALMENTE SI SU CASO TRATA DE TEMAS RESPECTO A NINOS, MANTENIMIENTO ECONOMICO DE NINOS, MANUTENCION MATRIMONIAL, RETIRO O BENEFICIOS DE PENSION, ACTIVOS U OBLIGACIONES.

___ YO PUEDO LEER ESPANOL.

___ YO NO PUEDO LEER ESPANOL. ESTE AVISO FUE LEIDO A MI POR {*NOMBRE*} ________ EN {*IDIOMA*} ________.

____

FIRMA

If information is provided by telephone, the notice of limitation of services provided shall be heard by all callers prior to speaking to self-help staff.

(i) Exemption. Self-help personnel are not required to complete Florida Family Law Rules of Procedure Form 12.900(a), Disclosure From Nonlawyer, as required by rule 10–2.1, Rules Regulating The Florida Bar. The provisions in rule 10–2.1, Rules Regulating The Florida Bar, which require a nonlawyer to include the nonlawyer's name and identifying information on a form if the nonlawyer assisted in the completion of a form, are not applicable to self-help personnel unless the self-help personnel recorded the information on the form as authorized by this rule.

(j) Availability of Services. Self-help programs are available to all self-represented litigants in family law cases.

(k) Cost of Services. Self-help programs, as authorized by statute, may require self-represented litigants to pay the cost of services provided for by this rule, provided that the charge for persons who are indigent is substantially reduced or waived.

(*l*) Records. All records made or received in connection with the official business of a self-help program are judicial records and access to such records shall be governed by Florida Rule of Judicial Administration 2.420.

(m) Domestic, Repeat, Dating, and Sexual Violence, and Stalking Exclusion. Nothing in this rule shall restrict services provided by the clerk of the court or family or injunctions for protection intake personnel pursuant to rule 12.610.

Added Dec. 3, 1998, effective Jan. 1, 1999 (725 So.2d 365). Amended Sept. 21, 2000 (810 So.2d 1); July 10, 2003 (853 So.2d 303); June 2, 2005 (905 So.2d 865); Oct. 16, 2008, effective Jan. 1, 2009 (995 So.2d 407); July 12, 2012, effective Oct. 1, 2012 (95 So.3d 126).

Commentary

1998 Adoption. It should be emphasized that the personnel in the self-help programs should not be providing legal advice to self-represented litigants. Self-help personnel should not engage in any activities that constitute the practice of law or inadvertently create an attorney-client relationship. Self-help programs should consistently encourage self-represented litigants to seek legal advice from a licensed attorney. The provisions of this rule only apply to programs established by the chief judge.

Subdivision (b). This rule applies only to assistance offered in family law cases. The types of family law cases included in a family law division may vary based on local rule and it is anticipated that a local rule establishing a self-help program may also exclude types of family law cases from the self-help program. Programs may operate with lawyer personnel, nonlawyer personnel, or a combination thereof.

Subdivision (c)(2). The self-help program is encouraged to cooperate with the local bar to develop a workable system to provide this information. The program may maintain information about members of The Florida Bar who are willing to provide services to self-represented litigants. The program may not show preference for a particular service, program, or attorney.

Subdivision (c)(3). In order to avoid the practice of law, the self-help personnel should not recommend a specific course of action.

Subdivision (c)(5). Self-help personnel should not suggest the specific information to be included in the blanks on the forms. Oral communications between the self-help personnel and the self-represented litigant should be focused on the type of information the form is designed to elicit.

Subdivision (c)(8). Self-help personnel should be familiar with the court rules and the most commonly used statutory provisions. Requests for information beyond these commonly used statutory provisions would require legal research, which is prohibited by subdivision (d)(8).

Subdivision (c)(9). Self-help personnel can have access to the court's docket and can provide information from the docket to the self-represented litigant.

Subdivision (f). Because an attorney-client relationship is not formed, the information provided by a self-represented litigant is not confidential or privileged.

Subdivision (g). Because an attorney-client relationship is not formed, there is no conflict in providing the limited services authorized under this rule to both parties.

Subdivision (h). It is intended that self-represented litigants who receive services from a self-help program understand that they are not receiving legal services. One purpose of the disclosure is to prevent an attorney-client relationship from being formed. In addition to the signed disclosure, it is recommended that each program post the disclosure in a prominent place in the self-help program. The written disclosure should be available and posted in the languages that are in prevalent use in the county.

Subdivision (i). This provision is to clarify that nonlawyer personnel are not required to use Florida Family Law Rules of Procedure Form 12.900(a) because the information is included in the disclosure required by this rule. Self–help personnel are required to include their name and identifying information on any form on which they record information for a self-represented litigant.

SECTION II. FAMILY LAW FORMS, COMMENTARY, AND INSTRUCTIONS

Form	
12.941(b).	Temporary Injunction to Prevent Removal of Minor Child(ren) and/or Denial of Passport Services (Ex Parte).
12.941(c).	Temporary Injunction to Prevent Removal of Minor Child(ren) and/or Denial of Passport Services (After Notice).
12.941(d).	Emergency Verified Motion for Child Pick–Up Order.
12.941(e).	Order to Pick-Up Minor Child(ren).
12.942(a).	Motion for Appointment of Guardian Ad Litem.
12.942(b).	Order Appointing Guardian Ad Litem.
12.943.	Motion to Deviate from Child Support Guidelines.
12.944(a).	Motion for Testimony and Attendance of Minor Child(ren).
12.944(b).	Order for Testimony and Attendance of Minor Child(ren).
12.947(a).	Motion for Temporary Support, Time-Sharing, and Other Relief with Dependent or Minor Child(ren).
12.947(b).	Temporary Order of Support, Time-Sharing, and Other Relief with Dependent or Minor Child(ren).
12.947(c).	Motion for Temporary Support and Other Relief with No Dependent or Minor Child(ren).
12.947(d).	Order for Temporary Support and Other Relief with no Dependent or Minor Child(ren).
12.950(a).	Agreement for Relocation With Minor Child(ren).
12.950(b).	Motion for Order Permitting Relocation With Agreement.
12.950(c).	Petition for Dissolution of Marriage With Dependent or Minor Child(ren) and Relocation.
12.950(d).	Supplemental Petition to Permit Relocation With Minor Child(ren).
12.950(e).	Motion for Temporary Order Granting Relocation.
12.950(f).	Temporary Order Granting/Denying Relocation.
12.950(g).	Motion for Civil Contempt and/or Return of Child(ren).
12.950(h).	Order on Motion for Civil Contempt for Relocation and/or Return of Child(ren).
12.950(i).	Final Judgment/Supplemental Final Judgment Granting Relocation.
12.950(j).	Final Judgment/Supplemental Final Judgment Denying Relocation.
12.951(a).	Petition to Disestablish Paternity and/or Terminate Child Support Obligation.
12.951(b).	Order Disestablishing Paternity and/or Terminating Child Support Obligation.
12.960.	Motion for Civil Contempt/Enforcement.
12.961.	Notice of Hearing on Motion for Contempt/Enforcement in Support Matters (Rule 12.615).
12.962.	Writ of Bodily Attachment (Child Support).
12.970(a).	Petition for Temporary Custody by Extended Family.
12.970(b).	Petition for Concurrent Custody by Extended Family.
12.970(c).	Waiver of Service of Process and Consent for Temporary Custody by Extended Family.
12.970(d).	Waiver of Service of Process and Consent for Concurrent Custody by Extended Family.
12.970(e).	Order Granting Petition for Temporary Custody by Extended Family.
12.970(f).	Order Granting Petition for Concurrent Custody by Extended Family.
12.980(a).	Petition for Injunction for Protection Against Domestic Violence.
12.980(b)(1).	Order Setting Hearing on Petition for Injunction for Protection Against Domestic Violence, Repeat Violence, Dating Violence, Sexual Violence, or Stalking, Without Issuance of an Interim Temporary Injunction.
12.980(b)(2).	Order Denying Petition for Injunction for Protection Against Domestic Violence, Repeat Violence, Dating Violence, or Sexual Violence, or Stalking.
12.980(c)(1).	Temporary Injunction for Protection Against Domestic Violence With Minor Child(ren).
12.980(c)(2).	Temporary Injunction for Protection Against Domestic Violence Without Minor Child(ren).
12.980(d)(1).	Final Judgment of Injunction for Protection Against Domestic Violence with Minor Child(ren) (After Notice).
12.980(d)(2).	Final Judgment of Injunction for Protection Against Domestic Violence Without Minor Child(ren) (After Notice).
12.980(e).	Order of Dismissal of Temporary Injunction for Protection Against ( ) Domestic Violence ( ) Repeat Violence ( ) Dating Violenc ( ) Sexual Violence ( ) Stalking.
12.980(f).	Petition for Injunction for Protection Against Repeat Violence.
12.980(g).	Supplemental Affidavit in Support of Petition for Injunction for Protection Against ( ) Domestic Violence ( ) Repeat Violence ( ) Dating Violence ( ) Sexual Violence ( ) Stalking.
12.980(h).	Request for Confidential Filing of Address.
12.980(i).	Motion for Extension of Injunction for Protection Against ( ) Domestic Violence ( ) Repeat Violence ( ) Dating Violence ( ) Sexual Violence ( ) Stalking.
12.980(j).	Motion for Modification of Injunction for Protection Against ( ) Domestic Violence ( ) Repeat Violence ( ) Dating Violence ( ) Sexual Violence ( ) Stalking.
12.980(k).	Temporary Injunction for Protection Against Repeat Violence.
12.980(*l*).	Final Judgment of Injunction for Protection Against Repeat Violence (After Notice).
12.980(m).	Order Extending Injunction for Protection Against ( ) Domestic Violence ( ) Repeat Violence ( ) Dating Violence ( ) Sexual Violence ( ) Stalking.
12.980(n).	Petition for Injunction for Protection Against Dating Violence.
12.980(*o*).	Temporary Injunction for Protection Against Dating Violence.
12.980(p).	Final Judgment of Injunction for Protection Against Dating Violence (After Notice).
12.980(q).	Petition for Injunction for Protection Against Sexual Violence.
12.980(r).	Temporary Injunction for Protection Against Sexual Violence.
12.980(s).	Final Judgment of Injunction for Protection Against Sexual Violence (After Notice).
12.980(t).	Petition for Injunction for Protection Against Stalking.

GENERAL INFORMATION

FAMILY LAW FORMS, COMMENTARY, AND INSTRUCTIONS
GENERAL INFORMATION FOR SELF-REPRESENTED LITIGANTS (09/13)

You should read this General Information thoroughly before taking any other steps to file your case or represent yourself in court. Most of this information is **not** repeated in the attached forms. This information should provide you with an overview of the court system, its participants, and its processes. It should be useful whether you want to represent yourself in a pending matter or have a better understanding of the way family court works. **This is not intended as a substitute for legal advice from an attorney. Each case has its own particular set of circumstances, and an attorney may advise you of what is best for you in your individual situation.**

These instructions are not the only place that you can get information about how a family case works. You may want to look at other books for more help. The Florida Statutes,

Florida Family Law Rules of Procedure, Florida Rules of Civil Procedure, and other legal information or books may be found at the public library or in a law library at your county courthouse or a law school in your area. If you are filing a petition for **Name Change** and/or **Adoption**, these instructions may not apply.

If the word(s) is printed in **bold**, this means that the word is being emphasized. Throughout these instructions, you will also find words printed in **bold** and **underlined**. This means that the definitions of these words may be found in the glossary of common family law terms at the end of this general information section.

Commentary

1995 Adoption. To help the many people in family law court cases who do not have attorneys to represent them (pro se litigants), the Florida Supreme Court added these simplified forms and directions to the Florida Family Law Rules of Procedure. The directions refer to the Florida Family Law Rules of Procedure or the Florida Rules of Civil Procedure. Many of the forms were adapted from the forms accompanying the Florida Rules of Civil Procedure. Practitioners should refer to the committee notes for those forms for rule history.

The forms were adopted by the Court pursuant to *Family Law Rules of Procedure*, 667 So. 2d 202 (Fla. 1995); *In re Petition for Approval of Forms Pursuant to Rule 10–1.1(b) of the Rules Regulating the Florida Bar—Stepparent Adoption Forms*, 613 So. 2d 900 (Fla. 1992); *Rules Regulating the Florida Bar—Approval of Forms*, 581 So. 2d 902 (Fla. 1991).

Although the forms are part of these rules, they are not all-inclusive, and additional forms, as necessary, should be taken from the Florida Rules of Civil Procedure as provided in Florida Family Law Rules of Procedure. Also, the following notice has been included to strongly encourage individuals to seek the advice, when needed, of an attorney who is a member in good standing of the Florida Bar.

1997 Amendment. In 1997, the Florida Family Law Forms were completely revised to simplify and correct the forms. Additionally, the appendices were eliminated, the instructions contained in the appendices were incorporated into the forms, and the introduction following the Notice to Parties was created. Minor changes were also made to the Notice to Parties set forth below.

NOTICE TO PARTIES WHO ARE NOT REPRESENTED BY AN ATTORNEY WHO IS A MEMBER IN GOOD STANDING OF THE FLORIDA BAR

If you have questions or concerns about these forms, instructions, commentary, the use of the forms, or your legal rights, it is strongly recommended that you talk to an attorney. If you do not know an attorney, you should call the lawyer referral service listed in the yellow pages of the telephone book under "Attorney." If you do not have the money to hire an attorney, you should call the legal aid office in your area. Because the law does change, the forms and information about them may have become outdated. You should be aware that changes may have taken place in the law or court rules that would affect the accuracy of the forms or instructions.

In no event will the Florida Supreme Court, The Florida Bar, or anyone contributing to the production of these forms or instructions be liable for any direct, indirect, or consequential damages resulting from their use.

FAMILY LAW PROCEDURES

Communication with the court. Ex parte communication is communication with the judge with only one party present. Judges are not allowed to engage in ex parte communication except in very limited circumstances, so, absent specific authorization to the contrary, you should not try to speak with or write to the judge in your case unless the other party is present or has been properly notified. **If you have something you need to tell the judge, you must ask for a hearing and give notice to the other party or file a written statement in the court file and send a copy of the written statement to the other party.**

Filing a case. A case begins with the filing of a **petition**. A petition is a written request to the court for some type of legal action. The person who originally asks for legal action is called the **petitioner** and remains the petitioner throughout the case.

A petition is given to the **clerk of the circuit court**, whose office is usually located in the county courthouse or a branch of the county courthouse. A case number is assigned and an official court file is opened. Delivering the petition to the clerk's office is called **filing** a case. A **filing fee** is usually required.

Once a case has been filed, a copy must be given to (served on) the respondent. The person against whom the original legal action is being requested is called the **respondent**, because he or she is expected to respond to the petition. The respondent remains the respondent throughout the case.

Service. When one party files a **petition**, **motion**, or other **pleading**, the other party must be "served" with a copy of the document. This means that the other party is given proper notice of the pending action(s) and any scheduled hearings. **Personal service** of the petition and summons on the respondent by a deputy sheriff or private process server is required in all **original petitions** and **supplemental petitions**, unless **constructive service** is permitted by law. Personal service may also be required in other actions by some judges. After initial service of the original or supplemental petition and summons by a deputy sheriff or private process server, service of most motions and other documents or papers filed in the case generally may be made by email, regular U.S. mail, or hand delivery. However, service by **certified mail** is required at other times so you have proof that the other party actually received the papers. The instructions with each form will advise you of the type of **service** required for that form. **If the other party is represented by an attorney, you should serve the attorney and send a copy to the other party, except for original or supplemental petitions, which must be personally served on the respondent.**

Other than the original or supplemental petitions, any time you file additional pleadings or motions in your case, you must provide a copy to the other party and include a **certificate of service**. Likewise, the other party must provide you with copies of everything that he or she files. Service of additional documents is usually completed by U.S. mail. For more information, see the instructions for **Certificate of Service (General)**, Florida Supreme Court Approved Family Law Form 12.914.

Forms for service of process are included in the Florida Family Law Forms, along with more detailed instructions and information regarding service. The instructions to those forms should be read carefully to ensure that you have the other party properly served. **If proper service is not obtained, the court cannot hear your case.**

Note: If you absolutely do not know where the other party to your case lives, or if the other party resides in another state, you may be able to use **constructive service**. However, if constructive service is used, other than granting a divorce, the court may only grant limited relief, which cannot include either alimony or child support. For more information on constructive service, see **Notice of Action for Dissolution of Marriage (No Child or Financial Support)**, Florida Supreme Court Approved Family Law Form 12.913(a)(1), **Notice of Action for Family Cases with Minor Child(ren)**, Florida Supreme Court Approved Family Law Form 12.913(a)(2), **Affidavit of Diligent Search and Inquiry**, Florida Family Law Rules of Procedure Form 12.913(b), and **Affidavit of Diligent Search**, Florida Family Law Rules of Procedure Form 12.913(c).. Additionally, if the other party is in the military service of the United States, additional steps for service may be required. See, for example, **Memorandum for Certificate of Military Service**, Florida Supreme Court Approved Family Law Form 12.912(a). In sum, the law regarding constructive service and service on an individual in the military is very complex and you may wish to consult an attorney regarding these issues.

Default . . . After being served with a petition or **counterpetition**, the other party has 20 days to file a response. If a response to a petition is not filed, the petitioner may file a **Motion for Default**, Florida Supreme Court Approved Family Law Form 12.922(a), with the clerk. This means that you may proceed with your case and set a **final hearing**, and a **judge** will make a decision, even if the other party will not cooperate. For more information, see rule 12.080(c), Florida Family Law Rules of Procedure.

Answer and Counterpetition . . . After being served, the respondent has 20 days to file an answer admitting or denying each of the allegations contained in the petition. In addition to an answer, the respondent may also file a counterpetition. In a counterpetition, the respondent may request the same or some other relief or action not requested by the petitioner. If the respondent files a counterpetition, the petitioner should then file an **Answer to Counterpetition**, Florida Supreme Court Approved Family Law Form 12.903(d), and either admit or deny the allegations in the respondent's counterpetition.

Mandatory disclosure . . . Rule 12.285, Florida Family Law Rules of Procedure, requires each party in a **dissolution of marriage** to exchange certain information and documents, and file a **Family Law Financial Affidavit**, Florida Family Law Rules of Procedure Form 12.902(b) or (c). Failure to make this required disclosure within the time required by the Florida Family Law Rules of Procedure may allow the court to dismiss the case or to refuse to consider the pleadings of the party failing to comply. This requirement also must be met in other family law cases, **except** adoptions, simplified dissolutions of marriage, enforcement proceedings, contempt proceedings, and proceedings for injunctions for domestic or repeat violence. The **Certificate of Compliance with Mandatory Disclosure**, Florida Family Law Rules of Procedure Form 12.932, lists the documents that must be given to the other party. For more information see rule 12.285, Florida Family Law Rules of Procedure, and the instructions to the **Certificate of Compliance with Mandatory Disclosure**, Florida Family Law Rules of Procedure Form 12.932.

Parenting Plan. If your case involves minor or dependent child(ren), a **Parenting Plan** shall be approved or established by the court. **Parenting Plan**, Florida Supreme Court Approved Family Law Form, 12.995(a), **Safety–Focused Parenting Plan**, Florida Supreme Court Approved Family Law Form 12.995(b), or **Relocation/Long Distance Parenting Plan**, Florida Supreme Court Approved Family Law Form 12.995(c). The Parenting Plan shall be developed and agreed to by the parents and approved by a court. **If the parents cannot agree, or if the agreed Parenting Plan is not approved, the court must establish a Parenting Plan.** The Parenting Plan shall contain a time-sharing schedule and should address the issues regarding the child(ren)'s education, health care, and physical, social, and emotional well-being.

Setting a hearing or trial. Generally, the court will have hearings on motions, final hearings on **uncontested** or **default** cases, and trials on contested cases. Before setting your case for **final hearing** or trial, certain requirements such as completing mandatory disclosure and filing certain papers and having them served on the other party must be met. These requirements vary depending on the type of case and the procedures in your particular jurisdiction. For further information, you should refer to the instructions for the type of form you are filing.

Next, you must obtain a hearing or trial date so that the court may consider your request. You should ask the clerk of court, or **family law intake staff** about the local procedure for setting a hearing or trial, which you should attend. These family law forms contain **orders** and **final judgments**, which the judge may use. You should ask the clerk of court or family law intake staff if you need to bring one of these forms with you to the hearing or trial. If so, you should type or print the heading, including the circuit, county, case number, division, and the parties' names, and leave the rest blank for the judge to complete at your hearing or trial.

Below are explanations of symbols or parts of different family law forms...

{specify}, {date}, {name(s)}, {street}, {city}, {state}, {phone}

Throughout these forms, you will find hints such as those above. These tell you what to put in the blank(s).

[one only] [all that apply]

These show how many choices you should check. Sometimes you may check only one, while other times you may check several choices. ( ) This also shows an area where you must make a choice. Check the ( ) in front of the choice that applies to you or your case.

IN THE CIRCUIT COURT OF THE ________(1)________ JUDICIAL CIRCUIT,
IN AND FOR ________(2)________ COUNTY, FLORIDA

Case No.: ________(3)________
Division: ________(4)________

________(5)________,
Petitioner,

and

________(6)________,
Respondent.

Line 1 The clerk of court can tell you the number of your judicial circuit. Type or print it here.
Line 2 Type or print your county name on line (2).
Line 3 If you are filing an initial petition or pleading, the Clerk of the Court will assign a case number after the case is filed. You should type or print this case number on all papers you file in this case.
Line 4 The clerk of the court can tell you the name of the division in which your case is being filed, and you should type or print it here. Divisions vary from court to court. For example, your case may be filed in the civil division, the family division, or the juvenile division.
Line 5 Type or print the legal name of the person who originally filed the case on line 5. This person is the petitioner because he/she is the one who filed the original petition.
Line 6 Type or print the other party's legal name on line 6. The other party is the respondent because he/she is responding to the petition.

I understand that I am swearing or affirming under oath to the truthfulness of the claims made in this petition and that the punishment for knowingly making a false statement includes fines and/or imprisonment.

Dated: ________(1)________ ________(2)________
Signature of Petitioner
Printed Name: ________(3)________
Address: ________(4)________
City, State, Zip: ________(5)________
Telephone Number: ________(6)________
Fax Number: ________(7)________
Email Address: ________(8)________

Some forms require that your signature be witnessed. You must sign the form in the presence of a **notary public** or deputy clerk (employee of the clerk of the court's office). When signing the form, you must have a valid photo identification unless the notary knows you personally. You should completely fill in all lines (1 & 3–8) except 2 with the requested information, if applicable. **Line 2, the signature line, must be signed in the presence of the notary public or deputy clerk.**

STATE OF FLORIDA
COUNTY OF ____________________

Sworn to or affirmed and signed before me on ____________ by ____________________.

____
NOTARY PUBLIC or DEPUTY CLERK

____
[Print, type, or stamp commissioned name of notary or clerk.]

___ Personally known
___ Produced identification
Type of identification produced ____________________

DO NOT SIGN OR FILL IN THIS PART OF ANY FORM. This section of the form is to be completed by the notary public who is witnessing your signature.

IF A NONLAWYER HELPED YOU FILL OUT THIS FORM, HE/SHE MUST FILL IN THE BLANKS BELOW:
[**fill in all** blanks] This form was prepared for the: *{either Petitioner or Respondent; or Husband or Wife}*
This form was completed with the assistance of:
*{name of individual }*________(1)____________________,
*{name of business}*____________(2)____________________,
{address} ____________________(3)____________________,
*{city}*___(4)__________,*{state}* __________(5), *{telephone number}* _(6)__________.

This section should be completed by anyone who helps you fill out these forms but is **not** an attorney who is a member in good standing of The Florida Bar, which means that he or she is not licensed to practice law in Florida.

Line 1 The **nonlawyer** who helps you should type or print his or her name on line 1.
Lines 2–6 The nonlawyer's business name, address, (including street, city, state, and telephone number) should be typed or printed on lines 2–6.

In addition, a **Disclosure from Nonlawyer**, Florida Family Law Rules of Procedure Form 12.900(a), should be completed if a nonlawyer assists you. The disclosure is available as a family law form and should be completed before the nonlawyer helps you. This is to be sure that you understand the role and limitations of a nonlawyer. You and the nonlawyer should keep a copy of this disclosure for your records.

FAMILY LAW GLOSSARY OF COMMON TERMS AND DEFINITIONS

Note: The following definitions are intended to be helpful, BUT they are not intended to constitute legal advice or address every possible meaning of the term(s) contained in this glossary.

Affidavit—a written statement in which the facts stated are sworn or affirmed to be true.

Alimony-spousal support which may be ordered by the court in a proceeding for dissolution of marriage. Types of alimony include: bridge-the-gap, durational, rehabilitative, or retroactive and may be either temporary or permanent. The court may order periodic payments, payment in lump sum, or both. In determining whether to award alimony, the court must determine whether either party has an actual need for alimony and whether the other party has the ability to pay. The court must consider the factors set forth in section 61.08, Florida Statutes, and must make certain written findings. An alimony award may not leave the paying party with significantly less net income than that of the receiving party without written findings of exceptional circumstances.

Answer—written response by a respondent that states whether he or she admits (agrees with) or denies (disagrees with) the allegations in the petition. Any allegations not specifically denied are considered to be admitted.

Appeal—asking a district court of appeal to review the decision in your case. There are strict procedural and time requirements for filing an appeal.

Asset—everything owned by you or your spouse, including property, cars, furniture, bank accounts, jewelry, life insurance policies, businesses, or retirement plans. An asset may be marital or non-marital, but that distinction is for the court to determine if you and your spouse do not agree.

Attorney—a person with special education and training in the field of law who is a member in good standing of The Florida Bar and licensed to practice law in Florida. An attorney is the only person who is allowed to give you legal advice. An attorney may file your case and represent you in court, or just advise you of your rights before you file your own case. In addition to advising you of your rights, an attorney may tell you what to expect and help prepare you for court. In family law matters, you are not entitled to a court-appointed lawyer, like a public defender in a criminal case. However, legal assistance is often available for those who are unable to hire a private attorney. You may consult the yellow pages of the telephone directory for a listing of legal aid or lawyer referral services in your area, or ask your local clerk of court or family law intake staff what services are available in your area. You may also obtain information from the Florida Supreme Court's Internet site located at http://www.flcourts.org.

Bond—money paid to the clerk of court by one party in a case, to be held and paid to an enjoined party in the event that the first party causes loss or damage of property as a result of wrongfully enjoining the other party.

Beneficiary Designation–Florida law provides that a beneficiary designation made by or on behalf of a party providing for the payment or transference of an asset or benefit upon his or her death to the other spouse is void when the final judgment dissolving or declaring a marriage invalid is signed, unless the final judgment specifically states otherwise. Federal law and other statutory provisions may also apply. This includes, but is not limited to, such assets as life insurance policies, annuities, employee benefit plans, individual retirement accounts, and payable-on-death accounts. Whether or not to continue a beneficiary designation is a complex area of the law and you may wish to consult with an attorney.

Bridge-the-Gap Alimony-spousal support which is ordered to assist a party to make the transition from being married to being single. Bridge-the-Gap alimony is designed to assist a party with legitimate, identifiable short-time needs; its length cannot exceed two years and it cannot be modified.

Central Depository-the office of the clerk of court that is responsible for collecting and disbursing court ordered alimony and child support payments. The depository also keeps payment records and files judgments if support is not paid.

Certificate of Service—a document that must be filed whenever a form you are using does not contain a statement for you to fill in showing to whom you are sending copies of the form. Florida Supreme Court Approved Family Law Form 12.914 is the certificate of service form and contains additional instructions.

Certified Copy—a copy of an order or final judgment, certified by the clerk of the circuit court to be an authentic copy.

Certified Mail—mail which requires the receiving party to sign as proof that they received it.

Child Support—money paid from one parent to the other for the benefit of their dependent or minor child(ren).

Clerk of the Circuit Court—elected official in whose office papers are filed, a case number is assigned, and case files are maintained. The clerk's office usually is located in the county courthouse.

Concurrent Custody—(for the purposes of a petition filed pursuant to chapter 751, Florida Statutes) means that an eligible extended family member is awarded custodial rights to care for a child or children concurrently with the child(ren)'s parent or parents.

Constructive Service—notification of the other party by newspaper publication or posting of notice at designated places when the other party cannot be located for personal service. You may also be able to use constructive service when the other party lives in another state. Constructive service is also called "service by publication." However, when constructive service is used, the relief the Court may grant is limited; that relief cannot include either alimony or child support. For more information on service, see the Instructions for Florida Family Law Rules of Procedure Forms 12.910(a) and 12.913(b) and Florida Supreme Court Approved Family Law Form 12.913(a).

Contested Issues—any or all issues upon which the parties are unable to agree and which must be resolved by the judge at a hearing or trial.

Contingent Asset—an asset that you **may** receive or get later, such as income, tax refund, accrued vacation or sick leave, a bonus, or an inheritance.

Contingent Liability—a liability that you **may** owe later, such as payments for lawsuits, unpaid taxes, or debts that you have agreed or guaranteed to pay if someone else does not.

Counterpetition—a written request to the court for legal action, which is filed by a respondent after being served with a petition.

Custody Order—a judgment or order incorporating a Parenting Plan is a child custody determination for the purposes of the Uniform Child Custody Jurisdiction and Enforcement Act, the International Child Abduction Remedies Act, 42 U.S.C. ss. 1601 et seq., the Parental Kidnapping Prevention Act, and the Convention on the Civil Aspects of International Child Abduction enacted at the Hague on October 25, 1980.

Default—a failure of a party to respond to the pleading of another party. This failure to respond may allow the court to decide the case without input from the party who did not appear or respond.

Delinquent—late.

Dependent Child(ren)—child(ren) who depend on their parent(s) for support either because they are under the age of 18, have a mental or physical disability that prevents them from supporting themselves, or are in high school, between the ages of 18 and 19, and performing in good faith with a reasonable expectation of graduation before the age of 19.

Deputy Clerk—an employee of the office of the clerk of court, which is usually located in the county courthouse or a branch of the county courthouse.

Dissolution of Marriage—divorce; a court action to end a marriage.

Durational Alimony-spousal support which is ordered to provide economic assistance for a set period of time following a marriage of short or moderate duration or following a marriage of long duration if there is no ongoing need for support on a permanent basis. Durational alimony terminates upon the death of either party or upon remarriage of the party receiving support. It may be modified or terminated, but cannot exceed the length of a marriage.

Electronic Communication –Contact, other than face-to-face contact, facilitated by tools such as telephones, electronic mail or email, webcams, video-conferencing equipment, and software or other wired or wireless technologies, or other means of communication to supplement fact-to face contact between a parent and that parent's minor child.

Enjoined—prohibited by the court from doing a specific act.

Ex Parte—communication with the judge by only one party. In order for a judge to speak with either party, the other party must have been properly notified and have an opportunity to be heard. If you have something you wish to tell the judge, you should ask for a hearing or file information in the clerk of court's office, with certification that a copy was sent to the other party.

Extended Family—(for the purposes of a petition filed pursuant to chapter 751, Florida Statutes) is a person who is either:

1) A relative of a minor child within the third degree by blood or marriage to the parent; OR

2) The stepparent of a minor child if the stepparent is currently married to the parent of the child and is not a party in a pending dissolution, separate maintenance, domestic violence, or other civil or criminal proceeding in any court of competent jurisdiction involving one or both of the child's parents as an adverse party.

Family Law Intake Staff—a court's employee(s) who is (are) available to assist you in filing a family law case. Family law intake staff are not attorneys and cannot give legal advice.

They may only assist you with filling out the form(s). Your local clerk's office can tell you if your county has such assistance available.

Filing—delivering a petition, response, motion, or other pleading in a court case to the clerk of court's office.

Filing Fee—an amount of money, set by law, that the petitioner must pay when filing a case. If you cannot afford to pay the fee, you must file an **Application for Determination of Civil Indigent Status**, to ask the clerk to file your case without payment of the fee. This form can be obtained from the clerk's office.

Final Hearing—trial in your case.

Financial Affidavit—a sworn statement that contains information regarding your income, expenses, assets, and liabilities.

Final Judgment—a written document signed by a judge and recorded in the clerk of the circuit court's office that contains the judge's decision in your case.

Guardian ad Litem—a neutral person who may be appointed by the court to evaluate or investigate your child's situation, and file a report with the court about what is in the best interests of your child(ren). Guardians do not "work for" either party. The guardian may interview the parties, visit their homes, visit the child(ren)'s school(s) and speak with teachers, or use other resources to make their recommendation.

Hearing—a legal proceeding before a judge or designated officer (general magistrate or hearing officer) on a motion.

Health Insurance-coverage under a fee-for-service arrangement, health care maintenance organization, or preferred provider organization, and other types of coverage available to either parent, under which medical services could be provided to a minor or dependent child.

Judge—an elected official who is responsible for deciding matters on which you and the other parties in your case are unable to agree. A judge is a neutral person who is responsible for ensuring that your case is resolved in a manner which is fair, equitable, and legal. **A judge is prohibited by law from giving you or the other party any legal advice, recommendations, or other assistance, and may not talk to either party unless both parties are present, represented, or at a properly scheduled hearing.**

Judicial Assistant—the judge's personal staff assistant.

Liabilities—everything owed by you or your spouse, including mortgages, credit cards, or car loans. A liability may be marital or nonmarital, but that distinction is for the court to determine if you and your spouse do not agree.

Lump Sum Alimony—money ordered to be paid by one spouse to another in a limited number of payments, often a single payment.

Mandatory Disclosure—items that must be disclosed by both parties except those exempted from disclosure by Florida Family Law Rule 12.285.

Marital Asset—generally, anything that you and/or your spouse acquired or received (by gift or purchase) during the marriage. For example, something you owned before your marriage **may** be nonmarital. An asset may only be determined to be marital by agreement of the parties or determination of the judge.

Marital Liability—generally, any debt that you and/or your spouse incurred during the marriage. A debt may only be determined to be nonmarital by agreement of the parties or determination of the judge.

Mediator—a person who is trained and certified to assist parties in reaching an agreement before going to court. Mediators do not take either party's side and are not allowed to give legal advice. They are only responsible for helping the parties reach an agreement and putting that agreement into writing. In some areas, mediation of certain family law cases may be required before going to court.

Modification—a change made by the court in an order or final judgment.

Motion—a request made to the court, other than a petition.

No Contact—a court order directing a party not speak to, call, send mail to, visit, or go near his or her spouse, ex-spouse, child(ren), or other family member.

Nonlawyer—a person who is not a member in good standing of The Florida Bar.

Nonmarital Asset—generally, anything owned separately by you or your spouse. An asset may only be determined to be nonmarital by either agreement of the parties or determination of the judge.

Nonmarital Liability—generally, any debt that you or your spouse incurred before your marriage or since your separation. A debt may only be determined to be nonmarital by either agreement of the parties or determination of the judge.

Nonparty—a person who is not the petitioner or respondent in a court case.

Notary Public—a person authorized to witness signatures on court-related forms.

Obligee—a person to whom money, such as child support or alimony, is owed.

Obligor—a person who is ordered by the court to pay money, such as child support or alimony.

Order—a written decision signed by a judge and filed in the clerk of the circuit court's office, that contains the judge's decision on part of your case, usually on a motion.

Original Petition—see **Petition**.

Parenting Course—a class that teaches parents how to help their child(ren) cope with divorce and other family issues.

Parenting Plan—a document created to govern the relationship between the parents relating to the decisions that must be made regarding the minor child(ren). The Parenting Plan must contain a timesharing schedule for the parents and child(ren) and shall address the issues concerning the minor child(ren). The issues concerning the minor child(ren) may include, but are not limited to, the child(ren)'s education, health care, and physical, social, and emotional well-being. In creating the Plan, all circumstances between the parents, including their historic relationship, domestic violence, and other factors must be taken into consideration. The Parenting Plan must be developed and agreed to by the parents and approved by the court. If the parents cannot agree to a Parenting Plan, or if the parents agreed to a plan that is not approved by the court, a Parenting Plan will be established by the court with or without the use of **parenting plan recommendations.**

Parenting Plan Recommendation—A nonbinding recommendation concerning one or more elements of a Parenting Plan made by a court-appointed mental health practitioner or other professional designated pursuant to either section 61.20 or 61.401, Florida Statutes, or Florida Family Law Rule of Procedure 12.363.

Party—a person involved in a court case, either as a petitioner or respondent.

Paternity Action—A lawsuit used to determine whether a designated individual is the father of a specific child or children.

Payor—an employer or other person who provides income to an obligor.

Permanent Alimony—spousal support ordered to provide for the needs and necessities of life as they were established during the marriage for a party who lacks the financial ability to meet his or her needs and necessities after dissolution of marriage. Permanent alimony is paid at a specified, periodic rate until: modification by a court order; the death of either party; or the remarriage of the party receiving alimony, whichever occurs first. Permanent alimony requires consideration of the factors set forth in section 61.08(2), Florida Statutes, and must include certain written findings by the court.

Personal Service—when a summons and a copy of a petition (or other pleading) that has been filed with the court are delivered by a deputy sheriff or private process server to the other party. Personal service is required for all petitions and supplemental petitions.

Petition—a written request to the court for legal action, which begins a court case.

Petitioner—the person who files a petition that begins a court case.

Pleading—a formal written statement of exactly what a party wants the court to do in a lawsuit or court action.

Pro Se or Self–Represented Litigant—a person who appears in court without the assistance of a lawyer.

Pro Se Coordinator—see **Family Law Intake Staff**.

Rehabilitative Alimony—spousal support ordered to be paid for a limited period of time to allow one of the parties an opportunity to complete a plan of education or training, according to a rehabilitative plan accepted by the court, so that he or she may better support himself or herself after dissolution of marriage.

Relocation—a change in the location of the principal residence of a parent or other person in accordance with section 61.13001, Florida Statutes.

Respondent—the person who is served with a petition requesting some legal action against him or her.

Scientific Paternity Testing—a medical test to determine who the father of a child is.

Service—the delivery of legal documents to a party. Service must be in accordance with Florida Rule of Judicial Administration 2.516.

Shared Parental Responsibility—an arrangement under which both parents have full parental rights and responsibilities for their child(ren), and the parents make major decisions affecting the welfare of the child(ren) jointly. Shared Parental Responsibility is presumptive in Florida.

Sole Parental Responsibility—a parenting arrangement under which the responsibility for the minor child(ren) is given to one parent by the court, with or without rights of time-sharing to the other parent.

State Disbursement Unit—the unit established and operated by the Title IV–D agency to provide one central address for the collection and disbursement of child support payments made in both Department of Revenue and non–Department of Revenue cases, in which the obligation is paid through an income deduction order.

Supervised Time–Sharing—a parenting arrangement under which time-sharing between a parent and his or her child(ren) is supervised by either a friend, family member, or a supervised visitation center.

Supplemental Petition—a petition that may be filed by either party after the judge has made a decision in a case and a final judgment or order has been entered. For example, a supplemental petition may be used to request that the court modify the previously entered final judgment or order.

Supportive Relationship–a relationship, defined in section 61.14(1)(b)1, Florida Statutes, existing between a spouse who receives alimony and a person with whom that spouse resides.

Time–Sharing Schedule—a timetable that must be included in the Parenting Plan that specifies the time, including overnights and holidays, that a minor child or children will spend with each parent. The timesharing schedule shall either be developed and agreed to by the parents of a minor child or children and is approved by the court, or established by the court if the parents cannot agree, or if their agreed-upon schedule is not approved by the court.

Trial—the final hearing in a contested case.

Uncontested—any and all issues on which the parties are able to agree and which are part of a marital settlement agreement.

Form 12.900(a). Disclosure From Nonlawyer

IN THE CIRCUIT COURT OF THE ____________ JUDICIAL CIRCUIT,
IN AND FOR ____________ COUNTY, FLORIDA

Case No.: ____________
Division: ____________

____________,
Petitioner,

and

____________,
Respondent.

DISCLOSURE FROM NONLAWYER

{Name} ____________ told me that he/she is a nonlawyer and may not give legal advice, cannot tell me what my rights or remedies are, cannot tell me how to testify in court, and cannot represent me in court.

Rule 10-2.1(b) of the Rules Regulating The Florida Bar defines a paralegal as a person who works under the supervision of a member of The Florida Bar and who performs specifically delegated substantive legal work for which a member of The Florida Bar is responsible. Only persons who meet the definition may call themselves paralegals. *{Name}*____________, informed me that he/she is not a paralegal as defined by the rule and cannot call himself/herself a paralegal.

*{Name}*____________, told me that he/she may only type the factual information provided by me in writing into the blanks on the form. Except for typing, *{name}*____________, may not tell me what to put in the form and may not complete the form for me. However, if using a form approved by the Supreme Court of Florida, *{name}*____________, may ask me factual questions to fill in the blanks on the form and may also tell me how to file the form.

[choose **one** only]
___ I can read English.
___ I cannot read English, but this disclosure was read to me [fill in **both** blanks] by *{name}*____________ in *{language}* ____________,which I understand.

Dated: ____________

____
Signature of Party

____
Signature of **NONLAWYER**
Printed Name: ____________
Name of Business: ____________
Address: ____________
____
Telephone Number: ____________

Florida Family Law Rules of Procedure Form 12.900(a), Disclosure From Nonlawyer (11/12)

INSTRUCTIONS FOR FLORIDA FAMILY LAW RULES OF PROCEDURE FORM 12.900(a), DISCLOSURE FROM NONLAWYER (11/12)

When should this form be used?

This form must be used when anyone who is **not** a lawyer in good standing with The Florida Bar helps you complete any Florida Family Law Form. Attorneys who are licensed to practice in other states but not Florida, or who have been disbarred or suspended from the practice of law in Florida, are nonlawyers for the purposes of the Florida Family Law Forms and instructions.

The nonlawyer must complete this form and both of you are to sign it before the nonlawyer assists you in completing any Family Law Form.

In addition, on any other form with which a nonlawyer helps you, the nonlawyer shall complete the nonlawyer section located at the bottom of the form unless otherwise specified in the instructions to the form. This is to protect you and be sure that you are informed in advance of the nonlawyer's limitations.

What should I do next?

A copy of this disclosure, signed by both the nonlawyer and the person, must be given to the person to retain and the nonlawyer must keep a copy in the person's file. The nonlawyer shall also keep copies for at least 6 years of all forms given to the person being assisted.

Special Notes

This disclosure form does **NOT** act as or constitute a waiver, disclaimer, or limitation of liability.

Added July 7, 1995, effective Jan. 1, 1996 (663 So.2d 1047). Renumbered from Form 12.900 and amended Sept. 1, 2000 (810 So.2d 1). Amended Feb. 9, 2006 (920 So.2d 1145); Nov. 15, 2012 (104 So.3d 314).

Form 12.900(b). Notice of Limited Appearance

IN THE CIRCUIT COURT OF THE ____________________ JUDICIAL CIRCUIT,
IN AND FOR ____________________ COUNTY, FLORIDA

Case No.: __________
Division: __________

____________________,
Petitioner,

and

____________________,
Respondent.

NOTICE OF LIMITED APPEARANCE

{Attorney's name} ____________________ files this Notice of Limited Appearance on behalf of *{name}* ____________________, [choose **one** only] ( ) Petitioner ( ) Respondent, for the following limited purpose(s). [choose **all** that apply]:

1. ___ The hearing set for *{date}* ____________________, at *{time}* __________ on the issue(s) of *{specify}* ____________________.

2. ___ To represent [check **one** only] ( ) Petitioner ( ) Respondent on the following issues throughout the proceedings:
   a. ___ Parental responsibility and time-sharing.
   b. ___ Equitable distribution of marital assets and liabilities.
   c. ___ Alimony.
   d. ___ Child support.
   e. ___ Other *{specify}*: ____________________

The clerk of the above-styled court is requested to enter this notice of record.

Copies of all future court papers should be served on the undersigned attorney at the address listed and on the [choose **one** only] ( ) Petitioner ( ) Respondent at *{name, address, e-mail address(es), telephone number, and fax number}* ____________________
____

I certify that a copy of this notice of limited appearance was: [check all used]
( ) e-mailed ( ) mailed ( ) faxed ( ) hand delivered to the person(s) listed below on
***{date}*_______________________.**

Other party or his/her attorney:
Name: ______________________________
Address: _____________________________
City, State, Zip: __________________________
Fax Number: ____________________________
E-mail Address(es): __________________________

____
Signature of Attorney
Printed Name: ____________________
Address: ________________________
City, State, Zip: ___________________
Telephone Number: _________________
E-mail Address(es): __________________
Florida Bar Number : _________________

____
Signature of Petitioner/Respondent
Printed Name: ____________________
Address: ________________________
City, State, Zip: ___________________
Telephone Number: _________________
E-mail Address(es): __________________

Florida Family Law Rules of Procedure Form 12.900(b), Notice of Limited Appearance (09/12)

INSTRUCTIONS FOR FLORIDA FAMILY LAW RULES OF PROCEDURE FORM 12.900(b), NOTICE OF LIMITED APPEARANCE (07/12)

When should this form be used?

This form should be used to provide notice to the court and the other **attorney** or **party** when an attorney is making a limited appearance for a client under Florida Family Law Rule of Procedure 12.040.

This form should be typed or printed in black ink. After completing and signing this form, the attorney should **file** the original with the **clerk of the circuit court** in the county in which the action is pending and keep a copy for his or her records.

What should I do next?

A copy of this form must be served on the other **party** or his or her **attorney** and on the attorney's client in the manner required by Florida Rule of Judicial Administration 2.516.

Where can I look for more information?

See Florida Family Law Rule of Procedure 12.040 and Florida Rule of Judicial Administration 2.516.

Added September 15, 2004 (883 So.2d 1285). Amended Oct. 16, 2008 (995 So.2d 445); Sept. 3, 2009 (19 So.3d 950); Oct. 18, 2012, effective, *nunc pro tunc*, Sept. 1, 2012 (102 So.3d 505).

Form 12.900(c). Consent to Limited Appearance by Attorney

IN THE CIRCUIT COURT OF THE ______________________ JUDICIAL CIRCUIT,
IN AND FOR ______________________ COUNTY, FLORIDA

Case No.: ______________________
Division: ______________________

______________________________,
Petitioner,

and

______________________________,
Respondent.

CONSENT TO LIMITED APPEARANCE BY ATTORNEY

{Name} ______________________________, the [check **one** only]
( ) Petitioner ( ) Respondent, consents to the limited representation by counsel,
{attorney's name} ______________________________, for the following limited purpose(s) [check **all** that apply]:

1. ____The hearing set for *{date}* ______________, at *{time}*________ on the issue(s) of *{specify}*
____.

2. ___To represent [check **one** only] ( ) Petitioner ( ) Respondent on the following issues throughout the proceedings:
   a. ___Parental responsibility and time-sharing.
   b. ___ Equitable distribution of marital assets and liabilities.
   c. ___ Alimony.
   d. ___ Child support.
   e. ___ Other *{specify}*:
   ____

The clerk of the above-styled court is requested to enter this notice of record.

I certify that a copy of this consent to limited appearance was: [check all used] ( ) e-mailed ( ) mailed ( ) faxed ( ) hand delivered to the person(s) listed below on *{date}* ________.

Other party or his/her attorney:
Name: ______________________
Address: ______________________
City, State, Zip: ______________________
Telephone Number: ______________________
Fax Number: ______________________
E-mail Address(es):______________________

Florida Family Law Rules of Procedure Form 12.900(c), Consent to Limited Appearance by Attorney (09/12)

____
Signature of Petitioner/Respondent
Printed Name: ____________________
Address: ____________________
City, State, Zip: ____________________
Telephone Number: ____________________
Fax Number: ____________________
E-mail Address(es): ____________________

IF A NONLAWYER HELPED YOU FILL OUT THIS FORM, HE/SHE MUST FILL IN THE BLANKS BELOW: [fill in all blanks] This form was prepared for the: *{choose only one}*
( ) Petitioner ( ) Respondent
This form was completed with the assistance of:
{name of individual} ____________________,
{name of business} ____________________,
{address} ____________________,
{city} ____________, *{state}* ______, *{telephone number}* ____________.

Florida Family Law Rules of Procedure Form 12.900(c), Consent to Limited Appearance by Attorney (09/12)

INSTRUCTIONS FOR FLORIDA FAMILY LAW RULES OF PROCEDURE FORM 12.900(c), CONSENT TO LIMITED APPEARANCE BY ATTORNEY (09/12)

When should this form be used?

This form should be used for a client to give consent when an **attorney** is making a limited appearance for the client under Florida Family Law Rule of Procedure 12.040.

This form should be typed or printed in black ink. After completing this form, the client should sign it. The attorney or client should then **file** it with the **clerk of the circuit court** in the county in which the action is pending. The attorney and client should each keep a copy for his or her records.

What should I do next?

A copy of this form must be served on the other **party** or his or her **attorney**. **Service** must be in accordance with Florida Rule of Judicial Administration 2.516.

Where can I look for more information?

See Florida Family Law Rule of Procedure 12.040.

Added September 15, 2004 (883 So.2d 1285). Amended Oct. 16, 2008 (995 So.2d 445); Sept. 3, 2009 (19 So.3d 950); Oct. 18, 2012, effective, *nunc pro tunc*, Sept. 1, 2012 (102 So.3d 505).

Form 12.900(d). Termination of Limited Appearance

IN THE CIRCUIT COURT OF THE ____________________ JUDICIAL CIRCUIT,
IN AND FOR ____________________ COUNTY, FLORIDA

Case No.: ____________________
Division: ____________________

____________________,
Petitioner,

and

____________________,
Respondent.

TERMINATION OF LIMITED APPEARANCE

{Attorney's name} ____________________, files this Termination of Limited Appearance on behalf of the **[check one only]** ( ) Petitioner ( ) Respondent, *{name}*, ____________________, and certifies that the proceeding or matter is concluded. The clerk of the above-styled court is requested to enter this Notice of Termination of Limited Appearance of record. Copies of all future court papers should be served on the **[check one only]** ( ) Petitioner ( ) Respondent at: *{name, address, e-mail address(es), fax number, and telephone number}* ____________________
____________________.

I certify that a copy of this termination of limited appearance was: [check all used] ( ) e-mailed ( ) mailed ( ) faxed ( ) hand delivered to the person(s) listed below on *{date}* ____________________.

Other party or his/her attorney:
Name: ____________________
Address: ____________________
City, State, Zip: ____________________
Fax Number: ____________________
E-mail Address(es): ____________________

Client Party:
Name: ____________________
Address: ____________________
City, State, Zip: ____________________
Telephone Number: ____________________
Fax Number: ____________________
E-mail Address(es): ____________________

Signature of Attorney
Printed Name: ______________________
Address: ______________________
City, State, Zip: ______________________
Telephone Number: ______________________
E-mail Address(es): ______________________
Florida Bar Number: ______________________

INSTRUCTIONS FOR FLORIDA FAMILY LAW RULES OF PROCEDURE FORM 12.900(d), TERMINATION OF LIMITED APPEARANCE (09/12)

When should this form be used?

This form should be used by an **attorney** who is terminating a limited appearance for a client under Florida Family Law Rule of Procedure 12.040.

This form should be typed or printed in black ink. After completing this form, the attorney should sign it and then **file** it with the **clerk of the circuit court** in the county in which the action is pending. The attorney should keep a copy for his or her records.

What should I do next?

A copy of this form must be served on the other **party** or his or her **attorney** and on the attorney's client. **Service** must be in accordance with Florida Rule of Judicial Administration 2.516.

Where can I look for more information?

See Florida Family Law Rule of Procedure 12.040.

Added September 15, 2004 (883 So.2d 1285). Amended Oct. 18, 2012, effective, *nunc pro tunc*, Sept. 1, 2012 (102 So.3d 505).

Form 12.900(e). Acknowledgment of Assistance by Attorney

{Name}, ______________________________, [check one only] (   ) Petitioner (   ) Respondent, certifies that he/she has received the assistance of the following attorney in the preparation of this document.

Attorney Name: ____________________
Address: ____________________
City, State, Zip: ____________________
Telephone Number: ____________________
E-mail Address(es): ____________________
Florida Bar Number: ____________________

Florida Family Law Rules of Procedure Form 12.900(e), Acknowledgment of Assistance by Attorney (09/12)

INSTRUCTIONS FOR FLORIDA FAMILY LAW RULES OF PROCEDURE FORM 12.900(e), ACKNOWLEDGMENT OF ASSISTANCE BY ATTORNEY (09/12)

When should this form be used?

This form should be added to the signature page of any petition, pleading, or motion when an attorney making a limited appearance under Florida Family Law Rule of Procedure 12.040 has assisted the petitioner or respondent in the preparation of the document. The petitioner or respondent should then sign the pleading and include his/her name and address.

Where can I get more information?

See the instructions to Florida Family Law Rules of Procedure Forms 12.900(b)–(d) and Rule 12.040.

Added September 15, 2004 (883 So.2d 1285). Amended Oct. 18, 2012, effective, *nunc pro tunc*, Sept. 1, 2012 (102 So.3d 505).

Form 12.900(f). Signature Block for Attorney Making Limited Appearance

Attorney for [check only one] ( ) Petitioner ( ) Respondent for the limited purpose of:
{specify matter or proceeding} ____ .

____
Signature of Attorney
Printed Name: ________________________
Address: ____________________________
City, State, Zip: ______________________
Telephone Number: ____________________
E-mail Address(es): ____________________
Florida Bar Number : ___________________

Petitioner/Respondent:
Name: ________________________________
Address: ______________________________
City, State, Zip: _________________________
Telephone Number: _______________________
E-mail Address(es): _______________________

Florida Family Law Rules of Procedure Form 12.900(f), Signature Block for Attorney Making Limited Appearance (09/12)

INSTRUCTIONS FOR FLORIDA FAMILY LAW RULES OF PROCEDURE FORM 12.900(f), SIGNATURE BLOCK FOR ATTORNEY MAKING LIMITED APPEARANCE (09/12)

When should this form be used?

This signature block should be used on any form filed with the court when the attorney is making a limited appearance under Florida Family Law Rule of Procedure 12.040.

Where can I look for more information?

See Florida Family Law Rule of Procedure 12.040(e).

Added September 15, 2004 (883 So.2d 1285). Amended Oct. 18, 2012, effective, *nunc pro tunc*, Sept. 1, 2012 (102 So.3d 505).

Form 12.900(g). Agreement Limiting Representation

AGREEMENT LIMITING REPRESENTATION

(This agreement is supplemental to the Attorney-Client fee agreement and is limited to addressing the consequences of Limited Legal Representation by an attorney in Florida)

TO THE CLIENT: THIS IS A LEGALLY BINDING CONTRACT. PLEASE READ IT CAREFULLY AND MAKE CERTAIN THAT YOU UNDERSTAND ALL OF THE TERMS AND CONDITIONS. YOU MAY TAKE THIS CONTRACT HOME WITH YOU, REVIEW IT WITH ANOTHER ATTORNEY IF YOU WISH, AND ASK ANY QUESTIONS YOU MAY HAVE BEFORE SIGNING.

EMPLOYMENT OF AN ATTORNEY FOR LIMITED REPRESENTATION REQUIRES THAT THE ATTORNEY AND CLIENT CAREFULLY AND THOROUGHLY REVIEW THE DUTIES AND RESPONSIBILITIES EACH WILL ASSUME. ANY LIMITED REPRESENTATION AGREEMENT SHOULD DESCRIBE, IN DETAIL, THE ATTORNEY'S DUTIES IN THE CLIENT'S INDIVIDUAL CASE.

1. **SERVICES/LIMITED SCOPE OF REPRESENTATION:** Client, *{name}* ____________________, employs Attorney, *{name}* ____________________ to provide representation only in the limited matter(s) described as follows:
____
____
____

2. **COMPLIANCE WITH CHAPTER 4 OF THE RULES REGULATING THE FLORIDA BAR:** Although legal assistance is limited, an attorney-client relationship exists, and the client is entitled to the standards of professional responsibility established by Chapter 4 of the Rules Regulating the Florida Bar, including confidentiality, competence, and diligence.

3. **COMPLIANCE WITH FLORIDA FAMILY LAW RULE OF PROCEDURE 12.040:** An Attorney hired to provide limited representation in court must comply with Florida Family Law Rule of Procedure 12.040, as follows:
   a. The attorney will file with the court a Notice of Limited Appearance, Florida Family Law Rules of Procedure Form 12.900(b), signed by the client, specifically limiting the attorney's appearance to the particular proceeding or matter in which the attorney appears.
   b. If the attorney seeks to withdraw from representation before the conclusion of a limited appearance, the attorney must:
      (1) File a motion with the court setting forth the reasons and serve that motion on the client and interested persons, and
      (2) Obtain approval of the court.
   c. At the conclusion of the proceeding or matter, the attorney's role terminates without the necessity of leave of court, on the attorney filing Termination of Limited Appearance, Florida Family Law Rules of Procedure Form 12.900(d). The notice shall include the names and last known addresses of the person(s) represented by the withdrawing attorney.
   d. THE CLIENT IS ADVISED THAT ANY OBJECTION TO THE ATTORNEY'S "TERMINATION OF LIMITED APPEARANCE" MUST BE MADE IN WRITING BY THE CLIENT BY PROVIDING THE JUDGE, THE

4. **ADDITIONAL SERVICES/REPRESENTATION:** The attorney and client may later determine that the attorney should provide additional limited services or assume full representation. The attorney may decline to provide additional services.
   a. If the attorney agrees to provide additional services, those additional services should be specifically listed in an amendment to this agreement, signed and dated by both the attorney and the client.
   b. If the attorney and client agree that the attorney shall serve as the client's attorney of record on all matters related to handling the client's case, the client and the attorney should indicate that agreement in an amendment to this agreement, signed and dated by both the attorney and the client.
   c. In either case, additional compliance with the notice requirement of Rule 12.040 will be required by the attorney.
   d. THE ATTORNEY AND THE CLIENT SHOULD NOT RELY ON VERBAL DISCUSSIONS OR VERBAL AGREEMENTS WHEN CHANGING THE TERMS OF THE ATTORNEY'S RESPONSIBILITY FOR REPRESENTATION.

5. **ATTORNEYS' FEES AND COURT COSTS:** The attorney and the client have made a separate agreement in writing as to payment of attorneys' fees and all costs associated with the case and the attorney's representation.

BY SIGNING THIS AGREEMENT YOU ACKNOWLEDGE THAT YOU HAVE CAREFULLY READ AND FULLY UNDERSTAND ALL OF THE FOREGOING TERMS, AND YOU INTEND TO BE LEGALLY BOUND BY THEM.

______________________ Attorney	______________________ Client
Name: ______________	Name: ______________
Address: ______________	Address: ______________
City, State, Zip: ______________	City, State, Zip: ______________
Telephone Number: ______________	Telephone Number: ______________
E-mail Address(es): ______________	E-mail Address(es): ______________
Florida Bar Number: ______________	
Date: ______________	Date: ______________

I HAVE BEEN PROVIDED A FULLY EXECUTED COPY OF THIS AGREEMENT LIMITING REPRESENTATION

____
Client

Florida Family Law Rules of Procedure Form 12.900(g), Agreement Limiting Representation (09/12)

INSTRUCTIONS FOR FLORIDA FAMILY LAW RULES OF PROCEDURE FORM 12.900(g), AGREEMENT LIMITING REPRESENTATION (09/12)

When should this form be used?

This form should be used as a "rider" or supplemental agreement, in addition to an Attorney–Client fee agreement, between the attorney and client when the attorney is making a limited appearance under Rules Regulating Florida Bar 4–1.2(c), 4–4.2(b), and 4–4.3(b) and Florida Family Law Rule of Procedure 12.040. A limited appearance means the attorney is not handling the whole case for the client, but is only being retained to do a specific part of the case.

Where can I look for more information?

See Rules Reg. Fla. Bar 4–1.2(c), 4–4.2(b), and 4–4.3(b) and Florida Family Law Rule of Procedure 12.040.

Added Oct. 16, 2008, effective Jan. 1, 2009 (995 So.2d 407). Amended Oct. 18, 2012, effective, *nunc pro tunc*, Sept. 1, 2012 (102 So.3d 505).

Form 12.900(h). Notice of Related Cases

IN THE CIRCUIT COURT OF THE ____________ JUDICIAL CIRCUIT,
IN AND FOR ____________________ COUNTY, FLORIDA

Case No.: ____________________
Division: ____________________

____________________,
Petitioner,

and

____________________,
Respondent.

NOTICE OF RELATED CASES

1. Petitioner submits this Notice of Related Cases as required by Florida Rule of Judicial Administration 2.545(d). A related case may be an open or closed civil, criminal, guardianship, domestic violence, juvenile delinquency, juvenile dependency, or domestic relations case. A case is "related" to this family law case if it involves any of the same parties, children, or issues and it is pending at the time the party files a family case; if it affects the court's jurisdiction to proceed; if an order in the related case may conflict with an order on the same issues in the new case; or if an order in the new case may conflict with an order in the earlier litigation.

[check **one** only]
___ **There are no related cases.**
___ **The following are the related cases (add additional pages if necessary):**

Related Case No. 1
Case Name(s): ____________________
Petitioner ____________________
Respondent ____________________
Case No.: ____________________ Division: ____________________

Type of Proceeding: [check **all** that apply]
____ Dissolution of Marriage
____ Custody
____ Child Support
____ Juvenile Dependency
____ Termination of Parental Rights
____ Domestic/Sexual/Dating/Repeat
____ Paternity
____ Adoption
____ Modification/Enforcement/Contempt Proceedings
____ Juvenile Delinquency
____ Criminal
____ Mental Health

Florida Family Law Rules of Procedure Form 12.900(h), Notice of Related Cases (11/13)

Violence or Stalking Injunctions ____ Other {specify}____________

State where case was decided or is pending: ____ Florida ____ Other: {specify}____________

Name of Court where case was decided or is pending (*for example, Fifth Circuit Court, Marion County, Florida*): ____________
Title of last Court Order/Judgment (if any): ____________
Date of Court Order/Judgment (if any): ____________

Relationship of cases [check **all** that apply]:
____ pending case involves same parties, children, or issues;
____ may affect court's jurisdiction;
____ order in related case may conflict with an order in this case;
____ order in this case may conflict with previous order in related case.
Statement as to the relationship of the cases: ____________
____
____

Related Case No. 2
Case Name(s): ____________
Petitioner ____________
Respondent ____________
Case No.: ____________ Division: ____________

Type of Proceeding: [check **all** that apply]
____ Dissolution of Marriage
____ Custody
____ Child Support
____ Juvenile Dependency
____ Termination of Parental Rights
____ Domestic/Sexual/Dating/Repeat Violence or Stalking Injunctions
____ Paternity
____ Adoption
____ Modification/Enforcement/Contempt Proceedings
____ Juvenile Delinquency
____ Criminal
____ Mental Health
____ Other {specify}____________

State where case was decided or is pending: ____ Florida ____ Other: {specify}____________

Name of Court where case was decided or is pending (*for example, Fifth Circuit Court, Marion County, Florida*): ____________
Title of last Court Order/Judgment (if any): ____________
Date of Court Order/Judgment (if any): ____________

Relationship of cases [check all that apply]:
____ pending case involves same parties, children, or issues;
____ may affect court's jurisdiction;
____ order in related case may conflict with an order in this case;
____ order in this case may conflict with previous order in related case.

Statement as to the relationship of the cases: ______________________________
____
____

Related Case No. 3
Case Name(s): ______________________________
Petitioner ______________________________
Respondent ______________________________
Case No.: ______________________ Division: ______________

Type of Proceeding: [check **all** that apply]
____ Dissolution of Marriage
____ Custody
____ Child Support
____ Juvenile Dependency
____ Termination of Parental Rights
____ Domestic/Sexual/Dating/Repeat Violence or Stalking Injunctions
____ Paternity
____ Adoption
____ Modification/Enforcement/Contempt Proceedings
____ Juvenile Delinquency
____ Criminal
____ Mental Health
____ Other *{specify}* ____________

State where case was decided or is pending: ____ Florida ____ Other: *{specify}* ____________

Name of Court where case was decided or is pending (*for example, Fifth Circuit Court, Marion County, Florida*): ______________________________
Title of last Court Order/Judgment (if any): ______________________________
Date of Court Order/Judgment (if any): ______________________________

Relationship of cases [check all that apply]:
____ Pending case involves same parties, children, or issues;
____ may affect court's jurisdiction;
____ Order in related case may conflict with an order in this case;
____ order in this case may conflict with previous order in related case.
Statement as to the relationship of the cases: ______________________________
____
____

Florida Family Law Rules of Procedure Form 12.900(h), Notice of Related Cases (11/13)

2. [check **one** only]

____ I **do not** request coordination of litigation in any of the cases listed above.

____ I **do** request coordination of the following cases: ________________________________
____
____

3. [check **all** that apply]

____ Assignment to one judge

____ Coordination of existing cases

will conserve judicial resources and promote an efficient determination of these cases because*:* ____.

4. The Petitioner acknowledges a continuing duty to inform the court of any cases in this or any other state that could affect the current proceeding.

Dated: ________________ ____________________________________

Petitioner's Signature
Printed Name: ____________________________
Address: ________________________________
City, State, Zip: __________________________
Telephone Number: ________________________
Fax Number: ______________________________
E-mail Address(es):________________________

CERTIFICATE OF SERVICE

I CERTIFY that I delivered a copy of this Notice of Related Cases to the ________________ County Sheriff's Department or a certified process server for service on the Respondent, and [**check all used]** ( ) e-mailed ( ) mailed ( ) hand delivered, a copy to *{name}*______________________, who is the [**check all that apply]** ( ) judge assigned to new case, ( ) chief judge or family law administrative judge, ( ) *{name}*______________________________ a party to the related case, ( ) *{name}* ___________________________, a party to the related case on *{date}* ______________________.

____
Signature of Petitioner/Attorney for Petitioner
Printed Name:_______________________
Address:___________________________
City, State, Zip:_____________________
Telephone Number:___________________

Florida Family Law Rules of Procedure Form 12.900(h), Notice of Related Cases (11/13)

Fax Number:____________________
E-mail Address(es):_______________
Florida Bar Number:______________

IF A NONLAWYER HELPED YOU FILL OUT THIS FORM, HE/SHE MUST FILL IN THE BLANKS BELOW:
[fill in **all** blanks] This form was prepared for the *{choose **only** one}*: ( ) Petitioner ( ) Respondent.
This form was completed with the assistance of:
*{name of individual}*____,
*{name of business}*____,
*{address}*____,
*{city}*___________*{state}*______, *{telephone number}*______________.

Florida Family Law Rules of Procedure Form 12.900(h), Notice of Related Cases (11/13)

INSTRUCTIONS FOR FLORIDA FAMILY LAW RULES OF PROCEDURE FORM 12.900(h), NOTICE OF RELATED CASES (11/13)

When should this form be used?

Florida Rule of Judicial Administration 2.545(d) requires the **petitioner** in a family law case to file with the court a notice of related cases, if any. Your circuit may also require this form to be filed even if there are no related cases. A case is considered related if

- it involves the same parties, children, or issues and is pending when the family law case is filed; or
- it affects the court's jurisdiction to proceed; or
- an order in the related case may conflict with an order on the same issues in the new case; or
- an order in the new case may conflict with an order in the earlier case.

This form is used to provide the required notice to the court.

This form should be typed or printed in black ink. It must be **filed** with the **clerk of the circuit court** with the initial pleading in the family law case.

What should I do next?

A copy of the form must be served on the presiding judges, either the chief judge or the family law administrative judge, and all parties in the related cases. You should also keep a copy for your records. **Service** must be in accordance with Florida Rule of Judicial Administration 2.516.

Where can I look for more information?

Before proceeding, you should read "General Information for Self–Represented Litigants" found at the beginning of these forms. The words that are in "**bold underline**" in these instructions are defined there. For further information, see Florida Rule of Judicial Administration 2.545(d).

Special notes . . .

Remember, a person who is NOT an attorney is called a nonlawyer. If a nonlawyer helps you fill out these forms, that person must give you a copy of a **Disclosure from Nonlawyer**, Florida Family Law Rules of Procedure Form 12.900(a), before he or she helps you. A nonlawyer helping you fill out these forms **must** also put his or her name, address, and telephone number on the bottom of the last page of every form he or she helps you complete.

Added Oct. 16, 2008, effective Jan. 1, 2009 (995 So.2d 407). Amended Oct. 18, 2012, effective, *nunc pro tunc*, Sept. 1, 2012 (102 So.3d 505); Nov. 14, 2013 (126 So.3d 228).

Form 12.901(a). Petition for Simplified Dissolution of Marriage

IN THE CIRCUIT COURT OF THE __________ JUDICIAL CIRCUIT,
IN AND FOR ____________________ COUNTY, FLORIDA

Case No.: ________________
Division: ________________

______________________________,
Husband,

and

______________________________,
Wife.

PETITION FOR SIMPLIFIED DISSOLUTION OF MARRIAGE

We, *{full legal name}* ____, Husband,

and *{full legal name}* ____, Wife, being sworn, certify that the following information is true:
[fill in **all** blanks]

1. We are both asking the Court for a dissolution of our marriage.
2. Husband lives in *{name}* __________ County, *{state}* __________, and has lived there since *{date}* __________. Wife lives in *{name}* ________________ County, *{state}* ____________, and has lived there since *{date}* ____________.
3. We were married to each other on *{date}* ____ in the city of *{city}* __________ in state of *{state}* __________, or country of *{country}* __________.
4. Our marriage is irretrievably broken.
5. We do not have any minor or dependent children together, the wife does not have any minor or dependent children born during the marriage, **and** the wife is not pregnant.
6. We have divided our assets (what we own) and our liabilities (what we owe) by agreement. We are satisfied with this agreement.

   *{Check **one** only}*

   ( ) Our marital settlement agreement, Florida Family Law Rules of Procedure Form 12.902(f)(3), is attached. This agreement was signed freely and voluntarily by each of us and we intend to be bound by it.

   ( ) Our marital settlement agreement is not in writing. We prefer to keep our financial agreements private.
7. *{Check **one** only}* ( ) yes ( ) no Wife wants to be known by her former name, which was *{full legal name}* ____.

8. We each certify that we have not been threatened or pressured into signing this petition. We each understand that the result of signing this petition may be a final judgment ending our marriage and allowing no further relief.
9. We each understand that **we both must come to the hearing** to testify about the things we are asking for in this petition.
10. We understand that we each may have legal rights as a result of our marriage and that by signing this petition we may be giving up those rights.
11. We ask the Court to end our marriage and approve our marital settlement agreement.

I understand that I am swearing or affirming under oath to the truthfulness of the claims made in this petition and that the punishment for knowingly making a false statement includes fines and/or imprisonment.

Dated: ____________________

____
Signature of HUSBAND
Printed Name: ____________________
Address: ____________________
City, State, Zip: ____________________
Telephone Number: ____________________
Fax Number: ____________________
E-mail Address(es): ____________________

STATE OF FLORIDA
COUNTY OF ____________________

Sworn to or affirmed and signed before me on ____________________ by ____________________.

____
NOTARY PUBLIC or DEPUTY CLERK

[Print, type, or stamp commissioned name of notary or deputy clerk.]

___ Personally known
___ Produced identification
Type of identification produced

Florida Family Law Rules of Procedure Form 12.901(a), Petition for Simplified Dissolution of Marriage (01/15)

I understand that I am swearing or affirming under oath to the truthfulness of the claims made in this petition and that the punishment for knowingly making a false statement includes fines and/or imprisonment.

Dated: ____________ ____

Signature of WIFE
Printed Name: ______________________________
Address: ______________________________
City, State, Zip: ______________________________
Telephone Number: ______________________________
Fax Number: ______________________________
E-mail Address(es): ______________________________

STATE OF FLORIDA
COUNTY OF

Sworn to or affirmed and signed before me on ________________ by ________________.

____
NOTARY PUBLIC or DEPUTY CLERK

[Print, type, or stamp commissioned name of notary or deputy clerk.]

___ Personally known
___ Produced identification
Type of identification produced

IF A NONLAWYER HELPED YOU FILL OUT THIS FORM, HE/SHE MUST FILL IN THE BLANKS BELOW: [fill in all blanks]
This form was prepared for: [choose only **one**] ( ) Husband ( ) Wife
This form was completed with the assistance of:
{name of individual} ______________________________,
{name of business} ______________________________,
{address} ______________________________,
{city} ________________, *{state}*______, *{telephone number}*________.

Florida Family Law Rules of Procedure Form 12.901(a), Petition for Simplified Dissolution of Marriage (01/15)

INSTRUCTIONS FOR FLORIDA FAMILY LAW RULES OF PROCEDURE FORM 12.901(a), PETITION FOR SIMPLIFIED DISSOLUTION OF MARRIAGE (01/15)

When should this form be used?

This form should be used when a husband and wife are filing for a simplified **dissolution of marriage**. You and/or your **spouse** must have lived in Florida for at least 6 months before filing for a dissolution in Florida. You may file a simplified dissolution of marriage in Florida if **all** of the following are true:

- You and your spouse agree that the marriage cannot be saved.
- You and your spouse have no minor or dependent child(ren) together, the wife does not have any minor or dependent children born during the marriage, and the wife is not now pregnant.
- You and your spouse have worked out how the two of you will divide the things that you both own (your **assets**) and who will pay what part of the money you both owe (your **liabilities**), and you are both satisfied with this division.
- You are not seeking support (**alimony**) from your spouse, and vice versa.
- You are willing to give up your right to **trial** and **appeal**.
- You and your spouse are both willing to go into the clerk's office to sign the petition (not necessarily together).
- You and your spouse are both willing to go to the **final hearing** (at the same time).

If you do not meet the criteria above, you must file a regular **petition** for dissolution of marriage.

This petition should be typed or printed in black ink. Each of you must sign the petition in the presence of a deputy clerk (in the clerk's office), although you do not have to go into the clerk's office at the same time. You will need to provide picture identification (valid driver's license or official identification card) for the clerk to witness your signatures.

What should I do next?

1. After completing this form, you should **file** the original with the **clerk of the circuit court** in the county where you live and keep a copy for your records.

You may document your agreement by signing a **Marital Settlement Agreement,** Florida Family Law Rules of Procedure Form 12.902(f)(3) and filing it with the **clerk of the circuit court** or you may agree that all of your assets (what you own) and liabilities (what you owe) have been disposed of by oral agreement.

2. You must prove to the court that the husband **and/or** wife has (have) lived in Florida for more than 6 months before filing the petition for dissolution of marriage. Residence can be proved by:

- a valid Florida driver's license, Florida identification card, or voter registration card issued to one of you at least 6 months prior to filing for dissolution of marriage; or
- the testimony of another person who knows that either you or your spouse has resided in Florida for more than 6 months and is available to testify in court; or
- an **affidavit**. To prove residence by affidavit, use an **Affidavit of Corroborating Witness,** Florida Supreme Court Approved Family Law Form 12.902(i). This form must be signed by a person who knows that either you or your spouse has lived in Florida for more than 6 months before the date that you filed the petition for dissolution of marriage. This affidavit may be signed in the presence of the clerk of the court or in the presence of a **notary public**, who must affix his or her seal at the proper place on the affidavit.

3. You must pay the appropriate **filing fees** to the clerk of the circuit court. If you and your spouse cannot afford to pay the filing fees, you may fill out an **Application for Determination of Civil Indigent Status**, and file it with your petition for dissolution of marriage. You may obtain this form from the clerk and he or she will determine whether you are eligible to have filing fees waived.

4. Either you or the clerk of court will need to complete a **Family Court Cover Sheet**, Florida Family Law Rules of Procedure Form 12.928. The clerk's office can provide this form.

5. You must obtain a date and time for a court appearance from the clerk of court. On that date, **you and your spouse must appear together before a judge**. You should complete a **Final Judgment of Simplified Dissolution of Marriage**, Florida Family Law Rules of Procedure Form 12.990(a), and bring it with you to the hearing. At that time, if all of the papers are in order, the judge may grant a final judgment dissolving your marriage under simplified dissolution of marriage procedures by signing the final judgment which you have provided.

6. If you fail to complete this procedure, the court may dismiss the case to clear its records.

Where can I look for more information?

Before proceeding, you should read "General Information for Self-Represented Litigants" found at the beginning of these forms. The words that are in "**bold underline**" in these instructions are defined there. For further information, see chapter 61, Florida Statutes, and Rule 12.105, Florida Family Law Rules of Procedure.

Special notes . . .

Remember, a person who is NOT an attorney is called a nonlawyer. If a nonlawyer helps you fill out these forms, that person must give you a copy of a **Disclosure from Nonlawyer**, Florida Family Law Rules of Procedure Form 12.900(a), before he or she helps you. A nonlawyer helping you fill out these forms also **must** put his or her name, address, and telephone number on the bottom of the last page of every form he or she helps you complete.

Added July 7, 1995, effective Jan. 1, 1996 (663 So.2d 1047). Amended Feb. 26, 1998, effective Mar. 16, 1998 (713 So.2d 1); Sept. 21, 2000 (810 So.2d 1); June 30, 2005, effective July 1, 2005 (910 So.2d 194); Nov. 3, 2011, effective, *nunc pro tunc,* Oct. 1, 2011 (78 So.3d 1045); Nov. 15, 2012, effective Nov. 15, 2012 (104 So.3d 314); Dec. 18, 2014, effective Jan. 1, 2015 (154 So.3d 301).

Form 12.901(b)(1). Petition for Dissolution of Marriage With Dependent or Minor Child(ren)

IN THE CIRCUIT COURT OF THE ______________________ JUDICIAL CIRCUIT,
IN AND FOR ______________________ COUNTY, FLORIDA

Case No.: ____________________
Division: ____________________

In re: The Marriage of:

______________________________,
Husband,

and

______________________________,
Wife.

PETITION FOR DISSOLUTION OF MARRIAGE WITH DEPENDENT OR MINOR CHILD(REN)

I, *{full legal name}* ____, the
{Choose only one}
_____ Husband _____ Wife, being sworn, certify that the following statements are true:

1. JURISDICTION/RESIDENCE

_____Husband _____ Wife _____ Both has (have) lived in Florida for at least 6 months before the filing of this Petition for Dissolution of Marriage.

2. The husband _____ is or _____ is not a member of the military service.

The wife _____ is or _____ is not a member of the military service.

3. MARRIAGE HISTORY

Date of marriage: *{month, day, year}* __________________
Date of separation: *{month, day, year}*_________________ (___Please indicate if approximate)
Place of marriage: *{county, state, country}* ____

4. DEPENDENT OR MINOR CHILD(REN)

*{Choose **all** that apply}*

a. _____ The wife is pregnant. Baby is due on: *{date}*
b. _____ The minor (under 18) child(ren) common to both parties are:

Name	**Birth date**

c._____ The minor child(ren) born or conceived during the marriage who are **not** common to both parties are:

Name **Birth date**

____

____

The birth father(s) of the above minor child(ren) is (are) *{name and address}* _______________

____

d._____The child(ren) common to both parties who are 18 or older but who are dependent upon the parties due to a mental or physical disability are:

Name **Birth date**

____

____

5. A completed Family Law Financial Affidavit, Florida Family Law Rules of Procedure Form 12.902(b) or (c) *{choose only **one**}* _____ is filed with this petition or _____ will be timely filed.

6. A completed Uniform Child Custody Jurisdiction and Enforcement Act (UCCJEA) Affidavit, Florida Supreme Court Approved Family Law Form 12.902(d), is filed with this petition. (You **must** complete and attach this form in a dissolution of marriage with minor child(ren)).

7. A completed Notice of Social Security Number, Florida Supreme Court Approved Family Law Form 12.902(j), is filed with this petition.

8. This petition for dissolution of marriage should be granted because:

*{Choose only **one**}*

a. _____ The marriage is irretrievably broken.

b. _____ One of the parties has been adjudged mentally incapacitated for a period of 3 years prior to the filing of this petition. A copy of the Judgment of Incapacity is attached.

SECTION I. MARITAL ASSETS AND LIABILITIES

1. _____There are no marital assets or liabilities.

OR

2. _____ There are marital assets or liabilities. All marital and nonmarital assets and liabilities are (or will be) listed in the financial affidavits, Florida Family Law Rules of Procedure Form 12.902(b) or (c), filed in this case.

*{Indicate **all** that apply}*

a._____ All marital assets and liabilities have been divided by a written agreement between the parties, which is attached, to be incorporated into the final judgment of dissolution of marriage. (The parties may use Marital Settlement Agreement for Dissolution of Marriage with Dependent or Minor Child(ren), Florida Supreme Court Approved Family Law Form 12.902(f)(1).

b.______ The Court should determine how the assets and liabilities of this marriage are to be distributed, under section 61.075, Florida Statutes.

c.______ Husband ______Wife should be awarded an interest in the other spouse's property because:
____
____
____
____

SECTION II. SPOUSAL SUPPORT (ALIMONY)

1. ______ **Husband ______Wife forever gives up his/her right to spousal support (alimony) from the other spouse.**

OR

2. ______ Husband ______Wife requests that the Court order the other spouse to pay the following spousal support (alimony) and claims that he or she has an actual need for the support that he or she is requesting **and that the other spouse has the ability to pay that support.** Spousal support (alimony) is requested in the amount of $__________ every ______ week ______ other week ______ month, beginning *{date}* ____________________ and continuing until *{date or event}* ____.

{Explain why the Court should order ____Husband ____Wife to pay, and any specific request(s) for type of alimony (temporary, permanent, bridge-the-gap, durational, rehabilitative, and/or lump sum}:
____
____
____
____
____.

3. ______Other provisions relating to alimony, including any tax treatment and consequences:
____
____
____.

4. ______ Husband ______ Wife requests life insurance on the other spouse's life, provided by that spouse, to secure such support.

SECTION III. PARENTING PLAN ESTABLISHING PARENTAL RESPONSIBILITY AND TIME-SHARING

1. The minor child(ren) currently reside(s) with ______ Mother ______Father ______ Other: *{explain}*
____

2. **Parental Responsibility.** It is in the child(ren)'s best interests that parental responsibility be: *{Choose only **one**}*

a. ______shared by both Father and Mother.

b. ____ awarded solely to _____ Father _____ Mother. Shared parental responsibility would be detrimental to the child(ren) because:____
____
____
____.

3. **Parenting Plan and Time-Sharing.**
It is in the best interests of the child(ren) that the family be ordered to comply with a Parenting Plan that _____ includes _____ does not include parental time-sharing with the child(ren). The Petitioner states that it is in the best interests of the child(ren) that:

*{Choose only **one**}*

a.____ The attached proposed Parenting Plan should be adopted by the court. The parties *{Choose only one}* _____ have _____ have **not** agreed to the Parenting Plan.

b.____ The court should establish a Parenting Plan with the following provisions:
____ No time-sharing for the _____ Father_____ Mother.
____ Limited time-sharing with the ____Father____Mother.
____ Supervised Time-Sharing for the _____ Father_____ Mother.
____ Supervised or third-party exchange of the child(ren).
____ Time-Sharing Schedule as follows:
____
____
____

4. Explain why this request is in the best interests of the child(ren):
____
____
____
____
____.

SECTION IV. CHILD SUPPORT
*{Choose **all** that apply}*

1. ____ Husband ____Wife requests that the Court award child support as determined by Florida's child support guidelines, section 61.30, Florida Statutes. A completed Child Support Guidelines Worksheet, Florida Family Law Rules of Procedure Form 12.902(e), _____ is, or _____ will be filed. Such support should be ordered retroactive to:
   a. ____ the date of separation *{date}* ________________________________.
   b. ____ the date of the filing of this petition.
   c. ____ other *{date}*____________ *{explain}* ____________________.

2. ____ Husband ____Wife requests that the Court award child support to be paid beyond the age of 18 years because:

a.____ the following child(ren) *{name(s)}* ____
is (are) dependent because of a mental or physical incapacity which began before the age of 18.
{explain} ____
____.

b.____ the following child(ren) *{name(s)}*_______________is (are) dependent in fact, is (are) in high school, and are between the ages of 18 and 19; said child(ren) is (are) performing in good faith with reasonable expectation of graduation before the age of 19.

3. ____Husband _____Wife requests that the Court award a child support amount that is more than or less than Florida's child support guidelines and understands that a Motion to Deviate from Child Support Guidelines, Florida Supreme Court Approved Family Law Form 12.943, **must** be filed before the Court will consider this request.

4. _____Husband _____Wife requests that medical/dental insurance for the minor child(ren) be provided by:
*{Choose only **one**}*
   a. ____ Husband.
   b. ____ Wife.

5. ____Husband ____ Wife requests that uninsured medical/dental expenses for the child(ren) be paid:
*{Choose only **one**}*
   a. ____by Husband.
   b. ____by Wife.
   c. ____by Husband and Wife equally [each pay one-half].
   d. ____according to the percentages in the Child Support Guidelines Worksheet, Florida Family Law Rules of Procedure Form 12.902(e).
   e. ____Other *{explain}*: ____
____
____

6. _____Husband ____Wife requests that life insurance to secure child support be provided by the other spouse.

SECTION V. OTHER

1. ____ Wife requests to be known by her former name, which was *{full legal name}*:
____.

2. Other relief *{specify}*:
____
____
____
____

SECTION VI. REQUEST (This section summarizes what you are asking the Court to include in the final judgment of dissolution of marriage.)

____Husband ___Wife requests that the Court enter an order dissolving the marriage **and**:
*{Indicate **all** that apply}*

1. ____distributing marital assets and liabilities as requested in Section I of this petition;

2. ____awarding spousal support (alimony) as requested in Section II of this petition;
3. ____adopting or establishing a Parenting Plan containing provisions for parental responsibility and time-sharing for the dependent or minor child(ren) common to both parties, as requested in Section III of this petition;
4. ____establishing child support for the dependent or minor child(ren) common to both parties, as requested in Section IV of this petition;
5. ____restoring Wife's former name as requested in Section V of this petition;
6. ____awarding other relief as requested in Section V of this petition; and any other terms the Court deems necessary.

I understand that I am swearing or affirming under oath to the truthfulness of the claims made in this petition and that the punishment for knowingly making a false statement includes fines and/or imprisonment.

Dated______________________________ ______________________________

Signature of _____ HUSBAND _____WIFE

Printed Name: ______________________________
Address: ______________________________
City, State, Zip: ______________________________
Telephone Number: ______________________________
Fax Number: ______________________________

Designated E-mail Address(es): ______________________________
____

STATE OF FLORIDA
COUNTY OF ______________________

Sworn to or affirmed and signed before me on __________ by______________________________.

____
NOTARY PUBLIC or DEPUTY CLERK

____
{Print, type, or stamp commissioned name of notary or deputy clerk.}
____ Personally known
____ Produced identification
Type of identification produced ______________________________

IF A NONLAWYER HELPED YOU FILL OUT THIS FORM, HE/SHE MUST FILL IN THE BLANKS BELOW:
[fill in **all** blanks] This form was prepared for the: *{choose only **one**}* ( ) Husband ( ) Wife
This form was completed with the assistance of:
*{name of individual}*______________________________,
*{name of business}*______________________________,

Florida Supreme Court Approved Family Law Form 12.901(b)(1), Petition for Dissolution of Marriage with Dependent or Minor Child(ren) (03/15)

{address} ____,
*{city}*____________________*{state}*______, *{zip code}*________, *{telephone number}* _________________.

INSTRUCTIONS FOR FLORIDA SUPREME COURT APPROVED FAMILY LAW FORM 12.901(b)(1), PETITION FOR DISSOLUTION OF MARRIAGE WITH DEPENDENT OR MINOR CHILD(REN) (03/15)

When should this form be used?

This form should be used when a husband or wife is filing for a **dissolution of marriage** and you and your spouse have a dependent or minor child(ren) together or the wife is pregnant. You and/or your **spouse** must have lived in Florida for at least 6 months before filing for a dissolution in Florida. You must **file** this form if the following is true:

- You and your spouse have a dependent or minor child(ren) together or the wife is pregnant.

This form should be typed or printed in black ink. After completing this form, you should sign the form before a **notary public or deputy clerk.** You should file the original with the **clerk of the circuit court** in the county where you live and keep a copy for your records. Because you are filing the **petition** in this proceeding, you may also be referred to as the **petitioner** and your spouse as the **respondent.**

IMPORTANT INFORMATION REGARDING E–FILING

The Florida Rules of Judicial Administration now require that all petitions, pleadings, and documents be filed electronically except in certain circumstances. **Self-represented litigants may file petitions or other pleadings or documents electronically; however, they are not required to do so.** If you choose to file your pleadings or other documents electronically, you must do so in accordance with Florida Rule of Judicial Administration 2.525, and you must follow the procedures of the judicial circuit in which you file. **The rules and procedures should be carefully read and followed.**

What should I do next?

For your case to proceed, you must properly notify your spouse of the **petition**. If you know where he or she lives, you should use **personal service**. If you absolutely do not know where he or she lives, you may use **constructive service**. You may also be able to use constructive service if your spouse resides in another state or country. However, if constructive service is used, other than granting a divorce, the court may only grant limited relief, which cannot include either spousal support (alimony) or child support. For more information on constructive service, see **Notice of Action for Family Cases with Minor Child(ren)**, Florida Supreme Court Approved Family Law Form 12.913(a)(2), and **Affidavit of Diligent Search and Inquiry**, Florida Family Law Rules of Procedure Form 12.913(b). If your spouse is in the military service of the United States, additional steps for service may be required. See, for example, **Memorandum for Certificate of Military Service**, Florida Supreme Court Approved Family Law Form 12.912(a) and **Affidavit of Military Service**, Florida Supreme Court Approved Family Law Form 12.912(b). In sum, the law regarding constructive service and service on an individual in the military service is very complex and you may wish to consult an attorney regarding these issues.

If personal service is used, your spouse has 20 days to answer after being served with your petition. Your case will then generally proceed in one of the following three ways:

DEFAULT. If after 20 days, your spouse has not filed an **answer**, you may file a **Motion for Default**, Florida Supreme Court Approved Family Law Form 12.922(a), with the clerk of court. Then, if you have filed all of the required papers, you may call the clerk, **family law intake staff**, or **judicial assistant** to set a **final hearing**. You must notify your spouse of the hearing by using a **Notice of Hearing (General)**, Florida Supreme Court Approved Family Law Form 12.923, or other appropriate notice of hearing form.

UNCONTESTED. If your spouse files an answer that agrees with everything in your petition or an answer and waiver, **and** you have complied with **mandatory disclosure** and filed all of the required papers, you may call the clerk, family law intake staff, or judicial assistant to set a final hearing. You must notify your spouse of the hearing by using a **Notice of Hearing (General)**, Florida Supreme Court Approved Family Law Form 12.923, or other appropriate notice of hearing form.

CONTESTED . . . If your spouse files an answer or an answer and **counterpetition**, which disagrees with or denies anything in your petition, **and** you are unable to settle the disputed issues, you should file a **Notice for Trial**, Florida Supreme Court Approved Family Law Form 12.924, after you have complied with mandatory disclosure and filed all of the required papers. Some circuits may require the completion of **mediation** before a final hearing may be set. You should contact the clerk, family law intake staff, or judicial assistant for instructions on how to set your case for trial (final hearing). If your spouse files an answer and counterpetition, you should answer the counterpetition within 20 days using an **Answer to Counterpetition**, Florida Supreme Court Approved Family Law Form 12.903(d).

Where can I look for more information?

Before proceeding, you should read General Information for Self–Represented Litigants found at the beginning of these forms. The words that are in **bold underline** in these instructions are defined there. For further information, see chapter 61, Florida Statutes.

IMPORTANT INFORMATION REGARDING E–SERVICE ELECTION

After the initial service of process of the petition or supplemental petition by the Sheriff or certified process server, the Florida Rules of Judicial Administration now require that all documents required or permitted to be served on the other party must be served by electronic mail (e-mail) except in certain circumstances. **You must strictly comply with the format requirements set forth in the Rules of Judicial Administration.**

SELF–REPRESENTED LITIGANTS MAY SERVE DOCUMENTS BY E–MAIL; HOWEVER, THEY ARE NOT REQUIRED TO DO SO. If a self-represented litigant elects to serve and receive documents by e-mail, the procedures must always be followed once the initial election is made.

To serve and receive documents by e-mail, you must designate your e-mail addresses by using the **Designation of Current Mailing and E-mail Address**, Florida Supreme Court Approved Family Law Form 12.915, and you must provide your e-mail address on each form on which your signature appears. Please **CAREFULLY** read the rules and instructions for: **Certificate of Service (General),** Florida Supreme Court Approved Family Law Form 12.914; **Designation of Current Mailing and E-mail Address**, Florida Supreme Court Approved Family Law Form 12.915; and Florida Rule of Judicial Administration 2.516.

Special notes . . .

If you do not have the money to pay the filing fee, you may obtain an Application for Determination of Civil Indigent Status from the clerk, fill it out, and the clerk will determine whether you are eligible to have filing fees deferred.

If you want to keep your address confidential because you are the victim of sexual battery, aggravated child abuse, aggravated stalking, harassment, aggravated battery, or domestic violence, do not enter the address, telephone, and fax information at the bottom of this form. Instead, file a **Request for Confidential Filing of Address**, Florida Supreme Court Approved Family Law Form 12.980(h).

With this form, you must also file the following:

- **Uniform Child Custody Jurisdiction and Enforcement Act (UCCJEA) Affidavit,** Florida Supreme Court Approved Family Law Form 12.902(d).
- **Child Support Guidelines Worksheet**, Florida Family Law Rules of Procedure Form 12.902(e), if you are asking that child support be ordered in the final judgment. (If you do not know your spouse's income, you may file this worksheet after his or her financial affidavit has been served on you.)
- **Affidavit of Corroborating Witness**, Florida Supreme Court Approved Family Law Form 12.902(i) OR photocopy of current Florida driver's license, Florida identification card, or voter's registration card (issue date of copied document must be at least six months before date case is actually filed with the clerk of the circuit court).
- **Marital Settlement Agreement for Dissolution of Marriage with Dependent or Minor Child(ren)**, Florida Supreme Court Approved Family Law Form 12.902(f)(1), if you and your spouse have reached an agreement on any or all of the issues.
- **Notice of Social Security Number**, Florida Supreme Court Approved Family Law Form 12.902(j).

• **Family Law Financial Affidavit**, Florida Family Law Rules of Procedure Form 12.902(b) or (c). (This must be filed with the petition if the petitioner seeks to establish child support. Otherwise, it must be filed within 45 days of service of the petition on the respondent.)

• **Certificate of Compliance with Mandatory Disclosure**, Florida Family Law Rules of Procedure Form 12.932. (This must be filed within 45 days of service of the petition on the respondent, if not filed at the time of the petition, unless you and your spouse have agreed not to exchange these documents.)

• **Parenting Plan**, Florida Supreme Court Approved Family Law Form 12.995(a), (b), or (c). If the parents have reached an agreement, a signed and notarized Parenting Plan should be attached. If the parents have not reached an agreement, a proposed Parenting Plan may be filed.

Parenting Plan and Time–Sharing . . . If you and your spouse are unable to agree on parenting arrangements and a time-sharing schedule, a judge will decide for you as part of establishing a Parenting Plan. The judge will decide the parenting arrangements and time-sharing based on the child(ren)'s best interests. Regardless of whether there is an agreement, the court reserves jurisdiction to modify issues relating to the minor child(ren). The judge may request a **parenting plan recommendation** or appoint a **guardian ad litem** in your case. This means that a neutral person will review your situation and report to the judge concerning parenting issues. The purpose of such intervention is to be sure that the best interests of the child(ren) is (are) being served. For more information, you may consult section 61.13, Florida Statutes.

A **parenting course** must be completed prior to entry of the final judgment. You should contact the clerk, family law intake staff, or judicial assistant about requirements for parenting courses where you live.

Listed below are some terms with which you should become familiar before completing your petition. **If you do not fully understand any of the terms below or their implications, you should speak with an attorney before going any further.**

- **Shared Parental Responsibility**
- **Sole Parental Responsibility**
- **Supervised Time–Sharing**
- **No contact**
- **Parenting Plan**
- **Parenting Plan Recommendation**
- **Time–Sharing Schedule**

Child Support . . . The court may order one parent to pay **child support** to assist the other parent in meeting the child(ren)'s material needs. **Both parents are required to provide financial support**, but one parent may be ordered to pay a portion of his or her support for the child(ren) to the other parent. Florida has adopted guidelines for determining the amount of child support to be paid. These guidelines are based on the combined income of **both** parents and take into account the financial contributions of both parents. You must file a **Family Law Financial Affidavit**, Florida Family Law Rules of Procedure Form 12.902(b) or (c), and your spouse will be required to do the same. From your financial affidavits, you should be able to calculate the amount of child support that should be paid using the **Child Support Guidelines Worksheet**, Florida Family Law Rules of Procedure Form 12.902(e). Because the child support guidelines take several factors into consideration, change over time, and vary from state to state, your child support obligation may be more or less than that of other people in seemingly similar situations.

Alimony . . . Alimony may be awarded to a spouse if the judge finds that he or she has an actual need for it and also finds that the other spouse has the ability to pay. **If you want alimony, you must request it in writing in the original petition or counterpetition. If you do not request alimony in writing before the final hearing, it is waived (you may not request it later).** You may request **permanent alimony, bridge-the-gap alimony, durational alimony, lump sum alimony**, or **rehabilitative alimony**.

Marital/Nonmarital Assets and Liabilities . . . Florida law requires an **equitable distribution** of **marital assets** and **marital liabilities**. "Equitable" does not necessarily mean "equal." Many factors, including child support, time-sharing, and alimony awards, may lead the court to make an unequal (but still equitable) distribution of assets and liabilities. **Nonmarital assets** and **nonmarital liabilities** are those assets and liabilities which the parties agree or the court determines belong to, or are the responsibility of, only one of the parties. If the parties agree or the court finds an asset or liability to be nonmarital, the judge will not consider it when distributing marital assets and liabilities.

Temporary Relief ... If you need temporary relief regarding temporary use of assets, temporary responsibility for liabilities, parental responsibility and time-sharing with child(ren), temporary child support, or temporary alimony, you may file a **Motion for Temporary Support and Time–Sharing with Dependent or Minor Child(ren)**, Florida Supreme Court Approved Family Law Form 12.947(a). For more information, see the instructions for that form.

Marital Settlement Agreement ... If you and your spouse are able to reach an agreement on any or all of the issues, you should file a **Marital Settlement Agreement for Dissolution of Marriage with Dependent or Minor Child(ren)**, Florida Supreme Court Approved Family Law Form 12.902(f)(1). Both of you must sign this agreement before a **notary public** or **deputy clerk**. Any issues on which you are unable to agree will be considered **contested** and settled by the judge at the final hearing.

Parenting Plan ... In all cases involving minor or dependent child(ren), a Parenting Plan shall be approved or established by the court. If you and your spouse have reached an agreement, you should file one of the following: **Parenting Plan**, Florida Supreme Court Approved Family Law Form 12.995(a), **Safety–Focused Parenting Plan**, Florida Supreme Court Approved Family Law Form 12.995(b), or **Relocation/Long–Distance Parenting Plan**, Florida Supreme Court Approved Family Law Form 12.995(c), which addresses the time-sharing schedule for the child(ren). If you have not reached an agreement, a proposed Parenting Plan may be filed. If the parties are unable to agree, a **Parenting Plan will be established by the court.**

Final Judgment Form ... These family law forms contain a **Final Judgment of Dissolution of Marriage with Dependent or Minor Child(ren)**, Florida Supreme Court Approved Family Law Form 12.990(c)(1), which the judge may use if your case is contested. If you and your spouse reach an agreement on all of the issues, the judge may use a **Final Judgment of Dissolution of Marriage with Dependent or Minor Child(ren) (Uncontested)**, Florida Supreme Court Approved Family Law Form 12.990(b)(1). You should check with the clerk, family law intake staff, or judicial assistant to see if you need to bring a final judgment with you to the hearing. If so, you should type or print the heading, including the circuit, county, case number, division, and the parties' names, and leave the rest blank for the judge to complete at your hearing or trial.

Nonlawyer ... Remember, a person who is NOT an attorney is called a nonlawyer. If a nonlawyer helps you fill out these forms, that person must give you a copy of a **Disclosure from Nonlawyer**, Florida Family Law Rules of Procedure Form 12.900(a), before he or she helps you. A nonlawyer helping you fill out these forms also **must** put his or her name, address, and telephone number on the bottom of the last page of every form he or she helps you complete.

Added Feb. 26, 1998, effective Mar. 16, 1998 (713 So.2d 1). Amended Sept. 21, 2000 (810 So.2d 1); June 30, 2005, effective July 1, 2005 (910 So.2d 194); March 26, 2009 (20 So.3d 173); Dec. 16, 2010 (59 So.3d 792); Nov. 3, 2011, effective, *nunc pro tunc*, Oct. 1, 2011 (78 So.3d 1045); May 24, 2012 (96 So.3d 217); July 3, 2013 (96 So.3d 217); March 26, 2015, effective March 26, 2015 (2015 WL 1343088).

Form 12.901(b)(2). Petition for Dissolution of Marriage with Property But No Dependent or Minor Child(ren)

IN THE CIRCUIT COURT OF THE ______________ JUDICIAL CIRCUIT,
IN AND FOR ______________ COUNTY, FLORIDA

Case No: ______________
Division: ______________

In re: the Marriage of:

______________________________,
Husband,

and

______________________________,
Wife.

PETITION FOR DISSOLUTION OF MARRIAGE WITH PROPERTY BUT NO DEPENDENT OR MINOR CHILD(REN)

I, *{full legal name}* ______________________________, the *[Choose **one** only]* ( ) Husband ( ) Wife, being sworn, certify that the following statements are true:

1. JURISDICTION/RESIDENCE
_____ Husband _____ Wife _____ Both has (have) lived in Florida for at least 6 months before the filing of this Petition for Dissolution of Marriage.

2. The husband _____ is or _____ is not a member of the military service.
The wife _____ is or _____ is not a member of the military service.

3. MARRIAGE HISTORY
Date of marriage: *{month, day, year}* ______________
Date of separation: *{month, day, year}* ______________ *{Please indicate if approximate}*
Place of marriage: *{county, state, country}* ______________________________

4. THERE ARE NO MINOR (under 18) OR DEPENDENT CHILD(REN) COMMON TO BOTH PARTIES AND THE WIFE IS NOT PREGNANT.

5. A completed Notice of Social Security Number, Florida Supreme Court Approved Family Law Form 12.902(j), is filed with this petition.

6. THIS PETITION FOR DISSOLUTION OF MARRIAGE SHOULD BE GRANTED BECAUSE:

a. _____ The marriage is irretrievably broken.

OR

b. _____ One of the parties has been adjudged mentally incapacitated for a period of 3 years before the filing of this petition. A copy of the Judgment of Incapacity is attached.

SECTION I. MARITAL ASSETS AND LIABILITIES

1. ____ There are no marital assets or liabilities.

OR

2. ____ There are marital assets or liabilities. All marital and nonmarital assets and liabilities are (or will be) listed in the financial affidavits, Florida Family Law Rules of Procedure Form 12.902(b) or (c), to be filed in this case.

*[Indicate **all** that apply]*

a. ____ All marital assets and debts have been divided by a written agreement between the parties, which is attached to be incorporated into the final judgment of dissolution of marriage. (The parties may use Marital Settlement Agreement for Simplified Dissolution of Marriage, Florida Family Law Rules of Procedure Form 12.902(f)(3) or Marital Settlement Agreement for Dissolution of Marriage with No Dependent or Minor Child(ren), Florida Supreme Court Approved Family Law Form 12.902(f)(2)).

b. ____ The Court should determine how the assets and liabilities of this marriage are to be distributed, under section 61.075, Florida Statutes.

c. ____Husband _____Wife should be awarded an interest in _____ the other spouse's property because:____
____
____.

SECTION II. SPOUSAL SUPPORT (ALIMONY)

1. ____ **Husband ____ Wife forever gives up his/her right to spousal support (alimony) from the other spouse.**

OR

2. ____ Husband ____Wife requests that the Court order the other spouse to pay the following spousal support (alimony) and claims that he or she has an actual need for the support that he or she is requesting **and that the other spouse has the ability to pay that support**. Spousal support (alimony) is requested in the amount of $ _________ every ( ) week ( ) other week ( ) month, beginning *{date}* ______________________________and continuing until *{date or event}*
____.

{Explain why the Court should order_____Husband_____Wife to pay and any specific request(s) for type of alimony (temporary, permanent, bridge-the-gap, durational, rehabilitative, and/or lump sum}:
____
____
____

____

____

____.

3.____Other provisions relating to alimony including any tax treatment and consequences:

____

____

____

____

4.____ Husband ____ Wife requests life insurance on the other spouse's life, provided by that spouse, to secure such support.

SECTION III. OTHER

1. ____Wife requests to be known by her former name, which was *{full legal name}*
____.

2. Other relief *{specify}*: ____.

____

____

SECTION IV. REQUEST

(This section summarizes what you are asking the Court to include in the final judgment of dissolution of marriage.)

____Husband ____Wife requests that the Court enter an order dissolving the marriage **and:**

[Indicate ***all*** *that apply]*

1. ____ distributing marital assets and liabilities as requested in Section I of this petition;

2. ____ awarding spousal support (alimony) as requested in Section II of this petition;

3. ____ restoring Wife's former name as requested in Section III of this petition;

4. ____ awarding other relief as requested in Section III of this petition; and any other terms the Court deems necessary.

Florida Supreme Court Approved Family Law Form 12.901(b)(2), Petition for Dissolution of Marriage with Property but No Dependent or Minor Child(ren) (03/15)

I understand that I am swearing or affirming under oath to the truthfulness of the claims made in this petition and that the punishment for knowingly making a false statement includes fines and/or imprisonment.

Dated: ______________________

Signature of ____ HUSBAND ____ WIFE
Printed Name: ______________________
Address: ______________________
City, State, Zip: ______________________
Telephone Number: ______________________
Fax Number: ______________________
Designated E-mail Address(es): ______________________

STATE OF FLORIDA
COUNTY OF ______________________

Sworn to or affirmed and signed before me on ______________ by ______________________.

____
NOTARY PUBLIC or DEPUTY CLERK

____
{Print, type, or stamp commissioned name of notary or deputy clerk.}

____ Personally known
____ Produced identification
____ Type of identification produced ______________________

IF A NONLAWYER HELPED YOU FILL OUT THIS FORM, HE/SHE MUST FILL IN THE BLANKS BELOW:
[fill in all blanks] This form was prepared for the: *{choose only one}* ( ) Husband ( ) Wife
This form was completed with the assistance of:
{name of individual} ______________________,
{name of business} ______________________,
{address} ______________________,
{city} ______________,*{state}* _____*{zip code}*___________, *{telephone number}* ______________.

Florida Supreme Court Approved Family Law Form 12.901(b)(2), Petition for Dissolution of Marriage with Property but No Dependent or Minor Child(ren) (03/15)

INSTRUCTIONS FOR FLORIDA SUPREME COURT APPROVED FAMILY LAW FORM 12.901(b)(2) PETITION FOR DISSOLUTION OF MARRIAGE WITH PROPERTY BUT NO DEPENDENT OR MINOR CHILD(REN) (03/15)

When should this form be used?

This form may be used when a husband or wife is filing for a **dissolution of marriage**, and the husband and wife have **marital assets** and/or **marital liabilities** but they do not have any dependent children nor is the wife pregnant. You and/or your **spouse** must have lived in Florida for at least 6 months before filing for a dissolution in Florida. If you and your spouse agree on all issues and both can attend the hearing, you may want to file a **Petition for Simplified Dissolution of Marriage,** Florida Family Law Rules of Procedure Form 12.901(a). However, you cannot file for a simplified dissolution of marriage if **any** of the following are true:

- You disagree about property, debts, or other matters and wish to have a judge settle them for you.
- Either you or your spouse is seeking support (**alimony**).
- You would like to ask questions and get documents concerning your spouse's income, expenses, assets, debts, or other matters before having a trial or settlement.
- You would like to reserve your rights to have any matters reconsidered or appeal the judge's decision.

This form should be typed or printed in black ink. After completing this form, you should sign the form before a **notary public** or **deputy clerk**. You should **file** the original with the **clerk of the circuit court** in the county where you live and keep a copy for your records. Because you are filing the **petition** in this proceeding, you may also be referred to as the **petitioner** and your spouse as the **respondent.**

IMPORTANT INFORMATION REGARDING E-FILING

The Florida Rules of Judicial Administration now require that all petitions, pleadings, and documents be filed electronically except in certain circumstances. **Self-represented litigants may file petitions or other pleadings or documents electronically; however, they are not required to do so.** If you choose to file your pleadings or other documents electronically, you must do so in accordance with Florida Rule of Judicial Administration 2.525, and you must follow the procedures of the judicial circuit in which you file. **The rules and procedures should be carefully read and followed.**

What should I do next?

For your case to proceed, you must properly notify your spouse of the **petition**. If you know where he or she lives, you should use **personal service**. If you absolutely do not know where he or she lives, you may use **constructive service**. You may also be able to use constructive service if your spouse resides in another state or country. However, if constructive service is used, other than granting a divorce, the court may only grant limited relief which cannot include spousal support (alimony). For more information on constructive service, see **Notice of Action for Dissolution of Marriage (No Child or Financial Support)**, Florida Supreme Court Approved Family Law Form 12.913(a)(1), and **Affidavit of Diligent Search and Inquiry**, Florida Family Law Rules of Procedure Form 12.913(b). If your spouse is in the military service of the United States, additional steps for service may be required. See, for example, **Memorandum for Certificate of Military Service**, Florida Supreme Court Approved Family Law Form 12.912(a) and **Affidavit of Military Service**, Florida Supreme Court Approved Family Law Form 12.912(b). In sum, the law regarding constructive service and service on an individual in the military service is very complex and you may wish to consult an attorney regarding these issues.

If personal service is used, your spouse has 20 days to answer after being served with your petition. Your case will then generally proceed in one of the following three ways:

DEFAULT . . . If after 20 days, your spouse has not filed an **answer**, you may file a **Motion for Default**, Florida Supreme Court Approved Family Law Form 12.922(a), with the clerk of court. Then, if you have filed all of the required papers, you may call the clerk, **family law**

intake staff, or **judicial assistant** to set a **final hearing**. You must notify your spouse of the hearing by using a **Notice of Hearing (General)**, Florida Supreme Court Approved Family Law Form 12.923, or other appropriate notice of hearing form.

UNCONTESTED ... If your spouse files an answer that agrees with everything in your petition or an answer and waiver, **and** you have complied with **mandatory disclosure** and filed all of the required papers, you may call the clerk, family law intake staff, or judicial assistant to set a final hearing. You must notify your spouse of the hearing by using a **Notice of Hearing (General)**, Florida Supreme Court Approved Family Law Form 12.923, or other appropriate notice of hearing form.

CONTESTED ... If your spouse files an answer or an answer and **counterpetition**, which disagrees with or denies anything in your petition, **and** you are unable to settle the disputed issues, you should file a **Notice for Trial**, Florida Supreme Court Approved Family Law Form 12.924, after you have complied with mandatory disclosure and filed all of the required papers. Some circuits may require the completion of **mediation** before a final hearing may be set. You should contact the clerk, family law intake staff, or judicial assistant for instructions on how to set your case for trial (final hearing). If your spouse files an answer and counterpetition, you should answer the counterpetition within 20 days using an **Answer to Counterpetition**, Florida Supreme Court Approved Family Law Form 12.903(d).

Where can I look for more information?

Before proceeding, you should read "General Information for Self–Represented Litigants" found at the beginning of these forms. The words that are in **bold underline** in these instructions are defined there. For further information, see chapter 61, Florida Statutes.

IMPORTANT INFORMATION REGARDING E–SERVICE ELECTION

After the initial service of process of the petition or supplemental petition by the Sheriff or certified process server, the Florida Rules of Judicial Administration now require that all documents required or permitted to be served on the other party must be served by electronic mail (e-mail) except in certain circumstances. **You must strictly comply with the format requirements set forth in the Rules of Judicial Administration.**

SELF–REPRESENTED LITIGANTS MAY SERVE DOCUMENTS BY E–MAIL; HOWEVER, THEY ARE NOT REQUIRED TO DO SO. If a self-represented litigant elects to serve and receive documents by e-mail, the procedures must always be followed once the initial election is made.

To serve and receive documents by e-mail, you must designate your e-mail addresses by using the **Designation of Current Mailing and E-mail Address**, Florida Supreme Court Approved Family Law Form 12.915, and you must provide your e-mail address on each form on which your signature appears. Please **CAREFULLY** read the rules and instructions for: **Certificate of Service (General),** Florida Supreme Court Approved Family Law Form 12.914; **Designation of Current Mailing and E-mail Address**, Florida Supreme Court Approved Family Law Form 12.915; and Florida Rule of Judicial Administration 2.516.

Special notes ...

If you do not have the money to pay the filing fee, you may obtain an Application for Determination of Civil Indigent Status from the clerk, fill it out, and the clerk will determine whether you are eligible to have filing fees deferred.

If you want to keep your address confidential because you are the victim of sexual battery, aggravated child abuse, aggravated stalking, harassment, aggravated battery, or domestic violence, do not enter the address, telephone, and fax information at the bottom of this form. Instead, file a **Request for Confidential Filing of Address**, Florida Supreme Court Approved Family Law Form 12.980(h).

With this form, you must also file the following:

- **Affidavit of Corroborating Witness**, Florida Supreme Court Approved Family Law Form 12.902(i) **OR** photocopy of current Florida driver's license, Florida identification card, or voter's registration card (issue date of copied document must be at least six months before date case is actually filed with the clerk of the circuit court).

• **Marital Settlement Agreement for Dissolution of Marriage with No Dependent or Minor Child(ren)**, Florida Supreme Court Approved Family Law Form 12.902(f)(2), if you and your spouse have reached an agreement on any or all of the issues.

• **Notice of Social Security Number,** Florida Supreme Court Approved Family Law Form 12.902(j).

• **Family Law Financial Affidavit**, Florida Family Law Rules of Procedure Form 12.902(b) or (c). (This must be filed within 45 days of service of the petition on the respondent, if not filed at the time of the petition.)

• **Certificate of Compliance with Mandatory Disclosure**, Florida Family Law Rules of Procedure Form 12.932. (This must be filed within 45 days of **service** of the petition on the respondent, if not filed at the time of the petition, unless you and your spouse have agreed not to exchange these documents.)

Alimony ... Alimony may be awarded to a spouse if the judge finds that he or she has an actual need for it and also finds that the other spouse has the ability to pay. **If you want alimony, you must request it in writing in the original petition or counterpetition. If you do not request alimony in writing before the final hearing, it is waived (you may not request it later).** You may request **permanent alimony, bridge-the-gap alimony, durational alimony, lump sum alimony**, or **rehabilitative alimony**.

Marital/Nonmarital Assets and Liabilities ... Florida law requires an **equitable distribution** of **marital assets** and **marital liabilities**. "Equitable" does not necessarily mean "equal." Many factors, including alimony awards, may lead the court to make an unequal (but still equitable) distribution of assets and liabilities. **Nonmarital assets** and **nonmarital liabilities** are those assets and liabilities which the parties agree or the court determines belong to, or are the responsibility of, only one of the parties. If the parties agree or the court finds an asset or liability to be nonmarital, the judge will not consider it when distributing marital assets and liabilities.

Temporary Relief ... If you need temporary relief regarding temporary use of assets, temporary responsibility for liabilities, or temporary alimony, you may file a **Motion for Temporary Support with No Dependent or Minor Child(ren)**, Florida Supreme Court Approved Family Law Form 12.947(c). For more information, see the instructions for that form.

Marital Settlement Agreement ... If you and your spouse are able to reach an agreement on any or all of the issues, you should file a **Marital Settlement Agreement for Dissolution of Marriage with Property But No Dependent or Minor Child(ren)**, Florida Supreme Court Approved Family Law Form 12.902(f)(2). Both husband and wife must sign this agreement before a **notary public** or **deputy clerk**. Any issues on which you are unable to agree will be considered **contested** and settled by the judge at the final hearing.

Final Judgment Form ... These family law forms contain a **Final Judgment of Dissolution of Marriage with Property but No Dependent or Minor Child(ren)**, Florida Supreme Court Approved Family Law Form 12.990(c)(2), which the judge may use if your case is contested. If you and your spouse reach an agreement on all of the issues, the judge may use a **Final Judgment of Dissolution of Marriage with Property but No Dependent or Minor Child(ren) (Uncontested)**, Florida Supreme Court Approved Family Law Form 12.990(b)(2). You should check with the clerk, family law intake staff, or judicial assistant to see if you need to bring a final judgment with you to the hearing. If so, you should type or print the heading, including the circuit, county, case number, division, and the parties' names, and leave the rest blank for the judge to complete at your hearing or trial.

Nonlawyer ... Remember, a person who is NOT an attorney is called a nonlawyer. If a nonlawyer helps you fill out these forms, that person must give you a copy of a **Disclosure from Nonlawyer**, Florida Family Law Rules of Procedure Form 12.900 (a), before he or she helps you. A nonlawyer helping you fill out these forms also **must** put his or her name, address, and telephone number on the bottom of the last page of every form he or she helps you complete.

Added Feb. 26, 1998, effective Mar. 16, 1998 (713 So.2d 1). Amended Sept. 21, 2000 (810 So.2d 1); June 30, 2005, effective July 1, 2005 (910 So.2d 194); Nov. 3, 2011, effective, *nunc pro tunc*, Oct. 1, 2011 (78 So.3d 1045); May 24, 2012 (96 So.3d 217); March 26, 2015, effective March 26, 2015 (2015 WL 1343088).

Form 12.901(b)(3). Petition for Dissolution of Marriage with No Dependent or Minor Child(ren) or Property

IN THE CIRCUIT COURT OF THE ______________________ JUDICIAL CIRCUIT,
IN AND FOR ____________________________ COUNTY, FLORIDA

In re: the Marriage of: Case No: ____________________
Division: ____________________

______________________________,
Husband,

and

______________________________,
Wife.

PETITION FOR DISSOLUTION OF MARRIAGE WITH NO DEPENDENT OR MINOR CHILD(REN) OR PROPERTY

I, *{full legal name}* ______________________________, the
[Choose only ***one****]* ____ Husband ____ Wife, being sworn, certify that the following statements are true:

1. JURISDICTION/RESIDENCE
____ Husband ____ Wife ____ Both has (have) lived in Florida for at least 6 months before the filing of this Petition for Dissolution of Marriage.

2. The husband _____ is or _____ is not a member of the military service.
The wife _____ is or _____ is not a member of the military service.

3. MARRIAGE HISTORY
Date of marriage: *{month, day, year}* ______________________________
Place of marriage: *{county, state, country}* ______________________________

4. THERE ARE NO MINOR (under 18) OR DEPENDENT CHILD(REN) COMMON TO BOTH PARTIES AND THE WIFE IS NOT PREGNANT.

5. A completed Notice of Social Security Number, Florida Supreme Court Approved Family Law Form 12.902(j), is filed with this petition.

6. THIS PETITION FOR DISSOLUTION OF MARRIAGE SHOULD BE GRANTED BECAUSE:

   a. _____ The marriage is irretrievably broken.

OR

   b. _____ One of the parties has been adjudged mentally incapacitated for a period of 3 years before the filing of this petition. A copy of the Judgment of Incapacity is attached.

7. THERE ARE NO MARITAL ASSETS OR LIABILITIES.

Florida Supreme Court Approved Law Form 12.901(b)(3), Petition for Dissolution of Marriage with No Dependent or Minor Child(ren) or Property (03/15)

8. _____**HUSBAND** _____**WIFE FOREVER GIVES UP HIS/HER RIGHTS TO SPOUSAL SUPPORT (ALIMONY) FROM THE OTHER SPOUSE.**

9. _____Wife requests to be known by her former name, which was *{full legal name}* ____.

10. Other relief *{specify}*: ____
____
____
____
____
____.

REQUEST

(This section summarizes what you are asking the Court to include in the final judgment of dissolution of marriage.)

_____Husband _____Wife requests that the Court enter an order dissolving the marriage **and:**

[Indicate all that apply]

1. ____ restoring Wife's former name as specified in paragraph 9 of this petition;

2. ____ awarding other relief as specified in paragraph 10 of this petition; and any other terms the Court deems necessary.

I understand that I am swearing or affirming under oath to the truthfulness of the claims made in this petition and that the punishment for knowingly making a false statement includes fines and/or imprisonment.

Dated: ____________________

____
Signature of _____ HUSBAND _____ WIFE
Printed Name: ____________________
Address: ____________________
City, State, Zip: ____________________
Telephone Number: ____________________
Fax Number: ____________________
Designated E-mail Address(es): ____________________

STATE OF FLORIDA
COUNTY OF ____________________

Sworn to or affirmed and signed before me on ____________ by____________________.

____
NOTARY PUBLIC or DEPUTY CLERK

Florida Supreme Court Approved Law Form 12.901(b)(3), Petition for Dissolution of Marriage with No Dependent or Minor Child(ren) or Property (03/15)

____
{Print, type, or stamp commissioned name of notary or deputy clerk.}
______ Personally known
______ Produced identification
______ Type of identification produced ____

IF A NONLAWYER HELPED YOU FILL OUT THIS FORM, HE/SHE MUST FILL IN THE BLANKS BELOW:
[fill in all blanks] This form was prepared for the: *{choose only **one**}* ( ) Husband ( ) Wife
This form was completed with the assistance of:
{name of individual} ____,
{name of business} ____,
{address} ____,
{city} __________________,*{state}* ______,*{zip code}*______________,*{telephone number}* _________.

INSTRUCTIONS FOR FLORIDA SUPREME COURT APPROVED FAMILY LAW FORM 12.901(b)(3) PETITION FOR DISSOLUTION OF MARRIAGE WITH NO DEPENDENT OR MINOR CHILD(REN) OR PROPERTY (03/15)

When should this form be used?

This form may be used when a husband or wife is filing for a **dissolution of marriage**, and the husband and wife have no **marital assets** and/or **marital liabilities** and they do not have any dependent children nor is the wife pregnant. You and/or your spouse must have lived in Florida for at least 6 months before filing for a dissolution in Florida. If you and your spouse agree on all issues and both can attend the hearing, you may want to file a **Petition for Simplified Dissolution of Marriage,** Florida Family Law Rules of Procedure Form 12.901(a). However, you may use this form if **all** of the following are true:

- You have no marital assets or marital debts.
- Neither you nor your spouse is seeking support (alimony).

This form should be typed or printed in black ink. After completing this form, you should sign the form before a **notary public** or **deputy clerk**. You should **file** the original with the **clerk of the circuit court** in the county where you live and keep a copy for your records. Because you are filing the **petition** in this proceeding, you may also be referred to as the **petitioner** and your spouse as the **respondent.**

IMPORTANT INFORMATION REGARDING E–FILING

The Florida Rules of Judicial Administration now require that all petitions, pleadings, and documents be filed electronically except in certain circumstances. **Self-represented litigants may file petitions or other pleadings or documents electronically; however, they are not required to do so.** If you choose to file your pleadings or other documents electronically, you must do so in accordance with Florida Rule of Judicial Administration 2.525, and you must follow the procedures of the judicial circuit in which you file. **The rules and procedures should be carefully read and followed.**

What should I do next?

For your case to proceed, you must properly notify your spouse of the **petition**. If you know where he or she lives, you should use **personal service**. If you absolutely do not know where he or she lives, you may use **constructive service**. You may also be able to use constructive service if your spouse resides in another state or country. However, if constructive service is used, other than granting a divorce, the court may only grant limited relief, which cannot include spousal support (alimony). For more information on constructive service, see **Notice of Action for Dissolution of Marriage (No Child or Financial Support)**, Florida Supreme Court Approved Family Law Form 12.913(a)(1), and **Affidavit of Diligent Search and Inquiry**, Florida Family Law Rules of Procedure Form 12.913(b). If your spouse is in the military service of the United States, additional steps for service may be required. See, for example, **Memorandum for Certificate of Military Service**, Florida Supreme Court Approved Family Law Form 12.912(a) and **Affidavit of Military Service**, Florida Supreme Court Approved Family Law Form 12.912(b). In sum, the law regarding constructive service and service on an individual in the military service is very complex and you may wish to consult an attorney regarding these issues.

If personal service is used, your spouse has 20 days to answer after being served with your petition. Your case will then generally proceed in one of the following three ways:

DEFAULT . . . If after 20 days, your spouse has not filed an **answer**, you may file a **Motion for Default**, Florida Supreme Court Approved Family Law Form 12.922(a), with the clerk of court. Then, if you have filed all of the required papers, you may call the clerk, **family law intake staff**, or **judicial assistant** to set a **final hearing**. You must notify your spouse of the hearing by using a **Notice of Hearing (General)**, Florida Supreme Court Approved Family Law Form 12.923, or other appropriate notice of hearing form.

UNCONTESTED . . . If your spouse files an answer that agrees with everything in your petition or an answer and waiver, **and** you have complied with **mandatory disclosure** and filed all of the required papers, you may call the clerk, family law intake staff, or judicial assistant to set a final hearing. You must notify your spouse of the hearing by using a **Notice of Hearing (General)**, Florida Supreme Court Approved Family Law Form 12.923, or other appropriate notice of hearing form.

CONTESTED ... If your spouse files an answer or an answer and **counterpetition**, which disagrees with or denies anything in your petition, **and** you are unable to settle the disputed issues, you should file a **Notice for Trial**, Florida Supreme Court Approved Family Law Form 12.924, after you have complied with mandatory disclosure and filed all of the required papers. Some circuits may require the completion of **mediation** before a final hearing may be set. You should contact the clerk, family law intake staff, or judicial assistant for instructions on how to set your case for trial (final hearing). If the your spouse files an answer and counterpetition, you should answer the counterpetition within 20 days using an **Answer to Counterpetition**, Florida Supreme Court Approved Family Law Form 12.903(d).

Where can I look for more information?

Before proceeding, you should read "General Information for Self-Represented Litigants" found at the beginning of these forms. The words that are in "**bold underline**" in these instructions are defined there. For further information, see chapter 61, Florida Statutes.

IMPORTANT INFORMATION REGARDING E-SERVICE ELECTION

After the initial service of process of the petition or supplemental petition by the Sheriff or certified process server, the Florida Rules of Judicial Administration now require that all documents required or permitted to be served on the other party must be served by electronic mail (e-mail) except in certain circumstances. **You must strictly comply with the format requirements set forth in the Rules of Judicial Administration.**

SELF-REPRESENTED LITIGANTS MAY SERVE DOCUMENTS BY E-MAIL; HOWEVER, THEY ARE NOT REQUIRED TO DO SO. If a self-represented litigant elects to serve and receive documents by e-mail, the procedures must always be followed once the initial election is made.

To serve and receive documents by e-mail, you must designate your e-mail addresses by using the **Designation of Current Mailing and E-mail Address**, Florida Supreme Court Approved Family Law Form 12.915, and you must provide your e-mail address on each form on which your signature appears. Please **CAREFULLY** read the rules and instructions for: **Certificate of Service (General),** Florida Supreme Court Approved Family Law Form 12.914; **Designation of Current Mailing and E-mail Address**, Florida Supreme Court Approved Family Law Form 12.915; and Florida Rule of Judicial Administration 2.516.

Special notes ...

If you do not have the money to pay the filing fee, you may obtain an Application for Determination of Civil Indigent Status from the clerk, fill it out, and the clerk will determine whether you are eligible to have filing fees deferred.

If you want to keep your address confidential because you are the victim of sexual battery, aggravated child abuse, aggravated stalking, harassment, aggravated battery, or domestic violence, do not enter the address, telephone, and fax information at the bottom of this form. Instead, file a **Request for Confidential Filing of Address**, Florida Supreme Court Approved Family Law Form 12.980(h).

With this form, you must also file the following:

- **Affidavit of Corroborating Witness**, Florida Supreme Court Approved Family Law Form 12.902(i) **OR** photocopy of current Florida driver's license, Florida identification card, or voter's registration card (issue date of copied document must be at least six months before date case is actually filed with the clerk of the circuit court).
- **Notice of Social Security Number**, Florida Supreme Court Approved Family Law Form 12.902(j).
- **Family Law Financial Affidavit**, Florida Family Law Rules of Procedure Form 12.902(b) or (c). (This must be filed within 45 days of service of the petition on the respondent, if not filed at the time of the petition.)

• **Certificate of Compliance with Mandatory Disclosure**, Florida Family Law Rules of Procedure Form 12.932. (This must be filed within 45 days of **service** of the petition on the respondent, if not filed at the time of the petition, unless you and your spouse have agreed not to exchange these documents.)

Final Judgment Form . . . These family law forms contain a **Final Judgment of Dissolution of Marriage with No Property or Minor Child(ren) (Uncontested)**, Florida Supreme Court Approved Family Law Form 12.990(b)(3). You should check with the clerk, family law intake staff, or judicial assistant to see if you need to bring a final judgment with you to the hearing. If so, you should type or print the heading, including the circuit, county, case number, division, and the parties' names, and leave the rest blank for the judge to complete at your hearing or trial.

Nonlawyer . . . Remember, a person who is NOT an attorney is called a nonlawyer. If a nonlawyer helps you fill out these forms, that person must give you a copy of a **Disclosure from Nonlawyer**, Florida Family Law Rules of Procedure Form 12.900(a), before he or she helps you. A nonlawyer helping you fill out these forms also **must** put his or her name, address, and telephone number on the bottom of the last page of every form he or she helps you complete.

Added Feb. 26, 1998, effective Mar. 16, 1998 (713 So.2d 1). Amended Sept. 21, 2000 (810 So.2d 1); Dec. 19, 2002 (836 So.2d 1019); June 30, 2005, effective July 1, 2005 (910 So.2d 194); Nov. 3, 2011, effective, *nunc pro tunc*, Oct. 1, 2011 (78 So.3d 1045); May 24, 2012 (96 So.3d 217); March 26, 2015, effective March 26, 2015 (2015 WL 1343088).

Form 12.902(b). Family Law Financial Affidavit (Short Form)

IN THE CIRCUIT COURT OF THE ____________________ JUDICIAL CIRCUIT,
IN AND FOR ____________________ COUNTY, FLORIDA

Case No.: ____________________
Division: ____________________

______________________________,
Petitioner,

and

______________________________,
Respondent.

FAMILY LAW FINANCIAL AFFIDAVIT (SHORT FORM)

(Under $50,000 Individual Gross Annual Income)

I, *{full legal name}*______________________________, being sworn, certify that the following information is true:

My Occupation: ______________________________

Employed by: ______________________________

Business Address: ______________________________

Pay rate: $ ________ ( ) every week ( ) every other week ( ) twice a month ( ) monthly ( ) other: ________

___ Check here if unemployed and explain on a separate sheet your efforts to find employment.

SECTION I. PRESENT MONTHLY GROSS INCOME:
All amounts must be MONTHLY. See the instructions with this form to figure out money amounts for anything that is NOT paid monthly. Attach more paper, if needed. Items included under "other" should be listed separately with separate dollar amounts.

1. $______ Monthly gross salary or wages
2. _______ Monthly bonuses, commissions, allowances, overtime, tips, and similar payments
3. _______ Monthly business income from sources such as self-employment, partnerships, close corporations, and/or independent contracts (gross receipts minus ordinary and necessary expenses required to produce income) (Attach sheet itemizing such income and expenses.)
4. _______ Monthly disability benefits/SSI
5. _______ Monthly Workers' Compensation
6. _______ Monthly Unemployment Compensation
7. _______ Monthly pension, retirement, or annuity payments
8. _______ Monthly Social Security benefits
9. ______ Monthly alimony actually received (Add 9a and 9b)

   9a. From this case: $ _______

Florida Family Law Rules of Procedure Form 12.902(b), Family Law Financial Affidavit (Short Form) (01/15)

9b. From other case(s): ________

10. ________ Monthly interest and dividends

11. ________Monthly rental income (gross receipts minus ordinary and necessary expenses required to produce income) (Attach sheet itemizing such income and expense items.)

12. ________ Monthly income from royalties, trusts, or estates

13. ________ Monthly reimbursed expenses and in-kind payments to the extent that they reduce personal living expenses

14. ________ Monthly gains derived from dealing in property (not including nonrecurring gains)

15. ________ Any other income of a recurring nature (list source) ________________

16. ____

17. $ ________ **TOTAL PRESENT MONTHLY GROSS INCOME** (Add lines 1–16)

PRESENT MONTHLY DEDUCTIONS:

18. $________Monthly federal, state, and local income tax (corrected for filing status and allowable dependents and income tax liabilities)

a. Filing Status ____________

b. Number of dependents claimed ________

19. ________ Monthly FICA or self-employment taxes

20. ________ Monthly Medicare payments

21. ________ Monthly mandatory union dues

22. ________ Monthly mandatory retirement payments

23. ________ Monthly health insurance payments (including dental insurance), excluding portion paid for any minor children of this relationship

24. ________ Monthly court-ordered child support actually paid for children from another relationship

25. ________Monthly court-ordered alimony actually paid (Add 25a and 25b)

25a. from this case: $ ________

25b. from other case(s):$ ________

26. $________ **TOTAL DEDUCTIONS ALLOWABLE UNDER SECTION 61.30, FLORIDA STATUTES** (Add lines 18 through 25).

27. $________ **PRESENT NET MONTHLY INCOME** (Subtract line 26 from line 17)

SECTION II. AVERAGE MONTHLY EXPENSES

Proposed/Estimated Expenses. If this is a dissolution of marriage case **and** your expenses as listed below do not reflect what you actually pay currently, you should write "estimate" next to each amount that is estimated.

A. HOUSEHOLD:

Mortgage or rent $ ______
Property taxes $ ______
Utilities $ ______
Telephone $ ______
Food $ ______
Meals outside home $ ______
Maintenance/Repairs $ ______
Other: $ ______

B. AUTOMOBILE

Gasoline $ ______
Repairs $ ______
Insurance $ ______

C. CHILD(REN)'S EXPENSES

Day care $ ______
Lunch money $ ______
Clothing $ ______
Grooming $ ______
Gifts for holidays $ ______
Medical/Dental (uninsured) $ ______
Other: ______________ $ ______

D. INSURANCE

Medical/Dental (if not listed on lines 23 or 45) $ ______
Child(ren)'s medical/dental $ ______
Life $ ______
Other: ______________ $ ______

E. OTHER EXPENSES NOT LISTED ABOVE

Clothing $ ______
Medical/Dental (uninsured) $ ______
Grooming $ ______
Entertainment $ ______
Gifts $ ______
Religious organizations $ ______
Miscellaneous $ ______
Other: $ ______
______________ $ ______
______________ $ ______
______________ $ ______
______________ $ ______

F. PAYMENTS TO CREDITORS

CREDITOR:	MONTHLY PAYMENT
______________	$ ______
______________	$ ______
______________	$ ______
______________	$ ______
______________	$ ______
______________	$ ______
______________	$ ______
______________	$ ______
______________	$ ______
______________	$ ______

28. $_______ **TOTAL MONTHLY EXPENSES** (add **ALL** monthly amounts in A through F above)

SUMMARY

29. $_______ **TOTAL PRESENT MONTHLY NET INCOME** (from line 27 of SECTION I. INCOME)
30. $_______ **TOTAL MONTHLY EXPENSES** (from line 28 above)
31. $_______ **SURPLUS** (If line 29 is more than line 30, subtract line 30 from line 29. This is the amount of your surplus. Enter that amount here.)
32. **($_______) (DEFICIT)** (If line 30 is more than line 29, subtract line 29 from line 30. This is the amount of your deficit. Enter that amount here.)

SECTION III. ASSETS AND LIABILITIES
Use the nonmarital column only if this is a petition for dissolution of marriage and you believe an item is "nonmarital," meaning it belongs to only one of you and should not be divided. You should indicate to whom you believe the item(s) or debt belongs. (Typically, you will only use this column if property/debt was owned/owed by one spouse before the marriage. See the **"General Information for Self-Represented Litigants"** found at the beginning of these forms and section 61.075(1), Florida Statutes, for definitions of "marital" and "nonmarital" assets and liabilities.)

A. ASSETS:

	DESCRIPTION OF ITEM(S). List a description of each separate item owned by you (and/or your spouse, if this is a petition for dissolution of marriage). LIST ONLY LAST 4 DIGITS OF ACCOUNT NUMBERS. Check the line next to any asset(s) which you are requesting the judge award to you.	**Current Fair Market Value**	**Nonmarital (check correct column)**	
			husband	wife
	Cash (on hand)	$		
	Cash (in banks or credit unions)			
	Stocks, Bonds, Notes			
	Real estate: (Home)			
	(Other)			
	Automobiles			
	Other personal property			
	Retirement plans (Profit Sharing, Pension, IRA, 401(k)s, etc.)			
	Other			
	Check here if additional pages are attached.			
Total Assets (add next column)		$		

B. LIABILITIES:

DESCRIPTION OF ITEM(S). List a description of each separate debt owed by you (and/or your spouse, if this is a petition for dissolution of marriage). **LIST ONLY LAST 4 DIGITS OF ACCOUNT NUMBERS. Check the line next to any debt(s) for which you believe you should be responsible.**		**Current Amount Owed**	**Nonmarital (check correct column)**	
			husband	wife
	Mortgages on real estate: First mortgage on home	$		
	Second mortgage on home			
	Other mortgages			
	Auto loans			
	Charge/credit card accounts			
	Other			
	____Check here if additional pages are attached.			
Total Debts (add next column)		$		

C. CONTINGENT ASSETS AND LIABILITIES:

INSTRUCTIONS: If you have any **POSSIBLE** assets (income potential, accrued vacation or sick leave, bonus, inheritance, etc.) or **POSSIBLE liabilities** (possible lawsuits, future unpaid taxes, contingent tax liabilities, debts assumed by another), you must list them here.

Contingent Assets **Check the line next to any contingent asset(s) which you are requesting the judge award to you.**		**Possible Value**	**Nonmarital (check correct column)**	
			husband	wife
		$		
Total Contingent Assets		$		

Contingent Liabilities **Check the line next to any contingent debt(s) for which you believe you should be responsible.**		**Possible Amount Owed**	**Nonmarital (check correct column)**	
			husband	wife
		$		
Total Contingent Liabilities		$		

Florida Family Law Rules of Procedure Form 12.902(b), Family Law Financial Affidavit (Short Form) (01/15)

SECTION IV. CHILD SUPPORT GUIDELINES WORKSHEET
(Florida Family Law Rules of Procedure Form 12.902(e), Child Support Guidelines Worksheet, MUST be filed with the court at or prior to a hearing to establish or modify child support. This requirement cannot be waived by the parties.)

[Check **one** only]
_____ **A Child Support Guidelines Worksheet IS or WILL BE filed in this case.** This case involves the establishment or modification of child support.
_____ **A Child Support Guidelines Worksheet IS NOT being filed in this case.** The establishment or modification of child support is not an issue in this case.

I certify that a copy of this document was [**check all used**]: ( ) e-mailed ( ) mailed ( ) faxed ( ) hand delivered to the person(s) listed below on *{date}* ____________________.

Other party or his/her attorney:
Name: ____________________
Address: ____________________
City, State, Zip: ____________________
Fax Number: ____________________
E-mail Address(es): ____________________
____

I understand that I am swearing or affirming under oath to the truthfulness of the claims made in this affidavit and that the punishment for knowingly making a false statement includes fines and/or imprisonment.

Dated: ____________________ ____________________
Signature of Party

Printed Name: ____________________
Address: ____________________
City, State, Zip: ____________________
Fax Number: ____________________
E-mail Address(es): ____________________
____

STATE OF FLORIDA
COUNTY OF ____________________

Sworn to or affirmed and signed before me on ____________ by ______________________________.

NOTARY PUBLIC or DEPUTY CLERK

____
[Print, type, or stamp commissioned name of notary or deputy clerk.]

____ Personally known
____ Produced identification
Type of identification produced ____________________

IF A NONLAWYER HELPED YOU FILL OUT THIS FORM, HE/SHE MUST FILL IN THE BLANKS BELOW:
[fill in **all** blanks] This form was prepared for the: *{choose only one}* ( ) Petitioner ( ) Respondent
This form was completed with the assistance of:
*{name of individual}*____,
*{name of business}*____,
*{address}*____,
{city} ____________,*{state}* ____________, *{telephone number}* ____________________.

Florida Family Law Rules of Procedure Form 12.902(b), Family Law Financial Affidavit (Short Form) (01/15)

INSTRUCTIONS FOR FLORIDA FAMILY LAW RULES OF PROCEDURE FORM 12.902(b), FAMILY LAW FINANCIAL AFFIDAVIT (SHORT FORM) (01/15)

When should this form be used?

This form should be used when you are involved in a family law case which requires a **financial affidavit and your individual gross income is UNDER $50,000 per year** unless:

(1) You are filing a simplified dissolution of marriage under rule 12.105 and both parties have waived the filing of a financial affidavit;

(2) You have no minor children, no support issues, and have filed a written settlement agreement disposing of all financial issues; or

(3) The court lacks jurisdiction to determine any financial issues.

This form should be typed or printed in black ink. After completing this form, you should sign the form before a **notary public** or **deputy clerk**. You should **file** the original with the **clerk of the circuit court** in the county where the **petition** was filed and keep a copy for your records.

What should I do next?

A copy of this form must be served on the other **party** in your case within 45 days of being served with the petition, if it is not served on him or her with your initial papers. **Service** must be in accordance with Florida Rule of Judicial Administration 2.516.

Where can I look for more information?

Before proceeding, you should read "General Information for Self–Represented Litigants" found at the beginning of these forms. The words that are in **"bold underline"** in these instructions are defined there. For further information, see Florida Family Law Rule of Procedure 12.285.

Special notes . . .

If you want to keep your address confidential because you are the victim of sexual battery, aggravated child abuse, aggravated stalking, harassment, aggravated battery, or domestic violence, do not enter the address, telephone, and fax information at the bottom of this form. Instead, file **Request for Confidential Filing of Address**, Florida Supreme Court Approved Family Law Form 12.980(h).

The affidavit must be completed using **monthly** income and expense amounts. If you are paid or your bills are due on a schedule which is not monthly, you must convert those amounts. Hints are provided below for making these conversions.

Hourly—If you are paid by the hour, you may convert your income to monthly as follows:

Hourly amount	×	Hours worked per week	=	Weekly amount
Weekly amount	×	52 Weeks per year	=	Yearly amount
Yearly amount	÷	12 Months per year	=	**Monthly Amount**

Daily—If you are paid by the day, you may convert your income to monthly as follows:

Daily amount	×	Days worked per week	=	Weekly amount
Weekly amount	×	52 Weeks per year	=	Yearly amount
Yearly amount	÷	12 Months per year	=	**Monthly Amount**

Weekly—If you are paid by the week, you may convert your income to monthly as follows:

Weekly amount	×	52 Weeks per year	=	Yearly amount
Yearly amount	÷	12 Months per year	=	**Monthly Amount**

Bi-weekly—If you are paid every two weeks, you may convert your income to monthly as follows:

Bi-weekly amount	×	26	=	Yearly amount
Yearly amount	÷	12 Months per year	=	**Monthly Amount**

Semi-monthly—If you are paid twice per month, you may convert your income to monthly as follows:

Semi-monthly amount	×	2	=	**Monthly Amount**

Expenses may be converted in the same manner.

Remember, a person who is NOT an attorney is called a nonlawyer. If a nonlawyer helps you fill out these forms, that person must give you a copy of a **Disclosure from Nonlawyer**, Florida Family Law Rules of Procedure Form 12.900(a), before he or she helps you. A nonlawyer helping you fill out these forms also **must** put his or her name, address, and telephone number on the bottom of the last page of every form he or she helps you complete.

Added July 7, 1995, effective Jan. 1, 1996 (663 So.2d 1047). Amended Feb. 26, 1998, effective Mar. 16, 1998 (713 So.2d 1); Sept. 21, 2000 (810 So.2d 1); July 10, 2003, effective Jan. 1, 2004 (853 So.2d 303); Sept. 28, 2006 (940 So.2d 409); Nov. 3, 2011, effective, *nunc pro tunc*, Oct. 1, 2011 (78 So.3d 1045); Oct. 18, 2012, effective, *nunc pro tunc*, Sept. 1, 2012 (102 So.3d 505); Dec. 18, 2014, effective Jan. 1, 2015 (154 So.3d 301).

Form 12.902(c). Family Law Financial Affidavit (Long Form)

IN THE CIRCUIT COURT OF THE ____________ JUDICIAL CIRCUIT,
IN AND FOR ____________ COUNTY, FLORIDA

Case No.: ____________
Division: ____________

____________________________,
Petitioner,

and

____________________________,
Respondent.

FAMILY LAW FINANCIAL AFFIDAVIT (LONG FORM)

($50,000 or more Individual Gross Annual Income)

I, *{full legal name}* ____________________________, being sworn, certify that the following information is true:

SECTION I. INCOME

1. My age is: ____________
2. My occupation is: ____________
3. I am currently

[Check all that apply]

a. ___ Unemployed

Describe your efforts to find employment, how soon you expect to be employed, and the pay you expect to receive: ____________________________

b. ___ Employed by: ____________________________

Address: ____________________________

City, State, Zip code: ____________ Telephone Number: ____________

Pay rate: $ ______ ( ) every week ( ) every other week ( ) twice a month ( ) monthly

( ) other: ____________________________

If you are expecting to become unemployed or change jobs soon, describe the change you expect and why and how it will affect your income: ____________________________

___ Check here if you currently have more than one job. List the information above for the second job(s) on a separate sheet and attach it to this affidavit.

c. ___ Retired. Date of retirement: ____________________________

Florida Family Law Rules of Procedure Form 12.902(c), Family Law Financial Affidavit (Long Form) (01/15)

Employer from whom retired: ______________________________
Address: ______________________________
City, State, Zip code: ______________ Telephone Number: __________

LAST YEAR'S GROSS INCOME: Your Income Other Party's Income *(if known)*
YEAR________ $ ________________ $ ____________

PRESENT MONTHLY GROSS INCOME:

All amounts must be MONTHLY. See the instructions with this form to figure out money amounts for anything that is NOT paid monthly. Attach more paper, if needed. Items included under "other" should be listed separately with separate dollar amounts.

1. $______ Monthly gross salary or wages
2. ______ Monthly bonuses, commissions, allowances, overtime, tips, and similar payments
3. ______ Monthly business income from sources such as self-employment, partnerships, close corporations, and/or independent contracts (Gross receipts minus ordinary and necessary expenses required to produce income.)(Attach sheet itemizing such income and expenses.)
4. ______ Monthly disability benefits/SSI
5. ______ Monthly Workers' Compensation
6. ______ Monthly Unemployment Compensation
7. ______ Monthly pension, retirement, or annuity payments
8. ______ Monthly Social Security benefits
9. ______ Monthly alimony actually received (Add 9a and 9b)
   9a. From this case: $________
   9b. From other case(s): ________
10. ______ Monthly interest and dividends
11. ______ Monthly rental income (gross receipts minus ordinary and necessary expenses required to produce income) (Attach sheet itemizing such income and expense items.)
12. ______ Monthly income from royalties, trusts, or estates
13. ______ Monthly reimbursed expenses and in-kind payments to the extent that they reduce personal living expenses (Attach sheet itemizing each item and amount.)
14. ______ Monthly gains derived from dealing in property (not including nonrecurring gains)
    Any other income of a recurring nature (identify source)
15. ____
16. ____
17. $________ **TOTAL PRESENT MONTHLY GROSS INCOME** (Add lines 1 through 16).

PRESENT MONTHLY DEDUCTIONS:
All amounts must be MONTHLY. See the instructions with this form to figure out money amounts for anything that is NOT paid monthly.

18. $______ Monthly federal, state, and local income tax (corrected for filing status and allowable dependents and income tax liabilities)
    a. Filing Status ______________
    b. Number of dependents claimed ______
19. ______ Monthly FICA or self-employment taxes
20. ______ Monthly Medicare payments
21. ______ Monthly mandatory union dues
22. ______ Monthly mandatory retirement payments

Florida Family Law Rules of Procedure Form 12.902(c), Family Law Financial Affidavit (Long Form) (01/15)

23. _______ Monthly health insurance payments (including dental insurance), excluding portion paid for any minor children of this relationship
24. _______ Monthly court-ordered child support actually paid for children from another relationship
25. _______ Monthly court-ordered alimony actually paid (Add 25a and 25b)
    25a. from this case: $ __________
    25b. from other case(s): __________

26. $_______ **TOTAL DEDUCTIONS ALLOWABLE UNDER SECTION 61.30, FLORIDA STATUTES** (Add lines 18 through 25).

27. $_______ **PRESENT NET MONTHLY INCOME** (Subtract line 26 from line 17).

SECTION II. AVERAGE MONTHLY EXPENSES

Proposed/Estimated Expenses. If this is a dissolution of marriage case **and** your expenses as listed below do not reflect what you actually pay currently, you should write "estimate" next to each amount that is estimated.

HOUSEHOLD:
1. $_______ Monthly mortgage or rent payments
2. _______ Monthly property taxes (if not included in mortgage)
3. _______ Monthly insurance on residence (if not included in mortgage)
4. _______ Monthly condominium maintenance fees and homeowner's association fees
5. _______ Monthly electricity
6. _______ Monthly water, garbage, and sewer
7. _______ Monthly telephone
8. _______ Monthly fuel oil or natural gas
9. _______ Monthly repairs and maintenance
10. _______ Monthly lawn care
11. _______ Monthly pool maintenance
12. _______ Monthly pest control
13. _______ Monthly misc. household
14. _______ Monthly food and home supplies
15. _______ Monthly meals outside home
16. _______ Monthly cable t.v.
17. _______ Monthly alarm service contract
18. _______ Monthly service contracts on appliances
19. _______ Monthly maid service

Other:
20. ____
21. ____
22. ____
23. ____
24. ____
25. $_______ **SUBTOTAL** (add lines 1 through 24).

AUTOMOBILE:

26. $_______ Monthly gasoline and oil
27. _______ Monthly repairs
28. _______ Monthly auto tags and emission testing
29. _______ Monthly insurance
30. _______ Monthly payments (lease or financing)
31. _______ Monthly rental/replacements
32. _______ Monthly alternative transportation (bus, rail, car pool, etc.)
33. _______ Monthly tolls and parking
34. _______ Other: ______________________________
35. $_______ **SUBTOTAL** (add lines 26 through 34)

MONTHLY EXPENSES FOR CHILDREN COMMON TO BOTH PARTIES:

36. $_______ Monthly nursery, babysitting, or day care
37. _______ Monthly school tuition
38. _______ Monthly school supplies, books, and fees
39. _______ Monthly after school activities
40. _______ Monthly lunch money
41. _______ Monthly private lessons or tutoring
42. _______ Monthly allowances
43. _______ Monthly clothing and uniforms
44. _______ Monthly entertainment (movies, parties, etc.)
45. _______ Monthly health insurance
46. _______ Monthly medical, dental, prescriptions (nonreimbursed only)
47. _______ Monthly psychiatric/psychological/counselor
48. _______ Monthly orthodontic
49. _______ Monthly vitamins
50. _______ Monthly beauty parlor/barber shop
51. _______ Monthly nonprescription medication
52. _______ Monthly cosmetics, toiletries, and sundries
53. _______ Monthly gifts from child(ren) to others (other children, relatives, teachers, etc.)
54. _______ Monthly camp or summer activities
55. _______ Monthly clubs (Boy/Girl Scouts, etc.)
56. _______ Monthly time-sharing expenses
57. _______ Monthly miscellaneous
58. $_______ **SUBTOTAL** (add lines 36 through 57)

MONTHLY EXPENSES FOR CHILD(REN) FROM ANOTHER RELATIONSHIP

(other than court-ordered child support)

59. $____
60. ____
61. ____
62. ____
63. $_______ **SUBTOTAL** (add lines 59 through 62)

Florida Family Law Rules of Procedure Form 12.902(c), Family Law Financial Affidavit (Long Form) (01/15)

MONTHLY INSURANCE:

64. $______ Health insurance (if not listed on lines 23 or 45)
65. ______ Life insurance
66. ______ Dental insurance

Other:

67. ______
68. ______
69. $______ **SUBTOTAL** (add lines 66 through 68, exclude lines 64 and 65)

OTHER MONTHLY EXPENSES NOT LISTED ABOVE:

70. $______ Monthly dry cleaning and laundry
71. ______ Monthly clothing
72. ______ Monthly medical, dental, and prescription (unreimbursed only)
73. ______ Monthly psychiatric, psychological, or counselor (unreimbursed only)
74. ______ Monthly non-prescription medications, cosmetics, toiletries, and sundries
75. ______ Monthly grooming
76. ______ Monthly gifts
77. ______ Monthly pet expenses
78. ______ Monthly club dues and membership
79. ______ Monthly sports and hobbies
80. ______ Monthly entertainment
81. ______ Monthly periodicals/books/tapes/CDs
82. ______ Monthly vacations
83. ______ Monthly religious organizations
84. ______ Monthly bank charges/credit card fees
85. ______ Monthly education expenses
86. ______ Other: (include any usual and customary expenses not otherwise mentioned in the items listed above)______
87. ______
88. ______
89. ______
90. $______ **SUBTOTAL** (add lines 70 through 89)

MONTHLY PAYMENTS TO CREDITORS: (only when payments are currently made by you on outstanding balances). List only last 4 digits of account numbers.

MONTHLY PAYMENT AND NAME OF CREDITOR(s):

91. $______
92. ______
93. ______
94. ______
95. ______
96. ______
97. ______
98. ______
99. ______
100. ______
101. ______
102. ______

Florida Family Law Rules of Procedure Form 12.902(c), Family Law Financial Affidavit (Long Form) (01/15)

103. ____

104. $_______ **SUBTOTAL** (add lines 91 through 103)

105. $_______ **TOTAL MONTHLY EXPENSES:**
(add lines 25, 35, 58, 63, 69, 90, and 104 of Section II, Expenses)

SUMMARY

106. $_______ **TOTAL PRESENT MONTHLY NET INCOME** (from line 27 of SECTION I. INCOME)

107. $_______ **TOTAL MONTHLY EXPENSES** (from line 105 above)

108. $_______ **SURPLUS** (If line 106 is more than line 107, subtract line 107 from line 106. This is the amount of your surplus. Enter that amount here.)

109. **($_______)(DEFICIT)** (If line 107 is more than line 106, subtract line 106 from line 107. This is the amount of your deficit. Enter that amount here.)

SECTION III. ASSETS AND LIABILITIES

A. **ASSETS (This is where you list what you OWN.)**

INSTRUCTIONS:

STEP 1: In column A, list a description of each separate item owned by you (and/or your spouse, if this is a petition for dissolution of marriage). Blank spaces are provided if you need to list more than one of an item.

STEP 2: If this is a petition for dissolution of marriage, check the line **in Column A** next to any item that you are requesting the judge award to you.

STEP 3: In column B, write what you believe to be the current fair market value of all items listed.

STEP 4: Use column C only if this is a petition for dissolution of marriage and you believe an item is "nonmarital," meaning it belongs to only one of you and should not be divided. You should indicate to whom you believe the item belongs. (Typically, you will only use Column C if property was owned by one spouse before the marriage. See the **"General Information for Self-Represented Litigants"** found at the beginning of these forms and section 61.075(1), Florida Statutes, for definitions of "marital" and "nonmarital" assets and liabilities.)

A ASSETS: DESCRIPTION OF ITEM(S) LIST ONLY LAST FOUR DIGITS OF ACCOUNT NUMBERS. Check the line next to any asset(s) which you are requesting the judge award to you.		B Current Fair Market Value	C Nonmarital (Check correct column)	
			husband	wife
	Cash (on hand)	$		
	Cash (in banks or credit unions)			
	Stocks/Bonds			

	Notes (money owed to you in writing)			
	Money owed to you (not evidenced by a note)			
	Real estate: (Home)			
	(Other)			
	Business interests			
	Automobiles			
	Boats			
	Other vehicles			
	Retirement plans (Profit Sharing, Pension, IRA, 401(k)s, etc.)			
	Furniture & furnishings in home			
	Furniture & furnishings elsewhere			
	Collectibles			

	Jewelry			
	Life insurance (cash surrender value)			
	Sporting and entertainment (T.V., stereo, etc.) equipment			
	Other assets:			
Total Assets (add column B)		$		

B. **LIABILITIES/DEBTS (This is where you list what you OWE.)**

INSTRUCTIONS:

STEP 1: **In column A**, list a description of each separate debt owed by you (and/or your spouse, if this is a petition for dissolution of marriage). Blank spaces are provided if you need to list more than one of an item.

STEP 2: If this is a petition for dissolution of marriage, check the line **in Column A** next to any debt(s) for which you believe you should be responsible.

STEP 3: **In column B**, write what you believe to be the current amount owed for all items listed.

STEP 4: **Use column C only if this is a petition for dissolution of marriage and you believe an item is "nonmarital," meaning the debt belongs to only one of you and should not be divided.** You should indicate to whom you believe the debt belongs. (Typically, you will only use Column C if the debt was owed by one spouse before the marriage. See the **"General Information for Self-Represented Litigants"** found at the beginning of these forms and section 61.075(1), Florida Statutes, for definitions of "marital" and "nonmarital" assets and liabilities.)

	A LIABILITIES: DESCRIPTION OF ITEM(S) **LIST ONLY LAST FOUR DIGITS OF ACCOUNT NUMBERS.** **Check the line next to any debt(s) for which you believe you should be responsible.**	B Current Amount Owed	C Nonmarital (Check correct column) husband	 wife
	Mortgages on real estate: First mortgage on home	$		
	Second mortgage on home			
	Other mortgages			
	Charge/credit card accounts			
	Auto loan			
	Auto loan			
	Bank/Credit Union loans			
	Money you owe (not evidenced by a note)			
	Judgments			
	Other:			
Total Debts (add column B)		$		

C. NET WORTH (excluding contingent assets and liabilities)

$_______**Total Assets** (enter total of Column B in Asset Table; Section A)
$_______**Total Liabilities** (enter total of Column B in Liabilities Table; Section B)
$_______**TOTAL NET WORTH (Total Assets minus Total Liabilities)**
(excluding contingent assets and liabilities)

D. CONTINGENT ASSETS AND LIABILITIES
INSTRUCTIONS:
If you have any **POSSIBLE assets** (income potential, accrued vacation or sick leave, bonus, inheritance, etc.) or **POSSIBLE liabilities** (possible lawsuits, future unpaid taxes, contingent tax liabilities, debts assumed by another), you must list them here.

A Contingent Assets **Check the line next to any contingent asset(s) which you are requesting the judge award to you.**		B Possible Value	C Nonmarital (Check correct column)	
			husband	wife
		$		
Total Contingent Assets		$		

A Contingent Liabilities **Check the line next to any contingent debt(s) for which you believe you should be responsible.**		B Possible Amount Owed	C Nonmarital (Check correct column)	
			husband	wife
		$		
Total Contingent Liabilities		$		

E. CHILD SUPPORT GUIDELINES WORKSHEET. Florida Family Law Rules of Procedure Form 12.902(e), Child Support Guidelines Worksheet, MUST be filed with the court at or prior to a hearing to establish or modify child support. This requirement cannot be waived by the parties.

[Check **one** only]

____**A Child Support Guidelines Worksheet IS or WILL BE filed in this case.** This case involves the establishment or modification of child support.

____**A Child Support Guidelines Worksheet IS NOT being filed in this case.** The establishment or modification of child support is not an issue in this case.

I certify that a copy of this financial affidavit was [check all used]: ( ) e-mailed ( ) mailed, ( ) faxed ( ) hand delivered to the person(s) listed below on *{date}* ____________.

Other party or his/her attorney:
Name: ____________________
Address: ____________________
City, State, Zip: ____________________
Fax Number: ____________________
E-mail Address(es): ____________________

I understand that I am swearing or affirming under oath to the truthfulness of the claims made in this affidavit and that the punishment for knowingly making a false statement includes fines and/or imprisonment.

Dated: ____________________

____
Signature of Party
Printed Name: ____________________
Address: ____________________
City, State, Zip: ____________________
Fax Number: ____________________
E-mail Address(es): ____________________
____

STATE OF FLORIDA
COUNTY OF ____________________

Sworn to or affirmed and signed before me on ____________ by ____________________.

____
NOTARY PUBLIC or DEPUTY CLERK

____
[Print, type, or stamp commissioned name of notary or deputy clerk]

_____ Personally known
_____ Produced identification
Type of identification produced____________________

Florida Family Law Rules of Procedure Form 12.902(c), Family Law Financial Affidavit (Long Form) (01/15)

IF A NONLAWYER HELPED YOU FILL OUT THIS FORM, HE/SHE MUST FILL IN THE BLANKS BELOW:
[fill in **all** blanks] This form was prepared for the: *{choose only **one**}* ( ) Petitioner ( ) Respondent
This form was completed with the assistance of:
*{name of individual}*______________________________,
{name of business} ______________________________,
{address} ______________________________,
{city} __________,*{state}*________, *{telephone number}* ________________.

Florida Family Law Rules of Procedure Form 12.902(c), Family Law Financial Affidavit (Long Form) (01/15)

INSTRUCTIONS FOR FLORIDA FAMILY LAW RULE OF PROCEDURE FORM 12.902(c), FAMILY LAW FINANCIAL AFFIDAVIT (LONG FORM)(01/15)

When should this form be used?

This form should be used when you are involved in a family law case which requires a **financial affidavit** and your individual gross income is $50,000 OR MORE per year unless:

(1) You are filing a simplified dissolution of marriage under rule 12.105 and both parties have waived the filing of financial affidavits;

(2) you have no minor children, no support issues, and have filed a written settlement agreement disposing of all financial issues; or

(3) the court lacks jurisdiction to determine any financial issues.

This form should be typed or printed in black ink. After completing this form, you should sign the form before a **notary public** or **deputy clerk**. You should then **file** the original with the **clerk of the circuit court** in the county where the **petition** was filed and keep a copy for your records.

What should I do next?

A copy of this form must be served on the other **party** in your case within 45 days of being served with the petition, if it is not served on him or her with your initial papers. **Service** must be in accordance with Florida Rule of Judicial Administration 2.516.

Where can I look for more information?

Before proceeding, you should read "General Information for Self-Represented Litigants" found at the beginning of these forms. The words that are in **"bold underline"** in these instructions are defined there. For further information, see Florida Family Law Rule of Procedure 12.285.

Special notes . . .

If you want to keep your address confidential because you are the victim of sexual battery, aggravated child abuse, aggravated stalking, harassment, aggravated battery, or domestic violence do not enter the address, telephone, and fax information at the bottom of this form. Instead, file **Request for Confidential Filing of Address**, Florida Supreme Court Approved Family Law Form 12.980(h).

The affidavit must be completed using **monthly** income and expense amounts. If you are paid or your bills are due on a schedule which is not monthly, you must convert those amounts. Hints are provided below for making these conversions.

Hourly—If you are paid by the hour, you may convert your income to monthly as follows:

Hourly amount	×	Hours worked per week	=	Weekly amount
Weekly amount	×	52 Weeks per year	=	Yearly amount
Yearly amount	÷	12 Months per year	=	**Monthly Amount**

Daily—If you are paid by the day, you may convert your income to monthly as follows:

Daily amount	×	Days worked per week	=	Weekly amount
Weekly amount	×	52 Weeks per year	=	Yearly amount
Yearly amount	÷	12 Months per year	=	**Monthly Amount**

Weekly—If you are paid by the week, you may convert your income to monthly as follows:

Weekly amount	×	52 Weeks per year	=	Yearly amount
Yearly amount	÷	12 Months per year	=	**Monthly Amount**

Bi-weekly—If you are paid every two weeks, you may convert your income to monthly as follows:

Bi-weekly amount	×	26	=	Yearly amount
Yearly amount	÷	12 Months per year	=	**Monthly Amount**

Semi-monthly—If you are paid twice per month, you may convert your income to monthly as follows:

Semi-monthly amount	**×**	**2**	**= Monthly Amount**

Expenses may be converted in the same manner.

Remember, a person who is NOT an attorney is called a nonlawyer. If a nonlawyer helps you fill out these forms, that person must give you a copy of a Disclosure from Nonlawyer, Florida Family Law Rules of Procedure Form 12.900(a), before he or she helps you. A nonlawyer helping you fill out these forms also must put his or her name, address, and telephone number on the bottom of the last page of every form he or she helps you complete.

Added Sept. 21, 2000 (810 So.2d 1). Amended Dec. 6, 2001 (817 So.2d 721); July 10, 2003, effective Jan. 1, 2004 (853 So.2d 303); Sept. 28, 2006 (940 So.2d 409); Nov. 3, 2011, effective, *nunc pro tunc*, Oct. 1, 2011 (78 So.3d 1045); Oct. 18, 2012, effective, *nunc pro tunc*, Sept. 1, 2012 (102 So.3d 505); Dec. 18, 2014, effective Jan. 1, 2015 (154 So.3d 301).

Form 12.902(d). Uniform Child Custody Jurisdiction and Enforcement Act (UCCJEA) Affidavit

IN THE CIRCUIT COURT OF THE ______________________ JUDICIAL CIRCUIT,
IN AND FOR ______________________ COUNTY, FLORIDA

Case No.: ______________
Division: ______________

______________________,
Petitioner,

and

______________________,
Respondent.

UNIFORM CHILD CUSTODY JURISDICTION AND ENFORCEMENT ACT (UCCJEA) AFFIDAVIT

I, *{full legal name}* ______________________________, being sworn, certify that the following statements are true:

1. The number of minor child(ren) subject to this proceeding is ____________. The name, place of birth, birth date, and sex of each child; the present address, periods of residence, and places where each child has lived **within the past five (5) years**; and the name, present address, and relationship to the child of each person with whom the child has lived during that time are:

THE FOLLOWING INFORMATION IS TRUE ABOUT CHILD # __1__:

Child's Full Legal Name: ______________________________
Place of Birth: ______________ Date of Birth: ______________ Sex: ______________

Child's Residence for the past 5 years:

Dates (From/To)	Address (including city and state) where child lived	Name and present address of person child lived with	Relationship to child
____/present*			
____/____			
____/____			
____/____			

Florida Supreme Court Approved Family Law Form 12.902(d), Uniform Child Custody Jurisdiction and Enforcement Act (UCCJEA) Affidavit (03/15)

____/____			
____/____			

*** If you are the petitioner in an injunction for protection against domestic violence case and you have filed a Request for Confidential Filing of Address, Florida Supreme Court Approved Family Law Form 12.980(h), you should write confidential in any space on this form that would require you to enter the address where you are currently living.**

THE FOLLOWING INFORMATION IS TRUE ABOUT CHILD # ____:

Child's Full Legal Name: ____
Place of Birth: ______________________ Date of Birth: ______________ Sex: ____________

Child's Residence for the past 5 years:

Dates (From/To)	Address (including city and state) where child lived	Name and present address of person child lived with	Relationship to child
______/present			
____/____			
____/____			
____/____			
____/____			
____/____			

THE FOLLOWING INFORMATION IS TRUE ABOUT CHILD # _____:

Child's Full Legal Name: ____
Place of Birth: ______________________ Date of Birth: ______________ Sex: ____________

Child's Residence for the past 5 years:

Dates (From/To)	Address (including city and state) where child lived	Name and present address of person child lived with	Relationship to child

____/present			
____/____			
____/____			
____/____			
____/____			
____/____			

2. **Participation in custody or time-sharing proceeding(s):**
*[Choose only **one**]*

____ I HAVE NOT participated as a party, witness, or in any capacity in any other litigation or custody proceeding in this or any other state, concerning custody of or time-sharing with a child subject to this proceeding.

____ I HAVE participated as a party, witness, or in any capacity in any other litigation or custody proceeding in this or another state, concerning custody of or time-sharing with a child subject to this proceeding. *Explain:*

a. Name of each child: ____________________
b. Type of proceeding: ____________________
c. Court and state: ____________________
d. Date of court order or judgment (if any): ____________________

3. **Information about custody or time-sharing proceeding(s):**
*[Choose only **one**]*

____ I HAVE NO INFORMATION of any custody or time-sharing proceeding pending in a court of this or any other state concerning a child subject to this proceeding.

____ I HAVE THE FOLLOWING INFORMATION concerning a custody or time-sharing proceeding pending in a court of this or another state concerning a child subject to this proceeding, other than set out in item 2. *Explain:*

e. Name of each child: ____________________
f. Type of proceeding: ____________________
g. Court and state: ____________________
h. Date of court order or judgment (if any): ____________________

4. **Persons not a party to this proceeding:**
*[Choose only **one**]*

Florida Supreme Court Approved Family Law Form 12.902(d), Uniform Child Custody Jurisdiction and Enforcement Act (UCCJEA) Affidavit (03/15)

____ I DO NOT KNOW OF ANY PERSON not a party to this proceeding who has physical custody or claims to have custody, visitation or time-sharing with respect to any child subject to this proceeding.

____ I KNOW THAT THE FOLLOWING NAMED PERSON(S) not a party to this proceeding has (have) physical custody or claim(s) to have custody, visitation, or time-sharing with respect to any child subject to this proceeding:

a. Name and address of person: ____
____
_____ has physical custody _____ claims custody rights _____ claims visitation or time-sharing
Name of each child: ____

b. Name and address of person: ____
____
_____ has physical custody _____ claims custody rights _____ claims visitation or time-sharing
Name of each child: ____

c. Name and address of person: ____
____
_____ has physical custody _____ claims custody rights _____ claims visitation or time-sharing
Name of each child: ____

5. Knowledge of prior child support proceedings:
[Choose only one]
_____The child(ren) described in this affidavit are NOT subject to existing child support order(s) in this or any state or territory.

Florida Supreme Court Approved Family Law Form 12.902(d), Uniform Child Custody Jurisdiction and Enforcement Act (UCCJEA) Affidavit (03/15)

_____The child(ren) described in this affidavit are subject to the following existing child support order(s):

a. Name of each child: ______________________________
b. Type of proceeding: ______________________________
c. Court and address: ______________________________
d. Date of court order/judgment (if any): ______________________________
e. Amount of child support paid and by whom: ______________________________

6. I acknowledge that I have a continuing duty to advise this Court of any custody, visitation or time-sharing, child support, or guardianship proceeding (including dissolution of marriage, separate maintenance, child neglect, or dependency) concerning the child(ren) in this state or any other state about which information is obtained during this proceeding.

I certify that a copy of this document was ( ) mailed ( ) faxed and mailed ( ) e-mailed ( ) hand delivered to the person(s) listed below on *{date}* ______________________________.

Other party or his/her attorney:
Name: ______________________________
Address: ______________________________
City, State, Zip: ______________________________
Fax Number: ______________________________
Designated E-mail Address(es):______________________________
____

I understand that I am swearing or affirming under oath to the truthfulness of the claims made in this affidavit and that the punishment for knowingly making a false statement includes fines and/or imprisonment.

Dated: ______________________________

____
Signature of Party
Printed Name: ______________________________
Address: ______________________________
City, State, Zip: ______________________________
Telephone Number: ______________________________
Fax Number: ______________________________
Designated E-mail Address(es):______________________________
____

STATE OF FLORIDA
COUNTY OF ______________________________

Florida Supreme Court Approved Family Law Form 12.902(d), Uniform Child Custody Jurisdiction and Enforcement Act (UCCJEA) Affidavit (03/15)

Sworn to or affirmed and signed before me on ______________ by ______________________________.

____
NOTARY PUBLIC or DEPUTY CLERK

____
[Print, type, or stamp commissioned name of notary or clerk.]
_____ Personally known
_____ Produced identification
Type of identification produced ______________________

IF A NONLAWYER HELPED YOU FILL OUT THIS FORM, HE/SHE MUST FILL IN THE BLANKS BELOW:
[fill in all blanks] This form was prepared for the: *{choose only one}* ( ) Husband ( ) Wife
This form was completed with the assistance of:
{name of individual} ____,
{name of business} ____,
{address}
{city} __________,*{state}* _____,*{zip code}* _______,*{telephone number}* ________.

Florida Supreme Court Approved Family Law Form 12.902(d), Uniform Child Custody Jurisdiction and Enforcement Act (UCCJEA) Affidavit (03/15)

INSTRUCTIONS FOR FLORIDA SUPREME COURT APPROVED FAMILY LAW FORM 12.902(d) UNIFORM CHILD CUSTODY JURISDICTION AND ENFORCEMENT ACT (UCCJEA) AFFIDAVIT (03/15)

When should this form be used?

This form should be used in any case involving custody of, visitation with, or time-sharing with any minor child(ren). This **affidavit** is **required** even if the custody of, visitation, or time-sharing with the minor child(ren) are not in dispute.

This form should be typed or printed in black ink. After completing this form, you should sign the form before a **notary public** or **deputy clerk**. You should then **file** the original with the **clerk of the circuit court** in the county where the petition was filed and keep a copy for your records.

IMPORTANT INFORMATION REGARDING E-FILING

The Florida Rules of Judicial Administration now require that all petitions, pleadings, and documents be filed electronically except in certain circumstances. **Self-represented litigants may file petitions or other pleadings or documents electronically; however, they are not required to do so.** If you choose to file your pleadings or other documents electronically, you must do so in accordance with Florida Rule of Judicial Administration 2.525, and you must follow the procedures of the judicial circuit in which you file. **The rules and procedures should be carefully read and followed.**

What should I do next?

A copy of this form must be mailed, e-mailed, or hand delivered to the other party in your case, if it is not served on him or her with your initial papers.

IMPORTANT INFORMATION REGARDING E-SERVICE ELECTION

After the initial service of process of the petition or supplemental petition by the Sheriff or certified process server, the Florida Rules of Judicial Administration now require that all documents required or permitted to be served on the other party must be served by electronic mail (e-mail) except in certain circumstances. **You must strictly comply with the format requirements set forth in the Rules of Judicial Administration.**

SELF-REPRESENTED LITIGANTS MAY SERVE DOCUMENTS BY E-MAIL; HOWEVER, THEY ARE NOT REQUIRED TO DO SO. If a self-represented litigant elects to serve and receive documents by e-mail, the procedures must always be followed once the initial election is made.

To serve and receive documents by e-mail, you must designate your e-mail addresses by using the **Designation of Current Mailing and E-mail Address**, Florida Supreme Court Approved Family Law Form 12.915, and you must provide your e-mail address on each form on which your signature appears. Please **CAREFULLY** read the rules and instructions for: **Certificate of Service (General),** Florida Supreme Court Approved Family Law Form 12.914; **Designation of Current Mailing and E-mail Address,** Florida Supreme Court Approved Family Law Form 12.915; and Florida Rule of Judicial Administration 2.516.

Where can I look for more information?

Before proceeding, you should read General Information for Self-Represented Litigants found at the beginning of these forms. The words that are in **bold underline** in these instructions are defined there. For further information, see sections 61.501–61.542, Florida Statutes.

Special notes . . .

Chapter 2008–61, Laws of Florida, effective October 1, 2008, eliminated such terms as custodial parent, noncustodial parent, primary residential parent, secondary residential parent, and visitation from Chapter 61, Florida Statutes. Instead, parents are to develop a Parenting Plan that includes, among other things, their time-sharing schedule with the minor child(ren). If the parents cannot agree, a parenting plan will be established by the Court.

However, because the UCCJEA uses the terms custody and visitation, they are included in this form.

If you are the petitioner in an injunction for protection against domestic violence case and you have filed a **Request for Confidential Filing of Address**, Florida Supreme Court Approved Family Law Form 12.980(h), you should write confidential in any space on this form that would require you to write the address where you are currently living.

Remember, a person who is NOT an attorney is called a nonlawyer. If a nonlawyer helps you fill out these forms, that person must give you a copy of a **Disclosure from Nonlawyer**, Florida Family Law Rules of Procedure Form 12.900(a), before he or she helps you. A nonlawyer helping you fill out these forms also **must** put his or her name, address, and telephone number on the bottom of the last page of every form he or she helps you complete.

Added February 26, 1998, effective Mar. 16, 1998 (713 So.2d 1). Amended Sept. 21, 2000 (810 So.2d 1); December 6, 2001 (817 So.2d 721); December 19, 2002 (836 So.2d 1019); March 26, 2009 (20 So.3d 173); Dec. 16, 2010 (59 So.3d 792); March 26, 2015, effective March 26, 2015 (2015 WL 1343088).

Form 12.902(e). Notice of Filing Child Support Guidelines Worksheet

IN THE CIRCUIT COURT OF THE ____________________ JUDICIAL CIRCUIT,
IN AND FOR ____________________ COUNTY, FLORIDA

Case No.: ____________________
Division: ____________________

______________________________,
Petitioner,

and

______________________________,
Respondent.

NOTICE OF FILING CHILD SUPPORT GUIDELINES WORKSHEET

PLEASE TAKE NOTICE, that *{name}*______________________________________, is filing his/her

Child Support Guidelines Worksheet attached and labeled Exhibit 1.

CERTIFICATE OF SERVICE

I certify that a copy of this Notice of Filing with the Child Support Guidelines Worksheet was **[check all used]**: ( ) e-mailed ( ) mailed ( ) faxed ( ) hand delivered to the person(s) listed below on *{date}*______________________.

Other party or his/her attorney:
Name: ______________________________
Address: ______________________________
City, State, Zip: ______________________________
Fax Number: ______________________________
E-mail Address(es): ______________________________

____
Signature of Party or his/her Attorney
Printed Name: ______________________________
Address: ______________________________
City, State, Zip: ______________________________
Fax Number: ______________________________
E-mail Address(es): ______________________________
Florida Bar Number: ______________________________

Florida Family Law Rules of Procedure Form 12.902(e), Child Support Guidelines Worksheet (09/12)

CHILD SUPPORT GUIDELINES WORKSHEET			
	A. FATHER	**B.** MOTHER	TOTAL
1. Present Net Monthly Income Enter the amount from line 27, Section I of Florida Family Law Rules of Procedure Form 12.902(b) or (c), Financial Affidavit.			
2. Basic Monthly Obligation There is (are) *{number}*_____ minor child(ren) common to the parties. Using the total amount from line 1, enter the appropriate amount from the child support guidelines chart.			
3. Percent of Financial Responsibility Divide the amount on line 1A by the total amount on line 1 to get Father's percentage of financial responsibility. Enter answer on line 3A. Divide the amount on line 1B by the total amount on line 1 to get Mother's percentage of financial responsibility. Enter answer on line 3B.	%	%	
4. Share of Basic Monthly Obligation Multiply the number on line 2 by the percentage on line 3A to get Father's share of basic obligation. Enter answer on line 4A. Multiply the number on line 2 by the percentage on line 3B to get Mother's share of basic obligation. Enter answer on line 4B.			
Additional Support — Health Insurance, Child Care & Other			
5. a. 100% of Monthly Child Care Costs [Child care costs should not exceed the level required to provide quality care from a licensed source. See section 61.30(7), Florida Statutes, for more information.]			
b. Total Monthly Child(ren)'s Health Insurance Cost [This is only amounts actually paid for health insurance on the child(ren).]			

Florida Family Law Rules of Procedure Form 12.902(e), Child Support Guidelines Worksheet (09/12)

CHILD SUPPORT GUIDELINES WORKSHEET			
	A. FATHER	B. MOTHER	TOTAL
c. Total Monthly Child(ren)'s Noncovered Medical, Dental and Prescription Medication Costs			
d. Total Monthly Child Care & Health Costs [Add lines 5a + 5b +5c].			
6. Additional Support Payments Multiply the number on line 5d by the percentage on line 3A to determine the Father's share. Enter answer on line 6A. Multiply the number on line 5d by the percentage on line 3B to determine the Mother's share. Enter answer on line 6B.			
Statutory Adjustments/Credits			
7. a. Monthly child care payments actually made			
b. Monthly health insurance payments actually made			
c. Other payments/credits actually made for any noncovered medical, dental and prescription medication expenses of the child(ren) not ordered to be separately paid on a percentage basis. (See section 61.30 (8), Florida Statutes)			
8. Total Support Payments actually made (Add 7a though 7c)			
9. **MINIMUM CHILD SUPPORT OBLIGATION FOR EACH PARENT** [Line 4 plus line 6; minus line 8]			
Substantial Time-Sharing (GROSS UP METHOD) If each parent exercises time-sharing at least 20 percent of the overnights in the year (73 overnights in the year), complete Nos. 10 through 21			
	A. FATHER	B. MOTHER	TOTAL
10. Basic Monthly Obligation x 150% [Multiply line 2 by 1.5]			

Florida Family Law Rules of Procedure Form 12.902(e), Child Support Guidelines Worksheet (09/12)

CHILD SUPPORT GUIDELINES WORKSHEET			
	A. FATHER	B. MOTHER	TOTAL
11. Increased Basic Obligation for each parent. Multiply the number on line 10 by the percentage on line 3A to determine the Father's share. Enter answer on line 11A. Multiply the number on line 10 by the percentage on line 3B to determine the Mother's share. Enter answer on line 11B.			
12. Percentage of overnight stays with each parent. The child(ren) spend(s) _______overnight stays with the Father each year. Using the number on the above line, multiply it by 100 and divide by 365. Enter this number on line 12A. The child(ren) spend(s) ______ overnight stays with the Mother each year. Using the number on the above line, multiply it by 100 and divide by 365. Enter this number on line 12B.	%	%	
13. Parent's support multiplied by other Parent's percentage of overnights. [Multiply line 11A by line 12B. Enter this number in 13A. Multiply line 11B by line 12A. Enter this number in 13B.]			
Additional Support — Health Insurance, Child Care & Other			
14. a. Total Monthly Child Care Costs [Child care costs should not exceed the level required to provide quality care from a licensed source. See section 61.30(7), Florida Statutes, for more information.]			
b. Total Monthly Child(ren)'s Health Insurance Cost [This is only amounts actually paid for health insurance on the child(ren).]			
c. Total Monthly Child(ren)'s Noncovered Medical, Dental and Prescription Medication Costs.			
d. Total Monthly Child Care & Health Costs [Add lines 14a + 14b + 14c.]			

Florida Family Law Rules of Procedure Form 12.902(e), Child Support Guidelines Worksheet (09/12)

CHILD SUPPORT GUIDELINES WORKSHEET			
	A. FATHER	B. MOTHER	TOTAL
15. Additional Support Payments. Multiply the number on line 14d by the percentage on line 3A to determine the Father's share. Enter answer on line 15A. Multiply the number on line 14d by the percentage on line 3B to determine the Mother's share. Enter answer on line 15B.			
Statutory Adjustments/Credits			
16. a. Monthly child care payments actually made			
b. Monthly health insurance payments actually made			
c. Other payments/credits actually made for any noncovered medical, dental and prescription medication expenses of the child(ren) not ordered to be separately paid on a percentage basis. [See section 61.30(8), Florida Statutes]			
17. Total Support Payments actually made [Add 16a though 16c]			
18. Total Additional Support Transfer Amount [Line 15 minus line 17; enter any negative number as zero)			
19. Total Child Support Owed from Father to Mother [Add line 13A plus line 18A]			
20. Total Child Support Owed from Mother to Father [Add line 13B plus line 18B]			
21. Actual Child Support to Be Paid. [Comparing lines 19 and 20, Subtract the smaller amount owed from the larger amount owed and enter the result in the column for the parent that owes the larger amount of support]	$		

ADJUSTMENTS TO GUIDELINES AMOUNT. If you or the other parent is requesting the Court to award a child support amount that is more or less than the child support guidelines, you must complete and file Motion to Deviate from Child Support Guidelines, Florida Supreme Court Approved Family Law Form 12.943.

Florida Family Law Rules of Procedure Form 12.902(e), Child Support Guidelines Worksheet (09/12)

[check **one** only]

a. ____ **Deviation from the guidelines amount is requested.** The Motion to Deviate from Child Support Guidelines, Florida Supreme Court Approved Family Law Form 12.943, is attached.

b. ____ **Deviation from the guidelines amount is NOT requested.** The Motion to Deviate from Child Support Guidelines, Florida Supreme Court Approved Family Law Form 12.943, is not attached.

IF A NONLAWYER HELPED YOU FILL OUT THIS FORM, HE/SHE MUST FILL IN THE BLANKS BELOW:
[fill in **all** blanks] This form was prepared for the: *{choose only **one**}* ( ) Petitioner ( ) Respondent
This form was completed with the assistance of:
{name of individual} ____,
{name of business} ____,
{address} ____,
{city} ______________________,*{state}* ,______ *{telephone number}*______________________.

INSTRUCTIONS FOR FLORIDA FAMILY LAW RULES OF PROCEDURE FORM 12.902(e), CHILD SUPPORT GUIDELINES WORKSHEET (09/12)

When should this form be used?

You should complete this worksheet if **child support** is being requested in your case. If you know the income of the other **party**, this worksheet should accompany your **financial affidavit**. If you do not know the other party's income, this form must be completed after the other party files his or her financial affidavit, and **serves** a copy on you.

This form should be typed or printed in black ink. You should file the original with the **clerk of the circuit court** in the county where your case is filed and keep a copy for your records.

What should I do next?

A copy of this form must be served on the other party in your case. **Service** must be in accordance with Florida Rule of Judicial Administration 2.516.

Where can I look for more information?

Before proceeding, you should read "General Information for Self–Represented Litigants" found at the beginning of these forms. The words that are in **"bold underline"** in these instructions are defined there. For further information, see section 61.30, Florida Statutes.

Special notes . . .

If you want to keep your address confidential because you are the victim of sexual battery, aggravated child abuse, aggravated stalking, harassment, aggravated battery or domestic violence, do not enter the address, telephone, and fax information at the bottom of this form. Instead, file **Request for Confidential Filing of Address**, Florida Supreme Court Approved Family Law Form 12.980(h).

The chart below contains the guideline amounts that you should use when calculating child support. This amount is based on the number of children and the combined income of the parents, and it is divided between the parents in direct proportion to their income or earning capacity. From time to time, some of the amounts in the child support guidelines chart will change. Be sure you have the most recent version of the chart before using it.

Because the guidelines are based on monthly amounts, it may be necessary to convert some income and expense figures from other frequencies to monthly. You should do this as follows:

If payment is twice per month	Payment amount	×	2	=	**Monthly amount**
If payment is every two weeks	Payment amount	×	26	=	Yearly amount due
	Yearly amount	÷	12	=	**Monthly amount**
If payment is weekly	Weekly amount	×	52	=	Yearly amount due
	Yearly amount	÷	12	=	**Monthly amount**

If you or the other parent request that the court award an amount that is different than the guideline amount, you must also complete and attach a **Motion to Deviate from Child Support Guidelines**, Florida Supreme Court Approved Family Law Form 12.943.

Remember, a person who is NOT an attorney is called a nonlawyer. If a nonlawyer helps you fill out these forms, that person must give you a copy of a **Disclosure from Nonlawyer**, Florida Family Law Rules of Procedure Form 12.900(a), before he or she helps you. A nonlawyer helping you fill out these forms also **must** put his or her name, address, and telephone number on the bottom of the last page of every form he or she helps you complete.

CHILD SUPPORT GUIDELINES CHART

Combined Monthly Available Income	One Child	Two Children	Three Children	Four Children	Five Children	Six Children
800.00	190	211	213	216	218	220
850.00	202	257	259	262	265	268
900.00	213	302	305	309	312	315
950.00	224	347	351	355	359	363
1000.00	235	365	397	402	406	410
1050.00	246	382	443	448	453	458
1100.00	258	400	489	495	500	505
1150.00	269	417	522	541	547	553
1200.00	280	435	544	588	594	600
1250.00	290	451	565	634	641	648
1300.00	300	467	584	659	688	695
1350.00	310	482	603	681	735	743
1400.00	320	498	623	702	765	790
1450.00	330	513	642	724	789	838
1500.00	340	529	662	746	813	869
1550.00	350	544	681	768	836	895
1600.00	360	560	701	790	860	920
1650.00	370	575	720	812	884	945
1700.00	380	591	740	833	907	971
1750.00	390	606	759	855	931	996
1800.00	400	622	779	877	955	1022
1850.00	410	638	798	900	979	1048
1900.00	421	654	818	923	1004	1074
1950.00	431	670	839	946	1029	1101
2000.00	442	686	859	968	1054	1128
2050.00	452	702	879	991	1079	1154
2100.00	463	718	899	1014	1104	1181
2150.00	473	734	919	1037	1129	1207
2200.00	484	751	940	1060	1154	1234
2250.00	494	767	960	1082	1179	1261
2300.00	505	783	980	1105	1204	1287
2350.00	515	799	1000	1128	1229	1314
2400.00	526	815	1020	1151	1254	1340
2450.00	536	831	1041	1174	1279	1367
2500.00	547	847	1061	1196	1304	1394
2550.00	557	864	1081	1219	1329	1420

Instructions for Florida Family Law Rules of Procedure Form 12.902(e), Child Support Guidelines Worksheet (09/12)

Combined Monthly Available Income	One Child	Two Children	Three Children	Four Children	Five Children	Six Children
2600.00	568	880	1101	1242	1354	1447
2650.00	578	896	1121	1265	1379	1473
2700.00	588	912	1141	1287	1403	1500
2750.00	597	927	1160	1308	1426	1524
2800.00	607	941	1178	1328	1448	1549
2850.00	616	956	1197	1349	1471	1573
2900.00	626	971	1215	1370	1494	1598
2950.00	635	986	1234	1391	1517	1622
3000.00	644	1001	1252	1412	1540	1647
3050.00	654	1016	1271	1433	1563	1671
3100.00	663	1031	1289	1453	1586	1695
3150.00	673	1045	1308	1474	1608	1720
3200.00	682	1060	1327	1495	1631	1744
3250.00	691	1075	1345	1516	1654	1769
3300.00	701	1090	1364	1537	1677	1793
3350.00	710	1105	1382	1558	1700	1818
3400.00	720	1120	1401	1579	1723	1842
3450.00	729	1135	1419	1599	1745	1867
3500.00	738	1149	1438	1620	1768	1891
3550.00	748	1164	1456	1641	1791	1915
3600.00	757	1179	1475	1662	1814	1940
3650.00	767	1194	1493	1683	1837	1964
3700.00	776	1208	1503	1702	1857	1987
3750.00	784	1221	1520	1721	1878	2009
3800.00	793	1234	1536	1740	1899	2031
3850.00	802	1248	1553	1759	1920	2053
3900.00	811	1261	1570	1778	1940	2075
3950.00	819	1275	1587	1797	1961	2097
4000.00	828	1288	1603	1816	1982	2119
4050.00	837	1302	1620	1835	2002	2141
4100.00	846	1315	1637	1854	2023	2163
4150.00	854	1329	1654	1873	2044	2185
4200.00	863	1342	1670	1892	2064	2207
4250.00	872	1355	1687	1911	2085	2229
4300.00	881	1369	1704	1930	2106	2251
4350.00	889	1382	1721	1949	2127	2273
4400.00	898	1396	1737	1968	2147	2295
4450.00	907	1409	1754	1987	2168	2317

Instructions for Florida Family Law Rules of Procedure Form 12.902(e), Child Support Guidelines Worksheet (09/12)

Combined Monthly Available Income	One Child	Two Children	Three Children	Four Children	Five Children	Six Children
4500.00	916	1423	1771	2006	2189	2339
4550.00	924	1436	1788	2024	2209	2361
4600.00	933	1450	1804	2043	2230	2384
4650.00	942	1463	1821	2062	2251	2406
4700.00	951	1477	1838	2081	2271	2428
4750.00	959	1490	1855	2100	2292	2450
4800.00	968	1503	1871	2119	2313	2472
4850.00	977	1517	1888	2138	2334	2494
4900.00	986	1530	1905	2157	2354	2516
4950.00	993	1542	1927	2174	2372	2535
5000.00	1000	1551	1939	2188	2387	2551
5050.00	1006	1561	1952	2202	2402	2567
5100.00	1013	1571	1964	2215	2417	2583
5150.00	1019	1580	1976	2229	2432	2599
5200.00	1025	1590	1988	2243	2447	2615
5250.00	1032	1599	2000	2256	2462	2631
5300.00	1038	1609	2012	2270	2477	2647
5350.00	1045	1619	2024	2283	2492	2663
5400.00	1051	1628	2037	2297	2507	2679
5450.00	1057	1638	2049	2311	2522	2695
5500.00	1064	1647	2061	2324	2537	2711
5550.00	1070	1657	2073	2338	2552	2727
5600.00	1077	1667	2085	2352	2567	2743
5650.00	1083	1676	2097	2365	2582	2759
5700.00	1089	1686	2109	2379	2597	2775
5750.00	1096	1695	2122	2393	2612	2791
5800.00	1102	1705	2134	2406	2627	2807
5850.00	1107	1713	2144	2418	2639	2820
5900.00	1111	1721	2155	2429	2651	2833
5950.00	1116	1729	2165	2440	2663	2847
6000.00	1121	1737	2175	2451	2676	2860
6050.00	1126	1746	2185	2462	2688	2874
6100.00	1131	1754	2196	2473	2700	2887
6150.00	1136	1762	2206	2484	2712	2900
6200.00	1141	1770	2216	2495	2724	2914
6250.00	1145	1778	2227	2506	2737	2927
6300.00	1150	1786	2237	2517	2749	2941
6350.00	1155	1795	2247	2529	2761	2954

Instructions for Florida Family Law Rules of Procedure Form 12.902(e), Child Support Guidelines Worksheet (09/12)

Combined Monthly Available Income	One Child	Two Children	Three Children	Four Children	Five Children	Six Children
6400.00	1160	1803	2258	2540	2773	2967
6450.00	1165	1811	2268	2551	2785	2981
6500.00	1170	1819	2278	2562	2798	2994
6550.00	1175	1827	2288	2573	2810	3008
6600.00	1179	1835	2299	2584	2822	3021
6650.00	1184	1843	2309	2595	2834	3034
6700.00	1189	1850	2317	2604	2845	3045
6750.00	1193	1856	2325	2613	2854	3055
6800.00	1196	1862	2332	2621	2863	3064
6850.00	1200	1868	2340	2630	2872	3074
6900.00	1204	1873	2347	2639	2882	3084
6950.00	1208	1879	2355	2647	2891	3094
7000.00	1212	1885	2362	2656	2900	3103
7050.00	1216	1891	2370	2664	2909	3113
7100.00	1220	1897	2378	2673	2919	3123
7150.00	1224	1903	2385	2681	2928	3133
7200.00	1228	1909	2393	2690	2937	3142
7250.00	1232	1915	2400	2698	2946	3152
7300.00	1235	1921	2408	2707	2956	3162
7350.00	1239	1927	2415	2716	2965	3172
7400.00	1243	1933	2423	2724	2974	3181
7450.00	1247	1939	2430	2733	2983	3191
7500.00	1251	1945	2438	2741	2993	3201
7550.00	1255	1951	2446	2750	3002	3211
7600.00	1259	1957	2453	2758	3011	3220
7650.00	1263	1963	2461	2767	3020	3230
7700.00	1267	1969	2468	2775	3030	3240
7750.00	1271	1975	2476	2784	3039	3250
7800.00	1274	1981	2483	2792	3048	3259
7850.00	1278	1987	2491	2801	3057	3269
7900.00	1282	1992	2498	2810	3067	3279
7950.00	1286	1998	2506	2818	3076	3289
8000.00	1290	2004	2513	2827	3085	3298
8050.00	1294	2010	2521	2835	3094	3308
8100.00	1298	2016	2529	2844	3104	3318
8150.00	1302	2022	2536	2852	3113	3328
8200.00	1306	2028	2544	2861	3122	3337
8250.00	1310	2034	2551	2869	3131	3347

Instructions for Florida Family Law Rules of Procedure Form 12.902(e), Child Support Guidelines Worksheet (09/12)

Combined Monthly Available Income	One Child	Two Children	Three Children	Four Children	Five Children	Six Children
8300.00	1313	2040	2559	2878	3141	3357
8350.00	1317	2046	2566	2887	3150	3367
8400.00	1321	2052	2574	2895	3159	3376
8450.00	1325	2058	2581	2904	3168	3386
8500.00	1329	2064	2589	2912	3178	3396
8550.00	1333	2070	2597	2921	3187	3406
8600.00	1337	2076	2604	2929	3196	3415
8650.00	1341	2082	2612	2938	3205	3425
8700.00	1345	2088	2619	2946	3215	3435
8750.00	1349	2094	2627	2955	3224	3445
8800.00	1352	2100	2634	2963	3233	3454
8850.00	1356	2106	2642	2972	3242	3464
8900.00	1360	2111	2649	2981	3252	3474
8950.00	1364	2117	2657	2989	3261	3484
9000.00	1368	2123	2664	2998	3270	3493
9050.00	1372	2129	2672	3006	3279	3503
9100.00	1376	2135	2680	3015	3289	3513
9150.00	1380	2141	2687	3023	3298	3523
9200.00	1384	2147	2695	3032	3307	3532
9250.00	1388	2153	2702	3040	3316	3542
9300.00	1391	2159	2710	3049	3326	3552
9350.00	1395	2165	2717	3058	3335	3562
9400.00	1399	2171	2725	3066	3344	3571
9450.00	1403	2177	2732	3075	3353	3581
9500.00	1407	2183	2740	3083	3363	3591
9550.00	1411	2189	2748	3092	3372	3601
9600.00	1415	2195	2755	3100	3381	3610
9650.00	1419	2201	2763	3109	3390	3620
9700.00	1422	2206	2767	3115	3396	3628
9750.00	1425	2210	2772	3121	3402	3634
9800.00	1427	2213	2776	3126	3408	3641
9850.00	1430	2217	2781	3132	3414	3647
9900.00	1432	2221	2786	3137	3420	3653
9950.00	1435	2225	2791	3143	3426	3659
10000.00	1437	2228	2795	3148	3432	3666

Instructions for Florida Family Law Rules of Procedure Form 12.902(e), Child Support Guidelines Worksheet (09/12)

Added Sept. 15, 2004 (883 So.2d 1285). Amended Oct. 16, 2008 (995 So.2d 445); Jan. 1, 2011 (48 So.3d 25); Nov. 3, 2011, effective, *nunc pro tunc*, Oct. 1, 2011 (78 So.3d 1045); Jan. 19, 2012 (80 So.3d 317); Oct. 18, 2012, effective, *nunc pro tunc*, Sept. 1, 2012 (102 So.3d 505).

Form 12.902(f)(1). Marital Settlement Agreement for Dissolution of Marriage with Dependent or Minor Child(ren)

IN THE CIRCUIT COURT OF THE ______________________ JUDICIAL CIRCUIT,
IN AND FOR ______________________ COUNTY, FLORIDA

Case No.: ____________
Division: ____________

In re: the Marriage of:

______________________,
Husband,

and

______________________,
Wife.

MARITAL SETTLEMENT AGREEMENT FOR DISSOLUTION OF MARRIAGE WITH DEPENDENT OR MINOR CHILD(REN)

We, *{Husband's full legal name}*______________________, and *{Wife's full legal name,*______________________ being sworn, certify that the following statements are true:

1. We were married to each other on *{date}* ______________________.

2. Because of irreconcilable differences in our marriage (no chance of staying together), we have made this agreement to settle once and for all what we owe to each other and what we can expect to receive from each other. Each of us states that nothing has been held back, that we have honestly included everything we could think of in listing our assets (everything we own and that is owed to us) and our debts (everything we owe), and that we believe the other has been open and honest in writing this agreement.

3. We have both filed a Family Law Financial Affidavit, Florida Family Law Rules of Procedure Form 12.902(b) or (c). Because we have voluntarily made full and fair disclosure to each other of all our assets and debts, we waive any further disclosure under rule 12.285, Florida Family Law Rules of Procedure.

4. Each of us agrees to execute and exchange any papers that might be needed to complete this agreement, including deeds, title certificates, etc.

SECTION I. MARITAL ASSETS AND LIABILITIES

A. Division of Assets. We divide our assets (everything we own and that is owed to us) as follows: Any personal item(s) not listed below is (are) the property of the party currently in possession of the item(s).

1. Wife shall receive as her own and Husband shall have no further rights or responsibilities regarding these assets:

ASSETS: DESCRIPTION OF ITEM(S) WIFE SHALL RECEIVE Please describe each item as clearly as possible. You do not need to list account numbers. Where applicable, include whether the name on any title/deed/account described below is wife's, husband's, or both.	Current Fair Market Value
Cash (on hand)	$
Cash (in banks/credit unions)	
Stocks/Bonds	
Notes (money owed to you in writing)	
Money owed to you (not evidenced by a note)	
Real estate: (Home)	
(Other)	
Business interests	
Automobiles	
Boats	
Other vehicles	
Retirement plans (Profit Sharing, Pension, IRA, 401(k)s, etc.)	
Furniture & furnishings in home	
Furniture & furnishings elsewhere	
Collectibles	

ASSETS: DESCRIPTION OF ITEM(S) WIFE SHALL RECEIVE **Please describe each item as clearly as possible.** **You do not need to list account numbers. Where applicable, include whether the name on any title/deed/account described below is wife's, husband's, or both.**	**Current Fair Market Value**
Jewelry	
Life insurance (cash surrender value)	
Sporting and entertainment (T.V., stereo, etc.) equipment	
Other assets	
Total Assets to Wife	$ ________

2. Husband shall receive as his own and Wife shall have no further rights or responsibilities regarding these assets:

ASSETS: DESCRIPTION OF ITEM(S) HUSBAND SHALL RECEIVE **Please describe each item as clearly as possible.** **You do not need to list account numbers. Where applicable, include whether the name on any title/deed/account described below is wife's, husband's or both.**	**Current Fair Market Value**
Cash (on hand)	$
Cash (in banks/credit unions)	
Stocks/Bonds	
Notes (money owed to you in writing)	
Money owed to you (not evidenced by a note)	

Florida Supreme Court Approved Family Law Form 12.902(f)(1), Marital Settlement Agreement for Dissolution of Marriage with Dependent or Minor Child(ren)(03/15)

ASSETS: DESCRIPTION OF ITEM(S) HUSBAND SHALL RECEIVE Please describe each item as clearly as possible. You do not need to list account numbers. Where applicable, include whether the name on any title/deed/account described below is wife's, husband's or both.	Current Fair Market Value
Real estate: (Home)	
(Other)	
Business interests	
Automobiles	
Boats	
Other vehicles	
Retirement plans (Profit Sharing, Pension, IRA, 401(k)s, etc.)	
Furniture & furnishings in home	
Furniture & furnishings elsewhere	
Collectibles	
Jewelry	
Life insurance (cash surrender value)	
Sporting and entertainment (T.V., stereo, etc.) equipment	
Other assets	

Florida Supreme Court Approved Family Law Form 12.902(f)(1), Marital Settlement Agreement for Dissolution of Marriage with Dependent or Minor Child(ren)(03/15)

ASSETS: DESCRIPTION OF ITEM(S) HUSBAND SHALL RECEIVE Please describe each item as clearly as possible. You do not need to list account numbers. Where applicable, include whether the name on any title/deed/account described below is wife's, husband's or both.	Current Fair Market Value
Total Assets to Husband	$ ______

B. Division of Liabilities/Debts. We divide our liabilities (everything we owe) as follows:

1. Wife shall pay as her own the following and will not at any time ask Husband to pay these debts/bills:

LIABILITIES: DESCRIPTION OF DEBT(S) TO BE PAID BY WIFE **Please describe each item as clearly as possible. You do not need to list account numbers. Where applicable, include whether the name on any mortgage, note, or account described below is wife's, husband's, or both**	**Monthly Payment**	**Current Amount Owed**
Mortgages on real estate: (Home)	$	$
(Other)		
Charge/credit card accounts		
Auto loan		
Auto loan		
Bank/credit union loans		
Money you owe (not evidenced by a note)		
Judgments		
Other		
Total Debts to Be Paid by Wife	$	$

Florida Supreme Court Approved Family Law Form 12.902(f)(1), Marital Settlement Agreement for Dissolution of Marriage with Dependent or Minor Child(ren)(03/15)

2. Husband shall pay as his own the following and will not at any time ask Wife to pay these debts/bills:

LIABILITIES: DESCRIPTION OF DEBT(S) TO BE PAID BY HUSBAND Please describe each item as clearly as possible. You do not need to list account numbers. Where applicable, include whether the name on any mortgage, note or account described below is wife's, husband's, or both.	**Monthly Payment**	**Current Amount Owed**
Mortgages on real estate: (Home)	$	$
(Other)		
Charge/credit card accounts		
Auto loan		
Auto loan		
Bank/credit union loans		
Money you owe (not evidenced by a note)		
Judgments		
Other		
Total Debts to Be Paid by Husband	$	$

C. Contingent Assets and Liabilities (listed in Section III of our Family Law Financial Affidavits) will be divided as follows:

____

____

____

Florida Supreme Court Approved Family Law Form 12.902(f)(1), Marital Settlement Agreement for Dissolution of Marriage with Dependent or Minor Child(ren)(03/15)

____.

D. Beneficiary Designation (Complete only if beneficiary designations continue after entry of Final Judgment of Dissolution of Marriage.)

_____The Husband and Wife agree that the designation providing for the payment or transfer at death of an interest in the assets set forth below to or for the benefit of the deceased party's former spouse **SHALL NOT BE VOID** as of the date of entry of the Final Judgment of Dissolution of Marriage.

The Final Judgment of Dissolution of Marriage shall provide that the designations set forth below remain in full force and effect:

_____1. The _____Husband _____Wife shall acquire or maintain the following assets for the benefit of the other spouse or child(ren) to be paid upon his/her death outright or in trust. This provision only applies if other assets fulfilling such requirement for the benefit of the other spouse or child(ren) do not exist upon his/her death and unless precluded by statute. *{Describe the assets with specificity}*:

____

____

____.

_____2. The _____Husband _____Wife shall not unilaterally terminate or modify the ownership of the following assets, or their disposition upon his/her death. *{Describe the assets with specificity}*: _______

____

____

____.

SECTION II. SPOUSAL SUPPORT (ALIMONY) (If you have not agreed on this matter, write n/a on the lines provided.)

1. **____Each of us forever gives up any right to spousal support (alimony) that we may have.**

OR

2. _____ HUSBAND_____ WIFE (hereinafter "Obligor") agrees to pay spousal support (alimony) in the amount of $ __________every _____ week _____ other week _____month, beginning *{date}* ____________and continuing until *{date or event}* _______________

____.

{Explain type of alimony (such as, permanent, bridge-the-gap, durational, rehabilitative, and/or lump sum) and any other specifics}: ____

____

____

3. _____ Other provisions relating to alimony, including any tax treatment and consequences:

____

____

4. Life insurance in the amount of $____________ to secure the above support, will be provided by the Obligor.

SECTION III. PARENTING PLAN ESTABLISHING PARENTAL RESPONSIBILITY AND TIME-SHARING

1. **The parties' minor child(ren) are:**

Name	**Birth date**

2. The parties shall have time-sharing and parental responsibility in accordance with the Parenting Plan attached as Exhibit _____.

SECTION IV. CHILD SUPPORT

1. _____ Wife ____ Husband (hereinafter "Obligor") will pay child support, under Florida's child support guidelines, section 61.30, Florida Statutes, to the other parent. The Child Support Guidelines Worksheet, Florida Family Law Rules of Procedure Form 12.902(e), is completed and attached.

Child support established at the rate of $__________ per month for the _____children *{total number of parties' minor or dependent children}* shall be paid commencing ____________________ *{month, day, year}* and terminating ____________________ *{month, day, year}*. Child support shall be paid in the amount of $ __________ per ___________ *{week, month, other}* which is consistent with the Obligor's current payroll cycle.

Upon the termination of the obligation of child support for one of the parties' children, child support in the amount of $____________ for the remaining ____ children *{total number of remaining children}* shall be paid commencing__________________ *{month, day, year}* and terminating __________________ *{month, day, year}*. This child support shall be paid in the amount of $ ________ per __________ *{week, month, other}* consistent with Obligor's current payroll cycle.

{Insert schedule for the child support obligation, including the amount, and commencement and termination dates, for the remaining minor or dependent children, which shall be payable as the obligation for each child ceases. Please indicate whether the schedule _____appears below or _____is attached as part of this form}

____
____
____
____
____

____

The Obligor shall pay child support until all the minor or dependent child(ren): reach the age of 18; become emancipated, marry, join the armed services, die, or become self-supporting; or until further order of the court or agreement of the parties. The child support obligation shall continue beyond the age of 18 and until high school graduation for any child who is: dependent in fact; between the ages of 18 and 19; and is still in high school, performing in good faith with a reasonable expectation of graduation before the age of 19.

If the child support amount above deviates from the guidelines by 5% or more, explain the reason(s) here: ____
____
____
____

2. **Child Support Arrearage.** There currently is a child support arrearage of $ ____________ for retroactive child support and/or $____________ for previously ordered unpaid child support. The total of $ ____________ in child support arrearage shall be repaid at the rate of $ __________ every _____week _____other week _____month, beginning *{date}* ____________________, until paid in full including statutory interest.

3. **Health Insurance.** _____ Wife _____ Husband will maintain health insurance for the parties' minor child(ren). The party providing coverage will provide insurance cards to the other party showing coverage. **OR** ( ) Health insurance is either not reasonable in cost or accessible to the child(ren) at this time. Any uninsured/ unreimbursed medical costs for the minor child(ren) shall be assessed as follows:

a. _____Shared equally by husband and wife.
b. _____Prorated according to the child support guideline percentages.
c. _____Other *{explain}*: ____________________________________

As to these uninsured/unreimbursed medical expenses, the party who incurs the expense shall submit a request for reimbursement to the other party within 30 days, and the other party, within 30 days of receipt, shall submit the applicable reimbursement for that expense, according to the schedule of reimbursement set out in this paragraph.

4. **Dental Insurance.**

____ Wife ____ Husband will maintain dental insurance for the parties' minor child(ren). The party providing coverage will provide insurance cards to the other party showing coverage

OR

_____ Dental insurance is either not reasonable in cost or accessible to the child(ren) at this time. Any uninsured/ unreimbursed dental costs for the minor child(ren) shall be assessed as follows:

a. _____Shared equally by husband and wife.
b._____Prorated according to the child support guideline percentages.
c._____Other *{explain}*: ____________________________________

As to these uninsured/unreimbursed dental expenses, the party who incurs the expense shall submit a request for reimbursement to the other party within 30 days, and the other party, within 30 days of receipt, shall submit the applicable reimbursement for that expense, according to the schedule of reimbursement set out in this paragraph.

5. **Life Insurance.** _____ Wife _______ Husband will maintain life insurance for the benefit of the parties' minor child(ren) in the amount of $ ____________ until the youngest child turns 18, becomes emancipated, marries, joins the armed services, or dies.

6. **IRS Income Tax Exemption(s).** The assignment of any tax exemptions for the child(ren) shall be as follows: *{explain}*

____

____.

The other parent will convey any applicable IRS form regarding the income tax exemption.

7. ______Other provisions relating to child support (e.g., uninsured medical/dental expenses, health or dental insurance, life insurance to secure child support, orthodontic payments, college fund, etc.):

____

____

____

____

____

____.

SECTION V. OTHER

____

____

____

____

____.

SECTION VI. We have not agreed on the following issues:

____

____

____

____

____

____

____.

Florida Supreme Court Approved Family Law Form 12.902(f)(1), Marital Settlement Agreement for Dissolution of Marriage with Dependent or Minor Child(ren)(03/15)

I certify that I have been open and honest in entering into this settlement agreement. I am satisfied with this agreement and intend to be bound by it.

Dated: ______________________

____
Signature of Husband
Printed Name: ______________________________
Address: ___________________________________
City, State, Zip: ____________________________
Telephone Number: __________________________
Fax Number: ________________________________
Designated E-mail Address(es): ______________
____

STATE OF FLORIDA
COUNTY OF ____________________

Sworn to or affirmed and signed before me on __________ by______________________.

____
NOTARY PUBLIC or DEPUTY CLERK

____
{Print, type, or stamp commissioned name of notary or deputy clerk.}
____ Personally known
____ Produced identification
____ Type of identification produced______________________

IF A NONLAWYER HELPED YOU FILL OUT THIS FORM, HE/SHE MUST FILL IN THE BLANKS BELOW:
[fill in all blanks] This form was prepared for the: *{choose only **one**}* ( ) Husband ( ) Wife
This form was completed with the assistance of:
{name of individual} ____,
{name of business} ____,
{address} ____,
{city} _____________,*{state}* _____,*{zip code}*__________,*{telephone number}* ______________.

Florida Supreme Court Approved Family Law Form 12.902(f)(1), Marital Settlement Agreement for Dissolution of Marriage with Dependent or Minor Child(ren)(03/15)

I certify that I have been open and honest in entering into this settlement agreement. I am satisfied with this agreement and intend to be bound by it.

Dated: ______________________

____

Signature of Wife
Printed Name: ______________________
Address: ______________________
City, State, Zip: ______________________
Telephone Number: ______________________
Fax Number: ______________________
Designated E-mail Address(es): ______________________
____

STATE OF FLORIDA
COUNTY OF ______________________

Sworn to or affirmed and signed before me on ____________ by______________________.

____
NOTARY PUBLIC or DEPUTY CLERK

____
{Print, type, or stamp commissioned name of notary or deputy clerk.}
____ Personally known
____ Produced identification
____ Type of identification produced ______________________

IF A NONLAWYER HELPED YOU FILL OUT THIS FORM, HE/SHE MUST FILL IN THE BLANKS BELOW:
[fill in all blanks] This form was prepared for the: *{choose only **one**}* ( ) Husband ( ) Wife
This form was completed with the assistance of:
{name of individual} ______________________,
{name of business} ______________________,
{address} ______________________,
{city} ____________,*{state}* _____,*{zip code}*__________,*{telephone number}* ________.

Florida Supreme Court Approved Family Law Form 12.902(f)(1), Marital Settlement Agreement for Dissolution of Marriage with Dependent or Minor Child(ren)(03/15)

INSTRUCTIONS FOR FLORIDA SUPREME COURT APPROVED FAMILY LAW FORM 12.902(f)(1) MARITAL SETTLEMENT AGREEMENT FOR DISSOLUTION OF MARRIAGE WITH DEPENDENT OR MINOR CHILD(REN)(03/15)

When should this form be used?

This form should be used when a **Petition for Dissolution of Marriage with Dependent or Minor Child(ren)**, Florida Supreme Court Approved Family Law Form 12.901(b)(1), has been **filed** and **the parties** have reached an agreement on some or all of the issues at hand.

This form should be typed or printed in black ink. **Both** parties must sign the agreement and have their signatures witnessed by a **notary public** or **deputy clerk**. After completing this form, you should **file** the original with the **clerk of the circuit court** in the county where the **petition** was filed and keep a copy for your records. You should then refer to the instructions for your petition, **answer**, or answer and **counterpetition** concerning the procedures for setting a hearing or **trial** (**final hearing**).

IMPORTANT INFORMATION REGARDING E–FILING

The Florida Rules of Judicial Administration now require that all petitions, pleadings, and documents be filed electronically except in certain circumstances. **Self-represented litigants may file petitions or other pleadings or documents electronically; however, they are not required to do so.** If you choose to file your pleadings or other documents electronically, you must do so in accordance with Florida Rule of Judicial Administration 2.525, and you must follow the procedures of the judicial circuit in which you file. **The rules and procedures should be carefully read and followed.**

Where can I look for more information?

Before proceeding, you should read General Information for Self–Represented Litigants found at the beginning of these forms. The words that are in **bold underline** in these instructions are defined there. For further information, see chapter 61, Florida Statutes, and the instructions for the petition and/or answer that were filed in this case.

IMPORTANT INFORMATION REGARDING E–SERVICE ELECTION

After the initial service of process of the petition or supplemental petition by the Sheriff or certified process server, the Florida Rules of Judicial Administration now require that all documents required or permitted to be served on the other party must be served by electronic mail (e-mail) except in certain circumstances. **You must strictly comply with the format requirements set forth in the Rules of Judicial Administration.**

SELF–REPRESENTED LITIGANTS MAY SERVE DOCUMENTS BY E–MAIL; HOWEVER, THEY ARE NOT REQUIRED TO DO SO. If a self-represented litigant elects to serve and receive documents by e-mail, the procedures must always be followed once the initial election is made.

To serve and receive documents by e-mail, you must designate your e-mail addresses by using the **Designation of Current Mailing and E-mail Address**, Florida Supreme Court Approved Family Law Form 12.915, and you must provide your e-mail address on each form on which your signature appears. Please **CAREFULLY** read the rules and instructions for: **Certificate of Service (General),** Florida Supreme Court Approved Family Law Form 12.914; **Designation of Current Mailing and E-mail Address**, Florida Supreme Court Approved Family Law Form 12.915; and Florida Rule of Judicial Administration 2.516.

Special notes . . .

With this form you must also file a **Child Support Guidelines Worksheet**, Florida Family Law Rules of Procedure Form 12.902(e), if not already filed.

This form does not act to transfer title to the property. Such transfer must be done by deed or supplemental final judgment.

Remember, a person who is NOT an attorney is called a nonlawyer. If a nonlawyer helps you fill out these forms, that person must give you a copy of a **Disclosure from Nonlawyer,** Florida Family Law Rules of Procedure Form 12.900 (a), before he or she helps you. A nonlawyer helping you fill out these forms also **must** put his or her name, address, and telephone number on the bottom of the last page of every form he or she helps you complete.

Added Sept. 21, 2000 (810 So.2d 1). Amended by March 26, 2009 (20 So.3d 173); Dec. 16, 2010 (59 So.3d 792); May 24, 2012 (96 So.3d 217); July 3, 2013 (117 So.3d 958); Sept. 4, 2013, effective Sept. 4, 2013 (122 So.3d 320); May 1, 2014, effective May 1, 2014 (138 So.3d 389); March 26, 2015, effective March 26, 2015 (2015 WL 1343088).

Form 12.902(f)(2). Marital Settlement Agreement for Dissolution of Marriage with Property But No Dependent or Minor Child(ren)

IN THE CIRCUIT COURT OF THE ______________________ JUDICIAL CIRCUIT,
IN AND FOR ______________________ COUNTY, FLORIDA

Case No.: ______________
Division: ____

In re: the Marriage of:

______________________,
Husband,

and

______________________,
Wife.

MARITAL SETTLEMENT AGREEMENT FOR DISSOLUTION OF MARRIAGE WITH PROPERTY BUT NO DEPENDENT OR MINOR CHILD(REN)

We, *{Husband's full legal name}*______________________ and *{Wife's full legal name}* ______________________, being sworn, certify that the following statements are true:

1. We were married to each other on *{date}* ______________________.

2. Because of irreconcilable differences in our marriage (no chance of staying together), we have made this agreement to settle once and for all what we owe to each other and what we can expect to receive from each other. Each of us states that nothing has been held back, that we have honestly included everything we could think of in listing our assets (everything we own and that is owed to us) and our debts (everything we owe), and that we believe the other has been open and honest in writing this agreement.

3. We have both filed a Family Law Financial Affidavit, Florida Family Law Rules of Procedure Form 12.902(b) or (c). Because we have voluntarily made full and fair disclosure to each other of all our assets and debts, we waive any further disclosure under rule 12.285, Florida Family Law Rules of Procedure.

4. Each of us agrees to execute and exchange any papers that might be needed to complete this agreement, including deeds, title certificates, etc.

SECTION I. MARITAL ASSETS AND LIABILITIES

A. Division of Assets. We divide our assets (everything we own and that is owed to us) as follows: Any personal item(s) not listed below is the property of the party currently in possession of the item(s).

1. Wife shall receive as her own and Husband shall have no further rights or responsibilities regarding these assets:

ASSETS: DESCRIPTION OF ITEM(S) WIFE SHALL RECEIVE Please describe each item as clearly as possible. You do not need to list account numbers. Where applicable, include whether the name on any title/deed/account described below is wife's, husband's, or both.	**Current Fair Market Value**
Cash (on hand)	$
Cash (in banks/credit unions)	
Stocks/Bonds	
Notes (money owed to you in writing)	
Money owed to you (not evidenced by a note)	
Real estate: (Home)	
(Other)	
Business interests	
Automobiles	
Boats	
Other vehicles	

Florida Supreme Court Approved Family Law Form 12.902(f)(2), Marital Settlement Agreement for Dissolution of Marriage with Property but No Dependent or Minor Child(ren) (03/15)

Retirement plans (Profit Sharing, Pension, IRA, 401(k)s, etc.)	
Furniture & furnishings in home	
Furniture & furnishings elsewhere	
Collectibles	
Jewelry	
Life insurance (cash surrender value)	
Sporting and entertainment (T.V., stereo, etc.) equipment	
Other assets	
Total Assets to Wife	**$** ____________

2. Husband shall receive as his own and Wife shall have no further rights or responsibilities regarding these assets:

ASSETS: DESCRIPTION OF ITEM(S) HUSBAND SHALL RECEIVE **Please describe each item as clearly as possible. You do not need to list account numbers. Where applicable, include whether the name on any title/deed/account described below is wife's, husband's or both.**	**Current Fair Market Value**
Cash (on hand)	$
Cash (in banks/credit unions)	

Stocks/Bonds	
Notes (money owed to you in writing)	
Money owed to you (not evidenced by a note)	
Real estate: (Home)	
(Other)	
Business interests	
Automobiles	
Boats	
Other vehicles	
Retirement plans (Profit Sharing, Pension, IRA, 401(k)s, etc.)	
Furniture & furnishings in home	
Furniture & furnishings elsewhere	
Collectibles	
Jewelry	
Life insurance (cash surrender value)	
Sporting and entertainment (T.V., stereo, etc.) equipment	

Florida Supreme Court Approved Family Law Form 12.902(f)(2), Marital Settlement Agreement for Dissolution of Marriage with Property but No Dependent or Minor Child(ren) (03/15)

Other assets	
Total Assets to Husband	$

B. Division of Liabilities/Debts. We divide our liabilities (everything we owe) as follows:

1. Wife shall pay as her own the following and will not at any time ask Husband to pay these debts/bills:

LIABILITIES: DESCRIPTION OF DEBT(S) TO BE PAID BY WIFE Please describe each item as clearly as possible. You do not need to list account numbers. Where applicable, include whether the name on any mortgage, note, or account described below is wife's, husband's, or both.	**Monthly Payment**	**Current Amount Owed**
Mortgages on real estate: (Home)	$	$
(Other)		
Charge/credit card accounts		
Auto loan		
Auto loan		
Bank/credit union loans		
Money you owe (not evidenced by a note)		
Judgments		

Florida Supreme Court Approved Family Law Form 12.902(f)(2), Marital Settlement Agreement for Dissolution of Marriage with Property but No Dependent or Minor Child(ren) (03/15)

Other		
Total Debts to Be Paid by Wife	$	$

2. Husband shall pay as his own the following and will not at any time ask Wife to pay these debts/bills:

LIABILITIES: DESCRIPTION OF DEBT(S) TO BE PAID BY HUSBAND **Please describe each item as clearly as possible. You do not need to list account numbers. Where applicable, include whether the name on any mortgage, note or account described below is wife's, husband's, or both.**	**Monthly Payment**	**Current Amount Owed**
Mortgages on real estate: (Home)	$	$
(Other)		
Charge/credit card accounts		
Auto loan		
Auto loan		
Bank/credit union loans		
Money you owe (not evidenced by a note)		
Judgments		
Other		
Total Debts to Be Paid by Husband	$	$

Florida Supreme Court Approved Family Law Form 12.902(f)(2), Marital Settlement Agreement for Dissolution of Marriage with Property but No Dependent or Minor Child(ren) (03/15)

C. **Contingent Assets and Liabilities (listed in Section III of our Family Law Financial Affidavits) will be divided as follows:**

____
____
____.

D. Beneficiary Designation (Complete only if beneficiary designations continue after entry of Final Judgment of Dissolution of Marriage.)

_____The Husband and Wife agree that the designation providing for the payment or transfer at death of an interest in the assets set forth below to or for the benefit of the deceased party's former spouse **SHALL NOT BE VOID** as of the date of entry of the Final Judgment of Dissolution of Marriage.

The Final Judgment of Dissolution of Marriage shall provide that the designations set forth below remain in full force and effect:

_____1. The _____Husband _____Wife shall acquire or maintain the following assets for the benefit of the other spouse or child(ren) to be paid upon his/her death outright or in trust. This provision only applies if other assets fulfilling such requirement for the benefit of the other spouse or child(ren) do not exist upon his/her death and unless precluded by statute. *{Describe the assets with specificity}*:
____
____
____.

_____2. The _____Husband _____Wife shall not unilaterally terminate or modify the ownership of the following assets, or their disposition upon his/her death. *{Describe the assets with specificity}*:_________
____
____
____.

SECTION II. SPOUSAL SUPPORT (ALIMONY) (If you have not agreed on this matter, write n/a on the lines provided.)

1. ____ **Each of us forever gives up any right to spousal support (alimony) that we may have.**

   OR

2. _____ HUSBAND _____ WIFE (hereinafter "Obligor") agrees to pay spousal support (alimony) in the amount of $______________every _____week _____other week _____ month, beginning

{date} ______________________ and continuing until *{date or event}* ______
____.

Explain type of alimony (permanent, bridge-the-gap, durational, rehabilitative, and/or lump sum) and any other specifics: ____
____
____
____.

3. ______Other provisions relating to alimony, including any tax treatment and consequences:
____
____
____
____

4. ____ Husband ____ Wife will provide life insurance in the amount of $______ to secure the above support.

SECTION III. OTHER

____
____
____
____
____
____.

SECTION IV. We have not agreed on the following issues:

____
____
____
____
____.

I certify that I have been open and honest in entering into this settlement agreement. I am satisfied with this agreement and intend to be bound by it.

Dated: ______________ ______________________________
Signature of Husband

Florida Supreme Court Approved Family Law Form 12.902(f)(2), Marital Settlement Agreement for Dissolution of Marriage with Property but No Dependent or Minor Child(ren) (03/15)

Printed Name: ______________________________
Address: ______________________________
City, State, Zip: ______________________________
Telephone Number: ______________________________
Fax Number: ______________________________
Designated E-mail Address(es): ______________________________
____

STATE OF FLORIDA
COUNTY OF ______________________

Sworn to or affirmed and signed before me on ____________ by ______________________________.

____
NOTARY PUBLIC or DEPUTY CLERK

____
{Print, type, or stamp commissioned name of notary or deputy clerk.}
____ Personally known
____ Produced identification
____ Type of identification produced ______________________________

IF A NONLAWYER HELPED YOU FILL OUT THIS FORM, HE/SHE MUST FILL IN THE BLANKS BELOW:
[fill in **all** blanks] This form was prepared for the: *{choose only **one**}* ( ) Husband ( ) Wife
This form was completed with the assistance of:
{name of individual} ______________________________,
{name of business} ______________________________,
{address} ______________________________,
{city} ______________,*{state}* ______,*{zip code}*____________,*{telephone number}* ______________.

I certify that I have been open and honest in entering into this settlement agreement. I am satisfied with this agreement and intend to be bound by it.

Dated: ______________________ ______________________________
Signature of Wife
Printed Name: ______________________________
Address: ______________________________
City, State, Zip: ______________________________
Telephone Number: ______________________________
Fax Number: ______________________________
Designated E-mail Address(es): ______________________
____

STATE OF FLORIDA
COUNTY OF ______________

Sworn to or affirmed and signed before me on __________ by______________________.

____
NOTARY PUBLIC or DEPUTY CLERK

____
{Print, type, or stamp commissioned name of notary or deputy clerk.}

____ Personally known
____ Produced identification
____ Type of identification produced ______________

IF A NONLAWYER HELPED YOU FILL OUT THIS FORM, HE/SHE MUST FILL IN THE BLANKS BELOW:
[fill in **all** blanks] This form was prepared for the: *{choose only **one**}* ( ) Husband ( ) Wife
This form was completed with the assistance of:
{name of individual} ______________________________,
{name of business} ______________________________,
{address} ______________________________,
{city} ______________,*{state}* _____,*{zip code}*__________,*{telephone number}* ______________.

Florida Supreme Court Approved Family Law Form 12.902(f)(2), Marital Settlement Agreement for Dissolution of Marriage with Property but No Dependent or Minor Child(ren) (03/15)

INSTRUCTIONS FOR FLORIDA SUPREME COURT APPROVED FAMILY LAW FORM 12.902(f)(2) MARITAL SETTLEMENT AGREEMENT FOR DISSOLUTION OF MARRIAGE WITH PROPERTY BUT NO DEPENDENT OR MINOR CHILD(REN)

(03/15)

When should this form be used?

This form should be used when a **Petition for Dissolution of Marriage with Property but no Dependent or Minor Child(ren)**, Florida Supreme Court Approved Family Law Form 12.901(b)(2), has been **filed** and the **parties** have reached an agreement on some or all of the issues at hand.

This form should be typed or printed in black ink. **Both** parties must sign the agreement and have their signatures witnessed by a **notary public** or **deputy clerk**. After completing this form, you should file the original with the **clerk of the circuit court** in the county where the **petition** was filed and keep a copy for your records. You should then refer to the instructions for your petition, **answer**, or answer and **counterpetition** concerning the procedures for setting a hearing or **trial** (**final hearing**).

IMPORTANT INFORMATION REGARDING E–FILING

The Florida Rules of Judicial Administration now require that all petitions, pleadings, and documents be filed electronically except in certain circumstances. **Self-represented litigants may file petitions or other pleadings or documents electronically; however, they are not required to do so.** If you choose to file your pleadings or other documents electronically, you must do so in accordance with Florida Rule of Judicial Administration 2.525, and you must follow the procedures of the judicial circuit in which you file. **The rules and procedures should be carefully read and followed.**

Where can I look for more information?

Before proceeding, you should read General Information for Self–Represented Litigants found at the beginning of these forms. The words that are in **bold underline** in these instructions are defined there. For further information, see chapter 61, Florida Statutes, and the instructions for the petition and/or answer that were filed in this case.

IMPORTANT INFORMATION REGARDING E–SERVICE ELECTION

After the initial service of process of the petition or supplemental petition by the Sheriff or certified process server, the Florida Rules of Judicial Administration now require that all documents required or permitted to be served on the other party must be served by electronic mail (e-mail) except in certain circumstances. **You must strictly comply with the format requirements set forth in the Rules of Judicial Administration.**

SELF–REPRESENTED LITIGANTS MAY SERVE DOCUMENTS BY E–MAIL; HOWEVER, THEY ARE NOT REQUIRED TO DO SO. If a self-represented litigant elects to serve and receive documents by e-mail, the procedures must always be followed once the initial election is made.

To serve and receive documents by e-mail, you must designate your e-mail addresses by using the **Designation of Current Mailing and E-mail Address**, Florida Supreme Court Approved Family Law Form 12.915, and you must provide your e-mail address on each form on which your signature appears. Please **CAREFULLY** read the rules and instructions for: **Certificate of Service (General)**, Florida Supreme Court Approved Family Law Form 12.914; **Designation of Current Mailing and E-mail Address**, Florida Supreme Court Approved Family Law Form 12.915; and Florida Rule of Judicial Administration 2.516.

Special notes . . .

This form does not act to transfer title to the property. Such transfer must be done by deed or supplemental final judgment.

Remember, a person who is NOT an attorney is called a nonlawyer. If a nonlawyer helps you fill out these forms, that person must give you a copy of a **Disclosure from Nonlawyer,**

Florida Family Law Rules of Procedure Form 12.900(a), before he or she helps you. A nonlawyer helping you fill out these forms also **must** put his or her name, address, and telephone number on the bottom of the last page of every form he or she helps you complete.

Added Sept. 21, 2000 (810 So.2d 1). Amended May 24, 2012 (96 So.3d 217); Sept. 4, 2013, effective Sept. 4, 2013 (122 So.3d 320); May 1, 2014, effective May 1, 2014 (138 So.3d 389); March 26, 2015, effective March 26, 2015 (2015 WL 1343088).

Form 12.902(f)(3). Marital Settlement Agreement for Simplified Dissolution of Marriage

IN THE CIRCUIT COURT OF THE ____________________ JUDICIAL CIRCUIT,
IN AND FOR ____________________ COUNTY, FLORIDA

Case No.: ____________________
Division: ____________________

In re: the Marriage of:

______________________________,
Petitioner,

and

______________________________,
Respondent.

MARITAL SETTLEMENT AGREEMENT FOR SIMPLIFIED DISSOLUTION OF MARRIAGE

We, *{Husband's full legal name}*____________________, and *{Wife's full legal name}* ______________________________, being sworn, certify that the following statements are true:

1. We were married to each other on *{date}* ____________________.

2. Because of irreconcilable differences in our marriage (no chance of staying together), we have made this agreement to settle once and for all what we owe to each other and what we can expect to receive from each other. Each of us states that nothing has been held back, that we have honestly included everything we could think of in listing our assets (everything we own and that is owed to us) and our debts (everything we owe), and that we believe the other has been open and honest in writing this agreement.

3. We have both filed a Family Law Financial Affidavit, Florida Family Law Rules of Procedure Form 12.902(b) or (c). Because we have voluntarily made full and fair disclosure to each other of all our assets and debts, we waive any further disclosure under rule 12.285, Florida Family Law Rules of Procedure.

4. Each of us agrees to execute and exchange any papers that might be needed to complete this agreement, including deeds, title certificates, etc.

SECTION I. MARITAL ASSETS AND LIABILITIES

A. Division of Assets. We divide our assets (everything we own and that is owed to us) as follows: Any personal item(s) not listed below is the property of the party currently in possession of the item(s).

1. Wife shall receive as her own and Husband shall have no further rights or responsibilities regarding these assets:

ASSETS: DESCRIPTION OF ITEM(S) WIFE SHALL RECEIVE (To avoid confusion at a later date, describe each item as clearly as possible. You do not need to list account numbers Where applicable, include whether the name on any title/deed/account described below is wife's, husband's, or both.	**Current Fair Market Value**
Cash (on hand)	$
Cash (in banks/credit unions)	
Stocks/Bonds	
Notes (money owed to you in writing)	
Money owed to you (not evidenced by a note)	
Real estate: (Home)	
(Other)	
Business interests	
Automobiles	
Boats	
Other vehicles	
Retirement plans (Profit Sharing, Pension, IRA, 401(k)s, etc.)	
Furniture & furnishings in home	

Florida Family Law Rules of Procedure Form 12.902(f)(3), Marital Settlement Agreement for Simplified Dissolution of Marriage (11/12)

Furniture & furnishings elsewhere	
Collectibles	
Jewelry	
Life insurance (cash surrender value)	
Sporting and entertainment (T.V., stereo, etc.) equipment	
Other assets	
Total Assets to Wife	$ ________

2. Husband shall receive as his own and Wife shall have no further rights or responsibilities regarding these assets:

ASSETS: DESCRIPTION OF ITEM(S) HUSBAND SHALL RECEIVE (To avoid confusion at a later date, describe each item as clearly as possible. You do not need to list account numbers Where applicable, include whether the name on any title/deed/account described below is wife's, husband's or both.	**Current Fair Market Value**
Cash (on hand)	$
Cash (in banks/credit unions)	
Stocks/Bonds	
Notes (money owed to you in writing)	
Money owed to you (not evidenced by a note)	

Real estate: (Home)	
(Other)	
Business interests	
Automobiles	
Boats	
Other vehicles	
Retirement plans (Profit Sharing, Pension, IRA, 401(k)s, etc.)	
Furniture & furnishings in home	
Furniture & furnishings elsewhere	
Collectibles	
Jewelry	
Life insurance (cash surrender value)	
Sporting and entertainment (T.V., stereo, etc.) equipment	
Other assets	
Total Assets to Husband	$__________

Florida Family Law Rules of Procedure Form 12.902(f)(3), Marital Settlement Agreement for Simplified Dissolution of Marriage (11/12)

B. Division of Liabilities/Debts. We divide our liabilities (everything we owe) as follows:

1. Wife shall pay as her own the following and will not at any time ask Husband to pay these debts/bills:

LIABILITIES: DESCRIPTION OF DEBT(S) TO BE PAID BY WIFE (To avoid confusion at a later date, describe each item as clearly as possible. You do not need to list account numbers Where applicable, include whether the name on any mortgage, note, or account described below is wife's, husband's, or both.)	**Monthly Payment**	**Current Amount Owed**
Mortgages on real estate: (Home)	$	$
(Other)		
Charge/credit card accounts		
Auto loan		
Auto loan		
Bank/credit union loans		
Money you owe (not evidenced by a note)		
Judgments		
Other		
Total Debts to Be Paid by Wife	$	$

2. Husband shall pay as his own the following and will not at any time ask Wife to pay these debts/bills:

LIABILITIES: DESCRIPTION OF DEBT(S) TO BE PAID BY HUSBAND (To avoid confusion at a later date, describe each item as clearly as possible. You do not need to list account numbers. Where applicable, include whether the name on any mortgage, note or account described below is wife's, husband's, or both.	Monthly Payment	Current Amount Owed
Mortgages on real estate: (Home)	$	$
(Other)		
Charge/credit card accounts		
Auto loan		
Auto loan		
Bank/credit union loans		
Money you owe (not evidenced by a note)		
Judgments		
Other		
Total Debts to Be Paid by Husband	$	$

C. Contingent Assets and Liabilities (listed in Section III of our Family Law Financial Affidavits) will be divided as follows:

____

____

____

____

____

Florida Family Law Rules of Procedure Form 12.902(f)(3), Marital Settlement Agreement for Simplified Dissolution of Marriage (11/12)

SECTION II. SPOUSAL SUPPORT (ALIMONY) Each of us forever gives up any right to spousal support (alimony) that we may have.

SECTION III. OTHER

____
____
____
____

I certify that I have been open and honest in entering into this settlement agreement. I am satisfied with this agreement and intend to be bound by it.

Dated: ________________

____
Signature of Husband
Printed Name: ________________________________
Address: ____________________________________
City, State, Zip: _____________________________
Telephone Number: ___________________________
Fax Number: _________________________________
E-mail Address(es): ___________________________

STATE OF FLORIDA
COUNTY OF

Sworn to or affirmed and signed before me on ______________ by ______________________.

____
NOTARY PUBLIC or DEPUTY CLERK

____
[Print, type, or stamp commissioned name of notary or clerk.]

_____ Personally known
_____ Produced identification
Type of identification produced

IF A NONLAWYER HELPED YOU FILL OUT THIS FORM, HE/SHE MUST FILL IN THE BLANKS BELOW:
[fill in all blanks] This form was prepared for the Husband who is the *{choose only* ***one****}* ( ) Petitioner ( ) Respondent.
This form was prepared with the assistance of:
{name of individual} ____,
{name of business} ____,
{address} ____,
{city} ____________________,*{state}* ________, *{telephone number}* ______________.

Florida Family Law Rules of Procedure Form 12.902(f)(3), Marital Settlement Agreement for Simplified Dissolution of Marriage (11/12)

I certify that I have been open and honest in entering into this settlement agreement. I am satisfied with this agreement and intend to be bound by it.

Dated: ____________________ ______________________________

Signature of Wife
Printed name:______________________________
Address:______________________________
City, State, Zip:______________________________
Telephone number:______________________________
Fax number______________________________
E-mail Address(es):______________________________

STATE OF FLORIDA
COUNTY OF

Sworn to or affirmed and signed before me on ____________ by ______.

____
NOTARY PUBLIC or DEPUTY CLERK

____
[Print, type, or stamp commissioned name of notary or clerk.]

_____ Personally known
_____ Produced identification
Type of identification produced

IF A NONLAWYER HELPED YOU FILL OUT THIS FORM, HE/SHE MUST FILL IN THE BLANKS BELOW:
[fill in **all** blanks] This form was prepared for the Wife who is the *{choose only **one**}* ( ) Petitioner ( ) Respondent.
This form was prepared with the assistance of:
*{name of individual}*______________________________,
*{name of business}*______________________________,
*{address}*______________________________,
*{city}*____________________,*{state}* ________, *{telephone number}* ____________.

INSTRUCTIONS FOR FLORIDA FAMILY LAW RULES OF PROCEDURE FORM 12.902(f)(3), MARITAL SETTLEMENT AGREEMENT FOR SIMPLIFIED DISSOLUTION OF MARRIAGE (11/12)

When should this form be used?

This form should be used when a **Petition for Simplified Dissolution of Marriage**, Florida Family Law Rules of Procedure Form 12.901(a), has been **filed** and the **parties** have reached an agreement on all of the issues at hand.

This form should be typed or printed in black ink. **Both** parties must sign the agreement and have their signatures witnessed by a **notary public** or **deputy clerk**. After completing this form, you should file the original with the **clerk of the circuit court** in the county where the **petition** was filed and keep a copy for your records. You should then refer to the instructions for your petition, **answer**, or answer and **counterpetition** concerning the procedures for setting a hearing or **trial** (**final hearing**).

Where can I look for more information?

Before proceeding, you should read General Information for Self-Represented Litigants found at the beginning of these forms. The words that are in **bold underline** in these instructions are defined there. For further information, see chapter 61, Florida Statutes, and the instructions for the petition which was filed in this case.

Special notes . . .

This form does not act to transfer title to the property. Such transfer must be done by deed or supplemental final judgment.

Remember, a person who is NOT an attorney is called a nonlawyer. If a nonlawyer helps you fill out these forms, that person must give you a copy of a **Disclosure from Nonlawyer**, Florida Family Law Rules of Procedure Form 12.900(a), before he or she helps you. A nonlawyer helping you fill out these forms also must put his or her name, address, and telephone number on the bottom of the last page of every form he or she helps you complete.

Added Sept. 21, 2000 (810 So.2d 1). Amended Nov. 15, 2012 (104 So.3d 314).

Form 12.902(i). Affidavit of Corroborating Witness

IN THE CIRCUIT COURT OF THE ______________ JUDICIAL CIRCUIT,
IN AND FOR ______________________ COUNTY, FLORIDA

Case No.: ______________________
Division: ______________________

__________________________,
Husband,

and

__________________________,
Wife.

AFFIDAVIT OF CORROBORATING WITNESS

I, *{full legal name}* ________________________, being sworn, certify that the following statements are true: I have known *{name}* ________________________ since *{approximate date}* ______________; to the best of my understanding the petition in this action was filed on *{date}* ________________; and I know of my own personal knowledge that this person has resided in the State of Florida for at least 6 months immediately before *{date}* ______________.

I understand that I am swearing or affirming under oath to the truthfulness of the claims made in this affidavit and that the punishment for knowingly making a false statement includes fines and/or imprisonment.

Dated: ______________________ ______________________
Signature of Corroborating Witness
Printed Name: ______________
Address: ______________
City, State, Zip: ______________
Telephone Number: ______________

STATE OF FLORIDA
COUNTY OF ______________________

Sworn to or affirmed and signed before me on ______________ by ______________.

____
NOTARY PUBLIC or DEPUTY CLERK

____
[Print, type, or stamp commissioned name of notary or clerk.]

____ Personally known
____ Produced identification

Florida Supreme Court Approved Family Law Form 12.902(i), Affidavit of Corroborating Witness (03/15)

Type of identification produced ____________________

IF A NONLAWYER HELPED YOU FILL OUT THIS FORM, HE/SHE MUST FILL IN THE BLANKS BELOW:
[fill in **all** blanks] This form was prepared for the: *{choose only **one**}* ( ) Husband ( ) Wife
This form was completed with the assistance of:
{name of individual} ____,
{name of business} ____,
{address} ____,
{city} ______________,*{state}* _____,*{zip code}*__________,*{telephone number}* __________.

INSTRUCTIONS FOR FLORIDA SUPREME COURT APPROVED FAMILY LAW FORM 12.902(i) AFFIDAVIT OF CORROBORATING WITNESS (03/15)

When should this form be used?

This form may be used to prove residency in a **dissolution of marriage** proceeding. To get a divorce in Florida, either the husband or the wife must have lived in Florida for at least 6 months before filing the petition. Residency may be proved by a valid Florida's driver's license, Florida identification card, or voter's registration card (issue date of document must be at least 6 months before the date the case is actually filed with the clerk of the circuit court), or the testimony or **affidavit** of someone other than you or your spouse. This form is used to prove residency by affidavit. The person signing this form must know that you have lived in the State of Florida for at least 6 months before the date you filed your **petition** for dissolution of marriage.

This form should be typed or printed in black ink, and signed in the presence of a **notary public** or **deputy clerk**. After completing this form, you should **file** the original with the **clerk of the circuit court** in the county where the petition was filed and keep a copy for you records.

IMPORTANT INFORMATION REGARDING E–FILING

The Florida Rules of Judicial Administration now require that all petitions, pleadings, and documents be filed electronically except in certain circumstances. **Self-represented litigants may file petitions or other pleadings or documents electronically; however, they are not required to do so.** If you choose to file your pleadings or other documents electronically, you must do so in accordance with Florida Rule of Judicial Administration 2.525, and you must follow the procedures of the judicial circuit in which you file. **The rules and procedures should be carefully read and followed.**

What should I do next?

A copy of this form must be mailed, e-mailed, or hand delivered to the other party in your case, if it is not **served** on him or her with your initial papers.

IMPORTANT INFORMATION REGARDING E–SERVICE ELECTION

After the initial service of process of the petition or supplemental petition by the Sheriff or certified process server, the Florida Rules of Judicial Administration now require that all documents required or permitted to be served on the other party must be served by electronic mail (e-mail) except in certain circumstances. **You must strictly comply with the format requirements set forth in the Rules of Judicial Administration.**

SELF–REPRESENTED LITIGANTS MAY SERVE DOCUMENTS BY E–MAIL; HOWEVER, THEY ARE NOT REQUIRED TO DO SO. If a self-represented litigant elects to serve and receive documents by e-mail, the procedures must always be followed once the initial election is made.

To serve and receive documents by e-mail, you must designate your e-mail addresses by using the **Designation of Current Mailing and E-mail Address**, Florida Supreme Court Approved Family Law Form 12.915, and you must provide your e-mail address on each form on which your signature appears. Please **CAREFULLY** read the rules and instructions for: **Certificate of Service (General),** Florida Supreme Court Approved Family Law Form 12.914; **Designation of Current Mailing and E-mail Address**, Florida Supreme Court Approved Family Law Form 12.915; and Florida Rule of Judicial Administration 2.516.

Where can I look for more information?

Before proceeding, you should read General Information for Self–Represented Litigants found at the beginning of these forms. The words that are in **"bold underline"** in these instructions are defined there. For further information, see chapter 61, Florida Statutes.

Special notes . . .

Remember, a person who is NOT an attorney is called a nonlawyer. If a nonlawyer helps you fill out these forms, that person must give you a copy of a **Disclosure from Nonlawyer,** Florida Family Law Rules of Procedure Form 12.900(a), before he or she helps you. A nonlawyer helping you fill out these forms also **must** put his or her name, address, and telephone number on the bottom of the last page of every form he or she helps you complete.

Added Sept. 21, 2000 (810 So.2d 1). Amended Sept. 28, 2006 (940 So.2d 409); March 26, 2015, effective March 26, 2015 (2015 WL 1343088).

Form 12.902(j). Notice of Social Security Number

IN THE CIRCUIT COURT OF THE ______ JUDICIAL CIRCUIT,
IN AND FOR ____________ COUNTY, FLORIDA

Case No.: ____________________
Division: ____________________

______________________,
Petitioner,

and

______________________,
Respondent.

NOTICE OF SOCIAL SECURITY NUMBER

I, *{full legal name}* ____, certify that my social security number is ____________________, as required by the applicable section of the Florida Statutes. My date of birth is ____________________.

*[Choose **one** only]*

_____ 1. This notice is being filed in a dissolution of marriage case in which the parties have **no** minor children in common.

_____ 2. This notice is being filed in a paternity or child support case, or in a dissolution of marriage in which the parties have minor children in common. The minor child(ren)'s name(s), date(s) of birth, and social security number(s) is/are:

Name	Birth date	Social Security Number

{Attach additional pages if necessary.}

Florida Supreme Court Approved Family Law Form 12.902(j), Notice of Social Security Number (03/15)

Disclosure of social security numbers shall be limited to the purpose of administration of the Title IV-D program for child support enforcement.

Florida Supreme Court Approved Family Law Form 12.902(j), Notice of Social Security Number (03/15)

I understand that I am swearing or affirming under oath to the truthfulness of the claims made in this notice and that the punishment for knowingly making a false statement includes fines and/or imprisonment.

Dated: ____________________

____
Signature
Printed Name: ____

Address: ____________________________
City, State, Zip: ________________________
Telephone Number:_______________________
Fax Number: __________________________
Designated E-mail Address(es):___________________
____

STATE OF FLORIDA
COUNTY OF ________

Sworn to or affirmed and signed before me on by ______________________________________.

____
NOTARY PUBLIC or DEPUTY CLERK

____
[Print, type, or stamp commissioned name of notary or clerk]

___Personally known
___Produced identification
Type of identification produced ______________________

IF A NONLAWYER HELPED YOU FILL OUT THIS FORM, HE/SHE MUST FILL IN THE BLANKS BELOW:
[fill in **all** blanks] This form was prepared for the: *{choose only **one**}* ( ) Petitioner ( ) Respondent
This form was completed with the assistance of:
{name of individual} ____,
{name of business} ____,
{address} ____,
{city} ______________,*{state}* _____,*{zip code}*__________,*{telephone number}* ______________.

Florida Supreme Court Approved Family Law Form 12.902(j), Notice of Social Security Number (03/15)

INSTRUCTIONS FOR FLORIDA SUPREME COURT APPROVED FAMILY LAW FORM 12.902(j), NOTICE OF SOCIAL SECURITY NUMBER (03/15)

When should this form be used?

This form must be completed and filed by each party in all **paternity**, **child support**, and **dissolution of marriage** cases, regardless of whether the case involves a minor child(ren) and/or property.

This form should be typed or printed in black ink. After completing this form, you should **file** the original with the **clerk of the circuit court** in the county where your case was filed and keep a copy for your records.

IMPORTANT INFORMATION REGARDING E-FILING

The Florida Rules of Judicial Administration now require that all petitions, pleadings, and documents be filed electronically except in certain circumstances. **Self-represented litigants may file petitions or other pleadings or documents electronically; however, they are not required to do so.** If you choose to file your pleadings or other documents electronically, you must do so in accordance with Florida Rule of Judicial Administration 2.525, and you must follow the procedures of the judicial circuit in which you file. **The rules and procedures should be carefully read and followed.**

What should I do next?

A copy of this form must be mailed, e-mailed, or hand delivered to the other party in your case, if it is not **served** on him or her with your initial papers.

IMPORTANT INFORMATION REGARDING E-SERVICE ELECTION

After the initial service of process of the petition or supplemental petition by the Sheriff or certified process server, the Florida Rules of Judicial Administration now require that all documents required or permitted to be served on the other party must be served by electronic mail (e-mail) except in certain circumstances. **You must strictly comply with the format requirements set forth in the Rules of Judicial Administration.**

SELF-REPRESENTED LITIGANTS MAY SERVE DOCUMENTS BY E-MAIL; HOWEVER, THEY ARE NOT REQUIRED TO DO SO. If a self-represented litigant elects to serve and receive documents by e-mail, the procedures must always be followed once the initial election is made.

To serve and receive documents by e-mail, you must designate your e-mail addresses by using the **Designation of Current Mailing and E-mail Address**, Florida Supreme Court Approved Family Law Form 12.915, and you must provide your e-mail address on each form on which your signature appears. Please **CAREFULLY** read the rules and instructions for: **Certificate of Service (General),** Florida Supreme Court Approved Family Law Form 12.914; **Designation of Current Mailing and E-mail Address**, Florida Supreme Court Approved Family Law Form 12.915; and Florida Rule of Judicial Administration 2.516.

Where can I look for more information?

Before proceeding, you should read General Information for Self-Represented Litigants found at the beginning of these forms. The words that are in "**bold underline**" in these instructions are defined there. For further information, see chapter 61, Florida Statutes.

Special notes ...

If this is a domestic violence case and you want to keep your address confidential for safety reasons, do not enter the address, telephone, fax, or e-mail information at the bottom of this form. Instead, file a **Request for Confidential Filing of Address**, Florida Supreme Court Approved Family Law Form 12.980(i).

Remember, a person who is NOT an attorney is called a nonlawyer. If a nonlawyer helps you fill out these forms, that person must give you a copy of a **Disclosure from Nonlawyer**, Florida Family Law Rules of Procedure Form 12.900(a), before he or she helps you. A nonlawyer helping you fill out these forms also **must** put his or her name, address, and telephone number on the bottom of the last page of every form he or she helps you complete.

Added Sept. 21, 2000 (810 So.2d 1). Amended March 26, 2015, effective March 26, 2015 (2015 WL 1343088).

Form 12.903(a). Answer, Waiver, and Request for Copy of Final Judgment of Dissolution of Marriage

IN THE CIRCUIT COURT OF THE ____________________ JUDICIAL CIRCUIT,
IN AND FOR ____________________ COUNTY, FLORIDA

Case No: ____________________
Division: ____________________

In re: the Marriage of:

____________________________________,
Husband,

and

____________________________________,
Wife.

ANSWER, WAIVER, AND REQUEST FOR COPY OF FINAL JUDGMENT OF DISSOLUTION OF MARRIAGE

I, *{full legal name}* ______________________________, being sworn, certify that the following information is true:

1. I answer the Petition for Dissolution of Marriage filed in this action and admit all the allegations. By admitting all of the allegations in the petition, I agree to all relief requested in the petition including any requests regarding parenting and time-sharing, child support, alimony, distribution of marital assets and liabilities, and temporary relief.

2. I hereby waive notice of hearing as well as all future notices in connection with the Petition for Dissolution of Marriage, as filed and also waive my appearance at the final hearing.

3. I request that a copy of the Final Judgment of Dissolution of Marriage entered in this case be provided to me at the address below.

4. If this case involves minor child(ren), a completed Uniform Child Custody Jurisdiction and Enforcement Act (UCCJEA) Affidavit, Florida Supreme Court Approved Family Law Form 12.902(d), is filed with this answer.

5. A completed Notice of Social Security Number, Florida Supreme Court Approved Family Law Form 12.902(j), is filed with this answer.

6. A completed Family Law Financial Affidavit, Florida Family Law Rules of Procedure Form 12.902(b) or (c), _____ is filed with this answer or _____ will be timely filed.

I certify that a copy of this document was ( ) mailed ( ) faxed and mailed ( ) e-mailed ( ) hand delivered to the person(s) listed below on *{date}* ______________________.

Other party or his/her attorney:
Name: ______________________
Address: ______________________
City, State, Zip: ______________________
Fax Number: ______________________
Designated E-mail Address(es): ______________________

I understand that I am swearing or affirming under oath to the truthfulness of the claims made in this answer and that the punishment for knowingly making a false statement includes fines and/or imprisonment.

Dated: ______________________

Signature of ( ) HUSBAND ( ) WIFE
Printed Name: ______________________
Address: ______________________
City, State, Zip: ______________________
Telephone Number: ______________________
Fax Number: ______________________

Designated E-mail Address(es): ______________________

STATE OF FLORIDA
COUNTY OF ______________________

Sworn to or affirmed and signed before me on __________ by ______________________.

____
NOTARY PUBLIC or DEPUTY CLERK

____
[Print, type, or stamp commissioned name of notary or deputy clerk.]

___ Personally known
___ Produced identification
___ Type of identification produced ______________________

IF A NONLAWYER HELPED YOU FILL OUT THIS FORM, HE/SHE MUST FILL IN THE BLANKS BELOW:
[fill in **all** blanks] This form was prepared for the: *{choose only one}* ( ) Husband ( ) Wife
This form was completed with the assistance of:
{name of individual} ______________________,
{name of business} ______________________,
{address} ______________________,
{city} __________, *{state}* __________, *{zip code}* __________, *{telephone number}* __________.

Florida Supreme Court Approved Form 12.903(a), Answer, Waiver, and Request for Copy of Final Judgment of Dissolution of Marriage (03/15)

INSTRUCTIONS FOR FLORIDA SUPREME COURT APPROVED FAMILY LAW FORM 12.903(a)
ANSWER, WAIVER, AND REQUEST FOR COPY OF FINAL JUDGMENT OF DISSOLUTION OF MARRIAGE (03/15)

When should this form be used?

This form should be used when you have been served with a **petition** for **dissolution of marriage** and you do not wish to **contest** it or appear at a **hearing**. If you file this form, you are admitting all of the allegations in the **petition**, saying that you do not need to be notified of or appear at the **final hearing**, and that you would like a copy of the **final judgment** mailed to you.

This form should be typed or printed in black ink, and your signature should be witnessed by a **notary public** or **deputy clerk**. After completing this form, you should sign the form before a notary public. You should **file** the original with the **clerk of the circuit court** in the county where the petition was filed and keep a copy for your records. The person filing the **petition** in a dissolution of marriage proceeding is also referred to as the **petitioner** and his or her **spouse** as the **respondent.**

IMPORTANT INFORMATION REGARDING E–FILING

The Florida Rules of Judicial Administration now require that all petitions, pleadings, and documents be filed electronically except in certain circumstances. **Self-represented litigants may file petitions or other pleadings or documents electronically; however, they are not required to do so.** If you choose to file your pleadings or other documents electronically, you must do so in accordance with Florida Rule of Judicial Administration 2.525, and you must follow the procedures of the judicial circuit in which you file. **The rules and procedures should be carefully read and followed.**

What should I do next?

You have 20 days to **answer** after being **served** with your spouse's petition. A copy of this form, along with all of the other forms required with this **answer** and **waiver**, must be mailed, e-mailed, or hand delivered to your spouse.

IMPORTANT INFORMATION REGARDING E–SERVICE ELECTION

After the initial service of process of the petition or supplemental petition by the Sheriff or certified process server, the Florida Rules of Judicial Administration now require that all documents required or permitted to be served on the other party must be served by electronic mail (e-mail) except in certain circumstances. **You must strictly comply with the format requirements set forth in the Rules of Judicial Administration.**

SELF–REPRESENTED LITIGANTS MAY SERVE DOCUMENTS BY E–MAIL; HOWEVER, THEY ARE NOT REQUIRED TO DO SO. If a self-represented litigant elects to serve and receive documents by e-mail, the procedures must always be followed once the initial election is made.

To serve and receive documents by e-mail, you must designate your e-mail addresses by using the **Designation of Current Mailing and E-mail Address**, Florida Supreme Court Approved Family Law Form 12.915, and you must provide your e-mail address on each form on which your signature appears. Please **CAREFULLY** read the rules and instructions for: **Certificate of Service (General),** Florida Supreme Court Approved Family Law Form 12.914; **Designation of Current Mailing and E-mail Address**, Florida Supreme Court Approved Family Law Form 12.915; and Florida Rule of Judicial Administration 2.516.

Where can I look for more information?

Before proceeding, you should read General Information for Self–Represented Litigants found at the beginning of these forms. The words that are in **bold underline** in these instructions are defined there. For further information, see chapter 61, Florida Statutes.

Special notes . . .

With this form, you must also file the following:

- **Uniform Child Custody Jurisdiction and Enforcement Act (UCCJEA) Affidavit,** Florida Supreme Court Approved Family Law Form 12.902(d), if the case involves a dependent or minor child(ren).
- **Child Support Guidelines Worksheet**, Florida Family Law Rules of Procedure Form 12.902(e), if the case involves a dependent or minor child(ren). (If you do not know the other party's income, you may file this worksheet after his or her financial affidavit has been served on you).
- **Marital Settlement Agreement for Dissolution of Marriage with Dependent or Minor Child(ren)**, Florida Supreme Court Approved Family Law Form 12.902(f)(1), or **Marital Settlement Agreement for Dissolution of Marriage with No Dependent or Minor Child(ren)**, Florida Supreme Court Approved Family Law Form 12.902(f)(2), if you have reached an agreement on any or all of the issues.
- **Notice of Social Security Number**, Florida Supreme Court Approved Family Law Form 12.902(j).
- **Family Law Financial Affidavit,** Florida Family Law Rules of Procedure Form 12.902(b) or (c). (This must be filed within 45 days of service of the petition on you, if not filed at the time you file this answer.)
- **Certificate of Compliance with Mandatory Disclosure**, Florida Family Law Rules of Procedure Form 12.932. (This must be filed within 45 days of service of the petition on you, if not filed at the time you file this answer, unless you and the other party have agreed not to exchange these documents.)

Parenting Plan and Time–Sharing . . . By filing this answer and waiver, you are agreeing to any parenting plan and time-sharing requests in the petition. The judge may request a **parenting plan recommendation** or appoint a **guardian ad litem** in your case. This means that a neutral person will review your situation and report to the judge concerning parenting issues. The purpose of such intervention is to be sure that the best interests of the child(ren) is (are) being served. For more information, you may consult section 61.13, Florida Statutes.

A **parenting course** must be completed prior to entry of a final judgment. You should contact the clerk, family law intake staff, or judicial assistant about requirements for parenting courses where you live.

Listed below are some terms with which you should become familiar before completing your answer to the petition. **If you do not fully understand any of the terms below or their implications, you should speak with an attorney before going any further.**

- **Shared Parental Responsibility**
- **Sole Parental Responsibility**
- **Supervised Time–Sharing**
- **No contact**
- **Parenting Plan**
- **Parenting Plan Recommendation**
- **Time–Sharing Schedule**

Child Support . . . By filing this answer and waiver, you are agreeing to any child support requests in the petition. The court may order one parent to pay **child support** to assist the other parent in meeting the child(ren)'s material needs. **Both parents are required to provide financial support**, but one parent may be ordered to pay a portion of his or her support for the child(ren) to the other parent. Florida has adopted guidelines for determining the amount of child support to be paid. These guidelines are based on the combined income of **both** parents and take into account the financial contributions of both parents. You must file a **Family Law Financial Affidavit**, Florida Family Law Rules of Procedure Form 12.902(b) or (c), and your spouse will be required to do the same. From your financial affidavits, you should be able to calculate the amount of child support that should be paid using the **Child Support Guidelines Worksheet**, Florida Family Law Rules of Procedure Form 12.902(e). Because the child support guidelines take several factors into consideration, change over time, and vary from state to state, your child support obligation may be more or less than that of other people in seemingly similar situations.

Alimony . . . By filing this answer and waiver, you are agreeing to any alimony requests in the petition. Alimony may be awarded to one spouse if the judge finds that he or she has an actual need for it and also finds that the other spouse has the ability to pay. **If you want alimony, you must request it in writing in a counterpetition and should not use this form. If you do not request alimony in writing before the final hearing, it is waived**

(you may not request it later). You may request **permanent alimony**, **bridge-the-gap alimony, durational alimony, lump sum alimony**, or **rehabilitative alimony**.

Marital/Nonmarital Assets and Liabilities . . . Florida law requires an **equitable distribution** of **marital assets** and **marital liabilities**. "Equitable" does not necessarily mean "equal." Many factors, including child support, time-sharing and alimony awards, may lead the court to make an unequal (but still equitable) distribution of assets and liabilities. **Nonmarital assets** and **nonmarital liabilities** are those assets and liabilities which the parties agree or the court determines belong to, or are the responsibility of, only one of the parties. By filing this answer and waiver, you are agreeing to any requests in the petition regarding division of assets and liabilities.

Final Judgment . . . You should receive a copy of the Final Judgment in the mail. If, for some reason you do not, you should call the clerk's office to request a copy. It is important for you to review a copy of the Final Judgment in your case to see what happened and to know what you must do and what you are entitled to receive.

Nonlawyer . . . Remember, a person who is NOT an attorney is called a nonlawyer. If a nonlawyer helps you fill out these forms, that person must give you a copy of a **Disclosure from Nonlawyer**, Florida Family Law Rules of Procedure Form 12.900(a), before he or she helps you. A nonlawyer helping you fill out these forms also **must** put his or her name, address, and telephone number on the bottom of the last page of every form he or she helps you complete.

Added July 7, 1995, effective Jan. 1, 1996 (663 So.2d 1047). Amended Feb. 26, 1998, effective Mar. 16, 1998 (713 So.2d 1); Sept. 21, 2000 (810 So.2d 1); Dec. 19, 2002 (836 So.2d 1019); March 26, 2009 (20 So.3d 173); Dec. 16, 2010 (59 So.3d 792); May 24, 2012 (96 So.3d 217); March 26, 2015, effective March 26, 2015 (2015 WL 1343088).

Form 12.903(b). Answer to Petition for Dissolution of Marriage

IN THE CIRCUIT COURT OF THE ______________________ JUDICIAL CIRCUIT,
IN AND FOR ________________________ COUNTY, FLORIDA

Case No.: ____________________
Division: ____________________

______________________________,
Petitioner,

and

______________________________,
Respondent.

ANSWER TO PETITION FOR DISSOLUTION OF MARRIAGE

I, *{full legal name}* ____, Respondent, being sworn, certify that the following information is true:

1. I **agree** with Petitioner as to the allegations raised in the following numbered paragraphs in the Petition and, therefore, **admit** those allegations: *{indicate section and paragraph number}* ____

2. I **disagree** with Petitioner as to the allegations raised in the following numbered paragraphs in the Petition and, therefore, **deny** those allegations: *{indicate section and paragraph number}* ____

3. I currently am unable to admit or deny the allegations raised in the following paragraphs due to lack of information: *{indicate section and paragraph number}* ____

4. If this case involves a dependent or minor child(ren), a completed Uniform Child Custody Jurisdiction and Enforcement Act (UCCJEA) Affidavit, Florida Supreme Court Approved Family Law Form 12.902(d), is filed with this answer.

5. If this case involves a dependent or minor child(ren), a completed Child Support Guidelines Worksheet, Florida Family Law Rules of Procedure Form 12.902(e), is *[choose* ***one*** *only]*
_____ filed with this answer or _____ will be filed after the other party serves his or her financial affidavit.

6. If necessary a completed Notice of Social Security Number, Florida Supreme Court Approved Family Law Form 12.902(j), is filed with this answer.

7. A completed Family Law Financial Affidavit, Florida Family Law Rules of Procedure Form 12.902(b) or (c), *[Choose only* ***one****]* _____ is filed with this answer or _____ will be timely filed.

Florida Supreme Court Approved Family Law Form 12.903(b), Answer to Petition for Dissolution of Marriage (03/15)

I certify that a copy of this document was ( ) mailed ( ) faxed and mailed ( ) e-mailed ( ) hand delivered to the person(s) listed below on *{date}* ______________________.

Petitioner or his/her attorney:
Name: ______________________
Address: ______________________
City, State, Zip: ______________________
Fax Number: ______________________
Designated E-mail Address(es): ______________________
____

I understand that I am swearing or affirming under oath to the truthfulness of the claims made in this answer and that the punishment for knowingly making a false statement includes fines and/or imprisonment.

Dated: ______________________
____
Signature of Respondent
Printed Name: ______________________
Address: ______________________
City, State, Zip: ______________________
Telephone Number: ______________________
Fax Number: ______________________
Designated E-mail Address(es): ______________________
____

STATE OF FLORIDA
COUNTY OF ______________________

Sworn to or affirmed and signed before me on ______________ by ______________________.

____
NOTARY PUBLIC or DEPUTY CLERK

____
[Print, type, or stamp commissioned name of notary or clerk.]
___ Personally known
___ Produced identification
Type of identification produced ______________________

IF A NONLAWYER HELPED YOU FILL OUT THIS FORM, HE/SHE MUST FILL IN THE BLANKS BELOW:
[fill in all blanks] This form was prepared for the Respondent.
This form was completed with the assistance of:
{name of individual} ______________________,
{name of business} ______________________,

Florida Supreme Court Approved Family Law Form 12.903(b), Answer to Petition for Dissolution of Marriage (03/15)

{address} ____,
{city} ______________, *{state}* _____,*{zip code}*__________,*{telephone number}* ________________.

INSTRUCTIONS FOR FLORIDA SUPREME COURT APPROVED FAMILY LAW FORM 12.903(b) ANSWER TO PETITION FOR DISSOLUTION OF MARRIAGE (03/15)

When should this form be used?

This form should be used when you are responding to a **petition** for **dissolution of marriage** and you wish to admit or deny all of the allegations in the petition but you do not plan to file a **counterpetition** seeking relief. You can use this form to answer any petition for dissolution of marriage, whether or not there are minor child(ren).

This form should be typed or printed in black ink. After completing this form, you should sign the form before a **notary public** or **deputy clerk**. You should **file** the original with the **clerk of the circuit court** in the county where the petition was filed and keep a copy for your records. This must be done within 20 days of receiving the petition.

IMPORTANT INFORMATION REGARDING E-FILING

The Florida Rules of Judicial Administration now require that all petitions, pleadings, and documents be filed electronically except in certain circumstances. **Self-represented litigants may file petitions or other pleadings or documents electronically; however, they are not required to do so.** If you choose to file your pleadings or other documents electronically, you must do so in accordance with Florida Rule of Judicial Administration 2.525, and you must follow the procedures of the judicial circuit in which you file. **The rules and procedures should be carefully read and followed.**

What should I do next?

A copy of this form, along with all of the other forms required with this **answer**, must be mailed, e-mailed, or hand delivered to the other party in your case. You have 20 days to answer after being served with the other party's petition. After you file your answer, the case will generally proceed in one of the following two ways:

UNCONTESTED . . . If you file an answer that agrees with everything in the other party's petition **and** you have complied with **mandatory disclosure** and filed all of the required papers, either party may call the clerk, **family law intake staff**, or **judicial assistant** to set a **final hearing**. If you request the final hearing, you must notify the other party of the hearing by using a **Notice of Hearing (General)**, Florida Supreme Court Approved Family Law Form 12.923, or other appropriate notice of hearing form.

CONTESTED . . . If you file an answer which disagrees with or denies anything in the petition, **and** you are unable to settle the disputed issues, either party may file a **Notice for Trial**, Florida Supreme Court Approved Family Law Form 12.924, after you have complied with mandatory disclosure and filed all of the required papers. Some circuits may require the completion of **mediation** before a final hearing may be set. You should contact the clerk, family law intake staff, or judicial assistant for instructions on how to set your case for trial (final hearing).

Where can I look for more information?

Before proceeding, you should read "General Information for Self-Represented Litigants" found at the beginning of these forms. The words that are in **"bold underline"** in these instructions are defined there. See chapter 61, Florida Statutes, for more information.

IMPORTANT INFORMATION REGARDING E-SERVICE ELECTION

After the initial service of process of the petition or supplemental petition by the Sheriff or certified process server, the Florida Rules of Judicial Administration now require that all documents required or permitted to be served on the other party must be served by electronic mail (e-mail) except in certain circumstances. **You must strictly comply with the format requirements set forth in the Rules of Judicial Administration.**

SELF-REPRESENTED LITIGANTS MAY SERVE DOCUMENTS BY E-MAIL; HOWEVER, THEY ARE NOT REQUIRED TO DO SO. If a self-represented litigant elects to serve and receive documents by e-mail, the procedures must always be followed once the initial election is made.

To serve and receive documents by e-mail, you must designate your e-mail addresses by using the **Designation of Current Mailing and E-mail Address**, Florida Supreme Court Approved Family Law Form 12.915, and you must provide your e-mail address on each form on which your signature appears. Please **CAREFULLY** read the rules and instructions for: **Certificate of Service (General),** Florida Supreme Court Approved Family Law Form 12.914; **Designation of Current Mailing and E-mail Address**, Florida Supreme Court Approved Family Law Form 12.915; and Florida Rule of Judicial Administration 2.516.

Special notes . . .

With this form, you must also file the following:

- **Uniform Child Custody Jurisdiction and Enforcement Act (UCCJEA) Affidavit,** Florida Supreme Court Approved Family Law Form 12.902(d), if the case involves a dependent or minor child(ren).
- **Child Support Guidelines Worksheet**, Florida Family Law Rules of Procedure Form 12.902(e), if the case involves a dependent or minor child(ren). (If you do not know the other party's income, you may file this worksheet after his or her financial affidavit has been served on you).
- **Marital Settlement Agreement for Dissolution of Marriage with Dependent or Minor Child(ren)**, Florida Supreme Court Approved Family Law Form 12.902(f)(1), or **Marital Settlement Agreement for Dissolution of Marriage with Property but No Dependent or Minor Child(ren)**, Florida Supreme Court Approved Family Law Form 12.902(f)(2), if you have reached an agreement on any or all of the issues.
- **Notice of Social Security Number**, Florida Supreme Court Approved Family Law Form 12.902(j).
- **Family Law Financial Affidavit**, Florida Family Law Rules of Procedure Form 12.902(b) or (c). (This must be filed within 45 days of service of the petition on you, if not filed at the time you file this answer.)
- **Certificate of Compliance with Mandatory Disclosure**, Florida Family Law Rules of Procedure Form 12.932. (This must be filed within 45 days of **service** of the petition on you, if not filed at the time you file this answer, unless you and the other party have agreed not to exchange these documents.)

Parenting and Time-sharing ... If you and your **spouse** are unable to agree on parenting arrangements and a time-sharing schedule, a judge will decide for you as part of establishing a Parenting Plan. The judge will decide the parenting arrangements and time-sharing schedule based on the child(ren)'s best interests. Regardless of whether there is an agreement, the court reserves jurisdiction to modify issues relating to the minor child(ren). The judge may request a **parenting plan recommendation** or appoint a **guardian ad litem** in your case. This means that a neutral person will review your situation and report to the judge concerning parenting issues. The purpose of such intervention is to be sure that the best interests of the child(ren) is (are) being served. For more information, you may consult section 61.13, Florida Statutes.

A **parenting course** must be completed prior to the entry of a final judgment. You should contact the clerk, family law intake staff, or judicial assistant about requirements for parenting courses where you live.

Listed below are some terms with which you should become familiar before completing your answer to the petition. **If you do not fully understand any of the terms below or their implications, you should speak with an attorney before going any further.**

- **Shared Parental Responsibility**
- **Sole Parental Responsibility**
- **Supervised Time–Sharing**
- **No contact**
- **Parenting Plan**
- **Parenting Plan Recommendation**
- **Time–Sharing Schedule**

Child Support . . . The court may order one parent to pay **child support** to assist the other parent in meeting the child(ren)'s material needs. **Both parents are required to provide financial support**, but one parent may be ordered to pay a portion of his or her support for the child(ren) to the other parent. Florida has adopted guidelines for determining the amount of child support to be paid. These guidelines are based on the combined income of **both** parents and take into account the financial contributions of both parents and the number of overnights the child(ren) spend with each parent. You must file a **Family Law Financial Affidavit**, Florida Family Law Rules of Procedure Form 12.902(b) or (c), and your spouse will be required to do the same. From your financial affidavits, you should be able to calculate the amount of child support that should be paid using the **Child Support Guidelines Worksheet**, Florida Family Law Rules of Procedure Form 12.902(e). Because the child support guidelines take several factors into consideration, change over time, and vary from state to state, your child support obligation may be more or less than that of other people in seemingly similar situations.

Alimony . . . Alimony may be awarded to a spouse if the judge finds that he or she needs it and that the other spouse has the ability to pay it. **If you want alimony, you must request it in writing in a counterpetition.** Florida Supreme Court Approved Family Law Form 12.903(c)(1) (with dependent or minor child(ren)), or Florida Supreme Court Approved Family Law Form 12.903(c)(2) (no dependent or minor child(ren)). **If you do not request alimony in writing before the final hearing, it is waived (you may not request it later).**

Marital/Nonmarital Assets and Liabilities . . . Florida law requires an **equitable distribution** of <u>**marital assets**</u> and <u>**marital liabilities**</u>. "Equitable" does not necessarily mean "equal." Many factors, including child support, any parenting plan and time-sharing schedule, and alimony awards, may lead the court to make an unequal (but still equitable) distribution of assets and liabilities. <u>**Nonmarital assets**</u> and <u>**nonmarital liabilities**</u> are those assets and liabilities which the parties agree or the court determines belong to, or are the responsibility of, only one of the parties. If the parties agree or the court finds an asset or liability to be nonmarital, the judge will not consider it when distributing marital assets and liabilities.

Temporary Relief . . . If you need temporary relief regarding temporary use of assets, temporary responsibility for liabilities, parental responsibility and time-sharing with child(ren), temporary child support, or temporary alimony, you may file a **Motion for Temporary Support and Time–Sharing with Dependent or Minor Child(ren)**, Florida Supreme Court Approved Family Law Form 12.947(a), or, if there are no dependent or minor child(ren), **Motion for Temporary Support with No Dependent or Minor Child(ren)**, Florida Supreme Court Approved Family Law Form 12.947(c). For more information, see the instructions for these forms.

Marital Settlement Agreement . . . If you and your spouse are able to reach an agreement on any or all of the issues, you should file a **Marital Settlement Agreement for Dissolution of Marriage with Dependent or Minor Child(ren)**, Florida Supreme Court Approved Family Law Form 12.902(f)(1), or **Marital Settlement Agreement for Dissolution of Marriage with No Dependent or Minor Child(ren)**, Florida Supreme Court Approved Family Law Form 12.902(f)(2). Both parties must sign this agreement before a <u>**notary public**</u> or <u>**deputy clerk**</u>. Any issues on which you are unable to agree will be considered **contested** and settled by the judge at the final hearing.

Final Judgment Form . . . These family law forms contain a **Final Judgment of Dissolution of Marriage with Dependent or Minor Child(ren)**, Florida Supreme Court Approved Family Law Form 12.990(c)(1), and **Final Judgment of Dissolution of Marriage with Property but No Dependent or Minor Child(ren)**, Florida Supreme Court Approved Family Law Form 12.990(c)(2), which the judge may use if your case is contested. If you and your spouse reach an agreement on all of the issues, the judge may use **Final Judgment of Dissolution of Marriage with Dependent or Minor Child(ren) (Uncontested)**, Florida Supreme Court Approved Family Law Form 12.990(b)(1), **Final Judgment of Dissolution of Marriage with Property but No Dependent or Minor Child(ren) (Uncontested)**, Florida Supreme Court Approved Family Law Form 12.990(b)(2), or **Final Judgment of Dissolution of Marriage with No Property and No Dependent or Minor Child(ren)**, Florida Supreme Court Approved Family Law Form 12.990(b)(3). You should check with the clerk, family law intake staff, or judicial assistant to see if you need to bring a <u>**final judgment**</u> with you to the <u>**hearing**</u>. If so, you should type or print the heading, including the circuit, county, case number, division, and the parties' names, and leave the rest blank for the judge to complete at your hearing or trial.

Nonlawyer . . . Remember, a person who is NOT an attorney is called a nonlawyer. If a nonlawyer helps you fill out these forms, that person must give you a copy of a **Disclosure from Nonlawyer**, Florida Family Law Rules of Procedure Form 12.900(a), before he or she helps you. A nonlawyer helping you fill out these forms also **must** put his or her name, address, and telephone number on the bottom of the last page of every form he or she helps you complete.

Added July 7, 1995, effective Jan. 1, 1996 (663 So.2d 1047). Amended Feb. 26, 1998, effective Mar. 16, 1998 (713 So.2d 1); Sept. 21, 2000 (810 So.2d 1); Dec. 19, 2002 (836 So.2d 1019); March 26, 2009 (20 So.3d 173); Dec. 16, 2010 (59 So.3d 792); March 26, 2015, effective March 26, 2015 (2015 WL 1343088).

Form 12.903(c)(1). Answer to Petition and Counterpetition for Dissolution of Marriage With Dependent or Minor Child(ren)

IN THE CIRCUIT COURT OF THE __________ JUDICIAL CIRCUIT,
IN AND FOR __________ COUNTY, FLORIDA

Case No.: __________
Division: __________

In re: the Marriage of:

__________,
Husband,

and

__________,
Wife.

ANSWER TO PETITION AND COUNTERPETITION FOR DISSOLUTION OF MARRIAGE WITH DEPENDENT OR MINOR CHILD(REN)

I, *{full legal name}* __________, being sworn, certify that the following information is true:

ANSWER TO PETITION

1. I **agree** with the allegations raised in the following numbered paragraphs in the Petition and, therefore, **admit** those allegations: *{indicate section and paragraph number}* __________ __________.

2. I **disagree** with the allegations raised in the following numbered paragraphs in the Petition and, therefore, **deny** those allegations: *{indicate section and paragraph number}* __________ __________.

3. I currently am unable to admit or deny the following paragraphs due to lack of information: *{indicate section and paragraph number}* __________ __________.

COUNTERPETITION FOR DISSOLUTION OF MARRIAGE WITH MINOR CHILD(REN)

1. JURISDICTION/RESIDENCE

_____ Husband _____ Wife _____Both has (have) lived in Florida for at least 6 months before the filing of this Petition for Dissolution of Marriage.

2. Husband _____ is or _____ is not a member of the military service.

Wife _____ is or _____ is not a member of the military service.

3. MARRIAGE HISTORY

Date of marriage: *{month, day, year}* __________
Date of separation: *{month, day, year}* __________ (_____ Indicate if approximate)

Florida Supreme Court Approved Family Law Form 12.903(c)(1), Answer to Petition and Counterpetition for Dissolution of Marriage with Dependent or Minor Child(ren) (03/15)

Place of marriage: *{county, state, country}* ______________________________

4. DEPENDENT OR MINOR CHILD(REN)
   *[Indicate **all** that apply]*
   a. _____The wife is pregnant. Baby is due on: *{date}* __________________

   b. _____The minor (under 18) child(ren) common to both parties are:

Name	**Birth date**

   c. _____The minor child(ren) born or conceived during the marriage who are **not** common to both parties are:

Name	**Birth date**

The birth father(s) of the above minor child(ren) is (are) *{name and address}* ______________
____

   d. _____ The child(ren) common to both parties who are 18 or older but who are dependent upon the parties due to a mental or physical disability are:

Name	**Birth date**

5. A completed Uniform Child Custody Jurisdiction and Enforcement Act (UCCJEA) Affidavit Florida Supreme Court Approved Family Law Form 12.902(d), is filed with this counterpetition. (You **must** complete and attach this form in a dissolution of marriage with minor child(ren).

6. A completed Notice of Social Security Number, Florida Supreme Court Approved Family Law Form 12.902(j), is filed with this counterpetition.

7. A completed Family Law Financial Affidavit, Florida Family Law Rules of Procedure Form 12.902(b) or (c) _____ is filed or _____ will be timely filed.

8. This counterpetition for dissolution of marriage should be granted because:

   a. _____The marriage is irretrievably broken.

OR

b. _____One of the parties has been adjudged mentally incapacitated for a period of 3 years prior to the filing of this counterpetition. A copy of the Judgment of Incapacity is attached.

SECTION I. MARITAL ASSETS AND LIABILITIES

1. ____There are no marital assets or liabilities.

OR

2. _____There are marital assets or liabilities. All marital and nonmarital assets and liabilities are (or will be) listed in the financial affidavits, Florida Family Law Rules of Procedure Form 12.902(b) or (c), to be filed in this case.

*[Indicate **all** that apply]*

a. _____All marital assets and liabilities have been divided by a written agreement between the parties, which is attached to be incorporated into the final judgment of dissolution of marriage. (The parties may use Marital Settlement Agreement for Dissolution of Marriage with Dependent or Minor Child(ren), Florida Supreme Court Approved Family Law Form 12.902(f)(1)).

b. _____The Court should determine how the assets and liabilities of this marriage are to be distributed, under section 61.075, Florida Statutes.

c. _____ Husband _____Wife should be awarded an interest in the other spouse's property because: ____
____
____.

SECTION II. SPOUSAL SUPPORT (ALIMONY)

1. **_____Husband _____Wife forever gives up his/her right to spousal support (alimony) from the other spouse.**

OR

2. _____Husband _____Wife requests that the Court order the other spouse to pay the following spousal support (alimony) and claims that he or she has an actual need for the support that he or she is requesting **and that the other spouse has the ability to pay that support**. Spousal support (alimony) is requested in the amount of $______________ every _____ week _____ other week _____ month, beginning *{date}*_______________ and continuing until *{date or event}* ____.

{Explain why the Court should order _____Husband _____Wife to pay, and any specific request(s) for type of alimony (temporary, permanent, bridge-the-gap, durational, rehabilitative, and/or lump sum)}:
____
____
____

____
____
____
____
____

3. _____Other provisions relating to alimony including any tax treatment and consequences:
____
____.

4. ____Husband ____ Wife requests life insurance on the other spouse's life, provided by that spouse, to secure such support.

SECTION III. PARENTING PLAN ESTABLISHING PARENTAL RESPONSIBILITY AND TIME-SHARING

1. The minor child(ren) currently reside(s) with _____ Mother _____ Father _____ Other: *{explain}*
____

2. **Parental Responsibility.** It is in the child(ren)'s best interests that parental responsibility be: *[Choose only **one**]*
   a. _____shared by both Father and Mother.
   b. _____awarded solely to _____ Father _____ Mother. Shared parental responsibility would be detrimental to the child(ren) because: ______________________________
____
____
____.

3. **Parenting Plan and Time-Sharing.** It is in the best interests of the child(ren) that the family be ordered to comply with a Parenting Plan that _____ includes _____does not include parental time-sharing with the child(ren). The _____ Husband _____ Wife states that it is in the best interests of the child(ren) that:

*[Choose only **one**]*

   a. _____The attached proposed Parenting Plan should be adopted by the court. The parties _____have _____ have **not** agreed to the Parenting Plan.
   b. _____The court should establish a Parenting Plan with the following provisions:
   _____ No time-sharing for the _____ Father _____ Mother.
   _____ Limited time-sharing with the _____ Father _____ Mother.
   _____ Supervised time-sharing for the _____ Father _____ Mother.
   _____ Supervised or third-party exchange of the child(ren).
   _____ Time-sharing as follows: ______________________________
   ____
   ____
   ____

Explain why this request is in the best interests of the child(ren): ______________________________

____
____
____
____
____

SECTION IV. CHILD SUPPORT
*[Indicate **all** that apply]*

1. _____Husband _____Wife requests that the Court award child support as determined by Florida's child support guidelines, section 61.30, Florida Statutes. A completed Child Support Guidelines Worksheet, Florida Family Law Rules of Procedure Form 12.902(e), is, or will be filed. Such support should be ordered retroactive to:

   a. _____ the date of separation *{date}*_______________
   b. _____the date of the filing of this petition.
   c. _____other *{date}*_______________________*{explain}* _______________
____

2. _____Husband _____Wife requests that the Court award child support to be paid beyond the age of 18 years because:

   a. _____the following child(ren) *{name(s)}* ______________________________
____
is (are) dependent because of a mental or physical incapacity which began before the age of 18. *{explain}* ____

   b. _____the following child(ren) *{name(s)}* ______________________________ is (are) dependent in fact; is (are) in high school, and are between the ages of 18 and 19; said child(ren) is (are) performing in good faith with reasonable expectation of graduation before the age of 19.

3. _____Husband _____Wife requests that the Court award a child support amount that is more than or less than Florida's child support guidelines and understands that a Motion to Deviate from Child Support Guidelines, Florida Supreme Court Approved Family Law Form 12.943, **must** be filed before the Court will consider this request.

4. _____Husband _____Wife requests that medical/dental insurance for the minor child(ren) be provided by:
*[Choose only **one**]*
   a. _____Husband.
   b. _____Wife.

5. _____Husband _____Wife requests that uninsured medical/dental expenses for the child(ren) be paid:
*[Choose only **one**]*
   a. _____ by Husband.

b. _____ by Wife.
c. _____ by Husband and Wife each paying one-half.
d. _____ according to the percentages in the Child Support Guidelines Worksheet, Florida Family Law Rules of Procedure Form 12.902(e).
e. _____ Other {explain}:
____

6._____ Husband _____Wife requests that life insurance to secure child support be provided by:

a. _____Husband.
b. _____ Wife.
c. _____ Both.

SECTION V. OTHER

1. Wife requests to be known by her former name, which was *{full legal name}* :
____

2. Other relief *{specify}*: ____
____
____
____
____
____

SECTION VI. REQUEST

(This section summarizes what you are asking the Court to include in the final judgment of dissolution of marriage.)

I request that the Court enter an order dissolving the marriage **and**:
*[Indicate **all** that apply]*

1. _____ distributing marital assets and liabilities as requested in Section I of this petition;
2. _____ awarding spousal support (alimony) as requested in Section II of this petition;
3. _____ adopting or establishing a Parenting Plan containing provisions for parental responsibility and time-sharing for the dependent or minor child(ren) common to both parties, as requested in Section III of this petition;
4. _____ establishing child support for the dependent or minor child(ren) common to both parties, as requested in Section IV of this petition;
5. _____ restoring Wife's former name as requested in Section V of this petition;
6. _____ awarding other relief as requested in Section V of this petition; and any other terms the Court deems necessary.

I certify that a copy of this document was ( ) mailed ( ) faxed and mailed ( ) e-mailed ( ) hand-delivered to the person(s) listed below on *{date}* ___________________________.

Other party or his/her attorney:
Name: ______________________________________
Address: ____________________________________

Florida Supreme Court Approved Family Law Form 12.903(c)(1), Answer to Petition and Counterpetition for Dissolution of Marriage with Dependent or Minor Child(ren) (03/15)

City, State, Zip: ______________________________
Fax Number: ______________________________
Designated E-mail Address(es): ______________________________
____

Florida Supreme Court Approved Family Law Form 12.903(c)(1), Answer to Petition and Counterpetition for Dissolution of Marriage with Dependent or Minor Child(ren) (03/15)

I understand that I am swearing or affirming under oath to the truthfulness of the claims made in this answer and counterpetition and that the punishment for knowingly making a false statement includes fines and/or imprisonment.

____

Signature of _____ Husband _____ Wife
Printed Name: ______________________________
Address:
City, State, Zip:
Telephone Number: ______________________________
Fax Number: ______________________________
Designated E-mail Address(es): ______________________________
____

STATE OF FLORIDA
COUNTY OF ______________________________
Sworn to or affirmed and signed before me on __________ by __________.

____
NOTARY PUBLIC or DEPUTY CLERK

____
{Print, type, or stamp commissioned name of notary or clerk.}
_____ Personally known
_____ Produced identification
Type of identification produced ______________________________

IF A NONLAWYER HELPED YOU FILL OUT THIS FORM, HE/SHE MUST FILL IN THE BLANKS BELOW:
[fill in all blanks] This form was prepared for the: *{choose only one}* ( ) Husband ( ) Wife
This form was completed with the assistance of:
{name of individual} ______________________________,
{name of business} ______________________________,
{address} ______________________________,
{city} __________, *{state}* _____, *{zip code}* _____, *{telephone number}* _____.

Florida Supreme Court Approved Family Law Form 12.903(c)(1), Answer to Petition and Counterpetition for Dissolution of Marriage with Dependent or Minor Child(ren) (03/15)

INSTRUCTIONS FOR FLORIDA SUPREME COURT APPROVED FAMILY LAW FORM 12.903(c)(1) ANSWER TO PETITION AND COUNTERPETITION FOR DISSOLUTION OF MARRIAGE WITH DEPENDENT OR MINOR CHILD(REN) (03/15)

When should this form be used?

This form should be used when you are responding to a **petition** for **dissolution of marriage** with dependent or minor child(ren) and you are asking the court for something not contained in the petition. The **answer** portion of this form is used to admit or deny the allegations contained in the petition, and the **counterpetition** portion of this form is used to ask for whatever you want the court to do for you.

This form should be typed or printed in black ink. After completing this form, you should sign the form before a **notary public** or **deputy clerk**. You should **file** the original with the **clerk of the circuit court** in the county where the petition was filed and keep a copy for your records. The person filing the **petition** in a dissolution of marriage proceeding is also referred to as the **petitioner** and his or her **spouse** as the **respondent.** The person filing a **counterpetition** is also referred to as the **counterpetitioner** and his or her spouse as the **counterrespondent.**

IMPORTANT INFORMATION REGARDING E–FILING

The Florida Rules of Judicial Administration now require that all petitions, pleadings, and documents be filed electronically except in certain circumstances. **Self-represented litigants may file petitions or other pleadings or documents electronically; however, they are not required to do so.** If you choose to file your pleadings or other documents electronically, you must do so in accordance with Florida Rule of Judicial Administration 2.525, and you must follow the procedures of the judicial circuit in which you file. **The rules and procedures should be carefully read and followed.**

What should I do next?

You have 20 days to answer after being served with your spouse's petition. A copy of this form must be mailed, e-mailed, or hand delivered to your spouse. After you file an answer and counterpetition your case will then generally proceed as follows:

The other party is required to answer your counterpetition within 20 days using an **Answer to Counterpetition**, Florida Supreme Court Approved Family Law Form 12.903(d).

UNCONTESTED . . . Your dissolution is uncontested if you and your spouse agree on all issues raised in the petition and the counterpetition. If this is the case, **and** you and the other party have complied with **mandatory disclosure** and filed all of the required papers, either party may call the clerk, **family law intake staff**, or **judicial assistant** to set a **final hearing**. If you request the hearing, you must notify the other party of the hearing by using a **Notice of Hearing (General)**, Florida Supreme Court Approved Family Law Form 12.923, or other appropriate notice of hearing form.

CONTESTED . . . Your dissolution is contested if you and your spouse disagree on any issue raised in the petition or counterpetition. If you are unable to settle the disputed issues, either party may file a **Notice for Trial**, Florida Supreme Court Approved Family Law Form 12.924, after you have complied with mandatory disclosure and filed all of the required papers. Some circuits may require the completion of **mediation** before a final hearing may be set. You should contact the clerk, family law intake staff, or judicial assistant for instructions on how to set your case for **trial** (final hearing).

Where can I look for more information?

Before proceeding, you should read General Information for Self–Represented Litigants found at the beginning of these forms. The words that are in **bold underline** in these instructions are defined there. For further information, see chapter 61, Florida Statutes.

IMPORTANT INFORMATION REGARDING E–SERVICE ELECTION

After the initial service of process of the petition or supplemental petition by the Sheriff or certified process server, the Florida Rules of Judicial Administration now require that all documents required or permitted to be served on the other party must be served by electronic mail (e-mail) except in certain circumstances. **You must strictly comply with the format requirements set forth in the Rules of Judicial Administration.**

SELF–REPRESENTED LITIGANTS MAY SERVE DOCUMENTS BY E–MAIL; HOWEVER, THEY ARE NOT REQUIRED TO DO SO. If a self-represented litigant elects to serve and receive documents by e-mail, the procedures must always be followed once the initial election is made.

To serve and receive documents by e-mail, you must designate your e-mail addresses by using the **Designation of Current Mailing and E-mail Address**, Florida Supreme Court Approved Family Law Form 12.915, and you must provide your e-mail address on each form on which your signature appears. Please **CAREFULLY** read the rules and instructions for: **Certificate of Service (General),** Florida Supreme Court Approved Family Law Form 12.914; **Designation of Current Mailing and E-mail Address,** Florida Supreme Court Approved Family Law Form 12.915; and Florida Rule of Judicial Administration 2.516.

Special notes . . .

With this form, you must also file the following:

- **Uniform Child Custody Jurisdiction and Enforcement Act (UCCJEA) Affidavit,** Florida Supreme Court Approved Family Law Form 12.902(d)
- **Child Support Guidelines Worksheet**, Florida Family Law Rules of Procedure Form 12.902(e). (If you do not know the other party's income, you may file this worksheet after his or her financial affidavit has been served on you.)
- **Affidavit of Corroborating Witness**, Florida Supreme Court Approved Family Law Form 12.902(i) **OR** photocopy of current Florida driver's license, Florida identification card, or voter's registration card (issue date of copied document must be at least six months before date case is actually filed with the clerk of the circuit court).
- **Marital Settlement Agreement for Dissolution of Marriage with Dependent or Minor Child(ren)**, Florida Supreme Court Approved Family Law Form 12.902(f)(1), if you have reached an agreement on any or all of the issues.
- **Parenting Plan**, Florida Supreme Court Approved Family Law Form 12.9.995(a), **Safety–Focused Parenting Plan**, Form 12.995(b), or **Relocation/Long–Distance Parenting Plan**, Form 12.995(c). If the parents have reached an agreement, a signed and notarized Parenting Plan should be attached. If the parents have not reached an agreement, a proposed Parenting Plan **may** be filed.
- **Notice of Social Security Number**, Florida Supreme Court Approved Family Law Form 12.902(j).
- **Family Law Financial Affidavit**, Florida Family Law Rules of Procedure Form 12.902(b) or (c). (This must be filed within 45 days of service of the petition on you, if not filed at the time you file this answer.)
- **Certificate of Compliance with Mandatory Disclosure**, Florida Family Law Rules of Procedure Form 12.932. (This must be filed within 45 days of **service** of the petition on you, if not filed at the time you file this answer, unless you and the other party have agreed not to exchange these documents.)

Parenting Plan and Time–Sharing . . . If you and your spouse are unable to agree on parenting arrangements and a time-sharing schedule, a **judge** will decide for you as part of establishing a Parenting Plan. The judge will decide the parenting arrangements and time-sharing schedule based on the child(ren)'s best interests. Regardless of whether there is an agreement, the court reserves jurisdiction to modify issues relating to the minor child(ren). The judge may request a **parenting plan recommendation** or appoint a **guardian ad litem** in your case. This means that a neutral person will review your situation and report to the judge concerning parenting issues. The purpose of such intervention is to be sure that the best interests of the child(ren) is (are) being served. For more information, you may consult section 61.13, Florida Statutes.

A **parenting course** must be completed prior to entry of the final judgment. You should contact the clerk, family law intake staff, or judicial assistant about requirements for parenting courses or mediation where you live.

Listed below are some terms with which you should become familiar before completing your petition. **If you do not fully understand any of the terms below or their implications, you should speak with an attorney before going any further.**

- Shared Parental Responsibility
- Sole Parental Responsibility
- Supervised Time–Sharing
- No contact
- Parenting Plan
- Parenting Plan Recommendation
- Time–Sharing Schedule

Child Support . . . The court may order one parent to pay child support to assist the other parent in meeting the child(ren)'s material needs. **Both parents are required to provide financial support**, but one parent may be ordered to pay a portion of his or her support for the child(ren) to the other parent. Florida has adopted guidelines for determining the amount of child support to be paid. These guidelines are based on the combined income of **both** parents and take into account the financial contributions of both parents. You must file a **Family Law Financial Affidavit**, Florida Family Law Rules of Procedure Form 12.902(b) or (c), and your spouse will be required to do the same. From your financial affidavits, you should be able to calculate the amount of child support that should be paid using the **Child Support Guidelines Worksheet**, Florida Family Law Rules of Procedure Form 12.902(e). Because the child support guidelines take several factors into consideration, change over time, and vary from state to state, your child support obligation may be more or less than that of other people in seemingly similar situations.

Alimony . . . Alimony may be awarded to a spouse if the judge finds that he or she has an actual need for it and that the other spouse has the ability to pay. **If you want alimony, you must request it in writing in your counterpetition. If you do not request alimony in writing before the final hearing, it is waived (you may not request it later).** You may request permanent alimony, bridge-the-gap alimony, durational alimony, lump sum alimony, or rehabilitative alimony.

Marital/Nonmarital Assets and Liabilities . . . Florida law requires an **equitable distribution** of **marital assets** and **marital liabilities**. Equitable does not necessarily mean equal. Many factors, including child support, time-sharing and alimony awards, may lead the court to make an unequal (but still equitable) distribution of assets and liabilities. **Nonmarital assets** and **nonmarital liabilities** are those assets and liabilities which the parties agree or the court determines belong to, or are the responsibility of, only one of the parties. If the parties agree or the court finds an asset or liability to be nonmarital, the judge will not consider it when distributing marital assets and liabilities.

Parenting Plan . . . In all cases involving minor or dependent child(ren), a Parenting Plan shall be approved or established by the court. If you and your spouse have reached an agreement, you should file **Parenting Plan**, Florida Supreme Court Approved Family Law Form 12.995(a), 12.995(b), or 12.995(c), which addresses the time-sharing schedule for the child(ren). If you have not reached an agreement, a proposed Parenting Plan **may** be filed. **If you and your spouse cannot agree, a Parenting Plan will be established by the court.**

Temporary Relief . . . If you need temporary relief regarding temporary use of assets, temporary responsibility for liabilities, parental responsibility and time-sharing with child(ren), temporary child support, or temporary alimony, you may file a **Motion for Temporary Support and Time–Sharing with Dependent or Minor Child(ren)**, Florida Supreme Court Approved Family Law Form 12.947(a). For more information, see the instructions for that form.

Marital Settlement Agreement . . . If you and your spouse are able to reach an agreement on any or all of the issues, you should file a **Marital Settlement Agreement for Dissolution of Marriage with Dependent or Minor Child(ren)**, Florida Supreme Court Approved Family Law Form 12.902(f)(1). Both of you must sign this agreement before a **notary public** or **deputy clerk**. Any issues on which you are unable to agree will be considered **contested** and settled by the judge at the final hearing.

Final Judgment Form . . . These family law forms contain a **Final Judgment of Dissolution of Marriage with Dependent or Minor Child(ren)**, Florida Supreme Court Approved Family Law Form 12.990(c)(1), which the judge may use if your case is contested. If you and your spouse reach an agreement on all of the issues, the judge may use a **Final Judgment of Dissolution of Marriage with Dependent or Minor Child(ren) (Uncontested)**, Florida Supreme Court Approved Family Law Form 12.990(b)(1). You should check with the clerk, family law intake staff, or judicial assistant to see if you need to bring a final judgment with you to the hearing. If so, you should type or print the heading, including the circuit, county, case number, division, and the parties' names, and leave the rest blank for the judge to complete at your hearing or trial.

Nonlawyer . . . Remember, a person who is NOT an attorney is called a nonlawyer. If a nonlawyer helps you fill out these forms, that person must give you a copy of a **Disclosure from Nonlawyer,** Florida Family Law Rules of Procedure Form 12.900(a), before he or she helps you. A nonlawyer helping you fill out these forms also **must** put his or her name, address, and telephone number on the bottom of the last page of every form he or she helps you complete.

Added Sept. 21, 2000 (810 So.2d 1). Amended Dec. 19, 2002 (836 So.2d 1019); March 26, 2009 (20 So.3d 173); Dec. 16, 2010 (59 So.3d 792); Nov. 3, 2011, effective, *nunc pro tunc*, Oct. 1, 2011 (78 So.3d 1045); May 24, 2012 (96 So.3d 217); March 26, 2015, effective March 26, 2015 (2015 WL 1343088).

Form 12.903(c)(2). Answer to Petition and Counterpetition for Dissolution of Marriage With Property but no Dependent or Minor Child(ren)

IN THE CIRCUIT COURT OF THE ________ JUDICIAL CIRCUIT,
IN AND FOR ________ COUNTY, FLORIDA

Case No: ________
Division: ________

In re: the Marriage of

________,
Husband,

and

________,
Wife.

ANSWER TO PETITION AND COUNTERPETITION FOR DISSOLUTION OF MARRIAGE WITH PROPERTY BUT NO DEPENDENT OR MINOR CHILD(REN)

I, *{full legal name}* ________________, being sworn, certify that the following information is true:

ANSWER TO PETITION

1. I **agree** with the allegations raised in the following numbered paragraphs in the Petition and, therefore, **admit** those allegations: *{indicate section and paragraph number}*
____
____.

2. I **disagree** with the allegations raised in the following numbered paragraphs in the Petition and, therefore, **deny** those allegations: *{indicate section and paragraph number}*
____
____.

3. I currently am unable to admit or deny the following paragraphs due to lack of information: *{indicate section and paragraph number}*
____
____.

COUNTERPETITION FOR DISSOLUTION OF MARRIAGE WITH PROPERTY BUT NO DEPENDENT OR MINOR CHILD(REN)

1. JURISDICTION/RESIDENCE
_____ Husband _____ Wife _____ Both has (have) lived in Florida for at least 6 months before the filing of this Petition for Dissolution of Marriage.

2. Petitioner _____ is or _____ is not a member of the military service.
Respondent _____ is or _____ is not a member of the military service.

3. MARRIAGE HISTORY
Date of marriage: *{month, day, year}* ____________________
Date of separation: *{month, day, year}* ____________________ (____ Indicate if approximate)
Place of marriage: *{county, state, country}* ____________________

4. THERE ARE NO MINOR (UNDER 18) OR DEPENDENT CHILD(REN) COMMON TO BOTH PARTIES AND THE WIFE IS NOT PREGNANT.

5. A completed Notice of Social Security Number, Florida Supreme Court Approved Family Law Form 12.902(j), is filed with this counterpetition.

6. This counterpetition for dissolution of marriage should be granted because:

   a. _____ The marriage is irretrievably broken.

OR

   b. _____ One of the parties has been adjudged mentally incapacitated for a period of 3 years prior to the filing of this counterpetition. A copy of the Judgment of Incapacity is attached.

SECTION I. MARITAL ASSETS AND LIABILITIES
*[Choose only **one**]*

1. _____ There are no marital assets or liabilities.

2. _____ There are marital assets or liabilities. All marital and nonmarital assets and liabilities are (or will be) listed in the financial affidavits, Florida Family Law Rules of Procedure Form 12.902(b) or (c), to be filed in this case.

*[Indicate **all** that apply]*

   a. _____ All marital assets and liabilities have been divided by a written agreement between the parties, which is attached to be incorporated into the final judgment of dissolution of marriage. (The parties may use Marital Settlement Agreement for Dissolution of Marriage with No Dependent or Minor Child(ren), Florida Supreme Court Approved Family Law Form 12.902(f)(2).

   b. ______The Court should determine how the assets and liabilities of this marriage are to be distributed, under section 61.075, Florida Statutes.

   c. _____ Husband _____Wife should be awarded an interest in the other spouse's property because: ____
____
____
____
____.

Florida Supreme Court Approved Family Law Form 12.903(c)(2), Answer to Petition and Counterpetition for Dissolution of Marriage with Property but No Dependent or Minor Child(ren) (03/15)

SECTION II. SPOUSAL SUPPORT (ALIMONY)

1. **_____ Husband _____Wife forever gives up his/her right to spousal support (alimony) from the other spouse.**

OR

2. _____ Husband _____Wife requests that the Court order the other spouse to pay the following spousal support (alimony) and claims that he or she has an actual need for the support that he or she is requesting **and that the other spouse has the ability to pay that support**. Spousal support (alimony) is requested in the amount of $_______________ every _____ week _____ other week _____ month, beginning *{date}* _______________________ and continuing until *{date or event}* ____.

Explain why the Court should order _____Husband _____Wife to pay, and any specific request(s) for type of alimony (temporary, permanent, bridge-the-gap, durational, rehabilitative, and/or lump sum):
____
____
____
____.

3. ___Other provisions relating to alimony including any tax treatment or consequences:
____
____
____

4. _____Husband _____ Wife requests life insurance on the other spouse's life, provided by that spouse, to secure such support

SECTION III. OTHER

1. Wife requests to be known by her former name, which was *{full legal name}*
____.

2. Other relief *{specify}*:
____
____
____
____
____
____

SECTION IV. REQUEST (This section summarizes what you are asking the Court to include in the final judgment of dissolution of marriage.)

Florida Supreme Court Approved Family Law Form 12.903(c)(2), Answer to Petition and Counterpetition for Dissolution of Marriage with Property but No Dependent or Minor Child(ren) (03/15)

_____Husband _____Wife requests that the Court enter an order dissolving the marriage **and**:

1. ____ distributing marital assets and liabilities as requested in Section I of this petition;
2. ____ awarding spousal support (alimony) as requested in Section II of this petition;
3. ____ restoring Wife's former name as requested in Section III of this petition;
4. ____ awarding other relief as requested in Section III of this petition; and any other terms the Court deems necessary.

I certify that a copy of this document was _____ mailed _____ faxed and mailed
( ) e-mailed ( ) hand delivered to the person(s) listed below on *{date}*__________________.

Other party or his/her attorney:
Printed Name: ______________________________
Address: ______________________________
City, State, Zip: ______________________________
Fax Number: ______________________________
Designated E-mail Address(es):______________________________

I understand that I am swearing or affirming under oath to the truthfulness of the claims made in this answer and counterpetition and that the punishment for knowingly making a false statement includes fines and/or imprisonment.

Dated: ______________________ ______________________________
Signature of ( ) Husband ( )Wife
Printed Name: ______________________________
Address:______________________________
City, State, Zip:______________________________
Telephone Number:______________________________
Fax Number: ______________________________
Designated E-mail Address(es): ______________________________
____

STATE OF FLORIDA
COUNTY OF ____________________

Sworn to or affirmed and signed before me on ___________ by______________________________.

____
NOTARY PUBLIC or DEPUTY CLERK

____
{Print, type, or stamp commissioned name of notary or deputy clerk.}
____ Personally known
____ Produced identification
____ Type of identification produced ______________________________

Florida Supreme Court Approved Family Law Form 12.903(c)(2), Answer to Petition and Counterpetition for Dissolution of Marriage with Property but No Dependent or Minor Child(ren) (03/15)

IF A NONLAWYER HELPED YOU FILL OUT THIS FORM, HE/SHE MUST FILL IN THE BLANKS BELOW:
[fill in **all** blanks] This form was prepared for the: *{choose only* ***one****}* ( ) Husband ( ) Wife
This form was completed with the assistance of:
{name of individual} ____,
{name of business} ____,
{address} ____,
{city} ______________, *{state}* _____, *{zip code}* ___________, *{telephone number}* __________.

Florida Supreme Court Approved Family Law Form 12.903(c)(2), Answer to Petition and Counterpetition for Dissolution of Marriage with Property but No Dependent or Minor Child(ren) (03/15)

INSTRUCTIONS FOR FLORIDA SUPREME COURT APPROVED FAMILY LAW FORM 12.903(c)(2) ANSWER TO PETITION AND COUNTERPETITION FOR DISSOLUTION OF MARRIAGE WITH PROPERTY BUT NO DEPENDENT OR MINOR CHILD(REN) (03/15)

When should this form be used?

This form should be used when you are responding to a **petition** for **dissolution of marriage** with property but no dependent or minor child(ren) and you are asking the court for something not contained in the petition. The **answer** portion of this form is used to admit or deny the allegations contained in the petition, and the **counterpetition** portion of this form is used to ask for whatever you want the court to do for you.

This form should be typed or printed in black ink. After completing this form, you should sign the form before a **notary public** or **deputy clerk**. You should **file** the original with the **clerk of the circuit court** in the county where the petition was filed and keep a copy for your records. The person filing the **petition** in a dissolution of marriage proceeding is also referred to as the **petitioner** and his or her **spouse** as the **respondent**. The person filing the **counterpetition** is referred to as the **counterpetitioner** and his or her spouse as the **counterrespondent.**

IMPORTANT INFORMATION REGARDING E–FILING

The Florida Rules of Judicial Administration now require that all petitions, pleadings, and documents be filed electronically except in certain circumstances. **Self-represented litigants may file petitions or other pleadings or documents electronically; however, they are not required to do so.** If you choose to file your pleadings or other documents electronically, you must do so in accordance with Florida Rule of Judicial Administration 2.525, and you must follow the procedures of the judicial circuit in which you file. **The rules and procedures should be carefully read and followed.**

What should I do next?

You have 20 days to answer after being served with your spouse's petition. A copy of this form must be mailed, e-mailed, or hand delivered to your spouse. After you file an answer and counterpetition your case will then generally proceed as follows:

Your spouse is required to answer your counterpetition within 20 days using an **Answer to Counterpetition**, Florida Supreme Court Approved Family Law Form 12.903(d).

UNCONTESTED ... Your dissolution is uncontested if you and your spouse agree on all issues raised in the petition and the counterpetition. If this is the case, **and** you and the other party have complied with **mandatory disclosure** and filed all of the required papers, either party may call the clerk, **family law intake staff**, or **judicial assistant** to set a **final hearing**. If you request the hearing, you must notify the other party of the hearing by using a **Notice of Hearing (General)**, Florida Supreme Court Approved Family Law Form 12.923, or other appropriate notice of hearing form.

CONTESTED ... Your dissolution is contested if you and your spouse disagree on any issue raised in the petition or counterpetition. If you are unable to settle the disputed issues, either spouse may file a **Notice for Trial**, Florida Supreme Court Approved Family Law Form 12.924, after you have complied with mandatory disclosure and filed all of the required papers. Some circuits may require the completion of **mediation** before a final hearing may be set. You should contact the clerk, family law intake staff, or judicial assistant for instructions on how to set your case for **trial** (final hearing).

Where can I look for more information?

Before proceeding, you should read General Information for Self–Represented Litigants found at the beginning of these forms. The words that are in **bold underline** in these instructions are defined there. For further information, see chapter 61, Florida Statutes.

IMPORTANT INFORMATION REGARDING E–SERVICE ELECTION

After the initial service of process of the petition or supplemental petition by the Sheriff or certified process server, the Florida Rules of Judicial Administration now require that all

documents required or permitted to be served on the other party must be served by electronic mail (e-mail) except in certain circumstances. **You must strictly comply with the format requirements set forth in the Rules of Judicial Administration.**

SELF–REPRESENTED LITIGANTS MAY SERVE DOCUMENTS BY E–MAIL; HOWEVER, THEY ARE NOT REQUIRED TO DO SO. If a self-represented litigant elects to serve and receive documents by e-mail, the procedures must always be followed once the initial election is made.

To serve and receive documents by e-mail, you must designate your e-mail addresses by using the **Designation of Current Mailing and E-mail Address**, Florida Supreme Court Approved Family Law Form 12.915, and you must provide your e-mail address on each form on which your signature appears. Please **CAREFULLY** read the rules and instructions for: **Certificate of Service (General),** Florida Supreme Court Approved Family Law Form 12.914; **Designation of Current Mailing and E-mail Address**, Florida Supreme Court Approved Family Law Form 12.915; and Florida Rule of Judicial Administration 2.516.

Special notes . . .

With this form, you must also file the following:

- **Affidavit of Corroborating Witness**, Florida Supreme Court Approved Family Law Form 12.902(i) **OR** photocopy of current Florida driver's license, Florida identification card, or voter's registration card (issue date of copied document must be at least six months before date case is actually filed with the clerk of the circuit court).
- **Marital Settlement Agreement for Dissolution of Marriage with No Dependent or Minor Child(ren)**, Florida Supreme Court Approved Family Law Form 12.902(f)(2), if you have reached an agreement on any or all of the issues.
- **Notice of Social Security Number**, Florida Supreme Court Approved Family Law Form 12.902(j).
- **Family Law Financial Affidavit**, Florida Family Law Rules of Procedure Form 12.902(b) or (c). (This must be filed within 45 days of **service** of the petition on you, if not filed at the time you file this answer.)
- **Certificate of Compliance with Mandatory Disclosure**, Florida Family Law Rules of Procedure Form 12.932. (This must be filed within 45 days of **service** of the petition on you, if not filed at the time you file this answer, unless you and the other party have agreed not to exchange these documents.)

Alimony . . . **Alimony** may be awarded to one spouse if the judge finds that he or she has an actual need for it and also finds that the other spouse has the ability to pay. **If you want alimony, you must request it in writing in your counterpetition. If you do not request alimony in writing before the final hearing, it is waived (you may not request it later).** You may request **permanent alimony, bridge-the-gap alimony, durational alimony, lump sum alimony**, or **rehabilitative alimony**.

Marital/Nonmarital Assets and Liabilities . . . Florida law requires an **equitable distribution** of **marital assets** and **marital liabilities**. Equitable does not necessarily mean equal. Many factors, including alimony awards, may lead the court to make an unequal (but still equitable) distribution of assets and liabilities. **Nonmarital assets** and **nonmarital liabilities** are those assets and liabilities which the parties agree or the court determines belong to, or are the responsibility of, only one of the parties. If the parties agree or the court finds an asset or liability to be nonmarital, the judge will not consider it when distributing marital assets and liabilities.

Temporary Relief . . . If you need temporary relief regarding temporary use of assets, temporary responsibility for liabilities, or temporary alimony, you may file a **Motion for Temporary Support with No Dependent or Minor Child(ren)**, Florida Supreme Court Approved Family Law Form 12.947(c). For more information, see the instructions for that form.

Marital Settlement Agreement . . . If you and your spouse are able to reach an agreement on any or all of the issues, you should file a **Marital Settlement Agreement for Dissolution of Marriage with No Dependent or Minor Child(ren)**, Florida Supreme Court Approved Family Law Form 12.902(f)(2). Both of you must sign this agreement before a notary public. Any issues on which you are unable to agree will be considered **contested** and settled by the judge at the final hearing.

<u>Final Judgment Forms</u> . . . These family law forms contain a **Final Judgment of Dissolution of Marriage with Property but No Dependent or Minor Child(ren)**, Florida Supreme Court Approved Family Law Form 12.990(c)(2), which the judge may use if your case is contested. If you and your spouse reach an agreement on all of the issues, the judge may use a **Final Judgment of Dissolution of Marriage with Property but No Dependent or Minor Child(ren) (Uncontested)**, Florida Supreme Court Approved Family Law Form 12.990(b)(2). You should check with the clerk, family law intake staff, or judicial assistant to see if you need to bring a final judgment with you to the hearing. If so, you should type or print the heading, including the circuit, county, case number, division, and the parties' names, and leave the rest blank for the judge to complete at your hearing or trial.

Nonlawyer . . . Remember, a person who is NOT an attorney is called a nonlawyer. If a nonlawyer helps you fill out these forms, that person must give you a copy of a **Disclosure from Nonlawyer**, Florida Family Law Rules of Procedure Form 12.900(a), before he or she helps you. A nonlawyer helping you fill out these forms also **must** put his or her name, address, and telephone number on the bottom of the last page of every form he or she helps you complete.

Added Sept. 21, 2000 (810 So.2d 1). Amended Nov. 3, 2011, effective, *nunc pro tunc*, Oct. 1, 2011 (78 So.3d 1045); May 24, 2012 (96 So.3d 217); March 26, 2015, effective March 26, 2015 (2015 WL 1343088).

Form 12.903(c)(3). Answer to Petition and Counterpetition for Dissolution of Marriage with no Dependent or Minor Child(ren) or Property

IN THE CIRCUIT COURT OF THE ________ JUDICIAL CIRCUIT,
IN AND FOR ________________ COUNTY, FLORIDA

Case No.: ____________
Division: ____________

______________________________,
Husband,

and

______________________________,
Wife.

ANSWER TO PETITION AND COUNTERPETITION FOR DISSOLUTION OF MARRIAGE WITH NO DEPENDENT OR MINOR CHILD(REN) OR PROPERTY

I, *{full legal name}*____, Respondent, being sworn, certify that the following information is true:

ANSWER TO PETITION

1. I **agree** with Petitioner as to the allegations raised in the following numbered paragraphs in the Petition and, therefore, **admit** those allegations: *{indicate section and paragraph number}* ____________ ____.

2. I **disagree** with Petitioner as to the allegations raised in the following numbered paragraphs in the Petition and, therefore, **deny** those allegations: *{indicate section and paragraph number}* ____________ ____.

3. I currently am unable to admit or deny the following paragraphs due to lack of information: *{indicate section and paragraph number}* ____ ____.

COUNTERPETITION FOR DISSOLUTION OF MARRIAGE WITH NO DEPENDENT OR MINOR CHILD(REN) OR PROPERTY

1. JURISDICTION/RESIDENCE
_____Husband _____ Wife _____ Both has (have) lived in Florida for at least 6 months before the filing of this Petition for Dissolution of Marriage.

2. Petitioner _____ is or _____ is not a member of the military service.

Florida Supreme Court Approved Family Law Form 12.903(c)(3), Answer to Petition and Counterpetition for Dissolution of Marriage with No Dependent or Minor Child(ren) or Property (03/15)

Respondent _____ is or _____ is not a member of the military service.

3. MARRIAGE HISTORY
Date of marriage: *{month, day, year}* ______________________
Place of marriage: *{city, state, country}* ______________________
Date of separation: *{month, day, year}* ______________________ (_____Indicate if approximate)

4. THERE ARE NO MINOR (under 18) OR DEPENDENT CHILD(REN) COMMON TO BOTH PARTIES AND THE WIFE IS NOT PREGNANT.

5. A completed Notice of Social Security Number, Florida Supreme Court Approved Family Law Form 12.902(j), is filed with this counterpetition.

6. THIS COUNTERPETITION FOR DISSOLUTION OF MARRIAGE SHOULD BE GRANTED BECAUSE:

a. _____The marriage is irretrievably broken.

OR

b. _____One of the parties has been adjudged mentally incapacitated for a period of 3 years before the filing of this counterpetition. A copy of the Judgment of Incapacity is attached.

7. THERE ARE NO MARITAL ASSETS OR LIABILITIES.

8. **RESPONDENT FOREVER GIVES UP HIS/HER RIGHTS TO SPOUSAL SUPPORT (ALIMONY) FROM PETITIONER.**

9. _____ *[If Respondent is also the Wife]*, Wife wants to be known by her former name, which was *{full legal name}* ______________________.

10. Other relief *{specify}*: ______________________
____
____
____
____
____
____
____
____

REQUEST
(This section summarizes what you are asking the Court to include in the final judgment of dissolution

Florida Supreme Court Approved Family Law Form 12.903(c)(3), Answer to Petition and Counterpetition for Dissolution of Marriage with No Dependent or Minor Child(ren) or Property (03/15)

of marriage.)
Respondent requests that the Court enter an order dissolving the marriage **and:**

1. ______restoring Wife's former name as specified in paragraph 9 of this petition;

2. _____ awarding other relief as specified in paragraph 10 of this petition; and any other terms the Court deems necessary.

I certify that a copy of this document was ( ) mailed ( ) faxed and mailed ( ) e-mailed ( ) hand delivered to the person(s) listed below on *{date}* ______________________________.

Petitioner or his/her attorney:
Name: ______________________________
Address: ______________________________
City, State, Zip: ______________________________
Fax Number: ______________________________
Designated E-mail Address(es): ______________________________

I understand that I am swearing or affirming under oath to the truthfulness of the claims made in this answer and counterpetition and that the punishment for knowingly making a false statement includes fines and/or imprisonment.

Dated: ____________________ ______________________________
Signature of Respondent
Printed Name: ______________________________
Address: ______________________________
City, State, Zip: ______________________________
Telephone Number: ______________________________
Fax Number: ______________________________
Designated E-mail Address(es): ______________________________
____

STATE OF FLORIDA
COUNTY OF

Sworn to or affirmed and signed before me on ______________ by ______________________________.

____
NOTARY PUBLIC or DEPUTY CLERK

Florida Supreme Court Approved Family Law Form 12.903(c)(3), Answer to Petition and Counterpetition for Dissolution of Marriage with No Dependent or Minor Child(ren) or Property (03/15)

____
[Print, type, or stamp commissioned name of notary or clerk.]
____ Personally known
____ Produced identification
Type of identification produced

IF A NONLAWYER HELPED YOU FILL OUT THIS FORM, HE/SHE MUST FILL IN THE BLANKS BELOW:
[fill in all blanks] This form was prepared for the *{choose only one}* ( ) Husband ( ) Wife.
This form was completed with the assistance of:
{name of individual} ______________________________________,
{name of business} ______________________________________,
{address} ______________________________________,
{city} ________, *{state}* ______, *{zip code}* ________, *{telephone number}* ________.

Florida Supreme Court Approved Family Law Form 12.903(c)(3), Answer to Petition and Counterpetition for Dissolution of Marriage with No Dependent or Minor Child(ren) or Property (03/15)

INSTRUCTIONS FOR FLORIDA SUPREME COURT APPROVED FAMILY LAW FORM 12.903(c)(3) ANSWER TO PETITION AND COUNTERPETITION FOR DISSOLUTION OF MARRIAGE WITH NO DEPENDENT OR MINOR CHILD(REN) OR PROPERTY (03/15)

When should this form be used?

This form should be used when you are responding to a **petition** for **dissolution of marriage** with no dependent or minor child(ren) or property and you are asking the court for something not contained in the petition. The **answer** portion of this form is used to admit or deny the allegations contained in the petition, and the **counterpetition** portion of this form is used to ask for whatever you want the court to do for you such as restoring your former name.

This form should be typed or printed in black ink. After completing this form, you should sign the form before a **notary public** or **deputy clerk**. You should **file** the original with the **clerk of the circuit court** in the county where the petition was filed and keep a copy for your records.

IMPORTANT INFORMATION REGARDING E–FILING

The Florida Rules of Judicial Administration now require that all petitions, pleadings, and documents be filed electronically except in certain circumstances. **Self-represented litigants may file petitions or other pleadings or documents electronically; however, they are not required to do so.** If you choose to file your pleadings or other documents electronically, you must do so in accordance with Florida Rule of Judicial Administration 2.525, and you must follow the procedures of the judicial circuit in which you file. **The rules and procedures should be carefully read and followed.**

What should I do next?

You have 20 days to answer after being served with the other party's petition. A copy of this form must be mailed, e-mailed, or hand delivered to the other party. After you file an answer and counterpetition your case will then generally proceed as follows:

The other party is required to answer your counterpetition within 20 days using an **Answer to Counterpetition**, Florida Supreme Court Approved Family Law Form 12.903(d).

UNCONTESTED . . . Your dissolution is uncontested if you and your spouse agree on all issues raised in the petition and the counterpetition. If this is the case, **and** you and the other party have complied with **mandatory disclosure** and filed all of the required papers, either party may call the clerk, **family law intake staff**, or **judicial assistant** to set a **final hearing**. If you request the hearing, you must notify the other party of the hearing by using a **Notice of Hearing (General)**, Florida Supreme Court Approved Family Law Form 12.923, or other appropriate notice of hearing form.

CONTESTED . . . Your dissolution is contested if you and your spouse disagree on any issues raised in the petition or counterpetition. If you are unable to settle the disputed issues, either party may file a **Notice for Trial**, Florida Supreme Court Approved Family Law Form 12.924, after you have complied with mandatory disclosure and filed all of the required papers. Some circuits may require the completion of **mediation** before a final hearing may be set. You should contact the clerk, family law intake staff, or judicial assistant for instructions on how to set your case for **trial** (final hearing).

Where can I look for more information?

Before proceeding, you should read General Information for Self–Represented Litigants found at the beginning of these forms. The words that are in **bold underline** in these instructions are defined there. For further information, see chapter 61, Florida Statutes.

IMPORTANT INFORMATION REGARDING E–SERVICE ELECTION

After the initial service of process of the petition or supplemental petition by the Sheriff or certified process server, the Florida Rules of Judicial Administration now require that all documents required or permitted to be served on the other party must be served by electronic mail (e-mail) except in certain circumstances. **You must strictly comply with the format requirements set forth in the Rules of Judicial Administration.**

SELF-REPRESENTED LITIGANTS MAY SERVE DOCUMENTS BY E-MAIL; HOWEVER, THEY ARE NOT REQUIRED TO DO SO. If a self-represented litigant elects to serve and receive documents by e-mail, the procedures must always be followed once the initial election is made.

To serve and receive documents by e-mail, you must designate your e-mail addresses by using the **Designation of Current Mailing and E-mail Address**, Florida Supreme Court Approved Family Law Form 12.915, and you must provide your e-mail address on each form on which your signature appears. Please **CAREFULLY** read the rules and instructions for: **Certificate of Service (General),** Florida Supreme Court Approved Family Law Form 12.914; **Designation of Current Mailing and E-mail Address**, Florida Supreme Court Approved Family Law Form 12.915; and Florida Rule of Judicial Administration 2.516.

Special notes ...

With this form, you must also file the following:

- **Affidavit of Corroborating Witness**, Florida Supreme Court Approved Family Law Form 12.902(i) **OR** photocopy of current Florida driver's license, Florida identification card, or voter's registration card (issue date of copied document must be at least six months before date case is actually filed with the clerk of the circuit court).
- **Notice of Social Security Number**, Florida Supreme Court Approved Family Law Form 12.902(j).
- **Family Law Financial Affidavit**, Florida Family Law Rules of Procedure Form 12.902(b) or (c). (This must be filed within 45 days of service of the petition on you, if not filed at the time you file this answer.)
- **Certificate of Compliance with Mandatory Disclosure**, Florida Family Law Rules of Procedure Form 12.932. (This must be filed within 45 days of **service** of the petition on you, if not filed at the time you file this answer, unless you and the other party have agreed not to exchange these documents.)

Alimony ... By using this form, you are forever giving up your rights to spousal support (alimony) from petitioner. Alimony may be awarded to a spouse if the judge finds that he or she needs it and that the other spouse has the ability to pay it. **If you want alimony, you must request it in writing** in an appropriate answer and counterpetition (see the other answer and counterpetition forms included in these forms for the appropriate form).

Marital/Nonmarital Assets and Liabilities ... By using this form, you are stating that there are no **marital assets** and/or **liabilities**.

Final Judgment Form ... These family law forms contain a **Final Judgment of Dissolution of Marriage with No Property or Minor Child(ren) (Uncontested)**, Florida Supreme Court Approved Family Law Form 12.990(b)(3). You should check with the clerk, family law intake staff, or judicial assistant to see if you need to bring a final judgment with you to the hearing. If so, you should type or print the heading, including the circuit, county, case number, division, and the parties' names, and leave the rest blank for the judge to complete at your hearing or trial.

Nonlawyer ... Remember, a person who is NOT an attorney is called a nonlawyer. If a nonlawyer helps you fill out these forms, that person must give you a copy of a **Disclosure from Nonlawyer**, Florida Family Law Rules of Procedure Form 12.900(a), before he or she helps you. A nonlawyer helping you fill out these forms also **must** put his or her name, address, and telephone number on the bottom of the last page of every form he or she helps you complete.

Added Sept. 21, 2000 (810 So.2d 1). Amended March 26, 2015, effective March 26, 2015 (2015 WL 1343088).

Form 12.903(d). Answer to Counterpetition

IN THE CIRCUIT COURT OF THE ______ JUDICIAL CIRCUIT,
IN AND FOR __________ COUNTY, FLORIDA

Case No.: __________
Division: __________

______________________________,
Petitioner/Counterrespondent,

and

______________________________,
Respondent/Counterpetitioner.

ANSWER TO COUNTERPETITION

I, *{full legal name}* ______________________, being sworn, certify that the following information is true:

1. I **agree** with Respondent as to the allegations raised in the following numbered paragraphs in the Counterpetition and, therefore, **admit** those allegations: *{indicate section and paragraph number}* ____.
2. I **disagree** with Respondent as to the allegations raised in the following numbered paragraphs in the Counterpetition and, therefore, **deny** those allegations: *{indicate section and paragraph number}* ____.
3. I am currently unable to admit or deny the following paragraphs due to lack of information: *{indicate section and paragraph number}* ______________________.

I certify that a copy of this document was ( ) mailed ( ) faxed and mailed ( ) e-mailed ( ) hand-delivered to the person(s) listed below on *{date}* ______________________.

Respondent or his/her attorney:
Name: ______________________
Address: ______________________
City, State, Zip: ______________________

Florida Supreme Court Approved Family Law Form 12.903(d), Answer to Counterpetition (03/15)

Fax Number: ____________________________
Designated E-mail Address(es): __________________

I understand that I am swearing or affirming under oath to the truthfulness of the claims made in this answer and that the punishment for knowingly making a false statement includes fines and/or imprisonment.

Dated: ________________

____
Signature of Petitioner
Printed Name: ____
Address: ____
City, State, Zip: ____
Telephone Number: ____
Fax Number: ____
Designated E-mail Address(es): ____
____

STATE OF FLORIDA
COUNTY OF ________________

Sworn to or affirmed and signed before me on ____________ by ________________________.

____
NOTARY PUBLIC or DEPUTY CLERK

____
[Print, type, or stamp commissioned name of notary or clerk.]

____ Personally known
____ Produced identification
Type of identification produced ____________

IF A NONLAWYER HELPED YOU FILL OUT THIS FORM, HE/SHE MUST FILL IN THE BLANKS BELOW:
[fill in all blanks] This form was prepared for the Petitioner.
This form was completed with the assistance of:
{name of individual} ____,
{name of business} ____,
{address} ____,
{city} ________,*{state}* ________,*{zip code}* ________, *{telephone number}* ________.

Florida Supreme Court Approved Family Law Form 12.903(d), Answer to Counterpetition (03/15)

INSTRUCTIONS FOR FLORIDA SUPREME COURT APPROVED FAMILY LAW FORM 12.903(d) ANSWER TO COUNTERPETITION (03/15)

When should this form be used?

This form should be used by a **petitioner** to respond to the **respondent's** **counterpetition.** You should use this form to admit or deny the allegations contained in the counterpetition.

This form should be typed or printed in black ink. After completing this form, you should sign the form before a **notary public** or **deputy clerk**. You should **file** the original with the **clerk of the circuit court** in the county where the case is filed and keep a copy for your records.

IMPORTANT INFORMATION REGARDING E–FILING

The Florida Rules of Judicial Administration now require that all petitions, pleadings, and documents be filed electronically except in certain circumstances. **Self-represented litigants may file petitions or other pleadings or documents electronically; however, they are not required to do so.** If you choose to file your pleadings or other documents electronically, you must do so in accordance with Florida Rule of Judicial Administration 2.525, and you must follow the procedures of the judicial circuit in which you file. **The rules and procedures should be carefully read and followed.**

What should I do next?

You have 20 days to answer after being served with the other party's counterpetition. A copy of this form must be mailed, e-mailed, or hand delivered to the other party.

To proceed with your case, you should refer to the instructions to your petition regarding setting a case for trial under UNCONTESTED and CONTESTED.

Where can I look for more information?

Before proceeding, you should read General Information for Self–Represented Litigants found at the beginning of these forms. The words that are in **bold underline** in these instructions are defined there.

IMPORTANT INFORMATION REGARDING E–SERVICE ELECTION

After the initial service of process of the petition or supplemental petition by the Sheriff or certified process server, the Florida Rules of Judicial Administration now require that all documents required or permitted to be served on the other party must be served by electronic mail (e-mail) except in certain circumstances. **You must strictly comply with the format requirements set forth in the Rules of Judicial Administration.**

SELF–REPRESENTED LITIGANTS MAY SERVE DOCUMENTS BY E–MAIL; HOWEVER, THEY ARE NOT REQUIRED TO DO SO. If a self-represented litigant elects to serve and receive documents by e-mail, the procedures must always be followed once the initial election is made.

To serve and receive documents by e-mail, you must designate your e-mail addresses by using the **Designation of Current Mailing and E-mail Address**, Florida Supreme Court Approved Family Law Form 12.915, and you must provide your e-mail address on each form on which your signature appears. Please **CAREFULLY** read the rules and instructions for: **Certificate of Service (General),** Florida Supreme Court Approved Family Law Form 12.914; **Designation of Current Mailing and E-mail Address**, Florida Supreme Court Approved Family Law Form 12.915; and Florida Rule of Judicial Administration 2.516.

Special notes ...

Remember, a person who is NOT an attorney is called a nonlawyer. If a nonlawyer helps you fill out these forms, that person must give you a copy of a **Disclosure from Nonlawyer,** Florida Family Law Rules of Procedure Form 12.900(a), before he or she helps you. A nonlawyer helping you fill out these forms also **must** put his or her name, address, and telephone number on the bottom of the last page of every form he or she helps you complete.

Added Feb. 26, 1998, effective Mar. 16, 1998 (713 So.2d 1). Amended Sept. 21, 2000 (810 So.2d 1); May 24, 2012 (96 So.3d 217); March 26, 2015, effective March 26, 2015 (2015 WL 1343088).

Form 12.903(e). Answer to Supplemental Petition

IN THE CIRCUIT COURT OF THE ________________________ JUDICIAL CIRCUIT,
IN AND FOR ________________________ COUNTY, FLORIDA

Case No.: ____________________
Division: ____________________

________________________________,
Petitioner,

and

________________________________,
Respondent.

ANSWER TO SUPPLEMENTAL PETITION

I, *{full legal name}* ____, being sworn, certify that the following information is true:

1. I **agree** with Petitioner as to the allegations raised in the following numbered paragraphs in the Supplemental Petition and, therefore, **admit** those allegations: *{indicate section and paragraph number}* ____
2. I **disagree** with Petitioner as to the allegations raised in the following numbered paragraphs in the Supplemental Petition and, therefore, **deny** those allegations: *{indicate section and paragraph number}* ____
3. I currently am unable to admit or deny the following paragraphs due to lack of information: *{indicate section and paragraph number}* ____
4. If not previously filed in this case, a completed Family Law Financial Affidavit, Florida Family Law Rules of Procedure Form 12.902(b) or (c) _____ is filed with this answer, or _____ will be timely filed.
5. If not previously filed in this case, a completed Notice of Social Security Number, Florida Supreme Court Approved Family Law Form 12.902(j), is filed with this answer.
6. _____*{If applicable}* This case involves minor child(ren), and a completed Uniform Child Custody Jurisdiction and Enforcement Act (UCCJEA) Affidavit, Florida Supreme Court Approved Family Law Form 12.902(d), is filed with this answer.
7. _____*{If applicable}* This case involves child support, and a completed Child Support Guidelines Worksheet, Florida Family Law Rules of Procedure Form 12.902(e),_____ is filed or _____ will be timely filed with the court.

I certify that a copy of this document was ( ) mailed ( ) faxed and mailed ( ) e-mailed ( ) hand delivered to the person(s) listed below on *{date}* ______________________.

Petitioner or his/her attorney:
Name: ______________________
Address: ______________________
City, State, Zip: ______________________
Fax Number: ______________________
Designated E-mail Address(es): ______________________
____

I understand that I am swearing or affirming under oath to the truthfulness of the claims made in this answer and that the punishment for knowingly making a false statement includes fines and/or imprisonment.

Dated: ______________________

____
Signature of Respondent
Printed Name: ______________________
Address: ______________________
City, State, Zip: ______________________
Telephone Number: ______________________
Fax Number: ______________________
Designated E-mail Address(es): ______________________
____

STATE OF FLORIDA
COUNTY OF ______________________

Sworn to or affirmed and signed before me on __________ by ______________________.

____
NOTARY PUBLIC or DEPUTY CLERK

____
[Print, type, or stamp commissioned name of notary or clerk.]
_____ Personally known
_____ Produced identification
Type of identification produced ______________________

IF A NONLAWYER HELPED YOU FILL OUT THIS FORM, HE/SHE MUST FILL IN THE BLANKS BELOW:
[fill in all blanks] This form was prepared for the Respondent.
This form was completed with the assistance of:
{name of individual} ______________________,
{name of business} ______________________,

Florida Supreme Court Approved Family Law Form 12.903(e), Answer to Supplemental Petition (03/15)

*{address}*____,
{city} ______________,*{state}* _____, *{zip code}*____________________, *{telephone number}* ________________.

INSTRUCTIONS FOR FLORIDA SUPREME COURT APPROVED FAMILY LAW FORM 12.903(e), ANSWER TO SUPPLEMENTAL PETITION (03/15)

When should this form be used?

This form should be used when you are responding to a **supplemental petition** for modification of Parenting Plan, time-sharing schedule, child support, or alimony. This form is used to admit or deny all of the allegations in the supplemental petition if you do not plan to file a **counterpetition**. There is no form for a counterpetition to a supplemental petition in these Family Law Forms. If you want to file a counterpetition to a supplemental petition you will need to either seek legal assistance or create a form yourself. You may construct an answer and counterpetition using the pertinent sections contained in the **Answer to Petition and Counterpetition for Dissolution of Marriage with Dependent or Minor Child(ren)**, Florida Supreme Court Approved Family Law Form 12.903(c)(1), or **Answer to Petition and Counterpetition for Dissolution of Marriage with Property but No Dependent or Minor Child(ren)**, Florida Supreme Court Approved Family Law Form 12.903(c)(2).

This form should be typed or printed in black ink. After completing this form, you should sign the form before a **notary public** or **deputy clerk**. You should **file** the original with the **clerk of the circuit court** in the county where the case was filed and keep a copy for your records. This must be done within 20 days of receiving the supplemental petition.

IMPORTANT INFORMATION REGARDING E–FILING

The Florida Rules of Judicial Administration now require that all petitions, pleadings, and documents be filed electronically except in certain circumstances. **Self-represented litigants may file petitions or other pleadings or documents electronically; however, they are not required to do so.** If you choose to file your pleadings or other documents electronically, you must do so in accordance with Florida Rule of Judicial Administration 2.525, and you must follow the procedures of the judicial circuit in which you file. **The rules and procedures should be carefully read and followed.**

What should I do next?

A copy of this form, along with all of the other forms required with this **answer**, must be mailed, e-mailed, or hand delivered to the other party in your case. Regardless of whether you file a counterpetition, you have 20 days to answer after being served with the other **party**'s supplemental petition. After you file your answer, the case will generally proceed in one of the following two ways:

UNCONTESTED . . . If you file an answer that agrees with everything in the other party's supplemental petition **and** you have complied with **mandatory disclosure** and filed all of the required papers, either party may call the clerk, **family law intake staff**, or **judicial assistant** to set a **final hearing**. If you request the hearing, you must notify the other party of the hearing by using a **Notice of Hearing (General)**, Florida Supreme Court Approved Family Law Form 12.923, or other appropriate notice of hearing form.

CONTESTED . . . If you file an answer which disagrees with or denies anything in the supplemental petition, **and** you are unable to settle the disputed issues, either party may file a **Notice for Trial**, Florida Supreme Court Approved Family Law Form 12.924, after you have complied with mandatory disclosure and filed all of the required papers. Some circuits may require the completion of **mediation** before a final hearing may be set. If you request the hearing, you should contact the clerk, family law intake staff, or judicial assistant for instructions on how to set your case for trial (final hearing).

Where can I look for more information?

Before proceeding, you should read "General Information for Self–Represented Litigants" found at the beginning of these forms. The words that are in "**bold underline**" in these instructions are defined there. See chapter 61, Florida Statutes, for more information.

IMPORTANT INFORMATION REGARDING E–SERVICE ELECTION

After the initial service of process of the petition or supplemental petition by the Sheriff or certified process server, the Florida Rules of Judicial Administration now require that all

documents required or permitted to be served on the other party must be served by electronic mail (e-mail) except in certain circumstances. **You must strictly comply with the format requirements set forth in the Rules of Judicial Administration.**

SELF–REPRESENTED LITIGANTS MAY SERVE DOCUMENTS BY E–MAIL; HOWEVER, THEY ARE NOT REQUIRED TO DO SO. If a self-represented litigant elects to serve and receive documents by e-mail, the procedures must always be followed once the initial election is made.

To serve and receive documents by e-mail, you must designate your e-mail addresses by using the **Designation of Current Mailing and E-mail Address**, Florida Supreme Court Approved Family Law Form 12.915, and you must provide your e-mail address on each form on which your signature appears. Please **CAREFULLY** read the rules and instructions for: **Certificate of Service (General),** Florida Supreme Court Approved Family Law Form 12.914; **Designation of Current Mailing and E-mail Address**, Florida Supreme Court Approved Family Law Form 12.915; and Florida Rule of Judicial Administration 2.516.

Special notes . . .

With this form, you must also file the following:

- **Uniform Child Custody Jurisdiction and Enforcement Act (UCCJEA) Affidavit,** Florida Supreme Court Approved Family Law Form 12.902(d), if the case involves child(ren).
- **Child Support Guidelines Worksheet**, Florida Family Law Rules of Procedure Form 12.902(e), if child support is an issue. (If you do not know the other party's income, you may file this worksheet after his or her financial affidavit has been served on you.)
- **Settlement Agreement**, if you have reached an agreement on any or all of the issues. Although there is no form for this in these Florida Family Law Forms, you may construct a settlement agreement using the pertinent sections contained in **Marital Settlement Agreement for Dissolution of Marriage with Dependent or Minor Child(ren),** Florida Supreme Court Approved Family Law Form 12.902(f)(1), or **Marital Settlement Agreement for Dissolution of Marriage with [Property but] No Dependent or Minor Child(ren)**, Florida Supreme Court Approved Family Law Form 12.902(f)(2).
- **Notice of Social Security Number**, Florida Supreme Court Approved Family Law Form 12.902(j), if not previously filed.
- **Family Law Financial Affidavit**, Florida Family Law Rules of Procedure Form 12.902(b) or (c). (This must be filed within 45 days of service of the supplemental petition on you, if not filed at the time you file your answer.)
- **Certificate of Compliance with Mandatory Disclosure,** Florida Family Law Rules of Procedure Form 12.932. (This must be filed within 45 days of **service** of the supplemental petition on you, if not filed at the time of you file your answer, unless you and the other party have agreed not to exchange these documents.)

Parenting and Time–Sharing . . . If you and the other party are unable to agree on parenting arrangements and a time-sharing schedule, a judge will decide for you as part of establishing a Parenting Plan. The judge will decide the parenting arrangements and timesharing schedule based on the child(ren)'s best interests. Regardless of whether there is an agreement, the court reserves jurisdiction to modify issues relating to the minor child(ren).

The judge may request a **parenting plan recommendation** or appoint a **guardian ad litem** in your case. This means that a neutral person will review your situation and report to the judge concerning parenting issues. The purpose of such intervention is to be sure that the best interests of the child(ren) is (are) being served. For more information, you may consult section 61.13, Florida Statutes. A **parenting course** may be required prior to entry of a final judgment. You should contact the clerk, family law intake staff, or judicial assistant about requirements for parenting courses or mediation where you live.

Listed below are some terms with which you should become familiar before completing your supplemental petition. **If you do not fully understand any of the terms below or their implications, you should speak with an attorney before going any further.**

Shared Parental Responsibility

Sole Parental Responsibility

Supervised Time–Sharing

No contact

Parenting Plan

Parenting Plan Recommendation

Time–Sharing Schedule

Child Support . . . If this case involves child support issues, the court may order one parent to pay child support to assist the other parent in meeting the child(ren)'s material needs. **Both parents are required to provide financial support**, but one parent may be ordered to pay a portion of his or her support for the child(ren) to the other parent. Florida has adopted guidelines for determining the amount of child support to be paid. These guidelines are based on the combined income of **both** parents and take into account the financial contributions of both parents. You must file a **Family Law Financial Affidavit**, Florida Family Law Rules of Procedure Form 12.902(b) or (c), and the other parent will be required to do the same. From your financial affidavits, you should be able to calculate the amount of child support that should be paid using the **Child Support Guidelines Worksheet**, Florida Family Law Rules of Procedure Form 12.902(e). Because the child support guidelines take several factors into consideration, change over time, and vary from state to state, your child support obligation may be more or less than that of other people in seemingly similar situations.

Temporary Relief . . . If you need temporary relief regarding parental responsibility and time-sharing with child(ren), child support or alimony, you may file a **Motion for Temporary Support with Dependent or Minor Child(ren)**, Florida Supreme Court Approved Family Law Form 12.947(a) or, if you need temporary relief regarding alimony and there are no dependent or minor child(ren), you may file a **Motion for Temporary Support with No Dependent or Minor Child(ren)**, Florida Supreme Court Approved Family Law Form 12.947(c). For more information, see the instructions for these forms.

Settlement Agreement . . . If you and the other party are able to reach an agreement on any or all of the issues, you should file a Settlement Agreement. Although there is no form for this in these Florida Family Law Forms, you may construct a settlement agreement using the pertinent sections contained in **Marital Settlement Agreement for Dissolution of Marriage with Dependent or Minor Child(ren)**, Florida Supreme Court Approved Family Law Form 12.902(f)(1), or **Marital Settlement Agreement for Dissolution of Marriage with No Dependent or Minor Child(ren)**, Florida Supreme Court Approved Family Law Form 12.902(f)(2). Both parties must sign this agreement before a notary public or deputy clerk. Any issues on which you are unable to agree will be considered contested and settled by the judge at the final hearing.

Final Judgment Form . . . These family law forms contain a **Supplemental Final Judgment Modifying Parental Responsibility, Visitation, or Parenting Plan/Time–Sharing Schedule or Other Relief**, Florida Supreme Court Approved Family Law Form 12.993(a), a **Supplemental Final Judgment Modifying Child Support**, Florida Supreme Court Approved Family Law Form 12.993(b), and a **Supplemental Final Judgment Modifying Alimony**, Florida Supreme Court Approved Family Law Form 12.993(c), which the judge may use, as appropriate. You should check with the clerk, family law intake staff, or judicial assistant to see if you need to bring a final judgment with you to the hearing. If so, you should type or print the heading, including the circuit, county, case number, division, and the parties' names, and leave the rest blank for the judge to complete at your hearing or trial.

Nonlawyer . . . Remember, a person who is NOT an attorney is called a nonlawyer. If a nonlawyer helps you fill out these forms, that person must give you a copy of a **Disclosure from Nonlawyer**, Florida Family Law Rules of Procedure Form 12.900(a), before he or she helps you. A nonlawyer helping you fill out these forms also **must** put his or her name, address, and telephone number on the bottom of the last page of every form he or she helps you complete.

Added Sept. 21, 2000 (810 So.2d 1). Amended Dec. 19, 2002 (836 So.2d 1019); March 26, 2009 (20 So.3d 173); Dec. 16, 2010 (59 So.3d 792); March 26, 2015, effective March 26, 2015 (2015 WL 1343088).

Form 12.904(a). Petition for Support Unconnected with Dissolution of Marriage with Dependent or Minor Child(ren)

IN THE CIRCUIT COURT OF THE ____________________ JUDICIAL CIRCUIT,
IN AND FOR ____________________ COUNTY, FLORIDA

In re: the Marriage of:

Case No: ____________________
Division: ____________________

____________________________________,
Husband,
and

____________________________________,
Wife.

PETITION FOR SUPPORT UNCONNECTED WITH DISSOLUTION OF MARRIAGE WITH DEPENDENT OR MINOR CHILD(REN)

I, *{full legal name}*____, the ( ) Husband ( ) Wife, the Petitioner, being sworn, certify that the following statements are true:

1. JURISDICTION
_____ Husband _____ Wife _____ Both live in Florida at the filing of this Petition for Support Unconnected with Dissolution of Marriage, which is filed pursuant to section 61.09, Florida Statutes.

2. Husband _____ is or _____ is not a member of the military service.
Wife _____ is or _____ is not a member of the military service.

3. MARRIAGE HISTORY
Date of marriage: *{month, day, year}* ____________________
Date of separation: *{month, day, year}* ________________ (___Indicate if approximate)

4. MINOR CHILD(REN)
*[Indicate **all** that apply]*
a. ____The wife is pregnant. The baby is due on: *{date}* ____________________.
b. ____The minor (under 18) child(ren) common to both parties are:

Name	Birth date

c. The minor child(ren) born or conceived during the marriage who are **not** common to both parties are:

Florida Supreme Court Approved Family Law Form 12.904(a), Petition for Support Unconnected with Dissolution of Marriage with Dependent or Minor Child(ren) (03/15)

Name **Birth date**

____

____

____

____

____

The birth father(s) of the above minor child(ren) is (are) *{name and address}* ______________________

____

d. ____The child(ren) common to both parties who are 18 or older but who are dependent upon the parties due to a mental or physical incapacity are:

Name **Birth date**

____

____

5. A completed Notice of Social Security Number, Florida Supreme Court Approved Family Law Form 12.902(j), is filed with this petition.

6. A completed Family Law Financial Affidavit, Florida Family Law Rules of Procedure Form 12.902(b) or (c) _____ is filed with this petition or _____ will be timely filed.

7. A completed Child Support Guidelines Worksheet, Florida Family Law Rules of Procedure Form 12.902(e) _____ is filed with this petition, or _____ will be timely filed.

8. A completed Uniform Child Custody Jurisdiction and Enforcement Act (UCCJEA) Affidavit, Florida Supreme Court Approved Family Law Form 12.902(d), is filed with this petition.

SECTION I. SPOUSAL SUPPORT (ALIMONY)

1. ____Husband ____ Wife does not request spousal support (alimony) from the other spouse at this time.

OR

2. ____ Husband ____Wife has the ability to contribute to the maintenance of the other spouse and has failed to do so.____ Husband ____Wife requests that the Court order the other spouse to pay the following spousal support (alimony) and claims that he or she has a need for the support that he or she is requesting. Spousal support (alimony) is requested in the amount of $______________ every _____ week _____ other week _____ month, beginning *{date}* ______________________, and continuing until *{date or event}* ______________________.

Explain why the Court should order ____ Husband ____ Wife to pay and any specific request(s) for type of alimony (temporary, permanent, rehabilitative, bridge-the-gap, durational, and/or lump sum):____

____

____

____

____

____

Florida Supreme Court Approved Family Law Form 12.904(a), Petition for Support Unconnected with Dissolution of Marriage with Dependent or Minor Child(ren) (03/15)

____
____.

3. ____Other provisions relating to alimony including any tax treatment and consequences:
____
____
____

4. _____Husband ____ Wife requests life insurance on the other spouse's life, provided by that spouse, to secure such support.

SECTION II. CHILD SUPPORT

1. ____ Husband ____Wife has the ability to contribute to the maintenance of his or her minor child(ren) and has failed to do so. Based upon the time-sharing schedule, the ____Husband _____Wife is entitled to child support.

*[Indicate **all** that apply]*

2. ____Husband ____Wife requests that the Court award child support as determined by Florida's child support guidelines, section 61.30, Florida Statutes.

3. ____ Husband ____ Wife requests that the Court award child support to be paid beyond the age of 18 years by ____Husband ____Wife because:

a.____the following child(ren), *{name(s)}*____, is (are) dependent because of a mental or physical incapacity which began prior to the age of 18 *{explain}*: ____
____
____

b.____the following child(ren), *{name(s)}*____, is (are) dependent in fact, is (are) in high school and is (are) between the ages of 18 and 19; said child(ren) is (are) performing in good faith with a reasonable expectation of graduation before the age of 19.

4. ____ Husband ____ Wife requests that medical/dental insurance for the minor child(ren) be provided by: ***[Choose only one]***
   a. ____ Husband.

   b. ____ Wife.

5. ____ Husband ____ Wife requests that uninsured medical/dental expenses for the child(ren) be paid: ***[Choose only one]***

   a. ____ by Husband.

   b. ____ by Wife.

   c. ____ by Husband and Wife each paying one-half.

   d. _____according to the percentages in the Child Support Guidelines Worksheet, Florida Family Law Rules of Procedure Form 12.902(e).

e. ____Other *{explain}*: ____.

6. _____Husband ____ Wife requests that life insurance to secure child support be provided by:

a._____Husband

b._____Wife

c._____Both

SECTION III. OTHER RELIEF

____
____
____
____
____

SECTION IV. REQUEST

(This section summarizes what you are asking the Court to include in the order for support.)

____ Husband ____ Wife requests that the Court enter an order establishing support **and:**

*[Indicate **all** that apply]*

a. ____ awarding spousal support (alimony) as requested in Section I of this petition;

b. ____ establishing child support for the minor child(ren) common to both parties, as requested in Section II of this petition;

c. ____ awarding other relief as requested in Section III of this petition; and any other items the Court deems necessary.

I understand that I am swearing or affirming under oath to the truthfulness of the claims made in this petition and that the punishment for knowingly making a false statement includes fines and/or imprisonment.

Dated: ______________________ ______________________________

Signature of ( ) Husband ( ) Wife

Printed Name: ______________________________
Address: ______
City, State, Zip: _
Telephone Number: ___
Fax Number: ______________________________
Designated E-mail Address(es): ______________________________
____

Florida Supreme Court Approved Family Law Form 12.904(a), Petition for Support Unconnected with Dissolution of Marriage with Dependent or Minor Child(ren) (03/15)

STATE OF FLORIDA
COUNTY OF ________________

Sworn to or affirmed and signed before me on ________ by ______________________.

____
NOTARY PUBLIC or DEPUTY CLERK

____
[Print, type, or stamp commissioned name of notary or deputy clerk.]
____ Personally known
____ Produced identification
____ Type of identification produced ______________

IF A NONLAWYER HELPED YOU FILL OUT THIS FORM, HE/SHE MUST FILL IN THE BLANKS BELOW:
[fill in all blanks] This form was prepared for the: *{choose only **one**}* ( ) Husband ( ) Wife
This form was completed with the assistance of:
*{name of individual}*______________________________,
*{name of business}*______________________________,
*{address}*______________________________,
*{city}*__________, *{state}*____, *{zip code}*__________, *{telephone number}*__________.

Florida Supreme Court Approved Family Law Form 12.904(a), Petition for Support Unconnected with Dissolution of Marriage with Dependent or Minor Child(ren) (03/15)

INSTRUCTIONS FOR FLORIDA SUPREME COURT APPROVED FAMILY LAW FORM 12.904(a), PETITION FOR SUPPORT UNCONNECTED WITH DISSOLUTION OF MARRIAGE WITH DEPENDENT OR MINOR CHILD(REN) (03/15)

When should this form be used?

This form may be used to ask the court to enter a support **order** if your spouse has the ability to contribute to you and your minor child(ren), but has failed to do so. You can **only** use this form if a **dissolution of marriage** has not been filed **and** based upon the time-sharing schedule, you are entitled to support. If a petition for dissolution of marriage has been filed, you should file a **Motion for Temporary Support and Time–Sharing with Dependent or Minor Child(ren)**, Florida Supreme Court Approved Family Law Form 12.947(a), instead of using this **petition**. Also, if you are requesting that an order be entered for you to pay support to your spouse, you should not file this form.

This petition cannot address the issues of property, debts, or parental responsibility and timesharing with child(ren). It only deals with **alimony** and **child support**.

This form should be typed or printed in black ink. After completing this form, you should sign the form before a **notary public** or **deputy clerk**. You should **file** the original with the **clerk of the circuit court** in the county where you live and keep a copy for your records. Because you are filing this **petition,** you are also referred to as the **petitioner** and your spouse as the **respondent.**

IMPORTANT INFORMATION REGARDING E–FILING

The Florida Rules of Judicial Administration now require that all petitions, pleadings, and documents be filed electronically except in certain circumstances. **Self-represented litigants may file petitions or other pleadings or documents electronically; however, they are not required to do so.** If you choose to file your pleadings or other documents electronically, you must do so in accordance with Florida Rule of Judicial Administration 2.525, and you must follow the procedures of the judicial circuit in which you file. **The rules and procedures should be carefully read and followed.**

What should I do next?

For your case to proceed, you must properly notify your spouse of the petition. Because this petition concerns child support and alimony, you should use **personal service**. If your spouse is in the military service of the United States, additional steps for service may be required. See, for example, **Memorandum for Certificate of Military Service**, Florida Supreme Court Approved Family Law Form 12.912(a) and **Affidavit of Military Service**, Florida Supreme Court Approved Family Law Form 12.912(b). Service on a spouse who is in the military can be complicated; therefore, you may wish to consult an attorney regarding this issue.

Your spouse has 20 days to **answer** after being served with your petition. Your case will then generally proceed in one of the following three ways:

DEFAULT. If after 20 days, no answer has been filed, you may file a **Motion for Default**, Florida Supreme Court Approved Family Law Form 12.922(a), with the clerk of court. Then, if you have filed all of the required papers, you may call the clerk, **family law intake staff**, or **judicial assistant** to set a **final hearing**. You must notify your spouse of the hearing by using a **Notice of Hearing (General)**, Florida Supreme Court Approved Family Law Form 12.923, or other appropriate notice of hearing form.

UNCONTESTED. If your spouse files an answer that agrees with everything in your petition or an answer and waiver, **and** you have complied with **mandatory disclosure** and filed all of the required papers, you may call the clerk, family law intake staff, or judicial assistant to set a final hearing. You must notify your spouse of the hearing by using a **Notice of Hearing (General)**, Florida Supreme Court Approved Family Law Form 12.923, or other appropriate notice of hearing form.

CONTESTED. If your spouse files an answer or an answer and **counterpetition**, which disagrees with or denies anything in your petition, **and** you are unable to settle the disputed issues, you should file a **Notice for Trial**, Florida Supreme Court Approved Family Law

Form 12.924, after you have complied with mandatory disclosure and filed all of the required papers. Some circuits may require the completion of **mediation** before a final hearing may be set. Then you should contact the clerk, family law intake staff, or judicial assistant for instructions on how to set your case for **trial** (final hearing). If your spouse files an answer and counterpetition, you should answer the counterpetition within 20 days using an **Answer to Counterpetition**, Florida Supreme Court Approved Family Law Form 12.903(d).

Where can I look for more information?

Before proceeding, you should read "General Information for Self-Represented Litigants" found at the beginning of these forms. The words that are in **bold underline** in these instructions are defined there. For further information, see section 61.09, Florida Statutes.

IMPORTANT INFORMATION REGARDING E-SERVICE ELECTION

After the initial service of process of the petition or supplemental petition by the Sheriff or certified process server, the Florida Rules of Judicial Administration now require that all documents required or permitted to be served on the other party must be served by electronic mail (e-mail) except in certain circumstances. **You must strictly comply with the format requirements set forth in the Rules of Judicial Administration.**

SELF-REPRESENTED LITIGANTS MAY SERVE DOCUMENTS BY E-MAIL; HOWEVER, THEY ARE NOT REQUIRED TO DO SO. If a self-represented litigant elects to serve and receive documents by e-mail, the procedures must always be followed once the initial election is made.

To serve and receive documents by e-mail, you must designate your e-mail addresses by using the **Designation of Current Mailing and E-mail Address**, Florida Supreme Court Approved Family Law Form 12.915, and you must provide your e-mail address on each form on which your signature appears. Please **CAREFULLY** read the rules and instructions for: **Certificate of Service (General),** Florida Supreme Court Approved Family Law Form 12.914; **Designation of Current Mailing and E-mail Address**, Florida Supreme Court Approved Family Law Form 12.915; and Florida Rule of Judicial Administration 2.516.

Special notes . . .

If you do not have the money to pay the filing fee, you may obtain an Application for Determination of Civil Indigent Status from the clerk, fill it out, and the clerk will determine whether you are eligible to have filing fees deferred.

With this form you must also file the following:

- **Notice of Social Security Number**, Florida Supreme Court Approved Family Law Form 12.902(j).
- **Uniform Child Custody Jurisdiction and Enforcement Act (UCCJEA) Affidavit**, Florida Supreme Court Approved Family Law Form 12.902(d), if the case involves minor or dependent child(ren).
- **Family Law Financial Affidavit**, Florida Family Law Rules of Procedure Form 12.902(b) or (c).
- **Certificate of Compliance with Mandatory Disclosure**, Florida Family Law Rules of Procedure Form 12.932. (This must be filed within 45 days of **service** of the petition on the respondent, if not filed at the time of the petition, unless you and the other party have agreed not to exchange these documents.)
- **Child Support Guidelines Worksheet**, Florida Family Law Rules of Procedure Form 12.902(e), if you are asking that child support be ordered in the final judgment. (If you do not know the other party's income, you may file this worksheet after his or her financial affidavit has been served on you.)

Alimony. Alimony may be awarded to a spouse if the judge finds that he or she has an actual need for it and that the other spouse has the ability to pay. **If you want alimony, you must request it in writing in the original petition. If you do not request alimony in writing before the final hearing, it is waived (you may not request it later).** You may request **permanent alimony, bridge-the-gap alimony, durational alimony, lump sum alimony,** or **rehabilitative alimony.**

Child Support. The court may order one parent to pay child support to assist the other parent in meeting the child(ren)'s material needs. **Both parents are required to provide**

financial support, but one parent may be ordered to pay a portion of his or her support for the child(ren) to the other parent. Florida has adopted guidelines for determining the amount of child support to be paid. These guidelines are based on the combined income of **both** parents and take into account the financial contributions of both parents and the number of overnights the child(ren) spend with each parent. You must file a **Family Law Financial Affidavit**, Florida Family Law Rules of Procedure Form 12.902(b) or (c), and your spouse will be required to do the same. From your financial affidavits, you should be able to calculate the amount of child support that should be paid using the **Child Support Guidelines Worksheet**, Florida Family Law Rules of Procedure Form 12.902(e). Because the child support guidelines take several factors into consideration, change over time, and vary from state to state, your child support obligation may be more or less than that of other people in seemingly similar situations.

Temporary Relief. If you need temporary relief regarding child support or temporary alimony, you may file a **Motion for Temporary Support and Time–Sharing with Dependent or Minor Child(ren)**, Florida Supreme Court Approved Family Law Form 12.947(a). For more information, see the instructions for that form.

Final Judgment Forms. These family law forms contain a **Final Judgment of Support Unconnected with Dissolution of Marriage with Dependent or Minor Child(ren)**, Florida Supreme Court Approved Family Law Form 12.994(a), which the judge may use if your case is contested. You should check with the clerk, family law intake staff, or judicial assistant to see if you need to bring a final judgment with you to the hearing. If so, you should type or print the heading, including the circuit, county, case number, division, and the parties' names, and leave the rest blank for the judge to complete at your hearing or trial.

Nonlawyer. Remember, a person who is NOT an attorney is called a nonlawyer. If a nonlawyer helps you fill out these forms, that person must give you a copy of a **Disclosure from Nonlawyer**, Florida Family Law Rules of Procedure Form 12.900(a), before he or she helps you. A nonlawyer helping you fill out these forms also **must** put his or her name, address, and telephone number on the bottom of the last page of every form he or she helps you complete.

Added July 7, 1995, effective Jan. 1, 1996 (663 So.2d 1047). Amended Feb. 26, 1998, effective Mar. 16, 1998 (713 So.2d 1); Sept. 21, 2000 (810 So.2d 1); Dec. 19, 2002 (836 So.2d 1019); June 30, 2005, effective July 1, 2005 (910 So.2d 194); March 26, 2009 (20 So.3d 173); Dec. 16, 2010 (59 So.3d 792); Nov. 3, 2011, effective, *nunc pro tunc*, Oct. 1, 2011 (78 So.3d 1045); May 24, 2012 (96 So.3d 217); July 3, 2013 (117 So.3d 958); March 26, 2015, effective March 26, 2015 (2015 WL 1343088).

Form 12.904(b). Petition for Support Unconnected with Dissolution of Marriage with no Dependent or Minor Child(ren)

IN THE CIRCUIT COURT OF THE ____________________ JUDICIAL CIRCUIT,
IN AND FOR ______________________________ COUNTY, FLORIDA

In re: the Marriage of:

Case No: ________________________
Division: ________________________

______________________________,
Husband,
and

______________________________,
Wife.

PETITION FOR SUPPORT UNCONNECTED WITH DISSOLUTION OF MARRIAGE WITH NO DEPENDENT OR MINOR CHILD(REN)

I, *{full legal name}* ____, the *[Choose only one]* _____ Husband _____ Wife, being sworn, certify that the following statements are true:

1. JURISDICTION
_____ Husband _____ Wife _____ Both live in Florida at the filing of this Petition for Support Unconnected with Dissolution of Marriage, which is filed pursuant to section 61.09, Florida Statutes.

2. Husband _____ is or _____ is not a member of the military service.
Wife _____ is or _____ is not a member of the military service.

3. MARRIAGE HISTORY
Date of marriage: *{month, day, year}* ____________________
Date of separation: *{month, day, year}* ____________________ (____Indicate if approximate)

4. A completed Family Law Financial Affidavit, Florida Family Law Rules of Procedure Form 12.902(b) or (c), _____ is filed with this petition or _____ will be timely filed.

5. A completed Notice of Social Security Number, Florida Supreme Court Approved Family Law Form 12.902(j), _____ is filed with this petition or _____ will be timely filed.

SECTION I. SPOUSAL SUPPORT (ALIMONY)

1. ____ Husband ____ Wife has the ability to contribute to the maintenance of the other spouse and has failed to do so. _____ Husband _____ Wife requests that the Court order the other spouse to pay the following spousal support (alimony) and claims that he or she has a need for the support that he or she is requesting and that the other spouse has the ability to pay. Spousal support (alimony) is requested in the amount of $__________ every _____ week _____ other week _____ month, beginning *{date}* ______________, and continuing until *{date or event}* ____________________
____.

Florida Supreme Court Approved Family Law Form 12.904(b), Petition for Support Unconnected with Dissolution of Marriage with No Dependent or Minor Child(ren) (03/15)

Explain why the Court should order ____ Husband ____Wife to pay and any specific request(s) for type of alimony (temporary, permanent, bridge-the-gap, durational, rehabilitative, and/or lump sum):
____
____
____
____
____
____.

2. _____ Other provisions relating to alimony including any tax treatment and consequences:
____
____
____.

3. ___ Husband ___ Wife requests life insurance on the other spouse's life, provided by that spouse, to secure such support.

SECTION II. OTHER RELIEF

____
____
____
____

SECTION III. REQUEST (This section summarizes what you are asking the Court to include in the order for support.)

____ Husband ____ Wife requests that the Court enter an order establishing support **and**:
*[Indicate **all** that apply]*

a. ____ awarding spousal support (alimony) pursuant to Section I of this petition;

b. ____ awarding other relief as specified in Section II of this petition; and any other terms the Court deems necessary.

I understand that I am swearing or affirming under oath to the truthfulness of the claims made in this petition and that the punishment for knowingly making a false statement includes fines and/or imprisonment.

Dated: ____________________ ______________________________

Signature of _____ Husband _____ Wife

Printed Name: ______________________________

Address: ______________________________

City, State, Zip: ______________________________

Telephone Number: ______________________________

Fax Number: ______________________________

Designated E-mail Addresses): ______________________________

____

STATE OF FLORIDA

COUNTY OF ____________________

Sworn to or affirmed and signed before me on __________ by ______________________________.

____

NOTARY PUBLIC or DEPUTY CLERK

____

[Print, type, or stamp commissioned name of notary or deputy clerk.]

____ Personally known

____ Produced identification

____ Type of identification produced ______________________________

IF A NONLAWYER HELPED YOU FILL OUT THIS FORM, HE/SHE MUST FILL IN THE BLANKS BELOW:

[fill in **all** blanks] This form was prepared for the: *{choose only **one**}* ( ) Husband ( ) Wife

This form was completed with the assistance of:

{name of individual} ______________________________,

{name of business} ______________________________,

{address} ______________________________,

{city} ______________,*{state}* _____, *{zip code}*__________, *{telephone number}* ______________.

Florida Supreme Court Approved Family Law Form 12.904(b), Petition for Support Unconnected with Dissolution of Marriage with No Dependent or Minor Child(ren) (03/15)

INSTRUCTIONS FOR FLORIDA SUPREME COURT APPROVED FAMILY LAW FORM 12.904(b), PETITION FOR SUPPORT UNCONNECTED WITH DISSOLUTION OF MARRIAGE WITH NO DEPENDENT OR MINOR CHILD(REN)(03/15)

When should this form be used?

This form may be used if a **dissolution of marriage** has not been filed, and you are requesting **alimony**. If a petition for dissolution has been filed, you should file a **Motion for Temporary Support with No Dependent or Minor Child(ren)**, Florida Supreme Court Approved Family Law Form 12.947(c), instead of using this **petition**. Also, if you are requesting that an order be entered for you to pay support to your spouse, you should not file this form.

This petition does not address the issues of property or debts. It only deals with alimony.

This form should be typed or printed in black ink. After completing this form, you should sign the form before a **notary public** or **deputy clerk**. You should **file** the original with the **clerk of the circuit court** in the county where you live and keep a copy for your records. Because you are filing the **petition** in this proceeding, you are also referred to as the **petitioner** and your **spouse** as the **respondent.**

IMPORTANT INFORMATION REGARDING E-FILING

The Florida Rules of Judicial Administration now require that all petitions, pleadings, and documents be filed electronically except in certain circumstances. **Self-represented litigants may file petitions or other pleadings or documents electronically; however, they are not required to do so.** If you choose to file your pleadings or other documents electronically, you must do so in accordance with Florida Rule of Judicial Administration 2.525, and you must follow the procedures of the judicial circuit in which you file. **The rules and procedures should be carefully read and followed.**

What should I do next?

For your case to proceed, you must properly notify your spouse of the petition. Because this petition concerns alimony, you should use **personal service**. If your spouse is in the military service of the United States, additional steps for service may be required. See, for example, **Memorandum for Certificate of Military Service**, Florida Supreme Court Approved Family Law Form 12.912(a) and **Affidavit of Military Service**, Florida Supreme Court Approved Family Law Form 12.912(b). Service on a spouse who is in the military can be complicated; therefore, you may wish to consult an attorney regarding this issue.

Your spouse has 20 days to **answer** after being served with your petition. Your case will then generally proceed in one of the following three ways:

DEFAULT ... If after 20 days, no answer has been filed, you may file a **Motion for Default**, Florida Supreme Court Approved Family Law Form 12.922(a), with the clerk of court. Then, if you have filed all of the required papers, you may call the clerk, **family law intake staff**, or **judicial assistant** to set a **final hearing**. You must notify your spouse of the hearing by using a **Notice of Hearing (General)**, Florida Supreme Court Approved Family Law Form 12.923, or other appropriate notice of hearing form.

UNCONTESTED ... If your spouse files an answer that agrees with everything in your petition or an answer and waiver, **and** you have complied with **mandatory disclosure** and filed all of the required papers, you may call the clerk, family law intake staff, or judicial assistant to set a final hearing. You must notify your spouse of the hearing by using a **Notice of Hearing (General)**, Florida Supreme Court Approved Family Law Form 12.923, or other appropriate notice of hearing form.

CONTESTED ... If your spouse files an answer or an answer and **counterpetition**, which disagrees with or denies anything in your petition, **and** you are unable to settle the disputed issues, you should file a **Notice for Trial**, Florida Supreme Court Approved Family Law Form 12.924, after you have complied with mandatory disclosure and filed all of the required papers. Some circuits may require the completion of **mediation** before a final hearing may be set. Then you should contact the clerk, family law intake staff, or judicial assistant for instructions on how to set your case for **trial** (final hearing). If your spouse files an answer and counterpetition, you should answer the counterpetition within 20 days using an **Answer to Counterpetition**, Florida Supreme Court Approved Family Law Form 12.903(d).

Where can I look for more information?

Before proceeding, you should read General Information for Self-Represented Litigants found at the beginning of these forms. The words that are in **bold underline** in these instructions are defined there. For further information, see section 61.09, Florida Statutes.

IMPORTANT INFORMATION REGARDING E-SERVICE ELECTION

After the initial service of process of the petition or supplemental petition by the Sheriff or certified process server, the Florida Rules of Judicial Administration now require that all documents required or permitted to be served on the other party must be served by electronic mail (e-mail) except in certain circumstances. **You must strictly comply with the format requirements set forth in the Rules of Judicial Administration.**

SELF-REPRESENTED LITIGANTS MAY SERVE DOCUMENTS BY E-MAIL; HOWEVER, THEY ARE NOT REQUIRED TO DO SO. If a self-represented litigant elects to serve and receive documents by e-mail, the procedures must always be followed once the initial election is made.

To serve and receive documents by e-mail, you must designate your e-mail addresses by using the **Designation of Current Mailing and E-mail Address**, Florida Supreme Court Approved Family Law Form 12.915, and you must provide your e-mail address on each form on which your signature appears. Please **CAREFULLY** read the rules and instructions for: **Certificate of Service (General),** Florida Supreme Court Approved Family Law Form 12.914; **Designation of Current Mailing and E-mail Address**, Florida Supreme Court Approved Family Law Form 12.915; and Florida Rule of Judicial Administration 2.516.

Special notes . . .

If you do not have the money to pay the filing fee, you may obtain an Application for Determination of Civil Indigent Status from the clerk, fill it out, and the clerk will determine whether you are eligible to have filing fees deferred.

With this form you must also file the following:

- **Notice of Social Security Number**, Florida Supreme Court Approved Family Law Form 12.902(j).
- **Family Law Financial Affidavit**, Florida Family Law Rules of Procedure Form 12.902(b) or (c). (This must be filed within 45 days of service of the petition on the respondent, if not filed at the time of the petition.)
- **Certificate of Compliance with Mandatory Disclosure**, Florida Family Law Rules of Procedure Form 12.932. (This must be filed within 45 days of **service** of the petition on the respondent, if not filed at the time of the petition, unless you and the other party have agreed not to exchange these documents.)

Alimony . . . Alimony may be awarded to a spouse if the judge finds that he or she has an actual need for it and that the other spouse has the ability to pay. **If you want alimony, you must request it in writing in the original petition. If you do not request alimony in writing before the final hearing, it is waived (you may not request it later).** You may request **permanent alimony, bridge-the-gap alimony, durational alimony, lump sum alimony**, or **rehabilitative alimony**.

Temporary Relief . . . If you need temporary relief regarding alimony, you may file a **Motion for Temporary Support with No Dependent or Minor Child(ren)**, Florida Supreme Court Approved Family Law Form 12.947(c). For more information, see the instructions for that form.

Final Judgment Forms . . . These family law forms contain a **Final Judgment of Support Unconnected with Dissolution of Marriage with No Dependent or Minor Child(ren)**, Florida Supreme Court Approved Family Law Form 12.994(b), which the judge may use if your case is contested. You should check with the clerk, family law intake staff, or judicial assistant to see if you need to bring a final judgment with you to the hearing. If so, you should type or print the heading, including the circuit, county, case number, division, and the parties' names, and leave the rest blank for the judge to complete at your hearing or trial.

Nonlawyer . . . Remember, a person who is NOT an attorney is called a nonlawyer. If a nonlawyer helps you fill out these forms, that person must give you a copy of a **Disclosure from Nonlawyer**, Florida Family Law Rules of Procedure Form 12.900(a), before he or she helps you. A nonlawyer helping you fill out these forms also **must** put his or her name, address, and telephone number on the bottom of the last page of every form he or she helps you complete.

Added July 7, 1995, effective Jan. 1, 1996 (663 So.2d 1047). Amended Feb. 26, 1998, effective Mar. 16, 1998 (713 So.2d 1); Sept. 21, 2000 (810 So.2d 1); June 30, 2005, effective July 1, 2005 (910 So.2d 194); Nov. 3, 2011, effective, *nunc pro tunc*, Oct. 1, 2011 (78 So.3d 1045); May 24, 2012 (96 So.3d 217); July 3, 2013 (117 So.3d 958); March 26, 2015, effective March 26, 2015 (2015 WL 1343088).

Form 12.905(a). Supplemental Petition to Modify Parental Responsibility, Visitation, or Parenting Plan/Time-Sharing Schedule and Other Relief

IN THE CIRCUIT COURT OF THE ______________________ JUDICIAL CIRCUIT,
IN AND FOR ______________________ COUNTY, FLORIDA

Case No.: ______________________
Division: ______________________

______________________________,
Petitioner,

and

______________________________,
Respondent.

SUPPLEMENTAL PETITION TO MODIFY PARENTAL RESPONSIBILITY, VISITATION, OR PARENTING PLAN/TIME-SHARING SCHEDULE AND OTHER RELIEF

I, *{full legal name}* ______________________ ______________________________, being sworn, certify that the following information is true:

1. The parties to this action were granted a final judgment of _____ dissolution of marriage _____ paternity on *{date}* __________________. A copy of the final judgment and any modification(s) is attached.

2. Paragraph(s)____________________of the _____ final judgment or _____ most recent modification thereof describes the present parental responsibility, visitation, or Parenting Plan/Time-Sharing schedule.

3. Since the final judgment or last modification thereof, there has been a substantial, material and unanticipated change in circumstances, requiring a modification of the parental responsibility, visitation, or Parenting Plan/Time-Sharing schedule. Those changes are as follows: *{explain}*
____
____
____
____
____
____
____
____

4. I ask the Court to modify the parental responsibility, visitation, Parenting Plan or Time-Sharing schedule as follows: *{explain}*
____

Florida Supreme Court Approved Family Law Form 12.905(a), Supplemental Petition to Modify Parental Responsibility, Visitation, or Parenting Plan/Time-Sharing Schedule and Other Relief (03/15)

____
____
______________________.This modification is in the best interests of the child(ren) because: *{explain}*
____
____
____
____.

5. Petitioner _____ requests _____ does not request that child support be modified, consistent with the modification of the Parenting Plan/Time-Sharing schedule.

6. If necessary, a Child Support Guidelines Worksheet, Florida Family Law Rules of Procedure Form 12.902(e), ______is, or _____ will be filed.

7. A completed Family Law Financial Affidavit, Florida Family Law Rules of Procedure Form 12.902(b) or (c), is ______, or ______ will be, filed.

8. A completed Uniform Child Custody Jurisdiction and Enforcement Act (UCCJEA) Affidavit, Florida Supreme Court Approved Family Law Form 12.902(d), is filed with this petition.

9. If not previously filed in this case, a completed Notice of Social Security Number, Florida Supreme Court Approved Family Law Form 12.902(j), is filed with this petition.

10. Other: ____
____
____
____
____.

Florida Supreme Court Approved Family Law Form 12.905(a), Supplemental Petition to Modify Parental Responsibility, Visitation, or Parenting Plan/Time-Sharing Schedule and Other Relief (03/15)

I understand that I am swearing or affirming under oath to the truthfulness of the claims made in this petition and that the punishment for knowingly making a false statement includes fines and/or imprisonment.

Dated: ______________ ____
Signature of Petitioner

Printed Name: ______________________________
Address: __________________________________
City, State, Zip: ____________________________
Telephone Number: ___________________________
Fax Number: _______________________________
Designated E-mail Address(es):__________________

STATE OF FLORIDA
COUNTY OF ______________

Sworn to or affirmed and signed before me on _______ by______________________________

____
NOTARY PUBLIC or DEPUTY CLERK

____
[Print, type, or stamp commissioned name of notary or deputy clerk.]

_____ Personally known
_____ Produced identification
Type of identification produced ___________________________

IF A NONLAWYER HELPED YOU FILL OUT THIS FORM, HE/SHE MUST FILL IN THE BLANKS BELOW:
[fill in all blanks] This form was prepared for the Petitioner.
This form was completed with the assistance of:
{name of individual} ____,

Florida Supreme Court Approved Family Law Form 12.905(a), Supplemental Petition to Modify Parental Responsibility, Visitation, or Parenting Plan/Time-Sharing Schedule and Other Relief (03/15)

{name of business} ____,
{address} ____,
{city} ________________,*{state}* ______,*{zip code}* ____________, *{telephone number}* ____________.

Florida Supreme Court Approved Family Law Form 12.905(a), Supplemental Petition to Modify Parental Responsibility, Visitation, or Parenting Plan/Time-Sharing Schedule and Other Relief (03/15)

INSTRUCTIONS FOR FLORIDA SUPREME COURT APPROVED FAMILY LAW FORM 12.905(a), SUPPLEMENTAL PETITION TO MODIFY PARENTAL RESPONSIBILITY, VISITATION OR PARENTING PLAN/ TIME–SHARING SCHEDULE AND OTHER RELIEF (03/15)

When should this form be used?

This form should be used when you are asking the court to change the current parental responsibility, visitation, and/or Parenting Plan/time-sharing schedule. A determination of parental responsibility, a Parenting Plan and a time-sharing schedule may not be modified without a showing of a substantial, material, and unanticipated change in circumstances and a determination that the modification is in the best interests of the child(ren).

This form should be typed or printed in black ink. After completing this form, you should sign the form before a **notary public** or **deputy clerk**. You should **file** this form in the county where the original order or judgment was entered. If the order or judgment was entered in another state, or if the child(ren) live(s) in another state, you should speak with an **attorney** about where to file this form. You should file the original with the **clerk of the circuit court** and keep a copy for your records.

IMPORTANT INFORMATION REGARDING E–FILING

The Florida Rules of Judicial Administration now require that all petitions, pleadings, and documents be filed electronically except in certain circumstances. **Self-represented litigants may file petitions or other pleadings or documents electronically; however, they are not required to do so.** If you choose to file your pleadings or other documents electronically, you must do so in accordance with Florida Rule of Judicial Administration 2.525, and you must follow the procedures of the judicial circuit in which you file. **The rules and procedures should be carefully read and followed.**

What should I do next?

For your case to proceed, you must properly notify the other party in your case of the **supplemental petition**. If you know where he or she lives, you should use **personal service**. If you absolutely do not know where he or she lives, you may use **constructive service**. You may also be able to use constructive service if the other party resides in another state or country. However, if constructive service is used, other than granting a dissolution of marriage, the court may only grant limited relief. For more information on constructive service, see **Notice of Action for Family Cases with Minor Child(ren)**, Florida Supreme Court Approved Family Law Form 12.913(a),(2) and **Affidavit of Diligent Search and Inquiry**, Florida Family Law Rules of Procedure Form 12.913(b). If the other party is in the military service of the United States, additional steps for service may be required. See, for example, **Memorandum for Certificate of Military Service**, Florida Supreme Court Approved Family Law Form 12.912(a). In sum, the law regarding constructive service and service on an individual in the military service is very complex and you may wish to consult an attorney regarding these issues.

If personal service is used, the other party has 20 days to **answer** after being served with your supplemental petition. Your case will then generally proceed in one of the following three ways:

DEFAULT . . . If after 20 days, no answer has been filed, you may file a **Motion for Default**, Florida Supreme Court Approved Family Law Form 12.922(a), with the clerk of court. Then, if you have filed all of the required papers, you may call the clerk, **family law intake staff**, or **judicial assistant** to set a **final hearing**. You must notify the other party of the hearing by using a **Notice of Hearing (General)**, Florida Supreme Court Approved Family Law Form 12.923, or other appropriate notice of hearing form.

UNCONTESTED . . . If the **respondent** files an answer that agrees with everything in your supplemental petition or an answer and waiver, **and** you have complied with **mandatory disclosure** and filed all of the required papers, you may call the clerk, family law intake staff, or judicial assistant to set a final hearing. You must notify the other party of the hearing by using a **Notice of Hearing (General)**, Florida Supreme Court Approved Family Law Form 12.923, or other appropriate notice of hearing form.

CONTESTED . . . If the respondent files an answer or an answer and **counterpetition**, which disagrees with or denies anything in your supplemental petition, **and** you are unable to settle the disputed issues, you should file a **Notice for Trial**, Florida Supreme Court Approved Family Law Form 12.924, after you have complied with mandatory disclosure and filed all of the required papers. Some circuits may require the completion of **mediation** before a final hearing may be set. Then you should contact the clerk, family law intake staff, or judicial assistant for instructions on how to set your case for **trial** (final hearing). If the respondent files an answer and counterpetition, you should answer the counterpetition within 20 days using an **Answer to Counterpetition**, Florida Supreme Court Approved Family Law Form 12.903(d).

Where can I look for more information?

Before proceeding, you should read "General Information for Self-Represented Litigants" found at the beginning of these forms. The words that are in **"bold underline"** in these instructions are defined there. For further information, see chapter 61, Florida Statutes.

IMPORTANT INFORMATION REGARDING E-SERVICE ELECTION

After the initial service of process of the petition or supplemental petition by the Sheriff or certified process server, the Florida Rules of Judicial Administration now require that all documents required or permitted to be served on the other party must be served by electronic mail (e-mail) except in certain circumstances. **You must strictly comply with the format requirements set forth in the Rules of Judicial Administration.**

SELF-REPRESENTED LITIGANTS MAY SERVE DOCUMENTS BY E-MAIL; HOWEVER, THEY ARE NOT REQUIRED TO DO SO. If a self-represented litigant elects to serve and receive documents by e-mail, the procedures must always be followed once the initial election is made.

To serve and receive documents by e-mail, you must designate your e-mail addresses by using the **Designation of Current Mailing and E-mail Address**, Florida Supreme Court Approved Family Law Form 12.915, and you must provide your e-mail address on each form on which your signature appears. Please **CAREFULLY** read the rules and instructions for: **Certificate of Service (General),** Florida Supreme Court Approved Family Law Form 12.914; **Designation of Current Mailing and E-mail Address**, Florida Supreme Court Approved Family Law Form 12.915; and Florida Rule of Judicial Administration 2.516.

Special notes . . .

If you do not have the money to pay the filing fee, you may obtain an Application for Determination of Civil Indigent Status from the clerk, fill it out, and the clerk will determine whether you are eligible to have filing fees deferred.

With this form, you must also file the following:

- **Uniform Child Custody Jurisdiction and Enforcement Act (UCCJEA) Affidavit,** Florida Supreme Court Approved Family Law Form 12.902(d).
- **Child Support Guidelines Worksheet**, Florida Family Law Rules of Procedure Form 12.902(e) if you are seeking to modify child support. (If you do not know the other party's income, you may file this worksheet after his or her financial affidavit has been served on you.)
- **Parenting Plan**, Florida Supreme Court Approved Family Law Form, 12.995(a) or 12.995(b). If the parties have reached an agreement, the Parenting Plan should be signed by both parties. If you have not reached an agreement, a proposed Parenting Plan may be filed. **Notice of Social Security Number**, Florida Supreme Court Approved Family Law Form 12.902(j), if not previously filed.
- **Family Law Financial Affidavit**, Florida Family Law Rules of Procedure Form 12.902(b) or (c). **Certificate of Compliance with Mandatory Disclosure,** Florida Family Law Rules of Procedure Form 12.932 if you are seeking to modify child support. (This must be filed within 45 days of **service** of the supplemental petition on the respondent, if not filed at the time of the supplemental petition, unless you and the other party have agreed not to exchange these documents.)

Parenting Plan and Time-Sharing . . . If you and the respondent are unable to agree on parenting arrangements and a time-sharing schedule, a judge will decide for you as part of establishing a Parenting Plan. The judge will decide the parenting arrangements and time-sharing schedule based on the child(ren)'s best interests. Regardless of whether there is an agreement, the court reserves jurisdiction to modify issues relating to the minor child(ren).

The judge may request a **parenting plan recommendation** or appoint a **guardian ad litem** in your case. This means that a neutral person will review your situation and report to the judge concerning parenting issues. The purpose of such intervention is to be sure that the best interests of the child(ren) is (are) being served. For more information, you may consult section 61.13, Florida Statutes.

A **parenting course** may be required prior to entry of a final judgment. You should contact the clerk, family law intake staff, or judicial assistant about requirements for parenting courses or mediation where you live.

Listed below are some terms with which you should become familiar before completing your supplemental petition. **If you do not fully understand any of the terms below or their implications, you should speak with an attorney before going any further.**

- **Shared Parental Responsibility**
- **Sole Parental Responsibility**
- **Supervised Time–Sharing**
- **No contact**
- **Parenting Plan**
- **Parenting Plan Recommendation**
- **Time–Sharing Schedule**

Child Support . . . The court may order one parent to pay **child support** to assist the other parent in meeting the child(ren)'s material needs. **Both parents are required to provide financial support**, but one parent may be ordered to pay a portion of his or her support for the child(ren) to the other parent. Florida has adopted guidelines for determining the amount of child support to be paid. These guidelines are based on the combined income of **both** parents and take into account the financial contributions of both parents and the number of overnights the child(ren) spend with each parent. You must file a **Family Law Financial Affidavit**, Florida Family Law Rules of Procedure Form 12.902(b) or (c), and the other parent will be required to do the same. From your financial affidavits, you should be able to calculate the amount of child support that should be paid using the **Child Support Guidelines Worksheet**, Florida Family Law Rules of Procedure Form 12.902(e). Because the child support guidelines take several factors into consideration, change over time, and vary from state to state, your child support obligation may be more or less than that of other people in seemingly similar situations.

Temporary Relief . . . If you need temporary relief regarding parental responsibility and time-sharing with child(ren), or temporary child support, you may file a **Motion for Temporary Support and Time–Sharing with Dependent or Minor Child(ren)**, Florida Supreme Court Approved Family Law Form 12.947(a). For more information, see the instructions for that form.

Settlement Agreement . . . If you and the respondent are able to reach an agreement on any or all of the issues, you should file a Settlement Agreement. Although there is no form for this in these Florida Family Law Forms, you may construct a settlement agreement using the pertinent sections contained in **Marital Settlement Agreement for Dissolution of Marriage with Dependent or Minor Child(ren)**, Florida Supreme Court Approved Family Law Form 12.902(f)(1). Both parties must sign this agreement before a **notary public**. Any issues on which you are unable to agree will be considered **contested** and settled by the judge at the final hearing.

Final Judgment Form . . . These family law forms contain a **Supplemental Final Judgment Modifying Parental Responsibility, Visitation, or Parenting Plan/Time–Sharing Schedule And Other Relief**, Florida Supreme Court Approved Family Law Form 12.993(a), which the judge may use. You should check with the clerk, family law intake staff, or judicial assistant to see if you need to bring it with you to the hearing. If so, you should type or print the heading, including the circuit, county, case number, division, and the parties' names, and leave the rest blank for the judge to complete at your hearing or trial.

Nonlawyer ... Remember, a person who is NOT an attorney is called a nonlawyer. If a nonlawyer helps you fill out these forms, that person must give you a copy of a **Disclosure from Nonlawyer**, Florida Family Law Rules of Procedure Form 12.900(a), before he or she helps you. A nonlawyer helping you fill out these forms also **must** put his or her name, address, and telephone number on the bottom of the last page of every form he or she helps you complete.

Added Sept. 21, 2000 (810 So.2d 1). Amended Dec. 19, 2002 (836 So.2d 1019); June 30, 2005, effective July 1, 2005 (910 So.2d 194); April 24, 2008 (981 So.2d 1198); March 26, 2009 (20 So.3d 173); Dec. 16, 2010 (59 So.3d 792); March 26, 2015, effective March 26, 2015 (2015 WL 1343088).

Form 12.905(b). Supplemental Petition for Modification of Child Support

IN THE CIRCUIT COURT OF THE ______________ JUDICIAL CIRCUIT,
IN AND FOR ______________ COUNTY, FLORIDA

Case No.: ______________
Division: ______________

______________,
Petitioner,

and

______________,
Respondent.

SUPPLEMENTAL PETITION FOR MODIFICATION OF CHILD SUPPORT

I, *{full legal name}* ______________, being sworn, certify that the following information is true:

1. The parties to this action were granted a final judgment _____ of dissolution of marriage _____ of paternity _____ for support unconnected with a dissolution of marriage _____ Other *[describe]* ______________ on *{date}* ______________.
A copy of the final judgment and any modification(s) is attached.

2. Paragraph(s) ______________ of the _____ final judgment or _____ most recent modification thereof establishes the present child support at $______________ every _____ week _____ other week _____ month, beginning on *{date}* ______________.

3. Since the final judgment or most recent modification thereof, there has been a substantial change in circumstances, requiring a modification in child support. This change in circumstance is as follows: *{explain}* ______________
____
____
____
____
____
____
____
______________.

4. I ask the Court to modify child support as follows: *{explain}* ______________
____
____
____
____
____
____

Florida Supreme Court Approved Family Law Form 12.905(b), Supplemental Petition for Modification of Child Support (03/15)

____.

5. This change is in the best interests of the child(ren) because: *{explain}* ______________
____
____
____
____
____
____.

6. A completed Family Law Financial Affidavit, Florida Family Law Rules of Procedure Form 12.902(b) or (c), is _____, or _____will be, filed.

7. If not previously filed in this case, a completed Notice of Social Security Number, Florida Supreme Court Approved Family Law Form 12.902(j), is filed.

8. A Child Support Guidelines Worksheet, Florida Family Law Rules of Procedure Form 12.902(e), _____ is, or _____ will be, filed.

9. Other:____
____.

I understand that I am swearing or affirming under oath to the truthfulness of the claims made in this petition and that the punishment for knowingly making a false statement includes fines and/or imprisonment.

Dated: ____________________

____
Signature of Petitioner
Printed Name: ____________________
Address: ____________________
City, State, Zip: ____________________
Telephone Number: ____________________
Fax Number: ____________________
Designated E-mail Address(es):____________________
____

STATE OF FLORIDA
COUNTY OF ____________________

Sworn to or affirmed and signed before me on ________ by__________________________________.

____
NOTARY PUBLIC or DEPUTY CLERK

____
[Print, type, or stamp commissioned name of notary or deputy clerk.]

_____ Personally known
_____ Produced identification
Type of identification produced ____________________

Florida Supreme Court Approved Family Law Form 12.905(b), Supplemental Petition for Modification of Child Support (03/15)

IF A NONLAWYER HELPED YOU FILL OUT THIS FORM, HE/SHE MUST FILL IN THE BLANKS BELOW:
[fill in all blanks] This form was prepared for the Petitioner.
This form was completed with the assistance of:
{name of individual} ____,
{name of business} ____,
{address} ____,
{city} __________,*{state}* _______,*{zip code}*__________, *{telephone number}* __________.

INSTRUCTIONS FOR FLORIDA SUPREME COURT APPROVED FAMILY LAW FORM 12.905(b) SUPPLEMENTAL PETITION FOR MODIFICATION OF CHILD SUPPORT (03/15)

When should this form be used?

This form should be used when you are asking the court to change a current court-ordered **child support** obligation. The court can change a child support **order** or **judgment** if the judge finds that there has been a **substantial change in the circumstances** of the parties and the change is in the **child(ren)'s best interests**.

This form should be typed or printed in black ink. After completing this form, you should sign the form before a **notary public** or **deputy clerk**. You should **file** this form in the county where the original order was entered. If the order was entered in another state, or if the child(ren) live(s) in another state, you should speak with an **attorney** about where to file this form. You should file the original with the **clerk of the circuit court** and keep a copy for your records.

IMPORTANT INFORMATION REGARDING E–FILING

The Florida Rules of Judicial Administration now require that all petitions, pleadings, and documents be filed electronically except in certain circumstances. **Self-represented litigants may file petitions or other pleadings or documents electronically; however, they are not required to do so.** If you choose to file your pleadings or other documents electronically, you must do so in accordance with Florida Rule of Judicial Administration 2.525, and you must follow the procedures of the judicial circuit in which you file. **The rules and procedures should be carefully read and followed.**

What should I do next?

For your case to proceed, you must properly notify the other party in your case of the **supplemental petition**. If you know where he or she lives, you should use **personal service.** If you absolutely do not know where he or she lives, you may use **constructive service**. You may also be able to use constructive service if the other party resides in another state or country. However, if constructive service is used, other than granting a divorce, the court may only grant limited relief. For more information on constructive service, see **Notice of Action for Family Cases with Minor Child(ren)**, Florida Supreme Court Approved Family Law Form 12.913(a)(2), and **Affidavit of Diligent Search and Inquiry**, Florida Family Law Rules of Procedure Form 12.913(b). If the other party is in the military service of the United States, additional steps for service may be required. See, for example, **Memorandum for Certificate of Military Service**, Florida Supreme Court Approved Family Law Form 12.912(a). In sum, the law regarding constructive service and service on an individual in the military service is very complex and you may wish to consult an attorney regarding these issues.

If personal service is used, the other party has 20 days to **answer** after being served with your supplemental petition. Your case will then generally proceed in one of the following three ways:

DEFAULT . . . If after 20 days, no answer has been filed, you may file a **Motion for Default**, Florida Supreme Court Approved Family Law Form 12.922(a), with the clerk of court. Then, if you have filed all of the required papers, you may call the clerk, **family law intake staff**, or **judicial assistant** to set a **final hearing**. You must notify the other party of the hearing by using a **Notice of Hearing (General)**, Florida Supreme Court Approved Family Law Form 12.923, or other appropriate notice of hearing form.

UNCONTESTED . . . If the **respondent** files an answer that agrees with everything in your supplemental petition or an answer and waiver, **and** you have complied with **mandatory disclosure** and filed all of the required papers, you may call the clerk, family law intake staff, or judicial assistant to set a final hearing. You must notify the other party of the hearing by using a **Notice of Hearing (General)**, Florida Supreme Court Approved Family Law Form 12.923, or other appropriate notice of hearing form.

CONTESTED . . . If the respondent files an answer or an answer and **counterpetition**, which disagrees with or denies anything in your supplemental petition, **and** you are unable to settle the disputed issues, you should file a **Notice for Trial**, Florida Supreme Court Approved Family Law Form 12.924, after you have complied with mandatory disclosure and filed all of the required papers. Some circuits may require the completion of **mediation** before a final hearing may be set. Then you should contact the clerk, family law intake staff, or judicial assistant for instructions on how to set your case for **trial** (final hearing). If the respondent files an answer and counterpetition, you should answer the counterpetition within 20 days using an **Answer to Counterpetition**, Florida Supreme Court Approved Family Law Form 12.903(d).

Where can I look for more information?

Before proceeding, you should read "General Information for Self–Represented Litigants" found at the beginning of these forms. The words that are in "**bold underline**" in these instructions are defined there. For further information, see chapter 61, Florida Statutes.

IMPORTANT INFORMATION REGARDING E–SERVICE ELECTION

After the initial service of process of the petition or supplemental petition by the Sheriff or certified process server, the Florida Rules of Judicial Administration now require that all documents required or permitted to be served on the other party must be served by electronic mail (e-mail) except in certain circumstances. **You must strictly comply with the format requirements set forth in the Rules of Judicial Administration.**

SELF–REPRESENTED LITIGANTS MAY SERVE DOCUMENTS BY E–MAIL; HOWEVER, THEY ARE NOT REQUIRED TO DO SO. If a self-represented litigant elects to serve and receive documents by e-mail, the procedures must always be followed once the initial election is made.

To serve and receive documents by e-mail, you must designate your e-mail addresses by using the **Designation of Current Mailing and E-mail Address**, Florida Supreme Court Approved Family Law Form 12.915, and you must provide your e-mail address on each form on which your signature appears. Please **CAREFULLY** read the rules and instructions for: **Certificate of Service (General),** Florida Supreme Court Approved Family Law Form 12.914; **Designation of Current Mailing and E-mail Address**, Florida Supreme Court Approved Family Law Form 12.915; and Florida Rule of Judicial Administration 2.516.

Special notes . . .

If you do not have the money to pay the filing fee, you may obtain an Application for Determination of Civil Indigent Status from the clerk, fill it out, and the clerk will determine whether you are eligible to have filing fees deferred.

With this form, you must also file the following:

- **Child Support Guidelines Worksheet**, Florida Family Law Rules of Procedure Form 12.902(e). (If you do not know the other party's income, you may file this worksheet after his or her financial affidavit has been served on you.)
- **Settlement Agreement**, if you have reached an agreement on any or all of the issues. Although there is no form for this in these Florida Family Law Forms, you may construct a settlement agreement using the pertinent sections contained in **Marital Settlement Agreement for Dissolution of Marriage with Dependent or Minor Child(ren)**, Florida Supreme Court Approved Family Law Form 12.902(f)(1).
- **Notice of Social Security Number**, Florida Supreme Court Approved Family Law Form 12.902(j), if not previously filed.
- **Family Law Financial Affidavit**, Florida Family Law Rules of Procedure Form 12.902(b) or (c). **Certificate of Compliance with Mandatory Disclosure**, Florida Family Law Rules of Procedure Form 12.932. (This must be filed within 45 days of **service** of the supplemental petition on the respondent, if not filed at the time of the supplemental petition, unless you and the other party have agreed not to exchange these documents.)

Child Support . . . The court may order one parent to pay **child support** to assist the other parent in meeting the child(ren)'s material needs. **Both parents are required to provide financial support**, but one parent may be ordered to pay a portion of his or her support for the child(ren) to the other parent. Florida has adopted guidelines for determining the amount of child support to be paid. These guidelines are based on the combined income of **both** parents and take into account the financial contributions of both parents. You must file a **Family Law Financial Affidavit**, Florida Family Law Rules of Procedure Form 12.902(b) or (c), and the other parent will be required to do the same. From your financial affidavits, you should be able to calculate the amount of child support that should be paid using the **Child Support Guidelines Worksheet**, Florida Family Law Rules of Procedure Form 12.902(e). Because the child support guidelines take several factors into consideration, change over time, and vary from state to state, your child support obligation may be more or less than that of other people in seemingly similar situations.

Temporary Relief . . . If you need temporary relief regarding child support, you may file a **Motion for Temporary Support and Time–Sharing with Dependent or Minor Child(ren)**, Florida Supreme Court Approved Family Law Form 12.947(a). For more information, see the instructions for that form.

Settlement Agreement . . . If you and the respondent are able to reach an agreement on any or all of the issues, you should file a Settlement Agreement. Although there is no form for this in these Florida Family Law Forms, you may construct a settlement agreement using the pertinent sections contained in

Marital Settlement Agreement for Dissolution of Marriage with Dependent or Minor Child(ren), Florida Supreme Court Approved Family Law Form 12.902(f)(1). Both parties must sign this agreement before a **notary public** or **deputy clerk.** Any issues on which you are unable to agree will be considered **contested** and settled by the judge at the final hearing.

Final Judgment Form . . . These family law forms contain a **Supplemental Final Judgment Modifying Child Support**, Florida Supreme Court Approved Family Law Form 12.993(b), which the judge may use. You should check with the clerk, family law intake staff, or judicial assistant to see if you need to bring it with you to the hearing. If so, you should type or print the heading, including the circuit, county, case number, division, and the parties' names, and leave the rest blank for the judge to complete at your hearing or trial.

Nonlawyer . . . Remember, a person who is NOT an attorney is called a nonlawyer. If a nonlawyer helps you fill out these forms, that person must give you a copy of a **Disclosure from Nonlawyer**, Florida Family Law Rules of Procedure Form 12.900(a), before he or she helps you. A nonlawyer helping you fill out these forms also **must** put his or her name, address, and telephone number on the bottom of the last page of every form he or she helps you complete.

Added Sept. 21, 2000 (810 So.2d 1). Amended June 30, 2005, effective July 1, 2005 (910 So.2d 194); March 26, 2009 (20 So.3d 173); Dec. 16, 2010 (59 So.3d 792); March 26, 2015, effective March 26, 2015 (2015 WL 1343088).

Form 12.905(c). Supplemental Petition for Modification of Alimony

IN THE CIRCUIT COURT OF THE ______________________ JUDICIAL CIRCUIT,
IN AND FOR ______________________ COUNTY, FLORIDA

Case No.: ______________________
Division: ______________________

______________________,
Petitioner,

______________________,
Respondent.

SUPPLEMENTAL PETITION FOR MODIFICATION OF ALIMONY

I, *{full legal name}* ______________________, being sworn, certify that the following information is true:

1. The parties to this action were granted a final judgment ( ) of dissolution of marriage ( ) for support unconnected with a dissolution of marriage on *{date}* ______________________. A copy of the final judgment and any modification(s) is attached.

2. Paragraph(s) ____________ of the _____ final judgment or _____ most recent modification thereof establishes the present alimony at $ ____________ every _____ week _____ other week _____ month, beginning on *{date}* ______________________.

3. Since the final judgment or most recent modification thereof, there has been a substantial change in circumstances, requiring a modification in alimony. This change in circumstance is as follows: *{explain}* ______________________
____
____
____
____
____
____
____
____
____
____
____
____
____.

4. I ask the Court to modify alimony as follows: *{explain}* ______________________
____
____
____

Florida Supreme Court Approved Family Law Form 12.905(c), Supplemental Petition for Modification of Alimony (03/15)

____
____
____
____
____.

5. A completed Family Law Financial Affidavit, Florida Family Law Rules of Procedure Form 12.902(b) or (c), is ______ , or ______will be, filed.

6. Other: ____
____
____

I understand that I am swearing or affirming under oath to the truthfulness of the claims made in this petition and that the punishment for knowingly making a false statement includes fines and/or imprisonment.

Dated: ______________________ ______________________________________
Signature of PETITIONER
Printed Name: ______________________________
Address: ___________________________________
City, State, Zip: ____________________________
Telephone Number: __________________________
Fax Number: _______________________________
Designated E-mail Address(es): _______________
____

STATE OF FLORIDA
COUNTY OF ____________________

Sworn to or affirmed and signed before me on ____________ by________________________________.

____
NOTARY PUBLIC or DEPUTY CLERK

____
[Print, type, or stamp commissioned name of notary or deputy clerk.]
____ Personally known
____ Produced identification
Type of identification produced ______________________________

IF A NONLAWYER HELPED YOU FILL OUT THIS FORM, HE/SHE MUST FILL IN THE BLANKS BELOW:

Florida Supreme Court Approved Family Law Form 12.905(c), Supplemental Petition for Modification of Alimony (03/15)

[fill in all blanks] This form was prepared for the: *{choose only **one**}* ( ) Petitioner ( ) Respondent
This form was completed with the assistance of:
{name of individual} ____,
{name of business} ____,
{address} ____,
{city} ____________,*{state}* ______, *{zip code}* ________, *{telephone number}* ________.

INSTRUCTIONS FOR FLORIDA SUPREME COURT APPROVED FAMILY LAW FORM 12.905(c), SUPPLEMENTAL PETITION FOR MODIFICATION OF ALIMONY (03/15)

When should this form be used?

This form should be used when you are asking the court to change a current court-ordered **alimony** obligation. The court can change an order for temporary, permanent periodic, durational, and rehabilitative alimony if the judge finds that there has been a **substantial change in the circumstances** of the parties. Lump sum and bridge-the-gap alimony cannot be modified.

This form should be typed or printed in black ink. After completing this form, you should sign the form before a **notary public** or **deputy clerk**. You should **file** this form in the county where the original order was entered. If the order was entered in another state, or if the respondent lives in another state, you should speak with an **attorney** about where to file this form. You should file the original with the **clerk of the circuit court** and keep a copy for your records. Because you are filing the **petition** in this proceeding, you are also referred to as the **petitioner** and your **spouse** as the **respondent.**

IMPORTANT INFORMATION REGARDING E-FILING

The Florida Rules of Judicial Administration now require that all petitions, pleadings, and documents be filed electronically except in certain circumstances. **Self-represented litigants may file petitions or other pleadings or documents electronically; however, they are not required to do so.** If you choose to file your pleadings or other documents electronically, you must do so in accordance with Florida Rule of Judicial Administration 2.525, and you must follow the procedures of the judicial circuit in which you file. **The rules and procedures should be carefully read and followed.**

What should I do next?

For your case to proceed, you must properly notify the other party in your case of the **supplemental petition**. Because this petition concerns alimony, you should use **personal service**. If the other party is in the military service of the United States, additional steps for service may be required. See, for example, **Memorandum for Certificate of Military Service**, Florida Supreme Court Approved Family Law Form 12.912(a) and **Affidavit of Military Service**, Florida Supreme Court Approved Family Law Form 12.912(b). In sum, the law regarding constructive service and service on an individual in the military service is very complex and you may wish to consult an attorney regarding this issue.

If personal service is used, the other party has 20 days to **answer** after being served with your supplemental petition. Your case will then generally proceed in one of the following three ways:

DEFAULT . . . If after 20 days, no answer has been filed, you may file a **Motion for Default**, Florida Supreme Court Approved Family Law Form 12.922(a), with the clerk of court. Then, if you have filed all of the required papers, you may call the clerk, **family law intake staff**, or **judicial assistant** to set a **final hearing**. You must notify the other party of the hearing by using a **Notice of Hearing (General)**, Florida Supreme Court Approved Family Law Form 12.923, or other appropriate notice of hearing form.

UNCONTESTED . . . If the **respondent** files an answer that agrees with everything in your supplemental petition or an answer and waiver, **and** you have complied with **mandatory disclosure** and filed all of the required papers, you may call the clerk, family law intake staff, or judicial assistant to set a final hearing. You must notify the other party of the hearing by using a **Notice of Hearing (General)**, Florida Supreme Court Approved Family Law Form 12.923, or other appropriate notice of hearing form.

CONTESTED . . . If the **respondent** files an answer or an answer and **counterpetition**, which disagrees with or denies anything in your supplemental petition, **and** you are unable to settle the disputed issues, you should file a **Notice for Trial**, Florida Supreme Court Approved Family Law Form 12.924, after you have complied with mandatory disclosure and filed all of the required papers. Some circuits may require the completion of **mediation** before a final hearing may be set. Then you should contact the clerk, family law intake staff, or judicial assistant for instructions on how to set your case for **trial** (final hearing). If the respondent files an answer and counterpetition, you should answer the counterpetition within 20 days using an **Answer to Counterpetition**, Florida Supreme Court Approved Family Law Form 12.903(d).

Where can I look for more information?

Before proceeding, you should read General Information for Self–Represented Litigants found at the beginning of these forms. The words that are in **bold underline** in these instructions are defined there. For further information, see chapter 61, Florida Statutes.

IMPORTANT INFORMATION REGARDING E–SERVICE ELECTION

After the initial service of process of the petition or supplemental petition by the Sheriff or certified process server, the Florida Rules of Judicial Administration now require that all documents required or permitted to be served on the other party must be served by electronic mail (e-mail) except in certain circumstances. **You must strictly comply with the format requirements set forth in the Rules of Judicial Administration.**

SELF–REPRESENTED LITIGANTS MAY SERVE DOCUMENTS BY E–MAIL; HOWEVER, THEY ARE NOT REQUIRED TO DO SO. If a self-represented litigant elects to serve and receive documents by e-mail, the procedures must always be followed once the initial election is made.

To serve and receive documents by e-mail, you must designate your e-mail addresses by using the **Designation of Current Mailing and E-mail Address**, Florida Supreme Court Approved Family Law Form 12.915, and you must provide your e-mail address on each form on which your signature appears. Please **CAREFULLY** read the rules and instructions for: **Certificate of Service (General),** Florida Supreme Court Approved Family Law Form 12.914; **Designation of Current Mailing and E-mail Address**, Florida Supreme Court Approved Family Law Form 12.915; and Florida Rule of Judicial Administration 2.516.

Special notes . . .

If you do not have the money to pay the filing fee, you may obtain an Application for Determination of Civil Indigent Status from the clerk, fill it out, and the clerk will determine whether you are eligible to have filing fees deferred.

With this form you must also file the following and serve a copy on the other party:

- **Settlement Agreement**, if you have reached an agreement on any or all of the issues. Although there is no form for this in these Florida Family Law Forms, you may construct a settlement agreement using the pertinent sections contained in **Marital Settlement Agreement for Dissolution of Marriage with Dependent or Minor Child(ren)**, Florida Supreme Court Approved Family Law Form 12.902(f)(1), or Marital **Settlement Agreement for Dissolution of Marriage with No Dependent or Minor Child(ren)**, Florida Supreme Court Approved Family Law Form 12.902(f)(2).

- **Family Law Financial Affidavit**, Florida Family Law Rules of Procedure Form 12.902(b) or (c).

- **Certificate of Compliance with Mandatory Disclosure,** Florida Family Law Rules of Procedure Form 12.932. (This must be filed within 45 days of service of the supplemental petition on the other party, if not filed at the time of the supplemental petition, unless you and the other party have agreed not to exchange these documents.)

Alimony . . . In order to modify an order for alimony, a **judge** must find that there has been a substantial change in circumstances.

Temporary Relief . . . If you need temporary relief regarding modification of alimony, you may file a **Motion for Temporary Support with Dependent or Minor Child(ren)**, Florida Supreme Court Approved Family Law Form 12.947(a), or **Motion for Temporary Support with No Dependent or Minor Child(ren)**, Florida Supreme Court Approved Family Law Form 12.947(d), whichever is appropriate. For more information, see the instructions for those forms.

Settlement Agreement . . . If you and the respondent are able to reach an agreement on any or all of the issues, you should file a Settlement Agreement. Although there is no form for this in these Florida Family Law Forms, you may construct a settlement agreement using the pertinent sections contained in **Marital Settlement Agreement for Dissolution of Marriage**

with Dependent or Minor Child(ren), Florida Supreme Court Approved Family Law Form 12.902(f)(1), or **Marital Settlement Agreement for Dissolution of Marriage with No Dependent or Minor Child(ren)**, Florida Supreme Court Approved Family Law Form 12.902(f)(2). Both parties must sign this agreement before a notary public. Any issues on which you are unable to agree will be considered contested and settled by the judge at the final hearing.

Final Judgment Form . . . These family law forms contain a **Supplemental Final Judgment Modifying Alimony**, Florida Supreme Court Approved Family Law Form 12.993(c), which the judge may use. You should check with the clerk, family law intake staff, or judicial assistant to see if you need to bring it with you to the hearing. If so, you should type or print the heading, including the circuit, county, case number, division, and the parties' names, and leave the rest blank for the judge to complete at your hearing or trial.

Nonlawyer . . . Remember, a person who is NOT an attorney is called a nonlawyer. If a nonlawyer helps you fill out these forms, that person must give you a copy of a **Disclosure from Nonlawyer**, Florida Family Law Rules of Procedure Form 12.900(a), before he or she helps you. A nonlawyer helping you fill out these forms also **must** put his or her name, address, and telephone number on the bottom of the last page of every form he or she helps you complete.

Added Sept. 21, 2000 (810 So.2d 1). Amended June 30, 2005, effective July 1, 2005 (910 So.2d 194); May 24, 2012 (96 So.3d 217); March 26, 2015, effective March 26, 2015 (2015 WL 1343088).

Form 12.905(d). Supplemental Petition for Temporary Modification of Parenting Issues for Child(ren) of Parent Activated, Deployed, or Temporarily Assigned to Military Service

IN THE CIRCUIT COURT OF THE ______________ JUDICIAL CIRCUIT,
IN AND FOR ____________________________ COUNTY, FLORIDA

Case No: ______________________
Division: ______________________

_______________________________,
Petitioner,
And

_______________________________,
Respondent.

SUPPLEMENTAL PETITION FOR TEMPORARY MODIFICATION OF PARENTING ISSUES FOR CHILD(REN) OF PARENT ACTIVATED, DEPLOYED, OR TEMPORARILY ASSIGNED TO MILITARY SERVICE

I, *{full legal name}* ____________________________________, being sworn, certify that the following information is true:

1. The parties to the action, *{names}* ______________________________, were granted a final judgment of *[Choose **one** only]* _____ dissolution of marriage _____ paternity on *{date}* ____________, _____ other *{describe}*____.

A copy/copies of the final judgment or any modification(s) is/are attached.

2. Paragraph(s) ______ of the *[Choose **one** only]* _____ final judgment or _____ most recent modification of it grants custody, primary care, or time-sharing of the minor child(ren), *{name(s)}* ________________________, with *{name of parent}* ____________________________________.

3. The parent, *{name}* ____, is: *[Choose **all** that apply]*

_____ activated
_____ deployed
_____ temporarily assigned to military service.

4. The parent, *{name}* ___________________________, is temporarily unable to continue the current parenting plan and time-sharing schedule with the minor child(ren) during the period of time that the parent is *[Choose **all** that apply]*

_____ activated
_____ deployed
_____ temporarily assigned to military service.

5. I ask the court to temporarily modify/amend the parental responsibility and time-sharing schedule of the minor child(ren) during the period of time that the parent, *{name}* ____________________, is

Florida Supreme Court Approved Family Law Form 12.905(d), Supplemental Petition for Temporary Modification of Parenting Issues for Child(ren) of Parent Activated, Deployed, or Temporarily Assigned to Military Service (03/15)

*[Choose **all** that apply]*
_____ activated
_____ deployed
_____ temporarily assigned to military service as follows:
*{explain}*____
____
____
____.

6. This temporary modification/amendment is in the best interests of the child(ren).

7. I ask that the court adopt _____ the attached temporary Parenting Plan _____ time-sharing schedule set forth below during the time that the parent is *[Choose **all** that apply]*
_____ activated
_____deployed
_____ temporarily assigned to military service:
____
____
____.

8. If the requested modification/amendment is granted, Petitioner requests that child support be temporarily modified/amended, consistent with the temporary modification/amendment of the Parenting Plan and time-sharing schedule. A Child Support Guidelines Worksheet, Florida Family Law Rules of Procedure Form 12.902(e) is, or will be, filed if a modification of child support is requested.

9. A completed Family Law Financial Affidavit, Florida Family Law Rules of Procedure Form 12.902(b) or (c) is filed with this Petition.

10. A completed Uniform Child Custody Jurisdiction and Enforcement Act (UCCJEA) Affidavit, Florida Supreme Court Approved Family Law Form 12.902(d), is filed with this petition.

11. Other: ____
____
____
____
____

I understand that I am swearing or affirming under oath to the truthfulness of the claims made in this petition and that the punishment for knowingly making a false statement includes fines and/or imprisonment.

Dated:_______________________ _______________________
Signature of PETITIONER

Florida Supreme Court Approved Family Law Form 12.905(d), Supplemental Petition for Temporary Modification of Parenting Issues for Child(ren) of Parent Activated, Deployed, or Temporarily Assigned to Military Service (03/15)

Printed Name:____________________
Address:____________________
City, State, Zip:____________________
Telephone Number:____________________
Fax Number:____________________
Designated E-mail Address(es):____________________
____

STATE OF FLORIDA
COUNTY OF ____________________

Sworn to or affirmed and signed before me on ____________ by ____________________________.

____
NOTARY PUBLIC or DEPUTY CLERK

____
[Print, type, or stamp commissioned name of notary or deputy clerk.]

____ Personally known
____ Produced identification
____ Type of identification produced ____________________________

IF A NONLAWYER HELPED YOU FILL OUT THIS FORM, HE/SHE MUST FILL IN THE BLANKS BELOW:
[fill in all blanks] This form was prepared for the Petitioner.
This form was completed with the assistance of:
{name of individual} ____,
*{name of business}*____,
{address} ____,
{city} ________,*{state}* ________, *{zip code}*________, *{telephone number}* __________.

Florida Supreme Court Approved Family Law Form 12.905(d), Supplemental Petition for Temporary Modification of Parenting Issues for Child(ren) of Parent Activated, Deployed, or Temporarily Assigned to Military Service (03/15)

INSTRUCTIONS FOR FLORIDA SUPREME COURT APPROVED FAMILY LAW FORM 12.905(d) SUPPLEMENTAL PETITION FOR TEMPORARY MODIFICATION OF PARENTING ISSUES FOR CHILD(REN) OF PARENT ACTIVATED, DEPLOYED, OR TEMPORARILY ASSIGNED TO MILITARY SERVICE (03/15)

When should this form be used?

This form should be used when a parent seeks a temporary modification of an order establishing custody, visitation, a parenting plan, or time-sharing schedule because the parent is activated, deployed, or temporarily assigned to military service and the parent's ability to comply with the prior order (s) and time-sharing schedule is materially affected.

This form should be typed or printed in black ink. After completing this form, you should sign the form before a **notary public** or **deputy clerk**. You should file the original with the **clerk of the circuit court** in the county where you live and keep a copy for your records. This form and these instructions do not apply to modification of temporary orders.

IMPORTANT INFORMATION REGARDING E-FILING

The Florida Rules of Judicial Administration now require that all petitions, pleadings, and documents be filed electronically except in certain circumstances. **Self-represented litigants may file petitions or other pleadings or documents electronically; however, they are not required to do so.** If you choose to file your pleadings or other documents electronically, you must do so in accordance with Florida Rule of Judicial Administration 2.525, and you must follow the procedures of the judicial circuit in which you file. **The rules and procedures should be carefully read and followed.**

What should I do next?

For your case to proceed, you must properly notify the other party in your case of the **supplemental petition**. If you know where he or she lives, you should use **personal service.** If you absolutely do not know where he or she lives, you may use **constructive service**. You may also be able to use constructive service if the other party resides in another state or country. However, if constructive service is used, other than granting dissolution of marriage, the court may only grant limited relief. For more information on constructive service, see **Notice of Action for Family Cases with Minor Child(ren)**, Florida Supreme Court Approved Family Law Form 12.913(a)(2), and **Affidavit of Diligent Search and Inquiry**, Florida Family Law Rules of Procedure Form 12.913(b). If the other party is in the military service of the United States, additional steps for service may be required. See, for example, **Memorandum for Certificate of Military Service**, Florida Supreme Court Approved Family Law Form 12.912(a). In sum, the law regarding constructive service and service on an individual in the military service is very complex and you may wish to consult an attorney regarding these issues.

If personal service is used, the other party has 20 days to **answer** after being served with your supplemental petition. Your case will then generally proceed in one of the following three ways:

DEFAULT . . . If after 20 days, no answer has been filed, you may file a **Motion for Default**, Florida Supreme Court Approved Family Law Form 12.922(a), with the clerk of court. Then, if you have filed all of the required papers, you may call the clerk, **family law intake staff**, or **judicial assistant** to set a **final hearing**. You must notify the other party of the hearing by using a **Notice of Hearing (General)**, Florida Supreme Court Approved Family Law Form 12.923, or other appropriate notice of hearing form.

UNCONTESTED . . . If the **respondent** files an answer that agrees with everything in your supplemental petition or an answer and waiver, **and** you have complied with **mandatory disclosure** and filed all of the required papers, you may call the clerk, family law intake staff, or judicial assistant to set a final hearing. You must notify the other party of the hearing by using a **Notice of Hearing (General)**, Florida Supreme Court Approved Family Law Form 12.923, or other appropriate notice of hearing form.

CONTESTED . . . If the respondent files an answer or an answer and **counterpetition**, which disagrees with or denies anything in your supplemental petition, **and** you are unable to settle the disputed issues, you should file a **Notice for Trial**, Florida Supreme Court Approved Family Law Form 12.924, after you have complied with mandatory disclosure and filed all of the required papers. Some circuits may require the completion of **mediation** before a final hearing may be set. Then you should contact the clerk, family law intake staff, or judicial assistant for instructions on how to set your case for **trial** (final hearing). If the respondent files an answer and counterpetition, you should answer the counterpetition within 20 days using an **Answer to Counterpetition**, Florida Supreme Court Approved Family Law Form 12.903(d).

Where can I look for more information?

Before proceeding, you should read General Information for Self-Represented Litigants found at the beginning of these forms. The words that are in **"bold underline"** in these instructions are defined there. For further information, see section 61.13002, Florida Statutes.

IMPORTANT INFORMATION REGARDING E-SERVICE ELECTION

After the initial service of process of the petition or supplemental petition by the Sheriff or certified process server, the Florida Rules of Judicial Administration now require that all documents required or permitted to be served on the other party must be served by electronic mail (e-mail) except in certain circumstances. **You must strictly comply with the format requirements set forth in the Rules of Judicial Administration.**

SELF-REPRESENTED LITIGANTS MAY SERVE DOCUMENTS BY E-MAIL; HOWEVER, THEY ARE NOT REQUIRED TO DO SO. If a self-represented litigant elects to serve and receive documents by e-mail, the procedures must always be followed once the initial election is made.

To serve and receive documents by e-mail, you must designate your e-mail addresses by using the **Designation of Current Mailing and E-mail Address**, Florida Supreme Court Approved Family Law Form 12.915, and you must provide your e-mail address on each form on which your signature appears. Please **CAREFULLY** read the rules and instructions for: **Certificate of Service (General),** Florida Supreme Court Approved Family Law Form 12.914; **Designation of Current Mailing and E-mail Address**, Florida Supreme Court Approved Family Law Form 12.915; and Florida Rule of Judicial Administration 2.516.

Special notes . . .

If you do not have the money to pay the filing fee, you may obtain an Application for Determination of Civil Indigent Status from the clerk, fill it out, and the clerk will determine whether you are eligible to have filing fees deferred.

With this form, you must also file the following:

- **Uniform Child Custody Jurisdiction and Enforcement Act (UCCJEA) Affidavit,** Florida Supreme Court Approved Family Law Form 12.902(d).
- **Child Support Guidelines Worksheet**, Florida Family Law Rules of Procedure Form 12.902(e), if you are seeking modification of the child support obligation. (If you do not know the other party's income, you may file this worksheet after his or her financial affidavit has been served on you.)
- **Settlement Agreement**, if you have reached an agreement on any or all of the issues. Although there is no form for this in these Florida Family Law Forms, you may construct a settlement agreement using the pertinent sections contained in **Marital Settlement Agreement for Dissolution of Marriage with Dependent or Minor Child(ren)**, Florida Supreme Court Approved Family Law Form 12.902(f)(1).
- **Notice of Social Security Number**, Florida Supreme Court Approved Family Law Form 12.902(j), if not previously filed.
- **Family Law Financial Affidavit**, Florida Family Law Rules of Procedure Form 12.902(b) or (c), if you are seeking modification of the child support obligation.
- **Parenting Plan**, Florida Supreme Court Approved Family Law Form, 12.995(a), (b), or (c). If the parties have reached an agreement, a signed and notarized Parenting Plan should be attached. If you have not reached an agreement, a proposed Parenting Plan may be filed.
- **Certificate of Compliance with Mandatory Disclosure**, Florida Family Law Rules of Procedure Form 12.932, if you are seeking modification of the child support obligation.

(This must be filed within 45 days of service of the supplemental petition on the respondent, if not filed at the time of the supplemental petition, unless you and the other party have agreed not to exchange these documents.)

Temporary Judgment Form ... These family law forms contain a **Supplemental Temporary Judgment Modifying Parenting Issues for Children of a Parent Activated, Deployed or Temporarily Assigned to Military Service** Florida Supreme Court Approved Family Law Form 12.993(d)), which the judge may use. You should check with the clerk, family law intake staff, or judicial assistant to see if you need to bring it with you to the hearing. If so, you should type or print the heading, including the circuit, county, case number, division, and the parties' names, and leave the rest blank for the judge to complete at your hearing or trial.

Nonlawyer ... Remember, a person who is NOT an attorney is called a nonlawyer. If a nonlawyer helps you fill out these forms, that person must give you a copy of a **Disclosure from Nonlawyer**, Florida Family Law Rules of Procedure Form 12.900(a), before he or she helps you. A nonlawyer helping you fill out these forms also **must** put his or her name, address, and telephone number on the bottom of the last page of every form he or she helps you complete.

Added July 12, 2007 (962 So.2d 302). Amended March 26, 2009 (20 So.3d 173); Dec. 16, 2010 (59 So.3d 792); Nov. 3, 2011, effective, *nunc pro tunc*, Oct. 1, 2011 (78 So.3d 1045); March 26, 2015, effective March 26, 2015 (2015 WL 1343088).

Form 12.910(a). Summons: Personal Service on an Individual

IN THE CIRCUIT COURT OF THE ____________ JUDICIAL CIRCUIT,
IN AND FOR ____________ COUNTY, FLORIDA

Case No.: ____________
Division: ____________

____________,
Petitioner,

and

____________,
Respondent.

SUMMONS: PERSONAL SERVICE ON AN INDIVIDUAL
ORDEN DE COMPARECENCIA: SERVICIO PERSONAL EN UN INDIVIDUO
CITATION: L'ASSIGNATION PERSONAL SUR UN INDIVIDUEL

TO/PARA/A: *{enter other party's full legal name}* ____________,
{address (including city and state)/location for service} ____________.

IMPORTANT

A lawsuit has been filed against you. You have **20 calendar days** after this summons is served on you to file a written response to the attached complaint/petition with the clerk of this circuit court, located at: *{street address}* ____________.
A phone call will not protect you. Your written response, including the case number given above and the names of the parties, must be **filed** if you want the Court to hear your side of the case.

If you do not file your written response on time, you may lose the case, and your wages, money, and property may be taken thereafter without further warning from the Court. There are other legal requirements. You may want to call an attorney right away. If you do not know an attorney, you may call an attorney referral service or a legal aid office (listed in the phone book).

If you choose to file a written response yourself, at the same time you file your written response to the Court, you must also serve a copy of your written response on the party serving this summons at:

{Name and address of party serving summons} ____________
____________.

If the party serving summons has designated e-mail address(es) for service or is represented by an attorney, you may designate e-mail address(es) for service by or on you. Service must be in accordance with Florida Rule of Judicial Administration 2.516.

Copies of all court documents in this case, including orders, are available at the Clerk of the Circuit Court's office. You may review these documents, upon request.

Florida Family Law Rules of Procedure Form 12.910(a), Summons: Personal Service on an Individual (09/12)

You must keep the Clerk of the Circuit Court's office notified of your current address. (You may file Designation of Current Mailing and E-mail Address, Florida Supreme Court Approved Family Law Form 12.915.) Future papers in this lawsuit will be served at the address on record at the clerk's office.

WARNING: Rule 12.285, Florida Family Law Rules of Procedure, requires certain automatic disclosure of documents and information. Failure to comply can result in sanctions, including dismissal or striking of pleadings.

IMPORTANTE

Usted ha sido demandado legalmente. Tiene veinte (20) dias, contados a partir del recibo de esta notificacion, para contestar la demanda adjunta, por escrito, y presentarla ante este tribunal. Localizado en: ______________________________. Una llamada telefonica no lo protegera. Si usted desea que el tribunal considere su defensa, debe presentar su respuesta por escrito, incluyendo el numero del caso y los nombres de las partes interesadas. Si usted no contesta la demanda a tiempo, pudiese perder el caso y podria ser despojado de sus ingresos y propiedades, o privado de sus derechos, sin previo aviso del tribunal. Existen otros requisitos legales. Si lo desea, usted puede consultar a un abogado inmediatamente. Si no conoce a un abogado, puede llamar a una de las oficinas de asistencia legal que aparecen en la guia telefonica.

Si desea responder a la demanda por su cuenta, al mismo tiempo en que presente su respuesta ante el tribunal, usted debe enviar por correo o entregar una copia de su respuesta a la persona denominada abajo.

Si usted elige presentar personalmente una respuesta por escrito, en el mismo momento que usted presente su respuesta por escrito al Tribunal, usted debe enviar por correo o llevar una copia de su respuesta por escrito a la parte entregando esta orden de comparencencia a:

Nombre y direccion de la parte que entrega la orden de comparencencia: ____________________

____.

Copias de todos los documentos judiciales de este caso, incluyendo las ordenes, estan disponibles en la oficina del Secretario de Juzgado del Circuito [Clerk of the Circuit Court's office]. Estos documentos pueden ser revisados a su solicitud.

Usted debe de manener informada a la oficina del Secretario de Juzgado del Circuito de su direccion actual. (Usted puede presentar _______ el Formulario: Ley de Familia de la Florida 12.915, Florida Supreme Court Approved Family Law Form 12.915, Designation of Current Mailing and E-mail Address.) Los papelos que se presenten en el futuro en esta demanda judicial seran env ados por correo a la direccion que este registrada en la oficina del Secretario.

ADVERTENCIA: Regla 12.285 (Rule 12.285), de las Reglas de Procedimiento de Ley de Familia de la Florida [Florida Family Law Rules of Procedure], requiere cierta revelacion automatica de documentos e informacion. El incumplimient, puede resultar en sanciones, incluyendo la desestimacion o anulacion de los alegatos.

IMPORTANT

Florida Family Law Rules of Procedure Form 12.910(a), Summons: Personal Service on an Individual (09/12)

Des poursuites judiciaries ont ete entreprises contre vous. Vous avez 20 jours consecutifs a partir de la date de l'assignation de cette citation pour deposer une reponse ecrite a la plainte ci-jointe aupres de ce tribunal. Qui se trouve a: *{L'Adresse}* ______________________. Un simple coup de telephone est insuffisant pour vous proteger; vous etes obliges de deposer votre reponse ecrite, avec mention du numero de dossier ci-dessus et du nom des parties nommees ici, si vous souhaitez que le tribunal entende votre cause. Si vous ne deposez pas votre reponse ecrite dans le delai requis, vous risquez de perdre la cause ainsi que votre salaire, votre argent, et vos biens peuvent etre saisis par la suite, sans aucun preavis ulterieur du tribunal. Il y a d'autres obligations juridiques et vous pouvez requerir les services immediats d'un avocat. Si vous ne connaissez pas d'avocat, vous pourriez telephoner a un service de reference d'avocats ou a un bureau d'assistance juridique (figurant a l'annuaire de telephones).

Si vous choisissez de deposer vous-meme une reponse ecrite, il vous faudra egalement, en meme temps que cette formalite, faire parvenir ou expedier une copie au carbone ou une photocopie de votre reponse ecrite a la partie qui vous depose cette citation.

Nom et adresse de la partie qui depose cette citation: ______________________

Les photocopies de tous les documents tribunals de cette cause, y compris des arrets, sont disponible au bureau du greffier. Vous pouvez revue ces documents, sur demande.

Il faut aviser le greffier de votre adresse actuelle. (Vous pouvez deposer Florida Supreme Court Approved Family Law Form 12.915, Designation of Current Mailing and E-mail Address.) Les documents de l'avenir de ce proces seront envoyer a l'adresse que vous donnez au bureau du greffier.

ATTENTION: La regle 12.285 des regles de procedure du droit de la famille de la Floride exige que l'on remette certains renseignements et certains documents a la partie adverse. Tout refus de les fournir pourra donner lieu a des sanctions, y compris le rejet ou la suppression d'un ou de plusieurs actes de procedure.

THE STATE OF FLORIDA
TO EACH SHERIFF OF THE STATE: You are commanded to serve this summons and a copy of the complaint in this lawsuit on the above-named person.

DATED: ______________________

CLERK OF THE CIRCUIT COURT

(SEAL)

By: ______________________
Deputy Clerk

Florida Family Law Rules of Procedure Form 12.910(a), Summons: Personal Service on an Individual (09/12)

INSTRUCTIONS FOR FLORIDA FAMILY LAW RULES OF PROCEDURE FORM 12.910(a), SUMMONS: PERSONAL SERVICE ON AN INDIVIDUAL (09/12)

When should this form be used?

This form should be used to obtain **personal service** on the other **party** when you begin your lawsuit. **Service** is required for **all** documents filed in your case. Service means giving a copy of the required papers to the other party using the procedure that the law requires. Generally, there are two ways to make service: (1) personal service, or (2) service by e-mail, mail, or hand delivery. A third method for service is called **constructive service**; however, the relief a court may grant may be limited in a case where constructive service has been used.

The law requires that certain documents be served by **personal service** if personal service is possible. **Personal service** means that a summons (this form) and a copy of the forms you are filing with the court that must be personally served are delivered by a deputy sheriff or private process server

- directly to the other party, **or**
- to someone over the age of fifteen with whom the other party lives.

Personal service is required for **all petitions**, including petitions for modification. You cannot serve these papers on the other party yourself or by mail or hand delivery. Personal service must be made by the sheriff's department in the county where the other party lives or works or by a private process server certified in the county where the other party lives or works.

In many counties, there are private process servers who, for a fee, will personally serve the summons and other documents that require personal service. You should look under **process servers** in the yellow pages of the telephone book for a list of private process servers in your area. You may use a private process server to serve any paper required to be personally served in a family law case **except** a petition for injunction for protection against domestic or repeat violence.

How do I start?

When you begin your lawsuit, you need to complete this form (summons) and a **Process Service Memorandum**, Florida Supreme Court Approved Family Law Form 12.910(b). The forms should be typed or printed legibly in black ink. Next, you will need to take these forms and, if you have not already done so, **file** your petition with the **clerk of the circuit court** in the county where you live. You should keep a copy of the forms for your records. The clerk will sign the summons, and then the summons, a copy of the papers to be served, and the process service memorandum must be delivered to the appropriate sheriff's office or to a private process server for service on the other party.

IF THE OTHER PARTY LIVES IN THE COUNTY WHERE SUIT IS FILED: Ask the clerk in your county about any local procedures regarding service. Generally, if the other party lives in the county in which you are filing suit and you want the sheriff's department to serve the papers, you will file the summons along with a **Process Service Memorandum**, Florida Supreme Court Approved Family Law Form 12.910(b), with the clerk and the clerk will forward those papers to the sheriff for service. Make sure that you attach a copy of the papers you want personally served to the summons. You may also need to provide the sheriff with a stamped envelope addressed to you. This will allow the sheriff to send the proof of service to you, after the sheriff serves your papers on the other party. However, in some counties the sheriff may send the proof of service directly to the clerk. If you are instructed to supply a self-addressed, stamped envelope and you receive the proof of service, you should file the proof of service with the clerk after you receive it from the sheriff. Also, you will need to find out how much the sheriff charges to serve the papers. Personal checks are not accepted. You should attach to the summons a cashier's check or money order made payable to the sheriff, and either give it to the clerk for delivery to the sheriff or send all of the paperwork and the fee to the sheriff yourself. The clerk will tell you which procedure to use. The costs for service may be waived if you are indigent.

If you want a private process server to serve the other party, you should still bring the summons to the clerk's office and have the clerk sign it for you. You should deliver the summons, along with the copy of your initial petition and any other papers to be served, and a **Process Service Memorandum**, Florida Supreme Court Approved Family Law Form 12.910(b), to the private process server. The private process server will charge you a fee for serving the papers. After service is complete, proof of service by the private process server must be filed with the clerk. You should discuss how this will occur with the private process server.

IF THE OTHER PARTY LIVES IN ANOTHER COUNTY: If the other party lives in another county, service needs to be made by a sheriff in the county where the other party lives or by a private process server certified in the county where the other party lives. Make sure that you attach a copy of the papers you want personally served to the summons as well as the **Process Service Memorandum**, Florida Supreme Court Approved Family Law Form 12.910(b). If you want the sheriff to serve the papers, the clerk may send your papers to that sheriff's office for you, or you may have to send the papers yourself. The clerk will tell you which procedure to use. Either way, you will need to provide the sheriff with a stamped envelope addressed to you. This will allow the sheriff to send the proof of service to you, after the sheriff serves your papers on the other party. You should file the proof of service with the clerk after you receive it from the sheriff. Also, you will need to find out how much the sheriff charges to serve the papers. Personal checks are not accepted. You should attach to the summons a cashier's check or money order made payable to the sheriff, and either give it to the clerk for delivery to the sheriff or send all of the paperwork and the fee to the sheriff yourself. The clerk will tell you which procedure to use. The costs for service may be waived if you are indigent.

If you want a private process server to serve the other party, you should still bring the summons to the clerk's office where the clerk will sign it for you. You should deliver the summons, along with the copy of your initial petition and any other papers to be served, and a **Process Service Memorandum**, Florida Supreme Court Approved Family Law Form 12.910(b), to the private process server. The private process server will charge you a fee for serving the papers. After service is complete, proof of service by the private process server must be filed with the clerk. You should discuss how this will occur with the private process server.

IF THE OTHER PARTY CANNOT BE LOCATED OR DOES NOT LIVE IN FLORIDA: If, after you have made a diligent effort to locate the other party, you absolutely cannot locate the other party, you may serve the other party by publication. Service by publication is also known as <u>constructive service</u>. You may also be able to use constructive service if the other party does not live in Florida. **However, Florida courts have only limited jurisdiction over a party who is served by constructive service and may have only limited jurisdiction over a party living outside of Florida regardless of whether that party is served by constructive or personal service**; that is, the judge's power to order the other party to do certain things may be limited. For example, the judge may be able to grant your request for a divorce, but the judge may not be able to address issues such as child support, spousal support (alimony), or division of property or debts.

Regardless of the type of service used, if the other party once lived in Florida but is living outside of Florida now, you should include in your petition a statement regarding the length of time the party lived in Florida, if any, and when. For example: Respondent last lived in Florida from {*date*} __________ to {*date*} __________.

This area of the law is very complex and you may need to consult with an attorney regarding the proper type of service to be used in your case if the other party does not live in Florida or cannot be located.

What happens when the papers are served on the other party?

The date and hour of service are written on the original summons and on all copies of it by the person making the service. The person who delivers the summons and copies of the petition must file a proof of service with the clerk or provide a proof of service to you for filing with the court. **It is your responsibility to make sure the proof of service has been returned to the clerk and placed in your case file.**

Where can I look for more information?

Before proceeding, you should read General Information for Self–Represented Litigants found at the beginning of these forms. For further information regarding service of process, see chapters 48 and 49, Florida Statutes, and rule 1.070, Florida Rules of Civil Procedure, as well as the instructions for **Notice of Action for Dissolution of Marriage (No Child or Financial Support)**, Florida Supreme Court Approved Family Law Form 12.913(a)(1), **Notice of Action for Family Cases with Minor Child(ren),** Florida Supreme Court Approved Family Law Form 12.913(a)(2), **Affidavit of Diligent Service and Inquiry**, Florida Family Law Rules of Procedure Form 12.913(b), and **Affidavit of Diligent Search,** Florida Family Law Rules of Procedure Form 12.913(c).

Special notes ...

If you have been unable to obtain proper service on the other party within **120 days** after filing your lawsuit, the court will dismiss your lawsuit against the other party unless you can show the court a good reason why service was not made within **120 days**. For this reason, if you had the local sheriff serve the papers, you should check with the clerk every couple of weeks after completing the service papers to see if service has been completed. You may need to supply the sheriff with a new or better address. If you had a private process server or a sheriff in another county serve the papers, you should be in contact with that person or sheriff until you receive proof of service from that person or sheriff. You should then file the proof of service with the clerk immediately.

If the other party fails to respond, i.e., fails to file a written response with the court, within **20 days** after the service of the summons, you are entitled to request a **default**. See the instructions to **Motion for Default**, Florida Supreme Court Approved Family Law Form 12.922 (a), and **Default**, Florida Supreme Court Approved Family Law Form 12.922(b), for further information. You will need to file an **Affidavit of Military Service**, Florida Supreme Court Approved Family Law Form 12.912(b), before a default may be granted.

Remember, a person who is NOT an attorney is called a nonlawyer. If a nonlawyer helps you fill out these forms, that person must give you a copy of **Disclosure from Nonlawyer**, Florida Family Law Rules of Procedure Form 12.900(a), before he or she helps you. A nonlawyer helping you fill out these forms also **must** put his or her name, address, and telephone number on the bottom of the last page of every form he or she helps you complete.

Added July 1, 1995, effective Jan. 1, 1996 (663 So.2d 1047). Amended Feb. 26, 1998, effective Mar. 16, 1998 (713 So.2d 1); Sept. 21, 2000 (810 So.2d 1); Oct. 29, 2000 (783 So.2d 937); Oct. 18, 2012, effective, *nunc pro tunc*, Sept. 1, 2012 (102 So.3d 505).

Form 12.910(b). Process Service Memorandum

IN THE CIRCUIT COURT OF THE ________ JUDICIAL CIRCUIT,
IN AND FOR ______________ COUNTY, FLORIDA

Case No.: ______________
Division: ______________

______________________________,
Petitioner,
and

______________________________,
Respondent.

PROCESS SERVICE MEMORANDUM

TO: ____ Sheriff of ______________ County, Florida; ____________ Division
____ Private process server: ______________________________

Please serve the *{name of document(s)}* ______________________________

____

in the above-styled cause upon:
Party: *{full legal name}* ______________________________
Address or location for service: ______________________________

____

Work Address: ______________________________

____

If the party to be served owns, has, and/or is known to have guns or other weapons, describe what type of weapon(s): ______________________________

SPECIAL INSTRUCTIONS: ______________________________

____

____

____

Dated: ______________ ______________________________
Signature of Party
*Printed Name: ______________________________
*Address: ______________________________
*City, State, Zip: ______________________________
*Telephone Number: ______________________________
*Fax Number: ______________________________
*Designated E-mail Address(es): ______________________________

Florida Supreme Court Approved Family Law Form 12.910(b), Process Service Memorandum (03/15)

* Please see the Special Notes section in the instructions to this form regarding Florida Supreme Court Approved Family Law Form 12.980(h), Request for Confidential Filing of Address, which may be used if you need to keep your addresses or telephone numbers confidential for safety reasons.

IF A NONLAWYER HELPED YOU FILL OUT THIS FORM, HE/SHE MUST FILL IN THE BLANKS BELOW:
[fill in all blanks] This form was prepared for the: *{choose only one}* ( ) Petitioner ( ) Respondent
This form was completed with the assistance of:
*{name of individual}*______________________________,
*{name of business}*______________________________,
*{address}*______________________________,
{city} ______________,*{state}* ___, *{zip code}* ________,*{telephone number}* ______________.

Florida Supreme Court Approved Family Law Form 12.910(b), Process Service Memorandum (03/15)

INSTRUCTIONS FOR FLORIDA SUPREME COURT APPROVED FAMILY LAW FORM 12.910(b), PROCESS SERVICE MEMORANDUM (03/15)

When should this form be used?

You should use this form to give the sheriff's department (or private process server) instructions for serving the other party in your case with the **Summons: Personal Service on an Individual**, Florida Family Law Rules of Procedure Form 12.910(a), and other papers to be served. On this form you can tell the sheriff's department the best times to find the person at work and/or at home. You can also include a map to the other person's home or work place to help the sheriff find the person and deliver the summons. Do not forget to attach to the summons a copy of your initial petition and any other papers you want personally served on the other party.

This form should be typed or printed in black ink. After completing this form, you should **file** the original with the **clerk of the circuit court** in the county where your petition was filed and attach a copy to the **Summons: Personal Service on an Individual**, Florida Family Law Rules of Procedure Form 12.910(a). You should also keep a copy for your records.

IMPORTANT INFORMATION REGARDING E–FILING

The Florida Rules of Judicial Administration now require that all petitions, pleadings, and documents be filed electronically except in certain circumstances. **Self-represented litigants may file petitions or other pleadings or documents electronically; however, they are not required to do so.** If you choose to file your pleadings or other documents electronically, you must do so in accordance with Florida Rule of Judicial Administration 2.525, and you must follow the procedures of the judicial circuit in which you file. **The rules and procedures should be carefully read and followed.**

Where can I look for more information?

Before proceeding, you should read General Information for Self–Represented Litigants found at the beginning of these forms. You should read the instructions for **Summons: Personal Service on an Individual**, Florida Family Law Rules of Procedure Form 12.910(a), for additional information.

IMPORTANT INFORMATION REGARDING E–SERVICE ELECTION

After the initial service of process of the petition or supplemental petition by the Sheriff or certified process server, the Florida Rules of Judicial Administration now require that all documents required or permitted to be served on the other party must be served by electronic mail (e-mail) except in certain circumstances. **You must strictly comply with the format requirements set forth in the Rules of Judicial Administration.**

SELF–REPRESENTED LITIGANTS MAY SERVE DOCUMENTS BY E–MAIL; HOWEVER, THEY ARE NOT REQUIRED TO DO SO. If a self-represented litigant elects to serve and receive documents by e-mail, the procedures must always be followed once the initial election is made.

To serve and receive documents by e-mail, you must designate your e-mail addresses by using the **Designation of Current Mailing and E-mail Address**, Florida Supreme Court Approved Family Law Form 12.915, and you must provide your e-mail address on each form on which your signature appears. Please **CAREFULLY** read the rules and instructions for: **Certificate of Service (General),** Florida Supreme Court Approved Family Law Form 12.914; **Designation of Current Mailing and E-mail Address**, Florida Supreme Court Approved Family Law Form 12.915; and Florida Rule of Judicial Administration 2.516.

Special notes . . .

If you fear that disclosing your address would put you in danger because you are the victim of sexual battery, aggravated child abuse, stalking, aggravated stalking, harassment, aggravated battery, or domestic violence, you should complete a **Request for Confidential Filing of Address**, Florida Supreme Court Approved Family Law Form 12.980(h), file it with the clerk, and write confidential in the space provided on the petition.

Nonlawyer. Remember, a person who is NOT an attorney is called a nonlawyer. If a nonlawyer helps you fill out these forms, that person must give you a copy of **Disclosure from Nonlawyer**, Florida Family Law Rules of Procedure Form 12.900 (a), before he or she helps you. A nonlawyer helping you fill out these forms also **must** put his or her name, address, and telephone number on the bottom of the last page of every form he or she helps you complete.

Added July 1, 1995, effective Jan. 1, 1996 (663 So.2d 1047). Amended Feb. 26, 1998, effective Mar. 16, 1998 (713 So.2d 1); Sept. 21, 2000 (810 So.2d 1); March 26, 2015, effective March 26, 2015 (2015 WL 1343088).

Form 12.912(a). Memorandum for Certificate of Military Service

IN THE CIRCUIT COURT OF THE _________ JUDICIAL CIRCUIT,
IN AND FOR _______________________ COUNTY, FLORIDA

Case No.: ___________________
Division: ___________________

_________________________________,
Petitioner,

and

_________________________________,
Respondent.

MEMORANDUM FOR CERTIFICATE OF MILITARY SERVICE

TO: ( ) USCG Commander, Personnel Service Center, Attn: PSD-MR, 4200 Wilson Blvd, Suite 1100, Arlington, VA 22203

( ) HQ AFPC/DPDXIDL, Attn: World Wide Locator, 550 C. Street West, Suite 50, Randolph AFB, TX 78150-4752

( ) Bureau of Naval Personnel, PERS-312E, 5720 Integrity Drive, Millington, TN 38055-3120

( ) CMC, HQ, (MMSB17), 2008 Elliot Road, Room 201, Quantico, VA 22134

( ) Public Health Service: Attn: Director, Division of Commissioned Corps Officer Support http://dcp.psc.gov/ad_search.asp

( ) Army World Wide Locator Service, Enlisted Records and Evaluation Center, 8899 East 56th Street, Indianapolis, IN 46249-5301

RE: ________________________________ ________________________________
{Name of Respondent} *{Respondent's Social Security Number}*

This case involves a family matter. It is imperative that a determination be made whether the above-named individual, who has an interest in these proceedings, is presently in the military service of the United States, and the dates of induction and discharge, if any. This information is requested under the Servicemembers Civil Relief Act (formerly known as Soldiers' and Sailors' Civil Relief Act of 1940). Please supply verification as soon as possible. My check for $___________ for your search fee and a self-addressed, stamped envelope are enclosed.

Florida Supreme Court Approved Family Law Form 12.912(a), Memorandum for Certificate of Military Service (03/15)

Dated: ____
Signature of Petitioner

Printed Name: ______________________
Address: ____
City, State, Zip: ______________________
Telephone Number: ______________________
Fax Number: ______________________
Designated E-mail Address(es): ______________________
____

IF A NONLAWYER HELPED YOU FILL OUT THIS FORM, HE/SHE MUST FILL IN THE BLANKS BELOW:
[fill in **all** blanks] This form was prepared for the Petitioner.
This form was completed with the assistance of:
{name of individual} ____,
{name of business} ____,
{address} ____,
{city} ____________, *{state}* ____, *{zip code}* ________, *{telephone number}* ____________.

Florida Supreme Court Approved Family Law Form 12.912(a), Memorandum for Certificate of Military Service (03/15)

INSTRUCTIONS FOR FLORIDA SUPREME COURT APPROVED FAMILY LAW FORM 12.912(a) MEMORANDUM FOR CERTIFICATE OF MILITARY SERVICE (03/15)

When should this form be used?

This form should be used if you **KNOW OR DO NOT KNOW** whether the other party in your case is on active duty in a branch of the military service of the United States. "Active duty" includes reserve personnel of the Army, Navy, Air Force, Marine Corps, and Coast Guard, and members of the Florida National Guard who have been called to active duty for more than thirty (30) days. Even if you believe that the other party **has never** or **would never** join the military, you must show the court proof that he or she is not a member of the military. Therefore, you may need to use this form to provide the court with such proof. See the instructions for an **Affidavit of Military Service**, Florida Supreme Court Approved Family Law Form 12.912(b), for additional information.

Servicemembers Civil Relief Act (SCRA) Certificates:

For information on obtaining certificates of service or non-service under the Servicemembers Civil Relief Act (SCRA)(formerly known as Soldiers' and Sailors' Civil Relief Act of 1940), please refer to the following websites: http://www.defense.gov or www.dfas.mil.

You may also fill out this form and **mail one copy to each** of the military branches listed below. You may be charged a service fee by each military service branch for their response. Please refer to the websites and/or phone numbers listed below for help in determining the amount of each military branch's fee and to verify its current mailing address.

COAST GUARD: USCG Commander, Personnel Service Center, Attn: PSD–MR, 4200 Wilson Blvd., Suite 1100, Arlington VA 22203 Phone 1–866–772–8724 NOTE: All requests must be in writing. www.uscg.mil/hq/cgpc/home/locator/html.

AIR FORCE: HQ AFPC/DPDXIDL, Attn: World Wide Locator, 550 C Street, West, Suite 50, Randolph AFB, TX 78150–4752, Phone: (210) 565–2660, NOTE: Requests will be taken by phone. www.af.mil

NAVY: Bureau of Naval Personnel, PERS–312E, 5720 Integrity Drive, Millington, TN 38055–3120, Phone: (901) 874–5111 www.npc.navy.mil NOTE: Requests will be taken by phone.

MARINE CORPS: CMC HQ (MMSB17), 2008 Elliot Road, Room 201, Quantico, VA 22134 Phone: (703)784–3941 NOTE: All requests must be in writing.

PUBLIC HEALTH SERVICE: Attn: Director, Division of Commissioned Corps Officer Support, http://dcp.psc.gov/ad_search.asp NOTE: Please direct all inquiries to the website.

ARMY: Army World Wide Locator Service, Enlisted Records and Evaluation Center, 8899 East 56th Street, Indianapolis, IN 46249–5301, Phone: (1–866) 771–6357, fax: (317) 510–3685 NOTE: All requests must be in writing.

This form should be typed or printed in black ink. You should complete this form for each branch of the United States' military listed above, and mail the form to each branch with a **check for the appropriate amount and a stamped, self-addressed envelope.** You should keep a copy of the form for your records. After you have received a verification of military status from each branch, you will need to attach those verifications to an **Affidavit of Military Service**, Florida Supreme Court Approved Family Law Form 12.912(b), for filing with the clerk.

Special notes ...

Remember, a person who is NOT an attorney is called a nonlawyer. If a nonlawyer helps you fill out these forms, that person must give you a copy of **Disclosure from Nonlawyer**, Florida Family Law Rules of Procedure Form 12.900(a), before he or she helps you. A nonlawyer helping you fill out these forms also **must** put his or her name, address, and telephone number on the bottom of the last page of every form he or she helps you complete.

Added July 7, 1995, effective Jan. 1, 1996 (663 So.2d 1047). Amended Feb. 26, 1998, effective Mar. 16, 1998 (713 So.2d 1); Sept. 21, 2000 (810 So.2d 1); Dec. 2, 2010 (50 So.3d 595); March 26, 2015, effective March 26, 2015 (2015 WL 1343088).

Form 12.912(b). Affidavit of Military Service

IN THE CIRCUIT COURT OF THE ______ JUDICIAL CIRCUIT,
IN AND FOR ____________________ COUNTY, FLORIDA

Case No.: ____________
Division: ____________

______________________________,
Petitioner,

and

______________________________,
Respondent.

AFFIDAVIT OF MILITARY SERVICE

I, *{full legal name}* ______________________________, am the Petitioner in this case. To support my application for a default judgment and to comply with the Servicemembers Civil Relief Act (SCRA) (formerly known as Soldiers' and Sailors' Civil Relief Act of 1940), I swear or affirm that the following information is true:

{Please choose only one}

1. ____I know of my own personal knowledge that the Respondent **IS** on active duty in the military service of the United States.

2. _____ I know of my own personal knowledge that Respondent **IS NOT** now on active duty in the military service of the United States, nor has the Respondent been on active military service of the United States within a period of thirty (30) days immediately before this date. "Active Service" includes reserve members of the Army, Navy, Air Force, Coast Guard, and Marines who have been ordered to report for active duty and members of the Florida National Guard who have been ordered to report to active duty for a period of more than thirty (30) days.

3. _____ I have contacted the military services of the United States and the U.S. Public Health Service and have obtained certificates showing that the Respondent is not on active duty status. These certificates are attached.

4. _____ I have attempted to determine the military status of the Respondent, but do not have sufficient information. This is what I have done to determine whether or not Respondent is on active duty in the United States military:

____
____
____

Florida Supreme Court Approved Family Law Form 12.912(b), Affidavit of Military Service (03/15)

____
____.

I have no reason to believe that s/he is on active duty at this time.

I understand that I am swearing or affirming under oath to the truthfulness of the claims made in this affidavit and that the punishment for knowingly making a false statement includes fines and/or imprisonment.

Dated:____________________ ______________________________

Signature of Petitioner

Printed Name: ____________________________
Address:____________________________
City, State, Zip: ____________________________
Telephone Number: ____________________________
Fax Number: ____________________________
Designated E-mail Address(es):____________________
____

STATE OF FLORIDA
COUNTY OF ____________________

Sworn to or affirmed and signed before me on __________ by ______________________________.

____
NOTARY PUBLIC or DEPUTY CLERK

____
[Print, type, or stamp commissioned name of notary or clerk.]

_____ Personally known

_____ Produced identification

_____ Type of identification produced ______________________________.

IF A NONLAWYER HELPED YOU FILL OUT THIS FORM, HE/SHE MUST FILL IN THE BLANKS BELOW:
[fill in all blanks] This form was prepared for the Petitioner.
This form was completed with the assistance of:
{name of individual}, ______________________________,
*{name of business}*______________________________,
{address} ______________________________,

Florida Supreme Court Approved Family Law Form 12.912(b), Affidavit of Military Service (03/15)

*{city}*__________________,*{state}* _____, *{zip code}*_________,*{telephone number}*_________________.

Florida Supreme Court Approved Family Law Form 12.912(b), Affidavit of Military Service (03/15)

INSTRUCTIONS FOR FLORIDA SUPREME COURT APPROVED FAMILY LAW FORM 12.912(b), AFFIDAVIT OF MILITARY SERVICE (03/15)

When should this form be used?

An Affidavit of Military Service is required in every case where the Respondent has not filed an answer or appearance. The purpose is to protect the men and women serving in the U.S. military from having a court judgment entered against them without first receiving notice of the lawsuit and a chance to defend the case.

You should use this form when ALL of the following statements are true:

- The other person in your case has been served, whether by **personal service** or **constructive service**.
- The other person in your case has not responded to your petition.
- You are requesting that the court enter a default judgment against the other person.

This form should be typed or printed in black ink. After completing this form, you should sign the form before a **notary public** or **deputy clerk**. You must **file** the original of this form with the **clerk of the circuit court** when you file your **Motion for Default**, Florida Supreme Court Approved Family Law Form 12.922(a). You must also attach copies of all verifications of nonmilitary service that you received from each branch of the United States' military service. You should keep a copy for your records.

IMPORTANT INFORMATION REGARDING E–FILING

The Florida Rules of Judicial Administration now require that all petitions, pleadings, and documents be filed electronically except in certain circumstances. **Self-represented litigants may file petitions or other pleadings or documents electronically; however, they are not required to do so.** If you choose to file your pleadings or other documents electronically, you must do so in accordance with Florida Rule of Judicial Administration 2.525, and you must follow the procedures of the judicial circuit in which you file. **The rules and procedures should be carefully read and followed.**

IMPORTANT INFORMATION REGARDING E–SERVICE ELECTION

After the initial service of process of the petition or supplemental petition by the Sheriff or certified process server, the Florida Rules of Judicial Administration now require that all documents required or permitted to be served on the other party must be served by electronic mail (e-mail) except in certain circumstances. **You must strictly comply with the format requirements set forth in the Rules of Judicial Administration.**

SELF–REPRESENTED LITIGANTS MAY SERVE DOCUMENTS BY E–MAIL; HOWEVER, THEY ARE NOT REQUIRED TO DO SO. If a self-represented litigant elects to serve and receive documents by e-mail, the procedures must always be followed once the initial election is made.

To serve and receive documents by e-mail, you must designate your e-mail addresses by using the **Designation of Current Mailing and E-mail Address**, Florida Supreme Court Approved Family Law Form 12.915, and you must provide your e-mail address on each form on which your signature appears. Please **CAREFULLY** read the rules and instructions for: **Certificate of Service (General),** Florida Supreme Court Approved Family Law Form 12.914; **Designation of Current Mailing and E-mail Address**, Florida Supreme Court Approved Family Law Form 12.915; and Florida Rule of Judicial Administration 2.516.

Special notes . . .

Remember, a person who is NOT an attorney is called a nonlawyer. If a nonlawyer helps you fill out these forms, that person must give you a copy of **Disclosure from Nonlawyer**, Florida Family Law Rules of Procedure Form 12.900 (a), before he or she helps you. A nonlawyer helping you fill out these forms also **must** put his or her name, address, and telephone number on the bottom of the last page of every form he or she helps you complete.

Added July 7, 1995, effective Jan. 1, 1996 (663 So.2d 1047). Amended Feb. 26, 1998, effective Mar. 16, 1998 (713 So.2d 1); Sept. 21, 2000 (810 So.2d 1); Dec. 2, 2010 (50 So.3d 595); March 26, 2015, effective March 26, 2015 (2015 WL 1343088).

Form 12.913(a)(1). Notice of Action for Dissolution of Marriage (No Child or Financial Support)

IN THE CIRCUIT COURT OF THE __________ JUDICIAL CIRCUIT,
IN AND FOR ______________________________ COUNTY, FLORIDA

Case No.________________________
Division: ________________________

_____________________________,
Petitioner

and

_____________________________,
Respondent.

NOTICE OF ACTION FOR DISSOLUTION OF MARRIAGE (NO CHILD OR FINANCIAL SUPPORT)

TO: *{name of Respondent}* ____
{Respondent's last known address} ________________________________

YOU ARE NOTIFIED that an action for dissolution of marriage has been filed against you and that you are required to serve a copy of your written defenses, if any, to it on *{name of Petitioner}* ____,
whose address is ____
on or before *{date}* __________________, and file the original with the clerk of this Court at *{clerk's address}* ____,
before service on Petitioner or immediately thereafter. **If you fail to do so, a default may be entered against you for the relief demanded in the petition.**

The action is asking the court to decide how the following real or personal property should be divided: *{insert "none" or, if applicable, the legal description of real property, a specific description of personal property, and the name of the county in Florida where the property is located}* ____

Copies of all court documents in this case, including orders, are available at the Clerk of the Circuit Court's office. You may review these documents upon request.

You must keep the Clerk of the Circuit Court's office notified of your current address. (You may file Designation of Current Mailing and E-Mail Address, Florida Supreme Court Approved Family Law Form 12.915.) Future papers in this lawsuit will be mailed or e-mailed to the address(es) on record at the clerk's office.

WARNING: Rule 12.285, Florida Family Law Rules of Procedure, requires certain automatic disclosure of documents and information. Failure to comply can result in sanctions, including dismissal or striking of pleadings.

Florida Supreme Court Approved Family Law Form 12.913(a)(1), Notice of Action for Dissolution of Marriage (No Child or Financial Support) (03/15)

Dated: ____________ CLERK OF THE CIRCUIT COURT

By: ______________________________
Deputy Clerk

IF A NONLAWYER HELPED YOU FILL OUT THIS FORM, HE/SHE MUST FILL IN THE BLANKS BELOW:
[fill in all blanks] This form was prepared for the Petitioner.
This form was completed with the assistance of:
{name of individual} ____,
{name of business} ____,
{address} ____,
{city} __________, *{state}* _____, *{zip code}* ________, *{telephone number}* ______________.

INSTRUCTIONS FOR FLORIDA SUPREME COURT APPROVED FAMILY LAW FORM 12.913(a)(1) NOTICE OF ACTION FOR DISSOLUTION OF MARRIAGE (NO CHILD OR FINANCIAL SUPPORT) (03/15)

When should this form be used?

This form may be used to obtain **constructive service** (also called service by publication) in a **dissolution of marriage** case that does not involve a minor child or financial support if you do not know where your **spouse** lives or if your spouse lives outside Florida and you are unable to obtain **personal service**. Constructive notice will allow the court to dissolve the marriage, but personal service is required before a court can order payment of financial support, such as **spousal** support (**alimony**) or costs. If you are asking the court to decide how real or personal property located in Florida should be divided, the **Notice of Action** must include a specific description of the property. If you use constructive service, the court can grant only limited relief because its jurisdiction is limited. This is a complicated area of the law and you should consult an attorney before using constructive service.

You should complete this form by typing or printing the appropriate information in black ink. You should insert your spouse's name and last known address and then **file** this form with the **clerk of the circuit court** in the county where your petition for dissolution of marriage was filed. You must also complete and file an **Affidavit of Diligent Search and Inquiry**, Florida Family Law Rules of Procedure Form 12.913(b). You should keep a copy for your records.

After the **Affidavit of Diligent Search and Inquiry**, Florida Family Law Rules of Procedure Form 12.913(b), is filed, the clerk will sign this form. The form must then be given to a qualified local newspaper in the county where the case is pending to be published once each week for four consecutive weeks. When in doubt, ask the clerk which newspapers in your area are "qualified." The newspaper will charge you for this service. If you cannot afford to pay the cost of publication of this notice in a qualified newspaper, you may ask the clerk to post the notice at a place designated for such postings. You will need to file an **Application for Determination of Civil Indigent Status,** which you can obtain from the clerk. If the clerk determines that you cannot afford these costs, the clerk will post the notice of action.

IMPORTANT INFORMATION REGARDING E–FILING

The Florida Rules of Judicial Administration now require that all petitions, pleadings, and documents be filed electronically except in certain circumstances. **Self-represented litigants may file petitions or other pleadings or documents electronically; however, they are not required to do so.** If you choose to file your pleadings or other documents electronically, you must do so in accordance with Florida Rule of Judicial Administration 2.525, and you must follow the procedures of the judicial circuit in which you file. **The rules and procedures should be carefully read and followed.**

Where can I look for more information?

Before proceeding, you should read "General Information for Self–Represented Litigants" found at the beginning of these forms. For further information, see rule 12.070, Florida Family Law Rules of Procedure, and chapter 49, Florida Statutes.

IMPORTANT INFORMATION REGARDING E–SERVICE ELECTION

After the initial service of process of the petition or supplemental petition by the Sheriff or certified process server, the Florida Rules of Judicial Administration now require that all documents required or permitted to be served on the other party must be served by electronic mail (e-mail) except in certain circumstances. **You must strictly comply with the format requirements set forth in the Rules of Judicial Administration.**

SELF–REPRESENTED LITIGANTS MAY SERVE DOCUMENTS BY E–MAIL; HOWEVER, THEY ARE NOT REQUIRED TO DO SO. If a self-represented litigant elects to serve and receive documents by e-mail, the procedures must always be followed once the initial election is made.

To serve and receive documents by e-mail, you must designate your e-mail addresses by using the **Designation of Current Mailing and E-mail Address**, Florida Supreme Court Approved

Family Law Form 12.915, and you must provide your e-mail address on each form on which your signature appears. Please **CAREFULLY** read the rules and instructions for: **Certificate of Service (General),** Florida Supreme Court Approved Family Law Form 12.914; **Designation of Current Mailing and E-mail Address,** Florida Supreme Court Approved Family Law Form 12.915; and Florida Rule of Judicial Administration 2.516.

Special notes . . .

If the other party fails to respond to your **petition** within the time limit stated in the notice of action that is published or posted, you are entitled to request a **default**. (See **Motion for Default**, Florida Supreme Court Approved Family Law Form 12.922(a), and **Default**, Florida Supreme Court Approved Family Law Form 12.922(b).)

Remember, a person who is NOT an attorney is called a nonlawyer. If a nonlawyer helps you fill out these forms, that person must give you a copy of **Disclosure from Nonlawyer**, Florida Family Law Rules of Procedure Form 12.900 (a), before he or she helps you. A nonlawyer helping you fill out these forms also **must** put his or her name, address, and telephone number on the bottom of the last page of every form he or she helps you complete.

Formerly Form 12.913(a), added July 7, 1995, effective Jan. 1, 1996 (663 So.2d 1047). Amended Feb. 26, 1998, effective Mar. 16, 1998 (713 So.2d 1); Sept. 21, 2000 (810 So.2d 1); June 30, 2005, effective July 1, 2005 (910 So.2d 194). Renumbered Form 12.913(a)(1) and amended March 15, 2012, effective *nunc pro tunc* Jan. 1, 2012 (84 So.3d 257). Amended March 26, 2015, effective March 26, 2015 (2015 WL 1343088).

Form 12.913(a)(2). Notice of Action for Family Cases with Minor Child(ren)

IN THE CIRCUIT COURT OF THE ______________ JUDICIAL CIRCUIT,
IN AND FOR ____________________ COUNTY, FLORIDA

Case No.: ________________________
Division: ________________________

______________________________,
Petitioner

and

______________________________,
Respondent.

NOTICE OF ACTION FOR

{Specify action} ____

TO: *{name of Respondent}* ____
{Respondent's last known address} ____

YOU ARE NOTIFIED that an action for *{identify the type of case}* ______________ has been filed against you and that you are required to serve a copy of your written defenses, if any, to it on *{name of Petitioner}* ____, whose address is ____ on or before *{date}* ______________, and file the original with the clerk of this Court at *{clerk's address}* ____ before service on Petitioner or immediately thereafter. **If you fail to do so, a default may be entered against you for the relief demanded in the petition.**

{If applicable, insert the legal description of real property, a specific description of personal property, and the name of the county in Florida where the property is located} ____
____.

Copies of all court documents in this case, including orders, are available at the Clerk of the Circuit Court's office. You may review these documents upon request.

You must keep the Clerk of the Circuit Court's office notified of your current address. (You may file Designation of Current Mailing and E-Mail Address, Florida Supreme Court Approved Family Law Form 12.915.) Future papers in this lawsuit will be mailed or e-mailed to the addresses on record at the clerk's office.

WARNING: Rule 12.285, Florida Family Law Rules of Procedure, requires certain automatic disclosure of documents and information. Failure to comply can result in sanctions, including dismissal or striking of pleadings.

Florida Supreme Court Approved Family Law Form 12.913(a)(2), Notice of Action For Family Cases With Minor Child(ren) (03/15)

Dated: ____________. CLERK OF THE CIRCUIT COURT

By: ______________________________
Deputy Clerk

IF A NONLAWYER HELPED YOU FILL OUT THIS FORM, HE/SHE MUST FILL IN THE BLANKS BELOW:
[fill in all blanks] This form was prepared for the Petitioner.
This form was completed with the assistance of:
{name of individual} ______________________________,
{name of business} ______________________________,
{address} ______________________________,
{city} ____________, *{state}* ____, *{zip code}* ________, *{telephone number}* ____________.

INSTRUCTIONS FOR FLORIDA SUPREME COURT APPROVED FAMILY LAW FORM 12.913(a)(2)
NOTICE OF ACTION FOR FAMILY CASES WITH MINOR CHILD(REN)
(03/15)

When should this form be used?

This form may be used to obtain **constructive service** (also called service by publication) in an action involving a parenting plan for a minor child under chapter 61, Florida Statutes; an action to determine temporary custody by extended family under chapter 751, Florida Statutes; and termination of a legal father's parental rights when another man is alleged to be the biological father. "Parenting plan" means a document created to govern the relationship between the parents relating to decisions that must be made regarding the minor child and must contain a time-sharing schedule for the parents and child. Section 61.046(14), Florida Statutes. You may use constructive service if you do not know where the other party lives or if the other party lives outside Florida and you are unable to obtain **personal service**. Constructive notice will allow the court to grant the relief requested, but personal service is required before a court can order payment or termination of **child support,** spousal support (**alimony**), or costs. If you are asking the court to decide how real or personal property located in Florida should be divided, the **Notice of Action** must include a specific description of the property. If you use constructive service, the court can grant only limited relief because its jurisdiction is limited. This is a complicated area of the law and you should consult an attorney before using constructive service.

You should complete this form by typing or printing the appropriate information in black ink. You must insert the other party's name and last known address and then **file** this form with the **clerk of the circuit court** in the county where your petition was filed. You must also complete and file an **Affidavit of Diligent Search and Inquiry**. Use Florida Family Law Rules of Procedure Form 12.913(b) unless you are serving the legal father in a paternity case where another man is alleged to be the biological father, in which case, you must use Form 12.913(c). You should keep a copy for your records.

IMPORTANT INFORMATION REGARDING E-FILING

The Florida Rules of Judicial Administration now require that all petitions, pleadings, and documents be filed electronically except in certain circumstances. **Self-represented litigants may file petitions or other pleadings or documents electronically; however, they are not required to do so.** If you choose to file your pleadings or other documents electronically, you must do so in accordance with Florida Rule of Judicial Administration 2.525, and you must follow the procedures of the judicial circuit in which you file. **The rules and procedures should be carefully read and followed.**

After the **Affidavit of Diligent Search and Inquiry**, Family Law Rules of Procedure Form 12.913(b) or 12.913(c), is filed, the clerk will sign this form. You will need to publish notice once each week for four consecutive weeks in a "qualified" newspaper in the county where the case is pending. When in doubt, ask the clerk which newspapers are "qualified." The newspaper will charge you for this service. If you cannot afford to pay the cost of publishing this notice, you may ask the clerk to post the notice at a place designated for such postings. You will need to file an **Application for Determination of Civil Indigent Status,** which you can obtain from the clerk. If the clerk determines that you cannot afford these costs, the clerk will post the notice of action. If your case involves termination of a legal father's parental rights when another man is alleged to be the biological father, you need to publish the notice only in the county where the legal father was last known to have resided. You are responsible for locating a "qualified" newspaper in the county where the other party last resided and paying the cost of publication.

Where can I look for more information?

Before proceeding, you should read "General Information for Self-Represented Litigants" found at the beginning of these forms. For further information, see rule 12.070, Florida Family Law Rules of Procedure, rule 1.070, Florida Rules of Civil Procedure, sections 61.501–61.542, Florida Statutes and chapter 49, Florida Statutes.

IMPORTANT INFORMATION REGARDING E–SERVICE ELECTION

After the initial service of process of the petition or supplemental petition by the Sheriff or certified process server, the Florida Rules of Judicial Administration now require that all documents required or permitted to be served on the other party must be served by electronic mail (e-mail) except in certain circumstances. **You must strictly comply with the format requirements set forth in the Rules of Judicial Administration.**

SELF–REPRESENTED LITIGANTS MAY SERVE DOCUMENTS BY E–MAIL; HOWEVER, THEY ARE NOT REQUIRED TO DO SO. If a self-represented litigant elects to serve and receive documents by e-mail, the procedures must always be followed once the initial election is made.

To serve and receive documents by e-mail, you must designate your e-mail addresses by using the **Designation of Current Mailing and E-mail Address**, Florida Supreme Court Approved Family Law Form 12.915, and you must provide your e-mail address on each form on which your signature appears. Please **CAREFULLY** read the rules and instructions for: **Certificate of Service (General),** Florida Supreme Court Approved Family Law Form 12.914; **Designation of Current Mailing and E-mail Address**, Florida Supreme Court Approved Family Law Form 12.915; and Florida Rule of Judicial Administration 2.516.

Special notes . . .

If the other party fails to respond to your **petition** within the time limit stated in the notice of action that is published or posted, you are entitled to request a **default**. (See **Motion for Default**, Florida Supreme Court Approved Family Law Form 12.922(a), and **Default**, Florida Supreme Court Approved Family Law Form 12.922(b).)

Remember, a person who is NOT an attorney is called a nonlawyer. If a nonlawyer helps you fill out these forms, that person must give you a copy of **Disclosure from Nonlawyer**, Florida Family Law Rules of Procedure Form 12.900(a), before he or she helps you. A nonlawyer helping you fill out these forms also **must** put his or her name, address, and telephone number on the bottom of the last page of every form he or she helps you complete.

Added March 15, 2012, effective *nunc pro tunc* Jan. 1, 2012 (84 So.3d 257). Amended March 26, 2015, effective March 26, 2015 (2015 WL 1343088).

Form 12.913(b). Affidavit of Diligent Search and Inquiry

IN THE CIRCUIT COURT OF THE ______________ JUDICIAL CIRCUIT,
IN AND FOR ______________ COUNTY, FLORIDA

Case No.: ______________
Division: ______________

______________,
Petitioner,

and

______________,
Respondent.

AFFIDAVIT OF DILIGENT SEARCH AND INQUIRY

I, *{full legal name}* ______________, being sworn, certify that the following information is true:

1. I have made diligent search and inquiry to discover the name and current residence of Respondent: *{Specify details of search}* **Refer to checklist below and identify all actions taken (any additional information included such as the date the action was taken and the person with whom you spoke is helpful) (attach additional sheet if necessary):**
[Check **all** that apply]

____ United States Post Office inquiry through Freedom of Information Act for current address or any relocations.

____ Last known employment of Respondent, including name and address of employer. You should also ask for any addresses to which W-2 Forms were mailed, and, if a pension or profit-sharing plan exists, then for any addresses to which any pension or plan payment is and/or has been mailed.

____ Unions from which Respondent may have worked or that governed his or her particular trade or craft.

____ Regulatory agencies, including professional or occupational licensing.

____ Names and addresses of relatives and contacts with those relatives, and inquiry as to Respondent's last known address. You are to follow up any leads of any addresses where Respondent may have moved. Relatives include, but are not limited to: parents, brothers, sisters, aunts, uncles, cousins, nieces, nephews, grandparents, great-grandparents, former in-laws, stepparents, stepchildren.

____ Information about the Respondent's possible death and, if dead, the date and location of the death.

____ Telephone listings in the last known locations of Respondent's residence.

____ Internet at http://www.switchboard.com or other Internet databank locator service. Please indicate if a public library assisted you in your search.

____ Law enforcement arrest and/or criminal records in the last known residential area of Respondent.

____ Highway Patrol records in the state of Respondent's last known address.

____ Department of Motor Vehicle records in the state of Respondent's last known address.

____ Department of Corrections records in the state of Respondent's last known address.

____ Title IV-D (child support enforcement) agency records in the state of Respondent's last known address.
____ Hospitals in the last known area of Respondent's residence.
____ Utility companies, which include water, sewer, cable TV, and electric, in the last known area of Respondent's residence.
____ Letters to the Armed Forces of the U.S. and their response as to whether or not there is any information about Respondent. (See Memorandum for Certificate of Military Service, Florida Supreme Court Approved Family Law Form 12.912(a).)
____ Tax Assessor's and Tax Collector's Office in the area where Respondent last resided.
____ Other: *{explain}* ____
____
____
____
____

2. The age of Respondent is [Choose only **one**] ( ) known *{enter age}* _____ **or** ( ) unknown.

3. **Respondent's current residence**
[Choose only **one**]
   a. ____Respondent's current residence is unknown to me.
   b. ____Respondent's current residence is in some state or country other than Florida.
   ____
   c. ____The Respondent, having residence in Florida, has been absent from Florida for more than 60 days prior to the date of this affidavit, or conceals him/her self so that process cannot be served personally upon him or her, and I believe there is no person in the state upon whom service of process would bind this absent or concealed Respondent.

4. **Respondent's last known address** as of *{date}*______________________________, was:
Address______________________City____________________State________Zip______
Telephone No. __________________Fax No.__________________.

Respondent's last known employment, as of *{date}*____________________________, was
Name of Employer____
Address_________________________City____________________State______Zip______
Telephone No._________________ Fax No.__________________

I understand that I am swearing or affirming under oath to the truthfulness of the claims made in this affidavit and that the punishment for knowingly making a false statement includes fines and/or imprisonment.

Dated: ____________________

Signature of Petitioner
Printed Name: ____________________
Address: ____________________
City, State, Zip: ____________________
Telephone Number: ____________________
Fax Number: ____________________
E-mail Address(es): ____________________

STATE OF FLORIDA
COUNTY OF

Sworn to or affirmed and signed before me on ____________________ by ____________________

____
NOTARY PUBLIC or DEPUTY CLERK

____
[Print, type, or stamp commissioned name of notary or clerk.]

____ Personally known
____ Produced identification
Type of identification produced ____________________

IF A NONLAWYER HELPED YOU FILL OUT THIS FORM, HE/SHE MUST FILL IN THE BLANKS BELOW:
[fill in all blanks]
This form was prepared for: *{choose only* ***one****}* ( ) Petitioner ( ) Respondent
This form was completed with the assistance of:
{name of individual} ____________________,
{name of business} ____________________,
{address} ____________________,
{city} ____________________,*{state}* ____________, *{telephone number}* ____________________.

INSTRUCTIONS FOR FLORIDA FAMILY LAW RULES OF PROCEDURE FORM 12.913(b), AFFIDAVIT OF DILIGENT SEARCH AND INQUIRY (11/12)

When should this form be used?

This form is to be used with **Notice of Action for Dissolution of Marriage (No Child or Financial Support)**, Florida Supreme Court Approved Family Law Form 12.913(a)(1) and **Notice of Action For Family Cases With Minor Child(ren)**, Form 12.913(a)(2), to obtain **constructive service** (also called service by publication).

The other party is entitled to actual notice of the proceedings when possible. When it is necessary to use constructive notice, it must be given in a way that is likely to provide actual notice. You must disclose the last known address of the other party. A last known address cannot be unknown. This form includes a checklist of places you can look for information on the location of the other party. While you do not have to look in all of these places, the court must believe that you have made a very serious effort to get information about the other party's location and that you have followed up on any information you received.

This form should be typed or printed in black ink. After completing this form, you should sign the form before a **notary public** or **deputy clerk**. You should **file** the original and a **Notice of Action for Dissolution of Marriage (No Child or Financial Support)**, Florida Supreme Court Approved Family Law Form 12.913(a)(1), or **Notice of Action For Family Cases With Minor Child(ren)**, Form 12.913(a)(2), with the **clerk of the circuit court** in the county where your petition is filed. You should keep a copy for your records.

Where can I look for more information?

Before proceeding, you should read "General Information for Self-Represented Litigants" found at the beginning of these forms. For further information, see rule 12.070, Florida Family Law Rules of Procedure and chapter 49, Florida Statutes.

Special notes . . .

Remember, a person who is NOT an attorney is called a nonlawyer. If a nonlawyer helps you fill out these forms, that person must give you a copy of **Disclosure from Nonlawyer**, Florida Family Law Rules of Procedure Form 12.900(a), before he or she helps you. A nonlawyer helping you fill out these forms also **must** put his or her name, address, and telephone number on the bottom of the last page of every form he or she helps you complete.

Added July 7, 1995, effective Jan. 1, 1996 (663 So.2d 1047). Amended Feb. 26, 1998, effective Mar. 16, 1998 (713 So.2d 1); Sept. 21, 2000 (810 So.2d 1); March 15, 2012, effective *nunc pro tunc* Jan. 1, 2012 (84 So.3d 257); Nov. 15, 2012 (104 So.3d 314).

Form 12.913(c). Affidavit of Diligent Search

IN THE CIRCUIT COURT OF THE ____________________ JUDICIAL CIRCUIT,
IN AND FOR ________________________ COUNTY, FLORIDA

Case No.: ______________
Division: ______________

__________________________________,
Petitioner,

and

__________________________________,
Respondent.

AFFIDAVIT OF DILIGENT SEARCH

I, *{full legal name}* ______________________________, being sworn, certify that the following information is true:

1. The last known address of the child(ren)'s legal father *{name}* __________________,
as of *{date}* ______________________________, was:
Address ______________ City __________ State __________ Zip ______
Telephone No. __________________ Fax No. ______________________.

His last known employment, as of *{date}* __________________, was:
Name of Employer
Address ______________ City __________ State __________ Zip ______
Telephone No. Fax No.

2. The legal father is over the age of 18.

3. The legal father's current residence is not known and cannot be determined, although I have made a diligent search and inquiry to locate him through the following:
You must search ALL of the following sources of information and state the results.
____ United States Post Office inquiry through the Freedom of Information Act for the legal father's current address or any previous address.
Result of search: ____
____ Last known employment of the legal father, including name and address of employer.
Result of search: ____

Florida Family Law Rules of Procedure Form 12.913(c), Affidavit of Diligent Search (11/12)

____ Regulatory agencies, including professional or occupational licensing, in the area where the legal father last resided.
Result of search:____

____ Names and addresses of relatives to the extent such can be reasonably obtained from the petitioner or other sources, contacts with those relatives and inquiry as to the legal father's last known address. You are to follow up any leads of any addresses where the legal father may have moved.
Result of search: ____

____ Information about the legal father's possible death and, if dead, the date and location.
Result of search:____

____ Telephone listings in the area where the legal father last resided.
Result of search: ____

____ Law enforcement agencies in the area where the legal father last resided.
Result of search: ____

____ Highway Patrol records in the state where the legal father last resided.
Result of search: ____

____ Department of Corrections records in the state where the legal father last resided.
Result of search: ____

____ Hospitals in the last known area of the legal father's residence.
Result of search: ____

____ Records of utility companies, which include water, sewer, cable TV, and electric in the last known area of the legal father's residence.
Result of search: ____

____ Records of the Armed Forces of the U.S. and their response as to whether or not there is any information about the legal father. (See Florida Supreme Court Approved Family Law Form 12.912(a), Memorandum for Certificate of Military Service.)
Result of search: ____

____ Records of the tax assessor's and tax collector's office in the area where the legal father last resided.
Result of search:____

____ Search of one Internet databank locator service.
Result of search: ____

____ Title IV-D (child support enforcement) agency records in the state of the legal father's last known address.
Result of search: ____

I understand that I am swearing or affirming under oath to the truthfulness of the claims made in this affidavit and that the punishment for knowingly making a false statement includes fines and/or imprisonment.

Dated:______________________________

____
Signature of Petitioner
Printed Name: ______________________________
Address: __________________________________
City, State, Zip: ______________________________
Telephone Number:___________________________
Fax Number: _______________________________
E-mail Address(es):__________________________

STATE OF FLORIDA
COUNTY OF _______________________

Sworn to or affirmed and signed before me on ____________ by _____________________________.

____
NOTARY PUBLIC or DEPUTY CLERK
[Print, type, or stamp commissioned name of notary or deputy clerk.]

____ Personally known
____ Produced identification
Type of identification produced ______________________________

IF A NONLAWYER HELPED YOU FILL OUT THIS FORM, HE/SHE MUST FILL IN THE BLANKS BELOW:
[fill in all blanks]
This form was prepared for: *{choose only **one**}* ( ) Petitioner ( ) Respondent
This form was completed with the assistance of:
{ name of individual} ____,
{name of business} ____,
{address} ____,
{city} _____________________,*{state}* ____________, *{telephone number}* ____________________.

INSTRUCTIONS FOR FLORIDA FAMILY LAW RULES OF PROCEDURE FORM 12.913(c), AFFIDAVIT OF DILIGENT SEARCH (11/12)

When should this form be used?

This form is to be used with **Notice of Action For Family Cases With Minor Child(ren)**, Florida Supreme Court Approved Family Law Form 12.913(a)(2), to obtain **constructive service** (also called service by publication) on the legal father in any action or proceeding to determine paternity which may result in termination of the legal father's parental rights.

The legal father is entitled to actual notice of the proceedings when possible. When it is necessary to use constructive notice, it must be given in a way that is likely to provide actual notice. You must disclose the last known address of the legal father. A last known address cannot be unknown. This form includes a checklist of places you must look for information on the location of the legal father. You have to look in all of these places, and the court must believe that you have made a very serious effort to get information about the person's location and that you have followed up on any information you received.

This form should be typed or printed in black ink. After completing this form, you should sign the form before a **notary public** or **deputy clerk**. You should **file** the original and a **Notice of Action For Family Cases With Minor Child(ren),** Florida Supreme Court Approved Family Law Form 12.913(a)(2), with the **clerk of the circuit court** in the county where your petition for dissolution of marriage is filed. You should keep a copy for your records.

Where can I look for more information?

Before proceeding, you should read General Information for Self–Represented Litigants found at the beginning of these forms. For further information, see rule 12.070, Florida Family Law Rules of Procedure, chapter 49, Florida Statutes, and section 409.257, Florida Statutes.

Special notes . . .

Remember, a person who is NOT an attorney is called a nonlawyer. If a nonlawyer helps you fill out these forms, that person must give you a copy of **Disclosure from Nonlawyer**, Florida Family Law Rules of Procedure Form 12.900(a), before he or she helps you. A nonlawyer helping you fill out these forms also **must** put his or her name, address, and telephone number on the bottom of the last page of every form he or she helps you complete.

July 12, 2007 (962 So.2d 302). Amended April 24, 2008 (981 So.2d 1189); March 15, 2012, effective *nunc pro tunc* Jan. 1, 2012 (84 So.3d 257); Nov. 15, 2012 (104 So.3d 314).

Form 12.914. Certificate of Service

IN THE CIRCUIT COURT OF THE ____________ JUDICIAL CIRCUIT,
IN AND FOR ____________ COUNTY, FLORIDA

Case No.: ____________
Division: ____________

____________,
Petitioner,

and

____________,
Respondent.

CERTIFICATE OF SERVICE

I certify that a copy of *{name of document(s)}* ____________
____
was ( ) mailed ( ) faxed and mailed ( ) e-mailed ( ) hand-delivered to the person listed below on *{date}* ____________.

Other party or his/her attorney:
Name: ____________
Address: ____________
City, State, Zip: ____________
Fax Number: ____________
Designated E-mail Address(es): ____________
____

____
Signature of Party
Printed Name: ____________
Address: ____________
City, State, Zip: ____________
Telephone Number: ____________
Fax Number: ____________
Designated E-mail Address(es): ____________
____

IF A NONLAWYER HELPED YOU FILL OUT THIS FORM, HE/SHE MUST FILL IN THE BLANKS BELOW:
[fill in **all** blanks] This form was prepared for the: *{choose only **one**}* ( ) Petitioner ( ) Respondent
This form was completed with the assistance of:
{name of individual} ____________,

Florida Supreme Court Approved Family Law Form 12.914, Certificate of Service (03/15)

*{name of business}*____,
*{address}*____,
{city} ________________,*{state}* ____,*{zip code}*___________,*{telephone number}* ____________________.

INSTRUCTIONS FOR FLORIDA SUPREME COURT APPROVED FAMILY LAW FORM 12.914 CERTIFICATE OF SERVICE (03/15)

When should this form be used?

After a petition or supplemental petition has been properly served (through either **personal service** or **constructive service**), both parties **must** serve copies of all additional documents or papers they **file** with the clerk on the other **party,** or his or her attorney, if he or she has one. Each time you file a document, you must certify that you provided the other party with a copy. Many of the Florida Family Law Forms already have a place above the signature line for this certification. It looks like this:

I certify that a copy of this document was ( ) mailed ( ) faxed and mailed ( ) e-mailed ( ) hand-delivered to the person(s) listed below on {*date*} __________.

Other party or his/her attorney:

Name: ____________________

Address: ____________________

City, State, Zip: ____________________

Fax Number: ____________________

Designated E-mail Address(es): ____________________

____

If a form you are filing has a certificate, you do not need to file a separate **Certificate of Service**, Florida Supreme Court Approved Family Law Form 12.914. However, **each time** you file a document that does **not** have a certificate like the one above, you must file a **Certificate of Service**, Florida Supreme Court Approved Family Law Form 12.914, and serve a copy of the document on the other party.

This form should be typed or printed in black ink. After completing this form (giving the name of each form, document, or paper filed), you should sign the form before a **notary public** or **deputy clerk**. You should file the original with the **clerk of the circuit court** in the county where your case was filed and keep a copy for your records.

IMPORTANT INFORMATION REGARDING E–FILING

The Florida Rules of Judicial Administration now require that all petitions, pleadings, and documents be filed electronically except in certain circumstances. **Self-represented litigants may file petitions or other pleadings or documents electronically; however, they are not required to do so.** If you choose to file your pleadings or other documents electronically, you must do so in accordance with Florida Rule of Judicial Administration 2.525, and you must follow the procedures of the judicial circuit in which you file. **The rules and procedures should be carefully read and followed.**

What should I do next?

The copy you are providing to the other party must be either mailed, e-mailed, or hand-delivered to the opposing party or his or her attorney on the same day indicated on the certificate of service. If it is mailed, it must be postmarked on the date indicated in the certificate of service.

IMPORTANT INFORMATION REGARDING E–SERVICE ELECTION

After the initial service of process of the petition or supplemental petition by the Sheriff or certified process server, the Florida Rules of Judicial Administration now require that all documents required or permitted to be served on the other party must be served by electronic mail (e-mail) except in certain circumstances. **You must strictly comply with the format requirements set forth in the Rules of Judicial Administration.**

SELF–REPRESENTED LITIGANTS MAY SERVE DOCUMENTS BY E–MAIL; HOWEVER, THEY ARE NOT REQUIRED TO DO SO. If a self-represented litigant elects to serve and receive documents by e-mail, the procedures must always be followed once the initial election is made.

To serve and receive documents by e-mail, you must designate your e-mail addresses by using the **Designation of Current Mailing and E-mail Address**, Florida Supreme Court Approved Family Law Form 12.915, and you must provide your e-mail address on each form on which your signature appears. Please **CAREFULLY** read the rules and instructions for: **Certificate of Service (General),** Florida Supreme Court Approved Family Law Form 12.914; **Designation of Current Mailing and E-mail Address**, Florida Supreme Court Approved Family Law Form 12.915; and Florida Rule of Judicial Administration 2.516.

Where can I look for more information?

Before proceeding, you should read General Information for Self–Represented Litigants found at the beginning of these forms. For more information, see rule 1.080, Florida Rules of Civil Procedure and rule 12.080, Florida Family Law Rules of Procedure.

Special notes

Remember, a person who is NOT an attorney is called a nonlawyer. If a nonlawyer helps you fill out these forms, that person must give you a copy of **Disclosure from Nonlawyer**, Florida Family Law Rules of Procedure Form 12.900(a), before he or she helps you. A nonlawyer helping you fill out these forms also **must** put his or her name, address, and telephone number on the bottom of the last page of every form he or she helps you complete.

Added July 7, 1995, effective Jan. 1, 1996 (663 So.2d 1047). Amended Feb. 26, 1998, effective Mar. 16, 1998 (713 So.2d 1); Sept. 21, 2000 (810 So.2d 1); March 26, 2015, effective March 26, 2015 (2015 WL 1343088).

Form 12.915. Designation of Current Mailing and E–Mail Address

IN THE CIRCUIT COURT OF THE ______________ JUDICIAL CIRCUIT,
IN AND FOR ______________ COUNTY, FLORIDA

Case No.: ______________
Division: ______________

______________________________,
Petitioner,

and

______________________________,
Respondent.

DESIGNATION OF CURRENT MAILING AND E-MAIL ADDRESS

I, *{full legal name}* ______________________________, being sworn, certify that my current mailing address is: *{Street}* ______________________________
{City} ______________, *{State}* ______________ *{Zip}* ______________
{Telephone No.} ______________ *{Fax No.}* ______________.

I designate as my current e-mail address(es): ______________________________
____

I understand that I must keep the clerk's office and the opposing party or parties notified of my current mailing and e-mail address(es) and that all future papers in this lawsuit will be served at the address(es) on record at the clerk's office.

I certify that a copy of this document was: ( ) e-mailed ( ) mailed ( ) faxed
( ) hand-delivered to the person(s) listed below on *{date}*______________.

Other party or his/her attorney:
Name: ______________
Address: ______________
City, State, Zip: ______________
Fax Number: ______________
Designated E-mail Address(es): ______________
____

Florida Supreme Court Approved Family Law Form 12.915, Designation of Current Mailing and E-mail Address (03/15)

Dated: _______________ ____

STATE OF FLORIDA
COUNTY OF
Sworn to or affirmed and signed before me on _________ by ______________________________.

____
NOTARY PUBLIC or DEPUTY CLERK

____
[Print, type, or stamp commissioned name of notary or clerk.]
___ Personally known
___ Produced identification
Type of identification produced ____________________

IF A NONLAWYER HELPED YOU FILL OUT THIS FORM, HE/SHE MUST FILL IN THE BLANKS BELOW:
[fill in all blanks] This form was prepared for the: *{choose only **one**}* ( ) Petitioner ( ) Respondent
This form was completed with the assistance of:
{name of individual} ______________________________,
{name of business} ______________________________,
{street} ______________________________,
{city} ______________,*{state}* ___, *{zip code}* ______,*{telephone number}* ______________.

Florida Supreme Court Approved Family Law Form 12.915, Designation of Current Mailing and E-mail Address (03/15)

INSTRUCTIONS FOR FLORIDA SUPREME COURT APPROVED FAMILY LAW FORM 12.915, DESIGNATION OF CURRENT MAILING AND E–MAIL ADDRESS (03/15)

When should this form be used?

This form should be used to inform the clerk and the other **party** of your current mailing and email address(es) or **any change of address**. It is very important that the court and the other party in your case have your correct address.

A party not represented by an attorney may choose to designate e-mail address(es) for **service.** A primary and up to two secondary e-mail addresses can be designated. If you do so and the other party is represented by an attorney or has also designated e-mail address(es) for service, e-mail will be the **exclusive means of service.**

If there is any change in your mailing or e-mail address(es), you must complete a new form, file it with the clerk, and serve a copy on any other party or parties in your case.

What should I do next?

This form should be typed or printed in black ink. After completing this form, you should **file** the original with the **clerk of the circuit court** in the county where your case is filed and keep a copy for your records. A copy of this form must be served on any other party in your case. **Service** must be in accordance with Florida Rule of Judicial Administration 2.516.

IMPORTANT INFORMATION REGARDING E–FILING

The Florida Rules of Judicial Administration now require that all petitions, pleadings, and documents be filed electronically except in certain circumstances. **Self-represented litigants may file petitions or other pleadings or documents electronically; however, they are not required to do so.** If you choose to file your pleadings or other documents electronically, you must do so in accordance with Florida Rule of Judicial Administration 2.525, and you must follow the procedures of the judicial circuit in which you file. **The rules and procedures should be carefully read and followed.**

IMPORTANT INFORMATION REGARDING E–SERVICE ELECTION

After the initial service of process of the petition or supplemental petition by the Sheriff or certified process server, the Florida Rules of Judicial Administration now require that all documents required or permitted to be served on the other party must be served by electronic mail (e-mail) except in certain circumstances. **You must strictly comply with the format requirements set forth in the Rules of Judicial Administration.**

SELF–REPRESENTED LITIGANTS MAY SERVE DOCUMENTS BY E–MAIL; HOWEVER, THEY ARE NOT REQUIRED TO DO SO. If a self-represented litigant elects to serve and receive documents by e-mail, the procedures must always be followed once the initial election is made.

To serve and receive documents by e-mail, you must designate your e-mail addresses by using the **Designation of Current Mailing and E-mail Address**, Florida Supreme Court Approved Family Law Form 12.915, and you must provide your e-mail address on each form on which your signature appears. Please **CAREFULLY** read the rules and instructions for: **Certificate of Service (General),** Florida Supreme Court Approved Family Law Form 12.914; **Designation of Current Mailing and E-mail Address**, Florida Supreme Court Approved Family Law Form 12.915; and Florida Rule of Judicial Administration 2.516.

Where can I look for more information?

Before proceeding, you should read General Information for Self–Represented Litigants found at the beginning of these forms. The words that are in **bold underline** in these instructions are defined there.

Special notes . . .

Remember, a person who is NOT an attorney is called a nonlawyer. If a nonlawyer helps you fill out these forms, that person must give you a copy of **Disclosure from Nonlawyer**, Florida

Family Law Rules of Procedure Form 12.900(a), before he or she helps you. A nonlawyer helping you fill out these forms also **must** put his or her name, address, and telephone number on the bottom of the last page of every form he or she helps you complete.

Added Feb. 26, 1998, effective Mar. 16, 1998 (713 So.2d 1). Amended Sept. 21, 2000 (810 So.2d 1); Oct. 18, 2012, effective, *nunc pro tunc*, Sept. 1, 2012 (102 So.3d 505); March 26, 2015, effective March 26, 2015 (2015 WL 1343088).

Form 12.920(a). Motion for Referral to General Magistrate

IN THE CIRCUIT COURT OF THE ____________________ JUDICIAL CIRCUIT,
IN AND FOR ____________________ COUNTY, FLORIDA

Case No: ____________________
Division: ____________________

______________________________,
Petitioner,

and

______________________________,
Respondent.

MOTION FOR REFERRAL TO GENERAL MAGISTRATE

I, *{full legal name}* ____________________________________, request that the Court enter an order referring this case to a general magistrate. The case should be referred to a general magistrate on the following issues: *{explain}*

____
____
____
____
____

I certify that a copy of this document was [check all used]: ( ) e-mailed ( ) mailed ( ) faxed ( ) hand delivered to the person(s) listed below on *{date}* ____________________.

Other party or his/her attorney:
Name: ____________________
Address: ____________________
City, State, Zip: ____________________
Fax Number: ____________________
E-mail Address(es): ____________________

____
Signature of Party or his/her attorney:
Printed Name: ____________________
Address: ____________________
City, State, Zip: ____________________
Telephone Number: ____________________
Fax Number: ____________________
E-mail Address(es): ____________________

Florida Family Law Rules of Procedure Form 12.920(a), Motion for Referral to General Magistrate (09/12)

Florida Bar Number:_______________

IF A NONLAWYER HELPED YOU FILL OUT THIS FORM, HE/SHE MUST FILL IN THE BLANKS BELOW:
[fill in **all** blanks] This form was prepared for the: *{choose only **one**}* ( ) Petitioner ( ) Respondent
This form was completed with the assistance of:
{name of individual} ____,
{name of business} ____,
{address} ____,
*{city}*_______________,*{state}*_______, *{telephone number}*_______________.

INSTRUCTIONS FOR FLORIDA FAMILY LAW RULES OF PROCEDURE FORMS 12.920(a), MOTION FOR REFERRAL TO GENERAL MAGISTRATE, 12.920(b), ORDER OF REFERRAL TO GENERAL MAGISTRATE, and 12.920(c), NOTICE OF HEARING BEFORE GENERAL MAGISTRATE (09/12)

When should this form be used?

A **general magistrate** is an attorney appointed by a **judge** to take testimony and recommend decisions on certain matters connected with a divorce. These recommendations are then reviewed by the judge and are generally approved unless contrary to the law or the facts of the case. The primary purposes of having general magistrates hear family law matters are to reduce the costs of litigation and to speed up cases. Either **party** may request that their case, or portions of their case, be heard by a general magistrate by filing **Motion for Referral to General Magistrate**, Florida Family Law Rules of Procedure Form 12.920(a). You must also prepare an **Order of Referral to General Magistrate**, Florida Family Law Rules of Procedure Form 12.920(b), to submit to the judge assigned to your case.

Many times, the court, either on its own motion or under current administrative orders of the court, may refer your case to a general magistrate. Even in those instances, you may be required to prepare and submit an **Order of Referral to General Magistrate**, Florida Family Law Rules of Procedure Form 12.920(b), to the judge.

Once a general magistrate has been appointed to your case, the general magistrate will assign a time and place for a **hearing** as soon as reasonably possible after the referral is made. The general magistrate will give notice of that hearing to each of the parties directly or will direct a party or attorney in the case to file and serve a notice of hearing on the other party. If you are asked to send the notice of hearing, you will need to use the form entitled **Notice of Hearing Before General Magistrate**, Florida Family Law Rules of Procedure Form 12.920(c). Regardless of who prepares the notice of hearing, the moving party (the one who requested referral to the general magistrate) is required to have the notice properly served on the other party.

These forms should be typed or printed in black ink. After completing this form, you should **file** the original with the **clerk of the circuit court** in the county where your case is filed and keep a copy for your records.

What should I do next?

If you are filing a **Motion for Referral to General Magistrate**, Florida Family Law Rules of Procedure Form 12.920(a), you need to send or deliver your motion directly to the judge assigned to your case, along with an **Order of Referral to General Magistrate**, Florida Family Law Rules of Procedure Form 12.920(b), and an addressed, stamped envelope for each party in the case. The judge will then either grant or deny the motion, usually without a hearing.

If you are required to submit an **Order of Referral to General Magistrate**, Florida Family Law Rules of Procedure Form 12.920(b), to the judge assigned to your case, you will need to send or deliver the order directly to the judge, along with addressed, stamped envelopes for each party in the case.

The party who prepares any of these forms must file the original with the clerk of the circuit court. A copy of the motion must be served on any other party in your case. **Service** must be in accordance with Florida Rule of Judicial Administration 2.516.

Where can I look for more information?

Before proceeding, you should read General Information for Self-Represented Litigants found at the beginning of these forms. The words that are in **bold underline** in these instructions are defined there. For further information, see Florida Family Law Rule of Procedure 12.490.

Special notes . . .

IMPORTANT: After the judge refers your case to a general magistrate, either party (including the party who was required to prepare and submit the Order of Referral) may object to the referral within 10 days of the date that the referral is made (if the Order of

Referral is served by mail, the parties have an additional 5 days within which to object to the referral). Every litigant is entitled to have his or her case heard by a judge. However, before you decide to object to an Order of Referral to General Magistrate, you should consider the potential extra costs and time delays that may result from having a judge hear your case instead of a general magistrate. You may want to speak with an attorney in your area who can assist you in making a more informed decision regarding whether you should file an objection to an Order of Referral to General Magistrate.

Remember, a person who is NOT an attorney is called a nonlawyer. If a nonlawyer helps you fill out these forms, that person must give you a copy of **Disclosure from Nonlawyer**, Florida Family Law Rules of Procedure Form 12.900(a), before he or she helps you. A nonlawyer helping you fill out these forms also **must** put his or her name, address, and telephone number on the bottom of the last page of every form he or she helps you complete.

Added July 7, 1995, effective Jan. 1, 1996 (663 So.2d 1047). Amended Feb. 26, 1998, effective Mar. 16, 1998 (713 So.2d 1); July 1, 1999 (759 So.2d 583); Sept. 21, 2000 (810 So.2d 1); Sept. 30, 2004, effective Oct. 1, 2004 (887 So.2d 1090); Sept. 28, 2011 (73 So.3d 213); Oct. 18, 2012, effective, *nunc pro tunc*, Sept. 1, 2012 (102 So.3d 505).

Form 12.920(b). Order of Referral to General Magistrate

IN THE CIRCUIT COURT OF THE ______________ JUDICIAL CIRCUIT,
IN AND FOR ______________ COUNTY, FLORIDA

Case No: ______________
Division: ______________

______________,
Petitioner,

and

______________,
Respondent.

ORDER OF REFERRAL TO GENERAL MAGISTRATE

THIS CASE IS REFERRED TO THE GENERAL MAGISTRATE on the following issues:

1. ______________
2. ______________
3. ______________
4. ______________

AND ANY OTHER MATTER RELATED THERETO.

IT IS FURTHER ORDERED that the above issues are referred to General Magistrate *{name}* ______________, for further proceedings, under rule 12.490 of the Florida Family Law Rules of Procedure and current administrative orders of the Court. Financial Affidavits, Florida Family Law Rules of Procedure Form 12.902(b) or (c), shall be filed in accordance with Florida Family Law Rule of Procedure 12.285. The General Magistrate is authorized to administer oaths and conduct hearings, which may include taking of evidence, and shall file a report and recommendations that contain findings of fact, conclusions of law, and the name of the court reporter, if any.

The General Magistrate shall assign a time for the proceedings as soon as reasonably possible after this referral is made and shall give notice to each of the parties either directly or by directing counsel or a party to file and serve a notice of hearing.

Counties within the State of Florida may have different rules. Please consult the ( ) Clerk of the Court ( ) Family Law Intake Staff ( ) other ______________ relating to this procedure.

Florida Family Law Rules of Procedure Form 12.920(b), Order of Referral to General Magistrate (09/12)

A REFERRAL TO A GENERAL MAGISTRATE REQUIRES THE CONSENT OF ALL PARTIES. YOU ARE ENTITLED TO HAVE THIS MATTER HEARD BY A JUDGE. IF YOU DO NOT WANT TO HAVE THIS MATTER HEARD BY THE GENERAL MAGISTRATE, YOU MUST FILE A WRITTEN OBJECTION TO THE REFERRAL WITHIN 10 DAYS OF THE TIME OF SERVICE OF THIS ORDER. IF THE TIME SET FOR THE HEARING IS LESS THAN 10 DAYS AFTER SERVICE OF THIS ORDER, THE OBJECTION MUST BE MADE BEFORE THE HEARING. IF THIS ORDER IS SERVED WITHIN THE FIRST 20 DAYS AFTER SERVICE OF PROCESS, THE TIME TO FILE AN OBJECTION IS EXTENDED TO THE TIME WITHIN WHICH A RESPONSIVE PLEADING IS DUE. FAILURE TO FILE A WRITTEN OBJECTION WITHIN THE APPLICABLE TIME PERIOD IS DEEMED TO BE A CONSENT TO THE REFERRAL.

If either party files a timely objection, this matter shall be returned to the undersigned judge with a notice stating the amount of time needed for hearing.

REVIEW OF THE REPORT AND RECOMMENDATIONS MADE BY THE GENERAL MAGISTRATE SHALL BE BY EXCEPTIONS AS PROVIDED IN RULE 12.490(f), FLORIDA FAMILY LAW RULES OF PROCEDURE. A RECORD, WHICH INCLUDES A TRANSCRIPT, MAY BE REQUIRED TO SUPPORT EXCEPTIONS.

YOU ARE ADVISED THAT IN THIS CIRCUIT:

a. ____ electronic recording is provided by the court. A party may provide a court reporter at that party's expense.

b. ____ a court reporter is provided by the court.

SHOULD YOU WISH TO SEEK REVIEW OF THE REPORT AND RECOMMENDATION MADE BY THE GENERAL MAGISTRATE, YOU MUST FILE EXCEPTIONS IN ACCORDANCE WITH RULE 12.490(f), FLORIDA FAMILY LAW RULES OF PROCEDURE. YOU WILL BE REQUIRED TO PROVIDE THE COURT WITH A RECORD SUFFICIENT TO SUPPORT YOUR EXCEPTIONS, OR YOUR EXCEPTIONS WILL BE DENIED. A RECORD ORDINARILY INCLUDES A WRITTEN TRANSCRIPT OF ALL RELEVANT PROCEEDINGS. THE PERSON SEEKING REVIEW MUST HAVE THE TRANSCRIPT PREPARED IF NECESSARY FOR THE COURT'S REVIEW.

ORDERED on ______________________________.

____
CIRCUIT JUDGE

COPIES TO:
Petitioner (or his or her attorney)
Respondent (or his or her attorney)
General Magistrate

Florida Family Law Rules of Procedure Form 12.920(b), Order of Referral to General Magistrate (09/12)

Added July 7, 1995, effective Jan. 1, 1996 (663 So.2d 1047). Amended Feb. 26, 1998, effective Mar. 16, 1998 (713 So.2d 1); July 1, 1999 (759 So.2d 583); Sept. 21, 2000 (810 So.2d 1); Sept. 30, 2004, effective Oct. 1, 2004 (887 So.2d 1090); Sept. 28, 2011 (73 So.3d 213); Oct. 18, 2012, effective, *nunc pro tunc*, Sept. 1, 2012 (102 So.3d 505).

Form 12.920(c). Notice of Hearing Before General Magistrate

IN THE CIRCUIT COURT OF THE ________ JUDICIAL CIRCUIT,
IN AND FOR ________ COUNTY, FLORIDA

Case No: ________
Division: ________

________________________,
Petitioner,

and

________________________,
Respondent.

NOTICE OF HEARING BEFORE GENERAL MAGISTRATE

[fill in all blanks]
TO: ________________________

There will be a hearing before General Magistrate *{name of general magistrate}* ________________,
on *{date}* __________, at *{time}* ___ m., in Room ________ of the ________________
Courthouse, on the following issues: ________________________
____
____

___ hour(s) ___ minutes have been reserved for this hearing.
PLEASE GOVERN YOURSELF ACCORDINGLY.

If the matter before the General Magistrate is a Motion for Civil Contempt/Enforcement, FAILURE TO APPEAR AT THE HEARING MAY RESULT IN THE COURT ISSUING A WRIT OF BODILY ATTACHMENT FOR YOUR ARREST. IF YOU ARE ARRESTED, YOU MAY BE HELD IN JAIL UP TO 48 HOURS BEFORE A HEARING IS HELD.

PLEASE GOVERN YOURSELF ACCORDINGLY.

This part to be filled out by the court or filled in with information you have obtained from the court:

If you are a person with a disability who needs any accommodation in order to participate in this proceeding, you are entitled, at no cost to you, to the provision of certain assistance. Please contact:

____
{identify applicable court personnel by name, address, and telephone number}

Florida Family Law Rules of Procedure Form 12.920(c), Notice of Hearing Before General Magistrate (09/12)

at least 7 days before your scheduled court appearance, or immediately upon receiving this notification if the time before the scheduled appearance is less than 7 days; if you are hearing or voice impaired, call 711.

SHOULD YOU WISH TO SEEK REVIEW OF THE REPORT AND RECOMMENDATION MADE BY THE GENERAL MAGISTRATE, YOU MUST FILE EXCEPTIONS IN ACCORDANCE WITH RULE 12.490(f), FLORIDA FAMILY LAW RULES OF PROCEDURE. YOU WILL BE REQUIRED TO PROVIDE THE COURT WITH A RECORD SUFFICIENT TO SUPPORT YOUR EXCEPTIONS, OR YOUR EXCEPTIONS WILL BE DENIED. A RECORD ORDINARILY INCLUDES A WRITTEN TRANSCRIPT OF ALL RELEVANT PROCEEDINGS. THE PERSON SEEKING REVIEW MUST HAVE THE TRANSCRIPT PREPARED IF NECESSARY FOR THE COURT'S REVIEW.

YOU ARE HEREBY ADVISED THAT IN THIS CIRCUIT:

a. _____electronic recording is provided by the court. A party may provide a court reporter at that party's expense.

b. _____ a court reporter is provided by the court.

If you are represented by an attorney or plan to retain an attorney for this matter you should notify the attorney of this hearing.

If this matter is resolved, the moving party shall contact the General Magistrate's Office to cancel this hearing.

I certify that a copy of this document was **[check all used]**: ( ) e-mailed ( ) mailed ( ) faxed ( ) hand delivered to the person(s) listed below on *{date}*______________________.

Other party or his/her attorney:
Name: ________________________________
Address: ________________________________
City, State, Zip: ________________________________
Fax Number: ________________________________
E-mail Address(es):________________________________

____
Signature of Party or his/her Attorney
Printed Name: ________________________
Address: ________________________
City, State, Zip:________________________
Telephone Number: ________________________
Fax Number: ________________________
E-mail Address(es):________________________
Florida Bar Number: ________________________

Florida Family Law Rules of Procedure Form 12.920(c), Notice of Hearing Before General Magistrate (09/12)

IF A NONLAWYER HELPED YOU FILL OUT THIS FORM, HE/SHE MUST FILL IN THE BLANKS BELOW:
[fill in **all** blanks] This form was prepared for the: *{choose only **one**}* ( ) Petitioner ( ) Respondent
This form was completed with the assistance of:
*{name of individual}*____,
*{name of business}*____,
*{address}*____,
*{city}*____________________*{state}*________, *{telephone number}*________________.

Florida Family Law Rules of Procedure Form 12.920(c), Notice of Hearing Before General Magistrate (09/12)

Added Feb. 26, 1998, effective Mar. 16, 1998 (713 So.2d 1). Amended July 1, 1999 (759 So.2d 583); Sept. 21, 2000 (810 So.2d 1); Sept. 30, 2004, effective Oct. 1, 2004 (887 So.2d 1090); Sept. 28, 2011 (73 So.3d 213); Oct. 18, 2012, effective, *nunc pro tunc*, Sept. 1, 2012 (102 So.3d 505).

Form 12.921. Notice of Hearing (Child Support Enforcement Hearing Officer)

IN THE CIRCUIT COURT OF THE ____________________ JUDICIAL CIRCUIT,
IN AND FOR ____________________ COUNTY, FLORIDA

Case No.: ____________________
Division: ____________________

______________________________________,
Petitioner,

and

______________________________________,
Respondent.

NOTICE OF HEARING
(CHILD SUPPORT ENFORCEMENT HEARING OFFICER)

TO: *{name of other party}*: ____
There will be a hearing before Child Support Enforcement Hearing Officer *{name}* ________________,
on *{date}* ________________, at *{time}* _____ m., in Room ______ of the ________________________
County Courthouse, on the following issues: ____
____.
_____ hour(s)/_____ minutes have been reserved for this hearing.

If the matter before the Child Support Enforcement Hearing Officer is a Motion for Civil Contempt/Enforcement, **FAILURE TO APPEAR AT THE HEARING MAY RESULT IN THE COURT ISSUING A WRIT OF BODILY ATTACHMENT FOR YOUR ARREST. IF YOU ARE ARRESTED, YOU MAY BE HELD IN JAIL UP TO 48 HOURS BEFORE A HEARING IS HELD.**

This part to be filled out by the court or filled in with information you have obtained from the court:

If you are a person with a disability who needs any accommodation in order to participate in this proceeding, you are entitled, at no cost to you, to the provision of certain assistance. Please contact:

____

{identify applicable court personnel by name, address, and telephone number} **at least 7 days before your scheduled court appearance, or immediately upon**

Florida Supreme Court Approved Family Law Form 12.921, Notice of Hearing (Child Support Enforcement Hearing Officer) (03/15)

receiving this notification if the time before the scheduled appearance is less than 7 days; if you are hearing or voice impaired, call 711.

If you are represented by an attorney or plan to retain an attorney for this matter, you should notify the attorney of this hearing.

If this matter is resolved, the moving party shall contact the hearing officer's office to cancel this hearing.

I certify that a copy of this document was ( ) mailed ( ) faxed and mailed ( ) e-mailed ( ) hand-delivered to the person(s) listed below on *{date}* ______________________.

Other party or his/her attorney:
Name: ____
Address: ______________________________________
City, State, Zip: ________________________________
Fax Number: ___________________________________
Designated E-mail Address(es): ___________________

____
Signature of Party
Printed Name: _________________________
Address: _____________________________
City, State, Zip: ________________________
Telephone Number: ______________________
Fax Number: ___________________________
Designated E-mail Address(es): ____________

IF A NONLAWYER HELPED YOU FILL OUT THIS FORM, HE/SHE MUST FILL IN THE BLANKS BELOW:
[fill in all blanks] This form was prepared for the: *{choose only **one**}* ( ) Petitioner ( ) Respondent
This form was completed with the assistance of:
{name of individual} ____,
{name of business} ____,
{address} ____,
{city} _______________, *{state}* ____, *{zip code}* __________, *{telephone number}* ______________.

Florida Supreme Court Approved Family Law Form 12.921, Notice of Hearing (Child Support Enforcement Hearing Officer) (03/15)

INSTRUCTIONS FOR FLORIDA SUPREME COURT APPROVED FAMILY LAW FORM 12.921, NOTICE OF HEARING (CHILD SUPPORT ENFORCEMENT HEARING OFFICER)(03/15)

When should this form be used?

A **child support enforcement hearing officer** is an attorney who has been appointed by administrative order of the court to take testimony and recommend decisions in cases involving the establishment, enforcement, and/or modification of **child support**. If your case only involves issues pertaining to child support, you cannot object to the referral of your case to a hearing officer.

Use this form anytime you have set a **hearing** before a child support enforcement hearing officer and have been instructed to send notice of the hearing to the other party. Before you fill out this form, you should coordinate a hearing time and date with the hearing officer and the other party. If the Department of Revenue is a party to the case, you may need to schedule your hearing time with the attorney for the Department of Revenue.

This form should be typed or printed in black ink. After completing this form, you should **file** the original with the **clerk of the circuit court** in the county where your case is filed and keep a copy for your records.

IMPORTANT INFORMATION REGARDING E-FILING

The Florida Rules of Judicial Administration now require that all petitions, pleadings, and documents be filed electronically except in certain circumstances. **Self-represented litigants may file petitions or other pleadings or documents electronically; however, they are not required to do so.** If you choose to file your pleadings or other documents electronically, you must do so in accordance with Florida Rule of Judicial Administration 2.525, and you must follow the procedures of the judicial circuit in which you file. **The rules and procedures should be carefully read and followed.**

What should I do next?

A copy of this form must be mailed, e-mailed, or hand-delivered to the other party in your case.

IMPORTANT INFORMATION REGARDING E-SERVICE ELECTION

After the initial service of process of the petition or supplemental petition by the Sheriff or certified process server, the Florida Rules of Judicial Administration now require that all documents required or permitted to be served on the other party must be served by electronic mail (e-mail) except in certain circumstances. **You must strictly comply with the format requirements set forth in the Rules of Judicial Administration.**

SELF-REPRESENTED LITIGANTS MAY SERVE DOCUMENTS BY E-MAIL; HOWEVER, THEY ARE NOT REQUIRED TO DO SO. If a self-represented litigant elects to serve and receive documents by e-mail, the procedures must always be followed once the initial election is made.

To serve and receive documents by e-mail, you must designate your e-mail addresses by using the **Designation of Current Mailing and E-mail Address**, Florida Supreme Court Approved Family Law Form 12.915, and you must provide your e-mail address on each form on which your signature appears. Please **CAREFULLY** read the rules and instructions for: **Certificate of Service (General)**, Florida Supreme Court Approved Family Law Form 12.914; **Designation of Current Mailing and E-mail Address**, Florida Supreme Court Approved Family Law Form 12.915; and Florida Rule of Judicial Administration 2.516.

Where can I look for more information?

Before proceeding, you should read General Information for Self Represented Litigants found at the beginning of these forms. For further information, See Rule 12.941, Florida Family Law Rules of Procedure.

Special notes . . .

An attorney who has been appointed by the court to serve as a child support enforcement hearing officer can also be appointed to serve as a general magistrate. If your case involves only child support issues, your case may properly be referred to a general magistrate acting as a child support enforcement hearing officer.

Remember, a person who is NOT an attorney is called a nonlawyer. If a nonlawyer helps you fill out these forms, that person must give you a copy of **Disclosure from Nonlawyer**, Florida Family Law Rules of Procedure Form 12.900 (a), before he or she helps you. A nonlawyer helping you fill out these forms also **must** put his or her name, address, and telephone number on the bottom of the last page of every form he or she helps you complete.

Added July 7, 1995, effective Jan. 1, 1996 (663 So.2d 1047). Amended Feb. 26, 1998, effective Mar. 16, 1998 (713 So.2d 1); July 1, 1999 (759 So.2d 583); Sept. 21, 2000 (810 So.2d 1); Sept. 30, 2004, effective Oct. 1, 2004 (887 So.2d 1090); Sept. 28, 2011 (73 So.3d 213); March 26, 2015, effective March 26, 2015 (2015 WL 1343088).

Form 12.922(a). Motion for Default

IN THE CIRCUIT COURT OF THE ________ JUDICIAL CIRCUIT,
IN AND FOR ______________ COUNTY, FLORIDA

Case No.: ______________________________
Division: ______________________________

________________________,
Petitioner,

and

________________________,
Respondent.

MOTION FOR DEFAULT

TO THE CLERK OF THE CIRCUIT COURT:

PLEASE ENTER A DEFAULT AGAINST RESPONDENT WHO HAS FAILED TO RESPOND TO THE PETITION.

I certify that a copy of this document was ( ) mailed ( ) faxed and mailed ( ) e-mailed ( ) hand-delivered to the person(s) listed below on *{date}* ______________________.

Other party or his/her attorney:
Name: ______________________________
Address: ______________________________
City, State, Zip: ______________________________
Fax Number: ______________________________
Designated E-mail Address(es): ______________________

____
Signature of Petitioner
Printed Name: ______________________________
Address: ______________________________
City, State, Zip: ______________________________
Telephone Number: ______________________________
Fax Number: ______________________________

Designated E-mail Address(es): ______________________

____

IF A NONLAWYER HELPED YOU FILL OUT THIS FORM, HE/SHE MUST FILL IN THE BLANKS BELOW:
[fill in **all** blanks] This form was prepared for the: *{choose only **one**}* ( ) Petitioner ( ) Respondent
This form was prepared with the assistance of:
{name of individual} ______________________________,
{name of business}
______________________________,
{address} ______________________________
______________________________,
{city} ____________, *{state}*____, *{zip code}*__________,*{telephone number}*______________.

Florida Supreme Court Approved Family Law Form 12.922(a), Motion for Default (03/15)

Added July 7, 1995, effective Jan. 1, 1996 (663 So.2d 1047). Amended Feb. 26, 1998, effective Mar. 16, 1998 (713 So.2d 1); Sept. 21, 2000 (810 So.2d 1); March 26, 2015, effective March 26, 2015 (2015 WL 1343088).

Form 12.922(b). Default

IN THE CIRCUIT COURT OF THE ______ JUDICIAL CIRCUIT,
IN AND FOR ____________________ COUNTY, FLORIDA

Case No.: ____________________
Division: ____________________

____________________________________,
Petitioner,

and

____________________________________,
Respondent.

DEFAULT

A default is entered in this action against Respondent for failure to serve or file a response or any paper as is required by law.

Dated: ____________________
CLERK OF THE CIRCUIT COURT
(SEAL)
By: ____________________________________
Deputy Clerk

I certify that a copy of this document was ( ) mailed ( ) faxed and mailed ( ) e-mailed ( ) hand-delivered to the person(s) listed below on *{date}*____________________________________.

Other party or his/her attorney:

Name: ____________________
Address: ____________________
City, State, Zip: ____________________
Fax Number: ____________________
Designated E-mail Address(es): ____________________

____
Signature of Petitioner
Printed Name: ____________________
Address: ____________________
City, State, Zip: ____________________
Telephone Number: ____________________
Fax Number: ____________________

Designated E-mail Address(es):____________________.

Florida Supreme Court Approved Family Law Form 12.922(b), Default (03/15)

IF A NONLAWYER HELPED YOU FILL OUT THIS FORM, HE/SHE MUST FILL IN THE BLANKS BELOW:
[fill in **all** blanks] This form was prepared for the: *{choose only **one**}* ( ) Petitioner ( ) Respondent
This form was completed with the assistance of:
{name of individual},____,
{name of business} ____,
{address} ____,
{city} __________________,*{state}*______,*{zip code}*____________,*{telephone number}* ______________.

Florida Supreme Court Approved Family Law Form 12.922(b), Default (03/15)

INSTRUCTIONS FOR FLORIDA SUPREME COURT APPROVED FAMILY LAW FORMS 12.922(a), MOTION FOR DEFAULT, AND 12.922(b), DEFAULT (03/15)

When should these forms be used?

If the other party has failed to file or serve any documents within 20 days after the date of service of your petition, you may ask the clerk of the circuit court to enter a default against him or her by filling out this form and filing it with the court. Generally, a default allows you to obtain an earlier final hearing to finish your case. Once the default is signed by the clerk, you can request a trial or final hearing in your case.

To obtain a default, you will need to complete **Motion for Default**, Florida Supreme Court Approved Family Law Form 12.922(a). You will then need to file your motion for default along with the **Default**, Florida Supreme Court Approved Family Law Form 12.922(b), so that the clerk can enter a default for you if your motion is proper.

This form should be typed or printed in black ink. After completing this form, you should file the original with the clerk of the circuit court in the county where you filed your petition and keep a copy for your records.

IMPORTANT INFORMATION REGARDING E–FILING

The Florida Rules of Judicial Administration now require that all petitions, pleadings, and documents be filed electronically except in certain circumstances. **Self-represented litigants may file petitions or other pleadings or documents electronically; however, they are not required to do so.** If you choose to file your pleadings or other documents electronically, you must do so in accordance with Florida Rule of Judicial Administration 2.525, and you must follow the procedures of the judicial circuit in which you file. **The rules and procedures should be carefully read and followed.**

What should I do next?

After the default has been entered, you must ask for a hearing, so that the judge can consider your petition. To do this, you must contact the clerk's office, family law intake staff, or judicial assistant to schedule a hearing and file a **Notice of Hearing (General)**, Florida Supreme Court Approved Family Law Form 12.923, with the clerk. A copy of the notice of hearing must be mailed, e-mailed, or hand-delivered to each party in the case. **You must send a notice of final hearing to the defaulted party.**

IMPORTANT INFORMATION REGARDING E–SERVICE ELECTION

After the initial service of process of the petition or supplemental petition by the Sheriff or certified process server, the Florida Rules of Judicial Administration now require that all documents required or permitted to be served on the other party must be served by electronic mail (e-mail) except in certain circumstances. **You must strictly comply with the format requirements set forth in the Rules of Judicial Administration.**

SELF–REPRESENTED LITIGANTS MAY SERVE DOCUMENTS BY E–MAIL; HOWEVER, THEY ARE NOT REQUIRED TO DO SO. If a self-represented litigant elects to serve and receive documents by e-mail, the procedures must always be followed once the initial election is made.

To serve and receive documents by e-mail, you must designate your e-mail addresses by using the **Designation of Current Mailing and E-mail Address**, Florida Supreme Court Approved Family Law Form 12.915, and you must provide your e-mail address on each form on which your signature appears. Please **CAREFULLY** read the rules and instructions for: **Certificate of Service (General),** Florida Supreme Court Approved Family Law Form 12.914; **Designation of Current Mailing and E-mail Address**, Florida Supreme Court Approved Family Law Form 12.915; and Florida Rule of Judicial Administration 2.516.

Where can I look for more information?

Before proceeding, you should read General Information for Self–Represented Litigants found at the beginning of these forms. For further information, see Florida Rules of Civil Procedure 1.500, concerning defaults and Rule 1.140, concerning the time within which a party can file an answer or other responsive pleading to a petition. See also Florida Family Law Rule of Procedure 12.080.

Special notes . . .

Remember, a person who is NOT an attorney is called a nonlawyer. If a nonlawyer helps you fill out these forms, that person must give you a copy of **Disclosure from Nonlawyer**, Florida Family Law Rules of Procedure Form 12.900 (a), before he or she helps you. A nonlawyer helping you fill out these forms also **must** put his or her name, address, and telephone number on the bottom of the last page of every form he or she helps you complete.

Added July 7, 1995, effective Jan. 1, 1996 (663 So.2d 1047). Amended Feb. 26, 1998, effective Mar. 16, 1998 (713 So.2d 1); Sept. 21, 2000 (810 So.2d 1); March 26, 2015, effective March 26, 2015 (2015 WL 1343088).

Form 12.922(c). Motion to Set Aside Default or Default Judgment

IN THE CIRCUIT COURT OF THE ________ JUDICIAL CIRCUIT,
IN AND FOR __________________ COUNTY, FLORIDA

Case No.: ____________________
Division: ____________________

_________________________________,
Petitioner,

and

_________________________________,
Respondent.

MOTION TO SET ASIDE DEFAULT OR DEFAULT JUDGMENT

I, *{full legal name}* ____________________, request that the Court enter an order to set aside the _____ Default _____ Default Judgment entered against me and that I be given the opportunity to present my views.

The Court should do this because:

1. I became aware of this Default/Default Judgment on *{date}* ____________________.

2. I found out about this in the following manner *{explain how you found out}*: ____________________
____
____
____
____
____

3. I did not answer or appear at the hearing because: ____________________
____
____
____
____
____

4. If I am given an opportunity, these are the defenses and arguments that I would like to tell the

court about: ____
____
____
____

I certify that a copy of this document was ( ) mailed ( ) faxed and mailed ( ) e-mailed ( ) hand-delivered to the person(s) listed below on *{date}* ______________________________.

Other party or his/her attorney:
Name: ______________________________
Address: ______________________________
City, State, Zip: ______________________________
Fax Number: ______________________________
Designated E-mail Address(es): ______________________________

I understand that I am swearing or affirming under oath to the truthfulness of the claims made in this motion and that the punishment for knowingly making a false statement includes fines and/or imprisonment.

Dated: ____________________

____
Signature of Respondent
Printed Name: ______________________________
Address: ______________________________
City, State, Zip: ______________________________
Telephone Number: ______________________________
Fax Number: ______________________________

Designated E-mail Address(es):
____

STATE OF FLORIDA
COUNTY OF

Sworn to or affirmed and signed before me on __________ by ______________________________.

____
NOTARY PUBLIC or DEPUTY CLERK

Supreme Court Approved Family Law Form 12.922(c), Motion to Set Aside Florida Default or Default Judgment (03/15)

____

[Print, type, or stamp commissioned name of notary or clerk.

____ Personally known

_____ Produced identification

Type of identification produced ______________________

IF A NONLAWYER HELPED YOU FILL OUT THIS FORM, HE/SHE MUST FILL IN THE BLANKS BELOW:

[fill in **all** blanks] This form was prepared for the: *{choose only **one**}* ( ) Petitioner ( ) Respondent

This form was completed with the assistance of:

{name of individual} ____,

{name of business} ____,

{address} ____,

{city} ____________,*{state}*______, *{zip code}*__________,*{telephone number}*______.

INSTRUCTIONS FOR FLORIDA SUPREME COURT APPROVED FAMILY LAW FORM 12.922(c), MOTION TO SET ASIDE DEFAULT OR DEFAULT JUDGMENT (03/15)

When should this form be used?

If a **default** or default judgment has been entered against you, and you believe, because of a mistake, inadvertence, excusable neglect, newly discovered evidence, or fraud, that it should not have been entered against you, you can use this form to request that the court set aside the default or default judgment.

This form should be typed or printed in black ink. After completing this form, you should sign the form before a **notary public** or **deputy clerk**. You should **file** the original with the **clerk of the circuit court** in the county where the default was entered and keep a copy for your records.

IMPORTANT INFORMATION REGARDING E-FILING

The Florida Rules of Judicial Administration now require that all petitions, pleadings, and documents be filed electronically except in certain circumstances. **Self-represented litigants may file petitions or other pleadings or documents electronically; however, they are not required to do so.** If you choose to file your pleadings or other documents electronically, you must do so in accordance with Florida Rule of Judicial Administration 2.525, and you must follow the procedures of the judicial circuit in which you file. **The rules and procedures should be carefully read and followed.**

What should I do next?

After you file this form with the clerk and serve a copy on the other party in the case, you must schedule a **hearing** so that the court can consider your motion. You should contact the clerk, **family law intake staff**, or **judicial assistant** to schedule a hearing. Once you have scheduled the hearing date and time, you will need to complete and send out a notice for that hearing. To do so, use **Notice of Hearing (General)**, Florida Supreme Court Approved Family Law Form 12.923, or other appropriate notice of hearing form.

IMPORTANT INFORMATION REGARDING E-SERVICE ELECTION

After the initial service of process of the petition or supplemental petition by the Sheriff or certified process server, the Florida Rules of Judicial Administration now require that all documents required or permitted to be served on the other party must be served by electronic mail (e-mail) except in certain circumstances. **You must strictly comply with the format requirements set forth in the Rules of Judicial Administration.**

SELF-REPRESENTED LITIGANTS MAY SERVE DOCUMENTS BY E-MAIL; HOWEVER, THEY ARE NOT REQUIRED TO DO SO. If a self-represented litigant elects to serve and receive documents by e-mail, the procedures must always be followed once the initial election is made.

To serve and receive documents by e-mail, you must designate your e-mail addresses by using the **Designation of Current Mailing and E-mail Address**, Florida Supreme Court Approved Family Law Form 12.915, and you must provide your e-mail address on each form on which your signature appears. Please **CAREFULLY** read the rules and instructions for: **Certificate of Service (General),** Florida Supreme Court Approved Family Law Form 12.914; **Designation of Current Mailing and E-mail Address**, Florida Supreme Court Approved Family Law Form 12.915; and Florida Rule of Judicial Administration 2.516.

Where can I look for more information?

Before proceeding, you should read General Information for Self-Represented Litigants found at the beginning of these forms. For further information, see Florida Family Law Rule of Procedure 12.540, and Florida Rules of Civil Procedure 1.500(d) and 1.540(d).

Special notes . . .

Remember, a person who is NOT an attorney is called a nonlawyer. If a nonlawyer helps you fill out these forms, that person must give you a copy of **Disclosure from Nonlawyer**, Florida Family Law Rules of Procedure Form 12.900 (a), before he or she helps you. A nonlawyer helping you fill out these forms also **must** put his or her name, address, and telephone number on the bottom of the last page of every form he or she helps you complete.

Added Feb. 26, 1998, effective Mar. 16, 1998 (713 So.2d 1). Amended Sept. 21, 2000 (810 So.2d 1); March 26, 2015, effective March 26, 2015 (2015 WL 1343088).

Form 12.923. Notice of Hearing (General)

IN THE CIRCUIT COURT OF THE ______________ JUDICIAL CIRCUIT,
IN AND FOR ______________ COUNTY, FLORIDA

Case No.: ______________
Division: ______________

______________________________,
Petitioner,

and

______________________________,
Respondent.

NOTICE OF HEARING (GENERAL)

[fill in **all** blanks]

TO: *{name of other party}*: ______________________________
There will be a hearing before Judge *{name}* ______________________________,
on *{date}* ______________, at *{time}* ________m., in Room _____ of the ______________
County Courthouse, on the following issues: ______________________________
____
______________________________.

_____ hour(s)/_____ minutes have been reserved for this hearing.

This part is to be filled out by the court or to be filled in with information you obtained from the court:

If you are a person with a disability who needs any accommodation in order to participate in this proceeding, you are entitled, at no cost to you, to the provision of certain assistance. Please contact:

____

{identify applicable court personnel by name, address, and telephone number} **at least 7 days before your scheduled court appearance, or immediately upon receiving this notification if the time before the scheduled appearance is less than 7 days; if you are hearing or voice impaired, call 711.**

Florida Supreme Court Approved Family Law Form 12.923, Notice of Hearing (General) (03/15)

If you are represented by an attorney or plan to retain an attorney for this matter, you should notify the attorney of this hearing.

If this matter is resolved, the moving party shall contact the judge's office to cancel this hearing.

I certify that a copy of this document was ( ) mailed ( ) faxed and mailed ( ) e-mailed ( ) hand-delivered to the person(s) listed below on *{date}*_______________________.

Other party or his/her attorney:
Name: ____
Address: _____________________________________
City, State, Zip: ______________________________
Fax Number: _________________________________
Designated E-mail Address: ___________________________

____
Signature of Party
Printed Name: ____
Address: ____
City, State, Zip: ____
Telephone Number: ____
Fax Number: ____
Designated E-mail Address(es): ____
____

IF A NONLAWYER HELPED YOU FILL OUT THIS FORM, HE/SHE MUST FILL IN THE BLANKS BELOW:
[fill in **all** blanks] This form was prepared for the: *{choose only **one**}* ( ) Petitioner ( ) Respondent
This form was completed with the assistance of:
{name of individual} ____,
{name of business} ____,
{address} ____,
{city} _________________, *{state}* _____, *{zip code}* __________, *{telephone number}* ______________.

Florida Supreme Court Approved Family Law Form 12.923, Notice of Hearing (General) (03/15)

INSTRUCTIONS FOR FLORIDA SUPREME COURT APPROVED FAMILY LAW FORM 12.923, NOTICE OF HEARING (GENERAL) (03/15)

When should this form be used?

Anytime you have set a hearing before a judge, you must send notice of the hearing to the other party.

IMPORTANT: If your hearing has been set before a general magistrate, you should use **Notice of Hearing Before General Magistrate**, Florida Family Law Rules of Procedure Form 12.920(c). If your hearing has been set before a child support enforcement hearing officer, you should use **Notice of Hearing (Child Support Hearing Officer)**, Florida Supreme Court Approved Family Law Form 12.921.

This form should be typed or printed in black ink. After completing this form, you should file the original with the clerk of the circuit court in the county where your case was filed and keep a copy for your records.

IMPORTANT INFORMATION REGARDING E–FILING

The Florida Rules of Judicial Administration now require that all petitions, pleadings, and documents be filed electronically except in certain circumstances. **Self-represented litigants may file petitions or other pleadings or documents electronically; however, they are not required to do so.** If you choose to file your pleadings or other documents electronically, you must do so in accordance with Florida Rule of Judicial Administration 2.525, and you must follow the procedures of the judicial circuit in which you file. **The rules and procedures should be carefully read and followed.**

What should I do next?

A copy of this form must be mailed, e-mailed, or hand delivered to the other party in your case. If a default has been entered, you must still send this form to the other party to notify the other party of the final hearing.

IMPORTANT INFORMATION REGARDING E–SERVICE ELECTION

After the initial service of process of the petition or supplemental petition by the Sheriff or certified process server, the Florida Rules of Judicial Administration now require that all documents required or permitted to be served on the other party must be served by electronic mail (e-mail) except in certain circumstances. **You must strictly comply with the format requirements set forth in the Rules of Judicial Administration.**

SELF–REPRESENTED LITIGANTS MAY SERVE DOCUMENTS BY E–MAIL; HOWEVER, THEY ARE NOT REQUIRED TO DO SO. If a self-represented litigant elects to serve and receive documents by e-mail, the procedures must always be followed once the initial election is made.

To serve and receive documents by e-mail, you must designate your e-mail addresses by using the **Designation of Current Mailing and E-mail Address**, Florida Supreme Court Approved Family Law Form 12.915, and you must provide your e-mail address on each form on which your signature appears. Please **CAREFULLY** read the rules and instructions for: **Certificate of Service (General),** Florida Supreme Court Approved Family Law Form 12.914; **Designation of Current Mailing and E-mail Address**, Florida Supreme Court Approved Family Law Form 12.915; and Florida Rule of Judicial Administration 2.516.

Where can I look for more information?

Before proceeding, you should read General Information for Self–Represented Litigants found at the beginning of these forms. For further information on serving notices of hearing, see rule 1.090(d), Florida Civil Rules of Procedure.

Special notes . . .

To set a hearing date and time, you will usually have to make a good-faith effort to coordinate a mutually convenient date and time for you, the other parties in the case, and the judge, except in certain emergency situations. Some circuits may have additional procedural requirements that you must follow when you notify the court and other parties of your scheduled hearing. Therefore, before you complete this form, you should contact the clerk's office, **family law intake staff**, or **judicial assistant** for information regarding the proper procedure to follow.

Remember, a person who is NOT an attorney is called a nonlawyer. If a nonlawyer helps you fill out these forms, that person must give you a copy of **Disclosure from Nonlawyer**, Florida Family Law Rules of Procedure Form 12.900 (a), before he or she helps you. A nonlawyer helping you fill out these forms also **must** put his or her name, address, and telephone number on the bottom of the last page of every form he or she helps you complete.

Added July 7, 1995, effective Jan. 1, 1996 (663 So.2d 1047). Amended Feb. 26, 1998, effective Mar. 16, 1998 (713 So.2d 1); Sept. 21, 2000 (810 So.2d 1); Sept. 30, 2004, effective Oct. 1, 2004 (887 So.2d 1090); Sept. 28, 2011 (73 So.3d 213); March 26, 2015, effective March 26, 2015 (2015 WL 1343088).

Form 12.924. Notice for Trial

IN THE CIRCUIT COURT OF THE _____ JUDICIAL CIRCUIT,
IN AND FOR ____________ COUNTY, FLORIDA

Case No.: ______________
Division: ______________

________________,
Petitioner,

and

________________,
Respondent.

NOTICE FOR TRIAL

Pursuant to Rule 12.440, Florida Family Law Rules of Procedure, the party signing below states that the case is ready to be set for trial. The estimated time needed for the parties to present their cases is: *{hours}* ______________.

I certify that a copy of this document was ( ) mailed ( ) faxed and mailed ( ) e-mailed ( ) hand-delivered to the person(s) listed below on *{date}* ________________________________.

Other party or his/her attorney:
Name: ________________________________
Address: ________________________________
City, State, Zip: ________________________
Fax Number: ______________________________
Designated E-mail Address(es): __________________

____
Signature of Party
Printed Name: ________________________________
Address: ________________________________
City, State, Zip: ________________________________
Telephone Number: ________________________________
Fax Number: ________________________________

Designated E-mail Address(es): ________________________________

Florida Supreme Court Approved Family Law Form 12.924, Notice for Trial (03/15)

IF A NONLAWYER HELPED YOU FILL OUT THIS FORM, HE/SHE MUST FILL IN THE BLANKS BELOW:
[fill in all blanks] This form was prepared for the: *{choose only one}* ( ) Petitioner ( ) Respondent
This form was completed with the assistance of:
{name of individual} ____,
{name of business} ____,
{address} ______________________
____,
{city} ________________,*{state}* ______,*{zip code}*________, *{telephone number}* __________.

INSTRUCTIONS FOR FLORIDA SUPREME COURT APPROVED FAMILY LAW FORM 12.924 NOTICE FOR TRIAL (03/15)

When should this form be used?

Generally, the court will have **trials** (or **final hearings**) in contested cases. This form is to be used to notify the court that your case is ready to be set for trial. Before setting your case for trial, certain requirements such as completing **mandatory disclosure** and **filing** certain papers and having them **served** on the other **party** must be met. These requirements vary depending on the type of case and the procedures in your particular circuit. In some circuits you must complete **mediation** or a **parenting course** before you can set a final hearing by using a **Notice of Hearing (General)**, Florida Supreme Court Approved Family Law Form 12.923, or other appropriate notice of hearing form. Other circuits may require that you set the trial using an **Order Setting Trial**. Contact the **clerk of the circuit court**, **family law intake staff**, or **judicial assistant** to determine how the **judge** assigned to your case sets trials. For further information, you should refer to the instructions for the type of form you are filing.

This form should be typed or printed in black ink. After completing this form, you should **file** the original with the clerk of the circuit court in the county where your case is filed and keep a copy for your records.

IMPORTANT INFORMATION REGARDING E–FILING

The Florida Rules of Judicial Administration now require that all petitions, pleadings, and documents be filed electronically except in certain circumstances. **Self-represented litigants may file petitions or other pleadings or documents electronically; however, they are not required to do so.** If you choose to file your pleadings or other documents electronically, you must do so in accordance with Florida Rule of Judicial Administration 2.525, and you must follow the procedures of the judicial circuit in which you file. **The rules and procedures should be carefully read and followed.**

What should I do next?

A copy of this form must be mailed, e-mailed, or hand-delivered to the other party in your case.

Where can I look for more information?

Before proceeding, you should read General Information for Self–Represented Litigants found at the beginning of these forms. For further information, see rule 12.440, Florida Family Law Rules of Procedure.

IMPORTANT INFORMATION REGARDING E–SERVICE ELECTION

After the initial service of process of the petition or supplemental petition by the Sheriff or certified process server, the Florida Rules of Judicial Administration now require that all documents required or permitted to be served on the other party must be served by electronic mail (e-mail) except in certain circumstances. **You must strictly comply with the format requirements set forth in the Rules of Judicial Administration.**

SELF–REPRESENTED LITIGANTS MAY SERVE DOCUMENTS BY E–MAIL; HOWEVER, THEY ARE NOT REQUIRED TO DO SO. If a self-represented litigant elects to serve and receive documents by e-mail, the procedures must always be followed once the initial election is made.

To serve and receive documents by e-mail, you must designate your e-mail addresses by using the **Designation of Current Mailing and E-mail Address**, Florida Supreme Court Approved Family Law Form 12.915, and you must provide your e-mail address on each form on which your signature appears. Please **CAREFULLY** read the rules and instructions for: **Certificate of Service (General)**, Florida Supreme Court Approved Family Law Form 12.914; **Designation of Current Mailing and E-mail Address**, Florida Supreme Court Approved Family Law Form 12.915; and Florida Rule of Judicial Administration 2.516.

Special notes . . .

These family law forms contain **orders** and **final judgments**, which the judge may use. You should ask the clerk of court, family law intake staff, or judicial assistant if you need to bring one of these forms with you to the hearing or trial. If so, you should type or print the heading, including the circuit, county, case number, division, and the parties' names, and leave the rest blank for the judge to complete at your hearing or trial.

Remember, a person who is NOT an attorney is called a nonlawyer. If a nonlawyer helps you fill out these forms, that person must give you a copy of a **Disclosure from Nonlawyer**, Florida Family Law Rules of Procedure Form 12.900 (a), before he or she helps you. A nonlawyer helping you fill out these forms also **must** put his or her name, address, and telephone number on the bottom of the last page of every form he or she helps you complete.

Added Feb. 26, 1998, effective Mar. 16, 1998 (713 So.2d 1). Amended Sept. 21, 2000 (810 So.2d 1); March 26, 2015, effective March 26, 2015 (2015 WL 1343088).

Form 12.927. Notice of Voluntary Dismissal

IN THE CIRCUIT COURT OF THE ______ JUDICIAL CIRCUIT,
IN AND FOR ______________ COUNTY, FLORIDA

Case No.: ______________
Division: ______________

______________________________,
Petitioner,

and

______________________________,
Respondent.

NOTICE OF VOLUNTARY DISMISSAL

I, *{full legal name}* ____, give notice that:
*[choose **one** only]*

a. _____ I am the Petitioner in this case and I voluntarily dismiss my petition.

b. _____ I am the Respondent in this case and I voluntarily dismiss my counterpetition.

I certify that a copy of this document was ( ) mailed ( ) faxed and mailed ( ) e-mailed ( ) hand delivered to the person(s) listed below on *{date}* ______________________.

Other party or his/her attorney:
Name: ______________________________
Address: ______________________________
City, State, Zip: ______________________________
Fax Number: ______________________________
Designated E-mail Address(es): ______________________________
____

____
Signature of Party
Printed Name: ______________________________
Address: ______________________________
City, State, Zip: ______________________________
Telephone Number: ______________________________
Fax Number: ______________________________
Designated E-mail

Florida Supreme Court Approved Family Law Form 12.927, Notice of Voluntary Dismissal (03/15)

Address(es):____

IF A NONLAWYER HELPED YOU FILL OUT THIS FORM, HE/SHE MUST FILL IN THE BLANKS BELOW:
[fill in **all** blanks] This form was prepared for the: *{choose only **one**}* ( ) Petitioner ( ) Respondent.
This form was completed with the assistance of:
{name of individual} ____,
{name of business} ____,
{address} ____,
{city} ____________, *{state}*______, *{zip code}*________,*{telephone number}* _____________.

INSTRUCTIONS FOR FLORIDA SUPREME COURT APPROVED FAMILY LAW FORM 12.927, NOTICE OF VOLUNTARY DISMISSAL (03/15)

When should this form be used?

If you are the **petitioner** in a case and you wish to discontinue (dismiss) the case, you may use this form to request that the court dismiss your **petition**. If you are the **respondent** in a case and you have filed a **counterpetition**, you may use this form to request that the court dismiss your counterpetition.

WARNING: If your case involves both a petition and a counterpetition, a notice of voluntary dismissal filed by one party will NOT dismiss the other party's petition or counterpetition. The other party also must file a notice of voluntary dismissal for the entire case to stop completely.

This form should be typed or printed in black ink. After completing this form, you should **file** the original with the **clerk of the circuit court** in the county where your case is filed and keep a copy for your records.

IMPORTANT INFORMATION REGARDING E–FILING

The Florida Rules of Judicial Administration now require that all petitions, pleadings, and documents be filed electronically except in certain circumstances. **Self–represented litigants may file petitions or other pleadings or documents electronically; however, they are not required to do so.** If you choose to file your pleadings or other documents electronically, you must do so in accordance with Florida Rule of Judicial Administration 2.525, and you must follow the procedures of the judicial circuit in which you file. **The rules and procedures should be carefully read and followed.**

What should I do next?

A copy of this form must be mailed, e-mailed or hand-delivered to each party in the case.

IMPORTANT INFORMATION REGARDING E–SERVICE ELECTION

After the initial service of process of the petition or supplemental petition by the Sheriff or certified process server, the Florida Rules of Judicial Administration now require that all documents required or permitted to be served on the other party must be served by electronic mail (e–mail) except in certain circumstances. **You must strictly comply with the format requirements set forth in the Rules of Judicial Administration.**

SELF–REPRESENTED LITIGANTS MAY SERVE DOCUMENTS BY E–MAIL; HOWEVER, THEY ARE NOT REQUIRED TO DO SO. If a self-represented litigant elects to serve and receive documents by e-mail, the procedures must always be followed once the initial election is made.

To serve and receive documents by e-mail, you must designate your e-mail addresses by using the **Designation of Current Mailing and E–mail Address**, Florida Supreme Court Approved Family Law Form 12.915, and you must provide your e-mail address on each form on which your signature appears. Please **CAREFULLY** read the rules and instructions for: **Certificate of Service (General),** Florida Supreme Court Approved Family Law Form 12.914; **Designation of Current Mailing and E–mail Address**, Florida Supreme Court Approved Family Law Form 12.915; and Florida Rule of Judicial Administration 2.516.

Where can I look for more information?

Before proceeding, you should read General Information for Self–Represented Litigants found at the beginning of these forms. For further information, see 12.420, Florida Family Law Rule of Procedure 12.420.

Special notes . . .

Remember, a person who is NOT an attorney is called a nonlawyer. If a nonlawyer helps you fill out these forms, that person must give you a copy of **Disclosure from Nonlawyer**, Florida Family Law Rules of Procedure Form 12.900 (a), before he or she helps you. A nonlawyer helping you fill out these forms also **must** put his or her name, address, and telephone number on the bottom of the last page of every form he or she helps you complete.

Added Feb. 26, 1998, effective Mar. 16, 1998 (713 So.2d 1). Amended Sept. 21, 2000 (810 So.2d 1); March 26, 2015, effective March 26, 2015 (2015 WL 1343088).

Form 12.928. Cover Sheet for Family Court Cases

COVER SHEET FOR FAMILY COURT CASES

I. Case Style

IN THE CIRCUIT COURT OF THE ______ JUDICIAL CIRCUIT,
IN AND FOR ________________ COUNTY, FLORIDA

Case No.: ________________
Judge: ________________

____
Petitioner

and

____
Respondent

II. Type of Action/Proceeding. Place a check beside the proceeding you are initiating. If you are simultaneously filing more than one type of proceeding against the same opposing party, such as a modification and an enforcement proceeding, complete a separate cover sheet for each action being filed. **If you are reopening a case, choose one of the three options below it.**

(A) ____ Initial Action/Petition
(B) ____ Reopening Case
  1. ____ Modification/Supplemental Petition
  2. ____ Motion for Civil Contempt/Enforcement
  3. ____ Other

III. Type of Case. If the case fits more than one type of case, select the most definitive.

(A) ____ Simplified Dissolution of Marriage
(B) ____ Dissolution of Marriage
(C) ____ Domestic Violence
(D) ____ Dating Violence
(E) ____ Repeat Violence
(F) ____ Sexual Violence
(G) ____ Stalking
(H) ____ Support IV-D (Department of Revenue, Child Support Enforcement)
(I) ____ Support Non-IV-D (**not** Department of Revenue, Child Support Enforcement)
(J) ____ UIFSA IV-D (Department of Revenue, Child Support Enforcement)
(K) ____ UIFSA Non-IV-D (**not** Department of Revenue, Child Support Enforcement)
(L) ____ Other Family Court
(M) ____ Adoption Arising Out Of Chapter 63

Florida Family Law Rules of Procedure Form 12.928, Cover Sheet for Family Court Cases
(11/13)

(N) ____ Name Change
(O) ____ Paternity/Disestablishment of Paternity
(P) ____ Juvenile Delinquency
(Q) ____ Petition for Dependency
(R) ____ Shelter Petition
(S) ____ Termination of Parental Rights Arising Out Of Chapter 39
(T) ____ Adoption Arising Out Of Chapter 39
(U) ____ CINS/FINS

IV. Rule of Judicial Administration 2.545(d) requires that a Notice of Related Cases Form, Family Law Form 12.900(h), be filed with the initial pleading/petition by the filing attorney or self-represented litigant in order to notify the court of related cases. Is Form 12.900(h) being filed with this Cover Sheet for Family Court Cases and initial pleading/petition?

____ No, to the best of my knowledge, no related cases exist.
____ Yes, all related cases are listed on Family Law Form 12.900(h).

ATTORNEY OR PARTY SIGNATURE

I CERTIFY that the information I have provided in this cover sheet is accurate to the best of my knowledge and belief.

Signature____ FL Bar No.: ________________
Attorney or party (Bar number, if attorney)

____ ________________________
(Type or print name) (E-mail Address(es))

____
Date

IF A NONLAWYER HELPED YOU FILL OUT THIS FORM, HE/SHE MUST FILL IN THE BLANKS BELOW: [fill in all blanks]

This form was prepared for the: *{choose only **one**}* ( ) Petitioner ( ) Respondent
This form was completed with the assistance of:
*{name of individual}*____,
*{name of business}*____,
*{address}*____,
*{city}*______________________________, *{state}*________, *{telephone number}*________.

INSTRUCTIONS FOR FLORIDA FAMILY LAW RULES OF PROCEDURE FORM 12.928, COVER SHEET FOR FAMILY COURT CASES (11/13)

When should this form be used?

The Cover Sheet for Family Court Cases and the information contained in it neither replace nor supplement the filing and service of pleadings or other documents as required by law. This form shall be filed by the petitioner/party opening or reopening a case for the use of the **clerk of the circuit court** for the purpose of reporting judicial workload data pursuant to Florida Statutes section 25.075.

This form should be typed or printed in black ink. The petitioner must **file** this cover sheet with the first pleading or motion filed to open or reopen a case in all domestic and juvenile cases.

What should I do next?

Follow these instructions for completing the form:

I. Case Style. Enter the name of the court, the appropriate case number assigned at the time of filing of the original petition, the name of the judge assigned (if applicable), and the name (last, first, middle initial) of the petitioner(s) and respondent(s).

II. Type of Action /Proceeding. Place a check beside the proceeding you are initiating. If you are simultaneously filing more than one type of proceeding against the same opposing party, such as a modification and an enforcement proceeding, complete a separate cover sheet for each action being filed.

(A) Initial Action/Petition

(B) Reopening Case. If you check "Reopening Case," indicate whether you are filing a modification or supplemental petition or an action for enforcement by placing a check beside the appropriate action/petition.

1. Modification/Supplemental Petition
2. Motion for Civil Contempt/ Enforcement
3. Other—All reopening actions not involving modification/supplemental petitions or petition enforcement.

III. Type of Case. Place a check beside the appropriate case. If the case fits more than one category, select the most definitive. Definitions of the categories are provided below.

(A) Simplified Dissolution of Marriage—petitions for the termination of marriage pursuant to Florida Family Law Rule of Procedure 12.105.

(B) Dissolution of Marriage—petitions for the termination of marriage pursuant to Chapter 61, Florida Statutes, other than simplified dissolution.

(C) Domestic Violence—all matters relating to injunctions for protection against domestic violence pursuant to section 741.30, Florida Statutes.

(D) Dating Violence—all matters relating to injunctions for protection against dating violence pursuant to section 784.046, Florida Statutes.

(E) Repeat Violence—all matters relating to injunctions for protection against repeat violence pursuant to section 784.046, Florida Statutes.

(F) Sexual Violence—all matters relating to injunctions for protection against sexual violence pursuant to section 784.046, Florida Statutes.

(G) Stalking—all matters relating to injunctions for protection against stalking pursuant to section 784.0485, Florida Statutes

(H) Support—IV–D—all matters relating to child or spousal support in which an application for assistance has been filed with the Department of Revenue, Child Support Enforcement under Title IV–D, Social Security Act, except for such matters relating to dissolution of marriage petitions (sections 409.2564, 409.2571, and 409.2597, Florida Statutes), paternity, or UIFSA.

(I) Support–Non IV–D—all matters relating to child or spousal support in which an application for assistance has **not** been filed under Title IV–D, Social Security Act.

(J) UIFSA—IV–D—all matters relating to Chapter 88, Florida Statutes, in which an application for assistance has been filed under Title IV–D, Social Security Act.

(K) UIFSA—Non IV–D—all matters relating to Chapter 88, Florida Statutes, in which an application for assistance has **not** been filed under Title IV–D, Social Security Act.

(L) Other Family Court—all matters involving time-sharing and/or parenting plans relating to minor child(ren), support unconnected with dissolution of marriage, annulment, delayed birth certificates pursuant to Florida Statutes section 382.0195, expedited affirmation of parental status pursuant to Florida Statutes section 742.16, termination of parental rights proceedings pursuant to Florida Statutes section 63.087, declaratory judgment actions related to premarital, marital, post-marital agreements, or other matters not included in the categories above.

(M) Adoption Arising Out Of Chapter 63—all matters relating to adoption pursuant to Chapter 63, Florida Statutes, excluding any matters arising out of Chapter 39, Florida Statutes.

(N) Name Change—all matters relating to name change, pursuant to section 68.07, Florida Statutes.

(O) Paternity/Disestablishment of Paternity—all matters relating to paternity pursuant to Chapter 742, Florida Statutes.

(P) Juvenile Delinquency—all matters relating to juvenile delinquency pursuant to Chapter 985, Florida Statutes.

(Q) Petition for Dependency—all matters relating to petitions for dependency.

(R) Shelter Petition—all matters relating to shelter petitions pursuant to Chapter 39, Florida Statutes.

(S) Termination of Parental Rights Arising Out Of Chapter 39—all matters relating to termination of parental rights pursuant to Chapter 39, Florida Statutes.

(T) Adoption Arising Out Of Chapter 39—all matters relating to adoption pursuant to Chapter 39, Florida Statutes.

(U) CINS/FINS—all matters relating to children in need of services (and families in need of services) pursuant to Chapter 984, Florida Statutes.

ATTORNEY OR PARTY SIGNATURE. Sign the Cover Sheet for Family Court Cases. Print legibly the name of the person signing the Cover Sheet for Family Court Cases. Attorneys must include a Florida Bar number. Insert the date the Cover Sheet for Family Court Cases is signed. Signature is a certification that filer has provided accurate information on the Cover Sheet for Family Court Cases.

Nonlawyer Remember, a person who is NOT an attorney is called a nonlawyer. If a nonlawyer helps you fill out these forms, that person must give you a copy of **Disclosure from Nonlawyer**, Florida Family Law Rules of Procedure Form 12.900(a), before he or she helps you. A nonlawyer helping you fill out these forms also **must** put his or her name, address, and telephone number on the bottom of the last page of every form he or she helps you complete.

Where can I look for more information?

Before proceeding, you should read "General Information for Self-Represented Litigants" found at the beginning of these forms. For further information, see Rule 12.100, Florida Family Law Rules of Procedure.

Added June 3, 2009, effective January 1, 2010 (15 So.3d 558). Amended October 15, 2009, effective January 1, 2010 (30 So.3d 477); Nov. 14, 2013 (126 So.3d 228).

Form 12.930(a). Notice of Service of Standard Family Law Interrogatories

IN THE CIRCUIT COURT OF THE ______________ JUDICIAL CIRCUIT,
IN AND FOR ______________ COUNTY, FLORIDA

Case No.: ______________
Division: ______________

______________________________,
Petitioner,

and

______________________________,
Respondent.

NOTICE OF SERVICE OF STANDARD FAMILY LAW INTERROGATORIES

I, *{full legal name}* ______________________________, have on *{date}* ______________,
served upon *{name of person served}* ______________________________,
to be answered under oath within 30 days after service, the Standard Family Law Interrogatories for [check **one** only]

( ) **Original or Enforcement Proceedings** ( ) **Modification Proceedings**

I am requesting that the following standard questions be answered: [check **all** that apply]

____1	____2	____3	____4	____5	____6	____7
Background Information	Education	Employment	Assets	Liabilities	Miscellaneous	Long Form Affidavit

In addition, I am requesting that the attached *{#}* ______________ questions be answered.

I certify that a copy of this document was [**check all used**]: ( ) e-mailed ( ) mailed ( ) faxed ( ) hand delivered to the person(s) listed below on *{date}* ______________.

Other party or his/her attorney:
Name: ______________
Address: ______________
City, State, Zip: ______________
Fax Number: ______________
E-mail Address(es): ______________

____
Signature of Party or his/her Attorney
Printed Name: ______________
Address: ______________
City, State, Zip: ______________
Telephone Number: ______________
Fax Number: ______________
E-mail Address(es): ______________

Florida Family Law Rules of Procedure Form 12.930(a), Notice of Service of Standard Family Law Interrogatories (09/12)

Florida Bar Number:________________________________

IF A NONLAWYER HELPED YOU FILL OUT THIS FORM, HE/SHE MUST FILL IN THE BLANKS BELOW:
[fill in **all** blanks] This form was prepared for the: *{choose only **one**}* ( ) Petitioner ( ) Respondent
This form was completed with the assistance of:
{name of individual} ____,
{name of business} ____,
{address} ____,
{city} ________________,*{state}* ____________, *{telephone number}* _________________________.

INSTRUCTIONS FOR FLORIDA FAMILY LAW RULES OF PROCEDURE FORM 12.930(a), NOTICE OF SERVICE OF STANDARD FAMILY LAW INTERROGATORIES (09/12)

When should this form be used?

You should use this form to tell the court that you are asking the other **party** in your case to answer certain standard questions in writing. These questions are called **interrogatories**, and they must relate to your case. The standard family law interrogatories are designed to supplement the information provided in the **Financial Affidavit**, Florida Family Law Rules of Procedure Form 12.902(b) or (c). You should carefully read the standard interrogatory forms, Florida Family Law Rules of Procedure Form 12.930(b) and (c), to determine which questions, if any, the other party needs to answer in order to provide you with information not covered by the financial affidavit forms.

This form should be typed or printed in black ink. You must indicate whether you are sending the interrogatories for original and enforcement proceedings **or** the interrogatories for modification proceedings. You must also indicate which questions you are asking the other party to answer. After completing this form you should **file** the original with the **clerk of the circuit court** in the county where your case was filed and keep a copy for your records.

What should I do next?

You must serve the other party with a copy of this form along with an original and a copy of the appropriate interrogatories, Florida Family Law Rules of Procedure Form 12.930(b) or (c), if service is by mail or hand delivery. You must serve a copy of this form and a copy of the interrogatories if service is by e-mail. **Service** must be in accordance with Florida Rule of Judicial Administration 2.516.

You may want to inform the other party of the following information:

As a general rule, within **30 days** after service of interrogatories, the other party must answer the questions in writing and serve you with the answers. **Service** of the answers must be in compliance with Florida Rule of Judicial Administration 2.516. His or her answers may be written on as many separate sheets of paper as necessary. He or she should number each page and indicate which question(s) he or she is answering, and be sure to make a copy for him/herself. All answers to these questions are made under oath or affirmation as to their truthfulness. Each question must be answered separately and as completely as the available information permits. The original of the answers to the interrogatories is to be provided to the requesting party. Do **not** file the original or a copy with the clerk of the circuit court except as provided in Florida Rule of Civil Procedure 1.340(e).

The other party may object to a question by writing the legal reason for the objection in the space provided. He or she may also ask the court for a protective order granting him or her permission not to answer certain questions and protecting him or her from annoyance, embarrassment, apprehension, or undue burden or expense. **If the other party fails to either answer or object to the questions within 30 days, he or she may be subject to court sanctions.**

Where can I look for more information?

Before proceeding, you should read General Information for Self–Represented Litigants found at the beginning of these forms. The words that are **bold underline** in these instructions are defined there. For further information, see Florida Family Law Rules of Procedure 12.280, 12.285, 12.340, and 12.380, and Florida Rules of Civil Procedure 1.280, 1.340, and 1.380.

Special notes . . .

Remember, a person who is NOT an attorney is called a nonlawyer. If a nonlawyer helps you fill out these forms, that person must give you a copy of **Disclosure from Nonlawyer**, Florida Family Law Rules of Procedure Form 12.900(a), before he or she helps you. A nonlawyer helping you fill out these forms also **must** put his or her name, address, and telephone number on the bottom of the last page of every form he or she helps you complete.

Added July 7, 1995, effective Jan. 1, 1996 (663 So.2d 1047). Amended Feb. 26, 1998, effective Mar. 16, 1998 (713 So.2d 1); Sept. 21, 2000 (810 So.2d 1); July 10, 2003, effective Jan. 1, 2004 (853 So.2d 303); Oct. 18, 2012, effective, *nunc pro tunc*, Sept. 1, 2012 (102 So.3d 505).

Form 12.930(b). Standard Family Law Interrogatories for Original or Enforcement Proceedings

IN THE CIRCUIT COURT OF THE ____________ JUDICIAL CIRCUIT,
IN AND FOR ____________ COUNTY, FLORIDA

Case No.: ____________________
Division: ____________________

______________________________,
Petitioner,

and

______________________________,
Respondent.

STANDARD FAMILY LAW INTERROGATORIES FOR ORIGINAL OR ENFORCEMENT PROCEEDINGS

TO BE COMPLETED BY THE PARTY SERVING THESE INTERROGATORIES
I am requesting that the following standard questions be answered: [check all that apply]

____1 Background Information ____2 Education ____3 Employment ____4 Assets ____5 Liabilities ____6 Miscellaneous ____7 Long Form Affidavit

In addition, I am requesting that the attached {#} ____________ questions be answered.

The answers to the following questions are intended to supplement the information provided in the Financial Affidavits, Florida Family Law Rules of Procedure Form 12.902(b) or (c). You should answer the group of questions indicated in the above shaded box. The questions should be answered in the blank space provided below each separately numbered question. If sufficient space is not provided, you may attach additional papers with the answers and refer to them in the space provided in the interrogatories. You should be sure to make a copy for yourself. Each question must be answered separately and as completely as the available information permits. All answers are to be made under oath or affirmation as to their truthfulness.

AFTER YOU ANSWER THE INTERROGATORIES, DO NOT FILE THE ORIGINAL WITH THE CLERK OF THE COURT. ALL PERSONAL INFORMATION CONTAINED IN THE COURT FILE BECOMES PUBLIC RECORD. INSTEAD, SERVE THE ORIGINAL OF THE ANSWERS TO THE INTERROGATORIES ON THE OTHER PARTY AND FILE FORM 12.930(d), NOTICE OF SERVICE OF ANSWERS TO INTERROGATORIES, WITH THE CLERK.

I, *{name of person answering interrogatories}* ______________________________, being sworn, certify that the following information is true:

1. **BACKGROUND INFORMATION:**
   a. State your full legal name and any other name by which you have been known.
   b. State your present residence and telephone numbers.

2. **EDUCATION:**
   a. List all business, commercial, and professional licenses that you have obtained.
   b. List all of your education including, but not limited to, vocational or specialized training, including the following:
      (1) name and address of each educational institution.
      (2) dates of attendance.
      (3) degrees or certificates obtained or anticipated dates of same.

3. **EMPLOYMENT:**
   a. For each place of your employment or self-employment during the last 3 years, state the following:
      (1) name, address, and telephone number of your employer.
      (2) dates of employment.
      (3) job title and brief description of job duties.
      (4) starting and ending salaries.
      (5) name of your direct supervisor.
      (6) all benefits received, including, for example, health, life, and disability insurance; expense account; use of automobile or automobile expense reimbursement; reimbursement for travel, food, or lodging expenses; payment of dues in any clubs or associations; and pension or profit sharing plans.

b. Other than as an employee, if you have been engaged in or associated with any business, commercial, or professional activity within the last 3 years that was not detailed above, state for each such activity the following:
(1) name, address, and telephone number of each activity.
(2) dates you were connected with such activity.
(3) position title and brief description of activities.
(4) starting and ending compensation.
(5) name of all persons involved in the business, commercial, or professional activity with you.
(6) all benefits and compensation received, including, for example, health, life, and disability insurance; expense account; use of automobile or automobile expense reimbursement; reimbursement for travel, food, or lodging expenses; payment of dues in any clubs or associations; and pension or profit sharing plans.

c. If you have been unemployed at any time during the last 3 years, state the dates of unemployment. If you have not been employed at any time in the last 3 years, give the information requested above in question 3.a for your last period of employment.

4. **ASSETS:**

a. **Real Estate.** State the street address, if any, and if not, the legal description of all real property that you own or owned during the last 3 years. For each property, state the following:
(1) the names and addresses of any other persons or entities holding any interest and their percentage of interest.
(2) the purchase price, the cost of any improvements made since it was purchased, and the amount of any depreciation taken.
(3) the fair market value on the date of your separation from your spouse.
(4) the fair market value on the date of the filing of the petition for dissolution of marriage.

b. **Tangible Personal Property.** List all items of tangible personal property that are owned by you or in which you have had any interest during the last 3 years including, but not limited to, motor vehicles, tools, furniture, boats, jewelry, art objects or other collections, and collectibles whose fair market value exceeds $100. For each item, state the following:

(1) the percentage and type of interest you hold.
(2) the names and addresses of any other persons or entities holding any interest.
(3) the date you acquired your interest.
(4) the purchase price.
(5) the present fair market value.
(6) the fair market value on the date of your separation from your spouse.
(7) the fair market value on the date of the filing of the petition for dissolution of marriage.

c. **Intangible Personal Property.** Other than the financial accounts (checking, savings, money market, credit union accounts, retirement accounts, or other such cash management accounts) listed in the answers to interrogatories 4.d and 4.e below, list all items of intangible personal property that are owned by you or in which you have had any ownership interest (including closed accounts) within the last 3 years, including but not limited to, partnership and business interests (including good will), deferred compensation accounts unconnected with retirement, including but not limited to stock options, sick leave, and vacation pay, stocks, stock funds, mutual funds, bonds, bond funds, real estate investment trust, receivables, certificates of deposit, notes, mortgages, and debts owed to you by another entity or person. For each item, state the following:
(1) the percentage and type of interest you hold.
(2) the names and addresses of any other persons or entities holding any interest and the names and addresses of the persons and entities who are indebted to you.
(3) the date you acquired your interest.
(4) the purchase price, acquisition cost, or loaned amount.
(5) the fair market value or the amounts you claim are owned by or owed to you:
(a) presently, at the time of answering these interrogatories.
(b) on the date of your separation from your spouse.
(c) on the date of the filing of the petition for dissolution of marriage.

You may comply with this interrogatory (4.c) by providing copies of all periodic (monthly, quarterly, semi-annual, or annual) account statements for each such account for the preceding 3 years. DO NOT FILE THESE DOCUMENTS IN THE COURT FILE. However, if the date of acquisition, the purchase price and the market valuations are not clearly reflected in the periodic statements which are furnished then these questions must be answered separately. You do not have to resubmit any periodic statements previously furnished under rule 12.285 (Mandatory Disclosure).

d. **Retirement Accounts:** List all information regarding each retirement account/plan, including but not limited to defined benefit plans, 401k, 403B, IRA accounts, pension plans, Florida Retirement System plans (FRS), Federal Government plans, money purchase plans, HR10 (Keogh) plans, profit sharing plans, annuities, employee savings plans, etc. that you have established and/or that have been established for you by you, your employer, or any previous employer. For each account, state the following:
(1) the name and last 4 digits of the account number of each account/plan and where it is located.
(2) the type of account/plan.
(3) the name and address of the fiduciary plan administrator/service representative.
(4) the fair market value of your interest in each account/plan.
(a) present value.
(b) value on the date of separation.
(c) value on the date of filing of the petition for dissolution of marriage
(5) whether you are vested or not vested; and if vested, in what amount, as of a certain date and the schedule of future vesting.
(6) the date at which you became/become eligible to receive some funds in this account/plan.
(7) monthly benefits of the account/plan if no fair market value is ascertained.
(8) beneficiary(ies) and/or alternate payee(s).

e. **Financial Accounts.** For all financial accounts (checking, savings, money market, credit union accounts, or other such cash management accounts) listed in your Financial Affidavit, in which you have had any legal or equitable interest, regardless of whether the interest is or was held in your own name individually, in your name with another person, or in any other name, give the following:
(1) name and address of each institution.
(2) name in which the account is or was maintained.
(3) the last 4 digits of account numbers.
(4) name of each person authorized to make withdrawals from the accounts.
(5) highest balance within each of the preceding 3 years.
(6) lowest balance within each of the preceding 3 years.

You may comply with this interrogatory (4.e) by providing copies of all periodic (monthly, quarterly, semi-annual, or annual) account statements for each such account for the preceding 3 years. DO NOT FILE THESE DOCUMENTS IN THE COURT FILE. You do not have to resubmit account statements previously furnished pursuant to rule 12.285 (Mandatory Disclosure).

f. **Closed Financial Accounts.** For all financial accounts (checking, savings, money market, credit union accounts, or other such cash management accounts) closed within the last 3 years, in which you have had any legal or equitable interest, regardless of whether the interest is or was held in your own name individually, in your name with another person, or in any other name, give the following:

(1) name and address of each institution.
(2) name in which the account is or was maintained.
(3) the last 4 digits of account numbers.
(4) name of each person authorized to make withdrawals from the accounts.
(5) date account was closed.

g. **Trust.** For any interest in an estate, trust, insurance policy, or annuity, state the following:
(1) If you are the beneficiary of any estate, trust, insurance policy, or annuity, give for each one the following:
(a) identification of the estate, trust, insurance policy, or annuity.
(b) the nature, amount, and frequency of any distributions of benefits.
(c) the total value of the beneficiaries' interest in the benefit.
(d) whether the benefit is vested or contingent.
(2) If you have established any trust or are the trustee of a trust, state the following:
(a) the date the trust was established.
(b) the names and addresses of the trustees.
(c) the names and addresses of the beneficiaries.
(d) the names and addresses of the persons or entities who possess the trust documents.
(e) each asset that is held in each trust, with its fair market value.

h. **Canceled Life Insurance Policies.** For all policies of life insurance within the preceding 3 years that you no longer hold, own, or have any interest in, state the following:
(1) name of company that issued the policy and last 4 digits of policy number.
(2) name, address, and telephone number of agent who issued the policy.
(3) amount of coverage.
(4) name of insured.
(5) name of owner of policy.
(6) name of beneficiaries.
(7) premium amount.
(8) date the policy was surrendered.
(9) amount, if any, of monies distributed to the owner.

i. **Name of Accountant, Bookkeeper, or Records Keeper.** State the names, addresses, and telephone numbers of your accountant, bookkeeper, and any other persons who possess your financial records, and state which records each possesses.

j. **Safe Deposit Boxes, Lock Boxes, Vaults, Etc.** For all safe deposit boxes, lock boxes, vaults, or similar types of depositories, state the following:

(1) The names and addresses of all banks, depositories, or other places where, at any time during the period beginning 3 years before the initiation of the action, until the date of your answering this interrogatory, you did any of the following:

(a) had a safe deposit box, lock box, or vault.

(b) were a signatory or co-signatory on a safe deposit box, lock box, or vault.

(c) had access to a safe deposit box, lock box, or vault.

(d) maintained property.

(2) The box or identification numbers and the name and address of each person who has had access to any such depository during the same time period.

(3) All persons who have possession of the keys or combination to the safe deposit box, lock box, or vault.

(4) Any items removed from any safe deposit boxes, lock boxes, vaults, or similar types of depositories by you or your agent during that time, together with the present location and fair market value of each item.

(5) All items in any safe deposit boxes, lock boxes, vaults, or similar types of depositories and fair market value of each item.

5. **LIABILITIES:**

a. **Loans, Liabilities, Debts, and Other Obligations.** For all loans, liabilities, debts, and other obligations (other than credit cards and charge accounts) listed in your Financial Affidavit, indicate for each the following:

(1) name and address of the creditor.

(2) name in which the obligation is or was incurred.

(3) last 4 digits of loan or account number, if any.

(4) nature of the security, if any.

(5) payment schedule.

(6) present balance and current status of your payments.

(7) total amount of arrearage, if any.

(8) balance on the date of your separation from your spouse.

(9) balance on the date of the filing of the petition for dissolution of marriage.

You may comply with this interrogatory (5.a) by providing copies of all periodic (monthly, quarterly, semi-annual, or annual) account statements for each such account for the preceding 3 years. DO NOT FILE THESE DOCUMENTS IN THE COURT FILE. You do not have to resubmit account statements previously furnished under rule 12.285 (Mandatory Disclosure).

b. **Credit Cards and Charge Accounts.** For all financial accounts (credit cards, charge accounts, or other such accounts) listed in your Financial Affidavit, in which you have had any legal or equitable interest, regardless of whether the interest is or was held in your own name individually, in your name with another person, or in any other name, give the following:

(1) name and address of the creditor.
(2) name in which the account is or was maintained.
(3) names of each person authorized to sign on the accounts.
(4) last 4 digits of account numbers.
(5) present balance and current status of your payments.
(6) total amount of arrearage, if any.
(7) balance on the date of your separation from your spouse.
(8) balance on the date of the filing of the petition for dissolution of marriage.
(9) highest and lowest balance within each of the preceding 3 years.

You may comply with this interrogatory (5.b) by providing copies of all periodic (monthly quarterly, semi-annual, or annual) account statements for each such account for the preceding 3 years. DO NOT FILE THESE DOCUMENTS IN THE COURT FILE. You do not have to resubmit account statements previously furnished under rule 12.285 (Mandatory Disclosure).

c. **Closed Credit Cards and Charge Accounts.** For all financial accounts (credit cards, charge accounts, or other such accounts) closed with no remaining balance, within the last 3 years, in which you have had any legal or equitable interest, regardless of whether the interest is or was held in your own name individually, in your name with another person, or in any other name, give the following:

(1) name and address of each creditor.
(2) name in which the account is or was maintained.
(3) last 4 digits of account numbers.
(4) names of each person authorized to sign on the accounts.
(5) date the balance was paid off.
(6) amount of final balance paid off.

You may comply with this interrogatory (5.c) by providing copies of all periodic (monthly, quarterly, semi-annual, or annual) account statements for each such account for the preceding

3 years. DO NOT FILE THESE DOCUMENTS IN THE COURT FILE. You do not have to resubmit account statements previously furnished under rule 12.285 (Mandatory Disclosure).

6. **MISCELLANEOUS:**
   a. If you are claiming an unequal distribution of marital property or enhancement or appreciation of nonmarital property, state the amount claimed and all facts upon which you rely in your claim.
   b. If you are claiming an asset or liability is nonmarital, list the asset or liability and all facts upon which you rely in your claim.
   c. If the mental or physical condition of a spouse or child is an issue, identify the person and state the name and address of all health care providers involved in the treatment of that person for said mental or physical condition.
   d. Detail your proposed parenting plan for the minor child(ren), including your proposed time-sharing schedule. Alternatively, attach a copy of your proposed parenting plan.
   e. If you are claiming that the other parent's time-sharing with the minor child(ren) should be limited, supervised, or otherwise restricted, or that you should have sole parental responsibility for the minor child(ren), with or without time-sharing with the other parent, or that you should have ultimate responsibility over specific aspects of the child(ren)'s welfare or that these responsibilities should be divided between you and the other parent, state your reasons and all facts which you rely upon to support your claim.

7. **LONG FORM AFFIDAVIT:** If you filed the short form affidavit, Florida Family Law Rules of Procedure Form 12.902(b), and you were specifically requested in the Notice of Service of Standard Family Law Interrogatories to file the Long Form Affidavit, Form 12.902(c), you must do so within the time to serve the answers to these interrogatories.

I certify that a copy of this document was [**check all used**]: ( ) e-mailed ( ) mailed ( ) faxed ( ) hand delivered to the person(s) listed below on *{date}* ________.

Other party or his/her attorney:
Name: ________________________
Address: ________________________
City, State, Zip: ________________________
Fax Number: ________________________
E-mail Address(es): ________________________

I understand that I am swearing or affirming under oath to the truthfulness of the answers to these interrogatories and that the punishment for knowingly making a false statement includes fines and/or imprisonment.

Dated: ________________________

____
Signature of Party
Printed Name: ________________________
Address: ________________________
City, State, Zip: ________________________
Telephone Number: ________________________
Fax Number: ________________________
E-mail Address(es): ________________________

STATE OF FLORIDA
COUNTY OF ________________________

Sworn to or affirmed and signed before me on ____________ by ________________________.

____
NOTARY PUBLIC or DEPUTY CLERK

____
[Print, type, or stamp commissioned name of notary or deputy clerk.]

___ Personally known
___ Produced identification
Type of identification produced ________________________

Florida Family Law Rules of Procedure Form 12.930(b), Standard Family Law Interrogatories for Original or Enforcement Proceedings (09/12)

IF A NONLAWYER HELPED YOU FILL OUT THIS FORM, HE/SHE MUST FILL IN THE BLANKS BELOW:
[fill in **all** blanks] This form was prepared for the: *{choose only **one**}* ( ) Petitioner ( ) Respondent
This form was completed with the assistance of:
{name of individual} ______________________________,
{name of business} ______________________________,
{address} ______________________________,
{city} ____________,*{state}* ______, *{telephone number}* ____________.

Florida Family Law Rules of Procedure Form 12.930(b), Standard Family Law Interrogatories for Original or Enforcement Proceedings (09/12)

INSTRUCTIONS FOR FLORIDA FAMILY LAW RULES OF PROCEDURE FORM 12.930(b), STANDARD FAMILY LAW INTERROGATORIES FOR ORIGINAL OR ENFORCEMENT PROCEEDINGS (09/12)

When should this form be used?

This form should be used to ask the other **party** in your case to answer certain standard questions in writing. These questions are called **interrogatories**, and they must relate to your case. If the other party fails to answer the questions, you may ask the **judge** to order the other party to answer the questions. (You cannot ask these questions before the **petition** has been **filed**.)

The questions in this form should be used in **original proceedings** or **enforcement proceedings** and are meant to supplement the information provided in the **Financial Affidavit**, Florida Family Law Rules of Procedure Form 12.902(b) or (c). You should read all of the questions in this form to determine which questions, if any, the other party needs to answer in order to provide you with information not covered in the financial affidavit forms. If there are questions to which you already know the answer, you may choose not to ask them.

This form should be typed or printed in black ink. You must complete the box at the beginning of this form to indicate which questions you are requesting that the other party answer.

You must serve the other party with an original and a copy of these interrogatories and a copy of the **Notice of Service of Standard Family Law Interrogatories**, Florida Family Law Rules of Procedure Form 12.930(a), if by mail or hand delivery. You must serve an original of these interrogatories and a copy of the **Notice**, if by e-mail. **Service** must be in accordance with Florida Rule of Judicial Administration 2.516.

You should also keep a copy for your records. You should not file this form with the clerk of the circuit court. However, you must file the **Notice of Service of Standard Family Law Interrogatories**, Florida Family Law Rules of Procedure 12.930(a), to tell the court that you have sent this form to the other party.

Where can I look for more information?

Before proceeding, you should read General Information for Self–Represented Litigants found at the beginning of these forms. The words that are in **bold underline** in these instructions are defined there. For further information, see the instructions for **Notice of Service of Standard Family Law Interrogatories**, Florida Family Law Rules of Procedure Form 12.930(a), Florida Family Law Rules of Procedure 12.280, 12.285, 12.340, and 12.380; and Florida Rules of Civil Procedure 1.280, 1.340, and 1.380.

Special notes . . .

In addition to the standard questions in this form, you may ask up to 10 additional questions. You should type or print legibly your additional questions on a separate sheet of paper and attach it to this form. If you want to ask more than 10 additional questions, you will need to get permission from the judge.

You may want to inform the other party of the following information: As a general rule, within **30 days** after service of interrogatories, the other party must answer the questions in writing and serve you with the answers. **Service** of the answers must be in accordance with Florida Rule of Judicial Administration 2.516. His or her answers shall be written in the blank space provided after each separately numbered interrogatory. If sufficient space is not provided, the answering party may attach additional papers with the answers and refer to them in the space provided in the interrogatories. He or she should be sure to make a copy for him/herself. All answers to these questions are made under oath or affirmation as to their truthfulness. Each question must be answered separately and as completely as the available information permits. The original of the answers to the interrogatories is to be provided to the requesting party. **DO NOT FILE THE ORIGINAL OR A COPY WITH THE CLERK OF THE COURT EXCEPT AS PROVIDED BY FLORIDA RULE OF CIVIL PROCEDURE 1.340(e) AND IN ACCORDANCE WITH THE REQUIREMENTS OF FLORIDA RULE OF JUDICIAL ADMINISTRATION 2.425.** The other party may object to a question by writing the legal reason for the objection in the space provided. He or she may also ask the court for a protective order granting him or her permission not to answer certain questions and protecting him or her from annoyance, embarrassment, apprehension, or undue burden or expense. If the other party fails to either answer or object to the questions within 30 days, he or she may be subject to court sanctions.

Remember, a person who is NOT an attorney is called a nonlawyer. If a nonlawyer helps you fill out these forms, that person must give you a copy of **Disclosure from Nonlawyer**, Florida Family Law Rules of Procedure Form 12.900(a), before he or she helps you. A nonlawyer helping you fill out these forms also **must** put his or her name, address, and telephone number on the bottom of the last page of every form he or she helps you complete.

Added July 7, 1995, effective Jan. 1, 1996 (663 So.2d 1047). Amended Feb. 26, 1998, effective Mar. 16, 1998 (713 So.2d 1); Sept. 21, 2000 (810 So.2d 1); Oct. 29, 2000 (783 So.2d 937); July 10, 2003, effective Jan. 1, 2004 (853 So.2d 303); Oct. 16, 2008 (995 So.2d 445); Sept. 3, 2009 (19 So.3d 950); Nov. 3, 2011, effective, *nunc pro tunc*, Oct. 1, 2011 (78 So.3d 1045); Oct. 18, 2012, effective, *nunc pro tunc*, Sept. 1, 2012 (102 So.3d 505).

Form 12.930(c). Standard Family Law Interrogatories for Modification Proceedings

IN THE CIRCUIT COURT OF THE ____________ JUDICIAL CIRCUIT,
IN AND FOR ____________ COUNTY, FLORIDA

Case No.: ____________
Division: ____________

____________________,
Petitioner,

and

____________________,
Respondent.

STANDARD FAMILY LAW INTERROGATORIES FOR MODIFICATION PROCEEDINGS

TO BE COMPLETED BY THE PARTY SERVING THESE INTERROGATORIES

I am requesting that the following standard questions be answered: [check all that apply]

___1	___2	___3	___4	___5	___6	___7
Background Information	Education	Employment	Assets	Liabilities	Miscellaneous	Long Form Affidavit

In addition, I am requesting that the attached {#} ____________ questions be answered.

The answers to the following questions are intended to supplement the information provided in the Financial Affidavits, Florida Family Law Rules of Procedure Form 12.902(b) or (c). You should answer the group of questions indicated in the above shaded box. The questions should be answered in the blank space provided below each separately numbered question. If sufficient space is not provided, you may attach additional papers with the answers and refer to them in the space provided in the interrogatories. You should be sure to make a copy for yourself. Each question must be answered separately and as completely as the available information permits. All answers are to be made under oath or affirmation as to their truthfulness.

AFTER YOU ANSWER THE INTERROGATORIES, DO NOT FILE THE ORIGINAL WITH THE CLERK OF THE COURT. ALL PERSONAL INFORMATION CONTAINED IN THE COURT FILE BECOMES PUBLIC RECORD. INSTEAD, SERVE THE ORIGINAL OF THE ANSWERS TO THE INTERROGATORIES ON THE OTHER PARTY AND FILE FORM 12.930(d), NOTICE OF SERVICE OF ANSWERS TO INTERROGATORIES, WITH THE CLERK.

I, *{name of person answering interrogatories}* ______________________________, being sworn, certify that the following information is true:

1. BACKGROUND INFORMATION:

a. State your full legal name and any other name by which you have been known.

b. State your present residence and telephone numbers.

2. EDUCATION:

a. List all business, commercial, and professional licenses that you have obtained since the entry of the Final Judgment sought to be modified.

b. List all of your education since the entry of the Final Judgment sought to be modified including, but not limited to, vocational or specialized training, including the following:

(1) name and address of each educational institution.

(2) dates of attendance.

(3) degrees or certificates obtained or anticipated dates of same.

3. EMPLOYMENT:

a. For each place of your employment or self-employment since the entry of the Final Judgment sought to be modified, state the following:

(1) name, address, and telephone number of your employer.

(2) dates of employment.

(3) job title and brief description of job duties.

(4) starting and ending salaries.

(5) name of your direct supervisor.

(6) all benefits received, including, for example, health, life, and disability insurance; expense account; use of automobile or automobile expense reimbursement; reimbursement for travel, food, or lodging expenses; payment of dues in any clubs or associations; and pension or profit sharing plans.

b. Other than as an employee, if you have been engaged in or associated with any business, commercial, or professional activity since the entry of the Final Judgment sought to be modified that was not detailed above, state for each such activity the following:
   (1) name, address, and telephone number of each activity.
   (2) dates you were connected with such activity.
   (3) position title and brief description of activities.
   (4) starting and ending compensation.
   (5) name of all persons involved in the business, commercial, or professional activity with you.
   (6) all benefits and compensation received, including, for example, health, life, and disability insurance; expense account; use of automobile or automobile expense reimbursement; reimbursement for travel, food, or lodging expenses; payment of dues in any clubs or associations; and pension or profit sharing plans.

c. If you have been unemployed at any time since the entry of the Final Judgment sought to be modified, state the dates of unemployment. If you have not been employed at any time since the entry of the Final Judgment sought to be modified, give the information requested above in question 3.a for your last period of employment.

4. **ASSETS:**

a. **Real Estate.** State the street address, if any, and if not, the legal description of all real property that you own or owned during the last 3 years, or since the entry of the Final Judgment sought to be modified, if shorter. For each property, state the following:
   (1) the names and addresses of any other persons or entities holding any interest and their percentage of interest.
   (2) the present fair market value.

b. **Tangible Personal Property.** List all items of tangible personal property that are owned by you or in which you have had any interest during the last 3 years, or since the entry of the Final Judgment sought to be modified, if shorter, including, but not limited to, motor vehicles, tools, furniture, boats, jewelry, art objects or other collections, and collectibles whose fair market value exceeds $100. For each item, state the following:

(1) the percentage and type of interest you hold.

(2) the names and addresses of any other persons or entities holding any interest.

(3) the present fair market value.

c. **Intangible Personal Property.** Other than the financial accounts (checking, savings, money market, credit union accounts, retirement accounts, or other such cash management accounts) listed in the answers to interrogatories 4.d and 4.e below, list all items of intangible personal property that are owned by you or in which you have had any ownership interest (including closed accounts) within the last 3 years, or since the entry of the Final Judgment sought to be modified, if shorter, including but not limited to, partnership and business interests (including good will), deferred compensation accounts unconnected with retirement, including but not limited to stock options, sick leave, and vacation pay, stocks, stock funds, mutual funds, bonds, bond funds, real estate investment trust, receivables, certificates of deposit, notes, mortgages, and debts owed to you by another entity or person. For each item, state the following:

(1) the percentage and type of interest you hold.

(2) the names and addresses of any other persons or entities holding any interest and the names and addresses of the persons and entities who are indebted to you

(3) the present fair market value or the amounts you claim are owned by or owed to you, at the time of answering these interrogatories.

You may comply with this interrogatory (4.c) by providing copies of all periodic (monthly, quarterly, semi-annual, or annual) account statements for each such account for the preceding 3 years, or since the entry of the Final Judgment sought to be modified, if shorter. DO NOT FILE THESE DOCUMENTS IN THE COURT FILE. However, if the date of acquisition, the purchase price and the market valuations are not clearly reflected in the periodic statements which are furnished, then these questions must be answered separately. You do not have to resubmit any periodic statements previously furnished under rule 12.285 (Mandatory Disclosure).

d. **Retirement Accounts:** List all information regarding each retirement account/plan, including but not limited to defined benefit plans, 401k, 403B, IRA accounts, pension plans, Florida Retirement System plans (FRS), Federal Government plans, money purchase plans, HR10 (Keogh) plans, profit sharing plans, annuities, employee savings plans, etc. that you have established and/or that have been established for you by you, your employer, or any previous employer. For each account, state the following:
(1) the name and last 4 digits of the account number of each account/plan and where it is located.
(2) the type of account/plan.
(3) the name and address of the fiduciary plan administrator/service representative.
(4) the present fair market value of your interest in each account/plan.
(5) whether you are vested or not vested; and if vested, in what amount, as of a certain date and the schedule of future vesting.
(6) the date at which you became/become eligible to receive some funds in this account/plan.
(7) monthly benefits of the account/plan if no fair market value is ascertained.
(8) beneficiary(ies) and/or alternate payee(s).

e. **Financial Accounts.** For all financial accounts (checking, savings, money market, credit union accounts, or other such cash management accounts) listed in your Financial Affidavit, in which you have had any legal or equitable interest, regardless of whether the interest is or was held in your own name individually, in your name with another person, or in any other name, give the following:
(1) name and address of each institution.
(2) name in which the account is or was maintained.
(3) last 4 digits of account numbers.
(4) names of each person authorized to make withdrawals from the accounts.
(5) highest balance within each of the preceding 3 years, or since the entry of the Final Judgment sought to be modified, if shorter.
(6) lowest balance within each of the preceding 3 years, or since the entry of the Final Judgment sought to be modified, if shorter.

You may comply with this interrogatory (4.e) by providing copies of all periodic (monthly, quarterly, semi-annual, or annual) account statements for each such account for the preceding 3 years, or since the entry of the Final Judgment sought to be modified, if shorter. DO NOT FILE THESE DOCUMENTS IN THE COURT FILE. You do not have to resubmit account statements previously furnished pursuant to rule 12.285 (Mandatory Disclosure).

f. **Closed Financial Accounts.** For all financial accounts (checking, savings, money market, credit union accounts, or other such cash management accounts) closed within the last 3 years, or since the entry of the Final Judgment sought to be modified, if shorter, in which you have had any legal or equitable interest, regardless of whether the interest is or was held in your own name individually, in your name with another person, or in any other name, give the following:
(1) name and address of each institution.
(2) name in which the account is or was maintained.
(3) last 4 digits of account numbers.
(4) name of each person authorized to make withdrawals from the accounts.
(5) date account was closed.

g. **Trust.** For any interest in an estate, trust, insurance policy, or annuity, state the following:
(1) If you are the beneficiary of any estate, trust, insurance policy, or annuity, give for each one the following:
(a) identification of the estate, trust, insurance policy, or annuity.
(b) the nature, amount, and frequency of any distributions of benefits.
(c) the total value of the beneficiaries' interest in the benefit.
(d) whether the benefit is vested or contingent.

(2) If you have established any trust or are the trustee of a trust, state the following:
(a) the date the trust was established.
(b) the names and addresses of the trustees.
(c) the names and addresses of the beneficiaries.
(d) the names and addresses of the persons or entities who possess the trust documents.
(e) each asset that is held in each trust, with its fair market value.

h. **Name of Accountant, Bookkeeper, or Records Keeper.** State the names, addresses, and telephone numbers of your accountant, bookkeeper, and any other persons who possess your financial records, and state which records each possesses.

5. **LIABILITIES:**

a. **Loans, Liabilities, Debts, and Other Obligations.** For all loans, liabilities, debts, and other obligations (other than credit cards and charge accounts) listed in your Financial Affidavit, indicate for each the following:
(1) name and address of the creditor.
(2) name in which the obligation is or was incurred.
(3) last 4 digits of loan or account number, if any.
(4) nature of the security, if any.
(5) payment schedule.
(6) present balance and current status of your payments.
(7) total amount of arrearage, if any.

You may comply with this interrogatory (5.a) by providing copies of all periodic (monthly, quarterly, semi-annual, or annual) account statements for each such account for the preceding 3 years, or since the entry of the Final Judgment sought to be modified, if shorter. DO NOT FILE THESE DOCUMENTS IN THE COURT FILE. You do not have to resubmit account statements previously furnished under rule 12.285 Mandatory Disclosure).

b. **Credit Cards and Charge Accounts.** For all financial accounts (credit cards, charge accounts, or other such accounts) listed in your Financial Affidavit, in which you have had any legal or equitable interest, regardless of whether the interest is or was held in your own name individually, in your name with another person, or in any other name, give the following:

(1) name and address of the creditor.
(2) name in which the account is or was maintained.
(3) name of each person authorized to sign on the accounts.
(4) last 4 digits of account numbers.
(5) present balance and current status of your payments.
(6) total amount of arrearage, if any.
(7) highest and lowest balance within each of the preceding 3 years, or since the entry of the Final Judgment sought to be modified, if shorter.

You may comply with this interrogatory (5.b) by providing copies of all periodic (monthly quarterly, semi-annual, or annual) account statements for each such account for the preceding 3 years, or since the entry of the Final Judgment sought to be modified, if shorter. DO NOT FILE THESE DOCUMENTS IN THE COURT FILE. You do not have to resubmit account statements previously furnished under rule 12.285 (Mandatory Disclosure).

c. **Closed Credit Cards and Charge Accounts.** For all financial accounts (credit cards, charge accounts, or other such accounts) closed with no remaining balance, within the last 3 years, or since the entry of the Final Judgment sought to be modified, if shorter, in which you have had any legal or equitable interest, regardless of whether the interest is or was held in your own name individually, in your name with another person, or in any other name, give the following:

(1) name and address of each creditor.
(2) name in which the account is or was maintained.
(3) last 4 digits of account numbers.
(4) name of each person authorized to sign on the accounts.
(5) date the balance was paid off.
(6) amount of final balance paid off.

You may comply with this interrogatory (5.c) by providing copies of all periodic (monthly, quarterly, semi-annual, or annual) account statements for each such account for the preceding 3 years, or since the entry of the Final Judgment sought to be modified, if shorter. DO NOT FILE THESE DOCUMENTS IN THE COURT FILE. You do not have to resubmit account statements previously furnished under rule 12.285 (Mandatory Disclosure).

Florida Family Law Rules of Procedure Form 12.930(c), Standard Family Law Interrogatories for Modification Proceedings (09/12)

6. **MISCELLANEOUS:**
   a. If you are claiming a diminished earning capacity since the entry of the Final Judgment sought to be modified as grounds to modify alimony or deviate from the child support established in your case, describe in detail how your earning capacity is lowered and state all facts upon which you rely in your claim. If unemployed, state how, why, and when you lost your job.
   b. If you are claiming a change in mental or physical condition since the entry of the Final Judgment sought to be modified as grounds to modify alimony or change the child support established in your case, describe in detail how your mental and/or physical capacity has changed and state all facts upon which you rely in your claim. Identify the change in your mental and/or physical capacity, and state the name and address of all health care providers involved in the treatment of this mental or physical condition.
   c. If you are requesting a change in shared or sole parental responsibility, ultimate decision-making, the time-sharing schedule, the parenting plan, or any combination thereof, for the minor child(ren), describe in detail the change in circumstances since the entry of the Final Judgment sought to be modified that you feel justify the requested change. State when the change of circumstances occurred, how the change or circumstances affects the child(ren), and why it is in the best interests of the child(ren) that the Court make the requested change. Attach your proposed parenting plan.
   d. If you do not feel the requested change in shared or sole parental responsibility, ultimate decision-making, the time-sharing schedule, the parenting plan, or any combination thereof, for the minor child(ren) is in their best interests, or if you feel there has not been a change in circumstances since the entry of the Final Judgment sought to be modified, describe in detail any facts since the entry of the Final Judgment sought to be modified that you feel justify the Court denying the requested change. State what requested change, if any, in shared or sole parenting responsibility, ultimate decision-making, the time-sharing schedule, or of the parenting plan is justified or agreeable to you and why it is in the best interests of the child(ren).

7. **LONG FORM AFFIDAVIT:** If you filed the Short Form Affidavit, Florida Family Law Rules of Procedure Form 12.902(b), and you were specifically requested in the Notice of Service of Standard Family Law Interrogatories to file the Long Form Affidavit, Form12.902(c), you must do so within the time to serve the answers to these interrogatories.

I certify that a copy of this document was **[check all used]:** ( ) e-mailed ( ) mailed ( ) faxed ( ) hand delivered to the person(s) listed below on *{date}*__________________________.

Other party or his/her attorney:
Name: __________________________________
Address: __________________________________
City, State, Zip: ______________________________
Fax Number: ________________________________
E-mail Address(es):____________________________

I understand that I am swearing or affirming under oath to the truthfulness of the answers to these interrogatories and that the punishment for knowingly making a false statement includes fines and/or imprisonment.

Dated: ____________________________

____
Signature of Party
Printed Name: __________________________________
Address: ____________________________________
City, State, Zip: ________________________________
Fax Number: __________________________________
E-mail Address(es):______________________________

STATE OF FLORIDA
COUNTY OF ____________________________

Sworn to or affirmed and signed before me on _______________ by __________________________.

Florida Family Law Rules of Procedure Form 12.930(c), Standard Family Law Interrogatories for Modification Proceedings (09/12)

NOTARY PUBLIC or DEPUTY CLERK

[Print, type, or stamp commissioned name of notary or deputy clerk.]

___ Personally known
___ Produced identification
Type of identification produced ____________________

IF A NONLAWYER HELPED YOU FILL OUT THIS FORM, HE/SHE MUST FILL IN THE BLANKS BELOW:
[fill in **all** blanks] This form was prepared for the: *{choose only **one**}* ( ) Petitioner ( ) Respondent
This form was completed with the assistance of:
{name of individual} ____________________,
{name of business} ____________________,
{address} ____________________,
{city} __________,*{state}* ______, *{telephone number}* __________.

Florida Family Law Rules of Procedure Form 12.930(c), Standard Family Law Interrogatories for Modification Proceedings (09/12)

INSTRUCTIONS FOR FLORIDA FAMILY LAW RULES OF PROCEDURE FORM 12.930(c), STANDARD FAMILY LAW INTERROGATORIES FOR MODIFICATION PROCEEDINGS (09/12)

When should this form be used?

This form should be used to ask the other **party** in your case to answer certain standard questions in writing. These questions are called **interrogatories**, and they must relate to your case. If the other party fails to answer the questions, you may ask the **judge** to order the other party to answer the questions. (You cannot ask these questions before the **petition** has been **filed**.)

The questions in this form should be used in **modification proceedings** and are meant to supplement the information provided in the **Financial Affidavit**, Florida Family Law Rules of Procedure Form 12.902(b) or (c). You should read all of the questions in this form to determine which questions, if any, the other party needs to answer in order to provide you with information not covered in the financial affidavit forms. If there are questions to which you already know the answer, you may choose not to ask them.

This form should be typed or printed in black ink. You must complete the box at the beginning of this form to indicate which questions you are requesting that the other party answer.

You must serve the other party with an original and a copy of these interrogatories and a copy of the **Notice of Service of Standard Family Law Interrogatories**, Florida Family Law Rules of Procedure Form 12.930(a), if by mail or hand delivery. You must serve an original of these interrogatories and a copy of the **Notice,** if by e-mail. **Service** must be in accordance with Florida Rule of Judicial Administration 2.516.

You should also keep a copy for your records. You should not file this form with the clerk of the circuit court. However, you must file the **Notice of Service of Standard Family Law Interrogatories**, Florida Family Law Rules of Procedure Form 12.930(a), to tell the court that you have sent this form to the other party.

After you receive the completed answers to the interrogatories, **DO NOT FILE THE ORIGINAL OR A COPY WITH THE CLERK OF THE COURT UNLESS THE ANSWERS ARE ADMITTED INTO EVIDENCE BY THE COURT AND ARE IN COMPLIANCE WITH FLORIDA RULE OF JUDICIAL ADMINISTRATION 2.425**

Where can I look for more information?

Before proceeding, you should read "General Information for Self–Represented Litigants" found at the beginning of these forms. The words that are in **bold underline** in these instructions are defined there.

For further information, see the instructions for **Notice of Service of Standard Family Law Interrogatories**, Florida Family Law Rules of Procedure Form 12.930(a), Florida Family Law Rules of Procedure 12.280, 12.285, 12.340, and 12.380; and Florida Rules of Civil Procedure 1.280, 1.340, and 1.380.

Special notes . . .

In addition to the standard questions in this form, you may ask up to 10 additional questions. You should type or print legibly your additional questions on a separate sheet of paper and attach it to this form. If you want to ask more than 10 additional questions, you will need to get permission from the judge.

You may want to inform the other party of the following information: As a general rule, within **30 days** after service of interrogatories, the other party must answer the questions in writing and serve you with the answers. **Service** of the answers must be in accordance with Florida Rule of Judicial Administration 2.516. His or her answers shall be written in the blank space provided after each separately numbered interrogatory. If sufficient space is not provided, the answering party may attach additional papers with the answers and refer to them in the space provided in the interrogatories. He or she should be sure to make a copy for him/herself. All answers to these questions are made under oath or affirmation as to their truthfulness. Each question must be answered separately and as completely as the available information permits. The original of the answers to the interrogatories is to be provided to the requesting party. **DO NOT FILE THE ORIGINAL OR A COPY WITH THE CLERK OF THE CIRCUIT COURT UNLESS THE ANSWERS ARE ADMITTED INTO EVIDENCE BY THE COURT AND ARE IN COMPLIANCE WITH THE REQUIREMENTS OF FLORIDA RULE OF JUDICIAL ADMINISTRATION 2.425.** The other party may object to a question by writing the legal reason for the objection in the space provided. He or she may also ask the court for a protective order granting him or her permission not to answer certain questions and protecting him or her from annoyance, embarrassment, apprehension, or undue burden or expense. If the other party fails to either answer or object to the questions within 30 days, he or she may be subject to court sanctions.

Remember, a person who is NOT an attorney is called a nonlawyer. If a nonlawyer helps you fill out these forms, that person must give you a copy of **Disclosure from Nonlawyer**, Florida Family Law Rules of Procedure Form 12.900(a), before he or she helps you. A nonlawyer helping you fill out these forms also **must** put his or her name, address, and telephone number on the bottom of the last page of every form he or she helps you complete.

Added Feb. 26, 1998, effective Mar. 16, 1998 (713 So.2d 1); Sept. 21, 2000 (810 So.2d 1); Oct. 29, 2000 (783 So.2d 937); July 10, 2003, effective Jan. 1, 2004 (853 So.2d 303). Amended Oct. 16, 2008, effective Jan. 1, 2009 (995 So.2d 407); Oct. 16, 2008 (995 So.2d 445); Sept. 3, 2009 (19 So.3d 950); Nov. 3, 2011, effective, *nunc pro tunc*, Oct. 1, 2011 (78 So.3d 1045); Oct. 18, 2012, effective, *nunc pro tunc*, Sept. 1, 2012 (102 So.3d 505).

Form 12.930(d). Notice of Service of Answers to Standard Family Law Interrogatories

IN THE CIRCUIT COURT OF THE ____________ JUDICIAL CIRCUIT,
IN AND FOR ____________ COUNTY, FLORIDA

Case No.: ____________
Division: ____________

____________,
Petitioner

and

____________,
Respondent.

NOTICE OF SERVICE OF ANSWERS TO STANDARD FAMILY LAW INTERROGATORIES

I, *{full legal name}*____________, have on *{date}*____________ served on *{name}*____________ fully completed and sworn answers to the standard family law interrogatories served on me, and additional interrogatories if requested. The interrogatories were for [check **one** only] ( ) original or enforcement proceedings ( ) modification proceedings.

I UNDERSTAND THAT I SHOULD NOT FILE THE ANSWERS TO INTERROGATORIES WITH THE CLERK OF THE CIRCUIT COURT EXCEPT AS PROVIDED BY FLORIDA RULE OF CIVIL PROCEDURE 1.340(e).

I certify that a copy of this document was [check all used] ( ) e-mailed ( ) mailed ( ) faxed ( ) hand delivered to the person(s) listed below on *{date}*____________.

Other party or his/her attorney:
Name: ____________
Address: ____________
City, State, Zip: ____________
Fax Number: ____________
E-mail Address(es):____________

Dated: ____________

____
Signature of Party
Printed Name: ____________
Address: ____________
City, State, Zip: ____________
Telephone Number: ____________
Fax Number: ____________
E-mail Address(es):____________

Florida Family Law Rules of Procedure Form 12.930(d), Notice of Service of Answers to Standard Family Law Interrogatories (11/12)

IF A NONLAWYER HELPED YOU FILL OUT THIS FORM, HE/SHE MUST FILL IN THE BLANKS BELOW:
[fill in all blanks]
This form was prepared for: *{choose only **one**}* ( ) Petitioner ( ) Respondent
This form was completed with the assistance of:
*{ name of individual}*____,
{name of business} ____,
*{address}*____,
*{city}*________________________, *{state}*_________, *{telephone number}*________________________.

Florida Family Law Rules of Procedure Form 12.930(d), Notice of Service of Answers to Standard Family Law Interrogatories (11/12)

INSTRUCTIONS FOR FLORIDA FAMILY LAW RULES OF PROCEDURE FORM 12.930(d), NOTICE OF SERVICE OF ANSWERS TO STANDARD FAMILY LAW INTERROGATORIES (11/12)

When should this form be used?

You should use this form to tell the court that you have responded to the other **party**'s request to answer certain standard questions (**interrogatories**) in writing.

This form should be typed or printed in black ink. You must indicate whether you are sending the answers to interrogatories for original and enforcement proceedings, Florida Family Law Rules of Procedure Form 12.930(b), or modification proceedings, Florida Family Law Rules of Procedure Form 12.930(c). You must also indicate whether you have additional questions that you were asked to answer. After completing this form you should **file** the original with the **clerk of the circuit court** in the county where your case was filed and keep a copy for your records.

What should I do next?

A copy of this form and the original completed answers to the interrogatories must be mailed or hand delivered to the other party in your case. However, **file** only this form with the clerk. **DO NOT FILE THE ORIGINAL ANSWERS TO THE INTERROGATORIES OR ANY ATTACHMENTS WITH THE CLERK UNLESS THEY ARE ADMITTED INTO EVIDENCE BY THE COURT AND ARE IN COMPLIANCE WITH FLORIDA RULE OF JUDICIAL ADMINISTRATION 2.425.**

Where can I look for more information?

Before proceeding, you should read **"General Information for Self–Represented Litigants" found at the beginning of these forms.** For further information see Florida Family Law Rules of Procedure Rules 12.280, 12.285, 12.340, and 12.380, and Florida Rules of Civil Procedure Rules 1.280, 1.340, and 1.380.

Special notes . . .

Remember, a person who is NOT an attorney is called a nonlawyer. If a nonlawyer helps you fill out these forms, that person must give you a copy of **Disclosure from Nonlawyer**, Florida Family Law Rules of Procedure Form 12.900(a), before he or she helps you. A nonlawyer helping you fill out these forms also **must** put his or her name, address, and telephone number on the bottom of the last page of every form he or she helps you complete.

Added Nov. 3, 2011, effective, *nunc pro tunc*, Oct. 1, 2011 (78 So.3d 1045). Amended Nov. 15, 2012 (104 So.3d 314).

Form 12.931(a). Notice of Production From Nonparty

IN THE CIRCUIT COURT OF THE ____________________ JUDICIAL CIRCUIT,
IN AND FOR ____________________ COUNTY, FLORIDA

Case No.: ____________________
Division: ____________________

____________________,
Petitioner,

and

____________________,
Respondent.

NOTICE OF PRODUCTION FROM NONPARTY

TO: ____________________
{all parties}

YOU ARE NOTIFIED that, after **10 days** from the date of service of this notice, the undersigned will apply to the clerk of this Court for issuance of the attached subpoena directed to *{name of person, organization, or agency}* ____________________, who is not a party, to produce the items listed at the time and place specified in the subpoena. Objections to the issuance of this subpoena must be filed with the clerk of the circuit court within **10 days**.

I certify that a copy of this document was ( ) mailed ( ) faxed and mailed ( ) e-mailed ( ) hand-delivered to the person(s) listed below on *{date}*____________________.

Other party or his/her attorney (if represented)	Other
Printed Name	Printed Name
Address	Address
City, State, Zip	City, State, Zip
Telephone (area code and number)	Telephone (area code and number)
Fax (area code and number)	Fax (area code and number)
Designated E-mail Address(es)	Designated E-mail Address(es)

Florida Supreme Court Approved Family Law Form 12.931(a) Notice of Production from Nonparty (03/15)

____
Signature of Party
Printed Name: ______________________________
Address: ___________________________________
City, State, Zip: ____________________________
Telephone Number: __________________________
Fax Number: _______________________________
Designated E-mail Address(es):_______________________

IF A NONLAWYER HELPED YOU FILL OUT THIS FORM, HE/SHE MUST FILL IN THE BLANKS BELOW:
[fill in **all** blanks] This form was prepared for the: *{choose only **one**}* ( ) Petitioner ( ) Respondent
This form was completed with the assistance of:
{name of individual},____,
{name of business} ____,
{address} ____
,
{city} __________, *{state}*________,*{zip code}*__________, *{telephone number}*____________
.

INSTRUCTIONS FOR SUPREME COURT APPROVED FAMILY LAW FORMS 12.931(a), NOTICE OF PRODUCTION FROM NONPARTY AND 12.931(b), SUBPOENA FOR PRODUCTION OF DOCUMENTS FROM NONPARTY (03/15)

When should these forms be used?

These forms should be used if you need copies of documents (for a purpose relating to your case) from a **nonparty** in your case. Both forms should be typed or printed in black ink.

Notice of Production from Nonparty, Florida Supreme Court Approved Family Law Form 12.931(a), is used to notify the other **party** in your case that in 10 days you are going to subpoena documents from a nonparty. **Subpoena for Production of Documents from Nonparty**, Florida Supreme Court Approved Family Law Form 12.931(b), is the actual subpoena directing the nonparty to produce specific documents. You must **file** the originals of these forms with the **clerk of the circuit court**. A copy of these forms must be mailed, e-mailed, **or** hand delivered to any other party in your case.

IMPORTANT INFORMATION REGARDING E–FILING

The Florida Rules of Judicial Administration now require that all petitions, pleadings, and documents be filed electronically except in certain circumstances. **Self–represented litigants may file petitions or other pleadings or documents electronically; however, they are not required to do so.** If you choose to file your pleadings or other documents electronically, you must do so in accordance with Florida Rule of Judicial Administration 2.525, and you must follow the procedures of the judicial circuit in which you file. **The rules and procedures should be carefully read and followed.**

IMPORTANT INFORMATION REGARDING E–SERVICE ELECTION

After the initial service of process of the petition or supplemental petition by the Sheriff or certified process server, the Florida Rules of Judicial Administration now require that all documents required or permitted to be served on the other party must be served by electronic mail (e–mail) except in certain circumstances. **You must strictly comply with the format requirements set forth in the Rules of Judicial Administration.**

SELF–REPRESENTED LITIGANTS MAY SERVE DOCUMENTS BY E–MAIL; HOWEVER, THEY ARE NOT REQUIRED TO DO SO. If a self–represented litigant elects to serve and receive documents by e-mail, the procedures must always be followed once the initial election is made.

To serve and receive documents by e-mail, you must designate your e-mail addresses by using the **Designation of Current Mailing and E–mail Address**, Florida Supreme Court Approved Family Law Form 12.915, and you must provide your e-mail address on each form on which your signature appears. Please **CAREFULLY** read the rules and instructions for: **Certificate of Service (General),** Florida Supreme Court Approved Family Law Form 12.914; **Designation of Current Mailing and E–mail Address**, Florida Supreme Court Approved Family Law Form 12.915; and Florida Rule of Judicial Administration 2.516.

What should I do next?

Ten days after you serve the **Notice of Production from Nonparty**, Florida Supreme Court Approved Family Law Form 12.931(a), on the other party in your case (15 days if service is by mail or e–mail), you should ask the clerk of the court to sign the subpoena. You should contact the deputy sheriff or private process server and have the subpoena **personally served** on the person named in the subpoena.

Where can I look for more information?

Before proceeding, you should read General Information for Self–Represented Litigants found at the beginning of these forms. Because these papers must also comply with rule 12.280, Florida Family Law Rule of Procedure, and rules 1.280, 1.350, 1.351, and 1.410, Florida Rules of Civil Procedure, you also should read those rules.

Special Notes

If the other party in your case objects in writing within **10 days** (allow an additional 5 days if served by mail or e–mail) of service of the **Notice of Production from Nonparty**, Florida Supreme Court Approved Family Law Form 12.931(a), you may not use this procedure to obtain documents from the nonparty unless and until the court orders otherwise.

The nonparty receiving the subpoena may charge you a reasonable fee for copies of the documents.

Remember, a person who is NOT an attorney is called a nonlawyer. If a nonlawyer helps you fill out these forms, that person must give you a copy of **Disclosure from Nonlawyer**, Florida Family Law Rules of Procedure Form 12.900 (a), before he or she helps you. A nonlawyer helping you fill out these forms also **must** put his or her name, address, and telephone number on the bottom of the last page of every form he or she helps you complete.

Added July 7, 1995, effective Jan. 1, 1996 (663 So.2d 1047). Amended Feb. 26, 1998, effective Mar. 16, 1998 (713 So.2d 1); Sept. 21, 2000 (810 So.2d 1); Mar. 25, 2004 (871 So.2d 113); Sept. 28, 2011 (73 So.3d 213); March 26, 2015, effective March 26, 2015 (2015 WL 1343088).

Form 12.931(b). Subpoena for Production of Documents From Nonparty

IN THE CIRCUIT COURT OF THE ______ JUDICIAL CIRCUIT,
IN AND FOR ______ COUNTY, FLORIDA

Case No.: ______________
Division: ______________

______________,
Petitioner,

and

______________,
Respondent.

SUBPOENA FOR PRODUCTION OF DOCUMENTS FROM NONPARTY

THE STATE OF FLORIDA
TO: ______________________________

YOU **MUST** go to *{place}*______________________, on *{date}* ______________, at *{time}* ________, a.m./p.m. and bring with you at that time and place the following:______________________________
____
______
____
______
____
______
____
______

These items will be inspected and may be copied at that time. You will not have to leave the original items.

You may obey this subpoena by providing readable copies of the items to be produced to the party **or** his/her attorney whose name appears on this subpoena on or before the scheduled date of production. You may condition the preparation of the copies upon payment in advance of the reasonable cost of preparation. If you mail or deliver the copies to the attorney whose name appears on this subpoena before the date indicated above, you do not have to appear in person.

You may be in contempt of court if you fail to: (1) appear as specified; (2) furnish the records instead

Florida Supreme Court Approved Family Law Form 12.931(b), Subpoena for Production from a Nonparty (03/15)

of appearing as provided above; or (3) object to this subpoena.

You can only be excused by the person whose name appears on this subpoena and, unless excused by that person of the Court, you shall respond as directed.

This part to be filled out by the court or filled in with information obtained from the court:

If you are a person with a disability who needs any accommodation in order to participate in this proceeding, you are entitled, at no cost to you, to the provision of certain assistance. Please contact:________________________

____

{identify applicable court personnel by name, address, and telephone number} **at least 7 days before your scheduled court appearance, or immediately upon receiving this notification if the time before the scheduled appearance is less than 7 days; if you are hearing or voice impaired, call 711.**

Dated:______________________

CLERK OF THE CIRCUIT COURT (SEAL)

By:____________________________________
Deputy Clerk

I CERTIFY that I gave notice to every other party to this action of my intent to serve a subpoena upon a person who is not a party to this action directing that person to produce documents or things without deposition. I also certify that no objection under Florida Rule of Civil Procedure 1.351 has been received by the undersigned within 10 days of service of this notice, if service was by hand-delivery or appropriate facsimile transmission, and within 15 days if service was by mail or e-mail.

Dated: __________________________

____
Signature of Party
Printed Name: ____
Address: ____
City, State, Zip: ____
Telephone Number: ____
Fax Number: ____
Designated E-mail Address(es): ____________________________

IF A NONLAWYER HELPED YOU FILL OUT THIS FORM, HE/SHE MUST FILL IN THE BLANKS BELOW:
[fill in all blanks] This form was prepared for the: *{choose only **one**}* ( ) Petitioner ( ) Respondent

Florida Supreme Court Approved Family Law Form 12.931(b), Subpoena for Production from a Nonparty (03/15)

This form was completed with the assistance of:
{name of individual } ______________________________,
{name of business} ______________________________,
{address} ______________________________,
{city}________________,{state}____, {zip code}__________, {telephone number}______________.

Florida Supreme Court Approved Family Law Form 12.931(b), Subpoena for Production from a Nonparty (03/15)

Added July 7, 1995, effective Jan. 1, 1996 (663 So.2d 1047). Amended Feb. 26, 1998, effective Mar. 16, 1998 (713 So.2d 1); Sept. 21, 2000 (810 So.2d 1); Mar. 25, 2004 (871 So.2d 113); Sept. 28, 2011 (73 So.3d 213); March 26, 2015, effective March 26, 2015 (2015 WL 1343088).

Form 12.932. Certificate of Compliance with Mandatory Disclosure

IN THE CIRCUIT COURT OF THE ________________ JUDICIAL CIRCUIT,
IN AND FOR ________________ COUNTY, FLORIDA

Case No.: ________________
Division: ________________

________________,
Petitioner,

and

________________,
Respondent.

CERTIFICATE OF COMPLIANCE WITH MANDATORY DISCLOSURE

ONLY THE ORIGINAL OF THIS COMPLETED FORM IS FILED WITH THE COURT. EXCEPT FOR THE FINANCIAL AFFIDAVIT AND CHILD SUPPORT GUIDELINES WORKSHEET, NO DOCUMENTS SHALL BE FILED IN THE COURT FILE WITHOUT A PRIOR COURT ORDER. THE DOCUMENTS LISTED BELOW ARE TO BE GIVEN TO THE OTHER PARTY.

I, *{full legal name}* ________________, certify that I have complied with the mandatory disclosure required by Florida Family Law Rule 12.285 as follows:

1. FOR TEMPORARY FINANCIAL RELIEF, ONLY:
The date the following documents were served: ________________.
[Check all that apply]

a. ____ Financial Affidavit
( ) Florida Family Law Rules of Procedure Form 12.902(b) (short form)
( ) Florida Family Law Rules of Procedure Form 12.902(c) (long form)

b. ____ All personal (1040) federal tax, gift tax, and intangible personal property tax returns for the preceding year; or
( ) Transcript of tax return as provided by IRS form 4506-T; or
( ) IRS forms W-2, 1099, and K-1 for the past year because the income tax return for the past year has not been prepared.

c. ____ Pay stubs or other evidence of earned income for the 3 months before the service of the financial affidavit.

2. FOR INITIAL, SUPPLEMENTAL, AND PERMANENT FINANCIAL RELIEF:
The date the following documents were served: ________________.
[Check all that apply]

a. ____ Financial Affidavit

( ) Florida Family Law Rules of Procedure Form 12.902(b) (short form)
( ) Florida Family Law Rules of Procedure Form 12.902(c) (long form)

b. ____ All personal (1040) federal and state income tax returns, gift tax returns, and intangible personal property tax returns for the preceding 3 years;
( ) IRS forms W-2, 1099, and K-1 for the past year because the income tax return for the past year has not been prepared.

c. ____ Pay stubs or other evidence of earned income for the 3 months before the service of the financial affidavit.

d. ___ A statement identifying the source and amount of all income for the 3 months before the service of the financial affidavit, if not reflected on the pay stubs produced.

e. ___ All loan applications and financial statements prepared for any purpose or used for any purpose within the 12 months preceding the service of the financial affidavit.

f. ___ All deeds to real estate in which I presently own or owned an interest within the past 3 years. All promissory notes in which I presently own or owned an interest within the last 12 months. All present leases in which I own an interest.

g. ___ All periodic statements for the last 3 months for all checking accounts and for the last year for all savings accounts, money market funds, certificates of deposit, etc.

h. ___ All brokerage account statements for the last 12 months.

i. ___ Most recent statement for any pension, profit sharing, deferred compensation, or retirement plan (for example, IRA, 401(k), 403(b), SEP, KEOGH, etc.) and summary plan description for any such plan in which I am a participant or alternate payee.

j. ___ The declaration page, the last periodic statement, and the certificate for any group insurance for all life insurance policies insuring my life or the life of me or my spouse.

k. ___ All health and dental insurance cards covering either me or my spouse and/or our dependent child(ren).

l. ___ Corporate, partnership, and trust tax returns for the last 3 tax years, in which I have an ownership or interest greater than or equal to 30%.

m. ___ All credit card and charge account statements and other records showing my (our) indebtedness as of the date of the filing of this action and for the prior 3 months. All promissory notes on which I presently owe or owed within the past year. All lease agreements I presently owe.

n. ___ All premarital and marital agreements between the parties to this case.

o. ___ If a modification proceeding, all written agreements entered into between the parties at any time since the order to be modified was entered.

p. ___ All documents and tangible evidence relating to claims for an unequal distribution of marital property, enhancement or appreciation in nonmarital property, or nonmarital status of an asset or debt.

q. ___ Any court order directing that I pay or receive spousal support (alimony) or child support.

I certify that a copy of this document was [**check all used**]: ( ) e-mailed ( ) mailed ( ) faxed ( ) hand delivered to the person(s) listed below on *{date}*________________.

Other party or his/her attorney:
Name: ____________________
Address: ____________________
City, State, Zip: ____________________
Fax Number: ____________________
E-mail Address(es): ____________________

I understand that I am swearing or affirming under oath to the accuracy of my compliance with the mandatory disclosure requirements of Florida Family Law Rule of Procedure 12.285 and that, unless otherwise indicated with specificity, this disclosure is complete. I further understand that the punishment for knowingly making a false statement or incomplete disclosure includes fines and/or imprisonment.

____
Signature of Party
Printed Name: ____________________
Address: ____________________
City, State, Zip: ____________________
Telephone Number: ____________________
Fax Number: ____________________
E-mail Address(es): ____________________

STATE OF FLORIDA
COUNTY OF ____________________

Sworn to or affirmed and signed before me on __________ by ____________________.

____
NOTARY PUBLIC or DEPUTY CLERK

____
[Print, type, or stamp commissioned name of notary or clerk.]

____ Personally known
____ Produced identification
Type of identification produced ____________________

IF A NONLAWYER HELPED YOU FILL OUT THIS FORM, HE/SHE MUST FILL IN THE BLANKS BELOW: [fill in all blanks] This form was prepared for the: *{choose only **one**}*
( ) Petitioner ( ) Respondent
This form was completed with the assistance of:
{name of individual} ____________________,
{name of business} ____________________,
{address} ____________________,
{city} __________, *{state}* ______, *{telephone number}* __________.

Florida Family Law Rules of Procedure Form 12.932, Certificate of Compliance with Mandatory Disclosure (09/12)

INSTRUCTIONS FOR FLORIDA FAMILY LAW RULES OF PROCEDURE FORM 12.932, CERTIFICATE OF COMPLIANCE WITH MANDATORY DISCLOSURE (09/12)

When should this form be used?

Mandatory disclosure requires each **party** in a **dissolution of marriage** case to provide the other party with certain financial information and documents. These documents must be served on the other party within 45 days of **service** of the petition for **dissolution of marriage** or supplemental petition for modification on the **respondent**. The mandatory disclosure rule applies to all original and **supplemental** dissolution of marriage cases, except simplified dissolution of marriage cases and cases where the respondent is served by **constructive service** and does not answer. You should use this form to notify the court and the other party that you have complied with the mandatory disclosure rule.

Each party must provide the other party with the documents listed in section 2 of this form if the relief being sought is permanent regardless of whether it is an initial or supplemental proceeding. ONLY THE ORIGINAL OF THE COMPLETED FORM IS FILED WITH THE COURT. EXCEPT FOR THE FINANCIAL AFFIDAVIT AND CHILD SUPPORT GUIDELINES WORKSHEET, NO DOCUMENTS SHALL BE FILED IN THE COURT FILE WITHOUT A PRIOR COURT ORDER. THE DOCUMENTS LISTED ON THE FORM ARE TO BE GIVEN TO THE OTHER PARTY. If your individual gross annual income is under $50,000, you should complete the **Family Law Financial Affidavit (Short Form)**, Florida Family Law Rules of Procedure Form 12.902(b). If your individual gross annual income is $50,000 or more, you should complete the **Family Law Financial Affidavit (Long Form)**, Florida Family Law Rules of Procedure Form 12.902(c).

In addition, there are separate mandatory disclosure requirements that apply to **temporary financial hearings**, which are listed in section 1 of this form. The party seeking temporary financial relief must serve these documents on the other party with the notice of temporary financial hearing. The responding party must serve the required documents on the party seeking temporary relief. Service by e-mail **or** mail shall be at least 7 days before the temporary financial relief hearing. Service by delivery shall be no later than 5:00 p.m., 2 business days before the hearing. Any documents that have already been served under the requirements for temporary or initial proceedings do not need to be reserved again in the same proceeding. If a supplemental petition is filed, seeking modification, then the mandatory disclosure requirements begin again.

This form should be typed or printed in black ink. After completing this form, you should **file** the original with the **clerk of the circuit court** in the county where your case is filed and keep a copy for your records. A copy of this form must be served on any other party in your case. **Service** must be in accordance with Florida Rule of Judicial Administration 2.516.

What should I do next?

After you have provided the other party all of the financial information and documents and have filed this form certifying that you have complied with this rule, you are under a continuing duty to promptly give the other party any information or documents that change your financial status or that make the information already provided inaccurate. You should not file with the clerk any of the documents listed in the certificate of compliance other than the financial affidavit and the child support guidelines worksheet. Refer to the instructions regarding the **petition** in your case to determine how you should proceed after filing this form.

Where can I look for more information?

Before proceeding, you should read "General Information for Self-Represented Litigants" found at the beginning of these forms. The words that are in **bold underline** in these instructions are defined there. For further information, see Florida Family Law Rule of Procedure 12. 285.

Special notes . . .

You may provide copies of required documents; however, the originals must be produced for inspection if the other party requests to see them.

Although the financial affidavits are based on individual gross income, either party may ask the other party to complete the **Family Law Financial Affidavit (Long Form),** Florida Family Law Rules of Procedure Form 12.902(c), by serving the appropriate interrogatory form. (See **Standard Family Law Interrogatories**, Florida Family Law Rules of Procedure Form 12.930(b) (original proceedings) or (c) (modification proceedings)).

Any portion of the mandatory disclosure rule may be modified by order of the **judge** or agreement of the parties. Therefore, you and your **spouse** may agree that you will not require each other to produce the documents required under the mandatory disclosure rule. This exception does **not** apply to the **Financial Affidavit**, Family Law Rules of Procedure Form 12.902(b) or (c), which is required in all cases and cannot be waived.

Remember, a person who is NOT an attorney is called a nonlawyer. If a nonlawyer helps you fill out these forms, that person must give you a copy of a **Disclosure from Nonlawyer**, Florida Family Law Rules of Procedure Form 12.900(a), before he or she helps you. A nonlawyer helping you fill out these forms also **must** put his or her name, address, and telephone number on the bottom of the last page of every form he or she helps you complete.

Added Feb. 26, 1998, effective Mar. 16, 1998 (713 So.2d 1). Amended Oct. 29, 1998, effective Feb. 1, 1999 (723 So.2d 208); Sept. 21, 2000 (810 So.2d 1); July 10, 2003, effective Jan. 1, 2004 (853 So.2d 303); Oct. 6, 2005, effective Jan. 1, 2006 (913 So.2d 545); Nov. 3, 2011, effective, *nunc pro tunc*, Oct. 1, 2011 (78 So.3d 1045); Jan. 19, 2012 (80 So.3d 317); Oct. 18, 2012, effective, *nunc pro tunc*, Sept. 1, 2012 (102 So.3d 505).

Form 12.940(d). Motion to Modify or Dissolve Temporary Injunction

IN THE CIRCUIT COURT OF THE ______________ JUDICIAL CIRCUIT,
IN AND FOR ______________ COUNTY, FLORIDA

Case No.: ______________
Division: ______________

______________,
Petitioner,
and

______________,
Respondent.

MOTION TO MODIFY OR DISSOLVE TEMPORARY INJUNCTION

_____ Petitioner _____ Respondent requests the Court to enter an order _____ dissolving the temporary injunction issued in the above styled case _____ modifying the temporary injunction issued in the above styled case in the following manner: ______________
______________.

I am the party against whom this temporary injunction has been granted and under rule 1.610, Florida Rules of Civil Procedure, I request that a hearing be held within 5 days after the filing of this motion.

I certify that a copy of this document was ( ) mailed ( ) faxed and mailed ( ) e-mailed ( ) hand delivered to the person(s) listed below on *{date}* ______________.

Other party or his/her attorney:
Name: ______________
Address: ______________
City, State, Zip: ______________
Fax Number: ______________
Designated E-mail Address(es): ______________
____

____
Signature of Party
Printed Name: ______________
Address: ______________
City, State, Zip: ______________
Telephone Number: ______________
Fax Number: ______________
Designated E-mail Address(es): ______________
____

IF A NONLAWYER HELPED YOU FILL OUT THIS FORM, HE/SHE MUST FILL IN THE BLANKS BELOW:
[fill in all blanks] This form was prepared for the: *{choose only one}* ( ) Petitioner ( ) Respondent
This form was completed with the assistance of:
{name of individual} ______________________________,
{name of business} ______________________________,
{address} ______________________________,
{city} __________,*{state}* ____, *{zip code}*________,*{telephone number}* __________.

INSTRUCTIONS FOR FLORIDA SUPREME COURT APPROVED FAMILY LAW FORM 12.940(d), MOTION TO MODIFY OR DISSOLVE TEMPORARY INJUNCTION (03/15)

When should this form be used?

If a temporary injunction, either ex parte or after a hearing, has been entered against you, you may use this form to ask the court to modify or dissolve that injunction. **This motion should not be used to dissolve a Temporary Injunction for Protection Against Domestic Violence.**

This form should be typed or printed in black ink. After completing this form, you should file the original with the clerk of the circuit court in the county where the injunction was entered and keep a copy for your records. You should ask the clerk to process your motion through their emergency procedures. A hearing will be held within 5 working days. You should ask for the date and time of your hearing and should file **Notice of Hearing (General)**, Florida Supreme Court Approved Family Law Form 12.923 or other appropriate notice of hearing form, and send a copy to the other party.

IMPORTANT INFORMATION REGARDING E–FILING

The Florida Rules of Judicial Administration now require that all petitions, pleadings, and documents be filed electronically except in certain circumstances. **Self–represented litigants may file petitions or other pleadings or documents electronically; however, they are not required to do so.** If you choose to file your pleadings or other documents electronically, you must do so in accordance with Florida Rule of Judicial Administration 2.525, and you must follow the procedures of the judicial circuit in which you file. **The rules and procedures should be carefully read and followed.**

What should I do next?

A copy of this form must be mailed, e-mailed, or hand delivered to the other party, along with a notice of hearing.

IMPORTANT INFORMATION REGARDING E–SERVICE ELECTION

After the initial service of process of the petition or supplemental petition by the Sheriff or certified process server, the Florida Rules of Judicial Administration now require that all documents required or permitted to be served on the other party must be served by electronic mail (e–mail) except in certain circumstances. **You must strictly comply with the format requirements set forth in the Rules of Judicial Administration.**

SELF–REPRESENTED LITIGANTS MAY SERVE DOCUMENTS BY E–MAIL; HOWEVER, THEY ARE NOT REQUIRED TO DO SO. If a self-represented litigant elects to serve and receive documents by e-mail, the procedures must always be followed once the initial election is made.

To serve and receive documents by e-mail, you must designate your e-mail addresses by using the **Designation of Current Mailing and E–mail Address**, Florida Supreme Court Approved Family Law Form 12.915, and you must provide your e-mail address on each form on which your signature appears. Please **CAREFULLY** read the rules and instructions for: **Certificate of Service (General)**, Florida Supreme Court Approved Family Law Form 12.914; **Designation of Current Mailing and E–mail Address**, Florida Supreme Court Approved Family Law Form 12.915; and Florida Rule of Judicial Administration 2.516.

Where can I look for more information?

Before proceeding, you should read "General Information for Self–Represented Litigants" found at the beginning of these forms. For further information, see chapter 61, Florida Statutes, and rule 1.610, Florida Rules of Civil Procedure.

Special notes . . .

If parental responsibility or time-sharing of a minor child(ren) is at issue, you must also file the following, if you have not already done so:

- **Uniform Child Custody Jurisdiction and Enforcement Act (UCCJEA) Affidavit,** Florida Supreme Court Approved Family Law Form 12.902(d).

Order ... These family law forms contain an **Order Dissolving Temporary Injunction**, Florida Supreme Court Approved Family Law Form 12.940(e), which the judge may use. You should check with the clerk, **family law intake staff**, or **judicial assistant** to see if you need to bring a blank order form with you to the hearing. If so, you should type or print the heading, including the circuit, county, case number, division, and the parties' names, and leave the rest blank for the judge to complete at your hearing or trial.

Remember, a person who is NOT an attorney is called a nonlawyer. If a nonlawyer helps you fill out these forms, that person must give you a copy of **Disclosure from Nonlawyer**, Florida Family Law Rules of Procedure Form 12.900(a), before he or she helps you. A nonlawyer helping you fill out these forms also **must** put his or her name, address, and telephone number on the bottom of the last page of every form he or she helps you complete.

Added Sept. 21, 2000 (810 So.2d 1). Amended Dec. 19, 2002 (836 So.2d 1019); March 26, 2009 (20 So.3d 173); Dec. 16, 2010 (59 So.3d 792); March 26, 2015, effective March 26, 2015 (2015 WL 1343088).

Form 12.940(e). Order Dissolving Temporary Injunction

IN THE CIRCUIT COURT OF THE ________ JUDICIAL CIRCUIT,
IN AND FOR ________ COUNTY, FLORIDA

Case No.: ____________
Division: ____________

______________________________,
Petitioner,
and

______________________________,
Respondent.

ORDER DISSOLVING TEMPORARY INJUNCTION

Upon _____Petitioner's _____ Respondent's motion and after hearing, the Court, being fully advised in the premises,

ORDERS that the temporary injunction entered on *{date}* ______________________________ in the above-styled case is hereby dissolved.

DONE AND ORDERED in ________________________, Florida, on *{date}* ____________________.

____
CIRCUIT JUDGE

I certify that a copy of *{name of document}* ________________________________was ( ) mailed ( ) faxed and mailed ( ) e-mailed ( ) hand-delivered to the parties and any other person(s) or entities listed below on *{date}* _______________:

____
By Clerk of Court, Designee, or Judicial Assistant

Petitioner (or his or her attorney)
Respondent (or his or her attorney)

U.S. Department of State
Office of Children's Issues
2201 "C" Street NW
CA/OCS/CI
Washington, D.C. 20520
Fax (202) 736-9133
preventabduction@state.gov

Florida Supreme Court Approved Family Law Form 12.940(e), Order Dissolving Temporary Injunction (03/15)

Added Sept. 21, 2000 (810 So.2d 1). Amended March 26, 2009 (20 So.3d 173); Dec. 16, 2010 (59 So.3d 792); March 26, 2015, effective March 26, 2015 (2015 WL 1343088).

Form 12.941(a). Verified Motion for Temporary Injunction to Prevent Removal of Minor Child(ren) and/or Denial of Passport Services

IN THE CIRCUIT COURT OF THE ________________ JUDICIAL CIRCUIT,
IN AND FOR ____________________ COUNTY, FLORIDA

Case No.: ________________
Division: ________________

______________________________,
Petitioner,

and

______________________________,
Respondent.

VERIFIED MOTION FOR TEMPORARY INJUNCTION TO PREVENT REMOVAL OF MINOR CHILD(REN) AND/OR DENIAL OF PASSPORT SERVICES

_____ Petitioner _____ Respondent requests the Court to enter a temporary injunction to prevent removal of the following listed minor child(ren) from the jurisdiction of this Court and deny passport services for the child(ren) and says:

1. The minor child(ren) subject to this request is (are):

Name	**Birth date**

2. The child(ren) has (have) been a resident(s) of ________________ County, Florida since *{date}* ________________.

3. A completed Uniform Child Custody Jurisdiction and Enforcement Act (UCCJEA) Affidavit, Florida Supreme Court Approved Family Law Form 12.902(d), _____is filed with this motion or _____ has already been filed.

4. It is in the best interests of the minor child(ren) that the Court order the following: *{Indicate **all** that apply}*

a. ___The child(ren) not be removed from the jurisdiction of this Court while litigation is pending because:________________________________

b. _____Passport services for the minor child(ren) be prohibited because:____

c. ____Existing passports for the minor child(ren) be immediately turned over to _____Petitioner _____ Respondent because: ____

5. This motion should be granted _____ with _____ without notice to the other party. *{If without notice, explain why there would be immediate and irreparable harm if the other party is given notice.}*
____.

WHEREFORE, _____ Petitioner _____ Respondent requests the following from the Court: *{Indicate **all** that apply}*

a. ____enter a temporary injunction to prevent removal of the child(ren) named above from the jurisdiction of this Court while this action is pending;
b. ____enter an order denying passport services for the minor child(ren);
c. ____enter an order requiring that any existing passports for the minor child(ren) be immediately delivered to _____ Petitioner _____ Respondent;
d. ____enter a temporary injunction without notice to the other party.

I certify that a copy of this document was ( ) mailed ( ) faxed and mailed ( ) e-mailed ( ) hand delivered to the person(s) listed below on *{date}* ______________________ or ( ) was **not** delivered to the person(s) listed below because ____.

Other party or his/her attorney:
Name: ______________________________
Address: ____________________________

Florida Supreme Court Approved Family Law Form 12.941(a), Verified Motion for Temporary Injunction to Prevent Removal of Minor Child(ren) and/or Denial of Passport Services (03/15)

City, State, Zip: ______________________________
Fax Number: ______________________________
Designated E-mail Address(es): ______________________________
____

I understand that I am swearing or affirming under oath to the truthfulness of the claims made in this verified motion and that the punishment for knowingly making a false statement includes fines and/or imprisonment.

Dated: ______________________ ______________________________
Signature of Party
Printed Name: ______________________________
Address: ______________________________
City, State, Zip: ______________________________
Telephone Number: ______________________________
Fax Number: ______________________________
Designated E-mail Address(es): ______________________________
____

STATE OF FLORIDA
COUNTY OF ______________________

Sworn to or affirmed and signed before me on ______________ by ______________________.

____
NOTARY PUBLIC or DEPUTY CLERK

____
[Print, type, or stamp commissioned name of notary or clerk.]
_____ Personally known
_____ Produced identification
Type of identification produced ______________________________

If the party filing this motion is represented by an attorney, the attorney must complete the following:

I, the undersigned attorney for the movant, hereby certify in that the following efforts have been made to give notice. *{if no efforts have been made, why}* ____________________
____
____
____
____
____
____

____
Signature
Printed Name: ____________________
Florida Bar Number: ____________________
Address: ____________________
City, State, Zip: ____________________
Telephone Number: ____________________
Fax Number: ____________________
Designated E-mail Address(es): ____________________
____

IF A NONLAWYER HELPED YOU FILL OUT THIS FORM, HE/SHE MUST FILL IN THE BLANKS BELOW:
[fill in **all** blanks] This form was prepared for the: *{choose only **one**}* ( ) Petitioner ( ) Respondent
This form was completed with the assistance of:
{name of individual} ____________________,
{name of business} ____________________
____________________,
{address} ____________________,
{city} ____________,*{state}* _____, *{zip code}*________,*{telephone number}*____________.

Florida Supreme Court Approved Family Law Form 12.941(a), Verified Motion for Temporary Injunction to Prevent Removal of Minor Child(ren) and/or Denial of Passport Services (03/15)

INSTRUCTIONS FOR FLORIDA SUPREME COURT APPROVED FAMILY LAW FORM 12.941(a), VERIFIED MOTION FOR TEMPORARY INJUNCTION TO PREVENT REMOVAL OF MINOR CHILD(REN) AND/OR DENIAL OF PASSPORT SERVICES (03/15)

When should this form be used?

You should use this form if you want the court to enter an **order** that your minor child(ren) is (are) not to be removed from the State of Florida while a case involving parenting or time-sharing is pending, that passport services for the minor child(ren) be prohibited, and/or that existing passports be turned over to you.

This form should be typed or printed in black ink. If you want the court to enter an **ex parte** order, without giving the other side advance notice of the hearing, you should explain your reasons in paragraph 5 of this form. After completing this form, you should sign the form before a **notary public**. You should **file** the original with the **clerk of the circuit court** in the county where your case is pending and keep a copy for your records. You should also ask the clerk to process your **motion** though their emergency procedures.

IMPORTANT INFORMATION REGARDING E–FILING

The Florida Rules of Judicial Administration now require that all petitions, pleadings, and documents be filed electronically except in certain circumstances. **Self–represented litigants may file petitions or other pleadings or documents electronically; however, they are not required to do so.** If you choose to file your pleadings or other documents electronically, you must do so in accordance with Florida Rule of Judicial Administration 2.525, and you must follow the procedures of the judicial circuit in which you file. **The rules and procedures should be carefully read and followed.**

What should I do next?

If the court enters an order without advance notice to the other party, you should take a **certified copy** of the order to the sheriff's office for further assistance. You must have this form and the court's order, served by **personal service** on the other party. You should read the court's order carefully. Look for directions in the order that apply to you and note the time and place of the **hearing** scheduled in the order. You should go to the hearing with whatever evidence you have regarding your motion.

If the court will not enter an order without advance notice to the other side, you should check with the clerk of court, **family law intake staff**, or **judicial assistant** for information on the local procedure for scheduling a hearing on your motion, unless the court sets a hearing in its order denying your request for an ex parte hearing. When you know the date and time of your hearing, you should file **Notice of Hearing (General)**, Florida Supreme Court Approved Family Law Form 12.923 or other appropriate notice of hearing form, and use personal service to notify the other party of your motion, the court's order, if any, and the hearing.

Where can I look for more information?

Before proceeding, you should read "General Information for Self–Represented Litigants" found at the beginning of these forms. For further information, see chapter 61, Florida Statutes, and rule 1.610, Florida Rules of Civil Procedure.

IMPORTANT INFORMATION REGARDING E–SERVICE ELECTION

After the initial service of process of the petition or supplemental petition by the Sheriff or certified process server, the Florida Rules of Judicial Administration now require that all documents required or permitted to be served on the other party must be served by electronic mail (e–mail) except in certain circumstances. **You must strictly comply with the format requirements set forth in the Rules of Judicial Administration.**

SELF–REPRESENTED LITIGANTS MAY SERVE DOCUMENTS BY E–MAIL; HOWEVER, THEY ARE NOT REQUIRED TO DO SO. If a self-represented litigant elects to serve and receive documents by e-mail, the procedures must always be followed once the initial election is made.

To serve and receive documents by e-mail, you must designate your e-mail addresses by using the **Designation of Current Mailing and E–mail Address**, Florida Supreme Court Approved Family Law Form 12.915, and you must provide your e-mail address on each form on which your signature appears. Please **CAREFULLY** read the rules and instructions for: **Certificate of Service (General),** Florida Supreme Court Approved Family Law Form 12.914; **Designation of Current Mailing and E–mail Address**, Florida Supreme Court Approved Family Law Form 12.915; and Florida Rule of Judicial Administration 2.516.

Special notes . . .

If you have an attorney, your attorney must certify in writing the efforts that have been made to give the other party notice, if no notice is given. The court may require you to post a **bond** as a condition of the injunction.

With this form you must also file the following, if you have not already done so, and provide a copy to the other party:

- **Uniform Child Custody Jurisdiction and Enforcement Act (UCCJEA) Affidavit,** Florida Supreme Court Approved Family Law Form 12.902(d).

Temporary Injunctions . . . These family law forms contain a **Temporary Injunction to Prevent Removal of Minor Child(ren) and/or Denial of Passport Services (Ex Parte),** Florida Supreme Court Approved Family Law Form 12.941(b), which the **judge** may use if he or she enters an order without a hearing, and a **Temporary Injunction to Prevent Removal of Minor Child(ren) and/or Denial of Passport Services (After Notice)**, Florida Supreme Court Approved Family Law Form 12.941(c), which the judge may use if he or she enters an order after a hearing. You should check with the clerk, family law intake staff, or judicial assistant to see if you need to bring a blank order form with you to the hearing. If so, you should type or print the heading, including the circuit, county, case number, division, and the parties' names, and leave the rest blank for the judge to complete at your hearing.

Remember, a person who is NOT an attorney is called a nonlawyer. If a nonlawyer helps you fill out these forms, that person must give you a copy of **Disclosure from Nonlawyer**, Florida Family Law Rules of Procedure Form 12.900 (a), before he or she helps you. A nonlawyer helping you fill out these forms also **must** put his or her name, address, and telephone number on the bottom of the last page of every form he or she helps you complete.

Added July 7, 1995, effective Jan. 1, 1996 (663 So.2d 1047). Amended Feb. 26, 1998, effective Mar. 16, 1998 (713 So.2d 1); Sept. 21, 2000 (810 So.2d 1); Dec. 19, 2002 (836 So.2d 1019); March 26, 2009 (20 So.3d 173); Dec. 16, 2010 (59 So.3d 792); March 26, 2015, effective March 26, 2015 (2015 WL 1343088).

Form 12.941(b). Temporary Injunction to Prevent Removal of Minor Child(ren) and/or Denial of Passport Services (Ex Parte)

IN THE CIRCUIT COURT OF THE ____________ JUDICIAL CIRCUIT,
IN AND FOR ______________________________ COUNTY, FLORIDA

Case No: ____________________
Division: ____________________

_________________________________,
Petitioner,
and

_________________________________,
Respondent.

TEMPORARY INJUNCTION TO PREVENT REMOVAL OF MINOR CHILD(REN) AND/OR DENIAL OF PASSPORT SERVICES (EX PARTE)

Upon verified motion of _____ Petitioner _____Respondent, the Court has jurisdiction of the parties and the subject matter and the Court being fully advised, it is ORDERED and ADJUDGED that:

NOTICE OF HEARING

This Temporary Injunction to Prevent Removal of Child(ren) has been issued without prior notice to Respondent. Pursuant to Rule 1.610, Florida Rules of Civil Procedure, the other party may file a motion to dissolve or modify this temporary injunction and a hearing will be scheduled within 5 days of that motion.

If no motion to dissolve is filed, Petitioner and Respondent are instructed that they are scheduled to appear and testify at a hearing regarding this matter on *{date}*__________________, at _____ a.m./p.m., when the Court will consider whether the Court should continue, modify, or dissolve this Temporary Injunction to Prevent Removal of Child(ren) and/or Denial of Passport Services, which would remain in effect until modified or dissolved by the Court, and whether other things should be ordered, including who should pay the filing fees and costs. The hearing will be before The Honorable *{name}*____, at *{room name/number, location, address, city}*
____, Florida.

IF PETITIONER AND/OR RESPONDENT DO (DOES) NOT APPEAR, THIS TEMPORARY INJUNCTION MAY BE CONTINUED IN FORCE, EXTENDED, OR DISMISSED, AND/OR OTHER ADDITIONAL ORDERS MAY BE ISSUED, INCLUDING THE IMPOSITION OF COURT COSTS.

Florida Supreme Court Approved Family Law Form 12.941(b), Temporary Injunction to Prevent Removal of Minor Child(ren) and/or Denial of Passport Services (Ex Parte) (03/15)

If you are a person with a disability who needs any accommodation in order to participate in this proceeding, you are entitled, at no cost to you, to the provision of certain assistance. Please contact:

____

{identify applicable court personnel by name, address, and telephone number} **at least 7 days before your scheduled court appearance, or immediately upon receiving this notification if the time before the scheduled appearance is less than 7 days; if you are hearing or voice impaired, call 711.**

FINDINGS

1. It appears from specific facts shown by verified motion that immediate and irreparable injury, loss, or damage will result to the minor child(ren) if a temporary injunction is not issued without notice to the other party.

2. _____ Petitioner's _____ Respondent's attorney has certified in writing any efforts made to give notice.

3. The reasons why notice should **not** be given are: ____
____
____
____

TEMPORARY INJUNCTION

*{Indicate **all** that apply}*

1. _____The following child(ren) shall not be removed from the jurisdiction of this Court during the pendency of this proceeding, or until further order of this Court:

Name	Birth date

2. _____ Petitioner _____Respondent shall not apply for any passports or passport services on behalf of the child(ren).

3. _____ Petitioner _____ Respondent shall immediately deliver any existing passports for the child(ren) to *{name}* ____.

4. The Court may enforce compliance with the terms of this injunction through civil and/or indirect criminal contempt proceedings, which may include arrest, incarceration, and/or the imposition of a fine.

5. Violation of this injunction may constitute criminal contempt of court.

6. Bond.
   a. _____ Bond is waived because this injunction is issued solely to prevent physical injury or abuse of a natural person.

   b. _____ This order is conditioned upon _____ Petitioner _____ Respondent posting bond in the sum of $ _________ with the clerk of this Court.

EXPIRATION.
This injunction shall remain in effect until the minor child(ren) reach(es) the age of 18, until the hearing scheduled herein, if any, or *{date}*______________________, whichever occurs first, unless modified by further order of this Court.

DONE AND ORDERED at ________________________, Florida on *{date}* _________________.

____
CIRCUIT JUDGE

I certify that a copy of the *{name of document(s)}* ____ was ( ) mailed ( ) faxed and mailed ( ) e-mailed ( ) hand-delivered to the parties and any other person(s) or entities listed below on *{date}*___________________________.

____
By: Clerk of Court, Designee, or Judicial Assistant

Petitioner (or his or her attorney)
Respondent (or his or her attorney)

U.S. Department of State
Office of Children's Issues
2201 "C" Street NW
CA/OCS/CI

Florida Supreme Court Approved Family Law Form 12.941(b), Temporary Injunction to Prevent Removal of Minor Child(ren) and/or Denial of Passport Services (Ex Parte) (03/15)

Washington, D.C. 20520
Fax (202) 736-9133
preventabduction@state.gov

Florida Supreme Court Approved Family Law Form 12.941(b), Temporary Injunction to Prevent Removal of Minor Child(ren) and/or Denial of Passport Services (Ex Parte) (03/15)

Added July 7, 1995, effective Jan. 1, 1996 (663 So.2d 1047). Amended Feb. 26, 1998, effective Mar. 16, 1998 (713 So.2d 1); Sept. 21, 2000 (810 So.2d 1); March 26, 2009 (20 So.3d 173); Dec. 16, 2010 (59 So.3d 792); Sept. 28, 2011 (73 So.3d 213); March 26, 2015, effective March 26, 2015 (2015 WL 1343088).

Form 12.941(c). Temporary Injunction to Prevent Removal of Minor Child(ren) and/or Denial of Passport Services (After Notice)

IN THE CIRCUIT COURT OF THE ______________ JUDICIAL CIRCUIT,
IN AND FOR ______________ COUNTY, FLORIDA

Case No.: ______________
Division:

______________________________,
Petitioner,

and

______________________________,
Respondent.

TEMPORARY INJUNCTION TO PREVENT REMOVAL OF MINOR CHILD(REN) AND/OR DENIAL OF PASSPORT SERVICES (AFTER NOTICE)

Upon verified motion of _____Petitioner _____ Respondent, the Court has jurisdiction of the parties and the subject matter and the Court being fully advised, it is ORDERED and ADJUDGED that:

*{Indicate **all** that apply}*

1. The following minor child(ren) shall not be removed from the jurisdiction of this Court during the pendency of this proceeding, or until further order of this Court:

Name	Birth date

2. _____ Petitioner _____Respondent shall not apply for any passports or passport services on behalf of the child(ren).

3. _____ Petitioner _____Respondent shall immediately deliver any existing passports for the child(ren) to *{name}* ____.

4. The Court may enforce compliance with the terms of this injunction through civil and/or indirect criminal contempt proceedings, which may include arrest, incarceration, and/or the imposition of a fine.

5. Violation of this injunction may constitute criminal contempt of court.

Florida Supreme Court Approved Family Law Form 12.941(c), Temporary Injunction to Prevent Removal of Minor Child(ren) and/or Denial of Passport Services (After Notice) (03/15)

6. **Bond.**
   a. _____Bond is waived because this injunction is issued solely to prevent physical injury or abuse of a natural person.
   b. _____This order is conditioned upon _____Petitioner _____Respondent posting bond in the sum of $ ____________________ with the clerk of this Court.

7. **Expiration.**
This temporary injunction shall remain in effect until the minor child(ren) reach(es) the age of 18, or until *{date}* ____________________, not to exceed one year from the date of this order, whichever occurs first, unless modified by further order of this Court.

DONE AND ORDERED at ______________________, Florida, on *{date}*_____________________.

____
CIRCUIT JUDGE

I certify that a copy of the *{name of document(s)}* ____________________ was ( ) mailed ( ) faxed and mailed ( ) e-mailed ( ) hand-delivered to the parties and any other person(s) or entities listed below on *{date}*_______________.

____
By: Clerk of Court, Designee, or Judicial Assistant

Petitioner (or his or her attorney)
Respondent (or his or her attorney)

U.S. Department of State
Office of Children's Issues
2201 "C" Street NW
CA/OCS/CI
Washington, D.C. 20520
Fax (202) 736-9133
preventabduction@state.gov

Florida Supreme Court Approved Family Law Form 12.941(c), Temporary Injunction to Prevent Removal of Minor Child(ren) and/or Denial of Passport Services (After Notice) (03/15)

Added Feb. 26, 1998, effective Mar. 16, 1998 (713 So.2d 1). Amended Sept. 21, 2000 (810 So.2d 1); March 26, 2009 (20 So.3d 173); Dec. 16, 2010 (59 So.3d 792); March 26, 2015, effective March 26, 2015 (2015 WL 1343088).

Form 12.941(d). Emergency Verified Motion for Child Pick-up Order

IN THE CIRCUIT COURT OF THE ______________ JUDICIAL CIRCUIT,
IN AND FOR ______________ COUNTY, FLORIDA

Case No.: ______________
Division: ______________

______________________________,
Petitioner,

and

______________________________,
Respondent.

EMERGENCY VERIFIED MOTION FOR CHILD PICK-UP ORDER

I, *{full legal name}* ______________________________, being sworn, certify that the following information is true:

1. This is a motion to enforce existing custody or time -sharing rights (as an operation of law or court-ordered) regarding the following minor child(ren):

Name	**Sex**	**Birth Date**	**Race**	**Physical Description**

2. Currently, the child(ren) subject to this motion is (are) in the physical possession of *{full legal name}* ______________________________
whose address or present physical location is: ______________________________
____
This individual's relationship to the minor child(ren) is: ______________________________
____

3. I _____ am _____ am not married to the person named in paragraph 2.

4. **Status of minor child(ren).** I have a superior right to custody of or time-sharing with the minor child(ren) over the person named in paragraph 2 because:
*{Indicate **all** that apply}*:

a. ____ **Custody or Time-Sharing has been established by a court.**
A final judgment or order awarding custody of or time-sharing with the minor child(ren) was made on *{date}*____________in *{name of court}* ________________
{case number} ________________. This order awarded custody of or specific time-sharing with the minor child(ren) to me. This final judgment or order applies to the following minor child(ren): *{list name(s) of the child(ren) or write all}*
____
____

A certified copy of said final judgment or order is attached, has not been modified, and is still in effect.
{Indicate if applicable} _____ This order is an out-of-state court order which is entitled to full faith and credit enforcement under the Uniform Child Custody Jurisdiction and Enforcement Act and/or the federal Parental Kidnaping Prevention Act.

b. _____ **Custody or time-sharing is established as an operation of law.** I am the birth mother of the minor child(ren) who was (were) born out of wedlock and there is no final judgment or order awarding custody of or time-sharing with the following minor child(ren): *{list name(s) of the child(ren) or write all}* ______________________________
____
____

1. ____ **Paternity has NOT been established.** A certified copy of the minor child(ren)'s birth certificate is attached and has not been amended.
2. ____ **Paternity has been established.** A certified copy of the final judgment of paternity, which shows no award of custody or time-sharing was made, is attached. This order has not been changed and is still in effect.

c. _____ Other: ____
____
____

5. A completed Uniform Child Custody Jurisdiction and Enforcement Act (UCCJEA) Affidavit, Florida Supreme Court Approved Family Law Form 12.902(d), is filed with this motion.

6. **Facts relating to the minor child(ren)'s current situation.**
*[Indicate **all** that apply]*

a. _____The person named in paragraph 2 wrongfully removed or wrongfully detained the minor child(ren) on *{date}* ____________ as follows:
____
____
____
____
_______ Please indicate here if you are attaching additional pages to continue these facts.

b. _____ I believe that the minor child(ren) is (are) in immediate danger of harm or removal

from this court's jurisdiction while with the person named in paragraph 2 based on the following: ____
____
____.

c. _____ The current location of the minor child(ren) is: *{choose only **one**}* ( ) unknown ( ) believed to be at the following address(es) with the following people *{list both the address and the people you believe will be there}*: ______________
____
____

7. Advance notice of this motion to the individual named in paragraph 2 should **not** be required because:
____
____
____
____
____

8. If needed, I can be contacted for notice of an emergency or expedited hearing at the following addresses/locations:
____
Name of Contact Person:
____
Address:
____
Telephone number(s) where I (or my designee) can be reached: *{give name of individual to call}* ____
Name of Contact Person: ______________________________________
Address: ____
Telephone number(s) where I (or my designee) can be reached: *{give name of individual to call}* ____

9. **Attorneys' Fees, Costs, and Suit Monies.**
[Indicate if applicable]
______I have filed this motion because of wrongful acts of the person listed in paragraph 2 above. I request that this Court award reasonable attorney's fees, costs, and suit monies as applicable or authorized under Florida law, the UCCJEA, and other legal authorities.

WHEREFORE, I request an Emergency Order to Pick-Up Minor Child(ren), without advance notice, directing all sheriffs of the State of Florida or other authorized law enforcement officers in this state or any other state to pick up the previously named minor child(ren) and deliver them to my physical custody.

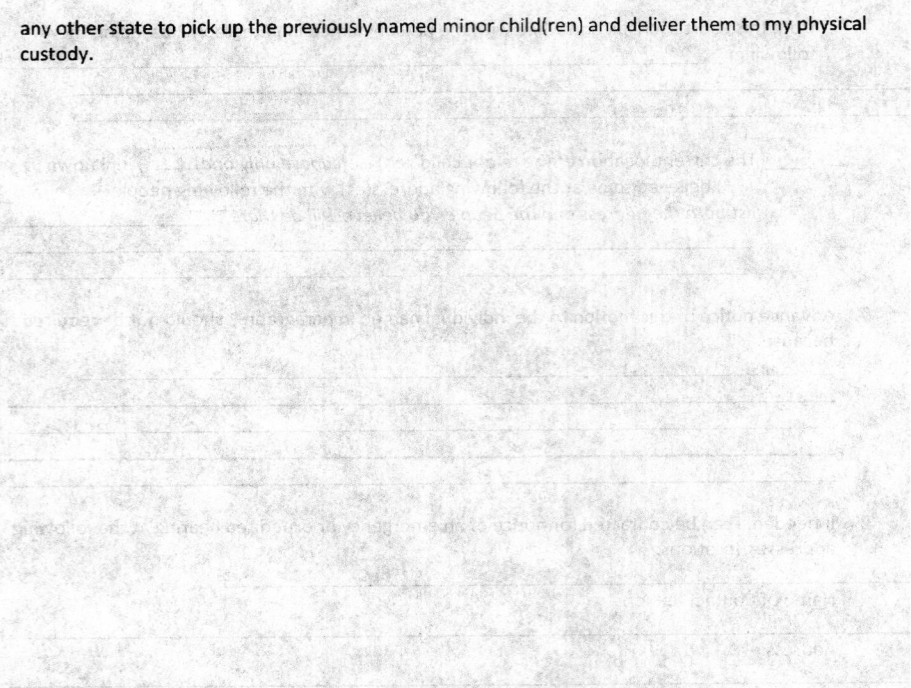

Florida Supreme Court Approved Family Law Form 12.941(d), Emergency Verified Motion for Child Pick-Up Order (03/15)

I understand that I am swearing or affirming under oath to the truthfulness of the claims made above and that the punishment for knowingly making a false statement includes fines and/or imprisonment.

Dated: ____________________

____
Signature of Party
Printed Name: ______________________________
Address: ______________________________
City, State, Zip: ______________________________
Telephone Number: ______________________________
Fax Number: ______________________________
Designated E-mail Address(es): ______________________________

STATE OF FLORIDA
COUNTY OF ____________
Sworn to or affirmed and signed before me on __________ by ______________

____
NOTARY PUBLIC or DEPUTY CLERK

____
[Print, type, or stamp commissioned name of notary or clerk.]
____ Personally known
____ Produced identification
Type of identification produced ______________

IF A NONLAWYER HELPED YOU FILL OUT THIS FORM, HE/SHE MUST FILL IN THE BLANKS BELOW:
[fill in all blanks] This form was prepared for the: *{choose only* ***one****}* ( ) Petitioner ( ) Respondent
This form was completed with the assistance of:
{name of individual} ______________________________,
{name of business} ______________________________,
{address} ______________________________,
{city} __________,*{state}* ___, *{zip code}*__________,*{telephone number}* __________.

Florida Supreme Court Approved Family Law Form 12.941(d), Emergency Verified Motion for Child Pick-Up Order (03/15)

INSTRUCTIONS FOR FLORIDA SUPREME COURT APPROVED FAMILY LAW FORM 12.941(d) EMERGENCY VERIFIED MOTION FOR CHILD PICK–UP ORDER (3/15)

When should this form be used?

You may use this form to request that the court enter an order directing the sheriff or other law enforcement officer to take a minor child(ren) from the person who currently has physical possession of the child(ren) and deliver the child(ren) to your physical custody or possession. **This form should only be used in an emergency by a person who has a pre-existing legal right to physical possession of a minor child.** This means that you already have a court order awarding you legal custody of or time-sharing with the child(ren) **OR** you are the birth mother of one or more children born out of wedlock and no court order has addressed any other person's parental rights. Before proceeding, you should read **General Information for Self–Represented Litigants** found at the beginning of these forms.

This form should be typed or printed in black ink. This form presumes that you want the court to enter an ex parte order without giving the other side advance notice of the hearing. You should explain your reasons for why such an ex parte order should be entered in paragraph 7 of this form. After completing this form, you should sign the form before a notary public or deputy clerk. You should file the original, along with all of the other forms required, with the clerk of the circuit court in the county where the child(ren) is (are) physically located and keep a copy for your records. You should also ask the clerk to process your motion though their emergency procedures.

IMPORTANT INFORMATION REGARDING E–FILING

The Florida Rules of Judicial Administration now require that all petitions, pleadings, and documents be filed electronically except in certain circumstances. **Self–represented litigants may file petitions or other pleadings or documents electronically; however, they are not required to do so.** If you choose to file your pleadings or other documents electronically, you must do so in accordance with Florida Rule of Judicial Administration 2.525, and you must follow the procedures of the judicial circuit in which you file. **The rules and procedures should be carefully read and followed.**

What should I do next?

If the court enters an order without advance notice to the other party, you should take a certified copy of the order to the sheriff's office for further assistance. You must have this form and the court's order served by personal service on the other party. You should read the court's order carefully. The order may require the sheriff to place the child(ren) somewhere other than in your physical possession. Look for directions in the order that apply to you and note the time and place of the hearing scheduled in the order. You should go to the hearing with whatever evidence you have regarding your motion.

If the court will not enter an order without advance notice to the other side, you should check with the clerk of court, judicial assistant, or family law intake staff for information on the local procedure for scheduling a hearing on your motion, unless the court sets a hearing in its order denying your request for an ex parte hearing. When you know the date and time of your hearing, you should file **Notice of Hearing (General)**, Florida Supreme Court Approved Family Law Form 12.923, and use personal service to notify the other party of your motion, the court's order, if any, and the hearing.

Special notes . . .

With this form you must also file the following:

- **Uniform Child Custody Jurisdiction and Enforcement Act (UCCJEA) Affidavit**, Florida Supreme Court Approved Family Law Form 12.902(d).
- A certified copy of the court order showing that you have legal custody of or time-sharing with the child(ren), if any.

OR

- A **certified copy** of the child(ren)'s birth certificate(s), if you are the birth mother of a child born out of wedlock and no court order addressing paternity exists.

OR

- A **certified copy** of any judgment establishing paternity, time-sharing with or custody of the minor child(ren).

Order . . . These family law forms contain an **Order to Pick–Up Minor Child(ren)**, Florida Supreme Court Approved Family Law Form 12.941(e), which the judge may use. You should check with the clerk, family law intake staff, or judicial assistant to see if you need to bring a blank order form with you to the hearing. If so, you should type or print the heading, including the circuit, county, case number, division, and the parties' names, and leave the rest blank for the judge to complete at your hearing.

Remember, a person who is NOT an attorney is called a nonlawyer. If a nonlawyer helps you fill out these forms, that person must give you a copy of **Disclosure from Nonlawyer**, Florida Family Law Rules of Procedure Form 12.900 (a), before he or she helps you. A nonlawyer helping you fill out these forms also **must** put his or her name, address, and telephone number on the bottom of the last page of every form he or she helps you complete.

Added Feb. 26, 1998, effective Mar. 16, 1998 (713 So.2d 1). Amended Oct. 29, 1998, effective Feb. 1, 1999 (723 So.2d 208); Sept. 21, 2000 (810 So.2d 1); Dec. 19, 2002 (836 So.2d 1019); March 26, 2009 (20 So.3d 173); Dec. 16, 2010 (59 So.3d 792); March 26, 2015, effective March 26, 2015 (2015 WL 1343088).

Form 12.941(e). Order to Pick-up Minor Child(ren)

IN THE CIRCUIT COURT OF THE ______________________ JUDICIAL CIRCUIT,
IN AND FOR ______________________ COUNTY, FLORIDA

Case No.: ______________
Division: ______________

______________________________,
Petitioner,

and

______________________________,
Respondent.

ORDER TO PICK-UP MINOR CHILD(REN)

An Emergency Verified Motion for Child Pick-Up Order has been filed by ____ Petitioner ____ Respondent, alleging facts which under existing law are determined to be sufficient to authorize taking into custody the minor child(ren) named below. Based on this motion, this Court makes the following findings, notices, and conclusions:

JURISDICTION
This Court has jurisdiction over issues surrounding the minor child(ren) listed below based on the following:

*{Choose **all** that apply}*

a. ____ This Court exercised and continues to exercise original jurisdiction over the minor children listed below under the Uniform Child Custody Jurisdiction and Enforcement Act (UCCJEA), specifically, section 61.514, Florida Statutes.

b. ____A certified out-of-state custody decree has been presented to this Court with a request for full faith and credit recognition and enforcement under the Parental Kidnapping Prevention Act, 28 U.S.C. Section 1738A. This Court has jurisdiction to enforce this decree under the UCCJEA, specifically sections 61.501-61.542, Florida Statutes.

c. ____ By operation of Florida law governing the custody of or time-sharing with child(ren) born out of wedlock, this Court has jurisdiction over the child(ren) listed below because this (these) child(ren) was (were) born in the State of Florida and no prior court action involving the minor child(ren) has addressed a putative father's rights to time-sharing or other parental rights. See sections 742.031 and 744.301, Florida Statutes.

d. ____ Pursuant to the UCCJEA, specifically section 61.516, Florida Statutes, this Court has jurisdiction to modify a custody decree of another state and has consulted with the Court which took initial jurisdiction over the minor child(ren) to determine this authority.

e. ____ Other: ____
____

Florida Supreme Court Approved Family Law Form 12.941(e), Order to Pick-Up Minor Child(ren) (03/15)

NOTICE OF HEARING

Because this Order to Pick-Up Minor Child(ren) has been issued without prior notice to the non-movant *{name}* ______________________________, all parties involved in this matter are informed that they are scheduled to appear and testify at a hearing regarding this matter on *{date}* ______________________, at {time} ________, at which time the Court will consider whether the Court should issue a further order in this case, and whether other things should be ordered, including who should pay the filing fees and costs. The hearing will be before the Honorable *{name}* ______________________________ at *{room name/number, location, address, city}* ____, Florida. If a party does not appear, this order may be continued in force, extended, or dismissed, and/or additional orders may be issued, including the imposition of court costs.

If you are a person with a disability who needs any accommodation in order to participate in this proceeding, you are entitled, at no cost to you, to the provision of certain assistance. Please contact:

____

{identify applicable court personnel by name, address, and telephone number} **at least 7 days before your scheduled court appearance, or immediately upon receiving this notification if the time before the scheduled appearance is less than 7 days; if you are hearing or voice impaired, call 711.**

ORDER

This Court **ORDERS AND DIRECTS** any and all sheriffs of the State of Florida (or any other authorized law enforcement officer in this state or in any other state) to immediately take into custody the minor child(ren) identified below from anyone who has possession and:

1. ____ **Place the minor child(ren) in the physical custody of** *{name}* ________________________ **who ( ) may ( ) may not remove the minor child(ren) from the jurisdiction of this Court.**

OR

____ **Accompany the minor child(ren) to the undersigned judge, if the minor child(ren) is (are) picked up during court hours, for immediate hearing on the issue of custody or time-sharing.** It is the intention of this Court that the nonmoving party, minor child(ren), and movant appear immediately upon service of this order before the undersigned judge, if available, or duty judge to conduct a hearing as to which party is entitled to lawful custody of the minor child(ren) at issue. It is not the intention of the court to turn over the child(ren) to the movant on an ex parte basis. Neither party should be permitted to remove the child(ren) from the jurisdiction of this Court pending a hearing. If unable to accomplish the above, the sheriff/officer shall take the child(ren) into custody and place them with the Department of Children and Family Services of the State of Florida pending an expedited hearing herein.

OR

____ **Place the minor child(ren) in the physical custody of** *{agency}* ____________________ **who shall contact the undersigned judge for an expedited hearing.** The sheriff/officer shall not delay the execution of this court order for any reason or permit the situation to arise where the nonmoving party is allowed to remove the child(ren) from the jurisdiction of this court.

2. **NEITHER PARTY OR ANYONE AT THEIR DIRECTION, EXCEPT PURSUANT TO THIS ORDER, MAY REMOVE THE CHILD(REN) FROM THE JURISDICTION OF THIS COURT PENDING FURTHER HEARING. SHOULD THE NONMOVING PARTY IN ANY WAY VIOLATE THE MANDATES OF THIS ORDER IN THE PRESENCE OF THE LAW ENFORCEMENT OFFICER, THIS OFFICER IS TO IMMEDIATELY ARREST AND INCARCERATE THE OFFENDING PARTY UNTIL SUCH TIME AS THE OFFENDING PARTY MAY BE BROUGHT BEFORE THIS COURT FOR FURTHER PROCEEDINGS.**

All sheriffs of the State for Florida are authorized and ORDERED to serve (and/or execute) and enforce this order in the daytime or in the nighttime and any day of the week, except as limited by this order above.

Except as limited by the above, if necessary, the sheriff/officer is authorized to take all reasonable, necessary, and appropriate measures to effectuate this order. The sheriff/officer shall not delay the execution of this order for any reason or permit the situation to arise where the child(ren) is (are) removed from the jurisdiction of this Court before execution of this order.

The minor child(ren) is (are) identified as follows:

Name	Sex	Birth date	Race	Physical Description

Current location/address of minor child(ren) or of party believed to have possession of the minor child(ren): ____

____

____

____

DONE AND ORDERED on at ____________________, Florida *{date}* ____________________.

____

CIRCUIT JUDGE

I certify that a copy of the *{name of document(s)}* ______________________________
was ( ) mailed ( ) faxed and mailed ( ) e-mailed ( ) hand-delivered to the parties listed below on *{date}*______________________________.

____
By: *{Clerk of the Court or designee}*

Petitioner (or his or her attorney)
Respondent (or his or her attorney)

Florida Supreme Court Approved Family Law Form 12.941(e), Order to Pick-Up Minor Child(ren) (03/15)

Added Feb. 26, 1998, effective Mar. 16, 1998 (713 So.2d 1). Amended Sept. 21, 2000 (810 So.2d 1); Dec. 6, 2001 (817 So.2d 721); Dec. 19, 2002 (836 So.2d 1019); March 26, 2009 (20 So.3d 173); Dec. 16, 2010 (59 So.3d 792); Sept. 28, 2011 (73 So.3d 213); March 26, 2015, effective March 26, 2015 (2015 WL 1343088).

Form 12.942(a). Motion for Appointment of Guardian Ad Litem

IN THE CIRCUIT COURT OF THE ______________________ JUDICIAL CIRCUIT,
IN AND FOR ______________________ COUNTY, FLORIDA

Case No.: ______________________
Division: ______________________

______________________________,
Petitioner,

and

______________________________,
Respondent.

MOTION FOR APPOINTMENT OF GUARDIAN AD LITEM

_____ Petitioner _____ Respondent requests that the Court enter an order appointing a guardian ad litem with all powers, privileges, and responsibilities authorized in section 61.403, Florida Statutes, and states:

1. The following minor child(ren) is (are) subject to this proceeding:

Name	**Birth date**	**Age**	**Sex**	**Location/Address**

2. Verified allegations of child abuse or neglect as defined in sections 39.01(2) or (45), Florida Statutes, _____ HAVE _____ HAVE NOT been made in this case.

3. The matters before the Court regarding the minor child(ren) are _____ establishment or _____ modification of:
   a. sole/shared parental responsibility
   b. Parenting Plan and time-sharing schedule
   c. Other:____

4. It is in the best interests of the minor child(ren) that a guardian ad litem be appointed to advance the best interests of the minor child(ren) because:
____
____
____
____.

I certify that a copy of this document was ( ) mailed ( ) faxed and mailed ( ) e-mailed ( ) hand delivered to the person(s) listed below on *{date}* ____________.

Other party or his/her attorney:
Name: ____________
Address: ____________
City, State, Zip: ____________
Fax Number: ____________
Designated E-mail Address(es): ____________

____
Signature of Party
Printed Name: ____________
Address: ____________
City, State, Zip: ____________
Telephone Number: ____________
Fax Number: ____________
Designated E-mail Address(es): ____________

IF A NONLAWYER HELPED YOU FILL OUT THIS FORM, HE/SHE MUST FILL IN THE BLANKS BELOW:
[fill in **all** blanks] This form was prepared for the: *{choose only one}* ( ) Petitioner ( ) Respondent
This form was completed with the assistance of:
{name of individual} ____________,
{name of business} ____________,
{address} ____________,
{city} ________,*{state}* ________, *{zip code}* ________,*{telephone number}* ________.

Florida Supreme Court Approved Family Law Form 12.942(a), Motion for Appointment of Guardian ad Litem (03/15)

INSTRUCTIONS FOR FLORIDA SUPREME COURT APPROVED FAMILY LAW FORM 12.942(a) MOTION FOR APPOINTMENT OF GUARDIAN AD LITEM (3/15)

When should this form be used?

This form may be used by either **party** in a family law case involving parenting, time-sharing, or **paternity** of a minor child(ren) to request that the judge appoint a **guardian ad litem** to represent the best interests of the minor child(ren). You should use this form if you feel that your child(ren) needs someone other than you to ensure that both the judicial system and the other **party**(ies) act(s) in the best interests of the child(ren). A guardian ad litem may be a volunteer who has been trained and certified by the State of Florida Guardian ad Litem Program **or** an **attorney** who is a member in good standing with The Florida Bar.

This form should be typed or printed in black ink. After completing this form, you should **file** the original with the **clerk of the circuit court** in the county where your case is filed and keep a copy for your records.

IMPORTANT INFORMATION REGARDING E-FILING

The Florida Rules of Judicial Administration now require that all petitions, pleadings, and documents be filed electronically except in certain circumstances. **Self-represented litigants may file petitions or other pleadings or documents electronically; however, they are not required to do so.** If you choose to file your pleadings or other documents electronically, you must do so in accordance with Florida Rule of Judicial Administration 2.525, and you must follow the procedures of the judicial circuit in which you file. **The rules and procedures should be carefully read and followed.**

What should I do next?

A copy of this form must be mailed, e-mailed, or hand delivered to the other party in your case.

It is possible that there will be a **hearing** on your motion. The **judge** may want to hear the reasons you feel an appointment of a guardian ad litem is necessary, or, the other party may object to your motion. If a hearing is required, check with the clerk of court, **family law court staff**, or **judicial assistant** for information on the local procedure for scheduling a hearing. When you know the date and time of your hearing, you should file **Notice of Hearing (General)**, Florida Supreme Court Approved Family Law Form 12.923, or other appropriate notice of hearing form, and provide a copy to the other party.

IMPORTANT INFORMATION REGARDING E-SERVICE ELECTION

After the initial service of process of the petition or supplemental petition by the Sheriff or certified process server, the Florida Rules of Judicial Administration now require that all documents required or permitted to be served on the other party must be served by electronic mail (e-mail) except in certain circumstances. **You must strictly comply with the format requirements set forth in the Rules of Judicial Administration.**

SELF-REPRESENTED LITIGANTS MAY SERVE DOCUMENTS BY E-MAIL; HOWEVER, THEY ARE NOT REQUIRED TO DO SO. If a self-represented litigant elects to serve and receive documents by e-mail, the procedures must always be followed once the initial election is made.

To serve and receive documents by e-mail, you must designate your e-mail addresses by using the **Designation of Current Mailing and E-mail Address**, Florida Supreme Court Approved Family Law Form 12.915, and you must provide your e-mail address on each form on which your signature appears. Please **CAREFULLY** read the rules and instructions for: **Certificate of Service (General),** Florida Supreme Court Approved Family Law Form 12.914; **Designation of Current Mailing and E-mail Address**, Florida Supreme Court Approved Family Law Form 12.915; and Florida Rule of Judicial Administration 2.516.

Where can I look for more information?

Before proceeding, you should read "General Information for Self-Represented Litigants" found at the beginning of these forms. You may also want to contact the Guardian ad Litem Program office in your area or see sections 61.401–405, Florida Statutes.

Special notes . . .

Order . . . These family law forms contain an **Order Appointing a Guardian ad Litem**, Florida Supreme Court Approved Family Law Form 12.942(b), which the judge may use. You should check with the clerk, family law intake staff, or judicial assistant to see if you need to bring a blank order form with you to the hearing. If so, you should type or print the heading, including the circuit, county, case number, division, and the parties' names, and leave the rest blank for the judge to complete at your hearing or trial.

Remember, a person who is NOT an attorney is called a nonlawyer. If a nonlawyer helps you fill out these forms, that person must give you a copy of **Disclosure from Nonlawyer**, Florida Family Law Rules of Procedure Form 12.900(a), before he or she helps you. A nonlawyer helping you fill out these forms also **must** put his or her name, address, and telephone number on the bottom of the last page of every form he or she helps you complete.

Added July 7, 1995, effective Jan. 1, 1996 (663 So.2d 1047). Amended Feb. 26, 1998, effective Mar. 16, 1998 (713 So.2d 1); Sept. 21, 2000 (810 So.2d 1); March 26, 2009 (20 So.3d 173); Dec. 16, 2010 (59 So.3d 792); March 26, 2015, effective March 26, 2015 (2015 WL 1343088).

Form 12.942(b). Order Appointing Guardian Ad Litem

IN THE CIRCUIT COURT OF THE ________________ JUDICIAL CIRCUIT,
IN AND FOR ________________ COUNTY, FLORIDA

Case No.: ________________
Division: ________________

________________________________,
Petitioner,

and

________________________________,
Respondent.

ORDER APPOINTING GUARDIAN AD LITEM

Upon _____ Petitioner's _____ Respondent's motion or the _____ Court's own motion to appoint a guardian ad litem for the minor child(ren) herein and the Court finding that:

a. _____ verified allegations of child abuse or neglect as defined in sections 39.01(2) or (45), Florida Statutes, have been made and are determined to be well-founded,

OR

b. _____ it is otherwise in the best interests of the child(ren) that a guardian ad litem be appointed to advance the best interests of the minor child(ren) because: ________________________________
____
____
____
____.

it is thereupon **ORDERED** as follows:

1. A guardian ad litem shall be appointed for the minor child(ren), *{name(s)}* ________________
____,
now residing at *{street address}* ________________________________.

2. The State of Florida Guardian ad Litem Program for the ________ Judicial Circuit shall assign a certified guardian ad litem for the minor child(ren). Upon filing of the Notice of Acceptance, the guardian ad litem can be served c/o Guardian ad Litem Program, *{address}* ________________
____.
Pursuant to the State of Florida Guardian ad Litem Standards of Operation adopted by the Supreme Court of Florida, if the Guardian ad Litem Program is appointed in the absence of a well-founded allegation of abuse or neglect, an automatic discharge by the Court will occur upon filing of a Motion to Discharge by the Program if the Program does not have sufficient volunteer and/or supervisory resources available to accommodate this appointment.

OR

{Name} ________________________________, an attorney in good standing with The Florida Bar, is appointed to serve as a private guardian ad litem for the above minor child(ren). The fees of the private guardian shall be paid by:

_____ Petitioner _____ Respondent _____ each party equally _____ other, *{specify}*
____.

3. The guardian ad litem is a party to any judicial proceeding from the date of this order until the date of discharge and shall have all of the powers, privileges, and responsibilities authorized in section 61.403, Florida Statutes, to the extent necessary to advance the best interests of the minor child(ren).

4. The guardian ad litem must be provided with copies of all pleadings, notices, stipulations, and other documents filed in this action and is entitled to reasonable notice before any action affecting the child(ren) is taken by either of the parties, their counsel, or the Court. The guardian ad litem is entitled, through counsel, to be present at any depositions, hearings, or other proceedings concerning the minor child(ren).

5. The guardian ad litem may investigate the allegations of the pleadings affecting the minor child(ren), and after proper notice may interview witnesses or any other person having information concerning the welfare of the minor child(ren).

6. The guardian ad litem shall maintain any information received from any source described in section 61.403(2), Florida Statutes, as confidential and shall not disclose such information except in reports to the Court served upon both parties to this cause and their counsel, or as directed by the Court.

7. The parties, or any other person entrusted by the parties with the care of the minor child(ren) shall allow the guardian ad litem access to the minor child(ren) at reasonable times and locations and no person shall obstruct the guardian ad litem from the minor child(ren).

8. The guardian ad litem shall submit his or her recommendations to the Court regarding any stipulation or agreement, whether incidental, temporary, or permanent, which affects the interest or welfare of the minor child(ren), within 10 days after the date the stipulation or agreement is served upon the guardian ad litem.

9. The guardian ad litem shall file a written report with the Court, which may include recommendations and a statement of the wishes of the minor child(ren). The report must be filed and served on all parties at least 20 days prior to the hearing at which it will be presented unless the Court waives such time period. The guardian ad litem's report shall address the following areas, subject to any conditions ordered by this Court:

a. ____ parental responsibility of child(ren);
b. ____ residence of child(ren);
c. ____ time-sharing including times and locations;
d. ____ appearance of child(ren) at depositions/hearings;
e. ____ relocation;
f. ____ best interests of child(ren) regarding scientific tests; and/or
g. ____ other ____
____
____

This appointment is subject to the following conditions: ______________________
____

Florida Supreme Court Approved Family Law Form 12.942(b), Order Appointing Guardian ad Litem (03/15)

____
____
____
____

10. The guardian ad litem is automatically discharged without further order 30 days after the entry of a final order or judgment in this proceeding, unless otherwise ordered by the Court.

DONE AND ORDERED at ________________________, Florida, on ____________________.

____
CIRCUIT JUDGE

I certify that a copy of the *{name of document(s)}* ____________________________________ was ( ) mailed ( ) faxed and mailed ( ) e-mailed ( ) hand-delivered to the parties and any other person(s) or entities listed below on *{date}*__________________.

____
By: *{Clerk of Court, Designee, or Judicial Assistant}*

Petitioner (or his or her attorney)
Respondent (or his or her attorney)
________ Guardian ad Litem Program
________ Other: ______________________________

Florida Supreme Court Approved Family Law Form 12.942(b), Order Appointing Guardian ad Litem (03/15)

Added July 7, 1995, effective Jan. 1, 1996 (663 So.2d 1047). Amended Feb. 26, 1998, effective Mar. 16, 1998 (713 So.2d 1); Sept. 21, 2000 (810 So.2d 1); March 26, 2009 (20 So.3d 173); Dec. 16, 2010 (59 So.3d 792); March 26, 2015, effective March 26, 2015 (2015 WL 1343088).

Form 12.943. Motion to Deviate from Child Support Guidelines

IN THE CIRCUIT COURT OF THE ______________________ JUDICIAL CIRCUIT,
IN AND FOR ______________________ COUNTY, FLORIDA

Case No.: ______________________
Division: ______________________

______________________,
Petitioner,

and

______________________,
Respondent.

MOTION TO DEVIATE FROM CHILD SUPPORT GUIDELINES

_____ Petitioner _____ Respondent requests that the Court enter an order granting the following:

SECTION I
[Choose A or B]

A.____ **MORE** child support than the amount required by the child support guidelines. The Court should order **MORE** child support than the amount required by the child support guidelines because of: *[Choose all that apply to your situation]*

1. ____Extraordinary medical, psychological, educational, or dental expenses;
2. ____Seasonal variations in one or both parent's income or expenses
3. ____Age(s) of the child(ren), taking into account the greater needs of older child(ren);
4. ____Special needs, such as costs that may be associated with the disability of a child or child(ren), that have traditionally been met within the family budget even though the fulfilling of those needs will cause support to exceed the presumptive amount established by the guidelines;
5. ____Total available assets of obligee, obligor, and the child(ren);
6. ____Impact of the Internal Revenue Service Child & Dependent Care Tax Credit, Earned Income Tax Credit, and dependency exemption and waiver of that exemption;
7. ____The Parenting Plan, such as where the child or children spend a significant amount of time, but less than 20 percent of the overnights, with one parent, thereby reducing the financial expenditures incurred by the other parent, or the refusal of a parent to become involved in the activities of the child(ren) has increased the financial expenditure incurred by the obligee;
8. ____The obligee parent's low income and ability to maintain the basic necessities of the home for the child(ren);
9. ____The likelihood that either parent will actually exercise the time-sharing schedule set forth in the parenting plan and/or whether all the children are exercising the same time-sharing schedule;

10. ____Any other adjustment that is needed to achieve an equitable result, which may include reasonable and necessary expenses or debts jointly incurred during the marriage.

Explain any items marked above: ____
____
____.

B.____ **LESS** child support than the amount required by the child support guidelines. The Court should order **LESS** child support than the amount required by the child support guidelines because of: *[Choose* ***all*** *that apply to your situation]*

1. ____ Extraordinary medical, psychological, educational, or dental expenses;
2. ____Independent income of child(ren), excluding the child(ren)'s SSI (supplemental security income)
3. ____Payment of support for a parent which has been regularly paid and for which there is a demonstrated need;
4. ____Seasonal variations in one or both parent's income or expenses;
5. ____Age of the child(ren), taking into account the greater needs of older child(ren);
6. ____ Total available assets of obligee, obligor, and child(ren);
7. _____Impact of the Internal Revenue Service Child & Dependent Care Tax Credit, Earned Income Tax Credit, and dependency exemption and waiver of that exemption;
8. ____ Application of the child support guidelines which requires the obligor to pay more than 55% of gross income for a single support order;
9. ____ Residency of subsequently born or adopted child(ren) with the obligor, include consideration of the subsequent spouse's income;
10. ____ The Parenting Plan, where the child(ren) spend a significant amount of time, but less than 20 percent of the overnights, with one parent, thereby reducing the financial expenditures incurred by the other parent; or the refusal of a parent to become involved in the activities of the child(ren)has reduced the financial expenditure of that parent;
11. ____Any other adjustment that is needed to achieve an equitable result, which may include reasonable and necessary expenses or debts jointly incurred during the marriage. Explain any items marked above:______________________________________
____
____.

SECTION II. INCOME AND ASSETS OF CHILD(REN) COMMON TO BOTH PARTIES

List the total of any independent income or assets of the child(ren) common to both parties (income from Social Security, gifts, stocks/bonds, employment, trust fund(s), investment(s), etc.). Attach an explanation.

TOTAL VALUE OF ASSETS OF CHILD(REN) $__________

TOTAL MONTHLY INCOME OF CHILD(REN) $__________

SECTION III. EXPENSES FOR CHILD(REN) COMMON TO BOTH PARTIES

All amounts must be MONTHLY. See the instructions with this form to figure out money amounts for anything that is NOT paid monthly. Attach more paper, if needed. Items included under "other" should be listed separately with separate dollar amounts.

1. $ _______ Monthly nursery, babysitting, or other child care
2. $ _______ Monthly after-school care
3. $ _______ Monthly school tuition
4. $ _______ Monthly school supplies, books, and fees
5. $ _______ Monthly after-school activities
6. $ _______ Monthly lunch money
7. $ _______ Monthly private lessons/tutoring
8. $ _______ Monthly allowance
9. $ _______ Monthly clothing
10. $ _______ Monthly uniforms
11. $ _______ Monthly entertainment (movies, birthday parties, etc.)
12. $ _______ Monthly health and dental insurance premiums
13. $ _______ Monthly medical, dental, prescription charges (unreimbursed)
14. $ _______ Monthly psychiatric/psychological/counselor (unreimbursed)
15. $ _______ Monthly orthodontic (unreimbursed)
16. $ _______ Monthly grooming
17. $ _______ Monthly non-prescription medications/cosmetics/toiletries/sundries
18. $ _______ Monthly gifts from children to others (other children, relatives, teachers, etc.)
19. $ _______ Monthly camp or other summer activities
20. $ _______ Monthly clubs (Boy/Girl Scouts, etc.) or recreational fees
21. $ _______ Monthly visitation expenses (for nonresidential parent)
    {Explain} ____
22. $ _______Monthly insurance (life, etc.)
    {explain}: ____

Other *{explain}*:

23. ____
24. ____
25. ____
26. $___________**TOTAL EXPENSES FOR CHILD(REN) COMMON TO BOTH PARTIES**
    (add lines 1 through 25)

Florida Supreme Court Approved Family Law Form 12.943, Motion to Deviate from Child Support Guidelines (03/15)

I have filed, will file, or am filing with this form the following additional documents:

1. Florida Family Law Family Law Financial Affidavit, Florida Family Law Rules of Procedure Form 12.902(b) or (c).
2. Child Support Guidelines Worksheet, Florida Family Law Rules of Procedure Form 12.902(e).

I certify that a copy of this document was ( ) mailed ( ) faxed and mailed ( ) e-mailed ( ) hand delivered to the person(s) listed below on *{date}* ____________.

Other party or his/her attorney:
Name: ____________
Address: ____________
City, State, Zip: ____________
Fax Number: ____________
Designated E-Mail Address(es): ____________
____

I understand that I am swearing or affirming under oath to the truthfulness of the claims made in this motion and that the punishment for knowingly making a false statement includes fines and/or imprisonment.

____
Signature of Party or his/her attorney

Printed Name: ____________
Address: ____________
City, State, Zip: ____________
Telephone Number: ____________
Fax Number: ____________
Designated E-mail Address(es): ____________
____

STATE OF FLORIDA
COUNTY OF ____________

Sworn to or affirmed and signed before me on ____________ by ____________

____
NOTARY PUBLIC or DEPUTY CLERK

____
[Print, type, or stamp commissioned name of notary or clerk.]
____ Personally known
____ Produced identification

Florida Supreme Court Approved Family Law Form 12.943, Motion to Deviate from Child Support Guidelines (03/15)

Type of identification produced_______________________________

IF A NONLAWYER HELPED YOU FILL OUT THIS FORM, HE/SHE MUST FILL IN THE BLANKS BELOW:
[fill in all blanks] This form was prepared for the: *{choose only **one**}* ( ) Petitioner ( ) Respondent
This form was completed with the assistance of:
{name of individual} _______________________________,
{name of business} _______________________________,
{address} _______________________________,
{city} __________, *{state}* ___, *{zip code}* ______, *{telephone number}* ________.

Florida Supreme Court Approved Family Law Form 12.943, Motion to Deviate from Child Support Guidelines (03/15)

INSTRUCTIONS FOR FLORIDA SUPREME COURT APPROVED FAMILY LAW FORM 12.943, MOTION TO DEVIATE FROM CHILD SUPPORT GUIDELINES (3/15)

When should this form be used?

Child support in Florida is determined by the child support guidelines found in section 61.30, Florida Statutes. The court, at its discretion, may raise or lower the child support guidelines amount by up to 5%. In addition, the court may raise or lower the guidelines support amount by more than 5%, if written reasons are given for the adjustment. The court may make these additional adjustments based on certain considerations, which are reflected in this form. You should review this form to determine if any of the reasons for adjusting the child support guidelines amount apply to your situation and you should complete this form **only** if you want the court to order **more child support or less child support** than the amount required by the child support guidelines.

This form should be typed or printed in black ink. After completing this form, you should **file** the original with the **clerk of the circuit court** in the county where your case is filed and keep a copy for your records.

IMPORTANT INFORMATION REGARDING E-FILING

The Florida Rules of Judicial Administration now require that all petitions, pleadings, and documents be filed electronically except in certain circumstances. **Self-represented litigants may file petitions or other pleadings or documents electronically; however, they are not required to do so.** If you choose to file your pleadings or other documents electronically, you must do so in accordance with Florida Rule of Judicial Administration 2.525, and you must follow the procedures of the judicial circuit in which you file. **The rules and procedures should be carefully read and followed.**

What should I do next?

A copy of this form must be mailed, e-mailed, or hand delivered to the other party in your case.

IMPORTANT INFORMATION REGARDING E-SERVICE ELECTION

After the initial service of process of the petition or supplemental petition by the Sheriff or certified process server, the Florida Rules of Judicial Administration now require that all documents required or permitted to be served on the other party must be served by electronic mail (e-mail) except in certain circumstances. **You must strictly comply with the format requirements set forth in the Rules of Judicial Administration.**

SELF-REPRESENTED LITIGANTS MAY SERVE DOCUMENTS BY E-MAIL; HOWEVER, THEY ARE NOT REQUIRED TO DO SO. If a self-represented litigant elects to serve and receive documents by e-mail, the procedures must always be followed once the initial election is made.

To serve and receive documents by e-mail, you must designate your e-mail addresses by using the **Designation of Current Mailing and E-mail Address**, Florida Supreme Court Approved Family Law Form 12.915, and you must provide your e-mail address on each form on which your signature appears. Please **CAREFULLY** read the rules and instructions for: **Certificate of Service (General)**, Florida Supreme Court Approved Family Law Form 12.914; **Designation of Current Mailing and E-mail Address**, Florida Supreme Court Approved Family Law Form 12.915; and Florida Rule of Judicial Administration 2.516.

Where can I look for more information?

Before proceeding, you should read General Information for Self-Represented Litigants found at the beginning of these forms. For further information, see section 61.30, Florida Statutes.

Special notes ...

More information on the child support guidelines as well as a chart for converting income and expenses to monthly amounts if paid or incurred on other than a monthly basis is contained in the instructions to **Florida Family Law Financial Affidavit,** Florida Family Law Rules of

Procedure Form 12.902(b) or (c), and the **Child Support Guidelines Worksheet,** Florida Family Law Rules of Procedure Form 12.902(e).

With this form you must also file the following, if not already filed:

- **Florida Family Law Financial Affidavit**, Florida Family Law Rules of Procedure Form 12.902(b) or (c).
- **Child Support Guidelines Worksheet,** Florida Family Law Rules of Procedure Form 12.902(e). (If you do not know the other party's income, you should file this worksheet as soon as you receive a copy of his or her **financial affidavit**.)

Remember, a person who is NOT an attorney is called a nonlawyer. If a nonlawyer helps you fill out these forms, that person must give you a copy of **Disclosure from Nonlawyer**, Florida Family Law Rules of Procedure Form 12.900 (a), before he or she helps you. A nonlawyer helping you fill out these forms also **must** put his or her name, address, and telephone number on the bottom of the last page of every form he or she helps you complete.

Added Feb. 26, 1998, effective Mar. 16, 1998 (713 So.2d 1). Amended July 1, 1999 (759 So.2d 583); Sept. 21, 2000 (810 So.2d 1); March 26, 2009 (20 So.3d 173); Dec. 16, 2010 (59 So.3d 792); Nov. 3, 2011, effective, *nunc pro tunc*, Oct. 1, 2011 (78 So.3d 1045); May 24, 2012 (96 So.3d 217); July 3, 2013 (117 So.3d 958); March 26, 2015, effective March 26, 2015 (2015 WL 1343088).

Form 12.944(a). Motion for Testimony and Attendance of Minor Child(ren)

IN THE CIRCUIT COURT OF THE __________ JUDICIAL CIRCUIT,
IN AND FOR __________ COUNTY, FLORIDA

Case No.: __________
Division: __________

______________________________,
Petitioner,

and

______________________________,
Respondent.

MOTION FOR TESTIMONY AND ATTENDANCE OF MINOR CHILD(REN)

____ Petitioner ____ Respondent requests that the Court enter an order authorizing one or more of the actions listed below related to the following minor child(ren):

Name	Birth date	Age

*[Indicate **all** that apply]*

1.____ Minor child(ren), *{name(s)}* ______________________________, be subpoenaed to appear at hearing now scheduled for *{date}* ______________________________.

2.____ Minor child(ren), *{name(s)}* ______________________________, attend deposition of *{name(s)}* now scheduled for*{date}* ______________ at *{location}* ______________________________.

3. ____ Minor child(ren)'s, *{name(s)}* ______________________________, deposition be taken on *{date}* ______________ at *{location}* ______________________________.

4. ____ Minor child(ren), *{name(s)}*______________________________, be brought to court to attend hearing now scheduled for *{date}* ______________________________ at *{location}* ______________________________.

5. ____ Minor child(ren), *{name(s)}* ______________________________, be brought to court to testify in a hearing now scheduled for *{date}* ______________________________ at *{location}* ______________________________.

Florida Supreme Court Approved Family Law Form 12.944(a), Motion for Testimony and Attendance of Minor Child(ren) (03/15)

The Court should do this because: ____
____
____
____
____
____
____.

I certify that a copy of this document was ( ) mailed ( ) faxed and mailed ( ) e-mailed ( ) hand delivered to the person(s) listed below on *{date}* ____________________________.

Other party or his/her attorney:
Name: ____________________________
Address: ____________________________
City, State, Zip: ____________________________
Fax Number: ____________________________
Designated E-mail Address(es): ____________________________

Signature of Party
Printed Name: ____________________________
Address: ____________________________
City, State, Zip: ____________________________
Telephone Number: ____________________________
Fax Number: ____________________________
Designated E-mail Address(es): ____________________________

IF A NONLAWYER HELPED YOU FILL OUT THIS FORM, HE/SHE MUST FILL IN THE BLANKS BELOW:
[fill in all blanks] This form was prepared for the *{choose only one}* ( ) Petitioner ( ) Respondent
This form was completed with the assistance of:
{name of individual} ____________________________,
{name of business} ____________________________,
{address} ____________________________,
{city} ______________,*{state}*______,*{zip code}* ________, *{telephone number}* ____________.

INSTRUCTIONS FOR FLORIDA SUPREME COURT APPROVED FAMILY LAW FORM 12.944(a), MOTION FOR TESTIMONY AND ATTENDANCE OF MINOR CHILD(REN) (03/15)

When should this form be used?

Rule 12.407, Florida Family Law Rules, provides that minor children may not be deposed (have their **deposition** taken), brought to court to appear as a **witness** or to attend a **hearing**, or **subpoenaed** to appear at a hearing without prior order of the court. This rule applies in all cases except when there is an emergency or the case is an uncontested adoption. You should use this form to request that the court enter an order authorizing a minor child(ren) to appear at a court proceeding.

This form should be typed or printed in black ink. After completing this form, you should **file** the original with the **clerk of the circuit court** in the county where your case is filed and keep a copy for your records.

IMPORTANT INFORMATION REGARDING E–FILING

The Florida Rules of Judicial Administration now require that all petitions, pleadings, and documents be filed electronically except in certain circumstances. **Self–represented litigants may file petitions or other pleadings or documents electronically; however, they are not required to do so.** If you choose to file your pleadings or other documents electronically, you must do so in accordance with Florida Rule of Judicial Administration 2.525, and you must follow the procedures of the judicial circuit in which you file. **The rules and procedures should be carefully read and followed.**

What should I do next?

A copy of this form must be mailed, e-mailed, or hand delivered to any other party(ies) in your case, including the guardian ad litem, if one has been appointed.

It is possible that there will be a hearing on your motion. The **judge** may want to hear the reasons you feel this motion should be granted, or the other party may object to your motion. If a hearing is required, check with the clerk of court, **judicial assistant**, or **family law intake staff** for information on the local procedure for scheduling a hearing. When you know the date and time of your hearing, you should file **Notice of Hearing (General)**, Florida Supreme Court Approved Family Law Form 12.923, or other appropriate notice of hearing form, and provide a copy to any other party.

Where can I look for more information?

Before proceeding, you should read General Information for Self–Represented Litigants found at the beginning of these forms. For further information, see rule 12.407, Florida Family Law Rules of Procedure.

IMPORTANT INFORMATION REGARDING E–SERVICE ELECTION

After the initial service of process of the petition or supplemental petition by the Sheriff or certified process server, the Florida Rules of Judicial Administration now require that all documents required or permitted to be served on the other party must be served by electronic mail (e–mail) except in certain circumstances. **You must strictly comply with the format requirements set forth in the Rules of Judicial Administration.**

SELF–REPRESENTED LITIGANTS MAY SERVE DOCUMENTS BY E–MAIL; HOWEVER, THEY ARE NOT REQUIRED TO DO SO. If a self-represented litigant elects to serve and receive documents by e-mail, the procedures must always be followed once the initial election is made.

To serve and receive documents by e-mail, you must designate your e-mail addresses by using the **Designation of Current Mailing and E–mail Address**, Florida Supreme Court Approved Family Law Form 12.915, and you must provide your e-mail address on each form on which your signature appears. Please **CAREFULLY** read the rules and instructions for: **Certificate of Service (General)**, Florida Supreme Court Approved Family Law Form 12.914; **Designation of Current Mailing and E–mail Address**, Florida Supreme Court Approved Family Law Form 12.915; and Florida Rule of Judicial Administration 2.516.

Special notes . . .

Remember, a person who is NOT an attorney is called a nonlawyer. If a nonlawyer helps you fill out these forms, that person must give you a copy of **Disclosure from Nonlawyer**, Florida Family Law Rules of Procedure Form 12.900 (a), before he or she helps you. A nonlawyer helping you fill out these forms also **must** put his or her name, address, and telephone number on the bottom of the last page of every form he or she helps you complete.

Added Feb. 26, 1998, effective Mar. 16, 1998 (713 So.2d 1). Amended Sept. 21, 2000 (810 So.2d 1); March 26, 2015, effective March 26, 2015 (2015 WL 1343088).

Form 12.944(b). Order for Testimony and Attendance of Minor Child(ren)

IN THE CIRCUIT COURT OF THE ________________ JUDICIAL CIRCUIT,
IN AND FOR ________________ COUNTY, FLORIDA

Case No.: ____________________
Division: ____________________

______________________________________,
Petitioner,

and

______________________________________,
Respondent.

ORDER FOR TESTIMONY AND APPEARANCE OF MINOR CHILD(REN)

Upon motion of ______ Petitioner _____ Respondent for testimony or attendance of minor child(ren) in these proceedings, and the Court finding that a showing of good cause has been made in support of the motion, it is

ORDERED that

{Indicate all that apply}

1. _____ Minor child(ren), *{name(s)}*____,
be subpoenaed to appear at hearing now scheduled for *{date}* ____________________________.

2. _____ Minor child(ren), *{name(s)}*
____,
attend deposition of *{name(s)}* ______________________________________ now scheduled for *{date}* ______________ at *{location}* ____.

3. _____ Minor child(ren)'s, *{name(s)}* ____,
deposition be taken on *{date}* ______________ at *{location}* ______________________________
____.

4. _____ Minor child(ren), *{name(s)}* ____
be brought to court to attend hearing now scheduled for *{date}* ________________ at *{location}*
____.

Florida Supreme Court Approved Family Law Form 12.944(b), Order for Testimony and Attendance of Minor Child(ren) (03/15)

5. ____Minor child(ren), *{name(s)}* ______________________________,
be brought to court to testify in a hearing now scheduled for *{date}* ____________ at *{location}*
____.

If the minor child or the person bringing the child is a person with a disability, who needs any accommodation in order to participate in this proceeding, either is entitled, at no cost to them, to the provision of certain assistance. Please contact:

____

{identify applicable court personnel by name, address, and telephone number} **at least 7 days before the scheduled court appearance, or immediately upon receiving this notification if the time before the scheduled appearance is less than 7 days; if you are hearing or voice impaired, call 711.**

Conditions or limitations concerning the minor child(ren), if any, include: ______________________
____
____
____
____
____
____
____
____

DONE AND ORDERED at ________________________, Florida on ______________________.

____

CIRCUIT JUDGE

I certify that a copy of the *{name of document}* ______________________________ was
( ) mailed ( ) faxed and mailed ( ) e-mailed ( ) hand-delivered to the parties and entities listed below on *{date}* ____________________________.

____

By: *{Clerk of court, designee, or judicial assistant}*

Florida Supreme Court Approved Family Law Form 12.944(b), Order for Testimony and Attendance of Minor Child(ren) (03/15)

Petitioner (or his or her attorney)
Respondent (or his or her attorney)

Florida Supreme Court Approved Family Law Form 12.944(b), Order for Testimony and Attendance of Minor Child(ren) (03/15)

Added Sept. 21, 2000 (810 So.2d 1). Amended Sept. 28, 2011 (73 So.3d 213); March 26, 2015, effective March 26, 2015 (2015 WL 1343088).

Form 12.947(a). Motion for Temporary Support, Time–Sharing, and Other Relief with Dependent or Minor Child(ren)

IN THE CIRCUIT COURT OF THE ______________________ JUDICIAL CIRCUIT,
IN AND FOR ______________________ COUNTY, FLORIDA

Case No.: ______________________
Division: ______________________

______________________________,
Petitioner,

and

______________________________,
Respondent.

MOTION FOR TEMPORARY SUPPORT, TIME-SHARING, AND OTHER RELIEF WITH DEPENDENT OR MINOR CHILD(REN)

The _____ Petitioner _____ Respondent requests that the Court enter an order granting the following temporary support:

*{Complete **all** that apply}*

1. **Assets and Liabilities.**
   a. _____**Award temporary exclusive use and possession of the marital home.** *{address}* _____
____

The Court should do this because: ____
____
____

   b. _____ **Award temporary use and possession of marital assets.** *{Specify, without giving account numbers}*
____
____

The Court should do this because: ____
____
____

   c. _____ **Enter a temporary injunction** prohibiting the parties from disposing of any marital assets, other than ordinary and usual expenses. *{Explain}* ______________
____
____

The Court should do this because: ____
____
____

Florida Supreme Court Approved Family Law Form 12.947(a), Motion for Temporary Support, Time-Sharing, and Other Relief with Dependent or Minor Child(ren) (03/15)

d. _____ **Require temporary payment of specific marital debts.** *{Explain without using account numbers}*______________________________

____

The Court should do this because: ______________________________

____

2. **Child(ren).**
   a. _____ Enter a temporary Parenting Plan with a time-sharing schedule for the parties' minor child(ren).
   b. _____ Enter a temporary injunction prohibiting the parties from permanently removing the child(ren) from the jurisdiction of the Court. The Court should do this because:

____

3. **Support.**
   a. _____ Award temporary child support of $ _______ per month.
   b. _____ Award temporary spousal support/alimony of $ __________ per month.

The Court should do this because: ______________________________

____

4. **Attorney's fees and costs.**
   a. _____ Award temporary attorney's fees of $ ____________.
   b. _____ Award temporary costs of $ __________.

The Court should do this because: ______________________________

____

5. **Other Relief.** *{specify}*______________________________

____

6. A completed Uniform Child Custody Jurisdiction and Enforcement Act (UCCJEA) Affidavit, Florida Supreme Court Approved Family Law Form 12.902(d), is filed with this motion or has already been filed with the Court.

7. A completed Notice of Social Security Number, Florida Supreme Court Approved Family Law Form 12.902(j), is filed with this motion or has already been filed with the Court.

8. I request that the Court hold a hearing on this matter and grant the relief specifically requested and any other relief this Court may deem just and proper.

I certify that a copy of this document was ( ) mailed ( ) faxed and mailed ( ) e-mailed ( ) hand delivered to the person(s) listed below on *{date}* ____________________.

Other party or his/her attorney:
Name: ________________________
Address: ________________________
City, State, Zip: ________________________
Fax Number: ________________________
Designated E-mail Address(es): ________________________
____

____
Signature of Party or his/her attorney
Printed Name: ________________________
Address: ________________________
City, State, Zip: ________________________
Telephone Number: ________________________
Fax Number: ________________________
Designated E-mail Address(es): ________________________
____

IF A NONLAWYER HELPED YOU FILL OUT THIS FORM, HE/SHE MUST FILL IN THE BLANKS BELOW:
[fill in **all** blanks] This form was prepared for the: *{choose only **one**}* ( ) Petitioner ( ) Respondent
This form was completed with the assistance of:
{name of individual} ________________________,
{name of business} ________________________,
{address} ________________________,
{city} ______________,*{state}* ______, *{zip code}* ________, *{telephone number}* ________________.

INSTRUCTIONS FOR FLORIDA SUPREME COURT APPROVED FAMILY LAW FORM 12.947(a), MOTION FOR TEMPORARY SUPPORT, TIME-SHARING, AND OTHER RELIEF WITH DEPENDENT OR MINOR CHILD(REN) (03/15)

When should this form be used?

This form may be used by:

(1) The **respondent** or the **petitioner** in a pending **dissolution of marriage** action. For you to use this form, a **petition** for dissolution of marriage must have already been filed. You should use this form to ask the court to award any of the following: temporary use of assets; temporary exclusive use of the marital home; temporary responsibility for liabilities/debts; temporary spousal support (**alimony**); temporary time-sharing schedule with minor child(ren); temporary **child support**; and other relief.

OR

(2) The petitioner in a pending action for support unconnected with dissolution. For you to use this form, a petition for support unconnected with dissolution of marriage must have already been filed. You should use this form to ask the court to award temporary spousal support (alimony) and/or temporary child support.

This form should be typed or printed in black ink. After completing this form, you should **file** the original with the **clerk of the circuit court** in the county where the petition for dissolution of marriage was filed and keep a copy for your records.

IMPORTANT INFORMATION REGARDING E-FILING

The Florida Rules of Judicial Administration now require that all petitions, pleadings, and documents be filed electronically except in certain circumstances. **Self-represented litigants may file petitions or other pleadings or documents electronically; however, they are not required to do so.** If you choose to file your pleadings or other documents electronically, you must do so in accordance with Florida Rule of Judicial Administration 2.525, and you must follow the procedures of the judicial circuit in which you file. **The rules and procedures should be carefully read and followed.**

What should I do next?

A copy of this form, along with all of the other forms required with this motion, must be mailed, e-mailed, or hand delivered to the other party in your case. When you have filed all of the required forms, you are ready to set a **hearing** on your motion. You should check with the clerk, **family law intake staff**, or **judicial assistant** for information on the local procedure for scheduling a hearing. When you know the date and time of your hearing, you should notify the other party using a **Notice of Hearing (General)**, Florida Supreme Court Approved Family Law Form 12.923, or other appropriate notice of hearing form.

IMPORTANT INFORMATION REGARDING E-SERVICE ELECTION

After the initial service of process of the petition or supplemental petition by the Sheriff or certified process server, the Florida Rules of Judicial Administration now require that all documents required or permitted to be served on the other party must be served by electronic mail (e-mail) except in certain circumstances. **You must strictly comply with the format requirements set forth in the Rules of Judicial Administration.**

SELF-REPRESENTED LITIGANTS MAY SERVE DOCUMENTS BY E-MAIL; HOWEVER, THEY ARE NOT REQUIRED TO DO SO. If a self-represented litigant elects to serve and receive documents by e-mail, the procedures must always be followed once the initial election is made.

To serve and receive documents by e-mail, you must designate your e-mail addresses by using the **Designation of Current Mailing and E-mail Address**, Florida Supreme Court Approved Family Law Form 12.915, and you must provide your e-mail address on each form on which your signature appears. Please **CAREFULLY** read the rules and instructions for: **Certificate of Service (General),** Florida Supreme Court Approved Family Law Form 12.914; **Designation of Current Mailing and E-mail Address**, Florida Supreme Court Approved Family Law Form 12.915; and Florida Rule of Judicial Administration 2.516.

Where can I look for more information?

Before proceeding, you should read General Information for Self–Represented Litigants found at the beginning of these forms. Words in **bold underline** in these instructions are defined there. For further information, see chapter 61, Florida Statutes, rule 12.285, Florida Family Law Rules of Procedure, and rule 1.610, Florida Rules of Civil Procedure.

Special notes . . .

If you use paragraph 1.c. of this form to ask the court to enter a temporary injunction, the court may require you to post a **bond**.

With this form you must also file the following, if not already filed:

- **Uniform Child Custody Jurisdiction and Enforcement Act (UCCJEA) Affidavit**, Florida Supreme Court Approved Family Law Form 12.902(d), if this case involves a minor or dependent child(ren).
- **Notice of Social Security Number**, Florida Supreme Court Approved Family Law Form 12.902(j).
- **Child Support Guidelines Worksheet**, Florida Family Law Rules of Procedure Form 12.902(e), if you are asking that temporary child support be ordered. (If you do not know the other party's income, you may file this worksheet as soon as a copy of his or her financial affidavit has been served on you.)

The parties seeking relief shall serve a financial affidavit (Florida Family Law Rules of Procedure Form 12.902 (b) or (c)) and certificate of compliance (Florida Family Law Rules of Procedure Form 12.932) with the notice of hearing on the motion for temporary support and time-sharing.

Parenting Plan . . . If you have reached an agreement on either a temporary Parenting Plan or time-sharing schedule, either one of the following proposed temporary Parenting Plans or a time-sharing schedule, signed by both parties, should be filed. **Parenting Plan,** Florida Supreme Court Approved Family Law Form 12.995(a), **Safety–Focused Parenting Plan,** Florida Supreme Court Approved Family Law Form 12.995(b), or **Relocation/Long Distance,** Florida Supreme Court Approved Family Law Form 12.995(c). If you have **not** reached an agreement, a proposed Parenting Plan or temporary time-sharing schedule may be filed for consideration by the Court.

Temporary Order . . . These family law forms contain a **Temporary Order for Support, Time–Sharing, and Other Relief with Dependent or Minor Child(ren),** Florida Supreme Court Approved Family Law Form 12.947(b), which the judge may use. You should check with the clerk, family law intake staff, or judicial assistant to see if you need to bring it with you to the hearing. If so, you should type or print the heading, including the circuit, county, case number, division, and the parties' names, and leave the rest blank for the judge to complete at your hearing.

Nonlawyer .... Remember, a person who is NOT an attorney is called a nonlawyer. If a nonlawyer helps you fill out these forms, that person must give you a copy of a **Disclosure from Nonlawyer**, Florida Family Law Rules of Procedure Form 12.900 (a), before he or she helps you. A nonlawyer helping you fill out these forms also **must** put his or her name, address, and telephone number on the bottom of the last page of every form he or she helps you complete.

Added Feb. 26, 1998, effective Mar. 16, 1998 (713 So.2d 1). Amended Sept. 21, 2000 (810 So.2d 1); Dec. 19, 2002 (836 So.2d 1019); March 26, 2009 (20 So.3d 173); Dec. 16, 2010 (59 So.3d 792); Nov. 3, 2011, effective, *nunc pro tunc*, Oct. 1, 2011 (78 So.3d 1045); May 24, 2012 (96 So.3d 217); March 26, 2015, effective March 26, 2015 (2015 WL 1343088).

Form 12.947(b). Temporary Order of Support, Time–Sharing, and Other Relief with Dependent or Minor Child(ren)

IN THE CIRCUIT COURT OF THE ______________________ JUDICIAL CIRCUIT,
IN AND FOR ______________________ COUNTY, FLORIDA

Case No.: ______________________
Division: ______________________

______________________,
Petitioner,

and

______________________,
Respondent.

TEMPORARY ORDER OF SUPPORT, TIME-SHARING, AND OTHER RELIEF WITH DEPENDENT OR MINOR CHILD(REN)

This cause came before this Court for a hearing on a Motion for Temporary Support, Time-Sharing, and Other Relief with Dependent or Minor Child(ren). The Court, having reviewed the file and heard the testimony, makes these findings of fact and ORDERS as follows:

The Court has jurisdiction over the subject matter and the parties.

SECTION I. MARITAL ASSETS AND LIABILITIES

A. Injunction.

1. _____ Petitioner _____ Respondent is (are) prohibited and enjoined from disposing of any marital assets without the written permission of the other party or a court order. If indicated here ____, the person(s) prohibited and enjoined from disposing of any marital assets may continue to pay all ordinary and usual expenses.
2. The Court may enforce compliance with the terms of this injunction through civil and/or indirect criminal contempt proceedings, which may include arrest, incarceration, and/or the imposition of a fine.
3. Violation of this injunction may constitute criminal contempt of court.
4. Bond. This order is conditioned upon _____ Petitioner _____ Respondent posting bond in the sum of $__________________ with the clerk of this Court.

B. Temporary Use of Assets.

1. The assets listed below are temporarily determined to be marital assets. Each party shall temporarily have the use of, as his/her own, the assets awarded in this section, and the other party shall temporarily have no further use of said assets. **Any personal property not listed below shall be for the use of party currently in possession of that item(s), and he or she may not dispose of that item(s) without the written permission of the other party or a court order.**

ASSETS: DESCRIPTION OF ITEM(S) (Please describe each item as clearly as possible. You do not have to list account numbers.)	Wife Shall Have Temporary Use	Husband Shall Have Temporary Use
Automobiles		
Furniture & furnishings in home		
Furniture & furnishings elsewhere		
Jewelry		
Business interests		
Other Assets		

C. **Temporary Responsibility for Liabilities/Debts.**

1. The liabilities listed below are temporarily determined to be marital. Each party shall pay as his or her own the marital liabilities indicated below and shall keep said payments current. The other party shall temporarily have no further responsibility for the payment of these debts.

LIABILITIES: DESCRIPTION OF DEBT(S)(Please describe each item as clearly as possible. You do not have to list account numbers.)	Current Amount Owed	Wife Shall Pay	Husband Shall Pay
Mortgages on real estate: (home)	$	$	$

Florida Supreme Court Approved Family Law Form 12.947(b), Temporary Order of Support, Time-Sharing, and Other Relief with Dependent or Minor Child(ren) (03/15)

LIABILITIES: DESCRIPTION OF DEBT(S)(Please describe each item as clearly as possible. You do not have to list account numbers.)	Current Amount Owed	Wife Shall Pay	Husband Shall Pay
Charge/credit card accounts			
Auto loan			
Auto loan			
Bank/Credit Union loans			
Money owed (not evidenced by a note)			
Other			

SECTION II. TEMPORARY EXCLUSIVE USE AND POSSESSION OF HOME

*[Indicate **all** that apply]*

1. _____ Petitioner _____Respondent shall have temporary exclusive use and possession of the dwelling located at: *{address}* ____
____
until: *{date or event}* ____
____.

2. _____ Petitioner _____Respondent may make a visit to the premises described in the paragraph above for the purpose of obtaining his or her clothing and items of personal health and hygiene and to obtain any items awarded in this order. This visit shall occur after notice to the person granted temporary exclusive use and possession of the dwelling and at the earliest convenience of both parties.

3. _____Other: ____
____
____

SECTION III. TEMPORARY PARENTAL RESPONSIBILITY AND TIME-SHARING WITH DEPENDENT OR MINOR CHILD(REN)

1. **Jurisdiction.** The Court has jurisdiction to determine temporary parental responsibility and time-sharing for the parties' minor child(ren) listed in paragraph 2 below.

2. **The parties' dependent or minor child(ren) is (are):**

Name	**Birth date**

3. **Temporary Parental Responsibility for the Minor Child(ren).**
*{Choose only **one**}*
   a. _____ The parties shall have temporary **shared parental responsibility** for the parties' minor child(ren).

   b. _____ Mother _____ Father shall have temporary **sole parental responsibility** for the parties' minor child(ren). Temporary shared parental responsibility would be detrimental to the child(ren) at this time because: ____
___
____
____.

   c. _____Mother_____Father shall have ultimate decision making authority regarding the following:____
____
____
_______.

   d. **Other provisions:** ____
____
____

4. **Temporary Time-sharing Schedule with Minor Child(ren).** The parent(s) shall have:
*{Choose only **one**}*
   a. _____ **reasonable** time-sharing schedule with the parties' minor child(ren) as agreed to by the parties, subject to any limitations in paragraph 5 below. The Court reserves jurisdiction to set a specific schedule.
   b. _____the following **specified time-sharing schedule** with the parties' minor child(ren), subject to any limitations set out in paragraph 5 below: *{specify days and times}*

____
____

Mother's Temporary Time-Sharing Schedule.
____
____
____
____.

Father's Temporary Time-sharing Schedule.
____
____
____
____.

c. _____ Time-sharing in accordance with the temporary **Parenting Plan attached as** Exhibit _____.

d. _____ Mother _____Father shall have **no contact** with the parties' minor child(ren) until further order of the Court, due to the existing conditions that are detrimental to the welfare of the minor child(ren): *{explain}:* ____
____
____

5. **Limitations on Time-sharing.** Neither parent shall take the child(ren) from the other parent, any child care provider, or other person entrusted by the other parent with the care of the child(ren) without the agreement of the other party during the other party's time-sharing. The above time-sharing shall be:

[Indicate if applicable]

a. _____ **supervised by a responsible adult** who is mutually agreeable to the parties. If the parties cannot agree, the supervising adult shall be: *{name}*________________________.

b. _____ at a **supervised visitation** center located at: *{address}* ____________________
____,

subject to the available times and rules of the supervised visitation center. The cost of such visits shall be paid by _____ Mother _____ Father _____ Both.

6. **Communication Arrangements, Parental Responsibility and Time-sharing with Minor Child(ren).**

[Indicate if applicable]

______The parties' communications to arrange time-sharing and discuss issues relating to the child(ren) (if temporary shared parenting, or time-sharing is provided in paragraph 3 above) are restricted as follows: _____ telephone, _____ fax, _____ e-mail, or _____ letter, _____ a responsible person shall coordinate the time-sharing arrangements of the minor child(ren). If the parties cannot agree, the responsible person shall be: *{name}* ____

other conditions for arrangements or discussions: *{explain}* ______________________________________
____
____
____.

7. **Exchange of Minor Child(ren).** The exchange of the minor child(ren) shall be on time as scheduled and as agreed to by the parties. The following conditions, if indicated below, shall also apply.

*{Indicate **all** that apply}*

a. _____ The parties shall temporarily exchange the child(ren) at the following location(s): ___
___

b. _____ Mother _____Father shall not get out of the vehicle, and the other parent shall not approach the vehicle, during the time the child(ren) are exchanged.

c. _____ A responsible person shall conduct all exchanges of the child(ren). ( ) Mother ( ) Father shall not be present during the exchange. If the parties cannot agree, the responsible person shall be: *{name}* ____________

d. _____ Other conditions for exchange of the child(ren) are as follows: ____________________
___
___
___

8. _____ **Injunction Prohibiting Removing the Child(ren).** The Court hereby temporarily prohibits and enjoins the _____ Mother _____Father _____ Both from removing the minor child(ren) from the State of Florida without a court order or the written consent of the other party.

9. _____ **Other Temporary Provisions Relating to the Minor Child(ren).**
____
____
____
____
____
____
____
____
____

SECTION IV. TEMPORARY ALIMONY

1. _____ The Court denies the request(s) for temporary alimony.

OR

2. _____ The Court finds that there is a need for, and that _____ Petitioner _____ Respondent, hereinafter Obligor, has/had the present ability to pay temporary alimony as follows: *{Indicate **all** that apply}*

   a. ____ **Temporary Periodic.** Obligor shall pay temporary periodic alimony to Obligee in the amount of $_______ per month, payable _____ in accordance with Obligor's employer's payroll cycle, and in any event, at least once a month ____ other *{explain}*

____,
beginning *{date}* ____________________. This temporary periodic alimony shall continue until modified by court order, the death of either party, or until, ______________________, *{date or event}* whichever occurs first.

   b. _____ **Retroactive.** Obligor shall pay retroactive alimony in the amount of $_________ for the period of *{date}* ___________ through *{date}* ______________, which shall be paid pursuant to paragraph 4 below.

3. **Reasons for Awarding/Denying Temporary Alimony Award.**

The reasons for awarding/denying temporary alimony are as follows:

   a. _____ length of the marriage of the party receiving temporary alimony: years________;
   b. _____ age of party receiving temporary alimony: _______ years;
   c. _____ health of party receiving temporary alimony: _____ excellent _____ good ____ poor _____ other____;
   d. _____ other factors ____
____
____
____

_______ Please indicate here if additional pages are attached.

4. **Retroactive Alimony.** _____ Petitioner _____ Respondent shall pay to the other party the temporary retroactive alimony of $__________, as of *{date}* __________. This amount shall be paid in the amount of $__________ per month, payable in accordance with Obligor's employer's payroll cycle, and in any event at least once a month ( ) other *{explain}* _______
____
beginning: *{date}* __________________________, until paid in full including statutory interest.

5. **Insurance.**
*{Indicate **all** that apply}*

a. _____ **Health Insurance.** _____ Petitioner _____ Respondent shall temporarily be required to pay health insurance premiums for the other party not to exceed $_________ per month. Further, _____ Petitioner _____ Respondent shall pay any reasonable and necessary uninsured medical costs for the other party not exceed $_________ per year. As to these uninsured medical expenses, the party who is entitled to reimbursement of the uninsured medical expense shall submit request for reimbursement to the other party within 30 days, and the other party shall, within 30 days after receipt, submit the applicable reimbursement for that expense.

b. _____ **Life Insurance (to secure payment of support).** To secure the temporary alimony obligations set forth in this order, the Obligor shall temporarily maintain life insurance on his/her life, naming the Obligee as the sole irrevocable beneficiary, so long as reasonably available. This temporary insurance shall be in the amount of at least $_____________ and shall remain in effect until this temporary obligation for alimony terminates.

6. _____Other provisions relating to temporary alimony including any tax treatment and consequences: ____

SECTION V. TEMPORARY CHILD SUPPORT

1. The Court finds that there is a need for temporary child support and that the _____ Mother _____ Father (hereinafter Obligor) has the present ability to pay child support.

The amounts in the Child Support Guidelines Worksheet, Florida Family Law Rules of Procedure Form 12.902(e), filed by the _____ Mother _____ Father are correct

OR

The Court makes the following findings:
The Mother's net monthly income is $___________.
The Father's net monthly income is $______________.
Monthly child care costs are $________________.
Monthly health/dental insurance costs are $__________.

2. **Amount.**

Child support established at the rate of $__________per month for the _____children *{total number of minor or dependent children}* shall be paid commencing _______________ *{month, day, year}* and terminating ______________________ *{month, day, year}*. Child support shall be paid in the amount of $__________ per ________ *{week, month, other}* which is consistent with the Obligor's current payroll cycle.

Upon the termination of the obligation of child support for one of the parties' children, child support in the amount of $________ for the remaining ______children *{number of remaining children}* shall be paid commencing _______________ *{month, day, year}* and terminating _______________ *{month, day, year}*. This child support shall be paid in the amount of $ _______ per _________ *{week,* *month, other}* consistent with Obligor's current payroll cycle.

{Insert schedule for the child support obligation, including the amount, and commencement and termination dates, for the remaining minor or dependent children, which shall be payable as the obligation for each child ceases. Please indicate whether the schedule ____appears below or____ is attached as part of this form}

____
____
____
____
____
____.

The Obligor shall pay child support until all of the minor or dependent children: reach the age of 18; become emancipated, marry, join the armed services, die, or become self-supporting; or until further order of the court or agreement of the parties. The child support obligation shall continue beyond the age of 18 and until high school graduation for any child who is dependent in fact, between the ages of 18 and 19, and is still in high school performing in good faith with a reasonable expectation of graduation before age 19.

If the temporary child support ordered deviates from the guidelines by more than 5%, the factual findings which support that deviation are: ____
____
____.

3. **Retroactive Child Support.**
{Indicate if applicable}

_____Mother _____ Father shall pay to the other party the temporary retroactive child support of $_________, as of *{date}* __________________. This amount shall be paid in the amount of $_________ per month, payable in accordance with Obligor's employer's payroll cycle, and in any event at least once a month ( ) other *{explain}* _________________
beginning *{date}* _______________, until paid in full including statutory interest.

4. **Insurance.**
*[Indicate **all** that apply)]*

_____**Health/Dental Insurance.** _____ Mother _____ Father shall be required to temporarily maintain_____health _____dental insurance for the parties' minor child(ren), so long as reasonable in cost and accessible to the child(ren). The party providing insurance shall be required to convey cards showing coverage to the other party.

OR

_____ Health _____ dental insurance is not reasonable in cost or accessible to the child(ren) at this time.

Florida Supreme Court Approved Family Law Form 12.947(b), Temporary Order of Support, Time-Sharing, and Other Relief with Dependent or Minor Child(ren) (03/15)

_____Reasonable and necessary **uninsured medical/dental/prescription drug costs** for the minor child(ren) shall temporarily be assessed as follows:
_____ Shared equally by both parents.
_____ Prorated according to the child support guideline percentages.
_____ Other *{explain}*: ____
____

As to these uninsured medical/dental/prescription drug expenses, the party who incurs the expense shall submit request for reimbursement to the other party within 30 days, and the other party, within 30 days of receipt, shall submit the applicable reimbursement for that expense, according to the schedule of reimbursement set out in this paragraph.

5. _____**Life Insurance (to secure payment of support).** To secure the temporary child support obligations in this order, _____ Petitioner _____ Respondent _____ Each party shall temporarily maintain life insurance, in an amount of at least $__________, on _____ his life _____ her life _____ his/her life naming the _____ minor child(ren) as the beneficiary (ies) **OR** naming the _____ Mother _____ Father_____ other *{name}*: ______________________________ as trustee for the minor child(ren), so long as reasonably available. The obligation to maintain the life insurance coverage shall continue until the Court orders otherwise or until *{date/event}* ____
________.

6. IRS Income Tax Exemption(s). The assignment of any tax exemption for the child(ren) shall be as follows: ____
____.

7. ____Other provisions relating to temporary child support: _______________________
____

SECTION VI. METHOD OF PAYMENT

Obligor shall pay any temporary court-ordered child support/alimony and arrears, if any, as follows:

1. **Place of Payment**

   a. _____ Obligor shall pay temporary court-ordered support directly to either the State Disbursement Unit or the central depository, as required by statute, along with any fee required by statute.

   b. _____ Both parties have requested and the court finds that it is in the best interests of the child(ren) that temporary support payments need not be directed through either the State Disbursement Unit or the central depository at this time; however, either party may subsequently apply, pursuant to section 61.13(1)(d)3, Florida Statutes, to require payments through either the State Disbursement Unit or the central depository.

Florida Supreme Court Approved Family Law Form 12.947(b), Temporary Order of Support, Time-Sharing, and Other Relief with Dependent or Minor Child(ren) (03/15)

2. **Income Deduction.**

_____ **Immediate.** Obligor shall pay through income deduction, pursuant to a separate Income Deduction Order which shall be effective immediately. Obligor is individually responsible for paying this temporary support obligation until all of said support is deducted from Obligor's income. Until temporary support payments are deducted from Obligor's paycheck, Obligor is responsible for making timely payments directly to the State Disbursement Unit or the Obligee, as previously set forth in this order.

_____ **Deferred.** Income deduction is ordered this day, but it shall not be effective until a delinquency of $__________, or, if not specified, an amount equal to one month's obligation occurs. Income deduction is not being implemented immediately based on the following findings: Income deduction is **not** in the best interests of the child(ren) because: *{explain}*
____
____
____

AND
there is proof of timely payment of a previously ordered obligation without an income deduction order in cases of modification,
AND
_____ there is an agreement by the Obligor to advise the Title IV-D agency, the clerk of court, and the Obligee of any change in Payor and/or health insurance
OR
_____ there is a signed written agreement providing an alternative arrangement between the Obligor and the Obligee and, at the option of the IV-D agency, by the IV-D agency in IV-D cases in which there is an assignment of support rights to the state, reviewed and entered in the record by the court.

3. **Bonus/one-time payments.** _____ All _____% _____ No income paid in the form of a bonus or other similar one-time payment, up to the amount of any arrearage or the remaining balance thereof owed pursuant to this order, shall be forwarded to the Obligee pursuant to the payment method prescribed above.

4. **Other provisions relating to method of payment.** _______________________________
____
____

SECTION VII. TEMPORARY ATTORNEY'S FEES, COSTS, AND SUIT MONEY

1. _____Petitioner's _____Respondent's request(s) for temporary attorney's fees, costs, and suit money is (are) denied because _______________________________
____

2. _____ The Court finds there is a need for and an ability to pay temporary attorney's fees, costs, and suit money. _____ Petitioner _____ Respondent is hereby ordered to pay to the other party $__________ in temporary attorney's fees, and $__________ in costs. The Court further finds that the temporary attorney's fees awarded are based on the reasonable rate of $__________ per hour and _______reasonable hours. Other provisions relating to temporary attorney's fees, costs, and suit money are as follows: ____
____
____
_______.

SECTION VIII. OTHER PROVISIONS

Other Provisions: ____
____
____
____.

DONE AND ORDERED in _______________________, Florida on *{date}* _______________.

____
CIRCUIT JUDGE

I certify that a copy of this *{name of document(s)}* _______________________ was
( ) mailed ( ) faxed and mailed ( ) e-mailed ( ) hand-delivered to the parties or entities listed below on *{date}*_______________________.

____
By: *{Clerk of Court or designee}*

Petitioner (or his or her attorney)
Respondent (or his or her attorney)
_____State Disbursement Unit
_____Central depository

Florida Supreme Court Approved Family Law Form 12.947(b), Temporary Order of Support, Time-Sharing, and Other Relief with Dependent or Minor Child(ren) (03/15)

_____Other: ________________________________

Florida Supreme Court Approved Family Law Form 12.947(b), Temporary Order of Support, Time-Sharing, and Other Relief with Dependent or Minor Child(ren) (03/15)

Added Feb. 26, 1998, effective Mar. 16, 1998 (713 So.2d 1). Amended July 1, 1999 (717 So.2d 914); Sept. 21, 2000 (810 So.2d 1); March 26, 2009 (20 So.3d 173); Dec. 16, 2010 (59 So.3d 792); Nov. 3, 2011, effective, *nunc pro tunc*, Oct. 1, 2011 (78 So.3d 1045); May 24, 2012 (96 So.3d 217); July 3, 2013 (117 So.3d 958); March 26, 2015, effective March 26, 2015 (2015 WL 1343088).

Form 12.947(c). Motion for Temporary Support and Other Relief with No Dependent or Minor Child(ren)

IN THE CIRCUIT COURT OF THE ____________________ JUDICIAL CIRCUIT,
IN AND FOR ____________________________ COUNTY, FLORIDA

Case No: ______________________
Division: ______________________

________________________________,
Petitioner,
and

________________________________,
Respondent.

MOTION FOR TEMPORARY SUPPORT AND OTHER RELIEF WITH NO DEPENDENT OR MINOR CHILD(REN)

_____ Petitioner _____ Respondent requests that the Court enter an order granting the following temporary support:

*{Complete **all** that apply}*

1. **Assets and Liabilities.**

a. _____ **Award temporary exclusive use and possession of the marital home.** *{address}* ______
____
The Court should do this because: _______________________________________
____
____

b. _____ **Award temporary use and possession of marital assets.** *{Specify, without using account numbers}* ____
____
____
____
The Court should do this because: _______________________________________
____
____.

c. _____ **Enter a temporary injunction** prohibiting the parties from disposing of any marital assets, other than ordinary and usual expenses. *{Explain}* ______________________________
____
____

Florida Supreme Court Approved Family Law Form 12.947(c), Motion for Temporary Support and Other Relief with No Dependent or Minor Child(ren) (03/15)

The Court should do this because: ____
____
____

d. _____ Require temporary payment of specific marital debts. *{Explain, without using account numbers}*
____
____
____

The Court should do this because: ____
____
____

2. **Support.** Award temporary spousal support/alimony of $___________ per month.
The Court should do this because: ____
____
____

3. Other provisions relating to alimony including any tax treatment and consequences:____
____
____

4. **Attorney's fees and costs.**

a. _____ Award temporary attorney's fees of $__________.

b. _____ Award temporary costs of $__________.

The Court should do this because: ____
____
____

5. **Other Relief.** *{specify}*____
____
____
____
____

6. A completed Certificate of Compliance with Mandatory Disclosure, Florida Family Law Rules of Procedure Form 12.932, is filed with this motion or has already been filed with the Court.

7. A completed Notice of Social Security Number, Florida Supreme Court Approved Family Law Form 12.902(j), is filed with this motion or has already been filed with the Court.

I request that the Court hold a hearing on this matter and grant the relief specifically requested and any other relief this Court may deem just and proper.

Florida Supreme Court Approved Family Law Form 12.947(c), Motion for Temporary Support and Other Relief with No Dependent or Minor Child(ren) (03/15)

I certify that a copy of this document was ( ) mailed ( ) faxed and mailed ( ) e-mailed ( ) hand delivered to the person(s) listed below on *{date}* ______________.

Other party or his/her attorney:
Name: ______________________________
Address: ______________________________
City, State, Zip: ______________________________
Fax Number: ______________________________
Designated E-mail Address(es): ______________________________

____
Signature of Party or his/her attorney
Printed Name: ______________________________
Address: ______________________________
City, State, Zip: ______________________________
Telephone Number: ______________________________
Fax Number: ______________________________
Designated E-mail Address(es): ______________________________

IF A NONLAWYER HELPED YOU FILL OUT THIS FORM, HE/SHE MUST FILL IN THE BLANKS BELOW:
[fill in all blanks] This form was prepared for the: *{choose only one}* ( ) Petitioner ( ) Respondent
This form was completed with the assistance of:
{name of individual} ______________________________,
{name of business} ______________________________,
{address} ______________________________,
{city} ______________,*{state}* ____,*{zip code}* ______ *{telephone number}* ______________.

Florida Supreme Court Approved Family Law Form 12.947(c), Motion for Temporary Support and Other Relief with No Dependent or Minor Child(ren) (03/15)

INSTRUCTIONS FOR FLORIDA SUPREME COURT APPROVED FAMILY LAW FORM 12.947(c) MOTION FOR TEMPORARY SUPPORT AND OTHER RELIEF WITH NO DEPENDENT OR MINOR CHILD(REN)(03/15)

When should this form be used?

This form may be used by:

(1) the **respondent** or the **petitioner** in a pending **dissolution of marriage** action. For you to use this form, a **petition** for dissolution of marriage must have already been filed. You should use this form to ask the court to award any of the following: temporary use of assets; temporary exclusive use of the marital home; temporary responsibility for liabilities/debts; temporary spousal support (**alimony**); and other relief.

OR

(2) the petitioner in a pending action for support unconnected with a dissolution. For you to use this form, a petition for support unconnected with a dissolution of marriage must have already been filed. You should use this form to ask the court to award temporary spousal support (alimony).

This form should be typed or printed in black ink. After completing this form, you should **file** the original with the **clerk of the circuit court** in the county where the petition for dissolution of marriage was filed and keep a copy for your records.

IMPORTANT INFORMATION REGARDING E–FILING

The Florida Rules of Judicial Administration now require that all petitions, pleadings, and documents be filed electronically except in certain circumstances. **Self–represented litigants may file petitions or other pleadings or documents electronically; however, they are not required to do so.** If you choose to file your pleadings or other documents electronically, you must do so in accordance with Florida Rule of Judicial Administration 2.525, and you must follow the procedures of the judicial circuit in which you file. **The rules and procedures should be carefully read and followed.**

What should I do next?

A copy of this form, along with all of the other forms required with this motion, must be mailed, e-mailed, or hand delivered to the other party in your case. When you have filed all of the required forms, you are ready to set a hearing on your motion. You should check with the clerk, **family law intake staff**, or **judicial assistant** for information on the local procedure for scheduling a hearing. When you know the date and time of your hearing, you should notify the other party using a **Notice of Hearing (General)**, Florida Supreme Court Approved Family Law Form 12.923, or other appropriate notice of hearing form.

IMPORTANT INFORMATION REGARDING E–SERVICE ELECTION

After the initial service of process of the petition or supplemental petition by the Sheriff or certified process server, the Florida Rules of Judicial Administration now require that all documents required or permitted to be served on the other party must be served by electronic mail (e–mail) except in certain circumstances. **You must strictly comply with the format requirements set forth in the Rules of Judicial Administration.**

SELF–REPRESENTED LITIGANTS MAY SERVE DOCUMENTS BY E–MAIL; HOWEVER, THEY ARE NOT REQUIRED TO DO SO. If a self-represented litigant elects to serve and receive documents by e-mail, the procedures must always be followed once the initial election is made.

To serve and receive documents by e-mail, you must designate your e-mail addresses by using the **Designation of Current Mailing and E–mail Address**, Florida Supreme Court Approved Family Law Form 12.915, and you must provide your e-mail address on each form on which your signature appears. Please **CAREFULLY** read the rules and instructions for: **Certificate of Service (General),** Florida Supreme Court Approved Family Law Form 12.914; **Designation of Current Mailing and E–mail Address**, Florida Supreme Court Approved Family Law Form 12.915; and Florida Rule of Judicial Administration 2.516.

Where can I look for more information?

Before proceeding, you should read General Information for Self–Represented Litigants found at the beginning of these forms. Words in **bold underline** in these instructions are defined there. For further information, see chapter 61, Florida Statutes, rule 12.285, Florida Family Law Rules of Procedure, and rule 1.610, Florida Rules of Civil Procedure.

Special notes . . .

If you use paragraph 1.c. of this form to ask the court to enter a temporary injunction, the court may require you to post a **bond**.

With this form you must also file the following, if not already filed:

- **Family Law Financial Affidavit**, Florida Family Law Rules of Procedure Form 12.902(b) or (c). (This must be filed within 45 days if not filed at the time of the petition.)
- **Notice of Social Security Number**, Florida Supreme Court Approved Family Law Form 12.902(j).
- **Certificate of Compliance with Mandatory Disclosure**, Florida Family Law Rules of Procedure Form 12.932.

Temporary Order . . . These family law forms contain an **Order for Temporary Support and Other Relief with No Dependent or Minor Child(ren)**, Florida Supreme Court Approved Family Law Form 12.947(d), which the judge may use. You should check with the clerk, family law intake staff, or judicial assistant to see if you need to bring it with you to the hearing. If so, you should type or print the heading, including the circuit, county, case number, division, and the parties' names, and leave the rest blank for the judge to complete at your hearing.

Nonlawyer . . . Remember, a person who is NOT an attorney is called a nonlawyer. If a nonlawyer helps you fill out these forms, that person must give you a copy of a **Disclosure from Nonlawyer**, Florida Family Law Rules of Procedure Form 12.900 (a), before he or she helps you. A nonlawyer helping you fill out these forms also **must** put his or her name, address, and telephone number on the bottom of the last page of every form he or she helps you complete.

Added Sept. 21, 2000 (810 So.2d 1). Amended Nov. 3, 2011, effective, *nunc pro tunc*, Oct. 1, 2011 (78 So.3d 1045); May 24, 2012 (96 So.3d 217); March 26, 2015, effective March 26, 2015 (2015 WL 1343088).

Form 12.947(d). Order for Temporary Support and Other Relief with No Dependent or Minor Child(ren)

IN THE CIRCUIT COURT OF THE _______________ JUDICIAL CIRCUIT,
IN AND FOR ______________________________ COUNTY, FLORIDA

Case No: ______________________
Division: ______________________

_________________________________,
Petitioner,

and

_________________________________,
Respondent.

ORDER FOR TEMPORARY SUPPORT AND OTHER RELIEF WITH NO DEPENDENT OR MINOR CHILD(REN)

This cause came before this Court for a hearing on a Motion for Temporary Support and Other Relief with No Dependent or Minor Child(ren). The Court, having reviewed the file and heard the testimony, makes these findings of fact and ORDERS as follows:

The Court has jurisdiction over the subject matter and the parties.

SECTION I. MARITAL ASSETS AND LIABILITIES

A. Injunction.

1. _____ Petitioner _____ Respondent is (are) prohibited and enjoined from disposing of any marital assets without the written permission of the other party or a court order. If indicated here ( ), the person(s) prohibited and enjoined from disposing of any marital assets may continue to pay all ordinary and usual expenses.

2. The Court may enforce compliance with the terms of this injunction through civil and/or indirect criminal contempt proceedings, which may include arrest, incarceration, and/or the imposition of a fine.

3. Violation of this injunction may constitute criminal contempt of court.

4. Bond. This order is conditioned upon _____ Petitioner _____ Respondent posting bond in the sum of $__________ with the clerk of this Court.

B. Temporary Use of Assets.

1. The assets listed below are temporarily determined to be marital assets. Each party shall temporarily have the use of, as his/her own, the assets awarded in this section, and the other party shall temporarily have no further use of said assets. **Any personal property not listed**

below shall be for the use of party currently in possession of that item(s), and he or she may not dispose of that item(s) without the written permission of the other party or a court order.

ASSETS: DESCRIPTION OF ITEM(S) (Please describe each item as clearly as possible. You do not need to list account numbers.)	**Wife Shall Have Temporary Use**	**Husband Shall Have Temporary Use**
Automobiles		
Furniture & furnishings in home		
Furniture & furnishings elsewhere		
Jewelry		
Business interests		
Other Assets		

C. Temporary Responsibility for Liabilities/Debts.

1. The liabilities listed below are temporarily determined to be marital. Each party shall pay as his or her own the marital liabilities indicated below and shall keep said payments current. The other party shall temporarily have no further responsibility for the payment of these debts.

LIABILITIES: DESCRIPTION OF DEBT(S) (Please describe each item as clearly as possible. You do not need to list account numbers.)	Current Amount Owed	Wife Shall Pay	Husband Shall Pay
Mortgages on real estate: (home)	$	$	$
Charge/credit card accounts			
Auto loan			
Auto loan			
Bank/Credit Union loans			
Money owed (not evidenced by a note)			
Other			

SECTION II. TEMPORARY EXCLUSIVE USE AND POSSESSION OF HOME

*{Indicate **all** that apply}*

1. _____Petitioner _____ Respondent shall have temporary exclusive use and possession of the dwelling located at: *{address}* ____
until *{date or event}* ____.

2. _____ Petitioner _____Respondent may make a visit to the premises described in the paragraph above for the purpose of obtaining his or her clothing and items of personal health and hygiene and to obtain any items awarded in this order. This visit shall occur after notice to the person granted temporary exclusive use and possession of the dwelling and at the earliest convenience of both parties.

3. _____ Other: ____
____.

SECTION III. TEMPORARY ALIMONY

1. _____ The Court denies the request(s) for temporary alimony.

OR

2. _____The Court finds that there is a need for, and that _____ Petitioner _____ Respondent, hereinafter Obligor, has/had the present ability to pay, temporary alimony as follows:

*{Choose **all** that apply}*

a. _____ **Temporary Periodic.** Obligor shall pay temporary periodic alimony to Obligee in the amount of $__________ per month, payable ( ) in accordance with Obligor's employer's payroll cycle, and in any event, at least once a month ( ) other *{explain}* ______________
____,
beginning *{date}* __________. This temporary periodic alimony shall continue until modified by court order, the death of either party, or until ____
________________________________ *{date or event}* whichever occurs first.

b. _____ **Retroactive.** Obligor shall pay retroactive alimony in the amount of $__________ for the period of *{date}* __________________ through *{date}* _______________, which shall be paid pursuant to paragraph 4 below.

3. **Reasons for Awarding/Denying Temporary Alimony Award.** The reasons for awarding/denying temporary alimony are as follows:

a_____ length of the marriage of the party receiving temporary alimony: ______ years;

b._____ age of party receiving temporary alimony: _________;

c._____health of party receiving temporary alimony: _____ excellent _____good _____ poor _____ other ____;

d._____ other factors ____
____
____
____

____ Please indicate here if additional pages are attached.

4. **Retroactive Alimony.** _____ Petitioner _____ Respondent shall pay to the other party the temporary retroactive alimony of $_____________, as of *{date}* __________. This amount shall be paid in the amount of $__________ per month, payable in accordance with Obligor's employer's payroll cycle, and in any event at least once a month ( ) other *{explain}*: ______
____,
beginning *{date}* _______________, until paid in full including statutory interest.

Florida Supreme Court Approved Family Law Form 12.947(d), Order for Temporary Support and Other Relief With No Dependent or Minor Child(ren) (03/15)

5. **Insurance.**

[Indicate all that apply]

a. _____ **Health Insurance.** _____ Petitioner _____ Respondent shall temporarily be required to pay health insurance premiums for the other party not to exceed $__________ per month. Further, _____ Petitioner _____ Respondent shall pay any reasonable and necessary uninsured medical costs for the other party not exceed $______________per year. As to these uninsured medical expenses, the party who is entitled to reimbursement of the uninsured medical expense shall submit request for reimbursement to the other party within 30 days, and the other party shall, within 30 days after receipt, submit the applicable reimbursement for that expense.

b. _____ **Life Insurance (to secure payment of support).** To secure the temporary alimony obligations set forth in this order, the Obligor shall temporarily maintain any existing life insurance coverage on his/her life naming the Obligee as the sole irrevocable beneficiary, so long as reasonably available. This temporary insurance shall be in the amount of at least $__________ and shall remain in effect until this temporary obligation for alimony terminates.

6. _____ **Other provisions relating to temporary alimony including any tax treatment and consequences:** ____
____
____.

SECTION IV. METHOD OF PAYMENT

Obligor shall pay any temporary court-ordered alimony and arrears, if any, as follows:

1. **Place of Payment.**

[Indicate if applies]

a. _____ Obligor shall pay temporary court-ordered support directly to either the State Disbursement Unit or the central depository, as required by statute, along with any fee required by statute.

b. _____ Both parties have requested and the court finds that it is in the best interests that temporary support payments need not be directed through either the State Disbursement Unit or the central depository at this time; however, either party may subsequently apply, pursuant to section 61.13(1)(d)3, Florida Statutes, to require payments through either the State Disbursement Unit or the central depository.

2. **Income Deduction.**

[If applicable]

a. _____ **Immediate.** Obligor shall pay through income deduction, pursuant to a separate Income Deduction Order which shall be effective immediately. Obligor is individually responsible for paying this temporary support obligation until all of said support is deducted from Obligor's income. Until support payments are deducted from Obligor's paycheck, Obligor is responsible for making timely payments directly to the State Disbursement Unit or the Obligee, as previously set forth in this order.

b. _____ **Deferred.** Income deduction is ordered this day, but it shall not be effective until a delinquency of $__________, or, if not specified, an amount equal to one month's obligation occurs. Income deduction is not being implemented immediately based on the following findings: there are no minor child(ren) common to the parties,

AND

there is proof of timely payment of a previously ordered obligation without an income deduction order in cases of modification,

AND

_____ there is an agreement by the Obligor to advise the Title IV-D agency, the clerk of court, and the Obligee of any change in Payor and/or health insurance **OR** ( ) there is a signed written agreement providing an alternative arrangement between the Obligor and the Obligee and, at the option of the IV-D agency, by the IV-D agency in IV-D cases in which there is an assignment of support rights to the state, reviewed and entered in the record by the court.

3. **Bonus/one-time payments.** _____ All ______% _____ No income paid in the form of a bonus or other similar one-time payment, up to the amount of any arrearage or the remaining balance thereof owed pursuant to this order, shall be forwarded to the Obligee pursuant to the payment method prescribed above.

4. **Other provisions relating to method of temporary payment:** ______________________________
____
____.

SECTION V. TEMPORARY ATTORNEY'S FEES, COSTS, AND SUIT MONEY

1. _____ Petitioner's _____ Respondent's request(s) for temporary attorney's fees, costs, and suit money is (are) denied because ____
____.

2. _____ The Court finds there is a need for and an ability to pay temporary attorney's fees, costs, and suit money. _____ Petitioner _____ Respondent is hereby ordered to pay to the other party $__________ in temporary attorney's fees, and $__________ in costs. The Court further finds that the temporary attorney's fees awarded are based on the reasonable rate of $__________ per hour and _____reasonable hours. Other provisions relating to temporary attorney fees, costs, and suit money are as follows: ____
____
____.

SECTION VI. OTHER PROVISIONS

Other Provisions: ____
____

____
____.

DONE AND ORDERED in ______________________, Florida, on *{date}* ________________.

____
CIRCUIT JUDGE

I certify that a copy of this *{name of document}*________________________
was ( ) mailed ( ) faxed and mailed ( ) e-mailed ( ) hand-delivered to the parties or entities listed below on *{date}*______________________________.

by______________________________
{Clerk of Court or designee}

Petitioner (or his or her attorney)
Respondent (or his or her attorney)
State Disbursement Unit
Other: ________________________

Florida Supreme Court Approved Family Law Form 12.947(d), Order for Temporary Support and Other Relief With No Dependent or Minor Child(ren) (03/15)

Added Sept. 21, 2000 (810 So.2d 1). Amended Nov. 3, 2011, effective, *nunc pro tunc*, Oct. 1, 2011 (78 So.3d 1045); May 24, 2012 (96 So.3d 217); July 3, 2013 (117 So.3d 958); March 26, 2015, effective March 26, 2015 (2015 WL 1343088).

Form 12.950(a). Agreement for Relocation with Minor Child(ren)___ Including or ___ Not Including Modification of Child Support

IN THE CIRCUIT COURT OF THE ________________ JUDICIAL CIRCUIT,
IN AND FOR ____________________ COUNTY, FLORIDA

Case No: ____________
Division: ____________

______________________________,
Petitioner,

And

______________________________,
Respondent.

AGREEMENT FOR RELOCATION WITH MINOR CHILD(REN) ____INCLUDING OR ____ NOT INCLUDING MODIFICATION OF CHILD SUPPORT

I, *{full legal name}* ______________________, (Petitioner) and I, *{full legal name}* ______________________________, (Respondent) being sworn, certify that the following information is true:

1. The parties to this action were granted a final judgment of ____ dissolution of marriage ____ paternity on *{date}* ______________. A copy of the final judgment and any modification(s) is/are attached.

2. *{If Applicable}*. The following other person is an individual who is not a parent, but with whom the child resides pursuant to a court order, or who has the right of access to, time-sharing with, of visitation with the child(ren)______________________________.

3. Paragraph(s)________________of the ____ final judgment or ____ most recent modification thereof describes the present custody, visitation, or time-sharing schedule.

4. The dependent or minor child(ren) referred to in this Agreement are:

Name(s)	**Birth Date(s)**

SECTION I. RELOCATION

A. Since the final judgment or last modification thereof, there has been a substantial change in circumstances, requiring a modification of the present visitation, Parenting Plan, or time-sharing schedule. Both parties agree and stipulate to the following terms regarding modification to allow the ____________________to relocate with the minor child (ren) and modify the terms regarding visitation or time-sharing, with or without a hearing.

B. The following relocation information is true and correct:

1. The location of the intended new residence, including the state, city, and physical address, if known, is: ____
____
____.

2. The mailing address of the new physical residence, if not the same as the physical address, is: ____.

3. The home telephone number of the intended new residence, if known, is:___________.

4. The date of the intended move or proposed relocation is: ____________________.

SECTION II: PARENTAL RESPONSIBILITY AND TIME-SHARING SCHEDULE *{Choose only* ***one****}*

1.____ Parental Responsibility and Time-Sharing shall remain the same as previously set out in the: ____ Final Judgment of Dissolution, ____ Final Judgment of Paternity or subsequent ____ Other *{title of supplemental order or judgment}*________________________ dated __________________________ and will continue without modification;

OR

2.____ The parties shall comply with the Parenting Plan which is attached and incorporated herein as Exhibit ____.

OR

3.____ The parties shall comply with the following Parenting Plan and time-sharing schedule:

A. **JURISDICTION**

The United States is the country of habitual residence of the child(ren).

The State of Florida is the child(ren)'s home state for the purposes of the Uniform Child Custody Jurisdiction and Enforcement Act.

This Parenting Plan is a child custody determination for the purposes of the Uniform Child Custody Jurisdiction and Enforcement Act, the International Child Abduction Remedies Act, 42 U.S.C. Sections 11601 et seq., the Parental Kidnapping Prevention Act, and the Convention on the Civil Aspects of International Child Abduction enacted at the Hague on October 25, 1980, and for all other state and federal laws.

Other: ____.

Florida Supreme Court Approved Family Law Form 12.950(a), Agreement for Relocation with Minor Child(ren) (03/15)

B. **PARENTAL RESPONSIBILITY AND DECISION MAKING**

1. **Parental Responsibility** *{Choose only one}*

a.______Shared Parental Responsibility.
It is in the best interests of the child(ren) that the parents confer and **jointly** make all major decisions affecting the welfare of the child(ren). Major decisions include, but are not limited to, decisions about the child(ren)'s education, healthcare, and other responsibilities unique to this family.

OR

b.______Shared Parental Responsibility with Decision Making Authority.
It is in the best interests of the child(ren) that the parents confer and attempt to agree on the major decisions involving the child(ren). If the parents are unable to agree, the authority for making major decisions regarding the child(ren) shall be as follows:

Education/Academic decisions	____ Mother	____ Father
Non-emergency health care	____ Mother	____ Father
____________________________	____ Mother	____ Father
____________________________	____ Mother	____ Father
____________________________	____ Mother	____ Father

OR

c.______Sole Parental Responsibility:
It is in the best interests of the child(ren) that the ____ Mother ____ Father shall have sole authority to make major decisions for the child(ren.) It is detrimental to the child(ren) for the parents to share decision making because: ____.

2. **Day-to-Day Decisions**
Unless otherwise specified in this Parenting Plan, each parent shall make decisions regarding day-to-day care and control of each child, including the performance of daily tasks, while the child is with that parent. Regardless of the allocation of decision making in the Parenting Plan, either parent may make emergency decisions affecting the health or safety of the child(ren) when the child is residing with that parent. A parent who makes an emergency decision shall share the decision with the other parent as soon as reasonably possible.

3. **Extracurricular Activities** ***{Choose all that apply}***

a.______Either parent may register the child(ren) and allow them to participate in the activity of the child(ren)'s choice.

b._____The parents must mutually agree to all extra-curricular activities.

c._____The costs of the extra-curricular activities shall be paid by:
Mother ______% Father _______%

d._____The uniforms and equipment required for the extra-curricular activities shall be paid by: Mother _______ % Father ________%

e._____Other: ____.

C. **INFORMATION SHARING. Unless Otherwise Indicated or Ordered by the Court:**

1. Unless otherwise prohibited by law, both parents shall have access to medical and school records pertaining to the child(ren) and shall be permitted to independently consult with any and all professionals involved with the child(ren). The parents shall cooperate with each other in sharing information related to the health, education, and welfare of the child(ren) and they shall sign any necessary documentation ensuring that both parents have access to said records.

2. Each parent shall be responsible for obtaining records and reports directly from the school and health care providers.

3. Both parents have equal rights to inspect and receive governmental agency and law enforcement records concerning the child(ren).

4. Both parents shall have equal and independent authority to confer with the child(ren)'s school, day care, health care providers, and other programs with regard to the child(ren)'s educational, emotional, and social progress.

5. Both parents shall be listed as "emergency contacts" for the child(ren).

6. Each parent has a continuing responsibility to provide a residential and mailing address, and contact telephone number(s) to the other parent. Each parent shall notify the other parent in writing within 24 hours of any changes. Each parent shall notify the court in writing within seven (7) days of any changes.

7. Other: ____.

D. **SCHEDULING**

1. **School Calendar**
If necessary, on or before ____________ of each year, both parents should obtain a copy of the school calendars for the next school year. The parents shall discuss the calendars and the time-sharing schedule so that any differences or questions can be resolved.

The parents shall follow the school calendar of: *{Choose **all** that apply}*

_____ the oldest child
_____ the youngest child
_____ the school calendar for _______________ County
_____ the school calendar for __________________ School

2. **Academic Break Definition**
When defining academic break periods, the period shall begin at the end of the last scheduled day of classes before the holiday or break and shall end on the first day of regularly scheduled classes after the holiday or break.

3. **Schedule Changes** *{Choose **all** that apply}*

a._____A parent making a request for a schedule change will make the request as soon as possible, but in any event, except in cases of emergency, no less than _______________ before the change is to occur.

b._____A parent requesting a change of schedule shall be responsible for any additional child care, or transportation costs caused by the change.

c._____Other ____.

E. **TIME-SHARING SCHEDULE**

1. **Weekday and Weekend Schedule**
The following schedule shall apply beginning on _________________ with the _____ Mother _____ Father and continue as follows:

The child(ren) shall spend time with the **Mother** on the following dates and times:
WEEKENDS: _____ Every _____ Every Other _____ Other (*specify*): ____________
From ______________________________ to ______________________________
WEEKDAYS: Specify days ____
From ______________________________ to ______________________________
OTHER: (Specify) ____
____
____.

The child(ren) shall spend time with the **Father** on the following dates and times:
WEEKENDS: _____ Every _____ Every Other _____ Other *{specify}*: ____________
From ______________________________ to ______________________________
WEEKDAYS: *{Specify days}* ____
From ______________________________ to ______________________________
OTHER: *{specify}* ____
____

____.

The child(ren) shall spend time with ______________________on the following dates and times:
WEEKENDS: ____ Every ____ Every Other ____ Other *{specify}*:______________
From ________________________________to______________________________
WEEKDAYS: *{Specify days}*____
From_________________________________to______________________________
OTHER: *{specify}* ____
____
____

Please indicate below if there is a different time-sharing schedule for any child. Complete a separate Attachment for each child for whom there is a different time-sharing schedule.

____ There is a different time-sharing schedule for the following child(ren) in Attachment ____.

______________________, and ______________________.
(Name of Child) (Name of Child)

2. **Holiday Schedule** *{Choose only **one**}*

a.____ No holiday time sharing shall apply. The regular time-sharing schedule set forth above shall apply.

b.____ Holiday time-sharing shall be as the parties agree.

c.____ Holiday time-sharing shall be in accordance with the following schedule. The holiday schedule will take priority over the regular weekday, weekend, and summer schedules. Fill in the blanks with Mother or Father to indicate where the child(ren) will be for the holidays. Provide the beginning and ending times. If a holiday is not specified as even, odd, or every year with one parent, then the child(ren) will remain with the parent in accordance with the regular schedule

Holidays	**Even Years**	**Odd Years**	**Every Year**	**Begin/End Time**
Mother's Day	________	________	________	________
Father's Day	________	________	________	________
President's Day	________	________	________	________
Martin Luther King Day	____	________	________	________
Easter	____	________	________	________
Passover	____	________	________	________
Memorial Day Weekend	____	________	________	________
4th of July	____	________	________	________
Labor Day Weekend	____	________	________	________

Columbus Day Weekend	____	________	________	____________
Halloween	____	________	________	____________
Thanksgiving	____	________	________	____________
Veteran's Day	____	________	________	____________
Hanukkah	____	________	________	____________
Yom Kippur	____	________	________	____________
Rosh Hashanah	____	________	________	____________
Child(ren)'s Birthdays	____	________	________	____________
________________			________	____________

3. **Winter Break**

A. Winter Break *{Choose only **one**}*

1._____The ____Mother ____ Father shall have the child(ren) from the day and time school is dismissed until December _____ at _____ a.m./p. m in ____odd-numbered years ____ even-numbered years ____ every year. The other parent will have the children for the second portion of the Winter Break. The parties shall alternate the arrangement each year.

2._____The ____ Mother ____ Father shall have the child(ren) for the entire Winter Break during ____ odd-numbered years ____ even-numbered years ____ every year.

3._____Other:
____
____
____.

B. Specific Winter Holidays

If not addressed above, the specific Winter Holidays such as Christmas, New Year's Eve, Hanukkah, Kwanzaa, etc. shall be shared as follows:
____
____
____
____.

4. **Spring Break** *{Choose only **one**}*

a._____The parents shall follow the regular schedule.

b._____The parents shall alternate the entire Spring Break with the Mother having the child(ren) during the _____ odd-numbered _____ even-numbered years.

c._____The _____ Father _____ Mother shall have the child(ren) for the entire Spring Break every year.

d._____The Spring Break will be evenly divided. The first half of the Spring Break will go to the parent whose regularly scheduled weekend falls on the first half and the second half going to the parent whose weekend falls during the second half.

e._____Other: ______________________________________

5. **Summer Break** *{Choose only **one**}*

a._____The parents shall follow the regular schedule through the summer.

b._____The _____ Mother _____Father shall have the entire Summer Break from ___________ after school is out until ______________ before school starts.

c._____The parents shall equally divide the Summer Break. During____ odd-numbered years____ even-numbered years, the _____Mother _____ Father shall have the child(ren) from ___________after school is out until______________. The other parent shall have the child(ren) for the second half of the summer break. The parents shall alternate the first and second halves of Summer Break each year unless otherwise agreed. During the extended periods of time-sharing, the other parent shall have the child(ren)__________________.

d._____Other:____.

6. **Number of Overnights:**

Based upon the time-sharing schedule, the Mother has a total of _____ overnights per year and the Father has a total of _____ overnights per year. **Note: The two numbers must equal 365.**

F. **TRANSPORTATION AND EXCHANGE OF CHILD(REN)**

Both parents shall have the child(ren) ready on time with sufficient clothing packed and ready at the agreed upon time of exchange. All necessary information and medicines will accompany the child(ren).

The parties shall exchange travel information and finalize travel plans at least_____ days in advance of the date of travel. Except in cases of emergency, any parent requesting a change of travel plans after the date of finalization shall be solely responsible for any additional costs.

1. **Automobile Transportation and Exchange**

If a parent is more than _____ minutes late without contacting the other parent to make other arrangements, the parent with the child(ren) may proceed with other plans and activities. *{Choose only one}*

a._____ The _____ Mother _____ Father shall provide all transportation.

b._____ The _____ Mother _____ Father shall pick up the child(ren) at the beginning of the visit and the other parent shall pick up the child(ren) at the end of the visit. The exchange shall take place:

c._____ At the parents' homes unless otherwise agreed

d._____ At the following location unless the parties agree in advance to a different place____.

e._____ The parents shall meet at the following central location: ____.

f. Other: ____.

2. **Airplane and Other Public Transportation and Exchange**

Airline regulations govern the age at which a child may fly unescorted. An older child or children may fly under such regulations as each airline may establish.

Airline reservations should be made well in advance, and preferably non-stop.

All flight information shall be sent to the other party(ies) at least _____ days in advance of the flight by the party purchasing the tickets.

If the child(ren) are flying accompanied by a party, the parent picking up the child(ren) shall exchange the child(ren) with the other parent at ____________________ and the parent returning the child(ren) shall exchange the child(ren) at ____________________.

If the exchange is to be made at the airport, the party flying in to pick up or drop off the child(ren) from/to the airport must notify the other party of any flight delays.

Unless otherwise agreed in advance, if the child(ren) are flying unaccompanied, the parent taking the child(ren) to the airport must call the other parent immediately upon departure to notify the other parent that the child(ren) is/are arriving, and the parent who meets the child(ren) must immediately notify the other parent upon the child(ren)'s arrival. *{Indicate all that apply}*

a._____ Until a child reaches the age of _____, the parties agree that the child(ren) shall take a direct flight and/or fly accompanied by ____________________.

b._____ Once a child reaches the age of _____ the child shall be permitted to fly accompanied by an airline employee.

c._____Once a child reached the age of ____ the child shall be permitted to fly unescorted.

d._____Other: ____.

3. **Costs of Airline and Other Public Transportation**

The parents shall work together to purchase the most convenient and least expensive tickets.

Unless otherwise agreed or in the case of an unavoidable emergency, any costs incurred by a missed travel connection shall be the sole responsibility of the parent who failed to timely deliver the child(ren) to the missed connection. *{Indicate all that apply}*

a._____Transportation costs are included in the Child Support Worksheets and/or the Order for Child Support and should not be included here.

b._____The Mother shall pay ______% and the Father shall pay ______% of the transportation costs.

c._____The Mother shall pay ______% and the Father shall pay _____% of the transportation costs for an adult to accompany the child(ren) during travel.

d._____If the parents are sharing travel costs, the non-purchasing parent shall reimburse the other parent within _____ days of receipt of documentation establishing the travel costs.

e._____Other: ____.

4. **Foreign and Out-Of-State Travel** *{Indicate all that apply}*

a._____Either parent may travel within the United States with the child(ren) during his/her time-sharing. The parent traveling with the child(ren) shall give the other parent at least _____ days written notice before traveling out of state unless there is an emergency, and shall provide the other parent with a detailed itinerary, including locations and telephone numbers where the child(ren) and parent can be reached at least _____ days prior to traveling.

b._____Either parent may travel out of the country with the child(ren) during his/her time-sharing. At least _____ days prior to traveling, the parent shall provide a detailed itinerary, including locations, and telephone numbers where the child(ren) and parent may be reached during the trip. Each parent agrees to provide whatever documentation is necessary for the other parent to take the child(ren) out of the country.

c._____If a parent wishes to travel out of the country with the child(ren), he/she shall

provide the following security for the return of the child(ren) ______________
____
____.

d.______Other ____.

5. **Other travel and exchange arrangements:**
____
____
____

G. **EDUCATION**

1. **School designation.** For purposes of school boundary determination and registration, the_____ Mother's ______Father's address shall be designated.

2. *{If Applicable}* The following provisions are made regarding private or home schooling:
____
____
____.

3. **Other.** ____
____
____

H. **DESIGNATION FOR OTHER LEGAL PURPOSES**

The child(ren) named in this Relocation Agreement are scheduled to reside the majority of the time with the _____ Mother ______ Father. This majority designation is **SOLELY** for purposes of all other state and federal laws which require such a designation. **This designation does not affect either parent's rights or responsibilities under this Relocation Agreement.**

I. **COMMUNICATION**

1. **Between Parents**

All communications regarding the child(ren) shall be between the parents. The parents shall not use the child(ren) as messengers to convey information, ask questions, or set up schedule changes.

The parents shall communicate with each other by: *{Indicate* ***all*** *that apply}*

a.______in person
b.______by telephone
c.______by letter
d.______by e-mail

e._____Other: ____.

2. **Between Parent and Child(ren)**

Both parents shall keep contact information current. Telephone or other electronic communication between the child(ren) and the other parent shall not be monitored by or interrupted by the other parent. "Electronic communication" includes telephones, electronic mail or e-mail, webcams, video-conferencing equipment and software or other wired or wireless technologies or other means of communication to supplement face to face contact.

The child(ren) may have _____ telephone ____ e-mail _____ other electronic communication in the form of ________________________ with the other parent: (Choose only **one**)

a.____ Anytime
b.____ Every day during the hours of _________________ to _______________________.
c.____ On the following days____
during the hours of _______________________ to _______________________.
d.____ Other: ____.

3. **Costs of Electronic Communication** shall be addressed as follows:
____
____
____

J. **CHANGES OR MODIFICATIONS OF THE PARENTING PLAN**

Temporary changes may be made informally without a written document. When the parents do not agree, the Parenting Plan remains in effect until further order of the court.

Any substantial changes to the Parenting Plan must be sought through the filing of a supplemental petition for modification.

K. **DISPUTES OR CONFLICT RESOLUTION**

Parents shall attempt to cooperatively resolve any disputes which may arise over the terms of the Parenting Plan. The parents may wish to use mediation or other dispute resolution methods and assistance, such as Parenting Coordinators and Parenting Counselors, before filing a court action.

SECTION III: CHILD SUPPORT AND INSURANCE

A. If the requested modification is granted, the parties:

1._____ agree that child support should be modified, consistent with the modification of the time-sharing schedule
2.____ agree that child support will NOT be modified.

Florida Supreme Court Approved Family Law Form 12.950(a), Agreement for Relocation with Minor Child(ren) (03/15)

B. The ____ Mother ____ Father (hereinafter "Obligor") will pay child support, under Florida's child support guidelines, section 61.30, Florida Statutes, to the other parent. The Child Support Guidelines Worksheet, Florida Family Law Rules of Procedure Form 12.902(e), is completed and attached.

This parent shall be obligated to pay child support at the rate of $____________, per month for the ______children *{number of parties' minor or dependent children}* beginning *{month, day, year}* ____________________ and terminating ____________________*{month, day, year}*. Child support shall be paid in the amount of $____________ per ____________*{week, month, other}*, which is consistent with the Obligor's current payroll cycle.

Upon the termination of the obligation of child support for one of the parties' children, child support in the amount of $________________ for the remaining_________ children *{total number of remaining children}* shall be paid beginning ___________________ *{month, day, year}* and terminating ______________________ *{month, day, year}*. This child support shall be paid in the amount of $________________ per _____________ *{week, month, other}* consistent with the Obligor's current payroll cycle.

{Insert schedule for the child support obligation, including the amount, and commencement and termination dates, for the remaining minor or dependent children, which shall be payable as the obligation for each child ceases. Please indicate whether the schedule either______ appears below or______ is attached as part of this form.

The Obligor shall pay child support until all the minor or dependent children: reach the age of 18, become emancipated, marry, die, joins the armed services; or become self-supporting; or until further order of the court or agreement of the parties. The child support obligation shall continue beyond the age of 18, and until high school graduation for any child who is: dependent in fact; between the ages of 18 and 19; and is still in high school, performing in good faith with a reasonable expectation of graduation before the age of 19.

If the child support amount above deviates from the guidelines by 5% or more, explain the reason(s) here:

____
____
____.

C. **Child Support Arrearage.** There currently is a child support arrearage of $ ____________ for retroactive child support and/or $______________ for previously ordered unpaid child support. The total of $ ______________ in child support arrearage shall be repaid at the rate of $ _______________every ____ week ____ other week ____ month, beginning *{date}* ________________, until paid in full including statutory interest.

D. **Health Insurance.**

1.____The ____ Mother ____ Father will maintain health insurance for the parties' minor child(ren). The party providing health insurance will provide insurance cards to the other party showing coverage.

OR

2.____ Health insurance is either not reasonable in cost or accessible to the child(ren) at this time. Any uninsured/ unreimbursed medical costs for the minor child(ren) shall be assessed as follows:
a.____Shared equally by both parents.
b.____Prorated according to the child support guideline percentages.
c.____Other *{explain}*: ____

As to these uninsured/unreimbursed medical expenses, the party who incurs the expense shall submit a request for reimbursement to the other party within 30 days, and the other party, within 30 days of receipt, shall submit the applicable reimbursement for that expense, according to the schedule of reimbursement set out in this paragraph.

E. **Dental Insurance.**
1.____The ____ Mother ____ Father will maintain dental insurance for the parties' minor child(ren). The party providing dental insurance will provide insurance cards to the other party showing coverage.

OR

2.____ Dental insurance is either not reasonable in cost or available to the children at this time. Any uninsured/unreimbursed dental costs for the minor child(ren) shall be assessed as follows:
d.______Shared equally by both parents.
e.______Prorated according to the child support guideline percentages.
f. ______Other *{explain}*:
____

As to these uninsured/unreimbursed dental expenses, the party who incurs the expense shall submit a request for reimbursement to the other party within 30 days, and the other party, within 30 days of receipt, shall submit the applicable reimbursement for that expense, according to the schedule of reimbursement set out in this paragraph.

F. **Life Insurance.**
The ____ Mother ____ Father shall be required to maintain life insurance coverage for the benefit of the parties' minor child(ren) in the amount of $ ________________ until the youngest child turns 18, becomes emancipated, marries, joins the armed services, or dies.

SECTION IV: OTHER
____
____
____

Florida Supreme Court Approved Family Law Form 12.950(a), Agreement for Relocation with Minor Child(ren) (03/15)

____

____

I certify that I have been open and honest in entering into this relocation agreement. I am satisfied with this agreement and intend to be bound by it.

Dated: ____________________

____
Signature of Mother

Printed Name: ____________________
Address: ____________________
City, State, Zip: ____________________
Telephone Number: ____________________
Fax Number: ____________________
Designated E-mail Address(es): ____________________
____

STATE OF FLORIDA
COUNTY OF ____________________

Sworn to or affirmed and signed before me on __________ by____________________.

____
NOTARY PUBLIC or DEPUTY CLERK

____
[Print, type, or stamp commissioned name of notary or deputy clerk.]

____ Personally known
____ Produced identification
____ Type of identification produced ____________________

I certify that I have been open and honest in entering into this relocation agreement. I am satisfied with this agreement and intend to be bound by it.

Dated: ______________________ ______________________________
Signature of Father

Printed Name: ______________________
Address: ______________________
City, State, Zip: ______________________
Telephone Number: ______________________
Fax Number: ______________________
Designated E-mail Address(es): ______________________
____

STATE OF FLORIDA
COUNTY OF ______________________

Sworn to or affirmed and signed before me on __________ by ______________________.

____
NOTARY PUBLIC or DEPUTY CLERK

____
[Print, type, or stamp commissioned name of notary or deputy clerk.]

____ Personally known
____ Produced identification
____ Type of identification produced ______________________

IF A NONLAWYER HELPED YOU FILL OUT THIS FORM, HE/SHE MUST FILL IN THE BLANKS BELOW: [fill in all blanks]
This form was prepared for the: *{choose only one}* _______Mother ______Father.
This form was completed with the assistance of:
{name of individual} ______________________,
{name of business} ______________________,
{address} ______________________,
{city} ____________, *{state}*___, *{zip code}* _________,*{telephone number}* ______________.

Florida Supreme Court Approved Family Law Form 12.950(a), Agreement for Relocation with Minor Child(ren) (03/15)

INSTRUCTIONS FOR FLORIDA SUPREME COURT APPROVED FAMILY LAW FORM 12.950(a) AGREEMENT FOR RELOCATION WITH MINOR CHILD(REN) (03/15)

When should this form be used?

This form should be used when the parents and every other person entitled to access to, visitation, or time-sharing with the minor child(ren) are in agreement and are asking the court to permit the relocation of the child(ren)'s principal residence. "Other Person" means an individual who is not the parent, but with whom the child resides pursuant to court order, or who has the right of access to, time-sharing with, or visitation with the child(ren). This form can be used at any time after either a petition or supplemental petition to relocate has been filed and the parties reach an agreement; OR can be used when the parties are in agreement and there is an existing cause of action, judgment, or decree of record pertaining to the child(ren)'s residence or time-sharing schedule. Either an agreement for relocation or a petition to relocate is required when:

1. You plan to relocate the child(ren)'s residence more than 50 miles from the child(ren)'s principal residence at the time of the last order which established or modified either a Parenting Plan or time-sharing schedule or at the time of filing of the pending action.
2. The court has not already entered an order granting permission to relocate.
3. The relocation will be for a period of 60 consecutive days or more, not including any absence for purposes of vacation, education, or health care for the child(ren).
4. Your order or final judgment defining custody, primary residence, the Parenting Plan, or time-sharing was entered before October 1, 2009 and the order does not expressly govern the relocation of the child(ren); or was entered on or after October 1, 2009, or your case was pending on October 1, 2009.
5. If the visitation or time-sharing schedule will change due to the relocation, a Parenting Plan with a time-sharing schedule must be included with the Agreement. Regardless of whether there is an agreement, the court reserves jurisdiction to modify issues relating to the minor child(ren).

This form should be typed or printed in black ink. **You must fill in all sections of the form.** If you are an "other person" entitled to access, visitation, or time-sharing with the child(ren), substitute your name for Mother or Father in the form and "parties" for "parents." After completing the form, you should sign the form before a notary public or deputy clerk.

IMPORTANT INFORMATION REGARDING E-FILING

The Florida Rules of Judicial Administration now require that all petitions, pleadings, and documents be filed electronically except in certain circumstances. **Self–represented litigants may file petitions or other pleadings or documents electronically; however, they are not required to do so.** If you choose to file your pleadings or other documents electronically, you must do so in accordance with Florida Rule of Judicial Administration 2.525, and you must follow the procedures of the judicial circuit in which you file. **The rules and procedures should be carefully read and followed.**

What should I do next?

For your case to proceed, you must properly notify the court by filing the original of the Agreement and a **Motion for Order Permitting Relocation by Agreement**, Florida Supreme Court Approved Family Law Form, 12.950 (b), with the clerk of the circuit court of one of the following: the circuit court which has jurisdiction in accordance with the Uniform Child Custody Jurisdiction and Enforcement Act; the circuit court in the county in which either parent and the child(ren) reside; or the circuit court in which the original action was adjudicated. If the order was entered in another state, or if the child(ren) live(s) in another state, you should speak with an attorney about where to file this form. You should file the original with the clerk of the circuit court and keep a copy for your records.

If the issue of the child(ren)'s physical residence is already before the court in an ongoing proceeding or through a judgment issued by the court, the court may enter an order adopting the Agreement without holding a hearing once both parties have signed it and neither has requested a hearing. When a hearing is not timely requested, the court shall presume that relocation is in the best interest of the child(ren) and may adopt the Agreement without holding a hearing.

If one or more of the parties to the Agreement timely requests a hearing in writing within 10 days after the date the Agreement is filed with the court, then you must notify the other party(ies) of the hearing by using a **Notice of Hearing (General)**, Florida Supreme Court Approved Family Law Form 12.923, or other appropriate notice of hearing form. The court will then enter an order after the hearing.

IMPORTANT INFORMATION REGARDING E–SERVICE ELECTION

After the initial service of process of the petition or supplemental petition by the Sheriff or certified process server, the Florida Rules of Judicial Administration now require that all documents required or permitted to be served on the other party must be served by electronic mail (e–mail) except in certain circumstances. **You must strictly comply with the format requirements set forth in the Rules of Judicial Administration.**

SELF–REPRESENTED LITIGANTS MAY SERVE DOCUMENTS BY E–MAIL; HOWEVER, THEY ARE NOT REQUIRED TO DO SO. If a self-represented litigant elects to serve and receive documents by e-mail, the procedures must always be followed once the initial election is made.

To serve and receive documents by e-mail, you must designate your e-mail addresses by using the **Designation of Current Mailing and E–mail Address**, Florida Supreme Court Approved Family Law Form 12.915, and you must provide your e-mail address on each form on which your signature appears. Please **CAREFULLY** read the rules and instructions for: **Certificate of Service (General)**, Florida Supreme Court Approved Family Law Form 12.914; **Designation of Current Mailing and E–mail Address**, Florida Supreme Court Approved Family Law Form 12.915; and Florida Rule of Judicial Administration 2.516.

Where can I look for more information?

Before proceeding, you should read "General Information for Self–Represented Litigants" found at the beginning of these forms. The words that are in "**bold underline**" in these instructions are defined there. For further information, see chapter 61, Florida Statutes.

If your case involves a modification of any provision relating to child support, you should also check with the clerk of the circuit court in the county in which you are filing this Agreement for Relocation to determine if any other forms must be filed.

If the parties agree to a modification of child support, the following forms should be filed with this Agreement:

- A Child Support Guidelines Worksheet, Florida Family Law Rules of Procedure Form 12.902(e),
- A completed Family Law Financial Affidavit, Florida Family Law Rules of Procedure Form 12.902(b) or (c).
- A completed Uniform Child Custody Jurisdiction and Enforcement Act (UCCJEA) Affidavit, Florida Supreme Court Approved Family Law Form 12.902(d).

Special notes . . .

The Agreement for Relocation with Minor Children must contain a **Parenting Plan** with a **time–sharing schedule**. At a minimum, the Parenting Plan must describe in adequate detail:

- How the parties will share and be responsible for the daily tasks associated with the upbringing of the child(ren),
- The time-sharing schedule that specifies the time that the minor child(ren) will spend with each parent and every other person entitled to access or time-sharing,
- A designation of who will be responsible for any and all forms of health care, school-related matters, including the address to be used for school-boundary determination and registration, and any other activities,
- The methods and technologies that the parents will use to communicate with the child(ren), and

- Any transportation arrangements related to access or time-sharing.

The best interests of the child(ren) is the primary consideration in the Parenting Plan. In creating the Parenting Plan, all circumstances between the parties, including the parties' historic relationship, domestic violence, and other factors must be taken into consideration. Determination of the best interests of the child(ren) shall be made by evaluating all of the factors affecting the welfare and interest of the particular minor child(ren) and the circumstances of the family as listed in s. 61.13(3), Florida Statutes.

This standard form does not include every possible issue that may be relevant to the facts of your case. The Parenting Plan should be as detailed as possible to address the time-sharing schedule. Additional provisions should be added to address all of the relevant factors. The parties should give special consideration to the age and needs of each child.

The Parenting Plan and time-sharing schedule may be set forth in the body of the Agreement for Relocation with Minor Children or may be attached as a separate document. You may attach a **Relocation/Long–Distance Parenting Plan**, Florida Supreme Court Approved Family Law Form 12.995(c), or similar form.

In developing the Parenting Plan, you may wish to consult or review other materials which are available at your local library, law library or through national and state family organizations.

Nonlawyer . . . Remember, a person who is NOT an attorney is called a nonlawyer. If a nonlawyer helps you fill out these forms, that person must give you a copy of a **Disclosure from Nonlawyer**, Florida Family Law Rules of Procedure Form 12.900(a), before he or she helps you. A nonlawyer helping you fill out these forms **must** put his or her name, address, and telephone number on the bottom of the last page of every form he or she helps you complete.

Added Sept. 30, 2010 (55 So.3d 381). Amended March 26, 2015, effective March 26, 2015 (2015 WL 1343088).

Form 12.950(b). Agreement for Relocation with Minor Child(ren)___ Including or ___ Not Including Modification of Child Support

IN THE CIRCUIT COURT OF THE ________________ JUDICIAL CIRCUIT,
IN AND FOR ________________________ COUNTY, FLORIDA

Case No: ____________________
Division: ____________________

____,
Petitioner,

And

____,
Respondent.

MOTION FOR ORDER PERMITTING RELOCATION WITH AGREEMENT

We, ____ Father, *{full legal name}*
____, Mother, *{full legal name}* and/or
____________________________________ *{full legal name}* of Other Person entitled to Access or Time-Sharing with child(ren), being sworn, certify that the following information is true: *{fill in all blanks}*

1. We are asking the Court to permit relocation of the minor child(ren) to a residence at least 50 miles from the child(ren)'s principal place of residence at the time of entry of the last order establishing or modifying time-sharing, or at the time of filing of the pending action.

2. There is an existing cause of action, judgment, decree of record pertaining the child(ren)'s residence or time-sharing schedule.

3. **WE CONSENT TO THE RELOCATION OF THE MINOR CHILD(REN)** to the following address:
____.

4. The dependent or minor child(ren) is (are):
Name(s) Birth Date(s)
____
____
____
____
____

5. **Agreement.** A written **Agreement for Relocation with Minor Child(ren)**, Florida Supreme Court Approved Family Law Form 12.950(a) or similar form, is filed with this motion which reflects consent to the relocation; defines an access or time-sharing schedule for the nonrelocating parent and any other persons who are entitled to access or time-sharing; and describes, if necessary, any transportation arrangements related to access or time-sharing.

6. The specific reasons for the proposed relocation of the child(ren) are:__________________________________
____

____
____
____
____

Attach additional sheets if necessary.

7. This modification is in the best interests of the child (ren) because: *{explain}* ________________
____
____
____
____

8. **Hearing.** We seek ratification of the agreement by court order: *{choose only **one**}*
a.____ With hearing
b.____ Without hearing

9. A completed Uniform Child Custody Jurisdiction and Enforcement Act (UCCJEA) Affidavit, Florida Supreme Court Approved Family Law Form 12.902(d), is filed with this Agreement.

10. If not previously filed in this case, a completed Notice of Social Security Number, Florida Supreme Court Approved Family Law Form 12.902(j), is filed with this Agreement.

I understand that I am swearing or affirming under oath to the truthfulness of the claims made in this motion and that the punishment for knowingly making a false statement includes fines and/or imprisonment.

Dated: ______________________

____
Signature of PETITIONER

Printed Name: ______________________
Address: ______________________
City, State, Zip: ______________________
Telephone Number: ______________________
Fax Number: ______________________
Designated E-mail Address(es): ______________________
____

STATE OF FLORIDA
COUNTY OF ____________

Sworn to or affirmed and signed before me on ________ by ______________________.

____
NOTARY PUBLIC or DEPUTY CLERK

____
[Print, type, or stamp commissioned name of notary or deputy clerk.]

____ Personally known
____ Produced identification
____ Type of identification produced ______________________

I understand that I am swearing or affirming under oath to the truthfulness of the claims made in this motion and that the punishment for knowingly making a false statement includes fines and/or imprisonment.

Dated: ______________________ ______________________________________

Signature of RESPONDENT

Printed Name: ______________________
Address: ______________________
City, State, Zip: ______________________
Telephone Number: ______________________
Fax Number: ______________________
Designated E-mail Address(es) ______________________
____

STATE OF FLORIDA
COUNTY OF ______________________

Sworn to or affirmed and signed before me on __________ by______________________.

____
NOTARY PUBLIC or DEPUTY CLERK

____
[Print, type, or stamp commissioned name of notary or deputy clerk.]

_____ Personally known
_____ Produced identification
_____ Type of identification produced ______________________

IF A NONLAWYER HELPED YOU FILL OUT THIS FORM, HE/SHE MUST FILL IN THE BLANKS BELOW:
[fill in **all** blanks] This form was prepared for the: *{choose only* ***one****}* ____Petitioner ____Respondent
This form was completed with the assistance of:
{name of individual ______________________________________,
{name of business} ______________________________________,
{address} ______________________________________,
{city} ______________,*{state}*____, *{zip code}* __________,*{telephone number}* __________.

INSTRUCTIONS FOR FLORIDA SUPREME COURT APPROVED FAMILY LAW FORM 12.950(b) MOTION FOR ORDER PERMITTING RELOCATION BY AGREEMENT (03/15)

When should this form be used?

This form should be used when the parents and every other person entitled to access to, visitation, or time-sharing with the minor child(ren) are in agreement and are asking the court to permit the relocation of the child(ren). "Other Person" means an individual who is not the parent, but with whom the child resides pursuant to court order, or who has the right of access to, time-sharing with, or visitation with the child(ren). You may file a Motion for Order Permitting Relocation with Agreement if the following are true:

- One of the parents or a person entitled to access to or time-sharing with the children wishes to relocate the child(ren) to a residence more than 50 miles from the child(ren)'s principal place of residence at the time of the last order establishing or modifying time-sharing or at time of filing of the pending action.
- There is an existing cause of action, judgment, or decree of record pertaining to the child(ren)'s residence or time sharing schedule.
- The parents and every other person entitled to access to or time-sharing with the children have signed a written agreement, **Agreement for Relocation with Minor Child(ren),** Florida Supreme Court Approved Family Law Form, 12.950(a), or similar form which:

1. Reflects the consent to the relocation;
2. Defines an access or time-sharing schedule for the non-relocating parent and any other persons who are entitled to access or time-sharing; and
3. Describes, if necessary, any transportation arrangements related to access or time-sharing.

- Your order regarding custody, primary residence, the parenting plan, time-sharing, or access to or with the child(ren) was entered before October 1, 2009 and the order does not expressly govern the relocation of the child(ren); was entered on or after October 1, 2009; or your case was pending on October 1, 2009.

This form should be typed or printed in black ink. **You must fill in all sections of the form**. If you are an "other person" entitled to access, visitation, or time-sharing with the child(ren), substitute your name for Mother or Father in the form. After completing the form, you should sign the form before a **notary public** or **deputy clerk.** You should **file** the form in the county where the original order or judgment was entered. If the order or judgment was entered in another state, or if the child(ren) live(s) in another state, you should speak with an **attorney** about where to file this form.

IMPORTANT INFORMATION REGARDING E–FILING

The Florida Rules of Judicial Administration now require that all petitions, pleadings, and documents be filed electronically except in certain circumstances. **Self–represented litigants may file petitions or other pleadings or documents electronically; however, they are not required to do so.** If you choose to file your pleadings or other documents electronically, you must do so in accordance with Florida Rule of Judicial Administration 2.525, and you must follow the procedures of the judicial circuit in which you file. **The rules and procedures should be carefully read and followed.**

IMPORTANT INFORMATION REGARDING E–SERVICE ELECTION

After the initial service of process of the petition or supplemental petition by the Sheriff or certified process server, the Florida Rules of Judicial Administration now require that all documents required or permitted to be served on the other party must be served by electronic mail (e–mail) except in certain circumstances. **You must strictly comply with the format requirements set forth in the Rules of Judicial Administration.**

SELF–REPRESENTED LITIGANTS MAY SERVE DOCUMENTS BY E–MAIL; HOWEVER, THEY ARE NOT REQUIRED TO DO SO. If a self-represented litigant elects to serve and receive documents by e-mail, the procedures must always be followed once the initial election is made.

To serve and receive documents by e-mail, you must designate your e-mail addresses by using the **Designation of Current Mailing and E-mail Address**, Florida Supreme Court Approved Family Law Form 12.915, and you must provide your e-mail address on each form on which your signature appears. Please **CAREFULLY** read the rules and instructions for: **Certificate of Service (General)**, Florida Supreme Court Approved Family Law Form 12.914; **Designation of Current Mailing and E-mail Address**, Florida Supreme Court Approved Family Law Form 12.915; and Florida Rule of Judicial Administration 2.516.

What should I do next?

After completing this form, you should file the original with the **clerk of the circuit court** where there is an existing cause of action, judgment, or decree of record pertaining to the child(ren)'s residence or time-sharing schedule and keep a copy for your records. The original Agreement for Relocation with Minor Child(ren) should be attached to Motion or filed with the clerk of the circuit court at the same time.

If both parties agree, the court may ratify the Agreement without the necessity of an evidentiary hearing. You should check with the clerk, family law intake staff, or judicial assistant for the proper way to submit the Motion and a proposed **Final Judgment/Supplemental Final Judgment Granting Relocation**, Florida Supreme Court Approved Family Law Form 12.950(i), to the judge. If one or more of the parties to the Agreement timely requests a hearing in writing within 10 days after the date the Agreement is filed with the court, then you must notify the other party(ies) of the hearing by using a **Notice of Hearing (General)**, Florida Supreme Court Approved Family Law Form 12.923, or other appropriate notice of hearing form. The court will then enter an order after hearing. If a hearing is not timely requested, the court shall presume that relocation is in the best interest of the child(ren) and may ratify the Agreement without an evidentiary hearing.

Where can I look for more information?

Before proceeding, you should read "General Information for Self-Represented Litigants" found at the beginning of these forms. The words that are in **"bold underline"** in these instructions are defined there. For further information, see chapter 61, Florida Statutes.

If your case involved a modification of any provision relating to child support, you should also check with the clerk of the circuit court in the county in which you are filing the Motion for Order Permitting Relocation with Minor Child(ren) and Agreement for Relocation with Minor Child(ren) to determine if any other forms must be filed.

Nonlawyer ... Remember, a person who is NOT an attorney is called a nonlawyer. If a nonlawyer helps you fill out these forms, that person must give you a copy of a **Disclosure from Nonlawyer**, Florida Family Law Rules of Procedure Former 12.900(a), before he or she helps you. A nonlawyer helping you fill out these forms **must** put his or her name, address, and telephone number on the bottom of the last page of every form he or she helps you complete.

Added Sept. 30, 2010 (55 So.3d 381). Amended March 26, 2015, effective March 26, 2015 (2015 WL 1343088).

Form 12.950(c). Petition for Dissolution of Marriage with Dependent or Minor Child(ren) and Relocation

IN THE CIRCUIT COURT OF THE ______________ JUDICIAL CIRCUIT,
IN AND FOR ______________ COUNTY, FLORIDA

Case No: ______________
Division: ______________

______________________________,
Husband,

And

______________________________,
Wife.

PETITION FOR DISSOLUTION OF MARRIAGE WITH DEPENDENT OR MINOR CHILD(REN) AND RELOCATION

I, *{full legal name}* ___, the
{Choose only one} ___ Husband ___ Wife, being sworn, certify that the following statements are true:

5. JURISDICTION/RESIDENCE
___ Husband ___ Wife ___ Both Spouses has/have lived in Florida for at least six (6) months before the filing of this Petition for Dissolution of Marriage.

6. The husband *{Choose only **one**}* ___ is ___ is not a member of the military service.
The wife *{Choose only **one**}* ___ is ___ is not a member of the military service.

7. MARRIAGE HISTORY
Date of marriage: *{month, day, year}*______________.
Place of marriage: *{city, county, state}*______________.
Date of separation: *{month, day, year}*______________ *(Please indicate if approximate)*.

8. DEPENDENT OR MINOR CHILD(REN)
*{Indicate **all** that apply}*
   c. ___ The wife is pregnant. Baby is due on: *{date}* ______________
   d. ___ The minor (under 18) child(ren) common to both parties are:

Name(s) **Birth Date(s)**
____
____
____
____
____

Florida Supreme Court Approved Family Law Form 12.950(c), Petition for Dissolution of Marriage with Dependent or Minor Child(ren) and Relocation (03/15)

e. _____The minor child(ren) born or conceived during the marriage who are **not** common to both parties are:

Name(s) **Birth Date(s)**

____

____

The birth father(s) of the above minor child(ren) is/are *{name(s) and address(es)}* ____________

____

____

f. ______ The child(ren) common to both parties who are 18 or older but who are dependent upon the parties due to a mental or physical disability are:

Name(s) **Birth Date(s)**

____

____

9. A completed **Family Law Financial Affidavit**, Florida Family Law Rules of Procedure Form 12.902(b) or (c) *{Choose only **one**}*____ has been filed or ____ will be filed.

10. A completed **Uniform Child Custody Jurisdiction and Enforcement Act (UCCJEA) Affidavit**, Florida Supreme Court Approved Family Law Form 12.902(d), is filed with this petition. (You **must** complete and attach this form in a dissolution of marriage with minor child(ren)).

11. A completed **Notice of Social Security Number**, Florida Supreme Court Approved Family Law Form 12.902(j), is filed with this petition.

12. This petition for dissolution of marriage should be granted because:
*{Choose only **one**}*

c. _____ The marriage is irretrievably broken.

d. _____ One of the parties has been adjudged mentally incapacitated for a period of 3 years prior to the filing of this petition. A copy of the Judgment of Incapacity is attached to this Petition.

SECTION I. MARITAL ASSETS AND LIABILITIES

*{Choose only **one**}*

3. _____ There are no marital assets or liabilities.

4. _____ There are marital assets or liabilities. All marital and nonmarital assets and liabilities are (or will be) listed in the financial affidavits, Florida Family Law Rules of Procedure Form 12.902(b) or (c), to be filed in this case.

*{Choose **all** that apply}*

a. _____ All marital assets and liabilities have been divided by a written agreement between the parties, which is attached, to be incorporated into the final judgment of dissolution of marriage. (The parties may use Marital Settlement Agreement for Dissolution of Marriage with Dependent or Minor Child(ren), Florida Supreme Court Approved Family Law Form 12.902(f)(1)).

b. _____ The Court should determine how the assets and liabilities of this marriage are to be distributed, under section 61.075, Florida Statutes.

c. _____Husband _______Wife should be awarded an interest in the other spouse's property because: ____
____
____
____.

SECTION II. SPOUSAL SUPPORT (ALIMONY)
*{Choose only **one**}*

1. _____ **Husband _____Wife forever gives up his/her right to spousal support (alimony) from the other spouse.**

2. _____ Husband _____Wife requests that the Court order the other spouse to pay the following spousal support (alimony) and claims that he or she has a need for the support that he or she is requesting **and that the other spouse has the ability to pay that support**. Spousal support (alimony) is requested in the amount of $__________ every _____ week _____ other week _____month, beginning *{date}*__________ and continuing until *{date or event}*
____.

Explain why the Court should order _____Husband _____Wife to pay and any specific request(s) for type of alimony (temporary, permanent, bridge-the-gap, durational, rehabilitative, and/or lump sum): ____
____
____
____
____
____
____.

{Indicate if applicable} _____ Husband _____Wife requests life insurance on the other spouse's life, provided by that spouse, to secure such support.

SECTION III. RELOCATION

1. The ____ Mother ____ Father seeks to relocate his/her residence to a place more than 50 miles from his/her place of residence at the time of filing of the Petition. The change of location is for a period of at least consecutive 60 days not including a temporary absence from the principal residence for purposes of vacation, education, or the provision of health care for the child(ren).

2. *{ If applicable}* The following other person is an individual who is not a parent but with whom the child resides pursuant to a court order, or who has the right of access to, time-sharing with, or visitation with the child(ren)____.

3. Pursuant to Section 61.13001(3), Florida Statutes, the following information is provided:

a. The location of the intended new residence, including the state, city, and physical address, if

known, is: ____
____
____

b. The mailing address of the new physical residence, if not the same as the physical address, is:
____
____
____

c. The home telephone number of the intended new residence, if known, is: ____________.

d. The date of the intended move or proposed relocation is: ____________________.

e. The specific reasons for the proposed relocation are:
____
____
____
____.

Attach additional sheets, if necessary.

f. One of the reasons for the proposed relocation is a job
____ Yes ____ No. A copy of the written job offer is attached to this Petition.

4. The relocation and time-sharing have been agreed to by the parties. *{Choose only one}* ____ Yes
____ No. If yes, attach a copy of the Agreement for Relocation to the Petition.

Failure to obtain an Order prior to the relocation renders the petition to relocate legally insufficient.

SECTION IV. PARENTING PLAN ESTABLISHING PARENTAL RESPONSIBILITY AND TIME-SHARING

1. The minor child(ren) currently reside(s) with ____ Mother ____ Father ____ Other Person: *{explain}* ____.

2. **Parental Responsibility.**
It is in the child(ren)'s best interests that parental responsibility be: *{Choose only one}*
c. ____ shared by both Father and Mother.

d. ____ awarded solely to ____ Father ____ Mother. Shared parental responsibility would be detrimental to the child(ren) because:____
____
____
____.

3. **Parenting Plan and Time-Sharing.**
It is in the best interests of the child(ren) that the family be ordered to comply with a Parenting Plan that ____ includes ____ does not include parental time-sharing with the child(ren). It is in the best interests of the child (ren) that:
{Choose only one}
a. ____ The attached proposed Parenting Plan should be adopted by the court. The parties:

_____ have _____ have **not** agreed to the Parenting Plan.

b. _____ The court should establish a Parenting Plan with the following provisions:
_____ No time-sharing for the ____ Father ____ Mother.
_____ Limited time-sharing with the ____ Father ____ Mother.
_____ Supervised Time-Sharing for the ____ Father ____ Mother.
_____ Supervised or third-party exchange of the child(ren).
____ Time-Sharing Schedule as follows:
____
____
____.

4. The proposed post-relocation transportation arrangements are as follows:
____
____
____
____
____.

5. Explain why the relocation time-sharing schedule is in the best interests of the child(ren):
____
____
____
____
____.

SECTION V. CHILD SUPPORT
{Indicate all that apply}

7. ____Husband ____Wife requests that the Court award child support as determined by Florida's child support guidelines, section 61.30, Florida Statutes. A completed Child Support Guidelines Worksheet, Florida Family Law Rules of Procedure Form 12.902(e), is, or will be filed. Such support should be ordered retroactive to:

d. ____ the date of separation *{date}* ____________
e. ____the date of the filing of this petition.
f. ____ other *{date}* ____________ *{explain}* ____________

8. ____ Husband _____Wife requests that the Court award child support to be paid beyond the age of 18 years because:

a. _____ the following child(ren): *{name(s)}* ____________________ is (are) dependent because of a mental or physical incapacity which began before the age of 18. *{explain}*____
____

b. _____ the following child(ren): *{name(s)}* ____________________ is (are) dependent in fact; is (are) in high school; between the ages of 18 and 19; and is (are) performing in good faith with reasonable expectation of graduation before the age of 19.

9. ____Husband _____Wife requests that the Court award a child support amount that is more than or less than Florida's child support guidelines. _____Husband _____Wife understands that Motion to Deviate from Child Support Guidelines, Florida Supreme Court Approved Family Law Form

12.943, **must** be filed before the court will consider this request.

10. ____Husband _____Wife requests that medical/dental insurance for the minor child(ren) be provided by:
*{Choose only **one**}*
c. ____ Father.
d. ____ Mother.

11. ____Husband _____Wife requests that uninsured medical/dental expenses for the child(ren) be paid: *{Choose only **one**}*
f. ____by Father.
g. ____by Mother.
h. ____by Father and Mother [each pay one-half].
i. ____according to the percentages in the Child Support Guidelines Worksheet, Florida Family Law Rules of Procedure Form 12.902(e).
j. ____Other *{explain}*: ____
____

12. ____Husband _____Wife requests that life insurance to secure child support be provided by:
a. ____Husband
b. ____Wife
c. ____Both.

SECTION VI. OTHER

3. *{If applicable}* _____Wife requests to be known by her former name, which was *{full legal name}*____.

4. Other relief *{specify}*:
____
____
____
____
____

SECTION VII. REQUEST (This section summarizes what you are asking the Court to include in the final judgment of dissolution of marriage.)

_____Husband _____Wife requests that the Court enter an order dissolving the marriage **and:**
*{Indicate **all** that apply}*

7. _____distribute marital assets and liabilities as requested in Section I of this petition;
8. _____award spousal support (alimony) as requested in Section II of this petition;
9. _____adopt or establish a Parenting Plan containing provisions for parental responsibility and time-sharing for the dependent or minor child(ren) common to both parties, as requested in Section IV of this petition;
10. _____permit relocation in accordance with Section III of this petition;
11. _____establish child support for the dependent or minor child(ren) common to both parties, as requested in Section V of this petition;
12. _____restore Wife's former name as requested in Section VI of this petition;

13. _____award other relief as requested in Section VI of this petition; and any other terms the Court deems necessary.

A RESPONSE TO THE PETITION OBJECTING TO THE RELOCATION MUST BE MADE IN WRITING, FILED WITH THE COURT, AND SERVED ON THE SPOUSE SEEKING TO RELOCATE WITHIN 20 DAYS AFTER SERVICE OF THIS PETITION TO RELOCATE. IF YOU FAIL TO TIMELY OBJECT TO THE RELOCATION, THE RELOCATION WILL BE ALLOWED, UNLESS IT IS NOT IN THE BEST INTERESTS OF THE CHILD, WITHOUT FURTHER NOTICE AND WITHOUT A HEARING.

The Response is in the form of an Answer and it must be sworn to under oath and must include the specific factual basis supporting the reasons for objecting to the relocation, including a statement of the amount of participation or involvement you currently have or have had in the life of the child(ren).

I understand that I am swearing or affirming under oath to the truthfulness of the claims made in this petition and that the punishment for knowingly making a false statement includes fines and/or imprisonment.

Dated: ________________________

____
Signature of _____ HUSBAND _____WIFE

Printed Name: ______________________________
Address: __________________________________
City, State, Zip: ____________________________
Telephone Number: __________________________
Fax Number: _______________________________
Designated E-mail Address(es):_______________

STATE OF FLORIDA
COUNTY OF ____________________

Sworn to or affirmed and signed before me on ____________ by______________________________.

____
NOTARY PUBLIC or DEPUTY CLERK

____
[Print, type, or stamp commissioned name of notary or deputy clerk.]

____ Personally known
____ Produced identification
____ Type of identification produced ____________________________

Florida Supreme Court Approved Family Law Form 12.950(c), Petition for Dissolution of Marriage with Dependent or Minor Child(ren) and Relocation (03/15)

IF A NONLAWYER HELPED YOU FILL OUT THIS FORM, HE/SHE MUST FILL IN THE BLANKS BELOW:
[fill in all blanks] This form was prepared for the _____Husband _____Wife
This form was completed with the assistance of:
{name of individual} ____,
{name of business} ____,
{address} ____,
{city} ______________,*{state}* ____, *{zip code}*__________,*{telephone number}* ________.

INSTRUCTIONS FOR FLORIDA SUPREME COURT APPROVED FAMILY LAW FORM 12.950(c), PETITION FOR DISSOLUTION OF MARRIAGE WITH DEPENDENT OR MINOR CHILD(REN) AND RELOCATION (03/15)

When should this form be used?

This form should be used when a husband or wife is filing for **dissolution of marriage,** there are dependent or minor children and pursuant to Section 61.13001, Florida Statutes:

1. You plan to relocate your residence more than 50 miles from the principal place of residence you have at the time of filing this petition; and

2. The change of location is for at least 60 consecutive days, not including a temporary absence from your principal place of residence for purposes of vacation, education or the provision of health care for the minor child(ren).

You and/or your **spouse** must have lived in Florida for at least 6 months before filing for dissolution of marriage in Florida.

This form should be typed or printed in black ink. After completing this form, you should sign the form before a **notary public** or **deputy clerk.** You should file the original with the **clerk of the circuit court** in the county where you live and keep a copy for your records.

IMPORTANT INFORMATION REGARDING E–FILING

The Florida Rules of Judicial Administration now require that all petitions, pleadings, and documents be filed electronically except in certain circumstances. **Self–represented litigants may file petitions or other pleadings or documents electronically; however, they are not required to do so.** If you choose to file your pleadings or other documents electronically, you must do so in accordance with Florida Rule of Judicial Administration 2.525, and you must follow the procedures of the judicial circuit in which you file. **The rules and procedures should be carefully read and followed.**

IMPORTANT INFORMATION REGARDING E–SERVICE ELECTION

After the initial service of process of the petition or supplemental petition by the Sheriff or certified process server, the Florida Rules of Judicial Administration now require that all documents required or permitted to be served on the other party must be served by electronic mail (e–mail) except in certain circumstances. **You must strictly comply with the format requirements set forth in the Rules of Judicial Administration.**

SELF–REPRESENTED LITIGANTS MAY SERVE DOCUMENTS BY E–MAIL; HOWEVER, THEY ARE NOT REQUIRED TO DO SO. If a self-represented litigant elects to serve and receive documents by e-mail, the procedures must always be followed once the initial election is made.

To serve and receive documents by e-mail, you must designate your e-mail addresses by using the **Designation of Current Mailing and E–mail Address**, Florida Supreme Court Approved Family Law Form 12.915, and you must provide your e-mail address on each form on which your signature appears. Please **CAREFULLY** read the rules and instructions for: **Certificate of Service (General),** Florida Supreme Court Approved Family Law Form 12.914; **Designation of Current Mailing and E–mail Address**, Florida Supreme Court Approved Family Law Form 12.915; and Florida Rule of Judicial Administration 2.516.

What should I do next?

For your case to proceed, you must properly notify your spouse and every other person entitled to access or time-sharing with the child(ren) of the petition. "Other Person" means an individual who is not the parent but with whom the child resides pursuant to court order, or who has the right of access to, time-sharing with, or visitation with the child(ren). If you know where he or she lives, you should use **personal service**. If you absolutely do not know where he or she lives, you may use **constructive service**. You may also be able to use constructive service if your spouse or the other person resides in another state or country. However, if constructive service is used, other than granting a divorce, the court may only grant limited relief. For more information on constructive service, see **Notice of Action for Dissolution of Marriage**, Florida Supreme Court Approved Family Law Form 12.913(a), and

Affidavit of Diligent Search and Inquiry, Florida Family Law Rules of Procedure Form 12.913(b). If your spouse is in the military service of the United States, additional steps for service may be required. See, for example, **Memorandum for Certificate of Military Service,** Florida Supreme Court Approved Family Law Form 12.912(a). In sum, the law regarding constructive service and service on an individual in the military service is very complex and you may wish to consult an attorney regarding these issues.

If personal service is used, the **respondent** has 20 days to answer after being served with your petition. Your case will then generally proceed in one of the following three ways:

DEFAULT. If after 20 days, your spouse has not filed an **answer**, you may file a **Motion for Default**, Florida Supreme Court Approved Family Law Form 12.922(a), with the clerk of court. Then, if you have filed all of the required papers, you may call the clerk, **family law intake staff**, or **judicial assistant** to set a **final hearing**. You must notify your spouse of the hearing by using a **Notice of Hearing (General)**, Florida Supreme Court Approved Family Law Form 12.923, or other appropriate notice of hearing form.

UNCONTESTED. If your spouse files an answer that agrees with everything in your petition or an answer and waiver, **and** you have complied with **mandatory disclosure** and filed all of the required papers, you may call the clerk, family law intake staff, or judicial assistant to set a final hearing. You must notify your spouse of the hearing by using a **Notice of Hearing (General)**, Florida Supreme Court Approved Family Law Form 12.923, or other appropriate notice of hearing form.

CONTESTED. If your spouse files an answer or an answer and **counterpetition**, which disagrees with or denies anything in your petition, **and** you are unable to settle the disputed issues, you should file a **Notice for Trial**, Florida Supreme Court Approved Family Law Form 12.924, after you have complied with mandatory disclosure and filed all of the required papers. Some circuits may require the completion of **mediation** before a final hearing may be set. You should contact the clerk, family law intake staff, or judicial assistant for instructions on how to set your case for trial (final hearing). If your spouse files an answer and counterpetition, you should answer the counterpetition within 20 days using an **Answer to Counterpetition**, Florida Supreme Court Approved Family Law Form 12.903(d).

Where can I look for more information?

Before proceeding, you should read "General Information for Self–Represented Litigants" found at the beginning of these forms. The words that are in **"bold underline"** in these instructions are defined there. For further information, see chapter 61, Florida Statutes.

Special notes . . .

If you do not have the money to pay the filing fee, you may obtain an Application for Determination of Civil Indigent Status from the clerk, fill it out, and the clerk will determine whether you are eligible to have filing fees deferred.

If you want to keep your address confidential because you are the victim of sexual battery, aggravated child abuse, aggravated stalking, harassment, aggravated battery, or domestic violence, do not enter the address, telephone, and fax information at the bottom of this form. Instead, file a **Request for Confidential Filing of Address**, Florida Supreme Court Approved Family Law Form 12.980(h).

With this form, you must also file the following:

- **Uniform Child Custody Jurisdiction and Enforcement Act (UCCJEA) Affidavit**, Florida Supreme Court Approved Family Law Form 12.902(d).
- **Child Support Guidelines Worksheet**, Florida Family Law Rules of Procedure Form 12.902(e), if you are asking that child support be ordered in the final judgment. (If you do not know your spouse's income, you may file this worksheet after his or her financial affidavit has been served on you.)
- **Affidavit of Corroborating Witness**, Florida Supreme Court Approved Family Law Form 12.902(i) OR photocopy of current Florida driver's license, Florida identification card, or voter's registration card (issue date of copied document must be at least six months before date case is actually filed with the clerk of the circuit court).
- **Marital Settlement Agreement for Dissolution of Marriage with Dependent or Minor Child(ren)**, Florida Supreme Court Approved Family Law Form 12.902(f)(1), if you and your spouse have reached an agreement on any or all of the issues.

- **Notice of Social Security Number**, Florida Supreme Court Approved Family Law Form 12.902(j).
- **Family Law Financial Affidavit**, Florida Family Law Rules of Procedure Form 12.902(b) or (c). (This must be filed with the petition if the petitioner seeks to establish child support. Otherwise, it must be filed within 45 days of service of the petition on the respondent.)
- **Certificate of Compliance with Mandatory Disclosure**, Florida Family Law Rules of Procedure Form 12.932. (This must be filed within 45 days of service of the petition on the respondent, if not filed at the time of the petition, unless you and your spouse have agreed not to exchange these documents.)
- **Parenting Plan**, Florida Supreme Court Approved Family Law Form 12.995(a), Safety–Focused Parenting Plan, Form 12.995(b), or Relocation/Long–Distance Parenting Plan, Form 12.995(c). If the parents have reached an agreement, a signed and notarized Parenting Plan should be attached. If the parents have not reached an agreement, a proposed Parenting Plan may be filed.

Updating Information. A parent or other person seeking to relocate has a continuing duty to provide current and updated information required by the relocation statute when that information becomes known.

Parenting Plan and Time–Sharing. If you and your spouse are unable to agree on parenting arrangements and a time-sharing schedule, a judge will decide for you as part of establishing a Parenting Plan. The judge will decide the parenting arrangements and time-sharing based on the child(ren)'s best interests. Regardless of whether there is an agreement, the court reserves jurisdiction to modify issues relating to the minor child(ren). The judge may request a **parenting plan recommendation** or appoint a **guardian ad litem** in your case. This means that a neutral person will review your situation and report to the judge concerning parenting issues. The purpose of such intervention is to be sure that the best interests of the child(ren) is (are) being served. For more information, you may consult section 61.13, Florida Statutes.

A **parenting course** must be completed prior to entry of the final judgment. You should contact the clerk, family law intake staff, or judicial assistant about requirements for parenting courses where you live.

Listed below are some terms with which you should become familiar before completing your petition. **If you do not fully understand any of the terms below or their implications, you should speak with an attorney before going any further.**

- **Shared Parental Responsibility**
- **Sole Parental Responsibility**
- **Supervised Time–Sharing**
- **No contact**
- **Parenting Plan**
- **Parenting Plan Recommendation**
- **Time–Sharing Schedule**

Child Support. The court may order one parent to pay **child support** to assist the other parent in meeting the child(ren)'s material needs. **Both parents are required to provide financial support**, but one parent may be ordered to pay a portion of his or her support for the child(ren) to the other parent. Florida has adopted guidelines for determining the amount of child support to be paid. These guidelines are based on the combined income of **both** parents and take into account the financial contributions of both parents. You must file a **Family Law Financial Affidavit**, Florida Family Law Rules of Procedure Form 12.902(b) or (c), and your spouse will be required to do the same. From your financial affidavits, you should be able to calculate the amount of child support that should be paid using the **Child Support Guidelines Worksheet**, Florida Family Law Rules of Procedure Form 12.902(e). Because the child support guidelines take several factors into consideration, change over time, and vary from state to state, your child support obligation may be more or less than that of other people in seemingly similar situations.

Alimony. Alimony may be awarded to a spouse if the judge finds that he or she needs it and that the other spouse has the ability to pay it. **If you want alimony, you must request it in**

writing in the original petition or counterpetition. If you do not request alimony in writing before the final hearing, it is waived (you may not request it later). You may request either **permanent alimony, bridge-the-gap alimony, durational alimony, lump sum alimony**, or **rehabilitative alimony**.

Marital/Nonmarital Assets and Liabilities. Florida law requires an **equitable distribution** of **marital assets** and **marital liabilities**. "Equitable" does not necessarily mean "equal." Many factors, including child support, time-sharing, and alimony awards, may lead the court to make an unequal (but still equitable) distribution of assets and liabilities. **Nonmarital assets** and **nonmarital liabilities** are those assets and liabilities which the parties agree or the court determines belong to, or are the responsibility of, only one of the parties. If the parties agree or the court finds an asset or liability to be nonmarital, the judge will not consider it when distributing marital assets and liabilities.

Temporary Relief. If you need temporary relief regarding temporary use of assets, temporary responsibility for liabilities, parental responsibility, relocation and time-sharing with child(ren), temporary child support, or temporary alimony, you may file a **Motion for Temporary Support and Time–Sharing with Dependent or Minor Child(ren)**, Florida Supreme Court Approved Family Law Form 12.947(a) and a **Motion for Temporary Relocation**, Florida Supreme Court Approved Family Law From 12.950(e). For more information, see the instructions for those forms.

Marital Settlement Agreement. If you and your spouse are able to reach an agreement on any or all of the issues, you should file a **Marital Settlement Agreement for Dissolution of Marriage with Dependent or Minor Child(ren)**, Florida Supreme Court Approved Family Law Form 12.902(f)(1). Both of you must sign this agreement before a **notary public** or **deputy clerk**. Any issues on which you are unable to agree will be considered **contested** and settled by the judge at the final hearing.

Parenting Plan. In all cases involving minor or dependent child(ren), a Parenting Plan shall be approved or established by the court. As you are seeking to relocate, the Parenting Plan must include a post-relocation schedule for access and time-sharing together with the necessary transportation arrangements. If you and your spouse have reached an agreement, you should file a **Parenting Plan**, Florida Supreme Court Approved Family Law Form 12.995(a), a **Safety–Focused Parenting Plan**, Florida Supreme Court Approved Family Law Form 12.995(b), or a **Relocation/Long–Distance Parenting Plan,** Florida Supreme Court Approved Family Law Form 12.995(c), which addresses the time-sharing schedule for the child(ren). If you have not reached an agreement, a proposed Parenting Plan may be filed. If the parties are unable to agree, a **Parenting Plan will be established by the court.**

Final Judgment Form. These family law forms contain a **Final Judgment of Dissolution of Marriage with Dependent or Minor Child(ren)**, Florida Supreme Court Approved Family Law Form 12.990(c)(1), which the judge may use if your case is contested. If you and your spouse reach an agreement on all of the issues, the judge may use a **Final Judgment of Dissolution of Marriage with Dependent or Minor Child(ren) (Uncontested)**, Florida Supreme Court Approved Family Law Form 12.990(b)(1). You should check with the clerk, family law intake staff, or judicial assistant to see if you need to bring a final judgment with you to the hearing. If so, you should type or print the heading, including the circuit, county, case number, division, and the parties' names, and leave the rest blank for the judge to complete at your hearing or trial.

Nonlawyer. Remember, a person who is NOT an attorney is called a nonlawyer. If a nonlawyer helps you fill out these forms, that person must give you a copy of a **Disclosure from Nonlawyer**, Florida Family Law Rules of Procedure Form 12.900(a), before he or she helps you. A nonlawyer helping you fill out these forms also **must** put his or her name, address, and telephone number on the bottom of the last page of every form he or she helps you complete.

Added Sept. 30, 2010 (55 So.3d 381). Amended March 26, 2015, effective March 26, 2015 (2015 WL 1343088).

Form 12.950(d). Supplemental Petition to Permit Relocation with Minor Child(ren)

IN THE CIRCUIT COURT OF THE ______________ JUDICIAL CIRCUIT,
IN AND FOR ______________________ COUNTY, FLORIDA

Case No: ______________
Division: ______________

______________________________,
Petitioner,

And

______________________________,
Respondent.

SUPPLEMENTAL PETITION TO PERMIT RELOCATION WITH MINOR CHILD(REN)

I, *{full legal name}* ______________________________, being sworn, certify that the following information is true:

1. The parties to this action were granted a final judgment of ____ dissolution of marriage ____ paternity on *{date}* ______________. A copy of the final judgment and any modification(s) is/are attached to this supplemental petition.

2. *{If applicable}* The following other person is an individual who is not a parent but with whom the child resides pursuant to court order, or who has the right of access to, time-sharing with, or visitation with the child(ren) ______________________________.

3. Paragraph(s) ______________ of the ____ final judgment or ____ most recent modification thereof describes the present custody, visitation, and/or time-sharing ordered.

4. The parties ______ have ______ have not reached an agreement on relocation. If yes, a copy of the agreement is attached to this supplemental petition.

5. The parties' dependent or minor child(ren) is (are):

Name	Birth Date

6. Since the final judgment or last modification thereof, there has been a substantial change in circumstances, requiring a modification of the present visitation or time-sharing schedule because I seek to relocate my principal residence at least 50 miles from my principal residence. Pursuant to Section 61.13001(3), Florida Statutes, the following information is provided:

a. The location of the intended new residence, including the state, city, and physical address, (if known), is:____

b. The mailing address of the new physical residence, if not the same as the physical address, is: ____

c. The home telephone number of the intended new residence, (if known), is: __________

d. The date of the intended move or proposed relocation is: ________________

7. The specific reasons for the proposed relocation are: ____.

Attach additional sheets if necessary.

8. One of the reasons for the proposed relocation is a job offer. *{Choose only **one**}* ____ Yes _____ No. The job offer is in writing. *{Choose only **one**}* _____ Yes _____ No. A copy of the written job offer is attached to this supplemental petition.

9. I ask the Court to modify access and time-sharing as follows: ____

10. This modification is in the best interests of the child(ren) because: *{explain}* ____.

11. If the requested modification is granted, Petitioner requests that child support be modified, consistent with the modification of visitation or time-sharing. A Child Support Guidelines Worksheet, Florida Family Law Rules of Procedure Form 12.902(e), is, or will be

filed. *{Choose only one}* _____ Yes _____ No.

12. I am requesting a temporary relief hearing to permit relocation prior to the final hearing. *{Choose only one}* _____ Yes _____ No. If yes, explain why you cannot wait for a final hearing date.
____
____
____
____.

Failure to obtain an Order prior to relocation renders the supplemental petition to relocate legally insufficient.

13. A completed **Family Law Financial Affidavit**, Florida Family Law Rules of Procedure Form 12.902(b) or (c), _____is, or _____will be, filed.

14. A completed **Uniform Child Custody Jurisdiction and Enforcement Act** (UCCJEA) Affidavit, Florida Supreme Court Approved Family Law Form 12.902(d), is filed with this petition.

15. If not previously filed in this case, a completed **Notice of Social Security Number,** Florida Supreme Court Approved Family Law Form 12.902(j), is filed with this petition.

16. Other: ____
____.

A RESPONSE TO THE SUPPLEMENTAL PETITION OBJECTING TO RELOCATION MUST BE MADE IN WRITING, FILED WITH THE COURT, AND SERVED ON THE PARENT OR OTHER PERSON SEEKING TO RELOCATE WITHIN 20 DAYS AFTER SERVICE OF THIS SUPPLEMENTAL PETITION TO RELOCATE. IF YOU FAIL TO TIMELY OBJECT TO THE RELOCATION, THE RELOCATION WILL BE ALLOWED, UNLESS IT IS NOT IN THE BEST INTERESTS OF THE CHILD, WITHOUT FURTHER NOTICE AND WITHOUT A HEARING.

A response is in the form of an Answer and it must be sworn to under oath and must include the specific factual basis supporting the reasons for objecting to the relocation, including a statement of the amount of participation or involvement you currently have or have had in the life of the child(ren).

I understand that I am swearing or affirming under oath to the truthfulness of the claims made in this petition and that the punishment for knowingly making a false statement includes fines and/or imprisonment.

Dated: ____________________ ______________________________
Signature of PETITIONER
Printed Name: ________________

Address:______________________
City, State, Zip:______________________
Telephone Number:______________________
Fax Number: ______________________
Designated E-mail Address(es):______________________

STATE OF FLORIDA
COUNTY OF ______________

Sworn to or affirmed and signed before me on __________ by ______________________.

____
NOTARY PUBLIC or DEPUTY CLERK

____
[Print, type, or stamp commissioned name of notary or deputy clerk.]

___ Personally known
___ Produced identification
___ Type of identification produced ______________________

IF A NONLAWYER HELPED YOU FILL OUT THIS FORM, HE/SHE MUST FILL IN THE BLANKS BELOW: [fill in all blanks] This form was prepared for the Petitioner.
This form was completed with the assistance of:
{name of individual} ______________________,
{name of business} ______________________,
{address} ______________________,
{city} ________,*{state}* ____, *{zip code}*______*{telephone number}* ________.

INSTRUCTIONS FOR FLORIDA SUPREME COURT APPROVED FAMILY LAW FORM 12.950(d) SUPPLEMENTAL PETITION TO PERMIT RELOCATION WITH MINOR CHILD(REN) (03/15)

When should this form be used?

This form should be used when you are asking the court to permit the relocation of the principal residence of the petitioner if:

1. You plan to relocate your residence more than 50 miles from your principal residence at the time of entry of the last order which established or modified primary residence, custody, visitation, or time-sharing;

2. The court has not entered an order granting permission to relocate.

3. The relocation will be for a period of 60 consecutive days or more, not including any absence for purposes of vacation, education, or health care for the child(ren).

4. Your order regarding custody, primary residence, visitation, time-sharing or parenting plan was entered before October 1, 2009 and the order does not expressly govern the relocation of the child(ren); was entered on or after October 1, 2006; or your case was pending on October 1, 2009.

This form should be typed or printed in black ink. **You must fill in all sections of the form.** After completing the form, you should sign the form before a **notary public** or **deputy clerk.** You should **file** this form in the county where the original order was entered. If the order was entered in another state, or if the child(ren) live(s) in another state, you should speak with an **attorney** about where to file this form. You should file the original with the **clerk of the circuit court** and keep a copy for your records.

IMPORTANT INFORMATION REGARDING E-FILING

The Florida Rules of Judicial Administration now require that all petitions, pleadings, and documents be filed electronically except in certain circumstances. **Self-represented litigants may file petitions or other pleadings or documents electronically; however, they are not required to do so.** If you choose to file your pleadings or other documents electronically, you must do so in accordance with Florida Rule of Judicial Administration 2.525, and you must follow the procedures of the judicial circuit in which you file. **The rules and procedures should be carefully read and followed.**

IMPORTANT INFORMATION REGARDING E-SERVICE ELECTION

After the initial service of process of the petition or supplemental petition by the Sheriff or certified process server, the Florida Rules of Judicial Administration now require that all documents required or permitted to be served on the other party must be served by electronic mail (e-mail) except in certain circumstances. **You must strictly comply with the format requirements set forth in the Rules of Judicial Administration.**

SELF-REPRESENTED LITIGANTS MAY SERVE DOCUMENTS BY E-MAIL; HOWEVER, THEY ARE NOT REQUIRED TO DO SO. If a self-represented litigant elects to serve and receive documents by e-mail, the procedures must always be followed once the initial election is made.

To serve and receive documents by e-mail, you must designate your e-mail addresses by using the **Designation of Current Mailing and E-mail Address**, Florida Supreme Court Approved Family Law Form 12.915, and you must provide your e-mail address on each form on which your signature appears. Please **CAREFULLY** read the rules and instructions for: **Certificate of Service (General),** Florida Supreme Court Approved Family Law Form 12.914; **Designation of Current Mailing and E-mail Address**, Florida Supreme Court Approved Family Law Form 12.915; and Florida Rule of Judicial Administration 2.516.

What should I do next?

For your case to proceed, you must properly notify the other parent and every other person entitled to, access, time-sharing, or visitation with the child(ren) in your case of the **supplemental petition**. "Other Person" means an individual who is not the parent but with whom the child resides pursuant to court order, or who has the right of access to, time-sharing with, or visitation with the child(ren). If you know where he or she lives, you should use **personal service**. If you absolutely do not know where he or she lives, you may use **constructive service**. You may also be able to use constructive service if the other party resides in another state or country. However, if constructive service is used, the court may only grant limited relief. For more information on constructive service, see **Notice of Action For**, Florida Supreme Court Approved Family Law Form 12.913(a)(2), and **Affidavit of Diligent Search and Inquiry**, Florida Family Law Rules of Procedure Form 12.913(b). If the other party is in the military service of the United States, additional steps for service may be required. See, for example, **Memorandum for Certificate of Military Service**, Florida Supreme Court Approved Family Law Form 12.912(a). The law regarding constructive service and service on an individual in the military service is very complex. If you have any questions about service, you may wish to consult an attorney regarding these issues.

If personal service is used, the other party has 20 days to **answer** after being served with your supplemental petition. Your case will then generally proceed in one of the following three ways:

DEFAULT . . . If after 20 days, no answer has been filed, you may file a **Motion for Default**, Florida Supreme Court Approved Family Law Form 12.922(a), with the clerk of court. Then, if you have filed all of the required papers, you may call the clerk, **family law intake staff**, or **judicial assistant** to set a **final hearing**. You must notify the other party of the hearing by using a **Notice of Hearing (General)**, Florida Supreme Court Approved Family Law Form 12.923, or other appropriate notice of hearing form.

UNCONTESTED . . . If the **respondent** files either an answer that agrees with everything in your supplemental petition or an answer and waiver, **and** you have complied with **mandatory disclosure** and filed all of the required papers, you may call the clerk, family law intake staff, or judicial assistant to set a final hearing. You must notify the other party of the hearing by using a **Notice of Hearing (General)**, Florida Supreme Court Approved Family Law Form 12.923, or other appropriate notice of hearing form.

CONTESTED . . . If the respondent files either an answer or an answer and **counterpetition**, which disagrees with or denies anything in your supplemental petition, **and** you are unable to settle the disputed issues, you should file a **Notice for Trial**, Florida Supreme Court Approved Family Law Form 12.924, after you have complied with mandatory disclosure and filed all of the required papers. Some circuits may require the completion of **mediation** before a final hearing may be set. Then you should contact the clerk, family law intake staff, or judicial assistant for instructions on how to set your case for **trial** (final hearing). If the respondent files an answer and counterpetition, you should answer the counterpetition within 20 days using an **Answer to Counterpetition**, Florida Supreme Court Approved Family Law Form 12.903(d).

Where can I look for more information?

Before proceeding, you should read "General Information for Self-Represented Litigants" found at the beginning of these forms. The words that are in "**bold underline**" in these instructions are defined there. For further information, see chapter 61, Florida Statutes.

Special notes . . .

If you do not have the money to pay the filing fee, you may obtain an Application for Determination of Civil Indigent Status from the clerk, fill it out, and the clerk will determine whether you are eligible to have filing fees deferred.

If there is a domestic violence case and you want to keep your address confidential for safety reasons, do not enter the address, telephone number, and fax information at the bottom of this form. Instead, file a **Request for Confidential Filing of Address**, Florida Supreme Court Approved Family Law Form 12.980(h).

With this form, you must also file the following:

- **Uniform Child Custody Jurisdiction and Enforcement Act (UCCJEA) Affidavit**, Florida Supreme Court Approved Family Law Form 12.902(d).
- **Child Support Guidelines Worksheet**, Florida Family Law Rules of Procedure Form 12.902(e). (If you do not know the other party's income, you may file this worksheet after his or her financial affidavit has been served on you.)

• **Agreement for Relocation,** if you have reached an agreement on any or all of the issues attach the proposed Agreement For Relocation with Minor Child(ren). Florida Supreme Court Approved Family Law 12.950(a). Both parties must sign this agreement before a **notary public**. Any issues on which you are unable to agree will be considered **contested** and settled by the judge at the final hearing.

• **Notice of Social Security Number**, Florida Supreme Court Approved Family Law Form 12.902(j), if not previously filed.

• **Family Law Financial Affidavit,** Florida Family Law Rules of Procedure Form 12.902(b) or (c).

• **Certificate of Compliance with Mandatory Disclosure**, Florida Family Law Rules of Procedure Form 12.932. (This must be filed within 45 days of **service** of the supplemental petition on the respondent, if not filed at the time of the supplemental petition, unless you and the other party have agreed not to exchange these documents.)

Updating Information. A parent or other person seeking to relocate has a continuing duty to provide current and updated information required by the relocation statute when that information becomes known.

Parenting and Time–Sharing ... If you and the other parent and every other person entitled to access to or time-sharing with the child(ren) are unable to agree on the parenting arrangements and a time-sharing schedule, a judge will decide for you as part of establishing a Parenting Plan. The judge will decide the parenting arrangements and a time-sharing schedule based upon the child(ren)'s best interests. Regardless of whether there is an agreement, the court reserves jurisdiction to modify issues relating to the minor child(ren).

Failure to obtain an Order prior to relocation renders the supplemental petition to relocate legally insufficient.

The judge may request a **parenting plan recommendation** or appoint a **guardian ad litem** in your case. This means that a neutral person will review your situation and report to the judge concerning parenting issues. The purpose of such intervention is to be sure that the best interests of the child(ren) is (are) being served. For more information, you may consult section 61.13, Florida Statutes.

If one has not already been completed, the court may require the completion of a **parenting course** before a final hearing is set. You should contact the clerk, family law intake staff, or judicial assistant about requirements for parenting courses or mediation where you live.

Child Support ... The court may order one parent to pay **child support** to assist the other parent in meeting the child(ren)'s material needs. **Both parents are required to provide financial support**, but one parent may be ordered to pay a portion of his or her support for the child(ren) to the other parent. Florida has adopted guidelines for determining the amount of child support to be paid. These guidelines are based on the combined income of **both** parents and take into account the financial contributions of both parents. You must file a **Family Law Financial Affidavit,** Florida Family Law Rules of Procedure Form 12.902(b) or (c), and the other parent will be required to do the same. From your financial affidavits, you should be able to calculate the amount of child support that should be paid using the **Child Support Guidelines Worksheet**, Florida Family Law Rules of Procedure Form 12.902(e). Because the child support guidelines take several factors into consideration, change over time, and vary from state to state, your child support obligation may be more or less than that of other people in seemingly similar situations.

Temporary Relief ... If you need temporary relief regarding relocation of the minor child(ren), complete paragraph eleven contained in the Supplemental Petition To Permit Relocation of Minor Child(ren).

Final Judgment Form ... These family law forms contain a **Final Judgment/Supplemental Final Judgment Permitting Relocation,** Florida Supreme Court Approved Family Law Form 12.950(i), which the judge may use. You should check with the clerk, family law intake staff, or judicial assistant to see if you need to bring it with you to the hearing. If so, you should type or print the heading, including the circuit, county, case number, division, and the parties' names, and leave the rest blank for the judge to complete at your hearing or trial.

Nonlawyer ... Remember, a person who is NOT an attorney is called a nonlawyer. If a nonlawyer helps you fill out these forms, that person must give you a copy of a **Disclosure**

from Nonlawyer, Florida Family Law Rules of Procedure Form 12.900(a), before he or she helps you. A nonlawyer helping you fill out these forms also **must** put his or her name, address, and telephone number on the bottom of the last page of every form he or she helps you complete.

Added Sept. 30, 2010 (55 So.3d 381). Amended March 26, 2015, effective March 26, 2015 (2015 WL 1343088).

Form 12.950(e). Motion for Temporary Order Granting Relocation

IN THE CIRCUIT COURT OF THE ________________ JUDICIAL CIRCUIT,
IN AND FOR __________________________ COUNTY, FLORIDA

Case No: ____________________
Division: ____________________

______________________________,
Petitioner,

And

______________________________,
Respondent.

MOTION FOR TEMPORARY ORDER GRANTING RELOCATION

The ____ Petitioner ____ Respondent requests that the Court enter a temporary order permitting relocation of the minor child(ren).

1. I have filed a Petition or a Supplemental Petition to Permit Relocation to the following:

a. The location of the intended new residence, including the state, city, and physical address, if known, is ____
____
____

b. The new principal residence is more than 50 miles from my principal place of residence at the time of the entry of the last order establishing or modifying time-sharing, or at the time of filing the pending action to establish or modify time-sharing. The change of location is at least 50 miles from that residence and is for at least 60 consecutive days.

c. The mailing address of the new physical residence, if not the same as the physical address, is:
____
____.

d. The home telephone number of the intended new residence, if known, is ______________.

e. The date of the intended move or proposed relocation is:________________________.

2. The dependent or minor child(ren) is (are):

Name	Birth Date

____
____

3. A petition or supplemental petition to relocate has been filed with the court and was served on the _____ Petitioner _____ Respondent _____ Other Person *{name}* ____________________ entitled to access or time-sharing with the child(ren) on ______________________________.

_____ A response objecting to the Relocation was filed
OR
_____ The time for filing a response has not passed as of the filing of this Motion.

4. The specific reasons for the proposed temporary relocation of the child(ren) are: ___________
____
____
____.
{Attach additional sheets if necessary.}

5. One of the reasons for the proposed temporary relocation is a job offer.
*{Choose **one** only}*_____Yes _____ No.
The job offer is in writing. *{Choose one only}* _____Yes _____No.
If yes, a copy of the written job offer is attached to this Motion.

6. I am requesting a temporary relief hearing to permit relocation and cannot wait for the final hearing because ____
____
____
____.

7. The temporary relocation is in the best interests of the child(ren) because: *{explain}* __________
____
____
____.

8. I ask the Court to temporarily establish or modify visitation or the time-sharing schedule as follows: *{explain}* ____
____
____
____.
____

9. *{Choose only **one**}* ____ Yes ____No. I ask the Court to temporarily modify child support, consistent with the modification of visitation or the time-sharing schedule. A Child Support Guidelines Worksheet, Florida Family Law Rules of Procedure Form 12.902(e), ____ is, or____ will be filed.

10. **Other Relief.** *{specify}*____
____
____
____

11. A completed Uniform Child Custody Jurisdiction and Enforcement Act (UCCJEA) Affidavit, Florida Supreme Court Approved Family Law Form 12.902(d), is filed with this motion or has already been filed with the Court.

12. A completed Family Law Financial Affidavit, Florida Family Law Rules of Procedure Form 12.902(b) or (c), is filed with this motion or has already been filed with the Court.

13. A completed Notice of Social Security Number, Florida Supreme Court Approved Family Law Form 12.902(j), is filed with this motion or has already been filed with the Court.

14. I request that the Court hold a hearing on this matter and grant the relief specifically requested and any other relief this Court may deem just and proper.

I certify that a copy of this document was ( ) mailed ( ) faxed and mailed ( ) e-mailed ( ) hand-delivered to the person(s) listed below on *{date}* ________________________________.

Other party or his/her attorney:
Name: ____
Address: ______________________________________
City, State, Zip: _________________________________
Fax Number: ____________________________________
Designated E-mail Address(es):_____________________
____

____
Signature of Party or his/her attorney
Printed Name: ________________________________
Address: ______________________________________
City, State, Zip: _________________________________
Telephone Number: ______________________________
Fax Number: ___________________________________
Designated E-mail Address(es):_____________________
____

IF A NONLAWYER HELPED YOU FILL OUT THIS FORM, HE/SHE MUST FILL IN THE BLANKS BELOW:
[fill in **all** blanks] This form was prepared for the *{choose only one}* ( ) Petitioner ( ) Respondent

Florida Supreme Court Approved Family Law Form 12.950(e), Motion for Temporary Order Granting Relocation (03/15)

This form was completed with the assistance of:
{name of individual} ____,
{name of business} ____,
{address} ____,
{city} ______________,*{state}* _____, *{zip code}*_________*{telephone number}* _____________.

INSTRUCTIONS FOR FLORIDA SUPREME COURT APPROVED FAMILY LAW FORM 12.950(e) MOTION FOR TEMPORARY ORDER GRANTING RELOCATION (03/15)

When should this form be used?

This form should be used when you have filed a Petition or Supplemental Petition to permit relocation of a child or children, or you are seeking relocation in a pending action. You should use this form to ask the court to permit a temporary relocation of the child(ren)'s principal residence, temporary modification of visitation or time-sharing, temporary modification of child support, and other relief before the court has had an opportunity to make a permanent decision on the question of relocation.

This form should be typed or printed in black ink. **You must fill in all sections of the form.** After completing this form, you should **file** the original with the **clerk of the circuit court** in the county where the Petition or Supplemental Petition for Modification to Permit Relocation with Minor Child(ren) was filed and keep a copy for your records.

IMPORTANT INFORMATION REGARDING E–FILING

The Florida Rules of Judicial Administration now require that all petitions, pleadings, and documents be filed electronically except in certain circumstances. **Self–represented litigants may file petitions or other pleadings or documents electronically; however, they are not required to do so.** If you choose to file your pleadings or other documents electronically, you must do so in accordance with Florida Rule of Judicial Administration 2.525, and you must follow the procedures of the judicial circuit in which you file. **The rules and procedures should be carefully read and followed.**

What should I do next?

A copy of this form, along with all of the other forms required with this motion, must be mailed, e-mailed, or hand-delivered to the other party in your case. When you have filed all of the required forms, you are ready to set a **hearing** on your motion. You should check with the clerk, **family law intake staff**, or **judicial assistant** for information on the local procedure for scheduling a hearing. When you know the date and time of your hearing, you should notify the other party using a **Notice of Hearing (General)**, Florida Supreme Court Approved Family Law Form 12.923, or other appropriate notice of hearing form.

IMPORTANT INFORMATION REGARDING E–SERVICE ELECTION

After the initial service of process of the petition or supplemental petition by the Sheriff or certified process server, the Florida Rules of Judicial Administration now require that all documents required or permitted to be served on the other party must be served by electronic mail (e–mail) except in certain circumstances. **You must strictly comply with the format requirements set forth in the Rules of Judicial Administration.**

SELF–REPRESENTED LITIGANTS MAY SERVE DOCUMENTS BY E–MAIL; HOWEVER, THEY ARE NOT REQUIRED TO DO SO. If a self-represented litigant elects to serve and receive documents by e-mail, the procedures must always be followed once the initial election is made.

To serve and receive documents by e-mail, you must designate your e-mail addresses by using the **Designation of Current Mailing and E–mail Address**, Florida Supreme Court Approved Family Law Form 12.915, and you must provide your e-mail address on each form on which your signature appears. Please **CAREFULLY** read the rules and instructions for: **Certificate of Service (General),** Florida Supreme Court Approved Family Law Form 12.914; **Designation of Current Mailing and E–mail Address**, Florida Supreme Court Approved Family Law Form 12.915; and Florida Rule of Judicial Administration 2.516.

Where can I look for more information?

Before proceeding, you should read "General Information for Self–Represented Litigants" found at the beginning of these forms. Words in "**bold underline**" in these instructions are defined there. For further information, see chapter 61, Florida Statutes.

Special notes . . .

If the temporary relocation of the child(ren) is approved, the court may require you to provide reasonable security, financial or otherwise, and guarantee that the court-ordered contact with the child(ren) will not be interrupted or interfered with by you.

If the relocation is not permitted and the child(ren) is/are relocated nevertheless, there could be serious consequences affecting the person violating the court order, including his or her parental responsibility and time-sharing or access with the child(ren)

With this form you must also file the following, **if not already filed**:

- **Uniform Child Custody Jurisdiction and Enforcement Act (UCCJEA) Affidavit**, Florida Supreme Court Approved Family Law Form 12.902(d).
- **Notice of Social Security Number**, Florida Supreme Court Approved Family Law Form 12.902(j).
- **Family Law Financial Affidavit**, Florida Family Law Rules of Procedure Form 12.902(b) or (c). (This must be filed within 45 days if not filed at the time of the petition.)
- **Child Support Guidelines Worksheet**, Florida Family Law Rules of Procedure Form 12.902(e), if you are asking for a temporary modification of child support. (If you do not know the other party's income, you may file this worksheet as soon as a copy of his or her financial affidavit has been served on you.)

Temporary Order . . . These family law forms contain a **Temporary Order Granting/Denying Relocation**, Florida Supreme Court Approved Family Law Form 12.950(f) which the judge may use. You should check with the clerk, family law intake staff, or judicial assistant to see if you need to bring it with you to the hearing. If so, you should type or print the heading, including the circuit, county, case number, division, and the parties' names, and leave the rest blank for the judge to complete at your hearing.

Nonlawyer. Remember, a person who is NOT an attorney is called a nonlawyer. If a nonlawyer helps you fill out these forms, that person must give you a copy of a **Disclosure from Nonlawyer**, Florida Family Law Rules of Procedure Form 12.900 (a), before he or she helps you. A nonlawyer helping you fill out these forms also **must** put his or her name, address, and telephone number on the bottom of the last page of every form he or she helps you complete.

Added Sept. 30, 2010 (55 So.3d 381). Amended March 26, 2015, effective March 26, 2015 (2015 WL 1343088).

Form 12.950(f). Temporary Order Granting/ Denying Relocation

IN THE CIRCUIT COURT OF THE __________ JUDICIAL CIRCUIT,
IN AND FOR ________________ COUNTY, FLORIDA

Case No:__________________
Division:_________________

____
Petitioner,

and

____
Respondent.

TEMPORARY ORDER GRANTING/ DENYING RELOCATION

The cause came before this Court for a hearing on a Motion for Temporary Order Permitting Relocation. The Court, having reviewed the file and heard the testimony, makes these findings of fact and ORDERS as follows:

SECTION I: FINDINGS

1. The Court has jurisdiction over the subject matter and the parties.

2. The last order establishing or modifying parental responsibility, visitation, or time-sharing was entered on *{date}*______________________.

3. The parties' dependent or minor child(ren) is/are:

Name	Birth Date

4. The ____ Petitioner ____ Respondent has filed a Motion for Temporary Order Permitting Relocation to *{address of intended new residence}*
____
____.

5. The new location is more than 50 miles from the principal place of residence at the time of the entry of the last order establishing or modifying the parenting plan or time-sharing schedule, or at the time of filing of the pending action, and the relocation is for a period of at least 60 consecutive days.

6. The other parent or person who is entitled to access, visitation, or time-sharing:

_____ has filed an Answer agreeing with the relocation;
_____ has filed an Answer objecting to the relocation;
_____ has failed to file a timely Answer.

SECTION II: GRANTING OF TEMPORARY ORDER PERMITTING RELOCATION
*[Please indicate **all** that apply]*

1. _____The Motion for Temporary Order Permitting Relocation is **GRANTED** as the Court finds: The petition to relocate was properly filed and is otherwise in compliance with the requirements of Section 61.13001(3), Florida Statutes;

AND

From an examination of the evidence presented at the preliminary hearing, there is a likelihood that at a final hearing the court will approve the relocation of the child, based upon the factors set forth in Section 61.13001(7), Florida Statutes.
Facts in support of finding:____
____
____
____

2. _____ **Security:** The Temporary Order Permitting Relocation ____ **IS** ____ **IS NOT** conditioned upon the ____ Petitioner ____ Respondent providing reasonable security by:
[If security is required, please indicate all that apply]
   a. _____ Posting bond in the amount of $______________ with the clerk of this Court;
   b. _____Providing:
   ____
   ____
   ____
   c. _____Guaranteeing that the court-ordered contact with the child(ren) will not be interrupted or interfered with by the relocating party by
   ____
   ____

3. _____ **Time-Sharing.** To ensure that the child(ren) has/have frequent, continuing, and meaningful contact, access, and time-sharing, the nonrelocating parent or person entitled to access shall have: *{Please choose only **one**}*

   a. _____ **reasonable time-sharing** with the parties' minor child(ren) after reasonable notice and as agreed to by the parties. The Court reserves jurisdiction to set a specific schedule;

   b. _____ the following **specified time-sharing** with the parties' minor child(ren):
   ____
   ____

____
____;

c. _____ **time-sharing** in accordance with the temporary **Parenting Plan** attached as Exhibit _____ and incorporated herein.

4. _____ **No Contact**. The _____ Petitioner _____ Respondent and/or _____ Other Person entitled to access or time-sharing shall have **no contact** with the parties' minor child(ren) until further court order, as such contact is detrimental to the welfare of the minor child(ren). *{Explain}*:
____
____
____

5. _____ **Communication** via telephone, Internet, web-cam, etc. with the parties' minor child(ren) subject to the following limitations *{if any}*____
____.

6. _____ **Exchange of Minor Child(ren)**. The exchange of the minor child(ren) shall be on time as scheduled by the parties. The following conditions, if checked below, shall also apply.

a. _____ The parties shall temporarily exchange the child(ren) at the following location(s):
____
____

b. _____ Other conditions for exchange of the child(ren) are as follows:
____
____

7. _____ **Costs of Transportation**

a. _____ The Petitioner shall pay ____% and the Respondent shall pay ____% of the post-relocation transportation costs.

b. _____ Other
____

8. _____ **Child Support.** The Court finds that based upon the Temporary Order Granting Relocation, the ____ Petitioner's____ Respondent's child support obligation should be temporarily modified in consideration of the costs of transportation and the respective net incomes of the parents. *[Please choose only **one**]*

a. _____ The amounts in the attached Child Support Guidelines Worksheet, Florida Family Law Rules of Procedure Form 12.902(e), filed by the _____ Petitioner _____ Respondent are correct.

OR

b. _____ The Court makes the following findings:
The Petitioner's net monthly income is $_______________.
The Respondent's net monthly income is $_______________.
Monthly child care costs are $_____________.
Monthly health/dental insurance costs are $_______________.
Transportation costs are $_________________.

9. _____ **Amount**. The Obligor's child support obligation shall be temporarily modified to $__________ per month payable _____ in accordance with Obligor's payroll cycle, and in any event, at least once a month _____ *{explain}* ____, commencing *{date}* ___________________ and continuing until further court order.

SECTION III: DENIAL OF TEMPORARY ORDER PERMITTING RELOCATION
*[Please indicate **all** that apply]*

1. _____The Motion for Temporary Order Permitting Relocation is **DENIED** because:

   a. _____The petition to relocate does not comply with subsection (3) of Section 61.13001, Florida Statutes;

   b. _____ The child(ren) has/have already been relocated without a written agreement of the parties or without court approval;

   c. _____ From an examination of the evidence presented at the preliminary hearing, there is a likelihood that upon final hearing, relocation of the child(ren) would not be approved.

   Facts in support of finding: ____
   ____
   ____.

2. _____ **Temporary Injunction Prohibiting Relocation of Child(ren)**
   The Court hereby temporarily prohibits and enjoins the _____ Petitioner _____ Respondent from relocating and removing the child(ren) from the jurisdiction of this Court during the pendency of this proceeding, or until further order of this Court.
   The Court may enforce compliance with this restraining order through civil and/or indirect criminal contempt proceedings, which may include arrest, incarceration, and/or the imposition of a fine.

3. _____ **Immediate Return of Child(ren)**
   The _____ Petitioner_____ Respondent has failed to comply with the relocation procedures set forth in Section 61.13001, Florida Statutes, and has relocated the child(ren) in violation of that section. The _____ Petitioner _____ Respondent **shall immediately return the child(ren)**

to the jurisdiction of this Court.

Failure to immediately return the child(ren) shall subject the non-complying party to contempt and other proceedings to compel return of the child(ren) and may be taken into account in any initial or post judgment action seeking a determination or modification of the parenting plan or time-sharing schedule.

SECTION IV: OTHER

1. Other Provisions: ____
____

2. The Court reserves jurisdiction to modify and enforce this Temporary Order regarding relocation.

3. Unless specifically modified by this Temporary Order, the provisions of all final judgments or orders remain in effect.

4. No weight shall be given to the decision to grant or deny the temporary relocation as a factor in reaching a final decision.

DONE AND ORDERED at ______________________, Florida, on ______________________.

____
CIRCUIT JUDGE

I certify that a copy of this Temporary Order Granting/Denying Relocation was ( ) mailed ( ) faxed and mailed ( ) e-mailed ( ) hand-delivered to the parties and any entities listed below on *{date}* ______________________

____
By: *{Clerk of court, designee, or Judicial Assistant}*

Florida Supreme Court Approved Family Law Form 12.950(f), Temporary Order Granting/Denying Relocation (03/15)

Petitioner (or his/her attorney)
Respondent (or his/her attorney)
Central Governmental Depository
Other:______________________

Florida Supreme Court Approved Family Law Form 12.950(f), Temporary Order Granting/Denying Relocation (03/15)

Added Sept. 30, 2010 (55 So.3d 381). Amended March 26, 2015, effective March 26, 2015 (2015 WL 1343088).

Form 12.950(g). Motion for Civil Contempt and/or Return of Child(ren)

IN THE CIRCUIT COURT OF THE ____________________ JUDICIAL CIRCUIT,
IN AND FOR ______________________________ COUNTY, FLORIDA

Case No: ________________________
Division: ________________________

_________________________________,
Petitioner,

And

_________________________________,
Respondent.

MOTION FOR CIVIL CONTEMPT AND/OR RETURN OF CHILD(REN)

_____ Petitioner _____ Respondent requests that the Court enter an order of civil contempt and/or an order for return of child(ren) against _____ Petitioner _____ Respondent because he/she has relocated with the parties' minor child(ren) or has taken other action with respect to relocation.

I. **NONCOMPLIANCE OR VIOLATION**

A. The other party in this case has willfully failed to comply with the: *{Choose only **one**}*

1.____ **Court order or judgment** entered on *{date}*______________________, by *{court, city, and state}*____.

____ Please indicate here if the judgment or order is not from this Court and attach a copy of the judgment or order to this motion.

2.____ **Written Agreement** of the parties.

3.____ **Relocation procedures** of Section 61.13001, Florida Statutes.

B. This order, judgment, agreement, or statute, required the other party in this case to do or not do the following: *{Explain what the other party was ordered to do or not do}*
____
____
____
____.

____ Please indicate here if additional pages are attached.

C. The other party in this case has willfully failed to comply with this order or judgment of the court , a written agreement, or the requirements of Section 61.13001,Florida Statutes: *{Explain what the other party has or has not done}*.____
____
____

Florida Supreme Court Approved Family Law Form 12.950(g), Motion for Civil Contempt And/Or Return of Child(ren) (03/15)

____.

____ Please indicate here if additional pages are attached.

II. **REQUEST FOR RELIEF OR SANCTION**

A. _____ There **IS** a prior court order or judgment and I respectfully request that the court issue an order holding the above-named person in civil contempt, if appropriate, and/or providing the following relief: *{Indicate all that apply}*

1. _____ordering the immediate return of the minor child(ren);
2. _____ granting a temporary order restraining the relocation of minor child(ren);
3. _____ enforcing or compelling compliance with the prior order or judgment;
4. _____ requiring the other party to pay costs and fees in connection with this motion;
5. _____ if the other party is found to be in civil contempt, ordering a compensatory fine;
6. _____ if the other party is found to be in civil contempt, ordering a coercive fine;
7. _____ if the other party is found to be in civil contempt, ordering incarceration of the other party after setting an appropriate purge;
8. _____ issuing a writ of bodily attachment as appropriate;
9. ____ awarding make-up time-sharing with minor child(ren) as follows *{explain}*

____

____

____

10. _____ awarding attorney's fees; and/or
11. _____ awarding other relief, including sanctions , *{explain}*:______________

____

____

OR

B. ___ There **is NO** prior court order; however, the above-named person has violated the requirements of Section 61.13001, Florida Statutes, and I respectfully request that the court issue an order providing the following relief:

1. _____ ordering the immediate return of the minor child(ren);
2. _____ granting a temporary order restraining the relocation of the minor child(ren);
3. _____ enforcing or compelling compliance with Section 61.13001, Florida Statutes;
4. _____ requiring the other party to pay costs and fees in connection with this motion;
5. _____ awarding make-up time-sharing with minor child(ren) as follows *{explain}*: _____

____

____

6. _____ awarding attorneys' fees; and/or
7. _____ awarding other relief, including sanctions, *{explain}*: ______________

____

____

Florida Supreme Court Approved Family Law Form 12.950(g), Motion for Civil Contempt And/Or Return of Child(ren) (03/15)

I certify that a copy of this document was ( ) mailed ( ) faxed and mailed
( ) e-mailed ( ) hand-delivered to the person(s) listed below on *{date}*________________.

Other party or his/her attorney:
Name:__________________________________
Address:________________________________
City, State, Zip:___________________________
Fax Number: _____________________________
Designated E-mail Address(es):__________________
____

I understand that I am swearing or affirming under oath to the truthfulness of the claims made in this motion and that the punishment for knowingly making a false statement includes fines and/or imprisonment.

Dated: ______________________ ____
Signature of Party

Printed Name: ______________________________
Address: ___________________________________
City, State, Zip: _____________________________
Telephone Number: __________________________
Fax Number: ________________________________
Designated E-mail Address(es):__________________
____

STATE OF FLORIDA
COUNTY OF ______________________

Sworn to or affirmed and signed before me on ____________ by______________________________________.

____
NOTARY PUBLIC or DEPUTY CLERK

____

[Print, type, or stamp commissioned name of notary or deputy clerk.]

____ Personally known
____ Produced identification
____ Type of identification produced ____________________

IF A NONLAWYER HELPED YOU FILL OUT THIS FORM, HE/SHE MUST FILL IN THE BLANKS BELOW:
[fill in all blanks] This form was prepared for the: *{choose only one}* ( ) Petitioner ( ) Respondent.
This form was completed with the assistance of:
{name of individual} ____________________,
{name of business} ____________________,
{address} ____________________,
{city} ________,*{state}* ___, *{zip code}* ______,*{telephone number}* ________.

INSTRUCTIONS FOR FLORIDA SUPREME COURT APPROVED FAMILY LAW FORM 12.950(g) MOTION FOR CIVIL CONTEMPT AND/OR RETURN OF CHILD(REN) (03/15)

When should this form be used?

You may use this form to ask the court to enforce a prior court **order**, **final judgment** or to request the return of a child(ren) who has been relocated in violation of Section 61.13001, Florida Statutes.

What should I do next?

To initiate a civil contempt/enforcement proceeding against a **party** who has relocated with a child contrary to the requirements of a prior court order, or is otherwise not complying with a prior court order concerning relocation, or in the event there has been a relocation in violation of Section 61.13001, Florida Statutes, you must file a **motion** with the court explaining what the party has failed to do. This form should be typed or printed in black ink. After completing this form, you should sign it before a **notary public** or **deputy clerk**. You should then **file** the original with the **clerk of the circuit court** in the county where your case was filed and keep a copy for your records.

IMPORTANT INFORMATION REGARDING E–FILING

The Florida Rules of Judicial Administration now require that all petitions, pleadings, and documents be filed electronically except in certain circumstances. **Self–represented litigants may file petitions or other pleadings or documents electronically; however, they are not required to do so.** If you choose to file your pleadings or other documents electronically, you must do so in accordance with Florida Rule of Judicial Administration 2.525, and you must follow the procedures of the judicial circuit in which you file. **The rules and procedures should be carefully read and followed.**

IMPORTANT INFORMATION REGARDING E–SERVICE ELECTION

After the initial service of process of the petition or supplemental petition by the Sheriff or certified process server, the Florida Rules of Judicial Administration now require that all documents required or permitted to be served on the other party must be served by electronic mail (e–mail) except in certain circumstances. **You must strictly comply with the format requirements set forth in the Rules of Judicial Administration.**

SELF–REPRESENTED LITIGANTS MAY SERVE DOCUMENTS BY E–MAIL; HOWEVER, THEY ARE NOT REQUIRED TO DO SO. If a self-represented litigant elects to serve and receive documents by e-mail, the procedures must always be followed once the initial election is made.

To serve and receive documents by e-mail, you must designate your e-mail addresses by using the **Designation of Current Mailing and E–mail Address**, Florida Supreme Court Approved Family Law Form 12.915, and you must provide your e-mail address on each form on which your signature appears. Please **CAREFULLY** read the rules and instructions for: **Certificate of Service (General),** Florida Supreme Court Approved Family Law Form 12.914; **Designation of Current Mailing and E–mail Address**, Florida Supreme Court Approved Family Law Form 12.915; and Florida Rule of Judicial Administration 2.516.

A copy of this form must be **personally served** by a sheriff or private process server or mailed*, e–mailed* **or** hand delivered to any other party(ies) in your case. *Please note that if notice is mailed or e-mailed, the court in certain circumstances may not consider mailing or e-mailing to be adequate notice. If you want to be sure, you should have the motion personally served. This is a technical area of the law; if you have any questions about it, you should consult a lawyer. For more information on personal service, see the instructions for **Summons: Personal Service on an Individual,** Florida Family Law Rules of Procedure Form 12.910(a).

The court will then set a **hearing**. You should check with the clerk of court, **judicial assistant**, or **family law intake staff** for information on the local procedure for scheduling a hearing. Once you know the time and date of the hearing, you will need to complete **Notice of Hearing on Motion for Contempt/Enforcement**, Florida Supreme Court Approved

Family Law Form 12.961, Florida Supreme Court Approved Family Law Form 12.921, or **Order of Referral to General Magistrate,** Florida Family Law Rules of Procedure Form 12.920(b), which will specify a time and place for a hearing on the issue. A copy of the form you used to schedule the hearing must be mailed, e-mailed, or hand-delivered to the other party. Again, if notice is mailed or e-mailed, the court in certain circumstances may not consider that to be adequate notice. If you want to be sure, you should have the notice personally served. This is a technical area of the law; if you have any questions about it, you should consult a lawyer. For more information on personal service, see the instructions for **Summons: Personal Service on an Individual,** Florida Family Law Rules of Procedure Form 12.910(a).

At the hearing, as in other civil proceedings, you, as the party seeking contempt or return of children, will have the burden of proof. The other party will have an opportunity to put on defenses, if any apply. If the judge finds the other party to be in willful contempt or in violation of Section 61.13001, Florida Statutes, the judge may order appropriate sanctions to compel compliance or return of the child(ren) by the other party, including jail, payment of attorneys' fees, suit money, court costs, coercive or compensatory fines, and may order any other relief permitted by law.

Where can I look for more information?

Before proceeding, you should read "General Information for Self–Represented Litigants" found at the beginning of these forms. See also section 61.14, Florida Statutes and rule 12.615, Florida Family Law Rules of Procedure.

Remember, a person who is NOT an attorney is called a nonlawyer. If a nonlawyer helps you fill out these forms, that person must give you a copy of **Disclosure from Nonlawyer,** Florida Family Law Rules of Procedure Form 12.900(a), before he or she helps you. A nonlawyer helping you fill out these forms also **must** put his or her name, address, and telephone number on the bottom of the last page of every form he or she helps you complete.

Added Sept. 30, 2010 (55 So.3d 381). Amended March 26, 2015, effective March 26, 2015 (2015 WL 1343088).

Form 12.950(h). Order on Motion for Civil Contempt for Relocation and/or Return of Child(ren)

IN THE CIRCUIT COURT OF THE ________________ JUDICIAL CIRCUIT,
IN AND FOR ______________________ COUNTY, FLORIDA

Case No: __________
Division:

_____________________________,
Petitioner,

And

_____________________________,
Respondent.

ORDER ON MOTION FOR CIVIL CONTEMPT FOR RELOCATION AND/OR RETURN OF CHILD(REN)

A Motion was filed by _____ Petitioner _____ Respondent for Civil Contempt for Improper Relocation and/or Return of the Minor Child(ren), and the Court finding as follows:

1. _____ Petitioner _____ Respondent has relocated with the parties' minor child(ren) more than 50 miles from the child(ren)'s principal place of residence at the time of the entry of the last order establishing or modifying the parenting plan or time-sharing schedule and the relocation places the child(ren) more than 50 miles away from either parent or other person entitled to access, time-sharing or visitation;

   a. _____ Contrary to a court order or judgment entered on *{date}* ______________, by this Court;

   b. _____ Contrary to a court order or judgment entered on *{date}* ______________, by *{court, city, and state}* ____.

   The order of the Court required the other party in this case to do or not do the following:
   ____
   ____
   ____
   ____.

   c. _____ Contrary to the relocation procedures set forth in Section 61.13001, Florida Statutes.

2. _____ Petitioner _____ Respondent has willfully failed to comply either with the order of the Court or with the requirements of Section 61.13001, Florida Statutes as follows:
____
____
____.

Based upon the above findings it is ORDERED AND ADJUDGED as follows:

Florida Supreme Court Approved Family Law Form 12.950 (h), Order on Motion for Civil Contempt for Relocation And/Or Return of Child(ren) (03/15)

3. _____ The Motion for Civil Contempt for Relocation/Return of Child is hereby **GRANTED.**

a. ____ Petitioner _____ Respondent is hereby ordered to immediately return the minor child(ren) to the jurisdiction of this Court.

b. ____ Petitioner _____ Respondent is hereby temporarily restrained from relocating with the minor child(ren), pending further order of this Court.

c. ____ This Court shall issue a Writ of Bodily Attachment against the _____Petitioner _____Respondent at the hearing on the Motion for Contempt.

d. ____ Petitioner _____ Respondent may purge himself/herself of the Contempt by immediately returning the minor child(ren) to the jurisdiction of this Court.

e. ____ Petitioner _____Respondent shall be awarded makeup time-sharing with the minor child(ren) as follows: ____
____
____.

f. ____ The following additional relief, including sanctions, is granted: ____
____.

OR

4. ____ The Motion For Civil Contempt For Relocation And/Or Return Of Child(ren) is hereby **DENIED.**

5. ____ **Attorney's Fees, Costs and Suit Money**

a. _____ Petitioner's _____ Respondent's request(s) for attorney's fees, costs, and suit money is/are denied because____
____.

OR

b. ______ The Court finds there is a need for and an ability to pay attorney's fees, costs, and suit money. _____Petitioner _____ Respondent is hereby ordered to pay to the other party $__________ in attorney's fees, and $__________ in costs. The Court further finds that the attorney's fees awarded are based on the reasonable rate of $_________ per hour and _______________reasonable hours. Other provisions relating to attorney fees, costs, and suit money are as follows: ____
____

DONE AND ORDERED at ___________________________, Florida, on ___________________________.

Florida Supreme Court Approved Family Law Form 12.950 (h), Order on Motion for Civil Contempt for Relocation And/Or Return of Child(ren) (03/15)

____
CIRCUIT JUDGE

I certify that a copy of the Order on Motion for Civil Contempt for Relocation and/or Return of Child(ren) was ( ) mailed ( ) faxed and mailed ( ) e-mailed ( ) hand-delivered to the parties and any entities listed below on *{date}* ______________________.

____
{Clerk of court, designee, or Judicial Assistant}

Petitioner (or his or her attorney)
Respondent (or his or her attorney)
Other Person (or his or her attorney)
____

Florida Supreme Court Approved Family Law Form 12.950 (h), Order on Motion for Civil Contempt for Relocation And/Or Return of Child(ren) (03/15)

Added Sept. 30, 2010 (55 So.3d 381). Amended March 26, 2015, effective March 26, 2015 (2015 WL 1343088).

Form 12.950(i). Final Judgment/Supplemental Final Judgment Granting Relocation

IN THE CIRCUIT COURT OF THE ____________________ JUDICIAL CIRCUIT,
IN AND FOR ________________________ COUNTY, FLORIDA

Case No: ____________________
Division: ____________________

______________________________,
Petitioner,

And

______________________________,
Respondent.

FINAL JUDGMENT/SUPPLEMENTAL FINAL JUDGMENT GRANTING RELOCATION

This cause came before this Court on a Petition/Supplemental Petition to relocate filed by (*name*) ______________________ the ______________________ of the child(ren). The Court makes these findings of fact and ORDERS as follows:

SECTION I. FINDINGS

1. The Court has jurisdiction over the subject matter and the parties.

2. The last judgment or order establishing or modifying parental responsibility, custody, visitation, or time-sharing (if any) was entered on (*date*)____________________.

3. ____ *{If Applicable}* A prior order or judgment in this cause expressly governs the issue of relocation of the child(ren).

4. The parties' dependent or minor child(ren) is (are):
Name(s) Birth Date(s)
____
____
____
____
____

5. The _____ Petitioner _____ Respondent _____Other Person entitled to access or time-sharing *{name}* ______________________ has filed a petition to relocate to *{location/or address}*____, a location more than 50 miles from his/her principal place of residence at the time of entry of the last order establishing or modifying time-sharing, or at the time of filing of the pending action to establish or modify time-sharing. The relocation is for a period of at least 60 consecutive days.

Florida Supreme Court Approved Family Law Form 12.950(i), Final Judgment/Supplemental Final Judgment Granting Relocation (03/15)

6. This judgment/supplemental judgment was entered: *{Choose only **one**}*
_____**After** a Hearing;

_____**Without** an evidentiary hearing due to the _____ written agreement of the parties or the _____ other party's failure to respond.

SECTION II. GRANTING REQUEST TO RELOCATE
The Court finds that the relocation IS **GRANTED** based upon:

*{Choose only **one**}*

1. _____**No response.** The other parent or person entitled to access to or time-sharing with the child(ren) failed to timely file a response objecting to the petition to relocate. The Court finds that the relocation is in the best interests of the child(ren) based upon the undisputed pleadings. The access or time-sharing schedule and post-relocation transportation arrangements contained within the petition are adopted by the Court.

2. _____**Agreement.** The parents or other person entitled to time-sharing with the child(ren) agree to the relocation and have signed a written agreement which consents to the relocation; defines the access or time-sharing schedule for the parents or any other persons entitled to access and time-sharing, and describes, if necessary, any post-relocation transportation arrangements relating to access or time-sharing. The Court finds that the relocation is in the best interests of the child(ren) based upon the pleadings and the Agreement.

   A copy of this Agreement is attached as Exhibit _______.

3. _____**Evidentiary Hearing.** The Court finds that the relocation is in the best interests of the child(ren) based upon the evidence presented at the evidentiary hearing. The Court has evaluated each of the factors enumerated in Section 61.13001(7), Florida Statutes, and **FINDS:**
   ____
   ____
   ____
   ____.

SECTION III.PARENTAL RESPONSIBILITY AND TIME-SHARING
*{Choose only **one**}*

1. _____**Time-Sharing.** The _____ Petitioner _____ Respondent _____ Other Person entitled to access or time-sharing shall have frequent, continuing, and meaningful contact, access, and time-sharing in accordance with:
   *{Choose only **one**}*
   a. _____the **Agreement for Relocation** attached as Exhibit _____and incorporated herein.
   b. _____the **Parenting Plan** attached as Exhibit _____ and incorporated herein.
   c. _____the following **specified time-sharing schedule:**
   ____
   ____
   ____

Florida Supreme Court Approved Family Law Form 12.950(i), Final Judgment/Supplemental Final Judgment

____
____

2. _____ **No Contact**. The _____ Petitioner _____ Respondent _____ Other Person entitled to access, visitation, or time-sharing shall have no contact with party's minor child(ren) until further order of the Court, as such contact is detrimental to the welfare of the minor child(ren). *{Explain}* ____
____
____.

SECTION IV: MODIFICATION OF CHILD SUPPORT
*{Indicate **all** that apply}*

1. _____ The Court finds that based upon the relocation, the _____ Petitioner's _____ Respondent's child support obligation should be modified in consideration of the costs of transportation and the respective net incomes of the parents.
*{Choose only **one**}*
   a. _____ The amounts in the Child Support Guidelines Worksheet, Florida Family Law Rules of Procedure Form 12.902(e), filed by the _____ Petitioner _____ Respondent are correct and are adopted by the Court.

   OR

   b. _____ The Court makes the following findings:
   The Petitioner's net monthly income is $____________.
   The Respondent's net monthly income is $____________.
   Monthly child care costs are $____________.
   Monthly health/dental insurance costs are $____________.
   Transportation costs are $____________.

2. _____ **Amount**. The Obligor's child support obligation shall be modified to $__________ per month for the _____ children *{total amount of parties' minor or dependent children}* commencing: *{month, day, year}* and terminating ____________ *{month, day, year}*. Child support shall be paid in the amount of $__________ per ________________ *{week, month, other}* consistent with Obligor's current payroll cycle.

Upon the termination of the obligation of child support for one of the parties' children, child support in the amount of $__________ for the remaining _____ children *{total number of remaining children}* shall be paid commencing ________________ *{month, day, year}* and terminating________________ *{month, day, year}*. This child support shall be paid in the amount of $________ per ________ *{week, month, other}* consistent with the Obligor's current payroll cycle.

{Insert schedule for the child support obligation, including the amount, and commencement and termination dates, for the remaining minor or dependent children, which shall be payable as the obligation for each child ceases. Please indicate whether the schedule ____ appears below or ____ is attached as part of this form.}
____
____

____
____
____
____

The Obligor shall pay child support until all of the minor or dependent children: reach the age of 18; become emancipated, marry, join the armed services, die, or become self-supporting; or until further order of the court or agreement of the parties. The child support obligation shall continue beyond the age of 18 and until high school graduation for any child who is dependent in fact, between the ages of 18 and 19, and is still in high school, performing in good faith with a reasonable expectation of graduation before the age of 19.

If the child support ordered deviates from the guidelines by more than 5%, the factual findings which support that deviation are: ______________________________
____
____

SECTION V. METHOD OF PAYMENT
Obligor shall pay modified child support as follows:

1. **Place of Payment.**

a. ____Obligor shall pay court-ordered support directly to either the State Disbursement Unit or the central depository, as required by statute, along with any fee required by statute.

b. ____Both parties have requested and the court finds that it is in the best interests of the child(ren) that support payments need not be directed through either the State Disbursement Unit or the central depository at this time; however, either party may subsequently apply, pursuant to section 61.13(1)(d)3, Florida Statutes, to require payment through either the State Disbursement Unit or the central depository.

2. **Income Deduction.**

a. ___**Immediate.** Obligor shall pay through income deduction, pursuant to a separate Income Deduction Order which shall be effective immediately. Obligor is individually responsible for paying this support obligation until all of said support is deducted from Obligor's income. Until support payments are deducted from Obligor's paycheck, Obligor is responsible for making timely payments directly to the State Disbursement Unit or the Obligee, as previously set forth in this order.

b. ___**Deferred.** Income deduction is ordered this day, but it shall not be effective until a delinquency of $__________, or, if not specified, an amount equal to one month's obligation occurs. Income deduction is not being implemented immediately based on the following findings: Income deduction is **not** in the best interests of the child(ren) because: *{explain}*
____
____
____,

AND

There is proof of timely payment of a previously ordered obligation without an Income Deduction Order in cases of modification,

AND

(   ) There is an agreement by the Obligor to advise the Title IV-D agency, the clerk of court, and the Obligee of any change in Payor and/or health insurance

OR

(   ) there is a signed written agreement providing an alternative arrangement between the Obligor and the Obligee and, at the option of the IV-D agency, by the IV-D agency in IV-D cases in which there is an assignment of support rights to the state, reviewed and entered in the record by the court.

SECTION VI. OTHER

1. _____**Other Provisions**

____
____
____
____.

2. _____The Court reserves jurisdiction to address all issues of time-sharing and parental responsibility, as well as to enforce or modify the provisions of this Judgment.

3. _____ Unless specifically modified herein, the provisions of all prior judgments or orders remain in effect.

DONE AND ORDERED at ________________________, Florida, on____________________.

____
CIRCUIT JUDGE

I certify that a copy of this Final Judgment/Supplemental Final Judgment Granting Relocation was (   ) mailed (   ) faxed and mailed (   ) e-mailed (   ) hand-delivered to the parties and any other persons or entities listed below on *{date}* ___________________________.

____
{Clerk of court, designee, or Judicial Assistant}

Petitioner (or his/her attorney)
Respondent (or his/her attorney)
Other Person (or his/her attorney)

Florida Supreme Court Approved Family Law Form 12.950(i), Final Judgment/Supplemental Final Judgment Granting Relocation (03/15)

State Disbursement Unit
Other:__________________________

Florida Supreme Court Approved Family Law Form 12.950(i), Final Judgment/Supplemental Final Judgment Granting Relocation (03/15)

Added Sept. 30, 2010 (55 So.3d 381). Amended March 26, 2015, effective March 26, 2015 (2015 WL 1343088).

Form 12.950(j). Final Judgment/Supplemental Final Judgment Denying Relocation

IN THE CIRCUIT COURT OF THE ________________ JUDICIAL CIRCUIT
IN AND FOR ________________________ COUNTY, FLORIDA

Case No: ____________
Division: ____________

______________________________,
Petitioner,

And

______________________________,
Respondent.

FINAL JUDGMENT/SUPPLEMENTAL FINAL JUDGMENT DENYING RELOCATION

This cause came before this Court on a Petition/Supplemental Petition to relocate filed by *{name}* ____________________ the ____________________ of the child(ren). The Court makes these findings of fact and ORDERS as follows:

SECTION I. FINDINGS

1. The Court has jurisdiction over the subject matter and the parties.

2. The last judgment or order establishing or modifying parental responsibility, custody, visitation, or time-sharing (if any) was entered on *{date}*________________________.

3. _____ *{If Applicable}* A prior order or judgment in this cause expressly governs the issue of relocation of the child(ren).

4. The parties' dependent or minor child(ren) is (are):

Name	Birth Date

5. The _____Petitioner _____Respondent _____Other Person entitled to access or time-sharing: *{name}*________________________________ has filed a petition to relocate to: *{location and/oraddress}*____,a location more than 50 miles from his/her principal place of residence at the time of entry of the last order establishing or modifying time-sharing, or at the time of filing of the pending action to establish or modify time-sharing. The relocation is for a period of more than 60 consecutive days.

The Court has evaluated each of the factors enumerated in Section 61.13001(7), Florida Statutes, and on the evidence presented, it is adjudged:

SECTION II. DENIAL OF REQUEST TO RELOCATE

The request to relocate is **DENIED** because:

1. _____ The Petition is legally insufficient as it fails to include a proposed revised post-relocation schedule for access and time-sharing that includes the necessary arrangements to effectuate time-sharing with the child(ren).

OR

2. _____ The requested relocation is not in the best interests of the child(ren).
Facts in support of finding:
____
____
____.

3. _____ **Order Requiring Return of Child(ren) if Parent and Child(ren) have Temporarily Relocated.**
The _____ Petitioner _____ Respondent _____ Other Person entitled to access to or time-sharing with the child(ren) shall **immediately return** the child(ren) to the jurisdiction of this Court. Failure to immediately return the child(ren) shall subject the non-complying party to contempt or other proceedings deemed necessary to compel return of the child(ren).

SECTION III. OTHER

1. ____ Other Provisions:
____
____
____.

2. _____ This Court reserves jurisdiction to address all issues of time-sharing and parental responsibility, as well as to enforce or modify the provisions of this Judgment.

3. _____ Unless specifically modified herein, the provisions of all prior judgments or orders remain in effect.

DONE AND ORDERED at _________________________, Florida on ______________________ .

____
CIRCUIT JUDGE

Florida Supreme Court Approved Family Law Form 12.950(j), Final Judgment/Supplemental Final Judgment Denying Relocation (03/15)

I certify that a copy of this Final Judgment/Supplemental Final Judgment Denying Relocation was ( ) mailed ( ) faxed and mailed ( ) e-mailed ( ) hand-delivered to the parties and any other persons or entities listed below on *{date}* ______________________.

____
{Clerk of court, designee, or Judicial Assistant}

Petitioner (or his/her attorney)
Respondent (or his/her attorney)
Other Person (or his/her attorney)
State Disbursement Unit

Florida Supreme Court Approved Family Law Form 12.950(j), Final Judgment/Supplemental Final Judgment Denying Relocation (03/15)

Added Sept. 30, 2010 (55 So.3d 381). Amended March 26, 2015, effective March 26, 2015 (2015 WL 1343088).

Form 12.951(a). Petition to Disestablish Paternity and/or Terminate Child Support Obligation

IN THE CIRCUIT COURT OF THE ______ JUDICIAL CIRCUIT,
IN AND FOR ______ COUNTY, FLORIDA

Case No.: ______
Division: ______

______,
Petitioner,

and

______,
Respondent.

PETITION TO DISESTABLISH PATERNITY AND/OR TERMINATE CHILD SUPPORT OBLIGATION

I, *{full legal name}* ______, certify that the following information is true.

1. **Paternity.** My paternity of the child(ren), *{name(s) and birth date(s)}* ______ ______ ______ was established by
*{Choose only **one**}*
a. ____operation of law because I was married to the child(ren)'s mother.
b. ____adjudication of paternity, entered by *{court}* ______ on *{date}* ______.
c. ____acknowledgment of paternity executed on *{date}* ______.
d. ____other: *{specify}* ______

A copy of any judgment is attached.

2. **Child support.** My child support obligation for the child(ren), *{name(s) and birth date(s)}*, ______ ______ was established by
*{Choose only **one**}*
a. ____a final judgment of dissolution of marriage, entered by *{court}* ______ ______ on *{date}* ______.
b. ____an administrative proceeding to establish child support in *{location}* ______ on *{date}* ______.
c. ____ a paternity proceeding in *{court}* ______ on *{date}* ______.
d. ____other *{specify}* ______

A copy of any judgment is attached.

Florida Supreme Court Approved Family Law Form 12.951(a), Petition to Disestablish Paternity and/or Terminate Child Support Obligation (03/15)

3. **Newly discovered evidence.** Newly discovered evidence concerning the paternity of this/these child(ren) has come to my knowledge since the initial paternity determination or establishment of the child support obligation. *{Explain}*
____
____
____
____

4. **Scientific tests.**

a. ____The results of scientific tests that are generally acceptable within the scientific community to show a probability of paternity, administered within 90 days prior to the filing of this petition, indicate that I cannot be the father of the child(ren) for whom support is required. A copy of the test results is attached.

b. _____ I did not have access to the child(ren) to have scientific testing performed before the filing of this petition and I request that the court order the child(ren) to be tested.

5. **Fulfillment of child support obligation.**
*{Choose only **one**}*
a. _____ I am current on all child support payments for the child(ren) for whom relief is sought.

b. _____I have substantially complied with my child support obligation for the child(ren) and any delinquency in my child support obligation for the child(ren) arose from my inability for just cause to pay the delinquent child support when the delinquent child support became due.

I ask the court to enter an order to:

*{Indicate **all** that apply}*

a. _____disestablish my paternity to *{name(s) of child(ren)}* ______________________
____

b. _____terminate my obligation to pay child support for *{name(s) of child(ren)}* ________
____

c. _____other: ____
____
____.

I certify that a copy of this document was ( ) mailed ( ) faxed and mailed ( ) e-mailed ( ) hand delivered to the person(s) listed below on *{date}* ______________.

Respondent or his/her attorney:
Name: ______________
Address: ______________
City, State, Zip: ______________
Fax Number: ______________
Designated E-mail Address(es): ______________

I understand that I am swearing or affirming under oath to the truthfulness of the claims made in this petition and that the punishment for knowingly making a false statement includes fines and/or imprisonment.

Dated: ______________

____
Signature of Petitioner
Printed Name: ______________
Address: ______________
City, State, Zip: ______________
Telephone Number: ______________
Fax Number: ______________
Designated E-mail Address(es): ______________

STATE OF FLORIDA
COUNTY OF ______________

Sworn to or affirmed and signed before me on ______________ by ______________.

____
NOTARY PUBLIC or DEPUTY CLERK

____
{Print, type, or stamp commissioned name of notary or deputy clerk.}

_____ Personally known
_____ Produced identification
Type of identification produced ______________

IF A NONLAWYER HELPED YOU FILL OUT THIS FORM, HE/SHE MUST FILL IN THE BLANKS BELOW: [fill in **all** blanks] This form was prepared for the Petitioner.
This form was completed with the assistance of:
{name of individual} ______________,
{name of business} ______________,
{address} ______________,
{city} ______ *{state}* ______, *{zip code}* ______, *{telephone number}* ______.

Florida Supreme Court Approved Family Law Form 12.951(a), Petition to Disestablish Paternity and/or Terminate Child Support Obligation (03/15)

INSTRUCTIONS FOR FLORIDA FAMILY LAW RULES OF PROCEDURE FORM 12.951(a) PETITION TO DISESTABLISH PATERNITY AND/OR TERMINATE CHILD SUPPORT OBLIGATION (03/15)

When should this form be used?

This form should be used by a man who wishes to disestablish paternity or terminate a child support obligation because he is not the biological father of the child(ren). The petition must be **filed**

- in the circuit court having jurisdiction over the child support obligation; or
- if the child support was determined administratively and has not been ratified by a court, in the circuit court in which the mother or legal guardian or custodian of the child(ren) resides; or
- if the mother or legal guardian or custodian no longer resides in the state, in the circuit court in the county in which the petitioner resides.

This form should be typed or printed in black ink. After completing the form, you should sign the form before a **notary public** or **deputy clerk.**

A copy of any judgment or order regarding paternity or child support and a copy of any scientific test results showing that you cannot be the father of the child(ren) must be attached to the petition and filed with the court.

IMPORTANT INFORMATION REGARDING E–FILING

The Florida Rules of Judicial Administration now require that all petitions, pleadings, and documents be filed electronically except in certain circumstances. **Self–represented litigants may file petitions or other pleadings or documents electronically; however, they are not required to do so.** If you choose to file your pleadings or other documents electronically, you must do so in accordance with Florida Rule of Judicial Administration 2.525, and you must follow the procedures of the judicial circuit in which you file. **The rules and procedures should be carefully read and followed.**

What should I do next?

The petition must be served on the mother or legal guardian or custodian of the child(ren). If the child support obligation was determined administratively and has not been ratified by a court, the petition must also be served on the Department of Revenue.

IMPORTANT INFORMATION REGARDING E–SERVICE ELECTION

After the initial service of process of the petition or supplemental petition by the Sheriff or certified process server, the Florida Rules of Judicial Administration now require that all documents required or permitted to be served on the other party must be served by electronic mail (e–mail) except in certain circumstances. **You must strictly comply with the format requirements set forth in the Rules of Judicial Administration.**

SELF–REPRESENTED LITIGANTS MAY SERVE DOCUMENTS BY E–MAIL; HOWEVER, THEY ARE NOT REQUIRED TO DO SO. If a self-represented litigant elects to serve and receive documents by e-mail, the procedures must always be followed once the initial election is made.

To serve and receive documents by e-mail, you must designate your e-mail addresses by using the **Designation of Current Mailing and E–mail Address**, Florida Supreme Court Approved Family Law Form 12.915, and you must provide your e-mail address on each form on which your signature appears. Please **CAREFULLY** read the rules and instructions for: **Certificate of Service (General),** Florida Supreme Court Approved Family Law Form 12.914; **Designation of Current Mailing and E–mail Address**, Florida Supreme Court Approved Family Law Form 12.915; and Florida Rule of Judicial Administration 2.516.

Where can I look for more information?

Before proceeding, you should read "General Information for Self–Represented Litigants" found at the beginning of these forms. For further information, see Section 742.18, Florida Statutes.

Special notes . . .

Remember, a person who is NOT an attorney is called a nonlawyer. If a nonlawyer helps you fill out these forms, that person must give you a copy of **Disclosure from Nonlawyer,** Florida Family Law Rules of Procedure Form 12.900(a), before he or she helps you. A nonlawyer helping you fill out these forms also **must** put his or her name, address, and telephone number on the bottom of the last page of every form he or she helps you complete.

Added Sept. 30, 2010 (55 So.3d 381). Amended March 26, 2015, effective March 26, 2015 (2015 WL 1343088).

Form 12.951(b). Order Disestablishing Paternity and/or Terminating Child Support Obligation

IN THE CIRCUIT COURT OF THE ________________ JUDICIAL CIRCUIT,
IN AND FOR ________________ COUNTY, FLORIDA

Case No.: ________________
Division: ________________

________________,
Petitioner,

and

________________,
Respondent.

ORDER DISESTABLISHING PATERNITY AND/OR TERMINATING CHILD SUPPORT OBLIGATION

This cause came before the court on *{date}* ________________ on *{full legal name}* ________________'s petition to *{Indicate **all** that apply}*

____ Disestablish paternity to *{child(ren)'s names and birth date(s)}* ________________
____
____

____ Terminate a child support obligation for *{child(ren)'s names and birth date(s)}* ________________
____
____

The court having been fully advised in the premises FINDS all of the following:

1. Newly discovered evidence relating to the paternity of the child(ren) has come to the petitioner's knowledge since the initial ____ paternity determination ____ establishment of a child support obligation.

2. Scientific tests that are generally acceptable within the scientific community to show a probability of paternity showing that the petitioner cannot be the father of the children were properly conducted.

3. The petitioner
*{Choose only **one**}*
____ is current on all child support payments for the child(ren).
____ has substantially complied with his child support obligation for the applicable child(ren) and any delinquency in his child support obligation arose from his inability for just cause to pay the delinquent child support when it became due.

4. The petitioner has not adopted the child.

Florida Supreme Court Approved Family Law Form 12.951(b), Order Disestablishing Paternity and/or Terminating Child Support Obligation (03/15)

5. The child(ren) was/were not conceived by artificial insemination while the petitioner and the child(ren)'s mother were married.

6. The petitioner did not act to prevent the biological father of the child(ren) from asserting his paternal rights with respect to the child(ren).

7. The child(ren) was/were younger than 18 years of age when the petition was filed.

8. Since learning that he is not the biological father of the child(ren), the petitioner has not

a. married the mother of the child(ren) while known as the reputed father in accordance with section 742.091, Florida Statutes, and voluntarily assumed the parental obligation and duty to pay child support;
b. acknowledged paternity in a sworn statement;
c. consented to be named as the child(ren)'s biological father on the child(ren)'s birth certificate(s);
d. voluntarily promised in writing to support the child(ren) and was required to support the child(ren) based on that promise;
e. received written notice from any state agency or any court directing him to submit to scientific testing which he disregarded; or
f. signed a voluntary acknowledgment of paternity as provided by section 742.10(4), Florida Statutes.

It is therefore ORDERED AND ADJUDGED:

*{Indicate **all** that apply}*

____ Petitioner's, *{name}* ______________________ paternity of *{name(s) of child(ren)}* ______________________ is disestablished.

____ Petitioner's, *{name}* ______________________ child support obligation to *{name(s) of child(ren)}* ______________________ is terminated.

DONE AND ORDERED ON ____________ in______________________, Florida

____
CIRCUIT JUDGE

Florida Supreme Court Approved Family Law Form 12.951(b), Order Disestablishing Paternity and/or Terminating Child Support Obligation (03/15)

I certify that a copy of the Order Disestablishing Paternity and/or Terminating Child Support Obligation was ( ) mailed ( ) faxed and mailed ( ) e-mailed ( ) hand-delivered to the parties and any entities listed below on *{date}* ______________________.

____
{Clerk of court, designee, or Judicial Assistant}

Petitioner
Respondent
Department of Revenue
Department of Health, Office of Vital Statistics
Court depositor/State Disbursement Unit
Other ____________________

Florida Supreme Court Approved Family Law Form 12.951(b), Order Disestablishing Paternity and/or Terminating Child Support Obligation (03/15)

Added Sept. 30, 2010 (55 So.3d 381). Amended March 26, 2015, effective March 26, 2015 (2015 WL 1343088).

Form 12.960. Motion for Civil Contempt/Enforcement

IN THE CIRCUIT COURT OF THE ______________ JUDICIAL CIRCUIT,
IN AND FOR ______________ COUNTY, FLORIDA

Case No.: ______________
Division: ______________

______________________,
Petitioner,

and

______________________,
Respondent.

MOTION FOR CIVIL CONTEMPT/ENFORCEMENT

_____ Petitioner _____ Respondent requests that the Court enter an order of civil contempt/enforcement against _____ Petitioner _____ Respondent in this case because:

1. A final judgment or order *{title of final judgment or order}* ______________ in this case was entered on *{date}* ______________, by *{court, city, and state}* ______________ ______________.
   _____ Please indicate here if the judgment or order is not from this Court and attach a copy.

2. This order of the Court required the other party in this case to do or not do the following: *{Explain what the other party was ordered to do or not do.}* ______________
   ____
   ____
   ____
   ____
   ____
   ____
   _____ Please indicate here if additional pages are attached.

3. The other party in this case has willfully failed to comply with this order of the Court: *{Explain what the other party has or has not done.}* ______________
   ____
   ____
   ____
   ____
   ____
   ____
   ____
   _____ Please indicate here if additional pages are attached.

4. I respectfully request that the Court issue an order holding the above-named person in civil contempt, if appropriate, and/or providing the following relief:

Florida Supreme Court Approved Family Law Form 12.960, Motion for Civil Contempt/Enforcement (03/15)

a. _____enforcing or compelling compliance with the prior order or judgment;
b. _____awarding a monetary judgment;
c. _____if a monetary judgment was included in the prior order, issuing a writ of execution or garnishment or other appropriate process;
d. _____awarding prejudgment interest;
e. _____requiring the other party to pay costs and fees in connection with this motion;
f. _____if the other party is found to be in civil contempt, ordering a compensatory fine;
g. _____if the other party is found to be in civil contempt, ordering a coercive fine;
h. _____if the other party is found to be in civil contempt, ordering incarceration of the other party with a purge;
i. _____issuing a writ of possession for real property, writ for possession of personal property, or other appropriate writ;
j. _____issuing a writ of bodily attachment if the other party fails to appear at the hearing set on this motion;
k. _____requiring the other party to make payments through the central governmental depository;
l. _____requiring the support payments to be automatically deducted from the other party's income or funds;
m. _____requiring the other party to seek employment;
n. _____awarding make-up time-sharing with minor child(ren) as follows *{explain}*: ___
____
____
____
____
____; and
o. _____awarding other relief *{explain}*: ____
____
____
____
____.

I certify that a copy of this document was: ( ) mailed ( ) faxed and mailed ( ) e-mailed ( ) hand-delivered to the person(s) listed below on *{date}* __________________.

Other party or his/her attorney:
Name: ____________________
Address: ____________________
City, State, Zip: ____________________
Fax Number: ____________________
Designated E-mail Address(es): ____________________
____

I understand that I am swearing or affirming under oath to the truthfulness of the claims made in this motion and that the punishment for knowingly making a false statement includes fines and/or imprisonment.

Dated: ____________________

____
Signature of Party
Printed Name: ____________________
Address: ____________________
City, State, Zip: ____________________
Telephone Number: ____________________
Fax Number: ____________________
Designated E-mail Address(es): ____________________
____

STATE OF FLORIDA
COUNTY OF ____________________

Sworn to or affirmed and signed before me on ______________ by ____________________.

____
NOTARY PUBLIC or DEPUTY CLERK

____
[Print, type, or stamp commissioned name of notary or clerk.]

____ Personally known
____ Produced identification
Type of identification produced ____________________

IF A NONLAWYER HELPED YOU FILL OUT THIS FORM, HE/SHE MUST FILL IN THE BLANKS BELOW:
[fill in **all** blanks] This form was prepared for the: *{choose only one}* ( ) Petitioner ( ) Respondent.
This form was completed with the assistance of:
{name of individual} ____________________,
{name of business} ____________________,
{address} ____________________,
{city} ____________,*{state}* ____, *{zip code}* ________,*{telephone number}* ____________.

Florida Supreme Court Approved Family Law Form 12.960, Motion for Civil Contempt/Enforcement (03/15)

INSTRUCTIONS FOR FLORIDA SUPREME COURT APPROVED FAMILY LAW FORM 12.960, MOTION FOR CIVIL CONTEMPT/ENFORCEMENT (03/15)

When should this form be used?

You may use this form to ask the court to enforce a prior court **order** or **final judgment**.

What should I do next?

To initiate a civil contempt/enforcement proceeding against a **party** who is not complying with a prior court order, you must file a **motion** with the court explaining what the party has failed to do. This form should be typed or printed in black ink. After completing this form, you should sign it before a **notary public** or **deputy clerk**. You should then **file** the original with the **clerk of the circuit court** in the county where your case was filed and keep a copy for your records.

IMPORTANT INFORMATION REGARDING E–FILING

The Florida Rules of Judicial Administration now require that all petitions, pleadings, and documents be filed electronically except in certain circumstances. **Self–represented litigants may file petitions or other pleadings or documents electronically; however, they are not required to do so.** If you choose to file your pleadings or other documents electronically, you must do so in accordance with Florida Rule of Judicial Administration 2.525, and you must follow the procedures of the judicial circuit in which you file. **The rules and procedures should be carefully read and followed.**

IMPORTANT INFORMATION REGARDING E–SERVICE ELECTION

After the initial service of process of the petition or supplemental petition by the Sheriff or certified process server, the Florida Rules of Judicial Administration now require that all documents required or permitted to be served on the other party must be served by electronic mail (e–mail) except in certain circumstances. **You must strictly comply with the format requirements set forth in the Rules of Judicial Administration.**

SELF–REPRESENTED LITIGANTS MAY SERVE DOCUMENTS BY E–MAIL; HOWEVER, THEY ARE NOT REQUIRED TO DO SO. If a self-represented litigant elects to serve and receive documents by e-mail, the procedures must always be followed once the initial election is made.

To serve and receive documents by e-mail, you must designate your e-mail addresses by using the **Designation of Current Mailing and E–mail Address**, Florida Supreme Court Approved Family Law Form 12.915, and you must provide your e-mail address on each form on which your signature appears. Please **CAREFULLY** read the rules and instructions for: **Certificate of Service (General),** Florida Supreme Court Approved Family Law Form 12.914; **Designation of Current Mailing and E–mail Address**, Florida Supreme Court Approved Family Law Form 12.915; and Florida Rule of Judicial Administration 2.516.

A copy of this form must be **personally served** by a sheriff or private process server or mailed,* e–mailed*, **or** hand delivered to any other party(ies) in your case. *Please note that if notice is mailed or e-mailed, the court in certain circumstances may not consider mailing or e-mailing, to be adequate notice. If you want to be sure, you should have the motion personally served. This is a technical area of the law; if you have any questions about it, you should consult a lawyer. For more information on personal service, see the instructions for **Summons: Personal Service on an Individual,** Florida Family Law Rules of Procedure Form 12.910(a).

The court will then set a **hearing**. You should check with the clerk of court, **judicial assistant**, or **family law intake staff** for information on the local procedure for scheduling a hearing. Once you know the time and date of the hearing, you will need to complete **Notice of Hearing on Motion for Contempt/Enforcement**, Florida Supreme Court Approved Family Law Form 12.961, or, if applicable, **Notice of Hearing (Child Support Enforcement Hearing Officer),** Florida Supreme Court Approved Family Law Form 12.921, or [**Notice of Hearing Before**] **General Magistrate,** Florida Family Law Rules of Procedure Form 12.920[(c)], which will specify a time and place for a hearing on the issue. A copy of this form must be mailed, e-mailed, or hand delivered to the other party. Again, if notice is mailed, the court in certain circumstances may not consider mailing or e-mailing to be adequate notice. If you want to be sure, you should have the notice personally served. This is a technical area of the law; if you have any questions about it, you should consult a lawyer. For more information on personal service, see the instructions for **Summons: Personal Service on an Individual,** Florida Family Law Rules of Procedure Form 12.910(a).

At the hearing, as in any other civil proceeding, you, as the moving party, will have the burden of proving the other party has not obeyed a prior court order. Once noncompliance is established, the other party will have an opportunity to show an inability to comply with the prior court order. If he or she is unable to do so, the judge may find the other party to be in contempt. If so, the judge may order appropriate sanctions to compel compliance by the other party, including jail, payment of attorneys' fees, suit money, or costs, and coercive or compensatory fines, and may order any other relief permitted by law.

Where can I look for more information?

Before proceeding, you should read "General Information for Self-Represented Litigants" found at the beginning of these forms. See also section 61.14, Florida Statutes and rule 12.615, Florida Family Law Rules of Procedure.

Remember, a person who is NOT an attorney is called a nonlawyer. If a nonlawyer helps you fill out these forms, that person must give you a copy of **Disclosure from Nonlawyer,** Florida Family Law Rules of Procedure Form 12.900(a), before he or she helps you. A nonlawyer helping you fill out these forms also **must** put his or her name, address, and telephone number on the bottom of the last page of every form he or she helps you complete.

Added July 1, 1999 (759 So.2d 583). Amended Sept. 21, 2000 (810 So.2d 1); Sept. 30, 2004, effective Oct. 1, 2004 (887 So.2d 1090); March 26, 2009 (20 So.3d 173); Dec. 16, 2010 (59 So.3d 792); March 26, 2015, effective March 26, 2015 (2015 WL 1343088).

Form 12.961. Notice of Hearing on Motion for Contempt/Enforcement in Support Matters (Rule 12.615)

IN THE CIRCUIT COURT OF THE ________________ JUDICIAL CIRCUIT,
IN AND FOR ________________ COUNTY, FLORIDA

Case No.: ____________________
Division: ____________________

______________________________,
Petitioner,

and

______________________________,
Respondent.

NOTICE OF HEARING ON MOTION FOR CONTEMPT/ENFORCEMENT IN SUPPORT MATTERS (RULE 12.615)

TO: *{name of other party}* ____

There will be a hearing before ______________________ *{name of judge or hearing officer}*, on *{date}*________________, at *{time}*______ m., in room ______ of the ________________ Courthouse, on the ____ Petitioner's ____ Respondent's Motion for Contempt in Support Matters. ___hour(s)/____minutes have been reserved for this hearing.

FAILURE TO APPEAR AT THE HEARING MAY RESULT IN THE COURT ISSUING A WRIT OF BODILY ATTACHMENT FOR YOUR ARREST. IF YOU ARE ARRESTED, YOU MAY BE HELD IN JAIL UP TO 48 HOURS BEFORE A HEARING IS HELD.

This part is to be filled out by the court or to be filled in with information obtained from the court:

If you are a person with a disability who needs any accommodation in order to participate in this proceeding, you are entitled, at no cost to you, to the provision of certain assistance. Please contact:

____

Florida Supreme Court Approved Family Law Form 12.961, Notice of Hearing on Motion for Contempt/ Enforcement (03/15)

{identify applicable court personnel by name, address, and telephone number } **at least 7 days before your scheduled court appearance, or immediately upon receiving this notification if the time before the scheduled appearance is less than 7 days; if you are hearing or voice impaired, call 711.**

If you are represented by an attorney or plan to retain an attorney for this matter, you should notify the attorney of this hearing.

If this matter is resolved, the moving party shall contact the judge or hearing officer's office to cancel this hearing.

I certify that a copy of this document was ( ) mailed ( ) faxed and mailed ( ) e-mailed ( ) hand delivered to the person(s) listed below on *{date}* _____________.

Other party or his/her attorney:
Name: __________________________________
Address: ________________________________
City, State, Zip: ___________________________
Fax Number: ______________________________
Designated E-mail Address(es):____________________

Dated: ____________________

____
Signature of Party
Printed Name: ____________________________
Address: ________________________________
City, State, Zip: __________________________
Telephone Number: ________________________
Fax Number: ______________________________
Designated E-mail Address(es):__________________

IF A NONLAWYER HELPED YOU FILL OUT THIS FORM, HE/SHE MUST FILL IN THE BLANKS BELOW:
[fill in **all** blanks] This form was prepared for the: *{choose only one}* ( ) Petitioner ( ) Respondent.
This form was completed with the assistance of:
{name of individual} ____,
*{name of business}*____,
*{address}*____,
{city} ______________, *{state}* ____, *{zip code}*___________, *{telephone number}* _______________.

Florida Supreme Court Approved Family Law Form 12.961, Notice of Hearing on Motion for Contempt/ Enforcement (03/15)

INSTRUCTIONS FOR FLORIDA SUPREME COURT APPROVED FAMILY LAW FORM 12.961 NOTICE OF HEARING ON MOTION FOR CONTEMPT/ENFORCEMENT (03/15)

When should this form be used?

Use this form anytime you have set a **hearing** on a **Motion for Contempt/Enforcement**, Florida Supreme Court Approved Family Law Form 12.960, for a support matter under rule 12.615, Florida Family Law Rules of Procedure. Before you fill out this form, you should coordinate a hearing time and date with the **judge** or **hearing officer** and the other party. If the Department of Revenue is a party to the case, you may need to schedule your hearing time with the attorney for the Department of Revenue.

If your case is to be heard by a child support enforcement hearing officer, the following information applies: A child support enforcement **hearing officer** is an attorney who has been appointed by administrative order of the court to take testimony and recommend decisions in cases involving the establishment, enforcement, and/or modification of **child support**, and the enforcement of alimony in conjunction with an ongoing child support arrearage order. If your case only involves issues pertaining to child support, you cannot object to the referral of your case to a hearing officer. If your case is going to be heard by a **general magistrate**, you should use **Notice of Hearing Before General Magistrate**, Florida Family Law Rules of Procedure Form 12.920(c).

This form should be typed or printed in black ink. After completing this form, you should **file** the original with the **clerk of the circuit court** in the county where your case was filed and keep a copy for your records.

IMPORTANT INFORMATION REGARDING E–FILING

The Florida Rules of Judicial Administration now require that all petitions, pleadings, and documents be filed electronically except in certain circumstances. **Self–represented litigants may file petitions or other pleadings or documents electronically; however, they are not required to do so.** If you choose to file your pleadings or other documents electronically, you must do so in accordance with Florida Rule of Judicial Administration 2.525, and you must follow the procedures of the judicial circuit in which you file. **The rules and procedures should be carefully read and followed.**

What should I do next?

A copy of this form must be **personally served** by a sheriff or private process server, mailed*, e–mailed*, **or** hand-delivered to any other party(ies) in your case. Please note that if notice is mailed, the court in certain circumstances may not consider mailing to be adequate notice. This is a technical area of the law; if you have any questions about it, you should consult a lawyer. For more information on personal service, see the instructions for **Summons: Personal Service on an Individual,** Florida Family Law Rules of Procedure Form 12.910(a).

IMPORTANT INFORMATION REGARDING E–SERVICE ELECTION

After the initial service of process of the petition or supplemental petition by the Sheriff or certified process server, the Florida Rules of Judicial Administration now require that all documents required or permitted to be served on the other party must be served by electronic mail (e–mail) except in certain circumstances. **You must strictly comply with the format requirements set forth in the Rules of Judicial Administration.**

SELF–REPRESENTED LITIGANTS MAY SERVE DOCUMENTS BY E–MAIL; HOWEVER, THEY ARE NOT REQUIRED TO DO SO. If a self-represented litigant elects to serve and receive documents by e-mail, the procedures must always be followed once the initial election is made.

To serve and receive documents by e-mail, you must designate your e-mail addresses by using the **Designation of Current Mailing and E-mail Address**, Florida Supreme Court Approved Family Law Form 12.915, and you must provide your e-mail address on each form on which your signature appears. Please **CAREFULLY** read the rules and instructions for: **Certificate of Service (General),** Florida Supreme Court Approved Family Law Form

12.914; **Designation of Current Mailing and E–mail Address**, Florida Supreme Court Approved Family Law Form 12.915; and Florida Rule of Judicial Administration 2.516.

Where can I look for more information?

Before proceeding, you should read General Information for Self–Represented Litigants found at the beginning of these forms. For further information, see rules 12.615 and 12.941, Florida Family Law Rules of Procedure.

Special notes

An attorney who has been appointed by the court to serve as a child support enforcement hearing officer can also be appointed to serve as a general magistrate. If your case involves only child support issues, your case properly may be referred to a general magistrate acting as a child support enforcement hearing officer.

Remember, a person who is NOT an attorney is called a nonlawyer. If a nonlawyer helps you fill out these forms, that person must give you a copy of **Disclosure from Nonlawyer**, Florida Family Law Rules of Procedure Form 12.900(a), before he or she helps you. A non-lawyer helping you fill out these forms also **must** put his or her name, address, and telephone number on the bottom of the last page of every form he or she helps you complete.

Added July 1, 1999 (759 So.2d 583). Amended Sept. 21, 2000 (810 So.2d 1); Sept. 30, 2004, effective Oct. 1, 2004 (887 So.2d 1090); Sept. 28, 2011 (73 So.3d 213); March 26, 2015, effective March 26, 2015 (2015 WL 1343088).

Form 12.962. Writ of Bodily Attachment (Child Support)

IN THE CIRCUIT COURT OF THE ________ JUDICIAL CIRCUIT,
IN AND FOR ________________ COUNTY, FLORIDA

Case No: ________________
Division: ________________

__________________________,
Petitioner,
and

__________________________,
Respondent.

WRIT OF BODILY ATTACHMENT
(Child Support)

TO ALL AND SINGULAR SHERIFFS AND OTHER AUTHORIZED LAW ENFORCEMENT PERSONNEL OF THE STATE OF FLORIDA

YOU ARE ORDERED to take into custody ________________________________ *{see attached Description Sheet}* and confine him/her in the county jail. The individual failed to appear before the court as ordered, failed to appear at a properly noticed hearing, and/or failed to comply with the previous order of the court which is attached and incorporated herein.

Service of this writ may be made on any day of the week and any time of the night or day, including Sunday and holidays.

YOU ARE FURTHER DIRECTED to bring this person before the court within 48 hours of execution of the writ for a hearing to determine the individual's present ability to pay support and, if so, whether the failure to pay such support is willful, pursuant to Rule 12.615(c)(2)(B), Florida Family Law Rules of Procedure.

NOTICE OF EXECUTION OF THIS WRIT SHALL IMMEDIATELY BE GIVEN TO THE FOLLOWING:
{Indicate all that apply}

____ The Office of the Judge/General Magistrate/Child Support Hearing Officer:
____
____

____ Counsel for the Department of Revenue:
____

____ Department of Revenue:
____

____ Other:

IT IS FURTHER ORDERED that the individual may purge this contempt and be immediately released from custody at any time by the payment of the sum of $______________________,
which includes (if applicable):
$ __________________, to be applied to unpaid support,
$ __________________, Sheriff's fee,
$__________________, Department of Revenue costs.
$ __________________, other

The court previously found in this proceeding that the individual had the ability to pay said sum. The Sheriff, or other authorized law enforcement personnel, executing this writ or having custody of the individual is authorized to assess and collect the actual costs associated with service of this writ and transportation of the individual pursuant to Section 61.11(2)(a), Florida Statutes.

PAYMENT SHALL BE MADE to the Sheriff of ________________________ County, Florida and shall be in the form of cash, cashier's check, certified funds, or money order. The purge payment, clearly marked with the individual's name and case number, and denoted as a purge payment shall be remitted to:
{Indicate which are applicable}:

_____ The Office of the Clerk of Circuit Court for ______________________, County, ____

_____ Other ____.

The Sheriff's office, or other authorized law enforcement personnel's office, receiving payment shall provide the individual with a written receipt acknowledging payment. The receipt must be carried by the individual for a period of at least 30 days as proof of payment.

If the individual pays the purge and secures his/her release, the Sheriff shall immediately notify: ____.

THIS ORDER SUPERSEDES ALL PRIOR CONFLICTING ORDERS.

DONE AND ORDERED in ___________ County, Florida this ____day of ___________, 20____.

____
CIRCUIT JUDGE

Florida Supreme Court Approved Family Law Form 12.962, Writ of Bodily Attachment (Child Support) (03/15)

I certify that a copy of this *{name of document}*____
was ( ) mailed ( ) faxed and mailed ( ) e-mailed ( ) hand-delivered to the parties or entities listed below on *{date}*________________________.

by________________________________
{Clerk of court or designee}

Petitioner (or his/her attorney)
Respondent (or his/her attorney)
Department of Revenue
Sheriff of ____________________County
Other:___________________________

DESCRIPTION SHEET

NAME: ______________________ DATE OF BIRTH: __________

OTHER NAMES THE INDIVIDUAL GOES BY (ALIASES OR NICKNAMES): __________

____

ADDRESS: ______________________________________

ALTERNATE ADDRESS: ____________________________

TELEPHONE: ______________ ALTERNATE PHONE: __________

SOCIAL SECURITY NUMBER: ______________ GENDER: ______ RACE: ______

HEIGHT: __________ WEIGHT: __________ EYE COLOR: __________

HAIR COLOR, LENGTH, STYLE: ____________________________

DISTINGUISHING MARKS, SCARS, TATTOOS: ____________________

OTHER CHARACTERISTICS: ______________________________

EMPLOYER: ______________________ EMPLOYER PHONE: __________

EMPLOYER ADDRESS: ____________________________________

VEHICLE (MAKE/MODEL): ________________________________

FLORIDA DRIVER'S LICENSE NUMBER: ______________________

Please use the space below for any additional information you would like to provide.

____

____

____

____

____

____

____

Florida Supreme Court Approved Family Law Form 12.962, Writ of Bodily Attachment (Child Support) (03/15)

Added Dec. 2, 2010 (50 So.3d 595). Amended Aug. 25, 2011 (70 So.3d 553); March 26, 2015, effective March 26, 2015 (2015 WL 1343088).

Form 12.970(a). Petition for Temporary Custody by Extended Family

IN THE CIRCUIT COURT OF THE ________ JUDICIAL CIRCUIT,
IN AND FOR ________________________ COUNTY, FLORIDA

Case No: ____________
Division: ____________

______________________________,
Petitioner,

and

______________________________,
Respondent/Mother,

______________________________,
Respondent/Father.

PETITION FOR TEMPORARY CUSTODY BY EXTENDED FAMILY

Petitioner, *{full legal name}* ______________________________, being sworn, certifies that the following information is true:

1. This is an action for temporary custody pursuant to Chapter 751, Florida Statutes.

2. Petitioner requests temporary custody of the following minor child(ren):

Name	Date of Birth	Current Address

3. Petitioner completed a **Uniform Child Custody Jurisdiction and Enforcement Act Affidavit**, Florida Supreme Court Approved Family Law Form 12.902(d), which was filed with this Petition. The affidavit includes the names and current addresses of the persons with whom the child(ren) has(have) lived during the past 5 years, the places where the child(ren) has(have) lived during the past 5 years, and information concerning any custody proceeding in this or any other state with respect to the child(ren). **If the Affidavit is not completely filled out, signed under oath, and filed with the Petition, the case may be dismissed without hearing.**

4. Petitioner is an extended family member who is: *{Choose **one** only}*

_____ Related to the minor child(ren) within the third degree by blood or marriage to a parent;

OR

_____ The stepparent of the minor child(ren), is married to the ____ Mother ____ Father and is not a party in a pending dissolution, separate maintenance, domestic violence, or other civil or criminal proceeding in any court of competent jurisdiction involving one or both of the child(ren)'s parents as an adverse party.

Florida Supreme Court Approved Family Law Form 12.970(a), Petition for Temporary Custody By Extended Family (03/15)

5. Petitioner's relationship to the minor child(ren) is: ______________________.

6. The residence and post office address of the Petitioner is: ______________________
____.

7. Petitioner is a proper person to be awarded temporary custody because: *{Choose **one** only}*
____ Petitioner has the signed, notarized consent from **both** of the child(ren)'s legal parents;
OR
____ Petitioner is caring full time for the child(ren) in the role of a substitute parent and the child(ren) currently live with the Petitioner.

If Petitioner does not have the signed consents from both parents or is not caring for the child(ren) full time as a substitute parent, Petitioner cannot obtain temporary custody under Chapter 751, Florida Statutes. Petitioner should consult an attorney about other options.

8. The legal mother of the child(ren) is ______________________, whose current address is: ____.

9. The legal father of the child(ren) is ______________________, whose current address is: ____.

10. The Consents of ______ Father **and/or** ______ Mother is/are attached to the Petition.
OR
{If Applicable} The Consent of the ______________ is not attached because that parent is deceased. A certified copy of the proof of death is attached.
OR
Consent has NOT been obtained from the parents. The specific acts or omissions of the parents which demonstrate that the parents have abused, abandoned, or neglected the child(ren) as defined in Chapter 39, Florida Statutes are: (attach additional sheets if necessary) __________
____
____
____
____.

11. Petitioner requests temporary custody be granted for the following period of time: __________
____.
The reasons that support this request are: ______________________________
____
____
____.

12. It is in the best interests of the child(ren) that the Petitioner have temporary custody of the child(ren) for the following reasons: ______________________________
____
____

Florida Supreme Court Approved Family Law Form 12.970(a), Petition for Temporary Custody By Extended Family (03/15)

____.

13. **ORDER OF PROTECTION**

_____ Petitioner **IS NOT** aware of any temporary or permanent order for protection entered on behalf of or against either parent, the Petitioner, or the child(ren) in Florida or any other jurisdiction.

OR

_____ Petitioner **IS** aware of the following temporary or permanent orders for protection entered on behalf of or against either parent, the Petitioner, or the child(ren) in Florida or any other jurisdiction. The court entering the order and the case number is: _______
____
____
____.

14. **TEMPORARY OR PERMANENT CHILD SUPPORT ORDERS**

_____ Petitioner **IS NOT** aware of any temporary or permanent orders for child support for the minor child(ren).

OR

_____ Petitioner **IS** aware of the following temporary or permanent order for child support for the minor child(ren). The court entering the order and the case number is:________
____
____
____.

15. **CHILD SUPPORT** *(Choose **one** only)*

(You must have proof or waiver of service of process upon the parent(s) or a Waiver of Service of Process and Consent for the court to consider an award for child support)

_____ Petitioner requests the court to order the parents to pay child support.

_____ Petitioner requests the court to redirect all or part of Mother's and/or Father's existing child support obligation to the Petitioner.

_____ Petitioner requests the court to redirect all or part of Mother's and/or Father's existing child support obligation to the Petitioner, and to award the Petitioner child support arrearages.

16. Petitioner ____ requests _____ does not request that the court establish reasonable visitation or a time-sharing schedule with the parents.

17. Other
____
____
____
____.

WHEREFORE, Petitioner requests that this Court grant the Petitioner temporary custody of the child(ren) subject to this proceeding; award the Petitioner other relief as requested; and award any other relief

Florida Supreme Court Approved Family Law Form 12.970(a), Petition for Temporary Custody By Extended Family (03/15)

that the Court deems necessary.

I understand that I am swearing or affirming under oath to the truthfulness of the claims made in this petition and that the punishment for knowingly making a false statement includes fines and/or imprisonment.

Dated:______________________________ ______________________________________
Signature of Petitioner

Printed Name: ____________________________
Address: ________________________________
City, State, Zip Code: ______________________
Telephone Number: _______________________
Number: ________________________________
E-Mail Address(es):_______________________
____

STATE OF FLORIDA
COUNTY OF ______________________________

Sworn to or affirmed and signed before me on ____________ by _________________________.

____
NOTARY PUBLIC OR DEPUTY CLERK

____
{Print, type, or stamp commissioned name of notary or deputy clerk.}

____ Personally known
____ Produced identification
Type of identification produced ______________________

IF A NONLAWYER HELPED YOU FILL OUT THIS FORM, HE/SHE MUST FILL IN THE BLANKS BELOW:
[fill in **all** blanks] This form was prepared for the Petitioner.
This form was completed with the assistance of:
{name of individual} ____,
{name of business} ____,
{address} ____,
{city} _________________, *{state}* ____,*{zip code}* ___________, *{telephone number}* _________.

INSTRUCTIONS FOR FLORIDA SUPREME COURT APPROVED FAMILY LAW FORM 12.970(a) PETITION FOR TEMPORARY CUSTODY BY EXTENDED FAMILY (03/15)

When should this form be used?

This form should be used by an extended family member to obtain temporary custody of a child or children pursuant to Chapter 751, Florida Statutes. This form **should not** be used if you are a parent seeking to establish parental responsibility or time-sharing with a child or children.

An **Extended Family Member** is:

A relative of a minor child within the third degree by blood or marriage to the parent;

OR

The stepparent of a minor child if the stepparent is currently married to the parent of the child and is not a party in a pending dissolution, separate maintenance, domestic violence, or other civil or criminal proceeding in any court of competent jurisdiction involving one or both of the child(ren)'s parents as an adverse party.

You may file a Petition for Temporary Custody if:

You have the signed, notarized consents of the child(ren)'s legal parents;

OR

You are an extended family member who is caring full time for the child(ren) in the role of a substitute parent and with whom the child(ren) is (are) presently living.

If one of the minor child(ren)'s parents objects to the Petition, the court shall grant the Petition only upon a finding, by clear and convincing evidence, that the child(ren)'s parent or parents are unfit to provide for the care and control of the child(ren). In determining that a parent is unfit, the court must find that the parent has abused, abandoned, or neglected the child(ren), as defined in Chapter 39, Florida Statutes. If you do not have the parents' consents **you should consult a family law attorney before you file your papers.**

If you do not meet the qualifications above, you should talk to an attorney about other options. You may also report any suspected abuse, abandonment, or neglect to the appropriate authorities.

This form should be typed or printed in black ink. After completing this form, you should sign the form before a notary public or deputy clerk. You should file the original with the clerk of the circuit court in the county where you live and keep a copy for your records.

IMPORTANT INFORMATION REGARDING E–FILING

The Florida Rules of Judicial Administration now require that all petitions, pleadings, and documents be filed electronically except in certain circumstances. **Self–represented litigants may file petitions or other pleadings or documents electronically; however, they are not required to do so.** If you choose to file your pleadings or other documents electronically, you must do so in accordance with Florida Rule of Judicial Administration 2.525, and you must follow the procedures of the judicial circuit in which you file. **The rules and procedures should be carefully read and followed.**

IMPORTANT INFORMATION REGARDING E–SERVICE ELECTION

After the initial service of process of the petition or supplemental petition by the Sheriff or certified process server, the Florida Rules of Judicial Administration now require that all documents required or permitted to be served on the other party must be served by electronic mail (e–mail) except in certain circumstances. **You must strictly comply with the format requirements set forth in the Rules of Judicial Administration.**

SELF–REPRESENTED LITIGANTS MAY SERVE DOCUMENTS BY E–MAIL; HOWEVER, THEY ARE NOT REQUIRED TO DO SO. If a self-represented litigant elects to serve and receive documents by e-mail, the procedures must always be followed once the initial election is made.

To serve and receive documents by e-mail, you must designate your e-mail addresses by using the **Designation of Current Mailing and E–mail Address**, Florida Supreme Court Approved Family Law Form 12.915, and you must provide your e-mail address on each form on which your signature appears. Please **CAREFULLY** read the rules and instructions for: **Certificate of Service (General),** Florida Supreme Court Approved Family Law Form 12.914; **Designation of Current Mailing and E–mail Address**, Florida Supreme Court Approved Family Law Form 12.915; and Florida Rule of Judicial Administration 2.516.

What should I do next?

IF YOU HAVE SIGNED AND NOTARIZED WAIVERS OF SERVICE OF PROCESS AND CONSENTS from the child(ren)'s mother and father, and the case is uncontested, you may call the clerk, **family law intake staff**, or **judicial assistant**, to set a **final hearing.** You must notify the child(ren)'s parents of the hearing by using a **Notice of Hearing (General)**, Florida Supreme Court Approved Family Law Form 12.923, or other appropriate notice of hearing form.

If one of the parents is deceased, you must file a certified copy of the proof of death.

IF YOU DO NOT HAVE SIGNED AND NOTARIZED WAIVERS OF SERVICE OF PROCESS AND CONSENTS from the child(ren)'s parents, you must properly notify the parents of the **petition**. If you know where he or she lives, you should use **personal service.** If you absolutely do not know where he or she lives after conducting a diligent search, you may use **constructive service.** You must complete all of the searches listed in the **Affidavit of Diligent Search and Inquiry**, Florida Family Law Rules of Procedure Form 12.913(b), and file the form with the clerk. You should seek legal advice on constructive service as this is a complicated area of the law. If the identity of one parent is unknown, you will need to seek legal advice to determine the proper way to serve an unknown parent. For more information, see Chapter 49, Florida Statutes.

If personal service is used, the **parents** have 20 days to answer after being served with your petition. Your case will generally proceed in one of the following ways:

DEFAULT . . . If after 20 days, no **answer** has been filed, you may file a **Motion for Default**, Florida Supreme Court Approved Family Law Form 12.922(a), with the clerk of court. You must file a **Notice for Trial**, Florida Supreme Court Approved Family Law Form 12.924. Then, if you have filed all of the required papers, you may call the clerk, **family law intake staff**, or **judicial assistant**, to set a **final hearing.** You must notify the child(ren)'s parents of the hearing by using a **Notice of Hearing (General)**, Florida Supreme Court Approved Family Law Form 12.923, or other appropriate notice of hearing form.

CONTESTED . . . If either parent files an answer which disagrees with or denies anything in your petition, and you are unable to settle the disputed issues, you must file a **Notice for Trial**, Florida Supreme Court Approved Family Law Form 12.924, to request a final hearing. Some circuits may require the completion of **mediation** before a final hearing may be set. You should contact the clerk, **family law intake staff**, or **judicial assistant** for instructions on how to set your case for **trial** (final hearing).

At any time, either or both of the child(ren)'s parents may petition the court to modify or terminate the order granting temporary custody. The court shall terminate the order upon a finding that the parent is a fit parent, or by the consent of the parties. The court may modify an order granting temporary custody if the parties consent or if the modification is in the best interest of the child(ren).

Where can I look for more information?

Before proceeding, you should read General Information for Self–Represented Litigants found at the beginning of these forms. The words that are in **bold underline** in these instructions are defined there. For further information, see Chapter 751 and Chapter 39, Florida Statutes.

Special Notes . . .

If you do not have the money to pay the filing fee, you may obtain an application for Determination of Civil Indigent Status, fill it out, and the clerk will determine whether you are eligible to have filing fees deferred.

With this petition, you must file the following and provide a copy to the other party:

- **Uniform Child Custody Jurisdiction and Enforcement Act (UCCJEA) Affidavit,** Florida Supreme Court Approved Family Law Form 12.902(d).

- **Notice of Related Cases**, Florida Family Law Rules of Procedure Form 12.900(h).
- **Family Court Cover Sheet**, Florida Family Law Rules of Procedure Form 12.928.
- **Non–Military Affidavit**, Florida Supreme Court Approved Family Law Form 12.912(b). (Required only for obtaining a default on petitions that have been personally or constructively served. Not required if both parents have signed a waiver and consent)

Remember, a person who is NOT an attorney is called a nonlawyer. If a nonlawyer helps you fill out these forms, that person must give you a copy of a **Disclosure from Nonlawyer**, Florida Family Law Rules of Procedure Form 12.900(a), before he or she helps you. A nonlawyer helping you fill out these forms **must** also put his or her name, address, and telephone number on the bottom of the last page of every form he or she helps you complete.

Added April 7, 2011 (60 So.3d 979). Amended March 26, 2015, effective March 26, 2015 (2015 WL 1343088).

Form 12.970(b). Petition for Concurrent Custody by Extended Family

IN THE CIRCUIT COURT OF THE ________ JUDICIAL CIRCUIT,
IN AND FOR ________________________ COUNTY, FLORIDA

Case No: ____________________
Division: ______________________

______________________________,
Petitioner,

and

______________________________,
Respondent/Mother,

______________________________,
Respondent/Father.

PETITION FOR CONCURRENT CUSTODY BY EXTENDED FAMILY

Petitioner, *{full legal name}* ______________________________, being sworn, certifies that the following information is true:

1. This is an action for concurrent custody pursuant to Chapter 751, Florida Statutes.

2. Petitioner requests concurrent custody of the following minor child(ren):
   Name Date of Birth Current Address
   ____
   ____
   ____
   ____

3. Petitioner completed a **Uniform Child Custody Jurisdiction and Enforcement Act Affidavit**, Florida Supreme Court Approved Family Law Form 12.902(d), which was filed with this Petition. The affidavit includes the names and current addresses of the persons with whom the child(ren) has (have) lived during the past 5 years, the places where the child(ren) has(have) lived during the past 5 years, and information concerning any custody proceeding in this or any other state with respect to the child(ren). **If the Affidavit is not completely filled out, signed under oath, and filed with the Petition, the case may be dismissed without a hearing.**

4. Petitioner is an extended family member who is: *{Choose **one** only}*
   _____ Related to the minor child(ren) within the third degree by blood or marriage to a parent;
   OR
   _____ The stepparent of the minor child(ren), is married to the ( )Mother ( )Father and is not a party in a pending dissolution, separate maintenance, domestic violence, or other civil or criminal proceeding in any court of competent jurisdiction involving one or both of the child(ren)'s parents as an adverse party.

Florida Supreme Court Approved Family Law Form 12.970(b), Petition for Concurrent Custody By Extended Family (03/15)

5. Petitioner's relationship to the minor child(ren) is: ______________________________.
6. The residence and post office address of the Petitioner is: ______________________________
______________________________.

7. The legal mother of the child(ren) is ______________________________, whose current address is: ______________________________.

8. The legal father of the child(ren) is ______________________________, whose current address is: ______________________________.

9. Petitioner currently has physical custody of the child(ren) and has had physical custody of the child(ren) for at least 10 days in any 30-day period within the last 12 months. Detail the time periods during the past 12 months when the child(ren) have resided with the Petitioner:
____
____
______________________________.

10. Petitioner does not have signed, written documentation from a parent which is sufficient to enable the Petitioner to do all of the things necessary to care for the child(ren).

11. *{If applicable}* Describe the type of documents, if any, provided by the parent or parents which enables the Petitioner to act on behalf of the child(ren): ______________________________
______________________________.

These documents are attached to this Petition as Exhibit ________.

12. Petitioner is unable to obtain or undertake the following services or actions without an order of custody:
____
____
____
______________________________.

13. The Consents of ______Father **and/or** ________ Mother is/are attached to the Petition.
OR
{If applicable} The Consent of the ______________ is not attached because that parent is deceased. A certified copy of the proof of death is attached.

14. Petitioner requests concurrent custody be granted for the following period of time:______________________________.
The reasons that support this request are: ______________________________
____
____
______________________________.

15. It is in the best interests of the child(ren) that the Petitioner have concurrent custody of the child(ren) for the following reasons: ______________________________

____
____
____.

16. **ORDER OF PROTECTION**

____ Petitioner **IS NOT** aware of any temporary or permanent order for protection entered on behalf of or against either parent, the Petitioner, or the child(ren) in Florida or any other jurisdiction.

OR

____ Petitioner **IS** aware of the following temporary or permanent orders for protection entered on behalf of or against either parent, the Petitioner, or the child(ren) in Florida or any other jurisdiction. The court entering the order and the case number is: ________
____
____
____.

17. **TEMPORARY OR PERMANENT CHILD SUPPORT ORDERS**

____ Petitioner **IS NOT** aware of any temporary or permanent orders for child support for the minor child(ren).

OR

____ Petitioner **IS** aware of the following temporary or permanent order for child support for the minor child(ren). The court entering the order and the case number is:______
____
____
____.

18. **CHILD SUPPORT (If Petitioner is seeking child support)** *{Choose one only}* (You must have proof of service upon or waiver of process by the parent(s) or a Waiver of Service of Process and Consent for the court to consider an award for child support)

____ Petitioner requests the court to order the parents to pay child support.

____ Petitioner requests the court to redirect all or part of Mother's and/or Father's existing child support obligation to the Petitioner.

____ Petitioner requests the court to redirect all or part of Mother's and/or Father's existing child support obligation to the Petitioner, **and** to award the Petitioner child support arrearages.

19. Petitioner ____ requests _____ does not request that the court establish reasonable visitation or a time-sharing schedule with the parents.

20. Other ____
____
____
____

WHEREFORE, Petitioner requests that this Court grant the Petitioner concurrent custody of the child(ren) subject to this proceeding; award the Petitioner other relief as requested; and award any other relief that the Court deems necessary.

I understand that I am swearing or affirming under oath to the truthfulness of the claims made in this petition and that the punishment for knowingly making a false statement includes fines and/or imprisonment.

Dated: ____________________________

____
Signature of Petitioner

Printed Name: ______________________
Address: __________________________
City, State, Zip Code: ________________
Telephone Number: _________________
Fax Number: _______________________
Designated E-mail Address(es): __________
____

STATE OF FLORIDA
COUNTY OF _______________________________

Sworn to or affirmed and signed before me on ______________ by ________________________.

____
NOTARY PUBLIC OR DEPUTY CLERK

____
Print, type, or stamp commissioned name of notary or deputy clerk.

____ Personally known
____ Produced identification
Type of identification produced ______________________

IF A NONLAWYER HELPED YOU FILL OUT THIS FORM, HE/SHE MUST FILL IN THE BLANKS BELOW:
[fill in **all** blanks] This form was prepared for the Petitioner.
This form was completed with the assistance of:
{name of individual} ____,
{name of business} ____,
{address} ____,
{city} ________________, *{state}* _____, *{zip code}*__________, *{telephone number}* ______________.

Florida Supreme Court Approved Family Law Form 12.970(b), Petition for Concurrent Custody By Extended Family (03/15)

INSTRUCTIONS FOR FLORIDA SUPREME COURT APPROVED FAMILY LAW FORM 12.970(b) PETITION FOR CONCURRENT CUSTODY BY EXPENDED FAMILY (03/15)

When should this form be used?

This form should be used by an **extended family member** to obtain concurrent custody of a child or children pursuant to Chapter 751, Florida Statutes. This form **should not** be used if you are a parent seeking to establish parental responsibility or time-sharing with a child or children. "Concurrent custody" means that an eligible extended family member is awarded custodial rights to care for a child or children concurrently with the child(ren)'s parent or parents.

An **Extended Family Member** is:

A relative of a minor child within the third degree by blood or marriage to the parent;

OR

The stepparent of a minor child if the stepparent is currently married to the parent of the child and is not a party in a pending dissolution, separate maintenance, domestic violence, or other civil or criminal proceeding in any court of competent jurisdiction involving one or both of the child(ren)'s parents as an adverse party.

You may file a Petition for Concurrent Custody if:

You have the signed, notarized consents of the child(ren)'s legal parents;

OR

You are an extended family member who is caring full time for the child(ren) in the role of a substitute parent and with whom the child(ren) is (are) presently living.

In addition, you must currently have physical custody of the child(ren) and have had physical custody of the child(ren) for at least 10 days in any 30–day period within the last 12 months; and not have signed, written documentation from a parent which is sufficient to enable you to do all the things necessary to care for the child(ren).

If you do not meet the qualifications above, you should talk to an attorney about other options. You may also report any suspected abuse, abandonment, or neglect to the appropriate authorities.

This form should be typed or printed in black ink. After completing this form, you should sign the form before a **notary public** or **deputy clerk**. You should **file** the original with the **clerk of the circuit court** in the county where you live and keep a copy for your records.

IMPORTANT INFORMATION REGARDING E–FILING

The Florida Rules of Judicial Administration now require that all petitions, pleadings, and documents be filed electronically except in certain circumstances. **Self–represented litigants may file petitions or other pleadings or documents electronically; however, they are not required to do so.** If you choose to file your pleadings or other documents electronically, you must do so in accordance with Florida Rule of Judicial Administration 2.525, and you must follow the procedures of the judicial circuit in which you file. **The rules and procedures should be carefully read and followed.**

IMPORTANT INFORMATION REGARDING E–SERVICE ELECTION

After the initial service of process of the petition or supplemental petition by the Sheriff or certified process server, the Florida Rules of Judicial Administration now require that all documents required or permitted to be served on the other party must be served by electronic mail (e–mail) except in certain circumstances. **You must strictly comply with the format requirements set forth in the Rules of Judicial Administration.**

SELF–REPRESENTED LITIGANTS MAY SERVE DOCUMENTS BY E–MAIL; HOWEVER, THEY ARE NOT REQUIRED TO DO SO. If a self-represented litigant elects to serve and receive documents by e-mail, the procedures must always be followed once the initial election is made.

To serve and receive documents by e-mail, you must designate your e-mail addresses by using the **Designation of Current Mailing and E–mail Address**, Florida Supreme Court Approved Family Law Form 12.915, and you must provide your e-mail address on each form on which your signature appears. Please **CAREFULLY** read the rules and instructions for: **Certificate of Service (General),** Florida Supreme Court Approved Family Law Form 12.914; **Designation of Current Mailing and E–mail Address**, Florida Supreme Court Approved Family Law Form 12.915; and Florida Rule of Judicial Administration 2.516.

What should I do next?

IF YOU HAVE SIGNED AND NOTARIZED WAIVERS OF SERVICE OF PROCESS AND CONSENTS from the child(ren)'s mother and father, you may call the clerk, **family law intake staff**, or **judicial assistant**, to set a **final hearing.** You must notify the child(ren)'s parents of the hearing by using a **Notice of Hearing (General)**, Florida Supreme Court Approved Family Law Form 12.923, or other appropriate notice of hearing form.

If one of the parents is deceased, you must file a certified copy of the proof of death.

If one of the minor child(ren)'s parents objects to the Petition for Concurrent Custody in writing, the court may not grant the petition even if the other parent consents, in writing, to the entry of the order. If a parent objects, you have the option of converting the Petition to a **Petition for Temporary Custody by Extended Family,** Florida Supreme Court Approved Family Law Form 12.970(a). If the Petition is not converted into a **Petition for Temporary Custody by Extended Family**, it shall be dismissed without prejudice.

At any time, the Petitioner or either or both of the child(ren)'s parents may move the court to terminate the order granting concurrent custody. The court shall terminate the order upon a finding that either or both of the child(ren)'s parents objects to the order. The fact that the order for concurrent custody has been terminated does not preclude any person who is otherwise eligible to petition for temporary custody from filing such petition.

Where can I look for more information?

Before proceeding, you should read General Information for Self–Represented Litigants found at the beginning of these forms. The words that are in **bold underline** in these instructions are defined there. For further information, see Chapter 751 and Chapter 39, Florida Statutes.

Special Notes . . .

If you do not have the money to pay the filing fee, you may obtain an application for Determination of Civil Indigent Status, fill it out, and the clerk will determine whether you are eligible to have filing fees deferred.

With this petition, you must file the following and provide a copy to the other party:

- **Uniform Child Custody Jurisdiction and Enforcement Act (UCCJEA) Affidavit,** Florida Supreme Court Approved Family Law Form 12.902(d).
- **Notice of Related Cases**, Florida Family Law Rules of Procedure Form 12.900(h).
- **Family Court Cover Sheet**, Florida Family Law Rules of Procedure Form 12.928.
- **Non–Military Affidavit**, Florida Supreme Court Approved Family Law Form 12.912(b). (Required only for obtaining a default on petitions that have been personally or constructively served. Not required if both parents have signed a waiver and consent.)

Remember, a person who is NOT an attorney is called a nonlawyer. If a nonlawyer helps you fill out these forms, that person must give you a copy of a **Disclosure from Nonlawyer,** Florida Family Law Rules of Procedure Form 12.900(a), before he or she helps you. A nonlawyer helping you fill out these forms must also put his or her name, address, and telephone number on the bottom of the last page of every form he or she helps you complete.

Added April 7, 2011 (60 So.3d 979). Amended March 26, 2015, effective March 26, 2015 (2015 WL 1343088).

Form 12.970(c). Waiver of Service of Process and Consent for Temporary Custody by Extended Family

IN THE CIRCUIT COURT OF THE ____________ JUDICIAL CIRCUIT,
IN AND FOR __________________________ COUNTY, FLORIDA

Case No: ____________________
Division: ____________________

_____________________________,
Petitioner,

and

_____________________________,
Respondent/Mother,

_____________________________,
Respondent/Father.

WAIVER OF SERVICE OF PROCESS AND CONSENT FOR TEMPORARY CUSTODY BY EXTENDED FAMILY

I, ____________________________________, the legal _____ Mother ____ Father of *{child(ren)'s name)s)}* ______________________________, having received a copy of the Petition for Temporary Custody by Extended Family filed herein and waived service of process, freely and voluntarily consent to the Petition filed by: *{Petitioner's Name}* ________________________.

I realize that by signing this document, I am consenting to the Petitioner having temporary legal custody of the minor child(ren) and that such temporary custody is in the best interest of the child(ren). Upon entry of an Order, the Petitioner shall be able to:

1. Consent to all necessary and reasonable medical and dental care for the child(ren), including nonemergency surgery and psychiatric care;

2. Secure copies of the child(ren)'s records, held by third parties, that are necessary for the care of the child(ren), including, but not limited to:
   a. Medical, dental, and psychiatric records;
   b. Birth Certificates and other records, and
   c. Educational records.

3. Enroll the child(ren) in school and grant or withhold consent for the child(ren) to be tested or placed in special school programs, including exceptional education; and

4. Do all other things necessary for the care of the child(ren).

Florida Supreme Court Approved Family Law Form 12.970(c), Waiver of Service of Process and Consent for Temporary Custody By Extended Family (03/15)

I realize that the custody of my child(ren) by the Petitioner is temporary and that I may, at any time, petition the court to return legal custody to me.

Dated: ____________________ ____

Signature of Parent
Printed Name: ______________________________
Address: ___________________________________
City, State, Zip Code: ______________________
Telephone Number: _________________________
Fax Number: _______________________________
Designated E-mail Address(es):_________________
____

STATE OF FLORIDA
COUNTY OF ____________________________________

Sworn to or affirmed and signed before me on ______________ by ________________________.

____
NOTARY PUBLIC OR DEPUTY CLERK

____
Print, type, or stamp commissioned name of notary or deputy clerk.

____ Personally known
____ Produced identification
Type of identification produced ____________________________

IF A NONLAWYER HELPED YOU FILL OUT THIS FORM, HE/SHE MUST FILL IN THE BLANKS BELOW:
[fill in all blanks] This form was prepared for the *{choose only one}* ( ) Petitioner ( ) Respondent.
This form was completed with the assistance of:
{name of individual} ____,
{name of business} ____,
{address} ____,
{city} ________________, *{state}* _____, *{zip code}* ________, *{telephone number}* ____________.

Florida Supreme Court Approved Family Law Form 12.970(c), Waiver of Service of Process and Consent for Temporary Custody By Extended Family (03/15)

INSTRUCTIONS FOR FLORIDA SUPREME COURT APPROVED FAMILY LAW FORM 12.970(c), WAIVER OF SERVICE OF PROCESS AND CONSENT FOR TEMPORARY CUSTODY BY EXTENDED FAMILY (03/15)

This form is to be completed and signed by a parent who agrees to grant temporary custody of a minor child or child(ren) to an **extended family member** and agrees to waive **service** of process. Service of process occurs when a summons and a copy of the petition (or other pleading) that has been filed with the court are delivered by a deputy or private process server.

An **Extended Family Member** is:

A relative of a minor child within the third degree by blood or marriage to the parent;

OR

The stepparent of a minor child if the stepparent is currently married to the parent of the child and is not a party in a pending dissolution, separate maintenance, domestic violence, or other civil or criminal proceeding in any court of competent jurisdiction involving one or both of the child(ren)'s parents as an adverse party.

This form should be typed or printed in black ink. After completing this form, you should sign the form before a **notary public** or **deputy clerk**. You should **file** the original with the **clerk of the circuit court** in the county where the **Petition for Temporary Custody by Extended Family,** Florida Supreme Court Approved Family Law Form 12.970(a) is filed and keep a copy for your records.

IMPORTANT INFORMATION REGARDING E-FILING

The Florida Rules of Judicial Administration now require that all petitions, pleadings, and documents be filed electronically except in certain circumstances. **Self-represented litigants may file petitions or other pleadings or documents electronically; however, they are not required to do so.** If you choose to file your pleadings or other documents electronically, you must do so in accordance with Florida Rule of Judicial Administration 2.525, and you must follow the procedures of the judicial circuit in which you file. **The rules and procedures should be carefully read and followed.**

Special notes . . .

Remember, a person who is NOT an attorney is called a nonlawyer. If a nonlawyer helps you fill out these forms, that person must give you a copy of a **Disclosure from Nonlawyer**, Florida Family Law Rules of Procedure Form 12.900(a), before he or she helps you. A nonlawyer helping you fill out these forms **must** also put his or her name, address, and telephone number on the bottom of the last page of every form he or she helps you complete.

Added April 7, 2011 (60 So.3d 979). Amended March 26, 2015, effective March 26, 2015 (2015 WL 1343088).

Form 12.970(d). Waiver of Service of Process and Consent for Concurrent Custody by Extended Family

IN THE CIRCUIT COURT OF THE ______________ JUDICIAL CIRCUIT,
IN AND FOR ____________________________ COUNTY, FLORIDA

Case No: ____________________
Division: ____________________

______________________________________,
Petitioner,

and

______________________________________,
Respondent/Mother,

______________________________________,
Respondent/Father.

WAIVER OF SERVICE OF PROCESS AND CONSENT FOR CONCURRENT CUSTODY BY EXTENDED FAMILY

I, ______________________________, the legal ____ Mother ____ Father of *{child(ren)'s name(s)}* ______________________________, having received a copy of the Petition for Concurrent Custody by Extended Family filed herein and waived service of process, freely and voluntarily consent to the Petition filed by *{Petitioner's Name}* ____________________.

I realize that by signing this document, I am consenting to the Petitioner having temporary concurrent custody of the minor child(ren) and that such concurrent custody is in the best interest of the child(ren). Upon entry of an Order, the Petitioner shall be able to:

1. Consent to all necessary and reasonable medical and dental care for the child(ren), including nonemergency surgery and psychiatric care;

2. Secure copies of the child(ren)'s records, held by third parties, that are necessary for the care of the child(ren), including, but not limited to:
   a. Medical, dental, and psychiatric records;
   b. Birth Certificates and other records, and
   c. Educational records.

3. Enroll the child(ren) in school and grant or withhold consent for the child(ren) to be tested or placed in special school programs, including exceptional education; and

4. Do all other things necessary for the care of the child(ren).

Florida Supreme Court Approved Family Law Form 12.970(d), Waiver of Service of Process and Consent for Concurrent Custody By Extended Family (03/15)

I realize that the concurrent custody of my child(ren) by the Petitioner is temporary and that I may, at any time, petition the court to return legal custody to me.

Dated: ____________________ ____________________
Signature of Parent

Printed Name: ____________________
Address: ____________________
City, State, Zip Code: ____________________
Telephone Number: ____________________
Fax Number: ____________________
Designated E-mail Address(es): ____________________
____

STATE OF FLORIDA
COUNTY OF ____________________

Sworn to or affirmed and signed before me on ____________ by ____________________.

____
NOTARY PUBLIC OR DEPUTY CLERK

____
Print, type, or stamp commissioned name of notary or deputy clerk.

____ Personally known
____ Produced identification
Type of identification produced ____________________

IF A NONLAWYER HELPED YOU FILL OUT THIS FORM, HE/SHE MUST FILL IN THE BLANKS BELOW:
[fill in all blanks] This form was prepared for the *{choose only **one**}* ( ) Petitioner ( ) Respondent.
This form was completed with the assistance of:
{name of individual} ____________________,
{name of business} ____________________,
{address} ____________________,
{city} ____________, *{state}* ____, *{zip code}* ____, *{telephone number}* ____________.

Florida Supreme Court Approved Family Law Form 12.970(d), Waiver of Service of Process and Consent for Concurrent Custody By Extended Family (03/15)

INSTRUCTIONS FOR FLORIDA SUPREME COURT APPROVED FAMILY LAW FORM 12.970(d), WAIVER OF SERVICE OF PROCESS AND CONSENT FOR CONCURRENT CUSTODY BY EXTENDED FAMILY (03/15)

This form is to be completed and signed by a parent who agrees to grant **concurrent custody** of a minor child or child(ren) to an **extended family member** and who agrees to waive **service** of process. Service of process occurs when a summons and a copy of the petition (or other pleading) that has been filed with the court are delivered by a deputy or private process server. "Concurrent custody" means that an eligible extended family member is awarded custodial rights to care for a child or children concurrently with the child(ren)'s parent or parents.

An **Extended Family Member** is:

A relative of a minor child within the third degree by blood or marriage to the parent;

OR

The stepparent of a minor child if the stepparent is currently married to the parent of the child and is not a party in a pending dissolution, separate maintenance, domestic violence, or other civil or criminal proceeding in any court of competent jurisdiction involving one or both of the child(ren)'s parents as an adverse party.

This form should be typed or printed in black ink. After completing this form, you should sign the form before a **notary public** or **deputy clerk**. You should **file** the original with the **clerk of the circuit court** in the county where the **Petition for Concurrent Custody by Extended Family,** Florida Supreme Court Approved Family Law Form 12.970(b) is filed and keep a copy for your records.

IMPORTANT INFORMATION REGARDING E–FILING

The Florida Rules of Judicial Administration now require that all petitions, pleadings, and documents be filed electronically except in certain circumstances. **Self–represented litigants may file petitions or other pleadings or documents electronically; however, they are not required to do so.** If you choose to file your pleadings or other documents electronically, you must do so in accordance with Florida Rule of Judicial Administration 2.525, and you must follow the procedures of the judicial circuit in which you file. **The rules and procedures should be carefully read and followed.**

Special notes . . .

Remember, a person who is NOT an attorney is called a nonlawyer. If a nonlawyer helps you fill out these forms, that person must give you a copy of a **Disclosure from Nonlawyer**, Florida Family Law Rules of Procedure Form 12.900(a), before he or she helps you. A nonlawyer helping you fill out these forms **must** also put his or her name, address, and telephone number on the bottom of the last page of every form he or she helps you complete.

Added April 7, 2011 (60 So.3d 979). Amended March 26, 2015, effective March 26, 2015 (2015 WL 1343088).

Form 12.970(e). Order Granting Petition for Temporary Custody by Extended Family

IN THE CIRCUIT COURT OF THE ____________________ JUDICIAL CIRCUIT
IN AND FOR ____________________ COUNTY, FLORIDA

Case No: ____________________
Division: ____________________

____________________________________,
Petitioner,

and

____________________________________,
Respondent/Mother

____________________________________,
Respondent/Father.

ORDER GRANTING PETITION FOR TEMPORARY CUSTODY BY EXTENDED FAMILY

This case came before this Court for a hearing on a Petition for Temporary Custody by Extended Family. The Court, having reviewed the file and heard the testimony, makes these findings of fact and reaches these conclusions of law:

SECTION I. FINDINGS:

1. The Court has jurisdiction over the subject matter and the parties.

2. The minor child(ren) at issue in this matter are:

Name	Date of Birth

3. The Petitioner, *{full legal name}* ____________________ is the *{extended family relationship}* ____________________ of the child(ren).

4. The Mother *{full legal name}* ____________________ of the child(ren):
   *{Choose **one** only}*
   ____ Filed a Waiver and Consent
   ____ Was served with the petition and failed to file an Answer

____ Is deceased as evidenced by: ______________________________
____ Objected to the petition. Based upon clear and convincing evidence, the Court finds that the Mother is unfit to provide for the care and control of the child(ren). Specifically, the Mother has abused, abandoned, or neglected the child(ren) as defined in Chapter 39, Florida Statutes. It is in the best interest of the child(ren) that the Petitioner have temporary custody because: *{facts in support of finding}* ____
____
____
____
____.

5. The Father *{full legal name}* ______________________________ of the child(ren): *{Choose **one** only}*
   ____ Filed a Waiver and Consent
   ____ Was served with the petition and failed to file an Answer
   ____ Is deceased as evidenced by: ______________________________
   ____ Objected to the petition. Based upon clear and convincing evidence, the Court finds that the Father is unfit to provide for the care and control of the child(ren). Specifically, the Father has abused, abandoned, or neglected the child(ren) as defined in Chapter 39, Florida Statutes. It is in the best interest of the child(ren) that the Petitioner have temporary custody because: *{facts in support of finding}*
   ____
   ____
   ____
   ____
   ____.

6. It is in the best interest of the child(ren) for the Petitioner to have temporary custody.

SECTION II: TEMPORARY CUSTODY

1. The Petitioner, ______________________________, is granted temporary custody of the minor child(ren).

2. The Petitioner shall have all the rights and responsibilities of a legal parent.

3. The Petitioner is authorized to make all reasonable and necessary decisions for the minor child(ren), including but not limited to:
   a) Consent to all necessary and reasonable medical and dental care for the child(ren), including nonemergency surgery and psychiatric care;

b) Secure copies of the child(ren)'s records, held by third parties, that are necessary for the care of the child(ren), including, but not limited to: medical, dental, and psychiatric records; birth certificates and other records; and educational records;

c) Enroll the child(ren) in school and grant or withhold consent for the child(ren) to be tested or placed in special school programs, including exceptional education; and

d) Do all other things necessary for the care of the child(ren).

SECTION III. TEMPORARY TIME-SHARING WITH MINOR CHILD(REN)

The parent(s) shall have: *{Choose **one** only}*

1. ____ **reasonable** time-sharing with the minor child(ren) as agreed to by the parties, subject to the following limitations: ____
____.

2. ____ the following **specified time-sharing schedule**: *{specify days and times}* ________
____.

Mother's Temporary Time-Sharing Schedule.

____
____
____.

Father's Temporary Time-Sharing Schedule.

____
____
____.

3. ____ Time-Sharing in accordance with the temporary **Parenting Plan** attached as Exhibit ___.

4. The____ Mother ____ Father shall have **No Contact** with the minor child(ren) until further order of the Court, due to existing conditions that are detrimental to the welfare of the minor child(ren): *{explain}* ____
____
____.

SECTION IV. CHILD SUPPORT

1. The Petitioner ____ did ____ did not request the establishment of child support.

2. ____ **If child support is requested,** the parents have received personal or substituted

service of process, the petition requests an order for support of the child(ren), and there is evidence of the parents' ability to pay the support ordered. The ____ Mother ____Father has the present ability to pay child support.

*{Choose **one** only}*

a. ____ The amounts in the Child Support Guidelines Worksheet, Florida Family Law Rules of Procedure Form 12.902(e) filed by the ____Mother ____ Father are correct;

OR

b. ____ The Court makes the following findings:
The Mother's net monthly income is $____________, (Child Support Guidelines ____%).
The Father's net monthly income is $____________, (Child Support Guidelines ____%)
Monthly child care costs are $____________.
Monthly health/dental insurance costs are $____________.

OR

c. The ____ Mother ____ Father is currently ordered to pay child support to the other parent in the amount of $____________ per ____________ as established in the case of *{style of case and number}* ____.

____ All of the child support or ____ a portion of the child support in the amount of $__________ shall be **redirected** to the Petitioner.

3. **Amount**

a) **Father's Obligation**

The Father shall be obligated to pay child support at the rate of $__________ per month for the ______ children *{total number of parties' minor or dependent children}* commencing ________________________ *{month, day, year}* and terminating ______________________ *{month, day, year}*.
Child support shall be paid in the amount of $__________ per __________ *{week, month, other}* which is consistent with the Father's current payroll cycle.

Upon the termination of the obligation of child support for one of the parties' children, child support in the amount of $______ for the remaining______ children *{total number of remaining children}* shall be paid commencing ____________ *{month, day, year}* and terminating ____________ *{month, day, year}*. This child support shall be paid in the amount of $__________ per ______ *{week, month, other}* consistent with the Father's current payroll cycle.

{Insert paragraph for the child support obligation, including the amount, and commencement and termination dates, for the remaining minor or dependent children, which shall be payable as the obligation for each child ceases.}

The Father shall pay child support until all minor or dependent children: reach the age of 18; become emancipated, marry, join the armed services, die, or become self-supporting; or until further order of the court or agreement of the parties. The child support obligation shall continue beyond the age of 18 and until high school graduation for any child who is dependent in fact, between the ages of 18 and 19, and is still in high school, performing in good faith with a reasonable expectation of graduation before the age of 19.

If the child support ordered deviates from the guidelines more than 5%, the factual findings which support that deviation are: ______________________________
____
____.

b) **Mother's Obligation**

The Mother shall be obligated to pay child support at the rate of $__________ per month for the ______ children *{total number of parties' minor or dependent children}* commencing ____________________ *{month, day, year}* and terminating ____________________ *{month, day, year}*. Child support shall be paid in the amount of $________ per ________ *{week, month, other}* consistent with the Mother's current payroll cycle.

Upon the termination of the obligation of child support for one of the parties' children, child support in the amount of $__________ for the remaining ______ children *{total number of remaining children}* shall be paid commencing ______________ *{month, day, year}* and terminating ____________________ *{month, day, year}*. This child support shall be paid in the amount of $__________ per ____________*{week, month, other}* consistent with the Mother's current payroll cycle.

{Insert paragraph for the child support obligation, including the amount, and commencement and termination dates, for the remaining minor or dependent children which shall be payable as the obligation for each child ceases.}

The Mother shall pay child support until all of the minor or dependent children: reach the age of 18; become emancipated, marry, join the armed services, die, or become self-supporting; or until further order of the court or agreement of the parties. The child support obligation shall continue beyond the age of 18 and until high school graduation for any child who is dependent in fact, between the ages of 18 and 19, and is still in high school, performing in good faith with a reasonable expectation of graduation before the age of 19.

If the child support ordered deviates from the guidelines more than 5%, the factual findings which support that deviation are: ______________________________
____.

4. **Arrearages/Retroactive Child Support**
   a) The _____ Mother _____ Father owes child support arrearages in the amount of $__________ as of *{date}* ______________ to the other parent. The child support arrearages shall be repaid in the amount of $_________ per month, payable _____ in accordance with the employer's payroll cycle, and in any event at least once per month _____other *{explain}* ______________________________ commencing *{date}* ______________, until paid in full including statutory interest.

   b) The _____ Mother _____ Father owes retroactive child support in the amount of $__________ as of *{date}* ______________ to the Petitioner. The retroactive child support shall be repaid in the amount of $_______ per month, payable _____ in accordance with the employer's payroll cycle, and in any event at least once per month _____other *{explain}* ______________________________ ______________________________ commencing *{date}* ______________, until paid in full including statutory interest.

5. **Insurance**
   *{Choose **all** that apply}*
   a) The _____ Mother _____ Father shall be required to maintain _____ health and/or _____ dental insurance for the parties' minor child(ren), so long as reasonable in cost and accessible to the child(ren). The party providing insurance shall be required to convey insurance cards demonstrating said coverage to the Petitioner and other parent.
   OR
   _____ Health and/or _____ dental insurance is either not reasonable in cost or accessible to the child(ren) at this time.

   b) _____ Reasonable and necessary uninsured medical/dental/prescription drug costs for the minor child(ren) shall be assessed as follows:
   _____ Shared equally by both parents.
   _____ Prorated according to the child support guidelines percentages.
   _____ Other *{explain}* ______________________

   As to these uninsured medical/dental/prescription drug expenses, the party who incurs the expense shall submit a request for reimbursement to the parent or parents within 30 days, and the parent or parents, within 30 days of receipt, shall submit the applicable reimbursement for that expense.

SECTION V. METHOD OF PAYMENT

The parent(s) shall pay court-ordered child support and arrearages, if any, as follows:

1. **Place of Payment**

   a) ____Parent(s) shall pay court-ordered support directly to either the State Disbursement Unit or the central depository, as required by statute, along with any fee required by statute.

   OR

   b) ____ The Petitioner and the Parent(s) have requested and the Court finds that it is in the best interest of the child(ren) that support payments need not be directed through either the State Disbursement Unit or the central depository at this time; however, any party may subsequently apply, pursuant to section 61.13(1)(d)(3), Florida Statutes, to require payment through either the State Disbursement Unit or the central depository.

2. **Income Deduction**
   (If applicable)

   a) ____ **Immediate.** _____ Mother _____ Father, hereinafter, Obligor(s), shall pay through income deduction, pursuant to a separate Income Deduction Order which shall be effective immediately. Obligor is individually responsible for paying this support obligation until all of said support is deducted from his/her income. Until support payments are deducted, the Obligor is responsible for making timely payments directly to the State Disbursement Unit or the Petitioner as previously set forth in this Order.

   b) ____ **Deferred.** Income deduction is ordered this day, but it shall not be effective until a delinquency of $_____________, or, if not specified, an amount equal to one month's obligation occurs. Income deduction is not being implemented immediately based on the following findings: Income deduction is **not** in the best interests of the child(ren) because: *{explain}* ____
   ____
   ____.

   AND

   There is proof of timely payment of a previously ordered obligation without an Income Deduction Order,

   AND

   _____ there is an agreement by the Obligor(s) to advise the Title IV-D agency, the clerk of court, and the Petitioner of any change in Payor and/or health insurance OR
   _____ there is a signed, written agreement providing an alternative arrangement between the Petitioner and the Obligor(s) and, at the option of the IV-D agency, by

the IV-D agency in IV-D cases in which there is an assignment of support rights to the state, reviewed and entered into the record by the court.

3. **Bonus/one-time payments.**
*{Choose **one** only}*

_____ All
_____ __________%
_____ No income paid in the form of a bonus or other similar one-time payment, up to the amount of any arrearage or the remaining balance thereof owed pursuant to this order, shall be forwarded to the Petitioner pursuant to the payment method prescribed above.

4. **Other provisions relating to method of payment:** ______________________________
____.

SECTION VI. ATTORNEY'S FEES, COSTS, AND SUIT MONEY
*{Choose **one** only}*

1. The ____ Petitioner's _____Respondents' request(s) for attorney's fees, costs, and suit money is (are) denied because ______________________________
____.

2. ____The Court finds there is a need for and ability to pay attorney's fees, costs, and suit money. _____ Petitioner _____ Respondent(s) is (are) ordered to pay the other party $__________ in attorney's fees, and $ __________ in costs. The Court further finds that the attorney's fees are awarded based on the reasonable rate of $______________ per hour and ________ reasonable hours. Other provisions relating to attorney's fees, costs, and suit money are as follows: ______________
____.

SECTION VII. OTHER PROVISIONS

1. **Other Provisions** ____
____
____
____.

2. The Court reserves jurisdiction to modify and enforce this Order for Temporary Custody.

Florida Supreme Court Approved Family Law Form 12.970(e), Order Granting Petition for Temporary Custody by Extended Family (03/15)

DONE AND ORDERED in ____________________, Florida on *{date}* ____________________

____
CIRCUIT JUDGE

I certify that a copy of this Order for Temporary Custody was:
( ) mailed ( ) faxed and mailed ( ) e-mailed ( ) hand-delivered to the parties and any entities listed below on *{date}* ______________________.

by ______________________________
{Clerk of court or designee}.

Petitioner (or his or her attorney)
Respondents (or his or her attorney)
_____State Disbursement Unit
_____Central Depository
_____Other ______________________________

Florida Supreme Court Approved Family Law Form 12.970(e), Order Granting Petition for Temporary Custody by Extended Family (03/15)

Added April 7, 2011 (60 So.3d 979). Amended March 15, 2012 (84 So.3d 274); March 26, 2015, effective March 26, 2015 (2015 WL 1343088).

Form 12.970(f). Order Granting Petition for Concurrent Custody by Extended Family

IN THE CIRCUIT COURT OF THE ________________________ JUDICIAL CIRCUIT
IN AND FOR ________________________ COUNTY, FLORIDA

Case No: ____________________
Division: ____________________

______________________________,
Petitioner,

and

______________________________,
Respondent/Father

______________________________,
Respondent/Mother.

ORDER GRANTING PETITION FOR CONCURRENT CUSTODY BY EXTENDED FAMILY

This case came before this Court for a hearing on a Petition for Concurrent Custody by Extended Family. The Court, having reviewed the file and heard the testimony, makes these findings of fact and reaches these conclusions of law:

SECTION I. FINDINGS:

1. The Court has jurisdiction over the subject matter and the parties.

2. The minor child(ren) at issue in this matter are:
   Name Date of Birth
   ____
   ____
   ____
   ____

3. The Petitioner, *{full legal name}* ______________________________ is the *{extended family relationship}* ______________________________ of the child(ren).

4. The Petitioner currently has physical custody of the child(ren) and has had physical custody of the child(ren) for at least 10 days in any 30-day period within the last 12 months.

5. The Petitioner does not have signed, written documentation from the parent(s) which is sufficient to enable the custodian to do all the things necessary to care for the child(ren) which are available to custodians who have an order for temporary custody by extended family.

6. The Mother *{full legal name}* ______________________________ of the child(ren): *{choose **one** only}*
____ Filed a Waiver and Consent
____ Was served with the petition and failed to file an Answer
____ Is deceased as evidenced by: ______________________________

7. The Father *{full legal name}* ______________________________ of the child(ren): *{choose **one** only}*
____ Filed a Waiver and Consent
____ Was served with the petition and failed to file an Answer
____ Is deceased as evidenced by: ______________________________

8. It is in the best interest of the child(ren) for the Petitioner to have concurrent custody.

SECTION II: CONCURRENT CUSTODY

1. The Petitioner, ______________________________, is granted concurrent custody of the minor child(ren).

2. The Petitioner shall have all the concurrent rights and responsibilities of a legal parent.

3. The Petitioner is authorized to make all reasonable and necessary decisions for the minor child(ren), including but not limited to:
   a) Consent to all necessary and reasonable medical and dental care for the child(ren), including nonemergency surgery and psychiatric care;

   b) Secure copies of the child(ren)'s records, held by third parties, that are necessary for the care of the child(ren), including, but not limited to: medical, dental, and psychiatric records; birth certificates and other records; and educational records,

   c) Enroll the child(ren) in school and grant or withhold consent for the child(ren) to be tested or placed in special school programs, including exceptional education; and

   d) Do all other things necessary for the care of the child(ren).

SECTION III. CHILD SUPPORT

1. The Petitioner ____ did ____ did not request the establishment of child support.

2. ____ **If child support is requested,** the parents have received personal or substituted service of process, the petition requests an order for support of the child(ren), and there is evidence of the parents' ability to pay the support ordered. The _____ Mother _____ Father has the present ability to pay child support.
{Choose one only}
a.____ The amounts in the Child Support Guidelines Worksheet, Florida Family Law Rules of Procedure Form 12.902(e) filed by the ( ) Mother ( ) Father are correct;
OR
b.____ The Court makes the following findings:
The Mother's net monthly income is $__________, (Child Support Guidelines ____%).
The Father's net monthly income is $__________, (Child Support Guidelines ____%)
Monthly child care costs are $__________.
Monthly health/dental insurance costs are $__________.
OR
c.____ The ( ) Mother ( ) Father is currently ordered to pay child support to the other parent in the amount of $__________ per __________ as established in the case of *{style of case and number}* ______________________________
______________________________.
_____ All of the child support or _____ a portion of the child support in the amount of $__________ shall be **redirected** to the Petitioner.

3. **Amount**
a) Father's Obligation
The Father shall be obligated to pay child support at the rate of $________ per month for the _____children *{total number of parties' minor or dependent children}* commencing __________ *{month, day, year}* and terminating __________ *{month, day, year}*. Child support shall be paid in the amount of $__________ per __________ *{week, month, other}* which is consistent with the Father's current payroll cycle.

Upon the termination of child support for one of the parties' children, child support in the amount of $__________ for the remaining _____ children *{total number of remaining children}* shall be paid commencing __________ *{month, day, year}* and terminating __________ *{month, day, year}*. This child support shall be paid in the amount of $__________ per __________*{week, month, other}* consistent with the Father's current payroll cycle.

Florida Supreme Court Approved Family Law Form 12.970(f), Order Granting Petition for Concurrent Custody by Extended Family (03/15)

{Insert paragraph for the child support obligation, including the amount, and commencement and termination dates, for the remaining minor or dependent children, which shall be payable as the obligation for each child ceases.}

The Father shall pay child support until all of the minor or dependent children: reach the age of 18, become emancipated, marry, join the armed services, die, or become self-supporting; or until further order of the court or agreement of the parties. The child support obligation shall continue beyond the age of 18 and until high school graduation for any child who is dependent in fact, between the ages of 18 and 19, and is still in high school, performing in good faith with a reasonable expectation of graduation before the age of 19.

If the child support ordered deviates from the guidelines more than 5%, the factual findings which support that deviation are: ________________________________
____
____.

b) Mother's Obligation

The Mother shall be obligated to pay child support at the rate of $____________ per month for the ________ children *{total number of parties' minor or dependent children}* commencing________________________ *{month, day, year}* and terminating ________________ *{month, day, year}*. Child support shall be paid in the amount of $__________per ______________ *{week, month, other}* consistent with the Mother's current payroll cycle.

Upon the termination of the obligation of child support for one of the parties' children, child support in the amount of $__________ for the remaining ______ children *{total number of remaining children}* shall be paid commencing ____________________ *{month, day, year}* and terminating ________________________ *month, day, year}*. This child support shall be paid in the amount of $______________ per ______________ *{week, month, other}* consistent with the Mother's current payroll cycle.

{Insert paragraph for the child support obligation, including the amount, and commencement and termination dates, for the remaining minor or dependent children, which shall be payable as the obligation for each child ceases.}

The Mother shall pay child support until all of the minor or dependent children: reach the age of 18; become emancipated, marry, join the armed services, die, or become self-supporting; or until further order of the court or agreement of the parties. The child support obligation shall continue beyond the age of 18 and until high school graduation for any child who is dependent in fact, between the ages of 18 and 19, and is still in high school, performing in good faith with a reasonable expectation of graduation before the age of 19.

If the child support ordered deviates from the guidelines more than 5%, the factual findings which support that deviation are:____
____
____.

4. **Arrearages/Retroactive Child Support**

c) The _____ Mother _____ Father owes child support arrearages in the amount of $__________ as of *{date}* _______________ to the other parent. The child support arrearages shall be repaid in the amount of $_______ per month, payable _____ in accordance with the employer's payroll cycle, and in any event at least once per month _____other *{explain}* ________________________________
_____
____
commencing *{date}* ___________________________, until paid in full including statutory interest.

d) The _____ Mother _____ Father owes retroactive child support in the amount of $__________ as of *{date}* _______________ to the Petitioner. The retroactive child support shall be repaid in the amount of $_______ per month, payable _____ in accordance with the employer's payroll cycle, and in any event at least once per month _____ other *{explain}* ________________________________
____
commencing *{date}* ___________________________, until paid in full including statutory interest.

5. **Insurance**

*{Choose **all** that apply}*

c) The _____ Mother _____ Father shall be required to maintain _____ health and/or _____ dental insurance for the parties' minor child(ren), so long as reasonable in cost and accessible to the child(ren). The party providing insurance shall be required to convey insurance cards demonstrating said coverage to the Petitioner and other parent.

OR

_____ Health and/or _____ dental insurance is either not reasonable in cost or accessible to the child(ren) at this time.

d) _____ Reasonable and necessary uninsured medical/dental/prescription drug costs for the minor child(ren) shall be assessed as follows:

_____ Shared equally by both parents.

Florida Supreme Court Approved Family Law Form 12.970(f), Order Granting Petition for Concurrent Custody by Extended Family (03/15)

_____ Prorated according to the child support guidelines percentages.
_____ Other *{explain}* ____

As to these uninsured medical/dental/prescription drug expenses, the party who incurs the expense shall submit a request for reimbursement to the parent or parents within 30 days, and the parent or parents, within 30 days of receipt, shall submit the applicable reimbursement for that expense.

SECTION IV. METHOD OF PAYMENT

The parent(s) shall pay court-ordered child support and arrearages, if any, as follows:

1. **Place of Payment**

a) _____Parents shall pay court-ordered support directly to either the State Disbursement Unit or the central depository, as required by statute, along with any applicable fee required by statute.

OR

b) ____The Petitioner and the Parents have requested and the court finds that it is in the best interest of the child(ren) that support payments need not be directed through either the State Disbursement Unit or the central depository at time; however, any party may subsequently apply, pursuant to 61.13(1)(d)(3), Florida Statutes, to require payment through either the State Disbursement Unit or the central depository.

2. **Income Deduction**
(If applicable)

a) _____ **Immediate.** _____ Mother _____ Father, hereinafter, Obligor(s), shall pay through income deduction, pursuant to a separate Income Deduction Order which shall be effective immediately. Obligor is individually responsible for paying this support obligation until all of said support is deducted from his/her income. Until support payments are deducted, the Obligor is responsible for making timely payments directly to the State Disbursement Unit or the Petitioner as previously set forth in this Order.

b) _____ **Deferred.** Income deduction is ordered this day, but it shall not be effective until a delinquency of $____________, or, if not specified, an amount equal to one month's obligation occurs. Income deduction is not being implemented immediately based on the following findings: Income deduction is **not** in the best interests of the child(ren) because: *{explain}*
____

______________________________________.

AND

There is proof of timely payment of a previously ordered obligation without an Income Deduction Order,

AND

_____ there is an agreement by the Obligor(s) to advise the Title IV-D agency, the clerk of court, and the Petitioner of any change in Payor and/or health insurance **OR**
_____ there is a signed, written agreement providing an alternative arrangement between the Petitioner and Obligor(s) and, at the option of the IV-D agency, by the IV-D agency in IV-D cases in which there is an assignment of support rights to the state, reviewed and entered into the record by the court.

3. **Bonus/one-time payments.**
*{Choose **one** only}*
_____ All
_____ __________%
_____ No income paid in the form of a bonus or other similar one-time payment, up to the amount of any arrearage or the remaining balance thereof owed pursuant to this order, shall be forwarded to the Petitioner pursuant to the payment method prescribed above.

4. **Other provisions relating to method of payment**: ______________________________________
____

SECTION V. ATTORNEY'S FEES, COSTS, AND SUIT MONEY
*{Choose **one** only}*

1. The _____ Petitioner's _____ Respondents' request(s) for attorney's fees, costs, and suit money is (are) denied because ______________________________________
______________________________________.

2. _____ The Court finds there is a need for and ability to pay attorney's fees, costs, and suit money. _____ Petitioner _____ Respondent(s) is (are) ordered to pay the other party $__________ in attorney's fees, and $__________ in costs. The Court further finds that the attorney's fees are awarded based on the reasonable rate of $__________ per hour and _____ reasonable hours. Other provisions relating to attorney's fees, costs, and suit money are as follows: ______________________________________
______________________________________.

SECTION VI. OTHER PROVISIONS

1. **Other Provisions** ____
____
____
____

2. The Court reserves jurisdiction to modify and enforce this Order for Concurrent Custody.

3. The granting of concurrent custody does not affect the ability of the child(ren)'s parent or parents to obtain physical custody of the child(ren) at any time.

DONE AND ORDERED in ____________________, Florida on *{date}* __________________

____
CIRCUIT JUDGE

I certify that a copy of this Order for Concurrent Custody was: ( ) mailed ( ) faxed and mailed ( ) e-mailed ( ) hand-delivered to the parties and any entities listed below on *{date}*____________________.

by____________________________

{Clerk of court or designee}

Petitioner (or his or her attorney)
Respondents (or his or her attorney)
_____State Disbursement Unit
_____Central Depository
_____Other ________________________________

Florida Supreme Court Approved Family Law Form 12.970(f), Order Granting Petition for Concurrent Custody by Extended Family (03/15)

Added April 7, 2011 (60 So.3d 979). Amended March 15, 2012 (84 So.3d 274); March 26, 2015, effective March 26, 2015 (2015 WL 1343088).

Form 12.980(a). Petition for Injunction for Protection Against Domestic Violence

IN THE CIRCUIT COURT OF THE ______________ JUDICIAL CIRCUIT,
IN AND FOR ______________ COUNTY, FLORIDA

Case No.: ______________
Division: ______________

______________,
Petitioner,
and

______________,
Respondent.

PETITION FOR INJUNCTION FOR PROTECTION AGAINST DOMESTIC VIOLENCE

I, *{full legal name}* ______________, being sworn, certify that the following statements are true:

SECTION I. PETITIONER
(This section is about you. It must be completed. However, **if you fear that disclosing your address to the respondent would put you in danger**, you should complete and file a **Request for Confidential Filing of Address**, Florida Supreme Court Approved Family Law Form 12.980(h), and write confidential in the space provided on this form for your address and telephone number.)

1. Petitioner's current address is: *{street address}* ______________
{city, state and zip code} ______________
Telephone Number: *{area code and number}* ______________
Physical description of Petitioner:
Race: ____ Sex: Male ____ Female ____ Date of Birth: ______________

2. Petitioner's attorney's name, address, and telephone number is: ______________
______________.
(If you do not have an attorney, write none.)

SECTION II. RESPONDENT
(This section is about the person you want to be protected from. It must be completed.)

1. Respondent's current address is: *{street address, city, state, and zip code}* ______________
______________.
Respondent's Driver's License number is: *{if known}* ______________.

Florida Supreme Court Approved Family Law Form 12.980(a), Petition for Injunction for Protection Against Domestic Violence (03/15)

2. Respondent is: *{Indicate all that apply}*

a. _____ the spouse of Petitioner. Date of Marriage: ______________________________
b. _____ the former spouse of Petitioner.
Date of Marriage: ______________________________
Date of Dissolution of Marriage: ______________________________
c. _____ related by blood or marriage to Petitioner.
Specify relationship: ______________________________
d. _____ a person who is or was living in one home with Petitioner, as if a family.
e._____ a person with whom Petitioner has a child in common, even if Petitioner and Respondent never were married or living together.

3. Petitioner has known Respondent since *{date}* ______________________________.

4. Respondent's last known place of employment: ______________________________
Employment address: ______________________________
Working hours: ______________________________

5. Physical description of Respondent:
Race: _____ Sex: Male _____ Female _____ Date of Birth: ______________________________
Height: ______ Weight: ______ Eye Color: ______ Hair Color: ______________________________
Distinguishing marks or scars: ______________________________
Vehicle: (make/model) ______________ Color: ________ Tag Number: ________

6. Other names Respondent goes by (aliases or nicknames): ______________________________

7. Respondent's attorney's name, address, and telephone number is: ______________________________
____

(If you do not know whether Respondent has an attorney, write unknown. If Respondent does not have an attorney, write none.)

SECTION III. CASE HISTORY AND REASON FOR SEEKING PETITION (This section must be completed.)

1. Has Petitioner ever received or tried to get an injunction for protection against domestic violence against Respondent in this or any other court?
_____ Yes _____ No If yes, what happened in that case? *{Include case number, if known}*
____
____

Florida Supreme Court Approved Family Law Form 12.980(a), Petition for Injunction for Protection Against Domestic Violence (03/15)

2. Has Respondent ever received or tried to get an injunction for protection against domestic violence against Petitioner in this or any other court?

_____ Yes _____ No If yes, what happened in that case? *{Include case number, if known}*

____

____.

3. Describe **any other** court case that is either going on now or that happened in the past, including a dissolution of marriage, paternity action, or child support enforcement action, **between Petitioner and Respondent** *{Include city, state, and case number, if known}*: _________

____.

4. Petitioner is either a victim of domestic violence or has reasonable cause to believe he or she is in imminent danger of becoming a victim of domestic violence because respondent has: *{mark all sections that apply and describe in the spaces below the incidents of violence or threats of violence, specifying when and where they occurred, including, but not limited to, locations such as a home, school, place of employment, or time-sharing exchange}*

a. _____committed or threatened to commit domestic violence defined in section 741.28, Florida Statutes, as any assault, aggravated assault, battery, aggravated battery, sexual assault, sexual battery, stalking, aggravated stalking, kidnapping, false imprisonment, or any criminal offense resulting in physical injury or death of one family or household member by another. With the exception of persons who are parents of a child in common, the family or household members must be currently residing or have in the past resided together in the same single dwelling unit.

b. _____previously threatened, harassed, stalked, or physically abused the petitioner.

c. _____attempted to harm the petitioner or family members or individuals closely associated with the petitioner.

d. _____threatened to conceal, kidnap, or harm the petitioner's child or children.

e. _____intentionally injured or killed a family pet.

f. _____used, or has threatened to use, against the petitioner any weapons such as guns or knives.

g. _____physically restrained the petitioner from leaving the home or calling law enforcement.

h. _____a criminal history involving violence or the threat of violence (if known).

i. _____another order of protection issued against him or her previously or from another jurisdiction (if known).

j. _____destroyed personal property, including, but not limited to, telephones or other communication equipment, clothing, or other items belonging to the petitioner.

k. _____engaged in any other behavior or conduct that leads the petitioner to have reasonable cause to believe he or she is in imminent danger of becoming a victim of domestic violence.

Below is a brief description of the latest act of violence or threat of violence that causes Petitioner to honestly fear imminent domestic violence by Respondent.
(Use additional sheets if necessary.)

On *{date}* ______________________, at *{location}* ______________________,
Respondent:
____
____
____
____
____
____
____
____
____
____
____
____
____
____

_______ Please indicate here if you are attaching additional pages to continue these facts.

5. **Additional Information**
*{Indicate **all** that apply}*
a.____Other acts or threats of domestic violence as described on attached sheet.
b.____This or other acts of domestic violence have been previously reported to *{person or agency}*: ______________________________
c.____ Respondent owns, has, and/or is known to have guns or other weapons.
Describe weapon(s): ______________________________
d. ____ Respondent has a drug problem.
e.____ Respondent has an alcohol problem.
f.____ Respondent has a history of mental health problems. If checked, answer the following, if known:
Has Respondent ever been the subject of a Baker Act proceeding? ____ Yes ____ No
Is Respondent supposed to take medication for mental health problems?

Florida Supreme Court Approved Family Law Form 12.980(a), Petition for Injunction for Protection Against Domestic Violence (03/15)

_____Yes _____No
If yes, is Respondent currently taking his/her medication? _____ Yes _____ No

SECTION IV. TEMPORARY EXCLUSIVE USE AND POSSESSION OF HOME (Complete this section **only** if you want the Court to grant you temporary exclusive use and possession of the home that you share with the Respondent.)

1. Petitioner claims the following about the home that Petitioner and Respondent share or that Petitioner left because of domestic violence:
*{Indicate **all** that apply}*

a.____ Petitioner needs the exclusive use and possession of the home that the parties share at *{street address}* ____,
{city, state, zip code} ____.

b.____Petitioner cannot get another safe place to live because: ____________________________
____
____
____
____.

c. ____If kept out of the home, Respondent has the money to get other housing or may live without money at *{street address}* ____,
{city, state, zip code} ____.

2. The home is:
*{Choose **one** only}*

a.____ owned or rented by Petitioner and Respondent jointly.

b.____ solely owned or rented by Petitioner.

c.____ solely owned or rented by Respondent.

SECTION V. TEMPORARY PARENTING PLAN WITH TEMPORARY TIME-SHARING SCHEDULE FOR MINOR CHILD(REN) (Complete this section **only** if you are asking the court to provide a temporary parenting plan, including a temporary time-sharing schedule with regard to, the minor child or children of the parties which might involve prohibiting or limiting time-sharing or requiring that it be supervised by a third party. You must be the natural parent, adoptive parent, or guardian by court order of the minor child(ren). If you are asking the court to provide a temporary parenting plan, including a temporary time-sharing schedule with regard to, the minor child or children of the parties which might involve prohibiting or limiting time-sharing or requiring that it be supervised by a third party, you must also complete and file a **Uniform Child Custody Jurisdiction and Enforcement Act (UCCJEA) Affidavit**, Florida Supreme Court Approved Family Law Form 12.902(d).)

Note: If the paternity of the minor child(ren) listed below has not been established through either marriage or court order, the Court may deny a request to provide a temporary parenting plan, including a temporary time-sharing schedule with regard to, the minor child or children, and/or a request for child support.

1. Petitioner is the natural parent, adoptive parent, or guardian by court order of the minor child(ren) whose name(s) and age(s) is (are) listed below.

Name **Birth date**

____

____

____

____

____

2. The minor child(ren) for whom Petitioner is asking the court to provide a temporary parenting plan, including a temporary time-sharing schedule with regard to:

*{Choose **one** only}*

a.____saw the domestic violence described in this petition happen.

b.____were at the place where the domestic violence happened but did not see it.

c.____were not there when the domestic violence happened this time but have seen previous acts of domestic violence by Respondent.

d.____have not witnessed domestic violence by Respondent.

3. Name **any other** minor child(ren) who were there when the domestic violence happened. Include child(ren)'s name, age, and parents' names. _______________

____

____

____

4. **Temporary Parenting Plan and Temporary Time-Sharing Schedule**

*{Indicate **all** that apply}*

a.____ Petitioner requests that the Court provide a temporary parenting plan, including a temporary time-sharing schedule with regard to, the minor child or children of the parties, as follows: ___________

____

____.

b.____ Petitioner requests that the Court order supervised exchange of the minor child(ren) or exchange through a responsible person designated by the Court. The following person is suggested as a responsible person for purposes of such exchange. *{Explain}:* ____.

c.____ Petitioner requests that the Court limit time-sharing by Respondent with the minor child(ren). *{Explain}:* ____
____.

d.____ Petitioner requests that the Court prohibit time-sharing by Respondent with the minor child(ren) because Petitioner genuinely fears that Respondent imminently will abuse, remove, or hide the minor child(ren) from Petitioner. *{Explain}:* ____
____.

e.____Petitioner requests that the Court allow only supervised time-sharing by Respondent with the minor child(ren). *Explain:* ____
____.

Supervision should be provided by a Family Visitation Center, or other *(specify)*:____

SECTION VI. TEMPORARY SUPPORT (Complete this section **only** if you are seeking financial support from the Respondent. You must also complete and file a **Family Law Financial Affidavit**, Florida Family Law Rules of Procedure Form 12.902(b) or (c), and **Notice of Social Security Number**, Florida Supreme Court Approved Family Law Form 12.902(j), if you are seeking child support. A **Child Support Guidelines Worksheet**, Florida Family Law Rules of Procedure Form 12.902(e), must be filed with the court at or prior to a hearing to establish or modify child support.) *{Indicate **all that apply**}*

1. ____Petitioner claims a need for the money he or she is asking the Court to make Respondent pay, and that Respondent has the ability to pay that money.

2. ____Petitioner requests that the Court order Respondent to pay the following temporary alimony to Petitioner. (Petitioner must be married to Respondent to ask for temporary alimony.) Temporary Alimony Requested $__________every: _____ week _____ other week _____ month.

3. _____Petitioner requests that the Court order Respondent to pay the following temporary child support to Petitioner. (The Respondent must be the natural parent, adoptive parent, or guardian by court order of the minor child(ren) for the court to order the Respondent to pay child support.) Temporary child support is requested in the amount of $____________ every: _____ week _____ other week _____ month.

SECTION VII. INJUNCTION (This section summarizes what you are asking the Court to include in the injunction. This section must be completed.)

1. Petitioner asks the Court to enter a TEMPORARY INJUNCTION for protection against domestic violence that will be in place from now until the scheduled hearing in this matter.

2. Petitioner asks the Court to enter, after a hearing has been held on this petition, a final judgment on injunction prohibiting Respondent from committing any acts of domestic violence against Petitioner **and:**

a. prohibiting Respondent from going to or within 500 feet of any place the Petitioner lives;

b. prohibiting Respondent from going to or within 500 feet of the Petitioner's place(s) of employment or school; the address of Petitioner's place(s) of employment or school is: ____
____.

c. prohibiting Respondent from contacting Petitioner by mail, by telephone, through another person, or in any other manner;

d. prohibiting Respondent from knowingly and intentionally going to or within 100 feet of Petitioner's motor vehicle.

e. prohibiting Respondent from defacing or destroying Petitioner's personal property.

*{Indicate **all** that apply}*

f. _____prohibiting Respondent from going to or within 500 feet of the following place(s) Petitioner or Petitioner's minor child(ren) must go often *{include address}*: _______________
____
____.

g._____ granting Petitioner temporary exclusive use and possession of the home Petitioner and

Respondent share;

h.____ granting Petitioner on a temporary basis 100% of the time sharing with the parties' minor child(ren);

i.____establishing a temporary parenting plan including a temporary time-sharing schedule for the parties' minor child(ren);

j.____granting temporary alimony for Petitioner;

k.____granting temporary child support for the minor child(ren);

l.____ordering Respondent to participate in treatment, intervention, and/or counseling services;

m.____referring Petitioner to a certified domestic violence center; and any other terms the Court deems necessary for the protection of Petitioner and/or Petitioner's child(ren), including injunctions or directives to law enforcement agencies, as provided in Section 741.30, Florida Statutes.

I UNDERSTAND THAT BY FILING THIS PETITION, I AM ASKING THE COURT TO HOLD A HEARING ON THIS PETITION, THAT BOTH RESPONDENT AND I WILL BE NOTIFIED OF THE HEARING, AND THAT I MUST APPEAR AT THE HEARING. I UNDERSTAND THAT IF EITHER RESPONDENT OR I FAIL TO APPEAR AT THE HEARING, WE WILL BE BOUND BY THE TERMS OF ANY INJUNCTION ISSUED AT THAT HEARING.

I HAVE READ EVERY STATEMENT MADE IN THIS PETITION, AND EACH STATEMENT IS TRUE AND CORRECT. I UNDERSTAND THAT THE STATEMENTS MADE IN THIS PETITION ARE BEING MADE UNDER PENALTY OF PERJURY, PUNISHABLE AS PROVIDED IN SECTION 837.02, FLORIDA STATUTES.

____________(initials)

Dated: ______________________

____

Signature of Petitioner
STATE OF FLORIDA
COUNTY OF ______________

Sworn to or affirmed and signed before me on ____________ by ______________________.

____

NOTARY PUBLIC or DEPUTY CLERK

Florida Supreme Court Approved Family Law Form 12.980(a), Petition for Injunction for Protection Against Domestic Violence (03/15)

{Print, type, or stamp commissioned name of notary or clerk.}

____ Personally known

____ Produced identification

Type of identification produced ____________________

Florida Supreme Court Approved Family Law Form 12.980(a), Petition for Injunction for Protection Against Domestic Violence (03/15)

INSTRUCTIONS FOR FLORIDA SUPREME COURT APPROVED FAMILY LAW FORM 12.980(a) PETITION FOR INJUNCTION FOR PROTECTION AGAINST DOMESTIC VIOLENCE (03/15)

When should this form be used?

If you are a victim of any act of domestic violence or have reasonable cause to believe that you are in imminent danger of becoming a victim of domestic violence, you can use this form to ask the court for a protective order prohibiting domestic violence. Because you are making a request to the court, you are called the **petitioner**. The person whom you are asking the court to protect you from is called the **respondent**. **Domestic violence includes**: assault, aggravated assault, battery, aggravated battery, sexual assault, sexual battery, stalking, aggravated stalking, kidnapping, false imprisonment, or any other criminal offense resulting in physical injury or death to petitioner by any of petitioner's family or household members. In determining whether you have reasonable cause to believe you are in imminent danger of becoming a victim of domestic violence, the court must consider all relevant factors alleged in the petition, including, but not limited to the following:

1. The history between the petitioner and the respondent, including threats, harassment, stalking, and physical abuse.
2. Whether the respondent has attempted to harm the petitioner or family members or individuals closely associated with the petitioner.
3. Whether the respondent has threatened to conceal, kidnap, or harm the petitioner's child or children.
4. Whether the respondent has intentionally injured or killed a family pet.
5. Whether the respondent has used, or has threatened to use, against the petitioner any weapons such as guns or knives.
6. Whether the respondent has physically restrained the petitioner from leaving the home or calling law enforcement.
7. Whether the respondent has a criminal history involving violence or the threat of violence.
8. The existence of a verifiable order of protection issued previously or from another jurisdiction.
9. Whether the respondent has destroyed personal property, including, but not limited to, telephones or other communications equipment, clothing, or other items belonging to the petitioner.
10. Whether the respondent engaged in any other behavior or conduct that leads the petitioner to have reasonable cause to believe that he or she is in imminent danger of becoming a victim of domestic violence.

The domestic violence laws only apply to your situation if the respondent is your **spouse**, former spouse, related to you by blood or marriage, living with you now or has lived with you in the past (if you are or were living as a family), or the other parent of your child(ren) whether or not you have ever been married or ever lived together. With the exception of persons who have a child in common, the family or household members must be currently residing together or have in the past resided together in the same single dwelling unit. If the respondent is not one of the above, you should look at **Petition for Injunction for Protection Against Repeat Violence**, Florida Supreme Court Approved Family Law Form 12.980(f), to determine if your situation will qualify for an injunction for protection against repeat violence, or **Petition for Injunction for Protection Against Dating Violence**, Florida Supreme Court Approved Family Law Form 12.980(n), to determine if your situation will qualify for an injunction for protection against dating violence, or **Petition for Injunction for Protection Against Sexual Violence,** Florida Supreme Court Approved Family Law Form 12.980(q), to determine if your situation will qualify for an injunction for protection against sexual violence.

If you are under the age of eighteen and you have never been married or had the disabilities of nonage removed by a court, then one of your parents, custodians, or your legal guardian must sign this petition with you.

This form should be typed or printed in black ink. You should complete this form (giving as much detail as possible) and sign it in front of a **notary public** or the **clerk of the circuit court** in the county where you live. The clerk will take your completed **petition** to a **judge**. You should keep a copy for your records. If you have any questions or need assistance completing this form, the clerk or **family law intake staff** will help you.

What should I do if the judge grants my petition?

If the facts contained in your petition convince the judge that you are a victim of domestic violence or that an **imminent danger of domestic violence** exists, the judge will sign either an immediate **Temporary Injunction for Protection Against Domestic Violence with Minor Child(ren)**, Florida Supreme Court Approved Family Law Form 12.980(c)(1) or an immediate **Temporary Injunction for Protection Against Domestic Violence without Minor Child(ren)**, Florida Supreme Court Approved Family Law Form 12.980(c)(2). A temporary injunction is issued without notice to the respondent. The clerk will give your petition, the temporary injunction, and any other papers filed with your petition to the sheriff or other law enforcement officer for **personal service** on the respondent. The temporary injunction will take effect immediately after the respondent is served with a copy of it. It lasts until a full **hearing** can be held or for a period of 15 days, whichever comes first. The court may extend the temporary injunction beyond 15 days for a good reason, which may include failure to obtain **service** on the respondent.

The temporary injunction is issued **ex parte**. This means that the judge has considered only the information presented by one side— YOU. The temporary injunction gives a date that you must appear in court for a hearing. At that hearing, you will be expected to testify about the facts in your petition. The respondent will be given the opportunity to testify at this hearing, also. At the hearing, the judge will decide whether to issue either a **Final Judgment of Injunction for Protection Against Domestic Violence with Minor Child(ren)(After Notice)**, Florida Supreme Court Approved Family Law Form 12.980(d)(1), or a **Final Judgment of Injunction for Protection Against Domestic Violence without Minor Child(ren)(After Notice),** Florida Supreme Court Approved Family Law Form 12.980(d)(2). Either of these final judgments will remain in effect for a specific time period or until modified or dissolved by the court. **If either you or the respondent do not appear at the final hearing, the temporary injunction may be continued in force, extended, or dismissed, and/or additional orders may be granted, including entry of a permanent injunction and the imposition of court costs. You and respondent will be bound by the terms of any injunction issued at the final hearing.**

IF EITHER YOU OR RESPONDENT DO NOT APPEAR AT THE FINAL HEARING, YOU WILL BOTH BE BOUND BY THE TERMS OF ANY INJUNCTION ISSUED IN THIS MATTER.

If the judge signs a temporary or final injunction, the clerk will provide you with the necessary copies. **Make sure that you keep one certified copy of the injunction with you at all times!**

What can I do if the judge denies my petition?

If your petition is denied solely on the grounds that it appears to the court that no imminent danger of domestic violence exists, the court will set a full hearing, at the earliest possible time, on your petition, unless you request that no hearing be set. The respondent will be notified by **personal service** of your petition and the hearing. If your petition is denied, you may: amend your petition by filing a **Supplemental Affidavit in Support of Petition for Injunction for Protection Against Domestic Violence, Repeat or Dating Violence**, Florida Family Law Form 12.980 (g); attend the hearing and present facts that support your petition; and/or dismiss your petition.

Where can I look for more information?

Before proceeding, you should read General Information for Self–Represented Litigants found at the beginning of these forms. The words that are in **bold underline** are defined in that section. The clerk of the circuit court or family law intake staff will help you complete any necessary domestic violence forms and can give you information about local domestic violence victim assistance programs, shelters, and other related services. You may also call the Domestic Violence Hotline at 1–800–500–1119. For further information, see Chapter 741, Florida Statutes, and Rule 12.610, Florida Family Law Rules of Procedure.

IMPORTANT INFORMATION REGARDING E–FILING

The Florida Rules of Judicial Administration now require that all petitions, pleadings, and documents be filed electronically except in certain circumstances. **Self-represented litigants may file petitions or other pleadings or documents electronically; however, they are not required to do so.** If you choose to file your pleadings or other documents electronically, you must do so in accordance with Florida Rule of Judicial Administration 2.525, and you must follow the procedures of the judicial circuit in which you file. **The rules and procedures should be carefully read and followed.**

IMPORTANT INFORMATION REGARDING E–SERVICE ELECTION

After the initial service of process of the petition or supplemental petition by the Sheriff or certified process server, the Florida Rules of Judicial Administration now require that all documents required or permitted to be served on the other party must be served by electronic mail (e-mail) except in certain circumstances. **You must strictly comply with the format requirements set forth in the Rules of Judicial Administration.**

SELF–REPRESENTED LITIGANTS MAY SERVE DOCUMENTS BY E–MAIL; HOWEVER, THEY ARE NOT REQUIRED TO DO SO. If a self-represented litigant elects to serve and receive documents by e-mail, the procedures must always be followed once the initial election is made.

To serve and receive documents by e-mail, you must designate your e-mail addresses by using the **Designation of Current Mailing and E-mail Address**, Florida Supreme Court Approved Family Law Form 12.915, and you must provide your e-mail address on each form on which your signature appears. Please **CAREFULLY** read the rules and instructions for: **Certificate of Service (General),** Florida Supreme Court Approved Family Law Form 12.914; **Designation of Current Mailing and E-mail Address**, Florida Supreme Court Approved Family Law Form 12.915; and Florida Rule of Judicial Administration 2.516.

Special notes . . .

With this form you may also need to file the following:

- **Uniform Child Custody Jurisdiction and Enforcement Act (UCCJEA) Affidavit**, Florida Supreme Court Approved Family Law Form 12.902(d), must be completed and filed if you are asking the court to determine issues with regard to your **parenting plan** or **time-sharing** for a minor child(ren).

- **Parenting plan** means a document created to govern the relationship between the parents relating to the decisions that must be made regarding the minor child(ren) and must contain a time-sharing schedule for the parents and child(ren). The issues concerning the minor child(ren) may include, but are not limited to, the child(ren)'s education, health care, and physical, social, and emotional well-being. In creating the plan, all circumstances between the parents, including their historic relationship, domestic violence, and other factors must be taken into consideration. The Parenting Plan shall be developed and agreed to by the parents and approved by a court, or, established by the court, with or without the use of a court-ordered parenting plan recommendation. If the parents cannot agree, or if the parents agreed to a plan that is not approved by the court, a Parenting Plan shall established by the court. **"Time-sharing schedule"** means a timetable that must be included in the Parenting Plan that specifies the time, including overnights and holidays, that a minor child will spend with each parent. If developed and agreed to by the parents of a minor child, it must be approved by the court. If the parents cannot agree, of if their agreed-upon schedule is not approved by the court, the schedule shall be established by the court.

- **Notice of Social Security Number**, Florida Supreme Court Approved Family Law Form 12.902(j), must be completed and filed if you are asking the court to determine issues of temporary child support.

- **Family Law Financial Affidavit**, Florida Family Law Rules of Procedure Form 12.902(b) or (c), must be completed and filed if you are seeking temporary alimony or temporary child support.

- **Child Support Guidelines Worksheet**, Florida Family Law Rules of Procedure Form 12.902(e), MUST be filed with the court at or prior to a hearing to establish or modify child support.

Additionally, if you fear that disclosing your address to the respondent would put you in danger, you should complete a **Request for Confidential Filing of Address**, Florida

Supreme Court Approved Family Law Form 12.980(h), and file it with the clerk of the circuit court and write confidential in the space provided on the petition.

Added as 12.980(b) July 7, 1995, effective Jan. 1, 1996 (663 So.2d 1047). Amended Feb. 26, 1998, effective Mar. 16, 1998 (713 So.2d 1); October 29, 1998, effective Feb. 1, 1999 (723 So.2d 208); Sept. 21, 2000 (810 So.2d 1); Oct. 3, 2002 (830 So.2d 72); Dec. 19, 2002 (836 So.2d 1019); May 15, 2003 (849 So.2d 1003). Renumbered from 12.980(b) Mar. 25, 2004 (871 So.2d 113). Amended March 26, 2009 (20 So.3d 173); Dec. 16, 2010 (59 So.3d 792); June 7, 2012 (93 So.3d 194); March 26, 2015, effective March 26, 2015 (2015 WL 1343088).

Form 12.980(b)(1). Order Setting Hearing on Petition for Injunction for Protection Against Domestic Violence, Repeat Violence, Dating Violence, Sexual Violence, or Stalking, without Issuance of an Interim Temporary Injunction

IN THE CIRCUIT COURT OF THE _____ JUDICIAL CIRCUIT,
IN AND FOR __________ COUNTY, FLORIDA

Case No.: __________
Division: __________

______________________________,
Petitioner,
and

______________________________,
Respondent.

ORDER SETTING HEARING ON PETITION FOR INJUNCTION FOR PROTECTION AGAINST ( ) DOMESTIC VIOLENCE ( ) REPEAT VIOLENCE ( ) DATING VIOLENCE ( ) SEXUAL VIOLENCE ( ) STALKING WITHOUT ISSUANCE OF AN INTERIM TEMPORARY INJUNCTION

A Petition for Injunction for Protection Against: Domestic Violence filed under section 741.30, Florida Statutes; Repeat, Dating, or Sexual Violence filed under section 784.046, Florida Statutes; or Stalking filed under section 784.0485, Florida Statutes, has been reviewed. This Court has jurisdiction of the parties and of the subject matter. Upon review of the Petition, this Court concludes that a **Temporary** Injunction for Protection Against Domestic Violence; Repeat, Dating, or Sexual Violence; or Stalking, pending the hearing scheduled below, **NOT** be entered at this time but that an injunction may be entered after the hearing, depending on the findings made by the Court at that time.

FINDINGS

The Court finds that based upon the facts, as stated in the Petition alone and without a hearing on the matter, there is no appearance of an immediate and present danger of domestic violence; repeat, dating, or sexual violence; or stalking, or that stalking exists. Therefore, there is not a sufficient factual basis upon which the court can enter a Temporary Injunction for Protection Against Domestic, Repeat, Dating, or Sexual Violence, or Stalking, prior to a hearing. A hearing is scheduled on the Petition for Injunction for Protection Against Domestic, Repeat, Dating, or Sexual Violence, or Stalking, in Section II of this Order. Petitioner may amend or supplement the Petition at any time to state further reasons why a Temporary Injunction should be ordered which would be in effect until the hearing scheduled below.

Florida Supreme Court Approved Family Law Form 12.980(b)(1), Order Setting Hearing on Petition for Injunction for Protection Against Domestic Violence, Repeat Violence, Dating Violence, Sexual Violence, or Stalking, without Issuance of an Interim Temporary Injunction (03/15)

NOTICE OF HEARING
Petitioner and Respondent are ordered to appear and testify at a hearing on the Petition for Injunction for Protection Against Domestic, Repeat, Dating, or Sexual Violence, or Stalking on: *{date}* ________, at ___ a.m./p.m. at *{location}*________________ at which time the Court will consider whether a Final Judgment of Injunction for Protection Against Domestic, Repeat, Dating, or Sexual Violence, or Stalking should be entered. If entered, the injunction will remain in effect until a fixed date set by the Court or until modified or dissolved by the Court. At the hearing, the Court will determine whether other things should be ordered, including, for example, such matters as time-sharing and support.

If Petitioner and/or Respondent do not appear, orders may be entered, including entry of a permanent injunction and the imposition of court costs. Petitioner and Respondent will be bound by the terms of any injunction or order issued at the final hearing.

IF EITHER PETITIONER OR RESPONDENT DO NOT APPEAR AT THE FINAL HEARING, HE OR SHE WILL BE BOUND BY THE TERMS OF ANY INJUNCTION OR ORDER ISSUED IN THIS MATTER.

All witnesses and evidence, if any, must be presented at this time. In cases where temporary support issues have been alleged in the pleadings, each party is ordered to bring his or her financial affidavit (Florida Family Law Rules of Procedure Form 12.902(b) or (c)), tax return, pay stubs, and other evidence of financial income to the hearing.

NOTICE: Because this is a civil case, there is no requirement that these proceedings be transcribed at public expense.

YOU ARE ADVISED THAT IN THIS COURT:

a. ____ a court reporter is provided by the court.

b. ____ electronic recording only is provided by the court. A party may arrange in advance for the services of and provide for a court reporter to prepare a written transcript of the proceedings at that party's expense.

c. ____ in repeat, dating, and sexual violence cases, no electronic recording or court reporting services are provided by the court. A party may arrange in advance for the services of and provide for a court reporter to prepare a written transcript of the proceedings at that party's expense.

A RECORD, WHICH INCLUDES A TRANSCRIPT, MAY BE REQUIRED TO SUPPORT AN APPEAL. THE PARTY SEEKING THE APPEAL IS RESPONSIBLE FOR HAVING THE TRANSCRIPT PREPARED BY A COURT REPORTER. THE TRANSCRIPT MUST BE FILED WITH THE REVIEWING COURT OR THE APPEAL MAY BE DENIED

If you are a person with a disability who needs any accommodation in order to participate in this proceeding, you are entitled, at no cost to you, to the provisions of certain assistance. Please contact: ____ *{identify applicable court personnel by name, address, and telephone number}* at least 7 days before your scheduled court appearance , or immediately upon receiving this notification if the time before the scheduled appearance is less than 7 days; if you are hearing or voice impaired, call 711.

Nothing in this order limits Petitioner's rights to dismiss the petition.

DONE AND ORDERED in ______________________, Florida, on ______________.

____
CIRCUIT JUDGE

COPIES TO:
Petitioner: _____ by hand delivery in open Court
_____ U.S. mail

Respondent: _____ forwarded to sheriff for service

Other: ______________________________________

I CERTIFY the foregoing is a true copy of the original **Order Setting Hearing on Petition for Injunction** as it appears on file in the office of the Clerk of the Circuit Court of ________________ County, Florida, and that I have furnished copies of this order as indicated above.

CLERK OF THE CIRCUIT COURT

(SEAL)
By: ______________________________________

Florida Supreme Court Approved Family Law Form 12.980(b)(1), Order Setting Hearing on Petition for Injunction for Protection Against Domestic Violence, Repeat Violence, Dating Violence, Sexual Violence, or Stalking, without Issuance of an Interim Temporary Injunction (03/15)

Deputy Clerk or Judicial Assistant

Added as 12.980(c)(1) Feb. 26, 1998, effective Mar. 16, 1998 (713 So.2d 1). Amended Sept. 21, 2000 (810 So.2d 1); May 15, 2003 (849 So.2d 1003). Renumbered from 12.980(c)(1) Mar. 25, 2004 (871 So.2d 113). Amended June 7, 2012 (93 So.3d 194); May 9, 2013 (113 So.3d 781); July 3, 2014, effective July 3, 2014 (142 So.3d 856); March 26, 2015, effective March 26, 2015 (2015 WL 1343088).

Form 12.980(b)(2). Order Denying Petition for Injunction for Protection Against Domestic Violence, Repeat Violence, Dating Violence, or Sexual Violence, or Stalking

IN THE CIRCUIT COURT OF THE ____________ JUDICIAL CIRCUIT,
IN AND FOR __________ COUNTY, FLORIDA

Case No.: ________________________________
Division: ________________________________

_______________________________________,
Petitioner,

and

_______________________________________,
Respondent.

ORDER DENYING PETITION FOR INJUNCTION FOR PROTECTION AGAINST ( ) DOMESTIC VIOLENCE ( ) REPEAT VIOLENCE ( ) DATING VIOLENCE ( ) SEXUAL VIOLENCE ( ) STALKING

The Court has reviewed the Petition for Injunction for Protection Against Domestic, Repeat, Dating, or Sexual Violence, or Stalking filed in this cause, and finds that Petitioner has failed to comply with one or more statutory requirements applicable to that petition, including the following:

1. _____ Petitioner has failed to allege in a petition for domestic violence that Respondent is a family or household member as that term is defined by Chapter 741, Florida Statutes.
2. _____ Petitioner has used a petition form other than that which is approved by the Court and the form used lacks the statutorily required components.
3. _____ Petitioner has failed to complete a mandatory portion of the petition.
4. _____ Petitioner has failed to sign the petition.
5. _____ Petitioner has failed to allege facts sufficient to support the entry of an injunction for protection against domestic, repeat, dating, or sexual violence; or stalking because:

_____
_____
_____
_____.

6. _____ Other: ____

_____
_____
_____.

It is therefore, ORDERED AND ADJUDGED that the petition is denied without prejudice to amend or supplement the petition to cure the above stated defects.

Florida Supreme Court Approved Family Law Form 12.980(b)(2), Order Denying Petition for Injunction for Protection Against Domestic Violence, Repeat Violence, Dating Violence, or Sexual Violence, or Stalking (03/15)

DONE AND ORDERED in_________________________, Florida, on ____________________.

____

CIRCUIT JUDGE

COPIES TO:
Petitioner:
_______ by hand delivery in open Court
_______ by U.S.mail
_____by e-mail to designated e-mail address(es)

I CERTIFY the foregoing is a true copy of the original **Order Denying Hearing on Petition for Injunction** as it appears on file in the office of the Clerk of the Circuit Court of __________________ County, Florida, and that I have furnished copies of this order as indicated above.

CLERK OF THE CIRCUIT COURT
(SEAL)
By: ____
{Deputy Clerk or Judicial Assistant}

Florida Supreme Court Approved Family Law Form 12.980(b)(2), Order Denying Petition for Injunction for Protection Against Domestic Violence, Repeat Violence, Dating Violence, or Sexual Violence, or Stalking (03/15)

Added as 12.980(c)(2) Feb. 26, 1998, effective Mar. 16, 1998 (713 So.2d 1). Amended Sept. 21, 2000 (810 So.2d 1); May 15, 2003 (849 So.2d 1003). Renumbered from 12.980(c)(2) Mar. 25, 2004 (871 So.2d 113). Amended June 7, 2012 (93 So.3d 194); May 9, 2013 (113 So.3d 781); March 26, 2015, effective March 26, 2015 (2015 WL 1343088).

Form 12.980(c)(1). Temporary Injunction for Protection Against Domestic Violence with Minor Child(ren)

IN THE CIRCUIT COURT OF THE ______________________ JUDICIAL CIRCUIT,
IN AND FOR ________________________ COUNTY, FLORIDA

Case No.: ________________________
Division: ________________________

________________________________,
Petitioner,

and

________________________________,
Respondent.

TEMPORARY INJUNCTION FOR PROTECTION AGAINST DOMESTIC VIOLENCE WITH MINOR CHILD(REN)

The Petition for Injunction for Protection Against Domestic Violence under section 741.30, Florida Statutes, and other papers filed in this Court have been reviewed. Under the laws of Florida, the Court has jurisdiction of the Petitioner and the subject matter and has jurisdiction of the Respondent upon service of the temporary injunction.

It is intended that this protection order meet the requirements of 18 U.S.C. Section 2265 and therefore intended that it be accorded full faith and credit by the court of another state or Indian tribe and enforced as if it were the order of the enforcing state or of the Indian tribe.

SECTION I. NOTICE OF HEARING

Because this Temporary Injunction for Protection Against Domestic Violence has been issued without prior notice to Respondent, the Petitioner and Respondent are instructed that they are scheduled to appear and testify at a hearing regarding this matter on *{date}* ____________________________, at ____ a.m./p.m., when the Court will consider whether to issue a Final Judgment of Injunction for Protection Against Domestic Violence, which would remain in effect until modified or dissolved by the Court, and whether other things should be ordered, including, for example, such matters as time-sharing and support. The hearing will be before The Honorable *{name}*________________________________, at *{room name/number, location, address, city}* ____ ____, Florida.

If Petitioner and/or Respondent do not appear, this temporary injunction may be continued in force, extended, dismissed, and/or additional orders may be granted, including entry of a permanent injunction and the imposition of court costs. Petitioner and Respondent will be bound by the terms of any injunction or order issued at the final hearing.

IF EITHER PETITIONER OR RESPONDENT DO NOT APPEAR AT THE FINAL HEARING, HE OR SHE WILL BE BOUND BY THE TERMS OF ANY INJUNCTION OR ORDER ISSUED IN THIS MATTER.

All witnesses and evidence, if any, must be presented at this time. In cases where temporary support issues have been alleged in the pleadings, each party is ordered to bring his or her financial affidavit Florida Family Law Rules of Procedure Form 12.902(b) or (c)), tax return, pay stubs, and other evidence of financial income to the hearing.

NOTICE: Because this is a civil case, there is no requirement that these proceedings be transcribed at public expense.

YOU ARE ADVISED THAT IN THIS COURT:

a. ____a court reporter is provided by the court.

b. ____an electronic recording only is provided by the court. A party may arrange in advance for the services of and provide for a court reporter to prepare a written transcript of the proceedings at that party's expense.

A RECORD, WHICH INCLUDES A TRANSCRIPT, MAY BE REQUIRED TO SUPPORT AN APPEAL. THE PARTY SEEKING THE APPEAL IS RESPONSIBLE FOR HAVING THE TRANSCRIPT PREPARED BY A COURT REPORTER. THE TRANSCRIPT MUST BE FILED WITH THE REVIEWING COURT OR THE APPEAL MAY BE DENIED.

If you are a person with a disability who needs any accommodation in order to participate in this proceeding, you are entitled, at no cost to you, to the provision of certain assistance. Please contact ____

{identify applicable court personnel by name, address, and phone number} **at least 7 days before your scheduled court appearance, or immediately upon receiving this notification if the time before the scheduled appearance is less than 7 days; if you are hearing impaired, call 711.**

SECTION II. FINDINGS

The statements made under oath by Petitioner make it appear that section 741.30, Florida Statutes, applies to the parties. It also appears that Petitioner is a victim of domestic violence by Respondent, and/or Petitioner has reasonable cause to believe he/she is in imminent danger of becoming a victim of domestic violence by Respondent, and that there is an immediate and present danger of domestic violence to Petitioner or persons lawfully with Petitioner.

SECTION III. TEMPORARY INJUNCTION AND TERMS

This injunction shall be effective until the hearing set above and in no event for longer than 15 days, unless extended by court order. If a final order of injunction is issued, the terms of this temporary injunction will be extended until service of the final injunction is effected upon Respondent. This injunction is valid and enforceable in all counties of the State of Florida. The terms of this injunction may not be changed by either party alone or by both parties together. Only the Court may modify the

terms of this injunction. Either party may ask the Court to change or end this injunction.

Any violation of this injunction, whether or not at the invitation of Petitioner or anyone else, may subject Respondent to civil or indirect criminal contempt proceedings, including the imposition of a fine or imprisonment. Certain willful violations of the terms of this injunction, such as: refusing to vacate the dwelling that the parties share; going to or being within 500 feet of Petitioner's residence, going to Petitioner's place of employment, school, or other place prohibited in this injunction; telephoning, contacting or communicating with Petitioner if prohibited by this injunction; knowingly or intentionally coming within 100 feet of Petitioner's motor vehicle, whether or not it is occupied; defacing or destroying Petitioner's personal property; refusing to surrender firearms or ammunition if ordered to do so by the court; or committing an act of domestic violence against Petitioner constitutes a misdemeanor of the first degree punishable by up to one year in jail, as provided by sections 775.082 and 775.083, Florida Statutes. In addition, it is a federal criminal felony offense, punishable by up to life imprisonment, depending on the nature of the violation, to cross state lines or enter Indian country for the purpose of engaging in conduct that is prohibited in this injunction. 18 U.S.C. Section 2262.

ORDERED and ADJUDGED:

1. **Violence Prohibited.** Respondent shall not commit, or cause any other person to commit, any acts of domestic violence against Petitioner. Domestic violence includes: assault, aggravated assault, battery, aggravated battery, sexual assault, sexual battery, stalking, aggravated stalking, kidnapping, false imprisonment, or any other criminal offense resulting in physical injury or death to Petitioner or any of Petitioner's family or household members. Respondent shall not commit any other violation of the injunction through an intentional unlawful threat, word or act to do violence to the Petitioner.

2. **No Contact. Respondent shall have no contact with Petitioner unless otherwise provided in this Section, or unless paragraph 14 below provides for contact connected with the temporary parenting plan and temporary time-sharing with respect to the minor child(ren).**

a. Unless otherwise provided herein, Respondent shall have no contact with Petitioner. Respondent shall not directly or indirectly contact Petitioner in person, by mail, e-mail, fax, telephone, through another person, or in any other manner. Further, Respondent shall not contact or have any third party contact anyone connected with Petitioner's employment or school to inquire about Petitioner or to send any messages to Petitioner. Unless otherwise provided herein, **Respondent shall not go to, in, or within 500 feet of:** Petitioner's current residence *{list address}* ______________________________

____

or any residence to which Petitioner may move; Petitioner's current or any subsequent place of employment *{list address of current employment}* ______________________________

______________________________or place where Petitioner attends school *{list address of school}*

____;

or the following other places (if requested by Petitioner) where Petitioner or Petitioner's minor child(ren) go often:____.

Respondent may not knowingly come within 100 feet of Petitioner's automobile at any time.

Florida Supreme Court Approved Family Law Form 12.980(c)(1), Temporary Injunction for Protection Against Domestic Violence with Minor Child(ren) (03/15)

b. _____Other provisions regarding contact: ____
____
____

3. **Firearms.**
*{Initial **all** that apply; write N/A **if does not** apply}*

a. _____Respondent shall not use or possess a firearm or ammunition.

b. _____Respondent shall surrender any firearms and ammunition in the Respondent's possession to the ______________ County Sheriff's Department until further order of the court.

c. _____Other directives relating to firearms and ammunition: ______________________________
____
____.

NOTE: RESPONDENT IS ADVISED THAT, IF A PERMANENT INJUNCTION FOR PROTECTION AGAINST DOMESTIC VIOLENCE IS ISSUED FOLLOWING A HEARING REGARDING THIS MATTER, IN MOST CASES IT WILL BE A VIOLATION OF SECTION 790.233, FLORIDA STATUTES, AND A FIRST DEGREE MISDEMEANOR, FOR RESPONDENT TO HAVE IN HIS OR HER CARE, CUSTODY, POSSESSION OR CONTROL ANY FIREARM OR AMMUNITION. ADDITIONALLY, IT WILL BE A FEDERAL CRIMINAL FELONY OFFENSE TO SHIP OR TRANSPORT IN INTERSTATE OR FOREIGN COMMERCE, OR POSSESS IN OR AFFECTING COMMERCE, ANY FIREARM OR AMMUNITION; OR TO RECEIVE ANY FIREARM OR AMMUNITION WHICH HAS BEEN SHIPPED OR TRANSPORTED IN INTERSTATE OR FOREIGN COMMERCE WHILE SUBJECT TO SUCH AN INJUNCTION. 18 U.S.C. SECTION 922(g)(8).

4. **Mailing Address or Designated E-Mail Address(es).** Respondent shall notify the Clerk of the Court of any change in either his or her mailing address, or designated e-mail address(es), within 10 days of the change. All further papers (excluding the final injunction, if entered without Respondent being present at the hearing, and pleadings requiring personal service) shall be served either by mail to Respondent's last known mailing address or by e-mail to Respondent's designated e-mail address(es). Service shall be complete upon mailing or e-mailing.

5. **Additional order(s) necessary to protect Petitioner from domestic violence:**
____
____
____
____
____
____.

TEMPORARY EXCLUSIVE USE AND POSSESSION OF HOME

*{Initial **all** that apply; write N/A **if does not** apply}*

6. ____**Possession of the Home.** ____ Petitioner ____ Respondent shall have temporary exclusive use and possession of the dwelling located at: ____
____.

7. ____**Transfer of Possession of the Home.** A law enforcement officer with jurisdiction over the home shall accompany ____ Petitioner ____ Respondent to the home, and shall place ____ Petitioner ____ Respondent in possession of the home.

8. ____**Personal Items.** ____ Petitioner ____ Respondent, **in the presence of a law enforcement officer**, may return to the premises described above ____ on *{date}*______________________, at ______a.m./p.m., or ____ at a time arranged with the law enforcement department with jurisdiction over the home, for the purpose of obtaining his or her clothing and items of personal health and hygiene and tools of the trade. A law enforcement officer with jurisdiction over the home from which these items are to be retrieved shall accompany ____ Petitioner ____ Respondent to the home and stand by to insure that he/she vacates the premises with only his/her personal clothing, toiletries, tools of the trade, and any items listed in paragraph 10 below. The law enforcement agency shall not be responsible for storing or transporting any property. **IF THE RESPONDENT IS NOT AWARDED POSSESSION OF THE HOME AND GOES TO THE HOME WITHOUT A LAW ENFORCEMENT OFFICER, IT IS A VIOLATION OF THIS INJUNCTION.**

9. ____ Petitioner ____ Respondent shall not damage or remove any furnishings or fixtures from the parties' former shared premises.

10. ____Other:____
____
____
____
____
____

TEMPORARY SUPPORT

Temporary support, if requested by Petitioner in the Petition for Injunction for Protection Against Domestic Violence, will be addressed by the Court after notice to Respondent and hearing on the matter.

TEMPORARY PARENTING PLAN WITH TIME-SHARING WITH MINOR CHILD(REN)

11. **Jurisdiction.** *{Initial **one** only}*

______ Jurisdiction to determine issues relating to parenting plan and time-sharing with respect to any minor child(ren) listed in paragraph 12 below is proper under the Uniform Child Custody Jurisdiction and Enforcement Act (UCCJEA).

______ Jurisdiction is exclusive to the dependency court, and accordingly no order is made herein. (Case Number ____________________________.)

12. **Temporary Order for 100% Time-Sharing With Respect to Minor Child(ren).** ___ Petitioner ___ Respondent shall, on a temporary basis, have 100% time sharing with respect to the parties' minor child(ren) listed below:

Name	**Birth date**

When requested by the parent to whom 100% time-sharing is awarded on a temporary basis herein, law enforcement officers shall use any and all reasonable and necessary force to physically deliver the minor child(ren) listed above to the parent to whom 100% time-sharing is awarded on a temporary basis herein. The other parent shall not take the child(ren) from the parent to whom 100% time-sharing is awarded on a temporary basis herein or any child care provider or other person entrusted by the parent to whom 100% time-sharing is awarded on a temporary basis herein with the care of the child(ren).

*{Initial **if** applies; write N/A **if does not** apply}*

______ Neither party shall remove the minor child(ren) from the State of Florida, which is the jurisdiction of this Court, prior to the hearing on this temporary injunction. Violation of this custody order may constitute a felony of the third degree under sections 787.03 and 787.04, Florida Statutes.

13. **Contact with Minor Child(ren).** Unless otherwise provided in paragraph 14 below, the ___ Petitioner ___ Respondent (i.e., the parent to whom 100% time-sharing is **not** awarded on a temporary basis herein) shall have **no contact** with the parties' minor child(ren) until further order of the Court.

14. **Other Additional Provisions Relating to the Minor Child(ren).**

____
____
____
____
____
____
____
____

SECTION IV. OTHER SPECIAL PROVISIONS

{This section to be used for inclusion of local provisions approved by the chief judge as provided in Florida Family Law Rule 12.610.}

____
____
____

SECTION V. DIRECTIONS TO LAW ENFORCEMENT OFFICER IN ENFORCING THIS INJUNCTION

{Unless ordered otherwise by the judge, all provisions in this injunction are considered mandatory provisions and should be interpreted as part of this injunction.}

1. The Sheriff of ________________ County, or any other authorized law enforcement officer, is ordered to serve this temporary injunction upon Respondent as soon as possible after its issuance.

2. **This injunction is valid in all counties of the State of Florida.** Violation of this injunction should be reported to the appropriate law enforcement agency. Law enforcement officers of the jurisdiction in which a violation of this injunction occurs shall enforce the provisions of this injunction and are authorized to arrest without warrant pursuant to section 901.15, Florida Statutes, for any violation of its provisions which constitutes a criminal act under section 741.31, Florida Statutes.

3. THIS INJUNCTION IS ENFORCEABLE IN ALL COUNTIES OF FLORIDA AND LAW ENFORCEMENT OFFICERS MAY EFFECT ARRESTS PURSUANT TO SECTION 901.15(6), FLORIDA STATUTES. The arresting agent shall notify the State Attorney's Office immediately after arrest.

4. **THIS IS A "CUSTODY ORDER" FOR PURPOSES OF THE UCCJEA AND ALL STATUTES MAKING IT A CRIME TO INTERFERE WITH CUSTODY UNDER CHAPTER 787 OF FLORIDA STATUTES AND OTHER SIMILAR STATUTES.**

5. **Reporting alleged violations.** If Respondent violates the terms of this injunction and there has not been an arrest, Petitioner may contact the Clerk of the Circuit Court of the county in which the violation occurred and complete an affidavit in support of the violation, or Petitioner may contact the State Attorney's office for assistance in filing an action for indirect civil contempt or indirect criminal contempt. Upon receiving such a report, the State Attorney is hereby appointed to prosecute such violations by indirect criminal contempt proceedings, or the State Attorney may decide to file a criminal charge, if warranted by the evidence.

DONE AND ORDERED at ______________________, Florida on ______________________.

____

CIRCUIT JUDGE

Florida Supreme Court Approved Family Law Form 12.980(c)(1), Temporary Injunction for Protection Against Domestic Violence with Minor Child(ren) (03/15)

COPIES TO:

Sheriff of ____________________ County

Petitioner: (or his or her attorney)
_____by U.S. Mail
_____by hand-delivery in open court
_____by e-mail to designated e-mail address(es)

Respondent:
_____ forwarded to the Sheriff for service

_____ State's Attorney's Office
_____ Other:______________________________

I CERTIFY the foregoing is a true copy of the original Temporary Injunction for Protection Against Domestic Violence with Minor Child(ren) as it appears on file in the office of the Clerk of the Circuit Court of ________________ County, Florida, and that I have furnished copies of this order as indicated above.

CLERK OF THE CIRCUIT COURT
(SEAL)
By: ____
{Deputy Clerk or Judicial Assistant}

Florida Supreme Court Approved Family Law Form 12.980(c)(1), Temporary Injunction for Protection Against Domestic Violence with Minor Child(ren) (03/15)

Added as 12.980(d)(1) Sept. 21, 2000 (810 So.2d 1). Amended Oct. 3, 2002 (830 So.2d 72); Dec. 19, 2002 (836 So.2d 1019); May 15, 2003 (849 So.2d 1003). Renumbered from 12.980(d)(1) Mar. 25, 2004 (871 So.2d 113). Amended March 26, 2009 (20 So.3d 173); Dec. 16, 2010 (59 So.3d 792); June 7, 2012 (93 So.3d 194); March 26, 2015, effective March 26, 2015 (2015 WL 1343088).

Form 12.980(c)(2). Temporary Injunction for Protection Against Domestic Violence Without Minor Child(ren)

IN THE CIRCUIT COURT OF THE __________ JUDICIAL CIRCUIT,
IN AND FOR __________________________ COUNTY, FLORIDA

Case No.: ______________
Division: ______________

______________________________,
Petitioner,
and

______________________________,
Respondent.

TEMPORARY INJUNCTION FOR PROTECTION AGAINST DOMESTIC VIOLENCE WITHOUT MINOR CHILD(REN)

The Petition for Injunction for Protection Against Domestic Violence under section 741.30, Florida Statutes, and other papers filed in this Court have been reviewed. Under the laws of Florida, the Court has jurisdiction of the Petitioner and the subject matter and has jurisdiction of the Respondent upon service of the temporary injunction.

It is intended that this protection order meet the requirements of 18 U.S.C. Section 2265 and therefore intended that it be accorded full faith and credit by the court of another state or Indian tribe and enforced as if it were the order of the enforcing state or of the Indian tribe.

SECTION I. NOTICE OF HEARING

Because this Temporary Injunction for Protection Against Domestic Violence has been issued without prior notice to Respondent, the Petitioner and Respondent are instructed that they are scheduled to appear and testify at a hearing regarding this matter on *{date}* ______________________________, at __________ a.m./p.m., when the Court will consider whether to issue a Final Judgment of Injunction for Protection Against Domestic Violence, which would remain in effect until modified or dissolved by the Court, and whether other things should be ordered, including, for example, such matters as support. The hearing will be before The Honorable *{name}* ______________________________, at *{room name/number, location, address, city}* ______________________________ ______________________________, Florida. If Petitioner and/or Respondent do not appear, this temporary injunction may be continued in force, extended, dismissed, and/or additional orders may be granted, including entry of a permanent injunction and the imposition of court costs. Petitioner and Respondent will be bound by the terms of any injunction or order issued at the final hearing.

IF EITHER PETITIONER OR RESPONDENT DO NOT APPEAR AT THE FINAL HEARING, HE OR SHE WILL BE BOUND BY THE TERMS OF ANY INJUNCTION OR ORDER ISSUED IN THIS MATTER.

Florida Supreme Court Approved Family Law Form 12.980(c)(2), Temporary Injunction for Protection Against Domestic Violence without Minor Child(ren) (03/15)

All witnesses and evidence, if any, must be presented at this time. In cases where temporary support issues have been alleged in the pleadings, each party is ordered to bring his or her financial affidavit (Florida Family Law Rules of Procedure Form 12.902(b) or (c)), tax return, pay stubs, and other evidence of financial income to the hearing.

NOTICE: Because this is a civil case, there is no requirement that these proceedings be transcribed at public expense.

YOU ARE ADVISED THAT IN THIS COURT:

a. ____ a court reporter is provided by the court.

b. ____ an electronic recording only is provided by the court. A party may arrange in advance for the services of and provide for a court reporter to prepare a written transcript of the proceedings at that party's expense.

A RECORD, WHICH INCLUDES A TRANSCRIPT, MAY BE REQUIRED TO SUPPORT AN APPEAL. THE PARTY SEEKING THE APPEAL IS RESPONSIBLE FOR HAVING THE TRANSCRIPT PREPARED BY A COURT REPORTER. THE TRANSCRIPT MUST BE FILED WITH THE REVIEWING COURT OR THE APPEAL MAY BE DENIED.

If you are a person with a disability who needs any accommodation in order to participate in this proceeding, you are entitled, at no cost to you, to the provision of certain assistance. Please contact ______________________________ *{identify applicable court personnel by name, address and telephone number}* at least 7 days before your scheduled court appearance, or immediately upon receiving this notification if the time before the scheduled appearance is less than 7 days; if you are hearing impaired, call 711.

SECTION II. FINDINGS

The statements made under oath by Petitioner make it appear that section 741.30, Florida Statutes, applies to the parties. It also appears that Petitioner is a victim of domestic violence by Respondent, and/or Petitioner has reasonable cause to believe he/she is in imminent danger of becoming a victim of domestic violence by Respondent, and that there is an immediate and present danger of domestic violence to Petitioner or persons lawfully with Petitioner.

SECTION III. TEMPORARY INJUNCTION AND TERMS

This injunction shall be effective until the hearing set above and in no event for longer than 15 days, unless extended by court order. If a final order of injunction is issued, the terms of this temporary injunction will be extended until service of the final injunction is effected upon Respondent. This injunction is valid and enforceable in all counties of the State of Florida. The terms of this injunction may not be changed by either party alone or by both parties together. Only the Court may modify the terms of this injunction. Either party may ask the Court to change or end this injunction.

Any violation of this injunction, whether or not at the invitation of Petitioner or anyone else, may subject Respondent to civil or indirect criminal contempt proceedings, including the imposition of a fine or imprisonment. Certain willful violations of the terms of this injunction, such as: refusing to vacate the dwelling that the parties share; going to or being within 500 feet of Petitioner's residence, going to Petitioner's place of employment, school, or other place prohibited in this injunction; telephoning, contacting or communicating with Petitioner if prohibited by this injunction; knowingly or intentionally coming within 100 feet of Petitioner's motor vehicle, whether or not it is occupied; defacing or destroying Petitioner's personal property; refusing to surrender firearms or ammunition if ordered to do so by the court; or committing an act of domestic violence against Petitioner constitutes a misdemeanor of the first degree punishable by up to one year in jail, as provided by sections 775.082 and 775.083, Florida Statutes. In addition, it is a federal criminal felony offense, punishable by up to life imprisonment, depending on the nature of the violation, to cross state lines or enter Indian country for the purpose of engaging in conduct that is prohibited in this injunction. 18 U.S.C. Section 2262.

ORDERED and ADJUDGED:

1. **Violence Prohibited.** Respondent shall not commit, or cause any other person to commit, any acts of domestic violence against Petitioner. Domestic violence includes: assault, aggravated assault, battery, aggravated battery, sexual assault, sexual battery, stalking, aggravated stalking, kidnapping, false imprisonment, or any other criminal offense resulting in physical injury or death to Petitioner or any of Petitioner's family or household members. Respondent shall not commit any other violation of the injunction through an intentional unlawful threat, word or act to do violence to the Petitioner.

2. **No Contact. Respondent shall have no contact with Petitioner unless otherwise provided in this section.**

a. Unless otherwise provided herein, Respondent shall have no contact with Petitioner. Respondent shall not directly or indirectly contact Petitioner in person, by mail, e-mail, fax, telephone, through another person, or in any other manner. Further, Respondent shall not contact or have any third party contact anyone connected with Petitioner's employment or school to inquire about Petitioner or to send any messages to Petitioner. Unless otherwise provided herein, **Respondent shall not go to, in, or within 500 feet of:** Petitioner's current residence *{list address}* ______________________________
____
or any residence to which Petitioner may move; Petitioner's current or any subsequent place of employment *{list address of current employment}* ______________________________
or place where Petitioner attends school *{list address of school}* ______________________________;

Florida Supreme Court Approved Family Law Form 12.980(c)(2), Temporary Injunction for Protection Against Domestic Violence without Minor Child(ren) (03/15)

or the following other places (if requested by Petitioner) where Petitioner or Petitioner's minor child(ren) go often: ____
____
____.

Respondent may not knowingly come within 100 feet of Petitioner's automobile at any time.
b. Other provisions regarding contact:
____
____
____.

3. **Firearms.**
*{Initial **all** that apply; write N/A **if does not** apply}*
a. ____Respondent shall not use or possess a firearm or ammunition.

b. _____Respondent shall surrender any firearms and ammunition in the Respondent's possession to the________________________ County Sheriff's Department until further order of the court.

c. _____Other directives relating to firearms and ammunition:_____________________________
____
____.

NOTE: RESPONDENT IS ADVISED THAT, IF A PERMANENT INJUNCTION FOR PROTECTION AGAINST DOMESTIC VIOLENCE IS ISSUED FOLLOWING A HEARING REGARDING THIS MATTER, IN MOST CASES IT WILL BE A VIOLATION OF SECTION 790.233, FLORIDA STATUTES, AND A FIRST DEGREE MISDEMEANOR, FOR RESPONDENT TO HAVE IN HIS OR HER CARE, CUSTODY, POSSESSION OR CONTROL ANY FIREARM OR AMMUNITION. ADDITIONALLY, IT WILL BE A FEDERAL CRIMINAL FELONY OFFENSE TO SHIP OR TRANSPORT IN INTERSTATE OR FOREIGN COMMERCE, OR POSSESS IN OR AFFECTING COMMERCE, ANY FIREARM OR AMMUNITION; OR TO RECEIVE ANY FIREARM OR AMMUNITION WHICH HAS BEEN SHIPPED OR TRANSPORTED IN INTERSTATE OR FOREIGN COMMERCE WHILE SUBJECT TO SUCH AN INJUNCTION. 18 U.S.C. SECTION 922(g)(8).

4. **Mailing Address or Designated E-Mail Address(es).** Respondent shall notify the Clerk of the Court of any change in either his or her mailing address, or designated e-mail address(es), within 10 days of the change. All further papers (excluding the final injunction, if entered without Respondent being present at the hearing, and pleadings requiring personal service) shall be served either by mail to Respondent's last known mailing address or by e-mail to Respondent's designated e-mail address(es). Service shall be complete upon mailing or e-mailing.

5. **Additional order(s) necessary to protect Petitioner from domestic violence:**
____
____
____
____

____.

TEMPORARY EXCLUSIVE USE AND POSSESSION OF HOME

*{Initial **all** that apply; write N/A **if does not** apply}*

6. ____**Possession of the Home.** ____ Petitioner ____ Respondent shall have temporary exclusive use and possession of ____.

7. ____ **Transfer of Possession of the Home.** A law enforcement officer with jurisdiction over the home shall accompany ____ Petitioner____ Respondent to the home, and shall place ____Petitioner ____ Respondent in possession of the home.

8. ____**Personal Items.** ____ Petitioner ____ Respondent, **in the presence of a law enforcement officer**, may return to the premises described above ________ on ________, at ________,a.m./p.m., or ____ at a time arranged with the law enforcement department with jurisdiction over the home, for the purpose of obtaining his or her clothing and items of personal health and hygiene and tools of the trade. A law enforcement officer with jurisdiction over the home from which these items are to be retrieved shall accompany ____ Petitioner

____ Respondent to the home and stand by to insure that he/she vacates the premises with only his/her personal clothing, toiletries, tools of the trade, and any items listed in paragraph 10 below. The law enforcement agency shall not be responsible for storing or transporting any property. **IF THE RESPONDENT IS NOT AWARDED POSSESSION OF THE HOME AND GOES TO THE HOME WITHOUT A LAW ENFORCEMENT OFFICER, IT IS A VIOLATION OF THIS INJUNCTION.**

9.____ Petitioner ____ Respondent shall not damage or remove any furnishings or fixtures from the parties' former shared premises.

10.____ Other: ____
____
____
____

TEMPORARY SUPPORT

Temporary support, if requested by Petitioner in the Petition for Injunction for Protection Against Domestic Violence, will be addressed by the Court after notice to Respondent and hearing on the matter.

SECTION IV. OTHER SPECIAL PROVISIONS

{This section to be used for inclusion of local provisions approved by the chief judge as provided in Florida Family Law Rule 12.610.}

____
____

____.

SECTION V. DIRECTIONS TO LAW ENFORCEMENT OFFICER IN ENFORCING THIS INJUNCTION
{Unless ordered otherwise by the judge, all provisions in this injunction are considered mandatory provisions and should be interpreted as part of this injunction.}

1. The Sheriff of ____________________ County, or any other authorized law enforcement officer, is ordered to serve this temporary injunction upon Respondent as soon as possible after its issuance.

2. **This injunction is valid in all counties of the State of Florida.** Violation of this injunction should be reported to the appropriate law enforcement agency. Law enforcement officers of the jurisdiction in which a violation of this injunction occurs shall enforce the provisions of this injunction and are authorized to arrest without warrant pursuant to section 901.15, Florida Statutes, for any violation of its provisions which constitutes a criminal act under section 741.31, Florida Statutes.

3. THIS INJUNCTION IS ENFORCEABLE IN ALL COUNTIES OF FLORIDA AND LAW ENFORCEMENT OFFICERS MAY EFFECT ARRESTS PURSUANT TO SECTION 901.15(6), FLORIDA STATUTES. The arresting agent shall notify the State Attorney's Office immediately after arrest.

4. **Reporting alleged violations.** If Respondent violates the terms of this injunction and there has not been an arrest, Petitioner may contact the Clerk of the Circuit Court of the county in which the violation occurred and complete an affidavit in support of the violation, or Petitioner may contact the State Attorney's office for assistance in filing an action for indirect civil contempt or indirect criminal contempt. Upon receiving such a report, the State Attorney is hereby appointed to prosecute such violations by indirect criminal contempt proceedings, or the State Attorney may decide to file a criminal charge, if warranted by the evidence.

DONE AND ORDERED in__________________________, Florida on ________________________.

____
CIRCUIT JUDGE

COPIES TO:

Sheriff of _________________ County

Petitioner: (or his or her attorney)
_____by U.S. Mail
_____ by hand-delivery in open court
_____by e-mail to designated e-mail address(es)

Respondent:
_____ forwarded to the sheriff for service

_____ State's Attorney's Office

_____ other:__________________________

I CERTIFY the foregoing is a true copy of the original Temporary Injunction for Protection Against Domestic Violence without Minor Child(ren) as it appears on file in the office of the Clerk of the Circuit Court of _________________ County, Florida, and that I have furnished copies of this order as indicated above.

CLERK OF THE CIRCUIT COURT

(SEAL)
By: ____

{Deputy Clerk or Judicial Assistant}

Florida Supreme Court Approved Family Law Form 12.980(c)(2), Temporary Injunction for Protection Against Domestic Violence without Minor Child(ren) (03/15)

Added as 12.980(d)(2) Sept. 21, 2000 (810 So.2d 1). Amended Oct. 3, 2002 (830 So.2d 72); May 15, 2003 (849 So.2d 1003). Renumbered from 12.980(d)(2) Mar. 25, 2004 (871 So.2d 113). Amended June 7, 2012 (93 So.3d 194); March 26, 2015, effective March 26, 2015 (2015 WL 1343088).

Form 12.980(d)(1). Final Judgment of Injunction for Protection Against Domestic Violence with Minor Child(ren) (After Notice)

IN THE CIRCUIT COURT OF THE ______________ JUDICIAL CIRCUIT,
IN AND FOR ______________ COUNTY, FLORIDA

Case No.: ______________
Division: ______________

______________,
Petitioner,
and

______________,
Respondent.

FINAL JUDGMENT OF INJUNCTION FOR PROTECTION AGAINST DOMESTIC VIOLENCE WITH MINOR CHILD(REN) (AFTER NOTICE)

The Petition for Injunction for Protection Against Domestic Violence under section 741.30, Florida Statutes, and other papers filed in this Court have been reviewed. The Court has jurisdiction of the parties and the subject matter.

It is intended that this protection order meet the requirements of 18 U.S.C. Section 2265 and therefore intended that it be accorded full faith and credit by the court of another state or Indian tribe and enforced as if it were the order of the enforcing state or of the Indian tribe.

SECTION I. HEARING

This cause came before the Court for a hearing to determine whether an Injunction for Protection Against Domestic Violence in this case should be:
_____ issued ____ modified ____ extended.

The hearing was attended by:
____ Petitioner
____ Respondent
____ Petitioner's Counsel
____ Respondent's Counsel

SECTION II. FINDINGS

On *{date}* ______________, a notice of this hearing was served on Respondent together with a copy of Petitioner's petition to this Court and the temporary injunction, if issued. Service was within the time required by Florida law, and Respondent was afforded an opportunity to be heard.

After hearing the testimony of each party present and of any witnesses, or upon consent of Respondent, the Court finds, based on the specific facts of this case, that Petitioner is a victim of domestic violence or has reasonable cause to believe that he/she is in imminent danger of becoming a victim of domestic violence by Respondent.

SECTION III. INJUNCTION AND TERMS

This injunction shall be in full force and effect until either ______ further order of the Court or ______ *{date}*____________________. This injunction is valid and enforceable in all counties of the State of Florida. The terms of this injunction may not be changed by either party alone or by both parties together. Only the Court may modify the terms of this injunction. Either party may ask the Court to change or end this injunction at any time.

Any violation of this injunction, whether or not at the invitation of Petitioner or anyone else, may subject Respondent to civil or indirect criminal contempt proceedings, including the imposition of a fine or imprisonment. Certain willful violations of the terms of this injunction, such as: refusing to vacate the dwelling that the parties share; going to or being within 500 feet of Petitioner's residence, going to Petitioner's place of employment, school, or other place prohibited in this injunction; telephoning, contacting or communicating with Petitioner if prohibited by this injunction; knowingly or intentionally coming within 100 feet of Petitioner's motor vehicle, whether or not it is occupied; defacing or destroying Petitioner's personal property; refusing to surrender firearms or ammunition if ordered to do so by the court; or committing an act of domestic violence against Petitioner constitutes a misdemeanor of the first degree punishable by up to one year in jail, as provided by sections 775.082 and 775.083, Florida Statutes. In addition, it is a federal criminal felony offense, punishable by up to life imprisonment, depending on the nature of the violation, to cross state lines or enter Indian country for the purpose of engaging in conduct that is prohibited in this injunction. 18 U.S.C. SECTION 2262.

ORDERED and ADJUDGED:

1. **Violence Prohibited.** Respondent shall not commit, or cause any other person to commit, any acts of domestic violence against Petitioner. Domestic violence includes: assault, aggravated assault, battery, aggravated battery, sexual assault, sexual battery, stalking, aggravated stalking, kidnapping, false imprisonment, or any other criminal offense resulting in physical injury or death to Petitioner or any of Petitioner's family or household members. Respondent shall not commit any other violation of the injunction through an intentional unlawful threat, word or act to do violence to the Petitioner.

2. **No Contact. Respondent shall have no contact with the Petitioner unless otherwise provided in this section, or unless paragraphs 13 through 19 below provide for contact connected with the temporary parenting plan and temporary time-sharing with respect to the minor child(ren).**

a. Unless otherwise provided herein, Respondent shall have no contact with Petitioner. Respondent shall not directly or indirectly contact Petitioner in person, by mail, e-mail, fax, telephone, through another person, or in any other manner. Further, Respondent shall not contact or have any third party contact anyone connected with Petitioner's employment or school to inquire about Petitioner or to send any messages to Petitioner. Unless otherwise provided herein, **Respondent shall not go to, in, or within 500 feet of:** Petitioner's current residence *{list address}*____________________

____
or any residence to which Petitioner may move; Petitioner's current or any subsequent place of employment *{list address of current employment}* ______________________________ ______________________________or place where Petitioner attends school *{list address of school}* ____;
or the following other places (if requested by Petitioner) where Petitioner or Petitioner's minor child(ren) go often:____
____
____
Respondent may not knowingly come within 100 feet of Petitioner's automobile at any time.

b.____Other provisions regarding contact: ______________________________
____
____.

3. **Firearms. Unless paragraph a. is initialed below, Respondent shall not have in his or her care, custody, possession or control any firearm or ammunition. It is a violation of section 790.233, Florida Statutes, and a first degree misdemeanor, for the respondent to have in his or her care, custody, possession or control any firearm or ammunition.**

*[Initial **if** applies; write N/A **if not** applicable]*

a.____Respondent is a state or local officer as defined in section 943.10(14), Florida Statutes, who holds an active certification, who receives or possesses a firearm or ammunition for use in performing official duties on behalf of the officer's employing agency and is not prohibited by the court from having in his or her care, custody, possession or control a firearm or ammunition. The officer's employing agency may prohibit the officer from having in his or her care, custody, possession or control a firearm or ammunition.

b.____Respondent shall surrender any firearms and ammunition in the Respondent's possession to the ______________________ County Sheriff's Department.

c.____Other directives relating to firearms and ammunition:
____
____
____.

NOTE: RESPONDENT IS ADVISED THAT IT IS A FEDERAL CRIMINAL FELONY OFFENSE TO SHIP OR TRANSPORT IN INTERSTATE OR FOREIGN COMMERCE, OR POSSESS IN OR AFFECTING COMMERCE, ANY FIREARM OR AMMUNITION; OR TO RECEIVE ANY FIREARM OR AMMUNITION WHICH HAS BEEN SHIPPED OR TRANSPORTED IN INTERSTATE OR FOREIGN COMMERCE WHILE SUBJECT TO SUCH AN INJUNCTION. 18 U.S.C. SECTION 922(g)(8).

4. **Evaluation/Counseling.**

*[Initial **all** that apply; write N/A **if does not** apply]*

a. The Court finds that Respondent has:

i. ____willfully violated the ex parte injunction;

ii. ____been convicted of, had adjudication withheld on, or pled nolo contendere to a crime involving violence or a threat of violence; and/or

iii. ____in this state or any other state, had at any time a prior injunction for protection against the Respondent after a hearing with notice.

Note: If Respondent meets any of the above enumerated criteria, the Court must order the Respondent to attend a batterers' intervention program unless it makes written factual findings stating why such a program would not be appropriate. See Section 741.30(6)(e), Florida Statutes.

____ a. Within ____10 days ______ days, (but no more than 10 days) of the date of this injunction, Respondent shall enroll in and thereafter without delay complete the following, and Respondent shall provide proof of such enrollment to the Clerk of Circuit Court within ____ 30 days or ____ days, (but no more than 30 days) of the date of this injunction:

i. ___A certified batterers' intervention program from a list of programs to be provided by the Court or any entity designated by the Court. Respondent shall also successfully complete any substance abuse or mental health evaluation that the assessing program counselor deems necessary as a predicate to completion of the batterers' intervention program.

ii. ____A substance abuse evaluation at:______________________________ or a similarly qualified facility and any substance abuse treatment recommended by that evaluation.

iii. ____A mental health evaluation by a licensed mental health professional at: ______________________________or any other similarly qualified facility and any mental health treatment recommended by that evaluation.

iv. ____Other:____
____.

____ b. ____Although Respondent meets the statutory mandate of attendance at a batterers' intervention program, the Court makes the following written findings as to why the condition of batterers' intervention program would be inappropriate: ______________
____
____
____.

c. ____Petitioner is referred to a certified domestic violence center and is provided with a list of certified domestic violence centers in this circuit, which Petitioner may contact.

5. **Mailing Address or Designated E-Mail Address(es).** Respondent shall notify the Clerk of the Court of any change in either his or her mailing address, or designated e-mail address(es), within 10 days of the change. All further papers (excluding pleadings requiring personal service) shall be served either by mail to Respondent's last known mailing address or by e-mail to Respondent's designated e-mail address(es). Service shall be complete upon mailing or e-mailing.

6. **Other provisions necessary to protect Petitioner from domestic violence:** ______________
____
______
______
______.

TEMPORARY EXCLUSIVE USE AND POSSESSION OF HOME
*[Initial if applies; write N/A **if not** applicable]*

7. ____**Possession of the Home.** ____ Petitioner ____ Respondent shall have temporary exclusive use and possession of the dwelling located at: ______________________________

8. ____**Transfer of Possession of the Home.** A law enforcement officer with jurisdiction over the home shall accompany ____ Petitioner ____ Respondent to the home, and shall place ____ Petitioner ____ Respondent in possession of the home.

9. ____**Personal Items.** ____ Petitioner ____ Respondent, **in the presence of a law enforcement officer**, may return to the premises described above on *{date}* ________________, at ________a.m./p.m., or ____ at a time arranged with the law enforcement department with jurisdiction over the home, accompanied by a law enforcement officer only, for the purpose of obtaining his or her clothing and items of personal health and hygiene and tools of the trade. A law enforcement officer with jurisdiction over the premises shall go with ___ Petitioner ___ Respondent to the home and stand by to insure that he/she vacates the premises with only his/her personal clothing, toiletries, tools of the trade, and any items listed in paragraph 10 below. The law enforcement agency shall not be responsible for storing or transporting any property. IF THE RESPONDENT IS NOT AWARDED POSSESSION OF THE HOME AND GOES TO THE HOME WITHOUT A LAW ENFORCEMENT OFFICER, IT IS A VIOLATION OF THIS INJUNCTION.

10. ____The following other personal possessions may also be removed from the premises at this time: ____
____.

11. ____Other: ____
____
____
______.

TEMPORARY PARENTING PLAN AND TIME-SHARING WITH MINOR CHILD(REN)

12. **Jurisdiction.**
[Initial one only]
______Jurisdiction to determine issues relating to parenting plan and time-sharing with respect_to any minor child(ren) listed in paragraph 13 below is proper under the Uniform Child Custody Jurisdiction and Enforcement Act (UCCJEA).

_____ Jurisdiction is exclusive to the dependency court, and accordingly no order is made herein. *{Case Number ______________________________.}*

13. **Temporary Parenting Plan for Minor Child(ren).** Except for that time-sharing (if any) specified for the other parent in paragraph 14, below, _____ Petitioner ____ Respondent shall on a temporary basis have 100% of the time-sharing with the parties' minor child(ren) listed below and shall have sole decision-making responsibility until further court order:

Name	**Birth date**

When requested by the parent to whom the majority of overnight time-sharing with the child(ren) is awarded on a temporary basis herein, in this case the _____ Petitioner _____ Respondent, law enforcement officers shall use any and all reasonable and necessary force to physically deliver the minor child(ren) listed above to the parent to whom the majority of overnight time-sharing with the child(ren) is awarded on a temporary basis herein. The other parent shall not take the child(ren) from the parent to whom the majority of overnight time-sharing with the child(ren) is awarded on a temporary basis herein or any child care provider or other person entrusted by the parent to whom the majority of overnight time-sharing with the child(ren) is awarded on a temporary basis herein with the care of the child(ren).

14. **Temporary Parenting Plan with Time-Sharing for Minor Child(ren).** The Petitioner and Respondent shall have time-sharing with the minor child(ren) on the following schedule:
{Initial one only}
a. ____ Petitioner ____ Respondent shall have 100% of time-sharing and ____ Petitioner ____ Respondent shall have 0% of time sharing with the child(ren) until further order of the Court. Until further order of the Court, all parenting decisions shall be made by the parent with 100% of the time-sharing.

Florida Supreme Court Approved Family Law Form 12.980(d)(1), Final Judgment of Injunction for Protection Against Domestic Violence with Minor Child(ren) (After Notice) (03/15)

b. ____ Petitioner ____ Respondent shall have time-sharing from __________ a.m./p.m. to ______a.m./p.m. on the following day(s)__________________________. The other parent will have the remaining time-sharing. ____.

c. ____Other: ____.

15. **Limitations on Time-Sharing.** The time-sharing specified in paragraph 14, above, for ____ Petitioner ____ Respondent with the child(ren) shall be:
*[Initial **all** that apply; write N/A **if does not** apply]*
a.______ unsupervised

b.______ supervised by the following specified responsible adult:______________________

c.______ at a supervised visitation center located at:
____,
and shall be subject to the available times and rules of the supervised visitation center. The cost associated with the services of the supervised visitation center shall be paid by the: *{choose **one**}* _____ parent to whom the majority of overnight time-sharing with the child(ren) is awarded on a temporary basis herein; _____ other parent; or _____ both parents: ______________________________________.
If specified, the level of supervision shall be:__________________________.

16. **Arrangements for Time-Sharing with Minor Child(ren).**
*{Initial **all** that apply; write N/A **if does not** apply}*
a. _____A responsible person shall coordinate the time-sharing arrangements with respect to the minor child(ren). If specified, the responsible person shall be: *{name}* ______________ ______________________________

b. _____Other conditions for time-sharing arrangements as follows: ______________ ______.

17. **Exchange of Minor Child(ren).**
*{Initial **all** that apply; write N/A **if does not** apply}*
a. _____The parties shall exchange the child(ren) at _____ school or daycare, or _____ at the following location(s): ____.

Florida Supreme Court Approved Family Law Form 12.980(d)(1), Final Judgment of Injunction for Protection Against Domestic Violence with Minor Child(ren) (After Notice) (03/15)

b. _____A responsible person shall conduct all exchanges of the child(ren). The _____ Petitioner _____ Respondent shall not be present during the exchange. If specified, the responsible person shall be: *{name}*____
____.

c. _____Other conditions for exchange as follows: ______________________________
____
____.

18. **Other Additional Provisions Relating to the Minor Child(ren).**
____
____
____
____
____
____
____.

TEMPORARY SUPPORT

19. **Temporary Alimony.**
*[Initial **all** that apply; write N/A **if does not apply**]*

a. _____The court finds that there is a need for temporary alimony and that _____ Petitioner _____ Respondent (hereinafter Obligor) has the present ability to pay alimony and shall pay temporary alimony to ____ Petitioner ____ Respondent (hereinafter Obligee) in the amount of $_________ per month, payable _____ in accordance with Obligor's employer's payroll cycle, and in any event, at least once a month _____ other *{explain}* ____
beginning *{date}* ____________________. This alimony shall continue until modified by court order, until a final judgment of dissolution of marriage is entered, until Obligee dies, until this injunction expires, or until *{date}* ______________, whichever occurs first.

b. _____ Petitioner _____ Respondent shall be required to maintain health insurance coverage for the other party. Any uncovered medical costs for the party awarded alimony shall be assessed as follows: ___
____.

c. _____Other provisions relating to alimony: __________________________________
____
____.

20. **Temporary Child Support.**
*{Initial **all** that apply; write N/A **if does not apply**}*

a. _____The Court finds that there is a need for temporary child support and that _____ Petitioner _____ Respondent (hereinafter Obligor) has the present ability to pay child support.

The amounts in the Child Support Guidelines Worksheet, Florida Family Law Form 12.902(e), filed by _____ Petitioner _____ Respondent are correct **OR** the Court makes the following findings:
The Petitioner's net monthly income is $ __________, (Child Support Guidelines %).
The Respondent's net monthly income is $__________, (Child Support Guidelines ______%). Monthly child care costs are $ __________________.
Monthly health/dental insurance costs are $________________.

b. _____**Amount.** Obligor shall pay temporary child support in the amount of $ ____________, per month payable _____ in accordance with Obligor's employer's payroll cycle, and in any event at least once a month _____other *{explain}*:____

____

beginning *{date}* ___________________________________, and continuing until further order of the court, or until *{date/event}* ____,
{explain} ____.
If the child support ordered deviates from the guidelines by more than 5%, the factual findings which support that deviation are:____
____.

c. ____ Petitioner ____ Respondent shall be required to maintain ____health ____ dental insurance coverage for the parties' minor child(ren) so long as it is reasonable in cost and accessible to the child(ren) **OR** ____ Health ____ dental insurance is either not reasonable in cost or accessible to the child(ren) at this time.

d. _____Any reasonable and necessary **uninsured medical/dental/prescription drug costs** for the minor child(ren) shall be assessed as follows:________________________________
____

e. _____Florida Supreme Court Approved Family Law Form 12.902(j), **Notice of Social Security Number**, is incorporated herein by reference.

f. _____Other provisions relating to child support: ______________________________
____
____

21. **Method of Payment.**
*[Initial **one** only]*
a. _____ Obligor shall pay any temporary court-ordered child support/alimony through income deduction, and such support shall be paid to either the State Disbursement Unit or the central depository. Obligor is individually responsible for paying this support obligation in the event that all or any portion of said support is not deducted from Obligor's income. Obligor shall also pay any service charge required by statute. Until child support/alimony payments are deducted from Obligor's paycheck pursuant to the Income Deduction Order, Obligor is responsible for making timely payments directly to either the State Disbursement Unit or the central depository.

b. ______ Temporary child support/alimony shall be paid through either the State Disbursement Unit or the central depository. Obligor shall also pay any service charge required by statute. Income deduction is **not** in the best interests of the child(ren) because: *{explain}* ____
____.

c. ______ Other provisions relating to method of payment: ____
____
____
____
____

SECTION IV. OTHER SPECIAL PROVISIONS
(This section to be used for inclusion of local provisions approved by the chief judge as provided in Florida Family Law Rule 12.610.)
____
____
____

SECTION V. DIRECTIONS TO LAW ENFORCEMENT OFFICER IN ENFORCING THIS INJUNCTION
{Unless ordered otherwise by the judge, all provisions in this injunction are considered mandatory provisions and should be interpreted as part of this injunction.}

1. **This injunction is valid in all counties of the State of Florida.** Violation of this injunction should be reported to the appropriate law enforcement agency. Law enforcement officers of the jurisdiction in which a violation of this injunction occurs shall enforce the provisions of this injunction and are authorized to arrest without warrant pursuant to section 901.15, Florida Statutes, for any violation of its provisions, except those regarding child support and/or alimony, which constitutes a criminal act under section 741.31, Florida Statutes. **When inconsistent with this order, any subsequent court order issued under Chapter 61 or Chapter 39, Florida Statutes, shall take precedence over this order on all matters relating to property division, alimony, parental responsibility, parenting plan, time-sharing, child custody, or child support.**

2. THIS INJUNCTION IS ENFORCEABLE IN ALL COUNTIES OF FLORIDA, AND LAW ENFORCEMENT OFFICERS MAY EFFECT ARRESTS PURSUANT TO SECTION 901.15(6), FLORIDA STATUTES. The arresting agent shall notify the State Attorney's Office immediately after arrest.

3. **Reporting alleged violations.** If Respondent violates the terms of this injunction and there has not been an arrest, Petitioner may contact the Clerk of the Circuit Court of the county in which the violation occurred and complete an affidavit in support of the violation, or Petitioner may contact the State Attorney's office for assistance in filing an action for indirect civil contempt or indirect criminal contempt. Upon receiving such a report, the State Attorney is hereby appointed to prosecute such violations by indirect criminal contempt proceedings, or the State Attorney may decide to file a criminal charge, if warranted by the evidence.

4. **Respondent, upon service of this injunction, shall be deemed to have knowledge of and to be**

bound by all matters occurring at the hearing and on the face of this injunction.

5. **The temporary injunction, if any, entered in this case is extended until such time as service of this injunction is effected upon Respondent.**

6. **THIS IS A "CUSTODY ORDER" FOR PURPOSES OF THE UCCJEA AND ALL STATUTES MAKING IT A CRIME TO INTERFERE WITH CUSTODY UNDER CHAPTER 787, FLORIDA STATUTES AND OTHER SIMILAR STATUTES.**

DONE AND ORDERED at ______________________, Florida, on ____________________.

____
CIRCUIT JUDGE

Sheriff of ______________________County

Petitioner (or his or her attorney):
____ by U. S. Mail
____ by hand delivery in open court (Petitioner must acknowledge receipt in writing on the face of the original order--see below.)
_____by e-mail to designated e-mail address(es)

Respondent (or his or her attorney):
____forwarded to sheriff for service
____ by hand delivery in open court (Respondent must acknowledge receipt in writing on the face of the original order--see below.)
____ by certified mail (may only be used when Respondent is present at the hearing and Respondent fails or refuses to acknowledge the receipt of a certified copy of this injunction.)

____ State Attorney's Office
____ Batterer's intervention program (if ordered)
____State Disbursement Unit (if ordered)
____Central Depository (if ordered)
____ Department of Revenue
____ Other____

I CERTIFY the foregoing is a true copy of the original Final Judgment of Injunction for Protection Against Domestic Violence with Minor Child(ren) as it appears on file in the office of the Clerk of the Circuit Court of ________________ County, Florida, and that I have furnished copies of this order as indicated above.
CLERK OF THE CIRCUIT COURT

Florida Supreme Court Approved Family Law Form 12.980(d)(1), Final Judgment of Injunction for Protection Against Domestic Violence with Minor Child(ren) (After Notice) (03/15)

(SEAL)
By: ______________________________
{Deputy Clerk or Judicial Assistant}

ACKNOWLEDGMENT

I, *{Name of Petitioner}*__________________________, acknowledge receipt of a certified copy of this Injunction for Protection.

Petitioner______________________________________

ACKNOWLEDGMENT

I, *{Name of Respondent}*__________________________, acknowledge receipt of a certified copy of this Injunction for Protection.

Respondent______________________________________

Florida Supreme Court Approved Family Law Form 12.980(d)(1), Final Judgment of Injunction for Protection Against Domestic Violence with Minor Child(ren) (After Notice) (03/15)

Added as 12.980 (e) July 1, 1995, effective Jan. 1, 1996 (663 So.2d 1047). Amended Feb. 26, 1998, effective Mar. 16, 1998 (713 So.2d 1). Renumbered as 12.980(e)(1) Sept. 21, 2000 (810 So.2d 1). Amended Oct. 3, 2002 (830 So.2d 72); Dec. 19, 2002 (836 So.2d 1019); May 15, 2003 (849 So.2d 1003). Renumbered from 12.980(e)(1) Mar. 25, 2004 (871 So.2d 113). Amended March 26, 2009 (20 So.3d 173); Dec. 16, 2010 (59 So.3d 792); June 7, 2012 (93 So.3d 194); March 26, 2015, effective March 26, 2015 (2015 WL 1343088).

Form 12.980(d)(2). Final Judgment of Injunction for Protection Against Domestic Violence Without Minor Child(ren) (After Notice)

IN THE CIRCUIT COURT OF THE ____________ JUDICIAL CIRCUIT,
IN AND FOR __________ COUNTY, FLORIDA

Case No.: ____________________
Division: ____________________

______________________________,
Petitioner,

and

______________________________,
Respondent.

FINAL JUDGMENT OF INJUNCTION FOR PROTECTION AGAINST DOMESTIC VIOLENCE WITHOUT MINOR CHILD(REN) (AFTER NOTICE)

The Petition for Injunction for Protection Against Domestic Violence under Section 741.30, Florida Statutes, and other papers filed in this Court have been reviewed. The Court has jurisdiction of the parties and the subject matter.

It is intended that this protection order meet the requirements of 18 U.S.C. Section 2265 and therefore intended that it be accorded full faith and credit by the court of another state or Indian tribe and enforced as if it were the order of the enforcing state or of the Indian tribe.

SECTION I. HEARING

This cause came before the Court for a hearing to determine whether an Injunction for Protection Against Domestic Violence in this case should be:

____ issued____ modified ____ extended.

The hearing was attended by:

_____ Petitioner
_____ Petitioner's Counsel
_____ Respondent
_____ Respondent's Counsel

SECTION II. FINDINGS

On *{date}* ______________________, a notice of this hearing was served on Respondent together with a copy of Petitioner's petition to this Court and the temporary injunction, if issued. Service was within the time required by Florida law, and Respondent was afforded an opportunity to be heard.

Florida Supreme Court Approved Family Law Form 12.980(d)(2), Final Judgment of Injunction for Protection Against Domestic Violence without Minor Child(ren) (After Notice) (03/15)

After hearing the testimony of each party present and of any witnesses, or upon consent of Respondent, the Court finds, based on the specific facts of this case, that Petitioner is a victim of domestic violence or has reasonable cause to believe that he/she is in imminent danger of becoming a victim of domestic violence by Respondent.

SECTION III. INJUNCTION AND TERMS

This injunction shall be in full force and effect until ____ further order of the Court or ____ *{date}*__________________________. This injunction is valid and enforceable in all counties of the State of Florida. The terms of this injunction may not be changed by either party alone or by both parties together. Only the Court may modify the terms of this injunction. Either party may ask the Court to change or end this injunction at any time.

Any violation of this injunction, whether or not at the invitation of Petitioner or anyone else, may subject Respondent to civil or indirect criminal contempt proceedings, including the imposition of a fine or imprisonment. Certain willful violations of the terms of this injunction, such as: refusing to vacate the dwelling that the parties share; going to or being within 500 feet of Petitioner's residence, going to Petitioner's place of employment, school, or other place prohibited in this injunction; telephoning, contacting or communicating with Petitioner if prohibited by this injunction; knowingly or intentionally coming within 100 feet of Petitioner's motor vehicle, whether or not it is occupied; defacing or destroying Petitioner's personal property; refusing to surrender firearms or ammunition if ordered to do so by the court; or committing an act of domestic violence against Petitioner constitutes a misdemeanor of the first degree punishable by up to one year in jail, as provided by sections 775.082 and 775.083, Florida Statutes. In addition, it is a federal criminal felony offense, punishable by up to life imprisonment, depending on the nature of the violation, to cross state lines or enter Indian country for the purpose of engaging in conduct that is prohibited in this injunction. 18 U.S.C. Section 2262.

ORDERED and ADJUDGED:

1. **Violence Prohibited.** Respondent shall not commit, or cause any other person to commit, any acts of domestic violence against Petitioner. Domestic violence includes: assault, aggravated assault, battery, aggravated battery, sexual assault, sexual battery, stalking, aggravated stalking, kidnapping, false imprisonment, or any other criminal offense resulting in physical injury or death to Petitioner or any of Petitioner's family or household members. Respondent shall not commit any other violation of the injunction through an intentional unlawful threat, word or act to do violence to the Petitioner.

2. **No Contact. Respondent shall have no contact with the Petitioner unless otherwise provided in this section.**

a. Unless otherwise provided herein, Respondent shall have no contact with Petitioner. Respondent shall not directly or indirectly contact Petitioner in person, by mail, e-mail, fax, telephone, through another person, or in any other manner. Further, Respondent shall not contact or have any third party

contact anyone connected with Petitioner's employment or school to inquire about Petitioner or to send any messages to Petitioner. Unless otherwise provided herein, **Respondent shall not go to, in, or within 500 feet of:** Petitioner's current residence *{list address}* ____________________
____
or any residence to which Petitioner may move; Petitioner's current or any subsequent place of employment *{list address of current employment}* ____________________
or place where Petitioner attends school *{list address of school}* ____________________;
or the following other places (if requested by Petitioner) where Petitioner or Petitioner's minor child(ren) go often: ____________________
____
____________________.
Respondent may not knowingly come within 100 feet of Petitioner's automobile at any time.

b. Other provisions regarding contact: ____________________
____
____

3. **Firearms. Unless paragraph a. is initialed below, Respondent shall not have in his or her care, custody, possession or control any firearm or ammunition. It is a violation of Section 790.233, Florida Statutes, and a first degree misdemeanor, for the Respondent to have in his or her care, custody, possession or control any firearm or ammunition.**

*{Initial if applies; write N/A **if not** applicable}*

a. ____Respondent is a state or local officer as defined in section 943.10(14), Florida Statutes, who holds an active certification, who receives or possesses a firearm or ammunition for use in performing official duties on behalf of the officer's employing agency and is not prohibited by the court from having in his or her care, custody, possession or control a firearm or ammunition. The officer's employing agency may prohibit the officer from having in his or her care, custody, possession or control a firearm or ammunition.

b. ____Respondent shall surrender any firearms and ammunition in the Respondent's possession to the ____________________ County Sheriff's Department.

c. ____Other directives relating to firearms and ammunition: ____________________
____
____

NOTE: RESPONDENT IS ADVISED THAT IT IS A FEDERAL CRIMINAL FELONY OFFENSE TO SHIP OR TRANSPORT IN INTERSTATE OR FOREIGN COMMERCE, OR POSSESS IN OR AFFECTING COMMERCE, ANY FIREARM OR AMMUNITION; OR TO RECEIVE ANY FIREARM OR AMMUNITION WHICH HAS BEEN SHIPPED OR TRANSPORTED IN INTERSTATE OR FOREIGN COMMERCE WHILE SUBJECT TO SUCH AN INJUNCTION. 18 U.S.C. SECTION 922(g)(8).

4. **Evaluation/Counseling.**
*{Initial **all** that apply; write N/A **if does not** apply}*

a. The Court finds that Respondent has:

i. ____willfully violated the ex parte injunction;

ii. ____been convicted of, had adjudication withheld on, or pled nolo contendere to a crime involving violence or a threat of violence; and/or

iii. ____in this state or any other state, had at any time a prior injunction for protection entered against the respondent after a hearing with notice.

Note: If Respondent meets any of the above enumerated criteria, the Court must order the Respondent to attend a batterers' intervention program unless it makes written factual findings stating why such a program would not be appropriate. See Section 741.30(6)(e), Florida Statutes.

b. Within ____10 days ____ days, (but no more than 10 days) of the date of this injunction, Respondent shall enroll in and thereafter without delay complete the following, and Respondent shall provide proof of such enrollment to the Clerk of Circuit Court within ____ 30 days ____ days, (but no more than 30 days) of the date of this injunction:

i. ____A certified batterers' intervention program from a list of programs to be provided by the Court or any entity designated by the Court. Respondent shall also successfully complete any substance abuse or mental health evaluation that the assessing program counselor deems necessary as a predicate to completion of the batterers' intervention program.

ii. ____A substance abuse evaluation at: ______________________________ or a similarly qualified facility and any substance abuse treatment recommended by that evaluation.

iii. ____A mental health evaluation by a licensed mental health professional at: ______________ ______________________or any other similarly qualified facility and any mental health treatment recommended by that evaluation.

iv. ____Other: ____
____

c. ____Although Respondent meets the statutory mandate of attendance at a batterers' intervention program, the Court makes the following written findings as to why the condition of batterers' intervention program would be inappropriate: ______________________________
____
____
____

d. ____Petitioner is referred to a certified domestic violence center and is provided with a list of certified domestic violence centers in this circuit, which Petitioner may contact.

5. **Mailing Address or Designated E-Mail Address(es).** Respondent shall notify the Clerk of the Court of any change in either his or her mailing address, or designated e-mail address(es), within 10 days of the change. All further papers (excluding pleadings requiring personal service) shall be served either by mail to Respondent's last known mailing address or by e-mail to Respondent's designated e-mail address(es). Service shall be complete upon mailing or emailing.

6. **Other provisions necessary to protect Petitioner from domestic violence:**______________________________
____
____
____
____
____
____

TEMPORARY EXCLUSIVE USE AND POSSESSION OF HOME
*[Initial **if** applies; write N/A **if not** applicable]*

7. ____**Possession of the Home.** ____ Petitioner ____ Respondent shall have temporary exclusive use and possession of the dwelling located at:______________________________
____.

8. ____**Transfer of Possession of the Home.** A law enforcement officer with jurisdiction over the home shall accompany ____ Petitioner ____ Respondent to the home, and shall place ____ Petitioner ____Respondent in possession of the home.

9. ____**Personal Items.** ____ Petitioner ____ Respondent, **in the presence of a law enforcement officer**, may return to the premises described above
____ on ______________________, at ______a.m./p.m., or
____ at a time arranged with the law enforcement department with jurisdiction over the home, accompanied by a law enforcement officer only, for the purpose of obtaining his or her clothing and items of personal health and hygiene and tools of the trade. A law enforcement officer with jurisdiction over the premises shall go with _____ Petitioner _____Respondent to the home and stand by to insure that he/she vacates the premises with only his/her personal clothing, toiletries, tools of the trade, and any items listed in paragraph 10 below. The law enforcement agency shall not be responsible for storing or transporting any property. **IF THE RESPONDENT IS NOT AWARDED POSSESSION OF THE HOME AND GOES TO THE HOME WITHOUT A LAW ENFORCEMENT OFFICER, IT IS A VIOLATION OF THIS INJUNCTION.**

10. ____The following other personal possessions may also be removed from the premises at this time: _

____.

11. ____Other: ____
____
____
____

TEMPORARY SUPPORT

12. **Temporary Alimony.**
*{Initial **all** that apply; write N/A **if does not** apply}*

a. ____The court finds that there is a need for temporary alimony and that ____ Petitioner ____Respondent (hereinafter Obligor) has the present ability to pay alimony and shall pay temporary alimony to ____ Petitioner ____ Respondent (hereinafter Obligee) in the amount of per month, payable ____ in accordance with Obligor's employer's payroll cycle, and in any event, at least once a month ____ other *{explain}* ____
____

beginning *{date}* ____________________. This alimony shall continue until modified by court order, until a final judgment of dissolution of marriage is entered, until Obligee dies, until this injunction expires, or until *{date}* __________________________, whichever occurs first.

b. ____The _____ Petitioner _____ Respondent shall be required to maintain health insurance coverage for the other party. Any uncovered medical costs for the party awarded alimony shall be assessed as follows: ____.

c. ____Other provisions relating to alimony: ______________________________
____

13. **Method of Payment.**
*[Initial **one** only]*

a. ____Obligor shall pay any temporary court-ordered alimony through income deduction, and such support shall be paid to either the State Disbursement Unit or the central depository. Obligor is individually responsible for paying this support obligation in the event that all or any portion of said support is not deducted from Obligor's income. Obligor shall also pay any service charge required by statute. Until alimony payments are deducted from Obligor's paycheck pursuant to the Income Deduction Order, Obligor is responsible for making timely payments directly to either the State Disbursement Unit or the central depository.

b. ___Temporary alimony shall be paid through either the State Disbursement Unit or the central depository. Obligor shall also pay any applicable service charge required by statute.

c. ____Other provisions relating to method of payment: ______________________
____

____
____.

SECTION IV. OTHER SPECIAL PROVISIONS

{This section to be used for inclusion of local provisions approved by the chief judge as provided in Florida Family Law Rule 12.610.}

____
____
____
____
____
________________________.

SECTION V. DIRECTIONS TO LAW ENFORCEMENT OFFICER IN ENFORCING THIS INJUNCTION

{Unless ordered otherwise by the judge, all provisions in this injunction are considered mandatory provisions and should be interpreted as part of this injunction.}

1. **This injunction is valid in all counties of the State of Florida.** Violation of this injunction should be reported to the appropriate law enforcement agency. Law enforcement officers of the jurisdiction in which a violation of this injunction occurs shall enforce the provisions of this injunction and are authorized to arrest without warrant pursuant to section 901.15, Florida Statutes, for any violation of its provisions, except those regarding child support and/or alimony, which constitutes a criminal act under section 741.31, Florida Statutes. **When inconsistent with this order, any subsequent court order issued under Chapter 61, Florida Statutes, shall take precedence over this order on all matters relating to property division, alimony, child custody, or child support.**

2. THIS INJUNCTION IS ENFORCEABLE IN ALL COUNTIES OF FLORIDA, AND LAW ENFORCEMENT OFFICERS MAY EFFECT ARRESTS PURSUANT TO SECTION 901.15(6), FLORIDA STATUTES. The arresting agent shall notify the State Attorney's Office immediately after arrest.

3. **Reporting alleged violations.** If Respondent violates the terms of this injunction and there has not been an arrest, Petitioner may contact the Clerk of the Circuit Court of the county in which the violation occurred and complete an affidavit in support of the violation, or Petitioner may contact the State Attorney's office for assistance in filing an action for indirect civil contempt or indirect criminal contempt. Upon receiving such a report, the State Attorney is hereby appointed to prosecute such violations by indirect criminal contempt

proceedings, or the State Attorney may decide to file a criminal charge, if warranted by the evidence.

4. Respondent, upon service of this injunction, shall be deemed to have knowledge of and to be bound by all matters occurring at the hearing and on the face of this injunction.

5. The temporary injunction, if any, entered in this case is extended until such time as service of this injunction is effected upon Respondent.

DONE AND ORDERED in ________________, Florida on ____________.

____
CIRCUIT JUDGE

Sheriff of ________________ County

Petitioner (or his or her attorney):
____ by U. S. Mail
____ by hand delivery in open court (Petitioner must acknowledge receipt in writing on the face of the original order--see below.)
____ by e-mail to designated e-mail address(es)

Respondent (or his or her attorney):
____ forwarded to sheriff for service
____ by hand delivery in open court (Respondent must acknowledge receipt in writing on the face of the original order--see below.)
____ by certified mail (may only be used when Respondent is present at the hearing and Respondent fails or refuses to acknowledge the receipt of a certified copy of this injunction.)

____ State Attorney's Office
____ Batterer's intervention program (if ordered)
____ State Disbursement Unit (if ordered)
____ Central Depository (if ordered)
____ Department of Revenue
____ Other______________________________

Florida Supreme Court Approved Family Law Form 12.980(d)(2), Final Judgment of Injunction for Protection Against Domestic Violence without Minor Child(ren) (After Notice) (03/15)

I CERTIFY that a copy of the original Final Judgment of Injunction for Protection Against Domestic Violence without Minor Child(ren) was ( ) mailed ( ) faxed and mailed ( ) e-mailed ( ) hand-delivered to the parties and any entities listed below on *{date}*_______________.

CLERK OF THE CIRCUIT COURT

(SEAL)
By: ____
Deputy Clerk or Judicial Assistant

Sheriff of _________________ County

Petitioner (or his or her attorney):
____ by U. S. Mail
____ by hand delivery in open court (Petitioner must acknowledge receipt in writing on the face of the original order--see below.)

Respondent (or his or her attorney):
____ forwarded to sheriff for service
____ by hand delivery in open court (Respondent must acknowledge receipt in writing on the face of the original order--see below.)
____ by certified mail (may only be used when Respondent is present at the hearing and Respondent fails or refuses to acknowledge the receipt of a certified copy of this injunction.)

____ State Attorney's Office
____ Batterer's intervention program (if ordered)
____ State Disbursement Unit (if ordered)
____ Central Depository (if ordered)
____ Department of Revenue
____ Other____

ACKNOWLEDGMENT

Florida Supreme Court Approved Family Law Form 12.980(d)(2), Final Judgment of Injunction for Protection Against Domestic Violence without Minor Child(ren) (After Notice) (03/15)

I, *{Name of Petitioner}*_________________________, acknowledge receipt of a certified copy of this Injunction for Protection.

____

Petitioner

ACKNOWLEDGMENT

I, *{Name of Respondent}*______________________________, acknowledge receipt of a certified copy of this Injunction for Protection.

____

Respondent

Florida Supreme Court Approved Family Law Form 12.980(d)(2), Final Judgment of Injunction for Protection Against Domestic Violence without Minor Child(ren) (After Notice) (03/15)

Added as 12.980(e) July 7, 1995, effective Jan. 1, 1996 (663 So.2d 1047). Amended Feb. 26, 1998, effective Mar. 16, 1998 (713 So.2d 1). Renumbered as 12.12.980(e)(2) Sept. 21, 2000 (810 So.2d 1). Amended Oct. 3, 2002 (830 So.2d 72); May 15, 2003 (849 So.2d 1003). Renumbered from 12.980(e)(2) Mar. 25, 2004 (871 So.2d 113). Amended June 7, 2012 (93 So.3d 194); March 26, 2015, effective March 26, 2015 (2015 WL 1343088).

Form 12.980(e). Order of Dismissal of Temporary Injunction for Protection Against ( ) Domestic Violence ( ) Repeat Violence ( ) Dating Violence ( ) Sexual Violence ( ) Stalking

IN THE CIRCUIT COURT OF THE _______ JUDICIAL CIRCUIT,
IN AND FOR ________________ COUNTY, FLORIDA

Case No.: ____________
Division: ____________

_______________________________,
Petitioner,
and

_______________________________,
Respondent.

ORDER OF DISMISSAL OF TEMPORARY INJUNCTION FOR PROTECTION AGAINST ( ) DOMESTIC VIOLENCE ( ) REPEAT VIOLENCE ( ) DATING VIOLENCE ( ) SEXUAL VIOLENCE ( ) STALKING

THIS CAUSE came before the Court on *{date}* __________, upon Petitioner's action for an injunction for protection against: domestic violence; repeat, dating, or sexual violence; or stalking. Based upon the following circumstances, the Court dismisses the Petition:

*{Indicate **all** that apply}*

a. _____ Petitioner failed to appear at the hearing scheduled in this cause.

b. _____ Petitioner appeared at the hearing but desires to voluntarily dismiss this action.

c. _____ The evidence presented is insufficient under Florida law (sections 741.30, 784.046, or 784.0485, Florida Statutes) to allow the Court to issue an injunction for protection against domestic, repeat, dating, or sexual violence; or stalking.

Accordingly, the case is dismissed without prejudice.

DONE AND ORDERED in______________________________, Florida on __________.

____
CIRCUIT JUDGE

Florida Supreme Court Approved Family Law Form 12.980(e), Order of Dismissal of Temporary Injunction for Protection Against Domestic Violence, Repeat Violence, Dating Violence, Sexual Violence, or Stalking (03/15)

COPIES TO:

Sheriff of ________________ County

Petitioner:
_____by U.S. Mail
_____ by hand delivery in open court
_____ by e-mail to designated e-mail address(es)

Respondent:
_____by U.S. Mail
_____by hand delivery in open court
_____ by e-mail to designated e-mail address(es)

_____State's Attorney's Office

_____Other:

I CERTIFY the foregoing is a true copy of the original **Order of Dismissal of Temporary Injunction** as it appears on file in the office of the Clerk of the Circuit Court of __________________ County, Florida, and that I have furnished copies of this order as indicated above.

CLERK OF THE CIRCUIT COURT

(SEAL)
By: ____
{Deputy Clerk or Judicial Assistant}

Florida Supreme Court Approved Family Law Form 12.980(e), Order of Dismissal of Temporary Injunction for Protection Against Domestic Violence, Repeat Violence, Dating Violence, Sexual Violence, or Stalking (03/15)

Added as 12.980(f) July 7, 1995, effective Jan. 1, 1996 (663 So.2d 1047). Amended Feb. 26, 1998, effective Mar. 16, 1998 (713 So.2d 1); Sept. 21, 2000 (810 So.2d 1); Oct. 3, 2002 (830 So.2d 72); May 15, 2003 (849 So.2d 1003). Renumbered from 12.980(f) Mar. 25, 2004 (871 So.2d 113). Amended June 7, 2012 (93 So.3d 194); May 9, 2013 (113 So.3d 781); March 26, 2015, effective March 26, 2015 (2015 WL 1343088).

Form 12.980(f). Petition for Injunction for Protection Against Repeat Violence

IN THE CIRCUIT COURT OF THE ________ JUDICIAL CIRCUIT,
IN AND FOR ____________________ COUNTY, FLORIDA

Case No.: ______________
Division: ______________

______________________________,
Petitioner,

and

______________________________,
Respondent.

PETITION FOR INJUNCTION FOR PROTECTION AGAINST REPEAT VIOLENCE

I, *{full legal name}*______________________________, being sworn, certify that the following statements are true:

SECTION I. PETITIONER
(This section is about you. It must be completed.)

1. Petitioner currently lives at the following address: *{address, city, state, zip code}* ______________________________.

*[Indicate **if** applicable]*
____**Petitioner seeks an injunction for protection on behalf of a minor child.** Petitioner is the parent or legal guardian of *{full legal name}*______________________, a minor child who is living at home.

2. Petitioner's attorney's name, address, and telephone number is: ______________________________.

(If you do not have an attorney, write "none.")

SECTION II. RESPONDENT
(This section is about the person you want to be protected from. It must be completed.)

1. Respondent currently lives at the following address: *{address, city, state, and zip code}* ______________________________.

Respondent's Driver's License number is: *{if known}* ______________________________.

2. Petitioner has known Respondent since: *{date}* ______________.

3. Respondent's last known place of employment: ______________________________
Employment address: ______________________________
Working hours: ______________________________

4. Physical description of Respondent:
Race: ________ Sex: Male _____ Female _____ Date of Birth: ______________________
Height: Weight: ______ Eye Color: __________ Hair Color: __
Distinguishing marks and/or scars: ______________________________
Vehicle: (make/model) ______________ Color: _______ Tag Number: ______________________

5. Other names Respondent goes by (aliases or nicknames): ______________________

6. Respondent's attorney's name, address, and telephone number is: ______________
____.
(If you do not know whether Respondent has an attorney, write "unknown." If Respondent does not have an attorney, write "none.")

SECTION III. CASE HISTORY AND REASON FOR SEEKING PETITION (This section must be completed.)

1. Has Petitioner ever received or tried to get an injunction for protection against domestic violence, repeat violence, dating violence, or sexual violence against Respondent in this or any other court?
_____ Yes _____ No If yes, what happened in that case? *{include case number, if known}*
____
____

2. Has Respondent ever received or tried to get an injunction for protection against domestic violence, repeat violence, dating violence, or sexual violence against Petitioner in this or any other court?
_____ Yes _____ No If yes, what happened in that case? *{include case number, if known}*
____
____

3. Describe **any other** court case that is either going on now or that happened in the past **between Petitioner and Respondent** *{include case number, if known}*:
____
____

4. Respondent has directed at least two incidents of violence, meaning assault, aggravated assault, battery, aggravated battery, sexual assault, sexual battery, stalking, aggravated stalking, kidnapping, or false imprisonment, or any criminal offense resulting in physical injury or death against Petitioner or a member of Petitioner's immediate family. One of these two incidents of violence has occurred within 6 months of the date of filing of this petition. The most recent incident (including date and location) is

described below.

On {date}____________________________, at {location}____,
Respondent ____
.

_____Please indicate here if you are attaching additional pages to continue these facts.

5. Other prior incidents (including dates and location) are described below:

On {date}____________________________, at {location}____,
Respondent ____
.

_____Please indicate here if you are attaching additional pages to continue these facts.

6. Petitioner genuinely fears repeat violence by Respondent. Explain:______________________________________

7. **Additional Information**

*[Choose **all** that apply]*

a. ____Respondent owns, has, and/or is known to have guns or other weapons.
Describe weapon(s): ____
____.

b. ____This or prior acts of repeat violence have been previously reported to: *{person or agency}* ____
____.

SECTION IV. INJUNCTION (This section must be completed.)

1. ____Petitioner asks the Court to enter a TEMPORARY INJUNCTION for protection against repeat violence that will be in place from now until the scheduled hearing in this matter.

2. ____Petitioner asks the Court to enter, after a hearing has been held on this petition, a final judgment of injunction prohibiting Respondent from committing any acts of violence against Petitioner **and**:

a. prohibiting Respondent from going to or within 500 feet of any place Petitioner lives;

b. prohibiting Respondent from going to or within 500 feet of Petitioner's place(s) of employment or the school that Petitioner attends; the address of Petitioner's place(s) of employment and/or school is:____
____;

c. prohibiting Respondent from contacting Petitioner by telephone, mail, by e-mail, in writing, through another person, or in any other manner;

d. ordering Respondent not to use or possess any guns or firearms;

*[Indicate **all** that apply]*

e. ____ prohibiting Respondent from going to or within 500 feet of the following place(s) Petitioner or Petitioner's immediate family must go to often: ______________________
____.

f. ____ prohibiting Respondent from knowingly and intentionally going to or within 100 feet of Petitioner's motor vehicle; and any other terms the Court deems necessary for the safety of Petitioner and Petitioner's immediate family.

I UNDERSTAND THAT BY FILING THIS PETITION, I AM ASKING THE COURT TO HOLD A HEARING ON THIS PETITION, THAT BOTH THE RESPONDENT AND I WILL BE NOTIFIED OF THE HEARING, AND THAT I MUST APPEAR AT THE HEARING. I UNDERSTAND THAT IF EITHER RESPONDENT OR I FAIL TO APPEAR AT THE FINAL HEARING, WE WILL BE BOUND BY THE TERMS OF ANY INJUNCTION OR ORDER ISSUED

AT THAT HEARING.

I UNDERSTAND THAT I AM SWEARING OR AFFIRMING UNDER OATH TO THE TRUTHFULNESS OF THE CLAIMS MADE IN THIS PETITION AND THAT THE PUNISHMENT FOR KNOWINGLY MAKING A FALSE STATEMENT INCLUDES FINES AND/OR IMPRISONMENT.

Dated: ____________________ ____________________
Signature of Petitioner

Printed Name: ____________________
Address: ____________________
City, State, Zip: ____________________
Telephone Number: ____________________
Fax Number: ____________________

Designated E-Mail Address(es): ____________________

STATE OF FLORIDA
COUNTY OF ____________________.

Sworn to or affirmed and signed before me on __________ by ____________________.

____
NOTARY PUBLIC or DEPUTY CLERK

____
{Print, type, or stamp commissioned name of notary or clerk}
_____ Personally known
_____ Produced identification
Type of identification produced ____________________

Florida Supreme Court Approved Family Law Form 12.980(f), Petition for Injunction for Protection Against Repeat Violence (03/15)

INSTRUCTIONS FOR FLORIDA SUPREME COURT APPROVED FAMILY LAW FORM 12.980(f) PETITION FOR INJUNCTION FOR PROTECTION AGAINST REPEAT VIOLENCE (03/15)

When should this form be used?

If you or a member of your immediate family are a victim of **repeat violence**, you can use this form to ask the court for a protective order prohibiting repeat violence. Repeat violence means that **two** incidents of violence have been committed against you or a member of your immediate family by another person, **one of which must have been within 6 months of filing this petition.** Repeat violence includes assault, aggravated assault, battery, aggravated battery, sexual assault, sexual battery, stalking, aggravated stalking, kidnapping, or false imprisonment, or any criminal offense resulting in physical injury or death. Because you are making a request to the court, you are called the **petitioner**. The person whom you are asking the court to protect you from is called the **respondent**. If you are under the age of eighteen and have never been married or had the disabilities of nonage removed by a court, one of your parents or your legal guardian must sign this petition on your behalf.

The parent or legal guardian of any minor child *who is living at home* may seek an injunction for protection against repeat violence on behalf of the minor child. With respect to a minor child who is living at home, the parent or legal guardian must have been an eye-witness to, or have direct physical evidence or **affidavits** from eye-witnesses of, the specific facts and circumstances that form the basis of the petition.

If the respondent is your **spouse**, former spouse, related to you by blood or marriage, living with you now or has lived with you in the past (if you are or were living as a family), or the other parent of your child(ren), whether or not you have ever been married or ever lived together, you should use **Petition for Injunction for Protection Against Domestic Violence**, Florida Supreme Court Approved Family Law Form 12.980(a), rather than this form.

This form should be typed or printed in black ink. You should complete this form (giving as much detail as possible) and sign it the presence of a notary or in front of the **clerk of the circuit court** in the county where you live. The clerk will take your completed petition to a **judge**. You should keep a copy for your records. If have any questions or need assistance completing this form, the clerk or **family law intake staff** will help you.

What should I do if the judge grants my petition?

If the facts contained in your petition convince the judge that you or a member of your immediate family are a victim of repeat violence and that an **immediate and present danger of repeat violence** to you or that family exists, the judge will sign a **Temporary Injunction for Protection Against Repeat Violence**, Florida Supreme Court Approved Family Law Form 12.980(k). A temporary injunction is issued without notice to the respondent. The clerk will give your **petition**, the temporary injunction, and any other papers filed with your petition to the sheriff or other law enforcement officer for **personal service** on the respondent. The temporary injunction will take effect immediately after the respondent is served with a copy of it. It lasts until a full **hearing** can be held or for a period of 15 days, whichever comes first. The court may extend the temporary injunction beyond 15 days for a good reason, which may include failure to obtain **service** on the respondent.

The temporary injunction is issued **ex parte**. This means that the judge has considered only the information presented by one side—YOU. Section I of the temporary injunction gives a date that you should appear in court for a hearing. You will be expected to testify about the facts in your petition. The respondent will be given the opportunity to testify at this hearing, also. At the hearing, the judge will decide whether to issue a **Final Judgment of Injunction for Protection Against Repeat Violence (After Notice)**, Florida Supreme Court Approved Family Law Form 12.980(*l*), which will remain in effect for a specific time period or until modified or dissolved by the court. **If you and/or the respondent do not appear, the temporary injunction may be continued in force, extended, or dismissed, and/or additional orders may be granted, including entry of a permanent injunction and the imposition of court costs. You and respondent will be bound by the terms of any injunction or order issued at the final hearing.**

IF EITHER YOU OR RESPONDENT DO NOT APPEAR AT THE FINAL HEARING, YOU WILL BOTH BE BOUND BY THE TERMS OF ANY INJUNCTION OR ORDER ISSUED IN THIS MATTER.

If the judge signs a temporary or final injunction, the clerk will provide you with the necessary copies. **Make sure that you keep one certified copy of the injunction with you at all times!**

What can I do if the judge denies my petition?

If your petition is denied on the grounds that it appears to the court that no immediate and present danger of repeat violence exists, the court will set a full hearing on your petition. The respondent will be notified by **personal service** of your petition and the hearing. If your petition is denied, you may: amend your petition by filing a **Supplemental Affidavit in Support of Petition for Injunction for Protection**, Florida Supreme Court Approved Family Law Form 12.980(g); attend the hearing and present facts that support your petition; and/or dismiss your petition.

Where can I look for more information?

Before proceeding, you should read General Information for Self-Represented Litigants found at the beginning of these forms. The words that are in **bold underline** are defined in that section. The clerk of the circuit court or **family law intake staff** will help you complete any necessary forms. For further information, see Section 784.046, Florida Statutes, and Rule 12.610, Florida Family Law Rules of Procedure.

IMPORTANT INFORMATION REGARDING E-FILING

The Florida Rules of Judicial Administration now require that all petitions, pleadings, and documents be filed electronically except in certain circumstances. **Self-represented litigants may file petitions or other pleadings or documents electronically; however, they are not required to do so.** If you choose to file your pleadings or other documents electronically, you must do so in accordance with Florida Rule of Judicial Administration 2.525, and you must follow the procedures of the judicial circuit in which you file. **The rules and procedures should be carefully read and followed.**

IMPORTANT INFORMATION REGARDING E-SERVICE ELECTION

After the initial service of process of the petition or supplemental petition by the Sheriff or certified process server, the Florida Rules of Judicial Administration now require that all documents required or permitted to be served on the other party must be served by electronic mail (e-mail) except in certain circumstances. **You must strictly comply with the format requirements set forth in the Rules of Judicial Administration.**

SELF-REPRESENTED LITIGANTS MAY SERVE DOCUMENTS BY E-MAIL; HOWEVER, THEY ARE NOT REQUIRED TO DO SO. If a self-represented litigant elects to serve and receive documents by e-mail, the procedures must always be followed once the initial election is made.

To serve and receive documents by e-mail, you must designate your e-mail addresses by using the **Designation of Current Mailing and E-mail Address**, Florida Supreme Court Approved Family Law Form 12.915, and you must provide your e-mail address on each form on which your signature appears. Please **CAREFULLY** read the rules and instructions for: **Certificate of Service (General),** Florida Supreme Court Approved Family Law Form 12.914; **Designation of Current Mailing and E-mail Address**, Florida Supreme Court Approved Family Law Form 12.915; and Florida Rule of Judicial Administration 2.516.

Added as 12.980(g) July 7, 1995, effective Jan. 1, 1996 (663 So.2d 1047). Amended Feb. 26, 1998, effective Mar. 16, 1998 (713 So.2d 1); July 1, 1999 (759 So.2d 583); Sept. 21, 2000 (810 So.2d 1); May 15, 2003 (849 So.2d 1003); July 8, 2004 (880 So.2d 579). Renumbered from 12.980(g) Mar. 25, 2004 (871 So.2d 113). Amended June 7, 2012 (93 So.3d 194); March 26, 2015, effective March 26, 2015 (2015 WL 1343088).

Form 12.980(g). Supplemental Affidavit in Support of Petition for Injunction for Protection Against ( ) Domestic Violence ( ) Repeat Violence ( ) Dating Violence ( ) Sexual Violence ( ) Stalking

IN THE CIRCUIT COURT OF THE __________ JUDICIAL CIRCUIT,
IN AND FOR ____________________ COUNTY, FLORIDA

Case No.: ____________________
Division: ____________________

____________________,
Petitioner,

and

____________________,
Respondent.

SUPPLEMENTAL AFFIDAVIT IN SUPPORT OF PETITION FOR INJUNCTION FOR PROTECTION AGAINST ( ) DOMESTIC VIOLENCE ( ) REPEAT VIOLENCE ( ) DATING VIOLENCE ( ) SEXUAL VIOLENCE ( ) STALKING

I, *{full legal name}* ______________________________, being sworn, certify that the following statements are true:
{Please complete all paragraphs that relate to your case}

1. On *{date}* __________________, at *{place and address}* ______________________________
______________________________, Respondent said or did the following things that hurt me or a member of my immediate family and made me afraid for my or my family member's safety:
____
____
____
____
____
____
____
____
____
____
____
____.

____ Please indicate here if you are attaching additional pages to continue these facts.

Florida Supreme Court Approved Family Law Form 12.980(g), Supplemental Affidavit in Support of Petition for Injunction for Protection Against Domestic, Repeat, Dating, or Sexual Violence, or Stalking (03/15)

2. On *{date}* ____________, at *{place and address}* ______________________
____,
the following event(s) took place: ____
____
____
____
____
____
____
____
____
____
____
____.

____ Please indicate here if you are attaching additional pages to continue these facts.

3. On *{date}* ______________ the following incidents of stalking occurred at the following locations: *{the locations may include, but need not be limited to, a home, school, or place of employment}* ____
____
____
____
____.

For cyberstalking, the following is a description of all evidence of contacts and/or threats made by Respondent in voice messages, texts, emails, or other electronic communication: ____
____
____
____
____.

____ Please indicate here if you are attaching additional pages to continue these facts.

4. _____Please indicate here if you are attaching copies of medical records for treatment you may have received for injuries referred to in your petition or in this supplemental affidavit, copies of any police or sheriff reports concerning incidents of violence involving you and Respondent, or any notice of inmate release.

Florida Supreme Court Approved Family Law Form 12.980(g), Supplemental Affidavit in Support of Petition for Injunction for Protection Against Domestic, Repeat, Dating, or Sexual Violence, or Stalking (03/15)

I understand that I am swearing or affirming under oath to the truthfulness of the claims made in this supplemental affidavit and that the punishment for knowingly making a false statement includes fines and/or imprisonment.

Dated: ________________

____
Signature of Petitioner

STATE OF FLORIDA
COUNTY OF

Sworn to or affirmed and signed before me on ____________ by __________________________.

____
NOTARY PUBLIC or DEPUTY CLERK

____
{Print, type, or stamp commissioned name of notary or clerk}

_____ Personally known
_____ Produced identification
Type of identification produced

Florida Supreme Court Approved Family Law Form 12.980(g), Supplemental Affidavit in Support of Petition for Injunction for Protection Against Domestic, Repeat, Dating, or Sexual Violence, or Stalking (03/15)

INSTRUCTIONS FOR FLORIDA SUPREME COURT APPROVED FAMILY LAW FORM 12.980(g) SUPPLEMENTAL AFFIDAVIT IN SUPPORT OF PETITION FOR INJUNCTION FOR PROTECTION AGAINST DOMESTIC, REPEAT, DATING, OR SEXUAL VIOLENCE, OR STALKING (03/15)

When should this form be used?

You may use this form if your **Petition for Injunction for Protection Against Domestic Violence**, Florida Supreme Court Approved Family Law Form 12.980(a), your **Petition for Injunction for Protection Against Repeat Violence**, Florida Supreme Court Approved Family Law Form 12.980(f), your **Petition for Injunction for Protection Against Dating Violence**, Florida Supreme Court Approved Family Law Form 12.980(n), your **Petition for Injunction for Protection Against Sexual Violence,** Florida Supreme Court Approved Family Law Form 12.890(q), or your **Petition for Injunction for Protection Against Stalking,** Florida Supreme Court Approved Family Law Form 12.980(t), was denied by the **judge**.

You should use this supplemental **affidavit** to add facts or clarify the facts you wrote in your original **petition**.

For a domestic violence case, you should include facts that establish that you have been a victim of violence or are in **imminent** danger of becoming a victim of violence from the **respondent**.

For a repeat violence case, you should include facts that establish that you or a member of your immediate family have or has been a victim of at least two prior incidents of violence, that one of those incidents occurred within the last six months and that there is an immediate and present risk of danger to you or a member of your immediate family.

For a dating violence case, you should include fact that establish that you have been a victim of violence or are in imminent danger of becoming a victim of violence from the **respondent** who is an individual with whom you have or have had a continuing and significant relationship of a romantic or intimate nature, to be determined by consideration of such facts as: whether the dating relationship existed within the past six months; whether the nature of the relationship included an expectation of affection or sexual involvement; and whether the frequency and type of interaction between you and the individual included involvement over time and on a continued basis. Dating violence does not include violence in a casual acquaintanceship or violence between individuals who have only engaged in ordinary fraternization in a business or social context.

For a sexual violence case, you should include facts that establish that you are a victim of sexual violence or the parent of a minor child living at home who is a victim of sexual violence, and that you have reported the sexual violence to law enforcement and are cooperating in the criminal proceeding if there is one. If the respondent was in state prison for sexual violence against you or the minor child and the respondent is out of prison or is getting out within 90 days of the petition, include that information in your supplemental affidavit, along with a copy of the notice of inmate release.

For a stalking case, you should include facts that establish that you are either a victim of stalking or cyberstalking, or that you are the parent or legal guardian of a minor child living at home who is a victim of stalking or cyberstalking. The facts must establish that stalking exists in order for the judge to order a temporary injunction for protection against stalking. Please be specific as to where the incidents of stalking took place. These locations may include, but need not be limited to, a home, school, or place of employment. For cyberstalking, please include a description of all evidence of contacts and/or threats made by the respondent in voice messages, texts, emails, or other electronic communication.

This form should be typed or printed in black ink. After completing this form, you should sign the form before a **notary public** or the **clerk of the circuit court**. You should then **file** the original with the clerk in the county where the petition was filed and keep a copy for your records.

IMPORTANT INFORMATION REGARDING E-FILING

The Florida Rules of Judicial Administration now require that all petitions, pleadings, and documents be filed electronically except in certain circumstances. **Self-represented litigants may file petitions or other pleadings or documents electronically; however, they are not required to do so.** If you choose to file your pleadings or other documents electronically, you must do so in accordance with Florida Rule of Judicial Administration 2.525, and you must follow the procedures of the judicial circuit in which you file. **The rules and procedures should be carefully read and followed.**

What should I do next?

After you complete this supplemental affidavit, the clerk will attach it to your original petition and all the documents will be submitted to the judge as your Amended Petition.

IMPORTANT INFORMATION REGARDING E-SERVICE ELECTION

After the initial service of process of the petition or supplemental petition by the Sheriff or certified process server, the Florida Rules of Judicial Administration now require that all documents required or permitted to be served on the other party must be served by electronic mail (e-mail) except in certain circumstances. **You must strictly comply with the format requirements set forth in the Rules of Judicial Administration.**

SELF-REPRESENTED LITIGANTS MAY SERVE DOCUMENTS BY E-MAIL; HOWEVER, THEY ARE NOT REQUIRED TO DO SO. If a self-represented litigant elects to serve and receive documents by e-mail, the procedures must always be followed once the initial election is made.

To serve and receive documents by e-mail, you must designate your e-mail addresses by using the **Designation of Current Mailing and E-mail Address**, Florida Supreme Court Approved Family Law Form 12.915, and you must provide your e-mail address on each form on which your signature appears. Please **CAREFULLY** read the rules and instructions for: **Certificate of Service (General),** Florida Supreme Court Approved Family Law Form 12.914; **Designation of Current Mailing and E-mail Address**, Florida Supreme Court Approved Family Law Form 12.915; and Florida Rule of Judicial Administration 2.516.

Added as 12.980(h) July 7, 1995, effective Jan. 1, 1996 (663 So.2d 1047). Amended Feb. 26, 1998, effective Mar. 16, 1998 (713 So.2d 1); Sept. 21, 2000 (810 So.2d 1); May 15, 2003 (849 So.2d 1003); July 8, 2004 (880 So.2d 579); June 30, 2005, effective July 1, 2005 (910 So.2d 194). Renumbered from 12.980(h) Mar. 25, 2004 (871 So.2d 113). Amended June 7, 2012 (93 So.3d 194); May 9, 2013 (113 So.3d 781); March 26, 2015, effective March 26, 2015 (2015 WL 1343088).

Form 12.980(h). Request for Confidential Filing of Address

IN THE CIRCUIT COURT OF THE ____________ JUDICIAL CIRCUIT,
IN AND FOR ____________ COUNTY, FLORIDA

Case No.: ______________________
Division: ______________________

______________________________,
Petitioner,
and

______________________________,
Respondent.

REQUEST FOR CONFIDENTIAL FILING OF ADDRESS

I, *{full legal name}* ______________________________, request that the Court maintain and hold as confidential, the following address:

Address ______________________________
____
City ______________ State ______________ Zip ______________
Telephone (area code and number) ______________________________

This request is being made for the purpose of keeping the location of my residence unknown for safety reasons pursuant to section 119.071(2)(j)1, section 784.0485(3)(b)1, Florida Statutes, or other statutory provision providing for the separate confidential filing for safety reasons.

Dated: ______________ ______________________________
Signature

CLERK'S CERTIFICATE AS TO REQUEST FOR CONFIDENTIAL FILING OF ADDRESS

I, ______________________________, as Clerk of the Circuit Court, do hereby certify that I received and filed the above and will keep the above address confidential, subsequent to further order of the Court relative to such confidentiality.

CLERK OF THE CIRCUIT COURT

(SEAL)

By: ______________________________
(Deputy Clerk)

Florida Supreme Court Approved Family Law Form 12.980(h), Request for Confidential Filing of Address (03/15)

INSTRUCTIONS FOR FLORIDA SUPREME COURT APPROVED FAMILY LAW FORM 12.980(h) REQUEST FOR CONFIDENTIAL FILING OF ADDRESS (03/15)

When should this form be used?

If you fear that disclosing your address would put you in danger because you are the victim of sexual battery, aggravated child abuse, stalking, aggravated stalking, harassment, aggravated battery, or domestic violence, you should complete this form and **file** it with the **clerk of the circuit court**.

This form should be typed or printed in black ink. After completing this form, you should **file** the original with the clerk of the circuit court in the county where your petition was filed and keep a copy for your records.

IMPORTANT INFORMATION REGARDING E-FILING

The Florida Rules of Judicial Administration now require that all petitions, pleadings, and documents be filed electronically except in certain circumstances. **Self-represented litigants may file petitions or other pleadings or documents electronically; however, they are not required to do so.** If you choose to file your pleadings or other documents electronically, you must do so in accordance with Florida Rule of Judicial Administration 2.525, and you must follow the procedures of the judicial circuit in which you file. **The rules and procedures should be carefully read and followed.**

Added as 12.980(i) Feb. 26, 1998, effective Mar. 16, 1998 (713 So.2d 1). Amended Sept. 21, 2000 (810 So.2d 1); May 15, 2003 (849 So.2d 1003); July 8, 2004 (880 So.2d 579); June 30, 2005, effective July 1, 2005 (910 So.2d 194). Renumbered from 12.980(i) Mar. 25, 2004 (871 So.2d 113). Amended Dec. 16, 2010 (59 So.3d 792); June 7, 2012 (93 So.3d 194); May 9, 2013 (113 So.3d 781); March 26, 2015, effective March 26, 2015 (2015 WL 1343088).

Form 12.980(i). Motion for Extension of Injunction for Protection Against ( ) Domestic Violence ( ) Repeat Violence ( ) Dating Violence ( ) Sexual Violence ( ) Stalking

IN THE CIRCUIT COURT OF THE ____________ JUDICIAL CIRCUIT,
IN AND FOR ________________________ COUNTY, FLORIDA

Case No.: ____________________

Division: ____________________

______________________________,
Petitioner,

and

______________________________,
Respondent.

MOTION FOR EXTENSION OF INJUNCTION FOR PROTECTION AGAINST ( ) DOMESTIC VIOLENCE ( ) REPEAT VIOLENCE ( ) DATING VIOLENCE ( ) SEXUAL VIOLENCE ( ) STALKING

I, *{full legal name}* ____________________________________, being sworn, certify that the following statements are true:

SECTION I. PETITIONER

(This section is about you. It must be completed; however, **if you fear that disclosing your address would put you in danger because you are the victim of sexual battery, aggravated child abuse, stalking, aggravated stalking, harassment, aggravated battery, or domestic violence**, you should complete and file a **Request for Confidential Filing of Address**, Florida Supreme Court Approved Family Law Form 12.980(h), and write "confidential" in the space provided on this form for your address and telephone number.)

1. Petitioner currently lives at the following address: *{street address}* ____________________
{city, state, and zip code} ____
Telephone Number: *{area code and number}* ______________________________________

2. Petitioner's attorney's name, address and telephone number is: ____________________
____.
(If you do not have an attorney, write "none.")

SECTION II. RESPONDENT

(This section is about the person you want to be protected from. It must be completed.)

New information about Respondent, since the current injunction was issued: (If known, write Respondent's new address, place of employment, physical description, vehicle, aliases or nicknames, or

Florida Supreme Court Approved Family Law Form 12.980(i), Motion for Extension of Injunction for Protection Against Domestic, Repeat, Dating or Sexual Violence; or Stalking (03/15)

attorney's name.) ____
____
____
____
____.

SECTION III. CASE HISTORY AND REASON FOR SEEKING EXTENSION OF INJUNCTION

1. Describe any attempts since the date of the current injunction by either Petitioner or Respondent to get an injunction for protection in this or any other court (other than the injunction you are asking to extend in this motion). ____
____
____.

2. Describe any other court cases (including city, state, and case numbers, if known) since the date of the current injunction between Petitioner and Respondent, including any cases involving the parties' minor child(ren), divorce, juvenile dependency, guardianship, or other civil or criminal cases. ________
____
____.

3. Petitioner requests that the previously entered injunction for protection against domestic violence, repeat violence, dating violence, sexual violence, or stalking, be extended for the following **specific** reasons: *{State **in detail** why you wish the injunction to remain in effect.}* ____________
____
____
____
____
____
____
____
____
____
____
____.

______Please indicate here if you are attaching additional pages to continue these facts.

4. Petitioner genuinely fears the continued threat of violence or stalking by Respondent.

SECTION IV. REQUESTED RELIEF

1. Petitioner understands that the Court will hold a hearing on this motion and that he or she must appear at the hearing.

2. Petitioner asks the Court to enter an order in this case that extends the previously entered injunction for a period of ( ) ______________ or ( ) until modified or dissolved by the court.

I certify that a copy of this document was ( ) mailed ( ) faxed and mailed ( ) e-mailed ( ) mailed by certified mail, return receipt requested, ( ) furnished to a law enforcement officer for personal service to the person(s) listed below on *{date}*______________________________.

Other party or his/her attorney:
Name:______________________________
Address:______________________________
City, State, Zip:______________________________
Fax Number:______________________________
Designated E-Mail Address(es):______________________________
____

I understand that I am swearing or affirming under oath to the truthfulness of the claims made in this motion and that the punishment for knowingly making a false statement includes fines and/or imprisonment.

Dated: ______________________

____
Signature of Petitioner

STATE OF FLORIDA
COUNTY OF

Sworn to or affirmed and signed before me on ______________ by ______________________.

____
NOTARY PUBLIC or DEPUTY CLERK

____
{Print, type, or stamp commissioned name of notary or clerk}
______ Personally known
______ Produced identification
Type of identification produced

Florida Supreme Court Approved Family Law Form 12.980(i), Motion for Extension of Injunction for Protection Against Domestic, Repeat, Dating or Sexual Violence; or Stalking (03/15)

INSTRUCTIONS FOR FLORIDA SUPREME COURT APPROVED FAMILY LAW FORM 12.980(i) MOTION FOR EXTENSION OF INJUNCTION FOR PROTECTION AGAINST DOMESTIC, REPEAT, DATING, OR SEXUAL VIOLENCE, OR STALKING (03/15)

When should this form be used?

If you are the **petitioner** on a previously entered injunction for protection against domestic violence, repeat violence, dating violence, sexual violence, or stalking, and that injunction will soon expire, you may use this form to request that the court **extend the injunction. You must file a motion for extension BEFORE the previously entered order expires.**

This form should be typed or printed in black ink. After completing this form, you should sign it before a notary public or the **clerk of the circuit court**. You should then **file** the original with the clerk in the county where the petition was filed and keep a copy for your records. If you have any questions or need assistance completing this form, the clerk or **family law intake staff** will help you.

What should I do next?

For your case to proceed, you will need to set a **hearing** on your motion. You must properly notify the other party of the motion and hearing. You should check with the clerk of court for information on the local procedure for scheduling a hearing. When you know the date and time of your hearing, you should file **Notice of Hearing (General)**, Florida Supreme Court Approved Family Law Form 12.923, or other appropriate notice of hearing form. You will need to serve a copy of your motion and Notice of Hearing on the other party by U.S. mail, e-mail, or hand delivery. Service of your motion must be in in[1] a manner that is reasonably calculated to apprise the other party of your motion and the hearing. Please note that if notice is mailed or e-mailed, the court in certain circumstances may not consider mailing or e-mailing to be adequate notice. If you want to be sure, you should consider using certified mail, return receipt requested, or having the motion personally served. This is a technical area of the law; if you have any questions about it, you should consult a lawyer. For more information on personal service, see the instructions for **Summons: Personal Service on an Individual,** Florida Family Law Rules of Procedure Form 12.910(a).

You will need to appear at the hearing on your motion. After the hearing, if the judge grants your motion, he or she will prepare an **Order Extending Injunction for Protection Against Domestic Violence, Repeat Violence, Dating Violence, or Sexual Violence, or Stalking, Florida Supreme Court Approved Family Law Form 12.980(m). After the judge signs the order, the clerk will provide you with the necessary copies. Make sure that you keep a certified copy of the previously entered injunction AND a certified copy of the order extending that injunction with you at all times.**

Where can I look for more information?

Before proceeding, you should read General Information for Self–Represented Litigants found at the beginning of these forms. The words that are in **bold underline** are defined in that section. The clerk of the circuit court or family law intake staff will help you complete any necessary domestic, repeat, dating, or sexual violence, or stalking forms and will answer any question that you may have.

IMPORTANT INFORMATION REGARDING E–FILING

The Florida Rules of Judicial Administration now require that all petitions, pleadings, and documents be filed electronically except in certain circumstances. **Self-represented litigants may file petitions or other pleadings or documents electronically; however, they are not required to do so.** If you choose to file your pleadings or other documents electronically, you must do so in accordance with Florida Rule of Judicial Administration 2.525, and you must follow the procedures of the judicial circuit in which you file. **The rules and procedures should be carefully read and followed.**

IMPORTANT INFORMATION REGARDING E–SERVICE ELECTION

After the initial service of process of the petition or supplemental petition by the Sheriff or certified process server, the Florida Rules of Judicial Administration now require that all

documents required or permitted to be served on the other party must be served by electronic mail (e-mail) except in certain circumstances. **You must strictly comply with the format requirements set forth in the Rules of Judicial Administration.**

SELF–REPRESENTED LITIGANTS MAY SERVE DOCUMENTS BY E–MAIL; HOWEVER, THEY ARE NOT REQUIRED TO DO SO. If a self-represented litigant elects to serve and receive documents by e-mail, the procedures must always be followed once the initial election is made.

To serve and receive documents by e-mail, you must designate your e-mail addresses by using the **Designation of Current Mailing and E-mail Address**, Florida Supreme Court Approved Family Law Form 12.915, and you must provide your e-mail address on each form on which your signature appears. Please **CAREFULLY** read the rules and instructions for: **Certificate of Service (General)**, Florida Supreme Court Approved Family Law Form 12.914; **Designation of Current Mailing and E-mail Address**, Florida Supreme Court Approved Family Law Form 12.915; and Florida Rule of Judicial Administration 2.516.

Special notes . . .

With this form you may also file a **Request for Confidential Filing of Address**, Florida Supreme Court Approved Family Law Form 12.980(h), if you fear that disclosing your address would put you in danger because you are the victim of sexual battery, aggravated child abuse, stalking, aggravated stalking, harassment, aggravated battery, or domestic violence, and you wish to keep your address confidential.

When completing this form, you should make sure that your reasons for requesting that the injunction be extended are stated clearly and that you include all relevant facts.

Added as 12.980(j) Feb. 26, 1998, effective Mar. 16, 1998 (713 So.2d 1). Amended July 1, 1999 (759 So.2d 583); Sept. 21, 2000 (810 So.2d 1); May 15, 2003 (849 So.2d 1003); July 8, 2004 (880 So.2d 579). Renumbered from 12.980(j) Mar. 25, 2004 (871 So.2d 113). Amended June 7, 2012 (93 So.3d 194); May 9, 2013 (113 So.3d 781); March 26, 2015, effective March 26, 2015 (2015 WL 1343088).

[1] So in original.

Form 12.980(j). Motion for Modification of Injunction for Protection Against ( ) Domestic Violence ( ) Repeat Violence ( ) Dating Violence ( ) Sexual Violence ( ) Stalking

IN THE CIRCUIT COURT OF THE ____________ JUDICIAL CIRCUIT,
IN AND FOR ____________________ COUNTY, FLORIDA

Case No.: ____________________

Division: ____________________

______________________________,
Petitioner,

and

______________________________,
Respondent.

MOTION FOR MODIFICATION OF INJUNCTION FOR PROTECTION AGAINST ( ) DOMESTIC VIOLENCE ( ) REPEAT VIOLENCE ( ) DATING VIOLENCE ( ) SEXUAL VIOLENCE ( ) STALKING

I, *{full legal name}* ______________________________________, being sworn, certify that the following statements are true:

SECTION I. MOVING PARTY

(This section is about you. It must be completed. However, **if you fear that disclosing your address would put you in danger because you are the victim of sexual battery, stalking, aggravated child abuse, aggravated stalking, harassment, aggravated battery, or domestic violence,** you should complete and file a **Request for Confidential Filing of Address**, Florida Supreme Court Approved Family Law Form 12.980(h), and write "confidential" in the space provided on this form for your address and telephone number.)

1. Moving Party is the _____ Petitioner _____ Respondent in this case.

2. Moving Party currently lives at the following address: *{street address}* ____________________
{city, state, and zip code} ____
Telephone Number: *{area code and number}* ______________________________

3. Moving Party's attorney's name, address and telephone number is: ____________________
____.
(If you do not have an attorney, write "none.")

SECTION II. NEW INFORMATION

New information since the previous injunction was issued: (If known, write the other party's new address, place of employment, physical description, vehicle, aliases or nicknames, or attorney's name.)
____
____
____
____
____
____.

SECTION III. CASE HISTORY AND REASON FOR SEEKING MODIFICATION OF INJUNCTION

1. Describe any attempts since the date of the current injunction by either Petitioner or Respondent to get an injunction for protection in this or any other court (other than the injunction you are asking to modify in this motion). ________________________________
____
____.

2. Describe any other court cases (including case numbers, if known) since the date of the current injunction between Petitioner and Respondent, including any cases involving the parties' minor child(ren), divorce, juvenile dependency, guardianship, or other civil or criminal cases. ________
____
____.

3. Moving Party requests that the previously entered injunction for protection against domestic violence, repeat violence, dating violence, sexual violence, or stalking, be modified for the following **specific** reasons: *{State why you wish the injunction to be changed.}* ____________________
____
____
____
____
____
____
____
____
____
____
____.

_____Please indicate here if you are attaching additional pages to continue these facts.

SECTION IV. REQUESTED RELIEF

1. Moving Party understands that the Court will hold a hearing on this motion and that he or she must appear at the hearing.

2. Moving Party asks the Court to enter an order in this case that modifies the previously entered injunction in the following ways: *{State how you wish the injunction to be changed.}* ____
____
____
____
____
____
____.

I certify that a copy of this document was ( ) mailed ( ) faxed and mailed ( ) e-mailed ( ) mailed by certified mail, return receipt requested, ( ) furnished to a law enforcement officer for personal service to the person(s) listed below on *{date}*______________________________.

Other party or his/her attorney:
Name:______________________________
Address:______________________________
City, State, Zip:______________________________
Fax Number:______________________________
Designated E-Mail Address(es):______________________________

I understand that I am swearing or affirming under oath to the truthfulness of the claims made in this motion and that the punishment for knowingly making a false statement includes fines and/or imprisonment.

Dated: ________________ ______________________________
Signature of Party

STATE OF FLORIDA
COUNTY OF

Sworn to or affirmed and signed before me on ____________ by ______________________________.

____
NOTARY PUBLIC or DEPUTY CLERK

Florida Supreme Court Approved Family Law Form 12.980(j), Motion for Modification of Injunction for Protection Against Domestic, Repeat, Dating or Sexual Violence, or Stalking (03/15)

____

{Print, type, or stamp commissioned name of notary or clerk}

_____ Personally known

_____ Produced identification

Type of identification produced ____________________

Florida Supreme Court Approved Family Law Form 12.980(j), Motion for Modification of Injunction for Protection Against Domestic, Repeat, Dating or Sexual Violence, or Stalking (03/15)

INSTRUCTIONS FOR FLORIDA SUPREME COURT APPROVED FAMILY LAW FORM 12.980(j) MOTION FOR MODIFICATION OF INJUNCTION FOR PROTECTION AGAINST DOMESTIC, REPEAT, DATING, OR SEXUAL VIOLENCE, OR STALKING (03/15)

When should this form be used?

This form may be used if you are a **party** to a previously entered injunction for protection against domestic, repeat, dating, or sexual violence, or stalking, and you want the court to **modify the terms** of the injunction. If you use this form, you are called the moving party.

This form should be typed or printed in black ink. After completing this form, you should sign the form before a **notary public** or the **clerk of the circuit court**. You should then file the original with the clerk in the county where the original petition was filed and keep a copy for your records. **You must file a motion for modification before the previously entered order expires.** If you have any questions or need assistance completing this form, the clerk or **family law intake staff** will help you.

What should I do next?

For your case to proceed, you will need to set a **hearing** on your motion. You must properly notify the other party of the motion and hearing. You should check with the clerk of court for information on the local procedure for scheduling a hearing. When you know the date and time of your hearing, you should file **Notice of Hearing (General)**, Florida Supreme Court Approved Family Law Form 12.923, or other appropriate notice of hearing form. You will need to serve a copy of your motion and Notice of Hearing on the other party. Service of your motion must be in in[1] a manner that is reasonably calculated to apprise the other party of your motion and the hearing. Please note that if notice is mailed or e-mailed, the court in certain circumstances may not consider mailing or e-mailing to be adequate notice. If you want to be sure, you should consider using certified mail, return receipt requested, or having the motion personally served. **If you are not represented by an attorney in this action, you must file proof that the other party personally received notice of your motion.** This is a technical area of the law; if you have any questions about it, you should consult a lawyer. For more information on personal service, see the instructions for **Summons: Personal Service on an Individual,** Florida Family Law Rules of Procedure Form 12.910(a).

You will need to appear at a hearing on your motion for modification of injunction. After the hearing, if the judge grants your motion, he or she will prepare a new injunction for protection that contains the modifications. After the judge signs the new injunction, the clerk will provide you with the necessary copies. **Make sure that you keep a certified copy of the new injunction with you at all times!**

Where can I look for more information?

Before proceeding, you should read General Information for Self–Represented Litigants found at the beginning of these forms. The words that are in **bold underline** are defined in that section. The clerk of the circuit court or family law intake staff will help you complete any necessary domestic, repeat, dating, or sexual violence; or stalking forms and will answer any question that you may have.

IMPORTANT INFORMATION REGARDING E–FILING

The Florida Rules of Judicial Administration now require that all petitions, pleadings, and documents be filed electronically except in certain circumstances. **Self-represented litigants may file petitions or other pleadings or documents electronically; however, they are not required to do so.** If you choose to file your pleadings or other documents electronically, you must do so in accordance with Florida Rule of Judicial Administration 2.525, and you must follow the procedures of the judicial circuit in which you file. **The rules and procedures should be carefully read and followed**

IMPORTANT INFORMATION REGARDING E–SERVICE ELECTION

After the initial service of process of the petition or supplemental petition by the Sheriff or certified process server, the Florida Rules of Judicial Administration now require that all documents required or permitted to be served on the other party must be served by electronic mail (e-mail) except in certain circumstances. **You must strictly comply with the format requirements set forth in the Rules of Judicial Administration.**

SELF–REPRESENTED LITIGANTS MAY SERVE DOCUMENTS BY E–MAIL; HOWEVER, THEY ARE NOT REQUIRED TO DO SO. If a self-represented litigant elects to serve and receive documents by e-mail, the procedures must always be followed once the initial election is made.

To serve and receive documents by e-mail, you must designate your e-mail addresses by using the **Designation of Current Mailing and E-mail Address**, Florida Supreme Court Approved Family Law Form 12.915, and you must provide your e-mail address on each form on which your signature appears. Please **CAREFULLY** read the rules and instructions for: **Certificate of Service (General),** Florida Supreme Court Approved Family Law Form 12.914; **Designation of Current Mailing and E-mail Address**, Florida Supreme Court Approved Family Law Form 12.915; and Florida Rule of Judicial Administration 2.516.

Special notes . . .

If the injunction you are seeking to modify is for domestic violence and you want the court to modify **alimony**, **child support**, or **time–sharing** of minor child(ren), you must establish that there has been a change in circumstance(s), as required by chapter 61, Florida Statutes, or chapter 741, Florida Statutes, as applicable, that requires this (these) modification(s). Be sure that you make these change(s) clear in your motion.

With this form you may also file the following:

- **Request for Confidential Filing of Address**, Florida Supreme Court Approved Family Law Form 12.980(h), if you fear that disclosing your address would put you in danger because you are the victim of sexual battery, aggravated child abuse, stalking, aggravated stalking, harassment, aggravated battery, or domestic violence, and you wish to keep your address confidential.
- **Uniform Child Custody Jurisdiction and Enforcement Act (UCCJEA) Affidavit**, Florida Supreme Court Approved Family Law Form 12.902(d), must be completed and attached if the modification(s) you are seeking involves temporary custody of any minor child(ren).
- **Family Law Financial Affidavit**, Florida Family Law Rules of Procedure Form 12.902(b) or (c), must be completed and attached if the modification(s) you are seeking involves temporary alimony or temporary child support.

When completing this form, you should make sure that your reasons for requesting that the injunction be modified are stated clearly and that you include all relevant facts.

Added as 12.980(k) Feb. 26, 1998, effective Mar. 16, 1998 (713 So.2d 1). Amended July 1, 1999 (759 So.2d 583); Sept. 21, 2000 (810 So.2d 1); Dec. 19, 2002 (836 So.2d 1019); May 15, 2003 (849 So.2d 1003). Renumbered from 12.980(k) Mar. 25, 2004 (871 So.2d 113). Amended June 7, 2012 (93 So.3d 194); May 9, 2013 (113 So.3d 781); March 26, 2015, effective March 26, 2015 (2015 WL 1343088).

[1] So in original.

Form 12.980(k). Temporary Injunction for Protection Against Repeat Violence

IN THE CIRCUIT COURT OF THE ______________ JUDICIAL CIRCUIT,
IN AND FOR ______ COUNTY, FLORIDA

Case No.: ______________________
Division: ______________________

______________________________,
Petitioner,
and

______________________________,
Respondent.

TEMPORARY INJUNCTION FOR PROTECTION AGAINST REPEAT VIOLENCE

The Petition for Injunction for Protection Against Repeat Violence under section 784.046, Florida Statutes, and other papers filed in this Court have been reviewed. Under the laws of Florida, the Court has jurisdiction of the petitioner and the subject matter and has jurisdiction of the respondent upon service of the temporary injunction. The term Petitioner as used in this injunction includes the person on whose behalf this injunction is entered.

It is intended that this protection order meet the requirements of 18 U.S.C. Section 2265 and therefore intended that it be accorded full faith and credit by the court of another state or Indian tribe and enforced as if it were the order of the enforcing state or of the Indian tribe.

SECTION I. NOTICE OF HEARING

Because this Temporary Injunction for Protection Against Repeat Violence has been issued without notice to Respondent, the Petitioner and Respondent are instructed that they are scheduled to appear and testify at a hearing regarding this matter on *{date}*____, at __________ a.m./p.m., when the Court will consider whether to issue a Final Judgment of Injunction for Protection Against Repeat Violence, which shall remain in effect until modified or dissolved by the Court, and whether other things should be ordered. The hearing will be before The Honorable *{name}* ____________________, at *{room name/number, location, address, city}* __________ ____, Florida.

If Petitioner and/or Respondent do not appear, this temporary injunction may be continued in force, extended, or dismissed, and/or additional orders may be granted, including entry of a permanent injunction and the imposition of court costs. All witnesses and evidence, if any, must be presented at this time. **Petitioner and Respondent will be bound by the terms of any injunction or order issued at the final hearing.**

IF EITHER PETITIONER OR RESPONDENT DO NOT APPEAR AT THE FINAL HEARING, HE OR SHE WILL BE BOUND BY THE TERMS OF ANY INJUNCTION OR ORDER ISSUED IN THIS MATTER.

Florida Supreme Court Approved Family Law Form 12.980(k), Temporary Injunction for Protection Against Repeat Violence (03/15)

NOTICE: Because this is a civil case, there is no requirement that these proceedings be transcribed at public expense.

YOU ARE ADVISED THAT IN THIS COURT:

a. ____ a court reporter is provided by the court.

b. ____ electronic recording only is provided by the court. A party may arrange in advance for the services of and provide for a court reporter to prepare a written transcript of the proceedings at that party's expense.

c. ____ neither electronic recording nor court reporting services are provided by the court. A party may arrange in advance for the services of and provide for a court reporter to prepare a written transcript of the proceedings at that party's expense.

A RECORD, WHICH INCLUDES A TRANSCRIPT, MAY BE REQUIRED TO SUPPORT AN APPEAL. THE PARTY SEEKING THE APPEAL IS RESPONSIBLE FOR HAVING THE TRANSCRIPT PREPARED BY A COURT REPORTER. THE TRANSCRIPT MUST BE FILED WITH THE REVIEWING COURT OR THE APPEAL MAY BE DENIED.

If you are a person with a disability who needs any accommodation in order to participate in this proceeding, you are entitled, at no cost to you, to the provision of certain assistance. Please contact ____ *{identify applicable court personnel by name, address, and telephone number}* at least 7 days before your scheduled court appearance, or immediately upon receiving this notification if the time before the scheduled appearance is less than 7 days; if you are hearing or voice impaired, call 711.

SECTION II. FINDINGS

The statements made under oath by Petitioner make it appear that Section 784.046, Florida Statutes, applies to the parties, that Petitioner is a victim of repeat violence and that an immediate and present danger of repeat violence exists to Petitioner or to a member of Petitioner's immediate family.

SECTION III. TEMPORARY INJUNCTION AND TERMS

This injunction shall be effective until the hearing set above and in no event for longer than 15 days, unless extended by court order. If a final order of injunction is issued, the terms of this temporary injunction will be extended until service of the final injunction is effected upon Respondent. This injunction is valid and enforceable in all counties of the State of Florida. The terms of this injunction

may not be changed by either party alone or by both parties together. Only the Court may modify the terms of this injunction. Either party may ask the Court to change or end this injunction.

Willful violation of the terms of this injunction, such as refusing to vacate the dwelling which the parties share, going to Petitioner's residence, place of employment, school, or other place prohibited in this injunction, telephoning, contacting or communicating with Petitioner, if prohibited by this injunction, or committing an act of repeat violence against Petitioner constitutes a misdemeanor of the first degree punishable by up to one year in jail, as provided by Sections 775.082 and 775.083, Florida Statutes.

Any party violating this injunction may be subject to civil or indirect criminal contempt proceedings, including the imposition of a fine or imprisonment, and also may be charged with a crime punishable by a fine, jail, or both, as provided by Florida Statutes.

ORDERED and ADJUDGED:

1. **Violence Prohibited.** Respondent shall not commit, or cause any other person to commit, any acts of violence against Petitioner, including assault, aggravated assault, battery, aggravated battery, sexual assault, sexual battery, stalking, aggravated stalking, kidnapping, or false imprisonment or any criminal offense resulting in physical injury or death. Respondent shall not commit any other violation of the injunction through an intentional unlawful threat, word, or act to do violence to the Petitioner.

2. **No Contact. Respondent shall have no contact with Petitioner unless otherwise provided in this section.**

a. Unless otherwise provided herein, Respondent shall have no contact with Petitioner. Respondent shall not directly or indirectly contact Petitioner in person, by mail, e-mail, fax, telephone, through another person, or in any other manner. Further, Respondent shall not contact or have any third party contact anyone connected with Petitioner's employment or school to inquire about Petitioner or to send any messages to Petitioner. Unless otherwise provided herein, **Respondent shall not go to, in, or within 500 feet of:** Petitioner's current residence *{list address}* ______________________________

____

or any residence to which Petitioner may move; Petitioner's current or any subsequent place of employment *{list address of current employment}*______________________________

or place where Petitioner attends school *{list address of school}*______________________

____

____

____.

*[Initial **if** applies; write N/A **if not** applicable]*

b. ____Respondent may not knowingly come within 100 feet of Petitioner's automobile at any time.

c. ____Other provisions regarding contact: ______________________________

____.

3. **Firearms.**

Florida Supreme Court Approved Family Law Form 12.980(k), Temporary Injunction for Protection Against Repeat Violence (03/15)

*[Initial **all** that apply; write N/A **if does not** apply]*

a. ____Respondent shall not use or possess a firearm or ammunition.

b. ____Respondent shall surrender any firearms and ammunition in Respondent's possession to the____________________ County Sheriff's Department.

c. ____Other directives relating to firearms and ammunition:________________________
____
____.

4. **Mailing Address or Designated E-Mail Address(es).** Respondent shall notify the Clerk of the Court of any change in either his or her mailing address, or designated e-mail address(es), within 10 days of the change. All further papers (excluding pleadings requiring personal service) shall be served either by mail to Respondent's last known mailing address or by e-mail to Respondent's designated e-mail address(es). Service by mail or e-mail shall be complete upon mailing.

5. **Additional order(s) necessary to protect Petitioner from repeat violence:**
____
____
____
____
____
____
____.

SECTION IV. OTHER SPECIAL PROVISIONS
{This section to be used for inclusion of local provisions approved by the chief judge as provided in Florida Family Law Rule 12.610.}
____
____
____.

SECTION V. DIRECTIONS TO LAW ENFORCEMENT OFFICER IN ENFORCING THIS INJUNCTION
{Unless ordered otherwise by the judge, all provisions in this injunction are considered mandatory provisions and should be interpreted as part of this injunction.}

1. The Sheriff of ________________ County, or any other authorized law enforcement officer, is ordered to serve this temporary injunction upon Respondent as soon as possible after its issuance.

2. **This injunction is valid and enforceable in all counties of the State of Florida.** Violation of this injunction should be reported to the appropriate law enforcement agency. Law enforcement officers of the jurisdiction in which a violation of this injunction occurs shall enforce the provisions of this injunction and are authorized to arrest without a warrant pursuant to Section 901.15, Florida Statutes, for any violation of its provisions, which constitutes a criminal act under Section 784.047, Florida

Statutes.

3. Should any Florida law enforcement officer having jurisdiction have probable cause to believe that Respondent has knowingly violated this injunction, the officer may arrest Respondent, confine him/her in the county jail without bail, and shall bring him/her before the Initial Appearance Judge on the next regular court day so that Respondent can be dealt with according to law. The arresting agent shall notify the State Attorney's Office immediately after arrest. THIS INJUNCTION IS ENFORCEABLE IN ALL COUNTIES OF FLORIDA AND LAW ENFORCEMENT OFFICERS MAY EFFECT ARRESTS PURSUANT TO SECTION 901.15(6), FLORIDA STATUTES.

4. **Reporting alleged violations.** If Respondent violates the terms of this injunction and there has not been an arrest, Petitioner may contact the Clerk of the Circuit Court of the county in which the violation occurred and complete an affidavit in support of the violation or Petitioner may contact the State Attorney's office for assistance in filing an action for indirect civil contempt or indirect criminal contempt. Upon receiving such a report, the State Attorney is hereby appointed to prosecute such violations by indirect criminal contempt proceedings, or the State Attorney may decide to file a criminal charge, if warranted by the evidence.

DONE AND ORDERED in ____________________, Florida on ____________________________.

____
CIRCUIT JUDGE

COPIES TO:

Sheriff of ____________________ County

Petitioner:
_____ by U.S. Mail
_____by hand delivery in open court
_____by e-mail to designated e-mail address(es)

Respondent:
_____ forwarded to the sheriff for service

_____State's Attorney's Office

_____Other:____________________

Florida Supreme Court Approved Family Law Form 12.980(k), Temporary Injunction for Protection Against Repeat Violence (03/15)

I CERTIFY the foregoing is a true copy of the original Temporary Injunction for Protection Against Repeat Violence as it appears on file in the office of the Clerk of the Circuit Court of ____________________ County, Florida, and that I have furnished copies of this order as indicated above.

CLERK OF THE CIRCUIT COURT

(SEAL)

By: ____

{Deputy Clerk or Judicial Assistant}

Florida Supreme Court Approved Family Law Form 12.980(k), Temporary Injunction for Protection Against Repeat Violence (03/15)

Added as 12.980(*l*) Feb. 26, 1998, effective Mar. 16, 1998 (713 So.2d 1). Amended Sept. 21, 2000 (810 So.2d 1); May 15, 2003 (849 So.2d 1003). Renumbered from 12.980(*l*) Mar. 25, 2004 (871 So.2d 113). Amended June 7, 2012 (93 So.3d 194); March 26, 2015, effective March 26, 2015 (2015 WL 1343088).

Form 12.980(*l*). Final Judgment of Injunction for Protection Against Repeat Violence (After Notice)

IN THE CIRCUIT COURT OF THE ______ JUDICIAL CIRCUIT,
IN AND FOR ____________ COUNTY, FLORIDA

Case No.: ____________________
Division: ____________________

______________________________,
Petitioner,
and

______________________________,
Respondent.

FINAL JUDGMENT OF INJUNCTION FOR PROTECTION AGAINST REPEAT VIOLENCE (AFTER NOTICE)

The Petition for Injunction for Protection Against Repeat Violence under Section 784.046, Florida Statutes, and other papers filed in this Court have been reviewed. The Court has jurisdiction of the parties and the subject matter. The term Petitioner as used in this injunction includes the person on whose behalf this injunction is entered.

It is intended that this protection order meet the requirements of 18 U.S.C. Section 2265 and therefore intended that it be accorded full faith and credit by the court of another state or Indian tribe and enforced as if it were the order of the enforcing state or of the Indian tribe.

SECTION I. HEARING

This cause came before the Court for a hearing to determine whether an Injunction for Protection Against Repeat Violence in this case should be:

____ issued ____ modified ____ extended.

The hearing was attended by:
_____ Petitioner
_____ Petitioner's Counsel
_____ Respondent
_____ Respondent's Counsel

SECTION II. FINDINGS

On *{date}* ________________, a notice of this hearing was served on Respondent together with a copy of Petitioner's petition to this Court and the temporary injunction, if issued. Service was within the time required by Florida law, and Respondent was afforded an opportunity to be heard.

Florida Supreme Court Approved Family Law Form 12.980(l), Final Judgment of Injunction for Protection Against Repeat Violence (After Notice) (03/15)

After hearing the testimony of each party present and of any witnesses, or upon consent of Respondent, the Court finds, based on the specific facts of this case, that Petitioner is a victim of repeat violence.

SECTION III. INJUNCTION AND TERMS

This injunction shall be in full force and effect until either ____ further order of the Court or ______ *{date}* ______________. This injunction is valid and enforceable throughout all counties in the State of Florida. The terms of this injunction may not be changed by either party alone or by both parties together. Only the Court may modify the terms of this injunction. Either party may ask the Court to change or end this injunction.

Willful violation of the terms of this injunction, such as refusing to vacate the dwelling which the parties share, going to Petitioner's residence, place of employment, school, or other place prohibited in this injunction, telephoning, contacting or communicating with Petitioner, if prohibited by this injunction, or committing an act of repeat violence against Petitioner constitutes a misdemeanor of the first degree punishable by up to one year in jail, as provided by Sections 775.082 and 775.083, Florida Statutes.

Any party violating this injunction shall be subject to civil or indirect criminal contempt proceedings, including the imposition of a fine or imprisonment, and also may be charged with a crime punishable by a fine, jail, or both, as provided by Florida Statutes.

ORDERED and ADJUDGED:

1. **Violence Prohibited.** Respondent shall not commit, or cause any other person to commit, any acts of violence against Petitioner, including assault, aggravated assault, battery, aggravated battery, sexual assault, sexual battery, stalking, aggravated stalking, kidnapping, or false imprisonment, or any criminal offense resulting in physical injury or death. Respondent shall not commit any other violation of the injunction through an intentional unlawful threat, word or act to do violence to the Petitioner.

2. **No Contact. Respondent shall have no contact with Petitioner unless otherwise provided in this section.**

a. Unless otherwise provided herein, Respondent shall have no contact with Petitioner. Respondent shall not directly or indirectly contact Petitioner in person, by mail, e-mail, fax, telephone, through another person, or in any other manner. Further, Respondent shall not contact or have any third party contact anyone connected with Petitioner's employment or school to inquire about Petitioner or to send any messages to Petitioner. Unless otherwise provided herein, **Respondent shall not go to, in, or within 500 feet of:** Petitioner's current residence *{list address}*______________________________ or any residence to which Petitioner may move; Petitioner's current or any subsequent place of

employment *{list address of current employment}*______________________________
or place where Petitioner attends school *{list address of school}*_______________________;
or the following other places (if requested by Petitioner) where Petitioner or Petitioner's minor child(ren) go often:____
____
____.

*{Initial **if** applies; write N/A **if not** applicable}*

b. _____Respondent may not knowingly come within 100 feet of Petitioner's automobile at any time.

c. _____Other provisions regarding contact: ____________________________________
____.

3. **Firearms.**
*{Initial **all** that apply; write N/A **if not** applicable}*
a._____ Respondent shall not use or possess a firearm or ammunition.

b. _____Respondent shall surrender any firearms and ammunition in the Respondent's possession to the_______________County Sheriff's Department.

c._____Other directives relating to firearms and ammunition:______________________
____

4. **Mailing Address or Designated E-Mail Address(es).** Respondent shall notify the Clerk of the Court of any change in either his or her mailing address, or designated e-mail address(es), within 10 days of the change. All further papers (excluding pleadings requiring personal service) shall be served by either mail or e-mail to Respondent's last known mailing address or by e-mail to Respondent's designated e-mail address(es). Service by mail or e-mail shall be complete upon mailing.

5. **Additional order(s) necessary to protect Petitioner from repeat violence:**__________
____
____
____
____
____
____
____
____
____.

SECTION IV. OTHER SPECIAL PROVISIONS

{This section to be used for inclusion of local provisions approved by the chief judge as provided in Florida Family Law Rule 12.610.}

____
____
____
____.

SECTION V. DIRECTIONS TO LAW ENFORCEMENT OFFICER IN ENFORCING THIS INJUNCTION

{Unless ordered otherwise by the judge, all provisions in this injunction are considered mandatory provisions and should be interpreted as part of this injunction.}

1. **This injunction is valid and enforceable in all counties of the State of Florida.** Violation of this injunction should be reported to the appropriate law enforcement agency. Law enforcement officers of the jurisdiction in which a violation of this injunction occurs shall enforce the provisions of this injunction and are authorized to arrest without a warrant pursuant to Section 901.15, Florida Statutes, for any violation of its provision, which constitutes a criminal act under Section 784.047, Florida Statutes.

2. Should any Florida law enforcement officer having jurisdiction have probable cause to believe that Respondent has knowingly violated this injunction, the officer may arrest Respondent, confine him/her in the county jail without bail, and shall bring him/her before the Initial Appearance Judge on the next regular court day so that Respondent can be dealt with according to law. The arresting agent shall notify the State Attorney's Office immediately after arrest. THIS INJUNCTION IS ENFORCEABLE IN ALL COUNTIES OF FLORIDA AND LAW ENFORCEMENT OFFICERS MAY EFFECT ARRESTS PURSUANT TO SECTION 901.15(6), FLORIDA STATUTES.

3. **Reporting alleged violations.** If Respondent violates the terms of this injunction and there has not been an arrest, Petitioner may contact the Clerk of the Circuit Court of the county in which the violation occurred and complete an affidavit in support of the violation or Petitioner may contact the State Attorney's office for assistance in filing an action for indirect civil contempt or indirect criminal contempt. Upon receiving such a report, the State Attorney is hereby appointed to prosecute such violations by indirect criminal contempt proceedings, or the State Attorney may decide to file a criminal charge, if warranted by the evidence.

4. Respondent, upon service of this injunction, shall be deemed to have knowledge of and to be bound by all matters occurring at the hearing and on the face of this injunction.

5. The temporary injunction, if any, entered in this case is extended until such time as service of this injunction is effected upon Respondent.

DONE AND ORDERED in ___________________________, Florida on _____________________________.

Florida Supreme Court Approved Family Law Form 12.980(*l*), Final Judgment of Injunction for Protection Against Repeat Violence (After Notice) (03/15)

____
CIRCUIT JUDGE
COPIES TO:
Sheriff of ______________________County

Petitioner (or his or her attorney):
____ by U. S. Mail
____ by hand delivery in open court (Petitioner must acknowledge receipt in writing on the face of the original order--see below.)
_____by e-mail to designated e-mail address(es)

Respondent (or his or her attorney):
____forwarded to sheriff for service
____ by hand delivery in open court (Respondent must acknowledge receipt in writing on the face of the original order--see below.)
____ by certified mail (may only be used when Respondent is present at the hearing and Respondent fails or refuses to acknowledge the receipt of a certified copy of this injunction.)

____ State Attorney's Office
____ Batterer's intervention program (if ordered)
____State Disbursement Unit (if ordered)
____Central Depository (if ordered)
____ Department of Revenue
____ Other______________________________________

I CERTIFY the foregoing is a true copy of the original Final Judgment of Injunction for Protection Against Repeat Violence as it appears on file in the office of the Clerk of the Circuit Court of ______________ County, Florida, and that I have furnished copies of this order as indicated above.

CLERK OF THE CIRCUIT COURT

(SEAL)
By: ______________________________________
{Deputy Clerk or Judicial Assistant}

ACKNOWLEDGMENT

I, *{Name of Petitioner}*________________________________, acknowledge receipt of a certified copy of this Injunction for Protection.

____
Petitioner

ACKNOWLEDGMENT

I, *{Name of Respondent}*________________________________, acknowledge receipt of a certified copy of this Injunction for Protection.

____
Respondent

Florida Supreme Court Approved Family Law Form 12.980(l), Final Judgment of Injunction for Protection Against Repeat Violence (After Notice) (03/15)

Added as 12.980(m) Feb. 26, 1998, effective Mar. 16, 1998 (713 So.2d 1). Amended Sept. 21, 2000 (810 So.2d 1); May 15, 2003 (849 So.2d 1003). Renumbered from 12.980(m) Mar. 25, 2004 (871 So.2d 113). Amended June 7, 2012 (93 So.3d 194); March 26, 2015, effective March 26, 2015 (2015 WL 1343088).

Form 12.980(m). Order Extending Injunction for Protection Against ( ) Domestic Violence ( ) Repeat Violence ( ) Dating Violence ( ) Sexual Violence ( ) Stalking

IN THE CIRCUIT COURT OF THE __________ JUDICIAL CIRCUIT,
IN AND FOR __________ COUNTY, FLORIDA

Case No.: __________
Division: __________

______________________________,
Petitioner
and

______________________________,
Respondent.

ORDER EXTENDING INJUNCTION FOR PROTECTION AGAINST ( ) DOMESTIC VIOLENCE ( ) REPEAT VIOLENCE ( ) DATING VIOLENCE ( ) SEXUAL VIOLENCE ( ) STALKING

THIS CAUSE came before the Court on *{date}* ______________________, upon Petitioner's motion for an extension of injunction for protection and it appearing to the Court as follows:

1.____**Ex parte.**
The claims in the motion for extension of injunction for protection make it appear to the Court that there is an immediate and present danger of domestic, repeat, dating, or sexual violence as required under section 741.30 or section 784.046, Florida Statutes, or that stalking exists, pursuant to section 784.0485, Florida Statutes. The previously entered injunction is extended until *{date}* __________. A full hearing on the petition is scheduled for *{date}* at _____ a.m./p.m. in ______________________ ______________________________________.

NOTICE: Because this is a civil case, there is no requirement that these proceedings be transcribed at public expense.

YOU ARE ADVISED THAT IN THIS COURT:

a. ____a court reporter is provided by the court.

b.____ electronic recording only is provided by the court. A party may arrange in advance for the services of and provide for a court reporter to prepare a written transcript of the proceedings at that party's expense.

c. ____If this is a repeat violence, dating violence, or sexual violence action, no electronic recording or court reporting services are provided by the court. A party may arrange in advance for the services of and provide for a court reporter to prepare a written transcript of the proceedings at that party's expense.

Florida Supreme Court Approved Family Law Form 12.980(m), Order Extending Injunction for Protection Against Domestic, Repeat, Dating or Sexual Violence, or Stalking (03/15)

A RECORD, WHICH INCLUDES A TRANSCRIPT, MAY BE REQUIRED TO SUPPORT AN APPEAL. THE PARTY SEEKING THE APPEAL IS RESPONSIBLE FOR HAVING THE TRANSCRIPT PREPARED BY A COURT REPORTER.

THE TRANSCRIPT MUST BE FILED WITH THE REVIEWING COURT OR THE APPEAL MAY BE DENIED.

If you are a person with a disability who needs any accommodation in order to participate in this proceeding, you are entitled, at no cost to you, to the provision of certain assistance. Please contact ______________________________

____

***{identify applicable court personnel by name, address, and telephone number}* at least 7 days before your scheduled court appearance, or immediately upon receiving this notification if the time before the scheduled appearance is less than 7 days; if you are hearing or voice impaired, call 711.**

2._____After notice and hearing.
Respondent was served with a copy of the temporary injunction, if applicable, and a notice of this hearing within the time required by Florida law and was afforded an opportunity to be heard. The notice and opportunity to be heard were sufficient to protect Respondent's right to due process. The following persons attended the hearing: ____ Petitioner ____ Respondent.

After hearing the testimony of each party present and of any witnesses, or upon consent of Respondent, the Court finds that Petitioner is a victim of domestic, repeat , dating , or sexual violence, or stalking, or reasonably fears that he/she will become a victim of domestic or dating violence from Respondent. The previously entered injunction is extended until *{date}*______________________________, or until further order of the Court.

DONE AND ORDERED in ____________________, Florida, on ____________________.

____
CIRCUIT JUDGE

Florida Supreme Court Approved Family Law Form 12.980(m), Order Extending Injunction for Protection Against Domestic, Repeat, Dating or Sexual Violence, or Stalking (03/15)

COPIES TO:
Sheriff of ________________ County

Petitioner (or his or her attorney):
_____ by U.S. Mail
_____ by hand delivery in open court
(Petitioner must acknowledge receipt in writing on the face of the original order—see below)
_____ by e-mail to designated address

Respondent (or his or her attorney):
_____forwarded to sheriff for service
_____ by hand delivery in open court
(Respondent must acknowledge receipt in writing on the face of the original order—see below)
_____ by certified mail (may only be used when Respondent is present at the hearing and Respondent fails or refuses to acknowledge the receipt of certified copy of this injunction)

_____State Attorney's Office

_____Other:

I CERTIFY the foregoing is a true copy of the original **Order Extending the Injunction for Protection** as it appears on file in the office of the Clerk of the Circuit Court of ____________________ County, Florida, and that I have furnished copies of this order as indicated above.

CLERK OF THE CIRCUIT COURT

(SEAL)

By: ________________________________
Deputy Clerk or Judicial Assistant

Florida Supreme Court Approved Family Law Form 12.980(m), Order Extending Injunction for Protection Against Domestic, Repeat, Dating or Sexual Violence, or Stalking (03/15)

ACKNOWLEDGMENT

I, *{Name of Petitioner}* ______________________________, acknowledge receipt of a certified copy of this Order Extending the Injunction for Protection.

____
Petitioner

ACKNOWLEDGMENT

I, *{Name of Respondent}* ______________________________, acknowledge receipt of a certified copy of this Order Extending the Injunction for Protection.

____
Respondent

Florida Supreme Court Approved Family Law Form 12.980(m), Order Extending Injunction for Protection Against Domestic, Repeat, Dating or Sexual Violence, or Stalking (03/15)

Added as 12.980(n) Feb. 26, 1998, effective Mar. 16, 1998 (713 So.2d 1). Amended Sept. 21, 2000 (810 So.2d 1); May 15, 2003 (849 So.2d 1003). Renumbered from 12.980(n) Mar. 25, 2004 (871 So.2d 113). Amended June 7, 2012 (93 So.3d 194); May 9, 2013 (113 So.3d 781); March 26, 2015, effective March 26, 2015 (2015 WL 1343088).

Form 12.980(n). Petition for Injunction for Protection Against Dating Violence

IN THE CIRCUIT COURT OF THE ________ JUDICIAL CIRCUIT,
IN AND FOR ____________ COUNTY, FLORIDA

Case No.: ______________________________
Division: ______________________________

______________,
Petitioner,

and

______________,
Respondent.

PETITION FOR INJUNCTION FOR PROTECTION AGAINST DATING VIOLENCE

I, *{full legal name}* ____, being sworn, certify that the following statements are true:

SECTION I. PETITIONER
(This section is about you. It must be completed.)

1. Petitioner currently lives at the following address: *{address, city, state, zip code}*____________
____.
Date of Birth of Petitioner: ________________________.
[Indicate if applicable]
_____ **Petitioner seeks an injunction for protection on behalf of a minor child.** Petitioner is the parent or legal guardian of *{full legal name}*______________________________, a minor child who is living at home.

2. Petitioner's attorney's name, address, and telephone number is: ____________________
____.
(If you do not have an attorney, write "none.")

SECTION II. RESPONDENT
(This section is about the person you want to be protected from. It must be completed.)

1. Respondent currently lives at the following address: *{address, city, state, and zip code}*__________
____
Respondent's Driver's License number is: *{if known}* ______________________________

2. Petitioner has known Respondent since *{date}*________________________________.

3. Respondent's last known place of employment:______________________________
Employment address:____
Working hours: ________________________

4. Physical description of Respondent:
Race: _____ Sex: Male ____ Female ____ Date of Birth:__________________
Height: _____ Weight: _____ Eye Color: _____ Hair Color:______________
Distinguishing marks and/or scars:
Vehicle: (make/model) ______________ Color: _________ Tag Number: ___________

5. Other names Respondent goes by (aliases or nicknames):__________________________
____.

6. Respondent's attorney's name, address, and telephone number is: ______________
____
(If you do not know whether Respondent has an attorney, write "unknown." If Respondent does not have an attorney, write "none.")

7. If Respondent is a minor, the address of Respondent's parent or legal guardian is:____________
____

SECTION III. CASE HISTORY AND REASON FOR SEEKING PETITION (This section must be completed.)

1. Have the Petitioner and Respondent been involved in a dating relationship within the past six months? _______Yes __________No

2. Describe the nature of the relationship between the Petitioner and Respondent *{include the length of time of the relationship, the romantic or intimate nature of the relationship, the frequency or type of interaction, and any other facts that characterize the relationship}*
____
____
____
____
____

____
____
____
____.

_____Please indicate here if you are attaching additional pages to continue these facts.

3. Has Petitioner ever received or tried to get an injunction for protection against domestic violence, dating violence, repeat violence, or sexual violence, or stalking against Respondent in this or any other court?
_____ Yes _____ No If yes, what happened in that case? *{Include case number, if known}*
____
____

4. Has Respondent ever received or tried to get an injunction for protection against domestic violence, dating violence, repeat violence, or sexual violence, or stalking against Petitioner in this or any other court?
_____ Yes _____ No If yes, what happened in that case? *{Include case number, if known}*__
____
____
____.

5. Describe **any other** court case that is either going on now or that happened in the past **between Petitioner and Respondent** *{Include case number, if known}*:__________
____
____
____
____.

6. Respondent has directed an incident of violence, meaning assault, aggravated assault, battery, aggravated battery, sexual assault, sexual battery, stalking, aggravated stalking, kidnapping, or false imprisonment, or any criminal offense resulting in physical injury or death against Petitioner or a minor child living at home. The incident (including date and location) is described below.
On *{date}*____________________________, at *{location}* ____________________,
Respondent ____
____
____
____
____
____
____
____

Florida Supreme Court Approved Family Law Form 12.980(n), Petition for Injunction for Protection Against Dating Violence (04/15)

____

____

____.

_____Please indicate here if you are attaching additional pages to continue these facts.

7. Other prior incidents (including dates and location) are described below:
On *{date(s)}* ______________________________, at *{location(s)}* ______________________________,
Respondent____

____.

_____Please indicate here if you are attaching additional pages to continue these facts.

8. **Imminent Danger**
*{Please complete **either** paragraph a or b below}*

a. _________Petitioner is a victim of dating violence and has reasonable cause to believe he or she is in **imminent danger** of becoming a victim of another act of dating violence. *{Explain what Respondent has done to make you a victim of dating violence and to make you fear that you are in **imminent danger** of becoming a victim of another act of dating violence.}*

____.

OR

b. _____Petitioner has reasonable cause to believe he or she is in **imminent danger** of becoming a victim of dating violence as demonstrated by the fact that Respondent has: *{Explain what Respondent has done that makes you fear that you are in **imminent danger** of becoming a victim of dating violence.}*

____

____

____

____

____

____.

9. **Additional Information**
*{Indicate **all** that apply}*
a.____ Respondent owns, has, and/or is known to have guns or other weapons.
Describe weapon(s):____

____

b.____ This or prior acts of dating violence have been previously reported to: *{person or agency}*
____

____.

SECTION IV. INJUNCTION
(This section must be completed.)

1. Petitioner asks the Court to enter a **TEMPORARY INJUNCTION** for protection against dating violence that will be in place from now until the scheduled hearing in this matter.

2. Petitioner asks the Court to enter an injunction prohibiting Respondent from committing any acts of violence against Petitioner and:
   a. prohibiting Respondent from going to or within 500 feet of any place Petitioner lives;
   b. prohibiting Respondent from going to or within 500 feet of Petitioner's place(s) of employment or the school that Petitioner attends; the address of Petitioner's place(s) of employment and/or school is:____
   ____;
   c. prohibiting Respondent from contacting Petitioner by telephone, mail, by e-mail, in writing, through another person, or in any other manner;
   d. ordering Respondent not to use or possess any guns or firearms;

*{Indicate **all** that apply}*
e. ____prohibiting Respondent from going to or within 500 feet of the following place(s) Petitioner or Petitioner's immediate family must go to often: _______________
____
____

____;

f. ____ prohibiting Respondent from knowingly and intentionally going to or within 100 feet of Petitioner's motor vehicle;

and any other terms the Court deems necessary for the safety of Petitioner and Petitioner's immediate family.

I UNDERSTAND THAT BY FILING THIS PETITION, I AM ASKING THE COURT TO HOLD A HEARING ON THIS PETITION, THAT BOTH THE RESPONDENT AND I WILL BE NOTIFIED OF THE HEARING, AND THAT I MUST APPEAR AT THE HEARING. I UNDERSTAND THAT IF EITHER RESPONDENT OR I FAIL TO APPEAR AT THE FINAL HEARING, WE WILL BE BOUND BY THE TERMS OF ANY INJUNCTION OR ORDER ISSUED AT THAT HEARING.

I UNDERSTAND THAT I AM SWEARING OR AFFIRMING UNDER OATH TO THE TRUTHFULNESS OF THE CLAIMS MADE IN THIS PETITION AND THAT THE PUNISHMENT FOR KNOWINGLY MAKING A FALSE STATEMENT INCLUDES FINES AND/OR IMPRISONMENT.

Dated:______________________________

____
Signature of Petitioner
Printed Name: ________________
Address: ____________________
City, State, Zip: ______________
Telephone Number: ____________
Fax Number: _________________
Designated E-Mail Address(es): ____________
____

STATE OF FLORIDA
COUNTY OF

Sworn to or affirmed and signed before me on ____________ by ________________________.

____
NOTARY PUBLIC or DEPUTY CLERK

____

Florida Supreme Court Approved Family Law Form 12.980(n), Petition for Injunction for Protection Against Dating Violence (04/15)

[Print, type, or stamp commissioned name of notary or clerk.]

___ Personally known
___ Produced identification
Type of identification produced ____________________

INSTRUCTIONS FOR FLORIDA SUPREME COURT APPROVED FAMILY LAW FORM 12.980(n) PETITION FOR INJUNCTION FOR PROTECTION AGAINST DATING VIOLENCE (04/15)

When should this form be used?

If you are a victim of **dating violence**, and have reasonable cause to believe you are in **imminent danger** of becoming the victim of another act of dating violence, **or** if you have reasonable cause to believe that you are in **imminent danger** of becoming a victim of dating violence, you can use this form to ask the court for a protective order prohibiting dating violence. Dating violence means violence between individuals who have or have had a continuing and significant relationship of a romantic or intimate nature. **The dating relationship must have existed within the past six months, the nature of the relationship must have been characterized by the expectation of affection or sexual involvement between the parties, and the frequency and type of interaction must have included that the persons have been involved over time and on a continuous basis during the course of the relationship. Dating violence does not include violence in a casual acquaintanceship or violence between individuals who only have engaged in ordinary fraternization in a business or social context.** Dating violence includes assault, aggravated assault, battery, aggravated battery, sexual assault, sexual battery, stalking, aggravated stalking, kidnapping, or false imprisonment, or any criminal offense resulting in physical injury or death. Because you are making a request to the court, you are called the **petitioner**. The person whom you are asking the court to protect you from is called the **respondent**. If you are under the age of eighteen and have never been married or had the disabilities of nonage removed by a court, one of your parents or your legal guardian must sign this petition on your behalf.

If you are filing on behalf of a child or children

The parent or legal guardian of any minor child *who is living at home* may seek an injunction for protection against dating violence on behalf of the minor child. With respect to a minor child who is living at home, if the party against whom the protective injunction is sought is also a parent, stepparent, or legal guardian, you, as the parent or legal guardian filing the petition, must have been an eye-witness to, or have direct physical evidence or **affidavits** from eye-witnesses of, the specific facts and circumstances that form the basis of the petition. If the party against whom the protective injunction is sought is a person **OTHER THAN** a parent, stepparent, or legal guardian of the minor child, you, as the parent or legal guardian filing the petition, must state why you have reasonable cause to believe that the minor child is a victim of dating violence.

Additional Information

If the respondent is your **spouse**, former spouse, related to you by blood or marriage, living with you now or has lived with you in the past (if you are or were living as a family), or the other parent of your child(ren), whether or not you have ever been married or ever lived together, you should use **Petition for Injunction for Protection Against Domestic Violence**, Florida Supreme Court Approved Family Law Form 12.980(a), rather than this form.

This form should be typed or printed in black ink. You should complete this form (giving as much detail as possible) and sign it the presence of a notary or in front of the **clerk of the circuit court** in the county where you live. The clerk will take your completed petition to a **judge**. You should keep a copy for your records. If you have any questions or need assistance completing this form, the clerk or **family law intake staff** will help you.

What should I do if the judge grants my petition?

If the facts contained in your petition convince the judge that an **immediate and present danger of dating violence** exists, the judge will sign a **Temporary Injunction for Protection Against Dating Violence**, Florida Supreme Court Approved Family Law Form 12.980(*o*). A temporary injunction is issued without notice to the respondent. The clerk will give your **petition**, the temporary injunction, and any other papers filed with your petition to the sheriff or other law enforcement officer for **personal service** on the respondent. The temporary injunction will take effect immediately after the respondent is served with a copy of it. It lasts until a full **hearing** can be held or for a period of 15 days, whichever comes first. The court may extend the temporary injunction beyond 15 days for a good reason, which may include failure to obtain **service** on the respondent.

The temporary injunction is issued **ex parte**. This means that the judge has considered only the information presented by one side—YOU. Section I of the temporary injunction gives a date that you should appear in court for a hearing. You will be expected to testify about the facts in your petition. The respondent will be given the opportunity to testify at this hearing, also. At the hearing, the judge will decide whether to issue a **Final Judgment of Injunction for Protection Against Dating Violence (After Notice)**, Florida Supreme Court Approved Family Law Form 12.980(p), which will remain in effect for a specific time period or until modified or dissolved by the court. **If you and/or the respondent do not appear, the temporary injunction may be continued in force, extended, or dismissed, and/or additional orders may be granted, including entry of a permanent injunction and the imposition of court costs. You and respondent will be bound by the terms of any injunction or order issued at the final hearing.**

IF EITHER YOU OR RESPONDENT DO NOT APPEAR AT THE FINAL HEARING, YOU WILL BOTH BE BOUND BY THE TERMS OF ANY INJUNCTION OR ORDER ISSUED IN THIS MATTER.

If the judge signs a temporary or final injunction, the clerk will provide you with the necessary copies. **Make sure that you keep one certified copy of the injunction with you at all times!**

What can I do if the judge denies my petition?

If your petition is denied on the grounds that it appears to the court that no immediate and present danger of dating violence exists, the court will set a full hearing on your petition. The respondent will be notified by **personal service** of your petition and the hearing. If your petition is denied, you may: amend your petition by filing a **Supplemental Affidavit in Support of Petition for Injunction for Protection**, Florida Supreme Court Approved Family Law Form 12.980(g); attend the hearing and present facts that support your petition; and/or dismiss your petition.

Where can I look for more information?

Before proceeding, you should read General Information for Self–Represented Litigants found at the beginning of these forms. The words that are in **bold underline** are defined in that section. The clerk of the circuit court or **family law intake staff** will help you complete any necessary forms. For further information, see Section 784.046, Florida Statutes, and Rule 12.610, Florida Family Law Rules of Procedure.

Added as 12.980(*o*) May 15, 2003 (849 So.2d 1003). Renumbered from 12.980(*o*) Mar. 25, 2004 (871 So.2d 113). Amended June 7, 2012 (93 So.3d 194); March 26, 2015, effective March 26, 2015 (2015 WL 1343088); April 23, 2015, effective April 23, 2015 (162 So.3d 964).

Form 12.980(*o*). Temporary Injunction for Protection Against Dating Violence

IN THE CIRCUIT COURT OF THE ____________ JUDICIAL CIRCUIT,
IN AND FOR ____________ COUNTY, FLORIDA

Case No.: ____________
Division: ____________

______________________________,
Petitioner,
and

______________________________,
Respondent.

TEMPORARY INJUNCTION FOR PROTECTION AGAINST DATING VIOLENCE

The Petition for Injunction for Protection Against Dating Violence under Section 784.046, Florida Statutes, and other papers filed in this Court have been reviewed. Under the laws of Florida, the Court has jurisdiction of the petitioner and the subject matter and has jurisdiction of the respondent upon service of the temporary injunction. The term Petitioner as used in this injunction includes the person on whose behalf this injunction is entered.

It is intended that this protection order meet the requirements of 18 U.S.C. Section 2265 and therefore intended that it be accorded full faith and credit by the court of another state or Indian tribe and enforced as if it were the order of the enforcing state or of the Indian tribe.

SECTION I. NOTICE OF HEARING

Because this Temporary Injunction for Protection Against Dating Violence has been issued without notice to Respondent, the Petitioner and Respondent are instructed that they are scheduled to appear and testify at a hearing regarding this matter on *{date}* ______________________________, at ________ a.m./p.m., when the Court will consider whether to issue a Final Judgment of Injunction for Protection Against Dating Violence, which shall remain in effect until modified or dissolved by the Court, and whether other things should be ordered. The hearing will be before The Honorable *{name}* ______________________________, at *{room name/number, location, address, city}* ______________________________ ______________________________, Florida.

If Petitioner and/or Respondent do not appear, this temporary injunction may be continued in force, extended, or dismissed, and/or additional orders may be granted, including entry of a permanent injunction and the imposition of court costs. All witnesses and evidence, if any, must be presented at this time. **Petitioner and Respondent will be bound by the terms of any injunction or order issued at the final hearing.**

IF EITHER PETITIONER OR RESPONDENT DO NOT APPEAR AT THE FINAL HEARING, HE OR SHE WILL BE

BOUND BY THE TERMS OF ANY INJUNCTION OR ORDER ISSUED IN THIS MATTER.
NOTICE: Because this is a civil case, there is no requirement that these proceedings be transcribed at public expense.

YOU ARE ADVISED THAT IN THIS COURT:

a._____a court reporter is provided by the court.

b._____electronic recording only is provided by the court. A party may arrange in advance for the services of and provide for a court reporter to prepare a written transcript of the proceedings at that party's expense.

c._____neither electronic recording nor court reporting services are provided by the court. A party may arrange in advance for the services of and provide for a court reporter to prepare a written transcript of the proceedings at that party's expense.

A RECORD, WHICH INCLUDES A TRANSCRIPT, MAY BE REQUIRED TO SUPPORT AN APPEAL. THE PARTY SEEKING THE APPEAL IS RESPONSIBLE FOR HAVING THE TRANSCRIPT PREPARED BY A COURT REPORTER. THE TRANSCRIPT MUST BE FILED WITH THE REVIEWING COURT OR THE APPEAL MAY BE DENIED.

If you are a person with a disability who needs any accommodation in order to participate in this proceeding, you are entitled, at no cost to you, to the provision of certain assistance. Please contact ____ *{identify applicable court personnel by name, address, and telephone number}* at least 7 days before your scheduled court appearance, or immediately upon receiving this notification if the time before the scheduled appearance is less than 7 days; if you are hearing or voice impaired, call 711.

SECTION II. FINDINGS

The statements made under oath by Petitioner make it appear that Section 784.046, Florida Statutes, applies to the parties, that Petitioner is a victim of dating violence and/or Petitioner has reasonable cause to believe he or she is in imminent danger of becoming a victim of an act of dating violence by Respondent, and that an immediate and present danger of dating violence exists to Petitioner or to a member of Petitioner's immediate family.

SECTION III. TEMPORARY INJUNCTION AND TERMS

This injunction shall be effective until the hearing set above and in no event for longer than 15 days,

unless extended by court order. If a final order of injunction is issued, the terms of this temporary injunction will be extended until service of the final injunction is effected upon Respondent. This injunction is valid and enforceable in all counties of the State of Florida. The terms of this injunction may not be changed by either party alone or by both parties together. Only the Court may modify the terms of this injunction. Either party may ask the Court to change or end this injunction.

Willful violation of the terms of this injunction, such as refusing to vacate the dwelling which the parties share, going to Petitioner's residence, place of employment, school, or other place prohibited in this injunction, telephoning, contacting or communicating with Petitioner, if prohibited by this injunction, or committing an act of dating violence against Petitioner constitutes a misdemeanor of the first degree punishable by up to one year in jail, as provided by Sections 775.082 and 775.083, Florida Statutes.

Any party violating this injunction may be subject to civil or indirect criminal contempt proceedings, including the imposition of a fine or imprisonment, and also may be charged with a crime punishable by a fine, jail, or both, as provided by Florida Statutes.

ORDERED and ADJUDGED:

1. **Violence Prohibited.** Respondent shall not commit, or cause any other person to commit, any acts of violence against Petitioner, including assault, aggravated assault, battery, aggravated battery, sexual assault, sexual battery, stalking, aggravated stalking, kidnapping, or false imprisonment, or any criminal offense resulting in physical injury or death. Respondent shall not commit any other violation of the injunction through an intentional unlawful threat, word, or act to do violence to the Petitioner.

2. **No Contact. Respondent shall have no contact with the Petitioner unless otherwise provided in this section.**

a. Unless otherwise provided herein, Respondent shall have no contact with Petitioner. Respondent shall not directly or indirectly contact Petitioner in person, by mail, e-mail, fax, telephone, through another person, or in any other manner. Further, Respondent shall not contact or have any third party contact anyone connected with Petitioner's employment or school to inquire about Petitioner or to send any messages to Petitioner. Unless otherwise provided herein, **Respondent shall not go to, in, or within 500 feet of:** Petitioner's current residence *{list address}*____

or any residence to which Petitioner may move; Petitioner's current or any subsequent place of employment *{list address of current employment}*____ or place where Petitioner attends school *{list address of school}*_; or the following other places (if requested by Petitioner) where Petitioner or Petitioner's minor child(ren) go often:____

{Initial if applies; write N/A if not applicable}

b. ____Respondent may not knowingly come within 100 feet of Petitioner's automobile at any time.

c. ____Other provisions regarding contact: ____
____
____

3. **Firearms.**

[Initial **all** that apply; write N/A **if does not** apply]

a. ____Respondent shall not use or possess a firearm or ammunition.

b. ____Respondent shall surrender any firearms and ammunition in Respondent's possession to the County Sheriff's Department.

c. ____Other directives relating to firearms and ammunition: ____________________________
____
____

4. **Mailing Address or Designated E-Mail Address(es).** Respondent shall notify the Clerk of the Court of any change in either his or her mailing address, or designated e-mail address(es), within 10 days of the change. All further papers (excluding pleadings requiring personal service) shall be served either by mail to Respondent's last known mailing address or by e-mail to Respondent's designated e-mail address(es). Service shall be complete upon mailing or e-mailing.

5. **Additional order(s) necessary to protect Petitioner from dating violence:**
____
____
____
____
____.

SECTION IV. OTHER SPECIAL PROVISIONS

{This section to be used for inclusion of local provisions approved by the chief judge as provided in Florida Family Law Rule 12.610.}
____
____
____

SECTION V. DIRECTIONS TO LAW ENFORCEMENT OFFICER IN ENFORCING THIS INJUNCTION

{Unless ordered otherwise by the judge, all provisions in this injunction are considered mandatory provisions and should be interpreted as part of this injunction.}

1. The Sheriff of ______________ County, or any other authorized law enforcement officer, is ordered to serve this temporary injunction upon Respondent as soon as possible after its issuance.

2. **This injunction is valid and enforceable in all counties of the State of Florida.** Violation of this injunction should be reported to the appropriate law enforcement agency. Law enforcement officers of the jurisdiction in which a violation of this injunction occurs shall enforce the provisions of this injunction and are authorized to arrest without a warrant pursuant to Section 901.15, Florida Statutes, for any violation of its provisions, which constitutes a criminal act under Section 784.047, Florida Statutes.

3. Should any Florida law enforcement officer having jurisdiction have probable cause to believe that Respondent has knowingly violated this injunction, the officer may arrest Respondent, confine him/her in the county jail without bail, and shall bring him/her before the Initial Appearance Judge on the next regular court day so that Respondent can be dealt with according to law. The arresting agent shall notify the State Attorney's Office immediately after arrest. THIS INJUNCTION IS ENFORCEABLE IN ALL COUNTIES OF FLORIDA AND LAW ENFORCEMENT OFFICERS MAY EFFECT ARRESTS PURSUANT TO SECTION 901.15(6), FLORIDA STATUTES.

4. **Reporting alleged violations.** If Respondent violates the terms of this injunction and there has not been an arrest, Petitioner may contact the Clerk of the Circuit Court of the county in which the violation occurred and complete an affidavit in support of the violation or Petitioner may contact the State Attorney's office for assistance in filing an action for indirect civil contempt or indirect criminal contempt. Upon receiving such a report, the State Attorney is hereby appointed to prosecute such violations by indirect criminal contempt proceedings, or the State Attorney may decide to file a criminal charge, if warranted by the evidence.

DONE AND ORDERED in ______________________________, Florida on ______________________________.

____
CIRCUIT JUDGE

COPIES TO:
Sheriff of ________________________ County
Petitioner:

Florida Supreme Court Approved Family Law Form 12.980(o), Temporary Injunction for Protection Against Dating Violence (03/15)

____ by U. S. Mail
____ by hand delivery in open court
_____ by e-mail to designated e-mail address(es)

Respondent:
_____ forwarded to sheriff for service

____ State Attorney's Office
_____ Other: ________________________

I CERTIFY the foregoing is a true copy of the original Temporary Injunction for Protection Against Dating Violence as it appears on file in the office of the Clerk of the Circuit Court of ______________County, Florida, and that I have furnished copies of this order as indicated above.

CLERK OF THE CIRCUIT COURT

(SEAL)

By:_____________________________________
{Deputy Clerk or Judicial Assistant}

Florida Supreme Court Approved Family Law Form 12.980(o), Temporary Injunction for Protection Against Dating Violence (03/15)

Added as 12.980(p) May 15, 2003 (849 So.2d 1003). Renumbered from 12.980(p) Mar. 25, 2004 (871 So.2d 113). Amended June 7, 2012 (93 So.3d 194); March 26, 2015, effective March 26, 2015 (2015 WL 1343088).

Form 12.980(p). Final Judgment of Injunction for Protection Against Dating Violence (After Notice)

IN THE CIRCUIT COURT OF THE ____ JUDICIAL CIRCUIT,
IN AND FOR ________________ COUNTY, FLORIDA

Case No.: ________________
Division: ________________

______________________________,
Petitioner,
and

______________________________,
Respondent.

FINAL JUDGMENT OF INJUNCTION FOR PROTECTION AGAINST DATING VIOLENCE (AFTER NOTICE)

The Petition for Injunction for Protection Against Dating Violence under Section 784.046, Florida Statutes, and other papers filed in this Court have been reviewed. The Court has jurisdiction of the parties and the subject matter. The term Petitioner as used in this injunction includes the person on whose behalf this injunction is entered.

It is intended that this protection order meet the requirements of 18 U.S.C. Section 2265 and therefore intended that it be accorded full faith and credit by the court of another state or Indian tribe and enforced as if it were the order of the enforcing state or of the Indian tribe.

SECTION I. HEARING

This cause came before the Court for a hearing to determine whether an Injunction for Protection Against Dating Violence in this case should be:

____ issued ____ modified ____ extended.

The hearing was attended by:
____ Petitioner
____ Petitioner's Counsel
____ Respondent
____ Respondent's Counsel

SECTION II. FINDINGS

On *{date}* ______________________, a notice of this hearing was served on Respondent together with a copy of Petitioner's petition to this Court and the temporary injunction, if issued. Service was within the time required by Florida law, and Respondent was afforded an opportunity to be heard.

Florida Supreme Court Approved Family Law Form 12.980(p), Final Judgment of Injunction for Protection Against Dating Violence (After Notice) (03/15)

After hearing the testimony of each party present and of any witnesses, or upon consent of Respondent, the Court finds, based on the specific facts of this case, that Petitioner is a victim of dating violence and/or Petitioner has reasonable cause to believe he or she is in imminent danger of becoming a victim of an act of dating violence by Respondent, and that an immediate and present danger of dating violence exists to Petitioner or to a member of Petitioner's immediate family.

SECTION III. INJUNCTION AND TERMS

This injunction shall be in full force and effect until ____ further order of the Court or ____ *{date}* ____________________________. This injunction is valid and enforceable throughout all counties in the State of Florida. The terms of this injunction may not be changed by either party alone or by both parties together. Only the Court may modify the terms of this injunction. Either party may ask the Court to change or end this injunction.

Willful violation of the terms of this injunction, such as refusing to vacate the dwelling which the parties share, going to Petitioner's residence, place of employment, school, or other place prohibited in this injunction, telephoning, contacting or communicating with Petitioner, if prohibited by this injunction, or committing an act of dating violence against Petitioner constitutes a misdemeanor of the first degree punishable by up to one year in jail, as provided by Sections 775.082 and 775.083, Florida Statutes.

Any party violating this injunction shall be subject to civil or indirect criminal contempt proceedings, including the imposition of a fine or imprisonment, and also may be charged with a crime punishable by a fine, jail, or both, as provided by Florida Statutes.

ORDERED and ADJUDGED:

1. **Violence Prohibited.** Respondent shall not commit, or cause any other person to commit, any acts of violence against Petitioner, including assault, aggravated assault, battery, aggravated battery, sexual assault, sexual battery, stalking, aggravated stalking, kidnapping, or false imprisonment, or any criminal offense resulting in physical injury or death. Respondent shall not commit any other violation of the injunction through an intentional unlawful threat, word or act to do violence to the Petitioner.

2. **No Contact. Respondent shall have no contact with Petitioner unless otherwise provided in this section.**

a. Unless otherwise provided herein, Respondent shall have no contact with Petitioner. Respondent shall not directly or indirectly contact Petitioner in person, by mail, e-mail, fax, telephone, through another person, or in any other manner. Further, Respondent shall not contact or have any third party contact anyone connected with Petitioner's employment or school to inquire about Petitioner or to send any messages to Petitioner. Unless otherwise provided herein, **Respondent shall not go to, in, or within 500 feet of:** Petitioner's current residence *{list address}*

____
____or any residence to which Petitioner may move; Petitioner's current or any subsequent place of employment *{list address of current employment}*____
or place where Petitioner attends school *{list address of school}* ____
______________________________; or the following other places (if requested by Petitioner) where Petitioner or Petitioner's minor child(ren) go often: ____________
____
____
____
____.

*{Initial **if** applies; write N/A **if not** applicable}*

b.____ Respondent may not knowingly come within 100 feet of Petitioner's automobile at any time.

c. ____Other provisions regarding contact: ______________________________
____
____
____.

3. **Firearms.**

*{Initial **all** that apply; write N/A **if does not** apply}*

a.____Respondent shall not use or possess a firearm or ammunition.

b.____Respondent shall surrender any firearms and ammunition in the Respondent's possession to the__________________ County Sheriff's Department.

c. ____Other directives relating to firearms and ammunition:______________________
____.

4. **Mailing Address or Designated E-Mail Address(es).** Respondent shall notify the Clerk of the Court of any change in either his or her mailing address, or designated e-mail address(es), within 10 days of the change. All further papers (excluding pleadings requiring personal service) shall be served either by mail to Respondent's last known mailing address or by e-mail to Respondent's designated e-mail address(es). Service shall be complete upon mailing or e-mailing.

5. **Additional order(s) necessary to protect Petitioner from dating violence:** ____________
____
____
____
____.

SECTION IV. OTHER SPECIAL PROVISIONS
{This section to be used for inclusion of local provisions approved by the chief judge as provided in Florida Family Law Rule 12.610.}

____
____
____.

SECTION V. DIRECTIONS TO LAW ENFORCEMENT OFFICER IN ENFORCING THIS INJUNCTION
{Unless ordered otherwise by the judge, all provisions in this injunction are considered mandatory provisions and should be interpreted as part of this injunction.}

1. **This injunction is valid and enforceable in all counties of the State of Florida.** Violation of this injunction should be reported to the appropriate law enforcement agency. Law enforcement officers of the jurisdiction in which a violation of this injunction occurs shall enforce the provisions of this injunction and are authorized to arrest without a warrant pursuant to Section 901.15, Florida Statutes, for any violation of its provision, which constitutes a criminal act under Section 784.047, Florida Statutes.

2. Should any Florida law enforcement officer having jurisdiction have probable cause to believe that Respondent has knowingly violated this injunction, the officer may arrest Respondent, confine him/her in the county jail without bail, and shall bring him/her before the Initial Appearance Judge on the next regular court day so that Respondent can be dealt with according to law. The arresting agent shall notify the State Attorney's Office immediately after arrest. THIS INJUNCTION IS ENFORCEABLE IN ALL COUNTIES OF FLORIDA AND LAW ENFORCEMENT OFFICERS MAY EFFECT ARRESTS PURSUANT TO SECTION 901.15(6), FLORIDA STATUTES.

3. **Reporting alleged violations.** If Respondent violates the terms of this injunction and there has not been an arrest, Petitioner may contact the Clerk of the Circuit Court of the county in which the violation occurred and complete an affidavit in support of the violation or Petitioner may contact the State Attorney's office for assistance in filing an action for indirect civil contempt or indirect criminal contempt. Upon receiving such a report, the State Attorney is hereby appointed to prosecute such violations by indirect criminal contempt proceedings, or the State Attorney may decide to file a criminal charge, if warranted by the evidence.

4. Respondent, upon service of this injunction, shall be deemed to have knowledge of and to be bound by all matters occurring at the hearing and on the face of this injunction.

5. The temporary injunction, if any, entered in this case is extended until such time as service of this injunction is effected upon Respondent.

DONE AND ORDERED in____________________________, Florida on ______________________.

____
CIRCUIT JUDGE

Florida Supreme Court Approved Family Law Form 12.980(p), Final Judgment of Injunction for Protection Against Dating Violence (After Notice) (03/15)

COPIES TO:
Sheriff of ____________ County

Petitioner (or his or her attorney):
____ by U. S. Mail
____ by hand delivery in open court (Petitioner must acknowledge receipt in writing on the face of the original order--see below)
______ by e-mail to designated e-mail address

Respondent (or his or her attorney):
____forwarded to sheriff for service
____ by hand delivery in open court (Respondent must acknowledge receipt in writing on the face of the original order--see below.)
____ by certified mail (may only be used when Respondent is present at the hearing and Respondent fails or refuses to acknowledge the receipt of a certified copy of this injunction.)

____ State Attorney's Office
____ Other____

I CERTIFY the foregoing is a true copy of the original Final Judgment of Injunction for Protection Against Dating Violence as it appears on file in the office of the Clerk of the Circuit Court of ____________ County, Florida, and that I have furnished copies of this order as indicated above.

CLERK OF THE CIRCUIT COURT

(SEAL)

By:______________________________
Deputy Clerk or Judicial Assistant

ACKNOWLEDGMENT

I, *{Name of Petitioner}*___________________________, acknowledge receipt of a certified copy of this Injunction for Protection.

Florida Supreme Court Approved Family Law Form 12.980(p), Final Judgment of Injunction for Protection Against Dating Violence (After Notice) (03/15)

____
Petitioner

ACKNOWLEDGMENT

I, *{Name of Respondent}* ______________________________, acknowledge receipt of a certified copy of this Injunction for Protection.

____
Respondent

Florida Supreme Court Approved Family Law Form 12.980(p), Final Judgment of Injunction for Protection Against Dating Violence (After Notice) (03/15)

Added as 12.980(q) May 15, 2003 (849 So.2d 1003). Renumbered from 12.980(q) Mar. 25, 2004 (871 So.2d 113). Amended June 7, 2012 (93 So.3d 194); March 26, 2015, effective March 26, 2015 (2015 WL 1343088).

Form 12.980(q). Petition for Injunction for Protection Against Sexual Violence

IN THE CIRCUIT COURT OF THE ________ JUDICIAL CIRCUIT,
IN AND FOR ____________________ COUNTY, FLORIDA

Case No.: ____________________
Division: ____________________

______________________________,
Petitioner,
and

______________________________,
Respondent.

PETITION FOR INJUNCTION FOR PROTECTION AGAINST SEXUAL VIOLENCE

I, *{full legal name}* ______________________________ being sworn, certify that the following statements are true:

SECTION I. PETITIONER
(This section is about you. It must be completed; however, **if you fear that disclosing your address to the respondent would put you in danger,** you should complete and file a Request for Confidential Filing of Address, Florida Supreme Court Approved Family Law Form 12.980(h), and write confidential in the space provided on this form for your address.)

1. Petitioner currently lives at the following address: *{address, city, state, zip code}* ____________
____
Date of Birth of Petitioner: ______________________________

{Indicate if applicable}
_____ **Petitioner seeks an injunction for protection on behalf of a minor child.**
Petitioner is the parent or legal guardian of *{full legal name}* ______________________,
a minor child who is living at home.

2. Petitioner's attorney's name, address, and telephone number is: ______________________
____
(If you do not have an attorney, write "none.")

SECTION II. RESPONDENT
(This section is about the person you want to be protected from. It must be completed.)

1. Respondent currently lives at the following address: *{address, city, state, and zip code}* ________

Family Supreme Court Approved Law Form 12.980(q), Petition for Injunction for Protection Against Sexual Violence (03/15)

____

Respondent's Driver's License number is: *{if known}* ____________________

2. Respondent's last known place of employment: ____________________
Employment address: ____________________
Working hours: ____________________

3. Physical description of Respondent:
Race: _____ Sex: Male _____ Female _____ Date of Birth: ____________________
Height: _____ Weight: _____ Eye Color: _____ Hair Color: ____________________
Distinguishing marks and/or scars: ____________________
Vehicle: (make/model) __________ Color: __________ Tag Number: ____________________

4. Other names Respondent goes by (aliases or nicknames): ____________________
____

5. Respondent's attorney's name, address, and telephone number is: ____________________
____

(If you do not know whether Respondent has an attorney, write "unknown." If Respondent does not have an attorney, write "none.")

6. If Respondent is a minor, the address of Respondent's parent or legal guardian is: __________
____

SECTION III. CASE HISTORY AND REASON FOR SEEKING PETITION
(This section must be completed.)

1. Petitioner has suffered sexual violence as shown by the fact that the Respondent has: *{describe the acts of violence}* ____________________
____
____
____
____
____.

_____ Please indicate here if you are attaching additional pages to continue these facts.

*{Indicate **all** that apply}*

a. _____ Petitioner reported the sexual violence to law enforcement and is cooperating in any criminal proceeding. The incident report number by law enforcement is: __________.

b. *{If there is a criminal case, include case number, if known}* ____________________.

Family Supreme Court Approved Law Form 12.980(q), Petition for Injunction for Protection Against Sexual Violence (03/15)

c. _____Respondent was sent to prison for committing sexual violence against Petitioner or Petitioner's minor child living at home and Respondent is out of prison or is getting out of prison within 90 days. The notice of inmate release is attached.

2. Has Petitioner ever received or tried to get an injunction for protection against domestic violence, dating violence, repeat violence, or sexual violence against Respondent in this or any other court?
_____ Yes _____No If yes, what happened in that case? *{Include case number, if known}*
____
____
____

3. Has Respondent ever received or tried to get an injunction for protection against domestic violence, dating violence, repeat violence, or sexual violence against Petitioner in this or any other court?
_____ Yes _____ No If yes, what happened in that case? *{Include case number, if known}*
____
____
____

4. Describe **any other** court case that is either going on now or that happened in the past **between Petitioner and Respondent** *{Include case number, if known}*:______________________
____
____
____

5. **Additional Information**
{Indicate all that apply}
a. ____Respondent owns, has, and/or is known to have guns or other weapons.
Describe weapon(s): ____

b. ____This or prior acts of violence have been previously reported to: *{person or agency}* ______
____

SECTION IV. INJUNCTION
(This section must be completed.)

1. Petitioner asks the Court to enter a TEMPORARY INJUNCTION for protection against sexual violence that will be in place from now until the scheduled hearing in this matter.

2. Petitioner asks the Court to enter an injunction prohibiting Respondent from committing any

acts of violence against Petitioner and:

a. prohibiting Respondent from going to or within 500 feet of any place Petitioner lives;

b. prohibiting Respondent from going to or within 500 feet of Petitioner's place(s) of employment or the school that Petitioner attends; the address of Petitioner's place(s) of employment and/or school is: ______________________________ __________;

c. prohibiting Respondent from contacting Petitioner by telephone, mail, by e-mail, in writing, through another person, or in any other manner;

d. ordering Respondent not to use or possess any guns or firearms;

*{Indicate **all** that apply}*

e. _____ prohibiting Respondent from going to or within 500 feet of the following place(s) Petitioner or Petitioner's immediate family must go to often: ______________________________ ______________________________ ______________________________;

f. _____ prohibiting Respondent from knowingly and intentionally going to or within 100 feet of Petitioner's motor vehicle;

AND any other terms the Court deems necessary for the safety of Petitioner and Petitioner's immediate family.

I UNDERSTAND THAT BY FILING THIS PETITION, I AM ASKING THE COURT TO HOLD A HEARING ON THIS PETITION, THAT BOTH THE RESPONDENT AND I WILL BE NOTIFIED OF THE HEARING, AND THAT I MUST APPEAR AT THE HEARING. I UNDERSTAND THAT IF EITHER RESPONDENT OF I FAIL TO APPEAR AT THE FINAL HEARING, WE WILL BE BOUND BY THE TERMS OF ANY INJUNCTION OR ORDER ISSUED AT THAT HEARING.

I UNDERSTAND THAT I AM SWEARING OR AFFIRMING UNDER OATH TO THE TRUTHFULNESS OF THE CLAIMS MADE IN THIS PETITION AND THAT THE PUNISHMENT FOR KNOWINGLY MAKING A FALSE STATEMENT INCLUDES FINES AND/OR IMPRISONMENT.

Dated: ______________________

____
Signature of Petitioner

Printed Name: ______________________
Address: ______________________

Florida Supreme Court Approved Family Law Form 12.980(q), Petition for Injunction for Protection Against Sexual Violence (03/15)

City, State, Zip: ____________________________
Telephone Number: ____________________________
Fax Number: ____________________________

Designated E-Mail Address(es): ____________________________

STATE OF FLORIDA
COUNTY OF ________________

Sworn to or affirmed and signed before me on __________________ by __________________.

____
NOTARY PUBLIC or DEPUTY CLERK

____
{Print, type, or stamp commissioned name of notary or clerk.}
______ Personally known
______ Produced identification
Type of identification produced ____________________

Florida Supreme Court Approved Family Law Form 12.980(q), Petition for Injunction for Protection Against Sexual Violence (03/15)

INSTRUCTIONS FOR FLORIDA SUPREME COURT APPROVED FAMILY LAW FORM 12.980(q) PETITION FOR INJUNCTION FOR PROTECTION AGAINST SEXUAL VIOLENCE (03/15)

When should this form be used?

If you are a victim of **sexual violence** or the parent or legal guardian of a minor child who is living at home and is a victim of sexual violence, you can use this form to ask the court for a protective order prohibiting sexual violence. Sexual violence means any one incident of:

- sexual battery, as defined in Chapter 794, Florida Statutes;
- a lewd or lascivious act, as defined in Chapter 800, Florida Statutes, committed upon or in the presence of a person younger than 16 years of age;
- luring or enticing a child, as described in Chapter 787, Florida Statutes;
- sexual performance by a child, as described in Chapter 827, Florida Statutes; or
- any other forcible felony wherein a sexual act is committed or attempted

In order to get an injunction you must have reported the sexual violence to a law enforcement agency and be cooperating in the criminal proceeding if there is one. It does not matter whether criminal charges based on the sexual violence have been filed, reduced, or dismissed by the state attorney's office. You may also seek an injunction for protection against sexual violence if the respondent was sent to prison for committing one of the sexual violence crimes listed above against you or your minor child living at home and respondent is out of prison or is getting out of prison within 90 days of your petition. Attach the notice of inmate release to your petition.

Because you are making a request to the court, you are called the **petitioner**. The person whom you are asking the court to protect you from is called the **respondent**. If you are seeking an injunction for protection against sexual violence on behalf of a minor child who is living at home, the parent or legal guardian must have been an eyewitness to, or have direct physical evidence or **affidavits** from eyewitnesses of, the specific facts and circumstances that form the basis of the petition. If you are under the age of eighteen and have never been married or had the disabilities of nonage removed by a court, one of your parents or your legal guardian must sign this petition on your behalf.

If the respondent is your **spouse**, former spouse, related to you by blood or marriage, living with you now or has lived with you in the past (if you are or were living as a family), or is the other parent of your child(ren) whether or not you have ever been married or ever lived together, you should use **Petition for Injunction for Protection Against Domestic Violence**, Florida Supreme Court Approved Family Law Form 12.980(a), rather than this form.

This form should be typed or printed in black ink. You should complete this form (giving as much detail as possible) and sign it the presence of a notary or in front of the **clerk of the circuit court** in the county where you live. The clerk will take your completed petition to a **judge**. You should keep a copy for your records. If you have any questions or need assistance completing this form, the clerk or **family law intake staff** will help you.

What should I do if the judge grants my petition?

If the facts contained in your petition convince the judge that an immediate and present danger of violence exists, the judge will sign a **Temporary Injunction for Protection Against Sexual Violence**, Florida Supreme Court Approved Family Law Form 12.980(r). A temporary injunction is issued without notice to the respondent. The clerk will give your **petition**, the temporary injunction, and any other papers filed with your petition to the sheriff or other law enforcement officer for **personal service** on the respondent. The temporary injunction will take effect immediately after the respondent is served with a copy of it. It lasts until a full **hearing** can be held or for a period of 15 days, whichever comes first, unless the **respondent** is incarcerated, and in such instance the temporary injunction is effective for 15 days following the date the **respondent** is released from incarceration. The court may extend the temporary injunction beyond 15 days for a good reason, which may include failure to obtain **service** on the respondent.

The temporary injunction is issued **ex parte**. This means that the judge has considered only the information presented by one side—YOU. Section I of the temporary injunction gives a date that you should appear in court for a hearing. You will be expected to testify about the facts in your petition. The respondent will be given the opportunity to testify at this hearing, also. At the hearing, the judge will decide whether to issue a **Final Judgment of Injunction for Protection Against Sexual Violence (After Notice)**, Florida Supreme Court Approved Family Law Form 12.980(s), which will remain in effect for a specific time period or until modified or dissolved by the court. **If you and/or the respondent do not appear, the temporary injunction may be continued in force, extended, or dismissed, and/or additional orders may be granted, including entry of a permanent injunction and the imposition of court costs. You and respondent will be bound by the terms of any injunction or order issued at the final hearing.**

IF EITHER YOU OR RESPONDENT DO NOT APPEAR AT THE FINAL HEARING, YOU WILL BOTH BE BOUND BY THE TERMS OF ANY INJUNCTION OR ORDER ISSUED IN THIS MATTER.

If the judge signs a temporary or final injunction, the clerk will provide you with the necessary copies. **Make sure that you keep one certified copy of the injunction with you at all times!**

What can I do if the judge denies my petition?

If your petition is denied on the grounds that it appears to the court that no immediate and present danger of sexual violence exists, the court will set a full hearing on your petition. The respondent will be notified by **personal service** of your petition and the hearing. If your petition is denied, you may: amend your petition by filing a **Supplemental Affidavit in Support of Petition for Injunction for Protection**, Florida Supreme Court Approved Family Law Form 12.980 (g); attend the hearing and present facts that support your petition; and/or dismiss your petition.

Where can I look for more information?

Before proceeding, you should read General Information for Self–Represented Litigants found at the beginning of these forms. The words that are in **bold underline** are defined in that section. The clerk of the circuit court or **family law intake staff** will provide you with necessary forms. For further information, see section 784.046, Florida Statutes.

IMPORTANT INFORMATION REGARDING E–FILING

The Florida Rules of Judicial Administration now require that all petitions, pleadings, and documents be filed electronically except in certain circumstances. **Self-represented litigants may file petitions or other pleadings or documents electronically; however, they are not required to do so.** If you choose to file your pleadings or other documents electronically, you must do so in accordance with Florida Rule of Judicial Administration 2.525, and you must follow the procedures of the judicial circuit in which you file. **The rules and procedures should be carefully read and followed.**

IMPORTANT INFORMATION REGARDING E–SERVICE ELECTION

After the initial service of process of the petition or supplemental petition by the Sheriff or certified process server, the Florida Rules of Judicial Administration now require that all documents required or permitted to be served on the other party must be served by electronic mail (e-mail) except in certain circumstances. **You must strictly comply with the format requirements set forth in the Rules of Judicial Administration.**

SELF–REPRESENTED LITIGANTS MAY SERVE DOCUMENTS BY E–MAIL; HOWEVER, THEY ARE NOT REQUIRED TO DO SO. If a self-represented litigant elects to serve and receive documents by e-mail, the procedures must always be followed once the initial election is made.

To serve and receive documents by e-mail, you must designate your e-mail addresses by using the **Designation of Current Mailing and E-mail Address**, Florida Supreme Court Approved Family Law Form 12.915, and you must provide your e-mail address on each form on which your signature appears. Please **CAREFULLY** read the rules and instructions for: **Certificate of Service (General)**, Florida Supreme Court Approved Family Law Form 12.914;

Designation of Current Mailing and E-mail Address, Florida Supreme Court Approved Family Law Form 12.915; and Florida Rule of Judicial Administration 2.516.

Special Notes . . .

If you fear that disclosing your address would put you in danger, you should complete a **Request for Confidential Filing of Address,** Florida Supreme Court Approved Family Law Form 12.980(h), and file it with the clerk of the circuit court and write confidential in the space provided for your address on the petition.

Added Mar. 25, 2004 (871 So.2d 113). Amended July 8, 2004 (880 So.2d 579); June 7, 2012 (93 So.3d 194); March 26, 2015, effective March 26, 2015 (2015 WL 1343088).

Form 12.980(r). Temporary Injunction for Protection Against Sexual Violence

IN THE CIRCUIT COURT OF THE ____________ JUDICIAL CIRCUIT,
IN AND FOR ______________________ COUNTY, FLORIDA

Case No.: ______________
Division: ______________

______________________________,
Petitioner,
and

______________________________,
Respondent.

TEMPORARY INJUNCTION FOR PROTECTION AGAINST SEXUAL VIOLENCE

The Petition for Injunction for Protection Against Sexual Violence under Section 784.046, Florida Statutes, and other papers filed in this Court have been reviewed. Under the laws of Florida, the Court has jurisdiction of the petitioner and the subject matter and has jurisdiction of the respondent upon service of the temporary injunction. The term Petitioner as used in this injunction includes the person on whose behalf this injunction is entered.

It is intended that this protection order meet the requirements of 18 U.S.C. Section 2265 and therefore intended that it be accorded full faith and credit by the court of another state or Indian tribe and enforced as if it were the order of the enforcing state or of the Indian tribe.

SECTION I. NOTICE OF HEARING

Because this Temporary Injunction for Protection Against Sexual Violence has been issued without notice to Respondent, the Petitioner and Respondent are instructed that they are scheduled to appear and testify at a hearing regarding this matter on *{date}* ____________________, at ________ a.m./p.m., when the Court will consider whether to issue a Final Judgment of Injunction for Protection Against Sexual Violence, which shall remain in effect until modified or dissolved by the Court, and whether other things should be ordered. The hearing will be before The Honorable *{name}*______________________, at *{room name/number, location, address, city}* ______________ ____, Florida. If Petitioner and/or Respondent do not appear, this temporary injunction may be continued in force, extended, or dismissed, and/or additional orders may be granted, including entry of a permanent injunction and the imposition of court costs. Petitioner and Respondent will be bound by the terms of any injunction or order issued at the final hearing. All witnesses and evidence, if any, must be presented at this time.

IF EITHER PETITIONER OR RESPONDENT DO NOT APPEAR AT THE FINAL HEARING, HE OR SHE WILL BE

BOUND BY THE TERMS OF ANY INJUNCTION OR ORDER ISSUED IN THIS MATTER.

NOTICE: Because this is a civil case, there is no requirement that these proceedings be transcribed at public expense.

YOU ARE ADVISED THAT IN THIS COURT:

a._____a court reporter is provided by the court.

b.____electronic recording only is provided by the court. A party may arrange in advance for the services of and provide for a court reporter to prepare a written transcript of the proceedings at that party's expense.

c.____ neither electronic recording nor court reporting services are provided by the court. A party may arrange in advance for the services of and provide for a court reporter to prepare a written transcript of the proceedings at that party's expense.

A RECORD, WHICH INCLUDES A TRANSCRIPT, MAY BE REQUIRED TO SUPPORT AN APPEAL. THE PARTY SEEKING THE APPEAL IS RESPONSIBLE FOR HAVING THE TRANSCRIPT PREPARED BY A COURT REPORTER. THE TRANSCRIPT MUST BE FILED WITH THE REVIEWING COURT OR THE APPEAL MAY BE DENIED.

If you are a person with a disability who needs any accommodation in order to participate in this proceeding, you are entitled, at no cost to you, to the provision of certain assistance. Please contact____ *{identify applicable court personnel by name, address, and telephone number}* at least 7 days before your scheduled court appearance, or immediately upon receiving this notification if the time before the scheduled appearance is less than 7 days; if you are hearing or voice impaired, call 711.

SECTION II. FINDINGS

The statements made under oath by Petitioner make it appear that Section 784.046, Florida Statutes, applies to the parties, that Petitioner is a victim of sexual violence by Respondent and meets the requirements for an injunction established by law.

SECTION III. TEMPORARY INJUNCTION AND TERMS

This injunction shall be effective until the hearing set above and in no event for longer than 15 days, unless extended by court order or unless the Respondent is incarcerated, and if incarcerated, shall be effective for 15 days following the date Respondent is released from incarceration. If a final order of

injunction is issued, the terms of this temporary injunction will be extended until service of the final injunction is effected upon Respondent. This injunction is valid and enforceable in all counties of the State of Florida. The terms of this injunction may not be changed by either party alone or by both parties together. Only the Court may modify the terms of this injunction. Either party may ask the Court to change or end this injunction.

Willful violation of the terms of this injunction, such as refusing to vacate the dwelling which the parties share, going to Petitioner's residence, place of employment, school, or other place prohibited in this injunction, telephoning, contacting or communicating with Petitioner, if prohibited by this injunction, or committing an act of sexual violence against Petitioner constitutes a misdemeanor of the first degree punishable by up to one year in jail, as provided by Sections 775.082 and 775.083, Florida Statutes.

Any party violating this injunction may be subject to civil or indirect criminal contempt proceedings, including the imposition of a fine or imprisonment and also may be charged with a crime punishable by a fine, jail, or both, as provided by Florida Statutes.

ORDERED and ADJUDGED:

1. **Violence Prohibited.** Respondent shall not commit, or cause any other person to commit, any acts of violence against Petitioner, including assault, aggravated assault, battery, aggravated battery, sexual assault, sexual battery, stalking, aggravated stalking, kidnapping, or false imprisonment, or any criminal offense resulting in physical injury or death. Respondent shall not commit any other violation of the injunction through an intentional unlawful threat, word, or act to do violence to Petitioner.

2. **No Contact. Respondent shall have no contact with the Petitioner unless otherwise provided in this section.**

a. Unless otherwise provided herein, Respondent shall have no contact with Petitioner. Respondent shall not directly or indirectly contact Petitioner in person, by mail, e-mail, fax, telephone, through another person, or in any other manner. Further, Respondent shall not contact or have any third party contact anyone connected with Petitioner's employment or school to inquire about Petitioner or to send any messages to Petitioner. Unless otherwise provided herein, **Respondent shall not go to, in, or within 500 feet of:** Petitioner's current residence *{list address}*____

____

or any residence to which Petitioner may move; Petitioner's current or any subsequent place of employment *{list address of current employment}* ______________________________________

____

or place where Petitioner attends school *{list address of school}* ______________________________

____;

or the following other places (if requested by Petitioner) where Petitioner or Petitioner's minor child(ren) go often:

____

____

____

____
____

*{Initial **if** applies; write N/A **if not** applicable}*

b. _____Respondent may not knowingly come within 100 feet of Petitioner's automobile at any time.

c. _____Other provisions regarding contact:_______________________________________
____.

3. **Firearms.**

*{Initial **all** that apply; write N/A **if does not** apply}*

a. ____Respondent shall not use or possess a firearm or ammunition.

b. ____Respondent shall surrender any firearms and ammunition in Respondent's possession to the ____________________County Sheriff's Department.

c. ____Other directives relating to firearms and ammunition: ____________________________
____
____.

4. **Mailing Address or Designated E-Mail Address(es).** Respondent shall notify the Clerk of the Court of any change in either his or her mailing address, or designated e-mail address(es), within 10 days of the change. All further papers (excluding pleadings requiring personal service) shall be served either by mail to Respondent's last known mailing address or by e-mail to Respondent's designated e-mail address(es). Service by mail shall be complete upon mailing or e-mailing.

5. **Additional order(s) necessary to protect Petitioner from sexual violence:**______________
____
____
____
____
____.

SECTION IV. OTHER SPECIAL PROVISIONS

{This section to be used for inclusion of local provisions approved by the chief judge as provided in Florida Family Law Rule 12.610.}

____
____
____

SECTION V. DIRECTIONS TO LAW ENFORCEMENT OFFICER IN ENFORCING THIS INJUNCTION

{Unless ordered otherwise by the judge, all provisions in this injunction are considered mandatory provisions and should be interpreted as part of this injunction.}

1. The Sheriff of _____________ County, or any other authorized officer, is ordered to serve this temporary injunction upon Respondent as soon as possible after its issuance.

2. **This injunction is valid and enforceable in all counties of the State of Florida.** Violation of this injunction should be reported to the appropriate law enforcement agency. Law enforcement officers of the jurisdiction in which a violation of this injunction occurs shall enforce the provisions of this injunction and are authorized to arrest without a warrant pursuant to section 901.15, Florida Statutes, for any violation of its provisions, which constitutes a criminal act under Section 784.047, Florida Statutes.

3. Should any Florida law enforcement officer having jurisdiction have probable cause to believe that Respondent has knowingly violated this injunction, the officer may arrest Respondent, confine him/her in the county jail without bail, and shall bring him/her before the Initial Appearance Judge on the next regular court day so that Respondent can be dealt with according to law. The arresting agent shall notify the State Attorney's Office immediately after arrest. THIS INJUNCTION IS ENFORCEABLE IN ALL COUNTIES OF FLORIDA AND LAW ENFORCEMENT OFFICERS MAY EFFECT ARRESTS PURSUANT TO SECTION 901.15(6), FLORIDA STATUTES.

4. **Reporting alleged violations.** If Respondent violates the terms of this injunction and there has not been an arrest, Petitioner may contact the Clerk of the Circuit Court of the county in which the violation occurred and complete an affidavit in support of the violation or Petitioner may contact the State Attorney's office for assistance in filing an action for indirect civil contempt or indirect criminal contempt. Upon receiving such a report, the State Attorney is hereby appointed to prosecute such violations by indirect criminal contempt proceedings, or the State Attorney may decide to file a criminal charge, if warranted by the evidence.

DONE AND ORDERED in ______________________, Florida on ______________________.

____
CIRCUIT JUDGE

COPIES TO:
Sheriff of ______________________ County

Petitioner: (or his or her attorney)
____ by U. S. Mail
____ by hand delivery in open court

Florida Supreme Court Approved Family Law Form 12.980(r), Temporary Injunction for Protection Against Sexual Violence (03/15)

____ by e-mail to designated e-mail address(es)

Respondent:
_____ forwarded to sheriff for service
____ State Attorney's Office
____ Other: ________________________

I CERTIFY the foregoing is a true copy of the original Temporary Injunction for Protection Against Sexual Violence as it appears on file in the office of the Clerk of the Circuit Court of ________________ County, Florida, and that I have furnished copies of this order as indicated above.

CLERK OF THE CIRCUIT COURT

(SEAL)

By: ________________________
Deputy Clerk or Judicial Assistant

Florida Supreme Court Approved Family Law Form 12.980(r), Temporary Injunction for Protection Against Sexual Violence (03/15)

Added Mar. 25, 2004 (871 So.2d 113). Amended July 8, 2004 (880 So.2d 579); June 7, 2012 (93 So.3d 194); March 26, 2015, effective March 26, 2015 (2015 WL 1343088).

Form 12.980(s). Final Judgment of Injunction for Protection Against Sexual Violence (After Notice)

IN THE CIRCUIT COURT OF THE _______ JUDICIAL CIRCUIT,
IN AND FOR _________________ COUNTY, FLORIDA

Case No.: ________________
Division: ________________

______________________________,
Petitioner,
and

______________________________,
Respondent.

FINAL JUDGMENT OF INJUNCTION FOR PROTECTION AGAINST SEXUAL VIOLENCE (AFTER NOTICE)

The Petition for Injunction for Protection Against Sexual Violence under Section 784.046, Florida Statutes, and other papers filed in this Court have been reviewed. The Court has jurisdiction of the parties and the subject matter. The term Petitioner as used in this injunction includes the person on whose behalf this injunction is entered.

It is intended that this protection order meet the requirements of 18 U.S.C. Section 2265 and therefore intended that it be accorded full faith and credit by the court of another state or Indian tribe and enforced as if it were the order of the enforcing state or of the Indian tribe.

SECTION I. HEARING

This cause came before the Court for a hearing to determine whether an Injunction for Protection Against Sexual Violence in this case should be:

____ issued ____ modified ____ extended.

The hearing was attended by:
____Petitioner
____Petitioner's Counsel
____Respondent
____Respondent's Counsel

SECTION II. FINDINGS

On *{date}* ____________________, a notice of this hearing was served on Respondent together with a copy of Petitioner's petition to this Court and the temporary injunction, if issued. Service was within the time required by Florida law, and Respondent was afforded an opportunity to be heard.

After hearing the testimony of each party present and of any witnesses, or upon consent of Respondent, the Court finds, based on the specific facts of this case, that Petitioner is a victim of sexual violence by Respondent and meets the requirements for an injunction established by law.

SECTION III. INJUNCTION AND TERMS

This injunction shall be in full force and effect until ____ further order of the Court or ____ *{date}* _____________________________. This injunction is valid and enforceable throughout all counties in the State of Florida. The terms of this injunction may not be changed by either party alone or by both parties together. Only the Court may modify the terms of this injunction. Either party may ask the Court to change or end this injunction.

Willful violation of the terms of this injunction, such as refusing to vacate the dwelling which the parties share, going to Petitioner's residence, place of employment, school, or other place prohibited in this injunction, telephoning, contacting or communicating with Petitioner, if prohibited by this injunction, or committing an act of sexual violence against Petitioner constitutes a misdemeanor of the first degree punishable by up to one year in jail, as provided by Sections 775.082 and 775.083, Florida Statutes.

Any party violating this injunction shall be subject to civil or indirect criminal contempt proceedings, including the imposition of a fine or imprisonment, and also may be charged with a crime punishable by a fine, jail, or both, as provided by Florida Statutes.

ORDERED and ADJUDGED:

1. **Violence Prohibited.** Respondent shall not commit, or cause any other person to commit, any acts of violence against Petitioner, including assault, aggravated assault, battery, aggravated battery, sexual assault, sexual battery, stalking, aggravated stalking, kidnapping, or false imprisonment, or any criminal offense resulting in physical injury or death. Respondent shall not commit any other violation of the injunction through an intentional unlawful threat, word or act to do violence to the Petitioner.

2. **No Contact. Respondent shall have no contact with Petitioner unless otherwise provided in this section.**

a. Unless otherwise provided herein, Respondent shall have no contact with Petitioner. Respondent shall not directly or indirectly contact Petitioner in person, by mail, e-mail, fax, telephone, through another person, or in any other manner. Further, Respondent shall not contact or have any third party contact anyone connected with Petitioner's employment or school to inquire about Petitioner or to send any messages to Petitioner. Unless otherwise provided herein, **Respondent shall not go to, in, or within 500 feet of:** Petitioner's current residence *{list address}*____
____
____or any residence to which Petitioner may move; Petitioner's current or any subsequent place of employment *{list address of current employment}*____

or place where Petitioner attends school *{list address of school}*____;

or the following other places (if requested by Petitioner) where Petitioner or Petitioner's minor child(ren) go often: ____.

*{Initial **if** applies; write N/A **if not** applicable}*

b.____ Respondent may not knowingly come within 100 feet of Petitioner's automobile at any time.

c. ____Other provisions regarding contact: ____.

3. **Firearms.**

*{Initial **all** that apply; write N/A **if does not** apply}*

a. ____Respondent shall not use or possess a firearm or ammunition.

b. ____Respondent shall surrender any firearms and ammunition in the Respondent's possession to the ____________________ County Sheriff's Department.

c. ____Other directives relating to firearms and ammunition: ____.

4. **Mailing Address or Designated E-Mail Address(es).** Respondent shall notify the Clerk of the Court of any change in either his or her mailing address, or designated e-mail address(es), within 10 days of the change. All further papers (excluding pleadings requiring personal service) shall be served either by mail to Respondent's last known mailing address or by e-mail to Respondent's designated e-mail address(es). Service shall be complete upon mailing or e-mailing.

5. **Additional order(s) necessary to protect Petitioner from sexual violence:** ____.

SECTION IV. OTHER SPECIAL PROVISIONS

{This section to be used for inclusion of local provisions approved by the chief judge as provided in Florida Family Law Rule 12.610.}

____

____

____.

SECTION V. DIRECTIONS TO LAW ENFORCEMENT OFFICER IN ENFORCING THIS INJUNCTION

{Unless ordered otherwise by the judge, all provisions in this injunction are considered mandatory provisions and should be interpreted as part of this injunction.}

1. **This injunction is valid and enforceable in all counties of the State of Florida.** Violation of this injunction should be reported to the appropriate law enforcement agency. Law enforcement officers of the jurisdiction in which a violation of this injunction occurs shall enforce the provisions of this injunction and are authorized to arrest without a warrant pursuant to Section 901.15, Florida Statutes, for any violation of its provision, which constitutes a criminal act under Section 784.047, Florida Statutes.

2. Should any Florida law enforcement officer having jurisdiction have probable cause to believe that Respondent has knowingly violated this injunction, the officer may arrest Respondent, confine him/her in the county jail without bail, and shall bring him/her before the Initial Appearance Judge on the next regular court day so that Respondent can be dealt with according to law. The arresting agent shall notify the State Attorney's Office immediately after arrest. THIS INJUNCTION IS ENFORCEABLE IN ALL COUNTIES OF FLORIDA AND LAW ENFORCEMENT OFFICERS MAY EFFECT ARRESTS PURSUANT TO SECTION 901.15(6), FLORIDA STATUTES.

3. **Reporting alleged violations.** If Respondent violates the terms of this injunction and there has not been an arrest, Petitioner may contact the Clerk of the Circuit Court of the county in which the violation occurred and complete an affidavit in support of the violation or Petitioner may contact the State Attorney's Office for assistance in filing an action for indirect civil contempt or indirect criminal contempt. Upon receiving such a report, the State Attorney is hereby appointed to prosecute such violations by indirect criminal proceedings, or the State Attorney may decide to file a criminal charge, if warranted by the evidence.

4. Respondent, upon service of this injunction, shall be deemed to have knowledge of and to be bound by all matters occurring at the hearing and on the face of this injunction.

5. The temporary injunction, if any, entered in this case is extended until such time as service of this injunction is effected upon Respondent.

DONE AND ORDERED in ______________________, Florida on ________________.

____

CIRCUIT JUDGE

Florida Supreme Court Approved Family Law Form 12.980(s), Final Judgment of Injunction for Protection Against Sexual Violence (After Notice) (03/15)

COPIES TO:
Sheriff of ____________ County

Petitioner (or his or her attorney):
____ by U. S. Mail
____ by hand delivery in open court (Petitioner must acknowledge receipt in writing on the face of the original order--see below.)
____ by e-mail to designated e-mail address

Respondent (or his or her attorney):
____ forwarded to sheriff for service
____ by hand delivery in open court (Respondent must acknowledge receipt in writing on the face of the original order--see below.)
____ by certified mail (may only be used when Respondent is present at the hearing and Respondent fails or refuses to acknowledge the receipt of a certified copy of this injunction.)

____ State Attorney's Office
____ Other ______________________

I CERTIFY the foregoing is a true copy of the original Final Judgment of Injunction for Protection Against Sexual Violence as it appears on file in the office of the Clerk of the Circuit Court of ____________ County, Florida, and that I have furnished copies of this order as indicated above.

CLERK OF THE CIRCUIT COURT

(SEAL)
By: ______________________________
Deputy Clerk or Judicial Assistant

ACKNOWLEDGMENT

I, *{Name of Petitioner}* ______________________, acknowledge receipt of a certified copy of this

Florida Supreme Court Approved Family Law Form 12.980(s), Final Judgment of Injunction for Protection Against Sexual Violence (After Notice) (03/15)

Injunction for Protection.

____
Petitioner

ACKNOWLEDGMENT

I, *{Name of Respondent}* ______________________, acknowledge receipt of a certified copy of this Injunction for Protection.

____
Respondent

Florida Supreme Court Approved Family Law Form 12.980(s), Final Judgment of Injunction for Protection Against Sexual Violence (After Notice) (03/15)

Added Mar. 25, 2004 (871 So.2d 113). Amended July 8, 2004 (880 So.2d 579); June 7, 2012 (93 So.3d 194); March 26, 2015, effective March 26, 2015 (2015 WL 1343088).

Form 12.980(t). Petition for Injunction for Protection Against Stalking

IN THE CIRCUIT COURT OF THE ________ JUDICIAL CIRCUIT,
IN AND FOR ____________________ COUNTY, FLORIDA

Case No.: ____________________
Division: ____________________

______________________________,
Petitioner,
and

______________________________,
Respondent.

PETITION FOR INJUNCTION FOR PROTECTION AGAINST STALKING

I, *{full legal name}*____, being sworn, certify that the following statements are true:

SECTION I. PETITIONER
(This section is about you. It must be completed; **however, if you require that your address be confidential for safety reasons,** you should complete and file a **Request for Confidential Filing of Address,** Florida Supreme Court Approved Family Law Form 12.980(h), and write confidential in the space provided on this form for your address and telephone number.)

1. Petitioner resides at the following address: *{address, city, state, zip code}* ________________
____.

{Indicate if applicable}
_____**Petitioner seeks an injunction for protection on behalf of a minor child.** Petitioner is the parent or legal guardian of *{full legal name}*______________________________,
a minor child who is living at home.

2. Petitioner's attorney's name, address, and telephone number is: ____________________
____.
(If you do not have an attorney, write "none.")

SECTION II. RESPONDENT
(This section is about the person you want to be protected from. It must be completed.)

1. Respondent resides at the following address: *{provide last known street address, city, state, and zip code}* ____
____.

2. Respondent's last known place of employment: ______________________
Employment address: ______________________
Working hours of Respondent: ______________________

3. Physical description of Respondent:
Race: ________ Sex: Male_____ Female_____ Date of Birth: ______________________
Height: Weight: _______ Eye Color: _________ Hair Color: ___
Distinguishing marks and/or scars: ______________________
Vehicle: (make/model)________ Color: ________ Tag Number *(if known)*________

4. Other names Respondent goes by (*aliases or nicknames*): ______________________
____

5. Respondent's attorney's name, address, and telephone number is: ______________________
____

(If you do not know whether Respondent has an attorney, write "unknown." If Respondent does not have an attorney, write "none.")

SECTION III. CASE HISTORY AND REASON FOR SEEKING PETITION (This section must be completed.)

1. Has Petitioner ever received or tried to get an injunction for protection against stalking against Respondent in this or any other court?
____ Yes ____ No If yes, what happened in that case? *{include case number, if known}*
____
______________________.

2. Has Respondent ever received or tried to get an injunction for protection against stalking against Petitioner in this or any other court?
____ Yes ____ No If yes, what happened in that case? *{include case number, if known}*________
____
______________________.

3. Describe any other court case that is either going on now or that happened in the past **between Petitioner and Respondent** *{include case number, if known}*: ______________________
____
______________________.

4. Petitioner is a victim of stalking because Respondent has: *{please mark all sections that apply}*
a. ____Committed stalking;
b. ____Previously threatened, harassed, stalked, cyberstalked, or physically abused the Petitioner;
c. ____Threatened to harm Petitioner or family members or individuals closely associated with Petitioner;

d. ____Intentionally injured or killed a family pet;
e. ____Used, or threatened to use, against Petitioner any weapons such as guns or knives;
f. ____A criminal history involving violence or the threat or violence, if known;
g. ____Another order of protection issued against him or her previously from another jurisdiction, if known;
h. ____ Destroyed personal property, including, but not limited to, telephones or other communication equipment, clothing, or other items belonging to Petitioner.

5. Below is a description of the specific incidents of stalking or cyberstalking: *{for cyberstalking, please include a description of all evidence of contacts and/or threats made by Respondent in voice messages, texts, emails, or other electronic communication}*
On *{dates}* ________________________ the following incidents of stalking occurred at the following locations:
{the locations may include, but need not be limited to, a home, school, or place of employment}
____
____
____
____.

_____Please indicate here if you are attaching additional pages to continue these facts.

6. **Additional Information**
____Respondent owns, has, and/or is known to have guns or other weapons.
Describe weapon(s) and where they may be located, if known: _______________________
____.

SECTION IV. INJUNCTION *{This section must be completed}*

1. Petitioner asks the Court to enter a **TEMPORARY INJUNCTION** for protection against stalking that will be in place from now until the scheduled hearing in this matter, which will immediately restrain Respondent from committing any acts of stalking, and which will provide any terms the Court deems necessary for the protection of a victim of stalking, including any injunctions or directives to law enforcement agencies.

2. Petitioner asks the Court to enter, after a hearing has been held on this petition, a **FINAL JUDGMENT** for protection against stalking prohibiting Respondent from committing any acts of stalking against Petitioner **and**:

a. prohibiting Respondent from going to or within 500 feet of any place Petitioner lives, or to any specified place regularly frequented by Petitioner and any named family members or individuals closely associated with Petitioner; ____
____;

b. prohibiting Respondent from going to or within 500 feet of Petitioner's place(s) of employment or the school that Petitioner attends; the address of Petitioner's place(s) of employment and/or school is:_____
____;

c. prohibiting Respondent from contacting Petitioner by telephone, mail, by e-mail, in writing, through another person, or in any other manner;

d. ordering Respondent that he or she shall not have in his or her care, custody, possession, or control any firearm or ammunition;

e. prohibiting Respondent from knowingly and intentionally going to or within 100 feet of Petitioner's motor vehicle, whether or not that vehicle is occupied;

3. Petitioner asks the Court to enter any other terms it deems necessary to protect Petitioner from stalking by Respondent.

I UNDERSTAND THAT BY FILING THIS PETITION, I AM ASKING THE COURT TO HOLD A HEARING ON THIS PETITION, THAT BOTH THE RESPONDENT AND I WILL BE NOTIFIED OF THE HEARING, AND THAT I MUST APPEAR AT THE HEARING. I UNDERSTAND THAT IF EITHER THE RESPONDENT OR I FAIL TO APPEAR AT THE FINAL HEARING, WE WILL BE BOUND BY THE TERMS OF ANY INJUNCTION OR ORDER ISSUED AT THAT HEARING.

I HAVE READ EVERY STATEMENT MADE IN THIS PETITION AND EACH STATEMENT IS TRUE AND CORRECT. I UNDERSTAND THAT THE STATEMENTS MADE IN THIS PETITION ARE BEING MADE UNDER PENALTY OF PERJURY, PUNISHABLE AS PROVIDED IN SECTION 837.02, FLORIDA STATUTES.

Dated: ____________

____
Signature of Petitioner
Printed Name: ____________
Address: ____________
City, State, Zip: ____________
Telephone Number: ____________

Designated E-Mail Address(es): ____________

STATE OF FLORIDA
COUNTY OF ____________

Sworn to or affirmed and signed before me on ____________ by ____________.

____
NOTARY PUBLIC or DEPUTY CLERK

____
[Print, type, or stamp commissioned name of notary or clerk.]
____ Personally known
____ Produced identification
____ Type of identification produced ____________

INSTRUCTIONS FOR FLORIDA SUPREME COURT APPROVED FAMILY LAW FORM 12.980(t) PETITION FOR INJUNCTION FOR PROTECTION AGAINST STALKING (03/15)

When should this form be used?

If you are a victim of stalking, you can use this form to ask the court for a protective order prohibiting stalking. Stalking means the repeated following, harassment, or cyberstalking of one person by another. Cyberstalk means to engage in a course of conduct to communicate, or to cause to be communicated, words, images, or language by or through the use of electronic mail or electronic communication, directed at a specific person, causing substantial emotional distress to that person and serving no legitimate purpose.

Because you are making a request to the court, you are called the **petitioner**. The person whom you are asking the court to protect you from is called the **respondent**. If you are under the age of eighteen and have never been married or had the disabilities of nonage removed by a court, and are living at home, one of your parents or your legal guardian must sign this petition on your behalf.

The parent or legal guardian of any minor child *who is living at home* may seek an injunction for protection against stalking on behalf of the minor child.

If the respondent is your **spouse**, former spouse, related to you by blood or marriage, living with you now or has lived with you in the past (if you are or were living as a family), or the other parent of your child(ren), whether or not you have ever been married or ever lived together, you may, instead, choose to use the **Petition for Injunction for Protection Against Domestic Violence**, Florida Supreme Court Approved Family Law Form 12.980(a), rather than this form.

This form should be typed or printed in black ink. You should complete this form (giving as much detail as possible) and sign it the presence of a notary or in front of the **clerk of the circuit court** in one of the following: the circuit where you currently or temporarily reside; the circuit where the respondent resides; or the circuit where the stalking occurred. The clerk will take your completed petition to a **judge**. You should keep a copy for your records. If have any questions or need assistance completing this form, the clerk or **family law intake staff** will help you. There is no filing fee for a petition for protection against stalking.

What should I do if the judge grants my petition?

If the facts contained in your petition convince the judge that stalking or cyberstalking exists, the judge will sign a **Temporary Injunction for Protection Against Stalking**, Florida Supreme Court Approved Family Law Form 12.980(u). A temporary injunction is issued without notice to the respondent. The clerk will give your **petition**, the temporary injunction, and any other papers filed with your petition to the sheriff or other law enforcement officer for **personal service** on the respondent. The temporary injunction will take effect immediately after the respondent is served with a copy of it. It lasts until a **hearing** can be held or for a period of 15 days, whichever comes first.

The court may extend the temporary injunction beyond 15 days for a good reason, which may include failure to obtain **service** on the respondent.

The temporary injunction is issued **ex parte**. This means that the judge has considered only the information presented by one side—YOU. Section I of the temporary injunction gives a date that you should appear in court for a hearing. You will be expected to testify about the facts in your petition. The respondent will be given the opportunity to testify at this hearing also. At the hearing, the judge will decide whether to issue a **Final Judgment of Injunction for Protection Against Stalking (After Notice)**, Florida Supreme Court Approved Family Law Form 12.980(v), which will remain in effect for a specific time period or until modified or dissolved by the court. **If either you or the respondent do not appear at the hearing, the temporary injunction may be continued in force, extended, or dismissed, and/or additional orders may be granted, including entry of a permanent injunction and the imposition of court costs. You and the respondent will be bound by the terms of any injunction or order issued at the final hearing.**

IF EITHER YOU OR THE RESPONDENT DO NOT APPEAR AT THE FINAL HEARING, YOU WILL BOTH BE BOUND BY THE TERMS OF ANY INJUNCTION OR ORDER ISSUED IN THIS MATTER.

If the judge signs a temporary or final injunction, the clerk will provide you with the necessary copies. **Make sure that you keep one certified copy of the injunction with you at all times!**

What can I do if the judge denies my petition or does not issue a Temporary Injunction?

If your petition is denied, you may amend your petition by filing a **Supplemental Affidavit in Support of Petition for Injunction for Protection**, Florida Supreme Court Approved Family Law Form 12.980(g). If the only ground for not granting an ex parte temporary injunction is no appearance of immediate and present danger of stalking, the court shall set a full hearing on your petition for injunction at the earliest possible time. The respondent will be notified by **personal service** of your petition and the hearing. You must attend the hearing, present facts, and bring evidence that supports your petition; failure to attend the hearing may result in dismissal of your petition.

Where can I look for more information?

Before proceeding, you should read General Information for Self–Represented Litigants found at the beginning of these forms. The words that are in **bold underline** are defined in that section. The clerk of the circuit court or **family law intake staff** will help you complete any necessary forms. For further information, see Section 784.0485, Florida Statutes, and Rule 12.610, Florida Family Law Rules of Procedure.

IMPORTANT INFORMATION REGARDING E–FILING

The Florida Rules of Judicial Administration now require that all petitions, pleadings, and documents be filed electronically except in certain circumstances. **Self-represented litigants may file petitions or other pleadings or documents electronically; however, they are not required to do so.** If you choose to file your pleadings or other documents electronically, you must do so in accordance with Florida Rule of Judicial Administration 2.525, and you must follow the procedures of the judicial circuit in which you file. **The rules and procedures should be carefully read and followed.**

IMPORTANT INFORMATION REGARDING E–SERVICE ELECTION

After the initial service of process of the petition or supplemental petition by the Sheriff or certified process server, the Florida Rules of Judicial Administration now require that all documents required or permitted to be served on the other party must be served by electronic mail (e-mail) except in certain circumstances. **You must strictly comply with the format requirements set forth in the Rules of Judicial Administration.**

SELF–REPRESENTED LITIGANTS MAY SERVE DOCUMENTS BY E–MAIL; HOWEVER, THEY ARE NOT REQUIRED TO DO SO. If a self-represented litigant elects to serve and receive documents by e-mail, the procedures must always be followed once the initial election is made.

To serve and receive documents by e-mail, you must designate your e-mail addresses by using the **Designation of Current Mailing and E-mail Address**, Florida Supreme Court Approved Family Law Form 12.915, and you must provide your e-mail address on each form on which your signature appears. Please **CAREFULLY** read the rules and instructions for: **Certificate of Service (General),** Florida Supreme Court Approved Family Law Form 12.914; **Designation of Current Mailing and E-mail Address**, Florida Supreme Court Approved Family Law Form 12.915; and Florida Rule of Judicial Administration 2.516.

Special Notes

If you require that your address be confidential for safety reasons, you should complete a **Request for Confidential Filing of Address**, Florida Supreme Court Approved Family Law Form 12.980(h), and file it with the clerk of the circuit. You should then write confidential in the space provided on the petition.

Added May 9, 2013 (113 So.3d 781). Amended March 26, 2015, effective March 26, 2015 (2015 WL 1343088).

Form 12.980(u). Temporary Injunction for Protection Against Stalking

IN THE CIRCUIT COURT OF THE ____________ JUDICIAL CIRCUIT,
IN AND FOR ____________________ COUNTY, FLORIDA

Case No.: ____________________
Division: ____________________

____________________________,
Petitioner,
and

____________________________,
Respondent.

TEMPORARY INJUNCTION FOR PROTECTION AGAINST STALKING

The Petition for Injunction for Protection Against Stalking under Section 784.0485, Florida Statutes, and other papers filed in this Court have been reviewed. Under the laws of Florida, the Court has jurisdiction of the Petitioner and the subject matter, and has jurisdiction of the Respondent upon service of the temporary injunction. The term Petitioner as used in this injunction includes the person on whose behalf this injunction is entered.

It is intended that this protection order meet the requirements of 18 U.S.C. Section 2265 and therefore intended that it be accorded full faith and credit by the court of another state or Indian tribe and enforced as if it were the order of the enforcing state or of the Indian tribe.

SECTION I. NOTICE OF HEARING

Because this Temporary Injunction for Protection Against Stalking has been issued without notice to Respondent, Petitioner and Respondent are instructed that they are scheduled to appear and testify at a hearing regarding this matter on *{date}* ____________________, at ____________ a.m./p.m., when the Court will consider whether it should issue a Final Judgment of Injunction for Protection Against Stalking, which shall remain in effect until modified or dissolved by the Court, and whether other things should be ordered. The hearing will be before The Honorable *{name}* ____________________, at the following address: ____ ____, Florida. If Petitioner and/or Respondent do not appear, this temporary injunction may be continued in force, extended, or dismissed, and/or additional orders may be granted, including entry of a permanent injunction and the imposition of court costs. All witnesses and evidence, if any, must be presented at this time. **Petitioner and Respondent will be bound by the terms of any injunction or order issued at the final hearing.**

IF EITHER PETITIONER OR RESPONDENT DO NOT APPEAR AT THE FINAL HEARING, HE OR SHE WILL BE BOUND BY THE TERMS OF ANY INJUNCTION OR ORDER ISSUED IN THIS MATTER.

NOTICE: Because this is a civil case, there is no requirement that these proceedings be transcribed at

public expense.
YOU ARE ADVISED THAT IN THIS COURT:

a.____ a court reporter is provided by the court.

b.____ electronic recording only is provided by the court. A party may arrange in advance for the services of and provide for a court reporter to prepare a written transcript of the proceedings at that party's expense.

A RECORD, WHICH INCLUDES A TRANSCRIPT, MAY BE REQUIRED TO SUPPORT AN APPEAL. THE PARTY SEEKING THE APPEAL IS RESPONSIBLE FOR HAVING THE TRANSCRIPT PREPARED BY A COURT REPORTER. THE TRANSCRIPT MUST BE FILED WITH THE REVIEWING COURT OR THE APPEAL MAY BE DENIED.

If you are a person with a disability who needs any accommodation in order to participate in this proceeding, you are entitled, at no cost to you, to the provision of certain assistance. Please contact________________________ ____ *{identify applicable court personnel by name, address, and telephone number}* at least 7 days before your scheduled court appearance, or immediately upon receiving this notification if the time before the scheduled appearance is less than 7 days; if you are hearing or voice impaired, call 711.

SECTION II. FINDINGS

The statements made under oath by Petitioner make it appear that Section 784.0485, Florida Statutes, applies to the parties, and that stalking exists.

SECTION III. TEMPORARY INJUNCTION AND TERMS

This injunction shall be in effect until the hearing set above and in no event for longer than 15 days, unless extended by court order. If a final order of injunction is issued, the terms of this temporary injunction will be extended until service of the final injunction is effected upon Respondent. This injunction is valid and enforceable in all counties of the State of Florida. The terms of this injunction may not be changed by either party alone or by both parties together. Only the Court may modify the terms of this injunction. Either party may ask the Court to change or end this injunction.

Willful violation of the terms of this injunction, such as: committing an act of stalking against Petitioner; going to or being within 500 feet of Petitioner's residence, place of employment, school, or other place prohibited in this injunction; knowingly and intentionally coming within 100 feet of Petitioner's motor vehicle, whether or not that vehicle is occupied; committing any other violation of this injunction through an intentional unlawful threat, word or act to do violence to Petitioner; telephoning, contacting or communicating with Petitioner, unless indirect contact through a third

party is specifically allowed by this injunction; defacing or destroying Petitioner's personal property, including Petitioner's motor vehicle; or refusing to surrender firearms or ammunition if ordered to so by the Court, constitutes a misdemeanor of the first degree punishable as provided by Sections 775.082 and 775.083, Florida Statutes.

Any party violating this injunction may be subject to civil or indirect criminal contempt proceedings, including the imposition of a fine or imprisonment, and also may be charged with a crime punishable by a fine, jail, or both, as provided by Florida Statutes.

ORDERED and ADJUDGED:

1. **Prohibited Actions.** Respondent shall not commit, or cause any other person to commit, any acts of stalking against Petitioner, including stalking, cyberstalking, aggravated stalking, or any criminal offense resulting in physical injury or death. Respondent shall not commit any other violation of this injunction through an intentional unlawful threat, word, or act to do violence to Petitioner.

2. **No Contact. Respondent shall have no contact with the Petitioner unless otherwise provided in this section.**

a. Unless otherwise provided herein, Respondent shall have **no** contact with Petitioner. Respondent shall not directly or indirectly contact Petitioner in person, by mail, e-mail, fax, telephone, through another person, or in any other manner, including any electronic means or use of social media. Further, Respondent shall not contact or have any third party contact anyone connected with Petitioner's employment or school to inquire about Petitioner or to send any messages to Petitioner. Unless otherwise provided herein, **Respondent shall not go to, in, or within 500 feet of:**

b. Petitioner's current residence *{list address}*____ or any residence to which Petitioner may move;

c. Petitioner's current or any subsequent place of employment *{list address of current employment}* ____

d. where Petitioner attends school *{list address of school}*____; or

e. the following other places (if requested by Petitioner) where Petitioner, specific members of Petitioner's family, or individuals closely associated with Petitioner, regularly frequent:____.

f. Respondent **shall not** knowingly and intentionally come within 100 feet of Petitioner's motor vehicle at any time, whether or not that vehicle is occupied;

g. Other provisions regarding contact: ____
____.

3. **Firearms.**
*{Initial **all** that apply; write N/A if not applicable}*

a. ____Respondent is a state or local officer, as defined in section 943.10(14), Florida Statutes, who holds an active certification, who receives or possesses a firearm or ammunition for use in performing official duties on behalf of the officer's employing agency, and is not prohibited by the court from having in his or her care, possession, or control any firearm or ammunition.

b. ____Respondent shall not use or possess a firearm or ammunition.

c. ____Respondent shall surrender any firearms and ammunition in the Respondent's possession to the__________________ County Sheriff's Department.

d. _____Other directives relating to firearms and ammunition: _____________________________
____
____
____

4. **Mailing Address.** Respondent shall notify the Clerk of the Court of any change in his or her mailing address within 10 days of the change. All further papers (excluding pleadings requiring personal service) shall be served by mail to Respondent's last known address of record. Such service by mail shall be complete upon mailing. Rule 12.080, Florida Family Law Rules of Procedure; Section 784.0485, Florida Statutes.

5. **Additional order(s) necessary to protect Petitioner from stalking:**
____
____
____
____

6. **Referral to Appropriate Services for Petitioner:**
Petitioner may contact the following services as needed:
____
____.

SECTION IV. OTHER SPECIAL PROVISIONS
(This section to be used for inclusion of local provisions approved by the chief judge as provided in Florida Family Law Rule 12.610.)
____

Florida Supreme Court Approved Family Law Form 12.980(u), Temporary Injunction for Protection Against Stalking (03/15)

____
____.

SECTION V. DIRECTIONS TO LAW ENFORCEMENT OFFICER IN ENFORCING THIS INJUNCTION
(Unless ordered otherwise by the judge, all provisions in this injunction are considered mandatory provisions and should be interpreted as part of this injunction.)

1. The Sheriff of ____________________County, or any other authorized law enforcement officer, is ordered to serve this temporary injunction upon Respondent as soon as possible after its issuance.

2. **This injunction is valid and enforceable in all counties of the State of Florida.** Violation of this injunction should be reported to the appropriate law enforcement agency. Law enforcement officers of the jurisdiction in which a violation of this injunction occurs shall enforce the provisions of this injunction and are authorized to arrest without a warrant pursuant to Section 901.15, Florida Statutes, for any violation of its provisions, which constitutes a criminal act under Section 784.0487, Florida Statutes.

3. **THIS INJUNCTION IS ENFORCEABLE IN ALL COUNTIES OF FLORIDA AND LAW ENFORCEMENT OFFICERS MAY EFFECT ARRESTS PURSUANT TO SECTION 901.15(6), FLORIDA STATUTES.** The arresting agent shall notify the State Attorney's Office immediately after arrest.

4. **Reporting alleged violations.** If Respondent violates the terms of this injunction and has not been arrested, Petitioner may contact the clerk of the circuit court of the county in which the violation is alleged to have occurred. The clerk shall assist Petitioner in preparing an affidavit in support of reporting the violation or direct Petitioner to the office operated by the court that has been designated by the chief judge of that circuit as the central intake point for violations of injunctions for protection where Petitioner can receive assistance in the preparation of the affidavit in support of the violation. The affidavit shall be immediately forwarded by the office assisting Petitioner to the state attorney of that circuit and to the judge designated by the chief judge as the recipient of affidavits of violations of an injunction. Procedures relating to reporting alleged violations are governed by section 784.0487, Florida Statutes.

DONE AND ORDERED in ____________________________, Florida, on ______________________.

____
CIRCUIT JUDGE

COPIES TO:
Sheriff of ____________________ County

Petitioner:
____ by U. S. Mail
____ by hand delivery in open court
Respondent:
____ forwarded to sheriff for service
____ State Attorney's Office
____ Other:

I CERTIFY the foregoing is a true copy of the original **Temporary Injunction for Protection Against Stalking** as it appears on file in the office of the Clerk of the Circuit Court of ________________ County, Florida, and that I have furnished copies of this order as indicated above.

CLERK OF THE CIRCUIT COURT

(SEAL)

By:______________________________
Deputy Clerk

Florida Supreme Court Approved Family Law Form 12.980(u), Temporary Injunction for Protection Against Stalking (03/15)

Added May 9, 2013 (113 So.3d 781). Amended July 3, 2014, effective July 3, 2014 (142 So.3d 856); March 26, 2015, effective March 26, 2015 (2015 WL 1343088).

Form 12.980(v). Final Judgment of Injunction for Protection Against Stalking (After Notice)

IN THE CIRCUIT COURT OF THE ______ JUDICIAL CIRCUIT,
IN AND FOR ___________________ COUNTY, FLORIDA

Case No.: ___________________
Division: ___________________

________________________________,
Petitioner,
and

________________________________,
Respondent.

FINAL JUDGMENT OF INJUNCTION FOR PROTECTION AGAINST STALKING (AFTER NOTICE)

The Petition for Injunction for Protection Against Stalking under Section 784.0485, Florida Statutes, and other papers filed in this Court have been reviewed. The Court has jurisdiction of the parties and the subject matter. The term Petitioner as used in this injunction includes the person on whose behalf this injunction is entered.

It is intended that this protection order meet the requirements of 18 U.S.C. Section 2265 and therefore intended that it be accorded full faith and credit by the court of another state or Indian tribe and enforced as if it were the order of the enforcing state or of the Indian tribe.

SECTION I. HEARING

This cause came before the Court for a hearing to determine whether an Injunction for Protection Against Stalking in this case should be:

____ issued ____ modified____ extended.

The hearing was attended by:
____Petitioner
____Petitioner's Counsel
____Respondent
____Respondent's Counsel

SECTION II. FINDINGS

On *{date}* ______________________, a notice of this hearing was served on Respondent together with a copy of Petitioner's petition to this Court and the temporary injunction, if issued. Service was within the

Florida Supreme Court Approved Family Law Form 12.980(v), Final Judgment of Injunction for Protection Against Stalking (After Notice) (03/15)

time required by Florida law, and Respondent was afforded an opportunity to be heard.

After hearing the testimony of each party present and of any witnesses, or upon consent of Respondent, the Court finds, based on the specific facts of this case, that Petitioner is a victim of stalking.

SECTION III. INJUNCTION AND TERMS

This injunction shall be in full force and effect until either ____ further order of the Court or ____ until *{date}* ____________________. This injunction is valid and enforceable throughout all counties in the State of Florida. The terms of this injunction may not be changed by either party alone or by both parties together. Only the Court may modify the terms of this injunction. Either party may ask the Court to change or end this injunction.

Willful violation of the terms of this injunction, such as: committing an act of stalking against Petitioner; going to or being within 500 feet of Petitioner's residence, place of employment, school, or other place prohibited in this injunction; knowingly and intentionally coming within 100 feet of Petitioner's motor vehicle, whether or not that vehicle is occupied; committing any other violation of this injunction through an intentional unlawful threat, word or act to do violence to Petitioner; telephoning, contacting or communicating with Petitioner, unless indirect contact through a third party is specifically allowed by this injunction; defacing or destroying Petitioner's personal property, including Petitioner's motor vehicle; having care, custody, use or possession of a firearm or ammunition unless authorized by section 790.233(3), Florida Statutes, constitutes a misdemeanor of the first degree punishable as provided by Sections 775.082 and 775.083, Florida Statutes.

Any party violating this injunction shall be subject to civil or indirect criminal contempt proceedings, including the imposition of a fine or imprisonment, and also may be charged with a crime punishable by a fine, jail, or both, as provided by Florida Statutes.

ORDERED and ADJUDGED:

1. **Prohibited Actions.** Respondent shall not commit, or cause any other person to commit, any acts of stalking against Petitioner, including stalking, cyberstalking, aggravated stalking, or any criminal offense resulting in physical injury or death. Respondent shall not commit any other violation of the injunction through an intentional unlawful threat, word or act to do violence to Petitioner.

2. **No Contact. Respondent shall have no contact with Petitioner unless otherwise provided in this section.**

a. Unless otherwise provided herein, Respondent shall have no contact with Petitioner. Respondent shall not directly or indirectly contact Petitioner in person, by mail, e-mail, fax, telephone, through another person, or in any other manner, including any electronic means or use of social media. Further, Respondent shall not contact or have any third party contact anyone connected with

Florida Supreme Court Approved Family Law Form 12.980(v), Final Judgment of Injunction for Protection Against Stalking (After Notice) (03/15)

Petitioner's employment or school to inquire about Petitioner or to send any messages to Petitioner.

Unless otherwise provided herein, **Respondent shall not go to, in, or within 500 feet of:**

b. Petitioner's current residence {list address} ______________________________

or any residence to which Petitioner may move;

c. Petitioner's current or any subsequent place of employment *{list address of current employment}* ______________________________;

d. Petitioner's school *{list address of school}* ______________________________; or

e. the following other place(s) regularly frequented by Petitioner and any named family members or individuals closely associated with Petitioner: ______________________________

f. Respondent shall not knowingly or intentionally come within 100 feet of Petitioner's motor vehicle, whether or not that vehicle is occupied;

g. Respondent shall not deface or destroy Petitioner's personal property, including Petitioner's motor vehicle.

h. Other provisions regarding contact: ______________________________
__________.

3. **Firearms.**

Unless paragraph a. is initialed below, Respondent shall not have in his or her care, custody, possession, or control any firearm or ammunition. It is a violation of section 790.233, Florida Statutes, and a first degree misdemeanor, for Respondent to have in his or her care, custody, possession or control any firearm or ammunition.

*{Initial **all** that apply; write N/A if not applicable}*

a. ______ Respondent is a state or local officer, as defined in section 943.10(14), Florida Statutes, who holds an active certification, who receives or possesses a firearm or ammunition for use in performing official duties on behalf of the officer's employing agency, and is not prohibited by the court from having in his or her care, custody, possession or control any firearm or ammunition.

b. ______ Respondent shall not use or possess a firearm or ammunition.

c. _____Respondent shall surrender any firearms and ammunition in the Respondent's possession to the__________________ County Sheriff's Department. Failure to surrender either firearms or ammunition if ordered to do so by the court constitutes a misdemeanor of the first degree, punishable as provided in section 775.082 or 775.083, Florida Statutes.

d. _____Other directives relating to firearms and ammunition: ____________________________________
____
____.

4. **Treatment, Intervention, or Counseling.**
*{Initial **if** applicable; write N/A if **not** applicable}*

a. _______Respondent shall participate in the treatment, intervention, or counseling specified below. Respondent shall pay for all services rendered: ________________________________
____
____.

b. Within _____ days of the date of this Injunction, Respondent shall enroll in, and thereafter complete without delay, the treatment, intervention, or counseling required in paragraph a. above. Respondent shall provide proof of such enrollment to the Clerk of the Court.

5. **Mailing Address or Designated E-Mail Address(es).** Respondent shall notify the Clerk of the Court of any change in either his or her mailing address, or designated e-mail address(es), within 10 days of the change. All further papers (excluding pleadings requiring personal service) shall be served either by mail to Respondent's last known mailing address or by e-mail to Respondent's designated e-mail address(es). Service shall be complete upon mailing or e-mailing.

6. **Additional provisions(s) necessary to protect Petitioner from stalking:**
____
____
____
____
____.

7. **Referral to Appropriate Services for Petitioner.** Petitioner may contact the following services as needed: ____
____
____.

SECTION IV. OTHER SPECIAL PROVISIONS
{This section to be used for inclusion of local provisions approved by the chief judge as provided in Florida Family Law Rule 12.610.}
____

____.

SECTION V. DIRECTIONS TO LAW ENFORCEMENT OFFICER IN ENFORCING THIS INJUNCTION
{Unless ordered otherwise by the judge, all provisions in this injunction are considered mandatory provisions and should be interpreted as part of this injunction.}

1. **This injunction is valid and enforceable in all counties of the State of Florida.** Violation of this injunction should be reported to the appropriate law enforcement agency. Law enforcement officers of the jurisdiction in which a violation of this injunction occurs shall enforce the provisions of this injunction and are authorized to arrest without a warrant pursuant to Section 901.15, Florida Statutes, for any violation of its provisions, which constitutes a criminal act under Section 784.0485, Florida Statutes.

2. **THIS INJUNCTION IS ENFORCEABLE IN ALL COUNTIES OF FLORIDA AND LAW ENFORCEMENT OFFICERS MAY EFFECT ARRESTS PURSUANT TO SECTION 901.15(6), FLORIDA STATUTES.** The arresting agent shall notify the State Attorney's Office immediately after arrest.

3. **Reporting alleged violations.** If Respondent violates the terms of this injunction and has not been arrested, Petitioner may contact the clerk of the circuit court of the county in which the violation is alleged to have occurred. The clerk shall assist Petitioner in preparing an affidavit in support of reporting the violation or direct Petitioner to the office operated by the court that has been designated by the chief judge of that circuit as the central intake point for violations of injunctions for protection where Petitioner can receive assistance in the preparation of the affidavit in support of the violation. The affidavit shall be immediately forwarded by the office assisting Petitioner to the state attorney of that circuit and to the judge designated by the chief judge as the recipient of affidavits of violations of an injunction. Procedures relating to reporting alleged violations are governed by section 784.0487, Florida Statutes.

4. Respondent, upon service of this injunction, shall be deemed to have knowledge of and to be bound by all matters occurring at the hearing and on the face of this injunction.

5. The temporary injunction, if any, entered in this case is extended until such time as service of this injunction is effected upon Respondent.

DONE AND ORDERED in______________________________, Florida, on ____________________.

____
CIRCUIT JUDGE

Florida Supreme Court Approved Family Law Form 12.980(v), Final Judgment of Injunction for Protection Against Stalking (After Notice) (03/15)

COPIES TO:
Sheriff of ____________________ County

Petitioner (or his or her attorney):
_____ by U. S. Mail
_____ by hand delivery in open court (Petitioner must acknowledge receipt in writing on the face of the original order--see below.)
_____ by e-mail to designated e-mail address(es)

Respondent (or his or her attorney):
_____forwarded to sheriff for service
_____ by hand delivery in open court (Respondent must acknowledge receipt in writing on the face of the original order--see below.)
_____ by certified mail (may only be used when Respondent is present at the hearing and Respondent fails or refuses to acknowledge the receipt of a certified copy of this injunction.)

_____ State Attorney's Office
_____ Other____________________________

I CERTIFY the foregoing is a true copy of the original **Final Judgment of Injunction for Protection Against Stalking** as it appears on file in the office of the Clerk of the Circuit Court of ______________________ County, Florida, and that I have furnished copies of this order as indicated above.

CLERK OF THE CIRCUIT COURT

(SEAL)

By:____
Deputy Clerk or Judicial Assistant

ACKNOWLEDGMENT

I, *{Name of Petitioner}* ___________________________, acknowledge receipt of a certified copy of this Final Judgment of Injunction for Protection Against Stalking.

Florida Supreme Court Approved Family Law Form 12.980(v), Final Judgment of Injunction for Protection Against Stalking (After Notice) (03/15)

____
Petitioner

ACKNOWLEDGMENT

I, *{Name of Respondent}* ____________________________, acknowledge receipt of a certified copy of this Final Judgment of Injunction for Protection Against Stalking.

____
Respondent

Added May 9, 2013 (113 So.3d 781). Amended March 26, 2015, effective March 26, 2015 (2015 WL 1343088).

Form 12.980(w). Petition by Affidavit for Order to Show Cause for a Violation of Final Judgment of Injunction for Protection Against ( ) Domestic Violence ( ) Repeat Violence ( ) Dating Violence ( ) Sexual Violence ( ) Stalking

IN THE CIRCUIT COURT OF THE ____________ JUDICIAL CIRCUIT,
IN AND FOR ________________________ COUNTY, FLORIDA

Case No.: ____________________

Division: ____________________

______________________________,
Petitioner,

and

______________________________,
Respondent.

PETITION BY AFFIDAVIT FOR ORDER TO SHOW CAUSE FOR A VIOLATION OF FINAL JUDGMENT OF INJUNCTION FOR PROTECTION AGAINST ( ) DOMESTIC VIOLENCE ( ) REPEAT VIOLENCE ( ) DATING VIOLENCE ( ) SEXUAL VIOLENCE ( ) STALKING

I, *{full legal name}* ____________________, being sworn, certify that I have actual knowledge of the following facts as set forth and the following statements are true:

1. The Court previously issued a *{Choose one only}*

a. ____ Final Judgment of Injunction for Protection Against Domestic Violence

b. ____ Final Judgment of Injunction for Protection Against Repeat Violence

c. ____ Final Judgment of Injunction for Protection Against Dating Violence

d. ____ Final Judgment of Injunction for Protection Against Sexual Violence

e. ____ Final Judgment of Injunction for Protection Against Stalking

in this case on *{date}* ____________.

The Final Judgment of Injunction for Protection was served on Respondent on *{date}* ____________.

2. On *{dates}* ____________________, at *{place and address}* ____________________
____,

the following event(s) took place: ____
____
____

Florida Supreme Court Approved Family Law Form 12.980(w), Petition By Affidavit for Order to Show Cause for a Violation of Final Judgment of Injunction for Protection Against Domestic, Repeat, Dating, or Sexual Violence, or Stalking (03/15)

_______________.

{For cyberstalking, please include a description of all evidence of contacts and/or threats made by Respondent in voice messages, texts, emails, or other electronic communication}

____
____
____
____.

_____Please indicate here if you are attaching additional pages to continue these facts.

3. Respondent has willfully violated the Injunction by: *{explain what Respondent did that violated the Order of Protection}*

____
____
____
____
_______.

_____Please indicate here if you are attaching additional pages to continue these facts.

5. ____ Please indicate here if you are attaching copies of medical records for treatment you may have received for injuries referred to in your affidavit, or copies of any police or sheriff reports concerning incidents of violence involving you and Respondent.

6. Respondent acted to impair, interfere with, delay, hinder, lessen the authority of, dignity of, and embarrass the cause of justice in a manner contemptuous of this court.

WHEREFORE, I respectfully request that the Court issue an Order to Show Cause, requiring Respondent to appear before the Court to show cause why Respondent should not be held in contempt of court for failure to abide by the terms and conditions of the Final Judgment of Injunction for Protection.

I understand that by filing this affidavit, I am asking the court to hold a hearing, that both Respondent and I will be notified of the hearing, and that I must appear at the hearing. In addition to my own testimony, I understand that I can bring other proof of the violation such as, for example, people who saw Respondent violate the order, pictures, medical records, police reports, or anything might help show the judge how Respondent violated the Final Judgment of Injunction for Protection.

I have read every statement made in this affidavit and each statement is true and correct. I understand that the statements made in this affidavit are being made under penalty of perjury, punishable as provided in Section 837.02, Florida Statutes and that the punishment for knowingly

making a false statement includes fines and/or imprisonment.

Dated: ____________________________

____
Signature of Petitioner

STATE OF FLORIDA
COUNTY OF ________________________

Sworn to or affirmed and signed before me on ____________ by ______________________________.

____
NOTARY PUBLIC or DEPUTY CLERK

____
{Print, type, or stamp commissioned name of notary or clerk.}

_____Personally known
_____Produced identification
Type of identification produced ____________________

I certify that a copy of this document was ( ) mailed ( ) faxed and mailed ( ) e-mailed ( ) hand delivered to the person(s) listed below on *{date}* ____________.

Other party or his/her attorney:
Name:______________________________
Address:____________________________
City, State, Zip:_____________________
Fax Number:_________________________
Designated E-mail Address(es):__________
____

Florida Supreme Court Approved Family Law Form 12.980(w), Petition By Affidavit for Order to Show Cause for a Violation of Final Judgment of Injunction for Protection Against Domestic, Repeat, Dating, or Sexual Violence, or Stalking (03/15)

IN THE CIRCUIT COURT OF THE ____________ JUDICIAL CIRCUIT,
IN AND FOR ____________________________ COUNTY, FLORIDA

Case No.: ____________________
Division: ____________________

______________________________________,
Petitioner,

and

______________________________________,
Respondent.

Description of Respondent:
Sex: __________ Eye color: __________ Height: __________ DOB: ______________
Race: __________ Hair color: __________ Weight: __________
Last known address: ____

ORDER TO SHOW CAUSE

This cause comes before the court for review based upon the alleged conduct of Respondent for the issuance of an Order to Show Cause directed to *{name}*______________________________ for violation of the Final Judgment of Injunction for Protection as is more specifically set forth in the **Petition By Affidavit For Order To Show Cause For a Violation Of Final Judgment Of Injunction For Protection,** a copy of which is attached hereto and made a part hereof.

NOW, THEREFORE, you, *{name}* ____, are hereby ORDERED to appear before this court before Judge *{name}*_________________________, on *{date}* __________________, at *{time}* ___.m., in Room ______ of the _______________Courthouse, located at ____, to be arraigned. A subsequent hearing will be scheduled requiring Respondent to show cause why he/she should not be held in contempt of this court for violation of the Final Judgment of Injunction for Protection as is stated in the attached **Petition By Affidavit For Order To Show Cause For a Violation of Final Judgment of Injunction For Protection**. Punishment, if imposed, may include a fine and incarceration. Should the court determine, based on the evidence presented at the hearing, that Respondent's conduct warrants sanctions for civil contempt in addition to or instead of indirect criminal contempt, the court reserves the right to find Respondent guilty of civil contempt and impose appropriate civil sanctions.

_____The court hereby appoints the State Attorney's Office to prosecute the case.

_____Respondent is advised that he/she is entitled to be represented by counsel.

If you are a person with a disability who needs any accommodation to participate in this proceeding, you are entitled, at no cost to you, to the

provision of certain assistance. Please contact: ____________________________

____

***{identify applicable court personnel by name, address, and telephone number}* at least 7 days before your scheduled court appearance, or immediately upon receiving this notification if the time before the scheduled appearance is less than 7 days; if you are hearing or voice impaired, call 711.**

IT IS FURTHER ORDERED that the Sheriff of this county serve this **Order to Show Cause** by delivering copies to Respondent, with proof of Sheriff's service.

DONE AND ORDERED in ______________ County, Florida, on *{date}* ______________.

____
Circuit Judge

Copies to:
Sheriff of ______________________ County

Petitioner or Counsel for Petitioner:
_____by U.S. Mail
_____by e-mail to designated e-mail address(es)

Respondent or Counsel for Respondent:
_____forwarded to the sheriff for service

___State Attorney's Office

I CERTIFY the foregoing is a true copy of the original Order to Show Cause as it appears on file in the office of the Clerk of the Circuit Court of ______________, County, Florida, and that I have furnished copies of this order as indicated above.

CLERK OF THE CIRCUIT COURT

____
By: Deputy Clerk or Judicial Assistant

Florida Supreme Court Approved Family Law Form 12.980(w), Petition By Affidavit for Order to Show Cause for a Violation of Final Judgment of Injunction for Protection Against Domestic, Repeat, Dating, or Sexual Violence, or Stalking (03/15)

INSTRUCTIONS FOR FLORIDA SUPREME COURT APPROVED FAMILY LAW FORM 12.980(w)
PETITION BY AFFIDAVIT FOR ORDER TO SHOW CAUSE FOR A VIOLATION OF FINAL JUDGMENT OF INJUNCTION FOR PROTECTION AGAINST DOMESTIC, REPEAT, DATING, OR SEXUAL VIOLENCE, OR STALKING (03/15)

When should this form be used?

You may use this form if you have a valid **Final Judgment of Injunction for Protection Against Domestic, Repeat, Dating, or Sexual Violence, or Stalking,** in force which has been violated. You should use this **affidavit** to state the essential facts which establish a violation of the Final Judgment of Injunction.

This form should be typed or printed in black ink. After completing this form, you should sign the form before a **notary public** or the **clerk of the circuit court**. You should then **file** the original with such clerk or judge as determined by the chief judge of your circuit to be the recipient of affidavits of violation, provide a copy to the state attorney of that circuit and keep a copy for your records.

IMPORTANT INFORMATION REGARDING E–FILING

The Florida Rules of Judicial Administration now require that all petitions, pleadings, and documents be filed electronically except in certain circumstances. **Self-represented litigants may file petitions or other pleadings or documents electronically; however, they are not required to do so.** If you choose to file your pleadings or other documents electronically, you must do so in accordance with Florida Rule of Judicial Administration 2.525, and you must follow the procedures of the judicial circuit in which you file. **The rules and procedures should be carefully read and followed.**

IMPORTANT INFORMATION REGARDING E–SERVICE ELECTION

After the initial service of process of the petition or supplemental petition by the Sheriff or certified process server, the Florida Rules of Judicial Administration now require that all documents required or permitted to be served on the other party must be served by electronic mail (e-mail) except in certain circumstances. **You must strictly comply with the format requirements set forth in the Rules of Judicial Administration.**

SELF–REPRESENTED LITIGANTS MAY SERVE DOCUMENTS BY E–MAIL; HOWEVER, THEY ARE NOT REQUIRED TO DO SO. If a self-represented litigant elects to serve and receive documents by e-mail, the procedures must always be followed once the initial election is made.

To serve and receive documents by e-mail, you must designate your e-mail addresses by using the **Designation of Current Mailing and E-mail Address**, Florida Supreme Court Approved Family Law Form 12.915, and you must provide your e-mail address on each form on which your signature appears. Please **CAREFULLY** read the rules and instructions for: **Certificate of Service (General),** Florida Supreme Court Approved Family Law Form 12.914; **Designation of Current Mailing and E-mail Address**, Florida Supreme Court Approved Family Law Form 12.915; and Florida Rule of Judicial Administration 2.516.

Formerly Form 12.980(r) May 15, 2003 (849 So.2d 1003). Renumbered as Form 12.890(t) March 25, 2004 (871 So.2d 113). Amended June 7, 2012 (93 So.3d 194). Renumbered as Form 12.980(w) and amended May 9, 2013 (113 So.3d 781). Amended March 26, 2015, effective March 26, 2015 (2015 WL 1343088).

Form 12.980(x). Order to Show Cause

IN THE CIRCUIT COURT OF THE ________ JUDICIAL CIRCUIT,
IN AND FOR ______________ COUNTY, FLORIDA

Case No.: ____________________

Division: ____________________

________________________,
Petitioner,

and

________________________,
Respondent.

Description of Respondent:
Sex: ____________ Eye color: __________
Race: ____________ Hair color: __________
Height: __________ Last known address: ____________________
Weight: __________ ______________________________
DOB: ____________

ORDER TO SHOW CAUSE

This cause comes before the court for review based upon the alleged conduct of Respondent for the issuance of an Order to Show Cause directed to *{name}*______________________________for violation of the Final Judgment of Injunction for Protection as is more specifically set forth in the **Petition By Affidavit For Order To Show Cause For a Violation Of Final Judgment Of Injunction For Protection,** a copy of which is attached hereto and made a part hereof.

NOW, THEREFORE, you, *{name}*______________________________, are hereby ORDERED to appear before this court before Judge *{name}* ____________________, on *{date}* ______________, at *{time}* ___.m., in Room _____ of the ____________Courthouse, located at ____________________, to be arraigned. A subsequent hearing will be scheduled requiring Respondent to show cause why he/she should not be held in contempt of this court for violation of the Final Judgment of Injunction for Protection as is stated in the attached **Petition By Affidavit For Order To Show Cause For a Violation of Final Judgment of Injunction For Protection**. Punishment, if imposed, may include a fine and incarceration. Should the court determine, based on the evidence presented at the hearing, that Respondent's conduct warrants sanctions for civil contempt in addition to or instead of indirect criminal contempt, the court reserves the right to find Respondent guilty of civil contempt and impose appropriate civil sanctions.

_____The court hereby appoints the State Attorney's Office to prosecute the case.

_____Respondent is advised that he/she is entitled to be represented by counsel.

If you are a person with a disability who needs any accommodation to participate in this proceeding, you are entitled, at no cost to you, to the provision of certain assistance. Please contact:________________________

____

***{identify applicable court personnel by name, address, and telephone number}* at least 7 days before your scheduled court appearance, or immediately upon receiving this notification if the time before the scheduled appearance is less than 7 days; if you are hearing or voice impaired, call 711.**

IT IS FURTHER ORDERED that the Sheriff of this county serve this **Order to Show Cause** by delivering copies to Respondent, with proof of Sheriff's service.

DONE AND ORDERED in ________________ County, Florida, on *{date}* _______________.

____
Circuit Judge

Copies to:
____ State Attorney
____ Petitioner or Counsel for Petitioner
____ Respondent or Counsel for Respondent

Florida Supreme Court Approved Family Law Form 12.980(x), Order to Show Cause (05/13)

Formerly Form 12.980(s), added May 15, 2003 (849 So.2d 1003). Renumbered as Form 12.980(u) March 25, 2004 (871 So.2d 113). Amended June 7, 2012 (93 So.3d 194). Renumbered as Form 12.980(x) and amended May 9, 2013 (113 So.3d 781).

Form 12.981(a)(1). Stepparent Adoption: Consent and Waiver by Parent

IN THE CIRCUIT COURT OF THE __________ JUDICIAL CIRCUIT,
IN AND FOR __________ COUNTY, FLORIDA

Case No.: __________
Division: __________

IN THE MATTER OF THE ADOPTION OF

____
{use name to be given to minor child(ren)} Adoptee(s).

CONSENT AND WAIVER BY PARENT

1. I, *{full legal name}* __________, am the *{Choose only one}* _____ father **or** _____ mother of the minor child(ren) subject to this consent who is/are:

	Child's Current Name	Gender	Birth date	Birthplace *{city, county, state}*
a.				
b.				
c.				
d.				
e.				
f.				

2. I relinquish all rights to, custody of, and time sharing with this (these) minor child(ren), *{name(s)}* __________, with full knowledge of the legal effect of the stepparent adoption and consent to the adoption by the child(ren)'s stepparent whose name is: *{Choose only one}*
   _____ *{name}* __________
   _____ not required for my granting of this consent.

3. I understand my legal rights as a parent and I understand that I do not have to sign this consent and release of my parental rights. I acknowledge that this consent is being given knowingly, freely, and voluntarily. I further acknowledge that my consent is not given under fraud or duress. I understand that there is a "grace period" in Florida during which I may revoke my consent. If the child to be adopted is older than 6 months at the time of consent, this grace period is for 3 days or until the child has been placed with the prospective adoptive parents, whichever is later. I understand that, in signing this consent, I am permanently and forever giving up all my parental rights to and interest in this (these) minor child(ren) and that this consent may only be withdrawn if the Court finds it was obtained by fraud or duress. I voluntarily, permanently relinquish all my parental rights to this (these) minor child(ren).

Florida Supreme Court Approved Family Law Form 12.981(a)(1), Stepparent Adoption: Consent and Waiver by Parent (03/15)

4. I consent, release, and give up permanently, of my own free will, my parental rights to this (these) minor child(ren), for the purpose of stepparent adoption.

5. I waive any further notice of the stepparent adoption proceeding.

6. I understand that pursuant to Chapter 63, Florida Statutes, "an action or proceeding of any kind to vacate, set aside, or otherwise nullify a judgment of adoption or an underlying judgment terminating parental rights on any ground may not be filed more than 1 year after entry of the judgment terminating parental rights."

7. I understand I have the right to choose a person who does not have an employment, professional, or personal relationship with the adoption entity or the prospective adoptive parents to be present when this affidavit is executed and to sign it as a witness. The witness I selected is: *{full legal name}* ______________________.

I understand that I am swearing or affirming under oath to the truthfulness of the claims made in this consent and waiver and that the punishment for knowingly making a false statement includes fines and/or imprisonment.

Dated: ______________________

Signature of Parent: ______________________
Printed Name: ______________________
Address: ______________________
City, State, Zip: ______________________
Telephone Number: ______________________
Fax Number: ______________________
Designated E-mail Address(es): ______________________
____

____
Signature of Witness
Printed Name: ______________________
Business Address: ______________________
Home Address: ______________________
Driver's License No.: ______________________
State ID Card No.: ______________________

____
Signature of Witness
Printed Name: ______________________
Business Address: ______________________
Home Address: ______________________
Driver's License No.: ______________________
State ID Card No.: ______________________

Florida Supreme Court Approved Family Law Form 12.981(a)(1), Stepparent Adoption: Consent and Waiver by Parent (03/15)

STATE OF FLORIDA
COUNTY OF

Sworn to or affirmed and signed before me on *{date}* ________ .

____
NOTARY PUBLIC or DEPUTY CLERK

____
{Print, type, or stamp commissioned name of notary or deputy clerk.}

____ Personally known
____ Produced identification
Type of identification produced

I hereby acknowledge receipt of a copy or duplicate original of this executed **Consent and Waiver.**

____
Signature of Parent

IF A NONLAWYER HELPED YOU FILL OUT THIS FORM, HE/SHE MUST FILL IN THE BLANKS BELOW:
[fill in **all** blanks] This form was prepared for the: *{choose only one}* ( ) Mother ( ) Father
This form was completed with the assistance of:
*{name of individual}*______________________________,
*{name of business}*______________________________,
*{address}*______________________________,
{city} ____________,*{state}* ____, *{zip code}*________ *{telephone number}*________.

INSTRUCTIONS FOR FLORIDA SUPREME COURT APPROVED FAMILY LAW FORM 12.981(a)(1)
STEPPARENT ADOPTION: CONSENT AND WAIVER BY PARENT (03/15)

When should this form be used?

This form is to be completed and signed by the parent who is giving up all rights to, custody of, and time-sharing with the minor child to be adopted. This consent shall not be executed before the birth of the minor child. For more information about consenting to adoption, you should refer to Chapter 63, Florida Statutes, and sections 63.062—63.082, Florida Statutes, in particular.

This form should be typed or printed in black ink. It must be signed in the presence of a **notary public** or **deputy clerk** and two witnesses other than the notary or clerk. You should **file** this form with the **Joint Petition for Adoption by Stepparent**, Florida Supreme Court Approved Family Law Form 12.981(b)(1).

After completing this form, you should hand deliver a copy or duplicate original to the parent giving consent and have them sign the original saying they received a copy. Then you should file the original with the **clerk of the circuit court** in the county where the **Joint Petition for Adoption by Stepparent**, Florida Supreme Court Approved Family Law Form 12.981(b)(1) is filed and keep a copy for your records.

IMPORTANT INFORMATION REGARDING E–FILING

The Florida Rules of Judicial Administration now require that all petitions, pleadings, and documents be filed electronically except in certain circumstances. **Self-represented litigants may file petitions or other pleadings or documents electronically; however, they are not required to do so.** If you choose to file your pleadings or other documents electronically, you must do so in accordance with Florida Rule of Judicial Administration 2.525, and you must follow the procedures of the judicial circuit in which you file. **The rules and procedures should be carefully read and followed.**

IMPORTANT INFORMATION REGARDING E–SERVICE ELECTION

After the initial service of process of the petition or supplemental petition by the Sheriff or certified process server, the Florida Rules of Judicial Administration now require that all documents required or permitted to be served on the other party must be served by electronic mail (e-mail) except in certain circumstances. **You must strictly comply with the format requirements set forth in the Rules of Judicial Administration.**

SELF–REPRESENTED LITIGANTS MAY SERVE DOCUMENTS BY E–MAIL; HOWEVER, THEY ARE NOT REQUIRED TO DO SO. If a self-represented litigant elects to serve and receive documents by e-mail, the procedures must always be followed once the initial election is made.

To serve and receive documents by e-mail, you must designate your e-mail addresses by using the **Designation of Current Mailing and E-mail Address**, Florida Supreme Court Approved Family Law Form 12.915, and you must provide your e-mail address on each form on which your signature appears. Please **CAREFULLY** read the rules and instructions for: **Certificate of Service (General),** Florida Supreme Court Approved Family Law Form 12.914; **Designation of Current Mailing and E-mail Address**, Florida Supreme Court Approved Family Law Form 12.915; and Florida Rule of Judicial Administration 2.516.

Special notes . . .

Remember, a person who is NOT an attorney is called a nonlawyer. If a nonlawyer helps you fill out these forms, that person must give you a copy of **Disclosure from Nonlawyer**, Florida Family Law Rules of Procedure Form 12.900 (a), before he or she helps you. A non-lawyer helping you fill out these forms also **must** put his or her name, address, and telephone number on the bottom of the last page of every form he or she helps you complete.

Added as 12.981(c)(1) Feb. 26, 1998, effective Mar. 16, 1998 (713 So.2d 1). Renumbered as 12.981(a)(2) and amended Mar. 28, 2002 (821 So.2d 263). Amended Oct. 3, 2002 (832 So.2d 684). Renumbered from 12.981(a)(2) Mar. 25, 2004 (870 So.2d 791). Amended March 26, 2009 (20 So.3d 173); Dec. 16, 2010 (59 So.3d 792); March 26, 2015, effective March 26, 2015 (2015 WL 1343088).

Form 12.981(a)(2). Stepparent Adoption: Consent of Adoptee

IN THE CIRCUIT COURT OF THE _______ JUDICIAL CIRCUIT,
IN AND FOR ____________ COUNTY, FLORIDA

Case No.: ____________
Division: ____________

IN THE MATTER OF THE ADOPTION OF

____
{use name to be given to the child(ren)} Adoptee(s).

CONSENT OF ADOPTEE

1. I, *{full legal name}* ______________________, being over the age of 12, consent to my adoption by *{name}* ______________________, to be his/her legal child and heir at law.

2. I have been told of my right to choose a person who does not have an employment, professional, or personal relationship with the adoption entity or prospective adoptive parents to be present when this affidavit is executed and to sign it as a witness. The witness I selected is: *{full legal name}* ______________________.

3. *{Choose only **one**}*

_____ I consent to my name being legally changed to *{specify}* ______________.

_____ I do **not** consent to a name change.

I understand that I am swearing or affirming under oath to the truthfulness of the claims made in this consent and that the punishment for knowingly making a false statement includes fines and/or imprisonment.

Dated: ______________

____
Signature of Adoptee
Printed Name: ______________
Address: ______________
City, State, Zip: ______________
Telephone Number: ______________
Fax Number: ______________
Designated E-mail Address(es): ______________

____

______________________	______________________
Signature of Witness	Signature of Witness
Printed Name: ______________	Printed Name: ______________
Business Address: ______________	Business Address: ______________
Home Address: ______________	Home Address: ______________
Driver's License No.: ______________	Driver's License No.: ______________
State ID Card No.: ______________	State ID Card No.: ______________

STATE OF FLORIDA
COUNTY OF ______________________

Sworn to or affirmed and signed before me on *{date}* ______________________.

____
NOTARY PUBLIC or DEPUTY CLERK

____
{Print, type, or stamp commissioned name of notary or deputy clerk.}

_____Personally known
_____Produced identification
Type of identification produced ______________________

IF A NONLAWYER HELPED YOU FILL OUT THIS FORM, HE/SHE MUST FILL IN THE BLANKS BELOW:
[fill in **all** blanks] This form was prepared for the *{choose only* ***one****}* ( ) adoptee ( ) stepparent
This form was completed with the assistance of:
{name of individual} ______________________,
{name of business} ______________________,
{address} ______________________,
{city} ______________,*{state}* ____,*{zip code}*________ *{telephone number}* ______________.

Florida Supreme Court Approved Family Law Form 12.981(a)(2), Stepparent Adoption: Consent of Adoptee (03/15)

INSTRUCTIONS FOR FLORIDA SUPREME COURT APPROVED FAMILY LAW FORM 12.981(a)(2)
STEPPARENT ADOPTION: CONSENT OF ADOPTEE (03/15)

When should this form be used?

This form must be completed and signed by the person being adopted, the adoptee, if he or she is over 12 years of age, unless the court, in the best interest of the minor excuses the minor's consent. It must be signed in the presence of a **notary public** or **deputy clerk** and two witnesses other than the notary public or deputy clerk.

This form should be typed or printed in black ink. After completing this form, you should **file** the original with the **clerk of the circuit court** in the county where the **Joint Petition for Adoption by Stepparent**, Florida Supreme Court Approved Family Law Form 12.981(b)(1) is filed and keep a copy for your records.

IMPORTANT INFORMATION REGARDING E-FILING

The Florida Rules of Judicial Administration now require that all petitions, pleadings, and documents be filed electronically except in certain circumstances. **Self-represented litigants may file petitions or other pleadings or documents electronically; however, they are not required to do so.** If you choose to file your pleadings or other documents electronically, you must do so in accordance with Florida Rule of Judicial Administration 2.525, and you must follow the procedures of the judicial circuit in which you file. **The rules and procedures should be carefully read and followed.**

Special notes . . .

Remember, a person who is NOT an attorney is called a nonlawyer. If a nonlawyer helps you fill out these forms, that person must give you a copy of **Disclosure from Nonlawyer**, Florida Family Law Rules of Procedure Form 12.900 (a), before he or she helps you. A nonlawyer helping you fill out these forms also must put his or her name, address, and telephone number on the bottom of the last page of every form he or she helps you complete.

Added as 12.981(b) July 1, 1995, effective Jan. 1, 1996 (663 So.2d 1047). Amended Feb. 26, 1998, effective Mar. 16, 1998 (713 So.2d 1); Sept. 21, 2000 (810 So.2d 1); Dec. 6, 2001 (817 So.2d 721). Renumbered as 12.981(a)(3) Mar. 28, 2002 (821 So.2d 263). Renumbered from 12.981(a)(3) Mar. 25, 2004 (870 So.2d 791). Amended March 26, 2015, effective March 26, 2015 (2015 WL 1343088).

Form 12.981(a)(3). Affidavit of Nonpaternity

IN THE CIRCUIT COURT OF THE ___ JUDICIAL CIRCUIT,
IN AND FOR __________ COUNTY, FLORIDA

Case No.: ____________________
Division: ____________________

IN THE MATTER OF THE ADOPTION OF

______________________________,
{use name to of the minor child(ren)} Adoptee(s)

AFFIDAVIT OF NONPATERNITY

I, *{full legal name}* ______________________, have personal knowledge of the facts stated in this affidavit and certify that the following statements are true:

2. I have been told that *{name}* ____________________ has a child. I do not wish to and shall not establish or claim paternity for this child, whose name is __________ and whose date of birth is ____________.
3. The child referenced in this affidavit was not conceived or born while the birth mother was married to me. I AM NOT MARRIED TO THE BIRTH MOTHER, nor do I intend to marry the birth mother.
4. The child has not been established to be my child in any court proceeding and I have not adopted this child.
5. I have no interest in assuming the responsibilities of parenthood for this child. I have not acknowledged and will not acknowledge in writing that I am the father of this child or will not institute court proceedings to establish the child as mine.
5. I do not object to any decision or arrangements the birth mother makes regarding this child, including adoption.
6. I understand my right to choose a person who does not have an employment, professional, or personal relationship with the adoption entity or the prospective adoptive parents to be present when this affidavit is executed and to sign it as a witness. The witness I selected is *{full legal name}* ____________________.
7. I am executing this affidavit freely and voluntarily and I understand that it can only be withdrawn if the court finds it was executed by fraud or duress.

I WAIVE NOTICE OF ANY AND ALL PROCEEDINGS TO TERMINATE PARENTAL RIGHTS OR FINALIZE AN ADOPTION UNDER CHAPTER 63, FLORIDA STATUTES.

Florida Supreme Court Approved Family Law Form 12.981(a)(3), Affidavit of Nonpaternity (03/15)

I understand that I am swearing or affirming under oath to the truthfulness of the claims made in this affidavit and that the punishment for knowingly making a false statement includes fines and/or imprisonment.

____
Signature
Printed Name: ______________________________
Address: ______________________________
City, State, Zip: ______________________________
Designated E-mail Address(es): ______________________________

______________________________	______________________________
Signature of Witness	Signature of Witness
Printed Name: ______________________________	Printed Name: ______________________________
Business Address: ______________________________	Business Address: ______________________________
Home Address: ______________________________	Home Address: ______________________________
Driver's License or State ID Card No.: ______________________________	Driver's License or State ID Card No.: ______________________________

STATE OF FLORIDA
COUNTY OF

Sworn to or affirmed and signed before me on *{date}* ______________

____
NOTARY PUBLIC or DEPUTY CLERK

____
[Print, type, or stamp commissioned name of notary or deputy clerk.]

___ Personally known
___ Produced identification
___ Type of identification produced

IF A NONLAWYER HELPED YOU FILL OUT THIS FORM, HE/SHE MUST FILL IN THE BLANKS BELOW:
[fill in **all** blanks] This form was prepared for the: *{choose only **one**}* ( ) parent or ( ) stepparent
This form was completed with the assistance of:
{name of individual} ______________________________,
{name of business} ______________________________,
{address} ______________________________,
{city} ______________,*{state}* ____, *{zip code}*__________,*{telephone number}* ______________.

Florida Supreme Court Approved Family Law Form 12.981(a)(3), Affidavit of Nonpaternity (03/15)

INSTRUCTIONS FOR FLORIDA SUPREME COURT APPROVED FAMILY LAW FORM 12.981(a)(3), AFFIDAVIT OF NONPATERNITY (03/15)

When should this form be used?

This form should be used when a stepfather is adopting his wife's minor child and the mother and father of the minor child(ren) were never married and paternity has not been established by a valid acknowledgment or court order. This Affidavit of Nonpaternity may be used instead of a consent form. This Affidavit may be executed before the birth of the minor child. The person signing the affidavit waives notice to all court proceedings after the date it is signed. After signing this affidavit, it may only be withdrawn if the court finds the affidavit was obtained by fraud or duress.

This form should be typed or printed in black ink. This form must be signed before a **notary public** or **deputy clerk** and two witnesses other than the notary or clerk. You should then **file** the original of this form with the **Joint Petition for Stepparent Adoption,** Florida Supreme Court Approved Family Law Form 12.981(b)(1).

IMPORTANT INFORMATION REGARDING E–FILING

The Florida Rules of Judicial Administration now require that petitions, pleadings, and documents be filed electronically except in certain circumstances. **Self-represented litigants may file petitions or other pleadings electronically; however, they are not required to do so.** If you choose to file your pleadings or other documents electronically, you must do so in accordance with Florida Rule of Judicial Administration 2.525, and you must follow the procedures of the judicial circuit in which you file. **The rules and procedures should be carefully read and followed.**

Special Notes

Remember—a person who is NOT an attorney is called a nonlawyer. If a nonlawyer helps you fill out these forms, that person must give you a copy of a **Disclosure from Nonlawyer,** Florida Family Law Rules of Procedure Form 12.900 (a), before he or she helps you. A nonlawyer helping you fill out these forms also **must** put his or her name, address, and telephone number on the bottom of the last page of every form he or she helps you complete.

Added as 12.981(a)(4) Mar. 28, 2002 (821 So.2d 263). Renumbered from 12.981(a)(4) Mar. 25, 2004 (870 So.2d 791). Amended March 26, 2015, effective March 26, 2015 (2015 WL 1343088).

Form 12.981(a)(4). Petition for Stepparent Adoption: Affidavit of Diligent Search

IN THE CIRCUIT COURT OF THE ____ JUDICIAL CIRCUIT,
IN AND FOR ____________ COUNTY, FLORIDA

Case No.: ____________
Division: ____________

IN THE MATTER OF THE ADOPTION OF

____
{use name to be given to the minor child(ren)} Adoptee(s).

PETITION FOR STEPPARENT ADOPTION: AFFIDAVIT OF DILIGENT SEARCH

I, *{full legal name}* ______________________________, being sworn, certify that the following information is true:

1. I am the child(ren)'s _____ mother _____ father.

2. The last known address of the child(ren)'s other parent *{name}* ____________________, as of *{date}* ____________________, was:

   ____
   Address City State Zip

   Telephone No. ______________ Fax No. ______________

   His/her last known employment, as of *{date}* ______________, was:

   ____
   Name of Employer

   ____
   Address City State Zip

   Telephone No. ______________ Fax No. ______________

3. The other parent is over the age of 18.

4. The other parent's current residence is not known and cannot be determined, although I have made a diligent search and inquiry to locate him/her through the following:

   You must search ALL of the following sources of information and state the results.

   _____United States Post Office inquiry through the Freedom of Information Act for the person's current address or any previous address.

   Result of search: ______________________________

   _____Last known employment of the other parent, including name and address of employer.

Florida Supreme Court Approved Family Law Form 12.981(a)(4), Petition for Stepparent Adoption: Affidavit of Diligent Search (03/15)

Result of search:
_____Regulatory agencies, including professional or occupational licensing, in the area where the other parent last resided.
Result of search: ____________________

_____Names and addresses of relatives to the extent such can be reasonably obtained from the petitioner or other sources, contacts with those relatives and inquiry as to the other parent's last known address. You are to follow up any leads of any addresses where the other parent may have moved.
Result of search: ____________________

_____Information about the other parent's possible death and, if dead, the date and location.
Result of search: ____________________

_____Telephone listings in the area where the other parent last resided.
Result of search: ____________________

_____Law enforcement agencies in the area where the other parent last resided.
Result of search: ____________________

_____Highway Patrol records in the state where the other parent last resided.
Result of search: ____________________

_____Department of Corrections records in the state where the other parent last resided.
Result of search: ____________________

_____Hospitals in the last known area of the other parent's residence.
Result of search: ____________________

_____Records of utility companies, which include water, sewer, cable TV, and electric in the last known area of the other parent's residence.
Result of search: ____________________

_____Records of the Armed Forces of the U.S. and their response as to whether or not there is any information about the other parent. (See Florida Supreme Court Approved Family Law Form 12.912(a), Memorandum for Certificate of Military Service.)
Result of search: ____________________

_____Records of the tax assessor's and tax collector's office in the area where the other parent last resided.
Result of search: ____________________

_____Search of one Internet databank locator service.
Result of search: ____________________

_____Title IV-D (child support enforcement) agency records in the state of the other parent's last known address.
Result of search: ____________________

{if applicable}:

_____ A search of the Putative Father Registry maintained by the Office of Vital Statistics of the Department of Health has been requested, and if granted, the certificate from the State Registrar will be filed in this action.

Florida Supreme Court Approved Family Law Form 12.981(a)(4), Petition for Stepparent Adoption: Affidavit of Diligent Search (03/15)

I understand that I am swearing or affirming under oath to the truthfulness of the claims made in this affidavit and that the punishment for knowingly making a false statement includes fines and/or imprisonment.

Dated: ____________________ ____________________
Signature of Petitioner

Printed Name: ____________________
Address: ____________________
City, State, Zip: ____________________
Telephone Number: ____________________
Fax Number: ____________________
Designated E-mail Address(es): ____________________

STATE OF FLORIDA
COUNTY OF

Sworn to or affirmed and signed before me on ________ by ____________________.

____
NOTARY PUBLIC or DEPUTY CLERK

____
[Print, type, or stamp commissioned name of notary deputy clerk.]

____ Personally known
____ Produced identification
Type of identification produced

IF A NONLAWYER HELPED YOU FILL OUT THIS FORM, HE/SHE MUST FILL IN THE BLANKS BELOW:
[fill in all blanks] This form was prepared for the petitioner.
This form was completed with the assistance of:
{name of individual} ____________________,
{name of business} ____________________,
{address} ____________________,
{city} ____________, *{state}* ___, *{zip code}* ________, *{telephone number}* ____________.

Florida Supreme Court Approved Family Law Form 12.981(a)(4), Petition for Stepparent Adoption: Affidavit of Diligent Search (03/15)

INSTRUCTIONS FOR FLORIDA SUPREME COURT APPROVED FAMILY LAW FORM 12.981(a)(4), STEPPARENT ADOPTION: AFFIDAVIT OF DILIGENT SEARCH (03/15)

When should this form be used?

Use this form to obtain **constructive service** (also called service by publication) in a proceeding for stepparent adoption, **Joint Petition for Adoption by Stepparent,** Florida Supreme Court Approved Family Law Form 12.981(b)(1), when any required consent is unavailable because the address or location of the person whose consent is required is not known and cannot be determined.

This form includes a checklist of places you must look for information on the location of the person whose rights you seek to terminate. You do have to look in all of these places, and the court must believe that you have made a very serious effort to get information about the person's location and that you have followed up on any information you received. Section 63.054, Florida Statutes, requires that in each adoption a search of Florida's Putative Father Registry must be conducted. You will need an order from the judge to do this, which you can request by filing a **Motion for Search of the Putative Father Registry,** Florida Supreme Court Approved Family Law Form 12.981(a)(6).

This form should be typed or printed in black ink. After completing this form, you should **file** the original with the **clerk of the circuit court** in the county where your **petition** was filed and keep a copy for your records.

IMPORTANT INFORMATION REGARDING E-FILING

The Florida Rules of Judicial Administration now require that all petitions, pleadings, and documents be filed electronically except in certain circumstances. **Self-represented litigants may file petitions or other pleadings or documents electronically; however, they are not required to do so.** If you choose to file your pleadings or documents electronically, you must do so in accordance with Florida Rule of Judicial Administration 2.525, and you must follow the procedures of the judicial circuit in which you file. **The rules and procedures should be carefully read and followed.**

Where can I look for more information?

Before proceeding, you should read General Information for Self-Represented Litigants found at the beginning of these forms. For further information, see rule 12.070, Florida Family Law Rules of Procedure and Rule 1.070, Florida Rules of Civil Procedure.

Special notes . . .

Remember, a person who is NOT an attorney is called a nonlawyer. If a nonlawyer helps you fill out these forms, that person must give you a copy of a **Disclosure from Nonlawyer,** Florida Family Law Rules of Procedure Form 12.900(a), before he or she helps you. A nonlawyer helping you fill out these forms also **must** put his or her name, address, and telephone number on the bottom of the last page of every form he or she helps you complete.

Added as 12.981(d) July 1, 1995, effective Jan. 1, 1996 (663 So.2d 1047). Amended Feb. 26, 1998, effective Mar. 16, 1998 (713 So.2d 1); Sept. 21, 2000 (810 So.2d 1). Renumbered as 12.981(a)(5) and amended Mar. 28, 2002 (821 So.2d 263). Amended Oct. 3, 2002 (832 So.2d 684). Renumbered from 12.981(a)(5) Mar. 25, 2004 (870 So.2d 791). Amended March 26, 2015, effective March 26, 2015 (2015 WL 1343088).

Form 12.981(a)(5). Indian Child Welfare Act Affidavit

IN THE CIRCUIT COURT OF THE ______ JUDICIAL CIRCUIT,
IN AND FOR ____________ COUNTY, FLORIDA

Case No.: ____________________
Division: ____________________

IN THE MATTER OF THE ADOPTION OF

______________________________,
{use name to be given to the minor child(ren)} Adoptee(s).

INDIAN CHILD WELFARE ACT AFFIDAVIT

I, *{full legal name}*______________________, being sworn, certify that the following statements are true:
Upon information and belief the child ______________________ *{name}* subject to this proceeding: *{choose **one** only}*

1._____is not an Indian child. The Indian Child Welfare Act does not apply to this proceeding.

2._____is an Indian child within the meaning of the Indian Child Welfare Act of 1978 (25 U.S.C. Section 1901 et seq.).

I certify that a copy of this document was ( ) mailed ( ) faxed and mailed ( ) e-mailed ( ) hand-delivered to the person(s) listed below on *{date}* ______________________.

Other party or his/her attorney:
Name:______________________
Address:______________________
City, State, Zip:______________________
Fax Number: ______________________
Designated E-mail Address(es): ______________

I understand that I am swearing or affirming under oath to the truthfulness of the claims made in this affidavit and that the punishment for knowingly making a false statement includes fines and/or imprisonment.

Dated: ________________

____
Signature of Party
Printed Name: ______________________
Address: ______________________
City, State, Zip: ______________________
Telephone Number: ______________________
Fax Number: ______________________
Designated E-mail Address(es):______________________

Florida Supreme Court Approved Family Law Form 12.981(a)(5), Indian Child Welfare Act Affidavit (03/15)

STATE OF FLORIDA
COUNTY OF

Sworn to or affirmed and signed before me on ________ by ______________________________.

____
NOTARY PUBLIC or DEPUTY CLERK

____
{Print, type, or stamp commissioned name of notary or clerk.}

_____ Personally known
_____ Produced identification
Type of identification produced ______________

IF A NONLAWYER HELPED YOU FILL OUT THIS FORM, HE/SHE MUST FILL IN THE BLANKS BELOW:
[fill in **all** blanks] This form was prepared for the: *{choose only **one**}* ( ) Petitioner ( ) Respondent
This form was completed with the assistance of:
{name of individual} ______________________________,
{name of business} ______________________________,
{address} ______________________________,
{city} ______________,*{state}* ____, *{zip code}*________, *{telephone number}* ____________.

INSTRUCTIONS FOR FLORIDA SUPREME COURT APPROVED FAMILY LAW FORM 12.981(a)(5), INDIAN CHILD WELFARE ACT AFFIDAVIT (03/15)

When should this form be used?

This form should be used in cases involving stepparent adoption of a child. This **affidavit** is **required.**

This form should be typed or printed in black ink. After completing this form, you should sign the form before a **notary public** or **deputy clerk**. You should then **file** the original with the **clerk of the circuit court** in the county where the petition was filed and keep a copy for your records.

IMPORTANT INFORMATION REGARDING E-FILING

The Florida Rules of Judicial Administration now require that all petitions, pleadings, and documents be filed electronically except in certain circumstances. **Self-represented litigants may file petitions or other pleading or documents electronically; however, they are not required to do so.** If you choose to file your pleadings or other documents electronically, you must do so in accordance with Florida Rule of Judicial Administration 2.525, and you must follow the procedures of the judicial circuit in which you file. **The rules and procedures should be carefully read and followed.**

What should I do next?

A copy of this form must be mailed, e-mailed, or hand delivered to the other party in your case, if it is not served on him or her with your initial papers.

IMPORTANT INFORMATION REGARDING E–SERVICE ELECTION

After the initial service of process of the petition or supplemental petition by the Sheriff or certified process server, the Florida Rules of Judicial Administration now require that all documents required or permitted to be served on the other party must be served by electronic mail (e-mail) except in certain circumstances. **You must strictly comply with the format requirements set forth in the Rules of Judicial Administration.**

SELF–REPRESENTED LITIGANTS MAY SERVE DOCUMENTS BY E–MAIL; HOWEVER, THEY ARE NOT REQUIRED TO DO SO. If a self-represented litigant elects to serve and receive documents by e-mail, the procedures must always be followed once the initial election is made.

To serve and receive documents by e-mail, you must designate your e-mail addresses by using the **Designation of Current Mailing and E-mail Address**, Florida Supreme Court Approved Family Law Form 12.915, and you must provide your e-mail address on each form on which your signature appears. Please **CAREFULLY** read the rules and instructions for: **Certificate of Service (General),** Florida Supreme Court Approved Family Law Form 12.914; **Designation of Current Mailing and E-mail Address**, Florida Supreme Court Approved Family Law Form 12.915; and Florida Rule of Judicial Administration 2.516.

Where can I look for more information?

Before proceeding, you should read General Information for Self–Represented Litigants found at the beginning of these forms. The words that are in **bold underline** in these instructions are defined there.

Special notes . . .

Remember, a person who is NOT an attorney is called a nonlawyer. If a nonlawyer helps you fill out these forms, that person must give you a copy of a **Disclosure from Nonlawyer**, Florida Family Law Rules of Procedure Form 12.900 (a), before he or she helps you. A nonlawyer helping you fill out these forms also **must** put his or her name, address, and telephone number on the bottom of the last page of every form he or she helps you complete.

Added as 12.981(a)(8) Oct. 3, 2002 (821 So.2d 263). Renumbered from 12.981(a)(8) Mar. 25, 2004 (870 So.2d 791). Amended March 26, 2015, effective March 26, 2015 (2015 WL 1343088).

Form 12.981(a)(6). Motion for Search of the Putative Father Registry

IN THE CIRCUIT COURT OF THE ______________________ JUDICIAL CIRCUIT,
IN AND FOR ______________________ COUNTY, FLORIDA

Case No.: ______________________
Division: ______________________

IN THE MATTER OF THE ADOPTION OF

______________________________________,
{use name to be given to the minor child} Adoptee.

MOTION FOR SEARCH OF THE PUTATIVE FATHER REGISTRY

Petitioner, *{full legal name}* ______________________________, files this Motion for Search of the Putative Father Registry, pursuant to Chapter 63, Florida Statutes, and states:

1. This is an action for adoption of a minor by the child's stepparent, who is the Petitioner. .

2. Section 63.054, Florida Statutes, requires that in every adoption, a search of the Putative Father Registry maintained by the Department of Health, Office of Vital Statistics be conducted. Section 63.0541, Florida Statutes, makes information maintained by the Registry confidential and exempt from public disclosure, except that it may be disclosed to adoption entities, registrant unmarried biological fathers, and the court, upon issuance of a court order concerning a petitioner acting pro se.

3. The Florida Putative Father Registry - Application for Search is completed and attached to this Motion.

WHEREFORE, I request that this Court enter an Order Granting Motion for Search of the Putative Father Registry.

Florida Supreme Court Approved Family Law Form 12.981(a)(6), Motion for Search of Putative Father Registry (03/15)

I understand that I am swearing or affirming under oath to the truthfulness of the claims made in this motion and that the punishment for knowingly making a false statement includes fines and/or imprisonment.

Dated:____________________ ____

Signature of Party

Printed Name:____________________________________
Address: ____
City, State, Zip:__________________________________
Telephone Number: _______________________________
Fax Number:
Designated E-mail Address(es): __________________
____

STATE OF FLORIDA
COUNTY OF ___________________________

Sworn to or affirmed and signed before me on__________________by__________________.

____
NOTARY PUBLIC or DEPUTY CLERK

____
{Print, type, or stamp commissioned name of notary or clerk.}

_____ Personally known
_____ Produced identification
Type of identification produced ___________________________

IF A NONLAWYER HELPED YOU FILL OUT THIS FORM, HE/SHE MUST FILL IN THE BLANKS BELOW:
[fill in all blanks] This form was prepared for the petitioner.
This form was completed with the assistance of:
*{name of individual}*____,
{name of business} ____,

Florida Supreme Court Approved Family Law Form 12.981(a)(6), Motion for Search of Putative Father Registry (03/15)

{address} ____,
*{city}*_______________,*{state}* ____, *{zip code}*___________, *{telephone number}*_____________.

Florida Supreme Court Approved Family Law Form 12.981(a)(6), Motion for Search of Putative Father Registry (03/15)

INSTRUCTIONS FOR FLORIDA SUPREME COURT APPROVED FAMILY LAW FORM 12.981(a)(6), MOTION FOR SEARCH OF THE PUTATIVE FATHER REGISTRY (03/15)

When should this form be used?

This form should be used when a stepparent is adopting his or her **spouse's** child. Section 63.054, Florida Statutes, requires that a search of Florida's Putative Father Registry be conducted in every adoption proceeding. The Office of Vital Statistics of the Department of Health has an application available called Florida Putative Father Registry—Application for Search which should be completed and attached to this form. The Office of Vital Statistics is allowed to charge for searching the registry. You may wish to contact that office in advance to find out what amount and method of payment will be accepted.

This form should be typed or printed in black ink. The name to be given to the adoptee **after** the adoption should be used in the heading of the **petition**. The stepparent is the **petitioner**, because he or she is the one who is asking the court for legal action. You must have your signature witnessed by a **notary public** or **deputy clerk**.

After completing this form, you should **file** the original with the **clerk of the circuit court** in the county where you have filed the **Joint Petition for Adoption by Stepparent,** Florida Supreme Court Approved Family Law Form 12.981(b)(1) and keep a copy for your records. These family law forms contain an **Order Granting Motion for Search of Putative Father Registry,** Florida Supreme Court Approved Family Law Form 12.981(a)(7), which the judge may use. You should check with the clerk, family law intake staff or judicial assistant to see if you need to provide this form order to the judge with your motion. If so, you should type or print the heading, including the circuit, county, case number, division, and the child(ren)'s name, and leave the rest blank for the judge to complete.

IMPORTANT INFORMATION REGARDING E–FILING

The Florida Rules of Judicial Administration now require that all petitions, pleadings, and documents be filed electronically except in certain circumstances. **Self-represented litigants may file petitions or other pleadings or documents electronically; however, they are not required to do so.** If you choose to file your pleadings or other documents electronically, you must do so in accordance with Florida Rule of Judicial Administration 2.525, and you must follow the procedures of the judicial circuit in which you file. **The rules and procedures should be carefully read and followed.**

What should I do next?

If the judge grants your motion, you will need to take the order, your completed application, and any fee to the Office of Vital Statistics. That office will conduct the search and file the results with the clerk of court. You may call the clerk's office to determine when the results have been filed in order to set a final hearing.

Where can I look for more information?

Before proceeding, you should read General Information for Self–Represented Litigants found at the beginning of these forms. See Chapter 63, Florida Statutes, and Florida Family Law Rule 12.200(a)(2) for further information.

IMPORTANT INFORMATION REGARDING E–SERVICE ELECTION

After the initial service of process of the petition or supplemental petition by the Sheriff or certified process server, the Florida Rules of Judicial Administration now require that all documents required or permitted to be served on the other party must be served by electronic mail (e-mail) except in certain circumstances. **You must strictly comply with the format requirements set forth in the Rules of Judicial Administration.**

SELF–REPRESENTED LITIGANTS MAY SERVE DOCUMENTS BY E–MAIL; HOWEVER, THEY ARE NOT REQUIRED TO DO SO. If a self-represented litigant elects to serve and receive documents by e-mail, the procedures must always be followed once the initial election is made.

To serve and receive documents by e-mail, you must designate your e-mail addresses by using the **Designation of Current Mailing and E-mail Address**, Florida Supreme Court Approved

Family Law Form 12.915, and you must provide your e-mail address on each form on which your signature appears. Please **CAREFULLY** read the rules and instructions for: **Certificate of Service (General),** Florida Supreme Court Approved Family Law Form 12.914; **Designation of Current Mailing and E-mail Address**, Florida Supreme Court Approved Family Law Form 12.915; and Florida Rule of Judicial Administration 2.516.

Special notes . . .

THIS ADOPTION MAY AFFECT THE ADOPTEE'S INHERITANCE.

Remember, a person who is NOT an attorney is called a nonlawyer. If a nonlawyer helps you fill out these forms, that person must give you a copy of a **Disclosure from Nonlawyer**, Florida Family Law Rules of Procedure Form 12.900 (a), before he or she helps you. A nonlawyer helping you fill out these forms also **must** put his or her name, address, and telephone number on the bottom of the last page of every form he or she helps you complete.

Added Mar. 25, 2004 (870 So.2d 791). Amended March 26, 2015, effective March 26, 2015 (2015 WL 1343088).

Form 12.981(a)(7). Order Granting Motion for Search of the Putative Father Registry

IN THE CIRCUIT COURT OF THE ________________ JUDICIAL CIRCUIT,
IN AND FOR ____________________________ COUNTY, FLORIDA

Case No.: ____________________
Division: ____________________

IN THE MATTER OF THE ADOPTION OF

____________________________________,
{use name to be given to the minor child} Adoptee.

ORDER GRANTING MOTION FOR SEARCH OF THE PUTATIVE FATHER REGISTRY

Upon consideration of Petitioner's Motion for Search of the Putative Father Registry, this Court finds:

1. This is an action for adoption of a minor by the child's stepparent, Petitioner, who is proceeding pro se.

2. Section 63.054, Florida Statutes, requires that in every adoption, a search of the Putative Father Registry maintained by the Department of Health, Office of Vital Statistics be conducted. Section 63.0541, Florida Statutes, makes information maintained by the Registry confidential and exempt, except that it may be disclosed to adoption entities, registrant unmarried biological fathers, the birth mother, and the court, upon issuance of a court order concerning a petitioner acting pro se.

NOW, THEREFORE, IT IS ORDERED THAT:

1. The Office of Vital Statistics, Department of Health shall conduct a search of the Putative Father Registry upon receipt of a completed application and payment of any authorized fee.

2. The State Registrar shall issue a certificate indicating the results of such search which shall be filed in this proceeding by transmitting the certificate to the clerk of court.

DONE and ORDERED on: ____________________ in __________________________, Florida.

____

Florida Supreme Court Approved Family Law Form 12.981(a)(7), Order Granting Motion for Search of Putative Father Registry (03/15)

Circuit Judge

I certify that a copy of the *{name of document(s)}*____
was ( ) mailed ( ) faxed and mailed ( ) e-mailed ( ) hand-delivered to the parties and to any other persons or entities listed below on *{date}* ____.

____
By: *Clerk of Court, Designee, or Judicial Assistant*

Petitioner (or his or her attorney)
Other: __________________________
State Registrar, Office of Vital Statistics

Florida Supreme Court Approved Family Law Form 12.981(a)(7), Order Granting Motion for Search of Putative Father Registry (03/15)

Added Mar. 25, 2004 (870 So.2d 791). Amended March 26, 2015, effective March 26, 2015 (2015 WL 1343088).

Form 12.981(b)(1). Joint Petition for Adoption by Stepparent

IN THE CIRCUIT COURT OF THE ______________ JUDICIAL CIRCUIT,
IN AND FOR ______________________ COUNTY, FLORIDA

Case No.: ______________________
Division: ______________________

IN THE MATTER OF THE ADOPTION OF

____,
{use name to be given to child(ren)} Adoptee(s).

JOINT PETITION FOR ADOPTION BY STEPPARENT

Petitioner, *{full legal name}* ______________________________ being sworn, joined by the above-named child(ren)'s _____ mother _____ father, *{full legal name}* ______________ ______________, being sworn, files this joint petition for adoption of the above-named minor child(ren), under chapter 63, Florida Statutes.

1. This is an action for adoption of a minor child(ren) by his or her (their) stepparent.

2. I desire to adopt the following child(ren):

	Name to be given to child(ren)	Birth date	Birthplace
a.			
b.			
c.			
d.			
e.			
f.			

A certified copy of the birth certificate(s) is/are attached.

3. The child(ren) has (have) resided with me since *{date}* ______________________. I wish to adopt the child(ren) because I would like to legally establish the parent-child relationship already existing between the child(ren) and me. Since the above date, I have been able to provide adequately for the material needs of the child(ren) and am able to continue doing so in the future, as well as to provide for the child(ren)'s mental and emotional well-being. Other reasons I wish to adopt the children are: ______________________
____
____

4. I am _________ years old, and have resided at *{street address}*, ______________ *{city}* ______________ *{county}* ____________ *{state}* _______ for _____ years.

5. I married the _____ father or _____ mother of the child(ren) on *{date}* ______________,

Florida Supreme Court Approved Family Law Form 12.981(b)(1), Joint Petition for Adoption by Stepparent (03/15)

in *{city}* ____________________, *{county}* ____________________, *{state}* ____________________.
The following are the dates and places of my dissolutions of marriage, if any:

Date Place

a. ____
b. ____

6. A completed **Uniform Child Custody Jurisdiction and Enforcement Act Affidavit (UCCJEA)**, Florida Supreme Court Approved Family Law Form 12.902(d), is filed with this petition.

7. A description and estimate of the value of any property of the adoptee(s) is as follows:
____
____
____
____.

8. Consent by the adoptee(s):
_____ is attached for: *Name(s)* ____________________
_____ is not required because the adoptee(s) is/are not 12 years of age: *Name(s)* ____________________
_____ was excused by the court for: *Name(s)* ____________________

9. The following person(s) is/are required to consent and the consent form or affidavit of nonpaternity is/are attached ____________________

10. The following person(s) whose consent is required has not consented. The facts/circumstances that excuse the lack of consent and would justify termination of this person's parental rights are:

Name Address Facts/circumstances
____
____
____
____

11. A copy of this Petition was served on all known persons whose consent is required but did not waive notice, as well as on all persons whose consent is required but did not provide consent. Proof of service is attached.

{Indicate if applicable}:

_____ A search of the Putative Father Registry maintained by the Office of Vital Statistics of the Department of Health has been requested, and if granted, the certificate from the State Registrar will be filed in this action.

WHEREFORE, I request that this Court terminate the parental rights of ____________________, *{name of parent whose rights are sought to be terminated}*, enter a Final Judgment of Adoption of the

Minor Child(ren) by Petitioner Stepparent and, as requested, change the name of the adoptee(s).

I understand that I am swearing or affirming under oath to the truthfulness of the claims made in this petition and that the punishment for knowingly making a false statement includes fines and/or imprisonment.

Dated: ______________________

____
Signature of Stepparent

Printed Name: ______________________
Address: ______________________
City, State, Zip: ______________________
Telephone Number: ______________________
Fax Number: ______________________
Designated E-mail Address(es): ______________________
____

STATE OF FLORIDA
COUNTY OF______________________

Sworn to or affirmed and signed before me on ______________ by ______________________

____
NOTARY PUBLIC or DEPUTY CLERK

____
[Print, type, or stamp commissioned name of notary or deputy clerk.]

_____ Personally known
_____ Produced identification
Type of identification produced ______________________

I understand that I am swearing or affirming under oath to the truthfulness of the claims made in this petition and that the punishment for knowingly making a false statement includes fines and/or imprisonment.

Dated:______________________________

____
Signature of ___ Mother ___ Father
Printed Name: ______________________________
Address: ______________________________
City, State, Zip: ______________________________
Telephone Number: ______________________________
Fax Number: ______________________________
Designated E-mail Address(es): ______________________________

STATE OF FLORIDA
COUNTY OF ______________________________

Sworn to or affirmed and signed before me on ________________ by ________________.

____
NOTARY PUBLIC or DEPUTY CLERK

____
[Print, type, or stamp commissioned name of notary or deputy clerk.]

___ Personally known
___ Produced identification
___ Type of identification produced ______________________________

IF A NONLAWYER HELPED YOU FILL OUT THIS FORM, HE/SHE MUST FILL IN THE BLANKS BELOW:
[fill in **all** blanks] This form was prepared for the: ( ) parent ( ) stepparent ( ) both.
This form was prepared with the assistance of:
{name of individual} ______________________________,
{name of business} ______________________________,
{address} ______________________________,
{city} ________________,*{state}*_______, *{zip code}*_________, *{telephone number}*_________.

Florida Supreme Court Approved Family Law Form 12.981(b)(1), Joint Petition for Adoption by Stepparent (03/15)

INSTRUCTIONS FOR FLORIDA SUPREME COURT APPROVED FAMILY LAW FORM 12.981(b)(1), JOINT PETITION FOR ADOPTION BY STEPPARENT (03/15)

When should this form be used?

This form should be used when a stepparent is adopting his or her **spouse**'s child. Both the stepparent and his or her spouse must sign this **petition**. You must attach all necessary consents or acknowledgments that apply to your case, as listed under the Special Notes section below. Florida Statutes require that consent to adoption be obtained from:

- The mother of the minor.
- The father of the minor if:

1. The minor was conceived or born while the father was married to the mother;
2. The minor is his child by adoption;
3. The minor has been established by a court proceeding to be his child;
4. He has filed an affidavit of paternity pursuant to section 382.013(2)(c) Florida Statutes; or
5. In the case of an unmarried biological father, he has acknowledged in writing, signed in the presence of a competent witness, that he is the father of the minor, has filed such acknowledgment with the Office of Vital Statistics of the Department of Health within the required timeframes, and has complied with the requirements of section 63.062(2), Florida Statutes.

Determining whether someone's consent is required, or when consent may not be required is a complicated issue and you may wish to consult an attorney. For more information about consenting to adoption, you should refer to Chapter 63, Florida Statutes, and sections 63.062–63.082 in particular.

This form should be typed or printed in black ink. The name to be given to the child(ren) **after** the adoption should be used in the heading of the petition. The stepparent is the **petitioner**, because he or she is the one who is asking the court for legal action. After completing this form, you and your spouse must sign it before a **notary public** or **deputy clerk**. You should then **file** the original and 1 copy with the **clerk of the circuit court** in the county where the minor resides unless the court changes the venue.

IMPORTANT INFORMATION REGARDING E–FILING

The Florida Rules of Judicial Administration now require that all petitions, pleadings, and documents be filed electronically except in certain circumstances. **Self-represented litigants may file petitions or other pleadings or documents electronically; however, they are not required to do so.** If you choose to file your pleadings or documents electronically, you must do so in accordance with Florida Rule of Judicial Administration 2.525, and you must follow the procedures of the judicial circuit in which you file. **The rules and procedures should be carefully read and followed.**

What should I do next?

For your case to proceed, you must have the written consent of the other birth parent and the child, if applicable. The **court** may choose not to require consent to an adoption in some circumstances. For more information about situations where consent may not be required, see section 63.064, Florida Statutes. If you are attempting to proceed without the consent of the other birth parent, you may wish to consult with an attorney. Section 63.054, Florida Statutes, requires that in each adoption proceeding, the Florida Putative Father Registry be searched. You will need an order from the judge to do this, which you can request by filing a **Motion for Search of the Putative Father Registry,** Florida Supreme Court Approved Family Law Form 12.981(a)(6).

When you have filed all of the required forms and met the requirements as outlined above, you are ready to set a **hearing** on your petition. You should check with the clerk of court, **family law intake staff** or the **judicial assistant** to set a **final hearing**. If all persons required to consent have consented and the consents/affidavits of nonpaternity have been filed with the court, the hearing may be held immediately. If not, notice of the hearing must be given as provided by the Rules of Civil Procedure. See Form 1.902, Florida Rules of Civil Procedure. If you know where the other birth parent lives, you should use **personal service.** If you absolutely do not know where he or she lives, you may use **constructive service.** In order to use constructive service you will need to complete and submit to the court **Stepparent Adoption: Affidavit of Diligent Search**, Florida Supreme Court Approved Family Law Form 12.981(a)(4). For more information about personal and constructive service, you should refer to the **"General Instructions for Self–Represented Litigants"** found at the beginning of these forms and the instructions to Florida Family Law Rules of Procedure Forms 12.910(a) and 12.913(b) and Florida Supreme Court Approved Family Law Form 12.913(a). However, the law regarding constructive service is very complex and you may wish to consult an attorney regarding that issue.

Where can I look for more information?

Before proceeding, you should read "General Information for Self–Represented Litigants" found at the beginning of these forms. See Chapter 63, Florida Statutes, and Florida Family Law Rule 12.200(a)(2) for further information.

IMPORTANT INFORMATION REGARDING E–SERVICE ELECTION

After the initial service of process of the petition or supplemental petition by the Sheriff or certified process server, the Florida Rules of Judicial Administration now require that all documents required or permitted to be served on the other party must be served by electronic mail (e-mail) except in certain circumstances. **You must strictly comply with the format requirements set forth in the Rules of Judicial Administration.**

SELF–REPRESENTED LITIGANTS MAY SERVE DOCUMENTS BY E–MAIL; HOWEVER, THEY ARE NOT REQUIRED TO DO SO. If a self-represented litigant elects to serve and receive documents by e-mail, the procedures must always be followed once the initial election is made.

To serve and receive documents by e-mail, you must designate your e-mail addresses by using the **Designation of Current Mailing and E-mail Address**, Florida Supreme Court Approved Family Law Form 12.915, and you must provide your e-mail address on each form on which your signature appears. Please **CAREFULLY** read the rules and instructions for: **Certificate of Service (General),** Florida Supreme Court Approved Family Law Form 12.914; **Designation of Current Mailing and E-mail Address,** Florida Supreme Court Approved Family Law Form 12.915; and Florida Rule of Judicial Administration 2.516.

Special notes . . .

With this petition you must file the following:

- Consent form executed by the birth parent, **Stepparent Adoption: Consent and Waiver by Parent,** Florida Supreme Court Approved Family Law Form 12.981(a)(1) or **Stepparent Adoption: Affidavit of Nonpaternity,** Florida Supreme Court Approved Family Law Form 12.981(a)(3).
- If any person whose consent is required is deceased, a certified copy of the death certificate must be attached to this Petition.
- Consent form executed by the minor child(ren), if the child(ren) is/are over 12 years of age, **Stepparent Adoption: Consent of Adoptee,** Florida Supreme Court Approved Family Law Form 12.981(a)(2). The court can excuse filing of this form under certain circumstances.
- Certified copy of the child(ren)'s birth certificate.
- **Uniform Child Custody Jurisdiction and Enforcement Act (UCCJEA) Affidavit,** Florida Supreme Court Approved Family Law Form 12.902(d).
- If applicable, **Stepparent Adoption: Motion for Search of the Putative Father Registry,** Florida Supreme Court Approved Family Law Form 12.981(a)(6).

These family law forms contain a **Final Judgment of Stepparent Adoption**, Florida Supreme Court Approved Family Law Form 12.981(b)(2), which the judge may use. You should check with the clerk, family law intake staff, or judicial assistant to see if you need to bring a final judgment form with you to the hearing. If so, you should type or print the heading, including the circuit, county case number, division, and the child(ren)'s names, and leave the rest blank for the judge to complete at your hearing. You should decide how many **certified copies** of the final judgment you will need and be prepared to obtain them after the hearing. There is a charge for certified copies, and the clerk can tell you how much. The file will be sealed after the final hearing, and then it will take an order from a judge to open the file and obtain a copy of the final judgment.

AN ADOPTIVE STEPPARENT WILL CONTINUE TO HAVE PARENTAL RIGHTS, INCLUDING CUSTODY AND TIME–SHARING, WHERE APPROPRIATE, IN THE EVENT OF A LATER DISSOLUTION OF MARRIAGE, AND MAY BE LIABLE FOR CHILD SUPPORT IN THE EVENT OF A LATER DISSOLUTION OF MARRIAGE. YOU COULD BE LIABLE IN LITIGATION FOR THE ACTIONS OF THE ADOPTEE(S). THIS ADOPTION MAY ALSO AFFECT THE ADOPTEE'S INHERITANCE.

Remember, a person who is NOT an attorney is called a nonlawyer. If a nonlawyer helps you fill out these forms, that person must give you a copy of a **Disclosure from Nonlawyer**, Florida Family Law Rules of Procedure Form 12.900 (a), before he or she helps you. A nonlawyer helping you fill out these forms also **must** put his or her name, address, and telephone number on the bottom of the last page of every form he or she helps you complete.

Added as 12.981(a)(1) Feb. 26, 1998, effective Mar. 16, 1998 (713 So.2d 1). Amended Sept. 21, 2000 (810 So.2d 1). Renumbered from 12.981(a)(1) and amended Mar. 28, 2002 (821 So.2d 263). Amended Oct. 3, 2002 (832 So.2d 684); Dec. 19, 2002 (836 So.2d 1019); Mar. 25, 2004 (870 So.2d 791); March 26, 2009 (20 So.3d 173); Dec. 16, 2010 (59 So.3d 792); March 26, 2015, effective March 26, 2015 (2015 WL 1343088).

Form 12.981(b)(2). Final Judgment of Stepparent Adoption

IN THE CIRCUIT COURT OF THE ________ JUDICIAL CIRCUIT,
IN AND FOR ______________________ COUNTY, FLORIDA

Case No.: ______________
Division: ______________

IN THE MATTER OF THE ADOPTION OF

_________________________________,
{use name to be given to child(ren)} Adoptee(s).

FINAL JUDGMENT OF STEPPARENT ADOPTION

Upon consideration of the Joint Petition for Adoption by Stepparent and the evidence presented, the Court finds that:

1. The Court has subject matter jurisdiction over the Joint Petition for Adoption by Stepparent.
2. The Court has jurisdiction over the minor child(ren) subject to the Joint Petition for Adoption by Stepparent.
3. Petitioner desires the permanent responsibility of a parent in this adoption.
4. There is no pending litigation regarding the child(ren) in Florida or in any other state, nor is there any other person not a party to these proceedings who has or claims to have physical custody or rights to the minor child(ren).
5. The consent of the birth _____mother _____ father who is not married to Petitioner is: *{Choose only **one**}*

_____ Attached to the petition
_____ Not required because he or she is deceased. A certified copy of the death certificate is attached.
_____ Waived because:
[Indicate all that apply]
_____ The parent has deserted the child without means of identification or has abandoned the child.
_____ The parent's rights have been terminated by a court of competent jurisdiction.
_____ The parent has been declared incompetent and restoration of competency is medically improbable.
_____ The legal guardian or lawful custodian of the adoptee(s), other than the birth parent, who has failed to respond in writing to a request for consent for a period of 60 days or the Court has examined the written reasons for withholding consent and has found the withholding of consent to be unreasonable.
_____ Other: ____.

Florida Supreme Court Approved Family Law Form 12.981(b)(2), Final Judgment of Stepparent Adoption (03/15)

6. The best interests of the child(ren) will be promoted by this adoption.

7. The minor child(ren) is (are) suitable for adoption by Petitioner.

NOW, THEREFORE, IT IS ORDERED that:

1. The minor child(ren) subject to the Petition is (are) declared to be the legal child(ren) of Petitioner,____ *{name}*

2. The minor child(ren) shall be the child(ren) and legal heir(s) at law of Petitioner, ____, *{name}* and shall be entitled to all rights and privileges, and subject to all obligations, of child(ren) born of Petitioner.

3. All legal relations between the adoptee(s) and the parent whose rights are being terminated and between the adoptee(s) and the relatives of that parent are terminated by this adoption, as are all parental rights and responsibilities of that birth parent.

4. This Final Judgment of Adoption creates a relationship between the adoptee(s) and Petitioner and all relatives of Petitioner that would have existed if the adoptee(s) was (were) a blood descendant of the Petitioner, born within wedlock, entitled to all rights and privileges thereof, and subject to all obligations of a child being born to Petitioner.

5. The minor child(ren) shall hereafter be known as *{full legal name(s)}*:
____
____
____
____

DONE AND ORDERED at ____________________, Florida on ____________.

____
CIRCUIT JUDGE

I certify that a copy of *{name of document(s)}* ______________________________was ( ) mailed ( ) faxed and mailed ( ) e-mailed ( ) hand-delivered to the parties and any persons or entities listed below on *{date}* ____________.

____
By: *Clerk of Court, Designee, or Judicial Assistant*

Florida Supreme Court Approved Family Law Form 12.981(b)(2), Final Judgment of Stepparent Adoption (03/15)

Petitioners (or their attorney)
Other: ______________________

Florida Supreme Court Approved Family Law Form 12.981(b)(2), Final Judgment of Stepparent Adoption (03/15)

Added as 12.981(g) July 1, 1995, effective Jan. 1, 1996 (663 So.2d 1047). Amended Feb. 26, 1998, effective Mar. 16, 1998 (713 So.2d 1); Sept. 21, 2000 (810 So.2d 1). Renumbered from 12.981(g) Mar. 28, 2002 (821 So.2d 263). Amended Mar. 25, 2004 (870 So.2d 791); March 26, 2009 (20 So.3d 173); Dec. 16, 2010 (59 So.3d 792); March 26, 2015, effective March 26, 2015 (2015 WL 1343088).

Form 12.981(c)(1). Petition for Adoption of Adult by Stepparent

IN THE CIRCUIT COURT OF THE ______________ JUDICIAL CIRCUIT,
IN AND FOR __________________________ COUNTY, FLORIDA

Case No.: ______________________________
Division: ______________________________

IN THE MATTER OF THE ADOPTION OF

__________________________________,
{use name to be given to adult} Adoptee.

PETITION FOR ADOPTION OF ADULT BY STEPPARENT

Petitioner, *{full legal name}* ____, files this petition for adoption of the above-named adult, pursuant to Chapter 63, Florida Statutes, and states:

1. This is an action for adoption of an adult by the adult's stepparent, Petitioner.

2. I desire to adopt *{adult's full legal name}* ____, who was born on *{date}* ____________________, at *{city, county, and state}* ________________ ____.

3. I desire to adopt the adult because: ____ ____ ____.

4. I am _____ years old, and I have resided at *{address}* ______________________________, ____________________________, Florida for ______ years.

5. The adoptee's name shall be:

6. The adoptee's birth parents are:

____
Father's Name Birth date

____

Address

Mother's Name Birth date

Address

7. **Notice.** Notice to the birth parents was made by:

8. **Consent.**
*{Indicate **all** that apply}*

a. _____ The consent of the adoptee is attached.
b. _____ The adoptee is married to *{full legal name of adoptee=s spouse}* ______________ ________________________________, and the consent of the spouse is attached.
c. _____ The adoptee is not married.

9. Written notice of this final hearing was provided to the parents or proof of service of process showing notice has been served on the parents is attached.

WHEREFORE, I request that this Court enter a Final Judgment of Adoption of the Adult by Petitioner Stepparent and change the name of the adoptee.

I understand that I am swearing or affirming under oath to the truthfulness of the claims made in this petition and that the punishment for knowingly making a false statement includes fines and/or imprisonment.

Dated: ____________________

____
Signature of Petitioner
Printed Name: ____________________
Address: ____________________
City, State, Zip: ____________________
Telephone Number: ____________________
Fax Number: ____________________
Designated E-mail Address(es):____________________
____

STATE OF FLORIDA
COUNTY OF

Sworn to or affirmed and signed before me on ____________ by ______________________.

Florida Supreme Court Approved Family Law Form 12.981(c)(1), Petition for Adoption of Adult by Stepparent (03/15)

____
NOTARY PUBLIC or DEPUTY CLERK

____
[Print, type, or stamp commissioned name of notary or clerk.]

____ Personally known
____ Produced identification
Type of identification produced

IF A NONLAWYER HELPED YOU FILL OUT THIS FORM, HE/SHE MUST FILL IN THE BLANKS BELOW:
[fill in **all** blanks] This form was prepared for the petitioner.
This form was completed with the assistance of:
*{name of individual}*____,
*{name of business}*____,
*{address}*____,
{city} ________________,*{state}* ______, *{zip code}*__________, *{telephone number}*_____________.

Florida Supreme Court Approved Family Law Form 12.981(c)(1), Petition for Adoption of Adult by Stepparent (03/15)

INSTRUCTIONS FOR FLORIDA SUPREME COURT APPROVED FAMILY LAW FORM 12.981(c)(1), PETITION FOR ADOPTION OF ADULT BY STEPPARENT (03/15)

When should this form be used?

This form should be used when a stepparent is adopting his or her **spouse's adult** child. You must obtain the written consent of the adult child to be adopted, as well as the written consent of his or her spouse (if married).

This form should be typed or printed in black ink. The name to be given to the adoptee **after** the adoption should be used in the heading of the **petition**. The stepparent is the **petitioner**, because he or she is the one who is asking the court for legal action. You must have your signature witnessed by a **notary public** or **deputy clerk**.

After completing this form, you should **file** the original with the **clerk of the circuit court** in the county where either you or the adoptee live and keep a copy for your records.

IMPORTANT INFORMATION REGARDING E–FILING

The Florida Rules of Judicial Administration now require that petitions, pleadings, and documents be filed electronically except in certain circumstances. **Self-represented litigants may file a petition or other pleadings electronically; however, they are not required to do so.** If you choose to file your petition, or other pleading or document electronically, you must do so in accordance with Florida Rule of Judicial Administration 2.525, and you must follow the procedures of the judicial circuit in which you file. **The rules and procedures should be carefully read and followed.**

What should I do next?

For your case to proceed, you must have the written consent of the adoptee, and his or her spouse if married. Consent of the birth parent is not required, but written notice of the final hearing on the adoption must be provided to the parents, if any, or proof of service of process must be filed showing notice has been served on the parents. If you know where they live, you must use **personal service**. If you absolutely do not know where they live, you may use **constructive service**. For more information about personal and constructive service, you should refer the **General Instructions for Self–Represented Litigants** found at the beginning of these forms and the instructions to Florida Family Law Rules of Procedure Forms 12.910(a) and 12.913(b) and Florida Supreme Court Approved Family Law Form 12.913(a). However, the law regarding constructive service is very complex and you may wish to consult an attorney regarding that issue.

When you have filed all of the required forms and met the requirements for consent as outlined above, you are ready to set a **hearing** on your petition. You should check with the clerk of court, **family law intake staff**, or **judicial assistant** to set a **final hearing**, and notify the other party(ies) using a **Notice of Hearing (General)**, Florida Supreme Court Approved Family Law Form 12.923, or other appropriate notice of hearing form.

IMPORTANT INFORMATION REGARDING E–SERVICE ELECTION

After the initial service of process of the petition or supplemental petition by the Sheriff or certified process server, the Florida Rules of Judicial Administration now require that all documents required or permitted to be served on the other party must be served by electronic mail (e-mail) except in certain circumstances. **You must strictly comply with the format requirements set forth in the Rules of Judicial Administration.**

SELF–REPRESENTED LITIGANTS MAY SERVE DOCUMENTS BY E–MAIL; HOWEVER, THEY ARE NOT REQUIRED TO DO SO. If a self-represented litigant elects to serve and receive documents by e-mail, the procedures must always be followed once the initial election is made.

To serve and receive documents by e-mail, you must designate your e-mail addresses by using the **Designation of Current Mailing and E-mail Address**, Florida Supreme Court Approved Family Law Form 12.915, and you must provide your e-mail address on each form on which your signature appears. Please **CAREFULLY** read the rules and instructions for: **Certificate of Service (General),** Florida Supreme Court Approved Family Law Form 12.914;

Designation of Current Mailing and E-mail Address, Florida Supreme Court Approved Family Law Form 12.915; and Florida Rule of Judicial Administration 2.516.

Where can I look for more information?

Before proceeding, you should read General Information for Self–Represented Litigants found at the beginning of these forms. See Chapter 63, Florida Statutes, and Florida Family Law Rule 12.200(a)(2) for further information.

Special notes . . .

With this petition you must file the following forms:

Stepparent Adoption: Consent of Adoptee, Florida Supreme Court Approved Family Law Form 12.981(a)(2)

Stepparent Adoption: Consent of Adult Adoptee's Spouse, Florida Supreme Court Approved Family Law Form 12.981(c)(2), if the adoptee is married

THIS ADOPTION MAY AFFECT THE ADOPTEE'S INHERITANCE.

Remember, a person who is NOT an attorney is called a nonlawyer. If a nonlawyer helps you fill out these forms, that person must give you a copy of a **Disclosure from Nonlawyer**, Florida Family Law Rules of Procedure Form 12.900(a), before he or she helps you. A nonlawyer helping you fill out these forms also **must** put his or her name, address, and telephone number on the bottom of the last page of every form he or she helps you complete.

Added as 12.981(a)(2) Feb. 26, 1998, effective Mar. 16, 1998 (713 So.2d 1). Amended Sept. 21, 2000 (810 So.2d 1). Renumbered from 12.981(a)(2) Mar. 28, 2002 (821 So.2d 263). Amended Oct. 3, 2002 (832 So.2d 684); Mar. 25, 2004 (870 So.2d 791); March 26, 2015, effective March 26, 2015 (2015 WL 1343088).

Form 12.981(c)(2). Stepparent Adoption: Consent of Adult Adoptee's Spouse

IN THE CIRCUIT COURT OF THE ______ JUDICIAL CIRCUIT,
IN AND FOR ____________ COUNTY, FLORIDA

Case No.: ______________________
Division: ______________________

IN RE: THE ADOPTION OF

______________________________,
{use name to be given to adult} Adoptee(s).

STEPPARENT ADOPTION: CONSENT OF ADULT ADOPTEE'S SPOUSE

1. I, *{full legal name}* ______________________, am the _____ wife _____ husband of *{full legal name}* ______________________, who Petitioner, *{full legal name}* ______________________ wishes to adopt.
2. I consent to the adoption of my spouse by Petitioner.
3. I understand my right to choose a person who does not have an employment, professional, or personal relationship with the adoption entity or the prospective adoptive parents to be present when this affidavit is executed and to sign it as a witness. The witness I selected is: *{full legal name}* ______________________.

I understand that I am swearing or affirming under oath to the truthfulness of the claims made in this consent and that the punishment for knowingly making a false statement includes fines and/or imprisonment.

Dated: ____________________

____
Signature of Spouse
Printed Name: ______________________
Address: ______________________
City, State, Zip: ______________________
Telephone Number: ______________________
Fax Number: ______________________
Designated E-mail Address(es): ______________________
____

____
Signature of Witness
Printed Name: ______________________
Business Address: ______________________
Home Address: ______________________

____
Signature of Witness
Printed Name: ______________________
Business Address: ______________________
Home Address: ______________________

Florida Supreme Court Approved Family Law Form 12.981(c)(2), Stepparent Adoption: Consent of Adult Adoptee's Spouse (03/15)

Driver's License or
State ID Card No.:______________________

Driver's License or
State ID Card No.:______________________

STATE OF FLORIDA
COUNTY OF

Sworn to or affirmed and signed before me on ____________ by ______________________.

____
NOTARY PUBLIC or DEPUTY CLERK

____
{Print, type, or stamp commissioned name of notary or deputy clerk.}

______ Personally known
______ Produced identification
Type of identification produced

IF A NONLAWYER HELPED YOU FILL OUT THIS FORM, HE/SHE MUST FILL IN THE BLANKS BELOW:
[fill in **all** blanks] This form was prepared for the ( ) stepparent ( ) adult adoptee's spouse.
This form was completed with the assistance of:
*{name of individual}*______________________,
*{name of business}*______________________,
*{address}*______________________,
*{city}*______________,*{state}*_____, *{zip code}*__________*{telephone number}*__________.

Florida Supreme Court Approved Family Law Form 12.981(c)(2), Stepparent Adoption: Consent of Adult Adoptee's Spouse (03/15)

INSTRUCTIONS FOR FLORIDA SUPREME COURT APPROVED FAMILY LAW FORM 12.981(c)(2), STEPPARENT ADOPTION: CONSENT OF ADULT ADOPTEE'S SPOUSE (03/15)

When should this form be used?

This form must be completed by the **spouse** of an adult who is being adopted.

This form should be typed or printed in black ink. After completing this form, the spouse of the adoptee should sign the form before a **notary public** or **deputy clerk**. You should **file** the original with the **clerk of the circuit court** in the county where the **petition** for adoption of an adult was filed and keep a copy for your records.

IMPORTANT INFORMATION REGARDING E–FILING

The Florida Rules of Judicial Administration now require that all petitions, pleadings, and documents be filed electronically except in certain circumstances. **Self-represented litigants may file petitions or other pleadings or documents electronically; however, they are not required to do so.** If you choose to file your pleading or other document electronically, you must do so in accordance with Florida Rule of Judicial Administration 2.525, and you must follow the procedures of the judicial circuit in which you file. **The rules and procedures should be carefully read and followed.**

Special notes ...

Remember, a person who is NOT an attorney is called a nonlawyer. If a nonlawyer helps you fill out these forms, that person must give you a copy of **Disclosure from Nonlawyer**, Florida Family Law Rules of Procedure Form 12.900 (a), before he or she helps you. A nonlawyer helping you fill out these forms also **must** put his or her name, address, and telephone number on the bottom of the last page of every form he or she helps you complete.

Added Feb. 26, 1998, effective Mar. 16, 1998 (713 So.2d 1). Amended Sept. 21, 2000 (810 So.2d 1); Mar. 25, 2004 (870 So.2d 791); March 26, 2015, effective March 26, 2015 (2015 WL 1343088).

Form 12.981(d)(1). Petition for Adoption Information

IN THE CIRCUIT COURT OF THE ______ JUDICIAL CIRCUIT,
IN AND FOR ______________ COUNTY, FLORIDA

Case No.: ________________
Division: ________________

IN RE: THE ADOPTION OF

______________________________,
Adoptee(s).

PETITION FOR ADOPTION INFORMATION

1. I, *{full legal name}* ______________________, am interested in this matter as:
*{choose **one** only}*
_____adult adoptee (over 18).
_____adoptive parent.
_____adult birth sibling.
_____other: *{specify}* ____.

2. The adoptee(s), *{name(s)}* ______________________________
was (were) born on *{date}* ______________________________.

3. I request nonidentifying information as to family medical history and social history of the adoptee(s) as follows:
*{indicate **all** that apply}*
_____If available, to be furnished to adoptive parents before finalization of the adoption.

_____If available, to be furnished to adoptee upon request after adoptee reaches majority.

4. The reason I am requesting disclosure of this information is: ______________________________
____
____.

I understand that I am swearing or affirming under oath to the truthfulness of the claims made in this petition and that the punishment for knowingly making a false statement includes fines and/or imprisonment.

Dated: ______________________ ______________________________
Signature of Petitioner
Printed Name: ______________________
Address: ______________________
City, State, Zip: ______________________
Telephone Number: ______________________

Fax Number: ______________________________
Designated E-mail Address(es): ____________________
____

STATE OF FLORIDA
COUNTY OF

Sworn to or affirmed and signed before me on ____________ by:

____
NOTARY PUBLIC or DEPUTY CLERK

____
{Print, type, or stamp commissioned name of notary or deputy clerk.}

_____Personally known
_____Produced identification
Type of identification produced

IF A NONLAWYER HELPED YOU FILL OUT THIS FORM, HE/SHE MUST FILL IN THE BLANKS BELOW:
[fill in all blanks] This form was prepared for the: *{choose only one}* ( ) adult adoptee
( ) adoptive parent ( ) adult birth sibling ( ) other *{specify}*____________.
This form was completed with the assistance of:
*{name of individual}*____________________________________,
{name of business} ____________________________________,
*{address}*____________________________________,
{city} ____________,*{state}* _____, *{zip code}* ________, *{telephone number}* ____________.

INSTRUCTIONS FOR FLORIDA SUPREME COURT APPROVED FAMILY LAW FORM 12.981(d)(1), PETITION FOR ADOPTION INFORMATION (03/15)

When should this form be used?

This form is used to request release of relevant medical or social information on an adoptee. You cannot use this form to find out the identity of birth parent(s).

This form should be typed or printed in black ink. After completing this form, you should sign the form before a **notary public** or **deputy clerk**. You should **file** the original with the **clerk of the circuit court** in the county where the adoption took place and keep a copy for your records.

IMPORTANT INFORMATION REGARDING E-FILING

The Florida Rules of Judicial Administration now require that all petitions, pleadings, and documents be filed electronically except in certain circumstances. **Self-represented litigants may file petitions or other pleadings or documents electronically; however, they are not required to do so.** If you choose to file your pleadings or other documents electronically, you must do so in accordance with Florida Rule of Judicial Administration 2.525, and you must follow the procedures of the judicial circuit in which you file. **The rules and procedures should be carefully read and followed.**

Special notes . . .

Remember, a person who is NOT an attorney is called a nonlawyer. If a nonlawyer helps you fill out these forms, that person must give you a copy of **Disclosure from Nonlawyer**, Florida Family Law Rules of Procedure Form 12.900 (a), before he or she helps you. A nonlawyer helping you fill out these forms also **must** put his or her name, address, and telephone number on the bottom of the last page of every form he or she helps you complete.

Added as 12.981(e) July 7, 1995, effective Jan. 1, 1996 (663 So.2d 1047). Amended Feb. 26, 1998, effective Mar. 16, 1998 (713 So.2d 1); Sept. 21, 2000 (810 So.2d 1). Renumbered from 12.981(e) Mar. 28, 2002 (821 So.2d 263). Amended March 26, 2015, effective March 26, 2015 (2015 WL 1343088).

Form 12.981(d)(2). Order Releasing Adoption Information

IN THE CIRCUIT COURT OF THE _______ JUDICIAL CIRCUIT,
IN AND FOR _____________ COUNTY, FLORIDA

Case No.: ______________________
Division: ______________________

IN RE: THE ADOPTION OF

______________________________,
Adoptee(s).

ORDER RELEASING ADOPTION INFORMATION

This case came before the Court upon the Petition for Adoption Information, and the Court being fully advised in the premises, it is **ORDERED:**

1. _____The Petitioner shall receive
   ______ a. nonidentifying information as to:
   ______ b. identifying information as to: ______________________________________.
   ______ c. all records relating to the adoption proceedings.

2. _____ The petition is denied in whole or in part because: ______________________
____.

DONE and ORDERED on _______________ in ______________________________, Florida.

____
CIRCUIT JUDGE

I certify that a copy of the *{name of document(s)}* ______________________________
was ( ) mailed ( ) faxed and mailed ( ) e-mailed ( ) hand-delivered to the parties and to any other persons or entities listed below on *{date}* ______________________________.

____
By: *Clerk of Court, Designee, or Judicial Assistant*

Petitioner (or his or her attorney)
Respondent (or his or her attorney)
Other:
____

Florida Supreme Court Approved Family Law Form 12.981(d)(2), Order Releasing Adoption Information (03/15)

Added as 12.981(f) July 7, 1995, effective Jan. 1, 1996 (663 So.2d 1047). Amended Feb. 26, 1998, effective Mar. 16, 1998 (713 So.2d 1); Sept. 21, 2000 (810 So.2d 1). Renumbered from 12.981(f) Mar. 28, 2002 (821 So.2d 263). Amended March 26, 2015, effective March 26, 2015 (2015 WL 1343088).

Form 12.982(a). Petition for Change of Name (Adult)

IN THE CIRCUIT COURT OF THE _________JUDICIAL CIRCUIT,
IN AND FOR_____________________COUNTY, FLORIDA

Case No.: ____________________
Division: ____________________

_______________________________,
Petitioner.

PETITION FOR CHANGE OF NAME (ADULT)

I, *{full legal name}* ____________________________, being sworn, certify that the following information is true:

1. My complete present name is: ____.
   I request that my name be changed to: ______________________________________.

2. I live in ________________ County, Florida, at *{street address}* _______________
   ____.

3. I was born on *{date}*_______________, in *{city}* _______________, *{county}* __________,
   {state} __________, *{country}* _______________.

4. My father's full legal name : ____.
   My mother's full legal name: ____.
   My mother's maiden name: ____.

5. I have lived in the following places since birth:
   Dates (to/from) Address

   _______/_________ ____
   _______/_________ ____
   _______/_________ ____
   _______/_________ ____

   (___ Please indicate here if you are continuing these facts on an attached page.)

6. **Family**
   *{Indicate **all** that apply}*
   a. _____ I am not married.
   b. _____ I am married. My spouse's full legal name is: ______________________________
   c. _____ I do not have child(ren).
   d. _____ The name(s), age(s), and address(es) of my child(ren) are as follows (all children, **including**

those over 18, must be listed):

Name *{last, first, middle initial}* **Age** **Address, City, State**

____
____
____
____
____

(______Please indicate here if you are continuing these facts on an attached page.)

7. **Former names**

*{Indicate **all** that apply}*

_____My name has never been changed **by a court**.

_____My name previously was changed **by court order** from ____________________
to ____________________ on *{date}* ____________________,
by *{court, city, and state}* ____________________.
A copy of the court order is attached.

_____My name previously was changed **by marriage** from ____________________
to ____________________ on *{date}* ____________________,
in *{city, county, and state}* ____________________.
A copy of the marriage certificate is attached.

_____I have never been known or called by any other name.

_____I have been known or called by the following other name(s):
{list name(s) and explain where you were known or called by such name(s)} ____________________
____
____.

8. **Occupation**

My occupation is: ____
I am employed at: *{company and address}* ____.

During the past 5 years, I have had the **following jobs**:

Dates (to/from)	Employer and employer's address
_____/_____	____________________
_____/_____	____________________
_____/_____	____________________
_____/_____	____________________
_____/_____	____________________

(______Please indicate here if you are continuing these facts on an attached page.)

9. **Business**

*{Choose **one** only}*
_____ I do not own and operate a business.
_____ I own and operate a business. The name of the business is: ____________________.
The street address is: ____________________.
My position with the business is: ____________________.
I have been involved with the business since: *{date}* ____________________.

10. **Profession**
*{Choose **one** only}*
_____I am not in a profession.
_____I am in a profession. My profession is: ____________________.
I have practiced this profession:

Dates (to/from)	Place and address
_____/_____	____________________
_____/_____	____________________
_____/_____	____________________
_____/_____	____________________
_____/_____	____________________

(_____ Please indicate here if you are continuing these facts on an attached page.)

11. **Education**
I have graduated from the following school(s):

Degree Received	Date of Graduation	School
_______	_______	____________________
_______	_______	____________________
_______	_______	____________________

(_______ Please indicate here if you are continuing these facts on an attached page.)

12. **Criminal History**
*{Choose **one** only}*
_____ I have never been arrested for or charged with, pled guilty or nolo contendere to, or been found to have committed a criminal offense, regardless of adjudication.
_____ I have a criminal history. In the past I have been arrested for or charged with, pled guilty or nolo contendere to, or been found to have committed a criminal offense, regardless of adjudication. The details of my criminal history are:

Date	City/State	Event (arrest, charge, plea, or adjudication)
_______	_______	____________________
_______	_______	____________________
_______	_______	____________________

(_______ Please indicate here if you are continuing these facts on an attached page.)

13. **Bankruptcy**

*{Choose **one** only}*
___I have never been adjudicated bankrupt.
___I was adjudicated bankrupt on *{date}* ________________, in *{city}* ________________________,
{county} ________________, *{state}* ______.
(___Please indicate here if you have filed additional bankruptcies, and explain on an attached page.)

14. **Creditor(s)' Judgments**
*{Choose **one** only}*
_____I have never had a money judgment entered against me by a creditor.
_____The following creditor(s)' money judgment(s) have been entered against me:

Date	Amount	Creditor	Court entering judgment and case number	if Paid *{date}*
______	_________	_________	_______________________________	
______	_________	_________	_______________________________	
______	_________	_________	_______________________________	
______	_________	_________	_______________________________	

(_______ Please indicate here if these facts are continued on an attached page.)

15. **Fingerprints and Criminal History Records Check**
Unless I am seeking to restore a former name, a copy of my fingerprints has been taken in a manner approved by the Department of Law Enforcement and submitted for a state and national criminal history records check. **I understand that I cannot request a hearing on my Petition until the Clerk of Court receives the results of the criminal history records check.**

16. I have no ulterior or illegal purpose for filing this petition, and granting it will not in any manner invade the property rights of others, whether partnership, patent, good will, privacy, trademark, or otherwise.

17. My civil rights have never been suspended, or, if my civil rights have been suspended, they have been fully restored.

I understand that I am swearing or affirming under oath to the truthfulness of the claims made in this petition and that the punishment for knowingly making a false statement includes fines and/or imprisonment.

Dated: ____________________ ____
Signature of PETITIONER

Printed Name: ______________________________
Address: ______________________________
City, State, Zip: ______________________________
Telephone Number: ______________________________
Fax Number: ______________________________
Designated E-mail Address(es):______________________________
____

Florida Supreme Court Approved Family Law Form 12.982(a), Petition for Change of Name (Adult) (03/15)

STATE OF FLORIDA
COUNTY OF ____________________

Sworn to or affirmed and signed before me on __________ by______________________________________.

____
NOTARY PUBLIC or DEPUTY CLERK

____
[Print, type, or stamp commissioned name of notary or deputy clerk.]

____ Personally known
____ Produced identification
____ Type of identification produced ______________________________

IF A NONLAWYER HELPED YOU FILL OUT THIS FORM, HE/SHE MUST FILL IN THE BLANKS BELOW:
[fill in **all** blanks] This form was prepared for the Petitioner.
This form was completed with the assistance of:
{name of individual} ____,
{name of business} ____,
{address} ____,
{city} ____________, *{state}* ______,*{ zip code}*______, *{telephone number}* ____________.

INSTRUCTIONS FOR FLORIDA SUPREME COURT APPROVED FAMILY LAW FORM 12.982(a)
PETITION FOR CHANGE OF NAME (ADULT) (03/15)

When should this form be used?

This form should be used when an adult wants the court to change his or her name. This form is **not** to be used in connection with a dissolution of marriage or for adoption of child(ren). If you want a change of name because of a **dissolution of marriage** or adoption of child(ren) that is not yet final, the change of name should be requested as part of that case.

This form should be typed or printed in black ink and must be signed before a **notary public** or **deputy clerk**. You should **file** the original with the **clerk of the circuit court** in the county where you live and keep a copy for your records.

IMPORTANT INFORMATION REGARDING E-FILING

The Florida Rules of Judicial Administration now require that all petitions, pleadings, and documents be filed electronically except in certain circumstances. **Self-represented litigants may file petitions or other pleadings or documents electronically; however, they are not required to do so.** If you choose to file your pleadings or other documents electronically, you must do so in accordance with Florida Rule of Judicial Administration 2.525, and you must follow the procedures of the judicial circuit in which you file. **The rules and procedures should be carefully read and followed.**

What should I do next?

Unless you are seeking to restore a former name, you must have fingerprints submitted for a state and national criminal records check. The fingerprints must be taken in a manner approved by the Department of Law Enforcement and must be submitted to the Department for a state and national criminal records check. **You may not request a hearing on the petition until the clerk of court has received the results of your criminal history records check.** The clerk of court can instruct you on the process for having the fingerprints taken and submitted, including information on law enforcement agencies or service providers authorized to submit fingerprints electronically to the Department of Law Enforcement. The process may take several weeks and you will have to pay for the cost of processing the fingerprints and conducting the state and national criminal history records check.

Next, you must obtain a **hearing** date for the court to consider your request. If you are seeking to restore a former name, a hearing on the petition MAY be held immediately after the petition is filed. The final hearing on any other petition for a name change may be held immediately after the clerk of court receives the results of your criminal history records check. You should ask the clerk of court, **family law intake staff**, or **judicial assistant** about the local procedure for setting a hearing. You may be required to attend the **final hearing**. Included in these forms is a **Final Judgment of Change of Name (Adult)**, Florida Supreme Court Approved Family Law Form 12.982(b), which the **judge** may use. You should check with the clerk, family law intake staff, or judicial assistant, to see if you need to bring a **final judgment** form with you. If so, you should type or print the heading, including the circuit, county, case number, division, and the parties' names, and leave the rest blank for the judge to complete at your hearing or trial.

If the judge grants your **petition**, he or she will sign this **order**. This officially changes your name. The clerk can provide you with **certified copies** of the signed order. There will be charges for the certified copies, and the clerk can tell you the amount of the charges.

Where can I look for more information?

Before proceeding, you should read General Information for Self-Represented Litigants found at the beginning of these forms. For further information, see Section 68.07, Florida Statutes.

IMPORTANT INFORMATION REGARDING E-SERVICE ELECTION

After the initial service of process of the petition or supplemental petition by the Sheriff or certified process server, the Florida Rules of Judicial Administration now require that all

documents required or permitted to be served on the other party must be served by electronic mail (e–mail) except in certain circumstances. **You must strictly comply with the format requirements set forth in the Rules of Judicial Administration.**

SELF–REPRESENTED LITIGANTS MAY SERVE DOCUMENTS BY E–MAIL; HOWEVER, THEY ARE NOT REQUIRED TO DO SO. If a self-represented litigant elects to serve and receive documents by e-mail, the procedures must always be followed once the initial election is made.

To serve and receive documents by e-mail, you must designate your e-mail addresses by using the **Designation of Current Mailing and E–mail Address**, Florida Supreme Court Approved Family Law Form 12.915, and you must provide your e-mail address on each form on which your signature appears. Please **CAREFULLY** read the rules and instructions for: **Certificate of Service (General),** Florida Supreme Court Approved Family Law Form 12.914; **Designation of Current Mailing and E–mail Address**, Florida Supreme Court Approved Family Law Form 12.915; and Florida Rule of Judicial Administration 2.516.

Special notes . . .

The heading of the form calls for the name of the **petitioner**. Your current legal name should be used, as you are the one who is asking the court for relief. The judicial circuit, case number, and division may be obtained from the clerk of court's office when you file the petition.

It may be helpful to compile a list of all of the people and/or places that will need a copy of your final judgment. This list may include the driver's license office, social security office, banks, schools, etc. A list will help you know how many copies of your order you should get from the clerk of court after your hearing.

Remember, a person who is NOT an attorney is called a nonlawyer. If a nonlawyer helps you fill out these forms, that person must give you a copy of a **Disclosure from Nonlawyer**, Florida Family Law Rules of Procedure Form 12.900 (a), before he or she helps you. A nonlawyer helping you fill out these forms also **must** put his or her name, address, and telephone number on the bottom of the last page of every form he or she helps you complete.

Added Feb. 26, 1998, effective Mar. 16, 1998 (713 So.2d 1). Amended Sept. 21, 2000 (810 So.2d 1); Nov. 24, 2004 (891 So.2d 1016); June 24, 2010 (50 So.3d 547); March 26, 2015, effective March 26, 2015 (2015 WL 1343088).

Form 12.982(b). Final Judgment of Change of Name (Adult)

IN THE CIRCUIT COURT OF THE ________ JUDICIAL CIRCUIT,
IN AND FOR ______________ COUNTY, FLORIDA

Case No.: ____________________
Division: ____________________

IN RE: THE NAME CHANGE OF

______________________________,
Petitioner.

FINAL JUDGMENT OF CHANGE OF NAME (ADULT)

This cause came before the Court on *{date}* ______________, for a hearing on Petition for Change of Name (Adult) under section 68.07, Florida Statutes, and it appearing to the Court that:

1. Petitioner is a bona fide resident of ______________ County, Florida;
2. Petitioner's request is not for any ulterior or illegal purpose; and
3. Granting this petition will not in any manner invade the property rights of others, whether partnership, patent, good will, privacy, trademark, or otherwise; it is

ORDERED that Petitioner's present name, ______________________________________,
is changed to ____,
by which Petitioner shall hereafter be known.

DONE and ORDERED ON ____________ in ________________________, Florida.

____
CIRCUIT JUDGE

I certify that a copy of the *{name of document(s)}* ______________________________
was ( ) mailed ( ) faxed and mailed ( ) e-mailed ( ) hand-delivered to the party(ies) listed below on *{date}* ______________________________.

Petitioner

Florida Supreme Court Approved Family Law Form 12.982(b), Final Judgment of Change of Name (Adult) (03/15)

Added Feb. 26, 1998, effective Mar. 16, 1998 (713 So.2d 1). Amended Sept. 21, 2000 (810 So.2d 1); March 26, 2015, effective March 26, 2015 (2015 WL 1343088).

Form 12.982(c). Petition for Change of Name (Minor Child(ren))

IN THE CIRCUIT COURT OF THE __________ JUDICIAL CIRCUIT,
IN AND FOR ________________________ COUNTY, FLORIDA

Case No.: ____________________
Division: ____________________

IN RE: THE NAME CHANGE OF

______________________________,
Petitioner/Father,

______________________________,
Petitioner/Mother.

PETITION FOR CHANGE OF NAME (MINOR CHILD(REN))

I/We, *{full legal name(s)}* ________________________, being sworn, certify that the following information is true:

I am/We are the birth or legal parent(s) or guardian of the minor child(ren) named in this petition. *{Choose* ***only one****}*

a. _____ There is only one minor child named in this petition.
b. _____ There are *{enter number of children}* __________ children named in this petition. The information on the first child is entered below. I/We have attached the completed supplemental forms for each other child.

The adult petitioner(s)'s fingerprints have been taken in a manner approved by the Department of Law Enforcement and submitted for a state and national criminal history records check. **I /We understand that I/we cannot request a hearing on my/our Petition until the clerk of court receives the results of the criminal history records check.**

A. **THE FOLLOWING INFORMATION IS TRUE ABOUT CHILD # __1__:**

1. **Minor child's complete present name is:**
   ____
   I/We request that this minor child's name be changed to:
   ____

2. The minor child lives in ____________ County, Florida, at *{street address}* ______________
   ____

PETITIONER(S) MUST INITIAL HERE __________

3. The minor child was born on *{date}* ________________, in *{city, county, state, country}* ______
____

4. The minor child's father's full legal name: ______________________________.
The minor child's mother's full legal name: ______________________________.
The minor child's mother's maiden name: ______________________________.

5. The minor child has lived in the following places since birth:

Dates (to/from) Address

_____/_____ ____

_____/_____ ____

_____/_____ ____

_____/_____ ____

_____/_____ ____

(____ Please indicate here if you are continuing these facts on an attached page.)

6. *{Choose **one** only}*

___ The minor child is not married.

___ The minor child is married to: *{full legal name}* ______________________________.

7. *{Choose **one** only}*

____ The minor child has no children.

____ The minor child is the parent of the following child(ren): {enter full name(s) and date(s) of birth} ______________________________.

8. **Former names.**

*{Indicate **all** that apply}*

____ The minor child's name has never been changed by a court.

____ The minor child's name previously was changed **by court order** from ______________
to ______________________ on *{date}* ______________________,
by *{court, city, and state}* ______________________________.

A copy of the court order is attached.

____ The minor child's name previously was changed **by marriage** from ______________
to ______________________ on *{date}* ______________________,
in *{city, county, and state}* ______________________________.

A copy of the marriage certificate is attached.

____ The minor child has never been known or called by any other name.

____ The minor child has been known or called by the following other name(s): *{list name(s) and explain where child was known or called by such name(s)}* ______________________________
____

PETITIONER(S) MUST INITIAL HERE ________

9. The minor child is not employed in an occupation or profession, does not own and operate a business, and has received no educational degrees. If the minor child has a job, explain: ______
____

10. **Criminal History.**
*{Choose **one** only}*
_____ The minor child has never been arrested for or charged with, pled guilty or nolo contendere to, or been found to have committed a criminal offense, regardless of adjudication.
_____ The minor child has a criminal history. In the past, the minor child was arrested for or charged with, pled guilty or nolo contendere to, or been found to have committed a criminal offense, regardless of adjudication. The details of the criminal history are:

Date	City/State	Event (arrest, charge, plea, or adjudication)

(_____ Please indicate here if you are continuing these facts on an attached page.)

11. **Money Judgments.**
*{Choose **one** only}*
_____ The minor child has never been adjudicated bankrupt, and no money judgment has ever been entered against him or her.
_____ The following money judgment(s) has been entered against him or her:

Date	Amount	Creditor	Court entering judgment and case number	*{date}* if Paid

B. **THE FOLLOWING INFORMATION IS TRUE ABOUT PETITIONER(S):**
_____ FATHER _____ MOTHER _____ GUARDIAN
_____ A Supplemental Form has been attached for the other parent or petitioner.

1. My complete present name is: ____
____

2. I live in _______________ County, Florida, at *{street address}* ______________________
____.

3. I have no ulterior or illegal purpose for filing this petition, and granting it will not in any manner invade the property rights of others, whether partnership, patent, good will, privacy, trademark, or otherwise.

PETITIONER(S) MUST INITIAL HERE ______
Florida Supreme Court Approved Family Law Form 12.982(c), Petition for Change of Name (Minor Child(ren)) (03/15)

4. My civil rights have never been suspended, or, if ever suspended, they have been fully restored.

PETITIONER(S) MUST INITIAL HERE ________

Florida Supreme Court Approved Family Law Form 12.982(c), Petition for Change of Name (Minor Child(ren)) (03/15)

I understand that I am swearing or affirming under oath to the truthfulness of the claims made in this petition and that the punishment for knowingly making a false statement includes fines and/or imprisonment.

Dated: ______________________________

Signature of Petitioner
Printed Name: ______________________
Address: ______________________
City, State, Zip: ______________________
Telephone Number: ______________________
Fax Number: ______________________
Designated E-mail Address(es): ______________________

____

STATE OF FLORIDA
COUNTY OF ______________________

Sworn to or affirmed and signed before me on ____________ by ______________________.

____
NOTARY PUBLIC or DEPUTY CLERK

____
{Print, type, or stamp commissioned name of notary or clerk.}

_____ Personally known
_____ Produced identification
Type of identification produced ______________________

IF A NONLAWYER HELPED YOU FILL OUT THIS FORM, HE/SHE MUST FILL IN THE BLANKS BELOW:
[fill in **all** blanks] This form was prepared for the Petitioner(s).
This form was completed with the assistance of:
{name of individual} ______________________,
{name of business} ______________________,
{address} ______________________,
{city} ______________________,*{state}* ___,*{zip code}* ________, *{telephone number}* ______________.

PETITIONER(S) MUST INITIAL HERE ________

ADULT SUPPLEMENTAL FORM FOR PETITION FOR CHANGE OF NAME (MINOR CHILDREN)

Case No.: ______________________

THE FOLLOWING INFORMATION IS TRUE ABOUT PETITIONER(S):
( ) FATHER ( ) MOTHER ( ) GUARDIAN

1. My complete present name is: ____
____

2. I live in ______________ County, Florida, at *{street address}* ________________________
____.

3. I have no ulterior or illegal purpose for filing this petition, and granting it will not in any manner invade the property rights of others, whether partnership, patent, good will, privacy, trademark, or otherwise.

4. My civil rights have never been suspended, or, if ever suspended, they have been fully restored.

I understand that I am swearing or affirming under oath to the truthfulness of the claims made in this petition and that the punishment for knowingly making a false statement includes fines and/or imprisonment.

Dated: ____

Signature of Petitioner
Printed Name: ______________________________
Address: ______________________________
City, State, Zip: ______________________________
Telephone Number: ______________________________
Fax Number: ______________________________
Designated E-mail Address(es): ______________________________

STATE OF FLORIDA
COUNTY OF ______________________________

Sworn to or affirmed and signed before me on ____________ by ______________________________.

____
NOTARY PUBLIC or DEPUTY CLERK

____
[Print, type, or stamp commissioned name of notary or clerk.]

_____ Personally known

PETITIONER(S) MUST INITIAL HERE ________

_____ Produced identification
Type of identification produced ___________________________

IF A NONLAWYER HELPED YOU FILL OUT THIS FORM, HE/SHE MUST FILL IN THE BLANKS BELOW:
[fill in **all** blanks] This form was prepared for the Petitioner(s).
This form was completed with the assistance of:
{name of individual} ____,
{name of business} ____,
{address} ____,
{city} ____________________,*{state}* ___,*{zip code}*__________, *{telephone number}* ____________.

PETITIONER(S) MUST INITIAL HERE ________

Florida Supreme Court Approved Family Law Form 12.982(c), Petition for Change of Name (Minor Child(ren)) (03/15)

SUPPLEMENTAL FORM FOR PETITION FOR CHANGE OF NAME (MINOR CHILD(REN))

Case No.: ____________________

THE FOLLOWING INFORMATION IS TRUE ABOUT CHILD #_____:

1. **Minor child's complete present name is:**
   ____.
   I/We request that minor child's name be changed to:
   ____.

2. The minor child lives in ____________ County, Florida, at *{street address}* ____________
   ____.

3. The minor child was born on *{date}* ____________________, in *{city, county, state, country}*
   ____.

4. The minor child's father's full legal name: ______________________________.
   The minor child's mother's full legal name: ______________________________.
   The minor child's mother's maiden name: ______________________________.

5. The minor child has lived in the following places since birth:
   Dates (to/from) Address
   ____________ / ____________________________________
   ____________ / ____________________________________
   ____________ / ____________________________________
   ____________ / ____________________________________
   ____________ / ____________________________________
   ____________ / ____________________________________
   (____ Please indicate here if you are continuing these facts on an attached page.)

6. [Choose **one** only]
   ____The minor child is not married.
   ____The minor child is married to: *{full legal name}* ______________________________.

7. [Choose **one** only]
   ____The minor child has no children.
   ____The minor child is the parent of the following child(ren): *{enter name(s) and date(s) of birth}*
   ____.

PETITIONER(S) MUST INITIAL HERE ________

8. **Former names**
[Choose all that apply]
___ The minor child's name has never been changed **by a court.**
___ The minor child's name previously was changed **by court order** from ____________________
to ____ on *{date}*____________________________,
by *{court, city, and state}* ____.
A copy of the court order is attached.
___ The minor child's name previously was changed **by marriage** from ____________________
to ____ on *{date}*____________________________,
in *{city, county, and state}* ____.
A copy of the marriage certificate is attached.
___ The minor child has never been known or called by any other name.
___ The minor child has been known or called by the following other name(s): *{list name(s) and explain where child was known or called by such name(s)}* ____________________________
____
____

9. The minor child is not employed in an occupation or profession, does not own and operate a business, and has received no educational degrees. If the minor child has a job, explain: _______
____.

10. **Criminal History**
[Choose **one** only]
___ The minor child has never been arrested for or charged with, pled guilty or nolo contendere to or been found to have committed a criminal offense, regardless of adjudication.
___ The minor child has a criminal history. In the past, the minor child was arrested for or charged with, pled guilty or nolo contendere to, or been found to have committed a criminal offense, regardless of adjudication. The details of the criminal history are:

Date	City/State	Event (arrest, charge, plea, or adjudication)

(____ Please indicate here if you are continuing these facts on an attached page.)

11. **Money Judgments**
[Choose **one** only]
_____ The minor child has never been adjudicated bankrupt, and no money judgment has ever been entered against him or her.
_____ The following money judgment(s) has (have) been entered against him or her:

Date	Amount	Creditor Court entering judgment and case number	*{date}* if Paid

PETITIONER(S) MUST INITIAL HERE ________

PETITIONER(S) MUST INITIAL HERE ______

INSTRUCTIONS FOR FLORIDA SUPREME COURT APPROVED FAMILY LAW FORM 12.982(c) PETITION FOR CHANGE OF NAME (MINOR CHILD(REN)) (03/15)

When should this form be used?

This form should be used when a parent or parents want the court to change the name of their minor child(ren). For the purposes of this proceeding, a person under the age of 18 is a minor. This form is not to be used in connection with an adoption, dissolution of marriage, or **paternity action**. If you want a change of name for your child(ren) because of an adoption or paternity action that is not yet final, the change of name should be requested as part of that case.

This form should be typed or printed in black ink and must be signed before a notary public or deputy clerk. You should file the original with the clerk of the circuit court, in the county where you live and keep a copy for your records. The **Petition** should only be completed by one Petitioner for one child. If you wish to change the name of more than one child or if there is more than one Petitioner, you should complete and file a Supplemental Form for Petition for Change of Name (Minor Child) for each child and/or a Supplemental Form for Petition for Change of Name. The supplemental form(s) is an attachment to the petition. **Be sure that the bottom of each page of each supplemental form is initialed by the petitioner(s).**

IMPORTANT INFORMATION REGARDING E–FILING

The Florida Rules of Judicial Administration now require that all petitions, pleadings, and documents be filed electronically except in certain circumstances. **Self–represented litigants may file petitions or other pleadings or documents electronically; however, they are not required to do so.** If you choose to file your pleadings or other documents electronically, you must do so in accordance with Florida Rule of Judicial Administration 2.525, and you must follow the procedures of the judicial circuit in which you file. **The rules and procedures should be carefully read and followed.**

IMPORTANT INFORMATION REGARDING E–SERVICE ELECTION

After the initial service of process of the petition or supplemental petition by the Sheriff or certified process server, the Florida Rules of Judicial Administration now require that all documents required or permitted to be served on the other party must be served by electronic mail (e–mail) except in certain circumstances. **You must strictly comply with the format requirements set forth in the Rules of Judicial Administration.**

SELF–REPRESENTED LITIGANTS MAY SERVE DOCUMENTS BY E–MAIL; HOWEVER, THEY ARE NOT REQUIRED TO DO SO. If a self-represented litigant elects to serve and receive documents by e-mail, the procedures must always be followed once the initial election is made.

To serve and receive documents by e-mail, you must designate your e-mail addresses by using the **Designation of Current Mailing and E–mail Address**, Florida Supreme Court Approved Family Law Form 12.915, and you must provide your e-mail address on each form on which your signature appears. Please **CAREFULLY** read the rules and instructions for: **Certificate of Service (General),** Florida Supreme Court Approved Family Law Form 12.914; **Designation of Current Mailing and E–mail Address**, Florida Supreme Court Approved Family Law Form 12.915; and Florida Rule of Judicial Administration 2.516.

What should I do next?

Unless you are seeking to restore a former name, each adult petitioner(s)'s fingerprints must be submitted for a state and national criminal history records check. The fingerprints must be taken in a manner approved by the Department of Law Enforcement. The fingerprints must be submitted to the Department of Law Enforcement for a state and national criminal history records check. **The Petitioner(s) may not request a hearing on the Petition until the copy of the fingerprints are filed and the clerk of court has received the results of the criminal history records check.** The clerk of court can instruct you on the process for having the fingerprints taken and submitted, including information on law enforcement agencies or service providers authorized to submit fingerprints electronically to the Department of Law Enforcement. The process may take several weeks and the parent or guardian of the minor must pay the cost of processing the fingerprints and conducting the state and national history records check.

If **both** parents agree to the change of name and live in the county where the change of name is sought, you may both file as **petitioners**. In this situation, **service** is not necessary, and you need only to set a **hearing**. You should ask the clerk of court, **family law intake staff**, or **judicial assistant** about the local procedure for setting a hearing.

If only one parent is a resident of the county where the change of name(s) is sought **or** only one parent asks for the child(ren)'s name(s) to be changed, the other parent must be notified and his or her consent obtained, if possible. If the other parent consents to the change of name, a **Consent for Change of Name (Minor Child(ren))**, Florida Supreme Court Approved Family Law Form 12.982(d), should be filed.

If the other parent does not consent to the change of name, you may still have a hearing on the petition **if** you have properly notified the other parent about your petition and the hearing. If you know where he or she lives, you must use **personal service**. If you absolutely do not know where he or she lives, you may use **constructive service**. For more information about personal and constructive service, you should refer [to] the **"General Instructions for Self-Represented Litigants"** found at the beginning of these forms and the instructions to Florida Family Law Rules of Procedure Forms 12.910(a) and 12.913(b) and Florida Supreme Court Approved Family Law Form 12.913(a). However, the law regarding constructive service is very complex and you may wish to consult an attorney regarding that issue.

Next, you must obtain a **final hearing** date for the court to consider your request. If you are seeking to restore a former name, a hearing on the petition MAY be held immediately after the petition is filed. The final hearing on any other petition for a name change may be held immediately after the clerk of court receives the results of your criminal history records check. You should ask the clerk of court, family law intake staff, or judicial assistant about the local procedure for setting a hearing. You may be required to attend the hearing. Included in these forms is a **Final Judgment of Change of Name (Minor Child(ren))**, Florida Supreme Court Approved Family Law Form 12.982(e), which may be used when a judge grants a change of name for a minor child(ren). If you attend the hearing, you should take the final judgment with you. You should complete the top part of the form, including the circuit, county, case number, division, and the name(s) of the petitioner(s) and leave the rest blank for the judge to complete. It should be typed or printed in black ink.

If the judge grants your petition, he or she will sign this **order**. This officially changes your child(ren)'s name(s). The clerk can provide you with **certified copies** of the signed order. There will be charges for the certified copies, and the clerk can tell you the amount of the charges.

Where can I look for more information?

Before proceeding, you should read "General Information for Self-Represented Litigants" found at the beginning of these forms. For further information, see section 68.07, Florida Statutes.

Special notes . . .

The heading of the form calls for the name(s) of the **petitioner(s)**. This means the parent(s) who is (are) requesting the change of their child(ren)'s name(s). The judicial circuit, case number, and division may be obtained from the clerk of court's office when you file the petition.

It may be helpful to compile a list of all of the people and places that will need a copy of the final judgment. This list may include the driver's license office, social security office, banks, schools, etc. A list will help you know how many copies of your order you should get from the clerk of court after your hearing.

Remember, a person who is NOT an attorney is called a nonlawyer. If a nonlawyer helps you fill out these forms, that person must give you a copy of a **Disclosure from Nonlawyer**, Florida Family Law Rules of Procedure Form 12.900(a), before he or she helps you. A nonlawyer helping you fill out these forms also **must** put his or her name, address, and telephone number on the bottom of the last page of every form he or she helps you complete.

Added Feb. 26, 1998, effective Mar. 16, 1998 (713 So.2d 1). Amended Sept. 21, 2000 (810 So.2d 1); Nov. 24, 2004 (891 So.2d 1016); Oct. 16, 2008, effective Jan. 1, 2009 (995 So.2d 407); June 24, 2010 (50 So.3d 547); March 26, 2015, effective March 26, 2015 (2015 WL 1343088).

Form 12.982(d). Consent for Change of Name (Minor Child(ren))

IN THE CIRCUIT COURT OF THE ______ JUDICIAL CIRCUIT,
IN AND FOR ______________ COUNTY, FLORIDA

Case No.: ______________
Division: ______________

IN RE: THE NAME CHANGE OF

______________________________,
Petitioner.

CONSENT FOR CHANGE OF NAME (MINOR CHILD(REN))

I, *{full legal name}* ______________________________, being sworn, certify that the following information is true:

I am the birth or legal ____ father ____ mother of the minor child(ren) named in this case, and I give consent for the following name changes:

Minor child(ren)'s complete present name(s):

(1) ______________________________
(2) ______________________________
(3) ______________________________
(4) ______________________________
(5) ______________________________
(6) ______________________________

I understand that I am swearing or affirming under oath to the truthfulness of the claims made in this consent and that the punishment for knowingly making a false statement includes fines and/or imprisonment.

Dated: ______________

____
Signature of Consenting Parent
Printed Name: ______________
Address: ______________
City, State, Zip: ______________
Telephone Number: ______________
Fax Number: ______________
Designated E-mail Address(es): ______________

Florida Supreme Court Approved Family Law Form 12.982(d), Consent for Change of Name (Minor Child(ren)) (03/15)

STATE OF FLORIDA
COUNTY OF

Sworn to or affirmed and signed before me on ____________ by ____________________.

____
NOTARY PUBLIC or DEPUTY CLERK

____
{Print, type, or stamp commissioned name of notary or clerk.}

_____Personally known
_____Produced identification
Type of identification produced

IF A NONLAWYER HELPED YOU FILL OUT THIS FORM, HE/SHE MUST FILL IN THE BLANKS BELOW:
[fill in all blanks] This form was prepared for the: *{choose one}* ( ) petitioner ( ) consenting parent
This form was completed with the assistance of:
{name of individual} ____________________,
{name of business} ____________________,
{address} ____________________,
{city} ____________,*{state}*_____,*{zip code}*_________, *{telephone number}* ____________.

Florida Supreme Court Approved Family Law Form 12.982(d), Consent for Change of Name (Minor Child(ren)) (03/15)

INSTRUCTIONS FOR FLORIDA SUPREME COURT APPROVED FAMILY LAW FORM 12.982(d), CONSENT FOR CHANGE OF NAME (MINOR CHILD(REN))(03/15)

When should this form be used

This form should be used when one parent consents to the other parent's **petition** to change the name of their minor child(ren). A parent who is not a **petitioner** in the case but is consenting to the change of name should complete this form and sign it in front of a **notary public** or **deputy clerk**.

This form should be typed or printed in black ink. After this form is signed and notarized, you should **file** it with the **clerk of the circuit court** in the county where the petition was filed and keep a copy for your records. This form should be attached to the **Petition for Change of Name (Minor Child(ren))**, Florida Supreme Court Approved Family Law Form 12.982(c), **if** obtained prior to the filing of the petition. Otherwise, it may be filed separately after it has been completed.

IMPORTANT INFORMATION REGARDING E–FILING

The Florida Rules of Judicial Administration now require that all petitions, pleadings, and documents be filed electronically except in certain circumstances. **Self–represented litigants may file petitions or other pleadings or documents electronically; however, they are not required to do so.** If you choose to file your pleadings or other documents electronically, you must do so in accordance with Florida Rule of Judicial Administration 2.525, and you must follow the procedures of the judicial circuit in which you file. **The rules and procedures should be carefully read and followed.**

Where can I look for more information?

Before proceeding, you should read General Information for Self–Represented Litigants found at the beginning of these forms. For further information see section 68.07, Florida Statutes, and the instructions for **Petition for Change of Name (Minor Child(ren))**, Florida Supreme Court Approved Family Law Form 12.982(c), or **Petition for Change of Name (Family)**, Florida Supreme Court Approved Family Law Form 12.982(f).

Special notes . . .

Remember, a person who is NOT an attorney is called a nonlawyer. If a nonlawyer helps you fill out these forms, that person must give you a copy of a **Disclosure from Nonlawyer**, Florida Family Law Rules of Procedure Form 12.900 (a), before he or she helps you. A nonlawyer helping you fill out these forms also **must** put his or her name, address, and telephone number on the bottom of the last page of every form he or she helps you complete.

Added Feb. 26, 1998, effective Mar. 16, 1998 (713 So.2d 1). Amended Sept. 21, 2000 (810 So.2d 1); March 26, 2015, effective March 26, 2015 (2015 WL 1343088).

Form 12.982(e). Final Judgment of Change of Name (Minor Child(ren))

IN THE CIRCUIT COURT OF THE _____ JUDICIAL CIRCUIT
IN AND FOR ____________ COUNTY, FLORIDA

Case No.: ____________________
Division: ____________________

IN RE: THE NAME CHANGE OF

______________,
Petitioner/Father,

______________,
Petitioner/Mother.

FINAL JUDGMENT OF CHANGE OF NAME (MINOR CHILD(REN))

This cause came before the Court on *{date}* ______________________, for a hearing on Petition for Change of Name under section 68.07, Florida Statutes, and it appearing to the Court that:

1. Petitioner(s) is (are) a bona fide resident(s) of ______________ County, Florida;

2. ______ Petitioners are the parents of the minor child(ren) named in the petition;

3. ______ Petitioner is the parent of the minor child(ren) named in the petition, and the other parent has been properly notified and has either consented or failed to respond;
______ Other: ____
____
____;

4. Petitioner's request is not for any ulterior or illegal purpose; and

5. Granting this petition will not in any manner invade the property rights of others, whether partnership, patent, good will, privacy, trademark, or otherwise; it is

ORDERED that the minor child(ren)'s
present name(s) ______________
(1) ______________________ by which they shall hereafter be known.
(2) ______________________ be changed to ___
(3) ______________________ (1) ______________________
(4) ______________________ (2) ______________________
(5) ______________________ (3) ______________________
(6) (4) ______________________
______________________ (5) ______________________

(6) ____

DONE and ORDERED ON ______________ in ______________________, Florida.

____
CIRCUIT JUDGE

I certify that a copy of the *{name of documents(s)}* ______________________________ was ( ) mailed ( ) faxed and mailed ( ) e-mailed ( ) hand-delivered to the parties and any other persons or entities listed below on *{date}* ______________________.

____
Clerk of Court, Designee, or Judicial Assistant

Petitioner(s) (or his, her, or their attorney)
Other: ______________________

Florida Supreme Court Approved Family Law Form 12.982(e), Final Judgment of Change of Name (Minor Child(ren)) (03/15)

Added Feb. 26, 1998, effective Mar. 16, 1998 (713 So.2d 1). Amended Sept. 21, 2000 (810 So.2d 1); March 26, 2015, effective March 26, 2015 (2015 WL 1343088).

Form 12.982(f). Petition for Change of Name (Family)

IN THE CIRCUIT COURT OF THE ________ JUDICIAL CIRCUIT,
IN AND FOR ____________________ COUNTY, FLORIDA

Case No.: ____________________
Division: ____________________

IN RE: THE NAME CHANGE OF

____________________,
Petitioner/Father,

____________________,
Petitioner/Mother.

PETITION FOR CHANGE OF NAME (FAMILY)

I/We, *{full legal name(s)}* _, ______________________________ being sworn, certify that the following information is true:

There are *{enter number}* _____ **adults named in this petition.** A supplemental form is attached for each adult not set out below.

There are *{enter number}* _____ **children named in this petition. I am/We are the birth or legal parents or guardian of the minor child(ren) named in this petition.** I/We have attached a completed supplemental form for each minor child.

Unless I am seeking to restore a former name, a copy of the fingerprints of each adult person seeking a name change in this petition has/have been taken in a manner approved by the Department of Law Enforcement, and submitted for a state and national criminal history records check. **I/We understand that I/We cannot request a hearing on my/our Petition until the clerk of court receives the results of the criminal history records check.**

THE FOLLOWING INFORMATION IS TRUE ABOUT PETITIONER:
_____ **HUSBAND** _____ **WIFE** _____ **GUARDIAN**
_____ **A Supplemental Form has been attached for the other parent or petitioner.**

1. My complete present name is:
   ____.
   I request that my name be changed to:
   ____.

2. I live in ______________ County, Florida, at *{street address}* ______________
   ____.

3. I was born on *{date}* ______________, in *{city}* ______________,
   {county} ______________, *{state}* ______________, *{country}* ______________.

Florida Supreme Court Approved Family Law Form 12.982(f), Petition for Change of Name (Family) (03/15)

4. My father's full legal name: ______________________________.
My mother's full legal name: ______________________________.
My mother's maiden name: ______________________________.

5. I have lived in the following places since birth:

Dates (to/from)	Address
______ / ______	______________________________
______ / ______	______________________________
______ / ______	______________________________
______ / ______	______________________________
______ / ______	______________________________
______ / ______	______________________________
______ / ______	______________________________

(____ Please indicate here if you are continuing these facts on an attached page.)

6. **Family**
*{Indicate **all** that apply}*
a. ____ I am not married.
b. ____ I am married. My spouse's full legal name is: ______________________________.
c. ____ I do not have child(ren).
d. ____ The name(s), age(s), and address(es) of my child(ren) are as follows (**all children, including those over 18**, must be listed):

Name *{last, first, middle initial}*	**Age**	**Address, City, State**

(____ Please indicate here if you are continuing these facts on an attached page.)

7. **Former names**
*{Indicate **all** that apply}*
____ My name has never been changed **by a court.**

____ My name previously was changed **by court order** from ______________________________
to ______________________________ on *{date}* ______________________________,
by *{court, city, and state}* ______________________________.
A copy of the court order is attached.

____ My name previously was changed **by marriage** from ______________________________
to ______________________________ on *{date}* ______________________________
in *{city, county, and state}* ______________________________.

A copy of the marriage certificate is attached.

_____ I have never been known or called by any other name.

_____ I have been known or called by the following other name(s): *{list name(s) and explain where you were known or called by such name(s)}*________________________________
____
____.

8. **Occupation**
My occupation is: ____.
I am employed at: *{company and address}* ________________________________
____.
During the past 5 years, I have had the following jobs:

Dates (to/from)	Employer and employer's address
____/____	________________________________
____/____	________________________________
____/____	________________________________
____/____	________________________________
____/____	________________________________

(____ Please indicate here if you are continuing these facts on an attached page.)

9. **Business**
*{Choose **one** only}*
_____I do not own and operate a business.

_____I own and operate a business. The name of the business is: ____________________.
The street address is: ____.
My position with the business is: ______________________________________.
I have been involved with the business since: *{date}* ____________________.

10. **Profession**
*{Choose **one** only}*
_____I am not in a profession.

_____I am in a profession. My profession is: ________________________________.
I have practiced this profession:

Dates (to/from)	Place and address
____/____	________________________________
____/____	________________________________
____/____	________________________________
____/____	________________________________

(____ Please indicate here if you are continuing these facts on an attached page.)

11. **Education**

I have graduated from the following school(s):

Degree Received	Date of Graduation	School

(____ Please indicate here if you are continuing these facts on an attached page.)

12. **Criminal History**

*{Choose **one** only}*

_____ I have never been arrested for or charged with, pled guilty or nolo contendere to, or have been found to have committed a criminal offense, regardless of adjudication.

_____ I have a criminal history. In the past I have been arrested for or charged with, pled guilty or nolo contendere to, or been found to have committed a criminal offense, regardless of adjudication. The details of my criminal history are:

Date	City/State	Event (arrest, charge, plea, or adjudication)

(____ Please indicate here if you are continuing these facts on an attached page.)

13. **Bankruptcy**

{Choose one only}

_____ I have never been adjudicated bankrupt.

_____ I was adjudicated bankrupt on *{date}* ______________, in *{city}* ______________, *{county}* ______________, *{state}* ______________.

(____ Please indicate here if you have had additional bankruptcies, and explain on an attached page.)

14. **Creditor(s)' Judgments**

*{Choose **one** only}*

_____ I have never had a money judgment entered against me by a creditor.

_____ The following creditor(s)' money judgment(s) have been entered against me:

Date	Amount	Creditor	Court entering judgment and case number	*{date}* if Paid

(____ Please indicate here if these facts are continued on an attached page.)

15. I have no ulterior or illegal purpose for filing this petition, and granting it will not in any manner invade the property rights of others, whether partnership, patent, good will, privacy, trademark, or otherwise.

16. My civil rights have never been suspended, or, if my civil rights have been suspended, they have been fully restored.

I understand that I am swearing or affirming under oath to the truthfulness of the claims made in this petition and that the punishment for knowingly making a false statement includes fines and/or imprisonment.

Dated: ____________

____
Signature of Petitioner
Printed Name: ____________________
Address: ____________________
City, State, Zip: ____________________
Telephone Number: ____________________
Fax Number: ____________________
Designated E-mail Address(es): ____________________
____

STATE OF FLORIDA
COUNTY OF ____________________
Sworn to or affirmed and signed before me on ____________ by ____________________.

____
NOTARY PUBLIC or DEPUTY CLERK

____
{Print, type, or stamp commissioned name of notary or clerk.}

_____ Personally known
_____ Produced identification
Type of identification produced ____________________

IF A NONLAWYER HELPED YOU FILL OUT THIS FORM, HE/SHE MUST FILL IN THE BLANKS BELOW:
[fill in **all** blanks] This form was prepared for the Petitioner.
This form was completed with the assistance of:
{name of individual} ____,
{name of business} ____,
{address} ____,
{city} ______________,*{state}*_____,*{zip code}*_____________, *{telephone number}* ______________.

ADULT SUPPLEMENTAL FORM FOR PETITION FOR CHANGE OF NAME (FAMILY)

Case No.: ______________________

THE FOLLOWING INFORMATION IS TRUE ABOUT PETITIONER:
( ) HUSBAND ( ) WIFE ( ) GUARDIAN

1. My complete present name is:
____.
I request that my name be changed to:
____.

2. I live in ______________ County, Florida, at *{street address}* ______________
____.

3. I was born on *{date}* ______________, in *{city}* ______________,
{county} ______________, *{state}* ______________, *{country}* ______________.

4. My father's full legal name: ______________________________.
My mother's full legal name: ______________________________.
My mother's maiden name: ______________________________.

5. I have lived in the following places since birth:

Dates (to/from)	Address
/	
/	
/	
/	
/	
/	
/	
/	
/	

(____ Please indicate here if you are continuing these facts on an attached page.)

6. **Family**{*[Indicate **all** that apply}*
   a. ____ I am not married.
   b. ____ I am married. My spouse's full legal name is: ______________________.
   c. ____ I do not have child(ren).
   d. ____ The name(s), age(s), and address(es) of my child(ren) are as follows (all children, **including those over 18**, must be listed):

PETITIONER(S) MUST INITIAL HERE ________

Name *{last, first, middle initial}* **Age** **Address, City, State**

____

____

____

____

(____ Please indicate here if you are continuing these facts on an attached page.)

7. **Former names**
*{Indicate **all** that apply}*
____My name has never been changed **by a court**.

____My name previously was changed **by court** order from ____________________
to ____________________ on *{date}* ____________________
by *{court, city, and state}* ____________________.
A copy of the court order is attached.

____My name previously was changed **by marriage** from ____________________
to ____________________ on *{date}* ____________________
in *{city, county, and state}* ____________________.
A copy of the marriage certificate is attached.

____I have never been known or called by any other name.

____I have been known or called by the following other name(s): *{list name(s) and explain where you were known or called by such name(s)}* ____________________

____

____

8. **Occupation**
My occupation is: ____________________.
I am employed at: *{company and address}* ____________________
____________________.

During the past 5 years, I have had the following jobs:

Dates (to/from)	Employer and employer's address
____/____	____________________
____/____	____________________
____/____	____________________
____/____	____________________
____/____	____________________
____/____	____________________
____/____	____________________

(____ Please indicate here if you are continuing these facts on an attached page.)

9. **Business**
*{indicate **all** that apply}*
____I do not own and operate a business.

PETITIONER(S) MUST INITIAL HERE ________

PETITIONER # ______, continued

____I own and operate a business. The name of the business is: ______________________.
The street address is: ______________________.
My position with the business is: ______________________.
I have been involved with the business since: *{date}* ______________________.

10. **Profession**
*{Indicate **all** that apply}*
____I am not in a profession.

____I am in a profession. My profession is: ______________________.
I have practiced this profession:

Dates (to/from)	Place and address
/	
/	
/	
/	

(___ Please indicate here if you are continuing these facts on an attached page.)

11. **Education**
I have graduated from the following school(s):

Degree Received	Date of Graduation	School

(___ Please indicate here if you are continuing these facts on an attached page.)

12. **Criminal History**
*{Choose **one** only}*
____I have never been arrested for or charged with, pled guilty or nolo contendere to, or been found to have committed a criminal offense, regardless of adjudication.

____I have a criminal history. In the past I have been arrested for or charged with, pled guilty or nolo contendere to, or been found to have committed a criminal offense, regardless of adjudication. The details of my criminal history are:

Date	City/State	Event (arrest, charge, plea, or adjudication)

(___ Please indicate here if you are continuing these facts on an attached page.)

13. **Bankruptcy**
*{Choose **one** only}*

PETITIONER(S) MUST INITIAL HERE ______

PETITIONER # _______, continued

___I have never been adjudicated bankrupt.

___I was adjudicated bankrupt on *{date}* _________________, in *{city}* _______________, *{county}* _________________________, *{state}* __________.

(___ Please indicate here if you have had additional bankruptcies, and explain on an attached page.)

14. **Creditors' Judgments**
*{Choose **one** only}*

___ I have never had a money judgment entered against me by a creditor.

___ The following creditor(s)' money judgment(s) have been entered against me:

Date	Amount	Creditor	Court entering judgment and case number	*{date}* if Paid

(____ Please indicate here if these facts are continued on an attached page.)

15. I have no ulterior or illegal purpose for filing this petition, and granting it will not in any manner invade the property rights of others, whether partnership, patent, good will, privacy, trademark, or otherwise.

16. My civil rights have never been suspended, or, if my civil rights have been suspended, they have been fully restored.

I understand that I am swearing or affirming under oath to the truthfulness of the claims made in this petition and that the punishment for knowingly making a false statement includes fines and/or imprisonment.

Dated: ____________________ ______________________________

Signature of Petitioner
Printed Name: ____________________
Address: ____________________
City, State, Zip: ____________________
Telephone Number: ____________________
Fax Number: ____________________
Designated E-mail Address(es):____________________

STATE OF FLORIDA
COUNTY OF ____________________
Sworn to or affirmed and signed before me on ____________ by ____________________.

____
NOTARY PUBLIC or DEPUTY CLERK

PETITIONER(S) MUST INITIAL HERE __________

Florida Supreme Court Approved Family Law Form 12.982(f), Supplemental Form for Petition for Change of Name (Family) (03/15)

PETITIONER # _______, continued

____
[Print, type, or stamp commissioned name of notary or clerk.]

_____ Personally known
_____ Produced identification
Type of identification produced ____________________

IF A NONLAWYER HELPED YOU FILL OUT THIS FORM, HE/SHE MUST FILL IN THE BLANKS BELOW:
[fill in **all** blanks] This form was prepared for the Petitioner.
This form was completed with the assistance of:
{name of individual} ____,
{name of business} ____,
{address} ____,
{city} ____________,*{state}*_____,*{zip code}*__________, *{telephone number}*__________.

PETITIONER(S) MUST INITIAL HERE __________

CHILD SUPPLEMENTAL FORM FOR PETITION FOR CHANGE OF NAME (FAMILY)

Case No.: ________________________________

THE FOLLOWING INFORMATION IS TRUE ABOUT MINOR CHILD # _____:

1. Minor child's complete present name is:
____
I/We request that minor child's name be changed to: ____________________________

2. The minor child lives in ______________ County, Florida, at *{street address}* ______________
____

3. The minor child was born on ____________________, in *{city, county, state, country}*
____.

4. The minor child's father's full legal name: ____________________________.
The minor child's mother's full legal name: ____________________________.
The minor child's mother's maiden name: ____________________________.

5. The minor child has lived in the following places since birth:

Dates (to/from)	Address
____________________ /	______________________________
____________________ /	______________________________
____________________ /	______________________________
____________________ /	______________________________
____________________ /	______________________________
____________________ /	______________________________
____________________ /	______________________________

(____ Please indicate here if continuing these facts on an attached page.)

6. *[Choose **one** only]*

____The minor child is not married

____The minor child is married to: *{full legal name}* ____________________________.

*[Choose **one** only]*

____ The minor child has no children.

____ The minor child is the parent of the following child(ren): *{enter name(s) and date(s) of birth}* ____.

7. Former names
*{Indicate **all** that apply}*

____The minor child's name has never been changed **by court order**.

____The minor child's name previously was changed **by court order** from:

PETITIONER(S) MUST INITIAL HERE __________

_______________________________ to _______________________________
on {date}_______________ {court, city, and state}_______________________
____.

A copy of the court order is attached.

____The minor child's name previously was changed by marriage from ______________ to ______________________________ on {date} ________, in {city, county, and state}____.

____The minor child has never been known or called by any other name.

____The minor child has been known or called by the following other name(s): *{list name(s) and explain where child was known or called by such name(s)}* ______________
____
____.

8. The minor child is not employed in an occupation or profession, does not own and operate a business, and has received no educational degrees. If the minor child has a job, explain:
____
____
____

9. Criminal History
{Choose ***one*** *only}*
____The minor child has never been arrested for or charged with, pled guilty or nolo contendere to, or been found to have committed a criminal offense, regardless of adjudication.

____The minor child has a criminal history. In the past, the minor child was arrested for or charged with, pled guilty or nolo contendere to, or been found to have committed a criminal offense, regardless of adjudication. The details of the criminal history are:

Date	City/State	Event (arrest, charge, plea, or adjudication)

(____ Please indicate here if you are continuing these facts on an attached page.)

10. Money Judgments
{Choose ***one*** *only}*
____The minor child has never been adjudicated bankrupt, and no money judgment has ever been entered against him or her.

____The following money judgment(s) has been entered against him or her:

Date	Amount	Creditor	Court entering judgment and case number *{date}* **if Paid**

PETITIONER(S) MUST INITIAL HERE

PETITIONER(S) MUST INITIAL HERE ________

Florida Supreme Court Approved Family Law Form 12.982(f), Supplemental Form for Petition for Change of Name (Family) (03/15)

INSTRUCTIONS FOR FLORIDA SUPREME COURT APPROVED FAMILY LAW FORM 12.982(f), PETITION FOR CHANGE OF NAME (FAMILY) (03/15)

When should this form be used?

This form should be used when a family wants the court to change its name. This form is **not** to be used in connection with a **dissolution of marriage**, **paternity**, or adoption action. If you want a change of name because of a dissolution of marriage, paternity, or adoption action that is not yet final, the change of name should be requested as part of that case. This form should be typed or printed in black ink and must be signed before a **notary public or deputy clerk**. You should **file** the original with the **clerk of the circuit court** in the county where you live and keep a copy for your records. The petition should only be completed for one adult. If you wish to change the name(s) of another adult and/or any child(ren), you should complete and file with the clerk of court the attached Supplemental Form(s) for Petition for Change of Name (Family) for each additional family member. **Be sure that the bottom of each page of each supplemental form is initialed.**

IMPORTANT INFORMATION REGARDING E–FILING

The Florida Rules of Judicial Administration now require that all petitions, pleadings, and documents be filed electronically except in certain circumstances. **Self–represented litigants may file petitions or other pleadings or documents electronically; however, they are not required to do so.** If you choose to file your pleadings or other documents electronically, you must do so in accordance with Florida Rule of Judicial Administration 2.525, and you must follow the procedures of the judicial circuit in which you file. **The rules and procedures should be carefully read and followed.**

IMPORTANT INFORMATION REGARDING E–SERVICE ELECTION

After the initial service of process of the petition or supplemental petition by the Sheriff or certified process server, the Florida Rules of Judicial Administration now require that all documents required or permitted to be served on the other party must be served by electronic mail (e–mail) except in certain circumstances. **You must strictly comply with the format requirements set forth in the Rules of Judicial Administration.**

SELF–REPRESENTED LITIGANTS MAY SERVE DOCUMENTS BY E–MAIL; HOWEVER, THEY ARE NOT REQUIRED TO DO SO. If a self-represented litigant elects to serve and receive documents by e-mail, the procedures must always be followed once the initial election is made.

To serve and receive documents by e-mail, you must designate your e-mail addresses by using the **Designation of Current Mailing and E–mail Address**, Florida Supreme Court Approved Family Law Form 12.915, and you must provide your e-mail address on each form on which your signature appears. Please **CAREFULLY** read the rules and instructions for: **Certificate of Service (General),** Florida Supreme Court Approved Family Law Form 12.914; **Designation of Current Mailing and E–mail Address**, Florida Supreme Court Approved Family Law Form 12.915; and Florida Rule of Judicial Administration 2.516.

What should I do next?

Unless you are seeking to restore a former name, each adult petitioner must have fingerprints submitted for a state and national criminal history records check. The fingerprints must be taken in a manner approved by the Department of Law Enforcement and must be submitted to the Department for a state and national criminal history records check. **You may not request a hearing on the petition until the clerk of court has received the results of your criminal history records check.** The clerk of court can instruct you on the process for having the fingerprints taken and submitted, including information on law enforcement agencies or service providers authorized to submit finger prints electronically to the Department of Law Enforcement. The process may take several weeks and you will have to pay for the cost of processing the fingerprints and conducting the state and national criminal history records check.

If any of the children for whom you are requesting this change of name are not the legal children of both adults filing this petition, you must obtain the consent of the legal parent(s).

A parent not named as a **petitioner** in this action may consent by submitting a **Consent for Change of Name (Minor Child(ren))**, Florida Supreme Court Approved Family Law Form 12.982(d).

If the other parent does not consent to the change of name, you may still have a **hearing** on the **petition if** you have properly notified the other parent about your petition and the hearing. If you know where he or she lives, you must use **personal service**. If you absolutely do not know where he or she lives, you may use **constructive service**. For more information about personal and constructive service, you should refer to the **General Instructions for Self–Represented Litigants** found at the beginning of these forms and the instructions to Florida Family Law Rules of Procedure Forms 12.910(a) and 12.913(b) and Florida Supreme Court Approved Family Law Form 12.913(a). The law on constructive service is very complex and you may wish to consult an attorney regarding constructive service.

Before a **final hearing** on your request may be held, you must obtain a date for the court to consider your request. If you are seeking to restore a former name, the final hearing on the petition MAY be held immediately after the petition is filed. The final hearing on any other petition for a name change may be held immediately after the clerk of court receives the results of your criminal history records check. You should ask the clerk of court, **family law intake staff**, or **judicial assistant** about the local procedure for setting a hearing. You may be required to attend the hearing. Included in these forms is a **Final Judgment of Change of Name (Family)**, Florida Supreme Court Approved Family Law Form 12.982(g), which may be used when a judge grants a change of name for a family. If you attend the hearing, you should take the **final judgment** form with you. You should complete the top part of this form, including the circuit, county, case number, division, the name(s) of the petitioner(s) and leave the rest blank for the judge to complete. It should be typed or printed in black ink.

If the judge grants your petition, he or she will sign this **order**. This officially changes your family's name. The clerk can provide you with **certified copies** of the signed order. There will be charges for the certified copies, and the clerk can tell you the amount of the charges.

Where can I look for more information?

Before proceeding, you should read "General Information for Self–Represented Litigants" found at the beginning of these forms. For further information, see section 68.07, Florida Statutes.

Special notes . . .

The heading of the form calls for the name(s) of the **petitioner**(s). This is (are) the parent(s) who is/are requesting the change of their family's name(s). The judicial circuit, case number, and division may be obtained from the clerk of court's office when you file the petition.

It may be helpful to compile a list of all of the people and places that will need a copy of the final judgment. This list may include the driver's license office, social security office, banks, schools, etc. A list will help you know how many copies of your order you should get from the clerk of court after your hearing.

Remember, a person who is NOT an attorney is called a nonlawyer. If a nonlawyer helps you fill out these forms, that person must give you a copy of a **Disclosure from Nonlawyer**, Florida Family Law Rules of Procedure Form 12.900(a), before he or she helps you. A nonlawyer helping you fill out these forms also **must** put his or her name, address, and telephone number on the bottom of the last page of every form he or she helps you complete.

Added Feb. 26, 1998, effective Mar. 16, 1998 (713 So.2d 1). Amended Sept. 21, 2000 (810 So.2d 1); Nov. 24, 2004 (891 So.2d 1016); Oct. 16, 2008, effective Jan. 1, 2009 (995 So.2d 407); June 24, 2010 (50 So.3d 547); March 26, 2015, effective March 26, 2015 (2015 WL 1343088).

Form 12.982(g). Final Judgment of Change of Name (Family)

IN THE CIRCUIT COURT OF THE ________ JUDICIAL CIRCUIT,
IN AND FOR ______________ COUNTY, FLORIDA

Case No.: ______________________________
Division: ______________________________

IN RE: THE NAME CHANGE OF

______________,
Petitioner/Father,

______________,
Petitioner/Mother.

FINAL JUDGMENT OF CHANGE OF NAME (FAMILY)

This cause came before the Court on *{date}* ________________, for a hearing on Petition for Change of Name under section 68.07, Florida Statutes, and it appearing to the Court that:

1. Petitioners are bona fide residents of ________________ County, Florida;

2. a.____Petitioners are the parents of the minor child(ren) named in the petition;
   b.____Petitioner is the parent of the minor child(ren) named in the petition, and the other parent has been properly notified and has either consented or failed to respond;
   c.____Other: ____
   ____;

3. Petitioner's request is not for any ulterior or illegal purpose; and

4. Granting this petition will not in any manner invade the property rights of others, whether partnership, patent, good will, privacy, trademark, or otherwise; it is

ORDERED that the:

present name(s)	be changed to
(1) ______________	(1) ______________
(2) ______________	(2) ______________
(3) ______________	(3) ______________
(4) ______________	(4) ______________
(5) ______________	(5) ______________
(6) ______________	(6) ______________

Florida Supreme Court Approved Family Law Form 12.982(g), Final Judgment of Change of Name (Family) (03/15)

by which they shall hereafter be known.

DONE AND ORDERED on ____________________ in ________________________________, Florida.

____
CIRCUIT JUDGE

I certify that a copy of the *{name of document(s)}* ______________________________
was ( ) mailed ( ) faxed and mailed ( ) e-mailed ( ) hand-delivered to the parties and any other persons or entities listed below on *{date}* ____________.

____
By: *Clerk of Court, Designee, or Judicial Assistant*

Petitioner(s) (or his/her/their attorney)
Other: ______________________________

Florida Supreme Court Approved Family Law Form 12.982(g), Final Judgment of Change of Name (Family) (03/15)

Added Feb. 26, 1998, effective Mar. 16, 1998 (713 So.2d 1). Amended Sept. 21, 2000 (810 So.2d 1); March 26, 2015, effective March 26, 2015 (2015 WL 1343088).

Form 12.983(a). Petition to Determine Paternity and for Related Relief

IN THE CIRCUIT COURT OF THE ______________ JUDICIAL CIRCUIT,
IN AND FOR ______________________________ COUNTY, FLORIDA

Case No: ____________________
Division: ____________________

______________________________,
Petitioner,

And

______________________________,
Respondent.

PETITION TO DETERMINE PATERNITY AND FOR RELATED RELIEF

Petitioner, *{full legal name}*______________________________, being sworn, certifies that the following information is true:

This is an action for paternity and to determine parental responsibility, time-sharing, and child support under chapter 742, Florida Statutes.

SECTION I.

1. Petitioner is the _____ Mother _____ Father of the following minor child(ren):

Name	Birth Date
1.	
2.	
3.	
4.	
5.	
6.	

2. Petitioner' s current address is: *{street address, city, state}* ______________________________
______________________________.

3. Respondent's current address is: *{street address, city, state}* ______________________________
____

4. Both parties are over the age of 18.

Florida Supreme Court Approved Family Law Form 12.983(a), Petition to Determine Paternity and for Related Relief (03/15)

5. Petitioner *{Choose only **one**}* _____ is _____ is not a member of the military service.
Respondent *{Choose only **one**}* _____ is _____ is not a member of the military service.

6. Neither Petitioner nor Respondent is mentally incapacitated.

7. A completed **Uniform Child Custody Jurisdiction and Enforcement Act (UCCJEA) Affidavit**, Florida Supreme Court Approved Family Law Form 12.902(d), is filed with this petition.

8. A completed **Notice of Social Security Number**, Florida Supreme Court Approved Family Law Form 12.902(j), is filed with this petition.

9. A completed **Family Law Financial Affidavit**, Florida Family Law Rules of Procedure Form 12.902(b) or (c), is, or will be, filed.

10. **Paternity Facts.**
*{Choose only **one**}*
a. _____Paternity has previously been established as a matter of law.

b. _____The parties engaged in sexual intercourse with each other in the month(s) of *{list month(s) and year(s)}* __________ in *{city and state}* __________
As a result of the sexual intercourse, _____ Petitioner _____ Respondent conceived and gave birth to the minor child(ren) named in paragraph 1. _____ Petitioner _____Respondent is the natural father of the minor child(ren). The mother _____ was _____ was not married at the time of the conception and/or birth of the minor child(ren) named in paragraph 1. If the mother was married, the name and address of her husband at the time of conception and/or birth is:
____
____

SECTION II. PARENTING PLAN ESTABLISHING PARENTAL RESPONSIBILITY AND TIME-SHARING

1. The minor child(ren) currently reside(s) with _____ Mother _____ Father _____ other: *{explain}*
____
____.

2. **Parental Responsibility.** It is in the child(ren)'s best interests that parental responsibility be:
*{Choose only **one**}*
a. _____ shared by both Father and Mother.

b. ____awarded solely to _____ Father _____ Mother. Shared parental responsibility would be detrimental to the child(ren) because: ____________________
____
____
____.

3. **Parenting Plan and Time-Sharing**. It is in the best interests of the child(ren) that the family be ordered to comply with a Parenting Plan that _____ includes _____does **not** include parental time-

sharing with the child(ren). The Petitioner states that it is in the best interests of the child(ren) that:
*{Choose only **one**}*

a. _____The attached proposed Parenting Plan should be adopted by the court.
The parties _____ have _____ have **not** agreed to the Parenting Plan.

b. _____ The court should establish a Parenting Plan with the following provisions:
1.____ No time-sharing for the _____ Father _____ Mother
2.____ Limited time-sharing with the _____ Father _____ Mother
3.____ Supervised time-sharing for the _____ Father _____ Mother.
4.____ Supervised or third-party exchange of the child(ren).
5.____ Time-sharing schedule as follows:
____
____
____

Explain why this schedule is in the best interests of the child(ren): ________
____
____
____

4. The minor child(ren) should
*{Choose only **one**}*
a. _____retain his/her (their) present name(s).

b. _____receive a change of name as follows:

present name(s)	be changed to
(1). ____________	(1). ____________
(2). ____________	(2). ____________
(3). ____________	(3). ____________
(4). ____________	(4). ____________
(5). ____________	(5). ____________
(6). ____________	(6). ____________

c. The name change would be in the best interest of the child(ren) because: ________
____

SECTION III. CHILD SUPPORT
{Indicate all that apply}

1. _____Petitioner requests that the Court award child support as determined by Florida's child support guidelines, section 61.30, Florida Statutes. A completed **Child Support Guidelines Worksheet**, Florida Family Law Rules of Procedure Form 12.902(e), is, or will be, filed. Such support should be ordered retroactive to:
*{Choose only **one**}*
a. _____the date when the parents did not reside together in the same household with the child, not to exceed a period of 24 months before the date of filing of this petition.

b. _____the date of the filing of this petition.

c. _____other: *{date}*_________________ *{Explain}* ___________________________
____

2. _____Petitioner requests that the Court award a child support amount that is more than or less than Florida's child support guidelines. Petitioner understands that a **Motion to Deviate from Child Support Guidelines**, Florida Supreme Court Approved Family Law Form 12.943, **must** be completed before the Court will consider this request.

3. _____Petitioner requests that medical/dental insurance for the minor child(ren) be provided by: *{Choose only **one**}*
a. _____Father.

b. _____Mother.

4. _____Petitioner requests that uninsured medical/dental expenses for the child(ren) be paid by: *{Choose only **one**}*
a. _____Father.
b. _____Mother.
c. _____Father and Mother each pay one-half.
d. _____Father and Mother each pay according to the percentages in the **Child Support Guidelines Worksheet**, Florida Family Law Rules of Procedure Form 12.902(e).
e. _____Other *{explain}*: ____
____
____

5. _____Petitioner requests that life insurance to secure child support be provided by: *[Choose only **one**]*
a. _____Father.
b. _____Mother.
c. _____Both

6. _____ Petitioner _____ Respondent _____ Both has (have) incurred medical expenses in the amount of $__________ on behalf of the minor child(ren), including hospital and other expenses incidental to the birth of the minor child(ren). There should be an appropriate allocation or apportionment of these expenses.

7. _____ Petitioner _____ Respondent _____ Both has (have) received past public assistance for this (these) minor child(ren).

PETITIONER'S REQUEST

1. Petitioner requests a hearing on this petition and understands that he or she must attend the hearing.
2. Petitioner requests that the Court enter an order that: *[Indicate **all** that apply]*
   a. ____establishes paternity of the minor child(ren), ordering proper scientific testing, if necessary;

b. _____adopts or establishes a Parenting Plan containing provisions for parental responsibility and time-sharing for the minor or dependent child(ren);
c. _____awards child support, including medical/dental insurance coverage for the minor child(ren);
d. _____determines the appropriate allocation or apportionment of all expenses incidental to the birth of the child(ren), including hospital and medical expenses;
e. _____determines the appropriate allocation or apportionment of all other past, present, and future medical and dental expenses incurred or to be incurred on behalf of the minor child(ren);
f. _____changes the child(ren)'s name(s);
g. _____other relief as follows: ____
____
____
____ and
grants such other relief as may be appropriate and in the best interests of the minor child(ren).

I understand that I am swearing or affirming under oath to the truthfulness of the claims made in this petition and that the punishment for knowingly making a false statement includes fines and/or imprisonment.

Dated: ______________________

____
Signature of PETITIONER
Printed Name: ______________________________
Address: __________________________________
City, State, Zip: ____________________________
Telephone Number: __________________________
Fax Number: _______________________________
Designated E-mail Address(es):_______________
____

STATE OF FLORIDA
COUNTY OF ____________________

Sworn to or affirmed and signed before me on ____________ by______________________________.

____
NOTARY PUBLIC or DEPUTY CLERK

____
{Print, type, or stamp commissioned name of notary or deputy clerk.}

_____ Personally known
_____Produced identification
_____ Type of identification produced ______________________________

IF A NONLAWYER HELPED YOU FILL OUT THIS FORM, HE/SHE MUST FILL IN THE BLANKS BELOW:
[fill in all blanks] This form was prepared for the Petitioner.
This form was completed with the assistance of:
{name of individual} ____,
{name of business} ____,
{address} ____,
{city} ____________,*{state}* _______,*{zip code}*_________, *{telephone number}* ____________.

Florida Supreme Court Approved Family Law Form 12.983(a), Petition to Determine Paternity and for Related Relief (03/15)

INSTRUCTIONS FOR FLORIDA SUPREME COURT APPROVED FAMILY LAW FORM 12.983(a), PETITION TO DETERMINE PATERNITY AND FOR RELATED RELIEF

(03/15)

When should this form be used?

This form should be used by a birth mother or father to ask the court to establish **paternity**, a **time–sharing schedule**, and/or **child support** of a minor child or children. This means that you are trying to legally establish who is the father of the child(ren).

This form should be typed or printed in black ink. After completing this form, you should sign the form before a **notary public** or **deputy clerk**. You should **file** the original with the **clerk of the circuit court** in the county where you live and keep a copy for your records.

IMPORTANT INFORMATION REGARDING E–FILING

The Florida Rules of Judicial Administration now require that all petitions, pleadings, and documents be filed electronically except in certain circumstances. **Self–represented litigants may file petitions or other pleadings or documents electronically; however, they are not required to do so.** If you choose to file your pleadings or other documents electronically, you must do so in accordance with Florida Rule of Judicial Administration 2.525, and you must follow the procedures of the judicial circuit in which you file. **The rules and procedures should be carefully read and followed.**

IMPORTANT INFORMATION REGARDING E–SERVICE ELECTION

After the initial service of process of the petition or supplemental petition by the Sheriff or certified process server, the Florida Rules of Judicial Administration now require that all documents required or permitted to be served on the other party must be served by electronic mail (e–mail) except in certain circumstances. **You must strictly comply with the format requirements set forth in the Rules of Judicial Administration.**

SELF–REPRESENTED LITIGANTS MAY SERVE DOCUMENTS BY E–MAIL; HOWEVER, THEY ARE NOT REQUIRED TO DO SO. If a self-represented litigant elects to serve and receive documents by e-mail, the procedures must always be followed once the initial election is made.

To serve and receive documents by e-mail, you must designate your e-mail addresses by using the **Designation of Current Mailing and E–mail Address**, Florida Supreme Court Approved Family Law Form 12.915, and you must provide your e-mail address on each form on which your signature appears. Please **CAREFULLY** read the rules and instructions for: **Certificate of Service (General),** Florida Supreme Court Approved Family Law Form 12.914; **Designation of Current Mailing and E–mail Address**, Florida Supreme Court Approved Family Law Form 12.915; and Florida Rule of Judicial Administration 2.516.

What should I do next?

For your case to proceed, you must properly notify the **respondent** of the **petition**. If you know where he or she lives, you should use **personal service**. If you absolutely do not know where he or she lives, you may use **constructive service**. However, if constructive service is used, the court may only grant limited relief. You should seek legal advice on constructive service in a paternity case. For more information see chapter 49, Florida Statutes, or you may contact Child Support Enforcement at the Florida Department of Revenue if you need assistance with your case.

If personal service is used, the **respondent** has 20 days to answer after being served with your petition. Your case will then generally proceed in one of the following three ways:

DEFAULT . . . If after 20 days, no **answer** has been filed, you may file a **Motion for Default**, Florida Supreme Court Approved Family Law Form 12.922(a), with the clerk of court. Then, if you have filed all of the required papers, you may call the clerk, **family law intake staff**, or **judicial assistant** to set a **final hearing**. You must notify the other party of the hearing by using a **Notice of Hearing (General)**, Florida Supreme Court Approved Family Law Form 12.923, or other appropriate notice of hearing form.

UNCONTESTED ... If the respondent files an answer that agrees with everything in your petition or an answer and waiver, **and** you have complied with **mandatory disclosure** and filed all of the required papers, you may call the clerk, family law intake staff, or judicial assistant to set a final hearing. You must notify the other party of the hearing by using a **Notice of Hearing (General)**, Florida Supreme Court Approved Family Law Form 12.923, or other appropriate notice of hearing form.

CONTESTED ... If the respondent files an answer or an answer and **counterpetition**, which disagrees with or denies anything in your petition, **and** you are unable to settle the disputed issues, you should file a **Notice for Trial**, Florida Supreme Court Approved Family Law Form 12.924, after you have complied with mandatory disclosure, completed the **scientific paternity testing**, if necessary, and filed all of the required papers. Then you should contact the clerk, family law intake staff, or judicial assistant for instructions on how to set your case for **trial** (final hearing). If the respondent files an answer and counterpetition, you should answer the counterpetition within 20 days using an **Answer to Counterpetition**, Florida Supreme Court Approved Family Law Form 12.983(d).

Where can I look for more information?

Before proceeding, you should read "General Information for Self-Represented Litigants" found at the beginning of these forms. The words that are in **"bold underline"** in these instructions are defined there. For further information, see chapter 742, Florida Statutes.

Special notes ...

If you do not have the money to pay the filing fee, you may obtain an Application for Determination of Civil Indigent Status, fill it out, and the clerk will determine whether you are eligible to have filing fees deferred.

More than one child of the same alleged father may be listed on a single petition. However, if you are filing a paternity action involving more than one possible father, a separate petition must be filed for each alleged father.

If the respondent files an answer denying that the person named in the petition is the child(ren)'s father, one of you should file a Motion for **Scientific Paternity Testing**, Florida Supreme Court Approved Family Law Form 12.983(e). This is used to ask the court to order a scientific test to determine who is the child(ren)'s father.

If the father signed papers at the hospital acknowledging that he was the father, paternity was established as a matter of law. This should be indicated on page 2, section 9a on this form.

If the paternity of a child who was conceived or born during a marriage is at issue, the court may appoint a **guardian ad litem** to assist the court in this matter and to protect the rights of child.

With this petition, you must file the following and provide a copy to the other party:

- **Uniform Child Custody Jurisdiction and Enforcement Act (UCCJEA) Affidavit**, Florida Supreme Court Approved Family Law Form 12.902(d).
- **Notice of Social Security Number**, Florida Supreme Court Approved Family Law Form 12.902(j).
- **Family Law Financial Affidavit**, Florida Family Law Rules of Procedure Form 12.902(b) or (c).
- **Certificate of Compliance with Mandatory Disclosure**, Florida Family Law Rules of Procedure Form 12.932. (This must be filed within 45 days, if not filed with the petition, unless you and the other party have agreed not to exchange these documents.)
- **Child Support Guidelines Worksheet**, Florida Family Law Rules of Procedure Form 12.902(e). (If you do not know the other party's income, you may file this worksheet after his or her financial affidavit has been filed.)
- **Parenting Plan**, Florida Supreme Court Approved Family Law Form, 12.995(a), 12.995(b), or 12.995(c). If the parents have reached an agreement, a signed and notarized Parenting Plan should be attached. If the parents have not reached an agreement, a proposed Parenting Plan **may** be filed.

Parenting Plan and Time-Sharing. If the parties are unable to agree on parenting arrangements and a time-sharing schedule, a judge will decide as part of establishing a

Parenting Plan. The judge will decide the parenting arrangements and time-sharing based on the child(ren)'s best interests. Regardless of whether there is an agreement between the parties, the court reserves jurisdiction to modify issues relating to minor or dependent child(ren).

The judge may request a **parenting plan recommendation** or appoint a **guardian ad litem** in your case. This means that a neutral person will review your situation and report to the judge concerning parenting issues. The purpose of such intervention is to be sure that the best interests of the child(ren) are being served. For more information, you may consult sections 61.401–61.405, Florida Statutes.

Listed below are some terms with which you should become familiar before completing your petition. **If you do not fully understand any of the terms below or their implications, you should speak with an attorney before going any further.**

- **Shared Parental Responsibility**
- **Sole Parental Responsibility**
- **Supervised Time–Sharing**
- **No contact**
- **Parenting Plan**
- **Parenting Plan Recommendation**
- **Time–Sharing Schedule**

Many circuits require that parents of a minor or dependent child(ren) who are involved in dissolution or paternity actions attend **mediation** before being allowed to schedule a final hearing. A **parenting course** must be completed prior to entry of the final judgment. You should check with your local clerk of court's office, family law intake staff, or judicial assistant for more information on the parenting course and mediation requirements in your area.

Child Support. The court may order one parent to pay **child support** to assist the other parent in meeting the child(ren)'s material needs. **Both parents are required to provide financial support**, but one parent may be ordered to pay a portion of his or her support for the child(ren) to the other parent.

Florida has adopted guidelines for determining the amount of child support to be paid. These guidelines are based on the combined income of **both** parents and take into account the financial contributions of both parents. You should file a **financial affidavit**, and the other parent will be required to do the same. From your financial affidavits, you should be able to calculate the amount of child support that should be paid. Because the child support guidelines take several factors into consideration, change over time, and vary from state to state, your child support obligation may be more or less than that of other people in seemingly similar situations.

Final Judgments. These family law forms contain a **Final Judgment of Paternity**, Florida Supreme Court Approved Family Law Form 12.983(g), which the judge may use. You should check with the clerk, family law intake staff, or judicial assistant to see if you need to bring it with you to the hearing. If so, you should type or print the heading, including the circuit, county, case number, division, and the parties' names, and leave the rest blank for the judge to complete at your hearing or trial.

Remember, a person who is NOT an attorney is called a nonlawyer. If a nonlawyer helps you fill out these forms, that person must give you a copy of a **Disclosure from Nonlawyer**, Florida Family Law Rules of Procedure Form 12.900 (a), before he or she helps you. A nonlawyer helping you fill out these forms also **must** put his or her name, address, and telephone number on the bottom of the last page of every form he or she helps you complete.

Added Feb. 26, 1998, effective Mar. 16, 1998 (713 So.2d 1). Amended July 1, 1999 (717 So.2d 914); Sept. 21, 2000 (810 So.2d 1); Dec. 19, 2002 (836 So.2d 1019); June 30, 2005 (910 So.2d 194); March 26, 2009 (20 So.3d 173); Dec. 16, 2010 (59 So.3d 792); Nov. 3, 2011, effective, *nunc pro tunc*, Oct. 1, 2011 (78 So.3d 1045); March 26, 2015, effective March 26, 2015 (2015 WL 1343088).

Form 12.983(b). Answer to Petition to Determine Paternity and for Related Relief

IN THE CIRCUIT COURT OF THE ______________ JUDICIAL CIRCUIT,
IN AND FOR ______________________ COUNTY, FLORIDA

Case No.: ______________
Division: ______________

______________________________,
Petitioner,

and

______________________________,
Respondent.

ANSWER TO PETITION TO DETERMINE PATERNITY AND FOR RELATED RELIEF

I, *{full legal name}* ______________________________, Respondent, being sworn, certify that the following information is true:

1. I **agree** with Petitioner as to the allegations raised in the following numbered paragraphs in the Petition and, therefore, **admit** those allegations: *{indicate section and paragraph number}* ______ ______________________________.
2. I **disagree** with Petitioner as to the allegations raised in the following numbered paragraphs in the Petition and, therefore, **deny** those issues: *{indicate section and paragraph number}* ______________________________.
3. I currently am unable to admit or deny the following paragraphs due to lack of information: *{indicate section and paragraph number}* ______________________________ ______________________________.
4. *[I applicable]* A completed **Uniform Child Custody Jurisdiction and Enforcement Act (UCCJEA) Affidavit**, Florida Supreme Court Approved Family Law Form 12.902(d), is filed with this answer as I disagree with the Affidavit filed by the Petitioner.
5. A completed **Notice of Social Security Number,** Florida Supreme Court Approved Family Law Form 12.902(j), is filed with this answer if one has not already been filed in this case.
6. A completed **Family Law Financial Affidavit**, Florida Family Law Rules of Procedure Form 12.902(b) or (c), ____ is, or ____ will be, filed.

I certify that a copy of this document was ( ) mailed ( ) faxed and mailed ( ) e-mailed ( ) hand delivered to the person(s) listed below on *{date}* ____________________________________.

Petitioner or his/her attorney:
Name: ____________________________________
Address: __________________________________
City, State, Zip: ____________________________
Fax Number: _______________________________
Designated E-mail Address(es): __________________
____

I understand that I am swearing or affirming under oath to the truthfulness of the claims made in this answer and that the punishment for knowingly making a false statement includes fines and/or imprisonment.

Dated:_______________________ ______________________________

Signature of Respondent
Printed Name: ______________________________
Address: ______________________________
City, State, Zip: ______________________________
Telephone Number: ______________________________
Fax Number: ______________________________
Designated E-mail Address(es):______________________________
____

STATE OF FLORIDA
COUNTY OF ______________________________

Sworn to or affirmed and signed before me on ____________ by ______________________________.

____
NOTARY PUBLIC or DEPUTY CLERK

____
{Print, type, or stamp commissioned name of notary or clerk.}

_____ Personally known
_____ Produced identification
Type of identification produced______________________________

IF A NONLAWYER HELPED YOU FILL OUT THIS FORM, HE/SHE MUST FILL IN THE BLANKS BELOW:
[fill in **all** blanks] This form was prepared for the: *{choose only **one**}* ( ) Petitioner ( ) Respondent.
This form was completed with the assistance of:
*{name of individual}*______________________________,
*{name of business}*______________________________,
{address} ______________________________,
{city} ____________, *{state}* ______, *{zip code}*________, *{telephone number}* ______________.

Florida Supreme Court Approved Family Law Form 12.983(b), Answer to Petition to Determine Paternity and for Related Relief (03/15)

INSTRUCTIONS FOR FLORIDA SUPREME COURT APPROVED FAMILY LAW FORM 12.983(b) ANSWER TO PETITION TO DETERMINE PATERNITY AND FOR RELATED RELIEF (03/15)

When should this form be used?

This form should be used when you are responding to a petition to determine paternity. You may use this form to admit or deny the allegations contained in the petition. However, if you wish to ask the court for things not included in the petition, such as, parental responsibility and time-sharing or child support, you should file an **Answer to Petition and Counterpetition to Determine Paternity and for Related Relief**, Florida Supreme Court Approved Family Law Form 12.983(c).

This form should be typed or printed in black ink. After completing this form, you should sign this form before a **notary public** or **deputy clerk**. You should then **file** the original with the **clerk of the circuit court** in the county where the petition was filed and keep a copy for your records.

IMPORTANT INFORMATION REGARDING E-FILING

The Florida Rules of Judicial Administration now require that all petitions, pleadings, and documents be filed electronically except in certain circumstances. **Self-represented litigants may file petitions or other pleadings or documents electronically; however, they are not required to do so.** If you choose to file your pleadings or other documents electronically, you must do so in accordance with Florida Rule of Judicial Administration 2.525, and you must follow the procedures of the judicial circuit in which you file. **The rules and procedures should be carefully read and followed.**

IMPORTANT INFORMATION REGARDING E-SERVICE ELECTION

After the initial service of process of the petition or supplemental petition by the Sheriff or certified process server, the Florida Rules of Judicial Administration now require that all documents required or permitted to be served on the other party must be served by electronic mail (e-mail) except in certain circumstances. **You must strictly comply with the format requirements set forth in the Rules of Judicial Administration.**

SELF-REPRESENTED LITIGANTS MAY SERVE DOCUMENTS BY E-MAIL; HOWEVER, THEY ARE NOT REQUIRED TO DO SO. If a self-represented litigant elects to serve and receive documents by e-mail, the procedures must always be followed once the initial election is made.

To serve and receive documents by e-mail, you must designate your e-mail addresses by using the **Designation of Current Mailing and E-mail Address**, Florida Supreme Court Approved Family Law Form 12.915, and you must provide your e-mail address on each form on which your signature appears. Please **CAREFULLY** read the rules and instructions for: **Certificate of Service (General)**, Florida Supreme Court Approved Family Law Form 12.914; **Designation of Current Mailing and E-mail Address**, Florida Supreme Court Approved Family Law Form 12.915; and Florida Rule of Judicial Administration 2.516.

What should I do next?

If you deny that the person named in the petition is the child(ren)'s father, a **Motion for Scientific Paternity Testing**, Florida Supreme Court Approved Family Law Form 12.983(e), should be filed. This is used to ask the court to order a scientific test to determine who is the child(ren)'s father.

You have 20 days to file an answer to the other party's petition. A copy of this form, along with all of the other forms required with this answer, must be mailed, e-mailed, **or** hand delivered to the other party in your case. After you file your answer, the case will generally proceed in one of the following two ways:

UNCONTESTED . . . This case is uncontested if you and the petitioner agree on all issues raised in the petition. If this is the case, **and** you and the other party have complied with **mandatory disclosure** and filed all of the required papers, either party may call the clerk, **family law intake staff**, or **judicial assistant** to set a **final hearing**. If you request the hearing, you must notify the other party of the hearing by using a **Notice of Hearing (General)**, Florida Supreme Court Approved Family Law Form 12.923, or other appropriate notice of hearing form.

CONTESTED ... This case is contested if you and the other party disagree on any issues raised in the petition. If you are unable to settle the disputed issues, either party may file a **Notice for Trial** Florida Supreme Court Approved Family Law Form 12.924, after you have complied with mandatory disclosure and filed all of the required papers. Some circuits may require the completion of **mediation** before a final hearing may be set. You should contact the clerk, family law intake staff, or judicial assistant for instructions on how to set your case for **trial** (final hearing).

Where can I look for more information?

Before proceeding, you should read General Information for Self–Represented Litigants found at the beginning of these forms. The words that are in **bold underline** in these instructions are defined there. For further information, see chapter 742, Florida Statutes.

Special notes ...

With this answer, you must file the following and provide a copy to the other party:

- **Uniform Child Custody Jurisdiction and Enforcement Act (UCCJEA) Affidavit,** Florida Supreme Court Approved Family Law Form 12.902(d).
- **Notice of Social Security Number**, Florida Supreme Court Approved Family Law Form 12.902(j).
- **Family Law Financial Affidavit,** Florida Family Law Rules of Procedure Form 12.902 (b) or (c). (This must be filed within 45 days of the **service** of the petition on you, if not filed at the time you file this answer.)
- **Certificate of Compliance with Mandatory Disclosure**, Florida Family Law Rules of Procedure Form 12.932. (This must be filed within 45 days of the **service** of the petition on you, if not filed at the time you file this answer, unless you and the other party have agreed not to exchange these documents.)
- **Child Support Guidelines Worksheet,** Florida Family Law Rules of Procedure Form 12.902(e). (If you do not know the other party's income, you may file this form after the other party files his or her financial affidavit.)

Many circuits require completion of **mediation** before being allowed to schedule a final hearing. A **parenting course** must be completed prior to entry of the final judgment. You should check with your local clerk, family law intake staff, or judicial assistant for more information on the parenting course and mediation requirements in your area.

Parenting Plan and Time–Sharing. If the parents are unable to agree on parenting arrangements and a time-sharing schedule, a judge will decide these issues as part of establishing a Parenting Plan. The judge will decide the parenting arrangements and time-sharing schedule based on the child(ren)'s best interests. Regardless of whether there is an agreement between the parties, the court reserves jurisdiction to modify issues relating to minor child(ren).

The judge may request a **parenting plan recommendation** or appoint a **guardian ad litem** in your case. This means that a neutral person will review your situation and report to the judge concerning parenting issues. The purpose of such intervention is to be sure that the best interests of the child(ren) are being served. For more information, you may consult sections 61.401 and 61.405, Florida Statutes.

Listed below are some terms with which you should become familiar before completing your answer. **If you do not fully understand any of the terms below or their implications, you should speak with an attorney before going any further.**

- **Shared Parental Responsibility**
- **Sole Parental Responsibility**
- **Supervised Time–Sharing**
- **No contact**
- **Parenting Plan**

- **Parenting Plan Recommendation**
- **Time–Sharing Schedule**

Child Support . . . The court may order one parent to pay **child support** to assist the other parent in meeting the child(ren)'s material needs. **Both parents are required to provide financial support**, but one parent may be ordered to pay a portion of his or her support for the child(ren) to the other parent. Florida has adopted guidelines for determining the amount of child support to be paid. These guidelines are based on the combined income of **both** parents and take into account the financial contributions of both parents. You should file a **financial affidavit**, and the other parent will be required to do the same. From your financial affidavits, you should be able to calculate the amount of child support that should be paid. Because the child support guidelines take several factors into consideration, change over time, and vary from state to state, your child support obligation may be more or less than that of other people in seemingly similar situations.

Final Judgments . . . These family law forms contain a **Final Judgment of Paternity**, Florida Supreme Court Approved Family Law Form 12.983(g), which the judge may use. You should check with the clerk, family law intake staff, or judicial assistant to see if you need to bring it with you to the hearing. If so, you should type or print the heading, including the circuit, county, case number, division, and the parties' names, and leave the rest blank for the judge to complete at your hearing or trial.

Remember, a person who is NOT an attorney is called a nonlawyer. If a nonlawyer helps you fill out these forms, that person must give you a copy of a **Disclosure from a Nonlawyer,** Florida Family Law Rules of Procedure Form 12.900 (a), before he or she helps you. A nonlawyer helping you fill out these forms also **must** put his or her name, address, and telephone number on the bottom of the last page of every form he or she helps you complete.

Added Feb. 26, 1998, effective Mar. 16, 1998 (713 So.2d 1). Amended Sept. 21, 2000 (810 So.2d 1); Dec. 19, 2002 (836 So.2d 1019); March 26, 2009 (20 So.3d 173); Dec. 16, 2010 (59 So.3d 792); March 26, 2015, effective March 26, 2015 (2015 WL 1343088).

Form 12.983(c). Answer to Petition and Counterpetition to Determine Paternity and for Related Relief

IN THE CIRCUIT COURT OF THE _______________ JUDICIAL CIRCUIT,
IN AND FOR ______________________________ COUNTY, FLORIDA

Case No: ______________
Division: ______________

______________________________,
Petitioner,

And

______________________________,
Respondent.

ANSWER TO PETITION AND COUNTERPETITION TO DETERMINE PATERNITY AND FOR RELATED RELIEF

I, *{full legal name}* ______________________________, Respondent, being sworn, certify that the following information is true:

ANSWER TO PETITION

1. I **agree** with Petitioner as to the allegations raised in the following numbered paragraphs in the Petition and, therefore, **admit** those allegations: *{indicate section and paragraph number}* ____.

2. I **disagree** with Petitioner as to the allegations raised in the following numbered paragraphs in the Petition and, therefore, **deny** those issues: *{indicate section and paragraph number}* ____.

3. I currently am unable to admit or deny the following paragraphs due to lack of information: *{indicate section and paragraph number}* ____.

COUNTERPETITION TO DETERMINE PATERNITY AND FOR RELATED RELIEF

SECTION I. PATERNITY

1. Respondent is the _____ mother _____ father of the following minor child(ren):

Name	Birth Date
(1). ______________________	______________________

Florida Supreme Court Approved Family Law Form 12.983(c), Answer to Petition and Counterpetition to Determine Paternity and for Related Relief (03/15)

(2). ____
(3). ____
(4). ____
(5). ____
(6). ____

2. Petitioner's current address is: *{street address, city, state}*
____
____.

3. Respondent's current address is: *{street address, city, state}*
____
____.

4. Both parties are over the age of 18.

5. Petitioner *{Choose only one}* _____ is _____ is not a member of the military service.

   Respondent *{Choose only one}* _____ is _____ is not a member of the military service.

6. Neither Petitioner nor Respondent is mentally incapacitated.

7. A completed Uniform Child Custody Jurisdiction and Enforcement Act (UCCJEA) Affidavit, Florida Supreme Court Approved Family Law Form 12.902(d), is filed with this counterpetition.

8. A completed Notice of Social Security Number, Florida Supreme Court Approved Family Law Form 12.902(j), is filed with this counterpetition.

9. A completed Family Law Financial Affidavit, Florida Family Law Rules of Procedure Form 12.902(b) or (c), _____ is, or _____ will be, filed.

10. **Paternity Facts.**
{Choose only ***one****}*
a. _____ Paternity has previously been established as a matter of law.

b. _____ The parties engaged in sexual intercourse with each other in the month(s) of *{list month(s) and year(s)}* ______________________________,
in: *{city and state}* ______________________________.
As a result of the sexual intercourse, _____ Petitioner _____ Respondent conceived and gave birth to the minor child(ren) named in paragraph 1. _____ Petitioner _____ Respondent is the natural father of the minor child(ren). The mother _____ was _____ was not married at the time of the conception and/or birth of the minor child(ren) named in paragraph l. If the mother was married, the name and address of her husband at the time of conception and/or birth is: ______________________________

____.

SECTION II. PARENTING PLAN ESTABLISHING PARENTAL RESPONSIBILITY AND TIME-SHARING

1. The minor child(ren) currently reside(s) with _____Mother _____ Father _____ Other: *{explain}*_ ____.

2. **Parental Responsibility.** It is in the child(ren)'s best interests that parental responsibility be: *{Choose only **one**}*
   a. _____ shared by both Father and Mother.

   b. _____ awarded solely to _____ Father _____ Mother. Shared parental responsibility would be detrimental to the child(ren) because:
   ____
   ____
   ____
   ____.

3. **Parenting Plan and Time-Sharing.** It is in the best interests of the child(ren) that the family be ordered to comply with a Parenting Plan that _____ includes _____ does not include parental time-sharing with the child(ren). The Respondent states that it is in the best interests of the child(ren) that:
   *{Choose only **one**}*
   a. _____The attached proposed Parenting Plan should be adopted by the court.
   The parties ( ) have ( ) have **not** agreed to the Parenting Plan.

   b. _____The court should establish a Parenting Plan with the following provisions:
   1.____ **No** time-sharing for the _____ Father _____ Mother.
   2.____ Limited time-sharing with the _____ Father _____ Mother.
   3.____ Supervised time-sharing for the _____ Father _____ Mother
   4.____ Supervised or third-party exchange for the child(ren).
   5.____ Time-sharing schedule as follows:
   ____
   ____
   ____.

4. **Explain why this request is in the best interest of the child(ren)**:_______________
____
____
____
____
____.

5. The minor child(ren) should:
*[Choose only **one**]*
a. ____retain his/her (their) present name(s).

b. _____ receive a change of name as follows:

present name(s)	be changed to:
1.________________	1.________________
2.________________	2.________________
3.________________	3.________________
4.________________	4.________________
5.________________	5.________________
6.________________	6.________________

SECTION III. CHILD SUPPORT

*[Indicate **all** that apply]*

1. Respondent requests that the court award child support as determined by Florida's child support guidelines, section 61.30, Florida Statutes. A completed **Child Support Guidelines Worksheet**, Florida Family Law Rules of Procedure Form 12.902(e), is, or will be, filed. Such support should be ordered retroactive to:

*[Choose only **one**]*
a. _____the date when the parents did not reside together in the same household with the child, not to exceed a period of 24 months before the date of filing of this counterpetition.

b. _____the date of the filing of this petition.

c. _____other: *{date}* ________________ *{Explain}* ________________
____.

2. ______Respondent requests that the Court award a child support amount that is more than or less than Florida's child support guidelines. Respondent understands that a **Motion to Deviate from Child Support Guidelines**,-Florida Supreme Court Approved Family Law Form 12.943, **must** be completed before the Court will consider this request.

3. ______Respondent requests that medical/dental insurance coverage for the minor child(ren) be provided by:

*[Choose only **one**]*
a. _____Father.

b. _____Mother.

4. _____Respondent requests that uninsured medical/dental expenses for the child(ren) be paid by: *[Choose only **one**]*

a. _____Father.
b. _____Mother.
c. _____Father and Mother each pay one-half.
d. _____Father and Mother each pay according to the percentages in the **Child Support Guidelines Worksheet**, Florida Family Law Rules of Procedure Form 12.902(e).
e. _____Other *{explain}*: ____

5. _____Respondent requests that life insurance to secure child support be provided by: *[Choose only **one**]*

a. _____Father.
b. _____Mother.
c. _____Both.

6. _____ Petitioner _____ Respondent _____ Both has (have) incurred medical expenses in the amount of $______________ on behalf of the minor child(ren), including hospital and other expenses incidental to the birth of the minor child(ren). There should be an appropriate allocation or apportionment of these expenses.

7. _____ Petitioner _____ Respondent _____ Both has (have) received past public assistance for this (these) minor child(ren).

RESPONDENT'S REQUEST

1. Respondent requests a hearing on this petition and understands that he or she must attend the hearing.

2. Respondent requests that the Court enter an order that: *[Choose **all** that apply]*

a. _____establishes paternity of the minor child(ren), ordering proper scientific testing, if necessary;
b. _____establishes a Parenting Plan containing provisions for parental responsibility and time-sharing for the minor or dependent child(ren);
c. _____awards child support, including medical/dental insurance coverage, for the minor child(ren);
d. _____determines the appropriate allocation or apportionment of all expenses incidental to the birth of the child(ren), including hospital and medical expenses;

e. _____determines the appropriate allocation or apportionment of all other past, present, and future medical and dental expenses incurred or to be incurred on behalf of the minor child(ren);

f. _____changes the child(ren)'s name(s); and

g. _____other relief as follows:____
____
____;

and grants such other relief as may be appropriate and in the best interests of the minor child(ren).

I certify that a copy of this document was ( ) mailed ( ) faxed and mailed ( ) e-mailed ( ) hand-delivered to the person(s) listed below on *{date}*________________.

Petitioner or his/her attorney:
Name:________________________________
Address:______________________________
City, State, Zip:_________________________
Fax Number:___________________________
Designated E-mail Address(es):_______________
____

I understand that I am swearing or affirming under oath to the truthfulness of the claims made in this answer and counterpetition and that the punishment for knowingly making a false statement includes fines and/or imprisonment.

Dated:____________________________ ______________________________________

Signature of Respondent/Counterpetitioner
Printed Name: ____________________________
Address: ________________________________
City, State, Zip: __________________________
Telephone Number: ________________________
Fax Number: _____________________________
Designated E-mail Address(es):_______________
____

STATE OF FLORIDA
COUNTY OF ____________________________

Sworn to or affirmed and signed before me on _____________ by ____________________________.

____
NOTARY PUBLIC or DEPUTY CLERK

Florida Supreme Court Approved Family Law Form 12.983(c), Answer to Petition and Counterpetition to Determine Paternity and for Related Relief (03/15)

____
{Print, type, or stamp commissioned name of notary or clerk.}

_____ Personally known
_____ Produced identification
Type of identification produced____________________________

IF A NONLAWYER HELPED YOU FILL OUT THIS FORM, HE/SHE MUST FILL IN THE BLANKS BELOW:
[fill in all blanks]This form was prepared for the Respondent/Counterpetitioner.
This form was completed with the assistance of:
*{name of individual}*____,
*{name of business}*____,
*{address}*____,
*{city}*_____________,*{state}*_____, *{zip code}*___________, *{telephone number}*__________.

INSTRUCTIONS FOR FLORIDA FAMILY LAW FORM 12.983(c), ANSWER TO PETITION AND COUNTERPETITION TO DETERMINE PATERNITY AND FOR RELATED RELIEF (03/15)

When should this form be used?

This form should be used when you are responding to a **petition** to determine **paternity** and asking the court for something different than what was in the petition, such as parental responsibility, time-sharing, and **child support**. The **answer** is used to admit or deny the allegations contained in the petition, and the **counterpetition** is used to ask for whatever you want the court to do for you. The other party has 20 days to answer your counterpetition after being served with your counterpetition.

This form should be typed or printed in black ink. After completing this form, you should sign the form before a **notary public** or **deputy clerk**. You should then **file** the original with the **clerk of the circuit court** in the county where the petition was filed and keep a copy for your records.

IMPORTANT INFORMATION REGARDING E-FILING

The Florida Rules of Judicial Administration now require that all petitions, pleadings, and documents be filed electronically except in certain circumstances. **Self–represented litigants may file petitions or other pleadings or documents electronically; however, they are not required to do so.** If you choose to file your pleadings or other documents electronically, you must do so in accordance with Florida Rule of Judicial Administration 2.525, and you must follow the procedures of the judicial circuit in which you file. **The rules and procedures should be carefully read and followed.**

IMPORTANT INFORMATION REGARDING E–SERVICE ELECTION

After the initial service of process of the petition or supplemental petition by the Sheriff or certified process server, the Florida Rules of Judicial Administration now require that all documents required or permitted to be served on the other party must be served by electronic mail (e–mail) except in certain circumstances. **You must strictly comply with the format requirements set forth in the Rules of Judicial Administration.**

SELF–REPRESENTED LITIGANTS MAY SERVE DOCUMENTS BY E–MAIL; HOWEVER, THEY ARE NOT REQUIRED TO DO SO. If a self-represented litigant elects to serve and receive documents by e-mail, the procedures must always be followed once the initial election is made.

To serve and receive documents by e-mail, you must designate your e-mail addresses by using the **Designation of Current Mailing and E–mail Address**, Florida Supreme Court Approved Family Law Form 12.915, and you must provide your e-mail address on each form on which your signature appears.

Please **CAREFULLY** read the rules and instructions for: **Certificate of Service (General)**, Florida Supreme Court Approved Family Law Form 12.914; **Designation of Current Mailing and E–mail Address**, Florida Supreme Court Approved Family Law Form 12.915; and Florida Rule of Judicial Administration 2.516.

What should I do next?

You have 20 days to file an answer or answer and counterpetition to the other party's petition. A copy of this form, along with all of the other forms required with this answer and counterpetition, must be mailed **or** hand delivered to the other party in your case.

If you deny that the person named in the petition is the child(ren)'s father, a **Motion for Scientific Paternity Testing** Florida Supreme Court Approved Family Law Form 12.983(e), should be filed. This is used to ask the court to order a scientific test to determine who is the child(ren)'s father.

After you file an answer and counterpetition, the case will then generally proceed as follows:

UNCONTESTED. This case is uncontested if you and the other party agree on all issues raised in the petition and the counterpetition. If this is the case, **and** you and the other party have complied with **mandatory disclosure** and filed all of the required papers, either party may call the clerk, **family law intake staff**, or **judicial assistant** to set a final hearing. If you request the hearing, you must notify the other party of the hearing by using a **Notice of Hearing (General)**, Florida Supreme Court Approved Family Law Form 12.923, or other appropriate notice of hearing form.

CONTESTED. This case is contested if you and the other party disagree on any issues raised in the petition or counterpetition. If you are unable to settle the disputed issues, either party may file a **Notice for Trial,** Florida Supreme Court Approved Family Law Form 12.924, after you have complied with mandatory disclosure and filed all of the required papers. Some circuits may require the completion of **mediation** before a final hearing may be set. You should contact the clerk, family law intake staff, or judicial assistant for instructions on how to set your case for **trial (final hearing)**.

Where can I look for more information?

Before proceeding, you should read General Information for Self–Represented Litigants" for some basic information. The words that are in **bold underline** in these instructions are defined there. For further information, see chapter 742, Florida Statutes.

Special notes ...

If the child(ren)'s father signed papers at the hospital acknowledging that he was the father, paternity was established as a matter of law. This should be indicated on page 2, section 10a of the counterpetition part of this form. With this answer, you must file the following:

- **Uniform Child Custody Jurisdiction and Enforcement Act (UCCJEA) Affidavit**, Florida Supreme Court Approved Family Law Form 12.902(d).
- **Notice of Social Security Number** Florida Supreme Court Approved Family Law Form 12.902(j).
- **Family Law Financial Affidavit**, Florida Family Law Rules of Procedure Form 12.902(b) or (c). (This must be filed within 45 days of **service** of the petition on you if not filed with this answer.)
- **Certificate of Compliance with Mandatory Disclosure** Florida Family Law Rules of Procedure Form 12.932. (This must be filed within 45 days of service of the petition on you, if not filed with this answer, unless you and the other party have agreed not to exchange these documents.)
- **Child Support Guidelines Worksheet**, Florida Family Law Rules of Procedure Form 12.902(e). (If you do not know the other party's income, you may file this worksheet after his or her financial affidavit has been filed.)
- **Parenting Plan**, Florida Supreme Court Approved Family Law Form 12.995(a), 12.995(b), or (c). If the parents have reached an agreement, a signed and notarized Parenting Plan should be attached. If the parents have not reached an agreement, a proposed Parenting Plan **may** be filed.

Many jurisdictions may require the completion of **mediation** before a final hearing may be set. A **parenting course** must be completed prior to entry of the final judgment. You should contact the office of your local clerk of court, family law intake staff, or the judicial assistant about requirements for parenting courses or mediation where you live.

Parenting Plan and Time–Sharing. If the parties are unable to agree on parenting arrangements and a time-sharing schedule, a judge will decide as part of establishing a Parenting Plan. The judge will decide the parenting arrangements and time-sharing schedule based on the child(ren)'s best interests. Regardless of whether there is an agreement between the parties, the court reserves jurisdiction to modify issues relating to minor child(ren).

The judge may request a **parenting plan recommendation** or appoint a **guardian ad litem** in your case. This means that a neutral person will review your situation and report to the judge concerning parenting issues. The purpose of such intervention is to be sure that the best interests of the child(ren) is being served. For more information, you may consult section 61.401 and 61.405, Florida Statutes.

Listed below are some terms with which you should become familiar before completing your answer and counterpetition. **If you do not fully understand any of the terms below or their implications, you should speak with an attorney before going any further.**

Shared Parental Responsibility

Sole Parental Responsibility

Supervised Time–Sharing

No contact

Parenting Plan

Parenting Plan Recommendations

Time–Sharing Schedule

Child Support. The court may order one parent to pay child support to assist the other parent in meeting the child(ren)'s material needs. **Both parents are required to provide financial support**, but one parent may be ordered to pay a portion of his or her support for the child(ren) to the other parent.

Florida has adopted guidelines for determining the amount of child support to be paid. These guidelines are based on the combined income of **both** parents and take into account the financial contributions of both parents. You should file a **financial affidavit**, and the other parent will be required to do the same. From your financial affidavits, you should be able to calculate the amount of child support that should be paid. Because the child support guidelines take several factors into consideration, change over time, and vary from state to state, your child support obligation may be more or less than that of other people in seemingly similar situations.

Parenting Plan. In all cases involving minor or dependent child(ren), a Parenting Plan shall be approved or established by the court. If the parties have reached an agreement, you should file a **Parenting Plan**, Florida Supreme Court Approved Family Law Form 12.995(a), 12.995(b), or 12.995(c) which addresses the time-sharing schedule for the child(ren). If you have not reached an agreement, a proposed Parenting Plan **may** be filed. **A Parenting Plan will be established by the court.**

Final Judgments. These family law forms contain a **Final Judgment of Paternity,** Florida Supreme Court Approved Family Law Form 12.983(g), which the judge may use. You should check with the clerk, family law intake staff, or judicial assistant to see if you need to bring it with you to the hearing. If so, you should type or print the heading, including the circuit, county, case number, division, and the parties' names, and leave the rest blank for the judge to complete at your hearing or trial.

Remember, a person who is NOT an attorney is called a nonlawyer. If a nonlawyer helps you fill out these forms, that person must give you a copy of a **Disclosure from Nonlawyer**, Florida Family Law Rules of Procedure Form 12.900 (a), before he or she helps you. A nonlawyer helping you fill out these forms also **must** put his or her name, address, and telephone number on the bottom of the last page of every form he or she helps you complete.

Added Feb. 26, 1998, effective Mar. 16, 1998 (713 So.2d 1). Amended July 1, 1999 (717 So.2d 914); Sept. 21, 2000 (810 So.2d 1); Dec. 19, 2002 (836 So.2d 1019); March 26, 2009 (20 So.3d 173); Dec. 16, 2010 (59 So.3d 792); Nov. 3, 2011, effective, *nunc pro tunc*, Oct. 1, 2011 (78 So.3d 1045); March 26, 2015, effective March 26, 2015 (2015 WL 1343088).

Form 12.983(d). Answer to Counterpetition

IN THE CIRCUIT COURT OF THE __________ JUDICIAL CIRCUIT,
IN AND FOR ______________________ COUNTY, FLORIDA

Case No.: ____________________
Division: ____________________

______________________________,
Petitioner/Counterrespondent,

and

______________________________,
Respondent/Counterpetitioner.

ANSWER TO COUNTERPETITION

I, *{full legal name}* ______________________________, Petitioner/Counterrespondent, being sworn, certify that the following information is true:

1. I **agree** with Petitioner as to the allegations raised in the following numbered paragraphs in the Petition and, therefore, **admit** those allegations: *{indicate section and paragraph number}* ______.
2. I **disagree** with Petitioner as to the allegations raised in the following numbered paragraphs in the Petition and, therefore, **deny** those issues: *{indicate section and paragraph number}* ______.
3. I currently am unable to admit or deny the following paragraphs due to lack of information: *{indicate section and paragraph number}* ______.

I certify that a copy of this document was ( ) mailed ( ) faxed and mailed ( ) e-mailed ( ) hand delivered to the person(s) listed below on *{date}* ______.

Respondent or his/her attorney:
Name: ______________________
Address: ______________________
City, State, Zip: ______________________
Fax Number: ______________________
Designated E-mail Address(es): ______________________

Florida Supreme Court Approved Family Law Form 12.983(d), Answer to Counterpetition (03/15)

I understand that I am swearing or affirming under oath to the truthfulness of the claims made in this answer and that the punishment for knowingly making a false statement includes fines and/or imprisonment.

Dated: ____________________ ____________________________________

Signature of Petitioner/Counterrespondent
Printed Name: ____________________
Address: ____________________
City, State, Zip: ____________________
Telephone Number: ____________________
Fax Number: ____________________
Designated E-mail Address(es): ____________________
____

STATE OF FLORIDA
COUNTY OF

Sworn to or affirmed and signed before me on ______________ by ____________________.

____
NOTARY PUBLIC or DEPUTY CLERK

____
[Print, type, or stamp commissioned name of notary or clerk.]

___ Personally known
___ Produced identification
Type of identification produced ____________________

IF A NONLAWYER HELPED YOU FILL OUT THIS FORM, HE/SHE MUST FILL IN THE BLANKS BELOW:
[fill in **all** blanks] This form was prepared for the: *{choose only one}* ( ) Petitioner ( ) Respondent.
This form was completed with the assistance of:
{name of individual} ____________________,
{name of business} ____________________,
{address} ____________________,
{city} __________,*{state}* ______, *{zip code}* ______, *{telephone number}* __________.

INSTRUCTIONS FOR FLORIDA SUPREME COURT APPROVED FAMILY LAW FORM 12.983(d), ANSWER TO COUNTERPETITION (03/15)

When should this form be used?

This form may be used by a **petitioner** to respond to the **respondent's counterpetition** in a **paternity** case. You may use this form to admit or deny the allegations contained in the respondent's counterpetition.

This form should be typed or printed in black ink. After completing this form, you should sign the form before a **notary public** or **deputy clerk**. You should then **file** the original with the **clerk of the circuit court** in the county where the petition was filed and keep a copy for your records.

IMPORTANT INFORMATION REGARDING E-FILING

The Florida Rules of Judicial Administration now require that all petitions, pleadings, and documents be filed electronically except in certain circumstances. **Self-represented litigants may file petitions or other pleadings or documents electronically; however, they are not required to do so.** If you choose to file your pleadings or other documents electronically, you must do so in accordance with Florida Rule of Judicial Administration 2.525, and you must follow the procedures of the judicial circuit in which you file. **The rules and procedures should be carefully read and followed.**

IMPORTANT INFORMATION REGARDING E-SERVICE ELECTION

After the initial service of process of the petition or supplemental petition by the Sheriff or certified process server, the Florida Rules of Judicial Administration now require that all documents required or permitted to be served on the other party must be served by electronic mail (e-mail) except in certain circumstances. **You must strictly comply with the format requirements set forth in the Rules of Judicial Administration.**

SELF-REPRESENTED LITIGANTS MAY SERVE DOCUMENTS BY E-MAIL; HOWEVER, THEY ARE NOT REQUIRED TO DO SO. If a self-represented litigant elects to serve and receive documents by e-mail, the procedures must always be followed once the initial election is made.

To serve and receive documents by e-mail, you must designate your e-mail addresses by using the **Designation of Current Mailing and E-mail Address**, Florida Supreme Court Approved Family Law Form 12.915, and you must provide your e-mail address on each form on which your signature appears. Please **CAREFULLY** read the rules and instructions for: **Certificate of Service (General),** Florida Supreme Court Approved Family Law Form 12.914; **Designation of Current Mailing and E-mail Address**, Florida Supreme Court Approved Family Law Form 12.915; and Florida Rule of Judicial Administration 2.516.

What should I do next?

A copy of this form must be mailed, e-mailed, **or** hand-delivered to the other party in your case.

If the respondent has denied that the person named in the petition is the father of the child(ren) and requested a **scientific paternity test**, you must now wait until the test is complete. You should then proceed according to the instructions in **Petition to Determine Paternity and for Related Relief**, Florida Supreme Court Approved Family Law Form 12.983(a).

Where can I look for more information?

Before proceeding, you should read General Information for Self-Represented Litigants found at the beginning of these forms. The words that are in **bold underline** in these instructions are defined there. For further information, see chapter 742, Florida Statutes.

Special notes . . .

Remember, a person who is NOT an attorney is called a nonlawyer. If a nonlawyer helps you fill out these forms, that person must give you a copy of a **Disclosure from Nonlawyer,**

Florida Family Law Rules of Procedure Form 12.900 (a), before he or she helps you. A nonlawyer helping you fill out these forms also **must** put his or her name, address, and telephone number on the bottom of the last page of every form he or she helps you complete.

Added Feb. 26, 1998, effective Mar. 16, 1998 (713 So.2d 1). Amended Sept. 21, 2000 (810 So.2d 1); March 26, 2015, effective March 26, 2015 (2015 WL 1343088).

Form 12.983(e). Motion for Scientific Paternity Testing

IN THE CIRCUIT COURT OF THE __________ JUDICIAL CIRCUIT,
IN AND FOR ____________________ COUNTY, FLORIDA

Case No.: ____________________
Division: ____________________

______________________________,
Petitioner,

and

______________________________,
Respondent.

MOTION FOR SCIENTIFIC PATERNITY TESTING

I, *{choose only one}* _____ Petitioner _____ Respondent certifies that the following information is true:

1. At this time, other than testimony, very little or no substantial proof of paternity or nonpaternity is available in this action.
2. I request, under section 742.12, Florida Statutes, that the Court enter an order for appropriate scientific testing of the biological samples of Petitioner and Respondent and the minor child(ren) listed below, so that a determination of paternity of the minor child(ren) can be made to a reasonable degree of medical certainty:

	Name	Birth Date
(1)		
(2)		
(3)		
(4)		
(5)		
(6)		

3. I request that the costs of the scientific testing initially be borne by ( ) Petitioner ( ) Respondent ( ) both Petitioner and Respondent.

I certify that a copy of this document was ( ) mailed ( ) faxed and mailed ( ) e-mailed ( ) hand delivered to the person(s) listed below on *{date}* ______________________________.

_____ **Petitioner or his/her attorney:**
_____ **Respondent or his/her attorney:**
Name: ______________________________
Address: ______________________________
City, State, Zip: ______________________________
Fax Number: ______________________________

Florida Supreme Court Approved Family Law Form 12.983(e), Motion for Scientific Paternity Testing (03/15)

Designated E-mail Address(es): ____________________

____

____
Signature of Party
Printed Name: ____________________
Address: ____________________
City, State, Zip: ____________________
Telephone Number: ____________________
Fax Number: ____________________
Designated E-mail Address(es): ____________________

____

STATE OF FLORIDA
COUNTY OF

Sworn to or affirmed and signed before me on __________ by __________.

____
NOTARY PUBLIC or DEPUTY CLERK

____
[Print, type, or stamp commissioned name of notary or clerk.]

____ Personally known
____ Produced identification
Type of identification produced

IF A NONLAWYER HELPED YOU FILL OUT THIS FORM, HE/SHE MUST FILL IN THE BLANKS BELOW:
[fill in all blanks] This form was prepared for the: *{choose only one}* ( ) Petitioner ( ) Respondent.
This form was completed with the assistance of:
{name of individual} ____________________,
{name of business} ____________________,
{address} ____________________,
{city} __________,*{state}* ______,*{zip code}* ________, *{telephone number}* __________.

INSTRUCTIONS FOR FLORIDA SUPREME COURT APPROVED FAMILY LAW FORM 12.983(e), MOTION FOR SCIENTIFIC PATERNITY TESTING (03/15)

When should this form be used?

This form should be used when the mother or alleged father wants the court to order a **scientific paternity test** to determine the **paternity** of a minor child(ren).

This form should be typed or printed in black ink. After completing this form, you should sign the form before a **notary public** or **deputy clerk**. You should **file** the original with the **clerk of the circuit court** in the county where the petition was filed and keep a copy for your records.

IMPORTANT INFORMATION REGARDING E–FILING

The Florida Rules of Judicial Administration now require that all petitions, pleadings, and documents be filed electronically except in certain circumstances. **Self–represented litigants may file petitions or other pleadings or documents electronically; however, they are not required to do so.** If you choose to file your pleadings or other documents electronically, you must do so in accordance with Florida Rule of Judicial Administration 2.525, and you must follow the procedures of the judicial circuit in which you file. **The rules and procedures should be carefully read and followed.**

IMPORTANT INFORMATION REGARDING E–SERVICE ELECTION

After the initial service of process of the petition or supplemental petition by the Sheriff or certified process server, the Florida Rules of Judicial Administration now require that all documents required or permitted to be served on the other party must be served by electronic mail (e–mail) except in certain circumstances. **You must strictly comply with the format requirements set forth in the Rules of Judicial Administration.**

SELF–REPRESENTED LITIGANTS MAY SERVE DOCUMENTS BY E–MAIL; HOWEVER, THEY ARE NOT REQUIRED TO DO SO. If a self-represented litigant elects to serve and receive documents by e-mail, the procedures must always be followed once the initial election is made.

To serve and receive documents by e-mail, you must designate your e-mail addresses by using the **Designation of Current Mailing and E–mail Address**, Florida Supreme Court Approved Family Law Form 12.915, and you must provide your e-mail address on each form on which your signature appears. Please **CAREFULLY** read the rules and instructions for: **Certificate of Service (General),** Florida Supreme Court Approved Family Law Form 12.914; **Designation of Current Mailing and E–mail Address**, Florida Supreme Court Approved Family Law Form 12.915; and Florida Rule of Judicial Administration 2.516.

What should I do next?

When you have filed this motion, you are ready to set a **hearing** on this motion. You should check with the clerk, **family law intake staff**, or **judicial assistant** for information on the local procedure for scheduling a hearing. When you know the date and time of your hearing, you should file a **Notice of Hearing (General)**, Florida Supreme Court Approved Family Law Form 12.923, or other appropriate notice of hearing form.

A copy of this motion and the Notice of Hearing must be mailed, e-mailed **or** hand-delivered to the other party in your case.

Where can I look for more information?

Before proceeding, you should read General Information for Self–Represented Litigants found at the beginning of these forms. The words that are in **bold underline** in these instructions are defined there. For further information, see chapter 742, Florida Statutes.

Special notes . . .

These family law forms contain an **Order on Motion for Scientific Paternity Testing**, Florida Supreme Court Approved Family Law Form 12.983(f), which the judge may use. You should check with the clerk, family law intake staff, or judicial assistant to see if you need to bring it with you to the hearing. If so, you should type or print the heading, including the circuit, county, case number, division, and the parties' names, and leave the rest blank for the judge to complete at your hearing or trial.

Remember, a person who is NOT an attorney is called a nonlawyer. If a nonlawyer helps you fill out these forms, that person must give you a copy of a **Disclosure from Nonlawyer**, Florida Family Law Rules of Procedure Form 12.900 (a), before he or she helps you. A nonlawyer helping you fill out these forms also **must** put his or her name, address, and telephone number on the bottom of the last page of every form he or she helps you complete.

Added Feb. 26, 1998, effective Mar. 16, 1998 (713 So.2d 1). Amended Sept. 21, 2000 (810 So.2d 1); March 26, 2015, effective March 26, 2015 (2015 WL 1343088).

Form 12.983(f). Order on Motion for Scientific Paternity Testing

IN THE CIRCUIT COURT OF THE ________ JUDICIAL CIRCUIT,
IN AND FOR ____________________ COUNTY, FLORIDA

Case No.: ____________________
Division: ____________________

______________________________,
Petitioner,

and

______________________________,
Respondent.

ORDER ON MOTION FOR SCIENTIFIC PATERNITY TESTING

This cause having come to be heard on *{date}* ________________________, upon a motion/stipulation for scientific paternity testing, and the Court having been fully advised in the premises, it is therefore FOUND:

1. That the Court has jurisdiction over the parties and subject matter of this action.

2. *{choose **one** only}*
   a.____That the natural mother of the dependent child(ren) at issue was not married to any individual at the time of conception or birth of the child(ren).
   b. _____ That the natural mother of the dependent child(ren) at issue was married to an individual other than the alleged father at the time of conception or birth of said child(ren); however, a court order has determined that said individual is not the child(ren)'s father.

It is therefore ORDERED:

3. The above motion is GRANTED.

4. Petitioner, Respondent, and the minor child(ren) shall appear for the purpose of appropriate scientific paternity testing:
   *{choose **one** only}*
   a. _____immediately.
   b. _____at _______ a.m./p.m. on *{date}* _________ at *{location}* ____________________________
   ____.
   c. _____ at a time and place to be specified by the Florida Department of Revenue. Appropriate scientific paternity testing on Petitioner, Respondent, and the minor child(ren) shall be in *{city}* _____ ______________________, Florida, with at least 30 days advance written notice. If the Florida Department of Revenue fails to notify the party(ies), the party(ies) shall contact the Florida Department of Revenue for further instructions.

Florida Supreme Court Approved Family Law Form 12.983(f), Order on Motion for Scientific Paternity Testing (03/15)

5. The costs of the scientific paternity testing shall be assessed (   ) at a later date (   ) against Petitioner (   ) against Respondent (   ) Other *{explain}* ______________________.

6. The test results, together with the opinions and conclusions of the test laboratory, shall be filed with the Court. Any objection to the test results must be made in writing and must be filed with the Court at least 10 days before the hearing. If no objection is filed, the test results shall be admitted into evidence with no further predicate. Nothing in this paragraph prohibits a party from calling an outside expert witness to refute or support the testing procedure or results or the mathematical theory on which they are based.

7. Test results are admissible in evidence and should be weighed along with other evidence of the paternity of the alleged father unless the statistical probability of paternity equals or exceeds 95 percent. A statistical probability of 95 percent or more creates a rebuttable presumption that the alleged father is the biological father of the child(ren). If the party fails to rebut the presumption of paternity, the Court may enter a summary judgment of paternity. If the test results show the alleged father cannot be the biological father, the case shall be dismissed with prejudice.

8. The Court reserves jurisdiction over the parties and the subject matter of this action to enforce the terms and provisions of this and all previous orders as well as to enter such other orders as may be just.

DONE AND ORDERED on ______________, in ______________, Florida.

____
CIRCUIT JUDGE

I CERTIFY that a copy of *{name of document(s)}* ______________ was (   ) mailed (   ) faxed and mailed (   ) e-mailed (   ) hand-delivered to the parties and any other person(s) or entities listed below on *{date}* ______________.

CLERK OF THE CIRCUIT COURT

(SEAL)

By: ______________________________
Deputy Clerk or Judicial Assistant

Petitioner (or his or her attorney)
Respondent (or his or her attorney)
Other: ______________________

Florida Supreme Court Approved Family Law Form 12.983(f), Order on Motion for Scientific Paternity Testing (03/15)

Added Feb. 26, 1998, effective Mar. 16, 1998 (713 So.2d 1). Amended Sept. 21, 2000 (810 So.2d 1); March 26, 2015, effective March 26, 2015 (2015 WL 1343088).

Form 12.983(g). Final Judgment of Paternity

IN THE CIRCUIT COURT OF THE ______________________ JUDICIAL CIRCUIT,
IN AND FOR ________________ COUNTY, FLORIDA

Case No.: ________________
Division: ________________

______________________________,
Petitioner,

and

______________________________,
Respondent.

FINAL JUDGMENT OF PATERNITY

This cause came before the Court upon a Petition to Determine Paternity and for Related Relief, under chapter 742, Florida Statutes. The Court having reviewed the file and having heard the testimony, makes these findings of fact and reaches these conclusions of law:

1. The Court has jurisdiction of the subject matter and the parties.

2. **Paternity.** *{Choose only one}* _____ By operation of law, _____ The Court finds that *{full legal name}* ____,
is the natural and biological father of the minor child(ren), listed below:

The parties' dependent or minor child(ren) is (are):

Name	**Birth date**

SECTION I. PARENTAL RESPONSIBILITY AND PARENTING PLAN ESTABLISHING TIME-SHARING WITH DEPENDENT OR MINOR CHILD(REN)

1. **Jurisdiction.** The Court has jurisdiction to determine parental responsibility and to adopt or establish a Parenting Plan with time-sharing with regard to the child(ren) listed in paragraph 2 above.

2. **Parental Responsibility and Parenting Plan for the Minor Child(ren).** *{Choose only one}*
   a. _____**Not adjudicated.** Since no request for relief was made in this action, parental

responsibility of and time-sharing with the minor child(ren) is governed by sections 742.031 and 744.301, Florida Statutes.

b. _____ **Parenting Plan**. The parties shall comply with the Parenting Plan which is attached hereto and incorporated herein as Exhibit _____.

SECTION II. CHILD SUPPORT

1. The Court finds that there is a need for child support and that the _____ Mother _____ Father (hereinafter Obligor) has the present ability to pay child support. The amounts in the **Child Support Guidelines Worksheet**, Florida Family Law Rules of Procedure Form 12.902(e), filed by the _____ Mother _____ Father are correct **OR** the Court makes the following findings:

   The Mother's net monthly income is $__________, (Child Support Guidelines _____%).
   The Father's net monthly income is $__________, (Child Support Guidelines _____%).
   Monthly child care costs are $__________.
   Monthly health/dental insurance costs are $__________.

2. **Amount.**
   Child support established at the rate of $__________ per month for the _______ children *{total number of parties' minor or dependent children}* shall be paid commencing _______________ *{month, day, year}* and terminating ________________ *{month, day, year}*. Child support shall be paid in the amount of $__________ per __________ *{week, month, other}* which is consistent with the Obligor's current payroll cycle.

   Upon the termination of the obligation of child support for one of the parties' oldest children, child support in the amount of $__________ for the remaining _____ children *{total number of remaining children}* shall be paid commencing ____________________ *{month, day, year}* and terminating ____________________ *{month, day, year}*. This child support shall be paid in the amount of $__________ per __________ *{week, month, other}* consistent with Obligor's current payroll cycle.

   {Insert schedule for the child support obligation, including the amount, and commencement and termination dates, for the remaining minor or dependent children, which shall be payable as the obligation for each child ceases. Please indicate whether the schedule ____ appears below or ____ is attached as part of this form.}

   ____
   ____
   ____
   ____
   ____
   ____

   The Obligor shall pay child support until all of the minor or dependent children: reach the age of 18; become emancipated, marry, join the armed services, die, or become self-supporting; or until further order of the court or agreement of the parties. The child support obligation shall continue beyond the age of 18 and until high school graduation for any child who is dependent in fact, between the ages of 18 and 19, and is still in high school, performing in good faith with a reasonable expectation of graduation before the age of 19.
   If the child support ordered deviates from the guidelines by more than 5%, the factual findings which support that deviation are: ____
   ____

3. **Arrearage/Retroactive Child Support.**

a. ____There is no retroactive child support or arrearage at the time of this Final Judgment.

b. ____ The _____ Mother _____ Father _____ both has (have) incurred medical expenses in the amount of $ __________ on behalf of the minor child(ren), including hospital and other expenses incidental to the birth of the minor child(ren). Petitioner shall pay ______%, Respondent shall pay _____%, which shall be paid as follows: _____ added to arrearage in paragraph c below _____other *{explain}* ____

____

c. ____The _____Mother _____ Father shall pay to the other party the child support arrearage of:

$________ for retroactive child support, as of *{date}*__________________________.

$_________ for previously ordered unpaid child support, as of *{date}* ______________.

$_________ for previously incurred medical expenses.

The total of $____________ in child support arrearage shall be repaid at the rate of $_____ per month, payable ( ) in accordance with Obligor's employer's payroll cycle, and in any event at least once a month ( ) other *{explain}* ______________________________

____,

beginning *{date}* ________________________, until paid in full including statutory interest.

4. **Insurance.**

*{Indicate **all** that apply}*

a. _____ **Health/Dental Insurance.** _____ Mother _____ Father shall be required to maintain:

_____ health and/or _____ dental insurance for the parties' minor child(ren), so long as it is reasonable in cost and accessible to the child(ren). The party providing insurance shall be required to convey insurance cards demonstrating said coverage to the other party;

OR

_____ health _____ dental insurance is not reasonable in cost or accessible to the child(ren) at this time.

b. Reasonable and necessary **uninsured medical/dental/prescription drug costs** for the minor child(ren) shall be assessed as follows:

_____ Shared equally by both parents.

_____ Prorated according to the child support guideline percentages.

_____ Other *{explain}*: ____

____

As to these uninsured medical/dental/prescription drug expenses, the party who incurs the expense shall submit request for reimbursement to the other party within 30 days, and the other party, within 30 days of receipt, shall submit the applicable reimbursement for that expense, according to the schedule of reimbursement set out in this paragraph.

5. _____**Life Insurance (to secure payment of support).** To secure the child support obligations in

this judgment, _____ Mother _____ Father _____ each party shall maintain life insurance coverage, in an amount of at least $____________, on _____ his life _____ her life _____ his/her life naming the _____ minor child(ren) as the beneficiary(ies) OR naming the _____ Mother _____Father _____other *{name}* ________________________________ as Trustee for the minor child(ren), so long as reasonably available. The obligation to maintain the life insurance coverage shall continue until the youngest child turns 18, becomes emancipated, marries, joins the armed services, dies, or otherwise becomes self-supporting.

6. _____**IRS Income Tax Exemption(s).** The assignment of any tax exemption(s) for the child(ren) shall be as follows: ____
____.
Further, each party shall execute any and all IRS forms necessary to effectuate the provisions of this paragraph.

7. **Other provisions relating to child support:** ______________________________
____
____

SECTION III. METHOD OF PAYMENT

Obligor shall pay court-ordered child support/alimony and arrears, if any, as follows:

1. **Place of Payment**

a. ____Obligor shall pay court-ordered support directly to either the State Disbursement Unit, or the central depository, as required by statute, along with any fee required by statute.
OR

b. ____Both parties have requested and the court finds that it is in the best interests of the child(ren) that support payments need not be directed through either the State Disbursement Unit or the central depository at this time; however, either party may subsequently apply, pursuant to section 61.13(1)(d)3, Florida Statutes, to require payments through either the State Disbursement Unit or the central depository.

2. **Income Deduction.**

a. ____**Immediate.** Obligor shall pay through income deduction, pursuant to a separate Income Deduction Order which shall be effective immediately. Obligor is individually responsible for paying this support obligation until all of said support is deducted from Obligor's income. Until support payments are deducted from Obligor's paycheck, Obligor is responsible for making timely payments directly to the State Disbursement Unit or the Obligee, as previously set forth in this order.

b. ____**Deferred.** Income deduction is ordered this day, but it shall not be effective until a delinquency of $__________, or, if not specified, an amount equal to one month's obligation occurs. Income deduction is not being implemented immediately based on the following findings: Income deduction is **not** in the best interests of the child(ren) because: *{explain}*
____
____

AND

there is proof of timely payment of a previously ordered obligation without an income deduction order in cases of modification,

AND

_____ there is an agreement by the Obligor to advise the Title IV-D agency, the clerk of court, and the Obligee of any change in Payor and/or health insurance

OR

_____ there is a signed written agreement providing an alternative arrangement between the Obligor and the Obligee and, at the option of the IV-D agency, by the IV-D agency in IV-D cases in which there is an assignment of support rights to the state, reviewed and entered in the record by the court.

3. **Bonus/one-time payments.** _____ All _____% _____ No income paid in the form of a bonus or other similar one-time payment, up to the amount of any arrearage or the remaining balance thereof owed pursuant to this order, shall be forwarded to Obligee pursuant to the payment method prescribed above.

4. **Other provisions relating to method of payment.** ______________________________________
____
____.

SECTION IV. CHILD(REN)'S NAME(S)

a. _____There shall be **no change** to the child(ren)'s name(s).

b. _____It is in the child(ren)'s best interests that the child(ren)'s present name(s): shall be changed to the following:

the child(ren)'s present name(s):	shall be changed to the following:
(1) ______________________	(1) ______________________
(2) ______________________	(2) ______________________
(3) ______________________	(3) ______________________
(4) ______________________	(4) ______________________
(5) ______________________	(5) ______________________
(6) ______________________	(6) ______________________

by which they shall hereafter be known

c. The name change is in the best interest(s) of the child(ren) because:______________________
____.

SECTION V. ATTORNEY'S FEES, COSTS, AND SUIT MONEY

1. _____ Petitioner's _____ Respondent's request(s) for attorney's fees, costs, and suit money is (are) denied because ____
____.

2. ____The Court finds there is a need for and an ability to pay attorney's fees, costs, and suit money. _____ Petitioner _____ Respondent is hereby ordered to pay to the other party $__________ in attorney's fees, and $__________ in costs. The Court further finds that the attorney's fees awarded are based on the reasonable rate of $_________ per hour and

__________ reasonable hours. Other provisions relating to attorney's fees, costs, and suit money are as follows:____
____
____.

3. The costs of the scientific paternity testing shall be assessed:
_____ against Petitioner
_____ against Respondent
_____ Other *{explain}* ____.

SECTION VI. OTHER PROVISIONS

1. **Other Provisions.** ____
____
____
____
____
____

The Court reserves jurisdiction to modify and enforce this Final Judgment.

DONE AND ORDERED at ____________________, Florida, on __________________.

____
CIRCUIT JUDGE

I CERTIFY that a copy of this *{name of document}*______________________________ was ( ) mailed ( ) faxed and mailed ( ) e-mailed ( ) hand-delivered to the parties or entities listed below on *{date}* ______________________________.

(SEAL)

By: _______________________________
{Clerk of court or designee}

Florida Supreme Court Approved Family Law Form 12.983(g), Final Judgment of Paternity (03/15)

Petitioner (or his or her attorney)
Respondent (or his or her attorney)
Central depository
State Disbursement Unit
____ Other: ______________________________

Added Feb. 26, 1998, effective Mar. 16, 1998 (713 So.2d 1). Amended July 1, 1999 (717 So.2d 914); Sept. 21, 2000 (810 So.2d 1); March 26, 2009 (20 So.3d 173); Dec. 16, 2010 (59 So.3d 792); May 24, 2012 (96 So.3d 217); July 3, 2013 (117 So.3d 958); March 26, 2015, effective March 26, 2015 (2015 WL 1343088).

Form 12.984(a). Order of Referral to Parenting Coordinator

IN THE CIRCUIT COURT OF THE ______________________ JUDICIAL CIRCUIT,
IN AND FOR ______________________________ COUNTY, FLORIDA

Case No: ______________________
Division: ______________________

______________________________,
Petitioner,

and

______________________________,
Respondent.

ORDER OF REFERRAL TO PARENTING COORDINATOR

The Court considered the ( ) motion of the court, ( ) joint motion of the parties, ( ) motion of a party, reviewed the court file, and considered the testimony presented. Based upon this information, the court **FINDS** that:

A. **Appropriateness of Process.** This matter is appropriate for parenting coordination and it is in the best interest of the child(ren).

B. **Parenting Coordination Process.** Parenting coordination is a child-focused alternative dispute resolution process whereby a parenting coordinator assists the parents in creating or implementing their parenting plan by facilitating the resolution of disputes, providing education and making recommendations to the parents; and, with the prior consent of the parents and approval of the court, making limited decisions within the scope of this order of referral.

C. **Parenting Coordinator.** A parenting coordinator is an impartial third person whose role is to assist the parents in successfully creating or implementing a parenting plan.

D. **Selection of Parenting Coordinator.** The parenting coordinator was selected by:
[Choose only one]
____ parties' agreement.
____ the court.

E. **History of Domestic Violence.** Based on testimony and evidence presented and a review of related court records, the court has determined:
[Choose all that apply]
____ There is no history of domestic violence.

____ There has been a history of domestic violence, and:

1. ____ Each party has had an opportunity to consult with an attorney or domestic violence advocate before this court has accepted the parties' consent; and

2. ____ Each party has consented to this referral and the consent has been given freely and voluntarily.

It is therefore, **ORDERED**:

1. **Parenting Coordinator.** The parties are referred to the following parenting coordinator for an initial period of ________months:

   Name: ________________________________
   Address: ________________________________
   ____
   Telephone: ________________________
   Fax Number: ________________________
   Email: ________________________________

   a. The parenting coordinator shall file a response to this Order within 30 days either accepting or declining the appointment. The response to the appointment must be in substantial compliance with Florida Family Law Rules of Procedure Form 12.984(b).

   b. The parties or their attorneys must provide to the parenting coordinator copies of all pleadings and orders related to domestic violence and any other pleadings and orders requested by the parenting coordinator related to parenting coordination.

2. **Meetings.** Unless prohibited herein as a domestic violence safeguard or by another court order, the parenting coordinator may meet with the parties and/or child(ren) together or separately, in person or by any electronic means.

3. **Domestic Violence Safeguards.** The parties shall adhere to all provisions of any injunction for protection or conditions of bail, probation, or a sentence arising from criminal proceedings. In addition to any safety measures the parenting coordinator deems necessary, the following domestic violence safeguards must be implemented:

   [Choose **all** that apply]
   ____ None are necessary.
   ____ No joint meetings
   ____ No direct negotiations
   ____ No direct communications
   ____ Other: ____

4. **Role, Responsibility, and Authority of Parenting Coordinator.** The parenting coordinator shall have the following role, responsibility, and authority:

   a. Assisting the parents in creating and implementing a parenting plan.

   b. Facilitating the resolution of disputes regarding the creation or implementation of the Parenting Plan.

c. Recommending to the parents strategies for creating or implementing the Parenting Plan. Such recommendations may include that one or both parents avail themselves of accessible and appropriate community resources, including, but not limited to, random drug screens, parenting classes, and individual psychotherapy or family counseling, if there is a history or evidence that such referrals are appropriate.

d. Recommending to the parents changes to the Parenting Plan.

e. Educating the parties to effectively:
   i. Parent in a manner that minimizes conflicts;
   ii. Communicate and negotiate with each other and their child(ren);
   iii. Develop and apply appropriate parenting skills;
   iv. Understand principles of child development and issues facing child(ren) when their parents no longer live together;
   v. Disengage from the other parent when engagement leads to conflicts and non-cooperation;
   vi. Identify the sources of their conflict with each other and work jointly to minimize conflict and lessen its deleterious effects on the child(ren); and,
   vii. Allow the child(ren) to grow up free from the threat of being caught in the middle of their parents' disputes.

f. Reporting or communicating with the court concerning nonconfidential matters as provided in paragraph 6 of this Order. In the event the parenting coordinator is unable to adequately perform the duties in accordance with the court's direction, the parenting coordinator shall file a written request for a status conference and the court shall set a timely status hearing. The request for status conference must be in substantial compliance with Florida Family Law Rules of Procedure Form 12.984(d). A report to the court of an emergency pursuant to section 61.125(8), Florida Statutes, must be in substantial compliance with Florida Family Law Rules of Procedure Form 12.984(c).

g. Communicating with the parties and their child(ren), separately or together, in person or by telephone, unless otherwise prohibited by court order or applicable law.

5. **Fees and Costs for Parenting Coordination.**
[Choose **all** that apply]

a. ____ The parties have consented to this referral to parenting coordination.

____ This order is without the consent of the parties, but the court has determined that the parties have the financial ability to pay the parenting coordination fees and costs.

b. ____The court allocates payment of fees and costs for parenting coordination as follows:
Hourly rate of compensation shall not exceed $____________, unless the parties otherwise agree.
____ % shall be paid by the Father.
____ % shall be paid by the Mother.
____ Other: ____

If a party causes the parenting coordinator to expend an unreasonable and unnecessary amount of time, that party may be held solely responsible for payment of the parenting coordinator's fees and costs for such time expended, and the court reserves jurisdiction to reallocate the payment of fees and costs in that event. Failure to pay the parenting coordinator's fees and costs in a timely manner may subject the party to sanctions for contempt of court.

6. **Confidentiality.** All communications made by, between, or among the parties and the parenting coordinator during parenting coordination sessions are confidential. The parenting coordinator and each party may not testify or offer evidence about communications made by a party or the parenting coordinator during the parenting coordination sessions, except if:

a. Necessary to identify, authenticate, confirm, or deny a written agreement entered into by the parties during parenting coordination.

b. The testimony or evidence is necessary to identify an issue for resolution by the court without otherwise disclosing communications made by any party or the parenting coordinator.

c. The testimony or evidence is limited to the subject of a party's compliance with this Order of Referral to Parenting Coordinator, orders for psychological evaluation, counseling ordered by the court or recommended by a health care provider, or for substance abuse testing or treatment.

d. The parenting coordinator reports that the case is no longer appropriate for parenting coordination.

e. The parenting coordinator reports that he or she is unable or unwilling to continue to serve and that a successor parenting coordinator should be appointed.

f. The testimony or evidence is necessary pursuant to section 61.125(5)(b) or section 61.125(8), Florida Statutes.

g. The parenting coordinator is not qualified to address or resolve certain issues in the case and a more qualified coordinator should be appointed.

h. The parties agree that the testimony or evidence be permitted.

i. The testimony or evidence is necessary to protect any person from future acts that would constitute domestic violence under Chapter 741, Florida Statutes; child abuse, neglect, or abandonment under Chapter 39, Florida Statutes; or abuse, neglect, or exploitation of an elderly or disabled adult under Chapter 825, Florida Statutes.

7. **Agreement on Nonconfidentiality.** The parties can agree to waive confidentiality of a specific communication or all communications. The waiver must be in writing, signed by the parties and their respective counsel. The waiver shall be filed with the court and a copy served on the parenting coordinator. Either party may revoke their waiver of confidentiality by providing

written notice signed by that party. The revocation shall be filed with the court and a copy served on the other party and the parenting coordinator.

8. **Scheduling.** Each party shall contact the parenting coordinator within 10 days of the date of this Order to schedule the first appointment. The parenting coordinator shall determine the schedule for subsequent appointments.

9. **Stipulation. Any written stipulation of parties to utilize the parenting coordination process filed with this court is incorporated into this Order.**

ORDERED ON *{date}* ________________________.

____
CIRCUIT JUDGE

Copies to:

_____Petitioner

_____Attorney for Petitioner

_____Respondent

_____Attorney for Respondent

_____Other:______________________________

Florida Family Law Rules of Procedure Form 12.984(a), Order of Referral to Parenting Coordinator (07/14)

Formerly Form 12.998, added Jan. 28, 2010 (27 So.3d 650). Renumbered Form 12.984(a) and amended July 3, 2014, effective July 3, 2014 (142 So.3d 831).

Form 12.984(b). Response by Parenting Coordinator

IN THE CIRCUIT COURT OF THE ____________________ JUDICIAL CIRCUIT,
IN AND FOR ______________________________ COUNTY, FLORIDA

Case No: ______________________
Division: ______________________

____________________________________,
Petitioner,

and

____________________________________,
Respondent.

RESPONSE BY PARENTING COORDINATOR

I, *{name}*____ notify the Court and affirm the following:

1. Acceptance.
   [Choose only **one**]
   a. ____ I accept the appointment as parenting coordinator.
   b. ____ I decline the appointment as parenting coordinator.

2. Qualifications.
   [Choose only **one**]
   a. ____ I meet the qualifications in section 61.125(4), Florida Statutes.
   b. ____ I do not meet the qualifications in section 61.125(4), Florida Statutes. However, the parties have chosen me by mutual consent and I believe I can perform the services of a parenting coordinator because: ____
   ____
   ____

3. I am not aware of any conflict, circumstance, or reason that renders me unable to serve as the parenting coordinator in this matter and I will immediately inform the court and the parties if such arises.

4. I understand my role, responsibility, and authority under the Order of Referral to Parenting Coordinator, Florida Family Law Rules of Procedure Form 12.984(a); section 61.125, Florida Statutes; Florida Family Law Rule of Procedure 12.742; and Rules for Qualified and Court Appointed Parenting Coordinators.

Florida Family Law Rules of Procedure Form 12.984(b), Response by Parenting Coordinator (07/14)

I hereby affirm the truth of the statements in this acceptance and understand that if I make any false representations in this acceptance, I am subject to sanctions by the Court.

______________________ Date

______________________________ Signature of Parenting Coordinator
Printed Name:______________________
Address: ______________________
City, State, Zip: ______________________
Telephone Number: ______________________
E-mail:______________________
Professional License # (if applicable) ______________
Professional Certification # (if applicable) ______________

Copies to:

_____Petitioner

_____Attorney for Petitioner

_____Respondent

_____Attorney for Respondent

_____Other: ______________________

IF A NONLAWYER HELPED YOU FILL OUT THIS FORM, HE/SHE MUST FILL IN THE BLANKS BELOW:
[fill in **all** blanks] This form was completed with the assistance of:
{name of individual} ______________________,
*{name of business}*______________________,
{address} ______________________,
{city} ______________,*{state}* __________,*{telephone number}* ______________.

INSTRUCTIONS FOR FLORIDA FAMILY LAW RULES OF PROCEDURE FORM 12.984(b) RESPONSE BY PARENTING COORDINATOR (07/14)

When should this form be used?

A person appointed as a parenting coordinator must accept or decline the appointment under Florida Family Law Rule of Procedure 12.742(e). If you accept the appointment, you must complete paragraphs 1(a) and 2 and sign it. If you decline the appointment, you must complete only paragraph 1(b) and sign the form. This form should be typed or printed in black ink.

Important Consideration Before Responding.

A Qualified Parenting Coordinator or other licensed mental health professional under Chapter 490 or 491, Florida Statutes, shall abide by the ethical and other professional standards imposed by his or her licensing authority, certification board, or both, as applicable.

A person who is not a Qualified Parenting Coordinator or a licensed mental health professional under Chapter 490 or 491, Florida Statutes, shall not accept an appointment to serve as parenting coordinator in a matter that presents an apparent or undisclosed conflict of interest. A conflict of interest arises when any relationship between the parenting coordinator and either party compromises or appears to compromise the parenting coordinator's ability to serve. The burden of disclosure of any potential conflict of interest rests on the parenting coordinator. Disclosure shall be made as soon as practical after the parenting coordinator becomes aware of the potential conflict of interest. If a parenting coordinator makes an appropriate disclosure of a conflict of interest or a potential conflict of interest, he or she may serve if all parties agree. However, if a conflict of interest substantially impairs a parenting coordinator's ability to serve, the parenting coordinator shall decline the appointment or withdraw regardless of the express agreement of the parties.

A parenting coordinator shall not provide any services to either party that would impair the parenting coordinator's ability to be neutral.

What should I do next?

After completing and signing this form, you must file the original with the clerk of the circuit court in the county in which the action is pending and keep a copy for your records. You must mail or hand-deliver a copy of this form to the attorney(s) for the parents or, if not represented by an attorney, to the parents.

Where can I look for more information?

Before proceeding, you should read "General Information for Self–Represented Litigants" found at the beginning of these forms. For more information, see section 61.125, Florida Statutes; Florida Family Law Rule of Procedure 12.742; Rules for Qualified and Court Appointed Parenting Coordinators; and the **Order of Referral to Parenting Coordinator**, Florida Family Law Rules of Procedure Form 12.984(a).

Special notes

Remember, a person who is NOT an attorney is called a nonlawyer. If a nonlawyer helps you fill out these forms, that person must give you a copy of **Disclosure from Nonlawyer**, Florida Family Law Rules of Procedure Form 12.900(a), before he or she helps you. A nonlawyer helping you fill out these forms also must put his or her name, address, and telephone number on the bottom of the last page of every form he or she helps you complete.

Formerly Form 12.984, added Jan. 28, 2010 (27 So.3d 650). Amended Nov. 15, 2012 (104 So.3d 314). Renumbered Form 12.984(b) and amended July 3, 2014, effective July 3, 2014 (142 So.3d 831).

Form 12.984(c). Parenting Coordinator Report of an Emergency

IN THE CIRCUIT COURT OF THE _______________ JUDICIAL CIRCUIT,
IN AND FOR ___________________________ COUNTY, FLORIDA

Case No: ___________________
Division: ___________________

_______________________________,
Petitioner,

and

_______________________________,
Respondent.

PARENTING COORDINATOR REPORT OF AN EMERGENCY

The undersigned parenting coordinator reports an emergency to the court:

1. _____ With notice to the parties. A party has obtained a final order or injunction of protection against domestic violence or has been arrested for an act of domestic violence as provided under chapter 741, F.S.
2. _____ Without notice to the parties pursuant to section 61.125 (8)(a), Florida Statutes, because: (choose all that apply)
   a. _____ There is a reasonable cause to suspect that a child will suffer or is suffering abuse, neglect, or abandonment as provided under chapter 39, Florida Statutes.
   b. _____ There is a reasonable cause to suspect a vulnerable adult has or is being abused, neglected, or exploited as provided under chapter 415, Florida Statutes.
   c. _____ A party, or someone acting on a party's behalf, is expected to wrongfully remove or is wrongfully removing the child from the jurisdiction of the court without prior approval or compliance with the requirements of section 61.13001, Florida Statutes.
3. Describe the emergency: ____
____
____.

VERIFICATION BY PARENTING COORDINATOR

I, ____ (name of parenting coordinator) do hereby swear or affirm that the facts contained in this Parenting Coordinator Report of an Emergency are true

Florida Family Law Rules of Procedure Form 12.984(c), Parenting Coordinator Report of an Emergency (07/14)

and correct to the best of my knowledge and belief.

Date

Signature of Parenting Coordinator
Printed Name:
Address:
City, State, Zip:
Telephone Number:
E-mail:
Professional License # (if applicable)
Professional Certification # (if applicable)

STATE OF FLORIDA
COUNTY OF

Sworn to or affirmed and signed before me on ________ by ________.

NOTARY PUBLIC or DEPUTY CLERK

[Print, type, or stamp commissioned name of notary or deputy clerk.]

____ Personally known
____ Produced identification
Type of identification produced ________

Copies to:

____ Presiding Judge

____ Petitioner

____ Attorney for Petitioner

____ Respondent

____ Attorney for Respondent

____ Other: ________

IF A NONLAWYER HELPED YOU FILL OUT THIS FORM, HE/SHE MUST FILL IN THE BLANKS BELOW:
[fill in all blanks] This form was completed with the assistance of:
{name of individual} ________,
{name of business} ________,
{address} ________,
{city} ________, *{state}* ________, *{telephone number}* ________.

Florida Family Law Rules of Procedure Form 12.984(c), Parenting Coordinator Report of an Emergency (07/14)

INSTRUCTIONS FOR FLORIDA FAMILY LAW RULES OF PROCEDURE FORM 12.984(c) PARENTING COORDINATOR REPORT OF AN EMERGENCY (07/14)

When should this form be used?

A person appointed as a parenting coordinator must immediately inform the court of an emergency situation pursuant to section 61.125(8), Florida Statutes. This form is used by the parenting coordinator to report an emergency with or without notice to the parties. It is critical to differentiate whether notice to the parties is required under the facts of any emergency.

Report With Notice. A parenting coordinator, upon information and belief, must immediately inform the court by affidavit or verified report of an emergency in which a party obtains a final order or injunction of protection against domestic violence or is arrested for an act of domestic violence as provided under chapter 741, Florida Statutes.

Report Without Notice. A parenting coordinator must immediately inform the court by affidavit or verified report of an emergency situation if:

1. There is a reasonable cause to suspect that a child will suffer or is suffering abuse, neglect, or abandonment as provided under chapter 39, Florida Statutes;

2. There is a reasonable cause to suspect a vulnerable adult has been or is being abused, neglected, or exploited as provided under chapter 415, Florida Statutes;

3. A party, or someone acting on a party's behalf, is expected to wrongfully remove or is wrongfully removing the child from the jurisdiction of the court without prior court approval or compliance with the requirements of section 61.13001, Florida Statutes. If the parenting coordinator suspects that the parent has relocated within the state to avoid domestic violence, the coordinator may not disclose the location of the parent and child unless required by court order.

This form should be typed or printed in black ink.

What should I do next?

After completing and signing this form, you must file the original with the clerk of the circuit court in the county in which the action is pending, provide a copy to the presiding judge, and keep a copy for your records.

Report With Notice. If notice to the parties is required under section 61.125(8)(b), Florida Statutes, you must also mail or hand deliver a copy of this form to attorney(s) for the parents or, if not represented by an attorney, to the parents.

Report Without Notice. If notice to the parties is not required, you must mail or hand-deliver a copy of this form to the Judge presiding over the case.

Where can I look for more information?

Before proceeding, you should read "General Information for Self–Represented Litigants" found at the beginning of these forms. For more information, see section 61.125, Florida Statutes; Florida Family Law Rule of Procedure 12.742; Rules for Qualified and Court Appointed Parenting Coordinators; and the **Order of Referral to Parenting Coordinator**, Florida Family Law Rules of Procedure Form 12.984(a).

Special notes

Remember, a person who is NOT an attorney is called a nonlawyer. If a nonlawyer helps you fill out these forms, that person must give you a copy of a **Disclosure from Nonlawyer**, Florida Family Law Rules of Procedure Form 12.900(a), before he or she helps you. A nonlawyer helping you fill out these forms also must put his or her name, address, and telephone number on the bottom of the last page of every form he or she helps you complete.

Added July 3, 2014, effective July 3, 2014 (142 So.3d 831).

Form 12.984(d). Parenting Coordinator Request for Status Conference

IN THE CIRCUIT COURT OF THE ______________ JUDICIAL CIRCUIT,
IN AND FOR ______________________ COUNTY, FLORIDA

Case No: ______________________
Division: ______________________

______________________________,
Petitioner,

and

______________________________,
Respondent.

PARENTING COORDINATOR REQUEST FOR STATUS CONFERENCE

The undersigned Parenting Coordinator requests a status conference in this case: (choose all that apply)

1. _____ To request direction from the court concerning: ______________________________
____
____.

2. _____ To request resolution by the court regarding: ______________________________
____
____.

3. _____ To report ____ petitioner's____ respondent's noncompliance with the Order of Referral to Parenting Coordinator, orders for psychological evaluation, counseling ordered by the court or recommended by a health care provider, or for substance abuse testing or treatment.

4. _____ To report that the case is no longer appropriate for parenting coordination.

5. _____ To report that the undersigned parenting coordinator is not qualified to address or resolve certain issues in this case and a more qualified successor parenting coordinator should be appointed.

6. _____ The undersigned parenting coordinator is unable or unwilling to continue to serve and a successor parenting coordinator should be appointed.

WHEREFORE, the undersigned Parenting Coordinator requests that a Status Conference be set by the Court.

Florida Family Law Rules of Procedure Form 12.984(d) Parenting Coordinator Request for Status Conference (07/14)

____
Date

____
Signature of Parenting Coordinator
Printed Name: ______________________________
Address: ______________________________
City, State, Zip: ______________________________
Telephone Number: ______________________________
E-mail: ______________________________
Professional License # (if applicable) ______________
Professional Certification # (if applicable) ____________

Copies to:

_____ Presiding Judge

_____ Petitioner

_____ Attorney for Petitioner

_____ Respondent

_____ Attorney for Respondent

_____ Other: ______________________________

IF A NONLAWYER HELPED YOU FILL OUT THIS FORM, HE/SHE MUST FILL IN THE BLANKS BELOW: [fill in all blanks] This form was completed with the assistance of:
{name of individual} ______________________________,
{name of business} ______________________________,
{address} ______________________________,
{city} ______________,*{state}* __________,*{telephone number}* ______________.

Florida Family Law Rules of Procedure Form 12.984(d) Parenting Coordinator Request for Status Conference (07/14)

INSTRUCTIONS FOR FLORIDA FAMILY LAW RULES OF PROCEDURE FORM 12.984(d) PARENTING COORDINATOR REQUEST FOR STATUS CONFERENCE (07/14)

When should this form be used?

A person appointed as a parenting coordinator may request a status conference with the judge and parties under Florida Family Law Rule of Procedure 12.742(1). This form is used when the parenting coordinator is unable to adequately perform the duties in accordance with the court's direction.

This form should be typed or printed in black ink.

What should I do next?

After completing and signing this form, you must file the original with the clerk of the circuit court in the county in which the action is pending, provide a copy to the presiding judge, and keep a copy for your records.

You must mail or hand-deliver a copy of this form to the attorney(s) for the parents or, if not represented by an attorney, to the parents.

Where can I look for more information?

Before proceeding, you should read "General Information for Self–Represented Litigants" found at the beginning of these forms. For more information, see section 61.125, Florida Statutes; Florida Family Law Rule of Procedure 12.742; Rules for Qualified and Court Appointed Parenting Coordinators; and the **Order of Referral to Parenting Coordinator**, Florida Family Law Rules of Procedure Form 12.984(a).

Special notes

Remember, a person who is NOT an attorney is called a nonlawyer. If a nonlawyer helps you fill out these forms, that person must give you a copy of **Disclosure from Nonlawyer**, Florida Family Law Rules of Procedure Form 12.900(a), before he or she helps you. A nonlawyer helping you fill out these forms also must put his or her name, address, and telephone number on the bottom of the last page of every form he or she helps you complete.

Added July 3, 2014, effective July 3, 2014 (142 So.3d 831).

Form 12.990(a). Final Judgment of Simplified Dissolution of Marriage

IN THE CIRCUIT COURT OF THE ________ JUDICIAL CIRCUIT,
IN AND FOR ________ COUNTY, FLORIDA

Case No.: ____________________
Division: ____________________

______________________________,
Petitioner,

and

______________________________,
Respondent.

FINAL JUDGMENT OF SIMPLIFIED DISSOLUTION OF MARRIAGE

This cause came before this Court for a hearing on the parties' Petition for Simplified Dissolution of Marriage. The Court, having reviewed the file and heard the testimony, makes these findings of fact and reaches these conclusions of law:

1. The Court has jurisdiction over the subject matter and the parties.
2. At least one party has been a resident of the State of Florida for more than 6 months immediately before filing the Petition for Simplified Dissolution of Marriage.
3. The parties have no minor or dependent children in common, and the wife is not pregnant.
4. The marriage between the parties is irretrievably broken. Therefore, the marriage between the parties is dissolved, and the parties are restored to the status of being single.
5. Marital Settlement Agreement.
[√ **one** only]
___ a. The parties have voluntarily entered into a Marital Settlement Agreement, and each has filed the required Financial Affidavit. Therefore, the Marital Settlement Agreement is filed as "Exhibit A" in this case and is ratified and made a part of this final judgment. The parties are ordered to obey all of its provisions.
___ b. There is no marital property or marital debts to divide, as the parties previously have divided all of their personal property. Therefore, each is awarded the personal property he or she presently has in his or her possession. Each party shall be responsible for any debts in his or her own name.
6. ( ) yes ( ) no The wife's former name of {*full legal name*} ____________________ is restored.
7. The Court reserves jurisdiction to enforce the marital settlement agreement.

ORDERED on ______________________.

____
CIRCUIT JUDGE

COPIES TO:
Petitioner (or his or her attorney)
Respondent (or his or her attorney)
Other: ____________

Added July 7, 1995, effective Jan. 1, 1996 (663 So.2d 1047). Amended Feb. 26, 1998, effective Mar. 16, 1998 (713 So.2d 1); Sept. 21, 2000 (810 So.2d 1).

Form 12.990(b)(1). Final Judgment of Dissolution of Marriage with Minor Child(ren) (Uncontested)

IN THE CIRCUIT COURT OF THE ______________________ JUDICIAL CIRCUIT,
IN AND FOR ______________________ COUNTY, FLORIDA

Case No.: ______________________
Division: ______________________

______________________,
Husband,

and

______________________,
Wife.

FINAL JUDGMENT OF DISSOLUTION OF MARRIAGE WITH MINOR CHILD(REN) (UNCONTESTED)

This cause came before this Court for a hearing on a Petition for Dissolution of Marriage. The Court, having reviewed the file and heard the testimony, makes these findings of fact and reaches these conclusions of law:

1. The Court has jurisdiction over the subject matter and the parties.

2. At least one party has been a resident of the State of Florida for more than 6 months immediately before filing the Petition for Dissolution of Marriage.

3. The marriage between the parties is irretrievably broken. Therefore, the marriage between the parties is dissolved, and the parties are restored to the status of being single.

4. Marital Settlement Agreement. The parties have voluntarily entered into a Marital Settlement Agreement and Parenting Plan, and each party has filed the required Family Law Financial Affidavit. Therefore, the Marital Settlement Agreement and Parenting Plan is filed as Exhibit A in this case and is ratified and made a part of this final judgment. The parties are ordered to obey all of the provisions.

5. The Court finds that the parties have the present ability to pay support as agreed to in the marital settlement agreement as ratified and made part of this final judgment.

6. *{If applicable}* The wife's former name of *{full legal name}* ______________________ ______________ is restored.

7. The Court reserves jurisdiction to modify and enforce this final judgment.

Florida Supreme Court Approved Family Law Form 12.990(b)(1), Final Judgment of Dissolution of Marriage with Minor Child(ren) (Uncontested) (03/15)

DONE AND ORDERED at ________________________, Florida, on __________________.

____
CIRCUIT JUDGE

I certify that a copy of the *{name of document(s)}* ________________________________
was ( ) mailed ( ) faxed and mailed ( ) e-mailed ( ) hand-delivered to the parties and any entities listed below on *{date}*__________________________.

by________________________________
{Clerk of court or designee}

Petitioner (or his or her attorney)
Respondent (or his or her attorney)
Other: ______________________________

Florida Supreme Court Approved Family Law Form 12.990(b)(1), Final Judgment of Dissolution of Marriage with Minor Child(ren) (Uncontested) (03/15)

Added Feb. 26, 1998, effective Mar. 16, 1998 (713 So.2d 1). Amended Sept. 21, 2000 (810 So.2d 1); March 26, 2009 (20 So.3d 173); Dec. 16, 2010 (59 So.3d 792); March 26, 2015, effective March 26, 2015 (2015 WL 1343088).

Form 12.990(b)(2). Final Judgment of Dissolution of Marriage with Property But No Dependent or Minor Child(ren) (Uncontested)

IN THE CIRCUIT COURT OF THE ______________________ JUDICIAL CIRCUIT,
IN AND FOR ______________________ COUNTY, FLORIDA

Case No.: ______________________
Division: ______________________

______________________________,
Husband,

and

______________________________,
Wife.

FINAL JUDGMENT OF DISSOLUTION OF MARRIAGE WITH PROPERTY BUT NO DEPENDENT OR MINOR CHILD(REN) (UNCONTESTED)

This cause came before this Court for a hearing on a Petition for Dissolution of Marriage. The Court, having reviewed the file and heard the testimony, makes these findings of fact and reaches these conclusions of law:

1. The Court has jurisdiction over the subject matter and the parties.
2. At least one party has been a resident of the State of Florida for more than 6 months immediately before filing the Petition for Dissolution of Marriage.
3. The parties have no minor or dependent children in common, and the wife is not pregnant.
4. The marriage between the parties is irretrievably broken. Therefore, the marriage between the parties is dissolved, and the parties are restored to the status of being single.
5. Marital Settlement Agreement. The parties have voluntarily entered into a Marital Settlement Agreement, and each has filed the required Family Law Financial Affidavit. Therefore, the Marital Settlement Agreement is filed as Exhibit _____ in this case and is ratified and made a part of this final judgment. The parties are ordered to obey all of its provisions.
6. The Court finds that the parties have the present ability to pay support as agreed to in the marital settlement agreement as ratified and made part of this final judgment.
7. *{If applicable}* The wife's former name of *{full legal name}* ______________________________ ______________ is restored.
8. The Court reserves jurisdiction to enforce this final judgment.

Florida Supreme Court Approved Family Law Form 12.990(b)(2), Final Judgment of Dissolution of Marriage with Property but No Dependent or Minor Child(ren) (Uncontested) (03/15)

DONE AND ORDERED in ____________________, Florida. on ______________.

____
CIRCUIT JUDGE

I certify that a copy of *{name of document(s)}* ______________________________
was ( ) mailed ( ) faxed and mailed ( ) e-mailed ( ) hand-delivered to the parties listed below on *{date}*__________________.

by______________________________
{Clerk of court or designee}

Petitioner (or his or her attorney)
Respondent (or his or her attorney)
Other: ______________________

Florida Supreme Court Approved Family Law Form 12.990(b)(2), Final Judgment of Dissolution of Marriage with Property but No Dependent or Minor Child(ren) (Uncontested) (03/15)

Added Feb. 26, 1998, effective Mar. 16, 1998 (713 So.2d 1). Amended Sept. 21, 2000 (810 So.2d 1); March 26, 2015, effective March 26, 2015 (2015 WL 1343088).

Form 12.990(b)(3). Final Judgment of Dissolution of Marriage with No Property or Dependent or Minor Child(ren) (Uncontested)

IN THE CIRCUIT COURT OF THE ______________________ JUDICIAL CIRCUIT,
IN AND FOR ______________________ COUNTY, FLORIDA

Case No.: ______________________
Division: ______________________

______________________,
Husband,

and

______________________,
Wife.

FINAL JUDGMENT OF DISSOLUTION OF MARRIAGE WITH NO PROPERTY OR DEPENDENT OR MINOR CHILD(REN) (UNCONTESTED)

This cause came before this Court for a hearing on a Petition for Dissolution of Marriage. The Court, having reviewed the file and heard the testimony, makes these findings of fact and reaches these conclusions of law:

1. The Court has jurisdiction over the subject matter and the parties.
2. At least one party has been a resident of the State of Florida for more than 6 months immediately before filing the Petition for Dissolution of Marriage.
3. The parties have no minor or dependent children in common, and the wife is not pregnant.
4. The marriage between the parties is irretrievably broken. Therefore, the marriage between the parties is dissolved, and the parties are restored to the status of being single.
5. There is no marital property or marital debts to divide, as the parties have previously divided all of their personal property. Therefore, each is awarded the personal property he or she presently has in his or her possession. Each party shall be responsible for any debts in his or her own name.
6. *{If applicable}* The wife's former name of *{full legal name}* ______________________ is restored.
7. The Court reserves jurisdiction to enforce this judgment.

DONE AND ORDERED in______________________, Florida, on ______________________.

____

Florida Supreme Court Approved Family Law Form 12.990(b)(3), Final Judgment of Dissolution of Marriage with No Property or Minor Child(ren) (Uncontested) (03/15)

CIRCUIT JUDGE

I certify that a copy of *{name of document(s)}* ______________________________
was ( ) mailed ( ) faxed and mailed ( ) e-mailed ( ) hand-delivered to the parties listed below on *{date}*__________________.

by______________________________
{Clerk of court or designee}

Petitioner (or his or her attorney)
Respondent (or his or her attorney)
Other: ______________________

Florida Supreme Court Approved Family Law Form 12.990(b)(3), Final Judgment of Dissolution of Marriage with No Property or Minor Child(ren) (Uncontested) (03/15)

Added Feb. 26, 1998, effective Mar. 16, 1998 (713 So.2d 1). Amended Sept. 21, 2000 (810 So.2d 1); March 26, 2015, effective March 26, 2015 (2015 WL 1343088).

Form 12.990(c)(1). Final Judgment of Dissolution of Marriage with Dependent or Minor Child(ren)

IN THE CIRCUIT COURT OF THE ______________________ JUDICIAL CIRCUIT,
IN AND FOR ______________________ COUNTY, FLORIDA

Case No.: ______________________
Division: ______________________

In re the Marriage of:

______________________________,
Husband,

and

______________________________,
Wife.

FINAL JUDGMENT OF DISSOLUTION OF MARRIAGE WITH DEPENDENT OR MINOR CHILD(REN)

This cause came before this Court for a trial on a Petition for Dissolution of Marriage. The Court, having reviewed the file and heard the testimony, makes these findings of fact and reaches these conclusions of law:

1. The Court has jurisdiction over the subject matter and the parties.
2. At least one party has been a resident of the State of Florida for more than 6 months immediately before filing the Petition for Dissolution of Marriage.
3. The marriage between the parties is irretrievably broken. Therefore, the marriage between the parties is dissolved, and the parties are restored to the status of being single.

SECTION I. MARITAL ASSETS AND LIABILITIES

A. **Date of Valuation of Property.** The assets and liabilities listed below are divided as indicated. The date of valuation of these assets and liabilities is, unless otherwise indicated:
   a. ____ date of filing petition for dissolution of marriage.
   b. ____ date of separation.
   c. ____ date of final hearing.
   d. ____ other: *{specify date}*______________________________

B. **Division of Assets.**
   1. **The assets listed below are nonmarital assets.** Each party shall keep, as his or her own, the

assets found to be nonmarital, and the other party shall have no further rights or responsibilities regarding these assets.

ASSETS: DESCRIPTION OF ITEM(S) Please describe each item as clearly as possible. You do not need to list account numbers.	Current Fair Market Value	Wife's Non-marital Property	Husband's Non-Marital Property
	$	$	$
Total Nonmarital Assets	$	$	$

2. **The assets listed below are marital assets.** Each party shall keep, as his or her own, the assets awarded in this section, and the other party shall have no further rights or responsibilities regarding these assets. **Any personal item(s) not listed below are awarded to the party currently in possession or control of the item(s).**

ASSETS: DESCRIPTION OF ITEM(S) Please describe each item as clearly as possible. You do not need to list account numbers.	Current Fair Market Value	Wife Shall Receive	Husband Shall Receive
Cash (on hand or in banks/credit unions)	$	$	$
Stocks/bonds			
Notes			
Business interests			
Real estate: (Home)			
Automobiles			

Florida Supreme Court Approved Family Law Form 12.990(c)(1), Final Judgment of Dissolution of Marriage with Dependent or Minor Child(ren) (03/15)

ASSETS: DESCRIPTION OF ITEM(S) **Please describe each item as clearly as possible.** **You do not need to list account numbers.**	**Current Fair Market Value**	**Wife Shall Receive**	**Husband Shall Receive**
Boats			
Furniture & furnishings			
Jewelry			
Life Insurance (cash surrender value)			
Retirement Plans (Profit sharing, Pension, IRA, 401(k)(s), etc.)			
Other assets			
Total Marital Assets	$	$	$

C. **Division of Liabilities/Debts.**

1. **The liabilities listed below are nonmarital liabilities** and, therefore, are owed as indicated. Each party shall owe, as his or her own, the liabilities found to be nonmarital, and the other party shall have no responsibilities regarding these debts.

LIABILITIES: DESCRIPTION OF DEBTS **Please describe each item as clearly as possible.** **You do not need to list account numbers.**	**Current Amount Owed**	**Wife's Non-Marital Liability**	**Husband's Non-Marital Liability**

LIABILITIES: DESCRIPTION OF DEBTS Please describe each item as clearly as possible. You do not need to list account numbers.	Current Amount Owed	Wife's Non-Marital Liability	Husband's Non-Marital Liability
	$	$	$
Total Nonmarital Liabilities	$	$	$

2. **The liabilities listed below are marital liabilities** and are divided as indicated. Each party shall hold the other party harmless and pay, as his or her own, the marital liabilities awarded below.

LIABILITIES: DESCRIPTION OF DEBTS Please describe each item as clearly as possible. You do not need to list account numbers.	Current Amount Owed	Wife Shall Pay	Husband Shall Pay
Mortgages on real estate: (Home)	$	$	$
(Other)			
Charge/Credit card accounts			
Auto loan			
Auto loan			
Bank. Credit Union loans			
Other			

Florida Supreme Court Approved Family Law Form 12.990(c)(1), Final Judgment of Dissolution of Marriage with Dependent or Minor Child(ren) (03/15)

LIABILITIES: DESCRIPTION OF DEBTS Please describe each item as clearly as possible. You do not need to list account numbers.	Current Amount Owed	Wife Shall Pay	Husband Shall Pay
Total Marital Liabilities			
	$	$	$

D. Contingent assets and liabilities will be divided as follows: ____________________________
____
____.

E. The distribution of assets and liabilities in this final judgment is equitable; if each party does not receive approximately one-half, the distribution is based on the following facts and reasoning:
____
____
____

F. Beneficiary Designation (By completing this section, the beneficiary designations continue after entry of Final Judgment of Dissolution of Marriage.)

The designation providing for the payment or transfer at death of an interest in the assets described below to or for the benefit of the deceased party's former spouse is **NOT VOID** as of the date of entry of the Final Judgment of Dissolution of Marriage.

The Final Judgment of Dissolution of Marriage shall provide that the designations set forth below remain in full force and effect:

_____1. The _____Husband _____Wife shall acquire or maintain the following assets for the benefit of the other spouse or child(ren), to be paid upon his/her death outright or in trust. This provision only applies if other assets fulfilling such requirement for the benefit of the other spouse or child(ren) do not exist upon his/her death and unless precluded by statute. *{Describe the assets with specificity}*:________
____
____
____.

_____2. The _____Husband _____Wife shall not unilaterally terminate or modify the ownership of the following assets, or their disposition upon his/her death. *{Describe the assets with specificity}*:________

____
____
____.

SECTION II. EXCLUSIVE USE AND POSSESSION OF HOME

*{Indicate **all** that apply}*

1. The____ Husband ____ Wife, as a condition of support, shall have exclusive use and possession of the dwelling located at the following address:______________________________
____
until: *{date or event}* ____
____
____
____.

2. The_____ Husband ____ Wife may make visits to the premises described in the paragraph above for the purpose of obtaining any items awarded in this Final Judgment. These visits shall occur after notice to the person granted exclusive use and possession of the dwelling and at the earliest convenience of both parties or as ordered in paragraph 4 below.

3. ____Upon the termination of the right of exclusive use and possession, the dwelling shall be sold and the net proceeds divided ____% to Husband and ____% to Wife, with the following credits and/or setoffs being allowed: ____
____
____
____.

4. ____Other: ____
____
____.

SECTION III. PARENTING PLAN ESTABLISHING PARENTAL RESPONSIBILITY AND TIME-SHARING WITH DEPENDENT OR MINOR CHILD(REN)

1. **Jurisdiction.** The Court has jurisdiction to determine parental responsibility, to establish or adopt a Parenting Plan, and a time-sharing schedule with regard to the minor child(ren) listed in paragraph 2 below.

2. **The parties' dependent or minor child(ren) is (are):**

Name	**Birth date**

3. **Parenting Plan.** The parties shall comply with the Parenting Plan which is attached and incorporated herein as Exhibit _____.

SECTION IV. ALIMONY

1. _____ The Court denies the request(s) for alimony;

OR

2. _____ The Court finds that ____ Husband ____ Wife, (hereinafter Obligee), has an actual need for, and that ____ Husband ____ Wife (hereinafter Obligor) has the present ability to pay, alimony as follows: *{Indicate **all** that apply}*

a. **Permanent Periodic.**

1. The Court finds that no other form of alimony is fair and reasonable under the circumstances of the parties.

2. As a marriage of: *{Choose only **one**}*

_______ **Long Duration** (17 years or greater) alimony is appropriate upon consideration of all relevant factors;

_______ **Moderate Duration** (greater than 7 years but less than 17) alimony is appropriate based upon clear and convincing evidence after consideration of all relevant factors; or

_______ **Short Duration** (less than 7 years) alimony is appropriate based upon the following exceptional circumstances: ____
____
____
____.

3. Obligor shall pay permanent periodic alimony to Obligee in the amount of $__________ per month, payable _____ in accordance with Obligor's employer's payroll cycle, and in any event, at least once a month _____ other *{explain}*
____
____
beginning *{date}* __________________. This alimony shall continue until modified by

court order, the death of either party, or remarriage of Obligee, whichever occurs first. The alimony may be modified or terminated based upon either a substantial change in circumstances, or the existence of a supportive relationship in accordance with section 61.14, Florida Statutes.

b._____ **Bridge-the-Gap.** Obligor shall pay bridge-the-gap alimony to Obligee in the amount of $________ per month, payable _____ in accordance with Obligor's employer's payroll cycle, and in any event, at least once a month or _____ other *{explain}*_____________________ beginning *{date}*____________________and continuing until: *{date}*__________________ *{a period not to exceed two (2) years}*; death of either party; or remarriage of the Obligee, whichever occurs first.

c.______**Rehabilitative.** Obligor shall pay rehabilitative alimony to Obligee in the amount of $__________ per month, payable _____ in accordance with Obligor's employer's payroll cycle, and in any event, at least once a month or _____ other *{explain}*_______________________ beginning *{date}*____________________. This rehabilitative alimony shall continue until: modified by court order; the death of either party; or until *{date/event}* ____________________ ____, whichever occurs first. The rehabilitative plan presented demonstrated the following: ________ ____ ____ ____.

d._____**Durational.** Obligor shall pay durational alimony to Obligee in the amount of $________ per month payable _____ in accordance with Obligor's employer's payroll cycle, and in any event, at least once a month _____ other *{explain}*_____________________________ beginning *{date}*____________________and terminating on *{date}*____________________, the death of either party, remarriage of the Obligee, or until modified by court order in accordance with section 61.08(7), Florida Statutes, whichever occurs first.

e._____**Lump Sum.** Obligor shall pay lump sum alimony to Obligee in the amount of $________, which shall be paid as follows:____ ____.

f. _____**Retroactive.** Obligor shall pay retroactive alimony in the amount of $__________ for the period of *{date}*________________,through *{date}* ________________, which shall be paid pursuant to paragraph 4 below.

3. **Reasons for _____ Awarding _____ Denying Alimony.** The Court has considered all of the following in awarding/denying alimony:
   a. The standard of living established during the marriage;
   b. The duration of the marriage;
   c. The age and the physical and emotional condition of each party;

d. The financial resources of each party, including the nonmarital and marital assets and liabilities distributed to each;

e. The earning capacities, educational levels, vocational skills, and employability of the parties and, when applicable, the time necessary for either party to acquire sufficient education or training to enable such party to find appropriate employment;

f. The contribution of each party to the marriage, including, but not limited to, services rendered homemaking, child care, education, and career building of the other party;

g. The responsibilities each party will have with regard to any minor or dependent children they have in common;

h. The tax treatment and consequences to both parties of any alimony award, including the designation of all or a portion of the payment as a nontaxable, nondeductible payment;

i. All sources of income available to either party, including income available to either party through investments of any asset held by that party and

j. Any other factor necessary to do equity and justice between the parties: *{explain}*
____
____
____
____
____.

_______ Please indicate here if additional pages are attached.

4. Arrearage/Retroactive Alimony.

a.____There is no alimony arrearage at the time of this Final Judgment.

OR

b. _____The _____ Husband _____ Wife shall pay to the other spouse the alimony arrearage of:
$____________ for retroactive alimony, as of *{date}*__________________;
$____________ for previously ordered unpaid alimony, as of *{date}* ______________.
The total of $ ________ in alimony arrearage shall be repaid in the amount of $_________ per month, payable _____ in accordance with Obligor's employer's payroll cycle, and in any event at least once a month or _____ other *{explain}* ______________________________
____
____
beginning *{date}*_________________________, until paid in full including statutory interest.

5.____ **Life Insurance (to secure payment of support).** To secure the alimony obligations set forth in this judgment, Obligor shall maintain life insurance on his/her life naming Obligee as the sole irrevocable beneficiary, so long as reasonably available. This insurance shall be in the amount of at least $___________ and shall remain in effect until the obligation for alimony terminates.

6. ____**Other provisions relating to alimony, including any tax treatment and consequences:**_

a. The award of alimony _____ does not _____ does leave the Obligor with significantly

less net income than the net income of the recipient/Obligee. If the award **does** leave the Obligor with significantly less net income than that of the Obligee, the Court finds the following exceptional circumstances: ____
____
____.

b. Other____
____
____.

SECTION V. CHILD SUPPORT

1. _____The Court finds that there is a need for child support and that the _____ Wife _____ Husband (hereinafter Obligor) has the present ability to pay child support. The amounts in the Child Support Guidelines Worksheet, Florida Family Law Rules of Procedure Form 12.902(e), filed by the ____ Wife ____ Husband are correct;

OR

_____The Court makes the following findings:
The Wife's net monthly income is $___________, (Child Support Guidelines____%).
The Husband's net monthly income is $___________, (Child Support Guidelines____%).
Monthly child care costs are $_______________.
Monthly health/dental insurance costs are $___________.

2. **Amount.**
Child support established at the rate of $__________per month for the _______children *{total number of parties' minor or dependent children}* shall be paid commencing _______________ *{month, day, year}* and terminating ______________________ *{month, day, year}*. Child support shall be paid in the amount of $ _______ per __________ *{week, month, other}* consistent with the Obligor's current payroll cycle.

Upon the termination of the obligation of child support for one of the parties' children, child support in the amount of $__________for the remaining _______children *{total number of remaining children}* shall be paid commencing ______________________ *{month, day, year}* and terminating______________________ *{month, day, year}*. This child support shall be paid in the amount of $_____per ________ *{week, month, other}* consistent with the Obligor's current payroll cycle.

{Insert schedule for the child support obligation, including the amount, and commencement and termination dates, for the remaining minor or dependent children, which shall be payable as the obligation for each child ceases. Please indicate whether the schedule _____appears below or _____is attached as part of this form.}

____

____

____

____

____

____

The Obligor shall pay child support until all of the minor or dependent children: reach the age of 18; become emancipated, marry, join the armed services, die, or become self-supporting; or until further order of the court or agreement of the parties. The child support obligation shall continue beyond the age of 18 and until high school graduation for any child who is dependent in fact, between the ages of 18 and 19, and is still in high school, performing in good faith with a reasonable expectation of graduation before the age of 19.

If the child support ordered deviates from the guidelines by more than 5%, the factual findings which support that deviation are: ______________________________

____

____

3. **Arrearage/Retroactive Child Support.**

a. ____There is no child support arrearage at the time of this Final Judgment.

OR

b. ____The____ Wife ____ Husband shall pay to the other spouse the child support arrearage of:
$________ for retroactive child support, as of *{date}* ______________;
$________ for previously ordered unpaid child support, as of *{date}* ________________.
The total of $___________ in child support arrearage shall be repaid in the amount of $__________ per month, payable _____ in accordance with Obligor's employer's payroll cycle, and in any event at least a month _____ other *{explain}* ___________________________

____

beginning *{date}*_________________________, until paid in full including statutory interest.

4. **Insurance.**

a. _____**Health/Dental Insurance.** _____ Wife _____ Husband shall be required to maintain _____health and/or _____ dental insurance for the parties' minor child(ren), so long as reasonable in cost and accessible to the child(ren). The party providing insurance shall be required to convey insurance cards demonstrating said coverage to the other party;

OR

_____ health and/or _____ dental insurance is not reasonable in cost or accessible to the child(ren) at this time.

b. _____Reasonable and necessary **uninsured medical/dental/prescription drug costs** for the minor child(ren) shall be assessed as follows:

_____ Shared equally by husband and wife.

_____ Prorated according to the child support guideline percentages.

_____ Other *{explain}*:

____

____

As to these uninsured medical/dental/prescription drug expenses, the party who incurs the expense shall submit request for reimbursement to the other party within 30 days, and the other party, within 30 days of receipt, shall submit the applicable reimbursement for that expense, according to the schedule of reimbursement set out in this paragraph.

5. ______**Life Insurance (to secure payment of support).** To secure the child support obligations in this judgment, _____ Husband _____Wife _____ Each party shall maintain life insurance, in an amount of at least $______________, on _____ his life _____ her life _____ naming minor child(ren) as the beneficiary(ies) **OR** naming the _____ Wife _____Husband_____other *{name}*____as Trustee for the minor child(ren), so long as reasonably available. The obligation to maintain the life insurance shall continue until the youngest child turns 18, becomes emancipated, marries, joins the armed services, dies, or becomes self-supporting.

6. **IRS Income Tax Exemption(s).** The assignment of any tax exemption(s) for the child(ren) shall be as follows: ____

____

____.

Each party shall execute any and all IRS forms necessary to effectuate the provisions of this paragraph.

7. **Other provisions relating to child support:** ______________________________________

____

____.

SECTION VI. METHOD OF PAYMENT

Obligor shall pay court-ordered child support/alimony and arrears, if any, as follows:

3. **Place of Payment.**

c. _____Obligor shall pay court-ordered support directly to either the State Disbursement Unit or the central depository, as required by statute, along with any fee required by statute.

d. _____Both parties have requested and the court finds that it is in the best interests of the child(ren) that support payments need not be directed through either the State Disbursement Unit or the central depository at this time; however, either party may subsequently apply, pursuant to section 61.13(1)(d)3, Florida Statutes, to require payment through either the State Disbursement Unit or the central depository.

4. **Income Deduction.**

c. _____**Immediate.** Obligor shall pay through income deduction, pursuant to a separate Income Deduction Order which shall be effective immediately. Obligor is individually responsible for paying this support obligation until all of said support is deducted from Obligor's income. Until support payments are deducted from Obligor's paycheck, Obligor is responsible for making timely payments directly to the State Disbursement Unit or the Obligee, as previously set forth in this order.

d. ______**Deferred.** Income deduction is ordered this day, but it shall not be effective until a delinquency of $__________, or, if not specified, an amount equal to one month's obligation occurs. Income deduction is not being implemented immediately based on the following findings: Income deduction is **not** in the best interests of the child(ren) because: *{explain}*
____
____
____,

AND

There is proof of timely payment of a previously ordered obligation without an Income Deduction Order in cases of modification,

AND

_____There is an agreement by the Obligor to advise the Title IV-D agency, the clerk of court, and the Obligee of any change in Payor and/or health insurance **OR**

_____there is a signed written agreement providing an alternative arrangement between the Obligor and the Obligee and, at the option of the IV-D agency, by the IV-D agency in IV-D cases in which there is an assignment of support rights to the state, reviewed and entered in the record by the court.

5. **Bonus/one-time payments.** _____ All ________% _____ No income paid in the form of a bonus or other similar one-time payment, up to the amount of any arrearage or the remaining balance thereof owed pursuant to this order, shall be forwarded to Obligee pursuant to the payment method prescribed above.

6. **Other provisions relating to method of payment.** ______________________________________
____
____.

SECTION VII. ATTORNEY'S FEES, COSTS, AND SUIT MONEY

1. _____ Husband's _____Wife's request(s) for attorney's fees, costs, and suit money is (are) denied

because: ____
____.

OR

2. _____The Court finds there is a need for and an ability to pay attorney's fees, costs, and suit money. _____ Husband _____ Wife is hereby ordered to pay to the other spouse $____________ in attorney's fees, and $ __________ in costs. The Court further finds that the attorney's fees awarded are based on the reasonable rate of $ __________ per hour and __________ reasonable hours. Other provisions relating to attorney's fees, costs, and suit money are as follows: ____
____.

SECTION VIII. OTHER PROVISIONS

1. **Former Name.** The wife's former name of *{full name}* ____________________________ is restored.

2. **Other Provisions.**
____
____
____.

3. The Court reserves jurisdiction to modify and enforce this Final Judgment.

DONE AND ORDERED at ____________________, Florida, on ____________________.

____
CIRCUIT JUDGE

I certify that a copy of this **Final Judgment of Dissolution** was ( ) mailed ( ) faxed and mailed ( ) e-mailed ( ) hand delivered to the parties listed below on *{date}* ____________________.

____
By *{clerk of court or designee}*

____Husband (or his attorney)
____Wife Respondent (or her attorney)
____Central Depository
____State Disbursement Unit
____Other ____________________________________

Florida Supreme Court Approved Family Law Form 12.990(c)(1), Final Judgment of Dissolution of Marriage with Dependent or Minor Child(ren) (03/15)

Added Feb. 26, 1998, effective Mar. 16, 1998 (713 So.2d 1). Amended July 1, 1999 (717 So.2d 914); Sept. 21, 2000 (810 So.2d 1); March 26, 2009 (20 So.3d 173); Dec. 16, 2010 (59 So.3d 792); May 24, 2012 (96 So.3d 217); July 3, 2013 (117 So.3d 958); Sept. 4, 2013, effective Sept. 4, 2013 (122 So.3d 320); May 1, 2014, effective May 1, 2014 (138 So.3d 389); March 26, 2015, effective March 26, 2015 (2015 WL 1343088).

Form 12.990(c)(2). Final Judgment of Dissolution of Marriage with Property but No Dependent or Minor Child(ren)

IN THE CIRCUIT COURT OF THE ________________ JUDICIAL CIRCUIT,
IN AND FOR __________ COUNTY, FLORIDA

Case No.: ______________________
Division: ______________________

In re the Marriage of:

____
Husband,

and

______________________,
Wife.

FINAL JUDGMENT OF DISSOLUTION OF MARRIAGE WITH PROPERTY BUT NO DEPENDENT OR MINOR CHILD(REN)

This cause came before this Court for a trial on a Petition for Dissolution of Marriage. The Court, having reviewed the file and heard the testimony, makes these findings of fact and reaches these conclusions of law:

1. The Court has jurisdiction over the subject matter and the parties.
2. At least one party has been a resident of the State of Florida for more than 6 months immediately before filing the Petition for Dissolution of Marriage.
3. The parties have no minor children in common, and the wife is not pregnant.
4. The marriage between the parties is irretrievably broken. Therefore, the marriage between the parties is dissolved and the parties are restored to the status of being single.

SECTION I. MARITAL ASSETS AND LIABILITIES

A. **Date of Valuation of Property.** The assets and liabilities listed below are divided as indicated. The date of valuation of these assets and liabilities is, unless otherwise indicated:

1.____ date of filing petition for dissolution of marriage ________________.
2.____ date of separation ____________________.
3. ____ date of final hearing ____________________.
4. ____ other: *{specify date}*____.

B. Division of Assets.

1. **The assets listed below are nonmarital assets.** Each party shall keep, as his or her own, the assets found to be nonmarital, and the other party shall have no further rights or responsibilities regarding these assets.

ASSETS: DESCRIPTION OF ITEM(S) Please describe each item as clearly as possible. You do not need to list account numbers.	Current Fair Market Value	Wife's Non marital Property	Husband's Non marital Property
	$	$	$
Total Nonmarital Assets	$	$	$

2. **The assets listed below are marital assets.** Each party shall keep, as his or her own, the assets awarded in this section, and the other party shall have no further rights or responsibilities regarding these assets. **Any personal item(s) not listed below are awarded to the party currently in possession or control of the item(s).**

ASSETS: DESCRIPTION OF ITEM(S) Please describe each item as clearly as possible. You do not need to list account numbers.	Current Fair Market Value	Wife Shall Receive	Husband Shall Receive
Cash (on hand or in banks/credit unions)	$	$	$
Stocks/bonds			
Notes			
Business interests			
Real estate: (Home)			
Automobiles			

Boats			
Furniture & furnishings			
Jewelry			
Life insurance (cash surrender value)			
Retirement Plans (Profit sharing, Pension, IRA, 401(k)s, etc.)			
Other assets			
Total Marital Assets	$	$	$

C. Division of Liabilities/Debts.

1. **The liabilities listed below are nonmarital liabilities** and, therefore, are owed as indicated. Each party shall owe, as his or her own, the liabilities found to be nonmarital, and the other party shall have no responsibilities regarding these debts.

LIABILITIES: DESCRIPTION OF DEBT(S) Please describe each item as clearly as possible. You do not need to list account numbers)	Current Amount Owed	Wife's Non-marital Liability	Husband's Non-marital Liability
	$	$	$
Total Nonmarital Liabilities	$	$	$

2. **The liabilities listed below are marital liabilities** and are divided as indicated. Each party shall hold the other party harmless and pay, as his or her own, the marital liabilities awarded below.

LIABILITIES: DESCRIPTION OF DEBT(S) Please describe each item as clearly as possible. You do not need to list account numbers.	Current Amount Owed	Wife Shall Pay	Husband Shall Pay
Mortgages on real estate: (Home)	$	$	$
(Other)			
Charge/credit card accounts			
Auto loan			
Auto loan			
Bank/Credit Union loans			
Other			

Florida Supreme Court Approved Family Law Form 12.990(c)(2), Final Judgment of Dissolution of Marriage with Property but No Dependent or Minor Child(ren) (03/15)

Total Marital Liabilities	$	$	$

D. Contingent assets and liabilities will be divided as follows: ______________________________

____

____

____

E. The distribution of assets and liabilities in this final judgment is equitable; if each party does not receive approximately one-half, the distribution is based on the following facts and reasoning:

____

____

____

____

F. Beneficiary Designation (By completing this section, the beneficiary designations continue after Entry of Final Judgment of Dissolution of Marriage.)

The designation providing for the payment or transfer at death of an interest in the assets described below to or for the benefit of the deceased party's former spouse is **NOT VOID** as of the date of entry of the Final Judgment of Dissolution of Marriage.

The Final Judgment of Dissolution of Marriage shall provide that the designations set forth below remain in full force and effect.

_____ 1. The _____ Husband _____Wife shall acquire or maintain the following assets for the benefit of the other spouse or child(ren) to be paid upon his/her death outright or in trust. This provision only applies if other assets fulfilling such requirement for the benefit of the other spouse or child(ren) do not exist upon his/her death and unless precluded by statute. *{Describe the assets with specificity}*

____

____

____.

_____2. The _____ Husband _____ Wife shall not unilaterally terminate or modify the ownership of

the following assets, or their disposition upon his/her death. *{Describe the assets with specificity}*
____
____
____
____.

SECTION II. EXCLUSIVE USE AND POSSESSION OF HOME

*{Indicate **all** that apply}*

1. _____ The _____ Husband _____ Wife, as a condition of support, shall have exclusive use and possession of the dwelling located at the following address:
____
until *{date or event}*____
____.

2. _____The_____ Husband _____Wife may make visits to the premises described in the paragraph above for the purpose of obtaining any items awarded in this Final Judgment. These visits shall occur after notice to the person granted exclusive use and possession of the dwelling and at the earliest convenience of both parties or as ordered in paragraph 4 below.

3. _____Upon the termination of the right of exclusive use and possession, the dwelling shall be sold and the net proceeds divided _______% to Husband and _______% to Wife, with the following credits and/or setoffs being allowed:_______________________
____
____.

4. _____Other: ____
____
____.

SECTION III. ALIMONY

1. _____ The Court denies the request(s) for alimony

   OR

2. _____ The Court finds that there is an actual need for, and that _____ Husband _____ Wife (hereinafter Obligor) has/had the present ability to pay, alimony as follows:

*{Indicate **all** that apply}*

a. _____ **Permanent Periodic.**

1. The Court finds that no other form of alimony is fair and reasonable under the

circumstances of the parties.

2. As a marriage of: ***{Choose only one}***

_____**Long Duration** (17 years or greater) alimony is appropriate upon consideration of all relevant factors;

_____**Moderate Duration** (greater than 7 years but less than 17) alimony is appropriate based upon clear and convincing evidence after consideration of all relevant factors; or

_____**Short Duration** (less than 7 years) alimony is appropriate based upon the following exceptional circumstances:_______________
____
____.

3. Obligor shall pay permanent periodic alimony to Obligee in the amount of $_________ per month, payable ____ in accordance with Obligor's employer's payroll cycle, and in any event, at least once a month or ____ other *{explain}*:_______________________________
____
beginning *{date}* _______________. This alimony shall continue until modified by court order, the death of either party, or remarriage of Obligee, whichever occurs first. The alimony may be modified or terminated based upon either a substantial change in circumstances or the existence of a supportive relationship in accordance with section 61.14, Florida Statutes.

b._____**Bridge-the-Gap.** Obligor shall pay bridge-the-gap alimony to Obligee in the amount of $_________ per month, payable _____ in accordance with Obligor's employer's payroll cycle, and in any event, at least once a month or _____ other *{explain}* ___________ beginning *{date}*_________________and continuing until *{date}*______________ *{a period not to exceed two years}*, the death of either party, or remarriage of the Obligee, whichever occurs first.

c._______**Rehabilitative.** Obligor shall pay rehabilitative alimony to Obligee in the amount of $_________ per month, payable _____ in accordance with Obligor's employer's payroll cycle, and in any event, at least once a month or _____other *{explain}*_____________ beginning *{date}* _____________. This rehabilitative alimony shall continue until modified by court order, the death of either party or until *{date/event}* ___________, whichever occurs first. The rehabilitative plan presented demonstrated the following:
____
____.

d._____**Durational.** Obligor shall pay durational alimony to Obligee in the amount of $_________ per month _____ payable in accordance with Obligor's employer's payroll cycle, and in any event, at least once a month or ____ *{explain}*________________________ beginning *{date}*___________ and terminating on *{date}*_______________, the death of either party, remarriage of Obligee, or until modified by court order in accordance with section 61.08(7), Florida Statutes, whichever occurs first.

e._____ **Lump Sum.** Obligor shall pay lump sum alimony to Obligee in the amount of $______________, which shall be paid as follows: ____.

f._____**Retroactive.** Obligor shall pay retroactive alimony in the amount of $____________ for the period of *{date}*____________________, through *{date}* _______________, which shall be paid pursuant to paragraph 4 below.

3. **Reasons for _____ Awarding _____ Denying Alimony.** The Court has considered all of the following in awarding/denying alimony:
   a. The standard of living established during the marriage;
   b. The duration of the marriage;
   c. The age and the physical and emotional condition of each party;
   d. The financial resources of each party, including, the nonmarital and the marital assets and liabilities distributed to each;
   e. The earning capacities, educational levels, vocational skills, and employability of the parties and, when applicable, the time necessary for either party to acquire sufficient education or training to enable such party to find appropriate employment;
   f. The contribution of each party to the marriage, including, but not limited to, services rendered in homemaking, child care, education, and career building of the other party;
   g. The tax treatment and consequences to both parties of any alimony award, including the designation of all or a portion of the payment as a nontaxable, nondeductible payment;
   h. All sources of income available to either party, including income available to either party through investments of any asset held by the party; and
   i. Any other factor necessary to do equity and justice between the parties: *{explain}*_________
   ____
   ____
   ____
   ____
   ____

   _______ Please indicate here if additional pages are attached.

4. **Arrearage/Retroactive Alimony.**

   a. ____ There is no alimony arrearage at the time of this Final Judgment.

   OR

b.____ The ____ Husband ____ Wife shall pay to the other party the alimony arrearage of:
$________ for retroactive alimony, as of *{date}* ________________;
$________ for previously ordered unpaid alimony, as of *{date}* ________________.
The total of $__________ in alimony arrearage shall be repaid in the amount of $_________ per month, payable ( ) in accordance with Obligor's employer's payroll cycle, and in any event at least once a month ( ) other *{explain}*____
____
beginning *{date}* ____________, until paid in full including statutory interest.

5. _____**Life Insurance (to secure payment of support).** To secure the alimony obligations set forth in this judgment, Obligor shall maintain life insurance coverage on his/her life naming Obligee as the sole irrevocable beneficiary, so long as reasonably available. This insurance shall be in the amount of at least $__________ and shall remain in effect until the obligation for alimony terminates.

6. _____**Other provisions relating to alimony, including any tax treatment and consequences:**

a. The award of alimony _____does not _____does leave the Obligor with significantly less net income than the net income of the recipient/Obligee. If yes, the court finds the following exceptional circumstances:____
____
____.

b. Other:____
____.

SECTION IV. METHOD OF PAYMENT

Obligor shall pay court-ordered alimony and arrears, if any, as follows:

1. **Place of Payment.**

a. _____ Obligor shall pay court-ordered support directly to either the State Disbursement Unit or the central depository, as required by statute, along with any fee required by statute.

b. _____ Both parties have requested and the court finds that support payments need not be directed through either the State Disbursement Unit or the central depository at this time at this time; however, either party may subsequently apply, pursuant to section 61.13(1)(d)3, Florida Statutes, to require payments through either the State Disbursement Unit or the central depository.

2. **Income Deduction.**

a. _____ **Immediate.** Obligor shall pay through income deduction, pursuant to a separate

Income Deduction Order which shall be effective immediately. Obligor is individually responsible for paying this support obligation until all of said support is deducted from Obligor's income. Until support payments are deducted from Obligor's paycheck, Obligor is responsible for making timely payments directly to the State Disbursement Unit or the Obligee, as previously set forth in this order.

b. _____ **Deferred.** Income Deduction is ordered this day, but it shall not be effective until a delinquency of $__________, or, if not specified, an amount equal to one month's obligation occurs. Income deduction is not being implemented immediately based on the following findings:

There are no minor or dependent child(ren) common to the parties,

AND

There is proof of timely payment of a previously ordered obligation without an Income Deduction Order in cases of modification,

AND

_____ There is an agreement by the Obligor to advise the Title IV-D agency, the clerk of court, and the Obligee of any change in Payor and/or health insurance **OR** _____ there is a signed written agreement providing an alternative arrangement between the Obligor and the Obligee and, at the option of the IV-D agency, by the IV-D agency in IV-D cases in which there is an assignment of support rights to the state, reviewed and entered in the record by the court.

3. **Bonus/one-time payments.** _____ All _____% _____ No income paid in the form of a bonus or other similar one-time payment, up to the amount of any arrearage or the remaining balance thereof owed pursuant to this order, shall be forwarded to Obligee pursuant to the payment method prescribed above.

4. **Other provisions relating to method of payment.** ____

SECTION V. ATTORNEY'S FEES, COSTS, AND SUIT MONEY

1. ____ Husband's ____ Wife's request(s) for attorney's fees, costs, and suit money is (are) denied because ____.

OR

2. _____ The Court finds there is a need for and an ability to pay attorney's fees, costs, and suit money. _____ Husband _____ Wife is hereby ordered to pay to the other spouse $____________ in attorney's fees, and $_______ in costs. The Court further finds that

the attorney's fees awarded are based on the reasonable rate of $________ per hour and ______ reasonable hours. Other provisions relating to attorney's fees, costs, and suit money are as follows:

____

____.

SECTION VI. OTHER PROVISIONS

1. **Former Name.** The wife's former name of *{full name}*____________________________ is restored.

2. **Other Provisions.**

____

____

____.

3. The Court reserves jurisdiction to modify and enforce this Final Judgment.

DONE AND ORDERED on ______________ in ______________________, Florida.

____

CIRCUIT JUDGE

I certify that a copy of this **Final Judgment of Dissolution** was ( ) mailed ( ) faxed and mailed ( ) e-mailed ( ) hand-delivered to the parties or entities listed below on *{date}*________________.

____

By: *{Clerk of court or designee}*

_____Husband (or his attorney)
_____Wife (or her attorney)
_____Central depository
_____State Disbursement Unit
_____Other: ____________________________

Florida Supreme Court Approved Family Law Form 12.990(c)(2), Final Judgment of Dissolution of Marriage with Property but No Dependent or Minor Child(ren) (03/15)

Added Feb. 26, 1998, effective Mar. 16, 1998 (713 So.2d 1). Amended July 1, 1999 (717 So.2d 914); Sept. 21, 2000 (810 So.2d 1); May 24, 2012 (96 So.3d 217); July 3, 2013 (117 So.3d 958); Sept. 4, 2013, effective Sept. 4, 2013 (122 So.3d 320); May 1, 2014, effective May 1, 2014 (138 So.3d 389); March 26, 2015, effective March 26, 2015 (2015 WL 1343088).

Form 12.993(a). Supplemental Final Judgment Modifying Parental Responsibility, Visitation, or Parenting Plan/Time–Sharing Schedule and Other Relief

IN THE CIRCUIT COURT OF THE ____________________ JUDICIAL CIRCUIT,
IN AND FOR COUNTY, ____________________ FLORIDA

Case No.: ____________________
Division: ____________________

____________________,
Petitioner,

and

____________________,
Respondent.

SUPPLEMENTAL FINAL JUDGMENT MODIFYING PARENTAL RESPONSIBILITY, VISITATION, OR PARENTING PLAN/TIME-SHARING SCHEDULE AND OTHER RELIEF

This cause came before this Court on a Supplemental Petition to Modify Parental Responsibility, Visitation, or Parenting Plan/Time-Sharing Schedule and Other Relief. The Court, having reviewed the file, having heard the testimony, and being otherwise fully advised, makes these findings of fact and reaches these conclusions of law:

SECTION I. FINDINGS

1. The Court has jurisdiction over the subject matter and the parties.

2. The last order establishing or modifying parental responsibility, visitation, a Parenting Plan, or time-sharing was entered on *{date}* ____________________.

3. There has been a substantial change in circumstances of the parties since the entry of the last order, specifically: ____________________
____
____
____
____
____
____________________.

4. It is in the best interests of the minor child(ren) that the current parental responsibility, visitation, time-sharing schedule or Parenting Plan be changed because: ____________________
____

Florida Supreme Court Approved Family Law Form 12.993(a), Supplemental Final Judgment Modifying Parental Responsibility, Visitation, or Parenting Plan/Time-Sharing Schedule and Other Relief (03/15)

____
____
____.

SECTION II. PARENTING PLAN ESTABLISHING PARENTAL RESPONSIBILITY AND TIME-SHARING WITH DEPENDENT OR MINOR CHILD(REN)

1. **Jurisdiction.** The Court has jurisdiction to determine parental responsibility, to establish or approve a Parenting Plan, and time-sharing with regard to the parties' minor child(ren) listed in paragraph 2 below.

2. **The parties' dependent or minor child(ren) is (are):**

Name	**Birth date**

3. **Parenting Plan.** The parties shall comply with the Parenting Plan which is attached and incorporated herein as Exhibit ______.

SECTION III. CHILD SUPPORT

1. **Modification of Child Support.**
*{Choose **one** only}*
   a. ______**The modification of parental responsibility or time-sharing entered above does not necessitate a modification of child support. The previous order or final judgment establishing or modifying child support shall remain in effect.**

   b. ______The Court finds that there is a need for modification of child support and that the ______Mother ______ Father (hereinafter Obligor) has the present ability to pay child support. The amounts in the Child Support Guidelines Worksheet, Florida Family Law Rules of Procedure Form 12.902(e), filed by the ______ Mother ______ Father are correct **OR** the Court makes the following findings:

   The Mother's net monthly income is $____________, (Child Support Guidelines _____%).
   The Father's net monthly income is $____________, (Child Support Guidelines _____%).
   Monthly child care costs are $______________.
   Monthly health/dental insurance costs are $__________.

2. **Amount.**

Child support established at the rate of $__________ per month for the _______children *{total number of parties' minor or dependent children}* shall be paid commencing __________ *{month, day, year}* and terminating ______________________________ *{month, day, year}*. Child support shall be paid in the amount of $____________per ____________ *{week, month, other}* which is consistent with the Obligor's current payroll cycle.

Upon the termination of the obligation of child support for one of the parties' children, child support in the amount of $_____________for the remaining _______ children *{total number of remaining children}* shall be paid commencing________________________________ *{month, day, year}* and terminating______________________________ *{month, day, year}*. This child support shall be paid in the amount of $__________ per __________ *{week, month, other}* consistent with the Obligor's current payroll cycle.

{Insert schedule for the child support obligation, including the amount, and commencement and termination dates, for the remaining minor or dependent children, which shall be payable as the obligation for each child ceases. Please indicate whether the schedule______appears below or _____ is attached as part of this form.}

____
____
____
____
____
____.

The Obligor shall pay child support until all of the minor or dependent child(ren): reach the age of 18; become emancipated, marry, join the armed services, die, or become self-supporting; or until further order of the court or agreement of the parties. The child support obligation shall continue beyond the age of 18 and until high school graduation for any child who is dependent in fact, between the ages of 18 and 19, and is still in high school, performing in good faith with a reasonable expectation of graduation before the age of 19.

If the child support ordered deviates from the guidelines by more than 5%, the factual findings which support that deviation are: ____
____
____

3. **Arrearage/Retroactive Child Support.**
*{Choose **one** only}*

a. _____There is no child support arrearage at the time of this Supplemental Final Judgment.

OR

b. _____The _____ Mother _____ Father shall pay to the other party the child support arrearage of:

$____________ for retroactive child support, as of *{date}*________________________.
$____________ for previously ordered unpaid child support, as of *{date}*__________________.
The total of $_______________ in child support arrearage shall be repaid in the amount of $_______________, per month payable ______ in accordance with Obligor's employer's payroll cycle, and in any event at least once a month _____ other *{explain}* __________________beginning *{date}*_____________________________ until paid in full including statutory interest.

4. **Insurance.**
[Indicate all that apply]

a. _____**Health/Dental Insurance.** _____ Mother _____ Father shall be required to maintain _____health and/or _____ dental insurance for the parties' minor child(ren), so long as reasonable in cost and accessible to the child(ren) . The party providing insurance shall be required to convey insurance cards demonstrating said coverage to the other party;

OR

_____ health and/or______ dental insurance is not reasonable in cost or accessible to the child(ren) at this time.

b. _____Reasonable and necessary **uninsured medical/dental/prescription drug costs** for the minor child(ren) shall be assessed as follows:
_____ Shared equally by both parents.
_____ Prorated according to the child support guideline percentages.
_____ Other *{explain}*: ____

As to these uninsured medical/dental/prescription drug expenses, the party who incurs the expense shall submit a request for reimbursement to the other party within 30 days, and the other party, within 30 days of receipt, shall submit the applicable reimbursement for that expense, according to the schedule of reimbursement set out in this paragraph.

5. ______**Life Insurance (to secure payment of support).** To secure the child support obligations in this judgment, ______ Mother ______ Father ______Each parent shall maintain life insurance, in an amount of at least $_______________, on ______ his life ______ her life ______ his/her life naming the _____ minor child(ren) as the beneficiary(ies) **OR** naming the _____ Mother _____ Father _____ other *{name}*_______________________________as Trustee for the minor child(ren), so long as reasonably available. The obligation to maintain the life insurance shall continue until the youngest child turns 18, becomes emancipated, marries, joins the armed services, dies, or becomes self-supporting.

6. ______**IRS Income Tax Exemption(s).** The assignment of any tax exemption(s) for the child(ren) shall be as follows: ____
____.

Further, each party shall execute any and all IRS forms necessary to effectuate the provisions of this paragraph.

7. **Other provisions relating to child support:** ____
____.

SECTION IV. METHOD OF PAYMENT

Obligor shall pay court-ordered child support and arrears, if any, as follows:

1. **Place of Payment.**

a. _____Obligor shall pay court-ordered support directly to either the State Disbursement Unit or the central depository, as required by statute, along with any fee required by statute.

b. _____Both parties have requested and the court finds that it is in the best interests of the child(ren) that support payments need not be directed through either the State Disbursement Unit or the central depository at this time; however, either party may subsequently apply, pursuant to section 61.13(1)(d)3, Florida Statutes, to require payments through either the State Disbursement Unit or the central depository.

2. **Income Deduction.**

a. ______**Immediate.** Obligor shall pay through income deduction, pursuant to a separate Income Deduction Order which shall be effective immediately. Obligor is individually responsible for paying this support obligation until all of said support is deducted from Obligor's income. Until support payments are deducted from Obligor's paycheck, Obligor is responsible for making timely payments directly to the State Disbursement Unit or the Obligee, as previously set forth in this order.

b. ______**Deferred.** Income deduction is ordered this day, but it shall not be effective until a delinquency of $____________, or, if not specified, an amount equal to one month's obligation occurs. Income deduction is not being implemented immediately based on the following findings: Income deduction is **not** in the best interests of the child(ren) because: *{explain}*
____
____,

AND

There is proof of timely payment of a previously ordered obligation without an income deduction order,

AND

_____ There is an agreement by the Obligor to advise the Title IV-D agency, the clerk of court, and the Obligee of any change in Payor and/or health insurance **OR**

_____ there is a signed written agreement providing an alternative arrangement between the Obligor and the Obligee and, at the option of the IV-D agency, by the IV-D agency in IV-D cases in which there is an assignment of support rights to the state, reviewed and entered in the record by the court.

3. **Bonus/one-time payments.** _____All __________% _____No income paid in the form of a bonus or other similar one-time payment, up to the amount of any arrearage or the remaining balance thereof owed pursuant to this order, shall be forwarded to the Obligee pursuant to the payment method prescribed above.

4. **Other provisions relating to method of payment.** ____.

SECTION V. ATTORNEY'S FEES, COSTS, AND SUIT MONEY

1. _____ Mother's _____ Father's request(s) for attorney's fees, costs, and suit money is (are) denied because ____.

2. _____The Court finds there is a need for and an ability to pay attorney's fees, costs, and suit money. _____ Mother _____ Father is hereby ordered to pay to the other party $____________ in attorney's fees, and $____________ in costs. The Court further finds that the attorney's fees awarded are based on the reasonable rate of $____________ per hour and ________ reasonable hours. Other provisions relating to attorney's fees, costs, and suit money are as follows: ____.

SECTION VI. OTHER

1. **Other Provisions.** ____.

2. The Court reserves jurisdiction to modify and enforce this Supplemental Final Judgment.

3. Unless specifically modified by this Supplemental Final Judgment, the provisions of all final judgments or orders in effect remain the same.

DONE AND ORDERED at __________________________, Florida, on _____________________.

____
CIRCUIT JUDGE

I certify that a copy of the *{name of document(s)}* ______________________________________ was: ( ) mailed ( ) faxed and mailed ( ) e-mailed ( ) hand-delivered to the parties and any entities listed below on *{date}*____________________________.

by____________________________________
{Clerk of court or designee}

_____Petitioner (or his or her attorney)
_____Respondent (or his or her attorney)
_____Central Depository
_____State Disbursement Unit
Other:___________________________

Florida Supreme Court Approved Family Law Form 12.993(a), Supplemental Final Judgment Modifying Parental Responsibility, Visitation, or Parenting Plan/Time-Sharing Schedule and Other Relief (03/15)

Added Feb. 26, 1998, effective Mar. 16, 1998 (713 So.2d 1). Amended July 1, 1999 (717 So.2d 914); Sept. 21, 2000 (810 So.2d 1); March 26, 2009 (20 So.3d 173); Dec. 16, 2010 (59 So.3d 792); May 24, 2012 (96 So.3d 217); July 3, 2013 (117 So.3d 958); March 26, 2015, effective March 26, 2015 (2015 WL 1343088).

Form 12.993(b). Supplemental Final Judgment Modifying Child Support

IN THE CIRCUIT COURT OF THE ______________________ JUDICIAL CIRCUIT,
IN AND FOR ______________________ COUNTY, FLORIDA

Case No.: ______________________
Division: ______________________

______________________,
Petitioner,

and

______________________,
Respondent.

SUPPLEMENTAL FINAL JUDGMENT MODIFYING CHILD SUPPORT

This cause came before this Court on a Supplemental Petition for Modification of Child Support. The Court, having heard the testimony and reviewed the file and financial affidavits of the parties and being otherwise fully advised, makes these findings of fact and reaches these conclusions of law:

SECTION I. FINDINGS

1. The Court has jurisdiction over the subject matter and the parties.

2. **The parties' dependent or minor child(ren) is (are):**

Name	Birth date

3. The last order awarding or modifying child support was entered on *{date}* ______________

4. There has been a substantial change in circumstances of the parties since the entry of the last order, specifically: ____
____
____
____
____
____.

5. It is in the best interests of the minor child(ren) that the current child support order be changed

because: ____
____
____
____.

SECTION II. CHILD SUPPORT

1. The Court finds that there is a need for modification of child support and that the _____ Mother _____ Father (hereinafter Obligor) has the present ability to pay child support. The amounts in the Child Support Guidelines Worksheet, Florida Family Law Rules of Procedure Form 12.902(e), filed by the _____ Mother _____ Father are correct **OR** the Court makes the following findings:

   The Mother's net monthly income is $___________, (Child Support Guidelines _____%).
   The Father's net monthly income is $___________, (Child Support Guidelines _____%).
   Monthly child care costs are $___________.
   Monthly health/dental insurance costs are $___________.

2. **Amount.**
   Child support established at the rate of $__________ per month for the _____children *{total number of parties' minor or dependent children}* shall be paid commencing__________ *{month, day, year}* and terminating__________ *{month, day, year}*. Child support shall be paid in the amount of $__________ per _____ *{week, month, other}* consistent with the Obligor's current payroll cycle.

   Upon the termination of the obligation of child support for one of the parties' children, child support in the amount of $__________for the remaining _____ children *{total number of remaining children}* shall be paid commencing__________ *{month, day, year}* and terminating __________ *month, day, year}*. This child support shall be paid in the amount of $__________ per __________ *{week, month, other}* consistent with the Obligor's current payroll cycle.

   {Insert schedule for the child support obligation, including the amount, and commencement and termination dates, for the remaining minor or dependent children, which shall be payable as the obligation for each child ceases. Please indicate whether the schedule _____ appears below or _____ is attached as part of this form.}
   ____
   ____
   ____

____

____

____.

The Obligor shall pay child support until all of the minor or dependent children: reach the age of 18; become emancipated, marry, join the armed services, die, or become self-supporting; or until further order of the court or agreement of the parties. The child support obligation shall continue beyond the age of 18 and until high school graduation for any child who is dependent in fact, between the ages of 18 and 19, and is still in high school, performing in good faith with a reasonable expectation of graduation before the age of 19.

If the child support ordered deviates from the guidelines by more than 5%, the factual findings which support that deviation are: ____
____
____.

3. **Arrearage/Retroactive Child Support.**

a. ____There is no child support arrearage at the time of this Supplemental Final Judgment.

OR

b. _____ Mother _____ Father shall pay to the other party the child support arrearage of:
$__________ for retroactive child support, as of *{date}* ______________________.
$__________ for previously ordered unpaid child support, as of *{date}* ______________.
The total of $__________ in child support arrearage shall be repaid in the amount of $________, per month payable _____ in accordance with his or her employer's payroll cycle, and in any event at least once a month _____ other *{explain}* ______________________________
beginning *{date}* ________________________, until paid in full including statutory interest.

4. **Insurance.**
*{Indicate **all** that apply}*

a. ______**Health/Dental Insurance.** _____ Mother _____ Father shall be required to maintain ______ health _____dental insurance for the parties' minor child(ren), so long as it is reasonable in cost and accessible to the child(ren). The party providing insurance shall be required to convey insurance cards demonstrating said coverage to the other party **OR** _____Health _____ Dental insurance is not reasonable in cost or accessible to the child(ren) at this time.

b. _____Reasonable and necessary **uninsured medical/dental/prescription costs** for the minor child(ren) shall be assessed as follows:
______ Shared equally by both parents.
______ Prorated according to the child support guideline percentages.

______ Other {explain}: ____

As to these uninsured medical/dental/prescription expenses, the party who incurs the expense shall submit a request for reimbursement to the other party within 30 days, and the other party, within 30 days of receipt, shall submit the applicable reimbursement for that expense, according to the schedule of reimbursement set out in this paragraph.

5. _____**Life Insurance (to secure payment of support).** To secure the child support obligations in this judgment, _____ Mother _____ Father _____ Each party shall maintain life insurance coverage, in an amount of at least $______________, on _____ his life _____ her life _____ his/her life naming the _____ minor child(ren) as the beneficiary(ies) **OR** naming the _____Mother _____ Father _____ other {name}______________________ as Trustee for the minor child(ren), so long as reasonably available. The obligation to maintain the life insurance coverage shall continue until the youngest child turns 18, becomes emancipated, marries, joins the armed services, dies or otherwise becomes self-supporting.

6. **IRS Income Tax Exemption(s).** The assignment of any tax exemption(s) for the child(ren) shall be as follows: ____
____.
Further, each party shall execute any and all IRS forms necessary to effectuate the provisions of this paragraph.

7. **Other provisions relating to child support:** ______________________________
____
____.

SECTION III. METHOD OF PAYMENT

1. **Place of Payment.**

a. _____Obligor shall pay court-ordered support directly to either the State Disbursement Unit or the central depository, as required by statute, along with any fee required by statute.

b. _____Both parties have requested and the court finds that it is in the best interests of the child(ren) that support payments need not be directed through either the State Disbursement Unit or the central depository at this time; however, either party may subsequently apply, pursuant to section 61.13(1)(d)3, Florida Statutes, to require payments through either the State Disbursement Unit or the central depository.

2. **Income Deduction.**

a. _____**Immediate.** Obligor shall pay through income deduction, pursuant to a separate Income Deduction Order which shall be effective immediately. Obligor is individually responsible for paying this support obligation until all of said support is deducted from Obligor's income. Until support payments are deducted from Obligor's paycheck, Obligor is responsible for making timely payments directly to the State Disbursement Unit or the Obligee, as previously set forth in this order.

b. _____**Deferred.** Income deduction is ordered this day, but it shall not be effective until a delinquency of $_____________, or, if not specified, an amount equal to one month's obligation occurs. Income deduction is not being implemented immediately based on the following findings:

Income deduction is **not** in the best interests of the child(ren) because: *{explain}* ___________
____
____,

AND

There is proof of timely payment of a previously ordered obligation without an Income Deduction Order,

AND

_____ There is an agreement by the Obligor to advise the Title IV-D agency, the clerk of court, and the Obligee of any change in Payor and/or health insurance

OR

_____ there is a signed written agreement providing an alternative arrangement between the Obligor and the Obligee and, at the option of the IV-D agency, by the IV-D agency in IV-D cases in which there is an assignment of support rights to the state, reviewed and entered in the record by the court.

3. **Bonus/one-time payments.** _____ All _____% _____ No income paid in the form of a bonus or other similar one-time payment, up to the amount of any arrearage or the remaining balance thereof owed pursuant to this order, shall be forwarded to the Obligee pursuant to the payment method prescribed above.

4. **Other provisions relating to method of payment** ___________________________
____.

SECTION IV. ATTORNEY'S FEES, COSTS, AND SUIT MONEY

1. _____ Mother's _____ Father's request(s) for attorney's fees, costs, and suit money is (are) denied because
____
____.

2. _____The Court finds there is a need for and an ability to pay attorney's fees, costs, and suit money. _____ Mother _____ Father is hereby ordered to pay to the other party $ _____________ in attorney's fees, and $_____________ in costs. The Court further finds

that the attorney's fees awarded are based on the reasonable rate of $__________ per hour and __________reasonable hours. Other provisions relating to attorney's fees, costs, and suit money are as follows:

____
____.

SECTION V. OTHER

1. **Other Provisions.** ____
____
____
____
____.

2. The Court reserves jurisdiction to modify and enforce this Supplemental Final Judgment.

3. Unless specifically modified by this Supplemental Final Judgment, the provisions of all final judgments or orders in effect remain the same.

DONE AND ORDERED at ____________________________, Florida, on ____________________.

____
CIRCUIT JUDGE

I certify that a copy of the *{name of document(s)}* ____ was ( ) mailed ( ) faxed and mailed ( ) e-mailed ( ) hand-delivered to the parties and any entities listed below on {*date*}____________________.

____
By: *{Clerk of court or designee}*

______Petitioner (or his or her attorney)
______Respondent (or his or her attorney)
______Central Depository
______State Disbursement Unit

Florida Supreme Court Approved Family Law Form 12.993(b), Supplemental Final Judgment Modifying Child Support (03/15)

______Other:______________________

Florida Supreme Court Approved Family Law Form 12.993(b), Supplemental Final Judgment Modifying Child Support (03/15)

Added Feb. 26, 1998, effective Mar. 16, 1998 (713 So.2d 1). Amended July 1, 1999 (717 So.2d 914); Sept. 21, 2000 (810 So.2d 1); March 26, 2009 (20 So.3d 173); Dec. 16, 2010 (59 So.3d 792); May 24, 2012 (96 So.3d 217); July 3, 2013 (117 So.3d 958); March 26, 2015, effective March 26, 2015 (2015 WL 1343088).

Form 12.993(c). Supplemental Final Judgment Modifying Alimony

IN THE CIRCUIT COURT OF THE ________________ JUDICIAL CIRCUIT,
IN AND FOR ________________ COUNTY, FLORIDA

Case No: ________________
Division: ________________

________________________________,
Petitioner,

and

________________________________,
Respondent.

SUPPLEMENTAL FINAL JUDGMENT MODIFYING ALIMONY

This cause came before this Court on a Supplemental Petition for Modification of Alimony. The Court, having heard the testimony and reviewed the file and the financial affidavits of the parties and being otherwise fully advised, makes these findings of fact and reaches these conclusions of law:

SECTION I. FINDINGS

1. The Court has jurisdiction over the subject matter and the parties.

2. The last order awarding or modifying alimony was entered on *{date}*________________.

3. There has been a substantial change in circumstances of the parties since entry of the last order, specifically: ____
____
____
____
____
____.

SECTION II. ALIMONY

1. _____The Court denies the request(s) for modification of alimony

OR

2. _____ The Court finds that there is a need to modify alimony and that _____ Petitioner _____ Respondent (hereinafter Obligor) has/had the present ability to pay alimony as follows:

*{Indicate **all** that apply}*

a. **Permanent Periodic.** The permanent periodic alimony is _____ modified _____ terminated based upon either _____ a substantial change in circumstances, **OR** _____ the existence of a supportive relationship in accordance with Section 61.14, Florida Statutes. Obligor shall pay modified permanent periodic alimony to Obligee in the amount of $_______ per month, payable _____ in accordance with Obligor's employer's payroll cycle, and in any event, at least once a month, or _____ other : *{explain}* ________________________

Florida Supreme Court Approved Family Law Form 12.993(c), Supplemental Final Judgment Modifying Alimony (03/15)

____
beginning *{date}* ________________________. This alimony shall continue until further modified by court order, the death of either party, or remarriage of Obligee, whichever occurs first

b. _____**Durational.** The durational alimony is _____ modified _____terminated based upon a substantial change in circumstances in accordance with section 61.08(7), Florida Statutes. If the length of the durational alimony is modified, the court finds that the following exceptional circumstances exist:____
____
Obligor shall pay modified durational alimony to Obligee in the amount of $_________ per month, payable _____ in accordance with Obligor's employer's payroll cycle, and in any event, at least once a month _____ other *{explain}*_________________________ beginning *{date}* ___________________, and terminating on *{date}*________________, the death of either party, remarriage of the Obligee, or until further modified by court order, whichever occurs first.

c. _____**Rehabilitative.** The rehabilitative alimony is _____ modified _____ terminated based upon: _____ a substantial change in circumstances, _____ noncompliance with the rehabilitative plan, or _____ completion of the rehabilitative plan. Obligor shall pay modified rehabilitative alimony to Obligee in the amount of $__________ per month, payable _____ in accordance with Obligor's employer's payroll cycle, and in any event, at least once a month, or _____ other *{explain}* ________________________ beginning *{date}* ____________________.
This modified rehabilitative alimony shall continue until modified further by court order, the death of either party or until *{date/event}* ____________________________, whichever occurs first. The rehabilitative plan presented demonstrated the following:
____
____
____
____.

d. _____**Retroactive.** Obligor shall pay retroactive alimony in the amount of $__________ for the period of *{date}* __________________, through *{date}* ____________________, which shall be paid pursuant to paragraph 4 below.

3. **Reasons for _____ Awarding _____Denying Modification of Alimony.** The Court has considered all of the following in awarding/denying the modification of alimony request:
   a. The standard of living established during the marriage;
   b. The duration of the marriage;
   c. The age and the physical and emotional condition of each party;
   d. The financial resources of each party, including, the nonmarital and the marital assets and liabilities distributed to each;
   e. The earning capacities, educational levels, vocational skills, and employability of the parties and when applicable, the time necessary for either party to acquire sufficient education or training to enable such party to find appropriate employment;
   f. The contribution of each party to the marriage, including, but not limited to, services rendered in homemaking, child care, education, and career building of the other party;

g. The tax treatment and consequences to both parties of any alimony award, including the designation of all or a portion of the payment as nontaxable, nondeductible payment;

h. All sources of income available to either party, including income available to either party through investments of any assets held by that party, and

i. _____Any other factor necessary to do equity and justice between the parties *{Explain}*

____

____

____

_____ Please indicate here if additional pages are attached.

4. Arrearage/Retroactive Alimony.

a. _____There is no alimony arrearage at the time of this Supplemental Final Judgment.

OR

b. _____The _____Petitioner _____Respondent shall pay to the other party the alimony arrearage of:

$____________for retroactive alimony, as of *{date}* ______________;

$____________for previously ordered unpaid alimony, as of *{date}* ______________.

The total of $____________ in alimony arrearage shall be repaid in the amount of $____________per month, payable _____ in accordance with Obligor's employer's payroll cycle, and in any event at least once a month _____ other *{explain}* ______________

____

beginning *{date}* ______________, until paid in full including statutory interest.

5. _____Life Insurance (to secure payment of support).

To secure the alimony obligations set forth in this judgment, Obligor shall maintain life insurance coverage on his/her life naming Obligee as the sole irrevocable beneficiary, so long as reasonably available. This insurance shall be in the amount of at least $____________ and shall remain in effect until the obligation for alimony terminates.

6. _____Other provisions relating to modification of alimony, including any tax treatment and consequences: ______________

____

____

____

____.

SECTION III. METHOD OF PAYMENT

1. Place of Payment

a. _____Obligor shall pay court-ordered support directly to either the State Disbursement Unit or the central depository, as required by statute, along with any fee required by statute.

b. _____Both parties have requested that support payments not be directed through either the

State Disbursement Unit or the central depository at this time; however, either party may subsequently apply to the depository pursuant to section 61.08, Florida Statutes, to require payments through either the State Disbursement Unit or the central depository.

2. **Income Deduction.**

a. _____**Immediate.** Obligor shall pay through income deduction, pursuant to a separate Income Deduction Order which shall be effective immediately. Obligor is individually responsible for paying this support obligation until all of said support is deducted from Obligor's income. Until support payments are deducted from Obligor's paycheck, Obligor is responsible for making timely payments directly to the State Disbursement Unit or the Obligee, as previously set forth in this order.

b. _____**Deferred.** Income Deduction is ordered this day, but it shall not be effective until a delinquency of $_______________, or, if not specified, an amount equal to one month's obligation occurs. Income deduction is not being implemented immediately based on the following findings:
There is (are) no minor or dependent child(ren) common to the parties,

AND

There is proof of timely payment of a previously ordered obligation without an Income Deduction Order,

AND

_____ There is an agreement by the Obligor to advise the Title IV-D agency, the clerk of court, and the Obligee of any change in Payor and/or health insurance

OR

_____ there is a signed written agreement providing an alternative arrangement between the Obligor and the Obligee and, at the option of the IV-D agency, by the IV-D agency in IV-D cases in which there is an assignment of support rights to the state, reviewed and entered in the record by the court.

3. **Bonus/one-time payments.** _____ All ______% _____ No income paid in the form of a bonus or other similar one-time payment, up to the amount of any arrearage of the remaining balance thereof owed pursuant to this order, shall be forwarded to the Obligee pursuant to the payment method prescribed above.

4. **Other provisions relating to method of payment.** ____________________________________
____
____
____.

SECTION IV. ATTORNEY'S FEES, COSTS, AND SUIT MONEY

1. _____ Petitioner's _____ Respondent's request(s) for attorney's fees, costs, and suit money is (are) denied because
____

____
____.

2. _____ The Court finds there is a need for and an ability to pay attorney's fees, costs, and suit money. _____ Petitioner _____ Respondent is hereby ordered to pay to the other party $_____________ in attorney's fees, and $________________ in costs. The Court further finds that the attorney's fees awarded are based on the reasonable rate of $__________ per hour and ______________ reasonable hours. Other provisions relating to attorney's fees, costs, and suit money are as follows:
____
____
____.

SECTION V. OTHER

1. **Other Provisions:** ____
____
____
____
____.

2. The Court reserves jurisdiction to modify and enforce this Supplemental Final Judgment.

3. Unless specifically modified by this Supplemental Final Judgment, the provisions of all final judgments or orders in effect remain the same.

DONE AND ORDERED on _________________ in _________________________, Florida.

____
CIRCUIT JUDGE

I certify that a copy of the *{name of document(s)}* ____
was ( ) mailed ( ) faxed and mailed ( ) e-mailed ( ) hand-delivered to the parties and any entities listed below on *{date}*__________________.

by_______________________________
{Clerk of court or designee}

____Petitioner (or his or her attorney)
____Respondent (or his or her attorney)
____Central Depository

Florida Supreme Court Approved Family Law Form 12.993(c), Supplemental Final Judgment Modifying Alimony (03/15)

____State Disbursement Unit
____Other:___________________________

Florida Supreme Court Approved Family Law Form 12.993(c), Supplemental Final Judgment Modifying Alimony (03/15)

Added Feb. 26, 1998, effective Mar. 16, 1998 (713 So.2d 1). Amended July 1, 1999 (717 So.2d 914); Sept. 21, 2000 (810 So.2d 1); May 24, 2012 (96 So.3d 217); July 3, 2013 (117 So.3d 958); March 26, 2015, effective March 26, 2015 (2015 WL 1343088).

Form 12.993(d). Supplemental Temporary Judgment Modifying Parenting Issues for Child(ren) of a Parent Activated, Deployed, or Temporarily Assigned to Military Service

IN THE CIRCUIT COURT OF THE ________________________ JUDICIAL CIRCUIT,
IN AND FOR ______________________ COUNTY, FLORIDA

Case No.: ______________________
Division: ______________________

______________________________,
Petitioner,

and

______________________________,
Respondent.

SUPPLEMENTAL TEMPORARY JUDGMENT MODIFYING PARENTING ISSUES FOR CHILD(REN) OF A PARENT ACTIVATED, DEPLOYED, OR TEMPORARILY ASSIGNED TO MILITARY SERVICE

This cause came before this Court on a Supplemental Petition for Temporary Modification of Custody or Parenting Plan/Time-Sharing Schedule for Child(ren) of a Parent Activated, Deployed, or Temporarily Assigned to Military Service. The Court, having reviewed the file, heard the testimony, and being otherwise fully advised, makes these findings of fact and reaches these conclusions of law:

SECTION I. FINDINGS

1. The Court has jurisdiction over the subject matter and the parties.

2. The last order establishing or modifying parental responsibility, visitation, or time-sharing was entered on *{date}* ______________________.

3. There is clear and convincing evidence that it is in the best interests of the minor child(ren) that the current order establishing parental responsibility, visitation, and time-sharing be temporarily modified as the _____ Mother _____ Father is activated, deployed, or temporarily assigned to military service. Specifically: ____
____
____
____.

SECTION II. TEMPORARY PARENTING PLAN ESTABLISHING PARENTAL RESPONSIBILITY AND TIME-SHARING WITH DEPENDENT OR MINOR CHILD(REN)

1. **Jurisdiction.** The Court has jurisdiction to determine parental responsibility, to establish or approve a Parenting Plan, and time-sharing with regards to the parties' minor child(ren) listed in paragraph 2 below.

2. **The parties' dependent or minor child(ren) is (are):**

Name	Birth date

3. **Parenting Plan.** The parties shall comply with the temporary Parenting Plan which is attached and incorporated herein as Exhibit _____.

SECTION III. CHILD SUPPORT

1. **Temporary Modification of Child Support.**
*{Choose **one** only}*

a. _____The _____ Mother's _____ Father's current obligation to pay child support is:

_____ Abated
_____ Suspended
_____ Modified to $______________ per ________________.

b. _____The Court finds that there is a need for temporary modification of child support and that the service member _____ Mother _____ Father (hereinafter Obligor) has the present ability to pay child support. The amounts in the Child Support Guidelines Worksheet, Florida Family Law Rules of Procedure Form 12.902(e), filed by the _____ Mother _____ Father are correct
OR the Court makes the following findings:

The Mother's net monthly income is $___________, (Child Support Guidelines ____ %).
The Father's net monthly income is $______________, (Child Support Guidelines_____%).
Monthly child care costs are $______________.
Monthly health/dental insurance costs are $__________________.

2. **Amount.**
Child support established at the rate of $___________per month for the _______children *{total number of parties' minor or dependent children}* shall be paid commencing ___________ *{month, day, year}* and terminating ___________

{month, day, year}. Child support shall be paid in the amount of $____________ per ____________ *{week, month, other}* which is consistent with the Obligor's current payroll cycle.

Upon the termination of the obligation of child support for one of the parties' children, child support in the amount of $____________ for the remaining _______ children *{total number of remaining children}* shall be paid commencing ____________________________ *{month, day, year}* and terminating __________________________ *{month, day, year}.* This child support shall be paid in the amount of $__________ per ____________ *{week, month, other}* consistent with the Obligor's current payroll cycle.

{Insert schedule for the child support obligation, including the amount, and commencement and termination dates, for the remaining minor or dependent children, which shall be payable as the obligation for each child ceases. Please indicate whether the schedule _____ appears below or _____ is attached as part of this form.}

____
____
____
____
____
____.

The Obligor shall pay child support until all of the minor or dependent children: reach the age of 18; become emancipated, marry, join the armed services, die, or become self-supporting; or until further order of the court or agreement of the parties. The child support obligation shall continue beyond the age of 18 and until high school graduation for any child who is dependent in fact, between the ages of 18 and 19, and is still in high school, performing in good faith with a reasonable expectation of graduation before the age of 19.

If the child support ordered deviates from the guidelines by more than 5%, the factual findings which support that deviation are: _______________________________________
____
____.

3. **Arrearage/Retroactive Child Support.**
{Choose one only}

a. _____There is no child support arrearage at the time of this Supplemental Temporary Judgment.
OR

b. _____The _____ Mother _____ Father shall pay to the other party the child support arrearage of:
$____________ for retroactive child support, as of *{date}* ________________.
$____________ for previously ordered unpaid child support, as of *{date}* ____________.
The total of $____________ in child support arrearage shall be repaid in the amount of

$__________, per month payable_____ in accordance with Obligor's employer's payroll cycle, and in any event at least once a month _____ other *{explain}* ______________________________

____

beginning *{date}* ______________, until paid in full including statutory interest.

4. **Insurance.**

a. _____**Health/Dental Insurance.**
*{Choose **one** only}*
_____The service member _____ Mother _____ Father shall enroll the child(ren) as a military dependent(s) with DEERs, TriCare, or other similar benefits available to military dependents as provided by the service member's branch or service and federal regulations;

OR

_____The _____ Mother _____ Father shall maintain _____ health and/or _____ dental insurance for the parties' minor child(ren), so long as it is reasonable in cost and accessible to the child(ren). The party providing insurance shall be required to convey insurance cards demonstrating said insurance to the other party;

OR

_____ Health _____Dental insurance is not reasonable in cost or accessible to the child(ren) at this time.

b. _____Reasonable and necessary **uninsured medical/dental/prescription drug costs** for the minor child(ren) shall be assessed as follows:
_____ Shared equally by both parents.
_____ Prorated according to the child support guideline percentages.
_____ Other *{explain}*: ______________________________
____
As to these uninsured medical/dental/prescription drug expenses, the party who incurs the expense shall submit a request for reimbursement to the other party within 30 days, and the other party, within 30 days of receipt, shall submit the applicable reimbursement for that expense, according to the schedule of reimbursement set out in this paragraph.

5. _____**Life Insurance (to secure payment of support).** To secure the child support obligations in this judgment, _____ Mother _____ Father _____Each party shall maintain life insurance, in an amount of at least $__________, on _____ his life _____ her life _____ his/her life naming the _____ minor child(ren) as the beneficiary(ies) **OR** naming the _____ Mother _____ Father _____ other *{name}* ____________________ as Trustee for the minor child(ren), so long as reasonably available. The obligation to maintain the life insurance coverage shall continue until the youngest child turns 18, becomes emancipated, marries, joins the armed services, dies, or otherwise becomes self-supporting.

6. _____**IRS Income Tax Exemption(s).** The assignment of any tax exemption(s) for the child(ren) shall

be as follows: ____
____.

Further, each party shall execute any and all IRS forms necessary to effectuate the provisions of this paragraph.

7. **Other provisions relating to child support:** ____
____
____.

SECTION IV. METHOD OF PAYMENT

Obligor shall pay court-ordered child support and arrears, if any, as follows:

1. **Place of Payment.**

   a. _____Obligor shall pay court-ordered support directly to either the State Disbursement Unit or the central depository, as required by statute, along with any fee required by statute.

   b. _____Both parties have requested and the court finds that it is in the best interests of the child(ren) that support payments need not be directed through either the State Disbursement Unit or the central depository at this time; however, either party may subsequently apply, pursuant to section 61.13(1)(d)3, Florida Statutes, to require payments through the State Disbursement Unit or the central depository.

2. **Income Deduction.**

   a. _____**Immediate.** Obligor shall pay through income deduction, pursuant to a separate Income Deduction Order which shall be effective immediately. Obligor is individually responsible for paying this support obligation until all of said support is deducted from Obligor's income. Until support payments are deducted from Obligor's paycheck, Obligor is responsible for making timely payments directly to the State Disbursement Unit or the Obligee, as previously set forth in this order.

   b. _____**Deferred.** Income deduction is ordered this day, but it shall not be effective until a delinquency of $______________, or, if not specified, an amount equal to one month's obligation occurs. Income deduction is not being implemented immediately based on the following findings:
   Income deduction is **not** in the best interests of the child(ren) because: *{explain}*
   ____
   ____

   AND

   _____ There is proof of timely payment of a previously ordered obligation without an Income Deduction Order,

AND

_____ There is an agreement by the Obligor to advise the Title IV-D agency, clerk of court and Obligee of any change in Payor and/or health insurance **OR** _____there is a signed written agreement providing an alternative arrangement between the Obligor and the Obligee and, at the option of the IV-D agency, by the IV-D agency in IV-D cases in which there is an assignment of support rights to the state, reviewed and entered in the record by the court.

3. **Bonus/one-time payments.** _____ All ______% _____ No income paid in the form of a bonus or other similar one-time payment, up to the amount of any arrearage or the remaining balance thereof owed pursuant to this order, shall be forwarded to the Obligee pursuant to the payment method prescribed above.

4. **Other provisions relating to method of payment.** ____
____
____.

SECTION V. ATTORNEY'S FEES, COSTS, AND SUIT MONEY

1. _____ Petitioner's _____ Respondent's request(s) for attorney's fees, costs, and suit money is (are) denied because ____
____.

OR

2. ______The Court finds there is a need for and an ability to pay attorney's fees, costs, and suit money. _____Petitioner _____ Respondent is hereby ordered to pay to the other party $__________ in attorney's fees, and $__________ in costs. The Court further finds that the attorney's fees awarded are based on the reasonable rate of $__________ per hour and __________ reasonable hours. Other provisions relating to attorney's fees, costs, and suit money are as follows: ____
____
____.

SECTION VI. OTHER

1. **Other Provisions.** ____
____
____
____
____.

2. The Court reserves jurisdiction to modify and enforce this Supplemental Temporary Judgment.

3. Unless specifically modified by this supplemental temporary judgment, the provisions of all final judgments or orders in effect remain the same.

DONE AND ORDERED at ________________________, Florida, on __________________.

____
CIRCUIT JUDGE

I certify that a copy of the {*name of document(s)*} ______________________________
was ( ) mailed ( ) faxed and mailed ( ) e-mailed ( ) hand-delivered to the parties and any entities listed below on {*date*}__________________.

____
by {*clerk of court or designee*}

_____Petitioner (or his or her attorney)
_____Respondent (or his or her attorney)
_____Central Depository
_____State Disbursement Unit
_____Other:_______________________

Florida Supreme Court Approved Family Law Form 12.993(d), Supplemental Temporary Judgment Modifying Parenting Issues for Child(ren) of a Parent Activated, Deployed, or Temporary Assigned to Military Service. (03/15)

Added March 26, 2009 (20 So.3d 173). Amended Dec. 16, 2010 (59 So.3d 792); May 24, 2012 (96 So.3d 217); July 3, 2013 (117 So.3d 958); March 26, 2015, effective March 26, 2015 (2015 WL 1343088).

Form 12.994(a). Final Judgment for Support Unconnected with Dissolution of Marriage with Dependent or Minor Child(ren)

IN THE CIRCUIT COURT OF THE ______________________ JUDICIAL CIRCUIT,
IN AND FOR ______________________ COUNTY, FLORIDA

Case No.: ______________________
Division: ______________________

______________________,
Husband,

and

______________________,
Wife.

FINAL JUDGMENT FOR SUPPORT UNCONNECTED WITH DISSOLUTION OF MARRIAGE WITH DEPENDENT OR MINOR CHILD(REN)

This cause came before this Court on a Petition for Support Unconnected with Dissolution of Marriage under section 61.09, Florida Statutes. The Court, having reviewed the file and heard the testimony, makes these findings of fact and reaches these conclusions of law:

1. The Court has jurisdiction over the subject matter and the parties.

2. The following child(ren) are common to the parties:

Name	**Birth date**

SECTION I. ALIMONY

1. _____The Court denies the request(s) for alimony.

   OR

2. _____The Court finds that there is a need for alimony and that _____Husband _____Wife has/had the ability to support his/her spouse and has failed to do so. ____Husband ____Wife(hereinafter Obligor) has the present ability to pay alimony as follows: *{Indicate all that apply}*

   a. _____**Permanent Periodic.**

Florida Supreme Court Approved Family Law Form 12.994(a), Final Judgment for Support Unconnected with Dissolution of Marriage with Dependent or Minor Child(ren) (03/15)

1. The court finds that no other form of alimony is fair and reasonable under the circumstances of the parties.
2. As a marriage of *{choose only one}*:

______**Long Duration** (17 years or greater) alimony is appropriate upon consideration of all relevant factors;

______**Moderate Duration** (greater than 7 years but less than 17) alimony is appropriate based upon clear and convincing evidence after consideration of all relevant factors; or

______**Short Duration** (less than 7 years) alimony is appropriate based upon the following exceptional circumstances:____
____
____.

3. Obligor shall pay permanent periodic alimony to Obligee in the amount of $ ______ per month, payable ______ in accordance with Obligor's employer's payroll cycle, and in any event, at least once a month or ______ other: *{explain}*____________________ beginning *{date}*______________. This alimony shall continue until modified by court order, the death of either party, or remarriage of Obligee, whichever occurs first. The alimony may be modified or terminated based upon either a substantial change in circumstances or the existence of a supportive relationship in accordance with section 61.14, Florida Statutes.

b.______**Bridge-the-Gap**. Obligor shall pay bridge-the-gap alimony to Obligee in the amount of $________ per month, payable ______ in accordance with Obligor's employer's payroll cycle, and in any event, at least once a month, or ______ other: *{explain}*____________________ beginning *{date}*____________________ and continuing until *{date}*____________________ *{a period not to exceed two (2) years}*, death of either party or remarriage of Obligee.

c.______**Rehabilitative.** Obligor shall pay rehabilitative alimony to Obligee in the amount of $__________ per month, payable ______ in accordance with Obligor's employer's payroll cycle, and in any event, at least once a month, or ______ other *{explain}* ____________________ beginning *{date}* ________________. This rehabilitative alimony shall continue until modified by court order, the death of either party or until *{date/event}*____________________, whichever occurs first. The rehabilitative plan presented demonstrated the following: ______
____
____
____.

d.______**Durational.** Obligor shall pay durational alimony to Obligee in the amount of $________ per month, payable ______ in accordance with Obligor's employer's payroll cycle, and in any event, at least once a month, or ____ other: *{explain}*__________________________ beginning *{date}*______________________ and terminating on *{date}*______________________, the death of either party, remarriage of Obligee or until modified by court order in accordance with section 61.08(7),Florida Statutes; whichever occurs first.

e.____ **Lump Sum.** Obligor shall pay lump sum alimony to Obligee in the amount of $________ which shall be paid as follows:____.

f.____ **Retroactive.** Obligor shall pay retroactive alimony in the amount of $ ____________ for the period of *{date}* ______________, through *{date}* __________________, which shall be paid pursuant to paragraph 4 below.

3. **Reasons for _____ Awarding _____ Denying Alimony.** The Court has considered all of the following in awarding/denying alimony:
   a. The standard of living established during the marriage;
   b. The duration of the marriage;
   c. The age and the physical and emotional condition of each party;
   d. The financial resources of each party, including the nonmarital and the marital assets and liabilities distributed to each;
   e. The earning capacities, educational levels, vocational skills, and employability of the parties and, when applicable, the time necessary for either party to acquire sufficient education or training to enable such party to find appropriate employment;
   f. The contribution of each party to the marriage, including, but not limited to, services rendered in homemaking, child care, education, and career building of the other party;
   g. The responsibilities each party will have with regard to any minor children they have in common;
   h. The tax treatment and consequences to both parties of any alimony award, including the designation of all or a portion of the payment as a nontaxable, nondeductible payment;
   i. All sources of income available to either party, including income available to either party through investments of any asset held by that party; and
   j. Any other factor necessary to do equity and justice between the parties: *{Explain}* ________
   ____
   ____
   ____
   ____
   ____

   _____ Please indicate here if additional pages are attached.

4. **Arrearage/Retroactive Alimony.**

   a. _____There is no alimony arrearage at the time of this Final Judgment.

   OR

   b. _____ Respondent shall pay to Petitioner the alimony arrearage of:

$________ for retroactive alimony, as of *{date}* __________.
$________ for previously ordered unpaid alimony, as of *{date}* __________.
The total of $_________ in alimony arrearage shall be repaid in the amount of $________ per month, payable _____ in accordance with Obligor's employer's payroll cycle, and in any event, at least once a month _____ other *{explain}* __________ beginning *{date}* ________________, until paid in full including statutory interest.

5. _____**Life Insurance (to secure payment of support).** To secure the alimony obligations set forth in this judgment, Obligor shall maintain life insurance on his/her life naming Obligee as the sole irrevocable beneficiary, so long as reasonably available. This insurance shall be in the amount of at least $____________ and shall remain in effect until the obligation for alimony terminates.

6. _____ **Other provisions relating to alimony including any tax treatment and consequences:**

a. The award of alimony _____ does not _____ does leave the Obligor with significantly less net income than the net income of the recipient/Obligee. If yes, the court finds the following exceptional circumstances:____.

b. Other:____.

SECTION II. CHILD SUPPORT

1. The Court finds that there is a need for child support and that the _____ Mother _____ Father (hereinafter Obligor) has the present ability to pay child support. The amounts in the Child Support Guidelines Worksheet, Florida Family Law Rules of Procedure Form 12.902(e), filed by the _____ Mother _____Father are correct **OR** the Court makes the following findings:

The Mother's net monthly income is $ __________, (Child Support Guidelines _____%).
The Father's net monthly income is $__________, (Child Support Guidelines _____%).
Monthly child care costs are $________.
Monthly health/dental insurance costs are $_________.

2. **Amount.**
Child support established at the rate of $__________ per month for the______children *{total number of parties' minor or dependent children}* shall be paid commencing __________ *{month, day, year}* and terminating ______________ *{month, day, year}*. Child support

shall be paid in the amount of $________ per ______________ *{week, month, other}* which is consistent with the Obligor's current payroll cycle.

Upon the termination of the obligation of child support for one of the parties' children, child support in the amount of $________ for the remaining ______ children *{total number of remaining children}* shall be paid commencing ____________________________*{month, day, year}* and terminating______________________________*{month, day, year}*. This child support shall be paid in the amount of $________per__________ *{week, month, other}* consistent with the Obligor's current payroll cycle.

{Insert schedule for the child support obligation, including the amount, and commencement and termination dates, for the remaining minor or dependent children, which shall be payable as the obligation for each child ceases. Please indicate whether the schedule _____appears below or _____ is attached as part of this form.}

____
____
____
____
____.

The Obligor shall pay child support until all of the minor or dependent children: reach the age of 18; become emancipated, marry, join the armed services, die, or become self-supporting; or until further order of the court or agreement of the parties. The child support obligation shall continue beyond the age of 18 and until high school graduation for any child who is dependent in fact, between the ages of 18 and 19, and is still in high school, performing in good faith with a reasonable expectation of graduation before the age of 19.

If the child support ordered deviates from the guidelines by more than 5%, the factual findings which support that deviation are: ____
____
____.

3. **Arrearage/Retroactive Child Support.**

a. _____ There is no child support arrearage at the time of this Final Judgment.

OR

b. _____ The _____ Mother _____ Father shall pay to the other party the child support for previously ordered unpaid child support, as of *{date}* _______________. The total of $__________of child support arrearage shall be repaid in the amount of $__________ per month, payable _____ in accordance with Obligor's employer's payroll cycle, and in any event, at least once a month _____ other *{explain}* _______________ beginning *{date}* ________________, until paid in full including statutory interest.

4. **Insurance.**
*{Indicate **all** that apply}*

a. **Health/Dental Insurance.** _____ Mother _____ Father shall be required to maintain _____ health and/or _____ dental insurance for the parties' minor child(ren), so long as it is reasonable in cost and accessible to the child(ren). The party providing insurance shall be required to convey insurance cards demonstrating said insurance to the other party.
OR
_____ Health _____ Dental insurance is either not reasonable in cost or accessible to the children at this time.

b. _____ Reasonable and necessary uninsured medical/dental/prescription drug costs for the minor child(ren) shall be assessed as follows:
_____ Shared equally by both parents.
_____ Prorated according to the child support guideline percentages.
_____ Other *{explain}*: ____
____
As to these uninsured medical/dental/prescription drug expenses, the party who incurs the expense shall submit a request for reimbursement to the other party within 30 days, and the other party, within 30 days of receipt, shall submit the applicable reimbursement for that expense, according to the schedule of reimbursement set out in this paragraph.

5. _____ **Life Insurance (to secure payment of support).** To secure the child support obligations in this judgment, _____ Mother _____ Father _____ Each party shall maintain life insurance, in an amount of at least $__________, on _____ his life _____ her life _____ his/her life naming the _____ minor child(ren) as the beneficiary(ies) **OR** naming _____ Mother _____ Father _____ other *{name}*____________________________ as Trustee for the minor child(ren). The obligation to maintain the life insurance coverage shall continue until the youngest child turns 18, becomes emancipated, marries, joins the armed services, dies, or becomes self-supporting.

6. **IRS Income Tax Exemption(s).** The assignment of any tax exemption(s) for the child(ren) shall be as follows: ____
____.
Further, each party shall execute any and all IRS forms necessary to effectuate the provisions of this paragraph.

7. **Other provisions relating to child support:** ____
____
____

SECTION III. METHOD OF PAYMENT

Obligor shall pay court-ordered child support/alimony and arrears, if any, as follows:

1. **Place of Payment.**

   a. _____ Obligor shall pay court-ordered support directly to either the State Disbursement Unit or the central depository, as required by statute, along with any fee required by statute.

   b. _____ Both parties have requested and the court finds that it is in the best interests of the child(ren) that support payments need not be directed through either the State Disbursement Unit or the central depository at this time; however, either party may subsequently apply, pursuant to section 61.08 or 61.13, Florida Statutes, to require payments through either the State Disbursement Unit or the central depository.

2. **Income Deduction.**

   a. _____ **Immediate.** Obligor shall pay through income deduction, pursuant to a separate Income Deduction Order which shall be effective immediately. Obligor is individually responsible for paying this support obligation until all of said support is deducted from Obligor's income. Until support payments are deducted from Obligor's paycheck, Obligor is responsible for making timely payments directly to the State Disbursement Unit or the Obligee, as previously set forth in this order.

   b. _____ **Deferred.** Income deduction is ordered this day, but it shall not be effective until a delinquency of $____________, or, if not specified, an amount equal to one month's obligation occurs. Income deduction is not being implemented immediately based on the following findings: Income deduction is **not** in the best interests of the child(ren) because: *{explain}* ____
   ____,

   AND

   _____ there is proof of timely payment of a previously ordered obligation without an Income Deduction Order in cases of modification,

   AND

   _____ there is an agreement by the Obligor to advise the Title IV-D agency, clerk of court, and Obligee of any change in Payor and/or health insurance

   OR

   _____ there is a signed written agreement providing an alternative arrangement between the Obligor and the Obligee and, at the option of the IV-D agency, by the IV-D agency in IV-D cases in which there is an assignment of support rights to the state, reviewed and entered in the record by the court.

3. **Bonus/one-time payments.** _____ All _____% _____ No income paid in the form of a bonus or other similar one-time payment, up to the amount of any arrearage or the remaining balance thereof owed pursuant to this order, shall be forwarded to the Obligee pursuant to the payment method prescribed above.

4. **Other provisions relating to method of payment.** ____
____
____

SECTION IV. ATTORNEY'S FEES, COSTS, AND SUIT MONEY

1. _____ Husband's _____ Wife's request(s) for attorney's fees, costs, and suit money is (are) denied because: ____
____.

2. _____ The Court finds there is a need for and an ability to pay attorney's fees, costs, and suit money. _____Husband _____ Wife is hereby ordered to pay to the other party $___________ in attorney's fees, and $___________ in costs. The Court further finds that the attorney's fees awarded are based on the reasonable rate of $___________per hour and _______ reasonable hours. Other provisions relating to attorney's fees, costs, and suit money are as follows:
____
____
____.

SECTION V. OTHER PROVISIONS

1. **Other Provisions:**
____
____
____
____
____
____.

2. The Court reserves jurisdiction to modify and enforce this Final Judgment.

DONE AND ORDERED at ______________________, Florida, on ______________________.

____
CIRCUIT JUDGE

I certify that a copy of the *{name of document(s)}* ______________________________ was ( ) mailed ( ) faxed and mailed ( ) e-mailed ( ) hand-delivered to the parties and any entities listed below on *{date}*______________________.

Florida Supreme Court Approved Family Law Form 12.994(a), Final Judgment for Support Unconnected with Dissolution of Marriage with Dependent or Minor Child(ren) (03/15)

____
By: {Clerk of court or designee}

_____Husband (or his attorney)
_____Wife (or her attorney)
_____Central Depository
_____State Disbursement Unit
_____Other: _______________

Florida Supreme Court Approved Family Law Form 12.994(a), Final Judgment for Support Unconnected with Dissolution of Marriage with Dependent or Minor Child(ren) (03/15)

Added July 7, 1995, effective Jan. 1, 1996 (663 So.2d 1047). Amended Feb. 26, 1998, effective Mar. 16, 1998 (713 So.2d 1); July 1, 1999 (717 So.2d 914); Sept. 21, 2000 (810 So.2d 1); March 26, 2009 (20 So.3d 173); Dec. 16, 2010 (59 So.3d 792); May 24, 2012 (96 So.3d 217); July 3, 2013 (117 So.3d 958); March 26, 2015, effective March 26, 2015 (2015 WL 1343088).

Form 12.994(b). Final Judgment for Support Unconnected with Dissolution of Marriage with No Dependent or Minor Child(ren)

IN THE CIRCUIT COURT OF THE _____ JUDICIAL CIRCUIT,
IN AND ________________ COUNTY, FLORIDA

In re the Marriage of:

Case No.: ________________
Division: ________________

________________________,
Husband,

and

________________________,
Wife.

FINAL JUDGMENT FOR SUPPORT UNCONNECTED WITH DISSOLUTION OF MARRIAGE WITH NO DEPENDENT OR MINOR CHILD(REN)

This cause came before this Court on a Petition for Support Unconnected with Dissolution of Marriage under section 61.09, Florida Statutes. The Court, having reviewed the file and heard the testimony, makes these findings of fact and reaches these conclusions of law:

1. The Court has jurisdiction over the subject matter and the parties.

2. The parties have no minor or dependent children in common, and the wife is not pregnant.

SECTION I. ALIMONY

1. _____The Court denies the request(s) for alimony.

OR

2. ____The Court finds that there is a need for alimony and that ____Husband ____Wife has/had the ability to support his/her spouse and has failed to do so. _____Husband _____Wife(hereinafter Obligor) has the present ability to pay alimony as follows: *{Indicate all that apply}*

   a. ______ **Permanent Periodic.**

Florida Supreme Court Approved Family Law Form 12.994(b), Final Judgment for Support Unconnected with Dissolution of Marriage with No Dependent or Minor Child(ren) (03/15)

1. The court finds that no other form of alimony is fair and reasonable under the circumstances of the parties.

2. As a marriage of **(choose one only):**

_____**Long Duration** (17 years or greater) alimony is appropriate upon consideration of all relevant factors;

_____**Moderate Duration** (greater than 7 years but less than 17) alimony is appropriate based upon clear and convincing evidence after consideration of all relevant factors; or

_____**Short Duration** (less than 7 years) alimony is appropriate based upon the following exceptional circumstances:____
____
____
____.

3. Obligor shall pay permanent periodic alimony to Obligee in the amount of $__________ per month, payable_____ in accordance with Obligor's employer's payroll cycle, and in any event, at least once a month, or _____ other: *{explain}*_____________________________ beginning *{date}*_______________. This alimony shall continue until modified by court order, the death of either party, or remarriage of Obligee, whichever occurs first. The alimony may be modified or terminated based upon either a substantial change in circumstances, or a supportive relationship in accordance with section 61.14, Florida Statutes.

b. _____**Bridge-the-Gap.** Obligor shall pay bridge-the-gap alimony to Obligee in the amount of $_____per month, payable_____ in accordance with Obligor's employer's payroll cycle, beginning *{date}*_______________and continuing until *{date}*_______________ *{a period not to exceed two years}*, remarriage of Obligee, or death of either party, whichever occurs first.

c. _____**Rehabilitative.** Obligor shall pay rehabilitative alimony to Obligee in the amount of $_______ per month, payable _____ in accordance with Obligor's employer's payroll cycle, and in any event, at least once a month _____ other *{explain}*_______________. beginning *{date}* _______________.This rehabilitative alimony shall continue until modified by court order, the death of either party or until *{date/event}* ___________________________
____.
whichever occurs first. The rehabilitative plan presented demonstrated the following: _______
____.

d. ______**Durational.** Obligor shall pay durational alimony to Obligee in the amount of $___________per month payable _____ in accordance with Obligor's employer's payroll cycle, and in any event, at least once a month, or _____ other *{explain}*___________________ beginning *{date}*__________________and terminating on *{date }*________________, remarriage of the Obligee, death of either party, or until modified by court order in accordance with section 61.08(7), Florida Statutes; whichever occurs first.

e. _____**Lump Sum.** Obligor shall pay lump sum alimony to Obligee in the amount of $__________which shall be paid as follows:_____________________________________ ____.

f.______**Retroactive.** Obligor shall pay retroactive alimony in the amount of $__________ for the period of *{date}*______________, through *{date}*________________, which shall be paid pursuant to paragraph 4 below.

3. **Reasons for _____ Awarding _____ Denying Alimony.** The Court has considered all of the following in awarding/denying alimony:
a. The standard of living established during the marriage;
b. The duration of the marriage;
c. The age and the physical and emotional condition of each party;
d. The financial resources of each party, including the nonmarital and the marital assets and liabilities distributed to each;
e. The earning capacities, educational levels, vocational skills, and employability of the parties and, when applicable, the time necessary for either party to acquire sufficient education or training to enable such party to find appropriate employment;
f. The contribution of each party to the marriage, including, but not limited to, services rendered in homemaking, child care, education, and career building of the other party;
g. The tax treatment and consequences to both parties of any alimony award, including the designation of all or a portion of the payment as nontaxable, nondeductible payment;
h. All sources of income available to either party, including income available to either party through investments of any asset held by the party; and
i. Any other factor necessary to do equity and justice between the parties *{Explain}*
____
____
____
____
____.
_____ Please indicate here if additional pages are attached.

4. **Arrearage/Retroactive Alimony.**

a. _____There is no alimony arrearage at the time of this Final Judgment.

OR

b._____Respondent shall pay to Petitioner the alimony arrearage of:

$__________ for retroactive alimony, as of *{date}* __________.
$__________ for previously ordered unpaid alimony, as of *{date}* __________.
The total of $________ in alimony arrearage shall be repaid in the amount of
$__________ per month, payable _____ in accordance with Obligor's employer's payroll cycle, and in any event at least once a month, _____ or other: *{explain}* __________
____
beginning *{date}* __________, until paid in full including statutory interest.

5. ______**Life Insurance (to secure payment of support).** To secure the alimony obligations set forth in this judgment, Obligor shall maintain life insurance coverage on his/her life naming Obligee as the sole irrevocable beneficiary, so long as reasonably available. This insurance shall be in the amount of at least $__________ and shall remain in effect until the obligation for alimony terminates.

6. ______**Other provisions relating to alimony including any tax treatment and consequences:**

a. The award of alimony _____ does not _____ does leave the Obligor with significantly less net income than the net income of the recipient/Obligee. If yes, the court finds the following exceptional circumstances: __________
____
__________.

b. Other __________
____
__________.

SECTION II. METHOD OF PAYMENT

Obligor shall pay court-ordered alimony and arrears, if any, as follows:

1. **Place of Payment**

a.______ Obligor shall pay court-ordered support directly to either the State Disbursement Unit or the central depository, as required by statute, along with any fee required by statute.

b._____ Both parties have requested and the court finds that support payments need not be directed through either the State Disbursement Unit or the central depository at this time; however, either party may subsequently apply, pursuant to section 61.13(1)(d)3, Florida Statutes, to require payments through either the State Disbursement Unit or the central depository.

2. **Income Deduction.**

a. _____**Immediate.** Obligor shall pay through income deduction, pursuant to a separate Income Deduction Order which shall be effective immediately. Obligor is individually responsible for paying this support obligation until all of said support is deducted from Obligor's income. Until support payments are deducted from Obligor's paycheck, Obligor is responsible for making timely payments directly to the State Disbursement Unit or the Obligee, as previously set forth in this order.

b._____**Deferred.** Income Deduction is ordered this day, but it shall not be effective until a delinquency of $______________, or, if not specified, an amount equal to one month's obligation occurs. Income deduction is not being implemented immediately based on the following findings:
There are no minor child(ren) common to the parties,

AND

There is proof of timely payment of a previously ordered obligation without an income deduction order in cases of modification,

AND

_____ There is an agreement by the Obligor to advise the Title IV-D agency, clerk of court, and Obligee of any change in Payor and/or health insurance
OR

_____ there is a signed written agreement providing an alternative arrangement between the Obligor and the Obligee and, at the option of the IV-D agency, by the IV-D agency in IV-D cases in which there is an assignment of support rights to the state, reviewed and entered in the record by the court.

3. **Bonus/One-Time Payments.** _____ All ______% _____ No income paid in the form of a bonus or other similar one-time payment, up to the amount of any arrearage or the remaining balance thereof owed pursuant to this order, shall be forwarded to the Obligee pursuant to the payment method prescribed above.

4. **Other provisions relating to method of payment:** ____
____
____.

SECTION III. ATTORNEY'S FEES, COSTS, AND SUIT MONEY

1. _____ Husband's _____ Wife's request(s) for attorney's fees, costs, and suit money is (are) denied because____
____.

2. The Court finds there is a need for and an ability to pay attorney's fees, costs, and suit

money. _____Husband _____Wife is hereby ordered to pay to the other party $__________ in attorney's fees, and $___________ in costs. The Court further finds that the attorney's fees awarded are based on the reasonable rate of $________ per hour and _______ reasonable hours. Other provisions relating to attorney's fees, costs, and suit money are as follows: ____.

SECTION IV. OTHER PROVISIONS

1. **Other Provisions.** ____.

2. The Court reserves jurisdiction to modify and enforce this Final Judgment.

DONE AND ORDERED on ________________________ in ____________________, Florida.

____
CIRCUIT JUDGE

I certify that a copy of the *{name of document(s)}* ______________________________ was ( ) mailed ( ) faxed and mailed ( ) e-mailed ( ) hand-delivered to the parties and any entities listed below on *{date}*____________________.

by______________________________
{Clerk of court or designee}

______Husband (or his attorney)
______Wife (or her attorney)

Florida Supreme Court Approved Family Law Form 12.994(b), Final Judgment for Support Unconnected with Dissolution of Marriage with No Dependent or Minor Child(ren) (03/15)

______Central Depository
______State Disbursement Unit
______Other: ____________________

Florida Supreme Court Approved Family Law Form 12.994(b), Final Judgment for Support Unconnected with Dissolution of Marriage with No Dependent or Minor Child(ren) (03/15)

Added July 7, 1995, effective Jan. 1, 1996 (663 So.2d 1047). Amended Feb. 26, 1998, effective Mar. 16, 1998 (713 So.2d 1); July 1, 1999 (717 So.2d 914); Sept. 21, 2000 (810 So.2d 1); May 24, 2012 (96 So.3d 217); July 3, 2013 (117 So.3d 958); March 26, 2015, effective March 26, 2015 (2015 WL 1343088).

Form 12.995(a). Parenting Plan

IN THE CIRCUIT COURT OF THE ____________________ JUDICIAL CIRCUIT
IN AND FOR ________________ COUNTY, FLORIDA

Case No: ________________

Division: ________________

____
Mother

and

____
Father

PARENTING PLAN

This parenting plan is: *{Choose only **one**}*

_____A Parenting Plan submitted to the court with the agreement of the parties.
_____A proposed Parenting Plan submitted by or on behalf of:
*{Parent's Name}*____.
_____A Parenting Plan established by the court.

This parenting plan is: *{Choose only **one**}*

_____A final Parenting Plan established by the court.
_____A temporary Parenting Plan established by the court.
_____A modification of a prior final Parenting Plan or prior final order.

I. PARENTS

Mother

Name:____
Address: ____
Telephone Number: ____________________________________
E-Mail: ____
_____ Address Unknown: *{Please indicate here if mother's address is unknown}*
_____ Address Confidential: *{Please indicate here if mother's address and phone numbers are confidential pursuant to either a _____ Final Judgment for Protection Against Domestic Violence, or _____ other court order ______________________________}.*

Father

Name:____
Address: ____
Telephone Number: ____________________________________
E-Mail: ____

_____ Address Unknown: *{Please indicate here if father's address is unknown}*

_____ Address Confidential: *{Please indicate here if father's address and phone numbers are confidential pursuant to either a _____ Final Judgment for Protection Against Domestic Violence or _____ other court order____.}*

II. CHILDREN: This parenting plan is for the following child(ren) born to, or adopted by the parties: *(add additional lines as needed)*

Name	Date of Birth

III. JURISDICTION

The United States is the country of habitual residence of the child(ren).

The State of Florida is the child(ren)'s home state for the purposes of the Uniform Child Custody Jurisdiction and Enforcement Act.

This Parenting Plan is a child custody determination for the purposes of the Uniform Child Custody Jurisdiction and Enforcement Act, the International Child Abduction Remedies Act, 42 U.S.C. Sections 11601 et seq., the Parental Kidnapping Prevention Act, and the Convention on the Civil Aspects of International Child Abduction enacted at the Hague on October 25, 1980, and for all other state and federal laws.

Other: ____.

IV. PARENTAL RESPONSIBILITY AND DECISION MAKING

4. **Parental Responsibility *{Choose only one}***

_____ **Shared Parental Responsibility.**
It is in the best interests of the child(ren) that the parents confer and **jointly** make all major decisions affecting the welfare of the child(ren). Major decisions include, but are not limited to, decisions about the child(ren)'s education, healthcare, and other responsibilities unique to this family.

OR

_____ **Shared Parental Responsibility with Decision Making Authority**

It is in the best interests of the child(ren) that the parents confer and attempt to agree on the major decisions involving the child(ren). If the parents are unable to agree, the authority for making major decisions regarding the child(ren) shall be as follows:

Education/Academic decisions _____ Mother _____ Father
Non-emergency health care _____ Mother _____ Father
Other: *{Specify}*____________ _____ Mother _____ Father
____________________ _____ Mother _____ Father
____________________ _____ Mother _____ Father

OR

_____ **Sole Parental Responsibility:**
It is in the best interests of the child(ren) that the ____ Mother ____ Father shall have sole authority to make major decisions for the child(ren.) It is detrimental to the child(ren) to have shared parental responsibility.

5. **Day-to-Day Decisions**
Unless otherwise specified in this plan, each parent shall make decisions regarding day-to-day care and control of each child while the child is with that parent. Regardless of the allocation of decision making in the parenting plan, either parent may make emergency decisions affecting the health or safety of the child(ren) when the child is residing with that parent. A parent who makes an emergency decision shall share the decision with the other parent as soon as reasonably possible.

6. **Extra-curricular Activities** *{Indicate all that apply}*

a._____ Either parent may register the child(ren) and allow them to participate in the activity of the child(ren)'s choice.

b._____ The parents must mutually agree to all extra-curricular activities.

c._____ and/or The parent with the minor child(ren) shall transport the minor child(ren) to from all mutually agreed upon extra-curricular activities, providing all necessary uniforms and equipment within the parent's possession.

d._____ The costs of the extra-curricular activities shall be paid by:
Mother _____% Father ________%

e._____ The uniforms and equipment required for the extra-curricular activities shall be paid by: Mother _______% Father _______%

f.____ Other:
{Specify}____
____.

V. **INFORMATION SHARING**. Unless otherwise indicated or ordered by the Court:

Unless otherwise prohibited by law, each parent shall have access to medical and school records and information pertaining to the child(ren) and shall be permitted to independently consult with any and all professionals involved with the child(ren). The parents shall cooperate with each other in sharing information related to the health, education, and welfare of the child(ren) and they shall sign any necessary documentation ensuring that both parents have access to said records.

Each parent shall be responsible for obtaining records and reports directly from the school and health care providers.

Both parents have equal rights to inspect and receive governmental agency and law enforcement records concerning the child(ren).

Both parents shall have equal and independent authority to confer with the child(ren)'s school, day care, health care providers, and other programs with regard to the child(ren)'s educational, emotional, and social progress.

Both parents shall be listed as "emergency contacts" for the child(ren).

Each parent has a continuing responsibility to provide a residential, mailing, and contact address and contact telephone number to the other parent. Each parent shall notify the other parent in writing within 24 hours of any changes. Each parent shall notify the court in writing within seven (7) days of any changes.

Other: ____
____.

VI. **SCHEDULING**

1. **School Calendar**
If necessary, on or before ______________ of each year, both parents should obtain a copy of the school calendar for the next school year. The parents shall discuss the calendars and the time-sharing schedule so that any differences or questions can be resolved.

The parents shall follow the school calendar of: *{Indicate all that apply}*
a._____the oldest child
b._____the youngest child
c._____ __________________ County
d._____ __________________ School

2. **Academic Break Definition**
When defining academic break periods, the period shall begin at the end of the last scheduled day of classes before the holiday or break and shall end on the first day of regularly scheduled classes after the holiday or break.

3. **Schedule Changes** *{Indicate all that apply}*

a._____A parent making a request for a schedule change will make the request as soon as possible, but in any event, except in cases of emergency, no less than ____________________before the change is to occur.

b._____A parent requesting a change of schedule shall be responsible for any additional child care, or transportation costs caused by the change.

c._____Other *{Specify}*____.

VII. TIME-SHARING SCHEDULE

1. **Weekday and Weekend Schedule**
The following schedule shall apply beginning on ______________________ with the _____ Mother _____ Father and continue as follows:

The child(ren) shall spend time with the **Mother** on the following dates and times:
WEEKENDS: _____ Every _____ Every Other _____ Other *{specify}* ______________
From________________________________ to ________________________________
WEEKDAYS: *{Specify days}* ____
From ___________________________________ to ________________________________
OTHER: *{Specify}* ____
____
____.

The child(ren) shall spend time with the **Father** on the following dates and times:
WEEKENDS: _____ Every _____ Every Other _____ Other *{specify}* ______________
From________________________________ to ________________________________
WEEKDAYS: *{Specify days}* ____

From ______________________________ to ________________
OTHER: *{Specify}* ____________________________________
____
____.

Please indicate if there is a different time sharing schedule for any child. Complete a separate Attachment for each child for whom there is a different time sharing schedule.

_____ There is a different time-sharing schedule for the following child(ren) in Attachment _______.

_______________________, and _______________________.
(Name of Child) (Name of Child)

2. **Holiday Schedule** *{Choose only one}*

a. _____No holiday time sharing shall apply. The regular time-sharing schedule set forth above shall apply.

b. _____Holiday time-sharing shall be as the parties agree.

c. _____Holiday time-sharing shall be in accordance with the following schedule. The Holiday schedule will take priority over the regular weekday, weekend, and summer schedules. Fill in the blanks with Mother or Father to indicate where the child(ren) will be for the holidays. Provide the beginning and ending times. If a holiday is not specified as even, odd, or every year with one parent, then the child(ren) will remain with the parent in accordance with the regular schedule

Holidays	Even Years	Odd Years	Every Year	Begin/End Time
Mother's Day	______	______	______	______
Father's Day	______	______	______	______
President's Day	______	______	______	______
M. L. King Day	______	______	______	______
Easter	______	______	______	______
Passover	______	______	______	______
Memorial Day Wkd	______	______	______	______
4th of July	______	______	______	______
Labor Day Wkd	______	______	______	______
Columbus Day Wkd	______	______	______	______
Halloween	______	______	______	______
Thanksgiving	______	______	______	______
Veteran's Day	______	______	______	______
Hanukkah	______	______	______	______
Yom Kippur	______	______	______	______

Rosh Hashanah __________ __________ __________ __________
Child(ren)'s
Birthdays: __________ __________ __________ __________

__________ __________ __________ __________ __________

__________ __________ __________ __________ __________

This holiday schedule may affect the regular Time-Sharing Schedule. Parents may wish to specify either or both of the following options:

d._____When the parents are using an alternating weekend plan and the holiday schedule would result in one parent having the child(ren) for three weekends in a row, the parents will exchange the following weekend, so that each has two weekends in a row before the regular alternating weekend pattern resumes.

e._____If a parent has the child(ren) on a weekend immediately before or after an unspecified holiday or non-school day, they shall have the child(ren) for the holiday or non-school day.

3. **Winter Break** *{Choose only **one**}*

a. _____The _____ Mother _____ Father shall have the child(ren) from the day and time school is dismissed until December __________ at ______ a.m./p. m in ____odd-numbered years _____ even-numbered years ____ every year. The other parent will have the children for the second portion of the Winter Break. The parties shall alternate the arrangement each year.

b.______The _____ Mother _____ Father shall have the child(ren) for the **entire** Winter Break during _____ odd-numbered years _____ even-numbered years _____ every year.

c._____Other: ____
____
____.

d. _____**Specific Winter Holidays**
If not addressed above, the specific Winter Holidays such as Christmas, New Year's Eve, Hanukkah, Kwanzaa, etc. shall be shared as follows:
____
____
____
____.

7. **Spring Break** *{Choose only **one**}*

a.______The parents shall follow the regular schedule.

b.____The parents shall alternate the entire Spring Break with the Mother having the child(ren) during the _____odd-numbered years _____even numbered years.

c._____The _____ Father _____ Mother shall have the child(ren) for the entire Spring Break every year.

d._____The Spring Break will be evenly divided. The first half of the Spring Break will go to the parent whose regularly scheduled weekend falls on the first half and the second half going to the parent whose weekend falls during the second half.

e._____Other: *{Specify}*____.

8. **Summer Break** *{Choose only **one**}*

a.____The parents shall follow the regular schedule through the summer.

b._____The _____ Mother _____ Father shall have the entire Summer Break from __________after school is out until _______________ before school starts.

c.____The parents shall equally divide the Summer Break as follows: During _____ odd-numbered years_____ even numbered years, the_____ Mother _____ Father shall have the children from __________after school is out until ______________. The other parent shall have the child(ren) for the second one-half of the Summer Break. The parents shall alternate the first and second one-halves each year unless otherwise agreed. During the extended periods of time-sharing, the other parent shall have the child(ren) ____.

d._____Other: *{Specify}*____ ____.

6. **Number of Overnights:**

Based upon the time-sharing schedule, the Mother has a total of _____ overnights per year and the Father has a total of _____overnights per year.
Note: The two numbers must equal 365.

7. _____**If not set forth above,** the parties shall have time-sharing in accordance with the schedule which is attached and incorporated herein.

VIII. TRANSPORTATION AND EXCHANGE OF CHILD(REN)

6. **Transportation** *{Choose only **one**}*

a.____The_____ Mother _____Father shall provide all transportation.

Florida Supreme Court Approved Family Law Form 12.995(a), Parenting Plan (03/15)

b. _____The parent beginning their time-sharing shall provide transportation for the child(ren).

c._____The parent ending their time-sharing shall provide transportation for the child(ren).

d._____Other: *{Specify}*____.

2. **Exchange**

Both parents shall have the child(ren) ready on time with sufficient clothing packed and ready at the agreed upon time of exchange. If a parent is more than ______ minutes late without contacting the other parent to make other arrangements, the parent with the child(ren) may proceed with other plans and activities. *{Choose only one}*:

a._____Exchanges shall be at Mother's and Father's homes unless both parents agree to a different meeting place.

b._____Exchanges shall occur at ____ unless both parties agree in advance to a different meeting place.

c._____Other: ____.

3. **Transportation Costs** *{Choose only one}*

a._____Transportation costs are included in the Child Support Worksheets and/or the Order for Child Support and should not be included here.

b._____The Mother shall pay ______% and the Father shall pay ______ % of the transportation costs.

c._____Other: ____.

4. **Foreign and Out-Of-State Travel** *{Indicate all that apply}*

a._____Either parent may travel within the United States with the child(ren) during his/her time-sharing. The parent traveling with the child(ren) shall give the other parent at least ____ days written notice before traveling out of state unless there is an emergency, and shall provide the other parent with a detailed itinerary, including locations and telephone numbers where the child(ren) and parent can be reached at least ____ days before traveling.

b._____Either parent may travel out of the country with the child(ren) during his/her time-sharing. At least ___ days prior to traveling, the parent shall provide a detailed itinerary, including locations, and telephone numbers where the child(ren) and parent may be reached during the trip. Each parent agrees to provide whatever documentation is necessary for the other parent to take the child(ren) out of the country.

c._____If a parent wishes to travel out of the country with the child(ren), he/she shall provide the following security for the return of the child

____

____.

d._____Other ____.

IX. EDUCATION

1. **School designation.**
For purposes of school boundary determination and registration, the_____ Mother's _____ Father's address shall be designated.

2. _____ *{If Applicable}* The following provisions are made regarding private or home schooling: ____
____
____.

3. **Other.** ____
____
____.

X. DESIGNATION FOR OTHER LEGAL PURPOSES

The child(ren) named in this Parenting Plan are scheduled to reside the majority of the time with the _____ Mother _____ Father. This majority designation is **SOLELY** for purposes of all other state and federal laws which require such a designation. **This designation does not affect either parent's rights and responsibilities under this Parenting Plan.**

XI. COMMUNICATION

1. **Between Parents**

All communications regarding the child(ren) shall be between the parents. The parents shall not use the child(ren) as messengers to convey information, ask questions, or set up schedule changes.

The parents shall communicate with each other: *{Indicate all that apply}*

_____in person
_____by telephone
_____by letter
_____by e-mail
_____Other: *{Specify}*_________________________.

2. **Between Parent and Child(ren)**

Both parents shall keep contact information current. Telephone or other electronic communication between the child(ren) and the other parent shall not be monitored by or interrupted by the other parent. "Electronic communication" includes telephones, electronic mail or e-mail, webcams, video-conferencing equipment and software or other wired or wireless technologies or other means of communication to supplement face to face contact.

The child(ren) may have _____ telephone _____ e-mail _____ other electronic communication in the form of _____________________ with the other parent: *{Choose only* ***one****}*

a._____Anytime
b._____Every day during the hours of _____________ to ____________________.
c._____On the following days____
during the hours of _________________________ to ___________________.
d._____Other: ____.

3. Costs of Electronic Communication shall be addressed as follows:
____
____
____.

XII. CHILD CARE *{Choose only* ***one****}*

a._____Each parent may select appropriate child care providers
b._____All child care providers must be agreed upon by both parents.
c._____Each parent must offer the other parent the opportunity to care for the child(ren) before using a child care provider for any period exceeding_______ hours.
d._____Other: *{Specify}*____.

XIII. CHANGES OR MODIFICATIONS OF THE PARENTING PLAN

Temporary changes to this Parenting Plan may be made informally without a written document; however, if the parties dispute the change, the Parenting Plan shall remain in effect until further order of the court.

Any substantial changes to the Parenting Plan must be sought through the filing of a supplemental petition for modification.

XIV. RELOCATION

Any relocation of the child(ren) is subject to and must be sought in compliance with section 61.13001, Florida Statutes.

XV. DISPUTES OR CONFLICT RESOLUTION

Parents shall attempt to cooperatively resolve any disputes which may arise over the terms of the Parenting Plan. The parents may wish to use mediation or other dispute resolution methods and assistance, such as Parenting Coordinators and Parenting Counselors, before filing a court action.

XVI. OTHER PROVISIONS

____
____
____
____
____
____
____.

SIGNATURE OF PARENTS

I certify that I have been open and honest in entering into this Parenting Plan. I am satisfied with this Plan and intend to be bound by it.

Dated: ________________________

____
Signature of Mother
Printed Name: ________________________
Address: ____________________________
City, State, Zip: _______________________
Telephone Number: _____________________
Fax Number: ____________________________

Designated E-mail Address(es):____________
____

STATE OF FLORIDA
COUNTY OF ____________

Sworn to or affirmed and signed before me on ____________ by ____________.

____
NOTARY PUBLIC or DEPUTY CLERK

____
{Print, type, or stamp commissioned name of notary or clerk.}

_____ Personally known
_____ Produced identification
Type of identification produced ____________

I certify that I have been open and honest in entering into this Parenting Plan. I am satisfied with this Plan and intend to be bound by it.

Dated:____________

____
Signature of Father
Printed Name: ____________
Address: ____________
City, State, Zip: ____________
Telephone Number: ____________
Fax Number: ____________
Designated E-mail Address(es):____________
____

STATE OF FLORIDA
COUNTY OF ____________

Sworn to or affirmed and signed before me on ____________ by ____________.

____
NOTARY PUBLIC or DEPUTY CLERK

____

Florida Supreme Court Approved Family Law Form 12.995(a), Parenting Plan (03/15)

{Print, type, or stamp commissioned name of notary or clerk.}

_____Personally known
______Produced identification
Type of identification produced ______________________________

IF A NONLAWYER HELPED YOU FILL OUT THIS FORM, HE/SHE MUST FILL IN THE BLANKS BELOW:
[fill in all blanks] This form was prepared for the: *{choose only one}* ( ) Mother ( ) Father
This form was completed with the assistance of:
{name of individual} ____,
{name of business} ____,
{address} ____,
{city} __________,*{state}* ______, *{zip code}* ________, *{telephone number}* __________.

Florida Supreme Court Approved Family Law Form 12.995(a), Parenting Plan (03/15)

INSTRUCTIONS FOR FLORIDA SUPREME COURT APPROVED FAMILY LAW FORM 12.995(a) PARENTING PLAN (03/15)

When should this form be used?

A **Parenting Plan** is required in all cases involving **time–sharing** with minor child(ren), even when time-sharing is not in dispute. The Parenting Plan must be developed and agreed to by the parents and approved by the court. If the parties cannot agree to a Parenting Plan or if the parents agreed to a plan that is not approved by the court, a Parenting Plan will be established by the court with or without the use of parenting plan recommendations. This form or a similar form should be used in the development of a Parenting Plan. If the case involves **supervised time–sharing**, the **Supervised/Safety Focused Parenting Plan**, Florida Supreme Court Approved Family Law Form 12.995(b) or a similar form should be used. If the case involves relocation, pursuant to Section 61.13001, Florida Statutes, then a **Relocation/Long Distance Parenting Plan,** Florida Supreme Court Approved Family Law Form 12.995(c) or a similar form should be used.

This form should be typed or printed in black ink. Please either delete or strike-through terms or paragraphs that are inappropriate or inapplicable to your agreement. If an agreement has been reached, **both** parties must sign the Parenting Plan and have their signatures witnessed by a **notary public** or **deputy clerk**. After completing this form, you should **file** the original with the **clerk of the circuit court** in the county where the **petition** was filed and keep a copy for your records. You should then refer to the instructions for your petition, **answer**, or answer and **counterpetition** concerning the procedures for setting a hearing or **trial** (**final hearing**). If the parents have not reached an agreement, a proposed Parenting Plan may be filed by either parent at the time of or any time prior to the final hearing. If an agreed Parenting Plan is not filed by the parties, the court shall establish a Plan.

IMPORTANT INFORMATION REGARDING E–FILING

The Florida Rules of Judicial Administration now require that all petitions, pleadings, and documents be filed electronically except in certain circumstances. **Self–represented litigants may file petitions or other pleadings or documents electronically; however, they are not required to do so.** If you choose to file your pleadings or other documents electronically, you must do so in accordance with Florida Rule of Judicial Administration 2.525, and you must follow the procedures of the judicial circuit in which you file. **The rules and procedures should be carefully read and followed.**

IMPORTANT INFORMATION REGARDING E–SERVICE ELECTION

After the initial service of process of the petition or supplemental petition by the Sheriff or certified process server, the Florida Rules of Judicial Administration now require that all documents required or permitted to be served on the other party must be served by electronic mail (e–mail) except in certain circumstances. **You must strictly comply with the format requirements set forth in the Rules of Judicial Administration.**

SELF–REPRESENTED LITIGANTS MAY SERVE DOCUMENTS BY E–MAIL; HOWEVER, THEY ARE NOT REQUIRED TO DO SO. If a self-represented litigant elects to serve and receive documents by e-mail, the procedures must always be followed once the initial election is made.

To serve and receive documents by e-mail, you must designate your e-mail addresses by using the **Designation of Current Mailing and E–mail Address**, Florida Supreme Court Approved Family Law Form 12.915, and you must provide your e-mail address on each form on which your signature appears. Please **CAREFULLY** read the rules and instructions for: **Certificate of Service (General),** Florida Supreme Court Approved Family Law Form 12.914; **Designation of Current Mailing and E–mail Address**, Florida Supreme Court Approved Family Law Form 12.915; and Florida Rule of Judicial Administration 2.516.

Where can I look for more information?

Before proceeding, you should read "General Information for Self–Represented Litigants" found at the beginning of these forms. The words that are in "**bold underline**" in these instructions are defined there. For further information, see chapter 61, Florida Statutes, and the instructions for the petition and/or answer that were filed in this case.

Special notes . . .

At a minimum, the **Parenting Plan** must describe in adequate detail:

- How the parties will share and be responsible for the daily tasks associated with the upbringing of the child(ren),
- The **time–sharing schedule** arrangements that specify the time that the minor child(ren) will spend with each parent,
- A designation of who will be responsible for any and all forms of health care, school-related matters, including the address to be used for school-boundary determination and registration, other activities, and
- The methods and technologies that the parents will use to communicate with the child(ren).

The best interests of the child(ren) is the primary consideration in the Parenting Plan. In creating the Parenting Plan, all circumstances between the parents, including their historic relationship, domestic violence, and other factors must be taken into consideration. Determination of the best interests of the child(ren) shall be made by evaluating all of the factors affecting the welfare and interest of the particular minor child(ren) and the circumstances of that family, as listed in section 61.13(3), Florida Statutes, including, but not limited to:

- The demonstrated capacity and disposition of each parent to facilitate and encourage a close and continuing parent-child relationship, to honor the time-sharing schedule, and to be reasonable when changes are required;
- The anticipated division of parental responsibilities after the litigation, including the extent to which parental responsibilities will be delegated to third parties;
- The demonstrated capacity and disposition of each parent to determine, consider, and act upon the needs of the child(ren) as opposed to the needs or desires of the parent;
- The length of time the child(ren) has lived in a stable, satisfactory environment and the desirability of maintaining continuity;
- The geographic viability of the parenting plan, with special attention paid to the needs of school-age children and the amount of time to be spent traveling to effectuate the parenting plan. This factor does not create a presumption for or against relocation of either parent with a child(ren);
- The moral fitness of the parents;
- The mental and physical health of the parents;
- The home, school, and community record of the child(ren);
- The reasonable preference of the child(ren), if the court deems the child(ren) to be of sufficient intelligence, understanding, and experience to express a preference;
- The demonstrated knowledge, capacity, and disposition of each parent to be informed of the circumstances of the minor child(ren), including, but not limited to, the child(ren)'s friends, teachers, medical care providers, daily activities, and favorite things;
- The demonstrated capacity and disposition of each parent to provide a consistent routine for the child(ren), such as discipline, and daily schedules for homework, meals, and bedtime;
- The demonstrated capacity of each parent to communicate with and keep the other parent informed of issues and activities regarding the minor child(ren), and the willingness of each parent to adopt a unified front on all major issues when dealing with the child(ren);
- Evidence of domestic violence, sexual violence, child abuse, child abandonment, or child neglect, regardless of whether a prior or pending action relating to those issues has been brought. If the court accepts evidence of prior or pending actions regarding domestic violence, sexual violence, child abuse, child abandonment, or child neglect, the court must specifically acknowledge in writing that such evidence was considered when evaluating the best interests of the child(ren);
- Evidence that either parent has knowingly provided false information to the court regarding any prior or pending action regarding domestic violence, sexual violence, child abuse, child abandonment, or child neglect;

- The particular parenting tasks customarily performed by each parent and the division or parental responsibilities before the institution of litigation and during the pending litigation, including the extent to which parenting responsibilities were undertaken by third parties;

- The demonstrated capacity and disposition of each parent to participate and be involved in the child(ren)'s school and extracurricular activities;

- The demonstrated capacity and disposition of each parent to maintain an environment for the child(ren) which is free from substance abuse;

- The capacity and disposition of each parent to protect the child(ren) from the ongoing litigation as demonstrated by not discussing the litigation with the child(ren), not sharing documents or electronic media related to the litigation with the child(ren), and refraining from disparaging comments about the other parent to the child)ren); and

- The developmental stages and needs of the child(ren) and the demonstrated capacity and disposition of each parent to meet the child(ren)'s developmental needs.

This standard form does not include every possible issue that may be relevant to the facts of your case. The Parenting Plan should be as detailed as possible to address the time-sharing schedule. Additional provisions should be added to address all of the relevant factors. The parties should give special consideration to the age and needs of each child.

In developing the Parenting Plan, you may wish to consult or review other materials which are available at your local library, law library or through national and state family organizations.

Remember, a person who is NOT an attorney is called a nonlawyer. If a nonlawyer helps you fill out these forms, that person must give you a copy of a **Disclosure from Nonlawyer**, Florida Family Law Rules of Procedure Form 12.900 (a), before he or she helps you. A nonlawyer helping you fill out these forms also **must** put his or her name, address, and telephone number on the bottom of the last page of every form he or she helps you complete.

Added March 26, 2009 (20 So.3d 173). Amended Dec. 16, 2010 (59 So.3d 792); Nov. 3, 2011, effective, *nunc pro tunc*, Oct. 1, 2011 (78 So.3d 1045); March 26, 2015, effective March 26, 2015 (2015 WL 1343088).

Form 12.995(b). Supervised/Safety-Focused Parenting Plan

IN THE CIRCUIT COURT OF THE ____________________ JUDICIAL CIRCUIT
IN AND FOR ________________ COUNTY, FLORIDA

Case No: ____________________
Division: ____________________

______________________________,
Mother,

and

______________________________,
Father.

SUPERVISED/SAFETY-FOCUSED PARENTING PLAN

This parenting plan is: *{Choose only one}*

____ A Parenting Plan submitted to the court with the agreement of the parties.

____ A proposed Parenting Plan submitted by or on behalf of: *{Parent's Name}*__________.

____ A Parenting Plan established by the court.

This parenting plan is: *{Choose only one}*

____ A final Parenting Plan established by the court.

____ A temporary Parenting Plan established by the court.

____ A modification of a prior final Parenting Plan or prior final order.

I. PARENTS

Mother

Name:____

Address:______________________________________

Telephone Number:_____________________________

E-Mail:_______________________________________

____ Address Unknown: *{Please indicate if mother's address is unknown}*

____ Address Confidential: *{Please indicate if mother's address and phone numbers are confidential pursuant to either a ____ Final Judgment for Protection Against Domestic Violence or other court order ______________________________.}*

Father

Name:____

Address:______________________________________

Telephone Number: _____________________________

E-Mail: _______________________________________

____ Address Unknown: *{Please indicate if father's address is unknown}*

____ Address Confidential: *{Please indicate if father's address and telephone numbers are* *confidential pursuant to either a _____ Final Judgment for Protection Against Domestic Violence or _____ other court order ____.)*

II. CHILDREN: This parenting plan is for the following child(ren) born to, or adopted by the parties: *(add additional lines as needed)*

Name Date of Birth

____

____

____

____

III. JURISDICTION

The United States is the country of habitual residence of the child(ren).

The State of Florida is the child(ren)'s home state for the purposes of the Uniform Child Custody Jurisdiction and Enforcement Act.

This Parenting Plan is a child custody determination for the purposes of the Uniform Child Custody Jurisdiction and Enforcement Act, the International Child Abduction Remedies Act, 42 U.S.C. Section 11601 et seq., the Parental Kidnapping Prevention Act, and the Convention on the Civil Aspects of International Child Abduction enacted at the Hague on October 25, 1980, and for other state and federal laws.

Other: ____.

IV. PARENTAL RESPONSIBILITY *{Choose only one}*

_____ **Sole** Parental Responsibility
It is in the best interests of the child(ren) that the_____ Mother _____ Father shall have **sole** authority to make major decisions for the child(ren.) It is detrimental to the child(ren) for the parents to have shared parental responsibility.

_____ **Shared** Parental Responsibility with Decision Making Authority
It is in the best interests of the child(ren) that the parents confer and attempt to agree on the major decisions involving the child(ren). If the parents are unable to agree, the authority for making major decisions regarding the child(ren) shall be as follows:

Education/Academic decisions	_____ Mother	_____ Father
Non-emergency health care	_____ Mother	_____ Father
____________________________	_____ Mother	_____ Father
____________________________	_____ Mother	_____ Father

______________________ ____ Mother ____ Father

_____**Other**: *(Explain)* ____.

V. TIME SHARING SCHEDULE *{Choose only one}*

____ **No Time-Sharing:** The _____ Mother _____Father shall have no contact with the child(ren) until further order of the court. All parenting decisions shall be made by the other parent.

1. _____ **Supervised Time-Sharing:** Whenever the child(ren) are with the _____ Mother _____ Father, the supervisor shall be present. The _____ Mother _____ Father has the right to spend time with the child(ren) even though the other parent will be making most, if not all, of the parenting decisions which are made on the child(ren)'s behalf. The time-sharing schedule shall be mutually agreed to between the parents, but not less than the schedule set forth below: *{Choose only one}*

   _____ hours per week. The place(s), and time(s) shall be set by the _____ Mother _____Father.

   _____ From ____ __m. to ____ __ m., on the following day(s) ____________________ ____.

2. _____ **Restricted Time-Sharing:** The _____ Mother _____ Father shall have time-sharing with the following restrictions. *{The restrictions should be described in detail such as time-sharing only in public places, no overnight visits, etc.}* The time-sharing schedule shall be mutually agreed upon between the parents, but not less than the schedule set forth below:______________________________________ ____ ____ ____.

3. _____ hours per week. The place(s), and time(s) shall be set by the _____Mother _____ Father.

4. ______Other: ____.

VI. SUPERVISOR AND SUPERVISION *{Choose only one}*

1. **Supervisor.** The person supervising the time-sharing shall: *{Choose only one}*
   _____ Be selected by the _____ Mother _____ Father.

_____ Be selected by the _____ Mother _____ Father, subject to the other parent's approval.

_____ Other: ____.

2. **Restrictions or Level of Supervision:** ______________________________
____
____.

3. **Costs of Supervision**

_____The costs of the supervision shall be paid by the _____ Mother _____ Father

_____Other: ____.

VII. LOCATION: *{Choose only one}*

The _____ Mother _____ Father shall spend his/her time-sharing with the child(ren) at the following location(s):

1. _____Supervised visitation center (*name and address of facility)* ____________________
____.

2. _____ ____________________________________ (*location*) or other location designated by the _____ Mother _____ Father

3. _____Any location designated by the _____ Mother _____ Father with the approval of the supervisor.

4. _____Other: ____.

VIII. DESIGNATION FOR OTHER LEGAL PURPOSES

1. The child(ren) named in this Safety-Focused Parenting Plan are scheduled to reside the majority of the time with the _____ Mother _____Father. This majority designation is **SOLELY** for purposes of all other state and federal statutes which require such a designation. **This designation does not affect either parent's rights and responsibilities under this parenting plan.**

2. For purposes of school boundary determination and registration, the _____ Mother's _____ Father's address shall be designated.

IX. TRANSPORTATION AND EXCHANGE OF CHILD(REN)

1. **Transportation**

The child(ren) shall not be driven in a car unless the driver has a valid driver's license, automobile insurance, seat belts, and child safety seats as required by Florida law.

The _____ Mother _____ Father or mutually agreed upon person shall be responsible for transporting the child(ren) to the exchange point. The child(ren) shall be picked up and/or returned to the exchange point by *{Choose only one}*

_____ The _____ Mother _____ Father with the supervisor present.

_____ The supervisor alone.

____ Other: ____.

2. **Exchange**

The exchange of the child(ren) shall occur at: *{Indicate all that apply}*

a._____ The site of the supervised visit.

b._____ A monitored exchange location *{specify name and address of facility}*________ ____.

c._____ Other: ____.

d._____ The _____ Mother _____ Father is prohibited from coming to the exchange point.

X. COMMUNICATION

1. **Between Parents**

All communications regarding the child(ren) shall be between the parents. The parents shall not use the child(ren) as messengers to convey information, ask questions, or set up schedule changes.

_____The parents shall communicate with each other: *{Indicate all that apply}*
_____in person
_____by telephone
_____by letter
_____by e-mail
_____Other: *{Specify}* ______________________________________.

_____ **No Communication**. Unless otherwise prohibited by court order, all information and communication regarding the child(ren) shall be exchanged via or through ____.

2. **Between Parent and Child(ren)**

The_____ Mother _____ Father *{Indicate all that apply}*

a._____Shall not telephone, write, or e-mail the child(ren) unless the contact is agreed to in advance by the other parent.

b._____May write or e-mail the child(ren) at any time. Each parent shall provide a contact address (and e-mail address if appropriate) to the other parent, unless other prohibited by court order.

c._____May call the child(ren) on the telephone _____ times per week. The call shall last no more than _____ minutes and shall take place between _____m. and _____ __ m. Each parent shall provide a telephone number to the other parent, unless otherwise prohibited by court order or law.

d._____ Long distance telephone calls made by the child(ren) to a parent shall be paid by ______________________. Each parent shall provide a telephone number to the other parent, unless otherwise prohibited by court order or law.

e._____Other: ____.

3. **Costs of Electronic Communication**

"Electronic communication" includes telephones, electronic mail or e-mail, webcams, video-conferencing equipment and software or other wired or wireless technologies or other means of communication to supplement face-to face contact.

The costs of electronic communication shall be addressed as follows:
____
____
____.

XI. ACCESS TO ACTIVITIES AND EVENTS

The _____ Mother _____ Father *{Choose only one}*

1._____Shall not attend the child(ren)'s activities and events, including but not limited to, school, athletic, and extra-curricular activities and events.

2._____May attend the child(ren)'s school, athletic, and extra-curricular activities and events.

3._____The _____ Mother _____ Father must stay _____ feet from the other parent and _____ feet from the child.

4._____ Other ____.

XII. CHILD(REN)'S SAFETY

The _____ Mother _____ Father shall follow the safety rules checked below.
(Indicate all that apply)

1._____There shall be no firearms in the home, car, or in the child(ren)'s presence during time-sharing.

2. _____No alcoholic beverages shall be consumed from twenty-four (24) hours before the child(ren) arrive until they are returned to the other parent.

3._____The child(ren) shall not be disciplined by corporal punishment.

4._____The following person(s) present a danger to the child(ren) and shall not be present during time-sharing: ____.

5._____Other: ____.

XIII. CHANGES OR MODIFICATIONS OF THE PARENTING PLAN

All changes to the Safety-Focused Parenting Plan must be pursuant to a court order.

XIV. OTHER PROVISIONS

____.

SIGNATURES OF PARENTS

I certify that I have been open and honest in entering into this Parenting Plan. I am satisfied with this Plan and intend to be bound by it.

Dated: ____________________ ______________________________

Signature of Mother
Printed Name: ______________________________
Address: ______________________________
City, State, Zip: ______________________________
Telephone Number: ______________________________
Fax Number: ______________________________
Designated E-mail Address(es): ______________________________

STATE OF FLORIDA
COUNTY OF ______________________________

Sworn to or affirmed and signed before me on ____________ by ______________________________.

____
NOTARY PUBLIC or DEPUTY CLERK

____
{Print, type, or stamp commissioned name of notary or clerk}

_____ Personally known

_____ Produced identification
Type of identification produced ______________________________

I certify that I have been open and honest in entering into this Parenting Plan. I am satisfied with this Plan and intend to be bound by it.

Dated: ______________________

____
Signature of Father
Printed Name: ______________
Address: ______________
City, State, Zip: ______________
Telephone Number: ______________
Fax Number: ______________
Designated E-mail Address(es): ______________

____

STATE OF FLORIDA
COUNTY OF ______________________

Sworn to or affirmed and signed before me on ______________ by ______________.

____
NOTARY PUBLIC or DEPUTY CLERK

____
{Print, type, or stamp commissioned name of notary or clerk.}

_____ Personally known
_____ Produced identification
Type of identification produced ______________

IF A NONLAWYER HELPED YOU FILL OUT THIS FORM, HE/SHE MUST FILL IN THE BLANKS BELOW:
[fill in all blanks] This form was prepared for the: *{choose only one}* ( ) Mother ( ) Father.
This form was completed with the assistance of:
{name of individual} ______________________________,
{name of business} ______________________________,
{address} ______________________________,
{city} ________,*{state}* _______, *{zip code}*__________,*{telephone number}* ______________.

INSTRUCTIONS FOR FLORIDA SUPREME COURT APPROVED FAMILY LAW FORM 12.995(b), SUPERVISED/SAFETY–FOCUSED PARENTING PLAN (03/15)

When should this form be used?

A **Parenting Plan** is required in all cases involving minor child(ren). This form or a similar form should be used in cases when you feel your child(ren) cannot be safely alone with the other parent or if you believe **shared parental responsibility** presents a detriment to the child(ren). In this case, a Parenting Plan must be developed that allows **time–sharing** with any minor child(ren), while providing protection for the child(ren). If safety or supervised time-sharing is not a concern, **Parenting Plan**, Florida Supreme Court Approved Family Law Form 12.995(a) or a similar form should be used. If the case involves relocation, pursuant to Section 61.13001, Florida Statutes, then **Relocation/Long Distance Parenting Plan,** Florida Supreme Court Approved Family Law Form 12.995(c) or a similar form should be used.

This form should be typed or printed in black ink. If an agreement has been reached, **both** parties must sign the Parenting Plan and have their signatures witnessed by a **notary public** or **deputy clerk**. After completing this form, you should **file** the original with the **clerk of the circuit court** in the county where the **petition** was filed and keep a copy for your records. You should then refer to the instructions for your petition, **answer**, or answer and **counterpetition** concerning the procedures for setting a hearing or **trial** (**final hearing**). If the parents have not reached an agreement, a proposed Parenting Plan may be filed by either parent at the time of or any time prior to the final hearing. If an agreed Parenting Plan is not filed by the parties, the court shall establish a Plan.

IMPORTANT INFORMATION REGARDING E–FILING

The Florida Rules of Judicial Administration now require that all petitions, pleadings, and documents be filed electronically except in certain circumstances. **Self–represented litigants may file petitions or other pleadings or documents electronically; however, they are not required to do so.** If you choose to file your pleadings or other documents electronically, you must do so in accordance with Florida Rule of Judicial Administration 2.525, and you must follow the procedures of the judicial circuit in which you file. **The rules and procedures should be carefully read and followed.**

IMPORTANT INFORMATION REGARDING E–SERVICE ELECTION

After the initial service of process of the petition or supplemental petition by the Sheriff or certified process server, the Florida Rules of Judicial Administration now require that all documents required or permitted to be served on the other party must be served by electronic mail (e–mail) except in certain circumstances. **You must strictly comply with the format requirements set forth in the Rules of Judicial Administration.**

SELF–REPRESENTED LITIGANTS MAY SERVE DOCUMENTS BY E–MAIL; HOWEVER, THEY ARE NOT REQUIRED TO DO SO. If a self-represented litigant elects to serve and receive documents by e-mail, the procedures must always be followed once the initial election is made.

To serve and receive documents by e-mail, you must designate your e-mail addresses by using the **Designation of Current Mailing and E–mail Address**, Florida Supreme Court Approved Family Law Form 12.915, and you must provide your e-mail address on each form on which your signature appears. Please **CAREFULLY** read the rules and instructions for: **Certificate of Service (General),** Florida Supreme Court Approved Family Law Form 12.914; **Designation of Current Mailing and E–mail Address**, Florida Supreme Court Approved Family Law Form 12.915; and Florida Rule of Judicial Administration 2.516.

Where can I look for more information?

Before proceeding, you should read "General Information for Self–Represented Litigants" found at the beginning of these forms. The words that are in **"bold underline"** in these instructions are defined there. For further information, see chapter 61, Florida Statutes, and the instructions for the petition and/or answer that were filed in this case.

Special notes . . .

If you fear that disclosing your address would put you in danger, you should complete a Request for Confidential Filing of Address, Florida Supreme Court Approved Form 12.980(h), file it with the clerk of the circuit court and write confidential in the space provided in the Parenting Plan.

At a minimum, the **Parenting Plan** must describe in adequate detail:

• How the parties will share and be responsible for the daily tasks associated with the upbringing of the child(ren),

• The **time–sharing schedule** arrangements that specify the time that the minor child(ren) will spend with each parent,

• A designation of who will be responsible for any and all forms of health care, school-related matters, including the address to be used for school-boundary determination and registration, other activities, and

• The methods and technologies that the parents will use to communicate with the child(ren).

The best interests of the child(ren) is the primary consideration in the Parenting Plan. In creating the Parenting Plan, all circumstances between the parents, including their historic relationship, domestic violence, and other factors must be taken into consideration. Determination of the best interests of the child(ren) shall be made by evaluating all of the factors affecting the welfare and interest of the particular minor child(ren) and the circumstances of that family, as listed in section 61.13(3), Florida Statutes, including, but not limited to:

• The demonstrated capacity and disposition of each parent to facilitate and encourage a close and continuing parent-child relationship, to honor the time-sharing schedule, and to be reasonable when changes are required;

• The anticipated division of parental responsibilities after the litigation, including the extent to which parental responsibilities will be delegated to third parties;

• The demonstrated capacity and disposition of each parent to determine, consider, and act upon the needs of the child(ren) as opposed to the needs or desires of the parent;

• The length of time the child(ren) has lived in a stable, satisfactory environment and the desirability of maintaining continuity;

• The geographic viability of the parenting plan, with special attention paid to the needs of school-age children and the amount of time to be spent traveling to effectuate the parenting plan. This factor does not create a presumption for or against relocation of either parent with a child(ren);

• The moral fitness of the parents;

• The mental and physical health of the parents;

• The home, school, and community record of the child(ren);

• The reasonable preference of the child(ren), if the court deems the child(ren) to be of sufficient intelligence, understanding, and experience to express a preference;

• The demonstrated knowledge, capacity, and disposition of each parent to be informed of the circumstances of the minor child(ren), including, but not limited to, the child(ren)'s friends, teachers, medical care providers, daily activities, and favorite things;

• The demonstrated capacity and disposition of each parent to provide a consistent routine for the child(ren), such as discipline, and daily schedules for homework, meals, and bedtime;

• The demonstrated capacity of each parent to communicate with and keep the other parent informed of issues and activities regarding the minor child(ren), and the willingness of each parent to adopt a unified front on all major issues when dealing with the child(ren);

• Evidence of domestic violence, sexual violence, child abuse, child abandonment, or child neglect, regardless of whether a prior or pending action relating to those issues has been brought. If the court accepts evidence of prior or pending actions regarding domestic violence, sexual violence, child abuse, child abandonment, or child neglect, the court must specifically acknowledge, in writing that such evidence was considered when evaluating the bests interests of the child(ren);

• Evidence that either parent has knowingly provided false information to the court regarding any prior or pending action regarding domestic violence, sexual violence, child abuse, child abandonment, or child neglect;

• The particular parenting tasks customarily performed by each parent and the division or parental responsibilities before the institution of litigation and during the pending litigation, including the extent to which parenting responsibilities were undertaken by third parties;

• The demonstrated capacity and disposition of each parent to participate and be involved in the child(ren)'s school and extracurricular activities;

• The demonstrated capacity and disposition of each parent to maintain an environment for the child(ren) which is free from substance abuse;

• The capacity and disposition of each parent to protect the child(ren) from the ongoing litigation as demonstrated by not discussing the litigation with the child(ren), not sharing documents or electronic media related to the litigation with the child(ren), and refraining from disparaging comments about the other parent to the child)ren); and

• The developmental stages and needs of the child(ren) and the demonstrated capacity and disposition of each parent to meet the child(ren)'s developmental needs.

This standard form does not include every possible issue that may be relevant to the facts of your case. The Parenting Plan should be as detailed as possible to address the time-sharing schedule. Additional provisions should be added to address all of the relevant factors. The parties should give special consideration to the age and needs of each child.

In developing the Parenting Plan, you may wish to consult or review other materials which are available at your local library, law library or through national and state family organizations.

Remember, a person who is NOT an attorney is called a nonlawyer. If a nonlawyer helps you fill out these forms, that person must give you a copy of a **Disclosure from Nonlawyer**, Florida Family Law Rules of Procedure Form 12.900 (a), before he or she helps you. A nonlawyer helping you fill out these forms also **must** put his or her name, address, and telephone number on the bottom of the last page of every form he or she helps you complete.

Added March 26, 2009 (20 So.3d 173). Amended Dec. 16, 2010 (59 So.3d 792); Nov. 3, 2011, effective, *nunc pro tunc*, Oct. 1, 2011 (78 So.3d 1045); March 26, 2015, effective March 26, 2015 (2015 WL 1343088).

Form 12.995(c). Relocation/Long–Distance Parenting Plan

IN THE CIRCUIT COURT OF THE ____________________ JUDICIAL CIRCUIT,
IN AND FOR ______________________________ COUNTY, FLORIDA

Case No: ________________
Division: ________________

__________________________________,
Petitioner,

And

__________________________________,
Respondent.

RELOCATION/LONG-DISTANCE PARENTING PLAN

This parenting plan is: *{Choose only* ***one****}*

_____ A Parenting Plan submitted to the court with the agreement of the parties.
_____ A proposed Parenting Plan submitted by or on behalf of: *{Name of Parent or Other Person}*____________________________.
_____ A Parenting Plan established by the court.

This parenting plan is: *{Choose only* ***one****}*

_____ A final Parenting Plan established by the court.
_____ A temporary Parenting Plan established by the court.
_____ A modification of a prior final Parenting Plan or prior final order.

I. PARTIES

Mother
Name:____
Address:____
Telephone Number: _________________________________
E-Mail: ____

Father
Name:____
Address:____
Telephone Number: _________________________________
E-Mail: ____

Other Person *{If Applicable}*
Name:____
Address:____
Telephone Number _________________________________
E-mail:____

Florida Supreme Court Approved Family Law Form 12.995(c), Relocation/Long Distance Parenting Plan (03/15)

II. **CHILDREN**: This parenting plan is for the following child(ren):
{Add additional lines as needed}

Name(s)	**Birth Date(s)**
____________	____________
____________	____________
____________	____________
____________	____________
____________	____________

III. **JURISDICTION**

The United States is the country of habitual residence of the child(ren).

The State of Florida is the child(ren)'s home state for the purposes of the Uniform Child Custody Jurisdiction and Enforcement Act.

This Parenting Plan is a child custody determination for the purposes of the Uniform Child Custody Jurisdiction and Enforcement Act, the International Child Abduction Remedies Act, 42 U.S.C. Sections 11601 et seq., the Parental Kidnapping Prevention Act, and the Convention on the Civil Aspects of International Child Abduction enacted at the Hague on October 25, 1980, and for all other state and federal laws.

Other: ____.

IV. **PARENTAL RESPONSIBILITY AND DECISION MAKING**

1. **Parental Responsibility** *{Choose only one}*

_____ **Shared** Parental Responsibility.
It is in the best interests of the child(ren) that the parties confer and **jointly** make all major decisions affecting the welfare of the child(ren). Major decisions include, but are not limited to, decisions about the child(ren)'s education, healthcare, and other responsibilities unique to this family.

_____ **Shared Parental** Responsibility with Decision Making Authority
It is in the best interests of the child(ren) that the parties confer and attempt to agree on the major decisions involving the child(ren). If the parties are unable to agree, the authority for making major decisions regarding the child(ren) shall be as follows:

Education/Academic decisions	____ Mother	____ Father	____ Other Person
Non-emergency health care	____ Mother	____ Father	____ Other Person
______________________	_____ Mother	____ Father	____ Other Person
______________________	____ Mother	____ Father	____ Other Person

Florida Supreme Court Approved Family Law Form 12.995(c), Relocation/Long Distance Parenting Plan (03/15)

_______________________ ____ Mother ____ Father ____ Other Person

_____ **Sole** Parental Responsibility:
It is in the best interests of the child(ren) that the _____ Mother _____ Father _____ Other Person shall have sole authority to make major decisions for the child(ren.) It is detrimental to the child(ren) for the parties to share decision making.

2. **Day-to-Day Decisions**
Unless otherwise specified in this plan, each party shall make decisions regarding day-to-day care and control of each child, including the performance of daily tasks, while the child is with that party. Regardless of the allocation of decision making in the Parenting Plan, any party may make emergency decisions affecting the health or safety of the child(ren) when the child is residing with that party. A party who makes an emergency decision shall share the decision with the other party as soon as reasonably possible.

3. **Extracurricular Activities** *(Indicate all that apply)*

i._____ Any party may register the child(ren) and allow them to participate in the activity of the child(ren)'s choice.

ii. _____ The parties must mutually agree to all extracurricular activities.

c. _____ The party with the minor child(ren) shall transport the minor child(ren) to and/or from all mutually agreed upon extra-curricular activities, providing all necessary uniforms and equipment within the party's possession.

d. _____ The costs of the extracurricular activities shall be paid by:
Mother _______% Father ________ %

e. _____ The uniforms and equipment required for the extracurricular activities shall be paid by:
Mother _____ % Father _______%

f. _____ Other: ____.

V. INFORMATION SHARING. Unless Otherwise Indicated or Ordered by the Court:

1. Unless otherwise prohibited by law, the parties shall have access to medical and school records, and information pertaining to the child(ren), and shall be permitted to independently consult with any and all professionals involved with the child(ren). The parties shall cooperate with each other in sharing information related to the health, education, and welfare of the child(ren) and they shall sign any necessary documentation ensuring that all parties have access to said records.

2. Each party shall be responsible for obtaining records and reports directly from the school and health care providers.

3. The parties have equal rights to inspect and receive governmental agency and law enforcement records concerning the child(ren).

4. The parties shall have equal and independent authority to confer with the child(ren)'s school, day care, health care providers, and other programs with regard to the child(ren)'s educational, emotional, and social progress.

5. The parties shall be listed as "emergency contacts" for the child(ren).

6. Each party has a continuing responsibility to provide a residential and mailing address, and contact telephone number (s) to the other parties. Each party shall notify the other parties in writing within 24 hours of any changes. Each party shall notify the court in writing within seven (7) days of any changes.

7. Other: ____
____.

VI. SCHEDULING

1. **School Calendar**

a. If necessary, on or before ______________ of each year, the parties should obtain a copy of the school calendar for the next school year. The parties shall discuss the calendars and the time-sharing schedule so that any differences or questions can be resolved.

b. The parties shall follow the school calendar of: *{Indicate **all** that apply}*

_____ the oldest child
_____ the youngest child
_____ ______________ County
_____ ________________ School

2. **Academic Break Definition**

When defining academic break periods, the period shall begin at the end of the last scheduled day of classes before the holiday or break and shall end on the first day of regularly scheduled classes after the holiday or break.

3. **Schedule Changes** *{Indicate **all** that apply}*

1. ______ A party making a request for a schedule change will make the request as soon as possible, but in any event, except in cases of emergency, no less than ______________ before the change is to occur.

2. ______ A party requesting a change of schedule shall be responsible for any additional child care, or transportation costs caused by the change.

3. ______ Other ____.

VII. TIME-SHARING SCHEDULE

1. **Weekday and Weekend Schedule**
The following schedule shall apply beginning on ________________________ with the _____ Mother _____ Father _____ *{If Applicable}* Other Person and continue as follows:

The child(ren) shall spend time with the **Mother** on the following dates and times:
WEEKENDS: _____ Every _____ Every Other _____ Other *{Specify}* :
____
From ______________________________ to ______________________________
WEEKDAYS: *{Specify days}* ______________________________________
From ______________________________ to ______________________________
OTHER: *{Specify}* ____
____
____

The child(ren) shall spend time with the **Father** on the following dates and times:
WEEKENDS: _____ Every _____ Every Other _____ Other *{Specify}*:
____
From______________________________ to ______________________________
WEEKDAYS: *{Specify days}* ______________________________________
From ______________________________ to ______________________________
OTHER: *{Specify}* ____
____
____

The child(ren) shall spend time with the **Other Person** *{If Applicable}* on the following dates and times:
WEEKENDS: _____ Every _____ Every Other _____ Other *{Specify}* :
____
From ______________________________to ______________________________
WEEKDAYS: *{Specify Days}*______________________________________
From ______________________________ to ______________________________
OTHER: *{Specify}* ____
____
____

Please indicate if there is a different time sharing schedule for any child. Complete a separate Attachment for each child for whom there is a different time sharing schedule.

_____ There is a different time-sharing schedule for the following child(ren) in Attachment _____.

______________________________, and ______________________________.
{Name of Child} *{Name of Child}*

Florida Supreme Court Approved Family Law Form 12.995(c), Relocation/Long Distance Parenting Plan (03/15)

2. **Holiday Schedule** *{Choose only* ***one****}*

a. _____No holiday time sharing shall apply. The regular time-sharing schedule set forth above shall apply.

b. _____Holiday time-sharing shall be as the parties agree.

c. _____Holiday time-sharing shall be in accordance with the following schedule. The Holiday schedule will take priority over the regular weekday, weekend, and summer schedules. Fill in the blanks with Mother, Father, or *{If Applicable}* Other Person to indicate where the child(ren) will be for the holidays. Provide the beginning and ending times. If a holiday is not specified as even, odd, or every year with one party, then the child(ren) will remain with the other party in accordance with the regular schedule

Holidays	Even Years	Odd Years	Every Year	Begin/End Time
Mother's Day	_____	_____	_____	_________
Father's Day	_____	_____	_____	_________
President's Day	_____	_____	_____	_________
Martin Luther King Day	_____	_____	_____	_________
Easter	_____	_____	_____	_________
Passover	_____	_____	_____	_________
Memorial Day Weekend	_____	_____	_____	_________
4th of July	_____	_____	_____	_________
Labor Day Weekend	_____	_____	_____	_________
Columbus Day Weekend	_____	_____	_____	_________
Halloween	_____	_____	_____	_________
Thanksgiving	_____	_____	_____	_________
Veteran's Day	_____	_____	_____	_________
Hanukkah	_____	_____	_____	_________
Yom Kippur	_____	_____	_____	_________
Rosh Hashanah	_____	_____	_____	_________
Child(ren)'s Birthdays	_____	_____	_____	_________
_____________	_____	_____	_____	_________
_____________	_____	_____	_____	_________

This holiday schedule may affect the regular time-sharing schedule. Parties may wish to specify one or more of the following options:

d_____ When the parties are using an alternating weekend plan and the holiday schedule would result in one party having the child(ren) for three weekends in a row, the parties will exchange the following weekend, so that each has two weekends in a row before the regular alternating weekend pattern resumes.

e. _____ If a party has the child(ren) on a weekend immediately before or after an unspecified holiday or non-school day, they shall have the child(ren) for the holiday or non-school day.

3. **Winter Break** *{choose only one}*

a. _____ The _____ Mother _____ Father _____ *{If Applicable}* Other Person shall have the child(ren) from the day and time school is dismissed until December ____ at ____ a.m./p. m in _____odd-numbered years _____ even-numbered years _____ every year. The other party will have the child(ren) for the second portion of the Winter Break. The parties shall alternate the arrangement each year.

b._____ The _____ Mother _____ Father _____ *{If Applicable}* Other Person shall have the child(ren) for the entire Winter Break during _____ odd-numbered years _____ even-numbered years _____ every year

c._____ Other:____

____

____

4. **Specific Winter Holidays**

If not addressed above, the specific Winter Holidays such as Christmas, New Year's Eve, Hanukkah, Kwanzaa, etc. shall be shared as follows:

____

____

____

____.

5. **Spring Break** *{Choose only one}*

a. _____The parties shall follow the regular schedule.

b. _____The parties shall alternate the entire Spring Break with the _____ Mother _____ Father _____ *{If Applicable}* Other Person having the child(ren) during the _____ odd-numbered _____ even-numbered years

c. _____The _____ Father _____ Mother _____ *{If Applicable}* Other Person shall have the child(ren) for the entire Spring Break every year.

d. _____The Spring Break will be evenly divided. The first half of the Spring Break will go to the party whose regularly scheduled weekend falls on the first half and the second half going to the party whose weekend falls during the second half.

e. _____Other: ____.

Florida Supreme Court Approved Family Law Form 12.995(c), Relocation/Long Distance Parenting Plan (03/15)

6. **Summer Break** *{Choose only one}*

a. _____ The parents shall follow the regular schedule through the summer.

b. _____ The _____ Mother _____ Father _____ *{If Applicable}* Other Person shall have the entire Summer Break from ______________________________ after school is out until ____________________ before school starts.

c. _____ The parties shall equally divide the Summer Break as follows:
____
____
____
____

d. _____ Other:
____
____.

7. **Number of Overnights:**

Based upon the time-sharing schedule, the Mother has a total of _____ overnights per year, the Father has a total of ____ overnights per year and *{If Applicable}* the Other Person has a total of _____ overnights per year. **Note: The total of these numbers must equal 365.**

8. **Attached Time-Sharing Schedule:**

_____**If not set forth above,** the parties shall have time-sharing in accordance with the schedule which is attached as Attachment ______and incorporated herein.

VIII. TRANSPORTATION AND EXCHANGE OF CHILD(REN)

1. The parties shall have the child(ren) ready on time with sufficient clothing packed and ready at the agreed upon time of exchange. All necessary information and medicines will accompany the child(ren).

2. The parties shall exchange travel information and finalize travel plans at least _______days in advance of the date of travel. Except in cases of emergency, any party requesting a change of travel plans after the date of finalization shall be solely responsible for any additional costs.

3. **Automobile Transportation and Exchange** *{Choose only one}*
If a party is more than ______minutes late without contacting the other party to make other arrangements, the party with the child(ren) may proceed with other plans and activities.

a._____ The _____ Mother _____Father _____ *{If Applicable}* Other Person shall provide all transportation.

b. _____ The _____ Mother _____Father _____ *{If Applicable}* Other Person shall pick up the child(ren) at the beginning of the visit and the other party shall pick up the child(ren) at the end of the visit. The exchange shall take place:

_____ At the parties' homes unless otherwise agreed

_____ At the following location unless the parties agree in advance to a different location:*{specify}*____.

_____ The parties shall meet at the following central location: *{specify}*____.

c. _____Other:____.

4. **Airplane and Other Public Transportation and Exchange**

Airline regulations govern the age at which a child may fly unescorted. An older child or children may fly under such regulations as each airline may establish.

a._____ Until a child reaches the age of ______, the parties agree that the child(ren) shall take a direct flight and/or fly accompanied by: _______________________.

b._____ Once a child reaches the age of ______, the child shall be permitted to fly accompanied by an airline employee.

c._____ Once a child reaches the age of ______, the child shall be permitted to fly unescorted.

d._____ Other: ____.

Airline reservations should be made well in advance and preferably, non-stop or direct.

All flight information shall be sent to the other party(ies) at least ______days in advance of the flight by the party purchasing the tickets.

If the child(ren) are flying accompanied by a party, the party picking up the child(ren) shall exchange the child(ren) with the other party at____________________ and the party returning the child(ren) shall exchange the children at ___________________________.
If the exchange is to be made at the airport, the party flying in to pick up or drop off the child(ren) from/to the airport must notify the other party of any flight delays.

Unless otherwise agreed in advance, the party taking the child(ren) to the airport must call the other party(ies) immediately upon departure to notify the other party(ies) that the child(ren) is/are arriving, and the party who meets the child(ren) must immediately notify the other party(ies) upon the child(ren)'s arrival.

5. **Costs of Airline and Other Public Transportation** *{Indicate all that apply}*

a. _____Ticket Purchase *{If Applicable}*:
The parties shall work together to purchase the most convenient and least expensive tickets.

After consultation among the parties, it shall be the responsibility of ____________________ to purchase the tickets by *{date}* ______________.
All parties entitled to access to, or time-sharing with the child(ren) shall be notified of the purchase by *{date}*______________.

Proof of the purchase and a copy of the itinerary (choose only **one**) [ ] shall be provided to all parties by *{date}*______________[ ] shall not be provided.

Unless otherwise agreed or in the case of an unavoidable emergency, any costs incurred by a missed travel connection shall be the sole responsibility of the party who failed to timely deliver the child(ren) to the missed connection.

b. _____Transportation costs are included in the Child Support Worksheets and/or the Order for Child Support and should not be included here.

c. _____Mother shall pay _____% Father shall pay _____% of the transportation costs.

d. _____Mother shall pay _____% Father shall pay _____% of the transportation costs for an adult to accompany the child(ren) during travel.

e. _____If the parties are sharing travel costs, the non-purchasing party shall reimburse the other party within ______days of receipt of documentation establishing the travel costs.

f. _____Other:____.

6. **Foreign and Out-Of-State Travel** *{Indicate all that apply}*

a. _____ The parties may travel within the United States with the child(ren) during his/her time-sharing. The party traveling with the child(ren) shall give the other party(ies) at least ____ days written notice before traveling out of state unless there is an emergency, and shall provide the other party(ies) with a detailed itinerary, including locations and telephone numbers where the child(ren) and party can be reached at least ____ days in advance of the date of travel.

b. _____A party may travel out of the country with the child(ren) during his/her time-sharing. At least ____ days in advance of the date of travel, the party shall provide a detailed itinerary, including locations, and telephone numbers where the child(ren) and party may be reached during the trip. Each party agrees to provide whatever documentation is necessary for the other party(ies) to take the child(ren) out of the country.

c. _____If a party wishes to travel out of the country with the child(ren), he/she shall provide the following security for the return of the child ________________ ____.

d. _____Other____.

7. **Other Travel and Exchange Arrangements:** ____________________________________ ____ ____

IX. EDUCATION

4. **School designation.** For purposes of school boundary determination and registration, the ____ Mother's _____ Father's _____ *{If Applicable}* Other Person's address shall be designated.

5. *{If Applicable}* The following provisions are made regarding private or home schooling: ____ ____ ____.

6. **Other.** ____ ____ ____.

X. DESIGNATION FOR OTHER LEGAL PURPOSES

The child(ren) named in this Parenting Plan are scheduled to reside the majority of the time with the _____ Mother _____ Father _____ *{If Applicable}* Other Person. This majority designation is **SOLELY** for purposes of all other state and federal laws which require such a designation. **This designation does not affect the rights or responsibilities of any party under this Parenting Plan.**

XI. COMMUNICATION

4. **Between Parties**

All communications regarding the child(ren) shall be between the parties. The parties shall not use the child(ren) as messengers to convey information, ask questions, or set up schedule changes.

The parties shall communicate with each other by: *{Indicate **all** that apply}*

_____ in person
_____ by telephone
_____ by letter
_____ by e-mail
_____ Other:____.

5. **Between Parties and Child(ren)**

The parties shall keep contact information current. Telephone or other electronic communication between the child(ren) and another party shall not be monitored by or interrupted by the other party. "Electronic communication" includes telephones, electronic mail or e-mail, webcams, video-conferencing equipment and software or other wired or wireless technologies or other means of communication to supplement face to face contact.

The child(ren) may have _____ telephone _____ e-mail _____ other electronic communication in the form of_____________________________ with the other party: *{Choose only **one**}*

_____ Anytime
_____ Every day during the hours of ______________ to ______________
_____ On the following days_____________________________________ during the hours of ______________ to ______________
_____ Other:____

6. **Costs of Electronic Communication** shall be addressed as follows:
____
____
____

XII. CHILD CARE *{Choose only **one**}*

1. _____ Each party may select appropriate child care providers
2. _____ All child care providers must be agreed upon by the parties.
3. _____ Each party must offer the other party the opportunity to care for the child(ren) before using a child care provider for any period exceeding _______ hours.
4. _____ Other ____.

XIII. CHANGES TO OR MODIFICATIONS OF THE PARENTING PLAN

Temporary changes may be made informally without a written document. When the parties do not agree, this Parenting Plan remains in effect until further order of the court.

Any substantial changes to the Parenting Plan must be sought through the filing of a supplemental petition for modification.

XIV. RELOCATION

Any relocation of the child(ren) is subject to and must be sought in compliance with Section 61.13001, Florida Statutes.

XV. DISPUTES OR CONFLICT RESOLUTION

The parties shall attempt to cooperatively resolve any disputes which may arise over the terms of the Parenting Plan. The parties may wish to use mediation or other dispute resolution methods and assistance, such as Parenting Coordinators and Parenting Counselors, before filing a court action.

XVI. OTHER PROVISIONS

____
____
____
____
____
____
____
____
____
____.

SIGNATURES OF PARTIES

I certify that I have been open and honest in entering into this Parenting Plan. I am satisfied with this plan and intend to be bound by it.

Dated: ____________________

____
Signature of Mother

Printed Name: ____________________
Address: ____________________
City, State, Zip: ____________________
Telephone Number: ____________________
Fax Number: ____________________
Designated E-mail Address(es): ____________________
____

STATE OF FLORIDA
COUNTY OF ____________________

Sworn to or affirmed and signed before me on __________ by ____________________.

____
NOTARY PUBLIC or DEPUTY CLERK

____
[Print, type, or stamp commissioned name of notary or deputy clerk.]

____ Personally known
____ Produced identification
____ Type of identification produced ____________________

I certify that I have been open and honest in entering into this Parenting Plan. I am satisfied with this plan and intend to be bound by it.

Dated: ______________________ ______________________________________

Signature of Father

Printed Name: ______________________

Address: ______________________

City, State, Zip: ______________________

Telephone Number: ______________________

Fax Number: ______________________

Designated E-mail Address(es): ______________________

____

STATE OF FLORIDA

COUNTY OF ______________________

Sworn to or affirmed and signed before me on __________ by______________________.

____

NOTARY PUBLIC or DEPUTY CLERK

____

[Print, type, or stamp commissioned name of notary or deputy clerk.]

____ Personally known

____ Produced identification

____ Type of identification produced ______________________________

I certify that I have been open and honest in entering into this Parenting Plan. I am satisfied with this plan and intend to be bound by it.

Florida Supreme Court Approved Family Law Form 12.995(c), Relocation/Long Distance Parenting Plan (03/15)

Dated: ____________________ ____________________________________

Signature of Other Person

Printed Name: ______________________

Address: __________________________

City, State, Zip: ____________________

Telephone Number: __________________

Fax Number: _______________________

Designated E-mail Address(es):_______________

____

STATE OF FLORIDA
COUNTY OF ____________________

Sworn to or affirmed and signed before me on __________ by____________________.

____

NOTARY PUBLIC or DEPUTY CLERK

____

[Print, type, or stamp commissioned name of notary or deputy clerk.]

____ Personally known
____ Produced identification
____ Type of identification produced ____________________

IF A NONLAWYER HELPED YOU FILL OUT THIS FORM, HE/SHE MUST FILL IN THE BLANKS BELOW: [fill in all blanks] This form was prepared for the: *{choose only one}* ( ) Mother ( ) Father ( ) Other Person.
This form was completed with the assistance of:
{name of individual} ____,
*{name of business}*____,
{address} ____,
{city} ________________, *{state}* _____,*{zip code}*_________,*{telephone number}* ______________.

INSTRUCTIONS FOR FLORIDA SUPREME COURT APPROVED FAMILY LAW FORM 12.995(c) RELOCATION/LONG DISTANCE PARENTING PLAN (03/15)

When should this form be used?

A **Parenting Plan** is required in all cases involving **time–sharing** with minor child(ren), even when time-sharing is not in dispute. The Parenting Plan must be developed and agreed to by the parents and every other person entitled to access or time-sharing with the child(ren) and approved by the court. "Other Person" means an individual who is not the parent, but with whom the child resides pursuant to court order, or who has the right of access to, time-sharing with or visitation with the child(ren). If the parties cannot agree to a Parenting Plan or if the parents agreed to a Plan that is not approved by the court, a Parenting Plan will be established by the court with or without the use of Parenting Plan Recommendations. This form or a similar form should be used in the development of a Parenting Plan when you are planning to relocate your or the child(ren)'s principal residence more than 50 miles from the principal place of residence:

- at the time of the last order either establishing or modifying time-sharing, or
- at the time of filing the pending action to either establish or modify time-sharing

This form should be typed or printed in black ink. If an agreement has been reached, **both** parties must sign the Parenting Plan and have their signatures witnessed by a **notary public** or **deputy clerk**. After completing this form, you should **file** the original with the **clerk of the circuit court** in the county where the **petition** was filed and keep a copy for your records. You should then refer to the instructions for your petition, **answer**, or answer and **counterpetition** concerning the procedures for setting a hearing or **trial** (**final hearing**). If an agreed Parenting Plan is not filed by the parties, the Court shall establish a Plan.

IMPORTANT INFORMATION REGARDING E–FILING

The Florida Rules of Judicial Administration now require that all petitions, pleadings, and documents be filed electronically except in certain circumstances. **Self–represented litigants may file petitions or other pleadings or documents electronically; however, they are not required to do so.** If you choose to file your pleadings or other documents electronically, you must do so in accordance with Florida Rule of Judicial Administration 2.525, and you must follow the procedures of the judicial circuit in which you file. **The rules and procedures should be carefully read and followed.**

IMPORTANT INFORMATION REGARDING E–SERVICE ELECTION

After the initial service of process of the petition or supplemental petition by the Sheriff or certified process server, the Florida Rules of Judicial Administration now require that all documents required or permitted to be served on the other party must be served by electronic mail (e–mail) except in certain circumstances. **You must strictly comply with the format requirements set forth in the Rules of Judicial Administration.**

SELF–REPRESENTED LITIGANTS MAY SERVE DOCUMENTS BY E–MAIL; HOWEVER, THEY ARE NOT REQUIRED TO DO SO. If a self-represented litigant elects to serve and receive documents by e-mail, the procedures must always be followed once the initial election is made.

To serve and receive documents by e-mail, you must designate your e-mail addresses by using the **Designation of Current Mailing and E–mail Address**, Florida Supreme Court Approved Family Law Form 12.915, and you must provide your e-mail address on each form on which your signature appears. Please **CAREFULLY** read the rules and instructions for: **Certificate of Service (General)**, Florida Supreme Court Approved Family Law Form 12.914; **Designation of Current Mailing and E–mail Address**, Florida Supreme Court Approved Family Law Form 12.915; and Florida Rule of Judicial Administration 2.516.

Where can I look for more information?

Before proceeding, you should read "General Information for Self–Represented Litigants" found at the beginning of these forms. The words that are in "**bold underline**" in these instructions are defined there. For further information, see chapter 61, Florida Statutes, and the instructions for the petition and/or answer that were filed in this case.

Special notes . . .

At a minimum, the **Relocation/Long Distance Parenting Plan** must describe in adequate detail:

- How the parties will share and be responsible for the daily tasks associated with the upbringing of the child(ren),
- The **time-sharing schedule** that specifies the time that the minor child(ren) will spend with each parent and every other person entitled to access or time-sharing,
- A designation of who will be responsible for any and all forms of health care, school-related matters, including the address to be used for school-boundary determination and registration, other activities,
- The methods and technologies that the parties will use to communicate with the child(ren), and
- Any transportation arrangements related to access or time-sharing.

The best interests of the child(ren) is the primary consideration in the Parenting Plan. In creating the Parenting Plan, all circumstances between the parties, including the parties' historic relationship, domestic violence, and other factors must be taken into consideration. Determination of the best interests of the child(ren) shall be made by evaluating all of the factors affecting the welfare and interest of the particular minor child(ren) and the circumstances of the family as listed in section 61.13(3), Florida Statutes, including, but not limited to:

- The demonstrated capacity and disposition of each party to facilitate and encourage a close and continuing parent-child relationship, to honor the timesharing schedule, and to be reasonable when changes are required;
- The anticipated division of parental responsibilities after the litigation, including the extent to which parental responsibilities will be delegated to third parties;
- The demonstrated capacity and disposition of each party to determine, consider, and act upon the needs of the child(ren) as opposed to the needs or desires of the parent;
- The length of time the child(ren) has lived in a stable, satisfactory environment and the desirability of maintaining continuity;
- The geographic viability of the parenting plan, with special attention paid to the needs of school-age children and the amount of time to be spent traveling to effectuate the parenting plan. This factor does not create a presumption for or against relocation of either party with a child(ren);
- The moral fitness of the parties;
- The mental and physical health of the parties;
- The home, school, and community record of the child(ren);
- The reasonable preference of the child(ren), if the court deems the child(ren) to be of sufficient intelligence, understanding, and experience to express a preference;
- The demonstrated knowledge, capacity, and disposition of each party to be informed of the circumstances of the minor child(ren), including, but not limited to, the child(ren)'s friends, teachers, medical care providers, daily activities, and favorite things;
- The demonstrated capacity and disposition of each party to provide a consistent routine for the child(ren), such as discipline, and daily schedules for homework, meals, and bedtime;
- The demonstrated capacity of each party to communicate with and keep the other part(y)ies informed of issues and activities regarding the minor child(ren), and the willingness of each party to adopt a unified front on all major issues when dealing with the child(ren);
- Evidence of domestic violence, sexual violence, child abuse, child abandonment, or child neglect, regardless of whether a prior or pending action relating to those issues has been brought. If the court accepts evidence of prior or pending actions regarding domestic violence, sexual violence, child abuse, child abandonment, or child neglect, the court must specifically acknowledge in writing that such evidence was considered when evaluating the best interests of the child(ren);

- Evidence that any party has knowingly provided false information to the court regarding any prior or pending action regarding domestic violence, sexual violence, child abuse, child abandonment, or child neglect;
- The particular parenting tasks customarily performed by each patty and the division of parental responsibilities before the institution of litigation and during the pending litigation, including the extent to which parenting responsibilities were undertaken by third parties;
- The demonstrated capacity and disposition of each party to participate and be involved in the child(ren)'s school and extracurricular activities;
- The demonstrated capacity and disposition of each party to maintain an environment for the child(ren) which is free from substance abuse;
- The capacity and disposition of each party to protect the child(ren) from the ongoing litigation as demonstrated by not discussing the litigation with the child(ren), not sharing documents or electronic media related to the litigation with the child(ren), and refraining from disp
- The developmental stages and needs of the child(ren) and the demonstrated capacity and disposition of each party to meet the child(ren)'s developmental needs.

This standard form does not include every possible issue that may be relevant to the facts of your case. The Parenting Plan should be as detailed as possible to address the time-sharing schedule. Additional provisions should be added to address all of the relevant factors. The parties should give special consideration to the age and needs of each child.

In developing the Parenting Plan, you may wish to consult or review other materials which are available at your local library, law library or through national and state family organizations.

Remember, a person who is NOT an attorney is called a nonlawyer. If a nonlawyer helps you fill out these forms, that person must give you a copy of a **Disclosure from Nonlawyer**, Florida Family Law Rules of Procedure Form 12.900 (a), before he or she helps you. A nonlawyer helping you fill out these forms also **must** put his or her name, address, and telephone number on the bottom of the last page of every form he or she helps you complete.

Added Sept. 30, 2010 (55 So.3d 381). Amended March 26, 2015, effective March 26, 2015 (2015 WL 1343088).

Form 12.996(a). Income Deduction Order (Non-Title IV–D Case)

IN THE CIRCUIT COURT OF THE ________ JUDICIAL CIRCUIT,
IN AND FOR ________ COUNTY, FLORIDA

Case No: ________
Division: ________

________________________,
Petitioner,

and

________________________,
Respondent.

INCOME DEDUCTION ORDER (Non–Title IV–D Case)

TO: ANY PRESENT OR SUBSEQUENT EMPLOYERS/PAYORS OF OBLIGOR
{*name*} ________________________

YOU ARE HEREBY ORDERED to make regular deductions from all income due and payable to the above-named obligor in accordance with the terms of this order as follows:

1. This Income Deduction Order shall be effective
[Choose only one]
____ immediately.
____ upon a delinquency in the amount of $ ________ but not to exceed one month's payment, pursuant to the order establishing, enforcing, or modifying the obligation.
____ beginning {*date*} ________________.

2. You shall deduct:
$ ___ per ___ for child support. Child support shall be automatically reduced or terminated consistent with the schedule in paragraph 7.
$ ________ per ________ for permanent alimony
$ ________ per ________ for rehabilitative alimony
$ ________ per ________ for ________ arrears totaling $ ______

The deduction for arrears shall be no less than 20% of the current support obligation. After the full amount of any arrears is paid, you shall deduct for attorneys' fees and costs owed until the full amount is paid.

$ ________ per ________ for attorneys' fees and costs totaling $ ____

$ ________ per ________ for State of Florida Disbursement Unit fee (4% of each payment not to exceed $5.25 per payment)
$ ________ Total amount of income to be deducted each pay period

3. You shall pay the deducted amount to the "State of Florida Disbursement Unit", and mail it to the State of Florida Disbursement Unit P.O. Box 8500, Tallahassee, FL 32314–8500, (tel.) (877) 769–0251. All payments must include the obligor's name (last, middle, first), obligor's social security number, obligee's name (last, middle, first), name of county where court order originated, and case number. All payments must be made by check, money order, cashier's check, certified check, or through the Internet with access provided by the State of

Florida www.floridasdu.com. No credit will be given for any payments made directly to the obligee without a court order permitting direct payments.

4. If a delinquency accrues after the order establishing, modifying, or enforcing the obligation has been entered and there is no order for repayment of the delinquency or a preexisting arrearage, a payor shall deduct an additional 20 percent of the current support obligation or other amount agreed to by the parties until the delinquency and any attorneys' fees and costs are paid in full. No deduction may be applied to attorneys' fees and costs until the delinquency is paid in full.

5. You shall not deduct in excess of the amounts allowed under the Consumer Credit Protection Act, 15 U.S.C. § 673(b), as amended.

6. You shall deduct (Choose only one) ( ) the full amount, ( ) ___ %, or ( ) none of the income which is payable to the obligor in the form of a bonus or other similar one-time payment, up to the amount of arrearage reported in the Income Deduction Order or the remaining balance thereof, and forward the payment to the State of Florida Disbursement Unit. For purposes of this subparagraph, "bonus" means a payment in addition to an obligor's usual compensation and which is in addition to any amounts contracted for or otherwise legally due and shall not include any commission payments due an obligor.

7. Child Support Reduction/Termination Schedule. Child support shall be automatically reduced or terminated as set forth in the following schedule:

Please list children by initials from eldest to youngest	[redacted]	Insert in this column the day, month, and year the child support obligation terminates for each designated child (see instructions)	[redacted]	Insert in this column the amount of child support for all minor children remaining (including designated child).
Child 1 (Eldest)	*From the effective date of this Income*		*child support for Child 1 and all other younger child(ren)*	

Initials & year of birth:	*Deduction Order **until** the following date:*		*should be paid in the following monthly amount:*	
Child 2 Initials & year of birth:	*After the date set forth in the row above until the following date:*		*child support for Child 2 and all other younger child(ren) should be paid in the following monthly amount:*	
Child 3 Initials & year of birth:	*After the date set forth in the row above until the following date:*		*child support for Child 3 and all other younger child(ren) should be paid in the following monthly amount:*	
Child 4 Initials & year of birth:	*After the date set forth in the row above until the following date:*		*child support for Child 4 and all other younger child(ren) should be paid in the following monthly amount:*	
Child 5 Initials & year of birth:	*After the date set forth in the row above until the following date:*		*child support for Child 5 and all other younger child(ren) should be paid in the following monthly amount:*	

(Continue on additional pages for additional children)

8. This Income Deduction Order shall remain in effect so long as the underlying order of support is effective or until further order of the court.

STATEMENT OF OBLIGOR'S RIGHTS, REMEDIES, AND DUTIES

9. The obligor is required to pay all amounts and fees specified within this Income Deduction Order.

10. The amounts deducted may not be in excess of that allowed under the Consumer Credit Protection Act, 15 U.S.C. § 1673(b) as amended.

11. This income deduction order applies to all of the obligor's current and subsequent payors and periods of employment.

12. A copy of the Income Deduction Order will be served upon the obligor's payor or payors.

13. Enforcement of the Income Deduction Order may only be contested on the ground of mistake of fact regarding the amount owed pursuant to the order establishing, enforcing, or modifying the obligation, the arrearages, or the identity of the obligor, the payor, or the obligee.

14. The obligor is required to notify the obligee and, when the obligee is receiving IV–D services, the IV–D agency, within 7 days of any changes in the obligor's address, payors, and the addresses of the obligor's payors.

15. In a Title IV–D case, if an obligation to pay current support is reduced or terminated due to emancipation of a child and the obligor owes an arrearage, retroactive support, delinquency, or costs, income deduction continues at the rate in effect immediately prior to emancipation until all arrearages, retroactive

support, delinquencies, and costs are paid in full or until the amount of withholding is modified.

ORDERED on ______________.

____
CIRCUIT JUDGE

COPIES TO:
Obligee
Obligor
Other: ______________________

INSTRUCTIONS FOR FLORIDA FAMILY LAW RULES OF PROCEDURE FORM 12.996(a), INCOME DEDUCTION ORDER (06/11)

When should this form be used?

This form should be used in non-Title IV–D cases when the court has ordered that support be paid by the **obligor's payor** through an income deduction order.

This form includes several blanks that must be filled in as applicable. The obligor is the person who is obligated to pay the support ordered by the court and the **obligee** is the person entitled to receive the support awarded by the court.

In Paragraph 1, one of the three lines must be checked off. The court order that establishes the support award and/or the settlement or mediation agreement entered into between the parties should state the effective date of the **Income Deduction Order**. The appropriate effective date should be checked off in Paragraph 1.

The blank lines in Paragraph 2 should be completed tracking the same terms of support as are in the court order that establishes the support award and/or the settlement or mediation agreement. The first blank in each line should state the amount of the support payment and the second blank in each line should state the time period that covers said support award. For example, if the child support is $100 per month the first blank would say $ *"100"* and the second blank in that line would say *"month"*. Similarly, if the payments are to be payable weekly, then the second blank would say *"week"*. If there are any arrearages owed at the time the **Income Deduction Order** is entered, they must be included in the line for arrears, along with the amount and frequency of the payments due for the arrears, which shall be no less than 20% of the current support obligation. All orders for immediate income deduction must be paid through the State Disbursement Unit. The actual dollar amount of the service fee for the support awarded in your case (4% of each payment not to exceed $5.25 per payment) should be included on the appropriate line.

Paragraph 6 must be completed to show what percentage, if any, of a one-time payment made to the obligor should be applied to any arrearage in support that may be due to the obligee.

You must complete the schedule in paragraph 7 to show the amount of child support for all the minor children at the time of the entry of this order and the amount of the child support that will be owed for any remaining child(ren) after one or more of the children are no longer entitled to receive child support. You should also show in the schedule the day, month, and year that the child support obligation terminates for each minor child. The date child support terminates should be listed as the child's 18th birthday unless the court has found that section 743.07(2), Florida Statues [1], applies, or the parties have otherwise agreed to a different date. You should use the record existing at the time of this order for the basis of computing all child support obligations.

What should I do next?

For this order to be effective, it must be signed by the **judge**. This form should be typed or printed in black ink. After completing this form, you must first send a copy to the other **party** or his or her **attorney**, if he or she is represented by an attorney, for approval or objection to the form before you send it to the judge assigned to your case. If the opposing party or his or her attorney, if represented, approves the form order, you may send the original proposed order and two copies to the judge assigned to your case with a letter telling the judge that you have first sent a copy of this proposed order to the opposing counsel or party, if unrepresented, and that they have no objection to the judge signing this order. If the other party or his or her attorney, if represented, has an objection to the proposed order as completed by you, you must tell the judge that you have sent a copy of this proposed order to the opposing party or his or her counsel, if represented, and that they specifically object to the entry of the proposed form **Income Deduction Order**. You must also send stamped self-addressed envelopes to the judge addressed to you and the opposing party or his or her attorney, if represented. You should keep a copy for your own records. If the judge signs the **Income Deduction Order**, the judge will mail you and the opposing party (or their attorney) copies of the signed order in the envelopes you provide to the court.

Where can I look for more information?

Before proceeding, you should read "General Information for Self-Represented Litigants" found at the beginning of these forms. The words that are in "**bold underline**" in these instructions are defined there. For further information see section 61.1301, Florida Statutes.

Special Instructions . . .

When the **Income Deduction Order** becomes effective (either immediately or delayed until arrearage), you must then also send a copy of the **Income Deduction Order** to the obligor's employer along with a **Notice to Payor,** Florida Family Law Rules of Procedure Form 12.996(b), for the **Income Deduction Order** to take effect.

It is your responsibility to determine what extra steps and/or forms, if any, must be taken, supplied, and/or filed to insure the **Income Deduction Order** is implemented.

Remember, a person who is NOT an attorney is called a nonlawyer. If a nonlawyer helps you fill out these forms, that person must give you a copy of a **Disclosure from Nonlawyer**, Florida Family Law Rules of Procedure Form 12.900(a), before he or she helps you. A nonlawyer helping you fill out these forms also **must** put his or her name, address, and telephone number on the bottom of the last page of every form he or she helps you complete.

Added March 4, 2010 (39 So.3d 227). Amended Sept. 23, 2010, effective Oct. 1, 2010 (48 So.3d 25); June 16, 2011 (66 So.3d 859).

[1] So in original.

Form 12.996(b). Notice to Payor

IN THE CIRCUIT COURT OF THE ____________________ JUDICIAL CIRCUIT,
IN AND FOR ____________________ COUNTY, FLORIDA

Case No.: ____________________
Division: ____________________

____________________________________,
Petitioner,

and

____________________________________,
Respondent.

NOTICE TO PAYOR

TO:
Name of Obligor's Payor: ______________________________
Payor's Address: ______________________________
____

RE:	Obligor	Obligee
Name:	______________________	______________________
Address:	______________________	______________________
	______________________	______________________

Obligor's social security number:______________________.
NOTE: The Obligor's social security number should be placed on the copy of the Notice to Payor that is mailed to the Obligor's Payor. This line should be left blank on the original Notice to Payor filed with the court.

YOU, THE PAYOR, ARE HEREBY NOTIFIED that, under section 61.1301, Florida Statutes, you have the responsibilities and rights set forth below with regard to the accompanying Income Deduction Order and/or any attachment(s):

1. You are required to deduct from the obligor's income the amount specified in the income deduction order, and in the case of a delinquency the amount specified in the notice of delinquency, and to pay that amount to the State of Florida Disbursement Unit. The amount actually deducted plus all administrative charges shall not be excess of the amount allowed under section 303(b) of the Consumer Credit Protection Act, 15 U.S.C. §1673(b) as amended.

2. You must implement income deduction no later than the first payment date which occurs more than 14 days after the date the income deduction order was served on you, and you shall conform the amount specified in the income deduction order or, in Title IV-D cases, the income deduction notice, to the obligor's pay cycle. The court should request at the time of the order that the payment cycle will reflect that of the obligor.

Florida Family Law Rules of Procedure Form 12.996(b), Notice to Payor (09/12)

3. You must forward, within 2 days after each date the obligor is entitled to payment from you, to the State of Florida Disbursement Unit, the amount deducted from the obligor's income, a statement as to whether the amount totally or partially satisfies the periodic amount specified in the income deduction order, or in Title IV-D cases, income deduction notice, and the specific date each deduction is made. If the IV-D agency is enforcing the order, you shall make these notifications to the agency.

4. If you fail to deduct the proper amount from the obligor's income, you are liable for the amount you should have deducted, plus costs, interest, and reasonable attorneys' fees;

5. You may collect up to $5 against the obligor's income to reimburse you for administrative costs for the first income deduction and up to $2 for each deduction thereafter.

6. The notice to payor, or, in Title IV-D cases, income deduction notice, and in the case of a delinquency, the notice of delinquency, are binding on you until further notice by the obligee, IV-D agency, or the court or until you no longer provide income to the obligor.

7. When you no longer provide income to the obligor, you shall notify the obligee and provide the obligor's last known address and the name and address of the obligor's new payor, if known. If you violate this provision, you are subject to a civil penalty not to exceed $250 for the first violation or $500 for any subsequent violation. If the IV-D agency is enforcing the order, you shall make these notifications to the agency instead of the obligee. Penalties shall be paid to the obligee or the IV-D agency, whichever is enforcing the income deduction order.

8. You shall not discharge, refuse to employ, or take disciplinary action against an obligor because of the requirement for income deduction. A violation of this provision subjects you to a civil penalty not to exceed $250 for the first violation or $500 for any subsequent violation. Penalties shall be paid to the obligee or the IV-D agency, whichever is enforcing the income deduction, if any alimony or child support obligation is owing. If no alimony or child support obligation is owing, the penalty shall be paid to the obligor.

9. The obligor may bring a civil action in the courts of this state against a payor who refuses to employ, discharges, or otherwise disciplines an obligor because of income deduction. The obligor is entitled to reinstatement of all wages and benefits lost, plus reasonable attorneys' fees and costs incurred.

10. The requirement for income deduction has priority over all other legal processes under state law pertaining to the same income and that payment, as required by the notice to payor or the income deduction notice, is a complete defense by the payor against any claims of the obligor or his or her creditors as to the sum paid.

11. When you receive notices to payor or income deduction notices requiring that the income of two or more obligors be deducted and sent to the same depository, the payor may combine the amounts that are to be paid to the depository in a single payment as long as the payments attributable to each obligor are clearly identified.

Florida Family Law Rules of Procedure Form 12.996(b), Notice to Payor (09/12)

12. If you receive more than one notice to payor or income deduction notice against the same obligor, the payor shall contact the court or, in Title IV-D cases, the Title IV-D agency for further instructions.

13. In a Title IV-D case, if an obligation to pay current support is reduced or terminated due to the emancipation of a child and the obligor owes an arrearage, retroactive support, delinquency, or costs, income deduction continues at the rate in effect immediately prior to emancipation until all arrearages, retroactive support, delinquencies, and costs are paid in full or until the amount of withholding is modified.

14. All notices to the obligee shall be sent to the address provided in this notice to payor, or any place thereafter the obligee requests in writing.

15. An employer who employed 10 or more employees in any quarter during the preceding state fiscal year or who was subject to and paid tax to the Department of Revenue in an amount of $20,000 or more shall remit support payments deducted pursuant to an income deduction order or income deduction notice and provide associated case data to the State Disbursement Unit by electronic means approved by the department. Payors who are required to remit support payments electronically can find more information on how to do so by accessing the State Disbursement Unit's website at www.floridasdu.com and clicking on "Payments." Payment options include Expert Pay, Automated Clearing House (ACH) credit through your financial institution, www.myfloridacounty.com, or Western Union. Payors may contact the SDU Customer Service Employer telephone line at 1-888-833-0743.

16. Additional information regarding the implementation of this Notice to Payor may be found at www.florida.sdu.com.

I certify that a copy of this document was [check all used]: ( ) e-mailed ( ) mailed ( ) faxed ( ) hand delivered to the person(s) listed below on *{date}*____________________.

Other party or his/her attorney:
Name: ____________________________
Address: ____________________________
City, State, Zip: ____________________________
Fax Number: ____________________________
E-mail Address(es): ____________________________

____
Signature of Party or his/her attorney
Printed Name: ____________________________
Address: ____________________________
City, State, Zip: ____________________________
Telephone Number: ____________________________

Florida Family Law Rules of Procedure Form 12.996(b), Notice to Payor (09/12)

Fax Number: ____________________
E-mail Address(es): ____________________
Florida Bar Number: ____________________

IF A NONLAWYER HELPED YOU FILL OUT THIS FORM, HE/SHE MUST FILL IN THE BLANKS BELOW:
[fill in all blanks] This form was prepared for the *{choose only one}* ( ) Petitioner ( ) Respondent
This form was completed with the assistance of:
{name of individual} ____________________,
{name of business} ____________________,
{street} ____________________,
{city} ________, *{state}* ________, *{telephone number}* ________.

Florida Family Law Rules of Procedure Form 12.996(b), Notice to Payor (09/12)

INSTRUCTIONS FOR FLORIDA FAMILY LAW RULES OF PROCEDURE FORM 12.996(b), NOTICE TO PAYOR (09/12)

When should this form be used?

This form should be used when an **Income Deduction Order** has been entered by the Court which is to take effect immediately.

This form should be typed or printed in black ink. After completing this form, the original of this form should be **filed** with the **clerk of the circuit court** in the county in which the action is pending. You should keep a copy for your own records.

What should I do next?

A copy of this form, and a copy of the Income Deduction Order, must be sent to the **obligor's** payor by certified mail, return receipt requested. The return receipt should be sent to the person that prepared this form so that it can filed with the clerk along with Florida Family Law Rules of Procedure Form 12.996(c), **Notice of Filing Return Receipt**.

A copy of this form must also be served on the other party or his or her attorney. **Service** must be in accordance with Florida Rule of Judicial Administration 2.516.

Where can I look for more information?

Before proceeding, you should read "General Information for Self-Represented Litigants" found at the beginning of these forms. The words that are in **"bold underline"** in these instructions are defined there. For further information, see section 61.1301, Florida Statutes.

Special Instructions . . .

The Obligor's social security number must be written on the copies of the Notice to Payor that are mailed to the Obligor's Payor and served on the other party or his or her attorney. The social security number should **not** be written on the copy of the Notice to Payor filed with the court.

Remember, a person who is NOT an attorney is called a nonlawyer. If a nonlawyer helps you fill out these forms, that person must give you a copy of a **Disclosure from Nonlawyer**, Florida Family Law Rules of Procedure Form 12.900(a), before he or she helps you. A nonlawyer helping you fill out these forms also **must** put his or her name, address, and telephone number on the bottom of the last page of every form he or she helps you complete.

Added March 4, 2010 (39 So.3d 227). Amended June Oct. 18, 2012, effective, *nunc pro tunc*, Sept. 1, 2012 (102 So.3d 505).

Form 12.996(c). Notice of Filing Return Receipt

IN THE CIRCUIT COURT OF THE ____________________ JUDICIAL CIRCUIT,
IN AND FOR ____________________ COUNTY, FLORIDA

Case No: ____________________
Division: ____________________

______________________________,
Petitioner,

and

______________________________,
Respondent.

NOTICE OF FILING RETURN RECEIPT

{Name} ______________________________, the **[check only one]** ( )Petitioner ( )Respondent, files the attached Return Receipt in reference to the Notice to Payor sent by certified mail to *{Payor's name}* ______________________________, the **[check only one]** ( ) Petitioner's ( ) Respondent's employer.

I certify that a copy of this document was [check all used]: ( ) e-mailed ( ) mailed ( ) faxed ( ) hand delivered to the persons(s) listed below on *{date}* ____________________.

Other party or his/her attorney:
Name: ______________________________
Address: ______________________________
City, State, Zip: ______________________________
Fax Number: ______________________________
E-mail Address(es): ______________________________

____
Signature of Party or his/her Attorney

Printed Name: ____________________
Address: ____________________
City, State, Zip: ____________________
Telephone Number: ____________________
Fax Number: ____________________
E-mail Address(es): ____________________
Florida Bar Number: ____________________

Florida Family Law Rules of Procedure Form 12.996(c), Notice of Filing Return Receipt (09/12)

IF A NONLAWYER HELPED YOU FILL OUT THIS FORM, HE/SHE MUST FILL IN THE BLANKS BELOW: [fill in **all** blanks] This form was prepared for the: *{choose only* ***one****}*
( ) Petitioner ( ) Respondent
This form was completed with the assistance of:
{name of individual} ______________________________,
{name of business} ______________________________,
{street} ______________________________,
{city} ______________, *{state}* ______, *{telephone number}* ______________.

Florida Family Law Rules of Procedure Form 12.996(c), Notice of Filing Return Receipt (09/12)

INSTRUCTIONS FOR FLORIDA FAMILY LAW RULES OF PROCEDURE FORM 12.996(c) NOTICE OF FILING RETURN RECEIPT (09/12)

When should this form be used?

This form should be used when an **Income Deduction Order**, Florida Family Law Rules of Procedure Form 12.996(a), is entered by the court and a **Notice to Payor**, Florida Family Law Rules of Procedure Form 12.996(b), has been sent by certified mail to the **obligor's payor**. When the post office returns the return receipt to you showing that the obligor's payor has received the **Notice to Payor**, you should type or print this form in black ink. After completing this form, you should sign it and attach the return receipt you received from the post office. The original of this form (and the attached return receipt) should be **filed** with the **clerk of the circuit court** in the county in which the action is pending. You should keep a copy for your own records.

What should I do next?

A copy of this form must also be served on the other party or his or her attorney. **Service** must be in accordance with Florida Rule of Judicial Administration 2.516.

Where can I look for more information?

Before proceeding, you should read "General Information for Self–Represented Litigants" found at the beginning of these forms. The words that are in **"bold underline"** in these instructions are defined there. For further information, see section 61.1301, Florida Statutes.

Special notes . . .

Remember, a person who is NOT an attorney is called a nonlawyer. If a nonlawyer helps you fill out these forms, that person must give you a copy of a **Disclosure from Nonlawyer**, Florida Family Law Rules of Procedure Form 12.900(a), before he or she helps you. A nonlawyer helping you fill out these forms also **must** put his or her name, address, and telephone number on the bottom of the last page of every form he or she helps you complete.

Added March 4, 2010 (39 So.3d 227). Amended Oct. 18, 2012, effective, *nunc pro tunc*, Sept. 1, 2012 (102 So.3d 505).

Form 12.996(d). Florida Addendum to Income Withholding Order

IN THE CIRCUIT COURT OF THE ____________________ JUDICIAL CIRCUIT,
IN AND FOR ____________________ COUNTY, FLORIDA

Case No: ____________
Division: ____________

______________________________,
Petitioner,

and

______________________________,
Respondent.

FLORIDA ADDENDUM TO INCOME WITHHOLDING ORDER

THE PAYOR, *{name}*______________________________, **IS HEREBY NOTIFIED** that, under sections 61.13 and 61.1301, Florida Statutes, you have the responsibilities and rights set forth below with regard to the Income Withholding Order/Notice for Support.

1. The Income Withholding Order/Notice for Support is enforceable against employers specifically listed upon the form as well as **all subsequent employers/payors** of Obligor, *{name}*____________________, *{address}*____________________.

2. You are required to deduct from the obligor's income the amount specified in the income withholding order, and in the case of a delinquency the amount specified in the notice of delinquency, and to pay that amount to the State of Florida Disbursement Unit. The amount actually deducted plus all administrative charges shall not be in excess of the amount allowed under section 303(b) of the Consumer Credit Protection Act, 15 U.S.C. Section 1673(b), as amended.

3. You must implement the income deduction no later than the first payment date which occurs more than 14 days after the date the income deduction order was served on you, and you shall conform the amount specified in the income withholding order to the obligor's pay cycle. The court should request at the time of the order that the payment cycle will reflect that of the obligor.

4. You must forward, within 2 days after each date the obligor is entitled to payment from you, to the State of Florida Disbursement Unit, the amount deducted from the obligor's income, a statement as to whether the amount totally or partially satisfies the periodic amount specified in the income withholding order, and the specific date each deduction is made. If the IV-D agency is enforcing the order, you shall make these notifications to the agency.

5. If you fail to deduct the proper amount from the obligor's income, you are liable for the amount you should have deducted, plus costs, interest, and reasonable attorneys' fees.

6. You may collect up to $5 against the obligor's income to reimburse you for the administrative costs for the first income deduction and up to $2 for each deduction thereafter.

7. The Income Withholding Order/Notice for Support is binding on you until further notice by court order or until you no longer provide income to the obligor.

8. When you no longer provide income to the obligor, you shall notify the obligee, *{name}*________________________, *{address}*______________________________________, and provide the obligor's last known address and the name and address of the obligor's new payor, if known, utilizing the form contained within the Income Withholding Order/Notice for Support. If you violate this provision, you are subject to a civil penalty not to exceed $250 for the first violation or $500 for any subsequent violation. If the IV-D agency is enforcing the order, you shall make these notifications to the agency instead of the obligee. Penalties shall be paid to the obligee or the IV-D agency, whichever is enforcing the income deduction order.

9. You shall not discharge, refuse to employ, or take disciplinary action against an obligor because of the requirement for income deduction. A violation of this provision subjects you to a civil penalty not to exceed $250 for the first violation or $500 for any subsequent violation. Penalties shall be paid to the obligee or the IV-D agency, whichever is enforcing the income deduction, if any alimony or child support obligation is owing. If no alimony or child support obligation is owing, the penalty shall be paid to the obligor.

10. The obligor may bring a civil action in the courts of this state against a payor who refuses to employ, discharges, or otherwise disciplines an obligor because of income deduction. The obligor is entitled to reinstatement of all wages and benefits lost, plus reasonable attorneys' fees and costs incurred.

11. In a Title IV-D case, if an obligation to pay current support is reduced or terminated due to the emancipation of a child and the obligor owes an arrearage, retroactive support, delinquency, or costs, income deduction continues at the rate in effect immediately prior to emancipation until all arrearages, retroactive support, delinquencies, and costs are paid in full or until the amount of withholding is modified.

12. All notices to the obligee shall be sent to the address provided in this notice to payor, or any place thereafter the obligee requests in writing.

13. An employer who employed 10 or more employees in any quarter during the preceding state fiscal year or who was subject to and paid tax to the Department of Revenue in an amount of $20,000 or more shall remit support payments deducted pursuant to an income deduction order or income deduction notice and provide associated case data to the State Disbursement Unit by electronic means approved by the department. Payors who are required to remit support payments electronically can find more information on how to do so by accessing the State Disbursement Unit's website at www.floridasdu.com and clicking on "Payments." Payment options include Expert Pay, Automated Clearing House (ACH) credit through your financial institution, www.myfloridacounty.com , or Western Union. Payors may contact the SDU Customer Service Employer telephone line at 1-888-883-0743.

14. The amount of arrears owed, if any, is $____________. You must withhold an additional twenty percent (20%) or more of the ongoing periodic obligation towards same at the rate of $________ per ____________ until full payment is made of any arrearage, attorneys' fees and costs—provided that no deduction shall be applied to attorneys' fees and costs until the full amount of any arrearage

is paid. If a delinquency accrues after the order establishing, modifying, or enforcing support has been entered and there is no existing order for repayment of the delinquency or a pre-existing arrearage, a payor shall deduct $________per ____________ (which represents an additional twenty percent (20%) of the current support obligation, or other amount agreed to by the parties) until the delinquency and any attorneys' fees and costs are paid in full. No deduction may be applied to attorneys' fees and costs until the delinquency is paid in full.

15. Pursuant to sections 61.13 and 61.1301, Florida Statutes, the amounts listed for payment on the Income Withholding Order must be varied by the employer/payor for bonus income, or similar one-time payment:

    You shall deduct [Choose only **one**] ( ) the full amount, ( ) ________%, or ( ) none of the income which is payable to the obligor in the form of a bonus or other similar one-time payment, up to the amount of arrearage reported in the Income Deduction Order or the remaining balance thereof, and forward the payment to the State of Florida Disbursement Unit. For purposes of this subparagraph, "bonus" means a payment in addition to an obligor's usual compensation and which is in addition to any amounts contracted for or otherwise legally due and shall not include any commission payments due an obligor.

16. Child Support Reduction/Termination Schedule. Child support amount listed on the IWO shall be automatically reduced or terminated as set forth in the following schedule:

Please list children by initials from eldest to youngest	[redacted]	**Insert in this column the day, month, and year the child support obligation terminates for each designated child (see instructions)**	[redacted]	**Insert in this column the amount of child support for all minor children remaining (including designated child).**
Child 1 (Eldest) Initials & year of birth:	*From the effective date of this Income Deduction Order* ***until*** *the following date:*		*child support for Child 1 and all other younger child(ren) should be paid in the following monthly amount:*	
Child 2 Initials & year of birth:	*After the date set forth in the row above until the following date:*		*child support for Child 2 and all other younger child(ren) should be paid in the following monthly amount:*	
Child 3 Initials & year of birth:	*After the date set forth in the row above until the*		*child support for Child 3 and all other younger child(ren) should be paid in the*	

	following date:		*following monthly amount:*	
Child 4 Initials & year of birth:	*After the date set forth in the row above until the following date:*		*child support for Child 4 and all other younger child(ren) should be paid in the following monthly amount:*	
Child 5 Initials & year of birth:	*After the date set forth in the row above until the following date:*		*child support for Child 5 and all other younger child(ren) should be paid in the following monthly amount:*	

(Continue on additional pages for additional children)

NOTE: This change only relates to the amount of the child support obligation portion of the payments listed in the first page of the Income Withholding Order. If there is a child support arrearage in a Title IV-D case, the amount will not be reduced due to the child no longer being eligible for support pursuant to paragraph 11 above.

17. Additional information regarding the implementation of income deduction may be found at www.floridasdu.com.

IF A NONLAWYER HELPED YOU FILL OUT THIS FORM, HE/SHE MUST FILL IN THE BLANKS BELOW
[fill in all blanks] This form was prepared for the: *{choose only one}* ( ) Petitioner ( ) Respondent
This form was completed with the assistance of:
*{name of individual}*______________________________,
*{name of business}*______________________________,
*{address}*______________________________,
*{city}*______________, *{state}*________, *{telephone number}*______________.

Florida Family Law Rules of Procedure Form 12.996(d), Florida Addendum to Income Withholding Order (07/13)

INSTRUCTIONS FOR FLORIDA FAMILY LAW RULES OF PROCEDURE FORM 12.996(d), FLORIDA ADDENDUM TO INCOME WITHHOLDING ORDER (7/13)

When should this form be used?

This form should be used when the court has ordered that support be paid by income deduction and OMB Form 0970–0154, Income Withholding for Support, has been used. This form must be added to the OMB form to provide provisions required for income deduction orders by Florida law.

This form should be typed or printed in black ink. It should be attached to the OMB form and **filed** with the clerk of the circuit court in the county in which your action is pending.

What should I do next?

A copy of this form and a copy of the OMB Income Withholding for Support form, signed by the judge, should be sent to the **obligor's** payor by certified mail, return receipt requested. The return receipt should be sent to the person who prepared this form, so that it can be filed with the court with Florida Family Law Rules of Procedure Form 12.996(c), **Notice of Filing Return Receipt.**

Where can I look for more information?

Before proceeding, you should read "General Information for Self–Represented Litigants" found at the beginning of these forms. The words that are in **"bold underline"** in these instructions are defined there. For further information see sections 61.13 and 61.1301, Florida Statutes.

Special Instructions . . .

When filling out an Income Withholding for Support form, please note the following additional instructions for that form:

1. The Remittance Identifier is the County Code for the county the case was heard in followed by the Case Number. A list of county codes is included with these instructions.

2. The FIPS code may be found on the attached list. Use the code for the County in which the case is pending.

Remember, a person who is NOT an attorney is called a nonlawyer. If a nonlawyer helps you fill out these forms, that person must give you a copy of a **Disclosure from Nonlawyer**, Florida Family Law Rules of Procedure Form 12.900(a), before he or she helps you. A nonlawyer helping you fill out these forms also **must** put his or her name, address, and telephone number on the bottom of the last page of every form he or she helps you complete.

FIPS and County Codes

COUNTY	FIPS	COUNTY CODE
ALACHUA	12001	01
BAKER	12003	02
BAY	12005	03
BRADFORD	12007	04
BREVARD	12009	05
BROWARD	12011	06
CALHOUN	12013	07
CHARLOTTE	12015	08
CITRUS	12017	09
CLAY	12019	10
COLLIER	12021	11
COLUMBIA	12023	12
DADE	12025	13
DESOTO	12027	14
DIXIE	12029	15
DUVAL	12031	16
ESCAMBIA	12033	17
FLAGER	12035	18

COUNTY	FIPS	COUNTY CODE
FRANKLIN	12037	19
GADSDEN	12039	20
GILCHRIST	12041	21
GLADES	12043	22
GULF	12045	23
HAMILTON	12047	24
HARDEE	12049	25
HENDRY	12051	26
HERNANDO	12053	27
HIGHLANDS	12055	28
HILLSBOROUGH	12057	29
HOLMES	12059	30
INDIAN RIVER	12061	31
JACKSON	12063	32
JEFFERSON	12065	33
LAFAYETTE	12067	34
LAKE	12069	35
LEE	12071	36

COUNTY	FIPS	COUNTY CODE
LEON	12073	37
LEVY	12075	38
LIBERTY	12077	39
MADISON	12079	40
MANATEE	12081	41
MARION	12083	42
MARTIN	12085	43
MONROE	12087	44
NASSAU	12089	45
OKALOOSA	12091	46
OKEECHOBEE	12093	47
ORANGE	12095	48
OSCEOLA	12097	49
PALM BEACH	12099	50
PASCO	12101	51

COUNTY	FIPS	COUNTY CODE
PINELLAS	12103	52
POLK	12105	53
PUTNAM	12107	54
ST. JOHNS	12109	55
ST. LUCIE	12111	56
SANTA ROSA	12113	57
SARASOTA	12115	58
SEMINOLE	12117	59
SUMTER	12119	60
SUWANNEE	12121	61
TAYLOR	12123	62
UNION	12125	63
VOLUSIA	12127	64
WAKULLA	12129	65
WALTON	12131	66
WASHINGTON	12133	67

Added June 28, 2012 (94 So.3d 558). Amended July 3, 2013 (121 So.3d 505).

INDEX TO
FLORIDA FAMILY LAW RULES OF PROCEDURE

FLORIDA RULES FOR CERTIFICATION AND REGULATION OF COURT REPORTERS

Omitted Rules

The Florida Rules for Certification and Regulation of Court Reporters were adopted by the Florida Supreme Court on December 24, 1998, effective July 1, 1999. The Florida Supreme Court held the rules in abeyance on December 7, 1999. See Amendments to Florida Rule of Judicial Administration 2.070 — Court Reporters, No. 92,300 (Fla. order filed Dec. 7, 1999). Because the rules have not been resubmitted by the Florida Rules of Judicial Administration Committee or reinstituted by the Florida Supreme Court, they have been omitted from publication.

FLORIDA RULES FOR CERTIFICATION AND REGULATION OF SPOKEN LANGUAGE COURT INTERPRETERS

Date Effective

Added effective July 1, 2006 (933 So.2d 504).

PART I. GENERAL PROVISIONS

Rule 14.100. Definitions

The following terms have the meanings shown as used in these rules:

(a) Court Interpreter. Any person providing spoken language court interpreting services during a court or court-related proceeding, except persons performing such services without remuneration on behalf of indigent persons in circumstances not requiring appointment of a court interpreter.

(b) Certified Court Interpreter. An interpreter who has completed all requirements for certification in accordance with these rules and holds a valid certificate issued by the Office of the State Courts Administrator.

(c) Language Skilled. A designation reserved for interpreters who have completed all requirements in accordance with these rules, but who are seeking certification in a spoken language for which there is no state-certifying examination, and hold a valid certificate issued by the Office of the State Courts Administrator.

(d) Provisionally Approved. A designation reserved for interpreters of spoken languages for which a state-certifying examination is available, who, although not yet certified, have passed the oral performance exam at a lesser qualifying prescribed level and hold a valid certificate issued by the Office of the State Courts Administrator.

(e) Duly Qualified Interpreter. An interpreter who is certified or language skilled, or, if a certified or language skilled interpreter is unavailable, a provisionally approved interpreter, as these terms are defined under subdivisions (b) through (d) above.

(f) Court. Any county, circuit or district court of this state or the Supreme Court of Florida.

(g) Court Proceeding. Any hearing or trial presided over by a state court judge, general magistrate, special magistrate, or hearing officer within the state courts system.

(h) Court–Related Proceeding. Any event, including, but not limited to, a deposition, mediation, arbitration, or examination, which occurs or could be made to occur as a result of a court order, subpoena, or general law, and for which the primary purpose is the communication or exchange of information related to a claim or defense in or the settlement of a pending or impending court case. However, a law enforcement investigation which does not yet involve the participation of the prosecuting authority shall not be considered a court-related proceeding.

(i) Board. The Court Interpreter Certification Board.

(j) Compliance Period. The two-year period beginning upon official designation as a certified, language skilled, or provisionally approved court interpreter.

(k) State–Certifying Examination. A full or abbreviated board-approved oral performance examination designed to objectively measure whether a candidate possesses the minimum levels of language knowledge and fluency and interpreting skills required to perform competently during court proceedings.

(*l*) Written Examination. An initial qualifying or screening examination designed to measure a candidate's literacy in English, familiarity with, and usage of, court-related terms, and/or knowledge of matters regarding interpreter ethics and related professional conduct.

(m) Full Oral Performance Examination. An oral examination which measures language knowledge and fluency in both English and non-English languages, as well as the ability to successfully render meaning in target and source languages in simultaneous interpretation, consecutive interpretation, and sight translation of documents.

(n) Abbreviated Oral Performance Examination. An oral examination assessing functional proficiency to competently interpret simultaneously in court from English to a non-English language, and prerequisite to which a candidate must satisfy board-approved oral proficiency interviews in both English and non-English languages.

(*o*) Oral Proficiency Interview. A standardized language proficiency interview assessing functional speaking ability in both English and non–English languages.

(p) Modes of Court Interpretation. Simultaneous interpretation, consecutive interpretation, and sight translation of documents in a court setting.

(q) Transcription. The process of preserving audio or videotaped sound files in written form, duplicating the original, together with its translation into the target language, and, when used for evidentiary purposes, produced in dual-language format with the original and translation appearing side-by-side.

(r) Translation. Converting a written text from one language into written text in another language.

Added June 29, 2006, effective July 1, 2006 (933 So.2d 504). Amended March 27, 2014, effective May 1, 2014 (136 So.3d 584); March 31, 2015, effective April 1, 2015, (159 So.3d 804).

Rule 14.110. Court Interpreter Certification Board

(a) Board Composition. The Court Interpreter Certification Board is created to supervise a process by which interpreters may become certified or otherwise duly qualified, and in accordance with which the conduct of all court-appointed persons engaged in spoken language interpreting in the courts shall be governed. The board shall be under the supervisory authority of the Supreme Court of Florida. It shall be composed of ten persons, appointed by the chief justice, as follows:

(1) two county court judges;

(2) three circuit court judges;

(3) three trial court administrators;

(4) one federally certified court interpreter; and

(5) one state certified court interpreter.

(b) Staff. Such staff as may be necessary to administer the program and permit the board to carry out its duties shall be provided by the Office of the State Courts Administrator insofar as funded by the Florida Legislature.

(c) Officers; Quorum. The chief justice shall appoint one of the board members to serve as chair. A majority of the board shall constitute a quorum.

(d) Vacancies. Any vacancy on the board shall be filled by appointment by the chief justice. A person appointed to fill a vacancy shall serve for the remainder of the term of the member being replaced.

(e) Terms. All terms shall be three years. Members shall be eligible for reappointment.

(f) Duties. The duties of the board shall include:

(1) registration, designation, regulation, and discipline of all court interpreters, and, upon failure to comply with these rules, suspension and revocation of registrations and acquired designations;

(2) authority to periodically review and adopt new or amended board operating procedures consistent with these rules;

(3) authority to make recommendations to the supreme court regarding language access issues and amendment of court rules relating to provision of spoken language court interpreting services; and

(4) performance of such other assignments relating to provision of spoken language court interpreting services as may be directed by the chief justice of the supreme court.

(g) Fees. The board shall have the authority to recommend to the supreme court such fees as the board may deem necessary to permit it to carry out its duties, including, but not limited to, orientation fees, examination fees, application fees, renewal fees, and late fees. All such fees shall be made payable to the State of Florida and shall be non-refundable.

(h) Records; Registry. The board shall maintain records and minutes of its meetings and all other official actions. It shall maintain a record of all continuing education credits earned by registered, certified, language skilled, and provisionally approved court interpreters. It shall also maintain separate registries containing the name and, as applicable, designation number, renewal date, and geographic areas where services are available for each registered and officially designated court interpreter.

(i) Expenses. Members of the board shall serve without compensation. However, they shall be reimbursed for all reasonable expenses incurred in the performance of their duties, in compliance with all rules and statutes governing such reimbursement.

Added June 29, 2006, effective July 1, 2006 (933 So.2d 504). Amended March 27, 2014, effective May 1, 2014 (136 So.3d 584); March 31, 2015, effective April 1, 2015, (159 So.3d 804).

PART II. INTERPRETER REGISTRATION AND DESIGNATIONS

Rule 14.200. Registration

Text of subrule (a) effective until October 1, 2015.

(a) Exclusive Designations. Individuals providing court interpreting services shall be designated certified court interpreters, language skilled, or provisionally approved upon qualifying in accordance with these rules. As a descriptive term employed in relation to the provision of court interpreting services, "duly qualified" refers exclusively to those persons who are certified or language skilled, or, if a certified or language skilled interpreter is unavailable, a provisionally approved interpreter.

Text of subrule (a) effective October 1, 2015.

(a) Registration. Court interpreters shall, prior to providing interpreter services, become registered with the Office of the State Courts Administrator.

(b) General Prerequisites. Unless otherwise provided, all applicants completing prerequisites for registration must:

(1) as an initial prerequisite, attend a two-day orientation program administered by the Office of the State Courts Administrator or board-approved training provider;

(2) pass a written examination approved by the board, which shall include an ethics component;

(3) submit an approved reporting form documenting completion of 20 hours of courtroom observation;

(4) take an oath to uphold the Code of Professional Conduct adopted in these rules;

(5) undergo and pass a background check according to standards prescribed by the board and published in board operating procedures;

(6) agree to obtain 16 credits of continuing education from a continuing education program approved by the board; and

(7) agree to diligently pursue designation as a certified, language skilled, or provisionally approved interpreter and, within the first year of any two-year registration period, submit to:

(i) at least 1 full oral performance examination approved by the board, or, in the event a full oral performance examination is unavailable, submit to a board-approved abbreviated oral examination and demonstrate functional speaking ability in English and a non-English language through oral proficiency interviews as a prerequisite to taking the abbreviated examination;

(ii) at least 1 approved oral proficiency interview in English and a non–English language for which there is no state-certifying examination as an assessment of functional speaking ability; or

(iii) at least 1 equivalent state-certifying examination in another state that is in accordance with board-approved requisites; and

(8) submit an application for registration and enclose an initial application fee in an amount set by the supreme court.

(c) Renewal. Registration under this rule shall be valid for a period of 2 years. Before any person's registration may be renewed, he or she must have completed 16 credits of continuing education through a board-approved program and comply again with subdivisions (b)(3) through (b)(7) of this rule. The board shall provide written notice of expiring registrations at least 90 days before expiration. Applications for renewal of registration must be accompanied by a fee in an amount set by the supreme court.

(d) Administrative Revocation. Registration shall be automatically revoked for any person who fails to submit to at least one of the foregoing examinations within the first year of any two-year registration period, except for registrants who have achieved the designation of certified, language skilled, or provisionally approved during a prior two-year registration period. A court interpreter whose registration is revoked under this subdivision shall not be eligible for registration for a period of 1 year following revocation and must thereafter comply with all requirements of subdivision (b) of this rule.

(e) Threshold Performance. Registration may be revoked at the discretion of the board for any person who fails to attain minimum scores, in accordance with standards prescribed by the board and published in board operating procedures, on the sight translation, simultaneous interpretation, and consecutive interpretation components during a single test administration as specified under subdivision (b)(7)(i) or (b)(7)(iii), or who fails to demonstrate satisfactory functional speaking ability as prescribed by the board during an oral proficiency interview under subdivision (b)(7)(ii).

(f) Persons Holding Valid Designation. A person holding the designation of certified, language skilled, or provisionally approved interpreter is deemed to be registered during the time he or she holds such designation. Renewal of the designation of certified, language skilled, or provisionally approved interpreter shall be governed by rule 14.230.

(g) Loss of Designation. Any certified, language skilled, or provisionally approved court interpreter whose designation expires, is suspended, or revoked shall be deemed unregistered on the 181st day following loss of designation, unless the board, in its discretion, sets a shorter period of time. Any person failing to renew registration within 181 days after loss of designation, or such lesser number of days as may be set by the board, shall cease providing interpreter services in all court and court-related proceedings.

Added June 29, 2006, effective July 1, 2006 (933 So.2d 504). Amended March 27, 2014, effective May 1, 2014 (136 So.3d 584); March 31, 2015, effective April 1, 2015, (159 So.3d 804); March 31, 2015, effective Oct. 1, 2015, (159 So.3d 804).

Rule 14.202. Exclusive Designations

Court interpreters shall be designated certified, language skilled, or provisionally approved upon qualifying in accordance with rules 14.205, 14.210, and 14.215.

Added March 31, 2015, effective April 1, 2015, (159 So.3d 804).

Rule 14.205. Certified Court Interpreter Designation

(a) Preferred Appointment, Retention, and Staffing. The certified court interpreter designation represents the highest qualified state-level interpreter designation and shall be the preferred designation in the selection, appointment, staffing, or private retention of court interpreters.

(b) Requirements. An applicant seeking designation as a certified court interpreter must:

Text of subrule (b)(1) effective until October 1, 2015.

(1) pass a full oral performance examination approved by the board, unless qualifying for a waiver of the examination requirement under rule 14.210, or, in the event a full oral performance examination is unavailable, pass a board-approved abbreviated oral examination and demonstrate functional speaking ability in English and non–English languages through oral proficiency interviews as a prerequisite to taking the abbreviated examination and qualifying for certification;

Text of subrule (b)(1) effective October 1, 2015.

(1) register under provisions of rule 14.200, complying with subdivisions 14.200(a), (b)(1) through (b)(6), and (b)(8);

(2) pass a board-approved full oral performance examination upon attaining a minimum score in accordance with standards prescribed by the board and published in board operating procedures, unless qualifying for a waiver of the examination requirement under rule 14.220;

(3) absent availability of a full oral performance examination, pass a board-approved abbreviated oral examination, attaining a minimum score in accordance with standards prescribed by the board and published in board operating procedures, and demonstrate functional speaking ability in English and a non-English language as prescribed by the board through oral proficiency interviews as a prerequisite to taking the abbreviated examination and qualifying for certification; and

(4) complete the process leading to designation within 2 years following submission of an application for registration, unless extended by the board in exceptional circumstances.

(c) Court–Employed Interpreters. Applicants who are selected as employee interpreters, but who are not certified at the time of court employment, shall become certified within 1 year of being employed in a court interpreting position. The one-year requirement may be modified by the board on a case-by-case basis, if necessary, only in exceptional circumstances.

Added March 27, 2014, effective May 1, 2014 (136 So.3d 584). Amended March 31, 2015, effective April 1, 2015, (159 So.3d 804); March 31, 2015, effective Oct. 1, 2015, (159 So.3d 804).

Rule 14.210. Language Skilled Designation

(a) Preferred Appointment, Retention, and Staffing. The language skilled designation represents the highest qualified state-level interpreter designation next beneath full certification and shall be the preferred designation over non-designated interpreters in the selection, appointment, staffing, or private retention of court interpreters in the area of the language skilled individual's linguistic expertise.

(b) Requirements. An applicant seeking designation as a language skilled court interpreter in a spoken language for which there is no state-certifying examination must:

Text of subrule (b)(1) effective until October 1, 2015.

(1) passing an approved oral proficiency interview in English and the non–English language as an assessment of functional speaking ability; and

Text of subrule (b)(1) effective October 1, 2015.

(1) register under provisions of rule 14.200, complying with subdivisions 14.200(a), (b)(1) through (b)(6), and (b)(8);

(2) pass an approved oral proficiency interview in English and a non-English language, attaining a minimum score in accordance with standards prescribed by the board and published in board operating procedures, as an assessment of functional speaking ability; and

(3) complete the process leading to designation within 2 years following submission of an application for registration, unless extended by the board in exceptional circumstances.

(c) Conditional Designation. In the event a language-specific state-certifying examination becomes available, a language skilled interpreters shall be required to take and pass the certifying examination within 2 years of notice of its availability. Failure to become certified within this two-year period shall result in loss of the language skilled designation, unless the board approves an extension in exceptional circumstances.

Former Rule 14.215 added March 27, 2014, effective May 1, 2014 (136 So.3d 584). Renumbered Rule 14.210 and amended March 31, 2015, effective April 1, 2015, (159 So.3d 804). Amended March 31, 2015, effective Oct. 1, 2015, (159 So.3d 804).

Rule 14.215. Provisionally Approved Designation

(a) Requirements. An individual not yet certified in a spoken language for which a state-certifying examination is available, but who has taken the oral performance exam, may be designated as provisionally approved upon:

Text of subrule (a)(1) effective until October 1, 2015.

(1) scoring a minimum 60 percent on each section of the oral exam and an overall 65 percent or greater;

Text of subrule (a)(1) effective October 1, 2015.

(1) registering under provisions of rule 14.200, complying with subdivisions 14.200(a), (b)(1) through (b)(6), and (b)(8);

(2) attaining minimum scores on each section of the oral exam in accordance with standards prescribed by the board and published in board operating procedures; and

(3) completing the process leading to designation within 2 years following submission of an application for registration, unless extended by the board in exceptional circumstances.

(b) Loss of Designation. Following designation as a provisionally approved interpreter, if the interpreter fails to become certified within 2 years, or within 1 year if the individual is employed in a court interpreting position, the interpreter will forfeit the designation unless the board approves an extension in exceptional circumstances.

Former Rule 14.220 added June 29, 2006, effective July 1, 2006 (933 So.2d 504). Amended March 27, 2014, effective May 1, 2014 (136 So.3d 584). Renumbered Rule 14.215 and amended March 31, 2015, effective April 1, 2015, (159 So.3d 804). Amended March 31, 2015, effective Oct. 1, 2015 (159 So.3d 804).

Rule 14.220. Waiver of Examination Requirement

(a) Federal Certification. Upon presentation of proof satisfactory to the board, the oral performance examination requirement shall be waived for anyone holding a federal courts certificate which is issued by the Administrative Office of the United States Courts and whose name appears on the registry of federally certified interpreters. No other component of certification is waived by this rule.

(b) Equivalent Examination. Upon presentation of proof satisfactory to the board, the examination requirement shall be waived for anyone who has passed an equivalent examination in another state and meets minimum qualifying board-approved requisites. No other component of registration, certification, language skilled, or provisionally approved designation is waived by this rule.

Added March 31, 2015, effective April 1, 2015, (159 So.3d 804).

Rule 14.225. Issuance of Certificates

Upon satisfactory completion of the specified requirements, the board shall issue a certificate for each official designation which shall include a designation number and date of issue. Letters confirming registration shall be issued to persons satisfying requirements under rule 14.200.

Added March 27, 2014, effective May 1, 2014 (136 So.3d 584). Amended March 31, 2015, effective April 1, 2015, (159 So.3d 804).

Rule 14.230. Renewal of Certificates

(a) Renewal. Once issued, the certificate for a certified court interpreter shall remain renewable unless suspended or revoked by the board. The language skilled designation may also be renewed conditioned upon continued unavailability of a state-certifying examination in the language for which this designation has been granted. Absent an extension of time granted only in exceptional circumstances, failure to become certified within 2 years, or 1 year for anyone employed in a court interpreting position, will result in forfeiture of a provisionally approved designation. Renewal of registration shall be undertaken as provided under rule 14.200(c).

(b) Biennial Renewal Fee. Each certified and language skilled court interpreter shall pay a biennial renewal fee in an amount set by the supreme court. A certificate shall be suspended automatically upon non-payment, but shall be reinstated upon application to the board, accompanied by payment and made within 60 days of the date of suspension. Upon expiration of the 60–day grace period, any request for reinstatement must be made in accordance with rule 14.450.

(c) Notification. The board shall notify all certified, language skilled, and provisionally approved court interpreters in writing of the expiration date of their certificates at least 90 days before such date.

Notice shall be given by regular United States mail, directed to the last mailing address on file with the board.

(d) Continued Status in Exceptional Circumstances. If the board determines exceptional circumstances warrant an extension of time within which a language skilled or provisionally approved interpreter may obtain certification, the interpreter will not forfeit the respective designation during the period of extension. A language skilled or provisionally approved interpreter who is granted an extension must, in lieu of a biennial renewal fee and as a condition of maintaining formal designation, pay a fee in an amount proportionate to the time of extension.

Added June 29, 2006, effective July 1, 2006 (933 So.2d 504). Amended March 27, 2014, effective May 1, 2014 (136 So.3d 584); March 31, 2015, effective April 1, 2015, (159 So.3d 804).

Rule 14.240. Maintenance of Official Designation

(a) Assignments. Each certified, language skilled, and provisionally approved court interpreter shall complete 20 law-related professional interpreting assignments, or a lesser number of assignments totaling no fewer than 40 hours, every two-year compliance period. Interpreters unable to complete this requirement because of a limited need for interpreting services in their language may be eligible, upon written request and board approval, for an extension of time or exemption. Officially designated state-level court interpreters who are employed by the courts in court interpreting positions may, in lieu of reporting discrete law-related professional assignments, provide proof of court employment and an affidavit averring compliance with this requirement.

(b) Continuing Education. Each certified, language skilled, and provisionally approved court interpreter shall earn 16 continuing education credits every two-year compliance period. Application for approval of continuing education credit shall be made in writing on a continuing education reporting form furnished by the board. Certified and language skilled interpreters renewing official designation shall return completed forms to the board with submission of renewal fees. Provisionally approved interpreters shall submit continuing education reporting forms to the board with applications for certification.

(c) Approved Programs. The board shall keep and maintain a list of approved continuing education programs. Approval of an educational program or activity not listed shall be at the board's discretion and subject to approval on a case-by-case basis.

Added June 29, 2006, effective July 1, 2006 (933 So.2d 504). Amended March 27, 2014, effective May 1, 2014 (136 So.3d 584).

PART III. CODE OF PROFESSIONAL CONDUCT

Rule 14.300. Professional Conduct

All court interpreters shall act in a professional manner in keeping with the Code of Professional Conduct as set forth herein. Failure to adhere to the Code may lead to disciplinary action. Disciplinary action is at the discretion of the board.

Added June 29, 2006, effective July 1, 2006 (933 So.2d 504). Amended March 27, 2014, effective May 1, 2014 (136 So.3d 584); March 31, 2015, effective April 1, 2015, (159 So.3d 804).

Rule 14.310. Accuracy and Completeness

Interpreters shall render a complete and accurate interpretation or sight translation, without altering, omitting, summarizing, or adding anything to what is stated or written, and without explanation.

Added June 29, 2006, effective July 1, 2006 (933 So.2d 504).

Committee Notes

The interpreter has a twofold duty: (1) to ensure that the proceedings in English reflect precisely what was said by a non-English speaking person, and (2) to place the non-English speaking person on an equal footing with those who understand English. This creates an obligation to conserve every element of information contained in a source language communication when it is rendered in the target language.

Therefore, interpreters are obligated to apply their best skills and judgment to preserve faithfully the meaning of what is said in court, including the style or register of speech. Verbatim, "word for word" or literal oral interpretations are not appropriate when they distort the meaning of the source language, but every spoken statement, even if it appears nonresponsive, obscene, rambling, or incoherent should be interpreted. This includes apparent misstatements and ambiguities.

Interpreters should never interject their own words, phrases, or expressions. If the need arises to explain an interpreting problem (for example, a term or phrase with no direct equivalent in the target language or a misunderstanding that only the interpreter can clarify), the interpreter should ask the court's permission to provide an explanation. Interpreters should convey the emotional emphasis of the speaker without reenacting or mimicking the speaker's emotions, or dramatic gestures. Sign language interpreters, however, must employ all of the visual cues that the language they are interpreting for requires, including facial expressions, body language, and hand gestures. Sign language interpreters, therefore, should ensure that court participants do not confuse these essential elements of the interpreted language with inappropriate interpreter conduct.

The obligation to preserve accuracy includes the interpreter's duty to correct any error of interpretation discovered by the interpreter during the proceeding. Interpreters should demonstrate their professionalism by objectively analyzing any challenge to their performance.

Rule 14.320. Representation of Qualifications

Interpreters shall accurately and completely represent their certifications, training, and pertinent experience.

Added June 29, 2006, effective July 1, 2006 (933 So.2d 504).

Committee Notes

Acceptance of a case by an interpreter conveys linguistic competency in legal settings. Withdrawing or being asked to withdraw from a case after it begins causes a disruption of court proceedings and is wasteful of scarce public resources. It is therefore essential that interpreters present a complete and truthful account of their training, certification and experience prior to appointment so the court can fairly evaluate their qualifications for delivering interpreting services.

Rule 14.330. Impartiality and Avoidance of Conflict of Interest

Interpreters shall be impartial and unbiased and shall refrain from conduct that may give an appearance of bias. Interpreters shall disclose any real or perceived conflict of interest.

Added June 29, 2006, effective July 1, 2006 (933 So.2d 504).

Committee Notes

The interpreter serves as an officer of the court, and the interpreter's duty in a court proceeding is to serve the court and the public to which the court is a servant. This is true regardless of whether the interpreter is publicly retained at government expense or retained privately at the expense of one of the parties.

The interpreter should avoid any conduct or behavior that presents the appearance of favoritism toward any of the parties. Interpreters should maintain professional relationships with their clients, and should not take an active part in any of the proceedings. The interpreter should discourage a non-English speaking party's personal dependence. During the course of the proceedings, interpreters should not converse with parties, witnesses, jurors, attorneys, or with friends of relatives of any party, except in the discharge of their official functions. It is especially important that interpreters, who are often familiar with attorneys or other members of the courtroom work group, including law enforcement officers, refrain from casual and personal conversation with anyone in the court that may convey an appearance of a special relationship or partiality to any of the court participants.

The interpreter should strive for professional detachment. Verbal and nonverbal displays of personal attitudes, prejudices, emotions, or opinions should be avoided at all times.

Should an interpreter become aware that a participant in the proceedings views the interpreter as having a bias or being biased, the interpreter should disclose that knowledge to the appropriate judicial authority and counsel. Any condition that interferes with the objectivity of an interpreter constitutes a conflict of interest. Before providing services in a matter, court interpreters must disclose any prior involvement to all parties and presiding officials, whether personal or professional, that could be reasonably construed as a conflict of interest. This disclosure should not include privileged or confidential information.

The following are examples including, but not limited to, circumstances that are presumed to create factual or apparent conflicts of interest for interpreters where interpreters should not serve:

(1) The interpreter is a friend, associate, or relative of a party or counsel for a party involved in the proceeding.

(2) The interpreter has served in an investigative capacity for any party involved in the proceeding.

(3) The interpreter has previously been retained by a law enforcement agency to assist in the preparation of the criminal case at issue.

(4) The interpreter or the interpreter's spouse or child has a financial interest in the subject matter in controversy or in a party to the proceeding, or any other interest that would be affected by the outcome of the case.

(5) The interpreter has been involved in the choice of a counsel or law firm for that case.

Interpreters should disclose to the court and other parties when they have previously been retained for private employment by one of the parties in the case.

An interpreter should not serve in any matter in which payment for his or her services is contingent upon the outcome of the case.

Court interpreters will not accept money or other consideration or favors of any nature or kind which might reasonably be interpreted as an attempt to influence their actions with respect to the discharge of their obligations except for the authorized payment for services.

An interpreter who is also an attorney should not serve in both capacities in the same matter. Interpreters should notify the presiding officer of any personal bias they may have involving any aspect of the proceeding. For example, an interpreter who has been the victim of a sexual assault may wish to be excused from interpreting in cases involving similar offenses.

Rule 14.340. Confidentiality and Restriction of Public Comment

Interpreters shall protect the confidentiality of all privileged and other confidential information. Furthermore, interpreters shall not publicly discuss, report, or offer an opinion concerning a matter in which they are or have been engaged, even when that information is not privileged or required by law to be confidential.

Added June 29, 2006, effective July 1, 2006 (933 So.2d 504).

Committee Notes

The interpreter must protect and uphold the confidentiality of all privileged information obtained during the course of her or his duties. It is especially important that the interpreter understand and uphold the attorney-client privilege, which requires confidentiality with respect to any communication between attorney and client.

This rule also applies to other types of privileged communications, except upon court order to the contrary.

Interpreters must also refrain from repeating or disclosing information obtained by them in the course of their employment that may be relevant to the legal proceeding.

In the event that an interpreter becomes aware of information that suggests imminent harm to someone or relates to a crime being committed during the course of the proceedings, the interpreter should immediately disclose the information to an appropriate authority within the judiciary who is not involved in the proceeding and seek advice in regard to the potential conflict in professional responsibility. An interpreter should never grant interviews to the media, make comments, or express personal opinions to any of the parties about any aspect of the case even after a verdict is rendered.

Rule 14.350. Professional Demeanor

Interpreters shall conduct themselves in a manner consistent with the dignity of the court and shall be as unobtrusive as possible.

Added June 29, 2006, effective July 1, 2006 (933 So.2d 504).

Committee Notes

Interpreters should know and observe the established protocol, rules, procedures, and dress code when delivering interpreting services. When speaking in English, interpreters should speak at a rate and volume that enables them to be heard and understood throughout the courtroom, but the interpreter's presence should otherwise be as unobtrusive as possible. Interpreters should work without drawing undue or inappropriate attention to themselves. Interpreters should dress in a manner that is consistent with the dignity of the proceeding of the court.

Interpreters shall refrain from making any type of referral. Interpreters shall adhere to all instructions given by the court in which their services are being used.

Rule 14.360. Scope of Practice

Interpreters shall limit themselves to interpreting or translating, and shall not give legal advice, express personal opinions to individuals for whom they are interpreting, or engage in any other activities which may be construed to constitute a service other than interpreting or translating while serving as an interpreter.

Added June 29, 2006, effective July 1, 2006 (933 So.2d 504).

Committee Notes

Since interpreters are responsible only for enabling others to communicate, they should limit themselves to the activity of interpreting or translating. Interpreters should refrain from initiating communications while interpreting unless it is necessary for assuring an accurate and faithful interpretation.

Interpreters may be required to initiate communications during a proceeding when they find it necessary to seek assistance in performing their duties. In this case, the interpreter should ask the Court's permission to initiate the communication. Examples of such circumstances include seeking direction when unable to understand or express a word or thought, requesting speakers to moderate their rate of communication or repeat or rephrase something, correcting their own interpreting errors, or notifying the court of reservations about their ability to satisfy an assignment competently. In such instances, they should make it clear that they are speaking for themselves. (This is achieved by using the third person—example: "The interpreter requests that the question be repeated, clarified, etc. . . .").

An interpreter may convey legal advice from an attorney to a person only while that attorney is giving it. An interpreter should not explain the purpose of forms, services, or otherwise act as counselors or advisors unless they are interpreting for someone who is acting in that official capacity. The interpreter may translate language on a form for a person who is filling out the form, but may not explain the form or its purpose for such a person.

The interpreter should not personally perform official acts that are the official responsibility of other court officers, including, but not limited to, court clerks, pretrial release investigators or interviewers, or probation counselors.

Rule 14.370. Assessing and Reporting Impediments to Performance

Interpreters shall assess their ability to deliver their services at all times. When interpreters have any reservation about their ability to satisfy an assignment competently, they shall immediately convey that reservation to the appropriate judicial authority.

Added June 29, 2006, effective July 1, 2006 (933 So.2d 504).

Committee Notes

If the communications mode or language of the non-English speaking person cannot be readily interpreted, the interpreter must immediately notify the appropriate judicial authority.

Interpreters should notify the appropriate judicial authority of any environmental or physical limitation that impedes or hinders their ability to deliver interpreting services adequately (for example, the court room is not quiet enough for the interpreter to hear or be heard by the non-English speaker, more than one person at a time is speaking, or principals or witnesses of the court are speaking at a rate of speed that is too rapid for the interpreter to adequately interpret). Sign language interpreters must ensure that they can both see and convey the full range of visual language elements that are necessary for communication, including facial expressions and body movement, as well as hand gestures.

Interpreters should notify the presiding officer of the need to take periodic breaks to maintain mental and physical alertness and prevent interpreter fatigue. Interpreters should recommend and encourage the use of team interpreting whenever necessary.

Interpreters are encouraged to make inquiries as to the nature of a case whenever possible before accepting an assignment. This enables interpreters to match more closely their professional qualifications, skills, and experience to potential assignments and more accurately assess their ability to satisfy those assignments competently. Even competent and experienced interpreters may encounter cases where routine proceedings suddenly involve technical or specialized terminology unfamiliar to the interpreter (for example, the unscheduled testimony of an expert witness). When such instances occur, interpreters should request a brief recess to familiarize themselves with the subject matter. If familiarity with the terminology requires extensive research, interpreters must inform the presiding officer.

Interpreters should refrain from accepting a case if they feel the language and subject matter of that case are likely to exceed their skills or capacities. Interpreters should feel no compunction about notifying the presiding officer if they feel unable to perform competently, due to lack of familiarity with terminology, preparation, or difficulty in understanding a witness or defendant. Because of the difficulty in translating sound recordings, the practice of doing so in court should be discouraged at all times. In certain instances, the presiding officer will order the interpreter to translate in court an audio recording. In such case, the interpreter should do it, but should state on the record that he or she cannot certify the accuracy of the translation.

Rule 14.380. Duty to Report Ethical Violations

Interpreters shall report any effort to impede or influence their compliance with any law, any provision of this Code, or any other official policy governing court interpreting and legal translating to the proper judicial authority.

Added June 29, 2006, effective July 1, 2006 (933 So.2d 504).

Committee Notes

Because the users of interpreting services frequently misunderstand the proper role of the interpreter, they may ask or expect the interpreter to perform duties or engage in activities that run counter to the provisions of this code or other laws, regulations, or policies governing court interpreters. It is incumbent upon the interpreter to inform such persons of his or her professional obligations. If, having been apprised of their obligations, the person persists in demanding that the interpreter violate them, the interpreter should turn to a supervisory interpreter, the judge, or another official with jurisdiction over interpreter matters to resolve the situation.

Interpreters must at all times during court proceedings interpret everything that is being said on the record, including, but not limited to jury instructions and comments made by the defendants or other participants in the proceeding unless directed to the contrary by the court on the record. Interpreters shall refrain from altering, amending, or omitting any statements made on the record even if asked by a court officer or any other party. Interpreters faced with such a request must immediately inform the party in question that this would constitute a direct violation of the interpreters' code of ethics and refuse to comply with such demand.

Rule 14.390. Professional Development

Interpreters shall continually improve their skills and knowledge and advance the profession through activities such as professional training, continuing education, and interaction with colleagues and specialists in related fields.

Added June 29, 2006, effective July 1, 2006 (933 So.2d 504).

Committee Notes

Interpreters must continually strive to increase their knowledge of the languages they work in professionally, including past and current trends in technical, vernacular, and regional terminology as well as their application within court proceedings.

Interpreters should keep informed of all statutes, rules of courts, and policies of the judiciary that relate to the performance of their professional duties. An interpreter should seek to elevate the standards of the profession through participation in workshops, professional meetings, interaction with colleagues, coursework, and reading current literature in the field.

PART IV. DISCIPLINE

Rule 14.400. Application

All court interpreters shall be subject to the disciplinary provisions under this part.

Added June 29, 2006, effective July 1, 2006 (933 So.2d 504). Amended March 27, 2014, effective May 1, 2014 (136 So.3d 584); March 31, 2015, effective April 1, 2015, (159 So.3d 804).

Rule 14.405. Suspension or Revocation

(a) Suspension or Revocation. Any official state-level interpreter designation or registration may be suspended or revoked.

(b) Cause. Any of the following may constitute cause:

(1) conviction of a felony or misdemeanor involving moral turpitude, dishonesty, or false statements;

(2) fraud, dishonesty, or corruption which is related to the functions and duties of a court interpreter;

(3) continued false or deceptive advertising after receipt of a cease and desist notice from the board;

(4) gross incompetence or unprofessional or unethical conduct;

(5) fraud or misrepresentation in obtaining or renewing any state-level court interpreter designation or registration;

(6) noncompliance with rule provisions directing completion of law-related professional interpreting assignments or continuing education requirements; or

(7) nonpayment of renewal or late fees.

Added March 27, 2014, effective May 1, 2014 (136 So.3d 584). Amended March 31, 2015, effective April 1, 2015, (159 So.3d 804).

Rule 14.410. Disciplinary Procedures

(a) Initiation. Disciplinary proceedings may be initiated by a standard form asserting a violation of these rules. The complaint shall be in writing under oath and filed with the Office of the State Courts Administrator. The board may initiate disciplinary proceedings on its own motion. The board shall be divided into an investigative committee and a hearing panel, as established by rules of the board.

(b) Facial Sufficiency. If a majority of the investigative committee, after an in-person or conference call meeting, finds that the allegations, if true, would constitute a violation of these rules, it shall send a copy of the complaint identifying the rule or rules alleged to have been violated to the court interpreter by certified United States mail directed to the last mailing address on file with the board. If the complaint is found to be facially insufficient, the complaint shall be dismissed without prejudice and the complainant and interpreter shall be so notified.

(c) Response. Within 30 days of the issuance of a finding of facial sufficiency, the court interpreter shall file a written response with the investigative committee. If no response is filed, the violations identified in the finding of facial sufficiency shall be deemed admitted.

(d) Review. Upon review of the complaint and the interpreter's response, if any, the investigative committee may find that no violation has occurred and dismiss the complaint. If the complaint is not dismissed, the investigative committee shall review the complaint, the response, if any, and any underlying documentation, to determine whether there is probable cause to believe that the alleged misconduct occurred and would constitute a violation of the rules. The investigative committee may conduct a further investigation if warranted. The investigative committee may also meet with the complainant and interpreter in an attempt to resolve the matter. Such resolution may include sanctions if agreed to by the interpreter.

(e) Probable Cause Found. If probable cause exists, the investigative committee may draft formal charges and forward such charges for a hearing. In the alternative, the investigative committee may decide not to pursue the case by filing a short and plain statement of the reason(s) for non-referral and so advise the complainant and the interpreter in writing. If formal charges are filed, they shall include a short and plain statement of the matters asserted in the complaint and references to the particular rules involved.

(f) Hearing Panel Review. Within 60 days after the filing of the formal charges, the hearing panel shall review the complaint, the finding of probable cause, and the response, if any, and decide whether to (i) dismiss the proceeding, (ii) issue a proposed disposition, or (iii) set a hearing. The hearing panel shall promptly send written notice of its decision to the court interpreter and to the complainant by certified United States mail, return receipt requested.

(g) No Hearing Demanded. A proposed disposition issued pursuant to subdivision (f)(ii) shall become final unless the court interpreter demands a hearing within 30 days of the date it was issued.

(h) Hearing Demanded. If the court interpreter demands a hearing in a timely manner, the hearing shall take place no less than 30 days nor more than 90 days from the date of notice pursuant to subdivision (f)(iii) or of the court interpreter's demand pursuant to subdivision (g).

(i) Legal Representation. The court interpreter may be represented by an attorney at any stage of the proceeding. The court interpreter shall be responsible for all of his or her costs and expenses, including attorney fees.

Added June 29, 2006, effective July 1, 2006 (933 So.2d 504). Amended March 27, 2014, effective May 1, 2014 (136 So.3d 584).

Rule 14.420. Disciplinary Hearings

(a) Pre–Hearing Discovery. Pre–hearing discovery shall not be permitted unless expressly authorized by the hearing panel, in response to a written request.

(b) Rules of Evidence. Strict rules of evidence shall not apply. The hearing panel may, in its discretion, consider any evidence presented, including affidavits, giving such evidence the weight it deems appropriate.

(c) Hearings to be Reported or Electronically Recorded. The hearing panel shall ensure that all hearings are reported or electronically recorded.

(d) Hearing Procedure. At the hearing, both the hearing panel and the court interpreter shall be afforded the opportunity to introduce documents and other relevant evidence, and to elicit sworn testimony.

(e) Hearing Panel Deliberations. Following the presentation of evidence, the hearing panel shall deliberate regarding its decision. Such deliberations shall take place in private.

(f) Finality of Decision; Rehearing. Unless the court interpreter files a request for rehearing within 30 days of the date of the decision, the decision shall become final without further action. If a timely request for rehearing is filed, the decision shall not become final until the request has been disposed of by written decision, a copy of which shall be sent to the court interpreter by certified United States mail.

Added June 29, 2006, effective July 1, 2006 (933 So.2d 504). Amended March 27, 2014, effective May 1, 2014 (136 So.3d 584).

Rule 14.430. Disciplinary Dispositions

(a) Burden of Proof. If the hearing panel finds that there is clear and convincing evidence that the court interpreter has violated one or more of these rules, it shall impose such discipline as it may deem appropriate, consistent with these rules.

(b) Vote Required; Notification. All decisions of the hearing panel shall be by majority vote, in writing and, if adverse to the court interpreter, shall contain factual findings supporting the decision. A copy of the decision shall be sent to the court interpreter by certified United States mail.

(c) Sanctions. Sanctions may consist of one or more of the following:

(1) a private reprimand;

(2) a public reprimand;

(3) the imposition of costs and expenses incurred by the hearing panel in connection with the proceeding, including investigative costs;

(4) restitution;

(5) a requirement that specified continuing education courses and/or additional law-related professional interpreting assignments be completed within a specified period of time;

(6) a requirement that one or more parts of a court interpreter examination be successfully taken or retaken;

(7) a limitation on the scope of practice or interpreting services;

(8) a requirement that work be supervised;

(9) suspension of registration or official state-level designation for a period not to exceed 1 year; or

(10) revocation of registration or official state-level designation.

Added June 29, 2006, effective July 1, 2006 (933 So.2d 504). Amended March 27, 2014, effective May 1, 2014 (136 So.3d 584); March 31, 2015, effective April 1, 2015, (159 So.3d 804).

Rule 14.440. Confidentiality of Disciplinary Proceeding

All complaints alleging misconduct against individuals subject to disciplinary action under these rules, including the interpreter's response, if any, and all other records made or received as part of the complaint procedure, are exempt from public disclosure under rule 2.420(c)(3)(B), Florida Rules of Judicial Administration, and shall remain confidential until a finding of probable cause or no probable cause is established, regardless of the outcome of any appeal.

Added June 29, 2006, effective July 1, 2006 (933 So.2d 504). Amended Oct. 16, 2008 (993 So.2d 507); March 27, 2014, effective May 1, 2014 (136 So.3d 584).

Rule 14.450. Reinstatement

A court interpreter whose registration or official state-level designation has been suspended or revoked may, at any time, apply in writing for reinstatement. Such request shall explain why the applicant believes that he or she should be reinstated, and shall be accompanied by a renewal fee in an amount set by the board. Whether to grant or to deny such a request shall rest in the sole and absolute discretion of the board. The board may impose such conditions upon reinstatement as it deems appropriate.

Added June 29, 2006, effective July 1, 2006 (933 So.2d 504). Amended March 27, 2014, effective May 1, 2014 (136 So.3d 584); March 31, 2015, effective April 1, 2015, (159 So.3d 804).

Rule 14.460. Chief Justice Review

(a) Right of Review. Any interpreter found to have committed a violation of these rules shall have a right of review of that action by the chief justice of the Supreme Court of Florida or the chief justice's designee, whose decision shall be final. An interpreter shall have no right of review of any resolution reached under rule 14.410(d).

(b) Rules of Procedure. The Florida Rules of Appellate Procedure, to the extent applicable and except as otherwise provided in this rule, shall control all appeals of interpreter disciplinary matters.

(1) The jurisdiction to seek review of disciplinary action shall be invoked by submitting an original and one copy of a Notice of Review of Interpreter Disciplinary Action to the chief justice within 30 days of the hearing panel's decision. A copy shall also be provided to the Board.

(2) The notice of review shall be substantially in the form prescribed by rule 9.900(a), Florida Rules of Appellate Procedure. A copy of the panel decision shall be attached to the notice.

(3) Appellant's initial brief, accompanied by an appendix as prescribed by rule 9.220, Florida Rules of Appellate Procedure, shall be served within 30 days of submitting the notice of review. Additional briefs shall be served as prescribed by rule 9.210, Florida Rules of Appellate Procedure.

(c) Standard of Review. The review shall be conducted in accordance with the following standard of review:

(1) The chief justice or the chief justice's designee shall review the findings and conclusions of the hearing panel using a competent substantial evidence standard, neither reweighing the evidence in the record nor substituting the reviewer's judgment for that of the hearing panel.

(2) Decisions of the chief justice or the chief justice's designee shall be final upon issuance of a mandate under rule 9.340, Florida Rules of Appellate Procedure.

Added June 29, 2006, effective July 1, 2006 (933 So.2d 504). Amended Oct. 16, 2008 (993 So.2d 507).

INDEX TO
FLORIDA RULES FOR CERTIFICATION AND REGULATION OF SPOKEN LANGUAGE COURT INTERPRETERS

CERTIFIED AND COURT INTERPRETERS

RULES FOR QUALIFIED AND COURT-APPOINTED PARENTING COORDINATORS

PART I. STANDARDS

PART I. STANDARDS

Rule 15.000. Applicability of Standards

These standards apply to all qualified parenting coordinators and court-appointed parenting coordinators. A qualified parenting coordinator is anyone who is qualified to serve as a parenting coordinator pursuant to the parenting coordination section of Chapter 61, Florida Statutes, and has been approved by the court to serve as a qualified parenting coordinator or to be on a qualified parenting coordination panel for any circuit.

Added July 3, 2014, effective July 3, 2014 (142 So.3d 831).

Rule 15.010. Parenting Coordination Defined

Parenting coordination is a child-focused alternative dispute resolution process whereby a parenting coordinator assists the parents in creating or implementing a parenting plan by facilitating the resolution of disputes between the parents by providing education, making recommendations, and, with the prior approval of the parents and the court, making limited decisions within the scope of the court's order of referral. For the purposes of these standards, "parent" refers to the child's mother, father, legal guardian, or other person who is acting as a parent and guardian.

Added July 3, 2014, effective July 3, 2014 (142 So.3d 831).

Rule 15.020. Parenting Coordination Concepts

Parenting coordination is a child-focused alternative dispute resolution process that emphasizes the needs and interests of children, parents and families. It is based on the concepts of communication, education, negotiation, facilitation, and problem-solving. The role of a parenting coordinator includes the integration of skills and core knowledge drawn primarily from the areas of mental health, law, and conflict resolution.

Added July 3, 2014, effective July 3, 2014 (142 So.3d 831).

Rule 15.030. Competence

(a) Professional Competence. Parenting coordinators shall acquire and maintain professional competence in parenting coordination. A parenting coordinator shall regularly participate in educational activities promoting professional growth.

(b) Circumstances Affecting Role. Parenting coordinators shall withdraw from the parenting coordination role if circumstances arise which impair the parenting coordinators' competency.

(c) Skill and Experience. A parenting coordinator shall decline an appointment, withdraw, or request appropriate assistance when the facts and circumstances of the case are beyond the parenting coordinator's skill or experience.

(d) Knowledge. A parenting coordinator shall maintain knowledge of all current statutes, court rules, local court rules, and court and administrative orders relevant to the parenting coordination process.

Added July 3, 2014, effective July 3, 2014 (142 So.3d 831).

Rule 15.040. Integrity

(a) Avoiding Dual Relationships. A parenting coordinator shall not accept the role of parenting coordinator if there has been a prior personal, professional or business relationship with the parties or their family members. A parenting coordinator shall not enter into a personal, professional or business relationship with the parties or their family members during the parenting coordination process or for a reasonable time after the parenting coordination process has concluded.

(b) Respect for Diversity. Parenting coordinators shall not allow their personal values, morals, or religious beliefs to undermine or influence the parenting coordination process or their efforts to assist the parents and children. If the parenting coordinator has personal, moral, or religious beliefs that will interfere with the process or the parenting coordinator's respect for persons involved in the parenting coordination process, the parenting coordinator shall decline the appointment or withdraw from the process.

(c) Inappropriate Activity. Parenting coordinators shall not engage in any form of harassment or exploitation of parents, children, students, trainees, supervisees, employees, or colleagues.

(d) Misrepresentation. A parenting coordinator shall not intentionally or knowingly misrepresent any material fact or circumstance in the course of conducting a parenting coordination process.

(e) Demeanor. A parenting coordinator shall be patient, dignified, and courteous during the parenting coordination process.

(f) Maintaining Integrity. A parenting coordinator shall not accept any engagement, provide any service, or perform any act that would compromise the parenting coordinator's integrity.

(g) Avoiding Coercion. A parenting coordinator shall not unfairly influence the parties as a means to achieve a desired result.

Added July 3, 2014, effective July 3, 2014 (142 So.3d 831).

Committee Notes

Any sexual relationship between a parenting coordinator and a party or a party's family member is a form of exploitation and creates a dual relationship and therefore would be considered a violation of these standards.

A parenting coordinator may at times direct a party's conduct. An example is when a parenting coordinator encourages compliance with a parenting plan by pointing out possible consequences of a party's course of action. However, the means to direct behavior should not include unfairly influencing the parties. Examples of unfairly influencing the parties include lying to the parties or exaggerating the parenting coordinator's power to influence the court.

Rule 15.050. Advice, Recommendations, and Information

(a) Informing Parties of Risks. Prior to a parenting coordinator making substantive recommendations to the parties regarding timesharing and parental responsibilities, the parenting coordinator should inform the parties of the inherent risk of making substantive recommendations without adequate data.

(b) Right to Independent Counsel. When a parenting coordinator believes a party does not understand or appreciate the party's legal rights or obligations, the parenting coordinator shall advise the party of the right to seek independent legal counsel.

Added July 3, 2014, effective July 3, 2014 (142 So.3d 831).

Rule 15.060. Impartiality

(a) Freedom from Favoritism and Bias. A parenting coordinator shall conduct the parenting coordination process in an impartial manner. Impartiality means freedom from favoritism or bias in word, action, and appearance.

(b) Disclosure. A parenting coordinator shall advise all parties of circumstances which may impact impartiality including but not limited to potential conflicts of interest bearing on possible bias, prejudice, or impartiality.

(c) Influence. A parenting coordinator shall not be influenced by outside pressure, bias, fear of criticism, or self-interest.

(d) Gifts. A parenting coordinator shall not give, accept or request a gift, favor, loan, or other item of value to or from a party, attorney, or any other person involved in and arising from any parenting coordination process.

(e) Prohibited Relationships. After accepting appointment, and for a reasonable period of time after the parenting coordination process has concluded, a parenting coordinator shall avoid entering into family, business, or personal relationships which could affect impartiality or give the appearance of partiality, bias, or influence.

(f) Withdrawal. A parenting coordinator shall withdraw from a parenting coordination process if the parenting coordinator can no longer be impartial.

Added July 3, 2014, effective July 3, 2014 (142 So.3d 831).

Rule 15.070. Conflicts of Interest

(a) Generally. A parenting coordinator shall not serve as a parenting coordinator in a matter that presents a clear or undisclosed conflict of interest. A conflict of interest arises when any relationship between the parenting coordinator and the parenting coordination participants or the subject matter of the dispute compromises or appears to compromise the parenting coordinator's impartiality.

(b) Disclosure. The burden of disclosure rests on the parenting coordinator. All such disclosures shall be made as soon as practical after the parenting coordinator becomes aware of the interest or relationship. After appropriate disclosure, the parenting coordinator may serve if all parties agree. However, if a conflict of interest clearly impairs a parenting coordinator's impartiality, the parenting coordinator shall withdraw regardless of the express agreement of the parties.

(c) Solicitation Prohibited. A parenting coordinator shall not use the parenting coordination process to solicit, encourage, or otherwise incur future professional services with any party.

Added July 3, 2014, effective July 3, 2014 (142 So.3d 831).

Committee Notes

The parenting coordination process may take place over a long period of time. Therefore, the parenting coordinator may initially accept an appointment where a potential conflict does not exist, but arises during the course of the parenting coordination process.

The disclosure requirements in this subdivision do not abrogate subdivision 15.040 (a) which prohibits a parenting coordinator from accepting the role of parenting coordinator if there has been a prior personal, professional or business relationship with the parties' or their family members. It is intended to address situations in which the conflict arises after the acceptance of appointment and encourage the timely disclosure to the parties.

Rule 15.080. Scheduling the Parenting Coordination Process

A parenting coordinator shall schedule parenting coordination sessions in a manner that provides adequate time for the process. A parenting coordinator shall perform parenting coordination services in a timely fashion, avoiding delays whenever possible.

Added July 3, 2014, effective July 3, 2014 (142 So.3d 831).

Rule 15.090. Compliance with Authority

A parenting coordinator shall comply with all statutes, court rules, local court rules, and court and administrative orders relevant to the parenting coordination process.

Added July 3, 2014, effective July 3, 2014 (142 So.3d 831).

Rule 15.100. Improper Influence

A parenting coordinator shall refrain from any activity that has the appearance of improperly influencing a court to secure an appointment to a case.

Added July 3, 2014, effective July 3, 2014 (142 So.3d 831).

Rule 15.110. Marketing Practices

(a) False or Misleading Marketing Practices. A parenting coordinator shall not engage in any marketing practice, including advertising, which contains false or misleading information. A parenting coordinator shall ensure that any marketing of the parenting coordinator's qualifications, services to be rendered, or the parenting coordination process is accurate and honest.

(b) Qualification. Any marketing practice in which a parenting coordinator indicates that such parenting coordinator is "qualified" is misleading unless the parenting coordinator indicates the Florida judicial circuits in which the parenting coordinator has been qualified.

(c) Prior Adjudicative Experience. Any marketing practice is misleading if the parenting coordinator states or implies that prior adjudicative experience, including, but not limited to, service as a judge, magistrate, or administrative hearing officer, makes one a better or more qualified parenting coordinator.

(d) Prohibited Claims or Promises. A parenting coordinator shall not make claims of achieving specific outcomes or promises implying favoritism for the purpose of obtaining business.

(e) Additional Prohibited Marketing Practices. A parenting coordinator shall not engage in any marketing practice that diminishes the importance of a party's right to self-determination or the impartiality of the parenting coordinator, or that demeans the dignity of the parenting coordination process or the judicial system.

Added July 3, 2014, effective July 3, 2014 (142 So.3d 831).

Committee Note

The roles of a parenting coordinator and an adjudicator are fundamentally distinct. The integrity of the judicial system may be impugned when the prestige of the judicial office is used for commercial purposes. When engaging in any parenting coordinator marketing practice, a former adjudicative officer should not lend the prestige of the judicial office to advance private interests in a manner inconsistent with this rule. For example, the depiction of a parenting coordinator in judicial robes or use of the word "judge" with or without modifiers to the parenting coordinator's name would be inappropriate. However, an accurate representation of the parenting coordinator's judicial experience would not be inappropriate.

Rule 15.120. Concurrent Standards

Other ethical standards to which a parenting coordinator may be professionally bound are not abrogated by these rules. In the course of performing parenting coordination services, however, these rules prevail over any conflicting ethical standards to which a parenting coordinator may otherwise be bound.

Added July 3, 2014, effective July 3, 2014 (142 So.3d 831).

Rule 15.130. Relationship with Other Professionals

A parenting coordinator shall respect the role of other professional disciplines in the parenting coordination process and shall promote cooperation between parenting coordinators and other professionals.

Added July 3, 2014, effective July 3, 2014 (142 So.3d 831).

Rule 15.140. Confidentiality

(a) Preservation of Confidentiality. A parenting coordinator shall maintain confidentiality of all communications made by, between, or among the parties and the parenting coordinator except when disclosure is required or permitted by law or court order. The parenting coordinator shall maintain confidentiality of all records developed or obtained during the parenting coordination process in accordance with law or court order.

(b) Use of Materials for Educational Purposes. A parenting coordinator shall not disclose the identity of the parents, children, or other persons involved in the parenting coordination process when information is used in teaching, writing, consulting, research, and public presentations.

(c) Record Keeping. A parenting coordinator shall maintain privacy in the storage and disposal of records and shall not disclose any identifying information when materials are used for research, training, or statistical compilations.

Added July 3, 2014, effective July 3, 2014 (142 So.3d 831).

Rule 15.150. Notice and Initial Session

(a) Notice of Fees. Prior to an initial meeting with the parties in a parenting coordination session, the parenting coordinator shall provide written notice of all fees, costs, methods of payment and collection.

(b) Initial Session. At the initial session a parenting coordinator shall, in person, describe the terms of the Order of Referral, if any, and inform the participants in writing of the following:

(1) the parenting coordination process, the role of the parenting coordinator and the prohibition against dual roles;

(2) parenting coordination is an alternative dispute resolution process wherein a parenting coordinator assists parents in creating or implementing a parenting plan;

(3) the parenting coordinator may provide education and make recommendations to the parties, and, with prior approval of the parents and the court, make non-substantive decisions;

(4) communications made during the parenting coordination session are confidential, except where disclosure is required or permitted by law;

(5) all fees, costs, methods of payment, and collections related to the parenting coordination process;

(6) the court's role in overseeing the parenting coordination process, including a party's right to seek court intervention;

(7) the party's right to seek legal advice; and

(8) the extent to which parties are required to participate in the parenting coordination process.

Added July 3, 2014, effective July 3, 2014 (142 So.3d 831).

Rule 15.160. Fees and Costs

A parenting coordinator holds a position of trust. Fees shall be reasonable and be guided by the following general principles:

(a) Changes in Fees, Costs, or Payments. Once services have begun, parenting coordinators shall provide advance written notice of any changes in fees or other charges.

(b) Maintenance of Financial Records. Parenting coordinators shall maintain the records necessary to support charges for services and expenses, and, upon request, shall make an accounting to the parents, their counsel, or the court.

(c) Equitable Service. Parenting coordinators shall provide the same quality of service to all parties regardless of the amount of each party's financial contribution.

(d) Basis for Charges. Charges for parenting coordination services based on time shall not exceed actual time spent or allocated.

(e) Costs. Charges for costs shall be for those actually incurred.

(f) Expenses. When time or expenses involve two or more parenting coordination processes on the same day or trip, the time and expense charges shall be prorated appropriately.

(g) Written Explanation of Fees. A parenting coordinator shall give the parties and their counsel a written explanation of any fees and costs prior to the parenting coordination process. The explanation shall include the:

(1) basis for and amount of any charges for services to be rendered, including minimum fees and travel time;

(2) amount charged for the postponement or cancellation of parenting coordination sessions and the circumstances under which such charges will be assessed or waived;

(3) basis and amount of charges for any other items; and

(4) parties' pro rata share of the parenting coordinator's fees and costs if previously determined by the court or agreed to by the parties.

(h) Maintenance of Records. A parenting coordinator shall maintain records necessary to support charges for services and expenses and, upon request, shall make an accounting to the parties, their counsel, or the court.

(i) Remuneration for Referrals. No commissions, rebates, or similar remuneration shall be given or received by a parenting coordinator for a parenting coordination referral.

(j) Contingency Fees Prohibited. A parenting coordinator shall not charge a contingent fee or base a fee on the outcome of the process.

Added July 3, 2014, effective July 3, 2014 (142 So.3d 831).

Rule 15.170. Records

(a) Documentation of Parenting Coordination Process. Parenting coordinators shall maintain all information and documents related to the parenting coordination process.

(b) Record Retention. Parenting coordinators shall maintain confidentiality and comply with applicable law when storing and disposing of parenting coordination records.

(c) Relocation or Closing the Parenting Coordination Practice. A parenting coordinator shall provide public notice of intent to relocate or close his or her practice. The notification shall include instructions on how parties' may obtain a copy of their records or arrange for their records to be transferred.

Added July 3, 2014, effective July 3, 2014 (142 So.3d 831).

Rule 15.180. Safety, Capacity, and Protection

(a) Monitoring. Parenting coordinators shall monitor the process for domestic violence, substance abuse, or mental health issues and take appropriate action to address any safety concerns.

(b) Injunctions for Protection. Parenting coordinators shall honor the terms of all active injunctions for protection and shall not seek to modify the terms of an injunction.

(c) Terminating Process Based on Safety Concerns. Parenting coordinators shall suspend the process and notify the court when the parenting coordinator determines it is unsafe to continue.

(d) Adjournment or Termination. A parenting coordinator shall adjourn or terminate a parenting coordination process if any party is incapable of participating meaningfully in the process.

Added July 3, 2014, effective July 3, 2014 (142 So.3d 831).

Rule 15.190. Education and Training

Parenting coordinators shall comply with any statutory, rule or court requirements relative to qualifications, training, and education.

Added July 3, 2014, effective July 3, 2014 (142 So.3d 831).

Rule 15.200. Responsibility to the Courts

(a) Candid with Referring Court. Parenting coordinators shall be candid, accurate, and responsive to the court concerning the parenting coordinators' qualifications, availability and other administrative matters.

(b) Providing Information to the Court. When parenting coordinators provide information to the court, parenting coordinators shall do so in a manner that is consistent with court rules and statutes. Parenting coordinators shall notify the referring court when the court orders conflict with the parenting coordinator's professional ethical responsibilities. Parenting coordinators shall notify the court when it is appropriate to terminate the process. A parenting coordinator shall be candid, accurate, and fully responsive to the court concerning the parenting coordinator's qualifications, availability, and other administrative matters.

Added July 3, 2014, effective July 3, 2014 (142 So.3d 831).

PART II. DISCIPLINE

Rule 15.210. Procedure

Any complaint alleging violations of the Rules For Qualified And Court–Appointed Parenting Coordinators, Part I: STANDARDS, shall be filed with the Dispute Resolution Center which shall be responsible for enforcing these Standards.

Added July 3, 2014, effective July 3, 2014 (142 So.3d 831).

INDEX TO

FLORIDA RULES FOR QUALIFIED AND COURT—APPOINTED PARENTING COORDINATORS

THE SUPREME COURT OF FLORIDA

MANUAL OF INTERNAL OPERATING PROCEDURES

Revision

Amended July 1989; February 2000; January 2002; April 2005; January 2009; May 2010; January 2014; February 2015.

INTRODUCTION

This manual of internal operating procedures is designed to: (1) assist practitioners; (2) orient new employees; (3) codify established practices and traditions; (4) protect and maintain the collegial decision-making process; and (5) make the judicial process more comprehensible to the general public. This manual neither supplants any of the Florida rules of court procedure nor creates any substantive or procedural rights. The Court continually reviews and improves internal procedures, and the manual is revised from time to time as new procedures are officially adopted. The latest version of this manual is always posted on the Court's website at http://www.floridasupremecourt.org/pub_info/documents/IOPs.pdf.

Section I. Court Structure.

A. Court Composition. The Supreme Court of Florida is composed of seven justices who serve terms of six years. Each justice, other than the chief justice, is authorized to employ three staff attorneys and one judicial assistant. The staff of the chief justice includes three staff attorneys, one of whom may serve as executive assistant to the chief justice; four judicial assistants; an inspector general and staff; a reporter of decisions; a director of the public information office and staff; and a central staff of attorneys, one of whom serves as the director of central staff, and a paralegal. Chambers for each justice, including the chief justice, are located on the fourth floor of the Supreme Court Building. Members of the public, including attorneys admitted to practice in Florida, are not permitted on the fourth floor unless they have obtained permission from a justice.

B. The Chief Justice. The chief justice is the administrative officer of the Court and the Florida judicial branch, responsible for the dispatch of the business of the Court and of the branch, and for directing the implementation of policies and priorities as determined by the Court for the operation of the Court and of the branch. The chief justice has the power to make temporary assignments of senior and active justices and judges to duty on any court for which they are qualified. The chief justice is chosen by a majority vote of the Court for a two-year term beginning in July of every even-numbered year and may serve successive terms limited to a total of eight years. The chief justice is selected based on managerial, administrative, and leadership abilities, without regard to seniority only. The chief justice may be removed by a vote of four justices. Whenever the chief justice is unavailable, the most senior justice available becomes the acting chief justice and may exercise all of the powers of that office.

C. The Administrative Justice. The administrative justice is appointed by the chief justice and has the authority to act on routine procedural motions and other case-related matters which do not require action by a panel of justices. The administrative justice advises the clerk's office and other Court staff on procedural issues which may arise in cases filed before the Court. One justice may serve as both administrative justice and administrative writ justice.

D. The Administrative Writ Justice. The administrative writ justice is appointed by the chief justice and has the authority to direct that certain clearly defined types of writ petitions be transferred to a more appropriate court. One justice may serve as both administrative justice and administrative writ justice.

E. The Clerk. The clerk of the Supreme Court serves at the Court's pleasure and has administrative and clerical responsibilities. The clerk is authorized to appoint a chief deputy clerk, who may discharge the duties of the clerk during the clerk's absence, and such other deputy clerks as the Court deems necessary. The clerk also supervises the Court's systems administrators. The clerk's office receives all documents and other papers filed with the Court. Office hours are 8 a.m. to 5 p.m., ET, Monday through Friday. Case–related questions should be directed to the clerk's office rather than to the office of any justice or the central staff attorneys. The telephone number for the clerk's office is 850–488–0125.

Generally, all Court records are open to public inspection except the work product of the justices and their staffs, vote and remark sheets placed in individual case files, justice assignment records maintained by the clerk's office, portions of case records sealed by a lower court, case files which are confidential under the rules of the Court, and internal case management data. Access to the Court's public records is governed by Florida Rule of Judicial Administration 2.420.

The Court's online docket, all briefs, and case disposition orders are posted on the Supreme Court clerk's office website located at http://www.floridasupremecourt.org/clerk/index.shtml.

F. The Marshal. The marshal of the Supreme Court serves at the Court's pleasure, is empowered to execute process of the Court throughout the state, and is the custodian of the Supreme Court Building, its furnishings, and grounds. The marshal is also responsible for Court security.

G. The Librarian. The librarian of the Supreme Court serves at the Court's pleasure. The Court's library is in the custody of the librarian, who has an assistant librarian, a technical services/documents librarian, an archivist, and an administrative assistant. The library uses a computerized cataloging system which is accessible to the public via the Court's website at http://library.flcourts.org/. The library is for the use of Court personnel at any time. Library hours for the public are from 8 a.m. to 5 p.m., ET, Monday through Friday.

H. State Courts Administrator. The Office of the State Courts Administrator has been created by the Court to serve the chief justice in carrying out his or her responsibilities as chief administrative officer of the Florida judiciary. The state courts administrator serves at the pleasure of the Court and is authorized with the approval of the Court to employ such assistants and clerical support personnel as are necessary.

I. Inspector General. The inspector general serves at the pleasure of the Court and reports directly to the chief justice. The inspector general is assigned specific duties and responsibilities for audit and investigation functions by section 20.055, Florida Statutes. The scope of these responsibilities encompasses the entire state courts system and includes advising in the development of performance measures, standards, and procedures for the evaluation of programs; reviewing actions taken to improve program performance and meet program standards; performing audits, investigations, and management reviews relating to programs and operations; recommending corrective actions; reviewing the progress made in implementing corrective action; and related duties.

J. Reporter of Decisions. The reporter of decisions serves at the pleasure of the Court and reports directly to the chief justice. The reporter of decisions reviews opinions prior to their release for technical and formal correctness, makes recommendations as to needed corrections, and coordinates the process of preparing opinions for release. The reporter of decisions works closely with the justices, their staffs, and the clerk's office in the process of releasing opinions to legal publishers, the press, and the public. The reporter of decisions assists the Court and clerk's office in the case management process and may also be assigned by the chief justice to assist the Court on various special projects.

K. Director of the Public Information Office. The director of the public information office serves at the pleasure of the Court and reports directly to the chief justice. The director of the public information office serves as public information officer and public spokesperson for the Court; coordinates Court communications with news media and the public at large; serves as the chief justice's communications officer; assists all of the justices in their public communications and public activities as required; supervises the Court's website; coordinates the broadcast of Court arguments; coordinates public events as required by the chief justice; and supervises the staff of the public information office, including a deputy director and the Court's web administrator. Press inquiries about the Court and its work should be directed to the public information office at publicinformation@flcourts.org or 850–414–7641.

L. Director of Central Staff. The director of central staff serves at the pleasure of the Court and reports directly to the chief justice in coordinating the responsibilities and assignments of the Court's central staff attorneys and paralegal. The director of central staff is authorized to hire and supervise attorneys and a paralegal whose positions on central staff have been authorized by the chief justice. The central staff director is also responsible for coordinating the rule-making process, advises on the Court's Internship Program for Distinguished Florida Law Students, and has other administrative duties as assigned by the chief justice.

M. Central Staff. The Court's central staff attorneys and paralegal serve at the pleasure of the Court and report to the chief justice through the central staff director. One of the chief justice's judicial assistants and a paralegal provides support for the Court's central staff attorneys. The central staff attorneys analyze issues raised in original proceedings, see section II(C) of this manual, and certain motions; at the discretion of the assigned justice, assist with attorney discipline, bar admission, standard jury instructions, and rule-amendment cases; and perform other duties as determined by the chief justice or the Court as a whole.

Section II. Internal Procedure for Handling Cases.

A. Mandatory Review.

1. *Statutory or Constitutional Invalidity.* Appeals involving decisions of the district courts of appeal holding invalid a state statute or a provision of the Florida Constitution are initially directed to the chief justice, once the briefs and record are filed, to determine if oral argument should be granted. If oral argument is granted, the case proceeds as described in section III(B) of this manual. If oral argument is denied, the case is sent to an assigned justice and the case proceeds in the same manner as a discretionary review case in which review has been granted without argument. (See section II(B)(1)(d) of this manual.) If a justice deems it important to hear argument on a case previously assigned without argument, the chief justice will customarily honor the request. If there is a question about jurisdiction, an order to show cause will issue. If no response to the order to show cause is filed and after approval by the administrative justice, an order of dismissal will be issued by the clerk's office. If a response is filed, the case will be assigned to a panel for direction.

When a party files a notice seeking appeal, the clerk's office determines whether the case is subject to administrative dismissal based on a lack of jurisdiction. If the clerk's office determines that the case is subject to administrative dismissal, pursuant to guidelines established by the Court, the case is docketed and automatically dismissed. In such cases, no rehearing is allowed. The clerk's office will administratively dismiss those cases in which a party seeks appeal from an unelaborated per curiam decision. See Jackson v. State, 926 So. 2d 1262 (Fla. 2006).

2. *Bond Validation Cases.* Appeals of final judgments entered in proceedings for the validation of bonds or certificates of indebtedness are directed to the chief justice, once the briefs are filed, to determine whether oral argument is appropriate. If oral argument is denied, the case proceeds in the same manner as a discretionary review case in which review is granted without oral argument. (See section II(B)(1)(d) of this manual.) If oral argument is granted, the case proceeds as described in section III(B) of this manual.

3. *Death Penalty Cases.*

(a) Initial appeals involving the imposition of the death penalty and appeals from the denial of postconviction relief (other than appeals from successive motions from denials of postconviction relief which are treated in the same manner as a discretionary review case in which review is granted without oral argument), whether or not accompanied by a request for oral argument, are automatically placed on the oral argument calendar at the earliest convenient date after the briefs and record are filed. Initial appeals are assigned by rotation. Pro se pleadings are not permitted in direct appeals. Such pleadings will be stricken by the clerk. See Davis v. State, 789 So. 2d 978 (Fla. 2001).

(b) Appeals in postconviction proceedings are assigned to the justice who was assigned to the initial appeal. If that justice is no longer on the Court, the postconviction proceeding will be assigned to his or her successor.

(c) Petitions seeking review of nonfinal orders in postconviction proceedings are assigned in the same manner as appeals in postconviction proceedings and are scheduled for argument only if a justice so requests. A response is not permitted and will be stricken unless ordered by the Court. A single justice may request a response or issue an order to show cause. After a response is filed or if the assigned justice votes to dismiss or deny the petition without a response, the case will be considered en banc.

(d) Original proceedings filed are assigned in the same manner as appeals in postconviction proceedings and are scheduled for argument only if a justice so requests. Cases scheduled for argument generally proceed as described in section III(B).

(e) Proceedings filed after a death warrant is signed are treated as a separate category for assignment purposes. Those proceedings are initially assigned to the justice who was originally assigned to the initial appeal or prior postconviction proceeding. If that justice is no longer on the Court, the case will be assigned to his or her successor. The initially assigned justice may elect to have the case reassigned, on a rotational basis, to a justice who has been assigned fewer death warrant cases.

4. *Public Service Commission.* Cases involving Public Service Commission action relating to rates or service of utilities providing electric, gas, or telephone service are initially examined by the chief justice, after the briefs and record are filed, to determine whether the case should be placed on the oral argument calendar. If the Court determines that oral argument is unnecessary, the case is assigned to a justice. The case then proceeds in the same manner as discretionary review cases in which the Court has granted review without argument. (See section II(B)(1)(d) of this manual.) If oral argument is grant-

ed, the case file is returned to the clerk's office and the procedure outlined in section III(B) of this manual is followed.

B. Discretionary Review.

1. *Discretionary Review of District Court of Appeal Decisions–Not Certified.*

(a) When a party files a notice seeking to invoke discretionary review, the clerk's office determines whether the case is subject to administrative dismissal based on a lack of jurisdiction. If the clerk's office determines that the case is subject to administrative dismissal, the case is docketed and automatically dismissed. In such cases, no rehearing is allowed. The clerk's office will administratively dismiss those cases in which a party seeks discretionary review from:

(1) a per curiam affirmance (PCA) without written opinion, see Jenkins v. State, 385 So. 2d 1356 (Fla. 1980);

(2) a per curiam affirmance (PCA) with a citation or citations to a rule of procedure, a statute, or a case not pending on review or a case that has not been quashed or reversed by the Court, see Dodi Publishing Co. v. Editorial America, S.A., 385 So. 2d 1369 (Fla. 1980);

(3) a per curiam denial of relief (PCD) without written opinion or other unelaborated denial of relief, see Stallworth v. Moore, 827 So. 2d 974 (Fla. 2002);

(4) a per curiam denial of relief (PCD), or other unelaborated denial of relief, with a citation or citations to a rule of procedure, a statute, or a case not pending on review or a case that has not been quashed or reversed by the Court, see Gandy v. State, 846 So. 2d 1141 (Fla. 2003); or

(5) a per curiam dismissal of a case without written opinion or other unelaborated dismissal of a case, see Wells v. State, 132 So. 3d 1110 (Fla. 2014).

(b) If the clerk's office determines that the case is not subject to administrative dismissal, the case is docketed and, when all jurisdictional briefs have been filed, assigned to a panel of five justices according to a rotation formula. The file is then sent to the office of the assigned justice on the panel. The assigned justice's office prepares a memorandum summarizing the basis for jurisdiction asserted in the jurisdictional briefs and analyzing whether a basis for exercising discretionary jurisdiction exists. The assigned justice's office sends the file, memorandum, the assigned justice's vote as to whether review should be granted and, if so, whether oral argument should be heard, and his or her vote on any motion for attorney fees that has been filed in the case to the clerk's office. The clerk's office electronically distributes copies of the briefs, memorandum, and any motion for attorney fees filed in the case to the offices of each of the other justices on the panel for a vote on whether review should be granted and, if so, whether oral argument should be heard, and for a vote on any motion for attorney fees and any other pending motions that have been filed in the case. Several possible actions result from the distribution of discretionary review cases.

(1) If at least four justices vote to deny discretionary review, an order is entered denying review, the case is closed, and the file is placed in storage.

(2) If at least four justices vote to grant review but four do not agree on the need for oral argument, the chief justice may decide whether to set the case for argument or may place the question of oral argument on the Court's next conference agenda.

(3) If at least four justices vote to grant review, the clerk's office notifies the parties.

(4) If at least four justices do not agree to either grant or deny discretionary review, the case is sent to the other two justices.

(c) If the Court decides to hear oral argument, the clerk schedules the argument for the earliest convenient date. In hearing oral argument, the Court follows the procedure outlined in section III(B) of this manual. After oral argument, the Court follows the procedure outlined in section IV of this manual.

(d) If the Court dispenses with oral argument, the case file is then sent to the assigned justice's office with a no request conference date set. Copies of the briefs are also distributed to the other members of the Court along with the no request conference date. The assigned justice's office summarizes and analyzes the issues raised in the briefs in a memorandum which is distributed to the justices prior to the no request conference. The case is placed on the designated conference for consideration by the Court. After conference, the assigned justice drafts a proposed opinion which is then electronically distributed to the other members of the Court, who vote on the merits and write any dissenting or concurring opinions or remarks deemed appropriate.

2. *Discretionary Review of District Court of Appeal Decisions—Certified.*

(a) Certified as Being of Great Public Importance. After the case is docketed, the case is assigned to a panel of five justices according to a rotation formula to determine whether the Court should exercise its discretion to hear the case and whether oral argument should be granted. A copy of the notice to invoke discretionary jurisdiction, along with a copy of the district court of appeal decision, is electronically distributed to the members of the panel for voting.

If review is denied, the case is closed and the file is placed in storage. If review is granted but oral argument is deemed to be unnecessary, the case then proceeds in the same manner as other discretionary review cases in which the Court has granted review without argument. (See section II(B)(1)(d) of this manual.) If oral argument is granted, the case is set for oral argument on the earliest convenient date after receipt of the briefs on the merits and record, and the case proceeds as described in section III(B) of this manual.

(b) Certified as Being in Conflict. After the case is docketed and all jurisdictional briefs have been filed, the case is assigned to a panel of five justices, according to a rotation formula, to determine whether the Court should exercise its discretion to hear the case and whether oral argument should be granted. Copies of the briefs are electronically distributed to the panel for voting.

If review is denied, the case is closed and the file is placed in storage. If review is granted but oral argument is deemed unnecessary, the case then proceeds in the same manner as other discretionary review cases in which the Court has granted review without argument. (See section II(B)(1)(d) of this manual.) If oral argument is granted, the case is set for oral argument on the earliest convenient date after receipt of the briefs on the merits and record, and the case proceeds as described in section III(B) of this manual.

3. *Discretionary Review of Trial Court Orders and Judgments Certified by the District Courts of Appeal.* When a district court of appeal certifies that a trial court order or judgment pending before it on appeal requires immediate resolution by the Supreme Court, no jurisdictional briefs are required. When the certification of the district court of appeal has been received, the Court considers at the next Court conference whether to accept jurisdiction. If review is granted, the record is brought up from the lower tribunal within ten days, and the case is processed in the same manner as a discretionary review case from a decision of a district court of appeal in which the Court has granted review. If review is declined, the case is transferred back to the district court of appeal.

4. *Discretionary Review of Certified Questions from the Supreme Court of the United States or United States Courts of Appeals.* Cases certifying a question from the Supreme Court of the United States or a United States Court of Appeals are initially examined by the chief justice after the briefs and record are filed to determine whether the case should be placed on the oral argument calendar. If oral argument is denied, the case is assigned to a justice. The case then proceeds in the same manner as discretionary review cases in which the Court has granted review without argument. (See section II(B)(1)(d) of this manual.) If oral argument is granted, the case file is returned to the clerk's office and the procedure outlined in section III(B) of this manual is followed.

5. *Notice to Invoke Discretionary Jurisdiction Citing Dual Basis for Jurisdiction.* Whenever a notice to invoke discretionary review is filed seeking dual basis for jurisdiction as to the same decision of a district court of appeal, the Court decides whether it has a basis for jurisdiction on any basis cited.

(a) Parties will automatically submit jurisdictional briefs addressing all jurisdictional bases sought, with the exception of review sought on a discretionary review case certified as being of great public importance, in which a briefing schedule will be issued by the Court.

(b) Once the case is perfected, it will proceed as would any other case in section II(B)(1)(b)–(d) and (B)(2) above.

6. *Appeals Filed in Combination With Notice to Invoke Discretionary Review.* Whenever both a notice of appeal and a notice to invoke discretionary review are filed as to the same decision of a district court of appeal, the two cases are automatically consolidated by the clerk. The case is then treated in the same fashion as a discretionary review case, and the Court decides whether it has any basis for jurisdiction.

7. *Motions for Rehearing Not Authorized.* Motions for rehearing or for clarification of the granting or denial of review in a discretionary review case are not authorized and are stricken by the clerk's office, at the direction of the administrative justice, as unauthorized. See Fla. R. App. P. 9.330.

C. Screening Mandatory Review and Discretionary Review Cases for Relatedness. Except for death penalty cases set forth in section II(A)(3) of this manual, the clerk's office screens incoming mandatory and discretionary review cases set forth in sections II(A) and (B) of this manual for any significant relationship to cases already pending before the Court. If the clerk's office finds no such relationship, the screened case proceeds as provided by those sections. If the clerk's office finds such a relationship, it may make any of the following recommendations to the assigned justice.

1. *Consolidate.* Consolidation may be warranted when the parties, issues, or facts of the cases are so intertwined or complementary that the ends of justice and administration of the law would be served by joint briefing and argument by the parties and simultaneous consideration and disposition by the Court or a panel thereof.

2. *Travel Together.* Cases that are not sufficiently intertwined or complementary to warrant consolidation may be sufficiently related such that simultaneous consideration of the cases by the Court or a panel thereof is warranted.

3. *Tag.* The clerk's office may determine that the Court's disposition of a case will likely be controlled or substantially impacted by its final disposition of a case already pending before the Court. The clerk's office

may recommend to the assigned justice that the case be "tagged" to the pending "lead" case. If the assigned justice agrees with the recommendation, then:

(a) The clerk's office issues an order staying the tag case until final disposition of the lead case.

(b) Upon final disposition of the lead case and the assigned justice's approval, the clerk's office lifts the stay in the tag case and issues an order directing the parties to show cause why the Court's or a panel thereof's disposition of the tag case should not be controlled by its disposition of the lead case.

(c) Upon filing of the parties' responses to the order to show cause, the tag case is submitted to the Court or a panel thereof, as appropriate, for consideration and disposition.

D. Original Proceedings.

1. *General.* Petitions for writs of mandamus, prohibition, quo warranto, and habeas corpus, and initial pleadings in other original proceedings are automatically docketed by the clerk's office and, if they are not administratively dismissed, in most cases are sent to central staff for a memorandum analyzing the issues. Non–routine petitions that raise significant issues and are appropriate for expedited handling are sent directly to the assigned justice's office for work up, which may seek input or assistance from central staff. Oral argument is set only if a justice so requests, regardless of whether a party has requested it.

2. *Writ Petitions.* Extraordinary writ proceedings are assigned to a justice by rotation. In an extraordinary writ proceeding, a single justice may transfer the case to one or more of the lower courts, authorize issuance of an order requesting a response from the respondent, or authorize issuance of an order to show cause unless the issuance of the order to show cause will automatically stay the proceedings below. If the assigned justice votes to dismiss or deny the petition or directs issuance of an order to show cause that will have the effect of staying the proceedings below, the clerk's office will automatically circulate the case to a panel of five justices. The clerk's office will also circulate the case to a panel of five justices for a vote on any matter if specifically requested to do so by the assigned justice. Once a panel has been assigned to an extraordinary writ proceeding, the case shall circulate to that panel on all matters until the case becomes final. If four of the justices on an extraordinary writ panel do not agree on a particular disposition, the case is automatically circulated to the two remaining justices on the Court.

3. *Filed by Former Death–Row Inmates.* Writ petitions that are filed by former death-row inmates whose death sentences were reduced to life in prison and which allege ineffective assistance of appellate counsel are assigned to the justice who was originally assigned to the initial appeal or prior postconviction proceeding. If that justice is no longer on the Court, the case will be assigned to his or her successor. All other writ petitions filed by former death-row inmates are handled as outlined in section II(C)(1) of this manual.

4. *Filed by Death–Row Inmates.* Original proceedings filed by death-row inmates are handled as outlined in section II(A)(3) of the manual.

5. *Automatic Transfer.* Certain clearly defined types of writ petitions that raise substantial issues of fact or present individualized issues that do not require immediate resolution by the Supreme Court or are not the type of case in which an opinion from the Supreme Court would provide important guiding principles for other courts of this State are automatically transferred to a more appropriate court. See Harvard v. Singletary, 733 So. 2d 1020 (Fla. 1999). However, in certain instances the Court will dismiss a petition without prejudice to refile in the appropriate court. See Williams v. Moore, 752 So. 2d 574 (Fla. 2000). Petitions appropriate for automatic transfer are identified by central staff and reviewed by the administrative justice, who directs their transfer.

6. *Automatic Dismissal; Rehearing Not Authorized.* When a party files an extraordinary writ petition, the clerk's office determines whether the party is seeking review of a district court of appeal decision and whether the case is subject to administrative dismissal based on a lack of jurisdiction. If the clerk's office determines that the case is subject to administrative dismissal, the case is docketed and automatically dismissed. In such cases, no rehearing is allowed. The clerk's office will administratively dismiss those cases in which a party seeks discretionary review from:

(a) a per curiam affirmance (PCA) without written opinion, see Grate v. State, 750 So. 2d 625 (Fla. 1999);

(b) a per curiam affirmance (PCA) without written opinion but with one or more citations to a rule of procedure, a statute, or a case not pending on review before the Court and that has not been quashed or reversed by the Court, see Persaud v. State, 838 So. 2d 529 (Fla. 2003);

(c) a per curiam denial of relief (PCD) without written opinion or other unelaborated denial of relief, see Stallworth v. Moore, 827 So. 2d 974 (Fla. 2002); or

(d) a per curiam denial of relief (PCD) without written opinion, or other unelaborated denial of relief, with one or more citations to a rule of procedure, a statute, or a case not pending on review before the Court and that has not been quashed or reversed by the Court, see Foley v. State, 969 So. 2d 283 (Fla. 2007).

7. *Automatic Dismissal; Rehearing Authorized.*

(a) Petitions seeking review of findings of no probable cause by The Florida Bar on complaints or grievances charging attorneys with professional misconduct are automatically dismissed by the clerk. See Tyson v. Florida Bar, 826 So. 2d 265 (Fla. 2002).

(b) Extraordinary writ petitions that seek affirmative relief relative to certain pending criminal proceedings in the trial court, where it is clear from the face of the petition or its attachments that the petitioner is represented by counsel in the pending proceedings below and is not seeking to discharge counsel in those proceedings, after the issuance of an order to show cause and either no response or a response conceding, are automatically dismissed by the clerk's office. See Logan v. State, 846 So. 2d 472 (Fla. 2003).

(c) Extraordinary writ petitions that seek affirmative relief relative to certain pending criminal proceedings in the district court, where it is clear from the face of the petition or its attachments that the petitioner is represented by counsel in the pending proceedings below and is not seeking to discharge counsel in those proceedings, after the issuance of an order to show cause and either no response or a response conceding, are automatically dismissed by the clerk's office. See Johnson v. State, 974 So. 2d 363 (Fla. 2008).

E. Regulation of the Legal Profession.

1. *Admission to The Florida Bar.* Petitions seeking review of action by the Florida Board of Bar Examiners are docketed by the clerk's office. Upon filing of a response from the Board and a reply thereto, the case is assigned by rotation.

2. *Disciplinary Proceedings.*

(a) Petitions for review of action recommended by a referee or the Board of Governors of The Florida Bar are treated in the same manner as discretionary review cases in which review has been granted without oral argument. (See section II(B)(1)(c) of this manual.) If the assigned justice determines that oral argument would assist the Court in deciding the issues in the case, the file is returned to the clerk's office and the procedure outlined in section III(B) of this manual is followed. If the action recommended by the referee is disbarment or if the Bar has filed a petition for review seeking disbarment, the petition shall be promptly circulated to a panel of five justices to determine whether oral argument should be granted. Uncontested referees' reports are routinely approved by clerk's order.

(b) When a party files a petition for review, but fails to file a timely and proper initial brief, and the opposing party does not file a motion to dismiss, the clerk's office will issue an order directing the party seeking review to file an initial brief within fifteen days. If the party does not comply within fifteen days by filing an initial brief in accordance with the Rules Regulating the Florida Bar, the Court will dismiss the petition for review. Such dismissal is not subject to reinstatement. The clerk's office will then process the case as an uncontested referee's report.

F. Regulation of the Judiciary. Upon filing, recommendations from the Judicial Qualifications Commission are examined promptly for procedural regularity. If a recommendation from the commission is found to be in compliance with the constitution and the commission's rules, the Court may issue an order to the affected justice or judge to show cause why the recommended action should not be taken. Once a response and reply thereto are filed, or if no response is requested, the case is treated in the same manner as a discretionary review case in which the Court has granted review without argument. (See section II(A)(1)(d) of this manual.) If oral argument is granted, the procedure outlined in section III(B) of this manual is followed. All Judicial Qualifications Commission filings with the Court are posted on the Court's website at http://www.floridasupremecourt.org/pub_info/jqc.shtml.

G. Rulemaking.

1. *General.* At the request of any justice, the Court, on its own motion, may adopt or amend rules. When the Court so acts, it generally will allow interested persons to file comments by a date certain. A specific effective date is usually designated by the Court. When the Court adopts or proposes a rule change in conjunction with a non-rule-amendment case, it will do so by means of an opinion in a separate case addressing only the rule amendment. The two opinions will reference each other and will be issued at the same time.

2. *Rules Regulating The Florida Bar.* Petitions to amend the Rules Regulating the Florida Bar are docketed and, in the discretion of the chief justice, either set for oral argument and processed as described in section III(B) of this manual or assigned to a justice and processed in the same manner as other cases assigned without oral argument. (See section II(B)(1)(d) of this manual.) At the assigned justice's discretion, central staff may assist with the case.

3. *Rules of Practice and Procedure.* Petitions to amend any of the procedural rules promulgated by the Court are docketed only if filed by The Florida Bar or a committee specially designated by the Court. Such cases are published for comments on the Proposed Rules page of the Supreme Court's website located at http://www.floridasupremecourt.org/decisions/proposed.shtml and, in the discretion of the assigned justice, either set for oral argument or processed in the same manner as a case assigned without oral argument, except that central staff may assist with the case. Other petitions to amend any procedural rule are referred by the clerk's office to the chair of the appropriate rules committee. Requests by the Court to rules committees for special consideration of proposed rule amendments are generally made on behalf of the Court by the clerk of the Court.

4. *Supreme Court Approved Family Law Forms.* The Court internally reviews, revises, and otherwise maintains the Supreme Court Approved Family Law Forms. The Court, on its own motion, makes technical and readability changes to these forms as necessary. For more substantial amendments, the Court seeks input from an informal Advisory Workgroup on the Florida Supreme Court Approved Family Law Forms. All amendments to the Supreme Court Approved Forms are adopted via written opinion, with previous publication for comment only when deemed necessary or desirable by the Court. See Amendments to the Fla. Family Law Rules of Pro. & Family Law Forms, 810 So. 2d 1, 14 (Fla. 2000). The Family Law Rules Forms are amended through the normal rulemaking process. See id.

5. *Liaison Appointments & Communications with Committees.* It is the policy of the Court to promote communication between the Court, The Florida Bar committees that advise the Court on court rules, Supreme Court committees authorized to propose changes to court rules or jury instructions, and any other entities, including The Florida Bar and the Florida Board of Bar Examiners, authorized to propose rule or jury instruction changes. Accordingly, the chief justice appoints a justice to serve as the Court's liaison to each of the various committees and, as deemed appropriate, designates committee member liaisons between Supreme Court committees and any Bar rules committee whose body of rules may be affected by the Supreme Court committees' proposals. The Court considers the free flow of information between the Court and the committees before proposed amendments are filed with the Court a necessary part of the Court's official administrative duties. The Court also authorizes prefiling communication between the committees or support staff to the committees and Court staff that assists the Court in processing proposed amendments. The Court has determined that this open communication promotes more efficient rule and jury instruction development and does not affect the integrity of the proceedings before the Court or advantage any participant in those proceedings. Accordingly, the justices of the Court and their staff are not ethically prohibited from these informal communications and will not be subject to disqualification upon the filing of the proposed amendments with the Court.

H. Advisory Opinions to the Governor and Attorney General.

1. *Governor.* When the governor requests the advice of the Court, the clerk immediately sends a copy of the request to each justice. As soon as practicable, the chief justice calls a conference for the purpose of determining whether the governor's question is answerable and, if so, whether oral argument is desired. If the Court decides the question is answerable, the Court permits briefs from all interested parties and allows oral argument at the earliest convenient date after briefs are required to be filed. If the Court decides the question is not answerable, a reply is drafted by the assigned justice, and the reply is circulated to the other justices for a vote.

2. *Attorney General.* When the attorney general requests an advisory opinion, it is handled in the same manner as above except that the Court does not have to determine if the question is answerable.

I. Cases Where Incorrect Legal Remedy Has Been Sought; Transfer; Unstyled Letters and Petitions. When a party seeking Supreme Court review has filed an appeal, a notice to invoke discretionary review, a petition for habeas corpus, or other pleading, but the pleading seeks an improper remedy, the Court will treat the case as if the proper remedy had been sought. When the case should have been filed in a district court of appeal or in a circuit court, the Supreme Court will transfer the case to the appropriate court, provided that the jurisdiction of the lower court was properly invoked and the filing was timely.

When an initial pleading is inadequate to notify the clerk of the nature of the case, the pleading is docketed as a notice to invoke discretionary review, if it can be ascertained that relief is sought from a ruling of a district court of appeal issued within the thirty-day jurisdictional filing period. The litigant is then notified by mail of both the need for a proper filing and the applicable rules of procedure. If the defect in pleading is not remedied within twenty days, the litigant is advised by mail that dismissal for lack of prosecution is imminent. Unless the litigant makes a supplementary filing within twenty days thereafter, the cause is dismissed. Defective pleadings from prison inmates are researched by central staff.

J. Untimely Filings. Untimely filings are docketed and immediately dismissed by the clerk's office with a form order stating that the case is subject to reinstatement if timeliness is established on proper motion filed within fifteen days.

K. Cases Affecting Children. It is the policy of the Court to expedite proceedings presenting time-sensitive issues affecting children. Pursuant to Florida Rules of Appellate Procedure 9.145 and 9.146, in all cases involving juvenile delinquency, dependency, or termination of parental rights, the file shall remain sealed in the office of the clerk when not in use by the Court and shall not be open to inspection except by the parties and their counsel or as otherwise ordered by the Court.

L. Stays and Relinquishments. Orders staying the proceedings and orders relinquishing jurisdiction to a lower tribunal will be for a specified period of time, e.g., ninety days. In all cases that are stayed in this Court pending action by an entity other than this Court or that are relinquished to a lower tribunal, the parties shall be required to submit regular status reports to the Court.

M. Sanctioning Abusive Litigants. When the Court determines that a litigant has repeatedly filed pleadings that are meritless, frivolous, abusive, or inappropriate for review by the Supreme Court or has otherwise abused the process of the Court, the Court disposes of the pleadings before it, retains jurisdiction, and orders the litigant to show cause why the Court should not sanction the litigant for the abusive filings. If the litigant fails to show cause, the Court issues an opinion sanctioning the litigant. When the litigant being sanctioned is a prisoner as defined under section 944.279, Florida Statutes, and the Court finds that the proceedings are frivolous or malicious or otherwise meet the requirements of the statute, the Court directs the Clerk of Court to forward a certified copy of the opinion making the required findings to the appropriate institution or facility to consider initiating disciplinary proceedings against the prisoner pursuant to the rules of the Department of Corrections.

Section III. Oral Arguments

A. Preargument Procedures. Oral arguments are routinely scheduled for one week of each month, except that no arguments are heard on state holidays or during the months of July and August. At least two months before the first day of the month in which oral argument has been scheduled, the clerk's office delivers the case file to the office of the assigned justice. The assigned justice's office summarizes and analyzes the issues raised in the briefs in a memorandum for use on the bench and distributes it to each justice no later than the Wednesday of the week preceding oral argument. The director of public information prepares a brief summary on each oral argument case, which is available to the public a few days prior to oral argument and is posted on the Supreme Court Public Information page of the Court's website located at http://www.floridasupremecourt.org/pub_info/summaries/index.shtml. The briefs are also posted there. These summaries are not official Court documents.

B. Oral Argument Procedures. On oral argument days, counsel appearing that day are required to sign in with the clerk's office starting thirty minutes before arguments are scheduled to begin. At this time coffee is available for counsel in the lawyers' lounge, and the justices may join counsel for conversation not relating to cases scheduled for argument.

Oral argument routinely begins at 9 a.m., ET, but may be scheduled by the chief justice to begin at other times. Oral argument on Fridays begins at 9 a.m., ET. Approximately ten minutes before arguments begin, the justices assemble in the robing room to don their robes for the bench. At the time arguments are to begin, the marshal announces that the Court is in session and the justices enter the courtroom from behind the bench, led by the chief justice or acting chief justice, in order of seniority. Retired justices or judges assigned to temporary duty on the Court enter last. Seating alternates from right to left based on seniority. All justices remain standing until the chief justice indicates that all justices are in place.

The chief justice controls the order of argument and the time allowed to any party. The division of time for argument between co-counsel or among multiple counsel on one side of a case, and between counsel's main presentation and rebuttal, is solely counsel's responsibility. In order to assist counsel, however, amber and red lights are mounted on the lectern. When the chief justice recognizes counsel, the allotted time begins. The amber light indicates that counsel has either (1) entered the time requested to be set aside for rebuttal, (2) gone into the time set aside for co-counsel's argument, or (3) entered the period of time near the end of argument when notice of the remaining time has been requested. The red light indicates that counsel's allotted time has expired, at which point counsel will be expected to relinquish the lectern. Any justice may ask questions or make comments at any time. The chief justice has discretion to authorize a recess during oral argument and by tradition has done so midway into the calendar. During this mid-morning recess, the justices will not meet with counsel.

At the conclusion of the calendar, the Court is adjourned. The justices leave the bench in the order in which they entered and reassemble in the conference room for a preliminary conference on the cases argued. No person may enter the conference room without the invitation of the full Court.

C. Electronic Recording and Broadcasts. Florida State University, through WFSU–TV, records all oral arguments on videotape, copies of which are available from WFSU–TV by calling 850–487–3170 or 800–322–WFSU. Except when preempted by legislative sessions, oral arguments are broadcast live via the AMC–3 satellite, KU band, at 87degrees west, transponder 18, virtual channel 802. The downlink frequency is 12046.750 MHz. The uplink frequency is 14348.500 MHz. The L–band frequency is 1296.750 MHz. The symbol rate is 7.32. The FEC is 3/4. The satellite may be preempted during legislative sessions and emergencies. Oral arguments are broadcast live on the Florida Channel, which is available statewide at the discretion of local cable providers. Arguments are also broadcast worldwide on the Internet in video and audio formats from a website jointly maintained with WFSU–TV (http://wfsu.org/gavel2gavel/). An archive of video and audio from previous arguments is maintained on the same website. The Court calendar, briefs, press summaries, and other information about cases and about using the Internet are posted on the Supreme Court Public Information page of the Court's website located at http://www.floridasupremecourt.org/pub_info/oralarguments.shtml.

Section IV. Consideration of Cases After Oral Argument.

After oral argument, the justices confer and take a tentative vote on the cases argued. The assigned justice is ordinarily the author of the Court's opinion or disposition order, and the case file is sent to that justice after conference. Once an opinion has been written, the assigned justice's office electronically distributes the opinion to the other justices, and the case file is delivered to the clerk's office. Each justice votes electronically, making any comments deemed appropriate. If a concurring, dissenting, or other separate opinion is written, the author's office electronically distributes copies to the other justices. When all participating justices have voted on all of the separate opinions in a case, the clerk's office determines whether there are four concurring votes for a decision. If not, the case is scheduled for discussion at the next regularly scheduled conference in order to reconcile the disparate views. If any justice has requested that the case be discussed at conference, the case is placed on the conference schedule.

When the clerk's office determines that a case has the necessary votes for release, the case is sent to the reporter of decisions for technical review. After technical review by the reporter of decisions, any needed technical changes are made at the direction of the author. Then the reporter of decisions returns the case to the clerk's office for release of the Court's opinion or a majority opinion and any separate opinions filed in the case.

Section V. Release of Opinions.

A. Routine Release. Copies of opinions ready for release to the public are electronically distributed to each justice no later than Thursday at noon. At any time before 10 a.m., ET, the following Thursday, any justice may direct the clerk not to release an opinion. Unless otherwise directed, on Thursday morning at 11 a.m., ET, the clerk electronically releases the opinions that were furnished to the justices the preceding Friday. Publishers other than the Court's official reporter may receive copies at the rate of fifty cents per page, and all other interested persons may receive copies at the cost of one dollar per page. Opinions are posted on the Court Opinions page of the Court's website located at http://www.floridasupremecourt.org/decisions/opinions.shtml by noon on the day they are released.

B. Special Release. Opinions may be released at any other time at the direction of the chief justice. When opinions are released at other times, the director of public information notifies the news media as soon as is practicable.

Section VI. Motions.

The chief justice and the administrative justice have authority to dispose of routine procedural motions, such as those seeking an extension of time, permission to file enlarged briefs, an expedited schedule, or a consolidation of cases. The chief justice and the chief justice's designee also have authority to grant requests for a stay during the pendency of a proceeding and a thirty-day stay of mandate pending review by the United States Supreme Court in order to allow counsel the opportunity to obtain a stay from that Court. Motions filed after a case has been assigned to a justice are ruled on by that justice.

Section VII. Rehearings.

Authorized motions for rehearing are considered by the justices who originally considered the case. Unauthorized and untimely motions for rehearing are sent to the administrative justice for his or her consideration.

Section VIII. Court Conferences.

The justices meet privately each Wednesday at 9 a.m., ET, unless the chief justice otherwise directs. The agenda for the conference is prepared by the chief justice's office. The chief justice may schedule additional conferences at his or her discretion. Minutes of the Court's conferences are prepared by a justice designated by the Court and are a record of the official action taken by the Court in conference on matters other than case dispositions. The minutes are submitted to the Court for approval at a subsequent conference. Case dispositions at conference result in a formal directive from the chief justice to the clerk that the opinions or appropriate orders be filed.

Section IX. Assignment of Cases.

Except as otherwise provided, all cases are assigned according to a rotation formula.

Section X. Recusals

When a justice is recused, the clerk will notify the justices of any recusals in advance of oral argument or the conference in which the case is scheduled. If four of the remaining justices cannot ultimately agree to a disposition, the chief justice may in certain cases assign a judge or senior judge to the case as a temporary "associate justice" under the procedures below. As a general rule, in such cases, reargument will not be scheduled because video and audio of the argument will be made available to the associate justice. The procedures of this subdivision do not apply where a majority of the Court agrees on the disposition of the case but a majority does not concur in a particular opinion.

A. Addition of Judge or Judges When Necessary for a Quorum. If fewer than five justices are able to participate in a case for any reason, the chief justice or the acting chief justice if the chief justice is unable to participate in the case shall assign a sufficient number of associate justices to create a quorum and may assign additional associate justices up to the maximum. Associate justices shall be assigned according to the procedure in subdivision D below.

B. Procedure in Discretionary Jurisdiction Cases. After the Court has accepted jurisdiction, if four justices cannot agree on a disposition, absent extraordinary circumstances, the Court will discharge jurisdiction. However, if four justices participating in the case agree that extraordinary circumstances exist that would justify deciding the case, the chief justice or the acting chief justice, if the chief justice is not participating in the case, shall invoke the procedure in subdivision D below.

C. Procedure in Mandatory Jurisdiction Cases. If the case is one within the Court's mandatory jurisdiction, the chief justice or the acting chief justice if the chief justice is unable to participate in the case shall invoke the procedure in subdivision D below.

D. Method of Selection. Associate justices shall be the chief judges of the district courts of appeal selected on a rotating basis from the lowest numbered court to the highest and repeating continuously. A district court shall be temporarily removed from the rotation if the case emanated from it. If more than one associate justice is needed, they shall be selected from separate district courts according to the numerical rotation. If the chief judge of a district court who would be assigned under this procedure is recused from the case or otherwise unavailable, the next most senior judge on that court (excluding senior judges) who is not recused shall replace the chief judge as associate justice.

RULES REGULATING THE FLORIDA BAR

Date Effective

The order of the Supreme Court adopting the Rules Regulating the Florida Bar, as modified upon rehearing petition (494 So.2d 977), provides:

"These rules will become effective at 12:01 a.m. on January 1, 1987. Thereafter, the Rules Regulating the Florida Bar shall govern the conduct of all members of the Florida Bar. All disciplinary cases pending as of 12:01 a.m. January 1, 1987 shall thereafter be processed in accordance with the procedures set forth in the Rules Regulating the Florida Bar."

CHAPTER 1. GENERAL

INTRODUCTION

The Supreme Court of Florida by these rules establishes the authority and responsibilities of The Florida Bar, an official arm of the court.

Amended July 23, 1992, effective Jan. 1, 1993 (605 So.2d 252).

1–1. NAME

The name of the body regulated by these rules shall be THE FLORIDA BAR.

1–2. PURPOSE

The purpose of The Florida Bar shall be to inculcate in its members the principles of duty and service to the public, to improve the administration of justice, and to advance the science of jurisprudence.

1–3. MEMBERSHIP

Rule 1–3.1. Composition

The membership of The Florida Bar shall be composed of all persons who are admitted by the Supreme Court of Florida to the practice of law in this state and who maintain their membership pursuant to these rules.

Amended March 30, 1989, effective March 31, 1989 (541 So.2d 110); July 23, 1992, effective Jan. 1, 1993 (605 So.2d 252).

Rule 1–3.2. Membership classifications

(a) Members in Good Standing. Members of The Florida Bar in good standing shall mean only those persons licensed to practice law in Florida who have paid annual membership fees or dues for the current year and who are not retired, resigned, delinquent, inactive, or suspended members.

(b) Conditionally Admitted Members. The Supreme Court of Florida may admit a person with a prior history of drug, alcohol, or psychological problems to membership in The Florida Bar and impose conditions of probation as the court deems appropriate upon that member. The period of probation shall be no longer than 5 years, or for such indefinite period of time as the court may deem appropriate by conditions in its order. The conditions may include, but not be limited to, participation in a rehabilitation program, periodic blood and urine analysis, periodic psychological examinations, or supervision by another member of The Florida Bar. The probation shall be monitored by The Florida Bar and the costs thereof shall be paid by the member on probation. A failure to observe the conditions of probation or a finding of probable cause as to conduct of the member committed during the period of probation may terminate the probation and subject the member to all available disciplinary sanctions. Proceedings to determine compliance with conditions of admission shall be processed in the same manner as matters of contempt provided elsewhere in these Rules Regulating The Florida Bar. If necessary, the court may assign a judicial referee to take testimony, receive evidence, and make findings of fact in the manner prescribed in the rule concerning procedures before a referee. The findings of the referee may be appealed as provided in the rule for procedures before the supreme court.

(c) Inactive Members. Inactive members of The Florida Bar shall mean only those members who have properly elected to be classified as inactive in the manner elsewhere provided.

Inactive members shall:

(1) pay annual membership fees as set forth in rule 1–7.3;

(2) be exempt from continuing legal education requirements;

(3) affirmatively represent their membership status as inactive members of The Florida Bar when any statement of Florida Bar membership is made;

(4) not hold themselves out as being able to practice law in Florida or render advice on matters of Florida law;

(5) not hold any position that requires the person to be a licensed Florida attorney;

(6) not be eligible for certification under the Florida certification plan;

(7) not vote in Florida Bar elections or be counted for purposes of apportionment of the board of governors;

(8) certify upon election of inactive status that they will comply with all applicable restrictions and limitations imposed on inactive members of The Florida Bar.

Failure of an inactive member to comply with all requirements thereof shall be cause for disciplinary action.

An inactive member may, at any time, apply for reinstatement to membership in good standing in the manner provided in rule 1–3.7.

Amended Dec. 4, 1986 (498 So.2d 914); March 30, 1989, effective March 31, 1989 (541 So.2d 110); Nov. 29, 1990, effective Jan. 1, 1991 (570 So.2d 940); July 23, 1992, effective Jan. 1, 1993 (605 So.2d 252); July 17, 1997 (697 So.2d 115); Sept. 24, 1998, effective Oct. 1, 1998 (718 So.2d 1179); Feb. 8, 2001 (795 So.2d 1); April 25, 2002 (820 So.2d 210).

Rule 1–3.3. Official Bar Name and Contact Information

Text of rule effective until October 1, 2015. See, also, rule effective October 1, 2015.

(a) Designation. Each member of The Florida Bar shall designate an official bar name, mailing address, business telephone number, and business e-mail address, if the member has one. If the physical location or street address is not the principal place of employment, the member must also provide an address for the principal place of employment.

(b) Changes. Each member shall promptly notify the executive director of any changes in any information required by this rule. The official bar name of each member of The Florida Bar shall be used in the course of the member's practice of law. Members may change their official bar name by sending a request to the Supreme Court of Florida. The court must approve all official bar name changes.

Amended Oct. 20, 1994 (644 So.2d 282); April 12, 2012, effective July 1, 2012 (101 So.3d 807).

Rule 1–3.3. Official Bar Name and Contact Information

Text of rule effective October 1, 2015. See, also, rule effective until October 1, 2015.

(a) Designation. Each member of The Florida Bar must designate an official bar name, mailing address, business telephone number, and business e-mail address. If the physical location or street address is not the principal place of employment, the member must also provide an address for the principal place of employment. The Florida Bar may excuse a bar member from the requirement of providing an e-mail address if the bar member has been excused by the court from e-service or the bar member demonstrates that the bar member has no e-mail account and lacks Internet service at the bar member's office.

(b) Changes. Each member must promptly notify the executive director of any changes in any information required by this rule. The official bar name of each member of The Florida Bar must be used in the course of the member's practice of law. Members may change their official bar name by sending a request to the Supreme Court of Florida. The court must approve all official bar name changes.

Amended Oct. 20, 1994 (644 So.2d 282); April 12, 2012, effective July 1, 2012 (101 So.3d 807); June 11, 2015, effective Oct. 1, 2015 (167 So.3d 412).

Rule 1–3.4. CLER delinquent members and CLER exempt members

(a) CLER Delinquent Members. Any member who is suspended by reason of failure to complete continuing legal education requirements shall be deemed a delinquent member. A delinquent member shall not engage in the practice of law in this state and shall not be entitled to any privileges and benefits accorded to members of The Florida Bar in good standing. Any member suspended for failure to complete continuing legal education requirements may be reinstated as elsewhere provided in these rules.

(b) CLER Exempt Members. Any member who is exempt from continuing legal education requirements (see rule 6–10.3(c)) shall not engage in the practice of law in this state; provided, however, that a member exempt from continuing legal education requirements by reason of active military service may practice law in Florida if required to do so as a part of assigned military duties.

Amended Oct. 10, 1991, effective Jan. 1, 1992 (587 So.2d 1121); July 23, 1992, effective Jan. 1, 1993 (605 So.2d 252).

Rule 1–3.5. Retirement

Any member of The Florida Bar may retire from The Florida Bar upon petition or other written request to, and approval of, the executive director. A retired member shall not practice law in this state except upon petition for reinstatement to, and approval of, the executive director; the payment of all membership fees, costs, or other amounts owed to The Florida Bar; and the completion of all outstanding continuing legal education or basic skills course requirements. A member who seeks and is approved to permanently retire shall not be eligible for reinstatement or readmission. A retired member shall be entitled to receive such other privileges as the board of governors may authorize.

A retired member shall remain subject to disciplinary action for acts committed before the effective date of retirement. Acts committed after retirement may be considered in evaluating the member's fitness to resume the practice of law in Florida as elsewhere stated in these Rules Regulating The Florida Bar.

If the executive director is in doubt as to disposition of a petition, the executive director may refer the petition to the board of governors for its action. Action of the executive director or board of governors denying a petition for retirement or reinstatement from retirement may be reviewed upon petition to the Supreme Court of Florida.

Amended Oct. 10, 1991, effective Jan. 1, 1992 (587 So.2d 1121); July 23, 1992, effective Jan. 1, 1993 (605 So.2d 252); June 27, 1996, effective July 1, 1996 (677 So.2d 272); Sept. 24, 1998, effective Oct. 1, 1998 (718 So.2d 1179); Feb. 8, 2001 (795 So.2d 1); Oct. 6, 2005, effective Jan. 1, 2006 (916 So.2d 655); April 12, 2012, effective July 1, 2012 (101 So.3d 807).

Rule 1–3.6. Delinquent Members

Any person now or hereafter licensed to practice law in Florida shall be deemed a delinquent member if the member:

(a) fails to pay membership fees;

(b) fails to comply with continuing legal education or basic skills course requirements;

(c) fails to pay the costs assessed in diversion or disciplinary cases within 30 days after the disciplinary decision or diversion recommendation becomes final, unless such time is extended by the board of governors for good cause shown;

(d) fails to make restitution imposed in diversion cases or disciplinary proceedings within the time specified in the order in such cases or proceedings;

(e) fails to pay fees imposed as part of diversion for more than 30 days after the diversion recommendation became final, unless such time is extended by the board of governors for good cause shown; or

(f) fails to pay an award entered in fee arbitration proceedings conducted under the authority stated elsewhere in these rules and 30 days or more have elapsed since the date on which the award became final.

Delinquent members shall not engage in the practice of law in Florida nor be entitled to any privileges and benefits accorded to members of The Florida Bar in good standing.

Amended Oct. 10, 1991, effective Jan. 1, 1992 (587 So.2d 1121); Sept. 24, 1998, effective Oct. 1, 1998 (718 So.2d 1179); May 20, 2004 (875 So.2d 448); Oct. 6, 2005, effective Jan. 1, 2006 (916 So.2d 655); Nov. 19, 2009, effective Feb. 1, 2010 (24 So.3d 63); April 12, 2012, effective July 1, 2012 (101 So.3d 807).

Rule 1–3.7. Reinstatement to Membership

Text of rule effective until October 1, 2015. See, also, rule effective October 1, 2015.

(a) Eligibility for Reinstatement. Members who have retired or been delinquent for a period of time not in excess of 5 years are eligible for reinstatement under this rule. Time will be calculated from the day of the retirement or delinquency.

Inactive members may also seek reinstatement under this rule.

(b) Petitions Required. A member seeking reinstatement must file a petition with the executive director setting forth the reason for inactive status, retirement, or delinquency and showing good cause why the petition for reinstatement should be granted. The petition must be on a form approved by the board of governors and the petitioner will furnish such information on such form as the board of governors may require. The petition must be accompanied by a nonrefundable reinstatement fee of $150 and payment of all arrearages unless adjusted by the executive director with concurrence of the executive committee for good cause shown. Inactive members are not required to pay the reinstatement fee. No member will be reinstated if, from the petition or from investigation conducted, the petitioner is not of good moral character and morally fit to practice law or if the member is delinquent with the continuing legal education or basic skills course requirements.

If the executive director is in doubt as to approval of a petition the executive director may refer the petition to the board of governors for its action. Action of the executive director or board of governors denying a petition for reinstatement may be reviewed upon petition to the Supreme Court of Florida.

(c) Members Who Have Retired or Been Delinquent for Less Than 5 Years, But More Than 3 Years. Members who have retired or been delinquent for less than 5 years, but more than 3 years, must have completed 10 hours of continuing legal education courses for each year or portion of a year that the member had retired or was deemed delinquent.

(d) Members Who Have Retired or Been Delinquent for 5 Years or More. Members who have retired or have been deemed delinquent for a period of 5 years or longer will not be reinstated under this rule and must be readmitted upon application to and approval by the Florida Board of Bar Examiners.

(e) Members Who Have Permanently Retired. Members who have permanently retired will not be reinstated under this rule.

(f) Members Delinquent 60 Days or Less. Reinstatement from membership fees delinquency accomplished within 60 days from the date of delinquency relates back to the date before the delinquency. Any member reinstated within the 60–day period is not subject to disciplinary sanction for practicing law in Florida during that time.

(g) Inactive Members. Inactive members may be reinstated to membership in good standing by petition filed with the executive director, in the form and as provided in (b) above, except:

(1) If the member has been inactive for greater than 5 years, has been authorized to practice law in another jurisdiction, and either actively practiced law in that jurisdiction or held a position that requires a license as a lawyer for the entire period of time, the member will be required to complete the Florida Law Update continuing legal education course as part of continuing legal education requirements.

(2) If the member has been inactive for greater than 5 years and does not meet the requirements of subdivision (1), the member will be required to complete the basic skills course requirement and the 30–hour continuing legal education requirement.

(3) An inactive member is not eligible for reinstatement until all applicable continuing legal education requirements have been completed and the remaining portion of membership fees for members in good standing for the current fiscal year have been paid.

Amended March 30, 1989, effective March 31, 1989 (541 So.2d 110); Oct. 10, 1991, effective Jan. 1, 1992 (587 So.2d 1121); Nov. 14, 1991, effective Jan. 1, 1992 (593 So.2d 1035); July 23, 1992, effective Jan. 1, 1993 (605 So.2d 252); Sept. 24, 1998, effective Oct. 1, 1998 (718 So.2d 1179); Feb. 8, 2001 (795 So.2d 1); Nov. 19, 2009, effective Feb. 1, 2010 (24 So.3d 63); April 12, 2012, effective July 1, 2012 (101 So.3d 807); May 29, 2014, effective June 1, 2014 (140 So.3d 541).

Rule 1–3.7. Reinstatement to Membership

Text of rule effective October 1, 2015. See, also, rule effective until October 1, 2015.

(a) Eligibility for Reinstatement. Members who have retired or been delinquent for a period of time not in excess of 5 years are eligible for reinstatement under this rule. Time will be calculated from the day of the retirement or delinquency.

Inactive members may also seek reinstatement under this rule.

(b) Petitions Required. A member seeking reinstatement must file a petition with the executive director setting forth the reason for inactive status, retirement, or delinquency and showing good cause why the petition for reinstatement should be granted. The petitioner must include all required information on a form approved by the board of governors. The petition must be accompanied by a nonrefundable reinstatement fee of $150 and payment of all arrearages unless adjusted by the executive director with concurrence of the executive committee for good cause shown. Inactive members are not required to pay the reinstatement fee. No member will be reinstated if, from the petition or from investigation conducted, the petitioner is not of good moral character and morally fit to practice law or if the member is delinquent with the continuing legal education or basic skills course requirements.

If the executive director is in doubt as to approval of a petition the executive director may refer the petition to the board of governors for its action. Action of the executive director or board of governors denying a petition for reinstatement may be reviewed on petition to the Supreme Court of Florida.

(c) Members Who Have Retired or Been Delinquent for Less Than 5 Years, But More Than 3 Years. Members who have retired or been delinquent for less than 5 years, but more than 3 years, must complete 10 hours of continuing legal education courses for each year or portion of a year that the member had retired or was deemed delinquent.

(d) Members Who Have Retired or Been Delinquent for 5 Years or More. Members who have retired or have been deemed delinquent for a period of 5 years or longer will not be reinstated under this rule and must be readmitted upon application to the Florida Board of Bar Examiners and approval by the Supreme Court of Florida.

(e) Members Who Have Permanently Retired. Members who have permanently retired will not be reinstated under this rule.

(f) Members Delinquent 60 Days or Less. Reinstatement from delinquency for payment of membership fees or completion of continuing legal education or basic skills course requirements approved within 60 days from the date of delinquency is effective on the last business day before the delinquency. Any member reinstated within the 60–day period is not subject to disciplinary sanction for practicing law in Florida during that time.

(g) Inactive Members. Inactive members may be reinstated to membership in good standing by petition filed with the executive director, in the form and as provided in (b) above, except:

(1) If the member has been inactive for greater than 5 years, has been authorized to practice law in another jurisdiction, and either actively practiced law in that jurisdiction or held a position that requires a license as a lawyer for the entire period of time, the member will be required to complete the Florida Law Update continuing legal education course as part of continuing legal education requirements.

(2) If the member has been inactive for greater than 5 years and does not meet the requirements of subdivision (1), the member will be required to complete the basic skills course requirement and the 30–hour continuing legal education requirement.

(3) An inactive member is not eligible for reinstatement until all applicable continuing legal education requirements have been completed and the remaining portion of membership fees for members in good standing for the current fiscal year have been paid.

Amended March 30, 1989, effective March 31, 1989 (541 So.2d 110); Oct. 10, 1991, effective Jan. 1, 1992 (587 So.2d 1121); Nov. 14, 1991, effective Jan. 1, 1992 (593 So.2d 1035); July 23, 1992, effective Jan. 1, 1993 (605 So.2d 252); Sept. 24, 1998, effective Oct. 1, 1998 (718 So.2d 1179); Feb. 8, 2001 (795 So.2d 1); Nov. 19, 2009, effective Feb. 1, 2010 (24 So.3d 63); April 12, 2012, effective July 1, 2012 (101 So.3d 807); May 29, 2014, effective June 1, 2014 (140 So.3d 541); June 11, 2015, effective Oct. 1, 2015 (167 So.3d 412).

Rule 1–3.8. Right to Inventory

(a) Appointment; Grounds; Authority. Whenever an attorney is suspended, disbarred, becomes a delinquent member, abandons a practice, disappears, dies, or suffers an involuntary leave of absence due to military service, catastrophic illness, or injury, and no partner, personal representative, or other responsible party capable of conducting the attorney's affairs is known to exist, the appropriate circuit court, upon proper proof of the fact, may appoint an attorney or attorneys to inventory the files of the subject attorney (hereinafter referred to as "the subject attorney") and to take such action as seems indicated to protect the interests of clients of the subject attorney.

(b) Maintenance of Attorney–Client Confidences. Any attorney so appointed shall not disclose any information contained in files so inventoried without the consent of the client to whom such file relates except as necessary to carry out the order of the court that appointed the attorney to make the inventory.

(c) Status and Purpose of Inventory Attorney. Nothing herein creates an attorney and client, fiduciary, or other relationship between the inventory attorney and the subject attorney. The purpose of appointing an inventory attorney is to avoid prejudice to clients of the subject attorney and, as a secondary result, prevent or reduce claims against the subject attorney for such prejudice as may otherwise occur.

(d) Rules of Procedure. The Florida Rules of Civil Procedure are applicable to proceedings under this rule.

(e) Designation of Inventory Attorney. Each member of the bar who practices law in Florida shall designate another member of The Florida Bar who has agreed to serve as inventory attorney under this rule; provided, however, that no designation is required with respect to any portion of the member's practice as an employee of a governmental entity. When the services of an inventory attorney become necessary, an authorized representative of The Florida Bar shall contact the designated member and determine the member's current willingness to serve. The designated member shall not be under any obligation to serve as inventory attorney.

Amended July 23, 1992, effective Jan. 1, 1993 (605 So.2d 252); July 17, 1997 (697 So.2d 115); Sept. 24, 1998, effective Oct. 1, 1998 (718 So.2d 1179); May 20, 2004 (875 So.2d 448); Oct. 6, 2005, effective Jan. 1, 2006 (916 So.2d 655); Nov. 19, 2009, effective Feb. 1, 2006 (24 So.3d 63).

Rule 1–3.9. Law faculty affiliates

Full-time faculty members in the employment of law schools in Florida approved by the American Bar Association who are admitted to practice and who are in good standing before a court of any state may become "law faculty affiliates" of The Florida Bar. Law faculty affiliates may participate in such activities of The Florida Bar as may be authorized by the board of governors, but shall not be entitled to engage in the practice of law, appear as attorneys before the courts of the state, or hold themselves out as possessing such entitlements.

Rule 1–3.10. Appearance by Non–Florida Lawyer in a Florida Court

(a) Non–Florida Lawyer Appearing in a Florida Court. A practicing lawyer of another state, in good standing and currently eligible to practice, may, upon association of a member of The Florida Bar and verified motion, be permitted to practice upon such conditions as the court deems appropriate under the circumstances of the case. Such lawyer shall comply with the applicable portions of this rule and the Florida Rules of Judicial Administration.

(1) *Application of Rules Regulating The Florida Bar.* Lawyers permitted to appear by this rule shall be subject to these Rules Regulating The Florida Bar while engaged in the permitted representation.

(2) *General Practice Prohibited.* Non–Florida lawyers shall not be permitted to engage in a general practice before Florida courts. For purposes of this rule more than 3 appearances within a 365–day period in separate representations shall be presumed to be a "general practice."

(3) *Effect of Professional Discipline or Contempt.* Non–Florida lawyers who have been disciplined or held in contempt by reason of misconduct committed while engaged in representation that is permitted by this rule shall thereafter be denied admission under this rule and the applicable provisions of the Florida Rules of Judicial Administration.

(b) Lawyer Prohibited From Appearing. No lawyer is authorized to appear pursuant to this rule or the applicable portions of the Florida Rules of Judicial Administration if the lawyer:

(1) is disbarred or suspended from practice in any jurisdiction;

(2) is a Florida resident, unless the attorney has an application pending for admission to The Florida Bar and has not previously been denied admission to The Florida Bar;

(3) is a member of The Florida Bar but ineligible to practice law;

(4) has previously been disciplined or held in contempt by reason of misconduct committed while engaged in representation permitted pursuant to this rule;

(5) has failed to provide notice to The Florida Bar or pay the filing fee as required by this rule; or

(6) is engaged in a "general practice" as defined elsewhere in this rule.

(c) Content of Verified Motion for Leave to Appear. Any verified motion filed under this rule or the applicable provisions of the Florida Rules of Judicial Administration shall include:

(1) a statement identifying all jurisdictions in which the lawyer is currently eligible to practice law;

(2) a statement identifying by date, case name, and case number all other matters in Florida state courts

in which pro hac vice admission has been sought in the preceding 5 years, and whether such admission was granted or denied;

(3) a statement identifying all jurisdictions in which the lawyer has been disciplined in any manner in the preceding 5 years and the sanction imposed, or all jurisdictions in which the lawyer has pending any disciplinary proceeding, including the date of the disciplinary action and the nature of the violation, as appropriate;

(4) a statement identifying the date on which the legal representation at issue commenced and the party or parties represented;

(5) a statement that all applicable provisions of this rule and the applicable provisions of the Florida Rules of Judicial Administration have been read and that the verified motion complies with those rules;

(6) the name, record bar address, and membership status of the Florida Bar member or members associated for purposes of the representation;

(7) a certificate indicating service of the verified motion upon all counsel of record in the matter in which leave to appear pro hac vice is sought and upon The Florida Bar at its Tallahassee office accompanied by a nonrefundable $250 filing fee made payable to The Florida Bar or notice of the waiver of the fee; and

(8) a verification by the lawyer seeking to appear pursuant to this rule or the applicable provisions of the Florida Rules of Judicial Administration and the signature of the Florida Bar member or members associated for purposes of the representation.

Amended Feb. 8, 2001 (795 So.2d 1); May 12, 2005, effective Jan. 1, 2006 (907 So.2d 1138); Nov. 19, 2009, effective Feb. 1, 2010 (24 So.3d 63).

Comment

Subdivision (a)(2) defines and prohibits the general practice before Florida courts by non-Florida lawyers. For purposes of this rule, an "appearance" means the initial or first appearance by that non-Florida lawyer in a case pending in a Florida court, and includes appearing in person or by telephone in court or filing a pleading, motion or other document with the court. A non-Florida lawyer making an appearance in a Florida court is required to comply with rule 2.510 of the Florida Rules of Judicial Administration.

This rule does not prohibit a non-Florida lawyer from participating in more than 3 cases during any 365–day period; instead, it prohibits a non-Florida lawyer from making an initial or first appearance in more than 3 cases during any 365–day period.

Example: The following example illustrates the application of this rule to a non-Florida lawyer's appearances. Assume for this example that a lawyer licensed to practice in Georgia only has been admitted pro hac vice pursuant to Fla. R. Jud. Admin. 2.510 in 3 separate Florida cases on the following dates: January 10, 2008; February 3, 2008; and February 20, 2008.

(1) In this example, the lawyer would be prohibited from seeking to appear pro hac vice under Fla. R. Jud. Admin. 2.510 in another separate representation until the expiration of the 365–day period from his or her oldest of the 3 appearances (i.e., until January 10, 2009).

(2) In this example, the lawyer would be permitted under this rule to seek to appear pro hac vice in a new case on January 10, 2009 even if the 3 cases in which he or she made an appearance are still active.

(3) In this example, the lawyer could seek to appear pro hac vice in yet another new case on February 3, 2009. The fact that the lawyer's cases in which he or she appeared on January 10, 2008, February 3, 2008, February 20, 2008, and January 1, 2009 are still active would not prohibit that lawyer from seeking to appear in the new case on February 3, 2009, because, as of that date, the lawyer would have only made an initial appearance in 2 prior cases within that preceding 365–day period (i.e., on February 20, 2008 and January 1, 2009). Thus, under this rule, a non-Florida lawyer could have pending more than 3 cases for which he or she has appeared at any given time, as the restriction on general practice relates to the making of an initial appearance within a 365–day period and not to whether any such case is still active following the expiration of 365 days.

(4) Similarly, in the above example, if the non-Florida lawyer's 3 cases are all resolved by April 1, 2008, that lawyer would still be prohibited from seeking to make a new appearance until the expiration of the oldest of the 3 prior appearances (i.e., until January 10, 2009).

The purpose of this comment is to explain what constitutes an "appearance" under this rule and how to calculate the number of appearances in any 365–day period. This comment and the rule itself do not require a Florida court to grant any specific request to appear under Fla. R. Jud. Admin. 2.510 if the non-Florida lawyer meets the requirements of subdivision (a)(2). In all such cases, the decision of whether a non-Florida lawyer may appear in a case under Fla. R. Jud. Admin. 2.510 is within the discretion of the court.

This rule is not applicable to appearances in federal courts sitting in Florida, as appearances before each of those courts are regulated by the rules applicable to those courts. Further, an appearance in a federal court sitting in Florida does not constitute an "appearance" as contemplated by subdivision (a)(2), because subdivision (a)(2) applies only to appearances before Florida state courts.

Rule 1–3.11. Appearance by non-Florida Lawyer in an Arbitration Proceeding in Florida

(a) Non–Florida Lawyer Appearing in an Arbitration Proceeding in Florida. A lawyer currently eligible to practice law in another United States jurisdiction or a non–United States jurisdiction may appear in an arbitration proceeding in this jurisdiction if the appearance is:

(1) for a client who resides in or has an office in the lawyer's home state; or

(2) where the appearance arises out of or is reasonably related to the lawyer's practice in a jurisdiction in which the lawyer is admitted to practice; and

(3) the appearance is not one that requires pro hac vice admission.

Such lawyer shall comply with the applicable portions of this rule and of rule 4-5.5.

(b) Lawyer Prohibited from Appearing. No lawyer is authorized to appear pursuant to this rule if the lawyer:

(1) is disbarred or suspended from practice in any jurisdiction;

(2) is a Florida resident;

(3) is a member of The Florida Bar but ineligible to practice law;

(4) has previously been disciplined or held in contempt by reason of misconduct committed while engaged in representation permitted pursuant to this rule;

(5) has failed to provide notice to The Florida Bar or pay the filing fee as required by this rule, except that neither notice to The Florida Bar nor a fee shall be required for lawyers appearing in international arbitrations; or

(6) is engaged in a "general practice" as defined elsewhere in these rules.

(c) Application of Rules Regulating the Florida Bar. Lawyers permitted to appear by this rule shall be subject to these Rules Regulating the Florida Bar while engaged in the permitted representation, including, without limitation, rule 4-5.5.

(d) General Practice Prohibited. Non-Florida lawyers shall not be permitted to engage in a general practice pursuant to this rule. In all arbitration matters except international arbitration, a lawyer who is not admitted to practice law in this jurisdiction who files more than 3 demands for arbitration or responses to arbitration in separate arbitration proceedings in a 365-day period shall be presumed to be engaged in a "general practice."

(e) Content of Verified Statement for Leave to Appear. In all arbitration proceedings except international arbitrations, prior to practicing pursuant to this rule, the non-Florida lawyer shall file a verified statement with The Florida Bar and serve a copy of the verified statement on opposing counsel, if known. If opposing counsel is not known at the time the verified statement is filed with The Florida Bar, the non-Florida lawyer shall serve a copy of the verified statement on opposing counsel within 10 days of learning the identity of opposing counsel. The verified statement shall include:

(1) a statement identifying all jurisdictions in which the lawyer is currently eligible to practice law including the attorney's bar number(s) or attorney number(s);

(2) a statement identifying by date, case name, and case number all other arbitration proceedings in which the non-Florida lawyer has appeared in Florida in the preceding 5 years; however, if the case name and case number are confidential pursuant to an order, rule, or agreement of the parties, this information does not need to be provided and only the dates of prior proceedings must be disclosed;

(3) a statement identifying all jurisdictions in which the lawyer has been disciplined in any manner in the preceding 5 years and the sanction imposed, or in which the lawyer has pending any disciplinary proceeding, including the date of the disciplinary action and the nature of the violation, as appropriate;

(4) a statement identifying the date on which the legal representation at issue commenced and the party or parties represented; however, if the name of the party or parties is confidential pursuant to an order, rule, or agreement of the parties, this information does not need to be provided and only the date on which the representation commenced must be disclosed;

(5) a statement that all applicable provisions of this rule have been read and that the verified statement complies with this rule;

(6) a certificate indicating service of the verified statement upon all counsel of record in the matter and upon The Florida Bar at its Tallahassee office accompanied by a nonrefundable $250.00 filing fee made payable to The Florida Bar; however, such fee may be waived in cases involving indigent clients; and

(7) a verification by the lawyer seeking to appear pursuant to this rule.

Added May 12, 2005, effective Jan. 1, 2006 (907 So.2d 1138). Amended Sept. 11, 2008, effective Jan. 1, 2009 (991 So.2d 842).

Comment

This rule applies to arbitration proceedings held in Florida where 1 or both parties are being represented by a lawyer admitted in another United States jurisdiction or a non-United States jurisdiction. For the most part, the rule applies to any type of arbitration proceeding and any matter being arbitrated. However, entire portions of subdivision (d) and subdivision (e) do not apply to international arbitrations. For the purposes of this rule, an international arbitration is defined as the arbitration of disputes between 2 or more persons at least 1 of whom is a nonresident of the United States or between 2 or more persons all of whom are residents of the United States if the dispute (1) involves property located outside the United States, (2) relates to a contract or other agreement which envisages performance or enforcement in whole or in part outside the United States, (3) involves an investment outside the United States or the ownership, management, or operation of a business entity through which such an investment is effected or any agreement pertaining to any interest in such an entity, (4) bears some other relation to 1 or more foreign countries, or (5) involves 2 or more persons at least 1 of whom is a foreign state as defined in 28 U.S.C. § 1603. International arbitration does not include the arbitration of any dispute pertaining to the ownership, use, development, or possession of, or a lien of record upon, real property located in Florida or any dispute involving domestic relations.

The exceptions provided in this rule for international arbitrations in no way exempt lawyers not admitted to The Florida Bar and appearing in Florida courts from compliance with the provisions of rule 1–3.10 and any applicable rules of judicial administration, regardless of whether the court proceeding arises out of or is related to the subject of a dispute in an international arbitration. For example, a lawyer not a member of The Florida Bar could not appear in a Florida court or confirm or vacate an award resulting from an international arbitration without being authorized to appear pro hac vice and without complying with all requirements contained in rule 1–3.10 and the applicable rules of judicial administration.

1–4. BOARD OF GOVERNORS

Rule 1–4.1. Composition of board of governors

The board of governors shall be the governing body of The Florida Bar. It shall have 52 members, 51 of whom shall be voting members, and shall consist of the president and the president-elect of The Florida Bar, president and president-elect (who shall vote only in the absence of the president) of the young lawyers division, representatives elected by and from the members of The Florida Bar in good standing, and 2 residents of the state of Florida who are not members of The Florida Bar. There shall be at least 1 representative from each judicial circuit and at least 1 representative from among the members in good standing residing outside of the state of Florida, all of whom shall be apportioned among and elected from the judicial circuits and the nonresident membership, on the basis of the number of members in good standing residing in each circuit and outside of the state. The formula for determining the number of representatives apportioned to and elected from each judicial circuit and the nonresident membership, and all other matters concerning election and term of office for members of the board of governors, shall be prescribed in chapter 2.

Amended Dec. 10, 1987, effective Jan. 1, 1988 (518 So.2d 251); July 23, 1992, effective Jan. 1, 1993 (605 So.2d 252); July 17, 1997 (697 So.2d 115); Sept. 24, 1998, effective Oct. 1, 1998 (718 So.2d 1179).

Rule 1–4.2. Authority; supervision

(a) Authority and Responsibility. The board of governors shall have the authority and responsibility to govern and administer The Florida Bar and to take such action as it may consider necessary to accomplish the purposes of The Florida Bar, subject always to the direction and supervision of the Supreme Court of Florida.

(b) Duty to Furnish Information to Court. The board of governors shall furnish to each member of the Supreme Court of Florida the following:

(1) The minutes of each meeting of the board of governors of The Florida Bar and each meeting of its executive committee except when acting in a prosecutorial role in a disciplinary or unlicensed practice of law matter.

(2) Any written report of any section, committee, or division of The Florida Bar submitted to the board of governors that is either accepted or adopted by the board.

(3) All rules, policies, or procedures adopted by the board of governors under the authority granted to the board by the court.

(4) Such additional information and material as may be requested by any member of the court.

(c) Powers of Court. The Supreme Court of Florida may at any time ratify or amend action taken by the board of governors under these rules, order that actions previously taken be rescinded, or otherwise direct the actions and activities of The Florida Bar and its board of governors.

Amended July 23, 1992, effective Jan. 1, 1993 (605 So.2d 252).

Rule 1–4.3. Committees

Text of rule effective until October 1, 2015. See, also, rule effective October 1, 2015.

The board of governors shall create an executive committee composed of the president, president-elect, chairs of the budget, communications, disciplinary review, and legislation committees, president of the young lawyers division, 2 members of the board appointed by the president, and 3 members of the board elected by the board to act upon such matters as arise and require disposition between meetings of the board; a budget committee composed of 9 members with 3–year staggered terms; grievance committees as provided for in chapter 3; unlicensed practice of law committees as provided for in chapter 10; and a professional ethics committee.

Amended May 12, 1988 (525 So.2d 868); amended July 23, 1992, effective Jan. 1, 1993 (605 So.2d 252); June 27, 1996, effective July 1, 1996 (677 So.2d 272); Nov. 19, 2009, effective Feb. 1, 2010 (24 So.3d 63).

Rule 1–4.3. Committees

Text of rule effective October 1, 2015. See, also, rule effective until October 1, 2015.

The board of governors will create an executive committee composed of the president, president-elect, chairs of the budget, communications, disciplinary review, program evaluation and legislation committees, president of the young lawyers division, 2 members of the board appointed by the president, and 3 members of the board elected by the board to act on matters that arise and require disposition between meetings of the board; a budget committee composed of 9 members with 3–year staggered terms; grievance committees as provided for in chapter 3; unlicensed practice of law committees as provided for in chapter 10; and a professional ethics committee.

Amended May 12, 1988 (525 So.2d 868); amended July 23, 1992, effective Jan. 1, 1993 (605 So.2d 252); June 27, 1996, effective July 1, 1996 (677 So.2d 272); Nov. 19, 2009, effective Feb. 1, 2010 (24 So.3d 63); May 21, 2015, effective Oct. 1, 2015 (164 So.3d 1217).

Rule 1–4.4. Board committees

The board may create and abolish additional committees as it may consider necessary to accomplish the purposes of The Florida Bar.

Rule 1–4.5. Sections

The board of governors may create and abolish sections as it may consider necessary or desirable to accomplish the purposes and serve the interests of The Florida Bar and of the sections and shall prescribe the powers and duties of such sections. The bylaws of any section shall be subject to approval of the board of governors.

1–5. OFFICERS

Rule 1–5.1. Officers

The officers of The Florida Bar shall be a president, a president-elect, and an executive director.

Rule 1–5.2. Duties

Chapter 2 shall prescribe the duties, terms of office, qualifications, and manner of election or selection of officers of The Florida Bar.

1–6. MEETINGS OF THE FLORIDA BAR

Rule 1–6.1. Annual meeting

An annual meeting of The Florida Bar shall be held each fiscal year at such time as may be designated by the board of governors.

Rule 1–6.2. Special meetings

Special meetings of The Florida Bar may be held at such times and places as may be determined by the board of governors or upon petition of 5 percent of the membership of The Florida Bar.

Amended July 23, 1992, effective Jan. 1, 1993 (605 So.2d 252).

Rule 1–6.3. Notice; rules of procedure

The manner of notice and rules of procedure for all meetings of The Florida Bar shall be prescribed in chapter 2.

1–7. MEMBERSHIP FEES AND FISCAL CONTROL

Rule 1–7.1. Budget

The board of governors shall adopt a proposed budget for The Florida Bar in advance of each fiscal year, publish such proposed budget in a publication of The Florida Bar generally circulated to members, and thereafter adopt a budget for the succeeding fiscal year. The budget adopted by the board of governors shall be filed with the Supreme Court of Florida 30 days prior to the beginning of each fiscal year and shall be deemed approved and become the budget of The Florida Bar unless rejected by the Supreme Court of Florida within said 30–day period or until amended by the board of governors in accordance with rule 2–6.12.

Amended July 23, 1992, effective Jan. 1, 1993 (605 So.2d 252).

Rule 1–7.2. Officers' salary

No member of the board of governors and no officer of The Florida Bar other than the executive director shall receive a fee or salary from The Florida Bar.

Rule 1–7.3. Membership Fees

(a) Membership Fees Requirement. On or before July 1 of each year, every member of The Florida Bar, except those members who have retired, resigned, been disbarred, or been classified as inactive members pursuant to rule 3–7.13, must pay annual membership fees to The Florida Bar in the amount of $265 per annum. Every member of The Florida Bar must pay the membership fee and concurrently file a fee statement with any information the board of governors requires.

(b) Prorated Membership Fees. Membership fees will be prorated for anyone admitted to The Florida Bar after July 1 of any fiscal year. The prorated amount will be based on the number of full calendar months remaining in the fiscal year at the time of their admission.

Unpaid prorated membership fees will be added to the next annual membership fees bill with no penalty to the member. The Florida Bar must receive the combined prorated and annual membership fees payment on or before August 15 of the first full year fees are due unless the member elects to pay by installment.

(c) Installment Payment of Membership Fees. Members of The Florida Bar may elect to pay annual membership fees in 3 equal installments as follows:

(1) in the second and third year of their admission to The Florida Bar;

(2) if the member is employed by a federal, state, or local government in a non-elected position that requires the individual to maintain membership in good standing within The Florida Bar; or

(3) if the member is experiencing an undue hardship.

A member must notify The Florida Bar of the intention to pay membership fees in installments. The first installment payment must be postmarked no later than August 15. The second and third installment payments must be postmarked no later than November 1 and February 1, respectively.

Second and/or third installment payments postmarked after their respective due date(s) are subject to a one-time late charge of $50. The late charge must accompany the final payment. The executive director with concurrence of the executive committee may adjust the late charge.

The executive director will send written notice to the last official bar address of each member who has not paid membership fees and late fees by February 1. Written notice may be by registered or certified mail, or by return receipt electronic mail. The member will be a delinquent member if membership fees and late charges are not paid by March 15. The executive director with concurrence of the executive committee may adjust these fees or due date for good cause.

Each member who elects to pay annual membership fees in installments may be charged an additional administrative fee set by the board of governors to defray the costs of this activity.

(d) Election of Inactive Membership. A member in good standing may elect to be classified as an inactive member. This election must be indicated on the annual membership fees statement and received by The Florida Bar by August 15. If the annual membership fees statement is received after August 15, the member's right to inactive status is waived until the next fiscal year. Inactive classification will continue from fiscal year to fiscal year until the member is reinstated as a member in good standing who is eligible to practice law in Florida. The election of inactive status is subject to the restrictions and limitations provided elsewhere in these rules.

Membership fees for inactive members are $175 per annum.

(e) Late Payment of Membership Fees. Payment of annual membership fees must be postmarked no later than August 15. Membership fees payments postmarked after August 15 must be accompanied by a late charge of $50. The executive director will send written notice to the last official bar address of each member whose membership fees have not been paid by August 15. Written notice may be by registered or certified mail, or by return receipt electronic mail. The member is considered a delinquent member upon failure to pay membership fees and any late charges by September 30, unless adjusted by the executive director with concurrence of the executive committee.

(f) Membership Fees Exemption for Activated Reserve Members of the Armed Services. Members of The Florida Bar engaged in reserve military service in the Armed Forces of the United States who are called to active duty for 30 days or more during the bar's fiscal year are exempt from the payment of membership fees. The Armed Forces of the United States includes the United States Army, Air Force, Navy, Marine Corps, Coast Guard, as well as the Army National Guard, Army Reserve, Navy Reserve, Marine Corps Reserve, the Air National Guard of the United States, the Air Force Reserve, and the Coast Guard Reserve. Requests for an exemption must be made within 15 days before the date that membership fees are due each year or within 15 days of activation to duty of a reserve member. To the extent membership fees were paid despite qualifying for this exemption, such membership fee will be reimbursed by The Florida Bar within 30 days of receipt of a member's request for exemption. Within 30 days of leaving active duty status, the member must report to The Florida Bar that he or she is no longer on active duty status in the United States Armed Forces.

Amended March 30, 1989, effective March 31, 1989 (541 So.2d 110); June 8, 1989 (544 So.2d 193); June 14, 1990 (562 So.2d 343); July 23, 1992, effective Jan. 1, 1993 (605 So.2d 252); Feb. 17, 1994 (632 So.2d 597); June 27, 1996, effective July 1, 1996 (677 So.2d 272); July 17, 1997 (697 So.2d 115); Sept. 24, 1998, effective Oct. 1, 1998 (718 So.2d 1179); Feb. 8, 2001 (795 So.2d 1); June 4, 2001 (797 So.2d 550); May 20, 2004 (875 So.2d 448); Oct. 6, 2005, effective Jan. 1, 2006 (916 So.2d 655); Dec. 20, 2007, effective March 1, 2008 (978 So.2d 91); May 29, 2014, effective June 1, 2014 (140 So.3d 541).

Rule 1–7.4. Procedures

Other matters relating to the budget and fiscal control shall be governed by chapter 2.

Rule 1–7.5. Retired, Inactive, Delinquent Members

A member who is retired, inactive, or delinquent shall not practice law in this state until reinstated as provided in these rules.

Amended March 30, 1989, effective March 31, 1989 (541 So.2d 110); July 23, 1992, effective Jan. 1, 1993 (605 So.2d 252); Nov. 19, 2009, effective Feb. 1, 2010 (24 So.3d 63).

1–8. PROGRAMS AND FUNCTIONS

Rule 1–8.1. Responsibility of board of governors

Among its other duties, the board of governors is charged with the responsibility of enforcing the Rules of Discipline and the Rules of Professional Conduct.

Rule 1–8.2. Unlicensed practice of law

The board of governors shall act as an arm of the Supreme Court of Florida for the purpose of seeking to prohibit the unlicensed practice of law by investigating, prosecuting, and reporting to this court and to appropriate authorities incidents involving the unlicensed practice of law in accordance with chapter 10.

Amended July 23, 1992, effective Jan. 1, 1993 (605 So.2d 252).

Rule 1–8.3. Board of legal specialization and education

The board of governors shall establish the board of legal specialization and education to function as a central administrative board to oversee specialization regulation in Florida in accordance with chapter 6.

Amended July 23, 1992, effective Jan. 1, 1993 (605 So.2d 252).

Rule 1–8.4. Clients' Security Fund

The board of governors may provide monetary relief to persons who suffer reimbursable losses as a result of misappropriation, embezzlement, or other wrongful taking or conversion of money or other property in accordance with chapter 7.

Amended April 12, 2012, effective July 1, 2012 (101 So.3d 807).

1–9. YOUNG LAWYERS DIVISION

Rule 1–9.1. Creation

There shall be a division of The Florida Bar known as the Young Lawyers Division composed of all members in good standing under the age of 36 and all members in good standing who have not been admitted to the practice of law in any jurisdiction for more than 5 years.

Amended July 23, 1992, effective Jan. 1, 1993 (605 So.2d 252).

Rule 1–9.2. Powers and duties

The division shall have such powers and duties as shall be prescribed by the board of governors of The Florida Bar.

Rule 1–9.3. Bylaws

The bylaws of the division shall be subject to approval of the board of governors.

1–10. RULES OF PROFESSIONAL CONDUCT

Rule 1–10.1. Compliance

All members of The Florida Bar shall comply with the terms and the intent of the Rules of Professional Conduct as established and amended by this court.

Amended July 23, 1992, effective Jan. 1, 1993 (605 So.2d 252).

1–11. BYLAWS

Rule 1–11.1. Generally

Bylaws, contained in chapter 2, not inconsistent with these rules shall govern the method and manner by which the requirements of these Rules Regulating The Florida Bar are met.

Rule 1–11.2. Notice of amendment

Notice of consideration of proposed amendments to chapter 2 by the board of governors of The Florida Bar shall be given to the members of The Florida Bar. Amendments to chapter 2 adopted by the board of governors shall become effective 50 days after the amendment and proof of the prescribed publication are filed with the Supreme Court of Florida unless a later effective date is provided for by the board of governors or unless otherwise ordered by the court. The court will consider objections to amendments to chapter 2 adopted by the board of governors that are filed with the court before the effective date of the amendment.

Former Rule 1–11.3. Renumbered and amended July 23, 1992, effective Jan. 1, 1993 (605 So.2d 252).

Rule 1–11.3. Supervision by Court

This court may at any time amend chapter 2 or modify amendments to chapter 2 adopted by the board of governors or order that amendments to chapter 2 not become effective or become effective at some date other than provided for in this rule.

Former Rule 1–11.4. Renumbered and amended July 23, 1992, effective Jan. 1, 1993 (605 So.2d 252).

1–12. AMENDMENTS

Rule 1–12.1. Amendment to Rules; Authority; Notice; Procedures; Comments

(a) Authority to Amend. The board of governors of The Florida Bar shall have the authority to amend chapters 7 and 9, as well as the standards for the individual areas of certification within chapter 6 of these Rules Regulating The Florida Bar, consistent with the notice, publication, and comments requirements provided below. Only the Supreme Court of Florida shall have the authority to amend all other chapters of these Rules Regulating The Florida Bar.

(b) Proposed Amendments. Any member of The Florida Bar in good standing or a section or committee of The Florida Bar may request the board of governors to consider an amendment to these Rules Regulating The Florida Bar.

(c) Board Review of Proposed Amendments. The board of governors shall review proposed amendments by referral of the proposal to an appropriate committee thereof for substantive review. After substantive review, an appropriate committee of the board shall review the proposal for consistency with these rules and the policies of The Florida Bar. After completion of review, a recommendation concerning the proposal shall be made to the board.

(d) Notice of Proposed Board Action. Notice of the proposed action of the board on a proposed amendment shall be given in an edition of The Florida Bar News and on The Florida Bar website that is published prior to the meeting of the board at which the board action is taken. The notice shall identify the rule(s) to be amended and shall state in general terms the nature of the proposed amendments.

(e) Comments by Members. Any member may request a copy of the proposed amendments and may file written comments concerning them. The comments shall be filed with the executive director sufficiently in advance of the board meeting to allow for copying and distribution to the members of the board.

(f) Approval of Amendments. Amendments to other than chapters 7 and 9, as well as the standards for the individual areas of certification within chapter 6 of these Rules Regulating The Florida Bar shall be by petition to the Supreme Court of Florida. Petitions to amend these Rules Regulating The Florida Bar may be filed by the board of governors or by 50 members in good standing, provided that any amendments proposed by members of the bar shall be filed 90 days after filing them with The Florida Bar.

(g) Notice of Intent to File Petition. Notice of intent to file a petition to amend these Rules Regulating The Florida Bar shall be published in The Florida Bar News and on The Florida Bar website at least 30 days before the filing of the petition. The notice shall set forth the text of the proposed amendments, state the date the petition will be filed, and state that any comments or objections must be filed within 30 days of filing the petition. A copy of all comments or objections shall be served on the executive director of The Florida Bar and any persons who may have made an appearance in the matter.

(h) Action by the Supreme Court of Florida. The court shall review all proposed amendments filed under this rule and such amendments shall not become effective until an order is issued approving them. Final action of the court shall be reported in The Florida Bar News and on The Florida Bar website.

(i) Waiver. On good cause shown, the court may waive any or all of the provisions of this rule.

Amended Oct. 10, 1991, effective Jan. 1, 1992 (587 So.2d 1121); July 23, 1992, effective Jan. 1, 1993 (605 So.2d 252); July 1, 1993 (621 So.2d 1032); July 20, 1995 (658 So.2d 930); Nov. 19, 2009, effective Feb. 1, 2010 (24 So.3d 63); April 12, 2012, effective July 1, 2012 (101 So.3d 807).

1–13. TIME

Rule 1–13.1. Time

Text of rule effective until October 1, 2015. See, also, rule effective October 1, 2015.

(a) Computation. In computing any period of time prescribed or allowed by the Rules Regulating The Florida Bar, the day of the act, event, or default from which the designated period of time begins to run shall not be included. The last day of the period so computed shall be included unless it is a Saturday, Sunday, or legal holiday, in which event the period shall run until the end of the next day that is not a Saturday, Sunday, or legal holiday.

(b) Additional Time After Service by Mail. When a person has the right or is required to do some act or take some proceeding within a prescribed period after service of a notice or other paper and the notice or paper is served by mail, 5 days shall be added to the prescribed period.

Added Oct. 10, 1991, effective Jan. 1, 1992 (587 So.2d 1121). Amended July 23, 1992, effective Jan. 1, 1993 (605 So.2d 252).

Rule 1–13.1. Time

Text of rule effective October 1, 2015. See, also, rule effective until October 1, 2015.

(a) Computation. In computing any period of time prescribed or allowed by the Rules Regulating The Florida Bar, the day of the act, event, or default from which the designated period of time begins to run will not be included. The last day of the period so computed will be included unless it is a Saturday, Sunday, or legal holiday, in which event the period will run until the end of the next day that is not a Saturday, Sunday, or legal holiday.

(b) Additional Time after Service by Mail or E-mail. When a person has the right or is required to do some act or take some proceeding within a prescribed period after service of a notice or other paper and the notice or paper is served by mail or e-mail, 5 days will be added to the prescribed period.

Added Oct. 10, 1991, effective Jan. 1, 1992 (587 So.2d 1121). Amended July 23, 1992, effective Jan. 1, 1993 (605 So.2d 252); May 21, 2015, effective Oct. 1, 2015 (164 So.3d 1217).

1–14. RECORDS

Rule 1–14.1. Access to Records

(a) Confidential Records. All records specifically designated confidential by court rules, the Florida or United States Constitution, statutes, attorney work product, and attorney-client communications shall be confidential. In the event that The Florida Bar objects to production, these records shall not be produced without order of the Supreme Court of Florida or some person designated by the supreme court to decide whether the records should be disclosed.

(b) Records Confidential under Applicable Law. All records in the possession of The Florida Bar that are confidential under applicable rule or law when made or received shall remain confidential and shall not be produced by the bar, except as authorized by rule or law or pursuant to order of the Supreme Court of Florida.

(c) Rules of Procedure and Florida Evidence Code; Applicability. Except as otherwise provided in these Rules Regulating The Florida Bar, any restrictions to production of records contained in the Florida Evidence Code (chapter 90, Florida Statutes, as amended), Florida Rules of Civil Procedure, or Florida Rules of Criminal Procedure shall apply to requests for access to the records of The Florida Bar.

(d) Access to Records; Notice; Costs of Production. Any records of The Florida Bar that are not designated confidential by these Rules Regulating The Florida Bar shall be available for inspection or production to any person upon reasonable notice and upon payment of the cost of reproduction of the records.

Added October 29, 1992 (608 So.2d 472).

CHAPTER 2. BYLAWS OF THE FLORIDA BAR

2-1. SEAL, EMBLEMS, AND SYMBOLS

Bylaw 2-1.1. Seal

The official seal of The Florida Bar shall be inscribed "The Florida Bar" on upper circular portion, "1950" on lower circular portion, with the official state seal occupying center portion.

Amended March 2, 1988.

Bylaw 2-1.2. Usage

The usages of the seal, emblems, or other symbols of The Florida Bar shall be determined by the board of governors.

Amended March 2, 1988; effective Feb. 8, 2001 (795 So.2d 1).

2-2. MEMBERSHIP

Bylaw 2-2.1. Attaining membership

Persons shall initially become a member of The Florida Bar, in good standing, only upon certification by the Supreme Court of Florida in accordance with the rules governing the Florida Board of Bar Examiners and administration of the required oath.

Amended March 2, 1988; amended July 23, 1992, effective Jan. 1, 1993 (605 So.2d 252).

Bylaw 2-2.2. Law faculty affiliates

Law faculty affiliates shall pay fees as set by the board of governors, shall be entitled to receive The Florida Bar Journal and The Florida Bar News, and shall have such other privileges and benefits of members of The Florida Bar as the board of governors shall authorize. The executive director shall issue to law faculty affiliates such special identification card as may be authorized by the board of governors.

Amended March 2, 1988.

Bylaw 2–2.3. List of members

The executive director shall furnish the chief judge of each circuit and the clerk of each court a list of all members in good standing and a list of all inactive members and shall furnish corrections and additions to such lists as occasion may require.

Amended March 2, 1988; March 30, 1989, effective March 31, 1989 (541 So.2d 110).

2–3. BOARD OF GOVERNORS

Bylaw 2–3.1. Generally

The board of governors shall be the governing body of The Florida Bar. The board of governors shall have the power and duty to administer the Rules Regulating The Florida Bar, including the power to employ necessary personnel. Subject to the authority of the Supreme Court of Florida, the board of governors, as the governing body of The Florida Bar, shall be vested with exclusive power and authority to formulate, fix, determine, and adopt matters of policy concerning the activities, affairs, or organization of The Florida Bar. The board of governors shall be charged with the duty and responsibility of enforcing and carrying into effect the provisions of the Rules Regulating The Florida Bar and the accomplishment of the aims and purposes of The Florida Bar. The board of governors shall direct the manner in which all funds of The Florida Bar are disbursed and the purposes therefor and shall adopt and approve a budget for each fiscal year. The board of governors shall perform all other duties imposed under the Rules Regulating The Florida Bar and shall have full power to exercise such functions as may be necessary, expedient, or incidental to the full exercise of any powers bestowed upon the board of governors by said rules or any amendment thereto or by this chapter.

Amended March 2, 1988; July 23, 1992, effective Jan. 1, 1993 (605 So.2d 252).

Bylaw 2–3.2. Powers

(a) Authority of Board; Supervision by Court. Subject to the continued direction and supervision by the Supreme Court of Florida, the board of governors may, by amendment to this chapter, take all necessary action to make nominations and appointments where authorized, support the Florida Bar Foundation, and create or abolish programs.

(b) Nomination and Appointment by Board. The board of governors may make nominations to or appointments to associations or other entities as required by the Rules Regulating The Florida Bar, this chapter, and any rules or policies adopted by the board of governors in accordance therewith or as required by law.

(c) Florida Bar Foundation. The board of governors may support the foundation known as The Florida Bar Foundation for charitable, scientific, literary, and educational purposes.

(d) Programs. The board of governors may establish, maintain, and supervise:

(1) a lawyer referral service;

(2) programs for providing continuing legal education for its members;

(3) the production of various print or electronic media for its members, affiliates, and the public;

(4) a program for providing information and advice to the courts and all other branches of government concerning current law and proposed or contemplated changes in the law;

(5) a program of cooperation with the faculty of accredited Florida law schools;

(6) a program for providing pre-paid legal services;

(7) a program for providing advice and educational information to members of the bar concerning the operation and management of law offices;

(8) programs for promoting and supporting the bar's public service obligations and activities, including, but not limited to, pro bono services support and law related education;

(9) programs for the development and provision of benefits and services to bar members, including, but not limited to, insurance benefits and association member discounts on goods and services;

(10) a program or funding for a program to provide for identification of and assistance to members of The Florida Bar who suffer from impairment related to chemical dependency or psychological problems;

(11) a program for providing enhanced opportunities and participation in the profession to minority members of the bar;

(12) a program to enhance the levels of professionalism within the courts, law schools, and the legal profession; and

(13) programs for providing information or discussion about lawyers and the legal system.

Amended March 2, 1988; April 13, 1989; July 23, 1992, effective Jan. 1, 1993 (605 So.2d 252); Sept. 24, 1998, effective Oct. 1, 1998 (718 So.2d 1179).

Bylaw 2–3.3. Formula for apportionment of members of board of governors

(a) Nonresident Representation. As used in these bylaws, "judicial circuit" and "circuit" shall include a hypothetical out-of-state judicial circuit with a circuit population equal to 50% of the number of members of The Florida Bar in good standing residing outside of the state of Florida.

(b) Apportionment Formula. The formula for determining the number of representatives apportioned to and elected from each judicial circuit shall be as follows:

(1) *Determination of Median Circuit Population.* Determine the median number of members in good standing residing in the judicial circuits ("the median circuit population") by ranking the judicial circuits in order of the number of members in good standing residing in each circuit and determining the number of members in good standing residing in the judicial circuit that is ranked exactly midway between the circuit with the largest number of members and the circuit with the smallest number of members or, if there is an even number of circuits, calculating the average membership of the 2 circuits that are ranked midway between the circuit with the largest number of members and the circuit with the smallest number of members.

(2) *Apportionment of Representatives Among the Judicial Circuits.* Apportion representatives among the judicial circuits by assigning to each judicial circuit the number of representatives equal to the quotient obtained by dividing the number of members in good standing residing in that circuit by the median circuit population and rounding to the nearest whole number.

(3) *Determination of Deviation From Median Circuit Population.* Determine the relative deviation of each circuit's proportionate representation from the median circuit population by (A) calculating the number of resident members per representative so apportioned, rounded to the nearest whole number, (B) subtracting from that number the median circuit population, (C) dividing the difference by the median circuit population, and (D) converting the quotient so obtained to the equivalent percentile.

(4) *Adjustment to Deviation From Median Circuit Population.* Determine whether each circuit's relative deviation from the median circuit population would be reduced by adding or subtracting 1 representative, and, if so, add or subtract 1 representative as indicated.

(5) *Minimum Guaranteed Representatives.* Assign 1 representative to each judicial circuit not otherwise qualifying for a representative under the calculations made in subdivisions (1) and (2).

(6) *Increase or Reduction in Number of Representatives to Achieve Required Board Size.* If the total number of representatives assigned to the judicial circuits as a result of the steps set forth in subdivisions (1) through (5), when added to the number of officers and other representatives who are members of the board by virtue of the provisions of rule 1–4.1, would result in a board of greater or fewer than 51 voting persons, increase or reduce the number of voting members of the board to exactly 51 voting persons by (A) determining which judicial circuit among those to which more than 1 representative has been apportioned would have the smallest relative deviation from the median circuit population after the gain or loss of 1 representative, (B) adding or subtracting 1 representative from that circuit, as indicated, and (C) repeating those 2 steps as necessary until the total number of voting board members is increased or reduced to exactly 51.

Amended Dec. 10, 1987, effective Jan. 1, 1988 (518 So.2d 251); March 2, 1988; July 23, 1992, effective Jan. 1, 1993 (605 So.2d 252); July 17, 1997 (697 So.2d 115); Sept. 24, 1998, effective Oct. 1, 1998 (718 So.2d 1179).

Bylaw 2–3.4. Annual Apportionment

(a) Certification of Membership by Executive Director. The executive director shall each year as of October 1 determine from the official records of The Florida Bar the number of members, in good standing, of The Florida Bar residing in each judicial circuit and outside the State of Florida. For purposes of these rules, residency shall be determined by a member's official bar address. The executive director shall thereafter determine by application of the formula in bylaw 2–3.3 the number of members of the board of governors to serve from each judicial circuit. The executive director shall file a certificate setting forth the above information with the clerk of the Supreme Court of Florida and shall cause a copy of such certificate to be published in The Florida Bar News on or before November 1 of each year and shall include the names of those incumbent board of governors' representatives who have advised the executive director of their intentions to seek reelection in accordance with the provisions of subdivision (b). The certificate shall be published in the format of bylaw 2–3.5(a). The reapportionment established by the terms of such certificate shall automatically amend bylaw 2–3.5(a) on December 1 unless the Supreme Court of Florida orders otherwise.

(b) Members' Intentions to Seek Reelection. Board of governors' members, in a nonbinding notification tendered to The Florida Bar no later than October 1 in the final year of their term of office, shall advise the executive director of their intentions to seek reelection to a new term. The executive director shall cause such information to be published in The Florida Bar News within the certification of board of governors' membership specified in subdivision (a).

(c) Elected Members to Serve Full Term. No elected member of the board of governors shall serve less than the full term to which elected by reason of any reapportionment required by subdivision (a).

Amended March 2, 1988; July 23, 1992, effective Jan. 1, 1993 (605 So.2d 252); July 20, 1995 (658 So.2d 930).

Bylaw 2–3.5. Nomination of members

(a) Staggered Terms. Elections shall be held and appointments made in even-numbered years for the following board of governors' representatives:

Circuit (seat #)
1
2(2)
3
4(1)
6(1)
7
9(1)
9(3)
10
11(1)
11(3)
11(5)
11(7)
11(9)
13(1)
14
15(1)
15(3)
17(1)
17(4)
18
20
nonresident (2)
nonresident (4)
public member (2)

Elections shall be held and appointments made in odd-numbered years for the following board of governors' representatives:

Circuit (seat #)
2(1)
4(2)
5
6(2)
8
9(2)
11(2)
11(4)
11(6)
11(8)
11(10)
12(1)
13(2)
13(3)
15(2)
16
17(2)
17(3)
17(5)
19
nonresident (1)
nonresident (3)
public member (1)

As additions or deletions of circuit representatives resulting from the application of the formula provided in this rule necessitate changes in the lists set forth above, both in circuit and office numbers, such changes shall be made by the executive director as appropriate and shall be published in The Florida Bar News on or before November 1.

(b) Time for Filing Nominating Petitions. Nominations for the election of representatives on the board of governors from each judicial circuit shall be made by written petition signed by not fewer than 5 members of The Florida Bar in good standing. In each circuit in which there is more than 1 representative to be elected, the offices of the representatives shall be designated numerically, with the executive director making whatever adjustments are necessary to reflect changes resulting from the annual certification, and a nominating petition shall state the number of the office sought by a nominee. Any number of candidates may be nominated on a single petition, and any number of petitions may be filed, but all candidates named in a petition and all members signing such petition shall have their official bar address in the judicial circuit that the candidate is nominated to represent and shall be members of The Florida Bar in good standing. Nominations for election of a nonresident member of the board of governors shall be by written petition signed by not fewer than 5 nonresident members of The Florida Bar in good standing. Nominees shall endorse their written acceptance on such petitions but no nominee shall accept nomination for more than 1 office. All nominating petitions shall be filed with the executive director at the headquarters office on or before 5:00 p.m., December 15 prior to the year of election. Filing by facsimile is permitted but shall occur only when transmission is complete. On a date to be fixed by the executive director the nominating petitions shall be canvassed and tabulated by the executive director who shall thereupon certify in writing the names of all members who have been properly nominated and file such certificate with the clerk of the Supreme Court of Florida.

(c) Nomination and Appointment of Nonlawyer Members. The board of governors' members who are not members of The Florida Bar shall be chosen and appointed by the Supreme Court of Florida from the list of nominees to be filed with the court by the board of governors. The board of governors of The Florida Bar by majority vote shall nominate 3 persons for each nonlawyer seat and shall file the nominations with the Supreme Court of Florida on or before April 15 of the appointment year for that seat. The 2 nonlawyer members shall serve staggered terms of 2 years and shall serve no more than 2 terms.

Amended Dec. 10, 1987, effective Jan. 1, 1988 (518 So.2d 251); March 2, 1988; July 23, 1992, effective Jan. 1, 1993 (605 So.2d 252); Oct. 20, 1994 (644 So.2d 282); July 20, 1995 (658 So.2d 930); July 17, 1997 (697 So.2d 115).

Bylaw 2-3.6. Election

Voting shall be by secret ballot. The executive director shall prepare and cause to be printed a sufficient number of ballots for the election of nonresident board members and for each judicial circuit office for which an election is to be held. One of such ballots shall be mailed to each member of The Florida Bar in good standing in each of such judicial circuits and to each nonresident member of The Florida Bar in good standing in the case of election of a nonresident board member. The records of the executive director shall be conclusive in determining the members entitled to receive such ballots. When more than one office is to be filled, the offices shall be listed on the ballots in numerical order. The names of candidates on the ballots shall be listed alphabetically for each office. The ballots shall be mailed on or before March 1. Only voted ballots received by the executive director prior to midnight on March 21 shall be counted or tabulated. Immediately after March 21, the executive director shall canvass and tabulate the ballots received, certify the results of the election, and file such certificate with the clerk of the Supreme Court of Florida. Failure to make a nomination shall result in a vacancy to be filled in accordance with the provisions of bylaw 2-3.9. The candidate for an office receiving a majority of the votes cast for the office shall be declared elected. In the event no candidate receives such majority there shall be a runoff election between the 2 candidates receiving the highest number of votes. The ballots for the runoff shall be mailed on or before April 1 and the voted ballots shall be received by the executive director prior to midnight on April 22. The ballots shall be counted and the results certified as provided for the first election. In the event that only 1 candidate has been nominated for a particular office on the board of governors, such candidate shall be declared elected. Results of the election shall be furnished by the executive director to the officers, members of the board of governors, and all candidates and may be furnished to any other interested persons upon their request.

Amended March 2, 1988; July 23, 1992, effective Jan. 1, 1993 (605 So.2d 252); July 20, 1995 (658 So.2d 930).

Bylaw 2-3.7. Term

The term of office for those persons regularly elected or appointed is 2 years and thereafter until a successor's term commences. The term commences at the conclusion of the annual meeting of The Florida Bar following election or appointment to office. The term of office for those persons elected or appointed to fill a vacancy shall run for the balance of the term.

Amended March 2, 1988; July 23, 1992, effective Jan. 1, 1993 (605 So.2d 252).

Bylaw 2-3.8. Removal

Any member of the board of governors may be removed for cause by resolution adopted by two-thirds of the entire membership of the board of governors.

Amended March 2, 1988.

Bylaw 2-3.9. Vacancy

Except for nonlawyer members, in the event of a vacancy on the board of governors the vacancy shall be filled by a special election within the framework of the pertinent election procedures presently existing under these rules relating to the election of members of the board of governors. Notice of the vacancy and the special election shall be given by publication in The Florida Bar News, which notice shall provide that nominating petitions must be filed within 30 days of the date of the publication of the notice with the executive director. The special election shall be held not less than 30 days and not more than 45 days after the publication of the notice. The procedures set forth in these rules for election shall be followed as closely as possible. In the event of a vacancy on the board of governors for a nonlawyer member, the vacancy shall be filled by special nomination and appointment in accordance with the provisions of bylaw 2-3.5(c).

Amended March 2, 1988; July 23, 1992, effective Jan. 1, 1993 (605 So.2d 252).

Bylaw 2-3.10. Meetings

The board of governors shall hold 6 regular meetings each year, at least 1 of which shall be held at The Florida Bar Center. Subject to the approval of the board of governors, the places and times of such meetings shall be determined by the president, who may make such designation while president-elect. Special meetings shall be held at the direction of the executive committee or the board of governors. Any member of The Florida Bar in good standing may attend meetings at any time except during such times as the board shall be in executive session concerning disciplinary matters, personnel matters, member objections to legislative positions of The Florida Bar, or receiving attorney-client advice. Minutes of all meetings shall be kept by the executive director.

Amended March 2, 1988; March 26, 1991; July 23, 1992, effective Jan. 1, 1993 (605 So.2d 252).

Bylaw 2-3.11. Quorum

A majority of the members of the board of governors shall constitute a quorum for the transaction of business at all meetings.

Amended March 2, 1988.

Bylaw 2-3.12. Executive committee

Unless otherwise limited by these rules, the executive committee shall have full power and authority to exercise the function of the board of governors to the extent authorized by the board of governors on any specific matter, and on any other matter that necessarily must be determined between meetings of the board of governors.

The executive committee shall notify the board of governors at the next meeting of all actions taken by the executive committee during the interim between meetings of the board of governors. Unless modified by the board of governors at such meeting, actions of the executive committee shall be final.

Amended March 2, 1988; July 23, 1992, effective Jan. 1, 1993 (605 So.2d 252).

2–4. OFFICERS

Bylaw 2–4.1. Duties of president

The president shall conduct and preside at all meetings of The Florida Bar and the board of governors. The president shall be the official spokesperson for The Florida Bar and the board of governors. Unless otherwise provided herein, the president shall appoint all committees. The president shall be the chief executive of The Florida Bar and shall be vested with full power to exercise whatever functions may be necessary or incident to the full exercise of any power bestowed upon the president by the board of governors consistent with the provisions of these Rules Regulating The Florida Bar. It shall be the duty and obligation of the president to furnish leadership in the accomplishment of the aims and purposes of The Florida Bar.

Amended March 2, 1988; July 23, 1992, effective Jan. 1, 1993 (605 So.2d 252).

Bylaw 2–4.2. Duties of president-elect

It shall be the duty of the president-elect to render every assistance and cooperation to the president and provide the president with the fullest measure of counsel and advice. The president-elect shall be familiarized with all activities and affairs of The Florida Bar and shall have such other duties as may be assigned to the president-elect by the board of governors. In the event the president-elect is absent or unable to act, or in the event of the president-elect's death, disability, or resignation, the board of governors shall select an acting president-elect to hold office until a successor shall have been elected by the members of The Florida Bar in good standing at a special election held pursuant to the direction of the board of governors.

Amended March 2, 1988.

Bylaw 2–4.3. Duties of executive director

The executive director shall be chosen by the board of governors and shall perform all duties usually required of a secretary and a treasurer and such other duties as may be assigned by the board of governors. The executive director shall serve as publisher of The Florida Bar Journal and The Florida Bar News and as director of public relations until otherwise directed by the board of governors. The executive director shall keep the records of The Florida Bar and the board of governors. The executive director shall maintain and be in charge of the offices and shall devote full time to the work of The Florida Bar. The board shall fix the executive director's salary and other benefits and emoluments of office.

Amended March 2, 1988; July 23, 1992, effective Jan. 1, 1993 (605 So.2d 252).

Bylaw 2–4.4. Qualifications for office

Only members of The Florida Bar in good standing shall be eligible to hold any elective office in The Florida Bar. No officer shall engage in political activity on behalf of a candidate for public office except in furtherance of the objectives of The Florida Bar and with the approval of the board of governors.

Amended March 2, 1988.

Bylaw 2–4.5. Nominations for President–Elect

(a) Policies. The Board of Governors of The Florida Bar is hereby authorized to adopt standing policies that govern the conduct of candidates and aspirants seeking support for their nomination as candidates, which shall include creation of a committee to oversee the conduct of such individuals and promulgation of sanctions for failure to comply with these rules or the policies adopted by authority hereof.

(b) Nominations Process. Any member of The Florida Bar in good standing may be nominated as a candidate for president-elect by petition signed by not fewer than 1 percent of the members of The Florida Bar in good standing. Such nominating petitions shall be filed with the executive director at the headquarters office on or after November 15 and on or before 5:00 p.m., eastern time, December 15 of the year preceding the election. Nominees shall endorse their written acceptance upon such petition. In the event that no member of The Florida Bar in good standing shall be nominated, the board of governors shall thereafter nominate at least 1 candidate for the office of president-elect.

Amended March 2, 1988; April 2, 1992 (597 So.2d 792); April 11, 1996 (672 So.2d 516); March 23, 2000 (763 So.2d 1002); Nov. 19, 2009, effective Feb. 1, 2010 (24 So.3d 63).

Bylaw 2–4.6. Election of president-elect

The members of The Florida Bar in good standing shall elect annually a president-elect, who shall become president at the conclusion of the annual meeting following the term as president-elect.

Only those members who are members in good standing as of February 15 are eligible to vote in the initial election. If a runoff election is necessary, only those members who are members in good standing as of March 15 are eligible to vote in the runoff election.

Ballots for election of president-elect shall be mailed on or before March 1 to each eligible member of The Florida Bar. Ballots shall be mailed to the member's record bar address. The names of the candidates for the office of president-elect shall be printed on the ballot in alphabetical order. Only those ballots received by The Florida Bar or its representative prior to midnight, eastern time, March 21 shall be counted.

Immediately after March 21, the executive director shall canvass and tabulate the ballots received prior to midnight, eastern time, March 21, certify the results of the election, and file such certificate with the clerk of the Supreme Court of Florida. The candidate who receives the majority of the votes cast shall be declared elected.

In the event no candidate receives a majority of the votes cast, a runoff election between the 2 candidates receiving the highest number of votes shall be held. Ballots for the runoff election shall be mailed on or before April 1 to each eligible member of The Florida Bar. The runoff ballots shall be mailed to the member's record bar address. The names of the runoff candidates shall be printed on the ballot in alphabetical order. Only ballots received by The Florida Bar or its representative prior to midnight, eastern time, April 22 shall be counted.

Immediately after April 22, the executive director shall canvass and tabulate the ballots received prior to midnight, eastern time, April 22, certify the results, and file such certificate with the clerk of the Supreme Court of Florida. The runoff candidate receiving a majority of the votes cast shall be declared elected.

The executive director shall furnish the results of the election to the officers and members of the board of governors of The Florida Bar, as well as to the candidates and, upon request, to any other interested person.

Amended March 2, 1988; April 2, 1992 (597 So.2d 792); July 23, 1992, effective Jan. 1, 1993 (605 So.2d 252); April 11, 1996 (672 So.2d 516).

Bylaw 2-4.7. President's absence

In the event the president is absent or unable to act, the president's duties shall be performed by the president-elect; and in the event of the death or resignation of the president, the president-elect shall serve as president during the remainder of the term of office thus vacated and then shall serve as president for the term for which elected. In the event of the death or disability of both the president and the president-elect, the board of governors shall elect an acting president of The Florida Bar to hold office until the next succeeding annual meeting.

Amended March 2, 1988; July 23, 1992, effective Jan. 1, 1993 (605 So.2d 252).

Bylaw 2-4.8. Prohibition against service on board of governors and as president or president-elect

In the event that a member of the board of governors shall become either the president or the president-elect of The Florida Bar such member shall not serve on the board of governors except as president or president-elect and the office of that member shall become vacant and shall be filled in accordance with the provisions of this chapter.

Amended March 2, 1988.

2-5. MEETINGS

Bylaw 2-5.1. Annual meeting

A program for the annual meeting of The Florida Bar shall be prepared by the president, with the advice and consent of the board of governors. Such program, when approved by the board of governors, shall be the order of business for the annual meeting and such order of business shall not be altered, except by consent of two-thirds of the members in good standing present and voting. Only the president, with the advice and consent of the board of governors, shall have the authority to extend invitations to nonmembers to attend the annual meeting as honored guests or speakers at the expense of The Florida Bar. No section or committee shall create any debt of The Florida Bar in connection with an annual meeting without prior approval of the board of governors. All papers, addresses, and reports read before or submitted at a meeting shall become the property of The Florida Bar and may be published by The Florida Bar. A registration fee for attendance at the annual meeting may be fixed by the board of governors to defray the costs and expenses in connection with such meeting.

Amended March 2, 1988.

Bylaw 2-5.2. Rules of procedure

Only members of The Florida Bar in good standing shall be entitled to vote at the annual meeting. A resolution for consideration at the annual meeting may be proposed by any member in good standing or by the resolutions committee, provided that the resolution shall be presented, handled in accordance with procedures that shall be established by the board of governors, and published in The Florida Bar Journal or The Florida Bar News a reasonable length of time prior to each annual meeting. Unless indicated on the official program, no person shall speak for more than 10 minutes or more than twice on any matter, except upon consent of a majority of the members in good standing present and voting at the meeting. Members of the bar of any foreign country or any state, district, or territory, who are not members of The

Florida Bar, may be accorded the privilege of the floor at any annual meeting.

Amended March 2, 1988; July 23, 1992, effective Jan. 1, 1993 (605 So.2d 252).

2-6. FISCAL MANAGEMENT

Bylaw 2-6.1. Expenditures

Within the parameters of the budget filed with the Supreme Court of Florida, the board of governors shall be vested with exclusive powers, authority, and control over all funds, property, and assets of The Florida Bar and the method and purpose of expenditure of all funds.

Amended March 2, 1988.

Bylaw 2-6.2. Fiscal year

The fiscal year of The Florida Bar shall commence on July 1 of each year.

Amended March 2, 1988.

Bylaw 2-6.3. Annual budget

The board of governors, with the advice and counsel of the budget committee, shall adopt an annual budget of The Florida Bar, setting forth the anticipated revenues and expenditures for the fiscal year.

Amended March 2, 1988.

Bylaw 2-6.4. Budget committee

The budget committee shall consist of 9 members having staggered terms. The president-elect, with the approval of the board of governors, shall appoint 3 members to 3-year terms, shall fill vacancies for the balance of a term, and shall name a chair-elect from the members of the committee. The chair-elect shall become chair when the president-elect becomes president and the chair shall serve as a tenth member of the committee if the chair's term on the committee would otherwise expire.

Amended March 2, 1988; July 23, 1992, effective Jan. 1, 1993 (605 So.2d 252).

Bylaw 2-6.5. Notice of budget committee hearings

The executive director shall publish a notice in The Florida Bar Journal or The Florida Bar News not later than a March issue giving notice of meetings of the budget committee in each of the districts of the district courts of appeal to receive suggestions from members of The Florida Bar for the preparation of the budget for the succeeding fiscal year. Such meetings shall be held not earlier than the fifteenth day of the month succeeding the month in which the notice is published. Written notice of intent to appear at such meetings must be received by the executive director at least 10 days prior to the date of the meeting. If no person files such a notice, the meeting may be canceled.

Amended March 2, 1988; July 23, 1992, effective Jan. 1, 1993 (605 So.2d 252).

Bylaw 2-6.6. Tentative budget of budget committee

At the meeting announced by such published notice, the budget committee shall hear and receive suggestions from members of The Florida Bar for the preparation of the budget for The Florida Bar for the succeeding fiscal year. The manner of filing and hearing such suggestions shall be set forth in the notice. After consideration of the suggestions received, the budget committee shall prepare a tentative budget for the succeeding fiscal year, which shall be filed with the executive director.

Amended March 2, 1988.

Bylaw 2-6.7. Proposed budget of board of governors

The board of governors, after considering the tentative budget prepared by the budget committee, shall adopt a proposed budget for the succeeding fiscal year in time to allow publication thereof not later than an April issue of The Florida Bar Journal or The Florida Bar News.

Amended March 2, 1988.

Bylaw 2-6.8. Membership fees

The membership fees for members of The Florida Bar shall be included in the proposed budget filed by The Florida Bar in the Supreme Court of Florida.

Amended March 2, 1988; Sept. 24, 1998, effective Oct. 1, 1998 (718 So.2d 1179).

Bylaw 2-6.9. Notice of board of governors hearing upon proposed budget

The executive director shall publish a notice in The Florida Bar Journal or The Florida Bar News not later than an April issue giving notice of a meeting of the board of governors to be held no earlier than the fifteenth day of the month succeeding the month the notice is published. Such notice shall contain the proposed budget and shall advise that the proposed budget shall become final unless written objections to any item or items therein shall be filed by members of The Florida Bar with the executive director on or before the tenth day of the month following the month of publication.

Amended March 2, 1988.

Bylaw 2–6.10. Hearing and adoption of budget by board of governors

If written objections to any item or items of the proposed budget are filed by members of The Florida Bar within the time provided, a hearing thereon shall be held by the board of governors at the time and place provided in such notice. After such hearing the board of governors shall consider the objections filed and upon consideration thereof the board may amend the proposed budget within the scope of the objections.

Amended March 2, 1988.

Bylaw 2–6.11. Filing of budget with the Supreme Court of Florida

The budget proposed by the board of governors shall be filed with the supreme court on or before June 1 and shall become effective unless rejected by the court within 30 days.

Amended March 2, 1988; July 23, 1992, effective Jan. 1, 1993 (605 So.2d 252).

Bylaw 2–6.12. Amendment of the budget

The board of governors, in its discretion from time to time, may amend the budget in order to provide funds for needed expenditures; provided, however, that the total of increases in items of the budget made by amendment, including new items created by such amendments, shall not exceed 10 percent of the total income of The Florida Bar for the current fiscal year as anticipated at the time of the amendment. If a proposed amendment shall cause the total of increases in items of the budget made by amendment to exceed such limitation, a hearing upon objections to any item or items therein shall be held by the board of governors in like manner as that provided for the proposed budget. The executive director shall publish a notice in The Florida Bar Journal or The Florida Bar News giving notice of a board of governors meeting to be held no earlier than the fifteenth day of the month succeeding the month in which the notice is published. Such notice shall contain the proposed amendment and shall advise that the proposed amendment shall become final unless written objections to any item or items therein shall be filed by members of The Florida Bar with the executive director on or before the tenth day of the month following the month of publication. If the proposed amendment is adopted by the board of governors in whole or in part, the amendment of the budget shall be filed with the Supreme Court of Florida within the month following the month in which the amendment is adopted.

Amended March 2, 1988; July 23, 1992, effective Jan. 1, 1993 (605 So.2d 252).

Bylaw 2–6.13. Appropriations of the budget

Each item of the budget shall be deemed a fixed appropriation, subject only to amendment as provided. All uncommitted balances of appropriations except appropriated restrictions of fund balances shall revert at the end of each fiscal year to the funds from which appropriated. No uncommitted appropriations other than those for the clients' security fund shall continue beyond the fiscal year for which the budget containing the appropriation is adopted.

Amended March 2, 1988.

Bylaw 2–6.14. Disbursements

The appropriations of the budget shall be disbursed by the executive director in the executive director's capacity as treasurer of The Florida Bar in accordance with this chapter. The executive director shall make such disbursements as are required to pay the obligations and expenses of The Florida Bar made within the provisions of the budget.

Amended March 2, 1988; July 23, 1992, effective Jan. 1, 1993 (605 So.2d 252).

Bylaw 2–6.15. Continuation of funding

Any program that calls for an expenditure of funds in excess of $10,000 during any fiscal year shall not be continued beyond the last day of the second of 2 fiscal years unless such program is specifically authorized by this or other chapters of the Rules Regulating The Florida Bar.

Amended March 2, 1988; July 23, 1992, effective Jan. 1, 1993 (605 So.2d 252).

Bylaw 2–6.16. Accounting and audit

The board of governors shall cause books and accounts to be kept in accordance with good accounting practices. Such records shall be audited annually by a certified public accountant authorized to practice in the State of Florida, and a copy of the audit shall be filed forthwith with the Supreme Court of Florida. Within a reasonable time after completion of the audit a condensed summary thereof shall be published in The Florida Bar Journal or The Florida Bar News and a copy filed with the Supreme Court of Florida.

Amended March 2, 1988.

2–7. SECTIONS AND DIVISIONS

Bylaw 2–7.1. Rules applicable to sections and divisions

All sections and divisions are governed by the provisions of the Rules Regulating The Florida Bar, this chapter, and the bylaws of the sections and divisions as approved by the board of governors and have the scope, powers, duties, and functions expressed in those documents.

Amended March 2, 1988; April 2, 1992 (597 So.2d 792).

Bylaw 2-7.2. Duties

It is the duty of each section and division, as an integral part of The Florida Bar, to work in cooperation with the board of governors and under its supervision toward accomplishment of the aims and purposes of The Florida Bar and of that section or division.

Amended March 2, 1988; April 2, 1992 (597 So.2d 792).

Bylaw 2-7.3. Creation of Sections and Divisions

Text of bylaw effective until October 1, 2015. See, also, bylaw effective October 1, 2015.

Sections and divisions may be created or abolished by the board of governors as deemed necessary or desirable.

(a) Sections. The following sections of The Florida Bar have been created by the board of governors:

(1) Administrative Law Section;

(2) Alternative Dispute Resolution Section;

(3) Appellate Practice Section;

(4) Business Law Section;

(5) City, County and Local Government Law Section;

(6) Criminal Law Section;

(7) Elder Law Section;

(8) Entertainment, Arts, and Sports Law Section;

(9) Environmental and Land Use Law Section;

(10) Equal Opportunities Law Section;

(11) Family Law Section;

(12) General Practice, Solo and Small Firm Section;

(13) Government Lawyer Section;

(14) Health Law Section;

(15) International Law Section;

(16) Labor and Employment Law Section;

(17) Public Interest Law Section;

(18) Real Property, Probate, and Trust Law Section;

(19) Tax Section;

(20) Trial Lawyers Section; and

(21) Workers' Compensation Section.

(b) Divisions. The following divisions of The Florida Bar have been created by the board of governors:

(1) Out-of-State Division; and

(2) Young Lawyers Division.

Amended March 2, 1988; March 30, 1990; April 2, 1992 (597 So.2d 792); July 23, 1992, effective Jan. 1, 1993 (605 So.2d 252); July 20, 1995 (658 So.2d 930); June 27, 1996, effective July 1, 1996 (677 So.2d 272); July 17, 1997 (697 So.2d 115); Feb. 8, 2001 (795 So.2d 1); Dec. 20, 2007, effective March 1, 2008 (978 So.2d 91); Nov. 19, 2009, effective Feb. 1, 2010 (24 So.3d 63); March 27, 2014, effective June 1, 2014 (140 So.3d 541).

Bylaw 2-7.3. Creation of Sections and Divisions

Text of bylaw effective October 1, 2015. See, also, bylaw effective until October 1, 2015.

Sections and divisions may be created or abolished by the board of governors as deemed necessary or desirable. The Florida Bar will maintain current lists of its sections and divisions and will post the lists on its website.

Amended March 2, 1988; March 30, 1990; April 2, 1992 (597 So.2d 792); July 23, 1992, effective Jan. 1, 1993 (605 So.2d 252); July 20, 1995 (658 So.2d 930); June 27, 1996, effective July 1, 1996 (677 So.2d 272); July 17, 1997 (697 So.2d 115); Feb. 8, 2001 (795 So.2d 1); Dec. 20, 2007, effective March 1, 2008 (978 So.2d 91); Nov. 19, 2009, effective Feb. 1, 2010 (24 So.3d 63); March 27, 2014, effective June 1, 2014 (140 So.3d 541); May 21, 2015, effective Oct. 1, 2015 (164 So.3d 1217).

Bylaw 2-7.4. Procedure for creation of sections and divisions

Those seeking approval of the board of governors to establish a section or division shall prepare and submit proposed bylaws for approval by the board of governors. They shall also inform the board of governors of the justification for establishing the section or division, the proposed dues, proposed budgeting, and proposed function and program of the section or division.

Amended March 2, 1988; April 2, 1992 (597 So.2d 792).

Bylaw 2-7.5. Legislative action of sections and divisions

(a) Limits of Legislative Involvement. Sections and divisions may be involved in legislation that is significant to the judiciary, the administration of justice, or the fundamental legal rights of the public or interests of the section or division or its programs and functions.

(b) Procedure to Determine Legislative Policy. Sections and divisions shall be required to adopt and follow a reasonable procedure, approved by the board of governors, for determination of legislative policy on any legislation.

(c) Notice to Executive Director. Sections and divisions shall notify the executive director immediately of determination of any section or division action regarding legislation.

(d) Identification of Action. Any legislative action taken by a section or division shall be clearly identified as the action of the section or division and not that of The Florida Bar.

Amended March 2, 1988; April 2, 1992 (597 So.2d 792).

2-8. COMMITTEES

Bylaw 2-8.1. Establishment and appointment of committees

In addition to those committees established elsewhere under this chapter or other chapters of the Rules Regulating The Florida Bar, the board of governors shall create such committees as it may deem advisable and necessary from time to time. The board of governors may dissolve a committee when it deems that the work of the committee has been completed or is no longer necessary. The board of governors may provide for members of any committee to serve for staggered terms beyond the current administrative year. Any vacancies in these committees shall be filled for the unexpired portion in order to provide a regular rotation of committee members. Before June 1 of each year, the president-elect shall appoint all committee members (except for grievance and unlicensed practice of law), who shall serve for the ensuing administrative year. The president-elect shall report the membership of committees to the board of governors and shall, with the advice and consent of the board of governors, name and designate the chair and vice-chair of each committee. Persons who are not members of The Florida Bar may be appointed to committees with the advice and consent of the board of governors. The president shall fill vacancies occurring in the membership of the committees for the remainder of the unexpired term and may remove or appoint additional members to a committee.

Amended March 2, 1988; July 23, 1992, effective Jan. 1, 1993 (605 So.2d 252).

Bylaw 2-8.2. Committee operations

Each committee shall select from its membership such officers other than the chair and vice-chair as it deems advisable and subcommittees may be designated by the chair from the membership of the committee. Each committee shall meet at such times and places as may be designated by the chair or vice-chair. Each committee shall file with the president and executive director all minutes, annual reports, and procedures and recommendations and such interim reports as desired or may be requested by the president or board of governors. No action, report, or recommendation of any committee shall be binding upon The Florida Bar unless adopted and approved by the board of governors.

Amended March 2, 1988; July 23, 1992, effective Jan. 1, 1993 (605 So.2d 252).

Bylaw 2-8.3. Standing and special committees

The board of governors shall determine and designate which committees shall be considered as standing committees (permanent) and which committees shall be considered as special committees (temporary or limited) and shall define the specific powers, duties, functions, and scope thereof.

Amended March 2, 1988.

Bylaw 2-8.4. Committee finances

No committee shall incur any debt payable by The Florida Bar without prior approval of the executive director. Each committee shall file with the executive director a detailed statement setting forth any funds needed or required in connection with the work of such committee during the ensuing administrative year for consideration by and inclusion in the annual budget of The Florida Bar after approval by the board of governors.

Amended March 2, 1988.

2-9. POLICIES AND RULES

Bylaw 2-9.1. Authority of board of governors

In order to accomplish the purposes of The Florida Bar and implement the Rules Regulating The Florida Bar, including this chapter, the board of governors shall have the power and authority to establish policies and rules of procedure on the subjects and in the manner provided in this rule.

Amended March 2, 1988.

Bylaw 2-9.2. Standing board policies

The board of governors shall adopt standing board policies governing the internal administration and operation of The Florida Bar and the board of governors. The board of governors may adopt, amend, or rescind standing board policies by a majority vote of the membership of the board of governors provided any amendment to any standing board policy shall not be effective until 30 days after adoption. Such standing board policies may be adopted, rescinded, or amended by a majority vote of those present at any regular meeting of the board of governors provided advance written notice is given to the members of the board of governors of the proposed adoption, repeal, or amendment of any standing board policy. The provision of any standing board policy may be waived by a two-thirds vote of those present at any regular meeting of the board of governors.

Amended March 2, 1988; July 23, 1992, effective Jan. 1, 1993 (605 So.2d 252).

Bylaw 2-9.3. Legislative policies

(a) Adoption of Rules of Procedure and Legislative Positions. The board of governors shall adopt and may repeal or amend rules of procedure governing the legislative activities of The Florida Bar in the same manner as provided in bylaw 2-9.2; provided, however, that the adoption of any legislative position shall require the affirmative vote of two-thirds of those present and voting at any regular meeting of the board of governors or two-thirds of the executive committee or by the president, as provided in the rules of procedure governing legislative activities.

(b) Publication of Legislative Positions. The Florida Bar shall publish notice of adoption of legislative positions in The Florida Bar News, in the issue immediately following the board meeting at which the positions were adopted.

(c) Objection to Legislative Positions of The Florida Bar.

(1) Any member in good standing of The Florida Bar may, within 45 days of the date of publication of notice of adoption of a legislative position, file with the executive director a written objection to a particular position on a legislative issue. The identity of an objecting member shall be confidential unless made public by The Florida Bar or any arbitration panel constituted under these rules upon specific request or waiver of the objecting member. Failure to object within this time period shall constitute a waiver of any right to object to the particular legislative issue.

(2) After a written objection has been received, the executive director shall promptly determine the pro rata amount of the objecting member's membership fees at issue and such amount shall be placed in escrow pending determination of the merits of the objection. The escrow figure shall be independently verified by a certified public accountant.

(3) Upon the deadline for receipt of written objections, the board of governors shall have 45 days in which to decide whether to give a pro rata refund to the objecting member(s) or to refer the action to arbitration.

(4) In the event the board of governors orders a refund, the objecting member's right to the refund shall immediately vest although the pro rata amount of the objecting member's membership fees at issue shall remain in escrow for the duration of the fiscal year and until the conclusion of The Florida Bar's annual audit as provided in bylaw 2–6.16, which shall include final independent verification of the appropriate refund payable. The Florida Bar shall thereafter pay the refund within 30 days of independent verification of the amount of refund, together with interest calculated at the statutory rate of interest on judgments as of the date the objecting member's membership fees at issue were received by The Florida Bar, for the period commencing with such date of receipt of the membership fees and ending on the date of payment of the refund by The Florida Bar.

(d) Composition of Arbitration Panel. Objections to legislative positions of The Florida Bar may be referred by the board of governors to an arbitration panel comprised of 3 members of The Florida Bar, to be constituted as soon as practicable following the decision by the board of governors that a matter shall be referred to arbitration.

The objecting member shall be allowed to choose 1 member of the arbitration panel, The Florida Bar shall appoint the second panel member, and those 2 members shall choose a third member of the panel who shall serve as chair. In the event the 2 members of the panel are unable to agree on a third member, the chief judge of the Second Judicial Circuit of Florida shall appoint the third member of the panel.

(e) Procedures for Arbitration Panel.

(1) Upon a decision by the board of governors that the matter shall be referred to arbitration, The Florida Bar shall promptly prepare a written response to the objection and serve a copy on the objecting member. Such response and objection shall be forwarded to the arbitration panel as soon as the panel is properly constituted. Venue for any arbitration proceedings conducted pursuant to this rule shall be in Leon County, Florida; however, for the convenience of the parties or witnesses or in the interest of justice, the proceedings may be transferred upon a majority vote of the arbitration panel. The chair of the arbitration panel shall determine the time, date, and place of any proceeding and shall provide notice thereof to all parties. The arbitration panel shall thereafter confer and decide whether The Florida Bar proved by the greater weight of evidence that the legislative matters at issue are constitutionally appropriate for funding from mandatory Florida Bar membership fees.

(2) The scope of the arbitration panel's review shall be to determine solely whether the legislative matters at issue are within those acceptable activities for which compulsory membership fees may be used under applicable constitutional law.

(3) The proceedings of the arbitration panel shall be informal in nature and shall not be bound by the rules of evidence. If requested by an objecting member who is a party to the proceedings, that party and counsel, and any witnesses, may participate telephonically, the expense of which shall be advanced by the requesting party. The decision of the arbitration panel shall be binding as to the objecting member and The Florida Bar. If the arbitration panel concludes the legislative matters at issue are appropriately funded from mandatory membership fees, there shall be no refund and The Florida Bar shall be free to expend the objecting member's pro rata amount of membership fees held in escrow. If the arbitration panel determines the legislative matters at issue are inappropriately funded from mandatory membership fees, the panel shall order a refund of the pro rata amount of membership fees to the objecting member.

(4) The arbitration panel shall thereafter render a final written report to the objecting member and the board of governors within 45 days of its constitution.

(5) In the event the arbitration panel orders a refund, the objecting member's right to the refund

shall immediately vest although the pro rata amount of the objecting member's membership fees at issue shall remain in escrow until paid. Within 30 days of independent verification of the amount of refund, The Florida Bar shall provide such refund together with interest calculated at the statutory rate of interest on judgments as of the date the objecting member's membership fees at issue were received by The Florida Bar, for the period commencing with such date of receipt of the membership fees and ending on the date of payment of the refund by The Florida Bar.

(6) Each arbitrator shall be compensated at an hourly rate equal to that of a circuit court judge based on services performed as an arbitrator pursuant to this rule.

(7) The arbitration panel shall tax all legal costs and charges of any arbitration proceeding conducted pursuant to this rule, to include arbitrator expenses and compensation, in favor of the prevailing party and against the nonprevailing party. When there is more than one party on one or both sides of an action, the arbitration panel shall tax such costs and charges against nonprevailing parties as it may deem equitable and fair.

(8) Payment by The Florida Bar of the costs of any arbitration proceeding conducted pursuant to this bylaw, net of costs taxed and collected, shall not be considered to be an expense for legislative activities, in calculating the amount of membership fees refunded pursuant to this bylaw.

Amended March 2, 1988; June 2, 1988 (526 So.2d 688); March 26, 1991; July 23, 1992, effective Jan. 1, 1993 (605 So.2d 252); Sept. 24, 1998, effective Oct. 1, 1998 (718 So.2d 1179); April 25, 2002 (820 So.2d 210).

Bylaw 2-9.4. Ethics

(a) Rules of Procedure. The board of governors shall adopt rules of procedure governing the manner in which opinions on professional ethics may be solicited by members of The Florida Bar, issued by the staff of The Florida Bar or by the professional ethics committee, circulated or published by the staff of The Florida Bar or by the professional ethics committee, and appealed to the board of governors of The Florida Bar.

(b) Amendment. The adoption of, repeal of, or amendment to the rules authorized by subdivision (a) shall be effective only under the following circumstances:

(1) The proposed rule, repealer, or amendment shall be approved by a majority vote of the board of governors at any regular meeting of the board of governors.

(2) The proposal thereafter shall be published in The Florida Bar News at least 20 days preceding the next regular meeting of the board of governors.

(3) The proposal shall thereafter receive a majority vote of the board of governors at its meeting following publication as herein required.

(c) Waiver. The rules of procedure adopted as required in subdivision (a) may be temporarily waived as to any particular matter only upon unanimous vote of those present at any regular meeting of the board of governors.

(d) Confidentiality. Each advisory opinion issued by Florida Bar ethics counsel shall be identified as a "staff opinion" and shall be available for inspection or production. The names and any identifying information of any individuals mentioned in a staff opinion shall be deleted before the staff opinion is released to anyone other than the member of The Florida Bar making the original request for the advisory opinion.

(e) Disqualification as Attorney Due to Conflict.

(1) *Members of the Professional Ethics Committee (PEC), Members of the Board of Governors, and Employees of The Florida Bar.* No member of the PEC, the board of governors, or employee of The Florida Bar shall represent a party other than The Florida Bar in proceedings for the issuance of opinions on professional ethics authorized under these Rules Regulating The Florida Bar.

(2) *Former Members of the PEC, Former Board Members, and Former Employees.* No former member of the PEC, former member of the board of governors, or former employee of The Florida Bar shall represent any party other than The Florida Bar in proceedings for the issuance of opinions on professional ethics authorized under these rules if personally involved to any degree in the matter while a member of the PEC, a member of the board of governors, or an employee of The Florida Bar.

A former member of the PEC, former member of the board of governors, or former employee of The Florida Bar who did not participate personally in any way in the matter or any related matter in which the attorney seeks to be a representative, and who did not serve in a supervisory capacity over such matter, shall not represent any party except The Florida Bar in proceedings for the issuance of opinions on professional ethics authorized under these rules for 1 year after such service without the express consent of the board.

(3) *Partners, Associates, Employers, or Employees of the Firms of PEC Members or Board of Governors Members Precluded From Representing Parties Other Than The Florida Bar.* Members of the firms of board of governors members or PEC members shall not represent any party other than The Florida Bar in proceedings for the issuance of opinions on professional ethics authorized under these rules without the express consent of the board.

(4) *Partners, Associates, Employers, or Employees of the Firms of Former PEC Members or Former Board of Governors Members Precluded From Representing Parties Other Than The Florida Bar.* Attor-

neys in the firms of former board of governors members or former PEC members shall not represent any party other than The Florida Bar in proceedings for the issuance of opinions on professional ethics authorized under these rules for 1 year after the former member's service without the express consent of the board.

Amended March 2, 1988; July 23, 1992, effective Jan. 1, 1993 (605 So.2d 252); Oct. 29, 1992 (608 So.2d 472); May 20, 2004 (875 So.2d 448).

Bylaw 2-9.5. Administrative policies

The executive director may adopt such policies or procedures necessary to govern the administrative operation of The Florida Bar and The Florida Bar staff, provided all policies of a continuing nature are in writing and a copy of all such policies is furnished to each member of the board of governors and available for inspection by any member of The Florida Bar at all reasonable times.

Amended March 2, 1988; July 23, 1992, effective Jan. 1, 1993 (605 So.2d 252).

Bylaw 2-9.6. Rules of order

The current edition of Robert's Rules of Order shall be the rules that govern the conduct of all meetings of The Florida Bar, its board of governors, its sections, divisions, and committees.

Amended March 2, 1988; July 23, 1992, effective Jan. 1, 1993 (605 So.2d 252).

Bylaw 2-9.7. Insurance for members of board of governors, officers, grievance committee members, UPL committee members, clients' security fund committee members, and employees

Appropriate insurance coverage for members of the board of governors, officers of The Florida Bar, members of UPL, clients' security fund, and grievance committees, and employees of The Florida Bar shall be provided as authorized by the budget committee and included in the budget. To the extent the person is not covered by insurance, The Florida Bar shall indemnify any officer, board member, UPL, clients' security fund, or grievance committee member, or employee of The Florida Bar who was or is a party, or is threatened to be made a party to any threatened, pending, or completed action, suit, or proceeding, whether civil, criminal, administrative, or investigative (other than an action by The Florida Bar), by reason of the fact that the person is or was an officer, board member, UPL, clients' security fund, or grievance committee member, or employee of The Florida Bar, against expenses (including attorneys' fees), judgments, fines, and amounts paid in settlement, actually and reasonably incurred by the person in connection with such action, suit, or proceeding, including any appeal thereof, if the person acted in good faith and in a manner reasonably believed to be in, or not opposed to, the best interests of The Florida Bar, and with respect to any criminal action or proceeding, had no reasonable cause to believe the conduct was unlawful. The termination of any action, suit, or proceeding by judgment, order, settlement, or conviction or upon a plea of nolo contendere or its equivalent shall not of itself create a presumption that the person did not act in good faith and in a manner that the person reasonably believed to be in, or not opposed to, the best interests of The Florida Bar, or with respect to any criminal action or proceeding, had reasonable cause to believe that the conduct was unlawful.

Added March 9, 1987. Amended March 2, 1988; July 23, 1992, effective Jan. 1, 1993 (605 So.2d 252); Oct. 20, 1994 (644 So.2d 282).

Bylaw 2-9.8. Law office management assistance service

The board of governors hereby creates the law office management assistance service and shall adopt standing board policies, as provided in bylaw 2-9.2, that shall govern the operation of the service.

Added effective April 13, 1989. Amended July 23, 1992, effective Jan. 1, 1993 (605 So.2d 252); Sept. 24, 1998, effective Oct. 1, 1998 (718 So.2d 1179).

Bylaw 2-9.9. Public interest programs

The board of governors hereby creates a program for promoting and supporting public service activities, which shall include, but not be limited to, pro bono services support and law related education.

Added effective April 13, 1989.

Bylaw 2-9.10. Member benefits program

The board of governors hereby creates a program for developing and providing benefits to members of the Bar, which shall include, but not be limited to, insurance and discounts on goods and/or services.

Added effective April 13, 1989.

Bylaw 2-9.11. Assistance to members suffering from impairment related to chemical dependency or psychological problems

The Florida Bar shall create or fund a program for the identification of its members who suffer from impairment related to chemical dependency or psychological problems that affect their professional performance or practice of law, and the assistance of those members in overcoming such dependency or problems.

Added effective April 13, 1989. Amended Sept. 24, 1998, effective Oct. 1, 1998 (718 So.2d 1179); amended effective Feb. 8, 2001 (795 So.2d 1).

2–10. AMENDMENTS

Bylaw 2–10.1. Proposed amendments

Amendments to these bylaws may be made in the manner set forth in rule 1–12.1.

Amended April 13, 1987, effective May 26, 1987; Aug. 7, 1987; March 2, 1988; Oct. 10, 1991, effective Jan. 1, 1992 (587 So.2d 1121); July 23, 1992, effective Jan. 1, 1993 (605 So.2d 252).

FLORIDA BAR PROCEDURES FOR RULING ON QUESTIONS OF ETHICS

Explanatory Note

Revised and adopted May 24, 2002.
Revised October 5, 2007.
The Florida Bar Procedures for Ruling on Questions of Ethics are not part of the Rules Regulating The Florida Bar. Instead, the Board of Governors of The Florida Bar has adopted these Procedures pursuant to Bylaw 2–9.4. The Procedures have been inserted at the end of Chapter 2 to assist practitioners using this Chapter.

Rule 1. Application; Scope; and Usage

These procedures are adopted pursuant to rule 2–9.4, Rules Regulating The Florida Bar, and govern the manner in which ethics opinions are issued and reviewed by The Florida Bar. These procedures do not apply to review of lawyer advertisements.

Staff opinions, professional ethics committee opinions, and opinions of the board of governors are advisory only and shall not be the basis for action by grievance committees, referees, or the board of governors except upon application of the respondent in disciplinary proceedings. If a respondent's defense includes reliance on the receipt of a staff opinion, ethics counsel may release to the bar counsel, grievance committee, referee, or board of governors information concerning the opinion or the request therefor that would otherwise be confidential under these rules. Information concerning requests for staff opinions shall be confidential, except as otherwise provided in bylaw 2–9.4 and these procedures. If public statements are made by the inquirer about any advisory opinion or opinion request, confidentiality of the request and the opinion is waived and ethics counsel may disclose the opinion and information relating to the request.

The advisory opinion process should not be used to circumvent procedures to adopt or amend Rules Regulating The Florida Bar.

Amended Aug. 11–14, 2004, by the Board of Governors of The Florida Bar; Oct. 5, 2007, by the Board of Governors of The Florida Bar.

Rule 2. Authority to Issue Ethics Opinions

Ethics counsel and assistant ethics counsel, the professional ethics committee, and the board of governors shall have the authority to issue ethics opinions in the type and manner as set forth in these procedures.

(a) Ethics Counsel and Assistant Ethics Counsel. Ethics counsel and assistant ethics counsel may render oral and written opinions that shall be identified as "staff opinions." Staff opinions shall be issued only to the members of The Florida Bar in good standing inquiring as to their own contemplated conduct.

(1) Staff opinions shall not be issued if it is known to staff that the inquiry:

(A) is made by a person who is not a member of The Florida Bar in good standing;

(B) concerns past conduct of the inquirer;

(C) involves the conduct of an attorney other than the inquirer;

(D) asks a question of law;

(E) asks a question of rule or court procedure; or

(F) is the subject of a proceeding brought under the Rules Regulating The Florida Bar.

(2) Staff may decline to issue an opinion if the inquiry:

(A) is the subject of current litigation; or

(B) asks a question for which there is no previous precedent or underlying bar policy on which to base an opinion.

(b) Professional Ethics Committee. ***The professional ethics committee (hereinafter referred to as PEC) may render written opinions, amend existing opinions, or withdraw existing opinions:***

(1) upon appeal of a written staff opinion by the inquiring attorney;

(2) upon request of the board of governors regarding application of the Rules of Professional Conduct to a particular set of facts;

(3) upon review of staff opinions by the PEC; or

(4) upon review of existing advisory ethics opinions by the PEC. Opinions of the PEC shall be identified as advisory ethics opinions.

(c) Board of Governors. The board of governors may render written opinions, amend existing opinions, or withdraw existing opinions:

(1) upon appeal of a PEC action; and

(2) upon its own initiative when the board of governors determines that the application of the Rules of Professional Conduct to a particular set of facts is likely to be of widespread interest or unusual importance to a significant number of Florida Bar members. Opinions of the board of governors shall be identified as advisory ethics opinions.

Amended Aug. 11–14, 2004, by the Board of Governors of The Florida Bar; Oct. 5, 2007, by the Board of Governors of The Florida Bar.

Rule 3. Procedures for Issuance of and Declining to Issue Staff Opinions

(a) Request for Staff Opinion.

(1) Oral Staff Opinions. Members in good standing may request an oral staff opinion by calling ethics counsel in Tallahassee, at 1–800–235–8619 or 1–850–561–5780. Oral opinions may be confirmed in writing only in accord with the procedures for issuance of written staff opinions. All information relating to the request for an oral staff opinion shall be confidential as provided elsewhere in these procedures.

(2) Written Staff Opinions. Members in good standing may request a written staff opinion by writing Ethics Counsel, The Florida Bar, 651 East Jefferson Street, Tallahassee, Florida 32399–2300 or by electronic mail to eto@flabar.org. All requests for written staff opinions shall set forth all operative facts upon which the request is based and contain an affirmative statement that the criteria of procedure 2(a) are met. All material and information relating to the request for a written staff opinion shall be confidential as provided elsewhere in these procedures.

(b) Declining to Issue Staff Opinions. Ethics counsel shall decline to issue a staff opinion if any criteria of procedure 2(a)(1) apply. Ethics counsel may decline to issue a staff opinion if any criteria of procedure 2(a)(2) apply.

(c) Form for Written Staff Opinion. Written staff opinions shall not reveal the identity of the inquirer and any other persons or entities involved in the inquiry.

(d) Appeal to PEC. Members requesting a written staff opinion may appeal the opinion or the decision not to issue the opinion to the PEC as provided elsewhere in these procedures. Appeals to the PEC shall be public information. Oral staff opinions and decisions not to issue an oral opinion may not be appealed.

(e) Monitoring Written Staff Opinions. A copy of each written staff opinion shall be provided to the chair of the PEC who shall assign same to members of the PEC or a subcommittee for determination of the exercise of the PEC's initiative review.

Amended Aug. 11–14, 2004, by the Board of Governors of The Florida Bar; Oct. 5, 2007, by the Board of Governors of The Florida Bar.

Rule 4. Procedure for Issuance of PEC Opinions

(a) Scheduling PEC Review. Timely appeals, requests of the board of governors, PEC review of staff opinions, and PEC review of existing advisory ethics opinions shall be scheduled for PEC consideration at the next meeting of the PEC if the appeal, request, or review is made more than 30 days in advance of such meeting and any official notice requirements are met.

(b) Authority of PEC Chair. The chair of the PEC shall have the discretion to determine the order of the agenda, time allocated to each matter, and whether personal appearances may be allowed. In addition, the chair may appoint a subcommittee to conduct the review.

(c) Notice of PEC Review. In the event that the PEC decides to consider rendering a written opinion for publication at the request of the board of governors, upon PEC review of staff opinions, or upon PEC review of existing formal opinions, the PEC shall publish in The Florida Bar *News* an official notice of its intent to consider rendering a written opinion. The notice shall state the time and place at which the PEC's deliberations will occur and shall invite written comments from interested bar members. Initial publication shall identify the subject matter of the issue and any proposed text, if then available, and invite written comment. If an opinion is issued, the PEC shall publish an official notice of the adoption of the advisory ethics opinion in The Florida Bar *News*, including the full text of the opinion. Any subsequent notice shall contain the full text of any revised advisory ethics opinion.

(d) Comments. Any member in good standing may file written comment with ethics counsel within 30 days of the date of publication of official notice of the PEC's intent to consider rendering a proposed advisory opinion, official notice of the PEC's adoption of an advisory ethics opinion, or official notice that the PEC has revised a proposed advisory ethics opinion.

All comments filed under this subdivision shall be in the form of written statements with relevant facts, arguments in support, and citations to relevant authority, if any.

(e) Record on Review. Ethics counsel shall prepare and distribute to the PEC a file on each matter for review. Any person may request and receive a copy of the file. Ethics counsel may charge a reasonable fee for providing copies in accord with established, general bar policies.

(1) *Appeals of Written Staff Opinions.* The file shall include the original request for the opinion, the written staff opinion, and the written request for PEC review.

(2) *Requests of Board of Governors.* The file shall include the request, relevant material and authorities, any proposed text for consideration, and any timely comments.

(3) *Review of Staff Opinions.* The file shall include the original request for the opinion, the written staff opinion, and the written request for PEC review.

(4) *Review of Existing Advisory Ethics Opinions.* The file shall include the existing advisory ethics opinion, relevant material and authorities, and the written request for PEC review.

(f) PEC Action. ***By majority vote of those present, the PEC may:***

(1) *Appeals of Written Staff Opinions.*

(A) affirm the opinion, in whole or in part;

(B) reverse the opinion, in whole or in part;

(C) return the opinion to ethics counsel with instructions as to redrafting; or

(D) determine to issue, amend, or withdraw an advisory ethics opinion.

(2) *Requests of Board of Governors.*

(A) decline to issue an advisory ethics opinion;

(B) agree to issue, amend, or withdraw an advisory ethics opinion; or

(C) provide informal information or comments to the inquirer.

(3) *Review of Staff Opinions.*

(A) affirm the opinion, in whole or in part;

(B) reverse the opinion, in whole or in part;

(C) return the opinion to ethics counsel with instructions as to redrafting; or

(D) determine to issue, amend, or withdraw an advisory ethics opinion.

(4) *Review of Existing Advisory Ethics Opinions.*

(A) affirm the advisory ethics opinion, in whole or in part;

(B) reverse the advisory opinion, in whole or in part; or

(C) determine to issue, amend, or withdraw an advisory ethics opinion.

(g) Notice of PEC Action. Notice of PEC action shall advise about the procedures for requesting review by the Board Review Committee on Professional Ethics. Notice of PEC action regarding formal opinions of the PEC shall be published in The Florida Bar News. Notice of the PEC's actions shall be provided by ethics counsel to:

(1) *Appeals of Written Staff Opinions.* The inquiring member who appealed a written staff opinion;

(2) *Requests of Board of Governors.* The inquirer, all members who timely commented on a referral from the board of governors and the bar's executive director;

(3) *Review of Staff Opinions.* All members who timely commented on notice of the PEC's review of staff opinions.

(4) *Review of Existing Advisory Ethics Opinions.* All members who timely commented on notice of the PEC's review of existing advisory ethics opinions.

(h) Appeal of PEC Action. Any member who timely commented to the PEC and any member who timely appealed a written staff opinion may appeal action of the PEC to the board of governors as provided elsewhere in these procedures.

Amended Aug. 11–14, 2004, by the Board of Governors of The Florida Bar; Oct. 5, 2007, by the Board of Governors of The Florida Bar.

Rule 5. Procedure for Review of PEC Action

(a) Referral to Board Review Committee on Professional Ethics. Timely appeals from PEC action shall be referred to the Board Review Committee on Professional Ethics (hereinafter BRC).

(b) Scheduling BRC Review. Timely appeals from PEC action shall be scheduled for BRC consideration at the next meeting of the BRC if the appeal or request is made more than 30 days in advance of such meeting.

(c) Authority of BRC Chair. The chair of the BRC shall have the discretion to determine the order of the agenda, time allocated to each matter, and whether personal appearances may be allowed. In addition, the chair may appoint a subcommittee to conduct the review.

(d) Record on Review. Ethics counsel shall prepare and distribute to the BRC a file on each matter for review. Any person may request and receive a copy of the file. Ethics counsel may charge a reasonable fee for providing copies in accord with established, general bar policies. The file shall include the record before the PEC and the request for BRC review.

(e) BRC Action. By majority vote of those present, the BRC may:

(1) affirm the PEC action, in whole or in part;

(2) reverse the PEC action, in whole or in part; or

(3) return the matter to the PEC with instructions as to redrafting.

(f) Review of BRC Action. The BRC shall report its actions to the board. By majority vote of those present, the board may:

(1) affirm the PEC action, in whole or in part;

(2) reverse the PEC action, in whole or in part; or

(3) return the matter to the PEC with instructions as to redrafting.

(g) Notice of Board of Governors Action. Notice of board of governors action regarding formal advisory opinions shall be published in The Florida Bar News. Notice of the board's actions shall be provided by ethics counsel to the members who timely requested board of governors review.

Amended Aug. 11–14, 2004, by the Board of Governors of The Florida Bar; Oct. 5, 2007, by the Board of Governors of The Florida Bar.

Rule 6. Procedure for Issuance of Board of Governors Opinions

(a) Referral to BRC. Board of governors decisions to render an advisory ethics opinion shall be referred to the BRC to develop a specific set of facts upon which the opinion will be based, comply with notice provisions in this procedure, and adopt a written advisory opinion applying the Rules of Professional Conduct to the set of facts.

(b) Scheduling BRC Review. Advisory ethics opinions shall be scheduled for BRC consideration if the decision to consider rendering an opinion is made more than 30 days in advance of such meeting and any official notice requirements are met.

(c) Authority of BRC Chair. The chair of the BRC shall have the discretion to determine the order of the agenda, time allocated to each matter, and whether personal appearances may be allowed. In addition, the chair may appoint a subcommittee to conduct the review.

(d) Notice of BRC Opinion. In the event that the board of governors refers an issue to the BRC to render a written opinion for publication, the BRC shall publish in The Florida Bar News an official notice of its intent to consider rendering a written opinion. The notice shall state the time and place at which the BRC's deliberations will occur and shall invite written comments from interested bar members. Initial publication shall identify the subject matter of the issue and any proposed text, if then available, and invite written comment. If an opinion is issued, the BRC shall publish an official notice of the adoption of the advisory ethics opinion in The Florida Bar News, including the full text of the opinion. Any subsequent notice shall contain the full text of any revised advisory ethics opinion.

(e) Comments. Any member in good standing may file written comment with ethics counsel within 30 days of the date of publication of official notice of the BRC's intent to consider rendering a proposed advisory opinion, official notice of the BRC's adoption of an advisory ethics opinion, or official notice that the BRC has revised a proposed advisory ethics opinion.

All comments filed under this subdivision shall be in the form of written statements with relevant facts, arguments in support, and citations to relevant authority, if any.

(f) Record on Review. Ethics counsel shall prepare and distribute to the BRC a file on each matter for review. Any person may request and receive a copy of the file. Ethics counsel may charge a reasonable fee for providing copies in accord with established, general bar policies. The file shall contain the statement of facts upon which the proposed advisory opinion will be made, relevant material and authorities, and the text of the proposed advisory opinion, if then available.

(g) BRC Action. By majority vote of those present, the BRC may:

(1) determine to issue an opinion; or

(2) determine not to issue an opinion.

(h) Review of BRC Action. The BRC shall report its actions to the board. By majority vote of those present, the board may:

(1) affirm the BRC action, in whole or in part;

(2) reverse the BRC action, in whole or in part; or

(3) return the matter to the BRC with instructions as to redrafting.

(i) Notice of Board of Governors Action. Notice of board of governors action regarding formal advisory opinions shall be published in The Florida Bar News. Notice of the board's actions shall be provided by ethics counsel to the members who timely filed comments.

Amended Aug. 11–14, 2004, by the Board of Governors of The Florida Bar; Oct. 5, 2007, by the Board of Governors of The Florida Bar.

Rule 7. Time for Appeals

All appeals allowed under these procedures shall be commenced by mailing the required items to Ethics

Counsel, The Florida Bar, 651 East Jefferson Street, Tallahassee, Florida 32399–2300, within 30 days of the date on the notice of the action that is the subject of the appeal. Failure to timely commence an appeal shall bar the appeal.

Amended Aug. 11–14, 2004, by the Board of Governors of The Florida Bar; Oct. 5, 2007, by the Board of Governors of The Florida Bar.

CHAPTER 3. RULES OF DISCIPLINE

3–1. PREAMBLE

Rule 3–1.1. Privilege to practice

A license to practice law confers no vested right to the holder thereof but is a conditional privilege that is revocable for cause.

Amended July 23, 1992, effective Jan. 1, 1993 (605 So.2d 252).

Rule 3–1.2. Generally

The Supreme Court of Florida has the inherent power and duty to prescribe standards of conduct for lawyers, to determine what constitutes grounds for discipline of lawyers, to discipline for cause attorneys admitted to practice law in Florida, and to revoke the license of every lawyer whose unfitness to practice law has been duly established.

3-2. DEFINITIONS

Rule 3-2.1. Generally

Wherever used in these rules the following words or terms shall have the meaning herein set forth unless the use thereof shall clearly indicate a different meaning:

(a) Bar Counsel. A member of The Florida Bar representing The Florida Bar in any proceeding under these rules.

(b) The Board or the Board of Governors. The board of governors of The Florida Bar.

(c) Complainant or Complaining Witness. Any person who has complained of the conduct of any member of The Florida Bar to any officer or agency of The Florida Bar.

(d) This Court or the Court. The Supreme Court of Florida.

(e) Court of this State. A state court authorized and established by the constitution or laws of the state of Florida.

(f) Diversion to Practice and Professionalism Enhancement Programs. The removal of a disciplinary matter from the disciplinary system and placement of the matter in a skills enhancement program in lieu of a disciplinary sanction.

(g) Executive Committee. The executive committee of the board of governors of The Florida Bar.

(h) Executive Director. The executive director of The Florida Bar.

(i) Practice and Professionalism Enhancement Programs. Programs operated either as a diversion from disciplinary action or as a part of a disciplinary sanction that are intended to provide educational opportunities to members of the bar for enhancing skills and avoiding misconduct allegations.

(j) Probable Cause. A finding by an authorized agency that there is cause to believe that a member of The Florida Bar is guilty of misconduct justifying disciplinary action.

(k) Referral to Practice and Professionalism Enhancement Programs. Placement of a lawyer in skills enhancement programs as a disciplinary sanction.

***(l)* Referee.** A judge or retired judge appointed to conduct proceedings as provided under these rules.

(m) Respondent. A member of The Florida Bar or an attorney subject to these rules who is accused of misconduct or whose conduct is under investigation.

(n) Staff Counsel. A lawyer employee of The Florida Bar designated by the executive director and authorized by these Rules Regulating The Florida Bar to approve formal complaints, conditional guilty pleas for consent judgments, and diversion recommendations and to make appointment of bar counsel.

***(o)* Chief Branch Discipline Counsel.** Chief branch discipline counsel is the counsel in charge of a branch office of The Florida Bar. Any counsel employed by The Florida Bar may serve as chief branch discipline counsel at the direction of the regularly assigned chief branch discipline counsel or staff counsel.

(p) Designated Reviewer. The designated reviewer is a member of the board of governors responsible for review and other specific duties as assigned with respect to a particular grievance committee or matter. The designated reviewer for a special grievance committee will be selected by the president and approved by the board.

(q) Final Adjudication. A decision by the authorized disciplinary authority or court issuing a sanction for professional misconduct that is not subject to judicial review except on direct appeal to the Supreme Court of the United States.

Amended July 23, 1992, effective Jan. 1, 1993 (605 So.2d 252); Oct. 20, 1994 (644 So.2d 282); April 25, 2002 (820 So.2d 210); May 20, 2005, effective Jan. 1, 2006 (907 So.2d 1138); Oct. 6, 2005, effective Jan. 1, 2006 (916 So.2d 655); Dec. 20, 2007, effective March 1, 2008 (978 So.2d 91); Nov. 19, 2009, effective Feb. 1, 2010 (24 So.3d 63).

3-3. JURISDICTION TO ENFORCE RULES

Rule 3-3.1. Supreme Court of Florida; disciplinary agencies

The exclusive jurisdiction of the Supreme Court of Florida over the discipline of persons admitted to the practice of law shall be administered in the following manner subject to the supervision and review of the court. The following entities are hereby designated as agencies of the Supreme Court of Florida for this purpose and with the following responsibilities, jurisdiction, and powers. The board of governors, grievance committees, and referees shall have such jurisdiction and powers as are necessary to conduct the proper and speedy disposition of any investigation or cause, including the power to compel the attendance of witnesses, to take or cause to be taken the deposition of witnesses, and to order the production of books, records, or other documentary evidence. Each member of such agencies has power to administer oaths and affirmations to witnesses in any matter within the jurisdiction of the agency.

Amended July 23, 1992, effective Jan. 1, 1993 (605 So.2d 252).

Rule 3-3.2. Board of Governors of The Florida Bar

(a) Responsibility of Board. The board is assigned the responsibility of maintaining high ethical standards among the members of The Florida Bar. The board shall supervise and conduct disciplinary proceedings in accordance with the provisions of these rules.

(b) Authority to File a Formal Complaint. No formal complaint shall be filed by The Florida Bar in disciplinary proceedings against a member of the bar unless 1 of the following conditions has been met:

(1) *Finding of Probable Cause.* A formal complaint may be filed if there has been a finding under these rules that probable cause exists to believe that the respondent is guilty of misconduct justifying disciplinary action;

(2) *Emergency Suspension or Probation.* A formal complaint may be filed if the member is the subject of an order of emergency suspension or emergency probation that is based on the same misconduct that is the subject matter of the formal complaint;

(3) *Felony Determination or Adjudication.* A formal complaint may be filed if the respondent has been determined or adjudged to be guilty of the commission of a felony;

(4) *Discipline In Another Jurisdiction.* A formal complaint may be filed if the respondent has been disciplined by another entity having jurisdiction over the practice of law;

(5) *Felony Charges.* A formal complaint may be filed if a member has been charged with commission of a felony under applicable law that warrants the imposition of discipline and if the chair of the grievance committee agrees. A decision of the grievance committee chair to not file a formal complaint shall be reviewed by the full grievance committee. The grievance committee may affirm or reverse the decision.

(6) *Discipline on Action of the Florida Judicial Qualifications Commission.* A formal complaint may be filed if the Supreme Court of Florida has adjudged the respondent guilty of judicial misconduct in an action brought by the Florida Judicial Qualifications Commission, the respondent is no longer a judicial officer, and the facts warrant imposing disciplinary sanctions.

(c) Executive Committee. All acts and discretion required by the board under these Rules of Discipline may be exercised by its executive committee between meetings of the board as may from time to time be authorized by standing board of governors' policies.

Amended March 16, 1990, effective March 17, 1990 (558 So.2d 1008); July 23, 1992, effective Jan. 1, 1993 (605 So.2d 252); Nov. 19, 2009, effective Feb. 1, 2010 (24 So.3d 63).

Rule 3-3.3. Counsel for The Florida Bar

(a) Authority of Board of Governors. The board may employ staff counsel and bar counsel for The Florida Bar to perform such duties, as may be assigned, under the direction of the executive director.

(b) Appointment of Bar Counsel. Staff counsel may designate members of The Florida Bar to serve as bar counsel to represent The Florida Bar in disciplinary proceedings.

(c) Appointment of Board Members Limited. A member of the board may represent The Florida Bar on any review proceeding under rule 3-7.7.

(d) Appointment of Grievance Committee Members Limited. A member of a grievance committee may represent the bar in any proceeding before a referee and any review by the supreme court under rule 3-7.7 if the case was not considered by the grievance committee on which the member serves.

(e) Compensation. Bar counsel may be compensated in accordance with budgetary policies adopted by the board.

Amended July 23, 1992, effective Jan. 1, 1993 (605 So.2d 252); April 25, 2002 (820 So.2d 210); Nov. 19, 2009, effective Feb. 1, 2010 (24 So.3d 63).

Rule 3-3.4. Grievance Committees

There shall be such grievance committees as are herein provided, each of which shall have the authority and jurisdiction required to perform the functions hereinafter assigned to it and which shall be constituted and appointed as follows:

(a) Circuit Grievance Committees. There shall be at least 1 grievance committee for each judicial circuit of this state and as many more as shall be found desirable by the board. Such committees shall be designated as judicial circuit grievance committees, and in circuits having more than 1 committee they shall be identified by alphabetical designation in the order of creation. Such committees shall be continuing bodies notwithstanding changes in membership, and they shall have jurisdiction and the power to proceed in all matters properly before them.

(b) Special Grievance Committees. The board may from time to time appoint grievance committees for the purpose of such investigations as may be assigned in accordance with these rules. Such committees shall continue only until the completion of tasks assigned, and they shall have jurisdiction and power to proceed in all matters so assigned to them. All provisions concerning grievance committees shall be applicable to special grievance committees except those concerning terms of office and other restrictions thereon as may be imposed by the board. Any vacancies occurring in such a committee shall be filled by the board, and such changes in members shall not affect the jurisdiction and power of the committee to proceed in all matters properly before it.

(c) Membership, Appointment, and Eligibility. Each grievance committee shall be appointed by the board and shall consist of not fewer than 3 members. At least one-third of the committee members shall be nonlawyers. All appointees shall be of legal age and, except for special grievance committees, shall be residents of the circuit or have their principal office in the circuit. The lawyer members of the committee shall have been members of The Florida Bar for at least 5 years.

No member of a grievance committee shall perform any grievance committee function when that member:

(1) is related by blood or marriage to the complainant or respondent;

(2) has a financial, business, property, or personal interest in the matter under consideration or with the complainant or respondent;

(3) has a personal interest that could be affected by the outcome of the proceedings or that could affect the outcome; or

(4) is prejudiced or biased toward either the complainant or the respondent.

Upon notice of the above prohibitions the affected members should recuse themselves from further proceedings. The grievance committee chair shall have the power to disqualify any member from any proceeding in which any of the above prohibitions exist and are stated of record or in writing in the file by the chair.

(d) Terms. The terms of the members shall be for 1 year from the date of administration of the oath of service on the grievance committee or until such time as their successors are appointed and qualified. Continuous service of a member shall not exceed 3 years. A member shall not be reappointed for a period of 3 years after the end of the member's term; provided, however, the expiration of the term of any member shall not disqualify such member from concluding any investigation or participating in disposition of cases that were pending before the committee when the member's term expired. A member who continues to serve on the grievance committee under the authority of this subdivision shall not be counted as a member of the committee when calculating the minimum number of public members required by this rule.

(e) Officers. There shall be a chair and vice-chair designated by the designated reviewer of that committee. The chair and vice-chair shall be members of The Florida Bar.

(f) Oath. Each new member of a committee shall subscribe to an oath to fulfill the duties of the office. Such oaths shall be filed with the executive director and placed with the official records of The Florida Bar.

(g) Removal. Any member may be removed from office by the designated reviewer of that committee or the board.

(h) Grievance Committee Meetings. Grievance committees should meet at regularly scheduled times, not less frequently than quarterly each year, and either the chair or vice-chair may call special meetings. Grievance committees should meet at least monthly during any period when the committee has 1 or more pending cases assigned for investigation and report. The time, date, and place of regular monthly meetings should be set in advance by agreement between the committee and chief branch discipline counsel.

Amended June 8, 1989 (544 So.2d 193); July 23, 1992, effective Jan. 1, 1993 (605 So.2d 252); April 25, 2002 (820 So.2d 210); Oct. 6, 2005, effective Jan. 1, 2006 (916 So.2d 655).

Rule 3–3.5. Circuit court jurisdiction

The jurisdiction of the circuit courts shall be concurrent with that of The Florida Bar under these Rules of Discipline. The forum first asserting jurisdiction in a disciplinary matter shall retain the same to the exclusion of the other until the final determination of the cause.

3–4. STANDARDS OF CONDUCT

Rule 3–4.1. Notice and Knowledge of Rules; Jurisdiction Over Lawyers of Other States and Foreign Countries

Every member of The Florida Bar and every lawyer of another state or foreign country who provides or offers to provide any legal services in this state is within the jurisdiction and subject to the disciplinary authority of this court and its agencies under this rule and is charged with notice and held to know the provisions of this rule and the standards of ethical and professional conduct prescribed by this court. Jurisdiction over a lawyer of another state who is not a member of The Florida Bar is limited to conduct as a lawyer in relation to the business for which the lawyer was permitted to practice in this state and the privilege in the future to practice law in the state of Florida. When The Florida Bar disciplines a lawyer that the bar is aware has bar membership in a European Union (E.U.) nation, the bar will notify the appropriate E.U. representative. The bar will use forms adopted by the Council of Laws and Bar Societies of Europe (CCBE) and the Conference of Chief Justices of the United States.

Amended July 23, 1992, effective Jan. 1, 1993 (605 So.2d 252); May 12, 2005, effective Jan. 1, 2006 (907 So.2d 1138); May 29, 2014, effective June 1, 2014 (140 So.3d 541).

Rule 3–4.2. Rules of Professional Conduct

Violation of the Rules of Professional Conduct as adopted by the rules governing The Florida Bar is a cause for discipline.

Rule 3–4.3. Misconduct and minor misconduct

The standards of professional conduct to be observed by members of the bar are not limited to the observance of rules and avoidance of prohibited acts, and the enumeration herein of certain categories of misconduct as constituting grounds for discipline shall not be deemed to be all-inclusive nor shall the failure to specify any particular act of misconduct be construed as tolerance thereof. The commission by a lawyer of any act that is unlawful or contrary to honesty and justice, whether the act is committed in the course of the attorney's relations as an attorney or otherwise, whether committed within or outside the state of Florida, and whether or not the act is a felony or misdemeanor, may constitute a cause for discipline.

Amended July 23, 1992, effective Jan. 1, 1993 (605 So.2d 252).

Rule 3–4.4. Criminal misconduct

Unless modified or stayed by the Supreme Court of Florida as provided elsewhere herein, a determination or judgment of guilt of a member of The Florida Bar by a court of competent jurisdiction of any crime or offense that is a felony under the laws of such jurisdiction is cause for automatic suspension from the practice of law in Florida. In addition, whether the alleged misconduct constitutes a felony or misdemeanor The Florida Bar may initiate disciplinary action regardless of whether the respondent has been tried, acquitted, or convicted in a court for the alleged criminal offense; however, the board may, in its discretion, withhold prosecution of disciplinary proceedings pending the outcome of criminal proceedings against the respondent. The acquittal of the respondent in a criminal proceeding shall not necessarily be a bar to disciplinary proceedings nor shall the findings, judgment, or decree of any court in civil proceedings necessarily be binding in disciplinary proceedings.

Amended July 23, 1992, effective Jan. 1, 1993 (605 So.2d 252).

Rule 3–4.5. Removal From Judicial Office by the Supreme Court of Florida

Whenever a judge is removed from office by the Supreme Court of Florida on the basis of a Judicial Qualifications Commission proceeding, the removal order, when the record in such proceedings discloses the appropriate basis, may also order the suspension of the judge as an attorney pending further proceedings hereunder.

When the Judicial Qualifications Commission files a recommendation that a judge be removed from office, The Florida Bar may seek leave to intervene in the proceedings before the Supreme Court of Florida. If intervention is granted, The Florida Bar may seek disciplinary action in the event the judge is removed by the court.

Amended March 23, 2000 (763 So.2d 1002).

Rule 3–4.6. Discipline by Foreign or Federal Jurisdiction; Choice of Law

(a) **Disciplinary Authority.** An attorney admitted to practice in this jurisdiction is subject to the disciplinary authority of this jurisdiction, regardless of where the attorney's conduct occurs. An attorney may be subject to the disciplinary authority of both this jurisdiction and another jurisdiction for the same conduct. A final adjudication in a disciplinary proceeding by a court or other authorized disciplinary agency of another jurisdiction, state or federal, that an attorney licensed to practice in that jurisdiction is guilty of misconduct justifying disciplinary action shall be considered as conclusive proof of such misconduct in a disciplinary proceeding under this rule.

(b) **Choice of Law.** In any exercise of the disciplinary authority of this jurisdiction, the rules of professional conduct to be applied shall be as follows:

(1) for conduct in connection with a matter pending before a tribunal, the rules of the jurisdiction in which the tribunal sits, unless the rules of the tribunal provide otherwise; and

(2) for any other conduct, the rules of the jurisdiction in which the attorney's conduct occurred, or, if the predominant effect of the conduct is in a different jurisdiction, the rules of that jurisdiction shall be applied to the conduct.

Amended May 12, 2005, effective Jan. 1, 2006 (907 So.2d 1138).

Rule 3–4.7. Oath

Violation of the oath taken by an attorney to support the constitutions of the United States and the State of Florida is ground for disciplinary action. Membership in, alliance with, or support of any organization, group, or party advocating or dedicated to the overthrow of the government by violence or by any means in violation of the Constitution of the United States or constitution of this state shall be a violation of the oath.

3–5. TYPES OF DISCIPLINE

Rule 3–5.1. Generally

Text of rule effective until October 1, 2015. See, also, rule effective October 1, 2015.

A judgment entered, finding a member of The Florida Bar guilty of misconduct, shall include one or more of the following disciplinary measures:

(a) **Admonishments.** A Supreme Court of Florida order finding minor misconduct and adjudging an admonishment may direct the respondent to appear before the Supreme Court of Florida, the board of governors, grievance committee, or the referee for administration of the admonishment. A grievance committee report and finding of minor misconduct or the board of governors, upon review of such report, may direct the respondent to appear before the board of governors or the grievance committee for administration of the admonishment. A memorandum of administration of an admonishment shall thereafter be made a part of the record of the proceeding.

(b) Minor Misconduct. Minor misconduct is the only type of misconduct for which an admonishment is an appropriate disciplinary sanction.

(1) *Criteria.* In the absence of unusual circumstances misconduct shall not be regarded as minor if any of the following conditions exist:

(A) the misconduct involves misappropriation of a client's funds or property;

(B) the misconduct resulted in or is likely to result in actual prejudice (loss of money, legal rights, or valuable property rights) to a client or other person;

(C) the respondent has been publicly disciplined in the past 3 years;

(D) the misconduct involved is of the same nature as misconduct for which the respondent has been disciplined in the past 5 years;

(E) the misconduct includes dishonesty, misrepresentation, deceit, or fraud on the part of the respondent; or

(F) the misconduct constitutes the commission of a felony under applicable law.

(2) *Discretion of Grievance Committee.* Despite the presence of 1 or more of the criteria described in subdivision (1) above, a grievance committee may recommend an admonishment for minor misconduct or diversion to a practice and professionalism enhancement program when unusual circumstances are present. When the grievance committee recommends an admonishment for minor misconduct or diversion to a practice and professionalism enhancement program under such circumstances, its report shall contain a detailed explanation of the circumstances giving rise to the committee's recommendation.

(3) *Recommendation of Minor Misconduct.* If a grievance committee finds the respondent guilty of minor misconduct or if the respondent shall admit guilt of minor misconduct and the committee concurs, the grievance committee shall file its report recommending an admonishment, the manner of administration, the taxing of costs, and an assessment or administrative fee in the amount of $1,250 against the respondent. The report recommending an admonishment shall be forwarded to staff counsel and the designated reviewer for review. If staff counsel does not return the report to the grievance committee to remedy a defect therein, or if the report is not referred to the disciplinary review committee by the designated reviewer [as provided in rule 3-7.5(b)], the report shall then be served on the respondent by bar counsel. The report and finding of minor misconduct shall become final unless rejected by the respondent within 15 days after service of the report. If rejected by the respondent, the report shall be referred to bar counsel and referee for trial on complaint of minor misconduct to be prepared by bar counsel as in the case of a finding of probable cause. If the report of minor misconduct is not rejected by the respondent, notice of the finding of minor misconduct shall be given, in writing, to the complainant.

(4) *Rejection of Minor Misconduct Reports.* The rejection by the board of governors of a grievance committee report of minor misconduct, without dismissal of the case, or remand to the grievance committee, shall be deemed a finding of probable cause. The rejection of such report by a respondent shall be deemed a finding of probable cause for minor misconduct. Upon trial before a referee following rejection by a respondent of a report of minor misconduct, the referee may recommend any discipline authorized under these rules.

(5) *Admission of Minor Misconduct.* Within 15 days after a finding of probable cause by a grievance committee, a respondent may tender a written admission of minor misconduct to bar counsel or the grievance committee. An admission of minor misconduct may be conditioned upon acceptance by the grievance committee, but the respondent may not condition the admission of minor misconduct upon the method of administration of the admonishment or upon nonpayment of costs incurred in the proceedings. Such an admission may be tendered after a finding of probable cause (but before the filing of a complaint) only if such an admission has not been previously tendered. If the admission is tendered after a finding of probable cause, the grievance committee may consider such admission without further evidentiary hearing and may either reject the admission, thereby affirming its prior action, or accept the admission and issue its report of minor misconduct. If a respondent's admission is accepted by the grievance committee, the respondent may not thereafter reject a report of the committee recommending an admonishment for minor misconduct. If the admission of minor misconduct is rejected, such admission shall not be considered or used against the respondent in subsequent proceedings.

(c) Probation. The respondent may be placed on probation for a stated period of time of not less than 6 months nor more than 5 years or for an indefinite period determined by conditions stated in the order. The judgment shall state the conditions of the probation, which may include but are not limited to the following:

(1) completion of a practice and professionalism enhancement program as provided elsewhere in these rules;

(2) supervision of all or part of the respondent's work by a member of The Florida Bar;

(3) the making of reports to a designated agency;

(4) the satisfactory completion of a course of study or a paper on legal ethics approved by the Supreme Court of Florida;

(5) such supervision over fees and trust accounts as the court may direct; or

(6) restrictions on the ability to advertise legal services, either in type of advertisement or a general prohibition for a stated period of time, in cases in which rules regulating advertising have been violated or the legal representation in which the misconduct occurred was obtained by advertising.

The respondent will reimburse the bar for the costs of supervision. Upon failure of a respondent to comply with the conditions of the probation or a finding of probable cause as to conduct of the respondent committed during the period of probation, the respondent may be punished for contempt on petition by The Florida Bar, as provided elsewhere in these Rules Regulating The Florida Bar. An order of the court imposing sanctions for contempt under this rule may also terminate the probation previously imposed.

(d) Public Reprimand. A public reprimand shall be administered in the manner prescribed in the judgment but all such reprimands shall be reported in the Southern Reporter. Due notice shall be given to the respondent of any proceeding set to administer the reprimand. The respondent shall appear personally before the Supreme Court of Florida, the board of governors, any judge designated to administer the reprimand, or the referee, if required, and such appearance shall be made a part of the record of the proceeding.

(e) Suspension. The respondent may be suspended from the practice of law for a definite period of time or an indefinite period thereafter to be determined by the conditions imposed by the judgment. During such suspension the respondent shall continue to be a member of The Florida Bar but without the privilege of practicing. A suspension of 90 days or less shall not require proof of rehabilitation or passage of the Florida bar examination and the respondent shall become eligible for all privileges of members of The Florida Bar upon the expiration of the period of suspension. A suspension of more than 90 days shall require proof of rehabilitation and may require passage of all or part of the Florida bar examination and the respondent shall not become eligible for all privileges of members of The Florida Bar until the court enters an order reinstating the respondent to membership in The Florida Bar. No suspension shall be ordered for a specific period of time in excess of 3 years.

Unless waived or modified by the court on motion of the respondent showing good cause, an order or opinion imposing a suspension of 90 days or less shall include a provision that prohibits the respondent from accepting new business from the date of the order or opinion until the end of the term of the suspension and shall provide that the suspension is effective 30 days from the date of the order or opinion so that the respondent may close out the practice of law and protect the interests of existing clients.

Unless waived or modified by the court on motion of the respondent showing good cause, an order or opinion imposing a suspension of more than 90 days shall include a provision that prohibits the respondent from accepting new business from the date of the order or opinion until the date of the court's order of reinstatement and shall provide that the suspension is effective 30 days from the date of the order or opinion so that the respondent may close out the practice of law and protect the interests of existing clients.

(f) Disbarment. A judgment of disbarment terminates the respondent's status as a member of the bar. Permanent disbarment shall preclude readmission. A former member who has not been permanently disbarred may only be admitted again upon full compliance with the rules and regulations governing admission to the bar. Except as might be otherwise provided in these rules, no application for readmission may be tendered within 5 years after the date of disbarment or such longer period as the court might determine in the disbarment order and thereafter until all court-ordered restitution and outstanding disciplinary costs have been paid.

Disbarment is the presumed sanction for lawyers found guilty of theft from a lawyer's trust account or special trust funds received or disbursed by a lawyer as guardian, personal representative, receiver, or in a similar capacity such as trustee under a specific trust document. A respondent found guilty of such theft shall have the opportunity to offer competent, substantial evidence to rebut the presumption that disbarment is appropriate.

Unless waived or modified by the court on motion of the respondent, an order or opinion imposing disbarment shall include a provision that prohibits the respondent from accepting new business from the date of the order or opinion and shall provide that the disbarment is effective 30 days from the date of the order or opinion so that the respondent may close out the practice of law and protect the interests of existing clients.

(g) Disciplinary Revocation. A disciplinary revocation is tantamount to a disbarment. A respondent may petition for disciplinary revocation in lieu of defending against allegations of disciplinary violations. If accepted by the Supreme Court of Florida, a disciplinary revocation terminates the respondent's status as a member of the bar. A former bar member whose disciplinary revocation has been accepted may only be admitted again upon full compliance with the rules and regulations governing admission to the bar. Like disbarment, disciplinary revocation terminates the respondent's license and privilege to practice law and requires readmission to practice under the Rules of the Supreme Court Relating to Admissions to the Bar. No application for readmission may be tendered until the later of 5 years after the date of the order of the Supreme Court of Florida granting the petition for disciplinary revocation, or such other period of time in excess of 5 years contained in said order.

(h) Notice to Clients. Upon service on the respondent of an order of disbarment, disbarment on consent, disciplinary revocation, suspension, emergency suspension, emergency probation, or placement on the inactive list for incapacity not related to misconduct, the respondent shall, unless this requirement is waived or modified in the court's order, forthwith furnish a copy of the order to:

(1) all of the respondent's clients with matters pending in the respondent's practice;

(2) all opposing counsel or co-counsel in the matters listed in (1), above; and

(3) all courts, tribunals, or adjudicative agencies before which the respondent is counsel of record.

Within 30 days after service of the order the respondent shall furnish bar counsel with a sworn affidavit listing the names and addresses of all persons and entities that have been furnished copies of the order.

(i) Forfeiture of Fees. An order of the Supreme Court of Florida or a report of minor misconduct adjudicating a respondent guilty of entering into, charging, or collecting a fee prohibited by the Rules Regulating The Florida Bar may order the respondent to forfeit the fee or any part thereof. In the case of a clearly excessive fee, the excessive amount of the fee may be ordered returned to the client, and a fee otherwise prohibited by the Rules Regulating The Florida Bar may be ordered forfeited to The Florida Bar Clients' Security Fund and disbursed in accordance with its rules and regulations.

(j) Restitution. In addition to any of the foregoing disciplinary sanctions and any disciplinary sanctions authorized elsewhere in these rules, the respondent may be ordered or agree to pay restitution to a complainant or other person if the disciplinary order finds that the respondent has received a clearly excessive, illegal, or prohibited fee or that the respondent has converted trust funds or property. In such instances the amount of restitution shall be specifically set forth in the disciplinary order or agreement and shall not exceed the amount by which a fee is clearly excessive, in the case of a prohibited or illegal fee shall not exceed the amount of such fee, or in the case of conversion shall not exceed the amount of the conversion established in disciplinary proceedings. The disciplinary order or agreement shall also state to whom restitution shall be made and the date by which it shall be completed. Failure to comply with the order or agreement shall not preclude further proceedings under these rules.

Amended March 16, 1990, effective March 17, 1990 (558 So.2d 1008); Dec. 21, 1990, effective Jan. 1, 1991 (571 So.2d 451); Nov. 14, 1991, effective Jan. 1, 1992 (593 So.2d 1035); July 23, 1992, effective Jan. 1, 1993 (605 So.2d 252); July 1, 1993 (621 So.2d 1032); Oct. 20, 1994 (644 So.2d 282); Sept. 24, 1998, effective Oct. 1, 1998 (718 So.2d 1179); Feb. 8, 2001 (795 So.2d 1); Oct. 6, 2005, effective Jan. 1, 2006 (916 So.2d 655); March 22, 2007, effective June 1, 2007 (952 So.2d 1185); Dec. 20, 2007, effective March 1, 2008 (978 So.2d 91); April 12, 2012, effective July 1, 2012 (101 So.3d 807).

Rule 3–5.1. Generally

Text of rule effective October 1, 2015. See, also, rule effective until October 1, 2015.

A judgment entered, finding a member of The Florida Bar guilty of misconduct, will include 1 or more of the following disciplinary measures:

(a) Admonishments. A Supreme Court of Florida order finding minor misconduct and adjudging an admonishment may direct the respondent to appear before the Supreme Court of Florida, the board of governors, grievance committee, or the referee for administration of the admonishment. A grievance committee report and finding of minor misconduct or the board of governors, on review of the report, may direct the respondent to appear before the board of governors or the grievance committee for administration of the admonishment. A memorandum of administration of an admonishment will be made a part of the record of the proceeding after the admonishment is administered.

(b) Minor Misconduct. Minor misconduct is the only type of misconduct for which an admonishment is an appropriate disciplinary sanction.

(1) *Criteria.* In the absence of unusual circumstances misconduct will not be regarded as minor if any of the following conditions exist:

(A) the misconduct involves misappropriation of a client's funds or property;

(B) the misconduct resulted in or is likely to result in actual prejudice (loss of money, legal rights, or valuable property rights) to a client or other person;

(C) the respondent has been publicly disciplined in the past 3 years;

(D) the misconduct involved is of the same nature as misconduct for which the respondent has been disciplined in the past 5 years;

(E) the misconduct includes dishonesty, misrepresentation, deceit, or fraud on the part of the respondent; or

(F) the misconduct constitutes the commission of a felony under applicable law.

(2) *Discretion of Grievance Committee.* A grievance committee may recommend an admonishment for minor misconduct or diversion to a practice and professionalism enhancement program when unusual circumstances are present, despite the presence of 1 or more of the criteria described in subpart (1) of this rule. When the grievance committee recommends an admonishment for minor misconduct or diversion to a practice and professionalism enhancement program under these circumstances, its report will contain a detailed explanation of the circumstances giving rise to the committee's recommendation.

(3) *Recommendation of Minor Misconduct.* If a grievance committee finds the respondent guilty of

minor misconduct or if the respondent admits guilt of minor misconduct and the committee concurs, the grievance committee will file its report recommending an admonishment, the manner of administration, the taxing of costs, and an assessment or administrative fee in the amount of $1,250 against the respondent. The report recommending an admonishment will be forwarded to staff counsel and the designated reviewer for review. If staff counsel does not return the report to the grievance committee to remedy a defect in the report, or if the report is not referred to the disciplinary review committee by the designated reviewer [as provided in rule 3–7.5(b)], the report will then be served on the respondent by bar counsel. The report and finding of minor misconduct becomes final unless rejected by the respondent within 15 days after service of the report. If rejected by the respondent, the report will be referred to bar counsel and referee for trial on complaint of minor misconduct to be prepared by bar counsel as in the case of a finding of probable cause. If the report of minor misconduct is not rejected by the respondent, notice of the finding of minor misconduct will be given, in writing, to the complainant.

(4) *Rejection of Minor Misconduct Reports.* The rejection by the board of governors of a grievance committee report of minor misconduct, without dismissal of the case, or remand to the grievance committee, is deemed a finding of probable cause. The rejection of a report by a respondent is deemed a finding of probable cause for minor misconduct. At trial before a referee following rejection by a respondent of a report of minor misconduct, the referee may recommend any discipline authorized under these rules.

(5) *Admission of Minor Misconduct.* A respondent may tender a written admission of minor misconduct to bar counsel or to the grievance committee within 15 days after a finding of probable cause by a grievance committee. An admission of minor misconduct may be conditioned on acceptance by the grievance committee, but the respondent may not condition the admission of minor misconduct on the method of administration of the admonishment or on nonpayment of costs incurred in the proceedings. An admission may be tendered after a finding of probable cause (but before the filing of a complaint) only if an admission has not been previously tendered. If the admission is tendered after a finding of probable cause, the grievance committee may consider the admission without further evidentiary hearing and may either reject the admission, affirming its prior action, or accept the admission and issue its report of minor misconduct. If a respondent's admission is accepted by the grievance committee, the respondent may not later reject a report of the committee recommending an admonishment for minor misconduct. If the admission of minor misconduct is rejected, the admission may not be considered or used against the respondent in subsequent proceedings.

(c) Probation. The respondent may be placed on probation for a stated period of time of not less than 6 months nor more than 5 years or for an indefinite period determined by conditions stated in the order. The judgment will state the conditions of the probation, which may include but are not limited to the following:

(1) completion of a practice and professionalism enhancement program as provided elsewhere in these rules;

(2) supervision of all or part of the respondent's work by a member of The Florida Bar;

(3) required reporting to a designated agency;

(4) satisfactory completion of a course of study or a paper on legal ethics approved by the Supreme Court of Florida;

(5) supervision over fees and trust accounts as the court directs; or

(6) restrictions on the ability to advertise legal services, either in type of advertisement or a general prohibition for a stated period of time, in cases in which rules regulating advertising have been violated or the legal representation in which the misconduct occurred was obtained by advertising.

The respondent will reimburse the bar for the costs of supervision. The respondent may be punished for contempt on petition by The Florida Bar, as provided elsewhere in these Rules Regulating The Florida Bar, on failure of a respondent to comply with the conditions of the probation or a finding of probable cause as to conduct of the respondent committed during the period of probation. An order of the court imposing sanctions for contempt under this rule may also terminate the probation previously imposed.

(d) Public Reprimand. A public reprimand will be administered in the manner prescribed in the judgment but all reprimands will be reported in the Southern Reporter. Due notice will be given to the respondent of any proceeding set to administer the reprimand. The respondent must appear personally before the Supreme Court of Florida, the board of governors, any judge designated to administer the reprimand, or the referee, if required, and this appearance will be made a part of the record of the proceeding.

(e) Suspension. The respondent may be suspended from the practice of law for a period of time to be determined by the conditions imposed by the judgment or order or until further order of the court. During this suspension the respondent continues to be a member of The Florida Bar but without the privilege of practicing. A suspension of 90 days or less does not require proof of rehabilitation or passage of the Florida bar examination and the respondent will become eligible for all privileges of members of The Florida Bar on the expiration of the period of suspension. A suspension of more than 90 days requires proof of rehabilitation and may require passage of all or part of the Florida bar examination and the respondent will not become eligible for all privileges of members of The Florida Bar until the court enters an order reinstating the respondent to membership in The Florida Bar. No suspension will be ordered for a specific period of time more than 3 years.

An order or opinion imposing a suspension of 90 days or less will include a provision that prohibits the respondent from accepting new business from the date of the order or opinion until the end of the term of the suspension and will provide that the suspension is effective 30 days from the date of the order or opinion so that the respondent may close out the practice of law and protect the interests of existing clients, unless the court orders otherwise.

An order or opinion imposing a suspension of more than 90 days will include a provision that prohibits the respondent from accepting new business from the date of the order or opinion until the date of the court's order of reinstatement and will provide that the suspension is effective 30 days from the date of the order or opinion so that the respondent may close out the practice of law and protect the interests of existing clients, unless the court orders otherwise.

(f) Disbarment. A judgment of disbarment terminates the respondent's status as a member of the bar. Permanent disbarment precludes readmission. A former member who has not been permanently disbarred may only be admitted again on full compliance with the rules and regulations governing admission to the bar. Except as otherwise provided in these rules, no application for readmission may be tendered within 5 years after the date of disbarment or a longer period ordered by the court in the disbarment order or at any time after that date until all court-ordered restitution and outstanding disciplinary costs have been paid.

Disbarment is the presumed sanction for lawyers found guilty of theft from a lawyer's trust account or special trust funds received or disbursed by a lawyer as guardian, personal representative, receiver, or trustee. A respondent found guilty of theft will have the opportunity to offer competent, substantial evidence to rebut the presumption that disbarment is appropriate.

Unless waived or modified by the court on motion of the respondent, an order or opinion imposing disbarment will include a provision that prohibits the respondent from accepting new business from the date of the order or opinion and will provide that the disbarment is effective 30 days from the date of the order or opinion so that the respondent may close out the practice of law and protect the interests of existing clients.

(g) Disciplinary Revocation. A disciplinary revocation is tantamount to a disbarment. A respondent may petition for disciplinary revocation in lieu of defending against allegations of disciplinary violations. If accepted by the Supreme Court of Florida, a disciplinary revocation terminates the respondent's status as a member of the bar. A former bar member whose disciplinary revocation has been accepted may only be admitted again upon full compliance with the rules and regulations governing admission to the bar. Like disbarment, disciplinary revocation terminates the respondent's license and privilege to practice law and requires readmission to practice under the Rules of the Supreme Court Relating to Admissions to the Bar. No application for readmission may be tendered until the later of 5 years after the date of the order of the Supreme Court of Florida granting the petition for disciplinary revocation, or such other period of time in excess of 5 years contained in said order.

(h) Notice to Clients. Unless the court orders otherwise, when the respondent is served with an order of disbarment, disbarment on consent, disciplinary revocation, suspension, emergency suspension, emergency probation, or placement on the inactive list for incapacity not related to misconduct, the respondent must, immediately furnish a copy of the order to:

(1) all of the respondent's clients with matters pending in the respondent's practice;

(2) all opposing counsel or co-counsel in the matters listed in (1), above;

(3) all courts, tribunals, or adjudicative agencies before which the respondent is counsel of record; and

(4) all state, federal, or administrative bars of which respondent is a member.

Within 30 days after service of the order the respondent must furnish bar counsel with a sworn affidavit listing the names and addresses of all persons and entities that have been furnished copies of the order.

(i) Forfeiture of Fees. An order of the Supreme Court of Florida or a report of minor misconduct adjudicating a respondent guilty of entering into, charging, or collecting a fee prohibited by the Rules Regulating The Florida Bar may order the respondent to forfeit the fee or any part thereof. In the case of a clearly excessive fee, the excessive amount of the fee may be ordered returned to the client, and a fee otherwise prohibited by the Rules Regulating The Florida Bar may be ordered forfeited to The Florida Bar Clients' Security Fund and disbursed in accordance with its rules and regulations.

(j) Restitution. In addition to any of the foregoing disciplinary sanctions and any disciplinary sanctions authorized elsewhere in these rules, the respondent may be ordered or agree to pay restitution to a complainant or other person if the disciplinary order finds that the respondent has received a clearly excessive, illegal, or prohibited fee or that the respondent has converted trust funds or property. The amount of restitution will be specifically set forth in the disciplinary order or agreement and will not exceed the amount by which a fee is clearly excessive, in the case of a prohibited or illegal fee will not exceed the amount of the fee, or in the case of conversion will not exceed the amount of the conversion established in disciplinary proceedings. The disciplinary order or agreement will also state to whom restitution must be made and the date by which it must be completed. Failure to comply with the order or agreement will cause the respondent to become a delinquent member and will not preclude further proceedings under these rules. The respondent must provide the bar with telephone numbers and current addresses of all individuals or entities to whom the respondent is ordered to pay restitution.

Amended March 16, 1990, effective March 17, 1990 (558 So.2d 1008); Dec. 21, 1990, effective Jan. 1, 1991 (571 So.2d 451); Nov. 14, 1991, effective Jan. 1, 1992 (593 So.2d 1035); July 23, 1992, effective Jan. 1, 1993 (605 So.2d 252); July 1, 1993 (621 So.2d 1032); Oct. 20, 1994 (644 So.2d 282); Sept. 24, 1998, effective Oct. 1, 1998 (718 So.2d 1179); Feb. 8, 2001 (795 So.2d 1); Oct. 6, 2005, effective Jan. 1, 2006 (916 So.2d 655); March 22, 2007, effective June 1, 2007 (952 So.2d 1185); Dec. 20, 2007, effective March 1, 2008 (978 So.2d 91); April 12, 2012, effective July 1, 2012 (101 So.3d 807); June 11, 2015, effective Oct. 1, 2015 (167 So.3d 412).

Rule 3–5.2. Emergency Suspension and Interim Probation or Interim Placement on the Inactive List for Incapacity not Related to Misconduct

Text of rule effective until October 1, 2015. See, also, rule effective October 1, 2015.

(a) Petition for Emergency Suspension.

(1) *Great Public Harm.* On petition of The Florida Bar, authorized by its president, president-elect, or executive director, supported by 1 or more affidavits demonstrating facts personally known to the affiants that, if unrebutted, would establish clearly and convincingly that an attorney appears to be causing great public harm, the Supreme Court of Florida may issue an order suspending said attorney on an emergency basis.

(2) *Discipline by Foreign Jurisdiction.* On petition of The Florida Bar, authorized by its president, president-elect, or executive director, supported by a certified copy of an order of a foreign disciplinary jurisdiction suspending or disbarring an attorney from the practice of law, the Supreme Court of Florida may issue an order suspending the attorney on an emergency basis. *See* subdivision (*l*) of rule 3–7.2.

A petition for emergency suspension shall also constitute a formal complaint. The respondent shall have 20 days after docketing by the Supreme Court of Florida of its order granting the bar's petition for emergency suspension in which to file an answer and any affirmative defenses to the bar's petition.

(b) Petition for Interim Probation or Interim Placement on the Inactive List for Incapacity Not Related to Misconduct. On petition of The Florida Bar, authorized by its president, president-elect, or executive director, supported by 1 or more affidavits demonstrating facts personally known to the affiants that, if unrebutted, would establish clearly and convincingly that conditions or restrictions on a lawyer's privilege to practice law in Florida are necessary for protection of the public, the Supreme Court of Florida may issue an order placing said lawyer on interim probation, the conditions of which shall be as provided in rule 3–5.1(c); or placing the lawyer on the inactive list for incapacity not related to misconduct as provided in rule 3–7.13. This petition shall also constitute the formal complaint. The respondent shall have 20 days after docketing by the Supreme Court of Florida of its order granting the bar's petition for interim probation in which to file an answer and any affirmative defenses to the bar's petition.

(c) Trust Accounts. Any order of emergency suspension or probation that restricts the attorney in maintaining a trust account shall, when served on any bank or other financial institution maintaining an account against which said attorney may make withdrawals, serve as an injunction to prevent said bank or financial institution from making further payment from such account or accounts on any obligation except in accordance with restrictions imposed by the court.

(d) New Cases and Existing Clients. Any order of emergency suspension issued under this rule shall immediately preclude the attorney from accepting any new cases and unless otherwise ordered permit the attorney to continue to represent existing clients for only the first 30 days after issuance of such emergency order. Any fees paid to the suspended attorney during the 30–day period shall be deposited in a trust account from which withdrawals may be made only in accordance with restrictions imposed by the court.

(e) Motions for Dissolution. The lawyer may move at any time for dissolution or amendment of an emergency order by motion filed with the Supreme Court of Florida, a copy of which will be served on bar counsel. Such motion shall not stay any other proceedings and applicable time limitations in the case and, unless the motion fails to state good cause or is procedurally barred as an invalid successive motion, shall immediately be assigned to a referee designated by the chief justice. The filing of such motion shall not stay the operation of an order of emergency suspension or interim probation entered under this rule.

(f) Appointment of Referee. Upon entry of an order of suspension or interim probation, as provided above, the Supreme Court of Florida shall promptly appoint or direct the appointment of a referee.

(g) Hearing on Petition to Terminate or Modify Suspension. The referee shall hear a motion to terminate or modify a suspension or interim probation imposed under this rule within 7 days of assignment and submit a report and recommendation to the Supreme Court of Florida within 7 days of the date of the hearing. The referee shall recommend dissolution or amendment, whichever is appropriate, to the extent that bar counsel cannot demonstrate a likelihood of prevailing on the merits on any element of the underlying rule violations.

(h) Successive Motions Prohibited. Successive motions for dissolution shall be summarily dismissed by the Supreme Court of Florida to the extent that they raise issues that were or with due diligence could have been raised in a prior motion.

(i) Review by the Supreme Court of Florida. Upon receipt of the referee's recommended order on the motion for dissolution or amendment, the Supreme Court of Florida shall review and act upon the referee's findings and recommendations.

(j) Hearings on Issues Raised in Petitions for Emergency Suspension or Interim Probation and Sanctions. Once the Supreme Court of Florida has granted a petition for emergency suspension or interim probation as set forth in this rule, the referee appointed by the court shall hear the matter in the same manner as provided in rule 3–7.6, except that the referee shall hear the matter after the lawyer charged shall have answered the charges in the petition for emergency suspension or interim probation or when the time has expired for filing an answer. The referee shall issue a final report and recommendation within 90 days of appointment. If the time limit specified in this subdivision is not met, that portion of an emergency order imposing a suspension or interim probation shall be automatically dissolved, except upon order of the Supreme Court of Florida, provided that any other appropriate disciplinary action on the underlying conduct still may be taken.

(k) Proceedings in the Supreme Court of Florida. Consideration of the referee's report and recommendation shall be expedited in the Supreme Court of Florida. If oral argument is granted, the chief justice shall schedule oral argument as soon as practicable.

(*l*) Waiver of Time Limits. The respondent may at any time waive the time requirements set forth in this rule by written request made to and approved by the referee assigned to hear the matter.

Former Rule 3–5.1(g) redesignated as new Rule 3–5.2 and amended Nov. 14, 1991, effective Jan. 1, 1992 (593 So.2d 1035). Amended July 23, 1992, effective Jan. 1, 1993 (605 So.2d 252); April 25, 2002 (820 So.2d 210); June 29, 2006, effective August 1, 2006 (933 So.2d 498); April 12, 2012, effective July 1, 2012 (101 So.3d 807).

Rule 3–5.2. Emergency Suspension and Interim Probation or Interim Placement on the Inactive List for Incapacity Not Related to Misconduct

Text of rule effective October 1, 2015. See, also, rule effective until October 1, 2015.

(a) Petition for Emergency Suspension.

(1) *Great Public Harm.* On petition of The Florida Bar, authorized by its president, president-elect, or executive director, supported by 1 or more affidavits demonstrating facts personally known to the affiants that, if unrebutted, would establish clearly and convincingly that a lawyer appears to be causing great public harm, the Supreme Court of Florida may issue an order suspending the lawyer on an emergency basis.

(2) *Discipline by Foreign Jurisdiction.* On petition of The Florida Bar, authorized by its president, president-elect, or executive director, supported by a certified copy of an order of a foreign disciplinary jurisdiction suspending or disbarring a lawyer from the practice of law, the Supreme Court of Florida may issue an order suspending the lawyer on an emergency basis. See subdivision (*l*) of rule 3–7.2.

A petition for emergency suspension will also constitute a formal complaint. The respondent will have 20 days after docketing by the Supreme Court of Florida of its order granting the bar's petition for emergency suspension in which to file an answer and any affirmative defenses to the bar's petition.

(b) Petition for Interim Probation or Interim Placement on the Inactive List for Incapacity Not Related to Misconduct. The Supreme Court of Florida may issue an order placing a lawyer on interim probation, under the conditions provided in subdivision (c) of rule 3–5.1 or placing the lawyer on the inactive list for incapacity not related to misconduct as provided in rule 3–7.13. Such order may be issued upon petition of The Florida Bar, authorized by its president, president-elect, or executive director, supported by 1 or more affidavits demonstrating facts personally known to the affiants that, if unrebutted, would establish clearly and convincingly that conditions or restrictions on a lawyer's privilege to practice law in Florida are necessary for protection of the public. This petition will also constitute the formal complaint. The respondent will have 20 days after docketing by the Supreme Court of Florida of its order granting the bar's petition for interim probation in which to file an answer and any affirmative defenses to the bar's petition.

(c) Trust Accounts. Any order of emergency suspension or probation that restricts the attorney in maintaining a trust account will be served on the respondent and any bank or other financial institution maintaining an account against which the respondent may make withdrawals. The order will serve as an injunction to prevent the bank or financial institution from making further payment from the trust account or accounts on any obligation except in accordance with restrictions imposed by the court through subsequent orders issued by a court-appointed referee. Bar counsel will serve a copy of the Supreme Court of Florida's order freezing a lawyer's trust account via first class mail on the bank(s) in which the respondent's trust account is held.

(1) The court's order appointing a referee under this rule may authorize the referee to determine enti-

tlement to funds in the frozen trust account. Any client or third party claiming to be entitled to funds in the frozen trust account must file a petition requesting release of frozen trust account funds with the referee appointed in the case, accompanied by proof of entitlement to the funds.

(2) Bar counsel and bar auditors will provide information to the appointed referee from bar audits and other existing information regarding persons claiming ownership of frozen trust account funds. The bar will notify persons known to bar staff in writing via regular first class mail of their possible interest in funds contained in the frozen trust account. The notices will include a copy of the form of a petition requesting release of frozen trust account funds, to be filed with the referee and instructions for completing the form. The bar will publish, in the local county or city newspaper published where the lawyer practiced before suspension, a notice informing the public that the lawyer's trust account has been frozen and those persons with claims on the funds should contact listed bar counsel within 30 days after publication whenever possible.

(A) If there are no responses to the notices mailed and published by the bar within 90 days from the date of the notice or if the amount in the frozen trust account is over $100,000, a receiver may be appointed by the referee to determine the person rightfully entitled to the frozen trust funds. The receiver will be paid from the corpus of the trust funds unless the referee orders otherwise.

(B) In all other instances, a referee shall determine who is entitled to funds in the frozen trust account, unless the amount in the frozen trust account is $5,000 or less and no persons with potential entitlement to frozen trust account funds respond to the bar's mailed or published notices within 90 days from the date of the notice. In such event, the funds will be unfrozen.

(d) Referee Review of Frozen Trust Account Petitions. The referee will determine when and how to pay the claim of any person entitled to funds in the frozen trust account after reviewing the bar's audit report, the lawyer's trust account records, the petitions filed or the receiver's recommendations. If the bar's audit report or other reliable evidence shows that funds have been stolen or misappropriated from the lawyer's trust account, then the referee may hold a hearing. Subchapter 3–7 will not apply to a referee hearing under this rule. No pleadings will be filed, only petitions requesting release of frozen trust account funds. The parties to this referee proceeding will be those persons filing a petition requesting release of frozen trust account funds. The bar will not be a party to the proceeding. The referee's order will be the final order in the matter unless one of the parties petitions for review of the referee's order to the Supreme Court of Florida. The sole issue before the referee will be determination of ownership of the frozen trust account funds. The referee will determine the percentage of monies missing from the respondent's trust account and the amounts owing to those petitioners requesting release of frozen trust account funds. A pro rata distribution is the method of distribution when there are insufficient funds in the account to pay all claims in full. The referee's decision is subject only to direct petition for review of the referee's final order by a party claiming an ownership interest in the frozen trust funds. The petition for review must be filed within 60 days of the referee's final order. The schedule for filing of briefs in the appellate process will be as set forth in subchapter 3–7 of these rules.

(e) Separate Funds in Frozen Trust Accounts. The referee will order return of any separate funds to their rightful owner(s) in full upon their filing a petition requesting release of frozen trust account funds with proof of entitlement to the funds. Separate funds are monies deposited into the respondent's trust account after the misappropriation, which are not affected by the misappropriation, and funds that have been placed into a separate segregated individual trust account under the individual client's tax identification number.

(f) New Cases and Existing Clients. Any order of emergency suspension issued under this rule will immediately preclude the attorney from accepting any new cases and unless otherwise ordered permit the attorney to continue to represent existing clients for only the first 30 days after issuance of an emergency order. Any fees paid to the suspended attorney during the 30–day period will be deposited in a trust account from which withdrawals may be made only in accordance with restrictions imposed by the court.

(g) Motions for Dissolution. The lawyer may move at any time for dissolution or amendment of an emergency order by motion filed with the Supreme Court of Florida, a copy of which will be served on bar counsel. The motion will not stay any other proceedings and applicable time limitations in the case and, unless the motion fails to state good cause or is procedurally barred as an invalid successive motion, will immediately be assigned to a referee designated by the chief justice. The filing of the motion will not stay the operation of an order of emergency suspension or interim probation entered under this rule.

(h) Appointment of Referee. On entry of an order of suspension or interim probation, as provided above, the Supreme Court of Florida will promptly appoint or direct the appointment of a referee. On determination that funds have been misappropriated from a lawyer's trust account as provided above, the Supreme Court of Florida will promptly appoint or direct the appointment of a referee.

(i) Hearing on Petition to Terminate or Modify Suspension. The referee will hear a motion to terminate or modify a suspension or interim probation imposed under this rule within 7 days of assignment and submit a report and recommendation to the Supreme Court of Florida within 7 days of the date of the hearing. The referee will recommend dissolution or amendment, whichever is appropriate, to the extent that bar counsel cannot demonstrate a likelihood of prevailing on the merits on any element of the underlying rule violations.

(j) Successive Motions Prohibited. Successive motions for dissolution will be summarily dismissed by the Supreme Court of Florida to the extent that they raise issues that were or with due diligence could have been raised in a prior motion.

(k) Review by the Supreme Court of Florida. On receipt of the referee's recommended order on the motion for dissolution or amendment, the Supreme Court of Florida will review and act upon the referee's findings and recommendations regarding emergency suspensions and interim probations. This subdivision does not apply to a referee's final order to determine ownership of funds in frozen trust accounts. These final orders of referee are reviewable by the Supreme Court of Florida only if a party timely files a petition for review pursuant to this rule. Briefing schedules following the petition for review will be as set forth in subchapter 3-7 of these rules.

(*l*) Hearings on Issues Raised in Petitions for Emergency Suspension or Interim Probation and Sanctions. Once the Supreme Court of Florida has granted a petition for emergency suspension or interim probation as set forth in this rule, the referee appointed by the court will hear the matter in the same manner as provided in rule 3-7.6, except that the referee will hear the matter after the lawyer charged has answered the charges in the petition for emergency suspension or interim probation or when the time has expired for filing an answer. The referee will issue a final report and recommendation within 90 days of appointment. If the time limit specified in this subdivision is not met, that portion of an emergency order imposing a suspension or interim probation will be automatically dissolved, except upon order of the Supreme Court of Florida, provided that any other appropriate disciplinary action on the underlying conduct still may be taken.

(m) Proceedings in the Supreme Court of Florida. Consideration of the referee's report and recommendation regarding emergency suspension and interim probation will be expedited in the Supreme Court of Florida. If oral argument is granted, the chief justice will schedule oral argument as soon as practicable.

(n) Waiver of Time Limits. The respondent may at any time waive the time requirements set forth in this rule by written request made to and approved by the referee assigned to hear the matter.

Former Rule 3-5.1(g) redesignated as new Rule 3-5.2 and amended Nov. 14, 1991, effective Jan. 1, 1992 (593 So.2d 1035). Amended July 23, 1992, effective Jan. 1, 1993 (605 So.2d 252); April 25, 2002 (820 So.2d 210); June 29, 2006, effective August 1, 2006 (933 So.2d 498); April 12, 2012, effective July 1, 2012 (101 So.3d 807); June 11, 2015, effective Oct. 1, 2015 (167 So.3d 412).

Rule 3-5.3. Diversion of Disciplinary Cases to Practice and Professionalism Enhancement Programs

Text of rule effective until October 1, 2015. See, also, rule effective October 1, 2015.

(a) Authority of Board. The board of governors is hereby authorized to establish practice and professionalism enhancement programs to which eligible disciplinary cases may be diverted as an alternative to disciplinary sanction.

(b) Types of Disciplinary Cases Eligible for Diversion. Disciplinary cases that otherwise would be disposed of by a finding of minor misconduct or by a finding of no probable cause with a letter of advice are eligible for diversion to practice and professionalism enhancement programs.

(c) Limitation on Diversion. A respondent who has been the subject of a prior diversion within 7 years shall not be eligible for diversion.

(d) Approval of Diversion of Cases at Staff or Grievance Committee Level Investigations. The bar shall not offer a respondent the opportunity to divert a disciplinary case that is pending at staff or grievance committee level investigations to a practice and professionalism enhancement program unless staff counsel, the grievance committee chair, and the designated reviewer concur.

(e) Contents of Diversion Recommendation. If a diversion recommendation is approved as provided in subdivision (d), the recommendation shall state the practice and professionalism enhancement program(s) to which the respondent shall be diverted, shall state the general purpose for the diversion, and the costs thereof to be paid by the respondent.

(f) Service of Recommendation on and Review by Respondent. If a diversion recommendation is approved as provided in subdivision (d), the recommendation shall be served on the respondent who may accept or reject a diversion recommendation in the same manner as provided for review of recommendations of minor misconduct. The respondent shall not have the right to reject any specific requirement of a practice and professionalism enhancement program.

(g) Effect of Rejection of Recommendation by Respondent. In the event that a respondent rejects a diversion recommendation the matter shall be returned for further proceedings under these rules.

(h) Diversion at Trial Level.

(1) *Agreement of the Parties.* A referee may recommend diversion of a disciplinary case to a practice and professionalism enhancement program if the bar approves diversion and the respondent agrees. The procedures for approval of conditional pleas provided elsewhere in these rules shall apply to diversion at the trial level.

(2) *After Submission of Evidence.* A referee may recommend diversion of a disciplinary case to a prac-

tice and professionalism enhancement program if, after submission of evidence, but before a finding of guilt, the referee determines that, if proven, the conduct alleged to have been committed by the respondent is not more serious than minor misconduct.

(3) *Costs of Practice and Professionalism Enhancement Program.* A referee's recommendation of diversion to a practice and professionalism enhancement program shall state the costs thereof to be paid by the respondent.

(4) *Appeal of Diversion Recommendation.* The respondent and the bar shall have the right to appeal a referee's recommendation of diversion, except in the case of diversion agreed to under subdivision (h)(1).

(5) *Authority of Referee to Refer a Matter to a Practice and Professionalism Enhancement Program.* Nothing in this rule shall preclude a referee from referring a disciplinary matter to a practice and professionalism enhancement program as a part of a disciplinary sanction.

(i) Effect of Diversion. When the recommendation of diversion becomes final, the respondent shall enter the practice and professionalism enhancement program(s) and complete the requirements thereof. Upon respondent's entry into a practice and professionalism enhancement program, the bar shall terminate its investigation into the matter and its disciplinary files shall be closed indicating the diversion. Diversion into the practice and professionalism enhancement program shall not constitute a disciplinary sanction.

(j) Effect of Completion of the Practice and Professionalism Enhancement Program. If a respondent successfully completes all requirements of the practice and professionalism enhancement program(s) to which the respondent was diverted, the bar's file shall remain closed.

(k) Effect of Failure to Complete the Practice and Professionalism Enhancement Program. If a respondent fails to fully complete all requirements of the practice and professionalism enhancement program(s) to which the respondent was diverted, including the payment of costs thereof, the bar may reopen its disciplinary file and conduct further proceedings under these rules. Failure to complete the practice and professionalism enhancement program shall be considered as a matter of aggravation when imposing a disciplinary sanction.

(*l*) Costs of Practice and Professionalism Enhancement Programs. The Florida Bar shall annually determine the costs of practice and professionalism enhancement programs and publish the amount of the costs thereof that shall be assessed against and paid by a respondent.

Added Oct. 20, 1994 (644 So.2d 282). Amended April 25, 2002 (820 So.2d 210); May 20, 2004 (875 So.2d 448).

Rule 3–5.3. Diversion of Disciplinary Cases to Practice and Professionalism Enhancement Programs

Text of rule effective October 1, 2015. See, also, rule effective until October 1, 2015.

(a) Authority of Board. The board of governors is hereby authorized to establish practice and professionalism enhancement programs to which eligible disciplinary cases may be diverted as an alternative to disciplinary sanction.

(b) Types of Disciplinary Cases Eligible for Diversion. Disciplinary cases that otherwise would be disposed of by a finding of minor misconduct or by a finding of no probable cause with a letter of advice are eligible for diversion to practice and professionalism enhancement programs.

(c) Limitation on Diversion. A respondent who has been the subject of a prior diversion is not eligible for diversion for the same type of rule violation for a period of 5 years after the earlier diversion. However, a respondent who has been the subject of a prior diversion and then is alleged to have violated a completely different type of rule at least 1 year after the initial diversion, will be eligible for a practice and professionalism enhancement program.

(d) Approval of Diversion of Cases at Staff or Grievance Committee Level Investigations. The bar shall not offer a respondent the opportunity to divert a disciplinary case that is pending at staff or grievance committee level investigations to a practice and professionalism enhancement program unless staff counsel, the grievance committee chair, and the designated reviewer concur.

(e) Contents of Diversion Recommendation. If a diversion recommendation is approved as provided in subdivision (d), the recommendation shall state the practice and professionalism enhancement program(s) to which the respondent shall be diverted, shall state the general purpose for the diversion, and the costs thereof to be paid by the respondent.

(f) Service of Recommendation on and Review by Respondent. If a diversion recommendation is approved as provided in subdivision (d), the recommendation shall be served on the respondent who may accept or reject a diversion recommendation in the same manner as provided for review of recommendations of minor misconduct. The respondent shall not have the right to reject any specific requirement of a practice and professionalism enhancement program.

(g) Effect of Rejection of Recommendation by Respondent. In the event that a respondent rejects a diversion recommendation the matter shall be returned for further proceedings under these rules.

(h) Diversion at Trial Level.

(1) *Agreement of the Parties.* A referee may recommend diversion of a disciplinary case to a practice and professionalism enhancement program if the bar

approves diversion and the respondent agrees. The procedures for approval of conditional pleas provided elsewhere in these rules shall apply to diversion at the trial level.

(2) *After Submission of Evidence.* A referee may recommend diversion of a disciplinary case to a practice and professionalism enhancement program if, after submission of evidence, but before a finding of guilt, the referee determines that, if proven, the conduct alleged to have been committed by the respondent is not more serious than minor misconduct.

(3) *Costs of Practice and Professionalism Enhancement Program.* A referee's recommendation of diversion to a practice and professionalism enhancement program shall state the costs thereof to be paid by the respondent.

(4) *Appeal of Diversion Recommendation.* The respondent and the bar shall have the right to appeal a referee's recommendation of diversion, except in the case of diversion agreed to under subdivision (h)(1).

(5) *Authority of Referee to Refer a Matter to a Practice and Professionalism Enhancement Program.* Nothing in this rule shall preclude a referee from referring a disciplinary matter to a practice and professionalism enhancement program as a part of a disciplinary sanction.

(i) Effect of Diversion. When the recommendation of diversion becomes final, the respondent shall enter the practice and professionalism enhancement program(s) and complete the requirements thereof. Upon respondent's entry into a practice and professionalism enhancement program, the bar shall terminate its investigation into the matter and its disciplinary files shall be closed indicating the diversion. Diversion into the practice and professionalism enhancement program shall not constitute a disciplinary sanction.

(j) Effect of Completion of the Practice and Professionalism Enhancement Program. If a respondent successfully completes all requirements of the practice and professionalism enhancement program(s) to which the respondent was diverted, the bar's file shall remain closed.

(k) Effect of Failure to Complete the Practice and Professionalism Enhancement Program. If a respondent fails to fully complete all requirements of the practice and professionalism enhancement program(s) to which the respondent was diverted, including the payment of costs thereof, the bar may reopen its disciplinary file and conduct further proceedings under these rules. Failure to complete the practice and professionalism enhancement program shall be considered as a matter of aggravation when imposing a disciplinary sanction.

(*l*) Costs of Practice and Professionalism Enhancement Programs. The Florida Bar shall annually determine the costs of practice and professionalism enhancement programs and publish the amount of the costs thereof that shall be assessed against and paid by a respondent.

Added Oct. 20, 1994 (644 So.2d 282). Amended April 25, 2002 (820 So.2d 210); May 20, 2004 (875 So.2d 448); June 11, 2015, effective Oct. 1, 2015 (167 So.3d 412).

Comment

As to subdivision (c) of 3-5.3, a lawyer who agreed to attend the Advertising Workshop in 1 year would not be eligible for another such diversion for an advertising violation for a period of 5 years following the first diversion. However, that same lawyer would be eligible to attend the Advertising Workshop 1 year and a Trust Account Workshop for a completely different violation 1 year after the first diversion is completed.

Rule 3-5.4. Publication of Discipline

(a) Nature of Sanctions. All disciplinary sanctions, as defined in rules 3-5.1 and 3-5.2, or their predecessors, of these Rules Regulating The Florida Bar in disciplinary cases opened after March 16, 1990 are public information. Admonishments for minor misconduct entered in disciplinary cases opened on or before March 16, 1990 are confidential.

(b) Disclosure on Inquiry. All public disciplinary sanctions shall be disclosed upon inquiry.

(c) Manner of Publication. Unless otherwise directed by the court, and subject to the exceptions set forth below, all public disciplinary sanctions may be published for public information in print or electronic media.

(d) Limited Exception for Admonishments Issued by the Supreme Court of Florida. All admonishments issued by the court containing the heading "Not to be Published" shall not be published in the official court reporter and shall not be published in *The Florida Bar News*.

"Not to be Published" does not have the same meaning as "confidential." The Florida Bar may post information regarding specific orders of admonishment on the Bar's website. Further, the Bar may provide information regarding an admonishment upon inquiry.

Added Nov. 19, 2009, effective Feb. 1, 2010 (24 So.3d 63).

Comment

All disciplinary sanctions as defined in rules 3-5.1 and 3-5.2, or their predecessors, entered in cases opened on or after March 17, 1990 are public information. Therefore, an inquiry into the conduct of a member of the bar will result in a disclosure of all such sanctions.

The public policy of this state is to provide reasonable means of access to public information. In furtherance of this policy, this rule is enacted so that all persons may understand what public information concerning lawyer disciplinary sanctions is available and in what format. This rule does not alter current court procedure or other requirements.

Admonishments are issued for minor misconduct and are the lowest form of disciplinary sanction. An admonishment is often issued for technical rule violations or for rule violations that did not result in harm. The court's orders imposing admonishments contain the heading "Not to be Published" and this rule directs that those admonishments not be published in *Southern Reporter* and directs The Florida Bar not to publish those admonishments in its newspaper, *The Florida Bar News*. The court does so in order to maintain a tangible difference between the sanctions of admonishment and public reprimand.

This rule does not bar disclosure of admonishments upon inquiry, whether written, oral, or electronic, and does not bar publication of admonishments on any website of The Florida Bar.

3–6. EMPLOYMENT OF CERTAIN LAWYERS OR FORMER LAWYERS

Rule 3–6.1. Generally

(a) Authorization and Application. Except as limited in this rule, persons or entities providing legal services may employ suspended lawyers and former lawyers who have been disbarred or whose disciplinary resignations or disciplinary revocations have been granted by the Florida Supreme Court [for purposes of this rule such lawyers and former lawyers are referred to as "individual(s) subject to this rule"] to perform those services that may ethically be performed by nonlawyers employed by authorized business entities.

An individual subject to this rule is considered employed by an entity providing legal services if the individual is a salaried or hourly employee, volunteer worker, or an independent contractor providing services to the entity.

(b) Employment by Former Subordinates Prohibited for a Period of 3 Years. An individual subject to this rule may not, for a period of 3 years from the entry of the order pursuant to which the suspension, disciplinary revocation, or disbarment became effective, or until the individual is reinstated or readmitted to the practice of law, whichever occurs sooner, be employed by or work under, the supervision of another lawyer who was supervised by the individual at the time of or subsequent to the acts giving rise to the order.

(c) Notice of Employment Required. Before employment commences, the entity must provide The Florida Bar with a notice of employment and a detailed description of the intended services to be provided by the individual subject to this rule.

(d) Prohibited Conduct.

(1) *Direct Client Contact.* Individuals subject to this rule must not have direct contact with any client. Direct client contact does not include the participation of the individual as an observer in any meeting, hearing, or interaction between a supervising lawyer and a client.

(2) *Trust Funds or Property.* Individuals subject to this rule must not receive, disburse, or otherwise handle trust funds or property.

(3) *Practice of Law.* Individuals subject to this rule must not engage in conduct that constitutes the practice of law and such individuals must not hold themselves out as being eligible to do so.

(e) Quarterly Reports by Individual and Employer Required. The individual subject to this rule and employer must submit sworn information reports to The Florida Bar. Such reports must be filed quarterly, based on the calendar year, and include statements that no aspect of the work of the individual subject to this rule has involved the unlicensed practice of law, that the individual subject to this rule has had no direct client contact, that the individual subject to this rule did not receive, disburse, or otherwise handle trust funds or property, and that the individual subject to this rule is not being supervised by a lawyer whom the individual subject to this rule supervised within the 3 years immediately previous to the date of the suspension, disbarment, disciplinary resignation, or disciplinary revocation.

Amended March 16, 1990, effective March 17, 1990 (558 So.2d 1008); July 23, 1992, effective Jan. 1, 1993 (605 So.2d 252); Sept. 24, 1998, effective Oct. 1, 1998 (718 So.2d 1179); May 20, 2004 (875 So.2d 448); Oct. 6, 2005, effective Jan. 1, 2006 (916 So.2d 655); Dec. 20, 2007, effective March 1, 2008 (978 So.2d 91); Nov. 19, 2009, effective Feb. 1, 2010 (24 So.3d 63); April 12, 2012, effective July 1, 2012 (101 So.3d 807); May 29, 2014, effective June 1, 2014 (140 So.3d 541).

3–7. PROCEDURES

Rule 3–7.1. Confidentiality

Text of rule effective until October 1, 2015. See, also, rule effective October 1, 2015.

(a) Scope of Confidentiality. All matters including files, preliminary investigation reports, interoffice memoranda, records of investigations, and the records in trials and other proceedings under these rules, except those disciplinary matters conducted in circuit courts, are property of The Florida Bar. All of those matters are confidential and will not be disclosed except as provided in these rules. When disclosure is permitted under these rules, it will be limited to information concerning the status of the proceedings and any information that is part of the public record as defined in these rules.

Unless otherwise ordered by this court or the referee in proceedings under these rules, nothing in these rules will prohibit the complainant, respondent, or any witness from disclosing the existence of proceedings under these rules, or from disclosing any documents or correspondence served on or provided to those persons.

(1) *Pending Investigations.* Disciplinary matters pending at the initial investigatory and grievance committee levels are treated as confidential by The Florida Bar, except as provided in rules 3–7.1(e) and (k).

(2) *Minor Misconduct Cases.* Any case in which a finding of minor misconduct has been entered by action of the grievance committee or board is public information.

(3) *Probable Cause Cases.* Any disciplinary case in which a finding of probable cause for further disciplinary proceedings has been entered is public information. For purposes of this subdivision a finding of probable cause is deemed in those cases authorized by rule 3–3.2(a), for the filing of a formal complaint without the prior necessity of a finding of probable cause.

(4) *No Probable Cause Cases.* Any disciplinary case that has been concluded by a finding of no probable cause for further disciplinary proceedings is public information.

(5) *Diversion or Referral to Grievance Mediation Program.* Any disciplinary case that has been concluded by diversion to a practice and professionalism enhancement program or by referral to the grievance mediation program is public information upon the entry of such a recommendation.

(6) *Contempt Cases.* Contempt proceedings authorized elsewhere in these rules are public information even though the underlying disciplinary matter is confidential as defined in these rules.

(7) *Incapacity Not Involving Misconduct.* Proceedings for placement on the inactive list for incapacity not involving misconduct are public information upon the filing of the petition with the Supreme Court of Florida.

(8) *Petition for Emergency Suspension or Probation.* Proceedings seeking a petition for emergency suspension or probation are public information.

(9) *Proceedings on Determination or Adjudication of Guilt of Criminal Misconduct.* Proceedings on determination or adjudication of guilt of criminal misconduct, as provided elsewhere in these rules, are public information.

(10) *Professional Misconduct in Foreign Jurisdiction.* Proceedings based on disciplinary sanctions entered by a foreign court or other authorized disciplinary agency, as provided elsewhere in these rules, are public information.

(11) *Reinstatement Proceedings.* Reinstatement proceedings, as provided elsewhere in these rules, are public information.

(12) *Disciplinary Resignations.* Proceedings involving petitions for disciplinary resignation, as provided elsewhere in these rules, are public information.

(b) Public Record. The public record consists of the record before a grievance committee, the record before a referee, the record before the Supreme Court of Florida, and any reports, correspondence, papers, recordings, and/or transcripts of hearings furnished to, served on, or received from the respondent or the complainant.

(c) Circuit Court Proceedings. Proceedings under rule 3–3.5 are public information.

(d) Limitations on Disclosure. Any material provided to The Florida Bar that is confidential under applicable law will remain confidential and will not be disclosed except as authorized by the applicable law. If this type of material is made a part of the public record, that portion of the public record may be sealed by the grievance committee chair, the referee, or the Supreme Court of Florida.

The procedure for maintaining the required confidentiality is set forth in subdivision (m) below.

(e) Response to Inquiry. Authorized representatives of The Florida Bar will respond to specific inquiries concerning matters that are in the public domain, but otherwise confidential under the rules, by acknowledging the status of the proceedings.

(f) Notice to Law Firms. When a disciplinary file is opened the respondent must disclose to the respondent's current law firm and, if different, the respondent's law firm at the time of the act or acts giving rise to the complaint, the fact that a disciplinary file has been opened. Disclosure must be in writing and in the following form:

> A complaint of unethical conduct against me has been filed with The Florida Bar. The nature of the allegations are ________. This notice is provided pursuant to rule 3–7.1(f) of the Rules Regulating The Florida Bar.

The notice must be provided within 15 days of notice that a disciplinary file has been opened and a copy of the above notice must be served on The Florida Bar.

(g) Production of Disciplinary Records Pursuant to Subpoena. The Florida Bar, pursuant to a valid subpoena issued by a regulatory agency, may provide any documents that are a portion of the public record, even if the disciplinary proceeding is confidential under these rules. The Florida Bar may charge a reasonable fee for identification of and photocopying the documents.

(h) Notice to Judges. Any judge of a court of record upon inquiry of the judge will be advised and, absent an inquiry, may be advised as to the status of a confidential disciplinary case and may be provided with a copy of documents in the file that would be part of the public record if the case was not confidential. The judge must maintain the confidentiality of the records and not otherwise disclose the status of the case.

(i) Evidence of Crime. The confidential nature of these proceedings does not preclude the giving of any information or testimony to authorities authorized to investigate alleged criminal activity.

(j) Chemical Dependency and Psychological Treatment. That a lawyer has voluntarily sought, received, or accepted treatment for chemical dependency or psychological problems is confidential and will not be admitted as evidence in disciplinary proceedings under these rules unless agreed to by the attorney who sought the treatment.

For purposes of this subdivision, a lawyer is deemed to have voluntarily sought, received, or accepted treatment for chemical dependency or psychological problems if the lawyer was not under compulsion of law or rule to do so, or if the treatment is not a part of conditional admission to The Florida Bar or of a disciplinary sanction imposed under these rules.

It is the purpose of this subdivision to encourage lawyers to voluntarily seek advice, counsel, and treatment available to lawyers, without fear that the fact it is sought or rendered will or might cause embarrassment in any future disciplinary matter.

(k) Response to False or Misleading Statements. If public statements that are false or misleading are made about any otherwise confidential disciplinary case, The Florida Bar may disclose all information necessary to correct such false or misleading statements.

(*l*) Disclosure by Waiver of Respondent. Upon written waiver executed by a respondent, The Florida Bar may disclose the status of otherwise confidential disciplinary proceedings and provide copies of the public record to:

(1) the Florida Board of Bar Examiners or the comparable body in other jurisdictions for the purpose of evaluating the character and fitness of an applicant for admission to practice law in that jurisdiction; or

(2) Florida judicial nominating commissions or the comparable body in other jurisdictions for the purpose of evaluating the character and fitness of a candidate for judicial office; or

(3) The Florida Bar Board of Legal Specialization and Education and any of its certification committees for the purpose of evaluating the character and fitness of a candidate for board certification or recertification; or

(4) the governor of the State of Florida for the purpose of evaluating the character and fitness of a nominee to judicial office.

(m) Maintaining Confidentiality Required by Rule or Law. The bar will maintain confidentiality of documents and records in its possession and control as required by applicable federal or state law in accordance with the requirements of Fla. R. Jud. Admin. 2.420. It will be the duty of respondents and other persons submitting documents and information to the bar to notify bar staff that such documents or information contain material that is exempt from disclosure under applicable rule or law and to request that such exempt material be protected and not be considered public record. Requests to exempt from disclosure all or part of any documents or records must be accompanied by reference to the statute or rule applicable to the information for which exemption is claimed.

Amended Oct. 22, 1987, effective Jan. 1, 1988 (519 So.2d 971); March 16, 1990, effective March 17, 1990 (558 So.2d 1008); Oct. 10, 1991, effective Jan. 1, 1992 (587 So.2d 1121); July 23, 1992, effective Jan. 1, 1993 (605 So.2d 252); Oct. 20, 1994 (644 So.2d 282); Feb. 8, 2001 (795 So.2d 1); May 20, 2004 (875 So.2d 448); Oct. 6, 2005, effective Jan. 1, 2006 (916 So.2d 655); July 7, 2011, effective Oct. 1, 2011 (67 So.3d 1037); May 29, 2014, effective June 1, 2014 (140 So.3d 541).

Rule 3–7.1. Confidentiality

Text of rule effective October 1, 2015. See, also, rule effective until October 1, 2015.

(a) Scope of Confidentiality. All records including files, preliminary investigation reports, interoffice memoranda, records of investigations, and the records in trials and other proceedings under these rules, except those disciplinary matters conducted in circuit courts, are property of The Florida Bar. All of those matters are confidential and will not be disclosed except as provided in these rules. When disclosure is permitted under these rules, it will be limited to information concerning the status of the proceedings and any information that is part of the public record as defined in these rules.

Unless otherwise ordered by this court or the referee in proceedings under these rules, nothing in these rules prohibits the complainant, respondent, or any witness from disclosing the existence of proceedings under these rules, or from disclosing any documents or correspondence served on or provided to those persons except where disclosure is prohibited in Chapter 4 of these rules or by statutes and caselaw regarding attorney-client privilege.

(1) *Pending Investigations.* Disciplinary matters pending at the initial investigatory and grievance committee levels are treated as confidential by The Florida Bar, except as provided in rules 3–7.1(e) and (k).

(2) *Minor Misconduct Cases.* Any case in which a finding of minor misconduct has been entered by action of the grievance committee or board is public information.

(3) *Probable Cause Cases.* Any disciplinary case in which a finding of probable cause for further disciplinary proceedings has been entered is public information. For purposes of this subdivision a finding of probable cause is deemed in those cases authorized by rule 3–3.2(a), for the filing of a formal complaint without the requirement of a finding of probable cause.

(4) *No Probable Cause Cases.* Any disciplinary case that has been concluded by a finding of no probable cause for further disciplinary proceedings is public information.

(5) *Diversion or Referral to Grievance Mediation Program.* Any disciplinary case that has been concluded by diversion to a practice and professionalism enhancement program or by referral to the grievance mediation program is public information on the entry of such a recommendation.

(6) *Contempt Cases.* Contempt proceedings authorized elsewhere in these rules are public information even if the underlying disciplinary matter is confidential as defined in these rules.

(7) *Incapacity Not Involving Misconduct.* Proceedings for placement on the inactive list for incapacity not involving misconduct are public information on the filing of the petition with the Supreme Court of Florida.

(8) *Petition for Emergency Suspension or Probation.* Proceedings seeking a petition for emergency suspension or probation are public information.

(9) *Proceedings on Determination or Adjudication of Guilt of Criminal Misconduct.* Proceedings on determination or adjudication of guilt of criminal misconduct, as provided elsewhere in these rules, are public information.

(10) *Professional Misconduct in Foreign Jurisdiction.* Proceedings based on disciplinary sanctions entered by a foreign court or other authorized disciplinary agency, as provided elsewhere in these rules, are public information.

(11) *Reinstatement Proceedings.* Reinstatement proceedings, as provided elsewhere in these rules, are public information.

(12) *Disciplinary Resignations and Disciplinary Revocations.* Proceedings involving petitions for disciplinary resignation or for disciplinary revocation as provided elsewhere in these rules, are public information.

(b) Public Record. The public record consists of the record before a grievance committee, the record before a referee, the record before the Supreme Court of Florida, and any reports, correspondence, papers, recordings, and/or transcripts of hearings furnished to, served on, or received from the respondent or the complainant.

(c) Circuit Court Proceedings. Proceedings under rule 3–3.5 are public information.

(d) Limitations on Disclosure. Any material provided to The Florida Bar that is confidential under applicable law will remain confidential and will not be disclosed except as authorized by the applicable law. If this type of material is made a part of the public record, that portion of the public record may be sealed by the grievance committee chair, the referee, or the Supreme Court of Florida.

The procedure for maintaining the required confidentiality is set forth in subdivision (m) below.

(e) Response to Inquiry. Authorized representatives of The Florida Bar will respond to specific inquiries concerning matters that are in the public domain, but otherwise confidential under the rules, by acknowledging the status of the proceedings.

(f) Notice to Law Firms. When a disciplinary file is opened the respondent must disclose to the respondent's current law firm and, if different, the respondent's law firm at the time of the act or acts giving rise to the complaint, the fact that a disciplinary file has been opened. Disclosure must be in writing and in the following form:

> A complaint of unethical conduct against me has been filed with The Florida Bar. The nature of the allegations are __________. This notice is provided pursuant to rule 3–7.1(f) of the Rules Regulating The Florida Bar.

The notice must be provided within 15 days of notice that a disciplinary file has been opened and a copy of the above notice must be served on The Florida Bar.

(g) Production of Disciplinary Records Pursuant to Subpoena. The Florida Bar, pursuant to a valid subpoena issued by a regulatory agency, may provide any documents that are a portion of the public record, even if the disciplinary proceeding is confidential under these rules. The Florida Bar may charge a reasonable fee for identification of and photocopying the documents.

(h) Notice to Judges. Any judge of a court of record upon inquiry of the judge will be advised and, absent an inquiry, may be advised as to the status of a confidential disciplinary case and may be provided with a copy of documents in the file that would be part of the public record if the case was not confidential. The judge must maintain the confidentiality of the records and not otherwise disclose the status of the case.

(i) Evidence of Crime. The confidential nature of these proceedings does not preclude the giving of any information or testimony to authorities authorized to investigate alleged criminal activity.

(j) Chemical Dependency and Psychological Treatment. That a lawyer has voluntarily sought, received, or accepted treatment for chemical dependency or psychological problems is confidential and will not be admitted as evidence in disciplinary proceedings under these rules unless agreed to by the attorney who sought the treatment.

For purposes of this subdivision, a lawyer is deemed to have voluntarily sought, received, or accepted treatment for chemical dependency or psychological problems if the lawyer was not under compulsion of law or rule to do so, or if the treatment is not a part of conditional admission to The Florida Bar or of a disciplinary sanction imposed under these rules.

It is the purpose of this subdivision to encourage lawyers to voluntarily seek advice, counsel, and treatment available to lawyers, without fear that the fact it is sought or rendered will or might cause embarrassment in any future disciplinary matter.

(k) Response to False or Misleading Statements. If public statements that are false or misleading are made about any otherwise confidential disciplinary case, The Florida Bar may disclose all information necessary to correct such false or misleading statements.

(*l*) Disclosure by Waiver of Respondent. Upon written waiver executed by a respondent, The Florida Bar may disclose the status of otherwise confidential disciplinary proceedings and provide copies of the public record to:

(1) the Florida Board of Bar Examiners or the comparable body in other jurisdictions for the purpose of evaluating the character and fitness of an applicant for admission to practice law in that jurisdiction; or

(2) Florida judicial nominating commissions or the comparable body in other jurisdictions for the purpose of evaluating the character and fitness of a candidate for judicial office; or

(3) The Florida Bar Board of Legal Specialization and Education and any of its certification committees for the purpose of evaluating the character and fitness of a candidate for board certification or recertification; or

(4) the governor of the State of Florida for the purpose of evaluating the character and fitness of a nominee to judicial office.

(m) Maintaining Confidentiality Required by Rule or Law. The bar will maintain confidentiality of documents and records in its possession and control as required by applicable federal or state law in accordance with the requirements of Fla. R. Jud. Admin. 2.420. It will be the duty of respondents and other persons submitting documents and information to the bar to notify bar staff that such documents or information contain material that is exempt from disclosure under applicable rule or law and to request that such exempt material be protected and not be considered public record. Requests to exempt from disclosure all or part of any documents or records must be accompanied by reference to the statute or rule applicable to the information for which exemption is claimed.

Amended Oct. 22, 1987, effective Jan. 1, 1988 (519 So.2d 971); March 16, 1990, effective March 17, 1990 (558 So.2d 1008); Oct. 10, 1991, effective Jan. 1, 1992 (587 So.2d 1121); July 23, 1992, effective Jan. 1, 1993 (605 So.2d 252); Oct. 20, 1994 (644 So.2d 282); Feb. 8, 2001 (795 So.2d 1); May 20, 2004 (875 So.2d 448); Oct. 6, 2005, effective Jan. 1, 2006 (916 So.2d 655); July 7, 2011, effective Oct. 1, 2011 (67 So.3d 1037); May 29, 2014, effective June 1, 2014 (140 So.3d 541); May 21, 2015, effective Oct. 1, 2015 (164 So.3d 1217).

Rule 3–7.2. Procedures Upon Criminal or Professional Misconduct; Discipline Upon Determination or Judgment of Guilt of Criminal Misconduct; Discipline on Removal from Judicial Office

(a) Definitions.

(1) *Judgment of Guilt.* For the purposes of these rules, "judgment of guilt" includes only those cases in which the trial court in the criminal proceeding enters an order adjudicating the respondent guilty of the offense(s) charged.

(2) *Determination of Guilt.* For the purposes of these rules, "determination of guilt" includes those cases in which the trial court in the criminal proceeding enters an order withholding adjudication of the respondent's guilt of the offense(s) charged, those cases in which the convicted lawyer has entered a plea of guilty to criminal charges, those cases in which the convicted lawyer has entered a no contest plea to criminal charges, those cases in which the jury has rendered a verdict of guilty of criminal charges, and those cases in which the trial judge in a bench trial has rendered a verdict of guilty of criminal charges.

(3) *Convicted Lawyer.* For the purposes of these rules, "convicted lawyer" means a lawyer who has had either a determination or judgment of guilt entered by the trial court in the criminal proceeding.

(b) Determination or Judgment of Guilt, Admissibility; Proof of Guilt. Determination or judgment of guilt of a member of The Florida Bar by a court of competent jurisdiction upon trial of or plea to any crime under the laws of this state, or under the laws under which any other court making such determination or entering such judgment exercises its jurisdiction, is admissible in proceedings under these rules and is conclusive proof of guilt of the criminal offense(s) charged for the purposes of these rules.

(c) Notice of Institution of Felony Criminal Charges. Upon the institution of a felony criminal charge against a member of The Florida Bar by the filing of an indictment or information the member must within 10 days of the institution of the felony criminal charges notify the executive director of The Florida Bar of such charges. Notice includes a copy of the document(s) evidencing institution of the charges.

If the state attorney whose office is assigned to a felony criminal case is aware that the defendant is a member of The Florida Bar, the state attorney must provide a copy of the indictment or information to the executive director.

(d) Notice of Determination or Judgment of Guilt of Felony Charges.

(1) *Trial Judge.* If any such determination or judgment is entered in a court of the State of Florida, the trial judge must, within 10 days of the date on which the determination or judgment is entered, give notice to the executive director of The Florida Bar and include a certified copy of the document(s) on which the determination or judgment was entered.

(2) *Clerk of Court.* If any such determination or judgment is entered in a court of the State of Florida, the clerk of that court must, within 10 days of the date on which the determination or judgment is entered, give notice to the executive director and include a certified copy of the document(s) on which the determination or judgment was entered.

(3) *State Attorney.* If the state attorney whose office is assigned to a felony criminal case is aware that the defendant is a member of The Florida Bar, the state attorney must give notice of the determination or judgment of guilt to the executive director and include a copy of the document(s) evidencing such determination or judgment.

(e) Notice by Members of Determination or Judgment of Guilt of All Criminal Charges. A member of The Florida Bar must within 10 days of entry of a determination or judgment for any criminal offense, which was entered on or after August 1, 2006, notify the executive director of The Florida Bar of such determination or judgment. Notice must include a copy of the document(s) on which such determination or judgment was entered.

(f) Suspension by Judgment of Guilt (Felonies). Upon receiving notice that a member of the bar has been determined to be or adjudicated guilty of a felony, the bar will file a "Notice of Determination or Judgment of Guilt" or a consent judgment for disbarment or disciplinary revocation in the Supreme Court of Florida. A copy of the document(s) on which the determination or judgment is based must be attached to the notice. Upon the filing of the notice with the Supreme Court of Florida and service of such notice upon the respondent, the respondent is suspended as a member of The Florida Bar as defined in rule 3–5.1(e).

(g) Petition to Modify or Terminate Suspension. At any time after the filing of a notice of determination or judgment of guilt, the respondent may file a petition with the Supreme Court of Florida to modify or terminate such suspension and must serve a copy of the petition on the executive director. The filing of such petition will not operate as a stay of the suspension imposed under the authority of this rule.

(h) Appointment of Referee. Upon the entry of an order of suspension, as provided above, the supreme court must promptly appoint or direct the appointment of a referee.

(1) *Hearing on Petition to Terminate or Modify Suspension.* The referee must hear a petition to terminate or modify a suspension imposed under this rule within 7 days of appointment and submit a report and recommendation to the Supreme Court of Florida within 7 days of the date of the hearing. The referee will recommend termination or modification of the suspension only if the suspended member can demonstrate that the member is not the convicted person or that the criminal offense is not a felony.

(2) *Hearing on Sanctions.* In addition to conducting a hearing on a petition to terminate or modify a suspension entered under this rule, the referee may also hear argument concerning the appropriate sanction to be imposed and file a report and recommendation with the supreme court in the same manner and form as provided in rule 3–7.6(m) of these rules. The hearing must be held and a report and recommendation filed with the supreme court within 90 days of assignment as referee.

The respondent may challenge the imposition of a sanction only on the grounds of mistaken identity or whether the conduct involved constitutes a felony under applicable law. The respondent may present relevant character evidence and relevant matters of mitigation regarding the proper sanction to be imposed. The respondent cannot contest the findings of guilt in the criminal proceedings. A respondent who entered a plea in the criminal proceedings is allowed to explain the circumstances concerning the entry of the plea for purposes of mitigation.

The report and recommendations of the referee may be reviewed in the same manner as provided in rule 3–7.7 of these rules.

(i) Appeal of Conviction. If an appeal is taken by the respondent from the determination or judgment in the criminal proceeding, the suspension will remain in effect during the appeal. If on review the cause is remanded for further proceedings, the suspension will remain in effect until the final disposition of the criminal cause unless modified or terminated by the Supreme Court of Florida as elsewhere provided.

Further, the suspension imposed will remain in effect until civil rights have been restored and until the respondent is reinstated.

(j) Expunction. Upon motion of the respondent, the Supreme Court of Florida may expunge a sanction entered under this rule when a final disposition of the criminal cause has resulted in acquittal or dismissal. A respondent who is the subject of a sanction that is expunged under this rule may lawfully deny or fail to acknowledge the sanction, except when the respondent is a candidate for election or appointment to judicial office, or as otherwise required by law.

(k) Waiver of Time Limits. The respondent may waive the time requirements set forth in this rule by written request made to and approved by the referee or supreme court.

(*l*) Professional Misconduct in Foreign Jurisdiction.

(1) *Notice of Discipline by a Foreign Jurisdiction.* A member of The Florida Bar who has submitted a disciplinary resignation or otherwise surrendered a license to practice law in lieu of disciplinary sanction, or has been disbarred or suspended from the practice of law by a court or other authorized disciplinary agency of another state or by a federal court must within 30 days after the effective date of the disciplinary resignation, disbarment or suspension file with the Supreme Court of Florida and the executive director of The Florida Bar a copy of the order or judgment effecting such disciplinary resignation, disbarment or suspension.

(2) *Effect of Adjudication or Discipline by a Foreign Jurisdiction.* On petition of The Florida Bar supported by a copy of a final adjudication by a foreign court or disciplinary authority, the Supreme Court of Florida may issue an order suspending on an emergency basis the member who is the subject of the final adjudication. All of the conditions not in conflict with this rule applicable to issuance of emergency suspension orders elsewhere within these Rules Regulating The Florida Bar are applicable to orders entered under this rule.

(m) Discipline Upon Removal From Judicial Office.

(1) *Notice of Removal.* If an order of the Supreme Court of Florida removes a member of The Florida Bar from judicial office for judicial misconduct, the clerk of the supreme court will forward a copy of the order of removal to the executive director of The Florida Bar.

(2) *Filing of Formal Complaint.* Upon receipt of an order removing a member from judicial office for judicial misconduct, the bar may file a formal complaint with the court and seek appropriate discipline.

(3) *Admissibility of Order; Conclusive Proof of Facts.* The order of removal is admissible in proceedings under these rules and is conclusive proof of the facts on which the judicial misconduct was found by the court.

(4) *Determination of Lawyer Misconduct.* The issue of whether the facts establishing the judicial misconduct also support a finding of lawyer misconduct are determined by the referee based on the record of the proceedings.

Amended July 23, 1992, effective Jan. 1, 1993 (605 So.2d 252); Sept. 24, 1998, effective Oct. 1, 1998 (718 So.2d 1179); April 25, 2002 (820 So.2d 210); May 12, 2005, effective January 1, 2006 (907 So.2d 1138); June 29, 2006, effective August 1, 2006 (933 So.2d 498); April 5, 2007 (954 So.2d 15); Nov. 19, 2009, effective Feb. 1, 2010 (24 So.3d 63); May 29, 2014, effective June 1, 2014 (140 So.3d 541).

Rule 3–7.3. Review of Inquiries, Complaint Processing, and Initial Investigatory Procedures

(a) Screening of Inquiries. Prior to opening a disciplinary file, bar counsel shall review the inquiry made and determine whether the alleged conduct, if proven, would constitute a violation of the Rules Regulating The Florida Bar warranting the imposition of discipline. If bar counsel determines that the facts allege a fee dispute which, if proven, would probably not constitute a clear violation under these rules, bar counsel may, with the consent of the complainant and respondent, refer the matter to The Florida Bar Grievance Mediation and Fee Arbitration Program under chapter 14. If bar counsel determines that the facts, if proven, would not constitute a violation of the Rules Regulating The Florida Bar warranting the imposition of discipline, bar counsel may decline to pursue the inquiry. A decision by bar counsel not to pursue an inquiry shall not preclude further action or review under the Rules Regulating The Florida Bar. The complainant and respondent shall be notified of a decision not to pursue an inquiry and shall be given the reasons therefor.

(b) Complaint Processing and Bar Counsel Investigation. If bar counsel decides to pursue an inquiry, a disciplinary file shall be opened and the inquiry shall be considered as a complaint, if the form requirement of subdivision (c) is met. Bar counsel shall investigate the allegations contained in the complaint.

(c) Form for Complaints. All complaints, except those initiated by The Florida Bar, shall be in writing and under oath. The complaint shall contain a statement providing:

Under penalty of perjury, I declare the foregoing facts are true, correct, and complete.

(d) Dismissal of Disciplinary Cases. Bar counsel may dismiss disciplinary cases if, after complete investigation, bar counsel determines that the facts show that the respondent did not violate the Rules Regulating The Florida Bar. Dismissal by bar counsel shall not preclude further action or review under the Rules Regulating The Florida Bar. Nothing in these rules shall preclude bar counsel from obtaining the concurrence of the grievance committee chair on the dismissal of a case or on dismissal of the case with issuance of a letter of advice as described elsewhere in these Rules Regulating The Florida Bar. If a disciplinary case is dismissed, the complainant shall be notified of the dismissal and shall be given the reasons therefor.

(e) Diversion to Practice and Professionalism Enhancement Programs. Bar counsel may recommend diversion of disciplinary cases as provided elsewhere in these rules if, after complete investigation, bar counsel determines that the facts show that the respondent's conduct did not constitute disciplinary violations more severe than minor misconduct.

(f) Referral to Grievance Committees. Bar counsel may refer disciplinary cases to a grievance committee for its further investigation or action as authorized elsewhere in these rules. Bar counsel may recommend specific action on a case referred to a grievance committee.

(g) Information Concerning Closed Inquiries and Complaints Dismissed by Staff. When bar counsel does not pursue an inquiry or dismisses a disciplinary case, such action shall be deemed a finding of no probable cause for further disciplinary proceedings and the matter shall become public information.

Added March 16, 1990, effective March 17, 1990 (558 So.2d 1008). Amended July 23, 1992, effective Jan. 1, 1993 (605 So.2d 252); Oct. 20, 1994 (644 So.2d 282); Sept. 24, 1998, effective Oct. 1, 1998 (718 So.2d 1179); July 7, 2011, effective Oct. 1, 2011 (67 So.3d 1037).

Rule 3–7.4. Grievance Committee Procedures

(a) Notice of Hearing. When notice of a grievance committee hearing is sent to the respondent, such notice shall be accompanied by a list of the grievance committee members.

(b) Complaint Filed With Grievance Committee. A complaint received by a committee direct from a complainant shall be reported to the appropriate bar counsel for docketing and assignment of a case number, unless the committee resolves the complaint within 10 days after receipt of the complaint. A written report to bar counsel shall include the following information: complainant's name and address, respondent's name, date complaint received by committee, copy of complaint letter or summary of the oral complaint made, and the name of the committee member assigned to the investigation. Formal investigation by a grievance committee may proceed after the matter has been referred to bar counsel for docketing.

(c) Investigation. A grievance committee is required to consider all charges of misconduct forwarded to the committee by bar counsel whether based upon a written complaint or not.

(d) Conduct of Proceedings. The proceedings of grievance committees may be informal in nature and the committees shall not be bound by the rules of evidence.

(e) No Delay for Civil or Criminal Proceedings. An investigation shall not be deferred or suspended without the approval of the board even though the respondent is made a party to civil litigation or is a defendant or is acquitted in a criminal action, notwithstanding that either of such proceedings involves the subject matter of the investigation.

(f) Counsel and Investigators. Upon request of a grievance committee, staff counsel may appoint a bar counsel or an investigator to assist the committee in an investigation. Bar counsel shall assist each grievance committee in carrying out its investigative and administrative duties and shall prepare status reports for the committee, notify complainants and respondents of committee actions as appropriate, and prepare all reports reflecting committee findings of probable cause, no probable cause, recommended discipline for minor misconduct, and letters of advice after no probable cause findings.

(g) Quorum, Panels, and Vote.

(1) *Quorum.* Three members of the committee, 2 of whom must be lawyers, shall constitute a quorum.

(2) *Panels.* The grievance committee may be divided into panels of not fewer than 3 members, 2 of whom must be lawyers. Division of the grievance committee into panels shall only be upon concurrence of the designated reviewer and the chair of the grievance committee. The 3–member panel shall elect 1 of its lawyer members to preside over the panel's actions. If the chair or vice-chair is a member of a 3–member panel, the chair or vice-chair shall be the presiding officer.

(3) *Vote.* All findings of probable cause and recommendations of guilt of minor misconduct shall be made by affirmative vote of a majority of the committee members present, which majority must number at least 2 members. There shall be no required minimum number of lawyer members voting in order to satisfy the requirements of this rule. The number of committee members voting for or against the committee report shall be recorded. Minority reports may be filed. A lawyer grievance committee member may not vote on the disposition of any matter in which that member served as the investigating member of the committee.

(h) Rights and Responsibilities of the Respondent. The respondent may be required to testify and to produce evidence as any other witness unless the respondent claims a privilege or right properly available to the respondent under applicable federal or state law. The respondent may be accompanied by counsel. At a reasonable time before any finding of probable cause or minor misconduct is made, the respondent shall be advised of the conduct that is being investigated and the rules that may have been violated. The respondent shall be provided with all materials considered by the committee and shall be given an opportunity to make a written statement, sworn or unsworn, explaining, refuting, or admitting the alleged misconduct.

(i) Rights of the Complaining Witness. The complaining witness is not a party to the disciplinary proceeding. Unless it is found to be impractical by the chair of the grievance committee due to unreasonable delay or other good cause, the complainant shall be granted the right to be present at any grievance committee hearing when the respondent is present before the committee. Neither unwillingness nor neglect of the complaining witness to cooperate, nor settlement, compromise, or restitution, will excuse the completion of an investigation. The complaining witness shall have no right to appeal.

(j) Finding of No Probable Cause.

(1) *Authority of Grievance Committee.* A grievance committee may terminate an investigation by finding that no probable cause exists to believe that the respondent has violated these rules. The committee may issue a letter of advice to the respondent in connection with the finding of no probable cause.

(2) *Notice of Committee Action.* Bar counsel shall notify the respondent and complainant of the action of the committee.

(3) *Effect of No Probable Cause Finding.* A finding of no probable cause by a grievance committee shall not preclude the reopening of the case and further proceedings therein.

(4) *Disposition of Committee Files.* Upon the termination of the grievance committee's investigation, the committee's file shall be forwarded to bar counsel for disposition in accord with established bar policy.

(k) Letter Reports in No Probable Cause Cases. Upon a finding of no probable cause, bar counsel will submit a letter report of the no probable cause finding to the complainant, presiding member, investigating member, and the respondent, including any documentation deemed appropriate by bar counsel and explaining why the complaint did not warrant further proceedings. Letters of advice issued by a grievance committee in connection with findings of no probable cause shall be signed by the presiding member of the committee. Letter reports and letters of advice shall not constitute a disciplinary sanction.

***(l)* Preparation, Forwarding, and Review of Grievance Committee Complaints.** If a grievance committee or the board of governors finds probable cause, the bar counsel assigned to the committee shall promptly prepare a record of its investigation and a formal complaint. The record before the committee shall consist of all reports, correspondence, papers, and/or recordings furnished to or received from the respondent, and the transcript of grievance committee meetings or hearings, if the proceedings were attended by a court reporter; provided, however, that the committee may retire into private session to debate the issues involved and to reach a decision as to the action to be taken. The formal complaint shall be approved by the member of the committee who presided in the proceeding. The formal complaint shall be in such form as shall be prescribed by the board. If the presiding member of the grievance committee disagrees with the form of the complaint, the presiding member may direct bar counsel to make changes accordingly. If bar counsel does not agree with the changes, the matter shall be referred to the designated reviewer of the committee for appropriate action. When a formal complaint by a grievance committee is not referred to the designated reviewer, or is not returned to the grievance committee for further action, the formal complaint shall be promptly forwarded to and reviewed by staff counsel. Staff counsel shall file the formal complaint and furnish a copy to the respondent. Staff counsel shall request the Chief Justice of the Supreme Court of Florida to assign a referee or to order the chief judge of the appropriate circuit to assign a referee to try the cause. A copy of the record shall be made available to the respondent at the respondent's expense.

If, at any time before the filing of a formal complaint, bar counsel, staff counsel, and the designated reviewer all agree that appropriate reasons indicate that the formal complaint should not be filed, the case may be returned to the grievance committee for further action.

(m) Recommendation of Admonishment for Minor Misconduct. If the committee recommends an admonishment for minor misconduct, the grievance committee report shall be drafted by bar counsel and signed by the presiding member. The committee report need only include: (1) the committee's recommendations regarding the admonishment, revocation of certification, and conditions of recertification; (2) the committee's recommendation as to the method of administration of the admonishment; (3) a summary of any additional charges that will be dismissed if the admonishment is approved; (4) any comment on mitigating, aggravating, or evidentiary matters that the committee believes will be helpful to the board in passing upon the admonishment recommendation; and (5) an admission of minor misconduct signed by the respondent, if the respondent has admitted guilt to minor misconduct. No record need be submitted with such a report. After the presiding member signs the grievance committee report, the report shall be returned to bar counsel. The report recommending an admonishment shall be forwarded to staff counsel and the designated reviewer for review. If staff counsel does not return the report to the grievance committee to remedy a defect therein, or if the designated reviewer does not present the same to the disciplinary review committee for action by the board, the report shall then be served on the respondent by bar counsel.

(n) Rejection of Admonishment. The order of admonishment shall become final unless rejected by the respondent within 15 days after service upon the respondent. If rejected by the respondent, the report shall be referred to bar counsel and referee for trial on complaint of minor misconduct to be prepared by bar counsel as in the case of a finding of probable cause.

***(o)* Recommendation of Diversion to Remedial Programs.** A grievance committee may recommend, as an alternative to issuing a finding of minor misconduct or no probable cause with a letter of advice, diversion of the disciplinary case to a practice and professionalism enhancement program as provided elsewhere in these rules. A respondent may reject the diversion recommendation in the same manner as provided in the rules applicable to rejection of findings of minor misconduct. In the event that a respondent rejects a recommendation of diversion, the matter shall be returned to the committee for further proceedings.

Former Rule 3–7.3 renumbered as Rule 3–7.4 and amended March 16, 1990, effective March 17, 1990 (558 So.2d 1008). Amended July 23, 1992, effective Jan. 1, 1993 (605 So.2d 252); Oct. 20, 1994 (644 So.2d 282); June 27, 1996, effective July 1, 1996 (677 So.2d 272); Feb. 8, 2001 (795 So.2d 1); April 25, 2002 (820 So.2d 210); Oct. 6, 2005, effective Jan. 1, 2006 (916 So.2d 655); Nov. 19, 2009, effective Feb. 1, 2010 (24 So.3d 63); July 7, 2011, effective Oct. 1, 2011 (67 So.3d 1037).

Rule 3–7.5. Procedures before the Board of Governors

(a) Review by the Designated Reviewer. Notice of grievance committee action recommending either diversion to a practice and professionalism enhancement program or finding no probable cause, no probable cause with a letter of advice, minor misconduct, or probable cause shall be given to the designated reviewer for review. The designated reviewer may request grievance committee reconsideration or refer the matter to the disciplinary review committee of the board of governors within 30 days of notice of grievance committee action. The request for a grievance committee reconsideration or referral to the disciplinary review committee shall be in writing and shall be submitted to bar counsel. For purposes of this subdivision letters, memoranda, handwritten notes, facsimile documents, and email shall constitute "in writing."

(1) *Requests for Grievance Committee Reconsideration.* If the designated reviewer requests grievance committee reconsideration, bar counsel shall forward the request to the chair of the grievance committee and shall give notice to the respondent and complainant that the request has been made. If the grievance committee agrees to reconsider the matter, the rule prescribing procedures before a grievance committee shall apply.

(2) *Referrals to Disciplinary Review Committee and Board of Governors.* If the designated reviewer refers the matter to the disciplinary review committee, bar counsel shall prepare and submit a discipline agenda item for consideration by the committee. Bar counsel shall give notice to respondent and complainant that the designated reviewer has made the referral for review.

(3) *Nature of Disciplinary Review Committee and Board of Governors Review.* The Florida Bar is a party in disciplinary proceedings and has no authority to adjudicate rights in those proceedings. Any such review on referral from a designated reviewer is in the nature of consultation on pending litigation and therefore is not subject to intervention by persons outside the relationship between the bar and its counsel.

(4) *Effect of Failure to Timely Make the Request for Reconsideration or Referral for Review.* If the designated reviewer fails to make the request for reconsideration or referral within the time prescribed, the grievance committee action shall become final.

(5) *Authority of Designated Reviewer to Make Recommendations.* When the designated reviewer makes a request for reconsideration or referral for review, the designated reviewer may recommend:

(A) referral of the matter to the grievance mediation program;

(B) referral of the matter to the fee arbitration program;

(C) closure of the disciplinary file by diversion to a component of the practice and professionalism enhancement program;

(D) closure of the disciplinary file by the entry of a finding of no probable cause;

(E) closure of the disciplinary file by the entry of a finding of no probable cause with a letter of advice;

(F) a finding of minor misconduct; or

(G) a finding of probable cause that further disciplinary proceedings are warranted.

(b) Review of Grievance Committee Matters. The disciplinary review committee shall review those grievance committee matters referred to it by a designated reviewer and shall make a report to the board. The disciplinary review committee may confirm, reject, or amend the recommendation of the designated reviewer in whole or in part. The report of the disciplinary review committee shall be final unless overruled by the board. Recommendations of the disciplinary review committee may include:

(1) referral of the matter to the grievance mediation program;

(2) referral of the matter to the fee arbitration program;

(3) closure of the disciplinary file by diversion to a component of the practice and professionalism enhancement program;

(4) closure of the disciplinary file by the entry of a finding of no probable cause;

(5) closure of the disciplinary file by the entry of a finding of no probable cause with a letter of advice;

(6) a finding of minor misconduct; or

(7) a finding of probable cause that further disciplinary proceedings are warranted.

(c) Board Action on Review of Designated Reviewer Recommendations. On review of a report and recommendation of the disciplinary review committee, the board of governors may confirm, reject, or amend the recommendation in whole or in part. Action by the board may include:

(1) referral of the matter to the grievance mediation program;

(2) referral of the matter to the fee arbitration program;

(3) closure of the disciplinary file by diversion to a component of the practice and professionalism enhancement program;

(4) closure of the disciplinary file by the entry of a finding of no probable cause;

(5) closure of the disciplinary file by the entry of a finding of no probable cause with a letter of advice;

(6) a finding of minor misconduct; or

(7) a finding of probable cause that further disciplinary proceedings are warranted.

(d) Notice of Board Action. Bar counsel shall give notice of board action to the respondent, complainant, and grievance committee.

(e) Finding of No Probable Cause. A finding of no probable cause by the board shall be final and no further proceedings shall be had in the matter by The Florida Bar.

(f) Control of Proceedings. Bar counsel, however appointed, shall be subject to the direction of the board at all times. The board, in the exercise of its discretion as the governing body of The Florida Bar, has the power to terminate disciplinary proceedings before a referee prior to the receipt of evidence by the referee, whether such proceedings have been instituted upon a finding of probable cause by the board or a grievance committee.

(g) Filing Service on Board of Governors. All matters to be filed with or served upon the board shall be addressed to the board of governors and filed with the executive director. The executive director or his designees shall be the custodians of the official records of The Florida Bar.

Former Rule 3–7.4 renumbered as Rule 3–7.5 and amended March 16, 1990, effective March 17, 1990 (558 So.2d 1008). Amended July 23, 1992, effective Jan. 1, 1993 (605 So.2d 252); April 25, 2002 (820 So.2d 210); May 20, 2004 (875 So.2d 448); Dec. 20, 2007, effective March 1, 2008 (978 So.2d 91); July 7, 2011, effective Oct. 1, 2011 (67 So.3d 1037).

Rule 3–7.6. Procedures Before a Referee

(a) Referees.

(1) *Appointment.* The chief justice shall have the power to appoint referees to try disciplinary cases and to delegate to a chief judge of a judicial circuit the power to appoint referees for duty in the chief judge's circuit. Such appointees shall ordinarily be active county or circuit judges, but the chief justice may appoint retired judges.

(2) *Minimum Qualifications.* To be eligible for appointment as a referee under this rule the judge must have previously served as a judicial referee in proceedings instituted under these rules before February 1, 2010, at 12:01 a.m., or must have received the referee training materials approved by the Supreme Court of Florida and certified to the chief judge that the training materials have been reviewed.

(b) Trial by Referee. When a finding has been made by a grievance committee or by the board that there is cause to believe that a member of The Florida Bar is guilty of misconduct justifying disciplinary action, and the formal complaint based on such finding of probable cause has been assigned by the chief justice for trial before a referee, the proceeding thereafter shall be an adversary proceeding that shall be conducted as hereinafter set forth.

(c) Pretrial Conference. Within 60 days of the order assigning the case to the referee, the referee shall conduct a pretrial conference. The purpose of the conference is to set a schedule for the proceedings, including discovery deadlines and a final hearing date. The referee shall enter a written order in the proceedings reflecting the schedule determined at the conference.

(d) Venue. The trial shall be held in the county in which an alleged offense occurred or in the county where the respondent resides or practices law or last practiced law in Florida, whichever shall be designated by the Supreme Court of Florida; provided, however, that if the respondent is not a resident of Florida and if the alleged offense is not committed in Florida, the trial shall be held in a county designated by the chief justice.

(e) Style of Proceedings. All proceedings instituted by The Florida Bar shall be styled "The Florida Bar, Complainant, v. ....(name of respondent).........., Respondent," and "In The Supreme Court of Florida (Before a Referee)."

(f) Nature of Proceedings.

(1) *Administrative in Character.* A disciplinary proceeding is neither civil nor criminal but is a quasi-judicial administrative proceeding. The Florida Rules of Civil Procedure apply except as otherwise provided in this rule.

(2) *Discovery.* Discovery shall be available to the parties in accordance with the Florida Rules of Civil Procedure.

(g) Bar Counsel. Bar counsel shall make such investigation as is necessary and shall prepare and prosecute with utmost diligence any case assigned.

(h) Pleadings. Pleadings may be informal and shall comply with the following requirements:

(1) *Complaint; Consolidation and Severance.*

(A) Filing. The complaint shall be filed in the Supreme Court of Florida.

(B) Content. The complaint shall set forth the particular act or acts of conduct for which the attorney is sought to be disciplined.

(C) Joinder of Charges and Respondents; Severance. A complaint may embrace any number of charges against 1 or more respondents, and charges may be against any 1 or any number of respondents; but a severance may be granted by the referee when the ends of justice require it.

(2) *Answer and Motion.* The respondent shall answer the complaint and, as a part thereof or by separate motion, may challenge only the sufficiency of the complaint and the jurisdiction of the forum. All other defenses shall be incorporated in the respondent's answer. The answer may invoke any proper privilege, immunity, or disability available to the respondent. All pleadings of the respondent must be filed within 20 days of service of a copy of the complaint.

(3) *Reply.* If the respondent's answer shall contain any new matter or affirmative defense, a reply thereto may be filed within 10 days of the date of service of a copy upon bar counsel, but failure to file such a reply shall not prejudice The Florida Bar. All affirmative allegations in the respondent's answer shall be considered as denied by The Florida Bar.

(4) *Disposition of Motions.* Hearings upon motions may be deferred until the final hearing, and, whenever heard, rulings thereon may be reserved until termination of the final hearing.

(5) *Filing and Service of Pleadings.*

(A) Prior to Appointment of Referee. Any pleadings filed in a case prior to appointment of a referee shall be filed with the Supreme Court of Florida and shall bear a certificate of service showing parties upon whom service of copies has been made. On appointment of referee, the Supreme Court of Florida shall notify the parties of such appointment and forward all pleadings filed with the court to the referee for action.

(B) After Appointment of Referee. All pleadings, motions, notices, and orders filed after appointment of a referee shall be filed with the referee and shall bear a certificate of service showing service of a copy on staff counsel and bar counsel of The Florida Bar and on all interested parties to the proceedings.

(6) *Amendment.* Pleadings may be amended by order of the referee, and a reasonable time shall be given within which to respond thereto.

(7) *Expediting the Trial.* If it shall be made to appear that the date of final hearing should be expedited in the public interest, the referee may, in the referee's discretion, shorten the time for filing pleadings and the notice requirements as provided in this rule.

(8) *Disqualification of Referee.* A referee may be disqualified from service in the same manner and to the same extent that a trial judge may be disqualified under existing law from acting in a judicial capacity. In the event of a disqualification, the chief judge of the appropriate circuit shall appoint a successor referee from that same circuit.

(i) Notice of Final Hearing. The cause may be set down for trial by either party or the referee upon not less than 10 days' notice. The trial shall be held as soon as possible following the expiration of 10 days from the filing of the respondent's answer, or if no answer is filed, then from the date when such answer is due.

(j) The Respondent. Unless the respondent claims a privilege or right properly available under applicable federal or state law, the respondent may be called as a witness by The Florida Bar to make specific and complete disclosure of all matters material to the issues. When the respondent is subpoenaed to appear and give testimony or to produce books, papers, or documents and refuses to answer or to produce such books, papers, or documents, or, having been duly sworn to testify, refuses to answer any proper question, the respondent may be cited for contempt of the court.

(k) Complaining Witness. The complaining witness is not a party to the disciplinary proceeding, and shall have no rights other than those of any other witness. However, unless it is found to be impractical due to unreasonable delay or other good cause, and after the complaining witness has testified during the case in chief, the referee may grant the complaining witness the right to be present at any hearing when the respondent is also present. A complaining witness may be called upon to testify and produce evidence as any other witness. Neither unwillingness nor neglect of the complaining witness to cooperate, nor settlement, compromise, or restitution will excuse failure to complete any trial. The complaining witness shall have no right to appeal.

***(l)* Parol Evidence.** Evidence other than that contained in a written attorney-client contract may not be used in proceedings conducted under the Rules Regulating The Florida Bar to vary the terms of that contract, except competent evidence other than that contained in a written fee contract may be used only if necessary to resolve issues of excessive fees or excessive costs.

(m) Referee's Report.

(1) *Contents of Report.* Within 30 days after the conclusion of a trial before a referee or 10 days after the referee receives the transcripts of all hearings, whichever is later, or within such extended period of time as may be allowed by the chief justice for good cause shown, the referee shall make a report and enter it as part of the record, but failure to enter the report in the time prescribed shall not deprive the referee of jurisdiction. The referee's report shall include:

(A) a finding of fact as to each item of misconduct of which the respondent is charged, which findings of fact shall enjoy the same presumption of correctness as the judgment of the trier of fact in a civil proceeding;

(B) recommendations as to whether the respondent should be found guilty of misconduct justifying disciplinary measures;

(C) recommendations as to the disciplinary measures to be applied;

(D) a statement of any past disciplinary measures as to the respondent that are on record with the executive director of The Florida Bar or that otherwise become known to the referee through evidence properly admitted by the referee during the course of the proceedings (after a finding of guilt, all evidence of prior disciplinary measures may be offered by bar counsel subject to appropriate objection or explanation by respondent); and

(E) a statement of costs incurred and recommendations as to the manner in which such costs should be taxed.

(2) *Filing.* The referee's report and record of proceedings shall in all cases be transmitted together to the Supreme Court of Florida. Copies of the report shall be served on the parties including staff counsel. Bar counsel will make a copy of the record, as furnished, available to other parties on request and payment of the actual costs of reproduction. The report of referee and record shall not be filed until the time for filing a motion to assess costs has expired and no motion has been filed or, if the motion was timely filed, until the motion has been considered and a ruling entered.

(n) The Record.

(1) *Recording of Testimony.* All hearings at which testimony is presented shall be attended by a court reporter who shall record all testimony. Transcripts of such testimony are not required to be filed in the matter, unless requested by a party, who shall pay the cost of transcription directly, or ordered by the referee, in which case the costs thereof are subject to assessment as elsewhere provided in these rules.

(2) *Contents.* The record shall include all items properly filed in the cause including pleadings, recorded testimony, if transcribed, exhibits in evidence, and the report of the referee.

(3) *Preparation and Filing.* The referee, with the assistance of bar counsel, shall prepare the record, certify that the record is complete, serve a copy of the index of the record on the respondent and The Florida Bar, and file the record with the office of the clerk of the Supreme Court of Florida.

(4) *Supplementing or Removing Items from the Record.* The respondent and The Florida Bar may seek to supplement the record or have items removed from the record by filing a motion with the referee for such purpose, provided such motion is filed within 15 days of the service of the index. Denial of a motion to supplement the record or to remove an item from the record may be reviewed in the same manner as provided for in the rule on appellate review under these rules.

***(o)* Plea of Guilty by Respondent.** At any time during the progress of disciplinary proceedings, a respondent may tender a plea of guilty.

(1) *Before Filing of Complaint.* If the plea is tendered before filing of a complaint by staff counsel, such plea shall be tendered in writing to the grievance committee or bar counsel.

(2) *After Filing of Complaint.* If the complaint has been filed against the respondent, the respondent may enter a plea of guilty thereto by filing the same in writing with the referee to whom the cause has been assigned for trial. Such referee shall take such testimony thereto as may be advised, following which the referee will enter a report as otherwise provided.

(3) *Unconditional.* An unconditional plea of guilty shall not preclude review as to disciplinary measures imposed.

(4) *Procedure.* Except as herein provided, all procedure in relation to disposition of the cause on pleas of guilty shall be as elsewhere provided in these rules.

(p) Cost of Review or Reproduction.

(1) The charge for reproduction, when photocopying or other reproduction is performed by the bar, for the purposes of these rules shall be as determined and published annually by the executive director. In addition to reproduction charges, the bar may charge a reasonable fee incident to a request to review disciplinary records or for research into the records of disciplinary proceedings and identification of documents to be reproduced.

(2) When the bar is requested to reproduce documents that are voluminous or is requested to produce transcripts in the possession of the bar, the bar may decline to reproduce the documents in the offices of the bar and shall inform the requesting person of the following options:

(A) purchase of the transcripts from the court reporter service that produced them;

(B) purchase of the documents from the third party from whom the bar received them; or

(C) designation of a commercial photocopy service to which the bar shall deliver the original documents to be copied, at the requesting party's expense, provided the photocopy service agrees to preserve and return the original documents and not to release them to any person without the bar's consent.

(q) Costs.

(1) *Taxable Costs.* Taxable costs of the proceedings shall include only:

(A) investigative costs, including travel and out-of-pocket expenses;

(B) court reporters' fees;

(C) copy costs;

(D) telephone charges;

(E) fees for translation services;

(F) witness expenses, including travel and out-of-pocket expenses;

(G) travel and out-of-pocket expenses of the referee;

(H) travel and out-of-pocket expenses of counsel in the proceedings, including of the respondent if acting as counsel; and

(I) an administrative fee in the amount of $1250 when costs are assessed in favor of the bar.

(2) *Discretion of Referee.* The referee shall have discretion to award costs and, absent an abuse of discretion, the referee's award shall not be reversed.

(3) *Assessment of Bar Costs.* When the bar is successful, in whole or in part, the referee may assess the bar's costs against the respondent unless it is shown that the costs of the bar were unnecessary, excessive, or improperly authenticated.

(4) *Assessment of Respondent's Costs.* When the bar is unsuccessful in the prosecution of a particular matter, the referee may assess the respondent's costs against the bar in the event that there was no justiciable issue of either law or fact raised by the bar.

(5) *Time for Filing Motion to Assess Costs.* A party shall file a statement of costs incurred in a referee proceeding and a request for payment of same within 15 days after written notice by the referee that the report of referee has been completed or at the time that a guilty plea for consent judgment is filed. Failure to timely file a motion, without good cause, shall be considered as a waiver of the right to request reimbursement of costs or to object to a request for reimbursement of costs. The party from whom costs are sought shall have 10 days from the date the motion was filed in which to serve an objection. Because costs may not be assessed against the respondent unless the bar is successful in some part and because costs may not be assessed against the bar unless the referee finds the lack of a justiciable issue of law or fact, this subdivision shall not be construed to require the filing of a motion to assess costs before the referee when doing so is not appropriate.

Amended April 20, 1989 (542 So.2d 982). Renumbered as Rule 3–7.6 and amended March 16, 1990, effective March 17, 1990 (558 So.2d 1008). Amended Feb. 13, 1992 (594 So.2d 735); July 23, 1992, effective Jan. 1, 1993 (605 So.2d 252); July 1, 1993 (621 So.2d 1032); Oct. 20, 1994 (644 So.2d 282); Sept. 24, 1998, effective Oct. 1, 1998 (718 So.2d 1179); March 23, 2000 (763 So.2d 1002); April 25, 2002 (820 So.2d 210); May 20, 2004 (875 So.2d 448); (Oct. 6, 2005, effective Jan. 1, 2006 (916 So.2d 655); Dec. 20, 2007, effective March 1, 2008 (978 So.2d 91); Nov. 19, 2009, effective Feb. 1, 2010 (24 So.3d 63); July 7, 2011, effective Oct. 1, 2011 (67 So.3d 1037).

Court Comment

A comprehensive referee's report under subdivision (m) is beneficial to a reviewing court so that the court need not make assumptions about the referee's intent or return the report to the referee for clarification. The referee's report should list and address each issue in the case and cite to available authority for the referee's recommendations concerning guilt and discipline.

Comment

Provisions for assessment of costs in proceedings before the Supreme Court of Florida are addressed in rule 3–7.7.

Rule 3–7.7. Procedures Before Supreme Court of Florida

All reports of a referee and all judgments entered in proceedings under these rules shall be subject to review by the Supreme Court of Florida in the following manner:

(a) Right of Review.

(1) Any party to a proceeding may procure review of a report of a referee or a judgment, or any specified portion thereof, entered under these rules.

(2) The Supreme Court of Florida shall review all reports and judgments of referees recommending probation, public reprimand, suspension, disbarment, or resignation pending disciplinary proceedings.

(3) A referee's report that does not recommend probation, public reprimand, suspension, disbarment, or resignation pending disciplinary proceedings, shall be final if not appealed.

(b) Appointment of Bar Counsel. The board or staff counsel, if authorized by the board, may appoint new or additional bar counsel to represent The Florida Bar on any review.

(c) Procedure for Review. Review by the Supreme Court of Florida shall be in accordance with the following procedures:

(1) *Notice of Intent to Seek Review of Report of Referee.* A party to a bar disciplinary proceeding wishing to seek review of a report of referee shall give notice of such intent within 60 days of the date on which the referee's report is docketed by the Clerk of the Supreme Court of Florida. Prompt written notice of the board's action, if any, shall be communicated to the respondent. The proceeding shall be commenced by filing with the Supreme Court of Florida notice of intent to seek review of a report of referee, specifying those portions of the report of a referee sought to be reviewed. Within 20 days after service of such notice of intent to seek review, the opposing party may file a cross-notice for review specifying any additional portion of the report that said party desires to be reviewed. The filing of such notice or cross-notice shall be jurisdictional as to a review to be procured as a matter of right, but the court may, in its discretion,

consider a late-filed notice or cross-notice upon a showing of good cause.

(2) *Record on Review.* The report and record filed by the referee shall constitute the record on review. If hearings were held at which testimony was heard, but no transcripts thereof were filed in the matter, the party seeking review shall order preparation of all such transcripts, file the original thereof with the court, and serve copies on the opposing party, on or before the time of filing of the initial brief, as provided elsewhere in this rule. The party seeking review shall be responsible for, and pay directly to the court reporter, the cost of preparation of transcripts. Failure to timely file and serve all of such transcripts may be cause for dismissal of the party's petition for review.

(3) *Briefs.* The party first seeking review shall file a brief in support of the notice of intent to seek review within 30 days of the filing of the notice. The opposing party shall file an answer brief within 20 days after the service of the initial brief of the party seeking review, which answer brief shall also support any cross-notice for review. The party originally seeking review may file a reply brief within 20 days after the service of the answer brief. The cross-reply brief, if any, shall be served within 20 days thereafter. Computation of time for filing briefs under this rule shall follow the applicable Florida Rules of Appellate Procedure. The form, length, binding, type, and margin requirements of briefs filed under this rule shall follow the requirements of Fla. R. App. P. 9.210.

(4) *Oral Argument.* Request for oral argument may be filed in any case wherein a party files a notice of intent to seek review at the time of filing the first brief. If no request is filed, the case will be disposed of without oral argument unless the court orders otherwise.

(5) *Burden.* Upon review, the burden shall be upon the party seeking review to demonstrate that a report of a referee sought to be reviewed is erroneous, unlawful, or unjustified.

(6) *Judgment of Supreme Court of Florida.*

(A) Authority. After review, the Supreme Court of Florida shall enter an appropriate order or judgment. If no review is sought of a report of a referee entered under the rules and filed in the court, the findings of fact shall be deemed conclusive and the disciplinary measure recommended by the referee shall be the disciplinary measure imposed by the court, unless the court directs the parties to submit briefs or oral argument directed to the suitability of the disciplinary measure recommended by the referee. A referee's report that becomes final when no review has been timely filed shall be reported in an order of the Supreme Court of Florida.

(B) Form. The judgment of the court shall include, where appropriate, judgment in favor of:

(i) the party to whom costs are awarded;

(ii) the person(s) to whom restitution is ordered; or

(iii) the person(s) to whom a fee is ordered to be forfeited.

(7) *Procedures on Motions to Tax Costs.* The court may consider a motion to assess costs if the motion is filed within 10 days of the entry of the court's order or opinion where the referee finds the respondent not guilty at trial and the supreme court, upon review, finds the respondent guilty of at least 1 rule violation and does not remand the case to the referee for further proceedings or where the respondent was found guilty at trial and the supreme court, upon review, finds the respondent not guilty of any rule violation. The party from whom costs are sought shall have 10 days from the date the motion was filed in which to serve an objection. Failure to timely file a petition for costs or to timely serve an objection, without good cause, shall be considered a waiver of request or objection to the costs and the court may enter an order without further proceedings. If an objection is timely filed, or the court otherwise directs, the motion shall be remanded to the referee. Upon remand, the referee shall file a supplemental report that shall include a statement of costs incurred and the manner in which the costs should be assessed. Any party may seek review of the supplemental report of referee in the same manner as provided for in this rule for other reports of the referee.

(d) Precedence of Proceedings. Notices of intent to seek review in disciplinary proceedings shall take precedence over all other civil causes in the Supreme Court of Florida.

(e) Extraordinary Writs. All applications for extraordinary writs that are concerned with disciplinary proceedings under these rules of discipline shall be made to the Supreme Court of Florida.

(f) Florida Rules of Appellate Procedure. To the extent necessary to implement this rule and if not inconsistent herewith, the Florida Rules of Appellate Procedure shall be applicable to notices of intent to seek review in disciplinary proceedings, provided service on The Florida Bar shall be accomplished by service on bar counsel and staff counsel.

(g) Contempt by Respondent. Whenever it is alleged that a respondent is in contempt in a disciplinary proceeding, a petition for an order to show cause why the respondent should not be held in contempt and the proceedings on such petition may be filed in and determined by the Supreme Court of Florida or as provided under rule 3–7.11(f).

(h) Pending Disciplinary Cases. If disbarment or disciplinary revocation is ordered by the court, dismissal without prejudice of other pending cases against the respondent may be ordered in the court's disbarment or disciplinary revocation order.

Former Rule 3–7.6 renumbered as Rule 3–7.7 March 16, 1990, effective March 17, 1990 (558 So.2d 1008). Amended July 23, 1992, effective Jan. 1, 1993 (605 So.2d 252); Sept. 24, 1998, effective Oct. 1, 1998 (718 So.2d 1179); April 25, 2002 (820 So.2d 210); Nov. 19, 2009, effective Feb. 1, 2010 (24 So.3d 63); April 12, 2012, effective July 1, 2012 (101 So.3d 807).

Comment

Subdivision (c)(7) of this rule applies to situations which arise when a referee finds a respondent not guilty but the supreme court, on review, finds the respondent guilty and does not remand the case back to the referee for further proceedings. *See*, e.g., *The Florida Bar v. Pape*, 918 So.2d 240 (Fla. 2005). A similar situation may also occur where a respondent is found guilty at trial, but not guilty by the supreme court on review of the referee's report and recommendation.

Rule 3–7.8. Procedures before a circuit court

(a) Filing of Motion. Whenever it shall be made known to any of the judges of the district courts of appeal or any judge of a circuit court or a county court in this state that a member of The Florida Bar practicing in any of the courts of the district or judicial circuit or county has been guilty of any unprofessional act as defined by these rules, such judge may direct the state attorney for the circuit in which the alleged offense occurred to make in writing a motion in the name of the State of Florida to discipline such attorney, setting forth in the motion the particular act or acts of conduct for which the attorney is sought to be disciplined.

(b) Copy Served Upon Respondent. Upon the filing of a motion in circuit court to discipline an attorney, a copy thereof shall be served upon the respondent attorney, and the respondent shall, within 20 days after the service thereof, file an answer thereto. A copy of such motion shall be filed with the executive director of The Florida Bar at the time of service upon the respondent.

(c) Trial Before a Circuit Judge. Upon the filing of the answer, the chief judge of the judicial circuit in which the alleged offense occurred shall designate a judge other than the judge who directed the filing of the motion to try said cause. Such judge shall conduct a hearing thereon and shall hear the evidence to be offered by the State of Florida and the respondent. A representative or representatives of The Florida Bar, appointed by the board, shall have the right to be present and to observe the proceedings. Upon the conclusion of the hearing, the judge shall enter such judgment of dismissal, reprimand, probation, suspension, or disbarment as shall be appropriate to the circumstances. The parties shall be entitled to compulsory process to force the attendance of any witnesses.

(d) Judgment Filed in Supreme Court of Florida. If the judgment be one of public reprimand, probation, suspension, or disbarment, 3 certified copies of the same shall be forthwith filed by the clerk of the trial court with the clerk of the Supreme Court of Florida. The clerk of the Supreme Court of Florida shall retain one copy for the court's records, deliver to the executive director of The Florida Bar one copy of the judgment for The Florida Bar's official records, and shall forthwith serve the third copy upon the respondent.

(e) Petition for Appellate Review. The respondent may appeal from a judgment entered by a circuit court. Such appeal shall be made in the manner provided by rule 3–7.7.

(f) Duty to Expedite Proceedings. It shall be the duty of the state attorney who is directed to file said motion to file the same promptly and to dispose of said controversy expeditiously.

(g) Readmission or Reinstatement. Readmission or reinstatement of attorneys disbarred or suspended by proceedings in circuit courts shall be governed as elsewhere provided in these rules.

(h) Reporting Misconduct to The Florida Bar. Nothing herein shall be construed to discourage or restrict the right and responsibility of a judge to refer to The Florida Bar the conduct of its members, which in the opinion of the judge, warrants investigation to determine if a violation of the Rules of Professional Conduct has occurred.

Former Rule 3–7.7 renumbered as Rule 3–7.8 March 16, 1990, effective March 17, 1990 (558 So.2d 1008). Amended July 23, 1992, effective Jan. 1, 1993 (605 So.2d 252).

Rule 3–7.9. Consent Judgment

Text of rule effective until October 1, 2015. See, also, rule effective October 1, 2015.

(a) Before Formal Complaint is Filed. If before a formal complaint is filed a respondent states a desire to plead guilty, bar counsel shall consult established board guidelines for discipline and confer with the designated reviewer. If bar counsel or the designated reviewer rejects the proposed consent judgment, the matter shall not be referred to the board of governors. If bar counsel and the designated reviewer approve the proposed consent judgment, the respondent shall be advised that bar counsel and the designated reviewer will recommend approval of the respondent's written plea, and the matter shall be placed on the agenda of the board of governors for its review. If the board of governors concurs in the consent judgment, bar counsel shall notify the respondent and file all necessary pleadings to secure approval of the plea. If a proposed consent judgment is rejected, bar counsel shall prepare and file a complaint as provided elsewhere in these rules.

(b) After Filing of Formal Complaint. If a respondent states a desire to plead guilty to a formal complaint that has been filed, staff counsel shall consult established board guidelines for discipline and confer with the designated reviewer. If staff counsel or the designated reviewer rejects the proposed consent judgment, the plea shall not be filed with the referee. If staff counsel and the designated reviewer approve the proposed consent judgment, the respondent shall be advised that staff counsel and the designated reviewer will recommend approval of the respondent's written plea and the consent judgment shall be filed with the referee. If the referee accepts the consent judgment, the referee shall enter a report and file same with the court as provided elsewhere in these rules. If the referee rejects the consent judgment, the matter shall proceed as provided in this chapter.

(c) Approval of Consent Judgments. Acceptance of any proposed consent judgment shall be conditioned on final approval by the Supreme Court of Florida, and the court's order will recite the disciplinary charges against the respondent.

(d) Content of Conditional Pleas. All conditional pleas shall show clearly by reference or otherwise the disciplinary offenses to which the plea is made. All conditional pleas in which the respondent agrees to the imposition of a suspension or disbarment shall include an acknowledgment that, unless waived or modified by the court on motion of the respondent, the court order accepting the conditional plea will contain a provision that prohibits the respondent from accepting new business from the date of the order or opinion and shall provide that the suspension or disbarment is effective 30 days from the date of the order or opinion so that the respondent may close out the practice of law and protect the interests of existing clients.

(e) Disbarment on Consent. A respondent may surrender membership in The Florida Bar in lieu of defending against allegations of disciplinary violations by agreeing to disbarment on consent. Disbarment on consent shall have the same effect as, and shall be governed by, the same rules provided for disbarment elsewhere in these Rules Regulating The Florida Bar.

Matters involving disbarment on consent shall be processed in the same manner as set forth in subdivisions (a) through (d) of this rule and elsewhere in these Rules Regulating The Florida Bar, except that a respondent may enter into a disbarment on consent without admitting any of the facts or rule violations alleged by the bar. In such event, the disbarment on consent shall set forth a brief recitation of the allegations underlying the disbarment on consent. This option shall only be available for disbarments on consent and not for any other type of consent judgment.

(f) Effect of Pleas on Certification. In negotiating consent judgments with a respondent or in recommending acceptance, rejection, or offer of a tendered consent judgment, staff counsel and designated reviewer shall consider and express a recommendation on whether the consent judgment shall include revocation of certification if held by the attorney and restrictions to be placed on recertification in such areas. When certification revocation is agreed to in a consent judgment, the revocation and any conditions on recertification will be reported to the legal specialization and education director for recording purposes.

Former Rule 3–7.8 renumbered as Rule 3–7.9 March 16, 1990, effective March 17, 1990 (558 So.2d 1008). Amended July 23, 1992, effective Jan. 1, 1993 (605 So.2d 252); Sept. 24, 1998, effective Oct. 1, 1998 (718 So.2d 1179); April 25, 2002 (820 So.2d 210); May 20, 2004 (875 So.2d 448); Oct. 6, 2005, effective Jan. 1, 2006 (916 So.2d 655); March 22, 2007, effective June 1, 2007 (952 So.2d 1185); April 12, 2012, effective July 1, 2012 (101 So.3d 807).

Rule 3–7.9. Consent Judgment

Text of rule effective October 1, 2015. See, also, rule effective until October 1, 2015.

(a) Before Formal Complaint is Filed. If before a formal complaint is filed a respondent states a desire to plead guilty, bar counsel shall consult established board guidelines for discipline and confer with the designated reviewer. If bar counsel or the designated reviewer rejects the proposed consent judgment, the matter shall not be referred to the board of governors. If bar counsel and the designated reviewer approve the proposed consent judgment, the respondent shall be advised that bar counsel and the designated reviewer will recommend approval of the respondent's written plea, and the matter shall be placed on the agenda of the board of governors for its review. If the board of governors concurs in the consent judgment, bar counsel shall notify the respondent and file all necessary pleadings to secure approval of the plea. If a proposed consent judgment is rejected, bar counsel shall prepare and file a complaint as provided elsewhere in these rules.

(b) After Filing of Formal Complaint. If a respondent states a desire to plead guilty to a formal complaint that has been filed, staff counsel shall consult established board guidelines for discipline and confer with the designated reviewer. If staff counsel or the designated reviewer rejects the proposed consent judgment, the plea shall not be filed with the referee. If staff counsel and the designated reviewer approve the proposed consent judgment, the respondent shall be advised that staff counsel and the designated reviewer will recommend approval of the respondent's written plea and the consent judgment shall be filed with the referee. If the referee accepts the consent judgment, the referee shall enter a report and file same with the court as provided elsewhere in these rules. If the referee rejects the consent judgment, the matter shall proceed as provided in this chapter.

(c) Approval of Consent Judgments. Acceptance of any proposed consent judgment shall be conditioned on final approval by the Supreme Court of

Florida, and the court's order will recite the disciplinary charges against the respondent.

(d) Content of Conditional Pleas. All conditional pleas shall show clearly by reference or otherwise the disciplinary offenses to which the plea is made. All conditional pleas in which the respondent agrees to the imposition of a suspension or disbarment shall include an acknowledgment that, unless waived or modified by the court on motion of the respondent, the court order accepting the conditional plea will contain a provision that prohibits the respondent from accepting new business from the date of the order or opinion and shall provide that the suspension or disbarment is effective 30 days from the date of the order or opinion so that the respondent may close out the practice of law and protect the interests of existing clients. A conditional plea may not permit a respondent to begin serving a suspension or disbarment until the Supreme Court of Florida issues an order or opinion approving the recommended discipline.

(e) Disbarment on Consent. A respondent may surrender membership in The Florida Bar in lieu of defending against allegations of disciplinary violations by agreeing to disbarment on consent. Disbarment on consent shall have the same effect as, and shall be governed by, the same rules provided for disbarment elsewhere in these Rules Regulating The Florida Bar.

Matters involving disbarment on consent shall be processed in the same manner as set forth in subdivisions (a) through (d) of this rule and elsewhere in these Rules Regulating The Florida Bar, except that a respondent may enter into a disbarment on consent without admitting any of the facts or rule violations alleged by the bar. In such event, the disbarment on consent shall set forth a brief recitation of the allegations underlying the disbarment on consent. This option shall only be available for disbarments on consent and not for any other type of consent judgment.

(f) Effect of Pleas on Certification. In negotiating consent judgments with a respondent or in recommending acceptance, rejection, or offer of a tendered consent judgment, staff counsel and designated reviewer shall consider and express a recommendation on whether the consent judgment shall include revocation of certification if held by the attorney and restrictions to be placed on recertification in such areas. When certification revocation is agreed to in a consent judgment, the revocation and any conditions on recertification will be reported to the legal specialization and education director for recording purposes.

Former Rule 3–7.8 renumbered as Rule 3–7.9 March 16, 1990, effective March 17, 1990 (558 So.2d 1008). Amended July 23, 1992, effective Jan. 1, 1993 (605 So.2d 252); Sept. 24, 1998, effective Oct. 1, 1998 (718 So.2d 1179); April 25, 2002 (820 So.2d 210); May 20, 2004 (875 So.2d 448); Oct. 6, 2005, effective Jan. 1, 2006 (916 So.2d 655); March 22, 2007, effective June 1, 2007 (952 So.2d 1185); April 12, 2012, effective July 1, 2012 (101 So.3d 807); June 11, 2015, effective Oct. 1, 2015 (167 So.3d 1217).

Rule 3–7.10. Reinstatement and Readmission Procedures

Text of rule effective until October 1, 2015. See, also, rule effective October 1, 2015.

(a) Reinstatement; Applicability. A lawyer who is ineligible to practice due to a court-ordered disciplinary suspension of 91 days or more or who has been placed on the inactive list for incapacity not related to misconduct may be reinstated to membership in good standing in The Florida Bar and be eligible to practice again pursuant to this rule. The proceedings under this rule are not applicable to any lawyer who is not eligible to practice law due to a delinquency as defined in rule 1–3.6 of these rules.

(b) Petitions; Form and Contents.

(1) *Filing.* The original petition for reinstatement and 1 copy must be in writing, verified by the petitioner, and addressed to and filed with the Supreme Court of Florida. A copy must be served on Staff Counsel, The Florida Bar, 651 East Jefferson Street, Tallahassee, Florida 32399–2300.

(2) *Form and Exhibits.* The petition must be in such form and accompanied by such exhibits as provided for elsewhere in this rule. The information required concerning the petitioner may include any or all of the following matters in addition to such other matters as may be reasonably required to determine the fitness of the petitioner to resume the practice of law: criminal and civil judgments; disciplinary judgments; copies of income tax returns together with consents to secure original returns; occupation during suspension and employment information; financial statements; and statement of restitution of funds that were the subject matter of disciplinary proceedings. In cases seeking reinstatement from incapacity, the petition must also include copies of all pleadings in the matter leading to placement on the inactive list and all such other matters as may be reasonably required to demonstrate the character and fitness of the petitioner to resume the practice of law.

(c) Deposit for Cost. The petition must be accompanied by proof of a deposit paid to The Florida Bar in such amount as the board of governors prescribes to ensure payment of reasonable costs of the proceedings, as provided elsewhere in this rule.

(d) Reference of Petition For Hearing. The chief justice will refer the petition for reinstatement to a referee for hearing; provided, however, that no such reference will be made until evidence is submitted showing that all costs assessed against the petitioner in all disciplinary or incapacity proceedings have been paid and restitution has been made.

(e) Bar Counsel. When a petition for reinstatement is filed, the board of governors or staff counsel, if authorized by the board of governors, may appoint bar counsel to represent The Florida Bar in the proceeding. The duties of such lawyers are to appear at the hearings and to prepare and present to the referee evidence that, in the opinion of the referee or such lawyer, should be considered in passing upon the petition.

(f) Determination of Fitness by Referee Hearing. The referee to whom the petition for reinstatement is referred must conduct the hearing as a trial, in the same manner, to the extent practical, as provided elsewhere in these rules. The matter to decide is the fitness of the petitioner to resume the practice of law. In determining the fitness of the petitioner to resume the practice of law, the referee will consider whether the petitioner has engaged in any disqualifying conduct, the character and fitness of the petitioner, and whether the petitioner has been rehabilitated, as further described in this subdivision. All conduct engaged in after the date of admission to The Florida Bar is relevant in proceedings under this rule.

(1) *Disqualifying Conduct.* A record manifesting a deficiency in the honesty, trustworthiness, diligence, or reliability of a petitioner may constitute a basis for denial of reinstatement. The following are considered disqualifying conduct:

(A) unlawful conduct;

(B) academic misconduct;

(C) making or procuring any false or misleading statement or omission of relevant information, including any false or misleading statement or omission on any application requiring a showing of good moral character;

(D) misconduct in employment;

(E) acts involving dishonesty, fraud, deceit, or misrepresentation;

(F) abuse of legal process;

(G) financial irresponsibility;

(H) neglect of professional obligations;

(I) violation of an order of a court;

(J) evidence of mental or emotional instability;

(K) evidence of drug or alcohol dependency;

(L) denial of admission to the bar in another jurisdiction on character and fitness grounds;

(M) disciplinary action by a lawyer disciplinary agency or other professional disciplinary agency of any jurisdiction;

(N) failure of a felony-suspended lawyer to submit proof that the affected lawyer's civil rights have been restored; and

(O) any other conduct that reflects adversely upon the character or fitness of the applicant.

(2) *Determination of Character and Fitness.* In addition to other factors in making this determination, the following factors should be considered in assigning weight and significance to prior conduct:

(A) age at the time of the conduct;

(B) recency of the conduct;

(C) reliability of the information concerning the conduct;

(D) seriousness of the conduct;

(E) factors underlying the conduct;

(F) cumulative effect of the conduct or information;

(G) evidence of rehabilitation;

(H) positive social contributions since the conduct;

(I) candor in the discipline and reinstatement processes; and

(J) materiality of any omissions or misrepresentations.

(3) *Elements of Rehabilitation.* Merely showing that an individual is now living as and doing those things that should be done throughout life, although necessary to prove rehabilitation, does not prove that the individual has undertaken a useful and constructive place in society. Any petitioner for reinstatement from discipline for prior misconduct is required to produce clear and convincing evidence of such rehabilitation including, but not limited to, the following elements:

(A) strict compliance with the specific conditions of any disciplinary, judicial, administrative, or other order, where applicable;

(B) unimpeachable character and moral standing in the community;

(C) good reputation for professional ability, where applicable;

(D) lack of malice and ill feeling toward those who by duty were compelled to bring about the disciplinary, judicial, administrative, or other proceeding;

(E) personal assurances, supported by corroborating evidence, of a desire and intention to conduct one's self in an exemplary fashion in the future;

(F) restitution of funds or property, where applicable; and

(G) positive action showing rehabilitation by such things as a person's community or civic service. Community or civic service is donated service or activity that is performed by someone or a group of people for the benefit of the public or its institutions.

The requirement of positive action is appropriate for persons seeking reinstatement to the bar as well as for applicants for admission to the bar because service to one's community is an essential obligation of members of the bar.

(4) *Educational Requirements.*

(A) In the case of a petitioner's ineligibility to practice for a period of 3 years or longer under this rule, the petitioner must demonstrate to the referee that the petitioner is current with changes and developments in the law:

(i) The petitioner must have completed at least 10 hours of continuing legal education courses for each year or portion of a year that the petitioner was ineligible to practice.

(ii) The petitioner may further demonstrate that the petitioner is current with changes and developments in the law by showing that the petitioner worked as a law clerk or paralegal or taught classes on legal issues during the period of ineligibility to practice.

(B) A petitioner who has been ineligible to practice for 5 years or more will not be reinstated under this rule until the petitioner has re-taken and passed the Florida portions of the Florida Bar Examination and the Multistate Professional Responsibility Examination (MPRE).

(g) Hearing; Notice; Evidence.

(1) *Notice.* The referee to whom the petition for reinstatement is referred will fix a time and place for hearing, and notice will be provided at least 10 days prior to the hearing to the petitioner, to lawyers representing The Florida Bar, and to such other persons as may be designated by the referee to whom the petition is referred.

(2) *Appearance.* Any persons to whom notice is given, any other interested persons, or any local bar association may appear before the referee in support of or in opposition to the petition at any time or times fixed for the hearings.

(3) *Failure of Petitioner to be Examined.* For the failure of the petitioner to submit to examination as a witness pursuant to notice given, the referee will dismiss the petition for reinstatement unless good cause is shown for such failure.

(4) *Summary Procedure.* If after the completion of discovery bar counsel is unable to discover any evidence on which denial of reinstatement may be based and if no other person provides same, bar counsel may, with the approval of the designated reviewer and staff counsel, stipulate to the issue of reinstatement, including conditions for reinstatement. The stipulation must include a statement of costs as provided elsewhere in these Rules Regulating the Florida Bar.

(5) *Evidence of Treatment or Counseling for Dependency or Other Medical Reasons.* If the petitioner has sought or received treatment or counseling for chemical or alcohol dependency or for other medical reasons that relate to the petitioner's fitness to practice law, the petitioner must waive confidentiality of such treatment or counseling for purposes of evaluation of the petitioner's fitness. The provisions of rule 3–7.1(d) are applicable to information or records disclosed under this subdivision.

(h) Prompt Hearing; Report. The referee to whom a petition for reinstatement has been referred by the chief justice will proceed to a prompt hearing, at the conclusion of which the referee will make and file with the Supreme Court of Florida a report that includes the findings of fact and a recommendation as to whether the petitioner is qualified to resume the practice of law. The referee must file the report and record in the Supreme Court of Florida.

(i) Review. Review of referee reports in reinstatement proceedings must be in accordance with rule 3–7.7.

(j) Recommendation of Referee and Judgment of the Court. If the petitioner is found unfit to resume the practice of law, the petition will be dismissed. If the petitioner is found fit to resume the practice of law, the referee will enter a report recommending, and the court may enter an order of, reinstatement of the petitioner in The Florida Bar; provided, however, that the reinstatement may be conditioned upon the payment of all or part of the costs of the proceeding and upon the making of partial or complete restitution to parties harmed by the petitioner's misconduct that led to the petitioner's suspension of membership in The Florida Bar or conduct that led to the petitioner's incapacity; and further provided, however, if suspension or incapacity of the petitioner has continued for more than 3 years, the reinstatement may be conditioned upon the furnishing of such proof of competency as may be required by the judgment in the discretion of the Supreme Court of Florida, which proof may include certification by the Florida Board of Bar Examiners of the successful completion of an examination for admission to The Florida Bar subsequent to the date of the suspension or incapacity.

(k) Successive Petitions. No petition for reinstatement may be filed within 1 year following an adverse judgment upon a petition for reinstatement filed by or on behalf of the same person. In cases of incapacity no petition for reinstatement may be filed within 6 months following an adverse judgment under this rule.

(*l*) Petitions for Reinstatement to Membership in Good Standing.

(1) *Availability.* Petitions for reinstatement under this rule are available to members placed on the inactive list for incapacity not related to misconduct and suspended members of the bar when the disciplinary judgment conditions their reinstatement upon a showing of compliance with specified conditions.

(2) *Style of Petition.* Petitions must be styled in the Supreme Court of Florida and an original and 1 copy filed with the court. A copy must be served on Staff Counsel, The Florida Bar, 651 East Jefferson Street, Tallahassee, Florida 32399–2300.

(3) *Contents of Petition.* The petition must be verified by the petitioner and accompanied by a written authorization to the District Director of the Inter-

nal Revenue Service, authorizing the furnishing of certified copies of the petitioner's tax returns for the past 5 years or since admission to the bar, whichever is greater. The authorization must be furnished on a separate sheet. The petition must have attached as an exhibit a true copy of all disciplinary judgments previously entered against the petitioner. It must also include the petitioner's statement concerning the following:

(A) name, age, residence, address, and number and relation of dependents of the petitioner;

(B) the conduct, offense, or misconduct upon which the suspension or incapacity was based, together with the date of such suspension or incapacity;

(C) the names and addresses of all complaining witnesses in any disciplinary proceedings that resulted in suspension; and the name and address of the referee or judge who heard such disciplinary proceedings or of the trial judge, complaining witnesses, and prosecuting lawyer, if suspension was based upon conviction of a felony or misdemeanor involving moral turpitude;

(D) the nature of the petitioner's occupation in detail since suspension or incapacity, with names and addresses of all partners, associates in business, and employers, if any, and dates and duration of all such relations and employments;

(E) a statement showing the approximate monthly earnings and other income of the petitioner and the sources from which all such earnings and income were derived during said period;

(F) a statement showing all residences maintained during said period, with names and addresses of landlords, if any;

(G) a statement showing all financial obligations of the petitioner including but not limited to amounts claimed, unpaid, or owing to The Florida Bar Clients' Security Fund or former clients at the date of filing of the petition, together with the names and addresses of all creditors;

(H) a statement of restitution made for any and all obligations to all former clients and The Florida Bar Clients' Security Fund and the source and amount of funds used for this purpose;

(I) a statement showing dates, general nature, and ultimate disposition of every matter involving the arrest or prosecution of the petitioner during the period of suspension for any crime, whether felony or misdemeanor, together with the names and addresses of complaining witnesses, prosecuting lawyers, and trial judges;

(J) a statement as to whether any applications were made during the period of suspension for a license requiring proof of good character for its procurement; and, as to each such application, the date and the name and address of the authority to whom it was addressed and its disposition;

(K) a statement of any procedure or inquiry, during the period of suspension, covering the petitioner's standing as a member of any profession or organization, or holder of any license or office, that involved the censure, removal, suspension, revocation of license, or discipline of the petitioner; and, as to each, the dates, facts, and the disposition and the name and address of the authority in possession of the record;

(L) a statement as to whether any charges of fraud were made or claimed against the petitioner during the period of suspension, whether formal or informal, together with the dates and names and addresses of persons making such charges;

(M) a concise statement of facts claimed to justify reinstatement to The Florida Bar;

(N) a statement showing the dates, general nature, and final disposition of every civil action in which the petitioner was either a party plaintiff or defendant, together with dates of filing of complaints, titles of courts and causes, and the names and addresses of all parties and of the trial judge or judges, and names and addresses of all witnesses who testified in said action or actions; and

(O) a statement showing what amounts, if any, of the costs assessed against the accused lawyer in the prior disciplinary proceedings against the petitioner have been paid by the petitioner and the source and amount of funds used for this purpose.

(4) *Comments on Petition.* Upon the appointment of a referee and bar counsel, copies of the petition will be furnished by the bar counsel to local board members, local grievance committees, and to such other persons as are mentioned in this rule. Persons or groups that wish to respond must direct their comments to bar counsel. The proceedings and finding of the referee will relate to those matters described in this rule and also to those matters tending to show the petitioner's rehabilitation, present fitness to resume the practice of law, and the effect of such proposed reinstatement upon the administration of justice and purity of the courts and confidence of the public in the profession.

(5) *Costs Deposit.* The petition must be accompanied by a deposit for costs of $500.

(m) Costs.

(1) *Taxable Costs.* Taxable costs of the proceedings must include only:

(A) investigative costs, including travel and out-of-pocket expenses;

(B) court reporters' fees;

(C) copy costs;

(D) telephone charges;

(E) fees for translation services;

(F) witness expenses, including travel and out-of-pocket expenses;

(G) travel and out-of-pocket expenses of the referee;

(H) travel and out-of-pocket expenses of counsel in the proceedings, including the petitioner if acting as counsel; and

(I) an administrative fee in the amount of $1250 when costs are assessed in favor of the bar.

(2) *Discretion of Referee.* The referee has discretion to award costs and absent an abuse of discretion the referee's award will not be reversed.

(3) *Assessment of Bar Costs.* The costs incurred by the bar in any reinstatement case may be assessed against the petitioner unless it is shown that the costs were unnecessary, excessive, or improperly authenticated.

(4) *Assessment of Petitioner's Costs.* The referee may assess the petitioner's costs against the bar in the event that there was no justiciable issue of either law or fact raised by the bar unless it is shown that the costs were unnecessary, excessive, or improperly authenticated.

(n) Readmission; Applicability. A former member who has been disbarred, disbarred on consent, or whose petition for disciplinary resignation or revocation has been accepted may be admitted again only upon full compliance with the rules and regulations governing admission to the bar. No application for readmission following disbarment, disbarment on consent, or disciplinary resignation or revocation may be tendered until such time as all restitution and disciplinary costs as may have been ordered or assessed have been paid together with any interest accrued.

(1) *Readmission After Disbarment.* Except as might be otherwise provided in these rules, no application for admission may be tendered within 5 years after the date of disbarment or such longer period of time as the court might determine in the disbarment order. An order of disbarment that states the disbarment is permanent precludes readmission to The Florida Bar.

(2) *Readmission After Disciplinary Resignation or Revocation.* A lawyer's petition for disciplinary resignation or revocation that states that it is without leave to apply for readmission will preclude any readmission. A lawyer who was granted a disciplinary resignation or revocation may not apply for readmission until all conditions of the Supreme Court order granting the disciplinary resignation or revocation have been complied with.

Former Rule 3–7.9 renumbered as Rule 3–7.10 March 16, 1990, effective March 17, 1990 (558 So.2d 1008). Amended July 23, 1992, effective Jan. 1, 1993 (605 So.2d 252); July 1, 1993 (621 So.2d 1032); Oct. 20, 1994 (644 So.2d 282); July 17, 1997 (697 So.2d 115); Sept. 24, 1998, effective Oct. 1, 1998 (718 So.2d 1179); Feb. 8, 2001 (795 So.2d 1); April 25, 2002 (820 So.2d 210); July 3, 2003 (850 So.2d 499); May 20, 2004 (875 So.2d 448); Oct. 6, 2005, effective Jan. 1, 2006 (916 So.2d 655); April 12, 2012, effective July 1, 2012 (101 So.3d 807); May 29, 2014, effective June 1, 2014 (140 So.3d 541).

Comment

To further illuminate the community service requirements of Rule 3–7.10(f)(3)(G), bar members can take guidance from the Florida Supreme Court's decision in *Florida Board of Bar Examiners re M.L.B.*, 766 So. 2d 994, 998–999 (Fla. 2000). The court held that rules requiring community service "contemplate and we wish to encourage positive actions beyond those one would normally do for self benefit, including, but certainly not limited to, working as a guardian ad litem, volunteering on a regular basis with shelters for the homeless or victims of domestic violence, or maintaining substantial involvement in other charitable, community, or educational organizations whose value system, overall mission and activities are directed to good deeds and humanitarian concerns impacting a broad base of citizens."

Court decisions dealing with reinstatements and other discipline provide further guidance as to what specific actions meet the test of community service. The court approved dismissal of a petition for reinstatement where the respondent had no community service and had devoted all her time during suspension to raising her young children. *Fla. Bar v. Tauler*, 837 So. 2d 413 (Fla. 2003). In a more recent decision, the court did not specifically mention lack of community service in denying reinstatement, but the respondent had shown no evidence of work for others outside his family in his petition. Respondent's community service consisted solely of taking care of his elderly parents and his small child. *Fla. Bar v. Juan Baraque*, 43 So. 3d 691 (Fla. 2010).

Rule 3–7.10. Reinstatement and Readmission Procedures

Text of rule effective October 1, 2015. See, also, rule effective until October 1, 2015.

(a) Reinstatement; Applicability. A lawyer who is ineligible to practice due to a court-ordered disciplinary suspension of 91 days or more or who has been placed on the inactive list for incapacity not related to misconduct may be reinstated to membership in good standing in The Florida Bar and be eligible to practice again pursuant to this rule. The proceedings under this rule are not applicable to any lawyer who is not eligible to practice law due to a delinquency as defined in rule 1–3.6 of these rules.

(b) Petitions; Form and Contents.

(1) *Filing.* The original petition for reinstatement must be verified by the petitioner and filed with the Supreme Court of Florida in compliance with the Florida Rules of Civil Procedure and the Florida Rules of Judicial Administration. A copy must be served on Staff Counsel, The Florida Bar, in compliance with applicable court rules. The petition for reinstatement may not be filed until the petitioner has completed at least 80% of the term of that lawyer's period of suspension.

(2) *Form and Exhibits.* The petition must be in the form and accompanied by the exhibits provided for elsewhere in this rule. The information required concerning the petitioner may include any or all of the following matters in addition to any other matters that may be reasonably required to determine the fitness of the petitioner to resume the practice of law: criminal and civil judgments; disciplinary judgments; copies of income tax returns together with consents to secure original returns; occupation during suspension and employment related information; financial statements; and statement of restitution of funds that were the subject matter of disciplinary proceedings. In cases seeking reinstatement from incapacity, the petition must also include copies of all pleadings in the matter leading to placement on the inactive list and all other matters reasonably required to demonstrate the character and fitness of the petitioner to resume the practice of law.

(c) Deposit for Cost. The petition must be accompanied by proof of a deposit paid to The Florida Bar in the amount the board of governors prescribes to ensure payment of reasonable costs of the proceedings, as provided elsewhere in this rule.

(d) Reference of Petition for Hearing. The chief justice will refer the petition for reinstatement to a referee for hearing; provided, however, that no such referral will be made until evidence is submitted showing that all costs assessed against the petitioner in all disciplinary or incapacity proceedings have been paid and restitution has been made.

(e) Bar Counsel. When a petition for reinstatement is filed, the board of governors or staff counsel, if authorized by the board of governors, may appoint bar counsel to represent The Florida Bar in the proceeding. The lawyer's duty is to appear at the hearings and to prepare and present to the referee evidence that, in the opinion of the referee or lawyer, will be considered in passing upon the petition.

(f) Determination of Fitness by Referee Hearing. The referee to whom the petition for reinstatement is referred must conduct the hearing as a trial, in the same manner, to the extent practical, as provided elsewhere in these rules. The referee must decide the fitness of the petitioner to resume the practice of law. In making this determination, the referee will consider whether the petitioner has engaged in any disqualifying conduct, the character and fitness of the petitioner, and whether the petitioner has been rehabilitated, as further described in this subdivision. All conduct engaged in after the date of admission to The Florida Bar is relevant in proceedings under this rule.

(1) *Disqualifying Conduct.* A record manifesting a deficiency in the honesty, trustworthiness, diligence, or reliability of a petitioner may constitute a basis for denial of reinstatement. The following are considered disqualifying conduct:

(A) unlawful conduct;

(B) academic misconduct;

(C) making or procuring any false or misleading statement or omission of relevant information, including any false or misleading statement or omission on any application requiring a showing of good moral character;

(D) misconduct in employment;

(E) acts involving dishonesty, fraud, deceit, or misrepresentation;

(F) abuse of legal process;

(G) financial irresponsibility;

(H) neglect of professional obligations;

(I) violation of an order of a court;

(J) evidence of mental or emotional instability;

(K) evidence of drug or alcohol dependency;

(L) denial of admission to the bar in another jurisdiction on character and fitness grounds;

(M) disciplinary action by a lawyer disciplinary agency or other professional disciplinary agency of any jurisdiction;

(N) failure of a felony-suspended lawyer to submit proof that the affected lawyer's civil rights have been restored; and

(*O*) any other conduct that adversely reflects on the character or fitness of the applicant.

(2) *Determination of Character and Fitness.* In addition to other factors in making this determination, the following factors will be considered in assigning weight and significance to prior conduct:

(A) age at the time of the conduct;

(B) recency of the conduct;

(C) reliability of the information concerning the conduct;

(D) seriousness of the conduct;

(E) factors underlying the conduct;

(F) cumulative effect of the conduct or information;

(G) evidence of rehabilitation;

(H) positive social contributions since the conduct;

(I) candor in the discipline and reinstatement processes; and

(J) materiality of any omissions or misrepresentations.

(3) *Elements of Rehabilitation.* Merely showing that an individual is now living as and doing those things that should be done throughout life, although necessary to prove rehabilitation, does not prove that the individual has undertaken a useful and constructive place in society. Any petitioner for reinstatement from discipline for prior misconduct is required to produce clear and convincing evidence of rehabilita-

tion including, but not limited to, the following elements:

(A) strict compliance with the specific conditions of any disciplinary, judicial, administrative, or other order, where applicable;

(B) unimpeachable character and moral standing in the community;

(C) good reputation for professional ability, where applicable;

(D) lack of malice and ill feeling toward those who by duty were compelled to bring about the disciplinary, judicial, administrative, or other proceeding;

(E) personal assurances, supported by corroborating evidence, of a desire and intention to conduct one's self in an exemplary fashion in the future;

(F) restitution of funds or property, where applicable; and

(G) positive action showing rehabilitation by such things as a person's community or civic service. Community or civic service is donated service or activity that is performed by someone or a group of people for the benefit of the public or its institutions.

The requirement of positive action is appropriate for persons seeking reinstatement to the bar as well as for applicants for admission to the bar because service to one's community is an essential obligation of members of the bar.

(4) *Educational Requirements.*

(A) In the case of a petitioner's ineligibility to practice for a period of 3 years or longer under this rule, the petitioner must demonstrate to the referee that the petitioner is current with changes and developments in the law:

(i) The petitioner must have completed at least 10 hours of continuing legal education courses for each year or portion of a year that the petitioner was ineligible to practice.

(ii) The petitioner may further demonstrate that the petitioner is current with changes and developments in the law by showing that the petitioner worked as a law clerk or paralegal or taught classes on legal issues during the period of ineligibility to practice.

(B) A petitioner who has been ineligible to practice for 5 years or more will not be reinstated under this rule until the petitioner has re-taken and provided proof in the lawyer's petition for reinstatement that the lawyer has passed both the Florida portions of the Florida Bar Examination and the Multistate Professional Responsibility Examination (MPRE).

(g) Hearing; Notice; Evidence.

(1) *Notice.* The referee to whom the petition for reinstatement is referred will fix a time and place for hearing, and notice of the hearing will be provided at least 10 days prior to the hearing to the petitioner, to lawyers representing The Florida Bar, and to other persons who may be designated by the appointed referee.

(2) *Appearance.* Any persons to whom notice is given, any other interested persons, or any local bar association may appear before the referee in support of or in opposition to the petition at any time or times fixed for the hearings.

(3) *Failure of Petitioner to be Examined.* For the failure of the petitioner to submit to examination as a witness pursuant to notice given, the referee will dismiss the petition for reinstatement unless good cause is shown for the failure.

(4) *Summary Procedure.* If after the completion of discovery bar counsel is unable to discover any evidence on which denial of reinstatement may be based and if no other person provides any relevant evidence, bar counsel may, with the approval of the designated reviewer and staff counsel, stipulate to the issue of reinstatement, including conditions for reinstatement. The stipulation must include a statement of costs as provided elsewhere in these Rules Regulating the Florida Bar.

(5) *Evidence of Treatment or Counseling for Dependency or Other Medical Reasons.* If the petitioner has sought or received treatment or counseling for chemical or alcohol dependency or for other medical reasons that relate to the petitioner's fitness to practice law, the petitioner must waive confidentiality of such treatment or counseling for purposes of evaluation of the petitioner's fitness. The provisions of rule 3-7.1(d) are applicable to information or records disclosed under this subdivision.

(h) Prompt Hearing; Report. The referee to whom a petition for reinstatement has been referred by the chief justice will proceed to a prompt hearing, at the conclusion of which the referee will make and file with the Supreme Court of Florida a report that includes the findings of fact and a recommendation as to whether the petitioner is qualified to resume the practice of law. The referee must file the report and record in the Supreme Court of Florida.

(i) Review. Review of referee reports in reinstatement proceedings must be in accordance with rule 3-7.7.

(j) Recommendation of Referee and Judgment of the Court. If the petitioner is found unfit to resume the practice of law, the petition will be dismissed. If the petitioner is found fit to resume the practice of law, the referee will enter a report recommending, and the court may enter an order of, reinstatement of the petitioner in The Florida Bar; provided, however, that the reinstatement may be conditioned on the payment of all or part of the costs of the proceeding and on the making of partial or complete restitution to parties harmed by the petitioner's misconduct that led to the petitioner's suspension of membership in The Florida Bar or conduct that led to the petitioner's incapacity; and, if suspension or incapacity of the petitioner has continued for more than 3 years, the reinstatement may be conditioned on proof of competency as may be required by the judgment in the discretion of the Supreme Court of Florida. Proof may include certification by the Florida Board of Bar Examiners of the successful completion of an examination for admission to The Florida Bar subsequent to the date of the suspension or incapacity.

(k) Successive Petitions. No petition for reinstatement may be filed within 1 year following an adverse judgment on a petition for reinstatement filed by or on behalf of the same person. In cases of incapacity no petition for reinstatement may be filed within 6 months following an adverse judgment under this rule.

(*l*) Petitions for Reinstatement to Membership in Good Standing.

(1) *Availability.* Petitions for reinstatement under this rule are available to members placed on the inactive list for incapacity not related to misconduct and suspended members of the bar when the disciplinary judgment conditions their reinstatement upon a showing of compliance with specified conditions.

(2) *Style of Petition.* Petitions must be styled in the Supreme Court of Florida and filed with the Supreme Court of Florida in accordance with the court's filing requirements, including e-filing requirements where applicable. A copy must be served on Staff Counsel, The Florida Bar, 651 East Jefferson Street, Tallahassee, Florida 32399–2300.

(3) *Contents of Petition.* The petition must be verified by the petitioner and accompanied by a written authorization to the District Director of the Internal Revenue Service, authorizing the furnishing of certified copies of the petitioner's tax returns for the past 5 years or since admission to the bar, whichever is greater. The authorization must be furnished on a separate sheet. The petition must have attached as an exhibit a true copy of all disciplinary judgments previously entered against the petitioner. It must also include the petitioner's statement concerning the following:

(A) name, age, residence, address, and number and relation of dependents of the petitioner;

(B) the conduct, offense, or misconduct on which the suspension or incapacity was based, together with the date of such suspension or incapacity;

(C) the names and addresses of all complaining witnesses in any disciplinary proceedings that resulted in suspension; and the name and address of the referee or judge who heard these disciplinary proceedings or of the trial judge, complaining witnesses, and prosecuting lawyer, if suspension was based on conviction of a felony or misdemeanor involving moral turpitude;

(D) the nature of the petitioner's occupation in detail since suspension or incapacity, with names and addresses of all partners, associates in business, and employers, if any, and dates and duration of all these relations and employments;

(E) a statement showing the approximate monthly earnings and other income of the petitioner and the sources from which all earnings and income were derived during this period;

(F) a statement showing all residences maintained during this period, with names and addresses of landlords, if any;

(G) a statement showing all financial obligations of the petitioner including but not limited to amounts claimed, unpaid, or owing to The Florida Bar Clients' Security Fund or former clients at the date of filing of the petition, together with the names and addresses of all creditors;

(H) a statement of restitution made for any and all obligations to all former clients and The Florida Bar Clients' Security Fund and the source and amount of funds used for this purpose;

(I) a statement showing dates, general nature, and ultimate disposition of every matter involving the arrest or prosecution of the petitioner during the period of suspension for any crime, whether felony or misdemeanor, together with the names and addresses of complaining witnesses, prosecuting lawyers, and trial judges;

(J) a statement as to whether any applications were made during the period of suspension for a license requiring proof of good character for its procurement; and, for each application, the date and the name and address of the authority to whom it was addressed and its disposition;

(K) a statement of any procedure or inquiry, during the period of suspension, covering the petitioner's standing as a member of any profession or organization, or holder of any license or office, that involved the censure, removal, suspension, revocation of license, or discipline of the petitioner; and, as to each, the dates, facts, and the disposition, and the name and address of the authority in possession of these records;

(L) a statement as to whether any charges of fraud were made or claimed against the petitioner during the period of suspension, whether formal or informal, together with the dates and names and addresses of persons making these charges;

(M) a concise statement of facts claimed to justify reinstatement to The Florida Bar;

(N) a statement showing the dates, general nature, and final disposition of every civil action in which the petitioner was either a party plaintiff or defendant, together with dates of filing of complaints, titles of courts and causes, and the names and addresses of all parties and of the trial judge or judges, and names and addresses of all witnesses who testified in this action or actions; and

(*O*) a statement showing what amounts, if any, of the costs assessed against the accused lawyer in the prior disciplinary proceedings against the petitioner have been paid by the petitioner and the source and amount of funds used for this purpose.

(4) *Comments on Petition.* On the appointment of a referee and bar counsel, copies of the petition will be furnished by the bar counsel to local board members, local grievance committees, and to other persons mentioned in this rule. Persons or groups that wish to respond must direct their comments to bar counsel. The proceedings and finding of the referee will relate to those matters described in this rule and also to those matters tending to show the petitioner's rehabilitation, present fitness to resume the practice of law, and the effect of the proposed reinstatement on the administration of justice and purity of the courts and confidence of the public in the profession.

(5) *Costs Deposit.* The petition must be accompanied by a deposit for costs of $500.

(m) Costs.

(1) *Taxable Costs.* Taxable costs of the proceedings must include only:

(A) investigative costs, including travel and out-of-pocket expenses;

(B) court reporters' fees;

(C) copy costs;

(D) telephone charges;

(E) fees for translation services;

(F) witness expenses, including travel and out-of-pocket expenses;

(G) travel and out-of-pocket expenses of the referee;

(H) travel and out-of-pocket expenses of counsel in the proceedings, including the petitioner if acting as counsel; and

(I) an administrative fee in the amount of $1250 when costs are assessed in favor of the bar.

(2) *Discretion of Referee.* The referee has discretion to award costs and absent an abuse of discretion the referee's award will not be reversed.

(3) *Assessment of Bar Costs.* The costs incurred by the bar in any reinstatement case may be assessed against the petitioner unless it is shown that the costs were unnecessary, excessive, or improperly authenticated.

(4) *Assessment of Petitioner's Costs.* The referee may assess the petitioner's costs against the bar in the event that there was no justiciable issue of either law or fact raised by the bar unless it is shown that the costs were unnecessary, excessive, or improperly authenticated.

(n) Readmission; Applicability. A former member who has been disbarred, disbarred on consent, or whose petition for disciplinary resignation or revocation has been accepted may be admitted again only upon full compliance with the rules and regulations governing admission to the bar. No application for readmission following disbarment, disbarment on consent, or disciplinary resignation or revocation may be tendered until such time as all restitution and disciplinary costs as may have been ordered or assessed have been paid together with any interest accrued.

(1) *Readmission After Disbarment.* Except as might be otherwise provided in these rules, no application for admission may be tendered within 5 years after the date of disbarment or such longer period of time as the court might determine in the disbarment order. An order of disbarment that states the disbarment is permanent precludes readmission to The Florida Bar.

(2) *Readmission After Disciplinary Resignation or Revocation.* A lawyer's petition for disciplinary resignation or revocation that states that it is without leave to apply for readmission will preclude any readmission. A lawyer who was granted a disciplinary resignation or revocation may not apply for readmission until all conditions of the Supreme Court order granting the disciplinary resignation or revocation have been complied with.

Former Rule 3-7.9 renumbered as Rule 3-7.10 March 16, 1990, effective March 17, 1990 (558 So.2d 1008). Amended July 23, 1992, effective Jan. 1, 1993 (605 So.2d 252); July 1, 1993 (621 So.2d 1032); Oct. 20, 1994 (644 So.2d 282); July 17, 1997 (697 So.2d 115); Sept. 24, 1998, effective Oct. 1, 1998 (718 So.2d 1179); Feb. 8, 2001 (795 So.2d 1); April 25, 2002 (820 So.2d 210); July 3, 2003 (850 So.2d 499); May 20, 2004 (875 So.2d 448); Oct. 6, 2005, effective Jan. 1, 2006 (916 So.2d 655); April 12, 2012, effective July 1, 2012 (101 So.3d 807); May 29, 2014, effective June 1, 2014 (140 So.3d 541); June 11, 2015, effective Oct. 1, 2015 (167 So.3d 412).

Comment

To further illuminate the community service requirements of Rule 3-7.10(f)(3)(G), bar members can take guidance from the Florida Supreme Court's decision in *Florida Board of Bar Examiners re M.L.B.*, 766 So. 2d 994, 998–999 (Fla. 2000). The court held that rules requiring community service "contemplate and we wish to encourage positive actions beyond those one would normally do for self benefit, including, but certainly not limited to, working as a guardian ad litem, volunteering on a regular basis with shelters for the homeless or victims of domestic violence, or maintaining substantial involvement in other charitable, community, or educational organizations whose value system, overall mission and activities are directed to good deeds and humanitarian concerns impacting a broad base of citizens."

Court decisions dealing with reinstatements and other discipline provide further guidance as to what specific actions meet the test of community service. The court approved dismissal of a petition for reinstatement where the respondent had no community service and had devoted all her time during suspension to raising her young children. *Fla. Bar v. Tauler*, 837 So. 2d 413 (Fla. 2003). In a more recent decision, the court did not specifically mention lack of community service in denying reinstatement, but the respondent had shown no evidence of work for others outside his family in his petition. Respondent's community service consisted solely of taking care of his elderly parents and his small child. *Fla. Bar v. Juan Baraque*, 43 So. 3d 691 (Fla. 2010).

Rule 3–7.11. General Rule of Procedure

Text of rule effective until October 1, 2015. See, also, rule effective October 1, 2015.

(a) Time is Directory. Except as provided herein, the time intervals required are directory only and are not jurisdictional. Failure to observe such directory intervals may result in contempt of the agency having jurisdiction or of the Supreme Court of Florida, but will not prejudice the offending party except where so provided.

(b) Process. Every member of The Florida Bar is charged with notifying The Florida Bar of a change of mailing address or military status. Mailing of registered or certified papers or notices prescribed in these rules to the last mailing address of an attorney as shown by the official records in the office of the executive director of The Florida Bar shall be sufficient notice and service unless this court shall direct otherwise. Every attorney of another state who is permitted to practice for the purpose of a specific case before a court of record of this state may be served by registered or certified mail addressed to said attorney in care of the Florida attorney who was associated or appeared with the attorney in the specific case for which the out-of-state attorney was permitted to practice or addressed to said attorney at any address listed by the attorney in the pleadings in such case.

Provided, however, when a person is represented by counsel service of process and notices shall be directed to counsel.

(c) Notice in Lieu of Process. Every member of The Florida Bar is within the jurisdiction of the Supreme Court of Florida and its agencies under these rules, and service of process is not required to obtain jurisdiction over respondents in disciplinary proceedings; but due process requires the giving of reasonable notice and such shall be effective by the service of the complaint upon the respondent by mailing a copy thereof by registered or certified mail return receipt requested to the last-known address of the respondent according to the records of The Florida Bar or such later address as may be known to the person effecting the service.

When the respondent is represented by counsel in the matter, due process is satisfied by the service of the complaint upon the respondent's counsel by mailing a copy thereof by registered or certified mail return receipt requested to the last known address of the respondent's counsel according to the records of The Florida Bar or such later address as may be known to the person effecting the service.

(d) Issuance of Subpoenas. Subpoenas for the attendance of witnesses and the production of documentary evidence other than before a circuit court shall be issued as follows:

(1) *Referees.* Subpoenas for the attendance of witnesses and production of documentary evidence before a referee shall be issued by the referee and shall be served in the manner provided by law for the service of process or by an investigator employed by The Florida Bar.

(2) *Grievance Committees.* Subpoenas for the attendance of witnesses and the production of documentary evidence shall be issued by the chair or vice-chair of a grievance committee in pursuance of an investigation authorized by the committee. Such subpoenas may be served by any member of such committee, by an investigator employed by The Florida Bar, or in the manner provided by law for the service of process.

(3) *Bar Counsel Investigations.* Subpoenas for the attendance of witnesses and the production of documentary evidence before bar counsel when same is conducting an initial investigation shall be issued by the chair or vice-chair of a grievance committee to which the matter will be assigned, if appropriate. Such subpoenas may be served by an investigator employed by The Florida Bar or in the manner provided by law for the service of process.

(4) *After Grievance Committee Action, But Before Appointment of Referee.* Subpoenas for the attendance of witnesses and the production of documentary evidence before bar counsel when same is conducting further investigation after action by a grievance committee, but before appointment of a referee, shall be issued by the chair or vice-chair of the grievance committee to which the matter was assigned. Such subpoenas may be served by an investigator employed by The Florida Bar or in the manner provided by law for the service of process.

(5) *Board of Governors.* Subpoenas for the attendance of witnesses and the production of documentary evidence before the board of governors shall be issued by the executive director and shall be served by an investigator employed by The Florida Bar or in the manner provided by law for the service of process.

(6) *Confidential Proceedings.* If the proceeding is confidential, a subpoena shall not name the respondent but shall style the proceeding as "Confidential Proceeding by The Florida Bar under the Rules of Discipline."

(7) *Contempt.*

(A) Generally. Any persons who without adequate excuse fail to obey such a subpoena served upon them may be cited for contempt of this court in the manner provided by this rule.

(B) Subpoenas for Trust Accounting Records. Members of the bar are under an obligation to maintain trust accounting records as required by these rules and, as a condition of the privilege of practicing law in Florida, may not assert any privilege personal to the lawyer that may be applicable to production of such records in any disciplinary proceedings under these rules.

(i) A respondent who has been found in willful noncompliance with a subpoena for trust accounting records may be cited for contempt under this rule only if the disciplinary agency that issued the subpoena shall have first found that no good cause existed for the respondent's failure to comply.

(ii) The disciplinary agency that issued the subpoena shall hear the issue of noncompliance and issue findings thereon within 30 days of a request for issuance of the notice of noncompliance.

(8) *Assistance to Other Lawyer Disciplinary Jurisdictions.* Upon receipt of a subpoena certified to be duly issued under the rules or laws of another lawyer disciplinary jurisdiction, the executive director may issue a subpoena directing a person domiciled or found within the state of Florida to give testimony and/or produce documents or other things for use in the other lawyer disciplinary proceedings as directed in the subpoena of the other jurisdiction. The practice and procedure applicable to subpoenas issued under this subdivision shall be that of the other jurisdiction, except that:

(A) the testimony or production shall be only in the county wherein the person resides or is employed, or as otherwise fixed by the executive director for good cause shown; and

(B) compliance with any subpoena issued pursuant to this subdivision and contempt for failure in this respect shall be sought as elsewhere provided in these rules.

(e) Oath of Witness. Every witness in every proceeding under these rules shall be sworn to tell the truth. Violation of this oath shall be an act of contempt of this court.

(f) Contempt. When a disciplinary agency, as defined elsewhere in these rules, finds that a person is in contempt under these rules, such person may be cited for contempt in the following manner:

(1) *Generally.*

(A) Petition for Contempt and Order to Show Cause. When a person is found in contempt by a disciplinary agency, bar counsel shall file a petition for contempt and order to show cause with the Supreme Court of Florida.

(B) Order to Show Cause; Suspension for Noncompliance with Subpoena for Trust Accounting Records. On review of a petition for contempt and order to show cause, the supreme court may issue an order directing the person to show cause why such person should not be held in contempt and appropriate sanctions imposed.

On review of a petition for contempt and order to show cause for noncompliance with a trust accounting subpoena the supreme court may also issue an order suspending the respondent from the practice of law in Florida until such time as the member fully complies with the subpoena and any further order of the court.

The order of the supreme court shall fix a time for a response.

(C) Response to Order to Show Cause.

(i) Generally. Any member subject to an order to show cause shall file a response as directed by the court.

(ii) Noncompliance with a Subpoena for Trust Account Records. Any member subject to an order to show cause for noncompliance with a subpoena for trust accounting records may request the court:

a. within 10 days of the filing of the petition for contempt and order to show cause, or such other time as the court may direct in the order to show cause, to withhold entry of an order of suspension; or

b. at any time after entry of an order of suspension, to terminate or modify the order of suspension. The court may terminate, modify, or withhold entry of an order of suspension if the member establishes good cause for failure to comply with the subpoena for trust account records.

(D) Failure to Respond to Order to Show Cause. Upon failure to timely respond to an order to show cause, the matters alleged in the petition shall be deemed admitted and the supreme court may enter a judgment of contempt and impose appropriate sanctions. Failure to respond may be an additional basis on which a judgment of contempt may be entered and sanctions imposed.

(E) Reply of The Florida Bar. When a timely response to an order to show cause is filed, The Florida Bar shall have 10 days, or such other time as the supreme court may order, from the date of filing in which to file a reply.

(F) Supreme Court Action. After expiration of the time to respond to an order to show cause and no response is timely filed, or after the reply of The Florida Bar has been filed, or the time therefore has expired without such filing, the supreme court shall review the matter and issue an appropriate judgment. Such judgment may include any sanction that a court may impose for contempt and, if the person found in contempt is a member of The Florida Bar, may include any disciplinary sanction authorized under these rules.

If the supreme court requires factual findings, the supreme court may direct appointment of a referee as elsewhere provided in these rules. Proceedings for contempt referred to a referee shall be processed in the same manner as disciplinary proceedings under these rules, including but not limited to the procedures provided therein for conditional guilty pleas for consent judgments. If the court determines it necessary to refer a request to terminate, modify, or withhold entry of an order of suspension based on a petition for contempt and order to show cause for noncompliance with a subpoena for trust account records to a referee for receipt of evidence, the referee proceedings shall be expedited and conducted in the same manner as proceedings before a referee on a petition to terminate, modify, or withhold an order of emergency suspension, as elsewhere provided in these rules.

(G) Preparation and Filing of Report of Referee and Record. The referee shall prepare and file a report and the record in cases brought under this rule. The procedures provided for in the rule on procedure before a referee elsewhere under these rules shall apply to the preparation, filing, and review of the record herein.

(H) Appellate Review of Report of Referee. Any party to the contempt proceedings may seek review of the report of referee in the manner provided in the rule on appellate review of disciplinary proceedings under these rules.

(2) *Failure to Respond to Official Bar Inquiries.*

(A) Petition for Contempt and Order to Show Cause. When a respondent is found in contempt by a disciplinary agency for failure to respond to an official bar inquiry without good cause shown, bar counsel shall file a petition for contempt and order to show cause with the Supreme Court of Florida.

(B) Response to Petition for Contempt and Order to Show Cause. The respondent shall have 10 days from the date of filing of a petition authorized by this subdivision in which to file a response.

(C) Supreme Court Action.

(i) Entry of Suspension Order. After a response has been filed, or the time for a response has expired, and unless otherwise ordered by the court, an order shall be entered suspending the respondent for failure to respond to an official bar inquiry until further order of the court.

(ii) Assignment to Referee. If the supreme court requires factual findings, the supreme court may direct appointment of a referee as elsewhere provided in these rules. Proceedings for contempt referred to a referee shall be processed in the same manner as disciplinary proceedings under these rules, including but not limited to the provisions provided for conditional guilty pleas for consent judgments.

(g) Court Reporters. Court reporters who are employees of The Florida Bar may be appointed to report any disciplinary proceeding. If the respondent objects at least 48 hours in advance of the matter to be recorded, an independent contract reporter may be retained. Reasonable costs for independent court reporter service shall be taxed to a respondent for payment to The Florida Bar.

(h) Disqualification as Trier and Attorney for Respondent Due to Conflict.

(1) *Grievance Committee Members, Members of the Board of Governors, and Employees of The Florida Bar.* No grievance committee member, member of the board of governors, or employee of The Florida Bar shall represent a party other than The Florida Bar in disciplinary proceedings authorized under these rules.

(2) *Former Grievance Committee Members, Former Board Members, and Former Employees.* No former member of a grievance committee, former member of the board of governors, or former employee of The Florida Bar shall represent any party other than The Florida Bar in disciplinary proceedings authorized under these rules if personally involved to any degree in the matter while a member of the grievance committee, the board of governors, or while an employee of The Florida Bar.

A former member of the board of governors, former member of any grievance committee, or former employee of The Florida Bar who did not participate personally in any way in the investigation or prosecution of the matter or in any related matter in which the attorney seeks to be a representative, and who did not serve in a supervisory capacity over such investigation or prosecution, shall not represent any party except The Florida Bar for 1 year after such service without the express consent of the board.

(3) *Partners, Associates, Employers, or Employees of the Firms of Grievance Committee Members or Board of Governors Members Precluded From Representing Parties Other Than The Florida Bar.* Members of the firms of grievance committee members or board members shall not represent any party other than The Florida Bar in disciplinary proceedings authorized under these rules without the express consent of the board.

(4) *Partners, Associates, Employers, or Employees of the Firms of Former Grievance Committee Members or Former Board of Governors Members Precluded From Representing Parties Other Than The Florida Bar.* Attorneys in the firms of former board members or former grievance committee members shall not represent any party other than The Florida Bar in disciplinary proceedings authorized under these rules for 1 year after the former member's service without the express consent of the board.

(i) Proceedings After Disbarment. The respondent may consent to or the court may order further proceedings after disbarment, which may include: an audit of trust, operating, or personal bank accounts, the cost of which may be assessed as provided elsewhere in these rules; a requirement for the respondent to provide a financial affidavit attesting to personal and business finances; and maintenance of a current mailing address for a stated period of time.

Former Rule 3–7.10 amended June 8, 1989 (544 So.2d 193). Renumbered as Rule 3–7.11 and amended March 16, 1990, effective March 17, 1990 (558 So.2d 1008). Amended July 23, 1992, effective Jan. 1, 1993 (605 So.2d 252); July 17, 1997 (697 So.2d 115); May 20, 2004 (875 So.2d 448); Oct. 6, 2005, effective Jan. 1, 2006 (916 So.2d 655); Dec. 20, 2007, effective March 1, 2008 (978 So.2d 91); Nov. 19, 2009, effective Feb. 1, 2010 (24 So.3d 63).

Rule 3–7.11. General Rules of Procedure

Text of rule effective October 1, 2015. See, also, rule effective until October 1, 2015.

(a) Time is Directory. Except as provided herein, the time intervals required are directory only and are not jurisdictional. Failure to observe such directory intervals may result in contempt of the agency having jurisdiction or of the Supreme Court of Florida, but will not prejudice the offending party except where so provided.

(b) Process. Every member of The Florida Bar is charged with notifying The Florida Bar of any change of mailing address, e-mail address (unless the lawyer has been excused by The Florida Bar or court from e-filing and e-service) and military status. The Florida Bar may serve notice of formal complaints in bar proceedings by U.S. Postal Service certified mail return receipt requested to the bar member's record bar address unless the Supreme Court of Florida directs other service. Every lawyer of another state who is admitted pro hac vice in a specific case before a court of record in Florida may be served by U.S. Postal Service certified mail return receipt requested addressed to the lawyer in care of the Florida lawyer who was associated or appeared with the lawyer admitted pro hac vice or addressed to the Florida lawyer at any address listed by the lawyer in the pleadings in the case.

Provided, however, when a person is represented by counsel, service of process and notices must be directed to counsel.

(c) Notice in Lieu of Process. Every member of The Florida Bar is within the jurisdiction of the Supreme Court of Florida and its agencies under these rules, and service of process is not required to obtain jurisdiction over respondents in disciplinary proceedings; but due process requires reasonable notice and this notice will be effected by service of the complaint on the respondent by mailing a copy of The Florida Bar's formal complaint by certified U.S. Postal Service mail return receipt requested to the respondent's record bar address or a more current address that may be known to the person serving the complaint or other process.

When the respondent is represented by counsel in a referee proceeding, due process is satisfied by service of the formal complaint on the respondent's counsel by mailing a copy by certified mail return receipt requested to the record bar address of the respondent's counsel or a more current address that may be known to the person serving the complaint.

All other correspondence between The Florida Bar and respondents or their counsel, including bar inquiries that require responses during the investigative stage of a disciplinary proceeding, may be made by e-mail to the respondent's record bar e-mail address or the record bar e-mail address of respondent's counsel. E-mail correspondence is encouraged in all instances except in service of a formal complaint or subpoena, or where a court directs otherwise. If a lawyer has been excused by The Florida Bar or court from e-filing and e-service, or service cannot be made by e-mail, service by first class postal mail is sufficient except where these rules or a court direct otherwise.

(d) Issuance of Subpoenas. Subpoenas for witnesses' attendance and the production of documentary evidence except before a circuit court must be issued as follows:

(1) *Referees.* Subpoenas for witnesses' attendance and production of documentary evidence before a referee must be issued by the referee and must be served either in the manner provided by law for the service of process or by an investigator employed by The Florida Bar.

(2) *Grievance Committees.* Subpoenas for witnesses' attendance and the production of documentary evidence must be issued by the chair or vice-chair of a grievance committee as part of an investigation authorized by the committee. These subpoenas may be served by any member of the grievance committee, by an investigator employed by The Florida Bar, or in the manner provided by law for service of process.

(3) *Bar Counsel Investigations.* Subpoenas for witnesses' attendance and the production of documentary evidence before bar counsel in an initial investigation must be issued by the chair or vice-chair of a grievance committee to which the matter will be assigned, if appropriate. These subpoenas may be served by an investigator employed by The Florida Bar or in the manner provided by law for the service of process.

(4) *After Grievance Committee Action, But Before Appointment of Referee.* Subpoenas for witnesses' attendance and the production of documentary evidence before bar counsel when conducting further investigation after action by a grievance committee, but before appointment of a referee, must be issued by the chair or vice-chair of the grievance committee to which the matter was assigned. These subpoenas may be served by an investigator employed by The

Florida Bar or in the manner provided by law for service of process.

(5) *Board of Governors.* Subpoenas for witnesses' attendance and the production of documentary evidence before the board of governors must be issued by the executive director and must be served by an investigator employed by The Florida Bar or in the manner provided by law for service of process.

(6) *Confidential Proceedings.* If the proceeding is confidential, a subpoena must not name the respondent but must style the proceeding as "Confidential Proceeding by The Florida Bar under the Rules of Discipline."

(7) *Contempt.*

(A) Generally. Any persons who, without adequate excuse, fail to obey a subpoena served on them under these rules, may be cited for contempt of this court in the manner provided by this rule.

(B) Subpoenas for Trust Accounting Records. Members of the bar are under an obligation to maintain trust accounting records as required by these rules and, as a condition of the privilege of practicing law in Florida, may not assert any privilege personal to the lawyer that may be applicable to production of these records in any disciplinary proceedings under these rules.

(i) A respondent who has been found in willful noncompliance with a subpoena for trust accounting records may be cited for contempt under this rule only if the disciplinary agency that issued the subpoena has found that no good cause existed for the respondent's failure to comply.

(ii) The disciplinary agency that issued the subpoena must hear the issue of noncompliance and issue findings on the noncompliance within 30 days of a request for issuance of the notice of noncompliance.

(8) *Assistance to Other Lawyer Disciplinary Jurisdictions.* On receipt of a subpoena certified to be issued under the rules or laws of another lawyer disciplinary jurisdiction, the executive director may issue a subpoena directing a person domiciled or found within the state of Florida to give testimony and/or produce documents or other evidence for use in the other jurisdiction's lawyer disciplinary proceedings as directed in the subpoena of the other jurisdiction. The practice and procedure applicable to subpoenas issued under this subdivision will be that of the other jurisdiction, except that:

(A) the testimony or production must be only in the county in which the person resides or is employed, or as otherwise fixed by the executive director for good cause shown; and

(B) compliance with any subpoena issued pursuant to this subdivision and contempt for failure in this respect must be sought under these rules.

(e) Oath of Witness. Every witness in every proceeding under these rules must be sworn to tell the truth. Violation of this oath is an act of contempt of this court.

(f) Contempt. When a disciplinary agency, as defined elsewhere in these rules, finds that a person is in contempt under these rules, that person may be cited for contempt in the following manner:

(1) *Generally.*

(A) Petition for Contempt and Order to Show Cause. When a person is found in contempt by a disciplinary agency, bar counsel must file a petition for contempt and order to show cause with the Supreme Court of Florida.

(B) Order to Show Cause; Suspension for Noncompliance with Subpoena for Trust Accounting Records. On review of a petition for contempt and order to show cause, the supreme court may issue an order directing the person to show cause why the person should not be held in contempt and appropriate sanctions imposed.

On review of a petition for contempt and order to show cause for noncompliance with a trust accounting subpoena, the supreme court may also issue an order suspending the respondent from the practice of law in Florida until the member fully complies with the subpoena and any further order of the court.

The order of the supreme court must fix a time for a response.

(C) Response to Order to Show Cause.

(i) Generally. Any member subject to an order to show cause must file a response as directed by the court.

(ii) Noncompliance with a Subpoena for Trust Account Records. Any member subject to an order to show cause for noncompliance with a subpoena for trust accounting records may request the court:

a. to withhold entry of an order of suspension, if filed within 10 days of the filing of the petition for contempt and order to show cause, or another time the court may direct in the order to show cause; or

b. to terminate or modify the order of suspension at any time after the order of suspension is issued. The court may terminate, modify, or withhold entry of an order of suspension if the member establishes good cause for failure to comply with the subpoena for trust account records.

(D) Failure to Respond to Order to Show Cause. On failure to timely respond to an order to show cause, the matters alleged in the petition are deemed admitted and the supreme court may enter a judgment of contempt and impose appropriate sanctions. Failure to respond may be an additional basis for the supreme court to enter a judgment of contempt and to impose sanctions.

(E) Reply of The Florida Bar. When a timely response to an order to show cause is filed, The Florida Bar will have 10 days, or another time period as the supreme court may order, from the date of filing to file a reply.

(F) Supreme Court Action. After the time to respond to an order to show cause has expired and no response is timely filed, or after the reply of The Florida Bar has been filed, or the time has expired without any filing, the supreme court will review the matter and issue an appropriate judgment. This judgment may include any sanction that a court may impose for contempt and, if the person found in contempt is a member of The Florida Bar, may include any disciplinary sanction authorized under these rules.

If the supreme court requires factual findings, the supreme court may direct appointment of a referee as provided in these rules. Proceedings for contempt referred to a referee must be processed in the same manner as disciplinary proceedings under these rules, including but not limited to the procedures provided in these rules for conditional guilty pleas for consent judgments. If the court determines it necessary to refer a request to terminate, modify, or withhold entry of an order of suspension based on a petition for contempt and order to show cause for noncompliance with a subpoena for trust account records to a referee for receipt of evidence, the referee proceedings must be expedited and conducted in the same manner as proceedings before a referee on a petition to terminate, modify, or withhold an order of emergency suspension, as provided in these rules.

(G) Preparation and Filing of Report of Referee and Record. The referee must prepare and file a report and the record in cases brought under this rule. The procedures provided for in the rule on procedure before a referee under these rules apply to the preparation, filing, and review of the record.

(H) Appellate Review of Report of Referee. Any party to the contempt proceedings may seek review of the report of referee in the manner provided in these rules for appellate review of disciplinary proceedings.

(2) *Failure to Respond to Official Bar Inquiries.*

(A) Petition for Contempt and Order to Show Cause. When a respondent is found in contempt by a disciplinary agency for failure to respond to an official bar inquiry without good cause shown, bar counsel must file a petition for contempt and order to show cause with the Supreme Court of Florida.

(B) Response to Petition for Contempt and Order to Show Cause. The respondent will have 10 days from the date of filing of a petition authorized by this subdivision to file a response.

(C) Supreme Court Action.

(i) Entry of Suspension Order. The court will enter an order suspending the respondent for failure to respond to an official bar inquiry after the respondent files a response to the order to show cause or the time for filing a response has expired, unless the court orders otherwise.

(ii) Assignment to Referee. If the supreme court requires factual findings, the supreme court may direct appointment of a referee as provided in these rules. Proceedings for contempt referred to a referee must be processed in the same manner as disciplinary proceedings under these rules, including but not limited to the provisions provided for conditional guilty pleas for consent judgments.

(g) Court Reporters. Court reporters who are employees of The Florida Bar may be appointed to report any disciplinary proceeding. If the respondent objects at least 48 hours in advance of the matter to be recorded, an independent contract reporter may be retained. Reasonable costs for independent court reporter service will be taxed to the respondent for payment to The Florida Bar.

(h) Disqualification as Trier and Lawyer for Respondent Due to Conflict.

(1) *Grievance Committee Members, Members of the Board of Governors, and Employees of The Florida Bar.* No grievance committee member, member of the board of governors, or employee of The Florida Bar may represent a party other than The Florida Bar in disciplinary proceedings authorized under these rules.

(2) *Former Grievance Committee Members, Former Board Members, and Former Employees.* No former member of a grievance committee, former member of the board of governors, or former employee of The Florida Bar may represent any party other than The Florida Bar in disciplinary proceedings authorized under these rules if personally involved to any degree in the matter while a member of the grievance committee, the board of governors, or while an employee of The Florida Bar.

A former member of the board of governors, former member of any grievance committee, or former employee of The Florida Bar who did not participate personally in any way in the investigation or prosecution of the matter or in any related matter in which the lawyer seeks to be a representative, and who did not serve in a supervisory capacity over the investigation or prosecution, may not represent any party except The Florida Bar for 1 year after this service without the express consent of the board.

(3) *Partners, Associates, Employers, or Employees of the Firms of Grievance Committee Members or Board of Governors Members Precluded From Representing Parties Other Than The Florida Bar.* Members of the firms of grievance committee members or

board members may not represent any party other than The Florida Bar in disciplinary proceedings authorized under these rules without the express consent of the board.

(4) *Partners, Associates, Employers, or Employees of the Firms of Former Grievance Committee Members or Former Board of Governors Members Precluded From Representing Parties Other Than The Florida Bar.* Lawyers in the firms of former board members or former grievance committee members may not represent any party other than The Florida Bar in disciplinary proceedings authorized under these rules for 1 year after the former member's service without the express consent of the board.

(i) Proceedings after Disbarment. The respondent may consent to or the court may order further proceedings after disbarment, which may include: an audit of trust, operating, or personal bank accounts, the cost of which may be assessed as provided in these rules; a requirement that the respondent provide a financial affidavit attesting to personal and business finances; and maintenance of a current mailing address for a stated period of time.

Former Rule 3–7.10 amended June 8, 1989 (544 So.2d 193). Renumbered as Rule 3–7.11 and amended March 16, 1990, effective March 17, 1990 (558 So.2d 1008). Amended July 23, 1992, effective Jan. 1, 1993 (605 So.2d 252); July 17, 1997 (697 So.2d 115); May 20, 2004 (875 So.2d 448); Oct. 6, 2005, effective Jan. 1, 2006 (916 So.2d 655); Dec. 20, 2007, effective March 1, 2008 (978 So.2d 91); Nov. 19, 2009, effective Feb. 1, 2010 (24 So.3d 63); May 21, 2015, effective Oct. 1, 2015 (164 So.3d 1217).

Rule 3–7.12. Disciplinary Revocation of Admission to the Florida Bar

If a disciplinary agency is investigating the conduct of a lawyer, or if such an agency has recommended probable cause, then disciplinary proceedings shall be deemed to be pending and a petition for disciplinary revocation may be filed pursuant to this rule. Disciplinary revocation is tantamount to disbarment in that both sanctions terminate the license and privilege to practice law and both require readmission to practice under the Rules of the Supreme Court Relating to Admissions to the Bar. A lawyer may seek disciplinary revocation of admission to The Florida Bar during the progress of disciplinary proceedings in the following manner:

(a) Petition for Disciplinary Revocation. The petition for disciplinary revocation shall be styled "In re (respondent's name)," titled "Petition for Disciplinary Revocation," filed with the Supreme Court of Florida and shall contain a statement of all past and pending disciplinary actions and criminal proceedings against the petitioner. The statement shall describe the charges made or those under investigation for professional misconduct, results of past proceedings, and the status of pending investigations and proceedings. The petition shall state whether it is with or without leave to apply for readmission to the bar. A copy of the petition shall be served upon the executive director of The Florida Bar.

(b) Judgment. Within 60 days after filing and service of the petition, The Florida Bar shall file with the Supreme Court of Florida its response to the petition either supporting or opposing the petition for disciplinary revocation. The bar's response shall be determined by the bar's board of governors. A copy of the response shall be served upon the petitioner. The Supreme Court of Florida shall consider the petition, any response, and the charges against the petitioner. The Supreme Court of Florida may enter judgment granting disciplinary revocation if it has been shown by the petitioner in a proper and competent manner that the public interest will not be adversely affected by the granting of the petition and that such will neither adversely affect the integrity of the courts nor hinder the administration of justice nor the confidence of the public in the legal profession. If otherwise, the petition shall be denied. If the judgment grants the disciplinary revocation, the judgment may require that the disciplinary revocation be subject to appropriate conditions. Such conditions may include, but shall not be limited to, requiring the petitioner to submit to a full audit of all client trust accounts, to execute a financial affidavit attesting to current personal and professional financial circumstances, and to maintain a current mailing address with the bar for a period of 5 years after the disciplinary revocation becomes final or such other time as the court may order.

(c) Delay of Disciplinary Proceedings. The filing of a petition for disciplinary revocation shall not stay the progress of the disciplinary proceedings without the approval of the bar's board of governors.

(d) Dismissal of Pending Disciplinary Cases. If disciplinary revocation is granted by the Supreme Court of Florida under this rule, such disciplinary revocation shall serve to dismiss all pending disciplinary cases.

(e) Costs of Pending Disciplinary Cases. The judgment of the court granting disciplinary revocation may impose a judgment for the costs expended by The Florida Bar in all pending disciplinary cases against the respondent. Such costs shall be of the types and amounts authorized elsewhere in these Rules Regulating The Florida Bar.

Added April 12, 2012, effective July 1, 2012 (101 So.3d 807).

Comment

The disciplinary revocation rule replaces the former disciplinary resignation rule, but with added safeguards. Disciplinary revocation is allowed for a minimum of 5 years up to permanent disciplinary revocation. The bar's response to all such petitions must be determined by the bar's board of governors. Disciplinary revocation, like the formerly allowed disciplinary resignation, is "tantamount to disbarment." *The Florida Bar* v. *Hale*, 762 So.2d 515, 517 (Fla. 2000). Like disbarred lawyers, lawyers whose licenses have been revoked pursuant to disciplinary revocation still remain subject to the continuing jurisdiction of the Supreme Court of Florida and must meet all requirements for readmission to bar membership. *The Florida Bar* v. *Ross*, 732 So.2d 1037, 1041 (Fla. 1998); *The Florida Bar* v. *Hale*, 762 So.2d 515, 517 (Fla. 2000).

Rule 3–7.13. Incapacity not Related to Misconduct

(a) Classification and Effect of Incapacity. Whenever an attorney who has not been adjudged incompetent is incapable of practicing law because of physical or mental illness, incapacity, or other infirmity, the attorney may be classified as an inactive member and shall refrain from the practice of law even though no misconduct is alleged or proved.

(b) Applicable Rules of Procedure. Proceedings under this rule shall be processed under the Rules of Discipline in the same manner as proceedings involving acts of misconduct, except that emergency or interim proceedings authorized under rule 3–5.2 shall be processed as stated in that rule.

(c) Reinstatement to Practice. A member who has been classified as inactive under this rule may be reinstated in the same manner as in proceedings for reinstatement after suspension for acts of misconduct.

(d) Proceedings Upon Adjudication of Incapacity or Hospitalization Under the Florida Mental Health Act or Under the Authority of Applicable Law. An attorney who has been adjudicated as incapacitated from the practice of law or is hospitalized under the Florida Mental Health Act or the authority of other applicable law concerning the capability of an attorney to practice law may be classified as an inactive member and shall refrain from the practice of law. Upon receipt of notice that a member has been adjudicated as incapacitated or is hospitalized under the Florida Mental Health Act or the authority of other applicable law concerning the capability of an attorney to practice law, The Florida Bar shall file notice thereof with the Supreme Court of Florida. Thereafter the court shall issue an order classifying the member as an inactive member.

If an order of restoration is entered by a court having jurisdiction or the attorney is discharged from hospitalization under the Florida Mental Health Act or the authority of other applicable law concerning the capability of an attorney to practice law, the attorney may be reinstated in the same manner as in proceedings for reinstatement after suspension for acts of misconduct.

(e) Proceedings Upon Consent to Incapacity. An attorney may consent to incapacity not for misconduct in the same manner as provided in rule 3–7.9 of these Rules Regulating The Florida Bar.

Former Rule 3–7.12 renumbered as Rule 3–7.13 March 16, 1990, effective March 17, 1990 (558 So.2d 1008). Amended July 23, 1992, effective Jan. 1, 1993 (605 So.2d 252); July 17, 1997 (697 So.2d 115); March 23, 2000 (763 So.2d 1002); Nov. 19, 2009, effective Feb. 1, 2010 (24 So.3d 63); April 12, 2012, effective July 1, 2012 (101 So.3d 807).

Rule 3–7.14. Florida statutes superseded

These Rules of Discipline shall supersede such parts of sections 454.18, 454.31, and 454.32, Florida Statutes (1991), as are in conflict herewith.

Former Rule 3–7.13 renumbered as Rule 3–7.14 March 16, 1990, effective March 17, 1990 (558 So.2d 1008). Amended July 23, 1992, effective Jan. 1, 1993 (605 So.2d 252).

Rule 3–7.15. Amendments

Petitions for revision of or amendments to chapter 3 will be entertained by this court when presented by the board of governors or by not fewer than 50 members in good standing of The Florida Bar. Notice of intention to file such petition together with a copy of the proposed amendment shall be published in The Florida Bar News not less than 30 days prior to the filing of such petition. The court will thereafter accept objections or comments on such petition.

Former Rule 3–7.14 renumbered as Rule 3–7.15 March 16, 1990, effective March 17, 1990 (558 So.2d 1008). Amended July 23, 1992, effective Jan. 1, 1993 (605 So.2d 252).

Rule 3–7.16. Limitation on Time to Bring Complaint

(a) Time for Inquiries, Complaints, and Reopened Cases. Inquiries raised or complaints presented by or to The Florida Bar under these rules shall be commenced within 6 years from the time the matter giving rise to the inquiry or complaint is discovered or, with due diligence, should have been discovered.

A reopened disciplinary investigation shall not be barred by this rule if the investigation is reopened within 1 year of the date on which the matter was closed, except that reopened investigations based on deferrals made in accord with bar policy and as authorized elsewhere in these Rules Regulating The Florida Bar shall not be barred if reopened within 1 year of the conclusion of the civil, criminal, or other proceedings on which deferral was based.

(b) Exception for Theft or Conviction of a Felony Criminal Offense. There shall be no limit on the time in which to present, reopen, or bring a matter alleging theft or conviction of a felony criminal offense by a member of The Florida Bar.

(c) Tolling Based on Fraud, Concealment, or Misrepresentation. In matters covered by this rule where it can be shown that fraud, concealment, or intentional misrepresentation of fact prevented the discovery of the matter giving rise to the inquiry or complaint, the limitation of time in which to bring or reopen an inquiry or complaint within this rule shall be tolled.

(d) Constitutional Officers. Inquiries raised or complaints presented by or to The Florida Bar about the conduct of a constitutional officer who is required to be a member in good standing of The Florida Bar shall be commenced within 6 years after the constitutional officer vacates office.

Added July 20, 1995 (658 So.2d 930). Amended March 23, 2000 (763 So.2d 1002); Dec. 20, 2007, effective March 1, 2008 (978 So.2d 91).

Rule 3–7.17. Vexatious Conduct and Limitation on Filings

(a) Definition. Vexatious conduct is conduct that amounts to abuse of the bar disciplinary process by use of inappropriate, repetitive, or frivolous actions or communications of any kind directed at or concerning any participant or agency in the bar disciplinary process such as the complainant, the respondent, a grievance committee member, the grievance committee, the bar, the referee, or the Supreme Court of Florida, or an agent, servant, employee, or representative of these individuals or agencies.

(b) Authority of the Court. Only the Supreme Court of Florida has the authority to enter an order under the provisions of this rule.

(c) Procedure.

(1) *Commencement.* Proceedings under this rule may be commenced on the court's own motion, by a report and recommendation of the referee, or a petition of The Florida Bar, acting for itself, the grievance committees or their members, authorized by its executive committee and signed by its executive director, demonstrating that an individual has abused the disciplinary process by engaging in vexatious conduct. The court may enter an order directing the individual(s) engaging in the vexatious conduct to show good cause why the court should not enter an order prohibiting continuation of the conduct and/or imposing limitations on future conduct.

(2) *Order To Show Cause.* The court, acting on its own motion, or on the recommendation of the referee or petition of the bar, may enter an order directing an individual to show cause why the court should not enter an order prohibiting continuation of the vexatious conduct and/or imposing limitations on future conduct. A copy of the order shall be served on the referee (if one has been appointed), the respondent, and The Florida Bar.

(3) *Response to Order to Show Cause.* The individual(s) alleged to have engaged in vexatious conduct shall have 15 days from service of the order to show cause, or such other time as the court may allow, in which to file a response. Failure to file a response in the time provided, without good cause, shall be a default and the court may, without further proceedings, enter an order prohibiting or limiting future communications or filings as set forth in this rule, or imposing any other sanction(s) that the court is authorized to impose. A copy of any response shall be served on a referee (if one has been appointed), the respondent, and The Florida Bar.

(4) *Reply.* The referee (if one has been appointed), the respondent, and The Florida Bar shall have 10 days from the filing of a response to an order to show cause entered under this rule in which to file a reply. Failure to file a reply in the time provided, without good cause, shall prohibit a reply.

(5) *Referral to Referee.* The court may refer proceedings under this rule to a referee for taking testimony and receipt of evidence. Proceedings before a referee under this subdivision shall be conducted in the same manner as proceedings before a referee as set forth in rule 3–7.6 of these rules.

(d) Court Order.

(1) *Rejection of Communications.* An order issued under this rule may contain provisions permitting the clerk of the Supreme Court of Florida, referee, The Florida Bar, and/or any other individual(s) or entity(ies) specified in the order to reject or block vexatious communications as specifically designated in the order. The order may authorize the individual(s), entity(ies), or group(s) specified in the order to block telephone calls made or electronic mail sent by an individual subject to an order issued under the authority of this rule.

(2) *Denial of Physical Access.* The order may deny access to specific physical areas or locations to an individual subject to an order issued under the authority of this rule. The order may also allow the individual(s), entity(ies), or group(s) specified in the order to deny access to those areas or locations.

(3) *Prohibition of or Limitation on Filings.* The order of the court may include a requirement that an individual subject to an order issued under the authority of this rule may be prohibited from submitting any future filings unless they are submitted solely by a member of The Florida Bar who is eligible to practice law or another person authorized to appear in the proceedings. If a person who is subject to an order issued under this rule is a member of The Florida Bar, that member may be prohibited from co-signing and submitting future filings.

(e) Violation of Order. Violation of an order issued under this rule shall be considered as a matter of contempt and processed as provided elsewhere in these Rules Regulating The Florida Bar.

Added Nov. 19, 2009, effective Feb. 1, 2010 (24 So.3d 63).

Comment

This rule is enacted to address circumstances involving repetitive conduct of the type that goes beyond conduct that is merely contentious and unsuccessful. This rule addresses conduct that negatively affects the finite resources of our court system, resources that must be reserved for resolution of genuine disputes. As recognized by the United States Supreme Court, "every paper filed with the Clerk of this Court, no matter how repetitious or frivolous, requires some portion of the institution's limited resources. A part of the court's responsibility is to see that these resources are allocated in a way that promotes the interests of justice." *In re McDonald*, 489 U.S. 180, 184 (1989).

This concept has also been recognized in bar disciplinary proceedings by the Supreme Court of Florida when the court stated: "Kandekore's actions create a drain on the Court's limited time, for with each filing the Court has, as it must, reviewed and considered repetitious and meritless arguments. Therefore, we conclude that a limitation on Kandekore's ability to file repeated challenges to his long-final sanctions would further the constitutional right of access because it would permit this Court to devote its finite resources to the consideration of legitimate claims filed by others." *The Florida Bar re. Kandekore*, 932 So.2d 1005, 1006 (Fla. 2006). Kandekore engaged in vexatious conduct after the court entered an order of disbarment.

The Supreme Court of Florida has also limited the ability of a lawyer to file further pleadings while that lawyer's disciplinary case(s) were in active litigation. *The Florida Bar v. Thompson*, 979 So.2d 917 (Fla. 2008).

3–8. FLORIDA BAR GRIEVANCE MEDIATION PROGRAM [DELETED]

CHAPTER 4. RULES OF PROFESSIONAL CONDUCT

PREAMBLE: A LAWYER'S RESPONSIBILITIES

Section
Preamble:. A Lawyer's Responsibilities.
Preamble:. A Lawyer's Responsibilities.

4–1. CLIENT–LAWYER RELATIONSHIP

Rule
4–1.1. Competence.
4–1.2. Objectives and Scope of Representation.
4–1.3. Diligence.
4–1.4. Communication.
4–1.5. Fees and Costs for Legal Services.
4–1.6. Confidentiality of Information.
4–1.6. Confidentiality of Information.
4–1.7. Conflict of Interest; Current Clients.
4–1.8. Conflict of Interest; Prohibited and Other Transactions.
4–1.9. Conflict of Interest; Former Client.
4–1.10. Imputation of Conflicts of Interest; General Rule.
4–1.11. Special Conflicts of Interest for Former and Current Government Officers and Employees.
4–1.12. Former Judge or Arbitrator, Mediator or Other Third–Party Neutral.
4–1.13. Organization as client.
4–1.14. Client under a disability.
4–1.15. Safekeeping property.
4–1.16. Declining or Terminating Representation.
4–1.17. Sale of Law Practice.
4–1.17. Sale of Law Practice.
4–1.18. Duties to Prospective Client.
4–1.18. Duties to Prospective Client.

4–2. COUNSELOR

4–2.1. Adviser.
4–2.3. Evaluation for Use by Third Persons.
4–2.4. Lawyer Serving as Third–Party Neutral.

4–3. ADVOCATE

4–3.1. Meritorious Claims and Contentions.
–3.2. Expediting litigation.
3. Candor Toward the Tribunal.
Fairness to Opposing Party and Counsel.
Impartiality and decorum of the tribunal.

Rule
4–3.6. Trial Publicity.
4–3.7. Lawyer as Witness.
4–3.8. Special responsibilities of a prosecutor.
4–3.9. Advocate in Nonadjudicative Proceedings.

4–4. TRANSACTIONS WITH PERSONS OTHER THAN CLIENTS

4–4.1. Truthfulness in statements to others.
4–4.2. Communication with Person Represented by Counsel.
4–4.3. Dealing with Unrepresented Persons.
4–4.4. Respect for Rights of Third Persons.
4–4.4. Respect for Rights of Third Persons.

4–5. LAW FIRMS AND ASSOCIATIONS

4–5.1. Responsibilities of Partners, Managers, and Supervisory Lawyers.
4–5.2. Responsibilities of a subordinate lawyer.
4–5.3. Responsibilities Regarding Nonlawyer Assistants.
4–5.3. Responsibilities Regarding Nonlawyer Assistants.
4–5.4. Professional Independence of a Lawyer.
4–5.5. Unlicensed Practice of Law; Multijurisdictional Practice of Law.
4–5.5. Unlicensed Practice of Law; Multijurisdictional Practice of Law.
4–5.6. Restrictions on Right to Practice.
4–5.7. Responsibilities regarding nonlegal services.
4–5.8. Procedures for Lawyers Leaving Law Firms and Dissolution of Law Firms.

4–6. PUBLIC SERVICE

4–6.1. Pro bono public service.
4–6.2. Accepting appointments.
4–6.3. Membership in legal services organization.
4–6.4. Law reform activities affecting client interests.
4–6.5. Voluntary Pro Bono Plan.
4–6.5. Voluntary Pro Bono Plan.

4–7. INFORMATION ABOUT LEGAL SERVICES

4–7.11. Application of Rules.
4–7.12. Required Content.

PREAMBLE: A LAWYER'S RESPONSIBILITIES

Preamble: A Lawyer's Responsibilities

Text of preamble effective until October 1, 2015. See, also, preamble effective October 1, 2015.

A lawyer, as a member of the legal profession, is a representative of clients, an officer of the legal system, and a public citizen having special responsibility for the quality of justice.

As a representative of clients, a lawyer performs various functions. As an adviser, a lawyer provides a client with an informed understanding of the client's legal rights and obligations and explains their practical implications. As an advocate, a lawyer zealously asserts the client's position under the rules of the adversary system. As a negotiator, a lawyer seeks a result advantageous to the client but consistent with requirements of honest dealing with others. As an evaluator, a lawyer acts by examining a client's legal affairs and reporting about them to the client or to others.

In addition to these representational functions, a lawyer may serve as a third-party neutral, a nonrepresentational role helping the parties to resolve a dispute or other matter. Some of these rules apply directly to lawyers who are or have served as third-party neutrals. See, e.g., rules 4–1.12 and 4–2.4. In addition, there are rules that apply to lawyers who are not active in the practice of law or to practicing lawyers even when they are acting in a nonprofessional capacity. For example, a lawyer who commits fraud in the conduct of a business is subject to discipline for engaging in conduct involving dishonesty, fraud, deceit, or misrepresentation. See rule 4–8.4.

In all professional functions a lawyer should be competent, prompt, and diligent. A lawyer should maintain communication with a client concerning the representation. A lawyer should keep in confidence information relating to representation of a client except so far as disclosure is required or permitted by the Rules of Professional Conduct or by law.

A lawyer's conduct should conform to the requirements of the law, both in professional service to clients and in the lawyer's business and personal affairs. A lawyer should use the law's procedures only for legitimate purposes and not to harass or intimidate others. A lawyer should demonstrate respect for the legal system and for those who serve it, including judges, other lawyers, and public officials. While it is a lawyer's duty, when necessary, to challenge the rectitude of official action, it is also a lawyer's duty to uphold legal process.

As a public citizen, a lawyer should seek improvement of the law, access to the legal system, the administration of justice, and the quality of service rendered by the legal profession. As a member of a learned profession, a lawyer should cultivate knowledge of the law beyond its use for clients, employ that knowledge in reform of the law, and work to strengthen legal education. In addition, a lawyer should further the public's understanding of and confidence in the rule of law and the justice system, because legal institutions in a constitutional democracy depend on popular participation and support to maintain their authority. A lawyer should be mindful of deficiencies in the administration of justice and of the fact that the poor, and sometimes persons who are not poor, cannot afford adequate legal assistance. Therefore, all lawyers should devote professional time and resources and use civic influence to ensure equal access to our system of justice for all those who because of economic or social barriers cannot afford or secure adequate legal counsel. A lawyer should aid the legal profession in pursuing these objectives and should help the bar regulate itself in the public interest.

Many of the lawyer's professional responsibilities are prescribed in the Rules of Professional Conduct and in substantive and procedural law. A lawyer is also guided by personal conscience and the approbation of professional peers. A lawyer should strive to attain the highest level of skill, to improve the law and the legal profession, and to exemplify the legal profession's ideals of public service.

A lawyer's responsibilities as a representative of clients, an officer of the legal system, and a public citizen are usually harmonious. Zealous advocacy is not inconsistent with justice. Moreover, unless violations of law or injury to another or another's property is involved, preserving client confidences ordinarily serves the public interest because people are more likely to seek legal advice, and thereby heed their legal obligations, when they know their communications will be private.

In the practice of law conflicting responsibilities are often encountered. Difficult ethical problems may arise from a conflict between a lawyer's responsibility to a client and the lawyer's own sense of personal honor, including obligations to society and the legal profession. The Rules of Professional Conduct often prescribe terms for resolving such conflicts. Within the framework of these rules, however, many difficult issues of professional discretion can arise. Such issues must be resolved through the exercise of sensitive professional and moral judgment guided by the basic principles underlying the rules. These principles include the lawyer's obligation to protect and pursue a client's legitimate interests, within the bounds of the law, while maintaining a professional, courteous, and civil attitude toward all persons involved in the legal system.

Lawyers are officers of the court and they are responsible to the judiciary for the propriety of their professional activities. Within that context, the legal profession has been granted powers of self-government. Self–regulation helps maintain the legal profession's independence from undue government domination. An independent legal profession is an important force in preserving government under law, for abuse of legal authority is more readily challenged by a profession whose members are not dependent on the executive and legislative branches of government for the right to practice. Supervision by an independent judiciary, and conformity with the rules the judiciary adopts for the profession, assures both independence and responsibility.

Thus, every lawyer is responsible for observance of the Rules of Professional Conduct. A lawyer should also aid in securing their observance by other lawyers. Neglect of these responsibilities compromises the independence of the profession and the public interest that it serves.

Scope:

The Rules of Professional Conduct are rules of reason. They should be interpreted with reference to the purposes of legal representation and of the law itself. Some of the rules are imperatives, cast in the terms of "shall" or "shall not." These define proper conduct for purposes of professional discipline. Others, generally cast in the term "may," are permissive and define areas under the rules in which the lawyer has discretion to exercise professional judgment. No disciplinary action should be taken when the lawyer chooses not to act or acts within the bounds of such discretion. Other rules define the nature of relationships between the lawyer and others. The rules are thus partly obligatory and disciplinary and partly constitutive and descriptive in that they define a lawyer's professional role.

The comment accompanying each rule explains and illustrates the meaning and purpose of the rule. The comments are intended only as guides to interpretation, whereas the text of each rule is authoritative. Thus, comments, even when they use the term "should," do not add obligations to the rules but merely provide guidance for practicing in compliance with the rules.

The rules presuppose a larger legal context shaping the lawyer's role. That context includes court rules and statutes relating to matters of licensure, laws defining specific obligations of lawyers, and substantive and procedural law in general. Compliance with the rules, as with all law in an open society, depends primarily upon understanding and voluntary compliance, secondarily upon reinforcement by peer and public opinion, and finally, when necessary, upon enforcement through disciplinary proceedings. The rules do not, however, exhaust the moral and ethical considerations that should inform a lawyer, for no worthwhile human activity can be completely defined by legal rules. The rules simply provide a framework for the ethical practice of law. The comments are sometimes used to alert lawyers to their responsibilities under other law.

Furthermore, for purposes of determining the lawyer's authority and responsibility, principles of substantive law external to these rules determine whether a client-lawyer relationship exists. Most of the duties flowing from the client-lawyer relationship attach only after the client has requested the lawyer to render legal services and the lawyer has agreed to do so. But there are some duties, such as that of confidentiality under rule 4–1.6, which attach when the lawyer agrees to consider whether a client-lawyer relationship shall be established. See rule 4–1.18. Whether a client-lawyer relationship exists for any specific purpose can depend on the circumstances and may be a question of fact.

Failure to comply with an obligation or prohibition imposed by a rule is a basis for invoking the disciplinary process. The rules presuppose that disciplinary assessment of a lawyer's conduct will be made on the basis of the facts and circumstances as they existed at the time of the conduct in question in recognition of the fact that a lawyer often has to act upon uncertain or incomplete evidence of the situation. Moreover, the rules presuppose that whether discipline should be imposed for a violation, and the severity of a sanction, depend on all the circumstances, such as the willfulness and seriousness of the violation, extenuating factors, and whether there have been previous violations.

Violation of a rule should not itself give rise to a cause of action against a lawyer nor should it create any presumption in such a case that a legal duty has been breached. In addition, violation of a rule does not necessarily warrant any other nondisciplinary remedy, such as disqualification of a lawyer in pending litigation. The rules are designed to provide guidance to lawyers and to provide a structure for regulating conduct through disciplinary agencies. They are not designed to be a basis for civil liability. Furthermore, the purpose of the rules can be subverted when they are invoked by opposing parties as procedural weapons. The fact that a rule is a just basis for a lawyer's self-assessment, or for sanctioning a lawyer under the administration of a disciplinary authority, does not imply that an antagonist in a collateral proceeding or transaction has standing to seek enforcement of the rule. Accordingly, nothing in the rules should be deemed to augment any substantive legal duty of lawyers or the extra-disciplinary consequences of violating such duty. Nevertheless, since the rules do establish standards of conduct by lawyers, a lawyer's violation of a rule may be evidence of a breach of the applicable standard of conduct.

Terminology:

"Belief" or "believes" denotes that the person involved actually supposed the fact in question to be true. A person's belief may be inferred from circumstances.

"Consult" or "consultation" denotes communication of information reasonably sufficient to permit the client to appreciate the significance of the matter in question.

"Confirmed in writing," when used in reference to the informed consent of a person, denotes informed consent that is given in writing by the person or a writing that a lawyer promptly transmits to the person confirming an oral informed consent. See "informed consent" below. If it is not feasible to obtain or transmit the writing at the time the person gives informed consent, then the lawyer must obtain or transmit it within a reasonable time thereafter.

"Firm" or "law firm" denotes a lawyer or lawyers in a law partnership, professional corporation, sole proprietorship, or other association authorized to practice law; or lawyers employed in the legal department of a corporation or other organization.

"Fraud" or "fraudulent" denotes conduct having a purpose to deceive and not merely negligent misrepresentation or failure to apprise another of relevant information.

"Informed consent" denotes the agreement by a person to a proposed course of conduct after the lawyer has communicated adequate information and explanation about the material risks of and reasonably available alternatives to the proposed course of conduct.

"Knowingly," "known," or "knows" denotes actual knowledge of the fact in question. A person's knowledge may be inferred from circumstances.

"Lawyer" denotes a person who is a member of The Florida Bar or otherwise authorized to practice in any court of the State of Florida.

"Partner" denotes a member of a partnership and a shareholder in a law firm organized as a professional corporation, or a member of an association authorized to practice law.

"Reasonable" or "reasonably" when used in relation to conduct by a lawyer denotes the conduct of a reasonably prudent and competent lawyer.

"Reasonable belief" or "reasonably believes" when used in reference to a lawyer denotes that the lawyer believes the matter in question and that the circumstances are such that the belief is reasonable.

"Reasonably should know" when used in reference to a lawyer denotes that a lawyer of reasonable prudence and competence would ascertain the matter in question.

"Screened" denotes the isolation of a lawyer from any participation in a matter through the timely imposition of procedures within a firm that are reasonably adequate under the circumstances to protect information that the isolated lawyer is obligated to protect under these rules or other law.

"Substantial" when used in reference to degree or extent denotes a material matter of clear and weighty importance.

"Tribunal" denotes a court, an arbitrator in a binding arbitration proceeding, or a legislative body, administrative agency, or other body acting in an adjudicative capacity. A legislative body, administrative agency, or other body acts in an adjudicative capacity when a neutral official, after the presentation of evidence or legal argument by a party or parties, will render a binding legal judgment directly affecting a party's interests in a particular matter.

"Writing" or "written" denotes a tangible or electronic record of a communication or representation, including handwriting, typewriting, printing, photostating, photography, audio or video recording, and e-mail. A "signed" writing includes an electronic sound, symbol or process attached to or logically associated with a writing and executed or adopted by a person with the intent to sign the writing.

Amended July 23, 1992, effective Jan. 1, 1993 (605 So.2d 252); March 23, 2006, effective May 22, 2006 (933 So.2d 417).

Comment

Confirmed in writing

If it is not feasible to obtain or transmit a written confirmation at the time the client gives informed consent, then the lawyer must obtain or transmit it within a reasonable time thereafter. If a lawyer has obtained a client's informed consent, the lawyer may act in reliance on that consent so long as it is confirmed in writing within a reasonable time thereafter.

Firm

Whether 2 or more lawyers constitute a firm above can depend on the specific facts. For example, 2 practitioners who share office space and occasionally consult or assist each other ordinarily would not be regarded as constituting a firm. However, if they present themselves to the public in a way that suggests that they are a firm or conduct themselves as a firm, they should be regarded as a firm for purposes of the rules. The terms of any formal agreement between associated lawyers are relevant in determining whether they are a firm, as is the fact that they have mutual access to information concerning the clients they serve. Furthermore, it is relevant in doubtful cases to consider the underlying purpose of the rule that is involved. A group of lawyers could be regarded as a firm for purposes of the rule that the same lawyer should not represent opposing parties in litigation, while it might not be so regarded for purposes of the rule that information acquired by 1 lawyer is attributed to another.

With respect to the law department of an organization, including the government, there is ordinarily no question that the members of the department constitute a firm within the meaning of the Rules of Professional Conduct. There can be uncertainty, however, as to the identity of the client. For example, it may not be clear whether the law department of a corporation represents a subsidiary or an affiliated corporation, as well as the corporation by which the members of the department are directly employed. A similar question can arise concerning an unincorporated association and its local affiliates.

Similar questions can also arise with respect to lawyers in legal aid and legal services organizations. Depending upon the structure of the organization, the entire organization or different components of it may constitute a firm or firms for purposes of these rules.

Fraud

When used in these rules, the terms "fraud" or "fraudulent" refer to conduct that has a purpose to deceive. This does not include merely negligent misrepresentation or negligent failure to apprise another of relevant information. For purposes of these rules, it is not necessary that anyone has suffered damages or relied on the misrepresentation or failure to inform.

Informed consent

Many of the Rules of Professional Conduct require the lawyer to obtain the informed consent of a client or other person (e.g., a former client or, under certain circumstances, a prospective client) before accepting or continuing representation or pursuing a course of conduct. See, e.g., rules 4–1.2(c), 4–1.6(a), 4–1.7(b), and 4–1.18. The communication necessary to obtain such consent will vary according to the rule involved and the circumstances giving rise to the need to obtain informed consent. The lawyer must make reasonable efforts to ensure that the client or other person possesses information reasonably adequate to make an informed decision. Ordinarily, this will require communication that includes a disclosure of the facts and circumstances giving rise to the situation, any explanation reasonably necessary to inform the client or other person of the material advantages and disadvantages of the proposed course of conduct and a discussion of the client's or other person's options and alternatives. In some circumstances it may be appropriate for a lawyer to advise a client or other person to seek the advice of other counsel. A lawyer need not inform a client or other person of facts or implications already known to the client or other person; nevertheless, a lawyer who does not personally inform the client or other person assumes the risk that the client or other person is inadequately informed and the consent is invalid. In determining whether the information and explanation provided are reasonably adequate, relevant factors include whether the client or other person is experienced in legal matters generally and in making decisions of the type involved, and whether the client or other person is independently represented by other counsel in giving the consent. Normally, such persons need less information and explanation than others, and generally a client or other person who is independently represented by other counsel in giving the consent should be assumed to have given informed consent.

Obtaining informed consent will usually require an affirmative response by the client or other person. In general, a lawyer may not assume consent from a client's or other person's silence. Consent may be inferred, however, from the conduct of a client or other person who has reasonably adequate information about the matter. A number of rules state that a person's consent be confirmed in writing. See, e.g., rule 4–1.7(b). For a definition of "writing" and "confirmed in writing," see terminology above. Other rules require that a client's consent be obtained in a writing signed by the client. See, e.g., rule 4–1.8(a). For a definition of "signed," see terminology above.

Screened

This definition applies to situations where screening of a personally disqualified lawyer is permitted to remove imputation of a conflict of interest under rules 4–1.11, 4–1.12, or 4–1.18.

The purpose of screening is to assure the affected parties that confidential information known by the personally disqualified lawyer remains protected. The personally disqualified lawyer should acknowledge the obligation not to communicate with any of the other lawyers in the firm with respect to the matter. Similarly, other lawyers in the firm who are working on the matter should be informed that the screening is in place and that they may not communicate with the personally disqualified lawyer with respect to the matter. Additional screening measures that are appropriate for the particular matter will depend on the circumstances. To implement, reinforce, and remind all affected lawyers of the presence of the screening, it may be appropriate for the firm to undertake such procedures as a written undertaking by the screened lawyer to avoid any communication with other firm personnel and any contact with any firm files or other materials relating to the matter, written notice and instructions to all other firm personnel forbidding any communication with the screened lawyer relating to the matter, denial of access by the screened lawyer to firm files or other materials relating to the matter, and periodic reminders of the screen to the screened lawyer and all other firm personnel.

In order to be effective, screening measures must be implemented as soon as practicable after a lawyer or law firm knows or reasonably should know that there is a need for screening.

Preamble: A Lawyer's Responsibilities

Text of preamble effective October 1, 2015.
See, also, preamble effective until October 1, 2015.

A lawyer, as a member of the legal profession, is a representative of clients, an officer of the legal system, and a public citizen having special responsibility for the quality of justice.

As a representative of clients, a lawyer performs various functions. As an adviser, a lawyer provides a client with an informed understanding of the client's legal rights and obligations and explains their practical implications. As an advocate, a lawyer zealously asserts the client's position under the rules of the adversary system. As a negotiator, a lawyer seeks a result advantageous to the client but consistent with requirements of honest dealing with others. As an evaluator, a lawyer acts by examining a client's legal affairs and reporting about them to the client or to others.

In addition to these representational functions, a lawyer may serve as a third-party neutral, a nonrepresentational role helping the parties to resolve a dispute or other matter. Some of these rules apply directly to lawyers who are or have served as third-party neutrals. See, e.g., rules 4–1.12 and 4–2.4. In addition, there are rules that apply to lawyers who are not active in the practice of law or to practicing lawyers even when they are acting in a nonprofessional capacity. For example, a lawyer who commits fraud in the conduct of a business is subject to discipline for engaging in conduct involving dishonesty, fraud, deceit, or misrepresentation. See rule 4–8.4.

In all professional functions a lawyer should be competent, prompt, and diligent. A lawyer should maintain communication with a client concerning the representation. A lawyer should keep in confidence information relating to representation of a client except so far as disclosure is required or permitted by the Rules of Professional Conduct or by law.

A lawyer's conduct should conform to the requirements of the law, both in professional service to clients and in the lawyer's business and personal affairs. A lawyer should use the law's procedures only for legitimate purposes and not to harass or intimidate others. A lawyer should demonstrate respect for the legal system and for those who serve it, including judges, other lawyers, and public officials. While it is a lawyer's duty, when necessary, to challenge the rectitude of official action, it is also a lawyer's duty to uphold legal process.

As a public citizen, a lawyer should seek improvement of the law, access to the legal system, the administration of justice, and the quality of service rendered by the legal profession. As a member of a learned profession, a lawyer should cultivate knowledge of the law beyond its use for clients, employ that knowledge in reform of the law, and work to strengthen legal education. In addition, a lawyer should further the public's understanding of and confidence in the rule of law and the justice system, because legal institutions in a constitutional democracy depend on popular participation and support to maintain their authority. A lawyer should be mindful of deficiencies in the administration of justice and of the fact that the poor, and sometimes persons who are not poor, cannot afford adequate legal assistance. Therefore, all lawyers should devote professional time and resources and use civic influence to ensure equal access to our system of justice for all those who because of economic or social barriers cannot afford or secure adequate legal counsel. A lawyer should aid the legal profession in pursuing these objectives and should help the bar regulate itself in the public interest.

Many of the lawyer's professional responsibilities are prescribed in the Rules of Professional Conduct and in substantive and procedural law. A lawyer is also guided by personal conscience and the approbation of professional peers. A lawyer should strive to attain the highest level of skill, to improve the law and the legal profession, and to exemplify the legal profession's ideals of public service.

A lawyer's responsibilities as a representative of clients, an officer of the legal system, and a public citizen are usually harmonious. Zealous advocacy is not inconsistent with justice. Moreover, unless violations of law or injury to another or another's property is involved, preserving client confidences ordinarily serves the public interest because people are more likely to seek legal advice, and heed their legal obligations, when they know their communications will be private.

In the practice of law, conflicting responsibilities are often encountered. Difficult ethical problems may arise from a conflict between a lawyer's responsibility to a client and the lawyer's own sense of personal honor, including obligations to society and the legal profession. The Rules of Professional Conduct often prescribe terms for resolving these conflicts. Within the framework of these rules, however, many difficult issues of professional discretion can arise. These issues must be resolved through the exercise of sensitive professional and moral judgment guided by the basic principles underlying the rules. These principles include the lawyer's obligation to protect and pursue a client's legitimate interests, within the bounds of the law, while maintaining a professional, courteous, and civil attitude toward all persons involved in the legal system.

Lawyers are officers of the court and they are responsible to the judiciary for the propriety of their professional activities. Within that context, the legal profession has been granted powers of self-government. Self-regulation helps maintain the legal profession's independence from undue government domination. An independent legal profession is an important force in preserving government under law, for abuse of legal authority is more readily challenged by a profession whose members are not dependent on the executive and legislative branches of government for the right to practice. Supervision by an independent judiciary, and conformity with the rules the judiciary adopts for the profession, assures both independence and responsibility.

Thus, every lawyer is responsible for observance of the Rules of Professional Conduct. A lawyer should also aid in securing their observance by other lawyers. Neglect of these responsibilities compromises the independence of the profession and the public interest that it serves.

Scope:

The Rules of Professional Conduct are rules of reason. They should be interpreted with reference to the purposes of legal representation and of the law itself. Some of the rules are imperatives, cast in the terms of "must," "must not," or "may not." These define proper conduct for purposes of professional discipline. Others, generally cast in the term "may," are permissive and define areas under the rules in which the lawyer has discretion to exercise professional judgment. No disciplinary action should be taken when the lawyer chooses not to act or acts within the bounds of that discretion. Other rules define the nature of relationships between the lawyer and others. The rules are thus partly obligatory and disciplinary and partly constitutive and descriptive in that they define a lawyer's professional role.

The comment accompanying each rule explains and illustrates the meaning and purpose of the rule. The comments are intended only as guides to interpretation, whereas the text of each rule is authoritative. Thus, comments, even when they use the term "should," do not add obligations to the rules but merely provide guidance for practicing in compliance with the rules.

The rules presuppose a larger legal context shaping the lawyer's role. That context includes court rules and statutes relating to matters of licensure, laws defining specific obligations of lawyers, and substantive and procedural law in general. Compliance with the rules, as with all law in an open society, depends primarily upon understanding and voluntary compliance, secondarily upon reinforcement by peer and public opinion, and finally, when necessary, upon enforcement through disciplinary proceedings. The rules do not, however, exhaust the moral and ethical considerations that should inform a lawyer, for no worthwhile human activity can be completely defined by legal rules. The rules simply provide a framework for the ethical practice of law. The comments are sometimes used to alert lawyers to their responsibilities under other law.

Furthermore, for purposes of determining the lawyer's authority and responsibility, principles of substantive law external to these rules determine whether a client-lawyer relationship exists. Most of the duties flowing from the client-lawyer relationship attach only after the client has requested the lawyer to render legal services and the lawyer has agreed to do so. But there are some duties, for example confidentiality under rule 4–1.6, which attach when the lawyer agrees to consider whether a client-lawyer relationship will be established. See rule 4–1.18. Whether a client-lawyer relationship exists for any specific purpose can depend on the circumstances and may be a question of fact.

Failure to comply with an obligation or prohibition imposed by a rule is a basis for invoking the disciplinary process. The rules presuppose that disciplinary assessment of a lawyer's conduct will be made on the basis of the facts and circumstances as they existed at the time of the conduct in question in recognition of the fact that a lawyer often has to act upon uncertain or incomplete evidence of the situation. Moreover, the rules presuppose that whether discipline should be imposed for a violation, and the severity of a sanction, depend on all the circumstances, such as the willfulness and seriousness of the violation, extenuating factors, and whether there have been previous violations.

Violation of a rule should not itself give rise to a cause of action against a lawyer nor should it create any presumption that a legal duty has been breached. In addition, violation of a rule does not necessarily warrant any other nondisciplinary remedy, such as disqualification of a lawyer in pending litigation. The rules are designed to provide guidance to lawyers and to provide a structure for regulating conduct through disciplinary agencies. They are not designed to be a basis for civil liability. Furthermore, the purpose of the rules can be subverted when they are invoked by opposing parties as procedural weapons. The fact that a rule is a just basis for a lawyer's self-assessment, or for sanctioning a lawyer under the administration of a disciplinary authority, does not imply that an antagonist in a collateral proceeding or transaction has standing to seek enforcement of the rule. Accordingly, nothing in the rules should be deemed to augment any substantive legal duty of lawyers or the extra-disciplinary consequences of violating a substantive legal duty. Nevertheless, since the rules do establish standards of conduct by lawyers, a lawyer's violation of a rule may be evidence of a breach of the applicable standard of conduct.

Terminology:

"Belief" or "believes" denotes that the person involved actually supposed the fact in question to be true. A person's belief may be inferred from circumstances.

"Consult" or "consultation" denotes communication of information reasonably sufficient to permit the client to appreciate the significance of the matter in question.

"Confirmed in writing," when used in reference to the informed consent of a person, denotes informed consent that is given in writing by the person or a writing that a lawyer promptly transmits to the person confirming an oral informed consent. See "informed consent" below. If it is not feasible to obtain or transmit the writing at the time the person gives informed consent, then the lawyer must obtain or transmit it within a reasonable time.

"Firm" or "law firm" denotes a lawyer or lawyers in a law partnership, professional corporation, sole proprietorship, or other association authorized to practice law; or lawyers employed in the legal department of a corporation or other organization.

"Fraud" or "fraudulent" denotes conduct having a purpose to deceive and not merely negligent misrepresentation or failure to apprise another of relevant information.

"Informed consent" denotes the agreement by a person to a proposed course of conduct after the lawyer has communicated adequate information and explanation about the material risks of and reasonably available alternatives to the proposed course of conduct.

"Knowingly," "known," or "knows" denotes actual knowledge of the fact in question. A person's knowledge may be inferred from circumstances.

"Lawyer" denotes a person who is a member of The Florida Bar or otherwise authorized to practice in any court of the State of Florida.

"Partner" denotes a member of a partnership and a shareholder in a law firm organized as a professional corporation, or a member of an association authorized to practice law.

"Reasonable" or "reasonably" when used in relation to conduct by a lawyer denotes the conduct of a reasonably prudent and competent lawyer.

"Reasonable belief" or "reasonably believes" when used in reference to a lawyer denotes that the lawyer believes the matter in question and that the circumstances are such that the belief is reasonable.

"Reasonably should know" when used in reference to a lawyer denotes that a lawyer of reasonable prudence and competence would ascertain the matter in question.

"Screened" denotes the isolation of a lawyer from any participation in a matter through the timely imposition of procedures within a firm that are reasonably adequate under the circumstances to protect information that the isolated lawyer is obligated to protect under these rules or other law.

"Substantial" when used in reference to degree or extent denotes a material matter of clear and weighty importance.

"Tribunal" denotes a court, an arbitrator in a binding arbitration proceeding, or a legislative body, administrative agency, or other body acting in an adjudicative capacity. A legislative body, administrative agency, or other body acts in an adjudicative capacity when a neutral official, after the presentation of evidence or legal argument by a party or parties, will render a binding legal judgment directly affecting a party's interests in a particular matter.

"Writing" or "written" denotes a tangible or electronic record of a communication or representation, including handwriting, typewriting, printing, photostating, photography, audio or video recording, and electronic communications. A "signed" writing includes an electronic sound, symbol or process attached to or logically associated with a writing and executed or adopted by a person with the intent to sign the writing.

Amended July 23, 1992, effective Jan. 1, 1993 (605 So.2d 252); March 23, 2006, effective May 22, 2006 (933 So.2d 417); May 21, 2015, effective Oct. 1, 2015 (164 So.3d 1217).

Comment

Confirmed in writing

If it is not feasible to obtain or transmit a written confirmation at the time the client gives informed consent, then the lawyer must obtain or transmit it within a reasonable time. If a lawyer has obtained a client's informed consent, the lawyer may act in reliance on that consent so long as it is confirmed in writing within a reasonable time.

Firm

Whether 2 or more lawyers constitute a firm above can depend on the specific facts. For example, 2 practitioners who share office space and occasionally consult or assist each other ordinarily would not be regarded as constituting a firm. However, if they present themselves to the public in a way that suggests that they are a firm or conduct themselves as a firm, they should be regarded as a firm for purposes of the rules. The terms of any formal agreement between associated lawyers are relevant in determining whether they are a firm, as is the fact that they have mutual access to information concerning the clients they serve. Furthermore, it is relevant in doubtful cases to consider the underlying purpose of the rule that is involved. A group of lawyers could be regarded as a firm for purposes of the rule that the same lawyer should not represent opposing parties in litigation, while it might not be so regarded for purposes of the rule that information acquired by 1 lawyer is attributed to another.

With respect to the law department of an organization, including the government, there is ordinarily no question that the members of the department constitute a firm within the meaning of the Rules of Professional Conduct. There can be uncertainty, however, as to the identity of the client. For example, it may not be clear whether the law department of a corporation represents a subsidiary or an affiliated corporation, as well as the corporation by which the members of the department are directly employed. A similar question can arise concerning an unincorporated association and its local affiliates.

Similar questions can also arise with respect to lawyers in legal aid and legal services organizations. Depending upon the structure of the organization, the entire organization or different components of it may constitute a firm or firms for purposes of these rules.

Fraud

When used in these rules, the terms "fraud" or "fraudulent" refer to conduct that has a purpose to deceive. This does not include merely negligent misrepresentation or negligent failure to apprise another of relevant information. For purposes of these rules, it is not necessary that anyone has suffered damages or relied on the misrepresentation or failure to inform.

Informed consent

Many of the Rules of Professional Conduct require the lawyer to obtain the informed consent of a client or other person (e.g., a former client or, under certain circumstances, a prospective client) before accepting or continuing representation or pursuing a course of conduct. See, e.g., rules 4–1.2(c), 4–1.6(a), 4–1.7(b), and 4–1.18. The communication necessary to obtain consent will vary according to the rule involved and the circumstances giving rise to the need to obtain informed consent. The lawyer must make reasonable efforts to ensure that the client or other person possesses information reasonably adequate to make an informed decision. Ordinarily, this will require communication that includes a disclosure of the facts and circumstances giving rise to the situation, any explanation reasonably necessary to inform the client or other person of the material advantages and disadvantages of the proposed course of conduct and a discussion of the client's or other person's options and alternatives. In some circumstances it may be appropriate for a lawyer to advise a client or other person to seek the advice of other counsel. A lawyer need not inform a client or other person of facts or implications already known to the client or other person; nevertheless, a lawyer who does not personally inform the client or other person assumes the risk that the client or other person is inadequately informed and the consent is invalid. In determining whether the information and explanation provided are reasonably adequate, relevant factors include whether the client or other person is experienced in legal matters generally and in making decisions of the type involved, and whether the client or other person is independently represented by other counsel in giving the consent. Normally, these persons need less information and explanation than others, and generally a client or other person who is independently represented by other counsel in giving the consent should be assumed to have given informed consent.

Obtaining informed consent will usually require an affirmative response by the client or other person. In general, a lawyer may not assume consent from a client's or other person's silence. Consent may be inferred, however, from the conduct of a client or other person who has reasonably adequate information about the matter. A number of rules state that a person's consent be confirmed in writing. See, e.g., rule 4–1.7(b). For a definition of "writing" and "confirmed in writing," see terminology above. Other rules require that a client's consent be obtained in a writing signed by the client. See, e.g., rule 4–1.8(a). For a definition of "signed," see terminology above.

Screened

This definition applies to situations where screening of a personally disqualified lawyer is permitted to remove imputation of a conflict of interest under rules 4–1.11, 4–1.12, or 4–1.18.

The purpose of screening is to assure the affected parties that confidential information known by the personally disqualified lawyer remains protected. The personally disqualified lawyer should acknowledge the obligation not to communicate with any of the other lawyers in the firm with respect to the matter. Similarly, other lawyers in the firm who are working on the matter should be informed that the screening is in place and that they may not communicate with the personally disqualified lawyer with respect to the matter. Additional screening measures that are appropriate for the particular matter will depend on the circumstances. To implement, reinforce, and remind all affected lawyers of the presence of the screening, it may be appropriate for the firm to undertake these procedures as a written undertaking by the screened lawyer to avoid any communication with other firm personnel and any contact with any firm files or other information, including information in electronic form, relating to the matter, written notice and instructions to all other firm personnel forbidding any communication with the screened lawyer relating to the matter, denial of access by the screened lawyer to firm files or other information, including information in electronic form, relating to the matter, and periodic reminders of the screen to the screened lawyer and all other firm personnel.

In order to be effective, screening measures must be implemented as soon as practicable after a lawyer or law firm knows or reasonably should know that there is a need for screening.

4–1. CLIENT–LAWYER RELATIONSHIP

Rule 4–1.1. Competence

A lawyer shall provide competent representation to a client. Competent representation requires the legal knowledge, skill, thoroughness, and preparation reasonably necessary for the representation.

Comment

Legal knowledge and skill

In determining whether a lawyer employs the requisite knowledge and skill in a particular matter, relevant factors include the relative complexity and specialized nature of the matter, the lawyer's general experience, the lawyer's training and experience in the field in question, the preparation and study the lawyer is able to give the matter, and whether it is feasible to refer the matter to, or associate or consult with, a lawyer of established competence in the field in question. In many instances the required proficiency is that of a general practitioner. Expertise in a particular field of law may be required in some circumstances.

A lawyer need not necessarily have special training or prior experience to handle legal problems of a type with which the lawyer is unfamiliar. A newly admitted lawyer can be as competent as a practitioner with long experience. Some important legal skills, such as the analysis of precedent, the evaluation of evidence and legal drafting, are required in all legal problems. Perhaps the most fundamental legal skill consists of determining what kind of legal problems a situation may involve, a skill that necessarily transcends any particular specialized knowledge. A lawyer can provide adequate representation in a wholly novel field through necessary study. Competent representation can also be provided through the association of a lawyer of established competence in the field in question.

In an emergency a lawyer may give advice or assistance in a matter in which the lawyer does not have the skill ordinarily required where referral to or consultation or association with another lawyer would be impractical. Even in an emergency, however, assistance should be limited to that reasonably necessary in the circumstances, for ill-considered action under emergency conditions can jeopardize the client's interest.

A lawyer may accept representation where the requisite level of competence can be achieved by reasonable preparation. This applies as well to a lawyer who is appointed as counsel for an unrepresented person. See also rule 4–6.2.

Thoroughness and preparation

Competent handling of a particular matter includes inquiry into and analysis of the factual and legal elements of the problem, and use of methods and procedures meeting the standards of competent practitioners. It also includes adequate preparation. The required attention and preparation are determined in part by what is at stake; major litigation and complex transactions ordinarily require more extensive treatment than matters of lesser complexity and consequence. The lawyer should consult with the client about the degree of thoroughness and the level of preparation required as well as the estimated costs involved under the circumstances.

Maintaining competence

To maintain the requisite knowledge and skill, a lawyer should keep abreast of changes in the law and its practice, engage in continuing study and education, and comply with all continuing legal education requirements to which the lawyer is subject.

Rule 4–1.2. Objectives and Scope of Representation

(a) Lawyer to Abide by Client's Decisions. Subject to subdivisions (c) and (d), a lawyer shall abide by a client's decisions concerning the objectives of representation, and, as required by rule 4–1.4, shall reasonably consult with the client as to the means by which they are to be pursued. A lawyer may take such action on behalf of the client as is impliedly authorized to carry out the representation. A lawyer shall abide by a client's decision whether to settle a matter. In a criminal case, the lawyer shall abide by the client's decision, after consultation with the lawyer, as to a plea to be entered, whether to waive jury trial, and whether the client will testify.

(b) No Endorsement of Client's Views or Activities. A lawyer's representation of a client, including representation by appointment, does not constitute an endorsement of the client's political, economic, social, or moral views or activities.

(c) Limitation of Objectives and Scope of Representation. If not prohibited by law or rule, a lawyer and client may agree to limit the objectives or scope of the representation if the limitation is reasonable under the circumstances and the client gives informed consent in writing. If the attorney and client agree to limit the scope of the representation, the lawyer shall advise the client regarding applicability of the rule prohibiting communication with a represented person.

(d) Criminal or Fraudulent Conduct. A lawyer shall not counsel a client to engage, or assist a client, in conduct that the lawyer knows or reasonably should know is criminal or fraudulent. However, a lawyer may discuss the legal consequences of any proposed course of conduct with a client and may counsel or assist a client to make a good faith effort to determine the validity, scope, meaning, or application of the law.

Amended July 23, 1992, effective Jan. 1, 1993 (605 So.2d 252); Nov. 13, 2003, effective Jan. 1, 2004 (860 So.2d 394); March 23, 2006, effective May 22, 2006 (933 So.2d 417).

Comment

Allocation of authority between client and lawyer

Subdivision (a) confers upon the client the ultimate authority to determine the purposes to be served by legal representation, within the limits imposed by law and the lawyer's professional obligations. Within those limits, a client also has a right to consult with the lawyer about the means to be used in pursuing those objectives. At the same time, a lawyer is not required to pursue objectives or employ means simply because a client may wish that the lawyer do so. A clear distinction between objectives and means sometimes cannot be drawn, and in many cases the client-lawyer relationship partakes of a joint undertaking. In questions of means, the lawyer should assume responsibility for technical and legal tactical issues but should defer to the client regarding such questions as the expense to be incurred and concern for third persons who might be adversely affected. Law defining the lawyer's scope of authority in litigation varies among jurisdictions. The decisions specified in subdivision (a), such as whether to settle a civil matter, must also be made by the client. See rule 4-1.4(a)(1) for the lawyer's duty to communicate with the client about such decisions. With respect to the means by which the client's objectives are to be pursued, the lawyer shall consult with the client as required by rule 4-1.4(a)(2) and may take such action as is impliedly authorized to carry out the representation.

On occasion, however, a lawyer and a client may disagree about the means to be used to accomplish the client's objectives. The lawyer should consult with the client and seek a mutually acceptable resolution of the disagreement. If such efforts are unavailing and the lawyer has a fundamental disagreement with the client, the lawyer may withdraw from the representation. See rule 4-1.16(b)(4). Conversely, the client may resolve the disagreement by discharging the lawyer. See rule 4-1.16(a)(3).

At the outset of a representation, the client may authorize the lawyer to take specific action on the client's behalf without further consultation. Absent a material change in circumstances and subject to rule 4-1.4, a lawyer may rely on such an advance authorization. The client may, however, revoke such authority at any time.

In a case in which the client appears to be suffering mental disability, the lawyer's duty to abide by the client's decisions is to be guided by reference to rule 4-1.14.

Independence from client's views or activities

Legal representation should not be denied to people who are unable to afford legal services or whose cause is controversial or the subject of popular disapproval. By the same token representing a client does not constitute approval of the client's views or activities.

Agreements limiting scope of representation

The scope of services to be provided by a lawyer may be limited by agreement with the client or by the terms under which the lawyer's services are made available to the client. When a lawyer has been retained by an insurer to represent an insured, for example, the representation may be limited to matters related to the insurance coverage. A limited representation may be appropriate because the client has limited objectives for the representation. In addition, the terms upon which representation is undertaken may exclude specific means that might otherwise be used to accomplish the client's objectives. Such limitations may exclude actions that the client thinks are too costly or that the lawyer regards as repugnant or imprudent, or which the client regards as financially impractical.

Although this rule affords the lawyer and client substantial latitude to limit the representation if not prohibited by law or rule, the limitation must be reasonable under the circumstances. If, for example, a client's objective is limited to securing general information about the law the client needs in order to handle a common and typically uncomplicated legal problem, the lawyer and client may agree that the lawyer's services will be limited to a brief consultation. Such a limitation, however, would not be reasonable if the time allotted was not sufficient to yield advice upon which the client could rely. In addition, a lawyer and client may agree that the representation will be limited to providing assistance out of court, including providing advice on the operation of the court system and drafting pleadings and responses. If the lawyer assists a pro se litigant by drafting any document to be submitted to a court, the lawyer is not obligated to sign the document. However, the lawyer must indicate "Prepared with the assistance of counsel" on the document to avoid misleading the court, which otherwise might be under the impression that the person, who appears to be proceeding pro se, has received no assistance from a lawyer. If not prohibited by law or rule, a lawyer and client may agree that any in-court representation in a family law proceeding be limited as provided for in Family Law Rule of Procedure 12.040. For example, a lawyer and client may agree that the lawyer will represent the client at a hearing regarding child support and not at the final hearing or in any other hearings. For limited in-court representation in family law proceedings, the attorney shall communicate to the client the specific boundaries and limitations of the representation so that the client is able to give informed consent to the representation.

Regardless of the circumstances, a lawyer providing limited representation forms an attorney-client relationship with the litigant, and owes the client all attendant ethical obligations and duties imposed by the Rules Regulating The Florida Bar, including, but not limited to, duties of competence, communication, confidentiality and avoidance of conflicts of interest. Although an agreement for limited representation does not exempt a lawyer from the duty to provide competent representation, the limitation is a factor to be considered when determining the legal knowledge, skill, thoroughness and preparation reasonably necessary for the representation. See rule 4-1.1.

An agreement concerning the scope of representation must accord with the Rules of Professional Conduct and law. For example, the client may not be asked to agree to representation so limited in scope as to violate rule 4-1.1 or to surrender the right to terminate the lawyer's services or the right to settle litigation that the lawyer might wish to continue.

Criminal, fraudulent, and prohibited transactions

A lawyer is required to give an honest opinion about the actual consequences that appear likely to result from a client's conduct. The fact that a client uses advice in a course of action that is criminal or fraudulent does not, of itself, make a lawyer a party to the course of action. However, a lawyer may not assist a client in conduct that the lawyer knows or reasonably should know to be criminal or fraudulent. There is a critical distinction between presenting an analysis of legal aspects of questionable conduct and recommending the means by which a crime or fraud might be committed with impunity.

When the client's course of action has already begun and is continuing, the lawyer's responsibility is especially delicate. The lawyer is required to avoid assisting the client, for example, by drafting or delivering documents that the lawyer knows are fraudulent or by suggesting how the wrongdoing might be concealed. A lawyer may not continue assisting a client in conduct that the lawyer originally supposed was legally proper but then discovers is criminal or fraudulent. The lawyer must, therefore, withdraw from the representation of the client in the matter. See rule 4–1.16(a). In some cases, withdrawal alone might be insufficient. It may be necessary for the lawyer to give notice of the fact of withdrawal and to disaffirm any opinion, document, affirmation, or the like. See rule 4–4.1.

Where the client is a fiduciary, the lawyer may be charged with special obligations in dealings with a beneficiary.

Subdivision (d) applies whether or not the defrauded party is a party to the transaction. For example, a lawyer must not participate in a transaction to effectuate criminal or fraudulent avoidance of tax liability. Subdivision (d) does not preclude undertaking a criminal defense incident to a general retainer for legal services to a lawful enterprise. The last sentence of subdivision (d) recognizes that determining the validity or interpretation of a statute or regulation may require a course of action involving disobedience of the statute or regulation or of the interpretation placed upon it by governmental authorities.

If a lawyer comes to know or reasonably should know that a client expects assistance not permitted by the Rules of Professional Conduct or other law or if the lawyer intends to act contrary to the client's instructions, the lawyer must consult with the client regarding the limitations on the lawyer's conduct. See rule 4–1.4(a)(5).

Rule 4–1.3. Diligence

A lawyer shall act with reasonable diligence and promptness in representing a client.

Comment

A lawyer should pursue a matter on behalf of a client despite opposition, obstruction, or personal inconvenience to the lawyer and take whatever lawful and ethical measures are required to vindicate a client's cause or endeavor. A lawyer must also act with commitment and dedication to the interests of the client and with zeal in advocacy upon the client's behalf. A lawyer is not bound, however, to press for every advantage that might be realized for a client. For example, a lawyer may have authority to exercise professional discretion in determining the means by which a matter should be pursued. See rule 4–1.2. The lawyer's duty to act with reasonable diligence does not require the use of offensive tactics or preclude the treating of all persons involved in the legal process with courtesy and respect.

A lawyer's workload must be controlled so that each matter can be handled competently.

Perhaps no professional shortcoming is more widely resented than procrastination. A client's interests often can be adversely affected by the passage of time or the change of conditions; in extreme instances, as when a lawyer overlooks a statute of limitations, the client's legal position may be destroyed. Even when the client's interests are not affected in substance, however, unreasonable delay can cause a client needless anxiety and undermine confidence in the lawyer. A lawyer's duty to act with reasonable promptness, however, does not preclude the lawyer from agreeing to a reasonable request for a postponement that will not prejudice the lawyer's client.

Unless the relationship is terminated as provided in rule 4–1.16, a lawyer should carry through to conclusion all matters undertaken for a client. If a lawyer's employment is limited to a specific matter, the relationship terminates when the matter has been resolved. If a lawyer has served a client over a substantial period in a variety of matters, the client sometimes may assume that the lawyer will continue to serve on a continuing basis unless the lawyer gives notice of withdrawal. Doubt about whether a client-lawyer relationship still exists should be clarified by the lawyer, preferably in writing, so that the client will not mistakenly suppose the lawyer is looking after the client's affairs when the lawyer has ceased to do so. For example, if a lawyer has handled a judicial or administrative proceeding that produced a result adverse to the client and the lawyer and the client have not agreed that the lawyer will handle the matter on appeal, the lawyer must consult with the client about the possibility of appeal before relinquishing responsibility for the matter. See rule 4–1.4(a)(2). Whether the lawyer is obligated to prosecute the appeal for the client depends on the scope of the representation the lawyer has agreed to provide to the client. See rule 4–1.2.

Rule 4–1.4. Communication

(a) Informing Client of Status of Representation. A lawyer shall:

(1) promptly inform the client of any decision or circumstance with respect to which the client's informed consent, as defined in terminology, is required by these rules;

(2) reasonably consult with the client about the means by which the client's objectives are to be accomplished;

(3) keep the client reasonably informed about the status of the matter;

(4) promptly comply with reasonable requests for information; and

(5) consult with the client about any relevant limitation on the lawyer's conduct when the lawyer knows or reasonably should know that the client expects assistance not permitted by the Rules of Professional Conduct or other law.

(b) Duty to Explain Matters to Client. A lawyer shall explain a matter to the extent reasonably necessary to permit the client to make informed decisions regarding the representation.

Amended July 23, 1992, effective Jan. 1, 1993 (605 So.2d 252); March 23, 2006, effective May 22, 2006 (933 So.2d 417).

Comment

Text of comment effective until October 1, 2015.

Reasonable communication between the lawyer and the client is necessary for the client to effectively participate in the representation.

Communicating with client

If these rules require that a particular decision about the representation be made by the client, subdivision (a)(1) requires that the lawyer promptly consult with and secure the client's consent prior to taking action unless prior discussions with the client have resolved what action the client wants the lawyer to take. For example, a lawyer who receives from opposing counsel an offer of settlement in a civil controversy or a proffered plea bargain in a criminal case must promptly inform the client of its substance unless the client has previously indicated that the proposal will be acceptable or unacceptable or has authorized the lawyer to accept or to reject the offer. See rule 4–1.2(a).

Subdivision (a)(2) requires the lawyer to reasonably consult with the client about the means to be used to accomplish the client's objectives. In some situations—depending on both the importance of the action under consideration and the feasibility of consulting with the client—this duty will require consultation prior to taking action. In other circumstances, such as during a trial when an immediate decision must be made, the exigency of the situation may require the lawyer to act without prior consultation. In such cases the lawyer must nonetheless act reasonably to inform the client of actions the lawyer has taken on the client's behalf. Additionally, subdivision (a)(3) requires that the lawyer keep the client reasonably informed about the status of the matter, such as significant developments affecting the timing or the substance of the representation.

A lawyer's regular communication with clients will minimize the occasions on which a client will need to request information concerning the representation. When a client makes a reasonable request for information, however, subdivision (a)(4) requires prompt compliance with the request, or if a prompt response is not feasible, that the lawyer, or a member of the lawyer's staff, acknowledge receipt of the request and advise the client when a response may be expected.

Explaining matters

The client should have sufficient information to participate intelligently in decisions concerning the objectives of the representation and the means by which they are to be pursued, to the extent the client is willing and able to do so.

Adequacy of communication depends in part on the kind of advice or assistance that is involved. For example, when there is time to explain a proposal made in a negotiation, the lawyer should review all important provisions with the client before proceeding to an agreement. In litigation a lawyer should explain the general strategy and prospects of success and ordinarily should consult the client on tactics that are likely to result in significant expense or to injure or coerce others. On the other hand, a lawyer ordinarily will not be expected to describe trial or negotiation strategy in detail. The guiding principle is that the lawyer should fulfill reasonable client expectations for information consistent with the duty to act in the client's best interests and the client's overall requirements as to the character of representation. In certain circumstances, such as when a lawyer asks a client to consent to a representation affected by a conflict of interest, the client must give informed consent, as defined in terminology.

Ordinarily, the information to be provided is that appropriate for a client who is a comprehending and responsible adult. However, fully informing the client according to this standard may be impracticable, for example, where the client is a child or suffers from mental disability. See rule 4–1.14. When the client is an organization or group, it is often impossible or inappropriate to inform every one of its members about its legal affairs; ordinarily, the lawyer should address communications to the appropriate officials of the organization. See rule 4–1.13. Where many routine matters are involved, a system of limited or occasional reporting may be arranged with the client.

Withholding information

In some circumstances, a lawyer may be justified in delaying transmission of information when the client would be likely to react imprudently to an immediate communication. Thus, a lawyer might withhold a psychiatric diagnosis of a client when the examining psychiatrist indicates that disclosure would harm the client. A lawyer may not withhold information to serve the lawyer's own interest or convenience or the interests or convenience of another person. Rules or court orders governing litigation may provide that information supplied to a lawyer may not be disclosed to the client. Rule 4–3.4(c) directs compliance with such rules or orders.

Text of comment effective October 1, 2015.

Reasonable communication between the lawyer and the client is necessary for the client to effectively participate in the representation.

Communicating with client

If these rules require that a particular decision about the representation be made by the client, subdivision (a)(1) requires that the lawyer promptly consult with and secure the client's consent prior to taking action unless prior discussions with the client have resolved what action the client wants the lawyer to take. For example, a lawyer who receives from opposing counsel an offer of settlement in a civil controversy or a proffered plea bargain in a criminal case must promptly inform the client of its substance unless the client has previously indicated that the proposal will be acceptable or unacceptable or has authorized the lawyer to accept or to reject the offer. See rule 4–1.2(a).

Subdivision (a)(2) requires the lawyer to reasonably consult with the client about the means to be used to accomplish the client's objectives. In some situations—depending on both the importance of the action under consideration and the feasibility of consulting with the client—this duty will require consultation prior to taking action. In other circumstances, such as during a trial when an immediate decision must be made, the exigency of the situation may require the lawyer to act without prior consultation. In such cases the lawyer must nonetheless act reasonably to inform the client of actions the lawyer has taken on the client's behalf. Additionally, subdivision (a)(3) requires that the lawyer keep the client reasonably informed about the status of the matter, such as significant developments affecting the timing or the substance of the representation.

A lawyer's regular communication with clients will minimize the occasions on which a client will need to request information concerning the representation. When a client makes a reasonable request for information, however, subdivision (a)(4) requires prompt compliance with the request, or if a prompt response is not feasible, that the lawyer, or a member of the lawyer's staff, acknowledge receipt of the request and advise the client when a response may be expected.

Lawyers have particular responsibilities in communicating with clients regarding changes in firm composition. See Rule 4–5.8.

Explaining matters

The client should have sufficient information to participate intelligently in decisions concerning the objectives of the representation and the means by which they are to be pursued, to the extent the client is willing and able to do so.

Adequacy of communication depends in part on the kind of advice or assistance that is involved. For example, when there is time to explain a proposal made in a negotiation, the lawyer should review all important provisions with the client before proceeding to an agreement. In litigation a lawyer should explain the general strategy and prospects of success and ordinarily should consult the client on tactics that are likely to result in significant expense or to injure or coerce others. On the other hand, a lawyer ordinarily will not be expected to describe trial or negotiation strategy in detail. The guiding principle is that the lawyer should fulfill reasonable client expectations for information consistent with the duty to act in the client's best interests and the client's overall requirements as to the character of representation. In certain circumstances, such as when a lawyer asks a client to consent to a representation affected by a conflict of interest, the client must give informed consent, as defined in terminology.

Ordinarily, the information to be provided is that appropriate for a client who is a comprehending and responsible adult. However, fully informing the client according to this standard may be impracticable, for example, where the client is a child or suffers from mental disability. See rule 4–1.14. When the client is an organization or group, it is often impossible or inappropriate to inform every one of its members about its legal affairs; ordinarily, the lawyer should address communications to the appropriate officials of the organization. See rule 4–1.13. Where many routine matters are involved, a system of limited or occasional reporting may be arranged with the client.

Withholding information

In some circumstances, a lawyer may be justified in delaying transmission of information when the client would be likely to react imprudently to an immediate communication. Thus, a lawyer might withhold a psychiatric diagnosis of a client when the examining psychiatrist indicates that disclosure would harm the client. A lawyer may not withhold information to serve the lawyer's own interest or convenience or the interests or convenience of another person. Rules or court orders governing litigation may provide that information supplied to a lawyer may not be disclosed to the client. Rule 4–3.4(c) directs compliance with such rules or orders.

Rule 4–1.5. Fees and Costs for Legal Services

(a) Illegal, Prohibited, or Clearly Excessive Fees and Costs. An attorney shall not enter into an agreement for, charge, or collect an illegal, prohibited, or clearly excessive fee or cost, or a fee generated by employment that was obtained through advertising or solicitation not in compliance with the Rules Regulating The Florida Bar. A fee or cost is clearly excessive when:

(1) after a review of the facts, a lawyer of ordinary prudence would be left with a definite and firm conviction that the fee or the cost exceeds a reasonable fee or cost for services provided to such a degree as to constitute clear overreaching or an unconscionable demand by the attorney; or

(2) the fee or cost is sought or secured by the attorney by means of intentional misrepresentation or fraud upon the client, a nonclient party, or any court, as to either entitlement to, or amount of, the fee.

(b) Factors to Be Considered in Determining Reasonable Fees and Costs.

(1) Factors to be considered as guides in determining a reasonable fee include:

(A) the time and labor required, the novelty, complexity, and difficulty of the questions involved, and the skill requisite to perform the legal service properly;

(B) the likelihood that the acceptance of the particular employment will preclude other employment by the lawyer;

(C) the fee, or rate of fee, customarily charged in the locality for legal services of a comparable or similar nature;

(D) the significance of, or amount involved in, the subject matter of the representation, the responsibility involved in the representation, and the results obtained;

(E) the time limitations imposed by the client or by the circumstances and, as between attorney and client, any additional or special time demands or requests of the attorney by the client;

(F) the nature and length of the professional relationship with the client;

(G) the experience, reputation, diligence, and ability of the lawyer or lawyers performing the service and the skill, expertise, or efficiency of effort reflected in the actual providing of such services; and

(H) whether the fee is fixed or contingent, and, if fixed as to amount or rate, then whether the client's ability to pay rested to any significant degree on the outcome of the representation.

(2) Factors to be considered as guides in determining reasonable costs include:

(A) the nature and extent of the disclosure made to the client about the costs;

(B) whether a specific agreement exists between the lawyer and client as to the costs a client is expected to pay and how a cost is calculated that is charged to a client;

(C) the actual amount charged by third party providers of services to the attorney;

(D) whether specific costs can be identified and allocated to an individual client or a reasonable basis exists to estimate the costs charged;

(E) the reasonable charges for providing in-house service to a client if the cost is an in-house charge for services; and

(F) the relationship and past course of conduct between the lawyer and the client.

All costs are subject to the test of reasonableness set forth in subdivision (a) above. When the parties have a written contract in which the method is established for charging costs, the costs charged thereunder shall be presumed reasonable.

(c) Consideration of All Factors. In determining a reasonable fee, the time devoted to the representation and customary rate of fee need not be the sole or controlling factors. All factors set forth in this rule should be considered, and may be applied, in justification of a fee higher or lower than that which would result from application of only the time and rate factors.

(d) Enforceability of Fee Contracts. Contracts or agreements for attorney's fees between attorney and client will ordinarily be enforceable according to the terms of such contracts or agreements, unless found to be illegal, obtained through advertising or solicitation not in compliance with the Rules Regulating The Florida Bar, prohibited by this rule, or clearly excessive as defined by this rule.

(e) Duty to Communicate Basis or Rate of Fee or Costs to Client. When the lawyer has not regularly represented the client, the basis or rate of the fee and costs shall be communicated to the client, preferably in writing, before or within a reasonable time after commencing the representation. A fee for legal services that is nonrefundable in any part shall be confirmed in writing and shall explain the intent of the parties as to the nature and amount of the nonrefundable fee. The test of reasonableness found in subdivision (b), above, applies to all fees for legal services without regard to their characterization by the parties.

The fact that a contract may not be in accord with these rules is an issue between the attorney and client and a matter of professional ethics, but is not the proper basis for an action or defense by an opposing party when fee-shifting litigation is involved.

(f) Contingent Fees. As to contingent fees:

(1) A fee may be contingent on the outcome of the matter for which the service is rendered, except in a matter in which a contingent fee is prohibited by subdivision (f)(3) or by law. A contingent fee agreement shall be in writing and shall state the method by which the fee is to be determined, including the percentage or percentages that shall accrue to the lawyer in the event of settlement, trial, or appeal, litigation and other expenses to be deducted from the recovery, and whether such expenses are to be deducted before or after the contingent fee is calculated. Upon conclusion of a contingent fee matter, the lawyer shall provide the client with a written statement stating the outcome of the matter and, if there is a recovery, showing the remittance to the client and the method of its determination.

(2) Every lawyer who accepts a retainer or enters into an agreement, express or implied, for compensation for services rendered or to be rendered in any action, claim, or proceeding whereby the lawyer's compensation is to be dependent or contingent in whole or in part upon the successful prosecution or settlement thereof shall do so only where such fee arrangement is reduced to a written contract, signed by the client, and by a lawyer for the lawyer or for the law firm representing the client. No lawyer or firm may participate in the fee without the consent of the client in writing. Each participating lawyer or law firm shall sign the contract with the client and shall agree to assume joint legal responsibility to the client for the performance of the services in question as if each were partners of the other lawyer or law firm involved. The client shall be furnished with a copy of the signed contract and any subsequent notices or consents. All provisions of this rule shall apply to such fee contracts.

(3) A lawyer shall not enter into an arrangement for, charge, or collect:

(A) any fee in a domestic relations matter, the payment or amount of which is contingent upon the securing of a divorce or upon the amount of alimony or support, or property settlement in lieu thereof; or

(B) a contingent fee for representing a defendant in a criminal case.

(4) A lawyer who enters into an arrangement for, charges, or collects any fee in an action or claim for personal injury or for property damages or for death or loss of services resulting from personal injuries based upon tortious conduct of another, including products liability claims, whereby the compensation is to be dependent or contingent in whole or in part upon the successful prosecution or settlement thereof shall do so only under the following requirements:

(A) The contract shall contain the following provisions:

(i) "The undersigned client has, before signing this contract, received and read the statement of client's rights and understands each of the rights set forth therein. The undersigned client has signed the statement and received a signed copy to refer to while being represented by the undersigned attorney(s)."

(ii) "This contract may be cancelled by written notification to the attorney at any time within 3 business days of the date the contract was signed, as shown below, and if cancelled the client shall not be obligated to pay any fees to the attorney for the work performed during that time. If the attorney has advanced funds to others in representation of the client, the attorney is entitled to be reimbursed for such amounts as the attorney has reasonably advanced on behalf of the client."

(B) The contract for representation of a client in a matter set forth in subdivision (f)(4) may provide for a contingent fee arrangement as agreed upon by the client and the lawyer, except as limited by the following provisions:

(i) Without prior court approval as specified below, any contingent fee that exceeds the following standards shall be presumed, unless rebutted, to be clearly excessive:

a. Before the filing of an answer or the demand for appointment of arbitrators or, if no answer is filed or no demand for appointment of arbitrators is made, the expiration of the time period provided for such action:

1. 33 1/3% of any recovery up to $1 million; plus

2. 30% of any portion of the recovery between $1 million and $2 million; plus

3. 20% of any portion of the recovery exceeding $2 million.

b. After the filing of an answer or the demand for appointment of arbitrators or, if no answer is filed or no demand for appointment of arbitrators is made, the expiration of the time period provided for such action, through the entry of judgment:

1. 40% of any recovery up to $1 million; plus

2. 30% of any portion of the recovery between $1 million and $2 million; plus

3. 20% of any portion of the recovery exceeding $2 million.

c. If all defendants admit liability at the time of filing their answers and request a trial only on damages:

1. 33 1/3% of any recovery up to $1 million; plus

2. 20% of any portion of the recovery between $1 million and $2 million; plus

3. 15% of any portion of the recovery exceeding $2 million.

d. An additional 5% of any recovery after institution of any appellate proceeding is filed or post-judgment relief or action is required for recovery on the judgment.

(ii) If any client is unable to obtain an attorney of the client's choice because of the limitations set forth in subdivision (f)(4)(B)(i), the client may petition the court in which the matter would be filed, if litigation is necessary, or if such court will not accept jurisdiction for the fee division, the circuit court wherein the cause of action arose, for approval of any fee contract between the client and an attorney of the client's choosing. Such authorization shall be given if the court determines the client has a complete understanding of the client's rights and the terms of the proposed contract. The application for authorization of such a contract can be filed as a separate proceeding before suit or simultaneously with the filing of a complaint. Proceedings thereon may occur before service on the defendant and this aspect of the file may be sealed. A petition under this subdivision shall contain a certificate showing service on the client and, if the petition is denied, a copy of the petition and order denying the petition shall be served on The Florida Bar in Tallahassee by the member of the bar who filed the petition. Authorization of such a contract shall not bar subsequent inquiry as to whether the fee actually claimed or charged is clearly excessive under subdivisions (a) and (b).

(iii) Subject to the provisions of 4–1.5(f)(4)(B)(i) and (ii) a lawyer who enters into an arrangement for, charges, or collects any fee in an action or claim for medical liability whereby the compensation is dependent or contingent in whole or in part upon the successful prosecution or settlement thereof shall provide the language of article

I, section 26 of the Florida Constitution to the client in writing and shall orally inform the client that:

a. Unless waived, in any medical liability claim involving a contingency fee, the claimant is entitled to receive no less than 70% of the first $250,000 of all damages received by the claimant, exclusive of reasonable and customary costs, whether received by judgment, settlement, or otherwise, and regardless of the number of defendants. The claimant is entitled to 90% of all damages in excess of $250,000, exclusive of reasonable and customary costs and regardless of the number of defendants.

b. If a lawyer chooses not to accept the representation of a client under the terms of article I, section 26 of the Florida Constitution, the lawyer shall advise the client, both orally and in writing of alternative terms, if any, under which the lawyer would accept the representation of the client, as well as the client's right to seek representation by another lawyer willing to accept the representation under the terms of article I, section 26 of the Florida Constitution, or a lawyer willing to accept the representation on a fee basis that is not contingent.

c. If any client desires to waive any rights under article I, section 26 of the Florida Constitution in order to obtain a lawyer of the client's choice, a client may do so by waiving such rights in writing, under oath, and in the form provided in this rule. The lawyer shall provide each client a copy of the written waiver and shall afford each client a full and complete opportunity to understand the rights being waived as set forth in the waiver. A copy of the waiver, signed by each client and lawyer, shall be given to each client to retain, and the lawyer shall keep a copy in the lawyer's file pertaining to the client. The waiver shall be retained by the lawyer with the written fee contract and closing statement under the same conditions and requirements provided in 4-1.5(f)(5).

WAIVER OF THE CONSTITUTIONAL RIGHT PROVIDED IN ARTICLE I, SECTION 26 OF THE FLORIDA CONSTITUTION

On November 2, 2004, voters in the State of Florida approved The Medical Liability Claimant's Compensation Amendment that was identified as Amendment 3 on the ballot. The amendment is set forth below:

The Florida Constitution

Article I, Section 26 is created to read "Claimant's right to fair compensation." In any medical liability claim involving a contingency fee, the claimant is entitled to receive no less than 70% of the first $250,000 in all damages received by the claimant, exclusive of reasonable and customary costs, whether received by judgment, settlement or otherwise, and regardless of the number of defendants. The claimant is entitled to 90% of all damages in excess of $250,000, exclusive of reasonable and customary costs and regardless of the number of defendants. This provision is self-executing and does not require implementing legislation.

The undersigned client understands and acknowledges that (initial each provision):

___ I have been advised that signing this waiver releases an important constitutional right; and

___ I have been advised that I may consult with separate counsel before signing this waiver; and that I may request a hearing before a judge to further explain this waiver; and

___ By signing this waiver I agree to an **increase in the attorney fee** that might otherwise be owed if the constitutional provision listed above is not waived. Without prior court approval, the increased fee that I agree to may be up to the maximum contingency fee percentages set forth in Rule Regulating The Florida Bar 4-1.5(f)(4)(B)(i). Depending on the circumstances of my case, the maximum agreed upon fee may range from 33 1/3% to 40% of any recovery up to $1 million; plus 20% to 30% of any portion of the recovery between $1 million and $2 million; plus 15% to 20% of any recovery exceeding $2 million; and

___ I have three (3) business days following execution of this waiver in which to cancel this waiver; and

___ I wish to engage the legal services of the lawyers or law firms listed below in an action or claim for medical liability the fee for which is contingent in whole or in part upon the successful prosecution or settlement thereof, but I am unable to do so because of the provisions of the constitutional limitation set forth above. In consideration of the lawyers' or law firms' agreements to represent me and my desire to employ the lawyers or law firms listed below, I hereby knowingly, willingly, and voluntarily waive any and all rights and privileges that I may have under the constitutional provision set forth above, as apply to the contingency fee agreement only. Specifically, I waive the percentage restrictions that are the subject of the constitutional provision and confirm the fee percentages set forth in the contingency fee agreement; and

___ I have selected the lawyers or law firms listed below as my counsel of choice in this matter and would not be able to engage their services without this waiver; and I expressly state that this waiver is made freely and voluntarily, with full knowledge of its terms, and that all questions have been answered to my satisfaction.

ACKNOWLEDGMENT BY CLIENT FOR PRESENTATION TO THE COURT

The undersigned client hereby acknowledges, under oath, the following:

I have read and understand this entire waiver of my rights under the constitutional provision set forth above.

I am not under the influence of any substance, drug, or condition (physical, mental, or emotional) that interferes with my understanding of this entire waiver in which I am entering and all the consequences thereof.

I have entered into and signed this waiver freely and voluntarily.

I authorize my lawyers or law firms listed below to present this waiver to the appropriate court, if required for purposes of approval of the contingency fee agreement. Unless the court requires my attendance at a hearing for that purpose, my lawyers or law firms are authorized to provide this waiver to the court for its consideration without my presence.

Dated this ___ day of _________, ___.
By: ______________________________

CLIENT

Sworn to and subscribed before me this ___ day of _______, ___ by _______, who is personally known to me, or has produced the following identification: _________.

____

Notary Public

My Commission Expires:
Dated this ___ day of _________, ___.
By: ______________________________

ATTORNEY

(C) Before a lawyer enters into a contingent fee contract for representation of a client in a matter set forth in this rule, the lawyer shall provide the client with a copy of the statement of client's rights and shall afford the client a full and complete opportunity to understand each of the rights as set forth therein. A copy of the statement, signed by both the client and the lawyer, shall be given to the client to retain and the lawyer shall keep a copy in the client's file. The statement shall be retained by the lawyer with the written fee contract and closing statement under the same conditions and requirements as subdivision (f)(5).

(D) As to lawyers not in the same firm, a division of any fee within subdivision (f)(4) shall be on the following basis:

(i) To the lawyer assuming primary responsibility for the legal services on behalf of the client, a minimum of 75% of the total fee.

(ii) To the lawyer assuming secondary responsibility for the legal services on behalf of the client, a maximum of 25% of the total fee. Any fee in excess of 25% shall be presumed to be clearly excessive.

(iii) The 25% limitation shall not apply to those cases in which 2 or more lawyers or firms accept substantially equal active participation in the providing of legal services. In such circumstances counsel shall apply to the court in which the matter would be filed, if litigation is necessary, or if such court will not accept jurisdiction for the fee division, the circuit court wherein the cause of action arose, for authorization of the fee division in excess of 25%, based upon a sworn petition signed by all counsel that shall disclose in detail those services to be performed. The application for authorization of such a contract may be filed as a separate proceeding before suit or simultaneously with the filing of a complaint, or within 10 days of execution of a contract for division of fees when new counsel is engaged. Proceedings thereon may occur before service of process on any party and this aspect of the file may be sealed. Authorization of such contract shall not bar subsequent inquiry as to whether the fee actually claimed or charged is clearly excessive. An application under this subdivision shall contain a certificate showing service on the client and, if the application is denied, a copy of the petition and order denying the petition shall be served on The Florida Bar in Tallahassee by the member of the bar who filed the petition. Counsel may proceed with representation of the client pending court approval.

(iv) The percentages required by this subdivision shall be applicable after deduction of any fee payable to separate counsel retained especially for appellate purposes.

(5) In the event there is a recovery, upon the conclusion of the representation, the lawyer shall prepare a closing statement reflecting an itemization of all costs and expenses, together with the amount of fee received by each participating lawyer or law firm. A copy of the closing statement shall be executed by all participating lawyers, as well as the client, and each shall receive a copy. Each participating lawyer shall retain a copy of the written fee contract and closing statement for 6 years after execution of the closing statement. Any contingent fee contract and closing statement shall be available for inspection at reasonable times by the client, by any other person upon judicial order, or by the appropriate disciplinary agency.

(6) In cases in which the client is to receive a recovery that will be paid to the client on a future structured or periodic basis, the contingent fee percentage shall be calculated only on the cost of the structured verdict or settlement or, if the cost is

unknown, on the present money value of the structured verdict or settlement, whichever is less. If the damages and the fee are to be paid out over the long term future schedule, this limitation does not apply. No attorney may negotiate separately with the defendant for that attorney's fee in a structured verdict or settlement when separate negotiations would place the attorney in a position of conflict.

(g) Division of Fees Between Lawyers in Different Firms. Subject to the provisions of subdivision (f)(4)(D), a division of fee between lawyers who are not in the same firm may be made only if the total fee is reasonable and:

(1) the division is in proportion to the services performed by each lawyer; or

(2) by written agreement with the client:

(A) each lawyer assumes joint legal responsibility for the representation and agrees to be available for consultation with the client; and

(B) the agreement fully discloses that a division of fees will be made and the basis upon which the division of fees will be made.

(h) Credit Plans. A lawyer or law firm may accept payment under a credit plan. No higher fee shall be charged and no additional charge shall be imposed by reason of a lawyer's or law firm's participation in a credit plan.

(i) Arbitration Clauses. A lawyer shall not make an agreement with a potential client prospectively providing for mandatory arbitration of fee disputes without first advising that person in writing that the potential client should consider obtaining independent legal advice as to the advisability of entering into an agreement containing such mandatory arbitration provisions. A lawyer shall not make an agreement containing such mandatory arbitration provisions unless the agreement contains the following language in bold print:

NOTICE: This agreement contains provisions requiring arbitration of fee disputes. Before you sign this agreement you should consider consulting with another lawyer about the advisability of making an agreement with mandatory arbitration requirements. Arbitration proceedings are ways to resolve disputes without use of the court system. By entering into agreements that require arbitration as the way to resolve fee disputes, you give up (waive) your right to go to court to resolve those disputes by a judge or jury. These are important rights that should not be given up without careful consideration.

STATEMENT OF CLIENT'S RIGHTS FOR CONTINGENCY FEES

Before you, the prospective client, arrange a contingent fee agreement with a lawyer, you should understand this statement of your rights as a client. This statement is not a part of the actual contract between you and your lawyer, but, as a prospective client, you should be aware of these rights:

1. There is no legal requirement that a lawyer charge a client a set fee or a percentage of money recovered in a case. You, the client, have the right to talk with your lawyer about the proposed fee and to bargain about the rate or percentage as in any other contract. If you do not reach an agreement with 1 lawyer you may talk with other lawyers.

2. Any contingent fee contract must be in writing and you have 3 business days to reconsider the contract. You may cancel the contract without any reason if you notify your lawyer in writing within 3 business days of signing the contract. If you withdraw from the contract within the first 3 business days, you do not owe the lawyer a fee although you may be responsible for the lawyer's actual costs during that time. If your lawyer begins to represent you, your lawyer may not withdraw from the case without giving you notice, delivering necessary papers to you, and allowing you time to employ another lawyer. Often, your lawyer must obtain court approval before withdrawing from a case. If you discharge your lawyer without good cause after the 3-day period, you may have to pay a fee for work the lawyer has done.

3. Before hiring a lawyer, you, the client, have the right to know about the lawyer's education, training, and experience. If you ask, the lawyer should tell you specifically about the lawyer's actual experience dealing with cases similar to yours. If you ask, the lawyer should provide information about special training or knowledge and give you this information in writing if you request it.

4. Before signing a contingent fee contract with you, a lawyer must advise you whether the lawyer intends to handle your case alone or whether other lawyers will be helping with the case. If your lawyer intends to refer the case to other lawyers, the lawyer should tell you what kind of fee sharing arrangement will be made with the other lawyers. If lawyers from different law firms will represent you, at least 1 lawyer from each law firm must sign the contingent fee contract.

5. If your lawyer intends to refer your case to another lawyer or counsel with other lawyers, your lawyer should tell you about that at the beginning. If your lawyer takes the case and later decides to refer it to another lawyer or to associate with other lawyers, you should sign a new contract that includes the new lawyers. You, the client, also have the right to consult with each lawyer working on your case and each lawyer is legally responsible to represent your interests and is legally responsible for the acts of the other lawyers involved in the case.

6. You, the client, have the right to know in advance how you will need to pay the expenses and the

legal fees at the end of the case. If you pay a deposit in advance for costs, you may ask reasonable questions about how the money will be or has been spent and how much of it remains unspent. Your lawyer should give a reasonable estimate about future necessary costs. If your lawyer agrees to lend or advance you money to prepare or research the case, you have the right to know periodically how much money your lawyer has spent on your behalf. You also have the right to decide, after consulting with your lawyer, how much money is to be spent to prepare a case. If you pay the expenses, you have the right to decide how much to spend. Your lawyer should also inform you whether the fee will be based on the gross amount recovered or on the amount recovered minus the costs.

7. You, the client, have the right to be told by your lawyer about possible adverse consequences if you lose the case. Those adverse consequences might include money that you might have to pay to your lawyer for costs and liability you might have for attorney's fees, costs, and expenses to the other side.

8. You, the client, have the right to receive and approve a closing statement at the end of the case before you pay any money. The statement must list all of the financial details of the entire case, including the amount recovered, all expenses, and a precise statement of your lawyer's fee. Until you approve the closing statement your lawyer cannot pay any money to anyone, including you, without an appropriate order of the court. You also have the right to have every lawyer or law firm working on your case sign this closing statement.

9. You, the client, have the right to ask your lawyer at reasonable intervals how the case is progressing and to have these questions answered to the best of your lawyer's ability.

10. You, the client, have the right to make the final decision regarding settlement of a case. Your lawyer must notify you of all offers of settlement before and after the trial. Offers during the trial must be immediately communicated and you should consult with your lawyer regarding whether to accept a settlement. However, you must make the final decision to accept or reject a settlement.

11. If at any time you, the client, believe that your lawyer has charged an excessive or illegal fee, you have the right to report the matter to The Florida Bar, the agency that oversees the practice and behavior of all lawyers in Florida. For information on how to reach The Florida Bar, call 850/561–5600, or contact the local bar association. Any disagreement between you and your lawyer about a fee can be taken to court and you may wish to hire another lawyer to help you resolve this disagreement. Usually fee disputes must be handled in a separate lawsuit, unless your fee contract provides for arbitration. You can request, but may not require, that a provision for arbitration (under Chapter 682, Florida Statutes, or under the fee arbitration rule of the Rules Regulating The Florida Bar) be included in your fee contract.

____
Client Signature

____
Date

____
Attorney Signature

____
Date

Amended Oct. 20, 1987, effective Jan. 1, 1988 (519 So.2d 971); Oct. 26, 1989 (550 So.2d 1120); Dec. 21, 1990, effective Jan. 1, 1991 (571 So.2d 451); July 23, 1992, effective Jan. 1, 1993 (605 So.2d 252); Oct. 20, 1994 (644 So.2d 282); July 20, 1995 (658 So.2d 930); Sept. 24, 1998, effective Oct. 1, 1998 (718 So.2d 1179); March 23, 2000 (763 So.2d 1002); Feb. 8, 2001 (795 So.2d 1); April 25, 2002 (820 So.2d 210); May 20, 2004 (875 So.2d 448); Oct. 6, 2005, effective Jan. 1, 2006 (916 So.2d 655); March 23, 2006, effective May 22, 2006 (933 So.2d 417); Sept. 28, 2006 (939 So.2d 1032); Dec. 20, 2007, effective March 1, 2008 (978 So.2d 91); Nov. 19, 2009, effective Feb. 1, 2010 (24 So.3d 63); April 12, 2012, effective July 1, 2012 (101 So.3d 807).

Comment

Bases or rate of fees and costs

When the lawyer has regularly represented a client, they ordinarily will have evolved an understanding concerning the basis or rate of the fee. The conduct of the lawyer and client in prior relationships is relevant when analyzing the requirements of this rule. In a new client-lawyer relationship, however, an understanding as to the fee should be promptly established. It is not necessary to recite all the factors that underlie the basis of the fee but only those that are directly involved in its computation. It is sufficient, for example, to state the basic rate is an hourly charge or a fixed amount or an estimated amount, or to identify the factors that may be taken into account in finally fixing the fee. Although hourly billing or a fixed fee may be the most common bases for computing fees in an area of practice, these may not be the only bases for computing fees. A lawyer should, where appropriate, discuss alternative billing methods with the client. When developments occur during the representation that render an earlier estimate substantially inaccurate, a revised estimate should be provided to the client. A written statement concerning the fee reduces the possibility of misunderstanding. Furnishing the client with a simple memorandum or a copy of the lawyer's customary fee schedule is sufficient if the basis or rate of the fee is set forth.

General overhead should be accounted for in a lawyer's fee, whether the lawyer charges hourly, flat, or contingent fees. Filing fees, transcription, and the like should be charged to the client at the actual amount paid by the lawyer. A lawyer may agree with the client to charge a reasonable amount for in-house costs or services. In-house costs include items such as copying, faxing, long distance telephone, and computerized research. In-house services include paralegal services, investigative services, accounting services, and courier services. The lawyer should sufficiently communicate with the client regarding the costs charged to the client so that the client understands the amount of costs being charged or the method for calculation of those costs. Costs appearing in sufficient detail on closing statements and approved by the parties to the transaction should meet the requirements of this rule.

Rule 4–1.8(e) should be consulted regarding a lawyer's providing financial assistance to a client in connection with litigation.

Lawyers should also be mindful of any statutory, constitutional, or other requirements or restrictions on attorneys' fees.

In order to avoid misunderstandings concerning the nature of legal fees, written documentation is required when any aspect of the fee is nonrefundable. A written contract provides a method to resolve misunderstandings and to protect the lawyer in the event of continued misunderstanding. Rule 4–1.5(e) does not require the client to sign a written document memorializing the terms of the fee. A letter from the lawyer to the client setting forth the basis or rate of the fee and the intent of the parties in regard to the nonrefundable nature of the fee is sufficient to meet the requirements of this rule.

All legal fees and contracts for legal fees are subject to the requirements of the Rules Regulating The Florida Bar. In particular, the test for reasonableness of legal fees found in rule 4–1.5(b) applies to all types of legal fees and contracts related to them.

Terms of payment

A lawyer may require advance payment of a fee but is obliged to return any unearned portion. See rule 4–1.16(d). A lawyer is not, however, required to return retainers that, pursuant to an agreement with a client, are not refundable. A lawyer may accept property in payment for services, such as an ownership interest in an enterprise, providing this does not involve acquisition of a proprietary interest in the cause of action or subject matter of the litigation contrary to rule 4–1.8(i). However, a fee paid in property instead of money may be subject to special scrutiny because it involves questions concerning both the value of the services and the lawyer's special knowledge of the value of the property.

An agreement may not be made whose terms might induce the lawyer improperly to curtail services for the client or perform them in a way contrary to the client's interest. For example, a lawyer should not enter into an agreement whereby services are to be provided only up to a stated amount when it is foreseeable that more extensive services probably will be required, unless the situation is adequately explained to the client. Otherwise, the client might have to bargain for further assistance in the midst of a proceeding or transaction. However, it is proper to define the extent of services in light of the client's ability to pay. A lawyer should not exploit a fee arrangement based primarily on hourly charges by using wasteful procedures. When there is doubt whether a contingent fee is consistent with the client's best interest, the lawyer should offer the client alternative bases for the fee and explain their implications. Applicable law may impose limitations on contingent fees, such as a ceiling on the percentage.

Prohibited contingent fees

Subdivision (f)(3)(A) prohibits a lawyer from charging a contingent fee in a domestic relations matter when payment is contingent upon the securing of a divorce or upon the amount of alimony or support or property settlement to be obtained. This provision does not preclude a contract for a contingent fee for legal representation in connection with the recovery of post-judgment balances due under support, alimony, or other financial orders because such contracts do not implicate the same policy concerns.

Contingent fee regulation

Subdivision (e) is intended to clarify that whether the lawyer's fee contract complies with these rules is a matter between the lawyer and client and an issue for professional disciplinary enforcement. The rules and subdivision (e) are not intended to be used as procedural weapons or defenses by others. Allowing opposing parties to assert noncompliance with these rules as a defense, including whether the fee is fixed or contingent, allows for potential inequity if the opposing party is allowed to escape responsibility for their actions solely through application of these rules.

Rule 4–1.5(f)(4) should not be construed to apply to actions or claims seeking property or other damages arising in the commercial litigation context.

Rule 4–1.5(f)(4)(B) is intended to apply only to contingent aspects of fee agreements. In the situation where a lawyer and client enter a contract for part noncontingent and part contingent attorney's fees, rule 4–1.5(f)(4)(B) should not be construed to apply to and prohibit or limit the noncontingent portion of the fee agreement. An attorney could properly charge and retain the noncontingent portion of the fee even if the matter was not successfully prosecuted or if the noncontingent portion of the fee exceeded the schedule set forth in rule 4–1.5(f)(4)(B). Rule 4–1.5(f)(4)(B) should, however, be construed to apply to any additional contingent portion of such a contract when considered together with earned noncontingent fees. Thus, under such a contract a lawyer may demand or collect only such additional contingent fees as would not cause the total fees to exceed the schedule set forth in rule 4–1.5(f)(4)(B).

The limitations in rule 4–1.5(f)(4)(B)(i)c. are only to be applied in the case where all the defendants admit liability at the time they file their initial answer and the trial is only on the issue of the amount or extent of the loss or the extent of injury suffered by the client. If the trial involves not only the issue of damages but also such questions as proximate cause, affirmative defenses, seat belt defense, or other similar matters, the limitations are not to be applied because of the contingent nature of the case being left for resolution by the trier of fact.

Rule 4–1.5(f)(4)(B)(ii) provides the limitations set forth in subdivision (f)(4)(B)(i) may be waived by the client upon approval by the appropriate judge. This waiver provision may not be used to authorize a lawyer to charge a client a fee that would exceed rule 4–1.5(a) or (b). It is contemplated that this waiver provision will not be necessary except where the client wants to retain a particular lawyer to represent the client or the case involves complex, difficult, or novel questions of law or fact that would justify a contingent fee greater than the schedule but not a contingent fee that would exceed rule 4–1.5(b).

Upon a petition by a client, the trial court reviewing the waiver request must grant that request if the trial court finds the client: (a) understands the right to have the limitations in rule 4–1.5(f)(4)(B) applied in the specific matter; and (b) understands and approves the terms of the proposed contract. The consideration by the trial court of the waiver petition is not to be used as an opportunity for the court to inquire into the merits or details of the particular action or claim that is the subject of the contract.

The proceedings before the trial court and the trial court's decision on a waiver request are to be confidential and not subject to discovery by any of the parties to the action or by any other individual or entity except The Florida Bar. However, terms of the contract approved by the trial court may be subject to discovery if the contract (without court approval) was subject to discovery under applicable case law or rules of evidence.

Rule 4–1.5(f)(4)(B)(iii) is added to acknowledge the provisions of Article 1, Section 26 of the Florida Constitution, and to create an affirmative obligation on the part of an attorney contemplating a contingency fee contract to notify a potential client with a medical liability claim of the limitations provided in that constitutional provision. This addition to the rule is adopted prior to any judicial interpretation of the meaning or scope of the constitutional provision and this rule is not intended to make any substantive interpretation of the meaning or scope of that provision. The rule also provides that a client who wishes to waive the rights of the constitutional provision, as those rights may relate to attorney's fees, must do so in the form contained in the rule.

Rule 4–1.5(f)(6) prohibits a lawyer from charging the contingent fee percentage on the total, future value of a recovery being paid on a structured or periodic basis. This prohibition does not apply if the lawyer's fee is being paid over the same length of time as the schedule of payments to the client.

Contingent fees are prohibited in criminal and certain domestic relations matters. In domestic relations cases, fees that include a bonus provision or additional fee to be determined at a later time and based on results obtained have been held to be impermissible contingency fees and therefore subject to restitution and disciplinary sanction as elsewhere stated in these Rules Regulating The Florida Bar.

Fees that provide for a bonus or additional fees and that otherwise are not prohibited under the Rules Regulating The Florida Bar can be effective tools for structuring fees. For example, a fee contract calling for a flat fee and the payment of a bonus based on the amount of property retained or recovered in a general civil action is not prohibited by these rules. However, the bonus or additional fee must be stated clearly in amount or formula for calculation of the fee (basis or rate). Courts have held that unilateral bonus fees are unenforceable. The test of reasonableness and other requirements of this rule apply to permissible bonus fees.

Division of fee

A division of fee is a single billing to a client covering the fee of 2 or more lawyers who are not in the same firm. A division of fee facilitates association of more than 1 lawyer in a matter in which neither alone could serve the client as well, and most often is used when the fee is contingent and the division is between a referring lawyer and a trial specialist. Subject to the provisions of subdivision (f)(4)(D), subdivision (g) permits the lawyers to divide a fee on either the basis of the proportion of services they render or by agreement between the participating lawyers if all assume responsibility for the representation as a whole and the client is advised and does not object. It does require disclosure to the client of the share that each lawyer is to receive. Joint responsibility for the representation entails the obligations stated in rule 4–5.1 for purposes of the matter involved.

Disputes over fees

Since the fee arbitration rule (chapter 14) has been established by the bar to provide a procedure for resolution of fee disputes, the lawyer should conscientiously consider submitting to it. Where law prescribes a procedure for determining a lawyer's fee, for example, in representation of an executor or administrator, a class, or a person entitled to a reasonable fee as part of the measure of damages, the lawyer entitled to such a fee and a lawyer representing another party concerned with the fee should comply with the prescribed procedure.

Referral fees and practices

A secondary lawyer shall not be entitled to a fee greater than the limitation set forth in rule 4–1.5(f)(4)(D)(ii) merely because the lawyer agrees to do some or all of the following: (a) consults with the client; (b) answers interrogatories; (c) attends depositions; (d) reviews pleadings; (e) attends the trial; or (f) assumes joint legal responsibility to the client. However, the provisions do not contemplate that a secondary lawyer who does more than the above is necessarily entitled to a larger percentage of the fee than that allowed by the limitation.

The provisions of rule 4–1.5(f)(4)(D)(iii) only apply where the participating lawyers have for purposes of the specific case established a co-counsel relationship. The need for court approval of a referral fee arrangement under rule 4–1.5(f)(4)(D)(iii) should only occur in a small percentage of cases arising under rule 4–1.5(f)(4) and usually occurs prior to the commencement of litigation or at the onset of the representation. However, in those cases in which litigation has been commenced or the representation has already begun, approval of the fee division should be sought within a reasonable period of time after the need for court approval of the fee division arises.

In determining if a co-counsel relationship exists, the court should look to see if the lawyers have established a special partnership agreement for the purpose of the specific case or matter. If such an agreement does exist, it must provide for a sharing of services or responsibility and the fee division is based upon a division of the services to be rendered or the responsibility assumed. It is contemplated that a co-counsel situation would exist where a division of responsibility is based upon, but not limited to, the following: (a) based upon geographic considerations, the lawyers agree to divide the legal work, responsibility, and representation in a convenient fashion. Such a situation would occur when different aspects of a case must be handled in different locations; (b) where the lawyers agree to divide the legal work and representation based upon their particular expertise in the substantive areas of law involved in the litigation; or (c) where the lawyers agree to divide the legal work and representation along established lines of division, such as liability and damages, causation and damages, or other similar factors.

The trial court's responsibility when reviewing an application for authorization of a fee division under rule 4–1.5(f)(4)(D)(iii) is to determine if a co-counsel relationship exists in that particular case. If the court determines a co-counsel relationship exists and authorizes the fee division requested, the court does not have any responsibility to review or approve the specific amount of the fee division agreed upon by the lawyers and the client.

Rule 4–1.5(f)(4)(D)(iv) applies to the situation where appellate counsel is retained during the trial of the case to assist with the appeal of the case. The percentages set forth in subdivision (f)(4)(D) are to be applicable after appellate counsel's fee is established. However, the effect should not be to impose an unreasonable fee on the client.

Credit Plans

Credit plans include credit cards. If a lawyer accepts payment from a credit plan for an advance of fees and costs, the amount must be held in trust in accordance with chapter 5, Rules Regulating The Florida Bar, and the lawyer must add the lawyer's own money to the trust account in an amount equal to the amount charged by the credit plan for doing business with the credit plan.

Rule 4–1.6. Confidentiality of Information

Text of rule effective until October 1, 2015. See, also, rule effective October 1, 2015.

(a) Consent Required to Reveal Information. A lawyer must not reveal information relating to representation of a client except as stated in subdivisions (b), (c), and (d), unless the client gives informed consent.

(b) When Lawyer Must Reveal Information. A lawyer must reveal such information to the extent the lawyer reasonably believes necessary:

(1) to prevent a client from committing a crime; or

(2) to prevent a death or substantial bodily harm to another.

(c) When Lawyer May Reveal Information. A lawyer may reveal such information to the extent the lawyer reasonably believes necessary:

(1) to serve the client's interest unless it is information the client specifically requires not to be disclosed;

(2) to establish a claim or defense on behalf of the lawyer in a controversy between the lawyer and client;

(3) to establish a defense to a criminal charge or civil claim against the lawyer based upon conduct in which the client was involved;

(4) to respond to allegations in any proceeding concerning the lawyer's representation of the client; or

(5) to comply with the Rules Regulating The Florida Bar.

(d) Exhaustion of Appellate Remedies. When required by a tribunal to reveal such information, a lawyer may first exhaust all appellate remedies.

(e) Limitation on Amount of Disclosure. When disclosure is mandated or permitted, the lawyer must disclose no more information than is required to meet the requirements or accomplish the purposes of this rule.

Amended July 23, 1992, effective Jan. 1, 1993 (605 So.2d 252); Oct. 20, 1994 (644 So.2d 282); March. 23, 2006, effective May 22, 2006 (933 So.2d 417); May 29, 2014, effective June 1, 2014 (140 So.3d 541).

Comment

The lawyer is part of a judicial system charged with upholding the law. One of the lawyer's functions is to advise clients so that they avoid any violation of the law in the proper exercise of their rights.

This rule governs the disclosure by a lawyer of information relating to the representation of a client during the lawyer's representation of the client. See rule 4–1.18 for the lawyer's duties with respect to information provided to the lawyer by a prospective client, rule 4–1.9(c) for the lawyer's duty not to reveal information relating to the lawyer's prior representation of a former client, and rules 4–1.8(b) and 4–1.9(b) for the lawyer's duties with respect to the use of such information to the disadvantage of clients and former clients.

A fundamental principle in the client-lawyer relationship is that, in the absence of the client's informed consent, the lawyer must not reveal information relating to the representation. See terminology for the definition of informed consent. This contributes to the trust that is the hallmark of the client-lawyer relationship. The client is thereby encouraged to seek legal assistance and to communicate fully and frankly with the lawyer even as to embarrassing or legally damaging subject matter. The lawyer needs this information to represent the client effectively and, if necessary, to advise the client to refrain from wrongful conduct. Almost without exception, clients come to lawyers in order to determine their rights and what is, in the complex of laws and regulations, deemed to be legal and correct. Based upon experience, lawyers know that almost all clients follow the advice given, and the law is upheld.

The principle of confidentiality is given effect in 2 related bodies of law, the attorney-client privilege (which includes the work product doctrine) in the law of evidence and the rule of confidentiality established in professional ethics. The attorney-client privilege applies in judicial and other proceedings in which a lawyer may be called as a witness or otherwise required to produce evidence concerning a client. The rule of client-lawyer confidentiality applies in situations other than those where evidence is sought from the lawyer through compulsion of law. The confidentiality rule applies not merely to matters communicated in confidence by the client but also to all information relating to the representation, whatever its source. A lawyer may not disclose such information except as authorized or required by the Rules Regulating The Florida Bar or by law. However, none of the foregoing limits the requirement of disclosure in subdivision (b). This disclosure is required to prevent a lawyer from becoming an unwitting accomplice in the fraudulent acts of a client. See also Scope.

The requirement of maintaining confidentiality of information relating to representation applies to government lawyers who may disagree with the policy goals that their representation is designed to advance.

Authorized disclosure

A lawyer is impliedly authorized to make disclosures about a client when appropriate in carrying out the representation, except to the extent that the client's instructions or special circumstances limit that authority. In litigation, for example, a lawyer may disclose information by admitting a fact that cannot properly be disputed or in negotiation by making a disclosure that facilitates a satisfactory conclusion.

Lawyers in a firm may, in the course of the firm's practice, disclose to each other information relating to a client of the firm, unless the client has instructed that particular information be confined to specified lawyers.

Disclosure adverse to client

The confidentiality rule is subject to limited exceptions. In becoming privy to information about a client, a lawyer may foresee that the client intends serious harm to another person. However, to the extent a lawyer is required or permitted to disclose a client's purposes, the client will be inhibited from revealing facts that would enable the lawyer to counsel against a wrongful course of action. While the public may be protected if full and open communication by the client is encouraged, several situations must be distinguished.

First, the lawyer may not counsel or assist a client in conduct that is criminal or fraudulent. See rule 4–1.2(d). Similarly, a lawyer has a duty under rule 4–3.3(a)(4) not to use false evidence. This duty is essentially a special instance of the duty prescribed in rule 4–1.2(d) to avoid assisting a client in criminal or fraudulent conduct.

Second, the lawyer may have been innocently involved in past conduct by the client that was criminal or fraudulent. In such a situation the lawyer has not violated rule 4–1.2(d), because to "counsel or assist" criminal or fraudulent conduct requires knowing that the conduct is of that character.

Third, the lawyer may learn that a client intends prospective conduct that is criminal. As stated in subdivision (b)(1), the lawyer must reveal information in order to prevent such consequences. It is admittedly difficult for a lawyer to "know" when the criminal intent will actually be carried out, for the client may have a change of mind.

Subdivision (b)(2) contemplates past acts on the part of a client that may result in present or future consequences that may be avoided by disclosure of otherwise confidential communications. Rule 4–1.6(b)(2) would now require the lawyer to disclose information reasonably necessary to prevent the future death or substantial bodily harm to another, even though the act of the client has been completed.

The lawyer's exercise of discretion requires consideration of such factors as the nature of the lawyer's relationship with the client and with those who might be injured by the client, the lawyer's own involvement in the transaction, and factors that may extenuate the conduct in question. Where practical the lawyer should seek to persuade the client to take suitable action. In any case, a disclosure adverse to the client's interest should be no greater than the lawyer reasonably believes necessary to the purpose.

Withdrawal

If the lawyer's services will be used by the client in materially furthering a course of criminal or fraudulent conduct, the lawyer must withdraw, as stated in rule 4–1.16(a)(1).

After withdrawal the lawyer is required to refrain from making disclosure of the client's confidences, except as otherwise provided in rule 4–1.6. Neither this rule nor rule 4–1.8(b) nor rule 4–1.16(d) prevents the lawyer from giving notice of the fact of withdrawal, and the lawyer may also withdraw or disaffirm any opinion, document, affirmation, or the like.

Where the client is an organization, the lawyer may be in doubt whether contemplated conduct will actually be carried out by the organization. Where necessary to guide conduct in connection with the rule, the lawyer may make inquiry within the organization as indicated in rule 4–1.13(b).

Dispute concerning lawyer's conduct

A lawyer's confidentiality obligations do not preclude a lawyer from securing confidential legal advice about the lawyer's personal responsibility to comply with these rules. In most situations, disclosing information to secure such advice will be impliedly authorized for the lawyer to carry out the representation. Even when the disclosure is not impliedly authorized, subdivision (c)(5) permits such disclosure because of the importance of a lawyer's compliance with the Rules of Professional Conduct.

Where a legal claim or disciplinary charge alleges complicity of the lawyer in a client's conduct or other misconduct of the lawyer involving representation of the client, the lawyer may respond to the extent the lawyer reasonably believes necessary to establish a defense. The same is true with respect to a claim involving the conduct or representation of a former client. The lawyer's right to respond arises when an assertion of such complicity has been made. Subdivision (c) does not require the lawyer to await the commencement of an action or proceeding that charges such complicity, so that the defense may be established by responding directly to a third party who has made such an assertion. The right to defend, of course, applies where a proceeding has been commenced. Where practicable and not prejudicial to the lawyer's ability to establish the defense, the lawyer should advise the client of the third party's assertion and request that the client respond appropriately. In any event, disclosure should be no greater than the lawyer reasonably believes is necessary to vindicate innocence, the disclosure should be made in a manner that limits access to the information to the tribunal or other persons having a need to know it, and appropriate protective orders or other arrangements should be sought by the lawyer to the fullest extent practicable.

If the lawyer is charged with wrongdoing in which the client's conduct is implicated, the rule of confidentiality should not prevent the lawyer from defending against the charge. Such a charge can arise in a civil, criminal, or professional disciplinary proceeding and can be based on a wrong allegedly committed by the lawyer against the client or on a wrong alleged by a third person; for example, a person claiming to have been defrauded by the lawyer and client acting together. A lawyer entitled to a fee is permitted by subdivision (c) to prove the services rendered in an action to collect it. This aspect of the rule expresses the principle that the beneficiary of a fiduciary relationship may not exploit it to the detriment of the fiduciary. As stated above, the lawyer must make every effort practicable to avoid unnecessary disclosure of information relating to a representation, to limit disclosure to those having the need to know it, and to obtain protective orders or make other arrangements minimizing the risk of disclosure.

Disclosures otherwise required or authorized

The attorney-client privilege is differently defined in various jurisdictions. If a lawyer is called as a witness to give testimony concerning a client, absent waiver by the client, rule 4–1.6(a) requires the lawyer to invoke the privilege when it is applicable. The lawyer must comply with the final orders of a court or other tribunal of competent jurisdiction requiring the lawyer to give information about the client.

The Rules of Professional Conduct in various circumstances permit or require a lawyer to disclose information relating to the representation. See rules 4–2.3, 4–3.3, and 4–4.1. In addition to these provisions, a lawyer may be obligated or permitted by other provisions of law to give information about a client. Whether another provision of law supersedes rule 4–1.6 is a matter of interpretation beyond the scope of these rules, but a presumption should exist against such a supersession.

Former client

The duty of confidentiality continues after the client-lawyer relationship has terminated. See rule 4–1.9 for the prohibition against using such information to the disadvantage of the former client.

Rule 4–1.6. Confidentiality of Information

Text of rule effective October 1, 2015. See, also, rule effective until October 1, 2015.

(a) Consent Required to Reveal Information. A lawyer must not reveal information relating to representation of a client except as stated in subdivisions (b), (c), and (d), unless the client gives informed consent.

(b) When Lawyer Must Reveal Information. A lawyer must reveal confidential information to the extent the lawyer reasonably believes necessary:

(1) to prevent a client from committing a crime; or

(2) to prevent a death or substantial bodily harm to another.

(c) When Lawyer May Reveal Information. A lawyer may reveal confidential information to the extent the lawyer reasonably believes necessary:

(1) to serve the client's interest unless it is information the client specifically requires not to be disclosed;

(2) to establish a claim or defense on behalf of the lawyer in a controversy between the lawyer and client;

(3) to establish a defense to a criminal charge or civil claim against the lawyer based on conduct in which the client was involved;

(4) to respond to allegations in any proceeding concerning the lawyer's representation of the client;

(5) to comply with the Rules Regulating The Florida Bar; or

(6) to detect and resolve conflicts of interest between lawyers in different firms arising from the lawyer's change of employment or from changes in the composition or ownership of a firm, but only if the revealed information would not compromise the attorney-client privilege or otherwise prejudice the client.

(d) Exhaustion of Appellate Remedies. When required by a tribunal to reveal confidential information, a lawyer may first exhaust all appellate remedies.

(e) Inadvertent Disclosure of Information. A lawyer must make reasonable efforts to prevent the inadvertent or unauthorized disclosure of, or unauthorized access to, information relating to the representation of a client.

(f) Limitation on Amount of Disclosure. When disclosure is mandated or permitted, the lawyer must disclose no more information than is required to meet the requirements or accomplish the purposes of this rule.

Amended July 23, 1992, effective Jan. 1, 1993 (605 So.2d 252); Oct. 20, 1994 (644 So.2d 282); March. 23, 2006, effective May 22, 2006 (933 So.2d 417); May 29, 2014, effective June 1, 2014 (140 So.3d 541); June 11, 2015, effective Oct. 1, 2015 (167 So.3d 412).

Comment

The lawyer is part of a judicial system charged with upholding the law. One of the lawyer's functions is to advise clients so that they avoid any violation of the law in the proper exercise of their rights.

This rule governs the disclosure by a lawyer of information relating to the representation of a client during the lawyer's representation of the client. See rule 4–1.18 for the lawyer's duties with respect to information provided to the lawyer by a prospective client, rule 4–1.9(c) for the lawyer's duty not to reveal information relating to the lawyer's prior representation of a former client, and rules 4–1.8(b) and 4–1.9(b) for the lawyer's duties with respect to the use of confidential information to the disadvantage of clients and former clients.

A fundamental principle in the client-lawyer relationship is that, in the absence of the client's informed consent, the lawyer must not reveal information relating to the representation. See terminology for the definition of informed consent. This contributes to the trust that is the hallmark of the client-lawyer relationship. The client is thereby encouraged to seek legal assistance and to communicate fully and frankly with the lawyer even as to embarrassing or legally damaging subject matter. The lawyer needs this information to represent the client effectively and, if necessary, to advise the client to refrain from wrongful conduct. Almost without exception, clients come to lawyers in order to determine their rights and what is, in the complex of laws and regulations, deemed to be legal and correct. Based on experience, lawyers know that almost all clients follow the advice given, and the law is upheld.

The principle of confidentiality is given effect in 2 related bodies of law, the attorney-client privilege (which includes the work product doctrine) in the law of evidence and the rule of confidentiality established in professional ethics. The attorney-client privilege applies in judicial and other proceedings in which a lawyer may be called as a witness or otherwise required to produce evidence concerning a client. The rule of client-lawyer confidentiality applies in situations other than those where evidence is sought from the lawyer through compulsion of law. The confidentiality rule applies not merely to matters communicated in confidence by the client but also to all information relating to the representation, whatever its source. A lawyer may not disclose confidential information except as authorized or required by the Rules Regulating The Florida Bar or by law. However, none of the foregoing limits the requirement of disclosure in subdivision (b). This disclosure is required to prevent a lawyer from becoming an unwitting accomplice in the fraudulent acts of a client. See also Scope.

The requirement of maintaining confidentiality of information relating to representation applies to government lawyers who may disagree with the policy goals that their representation is designed to advance.

Authorized disclosure

A lawyer is impliedly authorized to make disclosures about a client when appropriate in carrying out the representation, except to the extent that the client's instructions or special circumstances limit that authority. In litigation, for example, a lawyer may disclose information by admitting a fact that cannot properly be disputed or in negotiation by making a disclosure that facilitates a satisfactory conclusion.

Lawyers in a firm may, in the course of the firm's practice, disclose to each other information relating to a client of the firm, unless the client has instructed that particular information be confined to specified lawyers.

Disclosure adverse to client

The confidentiality rule is subject to limited exceptions. In becoming privy to information about a client, a lawyer may foresee that the client intends serious harm to another person. However, to the extent a lawyer is required or permitted to disclose a client's purposes, the client will be inhibited from revealing facts that would enable the lawyer to counsel against a wrongful course of action. While the public may be protected if full and open communication by the client is encouraged, several situations must be distinguished.

First, the lawyer may not counsel or assist a client in conduct that is criminal or fraudulent. See rule 4–1.2(d). Similarly, a lawyer has a duty under rule 4–3.3(a)(4) not to use false evidence. This duty is essentially a special instance of the duty prescribed in rule 4–1.2(d) to avoid assisting a client in criminal or fraudulent conduct.

Second, the lawyer may have been innocently involved in past conduct by the client that was criminal or fraudulent. In this situation the lawyer has not violated rule 4–1.2(d), because to "counsel or assist" criminal or fraudulent conduct requires knowing that the conduct is of that character.

Third, the lawyer may learn that a client intends prospective conduct that is criminal. As stated in subdivision (b)(1), the lawyer must reveal information in order to prevent these consequences. It is admittedly difficult for a lawyer to "know" when the criminal intent will actually be carried out, for the client may have a change of mind.

Subdivision (b)(2) contemplates past acts on the part of a client that may result in present or future consequences that may be avoided by disclosure of otherwise confidential communications. Rule 4–1.6(b)(2) would now require the lawyer to disclose information reasonably necessary to prevent the future death or substantial bodily harm to another, even though the act of the client has been completed.

The lawyer's exercise of discretion requires consideration of such factors as the nature of the lawyer's relationship with the client and with those who might be injured by the client, the lawyer's own involvement in the transaction, and factors that may extenuate the conduct in question. Where practical the lawyer should seek to persuade the client to take suitable action. In any case, a disclosure adverse to the client's interest should be no greater than the lawyer reasonably believes necessary to the purpose.

Withdrawal

If the lawyer's services will be used by the client in materially furthering a course of criminal or fraudulent conduct, the lawyer must withdraw, as stated in rule 4–1.16(a)(1).

After withdrawal the lawyer is required to refrain from making disclosure of the client's confidences, except as otherwise provided in rule 4–1.6. Neither this rule nor rule 4–1.8(b) nor rule 4–1.16(d) prevents the lawyer from giving notice of the fact of withdrawal, and the lawyer may also withdraw or disaffirm any opinion, document, affirmation, or the like.

Where the client is an organization, the lawyer may be in doubt whether contemplated conduct will actually be carried out by the organization. Where necessary to guide conduct in connection with the rule, the lawyer may make inquiry within the organization as indicated in rule 4–1.13(b).

Dispute concerning lawyer's conduct

A lawyer's confidentiality obligations do not preclude a lawyer from securing confidential legal advice about the lawyer's personal responsibility to comply with these rules. In most situations, disclosing information to secure this advice will be impliedly authorized for the lawyer to carry out the representation. Even when the disclosure is not impliedly authorized, subdivision (c)(5) permits this disclosure because of the importance of a lawyer's compliance with the Rules of Professional Conduct.

Where a legal claim or disciplinary charge alleges complicity of the lawyer in a client's conduct or other misconduct of the lawyer involving representation of the client, the lawyer may respond to the extent the lawyer reasonably believes necessary to establish a defense. The same is true with respect to a claim involving the conduct or representation of a former client. The lawyer's right to respond arises when an assertion of complicity has been made. Subdivision (c) does not require the lawyer to await the commencement of an action or proceeding that charges complicity, so that the defense may be established by responding directly to a third party who has made the assertion. The right to defend, of course, applies where a proceeding has been commenced. Where practicable and not prejudicial to the lawyer's ability to establish the defense, the lawyer should advise the client of the third party's assertion and request that the client respond appropriately. In any event, disclosure should be no greater than the lawyer reasonably believes is necessary to vindicate innocence, the disclosure should be made in a manner that limits access to the information to the tribunal or other persons having a need to know it, and appropriate protective orders or other arrangements should be sought by the lawyer to the fullest extent practicable.

If the lawyer is charged with wrongdoing in which the client's conduct is implicated, the rule of confidentiality should not prevent the lawyer from defending against the charge. A charge can arise in a civil, criminal, or professional disciplinary proceeding and can be based on a wrong allegedly committed by the lawyer against the client or on a wrong alleged by a third person; for example, a person claiming to have been defrauded by the lawyer and client acting together. A lawyer entitled to a fee is permitted by subdivision (c) to prove the services rendered in an action to collect it. This aspect of the rule expresses the principle that the beneficiary of a fiduciary relationship may not exploit it to the detriment of the fiduciary. As stated above, the lawyer must make every effort practicable to avoid unnecessary disclosure of information relating to a representation, to limit disclosure to those having the need to know it, and to obtain protective orders or make other arrangements minimizing the risk of disclosure.

Disclosures otherwise required or authorized

The attorney-client privilege is differently defined in various jurisdictions. If a lawyer is called as a witness to give testimony concerning a client, absent waiver by the client, rule 4–1.6(a) requires the lawyer to invoke the privilege when it is applicable. The lawyer must comply with the final orders of a court or other tribunal of competent jurisdiction requiring the lawyer to give information about the client.

The Rules of Professional Conduct in various circumstances permit or require a lawyer to disclose information relating to the representation. See rules 4–2.3, 4–3.3, and 4–4.1. In addition to these provisions, a lawyer may be obligated or permitted by other provisions of law to give information about a client. Whether another provision of law supersedes rule 4–1.6 is a matter of interpretation beyond the scope of these rules, but a presumption should exist against a supersession.

Detection of Conflicts of Interest

Subdivision (c)(6) recognizes that lawyers in different firms may need to disclose limited information to each other to detect and resolve conflicts of interest, for example, when a lawyer is considering an association with another firm, two or more firms are considering a merger, or a lawyer is considering the purchase of a law practice. See comment to rule 4–1.17. Under these circumstances, lawyers and law firms are permitted to disclose limited information, but only once substantive discussions regarding the new relationship have occurred. Any disclosure should ordinarily include no more than the identity of the persons and entities involved in a matter, a brief summary of the general issues involved, and information about whether the matter has terminated. Even this limited information, however, should be disclosed only to the extent reasonably necessary to detect and resolve conflicts of interest that might arise from the possible new relationship. The disclosure of any information is prohibited if it would compromise the attorney-client privilege or otherwise prejudice the client (e.g., the fact that a corporate client is seeking advice on a corporate takeover that has not been publicly announced; that a person has consulted a lawyer about the possibility of divorce before the person's intentions are known to the person's spouse; or that a person has consulted a lawyer about a criminal investigation that has not led to a public charge). Under those circumstances, subdivision (a) prohibits disclosure unless the client or former client gives informed consent. A lawyer's fiduciary duty to the lawyer's firm may also govern a lawyer's conduct when exploring an association with another firm and is beyond the scope of these rules.

Any information disclosed under this subdivision may be used or further disclosed only to the extent necessary to detect and resolve conflicts of interest. This subdivision does not restrict the use of information acquired by means independent of any disclosure under this subdivision. This subdivision also does not affect the disclosure of information within a law firm when the disclosure is otherwise authorized, for example, when a lawyer in a firm discloses information to another lawyer in the same firm to detect and resolve conflicts of interest that could arise in connection with undertaking a new representation.

Acting Competently to Preserve Confidentiality

Paragraph (e) requires a lawyer to act competently to safeguard information relating to the representation of a client against unauthorized access by third parties and against inadvertent or unauthorized disclosure by the lawyer or other persons who are participating in the representation of the client or who are subject to the lawyer's supervision. See rules 4–1.1, 4–5.1 and 4–5.3. The unauthorized access to, or the inadvertent or unauthorized disclosure of, information relating to the representation of a client does not constitute a violation of paragraph (e) if the lawyer has made reasonable efforts to prevent the access or disclosure. Factors to be considered in determining the reasonableness of the lawyer's efforts include, but are not limited to, the sensitivity of the information, the likelihood of disclosure if additional safeguards are not employed, the cost of employing additional safeguards, the difficulty of implementing the safeguards, and the extent to which the safeguards adversely affect the lawyer's ability to represent clients (e.g., by making a device or important piece of software excessively difficult to use). A client may require the lawyer to implement special security measures not required by this rule or may give informed consent to forgo security measures that would otherwise be required by this rule. Whether a lawyer may be required to take additional steps to safeguard a client's information in order to comply with other law, for example state and federal laws that govern data privacy or that impose notification requirements on the loss of, or unauthorized access to, electronic information, is beyond the scope of these rules. For a lawyer's duties when sharing information with nonlawyers outside the lawyer's own firm, see the comment to rule 4–5.3.

When transmitting a communication that includes information relating to the representation of a client, the lawyer must take reasonable precautions to prevent the information from coming into the hands of unintended recipients. This duty, however, does not require that the lawyer use special security measures if the method of communication affords a reasonable expectation of privacy. Special circumstances, however, may warrant special precautions. Factors to be considered in determining the reasonableness of the lawyer's expectation of confidentiality include the sensitivity of the information and the extent to which the privacy of the communication is protected by law or by a confidentiality agreement. A client may require the lawyer to implement special security measures not required by this rule or may give informed consent to the use of a means of communication that would otherwise be prohibited by this rule. Whether a lawyer may be required to take additional steps in order to comply with other law, for example state and federal laws that govern data privacy, is beyond the scope of these rules.

Former client

The duty of confidentiality continues after the client-lawyer relationship has terminated. See rule 4–1.9 for the prohibition against using such information to the disadvantage of the former client.

Rule 4–1.7. Conflict of Interest; Current Clients

(a) Representing Adverse Interests. Except as provided in subdivision (b), a lawyer must not represent a client if:

(1) the representation of 1 client will be directly adverse to another client; or

(2) there is a substantial risk that the representation of 1 or more clients will be materially limited by the lawyer's responsibilities to another client, a former client or a third person or by a personal interest of the lawyer.

(b) Informed Consent. Notwithstanding the existence of a conflict of interest under subdivision (a), a lawyer may represent a client if:

(1) the lawyer reasonably believes that the lawyer will be able to provide competent and diligent representation to each affected client;

(2) the representation is not prohibited by law;

(3) the representation does not involve the assertion of a position adverse to another client when the lawyer represents both clients in the same proceeding before a tribunal; and

(4) each affected client gives informed consent, confirmed in writing or clearly stated on the record at a hearing.

(c) Explanation to Clients. When representation of multiple clients in a single matter is undertaken, the consultation must include an explanation of the implications of the common representation and the advantages and risks involved.

(d) Lawyers Related by Blood, Adoption, or Marriage. A lawyer related by blood, adoption, or marriage to another lawyer as parent, child, sibling, or spouse must not represent a client in a representation directly adverse to a person who the lawyer knows is represented by the other lawyer except with the client's informed consent, confirmed in writing or clearly stated on the record at a hearing.

(e) Representation of Insureds. Upon undertaking the representation of an insured client at the expense of the insurer, a lawyer has a duty to ascertain whether the lawyer will be representing both the insurer and the insured as clients, or only the insured, and to inform both the insured and the insurer regarding the scope of the representation. All other Rules Regulating The Florida Bar related to conflicts of interest apply to the representation as they would in any other situation.

Amended July 23, 1992, effective Jan. 1, 1993 (605 So.2d 252); Jan. 23, 2003, effective July 1, 2003 (838 So.2d 1140); March 23, 2006, effective May 22, 2006 (933 So.2d 417); May 29, 2014, effective June 1, 2014 (140 So.3d 541).

Comment

Loyalty to a client

Loyalty and independent judgment are essential elements in the lawyer's relationship to a client. Conflicts of interest can arise from the lawyer's responsibilities to another client, a former client or a third person, or from the lawyer's own interests. For specific rules regarding certain conflicts of interest, see rule 4–1.8. For former client conflicts of interest, see rule 4–1.9. For conflicts of interest involving prospective clients, see rule 4–1.18. For definitions of "informed consent" and "confirmed in writing," see terminology.

An impermissible conflict of interest may exist before representation is undertaken, in which event the representation should be declined. If such a conflict arises after representation has been undertaken, the lawyer should withdraw from the representation. See rule 4–1.16. Where more than 1 client is involved and the lawyer withdraws because a conflict arises after representation, whether the lawyer may continue to represent any of the clients is determined by rule 4–1.9. As to whether a client-lawyer relationship exists or, having once been established, is continuing, see comment to rule 4–1.3 and scope.

As a general proposition, loyalty to a client prohibits undertaking representation directly adverse to that client's or another client's interests without the affected client's consent. Subdivision (a)(1) expresses that general rule. Thus, a lawyer ordinarily may not act as advocate against a person the lawyer represents in some other matter, even if it is wholly unrelated. On the other hand, simultaneous representation in unrelated matters of clients whose interests are only generally adverse, such as competing economic enterprises, does not require consent of the respective clients. Subdivision (a)(1) applies only when the representation of 1 client would be directly adverse to the other and where the lawyer's responsibilities of loyalty and confidentiality of the other client might be compromised.

Loyalty to a client is also impaired when a lawyer cannot consider, recommend, or carry out an appropriate course of action for the client because of the lawyer's other responsibilities or interests. The conflict in effect forecloses alternatives that would otherwise be available to the client. Subdivision (a)(2) addresses such situations. A possible conflict does not itself preclude the representation. The critical questions are the likelihood that a conflict will eventuate and, if it does, whether it will materially interfere with the lawyer's independent professional judgment in considering alternatives or foreclose courses of action that reasonably should be pursued on behalf of the client. Consideration should be given to whether the client wishes to accommodate the other interest involved.

Consultation and consent

A client may consent to representation notwithstanding a conflict. However, as indicated in subdivision (a)(1) with respect to representation directly adverse to a client and subdivision (a)(2) with respect to material limitations on representation of a client, when a disinterested lawyer would conclude that the client should not agree to the representation under the circumstances, the lawyer involved cannot properly ask for such agreement or provide representation on the basis of the client's consent. When more than 1 client is involved, the question of conflict must be resolved as to each client. Moreover, there may be circumstances where it is impossible to make the disclosure necessary to obtain consent. For example, when the lawyer represents different clients in related matters and 1 of the clients refuses to consent to the disclosure necessary to permit the other client to make an informed decision, the lawyer cannot properly ask the latter to consent.

Lawyer's interests

The lawyer's own interests should not be permitted to have adverse effect on representation of a client. For example, a lawyer's need for income should not lead the lawyer to undertake matters that cannot be handled competently and at a reasonable fee. See rules 4–1.1 and 4–1.5. If the probity of a lawyer's own conduct in a transaction is in serious question, it may be difficult or impossible for the lawyer to give a client detached advice. A lawyer may not allow related business interests to affect representation, for example, by referring clients to an enterprise in which the lawyer has an undisclosed interest.

Conflicts in litigation

Subdivision (a)(1) prohibits representation of opposing parties in litigation. Simultaneous representation of parties whose interests in litigation may conflict, such as co-plaintiffs or co-defendants, is governed by subdivisions (a), (b), and (c). An impermissible conflict may exist by reason of substantial discrepancy in the parties' testimony, incompatibility in positions in relation to an opposing party, or the fact that there are substantially different possibilities of settlement of the claims or liabilities in question. Such conflicts can arise in criminal cases as well as civil. The potential for conflict of interest in representing multiple defendants in a criminal case is so grave that ordinarily a lawyer should decline to represent more than 1 co-defendant. On the other hand, common representation of persons having similar interests is proper if the risk of adverse effect is minimal and the requirements of subdivisions (b) and (c) are met.

Ordinarily, a lawyer may not act as advocate against a client the lawyer represents in some other matter, even if the other matter is wholly unrelated. However, there are circumstances in which a lawyer may act as advocate against a client. For example, a lawyer representing an enterprise with diverse operations may accept employment as an advocate against the enterprise in an unrelated matter if doing so will not adversely affect the lawyer's relationship with the enterprise or conduct of the suit and if both clients consent upon consultation. By the same token, government lawyers in some circumstances may represent government employees in proceedings in which a government agency is the opposing party. The propriety of concurrent representation can depend on the nature of the litigation. For example, a suit charging fraud entails conflict to a degree not involved in a suit for a declaratory judgment concerning statutory interpretation.

A lawyer may represent parties having antagonistic positions on a legal question that has arisen in different cases, unless representation of either client would be adversely affected. Thus, it is ordinarily not improper to assert such positions in cases pending in different trial courts, but it may be improper to do so in cases pending at the same time in an appellate court.

Interest of person paying for a lawyer's service

A lawyer may be paid from a source other than the client, if the client is informed of that fact and consents and the arrangement does not compromise the lawyer's duty of loyalty to the client. See rule 4-1.8(f). For example, when an insurer and its insured have conflicting interests in a matter arising from a liability insurance agreement and the insurer is required to provide special counsel for the insured, the arrangement should assure the special counsel's professional independence. So also, when a corporation and its directors or employees are involved in a controversy in which they have conflicting interests, the corporation may provide funds for separate legal representation of the directors or employees, if the clients consent after consultation and the arrangement ensures the lawyer's professional independence.

Other conflict situations

Conflicts of interest in contexts other than litigation sometimes may be difficult to assess. Relevant factors in determining whether there is potential for adverse effect include the duration and intimacy of the lawyer's relationship with the client or clients involved, the functions being performed by the lawyer, the likelihood that actual conflict will arise, and the likely prejudice to the client from the conflict if it does arise. The question is often one of proximity and degree.

For example, a lawyer may not represent multiple parties to a negotiation whose interests are fundamentally antagonistic to each other, but common representation is permissible where the clients are generally aligned in interest even though there is some difference of interest among them.

Conflict questions may also arise in estate planning and estate administration. A lawyer may be called upon to prepare wills for several family members, such as husband and wife, and, depending upon the circumstances, a conflict of interest may arise. In estate administration the identity of the client may be unclear under the law of some jurisdictions. In Florida, the personal representative is the client rather than the estate or the beneficiaries. The lawyer should make clear the relationship to the parties involved.

A lawyer for a corporation or other organization who is also a member of its board of directors should determine whether the responsibilities of the 2 roles may conflict. The lawyer may be called on to advise the corporation in matters involving actions of the directors. Consideration should be given to the frequency with which such situations may arise, the potential intensity of the conflict, the effect of the lawyer's resignation from the board, and the possibility of the corporation's obtaining legal advice from another lawyer in such situations. If there is material risk that the dual role will compromise the lawyer's independence of professional judgment, the lawyer should not serve as a director.

Conflict charged by an opposing party

Resolving questions of conflict of interest is primarily the responsibility of the lawyer undertaking the representation. In litigation, a court may raise the question when there is reason to infer that the lawyer has neglected the responsibility. In a criminal case, inquiry by the court is generally required when a lawyer represents multiple defendants. Where the conflict is such as clearly to call in question the fair or efficient administration of justice, opposing counsel may properly raise the question. Such an objection should be viewed with caution, however, for it can be misused as a technique of harassment. See scope.

Family relationships between lawyers

Rule 4-1.7(d) applies to related lawyers who are in different firms. Related lawyers in the same firm are also governed by rules 4-1.9 and 4-1.10. The disqualification stated in rule 4-1.7(d) is personal and is not imputed to members of firms with whom the lawyers are associated.

The purpose of Rule 4-1.7(d) is to prohibit representation of adverse interests, unless informed consent is given by the client, by a lawyer related to another lawyer by blood, adoption, or marriage as a parent, child, sibling, or spouse so as to include those with biological or adopted children and within relations by marriage those who would be considered in-laws and stepchildren and stepparents.

Representation of insureds

The unique tripartite relationship of insured, insurer, and lawyer can lead to ambiguity as to whom a lawyer represents. In a particular case, the lawyer may represent only the insured, with the insurer having the status of a non-client third party payor of the lawyer's fees. Alternatively, the lawyer may represent both as dual clients, in the absence of a disqualifying conflict of interest, upon compliance with applicable rules. Establishing clarity as to the role of the lawyer at the inception of the representation avoids misunderstanding that may ethically compromise the lawyer. This is a general duty of every lawyer undertaking representation of a client, which is made specific in this context due to the desire to minimize confusion and inconsistent expectations that may arise.

Consent confirmed in writing or stated on the record at a hearing

Subdivision (b) requires the lawyer to obtain the informed consent of the client, confirmed in writing or clearly stated on the record at a hearing. With regard to being confirmed in writing, such a writing may consist of a document executed by the client or one that the lawyer promptly records and transmits to the client following an oral consent. See terminology. If it is not feasible to obtain or transmit the writing at the time the client gives informed consent, then the lawyer must obtain or transmit it within a reasonable time afterwards. See terminology. The requirement of a writing does not supplant the need in most cases for the lawyer to talk with the client, to explain the risks and advantages, if any, of representation burdened with a conflict of interest, as well as reasonably available alternatives, and to afford the client a reasonable opportunity to consider the risks and alternatives and to raise questions and concerns. Rather, the writing is required in order to impress upon clients the seriousness of the decision the client is being asked to make and to avoid disputes or ambiguities that might later occur in the absence of a writing.

Rule 4-1.8. Conflict of Interest; Prohibited and Other Transactions

(a) Business Transactions With or Acquiring Interest Adverse to Client. A lawyer shall not enter into a business transaction with a client or knowingly acquire an ownership, possessory, security, or other pecuniary interest adverse to a client, except a lien granted by law to secure a lawyer's fee or expenses, unless:

(1) the transaction and terms on which the lawyer acquires the interest are fair and reasonable to the client and are fully disclosed and transmitted in writing to the client in a manner that can be reasonably understood by the client;

(2) the client is advised in writing of the desirability of seeking and is given a reasonable opportunity to seek the advice of independent legal counsel on the transaction; and

(3) the client gives informed consent, in a writing signed by the client, to the essential terms of the transaction and the lawyer's role in the transaction, including whether the lawyer is representing the client in the transaction.

(b) Using Information to Disadvantage of Client. A lawyer shall not use information relating to representation of a client to the disadvantage of the client unless the client gives informed consent, except as permitted or required by these rules.

(c) Gifts to Lawyer or Lawyer's Family. A lawyer shall not solicit any substantial gift from a client, including a testamentary gift, or prepare on behalf of a client an instrument giving the lawyer or a person related to the lawyer any substantial gift unless the lawyer or other recipient of the gift is related to the client. For purposes of this subdivision, related persons include a spouse, child, grandchild, parent, grandparent, or other relative with whom the lawyer or the client maintains a close, familial relationship.

(d) Acquiring Literary or Media Rights. Prior to the conclusion of representation of a client, a lawyer shall not make or negotiate an agreement giving the lawyer literary or media rights to a portrayal or account based in substantial part on information relating to the representation.

(e) Financial Assistance to Client. A lawyer shall not provide financial assistance to a client in connection with pending or contemplated litigation, except that:

(1) a lawyer may advance court costs and expenses of litigation, the repayment of which may be contingent on the outcome of the matter; and

(2) a lawyer representing an indigent client may pay court costs and expenses of litigation on behalf of the client.

(f) Compensation by Third Party. A lawyer shall not accept compensation for representing a client from one other than the client unless:

(1) the client gives informed consent;

(2) there is no interference with the lawyer's independence of professional judgment or with the client-lawyer relationship; and

(3) information relating to representation of a client is protected as required by rule 4-1.6.

(g) Settlement of Claims for Multiple Clients. A lawyer who represents 2 or more clients shall not participate in making an aggregate settlement of the claims of or against the clients, or in a criminal case an aggregated agreement as to guilty or nolo contendere pleas, unless each client gives informed consent, in a writing signed by the client. The lawyer's disclosure shall include the existence and nature of all the claims or pleas involved and of the participation of each person in the settlement.

(h) Limiting Liability for Malpractice. A lawyer shall not make an agreement prospectively limiting the lawyer's liability to a client for malpractice unless permitted by law and the client is independently represented in making the agreement. A lawyer shall not settle a claim for such liability with an unrepresented client or former client without first advising that person in writing that independent representation is appropriate in connection therewith.

(i) Acquiring Proprietary Interest in Cause of Action. A lawyer shall not acquire a proprietary interest in the cause of action or subject matter of litigation the lawyer is conducting for a client, except that the lawyer may:

(1) acquire a lien granted by law to secure the lawyer's fee or expenses; and

(2) contract with a client for a reasonable contingent fee.

(j) Representation of Insureds. When a lawyer undertakes the defense of an insured other than a governmental entity, at the expense of an insurance company, in regard to an action or claim for personal injury or for property damages, or for death or loss of services resulting from personal injuries based upon tortious conduct, including product liability claims, the Statement of Insured Client's Rights shall be provided to the insured at the commencement of the representation. The lawyer shall sign the statement certifying the date on which the statement was provided to the insured. The lawyer shall keep a copy of the signed statement in the client's file and shall retain a copy of the signed statement for 6 years after the representation is completed. The statement shall be available for inspection at reasonable times by the insured, or by the appropriate disciplinary agency. Nothing in the Statement of Insured Client's Rights shall be deemed to augment or detract from any substantive or ethical duty of a lawyer or affect the extradisciplinary consequences of violating an existing substantive legal or ethical duty; nor shall any matter set forth in the Statement of Insured Client's Rights give rise to an independent cause of action or create any presumption that an existing legal or ethical duty has been breached.

STATEMENT OF INSURED CLIENT'S RIGHTS

An insurance company has selected a lawyer to defend a lawsuit or claim against you. This Statement of Insured Client's Rights is being given to you to assure that you are aware of your rights regarding your legal representation. This disclosure statement highlights many, but not all, of your rights when your legal representation is being provided by the insurance company.

1. *Your Lawyer.* If you have questions concerning the selection of the lawyer by the insurance company, you should discuss the matter with the insurance company and the lawyer. As a client, you have the right to know about the lawyer's education, training, and experience. If you ask, the lawyer should tell you specifically about the lawyer's actual experience dealing with cases similar to yours and give you this information in writing, if you request it. Your lawyer is responsible for keeping you reasonably informed regarding the case and promptly complying with your reasonable requests for information. You are entitled to be informed of the final disposition of your case within a reasonable time.

2. *Fees and Costs.* Usually the insurance company pays all of the fees and costs of defending the claim. If you are responsible for directly paying the lawyer for any fees or costs, your lawyer must promptly inform you of that.

3. *Directing the Lawyer.* If your policy, like most insurance policies, provides for the insurance company to control the defense of the lawsuit, the lawyer will be taking instructions from the insurance company. Under such policies, the lawyer cannot act solely on your instructions, and at the same time, cannot act contrary to your interests. Your preferences should be communicated to the lawyer.

4. *Litigation Guidelines.* Many insurance companies establish guidelines governing how lawyers are to proceed in defending a claim. Sometimes those guidelines affect the range of actions the lawyer can take and may require authorization of the insurance company before certain actions are undertaken. You are entitled to know the guidelines affecting the extent and level of legal services being provided to you. Upon request, the lawyer or the insurance company should either explain the guidelines to you or provide you with a copy. If the lawyer is denied authorization to provide a service or undertake an action the lawyer believes necessary to your defense, you are entitled to be informed that the insurance company has declined authorization for the service or action.

5. *Confidentiality.* Lawyers have a general duty to keep secret the confidential information a client provides, subject to limited exceptions. However, the lawyer chosen to represent you also may have a duty to share with the insurance company information relating to the defense or settlement of the claim. If the lawyer learns of information indicating that the insurance company is not obligated under the policy to cover the claim or provide a defense, the lawyer's duty is to maintain that information in confidence. If the lawyer cannot do so, the lawyer may be required to withdraw from the representation without disclosing to the insurance company the nature of the conflict of interest which has arisen. Whenever a waiver of the lawyer-client confidentiality privilege is needed, your lawyer has a duty to consult with you and obtain your informed consent. Some insurance companies retain auditing companies to review the billings and files of the lawyers they hire to represent policyholders. If the lawyer believes a bill review or other action releases information in a manner that is contrary to

your interests, the lawyer should advise you regarding the matter.

6. *Conflicts of Interest.* Most insurance policies state that the insurance company will provide a lawyer to represent your interests as well as those of the insurance company. The lawyer is responsible for identifying conflicts of interest and advising you of them. If at any time you believe the lawyer provided by the insurance company cannot fairly represent you because of conflicts of interest between you and the company (such as whether there is insurance coverage for the claim against you), you should discuss this with the lawyer and explain why you believe there is a conflict. If an actual conflict of interest arises that cannot be resolved, the insurance company may be required to provide you with another lawyer.

7. *Settlement.* Many policies state that the insurance company alone may make a final decision regarding settlement of a claim, but under some policies your agreement is required. If you want to object to or encourage a settlement within policy limits, you should discuss your concerns with your lawyer to learn your rights and possible consequences. No settlement of the case requiring you to pay money in excess of your policy limits can be reached without your agreement, following full disclosure.

8. *Your Risk.* If you lose the case, there might be a judgment entered against you for more than the amount of your insurance, and you might have to pay it. Your lawyer has a duty to advise you about this risk and other reasonably foreseeable adverse results.

9. *Hiring Your Own Lawyer.* The lawyer provided by the insurance company is representing you only to defend the lawsuit. If you desire to pursue a claim against the other side, or desire legal services not directly related to the defense of the lawsuit against you, you will need to make your own arrangements with this or another lawyer. You also may hire another lawyer, at your own expense, to monitor the defense being provided by the insurance company. If there is a reasonable risk that the claim made against you exceeds the amount of coverage under your policy, you should consider consulting another lawyer.

10. *Reporting Violations.* If at any time you believe that your lawyer has acted in violation of your rights, you have the right to report the matter to The Florida Bar, the agency that oversees the practice and behavior of all lawyers in Florida. For information on how to reach The Florida Bar call (850) 561–5839 or you may access the Bar at www.FlaBar.org.

IF YOU HAVE ANY QUESTIONS ABOUT YOUR RIGHTS, PLEASE ASK FOR AN EXPLANATION.

CERTIFICATE

The undersigned hereby certifies that this Statement of Insured Client's Rights has been provided to .... (name of insured/client(s)) .... by .... (mail/hand delivery) .... at .... (address of insured/client(s) to which mailed or delivered) ...., on ....(date) ....

____

[Signature of Attorney]

____

[Print/Type Name]

Florida Bar No.:

____

(k) Imputation of Conflicts. While lawyers are associated in a firm, a prohibition in the foregoing subdivisions (a) through (i) that applies to any one of them shall apply to all of them.

Amended July 23, 1992, effective Jan. 1, 1993 (605 So.2d 252); April 25, 2002 (820 So.2d 210); May 20, 2004 (875 So.2d 448); March 23, 2006, effective May 22, 2006 (933 So.2d 417); Nov. 19, 2009, effective Feb. 1, 2010 (24 So.3d 63).

Comment

Business transactions between client and lawyer

A lawyer's legal skill and training, together with the relationship of trust and confidence between lawyer and client, create the possibility of overreaching when the lawyer participates in a business, property, or financial transaction with a client. The requirements of subdivision (a) must be met even when the transaction is not closely related to the subject matter of the representation. The rule applies to lawyers engaged in the sale of goods or services related to the practice of law. See rule 4–5.7. It does not apply to ordinary fee arrangements between client and lawyer, which are governed by rule 4–1.5, although its requirements must be met when the lawyer accepts an interest in the client's business or other nonmonetary property as payment for all or part of a fee. In addition, the rule does not apply to standard commercial transactions between the lawyer and the client for products or services that the client generally markets to others, for example, banking or brokerage services, medical services, products manufactured or distributed by the client, and utilities services. In such transactions the lawyer has no advantage in dealing with the client, and the restrictions in subdivision (a) are unnecessary and impracticable. Likewise, subdivision (a) does not prohibit a lawyer from acquiring or asserting a lien granted by law to secure the lawyer's fee or expenses.

Subdivision (a)(1) requires that the transaction itself be fair to the client and that its essential terms be communicated to the client, in writing, in a manner that can be reasonably understood. Subdivision (a)(2) requires that the client also be advised, in writing, of the desirability of seeking the advice of independent legal counsel. It also requires that the client be given a reasonable opportunity to obtain such advice. Subdivision (a)(3) requires that the lawyer obtain the client's informed consent, in a writing signed by the client, both to the essential terms of the transaction and to the lawyer's role.

When necessary, the lawyer should discuss both the material risks of the proposed transaction, including any risk presented by the lawyer's involvement, and the existence of reasonably available alternatives and should explain why the advice of independent legal counsel is desirable. See terminology (definition of informed consent).

The risk to a client is greatest when the client expects the lawyer to represent the client in the transaction itself or when the lawyer's financial interest otherwise poses a significant risk that the lawyer's representation of the client will be materially limited by the lawyer's financial interest in the transaction. Here the lawyer's role requires that the lawyer must comply, not only with the requirements of subdivision (a), but also with the requirements of rule 4–1.7. Under that rule, the lawyer must disclose the risks associated with the lawyer's dual role as both legal adviser and participant in the transaction, such as the risk that the lawyer will structure the transaction or give legal advice in a way that favors the lawyer's interests at the expense of the client. Moreover, the lawyer must obtain the client's informed consent. In some cases, the lawyer's interest may be such that rule 4–1.7 will preclude the lawyer from seeking the client's consent to the transaction.

If the client is independently represented in the transaction, subdivision (a)(2) of this rule is inapplicable, and the subdivision (a)(1) requirement for full disclosure is satisfied either by a written disclosure by the lawyer involved in the transaction or by the client's independent counsel. The fact that the client was independently represented in the transaction is relevant in determining whether the agreement was fair and reasonable to the client as subdivision (a)(1) further requires.

Gifts to lawyers

A lawyer may accept a gift from a client, if the transaction meets general standards of fairness and if the lawyer does not prepare the instrument bestowing the gift. For example, a simple gift such as a present given at a holiday or as a token of appreciation is permitted. If a client offers the lawyer a more substantial gift, subdivision (c) does not prohibit the lawyer from accepting it, although such a gift may be voidable by the client under the doctrine of undue influence, which treats client gifts as presumptively fraudulent. In any event, due to concerns about overreaching and imposition on clients, a lawyer may not suggest that a substantial gift be made to the lawyer or for the lawyer's benefit, except where the lawyer is related to the client as set forth in subdivision (c). If effectuation of a substantial gift requires preparing a legal instrument such as a will or conveyance, however, the client should have the detached advice that another lawyer can provide and the lawyer should advise the client to seek advice of independent counsel. Subdivision (c) recognizes an exception where the client is related by blood or marriage to the donee or the gift is not substantial.

This rule does not prohibit a lawyer from seeking to have the lawyer or a partner or associate of the lawyer named as personal representative of the client's estate or to another potentially lucrative fiduciary position. Nevertheless, such appointments will be subject to the general conflict of interest provision in rule 4–1.7 when there is a significant risk that the lawyer's interest in obtaining the appointment will materially limit the lawyer's independent professional judgment in advising the client concerning the choice of a personal representative or other fiduciary. In obtaining the client's informed consent to the conflict, the lawyer should advise the client concerning the nature and extent of the lawyer's financial interest in the appointment, as well as the availability of alternative candidates for the position.

Literary rights

An agreement by which a lawyer acquires literary or media rights concerning the conduct of the representation creates a conflict between the interests of the client and the personal interests of the lawyer. Measures suitable in the representation of the client may detract from the publication value of an account of the representation. Subdivision (d) does not prohibit a lawyer representing a client in a transaction concerning literary property from agreeing that the lawyer's fee shall consist of a share in ownership in the property if the arrangement conforms to rule 4–1.5 and subdivision (a) and (i).

Financial assistance

Lawyers may not subsidize lawsuits or administrative proceedings brought on behalf of their clients, including making or guaranteeing loans to their clients for living expenses, because to do so would encourage clients to pursue lawsuits that might not otherwise be brought and because such assistance gives lawyers too great a financial stake in the litigation. These dangers do not warrant a prohibition on a lawyer advancing a client court costs and litigation expenses, including the expenses of diagnostic medical examination used for litigation purposes and the reasonable costs of obtaining and presenting evidence, because these advances are virtually indistinguishable from contingent fees and help ensure access to the courts. Similarly, an exception allowing lawyers representing indigent clients to pay court costs and litigation expenses regardless of whether these funds will be repaid is warranted.

Person paying for lawyer's services

Lawyers are frequently asked to represent a client under circumstances in which a third person will compensate the lawyer, in whole or in part. The third person might be a relative or friend, an indemnitor (such as a liability insurance company), or a co-client (such as a corporation sued along with one or more of its employees). Because third-party payers frequently have interests that differ from those of the client, including interests in minimizing the amount spent on the representation and in learning how the representation is progressing, lawyers are prohibited from accepting or continuing such representations unless the lawyer determines that there will be no interference with the lawyer's independent professional judgment and there is informed consent from the client. See also rule

4-5.4(d) (prohibiting interference with a lawyer's professional judgment by one who recommends, employs or pays the lawyer to render legal services for another).

Sometimes, it will be sufficient for the lawyer to obtain the client's informed consent regarding the fact of the payment and the identity of the third-party payer. If, however, the fee arrangement creates a conflict of interest for the lawyer, then the lawyer must comply with rule 4-1.7. The lawyer must also conform to the requirements of rule 4-1.6 concerning confidentiality. Under rule 4-1.7(a), a conflict of interest exists if there is significant risk that the lawyer's representation of the client will be materially limited by the lawyer's own interest in the fee arrangement or by the lawyer's responsibilities to the third-party payer (for example, when the third-party payer is a co-client). Under rule 4-1.7(b), the lawyer may accept or continue the representation with the informed consent of each affected client, unless the conflict is nonconsentable under that subdivision. Under rule 4-1.7(b), the informed consent must be confirmed in writing or clearly stated on the record at a hearing.

Aggregate settlements

Differences in willingness to make or accept an offer of settlement are among the risks of common representation of multiple clients by a single lawyer. Under rule 4-1.7, this is one of the risks that should be discussed before undertaking the representation, as part of the process of obtaining the clients' informed consent. In addition, rule 4-1.2(a) protects each client's right to have the final say in deciding whether to accept or reject an offer of settlement and in deciding whether to enter a guilty or nolo contendere plea in a criminal case. The rule stated in this subdivision is a corollary of both these rules and provides that, before any settlement offer or plea bargain is made or accepted on behalf of multiple clients, the lawyer must inform each of them about all the material terms of the settlement, including what the other clients will receive or pay if the settlement or plea offer is accepted. See also terminology (definition of informed consent). Lawyers representing a class of plaintiffs or defendants, or those proceeding derivatively, must comply with applicable rules regulating notification of class members and other procedural requirements designed to ensure adequate protection of the entire class.

Acquisition of interest in litigation

Subdivision (i) states the traditional general rule that lawyers are prohibited from acquiring a proprietary interest in litigation. This general rule, which has its basis in common law champerty and maintenance, is subject to specific exceptions developed in decisional law and continued in these rules, such as the exception for reasonable contingent fees set forth in rule 4-1.5 and the exception for certain advances of the costs of litigation set forth in subdivision (e).

This rule is not intended to apply to customary qualification and limitations in legal opinions and memoranda.

Representation of insureds

As with any representation of a client when another person or client is paying for the representation, the representation of an insured client at the request of the insurer creates a special need for the lawyer to be cognizant of the potential for ethical risks. The nature of the relationship between a lawyer and a client can lead to the insured or the insurer having expectations inconsistent with the duty of the lawyer to maintain confidences, avoid conflicts of interest, and otherwise comply with professional standards. When a lawyer undertakes the representation of an insured client at the expense of the insurer, the lawyer should ascertain whether the lawyer will be representing both the insured and the insurer, or only the insured. Communication with both the insured and the insurer promotes their mutual understanding of the role of the lawyer in the particular representation. The Statement of Insured Client's Rights has been developed to facilitate the lawyer's performance of ethical responsibilities. The highly variable nature of insurance and the responsiveness of the insurance industry in developing new types of coverages for risks arising in the dynamic American economy render it impractical to establish a statement of rights applicable to all forms of insurance. The Statement of Insured Client's Rights is intended to apply to personal injury and property damage tort cases. It is not intended to apply to workers' compensation cases. Even in that relatively narrow area of insurance coverage, there is variability among policies. For that reason, the statement is necessarily broad. It is the responsibility of the lawyer to explain the statement to the insured. In particular cases, the lawyer may need to provide additional information to the insured.

Because the purpose of the statement is to assist laypersons in understanding their basic rights as clients, it is necessarily abbreviated. Although brevity promotes the purpose for which the statement was developed, it also necessitates incompleteness. For these reasons, it is specifically provided that the statement shall not serve to establish any legal rights or duties, nor create any presumption that an existing legal or ethical duty has been breached. As a result, the statement and its contents should not be invoked by opposing parties as grounds for disqualification of a lawyer or for procedural purposes. The purpose of the statement would be subverted if it could be used in such a manner.

The statement is to be signed by the lawyer to establish that it was timely provided to the insured, but the insured client is not required to sign it. It is in the best interests of the lawyer to have the insured client sign the statement to avoid future questions, but it is considered impractical to require the lawyer to obtain the insured client's signature in all instances.

Establishment of the statement and the duty to provide it to an insured in tort cases involving personal injury or property damage should not be construed as lessening the duty of the lawyer to inform clients of their rights in other circumstances. When other types of insurance are involved, when there are other third-party payors of fees, or when multiple clients are represented, similar needs for fully informing clients exist, as recognized in rules 4–1.7(c) and 4–1.8(f).

Imputation of prohibitions

Under subdivision (k), a prohibition on conduct by an individual lawyer in subdivisions (a) through (i) also applies to all lawyers associated in a firm with the personally prohibited lawyer. For example, 1 lawyer in a firm may not enter into a business transaction with a client of another member of the firm without complying with subdivision (a), even if the first lawyer is not personally involved in the representation of the client.

Rule 4–1.9. Conflict of Interest; Former Client

A lawyer who has formerly represented a client in a matter must not afterwards:

(a) represent another person in the same or a substantially related matter in which that person's interests are materially adverse to the interests of the former client unless the former client gives informed consent;

(b) use information relating to the representation to the disadvantage of the former client except as these rules would permit or require with respect to a client or when the information has become generally known; or

(c) reveal information relating to the representation except as these rules would permit or require with respect to a client.

Amended July 23, 1992, effective Jan. 1, 1993 (605 So.2d 252); April 25, 2002 (820 So.2d 210); March 23, 2006, effective May 22, 2006 (933 So.2d 417); Nov. 19, 2009, effective Feb. 1, 2010 (24 So.3d 63); May 29, 2014, effective June 1, 2014 (140 So.3d 541).

Comment

After termination of a client-lawyer relationship, a lawyer may not represent another client except in conformity with this rule. The principles in rule 4–1.7 determine whether the interests of the present and former client are adverse. Thus, a lawyer could not properly seek to rescind on behalf of a new client a contract drafted on behalf of the former client. So also a lawyer who has prosecuted an accused person could not properly represent the accused in a subsequent civil action against the government concerning the same transaction.

The scope of a "matter" for purposes of rule 4–1.9(a) may depend on the facts of a particular situation or transaction. The lawyer's involvement in a matter can also be a question of degree. When a lawyer has been directly involved in a specific transaction, subsequent representation of other clients with materially adverse interests clearly is prohibited. On the other hand, a lawyer who recurrently handled a type of problem for a former client is not precluded from later representing another client in a wholly distinct problem of that type even though the subsequent representation involves a position adverse to the prior client. Similar considerations can apply to the reassignment of military lawyers between defense and prosecution functions within the same military jurisdiction. The underlying question is whether the lawyer was so involved in the matter that the subsequent representation can be justly regarded as a changing of sides in the matter in question.

Matters are "substantially related" for purposes of this rule if they involve the same transaction or legal dispute, or if the current matter would involve the lawyer attacking work that the lawyer performed for the former client. For example, a lawyer who has previously represented a client in securing environmental permits to build a shopping center would be precluded from representing neighbors seeking to oppose rezoning of the property on the basis of environmental considerations; however, the lawyer would not be precluded, on the grounds of substantial relationship, from defending a tenant of the completed shopping center in resisting eviction for nonpayment of rent.

Lawyers owe confidentiality obligations to former clients, and thus information acquired by the lawyer in the course of representing a client may not subsequently be used by the lawyer to the disadvantage of the client without the former client's consent. However, the fact that a lawyer has once served a client does not preclude the lawyer from using generally known information about that client when later representing another client. Information that has been widely disseminated by the media to the public, or that typically would be obtained by any reasonably prudent lawyer who had never represented the former client, should be considered generally known and ordinarily will not be disqualifying. The essential question is whether, but for having represented the former client, the lawyer would know or discover the information.

Information acquired in a prior representation may have been rendered obsolete by the passage of time. In the case of an organizational client, general knowledge of the client's policies and practices ordinarily will not preclude a subsequent representation; on the other hand, knowledge of specific facts gained in a prior representation that are relevant to the matter in question ordinarily will preclude such a representation. A former client is not required to reveal the confidential information learned by the lawyer in order to establish a substantial risk that the lawyer has confidential information to use in the subsequent matter. A conclusion about the possession of such information may be based on the nature of the services the lawyer provided the former client and information that would in ordinary practice be learned by a lawyer providing such services.

The provisions of this rule are for the protection of clients and can be waived if the former client gives informed consent. See terminology.

With regard to an opposing party's raising a question of conflict of interest, see comment to rule 4–1.7. With regard to disqualification of a firm with which a lawyer is associated, see rule 4–1.10.

Rule 4–1.10. Imputation of Conflicts of Interest; General Rule

(a) Imputed Disqualification of All Lawyers in Firm. While lawyers are associated in a firm, none of them may knowingly represent a client when any 1 of them practicing alone would be prohibited from doing so by rule 4–1.7 or 4–1.9 except as provided elsewhere in this rule, or unless the prohibition is based on a personal interest of the prohibited lawyer and does not present a significant risk of materially limiting the representation of the client by the remaining lawyers in the firm.

(b) Former Clients of Newly Associated Lawyer. When a lawyer becomes associated with a firm, the firm may not knowingly represent a person in the same or a substantially related matter in which that lawyer, or a firm with which the lawyer was associated, had previously represented a client whose interests are materially adverse to that person and about whom the lawyer had acquired information protected by rules 4–1.6 and 4–1.9(b) and (c) that is material to the matter.

(c) Representing Interests Adverse to Clients of Formerly Associated Lawyer. When a lawyer has terminated an association with a firm, the firm is not prohibited from thereafter representing a person with interests materially adverse to those of a client represented by the formerly associated lawyer unless:

(1) the matter is the same or substantially related to that in which the formerly associated lawyer represented the client; and

(2) any lawyer remaining in the firm has information protected by rules 4–1.6 and 4–1.9(b) and (c) that is material to the matter.

(d) Waiver of Conflict. A disqualification prescribed by this rule may be waived by the affected client under the conditions stated in rule 4–1.7.

(e) Government Lawyers. The disqualification of lawyers associated in a firm with former or current government lawyers is governed by rule 4–1.11.

Amended July 23, 1992, effective Jan. 1, 1993 (605 So.2d 252); March 23, 2006, effective May 22, 2006 (933 So.2d 417); July 7, 2011, effective Oct. 1, 2011 (67 So.3d 1037); May 29, 2014, effective June 1, 2014 (140 So.3d 541).

Comment

Definition of "firm"

With respect to the law department of an organization, there is ordinarily no question that the members of the department constitute a firm within the meaning of the Rules of Professional Conduct. However, there can be uncertainty as to the identity of the client. For example, it may not be clear whether the law department of a corporation represents a subsidiary or an affiliated corporation, as well as the corporation by which the members of the department are directly employed. A similar question can arise concerning an unincorporated association and its local affiliates.

Similar questions can also arise with respect to lawyers in legal aid. Lawyers employed in the same unit of a legal service organization constitute a firm, but not necessarily those employed in separate units. As in the case of independent practitioners, whether the lawyers should be treated as associated with each other can depend on the particular rule that is involved and on the specific facts of the situation.

Where a lawyer has joined a private firm after having represented the government, the situation is governed by rule 4–1.11(a) and (b); where a lawyer represents the government after having served private clients, the situation is governed by rule 4–1.11(c)(1). The individual lawyer involved is bound by the rules generally, including rules 4–1.6, 4–1.7, and 4–1.9.

Different provisions are thus made for movement of a lawyer from 1 private firm to another and for movement of a lawyer between a private firm and the government. The government is entitled to protection of its client confidences and, therefore, to the protections provided in rules 4–1.6, 4–1.9, and 4–1.11. However, if the more extensive disqualification in rule 4–1.10 were applied to former government lawyers, the potential effect on the government would be unduly burdensome. The government deals with all private citizens and organizations and thus has a much wider circle of adverse legal interests than does any private law firm. In these circumstances, the government's recruitment of lawyers would be seriously impaired if rule 4–1.10 were applied to the government. On balance, therefore, the government is better served in the long run by the protections stated in rule 4–1.11.

Principles of imputed disqualification

The rule of imputed disqualification stated in subdivision (a) gives effect to the principle of loyalty to the client as it applies to lawyers who practice in a law firm. Such situations can be considered from the premise that a firm of lawyers is essentially 1 lawyer for purposes of the rules governing loyalty to the client or from the premise that each lawyer is vicariously bound by the obligation of loyalty owed by each lawyer with whom the lawyer is associated. Subdivision (a) operates only among the lawyers currently associated in a firm. When a lawyer moves from 1 firm to another the situation is governed by subdivisions (b) and (c).

The rule in subdivision (a) does not prohibit representation where neither questions of client loyalty nor protection of confidential information are presented. Where 1 lawyer in a firm could not effectively represent a given client because of strong political beliefs, for example, but that lawyer will do no work on the case and the personal beliefs of the lawyer will not materially limit the representation by others in the firm, the firm should not be disqualified. On the other hand, if an opposing party in a case were owned by a lawyer in the law firm, and others in the firm would be materially limited in pursuing the matter because of loyalty to that lawyer, the personal disqualification of the lawyer would be imputed to all others in the firm.

The rule in subdivision (a) also does not prohibit representation by others in the law firm where the person prohibited from involvement in a matter is a nonlawyer, such as a paralegal or legal secretary. Such persons, however, ordinarily must be screened from any personal participation in the matter to avoid communication to others in the firm of confidential information that both the nonlawyers and the firm have a legal duty to protect. See terminology and rule 4–5.3.

Lawyers moving between firms

When lawyers have been associated in a firm but then end their association, however, the problem is more complicated. The fiction that the law firm is the same as a single lawyer is no longer wholly realistic. There are several competing considerations. First, the client previously represented must be reasonably assured that the principle of loyalty to the client is not compromised. Second, the rule of disqualification should not be so broadly cast as to preclude other persons from having reasonable choice of legal counsel. Third, the rule of disqualification should not unreasonably hamper lawyers from forming new associations and taking on new clients after having left a previous association. In this connection, it should be recognized that today many lawyers practice in firms, that many to some degree limit their practice to 1 field or another, and that many move from 1 association to another several times in their careers. If the concept of imputed disqualification were defined with unqualified rigor, the result would be radical curtailment of the opportunity of lawyers to move from 1 practice setting to another and of the opportunity of clients to change counsel.

Reconciliation of these competing principles in the past has been attempted under 2 rubrics. One approach has been to seek per se rules of disqualification. For example, it has been held that a partner in a law firm is conclusively presumed to have access to all confidences concerning all clients of the firm. Under this analysis, if a lawyer has been a partner in one law firm and then becomes a partner in another law firm, there is a presumption that all confidences known by a partner in the first firm are known to all partners in the second firm. This presumption might properly be applied in some circumstances, especially where the client has been extensively represented, but may be unrealistic where the client was represented only for limited purposes. Furthermore, such a rigid rule exaggerates the difference between a partner and an associate in modern law firms.

The other rubric formerly used for dealing with vicarious disqualification is the appearance of impropriety and was proscribed in former Canon 9 of the Code of Professional Responsibility. This rubric has a two-fold problem. First, the appearance of impropriety can be taken to include any new client-lawyer relationship that might make a former client feel anxious. If that meaning were adopted, disqualification would become little more than a question of subjective judgment by the former client. Second, since "impropriety" is undefined, the term "appearance of impropriety" is question-begging. It therefore has to be recognized that the problem of imputed disqualification cannot be properly resolved either by simple analogy to a lawyer practicing alone or by the very general concept of appearance of impropriety.

A rule based on a functional analysis is more appropriate for determining the question of vicarious disqualification. Two functions are involved: preserving confidentiality and avoiding positions adverse to a client.

Confidentiality

Preserving confidentiality is a question of access to information. Access to information, in turn, is essentially a question of fact in particular circumstances, aided by inferences, deductions, or working presumptions that reasonably may be made about the way in which lawyers work together. A lawyer may have general access to files of all clients of a law firm and may regularly participate in discussions of their affairs; it should be inferred that such a lawyer in fact is privy to all information about all the firm's clients. In contrast, another lawyer may have access to the files of only a limited number of clients and participate in discussion of the affairs of no other clients; in the absence of information to the contrary, it should be inferred that such a lawyer in fact is privy to information about the clients actually served but not information about other clients.

Application of subdivisions (b) and (c) depends on a situation's particular facts. In any such inquiry, the burden of proof should rest upon the firm whose disqualification is sought.

Subdivisions (b) and (c) operate to disqualify the firm only when the lawyer involved has actual knowledge of relevant information protected by rules 4–1.6 and 4–1.9(b) and (c). Thus, if a lawyer while with 1 firm acquired no knowledge or information relating to a particular client of the firm and that lawyer later joined another firm, neither the lawyer individually nor the second firm is disqualified from representing another client in the same or a related matter even though the interests of the 2 clients conflict.

Independent of the question of disqualification of a firm, a lawyer changing professional association has a continuing duty to preserve confidentiality of information about a client formerly represented. See rules 4–1.6 and 4–1.9.

Adverse positions

The second aspect of loyalty to client is the lawyer's obligation to decline subsequent representations involving positions adverse to a former client arising in substantially related matters. This obligation requires abstention from adverse representation by the individual lawyer involved, but does not properly entail abstention of other lawyers through imputed disqualification. Hence, this aspect of the problem is governed by rule 4–1. 9(a). Thus, if a lawyer left 1 firm for another, the new affiliation would not preclude the firms involved from continuing to represent clients with adverse interests in the same or related matters so long as the conditions of rule 4–1.10(b) and (c) concerning confidentiality have been met.

Rule 4–1.10(d) removes imputation with the informed consent of the affected client or former client under the conditions stated in rule 4–1.7. The conditions stated in rule 4–1.7 require the lawyer to determine that the representation is not prohibited by rule 4–1.7(b) and that each affected client or former client has given informed consent to the representation, confirmed in writing or clearly stated on the record. In some cases, the risk may be so severe that the conflict may not be cured by client consent. For a definition of informed consent, see terminology.

Where a lawyer is prohibited from engaging in certain transactions under rule 4–1.8, subdivision (k) of that rule, and not this rule, determines whether that prohibition also applies to other lawyers associated in a firm with the personally prohibited lawyer.

Rule 4–1.11. Special Conflicts of Interest for Former and Current Government Officers and Employees

(a) Representation of Private Client by Former Public Officer or Employee. A lawyer who has formerly served as a public officer or employee of the government:

(1) is subject to rule 4–1.9(b) and (c); and

(2) shall not otherwise represent a client in connection with a matter in which the lawyer participated personally and substantially as a public officer or employee, unless the appropriate government agency gives its informed consent, confirmed in writing, to the representation.

(b) Representation by Another Member of the Firm. When a lawyer is disqualified from representation under subdivision (a), no lawyer in a firm with which that lawyer is associated may knowingly undertake or continue representation in such a matter unless:

(1) the disqualified lawyer is timely screened from any participation in the matter and is directly apportioned no part of the fee therefrom; and

(2) written notice is promptly given to the appropriate government agency to enable it to ascertain compliance with the provisions of this rule.

(c) Use of Confidential Government Information. A lawyer having information that the lawyer knows is confidential government information about a person acquired when the lawyer was a public officer or employee may not represent a private client whose interests are adverse to that person in a matter in which the information could be used to the material disadvantage of that person. As used in this rule, the term "confidential government information" means information that has been obtained under governmental authority and which, at the time this rule is applied, the government is prohibited by law from disclosing to the public or has a legal privilege not to disclose and which is not otherwise available to the public. A firm with which that lawyer is associated may undertake or continue representation in the matter only if the disqualified lawyer is screened from any participation in the matter and is apportioned no part of the fee therefrom.

(d) Limits on Participation of Public Officer or Employee. A lawyer currently serving as a public officer or employee:

(1) is subject to rules 4–1.7 and 4–1.9; and

(2) shall not:

(A) participate in a matter in which the lawyer participated personally and substantially while in private practice or nongovernmental employment, unless the appropriate government agency gives its informed consent; or

(B) negotiate for private employment with any person who is involved as a party or as attorney for a party in a matter in which the lawyer is participating personally and substantially.

(e) Matter Defined. As used in this rule, the term "matter" includes:

(1) any judicial or other proceeding, application, request for a ruling or other determination, contract, claim, controversy, investigation, charge, accusation, arrest, or other particular matter involving a specific party or parties; and

(2) any other matter covered by the conflict of interest rules of the appropriate government agency.

Amended July 23, 1992, effective Jan. 1, 1993 (605 So.2d 252); March 23, 2006, effective May 22, 2006 (933 So.2d 417); July 7, 2011, effective Oct. 1, 2011 (67 So.3d 1037).

Comment

A lawyer who has served or is currently serving as a public officer or employee is personally subject to the rules of professional conduct, including the prohibition against concurrent conflicts of interest stated in rule 4–1.7. In addition, such a lawyer may be subject to statutes and government regulations regarding conflict of interest. Such statutes and regulations may circumscribe the extent to which the government agency may give consent under this rule. See terminology for definition of informed consent.

Subdivisions (a)(1), (a)(2), and (d)(1) restate the obligations of an individual lawyer who has served or is currently serving as an officer or employee of the government toward a former government or private client. Rule 4–1.10 is not applicable to the conflicts of interest addressed by this rule. Rather, subdivision (b) sets forth a special imputation rule for former government lawyers that provides for screening and notice. Because of the special problems raised by imputation within a government agency, subdivision (d) does not impute the conflicts of a lawyer currently serving as an officer or employee of the government to other associated government officers or employees, although ordinarily it will be prudent to screen such lawyers.

Subdivisions (a)(2) and (d)(2) apply regardless of whether a lawyer is adverse to a former client and are thus designed not only to protect the former client, but also to prevent a lawyer from exploiting public office for the advantage of another client. For example, a lawyer who has pursued a claim on behalf of the government may not pursue the same claim on behalf of a later private client after the lawyer has left government service, except when authorized to do so by the government agency under subdivision (a). Similarly, a lawyer who has pursued a claim on behalf of a private client may not pursue the claim on behalf of the government, except when authorized to do so by subdivision (d). As with subdivisions (a)(1) and (d)(1), rule 4–1.10 is not applicable to the conflicts of interest addressed by these subdivisions.

This rule represents a balancing of interests. On the one hand, where the successive clients are a government agency and another client, public or private, the risk exists that power or discretion vested in that agency might be used for the special benefit of the other client. A lawyer should not be in a position where benefit to the other client might affect performance of the lawyer's professional functions on behalf of the government. Also, unfair advantage could accrue to the other client by reason of access to confidential government information about the client's adversary obtainable only through the lawyer's government service. On the other hand, the rules governing lawyers presently or formerly employed by a government agency should not be so restrictive as to inhibit transfer of employment to and from the government. The government has a legitimate need to attract qualified lawyers as well as to maintain high ethical standards. Thus, a former government lawyer is disqualified only from particular matters in which the lawyer participated personally and substantially. The provisions for screening and waiver in subdivision (b) are necessary to prevent the disqualification rule from imposing too severe a deterrent against entering public service. The limitation of disqualification in subdivisions (a)(2) and (d)(2) to matters involving a specific party or parties, rather than extending disqualification to all substantive issues on which the lawyer worked, serves a similar function.

When a lawyer has been employed by 1 government agency and then moves to a second government agency, it may be appropriate to treat that second agency as another client for purposes of this rule, as when a lawyer is employed by a city and subsequently is employed by a federal agency. However, because the conflict of interest is governed by subdivision (d), the latter agency is not required to screen the lawyer as subdivision (b) requires a law firm to do. The question of whether 2 government agencies should be regarded as the same or different clients for conflict of interest purposes is beyond the scope of these rules. See rule 4–1.13 comment, government agency.

Subdivisions (b) and (c) contemplate a screening arrangement. See terminology (requirements for screening procedures). These subdivisions do not prohibit a lawyer from receiving a salary or partnership share established by prior independent agreement, but that lawyer may not receive compensation directly relating the attorney's compensation to the fee in the matter in which the lawyer is disqualified.

Notice, including a description of the screened lawyer's prior representation and of the screening procedures employed, generally should be given as soon as practicable after the need for screening becomes apparent.

Subdivision (c) operates only when the lawyer in question has knowledge of the information, which means actual knowledge; it does not operate with respect to information that merely could be imputed to the lawyer.

Subdivisions (a) and (d) do not prohibit a lawyer from jointly representing a private party and a government agency when doing so is permitted by rule 4–1.7 and is not otherwise prohibited by law.

For purposes of subdivision (e) of this rule, a "matter" may continue in another form. In determining whether 2 particular matters are the same, the lawyer should consider the extent to which the matters involve the same basic facts, the same or related parties, and the time elapsed.

Rule 4–1.12. Former Judge or Arbitrator, Mediator or Other Third–Party Neutral

(a) Representation of Private Client by Former Judge, Law Clerk, or Other Third–Party Neutral. Except as stated in subdivision (d), a lawyer shall not represent anyone in connection with a matter in which the lawyer participated personally and substantially as a judge or other adjudicative officer or law clerk to such a person or as an arbitrator, mediator, or other third-party neutral, unless all parties to the proceeding give informed consent, confirmed in writing.

(b) Negotiation of Employment by Judge, Law Clerk, or Other Third–Party Neutral. A lawyer shall not negotiate for employment with any person who is involved as a party or as attorney for a party in a matter in which the lawyer is participating personally and substantially as a judge or other adjudicative officer or as an arbitrator, mediator, or other third-party neutral. A lawyer serving as a law clerk to a judge or other adjudicative officer may negotiate for employment with a party or attorney involved in a matter in which the clerk is participating personally and substantially, but only after the lawyer has notified the judge or other adjudicative officer.

(c) Imputed Disqualification of Law Firm. If a lawyer is disqualified by subdivision (a), no lawyer in a firm with which that lawyer is associated may knowingly undertake or continue representation in the matter unless:

(1) the disqualified lawyer is timely screened from any participation in the matter and is directly apportioned no part of the fee therefrom; and

(2) written notice is promptly given to the parties and any appropriate tribunal to enable it to ascertain compliance with the provisions of this rule.

(d) Exemption for Arbitrator as Partisan. An arbitrator selected as a partisan of a party in a multimember arbitration panel is not prohibited from subsequently representing that party.

Amended July 23, 1992, effective Jan. 1, 1993 (605 So.2d 252); March 23, 2006, effective May 22, 2006 (933 So.2d 417).

Comment

This rule generally parallels rule 4–1.11. The term "personally and substantially" signifies that a judge who was a member of a multimember court, and thereafter left judicial office to practice law, is not prohibited from representing a client in a matter pending in the court, but in which the former judge did not participate. So also the fact that a former judge exercised administrative responsibility in a court does not prevent the former judge from acting as a lawyer in a matter where the judge had previously exercised remote or incidental administrative responsibility that did not affect the merits. Compare the comment to rule 4–1.11. The term "adjudicative officer" includes such officials as judges pro tempore, referees, special masters, hearing officers, and other parajudicial officers and also lawyers who serve as part-time judges. Compliance Canons A(2), B(2), and C of Florida's Code of Judicial Conduct provide that a part-time judge, judge pro tempore, or retired judge recalled to active service may not "act as a lawyer in a proceeding in which [the lawyer] has served as a judge or in any other proceeding related thereto." Although phrased differently from this rule, those rules correspond in meaning.

Like former judges, lawyers who have served as arbitrators, mediators, or other third-party neutrals may be asked to represent a client in a matter in which the lawyer participated personally and substantially. This rule forbids such representation unless all of the parties to the proceedings give their informed consent, confirmed in writing. See terminology. Other law or codes of ethics governing third-party neutrals may impose more stringent standards of personal or imputed disqualification. See rule 4–2.4.

Although lawyers who serve as third-party neutrals do not have information concerning the parties that is protected under rule 4–1.6, they typically owe the parties an obligation of confidentiality under law or codes of ethics governing third-party neutrals. Thus, subdivision (c) provides that conflicts of the personally disqualified lawyer will be imputed to other lawyers in a law firm unless the conditions of this subdivision are met.

Requirements for screening procedures are stated in terminology. Subdivision (c)(1) does not prohibit the screened lawyer from receiving a salary or partnership share established by prior independent agreement, but that lawyer may not receive compensation directly related to the matter in which the lawyer is disqualified.

Notice, including a description of the screened lawyer's prior representation and of the screening procedures employed, generally should be given as soon as practicable after the need for screening becomes apparent.

A Florida Bar member who is a certified or court-appointed mediator is governed by the applicable law and rules relating to certified and court-appointed mediators.

Rule 4–1.13. Organization as client

(a) Representation of Organization. A lawyer employed or retained by an organization represents the organization acting through its duly authorized constituents.

(b) Violations by Officers or Employees of Organization. If a lawyer for an organization knows that an officer, employee, or other person associated with the organization is engaged in action, intends to act, or refuses to act in a matter related to the representation that is a violation of a legal obligation to the organization or a violation of law that reasonably might be imputed to the organization and is likely to result in substantial injury to the organization, the lawyer shall proceed as is reasonably necessary in the best interest of the organization. In determining how to proceed, the lawyer shall give due consideration to the seriousness of the violation and its consequences, the scope and nature of the lawyer's representation, the responsibility in the organization and the apparent motivation of the person involved, the policies of the organization concerning such matters, and any other relevant considerations. Any measures taken shall be designed to minimize disruption of the organization and the risk of revealing information relating to the representation to persons outside the organization. Such measures may include among others:

(1) asking reconsideration of the matter;

(2) advising that a separate legal opinion on the matter be sought for presentation to appropriate authority in the organization; and

(3) referring the matter to higher authority in the organization, including, if warranted by the seriousness of the matter, referral to the highest authority that can act in behalf of the organization as determined by applicable law.

(c) Resignation as Counsel for Organization. If, despite the lawyer's efforts in accordance with subdivision (b), the highest authority that can act on behalf of the organization insists upon action, or a refusal to act, that is clearly a violation of law and is likely to result in substantial injury to the organization, the lawyer may resign in accordance with rule 4–1.16.

(d) Identification of Client. In dealing with an organization's directors, officers, employees, members, shareholders, or other constituents, a lawyer shall explain the identity of the client when the lawyer knows or reasonably should know that the organization's interests are adverse to those of the constituents with whom the lawyer is dealing.

(e) Representing Directors, Officers, Employees, Members, Shareholders, or Other Constituents of Organization. A lawyer representing an organization may also represent any of its directors, officers, employees, members, shareholders, or other constituents, subject to the provisions of rule 4–1.7. If the organization's consent to the dual representation is required by rule 4–1.7, the consent shall be given by an appropriate official of the organization other than the individual who is to be represented, or by the shareholders.

Amended July 23, 1992, effective Jan. 1, 1993 (605 So.2d 252); March 23, 2006, effective May 22, 2006 (933 So.2d 417).

Comment

The entity as the client

An organizational client is a legal entity, but it cannot act except through its officers, directors, employees, shareholders, and other constituents. Officers, directors, employees, and shareholders are the constituents of the corporate organizational client. The duties defined in this comment apply equally to unincorporated associations. "Other constituents" as used in this comment means the positions equivalent to officers, directors, employees, and shareholders held by persons acting for organizational clients that are not corporations.

When 1 of the constituents of an organizational client communicates with the organization's lawyer in that person's organizational capacity, the communication is protected by rule 4–1.6. Thus, by way of example, if an organizational client requests its lawyer to investigate allegations of wrongdoing, interviews made in the course of that investigation between the lawyer and the client's employees or other constituents are covered by rule 4–1.6. This does not mean, however, that constituents of an organizational client are the clients of the lawyer. The lawyer may not disclose to such constituents information relating to the representation except for disclosures explicitly or impliedly authorized by the organizational client in order to carry out the representation or as otherwise permitted by rule 4–1.6.

When constituents of the organization make decisions for it, the decisions ordinarily must be accepted by the lawyer even if their utility or prudence is doubtful. Decisions concerning policy and operations, including ones entailing serious risk, are not as such in the lawyer's province. However, different considerations arise when the lawyer knows that the organization may be substantially injured by action of a constituent that is in violation of law. In such a circumstance, it may be reasonably necessary for the lawyer to ask the constituent to reconsider the matter. If that fails, or if the matter is of sufficient seriousness and importance to the organization, it may be reasonably necessary for the lawyer to take steps to have the matter reviewed by a higher authority in the organization. Clear justification should exist for seeking review over the head of the constituent normally responsible for it. The stated policy of the organization may define circumstances and prescribe channels for such review, and a lawyer should encourage the formulation of such a policy. Even in the absence of organization policy, however, the lawyer may have an obligation to refer a matter to higher authority, depending on the seriousness of the matter and whether the constituent in question has apparent motives to act at variance with the organization's interest. Review by the chief executive officer or by the board of directors may be required when the matter is of importance commensurate with their authority. At some point it may be useful or essential to obtain an independent legal opinion.

The organization's highest authority to whom a matter may be referred ordinarily will be the board of directors or similar governing body. However, applicable law may prescribe that under certain conditions highest authority reposes elsewhere; for example, in the independent directors of a corporation.

Relation to other rules

The authority and responsibility provided in this rule are concurrent with the authority and responsibility provided in other rules. In particular, this rule does not limit or expand the lawyer's responsibility under rule 4–1.6, 4–1.8, 4–1.16, 4–3.3, or 4–4.1. If the lawyer's services are being used by an organization to further a crime or fraud by the organization, rule 4–1.2(d) can be applicable.

Government agency

The duty defined in this rule applies to governmental organizations. However, when the client is a governmental organization, a different balance may be appropriate between maintaining confidentiality and assuring that the wrongful official act is prevented or rectified, for public business is involved. In addition, duties of lawyers employed by the government or lawyers in military service may be defined by statutes and regulation. Defining precisely the identity of the client and prescribing the resulting obligations of such lawyers may be more difficult in the government context and is a matter beyond the scope of these rules. Although in some circumstances the client may be a specific agency, it may also be a branch of the government, such as the executive branch, or the government as a whole. For example, if the action or failure to act involves the head of a bureau, either the department of which the bureau is a part or the relevant branch of government may be the client for purposes of this rule. Moreover, in a matter involving the conduct of government officials, a government lawyer may have authority under applicable law to question such conduct more extensively than that of a lawyer for a private organization in similar circumstances. This rule does not limit that authority.

Clarifying the lawyer's role

There are times when the organization's interest may be or becomes adverse to those of 1 or more of its constituents. In such circumstances the lawyer should advise any constituent whose interest the lawyer finds adverse to that of the organization of the conflict or potential conflict of interest that the lawyer cannot represent such constituent and that such person may wish to obtain independent representation. Care must be taken to assure that the constituent understands that, when there is such adversity of interest, the lawyer for the organization cannot provide legal representation for that constituent and that discussions between the lawyer for the organization and the constituent may not be privileged.

Whether such a warning should be given by the lawyer for the organization to any constituent may turn on the facts of each case.

Dual representation

Subdivision (e) recognizes that a lawyer for an organization may also represent a principal officer or major shareholder.

Derivative actions

Under generally prevailing law, the shareholders or members of a corporation may bring suit to compel the directors to perform their legal obligations in the supervision of the organization. Members of unincorporated associations have essentially the same right. Such an action may be brought nominally by the organization, but usually is, in fact, a legal controversy over management of the organization.

The question can arise whether counsel for the organization may defend such an action. The proposition that the organization is the lawyer's client does not alone resolve the issue. Most derivative actions are a normal incident of an organization's affairs, to be defended by the organization's lawyer like any other suit. However, if the claim involves serious charges of wrongdoing by those in control of the organization, a conflict may arise between the lawyer's duty to the organization and the lawyer's relationship with the board. In those circumstances, rule 4–1.7 governs who should represent the directors and the organization.

Representing related organizations

Consistent with the principle expressed in subdivision (a) of this rule, a lawyer or law firm who represents or has represented a corporation (or other organization) ordinarily is not presumed to also represent, solely by virtue of representing or having represented the client, an organization (such as a corporate parent or subsidiary) that is affiliated with the client. There are exceptions to this general proposition, such as, for example, when an affiliate actually is the alter ego of the organizational client or when the client has revealed confidential information to an attorney with the reasonable expectation that the information would not be used adversely to the client's affiliate(s). Absent such an exception, an attorney or law firm is not ethically precluded from undertaking representations adverse to affiliates of an existing or former client.

Rule 4–1.14. Client under a disability

(a) Maintenance of Normal Relationship. When a client's ability to make adequately considered decisions in connection with the representation is impaired, whether because of minority, mental disability, or for some other reason, the lawyer shall, as far as reasonably possible, maintain a normal client-lawyer relationship with the client.

(b) Appointment of Guardian. A lawyer may seek the appointment of a guardian or take other protective action with respect to a client only when the lawyer reasonably believes that the client cannot adequately act in the client's own interest.

Amended July 23, 1992, effective Jan. 1, 1993 (605 So.2d 252).

Comment

The normal client-lawyer relationship is based on the assumption that the client, when properly advised and assisted, is capable of making decisions about important matters. When the client is a minor or suffers from a mental disorder or disability, however, maintaining the ordinary client-lawyer relationship may not be possible in all respects. In particular, an incapacitated person may have no power to make legally binding decisions. Nevertheless, a client lacking legal competence often has the ability to understand, deliberate upon, and reach conclusions about matters affecting the client's own well-being. Furthermore, to an increasing extent the law recognizes intermediate degrees of competence. For example, children as young as 5 or 6 years of age, and certainly those of 10 or 12, are regarded as having opinions that are entitled to weight in legal proceedings concerning their custody. So also, it is recognized that some persons of advanced age can be quite capable of handling routine financial matters while needing special legal protection concerning major transactions.

The fact that a client suffers a disability does not diminish the lawyer's obligation to treat the client with attention and respect. If the person has no guardian or legal representative, the lawyer often must act as de facto guardian. Even if the person does have a legal representative, the lawyer should as far as possible accord the represented person the status of client, particularly in maintaining communication.

If a legal representative has already been appointed for the client, the lawyer should ordinarily look to the representative for decisions on behalf of the client. If a legal representative has not been appointed, the lawyer should see to such an appointment where it would serve the client's best interests. Thus, if a disabled client has substantial property that should be sold for the client's benefit, effective completion of the transaction ordinarily requires appointment of a legal representative. In many circumstances, however, appointment of a legal representative may be expensive or traumatic for the client. Evaluation of these considerations is a matter of professional judgment on the lawyer's part.

If the lawyer represents the guardian as distinct from the ward and is aware that the guardian is acting adversely to the ward's interest, the lawyer may have an obligation to prevent or rectify the guardian's misconduct. See rule 4–1.2(d).

Disclosure of client's condition

Rules of procedure in litigation generally provide that minors or persons suffering mental disability shall be represented by a guardian or next friend if they do not have a general guardian. However, disclosure of the client's disability can adversely affect the client's interests. The lawyer may seek guidance from an appropriate diagnostician.

Rule 4–1.15. Safekeeping property

Compliance With Trust Accounting Rules. A lawyer shall comply with The Florida Bar Rules Regulating Trust Accounts.

Amended July 23, 1992, effective Jan. 1, 1993 (605 So.2d 252); April 25, 2002 (820 So.2d 210).

Rule 4–1.16. Declining or Terminating Representation

(a) When Lawyer Must Decline or Terminate Representation. Except as stated in subdivision (c), a lawyer shall not represent a client or, where representation has commenced, shall withdraw from the representation of a client if:

(1) the representation will result in violation of the Rules of Professional Conduct or law;

(2) the lawyer's physical or mental condition materially impairs the lawyer's ability to represent the client;

(3) the lawyer is discharged;

(4) the client persists in a course of action involving the lawyer's services that the lawyer reasonably believes is criminal or fraudulent, unless the client agrees to disclose and rectify the crime or fraud; or

(5) the client has used the lawyer's services to perpetrate a crime or fraud, unless the client agrees to disclose and rectify the crime or fraud.

(b) When Withdrawal Is Allowed. Except as stated in subdivision (c), a lawyer may withdraw from representing a client if:

(1) withdrawal can be accomplished without material adverse effect on the interests of the client;

(2) the client insists upon taking action that the lawyer considers repugnant, imprudent, or with which the lawyer has a fundamental disagreement;

(3) the client fails substantially to fulfill an obligation to the lawyer regarding the lawyer's services and has been given reasonable warning that the lawyer will withdraw unless the obligation is fulfilled;

(4) the representation will result in an unreasonable financial burden on the lawyer or has been rendered unreasonably difficult by the client; or

(5) other good cause for withdrawal exists.

(c) Compliance With Order of Tribunal. A lawyer must comply with applicable law requiring notice or permission of a tribunal when terminating a representation. When ordered to do so by a tribunal, a lawyer shall continue representation notwithstanding good cause for terminating the representation.

(d) Protection of Client's Interest. Upon termination of representation, a lawyer shall take steps to the extent reasonably practicable to protect a client's interest, such as giving reasonable notice to the client, allowing time for employment of other counsel, surrendering papers and property to which the client is entitled, and refunding any advance payment of fee or expense that has not been earned or incurred. The lawyer may retain papers and other property relating to or belonging to the client to the extent permitted by law.

Amended July 23, 1992, effective Jan. 1, 1993 (605 So.2d 252); May 20, 2004 (875 So.2d 448); March 23, 2006, effective May 22, 2006 (933 So.2d 417).

Comment

A lawyer should not accept representation in a matter unless it can be performed competently, promptly, without improper conflict of interest, and to completion. Ordinarily, a representation in a matter is completed when the agreed-upon assistance has been concluded. See rule 4–1.2, and the comment to rule 4–1.3.

Mandatory withdrawal

A lawyer ordinarily must decline or withdraw from representation if the client demands that the lawyer engage in conduct that is illegal or violates the Rules of Professional Conduct or law. The lawyer is not obliged to decline or withdraw simply because the client suggests such a course of conduct; a client may make such a suggestion in the hope that a lawyer will not be constrained by a professional obligation. Withdrawal is also mandatory if the client persists in a course of action that the lawyer reasonably believes is criminal or fraudulent, unless the client agrees to disclose and rectify the crime or fraud. Withdrawal is also required if the lawyer's services were misused in the past even if that would materially prejudice the client.

When a lawyer has been appointed to represent a client, withdrawal ordinarily requires approval of the appointing authority. See also rule 4–6. 2. Similarly, court approval or notice to the court is often required by applicable law before a lawyer withdraws from pending litigation. Difficulty may be encountered if withdrawal is based on the client's demand that the lawyer engage in unprofessional conduct. The court may request an explanation for the withdrawal, while the lawyer may be bound to keep confidential the facts that would constitute such an explanation. The lawyer's statement that professional considerations require termination of the representation ordinarily should be accepted as sufficient. Lawyers should be mindful of their obligations to both clients and the court under rules 4–1.6 and 4–3.3.

Discharge

A client has a right to discharge a lawyer at any time, with or without cause, subject to liability for payment for the lawyer's services. Where future dispute about the withdrawal may be anticipated, it may be advisable to prepare a written statement reciting the circumstances.

Whether a client can discharge appointed counsel may depend on applicable law. A client seeking to do so should be given a full explanation of the consequences. These consequences may include a decision by the appointing authority that appointment of successor counsel is unjustified, thus requiring the client to be self-represented.

If the client is mentally incompetent, the client may lack the legal capacity to discharge the lawyer, and in any event the discharge may be seriously adverse to the client's interests. The lawyer should make special effort to help the client consider the consequences and may take reasonably necessary protective action as provided in rule 4–1.14.

Optional withdrawal

A lawyer may withdraw from representation in some circumstances. The lawyer has the option to withdraw if it can be accomplished without material adverse effect on the client's interests. The lawyer also may withdraw where the client insists on taking action that the lawyer considers repugnant, imprudent, or with which the lawyer has a fundamental disagreement.

A lawyer may withdraw if the client refuses to abide by the terms of an agreement relating to the representation, such as an agreement concerning fees or court costs or an agreement limiting the objectives of the representation.

Assisting the client upon withdrawal

Even if the lawyer has been unfairly discharged by the client, a lawyer must take all reasonable steps to mitigate the consequences to the client. The lawyer may retain papers and other property as security for a fee only to the extent permitted by law.

Refunding advance payment of unearned fee

Upon termination of representation, a lawyer should refund to the client any advance payment of a fee that has not been earned. This does not preclude a lawyer from retaining any reasonable nonrefundable fee that the client agreed would be deemed earned when the lawyer commenced the client's representation. See also rule 4–1.5.

Rule 4–1.17. Sale of Law Practice

Text of rule effective until October 1, 2015. See, also, rule effective October 1, 2015.

A lawyer or a law firm may sell or purchase a law practice, or an area of practice, including good will, provided that:

(a) Sale of Practice or Area of Practice as an Entirety. The entire practice, or the entire area of practice, is sold to 1 or more lawyers or law firms authorized to practice law in Florida.

(b) Notice to Clients. Written notice is served by certified mail, return receipt requested, upon each of the seller's clients of:

(1) the proposed sale;

(2) the client's right to retain other counsel; and

(3) the fact that the client's consent to the substitution of counsel will be presumed if the client does not object within 30 days after being served with notice.

(c) Court Approval Required. If a representation involves pending litigation, there shall be no substitution of counsel or termination of representation unless authorized by the court. The seller may disclose, in camera, to the court information relating to the representation only to the extent necessary to obtain an order authorizing the substitution of counsel or termination of representation.

(d) Client Objections. If a client objects to the proposed substitution of counsel, the seller shall comply with the requirements of rule 4–1.16(d).

(e) Consummation of Sale. A sale of a law practice shall not be consummated until:

(1) with respect to clients of the seller who were served with written notice of the proposed sale, the 30-day period referred to in subdivision (b)(3) has expired or all such clients have consented to the substitution of counsel or termination of representation; and

(2) court orders have been entered authorizing substitution of counsel for all clients who could not be served with written notice of the proposed sale and whose representations involve pending litigation; provided, in the event the court fails to grant a substitution of counsel in a matter involving pending litigation, that matter shall not be included in the sale and the sale otherwise shall be unaffected. Further, the matters not involving pending litigation of any client who cannot be served with written notice of the proposed sale shall not be included in the sale and the sale otherwise shall be unaffected.

(f) Existing Fee Contracts Controlling. The purchaser shall honor the fee agreements that were entered into between the seller and the seller's clients. The fees charged clients shall not be increased by reason of the sale.

Added July 23, 1992, effective Jan. 1, 1993 (605 So.2d 252). Amended March 23, 2006, effective May 22, 2006 (933 So.2d 417).

Comment

The practice of law is a profession, not merely a business. Clients are not commodities that can be purchased and sold at will. In accordance with the requirements of this rule, when a lawyer or an entire firm sells the practice and other lawyers or firms take over the representation, the selling lawyer or firm may obtain compensation for the reasonable value of the practice as may withdrawing partners of law firms. See rules 4–5.4 and 4–5.6.

The requirement that all of the private practice, or all of an area of practice, be sold is satisfied if the seller in good faith makes the entire practice, or area of practice, available for sale to the purchasers. The fact that a number of the seller's clients decide not to be represented by the purchasers but take their matters elsewhere, therefore, does not result in a violation. Similarly, a violation does not occur merely because a court declines to approve the substitution of counsel in the cases of a number of clients who could not be served with written notice of the proposed sale.

Sale of entire practice or entire area of practice

The rule requires that the seller's entire practice, or an area of practice, be sold. The prohibition against sale of less than an entire practice area protects those clients whose matters are less lucrative and who might find it difficult to secure other counsel if a sale could be limited to substantial fee-generating matters. The purchasers are required to undertake all client matters in the practice, or practice area, subject to client consent or court authorization. This requirement is satisfied, however, even if a purchaser is unable to undertake a particular client matter because of a conflict of interest.

Client confidences, consent, and notice

Negotiations between seller and prospective purchaser prior to disclosure of information relating to a specific representation of an identifiable client do not violate the confidentiality provisions of rule 4–1.6 any more than do preliminary discussions concerning the possible association of another lawyer or mergers between firms, with respect to which client consent ordinarily is not required. Providing the prospective purchaser access to client-specific information relating to the representation and to the file, however, requires client consent or court authorization. See rule 4–1.6. Rule 4–1.17 provides that the seller must attempt to serve each client with written notice of the contemplated sale, including the identity of the purchaser and the fact that the decision to consent to the substitution of counsel or to make other arrangements must be made within 30 days. If nothing is heard within that time from a client who was served with written notice of the proposed sale, that client's consent to the substitution of counsel is presumed. However, with regard to clients whose matters involve pending litigation but who could not be served with written notice of the proposed sale, authorization of the court is required before the files and client-specific information relating to the representation of those clients may be disclosed by the seller to the purchaser and before counsel may be substituted.

A lawyer or law firm selling a practice cannot be required to remain in practice just because some clients cannot be served with written notice of the proposed sale. Because these clients cannot themselves consent to the substitution of counsel or direct any other disposition of their representations and files, with regard to clients whose matters involve pending litigation the rule requires an order from the court authorizing the substitution (or withdrawal) of counsel. The court can be expected to determine whether reasonable efforts to locate the client have been exhausted, and whether the absent client's legitimate interests will be served by authorizing the substitution of counsel so that the purchaser may continue the representation. Preservation of client confidences requires that the petition for a court order be considered in camera. If, however, the court fails to grant substitution of counsel in a matter involving pending litigation, that matter shall not be included in the sale and the sale may be consummated without inclusion of that matter.

The rule provides that matters not involving pending litigation of clients who could not be served with written notice may not be included in the sale. This is because the clients' consent to disclosure of confidential information and to substitution of counsel cannot be obtained and because the alternative of court authorization ordinarily is not available in matters not involving pending litigation. Although such matters shall not be included in the sale, the sale may be consummated without inclusion of those matters.

If a client objects to the proposed substitution of counsel, the rule treats the seller as attempting to withdraw from representation of that client and, therefore, provides that the seller must comply with the provisions of rule 4–1.16 concerning withdrawal from representation. Additionally, the seller must comply with applicable requirements of law or rules of procedure.

All the elements of client autonomy, including the client's absolute right to discharge a lawyer and transfer the representation to another, survive the sale of the practice or an area of practice.

Fee arrangements between client and purchaser

The sale may not be financed by increases in fees charged the clients of the practice. Existing agreements between the seller and the client as to fees and the scope of the work must be honored by the purchaser. This obligation of the purchaser is a factor that can be taken into account by seller and purchaser when negotiating the sale price of the practice.

Other applicable ethical standards

Lawyers participating in the sale of a law practice or a practice area are subject to the ethical standards applicable to involving another lawyer in the representation of a client for all matters pending at the time of the sale. These include, for example, the seller's ethical obligation to exercise competence in identifying a purchaser qualified to assume the practice and the purchaser's obligation to undertake the representation competently (see rule 4–1.1); the obligation to avoid disqualifying conflicts, and to secure the client's informed consent for those conflicts that can be agreed to (see rule 4–1.7 regarding conflicts and see the terminology section of the preamble for the definition of informed consent); and the obligation to protect information relating to the representation (see rules 4–1.6, 4–1.8(b), and 4–1.9(b) and (c)). If the terms of the sale involve the division between purchaser and seller of fees from matters that arise subsequent to the sale, the fee-division provisions of rule 4–1.5 must be satisfied with respect to such fees. These provisions will not apply to the division of fees from matters pending at the time of sale.

If approval of the substitution of the purchasing attorney for the selling attorney is required by the rules of any tribunal in which a matter is pending, such approval must be obtained before the matter can be included in the sale (see rule 4–1.16).

Applicability of this rule

This rule applies, among other situations, to the sale of a law practice by representatives of a lawyer who is deceased, disabled, or has disappeared. It is possible that a nonlawyer, who is not subject to the Rules of Professional Conduct, might be involved in the sale. When the practice of a lawyer who is deceased, is disabled, or has disappeared is being sold, the notice required by subdivision (b) of this rule must be given by someone who is legally authorized to act on the selling lawyer's behalf, such as a personal representative or a guardian. This is because the sale of a practice and transfer of representation involve legal rights of the affected clients.

Bona fide admission to, withdrawal from, or retirement from a law partnership or professional association, retirement plans and similar arrangements, and a sale of tangible assets of a law practice, do not constitute a sale or purchase governed by this rule.

Rule 4–1.17. Sale of Law Practice

Text of rule effective October 1, 2015. See, also, rule effective until October 1, 2015.

A lawyer or a law firm may sell or purchase a law practice, or an area of practice, including good will, provided that:

(a) Sale of Practice or Area of Practice as an Entirety. The entire practice, or the entire area of practice, is sold to 1 or more lawyers or law firms authorized to practice law in Florida.

(b) Notice to Clients. Written notice is served by certified mail, return receipt requested, on each of the seller's clients of:

(1) the proposed sale;

(2) the client's right to retain other counsel; and

(3) the fact that the client's consent to the substitution of counsel will be presumed if the client does not object within 30 days after being served with notice.

(c) Court Approval Required. If a representation involves pending litigation, there will be no substitution of counsel or termination of representation unless authorized by the court. The seller may disclose, in camera, to the court information relating to the representation only to the extent necessary to obtain an order authorizing the substitution of counsel or termination of representation.

(d) Client Objections. If a client objects to the proposed substitution of counsel, the seller must comply with the requirements of rule 4–1.16(d).

(e) Consummation of Sale. A sale of a law practice may not be consummated until:

(1) with respect to clients of the seller who were served with written notice of the proposed sale, the 30–day period referred to in subdivision (b)(3) has expired or all these clients have consented to the substitution of counsel or termination of representation; and

(2) court orders have been entered authorizing substitution of counsel for all clients who could not be served with written notice of the proposed sale and whose representations involve pending litigation; provided, in the event the court fails to grant a substitution of counsel in a matter involving pending litigation, that matter may not be included in the sale and the sale otherwise will be unaffected. Further, the matters not involving pending litigation of any client who cannot be served with written notice of the proposed sale may not be included in the sale and the sale otherwise will be unaffected.

(f) Existing Fee Contracts Controlling. The purchaser must honor the fee agreements that were entered into between the seller and the seller's clients. The fees charged clients may not be increased by reason of the sale.

Added July 23, 1992, effective Jan. 1, 1993 (605 So.2d 252). Amended March 23, 2006, effective May 22, 2006 (933 So.2d 417); June 11, 2015, effective Oct. 1, 2015 (167 So.3d 412).

Comment

The practice of law is a profession, not merely a business. Clients are not commodities that can be purchased and sold at will. In accordance with the requirements of this rule, when a lawyer or an entire firm sells the practice and other lawyers or firms take over the representation, the selling lawyer or firm may obtain compensation for the reasonable value of the practice as may withdrawing partners of law firms. See rules 4–5.4 and 4–5.6.

The requirement that all of the private practice, or all of an area of practice, be sold is satisfied if the seller in good faith makes the entire practice, or area of practice, available for sale to the purchasers. The fact that a number of the seller's clients decide not to be represented by the purchasers but take their matters elsewhere, therefore, does not result in a violation. Similarly, a violation does not occur merely because a court declines to approve the substitution of counsel in the cases of a number of clients who could not be served with written notice of the proposed sale.

Sale of entire practice or entire area of practice

The rule requires that the seller's entire practice, or an area of practice, be sold. The prohibition against sale of less than an entire practice area protects those clients whose matters are less lucrative and who might find it difficult to secure other counsel if a sale could be limited to substantial fee-generating matters. The purchasers are required to undertake all client matters in the practice, or practice area, subject to client consent or court authorization. This requirement is satisfied, however, even if a purchaser is unable to undertake a particular client matter because of a conflict of interest.

Client confidences, consent, and notice

Negotiations between seller and prospective purchaser prior to disclosure of information relating to a specific representation of an identifiable client do not violate the confidentiality provisions of rule 4–1.6 any more than do preliminary discussions concerning the possible association of another lawyer or mergers between firms, with respect to which client consent ordinarily is not required. See rule 4–1.6(c)(6). Providing the prospective purchaser access to detailed information relating to the representation, for example, the file, however, requires client consent or court authorization. See rule 4–1.6. Rule 4–1.17 provides that the seller must attempt to serve each client with written notice of the contemplated sale, including the identity of the purchaser and the fact that the decision to consent to the substitution of counsel or to make other arrangements must be made within 30 days. If nothing is heard within that time from a client who was served with written notice of the proposed sale, that client's consent to the substitution of counsel is presumed. However, with regard to clients whose matters involve pending litigation but who could not be served with written notice of the proposed sale, authorization of the court is required before the files and client-specific information relating to the representation of those clients may be disclosed by the seller to the purchaser and before counsel may be substituted.

A lawyer or law firm selling a practice cannot be required to remain in practice just because some clients cannot be served with written notice of the proposed sale. Because these clients cannot themselves consent to the substitution of counsel or direct any other disposition of their representations and files, with regard to clients whose matters involve pending litigation the rule requires an order from the court authorizing the substitution (or withdrawal) of counsel. The court can be expected to determine whether reasonable efforts to locate the client have been exhausted, and whether the absent client's legitimate interests will be served by authorizing the substitution of counsel so that the purchaser may continue the representation. Preservation of client confidences requires that the petition for a court order be considered in camera. If, however, the court fails to grant substitution of counsel in a matter involving pending litigation, that matter may not be included in the sale and the sale may be consummated without inclusion of that matter.

The rule provides that matters not involving pending litigation of clients who could not be served with written notice may not be included in the sale. This is because the clients' consent to disclosure of confidential information and to substitution of counsel cannot be obtained and because the alternative of court authorization ordinarily is not available in matters not involving pending litigation. Although these matters may not be included in the sale, the sale may be consummated without inclusion of those matters.

If a client objects to the proposed substitution of counsel, the rule treats the seller as attempting to withdraw from representation of that client and, therefore, provides that the seller must comply with the provisions of rule 4–1.16 concerning withdrawal from representation. Additionally, the seller must comply with applicable requirements of law or rules of procedure.

All the elements of client autonomy, including the client's absolute right to discharge a lawyer and transfer the representation to another, survive the sale of the practice or an area of practice.

Fee arrangements between client and purchaser

The sale may not be financed by increases in fees charged the clients of the practice. Existing agreements between the seller and the client as to fees and the scope of the work must be honored by the purchaser. This obligation of the purchaser is a factor that can be taken into account by seller and purchaser when negotiating the sale price of the practice.

Other applicable ethical standards

Lawyers participating in the sale of a law practice or a practice area are subject to the ethical standards applicable to involving another lawyer in the representation of a client for all matters pending at the time of the sale. These include, for example, the seller's ethical obligation to exercise competence in identifying a purchaser qualified to assume the practice and the purchaser's obligation to undertake the representation competently (see rule 4–1.1); the obligation to avoid disqualifying conflicts, and to secure the client's informed consent for those conflicts that can be agreed to (see rule 4–1.7 regarding conflicts and see the terminology section of the preamble for the definition of informed consent); and the obligation to protect information relating to the representation (see rules 4–1.6, 4–1.8(b), and 4–1.9(b) and (c)). If the terms of the sale involve the division between purchaser and seller of fees from matters that arise subsequent to the sale, the fee-division provisions of rule 4–1.5 must be satisfied with respect to these fees. These provisions will not apply to the division of fees from matters pending at the time of sale.

If approval of the substitution of the purchasing attorney for the selling attorney is required by the rules of any tribunal in which a matter is pending, approval must be obtained before the matter can be included in the sale (see rule 4–1.16).

Applicability of this rule

This rule applies, among other situations, to the sale of a law practice by representatives of a lawyer who is deceased, disabled, or has disappeared. It is possible that a nonlawyer, who is not subject to the Rules of Professional Conduct, might be involved in the sale. When the practice of a lawyer who is deceased, is disabled, or has disappeared is being sold, the notice required by subdivision (b) of this rule must be given by someone who is legally authorized to act on the selling lawyer's behalf, for example, a personal representative or a guardian. This is because the sale of a practice and transfer of representation involve legal rights of the affected clients.

Bona fide admission to, withdrawal from, or retirement from a law partnership or professional association, retirement plans and similar arrangements, and a sale of tangible assets of a law practice, do not constitute a sale or purchase governed by this rule.

Rule 4–1.18. Duties to Prospective Client

Text of rule effective until October 1, 2015. See, also, rule effective October 1, 2015.

(a) Prospective Client. A person who discusses with a lawyer the possibility of forming a client-lawyer relationship with respect to a matter is a prospective client.

(b) Confidentiality of Information. Even when no client-lawyer relationship ensues, a lawyer who has had discussions with a prospective client shall not use or reveal information learned in the consultation, except as rule 4–1.9 would permit with respect to information of a former client.

(c) Subsequent Representation. A lawyer subject to subdivision (b) shall not represent a client with interests materially adverse to those of a prospective client in the same or a substantially related matter if the lawyer received information from the prospective client that could be used to the disadvantage of that person in the matter, except as provided in subdivision (d). If a lawyer is disqualified from representation under this rule, no lawyer in a firm with which that lawyer is associated may knowingly undertake or continue representation in such a matter, except as provided in subdivision (d).

(d) Permissible Representation. When the lawyer has received disqualifying information as defined in subdivision (c), representation is permissible if:

(1) both the affected client and the prospective client have given informed consent, confirmed in writing; or

(2) the lawyer who received the information took reasonable measures to avoid exposure to more disqualifying information than was reasonably necessary to determine whether to represent the prospective client; and

(i) the disqualified lawyer is timely screened from any participation in the matter and is apportioned no part of the fee therefrom; and

(ii) written notice is promptly given to the prospective client.

Added March 23, 2006, effective May 22, 2006 (933 So.2d 417). Amended Nov. 19, 2009, effective Feb. 1, 2010 (24 So.3d 63).

Comment

Prospective clients, like clients, may disclose information to a lawyer, place documents or other property in the lawyer's custody, or rely on the lawyer's advice. A lawyer's discussions with a prospective client usually are limited in time and depth and leave both the prospective client and the lawyer free (and the lawyer sometimes required) to proceed no further. Hence, prospective clients should receive some but not all of the protection afforded clients.

Not all persons who communicate information to a lawyer are entitled to protection under this rule. A person who communicates information unilaterally to a lawyer, without any reasonable expectation that the lawyer is willing to discuss the possibility of forming a client-lawyer relationship, is not a "prospective client" within the meaning of subdivision (a).

It is often necessary for a prospective client to reveal information to the lawyer during an initial consultation prior to the decision about formation of a client-lawyer relationship. The lawyer often must learn such information to determine whether there is a conflict of interest with an existing client and whether the matter is one that the lawyer is willing to undertake. Subdivision (b) prohibits the lawyer from using or revealing that information, except as permitted by rule 4–1.9, even if the client or lawyer decides not to proceed with the representation. The duty exists regardless of how brief the initial conference may be.

In order to avoid acquiring disqualifying information from a prospective client, a lawyer considering whether to undertake a new matter should limit the initial interview to only such information as reasonably appears necessary for that purpose. Where the information indicates that a conflict of interest or other reason for non-representation exists, the lawyer should so inform the prospective client or decline the representation. If the prospective client wishes to retain the lawyer, and if consent is possible under rule 4–1.7, then consent from all affected present or former clients must be obtained before accepting the representation.

A lawyer may condition conversations with a prospective client on the person's informed consent that no information disclosed during the consultation will prohibit the lawyer from representing a different client in the matter. See terminology for the definition of informed consent. If the agreement expressly so provides, the prospective client may also consent to the lawyer's subsequent use of information received from the prospective client.

Even in the absence of an agreement, under subdivision (c), the lawyer is not prohibited from representing a client with interests adverse to those of the prospective client in the same or a substantially related matter unless the lawyer has received from the prospective client information that could be used to the disadvantage of the prospective client in the matter.

Under subdivision (c), the prohibition in this rule is imputed to other lawyers as provided in rule 4–1.10, but, under subdivision (d)(1), the prohibition and its imputation may be avoided if the lawyer obtains the informed consent, confirmed in writing, of both the prospective and affected clients. In the alternative, the prohibition and its imputation may be avoided if the conditions of subdivision (d)(2) are met and all disqualified lawyers are timely screened and written notice is promptly given to the prospective client. See terminology (requirements for screening procedures). Subdivision (d)(2)(i) does not prohibit the screened lawyer from receiving a salary or partnership share established by prior independent agreement, but that lawyer may not receive compensation directly related to the matter in which the lawyer is disqualified.

Notice, including a general description of the subject matter about which the lawyer was consulted, and of the screening procedures employed, generally should be given as soon as practicable after the need for screening becomes apparent.

The duties under this rule presume that the prospective client consults the lawyer in good faith. A person who consults a lawyer simply with the intent of disqualifying the lawyer from the matter, with no intent of possibly hiring the lawyer, has engaged in a sham and should not be able to invoke this rule to create a disqualification.

For the duty of competence of a lawyer who gives assistance on the merits of a matter to a prospective client, see rule 4–1.1. For a lawyer's duties when a prospective client entrusts valuables or papers to the lawyer's care, see chapter 5, Rules Regulating The Florida Bar.

Rule 4–1.18. Duties to Prospective Client

Text of rule effective October 1, 2015. See, also, rule effective until October 1, 2015.

(a) Prospective Client. A person who consults with a lawyer about the possibility of forming a client-lawyer relationship with respect to a matter is a prospective client.

(b) Confidentiality of Information. Even when no client-lawyer relationship ensues, a lawyer who has learned information from a prospective client may not use or reveal that information, except as rule 4–1.9 would permit with respect to information of a former client.

(c) Subsequent Representation. A lawyer subject to subdivision (b) may not represent a client with interests materially adverse to those of a prospective client in the same or a substantially related matter if the lawyer received information from the prospective client that could be used to the disadvantage of that person in the matter, except as provided in subdivision (d). If a lawyer is disqualified from representation under this rule, no lawyer in a firm with which that lawyer is associated may knowingly undertake or continue representation in the matter, except as provided in subdivision (d).

(d) Permissible Representation. When the lawyer has received disqualifying information as defined in subdivision (c), representation is permissible if:

(1) both the affected client and the prospective client have given informed consent, confirmed in writing; or

(2) the lawyer who received the information took reasonable measures to avoid exposure to more disqualifying information than was reasonably necessary to determine whether to represent the prospective client; and

(A) the disqualified lawyer is timely screened from any participation in the matter and is apportioned no part of the fee therefrom; and

(B) written notice is promptly given to the prospective client.

Added March 23, 2006, effective May 22, 2006 (933 So.2d 417). Amended Nov. 19, 2009, effective Feb. 1, 2010 (24 So.3d 63); May 21, 2015, effective Oct. 1, 2015 (164 So.3d 1217).

Comment

Prospective clients, like clients, may disclose information to a lawyer, place documents or other property in the lawyer's custody, or rely on the lawyer's advice. A lawyer's consultations with a prospective client usually are limited in time and depth and leave both the prospective client and the lawyer free (and the lawyer sometimes required) to proceed no further. Hence, prospective clients should receive some but not all of the protection afforded clients.

A person becomes a prospective client by consulting with a lawyer about the possibility of forming a client-lawyer relationship with respect to a matter. Whether communications, including written, oral, or electronic communications, constitute a consultation depends on the circumstances. For example, a consultation is likely to have occurred if a lawyer, either in person or through the lawyer's advertising in any medium, specifically requests or invites the submission of information about a potential representation without clear and reasonably understandable warnings and cautionary statements that limit the lawyer's obligations, and a person provides information in response. In contrast, a consultation does not occur if a person provides information to a lawyer in response to advertising that merely describes the lawyer's education, experience, areas of practice, and contact information, or provides legal information of general interest. A person who communicates information unilaterally to a lawyer, without any reasonable expectation that the lawyer is willing to discuss the possibility of forming a client-lawyer relationship, is not a "prospective client" within the meaning of subdivision (a).

It is often necessary for a prospective client to reveal information to the lawyer during an initial consultation prior to the decision about formation of a client-lawyer relationship. The lawyer often must learn this information to determine whether there is a conflict of interest with an existing client and whether the matter is one that the lawyer is willing to undertake. Subdivision (b) prohibits the lawyer from using or revealing that information, except as permitted by rule 4–1.9, even if the client or lawyer decides not to proceed with the representation. The duty exists regardless of how brief the initial conference may be.

In order to avoid acquiring disqualifying information from a prospective client, a lawyer considering whether to undertake a new matter should limit the initial consultation to only information as reasonably appears necessary for that purpose. Where the information indicates that a conflict of interest or other reason for non-representation exists, the lawyer should so inform the prospective client or decline the representation. If the prospective client wishes to retain the lawyer, and if consent is possible under rule 4–1.7, then consent from all affected present or former clients must be obtained before accepting the representation.

A lawyer may condition a consultation with a prospective client on the person's informed consent that no information disclosed during the consultation will prohibit the lawyer from representing a different client in the matter. See terminology for the definition of informed consent. If the agreement expressly so provides, the prospective client may also consent to the lawyer's subsequent use of information received from the prospective client.

Even in the absence of an agreement, under subdivision (c), the lawyer is not prohibited from representing a client with interests adverse to those of the prospective client in the same or a substantially related matter unless the lawyer has received from the prospective client information that could be used to the disadvantage of the prospective client in the matter.

Under subdivision (c), the prohibition in this rule is imputed to other lawyers as provided in rule 4–1.10, but, under subdivision (d)(1), the prohibition and its imputation may be avoided if the lawyer obtains the informed consent, confirmed in writing, of both the prospective and affected clients. In the alternative, the prohibition and its imputation may be avoided if the conditions of subdivision (d)(2) are met and all disqualified lawyers are timely screened and written notice is promptly given to the prospective client. See terminology (requirements for screening procedures). Subdivision (d)(2)(i) does not prohibit the screened lawyer from receiving a salary or partnership share established by prior independent agreement, but that lawyer may not receive compensation directly related to the matter in which the lawyer is disqualified.

Notice, including a general description of the subject matter about which the lawyer was consulted, and of the screening procedures employed, generally should be given as soon as practicable after the need for screening becomes apparent.

The duties under this rule presume that the prospective client consults the lawyer in good faith. A person who consults a lawyer simply with the intent of disqualifying the lawyer from the matter, with no intent of possibly hiring the lawyer, has engaged in a sham and should not be able to invoke this rule to create a disqualification.

For the duty of competence of a lawyer who gives assistance on the merits of a matter to a prospective client, see rule 4–1.1. For a lawyer's duties when a prospective client entrusts valuables or papers to the lawyer's care, see chapter 5, Rules Regulating The Florida Bar.

4–2. COUNSELOR

Rule 4–2.1. Adviser

In representing a client, a lawyer shall exercise independent professional judgment and render candid advice. In rendering advice, a lawyer may refer not only to law but to other considerations such as moral, economic, social, and political factors that may be relevant to the client's situation.

Comment

Scope of advice

A client is entitled to straightforward advice expressing the lawyer's honest assessment. Legal advice often involves unpleasant facts and alternatives that a client may be disinclined to confront. In presenting advice, a lawyer endeavors to sustain the client's morale and may put advice in as acceptable a form as honesty permits. However, a lawyer should not be deterred from giving candid advice by the prospect that the advice will be unpalatable to the client.

Advice couched in narrowly legal terms may be of little value to a client, especially where practical considerations, such as cost or effects on other people, are predominant. Purely technical legal advice, therefore, can sometimes be inadequate. It is proper for a lawyer to refer to relevant moral and ethical considerations in giving advice. Although a lawyer is not a moral adviser as such, moral and ethical considerations impinge upon most legal questions and may decisively influence how the law will be applied.

A client may expressly or impliedly ask the lawyer for purely technical advice. When such a request is made by a client experienced in legal matters, the lawyer may accept it at face value. When such a request is made by a client inexperienced in legal matters, however, the lawyer's responsibility as adviser may include indicating that more may be involved than strictly legal considerations.

Matters that go beyond strictly legal questions may also be in the domain of another profession. Family matters can involve problems within the professional competence of psychiatry, clinical psychology, or social work; business matters can involve problems within the competence of the accounting profession or of financial specialists. Where consultation with a professional in another field is itself something a competent lawyer would recommend, the lawyer should make such a recommendation. At the same time, a lawyer's advice at its best often consists of recommending a course of action in the face of conflicting recommendations of experts.

Offering advice

In general, a lawyer is not expected to give advice until asked by the client. However, when a lawyer knows that a client proposes a course of action that is likely to result in substantial adverse legal consequences to the client, the lawyer's duty to the client under rule 4–1.4 may require that the lawyer offer advice if the client's course of action is related to the representation. Similarly, when a matter is likely to involve litigation, it may be necessary under rule 4–1.4 to inform the client of forms of dispute resolution that might constitute reasonable alternatives to litigation. A lawyer ordinarily has no duty to initiate investigation of a client's affairs or to give advice that the client has indicated is unwanted, but a lawyer may initiate advice to a client when doing so appears to be in the client's interest.

Rule 4-2.2. Open/Vacant

Rule 4-2.3. Evaluation for Use by Third Persons

(a) When Lawyer May Provide Evaluation. A lawyer may provide an evaluation of a matter affecting a client for the use of someone other than the client if:

(1) the lawyer reasonably believes that making the evaluation is compatible with other aspects of the lawyer's relationship with the client; and

(2) the client gives informed consent.

(b) Limitation on Scope of Evaluation. In reporting the evaluation, the lawyer shall indicate any material limitations that were imposed on the scope of the inquiry or on the disclosure of information.

(c) Maintaining Client Confidences. Except as disclosure is required in connection with a report of an evaluation, information relating to the evaluation is otherwise protected by rule 4-1.6.

Amended July 23, 1992, effective Jan. 1, 1993 (605 So.2d 252); March 23, 2006, effective May 22, 2006 (933 So.2d 417).

Comment

Definition

An evaluation may be performed at the client's direction but for the primary purpose of establishing information for the benefit of third parties; for example, an opinion concerning the title of property rendered at the behest of a vendor for the information of a prospective purchaser or at the behest of a borrower for the information of a prospective lender. In some situations, the evaluation may be required by a government agency; for example, an opinion concerning the legality of the securities registered for sale under the securities laws. In other instances, the evaluation may be required by a third person, such as a purchaser of a business.

A legal evaluation should be distinguished from an investigation of a person with whom the lawyer does not have a client-lawyer relationship. For example, a lawyer retained by a purchaser to analyze a vendor's title to property does not have a client-lawyer relationship with the vendor. So also, an investigation into a person's affairs by a government lawyer, or by special counsel employed by the government, is not an evaluation as that term is used in this rule. The question is whether the lawyer is retained by the person whose affairs are being examined. When the lawyer is retained by that person, the general rules concerning loyalty to client and preservation of confidences apply, which is not the case if the lawyer is retained by someone else. For this reason, it is essential to identify the person by whom the lawyer is retained. This should be made clear not only to the person under examination, but also to others to whom the results are to be made available.

Duty to third person

When the evaluation is intended for the information or use of a third person, a legal duty to that person may or may not arise. That legal question is beyond the scope of this rule. However, since such an evaluation involves a departure from the normal client-lawyer relationship, careful analysis of the situation is required. The lawyer must be satisfied as a matter of professional judgment that making the evaluation is compatible with other functions undertaken in behalf of the client. For example, if the lawyer is acting as an advocate in defending the client against charges of fraud, it would normally be incompatible with that responsibility for the lawyer to perform an evaluation for others concerning the same or a related transaction. Assuming no such impediment is apparent, however, the lawyer should advise the client of the implications of the evaluation, particularly the lawyer's responsibilities to third persons and the duty to disseminate the findings.

Access to and disclosure of information

The quality of an evaluation depends on the freedom and extent of the investigation upon which it is based. Ordinarily, a lawyer should have whatever latitude of investigation seems necessary as a matter of professional judgment. Under some circumstances, however, the terms of the evaluation may be limited. For example, certain issues or sources may be categorically excluded or the scope of search may be limited by time constraints or the noncooperation of persons having relevant information. Any such limitations that are material to the evaluation should be described in the report. If, after a lawyer has commenced an evaluation, the client refuses to comply with the terms upon which it was understood the evaluation was to have been made, the lawyer's obligations are determined by law, having reference to the terms of the client's agreement and the surrounding circumstances. In no circumstances is the lawyer permitted to knowingly make a false statement of material fact or law in providing an evaluation under this rule. See rule 4-4.1.

Financial auditors' requests for information

When a question concerning the legal situation of a client arises at the instance of the client's financial auditor and the question is referred to the lawyer, the lawyer's response may be made in accordance with procedures recognized in the legal profession. Such a procedure is set forth in the American Bar Association Statement of Policy Regarding Lawyers' Responses to Auditors' Requests for Information, adopted in 1975.

Rule 4-2.4. Lawyer Serving as Third-Party Neutral

(a) Definition. A lawyer serves as a third-party neutral when the lawyer assists 2 or more persons who are not clients of the lawyer to reach a resolution of a dispute or other matter that has arisen between them. Service as a third-party neutral may include service as an arbitrator, a mediator, or in such other capacity as will enable the lawyer to assist the parties to resolve the matter.

(b) Communication With Unrepresented Parties. A lawyer serving as a third-party neutral must inform unrepresented parties that the lawyer is not representing them. When the lawyer knows or reasonably should know that a party does not understand the lawyer's role in the matter, the lawyer must explain the difference between the lawyer's role as a third-party neutral and a lawyer's role as one who represents a client.

Added March 23, 2006, effective May 22, 2006 (933 So.2d 417). Amended Nov. 19, 2009, effective Feb. 1, 2010 (24 So.3d 63); May 29, 2014, effective June 1, 2014 (140 So.3d 541).

Comment

Alternative dispute resolution has become a substantial part of the civil justice system. Aside from representing clients in dispute-resolution processes, lawyers often serve as third-party neutrals. A third-party neutral is a person, such as a mediator, arbitrator, conciliator, or evaluator, who assists the parties, represented or unrepresented, in the resolution of a dispute or in the arrangement of a transaction. Whether a third-party neutral serves primarily as a facilitator, evaluator, or decision-maker depends on the particular process that is either selected by the parties or mandated by a court.

The role of a third-party neutral is not unique to lawyers, although, in some court-connected contexts, only lawyers are allowed to serve in this role or to handle certain types of cases. In performing this role, the lawyer may be subject to court rules or other law that apply either to third-party neutrals generally or to lawyers serving as third-party neutrals. Lawyer–neutrals may also be subject to various codes of ethics, such as the Code of Ethics for Arbitration in Commercial Disputes prepared by a joint committee of the American Bar Association and the American Arbitration Association, or the Model Standards of Conduct for Mediators jointly prepared by the American Bar Association, the American Arbitration Association and Association for Conflict Resolution. A Florida Bar member who is a certified or court-appointed mediator is governed by the applicable law and rules relating to certified or court-appointed mediators.

Unlike nonlawyers who serve as third-party neutrals, lawyers serving in this role may experience unique problems as a result of differences between the role of a third-party neutral and a lawyer's service as a client representative. The potential for confusion is significant when the parties are unrepresented in the process. Thus, subdivision (b) requires a lawyer-neutral to inform unrepresented parties that the lawyer is not representing them. For some parties, particularly parties who frequently use dispute resolution processes, this information will be sufficient. For others, particularly those who are using the process for the first time, more information will be required. Where appropriate, the lawyer should inform unrepresented parties of the important differences between the lawyer's role as third-party neutral and a lawyer's role as a client representative, including the inapplicability of the attorney-client evidentiary privilege. The extent of disclosure required under this subdivision will depend on the particular parties involved and the subject matter of the proceeding, as well as the particular features of the dispute resolution process selected.

A lawyer who serves as a third-party neutral subsequently may be asked to serve as a lawyer representing a client in the same matter. The conflicts of interest that arise for both the individual lawyer and the lawyer's law firm are addressed in rule 4-1.12.

4-3. ADVOCATE

Rule 4-3.1. Meritorious Claims and Contentions

A lawyer shall not bring or defend a proceeding, or assert or controvert an issue therein, unless there is a basis in law and fact for doing so that is not frivolous, which includes a good faith argument for an extension, modification, or reversal of existing law. A lawyer for the defendant in a criminal proceeding, or the respondent in a proceeding that could result in incarceration, may nevertheless so defend the proceeding as to require that every element of the case be established.

Amended July 23, 1992, effective Jan. 1, 1993 (605 So.2d 252); March 23, 2006, effective May 22, 2006 (933 So.2d 417).

Comment

The advocate has a duty to use legal procedure for the fullest benefit of the client's cause, but also a duty not to abuse legal procedure. The law, both procedural and substantive, establishes the limits within which an advocate may proceed. However, the law is not always clear and never is static. Accordingly, in determining the proper scope of advocacy, account must be taken of the law's ambiguities and potential for change.

The filing of an action or defense or similar action taken for a client is not frivolous merely because the facts have not first been fully substantiated or because the lawyer expects to develop vital evidence only by discovery. What is required of lawyers, however, is that they inform themselves about the facts of their clients' cases and the applicable law and determine that they can make good faith arguments in support of their clients' positions. Such action is not frivolous even though the lawyer believes that the client's position ultimately will not prevail. The action is frivolous, however, if the lawyer is unable either to make a good faith argument on the merits of the action taken or to support the action taken by a good faith argument for an extension, modification, or reversal of existing law.

The lawyer's obligations under this rule are subordinate to federal or state constitutional law that entitles a defendant in a criminal matter to the assistance of counsel in presenting a claim or contention that otherwise would be prohibited by this rule.

Rule 4-3.2. Expediting litigation

A lawyer shall make reasonable efforts to expedite litigation consistent with the interests of the client.

Comment

Dilatory practices bring the administration of justice into disrepute. Although there will be occasions when a lawyer may properly seek a postponement for personal reasons, it is not proper for a lawyer to routinely fail to expedite litigation solely for the convenience of the advocates. Nor will a failure to expedite be reasonable if done for the purpose of frustrating an opposing party's attempt to obtain rightful redress or repose. It is not a justification that similar conduct is often tolerated by the bench and bar. The question is whether a competent lawyer acting in good faith would regard the course of action as having some substantial purpose other than delay. Realizing financial or other benefit from otherwise improper delay in litigation is not a legitimate interest of the client.

Rule 4-3.3. Candor Toward the Tribunal

(a) False Evidence; Duty to Disclose. A lawyer shall not knowingly:

(1) make a false statement of fact or law to a tribunal or fail to correct a false statement of material fact or law previously made to the tribunal by the lawyer;

(2) fail to disclose a material fact to a tribunal when disclosure is necessary to avoid assisting a criminal or fraudulent act by the client;

(3) fail to disclose to the tribunal legal authority in the controlling jurisdiction known to the lawyer to be directly adverse to the position of the client and not disclosed by opposing counsel; or

(4) offer evidence that the lawyer knows to be false. A lawyer may not offer testimony that the lawyer knows to be false in the form of a narrative unless so ordered by the tribunal. If a lawyer, the lawyer's client, or a witness called by the lawyer has offered material evidence and the lawyer comes to know of its falsity, the lawyer shall take reasonable remedial measures including, if necessary, disclosure to the tribunal. A lawyer may refuse to offer evidence that the lawyer reasonably believes is false.

(b) Criminal or Fraudulent Conduct. A lawyer who represents a client in an adjudicative proceeding and who knows that a person intends to engage, is engaging, or has engaged in criminal or fraudulent conduct related to the proceeding shall take reasonable remedial measures, including, if necessary, disclosure to the tribunal.

(c) Ex Parte Proceedings. In an ex parte proceeding a lawyer shall inform the tribunal of all material facts known to the lawyer that will enable the tribunal to make an informed decision, whether or not the facts are adverse.

(d) Extent of Lawyer's Duties. The duties stated in this rule continue beyond the conclusion of the proceeding and apply even if compliance requires disclosure of information otherwise protected by rule 4-1.6.

Amended March 8, 1990 (557 So.2d 1368); July 23, 1992, effective Jan. 1, 1993 (605 So.2d 252); April 21, 1994 (635 So.2d 968); May 20, 2004 (875 So.2d 448); Nov. 19, 2009, effective Feb. 1, 2010 (24 So.3d 63).

Comment

This rule governs the conduct of a lawyer who is representing a client in the proceedings of a tribunal. See terminology for the definition of "tribunal." It also applies when the lawyer is representing a client in an ancillary proceeding conducted pursuant to the tribunal's adjudicative authority, such as a deposition. Thus, for example, subdivision (a)(4) requires a lawyer to take reasonable remedial measures if the lawyer comes to know that a client who is testifying in a deposition has offered evidence that is false.

This rule sets forth the special duties of lawyers as officers of the court to avoid conduct that undermines the integrity of the adjudicative process. A lawyer acting as an advocate in an adjudicative proceeding has an obligation to present the client's case with persuasive force. Performance of that duty while maintaining confidences of the client is qualified by the advocate's duty of candor to the tribunal. Consequently, although a lawyer in an adversary proceeding is not required to present a disinterested exposition of the law or to vouch for the evidence submitted in a cause, the lawyer must not allow the tribunal to be misled by false statements of law or fact or evidence that the lawyer knows to be false.

Lawyers who represent clients in alternative dispute resolution processes are governed by the Rules of Professional Conduct. When the dispute resolution process takes place before a tribunal, as in binding arbitration (see terminology), the lawyer's duty of candor is governed by rule 4-3.3. Otherwise, the lawyer's duty of candor toward both the third-party neutral and other parties is governed by rule 4-4.1.

Representations by a lawyer

An advocate is responsible for pleadings and other documents prepared for litigation, but is usually not required to have personal knowledge of matters asserted therein, for litigation documents ordinarily present assertions by the client, or by someone on the client's behalf, and not assertions by the lawyer. Compare rule 4-3.1. However, an assertion purporting to be on the lawyer's own knowledge, as in an affidavit by the lawyer or in a statement in open court, may properly be made only when the lawyer knows the assertion is true or believes it to be true on the basis of a reasonably diligent inquiry. There are circumstances where failure to make a disclosure is the equivalent of an affirmative misrepresentation. The obligation prescribed in rule 4–1.2(d) not to counsel a client to commit or assist the client in committing a fraud applies in litigation. Regarding compliance with rule 4–1.2(d), see the comment to that rule. See also the comment to rule 4–8.4(b).

Misleading legal argument

Legal argument based on a knowingly false representation of law constitutes dishonesty toward the tribunal. A lawyer is not required to make a disinterested exposition of the law, but must recognize the existence of pertinent legal authorities. Furthermore, as stated in subdivision (a)(3), an advocate has a duty to disclose directly adverse authority in the controlling jurisdiction that has not been disclosed by the opposing party. The underlying concept is that legal argument is a discussion seeking to determine the legal premises properly applicable to the case.

False evidence

Subdivision (a)(4) requires that the lawyer refuse to offer evidence that the lawyer knows to be false, regardless of the client's wishes. This duty is premised on the lawyer's obligation as an officer of the court to prevent the trier of fact from being misled by false evidence. A lawyer does not violate this rule if the lawyer offers the evidence for the purpose of establishing its falsity.

If a lawyer knows that the client intends to testify falsely or wants the lawyer to introduce false evidence, the lawyer should seek to persuade the client that the evidence should not be offered. If the persuasion is ineffective and the lawyer continues to represent the client, the lawyer must refuse to offer the false evidence. If only a portion of a witness's testimony will be false, the lawyer may call the witness to testify but may not elicit or otherwise permit the witness to present the testimony that the lawyer knows is false.

The duties stated in this rule apply to all lawyers, including defense counsel in criminal cases.

The prohibition against offering false evidence only applies if the lawyer knows that the evidence is false. A lawyer's reasonable belief that evidence is false does not preclude its presentation to the trier of fact.

The rule generally recognized is that, if necessary to rectify the situation, an advocate must disclose the existence of the client's deception to the court. Such a disclosure can result in grave consequences to the client, including not only a sense of betrayal but also loss of the case and perhaps a prosecution for perjury. But the alternative is that the lawyer cooperate in deceiving the court, thereby subverting the truth-finding process that the adversary system is designed to implement. See rule 4–1.2(d). Furthermore, unless it is clearly understood that the lawyer will act upon the duty to disclose the existence of false evidence, the client can simply reject the lawyer's advice to reveal the false evidence and insist that the lawyer keep silent. Thus, the client could in effect coerce the lawyer into being a party to fraud on the court.

Remedial measures

If perjured testimony or false evidence has been offered, the advocate's proper course ordinarily is to remonstrate with the client confidentially if circumstances permit. In any case, the advocate should ensure disclosure is made to the court. It is for the court then to determine what should be done—making a statement about the matter to the trier of fact, ordering a mistrial, or perhaps nothing. If the false testimony was that of the client, the client may controvert the lawyer's version of their communication when the lawyer discloses the situation to the court. If there is an issue whether the client has committed perjury, the lawyer cannot represent the client in resolution of the issue and a mistrial may be unavoidable. An unscrupulous client might in this way attempt to produce a series of mistrials and thus escape prosecution. However, a second such encounter could be construed as a deliberate abuse of the right to counsel and as such a waiver of the right to further representation. This commentary is not intended to address the situation where a client or prospective client seeks legal advice specifically about a defense to a charge of perjury where the lawyer did not represent the client at the time the client gave the testimony giving rise to the charge.

Refusing to offer proof believed to be false

Although subdivision (a)(4) only prohibits a lawyer from offering evidence the lawyer knows to be false, it permits the lawyer to refuse to offer testimony or other proof that the lawyer reasonably believes is false. Offering such proof may reflect adversely on the lawyer's ability to discriminate in the quality of evidence and thus impair the lawyer's effectiveness as an advocate.

A lawyer may not assist the client or any witness in offering false testimony or other false evidence, nor may the lawyer permit the client or any other witness to testify falsely in the narrative form unless ordered to do so by the tribunal. If a lawyer knows that the client intends to commit perjury, the lawyer's first duty is to attempt to persuade the client to testify truthfully. If the client still insists on committing perjury, the lawyer must threaten to disclose the client's intent to commit perjury to the judge. If the threat of disclosure does not successfully persuade the client to testify truthfully, the lawyer must disclose the fact that the client intends to lie to the tribunal and, per 4–1.6, information sufficient to prevent the commission of the crime of perjury.

The lawyer's duty not to assist witnesses, including the lawyer's own client, in offering false evidence stems from the Rules of Professional Conduct, Florida statutes, and caselaw.

Rule 4–1.2(d) prohibits the lawyer from assisting a client in conduct that the lawyer knows or reasonably should know is criminal or fraudulent.

Rule 4–3.4(b) prohibits a lawyer from fabricating evidence or assisting a witness to testify falsely.

Rule 4–8.4(a) prohibits the lawyer from violating the Rules of Professional Conduct or knowingly assisting another to do so.

Rule 4–8.4(b) prohibits a lawyer from committing a criminal act that reflects adversely on the lawyer's honesty, trustworthiness, or fitness as a lawyer.

Rule 4–8.4(c) prohibits a lawyer from engaging in conduct involving dishonesty, fraud, deceit, or misrepresentation.

Rule 4–8.4(d) prohibits a lawyer from engaging in conduct that is prejudicial to the administration of justice.

Rule 4–1.6(b) requires a lawyer to reveal information to the extent the lawyer reasonably believes necessary to prevent a client from committing a crime.

This rule, 4–3.3(a)(2), requires a lawyer to reveal a material fact to the tribunal when disclosure is necessary to avoid assisting a criminal or fraudulent act by the client, and 4–3.3(a)(4) prohibits a lawyer from offering false evidence and requires the lawyer to take reasonable remedial measures when false material evidence has been offered.

Rule 4–1.16 prohibits a lawyer from representing a client if the representation will result in a violation of the Rules of Professional Conduct or law and permits the lawyer to withdraw from representation if the client persists in a course of action that the lawyer reasonably believes is criminal or fraudulent or repugnant or imprudent. Rule 4–1.16(c) recognizes that notwithstanding good cause for terminating representation of a client, a lawyer is obliged to continue representation if so ordered by a tribunal.

To permit or assist a client or other witness to testify falsely is prohibited by section 837.02, Florida Statutes (1991), which makes perjury in an official proceeding a felony, and by section 777.011, Florida Statutes (1991), which proscribes aiding, abetting, or counseling commission of a felony.

Florida caselaw prohibits lawyers from presenting false testimony or evidence. *Kneale v. Williams*, 30 So. 2d 284 (Fla. 1947), states that perpetration of a fraud is outside the scope of the professional duty of an attorney and no privilege attaches to communication between an attorney and a client with respect to transactions constituting the making of a false claim or the perpetration of a fraud. *Dodd v. The Florida Bar*, 118 So. 2d 17 (Fla. 1960), reminds us that "the courts are ... dependent on members of the bar to ... present the true facts of each cause ... to enable the judge or the jury to [decide the facts] to which the law may be applied. When an attorney ... allows false testimony ... [the attorney] ... makes it impossible for the scales [of justice] to balance. " See *The Fla. Bar v. Agar*, 394 So. 2d 405 (Fla. 1981), and *The Fla. Bar v. Simons*, 391 So. 2d 684 (Fla. 1980).

The United States Supreme Court in *Nix v. Whiteside*, 475 U.S. 157 (1986), answered in the negative the constitutional issue of whether it is ineffective assistance of counsel for an attorney to threaten disclosure of a client's (a criminal defendant's) intention to testify falsely.

Ex parte proceedings

Ordinarily, an advocate has the limited responsibility of presenting 1 side of the matters that a tribunal should consider in reaching a decision; the conflicting position is expected to be presented by the opposing party. However, in an ex parte proceeding, such as an application for a temporary injunction, there is no balance of presentation by opposing advocates. The object of an ex parte proceeding is nevertheless to yield a substantially just result. The judge has an affirmative responsibility to accord the absent party just consideration. The lawyer for the represented party has the correlative duty to make disclosures of material facts known to the lawyer and that the lawyer reasonably believes are necessary to an informed decision.

Rule 4–3.4. Fairness to Opposing Party and Counsel

A lawyer must not:

(a) unlawfully obstruct another party's access to evidence or otherwise unlawfully alter, destroy, or conceal a document or other material that the lawyer knows or reasonably should know is relevant to a pending or a reasonably foreseeable proceeding; nor counsel or assist another person to do any such act;

(b) fabricate evidence, counsel or assist a witness to testify falsely, or offer an inducement to a witness, except a lawyer may pay a witness reasonable expenses incurred by the witness in attending or testifying at proceedings; a reasonable, noncontingent fee for professional services of an expert witness; and reasonable compensation to a witness for time spent preparing for, attending, or testifying at proceedings;

(c) knowingly disobey an obligation under the rules of a tribunal except for an open refusal based on an assertion that no valid obligation exists;

(d) in pretrial procedure, make a frivolous discovery request or intentionally fail to comply with a legally proper discovery request by an opposing party;

(e) in trial, state a personal opinion about the credibility of a witness unless the statement is authorized by current rule or case law, allude to any matter that the lawyer does not reasonably believe is relevant or that will not be supported by admissible evidence, assert personal knowledge of facts in issue except when testifying as a witness, or state a personal opinion as to the justness of a cause, the culpability of a civil litigant, or the guilt or innocence of an accused;

(f) request a person other than a client to refrain from voluntarily giving relevant information to another party unless the person is a relative or an employee or other agent of a client, and it is reasonable to believe that the person's interests will not be adversely affected by refraining from giving such information;

(g) present, participate in presenting, or threaten to present criminal charges solely to obtain an advantage in a civil matter; or

(h) present, participate in presenting, or threaten to present disciplinary charges under these rules solely to obtain an advantage in a civil matter.

Amended July 23, 1992, effective Jan. 1, 1993 (605 So.2d 252); Oct. 20, 1994 (644 So.2d 282); Sept. 24, 1998, effective Oct. 1, 1998 (718 So.2d 1179); Oct. 6, 2005, effective Jan. 1, 2006 (916 So.2d 655); May 29, 2014, effective June 1, 2014 (140 So.3d 541).

Comment

The procedure of the adversary system contemplates that the evidence in a case is to be marshalled competitively by the contending parties. Fair competition in the adversary system is secured by prohibitions against destruction or concealment of evidence, improperly influencing witnesses, obstructive tactics in discovery procedure, and the like.

Documents and other items of evidence are often essential to establish a claim or defense. Subject to evidentiary privileges, the right of an opposing party, including the government, to obtain evidence through discovery or subpoena is an important procedural right. The exercise of that right can be frustrated if relevant material is altered, concealed, or destroyed. Applicable law in many jurisdictions makes it an offense to destroy material for the purpose of impairing its availability in a pending proceeding or one whose commencement can be foreseen. Falsifying evidence is also generally a criminal offense. Subdivision (a) applies to evidentiary material generally, including computerized information.

With regard to subdivision (b), it is not improper to pay a witness's expenses or to compensate an expert witness on terms permitted by law. The common law rule in most jurisdictions is that it is improper to pay an occurrence witness any fee for testifying and that it is improper to pay an expert witness a contingent fee.

Previously, subdivision (e) also proscribed statements about the credibility of witnesses. However, in 2000, the Supreme Court of Florida entered an opinion in *Murphy v. International Robotic Systems, Inc.*, 766 So. 2d 1010 (Fla. 2000), in which the court allowed counsel in closing argument to call a witness a "liar" or to state that the witness "lied."

There the court stated: "First, it is not improper for counsel to state during closing argument that a witness 'lied' or is a 'liar,' provided such characterizations are supported by the record." *Murphy*, id., at 1028. Members of the bar are advised to check the status of the law in this area.

Subdivision (f) permits a lawyer to advise employees of a client to refrain from giving information to another party, for the employees may identify their interests with those of the client. See also rule 4-4.2.

Rule 4-3.5. Impartiality and decorum of the tribunal

(a) Influencing Decision Maker. A lawyer shall not seek to influence a judge, juror, prospective juror, or other decision maker except as permitted by law or the rules of court.

(b) Communication with Judge or Official. In an adversary proceeding a lawyer shall not communicate or cause another to communicate as to the merits of the cause with a judge or an official before whom the proceeding is pending except:

(1) in the course of the official proceeding in the cause;

(2) in writing if the lawyer promptly delivers a copy of the writing to the opposing counsel or to the adverse party if not represented by a lawyer;

(3) orally upon notice to opposing counsel or to the adverse party if not represented by a lawyer; or

(4) as otherwise authorized by law.

(c) Disruption of Tribunal. A lawyer shall not engage in conduct intended to disrupt a tribunal.

(d) Communication With Jurors. A lawyer shall not:

(1) before the trial of a case with which the lawyer is connected, communicate or cause another to communicate with anyone the lawyer knows to be a member of the venire from which the jury will be selected;

(2) during the trial of a case with which the lawyer is connected, communicate or cause another to communicate with any member of the jury;

(3) during the trial of a case with which the lawyer is not connected, communicate or cause another to communicate with a juror concerning the case;

(4) after dismissal of the jury in a case with which the lawyer is connected, initiate communication with or cause another to initiate communication with any juror regarding the trial except to determine whether the verdict may be subject to legal challenge; provided, a lawyer may not interview jurors for this purpose unless the lawyer has reason to believe that grounds for such challenge may exist; and provided further, before conducting any such interview the lawyer must file in the cause a notice of intention to interview setting forth the name of the juror or jurors to be interviewed. A copy of the notice must be delivered to the trial judge and opposing counsel a reasonable time before such interview. The provisions of this rule do not prohibit a lawyer from communicating with members of the venire or jurors in the course of official proceedings or as authorized by court rule or written order of the court.

Amended July 23, 1992, effective Jan. 1, 1993 (605 So.2d 252).

Comment

Many forms of improper influence upon a tribunal are proscribed by criminal law. Others are specified in Florida's Code of Judicial Conduct, with which an advocate should be familiar. A lawyer is required to avoid contributing to a violation of such provisions.

The advocate's function is to present evidence and argument so that the cause may be decided according to law. Refraining from abusive or obstreperous conduct is a corollary of the advocate's right to speak on behalf of litigants. A lawyer may stand firm against abuse by a judge but should avoid reciprocation; the judge's default is no justification for similar dereliction by an advocate. An advocate can present the cause, protect the record for subsequent review, and preserve professional integrity by patient firmness no less effectively than by belligerence or theatrics.

Rule 4–3.6. Trial Publicity

(a) Prejudicial Extrajudicial Statements Prohibited. A lawyer shall not make an extrajudicial statement that a reasonable person would expect to be disseminated by means of public communication if the lawyer knows or reasonably should know that it will have a substantial likelihood of materially prejudicing an adjudicative proceeding due to its creation of an imminent and substantial detrimental effect on that proceeding.

(b) Statements of Third Parties. A lawyer shall not counsel or assist another person to make such a statement. Counsel shall exercise reasonable care to prevent investigators, employees, or other persons assisting in or associated with a case from making extrajudicial statements that are prohibited under this rule.

Amended July 23, 1992, effective Jan. 1, 1993 (605 So.2d 252); Oct. 20, 1994 (644 So.2d 282).

Comment

It is difficult to strike a balance between protecting the right to a fair trial and safeguarding the right of free expression. Preserving the right to a fair trial necessarily entails some curtailment of the information that may be disseminated about a party prior to trial, particularly where trial by jury is involved. If there were no such limits, the result would be the practical nullification of the protective effect of the rules of forensic decorum and the exclusionary rules of evidence. On the other hand, there are vital social interests served by the free dissemination of information about events having legal consequences and about legal proceedings themselves. The public has a right to know about threats to its safety and measures aimed at assuring its security. It also has a legitimate interest in the conduct of judicial proceedings, particularly in matters of general public concern. Furthermore, the subject matter of legal proceedings is often of direct significance in debate and deliberation over questions of public policy.

Rule 4–3.7. Lawyer as Witness

(a) When Lawyer May Testify. A lawyer shall not act as advocate at a trial in which the lawyer is likely to be a necessary witness on behalf of the client unless:

(1) the testimony relates to an uncontested issue;

(2) the testimony will relate solely to a matter of formality and there is no reason to believe that substantial evidence will be offered in opposition to the testimony;

(3) the testimony relates to the nature and value of legal services rendered in the case; or

(4) disqualification of the lawyer would work substantial hardship on the client.

(b) Other Members of Law Firm as Witnesses. A lawyer may act as advocate in a trial in which another lawyer in the lawyer's firm is likely to be called as a witness unless precluded from doing so by rule 4–1.7 or 4–1.9.

Amended July 23, 1992, effective Jan. 1, 1993 (605 So.2d 252); March 23, 2006, effective May 22, 2006 (933 So.2d 417).

Comment

Combining the roles of advocate and witness can prejudice the tribunal and the opposing party and can also involve a conflict of interest between the lawyer and client.

The trier of fact may be confused or misled by a lawyer serving as both advocate and witness. The combination of roles may prejudice another party's rights in the litigation. A witness is required to testify on the basis of personal knowledge, while an advocate is expected to explain and comment on evidence given by others. It may not be clear whether a statement by an advocate-witness should be taken as proof or as an analysis of the proof.

To protect the tribunal, subdivision (a) prohibits a lawyer from simultaneously serving as advocate and necessary witness except in those circumstances specified. Subdivision (a)(1) recognizes that if the testimony will be uncontested, the ambiguities in the dual role are purely theoretical. Subdivisions (a)(2) and (3) recognize that, where the testimony concerns the extent and value of legal services rendered in the action in which the testimony is offered, permitting the lawyers to testify avoids the need for a second trial with new counsel to resolve that issue. Moreover, in such a situation the judge has first-hand knowledge of the matter in issue; hence, there is less dependence on the adversary process to test the credibility of the testimony.

Apart from these 2 exceptions, subdivision (a)(4) recognizes that a balancing is required between the interests of the client and those of the tribunal and the opposing party. Whether the tribunal is likely to be misled or the opposing party is likely to suffer prejudice depends on the nature of the case, the importance and probable tenor of the lawyer's testimony, and the probability that the lawyer's testimony will conflict with that of other witnesses. Even if there is risk of such prejudice, in determining whether the lawyer should be disqualified, due regard must be given to the effect of disqualification on the lawyer's client. It is relevant that one or both parties could reasonably foresee that the lawyer would probably be a witness. The conflict of interest principles stated in rules 4–1.7, 4–1.9, and 4–1.10 have no application to this aspect of the problem.

Because the tribunal is not likely to be misled when a lawyer acts as advocate in a trial in which another lawyer in the lawyer's firm will testify as a necessary witness, subdivision (b) permits the lawyer to do so except in situations involving a conflict of interest.

In determining if it is permissible to act as advocate in a trial in which the lawyer will be a necessary witness, the lawyer must also consider that the dual role may give rise to a conflict of interest that will require compliance with rules 4–1.7 or 4–1.9. For example, if there is likely to be substantial conflict between the testimony of the client and that of the lawyer, the representation involves a conflict of interest that requires compliance with rule 4–1.7. This would be true even though the lawyer might not be prohibited by subdivision (a) from simultaneously serving as advocate and witness because the lawyer's disqualification would work a substantial hardship on the client. Similarly, a lawyer who might be permitted to simultaneously serve as an advocate and a witness by subdivision (a)(3) might be precluded from doing so by rule 4–1.9. The problem can arise whether the lawyer is called as a witness on behalf of the client or is called by the opposing party. Determining whether such a conflict exists is primarily the responsibility of the lawyer involved. If there is a conflict of interest, the lawyer must secure the client's informed consent. In some cases, the lawyer will be precluded from seeking the client's consent. See rule 4–1.7. If a lawyer who is a member of a firm may not act as both advocate and witness by reason of conflict of interest, rule 4–1.10 disqualifies the firm also. See terminology for the definition of "confirmed in writing" and "informed consent."

Subdivision (b) provides that a lawyer is not disqualified from serving as an advocate because a lawyer with whom the lawyer is associated in a firm is precluded from doing so by subdivision (a). If, however, the testifying lawyer would also be disqualified by rule 4–1.7 or 4–1.9 from representing the client in the matter, other lawyers in the firm will be precluded from representing the client by rule 4–1.10 unless the client gives informed consent under the conditions stated in rule 4–1.7.

Rule 4–3.8. Special responsibilities of a prosecutor

The prosecutor in a criminal case shall:

(a) refrain from prosecuting a charge that the prosecutor knows is not supported by probable cause;

(b) not seek to obtain from an unrepresented accused a waiver of important pre-trial rights such as a right to a preliminary hearing;

(c) make timely disclosure to the defense of all evidence or information known to the prosecutor that tends to negate the guilt of the accused or mitigates the offense, and, in connection with sentencing, disclose to the defense and to the tribunal all unprivileged mitigating information known to the prosecutor, except when the prosecutor is relieved of this responsibility by a protective order of the tribunal.

Amended July 23, 1992, effective Jan. 1, 1993 (605 So.2d 252).

Comment

A prosecutor has the responsibility of a minister of justice and not simply that of an advocate. This responsibility carries with it specific obligations such as making a reasonable effort to assure that the accused has been advised of the right to and the procedure for obtaining counsel and has been given a reasonable opportunity to obtain counsel so that guilt is decided upon the basis of sufficient evidence. Precisely how far the prosecutor is required to go in this direction is a matter of debate. Florida has adopted the American Bar Association Standards of Criminal Justice Relating to Prosecution Function. This is the product of prolonged and careful deliberation by lawyers experienced in criminal prosecution and defense and should be consulted for further guidance. See also rule 4–3.3(d) governing ex parte proceedings, among which grand jury proceedings are included. Applicable law may require other measures by the prosecutor and knowing disregard of these obligations or systematic abuse of prosecutorial discretion could constitute a violation of rule 4–8.4.

Subdivision (b) does not apply to an accused appearing pro se with the approval of the tribunal, nor does it forbid the lawful questioning of a suspect who has knowingly waived the rights to counsel and silence.

The exception in subdivision (c) recognizes that a prosecutor may seek an appropriate protective order from the tribunal if disclosure of information to the defense could result in substantial harm to an individual or to the public interest.

Rule 4–3.9. Advocate in Nonadjudicative Proceedings

A lawyer representing a client before a legislative body or administrative agency in a nonadjudicative proceeding shall disclose that the appearance is in a representative capacity and shall conform to the provisions of rules 4–3.3(a) through (d), and 4–3.4(a) through (c).

Amended March 23, 2006, effective May 22, 2006 (933 So.2d 417).

Comment

In representation before bodies such as legislatures, municipal councils, and executive and administrative agencies acting in a rule-making or policy-making capacity, lawyers present facts, formulate issues, and advance argument in the matters under consideration. The decision-making body, like a court, should be able to rely on the integrity of the submissions made to it. A lawyer appearing before such a body must deal with the tribunal honestly and in conformity with applicable rules of procedure. See rules 4–3.3(a) through (d), and 4–3.4(a) through (c).

Lawyers have no exclusive right to appear before nonadjudicative bodies, as they do before a court. The requirements of this rule therefore may subject lawyers to regulations inapplicable to advocates who are not lawyers. However, legislatures and administrative agencies have a right to expect lawyers to deal with them as they deal with courts.

This rule only applies when a lawyer represents a client in connection with an official hearing or meeting of a governmental agency or a legislative body to which the lawyer or the lawyer's client is presenting evidence or argument. It does not apply to representation of a client in a negotiation or other bilateral transaction with a governmental agency or in connection with an application for a license or other privilege or the client's compliance with generally applicable reporting requirements, such as the filing of income-tax returns. Nor does it apply to the representation of a client in connection with an investigation or examination of the client's affairs conducted by government investigators or examiners. Representation in such matters is governed by rules 4–4.1 through 4–4.4.

4–4. TRANSACTIONS WITH PERSONS OTHER THAN CLIENTS

Rule 4–4.1. Truthfulness in statements to others

In the course of representing a client a lawyer shall not knowingly:

(a) make a false statement of material fact or law to a third person; or

(b) fail to disclose a material fact to a third person when disclosure is necessary to avoid assisting a criminal or fraudulent act by a client, unless disclosure is prohibited by rule 4–1.6.

Amended July 23, 1992, effective Jan. 1, 1993 (605 So.2d 252).

Comment

Misrepresentation

A lawyer is required to be truthful when dealing with others on a client's behalf, but generally has no affirmative duty to inform an opposing party of relevant facts. A misrepresentation can occur if the lawyer incorporates or affirms a statement of another person that the lawyer knows is false. Misrepresentations can also occur by partially true but misleading statements or omissions that are the equivalent of affirmative false statements. For dishonest conduct that does not amount to a false statement or for misrepresentations by a lawyer other than in the course of representing a client, see rule 4–8.4.

Statements of fact

This rule refers to statements of fact. Whether a particular statement should be regarded as one of fact can depend on the circumstances. Under generally accepted conventions in negotiation, certain types of statements ordinarily are not taken as statements of material fact. Estimates of price or value placed on the subject of a transaction and a party's intentions as to an acceptable settlement of a claim are ordinarily in this category, and so is the existence of an undisclosed principal except where nondisclosure of the principal would constitute fraud. Lawyers should be mindful of their obligations under applicable law to avoid criminal and tortious misrepresentation.

Crime or fraud by client

Under rule 4–1.2(d), a lawyer is prohibited from counseling or assisting a client in conduct that the lawyer knows is criminal or fraudulent. Subdivision (b) states a specific application of the principle set forth in rule 4–1.2(d) and addresses the situation where a client's crime or fraud takes the form of a lie or misrepresentation. Ordinarily, a lawyer can avoid assisting a client's crime or fraud by withdrawing from the representation. Sometimes it may be necessary for the lawyer to give notice of the fact of withdrawal and to disaffirm an opinion, document, affirmation or the like. In extreme cases, substantive law may require a lawyer to disclose information relating to the representation to avoid being deemed to have assisted the client's crime or fraud. If the lawyer can avoid assisting a client's crime or fraud only by disclosing this information, then under subdivision (b) the lawyer is required to do so, unless the disclosure is prohibited by rule 4–1.6.

Rule 4–4.2. Communication with Person Represented by Counsel

(a) In representing a client, a lawyer must not communicate about the subject of the representation with a person the lawyer knows to be represented by another lawyer in the matter, unless the lawyer has the consent of the other lawyer. Notwithstanding the foregoing, a lawyer may, without such prior consent, communicate with another's client to meet the requirements of any court rule, statute or contract requiring notice or service of process directly on a person, in which event the communication is strictly restricted to that required by the court rule, statute or contract, and a copy must be provided to the person's lawyer.

(b) An otherwise unrepresented person to whom limited representation is being provided or has been provided in accordance with Rule Regulating the Florida Bar 4–1.2 is considered to be unrepresented for purposes of this rule unless the opposing lawyer knows of, or has been provided with, a written notice of appearance under which, or a written notice of time period during which, the opposing lawyer is to communicate with the limited representation lawyer as to the subject matter within the limited scope of the representation.

Amended Oct. 10, 1991, effective Jan. 1, 1992 (587 So.2d 1121); July 23, 1992, effective Jan. 1, 1993 (605 So.2d 252); Nov. 13, 2003, effective Jan. 1, 2004 (860 So.2d 394); May 20, 2004 (875 So.2d 448); May 29, 2014, effective June 1, 2014 (140 So.3d 541).

Comment

This rule contributes to the proper functioning of the legal system by protecting a person who has chosen to be represented by a lawyer in a matter against possible overreaching by other lawyers who are participating in the matter, interference by those lawyers with the client-lawyer relationship, and the uncounseled disclosure of information relating to the representation.

This rule applies to communications with any person who is represented by counsel concerning the matter to which the communication relates.

The rule applies even though the represented person initiates or consents to the communication. A lawyer must immediately terminate communication with a person if, after commencing communication, the lawyer learns that the person is one with whom communication is not permitted by this rule.

This rule does not prohibit communication with a represented person, or an employee or agent of such a person, concerning matters outside the representation. For example, the existence of a controversy between a government agency and a private party, or between 2 organizations, does not prohibit a lawyer for either from communicating with nonlawyer representatives of the other regarding a separate matter. Nor does this rule preclude communication with a represented person who is seeking advice from a lawyer who is not otherwise representing a client in the matter. A lawyer may not make a communication prohibited by this rule through the acts of another. See rule 4–8.4(a). Parties to a matter may communicate directly with each other, and a lawyer is not prohibited from advising a client concerning a communication that the client is legally entitled to make, provided that the client is not used to indirectly violate the Rules of Professional Conduct. Also, a lawyer having independent justification for communicating with the other party is permitted to do so. Permitted communications include, for example, the right of a party to a controversy with a government agency to speak with government officials about the matter.

In the case of a represented organization, this rule prohibits communications with a constituent of the organization who supervises, directs, or regularly consults with the organization's lawyer concerning the matter or has authority to obligate the organization with respect to the matter or whose act or omission in connection with the matter may be imputed to the organization for purposes of civil or criminal liability. Consent of the organization's lawyer is not required for communication with a former constituent. If a constituent of the organization is represented in the matter by the agent's or employee's own counsel, the consent by that counsel to a communication will be sufficient for purposes of this rule. Compare rule 4–3.4(f). In communication with a current or former constituent of an organization, a lawyer must not use methods of obtaining evidence that violate the legal rights of the organization. See rule 4–4.4.

The prohibition on communications with a represented person only applies in circumstances where the lawyer knows that the person is in fact represented in the matter to be discussed. This means that the lawyer has actual knowledge of the fact of the representation; but such actual knowledge may be inferred from the circumstances. See terminology. Thus, the lawyer cannot evade the requirement of obtaining the consent of counsel by closing eyes to the obvious.

In the event the person with whom the lawyer communicates is not known to be represented by counsel in the matter, the lawyer's communications are subject to rule 4–4.3.

Rule 4–4.3. Dealing with Unrepresented Persons

(a) In dealing on behalf of a client with a person who is not represented by counsel, a lawyer shall not state or imply that the lawyer is disinterested. When the lawyer knows or reasonably should know that the unrepresented person misunderstands the lawyer's role in the matter, the lawyer shall make reasonable efforts to correct the misunderstanding. The lawyer shall not give legal advice to an unrepresented person, other than the advice to secure counsel.

(b) An otherwise unrepresented person to whom limited representation is being provided or has been provided in accordance with Rule Regulating the Florida Bar 4–1.2 is considered to be unrepresented for purposes of this rule unless the opposing lawyer knows of, or has been provided with, a written notice of appearance under which, or a written notice of time period during which, the opposing lawyer is to communicate with the limited representation lawyer as to the subject matter within the limited scope of the representation.

Amended Nov. 13, 2003, effective Jan. 1, 2004 (860 So.2d 394); March 23, 2006, effective May 22, 2006 (933 So.2d 417).

Comment

An unrepresented person, particularly one not experienced in dealing with legal matters, might assume that a lawyer is disinterested in loyalties or is a disinterested authority on the law even when the lawyer represents a client. In order to avoid a misunderstanding, a lawyer will typically need to identify the lawyer's client and, where necessary, explain that the client has interests opposed to those of the unrepresented person. For misunderstandings that sometimes arise when a lawyer for an organization deals with an unrepresented constituent, see rule 4–1.13(d).

This rule does not prohibit a lawyer from negotiating the terms of a transaction or settling a dispute with an unrepresented person. So long as the lawyer has explained that the lawyer represents an adverse party and is not representing the person, the lawyer may inform the person of the terms on which the lawyer's client will enter into an agreement or settle a matter, prepare documents that require the person's signature and explain the lawyer's own view of the meaning of the document or the lawyer's view of the underlying legal obligations.

Rule 4–4.4. Respect for Rights of Third Persons

Text of rule effective until October 1, 2015. See, also, rule effective October 1, 2015.

(a) In representing a client, a lawyer shall not use means that have no substantial purpose other than to embarrass, delay, or burden a third person or knowingly use methods of obtaining evidence that violate the legal rights of such a person.

(b) A lawyer who receives a document relating to the representation of the lawyer's client and knows or reasonably should know that the document was inadvertently sent shall promptly notify the sender.

Amended July 23, 1992, effective Jan. 1, 1993 (605 So.2d 252); March 23, 2006, effective May 22, 2006 (933 So.2d 417).

Comment

Responsibility to a client requires a lawyer to subordinate the interests of others to those of the client, but that responsibility does not imply that a lawyer may disregard the rights of third persons. It is impractical to catalogue all such rights, but they include legal restrictions on methods of obtaining evidence from third persons and unwarranted intrusions into privileged relationships, such as the client-lawyer relationship.

Subdivision (b) recognizes that lawyers sometimes receive documents that were mistakenly sent or produced by opposing parties or their lawyers. If a lawyer knows or reasonably should know that such a document was sent inadvertently, then this rule requires the lawyer to promptly notify the sender in order to permit that person to take protective measures. Whether the lawyer is required to take additional steps, such as returning the original document, is a matter of law beyond the scope of these rules, as is the question of whether the privileged status of a document has been waived. Similarly, this rule does not address the legal duties of a lawyer who receives a document that the lawyer knows or reasonably should know may have been wrongfully obtained by the sending person. For purposes of this rule, "document" includes e-mail or other electronic modes of transmission subject to being read or put into readable form.

Some lawyers may choose to return a document unread, for example, when the lawyer learns before receiving the document that it was inadvertently sent to the wrong address. Where a lawyer is not required by applicable law to do so, the decision to voluntarily return such a document is a matter of professional judgment ordinarily reserved to the lawyer. See rules 4–1.2 and 4–1.4.

Rule 4–4.4. Respect for Rights of Third Persons

Text of rule effective October 1, 2015. See, also, rule effective until October 1, 2015.

(a) In representing a client, a lawyer may not use means that have no substantial purpose other than to embarrass, delay, or burden a third person or knowingly use methods of obtaining evidence that violate the legal rights of such a person.

(b) A lawyer who receives a document or electronically stored information relating to the representation of the lawyer's client and knows or reasonably should know that the document or electronically stored information was inadvertently sent must promptly notify the sender.

Amended July 23, 1992, effective Jan. 1, 1993 (605 So.2d 252); March 23, 2006, effective May 22, 2006 (933 So.2d 417); May 21, 2015, effective Oct. 1, 2015 (164 So.3d 1217).

Comment

Responsibility to a client requires a lawyer to subordinate the interests of others to those of the client, but that responsibility does not imply that a lawyer may disregard the rights of third persons. It is impractical to catalogue all these rights, but they include legal restrictions on methods of obtaining evidence from third persons and unwarranted intrusions into privileged relationships, such as the client-lawyer relationship.

Subdivision (b) recognizes that lawyers sometimes receive a document or electronically stored information that was mistakenly sent or produced by opposing parties or their lawyers. A document or electronically stored information is inadvertently sent when it is accidentally transmitted, such as when an e-mail or letter is misaddressed or a document or electronically stored information is accidentally included with information that was intentionally transmitted. If a lawyer knows or reasonably should know that a document or electronically stored information was sent inadvertently, then this rule requires the lawyer to promptly notify the sender in order to permit that person to take protective measures. Whether the lawyer is required to take additional steps, such as returning the document or electronically stored information, is a matter of law beyond the scope of these rules, as is the question of whether the privileged status of a document or electronically stored information has been waived. Similarly, this rule does not address the legal duties of a lawyer who receives a document that the lawyer knows or reasonably should know may have been wrongfully obtained by the sending person. For purposes of this rule, "document or electronically stored information" includes, in addition to paper documents, e-mail and other forms of electronically stored information, including embedded data (commonly referred to as "metadata"), that is subject to being read or put into readable form. Metadata in electronic documents creates an obligation under this rule only if the receiving lawyer knows or reasonably should know that the metadata was inadvertently sent to the receiving lawyer.

Some lawyers may choose to return a document or delete electronically stored information unread, for example, when the lawyer learns before receiving the document that it was inadvertently sent. Where a lawyer is not required by applicable law to do so, the decision to voluntarily return the document or delete electronically stored information is a matter of professional judgment ordinarily reserved to the lawyer. See rules 4–1.2 and 4–1.4.

4–5. LAW FIRMS AND ASSOCIATIONS

Rule 4–5.1. Responsibilities of Partners, Managers, and Supervisory Lawyers

(a) Duties Concerning Adherence to Rules of Professional Conduct. A partner in a law firm, and a lawyer who individually or together with other lawyers possesses comparable managerial authority in a law firm, shall make reasonable efforts to ensure that the firm has in effect measures giving reasonable assurance that all lawyers therein conform to the Rules of Professional Conduct.

(b) Supervisory Lawyer's Duties. Any lawyer having direct supervisory authority over another lawyer shall make reasonable efforts to ensure that the other lawyer conforms to the Rules of Professional Conduct.

(c) Responsibility for Rules Violations. A lawyer shall be responsible for another lawyer's violation of the Rules of Professional Conduct if:

(1) the lawyer orders the specific conduct or, with knowledge thereof, ratifies the conduct involved; or

(2) the lawyer is a partner or has comparable managerial authority in the law firm in which the other lawyer practices or has direct supervisory authority over the other lawyer, and knows of the conduct at a time when its consequences can be avoided or mitigated but fails to take reasonable remedial action.

Amended July 23, 1992, effective Jan. 1, 1993 (605 So.2d 252); Sept. 24, 1998, effective Oct. 1, 1998 (718 So.2d 1179); March 23, 2006, effective May 22, 2006 (933 So.2d 417).

Comment

Subdivision (a) applies to lawyers who have managerial authority over the professional work of a firm. See terminology. This includes members of a partnership, the shareholders in a law firm organized as a professional corporation, and members of other associations authorized to practice law; lawyers having comparable managerial authority in a legal services organization or a law department of an enterprise or government agency, and lawyers who have intermediate managerial responsibilities in a firm. Subdivision (b) applies to lawyers who have supervisory authority over the work of other lawyers in a firm.

Subdivision (a) requires lawyers with managerial authority within a firm to make reasonable efforts to establish internal policies and procedures designed to provide reasonable assurance that all lawyers in the firm will conform to the Rules of Professional Conduct. Such policies and procedures include those designed to detect and resolve conflicts of interest, identify dates by which actions must be taken in pending matters, account for client funds and property, and ensure that inexperienced lawyers are properly supervised.

Other measures that may be required to fulfill the responsibility prescribed in subdivision (a) can depend on the firm's structure and the nature of its practice. In a small firm of experienced lawyers, informal supervision and periodic review of compliance with the required systems ordinarily will suffice. In a large firm, or in practice situations in which difficult ethical problems frequently arise, more elaborate measures may be necessary. Some firms, for example, have a procedure whereby junior lawyers can make confidential referral of ethical problems directly to a designated supervising lawyer or special committee. See rule 4–5.2. Firms, whether large or small, may also rely on continuing legal education in professional ethics. In any event the ethical atmosphere of a firm can influence the conduct of all its members and the partners may not assume that all lawyers associated with the firm will inevitably conform to the rules.

Subdivision (c) expresses a general principle of personal responsibility for acts of another. See also rule 4–8.4(a).

Subdivision (c)(2) defines the duty of a partner or other lawyer having comparable managerial authority in a law firm, as well as a lawyer having supervisory authority over performance of specific legal work by another lawyer. Whether a lawyer has such supervisory authority in particular circumstances is a question of fact. Partners and lawyers with comparable authority have at least indirect responsibility for all work being done by the firm, while a partner or manager in charge of a particular matter ordinarily also has supervisory responsibility for the work of other firm lawyers engaged in the matter. Appropriate remedial action by a partner or managing lawyer would depend on the immediacy of that lawyer's involvement and the seriousness of the misconduct. A supervisor is required to intervene to prevent avoidable consequences of misconduct if the supervisor knows that the misconduct occurred. Thus, if a supervising lawyer knows that a subordinate misrepresented a matter to an opposing party in negotiation, the supervisor as well as the subordinate has a duty to correct the resulting misapprehension.

Professional misconduct by a lawyer under supervision could reveal a violation of subdivision (b) on the part of the supervisory lawyer even though it does not entail a violation of subdivision (c) because there was no direction, ratification, or knowledge of the violation.

Apart from this rule and rule 4–8.4(a), a lawyer does not have disciplinary liability for the conduct of a partner, shareholder, member of a limited liability company, officer, director, manager, associate, or subordinate. Whether a lawyer may be liable civilly or criminally for another lawyer's conduct is a question of law beyond the scope of these rules.

The duties imposed by this rule on managing and supervising lawyers do not alter the personal duty of each lawyer in a firm to abide by the Rules of Professional Conduct. See rule 4–5.2(a).

Rule 4–5.2. Responsibilities of a subordinate lawyer

(a) Rules of Professional Conduct Apply. A lawyer is bound by the Rules of Professional Conduct notwithstanding that the lawyer acted at the direction of another person.

(b) Reliance on Supervisor's Opinion. A subordinate lawyer does not violate the Rules of Professional Conduct if that lawyer acts in accordance with a supervisory lawyer's reasonable resolution of an arguable question of professional duty.

Amended July 23, 1992, effective Jan. 1, 1993 (605 So.2d 252).

Comment

Although a lawyer is not relieved of responsibility for a violation by the fact that the lawyer acted at the direction of a supervisor, that fact may be relevant in determining whether a lawyer had the knowledge required to render conduct a violation of the rules. For example, if a subordinate filed a frivolous pleading at the direction of a supervisor, the subordinate would not be guilty of a professional violation unless the subordinate knew of the document's frivolous character.

When lawyers in a supervisor-subordinate relationship encounter a matter involving professional judgment as to ethical duty, the supervisor may assume responsibility for making the judgment. Otherwise a consistent course of action or position could not be taken. If the question can reasonably be answered only 1 way, the duty of both lawyers is clear and they are equally responsible for fulfilling it. However, if the question is reasonably arguable, someone has to decide upon the course of action. That authority ordinarily reposes in the supervisor, and a subordinate may be guided accordingly. For example, if a question arises whether the interests of 2 clients conflict under rule 4–1.7, the supervisor's reasonable resolution of the question should protect the subordinate professionally if the resolution is subsequently challenged.

Rule 4–5.3. Responsibilities Regarding Nonlawyer Assistants

Text of rule effective until October 1, 2015. See, also, rule effective October 1, 2015.

(a) Use of Titles by Nonlawyer Assistants. A person who uses the title of paralegal, legal assistant, or other similar term when offering or providing services to the public must work for or under the direction or supervision of a lawyer or law firm.

(b) Supervisory Responsibility. With respect to a nonlawyer employed or retained by or associated with a lawyer or an authorized business entity as defined elsewhere in these Rules Regulating The Florida Bar:

(1) a partner, and a lawyer who individually or together with other lawyers possesses comparable managerial authority in a law firm, shall make reasonable efforts to ensure that the firm has in effect measures giving reasonable assurance that the person's conduct is compatible with the professional obligations of the lawyer;

(2) a lawyer having direct supervisory authority over the nonlawyer shall make reasonable efforts to ensure that the person's conduct is compatible with the professional obligations of the lawyer; and

(3) a lawyer shall be responsible for conduct of such a person that would be a violation of the Rules of Professional Conduct if engaged in by a lawyer if:

(A) the lawyer orders or, with the knowledge of the specific conduct, ratifies the conduct involved; or

(B) the lawyer is a partner or has comparable managerial authority in the law firm in which the person is employed, or has direct supervisory authority over the person, and knows of the conduct at a time when its consequences can be avoided or mitigated but fails to take reasonable remedial action.

(c) Ultimate Responsibility of Lawyer. Although paralegals or legal assistants may perform the duties delegated to them by the lawyer without the presence or active involvement of the lawyer, the lawyer shall review and be responsible for the work product of the paralegals or legal assistants.

Amended July 23, 1992, effective Jan. 1, 1993 (605 So.2d 252); April 25, 2002 (820 So.2d 210); March 23, 2006, effective May 22, 2006 (933 So.2d 417).

Comment

Lawyers generally employ assistants in their practice, including secretaries, investigators, law student interns, and paraprofessionals such as paralegals and legal assistants. Such assistants, whether employees or independent contractors, act for the lawyer in rendition of the lawyer's professional services. A lawyer must give such assistants appropriate instruction and supervision concerning the ethical aspects of their employment, particularly regarding the obligation not to disclose information relating to representation of the client. The measures employed in supervising nonlawyers should take account of the level of their legal training and the fact that they are not subject to professional discipline. If an activity requires the independent judgment and participation of the lawyer, it cannot be properly delegated to a nonlawyer employee.

Subdivision (b)(1) requires lawyers with managerial authority within a law firm to make reasonable efforts to establish internal policies and procedures designed to provide reasonable assurance that nonlawyers in the firm will act in a way compatible with the Rules of Professional Conduct. See comment to rule 4–5.1. Subdivision (b)(2) applies to lawyers who have supervisory authority over the work of a nonlawyer. Subdivision (b)(3) specifies the circumstances in which a lawyer is responsible for conduct of a nonlawyer that would be a violation of the Rules of Professional Conduct if engaged in by a lawyer.

Nothing provided in this rule should be interpreted to mean that a nonlawyer may have any ownership or partnership interest in a law firm, which is prohibited by rule 4–5.4. Additionally, this rule would not permit a lawyer to accept employment by a nonlawyer or group of nonlawyers, the purpose of which is to provide the supervision required under this rule. Such conduct is prohibited by rules 4–5.4 and 4–5.5.

Rule 4–5.3. Responsibilities Regarding Nonlawyer Assistants

Text of rule effective October 1, 2015. See, also, rule effective until October 1, 2015.

(a) Use of Titles by Nonlawyer Assistants. A person who uses the title of paralegal, legal assistant, or other similar term when offering or providing services to the public must work for or under the direction or supervision of a lawyer or law firm.

(b) Supervisory Responsibility. With respect to a nonlawyer employed or retained by or associated with a lawyer or an authorized business entity as defined elsewhere in these Rules Regulating The Florida Bar:

(1) a partner, and a lawyer who individually or together with other lawyers possesses comparable managerial authority in a law firm, must make reasonable efforts to ensure that the firm has in effect measures giving reasonable assurance that the person's conduct is compatible with the professional obligations of the lawyer;

(2) a lawyer having direct supervisory authority over the nonlawyer must make reasonable efforts to ensure that the person's conduct is compatible with the professional obligations of the lawyer; and

(3) a lawyer is responsible for conduct of such a person that would be a violation of the Rules of Professional Conduct if engaged in by a lawyer if the lawyer:

(A) orders or, with the knowledge of the specific conduct, ratifies the conduct involved; or

(B) is a partner or has comparable managerial authority in the law firm in which the person is employed, or has direct supervisory authority over the person, and knows of the conduct at a time when its consequences can be avoided or mitigated but fails to take reasonable remedial action.

(c) Ultimate Responsibility of Lawyer. Although paralegals or legal assistants may perform the duties delegated to them by the lawyer without the presence or active involvement of the lawyer, the lawyer must review and be responsible for the work product of the paralegals or legal assistants.

Amended July 23, 1992, effective Jan. 1, 1993 (605 So.2d 252); April 25, 2002 (820 So.2d 210); March 23, 2006, effective May 22, 2006 (933 So.2d 417); June 11, 2015, effective Oct. 1, 2015 (167 So.3d 412).

Comment

Lawyers generally employ assistants in their practice, including secretaries, investigators, law student interns, and paraprofessionals such as paralegals and legal assistants. Such assistants, whether employees or independent contractors, act for the lawyer in rendition of the lawyer's professional services. A lawyer must give such assistants appropriate instruction and supervision concerning the ethical aspects of their employment, particularly regarding the obligation not to disclose information relating to representation of the client. The measures employed in supervising nonlawyers should take account of the level of their legal training and the fact that they are not subject to professional discipline. If an activity requires the independent judgment and participation of the lawyer, it cannot be properly delegated to a nonlawyer employee.

Subdivision (b)(1) requires lawyers with managerial authority within a law firm to make reasonable efforts to ensure that the firm has in effect measures giving reasonable assurance that nonlawyers in the firm and nonlawyers outside the firm who work on firm matters act in a way compatible with the professional obligations of the lawyer. See comment to rule 1.1 (retaining lawyers outside the firm) and comment to rule 4–5.1 (responsibilities with respect to lawyers within a firm). Subdivision (b)(2) applies to lawyers who have supervisory authority over nonlawyers within or outside the firm. Subdivision (b)(3) specifies the circumstances in which a lawyer is responsible for conduct of nonlawyers within or outside the firm that would be a violation of the Rules of Professional Conduct if engaged in by a lawyer.

Nothing provided in this rule should be interpreted to mean that a nonlawyer may have any ownership or partnership interest in a law firm, which is prohibited by rule 4–5.4. Additionally, this rule does not permit a lawyer to accept employment by a nonlawyer or group of nonlawyers, the purpose of which is to provide the supervision required under this rule. This conduct is prohibited by rules 4–5.4 and 4–5.5.

Nonlawyers Outside the Firm

A lawyer may use nonlawyers outside the firm to assist the lawyer in rendering legal services to the client. Examples include the retention of an investigative or paraprofessional service, hiring a document management company to create and maintain a database for complex litigation, sending client documents to a third party for printing or scanning, and using an Internet-based service to store client information. When using these services outside the firm, a lawyer must make reasonable efforts to ensure that the services are provided in a manner that is compatible with the lawyer's professional obligations. The extent of this obligation will depend on the circumstances, including the education, experience and reputation of the nonlawyer; the nature of the services involved; the terms of any arrangements concerning the protection of client information; and the legal and ethical environments of the jurisdictions in which the services will be performed, particularly with regard to confidentiality. See also rules 4-1.1 (competence), 4-1.2 (allocation of authority), 4-1.4 (communication with client), 4-1.6 (confidentiality), 4-5.4 (professional independence of the lawyer), and 4-5.5 (unauthorized practice of law). When retaining or directing a nonlawyer outside the firm, a lawyer should communicate directions appropriate under the circumstances to give reasonable assurance that the nonlawyer's conduct is compatible with the professional obligations of the lawyer.

Where the client directs the selection of a particular nonlawyer service provider outside the firm, the lawyer ordinarily should agree with the client concerning the allocation of responsibility for monitoring as between the client and the lawyer. See Rule 1.2. When making this allocation in a matter pending before a tribunal, lawyers and parties may have additional obligations that are a matter of law beyond the scope of these rules.

Rule 4-5.4. Professional Independence of a Lawyer

(a) Sharing Fees with Nonlawyers. A lawyer or law firm shall not share legal fees with a nonlawyer, except that:

(1) an agreement by a lawyer with the lawyer's firm, partner, or associate may provide for the payment of money, over a reasonable period of time after the lawyer's death, to the lawyer's estate or to 1 or more specified persons;

(2) a lawyer who undertakes to complete unfinished legal business of a deceased lawyer may pay to the estate of the deceased lawyer that proportion of the total compensation that fairly represents the services rendered by the deceased lawyer;

(3) a lawyer who purchases the practice of a deceased, disabled, or disappeared lawyer may, in accordance with the provisions of rule 4-1.17, pay to the estate or other legally authorized representative of that lawyer the agreed upon purchase price;

(4) bonuses may be paid to nonlawyer employees for work performed, and may be based on their extraordinary efforts on a particular case or over a specified time period. Bonus payments shall not be based on cases or clients brought to the lawyer or law firm by the actions of the nonlawyer. A lawyer shall not provide a bonus payment that is calculated as a percentage of legal fees received by the lawyer or law firm; and

(5) a lawyer may share court-awarded fees with a nonprofit, pro bono legal services organization that employed, retained, or recommended employment of the lawyer in the matter.

(b) Qualified Pension Plans. A lawyer or law firm may include nonlawyer employees in a qualified pension, profit-sharing, or retirement plan, even though the lawyer's or law firm's contribution to the plan is based in whole or in part on a profit-sharing arrangement.

(c) Partnership with Nonlawyer. A lawyer shall not form a partnership with a nonlawyer if any of the activities of the partnership consist of the practice of law.

(d) Exercise of Independent Professional Judgment. A lawyer shall not permit a person who recommends, employs, or pays the lawyer to render legal services for another to direct or regulate the lawyer's professional judgment in rendering such legal services.

(e) Nonlawyer Ownership of Authorized Business Entity. A lawyer shall not practice with or in the form of a business entity authorized to practice law for a profit if:

(1) a nonlawyer owns any interest therein, except that a fiduciary representative of the estate of a lawyer may hold the stock or interest of the lawyer for a reasonable time during administration; or

(2) a nonlawyer is a corporate director or officer thereof or occupies the position of similar responsibility in any form of association other than a corporation; or

(3) a nonlawyer has the right to direct or control the professional judgment of a lawyer.

Amended June 8, 1989 (544 So.2d 193); July 23, 1992, effective Jan. 1, 1993 (605 So.2d 252); Oct. 20, 1994 (644 So.2d 282); June 27, 1996, effective July 1, 1996 (677 So.2d 272); Oct. 6, 2005, effective Jan. 1, 2006 (916 So.2d 655); March 23, 2006, effective May 22, 2006 (933 So.2d 417).

Comment

The provisions of this rule express traditional limitations on sharing fees. These limitations are to protect the lawyer's professional independence of judgment. Where someone other than the client pays the lawyer's fee or salary, or recommends employment of the lawyer, that arrangement does not modify the lawyer's obligation to the client. As stated in subdivision (d), such arrangements should not interfere with the lawyer's professional judgment.

This rule also expresses traditional limitations on permitting a third party to direct or regulate the lawyer's professional judgment in rendering legal services to another. See also rule 4-1.8(f) (lawyer may accept compensation from a third party as long as there is no interference with the lawyer's independent professional judgment and the client gives informed consent).

The prohibition against sharing legal fees with nonlawyer employees is not intended to prohibit profit-sharing arrangements that are part of a qualified pension, profit-sharing, or retirement plan. Compensation plans, as opposed to retirement plans, may not be based on legal fees.

Rule 4-5.5. Unlicensed Practice of Law; Multijurisdictional Practice of Law

Text of rule effective until October 1, 2015. See, also, rule effective October 1, 2015.

(a) Practice of Law. A lawyer shall not practice law in a jurisdiction other than the lawyer's home state, in violation of the regulation of the legal profession in that jurisdiction, or in violation of the regulation of the legal profession in the lawyer's home state or assist another in doing so.

(b) Prohibited Conduct. A lawyer who is not admitted to practice in Florida shall not:

(1) except as authorized by other law, establish an office or other regular presence in Florida for the practice of law;

(2) hold out to the public or otherwise represent that the lawyer is admitted to practice law in Florida; or

(3) appear in court, before an administrative agency, or before any other tribunal unless authorized to do so by the court, administrative agency, or tribunal pursuant to the applicable rules of the court, administrative agency, or tribunal.

(c) Authorized Temporary Practice by Lawyer Admitted in Another United States Jurisdiction. A lawyer admitted and authorized to practice law in another United States jurisdiction who has been neither disbarred or suspended from practice in any jurisdiction, nor disciplined or held in contempt in Florida by reason of misconduct committed while engaged in the practice of law permitted pursuant to this rule, may provide legal services on a temporary basis in Florida that:

(1) are undertaken in association with a lawyer who is admitted to practice in Florida and who actively participates in the matter; or

(2) are in or reasonably related to a pending or potential proceeding before a tribunal in this or another jurisdiction, if the lawyer is authorized by law or order to appear in such proceeding or reasonably expects to be so authorized; or

(3) are in or reasonably related to a pending or potential arbitration, mediation, or other alternative dispute resolution proceeding in this or another jurisdiction and the services are not services for which the forum requires pro hac vice admission:

(A) if the services are performed for a client who resides in or has an office in the lawyer's home state, or

(B) where the services arise out of or are reasonably related to the lawyer's practice in a jurisdiction in which the lawyer is admitted to practice; or

(4) are not within subdivisions (c)(2) or (c)(3), and

(A) are performed for a client who resides in or has an office in the jurisdiction in which the lawyer is authorized to practice, or

(B) arise out of or are reasonably related to the lawyer's practice in a jurisdiction in which the lawyer is admitted to practice.

(d) Authorized Temporary Practice by Lawyer Admitted in a Non-United States Jurisdiction. A lawyer who is admitted only in a non-United States jurisdiction who is a member in good standing of a recognized legal profession in a foreign jurisdiction whose members are admitted to practice as lawyers or counselors at law or the equivalent and are subject to effective regulation and discipline by a duly constituted professional body or a public authority, and who has been neither disbarred or suspended from practice in any jurisdiction nor disciplined or held in contempt in Florida by reason of misconduct committed while engaged in the practice of law permitted pursuant to this rule does not engage in the unlicensed practice of law in Florida when on a temporary basis the lawyer performs services in Florida that:

(1) are undertaken in association with a lawyer who is admitted to practice in Florida and who actively participates in the matter; or

(2) are in or reasonably related to a pending or potential proceeding before a tribunal held or to be held in a jurisdiction outside the United States if the lawyer is authorized by law or by order of the tribunal to appear in such proceeding or reasonably expects to be so authorized; or

(3) are in or reasonably related to a pending or potential arbitration, mediation, or other alternative dispute resolution proceeding held or to be held in Florida or another jurisdiction and the services are not services for which the forum requires pro hac vice admission:

(A) if the services are performed for a client who resides in or has an office in the jurisdiction in which the lawyer is admitted to practice, or

(B) where the services arise out of or are reasonably related to the lawyer's practice in a jurisdiction in which the lawyer is admitted to practice; or

(4) are not within subdivisions (d)(2) or (d)(3), and

(A) are performed for a client who resides or has an office in a jurisdiction in which the lawyer is authorized to practice to the extent of that authorization, or

(B) arise out of or are reasonably related to a matter that has a substantial connection to a jurisdiction in which the lawyer is authorized to practice to the extent of that authorization; or

(5) are governed primarily by international law or the law of a non-United States jurisdiction in which the lawyer is a member.

Amended July 23, 1992, effective Jan. 1, 1993 (605 So.2d 252); May 12, 2005, effective January 1, 2006 (907 So.2d 1138); Sept. 11, 2008, effective Jan. 1, 2009 (991 So.2d 842); April 12, 2012, effective July 1, 2012 (101 So.3d 807).

Comment

Subdivision (a) applies to unlicensed practice of law by a lawyer, whether through the lawyer's direct action or by the lawyer assisting another person. A lawyer may practice law only in a jurisdiction in which the lawyer is authorized to practice. A lawyer may be admitted to practice law in a jurisdiction on a regular basis or may be authorized by court rule or order or by law to practice for a limited purpose or on a restricted basis. Regardless of whether the lawyer is admitted to practice law on a regular basis or is practicing as the result of an authorization granted by court rule or order or by the law, the lawyer must comply with the standards of ethical and professional conduct set forth in these Rules Regulating the Florida Bar.

The definition of the practice of law is established by law and varies from one jurisdiction to another. Whatever the definition, limiting the practice of law to members of the bar protects the public against rendition of legal services by unqualified persons. This rule does not prohibit a lawyer from employing the services of paraprofessionals and delegating functions to them, so long as the lawyer supervises the delegated work and retains responsibility for their work. See rule 4-5.3. Likewise, it does not prohibit lawyers from providing professional advice and instruction to nonlawyers whose employment requires knowledge of law; for example, claims adjusters, employees of financial or commercial institutions, social workers, accountants, and persons employed in government agencies. In addition, a lawyer may counsel nonlawyers who wish to proceed pro se.

Other than as authorized by law, a lawyer who is not admitted to practice in Florida violates subdivision (b) if the lawyer establishes an office or other regular presence in Florida for the practice of law. Presence may be regular even if the lawyer is not physically present here. Such a lawyer must not hold out to the public or otherwise represent that the lawyer is admitted to practice law in Florida.

Subdivision (b) also prohibits a lawyer who is not admitted to practice in Florida from appearing in a Florida court, before an administrative agency, or before any other tribunal in Florida unless the lawyer has been granted permission to do so. In order to be granted the permission, the lawyer must follow the applicable rules of the court, agency, or tribunal including, without limitation, the Florida Rules of Judicial Administration governing appearance by foreign attorneys.

There are occasions in which a lawyer admitted and authorized to practice in another United States jurisdiction or in a non-United States jurisdiction may provide legal services on a temporary basis in Florida under circumstances that do not create an unreasonable risk to the interests of his or her clients, the public, or the courts. Subdivisions (c) and (d) identify such circumstances. This rule does not authorize a lawyer to establish an office or other regular presence in Florida without being admitted to practice generally here. Furthermore, no lawyer is authorized to provide legal services pursuant to this rule if the lawyer is disbarred or suspended from practice in any jurisdiction or has been disciplined or held in contempt in Florida by reason of misconduct committed while engaged in the practice of law permitted pursuant to this rule. The contempt must be final and not reversed or abated.

There is no single test to determine whether a lawyer's services are provided on a "temporary basis" in Florida and may therefore be permissible under subdivision (c). Services may be "temporary" even though the lawyer provides services in Florida on a recurring basis or for an extended period of time, as when the lawyer is representing a client in a single lengthy negotiation or litigation.

Subdivision (c) applies to lawyers who are admitted to practice law in any United States jurisdiction, which includes the District of Columbia and any state, territory, or commonwealth of the United States. The word "admitted" in subdivision (c) contemplates that the lawyer is authorized to practice in the jurisdiction in which the lawyer is admitted and excludes a lawyer who while technically admitted is not authorized to practice because, for example, the lawyer is on inactive status. Subdivision (d) applies to lawyers who are admitted to practice law in a non-United States jurisdiction if the lawyer is a member in good standing of a recognized legal profession in a foreign jurisdiction, the members of which are admitted to practice as lawyers or counselors at law or the equivalent and subject to effective regulation and discipline by a duly constituted professional body or a public authority. Due to the similarities between the subsections, they will be discussed together. Differences will be noted.

Subdivisions (c)(1) and (d)(1) recognize that the interests of clients and the public are protected if a lawyer admitted only in another jurisdiction associates with a lawyer licensed to practice in Florida. For these subdivisions to apply, the lawyer admitted to practice in Florida could not serve merely as a conduit for the out-of-state lawyer, but would have to share actual responsibility for the representation and actively participate in the representation. To the extent that a court rule or other law of Florida requires a lawyer who is not admitted to practice in Florida to obtain admission pro hac vice prior to appearing in court or before a tribunal or to obtain admission pursuant to applicable rule(s) prior to appearing before an administrative agency, this rule requires the lawyer to obtain that authority.

Lawyers not admitted to practice generally in Florida may be authorized by law or order of a tribunal or an administrative agency to appear before the tribunal or agency. This authority may be granted pursuant to formal rules governing admission pro hac vice or pursuant to formal rules of the agency. Under subdivision (c)(2), a lawyer does not violate this rule when the lawyer appears before a tribunal or agency pursuant to such authority. As with subdivisions (c)(1) and (d)(1), to the extent that a court rule or other law of Florida requires a lawyer who is not admitted to practice in Florida to obtain admission pro hac vice prior to appearing in court or before a tribunal or to obtain admission pursuant to applicable rule(s) prior to appearing before an administrative agency, this rule requires the lawyer to obtain that authority.

Subdivision (c)(2) also provides that a lawyer rendering services in Florida on a temporary basis does not violate this rule when the lawyer engages in conduct in anticipation of a proceeding or hearing in a jurisdiction in which the lawyer is authorized to practice law or in which the lawyer reasonably expects to be admitted pro hac vice. Examples of such conduct include meetings with the client, interviews of potential witnesses, and the review of documents. Similarly, a lawyer admitted only in another jurisdiction may engage in conduct temporarily in Florida in connection with pending litigation in another jurisdiction in which the lawyer is or reasonably expects to be authorized to appear, including taking depositions in Florida.

Subdivision (d)(2) is similar to subdivision (c)(2), however, the authorization in (d)(2) only applies to pending or potential proceedings before a tribunal to be held outside of the United States.

Subdivisions (c)(3) and (d)(3) permit a lawyer admitted to practice law in another jurisdiction to perform services on a temporary basis in Florida if those services are in or reasonably related to a pending or potential arbitration, mediation, or other alternative dispute resolution proceeding in this or another jurisdiction, if the services are performed for a client who resides in or has an office in the lawyer's home state, or if the services arise out of or are reasonably related to the lawyer's practice in a jurisdiction in which the lawyer is admitted to practice. The lawyer, however, must obtain admission pro hac vice in the case of a court-annexed arbitration or mediation if court rules or law so require. The lawyer must file a verified statement with The Florida Bar in arbitration proceedings as required by rule 1–3.11 unless the lawyer is appearing in an international arbitration as defined in the comment to that rule. A verified statement is not required if the lawyer first obtained the court's permission to appear pro hac vice and the court has retained jurisdiction over the matter. For the purposes of this rule, a lawyer who is not admitted to practice law in Florida who files more than 3 demands for arbitration or responses to arbitration in separate arbitration proceedings in a 365–day period shall be presumed to be providing legal services on a regular, not temporary, basis; however, this presumption shall not apply to a lawyer appearing in international arbitrations as defined in the comment to rule 1–3.11.

Subdivision (c)(4) permits a lawyer admitted in another jurisdiction to provide certain legal services on a temporary basis in Florida that are performed for a client who resides or has an office in the jurisdiction in which the lawyer is authorized to practice or arise out of or are reasonably related to the lawyer's practice in a jurisdiction in which the lawyer is admitted but are not within subdivisions (c)(2) or (c)(3). These services include both legal services and services that nonlawyers may perform but that are considered the practice of law when performed by lawyers. When performing services which may be performed by nonlawyers, the lawyer remains subject to the Rules of Professional Conduct.

Subdivisions (c)(3), (d)(3), and (c)(4) require that the services arise out of or be reasonably related to the lawyer's practice in a jurisdiction in which the lawyer is admitted. A variety of factors evidence such a relationship. The lawyer's client may have been previously represented by the lawyer, or may be resident in or have substantial contacts with the jurisdiction in which the lawyer is admitted. The matter, although involving other jurisdictions, may have a significant connection with that jurisdiction. In other cases, significant aspects of the lawyer's work might be conducted in that jurisdiction or a significant aspect of the matter may involve the law of that jurisdiction. The necessary relationship might arise when the client's activities or the legal issues involve multiple jurisdictions, such as when the officers of a multinational corporation survey potential business sites and seek the services of their lawyer in assessing the relative merits of each. In addition, the services may draw on the lawyer's recognized expertise developed through regular practice of law in a body of law that is applicable to the client's particular matter.

Subdivision (d)(4) permits a lawyer admitted in a non-United States jurisdiction to provide certain services on a temporary basis in Florida that are performed for a client who resides in or has an office in the jurisdiction where the lawyer is authorized to practice or arise out of or are reasonably related to a matter that has a substantial connection to a jurisdiction in which the lawyer is authorized to practice to the extent of that authorization but are not within subdivisions (d)(2) and (d)(3). The scope of the work the lawyer could perform under this provision would be limited to the services the lawyer may perform in the authorizing jurisdiction. For example, if a German lawyer came to the United States to negotiate on behalf of a client in Germany, the lawyer would be authorized to provide only those services that the lawyer is authorized to provide for that client in Germany. Subdivision (d)(5) permits a lawyer admitted in a non-United States jurisdiction to provide services in Florida that are governed primarily by international law or the law of a non-United States jurisdiction in which the lawyer is a member.

A lawyer who practices law in Florida pursuant to subdivisions (c), (d), or otherwise is subject to the disciplinary authority of Florida. A lawyer who practices law in Florida pursuant to subdivision (c) must inform the client that the lawyer is not licensed to practice law in Florida.

The Supreme Court of Florida has determined that it constitutes the unlicensed practice of law for a lawyer admitted to practice law in a jurisdiction other than Florida to advertise to provide legal services in Florida which the lawyer is not authorized to provide. The rule was adopted in 820 So. 2d 210 (Fla. 2002). The court first stated the proposition in 762 So. 2d 392, 394 (Fla. 1999). Subdivisions (c) and (d) do not authorize advertising legal services to prospective clients in Florida by lawyers who are admitted to practice in jurisdictions other than Florida. Whether and how lawyers may communicate the availability of their services to prospective clients in Florida is governed by rules 4–7.1 through 4–7.10.

A lawyer who practices law in Florida is subject to the disciplinary authority of Florida.

Rule 4–5.5. Unlicensed Practice of Law; Multijurisdictional Practice of Law

Text of rule effective October 1, 2015. See, also, rule effective until October 1, 2015.

(a) Practice of Law. A lawyer may not practice law in a jurisdiction other than the lawyer's home state, in violation of the regulation of the legal profession in that jurisdiction, or in violation of the regulation of the legal profession in the lawyer's home state or assist another in doing so.

(b) Prohibited Conduct. A lawyer who is not admitted to practice in Florida may not:

(1) except as authorized by other law, establish an office or other regular presence in Florida for the practice of law;

(2) hold out to the public or otherwise represent that the lawyer is admitted to practice law in Florida; or

(3) appear in court, before an administrative agency, or before any other tribunal unless authorized to do so by the court, administrative agency, or tribunal pursuant to the applicable rules of the court, administrative agency, or tribunal.

(c) Authorized Temporary Practice by Lawyer Admitted in Another United States Jurisdiction. A lawyer admitted and authorized to practice law in another United States jurisdiction who has been neither disbarred or suspended from practice in any jurisdiction, nor disciplined or held in contempt in Florida by reason of misconduct committed while engaged in the practice of law permitted pursuant to this rule, may provide legal services on a temporary basis in Florida that are:

(1) undertaken in association with a lawyer who is admitted to practice in Florida and who actively participates in the matter; or

(2) in or reasonably related to a pending or potential proceeding before a tribunal in this or another jurisdiction, if the lawyer is authorized by law or order to appear in the proceeding or reasonably expects to be so authorized; or

(3) in or reasonably related to a pending or potential arbitration, mediation, or other alternative dispute resolution proceeding in this or another jurisdiction, and the services are not services for which the forum requires pro hac vice admission:

(A) if the services are performed for a client who resides in or has an office in the lawyer's home state, or

(B) where the services arise out of or are reasonably related to the lawyer's practice in a jurisdiction in which the lawyer is admitted to practice; or

(4) not within subdivisions (c)(2) or (c)(3), and

(A) are performed for a client who resides in or has an office in the jurisdiction in which the lawyer is authorized to practice, or

(B) arise out of or are reasonably related to the lawyer's practice in a jurisdiction in which the lawyer is admitted to practice.

(d) Authorized Temporary Practice by Lawyer Admitted in a Non–United States Jurisdiction. A lawyer who is admitted only in a non-United States jurisdiction who is a member in good standing of a recognized legal profession in a foreign jurisdiction whose members are admitted to practice as lawyers or counselors at law or the equivalent and are subject to effective regulation and discipline by a duly constituted professional body or a public authority, and who has been neither disbarred or suspended from practice in any jurisdiction nor disciplined or held in contempt in Florida by reason of misconduct committed while engaged in the practice of law permitted pursuant to this rule does not engage in the unlicensed practice of law in Florida when on a temporary basis the lawyer performs services in Florida that are:

(1) undertaken in association with a lawyer who is admitted to practice in Florida and who actively participates in the matter; or

(2) in or reasonably related to a pending or potential proceeding before a tribunal held or to be held in a jurisdiction outside the United States if the lawyer is authorized by law or by order of the tribunal to appear in the proceeding or reasonably expects to be so authorized; or

(3) in or reasonably related to a pending or potential arbitration, mediation, or other alternative dispute resolution proceeding held or to be held in Florida or another jurisdiction and the services are not services for which the forum requires pro hac vice admission:

(A) if the services are performed for a client who resides in or has an office in the jurisdiction in which the lawyer is admitted to practice, or

(B) where the services arise out of or are reasonably related to the lawyer's practice in a jurisdiction in which the lawyer is admitted to practice; or

(4) not within subdivisions (d)(2) or (d)(3), and

(A) are performed for a client who resides or has an office in a jurisdiction in which the lawyer is authorized to practice to the extent of that authorization, or

(B) arise out of or are reasonably related to a matter that has a substantial connection to a jurisdiction in which the lawyer is authorized to practice to the extent of that authorization; or

(5) governed primarily by international law or the law of a non-United States jurisdiction in which the lawyer is a member.

Amended July 23, 1992, effective Jan. 1, 1993 (605 So.2d 252); May 12, 2005, effective January 1, 2006 (907 So.2d 1138); Sept. 11, 2008, effective Jan. 1, 2009 (991 So.2d 842); April 12, 2012, effective July 1, 2012 (101 So.3d 807); May 21, 2015, effective Oct. 1, 2015 (164 So.3d 1217).

Comment

Subdivision (a) applies to unlicensed practice of law by a lawyer, whether through the lawyer's direct action or by the lawyer assisting another person. A lawyer may practice law only in a jurisdiction in which the lawyer is authorized to practice. A lawyer may be admitted to practice law in a jurisdiction on a regular basis or may be authorized by court rule or order or by law to practice for a limited purpose or on a restricted basis. Regardless of whether the lawyer is admitted to practice law on a regular basis or is practicing as the result of an authorization granted by court rule or order or by the law, the lawyer must comply with the standards of ethical and professional conduct set forth in these Rules Regulating the Florida Bar.

The definition of the practice of law is established by law and varies from one jurisdiction to another. Whatever the definition, limiting the practice of law to members of the bar protects the public against rendition of legal services by unqualified persons. This rule does not prohibit a lawyer from employing the services of paraprofessionals and delegating functions to them, so long as the lawyer supervises the delegated work and retains responsibility for their work. See rule 4–5.3. Likewise, it does not prohibit lawyers from providing professional advice and instruction to nonlawyers whose employment requires knowledge of law; for example, claims adjusters, employees of financial or commercial institutions, social workers, accountants, and persons employed in government agencies. In addition, a lawyer may counsel nonlawyers who wish to proceed pro se.

Other than as authorized by law, a lawyer who is not admitted to practice in Florida violates subdivision (b) if the lawyer establishes an office or other regular presence in Florida for the practice of law. This prohibition includes establishing an office or other regular presence in Florida for the practice of the law of the state where the lawyer is admitted to practice. For example, a lawyer licensed to practice law in New York could not establish an office or regular presence in Florida to practice New York law. Such activity would constitute the unlicensed practice of law. However, for purposes of this rule, a lawyer licensed in another jurisdiction who is in Florida for vacation or for a limited period of time, may provide services to their clients in the jurisdiction where admitted as this does not constitute a regular presence. The lawyer must not hold out to the public or otherwise represent that the lawyer is admitted to practice law in Florida. Presence may be regular even if the lawyer is not physically present here.

Subdivision (b) also prohibits a lawyer who is not admitted to practice in Florida from appearing in a Florida court, before an administrative agency, or before any other tribunal in Florida unless the lawyer has been granted permission to do so. In order to be granted the permission, the lawyer must follow the applicable rules of the court, agency, or tribunal including, without limitation, the Florida Rules of Judicial Administration governing appearance by foreign lawyers. While admission by the Florida court or administrative agency for the particular case authorizes the lawyer's appearance in the matter, it does not act as authorization to allow the establishment of an office in Florida for the practice of law. Therefore, a lawyer licensed in another jurisdiction admitted in a case in Florida may not establish an office in Florida while the case is pending and the lawyer is working on the case.

There are occasions in which a lawyer admitted and authorized to practice in another United States jurisdiction or in a non-United States jurisdiction may provide legal services on a temporary basis in Florida under circumstances that do not create an unreasonable risk to the interests of his or her clients, the public, or the courts. Subdivisions (c) and (d) identify these circumstances. As discussed with regard to subdivision (b) above, this rule does not authorize a lawyer to establish an office or other regular presence in Florida without being admitted to practice generally here. Furthermore, no lawyer is authorized to provide legal services pursuant to this rule if the lawyer is disbarred or suspended from practice in any jurisdiction or has been disciplined or held in contempt in Florida by reason of misconduct committed while engaged in the practice of law permitted pursuant to this rule. The contempt must be final and not reversed or abated.

There is no single test to determine whether a lawyer's services are provided on a "temporary basis" in Florida and may therefore be permissible under subdivision (c). Services may be "temporary" even though the lawyer provides services in Florida on a recurring basis or for an extended period of time, as when the lawyer is representing a client in a single lengthy negotiation or litigation.

Subdivision (c) applies to lawyers who are admitted to practice law in any United States jurisdiction, which includes the District of Columbia and any state, territory, or commonwealth of the United States. The word "admitted" in subdivision (c) contemplates that the lawyer is authorized to practice in the jurisdiction in which the lawyer is admitted and excludes a lawyer who while technically admitted is not authorized to practice because, for example, the lawyer is on inactive status. Subdivision (d) applies to lawyers who are admitted to practice law in a non-United States jurisdiction if the lawyer is a member in good standing of a recognized legal profession in a foreign jurisdiction, the members of which are admitted to practice as lawyers or counselors at law or the equivalent and subject to effective regulation and discipline by a duly constituted professional body or a public authority. Due to the similarities between the subsections, they will be discussed together. Differences will be noted.

Subdivisions (c)(1) and (d)(1) recognize that the interests of clients and the public are protected if a lawyer admitted only in another jurisdiction associates with a lawyer licensed to practice in Florida. For these subdivisions to apply, the lawyer admitted to practice in Florida could not serve merely as a conduit for the out-of-state lawyer, but would have to share actual responsibility for the representation and actively participate in the representation. To the extent that a court rule or other law of Florida requires a lawyer who is not admitted to practice in Florida to obtain admission pro hac vice prior to appearing in court or before a tribunal or to obtain admission pursuant to applicable rule(s) prior to appearing before an administrative agency, this rule requires the lawyer to obtain that authority.

Lawyers not admitted to practice generally in Florida may be authorized by law or order of a tribunal or an administrative agency to appear before the tribunal or agency. This authority may be granted pursuant to formal rules governing admission pro hac vice or pursuant to formal rules of the agency. Under subdivision (c)(2), a lawyer does not violate this rule when the lawyer appears before a tribunal or agency pursuant to this authority. As with subdivisions (c)(1) and (d)(1), to the extent that a court rule or other law of Florida requires a lawyer who is not admitted to practice in Florida to obtain admission pro hac vice prior to appearing in court or before a tribunal or to obtain admission pursuant to applicable rule(s) prior to appearing before an administrative agency, this rule requires the lawyer to obtain that authority.

Subdivision (c)(2) also provides that a lawyer rendering services in Florida on a temporary basis does not violate this rule when the lawyer engages in conduct in anticipation of a proceeding or hearing in a jurisdiction in which the lawyer is authorized to practice law or in which the lawyer reasonably expects to be admitted pro hac vice. Examples of this conduct include meetings with the client, interviews of potential witnesses, and the review of documents. Similarly, a lawyer admitted only in another jurisdiction may engage in conduct temporarily in Florida in connection with pending litigation in another jurisdiction in which the lawyer is or reasonably expects to be authorized to appear, including taking depositions in Florida.

Subdivision (d)(2) is similar to subdivision (c)(2), however, the authorization in (d)(2) only applies to pending or potential proceedings before a tribunal to be held outside of the United States.

Subdivisions (c)(3) and (d)(3) permit a lawyer admitted to practice law in another jurisdiction to perform services on a temporary basis in Florida if those services are in or reasonably related to a pending or potential arbitration, mediation, or other alternative dispute resolution proceeding in this or another jurisdiction, if the services are performed for a client who resides in or has an office in the lawyer's home state, or if the services arise out of or are reasonably related to the lawyer's practice in a jurisdiction in which the lawyer is admitted to practice. The lawyer, however, must obtain admission pro hac vice in the case of a court-annexed arbitration or mediation if court rules or law so require. The lawyer must file a verified statement with The Florida Bar in arbitration proceedings as required by rule 1–3.11 unless the lawyer is appearing in an international arbitration as defined in the comment to that rule. A verified statement is not required if the lawyer first obtained the court's permission to appear pro hac vice and the court has retained jurisdiction over the matter. For the purposes of this rule, a lawyer who is not admitted to practice law in Florida who files more than 3 demands for arbitration or responses to arbitration in separate arbitration proceedings in a 365–day period is presumed to be providing legal services on a regular, not temporary, basis; however, this presumption does not apply to a lawyer appearing in international arbitrations as defined in the comment to rule 1–3.11.

Subdivision (c)(4) permits a lawyer admitted in another jurisdiction to provide certain legal services on a temporary basis in Florida that are performed for a client who resides or has an office in the jurisdiction in which the lawyer is authorized to practice or arise out of or are reasonably related to the lawyer's practice in a jurisdiction in which the lawyer is admitted but are not within subdivisions (c)(2) or (c)(3). These services include both legal services and services that nonlawyers may perform but that are considered the practice of law when performed by lawyers. When performing services which may be performed by nonlawyers, the lawyer remains subject to the Rules of Professional Conduct.

Subdivisions (c)(3), (d)(3), and (c)(4) require that the services arise out of or be reasonably related to the lawyer's practice in a jurisdiction in which the lawyer is admitted. A variety of factors evidence this relationship. The lawyer's client may have been previously represented by the lawyer, or may be resident in or have substantial contacts with the jurisdiction in which the lawyer is admitted. The matter, although involving other jurisdictions, may have a significant connection with that jurisdiction. In other cases, significant aspects of the lawyer's work might be conducted in that jurisdiction or a significant aspect of the matter may involve the law of that jurisdiction. The necessary relationship might arise when the client's activities or the legal issues involve multiple jurisdictions, for example, when the officers of a multinational corporation survey potential business sites and seek the services of their lawyer in assessing the relative merits of each. In addition, the services may draw on the lawyer's recognized expertise developed through regular practice of law in a body of law that is applicable to the client's particular matter.

Subdivision (d)(4) permits a lawyer admitted in a non-United States jurisdiction to provide certain services on a temporary basis in Florida that are performed for a client who resides in or has an office in the jurisdiction where the lawyer is authorized to practice or arise out of or are reasonably related to a matter that has a substantial connection to a jurisdiction in which the lawyer is authorized to practice to the extent of that authorization but are not within subdivisions (d)(2) and (d)(3). The scope of the work the lawyer could perform under this provision would be limited to the services the lawyer may perform in the authorizing jurisdiction. For example, if a German lawyer came to the United States to negotiate on behalf of a client in Germany, the lawyer would be authorized to provide only those services that the lawyer is authorized to provide for that client in Germany. Subdivision (d)(5) permits a lawyer admitted in a non-United States jurisdiction to provide services in Florida that are governed primarily by international law or the law of a non-United States jurisdiction in which the lawyer is a member.

A lawyer who practices law in Florida pursuant to subdivisions (c), (d), or otherwise is subject to the disciplinary authority of Florida. A lawyer who practices law in Florida pursuant to subdivision (c) must inform the client that the lawyer is not licensed to practice law in Florida.

The Supreme Court of Florida has determined that it constitutes the unlicensed practice of law for a lawyer admitted to practice law in a jurisdiction other than Florida to advertise to provide legal services in Florida which the lawyer is not authorized to provide. The rule was adopted in 820 So. 2d 210 (Fla. 2002). The court first stated the proposition in 762 So. 2d 392, 394 (Fla. 1999). Subdivisions (c) and (d) do not authorize advertising legal services in Florida by lawyers who are admitted to practice in jurisdictions other than Florida. Whether and how lawyers may communicate the availability of their services in Florida is governed by subchapter 4-7.

A lawyer who practices law in Florida is subject to the disciplinary authority of Florida.

Rule 4-5.6. Restrictions on Right to Practice

A lawyer shall not participate in offering or making:

(a) a partnership, shareholders, operating, employment, or other similar type of agreement that restricts the rights of a lawyer to practice after termination of the relationship, except an agreement concerning benefits upon retirement; or

(b) an agreement in which a restriction on the lawyer's right to practice is part of the settlement of a client controversy.

Amended July 23, 1992, effective Jan. 1, 1993 (605 So.2d 252); July 17, 1997 (697 So.2d 115); March 23, 2006, effective May 22, 2006 (933 So.2d 417).

Comment

An agreement restricting the right of lawyers to practice after leaving a firm not only limits their professional autonomy, but also limits the freedom of clients to choose a lawyer. Subdivision (a) prohibits such agreements except for restrictions incident to provisions concerning retirement benefits for service with the firm.

Subdivision (b) prohibits a lawyer from agreeing not to represent other persons in connection with settling a claim on behalf of a client.

This rule does not apply to prohibit restrictions that may be included in the terms of the sale of a law practice in accordance with the provisions of rule 4-1.17.

This rule is not a per se prohibition against severance agreements between lawyers and law firms. Severance agreements containing reasonable and fair compensation provisions designed to avoid disputes requiring time-consuming quantum merit analysis are not prohibited by this rule. Severance agreements, on the other hand, that contain punitive clauses, the effect of which are to restrict competition or encroach upon a client's inherent right to select counsel, are prohibited. The percentage limitations found in rule 4-1.5(f)(4)(D) do not apply to fees divided pursuant to a severance agreement. No severance agreement shall contain a fee-splitting arrangement that results in a fee prohibited by the Rules Regulating The Florida Bar.

Rule 4-5.7. Responsibilities regarding nonlegal services

(a) Services Not Distinct From Legal Services. A lawyer who provides nonlegal services to a recipient that are not distinct from legal services provided to that recipient is subject to the Rules Regulating The Florida Bar with respect to the provision of both legal and nonlegal services.

(b) Services Distinct From Legal Services. A lawyer who provides nonlegal services to a recipient that are distinct from any legal services provided to the recipient is subject to the Rules Regulating The Florida Bar with respect to the nonlegal services if the lawyer knows or reasonably should know that the recipient might believe that the recipient is receiving the protection of a client-lawyer relationship.

(c) Services by Nonlegal Entity. A lawyer who is an owner, controlling party, employee, agent, or otherwise is affiliated with an entity providing nonlegal services to a recipient is subject to the Rules Regulating The Florida Bar with respect to the nonlegal services if the lawyer knows or reasonably should know that the recipient might believe that the recipient is receiving the protection of a client-lawyer relationship.

(d) Effect of Disclosure of Nature of Service. Subdivision (b) or (c) does not apply if the lawyer makes reasonable efforts to avoid any misunderstanding by the recipient receiving nonlegal services. Those efforts must include advising the recipient, preferably in writing, that the services are not legal services and that the protection of a client-lawyer relationship does not exist with respect to the provision of nonlegal services to the recipient.

Added April 25, 2002 (820 So.2d 210).

Comment

For many years, lawyers have provided to their clients nonlegal services that are ancillary to the practice of law. A broad range of economic and other interests of clients may be served by lawyers participating in the delivery of these services. In recent years, however, there has been significant debate about the role the rules of professional conduct should play in regulating the degree and manner in which a lawyer participates in the delivery of nonlegal services. The ABA, for example, adopted, repealed, and then adopted a different version of ABA Model Rule 5.7. In the course of this debate, several ABA sections offered competing versions of ABA Model Rule 5.7.

One approach to the issue of nonlegal services is to try to substantively limit the type of nonlegal services a lawyer may provide to a recipient or the manner in which the services are provided. A competing approach does not try to substantively limit the lawyer's provision of nonlegal services, but instead attempts to clarify the conduct to which the Rules Regulating The Florida Bar apply and to avoid misunderstanding on the part of the recipient of the nonlegal services. This rule adopts the latter approach.

The potential for misunderstanding

Whenever a lawyer directly provides nonlegal services, there exists the potential for ethical problems. Principal among these is the possibility that the person for whom the nonlegal services are performed may fail to understand that the services may not carry with them the protection normally afforded by the client-lawyer relationship. The recipient of the nonlegal services may expect, for example, that the protection of client confidences, prohibitions against representation of persons with conflicting interests, and obligations of a lawyer to maintain professional independence apply to the provision of nonlegal services when that may not be the case. The risk of confusion is acute especially when the lawyer renders both types of services with respect to the same matter.

Providing nonlegal services that are not distinct from legal services

Under some circumstances, the legal and nonlegal services may be so closely entwined that they cannot be distinguished from each other. In this situation, confusion by the recipient as to when the protection of the client-lawyer relationship applies is likely to be unavoidable. Therefore, this rule requires that the lawyer providing the nonlegal services adhere to all of the requirements of the Rules Regulating The Florida Bar.

In such a case, a lawyer will be responsible for assuring that both the lawyer's conduct and, to the extent required elsewhere in these Rules Regulating The Florida Bar, that of nonlawyer employees comply in all respects with the Rules Regulating The Florida Bar. When a lawyer is obliged to accord the recipients of such nonlegal services the protection of those rules that apply to the client-lawyer relationship, the lawyer must take special care to heed the proscriptions of the Rules Regulating The Florida Bar addressing conflict of interest and to scrupulously adhere to the requirements of the rule relating to disclosure of confidential information. The promotion of the nonlegal services must also in all respects comply with the Rules Regulating The Florida Bar dealing with advertising and solicitation.

Subdivision (a) of this rule applies to the provision of nonlegal services by a lawyer even when the lawyer does not personally provide any legal services to the person for whom the nonlegal services are performed if the person is also receiving legal services from another lawyer that are not distinct from the nonlegal services.

Avoiding misunderstanding when a lawyer directly provides nonlegal services that are distinct from legal services

Even when the lawyer believes that his or her provision of nonlegal services is distinct from any legal services provided to the recipient, there is still a risk that the recipient of the nonlegal services will misunderstand the implications of receiving nonlegal services from a lawyer; the recipient might believe that the recipient is receiving the protection of a client-lawyer relationship. Where there is such a risk of misunderstanding, this rule requires that the lawyer providing the nonlegal services adhere to all the Rules Regulating The Florida Bar, unless exempted by other provisions of this rule.

Avoiding misunderstanding when a lawyer is indirectly involved in the provision of nonlegal services

Nonlegal services also may be provided through an entity with which a lawyer is somehow affiliated, for example, as owner, employee, controlling party, or agent. In this situation, there is still a risk that the recipient of the nonlegal services might believe that the recipient is receiving the protection of a client-lawyer relationship. Where there is such a risk of misunderstanding, this rule requires that the lawyer involved with the entity providing nonlegal services adhere to all the Rules Regulating The Florida Bar, unless exempted by another provision of this rule.

Avoiding the application of subdivisions (b) and (c)

Subdivisions (b) and (c) specify that the Rules Regulating The Florida Bar apply to a lawyer who directly provides or is otherwise involved in the provision of nonlegal services if there is a risk that the recipient might believe that the recipient is receiving the protection of a client- lawyer relationship. Neither the Rules Regulating The Florida Bar nor subdivisions (b) or (c) will apply, however, if pursuant to subdivision (d), the lawyer takes reasonable efforts to avoid any misunderstanding by the recipient. In this respect, this rule is analogous to the rule regarding respect for rights of third persons.

In taking the reasonable measures referred to in subdivision (d), the lawyer must communicate to the person receiving the nonlegal services that the relationship will not be a client-lawyer relationship. The communication should be made before entering into an agreement for the provision of nonlegal services, in a manner sufficient to assure that the person understands the significance of the communication, and preferably should be in writing.

The burden is upon the lawyer to show that the lawyer has taken reasonable measures under the circumstances to communicate the desired understanding. For instance, a sophisticated user of nonlegal services, such as a publicly held corporation, may require a lesser explanation than someone unaccustomed to making distinctions between legal services and nonlegal services, such as an individual seeking tax advice from a lawyer-accountant or investigative services in connection with a lawsuit.

The relationship between this rule and other Rules Regulating The Florida Bar

Even before this rule was adopted, a lawyer involved in the provision of nonlegal services was subject to those Rules Regulating The Florida Bar that apply generally. For example, another provision of the Rules Regulating The Florida Bar makes a lawyer responsible for fraud committed with respect to the provision of nonlegal services. Such a lawyer must also comply with the rule regulating business transactions with a client. Nothing in this rule (Responsibilities Regarding Nonlegal Services) is intended to suspend the effect of any otherwise applicable Rules Regulating The Florida Bar, such as the rules on personal conflicts of interest, on business transactions with clients, and engaging in conduct involving dishonesty, fraud, deceit, or misrepresentation.

In addition to the Rules Regulating The Florida Bar, principles of law external to the rules, for example, the law of principal and agent, may govern the legal duties owed by a lawyer to those receiving the nonlegal services.

Rule 4–5.8. Procedures for Lawyers Leaving Law Firms and Dissolution of Law Firms

(a) Contractual Relationship Between Law Firm and Clients. The contract for legal services creates the legal relationships between the client and law firm and between the client and individual members of the law firm, including the ownership of the files maintained by the lawyer or law firm. Nothing in these rules creates or defines those relationships.

(b) Client's Right to Counsel of Choice. Clients have the right to expect that they may choose counsel when legal services are required and, with few exceptions, nothing that lawyers and law firms do shall have any effect on the exercise of that right.

(c) Contact With Clients.

(1) *Lawyers Leaving Law Firms.* Absent a specific agreement otherwise, a lawyer who is leaving a law firm shall not unilaterally contact those clients of the law firm for purposes of notifying them about the anticipated departure or to solicit representation of the clients unless the lawyer has approached an authorized representative of the law firm and attempted to negotiate a joint communication to the clients concerning the lawyer leaving the law firm and bona fide negotiations have been unsuccessful.

(2) *Dissolution of Law Firm.* Absent a specific agreement otherwise, a lawyer involved in the dissolution of a law firm shall not unilaterally contact clients of the law firm unless, after bona fide negotiations, authorized members of the law firm have been unable to agree on a method to provide notice to clients.

(d) Form for Contact With Clients.

(1) *Lawyers Leaving Law Firms.* When a joint response has not been successfully negotiated, unilateral contact by individual members or the law firm shall give notice to clients that the lawyer is leaving the law firm and provide options to the clients to choose to remain a client of the law firm, to choose representation by the departing lawyer, or to choose representation by other lawyers or law firms.

(2) *Dissolution of Law Firms.* When a law firm is being dissolved and no procedure for contacting clients has been agreed upon, unilateral contact by members of the law firm shall give notice to clients that the firm is being dissolved and provide options to the clients to choose representation by any member of the dissolving law firm, or representation by other lawyers or law firms.

(3) *Liability for Fees and Costs.* In all instances, notice to the client required under this rule shall provide information concerning potential liability for fees for legal services previously rendered, costs expended, and how any deposits for fees or costs will be handled. In addition, if appropriate, notice shall be given that reasonable charges may be imposed to provide a copy of any file to a successor lawyer.

(e) Nonresponsive Clients.

(1) *Lawyers Leaving Law Firms.* In the event a client fails to advise the lawyers and law firm of the client's intention in regard to who is to provide future legal services when a lawyer is leaving the firm, the client shall be considered as remaining a client of the firm until the client advises otherwise.

(2) *Dissolution of Law Firms.* In the event a client fails to advise the lawyers of the client's intention in regard to who is to provide future legal services when a law firm is dissolving, the client shall be considered as remaining a client of the lawyer who primarily provided the prior legal services on behalf of the firm until the client advises otherwise.

Added Oct. 6, 2005, effective Jan. 1, 2006 (916 So.2d 655).

Comment

The current rule of law regarding ownership of client files is discussed in *Donahue v. Vaughn*, 721 So. 2d 356 (Fla. 5th DCA 1998), and *Dowda & Fields, P.A. v. Cobb*, 452 So. 2d 1140 (Fla. 5th DCA 1984). A lawyer leaving a law firm, when the law firm remains available to continue legal representation, has no right nor expectation to take client files without an agreement with the law firm to do so.

While clients have the right to choose counsel, such choice may implicate obligations. Those obligations may include a requirement to pay for legal services previously rendered and costs expended in connection with the representation as well as a reasonable fee for copying the client's file.

Whether individual members have any individual legal obligations to a client is a matter of contract law, tort law, or court rules that is outside the scope of rules governing lawyer conduct. Generally, individual lawyers have such obligations only if provided for in the contract for representation. Nothing in this rule or in the contract for representation may alter the ethical obligations that individual lawyers have to clients as provided elsewhere in these rules.

It is anticipated that in most instances a lawyer leaving a law firm and the law firm will engage in bona fide, good faith negotiations and craft a joint communication providing adequate information to the client so that the client may make a fully informed decision concerning future representation.

In those instances in which bona fide negotiations are unsuccessful, unilateral communication may be made by the departing lawyer or the law firm. In such circumstances, great care should be taken to meet the obligation of adequate communication and for this reason the specific requirements of subdivisions (d)(1) & (3) are provided.

Most law firms have some written instrument creating the law firm and specifying procedures to be employed upon dissolution of the firm. However, when such an instrument does not exist or does not adequately provide for procedures in the event of dissolution, the provisions of this rule are provided so that dissolution of the law firm does not disproportionately affect client rights.

As in instances of a lawyer departing a law firm, lawyers involved in the dissolution of law firms have a continuing obligation to provide adequate information to a client so that the client may make informed decisions concerning future representation.

The Florida Bar's Law Office Management Advisory Service has sample forms for notice to clients and sample partnership and other contracts that are available to members. The forms may be accessed on the bar's website, *www.flabar.org*, or by calling The Florida Bar headquarters in Tallahassee.

Lawyers involved in either a change in law firm composition or law firm dissolution may have duties to notify the court if the representation is in litigation. If the remaining law firm will continue the representation of the client, no notification of the change in firm composition to the court may be required, but such a notification may be advisable. If the departing lawyer will take over representation of the client, a motion for substitution of counsel or a motion by the firm to withdraw from the representation may be appropriate. If the departing lawyer and the law firm have made the appropriate request for the client to select either the departing lawyer or the law firm to continue the representation, but the client has not yet responded, the law firm should consider notifying the court of the change in firm composition, although under ordinary circumstances, absent an agreement to the contrary, the firm will continue the representation in the interim. If the departing lawyer and the law firm have agreed regarding who will continue handling the client's matters then, absent disagreement by the client, the agreement normally will determine whether the departing lawyer or the law firm will continue the representation.

4–6. PUBLIC SERVICE

Rule 4–6.1. Pro bono public service

(a) Professional Responsibility. Each member of The Florida Bar in good standing, as part of that member's professional responsibility, should (1) render pro bono legal services to the poor and (2) participate, to the extent possible, in other pro bono service activities that directly relate to the legal needs of the poor. This professional responsibility does not apply to members of the judiciary or their staffs or to government lawyers who are prohibited from performing legal services by constitutional, statutory, rule, or regulatory prohibitions. Neither does this professional responsibility apply to those members of the bar who are retired, inactive, or suspended, or who have been placed on the inactive list for incapacity not related to discipline.

(b) Discharge of the Professional Responsibility to Provide Pro Bono Legal Service to the Poor. The professional responsibility to provide pro bono legal services as established under this rule is aspirational rather than mandatory in nature. The failure to fulfill one's professional responsibility under this rule will not subject a lawyer to discipline. The professional responsibility to provide pro bono legal service to the poor may be discharged by:

(1) annually providing at least 20 hours of pro bono legal service to the poor; or

(2) making an annual contribution of at least $350 to a legal aid organization.

(c) Collective Discharge of the Professional Responsibility to Provide Pro Bono Legal Service to the Poor. Each member of the bar should strive to individually satisfy the member's professional responsibility to provide pro bono legal service to the poor. Collective satisfaction of this professional responsibility is permitted by law firms only under a collective satisfaction plan that has been filed previously with the circuit pro bono committee and only when providing pro bono legal service to the poor:

(1) in a major case or matter involving a substantial expenditure of time and resources; or

(2) through a full-time community or public service staff; or

(3) in any other manner that has been approved by the circuit pro bono committee in the circuit in which the firm practices.

(d) Reporting Requirement. Each member of the bar shall annually report whether the member has satisfied the member's professional responsibility to provide pro bono legal services to the poor. Each member shall report this information through a simplified reporting form that is made a part of the member's annual membership fees statement. The form will contain the following categories from which each member will be allowed to choose in reporting whether the member has provided pro bono legal services to the poor:

(1) I have personally provided ______ hours of pro bono legal services;

(2) I have provided pro bono legal services collectively by: (indicate type of case and manner in which service was provided);

(3) I have contributed $______ to: (indicate organization to which funds were provided);

(4) I have provided legal services to the poor in the following special manner: (indicate manner in which services were provided); or

(5) I have been unable to provide pro bono legal services to the poor this year; or

(6) I am deferred from the provision of pro bono legal services to the poor because I am: (indicate whether lawyer is: a member of the judiciary or judicial staff; a government lawyer prohibited by statute, rule, or regulation from providing services; retired, or inactive).

The failure to report this information shall constitute a disciplinary offense under these rules.

(e) Credit Toward Professional Responsibility in Future Years. In the event that more than 20 hours of pro bono legal service to the poor are provided and reported in any 1 year, the hours in excess of 20 hours may be carried forward and reported as such for up to 2 succeeding years for the purpose of determining whether a lawyer has fulfilled the professional responsibility to provide pro bono legal service to the poor in those succeeding years.

(f) Out-of-State Members of the Bar. Out-of-state members of the bar may fulfill their professional responsibility in the states in which they practice or reside.

Former Rule 4-6.1 deleted June 23, 1993, effective Oct. 1, 1993. New Rule 4-6.1 added June 23, 1993, eff. Oct. 1, 1993 (630 So.2d 501). Amended Sept. 24, 1998, effective Oct. 1, 1998 (718 So.2d 1179).

Comment

Pro bono legal service to the poor is an integral and particular part of a lawyer's pro bono public service responsibility. As our society has become one in which rights and responsibilities are increasingly defined in legal terms, access to legal services has become of critical importance. This is true for all people, be they rich, poor, or of moderate means. However, because the legal problems of the poor often involve areas of basic need, their inability to obtain legal services can have dire consequences. The vast unmet legal needs of the poor in Florida have been recognized by the Supreme Court of Florida and by several studies undertaken in Florida over the past two decades. The Supreme Court of Florida has further recognized the necessity of finding a solution to the problem of providing the poor greater access to legal service and the unique role of lawyers in our adversarial system of representing and defending persons against the actions and conduct of governmental entities, individuals, and nongovernmental entities. As an officer of the court, each member of The Florida Bar in good standing has a professional responsibility to provide pro bono legal service to the poor. Certain lawyers, however, are prohibited from performing legal services by constitutional, statutory, rule, or other regulatory prohibitions. Consequently, members of the judiciary and their staffs, government lawyers who are prohibited from performing legal services by constitutional, statutory, rule, or regulatory prohibitions, members of the bar who are retired, inactive, or suspended, or who have been placed on the inactive list for incapacity not related to discipline are deferred from participation in this program.

In discharging the professional responsibility to provide pro bono legal service to the poor, each lawyer should furnish a minimum of twenty hours of pro bono legal service to the poor annually or contribute $350 to a legal aid organization. "Pro bono legal service" means legal service rendered without charge or expectation of a fee for the lawyer at the time the service commences. Legal services written off as bad debts do not qualify as pro bono service. Most pro bono service should involve civil proceedings given that government must provide indigent representation in most criminal matters. Pro bono legal service to the poor is to be provided not only to those persons whose household incomes are below the federal poverty standard but also to those persons frequently referred to as the "working poor." Lawyers providing pro bono legal service on their own need not undertake an investigation to determine client eligibility. Rather, a good faith determination by the lawyer of client eligibility is sufficient. Pro bono legal service to the poor need not be provided only through legal services to individuals; it can also be provided through legal services to charitable, religious, or educational organizations whose overall mission and activities are designed predominantly to address the needs of the poor. For example, legal service to organizations such as a church, civic, or community service organizations relating to a project seeking to address the problems of the poor would qualify.

While the personal involvement of each lawyer in the provision of pro bono legal service to the poor is generally preferable, such personal involvement may not always be possible or produce the ultimate desired result, that is, a significant maximum increase in the quantity and quality of legal service provided to the poor. The annual contribution alternative recognizes a lawyer's professional responsibility to provide financial assistance to increase and improve the delivery of legal service to the poor when a lawyer cannot or decides not to provide legal service to the poor through the contribution of time. Also, there is no prohibition against a lawyer contributing a combination of hours and financial support. The limited provision allowing for collective satisfaction of the 20-hour standard recognizes the importance of encouraging law firms to undertake the pro bono legal representation of the poor in substantial, complex matters requiring significant expenditures of law firm resources and time and costs, such as class actions and post-conviction death penalty appeal cases, and through the establishment of full-time community or public service staffs. When a law firm uses collective satisfaction, the total hours of legal services provided in such substantial, complex matters or through a full-time community or public service staff should be credited among the firm's lawyers in a fair and reasonable manner as determined by the firm.

The reporting requirement is designed to provide a sound basis for evaluating the results achieved by this rule, reveal the strengths and weaknesses of the pro bono plan, and to remind lawyers of their professional responsibility under this rule. The fourth alternative of the reporting requirements allows members to indicate that they have fulfilled their service in some manner not specifically envisioned by the plan.

The 20–hour standard for the provision of pro bono legal service to the poor is a minimum. Additional hours of service are to be encouraged. Many lawyers will, as they have before the adoption of this rule, contribute many more hours than the minimum. To ensure that a lawyer receives credit for the time required to handle a particularly involved matter, this rule provides that the lawyer may carry forward, over the next 2 successive years, any time expended in excess of 20 hours in any 1 year.

Rule 4–6.2. Accepting appointments

A lawyer shall not seek to avoid appointment by a tribunal to represent a person except for good cause, such as when:

(a) representing the client is likely to result in violation of the Rules of Professional Conduct or of the law;

(b) representing the client is likely to result in an unreasonable financial burden on the lawyer; or

(c) the client or the cause is so repugnant to the lawyer as to be likely to impair the client-lawyer relationship or the lawyer's ability to represent the client.

Amended July 23, 1992, effective Jan. 1, 1993 (605 So.2d 252); June 23, 1993, eff. Oct. 1, 1993 (630 So.2d 501).

Comment

A lawyer ordinarily is not obliged to accept a client whose character or cause the lawyer regards as repugnant. The lawyer's freedom to select clients is, however, qualified. All lawyers have a responsibility to assist in providing pro bono public service as provided in these rules. See rule 4–6.1. In the course of fulfilling a lawyer's obligation to provide legal services to the poor, a lawyer should not avoid or decline representation of a client simply because a client is unpopular or involved in unpopular matters. Although these rules do not contemplate court appointment as a primary means of achieving pro bono service, a lawyer may be subject to appointment by a court to serve unpopular clients or persons unable to afford legal services.

For good cause a lawyer may seek to decline an appointment to represent a person who cannot afford to retain counsel or whose cause is unpopular. Good cause exists if the lawyer could not handle the matter competently, see rule 4–1.1, or if undertaking the representation would result in an improper conflict of interest, for example, when the client or the cause is so repugnant to the lawyer as to be likely to impair the client-lawyer relationship or the lawyer's ability to represent the client. A lawyer may also seek to decline an appointment if acceptance would be unreasonably burdensome, for example, when it would impose a financial sacrifice so great as to be unjust.

An appointed lawyer has the same obligations to the client as retained counsel, including the obligations of loyalty and confidentiality, and is subject to the same limitations on the client-lawyer relationship, such as the obligation to refrain from assisting the client in violation of the rules.

Rule 4–6.3. Membership in legal services organization

A lawyer may serve as a director, officer, or member of a legal services organization, apart from the law firm in which the lawyer practices, notwithstanding that the organization serves persons having interests adverse to the client of the lawyer. The lawyer shall not knowingly participate in a decision or action of the organization:

(a) if participating in the decision would be incompatible with the lawyer's obligations to a client under rule 4–1.7; or

(b) where the decision could have a material adverse effect on the representation of a client of the organization whose interests are adverse to a client of the lawyer.

Amended July 23, 1992, effective Jan. 1, 1993 (605 So.2d 252).

Comment

Lawyers should be encouraged to support and participate in legal service organizations. A lawyer who is an officer or a member of such an organization does not thereby have a client-lawyer relationship with persons served by the organization. However, there is potential conflict between the interests of such persons and the interests of the lawyer's clients. If the possibility of such conflict disqualified a lawyer from serving on the board of a legal services organization, the profession's involvement in such organizations would be severely curtailed.

It may be necessary in appropriate cases to reassure a client of the organization that the representation will not be affected by conflicting loyalties of a member of the board. Established, written policies in this respect can enhance the credibility of such assurances.

Rule 4–6.4. Law reform activities affecting client interests

A lawyer may serve as a director, officer, or member of an organization involved in reform of the law or its administration notwithstanding that the reform may affect the interests of a client of the lawyer. When the lawyer knows that the interests of a client may be materially affected by a decision in which the lawyer participates, the lawyer shall disclose that fact but need not identify the client.

Comment

Lawyers involved in organizations seeking law reform generally do not have a client-lawyer relationship with the organization. Otherwise, it might follow that a lawyer could not be involved in a bar association law reform program that might indirectly affect a client. See also rule 4–1.2(b). For example, a lawyer specializing in antitrust litigation might be regarded as disqualified from participating in drafting revisions of rules governing that subject. In determining the nature and scope of participation in such activities, a lawyer should be mindful of obligations to clients under other rules, particularly rule 4–1.7. A lawyer is professionally obligated to protect the integrity of the program by making an appropriate disclosure within the organization when the lawyer knows a private client might be materially affected.

Rule 4–6.5. Voluntary Pro Bono Plan

Text of rule effective until October 1, 2015. See, also, rule effective October 1, 2015.

(a) Purpose. The purpose of the voluntary pro bono attorney plan is to increase the availability of legal service to the poor. The following operating plan has as its goal the improvement of the availability of legal services to the poor and the expansion of present pro bono legal service programs. The following operating plan was implemented to accomplish this purpose and goal.

(b) Standing Committee on Pro Bono Legal Service. The president-elect of The Florida Bar is responsible for appointing a standing committee on pro bono legal service to the poor.

(1) *Composition of the Standing Committee.* The standing committee consists of no more than 25 members and include, but not be limited to:

(A) 5 members of the board of governors of The Florida Bar, 1 of whom is the chair or a member of the access to the legal system committee of the board of governors;

(B) 5 past or current directors of The Florida Bar Foundation;

(C) 1 trial judge and 1 appellate judge;

(D) 2 representatives of civil legal assistance providers;

(E) 2 representatives from local and statewide voluntary bar associations;

(F) 2 public members, 1 of whom shall be a representative of the poor

(G) the president or designee of the Board of Directors of Florida Legal Services, Inc.; and

(H) 1 representative of the out-of-state division of The Florida Bar.

(2) *Responsibilities of the Standing Committee.* The standing committee will:

(A) identify, encourage, support, and assist statewide and local pro bono projects and activities;

(B) receive reports from circuit committees submitted on standardized forms developed by the standing committee;

(C) review and evaluate circuit court pro bono plans;

(D) beginning in the first year in which individual attorney pro bono reports are due, submit an annual report as to the activities and results of the pro bono plan to the board of governors of The Florida Bar, The Florida Bar Foundation, and to the Supreme Court of Florida;

(E) present to the board of governors of The Florida Bar and to the Supreme Court of Florida any suggested changes or modifications to the pro bono rules.

(c) Circuit Pro Bono Committees. There will be 1 circuit pro bono committee in each of the judicial circuits of Florida. In each judicial circuit the chief judge of the circuit, or the chief judge's designee, shall appoint and convene the initial circuit pro bono committee and the committee will appoint its chair.

(1) *Composition of Circuit Court Pro Bono Committee.* Each circuit pro bono committee is composed of:

(A) the chief judge of the circuit or the chief judge's designee;

(B) to the extent feasible, 1 or more representatives from each voluntary bar association, including each federal bar association, recognized by The Florida Bar and 1 representative from each pro bono and legal assistance provider in the circuit, which representatives are nominated by the association or provider; and

(C) at least 1 public member and at least 1 client-eligible member, which members are nominated by the other members of the circuit pro bono committee.

Governance and terms of service are determined by each circuit pro bono committee. Replacement and succession members are appointed by the chief judge of the circuit or the chief judge's designee, upon nomination by the association, the provider organization or the circuit pro bono committee, as the case may be, as deemed appropriate or necessary to ensure an active circuit pro bono committee in each circuit.

(2) *Responsibilities of Circuit Pro Bono Committee.* The circuit pro bono committee will:

(A) prepare in written form a circuit pro bono plan after evaluating the needs of the circuit and making a determination of present available pro bono services;

(B) implement the plan and monitor its results;

(C) submit an annual report to The Florida Bar standing committee;

(D) use current legal assistance and pro bono programs in each circuit, to the extent possible, to implement and operate circuit pro bono plans and provide the necessary coordination and administrative support for the circuit pro bono committee;

(E) encourage more lawyers to participate in pro bono activities by preparing a plan that provides for various support and educational services for participating pro bono attorneys, which, to the extent possible, should include:

(i) intake, screening, and referral of prospective clients;

(ii) matching cases with individual attorney expertise, including the establishment of specialized panels;

(iii) resources for litigation and out-of-pocket expenses for pro bono cases;

(iv) legal education and training for pro bono attorneys in specialized areas of law useful in providing pro bono legal service;

(v) the availability of consultation with attorneys who have expertise in areas of law with respect to which a volunteer lawyer is providing pro bono legal service;

(vi) malpractice insurance for volunteer pro bono lawyers with respect to their pro bono legal service;

(vii) procedures to ensure adequate monitoring and follow-up for assigned cases and to measure client satisfaction; and

(viii) recognition of pro bono legal service by lawyers.

(d) Suggested Pro Bono Service Opportunities.[1] The following are suggested pro bono service opportunities that should be included in each circuit plan:

(1) representation of clients through case referral;

(2) interviewing of prospective clients;

(3) participation in pro se clinics and other clinics in which lawyers provide advice and counsel;

(4) acting as co-counsel on cases or matters with legal assistance providers and other pro bono lawyers;

(5) providing consultation services to legal assistance providers for case reviews and evaluations;

(6) participation in policy advocacy;

(7) providing training to the staff of legal assistance providers and other volunteer pro bono attorneys;

(8) making presentations to groups of poor persons regarding their rights and obligations under the law;

(9) providing legal research;

(10) providing guardian ad litem services;

(11) providing assistance in the formation and operation of legal entities for groups of poor persons; and

(12) serving as a mediator or arbitrator at no fee to the client-eligible party.

Added June 23, 1993, eff. Oct. 1, 1993 (630 So.2d 501). Amended Dec. 20, 2007, effective March 1, 2008 (978 So.2d 91); May 29, 2014, effective June 1, 2014 (140 So.3d 541).

[1] Suggested title added by Publisher.

Rule 4-6.5. Voluntary Pro Bono Plan

Text of rule effective October 1, 2015. See, also, rule effective until October 1, 2015.

(a) Purpose. The purpose of the voluntary pro bono attorney plan is to increase the availability of legal service to the poor. The following operating plan has as its goal the improvement of the availability of legal services to the poor and the expansion of present pro bono legal service programs. The following operating plan was implemented to accomplish this purpose and goal.

(b) Standing Committee on Pro Bono Legal Service. The president-elect of The Florida Bar is responsible for appointing a standing committee on pro bono legal service to the poor.

(1) *Composition of the Standing Committee.* The standing committee consists of no more than 25 members and includes, but is not limited to:

(A) 5 past or current members of the board of governors of The Florida Bar, 1 of whom is the chair or a member of the access to the legal system committee of the board of governors;

(B) 5 past or current directors of The Florida Bar Foundation;

(C) 1 trial judge and 1 appellate judge;

(D) 2 representatives of civil legal assistance providers;

(E) 2 representatives from local and statewide voluntary bar associations;

(F) 2 public members, 1 of whom is a representative of the poor;

(G) the president or designee of the Board of Directors of Florida Legal Services, Inc.;

(H) 1 representative of the Out-of-State division of The Florida Bar; and

(I) the president or designee of the Young Lawyers Division of The Florida Bar.

(2) *Responsibilities of the Standing Committee.* The standing committee will:

(A) identify, encourage, support, and assist statewide and local pro bono projects and activities;

(B) receive reports from circuit committees submitted on standardized forms developed by the standing committee;

(C) review and evaluate circuit court pro bono plans;

(D) beginning in the first year in which individual attorney pro bono reports are due, submit an annual report as to the activities and results of the pro bono plan to the board of governors of The Florida Bar, The Florida Bar Foundation, and to the Supreme Court of Florida;

(E) present to the board of governors of The Florida Bar and to the Supreme Court of Florida any suggested changes or modifications to the pro bono rules.

(c) Circuit Pro Bono Committees. There will be 1 circuit pro bono committee in each of the judicial circuits of Florida. In each judicial circuit the chief judge of the circuit, or the chief judge's designee, shall appoint and convene the initial circuit pro bono committee and the committee will appoint its chair.

(1) *Composition of Circuit Court Pro Bono Committee.* Each circuit pro bono committee is composed of:

(A) the chief judge of the circuit or the chief judge's designee;

(B) to the extent feasible, 1 or more representatives from each voluntary bar association, including each federal bar association, recognized by The Florida Bar and 1 representative from each pro bono and legal assistance provider in the circuit, which representatives are nominated by the association or provider; and

(C) at least 1 public member and at least 1 client-eligible member, which members are nominated by the other members of the circuit pro bono committee.

Governance and terms of service are determined by each circuit pro bono committee. Replacement and succession members are appointed by the chief judge of the circuit or the chief judge's designee, upon nomination by the association, the provider organization or the circuit pro bono committee, as the case may be, as deemed appropriate or necessary to ensure an active circuit pro bono committee in each circuit.

(2) *Responsibilities of Circuit Pro Bono Committee.* The circuit pro bono committee will:

(A) prepare in written form a circuit pro bono plan after evaluating the needs of the circuit and making a determination of present available pro bono services;

(B) implement the plan and monitor its results;

(C) submit an annual report to The Florida Bar standing committee;

(D) use current legal assistance and pro bono programs in each circuit, to the extent possible, to implement and operate circuit pro bono plans and provide the necessary coordination and administrative support for the circuit pro bono committee;

(E) encourage more lawyers to participate in pro bono activities by preparing a plan that provides for various support and educational services for participating pro bono attorneys, which, to the extent possible, should include:

(i) intake, screening, and referral of prospective clients;

(ii) matching cases with individual attorney expertise, including the establishment of specialized panels;

(iii) resources for litigation and out-of-pocket expenses for pro bono cases;

(iv) legal education and training for pro bono attorneys in specialized areas of law useful in providing pro bono legal service;

(v) consultation with attorneys who have expertise in areas of law with respect to which a volunteer lawyer is providing pro bono legal service;

(vi) malpractice insurance for volunteer pro bono lawyers with respect to their pro bono legal service;

(vii) procedures to ensure adequate monitoring and follow-up for assigned cases and to measure client satisfaction; and

(viii) recognition of pro bono legal service by lawyers.

(d) Pro Bono Service Opportunities. The following are suggested pro bono service opportunities that should be included in each circuit plan:

(1) represent clients through case referral;

(2) interview prospective clients;

(3) participate in pro se clinics and other clinics in which lawyers provide advice and counsel;

(4) act as co-counsel on cases or matters with legal assistance providers and other pro bono lawyers;

(5) provide consultation services to legal assistance providers for case reviews and evaluations;

(6) participate in policy advocacy;

(7) provide training to the staff of legal assistance providers and other volunteer pro bono attorneys;

(8) make presentations to groups of poor persons regarding their rights and obligations under the law;

(9) provide legal research;

(10) provide guardian ad litem services;

(11) provide assistance in the formation and operation of legal entities for groups of poor persons; and

(12) serve as a mediator or arbitrator at no fee to the client-eligible party.

Added June 23, 1993, eff. Oct. 1, 1993 (630 So.2d 501). Amended Dec. 20, 2007, effective March 1, 2008 (978 So.2d 91); May 29, 2014, effective June 1, 2014 (140 So.3d 541); May 21, 2015, effective Oct. 1, 2015 (164 So.3d 1217).

4–7. INFORMATION ABOUT LEGAL SERVICES

Rule 4–7.11. Application of Rules

(a) Type of Media. Unless otherwise indicated, this subchapter applies to all forms of communication in any print or electronic forum, including but not limited to newspapers, magazines, brochures, flyers, television, radio, direct mail, electronic mail, and Internet, including banners, pop-ups, websites, social networking, and video sharing media. The terms "advertising" and "advertisement" as used in chapter 4–7 refer to all forms of communication seeking legal employment, both written and spoken.

(b) Lawyers. This subchapter applies to lawyers, whether or not admitted to practice in Florida or other jurisdictions, who advertise that the lawyer provides legal services in Florida or who target advertisements for legal employment at Florida residents. The term "lawyer" as used in subchapter 4–7 includes 1 or more lawyers or a law firm. This rule does not permit the unlicensed practice of law or advertising that the lawyer provides legal services that the lawyer is not authorized to provide in Florida.

(c) Referral Sources. This subchapter applies to communications made to referral sources about legal services.

Added Jan. 31, 2013, effective May 1, 2013 (108 So.3d 609).

Comment

Websites

Websites are subject to the general lawyer advertising requirements in this subchapter and are treated the same as other advertising media. Websites of multistate firms present specific regulatory concerns. Subchapter 4–7 applies to portions of a multistate firm that directly relate to the provision of legal services by a member of the firm who is a member of The Florida Bar. Additionally, subchapter 4–7 applies to portions of a multistate firm's website that relate to the provision of legal services in Florida, e.g., where a multistate firm has offices in Florida and discusses the provision of legal services in those Florida offices. Subchapter 4–7 does not apply to portions of a multistate firm's website that relate to the provision of legal services by lawyers who are not admitted to The Florida Bar and who do not provide legal services in Florida. Subchapter 4–7 does not apply to portions of a multistate firm's website that relate to the provision of legal services in jurisdictions other than Florida.

Lawyers Admitted in Other Jurisdictions

Subchapter 4–7 does not apply to any advertisement broadcast or disseminated in another jurisdiction in which a Florida Bar member is admitted to practice if the advertisement complies with the rules governing lawyer advertising in that jurisdiction and is not broadcast or disseminated within the state of Florida or targeted at Florida residents. Subchapter 4–7 does not apply to such advertisements appearing in national media if the disclaimer "cases not accepted in Florida" is plainly noted in the advertisement. Subchapter 4–7 also does not apply to a website advertisement that does not offer the services of a Florida Bar member, a lawyer located in Florida, or a lawyer offering to provide legal services in Florida.

Subchapter 4–7 applies to advertisements by lawyers admitted to practice law in jurisdictions other than Florida who have established a regular and/or permanent presence in Florida for the practice of law as authorized by other law and who solicit or advertise for legal employment in Florida or who target solicitations or advertisements for legal employment at Florida residents.

For example, in the areas of immigration, patent, and tax, a lawyer from another jurisdiction may establish a regular or permanent presence in Florida to practice only that specific federal practice as authorized by federal law. Such a lawyer must comply with this subchapter for all advertisements disseminated in Florida or that target Florida residents for legal employment. Such a lawyer must include in all advertisements that the lawyer is "Not a Member of The Florida Bar" or "Admitted in [jurisdiction where admitted] Only" or the lawyer's limited area of practice, such as "practice limited to [area of practice] law." *See Fla. Bar v. Kaiser*, 397 So. 2d 1132 (Fla. 1981).

A lawyer from another jurisdiction is not authorized to establish a regular or permanent presence in Florida to practice law in an area in which that lawyer is not authorized to practice or to advertise for legal services the lawyer is not authorized to provide in Florida. For example, although a lawyer from another state may petition a court to permit admission pro hac vice on a specific Florida case, no law authorizes a pro hac vice practice on a general or permanent basis in the state of Florida. A lawyer cannot advertise for Florida cases within the state of Florida or target advertisements to Florida residents, because such an advertisement in and of itself constitutes the unlicensed practice of law.

A lawyer from another jurisdiction may be authorized to provide Florida residents legal services in another jurisdiction. For example, if a class action suit is pending in another state, a lawyer from another jurisdiction may represent Florida residents in the litigation. Any such advertisements disseminated within the state of Florida or targeting Florida residents must comply with this subchapter.

Rule 4–7.12. Required Content

(a) Name and Office Location. All advertisements for legal employment must include:

(1) the name of at least 1 lawyer, the law firm, the lawyer referral service if the advertisement is for the lawyer referral service, or the lawyer directory if the advertisement is for the lawyer directory, responsible for the content of the advertisement; and

(2) the city, town, or county of 1 or more bona fide office locations of the lawyer who will perform the services advertised.

(b) Referrals. If the case or matter will be referred to another lawyer or law firm, the advertisement must include a statement to such effect.

(c) Languages Used in Advertising. Any words or statements required by this subchapter to appear in an advertisement must appear in the same language in which the advertisement appears. If more than 1 language is used in an advertisement, any words or statements required by this subchapter must appear in each language used in the advertisement.

(d) Legibility. Any information required by these rules to appear in an advertisement must be reasonably prominent and clearly legible if written, or intelligible if spoken.

Added Jan. 31, 2013, effective May 1, 2013 (108 So.3d 609).

Comment

Name of Lawyer or Lawyer Referral Service

All advertisements are required to contain the name of at least 1 lawyer who is responsible for the content of the advertisement. For purposes of this rule, including the name of the law firm is sufficient. A lawyer referral service or lawyer directory must include its actual legal name or a registered fictitious name in all advertisements in order to comply with this requirement.

Geographic Location

For the purposes of this rule, a bona fide office is defined as a physical location maintained by the lawyer or law firm where the lawyer or law firm reasonably expects to furnish legal services in a substantial way on a regular and continuing basis.

An office in which there is little or no full-time staff, the lawyer is not present on a regular and continuing basis, and where a substantial portion of the necessary legal services will not be provided, is not a bona fide office for purposes of this rule. An advertisement cannot state or imply that a lawyer has offices in a location where the lawyer has no bona fide office. However, an advertisement may state that a lawyer is "available for consultation" or "available by appointment" or has a "satellite" office at a location where the lawyer does not have a bona fide office, if the statement is true.

Referrals to Other Lawyers

If the advertising lawyer knows at the time the advertisement is disseminated that the lawyer intends to refer some cases generated from an advertisement to another lawyer, the advertisement must state that fact. An example of an appropriate disclaimer is as follows: "Your case may be referred to another lawyer."

Language of Advertisement

Any information required by these rules to appear in an advertisement must appear in all languages used in the advertisement. If a specific disclaimer is required in order to avoid the advertisement misleading the viewer, the disclaimer must be made in the same language that the statement requiring the disclaimer appears.

Rule 4–7.13. Deceptive and Inherently Misleading Advertisements

A lawyer may not engage in deceptive or inherently misleading advertising.

(a) Deceptive and Inherently Misleading Advertisements. An advertisement is deceptive or inherently misleading if it:

(1) contains a material statement that is factually or legally inaccurate;

(2) omits information that is necessary to prevent the information supplied from being misleading; or

(3) implies the existence of a material nonexistent fact.

(b) Examples of Deceptive and Inherently Misleading Advertisements. Deceptive or inherently misleading advertisements include, but are not limited to advertisements that contain:

(1) statements or information that can reasonably be interpreted by a prospective client as a prediction or guaranty of success or specific results;

(2) references to past results unless such information is objectively verifiable, subject to rule 4–7.14;

(3) comparisons of lawyers or statements, words or phrases that characterize a lawyer's or law firm's skills, experience, reputation or record, unless such characterization is objectively verifiable;

(4) references to areas of practice in which the lawyer or law firm does not practice or intend to practice at the time of the advertisement;

(5) a voice or image that creates the erroneous impression that the person speaking or shown is the advertising lawyer or a lawyer or employee of the advertising firm. The following notice, prominently displayed would resolve the erroneous impression: "Not an employee or member of law firm";

(6) a dramatization of an actual or fictitious event unless the dramatization contains the following prominently displayed notice: "DRAMATIZATION. NOT AN ACTUAL EVENT." When an advertisement includes an actor purporting to be engaged in a particular profession or occupation, the advertisement must include the following prominently displayed notice: "ACTOR. NOT ACTUAL [. . .]";

(7) statements, trade names, telephone numbers, Internet addresses, images, sounds, videos or dramatizations that state or imply that the lawyer will engage in conduct or tactics that are prohibited by the Rules of Professional Conduct or any law or court rule;

(8) a testimonial:

(A) regarding matters on which the person making the testimonial is unqualified to evaluate;

(B) that is not the actual experience of the person making the testimonial;

(C) that is not representative of what clients of that lawyer or law firm generally experience;

(D) that has been written or drafted by the lawyer;

(E) in exchange for which the person making the testimonial has been given something of value; or

(F) that does not include the disclaimer that the prospective client may not obtain the same or similar results;

(9) a statement or implication that The Florida Bar has approved an advertisement or a lawyer, except a statement that the lawyer is licensed to practice in Florida or has been certified pursuant to chapter 6, Rules Regulating the Florida Bar; or

(10) a judicial, executive, or legislative branch title, unless accompanied by clear modifiers and placed subsequent to the person's name, in reference to a current, former or retired judicial, executive, or legislative branch official currently engaged in the practice of law. For example, a former judge may not state "Judge Doe (retired)" or "Judge Doe, former circuit judge." She may state "Jane Doe, Florida Bar member, former circuit judge" or "Jane Doe, retired circuit judge . . ."

Added Jan. 31, 2013, effective May 1, 2013 (108 So.3d 609).

Comment

Material Omissions

An example of a material omission is stating "over 20 years' experience" when the experience is the combined experience of all lawyers in the advertising firm. Another example is a lawyer who states "over 20 years' experience" when the lawyer includes within that experience time spent as a paralegal, investigator, police officer, or other nonlawyer position.

Implied Existence of Nonexistent Fact

An example of the implied existence of a nonexistent fact is an advertisement stating that a lawyer has offices in multiple states if the lawyer is not licensed in those states or is not authorized to practice law. Such a statement implies the nonexistent fact that a lawyer is licensed or is authorized to practice law in the states where offices are located.

Another example of the implied existence of a nonexistent fact is a statement in an advertisement that a lawyer is a founding member of a legal organization when the lawyer has just begun practicing law. Such a statement falsely implies that the lawyer has been practicing law longer than the lawyer actually has.

Predictions of Success

Statements that promise a specific result or predict success in a legal matter are prohibited because they are misleading. Examples of statements that impermissibly predict success include: "I will save your home," "I can save your home," "I will get you money for your injuries," and "Come to me to get acquitted of the charges pending against you."

Statements regarding the legal process as opposed to a specific result generally will be considered permissible. For example, a statement that the lawyer or law firm will protect the client's rights, protect the client's assets, or protect the client's family do not promise a specific legal result in a particular matter. Similarly, a statement that a lawyer will prepare a client to effectively handle cross-examination is permissible, because it does not promise a specific result, but describes the legal process.

Aspirational statements are generally permissible as such statements describe goals that a lawyer or law firm will try to meet. Examples of aspirational words include "goal," "strive," "dedicated," "mission," and "philosophy." For example, the statement, "My goal is to achieve the best possible result in your case," is permissible. Similarly, the statement, "If you've been injured through no fault of your own, I am dedicated to recovering damages on your behalf," is permissible.

Modifying language can be used to prevent language from running afoul of this rule. For example, the statement, "I will get you acquitted of the pending charges," would violate the rule as it promises a specific legal result. In contrast, the statement, "I will pursue an acquittal of your pending charges," does not promise a specific legal result. It merely conveys that the lawyer will try to obtain an acquittal on behalf of the prospective client. The following list is a nonexclusive list of words that generally may be used to modify language to prevent violations of the rule: try, pursue, may, seek, might, could, and designed to.

General statements describing a particular law or area of law are not promises of specific legal results or predictions of success. For example, the following statement is a description of the law and is not a promise of a specific legal result: "When the government takes your property through its eminent domain power, the government must provide you with compensation for your property."

Past Results

The prohibitions in subdivisions (b)(1) and (b)(2) of this rule preclude advertisements about results obtained on behalf of a client, such as the amount of a damage award or the lawyer's record in obtaining favorable verdicts, if the results are not objectively verifiable or are misleading, either alone or in the context in which they are used. For example, an advertised result that is atypical of persons under similar circumstances is likely to be misleading. A result that omits pertinent information, such as failing to disclose that a specific judgment was uncontested or obtained by default, or failing to disclose that the judgment is far short of the client's actual damages, is also misleading. Such information may create the unjustified expectation that similar results can be obtained for others without reference to the specific factual and legal circumstances. An example of a past result that can be objectively verified is that a lawyer has obtained acquittals in all charges in 4 criminal defense cases.

On the other hand, general statements such as, "I have successfully represented clients," or "I have won numerous appellate cases," may or may not be sufficiently objectively verifiable. For example, a lawyer may interpret the words "successful" or "won" in a manner different from the average prospective client. In a criminal law context, the lawyer may interpret the word "successful" to mean a conviction to a lesser charge or a lower sentence than recommended by the prosecutor, while the average prospective client likely would interpret the words "successful" or "won" to mean an acquittal.

Rule 4–1.6(a), Rules Regulating the Florida Bar, prohibits a lawyer from voluntarily disclosing any information regarding a representation without a client's informed consent, unless one of the exceptions to rule 4–1.6 applies. A lawyer who wishes to advertise information about past results must have the affected client's informed consent. The fact that some or all of the information a lawyer may wish to advertise is in the public record does not obviate the need for the client's informed consent.

Comparisons

The prohibition against comparisons that cannot be factually substantiated would preclude a lawyer from representing that the lawyer or the lawyer's law firm is "the best," or "one of the best," in a field of law.

On the other hand, statements that the law firm is the largest in a specified geographic area, or is the only firm in a specified geographic area that devotes its services to a particular field of practice are permissible if they are true, because they are comparisons capable of being factually substantiated.

Characterization of Skills, Experience, Reputation or Record

The rule prohibits statements that characterize skills, experience, reputation, or record that are not objectively verifiable. Statements of a character trait or attribute are not statements that characterize skills, experience, or record. For example, a statement that a lawyer is aggressive, intelligent, creative, honest, or trustworthy is a statement of a lawyer's personal attribute, but does not characterize the lawyer's skills, experience, reputation, or record. Such statements are permissible.

Descriptive statements characterizing skills, experience, reputation, or a record that are true and factually verified are permissible. For example, the statement "Our firm is the largest firm in this city that practices exclusively personal injury law," is permissible if true, because the statement is objectively verifiable. Similarly, the statement, "I have personally handled more appeals before the First District Court of Appeal than any other lawyer in my circuit," is permissible if the statement is true, because the statement is objectively verifiable.

Descriptive statements that are misleading are prohibited by this rule. Descriptive statements such as "the best," "second to none," or "the finest" will generally run afoul of this rule, as such statements are not objectively verifiable and are likely to mislead prospective clients as to the quality of the legal services offered.

Aspirational statements are generally permissible as such statements describe goals that a lawyer or law firm will try to meet. Examples of aspirational words include "goal," "dedicated," "mission," and "philosophy." For example, the statement, "I am dedicated to excellence in my representation of my clients," is permissible as a goal. Similarly, the statement, "My goal is to provide high quality legal services," is permissible.

Areas of Practice

This rule is not intended to prohibit lawyers from advertising for areas of practice in which the lawyer intends to personally handle cases, but does not yet have any cases of that particular type.

Dramatizations

A re-creation or staging of an event must contain a prominently displayed disclaimer, "DRAMATIZATION. NOT AN ACTUAL EVENT." For example, a re-creation of a car accident must contain the disclaimer. A re-enactment of lawyers visiting the re-construction of an accident scene must contain the disclaimer.

If an actor is used in an advertisement purporting to be engaged in a particular profession or occupation who is acting as a spokesperson for the lawyer or in any other circumstances where the viewer could be misled, a disclaimer must be used. However, an authority figure such as a judge or law enforcement officer, or an actor portraying an authority figure, may not be used in an advertisement to endorse or recommend a lawyer, or to act as a spokesperson for a lawyer under Rule 4–7.15.

Implying Lawyer Will Violate Rules of Conduct or Law

Advertisements which state or imply that the advertising lawyers will engage in conduct that violates the Rules of Professional Conduct are prohibited. The Supreme Court of Florida found that lawyer advertisements containing an illustration of a pit bull canine and the telephone number 1–800–pit-bull were false, misleading, and manipulative, because use of that animal implied that the advertising lawyers would engage in "combative and vicious tactics" that would violate the Rules of Professional Conduct. Fla. Bar v. Pape, 918 So. 2d 240 (Fla. 2005).

Testimonials

A testimonial is a personal statement, affirmation, or endorsement by any person other than the advertising lawyer or a member of the advertising lawyer's firm regarding the quality of the lawyer's services or the results obtained through the representation. Clients as consumers are well-qualified to opine on matters such as courtesy, promptness, efficiency, and professional demeanor. Testimonials by clients on these matters, as long as they are truthful and are based on the actual experience of the person giving the testimonial, are beneficial to prospective clients and are permissible.

Florida Bar Approval of Ad or Lawyer

An advertisement may not state or imply that either the advertisement or the lawyer has been approved by The Florida Bar. Such a statement or implication implies that The Florida Bar endorses a particular lawyer. Statements prohibited by this provision include, "This advertisement was approved by The Florida Bar." A lawyer referral service also may not state that it is a "Florida Bar approved lawyer referral service," unless the service is a not-for-profit lawyer referral service approved under chapter 8 of the Rules Regulating the Florida Bar.

Judicial, Executive, and Legislative Titles

This rule prohibits use of a judicial, executive, or legislative branch title, unless accompanied by clear modifiers and placed subsequent to the person's name, when used to refer to a current or former officer of the judicial, executive, or legislative branch. Use of a title before a name is inherently misleading in that it implies that the current or former officer has improper influence. Thus, the titles Senator Doe, Representative Smith, Former Justice Doe, Retired Judge Smith, Governor (Retired) Doe, Former Senator Smith, and other similar titles used as titles in conjunction with the lawyer's name are prohibited by this rule. This includes, but is not limited to, use of the title in advertisements and written communications, computer-accessed communications, letterhead, and business cards.

However, an accurate representation of one's judicial, executive, or legislative experience is permitted if the reference is subsequent to the lawyer's name and is clearly modified by terms such as "former" or "retired." For example, a former judge may state "Jane Doe, Florida Bar member, former circuit judge" or "Jane Doe, retired circuit judge."

As another example, a former state representative may not include "Representative Smith (former)" or "Representative Smith, retired" in an advertisement, letterhead, or business card. However, a former representative may state, "John Smith, Florida Bar member, former state representative."

Further, an accurate representation of one's judicial, executive, or legislative experience is permitted in reference to background and experience in biographies, curriculum vitae, and resumes if accompanied by clear modifiers and placed subsequent to the person's name, For example, the statement "John Jones was governor of the State of Florida from [. . . years of service . . .]" would be permissible.

Also, the rule governs attorney advertising. It does not apply to pleadings filed in a court. A practicing attorney who is a former or retired judge shall not use the title in any form in a court pleading. If a former or retired judge uses her previous title in a pleading, she could be sanctioned.

Rule 4-7.14. Potentially Misleading Advertisements

A lawyer may not engage in potentially misleading advertising.

(a) Potentially Misleading Advertisements. Potentially misleading advertisements include, but are not limited to:

(1) advertisements that are subject to varying reasonable interpretations, 1 or more of which would be materially misleading when considered in the relevant context;

(2) advertisements that are literally accurate, but could reasonably mislead a prospective client regarding a material fact;

(3) references to a lawyer's membership in, or recognition by, an entity that purports to base such membership or recognition on a lawyer's ability or skill, unless the entity conferring such membership or recognition is generally recognized within the legal profession as being a bona fide organization that makes its selections based upon objective and uniformly applied criteria, and that includes among its members or those recognized a reasonable cross-section of the legal community the entity purports to cover;

(4) a statement that a lawyer is board certified, a specialist, an expert, or other variations of those terms unless:

(A) the lawyer has been certified under the Florida Certification Plan as set forth in chapter 6, Rules Regulating the Florida Bar and the advertisement includes the area of certification and that The Florida Bar is the certifying organization;

(B) the lawyer has been certified by an organization whose specialty certification program has been accredited by the American Bar Association or The Florida Bar as provided elsewhere in these rules. A lawyer certified by a specialty certification program accredited by the American Bar Association but not The Florida Bar must include the statement "Not Certified as a Specialist by The Florida Bar" in reference to the specialization or certification. All such advertisements must include the area of certification and the name of the certifying organization; or

(C) the lawyer has been certified by another state bar if the state bar program grants certification on the basis of standards reasonably comparable to the standards of the Florida Certification Plan set forth in chapter 6 of these rules and the advertisement includes the area of certification and the name of the certifying organization.

In the absence of such certification, a lawyer may communicate the fact that the lawyer limits his or her practice to 1 or more fields of law; or

(5) information about the lawyer's fee, including those that indicate no fee will be charged in the absence of a recovery, unless the advertisement discloses all fees and expenses for which the client might be liable and any other material information relating to the fee. A lawyer who advertises a specific fee or range of fees for a particular service must honor the advertised fee or range of fees for at least 90 days unless the advertisement specifies a shorter period; provided that, for advertisements in the yellow pages

of telephone directories or other media not published more frequently than annually, the advertised fee or range of fees must be honored for no less than 1 year following publication.

(b) Clarifying Information. A lawyer may use an advertisement that would otherwise be potentially misleading if the advertisement contains information or statements that adequately clarify the potentially misleading issue.

Added Jan. 31, 2013, effective May 1, 2013 (108 So.3d 609).

Comment

Awards, Honors, and Ratings

Awards, honors and ratings are not subjective statements characterizing a lawyer's skills, experience, reputation or record. Instead, they are statements of objectively verifiable facts from which an inference of quality may be drawn. It is therefore permissible under the rule for a lawyer to list bona fide awards, honors and recognitions using the name or title of the actual award and the date it was given. If the award was given in the same year that the advertisement is disseminated or the advertisement references a rating that is current at the time the advertisement is disseminated, the year of the award or rating is not required.

For example, the following statements are permissible:

"John Doe is AV rated by Martindale–Hubbell. This rating is Martindale–Hubbell's highest rating."

"Jane Smith was named a 2008 Florida Super Lawyer by Super Lawyers Magazine."

Claims of Board Certification, Specialization or Expertise

This rule permits a lawyer or law firm to indicate areas of practice in communications about the lawyer's or law firm's services, provided the advertising lawyer or law firm actually practices in those areas of law at the time the advertisement is disseminated. If a lawyer practices only in certain fields, or will not accept matters except in such fields, the lawyer is permitted to indicate that. A lawyer who is not certified by The Florida Bar, by another state bar with comparable standards, or an organization accredited by the American Bar Association or The Florida Bar may not be described to the public as a "specialist," "specializing," "certified," "board certified," being an "expert," having "expertise," or any variation of similar import. A lawyer may indicate that the lawyer concentrates in, focuses on, or limits the lawyer's practice to particular areas of practice as long as the statements are true.

Certification is specific to individual lawyers; a law firm cannot be certified, and cannot claim specialization or expertise in an area of practice per subdivision (c) of rule 6–3.4. Therefore, an advertisement may not state that a law firm is certified, has expertise in, or specializes in any area of practice.

A lawyer can only state or imply that the lawyer is "certified," a "specialist," or an "expert" in the actual area(s) of practice in which the lawyer is certified. A lawyer who is board certified in civil trial law, may so state that, but may not state that the lawyer is certified, an expert in, or specializes in personal injury. Similarly, a lawyer who is board certified in marital and family law may not state that the lawyer specializes in divorce.

Fee and Cost Information

Every advertisement that contains information about the lawyer's fee, including a contingent fee, must disclose all fees and costs that the client will be liable for. If the client is, in fact, not responsible for any costs in addition to the fee, then no disclosure is necessary. For example, if a lawyer charges a flat fee to create and execute a will and there are no costs associated with the services, the lawyer's advertisement may state only the flat fee for that service.

However, if there are costs for which the client is responsible, the advertisement must disclose this fact. For example, if fees are contingent on the outcome of the matter, but the client is responsible for costs regardless of the matter's outcome, the following statements are permissible: "No Fee if No Recovery, but Client is Responsible for Costs," "No Fee if No Recovery, Excludes Costs," "No Recovery, No Fee, but Client is Responsible for Costs" and other similar statements.

On the other hand, if both fees and costs are contingent on the outcome of a personal injury case, the statements "No Fees or Costs If No Recovery" and "No Recovery—No Fees or Costs" are permissible.

Rule 4–7.15. Unduly Manipulative or Intrusive Advertisements

A lawyer may not engage in unduly manipulative or intrusive advertisements. An advertisement is unduly manipulative if it:

(a) uses an image, sound, video or dramatization in a manner that is designed to solicit legal employment by appealing to a prospective client's emotions rather than to a rational evaluation of a lawyer's suitability to represent the prospective client;

(b) uses an authority figure such as a judge or law enforcement officer, or an actor portraying an authority figure, to endorse or recommend the lawyer or act as a spokesperson for the lawyer;

(c) contains the voice or image of a celebrity, except that a lawyer may use the voice or image of a local announcer, disc jockey or radio personality who regularly records advertisements so long as the person recording the announcement does not endorse or offer a testimonial on behalf of the advertising lawyer or law firm; or

(d) offers consumers an economic incentive to employ the lawyer or review the lawyer's advertising; provided that this rule does not prohibit a lawyer from offering a discounted fee or special fee or cost structure as otherwise permitted by these rules and does not prohibit the lawyer from offering free legal advice or information that might indirectly benefit a consumer economically.

Added Jan. 31, 2013, effective May 1, 2013 (108 So.3d 609).

Comment

Unduly Manipulative Sounds and Images

Illustrations that are informational and not misleading are permissible. As examples, a graphic rendering of the scales of justice to indicate that the advertising lawyer practices law, a picture of the lawyer, or a map of the office location are permissible illustrations.

An illustration that provides specific information that is directly related to a particular type of legal claim is permissible. For example, a photograph of an actual medication to illustrate that the medication has been linked to adverse side effects is permissible. An x-ray of a lung that has been damaged by asbestos would also be permissible. A picture or video that illustrates the nature of a particular claim or practice, such as a person on crutches or in jail, is permissible.

An illustration or photograph of a car that has been in an accident would be permissible to indicate that the lawyer handles car accident cases. Similarly, an illustration or photograph of a construction site would be permissible to show either that the lawyer handles construction law matters or workers' compensation matters. An illustration or photograph of a house with a foreclosure sale sign is permissible to indicate that the lawyer handles foreclosure matters. An illustration or photograph of a person with a stack of bills to indicate that the lawyer handles bankruptcy is also permissible. An illustration or photograph of a person being arrested, a person in jail, or an accurate rendering of a traffic stop also is permissible. An illustration, photograph, or portrayal of a bulldozer to indicate that the lawyer handles eminent domain matters is permissible. Illustrations, photographs, or scenes of doctors examining x-rays are permissible to show that a lawyer handles medical malpractice or medical products liability cases. An image, dramatization, or sound of a car accident actually occurring would also be permissible, as long as it is not unduly manipulative.

Although some illustrations are permissible, an advertisement that contains an image, sound or dramatization that is unduly manipulative is not. For example, a dramatization or illustration of a car accident occurring in which graphic injuries are displayed is not permissible. A depiction of a child being taken from a crying mother is not permissible because it seeks to evoke an emotional response and is unrelated to conveying useful information to the prospective client regarding hiring a lawyer. Likewise, a dramatization of an insurance adjuster persuading an accident victim to sign a settlement is unduly manipulative, because it is likely to convince a viewer to hire the advertiser solely on the basis of the manipulative advertisement.

Some illustrations are used to seek attention so that viewers will receive the advertiser's message. So long as those illustrations, images, or dramatizations are not unduly manipulative, they are permissible, even if they do not directly relate to the selection of a particular lawyer.

Use of Celebrities

A lawyer or law firm advertisement may not contain the voice or image of a celebrity. A celebrity is an individual who is known to the target audience and whose voice or image is recognizable to the intended audience. A person can be a celebrity on a regional or local level, not just a national level. Local announcers or disc jockeys and radio personalities are regularly used to record advertisements. Use of a local announcer or disc jockey or a radio personality to record an advertisement is permissible under this rule as long as the person recording the announcement does not endorse or offer a testimonial on behalf of the advertising lawyer or law firm.

Rule 4–7.16. Presumptively Valid Content

The following information in advertisements is presumed not to violate the provisions of rules 4–7.11 through 4–7.15:

(a) Lawyers and Law Firms. A lawyer or law firm may include the following information in advertisements and unsolicited written communications:

(1) the name of the lawyer or law firm subject to the requirements of this rule and rule 4–7.21, a listing of lawyers associated with the firm, office locations and parking arrangements, disability accommodations, telephone numbers, website addresses, and electronic mail addresses, office and telephone service hours, and a designation such as "attorney" or "law firm";

(2) date of admission to The Florida Bar and any other bars, current membership or positions held in The Florida Bar or its sections or committees or those of other state bars, former membership or positions held in The Florida Bar or its sections or committees with dates of membership or those of other state bars, former positions of employment held in the legal profession with dates the positions were held, years of experience practicing law, number of lawyers in the advertising law firm, and a listing of federal courts and jurisdictions other than Florida where the lawyer is licensed to practice;

(3) technical and professional licenses granted by the state or other recognized licensing authorities and educational degrees received, including dates and institutions;

(4) military service, including branch and dates of service;

(5) foreign language ability;

(6) fields of law in which the lawyer practices, including official certification logos, subject to the requirements of subdivision (a)(4) of rule 4–7.14 regarding use of terms such as certified, specialist, and expert;

(7) prepaid or group legal service plans in which the lawyer participates;

(8) acceptance of credit cards;

(9) fee for initial consultation and fee schedule, subject to the requirements of subdivisions (a)(5) of rule 4–7.14 regarding cost disclosures and honoring advertised fees;

(10) common salutary language such as "best wishes," "good luck," "happy holidays," "pleased to announce," or "proudly serving your community";

(11) punctuation marks and common typographical marks;

(12) an illustration of the scales of justice not deceptively similar to official certification logos or The Florida Bar logo, a gavel, traditional renditions of Lady Justice, the Statue of Liberty, the American flag, the American eagle, the State of Florida flag, an unadorned set of law books, the inside or outside of a courthouse, column(s), diploma(s), or a photograph of the lawyer or lawyers who are members of, or employed by, the firm against a plain background such as a plain unadorned office or a plain unadorned set of law books.

(b) Lawyer Referral Services. A lawyer referral service may advertise its name, location, telephone number, the referral fee charged, its hours of operation, the process by which referrals are made, the areas of law in which referrals are offered, the geographic area in which the lawyers practice to whom those responding to the advertisement will be referred. A lawyer referral service approved by The Florida Bar under chapter 8 of the Rules Regulating the Florida Bar may advertise the logo of its sponsoring bar association and its nonprofit status.

Added Jan. 31, 2013, effective May 1, 2013 (108 So.3d 609).

Comment

The presumptively valid content creates a safe harbor for lawyers. A lawyer desiring a safe harbor from discipline may choose to limit the content of an advertisement to the information listed in this rule and, if the information is true, the advertisement complies with these rules. However, a lawyer is not required to limit the information in an advertisement to the presumptively valid content, as long as all information in the advertisement complies with these rules.

Rule 4–7.17. Payment for Advertising and Promotion

(a) Payment by Other Lawyers. No lawyer may, directly or indirectly, pay all or a part of the cost of an advertisement by a lawyer not in the same firm. Rule 4–1.5(f)(4)(D) (regarding the division of contingency fees) is not affected by this provision even though the lawyer covered by subdivision (f)(4)(D)(ii) of rule 4–1.5 advertises.

(b) Payment for Referrals. A lawyer may not give anything of value to a person for recommending the lawyer's services, except that a lawyer may pay the reasonable cost of advertising permitted by these rules, may pay the usual charges of a lawyer referral service, lawyer directory or other legal service organization, and may purchase a law practice in accordance with rule 4–1.17.

(c) Payment by Nonlawyers. A lawyer may not permit a nonlawyer to pay all or a part of the cost of an advertisement by that lawyer.

Added Jan. 31, 2013, effective May 1, 2013 (108 So.3d 609).

Comment

Paying for the Advertisements of Another Lawyer

A lawyer is not permitted to pay for the advertisements of another lawyer not in the same firm. This rule is not intended to prohibit more than 1 law firm from advertising jointly, but the advertisement must contain all required information as to each advertising law firm.

Paying Others for Recommendations

A lawyer is allowed to pay for advertising permitted by this rule and for the purchase of a law practice in accordance with the provisions of rule 4–1.17, but otherwise is not permitted to pay or provide other tangible benefits to another person for procuring professional work. However, a legal aid agency or prepaid legal services plan may pay to advertise legal services provided under its auspices. Likewise, a lawyer may participate in lawyer referral programs or lawyer directories and pay the usual fees charged by such programs, subject, however, to the limitations imposed by rules 4–7.22 and 4–7.23. This rule does not prohibit paying regular compensation to an assistant, such as a secretary or advertising consultant, to prepare communications permitted by this rule.

Rule 4–7.18. Direct Contact with Prospective Clients

(a) Solicitation. Except as provided in subdivision (b) of this rule, a lawyer may not:

(1) solicit, or permit employees or agents of the lawyer to solicit on the lawyer's behalf, professional employment from a prospective client with whom the lawyer has no family or prior professional relationship, in person or otherwise, when a significant motive for the lawyer's doing so is the lawyer's pecuniary gain. The term "solicit" includes contact in person, by telephone, telegraph, or facsimile, or by other communication directed to a specific recipient and includes any written form of communication, including any electronic mail communication, directed to a specific recipient and not meeting the requirements of subdivision (b) of this rule and rules 4–7.11 through 4–7.17 of these rules.

(2) enter into an agreement for, charge, or collect a fee for professional employment obtained in violation of this rule.

(b) Written Communication.

(1) A lawyer may not send, or knowingly permit to be sent, on the lawyer's behalf or on behalf of the lawyer's firm or partner, an associate, or any other lawyer affiliated with the lawyer or the lawyer's firm, a written communication directly or indirectly to a prospective client for the purpose of obtaining professional employment if:

(A) the written communication concerns an action for personal injury or wrongful death or otherwise relates to an accident or disaster involving the person to whom the communication is addressed or a relative of that person, unless the accident or disaster occurred more than 30 days prior to the mailing of the communication;

(B) the written communication concerns a specific matter and the lawyer knows or reasonably should know that the person to whom the communication is directed is represented by a lawyer in the matter;

(C) it has been made known to the lawyer that the person does not want to receive such communications from the lawyer;

(D) the communication involves coercion, duress, fraud, overreaching, harassment, intimidation, or undue influence;

(E) the communication violates rules 4–7.11 through 4–7.17 of these rules;

(F) the lawyer knows or reasonably should know that the physical, emotional, or mental state of the person makes it unlikely that the person would exercise reasonable judgment in employing a lawyer; or

(G) the communication concerns a request for an injunction for protection against any form of physical violence and is addressed to the respondent in the injunction petition, if the lawyer knows or reasonably should know that the respondent named in the injunction petition has not yet been served with notice of process in the matter.

(2) Written communications to prospective clients for the purpose of obtaining professional employment that are not prohibited by subdivision (b)(1) are subject to the following requirements:

(A) Such communications are subject to the requirements of 4–7.11 through 4–7.17 of these rules.

(B) Each page of such communication and the face of an envelope containing the communication must be reasonably prominently marked "advertisement" in ink that contrasts with both the background it is printed on and other text appearing on the same page. If the written communication is in the form of a self-mailing brochure or pamphlet, the "advertisement" mark must be reasonably prominently marked on the address panel of the brochure or pamphlet and on each panel of the inside of the brochure or pamphlet. If the written communication is sent via electronic mail, the subject line must begin with the word "Advertisement." Brochures solicited by clients or prospective clients need not contain the "advertisement" mark.

(C) Every written communication must be accompanied by a written statement detailing the background, training and experience of the lawyer or law firm. This statement must include information about the specific experience of the advertising lawyer or law firm in the area or areas of law for which professional employment is sought. Every written communication disseminated by a lawyer referral service must be accompanied by a written statement detailing the background, training, and experience of each lawyer to whom the recipient may be referred.

(D) If a contract for representation is mailed with the written communication, the top of each page of the contract must be marked "SAMPLE" in red ink in a type size one size larger than the largest type used in the contract and the words "DO NOT SIGN" must appear on the client signature line.

(E) The first sentence of any written communication prompted by a specific occurrence involving or affecting the intended recipient of the communication or a family member must be: "If you have already retained a lawyer for this matter, please disregard this letter."

(F) Written communications must not be made to resemble legal pleadings or other legal documents.

(G) If a lawyer other than the lawyer whose name or signature appears on the communication will actually handle the case or matter, or if the case or matter will be referred to another lawyer or law firm, any written communication concerning a specific matter must include a statement so advising the client.

(H) Any written communication prompted by a specific occurrence involving or affecting the intended recipient of the communication or a family member must disclose how the lawyer obtained the information prompting the communication. The disclosure required by this rule must be specific enough to enable the recipient to understand the extent of the lawyer's knowledge regarding the recipient's particular situation.

(I) A written communication seeking employment by a specific prospective client in a specific matter shall not reveal on the envelope, or on the outside of a self-mailing brochure or pamphlet, the nature of the client's legal problem.

(3) The requirements in subdivision (b)(2) of this rule do not apply to communications between lawyers, between lawyers and their own current and former clients, or between lawyers and their own family members.

Added Jan. 31, 2013, effective May 1, 2013 (108 So.3d 609).

Comment

Prior Professional Relationship

Persons with whom the lawyer has a prior professional relationship are exempted from the general prohibition against direct, in-person solicitation. A prior professional relationship requires that the lawyer personally had a direct and continuing relationship with the person in the lawyer's capacity as a professional. Thus, a lawyer with a continuing relationship as the patient of a doctor, for example, does not have the professional relationship contemplated by the rule because the lawyer is not involved in the relationship in the lawyer's professional capacity. Similarly, a lawyer who is a member of a charitable organization totally unrelated to the practice of law and who has a direct personal relationship with another member of that organization does not fall within the definition.

On the other hand, a lawyer who is the legal advisor to a charitable board and who has direct, continuing relationships with members of that board does have prior professional relationships with those board members as contemplated by the rule. Additionally, a lawyer who has a direct, continuing relationship with another professional where both are members of a trade organization related to both the lawyer's and the nonlawyer's practices would also fall within the definition. A lawyer's relationship with a doctor because of the doctor's role as an expert witness is another example of a prior professional relationship as provided in the rule.

A lawyer who merely shared a membership in an organization in common with another person without any direct, personal contact would not have a prior professional relationship for purposes of this rule. Similarly, a lawyer who speaks at a seminar does not develop a professional relationship within the meaning of the rule with seminar attendees merely by virtue of being a speaker.

Disclosing Where the Lawyer Obtained Information

In addition, the lawyer or law firm should reveal the source of information used to determine that the recipient has a potential legal problem. Disclosure of the information source will help the recipient to understand the extent of knowledge the lawyer or law firm has regarding the recipient's particular situation and will avoid misleading the recipient into believing that the lawyer has particularized knowledge about the recipient's matter if the lawyer does not. The lawyer or law firm must disclose sufficient information or explanation to allow the recipient to locate the information that prompted the communication from the lawyer.

Alternatively, the direct mail advertisement would comply with this rule if the advertisement discloses how much information the lawyer has about the matter. For example, a direct mail advertisement for criminal defense matters would comply if it stated that the lawyer's only knowledge about the prospective client's matter is the client's name, contact information, date of arrest and charge. In the context of securities arbitration, a direct mail advertisement would comply with this requirement by stating, if true, that the lawyer obtained information from a list of investors, and the only information on that list is the prospective client's name, address, and the fact that the prospective client invested in a specific company.

Group or Prepaid Legal Services Plans

This rule would not prohibit a lawyer from contacting representatives of organizations or groups that may be interested in establishing a group or prepaid legal plan for its members, insureds, beneficiaries, or other third parties for the purpose of informing such entities of the availability of, and details concerning, the plan or arrangement that the lawyer or the lawyer's law firm is willing to offer. This form of communication is not directed to a specific prospective client known to need legal services related to a particular matter. Rather, it is usually addressed to an individual acting in a fiduciary capacity seeking a supplier of legal services for others who may, if they choose, become clients of the lawyer. Under these circumstances, the activity that the lawyer undertakes in communicating with such representatives and the type of information transmitted to the individual are functionally similar to and serve the same purpose as advertising permitted under other rules in this subchapter.

Rule 4-7.19. Evaluation of Advertisements

(a) Filing Requirements. Subject to the exemptions stated in rule 4-7.20, any lawyer who advertises services shall file with The Florida Bar a copy of each advertisement at least 20 days prior to the lawyer's first dissemination of the advertisement. The advertisement must be filed at The Florida Bar headquarters address in Tallahassee.

(b) Evaluation by The Florida Bar. The Florida Bar will evaluate all advertisements filed with it pursuant to this rule for compliance with the applicable provisions set forth in rules 4-7.11 through 4-7.15 and 4-7.18(b)(2). If The Florida Bar does not send any communication to the filer within 15 days of receipt by The Florida Bar of a complete filing, or within 15 days of receipt by The Florida Bar of additional information when requested within the initial 15 days, the lawyer will not be subject to discipline by The Florida Bar, except if The Florida Bar subsequently notifies the lawyer of noncompliance, the lawyer may be subject to discipline for dissemination of the advertisement after the notice of noncompliance.

(c) Preliminary Opinions. A lawyer may obtain an advisory opinion concerning the compliance of a contemplated advertisement prior to production of the advertisement by submitting to The Florida Bar a draft or script that includes all spoken or printed words appearing in the advertisement, a description of any visual images to be used in the advertisement, and the fee specified in this rule. The voluntary prior submission does not satisfy the filing and evaluation requirements of these rules, but once completed, The Florida Bar will not charge an additional fee for evaluation of the completed advertisement.

(d) Opinions on Exempt Advertisements. A lawyer may obtain an advisory opinion concerning the compliance of an existing or contemplated advertisement intended to be used by the lawyer seeking the advisory opinion that is not required to be filed for review by submitting the material and fee specified in subdivision (h) of this rule to The Florida Bar, except that a lawyer may not file an entire website for review. Instead, a lawyer may obtain an advisory opinion concerning the compliance of a specific page, provision, statement, illustration, or photograph on a website.

(e) Facial Compliance. Evaluation of advertisements is limited to determination of facial compliance with rules 4–7.11 through 4–7.15 and 4–7.18(b)(2), and notice of compliance does not relieve the lawyer of responsibility for the accuracy of factual statements.

(f) Notice of Compliance and Disciplinary Action. A finding of compliance by The Florida Bar will be binding on The Florida Bar in a grievance proceeding unless the advertisement contains a misrepresentation that is not apparent from the face of the advertisement. The Florida Bar has a right to change its finding of compliance and in such circumstances must notify the lawyer of the finding of noncompliance, after which the lawyer may be subject to discipline for continuing to disseminate the advertisement. A lawyer will be subject to discipline as provided in these rules for:

(1) failure to timely file the advertisement with The Florida Bar;

(2) dissemination of a noncompliant advertisement in the absence of a finding of compliance by The Florida Bar;

(3) filing of an advertisement that contains a misrepresentation that is not apparent from the face of the advertisement;

(4) dissemination of an advertisement for which the lawyer has a finding of compliance by The Florida Bar more than 30 days after the lawyer has been notified that The Florida Bar has determined that the advertisement does not comply with this subchapter; or

(5) dissemination of portions of a lawyer's Internet website(s) that are not in compliance with rules 4–7.14 and 4–7.15 only after 15 days have elapsed since the date of The Florida Bar's notice of noncompliance sent to the lawyer's official bar address.

(g) Notice of Noncompliance. If The Florida Bar determines that an advertisement is not in compliance with the applicable rules, The Florida Bar will advise the lawyer that dissemination or continued dissemination of the advertisement may result in professional discipline.

(h) Contents of Filing. A filing with The Florida Bar as required or permitted by subdivision (a) must include:

(1) a copy of the advertisement in the form or forms in which it is to be disseminated, which is readily capable of duplication by The Florida Bar (e.g., video, audio, print media, photographs of outdoor advertising);

(2) a transcript, if the advertisement is in electronic format;

(3) a printed copy of all text used in the advertisement, including both spoken language and on-screen text;

(4) an accurate English translation of any portion of the advertisement that is in a language other than English;

(5) a sample envelope in which the written advertisement will be enclosed, if the advertisement is to be mailed;

(6) a statement listing all media in which the advertisement will appear, the anticipated frequency of use of the advertisement in each medium in which it will appear, and the anticipated time period during which the advertisement will be used;

(7) the name of at least 1 lawyer who is responsible for the content of the advertisement;

(8) a fee paid to The Florida Bar, in an amount of $150 for each advertisement timely filed as provided in subdivision (a), or $250 for each advertisement not timely filed. This fee will be used to offset the cost of evaluation and review of advertisements submitted under these rules and the cost of enforcing these rules; and

(9) additional information as necessary to substantiate representations made or implied in an advertisement if requested by The Florida Bar.

(i) Change of Circumstances; Refiling Requirement. If a change of circumstances occurs subsequent to The Florida Bar's evaluation of an advertisement that raises a substantial possibility that the advertisement has become false or misleading as a result of the change in circumstances, the lawyer must promptly re-file the advertisement or a modified advertisement with The Florida Bar at its headquarters address in Tallahassee along with an explanation of the change in circumstances and an additional fee set by the Board of Governors, which will not exceed $100.

(j) Maintaining Copies of Advertisements. A copy or recording of an advertisement must be submitted to The Florida Bar in accordance with the requirements of this rule, and the lawyer must retain a copy or recording for 3 years after its last dissemination along with a record of when and where it was used. If identical advertisements are sent to 2 or more prospective clients, the lawyer may comply with this requirement by filing 1 of the identical advertisements and retaining for 3 years a single copy together with a list of the names and addresses of persons to whom the advertisement was sent.

Added Jan. 31, 2013, effective May 1, 2013 (108 So.3d 609).

Comment

All advertisements must be filed for review pursuant to this rule, unless the advertisement is exempt from filing under rule 4–7.20. Even where an advertisement is exempt from filing under rule 4–7.20, a lawyer who wishes to obtain a safe harbor from discipline can submit the lawyer's advertisement that is exempt from the filing requirement and obtain The Florida Bar's opinion prior to disseminating the advertisement. A lawyer who files an advertisement and obtains a notice of compliance is therefore immune from grievance liability unless the advertisement contains a misrepresentation that is not apparent from the face of the advertisement. Subdivision (d) of this rule precludes a lawyer from filing an entire website as an advertising submission, but a lawyer may submit a specific page, provision, statement, illustration, or photograph on a website. A lawyer who wishes to be able to rely on The Florida Bar's opinion as demonstrating the lawyer's good faith effort to comply with these rules has the responsibility of supplying The Florida Bar with all information material to a determination of whether an advertisement is false or misleading.

Rule 4–7.20. Exemptions from the Filing and Review Requirement

The following are exempt from the filing requirements of rule 4–7.19:

(a) an advertisement in any of the public media that contains no illustrations and no information other than that set forth in rule 4–7.16;

(b) a brief announcement that identifies a lawyer or law firm as a contributor to a specified charity or as a sponsor of a public service announcement or a specified charitable, community, or public interest program, activity, or event, provided that the announcement contains no information about the lawyer or law firm other than the permissible content of advertisements listed in rule 4–7.16, and the fact of the sponsorship or contribution. In determining whether an announcement is a public service announcement, the following criteria may be considered:

(1) whether the content of the announcement appears to serve the particular interests of the lawyer or law firm as much as or more than the interests of the public;

(2) whether the announcement concerns a legal subject;

(3) whether the announcement contains legal advice; and

(4) whether the lawyer or law firm paid to have the announcement published;

(c) a listing or entry in a law list or bar publication;

(d) a communication mailed only to existing clients, former clients, or other lawyers;

(e) a written or recorded communication requested by a prospective client;

(f) professional announcement cards stating new or changed associations, new offices, and similar changes relating to a lawyer or law firm, and that are mailed only to other lawyers, relatives, close personal friends, and existing or former clients; and

(g) information contained on the lawyer's Internet website(s).

Added Jan. 31, 2013, effective May 1, 2013 (108 So.3d 609).

Rule 4–7.21. Firm Names and Letterhead

(a) False, Misleading, or Deceptive Firm Names. A lawyer may not use a firm name, letterhead, or other professional designation that violates rules 4–7.11 through 4–7.15.

(b) Trade Names. A lawyer may practice under a trade name if the name is not deceptive and does not imply a connection with a government agency or with a public or charitable legal services organization, does not imply that the firm is something other than a private law firm, and is not otherwise in violation of rules 4–7.11 through 4–7.15. A lawyer in private practice may use the term "legal clinic" or "legal services" in conjunction with the lawyer's own name if the lawyer's practice is devoted to providing routine legal services for fees that are lower than the prevailing rate in the community for those services.

(c) Advertising Under Trade Names. A lawyer may not advertise under a trade or fictitious name, except that a lawyer who actually practices under a trade name as authorized by subdivision (b) may use that name in advertisements. A lawyer who advertises under a trade or fictitious name is in violation of this rule unless the same name is the law firm name that appears on the lawyer's letterhead, business cards, office sign, and fee contracts, and appears with the lawyer's signature on pleadings and other legal documents.

(d) Law Firm with Offices in Multiple Jurisdictions. A law firm with offices in more than 1 jurisdiction may use the same name in each jurisdiction, but identification of the lawyers in an office of the firm must indicate the jurisdictional limitations on those not licensed to practice in the jurisdiction where the office is located.

(e) Name of Public Officer in Firm Name. The name of a lawyer holding a public office may not be used in the name of a law firm, or in communications on its behalf, during any substantial period in which the lawyer is not actively and regularly practicing with the firm.

(f) Partnerships and Business Entities. A name, letterhead, business card or advertisement may not imply that lawyers practice in a partnership or authorized business entity when they do not.

(g) Insurance Staff Attorneys. Where otherwise consistent with these rules, lawyers who practice law as employees within a separate unit of a liability insurer representing others pursuant to policies of liability insurance may practice under a name that does not constitute a material misrepresentation. In order for the use of a name other than the name of the insurer not to constitute a material misrepresentation, all lawyers in the unit must comply with all of the following:

(1) the firm name must include the name of a lawyer who has supervisory responsibility for all lawyers in the unit;

(2) the office entry signs, letterhead, business cards, websites, announcements, advertising, and listings or entries in a law list or bar publication bearing the name must disclose that the lawyers in the unit are employees of the insurer;

(3) the name of the insurer and the employment relationship must be disclosed to all insured clients and prospective clients of the lawyers, and must be disclosed in the official file at the lawyers' first appearance in the tribunal in which the lawyers appear under such name;

(4) the offices, personnel, and records of the unit must be functionally and physically separate from other operations of the insurer to the extent that would be required by these rules if the lawyers were private practitioners sharing space with the insurer; and

(5) additional disclosure should occur whenever the lawyer knows or reasonably should know that the lawyer's role is misunderstood by the insured client or prospective clients.

Added Jan. 31, 2013, effective May 1, 2013 (108 So.3d 609).

Comment

Misleading Firm Name

A firm may be designated by the names of all or some of its members, by the names of deceased members where there has been a continuing succession in the firm's identity, or by a trade name such as "Family Legal Clinic." Although the United States Supreme Court has held that legislation may prohibit the use of trade names in professional practice, use of such names in a law practice is acceptable so long as it is not misleading. If a private firm uses a trade name that includes a geographical name such as "Springfield Legal Clinic," an express disclaimer that it is not a public legal aid agency may be required to avoid a misleading implication. It may be observed that any firm name including the name of a deceased partner is, strictly speaking, a trade name. The use of such names to designate law firms has proven a useful means of identification. However, it is misleading to use the name of a lawyer not associated with the firm or a predecessor of the firm.

A sole practitioner may not use the term "and Associates" as part of the firm name, because it is misleading where the law firm employs no associates in violation of rule 4–7.13. *See Fla. Bar v. Fetterman*, 439 So. 2d 835 (Fla. 1983). Similarly, a sole practitioner's use of "group" or "team" implies that more than one lawyer is employed in the advertised firm and is therefore misleading.

Subdivision (a) precludes use in a law firm name of terms that imply that the firm is something other than a private law firm. Three examples of such terms are "academy," "institute" and "center." Subdivision (b) precludes use of a trade or fictitious name suggesting that the firm is named for a person when in fact such a person does not exist or is not associated with the firm. An example of such an improper name is "A. Aaron Able." Although not prohibited per se, the terms "legal clinic" and "legal services" would be misleading if used by a law firm that did not devote its practice to providing routine legal services at prices below those prevailing in the community for like services.

Trade Names

Subdivision (c) of this rule precludes a lawyer from advertising under a nonsense name designed to obtain an advantageous position for the lawyer in alphabetical directory listings unless the lawyer actually practices under that nonsense name. Advertising under a law firm name that differs from the firm name under which the lawyer actually practices violates both this rule and the prohibition against false, misleading, or deceptive communications as set forth in these rules.

With regard to subdivision (f), lawyers sharing office facilities, but who are not in fact partners, may not denominate themselves as, for example, "Smith and Jones," for that title suggests partnership in the practice of law.

All lawyers who practice under trade or firm names are required to observe and comply with the requirements of the Rules Regulating the Florida Bar, including but not limited to, rules regarding conflicts of interest, imputation of conflicts, firm names and letterhead, and candor toward tribunals and third parties.

Insurance Staff Lawyers

Some liability insurers employ lawyers on a full-time basis to represent their insured clients in defense of claims covered by the contract of insurance. Use of a name to identify these lawyers is permissible if there is such physical and functional separation as to constitute a separate law firm. In the absence of such separation, it would be a misrepresentation to use a name implying that a firm exists. Practicing under the name of a lawyer inherently represents that the identified person has supervisory responsibility. Practicing under a name prohibited by subdivision (f) is not permitted. Candor requires disclosure of the employment relationship on letterhead, business cards, and in certain other communications that are not presented to a jury. The legislature of the State of Florida has enacted, as public policy, laws prohibiting the joinder of a liability insurer in most such litigation, and Florida courts have recognized the public policy of not disclosing the existence of insurance coverage to juries. Requiring lawyers who are so employed to disclose to juries the employment relationship would negate Florida public policy. For this reason, the rule does not require the disclosure of the employment relationship on all pleadings and papers filed in court proceedings. The general duty of candor of all lawyers may be implicated in other circumstances, but does not require disclosure on all pleadings.

Rule 4-7.22. Lawyer Referral Services

(a) When Lawyers May Accept Referrals. A lawyer may not accept referrals from a lawyer referral service, and it is a violation of these Rules Regulating the Florida Bar to do so, unless the service:

(1) engages in no communication with the public and in no direct contact with prospective clients in a manner that would violate the Rules of Professional Conduct if the communication or contact were made by the lawyer;

(2) receives no fee or charge that constitutes a division or sharing of fees, unless the service is a not-for-profit service approved by The Florida Bar pursuant to chapter 8 of these rules;

(3) refers clients only to persons lawfully permitted to practice law in Florida when the services to be rendered constitute the practice of law in Florida;

(4) carries or requires each lawyer participating in the service to carry professional liability insurance in an amount not less than $100,000 per claim or occurrence;

(5) furnishes The Florida Bar, on a quarterly basis, with the names and Florida bar membership numbers of all lawyers participating in the service;

(6) furnishes The Florida Bar, on a quarterly basis, with the names of all persons authorized to act on behalf of the service;

(7) responds in writing, within 15 days, to any official inquiry by bar counsel when bar counsel is seeking information described in this subdivision or conducting an investigation into the conduct of the service or a lawyer who accepts referrals from the service;

(8) neither represents nor implies to the public that the service is endorsed or approved by The Florida Bar, unless the service is subject to chapter 8 of these rules;

(9) uses its actual legal name or a registered fictitious name in all communications with the public;

(10) affirmatively states in all advertisements that it is a lawyer referral service; and

(11) affirmatively states in all advertisements that lawyers who accept referrals from it pay to participate in the lawyer referral service.

(b) Responsibility of Lawyer. A lawyer who accepts referrals from a lawyer referral service is responsible for ensuring that any advertisements or written communications used by the service comply with the requirements of the Rules Regulating the Florida Bar, including the provisions of this subchapter.

(c) Definition of Lawyer Referral Service. A "lawyer referral service" is:

(1) any person, group of persons, association, organization, or entity that receives a fee or charge for referring or causing the direct or indirect referral of a potential client to a lawyer drawn from a specific group or panel of lawyers; or

(2) any group or pooled advertising program operated by any person, group of persons, association, organization, or entity wherein the legal services advertisements utilize a common telephone number or website and potential clients are then referred only to lawyers or law firms participating in the group or pooled advertising program.

A pro bono referral program, in which the participating lawyers do not pay a fee or charge of any kind to receive referrals or to belong to the referral panel, and are undertaking the referred matters without expectation of remuneration, is not a lawyer referral service within the definition of this rule.

Added Jan. 31, 2013, effective May 1, 2013 (108 So.3d 609).

Rule 4-7.23. Lawyer Directory

(a) Definition of Lawyer Directory. A lawyer directory is any person, group of persons, association, organization, or entity that receives any consideration, monetary or otherwise, given in exchange for publishing a listing of lawyers together in one place, such as a common Internet address, a book or pamphlet, a section of a book or pamphlet, in which all the participating lawyers and their advertisements are provided and the viewer is not directed to a particular lawyer or lawyers. A local or voluntary bar association that lists its members on its website or in its publications is not a lawyer directory under this rule. This rule does not apply to traditional telephone directories.

(b) When Lawyers May Advertise in a Directory. A lawyer may not advertise in a directory unless the directory:

(1) engages in no communication with the public and in no direct contact with prospective clients in a manner that would violate the Rules of Professional Conduct if the communication or contact were made by the lawyer;

(2) receives no fee or charge that constitutes a division or sharing of fees;

(3) lists only persons lawfully permitted to practice law in Florida when the services to be rendered constitute the practice of law in Florida;

(4) responds in writing, within 15 days, to any official inquiry by bar counsel when bar counsel is seeking information described in this subdivision or

conducting an investigation into the conduct of the directory or a lawyer who pays to be listed in the directory;

(5) neither represents nor implies to the public that the directory is endorsed or approved by The Florida Bar;

(6) uses its actual legal name or a registered fictitious name in all communications with the public; and

(7) affirmatively states in all advertisements that it is a legal directory or lawyer directory.

(c) Responsibility of Lawyer. A lawyer who advertises in a lawyer directory is responsible for ensuring that any advertisements or written communications used by the directory comply with the requirements of the Rules Regulating the Florida Bar, and that the directory is in compliance with the provisions of this subchapter. It is a violation of these Rules Regulating the Florida Bar and a failure of such responsibility if the lawyer knows or should have known that the directory is not in compliance with applicable rules or if the lawyer failed to seek information necessary to determine compliance.

Added Jan. 31, 2013, effective May 1, 2013 (108 So.3d 609).

4–8. MAINTAINING THE INTEGRITY OF THE PROFESSION

Rule 4–8.1. Bar Admission and Disciplinary Matters

An applicant for admission to the bar, or a lawyer in connection with a bar admission application or in connection with a disciplinary matter, shall not:

(a) knowingly make a false statement of material fact;

(b) fail to disclose a fact necessary to correct a misapprehension known by the person to have arisen in the matter or knowingly fail to respond to a lawful demand for information from an admissions or disciplinary authority, except that this rule does not require disclosure of information otherwise protected by rule 4–1.6; or

(c) commit an act that adversely reflects on the applicant's fitness to practice law. An applicant who commits such an act before admission, but which is discovered after admission, shall be subject to discipline under these rules.

Amended July 23, 1992, effective Jan. 1, 1993 (605 So.2d 252); Oct. 6, 2005, effective Jan. 1, 2006 (916 So.2d 655).

Comment

The duty imposed by this rule extends to persons seeking admission to the bar as well as to lawyers. Hence, if a person makes a material false statement in connection with an application for admission, it may be the basis for subsequent disciplinary action if the person is admitted and in any event may be relevant in a subsequent admission application. The duty imposed by this rule applies to a lawyer's own admission or discipline as well as that of others. Thus, it is a separate professional offense for a lawyer to knowingly make a misrepresentation or omission in connection with a disciplinary investigation of the lawyer's own conduct. Subdivision (b) of this rule also requires correction of any prior misstatement in the matter that the applicant or lawyer may have made and affirmative clarification of any misunderstanding on the part of the admissions or disciplinary authority of which the person involved becomes aware.

This rule is subject to the provisions of the fifth amendment of the United States Constitution and the corresponding provisions of the Florida Constitution. A person relying on such a provision in response to a question, however, should do so openly and not use the right of nondisclosure as a justification for failure to comply with this rule.

A lawyer representing an applicant for admission to the bar, or representing a lawyer who is the subject of a disciplinary inquiry or proceeding, is governed by the rules applicable to the client-lawyer relationship, including rule 4–1.6 and, in some cases, rule 4–3.3.

An applicant for admission may commit acts that adversely reflect on the applicant's fitness to practice law and which are discovered only after the applicant becomes a member of the bar. This rule provides a means to address such misconduct in the absence of such a provision in the Rules of the Supreme Court Relating to Admissions to the Bar.

Rule 4–8.2. Judicial and legal officials

(a) Impugning Qualifications and Integrity of Judges or Other Officers. A lawyer shall not make a statement that the lawyer knows to be false or with reckless disregard as to its truth or falsity concerning the qualifications or integrity of a judge, mediator, arbitrator, adjudicatory officer, public legal officer, juror or member of the venire, or candidate for election or appointment to judicial or legal office.

(b) Candidates for Judicial Office; Code of Judicial Conduct Applies. A lawyer who is a candidate for judicial office shall comply with the applicable provisions of Florida's Code of Judicial Conduct.

Amended June 8, 1989 (544 So.2d 193); July 23, 1992, effective Jan. 1, 1993 (605 So.2d 252).

Comment

Assessments by lawyers are relied on in evaluating the professional or personal fitness of persons being considered for election or appointment to judicial office and to public legal offices, such as attorney general, prosecuting attorney, and public defender. Expressing honest and candid opinions on such matters contributes to improving the administration of justice. Conversely, false statements by a lawyer can unfairly undermine public confidence in the administration of justice.

False statements or statements made with reckless disregard for truth or falsity concerning potential jurors, jurors serving in pending cases, or jurors who served in concluded cases undermine the impartiality of future jurors who may fear to execute their duty if their decisions are ridiculed. Lawyers may not make false statements or any statement made with the intent to ridicule or harass jurors.

When a lawyer seeks judicial office, the lawyer should be bound by applicable limitations on political activity.

To maintain the fair and independent administration of justice, lawyers are encouraged to continue traditional efforts to defend judges and courts unjustly criticized.

Rule 4–8.3. Reporting Professional Misconduct

(a) Reporting Misconduct of Other Lawyers. A lawyer who knows that another lawyer has committed a violation of the Rules of Professional Conduct that raises a substantial question as to that lawyer's honesty, trustworthiness, or fitness as a lawyer in other respects shall inform the appropriate professional authority.

(b) Reporting Misconduct of Judges. A lawyer who knows that a judge has committed a violation of applicable rules of judicial conduct that raises a substantial question as to the judge's fitness for office shall inform the appropriate authority.

(c) Confidences Preserved. This rule does not require disclosure of information:

(1) otherwise protected by rule 4–1.6;

(2) gained by a lawyer while serving as a mediator or mediation participant if the information is privileged or confidential under applicable law; or

(3) gained by a lawyer or judge while participating in an approved lawyers assistance program, unless the lawyer's participation in an approved lawyers assistance program is part of a disciplinary sanction, in which case a report about the lawyer who is participating as part of a disciplinary sanction shall be made to the appropriate disciplinary agency.

(d) Limited Exception for LOMAS Counsel. A lawyer employed by or acting on behalf of the Law Office Management Assistance Service (LOMAS) shall not have an obligation to disclose knowledge of the conduct of another member of The Florida Bar that raises a substantial question as to the other lawyer's fitness to practice, if the lawyer employed by or acting on behalf of LOMAS acquired the knowledge while engaged in a LOMAS review of the other lawyer's practice. Provided further, however, that if the LOMAS review is conducted as a part of a disciplinary sanction this limitation shall not be applicable and a report shall be made to the appropriate disciplinary agency.

Amended July 23, 1992, effective Jan. 1, 1993 (605 So.2d 252); effective Feb. 8, 2001 (795 So.2d 1); March 23, 2006, effective May 22, 2006 (933 So.2d 417); April 12, 2012, effective July 1, 2012 (107 So.3d 807).

Comment

Self-regulation of the legal profession requires that members of the profession initiate disciplinary investigation when they know of a violation of the Rules of Professional Conduct. Lawyers have a similar obligation with respect to judicial misconduct. An apparently isolated violation may indicate a pattern of misconduct that only a disciplinary investigation can uncover. Reporting a violation is especially important where the victim is unlikely to discover the offense.

A report about misconduct is not required where it would involve violation of rule 4–1.6. However, a lawyer should encourage a client to consent to disclosure where prosecution would not substantially prejudice the client's interests.

If a lawyer were obliged to report every violation of the rules, the failure to report any violation would itself be a professional offense. Such a requirement existed in many jurisdictions, but proved to be unenforceable. This rule limits the reporting obligation to those offenses that a self-regulating profession must vigorously endeavor to prevent. A measure of judgment is, therefore, required in complying with the provisions of this rule. The term "substantial" refers to the seriousness of the possible offense and not the quantum of evidence of which the lawyer is aware.

The duty to report professional misconduct does not apply to a lawyer retained to represent a lawyer whose professional conduct is in question. Such a situation is governed by the rules applicable to the client-lawyer relationship.

Generally, Florida statutes provide that information gained through a "mediation communication" is privileged and confidential, including information which discloses professional misconduct occurring outside the mediation. However, professional misconduct occurring during the mediation is not privileged or confidential under Florida statutes.

Information about a lawyer's or judge's misconduct or fitness may be received by a lawyer in the course of that lawyer's participation in an approved lawyers or judges assistance program. In that circumstance, providing for an exception to the reporting requirements of subdivisions (a) and (b) of this rule encourages lawyers and judges to seek treatment through such a program. Conversely, without such an exception, lawyers and judges may hesitate to seek assistance from these programs, which may then result in additional harm to their professional careers and additional injury to the welfare of clients and the public. These rules do not otherwise address the confidentiality of information received by a lawyer or judge participating in an approved lawyers assistance program; such an obligation, however, may be imposed by the rules of the program or other law.

Rule 4-8.4. Misconduct

A lawyer shall not:

(a) violate or attempt to violate the Rules of Professional Conduct, knowingly assist or induce another to do so, or do so through the acts of another;

(b) commit a criminal act that reflects adversely on the lawyer's honesty, trustworthiness, or fitness as a lawyer in other respects;

(c) engage in conduct involving dishonesty, fraud, deceit, or misrepresentation, except that it shall not be professional misconduct for a lawyer for a criminal law enforcement agency or regulatory agency to advise others about or to supervise another in an undercover investigation, unless prohibited by law or rule, and it shall not be professional misconduct for a lawyer employed in a capacity other than as a lawyer by a criminal law enforcement agency or regulatory agency to participate in an undercover investigation, unless prohibited by law or rule;

(d) engage in conduct in connection with the practice of law that is prejudicial to the administration of justice, including to knowingly, or through callous indifference, disparage, humiliate, or discriminate against litigants, jurors, witnesses, court personnel, or other lawyers on any basis, including, but not limited to, on account of race, ethnicity, gender, religion, national origin, disability, marital status, sexual orientation, age, socioeconomic status, employment, or physical characteristic;

(e) state or imply an ability to influence improperly a government agency or official or to achieve results by means that violate the Rules of Professional Conduct or other law;

(f) knowingly assist a judge or judicial officer in conduct that is a violation of applicable rules of judicial conduct or other law;

(g) fail to respond, in writing, to any official inquiry by bar counsel or a disciplinary agency, as defined elsewhere in these rules, when bar counsel or the agency is conducting an investigation into the lawyer's conduct. A written response shall be made:

(1) within 15 days of the date of the initial written investigative inquiry by bar counsel, grievance committee, or board of governors;

(2) within 10 days of the date of any follow-up written investigative inquiries by bar counsel, grievance committee, or board of governors;

(3) within the time stated in any subpoena issued under these Rules Regulating The Florida Bar (without additional time allowed for mailing);

(4) as provided in the Florida Rules of Civil Procedure or order of the referee in matters assigned to a referee; and

(5) as provided in the Florida Rules of Appellate Procedure or order of the Supreme Court of Florida for matters pending action by that court.

Except as stated otherwise herein or in the applicable rules, all times for response shall be calculated as provided elsewhere in these Rules Regulating The Florida Bar and may be extended or shortened by bar counsel or the disciplinary agency making the official inquiry upon good cause shown.

Failure to respond to an official inquiry with no good cause shown may be a matter of contempt and processed in accordance with rule 3-7.11(f) of these Rules Regulating The Florida Bar.

(h) willfully refuse, as determined by a court of competent jurisdiction, to timely pay a child support obligation; or

(i) engage in sexual conduct with a client or a representative of a client that exploits or adversely affects the interests of the client or the lawyer-client relationship.

If the sexual conduct commenced after the lawyer-client relationship was formed it shall be presumed that the sexual conduct exploits or adversely affects the interests of the client or the lawyer-client relationship. A lawyer may rebut this presumption by proving by a preponderance of the evidence that the sexual conduct did not exploit or adversely affect the interests of the client or the lawyer-client relationship.

The prohibition and presumption stated in this rule do not apply to a lawyer in the same firm as another lawyer representing the client if the lawyer involved in the sexual conduct does not personally provide legal services to the client and is screened from access to the file concerning the legal representation.

Amended July 23, 1992, effective Jan. 1, 1993 (605 So.2d 252); July 1, 1993 (621 So.2d 1032); July 1, 1993, eff. Jan. 1, 1994 (624 So.2d 720); Feb. 9, 1995 (649 So.2d 868); July 20, 1995 (658 So.2d 930); Sept. 24, 1998, effective Oct. 1, 1998 (718 So.2d 1179); Feb. 8, 2001 (795 So.2d 1); May 20, 2004 (875 So.2d 448); Oct. 6, 2005, effective Jan. 1, 2006 (916 So.2d 655); March 23, 2006, effective May 22, 2006 (933 So.2d 417); Nov. 19, 2009, effective Feb. 1, 2010 (24 So.3d 63).

Comment

Lawyers are subject to discipline when they violate or attempt to violate the Rules of Professional Conduct, knowingly assist or induce another to do so, or do so through the acts of another, as when they request or instruct an agent to do so on the lawyer's behalf. Subdivision (a), however, does not prohibit a lawyer from advising a client concerning action the client is legally entitled to take, provided that the client is not used to indirectly violate the Rules of Professional Conduct.

Many kinds of illegal conduct reflect adversely on fitness to practice law, such as offenses involving fraud and the offense of willful failure to file an income tax return. However, some kinds of offense carry no such implication. Traditionally, the distinction was drawn in terms of offenses involving "moral turpitude." That concept can be construed to include offenses concerning some matters of personal morality, such as adultery and comparable offenses, that have no specific connection to fitness for the practice of law. Although a lawyer is personally answerable to the entire criminal law, a lawyer should be professionally answerable only for offenses that indicate lack of those characteristics relevant to law practice. Offenses involving violence, dishonesty, breach of trust, or serious interference with the administration of justice are in that category. A pattern of repeated offenses, even ones of minor significance when considered separately, can indicate indifference to legal obligation.

A lawyer may refuse to comply with an obligation imposed by law upon a good faith belief that no valid obligation exists. The provisions of rule 4–1.2(d) concerning a good faith challenge to the validity, scope, meaning, or application of the law apply to challenges of legal regulation of the practice of law.

Subdivision (c) recognizes instances where lawyers in criminal law enforcement agencies or regulatory agencies advise others about or supervise others in undercover investigations, and provides an exception to allow the activity without the lawyer engaging in professional misconduct. The exception acknowledges current, acceptable practice of these agencies. Although the exception appears in this rule, it is also applicable to rules 4–4.1 and 4–4.3. However, nothing in the rule allows the lawyer to engage in such conduct if otherwise prohibited by law or rule.

Subdivision (d) of this rule proscribes conduct that is prejudicial to the administration of justice. Such proscription includes the prohibition against discriminatory conduct committed by a lawyer while performing duties in connection with the practice of law. The proscription extends to any characteristic or status that is not relevant to the proof of any legal or factual issue in dispute. Such conduct, when directed towards litigants, jurors, witnesses, court personnel, or other lawyers, whether based on race, ethnicity, gender, religion, national origin, disability, marital status, sexual orientation, age, socioeconomic status, employment, physical characteristic, or any other basis, subverts the administration of justice and undermines the public's confidence in our system of justice, as well as notions of equality. This subdivision does not prohibit a lawyer from representing a client as may be permitted by applicable law, such as, by way of example, representing a client accused of committing discriminatory conduct.

Lawyers holding public office assume legal responsibilities going beyond those of other citizens. A lawyer's abuse of public office can suggest an inability to fulfill the professional role of attorney. The same is true of abuse of positions of private trust such as trustee, executor, administrator, guardian, or agent and officer, director, or manager of a corporation or other organization.

A lawyer's obligation to respond to an inquiry by a disciplinary agency is stated in subdivision (g) of this rule and subdivision (h)(2) of rule 3–7.6. While response is mandatory, the lawyer may deny the charges or assert any available privilege or immunity or interpose any disability that prevents disclosure of a certain matter. A response containing a proper invocation thereof is sufficient under the Rules Regulating The Florida Bar. This obligation is necessary to ensure the proper and efficient operation of the disciplinary system.

Subdivision (h) of this rule was added to make consistent the treatment of attorneys who fail to pay child support with the treatment of other professionals who fail to pay child support, in accordance with the provisions of section 61.13015, Florida Statutes. That section provides for the suspension or denial of a professional license due to delinquent child support payments after all other available remedies for the collection of child support have been exhausted. Likewise, subdivision (h) of this rule should not be used as the primary means for collecting child support, but should be used only after all other available remedies for the collection of child support have been exhausted. Before a grievance may be filed or a grievance procedure initiated under this subdivision, the court that entered the child support order must first make a finding of willful refusal to pay. The child support obligation at issue under this rule includes both domestic (Florida) and out-of-state (URESA) child support obligations, as well as arrearages.

Subdivision (i) proscribes exploitation of the client or the lawyer-client relationship by means of commencement of sexual conduct. The lawyer-client relationship is grounded on mutual trust. A sexual relationship that exploits that trust compromises the lawyer-client relationship. Attorneys have a duty to exercise independent professional judgment on behalf of clients. Engaging in sexual relationships with clients has the capacity to impair the exercise of that judgment.

Sexual conduct between a lawyer and client violates this rule, regardless of when the sexual conduct began when compared to the commencement of the lawyer-client relationship, if the sexual conduct exploits the lawyer-client relationship, negatively affects the client's interest, creates a conflict of interest between the lawyer and client, or negatively affects the exercise of the lawyer's independent professional judgment in representing the client.

Subdivision (i) creates a presumption that sexual conduct between a lawyer and client exploits or adversely affects the interests of the client or the lawyer-client relationship if the sexual conduct is entered into after the lawyer-client relationship begins. A lawyer charged with a violation of this rule may rebut this presumption by a preponderance of the evidence that the sexual conduct did not exploit the lawyer-client relationship, negatively affect the client's interest, create a conflict of interest between the lawyer and client, or negatively affect the exercise of the lawyer's independent professional judgment in representing the client.

For purposes of this rule, a "representative of a client" is an agent of the client who supervises, directs, or regularly consults with the organization's lawyer concerning a client matter or has authority to obligate the organization with respect to the matter, or whose act or omission in connection with the matter may be imputed to the organization for purposes of civil or criminal liability.

Rule 4–8.5. Jurisdiction

A lawyer admitted to practice in this jurisdiction is subject to the disciplinary authority of this jurisdiction although engaged in practice elsewhere.

Comment

In modern practice lawyers frequently act outside the territorial limits of the jurisdiction in which they are licensed to practice, either in another state or outside the United States. In doing so, they remain subject to the governing authority of the jurisdiction in which they are licensed to practice. If their activity in another jurisdiction is substantial and continuous, it may constitute practice of law in that jurisdiction. See rule 4–5.5.

If the Rules of Professional Conduct in the 2 jurisdictions differ, principles of conflict of laws may apply. Similar problems can arise when a lawyer is licensed to practice in more than 1 jurisdiction.

Where the lawyer is licensed to practice law in 2 jurisdictions that impose conflicting obligations, applicable rules of choice of law may govern the situation. A related problem arises with respect to practice before a federal tribunal where the general authority of the states to regulate the practice of law must be reconciled with such authority as federal tribunals may have to regulate practice before them.

Comment amended July 23, 1992, effective Jan. 1, 1993 (605 So.2d 252).

Rule 4–8.6. Authorized Business Entities

(a) Authorized Business Entities. Lawyers may practice law in the form of professional service corporations, professional limited liability companies, sole proprietorships, general partnerships, or limited liability partnerships organized or qualified under applicable law. Such forms of practice are authorized business entities under these rules.

(b) Practice of Law Limited to Members of The Florida Bar. No authorized business entity may engage in the practice of law in the state of Florida or render advice under or interpretations of Florida law except through officers, directors, partners, managers, agents, or employees who are qualified to render legal services in this state.

(c) Qualifications of Managers, Directors and Officers. No person may serve as a partner, manager, director or executive officer of an authorized business entity that is engaged in the practice of law in Florida unless such person is legally qualified to render legal services in this state. For purposes of this rule the term "executive officer" includes the president, vice-president, or any other officer who performs a policy-making function.

(d) Violation of Statute or Rule. A lawyer who, while acting as a shareholder, member, officer, director, partner, proprietor, manager, agent, or employee of an authorized business entity and engaged in the practice of law in Florida, violates or sanctions the violation of the authorized business entity statutes or the Rules Regulating The Florida Bar will be subject to disciplinary action.

(e) Disqualification of Shareholder, Member, Proprietor, or Partner; Severance of Financial Interests. Whenever a shareholder of a professional service corporation, a member of a professional limited liability company, proprietor, or partner in a limited liability partnership becomes legally disqualified to render legal services in this state, said shareholder, member, proprietor, or partner must sever all employment with and financial interests in such authorized business entity immediately. For purposes of this rule the term "legally disqualified" does not include suspension from the practice of law for a period of time less than 91 days. Severance of employment and financial interests required by this rule will not preclude the shareholder, member, proprietor, or partner from receiving compensation based on legal fees generated for legal services performed during the time when the shareholder, member, proprietor, or partner was legally qualified to render legal services in this state. This provision will not prohibit employment of a legally disqualified shareholder, member, proprietor, or partner in a position that does not render legal service nor payment to an existing profit sharing or pension plan to the extent permitted in rules 3–6.1 and 4–5.4(a)(3), or as required by applicable law.

(f) Cessation of Legal Services. Whenever all shareholders of a professional service corporation, or all members of a professional limited liability company, the proprietor of a solo practice, or all partners in a limited liability partnership become legally disqualified to render legal services in this state, the authorized business entity must cease the rendition of legal services in Florida.

(g) Application of Statutory Provisions. Unless otherwise provided in this rule, each shareholder, member, proprietor, or partner of an authorized business entity will possess all rights and benefits and will be subject to all duties applicable to such shareholder, member, proprietor, or partner provided by the statutes pursuant to which the authorized business entity was organized or qualified.

Added June 8, 1989 (544 So.2d 193). Amended July 23, 1992, effective Jan. 1, 1993 (605 So.2d 252); June 27, 1996, effective July 1, 1996 (677 So.2d 272); Sept. 24, 1998, effective Oct. 1, 1998 (718 So.2d 1179); May 20, 2004 (875 So.2d 448); Oct. 6, 2005, effective Jan. 1, 2006 (916 So.2d 655); May 29, 2014, effective June 1, 2014 (140 So.3d 541).

Comment

In 1961 this court recognized the authority of the legislature to enact statutory provisions creating corporations, particularly professional service corporations. But this court also noted that "[e]nabling action by this Court is therefore an essential condition precedent to authorize members of The Florida Bar to qualify under and engage in the practice of their profession pursuant to The 1961 Act." *In Re The Florida Bar*, 133 So. 2d 554, at 555 (Fla. 1961).

The same is true today, whatever the form of business entity created by legislative enactment. Hence, this rule is adopted to continue authorization for members of the bar to practice law in the form of a professional service corporation, a professional limited liability company, or a limited liability partnership. This rule also permits a member of the bar to practice law as a sole proprietor or as a member of a general partnership. These types of entities are collectively referred to as authorized business entities.

Limitation on rendering legal services

No person may render legal services on behalf of an authorized business entity unless that person is otherwise authorized to do so via membership in the bar or through a motion for leave to appear. Neither the adoption of this rule nor the statutory provisions alter this limitation.

Employment by and financial interests in an authorized business entity

This rule and the statute require termination of employment of a shareholder, member, proprietor, or partner when same is "legally disqualified" to render legal services. The purpose of this provision is to prohibit compensation based on fees for legal services rendered at a time when the shareholder, member, proprietor, or partner cannot render the same type of services. Continued engagement in capacities other than rendering legal services with the same or similar compensation would allow circumvention of prohibitions of sharing legal fees with one not qualified to render legal services. Other rules prohibit the sharing of legal fees with nonlawyers and this rule continues the application of that type of prohibition. However, nothing in this rule or the statute prohibits payment to the disqualified shareholder, member, proprietor, or partner for legal services rendered while the shareholder, member, proprietor, or partner was qualified to render same, even though payment for the legal services is not received until the shareholder, member, proprietor, or partner is legally disqualified.

Similarly, this rule and the statute require the severance of "financial interests" of a legally disqualified shareholder, member, proprietor, or partner. The same reasons apply to severance of financial interests as those that apply to severance of employment. Other provisions of these rules proscribe limits on employment and the types of duties that a legally disqualified shareholder, member, proprietor, or partner may be assigned.

Practical application of the statute and this rule to the requirements of the practice of law mandates exclusion of short term, temporary removal of qualifications to render legal services. Hence, any suspension of less than 91 days, including membership fees delinquency suspensions, is excluded from the definition of the term. These temporary impediments to the practice of law are such that with the passage of time or the completion of ministerial acts, the member of the bar is automatically qualified to render legal services. Severe tax consequences would result from forced severance and subsequent reestablishment (upon reinstatement of qualifications) of all financial interests in these instances.

However, the exclusion of such suspensions from the definition of the term does not authorize the payment to the disqualified shareholder, member, proprietor, or partner of compensation based on fees for legal services rendered during the time when the shareholder, member, proprietor, or partner is not personally qualified to render such services. Continuing the employment of a legally disqualified shareholder, member, proprietor, or partner during the term of a suspension of less than 91 days requires the authorized business entity to take steps to avoid the practice of law by the legally disqualified shareholder, member, proprietor, or partner, the ability of the legally disqualified shareholder, member, proprietor, or partner to control the actions of members of the bar qualified to render legal services, and payment of compensation to the legally disqualified shareholder, member, proprietor, or partner based on legal services rendered while the legally disqualified shareholder, member, proprietor, or partner is not qualified to render them. Mere characterization of continued compensation, which is the same or similar to that the legally disqualified shareholder, member, proprietor, or partner received when qualified to render legal services, is not sufficient to satisfy the requirements of this rule.

Profit sharing or pension plans

To the extent that applicable law requires continued payment to existing profit sharing or pension plans, nothing in this rule or the statute may abridge such payments. However, if permitted under applicable law the amount paid to the plan for a legally disqualified shareholder, member, proprietor, or partner will not include payments based on legal services rendered while the legally disqualified shareholder, member, proprietor, or partner was not qualified to render legal services

Interstate practice

This rule permits members of The Florida Bar to engage in the practice of law with lawyers licensed to practice elsewhere in an authorized business entity organized under the laws of another jurisdiction and qualified under the laws of Florida (or vice–versa), but nothing in this rule is intended to affect the ability of non-members of The Florida Bar to practice law in Florida. See, e.g., *Fla. Bar v. Savitt*, 363 So. 2d 559 (Fla. 1978).

The terms qualified and legally disqualified are imported from the Professional Service Corporation Act (Chapter 621, Florida Statutes).

CHAPTER 5. RULES REGULATING TRUST ACCOUNTS

5-1. GENERALLY

5-1. GENERALLY

Rule 5-1.1. Trust Accounts

Text of rule effective until October 1, 2015. See, also, rule effective October 1, 2015.

(a) Nature of Money or Property Entrusted to Attorney.

(1) *Trust Account Required; Commingling Prohibited.* A lawyer shall hold in trust, separate from the lawyer's own property, funds and property of clients or third persons that are in a lawyer's possession in connection with a representation. All funds, including advances for fees, costs, and expenses, shall be kept in a separate bank or savings and loan association account maintained in the state where the lawyer's office is situated or elsewhere with the consent of the client or third person and clearly labeled and designated as a trust account. A lawyer may maintain funds belonging to the lawyer in the trust account in an amount no more than is reasonably sufficient to pay bank charges relating to the trust account.

(2) *Compliance With Client Directives.* Trust funds may be separately held and maintained other than in a bank or savings and loan association account if the lawyer receives written permission from the client to do so and provided that written permission is received before maintaining the funds other than in a separate account.

(3) *Safe Deposit Boxes.* If a member of the bar uses a safe deposit box to store trust funds or property, the member shall advise the institution in which the deposit box is located that it may include property of clients or third persons.

(b) Application of Trust Funds or Property to Specific Purpose. Money or other property entrusted to an attorney for a specific purpose, including advances for fees, costs, and expenses, is held in trust and must be applied only to that purpose. Money and other property of clients coming into the hands of an attorney are not subject to counterclaim or setoff for attorney's fees, and a refusal to account for and deliver over such property upon demand shall be deemed a conversion.

(c) Liens Permitted. This subchapter does not preclude the retention of money or other property upon which the lawyer has a valid lien for services nor does it preclude the payment of agreed fees from the proceeds of transactions or collection.

(d) Controversies as to Amount of Fees. Controversies as to the amount of fees are not grounds for disciplinary proceedings unless the amount demanded is clearly excessive, extortionate, or fraudulent. In a controversy alleging a clearly excessive, extortionate, or fraudulent fee, announced willingness of an attorney to submit a dispute as to the amount of a fee to a competent tribunal for determination may be considered in any determination as to intent or in mitigation of discipline; provided, such willingness shall not preclude admission of any other relevant admissible evidence relating to such controversy, including evidence as to the withholding of funds or property of the client, or to other injury to the client occasioned by such controversy.

(e) Notice of Receipt of Trust Funds; Delivery; Accounting. Upon receiving funds or other property in which a client or third person has an interest, a lawyer shall promptly notify the client or third person. Except as stated in this rule or otherwise permitted by law or by agreement with the client, a lawyer shall promptly deliver to the client or third person any funds or other property that the client or third person is entitled to receive and, upon request by the client or third person, shall promptly render a full accounting regarding such property.

(f) Disputed Ownership of Trust Funds. When in the course of representation a lawyer is in possession of property in which 2 or more persons (1 of whom may be the lawyer) claim interests, the property shall be treated by the lawyer as trust property, but the portion belonging to the lawyer or law firm shall be withdrawn within a reasonable time after it becomes due unless the right of the lawyer or law firm to receive it is disputed, in which event the portion in dispute shall be kept separate by the lawyer until the dispute is resolved. The lawyer shall promptly distribute all portions of the property as to which the interests are not in dispute.

(g) Interest on Trust Accounts (IOTA) Program.

(1) *Definitions.* As used herein, the term:

(A) "Nominal or short term" describes funds of a client or third person that, pursuant to subdivision (3), below, the lawyer has determined cannot earn income for the client or third person in excess of the costs to secure the income.

(B) "Foundation" means The Florida Bar Foundation, Inc.

(C) "IOTA account" means an interest or dividend-bearing trust account benefiting The Florida Bar Foundation established in an eligible institution for the deposit of nominal or short-term funds of clients or third persons.

(D) "Eligible Institution" means any bank or savings and loan association authorized by federal or state laws to do business in Florida and insured by the Federal Deposit Insurance Corporation, or any successor insurance corporation(s) established by federal or state laws, or any open-end investment company registered with the Securities and Exchange Commission and authorized by federal or state laws to do business in Florida, all of which must meet the requirements set out in subdivision (5), below.

(E) "Interest or dividend-bearing trust account" means a federally insured checking account or investment product, including a daily financial institution repurchase agreement or a money market fund. A daily financial institution repurchase agreement must be fully collateralized by, and an open-end money market fund must consist solely of, United States Government Securities. A daily financial institution repurchase agreement may be established only with an eligible institution that is deemed to be "well capitalized" or "adequately capitalized" as defined by applicable federal statutes and regulations. An open-end money market fund must hold itself out as a money market fund as defined by applicable federal statutes and regulations under the Investment Company Act of 1940, and have total assets of at least $250 million. The funds covered by this rule shall be subject to withdrawal upon request and without delay.

(2) *Required Participation.* All nominal or short-term funds belonging to clients or third persons that are placed in trust with any member of The Florida Bar practicing law from an office or other business location within the state of Florida shall be deposited into one or more IOTA accounts, unless the funds may earn income for the client or third person in excess of the costs incurred to secure the income, except as provided elsewhere in this chapter. Only trust funds that are nominal or short term shall be deposited into an IOTA account. The member shall certify annually, in writing, that the member is in compliance with, or is exempt from, the provisions of this rule.

(3) *Determination of Nominal or Short–Term Funds.* The lawyer shall exercise good faith judgment in determining upon receipt whether the funds of a client or third person are nominal or short term. In the exercise of this good faith judgment, the lawyer shall consider such factors as:

(A) the amount of a client's or third person's funds to be held by the lawyer or law firm;

(B) the period of time such funds are expected to be held;

(C) the likelihood of delay in the relevant transaction(s) or proceeding(s);

(D) the cost to the lawyer or law firm of establishing and maintaining an interest-bearing account or other appropriate investment for the benefit of the client or third person; and

(E) minimum balance requirements and/or service charges or fees imposed by the eligible institution.

The determination of whether a client's or third person's funds are nominal or short term shall rest in the sound judgment of the lawyer or law firm. No lawyer shall be charged with ethical impropriety or other breach of professional conduct based on the exercise of such good faith judgment.

(4) *Notice to Foundation.* Lawyers or law firms shall advise the Foundation, at Post Office Box 1553, Orlando, Florida 32802–1553, of the establishment of an IOTA account for funds covered by this rule. Such notice shall include: the IOTA account number as assigned by the eligible institution; the name of the lawyer or law firm on the IOTA account; the eligible institution name; the eligible institution address; and the name and Florida Bar attorney number of the lawyer, or of each member of The Florida Bar in a law firm, practicing from an office or other business location within the state of Florida that has established the IOTA account.

(5) *Eligible Institution Participation in IOTA.* Participation in the IOTA program is voluntary for banks, savings and loan associations, and investment companies. Institutions that choose to offer and maintain IOTA accounts must meet the following requirements:

(A) Interest Rates and Dividends. Eligible institutions shall maintain IOTA accounts which pay the highest interest rate or dividend generally available from the institution to its non-IOTA account customers when IOTA accounts meet or exceed the same minimum balance or other account eligibility qualifications, if any.

(B) Determination of Interest Rates and Dividends. In determining the highest interest rate or dividend generally available from the institution to its non-IOTA accounts in compliance with subdivision (5)(A), above, eligible institutions may consider factors, in addition to the IOTA account balance, customarily considered by the institution when setting interest rates or dividends for its customers, provided that such factors do not discriminate between IOTA accounts and accounts of non-IOTA customers, and that these factors do not include that the account is an IOTA account.

(C) Remittance and Reporting Instructions. Eligible institutions shall:

(i) calculate and remit interest or dividends on the balance of the deposited funds, in accordance with the institution's standard practice for non-IOTA account customers, less reasonable service charges or fees, if any, in connection with the deposited funds, at least quarterly, to the Foundation;

(ii) transmit with each remittance to the Foundation a statement showing the name of the lawyer or law firm from whose IOTA account the remittance is sent, the lawyer's or law firm's IOTA account number as assigned by the institution, the rate of interest applied, the period for which the remittance is made, the total interest or dividend earned during the remittance period, the amount and description of any service charges or fees assessed during the remittance period, and the net amount of interest or dividend remitted for the period; and

(iii) transmit to the depositing lawyer or law firm, for each remittance, a statement showing the amount of interest or dividend paid to the Foundation, the rate of interest applied, and the period for which the statement is made.

(6) *Small Fund Amounts.* The Foundation may establish procedures for a lawyer or law firm to maintain an interest-free trust account for client and third-person funds that are nominal or short term when their nominal or short-term trust funds cannot reasonably be expected to produce or have not produced interest income net of reasonable eligible institution service charges or fees.

(7) *Confidentiality and Disclosure.* The Foundation shall protect the confidentiality of information regarding a lawyer's or law firm's trust account obtained by virtue of this rule. However, the Foundation shall, upon an official written inquiry of The Florida Bar made in the course of an investigation conducted under these Rules Regulating The Florida Bar, disclose requested relevant information about the location and account numbers of lawyer or law firm trust accounts.

(h) Interest on Funds That Are Not Nominal or Short–Term. A lawyer who holds funds for a client or third person and who determines that the funds are not nominal or short-term as defined elsewhere in this subchapter shall not receive benefit from interest on funds held in trust.

(i) Unidentifiable Trust Fund Accumulations and Trust Funds Held for Missing Owners. When an attorney's trust account contains an unidentifiable accumulation of trust funds or property, or trust funds or property held for missing owners, such funds or property shall be so designated. Diligent search and inquiry shall then be made by the attorney to determine the beneficial owner of any unidentifiable accumulation or the address of any missing owner. If the beneficial owner of an unidentified accumulation is determined, the funds shall be properly identified as the lawyer's trust property. If a missing beneficial owner is located, the trust funds or property shall be paid over or delivered to the beneficial owner if the owner is then entitled to receive the same. Trust funds and property that remain unidentifiable and funds or property that are held for missing owners after being designated as such shall, after diligent search and inquiry fail to identify the beneficial owner or owner's address, be disposed of as provided in applicable Florida law.

(j) Disbursement Against Uncollected Funds. A lawyer generally may not use, endanger, or encumber money held in trust for a client for purposes of carrying out the business of another client without the permission of the owner given after full disclosure of the circumstances. However, certain categories of trust account deposits are considered to carry a limited and acceptable risk of failure so that disbursements of trust account funds may be made in reliance on such deposits without disclosure to and permission of clients owning trust account funds subject to possibly being affected. Except for disbursements based upon any of the 6 categories of limited-risk uncollected deposits enumerated below, a lawyer may not disburse funds held for a client or on behalf of that client unless the funds held for that client are collected funds. For purposes of this provision, "collected funds" means funds deposited, finally settled, and credited to the lawyer's trust account. Notwithstanding that a deposit made to the lawyer's trust account has not been finally settled and credited to the account, the lawyer may disburse funds from the trust account in reliance on such deposit:

(1) when the deposit is made by certified check or cashier's check;

(2) when the deposit is made by a check or draft representing loan proceeds issued by a federally or state-chartered bank, savings bank, savings and loan association, credit union, or other duly licensed or chartered institutional lender;

(3) when the deposit is made by a bank check, official check, treasurer's check, money order, or other such instrument issued by a bank, savings and loan association, or credit union when the lawyer has reasonable and prudent grounds to believe the instrument will clear and constitute collected funds in the lawyer's trust account within a reasonable period of time;

(4) when the deposit is made by a check drawn on the trust account of a lawyer licensed to practice in the state of Florida or on the escrow or trust account of a real estate broker licensed under applicable Florida law when the lawyer has a reasonable and prudent belief that the deposit will clear and constitute collected funds in the lawyer's trust account within a reasonable period of time;

(5) when the deposit is made by a check issued by the United States, the State of Florida, or any agency or political subdivision of the State of Florida;

(6) when the deposit is made by a check or draft issued by an insurance company, title insurance company, or a licensed title insurance agency authorized to do business in the state of Florida and the lawyer has a reasonable and prudent belief that the instrument will clear and constitute collected funds in the trust account within a reasonable period of time.

A lawyer's disbursement of funds from a trust account in reliance on deposits that are not yet collected funds in any circumstances other than those set forth above, when it results in funds of other clients being used, endangered, or encumbered without authorization, may be grounds for a finding of professional misconduct. In any event, such a disbursement is at the risk of the lawyer making the disbursement. If any of the deposits fail, the lawyer, upon obtaining knowledge of the failure, must immediately act to protect the property of the lawyer's other clients. However, if the lawyer accepting any such check personally pays the amount of any failed deposit or secures or arranges payment from sources available to the lawyer other than trust account funds of other clients, the lawyer shall not be considered guilty of professional misconduct.

(k) Overdraft Protection Prohibited. An attorney shall not authorize overdraft protection for any account that contains trust funds.

Amended July 20, 1989, effective Oct. 1, 1989 (547 So.2d 117); Oct. 10, 1991, effective Jan. 1, 1992 (587 So.2d 1121); July 23, 1992, effective Jan. 1, 1993 (605 So.2d 252); July 1, 1993 (621 So.2d 1032); July 20, 1995 (658 So.2d 930); April 24, 1997 (692 So.2d 181); June 14, 2001, effective July 14, 2001 (797 So.2d 551); April 25, 2002 (820 So.2d 210); May 20, 2004 (875 So.2d 448); March 23, 2006, effective May 22, 2006 (933 So.2d 417); Dec. 20, 2007, effective March 1, 2008 (978 So.2d 91); Nov. 19, 2009, effective Feb. 1, 2010 (24 So.3d 63); July 7, 2011, effective Oct. 1, 2011 (167 So.3d 1037).

Comment

A lawyer must hold property of others with the care required of a professional fiduciary. This chapter requires maintenance of a bank or savings and loan association account, clearly labeled as a trust account and in which only client or third party trust funds are held.

Securities should be kept in a safe deposit box, except when some other form of safekeeping is warranted by special circumstances.

All property that is the property of clients or third persons should be kept separate from the lawyer's business and personal property and, if money, in 1 or more trust accounts, unless requested otherwise in writing by the client. Separate trust accounts may be warranted when administering estate money or acting in similar fiduciary capacities.

A lawyer who holds funds for a client or third person and who determines that the funds are not nominal or short term as defined elsewhere in this subchapter should hold the funds in a separate interest-bearing account with the interest accruing to the benefit of the client or third person unless directed otherwise in writing by the client or third person.

Lawyers often receive funds from which the lawyer's fee will be paid. The lawyer is not required to remit to the client funds that the lawyer reasonably believes represent fees owed. However, a lawyer may not hold funds to coerce a client into accepting the lawyer's contention. The disputed portion of the funds must be kept in a trust account and the lawyer should suggest means for prompt resolution of the dispute, such as arbitration. The undisputed portion of the funds shall be promptly distributed.

Third parties, such as a client's creditors, may have lawful claims against funds or other property in a lawyer's custody. A lawyer may have a duty under applicable law to protect such third-party claims against wrongful interference by the client. When the lawyer has a duty under applicable law to protect the third-party claim and the third-party claim is not frivolous under applicable law, the lawyer must refuse to surrender the property to the client until the claims are resolved. However, a lawyer should not unilaterally assume to arbitrate a dispute between the client and the third party, and, where appropriate, the lawyer should consider the possibility of depositing the property or funds in dispute into the registry of the applicable court so that the matter may be adjudicated.

The Supreme Court of Florida has held that lawyer trust accounts may be the proper target of garnishment actions. See *Arnold, Matheny and Eagan, P.A. v. First American Holdings, Inc.*, 982 So.2d 628 (Fla. 2008).

The obligations of a lawyer under this chapter are independent of those arising from activity other than rendering legal services. For example, a lawyer who serves only as an escrow agent is governed by the applicable law relating to fiduciaries even though the lawyer does not render legal services in the transaction and is not governed by this rule.

Each lawyer is required to be familiar with and comply with the Rules Regulating Trust Accounts as adopted by the Supreme Court of Florida.

Money or other property entrusted to a lawyer for a specific purpose, including advances for fees, costs, and expenses, is held in trust and must be applied only to that purpose. Money and other property of clients coming into the hands of a lawyer are not subject to counterclaim or setoff for attorney's fees, and a refusal to account for and deliver over such property upon demand shall be a conversion. This does not preclude the retention of money or other property upon which a lawyer has a valid lien for services or to preclude the payment of agreed fees from the proceeds of transactions or collections.

Advances for fees and costs (funds against which costs and fees are billed) are the property of the client or third party paying same on a client's behalf and are required to be maintained in trust, separate from the lawyer's property. Retainers are not funds against which future services are billed. Retainers are funds paid to guarantee the future availability of the lawyer's legal services and are earned by the lawyer upon receipt. Retainers, being funds of the lawyer, may not be placed in the client's trust account.

The test of excessiveness found elsewhere in the Rules Regulating The Florida Bar applies to all fees for legal services including retainers, nonrefundable retainers, and minimum or flat fees.

Rule 5–1.1. Trust Accounts

Text of rule effective October 1, 2015. See, also, rule effective until October 1, 2015.

(a) Nature of Money or Property Entrusted to Attorney.

(1) *Trust Account Required; Location of Trust Account; Commingling Prohibited.* A lawyer must hold in trust, separate from the lawyer's own property, funds and property of clients or third persons that are in a lawyer's possession in connection with a representation. All funds, including advances for fees, costs, and expenses, must be kept in a separate bank or savings and loan association account maintained in the state where the lawyer's office is situated or elsewhere with the consent of the client or third person and clearly labeled and designated as a trust account except:

(A) A lawyer may maintain funds belonging to the lawyer in the lawyer's trust account in an amount no more than is reasonably sufficient to pay bank charges relating to the trust account; and

(B) A lawyer may deposit the lawyer's own funds into trust to replenish a shortage in the lawyer's trust account. Any deposits by the lawyer to cover trust account shortages must be no more than the amount of the trust account shortage, but may be less than the amount of the shortage. The lawyer must notify the bar's lawyer regulation department immediately of the shortage in the lawyer's trust account, the cause of the shortage, and the amount of the replenishment of the trust account by the lawyer.

(2) *Compliance with Client Directives.* Trust funds may be separately held and maintained other than in a bank or savings and loan association account if the lawyer receives written permission from the client to do so and provided that written permission is received before maintaining the funds other than in a separate account.

(3) *Safe Deposit Boxes.* If a lawyer uses a safe deposit box to store trust funds or property, the lawyer must advise the institution in which the deposit box is located that it may include property of clients or third persons.

(b) Application of Trust Funds or Property to Specific Purpose. Money or other property entrusted to an attorney for a specific purpose, including advances for fees, costs, and expenses, is held in trust and must be applied only to that purpose. Money and other property of clients coming into the hands of an attorney are not subject to counterclaim or setoff for attorney's fees, and a refusal to account for and deliver over such property upon demand shall be deemed a conversion.

(c) Liens Permitted. This subchapter does not preclude the retention of money or other property upon which the lawyer has a valid lien for services nor does it preclude the payment of agreed fees from the proceeds of transactions or collection.

(d) Controversies as to Amount of Fees. Controversies as to the amount of fees are not grounds for disciplinary proceedings unless the amount demanded is clearly excessive, extortionate, or fraudulent. In a controversy alleging a clearly excessive, extortionate, or fraudulent fee, announced willingness of an attorney to submit a dispute as to the amount of a fee to a competent tribunal for determination may be considered in any determination as to intent or in mitigation of discipline; provided, such willingness shall not preclude admission of any other relevant admissible evidence relating to such controversy, including evidence as to the withholding of funds or property of the client, or to other injury to the client occasioned by such controversy.

(e) Notice of Receipt of Trust Funds; Delivery; Accounting. Upon receiving funds or other property in which a client or third person has an interest, a lawyer shall promptly notify the client or third person. Except as stated in this rule or otherwise permitted by law or by agreement with the client, a lawyer shall promptly deliver to the client or third person any funds or other property that the client or third person is entitled to receive and, upon request by the client or third person, shall promptly render a full accounting regarding such property.

(f) Disputed Ownership of Trust Funds. When in the course of representation a lawyer is in possession of property in which 2 or more persons (1 of whom may be the lawyer) claim interests, the property shall be treated by the lawyer as trust property, but the portion belonging to the lawyer or law firm shall be withdrawn within a reasonable time after it becomes due unless the right of the lawyer or law firm to receive it is disputed, in which event the portion in dispute shall be kept separate by the lawyer until the dispute is resolved. The lawyer shall promptly distribute all portions of the property as to which the interests are not in dispute.

(g) Interest on Trust Accounts (IOTA) Program.

(1) *Definitions.* As used in this rule, the term:

(A) "Nominal or short term" describes funds of a client or third person that, pursuant to subdivision (3), below, the lawyer has determined cannot earn income for the client or third person in excess of the costs to secure the income.

(B) "Foundation" means The Florida Bar Foundation, Inc.

(C) "IOTA account" means an interest or dividend-bearing trust account benefiting The Florida Bar Foundation established in an eligible institution for the deposit of nominal or short-term funds of clients or third persons.

(D) "Eligible Institution" means any bank or savings and loan association authorized by federal or state laws to do business in Florida and insured by the Federal Deposit Insurance Corporation, or any successor insurance corporation(s) established by federal or state laws, or any open-end investment company registered with the Securities and Exchange Commission and authorized by federal or state laws to do business in Florida, all of which must meet the requirements set out in subdivision (5), below.

(E) "Interest or dividend-bearing trust account" means a federally insured checking account or investment product, including a daily financial institution repurchase agreement or a money market fund. A daily financial institution repurchase agreement must be fully collateralized by, and an open-end money market fund must consist solely of, United States Government Securities. A daily financial institution repurchase agreement may be established only with an eligible institution that is deemed to be "well capitalized" or "adequately capitalized" as defined by applicable federal statutes and regulations. An open-end money market fund must hold itself out as a money market fund as defined by applicable federal statutes and regulations under the Investment Company Act of 1940, and have total assets of at least $250 million. The funds covered by this rule shall be subject to withdrawal upon request and without delay.

(2) *Required Participation.* All nominal or short-term funds belonging to clients or third persons that are placed in trust with any member of The Florida Bar practicing law from an office or other business location within the state of Florida shall be deposited into one or more IOTA accounts, unless the funds may earn income for the client or third person in excess of the costs incurred to secure the income, except as provided elsewhere in this chapter. Only trust funds that are nominal or short term shall be deposited into an IOTA account. The member shall certify annually, in writing, that the member is in compliance with, or is exempt from, the provisions of this rule.

(3) *Determination of Nominal or Short–Term Funds.* The lawyer shall exercise good faith judgment in determining upon receipt whether the funds of a client or third person are nominal or short term. In the exercise of this good faith judgment, the lawyer shall consider such factors as:

(A) the amount of a client's or third person's funds to be held by the lawyer or law firm;

(B) the period of time such funds are expected to be held;

(C) the likelihood of delay in the relevant transaction(s) or proceeding(s);

(D) the cost to the lawyer or law firm of establishing and maintaining an interest-bearing account or other appropriate investment for the benefit of the client or third person; and

(E) minimum balance requirements and/or service charges or fees imposed by the eligible institution.

The determination of whether a client's or third person's funds are nominal or short term shall rest in the sound judgment of the lawyer or law firm. No lawyer shall be charged with ethical impropriety or other breach of professional conduct based on the exercise of such good faith judgment.

(4) *Notice to Foundation.* Lawyers or law firms shall advise the Foundation, at Post Office Box 1553, Orlando, Florida 32802–1553, of the establishment of an IOTA account for funds covered by this rule. Such notice shall include: the IOTA account number as assigned by the eligible institution; the name of the lawyer or law firm on the IOTA account; the eligible institution name; the eligible institution address; and the name and Florida Bar attorney number of the lawyer, or of each member of The Florida Bar in a law firm, practicing from an office or other business location within the state of Florida that has established the IOTA account.

(5) *Eligible Institution Participation in IOTA.* Participation in the IOTA program is voluntary for banks, savings and loan associations, and investment companies. Institutions that choose to offer and maintain IOTA accounts must meet the following requirements:

(A) Interest Rates and Dividends. Eligible institutions shall maintain IOTA accounts which pay the highest interest rate or dividend generally available from the institution to its non-IOTA account customers when IOTA accounts meet or exceed the same minimum balance or other account eligibility qualifications, if any.

(B) Determination of Interest Rates and Dividends. In determining the highest interest rate or dividend generally available from the institution to its non-IOTA accounts in compliance with subdivision (5)(A), above, eligible institutions may consider factors, in addition to the IOTA account balance, customarily considered by the institution when setting interest rates or dividends for its customers, provided that such factors do not discriminate between IOTA accounts and accounts of non-IOTA customers, and that these factors do not include that the account is an IOTA account.

(C) Remittance and Reporting Instructions. Eligible institutions shall:

(i) calculate and remit interest or dividends on the balance of the deposited funds, in accordance with the institution's standard practice for non-IOTA account customers, less reasonable service charges or fees, if any, in connection with the deposited funds, at least quarterly, to the Foundation;

(ii) transmit with each remittance to the Foundation a statement showing the name of the lawyer or law firm from whose IOTA account the remittance is sent, the lawyer's or law firm's IOTA account number as assigned by the institution, the rate of interest applied, the period for which the remittance is made, the total interest or dividend earned during the remittance period, the amount and description of any service charges or fees assessed during the remittance period, and the net amount of interest or dividend remitted for the period; and

(iii) transmit to the depositing lawyer or law firm, for each remittance, a statement showing the amount of interest or dividend paid to the Foundation, the rate of interest applied, and the period for which the statement is made.

(6) *Small Fund Amounts.* The Foundation may establish procedures for a lawyer or law firm to maintain an interest-free trust account for client and third-person funds that are nominal or short term when their nominal or short-term trust funds cannot reasonably be expected to produce or have not produced interest income net of reasonable eligible institution service charges or fees.

(7) *Confidentiality and Disclosure.* The Foundation shall protect the confidentiality of information regarding a lawyer's or law firm's trust account obtained by virtue of this rule. However, the Foundation shall, upon an official written inquiry of The Florida Bar made in the course of an investigation conducted under these Rules Regulating The Florida Bar, disclose requested relevant information about the location and account numbers of lawyer or law firm trust accounts.

(h) Interest on Funds That Are Not Nominal or Short–Term. A lawyer who holds funds for a client or third person and who determines that the funds are not nominal or short-term as defined elsewhere in this subchapter shall not receive benefit from interest on funds held in trust.

(i) Unidentifiable Trust Fund Accumulations and Trust Funds Held for Missing Owners. When an attorney's trust account contains an unidentifiable accumulation of trust funds or property, or trust funds or property held for missing owners, such funds or property shall be so designated. Diligent search and inquiry shall then be made by the attorney to determine the beneficial owner of any unidentifiable accumulation or the address of any missing owner. If the beneficial owner of an unidentified accumulation is determined, the funds shall be properly identified as the lawyer's trust property. If a missing beneficial owner is located, the trust funds or property shall be paid over or delivered to the beneficial owner if the owner is then entitled to receive the same. Trust funds and property that remain unidentifiable and funds or property that are held for missing owners after being designated as such shall, after diligent search and inquiry fail to identify the beneficial owner or owner's address, be disposed of as provided in applicable Florida law.

(j) Disbursement against Uncollected Funds. A lawyer generally may not use, endanger, or encumber money held in trust for a client for purposes of carrying out the business of another client without the permission of the owner given after full disclosure of the circumstances. However, certain categories of trust account deposits are considered to carry a limited and acceptable risk of failure so that disbursements of trust account funds may be made in reliance on such deposits without disclosure to and permission of clients owning trust account funds subject to possibly being affected. Except for disbursements based upon any of the 6 categories of limited-risk uncollected deposits enumerated below, a lawyer may not disburse funds held for a client or on behalf of that client unless the funds held for that client are collected funds. For purposes of this provision, "collected funds" means funds deposited, finally settled, and credited to the lawyer's trust account. Notwithstanding that a deposit made to the lawyer's trust account has not been finally settled and credited to the account, the lawyer may disburse funds from the trust account in reliance on such deposit:

(1) when the deposit is made by certified check or cashier's check;

(2) when the deposit is made by a check or draft representing loan proceeds issued by a federally or state-chartered bank, savings bank, savings and loan association, credit union, or other duly licensed or chartered institutional lender;

(3) when the deposit is made by a bank check, official check, treasurer's check, money order, or other such instrument issued by a bank, savings and loan association, or credit union when the lawyer has reasonable and prudent grounds to believe the instrument will clear and constitute collected funds in the lawyer's trust account within a reasonable period of time;

(4) when the deposit is made by a check drawn on the trust account of a lawyer licensed to practice in the state of Florida or on the escrow or trust account of a real estate broker licensed under applicable Florida law when the lawyer has a reasonable and prudent belief that the deposit will clear and constitute collected funds in the lawyer's trust account within a reasonable period of time;

(5) when the deposit is made by a check issued by the United States, the State of Florida, or any agency or political subdivision of the State of Florida;

(6) when the deposit is made by a check or draft issued by an insurance company, title insurance company, or a licensed title insurance agency authorized to do business in the state of Florida and the lawyer has a reasonable and prudent belief that the instrument will clear and constitute collected funds in the trust account within a reasonable period of time.

A lawyer's disbursement of funds from a trust account in reliance on deposits that are not yet collected funds in any circumstances other than those set forth above, when it results in funds of other clients being used, endangered, or encumbered without authorization, may be grounds for a finding of professional misconduct. In any event, such a disbursement is at the risk of the lawyer making the disbursement. If any of the deposits fail, the lawyer, upon obtaining knowledge of the failure, must immediately act to protect the property of the lawyer's other clients. However, if the lawyer accepting any such check personally pays the amount of any failed deposit or secures or arranges payment from sources available to the lawyer other than trust account funds of other clients, the lawyer shall not be considered guilty of professional misconduct.

(k) Overdraft Protection Prohibited. An attorney shall not authorize overdraft protection for any account that contains trust funds.

Amended July 20, 1989, effective Oct. 1, 1989 (547 So.2d 117); Oct. 10, 1991, effective Jan. 1, 1992 (587 So.2d 1121); July 23, 1992, effective Jan. 1, 1993 (605 So.2d 252); July 1, 1993 (621 So.2d 1032); July 20, 1995 (658 So.2d 930); April 24, 1997 (692 So.2d 181); June 14, 2001, effective July 14, 2001 (797 So.2d 551); April 25, 2002 (820 So.2d 210); May 20, 2004 (875 So.2d 448); March 23, 2006, effective May 22, 2006 (933 So.2d 417); Dec. 20, 2007, effective March 1, 2008 (978 So.2d 91); Nov. 19, 2009, effective Feb. 1, 2010 (24 So.3d 63); July 7, 2011, effective Oct. 1, 2011 (67 So.3d 1037); June 11, 2015, effective Oct. 1, 2015 (167 So.3d 412).

Comment

A lawyer must hold property of others with the care required of a professional fiduciary. This chapter requires maintenance of a bank or savings and loan association account, clearly labeled as a trust account and in which only client or third party trust funds are held.

Securities should be kept in a safe deposit box, except when some other form of safekeeping is warranted by special circumstances.

All property that is the property of clients or third persons should be kept separate from the lawyer's business and personal property and, if money, in 1 or more trust accounts, unless requested otherwise in writing by the client. Separate trust accounts may be warranted when administering estate money or acting in similar fiduciary capacities.

A lawyer who holds funds for a client or third person and who determines that the funds are not nominal or short term as defined elsewhere in this subchapter should hold the funds in a separate interest-bearing account with the interest accruing to the benefit of the client or third person unless directed otherwise in writing by the client or third person.

Lawyers often receive funds from which the lawyer's fee will be paid. The lawyer is not required to remit to the client funds that the lawyer reasonably believes represent fees owed. However, a lawyer may not hold funds to coerce a client into accepting the lawyer's contention. The disputed portion of the funds must be kept in a trust account and the lawyer should suggest means for prompt resolution of the dispute, such as arbitration. The undisputed portion of the funds shall be promptly distributed.

Third parties, such as a client's creditors, may have lawful claims against funds or other property in a lawyer's custody. A lawyer may have a duty under applicable law to protect such third-party claims against wrongful interference by the client. When the lawyer has a duty under applicable law to protect the third-party claim and the third-party claim is not frivolous under applicable law, the lawyer must refuse to surrender the property to the client until the claims are resolved. However, a lawyer should not unilaterally assume to arbitrate a dispute between the client and the third party, and, where appropriate, the lawyer should consider the possibility of depositing the property or funds in dispute into the registry of the applicable court so that the matter may be adjudicated.

The Supreme Court of Florida has held that lawyer trust accounts may be the proper target of garnishment actions. See *Arnold, Matheny and Eagan, P.A. v. First American Holdings, Inc.*, 982 So.2d 628 (Fla. 2008).

The obligations of a lawyer under this chapter are independent of those arising from activity other than rendering legal services. For example, a lawyer who serves only as an escrow agent is governed by the applicable law relating to fiduciaries even though the lawyer does not render legal services in the transaction and is not governed by this rule.

Each lawyer is required to be familiar with and comply with the Rules Regulating Trust Accounts as adopted by the Supreme Court of Florida.

Money or other property entrusted to a lawyer for a specific purpose, including advances for fees, costs, and expenses, is held in trust and must be applied only to that purpose. Money and other property of clients coming into the hands of a lawyer are not subject to counterclaim or setoff for attorney's fees, and a refusal to account for and deliver over such property upon demand shall be a conversion. This does not preclude the retention of money or other property upon which a lawyer has a valid lien for services or to preclude the payment of agreed fees from the proceeds of transactions or collections.

Advances for fees and costs (funds against which costs and fees are billed) are the property of the client or third party paying same on a client's behalf and are required to be maintained in trust, separate from the lawyer's property. Retainers are not funds against which future services are billed. Retainers are funds paid to guarantee the future availability of the lawyer's legal services and are earned by the lawyer upon receipt. Retainers, being funds of the lawyer, may not be placed in the client's trust account.

The test of excessiveness found elsewhere in the Rules Regulating The Florida Bar applies to all fees for legal services including retainers, nonrefundable retainers, and minimum or flat fees.

Rule 5–1.2. Trust Accounting Records and Procedures

Text of rule effective until October 1, 2015. See, also, rule effective October 1, 2015.

(a) Applicability. The provisions of these rules apply to all trust funds received or disbursed by members of The Florida Bar in the course of their professional practice of law as members of The Florida Bar except special trust funds received or disbursed by a lawyer as guardian, personal representative, receiver, or in a similar capacity such as trustee under a specific trust document where the trust funds are maintained in a segregated special trust account and not the general trust account and where this special trust position has been created, approved, or sanctioned by law or an order of a court that has authority or duty to issue orders pertaining to maintenance of such special trust account. These rules apply to matters in which a choice of laws analysis indicates that such matters are governed by the laws of Florida.

As set forth in this rule, "lawyer" denotes a person who is a member of The Florida Bar or otherwise authorized to practice in any court of the state of Florida. "Law firm" denotes a lawyer or lawyers in a private firm who handle client trust funds.

(b) Minimum Trust Accounting Records. Records may be maintained in their original format or stored in digital media as long as the copies include all data contained in the original documents and may be produced when required. The following are the minimum trust accounting records that must be maintained:

(1) a separate bank or savings and loan association account or accounts in the name of the lawyer or law firm and clearly labeled and designated as a "trust account";

(2) original or clearly legible copies of deposit slips if the copies include all data on the originals and, in the case of currency or coin, an additional cash receipts book, clearly identifying the date and source of all trust funds received and the client or matter for which the funds were received;

(3) original canceled checks or clearly legible copies of original canceled checks for all funds disbursed from the trust account, all of which must:

(A) be numbered consecutively;

(B) include all endorsements and all other data and tracking information; and

(C) clearly identify the client or case by number or name in the memo area of the check;

(4) other documentary support for all disbursements and transfers from the trust account including records of all electronic transfers from client trust accounts, including:

(A) the name of the person authorizing the transfer;

(B) the name of the recipient;

(C) confirmation from the banking institution confirming the number of the trust account from which money is withdrawn; and

(D) the date and time the transfer was completed.

(5) original or clearly legible digital copies of all records regarding all wire transfers into or out of the trust account, which at a minimum must include the receiving and sending financial institutions' ABA routing numbers and names, and the receiving and sending account holder's name, address and account number. If the receiving financial institution processes through a correspondent or intermediary bank, then the records must include the ABA routing number and name for the intermediary bank. The wire transfer information must also include the name of the client or matter for which the funds were transferred or received, and the purpose of the wire transfer, (e.g., "payment on invoice 1234" or "John Doe closing").

(6) a separate cash receipts and disbursements journal, including columns for receipts, disbursements, transfers, and the account balance, and containing at least:

(A) the identification of the client or matter for which the funds were received, disbursed, or transferred;

(B) the date on which all trust funds were received, disbursed, or transferred;

(C) the check number for all disbursements; and

(D) the reason for which all trust funds were received, disbursed, or transferred;

(7) a separate file or ledger with an individual card or page for each client or matter, showing all individual receipts, disbursements, or transfers and any unexpended balance, and containing:

(A) the identification of the client or matter for which trust funds were received, disbursed, or transferred;

(B) the date on which all trust funds were received, disbursed, or transferred;

(C) the check number for all disbursements; and

(D) the reason for which all trust funds were received, disbursed, or transferred; and

(8) all bank or savings and loan association statements for all trust accounts.

(c) Responsibility of Lawyers for Firm Trust Accounts and Reporting.

(1) Every law firm with more than 1 lawyer must have a written plan in place for supervision and compliance with this rule for each of the firm's trust account(s), which plan must be disseminated to each lawyer in the firm. The written plan must include the name(s) of the lawyer(s) who sign trust account checks for the law firm, the name(s) of the lawyer(s) who are responsible for reconciliation of the law firm's trust account(s) monthly and annually and the name(s) of the lawyer(s) who are responsible for answering any questions that lawyers in the firm may have about the firm's trust account(s). This written plan must be updated and re-issued to each lawyer in the firm whenever there are material changes to the plan, such as a change in the lawyer(s) signing trust account checks and/or reconciliation of the firm's trust account(s).

(2) Every lawyer is responsible for that lawyer's own actions regarding trust account funds subject to the requirements of chapter 4 of these rules. Any lawyer who has actual knowledge that the firm's trust account(s) or trust accounting procedures are not in compliance with chapter 5 may report the noncompliance to the managing partner or shareholder of the lawyer's firm. If the noncompliance is not corrected within a reasonable time, the lawyer must report the noncompliance to staff counsel for the bar if required to do so pursuant to the reporting requirements of chapter 4.

(d) Minimum Trust Accounting Procedures. The minimum trust accounting procedures that must be followed by all members of The Florida Bar (when a choice of laws analysis indicates that the laws of Florida apply) who receive or disburse trust money or property are as follows:

(1) The lawyer is required to make monthly:

(A) reconciliations of all trust bank or savings and loan association accounts, disclosing the balance per bank, deposits in transit, outstanding checks identified by date and check number, and any other items necessary to reconcile the balance per bank with the balance per the checkbook and the cash receipts and disbursements journal; and

(B) a comparison between the total of the reconciled balances of all trust accounts and the total of the trust ledger cards or pages, together with specific descriptions of any differences between the 2 totals and reasons for the differences.

(2) The lawyer is required to prepare an annual detailed list identifying the balance of the unexpended trust money held for each client or matter.

(3) The above reconciliations, comparisons, and listings must be retained for at least 6 years.

(4) The lawyer or law firm must authorize, at the time the account is opened, and request any bank or savings and loan association where the lawyer is a signatory on a trust account to notify Staff Counsel, The Florida Bar, 651 East Jefferson Street, Tallahassee, Florida 32399–2300, in the event the account is overdrawn or any trust check is dishonored or returned due to insufficient funds or uncollected funds, absent bank error.

(5) The lawyer must file with The Florida Bar between June 1 and August 15 of each year a trust accounting certificate showing compliance with these rules on a form approved by the board of governors. If the lawyer fails to file the trust accounting certificate, the lawyer will be deemed a delinquent member and ineligible to practice law.

(e) Electronic Wire Transfers. Authorized electronic transfers from a lawyer or law firm's trust account are limited to:

(1) money required to be paid to a client or third party on behalf of a client;

(2) expenses properly incurred on behalf of a client, such as filing fees or payment to third parties for services rendered in connection with the representation;

(3) money transferred to the lawyer for fees which are earned in connection with the representation and which are not in dispute; or

(4) money transferred from one trust account to another trust account.

(f) Record Retention. A lawyer or law firm that receives and disburses client or third-party funds or property must maintain the records required by this chapter for 6 years subsequent to the final conclusion of each representation in which the trust funds or property were received.

(g) Audits. Any of the following are cause for The Florida Bar to order an audit of a trust account:

(1) failure to file the trust account certificate required by rule 5–1.2(c)(5);

(2) return of a trust account check for insufficient funds or for uncollected funds, absent bank error;

(3) filing of a petition for creditor relief on behalf of a lawyer;

(4) filing of felony charges against a lawyer;

(5) adjudication of insanity or incompetence or hospitalization of a lawyer under The Florida Mental Health Act;

(6) filing of a claim against a lawyer with the Clients' Security Fund;

(7) when requested by the chair or vice chair of a grievance committee or the board of governors;

(8) upon court order; or

(9) upon entry of an order of disbarment, on consent or otherwise.

(h) Cost of Audit. Audits conducted in any of the circumstances enumerated in this rule will be at the cost of the lawyer audited only when the audit reveals that the lawyer was not in substantial compliance with the trust accounting requirements. It will be the obligation of any lawyer who is being audited to produce all records and papers concerning property and funds held in trust and to provide such explanations as may be required for the audit. Records of general accounts are not required to be produced except to verify that trust money has not been deposited in them. If it has been determined that trust money has been deposited into a general account, all of the transactions pertaining to any firm account will be subject to audit.

(i) Failure to Comply With Subpoena for Trust Accounting Records. Failure of a member to timely produce trust accounting records will be considered as a matter of contempt and process in the manner provided in subdivision (d) and (f) of rule 3–7.11, Rules Regulating The Florida Bar.

Amended Oct. 10, 1991, effective Jan. 1, 1992 (587 So.2d 1121); July 23, 1992, effective Jan. 1, 1993 (605 So.2d 252); July 17, 1997 (697 So.2d 115); April 25, 2002 (820 So.2d 210); July 3, 2003 (850 So.2d 499); May 20, 2004 (875 So.2d 448); Nov. 19, 2009, effective Feb. 1, 2010 (24 So.3d 63); April 12, 2012, effective July 1, 2012 (101 So.3d 807); May 29, 2014, effective June 1, 2014 (140 So.3d 541).

Rule 5–1.2. Trust Accounting Records and Procedures

Text of rule effective October 1, 2015. See, also, rule effective until October 1, 2015.

(a) Applicability. The provisions of these rules apply to all trust funds received or disbursed by members of The Florida Bar in the course of their professional practice of law as members of The Florida Bar except special trust funds received or disbursed by a lawyer as guardian, personal representative, receiver, or in a similar capacity such as trustee under a specific trust document where the trust funds are maintained in a segregated special trust account and not the general trust account and where this special trust position has been created, approved, or sanctioned by law or an order of a court that has authority or duty to issue orders pertaining to maintenance of such special trust account. These rules apply to matters in which a choice of laws analysis indicates that such matters are governed by the laws of Florida.

As set forth in this rule, "lawyer" denotes a person who is a member of The Florida Bar or otherwise authorized to practice in any court of the state of Florida. "Law firm" denotes a lawyer or lawyers in a private firm who handle client trust funds.

(b) Minimum Trust Accounting Records. Records may be maintained in their original format or stored in digital media as long as the copies include all data contained in the original documents and may be produced when required. The following are the minimum trust accounting records that must be maintained:

(1) a separate bank or savings and loan association account or accounts in the name of the lawyer or law firm and clearly labeled and designated as a "trust account";

(2) original or clearly legible copies of deposit slips if the copies include all data on the originals and, in the case of currency or coin, an additional cash receipts book, clearly identifying the date and source of all trust funds received and the client or matter for which the funds were received;

(3) original canceled checks or clearly legible copies of original canceled checks for all funds disbursed from the trust account, all of which must:

(A) be numbered consecutively;

(B) include all endorsements and all other data and tracking information; and

(C) clearly identify the client or case by number or name in the memo area of the check;

(4) other documentary support for all disbursements and transfers from the trust account including records of all electronic transfers from client trust accounts, including:

(A) the name of the person authorizing the transfer;

(B) the name of the recipient;

(C) confirmation from the banking institution confirming the number of the trust account from which money is withdrawn; and

(D) the date and time the transfer was completed.

(5) original or clearly legible digital copies of all records regarding all wire transfers into or out of the trust account, which at a minimum must include the receiving and sending financial institutions' ABA routing numbers and names, and the receiving and sending account holder's name, address and account number. If the receiving financial institution processes through a correspondent or intermediary bank, then the records must include the ABA routing number and name for the intermediary bank. The wire transfer information must also include the name of the client or matter for which the funds were transferred or received, and the purpose of the wire transfer, (e.g., "payment on invoice 1234" or "John Doe closing").

(6) a separate cash receipts and disbursements journal, including columns for receipts, disbursements, transfers, and the account balance, and containing at least:

(A) the identification of the client or matter for which the funds were received, disbursed, or transferred;

(B) the date on which all trust funds were received, disbursed, or transferred;

(C) the check number for all disbursements; and

(D) the reason for which all trust funds were received, disbursed, or transferred;

(7) a separate file or ledger with an individual card or page for each client or matter, showing all individual receipts, disbursements, or transfers and any unexpended balance, and containing:

(A) the identification of the client or matter for which trust funds were received, disbursed, or transferred;

(B) the date on which all trust funds were received, disbursed, or transferred;

(C) the check number for all disbursements; and

(D) the reason for which all trust funds were received, disbursed, or transferred; and

(8) all bank or savings and loan association statements for all trust accounts.

(c) Responsibility of Lawyers for Firm Trust Accounts and Reporting.

(1) Every law firm with more than 1 lawyer must have a written plan in place for supervision and compliance with this rule for each of the firm's trust account(s), which plan must be disseminated to each lawyer in the firm. The written plan must include the name(s) of the lawyer(s) who sign trust account checks for the law firm, the name(s) of the lawyer(s) who are responsible for reconciliation of the law firm's trust account(s) monthly and annually and the name(s) of the lawyer(s) who are responsible for answering any questions that lawyers in the firm may have about the firm's trust account(s). This written plan must be updated and re-issued to each lawyer in the firm whenever there are material changes to the plan, such as a change in the lawyer(s) signing trust account checks and/or reconciliation of the firm's trust account(s).

(2) Every lawyer is responsible for that lawyer's own actions regarding trust account funds subject to the requirements of chapter 4 of these rules. Any lawyer who has actual knowledge that the firm's trust account(s) or trust accounting procedures are not in compliance with chapter 5 may report the noncompliance to the managing partner or shareholder of the lawyer's firm. If the noncompliance is not corrected within a reasonable time, the lawyer must report the noncompliance to staff counsel for the bar if required to do so pursuant to the reporting requirements of chapter 4.

(d) Minimum Trust Accounting Procedures. The minimum trust accounting procedures that must be followed by all members of The Florida Bar (when a choice of laws analysis indicates that the laws of Florida apply) who receive or disburse trust money or property are as follows:

(1) The lawyer is required to make monthly:

(A) reconciliations of all trust bank or savings and loan association accounts, disclosing the balance per bank, deposits in transit, outstanding checks identified by date and check number, and any other items necessary to reconcile the balance per bank with the balance per the checkbook and the cash receipts and disbursements journal; and

(B) a comparison between the total of the reconciled balances of all trust accounts and the total of the trust ledger cards or pages, together with specific descriptions of any differences between the 2 totals and reasons for these differences.

(2) The lawyer is required to prepare an annual detailed list identifying the balance of the unexpended trust money held for each client or matter.

(3) The above reconciliations, comparisons, and listings must be retained for at least 6 years.

(4) The lawyer or law firm must authorize, at the time the account is opened, and request any bank or savings and loan association where the lawyer is a signatory on a trust account to notify Staff Counsel, The Florida Bar, 651 East Jefferson Street, Tallahassee, Florida 32399–2300, in the event the account is overdrawn or any trust check is dishonored or returned due to insufficient funds or uncollected funds, absent bank error.

(5) The lawyer must file with The Florida Bar between June 1 and August 15 of each year a trust accounting certificate showing compliance with these rules on a form approved by the board of governors. If the lawyer fails to file the trust accounting certificate, the lawyer will be deemed a delinquent member and ineligible to practice law.

(e) Electronic Wire Transfers. Authorized electronic transfers from a lawyer or law firm's trust account are limited to:

(1) money required to be paid to a client or third party on behalf of a client;

(2) expenses properly incurred on behalf of a client, such as filing fees or payment to third parties for services rendered in connection with the representation;

(3) money transferred to the lawyer for fees which are earned in connection with the representation and which are not in dispute; or

(4) money transferred from one trust account to another trust account.

(f) Record Retention. A lawyer or law firm that receives and disburses client or third-party funds or property must maintain the records required by this chapter for 6 years subsequent to the final conclusion of each representation in which the trust funds or property were received.

(1) On dissolution of a law firm or of any legal professional corporation, the partners shall make reasonable arrangements for the maintenance and reten-

tion of client trust account records specified in this rule.

(2) On the sale of a law practice, the seller must make reasonable arrangements for the maintenance and retention of trust account records specified in this rule consistent with other requirements regarding the sale of a law firm set forth in Chapter 4 of these rules.

(g) Audits. Any of the following are cause for The Florida Bar to order an audit of a trust account:

(1) failure to file the trust account certificate required by rule 5–1.2(c)(5);

(2) return of a trust account check for insufficient funds or for uncollected funds, absent bank error;

(3) filing of a petition for creditor relief on behalf of a lawyer;

(4) filing of felony charges against a lawyer;

(5) adjudication of insanity or incompetence or hospitalization of a lawyer under The Florida Mental Health Act;

(6) filing of a claim against a lawyer with the Clients' Security Fund;

(7) when requested by the chair or vice chair of a grievance committee or the board of governors;

(8) on court order; or

(9) on entry of an order of disbarment, on consent or otherwise.

(h) Cost of Audit. Audits conducted in any of the circumstances enumerated in this rule will be at the cost of the lawyer audited only when the audit reveals that the lawyer was not in substantial compliance with the trust accounting requirements. It will be the obligation of any lawyer who is being audited to produce all records and papers concerning property and funds held in trust and to provide such explanations as may be required for the audit. Records of general accounts are not required to be produced except to verify that trust money has not been deposited in them. If it has been determined that trust money has been deposited into a general account, all of the transactions pertaining to any firm account will be subject to audit.

(i) Failure to Comply With Subpoena for Trust Accounting Records. Failure of a member to timely produce trust accounting records will be considered as a matter of contempt and process in the manner provided in subdivision (d) and (f) of rule 3–7.11, Rules Regulating The Florida Bar.

Amended Oct. 10, 1991, effective Jan. 1, 1992 (587 So.2d 1121); July 23, 1992, effective Jan. 1, 1993 (605 So.2d 252); July 17, 1997 (697 So.2d 115); April 25, 2002 (820 So.2d 210); July 3, 2003 (850 So.2d 499); May 20, 2004 (875 So.2d 448); Nov. 19, 2009, effective Feb. 1, 2010 (24 So.3d 63); April 12, 2012, effective July 1, 2012 (101 So.3d 807); May 29, 2014, effective June 1, 2014 (140 So.3d 541); June 11, 2015, effective Oct. 1, 2015 (167 So.3d 412).

CHAPTER 6. LEGAL SPECIALIZATION AND EDUCATION PROGRAMS

6–1. GENERALLY

6–2. FLORIDA DESIGNATION PLAN (EXPIRED)

6–3. FLORIDA CERTIFICATION PLAN

6–4. STANDARDS FOR CERTIFICATION OF A BOARD CERTIFIED CIVIL TRIAL LAWYER

6–5. STANDARDS FOR CERTIFICATION OF A BOARD CERTIFIED TAX LAWYER

6–6. STANDARDS FOR CERTIFICATION OF A BOARD CERTIFIED MARITAL AND FAMILY LAWYER

6–1. GENERALLY

Rule 6–1.1. Composition of board

The board of legal specialization and education shall be composed of 16 members of The Florida Bar appointed by the president of The Florida Bar, with the advice and consent of the board of governors. Fifteen of the members shall hold office for 3 years and until their successors are appointed. These 15 members shall be appointed to staggered terms of office, and the initial appointees shall serve as follows: 5 members shall serve until June 30 next following their appointment, 5 members shall serve until the second June 30 following their appointment, and 5 members shall serve until the third June 30 following their appointment. One of the members shall be designated by the president as chair. In addition, 1 member shall also be the chair of the continuing legal education committee of The Florida Bar, although no person may be chair of both the board of legal specialization and education and continuing legal education committee of The Florida Bar. Any vacancy shall be filled in the manner provided for original appointments.

Amended Sept. 21, 1989, effective Oct. 1, 1989 (548 So.2d 1120); July 23, 1992, effective Jan. 1, 1993 (605 So.2d 252); June 27, 1996, effective July 1, 1996 (677 So.2d 272).

Rule 6–1.2. Public Notice

The Florida Bar may cause a public notice to be promulgated where and when it deems necessary, including, for example, telephone directory yellow pages, in substantially the following form:

NOTICE

FOR THE GENERAL INFORMATION OF THE PUBLIC

ATTORNEYS INDICATING "BOARD CERTIFIED," "SPECIALIST," OR "EXPERT" HAVE BEEN CERTIFIED BY THE FLORIDA BAR AS

HAVING SPECIAL KNOWLEDGE, SKILLS, AND PROFICIENCY IN THEIR AREAS OF PRACTICE AND HAVE BEEN EVALUATED BY THE BAR AS TO THEIR CHARACTER, ETHICS, AND REPUTATION FOR PROFESSIONALISM IN THE PRACTICE OF LAW.

ALL PERSONS ARE URGED TO MAKE THEIR OWN INDEPENDENT INVESTIGATION AND EVALUATION OF ANY ATTORNEY BEING CONSIDERED.

This notice published by The Florida Bar Board of Legal Specialization and Education, Telephone 850/561–5600, 651 East Jefferson Street, Tallahassee, Florida 32399–2300.

Amended Sept. 21, 1989, effective Oct. 1, 1989 (548 So.2d 1120); July 23, 1992, effective Jan. 1, 1993 (605 So.2d 252); June 27, 1996, effective July 1, 1996 (677 So.2d 272); Sept. 24, 1998, effective Oct. 1, 1998 (718 So.2d 1179); July 3, 2003 (850 So.2d 499); Dec. 20, 2007, effective March 1, 2008 (978 So.2d 91).

Rule 6–1.3. Liability

The Florida Bar shall assume no liability to any persons whomsoever by reason of the adoption and implementation of the designation or certification plans.

Amended Sept. 21, 1989, effective Oct. 1, 1989 (548 So.2d 1120).

Rule 6–1.4. Amendment

These rules may be amended in accordance with the procedures for amending the Rules Regulating The Florida Bar as provided in rule 1–12.1.

Amended Sept. 21, 1989, effective Oct. 1, 1989 (548 So.2d 1120); July 23, 1992, effective Jan. 1, 1993 (605 So.2d 252).

Rule 6–1.5. Disqualification as Attorney Due to Conflict

(a) Members of the BLSE, Members of the Certification Committees, Members of the Board of Governors, and Employees of The Florida Bar. No member of the BLSE, member of a certification committee, member of the board of governors, or employee of The Florida Bar shall represent a party other than The Florida Bar in certification proceedings authorized under these rules.

(b) Former Members of the BLSE, Former Members of the Certification Committees, Former Board Members, and Former Employees. No former member of the BLSE, former member of a certification committee, former member of the board of governors, or former employee of The Florida Bar shall represent any party other than The Florida Bar in certification proceedings authorized under these rules if personally involved to any degree in the matter while a member of the BLSE, certification committee, board of governors, or while an employee of The Florida Bar.

A former member of the BLSE, former member of a certification committee, former member of the board of governors, or former employee of The Florida Bar who did not participate personally in any way in the matter or in any related matter in which the attorney seeks to be a representative, and who did not serve in a supervisory capacity over such matter, shall not represent any party except The Florida Bar for 1 year after such service without the express consent of the board.

(c) Partners, Associates, Employers, or Employees of the Firms of BLSE Members, Certification Committee Members, or Board of Governors Members Precluded From Representing Parties Other Than The Florida Bar. Members of the firms of board of governors members, BLSE members, or certification committee members shall not represent any party other than The Florida Bar in certification proceedings authorized under these rules without the express consent of the board.

(d) Partners, Associates, Employers, or Employees of the Firms of Former BLSE Members, Former Certification Committee Members, or Former Board of Governors Members Precluded From Representing Parties Other Than The Florida Bar. Attorneys in the firms of former board of governors members, former BLSE members, or former certification committee members shall not represent any party other than The Florida Bar in certification proceedings authorized under these rules for 1 year after the former member's service without the express consent of the board.

Added May 20, 2004 (875 So.2d 448).

6–2. FLORIDA DESIGNATION PLAN (EXPIRED)

6–3. FLORIDA CERTIFICATION PLAN

Rule 6–3.1. Administration

The board of legal specialization and education shall have the authority and responsibility to administer the program for regulation of certification including:

(a) recommending to the board of governors areas in which certificates may be granted and providing procedures by which such areas may be determined, refined, or eliminated;

(b) recommending to the board of governors minimum, reasonable, and nondiscriminatory standards concerning education, experience, proficiency, and other relevant matters for granting certificates in areas of certification;

(c) providing procedures for the investigation and testing of the qualifications of applicants and certificate holders;

(d) awarding certificates to qualified applicants;

(e) encouraging law schools, the continuing legal education committee of The Florida Bar, voluntary bar associations, and other continuing legal education entities to develop and maintain a program of continuing legal education to meet the standards described by the plan;

(f) cooperating with other agencies of The Florida Bar in establishing and enforcing standards of professional conduct necessary for the recognition and regulation of certification;

(g) cooperating with the standing committee on specialization of the American Bar Association and with the agencies in other states engaged in the regulation of legal specialization;

(h) establishing policies, procedures, and appropriate fees to evaluate and accredit lawyer certifying organizations and programs;

(i) reporting as required, but at least annually, to the board of governors on the status and conditions of the plan;

(j) determining standards, rules, and regulations to implement these rules in accordance with the minimum standards prescribed by the Supreme Court of Florida; and

(k) delegating to The Florida Bar staff any of the administrative responsibilities of the board of legal specialization and education providing said board retains responsibility for staff decisions.

Amended effective Oct. 29, 1987 (515 So.2d 977); Sept. 21, 1989, effective Oct. 1, 1989 (548 So.2d 1120); July 23, 1992, effective Jan. 1, 1993 (605 So.2d 252); May 20, 2004 (875 So.2d 448).

Rule 6–3.2. Certification Committees

(a) Initial Certification Committees. For each certification area approved by the Supreme Court of Florida, a 9–member committee, bearing the name of the area, shall be appointed by the president of The Florida Bar, with the advice and consent of the board of governors. Initial committee appointees shall be eminent attorneys in each field, shall be members in good standing of The Florida Bar, shall have been admitted to The Florida Bar no less than 10 years, and must meet such other requirements as may in the future be promulgated by the board of legal specialization and education. Initial committee appointees shall be certified in the applicable area of practice by reason of appointment to that area's certification committee. The committee members shall hold office for 3 years and until their successors are appointed. The committee members shall be appointed to staggered terms of office, and the initial appointees shall serve as follows: 3 members shall serve until June 30 next following their appointment, 3 members shall serve until the second June 30 following their appointment, and 3 members shall serve until the third June 30 following their appointment.

(b) Subsequent Certification Committees. Subsequent certification committee appointees shall be appointed by the president-elect of The Florida Bar, must be certified in the area at the time of appointment, must be members in good standing of The Florida Bar, and must meet such other requirements as may be promulgated by the board of legal specialization and education. Upon the recommendation of the board of legal specialization and education and the approval of The Florida Bar Board of Governors, the composition of a certification committee may be adjusted to no fewer than 5 members or no more than 15 members. Committee members shall be appointed to staggered terms of office.

Amended Sept. 21, 1989, effective Oct. 1, 1989 (548 So.2d 1120); July 23, 1992, effective Jan. 1, 1993 (605 So.2d 252); July 1, 1993 (621 So.2d 1032); Feb. 8, 2001 (795 So.2d 1); April 12, 2012, effective July 1, 2012 (101 So.3d 807).

Rule 6–3.3. Jurisdiction of certification committees

Each certification committee shall be responsible for:

(a) proposing to the board of legal specialization and education criteria for the issuance or renewal of a certificate, which may include:

(1) experience;

(2) references;

(3) continuing legal education;

(4) examination, either oral or written or both;

(5) whether certificates may be issued without examination and on what basis; and

(6) other relevant matters;

(b) reviewing applications for certificates;

(c) reviewing and establishing testing procedures as may be deemed necessary for certification or recertification; and

(d) recommending to the board of legal specialization and education that certificates be issued to those individuals meeting both the minimum standards imposed by this plan and the particular standards for the area for which certification is sought.

Amended effective Oct. 29, 1987 (515 So.2d 977); Sept. 21, 1989, effective Oct. 1, 1989 (548 So.2d 1120); July 23, 1992, effective Jan. 1, 1993 (605 So.2d 252).

Rule 6–3.4. Limitations on the powers of the board of governors, the board of legal specialization and education, and the certification committees

(a) Limit on Right to Practice. No standard shall be approved that shall, in any way, limit the right of a certificate holder to practice law in all areas.

(b) Certification Not Required to Practice. No lawyer shall be required to be certified before practicing law in any particular area.

(c) Certification of Individuals Only. All requirements for and all benefits to be derived from certification are individual and may not be fulfilled by or attributed to a law firm of which the certified lawyer may be a member.

(d) Voluntary Nature of Plan. Participation in the plan shall be on a voluntary basis.

(e) Limit on Number of Certified Areas. The limit on the number of areas in which a lawyer may be certified shall be determined by such practical limits as are imposed by the requirements of "substantial involvement" and such other standards as may be established by the board of legal specialization and education.

(f) Rules Regulating The Florida Bar. No rules or standards shall be adopted in contravention of these Rules Regulating The Florida Bar.

Amended effective Oct. 29, 1987 (515 So.2d 977); Sept. 21, 1989, effective Oct. 1, 1989 (548 So.2d 1120); July 23, 1992, effective Jan. 1, 1993 (605 So.2d 252).

Rule 6–3.5. Standards for Certification

(a) Standards for Certification. The minimum standards for certification are prescribed below. Each area of certification established under this chapter may contain higher or additional standards if approved by the Supreme Court of Florida.

(b) Eligibility for Application. A member in good standing of The Florida Bar who is currently engaged in the practice of law and who meets the area's standards may apply for certification. From the date the application is filed to the date the certificate is issued, the applicant must continue to practice law and remain a member in good standing of The Florida Bar. The certificate issued by the board of legal specialization and education shall state that the lawyer is a "Board Certified (area of certification) Lawyer."

(c) Minimum Requirements for Qualifying for Certification With Examination. Minimum requirements for qualifying for certification by examination are as follows:

(1) A minimum of 5 years substantially engaged in the practice of law. The "practice of law" means legal work performed primarily for purposes of rendering legal advice or representation. Service as a judge of any court of record shall be deemed to constitute the practice of law. Employment by the government of the United States, any state (including subdivisions of the state such as counties or municipalities), or the District of Columbia, and employment by a public or private corporation or other business shall be deemed to constitute the practice of law if the individual was required as a condition of employment to be a member of the bar of any state or the District of Columbia. If otherwise permitted in the particular standards for the area in which certification is sought, the practice of law in a foreign nation state, U.S. territory, or U.S. protectorate, or employment in a position that requires as a condition of employment that the employee be licensed to practice law in such foreign nation state, U.S. territory, or U.S. protectorate, shall be counted as up to, but no more than, 3 of the 5 years required for certification.

(2) A satisfactory showing of substantial involvement in the particular area for which certification is sought during 3 of the last 5 years preceding the application for certification.

(3) A satisfactory showing of such continuing legal education in a particular field of law for which certification is sought as set by that area's standards but in no event less than 10 certification hours per year.

(4) Passing a written and/or oral examination applied uniformly to all applicants to demonstrate sufficient knowledge, skills, and proficiency in the area for which certification is sought and in the various areas relating to such field. The examination shall include professional responsibility and ethics. The award of an LL.M. degree from an approved law school in the area for which certification is sought within 8 years of application may substitute as the written examination required in this subdivision if the area's standards so provide.

(5) Current certification by an approved organization in the area for which certification is sought within 5 years of filing an application may, at the option of the certification committee, substitute as partial equivalent credit, including the written examination required in subdivision (c)(4). Approval will be by the board of legal specialization and education following a positive or negative recommendation from the certification committee.

(6) Peer review shall be used to solicit information to assess competence in the specialty field, and professionalism and ethics in the practice of law. To qualify for board certification, an applicant must be recognized as having achieved a level of competence indicating special knowledge, skills, and proficiency in handling the usual matters in the specialty field. The applicant shall also be evaluated as to character, ethics, and reputation for professionalism. An applicant otherwise qualified may be denied certification on the basis of peer review. Certification may also be withheld pending the outcome of any disciplinary complaint or malpractice action.

As part of the peer review process, the board of legal specialization and education and its area committees shall review an applicant's professionalism, ethics, and disciplinary record. Such review shall include both disciplinary complaints and malpractice actions. The process may also include solicitation of public input and independent inquiry apart from written references. Peer review is mandatory for all applicants and may not be eliminated by equivalents.

(d) Minimum Requirements for Qualification Without Examination. When certification without examination is available in an area, the minimum requirements for such certification are as follows:

(1) a minimum of 20 years in the practice on a full-time basis;

(2) a satisfactory showing of competence and substantial involvement in the particular area for which certification is sought during 5 of the last 10 years, including the year immediately preceding the application for certification. Substantial involvement in the particular area of law for the 1 year immediately preceding the application may be waived for good cause shown;

(3) a satisfactory showing of such continuing legal education in a particular field of law for which certification is sought as set by that area's standards but in no event less than 15 hours per year;

(4) satisfactory peer review and professional ethics record in accordance with subdivision (c)(6); and

(5) payment of any fees required by the plan.

(e) Certification Without Examination. When certification without examination is available in an area, it may be granted only:

(1) to individuals who apply within 2 years after the date on which the particular area is approved by the Supreme Court of Florida; or

(2) as otherwise permitted in the particular standards for the area for which certification is sought.

Amended Sept. 21, 1989, effective Oct. 1, 1989 (548 So.2d 1120); July 23, 1992, effective Jan. 1, 1993 (605 So.2d 252); July 1, 1993 (621 So.2d 1032); Sept. 24, 1998, effective Oct. 1, 1998 (718 So.2d 1179); Oct. 6, 2005, effective Jan. 1, 2006 (916 So.2d 655); Nov. 19, 2009, effective Feb. 1, 2010 (24 So.3d 63).

Rule 6–3.6. Recertification

(a) Duration of Certification. No certificate shall last for a period longer than 5 years.

(b) Minimum Standards for Proficiency. Each area of certification established under this chapter shall contain requirements and safeguards for the continued proficiency of any certificate holder. The following minimum standards shall apply:

(1) A satisfactory showing of substantial involvement during the period of certification in the particular area for which certification was granted.

(2) A satisfactory showing of such continuing legal education in the area for which certification is granted but in no event less than 50 credit hours during the 5–year period of certification.

(3) Satisfactory peer review and professional ethics record in accordance with rule 6–3.5(c)(6).

(4) Any applicant for recertification who is not, at the time of application for recertification, a member in good standing of The Florida Bar or any other bar or jurisdiction in which the applicant is admitted, as a result of discipline, disbarment, suspension, or resignation in lieu thereof, shall be denied recertification. The fact of a pending disciplinary complaint or malpractice action against an applicant for recertification shall not be the sole basis to deny recertification.

(5) The payment of any fees prescribed by the plan.

(c) Failure to Meet Standards for Recertification; Lapse of Certificate. Any applicant for recertification who has either failed to meet the standards for recertification or has allowed the certificate to lapse must meet all the requirements for initial certification as set out in the area's standards.

Amended Sept. 21, 1989, effective Oct. 1, 1989 (548 So.2d 1120); Oct. 10, 1991, effective Jan. 1, 1992 (587 So.2d 1121); July 23, 1992, effective Jan. 1, 1993 (605 So.2d 252); April 12, 2012, effective July 1, 2012 (107 So.3d 807).

Rule 6–3.7. Emeritus Specialist Status

(a) Purpose. The purpose of emeritus specialist status is to recognize the past and continuing contribution of a certified lawyer in the advancement of the speciality area through related career activities that do not constitute the actual practice of law. For purposes of this rule, the "practice of law" means legal work performed for purposes of rendering legal services, advice, or representation.

(b) Applicability. An applicant who seeks emeritus specialist status shall:

(1) be currently board certified by The Florida Bar;

(2) be a member of The Florida Bar in good standing;

(3) no longer be engaged in the practice of law; and

(4) otherwise comply with the applicable rules and policies governing emeritus specialist status.

(c) Qualifications. To qualify for emeritus specialist status, a member shall:

(1) not engage in the active practice of law;

(2) demonstrate integrity and professionalism, and submit to peer review as required by the board of legal specialization and education;

(3) promptly report to the board of legal specialization and education any disciplinary complaints or malpractice actions filed against the member;

(4) file the annual audit and pay the annual fee; and

(5) complete the required application and pay the specified fee.

(d) Communication. As an emeritus specialist, the member must:

(1) refrain from any written or oral communication that might be misconstrued as client solicitation for legal services; and,

(2) identify emeritus specialist status in all written or oral communication concerning board certification.

(e) Termination of Emeritus Specialist Status. At such time as the member elects to resume the practice of law, the member may regain recertification as a "certified specialist" upon:

(1) completion of all requirements for recertification within a time frame to be determined by the board of legal specialization and education; and

(2) completion of the required application and payment of the specified fee.

(f) Waiver. On special application and for good cause shown, the board of legal specialization and education may waive any portion of this rule if it determines such a waiver to be in the best interest of the certification program and emeritus status.

(g) Revocation. Existing rules relating to certification revocation shall also apply to emeritus specialist status.

(h) Exemption. During the 6 years following the effective date of this rule, any member formerly certified by The Florida Bar, whose certificate lapsed or was otherwise not renewed, may apply for emeritus status and qualify for an exemption from the provision that requires current certification. The applicant must demonstrate compliance with all other requirements of this rule. An applicant formerly certified by The Florida Bar, but whose certificate was revoked, is ineligible for this exemption.

Added Feb. 8, 2001 (795 So.2d 1); Oct. 6, 2005, effective Jan. 1, 2006 (916 So.2d 655).

Repeal

Order SC14–2107 (164 So.3d 1217), repeals this rule effective October 1, 2015.

Rule 6-3.8. Revocation of Certification

A certificate may be revoked by the board of legal specialization and education without hearing or advance notice for the following reasons:

(a) Termination of Area. If the program for certification in an area is terminated;

(b) Discipline. Disciplinary action is taken against a member pursuant to the Rules Regulating The Florida Bar;

(c) Criminal Action. When a member is found guilty, regardless of whether adjudication is imposed or withheld, of any crime involving dishonesty or a felony; or

(d) Miscellaneous. When it is determined, after hearing on appropriate notice, that:

(1) the certificate was issued to a lawyer who was not eligible to receive a certificate or who made any false representation or misstatement of material fact to the certification committee or the board of legal specialization and education;

(2) the certificate holder failed to abide by all rules and regulations governing the program promulgated by the board of governors or the board of legal specialization and education as amended from time to time, including any requirement or safeguard for continued proficiency;

(3) the certificate holder failed to pay any fee established by the plan;

(4) the certificate holder no longer meets the qualifications established by the plan or the board of legal specialization and education; or

(5) the certificate holder engaged in misconduct that is inconsistent with the demonstration of special knowledge, skills, proficiency, or ethical conduct and professionalism.

Amended effective Oct. 29, 1987 (515 So.2d 977); Sept. 21, 1989, effective Oct. 1, 1989 (548 So.2d 1120); July 23, 1992, effective Jan. 1, 1993 (605 So.2d 252). Renumbered and amended effective Feb. 8, 2001 (795 So.2d 1); Oct. 6, 2005, effective Jan. 1, 2006 (916 So.2d 655).

Rule 6-3.9. Manner of Certification

(a) Listing Area of Certification. A member having received a certificate in an area may list the area on the member's letterhead, business cards, and office door, in the yellow pages of the telephone directory, in approved law lists, and by such other means permitted by the Rules of Professional Conduct. The listing may be made by stating one or more of the following: "Board Certified (area of certification) Lawyer;" "Specialist in (area of certification);" or use of initials "B.C.S.," to indicate Board Certified Specialist. If the initials "B.C.S." are used, the area(s) in which the member is board certified must be identified; if used in court documents or a non-advertising context, the initials may stand alone.

(b) Members of Law Firms. No law firm may list an area of certification for the firm, but membership in the firm does not impair an individual's eligibility to list areas of certification in accordance with this chapter. Except for the firm listing in the telephone directory, a law firm may show next to the names of any firm members their certification area(s).

Amended Sept. 21, 1989, effective Oct. 1, 1989 (548 So.2d 1120); July 23, 1992, effective Jan. 1, 1993 (605 So.2d 252). Renumbered and amended effective Feb. 8, 2001 (795 So.2d 1). Amended Nov. 19, 2009, effective Feb. 1, 2010 (24 So.3d 63).

Rule 6-3.10. Right of Appeal

A lawyer who is refused certification or recertification, or whose certificate is revoked by the board of legal specialization and education, or any person who is aggrieved by a ruling or determination of that board shall have the right to appeal the ruling to the board of governors under such rules and regulations as it may prescribe. Exhaustion of this right of appeal shall be a condition precedent to judicial review by the Supreme Court of Florida. Such review shall be by petition for review in accordance with the procedures set forth in rule 9.100, Florida Rules of Appellate Procedure.

Amended effective Oct. 29, 1987 (515 So.2d 977); Sept. 21, 1989, effective Oct. 1, 1989 (548 So.2d 1120); July 23, 1992, effective Jan. 1, 1993 (605 So.2d 252). Renumbered and amended effective Feb. 8, 2001 (795 So.2d 1). Amended May 20, 2004 (875 So.2d 448).

Rule 6–3.11. Fees

Text of rule effective until October 1, 2015. See, also, rule effective October 1, 2015.

(a) Application Filing Fee. This fee is for the filing and review of an individual's certification or recertification application. This fee is not refundable.

(b) Examination/Certification Fee. This fee must be paid before the taking of the examination for certification or before an applicant who otherwise qualifies receives a certificate. This fee is not refundable.

(c) Annual Fee. This fee is assessed against each plan participant required to file an annual audit for a particular year. Collection of the fee shall coincide with the distribution of annual audit forms.

(d) Recertification Extension Fee. This fee is for extending the filing date of an application for recertification. This fee is not refundable.

(e) Challenge/Petition Filing Fee. This fee must accompany the filing of a challenge of an application denial or a petition for grade review. This fee is not refundable.

(f) Appeal Filing Fee. This fee must accompany the filing of an appeal. This fee is not refundable.

(g) Emeritus Application Fee. This fee must accompany the filing of an application for emeritus specialist status. This fee is not refundable.

(h) Course Evaluation Fee. This fee is assessed against course sponsors that seek continuing legal education credit hours required under the plan. This fee is not refundable.

(i) Individual Credit Approval Fee. This fee is assessed against applicants or plan participants to cover administrative costs of processing a credit request where a sponsor has not sought course approval under the plan.

Amended Sept. 21, 1989, effective Oct. 1, 1989 (548 So.2d 1120); July 23, 1992, effective Jan. 1, 1993 (605 So.2d 252); renumbered and amended effective Feb. 8, 2001 (795 So.2d 1). Amended ________, ____, by the Board of Governors of The Florida Bar.

Rule 6–3.11. Fees

Text of rule effective October 1, 2015. See, also, rule effective until October 1, 2015.

(a) Application Filing Fee. This fee is for the filing and review of an individual's certification or recertification application. This fee is not refundable.

(b) Examination/Certification Fee. This fee must be paid before taking the examination for certification or before an applicant who otherwise qualifies receives a certificate. This fee is not refundable.

(c) Annual Fee. This fee is assessed against each plan participant required to file an annual audit for a particular year. Collection of the fee coincides with the distribution of annual audit forms.

(d) Recertification Extension Fee. This fee is for extending the filing date of an application for recertification. This fee is not refundable.

(e) Challenge/Petition Filing Fee. This fee must accompany the filing of a challenge of an application denial or a petition for grade review. This fee is not refundable.

(f) Appeal Filing Fee. This fee must accompany the filing of an appeal. This fee is not refundable.

(g) Course Evaluation Fee. This fee is assessed against course sponsors that seek continuing legal education credit hours required under the plan. This fee is not refundable.

(h) Individual Credit Approval Fee. This fee is assessed against applicants or plan participants to cover administrative costs of processing a credit request where a sponsor has not sought course approval under the plan.

Amended Sept. 21, 1989, effective Oct. 1, 1989 (548 So.2d 1120); July 23, 1992, effective Jan. 1, 1993 (605 So.2d 252); renumbered and amended effective Feb. 8, 2001 (795 So.2d 1). Amended ________, ____, by the Board of Governors of The Florida Bar; May 21, 2015, effective Oct. 1, 2015 (164 So.3d 1217).

Rule 6–3.12. Confidentiality

All matters including but not limited to applications, references, tests and test scores, files, reports, investigations, hearings, findings, and recommendations shall be confidential so far as consistent with the effective administration of this plan, fairness to the applicant, and due process of law.

Amended Sept. 21, 1989, effective Oct. 1, 1989 (548 So.2d 1120). Renumbered and amended effective Feb. 8, 2001 (795 So.2d 1).

Rule 6–3.13. Amendments

Standards for individual areas of certification may be amended by the board of governors consistent with the notice and publication requirements set forth in rule 1–12.1.

Added July 1, 1993 (621 So.2d 1032). Renumbered and amended effective Feb. 8, 2001 (795 So.2d 1).

6–4. STANDARDS FOR CERTIFICATION OF A BOARD CERTIFIED CIVIL TRIAL LAWYER

Rule 6–4.1. Generally

A lawyer who is a member in good standing of The Florida Bar and who meets the standards prescribed below may be issued an appropriate certificate identifying the lawyer as a "Board Certified Civil Trial Lawyer." The purpose of the standards is to identify lawyers who practice civil trial law and have the special knowledge, skills, and proficiency, as well as the character, ethics, and reputation for professionalism, to be properly identified to the public as certified civil trial lawyers.

Amended Sept. 21, 1989, effective Oct. 1, 1989 (548 So.2d 1120); June 3, 2005, by the Board of Governors of The Florida Bar.

Rule 6–4.2. Definitions

(a) Civil Trial Law. "Civil trial law" is the practice of law dealing with litigation of civil controversies in all areas of substantive law before state courts, federal courts, administrative agencies, and arbitrators. In addition to actual pretrial and trial process, "civil trial law" includes evaluating, handling, and resolving civil controversies prior to the initiation of suit.

(b) Practice of Law. The "practice of law" for this area is defined as set out at rule 6–3.5(c)(1).

Amended Sept. 21, 1989, effective Oct. 1, 1989 (548 So.2d 1120); July 23, 1992, effective Jan. 1, 1993 (605 So.2d 252); May 21–22, 1998, by the Board of Governors of The Florida Bar.

Rule 6–4.3. Minimum Standards

(a) Substantial Involvement and Competence. To become certified as a civil trial lawyer, an applicant must demonstrate continuous substantial involvement and competence in civil trial law in accordance with the following standards.

(1) *Minimum Period of Practice.* The applicant must have actually practiced law for at least 5 years of which at least 50 percent has been spent actively participating in civil trial law. At least 3 years of this practice shall be immediately preceding application or, during those 3 years, the applicant may have served as a judge of a court of general civil jurisdiction (circuit court, federal district court, or a court of similar jurisdiction in another state) adjudicating civil trial matters.

(2) *Minimum Number of Matters.* The applicant must have handled the trials of a minimum of 15 contested civil cases, each involving substantial legal or factual issues, in courts of general jurisdiction (circuit court, federal district court, or a court of similar jurisdiction in other states). Of these 15 cases, 5 shall have been jury cases, 5 shall have been conducted by the applicant as lead counsel, and 5 shall have been submitted to the trier of fact on some or all of the issues. At least 5 of the 15 cases, including 2 jury cases and 2 cases conducted by the applicant as lead counsel, shall have been tried during the 5 years immediately preceding application. Matters deemed to be unacceptable are those that involve: mortgage foreclosure matters tried in less than 1 day, bankruptcy, family law, criminal law, workers' compensation, summary judgments, mediations, evidentiary hearings, preliminary injunctions, and appellate proceedings. (For purposes of this rule, a day shall be defined as a minimum of 6 hours). If an applicant is unable to submit 15 trials in courts of general jurisdiction, 3 substitutions may be submitted. For acceptance, such substitutions may include evidentiary hearings or preliminary injunctions lasting at least 1 day which must have involved substantial legal and factual issues, as determined by the civil trial certification committee. To be considered as a substitute for trial, the substituted matter must have been an adversarial proceeding which involved the taking of testimony and submission of evidence and must be binding on the parties. (For purposes of this rule, "binding" means that the parties are required to honor the court's decision unless and until the decision is overturned pursuant to law.) Completion of an advanced trial advocacy seminar, approved by the civil trial certification committee, either through teaching or attendance, that includes as part of its curriculum active participation by the applicant in simulated courtroom proceedings, may also substitute as 1 jury or non-jury trial.

(3) *Substantial Involvement and Competence.* The applicant must have substantial involvement in contested civil matters sufficient to demonstrate special competence as a civil trial lawyer within the 3 years immediately preceding application. Substantial involvement includes investigation, evaluation, pleading, discovery, taking of testimony, presentation of evidence, and argument of jury or nonjury cases. For good cause shown, the civil trial certification committee may waive 2 of the 3 years' substantial involvement for individuals who have served as judges of courts of general jurisdiction (circuit court, federal district court, or a court of similar jurisdiction in other states) adjudicating civil trial matters. In no event may the year immediately preceding application be waived.

(b) Peer Review. The applicant shall select and submit names and addresses of 6 lawyers, not associates or partners, as references to attest to the applicant's special competence and substantial involvement in civil trial practice, as well as the applicant's character, ethics, and reputation for professionalism. Individuals submitted as references shall be substantially involved in civil trial law and familiar with the applicant's practice. No less than 1 shall be a judge of a court of general jurisdiction (circuit court or federal district court) in the state of Florida before whom the applicant has appeared as an advocate in the 2 years immediately preceding the application. In addition, the civil trial certification committee may, at its option, send reference forms to other attorneys and judges. Peer review received on behalf of the applicant must be sufficient to demonstrate the applicant's competence, ethics, and professionalism in civil trial law.

(c) Education. The applicant shall complete at least 50 hours of approved continuing legal education in the field of civil trial law within the 3 years immediately preceding application. Such education shall be approved by The Florida Bar and may include such activity as:

(1) teaching a course in civil trial law;

(2) completion of a course in civil trial law;

(3) participation as a panelist or speaker in a symposium or similar program in civil trial law;

(4) attendance at a lecture series or similar program concerning civil trial law, sponsored by a qualified educational institution or bar group;

(5) authorship of a book or article on civil trial law, published in a professional publication or journal; or

(6) such other educational experience as the civil trial certification committee shall approve.

(d) Examination. The applicant must pass an examination applied uniformly to all applicants, to demonstrate sufficient knowledge, proficiency, and experience in civil trial law to justify the representation of special competence to the legal profession and the public.

Amended Sept. 21, 1989, effective Oct. 1, 1989 (548 So.2d 1120); July 23, 1992, effective Jan. 1, 1993 (605 So.2d 252); Feb. 17, 1995, by the Board of Governors of The Florida Bar; January 9–10, 1997, by the Board of Governors of The Florida Bar; May 21–22, 1998, by the Board of Governors of The Florida Bar; June 3, 2005, by the Board of Governors of The Florida Bar.

Rule 6–4.4. Recertification

To be eligible for recertification, an applicant must meet the following requirements:

(a) Substantial Involvement and Competence. The applicant must demonstrate continuous substantial involvement and competence in the practice of law, of which 50 percent has been spent in active participation in civil trial law throughout the period since the last date of certification. The demonstration of substantial involvement shall be made in accordance with the standards set forth in rule 6–4.3(a)(3).

(b) Minimum Number of Matters. The applicant must have handled the trial of:

(1) two contested civil cases in courts of general jurisdiction (circuit court, federal district court, or a court of similar jurisdiction in other states), of which at least 1 was a jury case conducted by the applicant as lead counsel. Matters deemed unacceptable are defined in rule 6–4.3(a)(2), however, the non-jury matter may include an evidentiary hearing or preliminary injunction as defined in rule 6–4.3(a)(2); or

(2) one jury trial as lead counsel lasting a minimum of 10 days. (For purposes of this rule, a day shall be defined as a minimum of 6 hours.)

(c) Trial Substitution. If the applicant has not participated as lead counsel in a jury trial, the applicant may substitute completion of an advanced trial advocacy seminar, either through teaching or attendance. The advanced trial advocacy seminar must be approved by the civil trial certification committee and include as part of its curriculum active participation by the applicant in simulated courtroom proceedings.

(d) Peer Review. The applicant shall submit the names and addresses of 3 lawyers, 1 of whom is currently board certified in the area of civil trial law, and 1 judge of a court of general jurisdiction (circuit court, federal district court, or a court of similar jurisdiction in another state), before whom the applicant has appeared as an advocate within the 2 years preceding application. Individuals submitted as references shall be sufficiently familiar with the applicant to attest to the applicant's special competence and substantial involvement in civil trial law, as well as the applicant's character, ethics, and reputation for professionalism, throughout the period since the last date of certification. The names of lawyers who currently practice in the applicant's law firm may not be submitted as references. The civil trial certification committee may, at its option, send reference forms to other attorneys and judges or authorize reference forms from other attorneys and judges. Peer review received on behalf of the applicant must be sufficient to demonstrate the applicant's competence, ethics, and professionalism in civil trial law.

(e) Education. The applicant must complete at least 50 hours of approved continuing legal education since the filing of the last application for certification. This requirement shall be satisfied by the applicant's participation in continuing legal education approved by The Florida Bar pursuant to rule 6–4.3(c)(1) through (6).

(f) Waiver of Compliance.

(1) On special application, for good cause shown, the civil trial certification committee may waive compliance with the substantial involvement criteria provided all other requirements of this rule have been complied with.

(2) On special application, for good cause shown, the civil trial certification committee may waive compliance with any portion of the trial and peer review criteria for an applicant who is an officer of any

judicial system (as defined in the Code of Judicial Conduct), including an officer such as a bankruptcy judge, special master, court commissioner, or magistrate, performing judicial functions on a full-time basis during any portion of the period since the last date of certification.

(3) On special application, for good cause shown, the civil trial certification committee may waive compliance with the trial criteria for an applicant who has been continuously certified as a civil trial lawyer for a period of 14 years or more.

Amended Sept. 21, 1989, effective Oct. 1, 1989 (548 So.2d 1120); Nov. 29, 1990, effective Oct. 1, 1989 (570 So.2d 1301); July 23, 1992, effective Jan. 1, 1993 (605 So.2d 252); Sept. 30–Oct. 1, 1993, by the Board of Governors of The Florida Bar; Feb. 17, 1995, by the Board of Governors of The Florida Bar; May 16–18, 1996, by the Board of Governors of The Florida Bar; Jan. 9–10, 1997, by the Board of Governors of The Florida Bar; May 21–22, 1998, by the Board of Governors of The Florida Bar; June 3, 2005, by the Board of Governors of The Florida Bar.

6–5. STANDARDS FOR CERTIFICATION OF A BOARD CERTIFIED TAX LAWYER

Rule 6–5.1. Generally

A lawyer who is a member in good standing of The Florida Bar and who meets the standards prescribed below may be issued an appropriate certificate identifying the lawyer as a "Board Certified Tax Lawyer." The purpose of the standards is to identify those lawyers who practice in the area of taxation and have the special knowledge, skills, and proficiency to be properly identified to the public as certified tax lawyers.

Amended Sept. 21, 1989, effective Oct. 1, 1989 (548 So.2d 1120).

Rule 6–5.2. Definitions

(a) Tax Law. "Tax law" means legal issues involving federal, state, or local income, estate, gift, ad valorem, excise, or other taxes.

(b) Practice of Law. The "practice of law" for this area is defined as set out rule 6–3.5(c)(1). Notwithstanding anything in the definition to the contrary, legal work done primarily for a purpose other than legal advice or representation (including, but not limited to, work related to the sale of insurance or retirement plans or work in connection with the practice of a profession other than the law) shall not be treated as the practice of law.

Amended Sept. 21, 1989, effective Oct. 1, 1989 (548 So.2d 1120); July 23, 1992, effective Jan. 1, 1993 (605 So.2d 252).

Rule 6–5.3. Minimum Standards

(a) Minimum Period of Practice. Every applicant shall have been engaged in the practice of law in the United States, or engaged in the practice of United States law while in a foreign country, and shall have been a member in good standing of the bar of any state of the United States or the District of Columbia for a period of 5 years as of the date of application.

(1) The years of practice of law need not be consecutive.

(2) Notwithstanding the definition of "practice of law" in rule 6–3.5(c)(1), receipt of an LL.M. degree in taxation (or such other related fields approved by the board of legal specialization and education and the tax certification committee) from an approved law school shall be deemed to constitute 1 year of the practice of law for purposes of the 5–year practice requirement (but not the 5–year bar membership requirement) under this subdivision. However, an applicant may not receive credit for more than 1 year of practice for any 12–month period under this subdivision; accordingly, for example, an applicant who, while being engaged in the practice of law, receives an LL.M. degree by attending night classes, would not receive credit for the practice of law requirement by virtue of having received the LL.M. degree.

(b) Substantial Involvement. Every applicant must demonstrate substantial involvement in the practice of tax law during the 3 years immediately preceding the date of application. Upon an applicant's request and the recommendation of the tax certification committee, the board of legal specialization and education may waive the requirement that the 3 years be "immediately preceding" the date of application if the board of legal specialization and education determines the waiver is warranted by special and compelling circumstances. Substantial involvement is defined as at least 500 hours per year in the practice of law in which an applicant has had substantial and direct participation in legal matters involving significant issues of tax law. An applicant must furnish information concerning the frequency of the applicant's work and the nature of the issues involved. For the purposes of this subdivision the "practice of law" shall be as defined in rule 6–3.5(c)(1), except that it shall also include time devoted to lecturing and/or authoring books or articles on tax law if the applicant was engaged in the practice of law during such period. Demonstration of compliance with this requirement shall be made initially through a form of questionnaire approved by the tax certification committee but written or oral supplementation may be required.

(c) Peer Review. Every applicant shall submit the names and addresses of 5 other attorneys who are familiar with the applicant's practice, not including attorneys who currently practice in the applicant's law firm, who can attest to the applicant's reputation for involvement in the field of tax law in accordance with rule 6–3.5(c)(6), as well as the applicant's character, ethics, and reputation for professionalism. The board of legal specialization and education or the tax certification committee may authorize references from persons other than attorneys in such cases as they deem appropriate. The board of legal specialization and education and the tax certification committee may also make such additional inquiries as they deem appropriate.

(d) Education. Every applicant must demonstrate that during the 3–year period immediately preceding the date of application, the applicant has met the continuing legal education requirements in tax law as follows. The required number of hours shall be established by the board of legal specialization and education and shall in no event be less than 90 hours. Credit for attendance at continuing legal education seminars shall be given only for programs that are directly related to tax law. The education requirement may be satisfied by 1 or more of the following:

(1) attendance at continuing legal education seminars meeting the requirements set forth above;

(2) lecturing at, and/or serving on the steering committee of, such continuing legal education seminars;

(3) authoring articles or books published in professional periodicals or other professional publications;

(4) teaching courses in "tax law" at an approved law school or other graduate level program presented by a recognized professional education association;

(5) completing such home study programs as may be approved by the board of legal specialization and education or the tax certification committee; or

(6) such other methods as may be approved by the board of legal specialization and education and the tax certification committee.

The board of legal specialization and education or the tax certification committee shall, by rule or regulation, establish standards applicable to this rule, including, but not limited to, the method of establishment of the number of hours allocable to any of the above-listed paragraphs. Such rules or regulations shall provide that hours shall be allocable to each separate but substantially different lecture, article, or other activity described in subdivisions (2), (3), and (4) above.

(e) Examination. Every applicant must pass a written examination designed to demonstrate sufficient knowledge, skills, and proficiency in the field of tax law to justify the representation of special competence to the legal profession and the public.

Amended effective Oct. 29, 1987 (515 So.2d 977); Sept. 21, 1989, effective Oct. 1, 1989 (548 So.2d 1120); July 23, 1992, effective Jan. 1, 1993 (605 So.2d 252); Dec. 7–8, 1993, by the Board of Governors of The Florida Bar; May 21–22, 1998, by the Board of Governors of The Florida Bar.

Rule 6–5.4. Recertification

To be eligible for recertification, an applicant must meet the following requirements:

(a) Substantial Involvement. A satisfactory showing, as determined by the board of legal specialization and education and the tax certification committee, of continuous and substantial involvement in the field of tax law throughout the period since the last date of certification. Demonstration of substantial involvement shall be in accordance with rule 6–5.3(b), except that the board of legal specialization and education and/or the tax certification committee may accept an affidavit from the applicant which attests to the applicant's proficiency in tax law consistent with the purpose of the substantial involvement requirement.

(b) Education. Demonstration that the applicant has completed at least 125 hours of continuing legal education since the filing of the last application for certification (or recertification). The continuing legal education must logically be expected to enhance the proficiency of attorneys who are board certified tax lawyers. If the applicant has not attained 125 hours of continuing legal education, but has attained more than 60 hours during such period, successful passage of the written examination given by the board of legal specialization and education to new applicants shall satisfy the continuing legal education requirements.

(c) Peer Review. Completion of the reference requirements set forth in rule 6–5.3(c).

(d) Examination. If, after reviewing the material submitted by an applicant for recertification, the board of legal specialization and education and the tax certification committee determine that the applicant may not meet the standards in tax law established under this chapter, the board of legal specialization and education and the tax certification committee may require, as a condition of recertification, that the applicant pass the written examination given by the board of legal specialization and education to new applicants.

Amended Oct. 29, 1987 (515 So.2d 977); Sept. 21, 1989, effective Oct. 1, 1989 (548 So.2d 1120); July 23, 1992, effective Jan. 1, 1993 (605 So.2d 252); May 21–22, 1998, by the Board of Governors of The Florida Bar; June 29, 2000, by the Board of Governors of The Florida Bar.

6–6. STANDARDS FOR CERTIFICATION OF A BOARD CERTIFIED MARITAL AND FAMILY LAWYER

Rule 6–6.1. Generally

A lawyer who is a member in good standing of The Florida Bar and who meets the standards prescribed below may be issued an appropriate certificate identifying the lawyer as "Board Certified in Marital and Family Law." The purpose of the standards is to identify those lawyers who practice marital and family law and have the special knowledge, skills, and proficiency, as well as the character, ethics, and reputation for professionalism to be properly identified to the public as board certified marital and family lawyers. The standards also contain provisions to allow judicial officers who regularly preside over marital and family law cases to achieve board certification in marital and family law.

Amended Sept. 21, 1989, effective Oct. 1, 1989 (548 So.2d 1120); Feb. 11, 1999, by the Board of Governors of The Florida Bar; Dec. 12, 2008, by the Board of Governors of The Florida Bar.

Rule 6–6.2. Definitions

(a) Marital and Family Law. "Marital and family law" is the practice of law dealing with legal problems arising from the family relationship of husband and wife and parent and child, including civil controversies arising from those relationships. In addition to actual pretrial and trial process, "marital and family law" includes evaluating, handling, and resolving such controversies prior to and during the institution of suit and postjudgment proceedings. The practice of marital and family law in the state of Florida is generally unique in that decisional, statutory, and procedural laws are specific to this state.

(b) Practice of Law. The "practice of law" for this area is defined as set out in rule 6–3.5(c)(1).

(c) Judicial Officers. "Judicial officers" shall include judges, general magistrates, special magistrates, child support hearing officers, and private triers of fact appointed by court order.

(d) Trial. A "trial" is defined as a matter submitted to and decided by the trier of fact for ultimate resolution by the court's rendition of a judgment or order on at least 1 issue aside from the dissolution of the parties' marriage. Further, the applicant must have, incident thereto, presided over as a judicial officer, or conducted as an advocate, at least 1 direct and 1 cross examination of at least 2 different witnesses, with the introduction into evidence of at least 1 exhibit. The applicant must have been responsible for all, or a majority of, the presentation of evidence and/or representation of the client if the matter was handled as an advocate.

(e) Substantial Involvement. "Substantial involvement" is defined as active participation in client interviewing, counseling, investigating, preparation of pleadings, participation in discovery beyond mandatory disclosure, taking of testimony, presentation of evidence, attendance at hearings, negotiations of settlement, attendance at mediation, drafting and preparation of marital settlement agreements, and argument and trial of marital and family law cases. Substantial involvement also includes active participation in the appeal of marital and family law cases.

Amended Sept. 21, 1989, effective Oct. 1, 1989 (548 So.2d 1120); July 23, 1992, effective Jan. 1, 1993 (605 So.2d 252); Feb. 11, 1999, by the Board of Governors of The Florida Bar; Dec. 12, 2008, by the Board of Governors of The Florida Bar.

Rule 6–6.3. Minimum Standards For Lawyer Applicants

(a) Minimum Period of Practice. The applicant must have at least 5 years of the actual practice of law immediately preceding application, of which at least 50 percent has been spent in active participation in marital and family law.

(b) Minimum Number of Cases. The applicant must demonstrate in the application trial experience and substantial involvement as set forth in subdivisions (1) and (2) below, in a minimum of 25 contested marital and family law cases in circuit courts during the 5–year period immediately preceding the date of application. All such cases must have involved substantial legal or factual issues other than the dissolution of marriage. In each of these 25 cases the applicant shall have been responsible for all or a majority of the presentation of evidence and representation of the client.

(1) At least 7 of the 25 cases must have been trials as defined in rule 6–6.2(d). An advanced trial advocacy seminar approved by the marital and family law certification committee, completed either by teaching, attendance, or a combination thereof, shall qualify as 1 of the 7 trials.

(2) The applicant shall have substantial involvement, as defined in rule 6–6.2(e), in at least 18 contested marital and family law cases sufficient to demonstrate special competence as a marital and family lawyer. Any trials in excess of the 7 trials meeting the criteria of subdivision (b)(1) of this rule shall automatically quality as substantial involvement cases.

(3) The determination of whether the applicant has sufficiently demonstrated substantial involvement in each case submitted shall be made on a qualitative basis by the marital and family law certification committee using the information provided by the applicant. The marital and family law certification committee reserves the right to seek additional information from the applicant as it deems necessary to make its determination that the minimum number of cases requirement has been met.

(c) Peer Review.

(1) The applicant shall submit names and addresses of 6 lawyers, who are neither current nor former associates or partners of the applicant within the 5–year period immediately preceding the date of application, as references to attest to the applicant's substantial competence and active involvement in the practice of marital and family law as well as the applicant's character, ethics, and reputation for professionalism. At least 3 of the lawyers shall be members of The Florida Bar, with their principal office located in the state of Florida. Such lawyers need not be Florida Bar board certified in marital and family law, however, they should be substantially involved in marital and family law and familiar with the applicant's practice. In addition, all lawyer references must have participated with the applicant, during the 5–year period immediately preceding the date of application, as either opposing or co-counsel in a marital and family law or juvenile dependency proceeding, involving some combination of discovery beyond mandatory disclosure, settlement negotiations, evidentiary hearings in excess of 3 hours, trials, and/or alternative dispute resolution mechanism such as collaborative law, mediation or arbitration. This requirement is to ensure meaningful comment on the applicant's most recent special knowledge, skills, proficiency, character, and reputation for professionalism in the practice of marital and family law, including the consideration of the needs of children and the family unit affected by the applicant's representation.

(2) The applicant shall submit the names and addresses of 3 judicial officers who have presided in circuit courts in the state of Florida and before whom the applicant has appeared as an advocate in a trial or an evidentiary hearing of at least 3 hours in length for a marital and family law and/or juvenile dependency case during the 5–year period immediately preceding the date of application.

(3) The marital and family law certification committee may, at its option, send reference forms to other attorneys and judicial officers, and make such other investigation as necessary to ensure that the applicant's special knowledge, skills, proficiency, character, and reputation for professionalism in the practice of marital and family law, including the consideration of the needs of children and the family, are befitting board certification in marital and family law.

(d) Education. The applicant must demonstrate completion of at least 75 credit hours of approved continuing legal education in the field of marital and family law during the 5–year period immediately preceding the date of application. At least 5 of the 75 credit hours must be in ethics, dispute resolution, collaborative law and/or mental health continuing legal education. Accreditation of educational hours is subject to policies established by the marital and family law certification committee or the board of legal specialization and education and may include such activity as:

(1) teaching a course in marital and family law;

(2) completion of a course in marital and family law;

(3) participation as a panelist or speaker in a symposium or similar program in marital and family law;

(4) attendance at a lecture series or similar program concerning marital and family law, sponsored by a qualified educational institution or bar group;

(5) authorship of a book or article on marital and family law, published in a professional publication or journal; and

(6) such other educational experience as the marital and family law certification committee or the board of legal specialization and education shall approve.

(e) Examination. The applicant must pass an examination applied uniformly to all applicants, to demonstrate sufficient knowledge, proficiency, experience, and professionalism in marital and family law to justify the representation of special competence to the legal profession and the public.

Amended Sept. 21, 1989, effective Oct. 1, 1989 (548 So.2d 1120); July 23, 1992, effective Jan. 1, 1993 (605 So.2d 252); Feb. 11, 1999, by the Board of Governors of The Florida Bar; Dec. 12, 2008, by the Board of Governors of The Florida Bar.

Rule 6–6.4. Minimum Standards for Judicial Officers

An applicant who has served as a judicial officer within the 5–year period immediately preceding the date of application may be eligible for board certification if the applicant complies with each of the following standards:

(a) Minimum Period of Practice or Judicial Service. The applicant must have devoted at least 50 percent of the applicant's practice or judicial labor to marital and family law cases during the 5–year period immediately preceding the date of application.

(b) Minimum Number of Cases. The applicant must demonstrate in the application trial experience and substantial involvement, as set forth in subdivisions (1) and (2) below, as a judicial officer who presided over, or who handled as an advocate, a minimum of 25 contested marital and family law cases in circuit courts during the 5–year period immediately preceding the date of application. All such cases must have involved substantial legal or factual issues other than the dissolution of marriage.

(1) At least 7 of the 25 cases must have been trials as defined in rule 6–6.2(d). The skill set inherent in presiding over a marital and family law case as a judicial officer encompasses all of the special knowledge, skills, and proficiency, as well as ethics, that the marital and family law certification committee finds sufficient to meet the trial requirements for certification. At a minimum, in each of the 7 cases, the applicant must have presided over a contested eviden-

tiary trial where at least 1 direct and 1 cross examination of at least 2 different witnesses was conducted and at least 1 piece of evidence was introduced as an exhibit. If the applicant handled the cases as an advocate, the applicant must have been responsible for all or a majority of the presentation of evidence and/or representation of the client. An advanced trial advocacy seminar approved by the marital and family law certification committee, completed either by teaching, attendance, or a combination thereof, shall qualify as 1 of the 7 trials.

(2) The applicant shall have substantial involvement, as defined in rule 6-6.2(e), in at least 18 contested marital and family law cases sufficient to demonstrate special competence in marital and family law. Any trials in excess of the 7 trials meeting the criteria of subdivision (b)(1) shall automatically qualify as substantial involvement cases.

(3) The determination of whether the applicant has sufficiently demonstrated substantial involvement in each case submitted shall be made on a qualitative basis by the marital and family law certification committee using the information provided by the applicant. The marital and family law certification committee reserves the right to seek additional information from the applicant as it deems necessary to make its determination that the minimum number of cases requirement has been met.

(c) Peer Review. The applicant shall submit names and addresses of 6 lawyers, who are neither current nor former associates or partners of the applicant within the 5-year period immediately preceding the date of application, as references to attest to the applicant's substantial competence and active involvement in marital and family law, as well as the applicant's character, ethics, and reputation for professionalism. At least 5 of the lawyers shall be members of The Florida Bar, with their principal office located in the state of Florida. Such lawyers need not be Florida Bar board certified in marital and family law, however, they should be substantially involved in marital and family law and familiar with the applicant's judicial service. This requirement is to ensure meaningful comment on the applicant's special knowledge, skills, proficiency, character, and reputation for professionalism in marital and family law, including the consideration of the needs of children and the family unit affected by the applicant's judicial service. Judicial references shall not be required.

(d) Education. The applicant shall comply with rule 6-6.3(d).

(e) Examination. The applicant must pass the examination required by rule 6-6.3(e).

Amended Sept. 21, 1989, effective Oct. 1, 1989 (548 So.2d 1120); July 23, 1992, effective Jan. 1, 1993 (605 So.2d 252); Oct. 31-Nov. 2, 1996, by the Board of Governors of The Florida Bar; Feb. 11, 1999, by the Board of Governors of The Florida Bar; ______, ____, by the Board of Governors of The Florida Bar; Dec. 12, 2008, by the Board of Governors of The Florida Bar.

Rule 6-6.5. Recertification

During the 5-year period immediately preceding the date of application, the applicant must demonstrate satisfaction of the following requirements for recertification:

(a) Minimum Period of Practice and/or Judicial Service. The applicant must have devoted at least 30 percent of the applicant's practice or judicial labor to marital and family law cases.

(b) Minimum Number of Cases. The applicant must demonstrate in the application trial experience and substantial involvement by handling as an advocate, or presiding over as a judicial officer, a minimum of 15 contested marital and family law cases in circuit courts. All such cases must have involved substantial legal or factual issues other than the dissolution of marriage.

(1) At least 5 of the 15 cases must have been trials as defined in rule 6-6.2(d). The skill set inherent in presiding over a marital and family law case as a judicial officer encompasses all of the special knowledge, skills, and proficiency, as well as ethics, that the marital and family law certification committee finds sufficient to meet the trial requirements for recertification. An advanced trial advocacy seminar approved by the marital and family law certification committee, completed either by teaching, attendance, or a combination thereof, shall qualify as one of the 5 trials.

(2) The applicant shall have substantial involvement, as defined in rule 6-6.2(e), in at least 10 contested marital and family law cases sufficient to demonstrate special competence as a marital and family lawyer or as a judicial officer presiding over marital and family law cases. Any trials in excess of the 5 trials meeting the criteria of subdivision (a)(1) shall automatically qualify as substantial involvement cases. The skill set inherent in presiding over a marital and family law case as a judicial officer encompasses all of the special knowledge, skills, and proficiency, as well as ethics, that the marital and family law certification committee finds sufficient to meet the substantial involvement requirements for recertification.

(3) The determination of whether the applicant has sufficiently demonstrated involvement in each case submitted shall be made on a qualitative basis by the marital and family law certification committee using the information provided by the applicant. The marital and family law certification committee reserves the right to seek additional information from the applicant as it deems necessary to make its determination that the minimum number of cases requirement has been met.

(4) On special application, for good cause shown, the marital and family law certification committee may waive compliance with rule 6-6.5(b)(1) and/or (2) for an applicant who has been continuously certified in marital and family law for a period of 14 years or more or who has demonstrated in the application an extraordinary contribution, as determined by the mar-

ital and family law certification committee after review, inquiry, and consideration thereof, to the field of marital and family law in Florida. The applicant shall be required to complete all sections of the application for recertification with the exception of schedule B–1.

(c) Education. The applicant must have completed at least 75 hours of approved continuing legal education in accordance with rule 6–6.3(d).

(d) Peer Review. The applicant must submit references and otherwise comply with rule 6–6.3(c) or 6–6.4(c). Judicial peer review is not required for judicial officers seeking recertification.

Amended Sept. 21, 1989, effective Oct. 1, 1989 (548 So.2d 1120); July 23, 1992, effective Jan. 1, 1993 (605 So.2d 252); Feb. 17, 1995, by the Board of Governors of The Florida Bar; Oct. 31-Nov. 2, 1996, by the Board of Governors of The Florida Bar; Feb. 11, 1999, by the Board of Governors of The Florida Bar; _______, ____, by the Board of Governors of The Florida Bar; Dec. 12, 2008, by the Board of Governors of The Florida Bar.

6–7. STANDARDS FOR CERTIFICATION OF A BOARD CERTIFIED WILLS, TRUSTS AND ESTATES LAWYER

Rule 6–7.1. Generally

A lawyer who is a member in good standing of The Florida Bar and who meets the standards prescribed below may be issued an appropriate certificate identifying the lawyer as a "Board Certified Wills, Trusts, and Estates Lawyer." The purpose of the standards is to identify those lawyers who practice in the area of wills, trusts, and estates and have demonstrated special knowledge, skills, and proficiency to be properly identified to the public as certified wills, trusts, and estates lawyers.

Amended Sept. 21, 1989, effective Oct. 1, 1989 (548 So.2d 1120); Oct. 10, 1991, effective Jan. 1, 1992 (587 So.2d 1121); July 1, 1993 (621 So.2d 1032).

Rule 6–7.2. Definitions

(a) Wills, Trusts, and Estates. "Wills, trusts and estates" is the practice of law dealing with all aspects of the analysis and planning for the conservation and disposition of estates, giving due consideration to the applicable tax consequences, both federal and state; the preparation of legal instruments to effectuate estate plans; administering estates, including tax related matters, both federal and state; and probate litigation.

(b) Practice of Law. The "practice of law" for this area is defined as set out in rule 6–3.5(c)(1). Notwithstanding anything in the definition to the contrary, legal work done primarily for any purpose other than legal advice or representation (including, but not limited to, work related to the sale of insurance or retirement plans or work in connection with the practice of a profession other than the law) shall not be treated as the practice of law. Service as a judge of any court of record shall be deemed to constitute the practice of law. Practice of law that otherwise satisfies these requirements but that is on a part-time basis will satisfy the requirement if the balance of the applicant's activity is spent as a teacher of wills, trusts and estates subjects in an accredited law school.

Amended Sept. 21, 1989, effective Oct. 1, 1989 (548 So.2d 1120); July 23, 1992, effective Jan. 1, 1993 (605 So.2d 252); July 1, 1993 (621 So.2d 1032).

Rule 6–7.3. Minimum standards

(a) Minimum Period of Practice. Every applicant shall have been engaged in the practice of law in the United States, or engaged in the practice of United States law while in a foreign country, and shall have been a member in good standing of the bar of any state of the United States or the District of Columbia for a period of 5 years as of the date of application.

Notwithstanding the definition of "practice of law" in rule 6–3.5(c)(1), receipt of an LL.M. degree in taxation or estate planning and probate (or such other related fields approved by the board and wills, trusts, and estates certification committee) from an approved law school shall be deemed to constitute 1 year of the practice of law for purposes of the 5–year practice requirement (but not the 5–year bar membership requirement) under this subdivision; provided, however, an applicant may not receive credit for more than 1 year of practice for any 12–month period under this subdivision; accordingly, for example, an applicant who, while being engaged in the practice of law, receives an LL.M. degree by attending night classes, would not receive credit for the practice of law requirement by virtue of having received the LL.M. degree.

(b) Substantial Involvement. Every applicant must demonstrate substantial involvement in the practice of law in estate planning, planning for incapacity, administration of estates and trusts, fiduciary and transfer taxation, probate and trust law, estates and trust litigation, and homestead law during the 5 years immediately preceding the date of application, including devoting not less than 40 percent of practice to estate planning, planning for incapacity, administration of estates and trusts, fiduciary and transfer taxation, probate and trust law, estates and trust litigation, and homestead law in this state during each of the 2 years immediately preceding application. Service as a judge in the probate division of the circuit court of this state during 6 months or more of a calendar year shall satisfy a year of substantial involvement. Except for the 2 years immediately preceding application, upon an applicant's request and the recommendation of the wills, trusts, and estates certification committee, the board of legal specialization and education may waive the requirement that the 5 years be "immediately preceding" the date of application if the board of legal specialization and education determines the waiver is warranted by special and compelling circumstances. Except for the 2 years immediately preceding application, receipt of an LL.M. degree in estate planning and probate (or such other degree containing substantial estate planning and probate content as approved by the board of legal specialization and education) from an approved law school may substitute for 1 year of substantial involvement. An applicant must furnish information concerning the frequency of work and the nature of the issues involved. For the purposes of this section the "practice of law" shall be as defined in rule 6–3.5(c)(1) except that it shall also include time devoted to lecturing and/or authoring books or articles on wills, trusts, and estates if the applicant was engaged in the practice of law during such period. Demonstration of compliance with this requirement shall be made initially through a form of questionnaire approved by the wills, trusts, and estates certification committee, but written or oral supplementation may be required.

(c) Peer Review. Every applicant shall submit the names and addresses of 5 other attorneys who are familiar with the applicant's practice, not including attorneys who currently practice in the applicant's law firm, who can attest to the applicant's reputation for professional competence and substantial involvement in the field of wills, trusts, and estates. The board of legal specialization and education and the wills, trusts, and estates certification committee may authorize references from persons other than attorneys in such cases as they deem appropriate. The board of legal specialization and education and the wills, trusts, and estates certification committee may also make such additional inquiries as they deem appropriate to complete peer review, as provided elsewhere in these rules.

(d) Education. Every applicant must demonstrate that, during the 3–year period immediately preceding the date of the application, the applicant has met the continuing legal education requirements in wills, trusts, and estates as follows. The required number of hours shall be established by the board of legal specialization and education and shall in no event be less than 90 hours. Credit for attendance at continuing legal education seminars shall be given only for programs that are directly related to wills, trusts and estates. The education requirement may be satisfied by 1 or more of the following:

(1) attendance at continuing legal education seminars meeting the requirements set forth above;

(2) lecturing at, and/or serving on the steering committee of, such continuing legal education seminars;

(3) authoring articles or books published in professional periodicals or other professional publications;

(4) teaching courses in estates and trusts, fiduciary administration, fiduciary and transfer taxation, and homestead law at an approved law school or other graduate level program presented by a recognized professional education association;

(5) completing such home study programs as may be approved by the board of legal specialization and education and the wills, trusts, and estates certification committee, subject to the limitation that no more than 50 percent of the required number of hours of education may be satisfied through home study programs; and

(6) such other methods as may be approved by the board of legal specialization and education and the wills, trusts, and estates certification committee.

The board of legal specialization and education and the wills, trusts, and estates certification committee shall, by rule or regulation, establish standards applicable to this rule, including, but not limited to, the method of establishment of the number of hours allocable to any of the above-listed subdivisions. Such rules or regulations shall provide that hours shall be allocable to each separate but substantially different lecture, article, or other activity described in subdivisions (2), (3), and (4) above.

(e) Examination. The applicant must pass an examination that will be practical and comprehensive and designed to demonstrate special knowledge, skills, and proficiency in estate planning, postmortem planning, planning for incapacity, administration of estates and trusts, fiduciary and transfer taxation, substantive and procedural aspects of probate and trust law, estates and trust litigation, homestead law, joint tenancies, tenancies by the entirety, conflicts of interest, and other ethical considerations. Such examination shall justify the representation of special competence to the legal profession and the public.

Amended Oct. 29, 1987 (515 So.2d 977); Sept. 21, 1989, effective Oct. 1, 1989 (548 So.2d 1120); Oct. 10, 1991, effective Jan. 1, 1992 (587 So.2d 1121); July 23, 1992, effective Jan. 1, 1993 (605 So.2d 252); July 1, 1993 (621 So.2d 1032).

Rule 6–7.4. Recertification

(a) Eligibility. Recertification must be obtained every 5 years. To be eligible for recertification, an applicant must meet the following requirements:

(1) A satisfactory showing, as determined by the board of legal specialization and education and the wills, trusts, and estates certification committee, of continuous and substantial involvement in wills, trusts, and estates law throughout the period since the last date of certification. The demonstration of substantial involvement of more than 40 percent during each year after certification or prior recertification shall be made in accordance with the standards set forth in rule 6–7.3(b).

(2) Completion of at least 125 hours of approved continuing legal education since the filing of the last application for certification. This requirement shall be satisfied by the applicant's participation in continuing legal education approved by The Florida Bar pursuant to rule 6–7.3(d)(1) through (6).

(3) Submission of the names and addresses of 3 individuals who are active in wills, trusts, and estates, including but not limited to lawyers, trust officers, certified public accountants, and judges who are familiar with the applicant's practice, excluding persons who are currently employed by or practice in the applicant's law firm, who can attest to the applicant's reputation for professional competence and substantial involvement in the field of wills, trusts, and estates law during the period since the last date of certification. The board of legal specialization and education or the wills, trusts, and estates certification committee may solicit references from persons other than those whose names are submitted by the applicant in such cases as they deem appropriate. The board of legal specialization and education or the wills, trusts, and estates certification committee may also make such additional inquiries as it deems appropriate.

(b) Denial of Recertification. The board of legal specialization and education may deny recertification based upon any information received from the peer review or from any individual referenced in subdivision (a)(3), above.

(c) Examination Requirement. If, after reviewing the material submitted by an applicant for recertification and the peer review, the wills, trusts, and estates certification committee determines the applicant may not meet the standards for wills, trusts, and estates certification established under this chapter, the wills, trusts, and estates certification committee may require, as a condition of recertification, that the applicant pass the examination given by the wills, trusts, and estates certification committee to new applicants.

Amended Oct. 29, 1987 (515 So.2d 977); Sept. 21, 1989, effective Oct. 1, 1989 (548 So.2d 1120); Oct. 10, 1991, effective Jan. 1, 1992 (587 So.2d 1121); July 23, 1992, effective Jan. 1, 1993 (605 So.2d 252); July 1, 1993 (621 So.2d 1032).

6–8. STANDARDS FOR CERTIFICATION OF A BOARD CERTIFIED CRIMINAL LAWYER

Rule 6–8.1. Generally

A lawyer who is a member in good standing of The Florida Bar and who meets the standards prescribed below may be issued an appropriate certificate identifying the lawyer as either a "Board Certified Criminal Trial Lawyer" or a "Board Certified Criminal Appellate Lawyer." An applicant may qualify for certification under both categories provided the applicant meets the standards for each category. The purpose of the standards is to identify those lawyers who practice criminal law and have the special knowledge, skills, and proficiency, as well as the character, ethics, and reputation for professionalism, to be properly identified to the public as certified criminal trial or appellate lawyers.

Amended Sept. 21, 1989, effective Oct. 1, 1989 (548 So.2d 1120); Feb. 11, 1999, by the Board of Governors of The Florida Bar; Aug. 17, 2007, by the Board of Governors of The Florida Bar.

Rule 6–8.2. Definitions and Committee

(a) Criminal Law. "Criminal law" is the practice of law dealing with the defense and prosecution of misdemeanor and felony crimes in state and federal trial and appellate courts.

(b) Practice of Law. The "practice of law" for this area is defined as set out in rule 6–3.5(c)(1).

(c) Criminal Law Certification Committee. At least 2 members of the "criminal law certification committee" shall be certified in criminal appellate law. At least 5 members shall be certified in criminal trial law.

(d) Trial. A "trial" shall be defined as substantially preparing a case for court, offering testimony or evidence (or cross-examination of witness[es]) in an adversarial proceeding before a trier of fact, and submission of a case to the trier of fact for determination of the ultimate fact of guilt or innocence.

A trial conducted under the Jimmy Ryce Act, section 394.911, *et seq.*, Florida Statutes, may count toward the trial requirement for initial certification or recertification. However, no more than 60 percent of the total trial requirement for criminal trial law certification or recertification may be based on Jimmy Ryce trials.

(e) Protracted Litigation. "Protracted litigation" shall be defined as litigation that proceeds on a long-term basis involving unusual and complicated legal or factual matters, extensive discovery, court hearings or trial, and by its very nature is so time consuming it precludes the applicant from meeting the numerical requirement.

Amended Sept. 21, 1989, effective Oct. 1, 1989 (548 So.2d 1120); July 23, 1992, effective Jan. 1, 1993 (605 So.2d 252); Feb. 11, 1999, by the Board of Governors of The Florida Bar; ________, ____, by the Board of Governors of The Florida Bar; Aug. 17, 2007, by the Board of Governors of The Florida Bar.

Rule 6–8.3. Criminal Trial; Minimum Standards

(a) Substantial Involvement and Competence. To become certified as a criminal trial lawyer, an applicant must demonstrate substantial involvement and competence in criminal trial law. Substantial involvement and competence shall include the following:

(1) At least 5 years of the actual practice of law of which at least 30 percent has been spent in active participation in criminal trial law. At least 3 years of this practice shall be immediately preceding application or, during those 3 years, the applicant may have served as a judge of a court of general jurisdiction adjudicating criminal trial matters.

(2) The trial of a minimum of 25 criminal cases. Of these 25 cases, at least 20 shall have been jury trials, tried to verdict, and at least 15 shall have involved felony charges; and at least 10 shall have been conducted by the applicant as lead counsel. At least 5 of the 25 cases shall have been tried during the 5 years immediately preceding application. On good cause shown, for satisfaction in part of the 25 criminal trials, the criminal law certification committee may consider involvement in protracted litigation as defined in rule 6–8.2(e).

(3) Submission of a criminal trial court memorandum or brief prepared and filed by the applicant within the 3 year period immediately preceding application. Such document shall be substantial in nature, state facts and argue various aspects of criminal law. The quality of this memorandum or brief will be considered in determining whether an applicant is qualified for certification.

(4) Within the 3 years immediately preceding application, the applicant's substantial involvement must be sufficient to demonstrate special competence as a criminal trial lawyer. Substantial involvement includes investigation, evaluation, pleading, discovery, taking of testimony, presentation of evidence, and argument of jury or non-jury cases. For good cause shown, the criminal law certification committee may waive 2 of the 3 years of substantial involvement for individuals who have served as judges. In no event may the year immediately preceding application be waived.

(b) Peer Review.

(1) The applicant shall submit the names and addresses of at least 4 lawyers, who are neither relatives nor current associates or partners, as references to attest to the applicant's substantial involvement and competence in criminal trial practice, as well as the applicant's character, ethics, and reputation for professionalism. Such lawyers shall be substantially involved in criminal trial law and familiar with the applicant's practice.

(2) The applicant shall submit the names and addresses of at least 2 judges before whom the applicant has appeared on criminal trial matters within the last 2 years, or before whom the applicant has tried a criminal trial to jury verdict, to attest to the applicant's substantial involvement and competence in criminal trial practice, as well as the applicant's character, ethics, and reputation for professionalism.

(3) Peer review received on behalf of the applicant shall be sufficient to demonstrate the applicant's competence in criminal trial law, character, ethics, and professionalism. The criminal law certification committee may, at its option, send reference forms to other attorneys and judges.

(c) Education. The applicant shall demonstrate that during the 3–years period immediately preceding the filing of an application, the applicant has met the continuing legal education requirements necessary for criminal trial certification. The required number of hours shall be established by the board of legal specialization and education and shall in no event be less than 45 hours. Accreditation of educational hours is subject to policies established by the criminal law certification committee or the board of legal specialization and education.

(d) Examination. Every applicant must pass an examination designed to demonstrate sufficient knowledge, skills, proficiency, and experience in criminal trial law, application of constitutional principles, and rules of criminal procedure to justify the representation of special competence to the legal profession and the public.

Amended June 18, 1987, effective July 1, 1987 (508 So.2d 1236); Sept. 21, 1989, effective Oct. 1, 1989 (548 So.2d 1120); July 23, 1992, effective Jan. 1, 1993 (605 So.2d 252); July 1, 1993 (621 So.2d 1032); April 14–15, 1994, by the Board of Governors of The Florida Bar; Feb. 11, 1999, by the Board of Governors of The Florida Bar; Aug. 17, 2007, by the Board of Governors of The Florida Bar.

Rule 6–8.4. Criminal Trial Recertification

During the 5–year period immediately preceding application, an applicant shall satisfy the following requirements for recertification:

(a) Substantial Involvement. The applicant shall demonstrate substantial involvement in the practice of law, of which at least 30 percent must have been spent in active participation in criminal trial law. Substantial involvement includes investigation, evaluation, pleading, discovery, taking of testimony, presentation of evidence, and argument of jury or non-jury cases.

(b) Criminal Trials.

Either as an advocate or as a judge, an applicant shall have completed the trial of a minimum of 5 criminal cases. Of these 5 cases, at least 4 shall have been jury trials and at least 3 shall have involved felony charges. On good cause shown, for satisfaction in part of the 5 criminal trials, the criminal law certification committee may consider, in its discretion, involvement in protracted litigation as defined in rule 6–8.3(a)(2)(e) or other such criteria as the committee may deem appropriate.

The proceedings that may serve as a trial for recertification purposes include, but are not limited to cases where the:

(1) result is "dismissal of charges" by the court upon a motion for judgment of acquittal at the close of the prosecution's case or thereafter;

(2) result is a "mistrial" or "plea." The case may be counted as a trial at the discretion of the committee provided the applicant offers sufficient information demonstrating substantial courtroom activity;

(3) case is a "violation of probation" or a proceeding involving post-conviction relief. The case may be counted as the 1 non-jury trial of the 5 trials for recertification if the applicant offers sufficient information demonstrating substantial courtroom activity;

(4) case is a "court martial" before a judge; however, discharge boards shall be considered non-jury;

(c) Education. The applicant shall demonstrate completion of at least 50 credit hours of approved continuing legal education for criminal trial law certification, in accordance with rule 6–8.3(c).

(d) Peer Review.

(1) The applicant shall submit the names and addresses of at least 4 lawyers, who are neither relatives nor current associates or partners, as references, to attest to the applicant's substantial involvement and competence in criminal trial practice, as well as the applicant's character, ethics, and reputation for professionalism. Such lawyers shall be substantially involved in criminal trial law and familiar with the applicant's practice.

(2) The applicant shall submit the names and addresses of at least 2 judges before whom the applicant has appeared on criminal trial matters within the last 2 years, or before whom the applicant has tried a criminal trial to jury verdict, to attest to the applicant's substantial involvement and competence in criminal trial practice, as well as the applicant's character, ethics, and reputation for professionalism.

(3) Peer review received on behalf of the applicant shall be sufficient to demonstrate the applicant's competence in criminal appellate law, character, ethics, and professionalism. The criminal law certification committee may, at its option, send reference forms to other attorneys and judges.

(e) Waiver of Compliance. On special application, for good cause shown, the criminal law certification committee may waive compliance with the trial criteria for an applicant who has been continuously certified as a criminal trial lawyer for a period of 14 years or more, provided the applicant:

(1) satisfies the peer review and education required in subdivisions (c) and (d) of this rule; and,

(2) demonstrates substantial involvement in criminal trial law defined, for purposes of this subdivision, as active participation in the litigation process, including the investigation and evaluation of criminal charges, involvement in pretrial processes such as discovery and motion practice, and the review of strategy and tactics for trial. The applicant shall describe the extent of substantial involvement, including courtroom and trial experience, since the last date of recertification.

Amended Sept. 21, 1989, effective Oct. 1, 1989 (548 So.2d 1120); Nov. 29, 1990, effective Oct. 1, 1989 (570 So.2d 1301); July 23, 1992, effective Jan. 1, 1993 (605 So.2d 252); Feb. 11, 1999, by the Board of Governors of The Florida Bar; Aug. 17, 2007, by the Board of Governors of The Florida Bar.

Rule 6–8.5. Criminal Appellate; Minimum Standards

(a) Substantial Involvement and Competence. To become certified as a criminal appellate lawyer, an applicant must demonstrate substantial involvement and competence in criminal appellate law. Substantial involvement and competence shall include:

(1) At least 5 years of the actual practice of law of which at least 30 percent has been spent in active participation in criminal appellate law. At least 3 years of this practice shall be immediately preceding application or, during those 3 years, the applicant may have served as a judge. The 5 years of criminal appellate practice shall include brief writing, motion practice, oral arguments, and extraordinary writs sufficient to demonstrate special competence as a criminal appellate lawyer.

(2) The representation of at least 25 criminal appellate actions. On good cause shown, for satisfaction in part of the 25 criminal appellate actions, the criminal law certification committee may consider involvement in protracted litigation as defined in subdivision 6–8.2(e). If any of the applicant's appellate actions occurred when the applicant was a judicial clerk/staff attorney and the rules of court prevent the applicant from enumerating those appellate actions, then the applicant shall obtain, from the applicant's judge, a letter stating the number of appellate actions in which the applicant participated while employed by the judge.

(3) Submission of 1 copy of the pleadings filed in 2 recent criminal appellate proceedings:

(4) Within the 3 years immediately preceding application, the applicant's substantial involvement must be sufficient to demonstrate special competence as a criminal appellate lawyer. Substantial involvement includes brief writing, motion practice, oral arguments, and extraordinary writs. For good cause shown, the criminal law certification committee may waive 2 of the 3 years' substantial involvement for individuals who have served as judges. In no event may the year immediately preceding application be waived.

(b) Peer Review.

(1) The applicant shall submit the names and addresses of at least 4 lawyers, who are neither relatives nor current associates or partners, as references to attest to the applicant's substantial involvement and competence in criminal appellate practice, as well as

the applicant's character, ethics, and reputation for professionalism. Such lawyers shall be substantially involved in criminal appellate law and familiar with the applicant's practice.

(2) The applicant shall submit the names and addresses of at least 2 judges before whom the applicant has appeared on criminal appellate matters within the last 2 years, to attest to the applicant's substantial involvement and competence in criminal appellate practice, as well as the applicant's character, ethics, and reputation for professionalism.

(3) Peer review received on behalf of the applicant shall be sufficient to demonstrate the applicant's competence in criminal appellate law, character, ethics, and professionalism. The criminal law certification committee may, at its option, send reference forms to other attorneys and judges.

(c) Education. The applicant shall demonstrate that during the 3–year–period immediately preceding the filing of an application, the applicant has met the continuing legal education requirements necessary for criminal appellate certification. The required number of hours shall be established by the board of legal specialization and education and shall in no event be less than 45 hours. Accreditation of educational hours is subject to policies established by the criminal law certification committee or the board of legal specialization and education.

(d) Examination. Every applicant must pass an examination designed to demonstrate sufficient knowledge, skills, proficiency, and experience in criminal appellate law, application of constitutional principles, and rules of criminal and appellate procedure to justify the representation of special competence to the legal profession and the public.

Amended June 18, 1987, effective July 1, 1987 (508 So.2d 1236); Sept. 21, 1989, effective Oct. 1, 1989 (548 So.2d 1120); July 23, 1992, effective Jan. 1, 1993 (605 So.2d 252); Feb. 11, 1999, by the Board of Governors of The Florida Bar; Aug. 17, 2007, by the Board of Governors of The Florida Bar.

Rule 6–8.6. Criminal Appellate Recertification

During the 5–year period immediately preceding application, an applicant shall satisfy the following requirements for recertification:

(a) Substantial Involvement. The applicant shall demonstrate substantial involvement in the practice of law, of which at least 30 percent must have been spent in active participation in criminal appellate law. Substantial involvement includes brief writing, motion practice, oral arguments, and extraordinary writs sufficient to demonstrate special competence as a criminal appellate lawyer.

(b) Appellate Actions. Either as an advocate or as a judge, an applicant shall have completed at least 10 criminal appellate actions. On good cause shown, for satisfaction in part of the 10 appellate actions, the criminal law certification committee may consider involvement in protracted litigation as defined in subdivision 6–8.2(e). If any of the applicant's criminal appellate actions occurred when the applicant was a judicial clerk/staff attorney and the rules of court prevent the applicant from enumerating those appellate actions, then the applicant shall obtain, from the applicant's judge, a letter stating the number of criminal appellate actions in which the applicant participated while employed by the judge.

(c) Education. The applicant shall demonstrate completion of at least 50 credit hours of approved continuing legal education for criminal appellate law certification, in accordance with rule 6–8.5(c).

(d) Peer Review.

(1) The applicant shall submit the names and addresses of at least 4 lawyers, who are neither relatives nor current associates or partners, as references, to attest to the applicant's substantial involvement and competence in criminal appellate practice, as well as the applicant's character, ethics, and reputation for professionalism. Such lawyers shall be substantially involved in criminal appellate law and familiar with the applicant's practice

(2) The applicant shall submit the names and addresses of at least 2 judges before whom the applicant has appeared on criminal appellate matters within the last 2 years, to attest to the applicant's substantial involvement and competence in criminal appellate practice, as well as the applicant's character, ethics, and reputation for professionalism.

(3) Peer review received on behalf of the applicant shall be sufficient to demonstrate the applicant's competence in criminal appellate law, character, ethics, and professionalism. The criminal law certification committee may, at its option, send reference forms to other attorneys and judges.

(e) Waiver of Compliance.

On special application, for good cause shown, the criminal law certification committee may waive compliance with the appellate action criteria for an applicant who has been continuously certified as a criminal appellate lawyer for a period of 14 years or more, provided the applicant:

(1) satisfies the peer review and education required in subdivisions (c) and (d) of this rule; and,

(2) demonstrates substantial involvement in criminal appellate law defined, for purposes of this subdivision, as active participation in the appellate process, including the investigation and evaluation of criminal appeals, and the review of strategy and tactics for appeals. The applicant shall describe the extent of substantial involvement, including briefs written and oral arguments attended, since the last date of recertification.

Amended Sept. 21, 1989, effective Oct. 1, 1989 (548 So.2d 1120); Nov. 29, 1990, effective Oct. 1, 1989 (570 So.2d 1301); July 23, 1992, effective Jan. 1, 1993 (605 So.2d 252); Feb. 11, 1999, by the Board of Governors of The Florida Bar; Aug. 17, 2007, by the Board of Governors of The Florida Bar.

6–9. STANDARDS FOR CERTIFICATION OF A BOARD CERTIFIED REAL ESTATE LAWYER

Rule 6–9.1. Generally

A lawyer who is a member in good standing of The Florida Bar and who meets the standards prescribed below may be issued an appropriate certificate identifying the lawyer as a "Board Certified Real Estate Lawyer." The purpose of the standards is to identify those lawyers who practice Florida real estate law and have the special knowledge, skills, and proficiency as well as the character, ethics, and reputation for professionalism, to be properly identified to the public as certified real estate lawyers. The practice of Florida real estate law is unique to the State of Florida because of the unique history, geographic features of the state, and the evolution of its constitutional, statutory, and decisional law. Accordingly, the standards require that lawyers seeking certification demonstrate a degree of practical knowledge and experience in Florida real estate law and transactions.

Amended Sept. 21, 1989, effective Oct. 1, 1989 (548 So.2d 1120); Jan. 30, 2004, by the Board of Governors of The Florida Bar..

Rule 6–9.2. Definitions

(a) Real Estate. "Real estate" is the practice of law, regardless of jurisdiction, dealing with matters relating to ownership and rights in real property including, but not limited to, the examination of titles, real estate conveyances and other transfers, leases, sales and other transactions involving real estate, condominiums, cooperatives, property owners associations and planned developments, interval ownership, zoning and land use planning regulation, real estate development and financing, real estate litigation, and the determination of property rights.

(b) Practice of Law. The "practice of law" for this area is defined as set out in rule 6–3.5(c)(1).

Amended Sept. 21, 1989, effective Oct. 1, 1989 (548 So.2d 1120); July 23, 1992, effective Jan. 1, 1993 (605 So.2d 252); Nov. 21, 1997, by the Board of Governors of The Florida Bar; Jan. 30, 2004, by the Board of Governors of The Florida Bar.

Rule 6–9.3. Minimum standards

(a) Minimum Period of Practice. Every applicant shall have been engaged in the practice of law in the United States, or engaged in the practice of United States law while in a foreign country, and shall have been a member in good standing of the bar of any state of the United States or the District of Columbia for a period of 5 years, 3 of which meet the requirements of 6–9.3(b) as of the date of filing an application. The years of law practice need not be consecutive.

(b) Substantial Involvement. Every applicant must demonstrate substantial involvement sufficient to show special knowledge, skills, and proficiency in the practice of real estate law during the 3 years immediately preceding the date of application. Substantial involvement is defined as including devoting at least 40 percent of one's practice to matters in which issues of real estate law are significant factors and in which the applicant had substantial and direct participation in those real estate issues. The applicant must also demonstrate that the applicant's real estate practice includes experience and involvement with Florida real estate law and transactions. Upon an applicant's request and the recommendation of the real estate certification committee, the board of legal specialization and education may waive the requirement that the 3 years be "immediately preceding" the date of application if the board of legal specialization and education determines the waiver is warranted by special and compelling circumstances. An applicant must furnish information concerning the frequency of the applicant's work and the nature of the issues involved. For the purposes of this subdivision, the "practice of law" shall be as defined in rule 6–3.5(c)(1), except that it shall also include time devoted to lecturing and/or authoring books or articles on fields of real estate law if the applicant was engaged in the practice of law during such period. Demonstration of compliance with this requirement shall be made initially through a form of questionnaire approved by the real estate certification committee, but written or oral supplementation may be required.

(c) Peer Review. Every applicant shall submit the names and addresses of 5 attorneys or judges, at least 3 of whom are licensed to practice law in Florida and are familiar with the applicant's practice, not including attorneys who currently practice in the applicant's law firm, who can attest to the applicant's reputation for involvement in Florida real estate law, as well as the applicant's character, ethics, and reputation for professionalism. The board of legal specialization and education and the real estate certification committee shall alternatively authorize references from persons, including non-Florida lawyers and judges and persons other than attorneys in such cases as they deem appropriate. The board of legal specialization and education and the real estate certification committee may also make such additional inquiries as they deem appropriate.

(d) Education. Every applicant must demonstrate that during the 3–year period immediately preceding the date of filing an application, the applicant has accumulated 45 hours of continuing legal education approved for credit in real estate law by the board of legal specialization and education. The board of legal specialization and education or the real estate law certification committee shall establish policies applicable to this rule.

(e) Examination. The applicant must pass a written examination that is practical, objective, and designed to demonstrate special knowledge, skills, and proficiency in real estate law to justify the representation of special competence to the legal profession and the public.

Amended effective Oct. 29, 1987 (515 So.2d 977); Sept. 21, 1989, effective Oct. 1, 1989 (548 So.2d 1120); July 23, 1992, effective Jan. 1, 1993 (605 So.2d 252); Jan. 30, 2004, by the Board of Governors of The Florida Bar.

Rule 6–9.4. Recertification

To be eligible for recertification, an applicant must meet the following requirements:

(a) Substantial Involvement. The applicant must make a satisfactory showing, as determined by the board of legal specialization and education and the real estate certification committee, of involvement in real estate law throughout the period since the last date of certification. The demonstration of substantial involvement of at least 40 percent during each year after certification prior to recertification shall be made in accordance with the standards set forth in rule 6–9.3(b).

(b) Continuing Legal Education Requirement. The applicant must show completion of at least 75 hours of accredited continuing legal education approved for credit in real estate law by the board of legal specialization and education since the filing of the last application for certification.

(c) Reference Requirement. An applicant for recertification shall submit the names and addresses of 5 attorneys or judges, at least 3 of whom are licensed to practice law in Florida and are familiar with the applicant's practice, not including lawyers who currently practice in the applicant's law firm, who can attest to the applicant's reputation for ability of practice and involvement in Florida real estate law as well as the applicant's character, ethics, and reputation for professionalism. The board of legal specialization and education and the real estate certification committee may also make such additional inquiries as they deem appropriate.

Amended effective Oct. 29, 1987 (515 So.2d 977); Sept. 21, 1989, effective Oct. 1, 1989 (548 So.2d 1120); July 23, 1992, effective Jan. 1, 1993 (605 So.2d 252); Jan. 30, 2004, by the Board of Governors of The Florida Bar.

6–10. CONTINUING LEGAL EDUCATION REQUIREMENT RULE

Rule 6–10.1. Continuing legal education requirement

(a) Preamble. It is of primary importance to the public and to the members of The Florida Bar that attorneys continue their legal education throughout the period of their active practice of law. To accomplish that objective, each member of The Florida Bar (hereinafter referred to as "member") shall meet certain minimum requirements for continuing legal education.

(b) Reporting Requirement. Each member except those exempt under rule 6–10.3(c)(4) and (5) shall report compliance with continuing legal education requirements in the manner set forth in the policies adopted for administration of this plan.

(c) Fees. The board of governors of The Florida Bar may require a reasonable fee to be paid to The Florida Bar in connection with each member's report concerning compliance with continuing legal education requirements.

(d) Rules. The board of legal specialization and education of The Florida Bar shall adopt policies necessary to implement continuing legal education requirements subject to the approval of the board of governors.

Added July 16, 1987, effective Jan. 1, 1988 (510 So.2d 585). Amended Sept. 21, 1989, effective Oct. 1, 1989 (548 So.2d 1120); July 23, 1992, effective Jan. 1, 1993 (605 So.2d 252).

Rule 6–10.2. Administration

(a) Board of Legal Specialization and Education. The board of legal specialization and education shall administer the continuing legal education requirements as herein provided. Any member affected by an adverse decision of the board of legal specialization and education may appeal as provided in rule 6–10.5.

(b) Delegation of Authority. The board of legal specialization and education may delegate to the staff of The Florida Bar any responsibility set forth herein, except that of granting a waiver or exemption from continuing legal education requirements.

(c) Scope of Board of Legal Specialization and Education Activities. The board of legal specialization and education shall cooperate with and answer inquiries from staff pertaining to continuing legal education requirements and make recommendations to the board of governors concerning continuing legal education requirements, including but not limited to:

(1) approved education courses;

(2) approved alternative education methods;

(3) number of hours' credit to be allowed for various education efforts;

(4) established educational standards for satisfaction and completion of approved courses;

(5) additional areas of education and/or practice approved for credit under continuing legal education requirements;

(6) modification or expansion of continuing legal education requirements;

(7) adoption of additional standards or regulations pertaining to continuing legal education requirements;

(8) amount of reporting or delinquency fees; and

(9) general administration of continuing legal education requirements.

(d) Maintenance of Records. The Florida Bar shall maintain a record of each member's compliance with continuing legal education requirements.

Added July 16, 1987, effective Jan. 1, 1988 (510 So.2d 585). Amended Sept. 21, 1989, effective Oct. 1, 1989 (548 So.2d 1120); Oct. 10, 1991, effective Jan. 1, 1992 (587 So.2d 1121); July 23, 1992, effective Jan. 1, 1993 (605 So.2d 252).

Rule 6–10.3. Minimum Continuing Legal Education Standards

(a) Applicability. Every member except those exempt under rule 6–10.3(c)(4) and (5) shall comply and report compliance with the continuing legal education requirement.

(b) Minimum Hourly Continuing Legal Education Requirements. Each member shall complete a minimum of 30 credit hours of approved continuing legal education activity every 3 years. Five of the 30 hours must be in approved legal ethics, professionalism, bias elimination, substance abuse, or mental illness awareness programs. Courses offering credit in professionalism must be approved by the center for professionalism. These 5 hours are to be included in, and not in addition to, the regular 30–hour requirement. If a member completes more than 30 hours during any reporting cycle, the excess credits cannot be carried over to the next reporting cycle.

(c) Exemptions. Eligibility for an exemption, in accordance with policies adopted under this rule, is available for;

(1) active military service;

(2) undue hardship;

(3) nonresident members not delivering legal services or advice on matters or issues governed by Florida law;

(4) members of the full-time federal judiciary who are prohibited from engaging in the private practice of law;

(5) justices of the Supreme Court of Florida and judges of the district courts of appeal, circuit courts, and county courts, and such other judicial officers and employees as may be designated by the Supreme Court of Florida; and,

(6) inactive members of The Florida Bar.

(d) Course Approval. Course approval shall be set forth in policies adopted pursuant to this rule. Special policies shall be adopted for courses sponsored by governmental agencies for employee attorneys that shall exempt such courses from any course approval fee and may exempt such courses from other requirements as determined by the board of legal specialization and education.

(e) Accreditation of Hours. Accreditation standards shall be set forth in the policies adopted under this rule. If a course is presented or sponsored by or has received credit approval from an organized state bar (whether integrated or voluntary), such course shall be deemed an approved course for purposes of this rule if the course meets the criteria for accreditation established by policies adopted under this rule.

(f) Full-time Government Employees. Credit hours shall be given full-time government employees for courses presented by governmental agencies. Application for credit approval may be submitted by the full-time government attorney before or after attendance, without charge.

(g) Skills Training Preadmission. The board of legal specialization and education may approve for CLER credit a basic skills or entry level training program developed and presented by a governmental entity. If approved, credit earned through attendance at such course, within 8 months prior to admission to The Florida Bar, shall be applicable under rule 6–10.3(b).

Added July 16, 1987, effective Jan. 1, 1988 (510 So.2d 585). Amended March 30, 1989, effective March 31, 1989 (541 So.2d 110); Sept. 21, 1989, effective Oct. 1, 1989 (548 So.2d 1120); Oct. 10, 1991, effective Jan. 1, 1992 (587 So.2d 1121); July 23, 1992, effective Jan. 1, 1993 (605 So.2d 252); July 17, 1997 (697 So.2d 115); Feb. 8, 2001 (795 So.2d 1); Nov. 19, 2009, effective Feb. 1, 2010 (24 So.3d 63).

Rule 6–10.4. Reporting Requirements

(a) Reports Required. Each member except those exempt under rule 6–10.3(c)(4) and (5) shall file a report showing compliance or noncompliance with the continuing legal education requirement. Such report shall be in the form prescribed by the board of legal specialization and education.

(b) Time for Filing. The report shall be filed with The Florida Bar no later than the last day of such member's applicable reporting period as assigned by The Florida Bar.

Added July 16, 1987, effective Jan. 1, 1988 (510 So.2d 585). Amended Sept. 21, 1989, effective Oct. 1, 1989 (548 So.2d 1120); Oct. 10, 1991, effective Jan. 1, 1992 (587 So.2d 1121); Nov. 19, 2009, effective Feb. 1, 2010 (24 So.3d 63).

Rule 6–10.5. Delinquency and Appeal

(a) Delinquency. If a member fails to complete and report the minimum required continuing legal education hours by the end of the applicable reporting period, the member shall be deemed delinquent in accordance with rule 1–3.6, Rules Regulating The Florida Bar.

(b) Appeal to the Board of Governors. A member deemed delinquent may appeal to the Board of Governors of The Florida Bar. Appeals to the board of governors shall be governed by the policies promulgated under these rules.

(c) Appeal to the Supreme Court of Florida. A decision of the board of governors may be appealed by the affected member to the Supreme Court of Florida. Such review shall be by petition for review in accordance with the procedures set forth in rule 9.100, Florida Rules of Appellate Procedure

(d) Exhaustion of Remedies. A member must exhaust each of the remedies provided under these rules in the order enumerated before proceeding to the next remedy.

(e) Tolling Time for Compliance. An appeal shall toll the time a member has for showing compliance with continuing legal education requirements.

Added July 16, 1987, effective Jan. 1, 1988 (510 So.2d 585). Amended Sept. 21, 1989, effective Oct. 1, 1989 (548 So.2d 1120); Oct. 10, 1991, effective Jan. 1, 1992 (587 So.2d 1121); July 23, 1992, effective Jan. 1, 1993 (605 So.2d 252); Nov. 19, 2009, effective Feb. 1, 2010 (24 So.3d 63).

Rule 6–10.6. Reinstatement

A member deemed delinquent for failure to meet the continuing legal education requirement may be reinstated in accordance with rule 1–3.7, Rules Regulating The Florida Bar.

Added July 16, 1987, effective Jan. 1, 1988 (510 So.2d 585). Amended Sept. 21, 1989, effective Oct. 1, 1989 (548 So.2d 1120); Feb. 15, 1990 (556 So.2d 1119); Oct. 10, 1991, effective Jan. 1, 1992 (587 So.2d 1121); Nov. 19, 2009, effective Feb. 1, 2010 (24 So.3d 63).

Rule 6–10.7. Confidentiality

Unless directed otherwise by the Supreme Court of Florida, the files, records, and proceedings of the board of legal specialization and education, as they relate to or arise out of any failure of a member to satisfy the continuing legal education requirements, shall be deemed confidential and shall not be disclosed, except in the furtherance of the duties of the board of legal specialization and education or upon request of the member, in writing, or as they may be introduced in the evidence or otherwise produced in proceedings under these rules. Nothing herein shall be construed to prohibit The Florida Bar from advising that a member has been suspended from the active practice of law for failure to meet continuing legal education requirements.

Added July 16, 1987, effective Jan. 1, 1988 (510 So.2d 585). Amended Sept. 21, 1989, effective Oct. 1, 1989 (548 So.2d 1120); July 23, 1992, effective Jan. 1, 1993 (605 So.2d 252).

Rule 6–10.8. Disciplinary Action

The board of legal specialization and education may refer misrepresentation of a material fact concerning compliance with or exemption from continuing legal education requirements for disciplinary proceedings under chapter 3 or chapter 4 of the Rules Regulating The Florida Bar.

Added July 16, 1987, effective Jan. 1, 1988 (510 So.2d 585). Amended Sept. 21, 1989, effective Oct. 1, 1989 (548 So.2d 1120).

6–11. STANDARDS FOR CERTIFICATION OF A BOARD CERTIFIED WORKERS' COMPENSATION LAWYER

Rule 6–11.1. Generally

A lawyer who is a member in good standing of The Florida Bar and who meets the standards prescribed below may be issued an appropriate certificate identifying the lawyer as a "Board Certified Workers' Compensation Lawyer." The purpose of the standards is to identify those lawyers who practice workers' compensation law and have the special knowledge, skills, and proficiency, as well as the character, ethics, and reputation for professionalism, to be properly identified to the public as certified workers' compensation lawyers.

Added June 18, 1987, effective July 1, 1987 (508 So.2d 1236). Amended Sept. 21, 1989, effective Oct. 1, 1989 (548 So.2d 1120); May 21–22, 1998, by the Board of Governors of The Florida Bar.

Rule 6–11.2. Definitions

(a) Workers' Compensation. "Workers' compensation" is the practice of law involving the analysis and litigation of problems or controversies arising out of the Florida Workers' Compensation Law (chapter 440, Florida Statutes).

(b) Practice of Law. The "practice of law" for this area is defined as set out in rule 6–3.5(c)(1).

(c) Trial. "Trial" shall be defined as the process of having carried a client's burden of going forward in either the prosecution or defense of a claim for any substantive benefit (including entitlement to an attorney's fee). Pretrial, settlement, lump sum, and motion hearings (including motions to be relieved of costs) shall not be considered trials. Substantial participation in a rule nisi petition and hearing for the enforcement of a workers' compensation order is a "trial" under this subsection, but no more than two such hearings may be used. Attorney fee hearings, on the sole issue of the quantum fees, cannot be considered as a contested workers' compensation case. Cases involving a merits hearing, with a later attorney fee hearing on the question of entitlement to an attorney's fee on the same merit issues, can count as only 1 case. Hearings and/or trials outside the jurisdiction of the Florida Office of the Judges of Compensation Claims, and appeals of these matters (including, but not limited to, federal workers' compensation matters, Federal Longshore and Harbor Workers' Compensation Act matters, and other circuit court actions, etc.) cannot be used to meet the trial, protracted litigation, or substantial equivalent requirements.

(d) Protracted Litigation. "Protracted litigation" shall be defined as litigation that involves unusual or complicated legal issues and extensive discovery, yet does not result in submission of the ultimate issue to the trier of fact, or substantial presentation in the appeal of workers' compensation cases.

(e) Substantial Equivalent. "Substantial equivalent" may be demonstrated by, but is not limited to, preparation and publication of legal articles and/or the presentation of lectures and seminars. For recertification only, an applicant may substitute 3 workers' compensation mediations, where the applicant has acted as mediator, to count as one "substantial equivalent" and the recertification applicant may substitute up to 3 substantial equivalents in this matter. What is or is not substantial equivalent and its relative value are within the sole discretion of the workers' compensation certification committee, but may not be substituted for more than 5 trials of workers' compensation cases.

Added June 18, 1987, effective July 1, 1987 (508 So.2d 1236). Amended Sept. 21, 1989, effective Oct. 1, 1989 (548 So.2d 1120); July 23, 1992, effective Jan. 1, 1993 (605 So.2d 252); Oct. 31–Nov. 2, 1996, by the Board of Governors of The Florida Bar; May 21–22, 1998, by the Board of Governors of The Florida Bar; ________, ____, by the Board of Governors of The Florida Bar.

Rule 6–11.3. Minimum Standards

(a) Substantial Involvement. To become certified as a workers' compensation lawyer, a lawyer must demonstrate substantial involvement in workers' compensation law. Substantial involvement shall include the following:

(1) At least 5 years of the actual practice of law of which at least 30 percent has been spent in active participation in workers' compensation law. At least 3 years of this practice shall be immediately preceding application or, during those 3 years, the applicant may have served as a judge of compensation claims adjudicating workers' compensation matters.

(2) The trial of a minimum of 25 contested workers' compensation cases. All such cases must have involved substantial legal or factual issues. In each of these 25 cases the applicant shall have been responsible for all or a majority of the presentation of evidence and representation of the client. As partial satisfaction of the requirement of 25 contested workers' compensation cases, the workers' compensation certification committee may substitute for "trials" their "substantial equivalent" appeals or cases involving protracted litigation of contested workers' compensation cases involving substantial legal or factual issues. Successful completion of a trial advocacy seminar, approved by the committee, that includes as a part of its curriculum active participation by the applicant in simulated courtroom proceedings may substitute as 1 contested workers' compensation case. The total number of cases that may be substituted for the minimum of 25 contested cases, including the successful completion of a trial advocacy seminar, cases of "substantial equivalent," appeals and cases of "protracted litigation" shall not exceed a total of 10, of which the cases of "protracted litigation" and/or appeals shall not exceed a total of 5 cases, and cases of "substantial equivalent" shall not exceed a total of 5 cases.

(3) Within the 3 years immediately preceding application, the applicant shall have substantial involvement in contested workers' compensation cases sufficient to demonstrate special competence as a workers' compensation lawyer. Substantial involvement includes investigation, evaluation, pleadings, discovery, taking of testimony, presentation of evidence and argument, and trial of workers' compensation cases. Substantial involvement also includes active participation in the appeal of workers' compensation cases. For good cause shown, the workers' compensation certification committee may waive up to 2 of the 3 years' substantial involvement for individuals who have served as judges of compensation claims adjudicating workers' compensation matters.

(b) Peer Review. The applicant shall select and submit names and addresses of 5 lawyers, not associates or partners, as references to attest to the applicant's special competence and substantial involvement in workers' compensation practice, as well as the applicant's character, ethics, and reputation for professionalism. Such lawyers themselves shall be involved in workers' compensation law and shall be familiar with the applicant's practice. No less than 1 shall be a judge of compensation claims before whom the applicant has appeared as an advocate in the trial of a workers' compensation case in the 2 years immediately preceding the application. In addition, the workers' compensation certification committee may, at its option, send reference forms to other attorneys and judges of compensation claims.

(c) Education. The applicant shall make a satisfactory showing that, within the 3 years immediately preceding application, the applicant has accumulated at least 45 hours of approved continuing legal education in the field of workers' compensation law.

(d) Examination. The applicant must pass an examination applied uniformly to all applicants to demonstrate sufficient knowledge, proficiency, and experience in workers' compensation law to justify the representation of special competence to the legal profession and the public.

Added June 18, 1987, effective July 1, 1987 (508 So.2d 1236). Amended Sept. 21, 1989, effective Oct. 1, 1989 (548 So.2d 1120); July 23, 1992, effective Jan. 1, 1993 (605 So.2d 252); July 28-29, 1994, by the Board of Governors of The Florida Bar; amended Jan. 26, 1996, by the Board of Governors of The Florida Bar; amended Oct. 31-Nov. 2, 1996, by the Board of Governors of The Florida Bar; amended May 21–22, 1998, by the Board of Governors of The Florida Bar; ________, ____, by the Board of Governors of The Florida Bar.

Rule 6-11.4. Judges of Compensation Claims

An applicant who is serving as a judge of compensation claims and applies for recertification while serving as a judge of compensation claims shall be deemed to have met the requirements of rule 6-11.5.

Added June 18, 1987, effective July 1, 1987 (508 So.2d 1236). Amended Sept. 21, 1989, effective Oct. 1, 1989 (548 So.2d 1120); July 23, 1992, effective Jan. 1, 1993 (605 So.2d 252); Oct. 31–Nov. 2, 1996, by the Board of Governors of The Florida Bar.

Rule 6-11.5. Recertification

To be eligible for recertification, an applicant must meet the following requirements:

(a) Substantial Involvement. The applicant shall demonstrate continuous and substantial involvement in the practice of law, of which 30 percent has been spent in active participation in workers' compensation law throughout the period since the last date of certification. The demonstration of substantial involvement shall be made in accordance with the standards set forth in rule 6-11.3(a)(3).

(b) Trial Requirement. The applicant must have completed trial of a minimum of 15 contested workers' compensation cases, or the substantial equivalent, since the filing of the last application for certification. All such cases must have involved substantial legal or factual issues. For good cause shown, as partial satisfaction for the requirement of 15 contested workers' compensation cases, the workers' compensation certification committee may substitute for "trials" their "substantial equivalent" or 5 cases involving appeals and/or protracted litigation of contested workers' compensation cases involving substantial legal or factual issues. The total number of cases that may be substituted for the minimum 15 contested cases, including cases of "substantial equivalent," appeals and cases of "protracted litigation," is a total of 10 cases, of which the total number of cases of "protracted litigation" and/or appeals, shall not exceed a total of 5 cases and cases of "substantial equivalent" shall not exceed a total of 5 cases. Attorney fee hearings, on the sole issue of the quantum fees, cannot be considered as a contested workers' compensation case. Cases involving a merits hearing, with a later attorney fee hearing in the question of entitlement to an attorney's fee on the same merit issues, can count as only 1 case. Hearings and/or trials outside the jurisdiction of the Florida Office of the Judges of Compensation Claims, and appeals of these matters (including, but not limited to, rule nisi, federal workers' compensation matters, Federal Longshore and Harbor Workers' Compensation Act matters, and other circuit court actions, etc.) cannot be used to meet the trial, protracted litigation, or substantial requirements.

(c) Peer Review. The applicant shall submit references as set forth in rule 6-11.3(b). The references submitted must be able to attest to the applicant's special competence and substantial involvement in workers' compensation practice, as well as the applicant's character, ethics, and professionalism, throughout the period since the last date of certification.

(d) Education. The applicant shall report completion of at least 75 hours of approved continuing legal education in workers' compensation law since the filing of the last application for certification.

(e) Waiver. On special application, for good cause shown, the workers' compensation certification committee may waive compliance with the 15 contested workers' compensation cases requirement for an applicant who has been continuously certified as a workers' compensation lawyer for a period of 14 years or more.

Added June 18, 1987 effective, July 1, 1987 (508 So.2d 1236). Amended Sept. 21, 1989, effective Oct. 1, 1989 (543 So.2d 1120); July 23, 1992, effective Jan. 1, 1993 (605 So.2d 252); July 28–29, 1994, by the Board of Governors of The Florida Bar; Jan. 26, 1996, by the Board of Governors of The Florida Bar; Oct. 31-Nov. 2, 1996, by the Board of Governors of The Florida Bar; May 21–22, 1998, by the Board of Governors of The Florida Bar; ______, ____, by the Board of Governors of The Florida Bar.

6-12. BASIC SKILLS COURSE REQUIREMENT RULE

Rule 6-12.1. Basic skills course requirement

(a) Preamble. It is of primary importance to the public and to the members of The Florida Bar that attorneys begin their legal careers with a thorough and practical understanding of the law. To accomplish that objective, each member of The Florida Bar (hereinafter referred to as "member") shall comply with the basic skills course requirement (hereinafter BSCR) through the completion of continuing legal education programs developed and presented by the Young Lawyers Division of The Florida Bar (hereinafter YLD). Oversight of member compliance with this rule shall be the responsibility of the board of legal specialization and education (hereinafter BLSE.)

(b) Applicability. Every member admitted to The Florida Bar after October 1, 1988 shall comply with the BSCR.

Added April 21, 1988, effective Oct. 1, 1988 (524 So.2d 634). Amended Sept. 21, 1989, effective Oct. 1, 1989 (548 So.2d 1120); July 23, 1992, effective Jan. 1, 1993 (605 So.2d 252); Dec. 18, 1997, effective Jan. 1, 1998 (702 So.2d 1258); Feb. 8, 2001 (795 So.2d 1).

Rule 6-12.2. Administration

(a) Responsibility. The YLD shall be responsible for the planning, content, and presentation of programs for BSCR compliance. The YLD shall also establish minimum quality standards for the Practicing with Professionalism program, to include instruction on discipline, ethics, professionalism, and responsibility to the public. The BLSE shall oversee member compliance with BSCR and adopt policies necessary for implementation. Such policies shall be subject to approval by the board of governors.

(b) Delegation of Authority. The BLSE may delegate to the staff of The Florida Bar any responsibility set forth herein, except that of denying a waiver or exemption from BSCR.

(c) Waiver. On special application and for good cause shown, the BLSE may adjust the time for completion, may waive compliance, or accept a substitute program, for either component of BSCR.

(d) Maintenance of Records. The Florida Bar shall maintain a record of each member's compliance with BSCR.

Added April 21, 1988, effective Oct. 1, 1988 (524 So.2d 634). Amended Sept. 21, 1989, effective Oct. 1, 1989 (548 So.2d 1120); July 23, 1992, effective Jan. 1, 1993 (605 So.2d 252); Dec. 18, 1997, effective Jan. 1, 1998 (702 So.2d 1258); Feb. 8, 2001 (795 So.2d 1).

Rule 6–12.3. Requirement

Text of rule effective until October 1, 2015. See, also, rule effective October 1, 2015.

(a) Course Components. Compliance with BSCR shall include:

(1) in-person attendance at a 1–day Practicing with Professionalism program sponsored by the YLD; and

(2) completion of 3 elective, basic, substantive continuing legal education programs sponsored by the YLD.

(b) Time for Completion. BSCR shall be completed as follows:

(1) the Practicing with Professionalism program shall be completed no sooner than 12 months prior to or no later than 12 months following admission to The Florida Bar; and

(2) the 3 elective, basic, substantive continuing legal education programs shall be completed during the member's initial 3–year continuing legal education requirement reporting cycle assigned upon admission to The Florida Bar.

Added April 21, 1988, effective Oct. 1, 1988 (524 So.2d 634). Amended Sept. 21, 1989, effective Oct. 1, 1989 (548 So.2d 1120); Feb. 15, 1990 (556 So.2d 1119); July 23, 1992, effective Jan. 1, 1993 (605 So.2d 252); Feb. 8, 2001 (795 So.2d 1); May 12, 2005 (903 So.2d 183); Feb. 4, 2010, effective March 6, 2010 (29 So.3d 288).

Rule 6–12.3. Requirement

Text of rule effective October 1, 2015. See, also, rule effective until October 1, 2015.

(a) Course Components. Compliance with BSCR includes:

(1) completion of a Practicing with Professionalism program sponsored by the YLD; and

(2) completion of 3 elective, basic, substantive continuing legal education programs sponsored by the YLD.

(b) Time for Completion. BSCR must be completed as follows:

(1) the Practicing with Professionalism program must be completed no sooner than 12 months prior to or no later than 12 months following admission to The Florida Bar; and

(2) the 3 elective, basic, substantive continuing legal education programs must be completed during the member's initial 3–year continuing legal education requirement reporting cycle assigned on admission to The Florida Bar.

Added April 21, 1988, effective Oct. 1, 1988 (524 So.2d 634). Amended Sept. 21, 1989, effective Oct. 1, 1989 (548 So.2d 1120); Feb. 15, 1990 (556 So.2d 1119); July 23, 1992, effective Jan. 1, 1993 (605 So.2d 252); Feb. 8, 2001 (795 So.2d 1); May 12, 2005 (903 So.2d 183); Feb. 4, 2010, effective March 6, 2010 (29 So.3d 288); June 11, 2015, effective Oct. 1, 2015, (167 So.3d 412).

Rule 6–12.4. Deferment and Exemption

(a) Deferment of Practicing with Professionalism Requirement.

(1) *Deferment Eligibility.* A member of The Florida Bar is eligible to defer compliance with the requirements of rule 6–12.3(a)(1), if:

(A) the member is on active military duty;

(B) compliance would create an undue hardship;

(C) the member is a nonresident member whose primary office is outside the state of Florida;

(D) the member elects inactive membership status in The Florida Bar; or

(E) the member is a full-time government employee who had benefitted from the deferment of the Practicing with Professionalism requirement as of its May 12, 2005, elimination, as long as the member continuously remains in government practice.

(2) *Deferment Expiration.* A deferment of the requirements of rule 6–12.3(a)(1) as provided under this rule shall expire at the time the member is no longer eligible for deferment. Upon expiration, a member must:

(A) promptly notify The Florida Bar in writing of the date deferment expired; and

(B) attend the Practicing with Professionalism program within 12 months of deferment expiration.

(b) Deferment of Basic Level YLD Courses.

(1) *Deferment Eligibility.* A member of The Florida Bar is eligible to defer compliance with the requirements of rule 6–12.3(a)(2) if:

(A) the member is on active military duty;

(B) compliance would create an undue hardship;

(C) the member is a nonresident member whose primary office is outside the state of Florida;

(D) the member is a full-time governmental employee; or

(E) the member elects inactive membership status in The Florida Bar.

(2) *Deferment Expiration.* A deferment of the requirements of rule 6–12.3(a)(2) as provided under this rule shall expire at the time the member is no longer eligible for deferment. Upon expiration, a member must:

(A) promptly notify The Florida Bar in writing of the date deferment expired; and

(B) complete 3 elective, basic, substantive continuing legal education programs sponsored by the YLD within 24 months of deferment expiration.

(c) Exemption.

(1) *Governmental Practice.* An exemption from rule 6–12.3(a)(1) shall be granted if a member who had benefitted from the deferment of the Practicing with Professionalism requirement as of its May 12, 2005, elimination has already or thereafter been continuously engaged in the practice of law for a Florida or federal governmental entity as a full-time governmental employee for a period of at least 6 years. An exemption from rule 6–12.3(a)(2) shall be granted if a member has been continuously engaged in the practice of law for a Florida or federal governmental entity as a full-time governmental employee for a period of at least 6 years.

(2) *Foreign Practice.* An exemption from rule 6–12.3(a)(2) shall be granted if a member has been continuously engaged in the practice of law (nongovernmental) in a foreign jurisdiction for a period of 5 years, can demonstrate completion of 30 hours of approved continuing legal education within the immediate 3-year period, and can attest that the continuing legal education completed has reasonably prepared the member for the anticipated type of practice in Florida.

Added Feb. 8, 2001 (795 So.2d 1). Amended May 12, 2005 (903 So.2d 183); Feb. 4, 2010, effective March 6, 2010 (29 So.3d 288).

Rule 6–12.5. Noncompliance and sanctions

(a) Notice of Noncompliance. If a member fails to comply with this rule, the member shall be deemed delinquent as provided elsewhere in the Rules Regulating The Florida Bar. The BLSE shall promptly send a notice of noncompliance to such member.

(b) Appeal to the Board of Governors. A delinquent member shall have the right to appeal the determination to the board of governors under such rules and regulations as it may prescribe.

(c) Appeal to the Supreme Court of Florida. A delinquent member shall have the right to appeal the determination of the board of governors to the Supreme Court of Florida under such rules and regulations as it may prescribe.

(d) Exhaustion of Remedies. A delinquent member must exhaust each of the remedies provided under these rules in the order enumerated before proceeding to the next remedy.

(e) Tolling Time. An appeal shall toll the determination of noncompliance and resulting delinquency until such time as all appeals have been completed or the time for taking same has expired.

Added April 21, 1988, effective Oct. 1, 1988 (524 So.2d 634). Amended Sept. 21, 1989, effective Oct. 1, 1989 (548 So.2d 1120); July 23, 1992, effective Jan. 1, 1993 (605 So.2d 252). Renumbered and amended Dec. 18, 1997, effective Jan. 1, 1998 (702 So.2d 1258). Renumbered and amended Feb. 8, 2001 (795 So.2d 1).

Rule 6–12.6. Reinstatement

Any member delinquent in completion of the BSCR may be reinstated by the executive director or board of governors upon a showing of compliance with the BSCR and payment of a uniform reinstatement fee, as established by the board of governors.

Added April 21, 1988, effective Oct. 1, 1988 (524 So.2d 634). Amended Sept. 21, 1989, effective Oct. 1, 1989 (548 So.2d 1120); July 23, 1992, effective Jan. 1, 1993 (605 So.2d 252). Renumbered and amended Dec. 18, 1997, effective Jan. 1, 1998 (702 So.2d 1258). Renumbered and amended Feb. 8, 2001 (795 So.2d 1).

Rule 6–12.7. Confidentiality

The files and records maintained regarding appeals conducted under this rule and any hearings in connection therewith shall be confidential until such time as the appeals process has concluded. If a member is deemed delinquent pursuant to this rule, that fact shall be public information.

Added April 21, 1988, effective Oct. 1, 1988 (524 So.2d 634). Amended Sept. 21, 1989, effective Oct. 1, 1989 (548 So.2d 1120); July 23, 1992, effective Jan. 1, 1993 (605 So.2d 252). Renumbered and amended Dec. 18, 1997, effective Jan. 1, 1998 (702 So.2d 1258). Renumbered and amended Feb. 8, 2001 (795 So.2d 1).

Rule 6–12.8. Disciplinary action

The BLSE may refer a member who makes a misrepresentation of a material fact concerning the BSCR for disciplinary investigation as provided elsewhere in these Rules Regulating The Florida Bar.

Added April 21, 1988, effective Oct. 1, 1988 (524 So.2d 634). Amended Sept. 21, 1989, effective Oct. 1, 1989 (548 So.2d 1120); July 23, 1992, effective Jan. 1, 1993 (605 So.2d 252). Renumbered and amended Dec. 18, 1997, effective Jan. 1, 1998 (702 So.2d 1258). Renumbered and amended Feb. 8, 2001 (795 So.2d 1).

6–13. STANDARDS FOR CERTIFICATION OF A BOARD CERTIFIED APPELLATE LAWYER

Rule 6–13.1. Generally

A lawyer who is a member in good standing of The Florida Bar and who meets the standards prescribed below may be issued an appropriate certificate identifying the lawyer as a "Board Certified Appellate Lawyer." The purpose of the standards is to identify those lawyers who engage in appellate practice and have the special knowledge, skills, and proficiency, as well as the character, ethics, and reputation for professionalism, to be properly identified to the public as certified appellate lawyers.

Adopted July 1, 1993 (621 So.2d 1032). Amended April 9, 1999, by the Board of Governors of The Florida Bar; Aug. 17, 2007, by the Board of Governors of The Florida Bar.

Rule 6–13.2. Definitions

(a) Appellate Practice. "Appellate practice" is the practice of law dealing with the recognition and preservation of error committed by lower tribunals, and the presentation of argument concerning the presence or absence of such error to state or federal appellate courts through brief writing, writ and motion practice, and oral argument. Appellate practice includes evaluation and consultation regarding potential appellate issues or remedies in connection with proceedings in the lower tribunal prior to the initiation of the appellate process.

(b) Appellate Action. "Appellate action" means an action filed in a state court, a federal district court, a United States court of appeals, or the Supreme Court of the United States seeking review of a decision of a lower tribunal.

(c) Practice of Law. The "practice of law" for this area is defined in rule 6–3.5(c)(1).

(d) Appellate Practice Certification Committee. The appellate practice certification committee may include 1 member presently serving as an appellate court judge from a Florida district court of appeal, the Supreme Court of Florida, a United States court of appeals, or the Supreme Court of the United States. Certification in appellate practice is preferred, but shall not be a requirement. Appointment shall otherwise be consistent with rule 6–3.2.

(e) Primary Responsibility. Having "primary responsibility" for filing a brief, petition, or response means having the most substantial and direct participation of all the lawyers contributing to that task. Only 1 lawyer may claim primary responsibility for any such task. Where primary responsibility is used to meet a requirement, the applicant must specifically identify any other lawyer who provided substantial assistance with the task and demonstrate, to the satisfaction of the appellate practice certification committee, that the applicant's level of participation was primary.

(f) Principal Briefs in Appeals. "Principal briefs in appeals" means the primary brief on the merits and excludes reply briefs, jurisdictional briefs, supplemental briefs, and amicus briefs. For good cause shown, the appellate practice certification committee may treat a reply brief, jurisdictional brief, supplemental brief, or amicus brief as a principal brief for the purpose of these rules, if the brief is substantial and reflects a level of effort and preparation comparable to that required to produce a principal brief.

(g) Petitions or Responses in Extraordinary Writ Cases. "Petitions or responses in extraordinary writ cases" refer to a petition or response to a petition that seeks a writ from an appellate court to challenge a ruling or the jurisdiction of a lower tribunal or administrative agency. The term includes a petition or response to a petition for a writ of certiorari filed in the Supreme Court of the United States. The term does not include any other petition or response to a petition that merely requests discretionary appellate review, such as a notice to invoke the discretionary jurisdiction of the Supreme Court of Florida, or for permission to appeal to a United States Court of Appeals an order of a district court pursuant to, for example, 28 U.S.C. § 1292(b) or Federal Rule of Civil Procedure 23(f).

(h) Good Cause. "Good cause" exceptions allow the appellate practice certification committee the discretion to waive technical compliance with the relevant requirement. The committee may allow certification or recertification of an individual where the applicant's proffered circumstances demonstrate that the applicant has, in the experience and judgment of the appellate practice certification committee, the special knowledge, skill, and proficiency, or the equivalent, the technical compliance that requirement is intended to demonstrate. The good cause exception will only be considered upon specific request by the applicant.

Added July 1, 1993 (621 So.2d 1032). Amended April 9, 1999, by the Board of Governors of The Florida Bar; August 17, 2007, by the Board of Governors of The Florida Bar; May 31, 2013, by the Board of Governors of The Florida Bar.

Rule 6–13.3. Minimum Standards

(a) Substantial Involvement. The applicant must have been engaged in the practice of law for at least 5 years. During the 3–year period immediately preceding the date of application, at least 30 percent of the applicant's practice must have been spent in substantial and direct involvement in appellate practice sufficient to demonstrate special competence as an appellate lawyer. For good cause shown, the appellate practice certification committee may waive up to 2 of the 3 years' substantial involvement for individuals who have served as appellate judges or as a clerk, career attorney, or staff attorney in an appellate court. Substantial involvement during the year immediately preceding the application will not be waived.

(b) Appellate Actions. During the 5–year period immediately preceding application, the applicant must have had sole or primary responsibility in at least 25 appellate actions for the filing of principal briefs in appeals, or the filing of petitions or responses in extraordinary writ cases.

(c) Oral Arguments. During the 5–year period immediately preceding application, the applicant must have presented at least 5 appellate oral arguments. The appellate practice certification committee may waive this requirement in particular instances, upon good cause shown.

(d) Education. During the 3–year period immediately preceding the filing of an application, the applicant must demonstrate completion of 45 credit hours of approved continuing legal education for appellate practice certification. Accreditation of educational hours is subject to policies established by the appellate practice certification committee or the board of legal specialization and education.

(e) Peer Review.

(1) The applicant must submit the names and addresses of at least 4 lawyers, who are neither relatives nor current associates or partners, as references to attest to the applicant's substantial involvement and competence in appellate practice, as well as the applicant's character, ethics, and reputation for professionalism. These lawyers must be involved in appellate practice and familiar with the applicant's practice.

(2) The applicant shall submit the names and addresses of at least 2 judges before whom the applicant has appeared on appellate matters within the last 2 years to attest to the applicant's substantial involvement and competence in appellate practice, as well as the applicant's character, ethics, and reputation for professionalism.

(3) The appellate practice certification committee may, at its option, send reference forms to other attorneys and judges.

(f) Examination. Every applicant must pass an examination designed to demonstrate sufficient knowledge, proficiency and experience in appellate practice—including the recognition, preservation, and presentation of trial error, and knowledge and application of the rules of appellate procedure applicable to state and federal appellate practice in Florida—to justify the representation of special competence to the legal profession and public.

Added July 1, 1993 (621 So.2d 1032). Amended Nov. 21, 1997; April 9, 1999, by the Board of Governors of The Florida Bar; August 17, 2007, by the Board of Governors of The Florida Bar; May 31, 2013, by the Board of Governors of The Florida Bar.

Rule 6–13.4. Recertification

During the 5–year period immediately preceding application, an applicant must satisfy the following requirements for recertification:

(a) Substantial Involvement. The applicant must demonstrate continuous and substantial involvement in the practice of law, of which at least 30 percent must have been spent in actual participation in appellate practice.

(b) Appellate Actions. The applicant must have had sole or primary responsibility in at least 15 appellate actions for the filing of principal briefs in appeals, or the filing of petitions or responses thereto in extraordinary writ cases. For good cause, the appellate practice certification committee may waive this requirement for applicants who have been continuously certified for 14 or more years.

(c) Oral Arguments. The applicant must have presented at least 5 appellate oral arguments. The appellate practice certification committee may waive this requirement upon good cause shown.

(d) Education. The applicant must demonstrate completion of at least 50 credit hours of approved continuing legal education for appellate practice certification. This requirement may be satisfied by the applicant's participation in at least 30 hours of continuing judicial education approved by the Supreme Court of Florida.

(e) Peer Review.

(1) The applicant must submit the names and addresses of at least 4 lawyers, who are neither relatives nor current associates or partners, as references to attest to the applicant's substantial involvement and competence in appellate practice, as well as the applicant's character, ethics, and reputation for professionalism. Such lawyers must be involved in appellate practice and familiar with the applicant's practice.

(2) The applicant must submit the names and addresses of at least 2 judges before whom the applicant has appeared on appellate matters within the last 2 years to attest to the applicant's substantial involvement and competence in appellate practice, as well as the applicant's character, ethics, and reputation for professionalism.

(3) The appellate practice certification committee may, at its option, send reference forms to other attorneys and judges.

(f) Judges.

(1) An applicant who is serving as an appellate court judge on a Florida district court of appeal, the Supreme Court of Florida, a United States court of appeals, or the United States Supreme Court, and who applies for recertification while serving as a judge of such court, will be deemed to have met the requirements of subdivisions (a)–(c) of this rule, and, for good cause shown, the appellate practice certification com-

mittee may waive compliance with the requirements of subdivision (e) of this rule.

(2) For an applicant who is subject to the Code of Judicial Conduct and who performs or has performed judicial functions on a full-time basis during a substantial portion of the period since the last date of certification, the appellate practice certification committee may waive compliance with the requirements of subdivisions (a)—(c) and (e) of this rule, for good cause shown, provided the applicant has complied with all other requirements for recertification.

(g) Good Cause. Subject to the requirements of rule 6–13.2(h), in determining good cause under this rule, the appellate practice certification committee will consider, if requested, the length of time the applicant has been certified; the applicant's supervisory responsibility for appellate actions or oral arguments since the date of the last certification application; the nature and complexity of the applicant's appellate actions since the last application for certification; the number of appellate actions in the applicant's career; and any health, career, or other factors that may have limited the number of appellate actions or oral arguments since the date of the last application for certification.

Added July 1, 1993 (621 So.2d 1032). Amended Nov. 21, 1997; April 9, 1999, by the Board of Governors of The Florida Bar; August 17, 2007, by the Board of Governors of The Florida Bar; May 22, 2008, by the Board of Governors of The Florida Bar; May 31, 2013, by the Board of Governors of The Florida Bar.

6–14. STANDARDS FOR CERTIFICATION OF A BOARD CERTIFIED HEALTH LAW ATTORNEY

Rule 6–14.1. Generally

A lawyer who is a member in good standing of The Florida Bar and who meets the standards prescribed below may be issued an appropriate certificate identifying the lawyer as a "Board Certified Health Law Attorney." The purpose of the standards is to identify those lawyers who practice in the area of health law and have the special knowledge, skills, and proficiency to be properly identified to the public as certified health law attorneys.

Added Sept. 1, 1994 (641 So.2d 1327). Amended Oct. 22, 1999, by the Board of Governors of The Florida Bar.

Rule 6–14.2. Definitions

(a) Health Law. "Health law" means legal issues involving federal, state, or local law, rules or regulations and health care provider issues, regulation of providers, legal issues regarding relationships between and among providers, legal issues regarding relationships between providers and payors, and legal issues regarding the delivery of health care services.

(b) Practice of Law. The "practice of law" for this area is defined as set out in rule 6–3.5(c)(1). Notwithstanding anything in the definition to the contrary, legal work done primarily for a purpose other than legal advice or representation (including, but not limited to, work related to the sale of insurance or retirement plans or work in connection with the practice of a profession other than the law) shall not be treated as the practice of law.

Added Sept. 1, 1994 (641 So.2d 1327). Amended Oct. 22, 1999, by the Board of Governors of The Florida Bar.

Rule 6–14.3. Minimum standards

(a) Minimum Period of Practice. Every applicant shall have been engaged in the practice of law in the United States, or engaged in the practice of United States law while in a foreign country, and shall have been a member in good standing of the bar of any state of the United States or the District of Columbia for a period of 5 years as of the date of application.

(1) The years of practice of law need not be consecutive.

(2) Notwithstanding the definition of "practice of law" in rule 6–3.5(c)(1), receipt of an LL.M. degree in health law (or such other related fields approved by the board of legal specialization and education and the health law certification committee) from an approved law school shall be deemed to constitute 1 year of the practice of law for purposes of the 5–year practice requirement (but not the 5–year bar membership requirement) under this subdivision. However, an applicant may not receive credit for more than 1 year of practice for any 12–month period under this subdivision; accordingly, for example, an applicant who, while being engaged in the practice of law, receives an LL.M. degree by attending night classes, would not receive credit for the practice of law requirement by virtue of having received the LL.M. degree.

(b) Substantial Involvement. Every applicant must demonstrate substantial involvement in the practice of health law during the 3 years immediately preceding the date of application. Upon an applicant's request and the recommendation of the health law certification committee, the board of legal specialization and education may waive the requirement that the 3 years be "immediately preceding" the date of application if the board of legal specialization and education determines the waiver is warranted by special and compelling circumstances. Substantial involvement means the applicant has devoted 40 percent or more of the applicant's practice to matters in which issues of health law are significant factors and in which the applicant had substantial and direct participation in those health law issues. An applicant must furnish information concerning the frequency of the applicant's work and the nature of the issues involved. For the purposes of this subdivision the "practice of law" shall be as defined in rule 6–3.5(c)(1), except that it shall also include time devoted to lecturing and/or authoring books or articles on health law if the applicant was engaged in the practice of law during such period. Demonstration of compliance with this requirement shall be made initially through a form of questionnaire approved by the health law certification committee but written or oral supplementation may be required.

(c) Peer Review. Every applicant shall submit the names and addresses of 5 other attorneys or judges who are familiar with the applicant's practice, not including attorneys who currently practice in the applicant's law firm, and who can attest to the applicant's reputation for involvement in the field of health law, as well as the applicant's character, ethics, and reputation for professionalism, in accordance with rule 6–3.5(c)(6). The board of legal specialization and education or the health law certification committee may authorize references from persons other than attorneys in such cases as they deem appropriate. The board of legal specialization and education and the health law certification committee may also make such additional inquiries as they deem appropriate.

(d) Education. Every applicant must demonstrate that during the 3–year period immediately preceding the date of application, the applicant has met the continuing legal education requirements in health law as follows. The required number of hours shall be established by the board of legal specialization and education and shall in no event be less than 60 hours, at least 18 hours of which must be obtained through attendance at continuing legal education seminars as described in subdivision (1) below. Credit for attendance at continuing legal education seminars shall be given only for programs that are directly related to health law. Subject to the requirements and limitations set forth above, the education requirement may be satisfied by 1 or more of the following:

(1) attendance at continuing legal education seminars meeting the requirements set forth above;

(2) lecturing at and/or preparation of outline material of such continuing legal education seminars;

(3) authoring articles or books published in professional periodicals or other professional publications;

(4) teaching courses in "health law" at an approved law school or other graduate or undergraduate level program presented by a recognized professional education association;

(5) completing such home study programs as may be approved by the board of legal specialization and education or the health law certification committee, subject to the limitation that no more than 50 percent of the required number of hours of education may be satisfied through home study programs; or

(6) such other methods as may be approved by the health law certification committee.

The board of legal specialization and education or the health law certification committee shall, by rule or regulation, establish standards applicable to this rule, including, but not limited to, the method of establishment of the number of hours allocable to any of the above-listed subdivisions. Such rules or regulations shall provide that hours shall be allocable to each separate but substantially different lecture, article, or other activity described in subdivisions (2), (3), and (4) above.

(e) Examination. Every applicant must pass a written examination designed to demonstrate sufficient knowledge, skills, and proficiency in the field of health law to justify the representation of special competence to the legal profession and the public.

Added Sept. 1, 1994 (641 So.2d 1327). Amended March 14–16, 1996, by the Board of Governors of The Florida Bar; Oct. 22, 1999, by the Board of Governors of The Florida Bar.

Rule 6–14.4. Recertification

To be eligible for recertification, an applicant must meet the following requirements:

(a) Substantial Involvement. Applicants must demonstrate a satisfactory showing, as determined by the board of legal specialization and education and the health law certification committee, of continuous and substantial involvement in the field of health law throughout the period since the last date of certification. The demonstration of substantial involvement shall be made in accordance with the standards set forth in rule 6–14.3(b), except that the board of legal specialization and education and the health law certification committee may accept an affidavit from the applicant attesting to the applicant's compliance with the substantial involvement requirement.

(b) Continuing Legal Education Requirement. Applicants must demonstrate the completion of at least 100 hours of continuing legal education since the filing of the last application for certification (or recertification). The continuing legal education must logically be expected to enhance the proficiency of attorneys who are board certified health law attorneys. If the applicant has not attained 100 hours of continuing legal education, but has attained more than 60 hours during such period, successful passage of the written examination given by the board of legal specialization and education to new applicants shall satisfy the continuing legal education requirements.

(c) Peer Review. Peer review shall be conducted in accordance with the standards set forth in rule 6–14.3(c).

(d) Examination Requirement. If, after reviewing the material submitted by an applicant for recertification, the board of legal specialization and education and the health law certification committee determine that the applicant may not meet the standards in health law established under this chapter, the board of legal specialization and education and the health law certification committee may require, as a condition of recertification, that the applicant pass the written examination given by the board of legal specialization and education to new applicants.

Added Sept. 1, 1994 (641 So.2d 1327). Amended Oct. 22, 1999, by the Board of Governors of The Florida Bar.

6–15. STANDARDS FOR CERTIFICATION OF A BOARD CERTIFIED IMMIGRATION AND NATIONALITY LAWYER

Rule 6–15.1. Generally

A lawyer who is a member in good standing of The Florida Bar and who meets the standards prescribed below may be issued an appropriate certificate identifying the lawyer as a "Board Certified Immigration and Nationality Lawyer." The purpose of the standards is to identify those lawyers who practice immigration and nationality law and have the special knowledge, skills, and proficiency to be properly identified to the public as certified immigration and nationality lawyers.

Added Sept. 1, 1994 (641 So.2d 1327).

Rule 6–15.2. Definitions

(a) Immigration and Nationality Law. "Immigration and nationality law" is the law dealing with all aspects of the United States Immigration and Nationality Act.

(b) Practice of Law. The "practice of law" for this area is defined as set out at rule 6–3.5(c)(1).

Added Sept. 1, 1994 (641 So.2d 1327).

Rule 6–15.3. Minimum standards

(a) Minimum Period of Practice. The applicant must have been engaged in the practice of law for at least 5 years preceding the date of application.

(b) Substantial Involvement. The applicant must demonstrate to the immigration and nationality certification committee substantial involvement in the practice of immigration and nationality law during the 3 years immediately preceding the date of application. Substantial involvement means that the applicant has devoted 40 percent or more of the applicant's practice to matters in which issues of immigration and nationality law are significant factors and in which the applicant had substantial and direct participation in those issues. Matters in which issues of immigration and nationality law are significant factors include, but are not limited to:

(1) the representation of clients before the United States Citizenship and Immigration Services and/or Customs and Border Patrol and/or Immigration and Customs Enforcement through either the preparation of petitions and applications for immigration benefits and discretionary relief or the appearance as counsel at deferred inspections, adjustment of status, and other interviews;

(2) the representation of clients before the Executive Office for Immigration Review during exclusion, deportation, removal, asylum only, bond proceedings, and appeals;

(3) the representation of clients before the Department of Labor through the preparation of Labor Certification Applications, Labor Condition Applications, and such other Department of Labor applications, petitions, and processes as are required in the Immigration and Nationality Act as a prerequisite for immigration benefits;

(4) the representation of clients before the Department of State in matters pertaining to the consular processing of visa applications; and

(5) the representation of clients in matters of original and appellate jurisdiction before United States district courts and United States courts of appeals concerning immigration and nationality matters.

The immigration and nationality certification committee may waive the 3 years immediately preceding the date of application requirement upon good cause shown.

(c) Peer Review. The applicant must submit to the immigration and nationality certification committee the names and addresses of 5 attorneys who are neither relatives nor current associates or partners, as references to attest to the applicant's reputation for substantial involvement and competence in the field of immigration and nationality law, as well as the applicant's character, ethics, and reputation for professionalism. No less than 1 reference shall be board certified in immigration and nationality law. The immigration and nationality law certification committee may authorize references from persons other than attorneys upon good cause shown.

(d) Education. The applicant must demonstrate completion of 50 credit hours of approved continuing legal education in immigration and nationality law during the 3–year period immediately preceding the date of application.

Accreditation of educational hours is subject to policies established by the immigration and nationality law certification committee or the board of legal specialization and education.

(e) Examination. The applicant must pass a written examination designed to demonstrate sufficient knowledge, skills, proficiency, and professionalism in the field of immigration and nationality law to justify the representation of special competence to the legal profession and the public.

Added Sept. 1, 1994 (631 So.2d 1327). Amended ______, ____, by the Board of Governors of The Florida Bar; Oct. 3, 2008, by the Board of Governors of The Florida Bar.

Rule 6-15.4. Recertification

During the 5-year period immediately preceding application, the applicant must satisfy the following requirements for recertification:

(a) Substantial Involvement. The applicants must demonstrate continuous and substantial involvement in the field of immigration and nationality law during the period since the last date of certification. The demonstration of substantial involvement shall be made in accordance with the standards set forth in rule 6-15.3(b). Upon good cause shown, the immigration and nationality law certification committee may waive all or any portion of the substantial involvement requirement if an applicant was or is currently a judge presiding over matters of immigration and nationality law.

(b) Education. The applicants must demonstrate completion of 100 credit hours of approved continuing legal education in immigration and nationality law. At least 60 of such hours shall be during the 3-year period immediately preceding the date of application. Accreditation of educational hours is subject to policies established by the immigration and nationality law certification committee or the board of legal specialization and education.

(c) Peer Review. Peer review shall be conducted in accordance with the standards set forth in rule 6-15.3(c).

(d) Examination Requirement. If the immigration and nationality law certification committee determines that the applicant does not meet the standards set forth in subdivision (b) of this rule, the immigration and nationality certification committee may, for good cause shown, require that the applicant pass the examination in lieu thereof.

Added Sept. 1, 1994 (631 So.2d 1327). Amended Jan. 26, 1996, by the Board of Governors of The Florida Bar; Oct. 3, 2008, by the Board of Governors of The Florida Bar.

6-16. STANDARDS FOR CERTIFICATION OF A BOARD CERTIFIED BUSINESS LITIGATION LAWYER

Rule 6-16.1. Generally

A lawyer who is a member in good standing of The Florida Bar and who meets the standards prescribed below may be issued d a certificate, identifying the lawyer as "Board Certified in Business Litigation." The purpose of the standards is to identify those lawyers who practice in the area of business litigation and have the special knowledge, skills, and proficiency, as well as the character, ethics, and reputation for professionalism, to be properly identified to the public as board certified business litigation lawyers.

Added July 20, 1995 (658 So.2d 930). Amended July 17-18, 1996, by the Board of Governors of The Florida Bar; September 18-20, 1997, by the Board of Governors of The Florida Bar; August 22, 2003, by the Board of Governors of The Florida Bar; January 31, 2014, by the Board of Governors of The Florida Bar.

Rule 6-16.2. Definitions

(a) Business Litigation. "Business litigation" is the practice of law dealing with the legal problems from commercial and business relationships, including litigation of controversies. "Business litigation" includes evaluating, handling, and resolving such controversies before state courts, federal courts, administrative agencies, mediators, and arbitrators. Matters not qualifying for business litigation include areas of practice dealing with personal injury, routine collection matters, marital and family law, or workers' compensation. Courts of "general jurisdiction" include state circuit courts, federal district courts, and courts of similar jurisdiction in other states, but not county courts.

(b) Practice of Law. The "practice of law" for this area is defined in subdivision (c)(1) of rule 6-3.5. The practice of law which otherwise satisfies these requirements but which is on a part-time basis will satisfy this requirement.

Added July 20, 1995 (658 So.2d 930). Amended July 17-18, 1996, by the Board of Governors of The Florida Bar; September 18-20, 1997, by the Board of Governors of The Florida Bar; August 22, 2003, by the Board of Governors of The Florida Bar; January 31, 2014, by the Board of Governors of The Florida Bar.

Rule 6-16.3. Minimum Standards

(a) Minimum Period of Practice. The applicant must have at least 5 years of the actual practice of law immediately preceding application, of which at least 30 percent has been spent in active participation in business litigation.

(b) Minimum Number of Matters. The applicant must have had substantial involvement in a minimum of 25 contested business litigation matters during the 5-year period immediately preceding application. These matters must have proceeded at least to the filing of a complaint or similar pleading and involve substantial legal or factual issues. At least 8 of the 25 matters must have been submitted to the trier of fact for resolution of 1 or more contested factual issues through the presentation of live testimony or other evidence at a hearing. The trier of fact includes any judge or jury of a court of general jurisdiction, an arbitration panel, administrative agency, bankruptcy court, or other similar body. At least 1 of the 8 matters must have been tried before a jury during the 10–year period immediately preceding application. If the applicant has not tried a business litigation matter before a jury, the business litigation certification committee may consider any civil dispute tried before a jury within the allowable time period to satisfy the jury trial requirement. "Submission to the trier of fact" and trial before a jury requires completion of the case in chief of the plaintiff, petitioner, or claimant. If the applicant has not participated in 8 matters submitted to the trier of fact for resolution, the applicant may substitute completion of an advanced trial advocacy seminar for 1 of the 8 matters, either by teaching, attendance, or any combination, provided that an advanced trial advocacy seminar may not be a substitute for the jury trial requirement. This seminar must be 3 full days, approved by the business litigation certification committee, and include as part of its curriculum active participation by the applicant in simulated courtroom proceedings. All course materials for the seminar must be submitted to the business litigation certification committee to be considered for substitute credit. The business litigation certification committee may consider involvement in protracted adversary proceedings to satisfy any of these requirements for good cause shown. A "protracted adversary proceeding" is a "business litigation" "matter which, by its very nature, is so time consuming as to preclude the applicant from meeting the requirements of this subdivision. In order to demonstrate compliance with the requirements of this section, the following criteria will be applicable:

(1) summary judgments will not count as 1 of the 8 matters submitted to the trier of fact;

(2) submission to the trier of fact and trial before a jury requires completion of the case in chief of the plaintiff, petitioner, or claimant;

(3) each preliminary injunction or other evidentiary hearing will count as 1 of the 8 matters submitted to the trier of fact; and,

(4) each matter in which the applicant supervises an associate will qualify the matter as 1 of the 25 but not as 1 of the 8 matters submitted to the trier of fact.

(c) Substantial Involvement. The applicant must have substantial involvement in contested business litigation cases sufficient to demonstrate special competence as a business litigation lawyer. Substantial involvement includes active participation in client interviewing, counseling and investigating, preparation of pleadings, participation in discovery, taking of testimony, presentation of evidence, negotiation of settlement, drafting and preparation of business litigation settlement agreements, and argument and trial of business law cases.

(d) Peer Review. The applicant must submit names and addresses of 5 lawyers, who are not the applicant's associates or partners, as references to attest to the applicant's special competence and substantial involvement in business litigation, as well as the applicant's character, ethics, and reputation for professionalism. The lawyers themselves must be substantially involved in business litigation and familiar with the applicant's practice. At least 1 of these references must be a judge or presiding officer of a court or other tribunal before whom the applicant has appeared as an advocate in a business litigation matter in the 2–year period immediately preceding the application. In addition, the business litigation certification committee may, at its option, send reference forms to other lawyers, judges, or officers and conduct such other investigation as necessary.

(e) Education. The applicant must demonstrate completion of at least 50 hours of approved continuing legal education in business litigation within the 3–year period immediately preceding the date of application. Accreditation of educational hours is subject to policies established by the business litigation certification committee or the board of legal specialization and education, and may include such activities as:

(1) teaching a course in business litigation;

(2) participation as a panelist or speaker in a symposium or similar program in business litigation;

(3) attendance at a lecture series or similar program concerning business litigation, sponsored by a qualified educational institution or bar group;

(4) authorship of a book or article on business litigation;

(5) attendance at a course dealing with trial practice procedures but in an area of law not considered business litigation as defined d in rule 6–16.2;

(6) attendance at seminars dealing with mediation or arbitration procedures and techniques;

(7) attendance at or participation in a "trial advocacy" workshop leader if the attorney participates in or attends the entire program; and,

(8) other educational activities approved by the business litigation certification committee.

(f) Examination. The applicant must pass an examination applied uniformly to all applicants to demonstrate sufficient knowledge, skills, experience, proficiency, and professionalism in business litigation to justify representation of special competence to the legal profession and to the public.

Added July 20, 1995 (658 So.2d 930). Amended July 17–18, 1996, by the Board of Governors of The Florida Bar; September 18–20, 1997, by the Board of Governors of The Florida Bar; June 29, 2000, by the Board of Governors of The Florida Bar; August 22, 2003, by the Board of Governors of The Florida Bar; June 2, 2006 effective June 5, 2006, by the Board of Governors of The Florida Bar; January 31, 2014, by the Board of Governors of The Florida Bar.

Rule 6–16.4. Recertification

During the 5–year period immediately preceding the date of application, the applicant must demonstrate satisfaction of the following requirements for recertification:

(a) Substantial Involvement. The applicant must demonstrate continuous and substantial involvement in the field of business litigation in accordance with the standards in subdivision (c) of rule 6–16.3.

(b) Minimum Number of Matters. The applicant must have had substantial involvement in a minimum of 25 contested business litigation matters. These matters must have proceeded at least to the filing of a complaint or similar pleading and involve substantial legal or factual issues. At least 5 of the 25 matters must have been submitted to the trier of fact for resolution of 1 or more contested factual issues through the presentation of live testimony or other evidence at a hearing, as described in subdivision (b) of rule 6–16.3. If the applicant has not participated in 5 matters submitted to the trier of fact for resolution, the applicant may substitute completion of an advanced trial advocacy seminar for 1 of the 5 required matters, either by teaching, attendance, or a combination. The seminar must be 3 full days, approved by the business litigation certification committee, and include as part of its curriculum active participation by the applicant in simulated courtroom proceedings. All course materials for the seminar must be submitted to the business litigation certification committee to be considered for substitute credit toward 1 of the 5 matters. The business litigation certification committee may consider involvement in protracted adversary proceedings, as defined in subdivision (b) of rule 6–16.3 to satisfy any of these requirements on good cause shown. In order to demonstrate compliance with the requirements of this section, the following criteria are applicable:

(1) summary judgments will not count as 1 of the 5 matters submitted to the trier of fact;

(2) submission to the trier of fact and trial before a jury requires completion of the case in chief of the plaintiff, petitioner, or claimant;

(3) each preliminary injunction or other evidentiary hearing counts as 1 of the 5 matters submitted to the trier of fact;

(4) each matter in which the applicant supervises an associate will qualify the matter as 1 of the 25 but not as 1 of the 5 matters submitted to the trier of fact.

The business litigation certification committee may waive compliance with the evidentiary hearing criteria for an applicant who has been continuously board certified as a business litigation lawyer for a period of 14 years or more on special application for good cause shown.

(c) Education. The applicant must have completed at least 50 hours of continuing legal education in the field of business litigation in accordance with subdivision (e) of rule 6–16.3.

(d) Peer Review. The applicant must satisfy the reference requirements in rule 616.3(d) and meet the standards in subdivision (c)(6) of rule 6–3.5.

(e) Judges. On special application, for good cause shown, an applicant who is serving as a judge and applies for recertification will have met the requirements of rule 6–16.4. The business litigation certification committee may waive compliance with any portion of the recertification criteria for an applicant who is an officer of any judicial system as defined in the Code of Judicial Conduct and who performs or has performed judicial functions on a full-time basis during a substantial portion of the period since the last date of certification.

Added July 20, 1995 (658 So.2d 930). Amended July 17–18, 1996, by the Board of Governors of The Florida Bar; September 18–20, 1997, by the Board of Governors of The Florida Bar; August 22, 2003, by the Board of Governors of The Florida Bar; June 2, 2006, effective June 5, 2006, by the Board of Governors of The Florida Bar; March 28, 2008, by the Board of Governors of The Florida Bar; January 31, 2014, by the Board of Governors of The Florida Bar.

6–17. STANDARDS FOR CERTIFICATION OF A BOARD CERTIFIED ADMIRALTY AND MARITIME LAWYER

Rule 6–17.1. Generally

A lawyer who is a member in good standing of The Florida Bar and who meets the standards prescribed below may be issued an appropriate certificate identifying the lawyer as a "Board Certified Admiralty and Maritime Lawyer." The purpose of the standards is to identify those lawyers who practice admiralty and maritime law and who have demonstrated special knowledge, skills and proficiency to be properly identified to the public as certified admiralty and maritime lawyers.

Added July 20, 1995 (658 So.2d 930).

Rule 6–17.2. Definitions

(a) Admiralty Law. "Admiralty and Maritime Law" is that distinct and separate practice of law dealing with the corpus of rules, concepts, and legal practices governing vessels, the shipping industry, the carrying of goods and passengers by water as well as related maritime concepts. Admiralty and maritime law includes the substantive law and procedural rules associated with the general maritime law of the United States, admiralty jurisdiction and procedure, personal injury and wrongful death of seamen and passengers aboard vessels, compensation for injury and wrongful death of longshoremen and harbor workers, government regulation of marine safety and the maritime industry, carriage of goods, charter parties, salvage, general average, collision, marine insurance, maritime liens, limitation of liability, marine pollution and environmental law, maritime arbitration, recreational vessels, vessel finance and documentation, international aspects of maritime practice as well as other maritime topics which because of their special history, as well as for historical and practical reasons, have been recognized as distinctly different from our modern system of common law and have been traditionally grouped and practiced as "admiralty and maritime law."

(b) Practice of Law. A minimum of 5 years in the practice of law including substantial involvement in the practice of admiralty and maritime law as set forth in rule 6–17.3(b). The term "practice of law" as used in these standards shall be as defined in rule 6-3.5(c)(1).

Added July 20, 1995 (658 So.2d 930). Amended Dec. 11, 1998, by the Board of Governors of The Florida Bar.

Rule 6–17.3. Minimum Standards

(a) Minimum Period of Practice. The applicant shall have been engaged in the practice of law in the United States, or engaged in the practice of United States law while in a foreign country, and shall have been a member in good standing of the bar of any state of the United States or the District of Columbia for period of 5 years as of the date of application.

Notwithstanding the definition of "practice of law" in rule 6–3.5(c)(1), receipt of an LL.M degree in admiralty law, ocean law, maritime law or such other related fields approved by the board of legal specialization and education and admiralty law certification committee from an approved law school shall be deemed to constitute 1 year of the practice of law for purposes of the 5–year practice requirement but not the 5–year bar membership requirement.

(b) Substantial Involvement. The applicant must demonstrate substantial involvement in the practice of admiralty and maritime law during the 5 years immediately preceding the date of application, including devoting not less than 35 percent of such practice to admiralty and maritime law during each of the 3 years immediately preceding the date of application. Except for the 3 years immediately preceding the date of application, upon the applicant's request and the recommendation of the admiralty and maritime law certification committee, the board of legal specialization and education may waive the requirement that the 5 years be "immediately preceding" the date of application if the board of legal specialization and education determines the waiver is warranted by special and compelling circumstances. Except for the 3 years immediately preceding the date of application, receipt of an LL.M degree in admiralty law, ocean law, maritime law (or such other degree containing substantial admiralty and maritime law content as approved by the board of legal specialization and education) from an approved law school may substitute for 1 year of substantial involvement. An applicant must furnish information concerning the frequency of work and the nature of issues involved. For the purposes of this section, the "practice of law" shall be as defined in rule 6–3.5(c)(1) except that it shall also include time devoted to lecturing and/or authoring books or articles on admiralty and maritime law if the applicant was engaged in the practice of law during such period. Demonstration of compliance with this requirement shall be made initially through a form of questionnaire approved by the admiralty law certification committee, but written or oral supplementation may be required.

(c) Peer Review. The applicant shall submit the names and addresses of 5 other attorneys who are familiar with the applicant's practice, not including attorneys who currently practice in the applicant's law firm, who can attest to the applicant's special competence and substantial involvement in the field of admiralty and maritime law, as well as the applicant's character, ethics, and reputation for professionalism. No less than 2 references shall be board certified in admiralty and maritime law or shall have, in the judgement of the committee, an established and recognized admiralty and maritime law practice. The board of legal specialization and education and admiralty law certification committee may authorize references from persons other than attorneys and may also make such additional inquiries as they deem appropriate to complete peer review, as provided elsewhere in these rules.

(d) Education. During the 3–year period immediately preceding the date of the application, the applicant must demonstrate completion of the continuing legal education requirements in admiralty and maritime law as follows. The required number of hours shall be established by the board of legal specialization and education and shall in no event be less than 50 hours. Credit for attendance at continuing legal education seminars shall be given only for programs that are directly related to admiralty and maritime law. The education requirement may be satisfied by one or more of the following:

(1) attendance at continuing legal education seminars meeting the requirements set forth above;

(2) lecturing at, and/or serving on the steering committee of, such continuing legal education seminars;

(3) authoring books or articles published in professional periodicals or other professional publications;

(4) teaching courses in admiralty and maritime law and related subjects at an approved law school or other graduate level program presented by a recognized professional education association;

(5) such other methods as may be approved by the board of legal specialization and education and the admiralty certification committee.

The board of legal specialization and education and the admiralty law certification committee shall, by rule or regulation, establish standards applicable to this rule, including, but not limited to, the method of establishment of the number of hours allocable to any of the above-listed subdivisions. Such rules or regulations shall provide that hours shall be allocable to each separate but substantially different lecture, article, or other activity described in subdivisions (2), (3), and (4) above.

(e) Examination. The applicant must pass an examination, applied uniformly to all applicants, that will be practical and comprehensive and designed to demonstrate special knowledge, skills, and proficiency in admiralty and maritime law topics including jurisdiction, procedure, personal injury and wrongful death, marine insurance and such other topics as may be selected by the admiralty certification committee. Such examination shall justify the representation of special competence in the field of admiralty law to the legal profession and the public.

Added July 20, 1995 (658 So.2d 930). Amended Dec. 11, 1998, by the Board of Governors of The Florida Bar; ______, ____, by the Board of Governors of The Florida Bar.

Rule 6–17.4. Recertification

Recertification shall be pursuant to the following standards:

(a) Substantial Involvement. A satisfactory showing, as determined by the board of legal specialization and education and the admiralty law certification committee, of continuous and substantial involvement in admiralty and maritime law throughout the period since the last date of certification. The demonstration of substantial involvement of at least 35 percent during each year of certification or prior recertification shall be made in accordance with the standards set forth in rule 6–17.3(b).

(b) Education. Completion of at least 55 hours of approved continuing legal education since the filing of the last application for certification. This requirement shall be satisfied by the applicant's participation in approved continuing legal education pursuant to rule 6–17.3(d)(1) through (5).

(c) Peer Review. Submission of the names and addresses of 3 individuals who are active in admiralty and maritime law, including but not limited to lawyers and judges who are familiar with the applicant's practice, excluding persons who are currently employed in the applicant's law firm, who can attest to the applicant's special competence and substantial involvement in the field of admiralty and maritime law, as well as the applicant's character, ethics, and reputation for professionalism, during the period since the last date of certification. The board of legal specialization and education or the admiralty law certification committee may solicit references from persons other than those whose names are submitted by the applicant and may also make additional inquiries as deemed appropriate.

(d) Examination. If, after reviewing the material submitted by an applicant for recertification and the peer review, the admiralty law certification committee determines the applicant may not meet the standards for admiralty law certification established under this chapter, the applicant may be required, as a condition of recertification, to pass the admiralty and maritime examination given to new applicants.

Added July 20, 1995 (658 So.2d 930). Amended Dec. 11, 1998, by the Board of Governors of The Florida Bar.

6–18. STANDARDS FOR CERTIFICATION OF A BOARD CERTIFIED CITY, COUNTY AND LOCAL GOVERNMENT LAWYER

Rule 6–18.1. Generally

A lawyer who is a member in good standing of The Florida Bar and who meets the standards prescribed below may be issued an appropriate certificate identifying the lawyer as "Board Certified City, County and Local Government Lawyer." The purpose of the standards is to identify those lawyers who practice city, county and local government law and have the special knowledge, skills, and proficiency to be properly identified to the public as certified city, county and local government lawyers.

Added July 20, 1995 (658 So.2d 930). Amended Oct. 22, 1999, by the Board of Governors of The Florida Bar.

Rule 6–18.2. Definitions

(a) City, County and Local Government Law. "City, County and Local Government Law" is the practice of law dealing with legal issues of county, municipal or other local governments, such as, but not limited to, special districts, agencies and authorities, including litigation in the federal and state courts and before administrative agencies; the preparation of laws, ordinances and regulations; and the preparation of legal instruments for or in behalf of city, county and local governments.

(b) Practice of Law. The "practice of law" for this area is defined as set out in rule 6–3.5(c)(1). Notwithstanding anything in the definition to the contrary, legal work done primarily for a purpose other than providing legal counsel or representation (including, but not limited to, work related to the administration of government or representing government as an elected official or as a state legislative lobbyist) shall not be treated as the practice of law.

Added July 20, 1995 (658 So.2d 930). Amended Oct. 22, 1999, by the Board of Governors of The Florida Bar.

Rule 6–18.3. Minimum Standards

(a) Minimum Period of Practice. The applicant shall have been engaged in the practice of law in the United States, or engaged in the practice of United States law while in a foreign country, and shall have been a member in good standing of the bar of any state of the United States or the District of Columbia for a period of 5 years as of the date of filing an application. The years of law practice need not be consecutive.

Notwithstanding the definition of "practice of law" in rule 6–3.5(c)(1), receipt of an LL.M. degree in urban affairs (or such other related fields approved by the board of legal specialization and education and the city, county and local government certification committee) from an approved law school shall be deemed to constitute 1 year of the practice of law for purpose of the 5–year practice requirement (but not the 5–year bar membership requirement) under this subsection. However, an applicant may not receive credit for more than 1 year of practice for any 12–month period under this subsection; accordingly, for example, an applicant who, while being engaged in the practice of law, receives an LL.M. degree by attending night classes, would not receive credit for the practice of law requirement by virtue of having received the LL.M. degree.

(b) Substantial Involvement. The applicant must demonstrate substantial involvement in the practice of Florida city, county and local government law during each of the 3 years immediately preceding the date of application. Upon an applicant's request and the recommendation of the city, county and local government certification committee, the board of legal specialization and education may waive the requirement that each of the 3 years be "immediately preceding" the date of application if the board of legal specialization and education determines the waiver is warranted by special and compelling circumstances. Substantial involvement means the applicant has devoted 40 percent or more of the applicant's practice to matters in which issues of Florida city, county and local government law are significant factors and in which the applicant had substantial and direct participation in those issues. An applicant must furnish information concerning the frequency of the applicant's work and the nature of the issues involved. For the purpose of this subsection the "practice of law" shall be as defined in rule 6–3.5(c)(1), except that it shall also include time devoted to lecturing and/or authoring books or articles on city, county and local government law if the applicant was otherwise engaged in the practice of law during such period. Demonstration of compliance with this requirement shall be made initially through a form of questionnaire approved by the city, county and local government certification committee but written or oral supplementation may be required.

(c) Peer Review. The applicant shall submit the names and addresses of 5 other attorneys who are familiar with the applicant's practice, not including attorneys who are currently employed by the same governmental entity as the applicant or who currently practice in the applicant's law firm, who can attest to the applicant's reputation for special competence and substantial involvement, as well as the applicant's character, ethics, and reputation for professionalism, in the field of city, county and local government law. Such lawyers themselves shall be substantially involved in Florida city, county and local government law. The board of legal specialization and education and the city, county and local government certification committee may authorize references from persons other than attorneys and may also make such additional inquiries as they deem appropriate to complete peer review, as provided elsewhere in these rules.

(d) Education. The applicant must demonstrate that during the 3–year period immediately preceding the date of application, the applicant has met the continuing legal education requirements in Florida city, county and local government law as follows: the required number of hours shall be established by the board of legal specialization and education and shall in no event be less than 60 hours. Credit for attendance at continuing legal education seminars shall be given only for programs that are directly related to Florida city, county and local government law. The education requirement may be satisfied by 1 or more of the following:

(1) attendance at continuing legal education seminars meeting the requirements set forth above;

(2) lecturing at, and/or serving on the steering committee of, such continuing legal education seminars;

(3) authoring articles or books published in professional periodicals or other professional publications;

(4) teaching courses in "city, county and local government law" at an approved law school or other graduate level program presented by a recognized professional education association;

(5) such other methods as may be approved by the board of legal specialization and education and the city, county and local government certification committee.

The board of legal specialization and education or the city, county and local government certification committee shall, by rule or regulation, establish standards applicable to this rule, including, but not limited to, the method of establishment of the number of hours allocable to any of the above listed paragraphs. Such rules or regulations shall provide that hours shall be allocable to each separate but substantially different lecture, article, or other activity described in subsections (2), (3), and (4) above.

(e) Examination. The applicant must pass a written examination, applied uniformly to all applicants, designed to demonstrate sufficient knowledge, skills, and proficiency in the field of Florida city, county and local government law to justify the representation of special competence to the legal profession and the public.

Added July 20, 1995 (658 So.2d 930). Amended Oct. 22, 1999, by the Board of Governors of The Florida Bar; ________, ____, by the Board of Governors of The Florida Bar.

Rule 6-18.4. Recertification

Recertification shall be pursuant to the following standards:

(a) Substantial Involvement. A satisfactory showing, as determined by the board of legal specialization and education and the city, county and local government certification committee, of continuous and substantial involvement in the field of Florida city, county and local government law throughout the period since the last date of certification. The demonstration of substantial involvement shall be made in accordance with the standards set forth in rule 6-18.3(b), except that the board of legal specialization and education and the city, county and local government certification committee may accept an affidavit from the applicant attesting to the applicant's compliance with the substantial involvement requirement.

(b) Education. Completion of at least 60 hours of continuing legal education since the filing of the last application for certification (or recertification). The continuing legal education must logically be expected to enhance the proficiency of attorneys who are board certified city, county and local government lawyers. If the applicant has not attained 60 hours of continuing legal education, but has attained more than 30 hours during such period, successful passage of the written examination given by the board of legal specialization and education to new applicants shall satisfy the continuing legal education requirements.

(c) Peer Review. The applicant shall submit the names and addresses of 3 other attorneys who are familiar with the applicant's practice, not including attorneys who are currently employed by the same governmental entity as the applicant or who currently practice in the applicant's law firm, who can attest to the applicant's reputation for special competence and substantial involvement, as well as the applicant's character, ethics, and reputation for professionalism, in the field of city, county and local government law. Such lawyers themselves shall be substantially involved in Florida city, county and local government law. The board of legal specialization and education and the city, county and local government certification committee may authorize references from persons other than attorneys and may also make such additional inquiries as they deem appropriate to complete peer review, as provided elsewhere in these rules.

(d) Examination. If, after reviewing the material submitted by an applicant for recertification, the board of legal specialization and education and the city, county and local government certification committee determine that the applicant may not meet the standards in city, county and local government law established under this chapter, the board of legal specialization and education and the city, county and local government certification committee may require, as a condition of recertification, that the applicant pass the written examination given by the board of legal specialization and education to new applicants.

Added July 20, 1995 (658 So.2d 930). Amended Oct. 22, 1999, by the Board of Governors of The Florida Bar; ________, ____, by the Board of Governors of The Florida Bar.

6-19. STANDARDS FOR CERTIFICATION OF A BOARD CERTIFIED AVIATION LAWYER

Rule 6-19.1. Generally

A lawyer who is a member in good standing of The Florida Bar and who meets the standards prescribed below may be issued an appropriate certificate identifying the lawyer as a "Board Certified Aviation Lawyer." The purpose of the standards is to identify those lawyers who practice aviation law and have the special knowledge, skills, and proficiency, as well as the character, ethics, and reputation for professionalism, to be properly identified to the public as board certified aviation lawyers.

Added July 20, 1995 (658 So.2d 930). Amended Oct. 3, 2008, by the Board of Governors of The Florida Bar.

Rule 6-19.2. Definitions

(a) Aviation Law. "Aviation law" includes all facets of the law dealing with the ownership, operation, maintenance, and use of aircraft, airports and airspace. It also involves licensing and aeromedical issues encompassed by the Federal Aviation Act and the associated federal aviation regulations promulgated thereunder. It also encompasses the laws that have been developed to regulate the use of outer space.

(b) Practice of Law. The "practice of law" for this area is defined as set out in rule 6-3.5(c)(1).

Added July 20, 1995 (658 So.2d 930).

Rule 6–19.3. Minimum Standards

(a) Minimum Period of Practice. The applicant shall have been engaged in the practice of law in the United States, or engaged in the practice of United States law while in a foreign country, and shall have been a member in good standing of the bar of any state of the United States or the District of Columbia for a period of 5 years as of the date of filing an application. The years of law practice need not be consecutive.

(b) Substantial Involvement. The applicant must demonstrate substantial involvement sufficient to show special knowledge, skills, and proficiency in the practice of aviation law during the 3 years immediately preceding the date of application. Substantial involvement is defined as including devoting at least 30 percent of one's practice to matters in which issues of aviation law are significant factors and in which the applicant had substantial and direct participation in those aviation issues. Upon the applicant's request and the recommendation of the aviation law certification committee, the board of legal specialization and education may waive the requirement that the 3 years be "immediately preceding" the date of application if the board of legal specialization and education determines the waiver is warranted by special and compelling circumstances.

The applicant must furnish information concerning the frequency of the applicant's work and the nature of the issues involved. For the purposes of this subdivision, the "practice of law" shall be as defined in rule 6–3.5(c)(1), except that it shall also include time devoted to lecturing and/or authoring books or articles on fields of aviation law if the applicant was engaged in the practice of law during such period.

Demonstration of compliance with this requirement shall be made initially in the form of a questionnaire approved by the aviation law certification committee, but written or oral supplementation may be required.

(c) Peer Review. The applicant shall submit the names and addresses of 5 attorneys or judges, who are neither relatives nor current associates or partners, who are familiar with the applicant's practice and who can attest to the applicant's special competence and substantial involvement in the field of aviation law, as well as the applicant's character, ethics, and reputation for professionalism. The board of legal specialization and education and the aviation law certification committee may authorize references from persons other than attorneys in such cases as deemed appropriate. The board of legal specialization and education and the aviation law certification committee may also make such additional inquiries as deemed appropriate.

(d) Education. The applicant must demonstrate that during the 3–year period immediately preceding the date of filing an application, the applicant has met the continuing legal education requirements necessary for aviation law. The required number of hours must be established by the board of legal specialization and education and must in no event be less than 60 hours. Accreditation of educational hours is subject to policies established by the aviation law certification committee or the board of legal specialization and education.

(e) Examination. The applicant must pass a written examination that is practical, objective, and designed to demonstrate special knowledge, skills, and proficiency in aviation law to justify the representation of special competence to the legal profession and the public.

Added July 20, 1995 (658 So.2d 930). Amended Oct. 3, 2008, by the Board of Governors of The Florida Bar.

Rule 6–19.4. Recertification

During the 5–year period immediately preceding application, an applicant must satisfy the following requirements for recertification:

(a) Substantial Involvement. The applicant must make a satisfactory showing, as determined by the board of legal specialization and education and the aviation law committee, of continuous and substantial involvement in aviation law throughout the period since the last date of certification. The demonstration of substantial involvement of at least 30 percent during the 5 years prior to recertification shall be made in accordance with the standards set forth in rule 6–19.3(b).

(b) Education. The applicant must show completion of at least 60 hours of accredited continuing legal education in aviation law since the filing of the last application for certification.

(c) Peer Review. The applicant shall submit the names and addresses of 3 attorneys or judges, who are neither relatives nor current associates or partners, who are familiar with the applicant's practice and who can attest to the applicant's special competence and substantial involvement in the field of aviation law, as well as the applicant's character, ethics, and reputation for professionalism. The board of legal specialization and education and the aviation law certification committee may also make such additional inquiries as deemed appropriate.

Added July 20, 1995 (658 So.2d 930). Amended ________, ____, by the Board of Governors of The Florida Bar; Oct. 3, 2008, by the Board of Governors of The Florida Bar.

6–20. STANDARDS FOR CERTIFICATION OF A BOARD CERTIFIED ELDER LAW LAWYER

Rule 6–20.1. Generally

A lawyer who is a member in good standing of The Florida Bar and who meets the standards prescribed below may apply to The Florida Bar board of legal specialization and education for a certificate identifying the lawyer as a "Board Certified Elder Law Attorney." The purpose of the standards is to identify those lawyers who practice in the area of elder law and who have the experience, knowledge, skills, and judgment to be properly identified to the public as certified elder law attorneys.

Added July 17, 1997 (697 So.2d 115).

Rule 6–20.2. Definitions

(a) [1] **Elder Law.** "Elder law" means legal issues involving health and personal care planning, including: advance directives; lifetime planning; family issues; fiduciary representation; capacity; guardianship; power of attorney; financial planning; public benefits and insurance; resident rights in long-term care facilities; housing opportunities and financing; employment and retirement matters; income, estate, and gift tax matters; estate planning; probate; nursing home claims; age or disability discrimination and grandparents' rights. The specialization encompasses all aspects of planning for aging, illness, and incapacity. Elder law clients are predominantly seniors, and the specialization requires a practitioner to be particularly sensitive to the legal issues impacting these clients.

Added July 17, 1997 (697 So.2d 115).

[1] This rule does not contain a "(b)".

Rule 6–20.3. Minimum standards

(a) Minimum Period of Practice. The applicant shall have been engaged in the practice of law in the United States, or engaged in the practice of United States law while in a foreign country, and shall have been a member in good standing of the bar of any state of the United States or the District of Columbia for a period of 5 years as of the date of filing an application. The years of law practice need not be consecutive.

(b) Substantial Involvement. The applicant must demonstrate substantial involvement in elder law as defined by the following:

(1) At least 5 years of law practice, of which at least 40 percent has been spent in active participation in elder law. At least 3 years of this practice shall be immediately preceding application.

(2) Substantial involvement means the applicant has devoted 40 percent or more of the applicant's practice to matters in which issues of elder law are significant factors and in which the applicant had substantial and direct participation in those elder law issues in each of the 3 years preceding the application. An applicant must furnish information concerning the frequency of the applicant's work and the nature of the issues involved. For the purposes of this subdivision the "practice of law" shall be defined in rule 6–3.5(c)(1), except that it shall also include time devoted to lecturing and/or authoring books or articles on elder law if the applicant was engaged in the practice of law during such period. Demonstration of compliance with this requirement shall be made initially through a form of questionnaire approved by the elder law certification committee but written or oral supplementation may be required.

(c) Practical Experience. During the 3 years immediately preceding the application, the applicant shall have provided legal services in at least 60 matters as follows:

(1) Forty must be in categories listed in (A) through (E) below, with at least 5 matters in each category.

(2) Ten of the matters must be in categories listed in (F) through (M) below. No more than 5 in any 1 category may be credited toward the total requirement of 60 matters.

(3) The remaining 10 matters may be in any category listed in (A) through (M) below, and are not subject to the limitation contained in parts (1) or (2) of this subdivision.

(4) As used in this subdivision, an applicant will be considered to have "provided legal services" if the applicant: provided advice (written or oral, but if oral, supported by substantial documentation in the client's file) tailored to and based on facts and circumstances specific to a particular client; drafted legal documents such as, but not limited to, wills, trusts, or health care directives, provided that those legal documents were tailored to and based on facts and circumstances specific to the particular client; prepared legal documents and took other steps necessary for the administration of a previously prepared legal directive such as, but not limited to, a will or trust; or provided representation to a party in contested litigation or administrative matters concerning an elder law issue.

(5) The categories are:

(A) Health and personal care planning, including giving advice regarding and preparing, advance medical directives (medical powers of attorney, living wills, and health care declarations) and counseling older persons, attorneys-in-fact, and families about medical and life-sustaining choices, and related personal life choices.

(B) Pre-mortem legal planning, including giving advice and preparing documents regarding wills, trusts, durable general or financial powers of attorney, real estate, gifting, and the financial and tax implications of any proposed action.

(C) Fiduciary representation, including seeking the appointment of, giving advice to, representing, or serving as executor, personal representative, attorney-in-fact, trustee, guardian, conservator, representative payee, or other formal or informal fiduciary.

(D) Legal capacity counseling, including advising how capacity is determined and the level of capacity required for various legal activities, and representing those who are or may be the subject of guardianship/conservatorship proceedings or other protective arrangements.

(E) Public benefits advice, including planning for and assisting in obtaining Medicare, Medicaid, Social Security, Supplemental Income, Veterans' benefits, and food stamps.

(F) Advice on insurance matters, including analyzing and explaining the types of insurance available, such as health, life, long-term care, home care, COBRA, medigap, long-term disability, dread disease, and burial/funeral policies.

(G) Resident rights advocacy, including advising patients and residents of hospitals, nursing facilities, continuing care facilities, and those cared for in their homes of their rights and appropriate remedies in matters such as admission, transfer and discharge policies, quality of care, and related issues.

(H) Housing counseling, including reviewing the options available and the financing of those options such as mortgage alternatives, renovation loan programs, life care contracts, and home equity conversion.

(I) Employment and retirement advice, including pensions, retiree health benefits, unemployment benefits, and other benefits.

(J) Income, estate, and gift tax advice, including consequences of plans made and advice offered.

(K) Counseling about tort claims against nursing homes.

(L) Counseling with regard to age and/or disability discrimination in employment and housing.

(M) Litigation and administrative advocacy in connection with any of the above matters, including will contests, contested capacity issues, elder abuse (including financial or consumer fraud), fiduciary administration, public benefits, nursing home torts, and discrimination.

(d) Peer Review. The applicant shall submit the names and addresses of 5 other attorneys who are familiar with the applicant's practice, not including attorneys who currently practice in the applicant's law firm, who can attest to the applicant's special competence and substantial involvement in the field of elder law. The board of legal specialization and education and elder law certification committee may authorize references from persons other than attorneys and may also make such additional inquiries as they deem appropriate to complete peer review, as provided elsewhere in these rules.

(e) Education. The applicant must demonstrate that during the 3–year period immediately preceding the date of application, the applicant has met the continuing legal education requirements in elder law as follows. The required number of hours shall be established by the board of legal specialization and education and shall in no event be less than 60 hours. Credit for attendance at continuing legal education seminars shall be given only for programs that are directly related to elder law. The education requirement may be satisfied by 1 or more of the following:

(1) attendance at continuing legal education seminars meeting the requirements set forth above;

(2) lecturing at, and/or serving on the steering committee of, such continuing legal education seminars;

(3) authoring articles or books published in professional periodicals or other professional publications;

(4) teaching courses in elder law at an approved law school or other graduate level program presented by a recognized professional education association;

(5) completing such home study programs as may be approved by the board of legal specialization and education or the elder law certification committee, subject to the limitation that no more than 50 percent of the required number of hours of education may be satisfied through home study programs; or

(6) such other methods as may be approved by the board of legal specialization and education and the elder law certification committee.

The elder law certification committee shall establish policies applicable to this subdivision, including, but not limited to, the method of establishment of the number of hours allocable to any of the preceding requirements. Such policies shall provide that hours shall be allocable to each separate but substantially different lecture, article, or other activity described in subdivisions (2), (3), and (4) above.

(f) Examination. The applicant must pass an examination designed to demonstrate sufficient knowledge, proficiency, and experience in elder law to justify the representation of special competence to the legal profession and the public.

(g) Exemption. Any applicant who as of the effective date of these standards is: currently certified by the National Elder Law Foundation and meets all other requirements set forth under subdivisions (a) through (e), shall be exempt from the examination. This exemption shall only be applicable with respect to any applicant meeting the aforesaid requirements and whose application is submitted within 2 years from the effective date of these standards.

Added July 17, 1997 (697 So.2d 115). Amended ______, ____, by the Board of Governors of The Florida Bar.

Rule 6-20.4. Recertification

To be eligible for recertification, an applicant must meet the following requirements:

(a) Substantial Involvement. Applicants must demonstrate a satisfactory showing as determined by the board of legal specialization and education and the elder law certification committee, of continuous and substantial involvement in the field of elder law throughout the period since the last date of certification. The demonstration of substantial involvement shall be made in accordance with the standards set forth in rule 6-20.3(b) and (c).

(b) Continuing Legal Education. Applicants must demonstrate the completion of at least 125 hours of continuing legal education since the filing of the last application for certification (or recertification). The continuing legal education must logically be expected to enhance the proficiency of attorneys who are board certified elder law attorneys. If the applicant has not attained 125 hours of continuing legal education, but has attained more than 75 hours during such period, successful passage of the written examination given by the board of legal specialization and education to new applicants shall satisfy the continuing legal education requirements.

(c) Peer Review. Peer review shall be conducted in accordance with the standards set forth in rule 6-20.3(d).

Added July 17, 1997 (697 So.2d 115).

6-21. STANDARDS FOR CERTIFICATION OF A BOARD CERTIFIED INTERNATIONAL LAWYER

Rule 6-21.1. Generally

A lawyer who is a member in good standing of The Florida Bar and who meets the standards prescribed below may be issued an appropriate certificate identifying the lawyer as a "Board Certified International Lawyer." The purpose of the standards is to identify those lawyers who practice in the area of international law and have the special knowledge, skills, and proficiency to be properly identified to the public as certified international lawyers.

Added Dec. 18, 1997, effective Jan. 1, 1998 (702 So.2d 1261). Amended April 9, 1999, by the Board of Governors of The Florida Bar.

Rule 6-21.2. Definitions

(a) International Law. "International law" is the practice of law dealing with issues, problems, or disputes arising from any and all aspects of the relations between or among states and international organizations as well as the relations between or among nationals of different countries, or between a state and a national of another state, including transnational business transactions, multinational taxation, customs, and trade. The term "international law" includes foreign and comparative law.

(b) Practice of Law. The "practice of law" for this area is defined as set out in rule 6-3.5(c)(1). Practice of law that otherwise satisfies these requirements but that is on a part-time basis will satisfy the requirement if the balance of the applicant's activity is spent as a teacher of international law subjects in an accredited law school.

Added Dec. 18, 1997, effective Jan. 1, 1998 (702 So.2d 1261). Amended April 9, 1999, by the Board of Governors of The Florida Bar.

Rule 6-21.3. Minimum Standards

(a) Minimum Period of Practice. The applicant shall have been engaged in the practice of law, either in the United States or abroad, and shall have been a member in good standing of the bar of any state of the United States or the District of Columbia, for a period of not less than 5 years as of the date of application. The years of law practice need not be consecutive. Receipt of an LL.M. degree in international law, as defined in rule 6-21.2(a), or in such other field as may be approved by the international law certification committee, shall be deemed to constitute 1 year of the practice of law requirement, but not the 5-year bar membership requirement, specified in this subdivision.

(b) Substantial Involvement. The applicant shall demonstrate substantial involvement in the practice of international law during each of the 3 years immediately preceding the date of application. Except for the 2 years immediately preceding application, receipt of an LL.M. degree, as defined in rule 6-21.2(a), may substitute for 1 year of substantial involvement. Substantial involvement shall mean that the applicant has devoted 50 percent or more of the applicant's practice to matters in which issues of international law played a significant role and in which the applicant had substantial and direct participation. For purposes of this subdivision, time devoted to lecturing on or writing about international law may be included. Although demonstration of compliance with this requirement shall be made initially through a form approved by the international law certification committee, the international law certification committee may at its option require written or oral supplementation.

(c) Education. The applicant shall demonstrate that during the 3-year period immediately preceding the date of application, the applicant has completed at least 60 hours of continuing legal education in the field of international law. This requirement can be met through: attendance at continuing legal education seminars on international law; satisfactory completion of graduate level law school courses while enrolled in an LL.M. program in international law or comparative law; satisfactory completion of graduate level law school courses involving international law aspects while enrolled in a graduate law program; lecturing at continuing legal education seminars on international law; authoring articles or books on international law; or teaching courses on international law at an accredited law school. The international law certification committee shall promulgate uniform regulations for the operation of the subdivision.

(d) Peer Review. The applicant shall submit the names and addresses of 5 other attorneys or judges who are familiar with the applicant's practice, excluding individuals who currently are employed by the same employer as the applicant, and who can attest to the applicant's special competence and substantial involvement in international law, as well as the applicant's character, ethics, and reputation for professionalism. The international law certification committee may at its option send reference forms to other attorneys and judges.

(e) Examination. The applicant shall take and pass an examination designed to demonstrate sufficient knowledge, skills, and proficiency in international law to justify the representation of special competence to the legal profession and the public.

Added Dec. 18, 1997, effective Jan. 1, 1998 (702 So.2d 1261). Amended April 9, 1999, by the Board of Governors of The Florida Bar; ______, ____, by the Board of Governors of The Florida Bar.

Rule 6-21.4. Recertification

Recertification shall be pursuant to the following standards:

(a) Substantial Involvement. The applicant shall demonstrate continuous and substantial involvement in the practice of international law throughout the period since the last date of certification. The demonstration of substantial involvement shall be made in accordance with the standards set forth in rule 6-21.3(b).

(b) Education. The applicant shall show completion of at least 75 hours of continuing legal education in international law since the filing of the last application for certification. In determining whether an applicant has satisfied this requirement, the standards set forth in rule 6-21.3(c) shall be followed.

(c) Peer Review. The applicant shall submit the names and addresses of 5 other attorneys or judges who are familiar with the applicant's practice, excluding individuals who currently are employed by the same employer as the applicant, and who can attest to the applicant's special competence and substantial involvement in international law, as well as the applicant's character, ethics, and reputation for professionalism. The international law certification committee may at its option send reference forms to other attorneys and judges.

(d) Examination. If, after reviewing the material submitted for recertification, the international law certification committee determines that the applicant may not meet the standards established by this chapter, it may require, as a condition of recertification, that the applicant take and pass the examination specified in rule 6-21.3(e).

Added Dec. 18, 1997, effective Jan. 1, 1998 (702 So.2d 1261). Amended April 9, 1999, by the Board of Governors of The Florida Bar.

6-22. STANDARDS FOR CERTIFICATION OF A BOARD CERTIFIED ANTITRUST AND TRADE REGULATION LAWYER

Rule 6-22.1. Generally

A lawyer who is a member in good standing of The Florida Bar and who meets the standards prescribed below may be issued an appropriate certificate identifying the lawyer as a "Board Certified Antitrust and Trade Regulation Lawyer." The purpose of the standards is to identify those lawyers who practice in the area of antitrust law, unfair methods of competition, and deceptive, unfair, or unconscionable trade practices and who have the special knowledge, skills, experience, and judgment, as well as the character, ethics, and reputation for professionalism, to be properly identified to the public as certified antitrust and trade regulation lawyers. Applicants shall be required to establish that they have a special ability as a consequence of broad and varied experience in antitrust and trade regulation law, including the following:

(a) a ready grasp of the substantive and procedural law bearing upon this area of practice;

(b) an awareness of and experience with the range of appropriate courses of action and remedies that can be invoked in aid of clients involved in such matters;

(c) a sound judgment in proposing solutions and approaches, so that proportion both as to expense and delay is maintained between the nature of the problem to be solved and the cost and elaborateness of the proposed response or solution; and

(d) an attitude of professionalism in every aspect of the applicant's approach to clients, courts, or administrative bodies, and fellow practitioners.

Added and amended March 23, 2000 (763 So.2d 1002). Amended Dec. 5, 2003, by the Board of Governors of The Florida Bar; Dec. 8, 2006, by the Governors of The Florida Bar.

Rule 6–22.2. Definitions

(a) Antitrust Law. "Antitrust law" covers the practice of law dealing with anticompetitive conduct or structure that may reduce consumer welfare in the United States. The primary federal antitrust laws are the Sherman Act, the Clayton Act, the Robinson–Patman Amendments to the Clayton Act, and the Federal Trade Commission Act. In addition, there are parallel state statutes. Generally, the practices that the antitrust laws are concerned with involve, but are not limited to: price fixes, limitations on production, division of markets, boycotts, attempts to monopolize and monopolization, tying of products, covenants to restrain trade, exclusive dealing contracts, price discrimination, and other exclusionary, predatory, or economically discriminatory activities.

(b) Trade Regulation Law. "Trade regulation law" covers the substantive area of law dealing with deceptive, unfair, or unconscionable acts or practices, and unfair methods of competition under the Federal Trade Commission Act and Florida's Deceptive and Unfair Trade Practices Act.

(c) Practice of Law. The "practice of law" for this area is defined as set forth in rule 6–3.5(c)(1).

(d) Contested Matters. "Contested matters" shall be defined as matters that were pending before an enforcement agency, a tribunal, or court that were adversarial and binding in which the applicant had a significant responsibility and personal involvement, and in which the applicant evaluated, handled, and resolved issues of fact and law in a dispute that involved antitrust or trade regulation law, either by reaching an adjudicated decision, or by achieving a settlement of a matter after it was the subject of substantial litigation or proceedings before an enforcement authority.

(e) Adjudicated Decision. An "adjudicated decision" on significant issues of antitrust or trade regulation law shall be defined as a decision resulting from a proceeding in which:

(1) a tribunal rendered a decision on a motion for temporary or preliminary injunction, or following an evidentiary hearing involving live testimony;

(2) a tribunal rendered a decision on a motion for summary judgment;

(3) a tribunal rendered a decision following briefing; or

(4) a tribunal or jury rendered a decision following a trial, or a court of appeals rendered a decision following an appeal. A single proceeding may generate multiple adjudicated decisions and an applicant shall receive credit for each such adjudicated decision as a separate contested matter; however, for purposes of certification, the number of adjudicated decisions from any single case within a 3–year period shall be limited to 2, absent extraordinary circumstances.

Added and amended March 23, 2000 (763 So.2d 1002). Amended Dec. 5, 2003, by the Board of Governors of The Florida Bar.

Rule 6–22.3. Minimum Standards

(a) Substantial Involvement and Competence. To become certified as an antitrust and trade regulation lawyer, an applicant must demonstrate continuous and substantial involvement and competence in substantive antitrust principles and deceptive, unfair, or unconscionable acts or practices in multiple areas of commerce. Substantial involvement and competence shall be demonstrated by:

(1) *Minimum Period of Practice.* The applicant must have actually practiced law for 5 years immediately preceding the filing of the application for certification, during which the applicant was involved in at least 8 matters that substantially involved antitrust or trade regulation law.

(2) *Minimum Number of Matters.* The applicant must have handled a minimum of 8 contested matters that involved representation of a client beyond counseling during the 10 years immediately preceding application. All such matters must have substantially involved legal and factual issues, and at least 50 percent of the matters must have involved federal antitrust law or state or federal trade regulation law. In each of these 8 matters, the applicant shall have had senior level responsibility for all or a majority of the counseling, advice, and supervision, of or involvement in: presentation of evidence, argument to the tribunal, and representation of the client. For satisfaction in whole or in part of the requirement of 8 contested matters, the antitrust and trade regulation certification committee shall consider involvement in protracted matters as separate matters on the following basis: every documented 300 hours of work on antitrust or trade regulation issues in a case shall be considered to be the equivalent of an additional matter for purposes of meeting the threshold of a minimum of 8 contested matters during the 10 years immediately preceding application. For good cause shown, for satisfaction in whole or in part of the requirement of 8 matters in which the applicant had senior level responsibility, the antitrust and trade regulation certification committee shall consider the following: (a) verified substantial involvement in matters involving antitrust law or trade regulation law at a government agency, and (b) in lieu of 2 contested matters, an applicant may submit a certificate of satisfactory completion of a nationally recognized trial advocacy course of at least a week's duration, in which the applicant's performance was, in whole or in part, recorded visually and critiqued by experienced trial lawyers.

(3) *Substantial Involvement.* The applicant shall have substantial involvement in matters involving federal antitrust, state or federal trade regulation law

sufficient to demonstrate special competence as an antitrust and trade regulation lawyer. Substantial involvement may be evidenced by active participation in client interviewing, counseling, evaluating, investigating, preparing pleadings, motions, and memoranda, participating in discovery, taking testimony, briefing issues, presenting evidence, negotiating settlement, drafting and preparing settlement agreements, and/or arguing, trying, or appealing cases involving antitrust law or trade regulation law.

(b) Peer Review. The applicant shall select and submit names and addresses of at least 5 lawyers or judges, who are neither relatives nor present or former associates or partners, as references to attest to the applicant's substantial involvement in antitrust and trade regulation law, as well as the applicant's character, ethics, and reputation for professionalism. Such lawyers should be substantially involved in antitrust and trade regulation law and familiar with the applicant's practice. In addition, the antitrust and trade regulation certification committee may, at its option, send reference forms to other attorneys, judges, or officers and make such other investigation and verification as necessary.

(c) Education. The applicant shall demonstrate completion of at least 50 hours of approved continuing legal education in the field of antitrust and trade regulation law within the 3 years preceding the date of application. Accreditation of educational hours is subject to policies established by the antitrust and trade regulation certification committee or the board of legal specialization and education.

(d) Examination. The applicant must pass an examination applied uniformly to all applicants to demonstrate sufficient knowledge, skills, and proficiency in antitrust and trade regulation law to justify representation of special competence to the legal profession and to the public. The award of an LL.M. degree from an approved law school in the area of antitrust or trade regulation law, within 8 years of application, may substitute as the written examination required by this subdivision. Any lawyer who is certified by The Florida Bar in business litigation or civil trial law, and who meets the minimum standards of subdivisions (a)–(c) of this rule, shall be exempted from the portion (if any) of the examination requirement of this subdivision that deals with the litigation process as distinguished from substantive law.

(e) Exemption. An applicant who has been substantially involved in antitrust and trade regulation law for a minimum of 20 years, in accordance with the standards set forth in rule 6–3.5(d) and subdivision (a)(3) of this rule, shall be exempt from the examination. This exemption only shall be applicable to those applicants who apply within 4 years of the effective date of the approval of this exemption and meet all other requirements for certification.

Added and amended March 23, 2000 (763 So.2d 1002). Amended Dec. 5, 2003, by the Board of Governors of The Florida Bar; Feb. 17, 2006, by the Board of Governors of The Florida Bar; Dec. 8, 2006, by the Board of Governors of The Florida Bar.

Rule 6–22.4. Recertification

During the 5-year period immediately preceding application, an applicant must satisfy the following requirements for recertification:

(a) Substantial Involvement. The applicant must show continuous and substantial involvement in the field of antitrust and trade regulation law. The demonstration of substantial involvement shall be made by showing that antitrust and trade regulation law comprises at least 30 percent of the applicant's practice, and that the applicant actively participated in client interviewing, counseling, evaluating, investigating, preparing pleadings, motions, and memoranda, participating in discovery, taking testimony, briefing issues, presenting evidence, negotiating settlement, drafting and preparing settlement agreements, and/or arguing, trying, or appealing cases involving antitrust or trade regulation law.

(b) Minimum Number of Matters. The applicant must have handled a minimum of 4 contested antitrust or trade regulation matters. All contested matters must have involved substantial legal or factual issues in the law of antitrust or trade regulation as determined by the certification committee. On good cause shown, for satisfaction in part of the 4 antitrust or trade regulation matters, the antitrust and trade regulation certification committee may consider involvement in protracted matters on the same basis as set forth in rule 6–22.3(a)(2).

(c) Peer Review. An applicant for recertification must submit the names and addresses of at least 3 lawyers and 1 federal or state judge or administrative law judge before whom the applicant has appeared as an advocate within the period since the last certification or recertification. Individuals used as references shall be sufficiently familiar with the applicant to attest to the applicant's special competence and substantial involvement in antitrust and trade regulation law, as well as the applicant's character, ethics, and reputation for professionalism. Lawyers who practiced law with the applicant during the recertification period and relatives may not be used as references. The antitrust and trade regulation certification committee may, at its option, send or authorize references to other attorneys, federal or state judges, or administrative law judges.

(d) Education. The applicant must demonstrate completion of at least 50 credit hours of approved continuing legal education for antitrust and trade regulation certification, in accordance with the standards set forth in rule 6–22.3(c).

(e) Waiver of Compliance. The antitrust and trade regulation certification committee may waive compliance with subdivisions (a)–(b) of this rule for:

(1) an applicant who has been continuously certified as an antitrust and trade regulation lawyer for a period of 14 years or more; or

(2) an applicant who, since the last certification or recertification, has become an officer of any judicial system (as defined in the Code of Judicial Conduct), including an officer such as a magistrate judge or administrative law judge, or who is a member of the Federal Trade Commission (or a member of its staff), or an assistant attorney general in the Antitrust Division of the Department of Justice (or a member of his or her staff), or an assistant attorney general in the Antitrust Division of a state attorney general's office on a full-time basis during the portion of the period since the last date of certification or recertification; or

(3) good cause shown.

Added and amended March 23, 2000 (763 So.2d 1002). Amended Dec. 15, 2003, by the Board of Governors of The Florida Bar; Aug. 26, 2005, by the Board of Governors of The Florida Bar; Dec. 8, 2006, by the Board of Governors of The Florida Bar.

6-23. STANDARDS FOR CERTIFICATION OF BOARD CERTIFIED LABOR AND EMPLOYMENT LAWYER

Rule 6-23.1. Generally

A lawyer who is a member in good standing of The Florida Bar and who meets the standards prescribed below may be issued an appropriate certificate identifying the lawyer as a "Board Certified Labor and Employment Lawyer." The purpose of the standards is to identify those lawyers who practice labor and employment law and who have demonstrated special knowledge, skills, and proficiency to be properly identified to the public as certified labor and employment lawyers.

Added and amended March 23, 2000 (763 So.2d 1002).

Rule 6-23.2. Definitions

(a) Labor and Employment Law. The practice of labor and employment law encompasses advice and representation concerning the application and interpretation of public and private sector labor and employment law principles, as well as employment discrimination and employment-related civil rights law. The diversity of this practice area is demonstrated by the experience requirements set forth in rule 6-23.3(c), however, competent practice in labor and employment law requires a thorough knowledge of all legal aspects of the employment relationship, both in the private and public sector. This knowledge is particularly necessary to fulfill the counseling obligations of attorneys toward their clients. This practice area encompasses both public and private sector collective bargaining and the many state and federal laws that apply to the employment relationship including, but not limited to:

(1) the National Labor Relations Act, as amended;

(2) the Fair Labor Standards Act;

(3) Florida's public sector collective bargaining laws and career service appeals;

(4) the Employment Retirement Income Security Act;

(5) the Family Medical Leave Act;

(6) Title VII of the 1964 Civil Rights Act and Florida's Civil Rights Act;

(7) the Americans With Disabilities Act;

(8) Occupational Safety and Health Act;

(9) the Age Discrimination in Employment Act; and

(10) the regulations promulgated thereunder.

(b) Practice of Law. The "practice of law" for this area is defined as set out in rule 6-3.5(c)(1).

Added and amended March 23, 2000 (763 So.2d 1002).

Rule 6-23.3. Minimum Standards

(a) Minimum Period of Practice. The applicant shall have at least 5 years of actual law practice of which at least 50 percent has been spent in active participation in labor and employment law. At least 5 years of this practice shall be immediately preceding the application for certification. An LL.M. in the field of labor and employment law may substitute for 1 of the 5 years of law practice required.

(b) Substantial Involvement. Substantial involvement means the applicant has devoted 50 percent or more of the applicant's practice to matters in which issues of labor and employment law are significant factors and in which the applicant had substantial and direct participation in those labor and employment law issues. An applicant must furnish information concerning the frequency of the applicant's work and the nature of the issues involved. Demonstration of this requirement shall be made initially through a form questionnaire approved by the labor and employment law certification committee, but written or oral supplementation may be required.

(c) Experience. The applicant shall have a total of 30 days acting as the primary attorney, judge, hearing officer, arbitrator, or mediator in litigation and/or administrative proceedings concerning labor and employment law issues, including but not limited to evidentiary hearings, arbitrations, collective bargaining, representing clients in relation to governmental agencies, mediations, court hearings, taking depositions, and oral arguments. Any such proceeding lasting less than 8 hours, but more than 5 hours, shall be credited a full day. Any such proceeding lasting less than 4 hours, but at least 1 hour, shall be credited a half day. This experience shall have been attained within the 5 years immediately preceding the filing of the application for certification.

(d) Peer Review. The applicant shall submit the names and addresses of 6 attorneys who are familiar with the applicant's practice, excluding attorneys who currently practice in the applicant's law firm, who can attest to the applicant's special competence and substantial involvement in the field of labor and employment law, as well as the applicant's character, ethics, and reputation for professionalism. The labor and employment law certification committee shall seek at least 3 additional secondary references. At least 1 of the 6 references shall be from a judge, arbitrator, mediator, or administrator before whom the applicant has appeared or practiced (or in the case of a mediator or arbitrator seeking certification, such references may be from attorneys who have appeared before the applicant) within the 2 years immediately preceding the application.

(e) Education. The applicant must demonstrate that during the 3–year period immediately preceding the date of the application, the applicant has met the continuing legal education requirements in labor and employment law. The required number of hours shall be established by the board of legal specialization and education and shall in no event be less than 60 hours. Credit for attendance at continuing legal education seminars shall be given only for programs that are directly related to labor and employment law. The board of legal specialization and education or the labor and employment law certification committee shall establish policies applicable to this rule. The education requirement may be satisfied by 1 or more of the following:

(1) attendance at continuing legal education seminars in labor and employment law;

(2) lecturing at continuing legal education seminars in labor and employment law;

(3) authoring articles, books, or other professional publications on labor and employment law;

(4) teaching courses in labor and employment law at an accredited law school or other graduate-level program presented by a recognized professional education association;

(5) completing such home study programs as may be approved by the board of legal specialization and education or the labor and employment law certification committee, subject to the limitation that no more than 50 percent of the required number of hours of education may be satisfied through home study programs; or

(6) such other methods as may be approved by the board of legal specialization and education and the labor and employment law certification committee.

(f) Examination. The applicant must pass an examination applied uniformly to all applicants, to demonstrate sufficient knowledge, proficiency, and experience in labor and employment law to justify the representation of special competence to the legal profession and the public. The examination will be comprehensive in scope and each applicant will be required to demonstrate at least some knowledge in each specific subject tested. However, applicants will be given the opportunity to emphasize their special knowledge in any 1 or more specific subject areas.

(g) Exemption. An applicant who has been substantially involved in labor and employment law for a minimum of 20 years, in accordance with the standards set forth in rules 6–3.5(d) and 6–23.3(b), shall be exempt from the examination. This exemption is only applicable to those applicants who apply within 2 years of the effective date of these standards and meet all other requirements for certification.

Added and amended March 23, 2000 (763 So.2d 1002). Amended Aug. 26, 2005, by the Board of Governors of The Florida Bar.

Rule 6–23.4. Recertification

Recertification shall be pursuant to the following standards:

(a) Substantial Involvement. The applicant shall demonstrate continuous and substantial involvement in labor and employment law throughout the period since filing the last application for certification. Substantial involvement means the applicant has devoted 50 percent or more of the applicant's practice to matters in which issues of labor and employment law are significant factors and in which the applicant had substantial and direct participation in those labor and employment law issues. An applicant must furnish information concerning the frequency of the applicant's work and the nature of the issues involved. Demonstration of this requirement shall be made initially through a form questionnaire approved by the labor and employment law certification committee, but written or oral supplementation may be required.

(b) Experience. The applicant shall have 25 days of involvement in contested matters involving labor and employment law issues throughout the period since filing the last application for certification. Applicants must have acted as the primary attorney, judge, hearing officer, arbitrator, or mediator in litigation and/or administrative proceedings concerning labor and employment law issues, including, but not limited to evidentiary hearings, arbitrations, collective bargaining, representing clients in relation to governmental agencies, mediations, court hearings, taking depositions, and oral arguments, throughout the period since filing the last application for certification. Any such proceeding lasting less than 8 hours, but more than 5 hours, shall be credited as a full day. Any such proceeding lasting less than 4 hours, but at least 1 hour, shall be credited as a half day.

Direct supervision of attorneys engaged in contested matters, as defined above, may be considered in determining compliance with this requirement.

(c) Education. The applicant shall complete no less than 75 hours of continuing legal education in the area of labor and employment law, since filing the last application for certification. Credit for attendance at continuing legal education seminars shall be given only for programs that are directly related to labor and employment law. The board of legal specialization and education or the labor and employment law certification committee shall establish policies applicable to this rule. The education requirement may be satisfied by 1 or more of the following:

(1) attendance at continuing legal education seminars in labor and employment law;

(2) lecturing at continuing legal education seminars in labor and employment law;

(3) authoring articles, books, or other professional publications on labor and employment law;

(4) teaching courses in labor and employment law at an accredited law school or other graduate-level program presented by a recognized professional education association;

(5) completing such home study programs as may be approved by the board of legal specialization and education or the labor and employment law certification committee, subject to the limitation that no more than 50 percent of the required number of hours of education may be satisfied through home study programs; or

(6) such other methods as may be approved by the board of legal specialization and education and the labor and employment law certification committee.

If the applicant has not attained 75 hours, successful passage of the examination given to new applicants for certification shall satisfy this requirement.

(d) Peer Review. The applicant shall submit the names and addresses of at least 3 attorneys and at least 1 judge, arbitrator, mediator, or administrator before whom the attorney has appeared or practiced since the last application for certification. The references may not include lawyers who currently practice in the applicant's law firm. Each reference must attest to the applicant's reputation for special competence and substantial involvement in the field of labor and employment law, as well as the applicant's character, ethics, and reputation for professionalism.

(e) Waiver of Compliance. For an applicant who has been continuously certified as a labor and employment lawyer for a period of 14 years or more, the labor and employment law certification committee may waive compliance with either the experience or substantial involvement criterion for recertification, for good cause shown and provided the applicant has complied with all other requirements for recertification.

Added and amended March 23, 2000 (763 So.2d 1002). Amended Aug. 26, 2005, by the Board of Governors of The Florida Bar.

6–24. STANDARDS FOR CERTIFICATION OF A BOARD CERTIFIED CONSTRUCTION LAW LAWYER

Rule 6–24.1. Generally

A lawyer who is a member in good standing of The Florida Bar and who meets the standards prescribed below may be issued an appropriate certificate identifying the lawyer as a "Board Certified Construction Lawyer." The purpose of the standards is to identify those lawyers who practice construction law and have the special knowledge, skills, and proficiency, as well as the character, ethics, and reputation for professionalism, to be properly identified to the public as certified construction lawyers.

Added May 20, 2004 (875 So.2d 448).

Rule 6–24.2. Definitions

(a) Construction Law. "Construction law" is the practice of law dealing with matters relating to the design and construction of improvements on private and public projects including, but not limited to, construction dispute resolution, contract negotiation, preparation, award and administration, lobbying in governmental hearings, oversight and document review, construction lending and insurance, construction licensing, and the analysis and litigation of problems arising out of the Florida Construction Lien Law, section 255.05, Florida Statutes, and the federal Miller Act, 40 U. S.C. § 270.

(b) Practice of Law. The "practice of law" for this area is set out in rule 6–3.5(c)(1).

(c) Construction Law Certification Committee. The construction law certification committee shall include a minimum of 3 members with experience in transactional construction law and 3 members with experience in construction law litigation.

Added May 20, 2004 (875 So.2d 448).

Rule 6–24.3. Minimum Standards

(a) Minimum Period of Practice. The applicant shall have been engaged in the practice of law in the United States, or engaged in the practice of United States law while in a foreign country, and shall have been a member in good standing of the bar of any state of the United States or the District of Columbia for a period of 5 years as of the date of filing an application. The years of law practice need not be consecutive.

(b) Substantial Involvement. To become certified as a construction lawyer, a lawyer must demonstrate substantial involvement in construction law. Substantial involvement shall include the following:

(1) At least 5 years of actual practice of law of which at least 40 percent has been spent in active participation in construction law. At least 3 years of this practice shall be immediately preceding application.

(2) Substantial involvement means the applicant has devoted 40 percent or more of the applicant's practice to matters in which issues of construction law are significant factors and in which the applicant had substantial and direct participation in those construction law issues. An applicant must furnish information concerning the frequency of the applicant's work and the nature of the issues involved. For the purposes of this subdivision the "practice of law" shall be as defined in rule 6–3.5(c)(1), except that it shall also include time devoted to lecturing and/or authoring books or articles on construction law if the applicant was engaged in the practice of law during such period. Demonstration of compliance with this requirement shall be made initially through a form of questionnaire approved by the construction law certification committee but written or oral supplementation may be required.

(c) Peer Review. The applicant shall submit the names and addresses of 5 attorneys who are familiar with the applicant's practice, not including attorneys who currently practice in the applicant's law firm, who can attest to the applicant's special competence and substantial involvement in the field of construction law, as well as the applicant's character, ethics, and reputation for professionalism. The board of legal specialization and education and the construction law certification committee may authorize references from persons other than attorneys and may also make such additional inquiries as deemed appropriate.

(d) Education. The applicant must demonstrate that during the 3–year period immediately preceding the date of application, the applicant has met the continuing legal education requirements in construction law as follows. The required number of hours shall be established by the board of legal specialization and education and shall in no event be less than 45 hours. Credit for attendance at continuing legal education seminars shall be given only for programs that are directly related to construction law. The education requirement may be satisfied by 1 or more of the following:

(1) attendance at continuing legal education seminars meeting the requirements set forth above;

(2) lecturing at, and/or serving on the steering committee of, such continuing legal education seminars;

(3) authoring articles or books published in professional periodicals or other professional publications;

(4) teaching courses in construction law at an approved law school or other graduate level program presented by a recognized professional education association;

(5) completing such home study programs as may be approved by the board of legal specialization and education or the construction law certification committee, subject to the limitation that no more than 50 percent of the required number of hours of education may be satisfied through home study programs; or

(6) such other methods as may be approved by the board of legal specialization and education and the construction law certification committee.

The board of legal specialization and education and the construction law certification committee shall establish policies applicable to this rule, including, but not limited to, approval of credit hours allocable to any of the above-listed continuing legal education activities. Such policies shall provide that credit hours shall be allocable to each separate but substantially different lecture, article, or other activity described in subdivisions (2), (3), and (4) above.

(e) Examination. The applicant must pass an examination, applied uniformly to all applicants, to demonstrate sufficient knowledge, proficiency, and experience in the practice of law applicable to the design and construction of projects in Florida construction law to justify the representation of special competence to the legal profession and the public.

Added May 20, 2004 (875 So.2d 448).

Rule 6–24.4. Recertification

Recertification shall be pursuant to the following standards:

(a) Substantial Involvement. A satisfactory showing, as determined by the board of legal specialization and education and the certification committee, of continuous and substantial involvement in construction law throughout the period since the last date of certification. The demonstration of substantial involvement of 40 percent or more during each year after certification or prior recertification shall be made in accordance with the standards set forth in rule 6–24.3(b).

(b) Education. Completion of at least 75 hours of continuing legal education since the last application for certification (or recertification). The continuing legal education must logically be expected to enhance the proficiency of attorneys who are board certified in construction law.

(c) Peer Review. An applicant for recertification shall submit the names and addresses of 5 attorneys or judges who are familiar with the applicant's practice, not including lawyers who currently practice in the applicant's law firm, who can attest to the applicant's reputation for special competence and substantial involvement in the field of construction law, as well as the applicant's character, ethics, and reputation for professionalism. The board of legal specialization and education and the construction law certification committee may also make such additional inquiries as they deem appropriate.

Added May 20, 2004 (875 So.2d 448).

6–25. STANDARDS FOR CERTIFICATION OF A BOARD CERTIFIED STATE AND FEDERAL GOVERNMENT AND ADMINISTRATIVE PRACTICE LAWYER

Rule 6–25.1. Generally

A lawyer who is a member in good standing of The Florida Bar and who meets the standards prescribed below may be issued an appropriate certificate identifying the lawyer as a "Board Certified State and Federal Government and Administrative Practice Lawyer." The purpose of the standards is to identify those lawyers who practice law before or on behalf of state and federal government entities and have the special knowledge, skills, and proficiency, as well as the character, ethics, and reputation for professionalism to be properly identified to the public as certified state and federal government and administrative practice lawyers.

Added July 6, 2006, effective August 1, 2006 (933 So.2d 1123).

Rule 6–25.2. Definitions

(a) State and Federal Government and Administrative Practice. "State and federal government and administrative practice" is the practice of law on behalf of public or private clients on matters including but not limited to rulemaking or adjudication associated with state or federal government entity actions such as contracts, licenses, orders, permits, policies, or rules. State and federal government and administrative practice also includes appearing before or presiding as an administrative law judge, arbitrator, hearing officer, or member of an administrative tribunal or panel over a dispute involving an administrative or government action.

(b) Government Entity. "Government entity" means any state agency, political subdivision, special district, or instrumentality of the state of Florida, and any federal agency, bureau, corporation, instrumentality or other government body of the United States, including the United States armed forces. This definition should be broadly construed.

(c) Lead Advocate. "Lead advocate" means serving as the primary attorney, whether as a team leader or alone, working on behalf of either a private party or a government entity. Service as a supervisor and signatory of legal documents, but without substantial participation in the preparation of those documents, does not constitute service as a lead advocate. Service in the role of lead advocate also includes presiding as an administrative law judge, arbitrator, hearing officer, or member of an administrative tribunal or panel over a dispute involving an administrative or government action.

(d) Practice of Law. The "practice of law" is defined as set forth in rule 6–3.5(c)(1).

(e) State and Federal Government and Administrative Practice Certification Committee. The state and federal government and administrative practice certification committee shall include at least 2 attorneys employed by government entities in Florida, at least 2 attorneys in private practice, at least 1 attorney with substantial experience in matters governed by the Federal Administrative Procedure Act, and at least 2 attorneys with substantial experience in government litigation.

Added July 6, 2006, effective August 1, 2006 (933 So.2d 1123). Amended effective December 10, 2010 by the Board of Governors of The Florida Bar.

Rule 6–25.3. Minimum Standards

(a) Minimum Period of Practice. The applicant must have been engaged in a state or federal government and administrative practice for at least 5 years preceding the date of application. The years of law practice need not be consecutive.

(b) Practice Requirements. The practice requirements shall be as follows:

(1) *Substantial Involvement.* The applicant must demonstrate substantial involvement in a state and federal government and administrative practice during 3 of the last 5 years immediately preceding application. Any applicant who meets the practical experience requirements in subdivisions 6–25.3(b)(2)(A)–(I) below is presumed to meet this requirement.

(2) *Practical Experience.* The applicant must demonstrate broad substantial practical experience in state or federal government and administrative practice by providing examples of service as the lead advocate on behalf of a private client or a government entity or instrumentality. Using the point values and limitations assigned below, the applicant's experience examples from the following actions must total at least 100 points and have been performed within 20 years preceding the filing of the application:

(A) administrative hearings, involving disputed issues of material fact [Section 120.57(1), Florida Statutes] and adjudicated through final order pursuant to the Florida Administrative Procedure Act, Chapter 120, Florida Statutes (5 points each);

(B) fully-adjudicated administrative actions or rulemaking proceedings pursuant to the Federal Administrative Procedure Act, 5 U.S.C. §§ 551–559, and other federal APA proceedings, including record review proceedings, pursuant to 5 U.S.C. §§ 701–706 (5 points each);

(C) any other fully-adjudicated state or federal administrative or civil proceeding before an administrative forum, hearing officer, magistrate, arbitrator, state or federal district, circuit or supreme court, or other forum, in which the applicant represents a party in a lawsuit brought by or against a government entity. Applicants are encouraged to identify cases involving state or federal constitutional or statutory matters, state or federal regulations, ethics, open government, public records, or sovereign immunity. Experience working on matters exclusively involving city, county, and local government law (such as code enforcement, municipal financing and licensing, local referenda, ordinances, and zoning) does not constitute practical experience for purposes of obtaining state and federal government and administrative practice certification (5 points each);

(D) rulemaking proceedings through rule adoption pursuant to the Florida Administrative Procedure Act, Chapter 120, Florida Statutes (3 points each);

(E) state or federal government or administrative actions as follows:

1. involvement in actions that are considered, pursuant to the Florida Administrative Procedure Act or the Federal Administrative Procedure Act, to provide a point of entry or otherwise create an opportunity for a person to seek to adjudicate legal rights in state or federal courts, or in an administrative forum. Examples may include, but are not limited to, policies, orders, emergency orders, permits, licenses, contracts, or other agency decisions, or intended decisions of state and federal government entities. Examples may not include documents requiring merely clerical completion (2 points each);

2. involvement as lead advocate in an administrative proceeding of the type identified herein, in which a written settlement agreement was negotiated and upon which the proceeding was terminated (2 points each);

3. involvement as lead advocate in an administrative proceeding of the type identified herein, in which a proposed administrative or government action or the challenge to the action was formally withdrawn (2 points each);

(F) other actions on behalf of state or federal government agencies, including military adjudicatory or rulemaking proceedings, that are the substantial equivalent of the practical experience categories identified herein, as determined at the sole discretion of the state and federal government and administrative practice certification committee after review of the application (1 to 4 points each);

(G) an advisory opinion issued by the Florida Commission on Ethics, Florida or United States Attorney General, or Supreme Court of Florida (1 point each);

(H) experience as legislative staff on a bill passed by the Florida Legislature and enacted into law within Chapters 119 (Public Records), 120 (Administrative Procedure Act), 286 (Open Meetings), or 287 (Procurement), Florida Statutes, or as staff for the Florida Legislature's Joint Administrative Procedures Committee on completed rulemaking initiatives (1 point each); or

(I) experience as judicial staff, or staff to an administrative law judge, arbitrator, hearing officer, or other administrative panel on fully-adjudicated cases consistent with this rule (1 point each).

The applicant may have a maximum of 40 points from examples within (F) through (I). If the applicant has no points within (A), (B), or (C), the applicant must have points from a minimum of 2 different categories within (D) through (I). The state and federal government and administrative practice certification committee may increase the number of points granted for activities of the type identified in subdivisions (b)(2)(A), (B), or (C), above, for good cause shown, such as an applicant's involvement as lead advocate in an administrative hearing that lasted more than 6 days.

(c) Peer Review. The applicant shall submit the names and addresses of 5 individuals, at least 4 of whom are attorneys and 1 of whom is a federal, state, or administrative law judge before whom the applicant has appeared within the 5 years immediately preceding application. Individuals who currently practice in the applicant's law firm or government entity may not be used as references. In lieu of a judicial reference, the applicant may provide the name and address of the head of a government entity (or a member of a collegial board that serves as the head of a government entity) if the applicant has advised or appeared before the person within the 5 years immediately preceding application. Administrative law judges or hearing officers applying for certification may offer the reference of an attorney who has appeared before them more than once, or, if appropriate, the reference of the chief administrative law judge or hearing officer. In all cases, at least 2 of the attorney references must be members of The Florida Bar. Individuals serving as references shall be sufficiently familiar with the applicant to attest to the applicant's special competence and substantial involvement in the field of state and federal government and administrative practice, as well as the applicant's character, ethics, and reputation for professionalism in the practice of law. The board of legal specialization and education and the state and federal government and administrative practice certification committee may authorize references from persons other than attorneys and may also make such additional inquiries as they deem appropriate to determine the applicant's qualifications for certification pursuant to this rule and rule 6-3.5(c)(6).

(d) Education. The applicant must demonstrate that during the 3-year period immediately preceding the date of application, the applicant has met the continuing legal education requirements in state and federal government and administrative practice. The required number of hours shall be established by the board of legal specialization and education and shall in no event be less than 50 hours for the 3 years immediately preceding the application for certification. Credit for attendance or speaking appearances at continuing legal education seminars shall be given only for programs that are directly related to state and federal government and administrative practice. In addition, the state and federal government and administrative practice certification committee may conclude that the education requirement is satisfied, in part, by 1 or more of the following:

(1) lecturing at continuing legal education seminars;

(2) authoring or editing articles or books published in professional periodicals or other professional publications;

(3) teaching courses directly related to state and federal government and administrative practice at an approved law school or other graduate level program presented by a recognized professional education association;

(4) completing such home study programs as may be approved by the board of legal specialization and education or the state and federal government and administrative practice certification committee, subject to the limitation that no more than 50 percent of the required number of hours of education may be satisfied through home study programs; or

(5) such other methods as may be approved by the board of legal specialization and education and the state and federal government and administrative practice certification committee.

The board of legal specialization and education or the state and federal government and administrative practice certification committee shall establish policies applicable to this rule including but not limited to the method of establishment of the number of hours allocable to any of the above-listed subdivisions. Such policies shall provide the hours that shall be allocable to each separate but substantially different lecture, article, or other activity described in subdivisions (1), (2), (3), and (4) above.

(e) Examination. The applicant must pass an examination applied uniformly to all applicants to demonstrate sufficient knowledge, proficiency, and experience in state and federal government and administrative practice to justify the representation of special competence to the legal profession and the public.

(f) Exemption. An applicant who has been substantially involved in state and federal government and administrative practice for a minimum of 20 years and who otherwise fulfills the standards set forth in rules 6-3.5(d) and 6-25.3(a)-(d), shall be exempt from the examination. This exemption is only applicable to those applicants who apply within the first 2 application filing periods from the effective date of these standards and who meet all other requirements for certification.

Added July 6, 2006, effective August 1, 2006 (933 So.2d 1123).

Rule 6-25.4. Recertification

Recertification shall be pursuant to the following standards:

(a) Substantial Involvement. A satisfactory showing, as determined by the board of legal specialization and education and the state and federal government and administrative practice certification committee, of continuous and substantial involvement in state and federal government and administrative practice throughout the period since the last date of certification or recertification. Any applicant who meets the practical experience and education requirements in paragraphs (b) and (c) below is presumed to meet this requirement.

(b) Practical Experience Requirement. An applicant seeking recertification must demonstrate involvement as the lead advocate on behalf of a private client or a government entity in state and federal government and administrative practice since certification or the last recertification, totaling at least 10 points as described in rule 6-25.3(b)(2)(A)-(I). For good cause shown, subject to approval by the board of legal specialization and education and the state and federal government and administrative practice certification committee, the 10-point requirement above may be waived for applicants who possess other extraordinary legal experience related to state and federal government and administrative practice. Examples of extraordinary experience may include: service as an administrative law judge; agency general counsel or other senior government attorney with supervisory responsibilities; representation of or membership on a committee working on substantial matters of state and federal government and administrative practice; and other appropriate legal experience described by the applicant.

(c) Education. The applicant must demonstrate completion of at least 90 hours of continuing legal education since the last application for certification or recertification. The continuing legal education hours must logically be expected to enhance the proficiency of attorneys who are board certified in state and federal government and administrative practice. If the applicant has not attained 90 hours of continuing legal education but has attained more than 60 hours during such period, successful passage of the examination given to new applicants shall satisfy the continuing legal education requirements. However, an applicant seeking recertification may also reduce the educational requirements in this subsection to 60 hours by demonstrating involvement as the lead advocate on behalf of a private client or a government entity in state and federal government and administrative practice since certification or the last recertification, totaling at least 25 points as described in rule 6–25.3(b)(2)(A)–(I).

(d) Peer Review. The applicant shall submit the names and addresses of 3 individuals, at least 2 of whom are attorneys and 1 of whom is a federal, state, or administrative law judge before whom the applicant has appeared within the past 5 years preceding the application. Individuals who currently practice in the applicant's law firm or government entity may not be used as references. In lieu of a judicial reference, the applicant may provide the name and address of the head of a government entity (or a member of a collegial board that serves as the head of a government entity) if the applicant has advised or appeared before the person within the 5 years preceding the application. At least 1 attorney reference must be a member of The Florida Bar. Individuals serving as references shall be sufficiently familiar with the applicant to attest to the applicant's special competence and substantial involvement in the field of state and federal government and administrative practice, as well as the applicant's character, ethics, and reputation for professionalism in the practice of law. The board of legal specialization and education and the state and federal government and administrative practice certification committee may authorize references from persons other than attorneys and may also make such additional inquiries as they deem appropriate to determine the applicant's qualifications for certification pursuant to this rule and rule 6–3.5(c)(6).

(e) Waiver of Compliance. Any applicant for recertification who at the time of application is serving and has served full time for 3 or more years as an administrative law judge, arbitrator, hearing officer, or member of an administrative tribunal or panel is deemed to meet the recertification criteria.

Added July 6, 2006, effective August 1, 2006 (933 So.2d 1123).

Rule 6–25.5. Manner of Listing Area of Certification

A member having received a certificate in state and federal government and administrative practice may list the area in the manner set forth under rule 6–3.9(a) or the listing may be abridged to indicate that the member is board certified in:

(1) state and federal government practice;

(2) state and federal administrative practice; or,

(3) Florida administrative practice.

A member who is certified pursuant to rule 6–25.3(f) and elects to have his or her listing limited to certification in state and federal administrative practice or Florida administrative practice shall have been certified with a minimum of 25 total points from examples in rule 6–25.3(b)(2)(A), (B), and (D).

Added July 6, 2006, effective August 1, 2006 (933 So.2d 1123). Amended effective December 10, 2010 by the Board of Governors of The Florida Bar.

6–26. STANDARDS FOR CERTIFICATION OF A BOARD CERTIFIED INTELLECTUAL PROPERTY LAWYER

Rule 6–26.1. Generally

A lawyer who is a member in good standing of The Florida Bar and who meets the standards prescribed below may be issued an appropriate certificate identifying the lawyer as a "Board Certified Intellectual Property Lawyer." The purpose of the standards is to identify those lawyers who practice intellectual property law and have the special knowledge, skills, and proficiency, as well as the character, ethics, and reputation for professionalism, to be properly identified to the public as certified intellectual property lawyers.

Added July 6, 2006, effective August 1, 2006 (933 So.2d 1123).

Rule 6–26.2. Definitions

(a) Patent Application Prosecution. "Patent application prosecution" covers the practice of law dealing with patent rights, and covers all aspects of the U. S. Patent Statutes, 35 U.S.C. §§ 1–376, as amended; the Rules of Practice in Patent Cases, 37 C.F.R. §§ 1.1—1.997, as amended; the American Inventors Protection Act of 1999, United States Patent and Trademark Office (USPTO) rules of practice, the Manual of Patent Examining Procedure (MPEP), the Patent Cooperation Treaty (as modified by any later court decisions or Official Gazette notices); the Assignment, Recording and Rights of Assignee, 37 C.F.R. §§ 3.1 -3.85, as amended; the Secrecy of Certain Inventions and Licenses to Export and File Application in Foreign Countries, 37 C.F.R. §§ 5.1—5.33, as amended; the Register of Government Interests in Patents, 37 C.F.R. § 3.58, as amended; and Representations of Others before the USPTO, 37 C.F.R. §§ 10.1—10.170, as amended, as well as representing clients in proceedings before the USPTO.

(1) A "patent" is a governmental grant derived from the United States Constitution to encourage innovation and a form of protected personal property under federal statute set forth in title 35 of the United States Code that guarantees the holder of a U.S.

patent a right to exclude others from making, using, offering to sell, selling, or importing an invention for a statutory period of years.

(2) "Patent matters" consist of the areas of knowledge required of attorneys registered to practice before the USPTO, including: rules, practice, and procedure; understanding how to draft claims and the ability to properly draft claims; knowledge about preparation and prosecution of patent applications based on education in and practical experience in engineering or science; understanding the application of patent laws to that endeavor; preparation of patentability opinions; filing and prosecuting patent applications, interferences, and re-issuances; preparing opinions concerning the validity and/or infringement of patents; prosecuting patent applications at the USPTO and in foreign jurisdictions; and the re-examination of patents.

(b) Patent Infringement Litigation. "Patent infringement litigation" covers the practice of law (including substantive law, evidence, and procedure) dealing with the litigation of patents in federal district courts and appeals to the federal circuit of the United States of America, and includes: Service of Process, 37 C.F.R. §§ 15.1—15.3; and Testimony of Employees and the Production of Documents in Legal Proceedings, 37 C.F.R. §§ 15.11—15.18. Infringement of a patent is a tort giving rise to a federal cause of action for a form of trespass. The grant of a patent by the USPTO carries with it the presumption of validity, including compliance with federal statutes. Invalidity is a defense to a claim for patent infringement and may be based on a number of factors, including: anticipation; obviousness; derivation; failure to disclose "best mode"; estoppel and laches; ineligible subject matter; lack of utility or operability; lack of enabling disclosure; claim indefiniteness; double patenting; inequitable conduct; violation of antitrust law; and non-infringement.

(1) "Contested matters" shall be defined as hearings before a tribunal or court that are adversarial, evidentiary, and binding in which the applicant has had a senior-level responsibility, and in which the applicant evaluated, handled, and resolved issues of fact and law in a dispute that involved a patent, either by reaching an adjudicated decision or by achieving a settlement before final adjudication or appeal.

(2) An "adjudicated decision" shall mean a decision resulting from a proceeding in which: a tribunal rendered a decision on a motion for preliminary injunction following an evidentiary hearing involving live testimony; a tribunal rendered a decision on a motion for summary judgment; a tribunal rendered a decision on significant issues of patent law following briefing (*e.g.*, a *Markman* hearing, a *Daubert* hearing, etc.); or a tribunal or jury rendered a decision following a trial, or the federal circuit court of appeals rendered a decision following an appeal. A single proceeding may generate multiple adjudicated decisions and an applicant shall receive credit for each such qualifying adjudicated decision as a separate contested matter; however, for purposes of certification, the number of adjudicated decisions from any single case shall be limited to 2.

(c) Trademark Law. "Trademark law" covers the practice of law dealing with all aspects of the Trademark Act of 1946 (the "Lanham Act"), as amended, 15 U.S.C. §§ 1051–1127, Trademark Counterfeiting Act of 1984, as amended, 18 U.S.C. § 2320, Tariff Act of 1930, as amended, 19 U.S.C. §§ 1337 and 1526, Chapter 495 of the Florida Statutes, as amended (the "Florida Trademark Law"), and common law principles, including: advising clients as to ownership, registration, transfer, validity, dilution, enforceability, and infringement of trademarks in the state of Florida, the United States and internationally; representing clients in proceedings before the USPTO and the Florida Department of State; and representing clients in proceedings in federal or state courts, or in arbitration, relating to the ownership, registration, licensing, transfer, validity, dilution, enforcement, and infringement of trademarks.

(1) A "trademark" is defined to include trademarks, service marks, certification marks, and collective marks. Each of these forms of marks shall have the meaning given in the Florida Trademark Law, Fla. Stat. § 495.011(1)–(4). A "trademark" is further defined to include trade dress as that term is used in the Restatement Third, Unfair Competition, Section 16, and domain names as that term is used in the Lanham Act, 15 U.S.C. § 1125(d).

(2) "Contested matters" shall be defined as hearings before a tribunal or court that are adversarial, evidentiary, and binding in which the applicant has had senior-level responsibility, and in which the applicant evaluated, handled, and resolved substantial issues of fact and law in a dispute that involved a trademark, either by reaching an adjudicated decision, or by achieving a settlement before final adjudication or appeal.

(3) An "adjudicated decision" shall mean a decision resulting from a proceeding in which: a tribunal rendered a decision on a motion for temporary or preliminary injunction following an evidentiary hearing involving live testimony; a tribunal rendered a decision on a motion for summary judgment; a tribunal rendered a decision on significant issues of trademark law following briefing in the USPTO; or a tribunal or jury rendered a decision following a trial. A single proceeding may generate multiple adjudicated decisions and an applicant shall receive credit for each such qualifying adjudicated decision as a separate contested matter; however, for purposes of certification, the number of adjudicated decisions from any single case shall be limited to 2.

(4) "Substantive refusal" shall be defined as refusals of trademark applications during *ex parte* USPTO

prosecution under Section 2 of the Lanham Act, 15 U.S.C. § 1052.

(d) Copyright Law. "Copyright law" covers the practice of law dealing with the protection of the works of the human intellect (literature, music, art, computer programs, etc.) under the copyright laws of the United States, including: subject matter; ownership; duration; registration; formalities; exclusive rights; transfers and licensing, including the rights and obligations of parties, appropriate terms and conditions in licensing contracts, antitrust and misuse constraints, international licensing considerations; contested matters relating to claims of infringement of copyrights and to disputes regarding the authorship, ownership, licensing, and transfer of copyrighted works, including infringement actions and defenses, remedies, jurisdiction and venue, jury considerations, federal preemption of state law; the Copyright Acts of 1909 and 1976, as amended; recent amendments to copyright law such as the Digital Millennium Copyright Act; and international aspects of copyright, including the Berne convention and other treaties on copyright and related subjects. The primary federal copyright law is contained in Title 17 of the United States Code. Generally, the practices that the copyright law is concerned with involve, but are not limited to, registration, licensing, transfer, and protection of copyrighted works.

(1) "Contested matters" shall be defined as hearings before a tribunal or court that were adversarial, evidentiary, and binding in which the applicant had a senior-level responsibility, and in which the applicant evaluated, handled, and resolved substantial issues of fact and law in a dispute that involved a copyright, either by reaching an adjudicated decision, or by achieving a settlement before final adjudication or appeal.

(2) An "adjudicated decision" shall mean a decision resulting from a proceeding in which: a tribunal rendered a decision on a motion for temporary or preliminary injunction following an evidentiary hearing involving live testimony; a tribunal rendered a decision on a motion for summary judgment; or a tribunal or jury rendered a decision following a trial. A single proceeding may generate multiple adjudicated decisions and an applicant shall receive credit for each such qualifying adjudicated decision as a separate contested matter, however, for purposes of certification, the number of adjudicated decisions from any single case shall be limited to 2.

(e) Practice of Law. The "practice of law" shall be defined as set forth in rule 6–3.5(c)(1) and rule 6–26.3(a).

(f) Intellectual Property Law Certification Committee. The intellectual property law certification committee shall consist of 9 members, including a minimum of 3 registered patent attorneys with experience in patent application prosecution, 2 members with experience in patent infringement litigation, 2 members with experience in trademark law, and 2 members with experience in copyright law.

Added July 6, 2006, effective August 1, 2006 (933 So.2d 1123).

Rule 6–26.3. Minimum Standards

(a) Minimum Period of Practice. The applicant shall have been engaged in the practice of law for at least 5 years immediately preceding the date of application. Notwithstanding the definition of "practice of law" in rule 6–3.5(c)(1), practicing "patent application prosecution," as defined in section 6–26.2(a), before the USPTO as a registered patent attorney or registered patent agent shall be deemed to constitute the practice of law for purposes of the 5–year practice requirement.

(b) Substantial Involvement. Substantial involvement means at least 30 percent of the applicant's practice during the 3 years immediately preceding application has been devoted to matters involving intellectual property law.

(c) Experience. During the 5 years immediately preceding application, the applicant must comply with the experience requirements in at least 1 of the following categories:

(1) *Patent Application Prosecution.* The applicant must have handled with senior-level responsibility a minimum of 40 patent matters that involved representation of a client. The quality of the applicant's work and the nature of the issues involved shall be a factor in determining eligibility for certification. Demonstration of compliance with this requirement shall be made initially through a form of questionnaire approved by the intellectual property law certification committee, but written or oral supplementation (including copies of work product) may be required. For good cause shown, for satisfaction in part of the 40 patent matters that involved representation of a client, verified substantial involvement in patent matters at a government agency may be considered. Verified substantial involvement in other areas of intellectual property law may also be considered to demonstrate overall proficiency.

(2) *Patent Infringement Litigation.* The applicant must have handled with senior-level responsibility a minimum of 5 contested matters in litigation or on appeal in which there was an adjudicated decision. Additionally, applicants shall have devoted a minimum of 800 hours per year to litigation matters generally, at least 300 hours per year of which shall have been devoted to patent infringement litigation; and applicant shall have, within the last 10 years, tried a patent infringement litigation matter to the close of testimony, verdict, or judgment. The applicant shall submit work product samples and a transcript (if available) in each such contested matter. For good cause shown, for satisfaction in part of the minimum requirements, verified substantial involvement in patent infringement litigation at a government agency may be considered. Verified substantial involvement in other

areas of intellectual property law may also be considered to demonstrate overall proficiency.

(3) *Trademark Law.* The applicant must have handled with senior-level responsibility either a minimum of 6 contested matters or 25 responses to substantive refusals, or a combination of the 2. Substantive refusals on which the applicant relies shall not have involved merely technical corrections, insignificant matters, or abandonment. The applicant shall submit work product samples and a transcript (if available) in each such contested matter. In addition, applicant must have engaged in at least 300 hours each year in the practice of law in which the applicant has had substantial senior-level participation in legal matters involving trademark law. Three contested matters involving in the aggregate no less than 50 hours of in-session hearing or trial shall satisfy the requirement of 6 contested matters. For good cause shown, for satisfaction in whole or in part of the requirement of 6 contested matters or 25 responses to substantive refusals, verified substantial involvement in a combination of contested matters and responses to substantive refusals shall be considered. For good cause shown, for satisfaction in part of the minimum requirements, verified substantial involvement in trademark matters at a government agency may be considered in lieu of representation of clients. Verified substantial involvement in other areas of intellectual property law may also be considered to demonstrate overall proficiency.

(4) *Copyright Law.* The applicant must have handled with senior-level responsibility a minimum of 40 substantive matters that involved representation of a client, with a minimum of 300 hours per year devoted to such matters. The ministerial preparation of a copyright registration is not considered a substantive matter for purposes of certification. The applicant shall submit work product samples and, if the applicant also relies upon participation in contested matters, the applicant shall submit transcripts (if available) in each such contested matter. For good cause shown, for satisfaction in part of the minimum requirements, verified substantial involvement in copyright matters at a government agency may be considered in lieu of representation of clients. Verified substantial involvement in other areas of intellectual property law may also be considered to demonstrate overall proficiency.

(d) Peer Review. The applicant shall select and submit the names and addresses of at least 6 lawyers or judges, who neither are relatives nor current associates, partners, or who otherwise practice law in an of-counsel relationship with the applicant, to serve as references. Such references will be contacted and requested to attest to the applicant's special competence and substantial involvement in intellectual property law, as well as to the applicant's character, ethics, and reputation for professionalism. Individuals submitted as references shall be substantially involved in intellectual property law and shall be familiar with the applicant's practice. In addition, other attorneys, judges, employees at government agencies, or other persons likely to be familiar with the applicant may be contacted as deemed necessary by the intellectual property law certification committee and the board of legal specialization and education.

(e) Education. The applicant must demonstrate that during the 3-year period immediately preceding the filing of an application, the applicant has met the continuing legal education requirements necessary for intellectual property law certification. The required number of hours shall be established by the board of legal specialization and education and shall in no event be less than 45 hours. Accreditation of educational hours shall be subject to policies established by the intellectual property law certification committee or the board of legal specialization and education and may be satisfied by participation in 1 or more of the following activities:

(1) attendance at continuing legal education seminars for which intellectual property law certification credit has been approved;

(2) teaching a course in intellectual property law;

(3) participation as a panelist or speaker in a symposium or similar program on intellectual property law;

(4) authorship of a book, chapter, or article on intellectual property law, published in a professional publication or journal;

(5) completing such home study programs as may be approved by the board of legal specialization and education or the intellectual property law certification committee, subject to the limitation that no more than 50 percent of the required number of hours of education may be satisfied through home study programs; and

(6) such other methods as may be approved by the board of legal specialization and education and the intellectual property law certification committee.

(f) Examination. The applicant must pass an examination applied uniformly to all applicants to demonstrate sufficient knowledge, proficiency, and experience in intellectual property law sufficient to justify certification of special competence to the legal profession and the public. The examination will be comprehensive in scope and each applicant will be required to demonstrate at least some knowledge in each specific subject tested. Applicants, however, will be given the opportunity to emphasize special knowledge in 1 or more specific subject areas.

(g) Exemption. An applicant may qualify for an exemption from the examination, or a portion thereof, as follows:

(1) an applicant currently a registered patent attorney in good standing with the USPTO shall not be required to take the section(s) of the examination on topics defined in rule 6-26.2(a), but must demonstrate

knowledge of substantive law pertaining to intellectual property;

(2) an applicant currently certified by The Florida Bar in civil trial or business litigation shall not be required to take the section of the examination on the litigation process, but must demonstrate knowledge of substantive law pertaining to intellectual property;

(3) an applicant who has been substantially involved in intellectual property law for a minimum of 20 years, in accordance with the standards set forth in rule 6–3.5(d), and who can demonstrate compliance with the experience requirements under rule 6–26.3(c), subdivisions (1), (2), (3), or (4) within a 10–year time frame, shall be exempt from the examination if all other requirements for certification are met. This exemption shall be applicable only to those applicants who apply by October 31, 2009.

Added July 6, 2006, effective August 1, 2006 (933 So.2d 1123). Amended Oct. 3, 2008, by the Board of Governors of The Florida Bar.

Rule 6–26.4. Recertification

To be eligible for recertification, an applicant must meet the following requirements:

(a) Substantial Involvement. The applicant must show continuous and substantial involvement in matters involving intellectual property law throughout the period since the last date of certification or recertification. The demonstration of substantial involvement shall be made by showing that intellectual property law comprises at least 30 percent of the applicant's practice.

(b) Experience. During the 5 years immediately preceding application, the applicant must comply with the experience requirements in at least 1 of the following categories:

(1) *Patent Application Prosecution.* The applicant must have handled with senior-level responsibility a minimum of 30 patent matters that involved representation of a client. For good cause shown, for satisfaction in part of the 30 patent matters, the applicant may provide verified substantial involvement in patent matters at a government agency in lieu of representation of clients. Verified substantial involvement in other areas of intellectual property law may also be considered to demonstrate overall proficiency.

(2) *Patent Infringement Litigation.* The applicant must have handled with senior-level responsibility a minimum of 5 contested matters in litigation or on appeal in which there was an adjudicated decision. The applicant may substitute completion of an approved, multi-day, intensive advocacy-training course where the applicant performed and was satisfactorily critiqued by recognized experts for 2 of the 5 contested matters. For good cause shown, for satisfaction in part of the 5 contested matters, the applicant may serve as a judge or an arbitrator in a contested matter involving an adjudicated decision concerning a patent, or may serve as an advocacy instructor in an intellectual property law continuing legal education program in lieu of senior-level responsibility as an advocate for a party. Verified substantial involvement in other areas of intellectual property law may also be considered to demonstrate overall proficiency.

(3) *Trademark Law.* The applicant must have handled either a minimum of 4 contested matters or 15 responses to substantive refusals of the application. In addition, an applicant must have engaged in at least 300 hours each year in the practice of law in which the applicant had substantial and direct senior-level participation in legal matters involving trademark law. Two contested matters involving in the aggregate no less than 2 days of in-session hearing or trial shall satisfy the requirement of 4 contested matters. For good cause shown, for satisfaction in whole or in part of the requirements, verified substantial involvement in a combination of contested matters and responses to substantive refusals resulting in allowance in satisfaction of the minimum number of matters shall be considered. The applicant may serve as a judge or an arbitrator in a contested matter involving an adjudicated decision concerning a trademark, or may serve as an advocacy instructor in an intellectual property continuing legal education program, in lieu of senior-level responsibility as an advocate for a party. Verified substantial involvement in other areas of intellectual property law may also be considered to demonstrate overall proficiency.

(4) *Copyright Law.* The applicant must have handled with senior-level responsibility a minimum of 30 matters that involved representation of a client. For good cause shown, for satisfaction in whole or in part of the requirement, the applicant may serve as a judge or an arbitrator in a contested matter involving an adjudicated decision concerning a copyright, or may serve as an advocacy instructor in an intellectual property law continuing legal education program in lieu of senior-level responsibility as an advocate for a party. Verified substantial involvement in other areas of intellectual property law may also be considered to demonstrate overall proficiency.

(c) Peer Review. The applicant must submit the names and addresses of at least 3 lawyers or judges, who neither are relatives nor current associates, partners, or who otherwise practice law in an of-counsel relationship with the applicant, to serve as references. Such references will be contacted and requested to attest to the applicant's special competence and substantial involvement in intellectual property law, as well as to the applicant's character, ethics, and reputation for professionalism in the practice of law. Individuals submitted as references shall be substantially involved in intellectual property law and shall be familiar with the applicant's practice. In addition, other attorneys, judges, employees at government agencies, or other persons likely to be familiar with the applicant may be contacted as deemed necessary by the intellectual property law certification committee and the board of legal specialization and education.

(d) Education. The applicant must have completed at least 50 hours of approved continuing legal education in intellectual property law, in accordance with the standards set forth in rule 6–26.3(e) since the filing of the last application for certification.

Added July 6, 2006, effective August 1, 2006 (933 So.2d 1123). Amended Oct. 3, 2008, by the Board of Governors of The Florida Bar.

6–27. STANDARDS FOR CERTIFICATION OF A BOARD CERTIFIED EDUCATION LAWYER

Rule 6–27.1. Generally

A lawyer who is a member in good standing of The Florida Bar and who meets the standards prescribed below may be issued an appropriate certificate identifying the lawyer as a "Board Certified Education Lawyer." The purpose of the standards is to identify those lawyers who practice in the area of education law and have the special knowledge, skills, and proficiency, as well as the character, ethics, and reputation for professionalism to be properly identified to the public as board certified education lawyers.

Added June 11, 2009 (11 So.3d 343).

Rule 6–27.2. Definitions

(a) Education Law. "Education law" means the practice of law involving the legal rights, responsibilities, procedures, and practices of "educational institutions," students, personnel employed by or on behalf of educational institutions, and the guardians and parents of students participating in education. The term "education law" shall also mean the practice of law on behalf of public or private clients in matters including, but not limited to: state, federal, and local laws, regulations, and proceedings involving student rights and student discipline; administrative law and rules regulating the operations of schools and education in Florida; charter schools; finance issues involving educational institutions, including bond indebtedness, certificates of participation, impact fees, and educational benefit districts; litigation involving educational institutions, including matters of sovereign immunity, civil rights in educational environments, including the civil rights of students and personnel in education; labor issues involving educational institutions, including standards of professional performance and practices involving personnel employed by or on behalf of educational institutions; private school contract matters and litigation involving private school entities; disability law, including § 504, Individuals With Disabilities Education Act, and the Americans With Disabilities Act; laws of general governance, including the Sunshine Law, Public Records Act, Code of Ethics for Public Officers and Officials, purchasing and bid issues; and construction, land use and development law as these areas relate to educational facilities. The purpose of education law certification is to identify lawyers who, although they may not practice substantially in each of these areas, nonetheless concentrate their practice of law in a wide variety of these categories of law in the educational environment, either on behalf of persons dealing with or receiving educational services, or as practitioners on behalf of educational institutions. "Education law" also includes presiding as an administrative law judge, arbitrator, hearing officer, judge or member of another tribunal or panel over a dispute involving education law issues.

(b) Educational Institution. "Educational institution" means any entity, private, public, for-profit or not-for-profit, that has appropriate licensure (or otherwise is legally authorized) as a provider of educational services and instruction, and is primarily devoted to the provision of education and instruction to persons of any age. Without limitation, examples of educational institutions shall be public school boards and school districts, public and private universities, community colleges, private schools, charter schools, and technical or trade schools.

(c) Lead Attorney. "Lead attorney" means one serving as the primary attorney, whether as a team leader or alone, working on behalf of either a private party or an educational institution. Service as a supervisor and signatory of legal documents, but without substantial participation in the preparation of those documents, does not constitute service as lead attorney. Service in the role of lead attorney also includes presiding as a judge, administrative law judge, arbitrator, hearing officer, or member of an administrative tribunal or panel hearing or presiding over a dispute involving a matter of education law.

(d) Practice of Law. "Practice of law" is defined as set forth in rule 6–3.5(c)(1).

Added June 11, 2009 (11 So.3d 343).

Rule 6–27.3. Minimum Standards

(a) Minimum Period of Practice. The applicant must have been engaged in the practice of education law for at least 5 years immediately preceding the date of application. Additionally, the applicant shall have been a member in good standing of the bar of any state of the United States or the District of Columbia for a period of 5 years as of the date of application.

(b) Substantial Involvement. The applicant must demonstrate substantial involvement in the practice of education law during at least 3 of the 5 years immediately preceding the date of application. An applicant who meets the practical experience requirements in subdivision (c) below shall be presumed to meet this requirement.

(c) Practical Experience. The applicant must demonstrate broad, substantial, practical experience in education law by providing examples of service as the lead attorney on behalf of a private or public client involved in education law issues. Using the point values and limitations assigned below, the applicant's examples from the following actions must total at least 50 points during the 5 years immediately preceding the date of application. Unless expressly permitted by the standard itself in the following subdivisions, an applicant may only take points under 1 subdivision for each project of work. By way of illustration, and as an example only, an applicant may not take points under both subdivisions (c)(3)(C) and (c)(4)(A) for writing an opinion letter and presenting that letter at a meeting of an educational institution. In cases where a project is subject to points in more than 1 category, and the rule does not expressly allow for points to be earned in more than 1 category, the applicant must elect the category under which the applicant wishes to receive points for such work.

To ensure a diversity of experience and involvement in the area of education law, the applicant cannot count more than the maximum points allowable for each section.

(1) The maximum points allowable for subdivision (1) are 30 points. Each item is worth 5 points or as otherwise indicated:

(A) The applicant participated in administrative hearings in which questions or matters of education law were at issue as lead attorney, including both formal and informal hearings (excluding student suspension hearings and expulsion hearings that are not appealed to a court) adjudicated through final order pursuant to the Florida Administrative Procedure Act, chapter 120, Florida Statutes. If the matter is appealed and the appeal is concluded by a court order or decision, or otherwise resolved after the case is fully briefed, the applicant will earn an additional 3 points. If the applicant is lead attorney in rulemaking proceedings covered in subdivision (c)(2)(A), the applicant shall receive 4 points for such work in addition to the points available under this subdivision.

(B) The applicant participated in other fully adjudicated administrative actions (including any formal arbitration or mediation proceeding) in which questions or matters of education law were at issue, as lead attorney for a client, including but not limited to labor/employment and rulemaking proceedings pursuant to the Federal Administrative Procedure Act, 5 U.S.C. §§ 551–559, and any arbitration agreement or federally required proceeding, including record review proceedings, pursuant to 5 U.S.C. §§ 701–706. If the matter is appealed and the appeal is concluded by a court or fully briefed to the court before the appeal is concluded, add 3 points for each. It is the intent of this standard that if the applicant is lead attorney in rulemaking proceedings covered in subdivision (c)(2)(A), the applicant shall receive 4 points for such work in addition to the points available under this subdivision.

(C) The applicant participated in fully adjudicated trial court proceedings as lead attorney in state or federal court, in which questions or matters of education law were at issue. If the matter is appealed and the appeal is concluded by a court or fully briefed to the court before the appeal is concluded, add 3 points for each.

(2) The maximum points allowable for subdivision (2) are 28 points. Each item is worth 4 points or as otherwise indicated:

(A) The applicant participated in rulemaking proceedings as lead attorney through rule adoption pursuant to Florida Administrative Procedure Act, chapter 120, Florida Statutes, which rulemaking involves a question or matter of education law or a rule on behalf of an educational institution.

(B) The applicant participated in administrative litigation, state or federal court litigation and arbitration, as lead attorney, resulting in settlement before final adjudication, and in which matter substantial questions or issues of education law were presented.

(C) The applicant conducted appeals as lead attorney in which the applicant either represented an educational institution or a party seeking relief against an educational institution on a question involving education law. This includes appellate matters that are settled on appeal, but only if the applicant, as lead attorney, filed at least 1 substantive brief in the appeal, including the appeal of student disciplinary matters pursuant to § 120.68, Florida Statutes.

(3) The maximum points allowable for subdivision (3) are 21 points. Each item is worth 3 points or as otherwise indicated:

(A) The applicant participated in student disciplinary hearings as a hearing officer or as lead attorney before a hearing officer or an educational institution which were not appealed.

(B) The applicant sought, on behalf of an educational institution as lead attorney, and obtained an advisory opinion from the Florida Commission on Ethics, Florida or United States Attorney General, or the Florida or United States Department of Education (and any constituent division thereof).

(C) The applicant appeared as lead attorney for a party or an educational institution before any governmental organization in a formal public meeting (Sunshine Meeting under § 286.011, Florida Statutes) including an appearance before an educational institution as lead attorney for such entity, involving a question of education law or a matter on behalf of an educational institution. Without limitation, this includes the applicant, as lead attorney, representing an educational institution before a local government or the Florida Department of Community Affairs on matters involving land use planning or zoning issues on behalf of an educational facility, appearing before a governmental entity or agency with regard to advocating a matter of interest to a client (either private or public) involving a question of education law or a matter of interest to an educational institution, and any other formal appearances before regulatory bodies and authorities with respect to a question of education law or matters of concern to an educational institution. This subdivision shall not apply and the applicant will not earn points when this appearance is in connection with another matter covered by another subdivision or practice for which points are awardable. By way of example, and for purposes of illustration only, an applicant will not earn points for appearing before an educational institution in an executive session to discuss pending litigation for which points are awarded under subdivision (c)(1)(C), nor will an applicant receive points when such appearance is in connection with a disciplinary hearing for which points are awardable under subdivision (c)(3)(A).

(D) The applicant participated in lobbying in support of a rule or law before any governmental authority, wherein the applicant is registered as a lobbyist with regard to a regulation or law involving education, education law, or a matter of concern to an educational institution. Each law or regulation for which the applicant has advocated before an authority shall constitute a separate matter of experience for accumulation of these points.

(E) The applicant conducted an investigation on behalf of an educational institution or represented a party being investigated, as lead attorney, during an investigation conducted by or on behalf of an educational institution. This includes all internal review procedures and work related to issues involving scientific misconduct, plagiarism, breach of test security, Institutional Review Board meetings, tenure, dismissal from or sanction of employment, and advising managerial staff or the governing body of an educational institution regarding such matters. Likewise, points in this category are awarded for each client involved in any of these types of matters in which the client is or may be adverse to an educational institution.

(F) The applicant participated in attempts to resolve through mediation or other negotiations a matter involving education law, as defined in rule 6–27.2(a), prior to filing before any tribunal.

(G) The applicant performed internal audits for an educational institution such as, but not limited to, assessing wage hour compliance, handbook review, etc.

(4) The maximum points allowable for subdivision (4) are 20 points. Each item is worth 2 points or as otherwise indicated:

(A) Two points will be awarded for each of the following actions on behalf of a client or educational institution involving a question of education law, to the extent such work is not covered by or included in the work under another subdivision of these standards: preparation of an opinion letter regarding a question or matter of education law; preparation of a contract involving educational services, technology, or other matters that will facilitate or allow for the delivery of educational services, or any agreement in which an educational institution is a party to the contract; or preparation of rules of procedure on behalf of an educational institution.

(d) Verification of Practical Experience Requirements. The education law certification committee will develop an application form to elicit specific information sufficient to verify the practical experience reported by the applicant. Due and appropriate regard will be made to preserve client and student-identifying confidences, but subject to the requirement of confidentiality, the application will provide for the applicant to identify case numbers for court and administrative litigation, parties in litigation (using initials with respect to student-identifying matters), the nature of the work performed, the dates on which the work was performed (or a period of time during which it was performed), the identity of any court or tribunal before which the work was performed, the results of the work, and the identity of any opposing attorney, as well as such other information the education law certification committee determines is reasonably required for the applicant to submit so that the practice requirements may be verified.

(e) Additional Points. The education law certification committee or the board of legal specialization and education may increase the number of points granted for activities of the type identified in subdivisions (c)(1)–(2), for good cause shown, such as the significant impact of a particular case on a question of education law.

(f) Peer Review. The applicant must submit the names and addresses of 5 individuals, at least 4 of whom are attorneys and 1 of whom is a federal, state, or administrative law judge before whom the applicant has appeared within the past 5 years preceding the date of application. In lieu of a judicial reference, the applicant may provide the name and address of the head of an educational institution (or a member of a collegiate body that serves as the head of the educational institution) if the applicant has advised or appeared before such person within the 5–year period preceding the date of application. The attorney references must be members of The Florida Bar, and may not be persons who practice currently in the applicant's law firm or, if the applicant is employed by an educational institution, the references may not be employed in the same law department at the same educational institution as the applicant at the time the application is filed. Individuals serving as references shall be sufficiently familiar with the applicant to attest to the applicant's special competence and substantial involvement in the field of education law, as well as the applicant's character, ethics, and reputation for professionalism. The board of legal specialization and education and the education law certification committee may authorize references from persons other than attorneys and may also make such additional inquiries as they deem appropriate to determine the qualifications of an applicant for certification pursuant to this rule and rule 6–3.5(c)(6).

(g) Education. The applicant must demonstrate completion of 50 credit hours of approved continuing legal education in education law during the 3–year period immediately preceding the date of application. Credit for attendance or speaking appearances at continuing legal education seminars shall be given only for programs that are directly related to education law, and such programs may include but are not limited to continuing legal education in the areas of civil rights, disability law, legal issues relevant to the governance and operations of educational institutions, including Sunshine, public records and Code of Ethics, government procurement law (including bid protests), government finance topics, trial practice topics, administrative law, and labor and employment law. Additionally, the education law certification committee may conclude that the education requirement is satisfied in part by 1 or more of the following:

(1) lecturing at or serving on the steering committee of continuing legal education seminars;

(2) authoring or editing articles or books published in professional periodicals or other professional publications on questions of education law;

(3) teaching courses related to education law at an approved law school or other graduate level program presented by a recognized professional education association;

(4) completing such home study program as may be approved by the board of legal specialization and education or the education law certification committee subject to the limitation that no more than 50 percent of the required number of hours of education may be satisfied through home study; or

(5) such other methods as may be approved by the board of legal specialization and education and the education law certification committee.

The board of legal specialization and education or the education law certification committee shall, by policy, establish standards applicable to this rule, including but not limited to the method of establishment of the credit hours applicable to any of the above listed subdivisions.

(h) Examination. The applicant must pass an examination administered uniformly to all applicants to demonstrate sufficient knowledge, skills, proficiency, experience, and professionalism in education law to justify the representation of special competence in education law to the legal profession and the public.

(i) Exemption. An applicant who has been substantially involved in education law for a minimum of 20 years and who otherwise fulfills the standards set forth in rules 6–3.5(d) and rules 6–27.3(a)–(g), shall be exempt from the examination. This exemption is only applicable to those applicants who apply within the first 2 application filing periods from the effective date of these standards.

Added June 11, 2009 (11 So.3d 343).

Rule 6–27.4. Recertification

During the 5–year period immediately preceding the date of application, the applicant must demonstrate satisfaction of the following requirements for recertification:

(a) Substantial Involvement. The applicant must demonstrate continuous and substantial involvement in education law throughout the period since the last date of certification or recertification. An applicant who meets the practical experience and education requirements in (b) below shall be presumed to meet this requirement.

(b) Practical Experience Requirement. The applicant must demonstrate involvement as lead attorney on behalf of a private client or educational institution in matters totaling at least 10 points as described in rule 6–27. 3(c) above. For good cause shown and at the discretion of the education law certification committee, the 10–point requirement may be waived for applicants who possess other extraordinary legal experience related to matters of education law. Examples of such extraordinary experience may include service as an administrative law judge, general counsel responsibility for an educational institution or other senior attorney experience with supervisory responsibilities on behalf of an educational institution, representation of or membership on a committee working on substantial matters of education law, teaching education law at the college level, and other appropriate legal experience described by the applicant and approved by the education law certification committee.

(c) Education. The applicant must demonstrate completion of at least 90 credit hours of approved continuing legal education for education law certification. If the applicant has not attained 90 credit hours of approved continuing legal education for education law certification, but has attained more than 60 hours during such period, successful passage of the examination given to new applicants will satisfy the education requirements. However, an applicant seeking recertification may also reduce the educational requirements in this subdivision to 60 hours by demonstrating involvement as lead attorney on behalf of a private client or an educational institution in matters of education law since certification or the last recertification, totaling at least 25 points as described in rule 6–27.3(c) above.

(d) Peer Review. The applicant must submit the names and addresses of 3 individuals, at least 2 of whom are attorneys and 1 of whom is a federal, state, or administrative law judge before whom the applicant has appeared during the 5–year period immediately preceding the date of application. In lieu of a judicial reference the applicant may provide the name and address of the head of an educational institution (or a member of a collegiate body that serves as the head of the educational institution) under circumstances where the applicant has advised or appeared before such person within the 5–year period immediately preceding the date of application. The attorney references must be members of The Florida Bar in good standing, and may not be members of the applicant's law firm or, if the applicant is employed by an educational institution, the references may not be employed in the same law department at the same educational institution as the applicant at the time the application is filed. Individuals serving as references must be sufficiently familiar with the applicant to attest to the applicant's special competence and substantial involvement in the field of education law, as well as the applicant's character, ethics, and reputation for professionalism. The board of legal specialization and education and the education law certification committee may authorize references from persons other than attorneys and may also make such additional inquiries as they deem appropriate to determine the applicant's qualifications for recertification pursuant to this rule and rule 6–3.5(c)(6).

(e) Waiver of Compliance. An applicant for recertification who, at the time of application is serving and has served full time for 3 or more years as an administrative law judge, is deemed to meet the recertification criteria in subdivisions 6–27.4(a) and (b).

Added June 11, 2009 (11 So.3d 343).

6–28. STANDARDS FOR CERTIFICATION OF A BOARD CERTIFIED ADOPTION LAWYER

Rule 6–28.1. Generally

A lawyer who is a member in good standing of The Florida Bar and who meets the standards prescribed below may be issued an appropriate certificate identifying the lawyer as a "Board Certified Adoption Lawyer." The purpose of the standards is to identify those lawyers who practice adoption law and have the special knowledge, skills, and proficiency, as well as the character, ethics, and reputation for professionalism, to be properly identified to the public as board certified adoption lawyers.

Added June 11, 2009 (11 So.3d 343).

Rule 6–28.2. Definitions

(a) Adoption Law. "Adoption law" is the practice of law dealing with the complexities and legalities of interstate and intrastate adoption placements, including civil controversies arising from termination of the biological parents' parental rights, the Indian Child Welfare Act, and interstate placements. In addition to the actual adoption placement, "adoption law" includes evaluating, handling, and resolving such controversies prior to the placement of a child for adoption and all post placement proceedings. The practice of adoption law in the state of Florida is generally unique in that decisional, statutory, and procedural laws are specific to this state.

(b) Practice of Law. "Practice of law" for this area is defined as set forth in rule 6–3.5(c)(1).

Added June 11, 2009 (11 So.3d 343).

Rule 6–28.3. Minimum Standards

(a) Minimum Period of Practice. The applicant must have at least 5 years of the actual practice of law, of which at least 50 percent has been spent in active participation in adoption law.

(b) Minimum Number of Cases. The applicant must demonstrate substantial involvement, as defined in subdivision (c) below, in a minimum of 50 adoption placements in circuit courts during the 5–year period immediately preceding the date of application. All such placements must have involved the placement of a minor child with an adoptive family who is not related to the child within the third degree of consanguinity or is not the minor child's stepparent. In each of these 50 adoption placements the applicant must have appeared before the court as the adoption entity, as defined in chapter 63, Florida Statutes, on behalf of the adoptive parents or as the lawyer for the adoption entity. In each of these 50 adoption placements, the applicant must have been responsible for all or a majority of the legal decisions concerning the minor child's adoption placement, termination of the biological and legal parents' parental rights, and finalization of the adoption. If the applicant does not meet the minimum requirement of 50 adoption placements, the applicant must demonstrate substantial involvement, as defined in subdivision (c) below, in a minimum of 15 contested adoption proceedings or appeals within the 5–year period immediately preceding the date of application. In each of these 15 contested adoption proceedings or appeals, the applicant must have been responsible for all or a majority of the legal decisions in each case.

(c) Substantial Involvement. The applicant must demonstrate, within the 5–year period immediately preceding the date of application, substantial involvement in the placement of minor children for adoption sufficient to demonstrate special competence as an adoption lawyer. Substantial involvement includes active participation in interviewing and counseling adoptive parents, providing full disclosure to adoptive parents regarding applicable law and the subject minor child, providing legally mandated disclosure to biological and legal parents, investigating issues necessary to assure a legally stable adoption placement, preparation of pleadings, providing notice to individuals legally entitled to notice, taking consents for adoption, presentation of evidence in termination of parental rights and adoption proceedings, attendance at hearings, preparation of interstate adoption documentation, and drafting and preparation of post placement communication agreements. Substantial involvement in a contested adoption proceeding requires that the applicant demonstrate responsibility for at least 50 percent of the legal work in preparing and presenting the case for any trial or evidentiary hearing for disposition by the trier of fact.

(d) Peer Review.

(1) The applicant must select and submit names and addresses of 6 lawyers, who neither are relatives nor current associates or partners, as references to attest to the applicant's substantial involvement and competence in adoption law, as well as the applicant's character, ethics, and reputation for professionalism. At least 3 of the lawyers shall be members of The Florida Bar, with their principal office located in the state of Florida. Such lawyers should be substantially involved in adoption law and familiar with the applicant's practice.

(2) The applicant must select and submit the names and addresses of 2 judges who have presided in circuit courts in the state of Florida before whom the applicant has appeared as an advocate or adoption entity in an adoption law case in the 2-year period immediately preceding the date of application.

(3) Peer review received on behalf of the applicant must be sufficient to demonstrate the applicant's competence, ethics, and professionalism in adoption law. In addition, the adoption law certification committee may, at its option, send reference forms to other attorneys and judges, and make such other investigation as necessary.

(e) Education. The applicant must demonstrate completion of at least 30 credit hours of approved continuing legal education in the field of adoption law during the 3-year period immediately preceding the date of application. Accreditation of educational hours shall be subject to policies established by the adoption law certification committee or the board of legal specialization and may include such activity as:

(1) teaching a course in adoption law;

(2) completion of a course in adoption law;

(3) participation as a panelist or speaker in a symposium or similar program in adoption law;

(4) attendance at a lecture series or similar program concerning adoption law, sponsored by a qualified educational institution or bar group;

(5) authorship of a book or article on adoption law, published in a professional publication or journal; and

(6) such other educational experience as the adoption law certification committee shall approve.

(f) Examination. The applicant must pass an examination administered uniformly to all applicants to demonstrate sufficient knowledge, skills, proficiency, experience, and professionalism in adoption law to justify the representation of special competence to the legal profession and the public.

Added June 11, 2009 (11 So.3d 343).

Rule 6-28.4. Recertification

During the 5-year period immediately preceding the date of application, the applicant must demonstrate satisfaction of the following requirements for recertification:

(a) Substantial Involvement. The applicant must have continuous and substantial involvement in the field of adoption law. The demonstration of substantial involvement shall be made in accordance with the definitional language set forth in subdivision 6-28.3(c).

(b) Minimum Number of Cases. The applicant must have had substantial involvement as defined in subdivision 6-28.3(c) in a minimum of 50 adoption law cases as follows:

(1) The applicant must have either presided over as a judge or general magistrate, or handled as an advocate, a minimum of 50 adoption placements. All such placements must have involved the placement of a minor child with an adoptive family who is not related to the child within the third degree of consanguinity or is not the minor child's stepparent. In each of these 50 adoption placements the applicant must have appeared before the court as the adoption entity, as defined in chapter 63, Florida Statutes, on behalf of the adoptive parents or as the lawyer for the adoption entity. In each of these 50 adoption placements, the applicant must have been responsible for all or a majority of the legal decisions concerning the minor child's adoption placement, termination of the biological and legal parents' parental rights, and finalization of the adoption. If the applicant does not meet the minimum requirement of 50 adoption placements, the applicant must demonstrate substantial involvement, as defined in subdivision (c) below, in a minimum of 15 contested adoption proceedings or appeals within the 5 years immediately preceding the date of application. In each of these 15 contested adoption proceedings or appeals, the applicant must have been responsible for all or a majority of the legal decisions in each case.

(2) The applicant must have either presided over as a judge or general magistrate, or handled as an advocate, a minimum of 50 adoption cases in which the applicant was substantially involved. Substantial in-

volvement includes active participation in interviewing and counseling adoptive parents, providing full disclosure to adoptive parents regarding applicable law and the subject minor child, providing legally mandated disclosure to biological and legal parents, investigating issues necessary to assure a legally stable adoption placement, preparation of pleadings, providing notice to individuals legally entitled to notice, taking consents for adoption, presentation of evidence in termination of parental rights and adoption proceedings, attendance at hearings, preparation of interstate adoption documentation, and drafting and preparation of post placement communication agreements. Substantial involvement in a contested adoption proceeding requires that the applicant demonstrate responsibility for at least 50 percent of the legal work in preparing and presenting the case for any trial or evidentiary hearing for disposition by the trier of fact.

(3) On special application, for good cause shown, the adoption law certification committee may waive compliance with rule 6–28.4(b)(1) or (2) or both for an applicant who has been continuously board certified in adoption law under these standards for a period of 14 years or more.

(c) Education. The applicant must demonstrate completion of 75 credit hours of approved continuing legal education in the field of adoption law. The continuing legal education must logically be expected to enhance the proficiency of attorneys who are board certified adoption lawyers. If the applicant has not attained 75 hours of approved continuing legal education but has attained more than 50 hours during such period, successful passage of the examination given to new applicants shall satisfy the continuing legal education requirements.

(d) Peer Review.

(1) The applicant must submit the names and addresses of 3 lawyers, who neither are relatives nor current associates or partners, as references to attest to the applicant's substantial involvement and competence in adoption law, as well as the applicant's character, ethics, and reputation for professionalism. Such lawyers shall be involved in adoption law and familiar with the applicant's practice.

(2) The applicant must submit the names and addresses of at least 2 judges before whom the applicant has appeared on adoption matters within the 2–year period immediately preceding the date of application to attest to the applicant's substantial involvement and competence in adoption law, as well as the applicant's character, ethics, and reputation for professionalism.

(3) The adoption law certification committee may, at its option, send reference forms to other attorneys and judges.

Added June 11, 2009 (11 So.3d 343).

6–29. STANDARDS FOR BOARD CERTIFICATION IN JUVENILE LAW

Effective Date

Order SC14–2107 (164 So.3d 1217), adopts this heading effective October 1, 2015.

Rule 6–29.1. Generally

Text of rule effective October 1, 2015.

A lawyer who is an active member in good standing of The Florida Bar and who meets the standards prescribed below may be issued a certificate identifying the lawyer as "Board Certified in Juvenile Law." The purpose of the standards is to identify those lawyers who practice juvenile law and have the special knowledge, skills, and proficiency, as well as the character, ethics, and reputation for professionalism, to be properly identified to the public as board certified in juvenile law.

Added May 21, 2015, effective Oct. 1, 2015 (164 So.3d 1217).

Rule 6–29.2. Definitions

Text of rule effective October 1, 2015.

(a) Juvenile Law. "Juvenile law" is the area of law that inherently and directly impacts children. It includes, but is not limited to, dependency, delinquency, and termination of parental rights matters. It does not include adoption matters or matters arising in the context of family law proceedings not consolidated with dependency or termination of parental rights matters.

(b) Trial. A "trial" is defined as substantially preparing a case for court, offering testimony or evidence, or cross-examination of witness(es), in an adversarial proceeding before a trier of fact, and submission of a case to the trier of fact for determination of the matter.

(c) Appellate proceeding. An "appellate proceeding" is defined as an action in a state or federal court seeking review of a decision of a lower tribunal.

(d) Practice of Law. The "practice of law" for this area is defined in rule 6–3.5(c)(1).

Added May 21, 2015, effective Oct. 1, 2015 (164 So.3d 1217).

Rule 6–29.3. Minimum Standards

Text of rule effective October 1, 2015.

(a) Minimum Period of Practice. The applicant must have been substantially engaged in the practice of law for at least 5 years immediately preceding the application date.

(b) Practice Requirements. The practice requirements are as follows:

(1) *Substantial Involvement.* The applicant must demonstrate substantial involvement in the practice of juvenile law during 3 of the last 5 years, immediately preceding application.

(2) *Practical Experience.* The applicant must demonstrate substantial practical experience in juvenile law by providing examples of service as the lead advocate on behalf of a governmental entity, a child, a parent, a guardian, a foster parent, or a child's relative with standing to litigate, in a minimum of 20 fully adjudicated trials or appellate proceedings arising from petitions for dependency, termination of parental rights, or delinquency. If at least 10 of the trials or appeals required by this provision occurred during the 5 years immediately preceding application, the requirements of rule 6–29.3(b)(1) are met.

(3) *Other Experience.* On good cause shown, the juvenile law certification committee may substitute other experience in juvenile law as defined for the portion of the trials or appellate proceedings as it deems appropriate. This experience may include, but is not limited to:

(A) handling school issues, including disciplinary issues and educational planning matters, participating in placement determinations, and the development of treatment and alternative plans;

(B) dealing with matters relating to governmental benefits;

(C) advocacy after termination of parental rights;

(D) advocacy before the Florida Department of Children and Families or other agencies;

(E) advocacy in juvenile delinquency matters other than trial or appellate proceedings;

(F) representation at administrative proceedings; and

(G) resolving health care matters.

(c) Peer Review.

(1) The applicant must submit the names and addresses of 6 lawyers, who are neither relatives nor current associates or partners nor who practice in the same governmental entity as the applicant. At least 4 of the references must be members of The Florida Bar. Individuals serving as references must have experience in juvenile law and be sufficiently familiar with the applicant to attest to the applicant's special competence in juvenile law, as well as the applicant's character, ethics, and reputation for professionalism in the practice of law.

(2) The applicant must submit the name and address of 1 judge before whom the applicant has appeared in a juvenile law matter within the 5–year period immediately preceding application to attest to the applicant's competence in juvenile law, as well as the applicant's character, ethics, and reputation for professionalism.

(3) The board of legal specialization and education and the juvenile law certification committee may authorize references from persons other than lawyers and may also make additional inquiries it deems appropriate to determine the applicant's qualifications for certification.

(d) Education. The applicant must demonstrate completion of 50 credit hours of approved continuing legal education in juvenile law during the 3–year period immediately preceding the date of application. Accreditation of educational hours is subject to policies established by the juvenile law certification committee or the board of legal specialization and education.

(e) Examination. The applicant must pass an examination administered uniformly to all applicants to demonstrate sufficient knowledge, proficiency, experience, and professionalism in juvenile law to justify the representation of special competence to the legal profession and the public.

(f) Exemption. An applicant who meets the standards set forth in subdivisions (a)—(d) of this rule and those of rule 6–3.5(d) are exempt from the examination. This exemption is only applicable to those applicants who apply within the first 2 application filing periods from the effective date of these standards.

Added May 21, 2015, effective Oct. 1, 2015 (164 So.3d 1217).

Rule 6–29.4. Recertification

Text of rule effective October 1, 2015.

During the 5–year period immediately preceding application, an applicant must satisfy the following requirements for recertification:

(a) Substantial Involvement. The applicant must demonstrate continuous and substantial involvement in juvenile law throughout the period since the last date of certification or recertification.

(b) Trials or Appellate Actions. The applicant must have had sole or primary responsibility in at least 10 trials or appellate actions involving juvenile law. When primary responsibility is used to meet this requirement, the applicant must specifically identify any co-counsel and demonstrate to the satisfaction of the juvenile law certification committee that the applicant's level of participation was substantial and direct. On good cause shown, the juvenile law certification committee may substitute other experience for any portion of the trials or appellate proceedings it deems appropriate. This experience may include, but is not limited to, the matters set forth in Rule 6–29.3(b)(3). Compliance with this provision constitutes a prima facie showing of compliance with the requirements of rule 6–29.4(a).

(c) Education. The applicant must demonstrate completion of at least 50 credit hours of approved continuing legal education in juvenile law certification. Accreditation of educational hours is subject to policies established by the juvenile law certification committee or the board of legal specialization and education.

(d) Peer Review.

(1) The applicant must submit the names and address of at least 4 lawyers who are neither relatives nor current associates or partners nor who practice in the same governmental entity as the applicant, as references to attest to the applicant's substantial involvement and competence in juvenile law, as well as the applicant's character, ethics, and reputation for professionalism. These lawyers must have experience in juvenile law and be familiar with the applicant's practice.

(2) The applicant must submit the name and address of at least 1 judge before whom the applicant has appeared within the last 5 years to attest to the applicant's competence in juvenile law, as well as the applicant's character, ethics, and reputation for professionalism.

(3) The juvenile law certification committee may, at its option, send reference forms to other lawyers and judges, as well as any other person the committee deems appropriate.

Added May 21, 2015, effective Oct. 1, 2015 (164 So.3d 1217).

STANDING POLICIES OF THE BOARD OF LEGAL SPECIALIZATION AND EDUCATION

100. ADMINISTRATION

200. FLORIDA CERTIFICATION PLAN

300. CERTIFICATION PROGRAM ACCREDITATION

400. APPEAL PROCEDURES

500. CLE ACCREDITATION

600. FLORIDA CONTINUING LEGAL EDUCATION REQUIREMENTS

Explanatory Note

Amended by the Board of Governors of The Florida Bar, April 27, 1982; August 4, 1982; September 11, 1987; January 22, 1988; August 14, 1998; December 11, 1998; February 11, 1999; October 22, 1999; June 29, 2000; June 2001; December 2001; September 2002; January 30, 2004; August 11–14, 2004; December 8–11, 2004; August 26, 2005; December 16, 2005; September 26, 2006; May 22, 2008; December 11, 2009; January 29, 2010; January 26, 2012.

Amendments to the approved areas of certification are incorporated within Standing Policy 2.02.

The Standing Policies of the Board of Legal Specialization and Education are not part of the Rules Regulating the Florida Bar. The Board of Legal Specialization and Education has adopted these Policies to implement Chapter 6 of the Rules Regulating the Florida Bar. The Policies are inserted following Chapter 6 in order to assist practitioners.

100. ADMINISTRATION

1.01. Board of Legal Specialization and Education

(a) Jurisdiction. The board of legal specialization and education (BLSE) has general jurisdiction over each certification committee and all matters pertaining to the administration of the Florida certification plan, the continuing legal education requirement (CLER), the basic skills course requirement (BSCR), and continuing legal education (CLE) accreditation as outlined in the Rules Regulating The Florida Bar, Chapter 6. Members are appointed by the bar president, for staggered terms and serve at the discretion of the board of governors.

(b) Rules and Policies. The BLSE has the authority to promulgate rules and policies, subject to approval by the Board of Governors of The Florida Bar (board of governors), to accomplish the responsibilities assigned to it as described in the previous section. These rules and policies will include, but not be limited to, the following:

(1) administration of the certification program;

(2) establishment of reasonable and nondiscriminatory standards concerning education, experience, proficiency, and other relevant matters for granting certification and recertification to lawyers in defined fields of law under the plan;

(3) establishment of procedures for the investigation and consideration of applicant qualifications for certification and recertification and awarding certificates of special knowledge, skills, and proficiency, as well as character, ethics, and reputation for professionalism, based on recommendations by a certification committee; and

(4) establishment of procedures and reasonable standards concerning the approval of continuing legal education, waivers, and other matters for determining compliance with the CLER and the BSCR.

(c) Policy Waiver. Subject to the continued direction and supervision by the board of governors, any provision of any policy may be waived by a two-thirds vote of those present at any meeting of the BLSE.

(d) BLSE Chair. The BLSE chair is designated by the president-elect to serve as the BLSE chair for a specified term. When the chair is absent, has requested recusal, or is otherwise unable or unavailable to serve, the vice chair or the chair's designee will perform the duties or exercise the discretion of the chair.

(e) Staff Duties. Staff will be responsible for all duties delegated by the BLSE as long as the BLSE retains responsibility for staff decisions. Such duties may include, but not be limited to:

(1) accepting applications;

(2) conducting preliminary review of applications;

(3) contacting candidates for certification and recertification for additional information or clarification;

(4) arranging meeting sites and preparing agenda(s) for the BLSE and certification committees;

(5) administering examinations; and

(6) processing and evaluating CLE credit requests in accordance with the BLSE's policies.

Amended Feb. 11, 1999, by the Board of Governors of The Florida Bar; Sept. 29, 2006, by the Board of Governors of The Florida Bar; Dec. 13, 2013, by the Board of Governors of The Florida Bar.

1.02. Administrative Procedure

(a) Meetings. The BLSE chair will designate meeting times and places and disseminate a calendar of meeting dates to the members at the beginning of each fiscal year.

(b) Quorum. Eight members will constitute a quorum of the BLSE for the transaction of business.

(c) Executive Session. The BLSE will be in executive session concerning matters deemed confidential under the rules. During executive session, only members of the BLSE and staff as designated by the BLSE chair may be admitted, except under limited circumstances. Other individuals will be permitted to appear before the BLSE during executive session as permitted by BLSE policy or at the direction of the BLSE chair. The extent of that appearance will be determined solely in the discretion of the BLSE chair.

(d) BLSE Subcommittees. The BLSE may establish subcommittees to assist in the administration of its duties. Such subcommittees may include, but are not limited to: executive, standards, rules and policies, national accreditation, strategic planning, and communications. The BLSE chair will appoint the members and leadership for each BLSE subcommittee.

(e) Meetings of the Executive Subcommittee. Minutes will be prepared for all executive subcommittee meetings. The minutes will be distributed to members of the BLSE along with other agenda materials prior to the next regularly scheduled meeting of the BLSE or as the executive subcommittee directs. The actions taken will not be final until the minutes are approved at the next regular meeting of the BLSE, or by teleconference as the BLSE chair determines necessary.

(f) Liaisons. The BLSE chair may appoint a BLSE liaison to each certification committee.

(g) Removal of Members. The chair of each certification committee or the BLSE chair may petition the president of The Florida Bar to remove a certification committee member for good cause shown. The BLSE chair may petition the president of The Florida Bar to remove a BLSE member for good cause shown. Good cause includes, but is not limited to, absence from 3 meetings or conference calls or a lack of participation in committee or BLSE activities and assignments in any 12–month period. If a member is recommended for removal from the BLSE or a certification committee, the member will be notified in advance.

(h) Ex Officio Members. The chair of each certification committee is an ex officio member of the BLSE and entitled to attend the BLSE meetings and to participate in discussions, but is not entitled to vote or to be counted in determining the existence of a quorum. Ex officio members may not be present for executive session matters before the BLSE unless otherwise permitted under these policies or by a two-thirds vote of the BLSE.

Amended Feb. 11, 1999, by the Board of Governors of The Florida Bar; Dec. 13, 2013, by the Board of Governors of The Florida Bar.

200. FLORIDA CERTIFICATION PLAN

2.01. Administration

(a) The BLSE. The BLSE bears ultimate responsibility in the certification of applicants. Its oversight of the certification committees will be in accordance with the Rules Regulating The Florida Bar and these policies to ensure minimum standards of the plan are met.

(b) Certification Committees. Each certification committee will operate under the Rules Regulating The Florida Bar and policies of the BLSE. The duties of each certification committee will include, but not be limited to:

(1) recommending the issuance, renewal, or denial of certificates;

(2) reviewing applications;

(3) establishing testing procedures;

(4) preparing, overseeing, administering, and grading the examination;

(5) developing policies subject to approval by the BLSE; and

(6) performing other duties deemed appropriate.

(c) LSE Director. The Legal Specialization and Education director (LSE director) will serve as the staff liaison to the BLSE.

(d) Staff. The BLSE and each certification committee will receive staff support to carry out the administrative responsibilities set forth in the Rules Regulating The Florida Bar. Staff support will be managed in accordance with the internal procedures of The Florida Bar. Among the responsibilities of the LSE director is to balance the effective administration of the program with practical fiscal considerations, including, but not limited to, whether in-person staff support at a meeting of a certification committee is necessary or may be accomplished by alternative conferencing methods.

Amended Dec. 13, 2013, by the Board of Governors of The Florida Bar.

2.02. Areas of Certification

(a) Supreme Court Approval. Each area of certification must be approved by the Supreme Court of Florida.

(b) Approved Areas. The areas of certification and the dates of approval are: tax (7/1/82); civil trial (7/1/82); marital and family law (7/1/84); wills, trusts and estates (7/1/85), criminal law (trial and appellate) (7/1/86); real estate (7/1/86); workers' compensation (7/1/87); appellate practice (7/1/93); health law (9/1/94); immigration and nationality law (9/1/94); admiralty and maritime (7/20/95); aviation (7/20/95); business litigation (7/20/95); city, county and local government (7/20/95); elder law (7/17/97); international law (12/18/97); antitrust and trade regulation (3/23/00); labor and employment law (3/23/00); construction law (5/20/04); intellectual property law (8/1/06); state and federal government and administrative practice (8/1/06); education law (6/11/09); and adoption law (6/11/09).

(c) Amendments to Area Standards. Each certification committee, in accordance with the Rules Regulating The Florida Bar, has the responsibility to recommend to the BLSE criteria for certification and recertification including, but not limited to, amendments to area standards. Before referral to the BLSE, any amendment to area standards will first be provided to the relevant bar section(s), division(s), and substantive law committee(s) of The Florida Bar with an invitation to comment. A 45-day response time will be suggested; however, reasonable accommodations to extend such period will be permitted to ensure a substantive review. Input received from section(s), division(s), and substantive law committee(s) of The Florida Bar will not be construed as a means to veto proposed changes, but merely to allow all those who have knowledge in a given field to offer substantive comment to ensure the continued maintenance of reasonable and uniform standards concerning education, experience, proficiency, and professionalism.

(d) Area Evaluation. Any certification area that does not reach 75 members by the end of the third year after implementation and maintain this number will be evaluated by the BLSE. Evaluation includes, but is not limited to, consideration of:

(1) the benefit of the area's existence for both the public and the profession;

(2) existing requirements to ensure they reflect practice standards common to the practice area and are attainable;

(3) examination statistics and the relative difficulty of passage in comparison to overall program average;

(4) the extent to which efforts have been made to stimulate participation;

(5) costs associated with administration; and

(6) the level of interest among those certified in certification committee service.

(e) Evaluation Results. The BLSE will conduct an annual review of certification areas that include fewer than 75 members and prepare a written report within 3 months of completing its evaluation, detailing its findings and recommendations for submission to the board of governors.

Amended Dec. 16, 2005, by the Board of Governors of The Florida Bar; May 22, 2008, by the Board of Governors of The Florida Bar; Dec. 13, 2013, by the Board of Governors of The Florida Bar.

2.03. New Certification Area Request

(a) Presentation. Any request for a new certification area will be presented to the BLSE. As the BLSE directs, staff will:

(1) poll the appropriate section(s), division(s), and substantive law committee(s) of The Florida Bar for input;

(2) contact other state bars or national certification organizations offering the same or similar specialization area; and

(3) notify the membership of the request by publication on The Florida Bar's web site for a minimum of 30 days to allow interested parties to respond.

(b) Consideration. New area proposals will be considered on a showing that the area is:

(1) an established and recognized area of legal practice in which certification would be of benefit to both the public and The Florida Bar; and

(2) projected to attain a 75 member threshold within the first 3 years of implementation.

(c) Application. An application for a new area must include, but is not limited to;

(1) letters of endorsement or petitions from a minimum of 100 members of The Florida Bar who would qualify under the proposed standards and who agree to seek certification on the area's establishment; and

(2) a letter of endorsement by a Florida Bar section, division, or substantive law committee.

(d) Preparation and Approval of Standards. The BLSE will review all information received. If there are sufficient facts to support establishment of the area, the BLSE will direct staff to assist the requestor in the preparation of proposed standards. On review and approval by the BLSE, the proposed standards must be approved by the board of governors. On approval by the board of governors, the standards must be approved by the Supreme Court of Florida before implementation.

Amended Dec. 16, 2005, by the Board of Governors of The Florida Bar; April 3, 2009, by the Board of Governors of The Florida Bar; Dec. 13, 2013, by the Board of Governors of The Florida Bar.

2.04. Fees

(a) Filing Fee. A fee must accompany each application submitted for certification or recertification. The fee amount will be set by the budget committee of the board of governors. Rejection or withdrawal of an application will not entitle an applicant to a refund of all or part of the fee.

(b) Examination/Certification Fee. A fee will be due and payable after an applicant has been notified of examination eligibility or before an applicant who otherwise qualifies receives a certificate. The fee amount will be set by the budget committee of the board of governors. Payment of the fee is required before taking the examination. The examination fee may be refunded only if written notification of cancellation is received by the LSE office at least 48 hours in advance of the examination date.

(c) Electronic Testing Fee. Each examinee that chooses to electronically complete a certification examination will pay an administrative surcharge to offset the expenses associated with the purchase of software, licensing agreements, consultant assistance, and testing site accommodations. The fee amount applicable to each examinee will be determined each year by the BLSE on the recommendation of the LSE director. Online registration must be complete at least 10 days in advance of the examination date. The electronic testing fee is non-refundable once the examinee has registered online.

(d) Annual Fee. An annual fee per area certified will be assessed against each board certified member, excluding those who are due to apply for recertification that year. Staff will bill each certified member, who is subject to pay the annual fee, between February 1 and May 31. Payment must be postmarked no later than 45 days from the invoice date or the member will be subject to a late fee. The fee amounts will be set by the budget committee of the board of governors. If payment is not received within an additional 30 days, staff will send written notice by registered or certified mail to the lawyer's Florida Bar membership address to advise that a recommendation to revoke certification will be forwarded to the BLSE under rule 6–3.8, Rules Regulating The Florida Bar.

(e) Reapplication Fee. A non-refundable fee must accompany each reapplication submitted. The fee amount will be set by the budget committee of the board of governors.

(f) Grade Review Petition Filing Fee. A non-refundable fee must accompany the filing of a grade review petition. The fee amount will be set by the budget committee of the board of governors.

(g) Lapse Reinstatement Fee. A non-refundable fee must accompany a request to reinstate certification on notification of a lapsed status. The fee amount will be set by the budget committee of the board of governors.

(h) Recertification File Extension Fee. A non-refundable fee must accompany an application for recertification file extension. The fee amount will be set by the budget committee of the board of governors.

(i) Emeritus Application Fee. A non-refundable fee must accompany an application for emeritus specialist status. The fee amount will be set by the budget committee of the board of governors.

(j) Fee Waiver or Modification. Any person seeking a fee waiver will file a written request with the LSE director detailing reasons for the waiver's necessity and any other information helpful to the BLSE. The BLSE will determine whether the waiver should be granted or the fee modified.

Amended Aug. 11–14, 2004, by the Board of Governors of The Florida Bar; Oct. 3, 2008, by the Board of Governors of The Florida Bar; Dec. 13, 2013, by the Board of Governors of The Florida Bar.

2.05. Applications

(a) Form and Content. Applications must be submitted on forms approved by the BLSE. Each question must be answered or shown as "not applicable." The applicant must swear that all information in the application(s) and any attachments are true and complete. Only complete applications will be substantively reviewed and the accuracy of the information verified.

(b) Revisions or Corrections. Applicants will be advised of their continuing obligation to notify the LSE department in writing of any change to any response in the application after filing.

(c) Supplemental Information. The BLSE or a certification committee may require an applicant to provide information in addition to that called for on the application form, including requiring an applicant to submit to a personal interview before the BLSE, the certification committee, any of its individual members, or any authorized representative. Failure to respond to a request for supplemental information will be considered a withdrawal of an application.

Amended Dec. 16, 2005, by the Board of Governors of The Florida Bar; May 22, 2008, by the Board of Governors of The Florida Bar; Dec. 13, 2013, by the Board of Governors of The Florida Bar.

2.06. Applicant Classifications

(a) Initial Applicants. An initial applicant must complete all requirements before filing an application; however:

(1) the examination will be completed after application filing;

(2) certain CLE requirements may be completed after application filing, if satisfactory proof of completion of the educational program is furnished to the BLSE before the application filing deadline; and

(3) the 5–year practice of law requirement may be completed after application filing, but no later than November 30 of the year in which application is made.

(b) Reapplicants. An applicant who is deemed eligible to sit for the examination by a certification committee, but who either declines to take or fails the examination, may apply as a reapplicant only during the next application filing period immediately following the year in which the applicant originally applied.

(c) Recertification Applicants. At the conclusion of the 5–year period of certification, a board certified member may apply as an applicant for recertification.

Amended Dec. 13, 2013, by the Board of Governors of The Florida Bar.

2.07. Application Filing Period and Dates of Certification and Recertification

(a) Initial and Reapplications. Unless an extension is granted by the BLSE, all applications must be postmarked by midnight of the last day of the application filing period to be considered for that annual class. Filing periods are as follows:

(1) *Cycle 1 Application Filing Period: July 1—August 31*

Aviation Law
Appellate Practice
Civil Trial Law
Marital and Family Law
Admiralty and Maritime Law
Tax Law
Immigration and Nationality Law
International Law
Elder Law
Labor and Employment Law
Adoption Law
Education Law

(2) *Cycle 2 Application Filing Period: September 1—October 31*

Criminal Trial Law/ Criminal Appellate Law
Workers' Compensation Law
Health Law
Wills, Trusts and Estates Law
Real Estate Law
Business Litigation
City, County and Local Government Law
Antitrust and Trade Regulation Law
Construction Law
Intellectual Property Law
State and Federal Government and Administrative Practice

(b) Date of Initial Certification. For applications filed for areas within the application filing period for cycle 1 above, (cycle 1 areas), the certification date is June 1 of the year following the filing of the application. For applications filed for areas within the application filing period for cycle 2 above, (cycle 2 areas), the certification date is August 1 of the year following the filing of the application.

(c) Recertification Application Filing Periods. Unless an extension is granted as provided elsewhere in these policies, all applications for recertification must be postmarked by midnight of the last day of the filing deadline. For cycle 1 areas, the filing deadline is May 31 at the conclusion of the 5–year period of certification. For cycle 2 areas, the filing deadline is July 31 at the conclusion of the 5–year period of certification.

(d) Recertification File Extension. A single 3–month recertification file extension will be granted if accompanied by a properly executed application for extension and payment of the appropriate fee. The extension will commence on the applicant's current certification expiration date. In executing the application for extension, the applicant must agree to complete all outstanding requirements for recertification and file the recertification application before the end of the 3–month extension. The applicant must confirm understanding that if the requirements are not met, no further extensions will be permitted and the fee may not be refunded.

(e) Date of Recertification. June 1 after the fifth year of certification is the effective date of recertification for cycle 1 areas. August 1 after the fifth year of certification is the effective date of recertification for cycle 2 areas.

Amended Dec. 13, 2013, by the Board of Governors of The Florida Bar.

2.08. Application Processing

(a) Review of Applications. Staff will conduct a preliminary review of each application before certification committee review.

(1) An applicant with a deficient application will be notified by staff in writing before certification committee review to correct or update any omissions.

(2) Only complete applications will be substantively reviewed by a certification committee.

(3) Omissions or inaccuracies in the completion and submission of application forms will be grounds for denial.

(b) Certification Retention. An applicant's certification status will remain intact throughout the period of recertification application review. If the application is denied by the BLSE, an applicant's certification status will continue only if the applicant seeks review under the appeal procedures set forth in the 400 series of these policies and, unless the BLSE's decision is reversed, certification status will automatically terminate upon completion of the appeal procedures.

(c) Pending Status.

(1) *Initial Application.* The application of an applicant for certification, who has an unresolved professional ethics matter, as described elsewhere in these policies, will be held in abeyance. The abeyance will not extend beyond 10 months from the filing deadline. If the matter remains unresolved at the end of the 10–month period, the application file will be considered withdrawn. The member will be advised and may reapply, without prejudice, during a future application filing cycle.

(2) *Recertification Application.* If an application for recertification has an unresolved professional ethics matter, as described elsewhere in these policies, the certification committee will consider the circumstances and recommend a course of action to the BLSE.

(d) Voluntary Withdrawal. An application for certification or recertification may be voluntarily withdrawn by an applicant. Notification of withdrawal must be in writing and must be received by the LSE director before an appeal under policy 4.04(a) is due.

Amended May 22, 2008, by the Board of Governors of The Florida Bar; Dec. 13, 2013, by the Board of Governors of The Florida Bar.

2.09. Professional Ethics and Competence

(a) Required Information. Each applicant is required to submit information for the time period specified in the application concerning the applicant's record of professional ethics and competence including, but not limited to:

(1) all instances of discipline;

(2) all disciplinary complaints currently pending;

(3) all instances in which a state or federal judge has found the applicant in contempt of court or otherwise adversely commented on the applicant's conduct;

(4) all malpractice claims made against the applicant (or against the applicant's firm that relate to the applicant's negligence) that resulted in a lawsuit filed, settlement paid, or appointment of a lawyer by the malpractice carrier to defend the applicant or the applicant's firm;

(5) all arrests, charges, convictions, or other dispositions of criminal matters; and

(6) any other matter that could adversely affect the applicant's membership in good standing with The Florida Bar or eligibility for board certification.

(b) Staff Review. Staff will check each applicant's record of professional ethics and competence before certification committee review and immediately before certification or recertification is granted. For all matters subject to lawyer regulation jurisdiction, staff will consult Florida Bar counsel for an update or status report for the application file.

(c) Certification Committee Review. Certification committee members will review each applicant's record of professional ethics and competence including, but not limited to, all instances of discipline and any unresolved complaints, and investigate all details of each complaint or matter. Staff counsel will be consulted, available files reviewed, and a hearing before the certification committee scheduled if necessary. Applications with pending matters related to professional ethics and competence will be held in a pending status or resolved as described elsewhere in these policies.

Former Rule 2.06 renumbered as Rule 2.09 and amended Dec. 13, 2013, by the Board of Governors of The Florida Bar.

2.10. Peer Review

(a) Applicant Submissions. Each applicant will submit names of lawyers and judges who can attest to the applicant's special competence and substantial involvement in the practice of law in which certification is sought, as well as the applicant's character, ethics, and reputation for professionalism, in accordance with the area standards and rule 6-3.5(c)(6).

(b) The BLSE and Certification Committee Inquiries. The BLSE or certification committee may solicit statements of reference from additional lawyers or judges at anytime during the application review process.

(c) Peer Review Statements. Statements of reference concerning applicants will be submitted on forms furnished by the BLSE.

(d) Exclusions. No applicant may submit the name of a board of governors member, a Florida Bar officer, an appeals committee member, BLSE member, certification committee member, or Justice of the Supreme Court of Florida to provide a statement of reference. The BLSE will not consider a statement of reference for an applicant from a board of governors member, Florida Bar officer, appeals committee member, BLSE member, certification committee member, or Justice of the Supreme Court of Florida.

Former Rule 2.08 amended May 22, 2008, by the Board of Governors of The Florida Bar. Renumbered as Rule 2.10 and amended Dec. 13, 2013, by the Board of Governors of The Florida Bar.

2.11. Approved Continuing Legal Education (CLE)

(a) Certification Credit. Unless otherwise specified below, the evaluation and accreditation of CLE activities for board certification is the responsibility of the certification committees and will be set forth in certification committee policies.

(b) Grade Review Panel Service. Participation on a grade review panel will entitle a member to certification credit equal to the amount of time devoted to the review and panel discussion of the examination question(s), model answer(s), and petition(s), provided the maximum amount does not exceed 5 credit hours per petition.

(c) Examination Question and Model Answer Drafting. Preparation of certification examination questions and corresponding model answers will entitle a member to certification credit equal to the amount of time devoted to the activity provided the maximum amount does not exceed 15 credit hours per year. If the activity occurs in connection with service on a certification committee, the certification committee chair will determine appropriate credit for each member in an amount not to exceed 15 credit hours per year. A maximum of 5 credit hours in ethics may be allocated as part of the 15 credit hours if the content of the question and model answer complies with the standards for ethics credit approval set forth elsewhere in these policies.

(d) Examination Pre–Tester. Participation as a pre-tester for a certification examination will entitle a member to certification credit equal to the amount of time devoted to answering examination questions and preparing the evaluation for committee review, provided the maximum amount does not exceed 10 credit hours.

(e) Proof of Completion. Applicants will certify attendance and completion of all programs they list toward meeting the educational requirements on the application.

(f) Overlap of Certification Credit Hours. Lawyers who are board certified in more than 1 area may apply certification credit hours to more than 1 area provided the hours are approved for the areas to which they are applied.

Former Rule 2.10 amended May 22, 2008, by the Board of Governors of The Florida Bar; Dec. 11, 2009, by the Board of Governors of The Florida Bar. Renumbered as Rule 2.11 and amended Dec. 13, 2013, by the Board of Governors of The Florida Bar.

2.12. Examination Preparation and Administration

(a) Examination Preparation and Review Courses.

(1) Certification committee members and members of the BLSE may attend or participate in any seminar intended as a preparatory or review course for a certification examination although they may not give instruction regarding, or otherwise comment on, any substantive legal matters relating to the examination. Certification committee members and members of the BLSE may participate in a preparatory review course to discuss in general terms, the following aspects of the certification process:

(A) development of examination questions;

(B) administration of examinations;

(C) grading/grading process of examinations;

(D) examinees' appeal rights and the procedures for appellate review; and

(E) available resources to study for examinations, such as available bibliographies. The certification committee may (but is not required to) provide 1 or more example questions used in past examinations, together with 1 or more model answers to the question. Any such question and answers used may not be used in any subsequent examination.

(2) The sponsor of any preparatory review course must:

(A) advise applicants and attendees in the course brochure and in any materials distributed to attendees that the course is developed and conducted without any endorsement by the BLSE or certification committees; and

(B) include a disclaimer in the course brochure and in any materials distributed to applicants and attendees consisting of substantially the following language:

This course is intended to provide a comprehensive review of the subject matter, and it may help candidates prepare for a certification examination. Those who have developed the program, however, have no information regarding the examination content other than the information contained in the examination specifications that are also provided to each examinee. Candidates for certification who take this course should not assume that the course material will cover all topics on the examination or that the examination will cover all topics in the course material.

(b) Examination Administration.

(1) *Examination Dates.* Unless otherwise adjusted by the BLSE, eligible applicants will successfully complete the examination as follows:

(A) for a cycle 1 area, the examination will be taken the following March;

(B) for a cycle 2 area, the examination will be taken the following May;

(C) subsequent examination opportunities will be subject to the limitations described elsewhere in these policies.

(2) *Location.* Each area examination will be conducted annually at the location(s) and on the date(s) as staff recommends subject to site availability, cost considerations, and the BLSE's approval.

(3) *Examinee Identification.* Staff must verify the identity of each examinee by requiring photographic identification on receipt of the examination materials.

(4) *Eligibility.* Only applicants deemed by the certification committee to have satisfied the application requirements will be eligible for examination.

(A) An applicant who is eligible to take the examination will have 2 consecutive opportunities to pass the examination. The first opportunity will be during the cycle in which the application was filed. The second opportunity will be subject to approval by the certification committee of a reapplication accompanied by the reapplication fee. The full examination fee must be paid for each examination taken.

(B) An applicant who does not obtain a passing score on the examination after 2 consecutive attempts is ineligible to reapply during the cycle year immediately following the second failure.

(C) The BLSE chair or vice-chair may permit an ineligible applicant to sit for an examination in instances in which:

(i) the certification committee requires additional time to investigate the applicant's qualifications; or

(ii) a disciplinary case against the applicant is pending; or

(iii) due to time constraints, the BLSE has not had an opportunity to consider the certification committee's recommendation.

(D) If an ineligible applicant is granted permission to take an examination:

(i) the examination fee must be paid in advance and may not be refunded;

(ii) the examination results may be released to the applicant but a passing grade may not be used as a basis to justify application approval;

(iii) and, if the applicant is unsuccessful on the examination, the examination may not be reviewed, nor may a petition for grade review be filed, unless the applicant is deemed to be an eligible applicant having satisfied all other requirements for certification;

(iv) and, if the applicant is successful on the examination, but is denied on the basis of the application, in lieu of challenging the application denial, the applicant may re-file in the next application filing cycle and, if approved, will not be subject to re-examination; and

(v) the applicant must acknowledge, in written form, understanding of and agreement with the above conditions before taking the examination.

(5) *Applicant Misconduct.* Failure to follow staff or administrator instructions pertaining to the examination or its administration will disqualify an applicant's examination and application.

(6) *Confidentiality.* To ensure and preserve the confidentiality of the certification testing process, all certification examinations, past, current, or proposed, and the model answers to such tests, will not be made available for inspection, copying, or use for any reason, except in those limited circumstances otherwise permitted by the BLSE's policies consistent with rule 6–3.12, Rules Regulating The Florida Bar.

Amended Dec. 16, 2005, by the Board of Governors of The Florida Bar; May 22, 2008, by the Board of Governors of The Florida Bar; Dec. 13, 2013, by the Board of Governors of The Florida Bar.

2.13. Grading, Review, and Petition Process

(a) Grading. The certification committees are responsible for grading all examinations. Each certification committee will regrade failed examinations before announcing examination results.

(b) Examination Results.

(1) *Passed Examination.* An applicant who passed an exam may not review the exam or obtain written test results. Examination results will be valid for 2 consecutive examinations. The first will be in the cycle in which the application was filed, and the second will be during the cycle immediately following.

(2) *Failed Examination.* Applicants who receive a failing grade may obtain their scores on written request.

(c) Examination Review.

(1) *Time and Location for Review.* Unless otherwise prohibited under these policies, an applicant who failed an examination may request an examination review. The review must be completed within 30 days of receipt of the certification committee's notification of the examination results. Examination review will take place at the location(s) and on the date(s) as established by the BLSE. The applicant may schedule an examination review at The Florida Bar office in Tallahassee during regular business hours during the 30–day period. An applicant may review the examination more than once, but no more than 3 times during the 30–day period.

(2) *Representation of Counsel.* The applicant may be represented by counsel in the examination review and grade review petition proceedings. If counsel is not board certified in the area in which the applicant failed the examination, counsel must execute a written agreement that counsel will not apply for certification in the area for 1 year following the applicant's examination review. For purposes of this provision, criminal appellate and criminal trial will be deemed a single certification area.

(3) *Acknowledgement of Non–disclosure.* An acknowledgement of non-disclosure and confidentiality must be executed by an applicant who requests examination review and the applicant's counsel, if present. The acknowledgment will bind the applicant and counsel throughout the review proceedings to maintain confidentiality in all matters disclosed in the review proceedings.

(4) *Items for Review.* On execution of the acknowledgment, the applicant and counsel may review only the following items: (i) a copy of the examination; (ii) the model answers, if any; and, (iii) the examinee's answer/test papers. Neither the applicant nor counsel may retain or copy any items made available at the examination review.

(d) Petition for Grade Review.

(1) *Commencement of Petition.* Within 30 days of the examination review, the applicant may file a petition for grade review with the LSE director. The petition must be accompanied by the non-refundable grade review filing fee. A petition received more than 30 days after the examination review will be returned. The petitioning applicant will be referred to as "petitioner" in the grade review proceedings.

(2) *Content of Petition.* The petition must specifically identify the answers that the petitioner wishes to challenge as graded incorrectly and must set forth the claimed grading error(s). The petition may include additional supporting authority to substantiate the claim of incorrect grading. The petition must neither disclose nor make any reference to the petitioner's identity except by use of the petitioner's assigned examination number. The petition must not include any reference to the petitioner's overall score or any reference to passing scores on other portions of the examination.

(3) *Certification Committee Consideration.* Within 10 days of a petition's filing, the LSE director will provide a copy of the petition to the relevant area certification committee chair and vice chair. If either

officer determines that the certification committee erred in the examination grading or a model answer construction, the certification committee will reconsider its grading of the examination challenged in the petition. The certification committee will also consider any other failed examinations that might be eligible to receive a passing score if the challenge in the petition is determined to be valid. The review will be completed within 30 days of the petition having been provided to the committee. Any comments on the petition, determined appropriate by the certification committee, must be in writing and submitted to the LSE director for dissemination to the petitioner and the grade review panel.

(e) Grade Review Panel.

(1) *Appointment of Members.* The BLSE chair must appoint a review panel (RP) consisting of 3 ad hoc appointees who are certified in the relevant area and appoint a BLSE member to serve as the RP's non-voting chair. No member of the RP may have had prior involvement with the examination for which a petition is filed either as a certification committee member, drafter, or grader.

(2) *Time for Review and Dissemination of Materials.* The petition and relevant materials will be forwarded to the RP within 60 days of receipt by the LSE director. Within 60 days of the RP's receipt of the petition, the RP must convene and issue a written recommendation on the petition. These time requirements will be tolled during any post-petition proceedings by the certification committee as provided elsewhere in these policies. The BLSE chair, for good cause shown, may extend the time for distribution of the petition and relevant materials to the RP or for issuance of the RP's written recommendation, but the RP's recommendation must be made before the registration deadline for the following year's examination. If an extension is granted, the petitioner will be notified by return receipt delivery to the petitioner's Florida Bar membership address.

(3) *Standard of Review.* The RP will review each question challenged to determine whether there is competent substantial evidence to support the certification committee's grading decisions. The RP's written recommendation will address each question challenged by indicating whether the points should remain as assigned or whether additional points should be awarded.

(4) *Procedure and Completion.*

(A) The LSE director will ensure that the grade review is accomplished anonymously and in accordance with these policies. All materials will be submitted to the RP without any identifying information and without any reference to the petitioner's overall score.

(B) The RP's written recommendation closes the grade review process.

(f) Appeal.

(1) On completion of the grade review, the petitioner may request that the BLSE review the RP's recommendation. The request must be filed within 10 days and will be considered by the BLSE at its next regularly scheduled meeting.

(2) The BLSE's jurisdiction is limited to claims of fraud, discrimination, arbitrary or capricious action in the grade review process.

(3) The BLSE will not consider whether the RP's recommendation is supported by competent substantial evidence.

(g) Ex Parte Contacts. No ex parte contacts may be made to members of the RP, the certification committee, or the BLSE in connection with or related to any grade review proceeding.

Former Rule 2.12 amended Dec. 16, 2005, by the Board of Governors of The Florida Bar; May 22, 2008, by the Board of Governors of The Florida Bar. Renumbered as Rule 2.13 and amended Dec. 13, 2013, by the Board of Governors of The Florida Bar.

2.14. Applicant Review Process for Certification or Recertification

(a) Certification Committee Review and Investigation.

(1) The certification committee will review an applicant's complete application and conduct further investigation as the certification committee deems necessary and appropriate to determine whether the applicant meets the requirements for certification or recertification. Investigation may include review of an application in an area other than that overseen by the committee.

(2) The area standards and policies for which certification or recertification is sought govern during the assigned committee's investigation and consideration.

(3) Any materials obtained by the certification committee that report or reference comments by members of the bench, The Florida Bar, or from any other source with respect to an applicant will be maintained as confidential.

(4) The BLSE chair will assign an application for recertification to another certification committee for consideration if the applicant is also a member of the certification committee to which the application is submitted.

(5) Certification committee members may not review applicants to whom they are related by consanguinity or affinity within the third degree. If a majority of the certification committee determines that a certification committee member cannot render a fair and impartial judgment on an applicant, that member may not review the applicant's file. The BLSE chair may direct that an applicant's file be reviewed by another certification committee.

(b) Recommendation of Approval. If the certification committee determines, by a preponderance of the evidence that the applicant meets the requirements for certification or recertification, the certification committee will recommend approval of the applicant to the BLSE.

(c) Notice that Recommendation of Denial is Under Consideration.

(1) If the certification committee determines, by a preponderance of the evidence, that the applicant has failed to meet the requirements for certification or recertification, the certification committee will provide the applicant written notice that its recommendation of denial is under consideration and will extend to the applicant an opportunity to provide additional supporting documentation.

(2) The written notice will identify at least 1 of the following bases for consideration of recommendation of denial:

(A) insufficient CLE credits;

(B) insufficient or unsatisfactory peer review;

(C) insufficient trials or other task requirements;

(D) insufficient substantial involvement in the practice area;

(E) unsatisfactory disciplinary or malpractice record; or

(F) action or conduct determined by the certification committee to be inconsistent with the special knowledge, skills, proficiency, character, ethics and reputation for professionalism that are required for board certification.

(d) Response to Notice that Recommendation of Denial is Under Consideration. If an applicant wishes to respond to the notice that a recommendation of denial is under consideration, the applicant may file additional supporting documentation to address the certification committee's concern(s) within 10 days of an applicant's receipt of the written notice. The submission may not exceed 25 pages in length, provided that the certification committee chair may allow a submission of no more than 50 pages on good cause shown.

(1) An applicant may not submit additional peer review assessments of any kind, but may submit to the certification committee the names of persons whom the applicant believes would be appropriate for additional peer review without representing the views of such persons. An applicant may advise potential reviewers that their names have been submitted to the certification committee, but should not offer an opinion as to the content of the reference statement or evaluation. Consistent with rule 6–3.12, Rules Regulating The Florida Bar, all peer review statements by members of the bench, The Florida Bar, or any other source will be maintained as confidential.

(2) Failure to respond to a written notice that a recommendation of denial is under consideration will be construed as a withdrawal of the application without the right to further review.

(e) Consideration of Response. The certification committee will consider the additional supporting documentation provided by the applicant and if the certification committee determines from such documentation that further investigation is warranted or appropriate, it will conduct further investigation as to the applicant's qualifications. The investigation may include soliciting additional peer review.

(f) Documentation. The certification committee is responsible for assembling documentation that will consist of the following:

(1) the application;

(2) all materials obtained or considered by the certification committee during its review, investigation, and consideration process; and

(3) additional supporting documentation provided by the applicant, or obtained by the certification committee, as permitted elsewhere under these policies.

(g) Notice of Recommendation. On review of all documentation, the certification committee will forward to the BLSE the documentation and the certification committee's written recommendation. Notice of the certification committee's recommendation will also be provided to the applicant. The recommendation will state at least 1 of the grounds set forth in policy 2.14(c)(2) as the basis for the certification committee's recommendation. If a member holds certification, or is an applicant for certification, in more than 1 area, the notice will specify that if the BLSE denies certification based on peer review, because the applicant's conduct is inconsistent with the character, ethics, and reputation for professionalism required of a board certified member, the BLSE will simultaneously determine whether to revoke or deny certification in the other area(s).

(h) The BLSE's Review of the Certification Committee's Recommendation.

(1) The BLSE will review the documentation and recommendation of the certification committee at the next regularly scheduled BLSE meeting that is set to take place not fewer than 20 days from the date of the recommendation.

(2) The BLSE's review will be limited to a determination of whether:

(A) the certification committee's recommendation is supported by competent substantial evidence in the documentation;

(B) the certification committee followed the requirements set forth in these policies in making its determination; and

(C) the applicant was afforded a full and fair opportunity to provide supplemental information to address the certification committee's expressed concerns.

(3) The BLSE may delegate initial review of the documentation and the certification committee's recommendation to a BLSE subcommittee. The subcom-

mittee will make a report to the BLSE for appropriate action at the scheduled meeting of the BLSE at which the certification committee's recommendation is considered.

(4) Based on its review, the BLSE will issue a decision. The BLSE's decision may: (i) grant certification or recertification; (ii) deny certification or recertification; or, (iii) remand the application to the certification committee for such further investigation or documentation as the BLSE may direct.

(5) The BLSE will provide written notice of its decision to the applicant and the committee chair, by certified mail, within 20 days after the BLSE's decision was made.

(i) Remand. If the application is remanded by the BLSE, the certification committee will have 60 days to conduct additional investigation or consideration as required by the BLSE and issue a new recommendation on certification or recertification. The 60–day time period for additional investigation or consideration may be extended by the BLSE chair for good cause shown.

(j) Procedures for Appearance Before the BLSE.

(1) *Request for Appearance.* Within 10 days of receipt of a decision by the BLSE denying certification or recertification, an applicant may submit a request for appearance before the BLSE to the LSE director. Within 10 days of receipt of a decision by the BLSE to grant certification or recertification, a certification committee chair, on behalf of the certification committee, may submit a request for appearance before the BLSE to the LSE director. If no request for appearance is timely filed, the applicant may proceed under policy 2.14(1).

(2) *Notice of Appearance.* On receipt of the request for appearance, the LSE director will issue a notice of appearance setting forth the date, time, and location of the next regularly scheduled BLSE meeting at which the applicant, a designated representative of the applicant, and the certification committee chair or the chair's committee designee, may appear in person or by teleconference. The notice will be served at least 20 days before the scheduled BLSE meeting.

(3) *Appearance Before BLSE.* The BLSE chair will afford the applicant and certification committee representative an opportunity for oral presentations. A maximum of 20 minutes, to be divided equally between the applicant and the certification committee representative, will be allowed for the hearing. No additional information or supporting documentation may be submitted by the applicant or the certification committee representative, either before or during the BLSE meeting, and the BLSE will disregard references to any materials that are not part of the documentation transmitted by the certification committee. The applicant may have a court reporter present during the hearing at the applicant's expense.

(4) *BLSE Consideration.* Following the hearing, the BLSE will consider the certification committee's recommendation in executive session, applying the standards set forth in section 2.14, de novo, without deference to the BLSE's initial decision.

(5) *Notice of Decision.* The BLSE will give notice, by certified mail, to the applicant and certification committee chair of its decision within 20 days of the BLSE meeting at which the hearing occurs.

(k) Finality of Decision. The BLSE's decision will close the application and peer review evaluation process.

(*l*) Appeal.

(1) Further review of the BLSE's decision by the applicant will be in accordance with the procedures set forth in the 400 series of the BLSE's policies.

(2) The appeal will be limited to whether the BLSE:

(A) followed the requirements in these policies and the Rules Regulating The Florida Bar in making its determination; and

(B) afforded the applicant a full and fair opportunity to be heard.

(3) There will be no further review of whether the certification committee's recommendation was supported by competent substantial evidence, nor will the appeal include further applications or peer review evaluations, or consideration of confidential peer review responses received by the certification committee or the BLSE.

(m) Ex Parte Contacts. Ex parte contacts with members of the certification committee, the BLSE, the AC or the board of governors in connection with the application review process are prohibited.

Former Rule 2.13 amended Aug. 26, 2005, by the Board of Governors of The Florida Bar; Dec. 16, 2005, by the Board of Governors of The Florida Bar; May 22, 2008, by the Board of Governors of The Florida Bar. Renumbered as Rule 2.14 and amended Dec. 13, 2013, by the Board of Governors of The Florida Bar.

2.15. Revocation

(a) Authority. Certification by the BLSE under the authority of the Rules Regulating The Florida Bar may be revoked by the BLSE.

(b) Automatic Revocation. The following will cause automatic revocation of board certification:

(1) An order imposing any discipline that terminates membership in The Florida Bar; and

(2) An order imposing a suspension of the practice of law.

On occurrence of either of the above, the member's certification is deemed immediately revoked without the necessity of any action by the BLSE and the member's name removed from any listings of board certified members. The BLSE will provide notice of revocation by mailing appropriate documents to the board certified member's Florida Bar membership address, by United States certified mail, return receipt requested, or by return receipt electronic mail.

(c) Discretionary Revocation. Other than those matters cited elsewhere in these policies that cause automatic revocation, the BLSE will consider revocation on the occurrence of any of the events described in rule 6–3.8, Rules Regulating The Florida Bar. The BLSE's determination must be based upon a preponderance of the evidence standard.

(d) Procedures for Discretionary Revocation.

(1) *Notice.* The BLSE will provide notice that the BLSE is considering revocation by mailing appropriate documents to the board certified member's Florida Bar membership address, by United States certified mail, return receipt requested or by return receipt electronic mail. The notice must specify the date on which the BLSE's consideration will occur and provide at least 20 days advance notice. If the member holds, or is applying for, certification in more than 1 area the notice must also specify that if the BLSE revokes certification on the basis of peer review determining that the applicant's conduct is inconsistent with the character, ethics, and reputation for professionalism required of a board certified member, the BLSE will simultaneously consider and determine whether to revoke or deny certification in the other area(s). On good cause shown by the board certified member, before the date of the BLSE's consideration, the consideration of revocation may be rescheduled once, and re-noticed. Time for response or request for appearance will be calculated based on this re-notice.

(2) *Response Required.* A board certified member must respond to the notice, in writing, within 10 days of receipt. The filing is limited to 25 pages unless extenuating circumstances are presented. The BLSE's chair may authorize up to 50 pages. Failure of a board certified member to respond timely, in writing, constitutes a waiver of all rights to respond and consent to the determination of the BLSE.

(3) *Request for Appearance.* A board certified member may appear before the BLSE to address the revocation consideration. The appearance will occur on the BLSE meeting date provided in the notice of consideration. No additional evidence may be taken at the meeting. Failure of a board certified member to make a timely request for an appearance constitutes a waiver of all rights to appear and consent to the determination of the BLSE.

(4) *Notice of Appearance.* On receipt of the request for appearance, the LSE director will issue a notice of appearance to confirm the date, time, and location of the meeting. The appearance may be in person or by teleconference. The board certified member may be accompanied by counsel and may have a court reporter present, at the member's expense.

(5) *Notice of Decision.* The BLSE will give notice of its decision to the member's Florida Bar membership address by United States certified mail, return receipt requested, or by return receipt electronic mail within 10 days of consideration of the board certified member's response and appearance, if held. The decision is final.

(6) *Appeal.* Further review of the BLSE's decision will be in accordance with the procedures set out in the 400 series of the BLSE policies. The appeal is limited to review of whether the BLSE afforded to the board certified member the procedural rights provided in these policies and pertinent Rules Regulating The Florida Bar.

(e) Interim Suspension of Certification. The BLSE may, at its discretion, suspend certification of any member who is under investigation for an offense related to professional integrity by any authority with jurisdiction, or who has been placed on probation from the practice of law by order of the Supreme Court of Florida. Notice of certification suspension will be sent to the board certified member's Florida Bar membership address, by United States certified mail, return receipt requested or by return receipt electronic mail. On occurrence of certification suspension, the member's name will be removed from any listings of board certified members. Following conclusion of the investigation or probation, the BLSE will either cancel the certification suspension or proceed to revoke certification. Recertification will be withheld during the certification suspension and, if the certification suspension is cancelled, the pending application will be processed immediately. Any member whose certification is suspended because of probation from the practice of law must promptly notify the BLSE of any change in the member's probation status.

Former Rule 2.16 amended Dec. 16, 2005, by the Board of Governors of The Florida Bar; May 22, 2008, by the Board of Governors of The Florida Bar. Renumbered as Rule 2.15 and amended Dec. 13, 2013, by the Board of Governors of The Florida Bar.

2.16. Lapse of Certification

(a) Authority. In accordance with rule 6–3.6(a), Rules Regulating The Florida Bar, no certificate will last for a period longer than 5 years. A lapse of certification may occur for reasons including, but not limited to, a member's failure to:

(1) file an application for recertification, or an extension request, by the application deadline;

(2) file an application for recertification by the extension deadline, if an extension has been granted by the BLSE; or

(3) respond as requested to supply additional information for application completion if confirmation of receipt of such request can be demonstrated by return

receipt delivery to the member's Florida Bar membership address.

(b) Lapse Notification. If a member allows a certificate to lapse, staff will send notification to the member by United States certified mail, return receipt requested, or by return receipt electronic mail to the member's Florida Bar membership address. The notice will advise that certification has lapsed, that the member's name has been removed from the listing of board certified members, that failure to respond to the notification within 30 days receipt constitutes acceptance of the lapse status and that any misleading indication as to the member's certification status may result in professional discipline.

(c) Lapse Removal Consideration. If requested by the member, and on payment of the lapse reinstatement fee, the lapse status may be removed if the member makes the request and submits the completed application, an extension request, or supplemental documentation as requested within 30 days receipt of the lapse notification, or payment of the lapse reinstatement fee. If the lapse status is removed, the application will be routinely processed as elsewhere provided in these policies.

Former Rule 2.19 added Oct. 3, 2008, by the Board of Governors of The Florida Bar. Renumbered as Rule 2.16 and amended Dec. 13, 2013, by the Board of Governors of The Florida Bar.

300. CERTIFICATION PROGRAM ACCREDITATION

3.01. Authority and Purpose

The BLSE shall have authority and responsibility to evaluate lawyer certifying organizations and programs and to define the conditions and procedures under which accreditation shall be granted, maintained, or revoked. Such review is intended to enable the BLSE to evaluate the objectives, standards, and procedures of such organizations and programs to ensure for the public the continued value of "certified," "board certified," "specialist," and "expert" as a means to identify lawyers who have demonstrated special competence, skills, and proficiency, as well as character, ethics, and professionalism in the practice of law.

Added Aug. 26, 2005, by the Board of Governors of The Florida Bar. Amended Dec. 11, 2009, by the Board of Governors of The Florida Bar.

3.02. Definitions

(a) "Accredited Organization" means an entity that has at least 1 program accredited by the BLSE to certify lawyers as specialists.

(b) "Applicant" means a certifying organization which applies to The Florida Bar BLSE for accreditation or re-accreditation.

(c) "Florida component" is knowledge, skill, and understanding of Florida law.

(d) "Florida plan" refers to the Florida Certification Plan, including the standards for each specialty area as set forth in chapter 6, Rules Regulating The Florida Bar.

(e) "Program," unless otherwise specified, means the process by which lawyers are certified as specialists in a certain area of law practice.

(f) "Specialty area" is the field of law in which lawyers are or are proposed to be certified as legal specialists.

(g) "Evaluation subcommittee" refers to the subcommittee convened to advise the BLSE in administering the accreditation of specialty certification programs for lawyers under these policies.

Added Aug. 26, 2005, by the Board of Governors of The Florida Bar. Amended Dec. 11, 2009, by the Board of Governors of The Florida Bar.

3.03. Eligibility for Accreditation

To be eligible to become an accredited organization, an applicant must:

(a) demonstrate its dedication to the identification of lawyers who possess an enhanced level of skill, expertise, and professionalism, and to the continued development and improvement of the professional competence of lawyers;

(b) demonstrate sufficient resources and personnel who, by experience, education and professional background, have the ability to direct such program(s) in a manner consistent with these policies;

(c) include a governing body, a majority of which are lawyers who have substantial involvement in the specialty area and are responsible for the review of lawyers for certification;

(d) define the specialty area(s) in which applicant certifies or proposes to certify lawyers as specialists in understandable terms for potential users of legal services in a manner that will not lead to confusion with other specialty areas;

(e) demonstrate that applicant organization's certification and recertification requirements are not arbitrary, can be clearly understood and easily applied, and that its programs operate in accordance with these policies;

(f) certify only lawyers who have satisfied each requirement and who continue to maintain such requirements comparable to, but no less than, those required for certification under the Florida plan;

(g) not require membership or completion of educational programs offered by any specific organization for certification; and,

(h) not discriminate against any lawyer seeking certification on the basis of race, religion, gender, sexual orientation, disability, or age.

Added Aug. 26, 2005, by the Board of Governors of The Florida Bar. Amended Dec. 11, 2009, by the Board of Governors of The Florida Bar.

3.04. Minimum Standards for Lawyer Certification

(a) [1]Applicant shall require lawyers to satisfy and maintain standards comparable to, but no less than, those required for certification under the Florida plan and, where the same or similar specialty area exists under the Florida plan, applicant shall require no less than the standards set forth for that specialty area, including passage of the Florida exam. If the area does not exist under the Florida Plan, specific and/or additional requirements shall include:

(1) *Substantial Involvement.* If determined appropriate by the BLSE, a Florida component shall be required to evidence experience and involvement specific to Florida law.

(2) *Peer Review.* Applicant, not the lawyer seeking certification, shall send and receive statements of reference. References must be from persons who are not related to the lawyer or who are not engaged in legal practice with the lawyer. Applicant shall further require and consider at least 2 statements of reference from individuals apart from those submitted by the lawyer. Statements of reference shall inquire at least into the reference's specialty area, familiarity with the specialty area, the length of time the reference has been practicing law and has known the lawyer, and the lawyer's qualifications, both generally and in the specialty field, as well as the lawyer's character, ethics, and professionalism.

(3) *Examination.* Applicant shall submit a copy of the written examination and must demonstrate that a lawyer seeking certification must pass such examination. The examination must be of suitable length and complexity to evaluate the lawyer's knowledge of substantive and procedural law in the specialty area. The examination shall include professional responsibility and ethics as relative to the specialty area. The examination shall also include evidence of a Florida component as determined appropriate by the BLSE. Applicant must also provide evidence of periodic review of the examination to ensure relevance to knowledge and skills needed in the specialty area as the law and practice methods develop over time, and evidence that appropriate measures are taken to protect the security of all examinations.

Added Aug. 26, 2005, by the Board of Governors of The Florida Bar. Amended Dec. 11, 2009, by the Board of Governors of The Florida Bar.

1 This policy does not contain a "(b)".

3.05. Minimum Standards for Lawyer Recertification

(a) [1]Applicant must have adopted a plan for recertification of all lawyers previously certified. Certification or recertification shall be valid for 5 years. While no examination shall be required for recertification, each certified lawyer must show continued competence in the specialty field in accordance with standards comparable to, but no less than, those required for recertification under the Florida plan and, where the same or similar specialty area exists under the Florida plan, applicant shall require no less than the standards set forth for that specialty area.

Added Aug. 26, 2005, by the Board of Governors of The Florida Bar. Amended Dec. 11, 2009, by the Board of Governors of The Florida Bar.

1 This policy does not contain a "(b)".

3.06. Applicant Procedural Requirements

(a) Applicant must provide a written review process whereby a lawyer has the opportunity to challenge a denial of eligibility, a denial of certification or recertification, or suspension or revocation of certification to an impartial decision maker.

(b) Applicant will require lawyers seeking certification or recertification to report to applicant, within the application, criminal or professional misconduct, judgments of guilt and/or disciplinary sanctions. Applicant will also require the lawyer seeking certification or recertification to report to applicant, within the application, whether the lawyer has either withdrawn an application for certification or recertification by The Florida Bar or had certification denied or revoked by The Florida Bar. Applicant will have procedures in place to revoke lawyer certification in instances of a disciplinary suspension, reprimand, disbarment, or criminal conviction. Applicant will revoke lawyer certification in instances of denial or revocation of certification by The Florida Bar. Applicant will further report such instances immediately to the BLSE.

Added Aug. 26, 2005, by the Board of Governors of The Florida Bar. Amended Dec. 11, 2009, by the Board of Governors of The Florida Bar.

3.07. Application for Accreditation

(a) Application shall be made to BLSE in a format prescribed by the BLSE with all information completed, including any supplemental documentation requested, along with the appropriate non-refundable processing fee.

(b) The application shall be accompanied by a listing of the names, bar numbers, specialty areas, and certification periods (beginning and ending dates) of Florida lawyers currently certified by applicant.

(c) The application shall be signed by an authorized representative of applicant.

(d) If applicant is accredited by the American Bar Association to certify lawyers as specialists, proof of such accreditation shall be provided with the application.

Added Aug. 26, 2005, by the Board of Governors of The Florida Bar. Amended Dec. 11, 2009, by the Board of Governors of The Florida Bar.

3.08. Evaluation Subcommittee

(a) It is responsibility of this subcommittee to conduct an independent evaluation of the qualifications of an applicant and each specialty program submitted and to recommend action to be taken on applications for accreditation.

(b) Appointment of the evaluation subcommittee shall be made by the BLSE chair and shall consist of up to 5 members including a member of the BLSE to serve as chair; a member of the relevant certification committee(s) (if applicable); person(s) knowledgeable in the specialty area(s); and, a person(s) knowledgeable in the administration and the operation of a program which certifies lawyers as specialists. If an applicant applies for accreditation in more than 1 specialty area, an experienced practitioner in each of the areas shall be appointed to the evaluation subcommittee.

(c) Unless otherwise extended, the evaluation subcommittee's responsibility shall end after final decision on an application has been made.

(d) Persons deemed to have a conflict of interest shall not serve on an evaluation subcommittee.

Added Aug. 26, 2005, by the Board of Governors of The Florida Bar. Amended Dec. 11, 2009, by the Board of Governors of The Florida Bar.

3.09. Evaluation Subcommittee Action

The evaluation subcommittee shall act by majority vote within 90 days after receipt of a complete application. The evaluation subcommittee shall:

(a) Recommend accreditation with or without conditions, if applicant has demonstrably satisfied all the requirements for accreditation as set forth in these policies; or request additional information; or

(b) Recommend denial if applicant fails to satisfy the requirements of these policies or has made material false representations or misstatements of material fact; and

(c) Provide written notice of its recommendation and the basis thereof to applicant, with a copy to the BLSE. A request for reconsideration may be made but must be in writing. It must state clearly and concisely any new or clarifying information addressing the basis for the denial and include all relevant evidence supporting the position of applicant. If no response is received within 30 days of the date of receipt of the notice, the recommendation shall be forwarded to the BLSE for action.

Added Aug. 26, 2005, by the Board of Governors of The Florida Bar. Amended Dec. 11, 2009, by the Board of Governors of The Florida Bar.

3.10. BLSE Action

The BLSE shall act on the recommendation of the evaluation subcommittee within 120 days after submission of the recommendation. The BLSE shall transmit its decision in writing to applicant.

Added Aug. 26, 2005, by the Board of Governors of The Florida Bar. Amended Dec. 11, 2009, by the Board of Governors of The Florida Bar.

3.11. Duration of Accreditation

Accreditation by the BLSE shall commence and remain in effect during the dates indicated on the notice of accreditation, unless terminated sooner pursuant to the earlier of the following occurrences:

(a) Termination of accreditation is requested in writing by the accredited organization and an acknowledgment letter sent by the BLSE stating the effective termination date; or

(b) Revocation of accreditation by the BLSE.

Added Aug. 26, 2005, by the Board of Governors of The Florida Bar. Amended Dec. 11, 2009, by the Board of Governors of The Florida Bar.

3.12. Advertisement of Accreditation

(a) In connection with advertisement of accreditation pursuant to these policies, an accredited organization must state in its Florida advertisement(s): "Accredited by The Florida Bar to certify lawyers in the specialty area(s) of [insert specialty fields]." If conditions are stated, the organization must also include: "under the following conditions [insert the conditions]."

(b) In connection with advertising the fact of certification by an accredited organization pursuant to these policies, a lawyer must state: "Certified Specialist in [insert specialty field) by (full name of the accredited organization.]"

(c) As to the accredited organization, a lawyer may, in addition, include "Accredited by The Florida Bar."

(d) A member of The Florida Bar may not hold himself or herself out as being certified by The Florida Bar or an accredited organization unless actually certified by those entities.

(e) A member of The Florida Bar certified by an organization whose accreditation is revoked pursuant to these policies may not advertise certification by that organization in Florida.

Added Aug. 26, 2005, by the Board of Governors of The Florida Bar. Amended Dec. 11, 2009, by the Board of Governors of The Florida Bar.

3.13. Revocation of Accreditation

An organization's accreditation may be revoked by the BLSE for the following reasons:

(a) Accreditation is granted contrary to these policies where the accredited organization made material false misrepresentations or misstatements of material facts; or

(b) The accredited organization no longer meets the standards for accreditation; or

(c) The accredited organization's advertisements are contrary to these rules; or

(d) The accredited organization fails to file any annual reports, fees, or respond to requests from the BLSE.

Added Aug. 26, 2005, by the Board of Governors of The Florida Bar. Amended Dec. 11, 2009, by the Board of Governors of The Florida Bar.

3.14. Revocation Process

Revocation of accreditation by the BLSE shall be pursuant to the following process:

(a) A notice of intended accreditation revocation shall be mailed to the accredited organization setting forth the proposed reasons for such action;

(b) Unless opposed, the action shall be effective 10 days from the receipt of such notice; or,

(c) If opposed, the accredited organization may contest the action by sending a written request to the BLSE setting forth the reasons review is sought and why such accreditation should remain intact. Such request shall be accompanied by all relevant evidence supporting the objections of the accredited organization.

(d) The BLSE shall consider the request and may hold hearings or investigate further as it deems appropriate. The ruling by the BLSE shall be final.

Added Aug. 26, 2005, by the Board of Governors of The Florida Bar. Amended Dec. 11, 2009, by the Board of Governors of The Florida Bar.

3.15. Annual Renewal

An accredited organization shall file an annual renewal. Failure to file shall result in revocation of accreditation. Annual renewals must be submitted in a format prescribed by the BLSE, shall be accompanied by the required processing fee, and shall include the following items:

(a) the certification examination that will be administered in the next testing session;

(b) sufficient documentation to show that the applicant continues to satisfy all requirements for accreditation set forth in Policy 3.04;

(c) an explanation of any changes to the applicant's standards or examination; and

(d) a complete list of the names and addresses of lawyers who have been certified or recertified as specialists in each program.

The renewal shall be signed and verified by an authorized representative of the accredited organization.

Added Aug. 26, 2005, by the Board of Governors of The Florida Bar. Amended Dec. 11, 2009, by the Board of Governors of The Florida Bar.

3.16. Fees

(a) The non-refundable application fee for accreditation shall be $1,500. If the organization is currently accredited by the American Bar Association, the non-refundable application fee shall be $1,000.

(b) The non-refundable annual renewal fee shall be $500 for each specialty area. Annual renewals received late shall be assessed an additional $250.

Added Aug. 26, 2005, by the Board of Governors of The Florida Bar. Amended Dec. 11, 2009, by the Board of Governors of The Florida Bar.

3.17. Disclosure of Information

(a) [1]Materials submitted by applicant as part of the accreditation process shall be deemed public information unless otherwise restricted by rule or policy. Examinations shall be kept confidential.

Added Aug. 26, 2005, by the Board of Governors of The Florida Bar. Amended Dec. 11, 2009, by the Board of Governors of The Florida Bar.

1 This policy does not contain a "(b)".

400. APPEAL PROCEDURES

4.01. Scope

These policies establish the review procedures by the board of governors of a request by any person who disagrees with a ruling or determination of the BLSE.

Amended Dec. 13, 2013, by the Board of Governors of The Florida Bar.

4.02. Appeals Committee of the Board of Governors

The appeals committee (AC) will consist of 7 members appointed by the president of The Florida Bar, 1 of whom will be designated as chair. At least 3 members will be members of the board of governors. The 7 members will be appointed to staggered terms of office, and the appointees will serve as follows: 2 members will serve until June 30 next following their appointment; 2 members will serve until the second June 30 following their appointment; and 3 members will serve until the third June 30 following their appointment.

Amended Dec. 13, 2013, by the Board of Governors of The Florida Bar.

4.03. Standard of Review

(a) Scope of Review. Review by the AC will be limited to whether the applicant or individual (appellant or petitioner) was provided the procedural rights set forth in the BLSE's policies and whether the

BLSE applied the correct procedural standards for approval or denial as provided elsewhere in these policies and by pertinent Rules Regulating The Florida Bar.

(b) Standard of Review. The appellant will have the burden of making a clear and convincing showing of arbitrary, capricious, or fraudulent denial of procedural rights or misapplication of the BLSE's policies or the Rules Regulating The Florida Bar.

Amended Dec. 13, 2013, by the Board of Governors of The Florida Bar.

4.04. Commencement of Proceedings

(a) Commencement of Appeal. An appeal will be commenced by filing a notice of appeal with the executive director of The Florida Bar, with a copy to the LSE director, within 45 days of receipt of the decision of the BLSE. A notice of appeal may be in the form of a letter, will be delivered by certified mail, and will be deemed filed upon receipt by the executive director of The Florida Bar. Failure to timely file will constitute a waiver of the right of appeal.

(b) Filing Fee. A fee will be paid when the notice of appeal is filed. The fee amount will be set by the budget committee of the board of governors.

(c) Contents of Notice of Appeal. The notice of appeal will identify the decision of the BLSE, by its date and nature that the appellant seeks to review. The notice of appeal will contain or be accompanied by a memorandum containing a statement of fact, argument limited to the standard described in policy 4.03, citations to authority, and a statement of relief sought.

Amended effective July 23, 2010, by the Board of Governors of The Florida Bar; Dec. 13, 2013, by the Board of Governors of The Florida Bar.

4.05. Response

A response to the appeal on behalf of the BLSE will be served on the appellant within 45 days after the appeal has been filed with the executive director of The Florida Bar. Service by mail will be complete on mailing. The response will contain statements of fact, an argument limited to the standard described in policy 4.03, citations to authority, and supporting material.

Amended Dec. 13, 2013, by the Board of Governors of The Florida Bar.

4.06. Right of Reply

(a) Time. The appellant may file a reply within 20 days of receipt of the response limited to rebuttal of matters argued in the response. Service by mail will be complete on mailing.

(b) Other Pleadings. No further pleadings will be permitted unless requested by the AC on its own initiative.

Amended Dec. 13, 2013, by the Board of Governors of The Florida Bar.

4.07. Evidence

No evidence will be presented on appeal that was not presented to the BLSE.

Amended Dec. 13, 2013, by the Board of Governors of The Florida Bar.

4.08. Computation of Time

In computing any period of time prescribed or allowed by these policies, Rule 2.154, Florida Rules of Judicial Administration, applies.

Amended Dec. 13, 2013, by the Board of Governors of The Florida Bar.

4.09. Consideration of Appeal

(a) Meeting. The AC will convene to consider the appeal at the next regularly scheduled meeting of the board of governors held no fewer than 20 days after the time for filing a reply by the appellant has expired or the filing of the reply, if a reply is filed. The chair of the AC will designate the time and place of the meeting and the LSE director will furnish notice of the meeting to the members of the AC, the appellant, and the BLSE. The notice will be provided at least 15 days before the date on which the AC is to convene. Members may participate telephonically and will be considered present.

(b) Record. The LSE director will furnish to the AC a copy of the decision of the BLSE; a copy of the notice of appeal and all supporting material filed by the appellant; a copy of the response; and a copy of the reply, if any. The record provided to the AC will not include any individual peer review references provided to or considered by the certification committee or the BLSE for performance of peer review evaluation.

(c) Oral Argument. The appellant will be entitled to present oral argument before the AC only if requested in the notice of appeal, memorandum in support, or reply. The BLSE will have the right to present oral argument only if requested by the appellant. If a request for oral argument is not made, the AC will make its decision solely on the basis of the record.

(d) Decision of the Appeals Committee. The decision of the AC will be by a majority of those present and voting. Four members of the AC present will constitute a quorum. The decision will become the order of the board of governors, unless reviewed and overruled by the board of governors.

(e) Notice of Decision. The AC will give notice, by certified mail, to the appellant and the BLSE of its decision within 30 days of the AC meeting.

Amended Dec. 13, 2013, by the Board of Governors of The Florida Bar.

4.10. Review by the Board of Governors

(a) Petition for Review. A petition for board of governors' review of an AC decision must be received by the executive director of The Florida Bar within 10 days of receipt of the AC's decision. The petition must demonstrate a clear and convincing showing of arbitrary, capricious, or fraudulent denial of procedural rights by the AC. Such petition must be briefly summarized and may not be accompanied by any materials already contained in the record before the AC.

(b) **Response.** The respondent may file a brief response within 10 days of the date the petition for review is filed with the executive director of The Florida Bar.

(c) **Procedures.** The board of governors will consider the petition for review and response at its next regular meeting. Oral argument will not be permitted. The decision of the board of governors will be by a majority of members voting, excluding the AC members who voted on the original decision.

(d) **Denial of Petition for Review.** If the petition for review is denied, the AC decision will stand as the decision of the board of governors.

(e) **Grant of Petition for Review.** If the petition for review is granted, the complete appellate record will be transmitted to the board of governors for consideration at its next regular meeting. If requested, oral argument may be permitted. In determining whether to uphold or reverse the AC decision, the standard of review will be clear and convincing error on the part of the AC. The decision of the board of governors will be by a majority of members voting, including the AC members who voted on the original decision.

(f) **Notice of Board of Governors Action.** The executive director of The Florida Bar will give notice of the board of governors' decision to the petitioner and respondent, by certified mail, or by return receipt electronic mail, within 20 days of the board of governors' meeting at which such decision was rendered.

(g) **Ex Parte Communications.** Because the appellate process is of a quasi-judicial nature, ex parte communications by anyone to members of the AC or the board of governors are prohibited.

Amended Dec. 13, 2013, by the Board of Governors of The Florida Bar.

4.11. Petition for Review to the Supreme Court of Florida

A petition for review may be filed with the Supreme Court of Florida, under rule 6–3.10, Rules Regulating The Florida Bar.

Amended Dec. 13, 2013, by the Board of Governors of The Florida Bar.

500. CLE ACCREDITATION

5.01. Accreditation Standards

(a) **Standards.** To be eligible for CLE accreditation, the course or activity must:

(1) have significant intellectual or practical content designed to increase or maintain the attorney's professional competence and skills as a lawyer;

(2) constitute an organized program of learning dealing with matters directly related to legal subjects and the legal profession;

(3) be conducted by an individual or group qualified by practical or academic experience;

(4) include materials that are prepared by an individual or group qualified by practical or academic experience; and

(5) be held in a setting physically suitable to the educational activity of the program.

(b) **Materials.** High quality and carefully prepared materials should be available to all attendees at or before the time the CLE activity is conducted. Materials are not suitable or readily available for some types of subjects, but the absence of materials for distribution should be an exception.

(c) **Level of Activity.**

(1) *Advanced.* An advanced CLE course is designed for the lawyer who practices primarily in the subject matter of the course.

(2) *Intermediate.* An intermediate CLE course is designed for the lawyer experienced in the subject matter of the course, but not necessarily at an advanced level. A survey course in which there have been recent, substantial changes will be deemed intermediate. In an intermediate course, some segments may be low, intermediate, or basic, and others high, intermediate, or advanced. In those instances, the course taken as a whole will be considered intermediate.

(3) *Basic.* A basic CLE course is designed for the lawyer with no experience or limited experience in the subject matter of the course. A survey course will be considered basic unless there are recent, significant changes in the law.

Amended Dec. 8–11, 2004, by the Board of Governors of The Florida Bar; May 22, 2008, by the Board of Governors of The Florida Bar; Dec. 13, 2013, by the Board of Governors of The Florida Bar.

5.02. Application Process

(a) **Course Accreditation.** To apply for course accreditation, the CLE provider must submit the application form with the course description, a detailed outline of the course content, a detailed time schedule, biographical information for each speaker, and the requisite accreditation fee(s). Staff may request additional materials such as copies of any course materials, i.e. books, electronic media, or handouts included in the course presentation.

(b) Incomplete Applications. A course will not be evaluated if the CLE provider does not submit all of the information required in the application or meet the requirements set forth in these policies. If the application is incomplete or if supplemental information is needed, staff will contact the CLE provider to request the necessary materials. Failure to respond to a request for supplemental information within 60 days will cause the application to be returned.

(c) Submission Deadline. An application for course accreditation must be submitted at least 30 days in advance of the first scheduled presentation or it will be subject to a late fee. The fee amount will be set by the budget committee of the board of governors.

(d) Rush Processing. An application for course accreditation submitted with a rush fee will be processed within 5 days of receipt. The fee amount will be set by the budget committee of the board of governors. If staff refers the course to the BLSE for review and processing cannot be completed within 10 days, the applicant's rush fee will be returned.

(e) Course Accreditation Fees. An application for course accreditation must be accompanied by a nonrefundable fee. The budget committee of the board of governors will set the course accreditation fee for each of the following CLE providers:

(1) state bar associations;

(2) local bar associations;

(3) federal, state, and local governmental agencies;

(4) law firms that offer courses for employee attorneys;

(5) CLE providers that offer courses at no cost to attendees; and,

(6) all other CLE providers.

(f) Co-sponsorship. A course sponsored by 2 or more CLE providers will not be eligible for accreditation at no charge unless each provider meets the criteria for accreditation at no charge. If more than 1 provider is subject to a fee, the higher fee amount is charged.

Amended Dec. 8–11, 2004, by the Board of Governors of The Florida Bar; Dec. 13, 2013, by the Board of Governors of The Florida Bar.

5.03. Evaluation

(a) Authority of Staff. Staff will evaluate all submissions for accreditation and grant or deny credit in accordance with the BLSE's policies or the certification committee's policies as approved by the BLSE. Staff will refer novel questions or matters of first impression to the BLSE or the relevant certification committee.

(b) Credit Hour Calculation. Fifty minutes of course time is equivalent to 1 credit hour. A course must be at least 25 minutes in length to qualify for a half hour of credit.

(c) Non-qualifying Time. Time devoted to breaks, meals, introductory, and welcoming remarks will not be included in the calculation of credit hours.

Amended Dec. 8–11, 2004, by the Board of Governors of The Florida Bar; Dec. 13, 2013, by the Board of Governors of The Florida Bar.

5.04. Notice of Evaluation

(a) Accreditation Granted. If accreditation is granted, staff will advise the CLE provider of the assigned course number, the credit hour(s) awarded, the categories to which the credit hours may be applied, the accreditation period and expiration date.

(b) Accreditation Period. The accreditation period of a course will not exceed 18 months from the date of the first course offering.

(c) Accreditation Denied. Staff will notify the CLE provider if accreditation is denied and state the basis for denial. The CLE provider may request BLSE review if staff denied accreditation.

Amended Dec. 8–11, 2004, by the Board of Governors of The Florida Bar; May 22, 2008, by the Board of Governors of The Florida Bar; Dec. 13, 2013, by the Board of Governors of The Florida Bar.

5.05. Revenue and Expense Distribution

All accreditation fee revenue and related expenses will be allocated and charged to the course approval cost center. Two–thirds of the year-end net profits will be distributed to the CLER program and one-third to the certification program.

Amended Dec. 8–11, 2004, by the Board of Governors of The Florida Bar; Aug. 17, 2007, by the Board of Governors of The Florida Bar; Dec. 10, 2010, by the Board of Governors of the Florida Bar; Dec. 13, 2013, by the Board of Governors of The Florida Bar.

5.06. Member Submission for Course Evaluation

A member may request credit for a course which has not been accredited. These requests apply only to credit hours toward the member's own CLER.

Amended Dec. 8–11, 2004, by the Board of Governors of The Florida Bar; May 22, 2008, by the Board of Governors of The Florida Bar; Dec. 13, 2013, by the Board of Governors of The Florida Bar.

5.07. Other CLE Format

(a) Electronic Media.

(1) CLE credit for study involving electronic media may be given in the same manner as for live CLE courses.

(b) Interactive CLE Activities. A CLE activity that allows lawyers to participate or interact with one another, fostering the free exchange of information and ideas, is creditable. Interactive CLE activities include those in which lawyers participate through some type of electronic medium, such as:

(1) teleconferencing seminars; or

(2) other CLE activities developed through advanced technology.

(c) Self-assessment Courses. Self-assessment courses may be awarded CLE credit if they are directly related to the practice of law and include a graded examination from the CLE provider. Staff will determine the number of hours awarded on a case-by-case basis after verifying the applicant passed the exam.

(d) Self-study Courses. To be eligible for accreditation, a self-study course must comply with the format design described in these policies and consist of more than reading materials.

Added May 22, 2008, by the Board of Governors of The Florida Bar. Amended Dec. 13, 2013, by the Board of Governors of The Florida Bar.

5.08. Credit Approval Guidelines

(a) Courses for Nonlawyers. A course designed primarily for participants other than lawyers will not receive CLE credit.

(b) Courses on Nonlaw Subjects. A course devoted to a non-legal subject may be approved if the applicant can demonstrate that the course will enhance the proficiency of a lawyer in the performance of legal services.

(c) Demonstrations and Moot Court. Trial and appeal demonstrations and moot court participation may receive up to 3 credit hours for each 50 minutes of participation. A member cannot claim more than 9 credit hours for these activities during a 3–year CLER reporting cycle.

(d) Law Office Management and Economics. A law office management and economics seminar may be awarded up to 10 credit hours per course. The course must include management principles such as trust accounting rules, docket control, prevention of client conflict, or integrating high-tech equipment into a law practice. A member cannot claim more than 10 credit hours for this activity during a 3–year CLER reporting cycle.

A course is ineligible to receive credit if the content includes only:

(1) the marketing of legal services (except for the discussion of the ethical restrictions on marketing and advertising);

(2) increasing profitability;

(3) networking with a prospective client;

(4) training non-legal presentation skills, writing, financial management, or organization skills.

(e) Computer Training. Computer training courses designed to enhance a member's ability to practice law may be awarded up to 3 credit hours per course. A member cannot claim more than 3 credit hours for this activity during a 3–year CLER reporting cycle. Topics on how to use social media or networking sites will be not eligible for credit.

(f) Self–Improvement Courses. Self-improvement courses designed to enhance human relations skills; offer practical assistance on how better to relate to clients, witnesses, and adversaries; or promote courtesy and thoughtfulness in the legal profession may be awarded up to 5 credit hours per course.

(g) Laws of Other Jurisdictions.

(1) Courses focused on laws or procedures of another state or territory of the United States or international law may be awarded credit. Bar staff will determine the number of hours awarded on a case-by-case basis.

(2) International legal tours may be awarded up to 10 credit hours if the applicant can demonstrate how the activity enhances the applicant's proficiency in the practice of law. The applicant must specify in the application how lawyer proficiency is enhanced. A member cannot claim more than 10 credit hours for this activity during a 3–year CLER reporting cycle.

(h) Legal Drafting. Courses on legal drafting may be awarded credit hours if the applicant can demonstrate that the course content reasonably relates to the preparation of legal documents. The number of hours awarded will be determined on a case-by-case basis. A member may not claim more than 15 hours for this activity during a 3–year CLER reporting cycle.

(i) Accreditation by a State Bar. The Florida Bar may accept CLE credits granted by another state bar provided the CLE activity meets accreditation criteria. Staff may adjust credit in accordance with these policies.

(j) College and University Courses. Approved law school and graduate law courses entitle a lawyer to receive 2 credit hours for each quarter hour assigned to the course or 3 credit hours for each semester hour assigned to the course.

Undergraduate courses are only eligible for credit it they qualify under another section of these policies.

Added Dec. 13, 2013, by the Board of Governors of The Florida Bar.

5.09. CLER Components Approval Guidelines

(a) General Credit Hours. General credit must include all approved CLE hours regardless of the category or topic to which the hours are assigned.

(b) Ethics. Credit may be awarded for courses that explore and address standards of conduct in the legal profession. Courses should also include aspirations that surpass ordinary expectations to further promote the ideals and goals of professionalism, such as the:

(1) independence of the lawyer in the context of the lawyer-client relationship;

(2) conflict between duty to client and duty to the system of justice;

(3) conflict in the duty to the client versus the duty to the other lawyer;

(4) responsibility of the lawyer to employ effective client communications and client relations skills in order to increase service to the client and foster understanding of expectations of the representation, including accessibility of the lawyer and agreement as to fees;

(5) lawyer's responsibilities as an officer of the court;

(6) misuse and abuse of discovery and litigation;

(7) lawyer's responsibility to perceive and protect the image of the profession;

(8) responsibility of the lawyer to the public generally and to public service; and

(9) duty of the lawyer to be informed about all forms of dispute resolution and to counsel clients accordingly.

(c) Professionalism. Credit in the category of professionalism is determined only by The Florida Bar's Center for Professionalism.

(d) Substance Abuse. Credit may be awarded for courses designed to enhance awareness and understanding of substance abuse and dependence disorders.

(1) Topics eligible for credit in this category include education regarding the mechanisms involved in substance abuse and dependence disorders as described in the Diagnostic and Statistical Manual of The American Psychiatric Association.

(2) Instruction may address the correlation between substance abuse/dependence disorders and professional misconduct, malpractice, and disciplinary actions; identification of the signs and symptoms of substance abuse/dependence disorders; types of intervention and treatment for substance abuse/dependence disorders among lawyers, including the lawyer assistance program available to Florida legal professionals.

(e) Mental Illness. Credit may be awarded for courses designed to enhance awareness and understanding of mental illness.

(1) Topics eligible for credit in this category include depression, manic-depression (bipolar disorder), schizophrenia, and anxiety disorders, including obsessive-compulsive disorders.

(2) Eligible courses must address relationships among mental illness, addiction, or substance abuse due to "self medication;" the prevention of suicide, aggressive behavior, criminal activities, and under achievement through prompt and faithful medical treatment; and the progressive deterioration of the brain and/or the increase in the severity of symptoms and accompanying problematic behaviors without proper medical treatment.

(f) Bias Elimination. Credit may be awarded for courses that address standards of conduct in the legal profession related to the recognition and elimination of bias, such as gender, ethnicity, religion, disabilities, age, or sexual orientation. Courses should educate lawyers as to the aspirations that surpass ordinary expectations to further promote the ideals and goals of professionalism.

Added Dec. 13, 2013, by the Board of Governors of The Florida Bar.

5.10. Individual Credit Approval Guidelines

(a) Lecturing. Satisfactory performance as a lecturer in an approved CLE seminar may entitle a lawyer to credit. The maximum credit awarded is calculated based on presentation time. Lawyers who:

(1) lecture at basic seminars may receive up to 3 credit hours for each 50 minutes of lecture time.

(2) lecture at intermediate seminars may receive up to 5 credit hours for each 50 minutes of lecture time.

(3) lecture at advanced seminars may receive up to 7.5 credit hours for each 50 minutes of lecture time.

(4) participate as a panel member or group discussion leader in a workshop may receive up to 3 credit hours for each 50 minutes of participation in an intermediate or advanced seminar or 2 credit hours for each 50 minutes of participation in a basic seminar.

(5) lecture at intermediate or advanced seminars may receive additional credit for extraordinary effort. Staff will determine additional credit on a case-by-case basis.

(6) repeat a lecture or performance at 1 or more locations are not entitled to additional credit.

(7) serve as a CLE program steering committee chair, co-chair, or course moderator are not entitled to credit. Introductory and welcoming remarks are also ineligible for credit.

(8) prepare a lecture outline for a CLE presentation are not entitled to additional credit beyond that granted for delivery of the lecture.

(b) College Teaching. CLE credit is available for lawyers who:

(1) teach in approved law school and graduate law courses may receive up to 4 credit hours for each quarter hour assigned to the course or up to 5 credit hours for each semester hour assigned to the course.

(2) teach an undergraduate course are eligible for credit if the course qualifies for credit under another section of these policies.

(3) repeat teaching a course during the lawyer's CLER reporting cycle are not entitled to additional credit.

(c) Writing.

(1) Lawyers who write articles, books, and chapters in books may receive credit when the material is accepted for publication in a professional publication or journal.

(2) Credit will be based on the time devoted to preparation, quality, originality, and scope of publication. No single publication approved for credit may exceed 50% of the total hours required for CLER compliance.

(3) When a publication has more than 1 author, credit may be awarded to each author or divided among them in a manner consistent with the facts presented by all the authors.

(4) Up to 10 credit hours may be awarded for the preparation of Florida bar examination questions.

(5) CLE publications steering committee members may receive up to 10 credit hours for their work. The staff editor's recommendation will be considered when determining the number of credits awarded.

(d) Standing Committee Service. CLE credit will not be awarded for ethics, grievance, standing, rules, or general committee participation unless otherwise provided elsewhere in these policies.

(e) Credit For Florida Bar Grievance Mediation Program. A program mediator who participates in mediation or co-mediation under The Florida Bar's Grievance Mediation Program may request and receive 1 ethics credit hour for each 50 minutes devoted to the mediation. The amount of credit received must not exceed 5 credit hours in a 3–year CLER reporting cycle.

(f) Legislative Service. A state or federal legislator may receive up to 10 general credit hours and 2 ethics credit hours for each full year of service during the applicable 3–year CLER reporting cycle.

(g) Executive Branch Service. A Florida governor, lieutenant governor, or a member of the Florida cabinet may receive up to 10 general credit hours and 2 ethics credit hours for each full year of service during the applicable 3-year CLER reporting cycle. An executive branch officer of another state may receive continuing legal education credit on a case-by-case basis.

(h) Justice Teaching Classroom Presentations. Justice Teaching presentations will be awarded CLE credit to support the Supreme Court of Florida's initiative to advance an understanding of Florida's justice system among elementary, middle school, and high school students. A member will receive 1 general credit hour for each presentation. The amount of credit received must not exceed 5 credit hours during a 3–year CLER reporting cycle.

(i) Adult Civics Teaching Presentations. The "Benchmarks: Raising the Bar on Civics Education" program will receive CLE credit to support The Florida Bar's initiative to teach the fundamentals of government and the courts to adult civic and community groups. A member will receive 1 ethics credit hour for each presentation. The amount of credit received must not exceed 3 credit hours in a 3–year CLER reporting cycle.

Added Dec. 13, 2013, by the Board of Governors of The Florida Bar.

5.11. Accreditation Revocation

CLE credit may be rescinded by the BLSE if it is determined that the course content or speaker credentials do not reflect the accreditation standards in these policies. For example, credit awarded to courses sponsored or delivered by speakers with court-imposed disciplinary sanctions may be revoked.

Former Rule 5.06 amended Dec. 8–11, 2004, by the Board of Governors of The Florida Bar; May 22, 2008, by the Board of Governors of The Florida Bar. Renumbered as Rule 5.11 and amended Dec. 13, 2013, by the Board of Governors of The Florida Bar.

5.12. Complimentary CLE

The Florida Bar will provide 10 hours of approved CLE material to each county law library or voluntary bar association in Florida each year, without charge or cost, to assist members in fulfilling the CLE requirement. Recipients must provide materials to all bar members without charge. An out-of-state bar association may request a copy of the CLE at no charge if the association provides the CLE at no cost to members of The Florida Bar.

Former Rule 5.07 added May 22, 2008, by the Board of Governors of The Florida Bar. Renumbered as Rule 5.12 Dec. 13, 2013, by the Board of Governors of The Florida Bar.

600. FLORIDA CONTINUING LEGAL EDUCATION REQUIREMENTS

6.01. Administration

These policies establish the reporting and compliance procedures for the administration of the Continuing Legal Education Requirement (CLER).

Amended Dec. 13, 2013, by the Board of Governors of The Florida Bar.

6.02. Reporting

(a) Reporting Date. Each newly admitted bar member will be assigned a date to report CLER completion. The report dates will be staggered to balance the number of members who report each month.

(b) Reporting Cycle. Each member must report compliance with the CLER, or eligibility for an exemption, by the last day of the member's assigned month. If a member is reinstated to practice law after retirement, disbarment, or an incapacitated membership status, the start date for the new reporting cycle will be the first day of reinstatement. A judge who returns to the practice of law may request a new reporting cycle.

(c) Reporting Compliance. Each member should use The Florida Bar's website to post and confirm CLE credit hours earned. If online posting is not used, the member must provide the following information regarding each CLE activity:

(1) title and sponsor;

(2) date and location;

(3) the member's involvement;

(4) number of earned CLE credit hours; and

(5) other activity constituting CLE credit.

(d) Reporting Affidavit. The bar will provide a reporting affidavit to a member who has not completed the CLER within 90 days of the member's reporting date. The member must complete the necessary hours for the current reporting cycle, update the affidavit, and return it to The Florida Bar by the member's reporting date. In lieu of returning the reporting affidavit, the member may update the member's CLER record through The Florida Bar's website.

(e) Supplemental Information. To ascertain compliance, the BLSE or staff may require the member to provide additional information.

(f) Exemptions. A member who seeks an exemption from the CLER under sections 6.02(f)(1), (2) or (3) must file a CLER exemption request form. Staff will review and confirm eligibility within 10 days of receipt of the request. If granted, the exemption will remain in effect until the member is no longer eligible.

(1) *Active Military Service.* A member on extended active military service during the applicable reporting period, who files a report establishing that status, is exempt from complying with the CLER. A member who is exempt under this section must not engage in the delivery of legal services within Florida or give advice on matters of Florida law except as required by the member's military duties.

(2) *Undue Hardship.* A member who establishes to the satisfaction of staff special circumstances which constitute undue hardship, may be exempt from complying with the CLER. The member must report, in the form prescribed, the special circumstances constituting undue hardship. On receipt of a timely filed report staff will determine whether an undue hardship exists. The member will be required to comply within 60 days if staff determines no undue hardship exists.

(3) *Non-resident Members.* A member who has permanently resided outside Florida, who has not practiced law in Florida, or provided advice or services on Florida law during the preceding year, may be exempt from complying with the CLER.

(4) *Full-time Federal Judiciary.* A member of the full-time federal judiciary, who is prohibited from engaging in the private practice of law, is exempt from complying with the CLER.

(5) *Florida Judiciary.* Justices of the Supreme Court of Florida and judges of the district courts of appeal, circuit and county courts, and judicial officers and employees designated by the Supreme Court of Florida are exempt from complying with the CLER.

(6) *Inactive Members.* A member whose Florida Bar membership status is inactive is exempt from complying with the CLER.

(7) *Pro rata Credit Hours.* A member exempt under sections 6.02(f)(1), (3) or (6) whose right to an exemption terminates prior to the end of the reporting period will be required to fulfill the CLE requirements based on the pro rata portion of the nonexempt reporting period. A member exempt under sections 6.02(f)(4) and (5) is not subject to this provision. Pro rata hours will be calculated in 10–hour increments, and any part of a 12–month period will be considered a full year requiring 10 hours.

Amended Dec. 13, 2013, by the Board of Governors of The Florida Bar.

6.03. Carry Over Prohibited

The member must complete the required CLE within the member's current reporting cycle to maintain active membership in the bar. CLE credit may not be counted for more than 1 reporting cycle and may not be carried forward to subsequent reporting cycles. Repeating a course during a member's CLER reporting cycle is not a basis for additional credit.

Amended Aug. 11–14, 2004, by the Board of Governors of The Florida Bar; Dec. 13, 2013, by the Board of Governors of The Florida Bar.

6.04. Evidence of Compliance

Completion of the requirement may be demonstrated through a member's online posting through The Florida Bar's website or the timely return of an executed reporting affidavit.

Amended Dec. 13, 2013, by the Board of Governors of The Florida Bar.

6.05. Notice of Delinquency and Appeal

A member who fails to comply with the CLER is delinquent the first day following the member's reporting date. The BLSE will notify members of their CLER delinquency by regular or electronic mail to the member's official bar address. A determination of noncompliance by the BLSE may be appealed under the 400 series of these policies.

Amended Dec. 13, 2013, by the Board of Governors of The Florida Bar.

6.06. Reinstatement

A delinquent member may petition for reinstatement under the Rules Regulating The Florida Bar.

Former Rule 6.05 renumbered as Rule 6.06 and amended Dec. 13, 2013, by the Board of Governors of The Florida Bar.

700. BASIC SKILLS COURSE REQUIREMENT

7.01. Administration

These policies establish the reporting and compliance procedures for the administration of the Basic Skills Course Requirement (BSCR).

Amended Aug. 11–14, 2004, by the Board of Governors of The Florida Bar; Dec. 13, 2013, by the Board of Governors of The Florida Bar.

7.02. Reporting and Compliance

Each member should use The Florida Bar's website to post and confirm BSCR courses earned. Course attendance records of The Florida Bar may also be evidence of compliance.

Amended Aug. 11–14, 2004, by the Board of Governors of The Florida Bar; Dec. 13, 2013, by the Board of Governors of The Florida Bar.

7.03. Deferment

(a) Establishment of Deferment. A member who seeks to defer compliance with either component of the BSCR must file a BSCR deferment request form. Staff will review and confirm eligibility within 10 days of receipt of the request. If granted, the deferment will remain in effect until the member is no longer eligible.

(1) *Active Military Service.* If active military duty is cited as the basis for deferral, the member must not engage in the delivery of legal services within Florida or give advice on matters of Florida law except as required by the member's military duties.

(2) *Government Service.* If governmental service is cited as the basis for deferral, the member must not engage in the delivery of legal services within Florida or give advice on matters of Florida law except as required by the member's governmental duties.

(3) *Undue Hardship.* If undue hardship is cited as the basis for deferral, the member must establish and report special circumstances which constitute undue hardship. On receipt of a timely-filed report staff will review the special circumstances and determine whether an undue hardship exists. If granted, the member may defer compliance from the BSCR for the applicable period. If denied, the member may request a 6–month extension for compliance.

Former Rule 7.02 amended Aug. 11–14, 2004, by the Board of Governors of The Florida Bar. Renumbered as Rule 7.03 and amended Dec. 13, 2013, by the Board of Governors of The Florida Bar.

7.04. Foreign Lawyers and Repetition of BSCR

If any conflict exists within these policies and rule 2.510, Florida Rules of Judicial Administration, rule 2.510 will control and govern foreign lawyers. A lawyer is not required to complete the BSCR more than once.

Amended Aug. 11–14, 2004, by the Board of Governors of The Florida Bar; Dec. 13, 2013, by the Board of Governors of The Florida Bar.

7.05. Exemption

A member who seeks an exemption from the BSCR must file a BSCR exemption request form. Staff will review and confirm eligibility within 10 days of receipt of the request. The member may request BLSE review within 14 days if staff recommends denial of the exemption.

Amended Aug. 11–14, 2004, by the Board of Governors of The Florida Bar; Dec. 13, 2013, by the Board of Governors of The Florida Bar.

7.06. Procedures on Noncompliance and Appeal

(a) Determination of noncompliance. Noncompliance will include, but not be limited to, failure to complete the BSCR, failure to establish eligibility for deferral, failure to request an extension for compliance, or failure to establish an exemption.

(b) Notice of delinquency. A member who fails to comply with the BSCR is delinquent the first day following the member's reporting date. The BLSE will notify members of their BSCR delinquency by regular or electronic mail to the member's official bar address.

(c) Appeals. A member may appeal a determination of noncompliance under the 400 series of these policies.

Former Rule 7.05 amended Aug. 11–14, 2004, by the Board of Governors of The Florida Bar. Renumbered as Rule 7.06 and amended Dec. 13, 2013, by the Board of Governors of The Florida Bar.

7.07. Reinstatement

A BSCR delinquent member may petition for reinstatement under the Rules Regulating The Florida Bar. A member may be conditionally reinstated and allowed an extension of 6 months to complete the BSCR if reasonable cause exists.

Former Rule 7.06 amended Aug. 11–14, 2004, by the Board of Governors of The Florida Bar. Renumbered as Rule 7.07 and amended Dec. 13, 2013, by the Board of Governors of The Florida Bar.

CHAPTER 7. CLIENTS' SECURITY FUND RULES

7–1. GENERALLY

Rule 7–1.1. Generally

The board of governors may provide monetary relief to persons who suffer reimbursable losses as a result of misappropriation, embezzlement, or other wrongful taking or conversion by a member of The Florida Bar of money or other property that comes into the possession or control of the member of The Florida Bar, including, but not limited to, attorney's fees.

Amended July 23, 1992, effective Jan. 1, 1993 (605 So.2d 252); July 1, 2009, by the Board of Governors of The Florida Bar.

Rule 7–1.2. Fund established

Pursuant to the authority granted by rule 1–8.4 of these Rules Regulating The Florida Bar, the board of governors hereby establishes a separate fund designated "Clients' Security Fund of The Florida Bar."

Rule 7–1.3. Administration

The fund shall be administered in accordance with regulations adopted by the board of governors.

Amended July 23, 1992, effective Jan. 1, 1993 (605 So.2d 252).

Rule 7–1.4. Definitions

For this rule the following terms shall have the following meanings:

(a) Claimant. "Claimant" means a person or persons or any legal entity that has filed a claim with The Florida Bar for a grant of monetary relief from the fund based on a claim that the person or entity has suffered a reimbursable loss.

(b) The Bar. "The bar" means The Florida Bar.

(c) The Board. "The board" means the board of governors of The Florida Bar.

(d) The Committee. The "committee" means the "Clients' Security Fund Committee," a standing committee of the bar.

(e) The Fund. "The fund" means the Clients' Security Fund of The Florida Bar.

(f) Reimbursable Loss. "Reimbursable loss" means a loss suffered by a claimant by reason of misappropriation, embezzlement, or other wrongful taking or conversion of money or other property by a member of The Florida Bar when acting: (1) as a lawyer; or (2) in a fiduciary capacity customary to the practice of law, i.e., a personal representative, trustee of an express trust, or guardian; or (3) as an escrow holder or other fiduciary having been designated as such by a client in the matter in which the loss arose or having been so appointed or selected as the result of an attorney and client relationship; provided, however, that such a relationship was not for a wrongful purpose and the claimant was not guilty of any bad faith in putting the money or other property in possession or control of the attorney.

(g) CSF Contribution. "CSF Contribution" means the total amount of the annual membership fee allocated to the fund as determined each fiscal year.

(h) Fee Claim. "Fee claim" means a reimbursable loss based on fees paid to a member of The Florida Bar for services to be rendered.

(i) Misappropriation Claim. "Misappropriation claim" means a reimbursable loss for misappropriation, embezzlement, or other wrongful taking or conversion of money or other property by a member of The Florida Bar.

Amended July 23, 1992, effective Jan. 1, 1993 (605 So.2d 252); July 1, 2009, by the Board of Governors of The Florida Bar.

7–2. COMMITTEE

Rule 7–2.1. Committee's duties

(a) Duties Assigned by Board. The committee shall have such duties in the administration of the fund as shall from time to time be prescribed by the board.

(b) Adoption of Regulations. The committee may adopt additional regulations for the efficient administration of the fund as approved by the board.

Amended July 23, 1992, effective Jan. 1, 1993 (605 So.2d 252).

Rule 7–2.2. Investigations

(a) Investigation Required. The committee shall investigate every claim for relief that appears to meet the requirements of this chapter. As part of the investigation, the committee may request the issuance of subpoenas for the production of documentary evidence before an investigating member of the committee or the committee. The subpoena will be issued by the designated reviewer assigned to that claim. The subpoena will be served by an investigator employed by The Florida Bar or in the manner provided by law for the service of process. Any persons who without adequate excuse fail to obey such a subpoena served upon them may be cited for contempt of the Supreme Court of Florida in the manner provided by rule 3–7.11.

(b) Payment of Meritorious Claims. The committee may approve for payment from the fund claims up to a limit of $10,000 unless, within 14 days from the date of assignment for review, the designated reviewer notifies fund staff to agenda the claim for board action. The board may otherwise approve for payment from the fund claims found to be meritorious and in accordance with the Clients' Security Fund Rules.

(c) Form for Claim. A form prescribed by The Florida Bar must be completed to initiate a claim.

Amended July 23, 1992, effective Jan. 1, 1993 (605 So.2d 252). Amended December 15, 2000 by the Board of Governors of The Florida Bar; May 29, 2009, effective July 1, 2009, by the Board of Governors of The Florida Bar; October 5, 2012, by the Board of Governors of The Florida Bar.

Rule 7–2.3. Payments

(a) Payment is Discretionary. If, in the judgment of the board or the committee, as the case may be, a reimbursable loss has been sustained by a claimant and the circumstances warrant relief, then, after taking into consideration the resources of the fund and the priority to be assigned to such claim, the committee or the board may, in the exercise of their respective discretion, as a matter of grace and not of right, grant monetary relief within the amount of their respective authority as set forth in rule 7–2.2(b).

(b) Determination of Amount and Manner of Payment. Such monetary relief shall be in such an amount as the board may determine and shall be payable in such a manner and upon such conditions and terms as the board shall prescribe.

(c) No Right to Payment. No claimant shall have any right, legal or equitable, contractual or statutory, to a grant of monetary relief from the fund, and neither a determination by the board to pay any portion or all of any claim, nor partial payment, shall vest any such right in the claimant.

Amended July 23, 1992, effective Jan. 1, 1993 (605 So.2d 252); Sept. 24, 1998, effective Oct. 1, 1998 (718 So.2d 1179); ________, ____, by the Board of Governors of The Florida Bar; July 1, 2009, by the Board of Governors of The Florida bar.

Rule 7–2.4. Prerequisites to payment

(a) Members in Good Standing. Payments from the fund will not be made unless the lawyer is suspended, deceased, placed on the inactive list for incapacity not related to misconduct, or has had the member's status as a member of The Florida Bar revoked or terminated. However, if the theft is by a nonlawyer employee of the lawyer or law firm, a payment may be made even if the lawyer remains in good standing.

(b) Complaints Required. The filing of a grievance complaint with The Florida Bar against the attorney claimed against may be required as a prerequisite to the consideration of a Clients' Security Fund claim.

Amended July 23, 1992, effective Jan. 1, 1993 (605 So.2d 252); Sept. 24, 1998, effective Oct. 1, 1998 (718 So.2d 1179); amended May 28, 2010, effective July 1, 2010, by the Board of Governors of The Florida Bar; amended July 25, 2014, effective July 25, 2014.

COMMENT

At times, the fund receives claims against an attorney where the theft was by a nonlawyer employee of the lawyer or law firm. As stated elsewhere in these rules, the fund may require that the claimant file a grievance complaint against the attorney. Rather than resulting in suspension or disbarment, the grievance may result in diversion, a finding of minor misconduct, or a finding of probable cause. Should this be the case, the attorney would remain in good standing. As the claimant hired the lawyer and/or law firm, the claimant should not be penalized for theft by a nonlawyer employee of the firm and discipline should not be imposed for the sole purpose of meeting a prerequisite to payment. Therefore, pursuant to this rule, the status of the attorney, in and of itself, will not act as a bar to payment of claims where the theft is by a nonlawyer employee of the lawyer or law firm. All other prerequisites to payment, including, but not limited to, exhaustion of remedies, apply to the claim and will be considered in analyzing the claim and recommending denial or payment. The prerequisite of exhaustion of remedies may include the claimant filing a suit against the lawyer, law firm, or nonlawyer employee.

Rule 7–2.5. Assignment in favor of bar

(a) Assignment as Prerequisite for Payment. As a condition precedent to the grant of monetary relief, the claimant shall make an assignment in favor of the bar of the subrogation rights or of the judgment (or the unsatisfied portion thereof) obtained by the claimant against the offending member or members of the bar, and the bar shall be entitled to be reimbursed to the extent of the amount of the relief granted with respect to such claim from the first moneys recovered by reason of such subrogation or assignment.

(b) Priority of Reimbursement to Bar. Ordinarily, as a matter of policy, however, in cases where the relief granted shall have been for less than the full amount that would have been allowable except for considerations of allocating available resources of the fund or other reasons related to the administration of the fund, the bar shall not be reimbursed for the amount of the relief granted with respect to such claim until and unless the last moneys shall be recovered by reason of such subrogation or assignment.

(c) Reassignment of Claim to Claimant. The bar shall have the right but shall be under no obligation to any claimant to seek recovery from the offending lawyer or lawyers of all or any portion of such claimant's claim; and if the bar elects not to pursue recovery, an claimant shall be entitled to receive from the bar, as the owner of the claim or judgment, a reassignment thereof sufficient to permit the applicant's collection thereof in the applicant's own name, provided that such reassignment shall reserve in favor of the bar a lien upon the proceeds of any recovery to the extent of the relief paid to the applicant from the fund. In the event of such reassignment, the applicant shall keep the bar fully informed of all the applicant's efforts to obtain recovery.

(d) Recoveries. Recoveries or repayments to the bar on account of payments from the fund will be restored to the fund.

Amended July 23, 1992, effective Jan. 1, 1993 (605 So.2d 252); July 1, 2009, by the Board of Governors of The Florida Bar.

7–3. FUNDS

Rule 7–3.1. Membership Fees Allocation

The board will allocate from the annual membership fees of the members of The Florida Bar up to $25 per member for the fund. In addition, the board will allocate up to $25.00 per motion to appear pro hac vice or verified statement in arbitration filed pursuant to rules 1–3.10 and 1–3.11.

Amended July 1, 2009, by the Board of Governors of The Florida Bar; April 19, 2013, effective July 1, 2013, by Board of Governors of The Florida Bar.

Rule 7–3.2. Gifts

The board is authorized to accept for the fund any contribution or gift offered to it for use in furtherance of the purposes of the fund.

Amended July 23, 1992, effective Jan. 1, 1993 (605 So.2d 252); Sept. 24, 1998, effective Oct. 1, 1998 (718 So.2d 1179); ________, ____, by the Board of Governors of The Florida Bar; July 1, 2009 by the Board of Governors of The Florida Bar.

7–4. AMENDMENTS

Rule 7–4.1. Generally

The clients' security fund rules may be amended in accordance with rule 1–12.1.

Amended Oct. 10, 1991, effective Jan. 1, 1992 (587 So.2d 1121); July 23, 1992, effective Jan. 1, 1993 (605 So.2d 252).

7–5. RECORDS

Rule 7–5.1. Access to Records

(a) Confidentiality. All matters, including, without limitation, claims proceedings (whether transcribed or not), files, preliminary and/or final investigation reports, correspondence, memoranda, records of investigation, and records of the committee and the board of governors involving claims for reimbursement from the clients' security fund are property of The Florida Bar and are confidential.

(b) Publication of Payment Information. After the board of governors has authorized payment of a claim, the bar may publish the nature of the claim, the amount of the reimbursement, and the name of the lawyer who is the subject of the claim. The name, address, and telephone number of the claimant shall remain confidential unless specific written permission has been granted by the claimant permitting disclosure.

(c) Response to Subpoena. The Florida Bar shall, pursuant to valid subpoena issued by a regulatory agency (including professional discipline agencies) or other law enforcement agencies, provide any documents that are otherwise confidential under this rule unless precluded by court order. The Florida Bar may charge a reasonable fee for the reproduction of the documents.

(d) Response to False or Misleading Statements. The Florida Bar may make any disclosure necessary to correct a false or misleading statement made concerning a claim.

(e) Statistical Information. Statistical information and/or analyses that are compiled by the bar from matters designated as confidential by this rule shall not be confidential.

(f) Evidence of Crime. The confidential nature of these proceedings will not preclude the giving of any information or testimony to authorities authorized to investigate alleged criminal activity.

Added October 29, 1992 (608 So.2d 472). Amended December 13, 2013, effective December 13, 2013, by the Board of Governors of The Florida Bar.

REGULATIONS OF THE CLIENTS' SECURITY FUND

REGULATIONS OF THE CLIENTS' SECURITY FUND

The Regulations of the Clients' Security Fund are not part of the Rules Regulating The Florida Bar. The Clients' Security Fund Committee has adopted these Regulations to implement Chapter 7 of the Rules Regulating The Florida Bar. The Regulations have been inserted following Chapter 7 in order to assist the practitioner.

Amended November 21, 1997, by the Board of Governors of The Florida Bar; October 29–30, 1998, by the Board of Governors of The Florida Bar; May 11, 2001, by the Board of Governors of The Florida Bar; July 1, 2009, by the Board of Governors of The Florida Bar; December 11, 2009, by the Board of Governor's of The Florida Bar; December 10, 2010, by the Board of Governor's of The Florida Bar.

In order to carry out the purposes and achieve the objectives of the provisions of chapter 7, Rules Regulating The Florida Bar, the Clients' Security Fund Committee, with the approval of the Board of Governors of The Florida Bar, promulgates the following regulations to serve as a guide, but not to bind, the operation of the Clients' Security Fund. The regulations may be amended by the committee with the approval of the board.

A. CLAIM PROCESSING.

1. The Clients' Security Fund Program shall serve as the staff agency for Clients' Security Fund matters with primary responsibility for (a) investigating and reporting on claims for amounts of $1,000 or less; (b) closing claims received which are clearly not covered by the Fund; (c) except as provided in chapter 7of the Rules Regulating The Florida Bar, closing claims when the underlying grievance matter has been closed by the bar without discipline, when the attorney remains a member in good standing, or the claimant has withdrawn the claim; (d) preparation of the committee agenda and recording the minutes of the committee meetings; (e) presentation of claims to the board of governors; (f) notifying claimants of ultimate disposition; (g) coordinating payouts with the finance and accounting department; (h) monitoring subrogation rights on previously paid claims; and (i) preparation of annual Fund reports.

2. Investigating members of the committee will prepare a written report on a form furnished by The Florida Bar on all claims assigned to each of them. The investigating member may recommend that the claim be: approved and provide a loss amount; denied and state all reasons for denial; or tabled or deferred and state the reason.

The committee will consider the claim at the next scheduled meeting. While the recommendation of the investigating member will be given deference, the committee may agree or disagree with the recommendation, including the loss amount.

The committee's recommendation will be forwarded to the designated reviewer. The designated reviewer will promptly review the report of the committee and report his or her recommendations to staff for inclusion in the agenda for the consideration of the board of governors. The designated reviewer may recommend that the claim be: approved and provide a loss amount; denied and state all reasons for denial; or sent back to the committee for further investigation. To the extent possible, guidance will be provided to the committee.

While the recommendation of the committee will be given deference, the designated reviewer may agree or disagree with the recommendation, including loss amount.

Upon receipt of the report of the designated reviewer, the claim will be placed on the agenda of the board of governors. The board of governors may recommend that the claim be: approved and provide a loss amount; denied and state all reasons for denial; or sent back to the committee for further investigation.

While the recommendation of the designated reviewer will be given deference, the board of governors may agree or disagree with the recommendation, including loss amount.

3. A claim against a member in good standing will be held until final disposition of the disciplinary matter. A claim alleging that a suspended lawyer took attorney's fees for legal services during the period of suspension will be processed in accordance with the rules and regulations. A claim alleging that a lawyer who has had the lawyer's status as a member of The Florida Bar revoked or terminated took attorney's fees after the lawyer's status was revoked or terminated will be closed by staff.

4. A claimant has a responsibility to respond to requests from staff for information that is necessary to process the claim. If a claimant fails to provide staff with the requested information after staff has made three attempts to obtain the information, staff may recommend to the chair of the CSF Committee that the claim be closed without further action. If the chair agrees, the claim will be closed without referral to the committee or designated reviewer.

COMMENT

When a claim is received by the Clients' Security Fund department, it is reviewed by staff for completeness. For example, staff will review the claim to determine whether proof of loss has been provided. Staff will write the claimant requesting any missing information that is necessary and an essential element to process the claim. The claimant is given 30 days to respond. If there is no response, staff will write again giving another 30 days. If there is no response to the second letter, staff will write a third letter once again giving the claimant 30 days to respond. The claimant is therefore given 90 days to provide information that is necessary and an essential element in processing a claim. If the claimant fails to respond after three attempts have been made, staff may recommend to the chair of the Clients' Security Fund Committee that the claim be closed. If the chair agrees, the claim will be closed without further review. Should the claimant provide the necessary information at a later date, the claim will be reopened. For purposes of determining whether the claim is timely, the date the claim was first filed will be used.

B. CLAIM PREREQUISITES.

1. No claim will be considered unless a claim for relief has been filed within 2 years after the date the disciplinary action becomes final. If the claim is against a deceased lawyer, the claim will not be considered unless it has been filed within 2 years of the date of the lawyer's death. For good cause shown, the board may, in its discretion, consider a claim filed out of time. In no event will a claim not filed within 4 years of the date the disciplinary order becomes final or the date of the lawyer's death be considered.

COMMENT

The regulation requires that a claim be filed within 2 years after the date the disciplinary action becomes final. If a claim is brought due to the death of the lawyer, the claim must be brought within 2 years after the date of the lawyer's death. However, for good cause shown, a claim filed beyond the 2 year period may be considered. The following are examples of good cause:

(i) conduct on the part of the lawyer such that the claimant was reasonably led to believe that the lawyer was working on the case, had not resolved the matter, or would reimburse the claimant for the loss; or

(ii) an award of restitution by a court or order by the supreme court that the lawyer must repay the claimant prior to reinstatement if the claimant reasonably relied on the award or order and delayed filing a claim in anticipation of reimbursement; or

(iii) conduct on the part of the claimant showing the claimant was trying to exhaust remedies.

However, even if good cause is found, a claim must be filed within 4 years from the date the disciplinary action becomes final or the date of the lawyer's death. Claims filed outside of this time period will be closed.

2. Claimants should reasonably exhaust other remedies before seeking reimbursement from the Clients' Security Fund. Other remedies include bonds, professional liability policies, third party responsibility, the defalcating attorney's partners and deceased attorney's estate. In determining whether a claimant has met this requirement, the factors which the committee may consider include, but are not limited to, the following;

(a) the availability of funds;

(b) the likelihood of collection;

(c) the amount of the loss;

(d) the ability of the claimant to retain legal counsel or to proceed pro se;

(e) the ability to locate the attorney.

3. The Clients' Security Fund Committee may require that the claimant file a complaint against the attorney with the appropriate state attorney's office; file a civil suit in an appropriate court; or cooperate with the committee in appropriate proceedings against such lawyer as prerequisites to the granting of relief from the Fund.

4. It is not a prerequisite to claims against deceased members that discipline was imposed or pending at the time of the death.

5. A claimant must provide credible evidence that the funds they seek to recover were in the attorney's possession or control before a claim may be approved. The following may be used to establish the payment or the amount of the payment or the amount of the loss:

(a) documentary evidence; or

(b) a finding by a court of competent jurisdiction; or

(c) an admission by the attorney; or

(d) a finding in an audit performed by a Florida Bar staff auditor

C. CLAIMS ORDINARILY DENIED.

1. Claims by relatives, partners, or other close associates of the attorney will ordinarily be denied.

2. Except as provided in chapter 7 of the Rules Regulation The Florida Bar, the Clients' Security Fund Committee will consider for payment only those claims arising out of a lawyer-client relationship.

3. Where the lawyer, unrelated to a lawyer and client relationship, is a personal representative, testamentary trustee, guardian or escrow agent for the claimant, and the lawyer's status as the personal representative, testamentary trustee, guardian or escrow agent is not due to or the result of an existing lawyer-client relationship with the claimant, the claim will be denied.

COMMENT

The existence of a lawyer-client relationship is central to the issue of whether a loss is reimbursable. If the lawyer is not acting in the capacity of a lawyer, the loss is not reimbursable. Therefore, if an individual is acting in a capacity unrelated to a lawyer-client relationship where their status as a lawyer is not material to the claim, the loss will be denied.

4. Claims by government agencies, institutional lenders, insurance companies, publicly owned entities including their subsidiaries and affiliates, entities which fail to disclose to the Clients' Security Fund Committee the names and addresses of their direct and indirect beneficial and record owners, and subrogees, brought on their behalf and not as representatives, will not ordinarily be considered for payment.

5. No claim shall be approved where the defalcating attorney was bonded in any capacity which protected the rights of the claimant, where the defalcating attorney was insured under a lawyers' professional liability policy or a policy of a similar nature which protected the rights of the claimant, or where the claim might be payable from any other source; provided, however, that the committee, may recommend payment of the difference of what the claimant received from the bond, insurance policy, or other source and the amount of the loss if the monies from the bond, insurance policy, or other source were exhausted and additional recovery cannot be sought from the bond, insurance policy, or other source.

COMMENT

Although the regulation allows the committee to recommend payment of the difference between what the claimant received and the loss under certain circumstances, if the claimant refuses or declines to participate in the settlement, the claim will be denied for failure to exhaust remedies.

6. If services were performed that were useful to the claimant, the claim may be denied.

An attorney may be deemed to have provided useful services to a client when, after accepting a fee from the client, the attorney:

(a) files a pleading or other document on behalf of the client that moves the client's case or matter forward or protects the client's interests, regardless of the quality of the pleading or other document; or

(b) engages in substantive communication about the matter for which the attorney was hired; or

(c) attends a court proceeding or proceedings that advance the case or cause of the client or protects the client's interests; or

(d) engages in investigation or discovery; or

(e) attends a mediation or arbitration or other alternative dispute resolution proceeding; or

(f) prepares a document or documents minimally suitable for use by the client in a legal proceeding or transactional matter; or

(g) provides legal advice and counsel to the client.

7. Investment advice given by the claimant's lawyer, although such advice may result in the loss of claimant's money, is not, in and of itself, a ground for seeking reimbursement from the Fund. Obtaining money or property from a claimant representing that it was to be used for investment purposes when no such investment was made, or any other theft or fraud committed by a lawyer, may be considered for reimbursement. In such circumstances the theft must be the result of a direct and current lawyer-client relationship.

COMMENT

Claims based on investment advice are ordinarily not reimbursable. Therefore, failure of an investment to perform as represented to or anticipated by the claimant is not a reimbursable loss. On the other hand, the theft or misappropriation of money or property by a lawyer where the lawyer represented to the claimant that the money or property would be used for an investment when no investment was made may be considered a reimbursable loss. In such circumstances the funds were obtained by fraud or a ruse for the purpose of being misappropriated by the lawyer. No investment existed nor was it the intent of the lawyer to invest the funds. As with all other claims, all claim prerequisites must be met including that the loss was the result of a direct and current lawyer-client relationship. Factors to consider in determining whether the loss was due to a direct and current lawyer-client relationship include the number, nature and timing of prior transactions between the claimant and the lawyer.

D. PAYMENT AND CAPS.

1. The maximum amount payable for an individual fee claim will be $5,000. Except as provided elsewhere in these regulations, fee claims may be paid

upon approval. Fee claims will be paid prior to misappropriation claims.

2. The maximum amount payable for a misappropriation claim will be $250,000. All approved misappropriation claims, except those with an approved loss amount of $1,000 or less, will be held for payment until the end of the fiscal year in which they were approved, at which time the approved misappropriation claims will be pooled for payment. Misappropriation claims with an approved loss amount of $1,000 or less may be paid on approval. The maximum amount available for payment of the pooled misappropriation claims will not exceed that fiscal year's CSF contribution less the sums used to pay approved fee claims and misappropriation claims with an approved loss amount of $1,000 or less. If there are not sufficient funds in the account to pay the remaining approved misappropriation claims, the remaining approved misappropriation claims will be paid on a pro rata basis with no individual claim exceeding a payment of $250,000.

3. No reimbursement on account of a claim shall be made from the fund unless and until the same has been authorized by the board or the committee and the claimant has executed assignments and other documents as may reasonably be requested by the board and the committee. As a condition to any payment staff may require such assurances as it deems appropriate to satisfy all conditions imposed upon any such payment, and to verify that payment is made to the proper party or representative of that party. Neither The Florida Bar, the board, the committee, nor staff shall incur any liability for nonpayment of claims or for erroneous payments.

4. If any approved payment remains unclaimed at the close of the fiscal year following the fiscal year in which the claim is approved, those funds will be returned to the fund. A final request for response will be sent to the claimant(s) prior to the return of the funds.

5. If it is determined that part of the money misappropriated by the attorney included sums to be used to pay a claimed lien, the amount of the lien will not be deducted from the loss. The claimant is liable for the lien.

E. ADMINISTRATIVE AND FISCAL.

1. The fund will operate on a fiscal year basis, concurrent with the fiscal year of The Florida Bar. Any sums remaining in the fund after all approved claims have been paid will be treated consistent with the Standing Board Policies.

2. An attorney representing a claimant shall be required to give to the committee a written statement that he or she will not accept a fee from the claimant for services rendered in connection with a claim against the Fund.

3. Publicity of Fund activities shall be at the discretion of the board of governors members and Clients' Security Fund Committee members in the circuit where an award is made.

4. An annual report detailing the financial activities of the Fund shall be prepared by staff, approved by the committee chair and published in The Florida Bar *Journal* or *News*.

CHAPTER 8. LAWYER REFERRAL RULE

8-1. GENERALLY

Rule 8-1.1. Statement of policy and purposes

Every citizen of the state should have access to the legal system. A person's access to the legal system is enhanced by the assistance of a qualified lawyer. Citizens often encounter difficulty in identifying and locating lawyers who are willing and qualified to consult with them about their legal needs. To this end bona fide not-for-profit state and local bar associations are uniquely qualified to provide lawyer referral services under supervision by The Florida Bar for the benefit of the public. It is the policy of The Florida Bar to support the establishment of local lawyer referral services and to encourage those services to: (a) make legal services readily available to the general public through a referral method that considers the client's financial circumstances, spoken language, geographical convenience, and the type and complexity of the client's legal problem; (b) provide information about lawyers and the availability of legal services that will aid in the selection of a lawyer; (c) inform the public when and where to seek legal services and provide an initial determination of whether those services are necessary or advisable; and (d) provide referral to consumer, government, and other agencies when the individual's best interests so dictate.

Amended July 23, 1992, effective Jan. 1, 1993 (605 So.2d 252).

8–2. REQUIREMENTS

Rule 8–2.1. Requirements for Establishing a Lawyer Referral Service Sponsored by a Local Bar Association

The Board of Governors of The Florida Bar may adopt such regulations as it deems desirable governing the establishment, operation, and termination of lawyer referral services operated by a local bar association.

No local bar association shall operate a lawyer referral service except upon application to and approval by the Board of Governors of The Florida Bar. No lawyer referral service shall be approved by The Florida Bar unless such lawyer referral service is offered primarily for the benefit of the public and unless such lawyer referral service is established and operated by a nonprofit organization exempt from federal taxation under section 501(c)(3), 501(c)(4), or 501(c)(6) of the Internal Revenue Code of 1986.

Amended July 23, 1992, effective Jan. 1, 1993 (605 So.2d 252); March 23, 2000 (763 So.2d 1002).

Rule 8–2.2. Contents of Application

An application by a local bar association to the Board of Governors of The Florida Bar for authority to operate a lawyer referral service shall be in writing and shall be filed with the executive director. Such application shall contain the following:

(a) Statement of Benefits. A statement of the benefits to the public to be achieved by the implementation of the lawyer referral service.

(b) Proof of Nonprofit Status. Proof that the referral service is established and operated by a nonprofit organization exempt from federal taxation under section 501(c)(3), 501(c)(4), or 501(c)(6) of the Internal Revenue Code of 1986.

(c) Submission and Content of Bylaws. The proposed bylaws or rules and regulations that will govern the lawyer referral service. The proposed bylaws shall include the following regulations:

(1) All members of the proposed referral service shall provide proof of professional liability insurance in the minimum amount of $100,000 unless the proposed lawyer referral service itself carries professional liability insurance in an amount not less than $100,000 per claim or occurrence.

(2) The proposed lawyer referral service shall accept membership applications only from attorneys who maintain an office in the geographic area served by the proposed lawyer referral service.

(3) The proposed lawyer referral service shall agree to maintain an alphabetical member list, updated quarterly, with The Florida Bar. In turn, The Florida Bar shall notify the service of any unresolved finding of probable cause against a member. When probable cause has been found at the local grievance committee level, and the lawyer referral service has been notified, such service shall be required to hold referral to the member in question until the matter is resolved. If the member is in good standing with The Florida Bar after the resolution of the matter, then the member may be returned to the service.

(d) Estimated Number of Panel Members. The estimated number of lawyers who will participate in the service.

(e) Number of Local Lawyers. The number of lawyers in the area.

(f) Statement of Need. A statement of the condition that evidences a need for such service in the area.

(g) Geographic Operational Area. The geographic area in which the proposed referral service will operate.

(h) Statement of Operation. A statement of how the lawyer referral service will be conducted.

(i) Statement of Fees. A statement of fees to be charged by the lawyer referral service, including, but not limited to, fees charged by the referral service to members of the public using such service and fees charged by the referral service or remitted to the referral service by member attorneys.

(j) Statement of No Discrimination. A statement that such lawyer referral service will be open for referral to the members of the public without regard to race, sex, national origin, or economic status.

(k) Statement of No Discrimination in Local Bar Membership. A statement that the local bar association is representative of the profession in the area of the service and is open to all members of the profession on an equal basis.

Amended July 23, 1992, effective Jan. 1, 1993 (605 So.2d 252); July 1, 1993 (621 So.2d 1032); March 23, 2000 (763 So.2d 1002).

Rule 8–2.3. Approval of Application

The board of governors may approve or disapprove the application to operate a lawyer referral service or it may call for additional information upon which to base its decision. No lawyer referral service shall be commenced by or on behalf of a local bar association until approval thereof has been communicated in writing from the Board of Governors of The Florida Bar.

Amended March 23, 2000 (763 So.2d 1002).

8–3. SUPERVISION

Rule 8–3.1. Supervision and reporting requirements

Any lawyer referral service approved by The Florida Bar and operated by a local bar association shall submit 3 quarterly reports and an annual report to The Florida Bar. The reports shall contain:

(a) a statement of the sources of income by category and amount;

(b) a statement of expenditures by category and amount;

(c) the number of attorneys who were members of the lawyer referral service for the reporting period and special panels, if any;

(d) the number of inquiries received by the referral service from members of the public during the reporting period;

(e) the number of referrals for legal services made by the service during the reporting period;

(f) the number of referrals for nonlegal services made by the service during the reporting period;

(g) a statement of the operation of the lawyer referral service, including the number of personnel employed and the means by which referrals are made by the service; and

(h) a statement of changes, if any, to the bylaws and regulations governing the lawyer referral service.

The annual report shall also contain a proposed budget for the next year and a statement of any material changes in the operation of the lawyer referral service since the filing of the initial application under rule 8–2.2 above.

The Florida Bar shall actively supervise the operation and conduct of all lawyer referral services established under this chapter and may require such other information as it deems necessary to determine the benefits of such service to the public and the achievement of the policies stated herein. The Florida Bar shall not make any charge to the local bar association or its lawyer referral service for such supervision.

Amended July 23, 1992, effective Jan. 1, 1993 (605 So.2d 252); July 1, 1993 (621 So.2d 1032).

8–4. REVOCATION

Rule 8–4.1. Revocation

Upon good cause shown, the board of governors may revoke the authority of any bar association to operate a lawyer referral service.

8–5. IMMUNITY

Rule 8–5.1. Generally

The members of The Florida Bar Lawyer Referral Service Committee and the staff of The Florida Bar Lawyer Referral Service, as well as local bar associations with a lawyer referral service approved under rule 8–2.1, including their directors, officers, lawyer referral service committees, and staff, shall have absolute immunity from civil liability for all acts in the course of their official duties in furtherance of this chapter.

Added and amended March 23, 2000 (763 So.2d 1002).

THE FLORIDA BAR LAWYER REFERRAL SERVICE RULES AND REGULATIONS

Explanatory Note

The Florida Bar Lawyer Referral Service Rules and Regulations are not part of The Rules Regulating The Florida Bar. The Rules and Regulations were adopted by the Board of Governors of The Florida Bar to implement Chapter 8 of the Rules Regulating The Florida Bar. These Rules and Regulations have been inserted following Chapter 8 in order to assist the practitioner.

Approved by the Board of Governors of The Florida Bar March 21, 1991

PREAMBLE

The Florida Bar recognizes that there exists a large group of persons of moderate means who believe that legal services are not readily available. In order to respond to the needs of those persons, it is the position of The Florida Bar that a lawyer referral service be established.

RULE I. OBJECTIVES

The immediate objective of The Florida Bar in the establishment of the Lawyer Referral Service, hereinafter referred to as the "Service," is to assist the general public by providing a way in which any person who can afford to pay a reasonable fee for legal services may be referred to a member of The Florida Bar.

As long range objectives, The Florida Bar seeks to:

A. Encourage lawyers to recognize the obligation to provide legal services to the general public.

B. Acquaint people in need of legal service with the value of consultation with a lawyer.

C. Acquaint lawyers with the fact that the needs of some clients suggest the use of a deferred payment plan.

RULE II. COMMITTEE

A Lawyer Referral Service Committee will be charged with the operation of the Service. It will be composed of not less than six members nor more than twenty-one members appointed by The Florida Bar president. The term for each member shall be for not less than one year nor more than three years. Appointments shall be staggered so the composition of the committee shall be divided, insofar as is practical, into equal numbers of one, two and three-year members. A chair and a vice chair will be selected by The Florida Bar president-elect.

RULE III. THE SERVICE

The Service will be operated from The Florida Bar Center in Tallahassee, utilizing members of the staff and under the general supervision of the Lawyer Referral Service Committee. A person seeking a lawyer will use a toll-free line maintained at The Florida Bar to be interviewed by a staff member, and a referral will be made to a panel member of the Service on a rotating basis upon the agreement of such person to pay an initial fee of $25, provided the initial consultation does not exceed one-half hour.

The Service shall not make referrals in any geographic area of the state where a local bar association lawyer referral service exists. In such cases, referrals will be made directly to the existing local bar association referral service.

RULE IV. FORMATION OF THE PARTICIPANT–MEMBER PANEL

A. Any Florida Bar member in good standing with no pending findings of probable cause by a grievance committee, who maintains an office in a county not served by any referral service sponsored by or affiliated with any local bar association, may qualify as a panel member.

B. Application for membership will be grouped by county.

C. (1) In submitting an application for membership on the panel, the applicant may list those areas of law which he or she is competent to handle. In accepting the registration of any applicant, the Service may require such information and certification as it deems necessary to have the applicant show membership in good standing with the Bar, qualification to practice and adherence to recognized ethical standards of the profession. The committee may conduct further investigation and require further information bearing upon the responsibility, capability, character and integrity of any applicant or panel member. Any applicant will be denied membership if the applicant has a grievance matter with a finding of probable cause pending with The Florida Bar or the Supreme Court of Florida at the time of initial application. The committee may also require such information as it deems necessary in accepting or continuing the membership of any applicant or panel member on any panel or panels that may be established.

(2) Any applicant may be denied membership and any panel member may be withdrawn from the Service if the attorney has:

a. willfully failed to pay any fee, render any report, or otherwise abide by the rules of the Service;

b. signed any application or other certification or report to the Service which shall be found to be untrue in any material respect. Such action may be taken by the vote of a majority of all members of the committee, only after a hearing on reasonable notice and an opportunity to be heard, and subject to the right of appeal to the Board of Governors of The Florida Bar.

Notwithstanding the foregoing, if at any time, the committee receives notice or information giving it reasonable grounds to believe that a panel member does not meet the required standards of responsibility, capability, character, and integrity, it may suspend a panel member from participation on the Service for such reasonable time as may be necessary.

(3) Any panel member will be automatically suspended from any further referrals upon the finding of probable cause by The Florida Bar in a grievance matter. A suspended panel member may apply for readmission to the panel upon the conclusion of any grievance proceeding and be readmitted at the committee's discretion.

D. A panel member, in filing an application as provided, agrees to:

(1) grant an initial half-hour office consultation for a fee of no more than $25 to any referred client on the Regular Panel;

(2) charge for further services only as agreed upon with the client in keeping with the stated objectives of the Service and the client's ability to pay;

(3) carry, and continue to carry, professional liability insurance with limits not less than $100,000;

(4) permit any dispute concerning fees arising from a referral to be submitted to binding arbitration if the client so petitions;

(5) grant all clients referred by the Service an appointment as soon as practicable after request is made;

(6) abide by all of the rules of the Service and indemnify and hold harmless The Florida Bar and any of its officers, members or employees from any and all claims, demands, actions, liability or loss which may arise from, or be incurred as a result of the operation of the Service or referrals of clients through the Service, or by applicant's failure to comply with any provision of the rules of the Service, or use of information contained in the application;

RULE V. FEE FOR MEMBERSHIP

Each panel member of the Service will pay to The Florida Bar, a nonrefundable, nonprorated annual membership fee of $125 each calendar year (January-December) or any portion thereof. Annual dues renewals are due on the first business day of January of each year.

RULE VI. REMITTANCE FEE STRUCTURE

If there is compensation for further services on Regular Panel cases, the panel member agrees to remit 10% of any attorneys' fees to the Service. All fees should be remitted with the Lawyer Referral Service Monthly Report. The 10% remittance fees are NOT required for referrals on the Low Fee, Elderly, Disability Law, and AIDS Law Panels, and for bankruptcy and Social Security cases.

RULE VII. WITHDRAWAL FROM MEMBERSHIP

A panel member may at any time, withdraw from participation on the Service upon five days written notice to The Florida Bar, but shall not thereby be entitled to a refund of the membership fee and shall not be relieved of the duty to dispose of, in accordance with standard practices, any pending case or obligation incurred during membership.

RULE VIII. OPERATION OF THE PANEL

A. Referrals will be made to members of the panel in rotation in the geographic area requested by the caller.

B. If the Service ascertains that a person being interviewed is presently represented by a lawyer, no referral will be made until a release is obtained from the client's lawyer.

C. Panel members will accept referrals for an initial consultation, however, should any referral give rise to a conflict of interest, or the attorney is unable to handle the case, the panel member should refer the client back to The Florida Bar Lawyer Referral Service. Nothing herein will be construed to obligate a panel member to accept employment beyond the initial consultation.

D. Florida Bar Referral Service panel members are not permitted to refer cases to other attorneys, and by virtue of their acceptance of membership, they acknowledge and agree to abide by this rule. Panel members who engage another attorney(s) to participate in a case with them, shall, to the extent practicable, associate an attorney who is already a member of the Service or who, as part of his/her participation in the file, agrees to become a member and/or satisfies the requirements of for same. Any association with another attorney shall only be done with the express written consent of the client and written acknowledgment by the client and the associating attorney of their understanding, of the Service participation in fees to be earned and the amount of the same. In addition, the original panel member must notify the director of the Service with the name, address and phone number of the associating attorney and shall be provided with a copy of the written consent signed by the associating attorney and the client which also acknowledges the fees to be paid to the Service. The original panel member, notwithstanding the fact that the associating attorney may also be a panel member, continues to be responsible for ensuring that the status of the case and the fees earned are reported and transmitted to the Service as required by the rules. The director is authorized to release the panel member of the responsibilities for reporting and remitting fees as to any referred matter upon a showing of good cause, in writing, as soon as the same is practicable.

E. If a Service member leaves a firm and leaves the Service cases with the firm after his/her departure, he/she will be responsible for ensuring that the status of all cases is reported to the Service and any fees due the Service are remitted in a timely manner. Former panel members will continue to receive the Outstanding Monthly Report and it will be their responsibility to contact their former firm and ask them to report the status of the cases to the Service and remit any fees due the Service.

F. A client will not be referred to an attorney outside the county where the client is located, unless the client either requests or agrees to such an arrangement.

G. It is the responsibility of panel members to notify the Service if there is a period of time of one week or more in which the attorney will be unavailable for referrals because of vacations, trials or other reasons.

RULE IX. ACKNOWLEDGMENT AND REPORT OF REFERRALS

Each panel member will be sent a Monthly Lawyer Referral Service Report on the 15th of each month. The panel member should complete it by indicating the status of each case and remit any fees due the Service and return it to the Bar within thirty (30) days. Failure to return the report within the time specified may justify the service in removing the member from the panel. Nothing herein will require any attorney to violate the attorney-client privilege.

RULE X. CONTACTING PROSPECTIVE CLIENTS

Panel members should not call prospective clients referred to them unless the prospective client calls them first. Calling a referred prospective client prior to the prospective client calling the lawyer is a violation of Rule 4-7.4(a) of the Rules Regulating The Florida Bar. Panel members should not send referred prospective clients any written communication prior to the prospective client contacting the lawyer. Prospective clients are informed of by the Service that no one will call them or send them anything before they contact the lawyer. A lawyer violating this rule may be subject to discipline.

RULE XI. RECORDS AND REVIEW

The Service will keep on file, a confidential record of all referrals and reports of panel members which will be subject to examination and inspection by the committee and officers of the Bar. All referrals will be reviewed on a quarterly basis.

RULE XII. PUBLICITY

The Service will be publicized in such manner, and to such extent, as will fulfill its objectives consistent with Florida Bar ethics and advertising rules.

STANDARDS AND GUIDELINES FOR BAR SPONSORED LAWYER REFERRAL SERVICES IN FLORIDA

Explanatory Note

The Standards and Guidelines for Bar Sponsored Lawyer Referral Services in Florida are not part of the Rules Regulating The Florida Bar. Instead, these Standards and Guidelines have been adopted by the Lawyer Referral Service Committee of The Florida Bar to implement Chapter 8 of the Rules Regulating The Florida Bar. The Publisher has inserted these Standards and Guidelines at the end of Chapter 8 to assist practitioners.

Approved by the Lawyer Referral Service Committee of The Florida Bar January 19, 1990

Including Amendments Received Through August 1, 2011

STANDARD I. PURPOSE

These standards and guidelines are established to assist The Florida Bar in supervising the operation and conduct of the Lawyer Referral Service of The Florida Bar, and those referral services operated by Voluntary Bar associations in Florida. The operation of all lawyer referral services in Florida are governed and authorized by the Rules Regulating The Florida Bar, promulgated by the Supreme Court, and shall be controlling in all respects. Specific requirements which are binding upon all bar sponsored lawyer referral services are contained in Rule 4–7.8 (Lawyer Referral Services) and Chapter 8 (Lawyer Referral Rule) of Rules Regulating The Florida Bar. All language contained herein is intended to be gender neutral.

STANDARD II. PLAN OF ORGANIZATION

(a) The Lawyer Referral Service committee of The Florida Bar is responsible for the supervision of all bar sponsored lawyer referral services in the State of Florida including but not limited to:

1. Providing liaison and assistance for all bar sponsored lawyer referral services operated within the state;

2. Promoting the establishment of metropolitan or regional bar sponsored Lawyer Referral Services to eliminate duplication of efforts;

3. Encouraging the adoption of minimum standards in the operation of bar sponsored Lawyer Referral Services to insure the availability of efficient, reliable, responsive and accessible services;

4. Assuring geographical coverage of the entire state;

5. Providing active supervision of the operation of all bar sponsored Lawyer Referral Services to insure compliance with the Rules Regulating The Florida Bar;

6. Receiving and consolidating the various reports from all bar sponsored Lawyer Referral Services and preparation and distribution of statistical reports concerning same.

(b) The Florida Bar Lawyer Referral Service shall be operated by the personnel of The Florida Bar and under the supervision of the Lawyer Referral Service Committee of The Florida Bar.

1. The membership of the committee (including the designation of chair-persons and vice chair-persons) shall be named by the President of The Florida Bar.

2. Committee members shall serve for rotating terms, and the period of appointment of each member should be long enough for the member to gain reasonable familiarity with the work of the Service. At least a majority of the members of the Committee shall be licensed to practice law in Florida. The president is encouraged to include on the Committee non-lawyer public representatives and representatives of local Lawyer Referral Services.

3. The Committee shall meet at regular intervals during the year.

4. The Committee shall formulate and adopt rules for the conduct and operation of the Service.

5. The Committee shall make or delegate all administrative decisions necessary in the operation of the Service.

6. The rules of the Service shall provide a mechanism for appeal of any action taken by the Committee.

7. The Committee may review at regular intervals the operation of and public response to the Service.

(c) Lawyer Referral Services sponsored by local bar associations may operate under the supervision of a local committee in a manner similar to that set out in (b) above.

STANDARD III. SERVICES TO BE PROVIDED AND GENERAL REQUIREMENTS FOR PARTICIPATION BY LAWYERS

(a) Each Service shall provide a panel or panels of lawyers to whom referrals of persons requesting the same can be made through the Service, in rotation, when practicable.

(b) The referral panel or panels or other services offered by the Lawyer Referral Service may be separate operations supervised by the Referral Service for which separate rules, regulations and fees may be established, depending upon the nature of the panel and other appropriate considerations.

(c) Lawyers may not be required to participate in all of such services in order to participate in any one of them; provided, however, that with respect to referral panels, lawyers may be required to participate on reduced fee or pro bono panels in order to participate in full fee generating panels.

(d) The Lawyer Referral Service shall encourage lawyers to participate in the Service. Only lawyers who are members of the Bar in good standing and licensed to practice in Florida may participate.

(e) Each participating lawyer shall agree that:

1. The information contained in the application or records of the Referral Service may be furnished to the Lawyer Referral Service Committee or its governing body as the need arises;

2. The member's name may be removed from any or all of the referral panels upon a vote of the majority of all of the members of the Lawyer Referral Service Committee; provided that the attorney has been accorded a reasonable opportunity to appear

before such committee and defend against such action and the right to appeal such action to the governing body of such Lawyer Referral Service committee (during which period further referrals may be suspended). In the event there is no Lawyer Referral Service committee, the governing body of the Lawyer Referral Service will resolve all disputes;

3. A panel member will pay to the Service all applicable fees and charges prescribed by the Service, if any;

4. The member will abide by all rules of the Service;

5. In the event of a dispute over attorney fees with a client referred by the Service the member agrees to submit the dispute to a local or state fee arbitration committee for resolution, if available.

STANDARD IV. THE REFERRAL PANELS

(a) Each service shall establish such number and variety of panels as the Lawyer Referral Service Committee determines will best enable the Service to make referrals in a manner which is responsive to individual client needs.

(b) Each Lawyer Referral Service may establish other separate panels including, but not limited to, a no-fee-to-indigents panel, a reduced-fee panel for referral of persons of modest or moderate means, a legal services for the aged panel, and a lawyer-to-lawyer consultation panel. In addition, each Lawyer Referral Service is encouraged to establish panels or subpanels so as to (a) facilitate referrals to a lawyer in the geographical vicinity of the person requesting the referral and (b) accommodate the non-English language needs of the community.

STANDARD V. ELIGIBILITY OF PANEL LAWYERS

All members of The Florida Bar in good standing are eligible to participate in the Lawyer Referral Service which services the area where the participating lawyer's office is located geographically, subject to the requirements of the Rules Regulating The Florida Bar and such additional requirements as the individual Lawyer Referral Service may require.

STANDARD VI. REFERRAL SERVICE PROCEDURES

(a) Procedures shall be established which assure that each referral is made in a fair and impartial manner to a member of an appropriate panel. Such procedures should be designed so as to respond to all circumstances of the client, including the subject of the legal problem presented, geographical convenience of the client, language needs and ability to pay for desired services.

(b) No referral shall be made on the basis of race, sex, age, religion or national origin.

(c) No referral shall be made by the referrer to the referrer, partners, family members, associates, or employees.

(d) If possible, each client-applicant should be interviewed by a lawyer or trained interviewer. The interview should be convenient to the client and may be conducted by telephone.

(e) The interviewer shall attempt to ascertain whether the client-applicant has a legal matter appropriate for referral. If so, the rules of the Service should assure that a referral is made. If the client-applicant does not have a legal matter appropriate for referral, the interviewer should be equipped to direct the client-applicant to a source which can provide help.

(f) The client-applicant will be informed, either orally or in writing, of the Service's applicable rules, including information about the first consultation fee, if any, to be paid by the client-applicant and the extent of legal services which will be rendered for such fee.

(g) If possible, the Service should arrange the time and place of the first consultation between the client-applicant and the lawyer. Such consultation should be made available as soon as possible after the initial interview.

(h) For many reasons the referred client and attorney may not establish an attorney client relationship. If the panel lawyer decided that special or different services are required and does not feel qualified to render such services, the member shall send the client-applicant back to the Service for another referral.

(i) The Service is encouraged to make regular and consistent attempts to follow up in a reasonable number of cases in order to obtain information which will enable the Service to find out whether appointments have been kept, whether the referred client was satisfied with the lawyer's handling of the case, whether the fee was within the client's means, and similar information. Information obtained by such follow-up procedures should be used to make such alterations in the operation of the Service as may appear desirable to the Committee from time to time.

(j) All Services shall comply with their application and rules and regulations as filed with The Florida Bar.

STANDARD VII. OPERATING FEES AND USE OF PROCEEDS

(a)[1] For participation in or use of the Service's referral panels, a Service may require that:

1. Each panel member pay to the Service a registration fee, "referral" fee (computed on a percentage basis or otherwise), or other like participating fee, or may require remittance to the Service of the initial

consultation fee, or any two or more of such fees, as a condition to panel membership; and/or

2. Each client-applicant pays a registration fee, initial consultation fee, or other like referral fee, or any two or more of such fees, as a condition to obtaining a referral;

provided, however, that no Lawyer Referral Service may require any fee or combination thereof, which is in conflict with statutory or other legal prohibitions against the award of attorney's fees or which is unreasonable, whether those fees be required of client-applicants, panel members or both. The primary criterion for determining whether a Service has failed to comply with this provision shall be whether the fee, or combination of fees, in question increases the client-applicant's cost for legal services beyond that which would normally be paid or decreases the quantity or quality of services which otherwise would have been received, but for the involvement of the Service.

1 This Standard does not contain a "(b)".

STANDARD VIII. PUBLICITY

(a) Each Service is encouraged to develop and maintain an active publicity program using communications media best designed to inform the general public in the area served of the existence, purpose and advantages of the Service and the kinds of information and services available. Whenever possible, the public should be informed as to when to seek legal services.

(b) The form and content of all publicity regarding the Service must be dignified and consistent with recognized principles of legal ethics within the applicable rules governing same in Florida and shall not be false, deceptive or misleading. All advertising shall identify the sponsor(s) of the Service.

(c) No publicity about the Service shall identify a particular lawyer participating in it.

(d) The Service is encouraged to make specific arrangements with legal aid programs, criminal justice agencies, hospitals, jails, courts, employers and other public and private agencies and institutions in the area served by the Service to assure the use of the Service by persons inquiring through such agencies and institutions.

STANDARD IX. VOLUNTARY WITHDRAWAL FROM MEMBERSHIP

(a) Prior to a panel member voluntarily withdrawing from a panel, the member shall notify the Lawyer Referral Service in writing including a report as to the status of all referral cases.

(b) Upon withdrawing a panel member shall remain obligated to complete all referred cases including payment of any fees due the Lawyer Referral Service.

CHAPTER 9. LEGAL SERVICES PLANS RULES AND REGULATIONS

9–1. GENERALLY

Rule 9–1.1. Authority

Pursuant to the provisions of bylaw 2–3.2(d), the Board of Governors of The Florida Bar hereby establishes these rules and regulations for the operation of legal services plans in this state.

Amended July 23, 1992, effective Jan. 1, 1993 (605 So.2d 252); July 20, 1995 (658 So.2d 930); April 2–4, 1998, by the Board of Governors of The Florida Bar.

Rule 9–1.2. Statement of Policy and Purposes

Every citizen of this state should have access to the legal system. A person's ability to gain such access is enhanced by the assistance of and representation by an attorney duly licensed to practice law in this state. However, many persons simply do not seek legal assistance because of a failure to recognize the existence of a legal problem, inability to locate an attorney, fears of excessive cost of legal representation, or other reason. To this end, it is the policy of The Florida Bar to support the concept and to actively encourage the establishment, operation, growth, and development of legal services plans as 1 means of increasing a person's ability to obtain legal services at an affordable cost in order to have the opportunity to better gain access to the legal system.

Amended July 23, 1992, effective Jan. 1, 1993 (605 So.2d 252); March 31–April 3, 1993, by the Board of Governors of The Florida Bar; Dec. 7–8, 1993, by the Board of Governors of The Florida Bar; April 2–4, 1998, by the Board of Governors of The Florida Bar.

Rule 9-1.3. Definitions

Unless otherwise described in this chapter, the following terms shall have the following described meanings:

(a) Bar. The bar shall mean The Florida Bar.

(b) Board. The board shall mean the Board of Governors of The Florida Bar.

(c) Committee. The committee shall mean the Prepaid Legal Services Committee, a standing committee of The Florida Bar.

(d) Group. Group shall mean an organization of 2 or more persons whose individual members are identifiable in terms of some common interest or affinity. Examples of groups shall include, but not be limited to, the following:

(1) churches;

(2) educational institutions;

(3) credit unions;

(4) employing units; and

(5) associations.

(e) Legal Services Plan. Legal services plan shall mean an arrangement whereby a sponsor contracts directly with a managing attorney for the provision of legal services to its members, hereinafter referred to as a plan. Lawyer referral services and legal aid societies shall be specifically excepted from this definition.

(f) Managing Attorney. Managing attorney shall mean a member in good standing of The Florida Bar who shall be the person responsible to the bar for the proper conduct and operation of a plan.

(g) Plan Attorney. Plan attorney shall mean a member in good standing of The Florida Bar who, upon contracting in writing directly with a managing attorney, shall provide legal services to plan participants under a plan.

(h) Plan Participant. Plan participant shall mean a member of a sponsor eligible to receive legal services under a plan.

(i) Sponsor. Sponsor shall mean a group that provides a plan for the benefit of its members.

Amended July 23, 1992, effective Jan. 1, 1993 (605 So.2d 252); Dec. 7–8, 1993, by the Board of Governors of The Florida Bar; April 2–4, 1998, by the Board of Governors of The Florida Bar.

9-2. REQUIREMENTS

Rule 9-2.1. Requirements For Establishing a Plan

A managing attorney shall not be permitted to operate a plan in this state without first obtaining approval by the board of governors to establish such plan. A managing attorney seeking to obtain board approval of a plan shall file with the committee a plan application pursuant to the requirements of this chapter.

Amended July 23, 1992, effective Jan. 1, 1993 (605 So.2d 252); April 2–4, 1998, by the Board of Governors of The Florida Bar.

Rule 9-2.2. Form and Content of Plan Application

A plan application shall consist of the following:

(a) Assurances by the Managing Attorney to the Bar. The managing attorney shall make the following assurances to the bar, in writing, executed on a form approved and adopted for use for such purpose by the committee:

(1) to exercise every reasonable effort in order to assure that the plan is operated in an ethical manner and is in compliance with the Rules Regulating The Florida Bar;

(2) to have a professional liability insurance policy issued in favor of the managing attorney in an amount not less than $100,000, and to attach to this form a copy of the declarations page of said policy;

(3) to take any and all steps reasonable and necessary in order to assure that there are a sufficient number of plan attorneys available in order to be able to adequately and properly perform the legal services to be provided under the plan;

(4) to file with the committee written notice of any proposed change to be made in any item described in the agreement described in subdivision (b).

(5) to not implement any proposed change described in subdivision (a)(4) without first obtaining the approval of the board;

(6) to file with the committee written notice of the termination of and cessation of operations by the plan within 10 days of such occurrence;

(7) to file with the committee a renewal request form approved and adopted for use for such purpose by the committee, as more particularly described in rule 9-2.5; and

(8) if applicable, to affirm and verify that the managing attorney and any specified members of the managing attorney's law firm shall be the sole plan attorney(s) under the plan.

Upon such affirmation and verification, the filing requirement of the agreement described in subdivision (c) shall be waived, and the managing attorney and any such specified members of the managing attorney's law firm shall each make an affirmative statement that the managing attorney and all such specified attorneys shall complete any and all legal services undertaken for and on behalf of a plan participant to the extent of the benefits provided under the plan in the event of the termination of the plan.

(b) Agreement by and between Managing Attorney and Sponsor. The managing attorney and sponsor shall both execute a written agreement which shall include, but not be limited to, the following:

(1) a detailed definition of who shall constitute a plan participant under the plan;

(2) a detailed description of any and all of the legal services to be provided under the plan;

(3) a detailed description of any and all of the legal services to be excluded under the plan;

(4) a detailed description of the geographic area in which the legal services shall be performed under the plan;

(5) the amount and method of payment of the fees to be paid to the managing attorney by the sponsor under the plan;

(6) the amount and method of payment of the fees to be paid to the managing attorney by the plan participants under the plan;

(7) a detailed description of the method of review and resolution of disputes and grievances arising under the plan;

(8) a method of termination of the agreement by either the managing attorney or the sponsor;

(9) an affirmative statement that the plan participant is the client under the plan and that the sponsor will have no influence whatsoever over the attorney-client relationship established thereunder;

(10) an affirmative statement that the plan participant is free to use a non-plan attorney, either at the plan participant's own expense or with reimbursement to be provided by either the managing attorney or the sponsor;

(11) a statement informing the plan participant that the plan participant may file a complaint with Staff Counsel, The Florida Bar, 651 East Jefferson Street, Tallahassee, Florida 32399–2300.

(12) A disclaimer announcement, as follows: "The Florida Bar does not guarantee in any way the success of the plan and gives no assurances of the quantity or quality of the legal services to be provided thereunder. Total responsibility for the delivery of legal services under the plan rests solely and entirely with the sponsor and the managing attorney and the plan attorneys."

(c) Agreement by and between Managing Attorney and Plan Attorney. The managing attorney and plan attorney shall both execute a written agreement which shall include, but not be limited to, the following:

(1) an assurance by the plan attorney to have a professional liability insurance policy issued in favor of the plan attorney in an amount not less than $100,000, and to attach to this agreement a copy of the declarations page of said policy;

(2) an affirmative statement that the plan attorney shall complete any and all legal services undertaken for and on behalf of a plan participant to the extent of the benefits provided under the plan in the event of the termination of the plan;

(3) a detailed description of any and all of the legal services to be performed by the plan attorney under the plan;

(4) a detailed description of the geographic area in which the legal services shall be performed by the plan attorney under the plan;

(5) the amount and method of payment of the fees to be paid to the plan attorney by the managing attorney under the plan;

(6) the amount and method of payment of the fees to be paid to the plan attorney by the plan participants under the plan;

(7) a detailed description of the method of review and resolution of disputes and grievances arising under the plan;

(8) a method of termination of the agreement by either the managing attorney or the plan attorney; and

(9) an affirmative statement that the plan participant is the client of the plan attorney and that neither the sponsor nor the managing attorney will have any influence whatsoever over the attorney-client relationship established by and between the plan participant and the plan attorney thereunder.

(d) Other Documents. Pursuant to the authority contained in rule 9–3. 3, the committee, in its discretion, may require other documents to be included in or filed with the plan application.

(e) Application Fee. Each plan application shall be accompanied by an application fee in the amount of $125 made payable to The Florida Bar.

Amended July 23, 1992, effective Jan. 1, 1993 (605 So.2d 252); March 31–April 3, 1993, by the Board of Governors of The Florida Bar; April 2–4, 1998, by the Board of Governors of The Florida Bar; July 3, 2003 (850 So.2d 499); Aug. 11–14, 2004, by the Board of Governors of The Florida Bar.

Rule 9–2.3. Review of Plan Application By the Committee

The plan application described in rule 9–2.2 shall be reviewed by both staff of the bar and a plan review subcommittee of the committee. Thereupon a report shall be provided to the committee at 1 of its regularly scheduled meetings. Upon consideration of said report, the committee, in its discretion, may:

(a) approve the plan application and thereupon make a recommendation to the board to approve said plan;

(b) approve the plan application conditionally upon requiring the managing attorney to file with the committee any requested additional or corrective information and, upon such compliance by the managing attorney, then make a recommendation to the board to approve said plan;

(c) require the managing attorney to file with the committee any requested additional or corrective information so that the committee may further review the plan application; or

(d) disapprove the plan application and thereupon advise the managing attorney of the reasons therefor.

Amended July 23, 1992, effective Jan. 1, 1993 (605 So.2d 252); March 31–April 3, 1993, by the Board of Governors of The Florida Bar; April 2–4, 1998, by the Board of Governors of The Florida Bar.

Rule 9–2.4. Approval of Plan By the Board

The committee shall request the board to place the committee's recommendation for approval of a plan on the agenda of a regularly scheduled meeting of the board. Upon consideration of the committee's recommendation for approval of a plan, the board in its discretion may either approve or disapprove the establishment of the plan. Thereupon the committee shall advise the managing attorney of the board's action.

Amended July 23, 1992, effective Jan. 1, 1993 (605 So.2d 252); April 2–4, 1998, by the Board of Governors of The Florida Bar.

Rule 9–2.5. Renewal

All plans approved by the board pursuant to this chapter shall be subject to renewal, as follows:

(a) If said approval is granted prior to July 1 of the year, then the managing attorney shall be required to file with the committee the plan's initial renewal request form as of December 31 of said year.

(b) If said approval is granted subsequent to July 1 of the year, then the managing attorney shall be required to file with the committee the plan's initial renewal request form as of December 31 of the following year.

(c) Subsequent to the filing of the initial renewal request form, the managing attorney shall file with the committee the plan's renewal request form as of December 31 of each and every year thereafter.

(d) Each renewal request form shall be accompanied by a renewal fee in the amount of $25 made payable to The Florida Bar.

Added April 2–4, 1998, by the Board of Governors of The Florida Bar.

Rule 9–2.6. Revocation

The board, in its discretion, may revoke any and all prior approval of a plan if the plan does not comply with any rule or regulation within these Rules Regulating The Florida Bar.

Added April 2–4, 1998, by the Board of Governors of The Florida Bar.

9–3. MISCELLANEOUS

Rule 9–3.1. Activities of Managing Attorneys

Managing attorneys and their employees or agents may:

(a) directly contact representatives or fiduciaries of groups for the purpose of informing them of the availability of a plan offered by the managing attorney;

(b) upon board approval of a plan, provide any written form of communication to members of the sponsor for the purpose of informing them of the availability of said plan and inviting them to become plan participants therein but only in accordance with the advertising and solicitation provisions of these Rules Regulating The Florida Bar; and

(c) do any and all things necessary and proper in order to fully and completely administer the plan.

Examples of permissible administrative activities shall include, but not be limited to, the compilation of the following:

(1) types of legal services performed;

(2) time expended per legal matter;

(3) number of plan participants receiving legal services under the plan; and

(4) the amount and method of payment of the fees paid to the plan attorney(s).

Notwithstanding any other provision herein to the contrary, the managing attorney is expressly prohibited from contracting with any third party of whatsoever type or kind to perform any administrative activities regarding the plan whatsoever.

Amended April 2–4, 1998, by the Board of Governors of The Florida Bar.

Rule 9–3.2. Limitation on Practice

Nothing in this chapter shall be construed as authorizing any limitation whatsoever on the practice of law not otherwise required of all attorneys licensed in this state.

Added April 2–4, 1998, by the Board of Governors of The Florida Bar.

Rule 9–3.3. Operating Rules and Regulations

Either the board or the committee, in its discretion, may from time to time adopt such operating rules and regulations deemed to be either reasonable or necessary governing the establishment, operation, or conduct of plans under this chapter.

Added April 2–4, 1998, by the Board of Governors of The Florida Bar.

Rule 9–3.4. Amendments

These rules and regulations for the operation of plans in this state may be amended pursuant to the provisions of the Rules Regulating The Florida Bar.

Added April 2–4, 1998, by the Board of Governors of The Florida Bar.

CHAPTER 10. RULES GOVERNING THE INVESTIGATION AND PROSECUTION OF THE UNLICENSED PRACTICE OF LAW

10–1. PREAMBLE

Rule 10–1.1. Jurisdiction

Pursuant to the provisions of article V, section 15, of the Florida Constitution, the Supreme Court of Florida has inherent jurisdiction to prohibit the unlicensed practice of law.

Amended July 9, 1987 (510 So.2d 596); June 20, 1991 (581 So.2d 901); July 23, 1992, effective Jan. 1, 1993 (605 So.2d 252).

Rule 10–1.2. Duty of The Florida Bar

The Florida Bar, as an official arm of the court, is charged with the duty of considering, investigating, and seeking the prohibition of matters pertaining to the unlicensed practice of law and the prosecution of alleged offenders. The court shall establish a standing committee on the unlicensed practice of law and at least 1 circuit committee on unlicensed practice of law in each judicial circuit.

Former Rule 10–1.1(c). Amended July 7, 1987 (510 So.2d 596). Redesignated as Rule 10–1.2 and amended July 23, 1992, effective Jan. 1, 1993 (605 So.2d 252).

10–2. DEFINITIONS

Rule 10–2.1. Generally

Text of rule effective until October 1, 2015. See, also, rule effective October 1, 2015.

Whenever used in these rules the following words or terms shall have the meaning herein set forth unless the use thereof shall clearly indicate a different meaning:

(a) Unlicensed Practice of Law. The unlicensed practice of law shall mean the practice of law, as prohibited by statute, court rule, and case law of the state of Florida.

(b) Paralegal or Legal Assistant. A paralegal or legal assistant is a person qualified by education, training, or work experience, who works under the supervision of a member of The Florida Bar and who performs specifically delegated substantive legal work for which a member of The Florida Bar is responsible. A nonlawyer or a group of nonlawyers may not offer legal services directly to the public by employing a lawyer to provide the lawyer supervision required under this rule. It shall constitute the unlicensed practice of law for a person who does not meet the definition of paralegal or legal assistant to use the title paralegal, legal assistant, or other similar term in offering to provide or in providing services directly to the public.

(c) Nonlawyer or Nonattorney. For purposes of this chapter, a nonlawyer or nonattorney is an individual who is not a member of The Florida Bar. This includes, but is not limited to, lawyers admitted in other jurisdictions, law students, law graduates, applicants to The Florida Bar, disbarred lawyers, and lawyers who have resigned from The Florida Bar. A suspended lawyer, while a member of The Florida Bar during the period of suspension as provided elsewhere in these rules, does not have the privilege of practicing law in Florida during the period of suspension. For purposes of this chapter, it shall constitute the unlicensed practice of law for a lawyer admitted in a state other than Florida to advertise to provide legal services in Florida which the lawyer is not authorized to provide.

(d) This Court or the Court. This court or the court shall mean the Supreme Court of Florida.

(e) Bar Counsel. Bar counsel is a member of The Florida Bar representing The Florida Bar in any proceeding under these rules.

(f) Respondent. A respondent is a nonlawyer who is accused of engaging in the unlicensed practice of law or whose conduct is under investigation.

(g) Referee. A referee is the judge or retired judge appointed to conduct proceedings as provided under these rules.

(h) Standing Committee. The standing committee is the committee constituted according to the directives contained in these rules.

(i) Circuit Committee. A circuit committee is a local unlicensed practice of law circuit committee.

(j) UPL Counsel. UPL counsel is the director of the unlicensed practice of law department and an employee of The Florida Bar employed to perform such duties, as may be assigned, under the direction of the executive director.

(k) UPL. UPL is the unlicensed practice of law.

(*l*) The Board or Board of Governors. The board or board of governors is the Board of Governors of The Florida Bar.

(m) Designated Reviewer. The designated reviewer is a member of the board of governors responsible for review and other specific duties as assigned by the board of governors with respect to a particular circuit committee or matter. If a designated reviewer recuses or is unavailable, any other board member may serve as designated reviewer in that matter. The designated reviewer will be selected, from time to time, by the board members from the circuit of such circuit committee. If circuits have an unequal number of circuit committees and board members, review responsibility will be reassigned, from time to time, to equalize workloads. On such reassignments responsibility for all pending cases from a particular committee passes to the new designated reviewer. UPL staff counsel will be given written notice of changes in the designated reviewing members for a particular committee.

(n) Executive Committee. The executive committee is the executive committee of the Board of Governors of The Florida Bar. All acts and discretion required by the board under these rules may be exercised by its executive committee between meetings of the board as may from time to time be authorized by standing policies of the board of governors.

Amended July 23, 1992, effective Jan. 1, 1993 (605 So.2d 252); July 20, 1995 (658 So.2d 930); June 27, 1996, effective July 1, 1996 (677 So.2d 272); Oct. 29, 1998, effective Feb. 1, 1999 (723 So.2d 208); April 25, 2002 (820 So.2d 210); Oct. 6, 2005, effective Jan. 1, 2006 (916 So.2d 655); Dec. 20, 2007, effective March 1, 2008 (978 So.2d 91); April 12, 2012, effective July 1, 2012 (101 So.3d 807).

Rule 10–2.1. Generally

Text of rule effective October 1, 2015. See, also, rule effective until October 1, 2015.

Whenever used in these rules the following words or terms shall have the meaning herein set forth unless the use thereof shall clearly indicate a different meaning:

(a) Unlicensed Practice of Law. The unlicensed practice of law shall mean the practice of law, as prohibited by statute, court rule, and case law of the state of Florida.

(b) Paralegal or Legal Assistant. A paralegal or legal assistant is a person qualified by education, training, or work experience, who works under the supervision of a member of The Florida Bar and who performs specifically delegated substantive legal work for which a member of The Florida Bar is responsible. A nonlawyer or a group of nonlawyers may not offer legal services directly to the public by employing a lawyer to provide the lawyer supervision required under this rule. It shall constitute the unlicensed practice of law for a person who does not meet the definition of paralegal or legal assistant to use the title paralegal, legal assistant, or other similar term in offering to provide or in providing services directly to the public.

(c) Nonlawyer or Nonattorney. For purposes of this chapter, a nonlawyer or nonattorney is an individual who is not a member of The Florida Bar. This includes, but is not limited to, lawyers admitted in other jurisdictions, law students, law graduates, applicants to The Florida Bar, disbarred lawyers, and lawyers who have resigned from The Florida Bar. A suspended lawyer, while a member of The Florida Bar during the period of suspension as provided elsewhere in these rules, does not have the privilege of practicing law in Florida during the period of suspension. For purposes of this chapter, it shall constitute the unlicensed practice of law for a lawyer admitted in a jurisdiction other than Florida to advertise to provide legal services in Florida which the lawyer is not authorized to provide.

(d) This Court or the Court. This court or the court shall mean the Supreme Court of Florida.

(e) Bar Counsel. Bar counsel is a member of The Florida Bar representing The Florida Bar in any proceeding under these rules.

(f) Respondent. A respondent is a nonlawyer who is accused of engaging in the unlicensed practice of law or whose conduct is under investigation.

(g) Referee. A referee is the judge or retired judge appointed to conduct proceedings as provided under these rules.

(h) Standing Committee. The standing committee is the committee constituted according to the directives contained in these rules.

(i) Circuit Committee. A circuit committee is a local unlicensed practice of law circuit committee.

(j) UPL Counsel. UPL counsel is the director of the unlicensed practice of law department and an employee of The Florida Bar employed to perform such duties, as may be assigned, under the direction of the executive director.

(k) UPL. UPL is the unlicensed practice of law.

(*l*) The Board or Board of Governors. The board or board of governors is the Board of Governors of The Florida Bar.

(m) Designated Reviewer. The designated reviewer is a member of the board of governors responsible for review and other specific duties as assigned by the board of governors with respect to a particular circuit committee or matter. If a designated reviewer recuses or is unavailable, any other board member may serve as designated reviewer in that matter. The designated reviewer will be selected, from time to time, by the board members from the circuit of such circuit committee. If circuits have an unequal number of circuit committees and board members, review responsibility will be reassigned, from time to time, to equalize workloads. On such reassignments responsibility for all pending cases from a particular committee passes to the new designated reviewer. UPL staff counsel will be given written notice of changes in the designated reviewing members for a particular committee.

(n) Executive Committee. The executive committee is the executive committee of the Board of Governors of The Florida Bar. All acts and discretion required by the board under these rules may be exercised by its executive committee between meetings of the board as may from time to time be authorized by standing policies of the board of governors.

Amended July 23, 1992, effective Jan. 1, 1993 (605 So.2d 252); July 20, 1995 (658 So.2d 930); June 27, 1996, effective July 1, 1996 (677 So.2d 272); Oct. 29, 1998, effective Feb. 1, 1999 (723 So.2d 208); April 25, 2002 (820 So.2d 210); Oct. 6, 2005, effective Jan. 1, 2006 (916 So.2d 655); Dec. 20, 2007, effective March 1, 2008 (978 So.2d 91); April 12, 2012, effective July 1, 2012 (101 So.3d 807); May 21, 2015, effective Oct. 1, 2015, (164 So.3d 1217).

Rule 10-2.2. Form Completion by a Nonlawyer

(a) Supreme Court Approved Forms. It shall not constitute the unlicensed practice of law for a nonlawyer to engage in limited oral communication to assist a self-represented person in the completion of blanks on a Supreme Court Approved Form. In assisting in the completion of the form, oral communication by nonlawyers is restricted to those communications reasonably necessary to elicit factual information to complete the blanks on the form and inform the self-represented person how to file the form. The nonlawyer may not give legal advice or give advice on remedies or courses of action. Legal forms approved by the Supreme Court of Florida which may be completed as set forth herein shall only include and are limited to the following forms, and any other legal form whether promulgated or approved by the Supreme Court is not a Supreme Court Approved Form for the purposes of this rule:

(1) forms which have been approved by the Supreme Court of Florida specifically pursuant to the

authority of rule 10–2.1(a) [formerly rule 10–1. 1(b)] of the Rules Regulating The Florida Bar;

(2) the Family Law Forms contained in the Florida Family Law Rules of Procedure; and

(3) the Florida Supreme Court Approved Family Law Forms contained in the Florida Family Law Rules of Procedure.

(b) Forms Which Have Not Been Approved by the Supreme Court of Florida.

(1) It shall not constitute the unlicensed practice of law for a nonlawyer to engage in a secretarial service, typing forms for self-represented persons by copying information given in writing by the self-represented person into the blanks on the form. The nonlawyer must transcribe the information exactly as provided in writing by the self-represented person without addition, deletion, correction, or editorial comment. The nonlawyer may not engage in oral communication with the self-represented person to discuss the form or assist the self-represented person in completing the form.

(2) It shall constitute the unlicensed practice of law for a nonlawyer to give legal advice, to give advice on remedies or courses of action, or to draft a legal document for a particular self-represented person. It also constitutes the unlicensed practice of law for a nonlawyer to offer to provide legal services directly to the public.

(c) As to All Legal Forms.

(1) Except for forms filed by the petitioner in an action for an injunction for protection against domestic or repeat violence, the following language shall appear on any form completed by a nonlawyer and any individuals assisting in the completion of the form shall provide their name, business name, address, and telephone number on the form:

This form was completed with the assistance of:
(Name of Individual)
(Name of Business)
(Address)
(Telephone Number)

(2) Before a nonlawyer assists a person in the completion of a form, the nonlawyer shall provide the person with a copy of a disclosure which contains the following provisions:

(Name) told me that he/she is a nonlawyer and may not give legal advice, cannot tell me what my rights or remedies are, cannot tell me how to testify in court, and cannot represent me in court.

Rule 10–2.1(b) of the Rules Regulating The Florida Bar defines a paralegal as a person who works under the supervision of a member of The Florida Bar and who performs specifically delegated substantive legal work for which a member of The Florida Bar is responsible. Only persons who meet the definition may call themselves paralegals. (Name) informed me that he/she is not a paralegal as defined by the rule and cannot call himself/herself a paralegal.

(Name) told me that he/she may only type the factual information provided by me in writing into the blanks on the form. Except for typing, (Name) may not tell me what to put in the form and may not complete the form for me. However, if using a form approved by the Supreme Court of Florida, (Name) may ask me factual questions to fill in the blanks on the form and may also tell me how to file the form.

.... I can read English

.... I cannot read English but this notice was read to me by (Name) in (Language) which I understand.

(3) A copy of the disclosure, signed by both the nonlawyer and the person, shall be given to the person to retain and the nonlawyer shall keep a copy in the person's file. The nonlawyer shall also retain copies for at least 6 years of all forms given to the person being assisted. The disclosure does not act as or constitute a waiver, disclaimer, or limitation of liability.

Added April 12, 2012, effective July 1, 2012 (101 So.3d 807).

10–3. STANDING COMMITTEE

Rule 10–3.1. Generally

Text of subrule (a) effective until July 1, 2015.

(a) Appointment and Terms. The standing committee shall be appointed by the court on advice of the board of governors of The Florida Bar and shall consist of 37 members, 18 of whom shall be nonlawyers. The board of governors is delegated the authority to appoint a chair and at least 1 vice-chair of the standing committee, both of whom may be nonlawyers. One–third of the members of the standing committee shall constitute a quorum. All appointments to the standing committee shall be for a term of 3 years. No member shall be appointed to more than 2 full consecutive terms. The members of the standing committee shall not be subject to removal by the court during their terms of office except for cause. Cause shall include unexcused failures to attend scheduled meetings, the number of which shall be set forth by the standing committee in an attendance policy.

Text of subrule (a) effective July 1, 2015.

(a) Appointment and Terms. Members of the standing committee on UPL are appointed by the Supreme Court of Florida, with advice from the Board of Governors of The Florida Bar. The committee must consist of 25 members, including 12 nonlawyers. The board appoints a chair and at least 1 vice-chair, who may be nonlawyers. All appointments to the standing committee are for a 3–year term. A member may not serve more than 2 full consecutive terms. One–third of the members of the standing committee constitutes a quorum. Members of the standing committee are not subject to removal by the court during their terms of office except for cause. Cause may include unexcused absences from scheduled meetings, the number to be set by the standing committee in an attendance policy.

(b) Recusal. A member of the standing committee must not perform any standing committee function when that member:

(1) is related by blood or marriage to the complainant or respondent;

(2) has a financial, business, property, or personal interest in the matter under consideration or with the complainant or respondent;

(3) has a personal interest that could be affected by the outcome of the proceedings or that could affect the outcome; or

(4) is prejudiced or biased toward either the complainant or the respondent.

Members should recuse themselves from participation in further proceedings on notice of any of the prohibitions. The standing committee chair may disqualify any member from any proceeding in which any of the above prohibitions exists. The chair must state the prohibition on the record or in writing in a file.

Amended July 23, 1992, effective Jan. 1, 1993 (605 So.2d 252); June 27, 1996, effective July 1, 1996 (677 So.2d 272); July 17, 1997 (697 So.2d 115); Dec. 20, 2007, effective March 1, 2008 (978 So.2d 91); May 29, 2014, effective June 1, 2014 and July 1, 2015 (140 So.3d 541).

Rule 10–3.2. Duties of the Standing Committee

It shall be the duty of the standing committee to receive and evaluate circuit committee reports and to determine whether litigation should be instituted in the court against any alleged offender. The standing committee may approve civil injunctive proceedings, indirect criminal contempt proceedings, or a combination of both, or such other action as may be appropriate. In addition, the duties of the standing committee shall include, but not be limited to:

(a) the consideration and investigation of activities that may, or do, constitute the unlicensed practice of law and exercising final authority to close cases not deemed by the standing committee to then warrant further action by The Florida Bar for unlicensed practice of law;

(b) the supervision of the circuit committees, which shall include, but not be limited to:

(1) prescribing rules of procedure for circuit committees;

(2) assigning reports of unlicensed practice of law for investigation;

(3) reassigning or withdrawing matters previously assigned;

(4) exercising final authority to close cases where UPL counsel or bar counsel objects to the closing of the case by the circuit committee;

(5) exercising final authority to accept a cease and desist affidavit in cases proposed to be resolved by cease and desist affidavit where UPL counsel or bar counsel objects to the acceptance of a cease and desist affidavit; and

(6) exercising final authority to accept a cease and desist affidavit and monetary penalty in cases proposed by the circuit committee to be resolved by a cease and desist affidavit that includes a monetary penalty not to exceed $500 per incident;

(7) joining with a circuit committee in a particular investigation;

(8) assigning staff investigators and bar counsel to conduct investigations on behalf of or in concert with the circuit committees; and

(9) suspending circuit committee members and chairs for cause and appointing a temporary circuit committee chair where there has been a suspension, resignation, or removal, pending the appointment of a permanent chair by the board of governors;

(c) the initiation and supervision of litigation, including the delegation of responsibility to bar counsel to prosecute such litigation;

(d) the giving of advice regarding the unlicensed practice of law policy to the officers, board of governors, staff, sections, or committees of The Florida Bar as requested; and

(e) furnishing any and all information, confidential records, and files regarding pending or closed investigations of unlicensed practice of law to any state or federal law enforcement or regulatory agency, United States Attorney, state attorney, the Florida Board of Bar Examiners and equivalent entities in other jurisdictions, and Florida bar grievance committees and equivalent entities in other jurisdictions where there is or may be a violation of state or federal law or the Rules of Professional Conduct of The Florida Bar.

Amended July 23, 1992, effective Jan. 1, 1993 (605 So.2d 252); June 27, 1996, effective July 1, 1996 (677 So.2d 272); March 23, 2000, (762 So.2d 1003); April 25, 2002 (820 So.2d 210).

Rule 10–3.3. Appointment and employment of UPL counsel and bar counsel

The board of governors shall employ UPL counsel, bar counsel, and other necessary employees, including investigators, to assist the standing committee to carry out its responsibilities as prescribed elsewhere in these rules. UPL counsel may appoint bar counsel to prosecute the cause before the referee.

Added July 23, 1992, effective Jan. 1, 1993 (605 So.2d 252). Amended June 27, 1996, effective July 1, 1996 (677 So.2d 272); July 17, 1997 (697 So.2d 115); April 25, 2002 (820 So.2d 210).

10–4. CIRCUIT COMMITTEES

Rule 10–4.1. Generally

(a) Appointment and Terms. Each circuit committee shall be appointed by the court on advice of the board of governors and shall consist of not fewer than 3 members, at least one-third of whom shall be nonlawyers. All appointees shall be residents of the circuit or have their principal office in the circuit. The terms of the members of circuit committees shall be for 3 years from the date of appointment by the court or until such time as their successors are appointed and qualified. Continuous service of a member shall not exceed 2 consecutive 3–year terms. A member shall not be reappointed for a period of 1 year after the end of the member's second term provided, however, the expiration of the term of any member shall not disqualify that member from concluding any investigations pending before that member. Any member of a circuit committee may be removed from office by the board of governors.

(b) Committee Chair. For each circuit committee there shall be a chair designated by the designated reviewer of that committee. A vice-chair and secretary may be designated by the chair of each circuit committee. The chair shall be a member of The Florida Bar.

(c) Quorum. Three members of the circuit committee or a majority of the members, whichever is less, shall constitute a quorum.

(d) Panels. The circuit committee may be divided into panels of not fewer than 3 members, 1 of whom must be a nonlawyer. Division of the circuit committee into panels shall only be upon concurrence of the designated reviewer and the chair of the circuit committee. The 3–member panel shall elect 1 of its members to preside over the panel's actions. If the chair or vice-chair of the circuit committee is a member of a 3–member panel, the chair or vice-chair shall be the presiding officer.

(e) Duties. It shall be the duty of each circuit committee to investigate, with dispatch, all reports of unlicensed practice of law and to make prompt report of its investigation and findings to bar counsel. In addition, the duties of the circuit committee shall include, but not be limited to:

(1) exercising final authority to close cases not deemed by the circuit committee to warrant further action by The Florida Bar except those cases to which UPL staff counsel objects to the closing of the case;

(2) exercising final authority to close cases proposed to be resolved by cease and desist affidavit except those cases to which UPL staff counsel objects to the acceptance of a cease and desist affidavit;

(3) forwarding to bar counsel for review by the standing committee recommendations for closing cases by a cease and desist affidavit that includes a monetary penalty not to exceed $500 per incident; and

(4) forwarding to UPL staff counsel recommendations for litigation to be reviewed by the standing committee.

(f) Circuit Committee Meetings. Circuit committees should meet at regularly scheduled times, not less frequently than quarterly each year. Either the chair or vice chair may call special meetings. Circuit committees should meet at least monthly during any period when the committee has 1 or more pending cases assigned for investigation and report. The time, date and place of regular monthly meetings should be set in advance by agreement between each committee and bar counsel.

(g) Recusal. No member of a circuit committee shall perform any circuit committee function when that member:

(1) is related by blood or marriage to the complainant or respondent;

(2) has a financial, business, property, or personal interest in the matter under consideration or with the complainant or respondent;

(3) has a personal interest that could be affected by the outcome of the proceedings or that could affect the outcome; or

(4) is prejudiced or biased toward either the complainant or the respondent.

Upon notice of any of the above prohibitions the affected members should recuse themselves from further proceedings. The circuit committee chair shall have the power to disqualify any member from any proceeding in which any of the above prohibitions exists and is stated of record or in writing in the file by the chair.

Amended July 23, 1992, effective Jan. 1, 1993 (605 So.2d 252); June 27, 1996, effective July 1, 1996 (677 So.2d 272); July 17, 1997 (697 So.2d 115); Sept. 24, 1998, effective Oct. 1, 1998 (718 So.2d 1179); March 23, 2000 (763 So.2d 1002); Feb. 8, 2001 (795 So.2d 1); April 25, 2002 (820 So.2d 210); May 20, 2004 (875 So.2d 448); Dec. 20, 2007, effective March 1, 2008 (978 So.2d 91).

10-5. COMPLAINT PROCESSING AND INITIAL INVESTIGATORY PROCEDURES

Rule 10-5.1. Complaint processing

(a) Complaints. All complaints alleging unlicensed practice of law, except those initiated by The Florida Bar, shall be in writing and signed by the complainant. The complaint shall contain a statement providing that:

Under penalties of perjury, I declare that I have read the foregoing document and that to the best of my knowledge and belief the facts stated in it are true.

(b) Review by Bar Counsel. Bar counsel shall review the complaint and determine whether the alleged conduct, if proven, would constitute a violation of the prohibition against engaging in the unlicensed practice of law. Bar counsel may conduct a preliminary, informal investigation to aid in this determination and, if necessary, may employ a Florida bar staff investigator to aid in the preliminary investigation. If bar counsel determines that the facts, if proven, would not constitute a violation, bar counsel may decline to pursue the complaint. A decision by bar counsel not to pursue a complaint shall not preclude further action or review under the Rules Regulating The Florida Bar. The complainant shall be notified of a decision not to pursue a complaint and shall be given the reasons therefor.

(c) Referral to Circuit Committee. Bar counsel may refer a UPL file to the appropriate circuit committee for further investigation or action as authorized elsewhere in these rules.

(d) Closing by Bar Counsel and Committee Chair. If bar counsel and a circuit committee chair concur in a finding that the case should be closed without a finding of unlicensed practice of law, the complaint may be closed on such finding without reference to the circuit committee or standing committee.

(e) Referral to Bar Counsel for Opening. A complaint received by a circuit committee or standing committee member directly from a complainant shall be reported to bar counsel for docketing and assignment of a case number. Should the circuit committee or standing committee member decide that the facts, if proven, would not constitute a violation of the unlicensed practice of law, the circuit committee or standing committee member shall forward this finding to bar counsel along with the complaint for notification to the complainant as outlined above. Formal investigation by a circuit committee may proceed after the matter has been referred to bar counsel for docketing.

Amended July 23, 1992, effective Jan. 1, 1993 (605 So.2d 252); July 17, 1997 (697 So.2d 115); April 25, 2002 (820 So.2d 210).

Rule 10-5.2. Disqualification as Attorney for Respondent Due to Conflict

(a) Members of the Standing Committee on UPL (Standing Committee), Members of the Circuit UPL Committees (Circuit Committees), Members of the Board of Governors, and Employees of The Florida Bar. No member of the standing committee, member of a circuit committee, member of the Board of Governors of The Florida Bar, or employee of The Florida Bar shall represent a party other than The Florida Bar in UPL proceedings authorized under these rules.

(b) Former Members of the Standing Committee, Former Members of the Circuit Committees, Former Board Members, and Former Employees. No former member of the standing committee, former member of a circuit committee, former member of the board of governors, or former employee of The Florida Bar shall represent any party other than The Florida Bar in UPL proceedings authorized under these rules if personally involved to any degree in the matter while a member of the standing committee, circuit committee, board of governors, or while an employee of The Florida Bar.

A former member of the standing committee, former member of a circuit committee, former member of the board of governors, or former employee of The Florida Bar who did not participate personally in any way in the matter or in any related matter in which the attorney seeks to be a representative, and who did not serve in a supervisory capacity over such matter, shall not represent any party except The Florida Bar for 1 year after such service without the express consent of the board.

(c) Partners, Associates, Employers, or Employees of the Firms of Standing Committee Members, Circuit Committee Members, or Board of Governors Members Precluded From Representing Parties Other Than The Florida Bar. Members of the firms of board of governors members, standing committee members, or circuit committee members shall not represent any party other than The Florida Bar in UPL proceedings authorized under these rules without the express consent of the board.

(d) Partners, Associates, Employers, or Employees of the Firms of Former Standing Committee Members, Former Circuit Committee Members, or Former Board of Governors Members Precluded From Representing Parties Other Than The Florida Bar. Attorneys in the firms of former board of governors members, former standing committee members, or former circuit committee members shall not represent any party other than The Florida Bar in UPL proceedings authorized under these rules for 1 year after the former member's service without the express consent of the board.

Added May 20, 2004 (875 So.2d 448).

10–6. PROCEDURES FOR INVESTIGATION

Rule 10–6.1. Taking of Testimony

(a) Conduct of Proceedings. The proceedings of circuit committees and the standing committee when testimony is taken may be informal in nature and the committees shall not be bound by the rules of evidence.

(b) Taking Testimony. Bar counsel, the standing committee, each circuit committee, and members thereof conducting investigations are empowered to take and have transcribed the testimony and evidence of witnesses. If the testimony is recorded stenographically or otherwise, the witness shall be sworn by any person authorized by law to administer oaths.

(c) Rights and Responsibilities of Respondent. The respondent may be required to appear and to produce evidence as any other witness unless the respondent claims a privilege or right properly available to the respondent under applicable federal or state law. The respondent may be accompanied by counsel.

(d) Rights of Complaining Witness. The complaining witness is not a party to the investigative proceeding although the complainant may be called as a witness should the matter come before a judge or a referee. The complainant may be granted the right to be present at any circuit committee proceeding when the respondent is present before the committee to give testimony. The complaining witness shall have no right to appeal the finding of the circuit committee.

Amended July 23, 1992, effective Jan. 1, 1993 (605 So.2d 252); July 17, 1997 (697 So.2d 115); April 25, 2002 (820 So.2d 210); Oct. 6, 2005, effective Jan. 1, 2006 (916 So.2d 655).

Rule 10–6.2. Subpoenas

(a) Issuance by Court. Upon receiving a written application of the chair of the standing committee or of a circuit committee or bar counsel alleging facts indicating that a person or entity is or may be practicing law without a license and that the issuance of a subpoena is necessary for the investigation of such unlicensed practice, the clerk of the circuit court in which the committee is located or the clerk of the Supreme Court of Florida shall issue subpoenas in the name, respectively, of the chief judge of the circuit or the chief justice for the attendance of any person or production of books and records or both before counsel or the investigating circuit committee or any member thereof at the time and place designated in such application. A like subpoena shall issue upon application by any person or entity under investigation.

(b) Failure to Comply. Failure to comply with any subpoena shall constitute a contempt of court and may be punished by the Supreme Court of Florida or by the circuit court of the circuit in which the subpoena was issued or where the contemnor may be found by such orders as may be necessary for the enforcement of the subpoena.

Added July 23, 1992, effective Jan. 1, 1993 (605 So.2d 252). Amended July 17, 1997 (697 So.2d 115); April 25, 2002 (820 So.2d 210); May 20, 2004 (875 So.2d 448); Oct. 6, 2005, effective Jan. 1, 2006 (916 So.2d 655); July 7, 2011, effective Oct. 1, 2011 (67 So.3d 1037).

Rule 10–6.3. Recommendations and Disposition of Complaints

(a) Circuit Committee Action. Upon concluding its investigation, the circuit committee shall report to bar counsel regarding the disposition of those cases closed, those cases where a cease and desist affidavit has been accepted, those cases where a cease and desist affidavit with monetary penalty has been recommended, and those cases where litigation is recommended. A majority of those present is required for all circuit committee recommendations; however, the vote may be taken by mail or telephone rather than at a formal meeting. All recommendations for a cease and desist affidavit with monetary penalty shall be reviewed by the standing committee for final approval. All recommendations for litigation under these rules shall be reviewed by the standing committee and a designated reviewer for final approval prior to initiating litigation.

(b) Action by Bar Counsel. Bar counsel shall review the disposition reports of the circuit committee. If bar counsel objects to any action taken by the circuit committee, bar counsel shall forward such objection to the circuit committee within 10 days of receipt of the circuit committee report. Bar counsel shall place the action and objection before the standing committee for review at its next scheduled meeting. The standing committee shall review the circuit committee action and the objection, and shall vote on the final disposition of the case. Once a case is closed or a cease and desist affidavit is accepted by the circuit committee or by the standing committee, bar counsel shall inform the complainant and, if contacted, the respondent of the disposition of the complaint.

(c) Review by Designated Reviewer. A designated reviewer shall review recommendations by the standing committee that litigation be initiated. The designated reviewer shall act on the recommendation within 21 days following the mailing date of the notice of standing committee action, otherwise the standing committee action shall become final. If the designated reviewer disagrees with all or any part of the recommendation for litigation, the designated reviewer shall make a report and recommendation to the board of governors and the board will make a final determination regarding the litigation.

Added July 23, 1992, effective Jan. 1, 1993 (605 So.2d 252). Amended June 27, 1996, effective July 1, 1996 (677 So.2d 272); March 23, 2000 (763 So.2d 1002); April 25, 2002 (820 So.2d 210); Nov. 19, 2009, effective Feb. 1, 2010 (24 So.3d 63); July 7, 2011, effective Oct. 1, 2011 (67 So.3d 1037).

10–7. PROCEEDINGS BEFORE A REFEREE

Rule 10–7.1. Proceedings for Injunctive Relief

(a) Filing Complaints. Complaints for civil injunctive relief shall be by petition filed in the Supreme Court of Florida by The Florida Bar in its name.

(b) Petitions for Injunctive Relief. Each such petition shall be processed in the Supreme Court of Florida in accordance with the following procedure:

(1) The petition shall not be framed in technical language but shall with reasonable clarity set forth the facts constituting the unlicensed practice of law. A demand for relief may be included in the petition but shall not be required.

(2) The court, upon consideration of any petition so filed, may issue its order to show cause directed to the respondent commanding the respondent to show cause, if there be any, why the respondent should not be enjoined from the unlicensed practice of law alleged, and further requiring the respondent to file with the court and serve upon UPL staff counsel within 20 days after service on the respondent of the petition and order to show cause a written answer admitting or denying each of the matters set forth in the petition. The legal sufficiency of the petition may, at the option of the respondent, be raised by motion to dismiss filed prior to or at the time of the filing of the answer. The filing of a motion to dismiss prior to the filing of an answer shall postpone the time for the filing of an answer until 10 days after disposition of the motion. The order and petition shall be served upon the respondent in the manner provided for service of process by Florida Rule of Civil Procedure 1.070(b). Service of all other pleadings shall be governed by the provisions of Florida Rule of Civil Procedure 1.080.

(3) Any party may request oral argument upon any question of law raised by the initial pleadings. The court may, in its discretion, set the matter for oral argument upon the next convenient motion day or at such time as it deems appropriate.

(4) If no response or defense is filed within the time permitted, the allegations of the petition shall be taken as true for purposes of that action. The court will then, upon its motion or upon motion of any party, decide the case upon its merits, granting such relief and issuing such order as might be appropriate; or it may refer the petition for further proceedings according to rule 10–7.1(b)(6).

(5) If a response or defense filed by a respondent raises no issue of material fact, any party, upon motion, may request summary judgment and the court may rule thereon as a matter of law.

(6) The court may, upon its motion or upon motion of any party, enter a judgment on the pleadings or refer questions of fact to a referee for determination.

(c) Proceedings Before the Referee. Proceedings before the referee shall be in accordance with the following:

(1) The proceedings shall be held in the county where the respondent resides or where the alleged offense was committed, whichever shall be designated by the court.

(2) Within 60 days of the order assigning the case to the referee, the referee shall conduct a case management conference. The purpose of the conference is to set a schedule for the proceedings, including discovery deadlines and a final hearing date. The referee shall enter a written order in the proceedings reflecting the schedule determined at the conference and, if civil penalties are requested, containing a notice to the respondent regarding the respondent's burden to show an inability to pay a civil penalty as set forth elsewhere in these rules.

(3) Subpoenas for the attendance of witnesses and the production of documentary evidence shall be issued in the name of the court by the referee upon request of a party. Failure or refusal to comply with any subpoena shall be contempt of court and may be punished by the court or by any circuit court where the action is pending or where the contemnor may be found, as if said refusal were a contempt of that court.

(4) The Florida Rules of Civil Procedure, including those provisions pertaining to discovery, not inconsistent with these rules shall apply in injunctive proceedings before the referee. The powers and jurisdiction generally reposed in the court under those rules may in this action be exercised by the referee. The Florida Bar may in every case amend its petition 1 time as of right, within 60 days after the filing of the order referring the matter to a referee.

(5) Review of interlocutory rulings of the referee may be had by petition to the court filed within 30 days after entry of the ruling complained of. A supporting brief or memorandum of law and a transcript containing conformed copies of pertinent portions of the record in the form of an appendix shall be

filed with the court by a party seeking such review. Any opposing party may file a responsive brief or memorandum of law and appendix containing any additional portions of the record deemed pertinent to the issues raised within 10 days thereafter. The petitioner may file a reply brief or memorandum of law within 5 days of the date of service of the opposing party's responsive brief or memorandum of law. Any party may request oral argument at the time that party's brief or memorandum of law is filed or due. Interlocutory review hereunder shall not stay the cause before the referee unless the referee or the court on its motion or on motion of any party shall so order.

(d) Referee's Report.

(1) *Generally.* At the conclusion of the hearing, the referee shall file a written report with the court stating findings of fact, conclusions of law, a statement of costs incurred and recommendations as to the manner in which costs should be taxed as provided elsewhere in this chapter, and a recommendation for final disposition of the cause which may include the imposition of a civil penalty not to exceed $1000 per incident and a recommendation for restitution as provided elsewhere in this chapter. The original record shall be filed with the report. Copies of the referee's report shall be served upon all parties by the referee at the time it is filed with the court.

(2) *Costs.* The referee shall have discretion to recommend the assessment of costs. Taxable costs of the proceeding shall include only:

(A) investigative costs;

(B) court reporters' fees;

(C) copy costs;

(D) telephone charges;

(E) fees for translation services;

(F) witness expenses, including travel and out-of-pocket expenses;

(G) travel and out-of-pocket expenses of the referee;

(H) travel and out-of-pocket expenses of counsel in the proceedings, including those of the respondent if acting as counsel; and

(I) any other costs which may properly be taxed in civil litigation.

(3) *Restitution.* The referee shall have discretion to recommend that the respondent be ordered to pay restitution. In such instances, the amount of restitution shall be specifically set forth in the referee's report and shall not exceed the amount paid to respondent by complainant(s). The referee's report shall also state the name(s) of the complainant(s) to whom restitution is to be made, the amount of restitution to be made, and the date by which it shall be completed. The referee shall have discretion over the timing of payments and over how those payments are to be distributed to multiple complainants. In determining the amount of restitution to be paid to complainant(s), the referee shall consider testimony and/or any documentary evidence that shows the amount paid to respondent by complainant(s) including:

(A) cancelled checks;

(B) credit card receipts;

(C) receipts from respondent; and

(D) any other documentation evidencing the amount of payment.

The referee shall also have discretion to recommend that restitution shall bear interest at the legal rate provided for judgments in this state. Nothing in this section shall preclude an individual from seeking redress through civil proceedings to recover fees or other damages.

(4) *Civil Penalty.* Except in cases where the parties have entered into a stipulated injunction, prior to recommending the imposition of a civil penalty, the referee shall determine whether the respondent has the ability to pay the penalty. The respondent has the burden to show the inability to pay a penalty. A respondent asserting an inability to pay shall file with the referee a completed affidavit containing the statutory financial information required to be submitted to the clerk of court when determining indigent status and stating that the affidavit is signed under oath and under penalty of perjury. In making a determination of whether the respondent has the ability to pay a penalty, the referee shall consider the applicable statutory criteria used by the clerk of court when determining indigent status and the applicable statutory factors considered by a court when reviewing that determination. If the referee finds that the respondent does not have the ability to pay a penalty, this shall be stated in the referee's report along with a recitation of the evidence upon which the referee made this finding. If the referee finds that the respondent does have the ability to pay a penalty, this shall be stated in the referee's report along with a recitation of the evidence upon which the referee made this finding.

(5) *Stipulated Injunction.* Should the parties enter into a stipulated injunction prior to the hearing, the stipulation shall be filed with the referee. The referee may approve the stipulation or reject the stipulation and schedule a hearing as provided elsewhere in these rules. If accepted, the stipulation and original record shall then be filed with the court for final approval of the stipulation and entry of an injunction. A written report as described in rule 10–7.1(d)(1) shall be filed by the referee along with the stipulation. The respondent may agree to pay restitution in the stipulation. In such instances the amount of restitution, to whom it shall be made, how payments are to be made, the date by which it shall be completed, and whether interest as provided elsewhere in this chapter will be paid, shall be specifically set forth in the stipulation.

(6) *Timing of Payment.* Should the referee recommend the imposition of restitution, costs, or a civil penalty, the respondent shall pay the award in the following order: restitution, costs, civil penalty.

(e) Record.

(1) *Contents.* The record shall include all items properly filed in the cause including pleadings, recorded testimony, if transcribed, exhibits in evidence, and the report of the referee.

(2) *Preparation and Filing.* The referee, with the assistance of bar counsel, shall prepare the record, certify that the record is complete, serve a copy of the index of the record on the respondent and The Florida Bar, and file the record with the office of the clerk of the Supreme Court of Florida.

(3) *Supplementing or Removing Items from the Record.* The respondent and The Florida Bar may seek to supplement the record or have items removed from the record by filing a motion with the referee for such purpose, provided such motion is filed within 15 days of the service of the index. Denial of a motion to supplement the record or to remove an item from the record may be reviewed in the same manner as provided for in the rule on appellate review under these rules.

(f) Review by the Supreme Court of Florida.

(1) Objections to the report of the referee shall be filed with the court by any party aggrieved, within 30 days after the filing of the report, or in the case where a party seeks review of a referee's denial to supplement or remove an item from the record, within 30 days after the court issues its ruling on that matter. Denial of a motion to supplement the record or to remove an item from the record may be reviewed in the same manner as provided for in the rule on appellate review under these rules.

If the objector desires, a brief or memorandum of law in support of the objections may be filed at the time the objections are filed. Any other party may file a responsive brief or memorandum of law within 20 days of service of the objector's brief or memorandum of law. The objector may file a reply brief or memorandum of law within 20 days of service of the opposing party's responsive brief or memorandum of law. Oral argument will be allowed at the court's discretion and will be governed by the provisions of the Florida Rules of Appellate Procedure.

(2) Upon the expiration of the time to file objections to the referee's report, the court shall review the report of the referee, together with any briefs or memoranda of law or objections filed in support of or opposition to such report. After review, the court shall determine as a matter of law whether the respondent has engaged in the unlicensed practice of law, whether the respondent's activities should be enjoined by appropriate order, whether costs should be awarded, whether restitution should be ordered, whether civil penalties should be awarded, and whether further relief shall be granted. Any order of the court that contains the imposition of restitution or civil penalties shall contain a requirement that the respondent send the restitution or penalty to the UPL Department of The Florida Bar. The restitution shall be made payable to the complainant(s) specified in the court's order. The Florida Bar shall remit all restitution received to the complainant(s). If The Florida Bar cannot locate the complainant(s) within 4 months, the restitution shall be returned to the respondent. The civil penalty shall be made payable to the Supreme Court of Florida. The Florida Bar shall remit all penalties received to the court. In the event respondent fails to pay the restitution as ordered by the court, The Florida Bar is authorized to file a petition for indirect criminal contempt as provided elsewhere in this chapter.

(g) Issuance of Preliminary or Temporary Injunction. Nothing set forth in this rule shall be construed to limit the authority of the court, upon proper application, to issue a preliminary or temporary injunction, or at any stage of the proceedings to enter any such order as the court deems proper when public harm or the possibility thereof is made apparent to the court, in order that such harm may be summarily prevented or speedily enjoined.

Amended July 9, 1987 (510 So.2d 596); July 23, 1992, effective Jan. 1, 1993 (605 So.2d 252); June 27, 1996, effective July 1, 1996 (677 So.2d 272); June 27, 1996 (685 So.2d 1203); Sept. 24, 1998, effective Oct. 1, 1998 (718 So.2d 1179); March 23, 2000 (763 So.2d 1002); April 25, 2002 (820 So.2d 210); May 20, 2004 (875 So.2d 448); Oct. 6, 2005, effective Jan. 1, 2006 (916 So.2d 655); Nov. 19, 2009, effective Feb. 1, 2010 (24 So.3d 63); July 7, 2011, effective Oct. 1, 2011 (67 So.3d 1037).

Rule 10-7.2. Proceedings for Indirect Criminal Contempt

Text of rule effective until October 1, 2015. See, also, rule effective October 1, 2015.

(a) Petitions for Indirect Criminal Contempt. Nothing within these rules prohibits or limits the right of the court to issue a permanent injunction in lieu of or in addition to any punishment imposed for an indirect criminal contempt.

(1) Upon receiving a sworn petition of the president, executive director of The Florida Bar, or the chair of the standing committee alleging facts indicating that a person, firm, or corporation is or may be unlawfully practicing law or has failed to pay restitution as provided elsewhere in this chapter, and containing a prayer for a contempt citation, the court may issue an order directed to the respondent, stating the essential allegations charged and requiring the respondent to appear before a referee appointed by the court to show cause why the respondent should not be held in contempt of this court for the unlicensed practice of law or for the failure to pay restitution as ordered. The referee must be a circuit judge of the state of Florida. The order must specify the time and

place of the hearing, and a reasonable time must be allowed for preparation of the defense after service of the order on the respondent.

(2) The respondent, personally or by counsel, may move to dismiss the order to show cause, move for a statement of particulars, or answer such order by way of explanation or defense. All motions and the answer must be in writing. A respondent's omission to file motions or answer will not be deemed an admission of guilt of the contempt charged.

(b) Indigency of Respondent. Any respondent who is determined to be indigent by the referee is entitled to the appointment of counsel.

(1) *Affidavit.* A respondent asserting indigency must file with the referee a completed affidavit containing the statutory financial information required to be submitted to the clerk of court when determining indigent status and stating that the affidavit is signed under oath and under penalty of perjury.

(2) *Determination.* After reviewing the affidavit and questioning the respondent, the referee must make one of the following determinations: the respondent is indigent or the respondent is not indigent. In making this determination, the referee must consider the applicable statutory criteria used by the clerk of court when determining indigent status and the applicable statutory factors considered by a court when reviewing that determination.

(c) Proceedings Before the Referee. Proceedings before the referee must be in accordance with the following:

(1) Venue for the hearing before the referee must be in the county where the respondent resides or where the alleged offense was committed, whichever is designated by the court.

(2) The court or referee may issue an order of arrest of the respondent if the court or referee has reason to believe the respondent will not appear in response to the order to show cause. The respondent will be admitted to bail in the manner provided by law in criminal cases.

(3) The respondent will be arraigned and enter a plea at the time of the hearing before the referee, or prior upon request. A subsequent hearing to determine the guilt or innocence of the respondent will follow a plea of not guilty. The date and time of the subsequent hearing will be set at the arraignment. The respondent is entitled to be represented by counsel, have compulsory process for the attendance of witnesses, and confront witnesses against the respondent. The respondent may testify in the respondent's own defense. No respondent may be compelled to testify. A presumption of innocence will be accorded the respondent. The Florida Bar, which will act as prosecuting authority, must prove guilt of the respondent beyond a reasonable doubt.

(4) Subpoenas for the attendance of witnesses and the production of documentary evidence will be issued in the name of the court by the referee upon request of a party. Failure or refusal to comply with any subpoena is a contempt of court and may be punished by the court or by any circuit court where the action is pending or where the contemnor may be found, as if said refusal were a contempt of that court.

(5) The referee will hear all issues of law and fact and all evidence and testimony presented will be transcribed.

(6) At the conclusion of the hearing, the referee will sign and enter of record a judgment of guilty or not guilty. There should be included in a judgment of guilty a recital of the facts constituting the contempt of which the respondent has been found and adjudicated guilty, and the costs of prosecution, including investigative costs and restitution, if any, will be included and entered in the judgment rendered against the respondent. The amount of restitution must be specifically set forth in the judgment and must not exceed the amount paid to respondent by complainant(s). The judgment must also state the name of the complainant(s) to whom restitution is to be made, the amount of restitution to be made, and the date by which it shall be completed. The referee has discretion over the timing of payments, over how those payments are to be distributed to multiple complainant(s), and whether restitution will bear interest at the legal rate provided for judgments in this state. In determining the amount of restitution to be paid to complainant(s), the referee will consider any documentary evidence that shows the amount paid to respondent by complainant(s), including cancelled checks, credit card receipts, receipts from respondent, and any other documentation evidencing the amount of payment. Nothing in this section precludes an individual from seeking redress through civil proceedings to recover fees or other damages.

(7) Prior to the pronouncement of a recommended sentence upon a judgment of guilty, the referee will inform the respondent of the accusation and judgment and afford the opportunity to present evidence of mitigating circumstances. The recommended sentence will be pronounced in open court and in the presence of the respondent.

(d) Record.

(1) *Contents.* The record must include all items properly filed in the cause including pleadings, recorded testimony, if transcribed, exhibits in evidence, and the report of the referee.

(2) *Preparation and Filing.* The referee, with the assistance of bar counsel, must prepare the record, certify that the record is complete, serve a copy of the index of the record on the respondent and The Florida Bar, and file the record with the office of the clerk of the Supreme Court of Florida.

(3) *Supplementing or Removing Items from the Record.* The respondent and The Florida Bar may seek to supplement the record or have items removed from the record by filing a motion with the referee for such purpose, provided such motion is filed within 15 days of the service of the index. Denial of a motion to supplement the record or to remove an item from the record may be reviewed in the same manner as provided for in the rule on appellate review under these rules.

(e) Review by the Supreme Court of Florida. The judgment and recommended sentence, upon a finding of "guilty," together with the entire record of proceedings must be forwarded to the Supreme Court of Florida for approval, modification, or rejection based upon the law. The respondent may file objections, together with a supporting brief or memorandum of law, to the referee's judgment and recommended sentence within 30 days of the date of filing with the court of the referee's judgment, recommended sentence, and record of proceedings, or in the case where a party seeks review of a referee's denial to supplement or remove an item from the record, within 30 days after the court issues its ruling on that matter. Denial of a motion to supplement the record or to remove an item from the record may be reviewed in the same manner as provided for in the rule on appellate review under these rules.

The Florida Bar may file a responsive brief or memorandum of law within 20 days after service of respondent's brief or memorandum of law. The respondent may file a reply brief or memorandum of law within 20 days after service of The Florida Bar's responsive brief or memorandum of law.

(f) Fine or Punishment. The punishment for an indirect criminal contempt under this chapter will be a fine not to exceed $2500, imprisonment of up to 5 months, or both.

(g) Costs and Restitution. The court may also award costs and restitution.

Added June 27, 1996, effective July 1, 1996 (677 So.2d 272). Amended July 17, 1997 (697 So.2d 115); Sept. 24, 1998, effective Oct. 1, 1998 (718 So.2d 1179); March 23, 2000 (763 So.2d 1002); Feb. 8, 2001 (795 So.2d 1); May 20, 2004 (875 So.2d 448); Oct. 6, 2005, effective Jan. 1, 2006 (916 So.2d 655); Dec. 20, 2007, effective March 1, 2008 (978 So.2d 91); Nov. 19, 2009, effective Feb. 1, 2010 (24 So.3d 63); July 7, 2011, effective Oct. 1, 2011 (67 So.3d 1037); May 29, 2014, effective June 1, 2014 (140 So.3d 541).

Rule 10–7.2. Proceedings for Indirect Criminal Contempt

Text of rule effective October 1, 2015. See, also, rule effective until October 1, 2015.

(a) Petitions for Indirect Criminal Contempt. Nothing within these rules prohibits or limits the right of the court to issue a permanent injunction in lieu of or in addition to any punishment imposed for an indirect criminal contempt.

(1) Upon receiving a sworn petition of the president, executive director of The Florida Bar, or the chair of the standing committee alleging facts indicating that a person, firm, or corporation is or may be unlawfully practicing law or has failed to pay restitution as provided elsewhere in this chapter, and containing a prayer for a contempt citation, the court may issue an order directed to the respondent, stating the essential allegations charged and requiring the respondent to appear before a referee appointed by the court to show cause why the respondent should not be held in contempt of this court for the unlicensed practice of law or for the failure to pay restitution as ordered. The referee must be a circuit judge of the state of Florida. The order must specify the time and place of the hearing, and a reasonable time must be allowed for preparation of the defense after service of the order on the respondent.

(2) The respondent, personally or by counsel, may move to dismiss the order to show cause, move for a statement of particulars, or answer the order by way of explanation or defense. All motions and the answer must be in writing. A respondent's omission to file motions or answer will not be deemed an admission of guilt of the contempt charged.

(b) Indigency of Respondent. Any respondent who is determined to be indigent by the referee is entitled to the appointment of counsel.

(1) *Affidavit.* A respondent asserting indigency must file with the referee a completed affidavit containing the statutory financial information required to be submitted to the clerk of court when determining indigent status and stating that the affidavit is signed under oath and under penalty of perjury.

(2) *Determination.* After reviewing the affidavit and questioning the respondent, the referee will determine whether the respondent is indigent or the respondent is not indigent.

In making this determination, the referee must consider the applicable statutory criteria used by the clerk of court when determining indigent status and the applicable statutory factors considered by a court when reviewing that determination.

(c) Proceedings Before the Referee. Proceedings before the referee must be in accordance with the following:

(1) Venue for the hearing before the referee must be in the county where the respondent resides or where the alleged offense was committed, whichever is designated by the court.

(2) The court or referee may issue an order of arrest of the respondent if the court or referee has reason to believe the respondent will not appear in response to the order to show cause. The respondent will be admitted to bail in the manner provided by law in criminal cases.

(3) The respondent will be arraigned and enter a plea at the time of the hearing before the referee, or prior on request. A subsequent hearing to determine the guilt or innocence of the respondent will follow a plea of not guilty. The date and time of the subsequent hearing will be set at the arraignment. The respondent is entitled to be represented by counsel, have compulsory process for the attendance of witnesses, and confront witnesses against the respondent. The respondent may testify in the respondent's own defense. No respondent may be compelled to testify. A presumption of innocence will be accorded the respondent. The Florida Bar acting as prosecuting authority must prove guilt of the respondent beyond a reasonable doubt.

(4) Subpoenas for the attendance of witnesses and the production of documentary evidence will be issued in the name of the court by the referee upon request of a party. Failure or refusal to comply with any subpoena is a contempt of court and may be punished by the court or by any circuit court where the action is pending or where the contemnor may be found, as if the refusal were a contempt of that court.

(5) The referee will hear all issues of law and fact and all evidence and testimony presented will be transcribed.

(6) At the conclusion of the hearing, the referee will sign and enter of record a judgment of guilty or not guilty. There should be included in a judgment of guilty a recital of the facts constituting the contempt of which the respondent has been found and adjudicated guilty, and the costs of prosecution, including investigative costs and restitution, if any, will be included and entered in the judgment rendered against the respondent. The amount of restitution must be specifically set forth in the judgment and must not exceed the amount paid to respondent by complainant(s). The judgment must also state the name of the complainant(s) to whom restitution is to be made, the amount of restitution to be made, and the date by which it must be completed. The referee has discretion over the timing of payments, over how those payments are to be distributed to multiple complainant(s), and whether restitution will bear interest at the legal rate provided for judgments in this state. In determining the amount of restitution to be paid to complainant(s), the referee will consider any documentary evidence that shows the amount paid to respondent by complainant(s), including cancelled checks, credit card receipts, receipts from respondent, and any other documentation evidencing the amount of payment. Nothing in this section precludes an individual from seeking redress through civil proceedings to recover fees or other damages.

(7) Prior to the pronouncement of a recommended sentence on a judgment of guilty, the referee will inform the respondent of the accusation and judgment and afford the opportunity to present evidence of mitigating circumstances. The recommended sentence will be pronounced in open court and in the presence of the respondent.

(d) Record.

(1) *Contents.* The record includes all items properly filed in the cause including pleadings, recorded testimony, if transcribed, exhibits in evidence, and the report of the referee.

(2) *Preparation and Filing.* The referee, with the assistance of bar counsel, must prepare the record, certify that the record is complete, serve a copy of the index of the record on the respondent and The Florida Bar, and file the record with the office of the clerk of the Supreme Court of Florida.

(3) *Supplementing or Removing Items from the Record.* The respondent and The Florida Bar may seek to supplement the record or have items removed from the record by filing a motion with the referee for that purpose, provided the motion is filed within 15 days of the service of the index. Denial of a motion to supplement the record or to remove an item from the record may be reviewed in the same manner as provided for in the rule on appellate review under these rules.

(e) Review by the Supreme Court of Florida. The judgment and recommended sentence, on a finding of "guilty," together with the entire record of proceedings must be forwarded to the Supreme Court of Florida for approval, modification, or rejection based upon the law. The petitioner or the respondent may file objections, together with a supporting brief or memorandum of law, to the referee's judgment and recommended sentence within 30 days of the date of filing with the court of the referee's judgment, recommended sentence, and record of proceedings, or in the case where a party seeks review of a referee's denial to supplement or remove an item from the record, within 30 days after the court issues its ruling on that matter. Denial of a motion to supplement the record or to remove an item from the record may be reviewed in the same manner as provided for in the rule on appellate review under these rules.

A responsive brief or memorandum of law may be filed within 20 days after service of the initial brief or memorandum of law. A reply brief or memorandum of law may be filed within 20 days after service of the responsive brief or memorandum of law.

(f) Fine or Punishment. The punishment for an indirect criminal contempt under this chapter will be a fine not to exceed $2500, imprisonment of up to 5 months, or both.

(g) Costs and Restitution. The court may also award costs and restitution.

Added June 27, 1996, effective July 1, 1996 (677 So.2d 272). Amended July 17, 1997 (697 So.2d 115); Sept. 24, 1998, effective Oct. 1, 1998 (718 So.2d 1179); March 23, 2000 (763 So.2d 1002); Feb. 8, 2001 (795 So.2d 1); May 20, 2004 (875 So.2d 448); Oct. 6, 2005, effective Jan. 1, 2006 (916 So.2d 655); Dec. 20, 2007, effective March 1, 2008 (978 So.2d 91); Nov. 19, 2009, effective Feb. 1, 2010 (24 So.3d 63); July 7, 2011, effective Oct. 1, 2011 (67 So.3d 1037); May 29, 2014, effective June 1, 2014 (140 So.3d 541); June 11, 2015, effective Oct. 1, 2015 (167 So.3d 412).

Rule 10-7.3. Enforcement of Award of Civil Penalty

If the respondent fails to pay the civil penalty within the time ordered by the court, The Florida Bar may conduct discovery in aid of execution. If the discovery shows that the respondent no longer has the ability to pay the civil penalty, The Florida Bar shall file with the court a motion to dissolve the civil penalty. The court may dissolve the civil penalty or may order that the penalty stand. If the discovery shows that the respondent has the ability to pay the civil penalty, The Florida Bar may file a petition for indirect criminal contempt as provided elsewhere in this chapter.

Added Nov. 19, 2009, effective Feb. 1, 2010 (24 So.3d 63).

10-8. CONFIDENTIALITY

Rule 10-8.1. Files

(a) Files Are Property of Bar. All matters, including files, preliminary investigation reports, interoffice memoranda, records of investigations, and the records in trials and other proceedings under these rules, except those unlicensed practice of law matters conducted in county or circuit courts, are property of The Florida Bar. All of those matters shall be confidential and shall not be disclosed except as provided in these rules. When disclosure is permitted under these rules, it shall be limited to information concerning the status of the proceedings and any information that is part of the UPL record as defined in these rules.

(b) UPL Record. The UPL record shall consist of the record before a circuit committee, the record before a referee, the record before the Supreme Court of Florida, and any reports, correspondence, papers, and recordings and transcripts of hearings and transcribed testimony furnished to, served on, or received from the respondent or the complainant. The record before the circuit committee shall consist of all reports, correspondence, papers, and recordings furnished to or received from the respondent and the transcript of circuit committee meetings or transcribed testimony, if the proceedings were attended by a court reporter; provided, however, that the committee may retire into private session to debate the issues involved and to reach a decision as to the action to be taken. The record before a referee and the record before the Supreme Court of Florida shall include all items properly filed in the cause including pleadings, transcripts of testimony, exhibits in evidence, and the report of the referee.

(c) Limitations on Disclosure. Any material provided to or promulgated by The Florida Bar that is confidential under applicable law shall remain confidential and shall not be disclosed except as authorized by the applicable law. If this type of material is made a part of the UPL record, that portion of the UPL record may be sealed by the circuit committee chair, the referee, or the court.

(d) Disclosure of Information. Unless otherwise ordered by this court or the referee in proceedings under this rule, nothing in these rules shall prohibit the complainant, respondent, or any witness from disclosing the existence of proceedings under these rules or from disclosing any documents or correspondence served on or provided to those persons.

(e) Response to Inquiry. Representatives of The Florida Bar, authorized by the board of governors, shall reply to inquiries regarding a pending or closed unlicensed practice of law investigation as follows:

(1) *Cases Opened Prior To November 1, 1992.* Cases opened prior to November 1, 1992, shall remain confidential.

(2) *Cases Opened On or After November 1, 1992.* In any case opened on or after November 1, 1992, the fact that an unlicensed practice of law investigation is pending and the status of the investigation shall be public information; however, the UPL record shall remain confidential except as provided in rule 10-8.1(e)(4).

(3) *Recommendations of Circuit Committee.* The recommendation of the circuit committee as to the disposition of an investigation opened on or after November 1, 1992, shall be public information; however, the UPL record shall remain confidential except as provided in rule 10-8.1(e)(4).

(4) *Final Action by Circuit Committee, Standing Committee, Designated Reviewer, and Bar Counsel.* The final action on investigations opened on or after November 1, 1992, shall be public information. The UPL record in cases opened on or after November 1, 1992, that are closed by the circuit committee, the standing committee, or bar counsel as provided elsewhere in these rules, cases where a cease and desist affidavit has been accepted, and cases where a litigation recommendation has been approved by a designated reviewer as provided elsewhere in these rules, shall be public information and may be provided upon specific inquiry except that information that remains confidential under rule 10-8.1(c). The Florida Bar may charge a reasonable fee for identification of and photocopying the documents.

(f) Production of UPL Records Pursuant to Subpoena. The Florida Bar, pursuant to a valid subpoena issued by a regulatory agency, may provide any documents that are a portion of the UPL record even if otherwise deemed confidential under these rules. The Florida Bar may charge a reasonable fee for identification of and photocopying the documents.

(g) Notice to Judges. Any judge of a court of record may be advised as to the status of a confidential unlicensed practice of law case and may be provided with a copy of the UPL record. The judge shall maintain the confidentiality of the matter.

(h) Response to False or Misleading Statements. If public statements that are false and misleading are made about any UPL case, The Florida Bar may make any disclosure necessary to correct such false or misleading statements.

(i) Providing Otherwise Confidential Material. Nothing contained herein shall prohibit The Florida Bar from providing otherwise confidential material as provided in rule 10–3.2(e).

Amended July 23, 1992, effective Jan. 1, 1993 (605 So.2d 252); October 29, 1992 (608 So.2d 472); July 17, 1997 (697 So.2d 115); Sept. 24, 1998, effective Oct. 1, 1998 (718 So.2d 1179); April 25, 2002 (820 So.2d 210); Oct. 6, 2005, effective Jan. 1, 2006 (916 So.2d 655); July 7, 2011, effective Oct. 1, 2011 (67 So.3d 1037).

10–9. ADVISORY OPINIONS

Rule 10-9.1. Procedures for Issuance of Advisory Opinions on the Unlicensed Practice of Law

(a) Definitions.

(1) *Committee.* The standing committee as constituted according to the directives contained in these rules.

(2) *Petitioner.* An individual or organization seeking guidance as to the applicability, in a hypothetical situation, of the state's prohibitions against the unlicensed practice of law.

(3) *Public Notice.* Publication in a newspaper of general circulation in the county in which the hearing will be held and in The Florida Bar News.

(4) *Court.* The Supreme Court of Florida (or such other court in the state of Florida as the supreme court may designate).

(b) Requests for Advisory Opinions. A petitioner requesting a formal advisory opinion concerning activities that may constitute the unlicensed practice of law shall do so by sending the request in writing addressed to The UPL Department, The Florida Bar, 651 East Jefferson Street, Tallahassee, Florida 32399–2300. The request for an advisory opinion shall state in detail to the extent practicable the operative facts upon which the request for opinion is based and contain the name and address of the petitioner. The request shall be reviewed by UPL staff counsel. If the request complies with the requirements of the rule as stated herein, the request will be placed on the agenda for the next scheduled meeting of the committee. At that meeting, the committee will determine whether to accept the request, such determination being within the discretion of the committee. Should the committee accept the request, a public hearing as provided in rule 10–9.1(f) shall be scheduled.

(c) Limitations on Opinions. No opinion shall be rendered with respect to any case or controversy pending in any court or tribunal in this jurisdiction and no informal opinion shall be issued except as provided in rule 10–9.1(g)(1). However, the committee shall issue a formal advisory opinion under circumstances described by the court in Harold Goldberg v. Merrill Lynch Credit Corporation, 35 So. 3d 905 (Fla. 2010), when the petitioner is a party to a lawsuit and that suit has been stayed or voluntarily dismissed without prejudice.

(d) Services of Voluntary Counsel. The committee shall be empowered to request and accept the voluntary services of a person licensed to practice in this state when the committee deems it advisable to receive written or oral advice regarding the question presented by the petitioner.

(e) Conflict of Interest. Committee members shall not participate in any matter in which they have either a material pecuniary interest that would be affected by a proposed advisory opinion or committee recommendation or any other conflict of interest that should prevent them from participating. However, no action of the committee will be invalid where full disclosure has been made and the committee has not decided that the member's participation was improper.

(f) Notice, Appearance, and Service.

(1) At least 30 days in advance of the committee meeting at which a hearing is to be held with respect to a potential advisory opinion, the committee shall give public notice of the date, time, and place of the hearing, provide a general description of the subject matter of the request and the bar website and address where a full copy of the question presented can be obtained, and invite written comments on the question. On the announced date the committee shall hold a public hearing at which any person affected shall be entitled to present oral testimony and be represented by counsel. Oral testimony by other persons may be allowed by the committee at its discretion. At the time of or prior to the hearing any other person shall be entitled to file written testimony on the issue before the committee. Additional procedures not inconsistent with this rule may be adopted by the committee.

(2) The committee shall issue either a written proposed advisory opinion, a letter that declines to issue an opinion, or an informal opinion as provided in rule 10–9.1(g)(1). No other form of communication shall be deemed to be an advisory opinion.

(3) A proposed advisory opinion shall be in writing and shall bear a date of issuance. The proposed opinion shall prominently bear a title indicating that it

is a proposed advisory opinion and a disclaimer stating that it is only an interpretation of the law and does not constitute final court action. The committee shall arrange for the publication of notice of filing the proposed advisory opinion and a summary thereof in The Florida Bar News within a reasonable time. Interested parties shall be furnished a copy of the full opinion upon request.

(g) Service and Judicial Review of Proposed Advisory Opinions.

(1) In the case of any proposed advisory opinion in which the standing committee concludes that the conduct in question is not the unlicensed practice of law, it shall decide, by a vote of a majority of the committee members present, either to publish the advisory opinion as provided in rule 10–9.1(f)(3) as an informal advisory opinion, or to file a copy of the opinion with the court as provided in rule 10–9.1(g)(2).

(2) In the case of any proposed advisory opinion in which the standing committee concludes that the conduct in question constitutes or would constitute the unlicensed practice of law, the committee shall file a copy of the opinion and all materials considered by the committee in adopting the opinion with the clerk of the court. The proposed advisory opinion, together with notice of the filing thereof, shall be furnished by certified mail to the petitioner.

(3) Within 30 days of the filing of the opinion, the petitioner may file objections and a brief or memorandum in support thereof, copies of which shall be served on the committee. Any other interested person may, within 30 days of the filing of the opinion, seek leave of the court to file and serve a brief, whether in support of or in opposition to the opinion, in accordance with this same procedure. The committee may file a responsive brief within 20 days of service of the initial brief. The petitioner, as well as other interested persons having leave of court, may file a reply brief within 10 days of service of the responsive brief. At its discretion, the court shall permit reasonable extension of these time periods. Oral argument will be allowed at the court's discretion. The Florida Rules of Appellate Procedure shall otherwise govern the above methods of filing, service, and argument.

(4) Upon the expiration of the time to file objections, briefs, and replies thereto, the court shall review the advisory opinion, regardless of whether any such objections are in fact made, together with any briefs or objections filed in support of or in opposition to such opinion. Upon review, it shall approve, modify, or disapprove the advisory opinion, and the ensuing opinion shall have the force and effect of an order of the court and be published accordingly. There shall be no further review of the opinion except as granted by the court in its discretion, upon petition to the court.

Amended July 23, 1992, effective Jan. 1, 1993 (605 So.2d 252); Feb. 8, 2001 (795 So.2d 1); July 3, 2003 (850 So.2d 499); May 20, 2004 (875 So.2d 448); Jan. 26, 2012, effective April 1, 2012 (82 So.3d 66).

10–10. IMMUNITY

Rule 10–10.1. Generally

The members of the standing committee and circuit committees, as well as staff persons and appointed voluntary counsel assisting those committees, shall have absolute immunity from civil liability for all acts in the course of their official duties.

Added July 23, 1992, effective Jan. 1, 1993 (605 So.2d 252).

10–11. AMENDMENTS

Rule 10–11.1. Generally

Rules governing the investigation and prosecution of the unlicensed practice of law may be amended in accordance with the procedures set forth in rule 1–12.1.

Added July 23, 1992, effective Jan. 1, 1993 (605 So.2d 252).

CHAPTER 11. RULES GOVERNING THE LAW SCHOOL PRACTICE PROGRAM

11–1. GENERALLY

11-1. GENERALLY

Rule 11-1.1. Purpose

The bench and the bar are primarily responsible for providing competent legal services for all persons, including those unable to pay for these services. As one means of providing assistance to lawyers who represent clients unable to pay for such services and to encourage law schools to provide clinical instruction in trial work of varying kinds, the following rules are adopted.

Amended April 21, 1994 (635 So.2d 968).

Rule 11-1.2. Activities

(a) Definition. A law school practice program is a credit-bearing clinical program coordinated by a law school in which students directly provide representation to clients in litigation under the supervision of a lawyer.

(b) Appearance in Court or Administrative Proceedings. An eligible law student may appear in any court or before any administrative tribunal in this state on behalf of any indigent person if the person on whose behalf the student is appearing has indicated in writing consent to that appearance and the supervising lawyer has also indicated in writing approval of that appearance. In those cases in which the indigent person has a right to appointed counsel, the supervising attorney shall be personally present at all critical stages of the proceeding. In all cases, the supervising attorney shall be personally present when required by the court or administrative tribunal who shall determine the extent of the eligible law student's participation in the proceeding.

(c) Appearance for the State in Criminal Proceedings. An eligible law student may also appear in any criminal matter on behalf of the state with the written approval of the state attorney or the attorney general and of the supervising lawyer. In such cases the supervising attorney shall be personally present when required by the court who shall determine the extent of the law student's participation in the proceeding.

(d) Appearance on Behalf of Governmental Officers or Entities. An eligible law student may also appear in any court or before any administrative tribunal in any civil matter on behalf of the state, state officers, or state agencies or on behalf of a municipality or county, provided that the municipality or county has a full-time legal staff, with the written approval of the attorney representing the state, state officer, state agency, municipality, or county. The attorney representing the state, state officer, state agency, municipality, or county shall supervise the law student and shall be personally present when required by the court or administrative tribunal, which shall determine the extent of the law student's participation in the proceeding.

(e) Filing of Consent and Approval. In each case the written consent and approval referred to above shall be filed in the record of the case and shall be brought to the attention of the judge of the court or the presiding officer of the administrative tribunal. If the client is the state attorney, state officer, or governmental entity, it shall be sufficient to file the written consent and approval with the clerk and each presiding judge once for the term of the student's participation.

(f) Fixing of Standards of Indigence. The board of governors shall fix the standards by which indigence is determined under this chapter upon the recommendation of the largest voluntary bar association located in the circuit in which a program is implemented hereunder.

Amended April 2, 1992 (596 So.2d 453); July 23, 1992, effective Jan. 1, 1993 (605 So.2d 252); April 21, 1994 (635 So.2d 968).

Rule 11-1.3. Requirements and Limitations

In order to make an appearance pursuant to this chapter, the law student must:

(a) have registered with the Florida Board of Bar Examiners as a certified legal intern registrant; have paid the $75 fee for such registration if the registration is completed within the first 250 days of the registrant's law school education or $150 if the registration is filed after the 250-day deadline; and have received a letter of clearance as to character and fitness from the Florida Board of Bar Examiners; any fee paid under this subdivision shall be deducted from the applicable application fee should the certified legal intern registrant subsequently decide to apply for admission to The Florida Bar;

(b) be duly enrolled in the United States in, and appearing as part of a law school practice program of, a law school approved by the American Bar Association;

(c) have completed legal studies amounting to at least 4 semesters or 6 quarters for which the student has received not less than 48 semester hours or 72 quarter hours of academic credit or the equivalent if the school is on some other basis;

(d) be certified by the dean of the student's law school as being of good character and competent legal ability and as being adequately trained to perform as a legal intern in a law school practice program;

(e) be introduced to the court in which the student is appearing by an attorney admitted to practice in that court;

(f) neither ask for nor receive any compensation or remuneration of any kind for the student's services from the person on whose behalf the student renders services, but this shall not prevent a state attorney, public defender, legal aid organization, or state officer or governmental entity from paying compensation to the eligible law student (nor shall it prevent any of the foregoing from making such charge for its services as it may otherwise require); and

(g) certify in writing that the student has read and is familiar with the Rules of Professional Conduct as adopted by this court and will abide by the provisions thereof.

Amended July 23, 1992, effective Jan. 1, 1993 (605 So.2d 252); April 21, 1994 (635 So.2d 968); July 5, 2007, effective Aug. 1, 2007 (964 So.2d 690).

Rule 11-1.4. Certification of Student

The certification of a student by the law school dean:

(a) Shall be filed with the clerk of this court, and, unless it is sooner withdrawn, it shall remain in effect until the expiration of 18 months after it is filed.

(b) May be withdrawn by the dean at any time by mailing a notice to that effect to the clerk of this court. It is not necessary that the notice state the cause for withdrawal.

(c) May be terminated by this court at any time without notice or hearing and without any showing of cause. Notice of the termination may be filed with the clerk of the court.

Amended July 23, 1992, effective Jan. 1, 1993 (605 So.2d 252); April 21, 1994 (635 So.2d 968).

Rule 11-1.5. Approval of Legal Aid Organization

Legal aid organizations that provide a majority of their legal services to the indigent and use law student interns pursuant to this chapter must be approved by the supreme court. A legal aid organization seeking approval shall file a petition with the clerk of the court certifying that it is a nonprofit organization and reciting with specificity:

(a) the structure of the organization and whether it accepts funds from its clients;

(b) the major sources of funds used by the organization;

(c) the criteria used to determine potential clients' eligibility for legal services performed by the organization;

(d) the types of legal and nonlegal services performed by the organization; and

(e) the names of all members of The Florida Bar who are employed by the organization or who regularly perform legal work for the organization.

Legal aid organizations approved on the effective date of this chapter need not reapply for approval, but all such organizations are under a continuing duty to notify the court promptly of any significant modification to their structure or sources of funds.

Added April 21, 1994 (635 So.2d 968). Amended July 5, 2007, effective Aug. 1, 2007 (964 So.2d 690).

Rule 11-1.6. Other Activities

(a) Preparation of Documents; Assistance of Indigents. In addition, an eligible law student may engage in other activities, under the general supervision of a member of the bar of this court, but outside the personal presence of that lawyer, including:

(1) preparation of pleadings and other documents to be filed in any matter in which the student is eligible to appear, but such pleadings or documents must be signed by the supervising lawyer;

(2) preparation of briefs, abstracts, and other documents to be filed in appellate courts of this state, but such documents must be signed by the supervising lawyer;

(3) except when the assignment of counsel in the matter is required by any constitutional provision, statute, or rule of this court, assistance to indigent inmates or correctional institutions or other persons who request such assistance in preparing applications for and supporting documents for postconviction relief. If there is an attorney of record in the matter, all such assistance must be supervised by the attorney of record, and all documents submitted to the court on behalf of such a client must be signed by the attorney of record.

(b) Identification of Student in Documents and Pleadings. Each document or pleading must contain the name of the eligible law student who has participated in drafting it. If the student participated in drafting only a portion of it, that fact may be mentioned.

(c) Participation in Oral Argument. An eligible law student may participate in oral argument in appellate courts but only in the presence of the supervising lawyer.

Former Rule 11-1.5. Amended July 23, 1992, effective Jan. 1, 1993 (605 So.2d 252). Renumbered and amended April 21, 1994 (635 So.2d 968).

Rule 11-1.7. Supervision

The member of the bar under whose supervision an eligible law student does any of the things permitted by this chapter shall:

(a) be a lawyer whose service as a supervising lawyer for this program is approved by the dean of the law school in which the law student is enrolled and who is a member of The Florida Bar in good standing;

(b) be a lawyer employed by a state attorney, public defender, an approved legal aid organization, a state officer, or a governmental entity enumerated in rule 11-1.2(d);

(c) assume personal professional responsibility for the student's guidance in any work undertaken and for supervising the quality of the student's work; and

(d) assist the student in the student's preparation to the extent the supervising lawyer considers it necessary.

Former Rule 11-1.6. Amended July 23, 1992, effective Jan. 1, 1993 (605 So.2d 252). Renumbered and amended April 21, 1994 (635 So.2d 968).

Rule 11-1.8. Miscellaneous

Nothing contained in this chapter shall affect the right of any person who is not admitted to the practice of law to do anything that the person might lawfully do prior to the adoption of this chapter.

Former Rule 11-1.7 Amended July 23, 1992, effective Jan. 1, 1993 (605 So.2d 252). Renumbered and amended April 21, 1994 (635 So.2d 968).

Rule 11-1.9. Continuation of Practice Program After Completion of Law School Program or Graduation

(a) Certification. A law student at an American Bar Association approved Florida law school who has filed an application for admission to The Florida Bar, has received an initial clearance letter as to character and fitness from the Florida Board of Bar Examiners, has completed a law school practice program awarding a minimum of 3 semester credit hours or the equivalent or requiring at least 200 hours of actual participation in the program, and has had certification withdrawn by the law school dean by reason of successful completion of the program or has graduated from law school following successful completion of the program may make appearances for any of the same supervisory authorities under the same circumstances and restrictions that were applicable to students in law school programs pursuant to this chapter if the supervising attorney:

(1) files a certification in the same manner and subject to the same limitations as that required to be filed by the law school dean and files a separate certificate of the dean stating that the law student has successfully completed the law school practice program. This certification may be withdrawn in the same manner as provided for the law school dean's withdrawal of certification. The maximum term of certification for graduates shall be 12 months from graduation; and

(2) further certifies that the attorney will assume the duties and responsibilities of the supervising attorney as provided by other provisions of this chapter.

(b) Graduates of Non-Florida Law Schools. A graduate of an American Bar Association approved non-Florida law school may qualify for continuation if the graduate has made application for admission to The Florida Bar and received a letter of initial clearance as to character and fitness from the Florida Board of Bar Examiners, and has successfully completed a clinical program in law school that met the definition of a law school practice program under rule 11-1.2(a) and that awarded a minimum of 3 semester hours or the equivalent or required at least 200 hours of actual participation in the program.

(c) Termination of Certification. Failure of a post-graduate certified legal intern to do any of the following shall result in the automatic termination of certification:

(1) failure to take the next available Florida bar examination;

(2) failure to take the second available Florida bar examination, if unsuccessful on the first administration;

(3) failure to pass every portion of the Florida bar examination by at least the second administration, if unsuccessful on the first administration; or

(4) denial of admission to The Florida Bar.

Former Rule 11-1.8. Amended June 4, 1992, (602 So.2d 914); July 23, 1992, effective Jan. 1, 1993 (605 So.2d 252). Renumbered and amended April 21, 1994 (635 So.2d 968). Amended July 5, 2007, effective Aug. 1, 2007 (964 So.2d 690).

Rule 11-1.10. Certification of Members of Out-of-State Bars

(a) Persons Authorized to Appear. A member of an out-of-state bar may practice law in Florida pursuant to this chapter if:

(1) the appearance is made as an employee of the attorney general, a state attorney, a public defender, or the capital collateral representative; and

(2) the member of an out-of-state bar has made application for admission to The Florida Bar; and

(3) the member of an out-of-state bar submits to the jurisdiction of the Supreme Court of Florida for disciplinary purposes; and

(4) the member of an out-of-state bar is in good standing with that bar and is not currently the subject of disciplinary proceedings.

(b) Term of Certification. The maximum term of certification under this section shall be 12 months from the date of certification; provided, however, that the certification may extend beyond 12 months if the certificate holder has passed the Florida bar examination and is awaiting the results of the character and fitness evaluation of the Florida Board of Bar Examiners. Certification may be withdrawn in the same manner as provided for the withdrawal of certification by a law school dean.

(c) Termination of Certification. Failure to take the next available Florida bar examination, failure of any portion of the Florida bar examination, or denial of admission to The Florida Bar shall terminate certification hereunder.

Added April 21, 1994 (635 So.2d 968).

CHAPTER 12. EMERITUS ATTORNEYS PRO BONO PARTICIPATION PROGRAM

12–1. GENERALLY

Rule 12–1.1. Purpose

Individuals admitted to the practice of law in Florida have a responsibility to provide competent legal services for all persons, including those unable to pay for such services. As one means of meeting these legal needs, the following rules establishing the emeritus attorneys pro bono participation program are adopted.

Amended July 23, 1992, effective Jan. 1, 1993 (605 So.2d 252).

Rule 12–1.2. Definitions

(a) Emeritus Attorney. An "emeritus attorney" is any person, who is retired from the practice of law in Florida or any other state or territory of the United States or the District of Columbia, or is an authorized house counsel certified by the Supreme Court of Florida and who:

(1) was engaged in the active practice of law for a minimum of 10 out of the 15 years immediately preceding the application to participate in the emeritus program, except that this requirement does not apply to authorized house counsel certified under chapter 17 of these rules;

(2) was a member in good standing of The Florida Bar or the entity governing the practice of law of any other state, territory, or the District of Columbia and has not been disciplined for professional misconduct by the bar or courts of any jurisdiction within the past 15 years;

(3) if not a retired member of The Florida Bar, has not failed the Florida bar examination 3 or more times;

(4) agrees to abide by the Rules of Professional Conduct and submit to the jurisdiction of the Supreme Court of Florida for disciplinary purposes;

(5) neither asks for nor receives compensation of any kind for the legal services to be rendered under this rule; and

(6) is certified under rule 12–1.5.

(b) Approved Legal Aid Organization. An "approved legal aid organization" for the purposes of this chapter is a not-for-profit legal aid organization that is approved by the Supreme Court of Florida. A legal aid organization seeking approval must file a petition with the clerk of the Supreme Court of Florida certifying that it is a not-for-profit organization and reciting with specificity:

(1) the structure of the organization and whether it accepts funds from its clients;

(2) the major sources of funds used by the organization;

(3) the criteria used to determine potential clients' eligibility for legal services performed by the organization;

(4) the types of legal and nonlegal services performed by the organization;

(5) the names of all members of The Florida Bar who are employed by the organization or who regularly perform legal work for the organization; and

(6) the existence and extent of malpractice insurance that will cover the emeritus attorney.

(c) Supervising Attorney. A "supervising attorney" as used in this chapter is a member in good standing of The Florida Bar who directs and supervises an emeritus attorney engaged in activities permitted by this chapter. The supervising attorney must:

(1) be employed by or be a participating volunteer for an approved legal aid organization; and

(2) assume personal professional responsibility for supervising the conduct of the matter, litigation, or administrative proceeding in which the emeritus attorney participates.

Amended July 23, 1992, effective Jan. 1, 1993 (605 So.2d 252); May 29, 2014, effective June 1, 2014 (140 So.3d 541).

Rule 12–1.3. Activities

(a) Permissible Activities. An emeritus attorney, in association with an approved legal aid organization and under the supervision of a supervising attorney, may perform the following activities:

(1) The emeritus attorney may appear in any court or before any administrative tribunal in this state on behalf of a client of an approved legal aid organization if the person on whose behalf the emeritus attorney is appearing has consented in writing to that appearance and a supervising attorney has given written approval for that appearance. The written consent and approval must be filed in the record of each case and brought

to the attention of a judge of the court or the presiding officer of the administrative tribunal.

(2) The emeritus attorney may prepare pleadings and other documents to be filed in any court or before any administrative tribunal in this state in any matter in which the emeritus attorney is involved. The supervising lawyer must sign all documents filed with the court.

(3) The emeritus attorney may engage in such other preparatory activities as are necessary for any matter in which the emeritus attorney is involved.

(b) Determination of Nature of Participation. The presiding judge or hearing officer may, in the judge's or officer's discretion, determine the extent of the emeritus attorney's participation in any proceedings before the court.

Amended July 23, 1992, effective Jan. 1, 1993 (605 So.2d 252); May 29, 2014, effective June 1, 2014 (140 So.3d 541).

Rule 12-1.4. Supervision and Limitations

(a) Supervision by Attorney. An emeritus attorney must perform all activities authorized by this chapter under the direct supervision of a supervising attorney.

(b) Representation of Bar Membership Status. Emeritus attorneys permitted to perform services are not, and must not represent themselves to be, active members of The Florida Bar licensed to practice law in this state.

(c) Payment of Expenses and Award of Fees. The prohibition against compensation for the emeritus attorney contained in rule 12-1.2(a)(5) will not prevent the approved legal aid organization from reimbursing the emeritus attorney for actual expenses incurred while rendering approved services. It does not prevent the approved legal aid organization from charging for its services as it may properly charge. The approved legal aid organization will be entitled to receive all court-awarded attorneys' fees for any representation rendered by the emeritus attorney.

Amended July 23, 1992, effective Jan. 1, 1993 (605 So.2d 252); May 29, 2014, effective June 1, 2014 (140 So.3d 541).

Rule 12-1.5. Certification

An emeritus attorney seeking to provide pro bono legal services must obtain approval from the Clerk of the Supreme Court of Florida by filing all of the following certificates:

(a) a certificate from an approved legal aid organization stating that the emeritus attorney is currently associated with that legal aid organization and that a Florida Bar member employed by or participating as a volunteer with that organization will assume the required duties of the supervising lawyer;

(b) a certificate from the highest court or agency in any state, territory, or district in which the emeritus attorney has been licensed to practice law, certifying that the emeritus attorney has fulfilled the requirements of active bar membership and has not been disciplined for professional misconduct by the bar or courts of that jurisdiction within the past 15 years. An authorized house counsel certified by the Supreme Court of Florida under chapter 17 of these rules need not provide this certificate; and

(c) a sworn statement by the emeritus attorney that the emeritus attorney:

(1) has read and will abide by the Rules of Professional Conduct as adopted by the Supreme Court of Florida;

(2) submits to the jurisdiction of the Supreme Court of Florida for disciplinary purposes as defined by chapter 3, Rules of Discipline, and by rules 12-1.2(a)(4) and 12-1.7, R. Regulating Fla. Bar; and

(3) will neither ask for nor receive compensation of any kind for the legal services authorized by this rule.

Amended July 23, 1992, effective Jan. 1, 1993 (605 So.2d 252); May 29, 2014, effective June 1, 2014 (140 So.3d 541).

Rule 12-1.6. Withdrawal of Certification

(a) Withdrawal of Permission to Perform Services. The emeritus attorney must immediately cease performing legal services if:

(1) the approved legal aid organization files a statement with the Clerk of the Supreme Court of Florida that:

(A) the emeritus attorney has ceased to be associated with the organization. This notice must be filed within 5 days after such association has ceased; or

(B) certification of such attorney is withdrawn. An approved legal aid organization may withdraw certification at any time and it is not necessary that the notice state the cause for such withdrawal.

The legal aid organization must mail a copy of the notice filed with the clerk of the Supreme Court of Florida to the emeritus attorney concerned; or

(2) the Supreme Court of Florida, in its discretion, at any time, revokes permission for the emeritus attorney to perform pro bono services. The Clerk of the Supreme Court of Florida must mail a copy of the statement to the emeritus attorney and the approved legal aid organization.

(3) The Florida Bar files a statement with the Supreme Court of Florida that the individual is no longer an authorized house counsel. The Florida Bar must mail a copy of the statement to the emeritus attorney involved.

(b) Notice of Withdrawal. If an emeritus attorney's certification is withdrawn for any reason, the supervising attorney must immediately file a notice of the withdrawal in the official file of each matter pending before any court or tribunal in which the emeritus attorney was involved.

Amended July 23, 1992, effective Jan. 1, 1993 (605 So.2d 252); May 29, 2014, effective June 1, 2014 (140 So.3d 541).

Rule 12-1.7. Discipline

The Supreme Court of Florida may impose appropriate proceedings and discipline under the Rules of Discipline or the Rules of Professional Conduct. In addition, the Supreme Court of Florida or the approved legal aid organization may, with or without cause, withdraw certification and the presiding judge or hearing officer for any matter in which the emeritus attorney has participated may hold the emeritus attorney in civil contempt for any failure to abide by the tribunal's orders.

Amended July 23, 1992, effective Jan. 1, 1993 (605 So.2d 252); May 29, 2014, effective June 1, 2014 (140 So.3d 541).

CHAPTER 13. AUTHORIZED LEGAL AID PRACTITIONERS RULE

13-1. GENERALLY

13-1. GENERALLY

Rule 13-1.1. Purpose

The purpose of this chapter is to expand the delivery of legal services to poor people. This chapter authorizes attorneys licensed to practice law in jurisdictions other than Florida to be certified to practice in Florida for up to 1 year while employed by a legal aid organization. The attorney so certified must take the next available Florida bar examination.

Added Oct. 22, 1987, effective Jan. 1, 1988 (519 So.2d 971). Amended July 23, 1992, effective Jan. 1, 1993 (605 So.2d 252).

Rule 13-1.2. Definitions

(a) Authorized Legal Aid Practitioner. An "authorized legal aid practitioner" is any person who:

(1) was engaged in the active practice of law for 3 years immediately preceding the application for certification under this chapter;

(2) is a member in good standing of the entity governing the practice of law of any other state or territory or the District of Columbia and has not been disciplined for professional misconduct by the bar or courts of any jurisdiction within the past 15 years;

(3) has not failed the Florida bar examination and has not been denied admission to the courts of any jurisdiction during the preceding 15 years;

(4) agrees to abide by the Rules Regulating The Florida Bar and submit to the jurisdiction of the Supreme Court of Florida for disciplinary purposes;

(5) neither asks for nor receives compensation of any kind from the person on whose behalf the practitioner renders legal services hereunder (this shall not prevent the approved legal aid organization from paying compensation to the attorney); and

(6) is certified under rule 13-1.5.

(b) Approved Legal Aid Organization. An "approved legal aid organization" for the purposes of this chapter is a not-for-profit legal aid organization that is approved by the Supreme Court of Florida as set forth herein. A legal aid organization seeking approval from the Supreme Court of Florida for the purposes of this chapter shall file a petition with the clerk of the Supreme Court of Florida certifying that it is a not-for-profit organization and stating with specificity:

(1) the structure of the organization and whether it accepts funds from its clients;

(2) the major sources of funds used by the organization;

(3) the criteria used to determine potential clients' eligibility for legal services performed by the organization;

(4) the types of legal and nonlegal services performed by the organization;

(5) the names of all members of The Florida Bar who are employed by the organization or who regularly perform legal work for the organization; and

(6) the existence and extent of malpractice insurance that will cover the authorized legal aid practitioner.

(c) Supervising Attorney. A "supervising attorney" as used herein is a member in good standing of The Florida Bar who directs and supervises an authorized legal aid practitioner engaged in activities permitted by this chapter. The supervising attorney must:

(1) be employed by or be a participating volunteer for an approved legal aid organization; and

(2) assume personal professional responsibility for supervising the conduct of the matter, litigation, or

administrative proceeding in which the authorized legal aid practitioner participates.

Added Oct. 22, 1987, effective Jan. 1, 1988 (519 So.2d 971). Amended July 23, 1992, effective Jan. 1, 1993 (605 So.2d 252).

Rule 13-1.3. Activities

(a) Permissible Activities. An authorized legal aid practitioner, in association with an approved legal aid organization and under the supervision of a supervising attorney, may perform the following activities:

(1) Appear in any court or before any administrative tribunal in this state on behalf of a client of an approved legal aid organization if the person on whose behalf the authorized legal aid practitioner is appearing has consented in writing to that appearance and a supervising attorney has given written approval for that appearance. The written consent and approval shall be filed in each case and shall be brought to the attention of a judge of the court or the presiding officer of the administrative tribunal.

(2) Prepare pleadings and other documents to be filed in any court or before any administrative tribunal in this state in any matter in which the authorized legal aid practitioner is involved. Such pleadings also shall be signed by the supervising attorney.

(3) Prepare legal documents, provide legal advice, and otherwise engage in the practice of law.

(4) Engage in such other preparatory activities as are necessary for any matter in which the practitioner is involved.

(b) Determination of Scope of Participation. The presiding judge or hearing officer may, in the judge's or officer's discretion, determine the extent of the authorized legal aid practitioner's participation in any proceeding.

Added Oct. 22, 1987, effective Jan. 1, 1988 (519 So.2d 971). Amended July 23, 1992, effective Jan. 1, 1993 (605 So.2d 252).

Rule 13-1.4. Supervision and limitations

(a) Supervision by Attorney. An authorized legal aid practitioner must perform all activities authorized by this chapter under the direct supervision of a supervising attorney.

(b) Representation of Bar Membership Status. Authorized legal aid practitioners permitted to perform services under this chapter are not, and shall not represent themselves to be, active members of The Florida Bar licensed to practice law in this state.

(c) Payment of Expenses and Award of Fees. The limitation on compensation for the authorized legal aid practitioner contained in rule 13-1.2(a)(5) shall not prevent the approved legal aid organization from reimbursing the authorized legal aid practitioner for actual expenses incurred while rendering services hereunder nor shall it prevent the approved legal aid organization from making such charges for its services as it may otherwise properly charge. The approved legal aid organization shall be entitled to receive all court-awarded attorney's fees for any representation rendered by the authorized legal aid practitioner.

Added Oct. 22, 1987, effective Jan. 1, 1988 (519 So.2d 971). Amended July 23, 1992, effective Jan. 1, 1993 (605 So.2d 252).

Rule 13-1.5. Certification

Permission for an authorized legal aid practitioner to perform services under this chapter shall become effective upon filing with and approval by the clerk of the Supreme Court of Florida of:

(a) A certification by an approved legal aid organization stating that the authorized legal aid practitioner is currently associated with that legal aid organization and that an attorney employed by or participating as a volunteer with that organization will assume the duties of the supervising attorney required hereunder.

(b) A certificate from the highest court or agency in the state, territory, or district in which the authorized legal aid practitioner is licensed to practice law certifying that the authorized legal aid practitioner is a member in good standing and has a clear disciplinary record as required by rule 13-1.2(a)(2). The certificate shall also advise of any pending complaints and/or investigations involving the authorized legal aid practitioner.

(c) A sworn statement by the authorized legal aid practitioner that the practitioner:

(1) has read and is familiar with chapter 4 of the Rules Regulating The Florida Bar as adopted by the Supreme Court of Florida and will abide by the provisions thereof;

(2) submits to the jurisdiction of the Supreme Court of Florida for disciplinary purposes, as defined by chapter 3 of the Rules Regulating The Florida Bar and by rule 13-1.7, and authorizes the practitioner's home state to be advised of any disciplinary action taken in Florida; and

(3) will take the next available Florida bar examination.

Added Oct. 22, 1987, effective Jan. 1, 1988 (519 So.2d 971). Amended July 23, 1992, effective Jan. 1, 1993 (605 So.2d 252).

Rule 13-1.6. Withdrawal or termination of certification

(a) Cessation of Permission to Perform Services. Permission to perform services under this chapter shall cease immediately upon the earliest of the following events:

(1) The passage of 1 year from the date of the authorized legal aid practitioner's certification by the court; provided, however, the certification of any authorized legal aid practitioner who has passed the Florida bar examination shall continue in effect until the date the practitioner is admitted to practice.

(2) Failure of the Florida bar examination.

(3) The filing with the clerk of the Supreme Court of Florida of a notice by the approved legal aid organization stating that:

(A) the authorized legal aid practitioner has ceased to be associated with the organization, which notice must be filed within 5 days after such association has ceased; or

(B) certification of such attorney is withdrawn. An approved legal aid organization may withdraw certification at any time and it is not necessary that the notice state the cause for such withdrawal. A copy of the notice filed with the clerk of the Supreme Court of Florida shall be mailed by the organization to the authorized legal aid practitioner concerned.

(4) The filing with the clerk of the Supreme Court of Florida of a notice by the Supreme Court of Florida, in its discretion, at any time, stating that permission to perform services under this chapter has been revoked. A copy of such notice shall be mailed by the clerk of the Supreme Court of Florida to the authorized legal aid practitioner involved and to the approved legal aid organization to which the practitioner had been certified. The certified legal aid attorney shall have 15 days to request reinstatement for good cause.

(b) Notice of Withdrawal of Certification. If an authorized legal aid practitioner's certification is withdrawn for any reason, the supervising attorney shall immediately file a notice of such action in the official file of each matter pending before any court or tribunal in which the authorized legal aid practitioner was involved.

Added Oct. 22, 1987, effective Jan. 1, 1988 (519 So.2d 971). Amended July 23, 1992, effective Jan. 1, 1993 (605 So.2d 252).

Rule 13-1.7. Discipline

(a) Contempt; Withdrawal of Certification. In addition to any appropriate proceedings and discipline that may be imposed by the Supreme Court of Florida under chapter 3 of these Rules Regulating The Florida Bar, the authorized legal aid practitioner shall be subject to the following disciplinary measures:

(1) the presiding judge or hearing officer for any matter in which the authorized legal aid practitioner has participated may hold the authorized legal aid practitioner in civil contempt for any failure to abide by such tribunal's order, in the same manner as any other person could be held in civil contempt; and

(2) the Supreme Court of Florida or the approved legal aid organization may, at any time, with or without cause, withdraw certification hereunder.

(b) Notice to Home State of Disciplinary Action. The Florida Bar shall notify the appropriate authority in the authorized legal aid attorney's home state of any disciplinary action taken against the authorized legal aid practitioner.

Added Oct. 22, 1987, effective Jan. 1, 1988 (519 So.2d 971). Amended July 23, 1992, effective Jan. 1, 1993 (605 So.2d 252).

CHAPTER 14. GRIEVANCE MEDIATION AND FEE ARBITRATION

14-1. ESTABLISHMENT

Rule 14-1.1. Establishment

The Florida Bar Grievance Mediation and Fee Arbitration Program (hereinafter "the program") is hereby established as a means to empower complainants and respondents to resolve disputes without the involvement of formal disciplinary processes.

Added April 6, 1989 (542 So.2d 975). Amended Nov. 14, 1991, effective Jan. 1, 1992 (593 So.2d 1035); July 23, 1992, effective Jan. 1, 1993 (605 So.2d 252); Oct. 20, 1994 (644 So.2d 282); May 20, 2004 (875 So.2d 448).

Rule 14-1.2. Jurisdiction

(a) Fee Arbitration. The program has jurisdiction to resolve disputes between members of The Florida Bar or between a member of The Florida Bar and a client or clients over a fee paid, charged, or claimed for legal services rendered by a member of The Florida Bar when the parties to the dispute agree to arbitrate under the program either by written contract that complies with the requirements of subdivision (i) of rule 4-1.5 or by a request for arbitration signed by all parties, or as a condition of probation or as a part of a discipline sanction as authorized elsewhere in these Rules Regulating The Florida Bar. Jurisdiction is limited to matters in which:

(1) there is no bona fide disputed issue of fact other than the amount of or entitlement to legal fees; and

(2) it is estimated by all parties that all the evidence bearing on the disputed issues of fact may be heard in 8 hours or less.

The program does not have jurisdiction to resolve disputes involving matters in which a court has taken jurisdiction to determine and award a reasonable fee to a party or that involve fees charged that constitute a violation of the Rules Regulating The Florida Bar, unless specifically referred to the program by the court or by bar counsel.

The program has authority to decline jurisdiction to resolve any particular dispute by reason of its complexity and protracted hearing characteristics.

(b) Grievance Mediation. The program has jurisdiction to mediate the issues in a disciplinary file referred to the program in which the public interest is satisfied by the resolution of the private rights of the parties to the mediation. The program does not have jurisdiction to resolve the issues in a disciplinary file if any issue involved in that file must remain for resolution within the disciplinary process.

Added April 6, 1989 (542 So.2d 975). Amended July 23, 1992, effective Jan. 1, 1993 (605 So.2d 252); May 20, 2004 (875 So.2d 448); April 12, 2012, effective July 1, 2012 (101 So.3d 807); May 29, 2014, effective June 1, 2014 (140 So.3d 541).

Rule 14-1.3. Authority of Board of Governors

The board of governors shall appoint a standing committee to administer the program and the board may adopt policies for implementation thereof.

Added April 6, 1989 (542 So.2d 975). Amended July 23, 1992, effective Jan. 1, 1993 (605 So.2d 252); May 20, 2004 (875 So.2d 448).

Rule 14-1.4. Application of Rules and Statutes

The Florida Arbitration Code (chapter 682, Florida Statutes), shall apply to arbitrations conducted under this chapter except as modified by or in conflict with these rules.

The Florida Rules for Certified and Court-Appointed Mediators shall apply to proceedings under this chapter unless otherwise stated herein or in conflict with the provisions of this rule or the Rules of Professional Conduct. A program mediator shall not report the misconduct of another member of The Florida Bar if the Florida Rules for Certified and Court-Appointed Mediators and applicable law preclude such report.

Added May 20, 2004 (875 So.2d 448).

14-2. STANDING COMMITTEE

Rule 14-2.1. Generally

(a) Appointment of Members; Quorum. The board of governors shall appoint a standing committee on grievance mediation and fee arbitration comprised of:

(1) 6 lawyers who are certified as mediators under this chapter;

(2) 3 nonlawyers who are certified as mediators under this chapter;

(3) 6 lawyers who are certified as arbitrators under this chapter; and

(4) 3 nonlawyers who are certified as arbitrators under this chapter.

The board of governors will appoint a chair and vice-chair of the committee from the members listed above. A majority of members of the committee constitutes a quorum. The lawyer members of the committee shall be members of The Florida Bar in good standing.

(b) Terms. All members shall be appointed for 3-year terms, each term commencing on July 1 of the year of appointment and ending on June 30 of the third year thereafter. Terms shall be staggered so that one-third of the members of the committee shall be appointed each year. No committee member may serve for more than 2 consecutive full terms.

(c) Duties. The standing committee shall administer the program, certify mediators and arbitrators for the program, promulgate necessary standards, forms, and documents, and make recommendations, as necessary, to the board of governors for changes in the program.

Added April 6, 1989 (542 So.2d 975). Amended July 23, 1992, effective Jan. 1, 1993 (605 So.2d 252); March 23, 2000 (763 So.2d 1002); May 20, 2004 (875 So.2d 448); Dec. 20, 2007, effective March 1, 2008 (978 So.2d 91).

14-3. CERTIFICATION OF PROGRAM MEDIATORS AND ARBITRATORS

Rule 14-3.1. Application Required

(a) Applications. Persons wishing to become program mediators or arbitrators shall apply to the committee for its review and certification. The committee shall promulgate standards and forms for certification hereunder. Membership in The Florida Bar shall not be required for certification.

(b) CLE Credit for Service. Members of The Florida Bar who are program mediators and arbitrators shall be entitled to a maximum of 5 hours of CLE credit in each reporting period in the area of ethics for service in the program as provided in the policies adopted under this chapter.

Added April 6, 1989 (542 So.2d 975). Amended July 23, 1992, effective Jan. 1, 1993 (605 So.2d 252); March 23, 2000 (763 So.2d 1002); May 20, 2004 (875 So.2d 448).

14-4. INSTITUTION OF PROCEEDINGS

Rule 14-4.1. Arbitration Proceedings

(a) Institution of Proceedings. All arbitration proceedings shall be instituted by the filing of a written consent to arbitration by written contract between the parties to the arbitration, or orders of this court in proceedings under these Rules Regulating The Florida Bar imposing a sanction or condition or probation, or by the consent form prescribed in the policies adopted under the authority of this chapter and signed by each party to the controversy.

(b) Position Statement and Relevant Documents. Each of the parties shall provide the arbitrator(s) with a concise statement of that party's position, including the amount claimed or in controversy, on the form prescribed and authorized by the standing committee. If there is a written contract regarding fees between the parties, a copy of that written contract shall accompany the request or submission.

(c) Referral by Intake Counsel or Bar Counsel. Intake counsel with the consent of the parties and concurrence of staff counsel, or bar counsel, with the consent of the parties, and the concurrence of the chief branch staff counsel, may refer appropriate cases to the fee arbitration program.

(d) Referral by Grievance Committees. Grievance committees, with concurrence of bar counsel and consent of the parties, may refer appropriate cases to the fee arbitration program.

(e) Referral by Board of Governors. The board of governors, with the agreement of the parties and upon review of a file referred to it as authorized elsewhere under these Rules Regulating The Florida Bar, may refer appropriate cases to the fee arbitration program if they meet the criteria established by the policies adopted under the authority of this chapter.

Added April 6, 1989 (542 So.2d 975). Amended July 23, 1992, effective Jan. 1, 1993 (605 So.2d 252); Oct. 20, 1994 (644 So.2d 282); May 20, 2004 (875 So.2d 448); Nov. 19, 2009, effective Feb. 1, 2010 (24 So.3d 63).

Rule 14-4.2. Grievance Mediation Proceedings

(a) Referral by Bar Counsel. Bar counsel, with the consent of the parties, may refer any file to the program that meets the criteria established by any policies adopted under the authority of this rule.

(b) Referral by Grievance Committees. Grievance committees, with concurrence of bar counsel and consent of the parties, may refer any file to the program that meets the criteria established by the policies adopted under the authority of this chapter.

(c) Referral by Board of Governors. The board of governors, upon review of a file referred to it as authorized elsewhere under the Rules Regulating The Florida Bar, may refer same to the program if it meets the criteria established by the policies adopted under the authority of this chapter.

(d) Referral by Referees. Referees, with concurrence of The Florida Bar, may refer any file to the program that meets the criteria established by the policies adopted under the authority of this chapter. Concurrence of The Florida Bar requires agreement of bar counsel and the member of the board of governors designated to review the disciplinary matter at issue.

(e) Referral by Order of Supreme Court of Florida. The Supreme Court of Florida may order referral of any file to the program that meets the criteria established by the policies adopted under the authority of this chapter.

Added May 20, 2004 (875 So.2d 448).

14-5. EFFECT OF AGREEMENT TO MEDIATE OR ARBITRATE AND FAILURE TO COMPLY

Rule 14-5.1. Effect of Referral to Mediation and Failure to Comply

(a) Closure of Disciplinary File. Upon referral for mediation of the issues involved in a disciplinary file, the disciplinary file shall be closed without the entry of a sanction and shall remain closed except as provided in subdivision (b), below:

(b) Effect of Respondent's Failure to Attend or Comply. It shall be a violation of the Rules Regulating The Florida Bar for a respondent to fail to attend an agreed-upon mediation conference without good cause. Likewise, it shall be a violation of the Rules Regulating The Florida Bar for a respondent to fail to fully comply with the terms of a written mediation agreement without good cause.

(c) Effect of Complainant's Failure to Attend. If a file referred for mediation is not fully resolved by reason of a complainant's failure to attend without good cause, the disciplinary file based thereon may remain closed.

Added April 6, 1989 (542 So.2d 975). Amended July 23, 1992, effective Jan. 1, 1993 (605 So.2d 252); May 20, 2004 (875 So.2d 448).

Rule 14-5.2. Effect of Agreement to Arbitrate and Failure to Comply

(a) Closure of Disciplinary File. A disciplinary file that involves only fee issues shall be closed without the entry of a sanction upon the entry of an agreement to arbitrate.

(b) Effect of Respondent's Failure to Attend or Comply. It shall be a violation of the Rules Regulating The Florida Bar for a respondent to fail to attend an agreed-upon arbitration conference without good cause. Likewise, it shall be a violation of the Rules Regulating The Florida Bar for a respondent to fail to fully comply with the terms of an arbitration award without good cause.

(c) Effect of Complainant's or Other Opposing Party's Failure to Attend. If a file referred for arbitration is not fully resolved by reason of a complainant's or other opposing party's failure to attend without good cause, the disciplinary file based thereon may remain closed.

Added May 20, 2004 (875 So.2d 448).

14-6. NATURE; ENFORCEMENT OF AWARD; EFFECT OF FAILURE TO PAY

Rule 14-6.1. Binding Nature; Enforcement; and Effect of Failure to Pay Award

(a) Binding Determination. The parties to a proceeding under these rules shall be bound by the terms of the arbitration award subject to those rights and procedures to set aside or modify the award provided by chapter 682, Florida Statutes, or by the terms of an agreement reached in mediation.

(b) Enforcement of Determination. In addition to any remedy authorized in this chapter, an arbitration award may be enforced as provided in chapter 682, Florida Statutes.

(c) Effect of Failure to Pay Award. Failure of a member of the bar to pay an award within 30 days of the date on which the award became final, without just cause for such failure, shall result in the member being delinquent and not authorized to practice law, as provided elsewhere in these rules defining delinquent members.

Added April 6, 1989 (542 So.2d 975). Amended July 23, 1992, effective Jan. 1, 1993 (605 So.2d 252); Renumbered from Rule 14-5.2 and amended May 20, 2004 (875 So.2d 448); Dec. 20, 2007, effective March 1, 2008 (978 So.2d 91); April 12, 2012, effective July 1, 2012 (101 So.3d 807).

14-7. IMMUNITY AND CONFIDENTIALITY

Rule 14-7.1. Immunity and Confidentiality

(a) Immunity. The members of the standing committee, mediators, arbitrators, staff of The Florida Bar, and appointed voluntary counsel assisting the committee, mediators, and arbitrators, shall have absolute immunity from civil liability for all acts in the course of their official duties.

(b) Confidentiality of Arbitration Proceedings and Records. All records, documents, files, proceedings, and hearings pertaining to fee arbitration under these rules shall be made available, upon inquiry, to anyone. Provided, however, that an arbitrator's mental processes shall not be subject to discovery and a panel of arbitrators may retire into executive session to consider the issues raised and to reach a decision as to an award.

(c) Confidentiality of Mediation Proceedings and Records. All records, documents, files, and proceedings pertaining to mediation under this chapter shall be made available only as provided in the Florida Rules for Certified and Court-Appointed Mediators and applicable law.

Added March 23, 2000 (763 So.2d 1002); Renumbered from Rule 14-5.3 and amended May 20, 2004 (875 So.2d 448).

FEE ARBITRATION PROCEDURAL RULES

Explanatory Note

These rules were added effective April 6, 1989 (542 So.2d 975), and were amended Nov. 11, 1989; Jan. 1990; Jan. 1991; July 23, 1992, effective Jan. 1, 1993 (605 So.2d 252); Oct. 20, 1994 (644 So.2d 282); Oct. 29-30, 1998, by the Board of Governors of The Florida Bar; Dec. 11, 1998, by the Board of Governors of The Florida Bar; May 20, 2004 (875 So.2d 448); Dec. 16, 2005 by the Board of Governors of The Florida Bar.

Rule I. Preamble

The following rules are those standards by which the program must conduct proceedings in fee arbitration matters.

Rule II. Selection of Arbitrators

(a) Referral to Arbitrators. Upon the filing of a written agreement wherein the parties agree to arbitrate under the provisions of Chapter 14, Rules Regulating The Florida Bar, or upon entry of an order by the Supreme Court of Florida requiring arbitration under that chapter, the matter will be referred to The Florida Bar's fee arbitration program.

Unless otherwise agreed by the parties the matter is referred to a sole arbitrator when the amount in controversy is $15,000 or less.

Unless otherwise agreed by the parties the matter is referred to a panel of 3 arbitrators, 1 of whom is designated panel chair for the case, if the amount in controversy exceeds $15,000.

The parties may stipulate to the use of 1 or 3 arbitrators without regard to the amount in controversy.

All 3–member panels will consist of at least 1 nonlawyer and 1 lawyer. This requirement may be waived by the parties.

(b) Eligibility to Serve. Any arbitrator designated as a sole arbitrator or panel member must disclose any reason why the arbitrator cannot ethically or conscientiously serve. When an arbitrator declines or is unable to serve, staff will designate another arbitrator. The standing committee chair has the authority to remove a sole arbitrator or panel member from hearing a particular matter if, in the judgment of the chair, the member should not serve.

(c) Postponements. If, at the time set for hearing by a panel, all members of the panel are not present, the panel chair, with the consent of the parties, may postpone the hearing or proceed with fewer than 3 members.

(d) Death or Inability to Serve. If any member of the panel dies or becomes unable to continue to serve while the matter is pending, but before an award has been made, a substitute panel member will be appointed by the panel chair unless the parties consent to proceed with the hearing. If a substitute panel member is appointed, the member will review the evidence admitted and recorded in the proceedings, if recorded. If not recorded, the review will consist of an examination of evidence admitted and oral summary by the panel chair followed by argument by the parties.

(e) Powers of Arbitrators. Arbitrators are vested with all the powers and assume all the duties granted and imposed upon arbitrators in accordance with chapter 682, Florida Statutes.

(f) Time. The panel or the sole arbitrator assigned will hold the hearing within 45 days after receipt of the assignment and will render the award within 10 days after the close of the hearing, unless extended by the chair of the standing committee for good cause. Failure of an arbitrator or panel to comply with these time requirements does not divest the arbitrator or panel of the authority to conduct proceedings authorized by these policies and applicable rules.

Rule III. Record of Proceedings

Any party may provide, at the party's cost, the service of a stenographer to record the proceedings. If the proceedings are transcribed, the arbitrators shall be promptly provided with a copy that shall be open to inspection by all of the parties to the arbitration. By stipulation of the parties, the proceedings may be recorded by tape recorder or other electronic means.

Rule IV. Hearings

(a) Setting and Notice of Hearing. The chair of the panel or the sole arbitrator, as the case may be, shall coordinate with the parties and panel members and thereafter fix a time and place for the hearing and shall cause written notice thereof to be served personally or by registered or certified mail on the parties to the arbitration at the address stated on the agreement to arbitration form not less than 10 days before the hearing. A copy of the notice of hearing shall be provided to the program administrator. A party's appearance at a scheduled hearing shall constitute a waiver of any deficiency in the notice of hearing.

(b) Absence of Party. The arbitration may proceed in the absence of a party who, after notice, fails to attend or to obtain a postponement from the panel chair or sole arbitrator. Postponement shall only be granted upon good cause shown. Despite the absence of a party or parties, no award shall be made without the submission of evidence to support the claim.

(c) Representation by Counsel. Each party has the right to be represented by counsel at any arbitration hearing.

(d) Presentation of Evidence. If all parties to the controversy so agree, they may waive an evidentiary hearing and may submit their positions and contentions in writing, together with exhibits, if any, to the arbitrators who shall render a final decision based on the information before them. The arbitrators shall require all parties and witnesses to be sworn before they testify. The arbitrators, if they so desire, may request opening statements and prescribe the order of proof. In any event, all parties shall be afforded a reasonable opportunity for the presentation of any evidence. Depositions shall be allowed only for the perpetuation of testimony. All other pre-hearing discovery is prohibited. The procedures for subpoenas and witness attendance shall be as prescribed in section 682.08, Florida Statutes as amended. Subpoenas may be enforced as provided in section 682.08, Florida Statutes, or as elsewhere provided in chapter 3 of the Rules Regulating The Florida Bar.

(e) Right of Party to Attend; Appearance by Telephone. All parties shall have the right to attend all hearings. The exclusion of other persons or witnesses shall be within the discretion of the arbitrators.

(f) Presiding Arbitrator. The arbitrators shall select 1 of their members as chair. The chair of the panel or the sole arbitrator shall preside at the hearing and shall rule on the admission and exclusion of evidence and on questions of procedure, and shall exercise all powers relating to the conduct of the hearing. The hearing should be informal in nature without strict observance of the rules of evidence or the Florida Rules of Civil Procedure.

(g) Factors to Consider Regarding Reasonable Fees. In reaching their decision, the arbitrators may consider all factors they deem relevant, including but not limited to the intention and understanding of the parties at the time the representation was undertaken as well as those factors for determining the reasonableness of a fee enumerated in rules 4–1.5(b) and (c), Rules of Professional Conduct.

Rule V. Closing of Hearings

The arbitrators shall specifically inquire of all parties whether they have any further evidence to submit in whatever form. If the answer is in the negative, the hearings shall be closed. The fee arbitration files shall be preserved for a period of 1 year from the date of submission of the award to the parties. Upon closure of the hearing, the arbitrator(s) may retire into executive session to consider the issues raised and reach a decision as to an award. The mental processes of the arbitrator(s) employed in reaching an award shall not be subject to discovery or use in any proceeding.

Rule VI. The Award

The decision of the arbitrators shall be expressed in a written award on the form prescribed by the standing committee, signed by the arbitrators, which shall include a brief explanation of the basis of the award and shall be submitted to the parties and the program administrator. If there is a dissent, it shall be signed separately but the award shall be binding if signed by a majority of the arbitrators. Unless the agreement to arbitrate or request for and notice of arbitration provides otherwise, the arbitrators may grant any lawful relief, including specific performance. An award may also be entered upon the consent of all the parties. Once the award is signed, the hearing may not be reopened except upon consent of all parties and the chair or sole arbitrator. The award may be confirmed, set aside, modified, or corrected only in accordance with chapter 682, Florida Statutes, as amended.

Rule VII. Standards for Certification and Training

(a) Eligibility. Persons eligible to be program arbitrators are:

(1) retired judges and justices of the courts of the State of Florida;

(2) persons who were members of circuit fee arbitration committees at the time of or prior to the merger of the grievance mediation and fee arbitration programs;

(3) persons who have served on a circuit grievance committee for 1 year or more; and

(4) any other person who, in the opinion of the committee, possesses the requisite education, training, or certification in alternative dispute resolution to be a program arbitrator.

Members of The Florida Bar must be members in good standing, and have no pending recommendation of minor misconduct or finding of probable cause to be eligible for appointment.

(b) Certification. The committee may certify applicants as program arbitrators if they meet the eligibility requirements stated above and have agreed to accept at least 2 referrals per calendar year.

The committee may decline to certify applicants who do not meet the eligibility requirements set forth above or have been found guilty of, pled guilty to, or been disciplined for misconduct that, in the opinion of the committee, renders those persons inappropriate for service as program arbitrators.

(c) Cessation of Referrals and Removal of Certification. A certified arbitrator shall not receive additional referrals where probable cause has been found against the arbitrator until the case has been disposed of. The standing committee may revoke certification of a program arbitrator for any reason that the committee might use to deny initial certification, and for any other reason that the committee believes would render a program arbitrator unfit.

(d) Reimbursement of Expenses. Program arbitrators are not compensated for time devoted to or travel incurred in connection with an arbitration conducted within the circuit in which the arbitrator resides. Program arbitrators who conduct arbitrations outside the circuit in which the arbitrator resides may be reimbursed for mileage at the rate approved by the budget committee to the Florida Bar. Program arbitrators may be reimbursed for out-of-pocket expenses that include, but are not limited to: court reporter fees; telephone calls; photocopying fees (at a maximum of $.25 per page); and translation services.

Rule VIII. Death or Incompetence of a Party

In the event of the death or adjudication of incompetency of a party during the course of arbitration but prior to the rendering of a decision, the proceeding shall abate upon the suggestion of death of a party or notice of adjudication of incompetency of a party, unless the personal representative or the guardian of the party consents to go forward. In the event of death or incompetence of a party after the close of the proceedings but prior to a decision, the decision rendered shall be binding upon the heirs, administrators, or executors of the deceased and on the estate and guardian of the incompetent.

GRIEVANCE MEDIATION POLICIES

Rule I. Adoption of Policies

Pursuant to the authority of chapter 14 of the Rules Regulating The Florida Bar, the board of governors hereby adopts The Florida Bar Grievance Mediation Policies (hereinafter "policies").

Rule II. Program Mediators

(a) Eligibility. Persons eligible to be program mediators are:

(1) Supreme Court of Florida certified mediators;

(2) retired judges and justices of the courts of the State of Florida;

(3) persons who were certified program mediators at or before the merger of the grievance mediation and fee arbitration programs; and

(4) any other person who, in the opinion of the committee, possesses the requisite education, training, or certification in alternative dispute resolution to be a program mediator.

Members of the bar must be a member in good standing and with no pending recommendation of minor misconduct or finding of probable cause to be eligible for appointment.

(b) Certification.

The committee may certify applicants as program mediators if they meet the eligibility requirements stated above and have agreed to accept at least 2 referrals per calendar year.

The committee may decline to certify applicants who do not meet the eligibility requirements set forth above or have been found guilty of, plead to, or been disciplined for misconduct that, in the opinion of the committee, renders those persons inappropriate for service as program mediators.

(c) Cessation of Referrals and Removal of Certification.

A certified mediator shall not receive additional referrals where probable cause has been found against the mediator, until the case has been disposed of. The committee may revoke certification of a program mediator for any reason that the committee might use to deny initial certification, and for any other reason that the committee believes would render a program mediator unfit.

(d) Reimbursement of Expenses.

Program mediators shall not be compensated for time devoted to and travel incurred in connection with a mediation conducted under the mediation program. Program mediators may be reimbursed for out-of-pocket expenses that include, but are not limited to:

telephone calls; photocopying fees (at a maximum of $.25 per page); and translation services.

Rule III. Guidelines for Referrals

No referral to mediation may be offered if any aspect of the matter must remain for resolution within the discipline system.

To assist those making referrals these factors should be considered:

(1) the severity of the alleged misconduct;

(2) whether dishonesty is involved;

(3) whether a pattern of possible misconduct is present;

(4) the nature of the ethical duty involved and whether the duty may yet be fulfilled;

(5) the public interest and protection thereof; and

(6) the interest of the complainant, the respondent and any third parties that are involved.

The following types of disciplinary cases are illustrative of disciplinary cases that may be considered for mediation:

(1) alleged refusal of a lawyer to timely return a clients file or copies thereof;

(2) alleged refusal of a lawyer to release a lien on a clients recovery in a case in which the lawyer has been succeeded by another counsel;

(3) alleged refusal of a lawyer to properly withdraw from representation upon discharge by the client;

(4) alleged failure of a lawyer to conclude legal representation by failure to prepare an essential dispositive document;

(5) alleged failure of a lawyer to comply with a letter of protection issued on behalf of a client;

(6) alleged failure of a lawyer to adequately communicate to a client not causing substantial harm to the client;

(7) alleged neglect by a lawyer which does not cause substantial harm;

(8) an alleged isolated instance of incompetence by a lawyer that is not part of a pattern of incompetence, when the act is not committed in conjunction with any other rule violation, and the lawyer has not been the subject of prior disciplinary sanction for incompetence; and

(9) any other matter involving the private rights of the complainant and respondent wherein the public interest is satisfied by a resolution that dismisses the disciplinary case without further bar action.

This list of illustrations is not intended to be an exclusive list, but rather is intended as a guide for those making referrals to the mediation program.

Rule IV. Procedures

(a) Co-mediation.

Co-mediation shall not be required, but may be utilized under appropriate circumstances. When co-mediation is employed, it is preferred that only 1 of the program mediators be a member of the bar.

(b) Records.

A record of all referrals and the result of each shall be maintained in accordance with The Florida Bar's record retention policy.

(c) Appearances at Mediation Conferences.

It is the policy of the bar that persons should personally attend mediation conferences. However, if special circumstances exist and the program mediator agrees, parties may be allowed to attend by telephone or video connection.

(d) Site of Mediation Conference.

Unless otherwise agreed upon by the parties and the program mediator(s), the mediation conference shall be held at the office of a program mediator.

(e) Right to Counsel.

Counsel shall be permitted at mediation conferences only if approved by the parties and agreed to by the program mediator(s).

(f) Time for Mediation.

If the program mediator(s) is(are) able to serve, the initial mediation conference shall be scheduled within 45 days of referral of the file. This time may be extended by agreement of the parties and the program mediator(s). Failure to meet this time requirement shall not divest the program mediator(s) of the authority to proceed otherwise.

(g) Report to The Florida Bar. At the conclusion of a mediation the program mediator shall report to the committee, limited to:

(1) reference to the matter by identification of the disciplinary file to which it pertains;

(2) reference to whether the matter settled without resort to a formal mediation conference;

(3) whether a formal mediation conference was held and, if so, when;

(4) the parties who attended and those who did not;

(5) whether the mediation resulted in complete settlement, partial settlement, or impasse; and

(6) in instances where disciplinary violations of a sort not proper for mediation are divulged or discovered, or a party to the mediation appears to the program mediator to be incompetent to participate in the mediation, a statement that the matter is no longer proper for mediation, without elaboration as to why.

Rule V. Cost of Mediation

There shall be no fee charged to any party to mediation conducted under this program.

CHAPTER 15. REVIEW OF LAWYER ADVERTISEMENTS AND SOLICITATIONS

15–1. GENERALLY

Rule 15–1.1. Purpose

The Florida Bar, as an official arm of the Supreme Court of Florida, is charged with the duty of enforcing the rules governing lawyer advertising and solicitation and with assisting members of The Florida Bar to advertise their services in a manner beneficial to both the public and the legal profession. The board of governors, pursuant to the authority vested in it under rule 2–8.3, shall create a standing committee on advertising to advise members of The Florida Bar on permissible advertising and solicitation practices. It shall be the duty of the committee to administer the advertising evaluation program set forth in subchapter 4–7.

Added Dec. 21, 1990, effective Jan. 1, 1991 (571 So.2d 451). Amended July 23, 1992, effective Jan. 1, 1993 (605 So.2d 252); April 25, 2002 (820 So.2d 210).

15–2. STANDING COMMITTEE ON ADVERTISING

Rule 15–2.1. Membership and terms

The standing committee on advertising shall consist of 4 members of The Florida Bar and 3 nonlawyers representing the public. Members of the committee shall be appointed by the president-elect of The Florida Bar, as provided in rule 2–8.1. The president-elect shall designate the chair and vice-chair, with the advice and consent of the board of governors. Members of the committee shall serve staggered 3–year terms. No member may serve more than 2 consecutive terms. A quorum shall consist of a majority of the members.

Added Dec. 21, 1990, effective Jan. 1, 1991 (571 So.2d 451). Amended July 23, 1992, effective Jan. 1, 1993 (605 So.2d 252).

Rule 15–2.2. Functions

It shall be the task of the committee to evaluate all advertisements filed with the committee for compliance with the rules governing advertising and solicitation and to provide written advisory opinions concerning compliance to the respective filers, to develop a handbook on advertising for the guidance of and dissemination to members of The Florida Bar, and to recommend to the board of governors from time to time such amendments to the Rules of Professional Conduct as the committee may deem advisable.

Added Dec. 21, 1990, effective Jan. 1, 1991 (571 So.2d 451). Amended July 23, 1992, effective Jan. 1, 1993 (605 So.2d 252).

Rule 15–2.3. Reimbursement for public members

The nonlawyer public members of the standing committee shall be reimbursed for reasonable travel and related expenses associated with attendance at meetings of the committee.

Added Dec. 21, 1990, effective Jan. 1, 1991 (571 So.2d 451). Amended July 23, 1992, effective Jan. 1, 1993 (605 So.2d 252).

Rule 15–2.4. Recusal of members

Members of the committee shall recuse themselves from consideration of any advertisement proposed or used by themselves or other lawyers in their firms.

Added Dec. 21, 1990, effective Jan. 1, 1991 (571 So.2d 451).

15–3. PROCEDURE

Rule 15–3.1. Meetings

The committee shall meet as often as is necessary to fulfill its duty to provide a prompt opinion regarding a submitted advertisement's compliance with the advertising and solicitation rules.

Added Dec. 21, 1990, effective Jan. 1, 1991 (571 So.2d 451).

Rule 15–3.2. Rules

The committee may adopt such procedural rules, subject to review by the board of governors, for its activities as may be required to enable the committee to fulfill its function.

Added Dec. 21, 1990, effective Jan. 1, 1991 (571 So.2d 451).

15–4. REPORT OF COMMITTEE

Rule 15–4.1. Generally

Within 3 months after the conclusion of the first year of the review program, the committee shall submit to the board of governors a report detailing the year's activities of the committee. The report shall include such information as the board of governors may require.

Added Dec. 21, 1990, effective Jan. 1, 1991 (571 So.2d 451). Amended July 23, 1992, effective Jan. 1, 1993 (605 So.2d 252).

Rule 15–4.2. Records

(a) Maintenance of Records. The committee shall keep records of its activities for 3 years.

(b) Public Access to Records. All records of the committee shall be open for public inspection and copying with the following exceptions:

(1) proposed advertisements and proposed direct mail communications filed for advisory review when the submitting attorney advises the committee that the materials constitute protected trade secrets or proprietary information;

(2) the media, frequency, and duration of an advertisement when the submitting attorney advises the committee that the information constitutes protected trade secrets or proprietary information;

(3) the names and addresses of recipient of direct mail communications;

(4) information made confidential by rule of the Supreme Court of Florida;

(5) attorney-client communications between the bar, its committees and staff and those attorneys retained by the bar in anticipation of, or during, civil litigation;

(6) work product prepared by an attorney retained by the bar in anticipation of, or during, civil litigation; and

(c) Inspection of Copyrighted Material. Copyrighted work may be inspected but not reproduced.

Added Dec. 21, 1990, effective Jan. 1, 1991 (571 So.2d 451). Amended July 23, 1992, effective Jan. 1, 1993 (605 So.2d 252); October 29, 1992 (608 So.2d 472).

FLORIDA BAR PROCEDURES FOR ISSUING ADVISORY OPINIONS RELATING TO LAWYER ADVERTISING OR SOLICITATION

Explanatory Note

The Florida Bar Procedures for Issuing Advisory Opinions Relating to Lawyer Advertising or Solicitation are not part of The Rules Regulating The Florida Bar. The Rules and Regulations were adopted by the Board of Governors of The Florida Bar to implement Chapter 15 of the Rules Regulating The Florida Bar. These Rules and Regulations have been inserted following Chapter 15 in order to assist the practitioner.

Revised and adopted by the Board of Governors on May 24, 2002. Revised October 5, 2007; August 5, 2013.

Rule 1. Application; Scope; and Usage

Staff opinions, standing committee on advertising opinions, and opinions of the board of governors are advisory only and are not the basis for action by grievance committees, referees, or the board of governors except upon application of the respondent in disciplinary proceedings. If a respondent's defense includes reliance on the receipt of a staff opinion, ethics counsel may release to the bar counsel, grievance committee, referee, or board of governors information concerning the opinion or the opinion request that would otherwise be confidential under these rules. Information concerning requests for staff opinions are confidential, except as otherwise provided in bylaw 2-9.4, Rule 15-4.2, and these procedures. If public statements are made by the inquirer about any advisory opinion or opinion request, confidentiality of the request and the opinion is waived and ethics counsel may disclose the opinion and information relating to the request.

The proposed advisory advertising opinion process should not be used to circumvent procedures to adopt or amend Rules Regulating The Florida Bar.

Amended Aug. 11–14, 2004, by the Board of Governors of The Florida Bar; Oct. 5, 2007, by the Board of Governors of The Florida Bar.

Rule 2. Authority to Issue Advertising Opinions

Ethics counsel and assistant ethics counsel, the standing committee on advertising, and the board of governors have the authority to evaluate attorney advertisements in accordance with rule 4-7.19 and to issue advisory advertising opinions in the type and manner as set forth in these procedures.

(a) Ethics Counsel and Assistant Ethics Counsel. Ethics counsel and assistant ethics counsel may render oral and written opinions that will be identified as "staff opinions." Staff opinions may be issued only to the members of The Florida Bar in good standing inquiring as to their own contemplated conduct.

(1) Staff opinions will not be issued if it is known to staff that the inquiry:

(A) is made by a person who is not a member of The Florida Bar in good standing;

(B) concerns past conduct of the inquirer;

(C) involves the conduct of an attorney other than the inquirer;

(D) asks a question of law;

(E) asks a question of rule or court procedure; or

(F) is the subject of a proceeding brought under the Rules Regulating The Florida Bar.

(2) Staff may decline to issue an opinion if the inquiry:

(A) is the subject of current litigation; or

(B) asks a question for which there is no previous precedent or underlying bar policy on which to base an opinion.

(b) Standing Committee on Advertising. The standing committee on advertising (SCA) may render written opinions, amend existing opinions, or withdraw existing opinions:

(1) on appeal of a written staff opinion by the inquiring attorney;

(2) on request of the board of governors regarding application of the attorney advertising rules to a particular set of facts;

(3) on review of staff opinions by the SCA; or

(4) on review of existing advisory advertising opinions by the SCA.

Opinions of the SCA shall be identified as advisory advertising opinions.

(c) Board of Governors. The board of governors may render written opinions, amend existing opinions, or withdraw existing opinions:

(1) on appeal of SCA action; and

(2) on its own initiative when the board of governors determines that the application of the attorney advertising rules to a particular set of facts is likely to be of widespread interest or unusual importance to a significant number of Florida Bar members.

Opinions of the board of governors will be identified as advisory advertising opinions.

Amended Aug. 11–14, 2004, by the Board of Governors of The Florida Bar; Oct. 5, 2007, by the Board of Governors of The Florida Bar.

Rule 3. Procedures for Issuance of and Declining to Issue Staff Opinions

(a) Request for Staff Opinion.

(1) *Oral Staff Opinions.* Members in good standing may request an oral staff opinion, other than an advertising filing required by rule 4-7.19, by calling ethics counsel in Tallahassee, at 1-800-235-8619 or 1-850-561-5780. Oral opinions may be confirmed in writing only in accord with the procedures for issuance of written staff opinions. All information relating to the request for an oral staff opinion shall be confidential as provided elsewhere in these procedures.

(2) *Written Staff Opinions.* Members in good standing may request a written staff opinion, other than an advertising filing required by rule 4-7.19, by writing Ethics Counsel, The Florida Bar, 651 East Jefferson Street, Tallahassee, Florida 32399-2300 or by electronic mail to eto@flabar.org. All requests for written staff opinions shall set forth all operative facts upon which the request is based and contain an affirmative statement that the criteria of procedure 2(a) are met. Except for advertising filings required by rule 4-7.19, all material and information relating to the request for a written staff opinion are confidential as provided elsewhere in these procedures.

(b) Declining to Issue Staff Opinions. Ethics counsel must decline to issue a staff opinion if any criteria of procedure 2(a)(1) apply. Ethics counsel may decline to issue a staff opinion if any criteria of procedure 2(a)(2) apply.

(c) Appeal to SCA. Members filing advertisements for evaluation under rule 4–7.19 or requesting a written staff opinion may appeal the opinion or the decision not to issue the opinion to the SCA as provided elsewhere in these procedures. Appeals to the SCA shall be public information. Oral staff opinions and decisions not to issue an oral opinion may not be appealed.

Amended Aug. 11–14, 2004, by the Board of Governors of The Florida Bar; Oct. 5, 2007, by the Board of Governors of The Florida Bar.

Rule 4. Procedure for Issuance of SCA Opinions

(a) Scheduling SCA Review. Timely appeals, requests of the board of governors, SCA review of staff opinions, and SCA review of existing advisory advertising opinions will be scheduled for SCA consideration at the next available meeting of the SCA if any official notice requirements are met.

(b) Authority of SCA Chair. The chair of the SCA has the discretion to determine the order of the agenda, time allocated to each matter, and whether personal appearances may be allowed. In addition, the chair may appoint a subcommittee to conduct the review.

(c) Notice of SCA Review.

(1) *Adoption and Modification of Opinions.* In the event that the SCA decides to consider rendering a written opinion for publication at the request of the board of governors, on SCA review of staff opinions, or on SCA review of existing formal opinions, the SCA must publish in The Florida Bar *News* an official notice of its intent to consider rendering a written opinion. The notice must state the time and place at which the SCA's deliberations will occur and must invite written comments from interested bar members. Initial publication must fully identify the subject matter of the issue and any proposed text, if then available, and invite written comment. If an opinion is issued, the SCA must publish an official notice of the adoption of the advisory advertising opinion in The Florida Bar *News*, including the full text of the opinion. Any subsequent notice must contain the full text of any revised advisory advertising opinion.

(2) *Withdrawal of Opinions.* In the event that the SCA decides to consider withdrawing an advisory advertising opinion, the SCA must publish in The Florida Bar *News* an official notice of its intent to consider withdrawing the advisory advertising opinion. The notice must state the time and place at which the SCA's deliberations will occur, summarize the advisory advertising opinion, and invite written comments from interested bar members.

(d) Comments. Any member in good standing may file written comment with ethics counsel within 30 days of the date of publication of official notice of the SCA's intent to consider rendering an advisory advertising opinions, official notice of the SCA's adoption of a proposed advisory advertising opinion, official notice that the SCA has revised a proposed advisory advertising opinion, or official notice that the SCA intends to withdraw an advisory advertising opinion.

All comments filed under this subdivision must be in the form of written statements with relevant facts, arguments in support, and citations to relevant authority, if any.

(e) Record on Review. Ethics counsel will prepare and distribute to the SCA a file on each matter for review. Any person may request and receive a copy of the file. Ethics counsel may charge a reasonable fee for providing copies in accord with established, general bar policies.

(1) *Appeals of Written Staff Opinions.* The file will include the original request for the opinion, the written staff opinion, and the written request for SCA review.

(2) *Requests of Board of Governors.* The file will include the request, relevant material and authorities, any proposed text for consideration, and any timely comments.

(3) *Review of Staff Opinions.* The file will include the original request for the opinion, the written staff opinion, and the written request for SCA review.

(4) *Review of Existing Advisory Advertising Opinions.* The file will include the existing advisory advertising opinion, relevant material and authorities, and the written request for SCA review.

(f) SCA Action. By majority vote of those present, the SCA may:

(1) *Appeals of Written Staff Opinions.*

(A) affirm the opinion, in whole or in part;

(B) reverse the opinion, in whole or in part;

(C) return the opinion to ethics counsel with instructions as to redrafting; or

(D) determine to issue, amend, or withdraw an advisory advertising opinion.

(2) *Requests of Board of Governors.*

(A) decline to issue an advisory advertising opinion;

(B) agree to issue, amend, or withdraw an advisory advertising opinion; or

(C) provide informal information or comments to the inquirer.

(3) *Review of Staff Opinions.*

(A) affirm the opinion, in whole or in part;

(B) reverse the opinion, in whole or in part;

(C) return the opinion to ethics counsel with instructions as to redrafting; or

(D) determine to issue, amend, or withdraw an advisory advertising opinion.

(4) *Review of Existing Advisory Advertising Opinions.*

(A) affirm the advisory advertising opinion, in whole or in part;

(B) reverse the advisory advertising opinion, in whole or in part;

(C) determine to issue, amend, or withdraw an advisory advertising opinion.

(g) Notice of SCA Action. Notice of SCA action regarding formal opinions of the SCA will be published in The Florida Bar *News*. Notice of the SCA's actions will be provided by ethics counsel to:

(1) *Appeals of Written Staff Opinions.* The inquiring member who requested review of a written staff opinion or an advertisement filed in accordance with rule 4–7.19;

(2) *Requests of Board of Governors.* The inquirer, all members who timely commented on a referral from the board of governors, any member who requests review within 30 days of the publication of the notice of SCA action, and the bar's executive director;

(3) *Review of Staff Opinions.* All members who timely commented on notice of the SCA's review of staff opinions;

(4) *Review of Existing Advisory Advertising Opinions.* All members who timely commented on notice of the SCA's review of existing advisory advertising opinions.

(h) Appeal of SCA Action. Any member who timely commented to the SCA and any member who timely appealed a written staff opinion may appeal action of the SCA to the board of governors as provided elsewhere in these procedures.

Amended Aug. 11–14, 2004, by the Board of Governors of The Florida Bar; Oct. 5, 2007, by the Board of Governors of The Florida Bar.

Rule 5. Procedure for Review of SCA Action

(a) Referral to Board Review Committee on Professional Ethics. Timely appeals from SCA action will be referred to the Board Review Committee on Professional Ethics (BRC).

(b) Scheduling BRC Review. Timely appeals will be scheduled for BRC consideration at the next meeting of the BRC if the appeal or request is made more than 30 days in advance of such meeting.

(c) Authority of BRC Chair. The chair of the BRC has the discretion to determine the order of the agenda, time allocated to each matter, and whether personal appearances may be allowed. In addition, the chair may appoint a subcommittee to conduct the review.

(d) Record on Review. Ethics counsel will prepare and distribute to the BRC a file on each matter for review. Any person may request and receive a copy of the file. Ethics counsel may charge a reasonable fee for providing copies in accord with established, general bar policies. The file will include the record before the SCA and the request for BRC review.

(e) BRC Action. By majority vote of those present, the BRC may:

(1) affirm the SCA action, in whole or in part;

(2) reverse the SCA action, in whole or in part; or

(3) return the matter to the SCA with instructions as to redrafting.

(f) Review of BRC Action. The BRC will report its actions to the board and the action will be placed on the agenda of the board for review and approval as a consent item if affirming SCA action. Any member of the board may request that any BRC action be taken up for discussion by the full board. By majority vote of those present, the board may:

(1) affirm the SCA action, in whole or in part;

(2) reverse the SCA action, in whole or in part; or

(3) return the matter to the SCA with instructions as to redrafting.

(g) Notice of Board of Governors Action. Notice of board of governors action regarding formal advisory advertising opinions will be published in The Florida Bar *News*. Notice of the board's actions will be provided by ethics counsel to the members who timely requested board of governors review.

Amended Aug. 11–14, 2004, by the Board of Governors of The Florida Bar; Oct. 5, 2007, by the Board of Governors of The Florida Bar.

Rule 6. Procedure for Issuance of Board of Governors Opinions

(a) Referral to BRC. Board of governors decisions to render an advisory advertising opinion will be referred to the BRC to develop a specific set of facts upon which the opinion will be based, comply with notice provisions in this procedure, and adopt a written advisory opinion applying the attorney advertising rules to the set of facts.

(b) Scheduling BRC Review. Advisory advertising opinions will be scheduled for BRC consideration if the decision to consider rendering an opinion is made more than 30 days in advance of such meeting and any official notice requirements are met.

(c) Authority of BRC Chair. The chair of the BRC has the discretion to determine the order of the agenda, time allocated to each matter, and whether personal appearances may be allowed. In addition, the chair may appoint a subcommittee to conduct the review.

(d) Notice of BRC Opinion. In the event that the board of governors refers an issue to the BRC to render a written opinion for publication, the BRC will publish in The Florida Bar *News* an official notice of its intent to consider rendering a written opinion. The notice will state the time and place at which the BRC's deliberations will occur and invite written comments from interested bar members. Initial publication will identify the subject matter of the issue and any proposed text, if then available, and invite written comment. If an opinion is issued, the BRC will publish an official notice of the adoption of the advisory advertising opinion in The Florida Bar *News*, including the full text of the opinion. Any subsequent notice will contain the full text of any revised advisory advertising opinion.

(e) Comments. Any member in good standing may file written comment with ethics counsel within 30 days of the date of publication of official notice of the BRC's intent to consider rendering a proposed advisory opinion, official notice of the BRC's adoption of an advisory opinion, or official notice that the BRC has revised a proposed advisory opinion.

All comments filed under this subdivision must be in the form of written statements with relevant facts, arguments in support, and citations to relevant authority, if any.

(f) Record on Review. Ethics counsel will prepare and distribute to the BRC a file on each matter for review. Any person may request and receive a copy of the file. Ethics counsel may charge a reasonable fee for providing copies in accord with established, general bar policies. The file will contain the statement of facts upon which the proposed advisory opinion will be made, relevant material and authorities, and the text of the proposed advisory opinion, if then available.

(g) BRC Action. By majority vote of those present, the BRC may:

(1) determine to issue an opinion; or

(2) determine not to issue an opinion.

(h) Review of BRC Action. The BRC will report its actions to the board. By majority vote of those present, the board may:

(1) affirm the BRC action, in whole or in part;

(2) reverse the BRC action, in whole or in part; or

(3) return the matter to the BRC with instructions as to redrafting.

(i) Notice of Board of Governors Action. Notice of board of governors action regarding formal advisory opinions will be published in The Florida Bar *News*. Notice of the board's actions will be provided by ethics counsel to the members who timely filed comments.

Amended Aug. 11–14, 2004, by the Board of Governors of The Florida Bar; Oct. 5, 2007, by the Board of Governors of The Florida Bar.

Rule 7. Time for Appeals

All appeals allowed under these procedures shall be commenced by mailing the required items to Ethics Counsel, The Florida Bar, 651 East Jefferson Street, Tallahassee, Florida 32399–2300, within 30 days of notice of the action that is the subject of the appeal. Failure to timely commence an appeal bars the appeal.

Amended Aug. 11–14, 2004, by the Board of Governors of The Florida Bar; Oct. 5, 2007, by the Board of Governors of The Florida Bar.

CHAPTER 16. FOREIGN LEGAL CONSULTANCY RULE

Rule

Rule 16–1.1. Purpose

The purpose of this chapter is to permit a person who is admitted to practice in a foreign country as an attorney, counselor at law, or the equivalent to act as a foreign legal consultant in the state of Florida. This chapter authorizes an attorney licensed to practice law in 1 or more foreign countries to be certified by the Supreme Court of Florida, without examination, to render services in this state as a legal consultant regarding the laws of the country in which the attorney is admitted to practice.

Added July 23, 1992, effective Jan. 1, 1993 (605 So.2d 252).

Rule 16–1.2. Definitions

A foreign legal consultant is any person who:

(a) has been admitted to practice in a foreign country as an attorney, counselor at law, or the equivalent for a period of not less than 5 of the 7 years immediately preceding the application for certification under this chapter;

(b) has engaged in the practice of law of such foreign country for a period of not less than 5 of the 7 years immediately preceding the application for certification under this chapter and has remained in good standing as an attorney, counselor at law, or the equivalent throughout said period;

(c) is admitted to practice in a foreign country whose professional disciplinary system for attorneys is generally consistent with that of The Florida Bar;

(d) has not been disciplined for professional misconduct by the bar or courts of any jurisdiction within 10 years immediately preceding the application for certification under this chapter and is not the subject of any such disciplinary proceeding or investigation pending at the date of application for certification under this chapter;

(e) has not been denied admission to practice before the courts of any jurisdiction based upon character or fitness during the 15-year period preceding application for certification under this chapter;

(f) has submitted, pursuant to requirements determined by the Supreme Court of Florida, an application for certification under this chapter and the appropriate fees;

(g) agrees to abide by the applicable Rules Regulating The Florida Bar and submit to the jurisdiction of the Supreme Court of Florida for disciplinary purposes;

(h) is over 26 years of age;

(i) maintains an office in the state of Florida for the rendering of services as a foreign legal consultant; and

(j) has satisfied, in all respects, the provisions of rule 16-1.4.

Added July 23, 1992, effective Jan. 1, 1993 (605 So.2d 252).

Rule 16-1.3. Activities

(a) Rendering Legal Advice. A person certified as a foreign legal consultant under this chapter may render legal services in the state of Florida; provided, however, that such services shall:

(1) be limited to those regarding the laws of the foreign country in which such person is admitted to practice as an attorney, counselor at law, or the equivalent;

(2) not include any activity or any service constituting the practice of the laws of the United States, the state of Florida, or any other state, commonwealth, or territory of the United States or the District of Columbia including, but not limited to, the restrictions that such person shall not:

(A) appear for another person as attorney in any court or before any magistrate or other judicial officer or before any federal, state, county, or municipal governmental agency, quasi-judicial, or quasi-governmental authority in the state of Florida, or prepare pleadings or any other papers in any action or proceedings brought in any such court, or before any such judicial officer, except as authorized in any rule of procedure relating to admission pro hac vice, or pursuant to administrative rule;

(B) prepare any deed, mortgage, assignment, discharge, lease, agreement of sale, or any other instrument affecting title to real property located in the United States, or personal property located in the United States, except where the instrument affecting title to such property is governed by the law of a jurisdiction in which the foreign legal consultant is admitted to practice as an attorney, counselor at law, or the equivalent;

(C) prepare any will or trust instrument affecting the disposition of any property located in the United States and owned by a resident thereof nor prepare any instrument relating to the administration of a decedent's estate in the United States;

(D) prepare any instrument with respect to the marital relations, rights, or duties of a resident of the United States or the custody or care of the children of such a resident;

(E) render professional legal advice on the law of the State of Florida, the United States, or any other state, subdivision, commonwealth, or territory of the United States, or the District of Columbia (whether rendered incident to the preparation of a legal instrument or otherwise); or

(F) render any legal services without utilizing a written retainer agreement that shall specify in bold type that the foreign legal consultant is not admitted to practice law in the state of Florida nor licensed to advise on the laws of the United States or any other state, commonwealth, territory, or the District of Columbia, unless so licensed, and that the practice of the foreign legal consultant is limited to the laws of the foreign country where such person is admitted to practice as an attorney, counselor at law, or the equivalent.

(b) Representing Status as Member of The Florida Bar. Foreign legal consultants certified to render services under this chapter shall not represent that they are admitted to The Florida Bar or licensed as an attorney or foreign legal consultant in another state, commonwealth, territory, or the District of Columbia, or as an attorney, counselor at law, or the equivalent in a foreign country, unless so licensed. Persons certified under this chapter shall not use any title other than "Foreign Legal Consultant, Not Admitted to Practice Law in Florida," although such person's authorized title and firm name in the foreign country in which the person is admitted to practice as an attorney, counselor at law, or the equivalent may be used if the title, firm name, and the name of the foreign country are stated together with the above-mentioned designation.

Foreign legal consultants certified under this chapter must provide clients with a letter disclosing the extent of professional liability insurance coverage maintained by the foreign legal consultant, if any, as well as an affirmative statement advising the client that any client aggrieved by the foreign legal consultant will not have access to the Clients' Security Fund of The Florida Bar. The letter must further include the list of activities that the foreign legal consultant certified under this chapter is prohibited from engaging in, as set out in rule 16-1.3(a)(2)(A)-(F).

Added July 23, 1992, effective Jan. 1, 1993 (605 So.2d 252).

Rule 16-1.4. Certification

(a) Commencement of Permission to Perform Services. Permission for a foreign legal consultant to render legal services under this chapter shall become effective upon the filing of an application and certification, with respect to an applicant, by the International Law Section of The Florida Bar, of the requirements of rules 16–1.2(a) through (j) and 16–1.3(a) and (b) herein. In addition to any other evidence that The Florida Bar, in its discretion, may require, the application shall include the filing and approval of:

(1) a duly authenticated certificate from the entity governing the practice of law in the foreign country in which the applicant is licensed to practice, which shall be accompanied by the official seal, if any, of such entity, and which shall certify:

(A) the entity's jurisdiction in such matters;

(B) the applicant's admission to practice in such foreign country and the date thereof;

(C) the applicant's good standing as an attorney, counselor at law, or the equivalent; and

(D) whether any charge or complaint has ever been filed against the applicant with such entity, and if so, the substance of each such charge or complaint and the adjudication or disposition thereof;

(2) a letter of recommendation signed by and with the official seal, if any, of 1 of the members of the executive body of such entity or from 1 of the judges of the highest court of law of such foreign country, certifying to the applicant's professional qualifications;

(3) a letter of recommendation from at least 2 attorneys, counselors at law, or the equivalent admitted in and practicing in such foreign country, setting forth the length of time, when, and under what circumstances they have known the applicant and their appraisal of the applicant's moral character;

(4) a letter of recommendation from at least 2 members in good standing of The Florida Bar, setting forth the length of time, when, and under what circumstances they have known the applicant and their appraisal of the applicant's moral character;

(5) a sworn statement by the applicant that the applicant:

(A) has read and is familiar with the Rules of Professional Conduct as adopted by the Supreme Court of Florida and will abide by, and be subject to, the provisions thereof;

(B) submits to the jurisdiction of the Supreme Court of Florida for disciplinary purposes, as defined in chapter 3 of these rules and rule 16–1.6. The statement by the applicant must also authorize notification to the entity governing the practice of law in the foreign country in which the applicant is licensed to practice of any disciplinary action taken against the applicant in Florida; and

(C) shall comply with the requirements of rule 16–1.3(b) regarding disclosure;

(6) a written commitment to notify the court of any resignation or revocation of the foreign legal consultant's admission to practice in the foreign country of admission, or in any other state or jurisdiction in which said consultant has been licensed as an attorney, counselor at law, or equivalent or as a foreign legal consultant, or of any censure, suspension, or expulsion in respect of such admission; and

(7) a duly acknowledged instrument setting forth the applicant's address within the state of Florida and designating the secretary of state as such person's agent upon whom process may be served, pursuant to applicable Florida law, with like effect as if served personally upon such applicant, in any action or proceeding thereafter brought against the applicant arising out of or based upon any legal services rendered or offered to be rendered by such applicant within or to the residents of the state of Florida, whenever after due diligence service cannot be made upon such applicant at such address.

(b) Annual Sworn Statement. A person certified under this chapter as a foreign legal consultant shall submit to The Florida Bar, on an annual basis, a sworn statement attesting to the foreign legal consultant's good standing as an attorney, counselor at law, or the equivalent in the foreign country in which such person is licensed to practice and shall also include with such statement an annual renewal fee equivalent to annual membership fees paid by members of The Florida Bar, in good standing, and such other evidence as The Florida Bar shall deem necessary to determine the continuing qualifications of the foreign legal consultant under this chapter.

Added July 23, 1992, effective Jan. 1, 1993 (605 So.2d 252). Amended Sept. 24, 1998, effective Oct. 1, 1998 (718 So.2d 1179).

Rule 16–1.5. Withdrawal or termination of certification

Permission to perform services under this chapter shall cease immediately upon the earliest of the following events:

(a) The filing of a notice by the Supreme Court of Florida, in its discretion, at any time, stating that permission to perform services under this chapter has been revoked. A copy of such notice shall be mailed by the clerk of the court to The Florida Bar and to the foreign legal consultant involved. The foreign legal consultant shall have 15 days to request reinstatement for good cause.

(b) The foreign country in which the foreign legal consultant is admitted to practice discontinues having a professional disciplinary system for attorneys that is generally consistent with that of The Florida Bar.

(c) The failure of the foreign legal consultant to comply with any applicable provisions of this chapter.

Added July 23, 1992, effective Jan. 1, 1993 (605 So.2d 252).

Rule 16–1.6. Discipline

(a) Discipline by Florida Courts. Each person licensed to practice as a foreign legal consultant under this chapter is expressly subject to the Rules of Professional Conduct and to continuing review of such consultant's qualifications to retain any license granted hereunder, and shall be subject to the disciplinary jurisdiction of the Supreme Court of Florida and the other courts of this state.

(b) Withdrawal of Certification. In addition to any appropriate proceedings and discipline that may be imposed by The Florida Bar or the Supreme Court of Florida under chapter 3 of the Rules Regulating The Florida Bar, the Supreme Court of Florida may, at any time, with or without cause, withdraw certification hereunder.

(c) Notification of Other Jurisdictions. The Florida Bar shall be authorized to notify each entity governing the practice of law in the foreign country in which the foreign legal consultant is licensed to practice law of any disciplinary action taken against the foreign legal consultant.

Added July 23, 1992, effective Jan. 1, 1993 (605 So.2d 252).

CHAPTER 17. AUTHORIZED HOUSE COUNSEL RULE

17-1. GENERALLY

17-1. GENERALLY

Rule 17-1.1. Purpose

The purpose of this chapter is to facilitate the relocation of persons employed by or to be employed by any business organization, as herein defined, for the purpose of undertaking, in whole or in part, activities, as herein defined, for such organizations. Notwithstanding the provisions of article I, section 1, Rules of the Supreme Court of Florida Relating to Admissions to the Bar, this chapter shall authorize attorneys licensed to practice in jurisdictions other than Florida to be permitted to undertake said activities in Florida while exclusively employed by a business organization without the requirement of taking the bar examination.

Added April 21, 1994 (635 So.2d 968).

Rule 17-1.2. Definitions

(a) Authorized House Counsel. An "authorized house counsel" is any person who:

(1) is exclusively employed by a business organization located in the state of Florida and is residing in Florida or relocating to the state of Florida in furtherance of such employment within 6 months of such application under this chapter and receives or shall receive compensation for activities performed for that business organization;

(2) has complied with rule 17-1.4; and

(3) has been certified as an authorized house counsel by the Supreme Court of Florida.

(b) Business Organization. A "business organization" for the purpose of this rule is a corporation, partnership, association or other legal entity (taken together with its respective parents, subsidiaries, and affiliates) authorized to transact business in this state that is not itself engaged in the practice of law or the rendering of legal services outside such organization, whether for a fee or otherwise, and does not charge or collect a fee for the representation or advice other than to entities comprising such organization by the activities of the authorized house counsel. For purposes of this rule, a "business organization" does not include:

(1) a governmental entity, governmental subdivision, political subdivision, or school board;

(2) or any other entity that has the authority to levy a tax.

Added April 21, 1994 (635 So.2d 968). Amended March 18, 1999 (746 So.2d 442); May 20, 2004 (875 So.2d 448); Dec. 20, 2007, effective March 1, 2008 (978 So.2d 91); Nov. 19, 2009, effective Feb. 1, 2010 (24 So.3d 63).

Rule 17-1.3. Activities

(a) Authorized Activities. An authorized house counsel, as an employee of a business organization, may provide legal services in the state of Florida to the business organization for which a registration is effective. Such activities are limited to:

(1) the giving of legal advice to the directors, officers, employees, and agents of the business organization with respect to its business and affairs;

(2) negotiating and documenting all matters for the business organization; and

(3) representation of the business organization in its dealings with any administrative agency or commission having jurisdiction; provided however, authorized house counsel may not make appearances as

counsel in any court, administrative tribunal, agency, or commission situated in the state of Florida unless the rules governing such court or body authorize the appearance, or the attorney is specially admitted by such court or body in a case;

(4) providing pro bono legal services under chapter 12 of these rules if certified as an emeritus attorney.

(b) Disclosure. In any communication with individual or organizations outside of the business organization, authorized house counsel must disclose that they are not licensed to practice law in the state of Florida. If the communication is in writing, authorized house counsel must disclose in writing the name of the business organization, their title or function, and that they are not licensed to practice law in the state of Florida. For example, the disclosure may state "J. Doe, XYZ Corporation, Authorized House Counsel, member .... (name of other state bar) .... only or not a member of The Florida Bar." In performing activities under this subdivision, authorized house counsel may not represent themselves as members of The Florida Bar or licensed to practice law in this state.

(c) Limitation on Representation. In no event will permitted activities include the individual or personal representation of any shareholder, owner, partner, officer, employee, servant, or agent in any matter or transaction or the giving of advice unless otherwise permitted or authorized by law, code, or rule or allowed by subdivision (a) of this rule.

(d) Opinions to Third Parties. An authorized house counsel may not express or render a legal judgment or opinion other than when representing the authorized house counsel's employer.

Added April 21, 1994 (635 So.2d 968). Amended March 23, 2000 (763 So.2d 1002); April 25, 2002 (820 So.2d 210); Dec. 20, 2007, effective March 1, 2008 (978 So.2d 91); May 29, 2014, effective June 1, 2014 (140 So.3d 541).

Rule 17-1.4. Registration

(a) Filing with The Florida Bar. The following shall be filed with The Florida Bar by an individual seeking to be certified as authorized house counsel:

(1) A certificate from an entity governing the practice of law in all United States jurisdictions in which the registrant is licensed to practice law certifying that the registrant is in active status and is a member in good standing; or is in inactive status. If in inactive status, the certificate must certify that the registrant is in voluntary inactive status and was not placed on inactive status involuntarily. If available, the registrant must provide a certificate of good standing in addition to the certificate regarding the registrant's inactive status.

(2) a sworn statement by the registrant that the registrant:

(A) has read and is familiar with chapters 4 and 17 of the Rules Regulating The Florida Bar as adopted by the Supreme Court of Florida and will abide by the provisions thereof;

(B) submits to the jurisdiction of the Supreme Court of Florida for disciplinary purposes, as defined in chapter 3 of the Rules Regulating The Florida Bar and rule 17-1.6 herein, and authorizes notification to or from the entity governing the practice of law of each state, territory, or the District of Columbia in which the registrant is licensed to practice law of any disciplinary action taken against the registrant; and

(C) is not subject to a disciplinary proceeding or outstanding order of reprimand, censure, or disbarment, permanent or temporary, for professional misconduct by the bar or courts of any jurisdiction and has not been permanently denied admission to practice before the bar of any jurisdiction based upon such person's character or fitness;

(3) a certificate from a business organization certifying that: it is qualified as set forth in subdivision (b) of rule 17-1.2; that it is aware that the registrant is not licensed to practice in Florida; and it is not relying upon The Florida Bar in any manner in employing the authorized house counsel;

(4) an appropriate registration application to The Florida Bar as promulgated by the executive director of The Florida Bar; and

(5) an appropriate remittance of a filing fee prescribed and set by the executive director of The Florida Bar in an amount not to exceed the amount applicable for admission to the bar examination for an attorney licensed in a state other than Florida.

(b) Review by The Florida Bar. Upon receipt of the items set forth in subdivision (a) of this rule, The Florida Bar shall review the items for compliance with this chapter. Any application not meeting the requirements of this chapter shall be sent back to the applicant.

(c) Certification by Court. Upon review of the application by The Florida Bar, The Florida Bar shall file with the clerk of the Supreme Court of Florida the name and address of those registrants complying with the provisions of subdivision (a) of this rule along with a request that the registrant be certified as authorized house counsel. Permission for authorized house counsel to perform services under this rule shall become effective upon approval of the request for certification by the clerk of the Supreme Court of Florida for a person employed in Florida or, if the registrant is not yet in Florida, the effective date of employment but not later than 6 months from the filing of the items set forth above.

(d) Annual Renewal. The registration pursuant to this section shall be annual in a manner consistent with that applicable to an attorney licensed to practice in the state of Florida including the annual fee therefor as if such authorized house counsel was so licensed, provided, however, such renewal shall include a statement that the registrant, if on active status, is in good standing in all states or United States territories in which licensed and is not subject to any disciplinary proceedings.

(e) Duty to Update. Should an individual certified as an authorized house counsel choose inactive status in 1 or more United States jurisdictions after certification, the authorized house counsel shall provide a certificate as required by subdivision (a)(1) of this rule.

Added April 21, 1994 (635 So.2d 968). Amended March 18, 1999 (746 So.2d 442); March 23, 2000 (763 So.2d 1002); May 20, 2004 (875 So.2d 448); Nov. 19, 2009, effective Feb. 1, 2010 (24 So.3d 63).

Rule 17-1.5. Termination or Withdrawal of Registration

(a) Cessation of Authorization to Perform Services. Authorization to perform services under this rule shall cease upon the earliest of the following events:

(1) the termination or resignation of employment with the business organization for which registration has been filed, provided, however, that if the authorized house counsel shall commence employment with another business organization within 30 days of the termination or resignation, authorization to perform services under this rule shall continue upon the filing with The Florida Bar of a certificate as set forth in subdivision (a)(3) of rule 17-1.4;

(2) the withdrawal of registration by the business organization;

(3) the withdrawal of registration by the authorized house counsel;

(4) the relocation of an authorized house counsel outside of Florida for a period greater than 180 days;

(5) disbarment or suspension from the practice of law, or involuntary placement on inactive status, by a court or other authorized disciplinary agency of another state or by a federal court; or

(6) the failure of authorized house counsel to comply with any applicable provision of this rule.

Notice of 1 of the events set forth in subdivision (a)(1)-(4) of this rule or a new certificate as provided in subdivision (a)(1) of this rule must be filed with The Florida Bar by the authorized house counsel within 30 days after such action. An authorized house counsel disbarred or suspended from the practice of law, or involuntarily placed on inactive status, by a court or other authorized disciplinary agency of another state or by a federal court shall within 30 days after the effective date of disbarment, or suspension, or involuntary placement on inactive status, file with The Florida Bar a copy of the order or judgment effecting such status. Failure to provide notice by the authorized house counsel shall be a basis for discipline pursuant to the Rules Regulating The Florida Bar.

(b) Notice of Termination of Authorization. Upon receipt of the notice required by subdivision (a) of this rule, The Florida Bar shall forward a request to the clerk of the Supreme Court of Florida that the authorization under this chapter be terminated. Notice of the termination shall be mailed by the clerk of the Supreme Court of Florida to The Florida Bar. The Florida Bar shall mail notice of the termination to the authorized house counsel and to the business organization employing the authorized house counsel.

(c) Reapplication. Nothing herein shall prevent an individual previously authorized as house counsel to reapply for authorization as set forth in rule 17-1.4.

Added April 21, 1994 (635 So.2d 968). Amended Sept. 24, 1998, effective Oct. 1, 1998 (718 So.2d 1179); March 18, 1999 (746 So.2d 442); Nov. 19, 2009, effective Feb. 1, 2010 (24 So.3d 63).

Rule 17-1.6. Discipline

(a) Termination of Authorization by Court. In addition to any appropriate proceedings and discipline that may be imposed by The Florida Bar or the Supreme Court of Florida under chapter 3 of the Rules Regulating The Florida Bar, the Supreme Court of Florida may, at any time, with cause, terminate an authorized house counsel's registration, temporarily or permanently.

(b) Notification to Other States. The Florida Bar shall be authorized to notify each entity governing the practice of law in the state, territory, or the District of Columbia in which the authorized house counsel is licensed to practice law of any disciplinary action against the authorized house counsel.

Added April 21, 1994 (635 So.2d 968).

Rule 17-1.7. Immunity from Prosecution

An authorized house counsel who has been duly registered under this rule shall not be subject to prosecution for the unlicensed practice of law for acting as counsel to a business organization prior to the effective date of this rule.

Added April 21, 1994 (635 So.2d 968). Amended May 20, 2004 (875 So.2d 448)

Rule 17-1.8. Amendment or revocation

The Supreme Court of Florida has the inherent power to amend or revoke this rule, in whole or in part, in accordance with the procedures for amending the Rules Regulating The Florida Bar.

Added April 21, 1994 (635 So.2d 968).

Rule 17-1.9. Continuing Legal Education Requirement

An individual certified as an authorized house counsel shall comply with rules 6-10.3, 6-10.4, and 6-12.3 of the Rules Regulating The Florida Bar unless the individual is eligible for an exemption to rule 6-12.3 pursuant to rule 6-12.4.

Added Nov. 19, 2009, effective Feb. 1, 2010 (24 So.3d 63).

CHAPTER 18. MILITARY LEGAL ASSISTANCE COUNSEL RULE

18-1. GENERALLY

18-1. GENERALLY

Rule 18-1.1. Purpose

Text of rule effective until October 1, 2015. See, also, rule effective October 1, 2015.

The purpose of this chapter is to expand the delivery of legal assistance services to military personnel stationed in the state of Florida. This chapter authorizes military attorneys licensed to practice law in jurisdictions other than Florida to be certified to practice before Florida courts while formally assigned as a legal assistance attorney at a military base in the state of Florida.

Added June 27, 1996, effective July 1, 1996 (677 So.2d 272). Amended March 23, 2000 (763 So.2d 1002).

Rule 18-1.1. Purpose

Text of rule effective October 1, 2015. See, also, rule effective until October 1, 2015.

The purpose of this chapter is to expand the delivery of legal assistance services to military personnel stationed in the state of Florida. This chapter authorizes military lawyers licensed to practice law in jurisdictions other than Florida to be certified to practice before Florida courts while formally assigned as a legal assistance lawyer at a military base in the state of Florida. Nothing contained in this chapter limits the scope of practice or services provided by legal assistance lawyers under Title 10, United States Code, section 1044, and applicable service regulations.

Added June 27, 1996, effective July 1, 1996 (677 So.2d 272). Amended March 23, 2000 (763 So.2d 1002); May 21, 2015, effective Oct. 1, 2015 (164 So.3d 1217).

Rule 18-1.2. Definitions

Text of rule effective until October 1, 2015. See, also, rule effective October 1, 2015.

(a) Authorized Legal Assistance Attorney. An "authorized legal assistance attorney" is any person who:

(1) is admitted to practice law by the highest court of another state, the District of Columbia, or a territory of the United States;

(2) is serving on active duty within the Department of Defense (including the National Guard while in federal service) or the Department of Transportation (with respect to the United States Coast Guard);

(3) is assigned to an installation, unit, and/or activity located within the geographic limitations of the courts of the state of Florida;

(4) has completed The Florida Bar Young Lawyers Division Practicing with Professionalism program (Basic Skills Course Requirement); and

(5) appears in connection with official duties as a legal assistance attorney.

(b) Approved Legal Assistance Office. An "approved legal assistance office" for the purposes of this chapter is a military command tasked with providing legal assistance as approved by the Department of Defense or Department of Transportation.

(c) Supervising Attorney. A "supervising attorney" as used herein is a member in good standing of The Florida Bar who supervises an authorized legal assistance attorney engaged in activities permitted by this chapter. The supervising attorney must:

(1) be employed by or be a participating volunteer for an approved legal assistance office (to specifically include military reserve attorneys); and

(2) assume personal professional responsibility for supervising the conduct of the matter, litigation, or administrative proceeding in which the authorized legal assistance attorney participates.

(d) Authorized Legal Assistance Client. An "authorized legal assistance client" is:

(1) an active duty military member who is assigned to an installation, unit, and/or activity located within

the state of Florida and who otherwise meets current income eligibility guidelines of the Legal Services Corporation;

(2) a military retiree who resides within the state of Florida and who otherwise meets current income eligibility guidelines of the Legal Services Corporation;

(3) the dependents of any active duty military member or retiree who are otherwise residents of the state of Florida and meet current income eligibility guidelines of the Legal Services Corporation; or

(4) for purposes of settling the affairs of an active duty military member who died while in active military service, the surviving family members of such decedent who are otherwise residents of the state of Florida.

Added June 27, 1996, effective July 1, 1996 (677 So.2d 272). Amended March 23, 2000 (763 So.2d 1002).

Rule 18–1.2. Definitions

Text of rule effective October 1, 2015. See, also, rule effective until October 1, 2015.

(a) Authorized Legal Assistance Lawyer. An "authorized legal assistance lawyer" is any person who:

(1) is admitted to practice law by the highest court of another state, the District of Columbia, or a territory of the United States;

(2) is serving on active duty within the Department of Defense (including the National Guard while in federal service) or the Department of Transportation (with respect to the United States Coast Guard);

(3) is assigned to an installation, unit, and/or activity located within the geographic limitations of the courts of the state of Florida; and

(4) completes The Florida Bar Young Lawyers Division Practicing with Professionalism program (Basic Skills Course Requirement) within the time required by rule 6–12.3; and

(5) appears in connection with official duties as a legal assistance lawyer.

(b) Approved Legal Assistance Office. An "approved legal assistance office" for the purposes of this chapter is a military command tasked with providing legal assistance as approved by the Department of Defense or Department of Transportation.

(c) Supervising Lawyer. A "supervising lawyer" is a member in good standing of The Florida Bar who supervises an authorized legal assistance lawyer engaged in activities permitted by this chapter. The supervising lawyer must:

(1) be employed by or be a participating volunteer for an approved legal assistance office (to specifically include military reserve lawyers); and

(2) assume personal professional responsibility for supervising the conduct of the matter, litigation, or administrative proceeding in which the authorized legal assistance lawyer participates.

(d) Authorized Legal Assistance Client. An "authorized legal assistance client" is:

(1) an active duty military member who is assigned to an installation, unit, and/or activity located within the state of Florida and who otherwise meets current income eligibility guidelines of the Legal Services Corporation;

(2) a military retiree who resides within the state of Florida and who otherwise meets current income eligibility guidelines of the Legal Services Corporation;

(3) the dependents of any active duty military member or retiree who are otherwise residents of the state of Florida and meet current income eligibility guidelines of the Legal Services Corporation; or

(4) the surviving family members who are Florida residents of an active duty military member who died while in active military service for purposes of settling the deceased military member's affairs.

Added June 27, 1996, effective July 1, 1996 (677 So.2d 272). Amended March 23, 2000 (763 So.2d 1002); May 21, 2015, effective Oct. 1, 2015 (164 So.3d 1217).

Rule 18–1.3. Activities

Text of rule effective until October 1, 2015. See, also, rule effective October 1, 2015.

(a) [1] Permissible Activities. An authorized legal assistance attorney, in association with an approved legal assistance office and under the supervision of a supervising attorney, may perform the following activities:

(1) appear in any court or before any administrative tribunal in this state on behalf of an authorized legal assistance client, provided the person on whose behalf the authorized legal assistance attorney is appearing has consented in writing to that appearance and a supervising attorney has given written approval for that appearance;

(2) prepare pleadings and other documents to be filed in any court or before any administrative tribunal in this state in any matter in which the authorized legal assistance attorney is involved, provided all notices of appearance, pleadings, and documents bear the attorney's name, the name of the bar to which admitted, that jurisdiction's bar number, and the legend "Rule 18 Military Legal Assistance Attorney"; or

(3) engage in such other preparatory activities as are necessary for any matter in which the authorized legal assistance attorney is involved.

Nothing contained herein shall limit the scope of services provided by legal assistance attorneys under Title 10, United States Code, section 1044, and applicable service regulations.

Added June 27, 1996, effective July 1, 1996 (677 So.2d 272). Amended March 23, 2000 (763 So.2d 1002).

[1] This rule does not contain a (b).

Rule 18–1.3. Activities

Text of rule effective October 1, 2015. See, also, rule effective until October 1, 2015.

(a) [1]**Permissible Activities.** An authorized legal assistance lawyer, in association with an approved legal assistance office and under the supervision of a supervising lawyer, may perform the following activities:

(1) appear in any court or before any administrative tribunal in this state on behalf of an authorized legal assistance client, provided the person on whose behalf the authorized legal assistance lawyer is appearing has consented in writing to that appearance and a supervising lawyer has given written approval for that appearance;

(2) prepare pleadings and other documents to be filed in any court or before any administrative tribunal in this state in any matter in which the authorized legal assistance lawyer is involved, provided all notices of appearance, pleadings, and documents bear the lawyer's name, the name of the bar to which admitted, that jurisdiction's bar number, and the legend "Rule 18 Military Legal Assistance Lawyer"; or

(3) engage in such other preparatory activities as are necessary for any matter in which the authorized legal assistance lawyer is involved.

Added June 27, 1996, effective July 1, 1996 (677 So.2d 272). Amended March 23, 2000 (763 So.2d 1002); May 21, 2015, effective Oct. 1, 2015 (164 So.3d 1217).

[1] This rule does not contain a (b).

Rule 18–1.4. Supervision and Limitations

Text of rule effective until October 1, 2015. See, also, rule effective October 1, 2015.

(a) Supervision by Attorney. An authorized legal assistance attorney must perform all activities authorized by this chapter under the supervision of a supervising attorney.

(b) Representation of Bar Membership Status. Authorized legal assistance attorneys permitted to perform services under this chapter are not, and shall not represent themselves to be, members in good standing of The Florida Bar licensed to practice law in this state.

(c) Range of Legal Issues for Which Representation is Permitted. An authorized legal assistance attorney may appear in court on behalf of authorized legal assistance clients provided the appearance is made concerning a civil matter limited to 1 of the following actions:

(1) all residential landlord/tenant disputes under applicable statutory law;

(2) all actions in small claims court;

(3) domestic relations matters limited solely to name changes, adoptions, paternity, dissolution, child custody, child/spousal support enforcement, or modification of prior judgments or orders;

(4) routine or statutory probate matters limited solely to summary administration and disposition of property without administration under applicable statutory law;

(5) all actions under the Florida Consumer Collection Practices Act;

(6) all actions under the Florida Motor Vehicle Repair Act; and

(7) any other proceedings if otherwise permitted by applicable law regarding appearances by foreign attorneys.

Added June 27, 1996, effective July 1, 1996 (677 So.2d 272). Amended July 17, 1997 (697 So.2d 115); March 23, 2000 (763 So.2d 1002).

Rule 18–1.4. Supervision and Limitations

Text of rule effective October 1, 2015. See, also, rule effective until October 1, 2015.

(a) Supervision by Lawyer. An authorized legal assistance lawyer must perform all activities authorized by this chapter under the supervision of a supervising lawyer.

(b) Representation of Bar Membership Status. Authorized legal assistance lawyers permitted to perform services are not, and may not represent themselves to be, members in good standing of The Florida Bar licensed to practice law in this state.

(c) Range of Legal Issues for Which Representation is Permitted. An authorized legal assistance lawyer may appear in court on behalf of authorized legal assistance clients provided the appearance is made concerning a civil matter limited to the following actions:

(1) all residential landlord/tenant disputes under applicable statutory law;

(2) all actions in small claims court;

(3) domestic relations matters limited solely to name changes, adoptions, paternity, dissolution, child custody, child/spousal support enforcement, or modification of prior judgments or orders;

(4) routine or statutory probate matters limited solely to summary administration and disposition of property without administration under applicable statutory law;

(5) all actions under the Florida Consumer Collection Practices Act;

(6) all actions under the Florida Motor Vehicle Repair Act; and

(7) any other proceedings if otherwise permitted by applicable law regarding appearances by foreign lawyers.

Added June 27, 1996, effective July 1, 1996 (677 So.2d 272). Amended July 17, 1997 (697 So.2d 115); March 23, 2000 (763 So.2d 1002); May 21, 2015, effective Oct. 1, 2015 (164 So.3d 1217).

Rule 18–1.5. Certification

Text of rule effective until October 1, 2015. See, also, rule effective October 1, 2015.

Permission for an authorized legal assistance attorney to perform services under this chapter shall become effective upon filing with and approval by the clerk of the Supreme Court of Florida of:

(a) a letter from the commanding officer of the approved legal assistance office stating that the authorized legal assistance attorney is currently assigned with that legal assistance office and that an attorney employed by or participating as a volunteer with that legal assistance office will assume the duties of the supervising attorney required hereunder;

(b) a certificate from the highest court or agency in the state, territory, or district in which the authorized legal assistance attorney is licensed to practice law certifying that the authorized legal assistance attorney is a member in good standing and has a clear disciplinary record, and advising of any pending complaints and/or investigations involving the authorized legal assistance attorney; and

(c) a sworn statement by the authorized legal assistance attorney that the attorney:

(1) has read and is familiar with chapter 4 of the Rules Regulating The Florida Bar as adopted by the Supreme Court of Florida and will abide by the provisions thereof;

(2) has completed The Florida Bar Young Lawyers Division Practicing with Professionalism program (Basic Skills Course Requirement); and

(3) submits to the jurisdiction of the Supreme Court of Florida for disciplinary purposes, as defined by chapter 3 and rule 18–1.7 of the Rules Regulating The Florida Bar, and authorizes the practitioner's home state to be advised of any disciplinary action taken in Florida.

Added June 27, 1996, effective July 1, 1996 (677 So.2d 272). Amended July 17, 1997 (697 So.2d 115); March 23, 2000 (763 So.2d 1002).

Rule 18–1.5. Certification

Text of rule effective October 1, 2015. See, also, rule effective until October 1, 2015.

Permission for an authorized legal assistance lawyer to perform services will become effective on approval by the clerk of the Supreme Court of Florida. The person seeking approval must file the following:

(a) a letter from the commanding officer of the approved legal assistance office stating that the authorized legal assistance lawyer is currently assigned with that legal assistance office and that a Florida Bar member employed by or participating as a volunteer with that legal assistance office will assume the required duties of the supervising lawyer;

(b) a certificate from the highest court or agency in any state, territory, or district in which the authorized legal assistance lawyer is licensed to practice law certifying that the authorized legal assistance lawyer is a member in good standing and has a clear disciplinary record, and advising of any pending complaints and/or investigations involving the authorized legal assistance lawyer; and

(c) a sworn statement by the authorized legal assistance lawyer that the lawyer:

(1) has read and will abide by chapter 4 of the Rules Regulating The Florida Bar as adopted by the Supreme Court of Florida;

(2) has completed or will complete The Florida Bar Young Lawyers Division Practicing with Professionalism program (Basic Skills Course Requirement) within the time required by rule 6–12.3; and

(3) submits to the jurisdiction of the Supreme Court of Florida for disciplinary purposes, as defined by chapter 3 and rule 18–1.7 of the Rules Regulating The Florida Bar, and authorizes the practitioner's home state to be advised of any disciplinary action taken in Florida.

Added June 27, 1996, effective July 1, 1996 (677 So.2d 272). Amended July 17, 1997 (697 So.2d 115); March 23, 2000 (763 So.2d 1002); May 21, 2015, effective Oct. 1, 2015 (164 So.3d 1217).

Rule 18–1.6. Withdrawal or Termination of Certification

(a) Cessation of Permission to Perform Services. Permission to perform services under this chapter shall cease immediately upon the earlier of the following events:

(1) the commanding officer of the approved legal assistance office filing a notice with the clerk of the Supreme Court of Florida stating that the authorized legal assistance attorney has ceased to be associated with the legal assistance office, which notice must be filed within 30 days after such association has ceased; or

(2) the filing with the clerk of the Supreme Court of Florida of a notice by the Supreme Court of Florida, in its discretion, at any time, stating that permission to perform services under this chapter has been revoked. A copy of such notice shall be mailed by the clerk of the Supreme Court of Florida to the authorized legal assistance attorney involved and to the approved legal assistance office to which the attorney had been certified. The decertified legal assistance attorney shall have 15 days upon receipt of notice to request reinstatement for good cause.

(b) Notice of Withdrawal of Certification. If an authorized legal assistance attorney's certification is withdrawn for any reason, the supervising attorney shall immediately file a notice of such action in the official file of each matter pending before any court or tribunal in which the authorized legal assistance attorney was involved.

Added June 27, 1996, effective July 1, 1996 (677 So.2d 272). Amended July 17, 1997 (697 So.2d 115); March 23, 2000 (763 So.2d 1002).

Rule 18-1.7. Discipline

(a) Contempt; Withdrawal of Certification. In addition to any appropriate proceedings and discipline that may be imposed by the Supreme Court of Florida under chapter 3 of the Rules Regulating The Florida Bar, the authorized legal assistance attorney shall be subject to the following disciplinary measures:

(1) the presiding judge or hearing officer for any matter in which the authorized legal assistance attorney has participated may hold the authorized legal assistance attorney in civil contempt for any failure to abide by such tribunal's order, in the same manner as any other person could be held in civil contempt; and

(2) the Supreme Court of Florida or the authorized legal assistance attorney may, at any time, with or without cause, withdraw certification hereunder.

(b) Notice to Home State of Disciplinary Action. The Florida Bar shall notify the appropriate authority in the authorized legal assistance attorney's home state of any disciplinary action taken against the authorized legal assistance attorney.

Added June 27, 1996, effective July 1, 1996 (677 So.2d 272). Amended July 17, 1997 (697 So.2d 115).

CHAPTER 19. CENTER FOR PROFESSIONALISM

Rule 19-1.1. Purpose

This rule is adopted in recognition of the importance of professionalism as the ultimate hallmark of the practice of law. The purpose of this rule is to create a center to identify and enunciate non-mandatory standards of professional conduct and encourage adherence thereto. These standards should involve aspirations higher than those required by the Rules of Professional Conduct.

Added Sept. 24, 1998, effective Oct. 1, 1998 (718 So.2d 1179).

Rule 19-1.2. Responsibility and Authority

The center's responsibilities and authority shall be to:

(a) consider efforts by lawyers and judges to improve the administration of justice;

(b) examine ways of educating the public about the system of justice;

(c) monitor and coordinate Florida's professionalism efforts in such institutional settings as its bar, courts, law schools, and law firms;

(d) monitor professionalism efforts in jurisdictions outside Florida;

(e) provide guidance and support to the continuing legal education department in its implementation and execution of the continuing legal education professionalism requirement;

(f) help implement a professionalism component of the basic skills course requirement;

(g) make recommendations to the supreme court and The Florida Bar concerning additional means by which professionalism can be enhanced;

(h) receive and administer gifts and grants; and

(i) assist in the implementation of the current professionalism enhancement program as it relates to professionalism issues.

Added Sept. 24, 1998, effective Oct. 1, 1998 (718 So.2d 1179).

Rule 19-1.3. Funding

Funding for the center on professionalism shall be from The Florida Bar general fund and in such amounts as shall be established by the board of governors.

Added Sept. 24, 1998, effective Oct. 1, 1998 (718 So.2d 1179).

Rule 19-1.4. Staffing, Operation, and Reporting Structure

The center shall be staffed by employees of The Florida Bar.

The physical location of the center shall be determined by the board of governors and the operation and reporting structure of the center shall be consistent with other Florida Bar programs.

Added Sept. 24, 1998, effective Oct. 1, 1998 (718 So.2d 1179).

Rule 19-1.5. Relationship to the Supreme Court Commission on Professionalism

The commission on professionalism has been established by administrative order of the Supreme Court of Florida and has been charged with the planning and implementation of an ongoing plan and policy to ensure that the fundamental ideals and values of the justice system and the legal profession are inculcated in all of those persons serving or seeking to serve in the system.

The center shall endeavor to assist the commission in this regard consistent with the center's funding, staffing, operational, and reporting structure.

Added Sept. 24, 1998, effective Oct. 1, 1998 (718 So.2d 1179).

CHAPTER 20. FLORIDA REGISTERED PARALEGAL PROGRAM

20–1. PREAMBLE

Rule 20–1.1. Purpose

The purpose of this chapter is to set forth a definition that must be met in order to use the title paralegal, to establish the requirements to become a Florida Registered Paralegal, and to establish the requirements to maintain Florida Registered Paralegal status. This chapter is not intended to set forth the duties that a paralegal may perform because those restrictions are set forth in the Rules of Professional Conduct and various opinions of the Professional Ethics Committee. Nothing contained herein shall be deemed relevant in charging or awarding fees for legal services rendered by nonlawyers under the supervision of a member of The Florida Bar, such fees being based on the nature of the services rendered and not the title of the person rendering the services.

Added Nov. 15, 2007, eff. Mar. 1, 2008 (969 So.2d 360).

20–2. DEFINITIONS

Rule 20–2.1. Generally

For purposes of this chapter, the following terms have the following meaning:

(a) Paralegal. A paralegal is a person with education, training, or work experience, who works under the direction and supervision of a member of The Florida Bar and who performs specifically delegated substantive legal work for which a member of The Florida Bar is responsible.

(b) Florida Registered Paralegal. A Florida Registered Paralegal is someone who meets the definition of paralegal and the requirements for registration as set forth elsewhere in these rules.

(c) Paralegal Work and Paralegal Work Experience. Paralegal work and paralegal work experience are specifically delegated substantive legal work performed by a person with education, training, or work experience under the direction and supervision of a member of The Florida Bar for which a member of The Florida Bar is responsible. In order to qualify as paralegal work or paralegal work experience for purposes of meeting the eligibility and renewal requirements, the paralegal must primarily perform paralegal work and the work must be continuous and recent. Recent paralegal work for the purposes of meeting the eligibility and renewal requirements means work performed during the previous 5 years in connection with an initial registration, and during the preceding year in the case of a registration renewal. Time spent performing clerical work is specifically excluded.

(d) Approved Paralegal Program. An approved paralegal program is a program approved by the American Bar Association (ABA) or a program that is in substantial compliance with the ABA guidelines by being an institutional member of the American Association for Paralegal Education (AAfPE) and accredited by a nationally recognized accrediting agency approved by the United States Department of Education.

(e) Employing or Supervising Lawyer. An employing or supervising lawyer is the lawyer having direct supervision over the work product of the paralegal or Florida Registered Paralegal.

(f) Board. The board is the Board of Governors of The Florida Bar.

(g) Respondent. A respondent is the individual whose conduct is under investigation.

(h) Designated Reviewer. The designated reviewer is a member of the board of governors appointed by the president of The Florida Bar from the district of the district paralegal committee and is responsible for review and other specific duties as assigned by the board of governors with respect to a particular district paralegal committee or matter. If a designated reviewer recuses or is unavailable, another board member from the district may be appointed by the president of The Florida Bar to serve as designated reviewer in that matter.

(i) Probable Cause. A finding of probable cause is a finding that there is cause to believe that a Florida Registered Paralegal is guilty of misconduct justifying disciplinary action.

(j) Bar Counsel. Bar counsel is a member of The Florida Bar representing The Florida Bar in any proceeding under these rules.

Added Nov. 15, 2007, eff. Mar. 1, 2008 (969 So.2d 360). Amended April 12, 2012, effective July 1, 2012 (101 So.3d 807); May 29, 2014, effective June 1, 2014 (140 So.3d 541).

20-3. ELIGIBILITY REQUIREMENTS

Rule 20-3.1. Requirements for Registration

In order to be a Florida Registered Paralegal under this chapter, an individual must meet 1 of the following requirements.

(a) Educational and Work Experience Requirements. A person may become a Florida Registered Paralegal by meeting 1 of the following education and paralegal work experience requirements:

(1) a bachelor's degree in paralegal studies from an approved paralegal program, plus a minimum of 1 year of paralegal work experience;

(2) a bachelor's degree or higher degree other than a juris doctorate from an institution accredited by a nationally recognized accrediting agency approved by the United States Department of Education or the Florida Department of Education, plus a minimum of 3 years of paralegal work experience;

(3) an associate's degree in paralegal studies from an approved paralegal program, plus a minimum of 2 years of paralegal work experience;

(4) an associate's degree from an institution accredited by a nationally recognized accrediting agency approved by the United States Department of Education or the Florida Department of Education, plus a minimum of 4 years of paralegal work experience; or

(5) a juris doctorate degree from an American Bar Association accredited institution, plus a minimum of 1 year of paralegal work experience.

(b) Certification. A person may become a Florida Registered Paralegal by obtaining 1 of the following certifications:

(1) successful completion of the Paralegal Advanced Competency Exam (PACE certification as offered by the National Federation of Paralegal Associations "NFPA") and good standing with NFPA; or

(2) successful completion of the Certified Legal Assistant/Certified Paralegal examination (CLA/CP certification as offered by the National Association of Legal Assistants "NALA") and good standing with NALA.

(c) Grandfathering Reapplication. A paralegal who was registered under the grandfathering provision on or prior to March 1, 2011, who resigns or whose registration is revoked may reapply based on work experience alone. The paralegal must provide work experience as defined elsewhere in these rules for 5 of the 8 years immediately preceding the date of reapplication.

Added Nov. 15, 2007, eff. Mar. 1, 2008 (969 So.2d 360). Amended July 7, 2011, effective Oct. 1, 2011 (67 So.3d 1037); May 29, 2014, effective June 1, 2014 (140 So.3d 541).

20–4. REGISTRATION

Rule 20–4.1. Generally

The following must be filed with The Florida Bar by an individual seeking to be registered as a Florida Registered Paralegal:

(a) Educational, Certification, or Experience Requirement.

(1) evidence that the individual has satisfied the requirements of rule 20–3.1(a) by supplying evidence of the degree and attestation from the employing or supervising lawyer(s) showing that the individual has the appropriate paralegal work experience; or

(2) a certificate showing that the individual has obtained 1 of the certifications set forth in rule 20–3.1(b) and attestation from the employing or supervising lawyer(s) showing that the individual is currently primarily performing paralegal work.

(b) Statement of Compliance. A sworn statement by the individual that the individual has read and will abide by the Code of Ethics and Responsibility set forth elsewhere in this chapter.

(c) Registration Fee. An appropriate registration fee set by the board.

(d) Review by The Florida Bar. Upon receipt of the items set forth in subdivision 20–4.1(a)–(c), The Florida Bar will review the items for compliance with this chapter. Any incomplete submissions will be returned. If the individual meets all of the requirements of this chapter, the individual will be added to the roll of Florida Registered Paralegals and a certificate evidencing such registration will be issued. If there is an open unlicensed practice of law complaint against the individual, the application will be held as pending until the investigation is resolved.

(e) Annual Renewal; Content and Registration Fee. Except as provided elsewhere in this rule, the registration pursuant to this subdivision will be annual and consistent with that applicable to a lawyer licensed to practice in the state of Florida. An annual registration fee will be set by the board in an amount not more than the annual fees paid by inactive members of The Florida Bar. The renewal must contain a statement that the individual is primarily performing paralegal work as defined elsewhere in this chapter and a statement that the individual is not ineligible for registration set forth elsewhere in this chapter. A Florida Registered Paralegal who is not primarily performing paralegal work is not eligible for renewal of the registration but may reapply for registration. If there is an open unlicensed practice of law complaint against the individual, renewal will be held as pending until the investigation is resolved.

(f) Installment Payment of Renewal Fee. If a Florida Registered Paralegal is employed by a federal, state, or local government, the Florida Registered Paralegal may elect to pay their annual renewal fee in 3 equal installments. The Florida Registered Paralegal's notice of election to pay the renewal fee in installments under this rule and the first installment payment must be postmarked no later than August 15. The second and third installment payments must be postmarked no later than November 1 and February 1, respectively.

Second and third installment payments postmarked after their respective due date(s) are subject to a one-time late charge of $50 per fiscal year, which shall accompany the final payment.

The Florida Bar will send written notice by registered or certified mail to the last official address of each Florida Registered Paralegal whose renewal fee and late fee have not been paid under this rule by February 1. Upon failure to pay renewal fees and any late charges under this rule by March 15, the individual's status as an Florida Registered Paralegal will be revoked.

Each Florida Registered Paralegal who elects to pay the annual renewal fee in installments under this rule may be charged an additional administrative fee to defray the costs of this activity as set by the Board of Governors.

(g) Renewal Fee Exemption for Activated Reserve Members of the Armed Services. Florida Registered Paralegals engaged in reserve military service in the Armed Forces of the United States who are called to active duty for 30 days or more during the bar's fiscal year are exempt from the payment of the annual renewal fee required under this rule. For purposes of this rule, the Armed Forces of the United States includes the United States Army, Air Force, Navy, Marine Corps, Coast Guard, as well as the Army National Guard, Army Reserve, Navy Reserve, Marine Corps Reserve, the Air National Guard of the United States, the Air Force Reserve, and the Coast Guard Reserve. Requests for an exemption must be made within 15 days before the date renewal fees are due each year or within 15 days of activation to duty of a reserve member. To the extent renewal fees were paid despite qualifying for this exemption, such renewal fee will be reimbursed by The Florida Bar within 30 days of receipt of a Florida Registered Paralegal's request for exemption. Within 30 days of leaving active duty status, the Florida Registered Paralegal must report to The Florida Bar that he or she is no longer on active duty status in the United States Armed Forces.

Added Nov. 15, 2007, eff. Mar. 1, 2008 (969 So.2d 360). Amended April 12, 2012, effective July 1, 2012 (101 So.3d 807); May 29, 2014, effective June 1, 2014 (140 So.3d 541).

20-5. INELIGIBILITY FOR REGISTRATION OR RENEWAL

Rule 20-5.1. Generally

The following individuals are ineligible for registration as a Florida Registered Paralegal or for renewal of a registration that was previously granted:

(a) a person who is currently suspended or disbarred or who has resigned in lieu of discipline from the practice of law in any state or jurisdiction;

(b) a person who has been convicted of a felony in any state or jurisdiction and whose civil rights have not been restored;

(c) a person who has been found to have engaged in the unlicensed (unauthorized) practice of law in any state or jurisdiction within 7 years of the date of application;

(d) a person whose registration or license to practice has been terminated or revoked for disciplinary reasons by a professional organization, court, disciplinary board, or agency in any jurisdiction;

(e) a person who is no longer primarily performing paralegal work as defined elsewhere in these rules;

(f) a person who fails to comply with prescribed continuing education requirements as set forth elsewhere in this chapter; or

(g) a person who is providing services directly to the public as permitted by case law and subchapter 10-2 of these rules.

Added Nov. 15, 2007, eff. Mar. 1, 2008 (969 So.2d 360). Amended April 12, 2012, effective July 1, 2012 (101 So.3d 807).

Rule 20-5.2. Duty to Update

An individual applying for registration as a Florida Registered Paralegal or who is registered as a Florida Registered Paralegal has a duty to inform The Florida Bar promptly of any fact or circumstance that would render the individual ineligible for registration or renewal.

Added Nov. 15, 2007, eff. Mar. 1, 2008 (969 So.2d 360).

20-6. CONTINUING EDUCATION

Rule 20-6.1. Generally

In order to maintain the status of Florida Registered Paralegal, a Florida Registered Paralegal must complete a minimum of 30 hours of continuing education every 3 years, 5 hours of which must be in legal ethics or professionalism. Courses approved for credit by The Florida Bar, the National Association of Legal Assistants (NALA), or the National Federation of Paralegal Associations (NFPA) will be deemed acceptable for purposes of this rule. To be eligible for re-registration, if a Florida Registered Paralegal resigns or has had his or her status revoked but is otherwise eligible for re-registration, the Florida Registered Paralegal must complete at least 10 hours of continuing education for each year the Florida Registered Paralegal was previously registered. The continuing education hours must be completed prior to the re-registration application and be posted on The Florida Bar website within 30 days of the effective date of re-registration, otherwise the new registration will be revoked and ineffective. Upon re-registration, the Florida Registered Paralegal will be given a new 3-year continuing education cycle.

Added Nov. 15, 2007, eff. Mar. 1, 2008 (969 So.2d 360). Amended May 29, 2014, effective June 1, 2014 (140 So.3d 541).

Comment

Continuing education is an important component of the Florida Registered Paralegal program and necessary to maintain the status of a Florida Registered Paralegal. If a Florida Registered Paralegal resigns or has had his or her status revoked at the end of a continuing education cycle without completing the necessary hours, the paralegal must show that he or she has completed a minimum of 10 hours of continuing education for each year of the immediately preceding term that the paralegal was registered. For example, if the paralegal was registered for 2 years, the paralegal must complete at least 20 hours of continuing education in order to re-register. The courses must be completed prior to the date the paralegal reapplies for Florida Registered Paralegal status. As an example, assume that a Florida Registered Paralegal was given a continuing education cycle that ran from January 1, 2011, to January 1, 2014, and the Florida Registered Paralegal resigned or had his or her status revoked in October 2013. If the paralegal reapplies for Florida Registered Paralegal status in February 2014, the paralegal must show 20 hours of continuing education credit completed between January 1, 2011, to January 1, 2014, to be eligible to re-register. Because a Florida Registered Paralegal must enter all course credits on The Florida Bar's website and access to the portion of the website where credits are posted is not available during the period the paralegal was not registered, the Florida Registered Paralegal will have 30 days after re-registration to enter the credits. Failure to timely enter the credits will result in the Florida Registered Paralegal's status being revoked. Upon re-registration, the Florida Registered Paralegal will be given a new continuing education cycle. The purpose of this rule is to ensure that a Florida Registered Paralegal continues his or her education. This is meant to avoid a situation where a Florida Registered Paralegal has not completed the continuing education requirement, resigns and then re-registers with a new 3-year cycle, having failed to complete the requisite hours when previously registered.

If a Florida Registered Paralegal resigns or has his or her status revoked during his or her continuing education cycle, the cycle will not reset. For example, assume a Florida Registered Paralegal has a continuing education cycle beginning January 1, 2011, and ending January 1, 2014. The Florida Registered Paralegal's status is revoked in October 2012, for failure to pay the annual renewal. If the paralegal reapplies and is re-registered in December 2012, the continuing education cycle will remain the same, and the Florida Registered Paralegal will have until January 1, 2014, to complete the necessary hours.

20-7. CODE OF ETHICS AND RESPONSIBILITY

Rule 20-7.1. Generally

A Florida Registered Paralegal shall adhere to the following Code of Ethics and Responsibility:

(a) Disclosure. A Florida Registered Paralegal shall disclose his or her status as a Florida Registered Paralegal at the outset of any professional relationship with a client, lawyers, a court or administrative agency or personnel thereof, and members of the general public. Use of the initials FRP meets the disclosure requirement only if the title paralegal also appears. For example, J. Doe, FRP, Paralegal. Use of the word "paralegal" alone also complies.

(b) Confidentiality and Privilege. A Florida Registered Paralegal shall preserve the confidences and secrets of all clients. A Florida Registered Paralegal must protect the confidences of a client, and it shall be unethical for a Florida Registered Paralegal to violate any statute or rule now in effect or hereafter to be enacted controlling privileged communications.

(c) Appearance of Impropriety or Unethical Conduct. A Florida Registered Paralegal should understand the attorney's Rules of Professional Conduct and this code in order to avoid any action that would involve the attorney in a violation of the rules or give the appearance of professional impropriety. It is the obligation of the Florida Registered Paralegal to avoid conduct that would cause the lawyer to be unethical or even appear to be unethical, and loyalty to the lawyer is incumbent upon the Florida Registered Paralegal.

(d) Prohibited Conduct. A Florida Registered Paralegal should not:

(1) establish attorney-client relationships, accept cases, set legal fees, give legal opinions or advice, or represent a client before a court or other tribunal, unless authorized to do so by the court or tribunal;

(2) engage in, encourage, or contribute to any act that could constitute the unlicensed practice of law;

(3) engage in the practice of law;

(4) perform any of the duties that attorneys only may perform nor do things that attorneys themselves may not do; or

(5) act in matters involving professional legal judgment since the services of an attorney are essential in the public interest whenever the exercise of such judgment is required.

(e) Performance of Services. A Florida Registered Paralegal must act prudently in determining the extent to which a client may be assisted without the presence of an attorney. A Florida Registered Paralegal may perform services for an attorney in the representation of a client, provided:

(1) the services performed by the paralegal do not require the exercise of independent professional legal judgment;

(2) the attorney is responsible for the client, maintains a direct relationship with the client, and maintains control of all client matters;

(3) the attorney supervises the paralegal;

(4) the attorney remains professionally responsible for all work on behalf of the client and assumes full professional responsibility for the work product, including any actions taken or not taken by the paralegal in connection therewith; and

(5) the services performed supplement, merge with, and become the attorney's work product.

(f) Competence. A Florida Registered Paralegal shall work continually to maintain integrity and a high degree of competency throughout the legal profession.

(g) Conflict of Interest. A Florida Registered Paralegal who was employed by an opposing law firm has a duty not to disclose any information relating to the representation of the former firm's clients and must disclose the fact of the prior employment to the employing attorney.

(h) Reporting Known Misconduct. A Florida Registered Paralegal having knowledge that another Florida Registered Paralegal has committed a violation of this chapter or code shall inform The Florida Bar of the violation.

Added Nov. 15, 2007, eff. Mar. 1, 2008 (969 So.2d 360). Amended July 7, 2011, effective Oct. 1, 2011 (67 So.3d 1037).

20-8. REVOCATION OF REGISTRATION

Preamble

The following rules and procedures shall apply to complaints against Florida Registered Paralegals:

Rule 20-8.1. Paralegal Committees

There shall be paralegal committees as are herein provided, each of which shall have the authority and jurisdiction required to perform the functions hereinafter assigned to the paralegal committee and which shall be constituted and appointed as follows:

(a) District Paralegal Committees. There shall be at least 1 paralegal committee for each appellate district of this state and as many more as shall be found desirable by the board. Such committees shall be continuing bodies notwithstanding changes in membership, and they shall have jurisdiction and the power to proceed in all matters properly before them.

(b) Membership, Appointment, and Eligibility. Each district paralegal committee shall consist of not fewer than 3 members, at least 1 of whom is a Florida Registered Paralegal and at least 1 of whom is a member of The Florida Bar. Members of district paralegal committees shall be nominated by the member of the board designated to review the actions of the committee and appointed by the board. All appointees shall be of legal age and shall be residents of the district or have their principal office in the district. For each district paralegal committee there shall be a chair designated by the designated reviewer of that committee. A vice-chair and secretary may be designated by the chair of each district committee.

(c) Terms. The terms of the members shall be for 3 years from the date of administration of the oath of service on the district paralegal committee or until such time as their successors are appointed and qualified. Continuous service of a member shall not exceed 6 years. A member shall not be reappointed for a period of 3 years after the end of the member's second term provided, however, the expiration of the term of any member shall not disqualify such member from concluding any investigation or participating in the disposition of cases that were pending before the committee when the member's term expired.

(d) Disqualification. No member of a district paralegal committee shall perform any district paralegal committee function when that member:

(1) is related by blood or marriage to the complainant or respondent;

(2) has a financial, business, property, or personal interest in the matter under consideration or with the complainant or respondent;

(3) has a personal interest that could be affected by the outcome of the proceedings or that could affect the outcome; or

(4) is prejudiced or biased toward either the complainant or the respondent.

Upon notice of the above prohibitions, the affected members should recuse themselves from further proceedings. The district paralegal committee chair shall have the power to disqualify any member from any proceeding in which any of the above prohibitions exists and is stated of record or in writing in the file by the chair.

(e) Removal. Any member may be removed from service by the designated reviewer of that committee or by the board.

(f) District Paralegal Committee Meetings. District paralegal committees should meet at regularly scheduled times, not less frequently than quarterly each year, and either the chair or vice-chair may call special meetings.

Added Nov. 15, 2007, eff. Mar. 1, 2008 (969 So.2d 360).

Rule 20-8.2. Duties and Authority

It is the duty of the district paralegal committees to receive and evaluate complaints against Florida Registered Paralegals. The district paralegal committees shall have the authority to remove or revoke an individual's registration as a Florida Registered Paralegal in accordance with the procedures set forth elsewhere in this chapter. A registration certificate issued pursuant to these rules may be suspended or revoked for any of the following reasons:

(a) conviction of a felony or of a misdemeanor involving moral turpitude, dishonesty, or false statement;

(b) fraud, dishonesty, or corruption that is related to the functions and duties of a Florida Registered Paralegal;

(c) gross incompetence or unprofessional or unethical conduct;

(d) willful, substantial, or repeated violation of any duty imposed by statute, rule, or order of court;

(e) fraud or misrepresentation in obtaining or renewing registration status;

(f) noncompliance with continuing education requirements;

(g) nonpayment of renewal fees; or

(h) violation of the Code of Ethics and Responsibility set forth elsewhere in these rules.

Added Nov. 15, 2007, eff. Mar. 1, 2008 (969 So.2d 360).

Rule 20-8.3. Complaint Processing

(a) Complaints. All complaints against a Florida Registered Paralegal may be initiated either by a sworn complaint asserting a violation of these rules or by The Florida Bar on its own motion.

(b) Review by Bar Counsel. Bar counsel shall review the complaint and determine whether the alleged conduct, if proven, would constitute a violation of these rules. Bar counsel may conduct a preliminary, informal investigation to aid in this determination and, if necessary, may employ a Florida Bar staff investigator to aid in the preliminary investigation. If bar counsel determines that the facts, if proven, would not constitute a violation, bar counsel may decline to pursue the complaint. The complainant shall be notified of a decision not to pursue a complaint and shall be given the reasons therefor.

(c) Closing by Bar Counsel and Committee Chair. Bar counsel may consult with the appropriate district paralegal committee chair to determine whether the alleged conduct of a complaint, if proven, would constitute a violation of these rules. If bar counsel and the district committee chair concur in a finding that the case should be closed, the complaint may be closed on such finding without referral to the district paralegal committee.

(d) Referral to District Paralegal Committee. Bar counsel may refer a file to the appropriate district paralegal committee for further investigation or action as authorized elsewhere in these rules.

(e) Notification of Violation. If a majority of the district paralegal committee finds probable cause to believe that a violation of these rules has occurred, bar counsel or the chair of the district paralegal committee will send written notice thereof to the Florida Registered Paralegal identifying the alleged violation. The notice shall be sent by certified U.S. mail directed to the last mailing address on file.

(f) Response to Notice of Violation. Within 30 days from the receipt of the notification, the Florida Registered Paralegal shall file a written response. If the Florida Registered Paralegal does not respond, the violations identified in the finding of probable cause shall be deemed admitted.

(g) Committee Review. After the filing of the written response to the finding of probable cause or following the expiration of the time within which to file a response if none is filed, the district paralegal committee shall review the complaint, the finding of probable cause, the response (if any), and any other pertinent materials, and decide whether to dismiss the proceeding or issue a proposed disposition. The committee shall promptly send written notice of its decision to the Florida Registered Paralegal by certified U.S. mail directed to the last mailing address on file.

Added Nov. 15, 2007, eff. Mar. 1, 2008 (969 So.2d 360).

Rule 20–8.4. Investigation

(a) Conduct of Proceedings. The proceedings of district paralegal committees when testimony is taken may be informal in nature and the committees shall not be bound by the rules of evidence.

(b) Taking Testimony. Bar counsel, each district paralegal committee, and members thereof conducting investigations are empowered to take and have transcribed the testimony and evidence of witnesses. If the testimony is recorded stenographically or otherwise, the witness shall be sworn by any person authorized by law to administer oaths.

(c) Rights and Responsibilities of Respondent. The respondent may be required to appear and to produce evidence as any other witness unless the respondent claims a privilege or right properly available to the respondent under applicable federal or state law. The respondent may be accompanied by counsel.

(d) Rights of Complaining Witness. The complaining witness is not a party to the investigation. The complainant may be granted the right to be present at any district paralegal committee proceeding when the respondent is present before the committee to give testimony. The complaining witness shall have no right to appeal the finding of the district paralegal committee.

Added Nov. 15, 2007, eff. Mar. 1, 2008 (969 So.2d 360).

Rule 20–8.5. Subpoenas

Subpoenas for the attendance of witnesses and the production of documentary evidence before a district paralegal committee shall be issued as follows:

(a) District Paralegal Committees. Subpoenas for the attendance of witnesses and the production of documentary evidence shall be issued by the chair or vice-chair of a district paralegal committee in pursuance of an investigation authorized by the committee.

(b) Bar Counsel Investigations. Subpoenas for the attendance of witnesses and the production of documentary evidence before bar counsel when bar counsel is conducting an initial investigation shall be issued by the chair or vice-chair of a district paralegal committee to which the matter will be assigned.

(c) Service. Subpoenas may be served by an investigator employed by The Florida Bar or in the manner provided by law for the service of process.

Added Nov. 15, 2007, eff. Mar. 1, 2008 (969 So.2d 360).

Rule 20–8.6. Disposition of Complaints

Upon concluding its investigation, the district paralegal committee shall determine which of the following action(s) should be taken:

(a) close the matter on a finding of no violation;

(b) require that a specified continuing education course be taken;

(c) accept an affidavit from the Florida Registered Paralegal acknowledging that the conduct surrounding the complaint was a violation of these rules and that the Florida Registered Paralegal will refrain from conduct that would create a violation of these rules;

(d) suspension of the Florida Registered Paralegal's registration certificate for a period not to exceed 1 year;

(e) revocation of registration certificate; or

(f) denial of request for renewal.

Added Nov. 15, 2007, eff. Mar. 1, 2008 (969 So.2d 360).

Rule 20-8.7. Review of District Paralegal Committee Action

(a) Review by the Designated Reviewer. Notice of district paralegal committee action recommending either revocation or denial of renewal shall be given to the designated reviewer for review. Upon review of the district paralegal committee action, the designated reviewer may affirm the action of the district paralegal committee, request the district paralegal committee to reconsider its action, or refer the district paralegal committee action to the disciplinary review committee of the board of governors for its review. The request for a district paralegal committee reconsideration or referral to the disciplinary review committee shall be in writing and must be made within 30 days of notice of the district paralegal committee action. If the designated reviewer fails to make the request for reconsideration or referral within the time prescribed, the district paralegal committee action shall become final.

(b) Review by Disciplinary Review Committee. The disciplinary review committee shall review those district paralegal committee matters referred to it by a designated reviewer or the district paralegal committee and shall make a report to the board. The disciplinary review committee may confirm, reject, or amend the recommendation of the designated reviewer in whole or in part. The report of the disciplinary review committee shall be final unless overruled by the board.

(c) Board Action on Recommendations of the Disciplinary Review Committee. On review of a report and recommendation of the disciplinary review committee, the board of governors may confirm, reject, or amend the recommendation in whole or in part.

(d) Notice of Board Action. Bar counsel shall give notice of board action to the respondent, complainant, and district paralegal committee.

(e) Filing Service on Board of Governors. All matters to be filed with or served upon the board shall be addressed to the board of governors and filed with the executive director. The executive director shall be the custodian of the official records of the Florida Registered Paralegal Program.

Added Nov. 15, 2007, eff. Mar. 1, 2008 (969 So.2d 360).

Rule 20-8.8. Files

(a) Files Are Property of Bar. All matters, including files, preliminary investigation reports, interoffice memoranda, records of investigations, and the records of other proceedings under these rules are property of The Florida Bar.

(b) Investigatory Record. The investigatory record shall consist of the record before a district paralegal committee and any reports, correspondence, papers, and recordings and transcripts of hearings and transcribed testimony furnished to, served on, or received from the respondent or the complainant or a witness before the district paralegal committee. The record before the district paralegal committee shall consist of all reports, correspondence, papers, and recordings furnished to or received from the respondent and the transcript of district paralegal committee meetings or transcribed testimony, if the proceedings were attended by a court reporter; provided, however, that the committee may retire into private session to debate the issues involved and to reach a decision as to the action to be taken.

(c) Limitations on Disclosure. Any material provided to or promulgated by The Florida Bar that is confidential under applicable law shall remain confidential and shall not be disclosed except as authorized by the applicable law. If this type of material is made a part of the investigatory record, that portion of the investigatory record may be sealed by the district paralegal committee chair.

(d) Disclosure of Information. Unless otherwise ordered by a court, nothing in these rules shall prohibit the complainant, respondent, or any witness from disclosing the existence of proceedings under these rules or from disclosing any documents or correspondence served on or provided to those persons.

(e) Response to Inquiry. Representatives of The Florida Bar, authorized by the board, shall reply to inquiries regarding a pending or closed investigation. The Florida Bar may charge a reasonable fee for copying documents consistent with applicable law.

(f) Production of Investigatory Records Pursuant to Subpoena. The Florida Bar, pursuant to a valid subpoena issued by a regulatory agency, may provide any documents that are a portion of the investigatory record even if otherwise deemed confidential under these rules. The Florida Bar may charge a reasonable fee for copying the documents consistent with applicable law.

(g) Response to False or Misleading Statements. If public statements that are false and misleading are made about any investigation brought pursuant to this chapter, The Florida Bar may make any disclosure consistent with applicable law necessary to correct such false or misleading statements.

(h) Providing Material to Other Agencies. Nothing contained herein shall prohibit The Florida Bar from providing material to any state or federal law enforcement or regulatory agency, United States Attorney, state attorney, the National Association of Legal Assistants or the National Federation of Paralegal Associations and equivalent organizations, the

Florida Board of Bar Examiners and equivalent entities in other jurisdictions, paralegal grievance committees and equivalent entities in other jurisdictions, and unlicensed practice of law committees and equivalent entities in other jurisdictions.

Added Nov. 15, 2007, eff. Mar. 1, 2008 (969 So.2d 360).

20–9. IMMUNITY

Rule 20–9.1. Generally

The members of the district paralegal committees, the board, bar staff and counsel assisting the committees, shall have absolute immunity from civil liability for all acts in the course of their official duties.

Added Nov. 15, 2007, eff. Mar. 1, 2008 (969 So.2d 360).

20–10. AMENDMENTS

Rule 20–10.1. Generally

Rules governing the Florida Registered Paralegal Program may be amended in accordance with the procedures set forth elsewhere in these rules.

Added Nov. 15, 2007, eff. Mar. 1, 2008 (969 So.2d 360).

FLORIDA STANDARDS FOR IMPOSING LAWYER SANCTIONS

Date Effective

Added effective January 1, 1987

Amended effective May 11, 2015

I. PREFACE

A. Background

In 1979, the American Bar Association published the Standards for Lawyer Discipline and Disability Proceedings. That book was a result of work by the Joint Committee on Professional Discipline of the American Bar Association. The Joint Committee was composed of members of the Judicial Administration Division and the Standing Committee on Professional Discipline of the American Bar Association. The task of the Joint Committee was to prepare standards for enforcement of discipline in the legal community.

The 1979 standards have been most helpful, and have been used by numerous jurisdictions as a frame of reference against which to compare their own disciplinary systems. Many jurisdictions have modified their procedures to comport with these suggested standards, and the Standing Committee on Professional Discipline of the American Bar Association has assisted state disciplinary systems in evaluating their programs in light of the approved standards.

It became evident that additional analysis was necessary in one important area — that of appropriate sanctions for lawyer misconduct. The American Bar Association Standards for Lawyer Discipline and Disability Proceedings (hereinafter "Standards for Lawyer Discipline") do not attempt to recommend the type of discipline to be imposed in any particular case. The Standards merely state that the discipline to be imposed should depend upon the facts and circumstances of the case, should be fashioned in light of the purpose of lawyer discipline, and may take into account aggravating or mitigating circumstances (Standard 7.1).

For lawyer discipline to be truly effective, sanctions must be based on clearly developed standards. Inappropriate sanctions can undermine the goals of lawyer discipline: sanctions which are too lenient fail to adequately deter misconduct and thus lower public confidence in the profession; sanctions which are too onerous may impair confidence in the system and deter lawyers from reporting ethical violations on the part of other lawyers. Inconsistent sanctions, either within a jurisdiction or among jurisdictions, cast doubt on the efficiency and the basic fairness of all disciplinary systems.

As an example of this problem of inconsistent sanctions, consider the range in levels of sanctions imposed for a conviction for failure to file federal income taxes. In one jurisdiction, in 1979, a lawyer who failed to file income tax returns for one year was suspended for one year, while, in 1980, a lawyer who failed to file income tax returns for two years was merely censured. Within a two-year period, the sanctions imposed on lawyers who converted their clients' funds included disbarment, suspension, and censure. The inconsistency of sanctions imposed by different jurisdictions for the same misconduct is even greater.

An examination of these cases illustrates the need for a comprehensive system of sanctions. In many cases, different sanctions are imposed for the same acts of misconduct, and the courts rarely provide any explanation for the selection of sanctions. In other cases, the courts may give reasons for their decisions, but their statements are too general to be useful. In still other cases, the courts may list specific factors to support a certain result, but they do not state whether these factors must be considered in every discipline case, nor do they explain whether these factors are entitled to equal weight.

The Joint Committee on Professional Sanctions (hereinafter "Sanctions Committee") was formed to address these problems by formulating standards to be used in imposing sanctions for lawyer misconduct. The Sanctions Committee was composed of members from the Judicial Administration Division and the Standing Committee on Professional Discipline. The mandate given was ambitious: the Committee was to examine the current range of sanctions imposed and to formulate standards for the imposition of appropriate sanctions.

In addressing this task, the Sanctions Committee recognized that any proposed standards should serve as a model which sets forth a comprehensive system of sanctions, but which leaves room for flexibility and creativity in assigning sanctions in particular cases of lawyer misconduct. These standards are designed to promote thorough, rational consideration of all factors relevant to imposing a sanction in an individual case. The standards attempt to ensure that such factors are given appropriate weight in light of the stated goals of lawyer discipline, and that only relevant aggravating and mitigating circumstances are considered at the appropriate time. Finally, the standards should help achieve the degree of consistency in the imposition of lawyer discipline necessary for fairness to the public and the bar.

While these standards will improve the operation of lawyer discipline systems, there is an additional factor which, though not the focus of this report, cannot be overlooked. In discussing sanctions for lawyer misconduct, this report assumes that all instances of unethical conduct will be brought to the attention of the disciplinary system. Experience indicates that such is not the case. In 1970, the ABA Special Committee on Evaluation of Disciplinary Enforcement (the Clark Committee), was charged with the responsibility for evaluating the effectiveness of disciplinary enforcement systems. The Clark Committee concluded that one of the most significant problems in lawyer discipline was the reluctance of lawyers and judges to report misconduct. That same problem exists today. It cannot be emphasized strongly enough that lawyers and judges must report unethical conduct to the appropriate disciplinary agency. Failure to render such reports is a disservice to the public and the legal profession.

Judges in particular should be reminded of their obligation to report unethical conduct to the disciplinary agencies. Under the ABA Code of Judicial Conduct, a judge is obligated to: "take or initiate appropriate disciplinary measures against a judge or lawyer for unprofessional conduct of which the judge may become aware." Frequently, judges take the position that there is no such need and that errant behavior of lawyers can be remedied solely by use of contempt proceedings and other alternative means. It must be emphasized that the goals of lawyer discipline are not properly and fully served if the judge who observes unethical conduct simply deals with it on an ad hoc basis. It may be proper and wise for a judge to use contempt powers in order to assure the court maintains control of the proceeding and punishes a law for abusive or obstreperous conduct in the court's presence. However, the lawyer discipline system is in addition to and serves purposes different from contempt powers and other mechanisms available to the judge. Only if all lawyer misconduct is in fact reported to the appropriate disciplinary agency can the legal profession have confidence that consistent sanctions are imposed for similar misconduct.

Consistency of sanctions depends on reporting of other types as well. The American Bar Association Center for Professional Responsibility has established a "National Discipline Data Bank" which collects statistics on the nature of ethical violations and sanctions imposed in lawyer discipline cases in all jurisdictions. The information available from the data bank is only as good as reports which reach it. It is vital that the data bank promptly receive complete, accurate and detailed information with regard to all discipline cases.

Finally, the purposes of lawyer sanctions can best be served, and the consistency of those sanctions enhanced, if courts and disciplinary agencies throughout the country articulate the reasons for sanctions imposed. Courts of record that impose lawyer discipline do a valuable service to the legal profession and the public when they issue opinions in lawyer discipline cases that explain the imposition of a specific sanction. The effort of the Sanctions Committee was made easier by the well-reasoned judicial opinions that were available. At the same time, the Sanctions Committee was frustrated by the fact that many jurisdictions do not publish lawyer discipline decisions, and that even published decisions are often summary in nature, failing to articulate the justification for the sanctions imposed.

B. Methodology

The Standards for Lawyer Sanctions have been developed after an explanation of all reported lawyer discipline cases from 1980 to June of 1984, where public discipline was imposed. In addition, eight jurisdictions, which represent a variety of disciplinary systems as well as diversity in geography and population size, were examined in depth. In these jurisdictions—Arizona, California, the District of Columbia, Florida, Illinois, New Jersey, North Dakota, and Utah—all published disciplinary cases from January of 1974 through June of 1984, were analyzed. In each case, data was collected concerning the type of offense, the sanction imposed, the policy considerations identified, and aggravating or mitigating circumstances noted by the court.

This data was examined to identify the patterns that currently exist among courts imposing sanctions and the policy considerations that guide the courts. In general, the courts were consistent in identifying the following policy considerations: protecting the public, ensuring the administration of justice, and maintaining the integrity of the profession. In the words of the California Supreme Court: "The purpose of a disciplinary proceeding is not punitive but to inquire into the fitness of the lawyer to continue in that capacity for the protection of the public, the courts, and the legal profession." However, the courts failed to articulate any theoretical framework for use in imposing sanctions.

In attempting to develop such a framework, the Sanctions Committee considered a number of options. The Committee considered the obvious possibility of identifying each and every type of misconduct in which a lawyer could engage, then suggesting either a recommended sanction or a range of recommended sanctions to deal with that particular misconduct. The Sanctions Committee unanimously rejected that option as being both theoretically simplistic and administratively cumbersome.

The Sanctions Committee next considered a[n ap]proach that dealt with general categories of la[wyer] misconduct and applied recommended sanctions [to] those types of misconduct depending on whether [or] not—and to what extent—the misconduct result[ed] from intentional or malicious acts of the lawye[r]. There is *some* merit in that approach; certainly, th[e] intentional or unintentional conduct of the lawyer is a relevant factor. Nonetheless, that approach was also abandoned after the Sanctions Committee carefully reviewed the purposes of lawyer sanctions. Solely focusing on the intent of the lawyer is not sufficient, and proposed standards must also consider the damage which the lawyer's misconduct causes to the client, the public, the legal system, and the profession. An approach which looked only at the extent of injury was also rejected as being too narrow.

The Committee adopted a model that looks first at the ethical duty and to whom it is owed, and then at the lawyer's mental state and the amount of injury caused by the lawyer's misconduct. (See Theoretical Framework, p. 5, for a detailed discussion of this approach.) Thus, one will look in vain for a section of this report which recommends a specific sanction for, say, improper contact with opposing party who are represented by counsel (Rule 4.2/ DR 7-104(A)(1)), or for any other specific misconduct. What one will find, however, is an organizational framework that provides recommendations as to the type of sanction that should be imposed based on violations of duties owed to clients, the public, the legal system, and the profession.

To provide support for this approach, the Sanctions Committee has offered as much specific data and guidance as possible from reported cases. Thus, with regard to each category of misconduct, the report provides the following:

-discussion of what types of sanctions have been imposed for similar misconduct in reported cases;
-discussion of policy reasons which are articulated in reported cases to support such sanctions; and
-finally, a recommendation as to the level of sanction imposed for the given misconduct, absent aggravating or mitigating circumstances.

While it is recognized that any individual case may present aggravating or mitigating factors which would lead to the imposition of a sanction different from that recommended, these standards present a model which can be used initially to categorize misconduct and to identify the appropriate sanction. The decision as to the effect of any aggravating or mitigating factors should come only after this initial determination of the sanction.

The Sanctions Committee also recognized that the imposition a sanction of suspension or disbarment does not conclude the matter. Typically, disciplined lawyers will request reinstatement or readmission. While this report does not include an in-depth study of readmission cases, a general rec- ...ncerning standards for reinstatement ...n appears as Standard 2.10.

II. THEORETICAL FRAMEWORK

Theoretical Framework

These standards are based on an analysis of the nature of the professional relationship. Historically, being a member of a profession has meant that an individual is some type of expert, possessing knowledge of high instrumental value such that the members of the community give the professional the power to make decisions for them. In the legal profession, the community has allowed the profession the right of self-regulation. As stated in the Preamble to the ABA Model Rules of Professional Conduct (hereinafter "Model Rules"), "[t]he legal profession's relative autonomy carries with it special responsibilities of self-government. The profession has a responsibility to assure that its regulations are conceived in the public interest and not in furtherance of parochial or self-interested concerns of the bar."

This view of the professional relationship requires lawyers to observe the ethical requirements that are set out in the Model Rules (or applicable standard in the jurisdiction where the lawyer is licensed). While the Model Rules define the ethical guidelines for lawyers, they do not provide any method for assigning sanction for ethical violations. The Committee developed a model which requires a court imposing sanctions to answer each of the following questions:

1) What ethical duty did the lawyer violate? (A duty to a client, the public, the legal system, or as a professional?)

2) What was the lawyer's mental state? (Did the lawyer act intentionally, knowingly, or negligently?)

3) What was the extent of the actual or potential injury caused by the lawyer's misconduct? (Was there a serious or potentially serious injury?) and

4) Are there any aggravating or mitigating circumstances?

In determining the nature of the ethical duty violated, the standards assume that the most important ethical duties are those obligations which a lawyer owes to clients. These include:

a) the duty of loyalty which (in the terms of the Model Rules and Code of Professional Responsibility) includes the duties to:

i. preserve the property of a client (Rule 1.15/ DR9–102),

ii. maintain client confidences (Rule 1.6/ DR4–101), and

iii. avoid conflicts of interest (Rules 1.7 through 1.13, 2.2, 3.7, 5.4(c) and 6.3/DR5–101 through DR5–105, DR9–101);

b) the duty of diligence (Rules 1.2, 1.3, 1.4/ DR6–101(A)(3));

c) the duty of competence (Rule 1.1/DR6–101(A)(1) and (2));

d) the duty of candor (Rule 8.4(c)/DR1–102(A)(4) and DR7–101(A)(3)).

In addition to duties owed to clients, the lawyer also owes duties to the general public. Members of the public are entitled to be able to trust lawyers to protect their property, liberty, and their lives. The community expects lawyers to exhibit the highest standards of honesty and integrity, and lawyers have a duty not to engage in conduct involving dishonesty, fraud, or interference with the administration of justice (Rules 8.2, 8.4(b) and (c)/DR1–102(A)(3), (4) and (5), DR8–101 through DR8–103, DR9–101(c)).

Lawyers also owe duties to the legal system. Lawyers are officers of the court, and must abide by the rules of substance and procedure which shape the administration of justice. Lawyers must always operate within the bounds of the law, and cannot create or use false evidence, or engage in any other illegal or improper conduct (Rules 3.1 through 3.6, 3.9, 4.1 through 4.4, 8.2, 8.4(d), (e) and (f)/DR7–102 through DR7–110).

Finally, lawyers owe other duties as a professional. Unlike the obligations mentioned above, these duties are not inherent in the relationship between the professional and the community. These duties do not concern the lawyer's basic responsibilities in representing clients, serving as an officer of the court, or maintaining the public trust, but include other duties relating to the profession. These ethical rules concern:

a) restrictions on advertising and recommending employment (Rules 7.1 through 7.5/DR2–101 through 2–104);

b) fees (Rules 1.5, 5.4 and 5.6/DR2–106, DR2–107, DR3–102);

c) assisting unauthorized practice (Rule 5.5/ DR3–101 through DR3–103 through DR3–103);

d) accepting, declining, or terminating representation (Rules 1.2, 1.14, 1.16/DR2–110); and

e) maintaining the integrity of the profession (Rules 8.1 and 8.3/DR1–101 and DR1–103).

The mental states used in this model are defined as follows. The most culpable mental state is that of intent, when the lawyer acts with the conscious objective or purpose to accomplish a particular result. The next most culpable mental state is that of knowledge, when the lawyer acts with conscious awareness of the nature or attendant circumstances of his or her conduct both without the conscious objective or purpose to accomplish a particular result. The least culpable mental state is negligence, when a lawyer fails to be aware of a substantial risk that circumstances exist or that a result will follow, which failure is a deviation from the standard of care that a reasonable lawyer would exercise in the situation.

The extent of the injury is defined by the type of duty violated and the extent of actual or potential harm. For example in a conversion case, the injury is determined by examining the extent of the client's actual or potential loss. In a case where lawyer tampers with a witness, the injury is measured by evaluating the level of interference or potential interference with the legal proceedings. In this model, the standards refer to various levels of injury: "serious injury," "injury," and "little or no injury." A reference to "injury" alone indicates any level of injury greater than "little or no" injury.

As an example of how this model works, consider two cases of conversion of a client's property. After concluding that the lawyers engaged in ethical misconduct, it is necessary to determine what duties were breached. In these cases, each lawyer breached the duty of loyalty owed to clients. To assign a sanction, however, it is necessary to go further, and to examine each lawyer's mental state and the extent of the injuries caused by the lawyer's actions.

In the first case, assume that the client gave the lawyer $100 as an advance against the costs of investigation. The lawyer took the money, deposited it in a personal checking account, and used it for personal expenses. In this case, where the lawyer acted intentionally and the client actually suffered an injury, the most severe sanction—disbarment—would be appropriate.

Contrast this with the case of a second lawyer, whose client delivered $100 to be held in a trust account. The lawyer, in a hurry to get to court, neglected to inform the secretary what to do with these funds and they were erroneously deposited into the lawyer's general office account. When the lawyer needed additional funds he drew against the general account. The lawyer discovered the mistake, and immediately replaced the money. In this case, where there was no actual injury and a potential for only minor injury, and where the lawyer was merely negligent, a less serious sanction should be imposed. The appropriate sanction would be at most either a public or private reprimand.

In each case, after making the initial determination as to the appropriate sanction, the court would then consider any relevant aggravating or mitigating factors (Standard 9). For example, the presence of aggravating factors, such as vulnerability of the victim or refusal to comply with an order to appear before the disciplinary agency, could increase the appropriate sanction. The presence of mitigating factors, such as absence of prior discipline or inexperience in the practice of law, could make a lesser sanction appropriate.

While there may be particular cases of lawyer misconduct that are not easily categorized, the standards are not designed to propose a specific sanction for each of the myriad of fact patterns in cases of lawyer misconduct. Rather, the standards provide a theoretical framework to guide the courts in imposing sanctions. The ultimate sanction imposed will depend on the presence of any aggravating or mitigating factors in that particular situation. The standards thus are not analogous to criminal determinate sentences, but are guidelines which give courts the flexibility to select the appropriate sanction in each particular case of lawyer misconduct.

The standards do not account for multiple charges of misconduct. The ultimate sanction imposed should at least be consistent with the sanction for the most serious instance of misconduct among a number of violations; it might well be and generally should be greater than the sanction for the most serious misconduct. Either a pattern of misconduct or multiple instances of misconduct should be considered as aggravating factors (see Standard 9.22).

III. STANDARDS FOR IMPOSING LAWYER SANCTIONS AND BLACK LETTER RULES AND COMMENTARY

The Board of Governors of The Florida Bar adopted an amended version of the ABA Standards for Imposing Lawyer Sanctions and thereby provided a format for Bar counsel, referees and the Supreme Court of Florida to consider each of these questions before recommending or imposing appropriate discipline:

1) duties violated;

2) the lawyer's mental state;

3) the potential or actual injury caused by the lawyer's misconduct;

4) the existence of aggravating or mitigating circumstances.

The Bar will use these standards to determine recommended discipline to referees and the court and to determine acceptable pleas under Rule 3–7.9.

For reference purposes, a list of the black letter rules is set out below.

A. Definitions

1) "Injury" is harm to a client, the public, the legal system, or the profession which results from a lawyer's misconduct. The level of injury can range from "serious" injury to "little or no" injury; a reference to "injury" alone indicates any level of injury greater than "little or no" injury.

2) "Intent" is the conscious objective or purpose to accomplish a particular result.

3) "Knowledge" is the conscious awareness of the nature or attendant circumstances of the conduct but without the conscious objective or purpose to accomplish a particular result.

4) "Negligence" is the failure of a lawyer to heed a substantial risk that circumstances exist or that a result will follow, which failure is a deviation from the standard care that a reasonable lawyer would exercise in the situation.

5) "Potential injury" is the harm to a client, the public, the legal system or the profession that is reasonably foreseeable at the time of the lawyer's misconduct, and which, but for some intervening factor or event, would probably have resulted from the lawyer's misconduct.

A. PURPOSE AND NATURE OF SANCTIONS

Standard 1.1. Purpose of Lawyer Discipline Proceedings

The purpose of lawyer discipline proceedings is to protect the public and the administration of justice from lawyers who have not discharged, will not discharge, or are unlikely to discharge their professional duties to clients, the public, the legal system, and the legal profession properly.

Commentary

While courts express their views on the purpose of lawyer sanctions somewhat differently, an examination of reported cases reveals surprising accord as to the basic purpose of discipline. As identified by the courts, the primary purpose is to protect the public. Second, the courts cite the need to protect the integrity of the legal system, and to insure the administration of justice. Another purpose is to deter further unethical conduct and, where appropriate, to rehabilitate the lawyer. A final purpose of imposing sanctions is to educate other lawyers and the public, thereby deterring unethical behavior among all members of the profession. As the courts have noted, while sanctions imposed on a lawyer obviously have a punitive aspect, nonetheless, it is not the purpose to impose such sanctions for punishment.

To achieve these purposes, sanctions for misconduct must apply to all licensed lawyers. Lawyers who are not actively practicing law, but who are serving in such roles as corporate officers, public officials, or law professors, do not lose their association with the legal profession because of their primary occupation. The public quite properly expects that anyone who is admitted to the practice of law, regardless of daily occupational activities, will conform to the minimum ethical standards of the legal profession. If the lawyer fails to meet these standards, appropriate sanctions should be imposed.

Standard 1.2. Public Nature of Lawyer Discipline Proceedings

Ultimate disposition of lawyer discipline should be public.

Commentary

Public disclosure of lawyer discipline, although not followed by a majority of jurisdictions, may enhance the public perception of the Bar. However, in the words of one court, "... the purpose of bar disciplinary proceedings is not to punish the respondent lawyer but to vindicate in the eyes of the public the overall reputation of the bar." Individual lawyers may prefer to avoid the embarrassment and stigma associated with a public sanction, but the profession as a whole will benefit. The more the public knows about how effectively the disciplinary system works, the more confidence they will have in that system. If there is approval of the system, it is hoped that public confidence in the profession's ability to discipline oneself will be assured.

Public identification of a lawyer who has been sanctioned serves other purposes as well. Where only some of the misconduct is known and more than one lawyer appears to be involved, announcement of the names of those who are sanctioned permits others' names to be cleared. Where the lawyer sanctioned is particularly prominent, public identification demonstrates that the system does not play favorites. Where the lawyer sanctioned may have caused injury to others who did not know they could complain, identification enables other victims to make themselves known.

Public sanctions also serve other members of the legal profession. When all sanctions are public, lawyers themselves can observe whether the system is operating fairly, treating consistently lawyers who are disciplined for similar misconduct. Public sanctions also educate other lawyers, and help deter misconduct by others in the profession. The preventive aspect of discipline cannot be overlooked.

Standard 1.3. Purpose of These Standards

These standards are designed for use in imposing a sanction or sanctions following a determination by clear and convincing evidence that a member of the legal profession has violated a provision of the Rules Regulating The Florida Bar. Descriptions in these standards of substantive disciplinary offenses are not intended to create grounds for determining culpability independent of those Rules. The Standards constitute a model, setting forth a comprehensive system for determining sanctions, permitting flexibility and creativity in assigning sanctions in particular cases of lawyer misconduct. They are designed to promote: (1) consideration of all factors relevant to imposing the appropriate level of sanctions in an individual case; (2) consideration of the appropriate weight of such factors in light of the stated goals of lawyer discipline; and (3) consistency in the imposition of disciplinary sanctions for the same or similar offenses within and among jurisdictions.

Commentary

The Rules Regulating The Florida Bar (or other standard under the laws of the particular jurisdiction) establish the ethical standards for lawyers, and lawyers who violate these standards are subject to discipline. When disciplinary proceedings are brought against lawyers alleged to have engaged in ethical misconduct, disciplinary counsel have the burden of proving misconduct by clear and convincing evidence. Following such a finding, the court or disciplinary agency should impose a sanction.

The Standards for Imposing Lawyer Sanctions are guidelines which are to be used by courts or disciplinary agencies in imposing sanctions following a finding of lawyer misconduct. These standards are not grounds for discipline, but, rather, constitute a model for the courts to follow in deciding what sanction to impose for proven lawyer misconduct. While these standards set forth a comprehensive model to be used in imposing sanctions, they also recognize that sanctions imposed must reflect the circumstances of each individual lawyer, and therefore provide for consideration of aggravating and mitigating circumstances in each case.

The Standards for Imposing Lawyer Sanctions are designed to promote consistency in the imposition of sanctions by identifying the relevant factors that courts should consider and then applying these factors to situations where lawyers have engaged in various types of misconduct. Because the Model Rules of Professional Conduct have been adopted by the American Bar Association as the ethical standards for the legal profession, the language of the Rules is used herein. However, because only a minority of jurisdictions have actually adopted the Rules, these Standards are phrased in terms of the fundamental duties owed to clients, the public, the legal system, and as a professional. This general language should make these standards applicable in all jurisdictions regardless of whether the jurisdiction chooses to adopt the Rules, the former Code of Professional Responsibility, or some combination of these standards.

B. SANCTIONS

Standard 2.1. Scope

A disciplinary sanction is imposed on a lawyer upon a finding or acknowledgment that the lawyer has engaged in professional misconduct.

Commentary

Sanctions in disciplinary matters are neither criminal nor civil but sui generis and imposed under authority of the state's highest court. Disciplinary sanctions are separate and apart from penalties which may be imposed solely for civil or criminal conduct, or contempt of court. Disciplinary sanctions do not include restrictions upon a lawyer's practice which may be imposed solely as a result of a lawyer's disability. For example, a lawyer who has not engaged in professional misconduct, but whose ability to practice law is impaired, as by alcoholism or mental illness, should be helped to limit his practice or transferred to inactive status; disciplinary sanctions should not be imposed. Disciplinary sanctions do not include penalties that may be imposed on lawyers who violate administrative rules or regulations applicable to members of the bar, such as by failing to pay dues or to attend mandatory continuing legal education programs.

Standard 2.2. Disbarment

Disbarment terminates the individual's status as a lawyer. Where disbarment is not permanent, procedures should be established for a lawyer who has been disbarred to apply for readmission, provided that:

1) no application should be considered for five years from the effective date of disbarment; and

2) the petition must show by clear and convincing evidence:

a) successful completion of the bar examination; and

b) rehabilitation and fitness to practice law.

Commentary

Disbarment is the most severe sanction, terminating the lawyer's ability to practice law. Disbarment enforces the purpose of discipline in that the public is protected from further practice by the lawyer; the reputation of the legal profession is protected by the action of the bench and bar in taking appropriate actions against unethical lawyers. Even though disbarment is reserved for the most serious cases, the majority of jurisdictions allow application for readmission after a period of time. For the protection of the public, however, the presumption should be against readmission, and, in order to insure that disbarment is in reality a more serious sanction than suspension, in no event should a lawyer even be considered for readmission until at least five years after the effective date of disbarment. After that time, a lawyer seeking to be readmitted to practice must show by clear and convincing evidence: successful completion of the bar examination, and rehabilitation and fitness to practice law.

Disbarment includes disbarment by consent, resignation in lieu of disbarment, and reciprocal disbarment. Although a lawyer who has been disbarred on consent or who has resigned in lieu of disbarment may not be readmitted any earlier than any other lawyer who has been disbarred, the fact that the lawyer resigned or was disbarred on consent is a factor that can be considered if the lawyer applies for readmission.

Standard 2.3. Suspension

Suspension is the removal of a lawyer from the practice of law for a specified minimum period of time. A suspension of ninety (90) days or less shall not require proof of rehabilitation or passage of the bar examination. A suspension of more than ninety (90) days shall require proof of rehabilitation and may require passage of all or part of The Florida Bar examination. No suspension shall be ordered for a specific period of time in excess of three (3) years.

Commentary

Suspension includes suspension by consent, resignation in lieu of suspension and reciprocal suspension. Although jurisdictions impose suspensions for various time periods, the Standards for Lawyer Discipline recommend that suspension be for a definite period of time not to exceed three (3) years. If the conduct is so egregious that a longer suspension seems warranted, the sanction of disbarment should be imposed.

In addition, the Standards draw a distinction between suspensions for ninety (90) days or less, and suspensions for more than ninety (90) days. Standard 6.4 states that a lawyer who has been suspended for ninety (90) days or less should be reinstated automatically (i.e., without establishing rehabilitation). However, a lawyer who has been suspended for more than ninety (90) days should not be reinstated without being required to show by clear and convincing evidence: rehabilitation, compliance with all applicable discipline or disability orders or rules, and fitness to practice law.

While the Standards for Lawyer Discipline currently provide for suspensions of less than six (6) months, short-term suspensions with automatic reinstatement are not an effective means of protecting the public. If a lawyer's misconduct is serious enough to warrant a suspension from practice, the lawyer should not be reinstated until rehabilitation can be established. While it may be possible in some cases for a lawyer to show rehabilitation in less than six (6) months, it is preferable to suspend a lawyer for at least six (6) months in order to insure effective demonstration of rehabilitation. In order to insure that administrative procedures do not extend the period of actual suspension beyond that imposed, however, expedited procedures should be established to reinstate immediately lawyers who show rehabilitation, compliance with rules and fitness to practice.

A six (6) month suspension is also necessary to protect clients. When shorter suspensions are imposed, lawyers can merely delay performing the requested services. If the lawyer eventually completes the work for the client and receives a fee, the suspension has only served to inconvenience the client. In reality a short-term suspension functions as a fine on the lawyer, and fines are prohibited by the Lawyer Standards (see Standard 6.14).

The amount of time for which a lawyer should be suspended, then, should generally be for a minimum of six (6) months. In no case should the time period prior to application for reinstatement be more than three (3) years. The specific period of time for the suspension should be determined after examining any aggravating or mitigating factors in the case. At the end of this time period the lawyer may apply for reinstatement, and the lawyer must show: rehabilitation, compliance with all applicable discipline or disability orders and rules, and fitness to practice law (see Standard 6.4).

Standard 2.4. Emergency Suspension

Emergency suspension is the temporary suspension of a lawyer from the practice of law pending imposition of final discipline. Emergency suspension includes:

1) suspension upon conviction of a "serious crime;" or

2) suspension when the lawyer's continuing conduct is or is likely to cause immediate and serious injury to a client or the public.

Commentary

The court should place a lawyer on emergency suspension immediately upon proof that the lawyer has been convicted of a "serious crime" or is causing great harm to the public. A "serious crime" is defined as any felony or any lesser crime a necessary element of which, as determined by the statutory or common law definition of such crime, involves interference with the administration of justice, false swearing, misrepresentation, fraud, extortion, misappropriation, theft; or an attempt or a conspiracy or solicitation of another to commit a "serious crime." An emergency suspension is necessary in such cases both to protect members of the public and to maintain public confidence in the legal profession. As explained in the commentary to Standard 6.5, of the Standards for Lawyer Discipline, it is difficult for members of the public to understand why a lawyer who has been convicted of stealing funds from a client can continue to handle client funds. Public confidence in the profession is strengthened when expedited procedures are available in such instances of lawyer misconduct.

Although due process does not require a hearing prior to imposing an emergency suspension following a criminal conviction, an opportunity to show cause as to why it should not be imposed should be available. An emergency suspension remains in effect until it is lifted by the court, or until the court imposes a final disciplinary sanction after compliance with relevant procedural rules.

An emergency suspension is also appropriate when the lawyer's continuing conduct is causing or is likely to cause immediate and serious injury to a client or the public. The commentary to Standard 6.5 cites the example of a lawyer who has displayed a pattern of misconduct, such as ongoing conversion of trust funds, as warranting emergency suspension. Emergency suspension is also appropriate where a lawyer abandons the practice of law.

(As explained above in Section 2.1, cases of lawyer disability are not included in the scope of this report. See Standard 12.1 in the Standards for Lawyer Discipline for a discussion of transfer to disability inactive status.)

Standard 2.5. Public Reprimand

Public reprimand is a form of public discipline which declares the conduct of the lawyer improper, but does not limit the lawyer's right to practice.

Commentary

Publicity enhances the effect of the discipline and emphasizes the concern of the court with all lawyer misconduct, not only serious ethical violations. A public reprimand is appropriate in cases where the lawyer's conduct, although violating ethical standards, is not serious enough to warrant suspension or disbarment. (See Definitions, Standards for Lawyer Discipline.) A public reprimand serves the useful purpose of identifying lawyers who have violated ethical standards, and, if accompanied by a published opinion, educates members of the bar as to these standards.

A public reprimand is not always sufficient to protect the public; it may also be appropriate to attach additional conditions to a public reprimand. When a lawyer lacks competence in one area of practice, for example, the court could impose a public reprimand and also require the lawyer to attend continuing education courses. In a case of neglect, the court could impose a public reprimand and probation, during which period of time the lawyer's diligence in handling client matters could be monitored.

Standard 2.6. Admonishment

Admonishment is the lowest form of discipline which declares the conduct of the lawyer improper, but does not limit the lawyer's right to practice.

Commentary

Although admonishment is the least serious of the formal disciplinary sanctions, the public is informed about the lawyers' misconduct, even though the ethical violation results in little or no injury to the client, the public, the legal system or the profession. However, disclosure of such information should help protect the public, while at the same time, avoid damage to a lawyer's reputation when future ethical violations seem unlikely. Public disclosure of an admonishment enhances the preventative nature of lawyer discipline.

Standard 2.7. Probation

Probation is a sanction that allows a lawyer to practice law under specified conditions. Probation can be imposed alone or in conjunction with any other disciplinary measure; probation can also be imposed as a condition of readmission or reinstatement.

Commentary

Probation is a sanction that should be imposed when a lawyer's right to practice law needs to be monitored or limited rather than suspended or revoked. The need for probation can arise under a variety of situations, and it can be imposed either alone or along with any other disciplinary measure. If probation is the sole sanction imposed, it can be either by public reprimand or admonishment, but the sanction should be public reprimand in any case in which the lawyer has violated a duty owed to a client, the public, or the legal system. Probation can also be imposed as a condition of readmission following disbarment or as a condition of reinstatement following a period of suspension from practice.

By imposing probation, the court allows a lawyer to continue to practice, but also requires the lawyer to meet certain conditions that will protect the public and will assist the lawyer to meet ethical obligations. Conditions of probation can include:

a) quarterly or semi-annual reports of caseload status, especially appropriate in neglect cases, see The Florida Bar v. Neale, 432 So.2d 50 (Fla. 1980);

b) supervision by a local disciplinary committee member, see In re Maragos, 285 N.W.2d 541 (N.D. 1979) and In re Hessberger, 96 Ill.2d 423, 451 N.E.2d 821 (1983);

c) periodic audits of trust accounts, especially appropriate in cases where lawyers improperly handle client funds, see The Florida Bar v. Montgomery, 418 So.2d 267 (Fla. 1982);

d) attendance at continuing education programs, especially appropriate in cases of incompetence, see The Florida Bar v. Glick, 383 So.2d 642 (Fla. 1980);

e) participation in alcohol or drug abuse programs, especially appropriate where the lawyer's abuse of alcohol or drugs was a significant cause of his misconduct, see Tenner v. State Bar, 28 Cal.3d 202, 617 P.2d 486, 168 Cal.Rptr. 333 (1980) and In re Heath, 296 Or. 683, 678 P.2d 736 (1984);

f) periodic physical or mental examinations, appropriate where the lawyer's physical or mental condition was a significant cause of his misconduct, see In re McCallum, 289 N.W.2d 146 (Minn. 1980) and In re Mudqe, 33 Cal.3d 152, 654 P.2d 1307J, 187 Cal.Rptr. 79 (1982);

g) passing the bar examination or the appropriate professional responsibility examination, see The Florida Bar v. Peterson, 418 So.2d 246 (Fla. 1982) and In re Morales, 35 Cal.3d 11, 671 P.2d 857, 196 Cal.Rptr. 353 (1983);

h) limitations on practice, see The Florida Bar v. Neely, 417 So.2d 957 (Fla. 1983); or

i) such other conditions as are appropriate for the misconduct.

Probation may be terminated by the court after the respondent has filed an affidavit of compliance with all conditions of probation and the court is satisfied that the need for probation no longer exists. In the event that a lawyer is charged with violating the conditions of probation, a hearing is needed to determine whether a violation has occurred. The disciplinary authority has the burden of establishing any such violation by clear and convincing evidence. Upon a finding that a lawyer has violated probation conditions, the court may extend the probation, impose a more severe sanction, or otherwise handle the matter.

Standard 2.8. Other Sanctions and Remedies

Other sanctions and remedies which may be imposed include:

a) restitution;

b) assessment of costs;

c) limitation upon practice;

d) appointment of a receiver;

e) requirement that the lawyer take the bar examination or professional responsibility examination;

f) requirement that the lawyer attend continuing education courses; and

g) other requirements that the state's highest court or disciplinary board deems consistent with the purposes of lawyer sanctions.

Commentary

These other sanctions and remedies are those that the court or the board may impose when it is deemed necessary to carry out the goals of the disciplinary system. The court should be creative and flexible in approaching those cases where there is some misconduct but where a severe sanction is not required. In less serious cases of incompetence, for example, a sanction requiring the lawyer to attend continuing legal education courses or to limit the lawyer's practice to handling certain types of cases may better protect the public than a period of suspension from practice. Fines are not an appropriate sanction (see Standard 6.14, Lawyer Standards).

Standard 2.9. Reciprocal Discipline

Reciprocal discipline is the imposition of a disciplinary sanction on a lawyer who has been disciplined in another jurisdiction.

Commentary

Public confidence in the profession is enhanced when lawyers who are admitted in more than one jurisdiction are prevented from avoiding the effect of discipline in one jurisdiction by practicing in another. Standard 10.2 of the Standards for Lawyer Discipline provides that a certified copy of the findings of fact in the disciplinary proceeding in the other jurisdiction should constitute conclusive evidence that the respondent committed the misconduct. Reciprocal discipline can be imposed without a hearing, but the court should provide the lawyer with an opportunity to raise a due process challenge or to show that a sanction different from the sanction imposed in the other jurisdiction is warranted. In order to facilitate the imposition of reciprocal discipline, bar counsel or other appropriate authority in each state should report all cases of public discipline to the ABA National Discipline Data Bank.

Standard 2.10. Readmission and Reinstatement

Procedures have been established to allow a disbarred lawyer to apply for readmission. Procedures have been established to allow a suspended lawyer to apply for reinstatement.

Commentary

Readmission occurs when a disbarred lawyer is returned to practice. Since the purpose of lawyer discipline is not punishment, readmission may be appropriate. However, in no event should a lawyer ever be considered for readmission until at least five years after the effective date of disbarment. After that time, a lawyer seeking to be readmitted to practice must show by clear and convincing evidence: rehabilitation, compliance with all applicable discipline or disability orders or rules, and fitness to practice law.

Reinstatement occurs when a suspended lawyer is returned to practice. Since the purpose of lawyer discipline is not punishment, reinstatement is appropriate when a lawyer can show rehabilitation. Application for reinstatement should not be permitted until expiration of the ordered period of suspension and generally not until at least six months after the effective date of suspension. A lawyer should not be reinstated unless he can show by clear and convincing evidence: rehabilitation, compliance with all applicable discipline or disability orders and rules and fitness to practice law (see Standard 6.4).

Conditional readmission and conditional reinstatement can occur when appropriate. Conditions that can be imposed include probation (see Standard 2.7) or other sanctions or remedies (see Standard 2.8).

C. FACTORS TO BE CONSIDERED IN IMPOSING SANCTIONS

STANDARD 3.0 GENERALLY

Standard 3.0. Generally

In imposing a sanction after a finding of lawyer misconduct, a court should consider the following factors:

a) the duty violated;

b) the lawyer's mental state;

c) the potential or actual injury caused by the lawyer's misconduct; and

d) the existence of aggravating or mitigating factors.

Commentary

This system for determining an initial sanction upon a finding of lawyer misconduct requires courts to examine four factors: the nature of the duty violated, the lawyer's mental state, the actual or potential injury resulting from the lawyer's misconduct, and the existence of aggravating or mitigating factors. As explained above (see Theoretical Framework, p. 5), a lawyer's misconduct may be a violation of a duty owed to a client, the public, the legal system, or the profession. The lawyer's mental state may be one of intent, knowledge, or negligence. The injury resulting from the lawyer's misconduct need not be actually realized; in order to protect the public, the court should also examine the potential for injury caused by the lawyer's misconduct. In a case where a lawyer intentionally converts client funds, for example, disbarment can be imposed even where there is no actual injury to any client (see 4.11). In other situations, the standards make distinctions between various levels of actual or potential injury; disbarment may be reserved for cases of serious or potentially serious injury, while admonition may be imposed only in cases where there is little or no actual or potential injury. In any case, however, the court may then take account of any particular aggravating or mitigating factors (see Standard 9.0 for a list of these factors).

STANDARD 4.0 VIOLATIONS OF DUTIES OWED TO CLIENTS

Introduction

This duty arises out of the nature of the basic relationship between the lawyer and the client. The lawyer is not required to accept all clients, but having agreed to perform services for a client, the lawyer has duties that arise under ethical rules, agency law, and under the terms of the contractual relationship with the individual client. The lawyer must preserve the property of a client, maintain client confidences, and avoid conflicts which will impair the lawyer's independent judgment. In addition, the lawyer must be competent to perform the services requested by the client. The lawyer must also be candid with the client during the course of the professional relationship.

Standard 4.1 Failure to Preserve the Client's Property

Absent aggravating or mitigating circumstances, and upon application of the factors set out in Standard 3.0, the following sanctions are generally appropriate in cases involving the failure to preserve client property:

4.11 Disbarment is appropriate when a lawyer intentionally or knowingly converts client property regardless of injury or potential injury.

Commentary

Some courts have held that disbarment is always the appropriate discipline when a lawyer knowingly converts client funds. For example, in the case of In re Wilson, 81 N.J. 451, 409 A.2d 1153 (1979), the Supreme Court of New Jersey discussed the rationale for imposing disbarment as a sanction on lawyers who misappropriate client funds:

> Like many rules governing the behavior of lawyers, this one has its roots in the confidence and trust which clients place in their attorneys. Having sought his advice and relying on his expertise, the client entrusts the lawyer with the transaction including the handling of the client's funds.
>
> Whether it be a real estate closing, the establishment of a trust, the purchase of a business, the investment of funds, the receipt of proceeds of litigation, or any one of a multitude of other situations, it is common-place that the work of lawyers involves possession of their client's funds . . . Whatever the need may be for the lawyer's handling of client's money, the client permits it because he trusts the lawyer . . . [T]here are few more egregious acts of professional misconduct of which an attorney can be guilty than the misappropriation of a client's funds held in trust. (citing In re Beckman, 79 N.J. 402, 404–05, 400 A.2d 792f 793 (1979)) . . . Recognition of the nature and gravity of the offense suggests only one result—disbarment (81 N.J. at 454–55, 409 A.2d at 1154–55).

California has held that disbarment is appropriate even absent knowing conversion when a lawyer is grossly negligent in dealing with client property. As the California Supreme Court observed, "[e]ven if (the attorney's) conduct were not willful and dishonest, gross carelessness and negligence constitute a violation of an attorney's oath faithfully to discharge his duties and involve moral turpitude," Chefsky v. State Bar, 36 Cal.3d 116, at 123, 680 P.2d 82 (1984).

Most courts, however, reserve disbarment for cases in which the lawyer uses the client's funds for the lawyer's own benefit. In Carter v. Ross, 461 A.2d 675 (R.I. 1983), for example, the lawyer took money from an estate and used it to pay office and personal expenses. The Rhode Island Supreme Court cited the Wilson case and imposed disbarment: "We, like our New Jersey colleagues, are convinced that continuing public confidence in the judicial system and the bar as a whole requires that the strictest discipline be imposed in misappropriation cases" (461 A.2d at 676). Similarly, in In re Freeman, 647 P.2d 820 (Kan. App. 1982), a lawyer was disbarred who caused checks from an insurance company to be issued to fictitious payees, and then converted that money for his own use. In these types of cases, where the lawyer's lack of integrity is clear, only the most compelling mitigating circumstances should justify a lesser sanction than disbarment.

In such cases, it may not even seem necessary to consider whether there is any injury to a client. Even though there will always be a potential injury to a client in such cases, the injury factor should still be considered. First, consideration of the extent of actual or potential injury can be important when it is especially serious: injury should be proved up at the disciplinary proceeding in order to make a record in the event that a lawyer applies for readmission. Second, even in jurisdictions where disbarment is permanent, consideration of injury reinforces the concept that a basic purpose of lawyer discipline is protection of the public. As the New York Supreme Court explained in a case where it imposed disbarment on a lawyer who misappropriated more than $31,000 from a client-descendant's estate by forging the administrator's signature on checks: "This result is called for by the duty to protect the public and to vindicate the public's trust in lawyers as custodians of clients' funds" (In re Marks, 72 A.D.2d 399, 401, 424 N.Y.S.2d 229, 230 (1980)). (Note: Lawyers who convert the property of persons other than their clients are covered by Standard 5.11.)

4.12 Suspension is appropriate when a lawyer knows or should know that he is dealing improperly with client property and causes injury or potential injury to a client.

Commentary

Suspension should be reserved for lawyers who engage in misconduct that does not amount to misappropriation or conversion. The most common cases involve lawyers who commingle client funds with their own, or fail to remit client funds promptly. While the court in In re Wilson, 81 N.J. 451, 409 A.2d 1153 (1979), defined misappropriation to include "any unauthorized use by the lawyer of clients' funds entrusted to him, . . . whether or not he derives any personal gain or benefit therefrom" (81 N.J. at 455, n.1., 409 A.2d at 1155, n.1), most courts do not impose disbarment on lawyers who merely commingle funds. As the Washington Supreme Court concluded, "We do not now nor have we ever held that trust account violations per se result in disbarment" (In re Salvesen, 94 Wash.2d 73, 79, 614 P.2d 1264, 1266 (1980)).

For example, in State v. Chartier, 234 Kan. 834, 676 P.2d 740 (1984), the lawyer commingled a client's funds, and failed to notify a client of receipt of garnishment proceeds. The court imposed an indefinite suspension, stating that the lawyer "knew, or should have known through the exercise of reasonable diligence" that the garnishment funds collected exceeded the amounts actually due (234 Kan, at 836, 676 P.2d at 742). Similarly, in Disciplinary Board of the Supreme Court v. Banks, 641 S.W.2d 501 (Tenn. 1982), the court imposed a one-year suspension where the lawyer took the client's money to invest but did not pay her interest on a regular basis or pay over the client's money upon her demand. The court noted that the lawyer did not intend to convert the client's funds to his own use: "At all times he acknowledged his responsibility for them and his indebtedness to her" (641 S.W.2d at 504). Because lawyers who commingle client's funds with their own subject the client's funds to the claims of creditors, commingling is a serious violation for which a period of suspension is appropriate even in cases when the client does not suffer a loss. As explained by the Illinois Supreme Court: "It is the risk of the loss of the funds while they are in the attorney's possession, and not only their actual loss, which the rule is designed to eliminate . . ." In re Bizar, 97 Ill.2d 127, 454 N.E.2d 271 (1983).

4.13 Public reprimand is appropriate when a lawyer is negligent in dealing with client property and causes injury or potential injury to a client.

Commentary

Public reprimand should be reserved for lawyers who are merely negligent in dealing with client property, and who cause little or no injury or potential injury to a client. Suspension or disbarment as applicable under Standards 4.11 and 4.12 and the commentary thereto is appropriate for lawyers who are grossly negligent. For example, lawyers who are grossly negligent in failing to establish proper accounting procedures should be suspended; public reprimand is appropriate for lawyers who simply fail to follow their established procedures. Public reprimand is also appropriate when a lawyer is negligent in training or supervising his or her office staff concerning proper procedures in handling client funds.

The courts have typically imposed public reprimands in cases when lawyers fail to maintain adequate trust accounting procedures, or neglect to return the client's property promptly. In The Florida Bar v. Golden, 401 So.2d 1340 (Fla. 1981), a public reprimand was imposed on a lawyer who failed to repay a loan made to him by a client for two years and who failed to keep adequate records of his trust accounting procedures. Similarly, in Carter v. Gallucci, 457 A.2d 269 (R.I. 1983), because of inadequate records, a lawyer failed to pay real estate taxes out of funds disbursed to him. He did subsequently pay the taxes, and the court imposed a public reprimand.

4.14 Admonishment is appropriate when a lawyer is negligent in dealing with client property and causes little or no actual or potential injury to a client or where there is a technical violation of trust account rules or where there is an unintentional mishandling of client property.

Commentary

Admonishment should be reserved for cases where the lawyer's negligence poses injury or potential injury to a client. An admonishment would be appropriate, for example, when a lawyer's sloppy bookkeeping practices make it difficult to determine the state of a client trust account, but where all client funds are actually properly maintained. Imposing an admonishment in such a case should serve as a warning to the lawyer to improve his or her accounting procedures, thus preventing any actual injury to any client.

Standard 4.2 Failure to Preserve the Client's Confidences

Absent aggravating or mitigating circumstances, and upon application of the factors set out in Standard

3.0, the following sanctions are generally appropriate in cases involving improper revelation of information relating to representation of a client:

4.21 Disbarment is appropriate when a lawyer, with the intent to benefit the lawyer or another, intentionally reveals information relating to representation of a client not otherwise lawfully permitted to be disclosed and this disclosure causes injury or potential injury to a client.

Commentary

Disbarment is warranted in situations when a lawyer intentionally abuses the client's trust by using the professional relationship to gain information which benefits the lawyer or another and which causes injury or potential injury to a client. Because the violation of a client's confidence poses such a serious threat to the lawyer-client relationship, disbarment should be imposed whenever the lawyer acts with the intent to benefit the lawyer or another. Neither a "serious" injury nor a "potentially serious" injury to a client need be proved; any injury to a client will be sufficient to impose disbarment. An example of a case where disbarment is appropriate occurred in In re Pool, No. 83–37 BD, Sup. J. Ct., Suff. Cty., Mass. (1984), where a defendant's lawyer gave a federal prosecutor information about the location of a safety deposit box containing incriminating evidence in order to gain access to obtain funds to cover the costs of investigation. In the words of the court, "[t]he disclosure of confidential information by a defense attorney to a prosecutor, without the client's consent, is a serious violation of the defense attorney's obligations" (Id. at 4). (Note: This situation should be distinguished from the situation where a lawyer is acting under a good faith belief that there is no choice but to reveal a client's confidence, as in a case where a lawyer is called to testify as to the whereabouts of the client in a divorce proceeding and the lawyer's answer involves facts learned in the lawyer-client relationship. Here, the lawyer's good faith belief that the law requires disclosure of the information would be a mitigating factor, see Standard 9.32(b)).

4.22 Suspension is appropriate when a lawyer knowingly reveals information relating to the representation of a client not otherwise lawfully permitted to be disclosed, and this disclosure causes injury or potential injury to a client.

Commentary

Suspension is appropriate when the lawyer is not intentionally using the professional relationship to benefit himself or another, but nevertheless knowingly breaches a client's confidence such that the client suffers injury or potential injury. An appropriate case for a suspension would involve a lawyer who knowingly revealed confidential information to the opposing party in litigation, with the result that the client's position was weakened.

4.23 Public reprimand is appropriate when a lawyer negligently reveals information relating to representation of a client not otherwise lawfully permitted to be disclosed and this disclosure causes injury or potential injury to a client.

Commentary

Public Reprimand should be imposed when a lawyer negligently breaches a client's confidence. Even when the client is not actually harmed, the potential for harm to the client and damage to the professional relationship is so significant that a public sanction should be imposed. In the words of one court: "This element of trust is the very essence of the attorney-client relationship" (Matter of Roache, 446 N.E.2d 1302, 1303 (Ind. 1983)). An appropriate case for a public reprimand would involve a lawyer who negligently leaves a client's documents in a conference room following a meeting, or who discusses a client matter in a public place.

4.24 Admonishment is appropriate when a lawyer negligently reveals information relating to representation of a client not otherwise lawfully permitted to be disclosed and this disclosure causes little or no actual or potential injury to a client.

Commentary

Maintaining a client's confidence is so fundamental to the professional relationship that it is inappropriate to impose an admonishment. At a minimum, a public reprimand should be imposed (see Standard 4.23).

Standard 4.3 Failure to Avoid Conflicts of Interest

Absent aggravating or mitigating circumstances, and upon application of the factors set out in Standard 3.0, the following sanctions are generally appropriate in cases involving conflicts of interest:

4.31 Disbarment is appropriate when a lawyer, without the informed consent of the client(s):

a) engages in representation of a client knowing that the lawyer's interests are adverse to the client's with the intent to benefit the lawyer or another, and causes serious or potentially serious injury to the client; or

b) simultaneously represents clients that the lawyer knows have adverse interests with the intent to benefit the lawyer or another, and causes serious or potentially serious injury to a client; or

c) represents a client in a matter substantially related to a matter in which the interests of a present or former client are materially adverse, and knowingly uses information relating to the representation of a client with the intent to benefit the lawyer or another, and causes serious or potentially serious injury to a client.

Commentary

The courts generally disbar lawyers who intentionally exploit the lawyer-client relationship by acquiring an ownership, possessory, security or other pecuniary interest adverse to a client without the client's understanding or consent. For example, in Matter of Easler, 269 S.E.2d 765 (S.C. 1980), a lawyer who engaged in a fraudulent scheme to obtain the client's property at a price well below market value was disbarred. The court noted that "in his attempt to acquire their property for his personal gain," the lawyer falsely notarized one of the client's signature, and took advantage of the "domestic and financial difficulties the McFarlins [the clients] were undergoing" (269 S.E.2d at 766). In In re Wolf, 82 N.J. 326, 413 A.2d 317 (1980), a widow retained the lawyer who had represented her husband during his lifetime to handle her husband's estate. When she asked the lawyer to suggest an investment for a portion of her inheritance, he suggested that she invest in property which was owned by a company in which he was a stockholder and officer. Knowing that his client was naive and inexperienced in business matters, he directed her to invest her money in property worth only half of what he represented to her, and did not inform her as to the status of the mortgage, the title, or unpaid real estate taxes. Later on, he failed to notify her of a foreclosure action on the property or to defend the action on her behalf. In the words of the court, "It is clear that he exploited his client for his own financial benefit. It was unthinkable in the first place for the respondent to have suggested such an investment, but, having done so, it was unconscionable for him to have continued to represent the widow. He should have insisted that she retain independent counsel or refused to consummate the transaction. Undoubtedly, independent counsel would never have allowed the widow to make this investment" (413 A.2d at 321). (Note: the lawyer, who was disbarred, also attempted to commit fraud on the court in order to secure a larger fee.) Similarly, in In re Hills, 296 Or. 526, 678 P.2d 262 (1984), the lawyer entered into a loan transaction with clients in which he intentionally misrepresented that funds were available to pay the note. He also entered into a partnership agreement with another client in which he misrepresented that the client would be a limited partner but, in fact, made the client a general partner. In neither of these cases did the lawyer advise the clients to seek independent legal counsel.

Disbarment is also appropriate in cases of multiple representation when a lawyer knowingly engages in conduct with the intent to benefit the lawyer or another. As one court has explained, "Although many ingredients go into the recipe for a successful lawyer-client relationship, one ingredient is indispensable: individual loyalty. The relationship cannot properly exist absent the lawyer's uncompromised commitment to the client's cause. DR5–105 aims to insure undivided loyalty in its absence, the lawyer cannot serve. The rule also seeks to maintain or increase public confidence in public institutions, for the appearance of impropriety that sometimes exists when a lawyer represents multiple clients . . . erodes public confidence in the legal profession." In re Jans, 295 Or. 289, 666 P.2d 830, 832 (1983). In In re Keast, 497 P.2d 103 (Mont. 1972), a lawyer represented a client charged with procuring girls for immoral purposes. Although the lawyer was named as one of the individuals for whom the girls were procured, he served as defense counsel in his client's criminal case. While this case was pending, the lawyer also filed an action for divorce against the client on behalf of the client's wife. The court imposed disbarment. In Stanley v. Board of Professional Responsibility, 640 S.W.2d 210 (Tenn. 1982), a lawyer was disbarred who represented both the victim and the defendant in a criminal matter. After learning about the crime from the victim, the lawyer misled the defendant into employing him when the lawyer knew that the victim no longer wished to prosecute. In the words of the court, "Stanley [the lawyer] deceived an immature youth and his naive parents. He compounded the deception with his lack of understanding of the proper role of a lawyer—which does not include a self-appointed role as a paraclete, comforter, helper, or hand-holder, under the guise of legal services and at a lawyer's compensation rate" (640 S.W.2d at 213). (Note: the lawyer also was involved in another conflict of interest by entering into usurious loan transactions with two other clients.)

Finally, disbarment is appropriate when a lawyer knowingly uses information relating to representation of a former client with the intent to benefit the lawyer or another, and causes serious or potentially serious injury to a client. Although such cases are rare, disbarment is warranted when there is such an intentional abuse of the lawyer-client relationship.

4.32 Suspension is appropriate when a lawyer knows of a conflict of interest and does not fully disclose to a client the possible effect of that conflict, and causes injury or potential injury to a client.

Commentary

Conflicts can take the form of a conflict between the lawyer and his or her client, between current clients, or between a former client and a present client. In the case of conflicts between a lawyer and a present client, suspension is appropriate when the lawyer knows that his or her interests may be or are likely to be adverse to that of the client, but does not fully disclose the conflict, and causes injury or potential injury to a client. For example, in In re Boyer, 295 Or. 624, 669 P.2d 326 (1983), the lawyer represented a client for a number of years, rendering both financial and legal advice. When another of his clients wanted to borrow money, the lawyer arranged for the first client to make a loan, and he prepared the note and a mortgage to secure the note, but the lawyer did not tell the first client either that such a loan might be usurious, and thus unenforceable, or that he had received a finder's fee from the second client for his efforts. The Oregon Supreme Court found that the lawyer violated DR5–101(A) in his representation of the first client, and suspended him for seven months. (Note: the court also found a violation of DR5–105(B).) Similarly, in Joseph E. Chabat, DP–161/80, DP 74/81 (Michigan Attorney Discipline Board, 1980), a lawyer in a divorce action was suspended for nine months when he lent himself money from the sale of a client's house and failed to advise the client to seek independent representation in regard to the loan.

Suspension is also appropriate when a lawyer knows of a conflict among several clients, but does not fully disclose the possible effect of the multiple representation, and causes injury or potential injury to one or more of the clients. For example, in State v. Callahan, 232 Kan. 136, 652 P.2d 708 (1982), the lawyer represented both the vendors and the purchaser in a land sale transaction. The lawyer failed to warn the vendors that they did not have a perfected security interest and failed to make full disclosure to the vendors of his close business and professional associations with the purchaser. The Supreme Court of Kansas imposed an indefinite suspension. Similarly, in Matter of Krakauer, 81 N.J. 32, 404 A.2d 1137 (1979), the New Jersey Supreme Court imposed a one-year suspension on a lawyer who represented both sides in a real estate transaction (and who also attempted to retain an unearned commission and called for a title search which was not ordered by the client).

Finally, suspension is appropriate when a lawyer knows or should know that the interests of a client are materially adverse to the interests of a former client in a substantially related matter, and causes injury or potential injury to the former or the subsequent client. For example, in In re LaPinska, 72 Ill.2d 461, 381 N.E.2d 700 (1978), the lawyer represented a contractor to secure title papers for a residence being sold. The lawyer, a city attorney, then represented the city in a suit brought by the purchasers of the residence against the contractor regarding a zoning violation of the property. When the purchasers complained about the leniency of the fine imposed on the contractor, the lawyer agreed to represent them in a civil suit against the contractor. Despite the fact that the lawyer had acted openly, and all the affected parties were aware of the dual representation, the Illinois Supreme Court suspended the lawyer for one year. Similarly, In re Odendahl, M.R. 2787 (Ill. 1982), the Illinois Supreme Court suspended a lawyer for one year when, while a state's attorney, he represented individuals in nine divorce proceedings in which support payments were due. In one case, he represented the wife to obtain the divorce, and then the husband, in a petition to reduce the support payments. In another case, he prosecuted a defendant for disorderly conduct and then filed an answer for him in a divorce suit by his wife. The court noted that four of these cases occurred after motions to disqualify had been filed against the lawyer and that he knew or should have known of the impropriety of his conduct.

4.33 Public reprimand is appropriate when a lawyer is negligent in determining whether the representation of a client may be materially affected by the lawyer's own interests, or whether the representation will adversely affect another client, and causes injury or potential injury to a client.

Commentary

The courts generally impose a public reprimand when a lawyer engages in a single instance of misconduct involving a conflict of interest when the lawyer has merely been negligent and there is no overreaching or serious injury to a client. For example, in State v. Swoyer, 228 Kan. 799, 619 P.2d 1166 (1980), a public censure [publicly reprimand] was imposed on a lawyer who was representing a client who owned his own business, and who also advised the client's former employee to sue the client for back wages. Although the lawyer stated that he was simply carrying out his client's wishes by attempting to secure payment for the employee, and that he merely advised her to file suit herself, the court found an ethical violation worthy of censure (public reprimand) since her petition was actually typed in the lawyer's office and filed by the lawyer. In a multiple representation situation, the court in Gendron v. State Bar of California, 35 Cal.3d 409, 673 P.2d 260, 197 Cal.3d 409, 673 P.2d 260, 197 Cal.Rptr. 590, (1983), imposed a public reprimand on a public defender who neglected to obtain written waiver of conflict forms from three defendants who were jointly charged with robbery. In Matter of Palmieri, 76 N.J. 51, 385 A.2d 856 (1978), a public reprimand was imposed on a lawyer who represented the seller of a supermarket when, with the buyers unable to hire a lawyer and upon the insistence of the seller, he also represented the buyers. Although the lawyer made full disclosure of the relevant facts and pitfalls of multiple representation, he later filed suit against the buyers and eventually had to withdraw when he was required to be a witness concerning the nature of the agreement between the parties.

Courts also impose public reprimands in cases of subsequent representation, for example, in In re Drendel, M.R. 1708 (Ill. 1975), a lawyer represented a client in a divorce suit against his wife, but the parties reconciled before the hearing and the case was dismissed. About eighteen months later, he represented the wife in a divorce action against the husband, but this suit was also dismissed. Similarly, in In re Lewis, M.R. 2766 (Ill. 1982), the lawyer represented the executor of a will and later, while employed in another office, represented a client who was the devisee of the residence property who filed a petition alleging misconduct by the executor. The court ordered the lawyer censured [publicly reprimanded], noting no evidence of secrecy, fraud, or financial benefit to the lawyer.

4.34 Admonishment is appropriate when a lawyer is negligent in determining whether the representation of a client may be materially affected by the lawyer's own interests, or whether the representation will adversely affect another client, and causes little or no injury or potential injury to a client.

Standard 4.4 Lack of Diligence

Absent aggravating or mitigating circumstances, and upon application of the factors set out in Standard 3.0, the following sanctions are generally appropriate in cases involving a failure to act with reasonable diligence and promptness in representing a client:

4.41 Disbarment is appropriate when:

a) a lawyer abandons the practice and causes serious or potentially serious injury to a client; or

b) a lawyer knowingly fails to perform services for a client and causes serious or potentially serious injury to a client; or

c) a lawyer engages in a pattern of neglect with respect to client matters and causes serious or potentially serious injury to a client.

Commentary

Lack of diligence can take a variety of forms. Some lawyers simply abandon their practices, leaving clients completely unaware that they have no legal representation and often leaving clients without any legal remedy. Other lawyers knowingly fail to perform services for a client, or engage in a pattern of misconduct, demonstrating by their behavior that they either cannot or will not conform to the required ethical standards.

Disbarment is appropriate in each of these situations. For example, in The Florida Bar v, Lehman, 417 So.2d 648 (Fla. 1982), a lawyer abandoned his practice and kept approximately 450 pending client matters. The clients suffered serious injuries; one client's statute of limitations ran, and many of the clients never recovered money paid to the lawyer as fees. See also: In re Cullinam, M.R. 2963 (Ill. 1983) (with other charges). In a case demonstrating a pattern of neglect, State v. Dixon, 233 Kan. 465, 664 P.2d 286 (1983), a lawyer was disbarred after having been disciplined for thirteen counts of neglect of probate cases, with each case involving a long period of neglect (Sixteen years, twenty-eight years, etc.). The court noted that, although there was no evidence of dishonesty on the part of the lawyer, disbarment was appropriate because "the extent of the neglect is extreme and had reached proportions never before considered by this court" (233 Kan. at 470, 644 P.2d at 289). See also; The Florida Bar v. Mitchell, 285 So.2d 96 (Fla.1980).

4.42 Suspension is appropriate when:

a) a lawyer knowingly fails to perform services for a client and causes injury or potential injury to a client; or

b) a lawyer engages in a pattern of neglect and causes injury or potential injury to a client.

Commentary

Suspension should be imposed when a lawyer knows that he is not performing the services requested by the client, but does nothing to remedy the situation, or when a lawyer engages in a pattern of neglect, with the result that the lawyer causes injury or potential injury to a client. Most cases involve lawyers who do not communicate with their clients. For example, in In re Earl J. Taylor, 666 Ill.2d 567, 363 N.E.2d 845 (1977), a lawyer was suspended for one year when he failed to appear at a criminal hearing to file a divorce action, and failed to prosecute a civil case. In the third case, the lawyer told the client that "he'd take care of everything," yet did not contact her or return her telephone calls. This last client suffered a default judgment, which forced her to settle and pay a second lawyer; the first two clients suffered the loss of the fee. See also: Hunt v. Disciplinary Board of the Alabama State Bar, 381 So.2d 52 (Ala. 1980); People v. Dixon, 616 P.2d 103 (Colo. 1980).

4.43 Public reprimand is appropriate when a lawyer is negligent and does not act with reasonable diligence in representing a client, and causes injury or potential injury to a client.

Commentary

Most courts impose a public reprimand when the lawyer is negligent. For example, in In re Logan, 70 N.J. 222, 358 A.2d 787 (1976), a lawyer who neglected a client matter was reprimanded when, knowing that a motion for reduction of alimony was dependent on the court's examination of his client's tax return, he failed to file a copy of the tax return with the court. See also: In re Donohue, 77 A.2d 112, 432 N.Y.S.2d 498 (1980), where a lawyer neglected an estate matter, but where the estate was eventually closed to the satisfaction of all parties and with no financial loss, and Louis Lan, DP–194180 (Mich. Atty. Dis. Board 1980), where the lawyer attempted to transfer cases to other lawyers without adequately communicating with his clients.

4.44 Admonishment is appropriate when a lawyer is negligent and does not act with reasonable diligence in representing a client, and causes little or no actual or potential injury to a client.

Standard 4.5 Lack of Competence

Absent aggravating or mitigating circumstances, and upon application of the factors set out in Standard 3.0, the following sanctions are generally appropriate in cases involving failure to provide competent representation to a client:

4.51 Disbarment is appropriate when a lawyer's course of conduct demonstrates that the lawyer does not understand the most fundamental legal doctrines or procedures, and the lawyer's conduct causes injury or potential injury to a client.

Commentary

Disbarment should be imposed on lawyers who are found to have engaged in multiple instances of incompetent behavior. Since disbarment is such a serious sanction, it should rarely be imposed on a lawyer who has demonstrated only a single instance of incompetence; rather, disbarment should be imposed on lawyers whose course of conduct demonstrates that they cannot or will not master the knowledge and skills necessary for minimally competent practice. For example, in The Florida Bar v. Blaha, 366 So.2d 443 (Fla. 1978), the court disbarred a lawyer who totally mishandled a guardianship and real estate transaction, and also filed a complaint for another client in the wrong court, such that relief was denied. In representing a third client, the lawyer mishandled a replevin action, filing replevin under old rules at a time when his client had not yet perfected a security interest necessary to support the action. As a result of this incompetence, the lawyer was eventually held in contempt and fined $3,000.00.

4.52 Suspension is appropriate when a lawyer engages in an area of practice in which the lawyer knowingly lacks competence, and causes injury or potential injury to a client.

Commentary

In order to protect the public, a suspension should be imposed in cases when a lawyer engages in practice in areas in which a lawyer knows that he or she is not competent. In such cases, it may also be appropriate to attach certain conditions to the suspension, such as a requirement that the lawyer pass the bar examination or limit his or her practice to certain areas. Such a situation arose in the case of Office of Disciplinary Counsel v. Henry, 664 S.W.2d 62 (Tenn. 1983), where the lawyer mishandled four cases in a relatively short period of time. In one case, the lawyer attempted to represent a client charged with murder. The lawyer had never handled any felony case before, and yet did not associate any lawyer with him. He made little investigation of the crime, and filed motions based on statutes which had been superseded. Further, he severely damaged his client's case by filing an "amended answer" to the indictment, following the form which would be filed in a civil action, which set forth his client's version of the homicide. The court imposed a two-year suspension with reinstatement conditioned "upon a showing that he has obtained a level of competence adequate to justify the issuance of a license" (664 S.W.2d at 64).

4.53 Public reprimand is appropriate when a lawyer:

a) demonstrates failure to understand relevant legal doctrines or procedures and causes injury or potential injury to a client; or

b) is negligent in determining whether the lawyer is competent to handle a legal matter and causes injury or potential injury to a client.

Commentary

Most courts impose public reprimands on lawyers who are incompetent. For example, in The Florida Bar v. Gray, 380 So.2d 1292 (Fla. 1980), the lawyer agreed to represent a client in a claim of violation of the truth in lending laws, but, although the evidence showed that he expected to become qualified in this area, he did not engage in sufficient study and investigation to become competent (only securing a number of laymen's publications). The court imposed a public reprimand. Similarly, in State ex rel. Nebraska State Bar Association v. Holscher, 193 Neb. 729, 230 N.W.2d 75 (1975), a county lawyer who filed a claim for services he rendered in foreclosing tax sale certificates without familiarizing himself with the statute prescribing the fee for such services received a public reprimand.

While public reprimand alone can be appropriate, a combination of public reprimand and probation is often a more productive approach. Probation can be very effective in assisting lawyers to improve their legal skills. The court can use probation creatively, imposing whatever conditions are necessary to assist that particular lawyer. It may be appropriate, for example, to require an inexperienced lawyer to associate with co-counsel. In The Florida Bar v. Glick, 383 So.2d 642 (Fla. 1980), the court imposed a public reprimand and one-year probation on a lawyer who mishandled a quiet title action. The court imposed the following conditions of probation: that the lawyer refrain from representing clients in real estate matters and that he complete 30 hours of approved continuing education courses in real property.

4.54 Admonishment is appropriate when a lawyer engages in an isolated instance of negligence in determining whether the lawyer is competent to handle a legal matter, and causes little or no injury to a client.

Standard 4.6 Lack of Candor

Absent aggravating or mitigating circumstances, and upon application of the factors set out in Standard 3.0, the following sanctions are generally appropriate in cases where the lawyer engages in fraud, deceit, or misrepresentation directed toward a client:

4.61 Disbarment is appropriate when a lawyer knowingly or intentionally deceives a client with the intent to benefit the lawyer or another regardless of injury or potential injury to the client.

Commentary

Disbarment is appropriate when a lawyer intentionally abuses the fiduciary relationship, making misrepresentations to a client in order to benefit himself or another regardless of injury or potential injury to a client. (For a discussion of lack of candor before a court, see Standard 6.1.) For example, in Matter of Wolfson, 313 N.W.2d 596 (Minn. 1981), the court disbarred a lawyer who asked a client to help him arrange for a loan, and who misrepresented that the loan was for medical treatment for his daughter, when the loan was actually used in his wife's business. The client personally guaranteed payment of the loan and, when the lawyer failed to repay it, the client had to institute legal action against the lawyer to obtain a $832.61 judgment. In imposing disbarment, the court stated that the lawyer had not "hesitated to use his knowledge and skill as a lawyer for improper purposes" (313 N.W.2d at 602). (Note: The lawyer had also engaged in acts of neglect and abuse of the legal process.) Similarly, in (anonymous) 49 Cal. State Bar J. 73 (1974), a lawyer was disbarred after he borrowed money from two clients, falsely leading them to believe that he was solvent, with the result that the clients received an unsecured promissory note. In Virginia State Bar ex rel. Eighth District Committee v. Fred W. Bender, Jr., No. 50228 (Va. App. Ct. 1981), the court revoked the license of a lawyer who intentionally overstated the number of hours he worked on a client's estate to make it appear that he was entitled to $9,500.00.

4.62 Suspension is appropriate when a lawyer knowingly deceives a client, and causes injury or potential injury to the client.

Commentary

Suspension is appropriate when a lawyer knowingly deceives a client, although not necessarily for his own direct benefit, and the client is injured. The most common cases are those in which a lawyer misrepresents the nature or the extent of services performed. For example, in Kentucky Bar Association v. Reed, 623 S.W.2d 228 (Ky. 1981), the court suspended a lawyer for one year when he misrepresented the status of three different cases and all three clients suffered injury (two clients suffered a summary judgment against them and another client was denied a settlement payment for an extensive period of time).

4.63 Public reprimand is appropriate when a lawyer negligently fails to provide a client with accurate or complete information, and causes injury or potential injury to the client.

Commentary

Public Reprimand is justified when the lawyer is merely negligent and there is injury or potential injury to a client. In Hawkins v. State Bar, 23 Cal.3d 622, 591 P.2d 524, 153 Cal.Rptr. 234 (1979), a lawyer received a public reproval [public reprimand] when he failed to fully explain to his clients the nature of a contingency interest which he possessed in insurance proceeds used to satisfy an adverse judgment against the clients in a personal injury action.

4.64 Admonishment is appropriate when a lawyer negligently fails to provide a client with accurate or complete information, and causes little or no actual or potential injury to the client.

STANDARD 5.0 VIOLATIONS OF DUTIES OWED TO THE PUBLIC

Standard 5.1 Failure to Maintain Personal Integrity

Absent aggravating or mitigating circumstances, and upon application of the factors set out in Standard 3.0, the following sanctions are generally appropriate in cases involving commission of a criminal act that reflects adversely on the lawyer's honesty, trustworthiness, or fitness as a lawyer in other respects, or in cases with conduct involving dishonesty, fraud, deceit, or misrepresentation:

5.11 Disbarment is appropriate when:

a) a lawyer is convicted of a felony under applicable law; or

b) a lawyer engages in serious criminal conduct, a necessary element of which includes intentional interference with the administration of justice, false swearing, misrepresentation, fraud, extortion, misappropriation, or theft; or

c) a lawyer engages in the sale, distribution or importation of controlled substances; or

d) a lawyer engages in the intentional killing of another; or

e) a lawyer attempts or conspires or solicits another to commit any of the offenses listed in sections (a)–(d); or

f) a lawyer engages in any other intentional conduct involving dishonesty, fraud, deceit, or misrepresentation that seriously adversely reflects on the lawyer's fitness to practice.

Commentary

A lawyer who engages in any of the illegal acts listed above has violated one of the most basic professional obligations to the public, the pledge to maintain personal honesty and integrity. This duty to the public is breached regardless of whether a criminal charge has been brought against the lawyer. In fact, this type of misconduct is so closely related to practice and poses such an immediate threat to the public that the lawyer should be suspended from the practice of law immediately pending a final determination of the ultimate discipline to be imposed (see Standards for Lawyer Discipline, Standard 6.5).

In imposing final discipline in such cases, most courts impose disbarment on lawyers who are convicted of serious felonies. As the court noted in a case where a lawyer was convicted of two counts of federal income tax evasion and one count of subornation of perjury, "we cannot ask the public to voluntarily comply with the legal system if we, as lawyers, reject its fairness and application to ourselves." In the Matter of Grimes, 414 Mich. 483, 326 N.W.2d 380 (1982). See also: In re Fry, 251 Ga. 247, 305 S.E.2d 590 (Ga. 1983), conviction of murder; Sixth District Committee of the Virginia State Bar v. Albert C. Hodgson, No. 80–18 (Va. Disciplinary Board, 1981), where a lawyer advised a client that he could make arrangements to have her husband killed in lieu of bringing a child custody suit.

5.12 Suspension is appropriate when a lawyer knowingly engages in criminal conduct which is not included within Standard 5.11 and that seriously adversely reflects on the lawyer's fitness to practice.

Commentary

Lawyers who engage in criminal conduct other than that described above in Standard 5.11 should be suspended in cases where their conduct seriously adversely reflects on their fitness to practice law. As in the case of disbarment, a suspension can be imposed even where no criminal charges have been filed against the lawyer. Not every lawyer who commits a criminal act should be suspended, however. As pointed out in the Model Rules of Professional Conduct:

Although a lawyer is personally answerable to the entire criminal law, a lawyer should be professionally answerable only for offenses that indicate lack of those characteristics relevant to law practice. Offenses involving violence, dishonesty, or breach of trust, or serious interference with the administration of justice are in that category. A pattern of repeated offenses, even ones of minor significance when considered separately, can indicate indifference to legal obligation.

The most common cases involved lawyers who commit felonies other than those listed above, such as the possession of narcotics or sexual assault. See: In re Robideau, 102 Wis.2d 16, 306 N.W.2d 1 (1981), suspension for three years for contributing to the delinquency of a minor and possession of a controlled substance; In re Lanier, 309 S.E.2d 754 (S.C. 1983), indefinite suspension for possession of marijuana; In re Safran, 18 Cal.3d 134, 554 P.2d 329, 133 Cal.Rptr. 9 (1976), suspension for three years for conviction of two counts of child molesting.

5.13 Public reprimand is appropriate when a lawyer knowingly engages in any other conduct that involves dishonesty, fraud, deceit, or misrepresentation and that adversely reflects on the lawyer's fitness to practice law.

Commentary

There are few situations not involving fraud or dishonesty which are sufficiently related to the practice of law to subject a lawyer to discipline. The Arizona Supreme court applied this standard in In re Johnson, 106 Ariz. 73, 471 P.2d 269 (1970), a case where a lawyer was charged with assault, stating that "isolated, trivial incidents of this kind not involving a fixed pattern of misbehavior find ample redress in the criminal and civil laws. They have none of the elements of moral turpitude, arising more out of the infirmities of human nature. They are not the appropriate subject matter of a solemn public reprimand by this court" (471 P.2d at 271). However, a pattern of repeated offenses, even ones of minor significance when considered separately, can indicate such indifference to legal obligation as to justify a public reprimand.

There can be situations, however, in which the lawyer's conduct is not even criminal, but, because it is directly related to his or her professional role, discipline is required. For example, in In re Lamberis, 93 Ill.2d 222, 443 N.E.2d 549 (1982), the court imposed censure [public reprimand] on a lawyer who knowingly plagiarized two published works in a thesis submitted in satisfaction of the requirements for a master's degree. The court noted that although the lawyer's conduct might appear to be "fairly distant from the practice of law," discipline was "appropriate and required because both the extent of the appropriated material and the purpose for which it was used evidence the respondent's complete disregard for values that are most fundamental in the legal profession" (443 N.E.2d at 551). Specifically, the lawyer's plagiarism displayed "an extreme cynicism toward the property rights of others," and a "lack of honesty which cannot go undisciplined, especially because honesty is so fundamental to the functioning of the legal profession" (443 N.E.2d at 551–52).

5.14 Admonishment is appropriate when a lawyer engages in any other conduct that reflects adversely on the lawyer's fitness to practice law.

Standard 5.2 Failure to Maintain the Public Trust

Absent aggravating or mitigating circumstances, and upon application of the factors set out in Standard 3.0, the following sanctions are generally appropriate in cases involving public officials who engage in conduct that is prejudicial to the administration of justice or who state or imply an ability to influence improperly a government agency or official:

5.21 Disbarment is appropriate when a lawyer in an official or governmental position knowingly misuses the position with the intent to obtain a significant benefit or advantage for himself or another, or with the intent to cause serious or potentially serious injury to a party or to the integrity of the legal process.

Commentary

The public officials who are subject to disbarment generally engage in conduct involving fraud and deceit, and are generally subject to criminal sanctions as well. For example, in In re Rosenthal, 73 Ill.2d 46, 382 N.E.2d 257 (1978), two lawyers were disbarred who participated in an extortion scheme to benefit their client as part of a zoning request. One of the lawyers was an Assistant Attorney General, a fact which the court emphasized as significant in imposing disbarment: "Despite his obligations as a law officer, he knowingly participated and furthered conduct which he knew to be illegal, and then, further, deliberately misled federal agents" (382 N.E.2d at 262). The court concluded, "corruption within government could not, in most instances, thrive but for those few attorneys, who, like respondents, are willing to tolerate such illegal activity if it will benefit their client. The practice of law is a privilege and demands a greater acceptance of responsibility and adherence to ethical standards than respondents have demonstrated" (382 N.E.2d at 261).

5.22 Suspension is appropriate when a lawyer in an official or governmental position knowingly fails to follow proper procedures or rules, and causes injury or potential injury to a party or to the integrity of the legal process.

Commentary

Suspension is an appropriate sanction when lawyers who are public officials knowingly act improperly, but not necessarily for their own benefit. For example, in In re DeLucia, 76 N.J. 329, 387 A.2d 362 (1978), a judge fixed a traffic ticket by entering a not guilty judgment when no hearing had been held. He later attempted to cover up his wrongdoing by preparing an affidavit with a backdated acknowledgment. Disciplinary proceedings were instituted after the lawyer had resigned from his part-time judgeship. The court imposed a one year suspension, noting that he did not personally benefit. Similarly, in In re Weishoff, 75 N.J. 326, 382

A.2d 632 (1978), the court held that a municipal prosecutor's knowing participation in an improper disposition of a traffic ticket warranted a one year suspension. In In re Vasser, 75 N.J. 357, 382 A.2d 1114 (1978), the court imposed a six-month suspension on a lawyer/part–time judge who improperly practiced law and also interceded in another court to obtain a postponement of a trial to give his client an advantage in an unrelated civil matter. The lawyer also used official court stationery with respect to a transaction relating solely to his private law practice. The court noted that "the instances of proved misconduct did not assume egregious proportions. His improper intercession in the neighboring municipal court apparently did not result in any tangible or lasting distortion of justice" (382 A.2d at 1117).

5.23 Public reprimand is appropriate when a lawyer in an official or governmental position negligently fails to follow proper procedures or rules, and causes injury or potential injury to a party or to the integrity of the legal process.

Commentary

In In re Shafir, 92 N.J. 138, 455 A.2d 1114 (1983), the court imposed a public reprimand on a county prosecutor who improperly placed his supervisor's signature on forms filed in plea bargaining cases. The lawyer stated that he believed he had explicit or implicit authority to sign what he thought were internal records and the disciplinary committee found that the lawyer "was not motivated by personal gain but only by a desire to move cases on his trial list" (455 A.2d at 1116). Similarly, in State v. Socolofsky, 233 Kan. 1020, 666 P.2d 725 (1983), the court imposed a public censure [public reprimand] on a county attorney who anonymously mailed to discharged members of a jury a copy of a newspaper article describing that the acquitted defendant had subsequently pled guilty to a misdemeanor charge of delivery of L.S.D. in an unrelated case. Some of the jurors who received the mailing were called for service only a month later. The lawyer testified that he would not have mailed the article had he realized that the jurors were to be called for further service, and, that in his experience as a prosecutor, "he had never seen jurors called back for further duty so soon" (666 P.2d at 726).

5.24 Admonishment is appropriate when a lawyer in an official or governmental position negligently fails to follow proper procedures or rules, and causes little or no actual or potential injury to a party or to the integrity of the legal process.

STANDARD 6.0 VIOLATIONS OF DUTIES OWED TO THE LEGAL SYSTEM

Standard 6.1 False Statements, Fraud, and Misrepresentation

Absent aggravating or mitigating circumstances, and upon application of the factors set out in Standard 3.0, the following sanctions are generally appropriate in cases involving conduct that is prejudicial to the administration of justice or that involves dishonesty, fraud, deceit, or misrepresentation to a court:

6.11 Disbarment is appropriate when a lawyer:

a) with the intent to deceive the court, knowingly makes a false statement or submits a false document; or

b) improperly withholds material information, and causes serious or potentially serious injury to a party, or causes a significant or potentially significant adverse effect on the legal proceeding.

Commentary

The lawyers who engage in these practices violate the most fundamental duty of an officer of the court. As the court noted in a case in which a criminal defense lawyer was disbarred for putting a client on the stand to testify falsely, "A lawyer's participation in the presentation of knowing false evidence is the clearest kind of ethical breach" (Board of Overseers of the Bar v. James Dineen, No. 83–46 (Me. 1983) at 41. In Office of Disciplinary Counsel v. Grigsby, 493 Pa. 194, 425 A.2d 730 (1981), a lawyer was disbarred where he filed a false sworn pleading in connection with a pending garnishment proceeding. The pleading stated that the funds in the lawyer's checking account belonged to clients and could not be reached. The lawyer's action to save his money from garnishment was both intentional and damaging to his creditors. Similarly, in Matter of Discipline of Agnew, 311 N.W.2d 869 (Minn. 1981), the court disbarred a lawyer who refused to return a client's documents after an initial consultation and, without the client's knowledge or consent, then instituted a suit on his behalf in which he made false allegations that the client had been harmed by the defendant. Because of the lawyer's actions, the client incurred legal bills of $8,000 and lost time appearing in court to obtain his own documents.

6.12 Suspension is appropriate when a lawyer knows that false statements or documents are being submitted to the court or that material information is improperly being withheld, and takes no remedial action.

Commentary

Suspension is appropriate when a lawyer has not acted with intent to deceive the court, but when he knows that material information is being withheld and does not inform the court. For example, in In re Nigohosian, 88 N.J. 308, 442 A.2d 1007 (1982), the court suspended a lawyer for six (6) months when he failed to disclose to the court or to opposing counsel the fact that he had previously conveyed property that was the subject of a settlement to someone else. The court noted that, while a lawyer does not have a continuing obligation to inform the court of the state of a client's assets, he "has a duty of disclosure of any significant fact" touching upon the status of an asset which is the subject matter of a stipulation before the court (442 A.2d at 1009).

6.13 Public reprimand is appropriate when a lawyer is negligent either in determining whether statements or documents are false or in taking remedial action when material information is being withheld.

Commentary

Public Reprimand is appropriate when a lawyer is merely negligent. For example, in Gilbert E. Meltry, D.P. 144/81 (Mich. Atty. Dis. Brd. 1981), the lawyer was publicly reprimanded where he accidentally filed a motion for a bond which contained inaccurate statements. Similarly, in In re Coughlin, 91 N.J. 374, 450 A.2d 1326 (1982), the court held that a public reprimand should be imposed on a lawyer who did not follow proper procedures in acknowledging a deed (neglecting to secure the grantor's acknowledgment in his presence). The court noted that "his actions were not grounded on any intent of self-benefit, nor was anyone harmed as a result of his actions" (450 A.2d at 1327). In Davidson v. State Bar, 17 Cal.3d 570, 551 P.2d 1211, 131 Cal.Rptr. 379 (1976), the court imposed a public reprimand on a lawyer who failed to disclose to the court the location of his client in a child custody case when his conduct occurred in confused circumstances caused by contradictory ex parte custody orders.

6.14 Admonishment is appropriate when a lawyer is negligent in determining whether submitted statements or documents are false or in failing to disclose material information upon learning of its falsity, and causes little or no actual or potential injury to a party, or causes little or no adverse or potentially adverse effect on the legal proceeding.

Standard 6.2 Abuse of the Legal Process

Absent aggravating or mitigating circumstances, and upon application of the factors set out in Standard 3.0, the following sanctions are generally appropriate in cases involving failure to expedite litigation or bring a meritorious claim, or failure to obey any obligation under the rules of a tribunal except for an open refusal based on an assertion that no valid obligation exists:

6.21 Disbarment is appropriate when a lawyer knowingly violates a court order or rule with the intent to obtain a benefit for the lawyer or another, and causes serious injury or potentially serious injury to a party or causes serious or potentially serious interference with a legal proceeding.

Commentary

Lawyers should be disbarred for intentionally misusing the judicial process to benefit the lawyer or another when the lawyer's conduct causes injury or potentially serious injury to a party, or serious or potentially serious interference with a legal proceeding. For example, in In the Matter of Daniel Friedland, 416 N.E.2d 433 (Ind. 1981), the lawyer filed charges against members of the Disciplinary Committee and witnesses in the lawyer disciplinary hearing. The lawyer attempted to use the lawsuit to intimidate and discredit those who administered and prosecuted grievances against him. In holding that the lawyer was not protected by the First Amendment, the court recognized the harm to judicial integrity. "It is the Constitutional duty of this Court, on behalf of sovereign interest, to preserve, manage, and safeguard the adjudicatory system of this State. The adjudicatory process cannot function when its officers misconstrue the purpose of litigation. The respondent attempted to influence the process through the use of threats and intimidation against the participants involved. This type of conduct must be enjoined to preserve the integrity of the system. The adjudicatory process, including disciplinary proceedings, must permit the orderly resolution of issues; Respondent's conduct impeded the order of this process" (416 N.E.2d at 438). See also: In re Crumpacker, 269 Ind. 630, 383 N.E.2d 36 (1978), where the court disbarred a lawyer who had engaged in nineteen acts of misconduct, including shouting at and verbally abusing witnesses and opposing counsel, taking an action merely to harass another, and generally using offensive tactics. In the words of the court, his misconduct showed that he was "a vicious, sinister person, tunnel-visioned by personal pique, willing to forego all professional responsibilities which conflict with acts of preconceived vengeance on personal enemies" (383 N.E.2d at 52).

6.22 Suspension is appropriate when a lawyer knowingly violates a court order or rule, and causes injury or potential injury to a client or a party, or causes interference or potential interference with a legal proceeding.

Commentary

In many cases, lawyers are suspended when they knowingly violate court orders. Such knowing violations can occur when a lawyer fails to comply with a court order that applies directly to him or her, as in the case of lawyers who do not comply with a divorce decree ordering spousal maintenance or child support. Suspension is also appropriate where the lawyer interferes directly with the legal process. For example, in In re Vincenti, 92 N.J. 591, 458 A.2d 1268 (1983), the court imposed a suspension for one year and until further order of court where the lawyer made repeated discourteous, insulting and degrading verbal attacks on the judge and his rulings which substantially interfered with the orderly trial process. The court noted that it was not confronted with "an isolated example of loss of composure brought on by the emotion of the moment; rather, the numerous instances of impropriety pervaded the proceedings over a period of three months" (458 A.2d at 1274).

6.23 Public reprimand is appropriate when a lawyer negligently fails to comply with a court order or rule, and causes injury or potential injury to a client or other party, or causes interference or potential interference with a legal proceeding.

Commentary

Most courts impose a public reprimand on lawyers who engage in misconduct at trial or who violate a court order or rule that causes injury or potential injury to a client or other party, or who cause interference or potential interference with a legal proceeding. For example, in McDaniel v. State of Arkansas, 640 S.W.2d 442 (Ark. 1982), a lawyer who failed to file briefs in a timely manner after having been given extensions received a public reprimand. In The Florida Bar v. Rosenberg, 387 So.2d 935 (Fla. 1980), the court imposed a public reprimand on a lawyer who used harassing delay tactics at trial and who also refused to send copies of documents to opposing counsel. Courts also impose public reprimands when lawyers neglect to respond to orders of the disciplinary agency. For example, in In re Minor, 658 P.2d 781 (Alaska 1983), the court imposed a public censure [public reprimand] on a lawyer who, because of poor office procedures, neglected to respond to a letter from the Alaska Bar Association.

6.24 Admonishment is appropriate when a lawyer negligently fails to comply with a court order or rule, and causes little or no injury to a party, or causes little or no actual or potential interference with a legal proceeding.

Standard 6.3 Improper Communications With Individuals in the Legal System

Absent aggravating or mitigating circumstances, and upon application of the factors set out in Standard 3.0, the following sanctions are generally appropriate in cases involving attempts to influence a witness, judge, juror, prospective juror or other official by means prohibited by law:

6.31 Disbarment is appropriate when a lawyer:

a) intentionally directly or indirectly tampers with a witness; or

b) makes an unauthorized ex parte communication with a judge or juror with intent to affect the outcome of the proceeding.

Commentary

Disbarment is warranted in cases where the lawyer uses fraud or undue influence to injure a party or to affect the outcome of a legal proceeding. For example, in In the Matter of Stroh, 97 Wash.2d 289, 644 P.2d 1161 (1982), a lawyer was disbarred when he was convicted of tampering with a witness. The court justified imposing disbarment on the following basis: "First, the crime of tampering with a witness strikes at the very core of the judicial system and therefore necessarily involves moral turpitude . . . An attorney presents his case almost entirely through the testimony of witnesses. Although an occasional witness may perjure him/herself the presentation of the opponent's other witnesses and effective cross-examination frequently reveals the falsehood before a fraud has been perpetrated upon the court. A witness, tampered by an attorney, however, becomes much more destructive to the search for truth. That witness, privy to the testimony of other witnesses, can avoid the pitfalls of contradiction and refutation by judicious fabrication. Vigorous cross-examination may become ineffective as the coached witness would know both the questions and the proper answers. In sum, the legal system is virtually defenseless against the united forces of a corrupt attorney and a perjured witness" (644 P.2d at 1165). Similarly, in Matter of Holman, 286 S.E.2d 1 (S.C. 1982), a lawyer was disbarred who was convicted of contempt of court based on a communication with a member of a jury selected for trial.

6.32 Suspension is appropriate when a lawyer engages in communication with an individual in the legal system when the lawyer knows that such communication is improper, and causes injury or potential injury to a party or causes interference or potential interference with the outcome of the legal proceeding.

Commentary

In the case of John Arnold Fitzgerald (Tenn. 1980) (unpublished decision), a lawyer was suspended for one year for threats to an opposing party. Similarly, in The Florida Bar v. Lopez, 406 So.2d 1100 (Fla. 1982), a lawyer was suspended for one year where he urged two parties he was suing on behalf of his client to change their testimony in exchange for general releases from prosecution. In imposing this sanction, the court rejected a referee's recommendation of a three month suspension with automatic reinstatement, stating, "We feel that a three-month suspension is insufficient to impress upon respondent, the bar, and the public our dissatisfaction with and distress over his conduct. If Mr. Lopez had been convicted in a court of this state of tampering with a witness, he would have been subject to a one-year term of imprisonment. Using the witness-tampering statute as a guideline, we find a one-year suspension appropriate in this case" (406 So.2d at 1102). In *The Florida Bar v. Mason*, 334 So.2d 1 (Fla. 1976), the court imposed a reprimand and suspension for one year and until proof of rehabilitation when a lawyer engaged in ex parte communications with justices of the Florida Supreme Court concerning the merits of a pending case and subsequently concealed his actions from opposing counsel.

6.33 Public reprimand is appropriate when a lawyer is negligent in determining whether it is proper to engage in communication with an individual in the legal system, and causes injury or potential injury to a party or interference or potential interference with the outcome of the legal proceeding.

Commentary

Most courts impose public reprimands on lawyers who engage in improper communications. For example, in In re McCaffrey, 549 P.2d 666 (Or. 1976), the court imposed a public reprimand on a lawyer who unknowingly improperly communicated with a party represented by a lawyer. Even though the lawyer claimed that he thought the party, the husband in a dispute of visitation, was representing himself, the court stated that discipline could be imposed in cases of misconduct that the rule is designed to prevent, and it is "immaterial whether the communication is an intentional or a negligent violation of the rule" (549 P.2d at 668).

6.34 Admonishment is appropriate when a lawyer negligently engages in an improper communication with an individual in the legal system, and causes little or no actual or potential injury to a party, or causes little or no actual or potential interference with the outcome of the legal proceeding.

STANDARD 7.0 VIOLATIONS OF OTHER DUTIES OWED AS A PROFESSIONAL

Absent aggravating or mitigating circumstances, and upon application of the factors set out in Standard 3.0, the following sanctions are generally appropriate in cases involving false or misleading communication about the lawyer or the lawyer's services, improper communication of fields of practice, improper solicitation of professional employment from a prospective client, unreasonable or improper fees, unlicensed practice of law, improper withdrawal from representation, or failure to report professional misconduct.

7.1 Disbarment is appropriate when a lawyer intentionally engages in conduct that is a violation of a duty owed as a professional with the intent to obtain a benefit for the lawyer or another, and causes serious or potentially serious injury to a client, the public, or the legal system.

Commentary

Disbarment should be imposed in cases when the lawyer knowingly engages in conduct that violates a duty owed as professional with the intent to benefit the lawyer or another, and which causes serious injury or potentially serious injury to a client, the public or the legal system. For example, disbarment is appropriate when a lawyer intentionally makes false material statements in his application for admission to the bar. For example, in In re W. Jason Mitan, 75 Ill.2d 118, 387 N.E.2d 278 (1979), cert. denied, 444 U.S. 916 (1979), the respondent made false statements and deliberately failed to disclose certain information on his application for admission to the bar. These false statements and omissions included his failure to disclose at least four of his previous addresses, the wrong birth date, his change of name, a previous marriage, a subsequent divorce, other law schools attended, application for admission to another state's bar, previous employers and occupations, prior civil suits and arrests, and conviction of a felony. The court felt that these falsehoods and omissions had a direct effect on the ability to practice law and be a competent member of the profession, and imposed disbarment.

7.2 Suspension is appropriate when a lawyer knowingly engages in conduct that is a violation of a duty owed as a professional and causes injury or potential injury to a client, the public, or the legal system.

Commentary

Suspension is appropriate when the lawyer knowingly violates a duty owed as a professional and causes injury or potential injury to a client, the public, or the legal system, even when a lawyer does not intentionally abuse the professional relationship by engaging in deceptive conduct. Suspension is appropriate, for example, when the lawyer did not mislead a client but engages in a pattern of charging excessive or improper fees. A suspension is also appropriate when a lawyer solicits employment knowing that the individual is in a vulnerable state. For example, in In re Teichner, 75 Ill.2d 88, 387 N.E.2d 265 (1979), the court suspended a lawyer for two years who was invited by a minister to speak to victims of a railway disaster, but who then contacted victims whom he knew were still in a vulnerable state as a result of the tragedy.

7.3 Public reprimand is appropriate when a lawyer negligently engages in conduct that is a violation of a duty owed as a professional and causes injury or potential injury to a client, the public, or the legal system.

Commentary

Public Reprimand is the appropriate sanction in most cases of a violation of a duty owed as a professional. Usually there is little or no injury to a client, the public, or the legal system, and the purposes of lawyer discipline will be best served by imposing a public sanction that helps educate the respondent lawyer and deter future violations. A public sanction also informs both the public and other members of the profession that this behavior is improper. For example, in Carter v. Falcarelli, 402 A.2d 1175 (RI 1979), the court imposed public censure [public reprimand] on a lawyer who failed to divulge the identity of another lawyer when matters had been forwarded and subsequently neglected.

Courts typically impose public reprimands when lawyers engage in a single instance of charging an excessive or improper fee. See In the Matter of Donald L., 444 N.E.2d 849 (Ind. 1983), the court imposed a public reprimand where the lawyer entered into an agreement for a contingent fee in a criminal case; Russell Jr., DP 63 (Mich. Atty. Dis. Brd., 1983), where a lawyer charged an excessive fee by improperly adding investigation costs; and The Florida Bar v. Sagrans, 388 So.2d 1040 (Fla. 1980), where the lawyer improperly split fees with a chiropractor.

Courts also impose public reprimands on lawyers who are negligent in supervising their employees. For example, in the case of Donald Franklin Kotter, 52 Calif. State Bar J. 552–3 (Cal. 1977), the court imposed a public reproval [public reprimand] on a lawyer who neglected properly to instruct his employees regarding what acts constitute solicitation.

7.4 Admonishment is appropriate when a lawyer is negligent in determining whether the lawyer's conduct violates a duty owed as a professional, and causes little or no actual or potential injury to a client, the public, or the legal system.

STANDARD 8.0 PRIOR DISCIPLINE ORDERS

Absent aggravating or mitigating circumstances, and upon application of the factors set out in Standard 3.0, the following sanctions are generally appropriate in cases involving prior discipline:

8.1 Disbarment is appropriate when a lawyer:

a) intentionally violates the terms of a prior disciplinary order and such violation causes injury to a client, the public, the legal system, or the profession; or

b) has been suspended for the same or similar misconduct, and intentionally engages in further similar acts of misconduct.

Commentary

Disbarment is warranted when a lawyer who has previously been disciplined intentionally violates the terms of that order and, as a result, causes injury to a client, the public, the legal system, or the profession. The most common case is one where a lawyer has been suspended but, nevertheless, practices law. The courts are generally in agreement in imposing disbarment in such cases. As the court explained in Matter of McInerney, 389 Mass. 528, 451 N.E.2d 401, 405 (1983), when the record establishes a lawyer's willingness to violate the terms of his suspension order, disbarment is appropriate "as a prophylactic measure to prevent further misconduct by the offending individual." See also: In re Reiser, M.R. 2269 (Ill. 1980), where a lawyer was disbarred when he continued to practice law in violation of an order of suspension and caused serious injury to a client by neglecting her legal matter.

Disbarment is also appropriate when a lawyer intentionally engages in the same or similar misconduct. For example, in Benson v. State Bar, 13 Cal.3d 581, 531 P.2d 1081, 119 Cal.Rptr. 297 (1975), the court disbarred a lawyer who induced a client to loan him money by making false representations and who then failed to repay the loan. The lawyer in that case had previously been suspended for one year (with a four-year probationary period) for misappropriation of client funds. See also: Matter of Friedland, 416 N.E.2d 433 (Ind. 1981).

8.2 Suspension is appropriate when a lawyer has been publicly reprimanded for the same or similar conduct and engages in further similar acts of misconduct that cause injury or potential injury to a client, the public, the legal system, or the profession.

Commentary

Lawyers should be suspended when they engage in the same or similar misconduct for which they were previously disciplined when that misconduct causes injury or potential injury to a client, the public, the legal system, or the profession. As the court noted in The Florida Bar v. Glick, 397 So.2d 1140, 1141 (Fla. 1981), "[W]e must deal more severely with an attorney who exhibits cumulative misconduct."

8.3 Public reprimand is appropriate when a lawyer:

a) negligently violates the terms of a prior disciplinary order and such violation causes injury or potential injury to a client, the public, the legal system, or the profession; or

b) has received an admonishment for the same or similar misconduct and engages in further similar acts of misconduct.

Commentary

Public Reprimands are most commonly imposed on lawyers who have been disciplined and engage in the same or similar acts of misconduct. For example, in Shalant v. State Bar of California, 33 Cal.3d 485, 658 P.2d 737, 189 Cal.Rptr. 374 (1983), the court imposed a public reproval [public reprimand] on a lawyer who failed to communicate with a client and who had received a private reproval for the same misconduct. See also: Matter of Davis, 280 S.E.2d 644 (S.C. 1981), where the court explained that a public reprimand for neglect was necessary because prior warnings for similar behavior were "ignored" (280 S.E.2d at 647).

8.4 Admonishment is not an appropriate sanction when a lawyer violates the terms of a prior disciplinary order or when a lawyer has engaged in the same or similar misconduct in the past.

Commentary

Admonishment is a sanction which should only be imposed in cases of minor misconduct, where the lawyer's acts cause little or no injury to a client, the public, the legal system, or the profession, and where the lawyer is unlikely to engage in further misconduct. Lawyers who do engage in additional similar acts of misconduct, or who violate the terms of a prior disciplinary order, have obviously not been deterred, and a more severe sanction should be imposed.

STANDARD 9.0 AGGRAVATION AND MITIGATION

Standard 9.1. Generally

After misconduct has been established, aggravating and mitigating circumstances may be considered in deciding what sanction to impose.

Commentary

Each disciplinary case involves unique facts and circumstances. In striving for fair disciplinary sanctions, consideration must necessarily be given to the facts pertaining to the professional misconduct and to any aggravating or mitigating factors (see Standards for Lawyer Discipline, Standard 7.1). Aggravating and mitigating circumstances generally relate to the offense at issue, matters independent of the specific offense but relevant to fitness to practice, or matters arising incident to the disciplinary proceeding.

Standard 9.2. Aggravation

9.21 Definition. Aggravation or aggravating circumstances are any considerations or factors that may justify an increase in the degree of discipline to be imposed.

9.22 Factors which may be considered in aggravation. Aggravating factors include:

a) prior disciplinary offenses; provided that after 7 or more years in which no disciplinary sanction has been imposed, a finding of minor misconduct shall not be considered as an aggravating factor;

b) dishonest or selfish motive;

c) a pattern of misconduct;

d) multiple offenses;

e) bad faith obstruction of the disciplinary proceeding by intentionally failing to comply with rules or orders of the disciplinary agency;

f) submission of false evidence, false statements, or other deceptive practices during the disciplinary process;

g) refusal to acknowledge wrongful nature of conduct;

h) vulnerability of victim;

i) substantial experience in the practice of law;

j) indifference to making restitution;

k) obstruction of fee arbitration awards by refusing or intentionally failing to comply with a final award.

Commentary

Cases citing each of the factors listed above include: (a) prior disciplinary offenses: Matter of Walton, 251 N.W.2d 762 (N.D. 1977), People v. Vernon, 660 P.2d 879 (Colo. 1982); (b) dishonest or selfish motive: In re: James H. Dineen, SJC–535 (Me. 1980); (c) pattern of misconduct: The Florida Bar v. Mavrides, 442 So.2d 220 (Fla. 1983), State v. Dixon, 233 Kan. 465, 664 P.2d 286 (1983); (d) multiple offenses: State ex rel. Oklahoma Bar Association v. Warzya, 624 P.2d 1068 (Okla. 1981), Ballard v. State Bar of California, 35 Cal.3d 274, 673 P.2d 226, 197 Cal.Rptr. 556 (1983); (e) bad faith obstruction of disciplinary proceedings: In re Brody, 65 Ill.2d 152, 357 N.E.2d 498 (1976), Committee on Prof. Ethics v. Broadsky, 318 N.W.2d 180 (Iowa 1982); (f) lack candor during the disciplinary process: In re Stillo, 68 Ill.2d 49, 368 N.E.2d 897 (1977), Weir v. State Bar, 23 Cal.3d 564, 591 P.2d 19, 152 Cal.Rptr. 921 (1979); (g) refusal to acknowledge wrongful nature of conduct: Greenbaum v. State Bar, 18 Cal.3d 893, 544 P.2d 921, 126 Cal. Rptr. 785 (1976), H. Parker Stanley v. Bd. of Professional Responsibility, 640 S.W.2d 210 (Tenn. 1982); (h) vulnerability of victim: People v. Lanza, 613 P.2d 337 (Colo. 1980); (i) substantial experience in the practice of law: John F. Buckley, 2 Mass. Atty. Dis. Rpt. 24 (1980); (j) indifference to making restitution: The Florida Bar v. Zinzell, 387 So.2d 346 (Fla. 1980); Bate v. State Bar of California, 34 Cal.3d 920, 671 P.2d 360, 196 Cal.Rptr. 209 (1983).

Standard 9.3 Mitigation

9.31 Definition. Mitigation or mitigating circumstances are any considerations or factors that may justify a reduction in the degree of discipline to be imposed.

9.32 Factors which may be considered in mitigation. Mitigating factors include:

a) absence of a prior disciplinary record;

b) absence of a dishonest or selfish motive;

c) personal or emotional problems;

d) timely good faith effort to make restitution or to rectify consequences of misconduct;

e) full and free disclosure to disciplinary board or cooperative attitude toward proceedings;

f) inexperience in the practice of law;

g) character or reputation;

h) physical or mental disability or impairment;

i) unreasonable delay in disciplinary proceeding provided that the respondent did not substantially contribute to the delay and provided further that the respondent has demonstrated specific prejudice resulting from that delay;

j) interim rehabilitation;

k) imposition of other penalties or sanctions;

l) remorse;

m) remoteness of prior offenses;

n) prompt compliance with a fee arbitration award.

Commentary

While the courts generally agree that each of these factors can be considered in mitigation, the courts differ on whether restitution is a mitigating factor. Some courts hold that restitution should not be considered. See Ambrose v. State Bar, 31 Cal.3d 184, 643 P.2d 486, 481 Cal.Rptr. 903 (1982); Oklahoma Bar Association v. Lowe, 640 P.2d 1361 (Okla. 1982), In re Galloway, 300 S.E. 2d 479 (S.C. 1983). Other courts do consider restitution. See People v. Luxford, 626 P.2d 675 (Colo. 1981); The Florida Bar v. Pincket, 398 So.2d 802 (Fla. 1980); In re Suernick, 100 Wis.2d 427, 321 N.W. 2d 298 (1982). While restitution should not be a complete defense to a charge of misconduct, the better policy is to allow a good faith effort to make restitution to be considered as a factor in mitigation. Such a policy will encourage lawyers to make restitution, reducing the degree of injury to the client and his conduct. Restitution which is made upon the lawyer's own initiative should be considered as mitigating; lawyers who make restitution prior to the initiation of disciplinary proceedings present the best case for mitigation, while lawyers who make restitution later in the proceedings present a weaker case.

Cases citing personal and emotional problems as mitigating factors include a wide range of difficulties, most often involving marital or financial problems. The factor which has been treated most inconsistently by the courts is (h): physical/mental disability or impairment. The cases include the following types of behaviors or conditions: alcoholism, The Florida Bar v. Ullensvang, 400 So.2d 969 (Fla. 1981); mental disorders, In re Weyrich, 339 N.W.2d 274 (Minn. 1983); drug abuse, In re Hansen, 318 N.W.2d 856 (Minn.1982). While most courts treat such disabilities or impairments as mitigating factors, it is important to note that the consideration of these factors does not completely excuse the lawyer's misconduct. In the words of the Illinois Supreme Court, "alcoholism is at most an extenuating circumstance, a mitigating fact, not an excuse." In re Driscoll, 85 Ill.2d 312, 423 N.E.2d 873, 874 (1981).

Cases citing each of the factors listed above include: (a) absence of a prior disciplinary record: In re Battin, 617 P.2d 1109, 168 Cal.Rptr. 477 (180), The Florida Bar v. Shannon, 398 So.2d 453 (Fla. 1981); (b) absence of selfish or dishonest motive: People ex rel. Goldberg v. Gordon, 607 P.2d 995 (Colo. 1980); (c) personal/emotional problems: In re Stout, 75 N.J. 321, 382 A.2d 630 (1981), Matter of Barron, 246 Ga. 327, 271 S.E.2d 474 (1980); (d) timely good faith effort to make restitution or to rectify consequences of misconduct: Matter of Byars, 628 S.E.2d 155 (Ga. 1980), Matter of Rubi, 133 Ariz. 491, 652 P.2d 1014 (1982); (e) full and free disclosure to disciplinary board/cooperative attitude toward proceedings: Matter of Shaw, 298 N.W.2d 133 (Minn. 1980), In the Matter of Rhame, 416 N.E.2d 823 (Ind. 1981); (f) inexperience in the practice of law: In re James M. Pool, No. 83–37 BD (Sup. Jud. Ct. Suffolk Cty., Mass. 1984); Matter of Price, 429 N.E.2d 961 (Ind. 1982); (g) character/reputation: Matter of Shaw, 298 N.W.2d 133 (Minn. 1980), In re Bizar, 97 Ill.2d 127, 454 N.E.2d 271 (1983); (h) physical/mental disability or impairment: The Florida Bar v. Routh, 414 So.2d 1023 (Fla. 1982), In re Hopper, 85 Ill.2d 318, 423 N.E.2d 900 (1981); (i) delay in disciplinary proceedings: Yokozeki v. State Bar, 11 Cal.3d 436, 521 P.2d 858, 113 Cal.Rptr. 602 (1974), The Florida Bar v. Thomson, 429 So.2d 2 (Fla. 1983); (j) interim rehabilitation: In re Barry, 90 N.J. 286, 447 A. 2d 923 (1982), Tenner v. State Bar of California, 617 P.2d 486, 168 Cal.Rptr. 333 (1980); (k) imposition of other penalties or sanctions: In re Lamberis, 93 Ill.2d 222, 443 N.E.2d 549 (1982), In re John E. Walsh, SJC–53.9 (Me. 1980); Matter of Garrett, 399 N.E.2d 369 (Ind. 1980); (*l*) remorse; In re Power, 91 N.J. 408, 451 A.2d 666 (1982), In re Nadler, 91 ll.2d 326, 438 N.E.2d 198 (1982); (m) remoteness of prior offenses: (no cases found).

Standard 9.4. Factors which are Neither Aggravating nor Mitigating

The following factors should not be considered as either aggravating or mitigating:

a) forced or compelled restitution;

b) agreeing to the client's demand for certain improper behavior or result;

c) withdrawal of complaint against the lawyer;

d) resignation prior to completion of disciplinary proceedings;

e) complainant's recommendation as to sanction;

f) failure of injured client to complain;

g) an award has been entered in a fee arbitration proceeding.

Commentary

While courts have considered each of these factors, the purposes of lawyer discipline are best served by viewing them as irrelevant to the imposition of a sanction. Lawyers who make restitution voluntarily and on their own initiative demonstrate both recognition of their ethical violation and their responsibility to the injured client or other party. Such conduct should be considered as mitigation (see Standard 8.32), even if the restitution is made in response to a complaint filed with the disciplinary agency. Lawyers who make restitution only after a disciplinary proceeding has been instituted against them, however, cannot be regarded as acting out of a sense of responsibility for their misconduct, but, instead, as attempting to circumvent the operation of the disciplinary system. Such conduct should not be considered in mitigation, See Fitzpatrick v. State Bar of California, 20 Cal.3d 73, 141 Cal.Rptr. 169, 569 P.2d 763 (1977); In re O'Bryant, 425 A.2d 1313 (D.C. 1981).

Similarly, mitigation should not include a lawyer's claim that "the client made me do it." Each lawyer is responsible for adhering to the ethical standards of the profession. Unethical conduct is much less likely to be deterred if lawyers can lessen or avoid the imposition of sanctions merely by blaming the client (see In re Price, 429 N.E.2d 961 (Ind. 1982); People v. Kennel, 648 P.2d 1065 (Colo. 1982)). In addition, neither the withdrawal of the complaint against the lawyer nor the lawyer's resignation prior to completion of disciplinary proceedings should mitigate the sanction imposed. In order for the public to be protected, sanctions must be imposed on lawyers who engage in unethical conduct. The mere fact that a complainant may have decided to withdraw a complaint should not result in a lesser sanction being imposed on a lawyer who has behaved unethically and from whom other members of the public need protection (see In re McWhorter, 405 Mich. 563, 275 N.W.2d 259 (1979), on reh'g, 407 Mich. 278, 284 N.W.2d 472 (1979)). Similarly, the lawyer's resignation is irrelevant; the purposes of deterrence and education can only be served if sanctions are imposed on all lawyers who violate ethical standards (see In re Johnson, 290 N.W.2d 604 (Minn. 1980) and In re Phillips, 452 A.2d 345 (D.C. 1982)).

The complainant's recommendation as to a sanction is a factor which should be neither aggravating nor mitigating. The consistency of sanctions cannot be assured if any individual's personal views concerning an appropriate sanction can either increase or decrease the severity of the sanction to be imposed by the court. Although the court should not consider the complainant's recommendation as to sanction, the complainant's feelings about the lawyer's misconduct need not be completely ignored. The complainant's views will be relevant and important in determining the amount of injury caused by the lawyer's misconduct, a factor which can be either aggravating (Standard 8.22(j)) or mitigating (Standard 8.32(i)).

Finally, the fact that an injured client has not complained should not serve as mitigation. The disciplinary system is designed to protect all members of the public. The fact that one injured person is willing to forgive and forget should not relieve or excuse the lawyer, who then has the capability of injuring others (see In re Krakauer, 81 N.J. 32, 404 A.2d 1137 (1979), State ex rel. Oklahoma Bar Association v. Braswell, 663 P.2d 1228 (Okla. 1983)).

STANDARD 10.0 STANDARDS FOR IMPOSING LAWYER SANCTIONS IN DRUG CASES

The following standard is to be used in the disposition of disciplinary cases involving "personal use and/or possession for personal use of controlled substances," *when no criminal conviction is obtained.* Standard 5.1 would remain in effect for felony convictions, sale or distribution violations and other criminal convictions.

10.1 Upon the initial contact between The Florida Bar and an accused attorney involving a disciplinary matter, the accused attorney will be advised of the existence of FLA, Inc., and informed that good faith, ongoing, supervised rehabilitation with FLA, Inc., (when appropriate) or a treatment program approved by FLA, Inc., (when appropriate) in an attempt at rehabilitation both prior to and subsequent to the case being forwarded to the grievance committee for investigation may be viewed as mitigation.

10.2 Absent aggravating or mitigating circumstances, a 91–day suspension followed by probation is appropriate when a lawyer engages in misdemeanor conduct involving controlled substances, regardless of the jurisdiction where such conduct occurs and regardless of whether or not the lawyer is formally prosecuted or convicted concerning said conduct.

10.3 Absent the existence of aggravating factors, the appropriate discipline for an attorney found guilty of felonious conduct as defined by Florida state law involving the personal use and/or possession of a controlled substance who has sought and obtained assistance from FLA, Inc., or a treatment program approved by FLA, Inc., as described in paragraph one above, would be as follows:

a) a suspension from the practice of law for a period of 91 days or 90 days if rehabilitation has been proven; and

b) a three-year period of probation, subject to possible early termination or extension of said probation, with a condition that the attorney enter into a rehabilitation contract with FLA, Inc., prior to reinstatement.

10.4 Reinstatement after the 91–day suspension imposed under either paragraph two or three above would take place on an expedited basis with a hearing before a referee.

The provisions of discipline enumerated in paragraphs two and three above would not be applicable to:

a) an accused attorney who has allegedly violated other disciplinary rules, i.e., theft of trust funds;

b) an accused attorney involved in conduct covered by Standard 5.11; and/or

c) an accused attorney where aggravating factors as defined below are found to exist.

Commentary

A lawyer whose ability to practice law may be impaired by alcohol or drug abuse should have a rehabilitative program available in which to seek treatment. The Florida Bar's program offering rehabilitative services is Florida Lawyers Assistance, Inc. (FLA, Inc.) A lawyer with an impairment problem may seek voluntary assistance by FLA, Inc., and this information will be kept confidential if the lawyer was not otherwise in the discipline system. However, if an accused attorney enters the discipline system in a case involving personal use and/or possession for personal use of a controlled substance, when no criminal conviction is obtained, The Florida Bar will advise the accused attorney of the existence of FLA, Inc. When appropriate, an attempt at rehabilitation may be viewed as mitigation. A lawyer engaging in a misdemeanor or felonious conduct, involving controlled substances, will be suspended from the practice of law. The length of the suspension may be influenced by mitigating and/or aggravating factors. However, a suspension may not be applicable to an accused attorney who has either allegedly violated other Rules Regulating The Florida Bar, such as theft of trust funds, or if the attorney was involved in conduct covered by Standard 5.11.

STANDARD 11.0 MITIGATING FACTORS

11.1 In addition to those matters of mitigation listed in Standard 9.32, good faith, ongoing supervised rehabilitation by the attorney, through FLA, Inc., and any treatment program(s) approved by FLA, Inc., whether or not the referral to said program(s) was initially made by FLA, Inc., occurring both before and after disciplinary proceedings have commenced may be considered as mitigation.

Commentary

The Florida Bar encourages all impaired attorneys to participate in FLA, Inc.'s supervised rehabilitation program or any treatment program(s) approved by FLA, Inc. The Florida Bar views such participation, occurring both before and after disciplinary proceedings have commenced, as mitigation.

STANDARD 12.0 AGGRAVATING FACTORS

12.1 In addition to those matters of aggravation listed in Standard 9.22, the following factors may be considered in aggravation:

a) involvement of client in the misconduct, irrespective of actual harm to the client;

b) actual harm to clients or third parties; and

c) refusal or failure by the attorney to obtain, in good faith, ongoing, supervised rehabilitation (where appropriate), even after investigation by the Bar and prior to hearing before the referee or entry of the consent judgment.

Commentary

The Florida Bar's commitment to rehabilitation is reflected in that the attorney's failure or refusal to participate in rehabilitation may be considered as aggravation. An aggravating factor may also include conduct by an attorney which results in actual harm to clients or third parties. Moreover, a client's involvement in the misconduct may be considered as aggravation whether or not the client was actually harmed.

STANDARD 13.0 STANDARDS FOR IMPOSING LAWYER SANCTIONS IN ADVERTISING AND SOLITATION[1] RULE VIOLATIONS

The following standard is to be used in the disposition of disciplinary cases involving violations of rules relating to lawyer advertising and solicitation. This standard is not intended to replace or alter the provisions of any other portions of the Florida Standards for Imposing Lawyer Sanctions. These standards are intended as a guide for bar counsel, the board of governors, referees, and the court in determining a recommendation or imposition of appropriate discipline. While the provisions of these standards shall be consulted in each applicable case, and should be applied consistently, these standards should not be viewed as a type of sentencing guideline from which no departure is authorized.

For purposes of these standards "negligently fails to file" includes only those circumstances in which the lawyer engaging in the activity has not previously filed an advertising or direct mail communication as required by applicable rules and is unaware of that requirement. All other circumstances described in these standards shall be considered as knowing action or knowing failure to act.

For purposes of this standard "solicitation" shall have the same meaning as "solicit" as that term is defined in the Rules Regulating The Florida Bar. The term also includes these actions when engaged in by an agent of the lawyer.

For purposes of this standard "direct mail communication" shall include written or electronic communications as described in the Rules Regulating The Florida Bar.

ADVERTISEMENTS

Absent mitigating or aggravating circumstances, and upon application of the factors set out in Standard 3.0, the following sanctions are generally appropriate in cases involving an advertisement that violates applicable rules:

13.1 Diversion to a practice and professionalism program or minor misconduct is appropriate:

a) when a lawyer fails to file an advertisement for review that is otherwise in compliance with applicable rules;

b) when a lawyer negligently fails to include the disclosure statement required for all non-exempt public print media advertisements and no other violation of applicable rules is involved;

c) when a lawyer fails to include one or more of the following in an advertisement, provided that no other violation of applicable rules is involved:

1) the name of at least 1 lawyer responsible for the content of the advertisement; or

2) the location of 1 or more bona fide offices of the lawyer or lawyers who will actually perform the services that are the subject of the advertisement; or

3) the required information in all applicable languages.

d) when an advertisement:

1) contains an illustration that is not objectively relevant to the need for legal services in specific matters, provided the illustration does not involve fraud, deceit, or misrepresentation;

2) contains a verbal or visual description, depiction, or portrayal that is not objectively relevant to the selection of an attorney, provided that the description, depiction, or portrayal does not involve fraud, deceit, misrepresentation or manipulation; or

3) contains a statement concerning fees for legal services but does not disclose the responsibility for costs associated with legal services;

4) contains a statement that characterizes the quality of legal services, except for information on request.

e) when an advertisement in the electronic media, provided no other violation of applicable rules exists:

1) is articulated in more than one human voice; or

2) contains prohibited background sound; or

3) uses the voice or image of a person other than a lawyer who is a member of the firm whose services are advertised; or

4) contains a prohibited background or location for the advertisement.

f) when an advertisement:

1) contains information concerning an area practice in which the lawyer does not currently engage in the practice of law;

2) states or implies that the lawyer is a specialist, unless the lawyer is certified by The Florida Bar or an organization whose certification program has been accredited by the ABA;

3) fails to contain an indication that the matter will be referred to another lawyer or law firm if that is the case;

4) sets forth a fee schedule that the lawyer fails to honor for at least one year for yellow pages and other advertisements that are published annually and at least ninety (90) days for other advertisements, unless the advertisement specifies a shorter period of time;

5) contains a law firm name that is prohibited by the Rules Regulating The Florida Bar;

6) contains a trade name that does not appear on the lawyer's letterhead, business cards, office sign, and fee contracts or does not appear with the lawyer's signature on pleadings and other documents;

7) is paid for, in whole or in part, by a lawyer who is not in a firm whose services are being advertised;

8) contains a statement concerning past success or otherwise creates an unjust expectation as to results that may be obtained;

9) contains statements comparing the services of the advertising lawyer to the services of other lawyers, unless the comparison may be factually substantiated;

10) contains a testimonial;

11) contains statements or claims that are potentially false and misleading;

12) contains statements or claims that are unsubstantiated; or

13) fails to disclose material information that is necessary to prevent the advertisement from being actually or potentially false or misleading.

g) when a lawyer negligently fails to file an advertisement for review and the advertisement contains a violation that does not constitute fraud, deceit, or misrepresentation.

h) when another violation of applicable rules is involved that does not constitute fraud, deceit, or misrepresentation and a lawyer negligently fails to include the disclosure statement required for all non-exempt public print media advertisements.

13.2 Public Reprimand is appropriate:

a) when a lawyer knowingly fails to include the disclosure statement required for all non-exempt public print media advertisements, provided that no violation of applicable rules constituting fraud, deceit, or misrepresentation is also involved.

b) when a lawyer knowingly fails to file multiple advertisements for review and the advertisements are otherwise in compliance with the applicable rules.

c) when a lawyer negligently fails to file an advertisement or for review and the advertisement involves fraud, deceit, or misrepresentation, but does not result in actual injury.

d) when another violation of applicable rules involving fraud, deceit or misrepresentation exists and the advertisement in the electronic media:

1) is articulated in more than one human voice; or

2) contains prohibited background sound; or

3) uses the voice or image of a person other than a lawyer who is a member of the firm whose services are advertised; or

4) contains a prohibited background or location for the advertisement.

13.3 Suspension is appropriate:

a) when a lawyer negligently fails to file an advertisement for review and the advertisement involves fraud, deceit, or misrepresentation, and results in potential for or actual injury;

b) when another violation of applicable rules is involved that constitutes fraud, deceit, or misrepresentation and a lawyer negligently fails to include the disclosure statement required for all non-exempt public print media advertisements;

c) when an advertisement:

1) contains a material misrepresentation or omission of facts necessary to avoid a material misrepresentation;

2) contains statements or implications that the lawyer may achieve results by means of violation of the Rules Regulating The Florida Bar;

3) contains statements that are directly or impliedly false or misleading; or

4) contains unfair or deceptive statements or claims.

13.4 Rehabilitation Suspension is appropriate:

a) when a lawyer knowingly fails to file an advertisement for review and the advertisement involves fraud, deceit, or misrepresentation that results in actual injury.

b) when another violation of applicable rules is involved that constitutes fraud, deceit, or misrepresentation and a lawyer knowingly fails to include the disclosure statement required for all non-exempt public print media advertisements.

DIRECT MAIL COMMUNICATIONS

13.5 Diversion to a practice and professionalism enhancement program or minor misconduct is appropriate:

a) when a lawyer fails to file a direct mail communication that is otherwise in compliance with applicable rules.

b) when a lawyer fails to include in a direct mail communication, provided that no other violation of applicable rules is involved:

1) the name of at least 1 lawyer responsible for the content of the direct mail communication;

2) the location of 1 or more bonafide offices of the lawyer or lawyers who will actually perform the services that are the subject of the direct mail communication;

3) the required information in all applicable languages;

4) the word "advertisement" in red ink on the first page of the direct mail communication, except for electronic mail communications;

5) the word "advertisement" in red ink in the lower left-hand corner of the envelope containing the direct mail communication, except for electronic mail communications;

6) the words "legal advertisement" as the subject line of an electronic mail communication;

7) a written statement detailing the background, training and experience of the lawyer or law firm;

8) information outlining the specific experience of the advertising lawyer or law firm in the area of law being advertised;

9) the word "SAMPLE" in red ink in type size 1 size larger than the largest type used in the contract if a contract is enclosed;

10) the words "DO NOT SIGN" on the signature line of a contract for legal services if a contract is enclosed;

11) as the first sentence of the direct mail communication: "If you have already retained a lawyer for this matter, please disregard this letter" if the direct mail communication is prompted by a specific occurrence; or

12) a statement advising the recipient how the lawyer obtained the information prompting the direct mail communication is prompted by a specific occurrence.

c) when a lawyer negligently fails to file a direct mail communication that violates applicable rules, but does not constitute fraud, deceit, or misrepresentation.

d) when a direct mail communication:

1) contains an illustration that is not objectively relevant to the need for legal services in specific matters, provided the illustration does not involve fraud, deceit, or misrepresentation;

2) contains a verbal or visual description, depiction, or portrayal that is not objectively relevant to the selection of an attorney, provided that the description, depiction, or portrayal does not involve fraud, deceit, misrepresentation or manipulation; or

3) contains a statement concerning fees for legal services but does not disclose the responsibility for costs associated with legal services;

4) contains a statement that characterizes the quality of legal service;

5) contains information concerning an area practice in which the lawyer does not currently engage in the practice of law;

6) states or implies that the lawyer is a specialist, unless the lawyer is certified by The Florida Bar or an organization whose certification program has been accredited by the ABA;

7) fails to contain an indication that the matter will be referred to another lawyer or law firm if that is the case;

8) sets forth a fee schedule that the lawyer fails to honor for at least 90 days unless the direct mail communication specifies a shorter period of time;

9) contains a law firm name that is prohibited by the Rules Regulating The Florida Bar;

10) contains a trade name that does not appear on the lawyer's letterhead, business cards, office sign, and fee contracts or does not appear with the lawyer's signature on pleadings and other documents;

11) is paid for, in whole or in part, by a lawyer who is not in a firm whose services are being advertised;

12) contains a statement concerning past success or otherwise creates an unjust expectation as to results that may be obtained;

13) contains statements comparing the services of the advertising lawyer to the services of other lawyers, unless the comparison may be factually substantiated;

14) contains a testimonial;

15) contains statements or claims that are potentially false and misleading;

16) contains statements or claims that are unsubstantiated; or

17) fails to disclose material information that is necessary to prevent the advertisement from being actually or potentially false or misleading.

e) when a lawyer knowingly fails to include the disclosure statement required for all non-exempt public print media direct mail communications, provided that no other violation of applicable rules is involved.

f) when a lawyer, provided that no other violation of applicable rules is involved:

1) sends a direct mail communication concerning a personal injury, wrongful death, accident or disaster within 30 days of the incident; or

2) sends a direct mail communication when the lawyer knows that the recipient does not want to receive direct mail communications from the lawyer; or

3) sends a direct mail communication when the lawyer knows or reasonably should know that the recipient is unlikely to use reasonable judgment in employing a lawyer because of the person's physical, emotional or mental state; or

4) sends a direct mail communication by registered mail or other restricted delivery; or

5) states or implies that the direct mail communication has received approval from The Florida Bar; or

6) sends a direct mail communication that resembles legal pleadings or legal documents, except for electronic mail communications; or

7) reveals the nature of the prospective client's legal problem on the outside of a direct mail communication if prompted by a specific occurrence, except for electronic mail communications.

13.6 Public Reprimand is appropriate:

a) when a lawyer fails to include 2 or more of the following required information, provided no other violation of applicable rules is involved:

1) the name of at least 1 lawyer responsible for the content of the direct mail communication; or

2) the location of 1 or more bonafide offices of the lawyer or lawyers who will actually perform the services that are the subject of the direct mail communication; or

3) the required information in all applicable languages; or

4) the word "advertisement" in red ink on the first page of the direct mail communication; or

5) the word "advertisement" in red ink in the lower left-hand corner of the envelope containing the direct mail communication; or

6) a written statement detailing the background, training and experience of the lawyer or law firm; or

7) information outlining the specific experience of the advertising lawyer or law firm in the area of law being advertised; or

8) the word "SAMPLE" in red ink in type size 1 size larger than the largest type used in the contract if a contract is enclosed; or

9) the words "DO NOT SIGN" on the signature line of a contract for legal services if a contract is enclosed; or

10) as the first sentence of the direct mail communication; "If you have already retained a lawyer for this matter, please disregard this letter" if the direct mail communication is prompted by a specific occurrence; or

11) an indication that the matter will be referred to another lawyer or law firm if that is the case; or

12) a statement advising the recipient how the lawyer obtained the information prompting the direct mail communication if the direct mail communication is prompted by a specific occurrence.

b) when a lawyer knowingly fails to file a direct mail communication that contains violation of applicable rules that does not constitute fraud, deceit, or misrepresentation.

c) when a lawyer negligently fails to file a direct mail communication for review and the direct mail communication involves fraud, deceit, or misrepresentation, but does not result in actual injury.

d) when a direct mail communication:

1) contains a material misrepresentation or omission of facts necessary to avoid a material misrepresentation;

2) contains statements or implications that the lawyer may achieve results by means of violation of the Rules Regulating The Florida Bar;

3) contains statements that are directly or impliedly false or misleading;

4) contains unfair or deceptive statements or claims.

13.7 Suspension is appropriate:

a) when a lawyer knowingly fails to file multiple direct mail communications (for this standard "multiple" shall include the same direct mail communication sent to more than one party) for review and the direct mail communications are otherwise in compliance with the applicable rules;

b) when a lawyer negligently fails to file a direct mail communication for review, the direct mail communication involves fraud, deceit, or misrepresentation, and results in actual injury.

13.8 Rehabilitation Suspension is appropriate:

a) when a lawyer negligently fails to file a direct mail communication for review and the direct mail communication involves fraud, deceit, or misrepresentation that results in actual injury.

SOLICITATION VIOLATIONS

Absent mitigating or aggravating circumstances, and upon application of the factors set out in Standard 3.0, the following sanctions are generally appropriate in cases of solicitation:

13.9 Diversion is appropriate:

a) when a lawyer negligently fails to adequately supervise employees or agents who engage in solicitation that does not involve fraud, deceit or misrepresentation, and results in no actual injury.

13.10 Public Reprimand is appropriate:

a) when a lawyer is negligent in supervising employees or agents who engage in solicitation involving fraud, deceit, or misrepresentation regardless of whether actual injury occurs.

b) when a lawyer knowingly and personally engages in solicitation that does not involve fraud, deceit, or misrepresentation or through an employee or agent, and results in no actual injury.

13.11 Suspension is appropriate:

a) when a lawyer knowingly engages in solicitation that does not involve fraud, deceit, or misrepresentation, that involves another violation of the Rules Regulating The Florida Bar, but results in no actual injury.

13.12 Rehabilitation Suspension is appropriate:

a) when a lawyer engages in solicitation that involves fraud, deceit, or misrepresentation, or another violation of the Rules Regulating The Florida Bar, and results in actual injury.

INFORMATION ON REQUEST

Absent mitigating and aggravating circumstances, and upon application of the factors set out in Standard 3.0, the following sanctions are generally appropriate for information provided to a prospective client on that person's request:

13.13 Diversion to a practice and professionalism enhancement program or minor misconduct is appropriate:

a) when information provided on request:

1) fails to disclose the name of at least 1 lawyer responsible for the content;

2) fails to disclose the location of 1 or more bonafide office locations of lawyer or law firm;

3) fails to disclose all jurisdictions in which the lawyers or members of the law firm are licensed to practice in a website or homepage sponsored by the lawyer or law firm;

4) contains an illustration that is not objectively relevant to the need for legal services in specific matters, provided the illustration does not involve fraud, deceit, or misrepresentation;

5) contains a verbal or visual description, depiction, or portrayal that is not objectively relevant to the selection of an attorney, provided that the description, depiction, or portrayal does not involve fraud, deceit, misrepresentation or manipulation; or

6) contains a statement concerning fees for legal services but does not disclose the responsibility for costs associated with legal services;

7) contains an illustration that is not objectively relevant to the need for legal services in specific matters, provided the illustration does not involve fraud, deceit, or misrepresentation;

8) contains a verbal or visual description, depiction, or portrayal that is not objectively relevant to the selection of an attorney, provided that the description, depiction, or portrayal does not involve fraud, deceit, misrepresentation or manipulation;

9) contains a statement concerning fees for legal services but does not disclose the responsibility for costs associated with legal service;

10) contains information concerning an area practice in which the lawyer does not currently engage in the practice of law;

11) states or implies that the lawyer is a specialist, unless the lawyer is certified by The Florida Bar or an organization whose certification program has been accredited by the ABA;

12) fails to contain an indication that the matter will be referred to another lawyer or law firm if that is the case;

13) sets forth a fee schedule that the lawyer fails to honor for at least one year for yellow pages and other advertisements that are published annually and at least 90 days for other advertisements and direct mail communications, unless the advertisement specifies a shorter period of time;

14) contains a law firm name that is prohibited by the Rules Regulating The Florida Bar;

15) contains a trade name that does not appear on the lawyer's letterhead, business cards, office sign, and fee contracts or does not appear with the lawyer's signature on pleadings and other documents;

16) is paid for, in whole or in part, by a lawyer who is not in a firm whose services are being advertised;

17) creates an unjustified expectation as to results that may be obtained;

18) contains statements comparing the services of the advertising lawyer to the services of other lawyers, unless the comparison may be factually substantiated;

19) contains a testimonial;

20) contains statements or claims that are potentially false and misleading;

21) contains statements or claims that are unsubstantiated; or

22) fails to disclose material information that is necessary to prevent the advertisement from being actually or potentially false or misleading.

13.14 Public Reprimand is appropriate:

a) when information on request involves a violation that constitutes fraud, deceit, or misrepresentation, and negligently:

1) fails to disclose the name of at least 1 lawyer responsible for the content;

2) fails to disclose the location of 1 or more bonafide office locations of lawyer or law firm;

3) fails to disclose all jurisdictions in which the lawyers or members of the law firm are licensed to practice in a website or home page sponsored by the lawyer or law firm.

b) when information on request:

1) contains a material misrepresentation or omission of facts necessary to avoid a material misrepresentation;

2) contains statements or implications that the lawyer may achieve results by means of violation of the Rules Regulating The Florida Bar;

3) contains statements that are directly or impliedly false or misleading;

4) contains unfair or deceptive statements or claims.

13.15 Suspension is appropriate:

a) when information on request involves a violation that constitutes fraud, deceit, or misrepresentation, and knowingly:

1) fails to disclose the name of at least 1 lawyer responsible for the content;

2) fails to disclose the location of 1 or more bonafide office locations of lawyer or law firm; or

3) fails to disclose all jurisdictions in which the lawyers or members of the law firm are licensed to practice in a website or home page sponsored by the lawyer or law firm.

FORFEITURE OF FEES

13.16 In addition to any sanction provided by these standards, the fee obtained from legal representation secured by use of an advertisement or direct mail communication that contains any knowing violation of applicable rules, other than knowing failure to file, or involves fraud, deceit, or misrepresentation may be forfeited as provided in the Rules Regulating The Florida Bar.

13.17 In addition to any sanction provided by these standards, the fee obtained from legal representation secured by direct solicitation, personally or by an agent, may be forfeited as provided in the Rules Regulating The Florida Bar.

MITIGATION AND AGGRAVATION

13.18 Mitigating and aggravating factors, as provided elsewhere in the Florida Standards For Imposing Lawyer Sanctions, are applicable to matters involving sanctions imposed for lawyer advertising and solicitation rule violations. In addition to those factors the following may be considered in mitigation:

a) the respondent had a good faith claim or belief that the advertisement or direct mail communication was exempt from the filing requirements;

b) no prior guidance in the form of a court order or opinion interpreting the applicable advertising or solicitation rules was available when the respondent disseminated the advertisement or direct mail communication in question and ethics counsel was unable to render an opinion.

c) the respondent sought guidance from The Florida Bar and followed the advice given in respect of advertising, direct mail communications, or solicitation, even though such advice may have ceased to be accurate or may have been erroneous at the time it was given.

[1] So in original.

CODE OF JUDICIAL CONDUCT

Date Effective

Adopted Sept. 29, 1994, effective Jan. 1, 1995 (643 So.2d 1037)

Preamble

Our legal system is based on the principle that an independent, fair and competent judiciary will interpret and apply the laws that govern us. The role of the judiciary is central to American concepts of justice and the rule of law. Intrinsic to all sections of this Code are the precepts that judges, individually and collectively, must respect and honor the judicial office as a public trust and strive to enhance and maintain confidence in our legal system. The judge is an arbiter of facts and law for the resolution of disputes and a highly visible symbol of government under the rule of law.

The Code of Judicial Conduct establishes standards for ethical conduct of judges. It consists of broad statements called Canons, specific rules set forth in Sections under each Canon, a Definitions Section, an Application Section and Commentary. The text of the Canons and the Sections, including the Definitions and Application Sections, is authoritative. The Commentary, by explanation and example, provides guidance with respect to the purpose and meaning of the Canons and Sections. The Commentary is not intended as a statement of additional rules. When the text uses "shall" or "shall not," it is intended to impose binding obligations the violation of which, if proven, can result in disciplinary action. When "should" or "should not" is used, the text is intended as hortatory and as a statement of what is or is not appropriate conduct but not as a binding rule under which a judge may be disciplined. When "may" is used, it denotes permissible discretion or, depending on the context, it refers to action that is not covered by specific proscriptions.

The Canons and Sections are rules of reason. They should be applied consistent with constitutional requirements, statutes, other court rules and decisional law and in the context of all relevant circumstances. The Code is not to be construed to impinge on the essential independence of judges in making judicial decisions.

The Code is designed to provide guidance to judges and candidates for judicial office and to provide a structure for regulating conduct through disciplinary agencies. It is not designed or intended as a basis for civil liability or criminal prosecution. Furthermore, the purpose of the Code would be subverted if the Code were invoked by lawyers for mere tactical advantage in a proceeding.

The text of the Canons and Sections is intended to govern conduct of judges and to be binding upon them. It is not intended, however, that every transgression will result in disciplinary action. Whether disciplinary action is appropriate, and the degree of discipline to be imposed, should be determined through a reasonable and reasoned application of the text and should depend on such factors as the seriousness of the transgression, whether there is a pattern of improper activity and the effect of the improper activity on others or on the judicial system.

The Code of Judicial Conduct is not intended as an exhaustive guide for the conduct of judges. They should also be governed in their judicial and personal conduct by general ethical standards. The Code is intended, however, to state basic standards which should govern the conduct of all judges and to provide guidance to assist judges in establishing and maintaining high standards of judicial and personal conduct.

Definitions

"Appropriate authority" denotes the authority with responsibility for initiation of disciplinary process with respect to the violation to be reported.

"Candidate." A candidate is a person seeking selection for or retention in judicial office by election or appointment. A person becomes a candidate for judicial office as soon as he or she makes a public announcement of candidacy, opens a campaign account as defined by Florida law, declares or files as a candidate with the election or appointment authority, or authorizes solicitation or acceptance of contributions or support. The term "candidate" has the same meaning when applied to a judge seeking election or appointment to nonjudicial office.

"Court personnel" does not include the lawyers in a proceeding before a judge.

"De minimis" denotes an insignificant interest that could not raise reasonable question as to a judge's impartiality.

"Economic interest" denotes ownership of a more than de minimis legal or equitable interest, or a relationship as officer, director, advisor, or other active participant in the affairs of a party, except that:

(i) ownership of an interest in a mutual or common investment fund that holds securities is not an economic interest in such securities unless the judge participates in the management of the fund or a proceeding pending or impending before the judge could substantially affect the value of the interest;

(ii) service by a judge as an officer, director, advisor, or other active participant in an educational, religious, charitable, fraternal, sororal, or civic organization, or service by a judge's spouse, parent, or child as an officer, director, advisor, or other active participant in any organization does not create an economic interest in securities held by that organization;

(iii) a deposit in a financial institution, the proprietary interest of a policy holder in a mutual insurance company, of a depositor in a mutual savings association, or of a member in a credit union, or a similar proprietary interest, is not an economic interest in the organization unless a proceeding pending or impending before the judge could substantially affect the value of the interest;

(iv) ownership of government securities is not an economic interest in the issuer unless a proceeding pending or impending before the judge could substantially affect the value of the securities.

"Fiduciary" includes such relationships as personal representative, administrator, trustee, guardian, and attorney in fact.

"Impartiality" or "impartial" denotes absence of bias or prejudice in favor of, or against, particular parties or classes of parties, as well as maintaining an open mind in considering issues that may come before the judge.

"Judge." When used herein this term means Article V, Florida Constitution judges and, where applicable, those persons performing judicial functions under the direction or supervision of an Article V judge.

"Knowingly," "knowledge," "known," or "knows" denotes actual knowledge of the fact in question. A person's knowledge may be inferred from circumstances.

"Law" denotes court rules as well as statutes, constitutional provisions, and decisional law.

"Member of the candidate's family" denotes a spouse, child, grandchild, parent, grandparent, or other relative or person with whom the candidate maintains a close familial relationship.

"Member of the judge's family" denotes a spouse, child, grandchild, parent, grandparent, or other relative or person with whom the judge maintains a close familial relationship.

"Member of the judge's family residing in the judge's household" denotes any relative of a judge by blood or marriage, or a person treated by a judge as a member of the judge's family, who resides in the judge's household.

"Nonpublic information" denotes information that, by law, is not available to the public. Nonpublic information may include but is not limited to: information that is sealed by statute or court order, impounded or communicated in camera; and information offered in grand jury proceedings, presentencing reports, dependency cases, or psychiatric reports.

"Political organization" denotes a political party or other group, the principal purpose of which is to further the election or appointment of candidates to political office.

"Public election." This term includes primary and general elections; it includes partisan elections, nonpartisan elections, and retention elections.

"Require." The rules prescribing that a judge "require" certain conduct of others are, like all of the rules in this Code, rules of reason. The use of the term "require" in that context means a judge is to exercise reasonable direction and control over the conduct of those persons subject to the judge's direction and control.

"Third degree of relationship." The following persons are relatives within the third degree of relationship: great-grandparent, grandparent, parent, uncle, aunt, brother, sister, child, grandchild, great-grandchild, nephew, or niece.

Amended Jan. 5, 2006 (918 So.2d 949).

Canon 1. A Judge Shall Uphold the Integrity and Independence of the Judiciary

An independent and honorable judiciary is indispensable to justice in our society. A judge should participate in establishing, maintaining, and enforcing high standards of conduct, and shall personally observe those standards so that the integrity and independence of the judiciary may be preserved. The provisions of this Code should be construed and applied to further that objective.

Amended Jan. 5, 2006 (918 So.2d 949).

Commentary

Deference to the judgments and rulings of courts depends upon public confidence in the integrity and independence of judges. The integrity and independence of judges depend in turn upon their acting without fear or favor. Although judges should be independent, they must comply with the law, including the provisions of this Code. Public confidence in the impartiality of the judiciary is maintained by the adherence of each judge to this responsibility. Conversely, violation of this Code diminishes public confidence in the judiciary and thereby does injury to the system of government under law.

Canon 2. A Judge Shall Avoid Impropriety and the Appearance of Impropriety in all of the Judge's Activities

A. A judge shall respect and comply with the law and shall act at all times in a manner that promotes public confidence in the integrity and impartiality of the judiciary.

B. A judge shall not allow family, social, political or other relationships to influence the judge's judicial conduct or judgment. A judge shall not lend the prestige of judicial office to advance the private interests of the judge or others; nor shall a judge convey or permit others to convey the impression that they are in a special position to influence the judge. A judge shall not testify voluntarily as a character witness.

C. A judge should not hold membership in an organization that practices invidious discrimination on the basis of race, sex, religion, or national origin. Membership in a fraternal, sororal, religious, or ethnic heritage organization shall not be deemed to be a violation of this provision.

Amended Jan. 5, 2006 (918 So.2d 949).

Commentary

Canon 2A. Irresponsible or improper conduct by judges erodes public confidence in the judiciary. A judge must avoid all impropriety and appearance of impropriety. A judge must expect to be the subject of constant public scrutiny. A judge must therefore accept restrictions on the judge's conduct that might be viewed as burdensome by the ordinary citizen and should do so freely and willingly. Examples are the restrictions on judicial speech imposed by Sections 3B(9) and (10) that are indispensable to the maintenance of the integrity, impartiality, and independence of the judiciary.

The prohibition against behaving with impropriety or the appearance of impropriety applies to both the professional and personal conduct of a judge. Because it is not practicable to list all prohibited acts, the proscription is necessarily cast in general terms that extend to conduct by judges that is harmful although not specifically mentioned in the Code. Actual improprieties under this standard include violations of law, court rules, or other specific provisions of this Code. The test for appearance of impropriety is whether the conduct would create in reasonable minds, with knowledge of all the relevant circumstances that a reasonable inquiry would disclose, a perception that the judge's ability to carry out judicial responsibilities with integrity, impartiality, and competence is impaired.

See also Commentary under Section 2C.

Canon 2B. Maintaining the prestige of judicial office is essential to a system of government in which the judiciary functions independently of the executive and legislative branches. Respect for the judicial office facilitates the orderly conduct of legitimate judicial functions. Judges should distinguish between proper and improper use of the prestige of office in all of their activities. For example, it would be improper for a judge to allude to his or her judgeship to gain a personal advantage such as deferential treatment when stopped by a police officer for a traffic offense. Similarly, judicial letterhead must not be used for conducting a judge's personal business, although a judge may use judicial letterhead to write character reference letters when such letters are otherwise permitted under this Code.

A judge must avoid lending the prestige of judicial office for the advancement of the private interests of others. For example, a judge must not use the judge's judicial position to gain advantage in a civil suit involving a member of the judge's family. In contracts for publication of a judge's writings, a judge should retain control over the advertising to avoid exploitation of the judge's office. As to the acceptance of awards, see Section 5D(5) and Commentary.

Although a judge should be sensitive to possible abuse of the prestige of office, a judge may, based on the judge's personal knowledge, serve as a reference or provide a letter of recommendation. However, a judge must not initiate the communication of information to a sentencing judge or a probation or corrections officer but may provide to such persons information for the record in response to a formal request.

Judges may participate in the process of judicial selection by cooperating with appointing authorities and screening committees seeking names for consideration, and by responding to official inquiries concerning a person being considered for a judgeship. See also Canon 7 regarding use of a judge's name in political activities.

A judge must not testify voluntarily as a character witness because to do so may lend the prestige of the judicial office in support of the party for whom the judge testifies. Moreover, when a judge testifies as a witness, a lawyer who regularly appears before the judge may be placed in the awkward position of cross-examining the judge. A judge may, however, testify when properly summoned. Except in unusual circumstances where the demands of justice require, a judge should discourage a party from requiring the judge to testify as a character witness.

Canon 2C. Florida Canon 2C is derived from a recommendation by the American Bar Association and from the United States Senate Committee Resolution, 101st Congress, Second Session, as adopted by the United States Senate Judiciary Committee on August 2, 1990.

Membership of a judge in an organization that practices invidious discrimination gives rise to perceptions that the judge's impartiality is impaired. Whether an organization practices invidious discrimination is often a complex question to which judges should be sensitive. The answer cannot be determined from a mere examination of an organization's current membership rolls but rather depends on the history of the organization's selection of members and other relevant factors, such as that the organization is dedicated to the preservation of religious, ethnic, or cultural values of legitimate common interest to its members, or that it is in fact and effect an intimate, purely private organization whose membership limitations could not be constitutionally prohibited. *See New York State Club Ass'n. Inc. v. City of New York*, 487 U.S. 1, 108 S.Ct. 2225, 101 L.Ed.2d 1 (1988); *Board of Directors of Rotary International v. Rotary Club of Duarte*, 481 U.S. 537, 107 S.Ct. 1940, 95 L.Ed.2d 474 (1987); *Roberts v. United States Jaycees*, 468 U.S. 609, 104 S.Ct. 3244, 82 L.Ed. 2d 462 (1984). Other relevant factors include the size and nature of the organization and the diversity of persons in the locale who might reasonably be considered potential members. Thus the mere absence of diverse membership does not by itself demonstrate a violation unless reasonable persons with knowledge of all the relevant circumstances would expect that the membership would be diverse in the absence of invidious discrimination. Absent such factors, an organization is generally said to discriminate invidiously if it arbitrarily excludes from membership on the basis of race, religion, sex, or national origin persons who would otherwise be admitted to membership.

This Canon is not intended to prohibit membership in religious and ethnic clubs, such as Knights of Columbus, Masons, B'nai B'rith, and Sons of Italy; civic organizations, such as Rotary, Kiwanis, and The Junior League; young people's organizations, such as Boy Scouts, Girl Scouts, Boy's Clubs, and Girl's Clubs; and charitable organizations, such as United Way and Red Cross.

Although Section 2C relates only to membership in organizations that invidiously discriminate on the basis of race, sex, religion or national origin, a judge's membership in an organization that engages in any discriminatory membership practices prohibited by the law of the jurisdiction also violates Canon 2 and Section 2A and gives the appearance of impropriety. In addition, it would be a violation of Canon 2 and Section 2A for a judge to arrange a meeting at a club that the judge knows practices invidious discrimination on the basis of race, sex, religion or national origin in its membership or other policies, or for the judge to regularly use such a club. Moreover, public manifestation by a judge of the judge's knowing approval of invidious discrimination on any basis gives the appearance of impropriety under Canon 2 and diminishes public confidence in the integrity and impartiality of the judiciary, in violation of Section 2A.

When a person who is a judge on the date this Code becomes effective learns that an organization to which the judge belongs engages in invidious discrimination that would preclude membership under Section 2C or under Canon 2 and Section 2A, the judge is permitted, in lieu of resigning, to make immediate efforts to have the organization discontinue its invidiously discriminatory practices, but is required to suspend participation in any other activities of the organization. If the organization fails to discontinue its invidiously discriminatory practices as promptly as possible (and in all events within a year of the judge's first learning of the practices), the judge is required to resign immediately from the organization.

Canon 3. A Judge Shall Perform the Duties of Judicial Office Impartially and Diligently

A. Judicial Duties in General.

The judicial duties of a judge take precedence over all the judge's other activities. The judge's judicial duties include all the duties of the judge's office prescribed by law. In the performance of these duties, the specific standards set forth in the following sections apply.

B. Adjudicative Responsibilities.

(1) A judge shall hear and decide matters assigned to the judge except those in which disqualification is required.

(2) A judge shall be faithful to the law and maintain professional competence in it. A judge shall not be swayed by partisan interests, public clamor, or fear of criticism.

(3) A judge shall require order and decorum in proceedings before the judge.

(4) A judge shall be patient, dignified, and courteous to litigants, jurors, witnesses, lawyers, and others with whom the judge deals in an official capacity, and shall require similar conduct of lawyers, and of staff, court officials, and others subject to the judge's direction and control.

(5) A judge shall perform judicial duties without bias or prejudice. A judge shall not, in the performance of judicial duties, by words or conduct manifest bias or prejudice, including but not limited to bias or prejudice based upon race, sex, religion, national origin, disability, age, sexual orientation, or socioeconomic status, and shall not permit staff, court officials, and others subject to the judge's direction and control to do so. This section does not preclude the consideration of race, sex, religion, national origin, disability, age, sexual orientation, socioeconomic status, or other similar factors when they are issues in the proceeding.

(6) A judge shall require lawyers in proceedings before the judge to refrain from manifesting, by words, gestures, or other conduct, bias or prejudice based upon race, sex, religion, national origin, disability, age, sexual orientation, or socioeconomic status, against parties, witnesses, counsel, or others. This Section 3B(6) does not preclude legitimate advocacy when race, sex, religion, national origin, disability, age, sexual orientation, socioeconomic status, or other similar factors are issues in the proceeding.

(7) A judge shall accord to every person who has a legal interest in a proceeding, or that person's lawyer, the right to be heard according to law. A judge shall not initiate, permit, or consider ex parte communications, or consider other communications made to the judge outside the presence of the parties concerning a pending or impending proceeding except that:

(a) Where circumstances require, ex parte communications for scheduling, administrative purposes, or emergencies that do not deal with substantive matters or issues on the merits are authorized, provided:

(i) the judge reasonably believes that no party will gain a procedural or tactical advantage as a result of the ex parte communication, and

(ii) the judge makes provision promptly to notify all other parties of the substance of the ex parte communication and allows an opportunity to respond.

(b) A judge may obtain the advice of a disinterested expert on the law applicable to a proceeding before the judge if the judge gives notice to the parties of the person consulted and the substance of the advice and affords the parties reasonable opportunity to respond.

(c) A judge may consult with other judges or with court personnel whose function is to aid the judge in carrying out the judge's adjudicative responsibilities.

(d) A judge may, with the consent of the parties, confer separately with the parties and their lawyers in an effort to mediate or settle matters pending before the judge.

(e) A judge may initiate or consider any ex parte communications when expressly authorized by law to do so.

(8) A judge shall dispose of all judicial matters promptly, efficiently, and fairly.

(9) A judge shall not, while a proceeding is pending or impending in any court, make any public comment that might reasonably be expected to affect its outcome or impair its fairness or make any nonpublic comment that might substantially interfere with a fair trial or hearing. The judge shall require similar abstention on the part of court personnel subject to the judge's direction and control. This Section does not prohibit judges from making public statements in the course of their official duties or from explaining for public information the procedures of the court. This Section does not apply to proceedings in which the judge is a litigant in a personal capacity.

(10) A judge shall not, with respect to parties or classes of parties, cases, controversies or issues likely to come before the court, make pledges, promises or commitments that are inconsistent with the impartial performance of the adjudicative duties of the office.

(11) A judge shall not commend or criticize jurors for their verdict other than in a court order or opinion in a proceeding, but may express appreciation to jurors for their service to the judicial system and the community.

(12) A judge shall not disclose or use, for any purpose unrelated to judicial duties, nonpublic information acquired in a judicial capacity.

C. Administrative Responsibilities.

(1) A judge shall diligently discharge the judge's administrative responsibilities without bias or prejudice and maintain professional competence in judicial administration, and should cooperate with other judges and court officials in the administration of court business.

(2) A judge shall require staff, court officials, and others subject to the judge's direction and control to observe the standards of fidelity and diligence that apply to the judge and to refrain from manifesting bias or prejudice in the performance of their official duties.

(3) A judge with supervisory authority for the judicial performance of other judges shall take reasonable measures to assure the prompt disposition of matters before them and the proper performance of their other judicial responsibilities.

(4) A judge shall not make unnecessary appointments. A judge shall exercise the power of appointment impartially and on the basis of merit. A judge shall avoid nepotism and favoritism. A judge shall not approve compensation of appointees beyond the fair value of services rendered.

D. Disciplinary Responsibilities.

(1) A judge who receives information or has actual knowledge that substantial likelihood exists that another judge has committed a violation of this Code shall take appropriate action.

(2) A judge who receives information or has actual knowledge that substantial likelihood exists that a lawyer has committed a violation of the Rules Regulating The Florida Bar shall take appropriate action.

(3) Acts of a judge, in the discharge of disciplinary responsibilities, required or permitted by Sections 3D(1) and 3D(2) are part of a judge's judicial duties and shall be absolutely privileged, and no civil action predicated thereon may be instituted against the judge.

E. Disqualification.

(1) A judge shall disqualify himself or herself in a proceeding in which the judge's impartiality might reasonably be questioned, including but not limited to instances where:

(a) the judge has a personal bias or prejudice concerning a party or a party's lawyer, or personal knowledge of disputed evidentiary facts concerning the proceeding;

(b) the judge served as a lawyer or was the lower court judge in the matter in controversy, or a lawyer with whom the judge previously practiced law served during such association as a lawyer concerning the matter, or the judge has been a material witness concerning it;

(c) the judge knows that he or she individually or as a fiduciary, or the judge's spouse, parent, or child wherever residing, or any other member of the judge's family residing in the judge's household has an economic interest in the subject matter in controversy or in a party to the proceeding or has any other more than de minimis interest that could be substantially affected by the proceeding;

(d) the judge or the judge's spouse, or a person within the third degree of relationship to either of them, or the spouse of such a person:

(i) is a party to the proceeding, or an officer, director, or trustee of a party;

(ii) is acting as a lawyer in the proceeding;

(iii) is known by the judge to have a more than de minimis interest that could be substantially affected by the proceeding;

(iv) is to the judge's knowledge likely to be a material witness in the proceeding;

(e) the judge's spouse or a person within the third degree of relationship to the judge participated as a lower court judge in a decision to be reviewed by the judge;

(f) the judge, while a judge or a candidate for judicial office, has made a public statement that commits, or appears to commit, the judge with respect to:

(i) parties or classes of parties in the proceeding;

(ii) an issue in the proceeding; or

(iii) the controversy in the proceeding.

(2) A judge should keep informed about the judge's personal and fiduciary economic interests, and make a reasonable effort to keep informed about the economic interests of the judge's spouse and minor children residing in the judge's household.

F. Remittal of Disqualification.

A judge disqualified by the terms of Section 3E may disclose on the record the basis of the judge's disqualification and may ask the parties and their lawyers to consider, out of the presence of the judge, whether to waive disqualification. If following disclosure of any basis for disqualification other than personal bias or prejudice concerning a party, the parties and lawyers, without participation by the judge, all agree the judge should not be disqualified, and the judge is then willing to participate, the judge may participate in the proceeding. The agreement shall be incorporated in the record of the proceeding.

Amended Jan. 23, 2003 (838 So.2d 521); Jan. 5, 2006 (918 So.2d 949).

Commentary

Canon 3B(4). The duty to hear all proceedings fairly and with patience is not inconsistent with the duty to dispose promptly of the business of the court. Judges can be efficient and business-like while being patient and deliberate.

Canon 3B(5). A judge must refrain from speech, gestures or other conduct that could reasonably be perceived as sexual harassment and must require the same standard of conduct of others subject to the judge's direction and control.

A judge must perform judicial duties impartially and fairly. A judge who manifests bias on any basis in a proceeding impairs the fairness of the proceeding and brings the judiciary into disrepute. Facial expression and body language, in addition to oral communication, can give to parties or lawyers in the proceeding, jurors, the media and others an appearance of judicial bias. A judge must be alert to avoid behavior that may be perceived as prejudicial.

Canon 3B(7). The proscription against communications concerning a proceeding includes communications from lawyers, law teachers, and other persons who are not participants in the proceeding, except to the limited extent permitted.

To the extent reasonably possible, all parties or their lawyers shall be included in communications with a judge.

Whenever presence of a party or notice to a party is required by Section 3B(7), it is the party's lawyer, or if the party is unrepresented, the party who is to be present or to whom notice is to be given.

An appropriate and often desirable procedure for a court to obtain the advice of a disinterested expert on legal issues is to invite the expert to file a brief as amicus curiae.

Certain ex parte communication is approved by Section 3B(7) to facilitate scheduling and other administrative purposes and to accommodate emergencies. In general, however, a judge must discourage ex parte communication and allow it only if all the criteria stated in Section 3B(7) are clearly met. A judge must disclose to all parties all ex parte communications described in Sections 3B(7)(a) and 3B(7)(b) regarding a proceeding pending or impending before the judge.

A judge must not independently investigate facts in a case and must consider only the evidence presented.

A judge may request a party to submit proposed findings of fact and conclusions of law, so long as the other parties are apprised of the request and are given an opportunity to respond to the proposed findings and conclusions.

A judge must make reasonable efforts, including the provision of appropriate supervision, to ensure that Section 3B(7) is not violated through law clerks or other personnel on the judge's staff.

If communication between the trial judge and the appellate court with respect to a proceeding is permitted, a copy of any written communication or the substance of any oral communication should be provided to all parties.

Canon 3B(8). In disposing of matters promptly, efficiently, and fairly, a judge must demonstrate due regard for the rights of the parties to be heard and to have issues resolved without unnecessary cost or delay. Containing costs while preserving fundamental rights of parties also protects the interests of witnesses and the general public. A judge should monitor and supervise cases so as to reduce or eliminate dilatory practices, avoidable delays, and unnecessary costs. A judge should encourage and seek to facilitate settlement, but parties should not feel coerced into surrendering the right to have their controversy resolved by the courts.

Prompt disposition of the court's business requires a judge to devote adequate time to judicial duties, to be punctual in attending court and expeditious in determining matters under submission, and to insist that court officials, litigants, and their lawyers cooperate with the judge to that end.

Canon 3B(9) and 3B(10). Sections 3B(9) and (10) restrictions on judicial speech are essential to the maintenance of the integrity, impartiality, and independence of the judiciary. A pending proceeding is one that has begun but not yet reached final disposition. An impending proceeding is one that is anticipated but not yet begun. The requirement that judges abstain from public comment regarding a pending or impending proceeding continues during any appellate process and until final disposition. Sections 3B(9) and (10) do not prohibit a judge from commenting on proceedings in which the judge is a litigant in a personal capacity, but in cases such as a writ of mandamus where the judge is a litigant in an official capacity, the judge must not comment publicly. The conduct of lawyers relating to trial publicity is governed by Rule 4–3.6 of the Rules Regulating The Florida Bar.

Canon 3B(10). Commending or criticizing jurors for their verdict may imply a judicial expectation in future cases and may impair a juror's ability to be fair and impartial in a subsequent case.

Canon 3C(4). Appointees of a judge include assigned counsel, officials such as referees, commissioners, special magistrates, receivers, mediators, arbitrators, and guardians and personnel such as clerks, secretaries, and bailiffs. Consent by the parties to an appointment or an award of compensation does not relieve the judge of the obligation prescribed by Section 3C(4). See also Fla.Stat. § 112.3135 (1991).

Canon 3D. Appropriate action may include direct communication with the judge or lawyer who has committed the violation, other direct action if available, or reporting the violation to the appropriate authority or other agency. If the conduct is minor, the Canon allows a judge to address the problem solely by direct communication with the offender. A judge having knowledge, however, that another judge has committed a violation of this Code that raises a substantial question as to that other judge's fitness for office or has knowledge that a lawyer has committed a violation of the Rules of Professional Conduct that raises a substantial question as to the lawyer's honesty, trustworthiness or fitness as a lawyer in other respects, is required under this Canon to inform the appropriate authority. While worded differently, this Code provision has the identical purpose as the related Model Code provisions.

Canon 3E(1). Under this rule, a judge is disqualified whenever the judge's impartiality might reasonably be questioned, regardless of whether any of the specific rules in Section 3E(1) apply. For example, if a judge were in the process of negotiating for employment with a law firm, the judge would be disqualified from any matters in which that law firm appeared, unless the disqualification was waived by the parties after disclosure by the judge.

A judge should disclose on the record information that the judge believes the parties or their lawyers might consider relevant to the question of disqualification, even if the judge believes there is no real basis for disqualification. The fact that the judge conveys this information does not automatically require the judge to be disqualified upon a request by either party, but the issue should be resolved on a case-by-case basis. Similarly, if a lawyer or party has previously filed a complaint against the judge with the Judicial Qualifications Commission, that the fact does not automatically require disqualification of the judge. Such disqualification should be on a case-by-case basis.

By decisional law, the rule of necessity may override the rule of disqualification. For example, a judge might be required to participate in judicial review of a judicial salary statute, or might be the only judge available in a matter requiring immediate judicial action, such as a hearing on probable cause or a temporary restraining order. In the latter case, the judge must disclose on the record the basis for possible disqualification and use reasonable efforts to transfer the matter to another judge as soon as practicable.

Canon 3E(1)(b). A lawyer in a government agency does not ordinarily have an association with other lawyers employed by that agency within the meaning of Section 3E(1)(b); a judge formerly employed by a government agency, however, should disqualify himself or herself in a proceeding if the judge's impartiality might reasonably be questioned because of such association.

Canon 3E(1)(d). The fact that a lawyer in a proceeding is affiliated with a law firm with which a relative of the judge is affiliated does not of itself disqualify the judge. Under appropriate circumstances, the fact that "the judge's impartiality might reasonably be questioned" under Section 3E(1), or that the relative is known by the judge to have an interest in the law firm that could be "substantially affected by the outcome of the proceeding" under Section 3E(1)(d)(iii) may require the judge's disqualification.

Canon 3E(1)(e). It is not uncommon for a judge's spouse or a person within the third degree of relationship to a judge to also serve as a judge in either the trial or appellate courts. However, where a judge exercises appellate authority over another judge, and that other judge is either a spouse or a relationship within the third degree, then this Code requires disqualification of the judge that is exercising appellate authority. This Code, under these circumstances, precludes the appellate judge from participating in the review of the spouse's or relation's case.

Canon 3F. A remittal procedure provides the parties an opportunity to proceed without delay if they wish to waive the disqualification. To assure that consideration of the question of remittal is made independently of the judge, a judge must not solicit, seek, or hear comment on possible remittal or waiver of the disqualification unless the lawyers jointly propose remittal after consultation as provided in the rule. A party may act through counsel if counsel represents on the record that the party has been consulted and consents. As a practical matter, a judge may wish to have all parties and their lawyers sign the remittal agreement.

Canon 4. A Judge is Encouraged to Engage in Activities to Improve the Law, the Legal System, and the Administration of Justice

A. A judge shall conduct all of the judge's quasi-judicial activities so that they do not:

(1) cast reasonable doubt on the judge's capacity to act impartially as a judge;

(2) undermine the judge's independence, integrity, or impartiality;

(3) demean the judicial office;

(4) interfere with the proper performance of judicial duties;

(5) lead to frequent disqualification of the judge; or

(6) appear to a reasonable person to be coercive.

B. A judge is encouraged to speak, write, lecture, teach and participate in other quasi-judicial activities concerning the law, the legal system, the administration of justice, and the role of the judiciary as an independent branch within our system of government, subject to the requirements of this Code.

C. A judge shall not appear at a public hearing before, or otherwise consult with, an executive or legislative body or official except on matters concerning the law, the legal system or the administration of justice or except when acting pro se in a matter involving the judge or the judge's interests.

D. A judge is encouraged to serve as a member, officer, director, trustee or non-legal advisor of an organization or governmental entity devoted to the improvement of the law, the legal system, the judicial branch, or the administration of justice, subject to the following limitations and the other requirements of this Code.

(1) A judge shall not serve as an officer, director, trustee or non-legal advisor if it is likely that the organization

(a) will be engaged in proceedings that would ordinarily come before the judge, or

(b) will be engaged frequently in adversary proceedings in the court of which the judge is a member or in any court subject to the appellate jurisdiction of the court of which the judge is a member.

(2) A judge as an officer, director, trustee or non-legal advisor, or as a member or otherwise:

(a) may assist such an organization in planning fund-raising and may participate in the management and investment of the organization's funds, but shall not personally or directly participate in the solicitation of funds, except that a judge may solicit funds from other judges over whom the judge does not exercise supervisory or appellate authority;

(b) may appear or speak at, receive an award or other recognition at, be featured on the program of, and permit the judge's title to be used in conjunction with an event of such an organization or entity, but if the event serves a fund-raising purpose, the judge may participate only if the event concerns the law, the legal system, or the administration of justice and the funds raised will be used for a law related purpose(s);

(c) may make recommendations to public and private fund-granting organizations on projects and programs concerning the law, the legal system or the administration of justice;

(d) shall not personally or directly participate in membership solicitation if the solicitation might reasonably be perceived as coercive;

(e) shall not make use of court premises, staff, stationery, equipment, or other resources for fund-raising purposes, except for incidental use for activities that concern the law, the legal system, or the administration of justice, subject to the requirements of this Code.

Amended May 22, 2008 (983 So.2d 550).

Commentary

Canon 4A. A judge is encouraged to participate in activities designed to improve the law, the legal system, and the administration of justice. In doing so, however, it must be understood that expressions of bias or prejudice by a judge, even outside the judge's judicial activities, may cast reasonable doubt on the judge's capacity to act impartially as a judge and may undermine the independence and integrity of the judiciary. Expressions which may do so include jokes or other remarks demeaning individuals on the basis of their race, sex, religion, national origin, disability, age, sexual orientation or socioeconomic status. See Canon 2C and accompanying Commentary.

Canon 4B. This canon was clarified in order to encourage judges to engage in activities to improve the law, the legal system, and the administration of justice. As a judicial officer and person specially learned in the law, a judge is in a unique position to contribute to the improvement of the law, the legal system, and the administration of justice, including, but not limited to, the improvement of the role of the judiciary as an independent branch of government, the revision of substantive and procedural law, the improvement of criminal and juvenile justice, and the improvement of justice in the areas of civil, criminal, family, domestic violence, juvenile delinquency, juvenile dependency, probate and motor vehicle law. To the extent that time permits, a judge is encouraged to do so, either independently or through a bar association, judicial conference or other organization dedicated to the improvement of the law. Support of pro bono legal services by members of the bench is an activity that relates to improvement of the administration of justice. Accordingly, a judge may engage in activities intended to encourage attorneys to perform pro bono services, including, but not limited to: participating in events to recognize attorneys who do pro bono work, establishing general procedural or scheduling accommodations for pro bono attorneys as feasible, and acting in an advisory capacity to pro bono programs. Judges are encouraged to participate in efforts to promote the fair administration of justice, the independence of the judiciary and the integrity of the legal profession, which may include the expression of opposition to the persecution of lawyers and judges in other countries.

The phrase "subject to the requirements of this Code" is included to remind judges that the use of permissive language in various sections of the Code does not relieve a judge from the other requirements of the Code that apply to the specific conduct.

Canon 4C. See Canon 2B regarding the obligation to avoid improper influence.

Canon 4D(1). The changing nature of some organizations and of their relationship to the law makes it necessary for a judge regularly to reexamine the activities of each organization with which the judge is affiliated to determine if it is proper for the judge to continue the affiliation. For example, the boards of some legal aid organizations now make policy decisions that may have political significance or imply commitment to causes that may come before the courts for adjudication.

Canon 4D(2). A judge may solicit membership or endorse or encourage membership efforts for an organization devoted to the improvement of the law, the legal system or the administration of justice as long as the solicitation cannot reasonably be perceived as coercive. Personal or direct solicitation of funds for an organization and personal or direct solicitation of memberships involve the danger that the person solicited will feel obligated to respond favorably to the solicitor if the solicitor is in a position of influence or control. A judge must not engage in direct, individual solicitation of funds or memberships in person, in writing or by telephone except in the following cases: 1) a judge may solicit for funds or memberships other judges over whom the judge does not exercise supervisory or appellate authority, 2) a judge may solicit other persons for membership in the organizations described above if neither those persons nor persons with whom they are affiliated are likely ever to appear before the court on which the judge serves and 3) a judge who is an officer of such an organization may send a general membership solicitation mailing over the judge's signature.

A judge may be a speaker or guest of honor at an organization's fund-raising event if the event concerns the law, the legal system, or the administration of justice, and the judge does not engage in the direct solicitation of funds. However, judges may not participate in or allow their titles to be used in connection with fund-raising activities on behalf of an organization engaging in advocacy if such participation would cast doubt on the judge's capacity to act impartially as a judge.

Use of an organization letterhead for fund-raising or membership solicitation does not violate Canon 4D(2) provided the letterhead lists only the judge's name and office or other position in the organization, and, if comparable designations are listed for other persons, the judge's judicial designation. In addition, a judge must also make reasonable efforts to ensure that the judge's staff, court officials and others subject to the judge's direction and control do not solicit funds on the judge's behalf for any purpose, charitable or otherwise.

Canon 5. A Judge Shall Regulate Extrajudicial Activities to Minimize the Risk of Conflict With Judicial Duties

A. Extrajudicial Activities in General. A judge shall conduct all of the judge's extra-judicial activities so that they do not:

(1) cast reasonable doubt on the judge's capacity to act impartially as a judge;

(2) undermine the judge's independence, integrity, or impartiality;

(3) demean the judicial office;

(4) interfere with the proper performance of judicial duties;

(5) lead to frequent disqualification of the judge; or

(6) appear to a reasonable person to be coercive.

B. Avocational Activities. A judge is encouraged to speak, write, lecture, teach and participate in other extrajudicial activities concerning non-legal subjects, subject to the requirements of this Code.

C. Governmental, Civic or Charitable Activities.

(1) A judge shall not appear at a public hearing before, or otherwise consult with, an executive or legislative body or official except on matters concerning the law, the legal system or the administration of justice or except when acting pro se in a matter involving the judge or the judge's interests.

(2) A judge shall not accept appointment to a governmental committee or commission or other governmental position that is concerned with issues of fact or

policy on matters other than the improvement of the law, the legal system, the judicial branch, or the administration of justice. A judge may, however, represent a country, state or locality on ceremonial occasions or in connection with historical, educational or cultural activities.

(3) A judge may serve as an officer, director, trustee or non-legal advisor of an educational, religious, charitable, fraternal, sororal or civic organization not conducted for profit, subject to the following limitations and the other requirements of this Code.

(a) A judge shall not serve as an officer, director, trustee or non-legal advisor if it is likely that the organization

(i) will be engaged in proceedings that would ordinarily come before the judge, or

(ii) will be engaged frequently in adversary proceedings in the court of which the judge is a member or in any court subject to the appellate jurisdiction of the court of which the judge is a member.

(b) A judge as an officer, director, trustee or non-legal advisor, or as a member or otherwise:

(i) may assist such an organization in planning fund-raising and may participate in the management and investment of the organization's funds, but shall not personally or directly participate in the solicitation of funds, except that a judge may solicit funds from other judges over whom the judge does not exercise supervisory or appellate authority;

(ii) shall not personally or directly participate in membership solicitation if the solicitation might reasonably be perceived as coercive;

(iii) shall not use or permit the use of the prestige of judicial office for fund-raising or membership solicitation.

D. Financial Activities.

(1) A judge shall not engage in financial and business dealings that

(a) may reasonably be perceived to exploit the judge's judicial position, or

(b) involve the judge in frequent transactions or continuing business relationships with those lawyers or other persons likely to come before the court on which the judge serves.

(2) A judge may, subject to the requirements of this Code, hold and manage investments of the judge and members of the judge's family, including real estate, and engage in other remunerative activity.

(3) A judge shall not serve as an officer, director, manager, general partner, advisor or employee of any business entity except that a judge may, subject to the requirements of this Code, manage and participate in:

(a) a business closely held by the judge or members of the judge's family, or

(b) a business entity primarily engaged in investment of the financial resources of the judge or members of the judge's family.

(4) A judge shall manage the judge's investments and other financial interests to minimize the number of cases in which the judge is disqualified. As soon as the judge can do so without serious financial detriment, the judge shall divest himself or herself of investments and other financial interests that might require frequent disqualification.

(5) A judge shall not accept, and shall urge members of the judge's family residing in the judge's household not to accept, a gift, bequest, favor or loan from anyone except for:

(a) a gift incident to a public testimonial, books, tapes and other resource materials supplied by publishers on a complimentary basis for official use, or an invitation to the judge and the judge's spouse or guest to attend a bar-related function or an activity devoted to the improvement of the law, the legal system or the administration of justice;

(b) a gift, award or benefit incident to the business, profession or other separate activity of a spouse or other family member of a judge residing in the judge's household, including gifts, awards and benefits for the use of both the spouse or other family member and the judge (as spouse or family member), provided the gift, award or benefit could not reasonably be perceived as intended to influence the judge in the performance of judicial duties;

(c) ordinary social hospitality;

(d) a gift from a relative or friend, for a special occasion, such as a wedding, anniversary or birthday, if the gift is fairly commensurate with the occasion and the relationship;

(e) a gift, bequest, favor or loan from a relative or close personal friend whose appearance or interest in a case would in any event require disqualification under Canon 3E;

(f) a loan from a lending institution in its regular course of business on the same terms generally available to persons who are not judges;

(g) a scholarship or fellowship awarded on the same terms and based on the same criteria applied to other applicants; or

(h) any other gift, bequest, favor or loan, only if: the donor is not a party or other person who has come or is likely to come or whose interests have come or are likely to come before the judge; and, if its value, or the aggregate value in a calendar year of such gifts, bequests, favors, or loans from a single source, exceeds $100.00, the judge reports it in the same manner as the judge reports gifts under Canon 6B(2).

E. Fiduciary Activities.

(1) A judge shall not serve as executor, administrator or other personal representative, trustee, guard-

ian, attorney in fact or other fiduciary, except for the estate, trust or person of a member of the judge's family, and then only if such service will not interfere with the proper performance of judicial duties.

(2) A judge shall not serve as a fiduciary if it is likely that the judge as a fiduciary will be engaged in proceedings that would ordinarily come before the judge, or if the estate, trust or ward becomes involved in adversary proceedings in the court on which the judge serves or one under its appellate jurisdiction.

(3) The same restrictions on financial activities that apply to a judge personally also apply to the judge while acting in a fiduciary capacity.

F. Service as Arbitrator or Mediator.

(1) A judge shall not act as an arbitrator or mediator or otherwise perform judicial functions in a private capacity unless expressly authorized by law or Court rule. A judge may, however, take the necessary educational and training courses required to be a qualified and certified arbitrator or mediator, and may fulfill the requirements of observing and conducting actual arbitration or mediation proceedings as part of the certification process, provided such program does not, in any way, interfere with the performance of the judge's judicial duties.

(2) A senior judge may serve as a mediator in a case in a circuit in which the senior judge is not presiding as a judge only if the senior judge is certified pursuant to rule 10.100, Florida Rules for Certified and Court–Appointed Mediators. Such senior judge may be associated with entities that are solely engaged in offering mediation or other alternative dispute resolution services but that are not otherwise engaged in the practice of law. However, such senior judge may not advertise, solicit business, associate with a law firm, or participate in any other activity that directly or indirectly promotes his or her mediation services and shall not permit an entity with which the senior judge associates to do so. A senior judge shall not serve as a mediator in any case in a circuit in which the judge is currently presiding as a senior judge. A senior judge who provides mediation services shall not preside over any case in the circuit where the mediation services are provided; however, a senior judge may preside over cases in circuits in which the judge does not provide mediation services. A senior judge shall disclose if the judge is being utilized or has been utilized as a mediator by any party, attorney, or law firm involved in the case pending before the senior judge. Absent express consent of all parties, a senior judge is prohibited from presiding over any case involving any party, attorney, or law firm that is utilizing or has utilized the judge as a mediator within the previous three years. A senior judge shall disclose any negotiations or agreements for the provision of mediation services between the senior judge and any of the parties or counsel to the case.

G. Practice of Law. A judge shall not practice law. Notwithstanding this prohibition, a judge may act pro se and may, without compensation, give legal advice to and draft or review documents for a member of the judge's family.

Amended Nov. 3, 2005, effective Jan. 1, 2006 (915 So.2d 145); May 22, 2008 (983 So.2d 550); June 19, 2014, effective Oct. 1, 2014 (141 So.3d 1172).

Commentary

Canon 5A. Complete separation of a judge from extra-judicial activities is neither possible nor wise; a judge should not become isolated from the community in which the judge lives. For that reason, judges are encouraged to participate in extrajudicial community activities.

Expressions of bias or prejudice by a judge, even outside the judge's judicial activities, may cast reasonable doubt on the judge's capacity to act impartially as a judge, and may undermine the independence and integrity of the judiciary. Expressions which may do so include jokes or other remarks demeaning individuals on the basis of their race, sex, religion, national origin, disability, age, sexual orientation or socioeconomic status. See Canon 2C and accompanying Commentary.

Canon 5B. In this and other sections of Canon 5, the phrase "subject to the requirements of this Code" is used, notably in connection with a judge's governmental, civic or charitable activities. This phrase is included to remind judges that the use of permissive language in various sections of the Code does not relieve a judge from the other requirements of the Code that apply to the specific conduct.

Canon 5C(1). See Canon 2B regarding the obligation to avoid improper influence.

Canon 5C(2). Canon 5C(2) prohibits a judge from accepting any governmental position except one relating to the law, legal system or administration of justice as authorized by Canon 4D. The appropriateness of accepting extrajudicial assignments must be assessed in light of the demands on judicial resources created by crowded dockets and the need to protect the courts from involvement in extrajudicial matters that may prove to be controversial. Judges should not accept governmental appointments that are likely to interfere with the effectiveness and independence of the judiciary.

Canon 5C(2) does not govern a judge's service in a nongovernmental position. See Canon 5C(3) permitting service by a judge with educational, religious, charitable, fraternal, sororal or civic organizations not conducted for profit. For example, service on the board of a public educational institution, unless it were a law school, would be prohibited under Canon 5C(2), but service on the board of a public law school or any private educational institution would generally be permitted under Canon 5C(3).

Canon 5C(3). Canon 5C(3) does not apply to a judge's service in a governmental position unconnected with the improvement of the law, the legal system or the administration of justice; see Canon 5C(2).

See Commentary to Canon 5B regarding use of the phrase "subject to the following limitations and the other requirements of this Code." As an example of the meaning of the phrase, a judge permitted by Canon 5C(3) to serve on the board of a fraternal institution may be prohibited from such service by Canons 2C or 5A if the institution practices invidious discrimination or if service on the board otherwise casts reasonable doubt on the judge's capacity to act impartially as a judge.

Service by a judge on behalf of a civic or charitable organization may be governed by other provisions of Canon 5 in addition to Canon 5C. For example, Canon 5G prohibits a judge from serving as a legal advisor to a civic or charitable organization.

Canon 5C(3)(a). The changing nature of some organizations and of their relationship to the law makes it necessary for a judge to regularly reexamine the activities of each organization with which the judge is affiliated in order to determine if it is proper for the judge to continue the affiliation. For example, in many jurisdictions charitable hospitals are now more frequently in court than in the past.

Canon 5C(3)(b). A judge may solicit membership or endorse or encourage membership efforts for a nonprofit educational, religious, charitable, fraternal, sororal or civic organization as long as the solicitation cannot reasonably be perceived as coercive and is not essentially a fund-raising mechanism. Personal or direct solicitation of funds for an organization and personal or direct solicitation of memberships involve the danger that the person solicited will feel obligated to respond favorably to the solicitor if the solicitor is in a position of influence or control. A judge must not engage in direct, individual solicitation of funds or memberships in person, in writing or by telephone except in the following cases: 1) a judge may solicit for funds or memberships other judges over whom the judge does not exercise supervisory or appellate authority, 2) a judge may solicit other persons for membership in the organizations described above if neither those persons nor persons with whom they are affiliated are likely ever to appear before the court on which the judge serves and 3) a judge who is an officer of such an organization may send a general membership solicitation mailing over the judge's signature.

Mere attendance at an event, whether or not the event serves a fund-raising purpose, does not constitute a violation of Canon 5C(3)(b). It is also generally permissible for a judge to pass a collection plate at a place of worship or for a judge to serve as an usher or food server or preparer, or to perform similar subsidiary and unadvertised functions at fund-raising events sponsored by educational, religious, charitable, fraternal, or civic organizations, so long as they do not entail direct or personal solicitation. However, a judge may not be a speaker, guest of honor, or otherwise be featured at an organization's fund-raising event, unless the event concerns the law, the legal system, or the administration of justice as authorized by Canon 4D(2)(b).

Use of an organization letterhead for fund-raising or membership solicitation does not violate Canon 5C(3)(b) provided the letterhead lists only the judge's name and office or other position in the organization, and, if comparable designations are listed for other persons, the judge's judicial designation. In addition, a judge must also make reasonable efforts to ensure that the judge's staff, court officials and others subject to the judge's direction and control do not solicit funds on the judge's behalf for any purpose, charitable or otherwise.

Canon 5D(1). When a judge acquires in a judicial capacity information, such as material contained in filings with the court, that is not yet generally known, the judge must not use the information for private gain. See Canon 2B; see also Canon 3B(11).

A judge must avoid financial and business dealings that involve the judge in frequent transactions or continuing business relationships with persons likely to come either before the judge personally or before other judges on the judge's court. In addition, a judge should discourage members of the judge's family from engaging in dealings that would reasonably appear to exploit the judge's judicial position. This rule is necessary to avoid creating an appearance of exploitation of office or favoritism and to minimize the potential for disqualification. With respect to affiliation of relatives of the judge with law firms appearing before the judge, see Commentary to Canon 3E(1) relating to disqualification.

Participation by a judge in financial and business dealings is subject to the general prohibitions in Canon 5A against activities that tend to reflect adversely on impartiality, demean the judicial office, or interfere with the proper performance of judicial duties. Such participation is also subject to the general prohibition in Canon 2 against activities involving impropriety or the appearance of impropriety and the prohibition in Canon 2B against the misuse of the prestige of judicial office. In addition, a judge must maintain high standards of conduct in all of the judge's activities, as set forth in Canon 1. See Commentary for Canon 5B regarding use of the phrase "subject to the requirements of this Code."

Canon 5D(2). This Canon provides that, subject to the requirements of this Code, a judge may hold and manage investments owned solely by the judge, investments owned solely by a member or members of the judge's family, and investments owned jointly by the judge and members of the judge's family.

Canon 5D(3). Subject to the requirements of this Code, a judge may participate in a business that is closely held either by the judge alone, by members of the judge's family, or by the judge and members of the judge's family.

Although participation by a judge in a closely-held family business might otherwise be permitted by Canon 5D(3), a judge may be prohibited from participation by other provisions of this Code when, for example, the business entity frequently appears before the judge's court or the participation requires significant time away from judicial duties. Similarly, a judge must avoid participating in a closely-held family business if the judge's participation would involve misuse of the prestige of judicial office.

Canon 5D(5). Canon 5D(5) does not apply to contributions to a judge's campaign for judicial office, a matter governed by Canon 7.

Because a gift, bequest, favor or loan to a member of the judge's family residing in the judge's household might be viewed as intended to influence the judge, a judge must inform those family members of the relevant ethical constraints upon the judge in this regard and discourage those family members from violating them. A judge cannot, however, reasonably be expected to know or control all of the financial or business activities of all family members residing in the judge's household.

Canon 5D(5)(a). Acceptance of an invitation to a law-related function is governed by Canon 5D(5)(a); acceptance of an invitation paid for by an individual lawyer or group of lawyers is governed by Canon 5D(5)(h).

A judge may accept a public testimonial or a gift incident thereto only if the donor organization is not an organization whose members comprise or frequently represent the same side in litigation, and the testimonial and gift are otherwise in compliance with other provisions of this Code. See Canons 5A(1) and 2B.

Canon 5D(5)(d). A gift to a judge, or to a member of the judge's family living in the judge's household, that is excessive in value raises questions about the judge's impartiality and the integrity of the judicial office and might require disqualification of the judge where disqualification would not otherwise be required. See, however, Canon 5D(5)(e).

Canon 5D(5)(h). Canon 5D(5)(h) prohibits judges from accepting gifts, favors, bequests or loans from lawyers or their firms if they have come or are likely to come before the judge; it also prohibits gifts, favors, bequests or loans from clients of lawyers or their firms when the clients' interests have come or are likely to come before the judge.

Canon 5E(3). The restrictions imposed by this Canon may conflict with the judge's obligation as a fiduciary. For example, a judge should resign as trustee if detriment to the trust would result from divestiture of holdings the retention of which would place the judge in violation of Canon 5D(4).

Canon 5F(1). Canon 5F(1) does not prohibit a judge from participating in arbitration, mediation or settlement conferences performed as part of judicial duties. An active judge may take the necessary educational and training programs to be certified or qualified as a mediator or arbitrator, but this shall not be a part of the judge's judicial duties. While such a course will allow a judge to have a better understanding of the arbitration and mediation process, the certification and qualification of a judge as a mediator or arbitrator is primarily for the judge's personal benefit. While actually participating in the mediation and arbitration training activities, care must be taken in the selection of both cases and locations so as to guarantee that there is no interference or conflict between the training and the judge's judicial responsibilities. Indeed, the training should be conducted in such a manner as to avoid the involvement of persons likely to appear before the judge in legal proceedings.

Canon 5F(2). The purpose of the admonitions in this canon is to ensure that the impartiality of a senior judge is not subject to question. Although a senior judge may act as a mediator or arbitrator in a circuit in which the judge is not presiding as a senior judge, attention must be given to relationships with lawyers and law firms which may require disclosure or disqualification. These provisions are intended to prohibit a senior judge from soliciting lawyers to use the senior judge's mediation services when those lawyers are or may be before the judge in proceedings where the senior judge is acting in a judicial capacity and to require a senior judge to ensure that entities with which the senior judge associates as a mediator abide by the same prohibitions on advertising or promoting the senior judge's mediation service as are imposed on the senior judge.

Canon 5G. This prohibition refers to the practice of law in a representative capacity and not in a pro se capacity. A judge may act for himself or herself in all legal matters, including matters involving litigation and matters involving appearances before or other dealings with legislative and other governmental bodies. However, in so doing, a judge must not abuse the prestige of office to advance the interests of the judge or the judge's family. See Canon 2B.

The Code allows a judge to give legal advice to and draft legal documents for members of the judge's family, so long as the judge receives no compensation. A judge must not, however, act as an advocate or negotiator for a member of the judge's family in a legal matter.

Canon 6. Fiscal Matters of a Judge Shall be Conducted in a Manner That Does Not Give the Appearance of Influence or Impropriety; a Judge Shall Regularly File Public Reports as Required by Article II, Section 8, of the Constitution of Florida, and Shall Publicly Report Gifts; Additional Financial Information Shall be Filed With the Judicial Qualifications Commission to Ensure Full Financial Disclosure

A. Compensation for Quasi–Judicial and Extrajudicial Services and Reimbursement of Expenses.

A judge may receive compensation and reimbursement of expenses for the quasi-judicial and extrajudicial activities permitted by this Code, if the source of such payments does not give the appearance of influencing the judge in the performance of judicial duties or otherwise give the appearance of impropriety, subject to the following restrictions:

(1) Compensation. Compensation shall not exceed a reasonable amount nor shall it exceed what a person who is not a judge would receive for the same activity.

(2) Expense Reimbursement. Expense reimbursement shall be limited to the actual cost of travel, food, and lodging reasonably incurred by the judge and, where appropriate to the occasion, to the judge's spouse. Any payment in excess of such an amount is compensation.

B. Public Financial Reporting.

(1) Income and Assets. A judge shall file such public report as may be required by law for all public officials to comply fully with the provisions of Article II, Section 8, of the Constitution of Florida. The form for public financial disclosure shall be that recommended or adopted by the Florida Commission on Ethics for use by all public officials. The form shall be filed with the Florida Commission on Ethics on the date prescribed by law, and a copy shall be filed simultaneously with the Judicial Qualifications Commission.

(2) Gifts. A judge shall file a public report of all gifts which are required to be disclosed under Canon 5D(5)(h) of the Code of Judicial Conduct. The report of gifts received in the preceding calendar year shall be filed with the Florida Commission on Ethics on or before July 1 of each year. A copy shall be filed simultaneously with the Judicial Qualifications Commission.

(3) Disclosure of Financial Interests Upon Leaving Office. A judge shall file a final disclosure statement within 60 days after leaving office, which report shall cover the period between January 1 of the year in which the judge leaves office and his or her last day of office, unless, within the 60–day period, the judge takes another public position requiring financial disclosure under Article II, Section 8, of the Constitution of Florida, or is otherwise required to file full and public disclosure for the final disclosure period. The form for disclosure of financial interests upon leaving office shall be that recommended or adopted by the Florida Commission on Ethics for use by all public officials. The form shall be filed with the Florida Commission on Ethics and a copy shall be filed simultaneously with the Judicial Qualifications Commission.

C. Confidential Financial Reporting to the Judicial Qualifications Commission.

To ensure that complete financial information is available for all judicial officers, there shall be filed with the Judicial Qualifications Commission on or before July 1 of each year, if not already included in the public report to be filed under Canon 6B(1) and (2), a verified list of the names of the corporations and other business entities in which the judge has a financial interest as of December 31 of the preceding year, which shall be transmitted in a separate sealed envelope, placed by the Commission in safekeeping, and not be opened or the contents thereof disclosed except in the manner hereinafter provided.

At any time during or after the pendency of a cause, any party may request information as to whether the most recent list filed by the judge or judges before whom the cause is or was pending contains the name of any specific person or corporation or other business entity which is a party to the cause or which has a substantial direct or indirect financial interest in its outcome. Neither the making of the request nor the contents thereof shall be revealed by the chair to any judge or other person except at the instance of the individual making the request. If the request meets the requirements hereinabove set forth, the chair shall render a prompt answer thereto and thereupon return the report to safekeeping for retention in accordance with the provisions hereinabove stated. All such requests shall be verified and transmitted to the chair of the Commission on forms to be approved by it.

D. Limitation of Disclosure.

Disclosure of a judge's income, debts, investments or other assets is required only to the extent provided in this Canon and in Sections 3E and 3F, or as otherwise required by law.

Commentary

Canon 6A. See Section 5D(5)(a)–(h) regarding reporting of gifts, bequests and loans.

The Code does not prohibit a judge from accepting honoraria or speaking fees provided that the compensation is reasonable and commensurate with the task performed. A judge should ensure, however, that no conflicts are created by the arrangement. Judges must not appear to trade on the judicial position for personal advantage. Nor should a judge spend significant time away from court duties to meet speaking or writing commitments for compensation. In addition, the source of the payment must not raise any question of undue influence or the judge's ability or willingness to be impartial.

Canon 6C. Subparagraph A prescribes guidelines for additional compensation and the reimbursement of expense funds received by a judge.

Subparagraphs B and C prescribe the three types of financial disclosure reports required of each judicial officer.

The first is the Ethics Commission's constitutionally required form pursuant to Article II, Section 8, of the Constitution. It must be filed each year as prescribed by law. The financial reporting period is for the previous calendar year. A final disclosure statement generally is required when a judge leaves office. The filing of the income tax return is a permissible alternative.

The second is a report of gifts received during the preceding calendar year to be filed publicly with the Florida Commission on Ethics. The gifts to be reported are in accordance with Canon 5D(5)(h). This reporting is in lieu of that prescribed by statute as stated in the Supreme Court's opinion rendered in In re Code of Judicial Conduct, 281 So. 2d 21 (Fla.1973). The form for this report is as follows:

Form 6A. Gift Disclosure

All judicial officers must file with the Florida Commission on Ethics a list of all gifts received during the preceding calendar year of a value in excess of $100.00 as provided in Canon 5D(5) and Canon 6B(2) of the Code of Judicial Conduct.

Name: ______________________

Telephone: ______________________

Address: ______________________

Position Held: ______________________

Please identify all gifts you received during the preceding calendar year of a value in excess of $100.00, as required by Canon 5D(5) and Canon 6B(2) of the Code of Judicial Conduct.

____

____

____

____

____

OATH

State of Florida

County of ____________

I, ________, the public official filing this disclosure statement, being first duly sworn, do depose on oath and say that the facts set forth in the above statement are true, correct, and complete to the best of my knowledge and belief.

____

(Signature of Reporting Official)

____

(Signature of Officer Authorized to Administer Oaths)

My Commission expires ________.
Sworn to and subscribed before me this ________ day of ________, 20__.

Commentary

The third financial disclosure report is prescribed in subparagraph C. This provision ensures that there will be complete financial information for all judicial officers available with the Judicial Qualifications Commission by requiring that full disclosure be filed confidentially with the Judicial Qualifications Commission in the event the limited disclosure alternative is selected under the provisions of Article II, Section 8.

The amendment to this Canon requires in 6B(2) a separate gift report to be filed with the Florida Commission on Ethics on or before July 1 of each year. The form to be used for that report is included in the commentary to Canon 6. It should be noted that Canon 5, as it presently exists, restricts and prohibits the receipt of certain gifts. This provision is not applicable to other public officials.

With reference to financial disclosure, if the judge chooses the limited disclosure alternative available under the provision of Article II, Section 8, of the Constitution of Florida, without the inclusion of the judge's Federal Income Tax Return, then the judge must file with the Commission a list of the names of corporations or other business entities in which the judge has a financial interest even though the amount is less than $1,000. This information remains confidential until a request is made by a party to a cause before the judge. This latter provision continues to ensure that complete financial information for all judicial officers is available with the Judicial Qualifications Commission and that parties who are concerned about a judge's possible financial interest have a means of obtaining that information as it pertains to a particular cause before the judge.

Canon 6D. Section 3E requires a judge to disqualify himself or herself in any proceeding in which the judge has an economic interest. See "economic interest" as explained in the Definitions Section. Section 5D requires a judge to refrain from engaging in business and from financial activities that might interfere with the impartial performance of judicial duties; Section 6B requires a judge to report all compensation the judge received for activities outside judicial office. A judge has the rights of any other citizen, including the right to privacy of the judge's financial affairs, except to the extent that limitations established by law are required to safeguard the proper performance of the judge's duties.

Canon 7. A Judge or Candidate for Judicial Office Shall Refrain From Inappropriate Political Activity

A. All judges and Candidates.

(1) Except as authorized in Sections 7B(2), 7C(2) and 7C(3), a judge or a candidate for election or appointment to judicial office shall not:

(a) act as a leader or hold an office in a political organization;

(b) publicly endorse or publicly oppose another candidate for public office;

(c) make speeches on behalf of a political organization;

(d) attend political party functions; or

(e) solicit funds for, pay an assessment to or make a contribution to a political organization or candidate, or purchase tickets for political party dinners or other functions.

(2) A judge shall resign from judicial office upon becoming a candidate for a non-judicial office either in a primary or in a general election, except that the judge may continue to hold judicial office while being a candidate for election to or serving as a delegate in a state constitutional convention if the judge is otherwise permitted by law to do so.

(3) A candidate for a judicial office:

(a) shall be faithful to the law and maintain professional competence in it, and shall not be swayed by partisan interests, public clamor, or fear of criticism;

(b) shall maintain the dignity appropriate to judicial office and act in a manner consistent with the impartiality, integrity, and independence of the judiciary, and shall encourage members of the candidate's family to adhere to the same standards of political conduct in support of the candidate as apply to the candidate;

(c) shall prohibit employees and officials who serve at the pleasure of the candidate, and shall discourage other employees and officials subject to the candidate's direction and control from doing on the candidate's behalf what the candidate is prohibited from doing under the Sections of this Canon;

(d) except to the extent permitted by Section 7C(1), shall not authorize or knowingly permit any other person to do for the candidate what the candidate is prohibited from doing under the Sections of this Canon;

(e) shall not:

(i) with respect to parties or classes of parties, cases, controversies, or issues that are likely to come before the court, make pledges, promises, or commitments that are inconsistent with the impartial performance of the adjudicative duties of the office; or

(ii) knowingly misrepresent the identity, qualifications, present position or other fact concerning the candidate or an opponent;

(iii) while a proceeding is pending or impending in any court, make any public comment that might reasonably be expected to affect its outcome or impair its fairness or make any nonpublic comment that might substantially interfere with a fair trial or hearing. This section does not apply to proceedings in which the judicial candidate is a litigant in a personal capacity.

(iv) commend or criticize jurors for their verdict, other than in a court pleading, filing or hearing in which the candidate represents a party in the proceeding in which the verdict was rendered.

(f) may respond to personal attacks or attacks on the candidate's record as long as the response does not violate Section 7A(3)(e).

B. Candidates Seeking Appointment to Judicial or Other Governmental Office.

(1) A candidate for appointment to judicial office or a judge seeking other governmental office shall not solicit or accept funds, personally or through a committee or otherwise, to support his or her candidacy.

(2) A candidate for appointment to judicial office or a judge seeking other governmental office shall not engage in any political activity to secure the appointment except that:

(a) such persons may:

(i) communicate with the appointing authority, including any selection or nominating commission or other agency designated to screen candidates;

(ii) seek support or endorsement for the appointment from organizations that regularly make recommendations for reappointment or appointment to the office, and from individuals; and

(iii) provide to those specified in Sections 7B(2)(a)(i) and 7B(2)(a)(ii) information as to his or her qualifications for the office;

(b) a non-judge candidate for appointment to judicial office may, in addition, unless otherwise prohibited by law:

(i) retain an office in a political organization,

(ii) attend political gatherings, and

(iii) continue to pay ordinary assessments and ordinary contributions to a political organization or candidate and purchase tickets for political party dinners or other functions.

C. Judges and Candidates Subject to Public Election.

(1) A candidate, including an incumbent judge, for a judicial office that is filled by public election between competing candidates shall not personally solicit campaign funds, or solicit attorneys for publicly stated support, but may establish committees of responsible persons to secure and manage the expenditure of funds for the candidate's campaign and to obtain public statements of support for his or her candidacy. Such committees are not prohibited from soliciting campaign contributions and public support from any person or corporation authorized by law. A candidate shall not use or permit the use of campaign contributions for the private benefit of the candidate or members of the candidate's family.

(2) A candidate for merit retention in office may conduct only limited campaign activities until such time as the judge certifies that the judge's candidacy has drawn active opposition. Limited campaign activities shall only include the conduct authorized by subsection C(1), interviews with reporters and editors of the print, audio and visual media, and appearances and speaking engagements before public gatherings and organizations. Upon mailing a certificate in writing to the Secretary of State, Division of Elections, with a copy to the Judicial Qualifications Commission, that the judge's candidacy has drawn active opposition, and specifying the nature thereof, a judge may thereafter campaign in any manner authorized by law, subject to the restrictions of subsection A(3). This includes candidates facing active opposition in a merit retention election for the same judicial office campaigning together and conducting a joint campaign designed to educate the public on merit retention and each candidate's views as to why he or she should be

retained in office, to the extent not otherwise prohibited by Florida law.

(3) A judicial candidate involved in an election or re-election, or a merit retention candidate who has certified that he or she has active opposition, may attend a political party function to speak in behalf of his or her candidacy or on a matter that relates to the law, the improvement of the legal system, or the administration of justice. The function must not be a fund raiser, and the invitation to speak must also include the other candidates, if any, for that office. The candidate should refrain from commenting on the candidate's affiliation with any political party or other candidate, and should avoid expressing a position on any political issue. A judicial candidate attending a political party function must avoid conduct that suggests or appears to suggest support of or opposition to a political party, a political issue, or another candidate. Conduct limited to that described above does not constitute participation in a partisan political party activity.

D. Incumbent Judges. A judge shall not engage in any political activity except (i) as authorized under any other Section of this Code, (ii) on behalf of measures to improve the law, the legal system or the administration of justice, or (iii) as expressly authorized by law.

E. Applicability. Canon 7 generally applies to all incumbent judges and judicial candidates. A successful candidate, whether or not an incumbent, is subject to judicial discipline for his or her campaign conduct; an unsuccessful candidate who is a lawyer is subject to lawyer discipline for his or her campaign conduct. A lawyer who is a candidate for judicial office is subject to Rule 4–8.2(b) of the Rules Regulating The Florida Bar.

F. Statement of Candidate for Judicial Office. Each candidate for a judicial office, including an incumbent judge, shall file a statement with the qualifying officer within 10 days after filing the appointment of campaign treasurer and designation of campaign depository, stating that the candidate has read and understands the requirements of the Florida Code of Judicial Conduct. Such statement shall be in substantially the following form:

STATEMENT OF CANDIDATE FOR JUDICIAL OFFICE

I, ______________, the judicial candidate, have received, have read, and understand the requirements of the Florida Code of Judicial Conduct.

____
Signature of Candidate

____
Date

Amended Aug. 24, 1995 (659 So.2d 692); May 30, 1996 (675 So.2d 111); Nov. 12, 1998 (720 So.2d 1079); Mar. 10, 2005 (897 So.2d 1262); Jan. 5, 2006 (918 So.2d 949); July 3, 2008, (985 So.2d 1073); June 11, 2015, effective June 11, 2015 (167 So.3d 399).

Commentary

Canon 7A(1). A judge or candidate for judicial office retains the right to participate in the political process as a voter.

Where false information concerning a judicial candidate is made public, a judge or another judicial candidate having knowledge of the facts is not prohibited by Section 7A(1) from making the facts public.

Section 7A(1)(a) does not prohibit a candidate for elective judicial office from retaining during candidacy a public office such as county prosecutor, which is not "an office in a political organization."

Section 7A(1)(b) does not prohibit a judge or judicial candidate from privately expressing his or her views on judicial candidates or other candidates for public office.

A candidate does not publicly endorse another candidate for public office by having that candidate's name on the same ticket.

Section 7A(1)(b) prohibits judges and judicial candidates from publicly endorsing or opposing candidates for public office to prevent them from abusing the prestige of judicial office to advance the interests of others. Section 7C(2) authorizes candidates facing active opposition in a merit retention election for the same judicial office to campaign together and conduct a joint campaign designed to educate the public on merit retention and each candidate's views as to why he or she should be retained in office, to the extent not otherwise prohibited by Florida law. Joint campaigning by merit retention candidates, as authorized under Section 7C(2), is not a prohibited public endorsement of another candidate under Section 7A(1)(b).

Canon 7A(3)(b). Although a judicial candidate must encourage members of his or her family to adhere to the same standards of political conduct in support of the candidate that apply to the candidate, family members are free to participate in other political activity.

Canon 7A(3)(e). Section 7A(3)(e) prohibits a candidate for judicial office from making statements that commit the candidate regarding cases, controversies or issues likely to come before the court. As a corollary, a candidate should emphasize in any public statement the candidate's duty to uphold the law regardless of his or her personal views. Section 7A(3)(e) does not prohibit a candidate from making pledges or promises respecting improvements in court administration. Nor does this Section prohibit an incumbent judge from making private statements to other judges or court personnel in the performance of judicial duties. This Section applies to any statement made in the process of securing judicial office, such as statements to commissions charged with judicial selection and tenure and legislative bodies confirming appointment.

Canon 7B(2). Section 7B(2) provides a limited exception to the restrictions imposed by Sections 7A(1) and 7D. Under Section 7B(2), candidates seeking reappointment to the same judicial office or appointment to another judicial office or other governmental office may apply for the appointment and seek appropriate support.

Although under Section 7B(2) non-judge candidates seeking appointment to judicial office are permitted during candidacy to retain office in a political organization, attend political gatherings and pay ordinary dues and assessments, they remain subject to other provisions of this Code during candidacy. See Sections 7B(1), 7B(2)(a), 7E and Application Section.

Canon 7C. The term "limited campaign activities" is not intended to permit the use of common forms of campaign advertisement which include, but are not limited to, billboards, bumperstickers, media commercials, newspaper advertisements, signs, etc. Informational brochures about the merit retention system, the law, the legal system or the administration of justice, and neutral, factual biographical sketches of the candidates do not violate this provision.

Active opposition is difficult to define but is intended to include any form of organized public opposition or an unfavorable vote on a bar poll. Any political activity engaged in by members of a judge's family should be conducted in the name of the individual family member, entirely independent of the judge and without reference to the judge or to the judge's office.

Canon 7D. Neither Section 7D nor any other section of the Code prohibits a judge in the exercise of administrative functions from engaging in planning and other official activities with members of the executive and legislative branches of government. With respect to a judge's activity on behalf of measures to improve the law, the legal system and the administration of justice, see Commentary to Section 4B and Section 4C and its Commentary.

Application of the Code of Judicial Conduct

This Code applies to justices of the Supreme Court and judges of the District Courts of Appeal, Circuit Courts, and County Courts.

Anyone, whether or not a lawyer, who performs judicial functions, including but not limited to a civil traffic infraction hearing officer, court commissioner, general or special magistrate, domestic relations commissioner, child support hearing officer, or judge of compensation claims, shall, while performing judicial functions, conform with Canons 1, 2A, and 3, and such other provisions of this Code that might reasonably be applicable depending on the nature of the judicial function performed.

Any judge responsible for a person who performs a judicial function should require compliance with the applicable provisions of this Code.

If the hiring or appointing authority for persons who perform a judicial function is not a judge then that authority should adopt the applicable provisions of this Code.

A. Civil Traffic Infraction Hearing Officer

A civil traffic infraction hearing officer:

(1) is not required to comply with Section 5C(2), 5D(2) and (3), 5E, 5F, and 5G, and Sections 6B and 6C.

(2) should not practice law in the civil or criminal traffic court in any county in which the civil traffic infraction hearing officer presides.

B. Retired/Senior Judge

(1) A retired judge eligible to serve on assignment to temporary judicial duty, hereinafter referred to as "senior judge," shall comply with all the provisions of this Code except Sections 5C(2), 5E, 5F(1), and 6A. A senior judge shall not practice law or serve as a mediator in a circuit in which the judge is presiding as a senior judge, and shall refrain from accepting any assignment in any cause in which the judge's present financial business dealings, investments, or other extra-judicial activities might be directly or indirectly affected.

(2) If a retired justice or judge does not desire to be assigned to judicial service, such justice or judge who is a member of The Florida Bar may engage in the practice of law and still be entitled to receive retirement compensation. The justice or judge shall then be entitled to all the rights of an attorney-at-law and no longer be subject to this Code.

Amended Nov. 3, 2005, effective Jan. 1, 2006 (915 So.2d 145); Jan. 5, 2006 (918 So.2d 949); June 19, 2014, effective Oct. 1, 2014 (141 So.3d 1172).

Commentary

Section A. Please see *In re Florida Rules of Practice and Procedure for Traffic Courts—Civil Traffic Infraction Hearing Officer Pilot Program,* 559 So. 2d 1101 (Fla.1990), regarding civil traffic infraction hearing officers.

Effective Date of Compliance

A person to whom this Code becomes applicable shall comply immediately with all provisions of this Code except Sections 5D(2), 5D(3) and 5E and shall comply with these Sections as soon as reasonably possible and shall do so in any event within the period of one year.

Commentary

If serving as a fiduciary when selected as judge, a new judge may, notwithstanding the prohibitions in Section 5E, continue to serve as fiduciary but only for that period of time necessary to avoid serious adverse consequences to the beneficiary of the fiduciary relationship and in no event longer than one year. Similarly, if engaged at the time of judicial selection in a business activity, a new judge may, notwithstanding the prohibitions in Section 5D(3), continue in that activity for a reasonable period but in no event longer than one year.

RULES OF THE SUPREME COURT RELATING TO ADMISSIONS TO THE BAR

Date Effective

Effective June 1, 1981 (397 So.2d 627)

Revision

Revised June 5, 1997 (695 So.2d 312). The Florida Supreme Court per curiam opinion of June 5, 1997, rewrote and reorganized the Rules of the Supreme Court Relating to Admissions to The Bar. The former configuration of seven articles was replaced with five rules. A number of substantive changes and deletions were also made.

Rule 1. General

1–10 Authority and Mission.

1–11 Introduction. The admission of attorneys to the practice of the profession of law is a judicial function.

1–12 Rules. The Rules of the Supreme Court Relating to Admissions to the Bar are reviewed, approved, and promulgated by the Supreme Court of Florida. Modifications to the rules require the filing of a petition with the Supreme Court of Florida and subsequent order by the court.

1–12.1 Deadlines on Weekend or Holiday. If a deadline described in these rules falls on a Saturday, Sunday, or holiday, then the deadline will be extended until the end of the next business day.

1–13 Florida Board of Bar Examiners. The Florida Board of Bar Examiners is an administrative agency of the Supreme Court of Florida created by the court to implement the rules relating to bar admission.

1–14 Background Investigations.

1–14.1 Purpose. The primary purposes of the character and fitness investigation before admission to The Florida Bar are to protect the public and safeguard the judicial system.

1–14.2 Responsibility. The board must ensure that each applicant has met the requirements of the rules with regard to character and fitness, education, and technical competence prior to recommending an applicant for admission.

1–15 Bar Examination.

1–15.1 Purpose. The primary purpose of the bar examination is to ensure that all who are admitted to The Florida Bar have demonstrated minimum technical competence.

1–15.2 Responsibility. The board is responsible for preparing, administering, and grading written examinations. Board members must be willing and available to discuss with applicants the purposes, policies, and procedures of the admissions process.

1–16 Admission Recommendations. Following each of its meetings, the board will recommend the admission of every applicant who has complied with all the requirements of the applicable rules, who has attained passing scores on the examination, and who has demonstrated the requisite character and fitness for admission.

1–20 Florida Board of Bar Examiners.

1–21 Membership. The Florida Board of Bar Examiners consists of 12 members of The Florida Bar and 3 public members who are not lawyers.

1–21.1 Additional Members. The board may submit to the court a request for additional members to serve, as necessary. The request and appointee recommendations must be submitted in the same manner as appointee recommendations under rules 1–22.2 and 1–23.2. The term of service of a member appointed under this rule will be as provided in rules 1–22.3 and 1–23.3 or as otherwise approved by the court.

1–22 Attorney Members.

1–22.1 Qualifications. Attorney members must be practicing attorneys with scholarly attainments and an affirmative interest in legal education and the requirements for admission to the bar. Attorney members must have been members of The Florida Bar for at least 5 years.

1–22.2 Appointments. The Florida Bar Board of Governors must submit to the court not less than 90 days before the expiration of the term of any attorney member of the board, or within 90 days of a vacancy, a group of 3 recommended appointees.

1–22.3 Term of Service. Appointments will be for no more than 5 years and the term of all appointments will extend to October 31 of the last year of the term. Any vacancy occurring during a term must be filled by appointment. No attorney appointed by the court as a result of a vacancy occurring during a term will be appointed for more than 5 years.

1–23 Public Members.

1–23.1 Qualifications. Public members must not be lawyers and must have an academic bachelor's degree. It is desirable that public members possess educational or work-related experience of value to the board such as educational testing, accounting, statistical analysis, medicine, psychology, or related sciences.

1–23.2 Appointments. A joint committee composed of 3 members of the board and 3 members of The Florida Bar Board of Governors must submit to the court not less than 90 days before the expiration of the term of any public member of the board, or within 90 days of a vacancy, a group of 3 recommended appointees.

1–23.3 Term of Service. Appointments will be for no more than 3 years and the term of all appointments will extend to October 31 of the last year of the term. Any vacancy occurring during a term must be filled by appointment. No public member appointed by the court as a result of a vacancy occurring during a term will be appointed for more than 3 years.

1–24 Board Members Emeritus.

1–24.1 Eligibility. A former member of the board may accept the designation of board member emeritus, if eligible under rule 1–34.

1–24.2 Purpose. To assist the board in fulfilling its investigative and adjudicative functions, a board member emeritus is authorized to participate as a member of an investigative or formal hearing panel as provided by rule 3–22 and 3–23.2. The formal hearing panel must consist of a majority of current members of the board. At least 1 member of an investigative hearing panel must be a current member of the board. All recommendations of investigative hearing panels must be approved by a quorum of the current board.

1–25 Officers.

1–25.1 Vice Chair. During the board meeting preceding November 1 of each year, the board must designate a vice chair who will hold office for a period of 1 year beginning on November 1. The designation will be determined by majority vote. In the event of an irreconcilable tie vote, the matter will be certified to the Supreme Court of Florida, and the court will designate the vice chair for the next year.

1–25.2 Chair. On November 1 of each succeeding year, the previously elected vice chair will become chair for a period of 1 year.

1–27 Office Location. The office of the board will be maintained in Tallahassee, Florida.

1–30 Board Member Responsibilities.

1–31 Tenure. A board member should be appointed for a fixed term but should be eligible for reappointment if the board member's work is of high quality. Members of the board should be appointed for staggered terms to ensure continuity of policy but with sufficient rotation to bring new views to the board and to ensure continuing interest in its work.

1–32 Devotion to Duty. A board member should be willing and able to devote whatever time is necessary to perform the duties of a board member.

1–33 Essential Conduct. A board member should be conscientious, studious, thorough, and diligent in learning the methods, problems, and progress of legal education, in preparing bar examinations, and in seeking to improve the examination, its administration, and requirements for admission to the bar. Each board member should be just and impartial in recommending the admission of applicants and should exhibit courage, judgment, and moral stamina in refusing to recommend applicants who lack adequate general and professional preparation or who lack good moral character.

1–34 Board Influences, Conflicting Duties, and Obligations. Board members should not have adverse interests, conflicting duties, inconsistent obligations, or improper considerations that will in any way interfere or appear to interfere with the proper administration of their functions. A member of the board or a board member emeritus may not serve as a judge of any court; a regular or adjunct professor of law; an instructor, advisor or in any capacity related to a bar review course, or in other activities involved with preparation of applicants for bar admission; or as a member of the governing or other policy-making board or committee of a law school or the university of which it is a part. A board member is not prohibited from service on the board or as an officer of alumni groups that support law schools or universities or from assisting them with fund raising activities.

1–35 Compensation. Board members will serve without compensation, but will be reimbursed for reasonable travel and subsistence expenses incurred in the performance of their services for the board.

1–40 Board Meetings.

1–41 Conducting Board Meetings. The board will meet in formal session throughout the State of Florida on a regularly scheduled basis to consider administrative, applicant, and registrant matters and to conduct investigative and formal hearings. Subject to the approval of the board, the place and time of meetings will be determined by the chair of the board.

1–42 Special Hearing Panels. Hearings may also be conducted by special hearing panels of the board convened at other times and places fixed by the board.

1–43 Telephone Conference Meetings. On reasonable notice, the chair of the board may conduct a meeting of the board by conference telephone call for routine administrative action or for emergency action.

1–50 Fiscal Authority.

1–51 Budget. The board will annually prepare a budget and submit it to the Supreme Court of Florida for approval.

1–51.1 Income. Subject to the approval of the court, the board may classify applicants and registrants, and fix the charges, fees, and expenses that will be paid by each.

1–51.2 Expenses. The board will make such disbursements as are required to pay the necessary expenses of the board.

1–52 Audit. The board will have an annual audit conducted by a certified public accountant. The annual audit must be filed with the Clerk of the Supreme Court of Florida.

1–53 Staffing. The board will employ an executive director and other assistants as it may deem necessary. It will provide for the compensation of employees and will pay expenses incurred in the performance of their official duties. All employees must be bonded as may be directed by the board.

1–60 Confidentiality.

1–61 Confidentiality. All information maintained by the board in the discharge of the responsibilities delegated to it by the Supreme Court of Florida is confidential, except as provided by these rules or otherwise authorized by the court.

1–62 Custodian of Records. All records including, but not limited to, registrant and applicant files, investigative reports, examination materials, and interoffice memoranda are the property of the Supreme Court of Florida, and the board will serve as custodian of all the records.

1–63 Release of Information. The board is authorized to disclose information relating to an individual registrant, applicant, or member of The Florida Bar, absent specific instructions from the court, in the following situations only.

1–63.1 Public Request. On request, the staff will confirm if a person has filed a Registrant Bar Application, Examination Application, or Bar Application with the board, and will provide the date of admission of any attorney admitted to The Florida Bar.

1–63.2 National Data Bank. The name, date of birth, Social Security number, and date of application will be provided for placement in a national data bank operated by, or on behalf of, the National Conference of Bar Examiners.

1–63.3 The Florida Bar. On written request from The Florida Bar for information relating to disciplinary proceedings, reinstatement proceedings, or unlicensed practice of law investigations, information will be provided with the exception of any information received by the board under the specific agreement of confidentiality or otherwise restricted by law.

1–63.4 National Conference of Bar Examiners or Foreign Bar Admitting Agency. On written request from the National Conference of Bar Examiners, or from foreign bar admitting agencies, foreign bar associations, or other similar agencies, when accompanied by an authorization and release executed by the person about whom information is sought, information will be provided with the exception of any information received by the board under a specific agreement of confidentiality or otherwise restricted by law.

1–63.5 Documents Filed by Registrant or Applicant. On written request from registrants or applicants for copies of documents previously filed by them, and copies of any documents or exhibits formally introduced into the record at an investigative or formal hearing before the board, and the transcript of hearings, copies will be provided. Costs of copies are set out below:

(a) The fee for a copy of any document or portion of a document is $25 for the first page and 50 cents for each additional page.

(b) The fee for a copy of the Bar Application or Registrant Bar Application is $50.

1–63.6 Documents Filed on Behalf of the Registrant or Applicant. On written request from registrants or applicants, copies of documents filed on their behalf, or at the request of the board with the written consent of the party submitting the documents, will be provided. If the documents would be independently available to the requesting registrant or applicant, then consent of the party submitting the documents will be deemed waived. The fees for requested copies are $25 for the first page and 50 cents for each additional page.

1–63.7 Grand Jury or Florida State Attorney. On service of a subpoena issued by a Federal or Florida grand jury, or Florida state attorney, in connection with a felony investigation only, information will be provided with the exception of any information that is otherwise restricted by law.

1–63.8 Third Parties. The board may divulge the following information to all sources contacted during the background investigation:

(a) name of applicant or registrant;

(b) former names;

(c) date of birth;

(d) current address; and

(e) Social Security number.

1–63.9 List of Candidates. Following the board's recommendation under rule 5–10 and the court's approval for an applicant's admission to The Florida Bar, the applicant's name and mailing address is public information.

1–64 Breach of Confidentiality. Whenever any person intentionally and without authority discloses confidential information maintained by the board, the person may be in contempt of the board. The board must report to the Supreme Court of Florida the fact that the person is in contempt of the board for proceedings against the person as the court may deem advisable.

1–65 Disclosure of Information. Unless otherwise ordered by the Supreme Court of Florida, the chair of the board, or the presiding officer at a hearing before the board, nothing in these rules prohibits any applicant or witness from disclosing the existence or nature of any proceeding under rule 3, or from disclosing any documents or correspondence served on, submitted by, or provided to the applicant or witness.

1–70 Immunity and Privilege.

1–71 Board and Employee Civil Immunity. The board and its members, employees, and agents are immune from all civil liability for damages for conduct and communications occurring in the performance and within the scope of their official duties relating to the examination, character and fitness qualification, and licensing of persons seeking to be admitted to the practice of law.

1–72 Immunity and Privilege for Information. Records, statements of opinion, and other information regarding an applicant for admission to The Florida Bar, communicated without malice to the board, its members, employees, or agents by any entity, including any person, firm, or institution, are privileged, and civil suits for damages predicated on those communications may not be instituted.

Added June 5, 1997 (695 So.2d 312). Amended June 4, 1998 (712 So.2d 766); March 20, 2003 (843 So.2d 245); October 18, 2007, eff. May 1, 2008 (967 So.2d 877); Dec. 16, 2010 (52 So.3d 652); Feb. 3, 2011 (54 So.3d 460); May 28, 2015, effective June 29, 2015, (165 So.3d 666); June 4, 2015, effective June 4, 2015 (166 So.3d 178).

Rule 2. Application requirements

2–10 Application Qualifications. To seek admission to The Florida Bar, a person must meet the qualifications, file the appropriate applications and fees as set out in this rule, and comply with rules 3 and 4.

2–12 Proof of Character and Fitness. All applicants seeking admission to The Florida Bar must produce satisfactory evidence of good moral character, an adequate knowledge of the standards and ideals of the profession, and proof that the applicant is otherwise fit to take the oath and to perform the obligations and responsibilities of an attorney. See rule 3, Background Investigation.

2–13 Prohibitions Against Application. A person is not eligible to apply for admission to The Florida Bar or for admission into the General Bar Examination unless the time period as indicated below has expired, or the required condition or status has been met.

2–13.1 Disbarred or Resigned Pending Disciplinary Proceedings. A person who has been disbarred from the practice of law, or who has resigned pending disciplinary proceedings and whose resignation from practice has been accepted by the Supreme Court of Florida, in proceedings based on conduct that occurred in Florida for the disbarment or resignation, will not be eligible to apply for readmission for a period of 5 years from the date of disbarment, or 3 years from the date of resignation, such other time as is set forth in any Florida rules of discipline, or longer period set for readmission by the Supreme Court of Florida. If the person's disbarment or disciplinary resignation is based on conduct that occurred in a foreign jurisdiction, then the person will not be eligible to apply for admission or readmission to The Florida Bar until the person is readmitted in the foreign jurisdiction in which the conduct that resulted in discipline occurred. Readmission must occur in the foreign jurisdiction in which the conduct occurred even if Florida imposed discipline prior to the imposition of discipline in the other jurisdiction and even if the person would otherwise be eligible for readmission under the terms of any Florida discipline.

2–13.15 Public Hearing. Once eligibility has been established, and following completion of the background investigation, the applicant who has been disbarred, or who has resigned pending disciplinary proceedings, will be required to appear for a formal hearing that is open to the public as provided by rule 3–22.7.

2–13.2 Suspension for Disciplinary Reasons. A person who has been suspended for disciplinary reasons from the practice of law in a foreign jurisdiction is not eligible to apply until expiration of the period of suspension. If the person's suspension occurred in the person's home state, then the person is not eligible to apply for admission to The Florida Bar until the person is reinstated to the practice of law in the person's home state.

2–13.25 Satisfaction of Court–Ordered Restitution and Disciplinary Costs. Except upon a showing of exceptional circumstances, a person who was disbarred, resigned with pending disciplinary proceedings, or was suspended in Florida or from a foreign jurisdiction will not be eligible to apply except on proof of satisfaction in full of any restitution and disciplinary costs. Restitution consists of the following:

(a) restitution imposed by a court in its order of disbarment, resignation, or suspension;

(b) restitution ordered by a court in any underlying criminal case that resulted in the disbarment, resignation, or suspension; and

(c) restitution owed for the payment of any claims by the Clients' Security Fund in Florida or by a similar bar fund in a foreign jurisdiction.

Exceptional circumstances may be established by showing that the applicant has made diligent, good-faith efforts to satisfy the restitution and costs obligation and has demonstrated a consistent commitment to fully satisfy the obligation; the applicant has entered a payment plan which insures satisfaction in full as soon as practicable; and the payment plan is necessary to protect the interests of any person or entity entitled to payment.

2–13.3 Convicted Felon. A person who has been convicted of a felony is not eligible to apply until the person's civil rights have been restored.

2–13.4 Serving Felony Probation. A person who is serving a sentence of felony probation, regardless of adjudication of guilt, is not eligible to apply until termination of the period of probation.

2–13.5 Found Unqualified by Board. Any applicant or registrant, who was previously denied admission by the board by a negotiated consent judgment or through a "Findings of Fact and Conclusions of Law" that has not been reversed by the Supreme Court of Florida, may reapply for admission by filing a new Bar Application after 2 years or such other period as may be set in the consent judgment or the Findings. The applicant or registrant will be eligible to take the General Bar Examination during the disqualification period.

2–14 Reapplications for Admission. Any applicant or registrant who was previously denied admission by the board by a negotiated consent judgment or through a "Findings of Fact and Conclusions of Law" that has not been reversed by the Supreme Court of Florida may reapply for admission by filing a new Bar Application after 2 years or such other period as may be set in the consent judgment or the Findings. The new application must be filed on the form available on the board's website with current references, submission of fingerprints in the format required by the board, any supplemental documents that the board may reasonably require, the applicable fee, and a detailed written statement describing the scope and character of the applicant's evidence of rehabilitation as required by rule 3–13. The statement must be sworn and may include corroborating evidence such as letters and affidavits. Thereafter, the board will determine at an investigative hearing, a formal hearing, or both, if the applicant's evidence of rehabilitation is clear and convincing and will make a recommendation as required by rule 3–23.6. In determining whether an applicant should appear before an investigative hearing panel, a formal hearing panel, or both, the board is clothed with broad discretion.

2–20 Applications and Fees.

2–21 Applications. Every applicant for admission to The Florida Bar must file with the board a Bar Application on the form available on the board's website. Law student registrants who register with the board under rule 2–21.2 must file a Registrant Bar Application and a Supplement to Registrant Bar Application. The Bar Application or Registrant Bar Application must be completed interactively online using instructions on the board's website.

2–21.1 Admission to General Bar Examination. A person who, prior to the applicable filing deadline specified in rule 4–42 or the applicable late filing deadline specified in rule 4–43, has not filed with the board the Bar Application (or, in the case of a law student registrant, the Registrant Bar Application and the Supplement to Registrant Bar Application) and paid the appropriate filing fees will not be permitted to take the General Bar Examination.

2–21.2 Registration. Law students are encouraged to register with the board within the first year of law school. Every law student intending to apply for admission to The Florida Bar, following the commencement of the study of law in an accredited law school, may register with the board by filing a Registrant Bar Application on the form available on the board's website accompanied by the applicable filing fee, and any supplemental documents that reasonably may be required by the board. See rule 2–23.1 for a schedule of fees. A basic character and fitness investigation will be conducted in areas of possible concern on each registrant. The Registrant Bar Application must be converted into a Bar Application by the filing of a Supplement to Registrant Bar Application available online on the board's website. Each law student registrant is encouraged to file the Supplement to Registrant Bar Application at the beginning of the student's final year in law school to ensure timely completion of the board's character and fitness investigation.

2–22 Character and Fitness Investigation. On the filing of a Bar Application or a Registrant Bar Application, the board will initiate a character and fitness investigation under these rules. When a law student registrant files a Supplement to Registrant Bar Application, the board will update the character and fitness investigation conducted following such student's filing of the Registrant Bar Application.

2–23 Application Fees. All fees are set by order of the Supreme Court of Florida and are subject to change by published order of the court. The total application fee is due and payable to the Florida Board of Bar Examiners by the applicant when filing the Bar Application, the Registrant Bar Application, or the Supplement to Registrant Bar Application, and no application will be considered complete without the full fee. Any fee paid by an applicant or registrant will not be refunded.

2–23.1 Student Registrant Fee. Except as provided below, every law student filing a Registrant Bar Application with the board must file with the completed Registrant Bar Application the fee of $400. For any law student who files a Registrant Bar Application by the deadlines established, discounted early registration fees are available as follows:

(a) *$100.* For those students who commence the study of law in:

(1) August or September and who file a Registrant Bar Application by the following January 15;

(2) January or February and who file a Registrant Bar Application by the following June 15; or

(3) May or June and who file a Registrant Bar Application by the following October 15.

(b) *$350.* For those students who commence the study of law in:

(1) August or September and who file a Registrant Bar Application by the following March 15;

(2) January or February and who file a Registrant Bar Application by the following August 15; or

(3) May or June and who file a Registrant Bar Application by the following December 15.

2–23.2 Student Applicant Fee. Applicants who did not file the Registrant Bar Application with the board as law students and who have not been admitted to the bar in any jurisdiction for a period in excess of 12 months, excluding time spent in military service of the United States, must file with the Bar Application the fee of $1,000.

2–23.3 Supplement to Registrant Bar Application Fee. Applicants who filed the Registrant Bar Application with the board as law students and who have not been admitted to the bar in any jurisdiction for a period in excess of 12 months, excluding time spent in military service of the United States, must file with the Supplement to Registrant Bar Application the applicable fee as follows:

(a) *Less than 5 years.* If the Supplement to Registrant Bar Application is filed within 5 years of the filing date of the original Registrant Bar Application, the fee is $600.

(b) *More than 5 years.* If the Supplement to Registrant Bar Application is filed more than 5 years after the filing of the original Registrant Bar Application, the fee is $1,000 as set forth in rule 2–23.2, less any fee previously paid.

2–23.4 Attorney Fee. Applicants who have been admitted to the bar in any jurisdiction for a period in excess of 12 months, excluding time spent in military service of the United States, must file with the Bar Application a fee based on the number of years the applicant has been admitted in another jurisdiction as follows:

(a) *Less than 5 years.* If the applicant has been admitted in another jurisdiction for more than 1 year but less than 5 years, the fee is $1,600.

(b) *5 or more but less than 10 years.* If the applicant has been admitted in another jurisdiction for 5 years or more but less than 10 years, the fee is $2,000.

(c) *10 or more but less than 15 years.* If the applicant has been admitted in another jurisdiction for 10 years or more but less than 15 years, the fee is $2,400.

(d) *15 or more years.* If the applicant has been admitted in another jurisdiction for 15 or more years, the fee is $3,000.

2–23.5 Fee Determination. The fee for an admitted attorney is determined by the date of the filing of the Bar Application and the status of the applicant on that date as it relates to his or her admission to the bar of any foreign jurisdiction or United States military service.

2–23.6 Disbarred Attorney Fee. Applicants applying for admission after disbarment or resignation pending disciplinary proceedings in Florida or in any other jurisdiction must file with the Bar Application the fee of $6,000.

2–28 Application Fee for Reapplication for Admission Based on Rehabilitation. Applicants or registrants who are reapplying for admission and asserting rehabilitation from prior conduct that resulted in a denial of admission through Findings of Fact and Conclusions of Law or Consent Judgment must file with the application a fee of $2,200.

2–29 Stale File Fee. An applicant whose Bar Application has been on file for more than 3 years is required to file a new Bar Application on the form available on the board's website with current references, submission of fingerprints in the format required by the board, any supplemental documents that the board may reasonably require, and the applicable fee.

(a) *If within 5 Years.* If filed within 5 years of the filing date of the last application filed, a fee of $525 is applicable.

(b) *If more than 5 Years.* If filed more than 5 years after the filing date of the last application filed, the full application fee under rules 2–23.2, 2–23.4, or 2–23.6 above is applicable.

2–30 Petitions Relating to Administrative Rulings.

2–30.1 Filed with the Board. Any applicant or registrant who is dissatisfied with an administrative decision of the board that does not concern character and fitness matters may petition the board for reconsideration of the decision. Applicants also may petition the board for a suspension or waiver of any bar admission rule or regulation. A petition seeking a suspension or waiver of a rule or seeking review of an administrative decision not related to a character and fitness recommendation may be presented in the form of a letter, must be filed with the board within 60 days after receipt of written notice of the board's action complained of, and must be filed with a fee of $75.

2–30.2 Filed with the Court. Any applicant or registrant who is dissatisfied with an administrative decision of the board that does not concern character and fitness matters may, within 60 days after receipt of written notice of that decision, file a petition with the Supreme Court of Florida for review of the action. If not inconsistent with these rules, the Florida Rules of Appellate Procedure are applicable to all proceedings filed in the Supreme Court of Florida. A copy of the petition must be served on the executive director of the board. The applicant seeking review must serve an initial brief within 30 days of the filing of the petition. The board will have 30 days to serve an answer brief after the service of the applicant's initial brief. The applicant may serve a reply brief within 30 days after the service of the answer brief.

Added June 5, 1997 (695 So.2d 312). Amended June 4, 1998 (712 So.2d 766); Jan. 6, 2000 (762 So.2d 435); March 20, 2003 (843 So.2d 245); October 18, 2007, eff. May 1, 2008 (967 So.2d 877); Dec. 16, 2010 (52 So.3d 652); Feb. 3, 2011 (54 So.3d 460).

Rule 3. Background investigation

3–10 Standards of an Attorney. An attorney should have a record of conduct that justifies the trust of clients, adversaries, courts, and others with respect to the professional duties owed to him or her.

3–10.1 Essential Eligibility Requirements. The board considers the following attributes to be essential for all applicants and registrants seeking admission to The Florida Bar:

(a) knowledge of the fundamental principles of law and their application;

(b) ability to reason logically and accurately analyze legal problems; and,

(c) ability to and the likelihood that, in the practice of law, one will:

(1) comply with deadlines;

(2) communicate candidly and civilly with clients, attorneys, courts, and others;

(3) conduct financial dealings in a responsible, honest, and trustworthy manner;

(4) avoid acts that are illegal, dishonest, fraudulent, or deceitful; and,

(5) comply with the requirements of applicable state, local, and federal laws, rules, and regulations; any applicable order of a court or tribunal; and the Rules of Professional Conduct.

3–11 Disqualifying Conduct. A record manifesting a lack of honesty, trustworthiness, diligence, or reliability of an applicant or registrant may constitute a basis for denial of admission. The revelation or discovery of any of the following may be cause for further inquiry before the board recommends whether the applicant or registrant possesses the character and fitness to practice law:

(a) unlawful conduct;

(b) academic misconduct;

(c) making or procuring any false or misleading statement or omission of relevant information, including any false or misleading statement or omission on the Bar Application, or any amendment, or in any testimony or sworn statement submitted to the board;

(d) misconduct in employment;

(e) acts involving dishonesty, fraud, deceit, or misrepresentation;

(f) abuse of legal process;

(g) financial irresponsibility;

(h) neglect of professional obligations;

(i) violation of an order of a court;

(j) evidence of mental or emotional instability;

(k) evidence of drug or alcohol dependency;

(*l*) denial of admission to the bar in another jurisdiction on character and fitness grounds;

(m) disciplinary action by a lawyer disciplinary agency or other professional disciplinary agency of any jurisdiction; or

(n) any other conduct that reflects adversely on the character or fitness of the applicant.

3–12 Determination of Present Character. The board must determine whether the applicant or registrant has provided satisfactory evidence of good moral character. The following factors, among others, will be considered in assigning weight and significance to prior conduct:

(a) age at the time of the conduct;

(b) recency of the conduct;

(c) reliability of the information concerning the conduct;

(d) seriousness of the conduct;

(e) factors underlying the conduct;

(f) cumulative effect of the conduct or information;

(g) evidence of rehabilitation;

(h) positive social contributions since the conduct;

(i) candor in the admissions process; and,

(j) materiality of any omissions or misrepresentations.

3–13 Elements of Rehabilitation. Any applicant or registrant who affirmatively asserts rehabilitation from prior conduct that adversely reflects on the person's character and fitness for admission to the bar must produce clear and convincing evidence of rehabilitation including, but not limited to, the following elements:

(a) strict compliance with the specific conditions of any disciplinary, judicial, administrative, or other order, where applicable;

(b) unimpeachable character and moral standing in the community;

(c) good reputation for professional ability, where applicable;

(d) lack of malice and ill feeling toward those who, by duty, were compelled to bring about the disciplinary, judicial, administrative, or other proceeding;

(e) personal assurances, supported by corroborating evidence, of a desire and intention to conduct one's self in an exemplary fashion in the future;

(f) restitution of funds or property, where applicable; and,

(g) positive action showing rehabilitation by occupation, religion, or community or civic service. Merely showing that an individual is now living as and doing those things he or she should have done throughout life, although necessary to prove rehabilitation, does not prove that the individual has undertaken a useful and constructive place in society. The requirement of positive action is appropriate for applicants for admission to The Florida Bar because service to one's community is an implied obligation of members of The Florida Bar.

3–14 Bar Application and Supporting Documentation.

3–14.1 Filed as an Applicant. Applicants are required to file complete and sworn Bar Applications. Transcripts required by this rule must be sent directly to the board from the educational institutions. The application will not be deemed complete until all of the following items have been received by the board:

(a) an authorization and release on a form available on the board's website requesting and directing the inspection of and furnishing to the board, or any of its authorized representatives, all relevant documents, records, or other information pertaining to the applicant, and releasing any person, official, or representative of a firm, corporation, association, organization, or institution from any and all liability in respect to the inspection or the furnishing of any information;

(b) a Certificate of Dean certifying the applicant's graduation from a law school accredited by the American Bar Association;

(c) an official transcript of academic credit from each law school attended including the law school certifying that the applicant has received the degree of bachelor of laws or doctor of jurisprudence;

(d) if the applicant received an undergraduate degree, then an official transcript from the institution that awarded the degree;

(e) if the applicant has been admitted to the practice of law in 1 or more jurisdictions, evidence satisfactory to the board that the applicant is in good standing in each jurisdiction, and a copy of the application for admission filed in each jurisdiction;

(f) an affidavit on a form available on the board's website attesting that the applicant has read Chapter 4, Rules of Professional Conduct, and Chapter 5, Rules Regulating Trust Accounts, of the Rules Regulating The Florida Bar; and,

(g) supporting documents and other information as may be required in the forms available on the board's website, and other documents, including additional academic transcripts, as the board may require.

3–14.2 Filed as a Registrant. A registrant is required to file a complete and sworn Registrant Bar Application. Transcripts required by this rule must be sent directly to the board from the educational institutions. The application will not be deemed complete until all of the following items have been received by the board:

(a) an authorization and release on a form available on the board's website requesting and directing the inspection of and furnishing to the board, or any of its authorized representatives, all relevant documents, records, or other information pertaining to the registrant, and releasing any person, official, or representative of a firm, corporation, association, organization, or institution from any and all liability in respect to the inspection or the furnishing of any information;

(b) if the applicant received an undergraduate degree, then an official transcript from the institution that awarded the degree; and

(c) supporting documents and other information as may be required in the forms available on the board's website, and other documents, including additional academic transcripts, as the board may require.

3–14.3 Defective Applications. A Bar Application or Registrant Bar Application initially filed in a defective condition (e.g., without notarization, without supporting documents, or having blank or incomplete items on the application) may delay the initiation or the processing of the background investigation. A Bar Application or Registrant Bar Application filed in a defective condition will be accepted, but a fee of $150 will be assessed.

3–14.4 Filing Timely Amendments. An application filed by an applicant or registrant is a continuing application and the applicant or registrant has an obligation to keep the responses to the questions current, complete, and correct by the filing of timely amendments to the application, on forms available on the board's website, until the date of an applicant's submission to the Oath of Attorney in Florida. An amendment to the application is considered timely when made within 30 days of any occurrence that would change or render incomplete any answer to any question on the application.

3–14.5 Timely Processing. In order to ensure timely processing of the background investigation, an applicant or registrant must be responsive to board requests for further information. The Bar Application or Registrant Bar Application must be vigorously pursued by the applicant or registrant.

3–14.6 Non–Compliance.

(a) An applicant's failure to respond to inquiry from the board within 90 days may result in termination of his or her Bar Application and require reapplication and payment of all fees as if the applicant were applying for the first time.

(b) A registrant's failure to respond to inquiry from the board within 90 days may result in cancellation of his or her application and require full payment of the student registrant fee.

3–15 Withdrawal of a Bar Application without Prejudice. An applicant or registrant may request withdrawal of a Bar Application without prejudice. The board will consider acceptance of the request, but may continue its investigative and adjudicative functions to conclusion.

3–16 Withdrawal of a Bar Application with Prejudice. An applicant or registrant may request withdrawal of a Bar Application with prejudice. The board will accept the withdrawal and immediately dismiss its investigative and adjudicative functions. An applicant or registrant who files a withdrawal with prejudice will be permanently barred from filing a subsequent application.

3–17 Extraordinary Investigative Expenses.

3–17.1 Transcript or Records Cost. The cost of a transcript or any record or document reasonably required by the board in the conduct of investigative or adjudicative functions will be paid by the applicant or registrant.

3–17.2 Petition for Extraordinary Expenses. On a showing of actual or anticipated extraordinary expenditures by the board, the Supreme Court of Florida may order any applicant or registrant to pay to the board additional sums including attorney's fees or compensation necessary in the conduct of an inquiry and investigation into the character and fitness and general qualifications of the applicant or registrant including the procurement and presentation of evidence and testimony at a formal hearing.

3–20 Investigative Process.

3–21 Inquiry Process. The board will conduct an investigation to determine the character and fitness of each applicant or registrant. In each investigation and inquiry, the board may obtain information pertaining to the character and fitness of the applicant or registrant and may take and hear testimony, administer oaths and affirmations, and compel by subpoena the attendance of witnesses and the production of documents.

3–21.1 Noncompliance with Subpoena Issued by the Board. Any person subpoenaed to appear and give testimony or to produce documents who refuses to appear to testify before the board, to answer any questions, or to produce documents, may be held in contempt of the board. The board will report the fact that a person under subpoena is in contempt of the board for proceedings that the Supreme Court of Florida may deem advisable.

3–22 Investigative Hearing. An applicant or registrant may be requested to appear for an investigative hearing. Investigative hearings will be informal but thorough, with the object of ascertaining the truth. Technical rules of evidence need not be observed. The admissibility of results of a polygraph examination will be determined in accordance with Florida law. An investigative hearing will be convened before a division of the board consisting of not fewer than 3 members of the board. Any member of the board may administer oaths and affirmations during the hearing.

3–22.1 Investigative Hearing Cost. Any applicant or registrant requested to appear for an investigative hearing must pay the administrative cost of $250.

3–22.2 Response and Selection of a Preferred Hearing Date. An applicant or registrant who has been requested to appear for an investigative hearing must promptly respond to written notice from the board and give notice of preferred dates. Failure to respond within 60 days will result in termination of the application for non-compliance as provided in rule 3–14.6.

3–22.3 Investigative Hearing Postponement. Postponement of a previously scheduled investigative hearing is permitted on written request and for good cause when accompanied by the following fee:

(a) **$75** if the request is received at least 31 days before the hearing date; or

(b) **$125** if the request is received less than 31 days before the hearing date.

3–22.4 Board Waiver of an Investigative Hearing. In cases where the facts are undisputed regarding an applicant's or registrant's prior conduct that adversely affects his or her character and fitness for admission to The Florida Bar, the board may forgo an investigative hearing and proceed directly with the execution of a Consent Agreement or the filing of Specifications as provided in rule 3–22.5.

3–22.5 Board Action Following an Investigative Hearing. After an investigative hearing, the board may make any of the following determinations:

(a) The applicant or registrant has established his or her qualifications as to character and fitness.

(b) The board will offer to the applicant or registrant a Consent Agreement in lieu of the filing of Specifications pertaining to drug, alcohol, or psychological problems and subject to provisions of rule 5–15. In a Consent Agreement, the board is authorized to recommend to the court the admission of the applicant who has agreed to abide by specified terms and conditions on admission to The Florida Bar.

(c) Further investigation into the applicant's or registrant's character and fitness is warranted.

(d) The board will file Specifications charging the applicant or registrant with matters that, if proven, would preclude a favorable finding by the board.

3–22.6 Investigative Hearing Transcript Cost. The cost of a transcript reasonably required by the board in the conduct of investigative or adjudicative functions must be paid by the applicant or registrant.

3–22.7 Public Hearing for Disbarred/Resigned Attorneys. All applicants who have been disbarred from the practice of law, or who have resigned pending disciplinary proceedings must appear before a quorum of the board for a formal hearing. The formal hearing will be open to the public, and the record produced at the hearing and the Findings of Fact and Conclusions of Law are public information and exempt from the confidentiality provision of rule 1–60.

3–23 Specifications. Specifications are formal charges filed in those cases where the board has cause to believe that the applicant or registrant is not qualified for admission to The Florida Bar. If the board votes to prepare and file Specifications, the Specifications are served on the applicant or registrant. The response to Specifications must be filed in the form of a sworn, notarized answer to the Specifications within 20 days from receipt of the Specifications.

3–23.1 Failure to File the Answer. If an applicant or registrant fails to file an answer to the Specifications within the 20–day deadline or within any extension of time allowed by the board, the Specifications will be deemed admitted. The board will enter Findings of Fact, finding the Specifications proven, and appropriate conclusions of law that may include a recommendation that the applicant not be admitted to The Florida Bar, or that the registrant has not established his or her qualifications as to character and fitness.

3–23.2 Formal Hearing. Any applicant or registrant who receives Specifications is entitled to a formal hearing before the board, representation by counsel at his or her own expense, disclosure by the Office of General Counsel of its witness and exhibit lists, cross-examination of witnesses, presentation of witnesses and exhibits on his or her own behalf, and access to the board's subpoena power. After receipt of the answer to Specifications, the board will provide notice of the dates and locations available for the scheduling of the formal hearing. Formal hearings are conducted before a panel of the board that will consist of not fewer than 5 members. The formal hearing panel will consist of members of the board other than those who participated in the investigative hearing. This provision may be waived with the consent of the applicant or registrant. The weight to be given all testimony and exhibits received in evidence at a formal hearing must be considered and determined by the board. The board is not bound by technical rules of evidence at a formal hearing. A judgment of guilt to either a felony or misdemeanor will constitute conclusive proof of the criminal offense(s) charged. An order withholding adjudication of guilt of a charged felony will constitute conclusive proof of the criminal offense(s) charged. An order withholding adjudication of guilt of a charged misdemeanor will be admissible evidence of the criminal offense(s) charged. The admissibility of results of a polygraph examination will be in accordance with Florida law.

3–23.3 Formal Hearing Cost. Any applicant or registrant who receives Specifications that require the scheduling of a formal hearing must pay the administrative cost of $600.

3–23.4 Selection of a Preferred Formal Hearing Date. The applicant or registrant and the board must agree on a date and location for the formal hearing. If the applicant or registrant fails to agree on 1 of the dates and locations proposed, the board will set the date and location of the hearing. If the applicant or registrant, without good cause, fails to attend the formal hearing, the Specifications will be deemed admitted. The board will enter Findings of Fact, finding the Specifications proven, and appropriate conclusions of law that may include a recommendation that the applicant not be admitted to The Florida Bar or that the registrant has not established his or her qualifications as to character and fitness.

3–23.5 Formal Hearing Postponement. Postponement of a previously scheduled formal hearing is permitted by written request and for good cause when accompanied by the following fee:

(a) $250 if request is received between 45 and 31 days before the hearing date; or

(b) $600 if the request is received less than 31 days before the hearing date.

3–23.6 Board Action Following Formal Hearing. Following the conclusion of a formal hearing, the board will promptly notify the applicant or registrant of its decision. The board may make any of the following recommendations:

(a) The applicant or registrant has established his or her qualifications as to character and fitness.

(b) The applicant be conditionally admitted to The Florida Bar in exceptional cases involving drug, alcohol, or psychological problems on the terms and conditions specified by the board and subject to the provisions of rule 5–15.

(c) The applicant's admission to The Florida Bar be withheld for a specified period of time not to exceed 2 years. At the end of the specified period of time, the board will recommend the applicant's admission if the applicant has complied with all special conditions outlined in the Findings of Fact and Conclusions of Law.

(d) The applicant or registrant has not established his or her qualifications as to character and fitness and that the applicant or registrant be denied admission to The Florida Bar. A 2–year disqualification period is presumed to be the minimum period of time required before an applicant or registrant may reapply for admission and establish rehabilitation. In a case involving significant mitigating circumstances, the board has the discretion to recommend that the applicant or registrant be allowed to reapply for admission within a specified period of less than 2 years. In a case involving significant aggravating factors (including but not limited to material omissions or misrepresentations in the application process), the board has the discretion to recommend that the applicant or registrant be disqualified from reapplying for admission for a specified period greater than 2 years, but not more than 5 years. In a case involving extremely grievous misconduct, the board has the discretion to recommend that the applicant or registrant be permanently prohibited from applying or reapplying for admission to The Florida Bar.

3–23.7 Findings of Fact and Conclusions of Law. In cases involving a recommendation other than under rule 3–23.6(a), the board will expeditiously issue its written Findings of Fact and Conclusions of Law. The Findings must be supported by competent, substantial evidence in the formal hearing record. The Findings, conclusions, and recommendation are subject to review by the Supreme Court of Florida as specified under rule 3–40. The Findings, conclusions, and recommendation are final, if not appealed, except in cases involving a favorable recommendation for applicants seeking readmission to the practice of law after having been disbarred or having resigned pending disciplinary proceedings. In those cases, the board will file a report containing its recommendation with the Supreme Court of Florida for final action by the court. Admission to The Florida Bar for those applicants will occur only by public order of the court. All reports, pleadings, correspondence, and papers received by the court in those cases are public information and exempt from the confidentiality provision of rule 1–60.

3–23.8 Formal Hearing Transcript Cost. The cost of a transcript reasonably required in the conduct of investigative or adjudicative functions must be paid by the applicant or registrant.

3–23.9 Negotiated Consent Judgments. Counsel for the board and an applicant or registrant may waive a formal hearing and enter into a proposed consent judgment. The consent judgment must contain a proposed resolution of the case under 1 of the board action recommendations specified above. If the consent judgment is approved by the full board, then the case will be resolved in accordance with the consent judgment without further proceedings.

3–30 Petition for Board Reconsideration. Any applicant or registrant who is dissatisfied with the recommendation concerning his or her character and fitness may, within 60 days from the date of the Findings of Fact and Conclusions of Law, file with the board a petition for reconsideration with a fee of $165. The petition must contain new and material evidence that by due diligence could not have been produced at the formal hearing. Evidence of rehabilitation as provided by rule 3–13 is not permitted in a petition for reconsideration. Only 1 petition for reconsideration may be filed.

3–40 Petition for Court Review.

3–40.1 Dissatisfied with Board's Recommendation. Any applicant or registrant who is dissatisfied with the recommendation concerning his or her character and fitness may petition the Supreme Court of Florida for review within 60 days from receipt of the Findings of Fact and Conclusions of Law or within 60 days of receipt of notice of the board's action on a petition filed under rule 3–30. If not inconsistent with these rules, the Florida Rules of Appellate Procedure are applicable to all proceedings filed in the Supreme Court of Florida. A copy of the petition must be served on the executive director of the board. The applicant seeking review must serve an initial brief within 30 days of the filing of the petition. The board will have 30 days to serve an answer brief after the service of the applicant's initial brief. The applicant may serve a reply brief within 30 days after the service of the answer brief. At the time of the filing of the answer brief, the executive director will transmit the record of the formal hearing to the court.

3–40.2 Dissatisfied with Length of Board's Investigation. Any applicant or registrant whose character and fitness investigation is not finished within 9 months from the date of submission of a completed Bar Application or Registrant Bar Application may petition the Supreme Court of Florida for an order directing the board to conclude its investigation. If not inconsistent with these rules, the Florida Rules of Appellate Procedure are applicable to all proceedings filed in the Supreme Court of Florida. A copy of the petition must be served on the executive director of the board. The board will have 30 days after the service of the petition to serve a response. The applicant may serve a reply within 30 days after the service of the board's response.

Added June 5, 1997 (695 So.2d 312). Amended June 4, 1998 (712 So.2d 766); March 20, 2003 (843 So.2d 245); October 18, 2007, eff. May 1, 2008 (967 So.2d 877); Dec. 10, 2009 (23 So.3d 1179); Dec. 16, 2010 (52 So.3d 652); Feb. 3, 2011 (54 So.3d 460).

Rule 4. Bar examination

4–10 General Information.

4–11 Florida Bar Examination. The Florida Bar Examination will consist of a General Bar Examination and the Multistate Professional Responsibility Examination (MPRE).

4–12 Requirement to Submit. All individuals who seek the privilege of practicing law in the State of Florida must take the Florida Bar Examination.

4–13 Technical Competence. All applicants seeking admission to The Florida Bar must produce satisfactory evidence of technical competence by passing all parts of the Florida Bar Examination.

4–13.1 Educational Qualifications.

(a) *Eligibility.* An applicant may take the MPRE prior to graduation from law school; however, the requirements of rule 4–18.1 are applicable. To be eligible to take any portion of the General Bar Examination, an applicant must either:

(1) complete the requirements for graduation, or receive the degree of bachelor of laws or doctor of jurisprudence, from an accredited law school or within 12 months of accreditation; or,

(2) be found educationally qualified under the alternative method of educational qualification provided in rule 4–13.4.

(b) *Proscribed Substitutions.* Except as provided in rule 4–13.4, none of the following may be substituted for the required degree from an accredited law school:

(1) private study, correspondence school, or law office training;

(2) age or experience; or,

(3) waived or lowered standards of legal training for particular persons or groups.

4–13.2 Definition of Accredited. An "accredited" law school is any law school approved or provisionally approved by the American Bar Association at the time of the applicant's graduation or within 12 months of the applicant's graduation.

4–13.3 Definition of Degree Requirements. The term "complete the requirements for graduation" refers to the time when completion of the requirements for graduation is recorded in the office of the law school dean or administrator.

4–13.4 Alternative Method of Educational Qualification.

(a) *Applicants Not Meeting Educational Qualifications.* An applicant who does not meet the educational qualifications in rule 4–13.1, must meet the following requirements:

(1) evidence as the board may require that the applicant was engaged in the practice of law for at least 10 years in the District of Columbia, in other states of the United States of America, or in federal courts of the United States or its territories, possessions, or protectorates, and was in good standing at the bar of the jurisdictions in which the applicant practiced; and

(2) a representative compilation of the work product in the field of law showing the scope and character of the applicant's previous experience and practice at the bar, including samples of the quality of the applicant's work, including pleadings, briefs, legal memoranda, contracts, or other working papers that the applicant considers illustrative of his or her expertise and academic and legal training. The representative compilation of the work product must be confined to the applicant's most recent 10 years of practice and must be complete and include all supplemental documents requested.

(b) *Deadline for Filing Work Product.* To be considered timely filed, the work product must be complete with all required supplemental documentation and filed by the filing deadline of the General Bar Examination as required by rule 4–42. Work product initially filed incomplete and perfected after the deadline will not be considered timely filed. Late or incomplete work product will be given consideration for admission into the next administration of the bar examination for which the deadline has not passed.

(c) *Acceptance of Work Product.* If a thorough review of the representative compilation of the work product and other materials submitted by the applicant shows that the applicant is a lawyer of high ability whose reputation for professional competence is above reproach, the board may admit the applicant to the General Bar Examination and accept score reports from the National Conference of Bar Examiners or its designee.

(d) *Board Discretion.* In evaluating academic and legal scholarship under subdivision (a), the board is clothed with broad discretion.

4–14 Dates of Administration. The General Bar Examination will be administered on the last Tuesday and Wednesday of February and July of each calendar year. The Multistate Professional Responsibility Examination is administered in March, August, and November of each year.

4–15 Location of Administration. The General Bar Examination will be held in locations in the State of Florida as the board may from time to time direct. The Multistate Professional Responsibility Examination (MPRE) is administered 3 times each year throughout the country at various locations selected by the National Conference of Bar Examiners or its designee.

4–16 Publication of Examination Topics and Study Materials. The board will publish the topics included on the bar examination and also make suggestions for the information and guidance of students to promote their studies.

4–16.1 Part A Examination Study Guide. The board will provide a bar examination study guide that includes essay questions from 2 previously administered General Bar Examinations, sample answers to the essay questions, and sample multiple-choice questions from Part A of the General Bar Examination. The study guide is available on the board's website.

4–16.2 Copies of Essay Answers. The board will provide, on request from an applicant, a copy of his or her answers to essay questions from a single General Bar Examination for the period of time from the release of the examination results until the administration of the next examination. The answers will not reflect any grading marks and will be forwarded on written request accompanied by a fee of $50.

4–17 Test Accommodations.

4–17.1 Accommodations. In accordance with the Americans with Disabilities Act, test accommodations are provided by the board at no additional cost to applicants.

4–17.2 Requests for Test Accommodations. Applicants seeking test accommodations because of disability must file a written petition for accommodations accompanied by supporting documentation or additional information as reasonably may be required on the forms available on the board's website. Receipt of requests for test accommodations and supporting documentation are subject to the deadline and late filing fees applicable to all examinees as set forth in rules 4–42.3 and 4–42.4.

4–18 Time Limitation on Passing Examination.

4–18.1 Twenty–Five Months. An applicant must successfully complete the General Bar Examination and the Multistate Professional Responsibility Examination (MPRE) within 25 months of the date of the administration of any part of the examination that is passed. If an applicant fails to pass all parts within 25 months of first passing any part, passing score(s) of individual parts older than 25 months are deleted.

4–18.2 Five Years. An applicant's passing scores on the Florida Bar Examination will be valid for a period of 5 years from the date of the administration of the last part of the Florida Bar Examination that he or she passed. If the 5–year period expires without admission, an applicant, except for good cause shown, will be required to retake the Florida Bar Examination and again pass all parts of the examination.

4–20 General Bar Examination. A portion of the General Bar Examination will consist of questions in the form of hypothetical fact problems requiring essay answers. Essay questions may not be labeled as to subject matter. Questions may be designed to require answers based on Florida case or statutory law of substantial importance. The General Bar Examination will consist of 2 parts (A and B). Part A will be a combination of essay and multiple-choice questions and Part B will be the Multistate Bar Examination (MBE).

4–21 Purpose. The General Bar Examination will test the applicant's ability to reason logically, to analyze accurately the problem presented, and to demonstrate a thorough knowledge of the fundamental principles of law and their application.

4–22 Part A. Part A will consist of 6 one-hour segments. One segment will include the subject of Florida Rules of Civil and Criminal Procedure and the Florida Rules of Judicial Administration 2.330, 2.420, 2.505, and 2.515. The remaining 5 segments, each of which will include no more than 3 subjects, will be selected from the following subjects including their equitable aspects:

(a) Florida constitutional law;

(b) federal constitutional law;

(c) business entities;

(d) wills and administration of estates;

(e) trusts;

(f) real property;

(g) evidence;

(h) torts;

(i) criminal law, constitutional criminal procedure, and juvenile delinquency;

(j) contracts;

(k) Articles 3 and 9 of the Uniform Commercial Code;

(*l*) family law and dependency;

(m) Chapter 4, Rules of Professional Conduct of the Rules Regulating The Florida Bar; and

(n) Chapter 5, Rules Regulating Trust Accounts of the Rules Regulating The Florida Bar; and

(*o*) professionalism.

4–23 Part B. Part B will be the Multistate Bar Examination (MBE) offered to each jurisdiction by the National Conference of Bar Examiners.

4–23.1 Transfer of Score. A score achieved by an applicant on the Multistate Bar Examination administered in a jurisdiction other than the State of Florida will not be transferred to or recognized by the board.

4–24 General Bar Examination Preparation and Grading. The board may use the services of expert drafters to prepare bar examination questions, either by arranging for the drafting services of qualified persons, including out-of-state law teachers, or by using the services of the National Conference of Bar Examiners or another national agency. The board may use the services of trained expert readers. Readers will be selected solely upon the qualifications of the individuals.

4–24.1 Essay Questions. Every essay question, whether drafted by the examiners or by expert drafters, will be thoroughly briefed on every point of law in the question and the question analyzed and approved by the board preceding inclusion of the question on the General Bar Examination.

4–24.2 Machine–Scored Questions. Every machine-scored item of Part A must specify authority for the best response, and every item and authority should be analyzed and approved by the board preceding inclusion of the item on the General Bar Examination.

4–25 Submission Methods. Applicants who take the General Bar Examination must do so for the sole purpose of fulfilling the admission requirements for The Florida Bar. An applicant may elect to take the General Bar Examination by either of the following methods:

(a) *Overall Method.* Overall method is used only if the applicant takes Parts A and B during the same administration of the General Bar Examination.

(b) *Individual Method.* Individual method is used if the applicant takes only 1 part of the General Bar Examination. Applicants who elect to take only 1 part of the General Bar Examination under the individual method may not combine a score attained on 1 part from 1 administration with a score on the other part from a different administration. Applicants may not take Part A only using this method unless they have previously taken the Multistate Bar Examination (MBE) in Florida.

4–25.1 Retention of Passing Status. If an applicant attains a passing scaled score on only 1 part and elects to take the overall method of the General Bar Examination as described above, the previous passing status will not be replaced by a failing status if the applicant fails to achieve a passing score on a subsequent submission effort.

4–26 Scoring Method. Each examination paper produced by an applicant on the General Bar Examination will be separately graded. Papers will be graded and reported by number and not by applicant's name. The name of the writer of the examination paper will not be revealed by the staff to the members of the board or readers or any source other than the Supreme Court of Florida. To ensure maximum uniformity in all grading of essay questions, the board will use the services of multiple calibrated readers.

4–26.1 Examination Scaling. The scores of each section of Part A will be converted to a common scale by a recognized statistical procedure so that each section is equally weighted. The sum of the converted section scores is the total score for Part A. All total scores attained by the applicants on Part A are converted to the same distribution as their Multistate Bar Examination (MBE) scaled scores. MBE scores (Part B) are the scaled scores on the MBE provided by the National Conference of Bar Examiners. Scaled scores are used in order to ensure that the standard of measurement of competence from examination to examination is not affected by the difficulty of the particular test or the ability of that particular group as distinguished from the general population of applicants.

4–26.2 Pass/Fail Line. Effective July 1, 2004, each applicant must attain a scaled score of 136 or better on Part A and on Part B under the individual method and an average of 136 or better under the overall method, or such scaled score as may be fixed by the court.

4–30 Multistate Professional Responsibility Examination. The Multistate Professional Responsibility Examination (MPRE) is the examination offered to jurisdictions by the National Conference of Bar Examiners.

4–31 Purpose. The purpose of the MPRE is to measure the applicant's knowledge of the ethical standards of the legal profession.

4–32 Applications and Filing Deadlines. Applications for admission into the Multistate Professional Responsibility Examination (MPRE) are distributed by and must be filed with the designee of the National Conference of Bar Examiners that administers the MPRE within the time limitations set by that authority.

4–33 Scoring Method. Each examination paper produced by an applicant on the MPRE will be separately graded. The raw score attained by each applicant will be converted to a scaled score by the National Conference of Bar Examiners or its designee in order to ensure that the standard of measurement of competence from examination to examination is not affected by the difficulty of the particular test or the ability of that particular group as distinguished from the general population of applicants.

4–33.1 Transfer of Score. The applicant must direct requests to transfer the score attained on the MPRE to the agency that administers the MPRE. Scores are transferred on a certificate supplied by the agency and must be forwarded directly by that agency to the board.

4–33.2 Pass/Fail Line. On the MPRE, each applicant must attain a scaled score of 80 or better, or such scaled score as may be fixed by the court.

4–40 Application for the General Bar Examination.

4–41 Application Requirements. By the applicable filing deadline prescribed in rule 4–42 or the late filing deadline prescribed in rule 4–43, each applicant desiring to take the General Bar Examination for the first time must submit to the board either the complete Bar Application or, in the case of law student registrants, the Supplement to Registrant Bar Application, the appropriate applicant filing fee, a current 2″ × 2″ photograph of the applicant, and submission of fingerprints in the format required by the board.

4–42 Examination Filing Deadlines.

4–42.1 **February Filing Deadline.** Timely applications for admission to the February administration of the General Bar Examination must be postmarked or received not later than November 15 prior to the examination.

4–42.2 **July Filing Deadline.** Timely applications for admission to the July administration of the General Bar Examination must be postmarked or received not later than May 1 prior to the examination.

4–42.3 **Deadline for Test Accommodations.** Petitions for accommodations and supporting documentation are subject to the examination filing deadline. Applicants seeking test accommodations must file the Bar Application, Supplement to Registrant Bar Application, or Reexamination Application, petition, and supporting documents by the examination filing deadline to avoid examination late filing fees.

4–42.4 **Cutoff for Test Accommodations.** To avoid an undue burden on the board while it is making final preparations for the administration of the bar examination, a minimum amount of time is required for the orderly processing of a request for accommodations. Except for emergency petitions as designated by the board, no request for test accommodations will be processed if postmarked or received after January 15 for the February examination or after June 15 for the July examination.

4–43 **Filing After the Deadline.** Applicants seeking late filing for a General Bar Examination will be permitted to do so on payment of an additional fee as set out below, completion of the Bar Application, Supplement to Registrant Bar Application, or Reexamination Application, and receipt of all supporting documents.

4–43.1 **$325.** If the Bar Application, Supplement to Registrant Bar Application, or Reexamination Application, as applicable, is postmarked or received on or before December 15 for the February examination or June 1 for the July examination, the fee is $325.

4–43.2 **$625.** If the Bar Application, Supplement to Registrant Bar Application, or Reexamination Application, as applicable, is postmarked or received after December 15 but on or before January 15 for the February examination, or after June 1 but on or before June 15 for the July examination, the fee is $625. No Bar Application, Supplement to Registrant Bar Application, Reexamination Application, appropriate applicant filing fee, 2" × 2" photograph, or submission of fingerprints will be deemed to have met the late filing deadline if postmarked after January 15 for the February examination, or after June 15 for the July examination.

4–44 **Computer Option.** Applicants are permitted the use of a laptop computer with software designated by the board to complete answers to the essay portion of the General Bar Examination. Applicants seeking to use a laptop computer must complete a form available on the board's website and pay a fee of $125.

4–45 **Examination Postponement.** Applicants seeking to postpone the taking of an individual part or the entire General Bar Examination must file a written request with the board. The applicable postponement fees based on the received date of the postponement request are set forth in rule 4–46 below. Applicants who fail to request a postponement or who untimely request a postponement received by the board after the commencement of the bar examination must reapply under rule 4–47.

4–46 **Reapplication after Postponement.** Applicants seeking to reapply after postponing as indicated above will be permitted admission into another General Bar Examination on filing with the board the Reexamination Application on the form available on the board's website and payment of the applicable postponement fee. To be timely filed, the completed application and appropriate fee must be postmarked or received by the examination filing deadline. If the Reexamination Application is not postmarked or received on or before the filing deadline or if filed incomplete, the appropriate examination late filing fee must be included. If requested by the board, an applicant will submit a current photograph. The fee payable with the Reexamination Application will be as follows:

(a) If the board receives the applicant's written notice of postponement under rule 4–45 at least 7 days before the commencement of the administration of the postponed examination, the fee is $100.

(b) If the board receives the applicant's written notice of postponement under rule 4–45 prior to but less than 7 days before the commencement of the administration of the postponed examination, the fee is $200.

4–47 **Examination Reapplication.** Applicants not covered by rule 4–46 and seeking to reapply for all or part of the General Bar Examination will be permitted admission into another General Bar Examination on filing a Reexamination Application on the form available on the board's website and payment of the reapplication fee of $450. To be timely filed, the completed Reexamination Application and fee must be postmarked or received by the examination filing deadline. If the Reexamination Application is not postmarked or received on or before the filing deadline or if filed incomplete, the appropriate examination late filing fee must be included. If requested by the board, an applicant will submit a current photograph.

4–50 **Examination Administration.**

4–51 **Rules of Conduct.** Applicants must abide by all rules governing the administration of the General Bar Examination as set out below.

4–51.1 **Possession or Use of Unauthorized Materials or Equipment.** Applicants must not possess or use any book bags, backpacks, purses, hats or baseball caps, notes, books, study materials, food or liquids, cellular telephones, beepers, watches or clocks with audible alarms, calculators, computers, or other electronic devices in the examination room without the prior written approval of the board.

4–51.2 Receipt of Unauthorized Aid. Applicants must not use answers or information from other applicants while taking the examination.

4–51.3 Observance of Examination Start/Stop Announcements. Applicants must not read questions on the examination prior to the announcement to begin the examination and must not continue to answer any questions after the announcement to stop because the session has ended.

4–51.4 Observance of Confidentiality of Machine–Scored Questions. Applicants must not remove any multiple-choice, machine-scored examination questions from the examination room or otherwise communicate the substance of any of those questions to persons who are employed by or associated with bar review courses.

4–52 Examination Proctors. The board may seek the assistance of other members of The Florida Bar in proctoring the bar examination.

4–60 Release of Examination Results.

4–61 Confidentiality. No information regarding applicants' scores will be released except as authorized by the rules or as directed by the Supreme Court of Florida.

4–62 General Bar Examination. The board will notify each person submitting to any part of the General Bar Examination whether the person has passed or failed any or all parts of the examination except any person whose grades have been impounded by the Supreme Court of Florida.

4–62.1 Impoundment of Examination Results. Results of the General Bar Examination will be impounded by the court if the applicant fails to pay the full balance of any application or examination late filing fee, or if the applicant is suspected of a violation of the examination administration rules of conduct.

4–62.2 Release of Impounded Examination Results. On submission of documentation that establishes that the applicant has paid all application and late fees, is determined not to have violated examination administration rules of conduct, and on payment of a $100 impoundment fee, the board will request the court to release the impounded grades.

4–62.3 Date of Release. The date for release of the results from the General Bar Examination will be set by the court. At that time, all applicants who have passed all parts of the examination, but who have not been recommended to the court for admission to The Florida Bar will be advised of the status of their Bar Application.

4–63 Multistate Professional Responsibility Examination. Applicants will be notified by letter whether their Multistate Professional Responsibility Examination (MPRE) scores transferred to Florida are accepted.

4–64 Investigation of Examination–Related Conduct. If the board has cause to believe that an applicant has violated any of the eligibility or conduct rules relating to the General Bar Examination, the board may conduct an investigation, hold hearings, and make Findings under rule 3–20.

4–65 Invalidation of Exam Scores.

4–65.1 Relating to Educational Qualifications. If an applicant is found by the board after an investigation under rule 3–20 to be in violation of rule 4–13.1, the results of the Florida Bar Examination will be invalidated. Once the results are invalidated and subsequent to providing evidence that all eligibility requirements have been met, the applicant will be permitted to resubmit to the General Bar Examination by filing a new application and the reapplication fee.

4–65.2 Relating to Work Product Submission or Rules of Conduct. If an applicant is found by the board after an investigation under rule 3–20 to have made a material misstatement or omission under rule 4–13.4, or to have violated the examination administration rules of conduct under rule 4–51, the results of the Florida Bar Examination will be invalidated. The applicant will not be eligible to submit another work product (if in violation of rule 4–13.4) or submit to another examination for a period of 5 years from the date that the board delivered its adverse Findings or the period of time set in the Findings.

Added June 5, 1997 (695 So.2d 312). Amended June 4, 1998 (712 So.2d 766); Jan. 6, 2000 (762 So.2d 435); March 20, 2003 (843 So.2d 245); October 18, 2007, eff. May 1, 2008 (967 So.2d 877); Dec. 9, 2010, eff. Dec. 9, 2010, with Rule 4–22 Part A, subsecs. (c), (i), (k), (*l*), and (*o*), eff. Dec. 9, 2012; Dec. 16, 2010 (52 So.3d 652); Feb. 3, 2011 (54 So.3d 460).

Rule 5. Recommendations and jurisdiction

5–10 Recommendations and Admission. Every applicant who has complied with the requirements of the applicable rules for admission into the Florida Bar Examination, attained passing scores on the examination, met the requirements as to character and fitness, complied with the requirements of the applicable rules for admission into The Florida Bar, and who is 18 years of age or older will be recommended by the Florida Board of Bar Examiners to the Supreme Court of Florida for admission to The Florida Bar.

5–11 Supreme Court Action. If the court is satisfied with the qualifications of each applicant recommended, an order of admission will be made and entered in the minutes of the court. The court will designate the manner that applicants will take the oath.

5–12 Induction Ceremonies. Formal induction ceremonies will be scheduled after each release of grades from the previous administration of the bar examination. The ceremonies will be held at the

Supreme Court of Florida or the First District Court of Appeal and at each of the other district courts of appeal. Attendance at an induction ceremony is voluntary.

5–13 Oath of Attorney. Any applicant who chooses not to attend an induction ceremony may take the oath before any resident Circuit Judge or other official authorized to administer oaths, such as a notary public. All applicants must present themselves for administration of the oath not later than 90 days from the date of notification of eligibility for admission by the Clerk of the Supreme Court of Florida.

5–13.1 Filing of the Oath. An executed copy of the Oath of Attorney must be filed with the board. Upon receipt of the oath, the board will certify the applicant and the date of admission to the Supreme Court of Florida and The Florida Bar. The Clerk will maintain a permanent register of all admitted persons.

5–13.2 Certificate of Admission. The Certificate of Admission and a printed reproduction of the Oath of Attorney will be issued without charge when the duly executed oath is received by the board. Additional certificates may be purchased for $25 each.

5–14 Board Jurisdiction after Admission. If, within 12 months of admission of an applicant to The Florida Bar, the board determines that a material misstatement or material omission in the application process of the applicant may have occurred, the board may conduct an investigation and hold hearings. After investigation and hearings, the board may make Findings and recommendations as to revocation of any license issued to the applicant and will file any Findings with the Supreme Court of Florida for final determination by the court.

5–15 Bar Jurisdiction after Admission. If an applicant is granted admission by the court under a Consent Agreement, then the terms and conditions of his or her admission will be administered by The Florida Bar. The board must provide The Florida Bar access to all information gathered by the board on a conditionally-admitted applicant, except information received by the board under a specific agreement of confidentiality or otherwise restricted by law. Conditional admission is limited to persons who will live in Florida, who will be engaged in the practice of law primarily in Florida, and who will be monitored in Florida during the entire period of conditional admission. If the applicant fails to abide by the terms and conditions of admission, including the requirement of living in Florida, The Florida Bar is authorized to institute proceedings consistent with the Rules Regulating The Florida Bar as to revocation of the license issued to the applicant under the Consent Agreement. The board must be notified of any disciplinary proceedings and have access to all information relating to the administration of a conditional admission, except information received by The Florida Bar under a specific agreement of confidentiality or otherwise restricted by law.

Added June 5, 1997 (695 So.2d 312). Amended October 18, 2007, eff. May 1, 2008 (967 So.2d 877); Dec. 10, 2009 (23 So.3d 1179); Feb. 3, 2011 (54 So.3d 460).

OATH OF ADMISSION

Oath of Admission to The Florida Bar

I do solemnly swear:

I will support the Constitution of the United States and the Constitution of the State of Florida;

I will maintain the respect due to courts of justice and judicial officers;

I will not counsel or maintain any suit or proceedings which shall appear to me to be unjust, nor any defense except such as I believe to be honestly debatable under the law of the land;

I will employ for the purpose of maintaining the causes confided to me such means only as are consistent with truth and honor, and will never seek to mislead the judge or jury by any artifice or false statement of fact or law;

I will maintain the confidence and preserve inviolate the secrets of my clients, and will accept no compensation in connection with their business except from them or with their knowledge and approval;

To opposing parties and their counsel, I pledge fairness, integrity, and civility, not only in court, but also in all written and oral communications;

I will abstain from all offensive personality and advance no fact prejudicial to the honor or reputation of a party or witness, unless required by the justice of the cause with which I am charged;

I will never reject, from any consideration personal to myself, the cause of the defenseless or oppressed, or delay anyone's cause for lucre or malice. So help me God.

Adopted by the Supreme Court Jan. 27, 1941 (145 Fla. 797, 798). Revised with amendments received through January 15, 2003. Amended Sept. 12, 2011, effective Sept. 12, 2011 (73 So.3d 149). Revised effective June 25, 2013.

CODE FOR RESOLVING PROFESSIONALISM COMPLAINTS

STANDARDS OF PROFESSIONALISM

Explanatory Note

Adopted June 6, 2013, effective June 6, 2013 (116 So.3d 280).

STANDARDS OF PROFESSIONALISM

Standards of Professionalism

Members of The Florida Bar shall not engage in unprofessional conduct. "Unprofessional conduct" means substantial or repeated violations of the *Oath of Admission to The Florida Bar, The Florida Bar Creed of Professionalism, The Florida Bar Ideals and Goals of Professionalism, The Rules Regulating The Florida Bar, or the decisions of The Florida Supreme Court.*

Unprofessional conduct, as defined above, in many instances will constitute a violation of one or more of the *Rules of Professional Conduct.* In particular, Rule 4–8.4(d) of *The Rules Regulating The Florida Bar* has been the basis for imposing discipline in such instances. *See generally, The Florida Bar v. Ratiner,* 46 So. 3d 35 (Fla. 2010); *The Florida Bar v. Abramson,* 3 So. 3d 964 (Fla. 2009); and *The Florida Bar v. Martocci,* 791 So. 2d 1074 (Fla. 2001).

Adopted June 6, 2013, effective June 6, 2013 (116 So.3d 280).

IMPLEMENTATION PROCEDURES

Section 1. Terminology

1.1. Standards of Professionalism: The Standards of Professionalism are set forth in the *Oath of Admission to The Florida Bar, The Florida Bar Creed of Professionalism, The Florida Bar Ideals and Goals of Professionalism, The Rules Regulating The Florida Bar* and the decisions of The Florida Supreme Court.

1.2. Complainant: The person who complains that an attorney's conduct has violated the Standards of Professionalism.

1.3. Respondent: The attorney whose behavior is the subject of the complaint.

1.4. Attorney Consumer Assistance and Intake Program (ACAP): The program of The Florida Bar which fields and screens complaints against members of The Florida Bar. Depending upon the nature and severity of the professionalism complaint, ACAP can resolve the complaint informally as provided herein or it can refer the matter to the appropriate branch office of The Florida Bar's Lawyer Regulation Department for further action.

1.5. Local Professionalism Panel: An entity independent of The Florida Bar which is established at the local level for the purpose of resolving complaints of alleged unprofessional conduct by attorneys practicing in that circuit.

1.6. Practice and Professionalism Enhancement Programs: The various programs of The Florida Bar which exist for use in diversion cases or as a condition of discipline. These programs include Ethics School, Professionalism Workshops, Law Office Management Assistance Service (LOMAS), Stress Management Workshop, Florida Lawyers Assistance, Inc., and the Trust Accounting Workshop.

Adopted June 6, 2013, effective June 6, 2013 (116 So.3d 280).

Section 2. Initiating Professionalism Complaints

2.1. Commencement of the Process: Any person may initiate a professionalism complaint against a member of The Florida Bar through a Local Professionalism Panel when available and appropriate, or through ACAP. Complaints received by a Local Professionalism Panel may be referred to ACAP at any time depending upon the nature and severity of the complaint.

Adopted June 6, 2013, effective June 6, 2013 (116 So.3d 280).

Section 3. Processing Professionalism Complaints Through ACAP

3.1. Complaints initiated through ACAP can be an informal request for assistance either through a telephone call or by a written request. The complaint can also be a formal complaint either under oath as required by Rule 3–7.3(c) of *The Rules Regulating The Florida Bar* or as an unsworn judicial referral as outlined in Standing Board Policy 15.91 of The Florida Bar. The Bar may also lodge a complaint on its own initiative.

3.2. Initial Screening.

3.2.1. Upon receipt of a complaint, ACAP will create a record of the request by obtaining the contact information for both the Complainant and the Respondent. The information will then be forwarded to an ACAP Attorney for Initial Screening.

3.2.2. If the ACAP Attorney determines that the concerns raised in the complaint could be resolved informally, the ACAP Attorney will contact the Respondent to discuss the professionalism issues and provide remedial guidance as necessary, or refer the complaint to a Local Professionalism Panel. If the matter cannot be resolved informally, the ACAP Attorney will contact the Complainant and explain any further available options.

3.2.3. Upon receipt of a complaint that cannot be resolved informally, the ACAP Attorney will determine whether the allegations, if proven, would constitute a violation of *The Rules of Professional Conduct* relating to professionalism. If the ACAP Attorney determines the facts as alleged would constitute a violation, an inquiry will be opened and the ACAP Attorney will investigate the allegations. If the ACAP Attorney determines the facts as alleged would not constitute a violation, the ACAP Attorney will advise the Complainant and the Respondent of the decision not to pursue an inquiry and will provide the reasons for doing so.

3.2.4. If the ACAP Attorney determines after investigation that the facts show the Respondent did not violate *The Rules of Professional Conduct*, the ACAP Attorney may dismiss the case after taking informal action if necessary, such as providing remedial guidance. The Complainant and Respondent will be notified of the dismissal and will be provided the reasons for doing so.

3.2.5. If the ACAP Attorney determines after investigation that a complaint warrants further action for a possible violation of one or more of *The Rules of Professional Conduct*, the ACAP Attorney will forward the matter to the appropriate branch office of The Florida Bar's Lawyer Regulation Department for further consideration.

3.3. Review at the Branch Level: Upon a referral to the branch office, branch Bar counsel may dismiss the case after further review and/or investigation, recommend Diversion to a Practice and Professionalism Enhancement Program in accordance with Rule 3–5.3(d) of *The Rules Regulating The Florida Bar*, or refer to a Grievance Committee for further investigation.

3.4. Review by the Grievance Committee: Upon referral and conclusion of the investigation, the Grievance Committee will make one of the following findings:

A. No probable cause;

B. No probable cause and include a letter of advice to the Respondent;

C. Recommendation of Diversion to one of the Practice and Professionalism Enhancement Programs;

D. Recommendation of Admonishment for Minor Misconduct; or

E. Probable cause. Probable cause under Rule 3–2.1 of *The Rules Regulating The Florida Bar* is a finding by an authorized agency that there is cause to believe that a member of The Florida Bar is guilty of misconduct justifying disciplinary action.

3.5. Confidentiality: The confidentiality of disciplinary investigations and proceedings is outlined in Rule 3–7.1 of *The Rules Regulating the Florida Bar*. Any record of informal attempts to resolve a dispute as outlined in paragraph 3.2.2. would also be subject to the provisions of Rule 3–7.1 except that notes of any telephonic communication between the ACAP Attorney and the Complainant, the Respondent, or any third party would be considered the work product of The Florida Bar and would remain confidential and not become part of the public record.

Adopted June 6, 2013, effective June 6, 2013 (116 So.3d 280).

Section 4. Immunity

4.1. Local Professionalism Panels and Circuit Committees on Professionalism: The members of the Local Professionalism Panels, staff persons assisting those panels, members of the Circuit Committees on Professionalism, and staff persons assisting those committees, shall have absolute immunity from civil liability for all acts in the course and scope of their official duties.

Added Jan. 29, 2015, effective Jan. 29, 2015 (156 So.3d 1034).

FLORIDA JUDICIAL QUALIFICATIONS COMMISSION RULES

Revision

The Florida Judicial Qualifications Commission adopted the following Rules on May 18, 1984, which were accepted without change by the Florida Supreme Court on September 13, 1984 (458 So.2d 1116). The rules supersede rules adopted by the Commission January 20, 1977, amended by the Supreme Court May 12, 1977 (346 So.2d 70) and revised November 9, 1978 (364 So.2d 471).

The Florida Judicial Qualifications Commission submitted revisions of these rules to the Florida Supreme Court, and the Court approved such revisions in its opinion of April 30, 1998 (719 So.2d 858).

The Florida Judicial Qualifications Commission submitted revisions of these rules to the Florida Supreme Court, and the Court approved such revisions in its opinion of August 2, 2012 (141 So.3d 132).

Rule 1. Scope and Title

These rules apply to all proceedings before the Judicial Qualifications Commission involving the discipline, retirement or removal of justices of the Supreme Court, and judges of the District Courts of Appeal, Circuit Courts, and County Courts pursuant to Article V, Section 12 of the Constitution of the State of Florida, as amended, and removal or disqualification of members of the Commission. These rules shall be known as Florida Judicial Qualifications Commission Rules and may be abbreviated as "FJQCR."

Rule 2. Definitions

In these rules, the singular shall include the plural and vice-versa, and any singular personal pronoun shall include both feminine and masculine genders, and unless the context or subject matter otherwise requires:

(1) "Commission" means the Judicial Qualifications Commission.

(2) "Investigative Panel" means a division of the Commission vested with the jurisdiction to receive or initiate complaints, conduct investigations, dismiss complaints, and, upon a vote of a simple majority of the panel, submit formal charges to the hearing panel. The chair of the Commission shall be its chair.

(3) "Hearing Panel" means a division of the Commission vested with the authority to receive and hear formal charges from the Investigative Panel. The Hearing Panel, by majority vote of its members may recommend to the Supreme Court that a judge be subject to appropriate discipline. Upon a two-thirds vote, the panel may recommend to the Supreme Court the removal of a judge, as provided in Article 5, § 12, of the Constitution of the State of Florida, or the involuntary retirement of a judge for any permanent disability that seriously interferes with the performance of judicial duties.

(4) "Judge" means a justice of the Supreme Court and a judge of the District Court of Appeal, Circuit Court and County Court.

(5) "Chair" includes the acting chair.

(6) "General Counsel" means any member of The Florida Bar designated by the Commission to serve as legal advisor to the Commission and Investigative Panel, and to perform such other duties as authorized by the Commission.

(7) "Counsel to the Hearing Panel" means any member(s) of The Florida Bar, designated by the

Hearing Panel to serve as legal advisor to the Hearing Panel.

(8) "Special Counsel" means any member(s) of The Florida Bar designated by the Investigative Panel to gather and present evidence before the Investigative Panel or the Hearing Panel with respect to the charges against a judge and to represent the Commission in any proceedings, related to the activities of the Commission.

(9) "Shall" is mandatory and "may" is permissive.

(10) "Mail" and "mailed" include ordinary, registered, certified, or other form of United States mail, personal delivery, and delivery by a commercial delivery service.

(11) "Executive Director" means a person designated by the Commission to supervise its staff and to render such services to the Commission and its several panels as required, provided, however, that the Executive Director and staff will provide only ministerial or similar services to facilitate the activities of the Hearing Panel.

(12) "Member" means a member of the Commission.

(13) "Supreme Court" means the Supreme Court of Florida.

Amended Aug. 2, 2012, effective Aug. 2, 2012 (141 So.3d 132).

Rule 3. Membership and Jurisdiction

(a) The membership of the Commission shall be as prescribed in Article V, Section 12 of the Constitution of the State of Florida and for such term as prescribed by general law. When a member ceases to be a member of the appointing body from which that member was appointed or whenever any member becomes otherwise ineligible to hold office, that person's membership on the Commission shall terminate. The Chair shall promptly notify the appointing authority of the vacancy. In the event of a vacancy the Chair of the Commission shall appoint a temporary replacement as provided in Rule 25.

(b) The Commission shall have such jurisdiction and powers as are necessary to conduct the proper and speedy disposition of any investigation or hearing, including the power to compel the attendance of witnesses, to take or to cause to be taken the deposition of witnesses, to order the production of books, records or other documentary evidence, and the power of contempt. In any matter within the jurisdiction of the Commission requiring the appearance of any person before the Commission or any member, any member shall have the power to issue subpoenas and to administer oaths and affirmations to such persons.

Amended Aug. 2, 2012, effective Aug. 2, 2012 (141 So.3d 132).

Rule 4. Officers of the Commission

The Commission shall elect a Chair and a Vice–Chair, each of whom shall serve for a term of two years. The Vice–Chair shall act as the chair of the Commission in the absence of the Chair. If both the Chair and the Vice–Chair are absent, then a majority of the members present may appoint a Chair Pro Tempore. The Commission may employ staff, including an executive director and General Counsel, and such other staff as necessary to carry out its duties. The Commission will consider and decide matters relating to budget and other business of the Commission not specifically assigned to its panels. The Hearing Panel may appoint Counsel to the Hearing Panel to serve as its legal advisor.

Amended Aug. 2, 2012, effective Aug. 2, 2012 (141 So.3d 132).

Rule 5. Quorum of Commission

(a) A quorum for the transaction of the Commission's executive business shall be eight members except as otherwise provided in these rules.

(b) A quorum of the Investigative Panel shall be not less than five members of that Panel.

(c) A quorum of the Hearing Panel shall be not less than five of the members of that Panel.

Rule 6. Investigative Panel Rules

(a) The Investigative Panel of the Commission, upon receiving factual information, not obviously unfounded or frivolous, or an individual complaint made under oath, indicating that a judge is guilty of willful or persistent failure to perform judicial duties, or conduct unbecoming a member of the judiciary demonstrating a present unfitness to hold office, or conduct violative of the Code of Judicial Conduct, or that the judge has a disability seriously interfering with the performance of the judge's duties, which is, or is likely to become, permanent in nature, may make an investigation to determine whether formal charges should be instituted.

(b) The judge has no right to be present or to be heard during an investigation, but before the Investigative Panel determines that there is probable cause to initiate formal charges, the judge shall be notified of the investigation, the general nature of the subject matter of the investigation, and shall be afforded reasonable opportunity to make a statement before the Investigative Panel, personally or by the judge's attorney(s), verbally or in writing, sworn or unsworn, explaining, refuting or admitting the alleged misconduct or disability, and to respond to questions from the Panel. The judge shall not have the right to present other oral testimony or evidence, nor the right of confrontation or cross-examination of any person interviewed, called or interrogated by the Investigative Panel; provided that the Investigative Panel in its sole discretion may receive and consider documentary evidence, including affidavits submitted by a judge. Such notification shall be given personally, by registered or certified mail, or by delivery by a commercial service, addressed to the judge at the judge's chambers or, if returned undelivered, at the judge's last known residence.

(c) The Investigative Panel shall have the right to require a judge to meet with it on an informal basis in reference to matters that relate to the judge's duties.

(d) When a judge has received a notice of investigation, or a notice to appear before the Investigative Panel, or has requested such notification, the judge shall be promptly notified in writing if the investigation does not disclose probable cause to warrant further proceedings.

(e) The Investigative Panel shall have access to all information from all executive, legislative and judicial agencies, including grand juries. At any time, on request of the Speaker of the House of Representatives, the Commission shall make available all information in possession of the Commission for use in consideration of impeachment.

(f) When the Investigative Panel finds probable cause that formal charges should be filed against the judge, the Investigative Panel shall file a Notice of Formal Charges with the Clerk of the Supreme Court. The Investigative Panel shall designate one or more Special Counsel who shall prepare appropriate papers and pleadings, gather and present evidence before the Hearing Panel with respect to the charges against the judge, and otherwise act as counsel in connection with the prosecution of the charges against the judge, including the representation of the Commission in connection with any Commission or judicial proceedings. The Investigative Panel shall cause to be served on the judge a copy of the Notice of Formal Charges. Such proceedings shall be styled:

"BEFORE THE FLORIDA JUDICIAL QUALIFICATIONS COMMISSION"

"Inquiry Concerning a Judge, The Honorable ________, No. ________"

"BEFORE THE FLORIDA JUDICIAL QUALIFICATIONS COMMISSION"

"Inquiry Concerning a Judge, No. ________"

(g) The notice shall be issued in the name of the Commission and specify in ordinary and concise language the charges against the judge and allege the essential facts upon which such charges are based, and shall advise the judge of the judge's right to file a written answer to the charges within 20 days after service of the notice upon the judge.

(h) Service of the notice shall be made personally, by registered or certified mail or by commercial delivery service, addressed to the judge at the judge's chambers or, if returned undelivered, at the judge's last known residence.

(i) After the notice has been filed, any notice or other material shall be mailed to the judge at the judge's chambers or residence address, or to the judge's attorney(s), if any.

(j) The Investigative Panel may reach agreement with a judge on discipline or disability, and such stipulation shall be transmitted directly to the Supreme Court to accept or reject. If rejected, such agreement shall be without prejudice to any party thereto.

Amended Aug. 2, 2012, effective Aug. 2, 2012 (141 So.3d 132).

Rule 7. Hearing Panel Rules

(a) The Hearing Panel shall receive, hear and determine formal charges from the Investigative Panel. The Chair of the Commission shall select one of its the Hearing Panel members as Chair.

(b) The Chair of the Hearing Panel shall dispose of all pre-trial motions. These motions may be heard by teleconference or be determined with or without hearings. The Chair's disposition of motions shall be subject to review by the full Hearing Panel.

Amended Aug. 2, 2012, effective Aug. 2, 2012 (141 So.3d 132).

Rule 8. Suspension of Judge

Before or after the filing of a Notice of Formal Charges, the Investigative Panel may, in its discretion, issue its order directed to the judge ordering the judge to show cause before it why that panel should not recommend to the Supreme Court that the judge be suspended from office, either with compensation or without compensation, while the inquiry is pending. The order to show cause shall be returnable before the Investigative Panel at a designated place and at a time certain, at which place and time the Investigative Panel shall consider the question of suspension and any action thereto. Thereafter, and upon the filing of a Notice of Formal Charges with the Supreme Court, the Investigative Panel, not less than two-thirds of its members concurring, may recommend to the Supreme Court that the judge be suspended from performing the duties of office, either with or without compensation, pending final determination of the inquiry. If the Investigative Panel recommends suspension, such recommendation shall have incorporated therein a record of the proceedings of the Investigative Panel in relation to the order to show cause.

Rule 9. Answer

Within 20 days after service of the Notice of Formal Charges, the judge may serve and file an Answer, a copy of which shall be served on the Chair of the Hearing Panel and the original of which shall be filed with the Clerk of the Supreme Court. If the judge desires that the final hearings be heard in the county of the judge's residence, the judge shall so demand in writing at the time the initial Answer is filed.

Amended Aug. 2, 2012, effective Aug. 2, 2012 (141 So.3d 132).

Rule 10. Filing

(a) Upon the filing of the Notice of Formal Charges against a judge with the Clerk of the Supreme Court of Florida, the Notice of Formal Charges and all subsequent proceedings before the Hearing Panel shall be public.

(b) The original of all pleadings subsequent to the Notice of Formal Charges shall be filed with the Clerk of the Supreme Court of Florida, which office is designated by the Commission for receiving, docketing, filing and making such records available for public inspection. A duplicate original of all pleadings filed in the proceedings shall be served on each party, with a copy to the Chair of the Hearing Panel.

Rule 11. Setting for Hearing

After the filing of an Answer or the expiration of the time for its filing, the Hearing Panel shall set a time and place for a hearing and shall give notice of such hearing at least 20 days prior to the date set. If the judge timely requests that the hearing be held in the county of the judge's residence, it shall be so held unless the Hearing Panel, by an affirmative vote of two-thirds of its members, determines otherwise.

Rule 12. Procedure

(a) Settlement Negotiations. Prior to commencement of the hearing to determine formal charges against a judge, the Investigative Panel retains the authority to enter into stipulations for proposed discipline with the judge or judge's representatives. After the commencement of the hearing to determine formal charges against a judge, the Hearing Panel shall have the authority to enter into stipulations for proposed discipline with the judge or judge's representative, which it shall incorporate into its recommendation to the Supreme Court.

(b) In all proceedings before the Hearing Panel, the Florida Rules of Civil Procedure shall be applicable except where inappropriate or as otherwise provided by these rules.

(c) Special Counsel shall, upon written demand of a party or counsel of record, promptly furnish the following:

The names and addresses of all witnesses whose testimony the Special Counsel expects to offer at the hearing, together with copies of all written statements and transcripts of testimony of such witnesses in the possession of the counsel or the Investigative Panel which are relevant to the subject matter of the hearing and which have not previously been furnished, except those documents confidential under the Constitution of the State. When good cause is shown this rule may be waived.

(d) At the time and place set for hearing, the Hearing Panel may proceed with the hearing whether or not the judge has filed an Answer or appears at the hearing.

Amended Aug. 2, 2012, effective Aug. 2, 2012 (141 So.3d 132).

Rule 13. Disability

Upon receiving information that a judge is suffering a possible physical or mental disability which seriously interferes with the performance of the judge's duties, the Investigative Panel, upon a majority vote, may order the judge to submit to a physical and/or mental examination and/or may give notice of formal charges pursuant to Rule 6, infra. If the judge fails to submit to such examination within the time ordered, the Investigative Panel may recommend to the Supreme Court that the judge be suspended without compensation until such time as the judge complies with the Investigative Panel's order.

Rule 14. Evidence

At a hearing before the Hearing Panel, legal evidence only shall be received and oral evidence shall be taken only on oath or affirmation.

Rule 15. Procedural Rights of Judge Before the Hearing Panel

(a) In all hearings before the Hearing Panel, a judge shall have the right and reasonable opportunity to defend against the charges by the introduction of evidence, to be represented by attorney(s), and to examine and cross-examine witnesses. The judge shall also have the right to the issuance of subpoenas for attendance of witnesses to testify or produce books, papers, and other evidentiary matter.

(b) When a transcript of the trial proceedings has been prepared at the expense of the Commission, a copy thereof shall be furnished without cost to the judge. The judge shall also have the right, without any order or approval, to have all or any portion of the proceedings transcribed at the judge's expense.

(c) If the judge is adjudicated to be incapacitated, the panel with jurisdiction shall appoint an attorney ad litem unless there is a duly appointed legal guardian authorized to represent the judge, or to appoint counsel to represent the judge. The guardian or attorney ad litem may claim and exercise any right and privilege and make any defense for the judge with the same force and effect as if claimed, exercised, or made by the judge, with capacity, and whenever these rules provide for the serving or giving notice or sending any matter to the judge, a copy of such notice or matter also shall be served, given or sent to the guardian or attorney ad litem.

Rule 16. Amendments to Notice or Answer

The Hearing Panel may in the interest of justice allow or require amendments to the Notice of Formal Charges and may allow amendments to the Answer. In case such amendment is made, the judge shall be given reasonable time both to answer the amendment and to prepare and present a defense against the matters charged. If requested by the judge, the Hearing Panel may refer to the Investigative Panel any new matter presented or alleged in such amendment, as to which there has been no previous finding of probable cause by the Investigative Panel.

Rule 17. Extension of Time

The Chair of the Hearing Panel may extend the time for filing an Answer or for the commencement of a hearing before the Hearing Panel.

Rule 18. Hearing Additional Evidence

The Hearing Panel may order a hearing for the taking of additional evidence at any time while the matter is pending before it. The order shall set the time and place of the hearing and shall indicate matters on which the evidence is to be taken. A copy of such order shall be sent by mail at least ten days prior to the date of the hearing.

Rule 19. Hearing Panel Vote

After conclusion of the hearing and consideration of the issues presented for decision, the Hearing Panel shall determine by vote the judge's guilt or innocence of formal charges. If the Hearing Panel determines by a two-thirds vote that the judge is guilty of one or more of the charges so specified, it shall then proceed to determine the discipline to be recommended. The vote of four members of the Hearing Panel shall be required to recommend removal of the judge from office or for medical retirement of a judge. Upon a simple majority vote of a quorum of the Hearing Panel, the Panel may recommend to the Supreme Court that the justice or judge be subject to other appropriate discipline. Failure to recommend the imposition of any penalty by the prescribed affirmative vote of the Hearing Panel shall constitute a dismissal of the proceedings.

Rule 20. Certification of Hearing Panel Recommendations to Supreme Court

If the Hearing Panel dismisses the formal charges, the Hearing Panel shall promptly file a copy of the dismissal order certified by the Chair of the Hearing Panel with the Clerk of the Supreme Court. Upon making a determination recommending discipline, retirement or removal of a judge, the Hearing Panel shall file a copy of the recommendation certified by the Chair of the Hearing Panel, together with a transcript and the findings and conclusions, with the Clerk of the Supreme Court and shall mail to the judge and to the judge's attorney(s) notice of such filing, together with a copy of such recommendations, findings and conclusions.

Rule 21. Review of Proceedings

(a) Non–Final. Non–final orders of the Hearing Panel are subject to immediate review only where it can be demonstrated that an order departs from the essential requirements of law, causing material injury to the petitioner, and leaving no adequate remedy after issuance of the Hearing Panel's report and recommendations. Review of such orders shall be by appropriate extraordinary writ, directly to the Supreme Court. In the absence of a stay the hearing shall proceed to a conclusion.

(b) To the extent necessary to implement this rule, the Florida Rules of Appellate Procedure and Rule 2.310 of the Florida Rules of Judicial Administration shall be applicable to reviews of Investigative and Hearing Panel proceedings by the Supreme Court.

Amended Aug. 2, 2012, effective Aug. 2, 2012 (141 So.3d 132).

Rule 22. Subpoenas

Subpoenas for the attendance of witnesses and the production of documentary evidence shall be issued as follows:

(a) For investigative purposes, subpoenas may be issued for the attendance of witnesses and the production of documents before the General Counsel or Special Counsel with respect to any potential violation of the Code of Judicial Conduct, and counsel is empowered to administer oaths to all who are summonsed to testify or who may voluntarily appear before counsel to testify as to any potential violations of the Canons of the Code of Judicial Conduct.

(b) Subpoenas for the attendance of witnesses and the production of documentary evidence for discovery, and for the appearance of any person before any panel of the Commission, may be issued by the General Counsel, Counsel to the Hearing Panel, or Special Counsel, and may be served in the manner provided by law for the service of witness subpoenas in a civil action.

(c) Contempt. Any person who, without adequate excuse, fails to obey such a subpoena of the Commission or a panel of the Commission served upon that person may be cited for contempt of the Commission in the manner provided in these rules.

Amended Aug. 2, 2012, effective Aug. 2, 2012 (141 So.3d 132).

Rule 23. Confidentiality of Proceedings

(a) Until formal charges against a judge are filed by the Investigative Panel of the Commission with the Clerk of the Supreme Court, all proceedings by or before the Commission shall be confidential. Upon a finding of probable cause and the filing by the Investigative Panel of the Commission with the Clerk of such formal charges against a judge, such charges and all further proceedings before the Hearing Panel shall be public.

(b) All notices, papers and pleadings mailed to a judge prior to formal charges being instituted shall be enclosed in a cover marked "confidential."

(c) Every witness in every proceeding under these Rules shall swear or affirm to tell the truth and not to disclose the existence of the proceeding, the subject matter thereof, or the identity of the judge until the proceeding is no longer confidential under these Rules. Violation of this oath shall be an act of contempt of the Commission.

(d) Violation of this Rule by a member of the Commission shall subject that member, after written notice and hearing, to removal from office by an affirmative vote of eight members of the Commission and shall constitute contempt of the Commission which may be enforced by appropriate proceedings in the Supreme Court of Florida. (See Rule 26.)

Amended Aug. 2, 2012, effective Aug. 2, 2012 (141 So.3d 132).

Rule 24. Interested Party

A judge who is a member of the Commission or of the Supreme Court shall be disqualified from participation in such capacity in any proceedings involving the judge's own discipline, retirement or removal.

Rule 25. Disqualification or Vacancy

(a) Whenever a judge against whom formal proceedings have been instituted, shall file with the Hearing Panel an affidavit that the judge fears the judge will not receive a fair hearing before the Hearing Panel on the charges because of the prejudice of one or more members of the Hearing Panel against the judge, and the facts stated as the basis for making the affidavit shall be supported in substance by affidavit of at least two reputable citizens of the State of Florida not kin to the judge or the judge's attorney, or if any member of the Hearing Panel shall voluntarily recuse himself, such member or members of the Hearing Panel shall proceed no further therein and shall be disqualified from hearing the charges. The affidavit shall state the facts and the reasons for the belief that any such prejudice exists, shall specify the member(s) of the Hearing Panel allegedly prejudiced and shall be filed not more than 15 days after service of the Notice of Formal Charges upon the judge charged.

(b) The Chair of the Commission shall request from each of the appointing authorities a list of four persons who may temporarily serve in the absence of incapacitated or disqualified members. The appointing authorities are the Conference of District Court of Appeal Judges, the Conference of Circuit Court Judges, the Conference of County Court Judges, the Board of Governors of The Florida Bar, and the Governor of Florida. Upon the disqualification of or in the absence of a member of the Hearing Panel, the replacement shall be chosen by the Chair from those listed by the appropriate appointing authority. Each such replacement shall be from the same category as the disqualified member(s) set forth in Section 12(a), Article V of the Constitution of the State of Florida.

(c) The judge may within 15 days after receiving notice of such ad hoc appointment, file a like affidavit as to that appointee, which shall be supported in substance by an affidavit of two citizens as set forth above, in which event the ad hoc appointee shall not be disqualified on account of alleged prejudice against the judge unless the appointee admits that it is then a fact that the appointee is prejudiced against the judge or unless a majority of the Hearing Panel, which may include any ad hoc appointee, holds that the appointee is prejudiced against the judge, in which event the same ad hoc appointment procedure set forth above shall be followed until a qualified person has been appointed.

(d) A judge moved against by the Commission may, by affidavit, suggest the disqualification of a member or members of the Commission unsupported by two citizens, but in such event the determination of the matter of disqualification shall be by majority vote of the panel having jurisdiction unless the person sought to be disqualified voluntarily recuses himself.

(e) Upon the vacancy of a position on the Commission due to resignation or ineligibility as a member of the Commission, or upon the failure of the appointing authority to timely appoint a constituent member, the Chair shall appoint an ad hoc member from a list provided by the appropriate appointing authority. Each such replacement shall be from the same category as the disqualified member(s) set forth in Section 12(a), Article V of the Constitution of the State of Florida, and shall serve only until the appointing authority selects a representative to fill the vacancy.

Amended Aug. 2, 2012, effective Aug. 2, 2012 (141 So.3d 132).

Rule 26. Contempt

Should any witness fail, without justification, to respond to the lawful subpoena of the Commission or, having responded, fail or refuse to answer all inquiries or to turn over evidence that has been lawfully subpoenaed, or should any person be guilty of disorderly or contemptuous conduct before any proceeding of the Commission, or should any person violate the confidentiality of a proceeding conducted prior to the filing of formal charges, a motion may be filed in the name of the Commission before the Circuit Court of the County in which the contemptuous act was committed, alleging the specific failure on the part of the witness or the specific disorderly or contemptuous act of the person which forms the basis of an alleged contempt of the Commission. Such motion shall pray for the issuance of an order to show cause before the Circuit Court why the Circuit Court should not find the person in contempt of the Commission and why that person should not be punished by the Court therefore. The Circuit Court shall issue such orders and judgments therein as the Court deems appropriate.

Amended Aug. 2, 2012, effective Aug. 2, 2012 (141 So.3d 132).

Rule 27. Appointments

The Chair of the Commission shall assign the members to the Investigative Panel and the Hearing Panel. The Chair shall appoint to the Investigative Panel four judges, two members of The Florida Bar and three non-lawyers. The Chair shall appoint to the Hearing

Panel two judges, two members of the Bar of Florida and two non-lawyers. The membership on the panels may change at a time and in a manner determined by the Chair, provided that no member shall vote as a member of both the Investigative Panel and Hearing Panel in the same proceeding.

SUPREME COURT JUDICIAL NOMINATING COMMISSION RULES OF PROCEDURE

Approval Date

Approved and Made Mandatory January, 1985

Revision

Amended September 10, 1997; November 7, 2002

Section I. Initial Procedure; Investigative Sources; Notice

Whenever a vacancy occurs on the Supreme Court, or in the office of Statewide Prosecutor, or in the office of Capital Collateral Regional Counsel the Supreme Court Judicial Nominating Commission (hereinafter referred to as the "Commission") shall receive and review applications submitted by those applicants who timely request consideration. Each such application shall be in substantial compliance with the approved form of the Commission and shall include a waiver of confidentiality of all materials deemed necessary by the Commission to adequately investigate each applicant including, but not limited to, disciplinary records of The Florida Bar, records of the Florida Board of Bar Examiners, credit records, records of any law enforcement agency and (where applicable) records of the Florida Judicial Qualifications Commission.

The Commission shall notify The Florida Bar, the county and the local bar associations (including minority and women's bar associations) within the jurisdiction where the vacancy exists and at least one newspaper of general circulation in such area of the existence of the vacancy and the deadline for applications.

The Commission may seek and shall receive information from interested persons and groups. All applications, and other written information received from or concerning applicants, and all interviews and proceedings of the Commission, except for deliberations by the Commission, shall be open to the public to the extent required by law.

Eleven copies of the application and all attachments shall be filed with the chair (or designee) by each applicant prior to the deadline for filing applications. One copy of each application with attachments shall be forwarded by the chair to the Judicial Nominating Commission Coordinator, The Florida Bar, Tallahassee, Florida and one to the Judicial Nominating Commission Coordinator, General Counsel, Office of the Governor. The Commission shall require appropriate financial disclosure information as part of the application. The Commission may require such additional information as it deems appropriate.

The application shall include a separate page asking applicants to identify their race, ethnicity and gender. Completion of this page shall be optional, and the page shall include an explanation that the information is requested for data collection purposes in order to assess and promote diversity in the judiciary. The chair of the Commission shall forward all such completed pages, along with the names of the nominees, to the JNC Coordinator at The Florida Bar.

Section II. Initial Screening

Within a reasonable time after notice is given of the existence of a vacancy, the Commission shall meet to consider applicants and to select those applicants to be interviewed.

All applications, and other written information received from or concerning applicants, and all interviews and proceedings of the Commission, except for deliberations by the Commission, shall be open to the public to the extent required by law.

Section III. Electronic Media and Still Photography Coverage of Judicial Nominating Commission Proceedings

(a) Subject at all times to the authority of the chairperson of the commission to: (i) control the conduct of proceedings before the commission; (ii) ensure decorum and prevent distractions; and (iii) ensure the fair administration of justice in the pending cause, electronic media and still photography coverage of the open commission proceedings shall be allowed in accordance with the following rule.

(b) Equipment and Personnel.

(1) Not more than 1 portable television camera (film camera—16mm sound on film (self blimped) or videotape electronic camera), operated by not more than 1 camera person, shall be permitted in any open commission proceeding.

(2) Not more than 1 still photographer, using not more than 2 still cameras with not more than 2 lenses for each camera and related equipment for print purposes, shall be permitted in any open commission proceeding.

(3) Not more than 1 audio system for radio broadcast purposes shall be permitted in any open commission proceeding. Audio pickup for all media purposes shall be accomplished from existing audio systems present in the commission meeting place. If no technically suitable audio system exists in the commission meeting place, microphones and related wiring essential for media purposes shall be unobtrusive and shall be located in places designated in advance of any proceeding by the chairperson in which the commission proceeding is located.

(4) Any "pooling" arrangements among the media required by these limitations on equipment and personnel shall be the sole responsibility of the media without calling upon the chairperson of the commission to mediate any dispute as to the appropriate media representative or equipment authorized to cover a particular proceeding. In the absence of advance media agreement on disputed equipment or personnel issues, the chairperson of the commission shall exclude all contesting media personnel from a proceeding.

(c) Sound and Light Criteria.

(1) Only television photographic and audio equipment that does not produce distracting sound or light shall be used to cover open commission proceedings. Specifically, such photographic and audio equipment shall produce no greater sound or light than the equipment designated in the Appendix to this rule, when such designated equipment is in good working order. No artificial lighting device of any kind shall be used in connection with the television camera.

(2) Only still camera equipment that does not produce distracting sound or light shall be used to cover open commission proceedings. Specifically, such still camera equipment shall produce no greater sound or light than a 35mm Leica "M" Series Rangefinder camera, and no artificial lighting device of any kind shall be used in connection with a still camera.

(3) It shall be the affirmative duty of media personnel to demonstrate to the chairperson of the commission adequately in advance of any proceeding that the equipment sought to be used meets the sound and light criteria enunciated in this rule. A failure to obtain advance approval for equipment shall preclude its use in the proceeding.

(d) Location of Equipment Personnel.

(1) Television camera equipment shall be positioned in such location in the meeting place of the commission as shall be designated by the chairperson. The area designated shall provide reasonable access to coverage. If and when areas remote from the commission proceedings permit reasonable access to coverage are provided, all television camera and audio equipment shall be positioned only in such area. Videotape recording equipment that is not a component part of a television camera shall be located in an area remote from the commission proceedings.

(2) A still camera photographer shall position himself or herself in such location in the meeting place of the commission as shall be designated by the chairperson. The area designated shall provide reasonable access to coverage. Still camera photographers shall assume a fixed position within the designated area and, once established in a shooting position, shall act so as not to call attention to themselves through further movement. Still camera photographers shall not be permitted to move about in order to obtain photographs of the commission proceedings.

(3) Broadcast media representatives shall not move about the meeting place of the commission while proceedings are in session, and microphones or taping equipment once positioned as required by subdivision (a)(3) shall not be moved during the pendency of the proceeding.

(e) Movement During Proceedings. News media photographic or audio equipment shall not be placed in or removed from the meeting place of the commission except before commencement or after adjournment of proceedings each day, or during a recess. Neither television film magazines nor still camera film or lenses shall be changed within the meeting place of the commission except during a recess in the proceeding.

(f) Commission Meeting Place Light Sources. With the concurrence of the chairperson of the commission in which the meeting is situated, modifications and additions may be made in light sources existing in the commission meeting place, provided such modifications or additions are installed and maintained without public expense and removed immediately, following the commission proceeding, all light sources returned to their original condition.

APPENDIX

FILM CAMERAS		16mm Sound of Film (self blimped)
1. Cinema Products	CP–16A–R	Sound Camera
2. Arriflex	16mm–16BL Model	Sound Camera
3. Frezzolini	16mm (LW16)	Sound on Film Camera

4.	Auricon	"Cini-Voice"	Sound Camera
5.	Auricon	"Pro-600"	Sound Camera
6.	General Camera	SS III	Sound Camera
7.	Eclair	Model ACL	Sound Camera
8.	General Camera	DGX	Sound Camera
9.	Wilcam Reflex	16mm	Sound Camera

VIDEOTAPE ELECTRONIC CAMERAS

1.	Ikegami	HL-77 HL-33 HL-35 HL-34 HL-51
2.	RCA	TK 76
3.	Sony	DXC-1600 Trinicon
4.	ASACA	ACC-2006
5.	Hitachi	SK 80 SK 90
6.	Hitachi	FP-3030
7.	Philips	LDK-25
8.	Sony BVP-200	ENG Camera
9.	Fernseh	Video Camera
10.	JVC-8800u	ENG Camera
11.	AKAI	CVC-150 VTS-150
12.	Panasonic	WV-308 NV-3085
13.	JVC	GC-4800u

VIDEOTAPE RECORDER/used with video cameras

1.	Ikegami	3800
2.	Sony	3800
3.	Sony	BVU-100
4.	Ampex	Video Recorder
5.	Panasonic	1 inch Video Recorder
6.	JVC	4400
7.	Sony	3800H

Section IV. Further Investigation; Interviews

Upon selection by the Commission of the applicants to be interviewed, the Commission shall further investigate the fitness and qualifications of each such applicant, utilizing all sources reasonably available within the time permitted by law. The Commission shall invite each such selected applicant to appear before a quorum of the Commission sitting as a whole to respond to questions by the Commission designed to determine the fitness of the applicant to serve on the Supreme Court, to serve as Statewide Prosecutor, or to serve as Capital Collateral Regional Counsel, as the case may be.

Prior to the interview of any applicant, each Commission member shall disclose to the remaining Commission members all negative information received by such member concerning any applicant.

At any time before its final vote is concluded, the Commission may request an applicant to reappear before the Commission to answer additional questions and to provide additional information.

Section V. Standards and Qualifications; Criteria

No person shall be recommended to the Governor or to the Attorney General for appointment unless the Commission finds such applicant to be fit for appointment after full and careful consideration. Consideration of applicants for appointment to the Supreme Court shall include, but not necessarily be limited to, the following criteria;

(a) Applicable statutory criteria

(b) Personal attributes

(1) Personal integrity

(2) Standing in community

(3) Sobriety

(4) Moral conduct

(5) Ethics

(6) Commitment to equal justice under law

(c) Competency and experience

(1) General health

(2) Physical disabilities

(3) Intelligence

(4) Knowledge of the law and judicial system

(5) Professional reputation

(6) Knowledge and experience of the Supreme Court

(7) Meets legal judicial requirements

(d) Judicial capabilities

(1) Patience

(2) Decisiveness

(3) Impartiality

(4) Courtesy

(5) Civility

(6) Industry and promptness

(7) Administrative ability

(8) Possible reaction to judicial power

(9) Temperament

(10) Independence

To the extent applicable, such criteria shall also be considered with relation to applicants for the position of Statewide Prosecutor and for the position of Capital Collateral Regional Counsel. Every application shall be reviewed to determine that the applicant meets all constitutional and statutory requirements; including Section 16.56, F.S. for Statewide Prosecutor, and Section 27.701, F.S. for Capital Collateral Regional Counsels.

Section VI. Final Selection of Nominees

Upon conclusion of all investigation reasonably conducted and obtained by the Commission and after the procedures set forth in Section IV have been completed, the Commission shall meet to select by majority vote qualified nominees from those persons having applied for such vacancy. For each vacancy on the Florida Supreme Court the commission shall select not less than three (3) but not more than six (6) nominees. For a vacancy in the office of Statewide Prosecutor or a vacancy in any office of Capital Collateral Regional Counsel the Commission shall select three (3) nominees. The Commission shall complete its work within thirty (30) days from the occurrence of the vacancy, unless the period is extended by the Governor. The names of nominees selected and recommended by the Commission for appointment to the Supreme Court shall be certified to the Governor in alphabetical order and a copy of all written investigative information and documents relating to each such nominee shall be furnished therewith. The names of such three (3) nominees selected and recommended by the Commission for appointment to the Office of the Statewide Prosecutor shall be certified to the Attorney General of the State of Florida in alphabetical order and a copy of all investigative information and documents relating to each such nominee shall be furnished therewith. The names of such three (3) nominees selected and recommended by the Commission for appointment as Capital Collateral Regional Counsel shall be certified to the Governor in alphabetical order and a copy of all investigative information and documents relating to each such nominee shall be furnished therewith.

Section VII. Procedure for Final Voting

1. Final voting procedures to nominate to the Governor or to the Attorney General qualified applicants from those interviewed will take place:

(a) After the Commissioners have had an opportunity to review the applications, supporting data, and all other pertinent information;

(b) After the applicants selected by the Commission to be interviewed have been interviewed to the satisfaction of a majority of the Commission members;

(c) After the applicants have been discussed to the satisfaction of a majority of the Commission members; and

(d) Without any straw vote, unofficial vote, tentative vote, or official vote until the above-described steps have been taken, except that this limitation shall not apply to a screening process to reduce the number of applicants to be interviewed.

2. All votes shall be cast by written, secret ballot. On the initial round of voting each Commissioner shall cast six (6) votes, one per applicant. Any applicant who receives two (2) votes shall continue to the next round of voting.

3. On each successive round(s) of voting, the number of votes cast by each Commissioner shall be reduced by one (1) and the minimum required to remain on the proposed list shall be raised by one (1) vote.

4. This process shall continue until only three (3) applicants remain on the list or, if there is a tie for third place, more than three (3) shall be permitted so long as it is less than six (6). If there are more than six (6) then there will be a vote among those tied for third place with each Commissioner casting one (1) vote and only the person who receives the most votes shall remain on the proposed list.

5. Following completion of the initial round of voting, any Commissioner can then move to reconsider an applicant who did not make the initial proposed list. If the motion is seconded, the Commission shall vote to reconsider the applicant. Once the list of all persons for reconsideration has been determined, the Commission shall then vote on the list of persons being reconsidered. For that ballot, the number of potential votes each Commissioner may cast will be determined by subtracting the number of applicants already on the proposed list from the number of six (6). No Commissioner shall be required to vote but may cast up to the number of votes as determined above not to exceed one vote per applicant. Any applicant who receives at least five votes shall be added to the proposed list until there are not more than six (6) applicants on the proposed list. If there is a tie for the last position, then the Commissioner shall vote on the tied applicants with each Commissioner casting one (1) vote, and the applicant with the most votes will be added to the proposed list.

6. After the proposed list is complete, any Commissioner may make a motion to remove anyone on the list. If it is seconded, a vote shall be cast on the applicant, with each Commissioner casting one (1) vote. If a majority of the Commissioners eligible to vote, vote in favor of the motion, the applicant shall be removed from the list.

7. Finally, a motion to declare the list final shall be made, seconded and if it receives a majority vote of the Commissioners, the final list shall then be complete and those names shall be submitted to the Governor.

Section VIII. Publication of Names of Nominees

The chair of the Commission shall make public the names of all persons recommended by the Commission for appointment by the Governor or by the Attorney General without indicating any preference of the Commission.

Section IX. Ethical Considerations

Judicial Nominating Commissioners hold positions of public trust. A Commissioner's conduct should not reflect discredit upon the judicial selection process or disclose partisanship or partiality in the consideration of applicants. Accordingly, a Commissioner shall not become an advocate for any applicant. Consideration of applicants shall be made impartially, and objectively.

A Commissioner shall disclose to other Commissioners present all personal, professional and business relationships with an applicant. In the event any applicant is a member of the judiciary, each member of the Commission shall disclose to the Commission all matters which he, she, or any of his or her clients have pending before such applicant. If a substantial conflict of interest is apparent, that Commissioner shall not vote on further consideration of any applicants so long as the applicant creating the conflict is under consideration during the selection of the initial three (3) nominees. In addition, the Commissioner shall not participate in the selection of any additional nominees so long as the applicant creating the conflict is eligible for consideration. The chair shall rule upon whether a substantial conflict of interest exists. All balloting by the Commission shall be by secret ballot and the chair shall be entitled to vote in all instances. Upon certification of the nominees to the Governor or to the Attorney General, no Commissioner shall contact the Governor or the Attorney General or any member of their offices or staffs, for the purpose of further influencing the Governor's or Attorney General's ultimate decision. However, if contacted by the Governor or Attorney General, or their offices or staffs, a Commissioner shall be entitled to answer questions about each nominee. No attempt should be made to rank nominees or to otherwise disclose a preference of the Commission.

Section X. Misconduct

Each Commissioner shall be accountable to the Governor, their appointing authority and the chair for compliance with these rules and the proper performance of their duties as a member of the Commission. Each Commissioner affirms that under these rules the Governor, their appointing authority or the chair may dispose of any written complaint alleging the misconduct of one or more Commissioners or of the Commission, limited only by Article IV, Section 7 of the Constitution of the State of Florida. Each Commissioner further acknowledges that pursuant to Article IV, Section 7 of the Constitution the Governor may suspend from office any Commission member for malfeasance, misfeasance, neglect of duty, drunkenness, incompetence, permanent inability to perform their official duties, or commission of a felony.

A complaint alleging the misconduct of one or more Commissioners (other than the chair) shall be reported in writing to the chair for action. Upon the chair's receipt of any such charges, the subject Commissioner(s) and the appointing authority of the subject Commissioner(s) shall be immediately notified thereof and thereafter kept continuously apprised of the status of such complaint through final disposition. The chair shall investigate any complaint if the allegations are in writing, signed by the complainant, and deemed sufficient by the chair. A complaint shall be deemed sufficient if the chair determines that it contains allegations which if proven would be a violation of these rules or reflects discredit on the judicial selection process. Prior to determining sufficiency the chair may require supporting information or documentation as necessary for that determination. Upon determination of sufficiency, each charge: (a) may be disposed of by the chair solely; or, (b) may be referred by the chair for disposition by the appointing authority of the subject Commissioner exclusively, or with the concurrence of the chair, but in consultation with the Governor, the appointing authority of the subject Commissioner, and all other members of the Commission. Disposition of a complaint shall include a hearing which affords the opportunity for the presentation of evidence by all interested parties to be evaluated by a clear and convincing standard of proof. Action shall be taken within 60 days of receipt of any written complaint and its final disposition shall be immediately reported to the appointing authority, the chair and the Governor.

A complaint alleging the misconduct only of the chair shall be reported in writing to the appointing authority of the chair for action. Upon the appointing authority's receipt of any such charges, the chair shall be immediately notified thereof and thereafter kept continuously apprised of his or her status through final disposition. The appointing authority shall investigate any complaint if the allegations are in writing, signed by the complainant, and deemed sufficient. A complaint shall be deemed sufficient if the appointing authority determines that it contains allegations which if proven would be a violation of these rules or reflects discredit upon the judicial selection process. Prior to determining sufficiency the appointing authority may require supporting information or documentation as necessary for that determination. Upon determination of sufficiency, each charge shall be disposed of by the appointing authority, with the concurrence of the Governor when not otherwise involved as appointing authority, and in consultation with all other members of the Commission. Disposition of a complaint shall include a hearing which affords the opportunity for the presentation of evidence by all interested parties to be evaluated by a clear and convincing standard of proof. Action shall be taken within 60 days of receipt of any written complaint and its final disposition shall be immediately reported to the Commission, the appointing authority and the Governor.

A complaint alleging the misconduct of the chair and one or more Commissioners shall be reported in writing to the Governor for action. Upon the Governor's receipt of any such charges, the chair and Commissioner(s) shall be immediately notified thereof and thereafter kept continuously apprised of their status through final disposition. The Governor shall investigate any complaint if the allegations are in writing, signed by the complainant, and deemed by the Governor to be sufficient. A complaint shall be deemed sufficient if the Governor determines that it contains allegations which if proven would be a violation of these rules or would reflect discredit on the judicial selection process. Prior to determining sufficiency the Governor may require supporting information or documentation as necessary for that determination. Upon determination of sufficiency each charge may be disposed of by the Governor solely, or may be referred by the Governor for disposition by the appointing authority of the chair or Commissioner, exclusively or with the concurrence of the Governor, but in consultation with both the appointing authority of the chair or Commissioner and with all other members of the Commission. Disposition of a complaint shall include a hearing which affords the opportunity for the presentation of evidence by all interested parties to be evaluated by a clear and convincing standard of proof. Action shall be taken within 60 days of receipt of any written complaint and its final disposition shall be immediately reported by the Governor to the appointing authority and members of the Commission.

Section XI. Annual Meeting; Selection of Chair; Local Rules; Safeguarding of Records

Annually, after July 1, the Commission shall designate a chair by majority vote to serve for one year and shall certify his or her name to the Governor. The chair's term shall end on July 1 of the next succeeding year or upon the election of his or her succession in office. The chair may be reappointed. After July 1st and the appointment of all Commission vacancies by the Governor and Board of Governors, the new Commission shall meet to elect by majority vote a vice chair who shall have at least two years remaining in their term. The vice chair shall automatically be nominated for chair at the next annual election held. Additional nominations of qualified persons for chair are allowed.

Within the first twelve months of appointment, each JNC appointee must complete an educational course designed to familiarize members with JNC rules and procedures. Training shall include segments regarding interviewing techniques and diversity sensitivity.

The Florida Bar (through its JNC Coordinator or other appropriate designated officer or employee) shall be the official depository and custodian of the records of the Commission.

The chair shall keep a permanent written record of all policies and procedures adopted by the Commission during his or her term and shall send a copy to the JNC Coordinator at The Florida Bar.

The Commission may adopt such additional operating rules, forms and notices as it may from time to time deem necessary, so long as they are not inconsistent with these rules. The Commission shall maintain continuous records of its proceedings. In order that such records may be safeguarded, the Commission after completing its deliberations and submitting its recommendations to the Governor, shall place all remaining applications, questionnaires and other investigative data in a file, sealed by the chair, and transmit the same to the office of The Florida Bar. Minutes of each meeting affecting the official formal actions taken by the Commission shall be prepared and signed by the chair. The same shall be delivered to the Florida Bar where the same shall be preserved in a permanent file. The files will be available on a continuous basis to the Commission upon request, but the files may be destroyed on a yearly basis.

At the conclusion of the chair's term, the files of all written records of adopted policies and procedures shall be turned over to the newly elected chair. A copy of the same shall be permanently retained by the Florida Bar.

Section XII. Amendments

These rules may be amended by majority vote of the members of the Commission.

UNIFORM RULES OF PROCEDURE FOR DISTRICT COURTS OF APPEAL JUDICIAL NOMINATING COMMISSIONS

Explanatory Note

These rules were promulgated by representatives from each of the District Courts of Appeal Judicial Nominating Commissions, meeting in open session on January 24, 1985 in Miami. The rules were amended in open session on January 11, 1989 in Orlando; April 3, 1992 in Tampa; January 29, 1993 in Tampa; December 7, 1994 in Tampa; January 22, 1997 in Miami; March 30, 2000 in Tampa and June 25, 2003 in Orlando.

Section I. Initial Procedure; Investigative Sources; Notice

Whenever a vacancy occurs in a judicial office within the jurisdiction of a judicial nominating commission, the appropriate commission shall actively seek, receive, and review the approved background statements submitted by those who voluntarily request consideration, and by those who otherwise consent in writing to such consideration by the commission. Each such background statement shall be in substantial compliance with the form provided for this purpose, and shall include a waiver of confidentiality of all material necessary to adequately investigate each applicant, including but not limited to, disciplinary records of The Florida Bar, records of the Florida Board of Bar Examiners, credit records, records maintained by any law enforcement agency, and records of the Florida Judicial Qualifications Commission. The commission shall notify The Florida Bar, the county or local bar associations (including minority and women's bar associations) within the jurisdiction where the vacancy exists, newspapers of general circulation in such area, and the electronic media, to the extent reasonably possible, of the existence of the vacancy and the deadline for applications. The commissions may seek and shall receive information from interested persons and groups.

Section II. Initial Screening

The commission shall require completion of the application for judicial nomination prescribed by the commission. The commission shall meet within a reasonable time after the deadline for applications to evaluate, classify, and list applicants as "most qualified" for further investigation and consideration. The list may be limited in number if agreed upon by 2/3 of the commissioner's voting. No person shall be classified as "most qualified" until the commission affirmatively determines that the applicant meets all legal requirements for that judicial office and that the applicant appears from the materials then available to the commission to possess the personal qualities and attributes of character, experience, judicial temperament, and professional competence essential to that judicial office.

Section III. Electronic Media and Still Photography Coverage of Judicial Nominating Commission Proceedings

Subject at all times to the authority of the chairperson of the commission to: (i) control the conduct of proceedings before the commission; (ii) ensure decorum and prevent distractions; and (iii) ensure the fair administration of justice in the pending cause, electronic media and still photography coverage of the open commission proceedings shall be allowed in accordance with Judicial Administration Rule 2.170.

Section IV. Further Investigation; Interviews

After selection of the "most qualified" list of applicants, the commission shall further investigate the fitness and qualifications of each applicant, utilizing all sources reasonably available within the time permitted by the Florida Constitution. In addition, the commission may invite each "most qualified" applicant to appear before a quorum of the commission sitting as a whole to respond to questions deemed pertinent to each applicant's fitness and qualifications to hold the judicial office. All applications, and other information received from or concerning applicants, and all interviews and proceedings of the commission, except for deliberations by the commission, shall be open to the public to the extent required by the Florida Constitution.

The application shall include a separate page asking applicants to identify their race, ethnicity and gender. Completion of this page shall be optional, and the page shall include an explanation that the information is requested for data collection purposes in order to assess and promote diversity in the judiciary. The chair of the Commission shall forward all such completed pages, along with the names of the nominees, to the JNC Coordinator at the Governor's Office.

At a point in the investigative and interview process deemed appropriate by the commission, the commission shall:

(a) Inquire as to an applicant's past and present affiliation with or membership in legal and nonlegal organizations and clubs that practice or have policy that restricts or has restricted during the time of the applicant's affiliation or membership on the basis of race, religion, national origin, or sex. If affiliation with or membership in a restrictive or discriminatory club or organization is disclosed, inquiry shall be made as to whether the applicant intends to continue such affiliation or membership if selected to serve on the bench.

(b) Inquire as to an applicant's medical status to determine whether he or she is physically capable of performing judicial duties. Such inquiry shall include questions regarding past and present history of drug or alcohol dependency and, if relevant, participation in treatment and rehabilitative programs.

(c) Require complete financial disclosure from the applicant.

Section V. Standards and Qualifications; Criteria

No nominee shall be recommended to the governor for appointment unless the commission finds that the nominee meets all constitutional and statutory requirements and is fit for appointment to the particular judicial office after full and careful consideration which consideration shall include but not necessarily limited to the following criteria:

(a) Personal attributes

(1) Personal integrity

(2) Standing in community

(3) Sobriety

(4) Moral conduct

(5) Ethics

(6) Commitment to equal justice under law

(b) Competency and experience

(1) General health, mental and physical

(2) Intelligence

(3) Knowledge of the law

(4) Professional reputation

(5) Knowledge of and experience in the court involved

(c) Judicial capabilities

(1) Patience

(2) Decisiveness

(3) Impartiality

(4) Courtesy

(5) Civility

(6) Industry and promptness

(7) Administrative ability

(8) Possible reaction to judicial power

(9) Temperament

(10) Independence

Section VI. Final Selection of Nominees

Upon conclusion of all investigation obtained by the commission, and after the "most qualified" applicants have been afforded the opportunity of a personal interview by the commission, the commission shall meet to evaluate the "most qualified" applicants. By majority vote, the commission shall select from the list of "most qualified" applicants who meet all legal requirements for the judicial office (no fewer than three and no more than six nominees for each vacancy in the judicial office). The names of such nominees selected by the commission shall be certified to the governor in alphabetical order, and a copy of all investigative information and documents relating to each such nominee shall be forwarded to the governor in a sealed container so that it is received no later than thirty days from the occurrence of a vacancy, unless the period is extended by the governor.

Section VII. Publication of Names of Nominees

The chair of the commission shall make public the names of all persons recommended for gubernatorial appointment, without indicating any preference of the commission.

Section VIII. Ethical Responsibilities

Judicial nominating commissioners hold positions of public trust. A commissioner's conduct should not reflect discredit upon the judicial selection process or disclose partisanship or partiality in the consideration of applicants. Consideration of applicants shall be made impartially and objectively.

A commissioner shall disclose to all other commissioners present all personal and business relationships with an applicant. If a substantial conflict of interest is apparent, that commissioner shall not vote on further consideration of any affected applicants. All balloting by the commission shall be by secret ballot and the chair shall be entitled to vote in all instances. Upon certification of a list of nominees to the governor, no commissioner shall contact the governor or any member of his office or staff, for the purpose of further influencing the governor's ultimate decision. However, if contacted by the governor, or his office or staff, a commissioner shall be entitled to answer questions about each nominee. No attempt should be made to rank such nominees or to otherwise disclose a preference of the commission.

Section IX. Misconduct

Each commissioner shall be accountable to the Governor, and the chair of their commission for compliance with these rules and the proper performance of their duties as a member of a judicial nominating commission. Each commissioner affirms that under these rules the Governor, and/or the chair of their commission may dispose of any written complaint alleging the misconduct of one or more commissioners or commissions, limited only by Article IV, Section 7 of the Constitution of the State of Florida. Each commissioner further acknowledges that pursuant to Article IV, Section 7 the Governor may suspend from office any commission member for malfeasance, misfeasance, neglect of duty, drunkenness, incompetence, permanent inability to perform their official duties, or commission of a felony.

A complaint alleging the misconduct of one or more commissioners (other than the chair) within a single judicial nominating commission shall be reported in writing to the chair of the affected commission for action. Upon the chair's receipt of any such charges, the subject commissioner(s) and the Governor shall be immediately notified thereof and thereafter kept continuously apprised of their status through final disposition. The chair shall investigate any complaint if the allegations are in writing, signed by the complainant, and deemed sufficient. A complaint is sufficient if the chair determines that it contains allegations which if proven would be a violation of these rules or reflects discredit on the judicial selection process. Prior to determining sufficiency the chair may require supporting information or documentation as necessary for that determination. Upon determination of sufficiency each charge may be disposed of by the chair solely, or may be referred by the chair for disposition by the Governor, exclusively or with the concurrence of the chair, but in consultation with all other members of the affected JNC who are not otherwise involved in the disposition. Disposition of a complaint shall include a hearing which affords the opportunity for the presentation of evidence to be evaluated by a clear and convincing standard of proof. Action shall be taken within 60 days of receipt of any written complaint and its final disposition shall be immediately reported.

A complaint alleging the sole misconduct of a judicial nominating commission chair shall be reported in writing to the Governor for action. Upon the Governor's receipt of any such charges, the subject chair shall be immediately notified thereof and thereafter kept continuously apprised of their status through final disposition. The Governor shall investigate any complaint if the allegations are in writing, signed by the complainant, and deemed sufficient. A complaint is sufficient if the Governor determines that it contains allegations which if proven would be a violation of these rules or reflects discredit upon the judicial selection process. Prior to determining sufficiency the Governor may require supporting information or documentation as necessary for that determination. Upon determination of sufficiency, each charge shall be disposed of by the Governor in consultation with all other members of the affected JNC who are not otherwise involved in the disposition. Disposition of a complaint shall include a hearing which affords the opportunity for the presentation of evidence to be evaluated by a clear and convincing standard of proof. Action shall be taken within 60 days of receipt of any written complaint and its final disposition shall be immediately reported.

A complaint alleging the misconduct of a judicial nominating commission chair and one or more commissioners of a judicial nominating commission shall be reported in writing to the Governor for action. Upon the Governor's receipt of any such charges, the subject chair and commissioner(s) shall be immediately notified thereof and thereafter kept continuously apprised of their status through final disposition. The Governor shall investigate any complaint if the allegations are in writing, signed by the complainant, and deemed sufficient. A complaint is sufficient if the Governor determines that it contains allegations which if proven would be a violation of these rules or reflects discredit on the judicial selection process. Prior to determining sufficiency the Governor may require supporting information or documentation as necessary for that determination. Upon determination of sufficiency each charge may be disposed of by the Governor solely, but in consultation with all other members of the affected JNC who are not otherwise involved in the disposition or the subjects of the alleged misconduct. Disposition of a complaint shall include a hearing which affords the opportunity for the presentation of evidence to be evaluated by a clear and convincing standard of proof. Action shall be taken within 60 days of receipt of any written complaint and its final disposition shall be immediately reported.

Section X. Annual Meeting; Selection of Chair; Local Rules; Safeguarding of Records

Annually, after July 1st, the commission shall meet to elect by a majority vote a chair. His or her term shall end on July 1 of the next succeeding year. The chair's term shall not exceed one year. After July 1st and the appointment of all commission vacancies by the Governor, the new commission shall meet to elect by majority vote a vice chair who shall have at least two years remaining in his or her term. Each commission shall certify the chair's name to the Governor. The vice chair shall automatically be nominated for chair at the next annual election held. Additional nominations of qualified persons for chair are allowed.

The chair shall keep a permanent written record of all policies and procedures adopted by the commission during his or her term.

Each commission may adopt such additional operating rules, forms and notices as it may from time to time deem necessary, so long as they are not inconsistent with these rules. Each commission shall maintain continuous records of its proceedings. In order that such records may be safeguarded, the commission after completing its deliberations and submitting its recommendations to the Governor, shall place all remaining applications, questionnaires and other investigative data in a file. The files will be available on a continuous basis to the commission upon request, but the files may be destroyed on a yearly basis.

At the conclusion of his or her term, the outgoing chair shall turn over to the newly elected chair all written records of adopted policies and procedures.

Within the first twelve months of appointment, each JNC appointee must complete an educational course designed to familiarize members with JNC rules and procedures. Training shall include segments regarding interviewing techniques and diversity sensitivity.

Section XI. Amendments

These rules may be amended by majority vote of the DCA Judicial Nominating Commissions voting by an authorized representative.

Upon written request of 25% of all DCA judicial nominating commissions, a meeting shall be convened within 90 days for the purpose of considering amendments to these rules.

UNIFORM RULES OF PROCEDURE FOR CIRCUIT JUDICIAL NOMINATING COMMISSIONS

Explanatory Note

These rules were promulgated by a majority of the circuit judicial nominating commissions, meeting in open session on January 24, 1985 in Miami. The rules were amended in open session on January 11, 1989 in Orlando; February 22, 1991 in Tampa; April 3, 1992 in Tampa; January 29, 1993 in Tampa; December 7, 1994 in Tampa; September 6, 1995 in Tampa; January 22, 1997 in Miami; March 30, 2000 in Tampa; and June 25, 2003 in Orlando.

A provision was contained in these rules stating that they take effect on January 8, 1985; however, the rules were promulgated by a majority of the circuit judicial nominating commissions on January 24, 1985.

Section I. Initial Procedure; Investigative Sources; Notice

Whenever a vacancy occurs in a judicial office within the jurisdiction of a judicial nominating commission, the appropriate commission shall actively seek, receive and review the approved background statements submitted by those who voluntarily request consideration, and by those who otherwise consent in writing to such consideration by the commission. The commission shall require completion of the application form attached hereto and incorporated herein, which shall include a waiver of confidentiality of all material necessary to adequately investigate each applicant, including but not limited to, disciplinary records of The Florida Bar, records of the Florida Board of Bar Examiners, credit records, records maintained by any law enforcement agency, and records of the Florida Judicial Qualifications Commission. The commission shall notify The Florida Bar, representative bar associations (including minority and women's bar associations) within the jurisdiction where the vacancy occurs and electronic media; and shall seek applications for nominations from all persons who meet the eligibility requirements in the Florida Constitution. The commissions may seek and shall receive information from interested persons and groups.

Section II. Screening Procedures

Within a reasonable time after notice is given of the existence of the vacancy, the commission shall meet to consider applicants. At this meeting the procedures for screening and voting upon applicant for said vacancy shall be determined.

Section III. Electronic Media and Still Photography Coverage of Judicial Nominating Commission Proceedings

Subject at all times to the authority of the chairperson of the commission to: (i) control the conduct of proceedings before the commission; (ii) ensure decorum and prevent distractions; and (iii) ensure the fair administration of justice in the pending cause, electronic media and still photography coverage of the open commission proceedings shall be allowed in accordance with Judicial Administrative Rule 2.170.

Section IV. Further Investigation; Interviews

The commission shall investigate the fitness and qualifications of each applicant, utilizing all sources reasonably available within the time permitted by the Florida Constitution. In addition, the commission may invite any applicant to appear before a quorum of the commission sitting as a whole to respond to questions deemed pertinent to each applicant's fitness and qualifications to hold the judicial office. All applications, and other information received from or concerning applicants, and all interviews and proceedings of the commission, except for deliberations by the commission, shall be open to the public to the extent required by the Florida Constitution or Florida Statutes.

The application shall include a separate page asking applicants to identify their race, ethnicity and gender. Completion of this page shall be optional, and the page shall include an explanation that the information is requested for data collection purposes in order to assess and promote diversity in the judiciary. The chair of the Commission shall forward all such completed pages, along with the names of the nominees, to the JNC Coordinator in the Governor's Office.

At a point in the investigative and interview process deemed appropriate by the commission, the commission shall require financial disclosure from the applicant.

Section V. Standards and Qualifications; Criteria

No nominee shall be recommended to the governor for appointment unless the commission finds that the nominee meets all constitutional and statutory requirements and is fit for appointment to the particular judicial office after full and careful consideration which consideration shall include but not necessarily limited to the following criteria:

(a) Personal attributes

(1) Personal integrity

(2) Standing in community

(3) Sobriety

(4) Moral conduct

(5) Ethics

(6) Commitment to equal justice under law

(b) Competency and experience

(1) General health, mental and physical

(2) Intelligence

(3) Knowledge of the law

(4) Professional Reputation

(5) Knowledge of and experience in the court involved

(c) Judicial capabilities

(1) Patience

(2) Decisiveness

(3) Impartiality

(4) Courtesy

(5) Civility

(6) Industry and promptness

(7) Administrative ability

(8) Possible reaction to judicial power

(9) Temperament

(10) Independence

Section VI. Final Selection of Nominees

By majority vote, the commission shall select no fewer than three and no more than six nominees from the list of applicants who meet the requirements of the Florida Constitution and all other legal requirements for the judicial office.

The names of such nominees selected by the commission shall be certified to the governor in alphabetical order, and a copy of all investigative information and documents relating to each such nominee shall be forwarded to the governor.

Section VII. Publication of Names of Nominees

The chairperson of the commission shall make public the names of all persons recommended for gubernatorial appointment, without indicating any preference of the commission.

Section VIII. Ethical Responsibilities

Judicial nominating commissioners hold positions of public trust. A commissioner's conduct should not reflect discredit upon the judicial selection process or disclose partisanship or partiality in the consideration of applicants. Consideration of applicants shall be made impartially and objectively.

A commissioner shall disclose to all other commissioners present all personal and business relationships with an applicant. If a substantial conflict of interest is apparent, that commissioner shall not vote on further consideration of any affected applicants. A Commissioner shall declare any conflict of interest that he/she has. Alternatively, upon motion by any Commissioner, a majority of all of the Commissioners may declare that a commissioner has a conflict of interest. The affected Commissioner may vote on the motion. All balloting by the commission shall be by secret ballot and the chair shall be entitled to vote in all instances. Upon certification of a list of nominees to the governor, no commissioner shall contact the governor or any member of his office or staff, for the purpose of further influencing the governor's ultimate decision. However, if contacted by the governor, or his office or staff, a commissioner shall be entitled to answer questions about each nominee. No attempt should be made to rank such nominees or to otherwise disclose a preference of the commission.

Section IX. Misconduct

Each commissioner shall be accountable to the Governor and the chair of their commission for compliance with these rules and the proper performance of their duties as a member of a judicial nominating commission. Each commissioner affirms that under these rules the Governor and/or the chair of their commission may dispose of any legally sufficient written complaint alleging the misconduct of one or more commissioners or commissions, limited only by Article IV, Section 7 of the Constitution of the State of Florida. Each commissioner further acknowledges that pursuant to Article IV, Section 7 the Governor may suspend from office any commission member for malfeasance, misfeasance, neglect of duty, drunkenness, incompetence, permanent inability to perform their official duties, or commission of a felony.

A complaint alleging the misconduct of one or more commissioners (other than the chair) within a single judicial nominating commission shall be reported in writing to the chair of the affected commission for action. Upon the chair's receipt of any such charges, the subject commissioner(s) and the Governor shall be immediately notified thereof and thereafter kept continuously apprised of their status through final disposition. The chair shall investigate any complaint if the allegations are in writing, signed by the complainant, and legally sufficient. A complaint is legally sufficient if the chair determines that it contains ultimate facts which show a violation of these rules or reflects discredit on the judicial selection process. Prior to determining legal sufficiency the chair may require supporting information or documentation as necessary for that determination. Upon determination of legal sufficiency each charge may be disposed of by the chair solely, or may be referred by the chair for disposition by the Governor, exclusively or with the concurrence of the chair, but in consultation with all other members of the affected JNC who are not otherwise involved in the disposition. Disposition of a complaint shall include a hearing which affords the opportunity for the presentation of evidence to be evaluated by a clear and convincing standard of proof. Action shall be taken within 60 days of receipt of any written complaint and its final disposition shall be immediately reported.

A complaint alleging the sole misconduct of a judicial nominating commission chair shall be reported in writing to the Governor for action. Upon the Governor's receipt of any such charges, the subject chair shall be immediately notified thereof and thereafter kept continuously apprised of their status through final disposition. The Governor shall investigate any complaint if the allegations are in writing, signed by the complainant, and legally sufficient. A complaint is legally sufficient if the Governor determines that it contains ultimate facts which show a violation of these rules or reflects discredit upon the judicial selection process. Prior to determining legal sufficiency the Governor may require supporting information or documentation as necessary for that determination. Upon determination of legal sufficiency, each charge shall be disposed of by the Governor in consultation with all other members of the affected JNC who are not otherwise involved in the disposition. Disposition of a complaint shall include a hearing which affords the opportunity for the presentation of evidence to be evaluated by a clear and convincing standard of proof. Action shall be taken within 60 days of receipt of any written complaint and its final disposition shall be immediately reported.

A complaint alleging the misconduct of a judicial nominating commission chair and one or more commissioners of a judicial nominating commission shall be reported in writing to the Governor for action. Upon the Governor's receipt of any such charges, the subject chair and commissioner(s) shall be immediately notified thereof and thereafter kept continuously apprised of their status through final disposition. The Governor shall investigate any complaint if the allegations are in writing, signed by the complainant, and legally sufficient. A complaint is legally sufficient if the Governor determines that it contains ultimate facts which show a violation of these rules or reflects discredit on the judicial selection process. Prior to determining legal sufficiency the Governor may require supporting information or documentation as necessary for that determination. Upon determination of legal sufficiency each charge may be disposed of by the Governor solely, or in consultation with all other members of the affected JNC who are not otherwise involved in the disposition or the subjects of the alleged misconduct. Disposition of a complaint shall include a hearing which affords the opportunity for the presentation of evidence to be evaluated by a clear and convincing standard of proof. Action shall be taken within 60 days of receipt of any written complaint and its final disposition shall be immediately reported.

Section X. Annual Meeting; Selection of Chairperson; Local Rules

On July 2 of each year or as soon thereafter as practicable, each commission shall designate a chairperson by majority vote to serve for one year and shall certify his or her name to the Governor. The chairperson shall be entitled to vote in all matters. His or her term shall end on July 1 of the next succeeding year. After July 1st and the appointment of all commission vacancies by the Governor, the new commission shall meet to elect by majority vote a vice chairperson who shall have at least two years remaining in his or her term. The vice chairperson shall automatically be nominated for chairperson at the next annual election held. Additional nominations of qualified persons for chairperson are allowed.

The chairperson shall keep a permanent written record of the minutes of all meetings of the commission, and all policies and procedures adopted by the commission, and all policies and procedures adopted by the commission during his or her term. At the conclusion of his or her term the outgoing chairperson shall turn over to the newly elected chairperson all minutes of meetings and written records of adopted policies and procedures. Each commission may adopt such additional operating rules, forms and notices as it may from time to time deem necessary, so long as they are not inconsistent with these rules.

Within the first twelve months of appointment, each JNC appointee must complete an educational course designed to familiarize members with JNC rules and procedures. Training shall include segments regarding interviewing techniques and diversity sensitivity.

Section XI. Amendments

These rules may be amended by majority vote of the circuit judicial nominating commissions, voting by an authorized representative.

Upon written request of 25% of all circuit judicial nominating commissions, a meeting shall be convened within 90 days for the purpose of considering amendments to these rules.

These rules became effective January 8, 1985. Amendments were made effective January 31, 1989 and February 22, 1991.